# Profiles
## of
# New York State

WITHDRAWN

# Profiles
## of
## New York State

# 2012-2013
## Eighth Edition

# Profiles
# of
# New York State

A UNIVERSAL REFERENCE BOOK

Grey House
Publishing

PUBLISHER: Leslie Mackenzie
EDITORIAL DIRECTOR: Laura Mars
EDITOR: David Garoogian
MARKETING DIRECTOR: Jessica Moody

Grey House Publishing, Inc.
4919 Route 22
Amenia, NY 12501
518.789.8700
FAX 845.373.6390
www.greyhouse.com
e-mail: books @greyhouse.com

*Profiles of New York State*
2 Volume Set (*New York State Directory* and *Profiles of New York State*)

ISBN: 978-1-59237-865-4
ISBN: 978-1-59237-864-7

# Table of Contents

**Introduction**
Introduction . . . . . . . . . . . . . . . . . . . . . . . . . . . . . . . . . . . . . . . . . vii

**About New York State**
State Emblems. . . . . . . . . . . . . . . . . . . . . . . . . . . . . . . . . . . . . . . . . ix
Photo Gallery . . . . . . . . . . . . . . . . . . . . . . . . . . . . . . . . . . . . . . . . . . xi
Government
    Brief History and Organization . . . . . . . . . . . . . . . . . . . . . . . . xv
    Congressional Districts (112th Congress) . . . . . . . . . . . . . . . . . xviii
    Percent of Population Who Voted for Barack Obama in 2008 . . . . . . . . . . xix
Land and Natural Resources
    State Summary . . . . . . . . . . . . . . . . . . . . . . . . . . . . . . . . . . . xxi
    New York State Energy Overview and Analysis . . . . . . . . . . . . . . . . . xxii
    Populated Places, Transportation and Physical Features. . . . . . . . . . . . . xxv
    Federal Lands and Indian Reservations . . . . . . . . . . . . . . . . . . . . . xxvi
    Satellite View . . . . . . . . . . . . . . . . . . . . . . . . . . . . . . . . . . . . xxvii
    Economic Losses from Hazard Events, 1960–2009. . . . . . . . . . . . . . . xxviii
    Hazard Losses, 1960–2009. . . . . . . . . . . . . . . . . . . . . . . . . . . . xxix
Demographic Maps
    Population. . . . . . . . . . . . . . . . . . . . . . . . . . . . . . . . . . . . . . xxxi
    Percent White . . . . . . . . . . . . . . . . . . . . . . . . . . . . . . . . . . . xxxii
    Percent Black . . . . . . . . . . . . . . . . . . . . . . . . . . . . . . . . . . . xxxiii
    Percent Asian . . . . . . . . . . . . . . . . . . . . . . . . . . . . . . . . . . . xxxiv
    Percent Hispanic . . . . . . . . . . . . . . . . . . . . . . . . . . . . . . . . . xxxv
    Median Age . . . . . . . . . . . . . . . . . . . . . . . . . . . . . . . . . . . . xxxvi
    Median Household Income . . . . . . . . . . . . . . . . . . . . . . . . . . . xxxvii
    Median Home Value . . . . . . . . . . . . . . . . . . . . . . . . . . . . . . xxxviii
    High School Graduates. . . . . . . . . . . . . . . . . . . . . . . . . . . . . . xxxix
    College Graduates . . . . . . . . . . . . . . . . . . . . . . . . . . . . . . . . . . xl
    Core-Based Statistical Areas and Counties . . . . . . . . . . . . . . . . . . . . xli

**User's Guides**
Profiles. . . . . . . . . . . . . . . . . . . . . . . . . . . . . . . . . . . . . . . . . . . . xliii
Education . . . . . . . . . . . . . . . . . . . . . . . . . . . . . . . . . . . . . . . . . . . lix
Ancestry and Ethnicity. . . . . . . . . . . . . . . . . . . . . . . . . . . . . . . . . . . lxiii
Climate. . . . . . . . . . . . . . . . . . . . . . . . . . . . . . . . . . . . . . . . . . . . lxxi

**Profiles**
Alphabetical by County/Place . . . . . . . . . . . . . . . . . . . . . . . . . . . . . . . 1
Alphabetical Place Index . . . . . . . . . . . . . . . . . . . . . . . . . . . . . . . . . 663
Comparative Statistics . . . . . . . . . . . . . . . . . . . . . . . . . . . . . . . . . . 679

**Education**
Public School Profile . . . . . . . . . . . . . . . . . . . . . . . . . . . . . . . . . . . 712
School District Rankings . . . . . . . . . . . . . . . . . . . . . . . . . . . . . . . . . 713
National Assessment of Educational Progress (NAEP). . . . . . . . . . . . . . . . . 741
State Report Card . . . . . . . . . . . . . . . . . . . . . . . . . . . . . . . . . . . . . 749

**Ancestry and Ethnicity**
State Profile . . . . . . . . . . . . . . . . . . . . . . . . . . . . . . . . . . . . . . . . 782
County Profiles. . . . . . . . . . . . . . . . . . . . . . . . . . . . . . . . . . . . . . . 783
Place Profiles . . . . . . . . . . . . . . . . . . . . . . . . . . . . . . . . . . . . . . . 845
Ancestry Group Rankings . . . . . . . . . . . . . . . . . . . . . . . . . . . . . . . . 889
Hispanic Origin Rankings . . . . . . . . . . . . . . . . . . . . . . . . . . . . . . . . 909
Racial Group Rankings . . . . . . . . . . . . . . . . . . . . . . . . . . . . . . . . . . 914

**Climate**

    State Physical Features and Climate Narrative . . . . . . . . . . . . . . . . . . . . . . . . 933
    State Reference Map . . . . . . . . . . . . . . . . . . . . . . . . . . . . . . . . . . . . . . . . . . . . 934
    State Relief Map . . . . . . . . . . . . . . . . . . . . . . . . . . . . . . . . . . . . . . . . . . . . . . . 935
    Weather Stations Map . . . . . . . . . . . . . . . . . . . . . . . . . . . . . . . . . . . . . . . . . . 936
    Weather Stations by County . . . . . . . . . . . . . . . . . . . . . . . . . . . . . . . . . . . . . . 937
    Weather Stations by City . . . . . . . . . . . . . . . . . . . . . . . . . . . . . . . . . . . . . . . . 938
    Weather Stations by Elevation . . . . . . . . . . . . . . . . . . . . . . . . . . . . . . . . . . . . 940
    National Weather Service Stations . . . . . . . . . . . . . . . . . . . . . . . . . . . . . . . . . 941
    Cooperative Weather Stations . . . . . . . . . . . . . . . . . . . . . . . . . . . . . . . . . . . . 950
    Weather Station Rankings . . . . . . . . . . . . . . . . . . . . . . . . . . . . . . . . . . . . . . . 959
    Significant Storm Events . . . . . . . . . . . . . . . . . . . . . . . . . . . . . . . . . . . . . . . . 970

# Introduction

This is the eighth edition of *Profiles of New York State—Facts, Figures & Statistics for 2,602 Populated Places in New York.* As with the other titles in our *State Profiles* series, it was built with content from Grey House Publishing's award-winning *Profiles of America*—a 4-volume compilation of data on more than 42,000 places in the United States. We have updated and included the New York chapter from *Profiles of America,* and added several new chapters of demographic information and ranking sections, so that *Profiles of New York State* is the most comprehensive portrait of the state of New York ever published.

*Profiles of New York State* provides data on all populated communities and counties in the state of New York for which the US Census provides individual statistics. This edition also includes profiles of 456 unincorporated places and neighborhoods (i.e. Bayside, Queens) based on US Census data by zip code and, for the first time, includes communities that span multiple zip codes.

This premier reference work includes five major sections that cover everything from **Education** to **Ethnic Backgrounds** to **Climate**. All sections include **Comparative Statistics** or **Rankings**. New to this edtion is a section called **About New York** at the front of the book, comprised of detailed narrative and colorful photos and maps. Here is an overview of each section:

## 1. About New York

This NEW 4-color section gives the researcher a real sense of the state and its history. It includes a Photo Gallery, and comprehensive sections on New York's Government, Land and Natural Resources, and Demographic Maps. With charts and maps, these 30 pages help to anchor the researcher to the state, both physically and politically.

## 2. Profiles

This section, organized by county, gives detailed profiles of 2,602 places plus 62 counties, based on Census 2010 and data from the American Community Survey. In addition, we have added current government statistics and original research, so that these profiles pull together statistical and descriptive information on every Census-recognized place in the state. Major fields of information include:

| | | | |
|---|---|---|---|
| *Geography* | *Housing* | *Education* | *Religion* |
| *Ancestry* | *Transportation* | *Population* | *Climate* |
| *Economy* | *Industry* | *Health* | |

In addition to place profiles, this section includes an **Alphabetical Place Index** and **Comparative Statistics** that compare New York's 100 largest communities by dozens of data points.

## 3. Education

This section begins with an **Educational State Profile,** summarizing number of schools, students, diplomas granted and educational dollars spent. Following the state profile are **School District Rankings** on 16 topics ranging from *Teacher/Student Ratios* to *High School Drop-Out Rates.* Following these rankings are statewide *National Assessment of Educational Progress (NAEP)* results and data from *The New York State Report Card*—an overview of student performance by subject, including easy-to-read charts and graphs.

## 4. Ancestry and Ethnicity

This section provides a detailed look at the ancestral, Hispanic and racial makeup of New York's 200+ ethnic categories. Data is ranked three ways: 1) by number, based on all places regardless of population; 2) by percent, based on all places regardless of population; 3) by percent, based on places with populations of 50,000 or more. You will discover, for example, that Rochester has the greatest number of *Laotians* in the state (668), and that 13.5% of the population of Harbor Hills are of *Armenian* ancestry.

## 5. Climate

Each state chapter includes a State Summary, three colorful maps and profiles of both National and Cooperative Weather Stations. In addition, you'll find Weather Station Rankings with hundreds of interesting details, such as Boonville 2 SSW reporting the highest annual snowfall with 197.5 inches.

This section also includes Significant Storm Event data from January 2000 through December 2009. Here you will learn that a flash flood caused $250 million in property damage in Delaware County in June 2006 and that excessive heat was responsible for 42 deaths in Southeast New York State in August 2006.

Note: The extensive **User's Guide** that follows **About New York** is segmented into four sections and examines, in some detail, each data field in the individual profiles and comparative sections for all chapters. It provides sources for all data points and statistical definitions as necessary.

# About New York State

**Governor** . . . . . . . . . . . . . . . . **Andrew M. Cuomo**
**Lieutenant Governor** . . . . . . . . . . . . . **Bob Duffy**
**518-474-8390**

## STATE EMBLEMS

State Animal . . . . . . . . . . . . . . . . . . . . . . . . . . . . . . Beaver
State Beverage. . . . . . . . . . . . . . . . . . . . . . . . . . . . . . Milk
State Bird . . . . . . . . . . . . . . . . . . . . . . . . Eastern Bluebird
State Bush . . . . . . . . . . . . . . . . Lilac bush (syringa vulgaris)
State Fish (fresh water) . . . . . . . . . . . . . . . . . . . Brook Trout
State Fish (salt water) . . . . . . Striped bass (morone Saxatilis)
State Flower . . . . . . . . . . . . . . . . . . . . . . . . . . . . . . . Rose
State Fossil . . . . . . . . . . . . . . . . . . . . . . Eurypterus Remipes
State Fruit . . . . . . . . . . . . . . . . . . . . . . . . . . . . . . . Apple
State Gem. . . . . . . . . . . . . . . . . . . . . . . . . . . . . . Garnet
State Insect . . . . . . . . . . . Lady bug (coccinella novemnotata)
State Motto . . . . . . . . . . . . . . . . . . . Excelsior (Ever Upward)
State Muffin. . . . . . . . . . . . . . . . . . . . Apple (genus malus)
State Reptile . . Common snapping turtle (chelydra serpentina)
State Shell. . . . . . . . . . . . . Bay scallop (argopecten irradians)
State Tree . . . . . . . . . . . . . . . . . . . . . . . . . Sugar maple

## CONTENTS

Photo Gallery . . . . . . . . . . . . . . . . . . . . . . . . . . . . . . . . . . xi
Government. . . . . . . . . . . . . . . . . . . . . . . . . . . . . . . . . . xv
Land and Natural Resources . . . . . . . . . . . . . . . . . . . . . xxi
Demographics . . . . . . . . . . . . . . . . . . . . . . . . . . . . . xxxi

*The Montauk Point Light is a lighthouse at the easternmost point of the state of New York. It was the first lighthouse to be built in the state, and is the fourth oldest active lighthouse in the United States. It was first lit in 1797.*

*Niagara Falls forms the international border between the Canadian province of Ontario and the state of New York. It is made up of three drops: Horseshoe Falls, above, the most powerful waterfall in North America; American Falls; and Bridal Veil Falls. Combined, they form the highest flow rate of any waterfall in the world.*

*Agriculture is an important industry in New York. The farm pictured above is typical of the more than 34,000 working dairy farms in the northern region of the state.*

*Grand Central Terminal in New York City was built in 1871 and is the largest train station in the world, by number of platforms. This commuter rail terminal station has two levels, with restaurants and shopping throughout. GCT is reportedly the world's sixth most visited tourist attraction, with approximately 21,600,000 visitors annually.*

*The Statue of Liberty stands on Liberty Island in New York Harbor. It was presented as a gift to the United States from France in 1884. One of the most visited attractions in the world, visitor access to the statue closed in October, 2011 to install a secondary staircase and other safety features. It's scheduled to reopen in late 2012.*

*The world's ultimate skyscraper city, New York is located in the state's southeast corner. In the 20th century, eight New York City skyscrapers held the title of the world's tallest building.*

# Government

## Brief History

New York harbor was visited by Verrazano in 1524, and the Hudson River was first explored by Henry Hudson in 1609. The Dutch settled here permanently in 1624 and for 40 years they ruled over the colony of New Netherland. It was conquered by the English in 1664 and was then named New York in honor of the Duke of York.

Existing as a colony of Great Britain for over a century, New York declared its independence on July 9, 1776, becoming one of the original 13 states of the Federal Union. The next year, on April 20, 1777, New York's first constitution was adopted.

In many ways, New York State was the principal battleground of the Revolutionary War. The Battle of Saratoga was the turning point of the Revolution leading to the French alliance and eventual victory. New York City, long occupied by British troops, was evacuated on November 25, 1783 where, on December 4 at Fraunces Tavern, General George Washington bade farewell to his officers.

During the Revolutionary War, an election for the first governor took place and George Clinton was inaugurated as Governor at Kingston, July 30, 1777. New York City became the first capital of the new nation, where President George Washington was inaugurated on April 30, 1789. Albany became the capital of the State in January 1797.

In following years, New York's economic and industrial growth encouraged the title "The Empire State," an expression possibly originated by George Washington in 1784.

The Erie Canal, completed in 1825, greatly enhanced the importance of the port of New York and caused populous towns and cities to spring up across the state. The Erie Canal was replaced by the Barge Canal in 1918, and the system of waterways was further expanded by the construction of the St. Lawrence Seaway.

Overland transportation grew rapidly from a system of turnpikes established in the early 1880s to the modern day Governor Thomas E. Dewey New York State Thruway. By 1853, railroads crossed the state in systems like the Erie and New York Central.

Located in New York harbor, the Statue of Liberty was formally presented to the U.S. Minister to France, Levi Parsons on July 4, 1884 by Ferdinand Lesseps, representing the Franco-American Union. President Grover Cleveland dedicated the Statue of Liberty on October 28, 1886, when the last rivet was put into place. Its famous inscription, "Give me your tired, your poor, your huddled masses yearning to breathe free," was the first symbol of America's mission.

The international character of New York City, the principal port for overseas commerce, and later for transcontinental and international airways, has been further enhanced by becoming the home of the United Nations, capital of the free world. Here the people of all nations and races come to discuss and try to solve the world's problems in a free and democratic climate.

As one of the wealthiest states, New York made tremendous strides in industry and commerce. The New York Stock Exchange, founded in 1792, has become the center of world finance. New York City also became a leading national center for art, music and literature, as exemplified by the Metropolitan Museum of Art, The Metropolitan Opera Company, and large publishing houses.

# Organization

New York's state government contains three branches: legislative, judicial and executive.

## The Legislative Branch

The legislative branch consists of a bicameral (two chamber) Legislature—a 62 member Senate and 150 member Assembly that, together, represent the 18 million citizens of the State. All members are elected for two-year terms.

## The Judicial Branch

The judicial branch comprises a range of courts (from trial to appellate) with various jurisdictions (from village and town courts to the State's highest court—the Court of Appeals). The State assumes the cost for all but the town and village courts.

The Judiciary functions under a Unified Court System whose organization, administration and financing are prescribed by the State Constitution and the Unified Court Budget Act. The Unified Court System has responsibility for peacefully and fairly resolving civil claims, family disputes, and criminal accusations, as well as providing legal protection for children, mentally-ill persons and others entitled to special protections.

## The Executive Branch

The executive branch of New York State government consists of 20 departments—the maximum number allowed by the State Constitution. This limitation came about as a result of constitutional reforms from the 1920s that were designed to make State government more manageable by eliminating many of the independently elected executive officers and curbing the creation of new departments. The 20 departments are:

- **Agriculture and Markets:** Serves agricultural producers and the consuming public. Promotes agriculture through various industry and export development programs; enforces food safety laws.
- **Audit and Control:** Maintains the State's accounts; pays the State's payrolls and bills; invests State funds; audits State agencies and local governments; and administers the State employee retirement system.
- **Banking:** Primary regulator for State-licensed and State-chartered financial entities operating in New York, including: domestic banks, foreign agencies, branch and representative offices, savings institutions and trust companies, mortgage bankers and brokers, check cashers and money transmitters. Ensures the safe and sound conduct of these businesses, maintains public confidence in the banking system and protects the public interest as well as the interests of depositors, creditors and shareholders.
- **Civil Service:** The central personnel agency for the Executive branch of State government. Provides the State of New York with a trained workforce; administers health, dental and insurance programs covering State employees and retirees as well as some local government employees; and provides technical services to the State's 102 municipal service agencies, covering approximately 392,000 local government employees.
- **Correctional Services:** Operates facilities for the custody and rehabilitation of inmates.
- **Economic Development:** Creates jobs and encourages economic prosperity by providing technical and financial assistance to businesses.
- **Education:** Supervises all educational institutions in the State, operates certain educational and cultural institutions, certifies teachers and certifies/licenses 44 other professions.
- **Environmental Conservation:** Administers programs designed to protect and improve the State's natural resources.
- **Executive:** Since the 1920s constitutional reforms, numerous agencies have been created within the Executive Department to accommodate various governmental functions. These include the Division of Veterans' Affairs (which advises veterans on services, benefits and entitlements, and administers payments of bonuses and annuities to blind veterans) and the Office of General Services (which provides centralized data processing, construction, maintenance and design services as well as printing, transportation and communication systems).

- **Family Assistance:** Promotes greater self-sufficiency by providing support services for needy families and adults that lead to self-reliance.
- **Health:** Protects and promotes the health of New Yorkers through enforcement of public health and related laws, and assurance of quality health care delivery.
- **Insurance:** Supervises and regulates all insurance business in New York State. Issues licenses to agents, brokers and consultants; conducts examinations of insurers; reviews complaints from policyholders; and approves corporate formations, mergers and consolidations.
- **Labor:** Helps New York work by preparing individuals for jobs; administering unemployment insurance, disability benefits and workers' compensation; and ensuring workplace safety.
- **Law:** Protects the rights of New Yorkers; represents the State in legal matters; and prosecutes violations of State law.
- **Mental Hygiene:** Provides services for individuals suffering from mental illness, developmental disabilities and/or substance abuse.
- **Motor Vehicles:** Registers vehicles, licenses drivers and promotes highway safety.
- **Public Service:** Ensures that all New Yorkers have access to reliable and low-cost utility services by promoting competition and reliability in utility services.
- **State:** Known as the keeper of records, the Department of State issues business licenses, enforces building codes, provides technical assistance to local governments and administers fire prevention and control services.
- **Taxation and Finance:** Collects taxes and administers the State's tax laws.
- **Transportation:** Coordinates and assists in the development and operation of highway, railroad, mass transit, port, waterway and aviation facilities.

## Elected Officers and Appointed Officials

Only four statewide government officers are directly elected:

- The Governor, who heads the Executive Department, and Lieutenant Governor (who are elected on a joint ballot).
- The State Comptroller, who heads the Department of Audit and Control.
- The Attorney General, who heads the Department of Law.

With a few exceptions, the Governor appoints the heads of all State departments and agencies of the executive branch. The exceptions include:

- The Commissioner of the State Education Department, who is appointed by and serves at the pleasure of the State Board of Regents.
- The Chancellor of the State University of New York, who is appointed by a Board of Trustees.
- The Chancellor of the City University of New York, who is appointed by a Board of Trustees.

## Local Governments

Geographically, New York State is divided into 62 counties (five of which are boroughs of New York City). Within these counties are 62 cities (including New York City), 932 towns, 555 villages and 697 school districts (including New York City). In addition to counties, cities, towns and villages, "special districts" meet local needs for fire and police protection, sewer and water systems or other services.

Local governments are granted the power to adopt local laws that are not inconsistent with the provisions of the State Constitution or other general law. The Legislature, in turn, may not pass any law that affects only one locality unless the governing body of that locality has first approved the bill—referred to as a home rule request—or unless a State interest exists.

*Source: New York State Division of the Budget, June 2012*

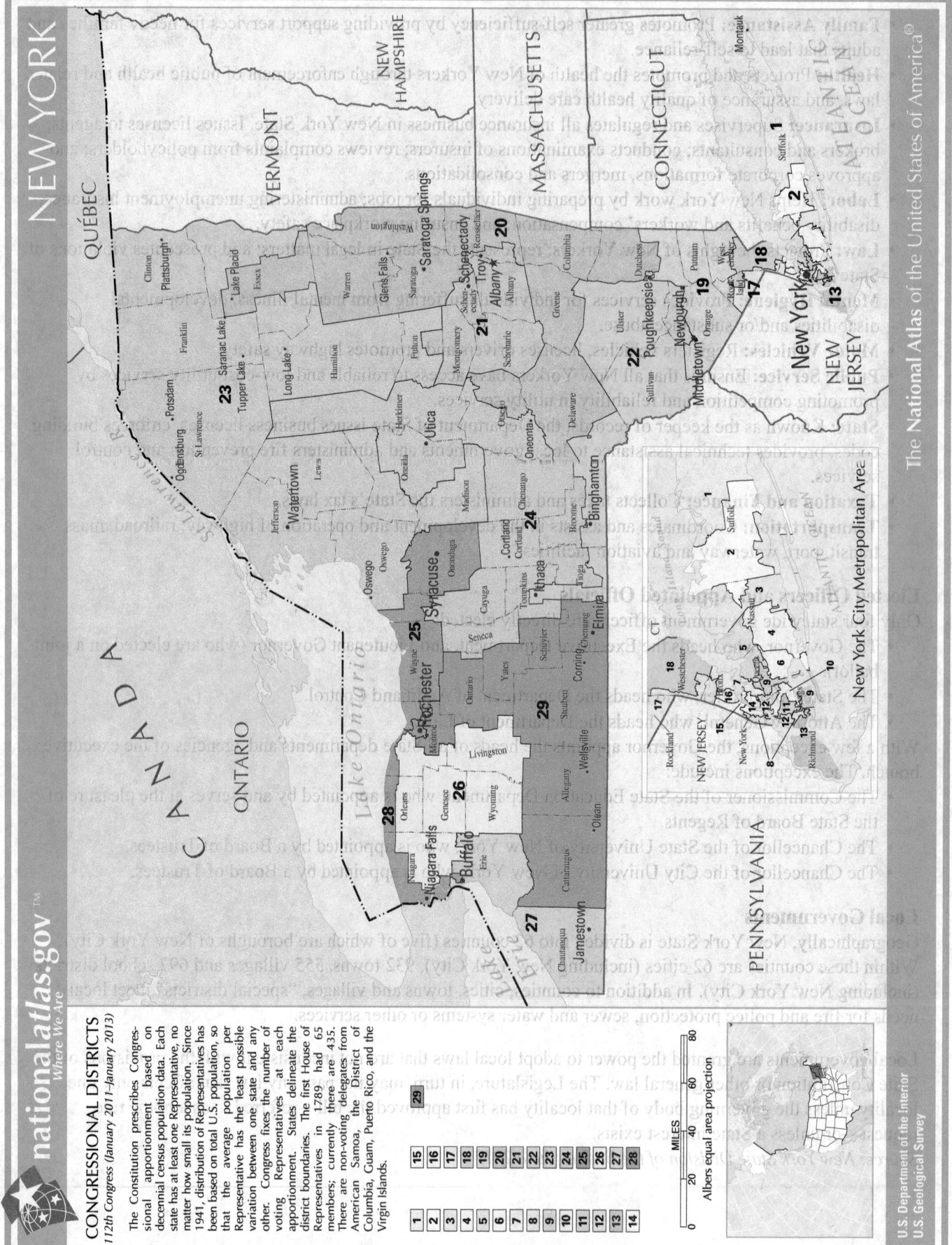

CONGRESSIONAL DISTRICTS
112th Congress (January 2011–January 2013)

The Constitution prescribes Congressional apportionment based on decennial census population data. Each state has at least one Representative, no matter how small its population. Since 1941, distribution of Representatives has been based on total U.S. population, so that the average population per Representative has the least possible variation between one state and any other. Congress fixes the number of voting Representatives at each apportionment. States delineate the district boundaries. The first House of Representatives in 1789 had 65 members; currently there are 435. There are non-voting delegates from American Samoa, the District of Columbia, Guam, Puerto Rico, and the Virgin Islands.

MILES

0    20    40    60    80

Albers equal area projection

NEW YORK

The National Atlas of the United States of America®

New York City Metropolitan Area

U.S. Department of the Interior
U.S. Geological Survey

## Percent of Population Who Voted for Barack Obama in 2008

**Legend (%)**
- 60.0 and Over
- 55.0 to 59.9
- 50.0 to 54.9
- 45.0 to 49.9
- 40.0 to 44.9
- Under 40.0

# Land and Natural Resources

| Topic | Value | Time Period |
|---|---|---|
| Total Surface Area (acres) | 31,360,800 | 2007 |
| Land | 30,070,900 | 2007 |
| Federal Land | 205,300 | 2007 |
| Owned | 164,132 | FY 2009 |
| Leased | 2,378 | FY 2009 |
| Otherwise Managed | 2,482 | FY 2009 |
| National Forest | 16,000 | September 2006 |
| National Wilderness | 1,380 | October 2011 |
| Non-Federal Land, Developed | 3,793,900 | 2007 |
| Non-Federal Land, Rural | 26,071,700 | 2007 |
| Water | 1,289,900 | 2007 |
| | | |
| National Natural Landmarks | 27 | December 2010 |
| National Historic Landmarks | 261 | December 2010 |
| National Register of Historic Places | 5,318 | December 2010 |
| National Parks | 22 | December 2010 |
| Visitors to National Parks | 17,506,355 | 2010 |
| Historic Places Documented by the National Park Service | 1,931 | December 2010 |
| Archeological Sites in National Parks | 266 | December 2010 |
| Threatened and Endangered Species in National Parks | 14 | December 2010 |
| Economic Benefit from National Park Tourism (dollars) | 340,054,000 | 2009 |
| | | |
| Conservation Reserve Program (acres) | 51,654 | October 2011 |
| Land and Water Conservation Fund Grants (dollars) | 232,947,093 | Since 1965 |
| Historic Preservation Grants (dollars) | 60,761,211 | 2010 |
| Community Conservation and Recreation Projects | 80 | Since 1987 |
| Federal Acres Transferred for Local Parks and Recreation | 5,952 | Since 1948 |
| | | |
| Crude Petroleum Production (millions of barrels) | Not Available | 2010 |
| Crude Oil Proved Reserves (millions of barrels) | Not Available | 2009 |
| Natural Gas Reserves (billions of cubic feet) | 196 | 2009 |
| Natural Gas Liquid Reserves (millions of barrels) | Not Available | 2008 |
| Natural Gas Marketed Production (billions of cubic feet) | 45 | 2009 |
| Coal Reserves (millions of short tons) | Not Available | 2009 |

**Sources:** *U.S. Department of the Interior, National Park Service, State Profiles, December 2010; United States Department of Agriculture, Natural Resources Conservation Service, 2007 National Resources Inventory; U.S. General Services Administration, Federal Real Property Council, FY 2009 Federal Real Property Report, September 2010; University of Montana, www.wilderness.net; U.S. Department of Agriculture, Farm Services Agency, Conservation Reserve Program, October 2011; U.S Census Bureau, 2012 Statistical Abstract of the United States*

# New York Energy Overview and Analysis

## Quick Facts

- The New York Harbor area between New York and New Jersey has a petroleum bulk terminal storage capacity of over 75 million barrels, making it the largest petroleum product hub in the Northeast.
- New York produces more hydroelectric power than any other State east of the Rocky Mountains.
- The 2,353-megawatt Robert Moses Niagara plant, harnessing power from the Niagara River, is one of the largest hydroelectric facilities in the world.
- Per capita energy consumption in New York is among the lowest in the Nation due in part to its widely used mass transportation systems.
- During the Northeast Blackout of August 2003, almost the entire State lost power and all four of New York's nuclear plants were shut down.
- A proposed pipeline could transport up to 10 million gallons of ethanol per day from production facilities in the Midwest to terminals in the Northeast, including New York Harbor.

## Analysis

### Resources and Consumption

New York has minor reserves of oil and conventional natural gas, found primarily in the far western part of the State near Lake Erie. The Marcellus shale formation, which contains unconventional shale gas, extends into the lower portion of the State.

Although New York's fossil fuel resources are limited, the State possesses considerable renewable energy potential. Several powerful rivers, including the Niagara and the Hudson, provide New York with some of the greatest hydropower resources in the Nation, and New York's Catskill and Adirondack mountains offer substantial wind power potential. In addition, parts of New York are densely forested, allowing for potential fuelwood harvesting.

Although New York's total energy consumption is among the highest in the United States, energy intensity and per capita energy consumption are among the lowest, due in part to the region's widely used mass transportation systems. The commercial and residential sectors lead State energy demand, while the transportation sector is also a major consumer.

### Petroleum

New York's petroleum products are supplied by refineries located in New Jersey and Pennsylvania, the Colonial Pipeline system from the Gulf Coast, and foreign imports that principally originate in Canada, the Caribbean, South America, North Africa, and Europe. Located in both New York and New Jersey, the New York Harbor area has a petroleum bulk terminal storage capacity of over 75 million barrels, making it the largest and most important petroleum product hub in the high-demand Northeast.

New York Harbor acts as a central distribution center for the region, and many of the petroleum products delivered to the Harbor are redistributed to smaller ports where they supply local demand. In particular, the Hudson River, which meets the Atlantic Ocean in New York Harbor, provides a major inland water route for petroleum product barges supplying eastern New York and parts of western New England. On the other side of the State, western New York product markets are primarily supplied from Canada at the Port of Buffalo, and via the Buckeye and Sunoco pipeline systems from Pennsylvania and the Midwest. The TEPPCO pipeline system from the Gulf Coast delivers mostly propane to upstate markets.

As in many northeastern urban areas, New York City and the surrounding metropolitan areas require reformulated gasoline blended with ethanol, and the New York Harbor area is the primary Northeast distribution hub for ethanol supplies. Ports located on the New Jersey side of New York Harbor receive ethanol rail shipments from the Midwest and marine imports from Brazil and the Caribbean, and then redistribute these supplies to markets throughout the Northeast. Another large ethanol storage facility serving the Northeast is located in Albany, New York. A proposed pipeline would transport up to 10 million gallons of ethanol per day from production facilities in Iowa, Illinois, Minnesota, and South Dakota to terminals in Pittsburgh, Philadelphia, and the New York Harbor.

New York, along with much of the Northeast, is vulnerable to distillate fuel oil shortages and price spikes during the winter months due to high demand for home heating. One-third of New York households use fuel oil as their primary energy source for home heating. In January and February 2000, distillate fuel oil prices in the Northeast rose sharply when extreme winter weather increased demand unexpectedly and hindered the arrival of new supply, as frozen rivers and high winds slowed the docking and unloading of barges and tankers. In July 2000, in order to reduce the risk of future shortages, the President directed the U.S. Department of Energy to establish the Northeast Heating Oil Reserve. The Reserve gives Northeast consumers adequate supplies for about 10 days, the time required for ships to carry heating oil from the Gulf of Mexico to New York Harbor. The Reserve's storage terminals are located at Perth Amboy, New Jersey, and Groton and New Haven, Connecticut.

### Natural Gas

Although western New York produces a small amount of natural gas, the vast majority of New York's natural gas supply is brought in via pipeline from other States and Canada. The Transcontinental and Tennessee Gas Transmission pipelines from the Gulf Coast and the Iroquois pipeline from Canada link up with local gas distribution networks that supply the New York City metropolitan area and Long Island. Numerous other gas transmission systems branch in from Pennsylvania and Canada to feed other parts of the State.

New York has moderate natural gas storage capacity, developed principally from depleted natural gas fields in the Appalachian Basin in western New York. These storage sites, along with those in Pennsylvania, Ohio, and West Virginia, are important for supplying the Northeast region, particularly during the peak demand winter season. New York's residential, commercial, and electric power sectors all consume large amounts of natural gas. To meet New York and Connecticut's growing demand for natural gas, particularly for electric power generation, an offshore liquefied natural gas (LNG) import terminal with a capacity of 2 billion cubic feet per day has been proposed in Federal waters on the Outer Continental Shelf south of Long Island, 25 miles away from New York Harbor.

## Coal, Electricity, and Renewables

Unlike many States, New York does not rely heavily on any one fuel for electricity generation. Nuclear power from New York's four nuclear plants and natural gas are the leading generation fuels, each typically accounting for about three-tenths of State generation. Hydroelectricity, coal, and petroleum each account for a substantial share of the power generated in the State, as well. New York also imports electricity from neighboring States and Canada.

The average New York household consumes about one-half the electricity of the average U.S. household, largely because few use electricity as their primary energy source for home heating and because demand for air-conditioning is low during the typically mild summer months.

Various failures led to major electricity outages affecting New York in 1965, 1977, and 2003. The August 2003 blackout was the most severe blackout in North American history, affecting an estimated 55 million people in the U.S. Northeast and eastern Canada. For safety reasons, nuclear power plants are required by Federal law to shut down if back-up power systems fail, and all four of New York's nuclear power plants were forced offline. As a result, almost the entire State lost power during the incident.

New York is a major hydroelectric power producer, and its hydroelectric generation is the highest of any State east of the Rocky Mountains. When New York's Robert Moses Niagara plant opened near the Niagara River in 1961, it was the largest hydroelectric generation facility in the world. Today, the 2,353-megawatt power plant is still New York's largest electricity generator. Nonhydroelectric renewable energy sources contribute only minimally to the State's power grid, although New York is one of the Nation's top generators of electricity from municipal solid waste and landfill gas. As of 2008, New York ranked among the top 10 States in photovoltaic solar power capacity and had become a substantial producer of wind energy by doubling its wind energy capacity between 2006 and 2008. In September 2004, the New York Public Service Commission adopted a renewable portfolio standard requiring 24 percent of the State's electricity to be generated from renewable sources by 2013.

*Source: U.S. Energy Information Administration, October 2009*

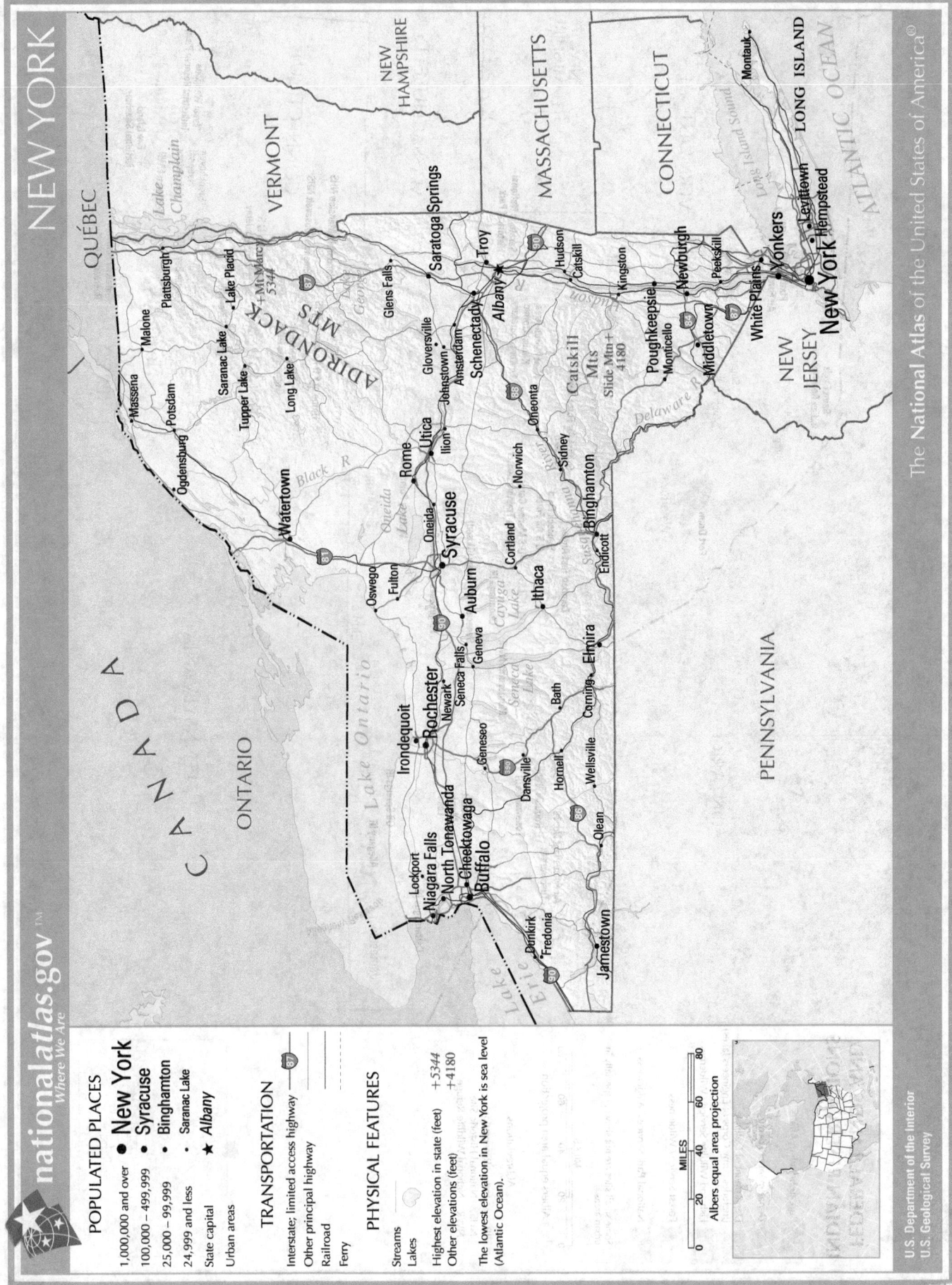

NEW YORK

POPULATED PLACES

● New York    1,000,000 and over
● Syracuse    100,000 – 499,999
● Binghamton    25,000 – 99,999
· Saranac Lake    24,999 and less
★ Albany    State capital
Urban areas

TRANSPORTATION

Interstate; limited access highway    —87—
Other principal highway
Railroad
Ferry

PHYSICAL FEATURES

Streams
Lakes

Highest elevation in state (feet)    +5344
Other elevations (feet)    +4180

The lowest elevation in New York is sea level (Atlantic Ocean).

MILES
0    20    40    60    80
Albers equal area projection

QUÉBEC
VERMONT
NEW HAMPSHIRE
MASSACHUSETTS
CONNECTICUT
LONG ISLAND
ATLANTIC OCEAN
NEW JERSEY
PENNSYLVANIA
CANADA
ONTARIO

Lake Champlain
Lake Ontario
Lake Erie

ADIRONDACK MTS
+Mt Marcy 5344

Catskill Mts
Slide Mtn +4180

Long Island Sound

Plattsburgh
Malone
Massena
Potsdam
Ogdensburg
Saranac Lake
Lake Placid
Tupper Lake
Long Lake
Watertown
Black R
Oneida Lake
Rome
Utica
Ilion
Oneida
Oswego
Fulton
Syracuse
Auburn
Cortland
Ithaca
Geneva
Seneca Falls
Newark
Rochester
Irondequoit
Geneseo
Dansville
Hornell
Wellsville
Olean
Jamestown
Fredonia
Dunkirk
Buffalo
Cheektowaga
North Tonawanda
Niagara Falls
Lockport
Bath
Corning
Elmira
Endicott
Binghamton
Sidney
Norwich
Oneonta
Johnstown
Amsterdam
Gloversville
Schenectady
Saratoga Springs
Glens Falls
Troy
Albany
Hudson
Catskill
Kingston
Poughkeepsie
Monticello
Middletown
Newburgh
Peekskill
White Plains
Yonkers
New York
Levittown
Hempstead
Montauk

Genesee River
Mohawk River
Susquehanna R
Delaware R
Hudson R
Cayuga Lake
Seneca Lake

The National Atlas of the United States of America®

U.S. Department of the Interior
U.S. Geological Survey

NEW YORK

QUÉBEC

VERMONT

NEW HAMPSHIRE

MASSACHUSETTS

CONNECTICUT

CANADA

ONTARIO

PENNSYLVANIA

NEW JERSEY

LONG ISLAND

ATLANTIC OCEAN

Lake Champlain

Lake Ontario

Lake Erie

St. Lawrence R.

Hudson

Delaware R.

Allegheny Reservoir

Plattsburgh
Plattsburgh Air Force Base (Closed)
Lake Placid
Saranac Lake
Tupper Lake
Long Lake
Potsdam
Ogdensburg
Saint Regis Indian Reservation

Saratoga Springs
Saratoga National Historical Park
Glens Falls
Troy
Albany ★
Schenectady
West Milton Area Knolls Atomic Power Laboratory

Griffiss Air Force Base (Closed)
Utica
Oneonta

Fort Drum
Watertown
Oswego

Camden Test Annex
Hancock Field U S Air Force
U S Marine Corps Reserve Training Center
Syracuse
Onondaga IR
Seneca Army Depot (Closed)
Cortland
Finger Lakes National Forest
Ithaca
Whitney Point Lake
Binghamton
Elmira
Corning

Rochester
Montezuma NWR

Iroquois NWR
Tonawanda IR
Mount Morris Lake
Oil Springs IR
Wellsville

Air Force Plant No. 38
Tuscarora IR
Niagara Falls
Buffalo
Cattaraugus IR
Allegany IR
Olean
Jamestown

Vanderbilt Mansion NHS
Eleanor Roosevelt NHS
Newburgh
West Point U S Military Academy
Home of F D Roosevelt NHS
Poughkeepsie
Shawangunk Grasslands NWR
Middletown
Wallkill River NWR
White Plains
Oyster Bay NWR
New York

Montauk
Naval Weapons Industrial Reserve Plant
Brookhaven National Laboratory
Wertheim NWR
Fire Island National Seashore
Levittown
Gateway National Recreation Area

The National Atlas of the United States of America®

nationalatlas.gov™
Where We Are

U.S. Department of the Interior
U.S. Geological Survey

## FEDERAL LANDS AND INDIAN RESERVATIONS

Bureau of Indian Affairs

Department of Energy

Department of Defense (includes Army Corps of Engineers lakes)

Fish and Wildlife Service / Wilderness

Forest Service / Wilderness

National Park Service / Wilderness

Some small sites are not shown, especially in urban areas.

MILES
0    20    40    60    80

Albers equal area projection

Abbreviations

IR    Indian Reservation
NHS   National Historic Site
NWR   National Wildlife Refuge

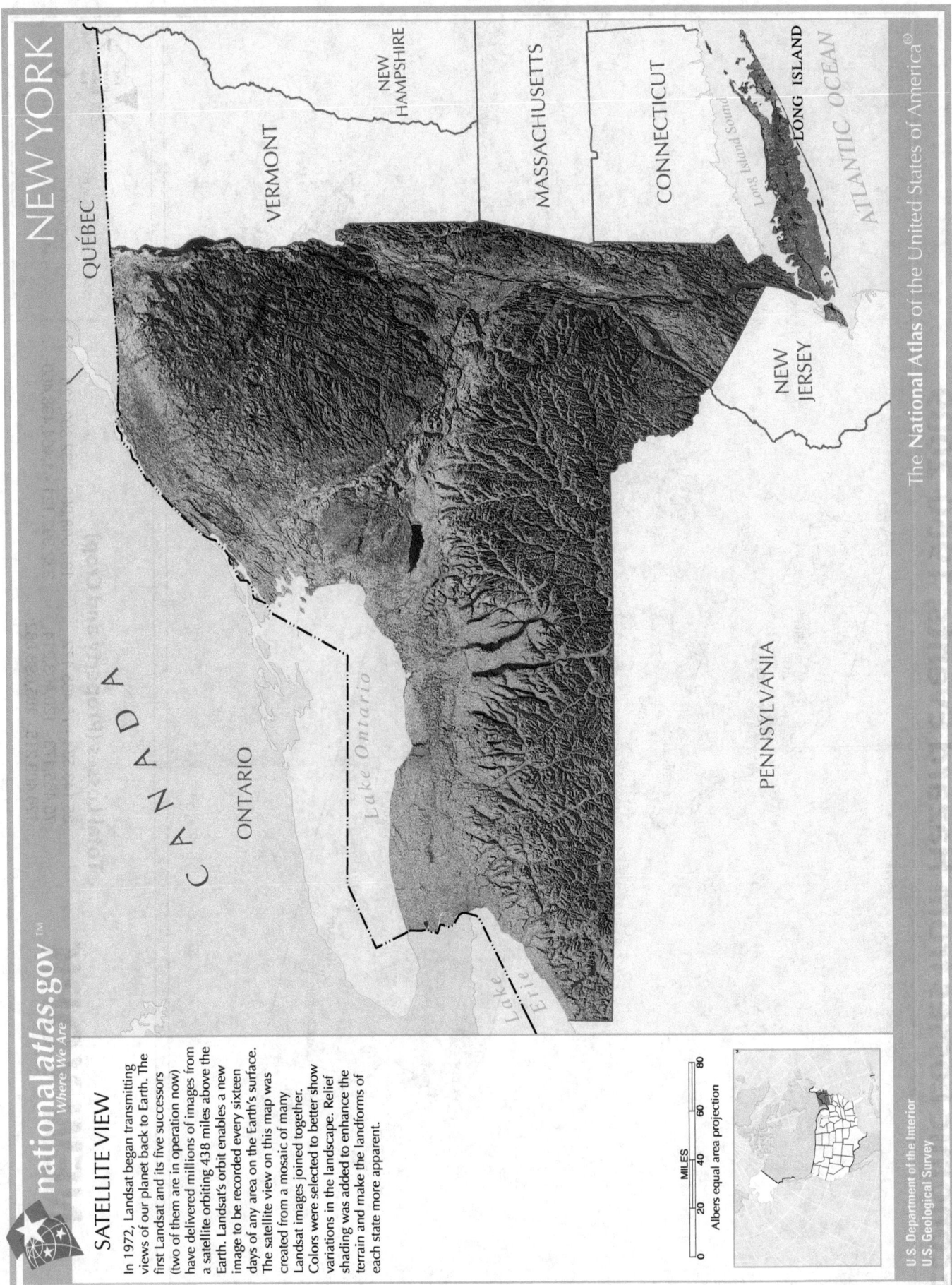

# NEW YORK

### SATELLITE VIEW

In 1972, Landsat began transmitting views of our planet back to Earth. The first Landsat and its five successors (two of them are in operation now) have delivered millions of images from a satellite orbiting 438 miles above the Earth. Landsat's orbit enables a new image to be recorded every sixteen days of any area on the Earth's surface. The satellite view on this map was created from a mosaic of many Landsat images joined together. Colors were selected to better show variations in the landscape. Relief shading was added to enhance the terrain and make the landforms of each state more apparent.

nationalatlas.gov ™
*Where We Are*

MILES
0    20    40    60    80
Albers equal area projection

The **National Atlas** of the United States of America®

U.S. Department of the Interior
U.S. Geological Survey

CANADA

QUÉBEC

ONTARIO

Lake Ontario

Lake Erie

VERMONT

NEW HAMPSHIRE

MASSACHUSETTS

CONNECTICUT

LONG ISLAND

Long Island Sound

ATLANTIC OCEAN

NEW JERSEY

PENNSYLVANIA

# Economic Losses from Hazard Events, 1960-2009

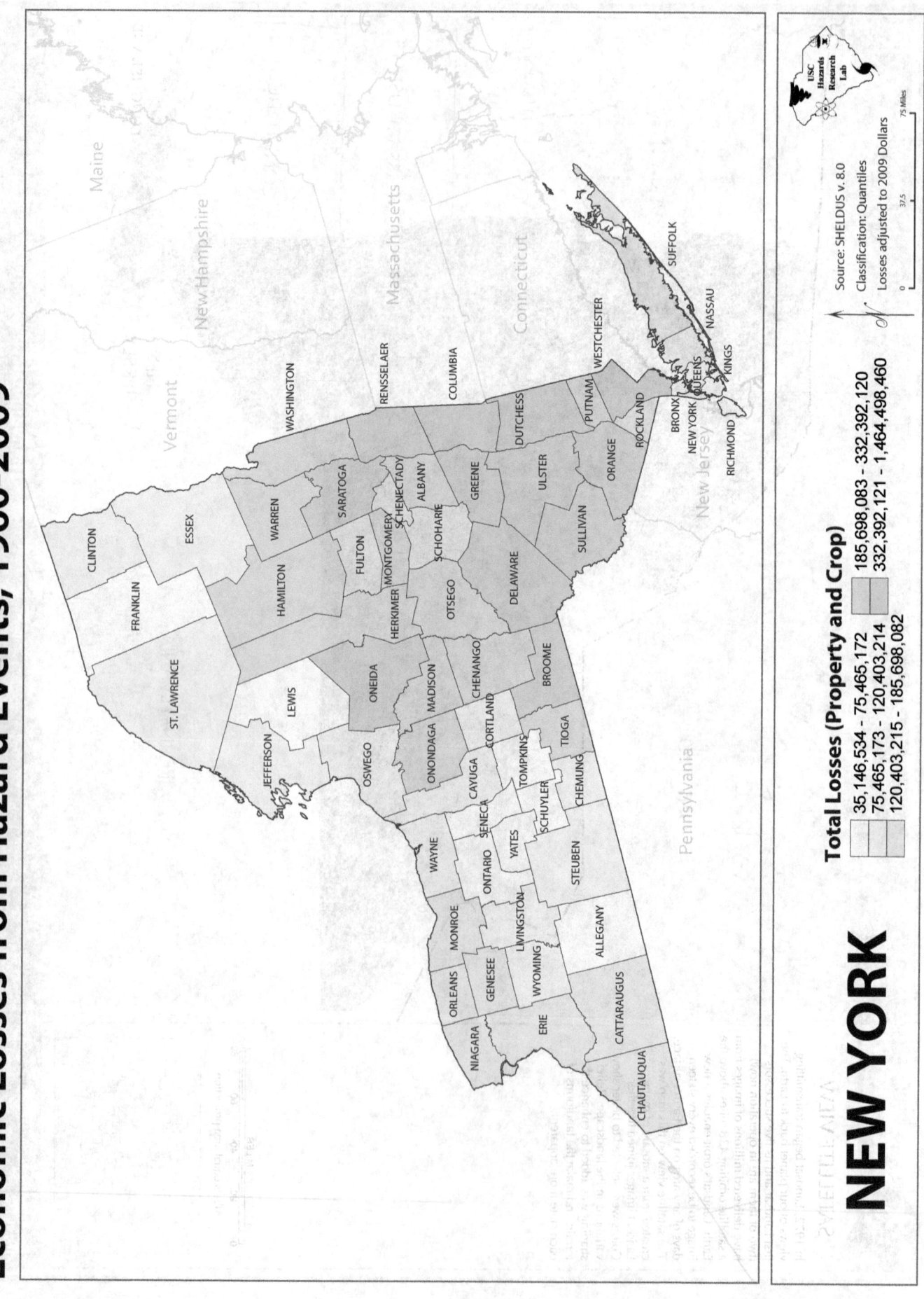

## NEW YORK

### Total Losses (Property and Crop)

| | |
|---|---|
| 35,146,534 - 75,465,172 | 185,698,083 - 332,392,120 |
| 75,465,173 - 120,403,214 | 332,392,121 - 1,464,498,460 |
| 120,403,215 - 185,698,082 | |

Source: SHELDUS v. 8.0
Classification: Quantiles
Losses adjusted to 2009 Dollars

USC Hazards Research Lab

0      37.5      75 Miles

# NEW YORK
## Hazard Losses, 1960-2009

### Distribution of Hazard Events
(number of events)

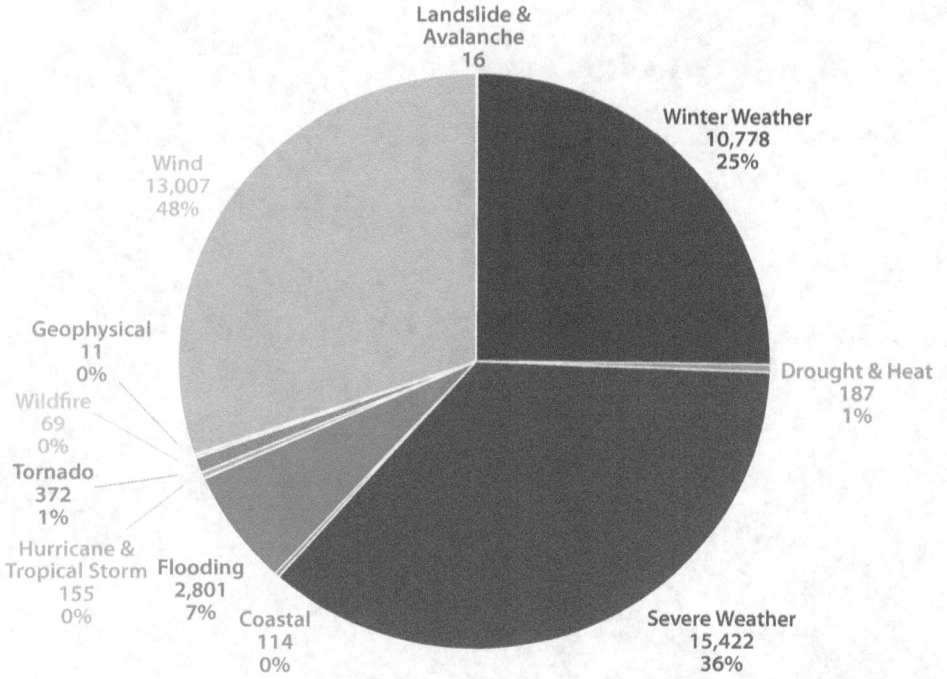

Landslide & Avalanche
16

Winter Weather
10,778
25%

Wind
13,007
48%

Drought & Heat
187
1%

Geophysical
11
0%

Wildfire
69
0%

Tornado
372
1%

Hurricane & Tropical Storm
155
0%

Flooding
2,801
7%

Coastal
114
0%

Severe Weather
15,422
36%

### Distribution of Losses by Hazard Type
(in 2009 USD million)

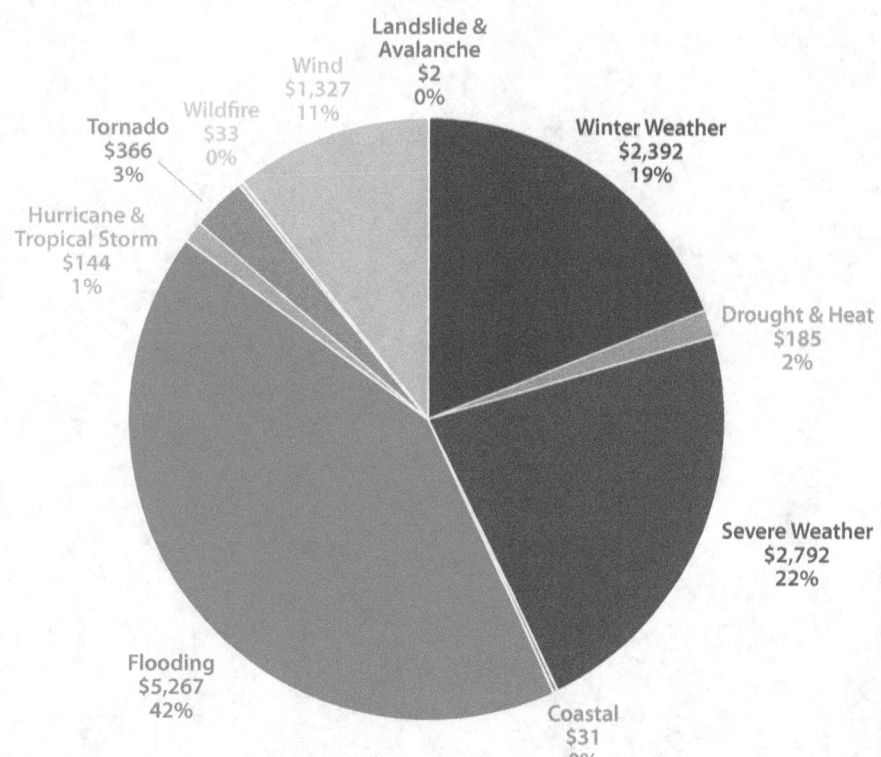

Landslide & Avalanche
$2
0%

Wind
$1,327
11%

Wildfire
$33
0%

Tornado
$366
3%

Winter Weather
$2,392
19%

Hurricane & Tropical Storm
$144
1%

Drought & Heat
$185
2%

Severe Weather
$2,792
22%

Flooding
$5,267
42%

Coastal
$31
0%

# Demographic Maps

## Population (2010)

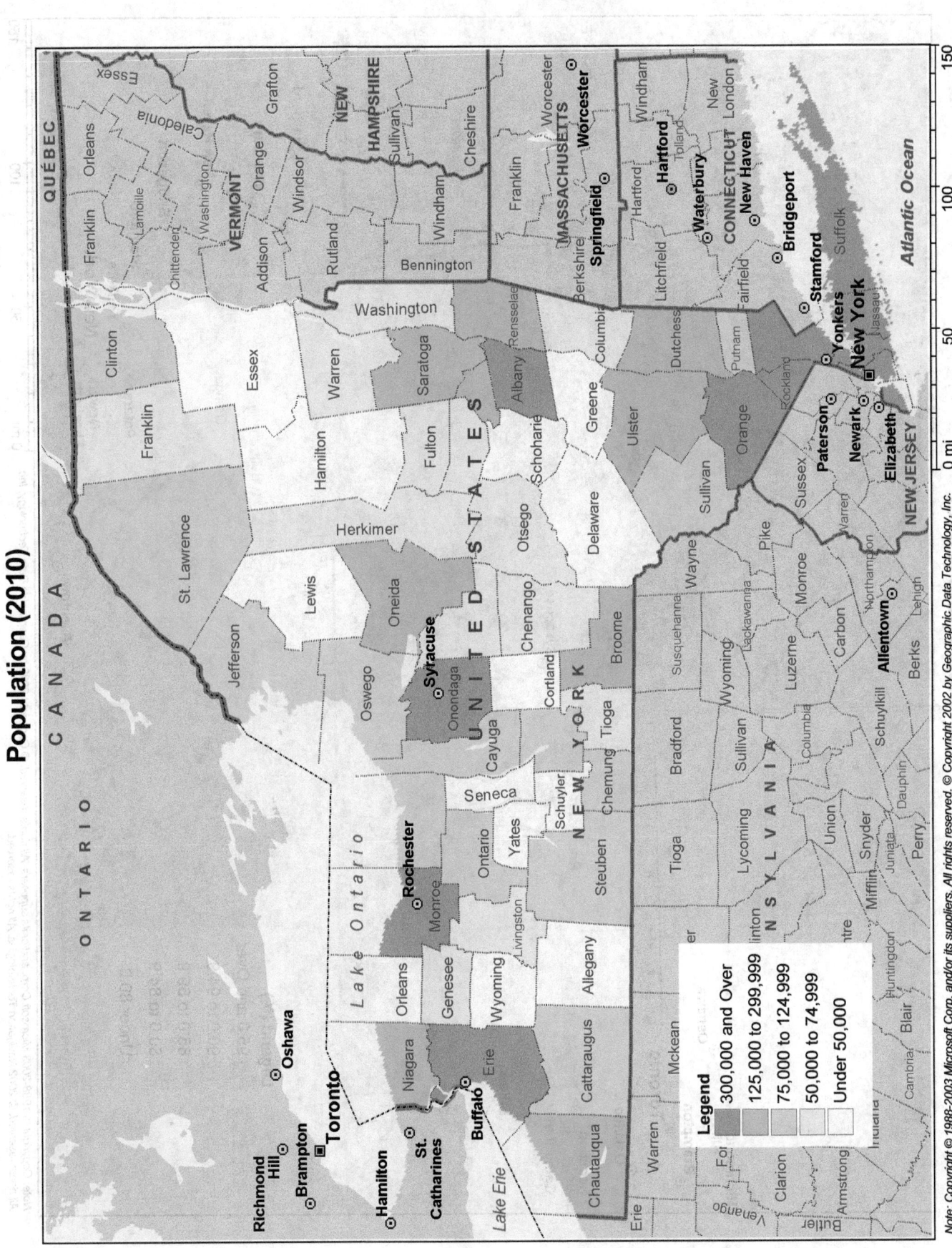

**Legend**
- 300,000 and Over
- 125,000 to 299,999
- 75,000 to 124,999
- 50,000 to 74,999
- Under 50,000

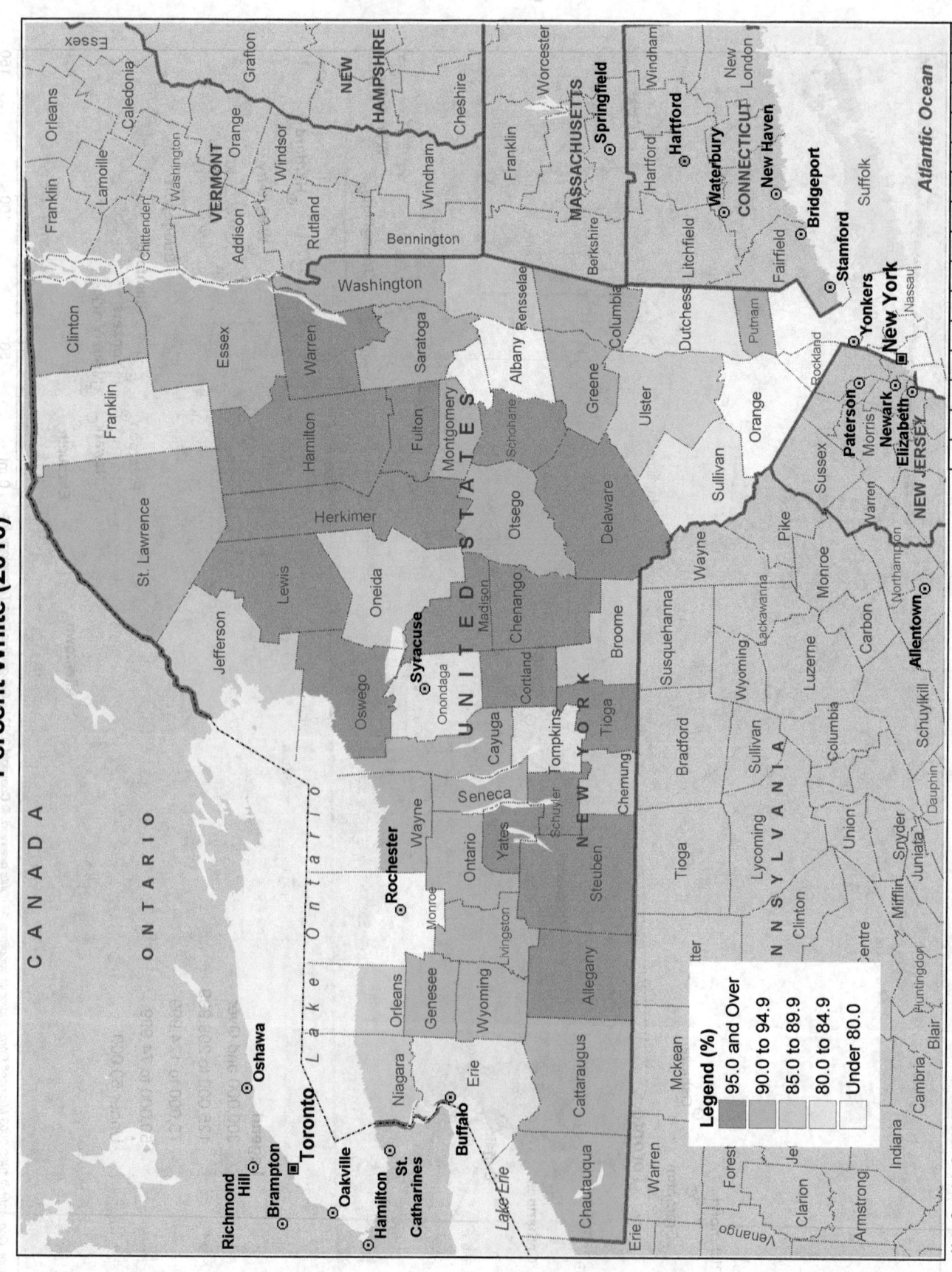

Percent White (2010)

Legend (%)

95.0 and Over
90.0 to 94.9
85.0 to 89.9
80.0 to 84.9
Under 80.0

# Percent Black (2010)

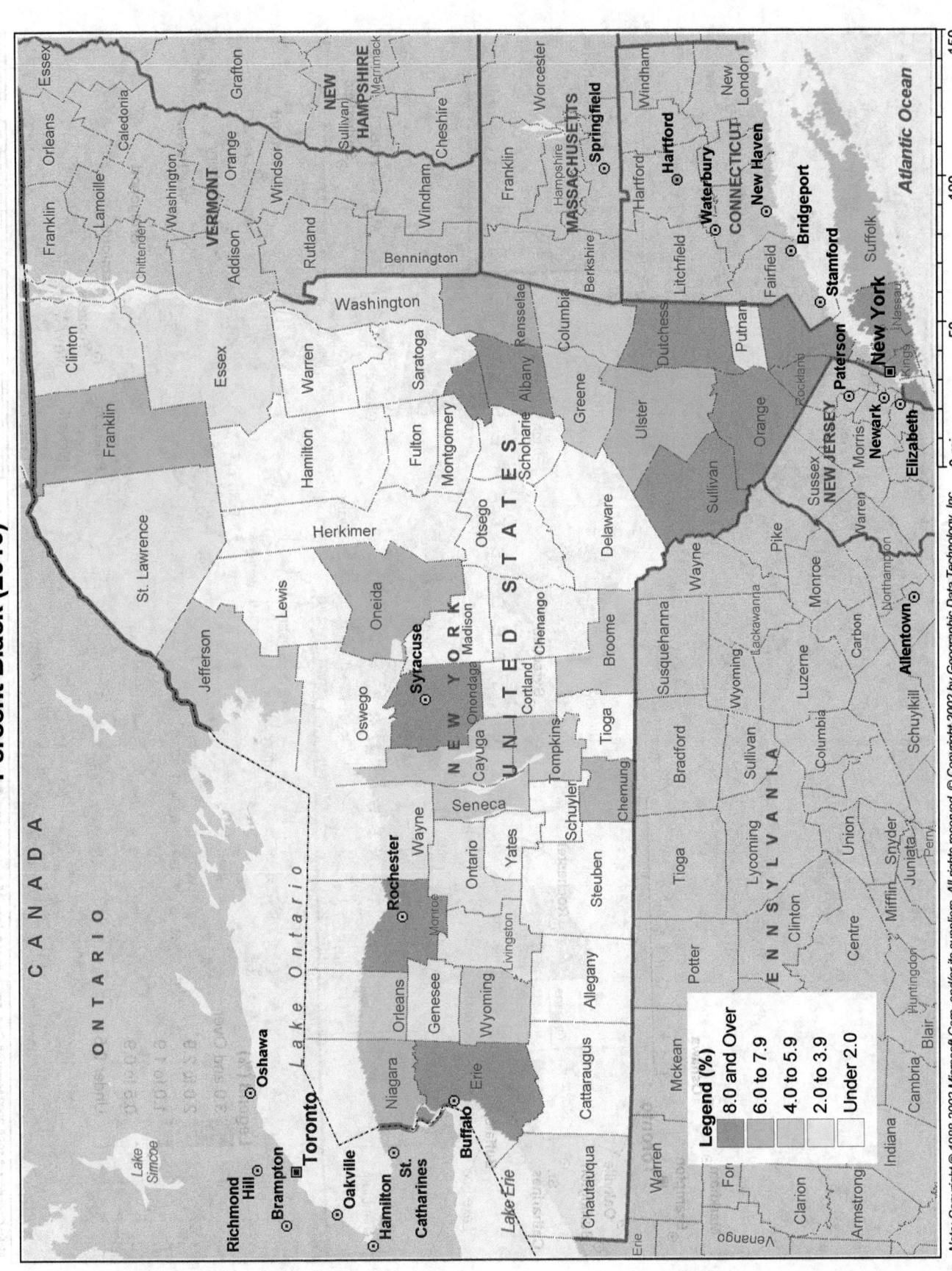

Legend (%)
- 8.0 and Over
- 6.0 to 7.9
- 4.0 to 5.9
- 2.0 to 3.9
- Under 2.0

# Percent Asian (2010)

**Legend (%)**

- 3.0 and Over
- 2.0 to 2.9
- 1.0 to 1.9
- 0.5 to 0.9
- Under 0.5

## Percent Hispanic (2010)

**Legend (%)**

- 8.0 and Over
- 6.0 to 7.9
- 4.0 to 5.9
- 2.0 to 3.9
- Under 2.0

# Median Age (2010)

**Legend (years)**

- 41.0 and Over
- 40.0 to 40.9
- 39.0 to 39.9
- 38.0 to 38.9
- Under 38.0

## Median Household Income (2010)

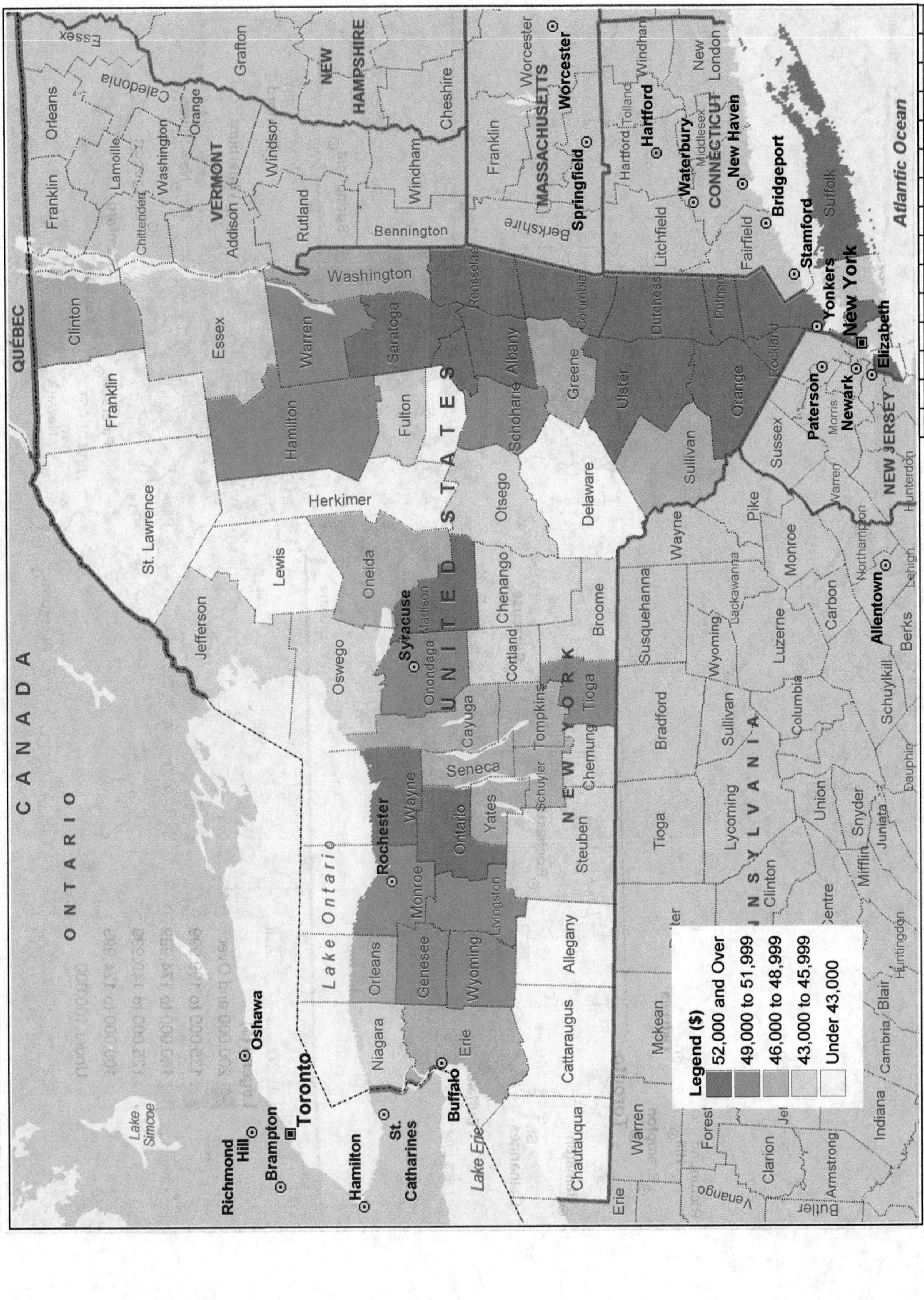

**Legend ($)**

- 52,000 and Over
- 49,000 to 51,999
- 46,000 to 48,999
- 43,000 to 45,999
- Under 43,000

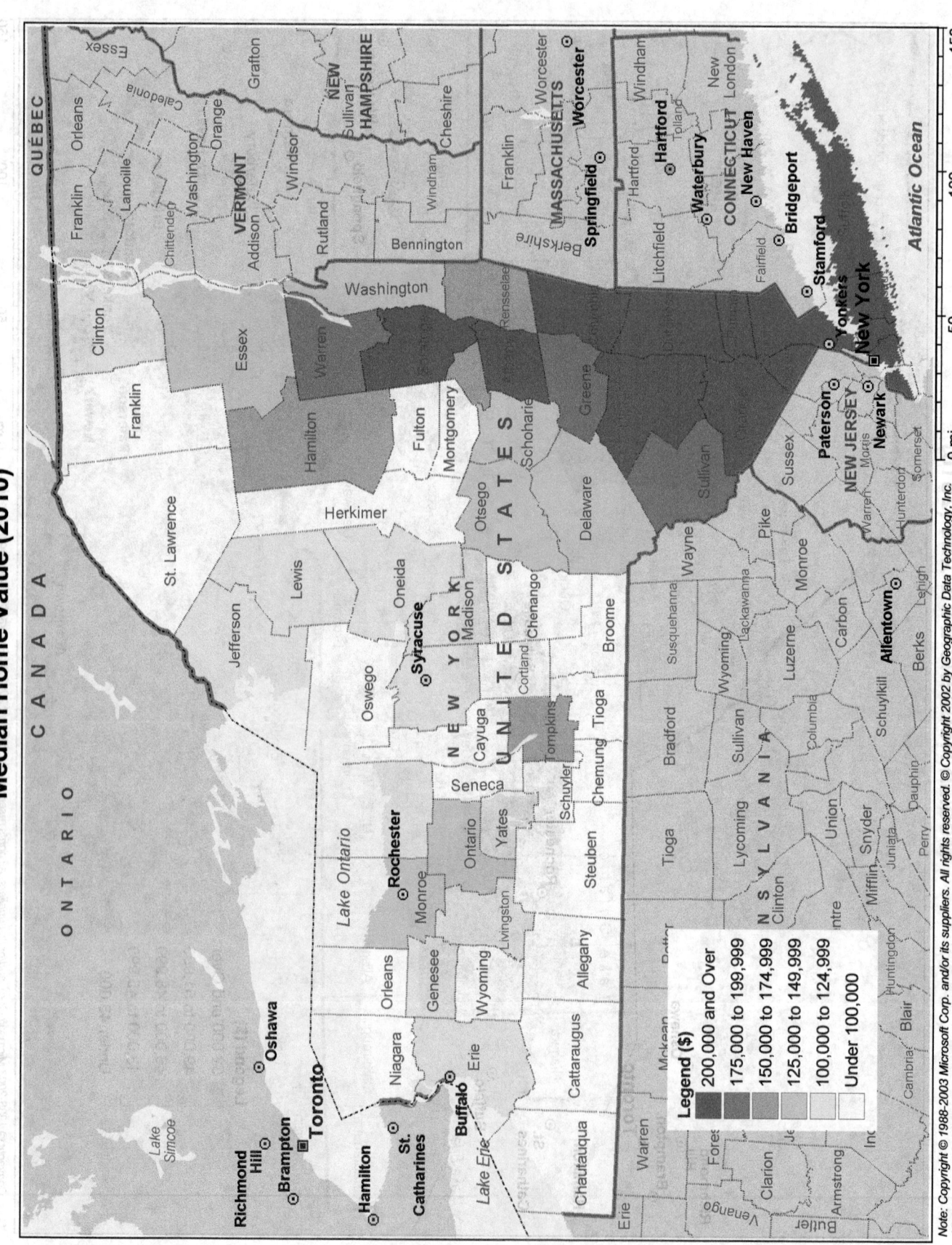

Median Home Value (2010)

Legend ($)

200,000 and Over
175,000 to 199,999
150,000 to 174,999
125,000 to 149,999
100,000 to 124,999
Under 100,000

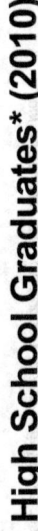

# High School Graduates* (2010)

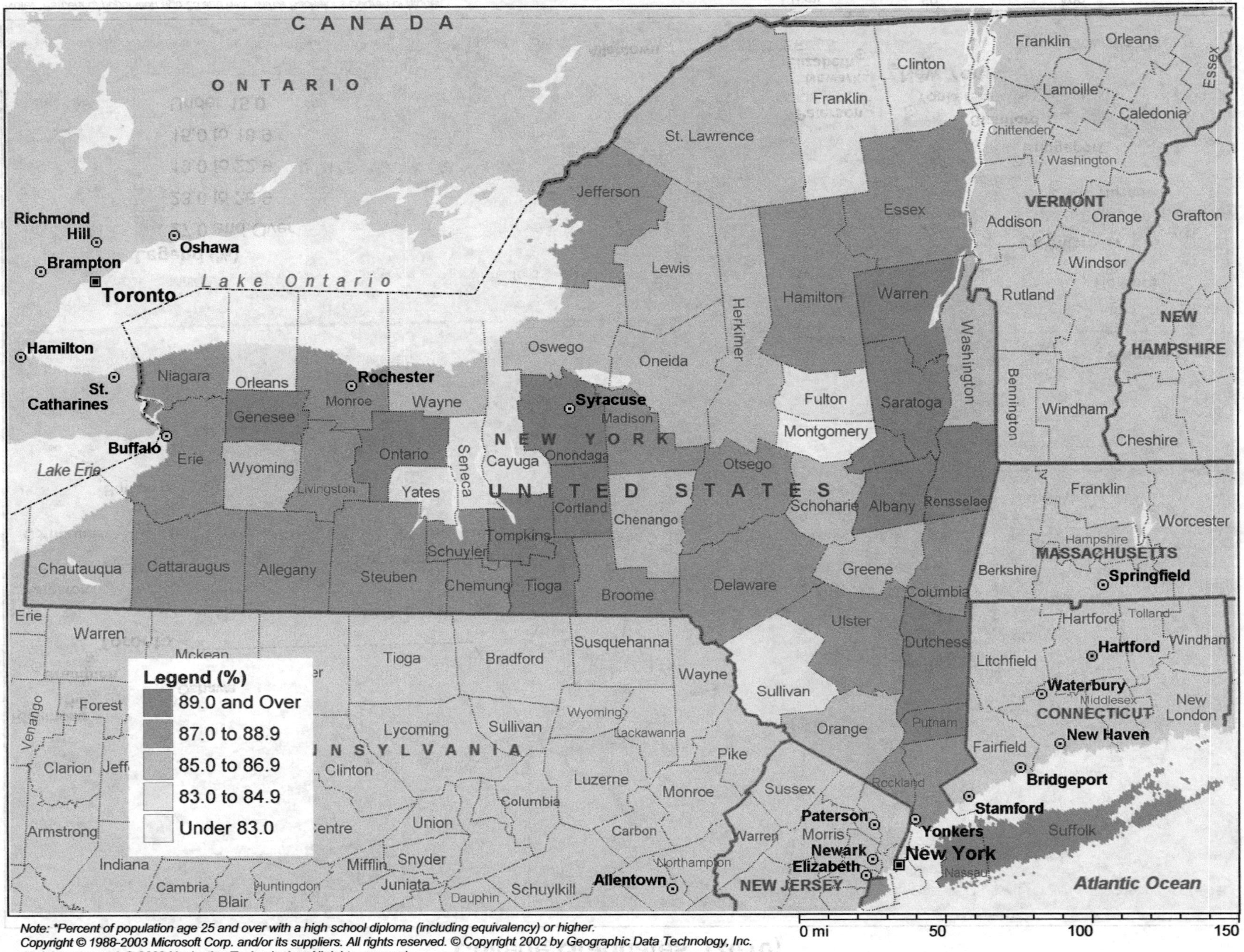

**Legend (%)**
- 89.0 and Over
- 87.0 to 88.9
- 85.0 to 86.9
- 83.0 to 84.9
- Under 83.0

## College Graduates* (2010)

**Legend (%)**

- 27.0 and Over
- 23.0 to 26.9
- 19.0 to 22.9
- 15.0 to 18.9
- Under 15.0

CANADA

ONTARIO

Richmond Hill

Brampton

Toronto

Oshawa

Hamilton

St. Catharines

Buffalo

Lake Simcoe

Lake Ontario

Lake Erie

Niagara

Erie

Chautauqua

Cattaraugus

Allegany

Steuben

Wyoming

Genesee

Orleans

Monroe

Wayne

Ontario

Yates

Seneca

Livingston

Rochester

VERMONT

NEW HAMPSHIRE

Essex

Caledonia

Orleans

Franklin

Lamoille

Washington

Grafton

Orange

Windsor

Chittenden

Addison

Rutland

Windsor

Sullivan

Cheshire

Bennington

Windham

Clinton

Franklin

Essex

Warren

Washington

Saratoga

Hamilton

Herkimer

Fulton

Montgomery

St. Lawrence

Jefferson

Lewis

Oswego

Oneida

Madison

Onondaga

Cayuga

Syracuse

Cortland

Tompkins

Chemung

Schuyler

Tioga

Chenango

Otsego

Schoharie

Albany

Rensselaer

Columbia

Greene

Delaware

Broome

NEW YORK

UNITED STATES

PENNSYLVANIA

McKean

Forest

Clarion

Venango

Warren

Cameron

Clinton

Centre

Tioga

Bradford

Sullivan

Lycoming

Union

Snyder

Mifflin

Juniata

Huntingdon

Blair

Cambria

Indiana

Jeff

Dauphin

Schuylkill

Northumberland

Susquehanna

Wayne

Pike

Wyoming

Lackawanna

Luzerne

Monroe

Carbon

Allentown

Northampton

NEW JERSEY

Sussex

Warren

Morris

Paterson

Newark

Elizabeth

MASSACHUSETTS

Franklin

Hampshire

Berkshire

Springfield

Hartford

Litchfield

Hartford

CONNECTICUT

Waterbury

New Haven

Windham

New London

Fairfield

Bridgeport

Stamford

New York

Yonkers

Rockland

Putnam

Dutchess

Ulster

Sullivan

Orange

Rockland

Nassau

Suffolk

Atlantic Ocean

0 mi          50          100          150

# NEW YORK - Core Based Statistical Areas and Counties

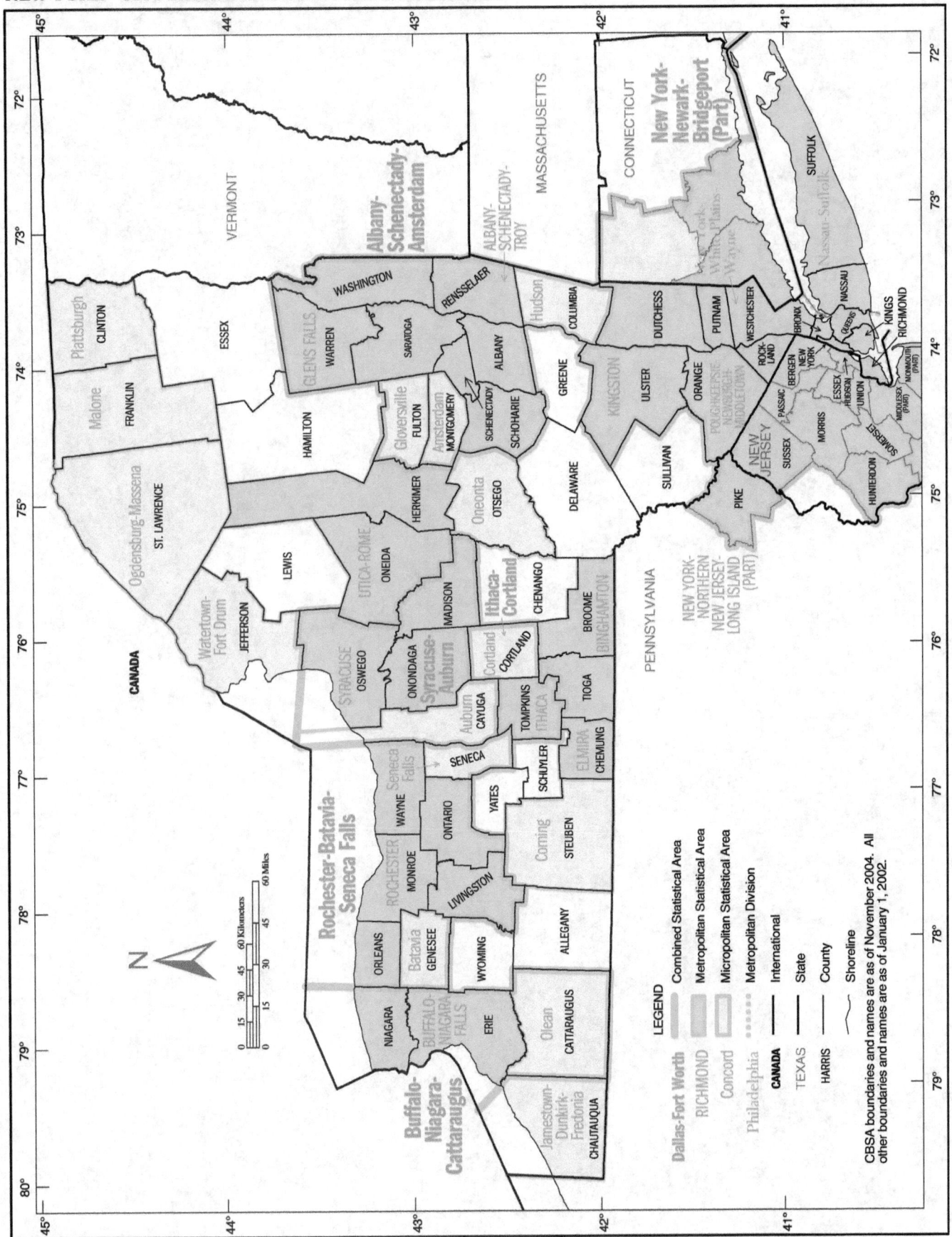

**NEW YORK - Core Based Statistical Areas and Counties**

U.S. DEPARTMENT OF COMMERCE Economics and Statistics Administration, U.S. Census Bureau

# User's Guide: Profiles

## Places Covered

**All 62 counties.**

**614 incorporated municipalities.** Municipalities are incorporated as either cities or villages.

**936 minor civil divisions** (towns and reservations in New York) for the states where the Census Bureau has determined that they serve as general-purpose governments. Those states are Connecticut, Maine, Massachusetts, Michigan, Minnesota, New Hampshire, New Jersey, New York, Pennsylvania, Rhode Island, Vermont, and Wisconsin. In some states incorporated municipalities are part of minor civil divisions and in some states they are independent of them.

**568 census designated places (CDP).** The U.S. Bureau of the Census defines a CDP as "a statistical entity, defined for each decennial census according to Census Bureau guidelines, comprising a densely settled concentration of population that is not within an incorporated place, but is locally identified by a name. CDPs are delineated cooperatively by state and local officials and the Census Bureau, following Census Bureau guidelines. Beginning with Census 2000 there are no size limits."

**476 unincorporated communities.** The communities included have statistics for their ZIP Code Tabulation Area (ZCTA) available from the Census Bureau. They are referred to as "postal areas." A ZCTA is a statistical entity developed by the Census Bureau to approximate the delivery area for a US Postal Service 5-digit or 3-digit ZIP Code in the US and Puerto Rico. A ZCTA is an aggregation of census blocks that have the same predominant ZIP Code associated with the mailing addresses in the Census Bureau's Master Address File. Thus, the Postal Service's delivery areas have been adjusted to encompass whole census blocks so that the Census Bureau can tabulate census data for the ZCTAs. ZCTAs do not include all ZIP Codes used for mail delivery and therefore do not precisely depict the area within which mail deliveries associated with that ZIP Code occur. Additionally, some areas that are known by a unique name, although they are part of a larger incorporated place, are also included as "postal areas."

**Eight communities** have mixed designations such as town/cdp or town/village.

For a more in-depth discussion of geographic areas, please refer to the Census Bureau's Geographic Areas Reference Manual at http://www.census.gov/geo/www/garm.html.

### Important Notes

- *Profiles of New York State* uses the term "community" to refer to all places except counties. The term "county" is used to refer to counties and county-equivalents. All places are defined as of the 2010 Census.

- Several states, including New York, have incorporated municipalities and minor civil divisions in the same county with the same name. Those communities are given separate entries (e.g. Adams, New York, in Jefferson County will be listed under both the village and town of Adams).

- The city of New York (composed of five coextensive counties/boroughs) has a unique format. Statistical information for the individual counties/boroughs can be found within the New York City entry. The five counties/boroughs are: Bronx County and Borough, Kings County and Brooklyn Borough, New York County and Manhattan Borough, Queens County and Borough, and Richmond County and Staten Island Borough.

- In each community profile, only school districts that have schools that are physically located within the community are shown. In addition, statistics for each school district cover the entire district, regardless of the physical location of the schools within the district.

- Special care should be taken when interpreting certain statistics for communities containing large colleges or universities. College students were counted as residents of the area in which they were living while attending college (as they have been since the 1950 census). One effect this may have is skewing the figures for population, income, housing, and educational attainment.

- Some information (e.g. unemployment rates) is available for both counties and individual communities. Other information is available for just counties (e.g. election results), or just individual communities (e.g. local newspapers).

- Some statistical information is available only for larger communities. In addition, the larger places are more apt to have services such as newspapers, airports, school districts, etc.

- For the most complete information on any community, you should also check the entry for the county in which the community is located. In addition, more information and services will be listed under the larger places in the county.

# Information for Incorporated Communities and Census Designated Places

## PHYSICAL CHARACTERISTICS

**Place Type:** Lists the type of place (city, town, village, borough, special city, CDP, township, plantation, gore, district, grant, location, reservation, or postal area). *Source: U.S. Census Bureau, Census 2010 and U.S. Postal Service, City State File.*

**Land and Water Area:** Land and water area in square miles. *Source: U.S. Census Bureau, Census 2010.*

**Latitude and Longitude:** Latitude and longitude in degrees. *Source: U.S. Census Bureau, Census 2010.*

**Elevation:** Elevation in feet. *Source: U.S. Geological Survey, Geographic Names Information System (GNIS).*

## HISTORY

**History:** Historical information. *Source: Columbia University Press, The Columbia Gazetteer of North America; Original research.*

## POPULATION

**Population:** 1990, 2000 and 2010 figures are a 100% count of population. *Source: U.S. Census Bureau, Census 2010.*

**Race/Hispanic Origin:** Figures are from Census 2010 and include the U.S. Census Bureau categories of White alone; Black alone; Asian alone; American Indian/Alaska Native alone; Native Hawaiian/Other Pacific Islander alone; Hispanic of any race. Alone refers to the fact that these figures are not in combination with any other race.

The concept of race, as used by the Census Bureau, reflects self-identification by people according to the race or races with which they most closely identify. These categories are socio-political constructs and should not be interpreted as being scientific or anthropological in nature. Furthermore, the race categories include both racial and national-origin groups.

- **African American or Black:** A person having origins in any of the Black racial groups of Africa. It includes people who indicated their race(s) as "Black, African Am., or Negro" or reported entries such as African American, Kenyan, Nigerian, or Haitian.

- **American Indian or Alaska Native:** A person having origins in any of the original peoples of North and South America (including Central America) and who maintains tribal affiliation or community attachment. This category includes people who indicated their race(s) as "American Indian or Alaska Native" or reported their enrolled or principal tribe, such as Navajo, Blackfeet, Inupiat, Yup'ik, or Central American Indian groups or South American Indian groups.

- **Asian:** A person having origins in any of the original peoples of the Far East, Southeast Asia, or the Indian subcontinent, including, for example, Cambodia, China, India, Japan, Korea, Malaysia, Pakistan, the Philippine Islands, Thailand, and Vietnam. It includes people who indicated their race(s) as "Asian" or reported entries such as "Asian Indian," "Chinese," "Filipino," "Korean," "Japanese," "Vietnamese," and "Other Asian" or provided other detailed Asian responses.

- **Native Hawaiian or Other Pacific Islander:** A person having origins in any of the original peoples of Hawaii, Guam, Samoa, or other Pacific Islands. It includes people who indicated their race(s) as "Pacific Islander" or reported entries such as "Native Hawaiian," "Guamanian or Chamorro," "Samoan," and "Other Pacific Islander" or provided other detailed Pacific Islander responses.

- **White:** A person having origins in any of the original peoples of Europe, the Middle East, or North Africa. It includes people who indicated their race(s) as "White" or reported entries such as Irish, German, Italian, Lebanese, Arab, Moroccan, or Caucasian.

- **Hispanic:** The data on the Hispanic or Latino population were derived from answers to a question that was asked of all people. The terms "Spanish," "Hispanic origin," and "Latino" are used interchangeably. Some respondents identify with all three terms while others may identify with only one of these three specific terms. Hispanics or Latinos who identify with the terms "Spanish," "Hispanic," or "Latino" are those who classify themselves in one of the specific Spanish, Hispanic, or Latino categories listed on the questionnaire ("Mexican," "Puerto Rican," or "Cuban") as well as those who indicate that they are "other Spanish/Hispanic/Latino." People who do not identify with one of the specific origins listed on the questionnaire but indicate that they are "other Spanish/Hispanic/Latino" are those whose origins are from Spain, the Spanish-speaking countries of Central or South America, the Dominican Republic, or people identifying themselves generally as Spanish, Spanish-American, Hispanic, Hispano, Latino, and so on. All write-in responses to the "other Spanish/Hispanic/Latino" category were coded. Origin can be viewed as the heritage, nationality group, lineage, or country of birth of the person or the person's parents or ancestors before their arrival in the United States. People who identify their origin as Spanish, Hispanic, or Latino may be of any race.

**Population Density:** Total population divided by the land area in square miles. *Source: U.S. Census Bureau, Census 2010.*

**Average Household Size:** Number of persons in the average household. *Source: U.S. Census Bureau, Census 2010.*

**Median Age:** Median age of the population. *Source: U.S. Census Bureau, Census 2010.*

**Male/Female Ratio:** Number of males per 100 females. *Source: U.S. Census Bureau, Census 2010.*

**Marital Status:** Percentage of population never married, now married, widowed, or divorced. *Source: U.S. Census Bureau, American Community Survey, 2006-2010 Five-Year Estimates.*

The marital status classification refers to the status at the time of enumeration. Data on marital status are tabulated only for the population 15 years old and over. Each person was asked whether they were "Now married," "Widowed," "Divorced," or "Never married." Couples who live together (for example, people in common-law marriages) were able to report the marital status they considered to be the most appropriate.

- **Never married.** Never married includes all people who have never been married, including people whose only marriage(s) was annulled.
- **Now married.** All people whose current marriage has not ended by widowhood or divorce. This category includes people defined as "separated."
- **Widowed.** This category includes widows and widowers who have not remarried.
- **Divorced.** This category includes people who are legally divorced and who have not remarried.

**Foreign Born:** Percentage of population who were not U.S. citizens at birth. Foreign-born people are those who indicated they were either a U.S. citizen by naturalization or they were not a citizen of the United States. *Source: U.S. Census Bureau, American Community Survey, 2006-2010 Five-Year Estimates.*

**Ancestry:** Largest ancestry groups reported (up to five). The data includes persons who report multiple ancestries. For example, if a person reported being Irish and Italian, they would be included in both categories. Thus, the sum of the percentages may be greater than 100%. *Source: U.S. Census Bureau, American Community Survey, 2006-2010 Five-Year Estimates.*

The data represent self-classification by people according to the ancestry group or groups with which they most closely identify. Ancestry refers to a person's ethnic origin or descent, "roots," heritage, or the place of birth of the person, the person's parents, or their ancestors before their arrival in the United States. Some ethnic identities, such as Egyptian or Polish, can be traced to geographic areas outside the United States, while other ethnicities such as Pennsylvania German or Cajun evolved in the United States.

The ancestry question was intended to provide data for groups that were not included in the Hispanic origin and race questions. Therefore, although data on all groups are collected, the ancestry data shown in these tabulations are for non-Hispanic and non-race groups. *See* Race/Hispanic Origin for information on Hispanic and race groups.

## ECONOMY

**Unemployment Rate:** Unemployment rate as of February 2012. Includes all civilians age 16 or over who were unemployed and looking for work. *Source: U.S. Department of Labor, Bureau of Labor Statistics, Local Area Unemployment Statistics.*

**Total Civilian Labor Force:** Total civilian labor force as of February 2012. Includes all civilians age 16 or over who were either employed, or unemployed and looking for work. *Source: U.S. Department of Labor, Bureau of Labor Statistics, Local Area Unemployment Statistics.*

**Single-Family Building Permits Issued:** Building permits issued for new single-family housing units in 2011. *Source: U.S. Census Bureau, Manufacturing and Construction Division.*

**Multi-Family Building Permits Issued:** Building permits issued for new multi-family housing units in 2011. *Source: U.S. Census Bureau, Manufacturing and Construction Division.*

Statistics on housing units authorized by building permits include housing units issued in local permit-issuing jurisdictions by a building or zoning permit. Not all areas of the country require a building or zoning permit. The statistics only represent those areas that do require a permit. Current surveys indicate that construction is undertaken for all but a very small percentage of housing units authorized by building permits. A major portion typically get under way during the month of permit issuance and most of the remainder begin within the three following months. Because of this lag, the housing unit authorization statistics do not represent the number of units actually put into construction for the period shown, and should therefore not be directly interpreted as "housing starts."

Statistics are based upon reports submitted by local building permit officials in response to a mail survey. They are obtained using Form C-404 const/www/c404.pdf, "Report of New Privately-Owned Residential Building or Zoning Permits Issued." When a report is not received, missing data are either (1) obtained from the Survey of Use of Permits (SUP) which is used to collect information on housing starts, or (2) imputed based on the assumption that the ratio of current month authorizations to those of a year ago should be the same for reporting and non-reporting places.

**Employment by Occupation:** Percentage of the employed civilian population 16 years and over in management, professional, service, sales, farming, construction, and production occupations. *Source: U.S. Census Bureau, American Community Survey, 2006-2010 Five-Year Estimates.*

- **Management** includes management, business, and financial operations occupations:
    Management occupations, except farmers and farm managers
    Farmers and farm managers
    Business and financial operations occupations:
        Business operations specialists
        Financial specialists

- **Professional** includes professional and related occupations:
    Computer and mathematical occupations
    Architecture and engineering occupations:
        Architects, surveyors, cartographers, and engineers
        Drafters, engineering, and mapping technicians
    Life, physical, and social science occupations
    Community and social services occupations
    Legal occupations
    Education, training, and library occupations
    Arts, design, entertainment, sports, and media occupations
    Healthcare practitioners and technical occupations:
        Health diagnosing and treating practitioners and technical occupations
        Health technologists and technicians

- **Service** occupations include:
    Healthcare support occupations
    Protective service occupations:
        Fire fighting, prevention, and law enforcement workers, including supervisors
        Other protective service workers, including supervisors
    Food preparation and serving related occupations
    Building and grounds cleaning and maintenance occupations
    Personal care and service occupations

- **Sales** and office occupations include:
    Sales and related occupations
    Office and administrative support occupations

- **Farming,** fishing, and forestry occupations

- **Construction,** extraction, and maintenance occupations include:

Construction and extraction occupations:
    Supervisors, construction, and extraction workers
    Construction trades workers
    Extraction workers
Installation, maintenance, and repair occupations

- **Production,** transportation, and material moving occupations include:
    Production occupations
    Transportation and material moving occupations:
        Supervisors, transportation, and material moving workers
        Aircraft and traffic control occupations
        Motor vehicle operators
        Rail, water, and other transportation occupations
        Material moving workers

## INCOME

**Per Capita Income:** Per capita income is the mean income computed for every man, woman, and child in a particular group. It is derived by dividing the total income of a particular group by the total population in that group. Per capita income is rounded to the nearest whole dollar. *Source: U.S. Census Bureau, American Community Survey, 2006-2010 Five-Year Estimates.*

**Median Household Income:** Includes the income of the householder and all other individuals 15 years old and over in the household, whether they are related to the householder or not. The median divides the income distribution into two equal parts: one-half of the cases falling below the median income and one-half above the median. For households, the median income is based on the distribution of the total number of households including those with no income. Median income for households is computed on the basis of a standard distribution and is rounded to the nearest whole dollar. *Source: U.S. Census Bureau, American Community Survey, 2006-2010 Five-Year Estimates.*

**Average Household Income:** Average household income is obtained by dividing total household income by the total number of households. *Source: U.S. Census Bureau, American Community Survey, 2006-2010 Five-Year Estimates.*

**Percent of Households with Income of $100,000 or more:** Percent of households with income of $100,000 or more. *Source: U.S. Census Bureau, American Community Survey, 2006-2010 Five-Year Estimates.*

**Poverty Rate:** Percentage of population with income below the poverty level. Based on individuals for whom poverty status is determined. Poverty status was determined for all people except institutionalized people, people in military group quarters, people in college dormitories, and unrelated individuals under 15 years old. *Source: U.S. Census Bureau, American Community Survey, 2006-2010 Five-Year Estimates.*

## TAXES

**Total City Taxes Per Capita:** Total city taxes collected divided by the population of the city. *Source: U.S. Census Bureau, State and Local Government Finances, 2009.*

Taxes include:

- Property Taxes
- Sales and Gross Receipts Taxes
- Federal Customs Duties
- General Sales and Gross Receipts Taxes
- Selective Sales Taxes (alcoholic beverages; amusements; insurance premiums; motor fuels; pari-mutuels; public utilities; tobacco products; other)
- License Taxes (alcoholic beverages; amusements; corporations in general; hunting and fishing; motor vehicles motor vehicle operators; public utilities; occupation and business, NEC; other)
- Income Taxes (individual income; corporation net income; other)
- Death and Gift
- Documentary & Stock Transfer
- Severance
- Taxes, NEC

**Total City Property Taxes Per Capita:** Total city property taxes collected divided by the population of the city. *Source: U.S. Census Bureau, State and Local Government Finances, 2009.*

Property Taxes include general property taxes, relating to property as a whole, taxed at a single rate or at classified rates according to the class of property. Property refers to real property (e.g. land and structures) as well as personal property; personal property can be either tangible (e.g. automobiles and boats) or intangible (e.g. bank accounts and stocks and bonds). Special property taxes, levied on selected types of property (e.g. oil and gas properties, house trailers, motor vehicles, and intangibles) and subject to rates not directly related to general property tax rates. Taxes based on income produced by property as a measure of its value on the assessment date.

## EDUCATION

**Educational Attainment:** Figures show the percent of population age 25 and over with:

- **High school diploma (including GED) or higher:** Includes people whose highest degree is a high school diploma or its equivalent, people who attended college but did not receive a degree, and people who received a college, university, or professional degree.
- **Bachelor's degree or higher:** Includes people who received a bachelor's, master's, doctorate, or professional degree.
- **Master's degree or higher:** Includes people who received a master's, doctorate, or professional degree. *Source: U.S. Census Bureau, American Community Survey, 2006-2010 Five-Year Estimates.*

**School Districts:** Lists the name of each school district, the grade range (PK=pre-kindergarten; KG=kindergarten), the student enrollment, and the district headquarters' phone number. In each community profile, only school districts that have schools that are physically located within the community are shown. In addition, statistics for each school district cover the entire district, regardless of the physical location of the schools within the district. *Source: U.S. Department of Education, National Center for Educational Statistics, Directory of Public Elementary and Secondary Education Agencies, 2009-10.*

**Four-year Colleges:** Lists the name of each four-year college, the type of institution (private or public; for-profit or non-profit; religious affiliation; historically black), the total student enrollment (Fall 2010), the general telephone number, and the annual tuition and fees for full-time, first-time undergraduate students (in-state and out-of-state). *Source: U.S. Department of Education, National Center for Educational Statistics, IPEDS College Data, 2011-12.*

**Two-year Colleges:** Lists the name of each two-year college, the type of institution (private or public; for-profit or non-profit; religious affiliation; historically black), the total student enrollment (Fall 2010), the general telephone number, and the annual tuition and fees for full-time, first-time undergraduate students (in-state and out-of-state). *Source: U.S. Department of Education, National Center for Educational Statistics, IPEDS College Data, 2011-12.*

**Vocational/Technical Schools:** Lists the name of each vocational/technical school, the type of institution (private or public; for-profit or non-profit; religious affiliation; historically black), the total student enrollment (Fall 2010), the general telephone number, and the annual tuition and fees for full-time students. *Source: U.S. Department of Education, National Center for Educational Statistics, IPEDS College Data, 2011-12.*

## HOUSING

**Homeownership Rate:** Percentage of housing units that are owner-occupied. *Source: U.S. Census Bureau, Census 2010.*

**Median Home Value:** Median value of all owner-occupied housing units as reported by the owner. Figures shown are 2010 estimates. *Source: U.S. Census Bureau, American Community Survey, 2006-2010 Five-Year Estimates.*

**Median Rent:** Median monthly contract rent on specified renter-occupied and specified vacant-for-rent units. Specified renter-occupied and specified vacant-for-rent units exclude 1-family houses on 10 acres or more. Contract rent is the monthly rent agreed to or contracted for, regardless of any furnishings, utilities, fees, meals, or services that may be included. For vacant units, it is the monthly rent asked for the rental unit at the time of enumeration. *Source: U.S. Census Bureau, American Community Survey, 2006-2010 Five-Year Estimates.*

**Median Year Structure Built:** Year structure built refers to when the building was first constructed, not when it was remodeled, added to, or converted. For mobile homes, houseboats, RVs, etc, the manufacturer's model year was assumed to be the year built. The data relate to the number of units built during the specified periods that were still in existence at the time of enumeration. *Source: U.S. Census Bureau, American Community Survey, 2006-2010 Five-Year Estimates.*

## HOSPITALS

Lists the hospital name and the number of licensed beds. *Source: Grey House Publishing, Directory of Hospital Personnel, 2010.*

## SAFETY

**Violent Crime Rate:** Number of violent crimes reported per 10,000 population. Violent crimes include murder, forcible rape, robbery, and aggravated assault. *Source: Federal Bureau of Investigation, Uniform Crime Reports 2010*

**Property Crime Rate:** Number of property crimes reported per 10,000 population. Property crimes include burglary, larceny-theft, and motor vehicle theft. *Source: Federal Bureau of Investigation, Uniform Crime Reports 2010*

## NEWSPAPERS

Lists the name, circulation and news focus of daily and weekly newspapers. Includes newspapers with offices located in the community profiled. *Source: MediaContactsPro 2010*

## TRANSPORTATION

**Commute to Work:** Percentage of workers 16 years old and over that use the following means of transportation to commute to work: car; public transportation; walk; work from home. *Source: U.S. Census Bureau, American Community Survey, 2006-2010 Five-Year Estimates.*

The means of transportation data for some areas may show workers using modes of public transportation that are not available in those areas (e.g. subway or elevated riders in a metropolitan area where there actually is no subway or elevated service). This result is largely due to people who worked during the reference week at a location that was different from their usual place of work (such as people away from home on business in an area where subway service was available) and people who used more than one means of transportation each day but whose principal means was unavailable where they lived (e.g. residents of non-metropolitan areas who drove to the fringe of a metropolitan area and took the commuter railroad most of the distance to work).

**Travel Time to Work:** Travel time to work for workers 16 years old and over. Reported for the following intervals: less than 15 minutes; 15 to 30 minutes; 30 to 45 minutes; 45 to 60 minutes; 60 minutes or more. *Source: U.S. Census Bureau, American Community Survey, 2006-2010 Five-Year Estimates.*

Travel time to work refers to the total number of minutes that it usually took the person to get from home to work each day during the reference week. The elapsed time includes time spent waiting for public transportation, picking up passengers in carpools, and time spent in other activities related to getting to work.

**Amtrak:** Indicates if Amtrak rail or bus service is available. Please note that the cities being served continually change. *Source: National Railroad Passenger Corporation, Amtrak National Timetable, 2012*

## AIRPORTS

Lists the local airport(s) along with type of service and hub size. *Source: U.S. Department of Transportation, Bureau of Transportation Statistics*

## ADDITIONAL INFORMATION CONTACTS

The following phone numbers are provided as sources of additional information: Chambers of Commerce; Economic Development Agencies; and Convention & Visitors Bureaus. Efforts have been made to provide the most recent area codes. However, area code changes may have occurred in listed numbers. *Source: Original research.*

# Information for Unincorporated Communities (Postal Areas)

## PHYSICAL CHARACTERISTICS

**Zip Code:** The statistics that follow cover the corresponding ZIP Code Tabulation Area (ZCTA). A ZCTA is a statistical entity developed by the Census Bureau to approximate the delivery area for a US Postal Service 5-digit or 3-digit ZIP Code in the US and Puerto Rico. A ZCTA is an aggregation of census blocks that have the same predominant ZIP Code associated with the mailing addresses in the Census Bureau's Master Address File. Thus, the Postal Service's delivery areas have been adjusted to encompass whole census blocks so that the Census Bureau can tabulate census data for the ZCTAs. ZCTAs do not include all ZIP Codes used for mail delivery and therefore do not precisely depict the area within which mail deliveries associated with that ZIP Code occur. Additionally, some areas that are known by a unique name, although they are part of a larger incorporated place, are also included as "postal areas." *Source: U.S. Census Bureau, Census 2010 and U.S. Postal Service, City State File.*

**Land and Water Area:** Land and water area in square miles. *Source: U.S. Census Bureau, Census 2010.*

**Latitude and Longitude:** Latitude and longitude in degrees. *Source: U.S. Census Bureau, Census 2010.*

**Elevation:** Elevation in feet. *Source: U.S. Geological Survey, Geographic Names Information System (GNIS).*

## POPULATION

**Population:** Figures are a 100% count of population. *Source: U.S. Census Bureau, Census 2010.*

**Population Density:** Total population divided by the land area in square miles. *Source: U.S. Census Bureau, Census 2010.*

**Race/Hispanic Origin:** Figures are from Census 2010 and include the U.S. Census Bureau categories of White alone; Black alone; Asian alone; American Indian/Alaska Native alone; Native Hawaiian/Other Pacific Islander alone; Hispanic of any race. Alone refers to the fact that these figures are not in combination with any other race.

The concept of race, as used by the Census Bureau, reflects self-identification by people according to the race or races with which they most closely identify. These categories are socio-political constructs and should not be interpreted as being scientific or anthropological in nature. Furthermore, the race categories include both racial and national-origin groups.

- **African American or Black:** A person having origins in any of the Black racial groups of Africa. It includes people who indicated their race(s) as "Black, African Am., or Negro" or reported entries such as African American, Kenyan, Nigerian, or Haitian.

- **American Indian or Alaska Native:** A person having origins in any of the original peoples of North and South America (including Central America) and who maintains tribal affiliation or community attachment. This category includes people who indicated their race(s) as "American Indian or Alaska Native" or reported their enrolled or principal tribe, such as Navajo, Blackfeet, Inupiat, Yup'ik, or Central American Indian groups or South American Indian groups.

- **Asian:** A person having origins in any of the original peoples of the Far East, Southeast Asia, or the Indian subcontinent, including, for example, Cambodia, China, India, Japan, Korea, Malaysia, Pakistan, the Philippine Islands, Thailand, and Vietnam. It includes people who indicated their race(s) as "Asian" or reported entries such as "Asian Indian," "Chinese," "Filipino," "Korean," "Japanese," "Vietnamese," and "Other Asian" or provided other detailed Asian responses.

- **Native Hawaiian or Other Pacific Islander:** A person having origins in any of the original peoples of Hawaii, Guam, Samoa, or other Pacific Islands. It includes people who indicated their race(s) as "Pacific Islander" or reported entries such as "Native Hawaiian," "Guamanian or Chamorro," "Samoan," and "Other Pacific Islander" or provided other detailed Pacific Islander responses.

- **White:** A person having origins in any of the original peoples of Europe, the Middle East, or North Africa. It includes people who indicated their race(s) as "White" or reported entries such as Irish, German, Italian, Lebanese, Arab, Moroccan, or Caucasian.

- **Hispanic:** The data on the Hispanic or Latino population were derived from answers to a question that was asked of all people. The terms "Spanish," "Hispanic origin," and "Latino" are used interchangeably. Some respondents identify with all three terms while others may identify with only one of these three specific terms. Hispanics or Latinos who identify with the terms "Spanish," "Hispanic," or "Latino" are those who classify themselves in one of the specific Spanish, Hispanic, or Latino categories listed on the questionnaire ("Mexican," "Puerto Rican," or "Cuban") as well as those who indicate that they are "other Spanish/Hispanic/Latino." People who do not identify with one of the specific origins listed on the questionnaire but indicate that they are "other Spanish/Hispanic/Latino" are those whose origins are from Spain, the Spanish-speaking countries of Central or South America, the Dominican Republic, or people identifying themselves generally as Spanish, Spanish-American, Hispanic, Hispano, Latino, and so on. All write-in responses to the "other Spanish/Hispanic/Latino" category were coded. Origin can be viewed as the heritage, nationality group, lineage, or country of birth of the person or the person's parents or ancestors before their arrival in the United States. People who identify their origin as Spanish, Hispanic, or Latino may be of any race.

**Average Household Size:** Number of persons in the average household. *Source: U.S. Census Bureau, Census 2010.*

**Median Age:** Median age of the population. *Source: U.S. Census Bureau, Census 2010.*

**Male/Female Ratio:** Number of males per 100 females. *Source: U.S. Census Bureau, Census 2010.*

**Homeownership Rate:** Percentage of housing units that are owner-occupied. *Source: U.S. Census Bureau, Census 2010.*

# Information for Counties

## PHYSICAL CHARACTERISTICS

**Physical Location:** Describes the physical location of the county. *Source: Columbia University Press, The Columbia Gazetteer of North America and original research.*

**Land and Water Area:** Land and water area in square miles. *Source: U.S. Census Bureau, Census 2010.*

**Time Zone:** Lists the time zone. *Source: Original research.*

**Year Organized:** Year the county government was organized. *Source: National Association of Counties*

**County Seat:** Lists the county seat. If a county has more than one seat, then both are listed. *Source: National Association of Counties*

**Metropolitan Area:** Indicates the metropolitan area the county is located in. Also lists all the component counties of that metropolitan area. The Office of Management and Budget (OMB) defines metropolitan and micropolitan statistical areas. The most current definitions are as of December 2009. *Source: U.S. Census Bureau.*

**Climate:** Includes all weather stations located within the county. Indicates the station name and elevation as well as the monthly average high and low temperatures, average precipitation, and average snowfall. The period of record is generally 1980-2009, however, certain weather stations contain averages going back as far as 1900. *Source: Grey House Publishing, Weather America: A Thirty-Year Summary of Statistical Weather Data and Rankings, 2010.*

## POPULATION

Population: 1990, 2000 and 2010 figures are a 100% count of population. *Source: U.S. Census Bureau, Census 2010.*

**Race/Hispanic Origin:** Figures are from Census 2010 and include the U.S. Census Bureau categories of White alone; Black alone; Asian alone; American Indian/Alaska Native alone; Native Hawaiian/Other Pacific Islander alone; Hispanic of any race. Alone refers to the fact that these figures are not in combination with any other race.

The concept of race, as used by the Census Bureau, reflects self-identification by people according to the race or races with which they most closely identify. These categories are socio-political constructs and should not be interpreted as being scientific or anthropological in nature. Furthermore, the race categories include both racial and national-origin groups.

- **African American or Black:** A person having origins in any of the Black racial groups of Africa. It includes people who indicated their race(s) as "Black, African Am., or Negro" or reported entries such as African American, Kenyan, Nigerian, or Haitian.

- **American Indian or Alaska Native:** A person having origins in any of the original peoples of North and South America (including Central America) and who maintains tribal affiliation or community attachment. This category includes people who indicated their race(s) as "American Indian or Alaska Native" or reported their enrolled or principal tribe, such as Navajo, Blackfeet, Inupiat, Yup'ik, or Central American Indian groups or South American Indian groups.

- **Asian:** A person having origins in any of the original peoples of the Far East, Southeast Asia, or the Indian subcontinent, including, for example, Cambodia, China, India, Japan, Korea, Malaysia, Pakistan, the Philippine Islands, Thailand, and Vietnam. It includes people who indicated their race(s) as "Asian" or reported entries such as "Asian Indian," "Chinese," "Filipino," "Korean," "Japanese," "Vietnamese," and "Other Asian" or provided other detailed Asian responses.

- **Native Hawaiian or Other Pacific Islander:** A person having origins in any of the original peoples of Hawaii, Guam, Samoa, or other Pacific Islands. It includes people who indicated their race(s) as "Pacific Islander" or reported entries such as "Native Hawaiian," "Guamanian or Chamorro," "Samoan," and "Other Pacific Islander" or provided other detailed Pacific Islander responses.

- **White:** A person having origins in any of the original peoples of Europe, the Middle East, or North Africa. It includes people who indicated their race(s) as "White" or reported entries such as Irish, German, Italian, Lebanese, Arab, Moroccan, or Caucasian.

- **Hispanic:** The data on the Hispanic or Latino population were derived from answers to a question that was asked of all people. The terms "Spanish," "Hispanic origin," and "Latino" are used interchangeably.

Some respondents identify with all three terms while others may identify with only one of these three specific terms. Hispanics or Latinos who identify with the terms "Spanish," "Hispanic," or "Latino" are those who classify themselves in one of the specific Spanish, Hispanic, or Latino categories listed on the questionnaire ("Mexican," "Puerto Rican," or "Cuban") as well as those who indicate that they are "other Spanish/Hispanic/Latino." People who do not identify with one of the specific origins listed on the questionnaire but indicate that they are "other Spanish/Hispanic/Latino" are those whose origins are from Spain, the Spanish-speaking countries of Central or South America, the Dominican Republic, or people identifying themselves generally as Spanish, Spanish-American, Hispanic, Hispano, Latino, and so on. All write-in responses to the "other Spanish/Hispanic/Latino" category were coded. Origin can be viewed as the heritage, nationality group, lineage, or country of birth of the person or the person's parents or ancestors before their arrival in the United States. People who identify their origin as Spanish, Hispanic, or Latino may be of any race.

**Population Density:** Total population divided by the land area in square miles. *Source: U.S. Census Bureau, Census 2010.*

**Average Household Size:** Number of persons in the average household. *Source: U.S. Census Bureau, Census 2010.*

**Median Age:** Median age of the population. *Source: U.S. Census Bureau, Census 2010.*

**Male/Female Ratio:** Number of males per 100 females. *Source: U.S. Census Bureau, Census 2010.*

## RELIGION

**Religion:** Lists the largest religious groups (up to six) based on the number of adherents divided by the population of the county. Adherents are defined as "all members, including full members, their children and the estimated number of other regular participants who are not considered as communicant, confirmed or full members." *Source: American Religious Bodies, 2010 U.S. Religion Census: Religious Congregations & Membership Study*

## ECONOMY

**Unemployment Rate:** Unemployment rate as of February 2012. Includes all civilians age 16 or over who were unemployed and looking for work. *Source: U.S. Department of Labor, Bureau of Labor Statistics, Local Area Unemployment Statistics.*

**Total Civilian Labor Force:** Total civilian labor force as of February 2012. Includes all civilians age 16 or over who were either employed, or unemployed and looking for work. *Source: U.S. Department of Labor, Bureau of Labor Statistics, Local Area Unemployment Statistics.*

**Leading Industries:** Lists the three largest industries (excluding government) based on the number of employees. *Source: U.S. Census Bureau, County Business Patterns 2008 (http://www.census.gov/epcd/cbp/view/cbpview.html).*

**Farms:** The total number of farms and the total acreage they occupy. *Source: U.S. Department of Agriculture, National Agricultural Statistics Service, 2007 Census of Agriculture (http://www.agcensus.usda.gov).*

**Companies that Employ 500 or more persons:** The numbers of companies that employ 500 or more persons. Includes private employers only. *Source: U.S. Census Bureau, County Business Patterns 2009*

**Companies that Employ 100–499 persons:** The numbers of companies that employ 100 - 499 persons. Includes private employers only. *Source: U.S. Census Bureau, County Business Patterns 2009*

**Companies that Employ 1–99 persons:** The numbers of companies that employ 1 - 99 persons. Includes private employers only. *Source: U.S. Census Bureau, County Business Patterns 2009*

**Black-Owned Businesses:** Number of businesses that are majority-owned by a Black or African-American person(s). Majority ownership is defined as having 51 percent or more of the stock or equity in the business. Black or African American is defined as a person having origins in any of the black racial groups of Africa, including those who consider themselves to be "Haitian." *Source: U.S. Census Bureau, 2007 Economic Census, Survey of Business Owners: Black-Owned Firms, 2007*

**Asian-Owned Businesses:** Number of businesses that are majority-owned by an Asian person(s). Majority ownership is defined as having 51 percent or more of the stock or equity in the business. *Source: U.S. Census Bureau, 2007 Economic Census, Survey of Business Owners: Asian-Owned Firms, 2007*

**Hispanic-Owned Businesses:** Number of businesses that are majority-owned by a person(s) of Hispanic or Latino origin. Majority ownership is defined as having 51 percent or more of the stock or equity in the business. Hispanic or Latino origin is defined as a person of Cuban, Mexican, Puerto Rican, South or Central American, or other Spanish culture or origin, regardless of race. *Source: U.S. Census Bureau, 2007 Economic Census, Survey of Business Owners: Hispanic-Owned Firms, 2007*

**Women-Owned Businesses:** Number of businesses that are majority-owned by a woman. Majority ownership is defined as having 51 percent or more of the stock or equity in the business. *Source: U.S. Census Bureau, 2007 Economic Census, Survey of Business Owners: Women-Owned Firms, 2007*

**Retail Sales per Capita:** Total dollar amount of estimated retail sales divided by the estimated population of the county in 2010. *Source: Editor & Publisher Market Guide 2010*

**Single-Family Building Permits Issued:** Building permits issued for new, single-family housing units in 2011. *Source: U.S. Census Bureau, Manufacturing and Construction Division*

**Multi-Family Building Permits Issued:** Building permits issued for new, multi-family housing units in 2011. *Source: U.S. Census Bureau, Manufacturing and Construction Division*

Statistics on housing units authorized by building permits include housing units issued in local permit-issuing jurisdictions by a building or zoning permit. Not all areas of the country require a building or zoning permit. The statistics only represent those areas that do require a permit. Current surveys indicate that construction is undertaken for all but a very small percentage of housing units authorized by building permits. A major portion typically get under way during the month of permit issuance and most of the remainder begin within the three following months. Because of this lag, the housing unit authorization statistics do not represent the number of units actually put into construction for the period shown, and should therefore not be directly interpreted as "housing starts."

Statistics are based upon reports submitted by local building permit officials in response to a mail survey. They are obtained using Form C-404 const/www/c404.pdf, "Report of New Privately-Owned Residential Building or Zoning Permits Issued." When a report is not received, missing data are either (1) obtained from the Survey of Use of Permits (SUP) which is used to collect information on housing starts, or (2) imputed based on the assumption that the ratio of current month authorizations to those of a year ago should be the same for reporting and non-reporting places.

## INCOME

**Per Capita Income:** Per capita income is the mean income computed for every man, woman, and child in a particular group. It is derived by dividing the total income of a particular group by the total population in that group. Per capita income is rounded to the nearest whole dollar. *Source: U.S. Census Bureau, American Community Survey, 2006-2010 Five-Year Estimates.*

**Median Household Income:** Includes the income of the householder and all other individuals 15 years old and over in the household, whether they are related to the householder or not. The median divides the income distribution into two equal parts: one-half of the cases falling below the median income and one-half above the median. For households, the median income is based on the distribution of the total number of households including those with no income. Median income for households is computed on the basis of a standard distribution and is rounded to the nearest whole dollar. *Source: U.S. Census Bureau, American Community Survey, 2006-2010 Five-Year Estimates.*

**Average Household Income:** Average household income is obtained by dividing total household income by the total number of households. *Source: U.S. Census Bureau, American Community Survey, 2006-2010 Five-Year Estimates.*

**Percent of Households with Income of $100,000 or more:** Percent of households with income of $100,000 or more. *Source: U.S. Census Bureau, American Community Survey, 2006-2010 Five-Year Estimates.*

**Poverty Rate:** Percentage of population with income below the poverty level. Based on individuals for whom poverty status is determined. Poverty status was determined for all people except institutionalized people, people in military group quarters, people in college dormitories, and unrelated individuals under 15 years old. *Source: U.S. Census Bureau, American Community Survey, 2006-2010 Five-Year Estimates.*

**Bankruptcy Rate:** The personal bankruptcy filing rate is the number of bankruptcies per thousand residents in 2011. Personal bankruptcy filings include both Chapter 7 (liquidations) and Chapter 13 (reorganizations) based on the county of residence of the filer. *Source: Federal Deposit Insurance Corporation, Regional Economic Conditions*

## TAXES

**Total County Taxes Per Capita:** Total county taxes collected divided by the population of the county. *Source: U.S. Census Bureau, State and Local Government Finances, 2009*

Taxes include:

- Property Taxes
- Sales and Gross Receipts Taxes
- Federal Customs Duties
- General Sales and Gross Receipts Taxes
- Selective Sales Taxes (alcoholic beverages; amusements; insurance premiums; motor fuels; pari-mutuels; public utilities; tobacco products; other)
- License Taxes (alcoholic beverages; amusements; corporations in general; hunting and fishing; motor vehicles motor vehicle operators; public utilities; occupation and business, NEC; other)
- Income Taxes (individual income; corporation net income; other)
- Death and Gift
- Documentary & Stock Transfer
- Severance
- Taxes, NEC

**Total County Property Taxes Per Capita:** Total county property taxes collected divided by the population of the county. *Source: U.S. Census Bureau, State and Local Government Finances, 2009*

Property Taxes include general property taxes, relating to property as a whole, taxed at a single rate or at classified rates according to the class of property. Property refers to real property (e.g. land and structures) as well as personal property; personal property can be either tangible (e.g. automobiles and boats) or intangible (e.g. bank accounts and stocks and bonds). Special property taxes, levied on selected types of property (e.g. oil and gas properties, house trailers, motor vehicles, and intangibles) and subject to rates not directly related to general property tax rates. Taxes based on income produced by property as a measure of its value on the assessment date.

## EDUCATION

**Educational Attainment:** Figures show the percent of population age 25 and over with:

- **High school diploma (including GED) or higher:** Includes people whose highest degree is a high school diploma or its equivalent, people who attended college but did not receive a degree, and people who received a college, university, or professional degree.
- **Bachelor's degree or higher:** Includes people who received a bachelor's, master's, doctorate, or professional degree.
- **Master's degree or higher:** Includes people who received a master's, doctorate, or professional degree. *Source: U.S. Census Bureau, American Community Survey, 2006-2010 Five-Year Estimates.*

## HOUSING

**Homeownership Rate:** Percentage of housing units that are owner-occupied. *Source: U.S. Census Bureau, Census 2010.*

**Median Home Value:** Median value of all owner-occupied housing units as reported by the owner. Figures shown are 2010 estimates. *Source: U.S. Census Bureau, American Community Survey, 2006-2010 Five-Year Estimates.*

**Median Rent:** Median monthly contract rent on specified renter-occupied and specified vacant-for-rent units. Specified renter-occupied and specified vacant-for-rent units exclude 1-family houses on 10 acres or more. Contract rent is the monthly rent agreed to or contracted for, regardless of any furnishings, utilities, fees, meals, or services that may be included. For vacant units, it is the monthly rent asked for the rental unit at the time of enumeration. *Source: U.S. Census Bureau, American Community Survey, 2006-2010 Five-Year Estimates.*

**Median Year Structure Built:** Year structure built refers to when the building was first constructed, not when it was remodeled, added to, or converted. For mobile homes, houseboats, RVs, etc, the manufacturer's model year was assumed to be the year built. The data relate to the number of units built during the specified periods that were still in existence at the time of enumeration. *Source: U.S. Census Bureau, American Community Survey, 2006-2010 Five-Year Estimates.*

## HEALTH AND VITAL STATISTICS

**Birth Rate:** Estimated number of births per 10,000 population in 2011. *Source: U.S. Census Bureau, Annual Components of Population Change, July 1, 2010 – July 1, 2011*

**Death Rate:** Estimated number of deaths per 10,000 population in 2011. *Source: U.S. Census Bureau, Annual Components of Population Change, July 1, 2010 – July 1, 2011*

**Age-adjusted Cancer Mortality Rate:** Number of age-adjusted deaths from cancer per 100,000 population in 2009. Cancer is defined as International Classification of Disease (ICD) codes C00 - D48.9 Neoplasms. *Source: Centers for Disease Control, CDC Wonder*

Age-adjusted death rates are weighted averages of the age-specific death rates, where the weights represent a fixed population by age. They are used because the rates of almost all causes of death vary by age. Age adjustment is a technique for "removing" the effects of age from crude rates, so as to allow meaningful comparisons across populations with different underlying age structures. For example, comparing the crude rate of heart disease in New York to that of California is misleading, because the relatively older population in New York will lead to a higher crude death rate, even if the age-specific rates of heart disease in New York and California are the same. For such a comparison, age-adjusted rates would be preferable. Age-adjusted rates should be viewed as relative indexes rather than as direct or actual measures of mortality risk.

Death rates based on counts of twenty or less (≤ 20) are flagged as "Unreliable". Death rates based on fewer than three years of data for counties with populations of less than 100,000 in the 2000 Census counts, are also flagged as "Unreliable" if the number of deaths is five or less (≤ 5).

**Air Quality Index:** The percentage of days in 2010 the AQI fell into the Good (0-50), Moderate (51-100), Unhealthy for Sensitive Groups (101-150), Unhealthy (151-199), and Very Unhealthy (200-299) ranges. Data covers January 2010 through December 2010. *Source: AirData: Access to Air Pollution Data, U.S. Environmental Protection Agency, Office of Air and Radiation*

The AQI is an index for reporting daily air quality. It tells you how clean or polluted your air is, and what associated health concerns you should be aware of. The AQI focuses on health effects that can happen within a few hours or days after breathing polluted air. EPA uses the AQI for five major air pollutants regulated by the Clean Air Act: ground-level ozone, particulate matter, carbon monoxide, sulfur dioxide, and nitrogen dioxide. For each of these pollutants, EPA has established national air quality standards to protect against harmful health effects.

The AQI runs from 0 to 500. The higher the AQI value, the greater the level of air pollution and the greater the health danger. For example, an AQI value of 50 represents good air quality and little potential to affect public health, while an AQI value over 300 represents hazardous air quality. An AQI value of 100 generally corresponds to the national air quality standard for the pollutant, which is the level EPA has set to protect public health. So, AQI values below 100 are generally thought of as satisfactory. When AQI values are above 100, air quality is considered to be unhealthy— at first for certain sensitive groups of people, then for everyone as AQI values get higher. Each category corresponds to a different level of health concern. For example, when the AQI for a pollutant is between 51 and 100, the health concern is "Moderate." Here are the six levels of health concern and what they mean:

- "Good" The AQI value for your community is between 0 and 50. Air quality is considered satisfactory and air pollution poses little or no risk.
- "Moderate" The AQI for your community is between 51 and 100. Air quality is acceptable; however, for some pollutants there may be a moderate health concern for a very small number of individuals. For example, people who are unusually sensitive to ozone may experience respiratory symptoms.
- "Unhealthy for Sensitive Groups" Certain groups of people are particularly sensitive to the harmful effects of certain air pollutants. This means they are likely to be affected at lower levels than the general public. For example, children and adults who are active outdoors and people with respiratory disease are at greater risk from exposure to ozone, while people with heart disease are at greater risk from carbon monoxide. Some people may be sensitive to more than one pollutant. When AQI values are between 101 and 150, members of sensitive groups may experience health effects. The general public is not likely to be affected when the AQI is in this range.

- "Unhealthy" AQI values are between 151 and 200. Everyone may begin to experience health effects. Members of sensitive groups may experience more serious health effects.
- "Very Unhealthy" AQI values between 201 and 300 trigger a health alert, meaning everyone may experience more serious health effects.
- "Hazardous" AQI values over 300 trigger health warnings of emergency conditions. The entire population is more likely to be affected.

**Number of Physicians:** The number of active, non-federal physicians per 10,000 population in 2008. *Source: Area Resource File (ARF) 2009-2010. U.S. Department of Health and Human Services, Health Resources and Services Administration, Bureau of Health Professions, Rockville, MD.*

**Number of Hospital Beds:** The number of hospital beds per 10,000 population in 2007. *Source: Area Resource File (ARF) 2009-2010. U.S. Department of Health and Human Services, Health Resources and Services Administration, Bureau of Health Professions, Rockville, MD.*

**Number of Hospital Admissions:** The number of hospital admissions per 10,000 population in 2007. *Source: Area Resource File (ARF) 2009-2010. U.S. Department of Health and Human Services, Health Resources and Services Administration, Bureau of Health Professions, Rockville, MD.*

## ELECTIONS

**Elections:** 2008 Presidential election results. *Source: Dave Leip's Atlas of U.S. Presidential Elections (http://www.uselectionatlas.org).*

## NATIONAL AND STATE PARKS

Lists National and State parks located in the area. *Source: U.S. Geological Survey, Geographic Names Information System.*

## ADDITIONAL INFORMATION CONTACTS

The following phone numbers are provided as sources of additional information: Chambers of Commerce; Economic Development Agencies; and Convention & Visitors Bureaus. Efforts have been made to provide the most recent area codes. However, area code changes may have occurred in listed numbers. *Source: Original research.*

# User's Guide: Education

## School District Rankings

**Number of Schools:** Total number of schools in the district. *Source: U.S. Department of Education, National Center for Education Statistics, Common Core of Data, Public Elementary/Secondary School Universe Survey: School Year 2009-2010.*

**Number of Teachers:** Teachers are defined as individuals who provide instruction to pre-kindergarten, kindergarten, grades 1 through 12, or ungraded classes, or individuals who teach in an environment other than a classroom setting, and who maintain daily student attendance records. Numbers reported are full-time equivalents (FTE). *Source: U.S. Department of Education, National Center for Education Statistics, Common Core of Data, Local Education Agency (School District) Universe Survey: School Year 2009-2010.*

**Number of Students:** A student is an individual for whom instruction is provided in an elementary or secondary education program that is not an adult education program and is under the jurisdiction of a school, school system, or other education institution. *Sources: U.S. Department of Education, National Center for Education Statistics, Common Core of Data, Local Education Agency (School District) Universe Survey: School Year 2009-2010 and Public Elementary/Secondary School Universe Survey: School Year 2009-2010*

**Individual Education Program (IEP) Students:** A written instructional plan for students with disabilities designated as special education students under IDEA-Part B. The written instructional plan includes a statement of present levels of educational performance of a child; statement of annual goals, including short-term instructional objectives; statement of specific educational services to be provided and the extent to which the child will be able to participate in regular educational programs; the projected date for initiation and anticipated duration of services; the appropriate objectives, criteria and evaluation procedures; and the schedules for determining, on at least an annual basis, whether instructional objectives are being achieved. *Source: U.S. Department of Education, National Center for Education Statistics, Common Core of Data, Local Education Agency (School District) Universe Survey: School Year 2009-2010*

**English Language Learner (ELL) Students:** Formerly referred to as Limited English Proficient (LEP). Students being served in appropriate programs of language assistance (e.g., English as a Second Language, High Intensity Language Training, bilingual education). Does not include pupils enrolled in a class to learn a language other than English. Also Limited-English-Proficient students are individuals who were not born in the United States or whose native language is a language other than English; or individuals who come from environments where a language other than English is dominant; or individuals who are American Indians and Alaskan Natives and who come from environments where a language other than English has had a significant impact on their level of English language proficiency; and who, by reason thereof, have sufficient difficulty speaking, reading, writing, or understanding the English language, to deny such individuals the opportunity to learn successfully in classrooms where the language of instruction is English or to participate fully in our society. *Source: U.S. Department of Education, National Center for Education Statistics, Common Core of Data, Local Education Agency (School District) Universe Survey: School Year 2009-2010*

**Students Eligible for Free Lunch Program:** The free lunch program is defined as a program under the National School Lunch Act that provides cash subsidies for free lunches to students based on family size and income criteria. *Source: U.S. Department of Education, National Center for Education Statistics, Common Core of Data, Public Elementary/Secondary School Universe Survey: School Year 2009-2010*

**Students Eligible for Reduced-Price Lunch Program:** A student who is eligible to participate in the Reduced-Price Lunch Program under the National School Lunch Act. *Source: U.S. Department of Education, National Center for Education Statistics, Common Core of Data, Public Elementary/Secondary School Universe Survey: School Year 2009-2010*

**Student/Teacher Ratio:** The number of students divided by the number of teachers (FTE). See Number of Students and Number of Teachers above for for information.

**Student/Librarian Ratio:** The number of students divided by the number of library and media support staff. Library and media support staff are defined as staff members who render other professional library and media services; also includes library aides and those involved in library/media support. Their duties include selecting, preparing, caring for, and making available to instructional staff, equipment, films, filmstrips, transparencies, tapes, TV programs, and similar materials maintained separately or as part of an instructional materials center. Also included are activities in the audio-visual center, TV studio, related-work-study areas, and services provided by audio-visual personnel.

Numbers are based on full-time equivalents. *Source: U.S. Department of Education, National Center for Education Statistics, Common Core of Data, Local Education Agency (School District) Universe Survey: School Year 2009-2010.*

**Student/Counselor Ratio:** The number of students divided by the number of guidance counselors. Guidance counselors are professional staff assigned specific duties and school time for any of the following activities in an elementary or secondary setting: counseling with students and parents; consulting with other staff members on learning problems; evaluating student abilities; assisting students in making educational and career choices; assisting students in personal and social development; providing referral assistance; and/or working with other staff members in planning and conducting guidance programs for students. The state applies its own standards in apportioning the aggregate of guidance counselors/directors into the elementary and secondary level components. Numbers reported are full-time equivalents. *Source: U.S. Department of Education, National Center for Education Statistics, Common Core of Data, Local Education Agency (School District) Universe Survey: School Year 2009-2010.*

**Current Spending per Student:** Expenditure for Instruction, Support Services, and Other Elementary/Secondary Programs. Includes salaries, employee benefits, purchased services, and supplies, as well as payments made by states on behalf of school districts. Also includes transfers made by school districts into their own retirement system. Excludes expenditure for Non-Elementary/Secondary Programs, debt service, capital outlay, and transfers to other governments or school districts. This item is formally called "Current Expenditures for Public Elementary/Secondary Education."

*Instruction:* Includes payments from all funds for salaries, employee benefits, supplies, materials, and contractual services for elementary/secondary instruction. It excludes capital outlay, debt service, and interfund transfers for elementary/secondary instruction. Instruction covers regular, special, and vocational programs offered in both the regular school year and summer school. It excludes instructional support activities as well as adult education and community services. Instruction salaries includes salaries for teachers and teacher aides and assistants.

*Support Services:* Relates to support services functions (series 2000) defined in Financial Accounting for Local and State School Systems (National Center for Education Statistics 2000). Includes payments from all funds for salaries, employee benefits, supplies, materials, and contractual services. It excludes capital outlay, debt service, and interfund transfers. It includes expenditure for the following functions:

- Business/Central/Other Support Services
- General Administration
- Instructional Staff Support
- Operation and Maintenance
- Pupil Support Services
- Pupil Transportation Services
- School Administration
- Nonspecified Support Services

Values shown are dollars per pupil per year. They were calculated by dividing the total dollar amounts by the fall membership. Fall membership is comprised of the total student enrollment on October 1 (or the closest school day to October 1) for all grade levels (including prekindergarten and kindergarten) and ungraded pupils. Membership includes students both present and absent on the measurement day. *Source: U.S. Department of Education, National Center for Education Statistics, Common Core of Data, School District Finance Survey (F-33), Fiscal Year 2007-2008.*

**Drop-out Rate:** A dropout is a student who was enrolled in school at some time during the previous school year; was not enrolled at the beginning of the current school year; has not graduated from high school or completed a state or district approved educational program; and does not meet any of the following exclusionary conditions: has transferred to another public school district, private school, or state- or district-approved educational program; is temporarily absent due to suspension or school-approved illness; or has died. The values shown cover grades 9 through 12. *Note: Drop-out rates are no longer available to the general public disaggregated by grade, race/ethnicity, and gender at the school district level. Beginning with the 2005–06 school year the CCD is reporting dropout data aggregated from the local education agency (district) level to the state level. This allows data users to compare event dropout rates across states, regions, and other jurisdictions. Source: U.S. Department of Education, National Center for Education Statistics, Common Core of Data, Local Education Agency (School District) Universe Survey Dropout and Completion Data, 2005-2006; U.S. Department of Education, National Center for Education Statistics, Common Core of Data, State Dropout and Completion Data File, 2008-2009*

**Average Freshman Graduation Rate (AFGR):** The AFGR is the number of regular diploma recipients in a given year divided by the average of the membership in grades 8, 9, and 10, reported 5, 4, and 3 years earlier, respectively. For example, the denominator of the 2008–09 AFGR is the average of the 8th-grade membership in 2004–05,

9th-grade membership in 2005–06, and 10th-grade membership in 2006–07. Ungraded students are prorated into these grades. Averaging these three grades provides an estimate of the number of first-time freshmen in the class of 2005–06 freshmen in order to estimate the on-time graduation rate for 2008–09.

*Caution in interpreting the AFGR.* Although the AFGR was selected as the best of the available alternatives, several factors make it fall short of a true on-time graduation rate. First, the AFGR does not take into account any imbalances in the number of students moving in and out of the nation or individual states over the high school years. As a result, the averaged freshman class is at best an approximation of the actual number of freshmen, where differences in the rates of transfers, retention, and dropping out in the three grades affect the average. Second, by including all graduates in a specific year, the graduates may include students who repeated a grade in high school or completed high school early and thus are not on-time graduates in that year. *Source: U.S. Department of Education, National Center for Education Statistics, Common Core of Data, Local Education Agency (School District) Universe Survey Dropout and Completion Data, 2008-2009; U.S. Department of Education, National Center for Education Statistics, Common Core of Data, State Dropout and Completion Data File, 2008-2009*

**Number of Diploma Recipients:** A student who has received a diploma during the previous school year or subsequent summer school. This category includes regular diploma recipients and other diploma recipients. A High School Diploma is a formal document certifying the successful completion of a secondary school program prescribed by the state education agency or other appropriate body. *Note: Diploma counts are no longer available to the general public disaggregated by grade, race/ethnicity, and gender at the school district level. Source: U.S. Department of Education, National Center for Education Statistics, Common Core of Data, Local Education Agency (School District) Universe Survey Dropout and Completion Data, 2008-2009; U.S. Department of Education, National Center for Education Statistics, Common Core of Data, State Dropout and Completion Data File, 2008-2009*

**Note:** n/a indicates data not available.

## State Educational Profile

Please refer to the District Rankings section in the front of this User's Guide for an explanation of data for all items except for the following:

**Average Salary:** The average salary for classroom teachers in 2011-2012. *Source: National Education Association, Rankings & Estimates: Rankings of the States 2011 and Estimates of School Statistics 2012*

**College Entrance Exam Scores:**

**Scholastic Aptitude Test (SAT).** *Note: Data covers the 2011 school year. The College Board strongly discourages the comparison or ranking of states on the basis of SAT scores alone. Source: The College Board, SAT Trends*

**American College Testing Program (ACT).** *ACT, 2011 ACT National and State Scores*

## National Assessment of Educational Progress (NAEP)

The National Assessment of Educational Progress (NAEP), also known as "the Nation's Report Card," is the only nationally representative and continuing assessment of what America's students know and can do in various subject areas. As a result of the "No Child Left Behind" legislation, all states are required to participate in NAEP.

For more information, visit the U.S. Department of Education, National Center for Education Statistics at http://nces.ed.gov/nationsreportcard.

# User's Guide: Ancestry and Ethnicity

## Places Covered

The ancestry and ethnicity profile section of this book covers the state, all counties, and all places with populations of 50,000 or more. Places included fall into one of the following categories:

**Incorporated Places.** Depending on the state, places are incorporated as either cities, towns, villages, boroughs, municipalities, independent cities, or corporations. A few municipalities have a form of government combined with another entity (e.g. county) and are listed as special cities or consolidated, unified, or metropolitan governments.

**Census Designated Places (CDP).** The U.S. Census Bureau defines a CDP as "a statistical entity," defined for each decennial census according to Census Bureau guidelines, comprising a densely settled concentration of population that is not within an incorporated place, but is locally identified by a name. CDPs are delineated cooperatively by state and local officials and the Census Bureau, following Census Bureau guidelines.

**Minor Civil Divisions** (called charter townships, districts, gores, grants, locations, plantations, purchases, reservations, towns, townships, and unorganized territories) for the states where the Census Bureau has determined that they serve as general-purpose governments. Those states are Connecticut, Maine, Massachusetts, Michigan, Minnesota, New Hampshire, New Jersey, New York, Pennsylvania, Rhode Island, Vermont, and Wisconsin. In some states incorporated municipalities are part of minor civil divisions and in some states they are independent of them.

**Note:** Several states have incorporated municipalities and minor civil divisions in the same county with the same name. Those communities are given separate entries (e.g. Burlington, New Jersey, in Burlington County will be listed under both the city and township of Burlington). A few states have Census Designated Places and minor civil divisions in the same county with the same name. Those communities are given separate entries (e.g. Bridgewater, Massachusetts, in Plymouth County will be listed under both the CDP and town of Bridgewater).

## Source of Data

The ethnicities shown in this book were compiled from two different sources. Data for Race and Hispanic Origin was taken from Census 2010 Summary File 1 (SF1) while Ancestry data was taken from the American Community Survey (ACS) 2006-2010 Five-Year Estimate. The distinction is important because SF1 contains 100-percent data, which is the information compiled from the questions asked of all people and about every housing unit. ACS estimates are compiled from a sampling of households. The 2006-2010 Five-Year Estimate is based on data collected from January 1, 2006 to December 31, 2010.

The American Community Survey (ACS) is a relatively new survey conducted by the U.S. Census Bureau. It uses a series of monthly samples to produce annually updated data for the same small areas (census tracts and block groups) formerly surveyed via the decennial census long-form sample. While some version of this survey has been in the field since 1999, it was not fully implemented in terms of coverage until 2006. In 2005 it was expanded to cover all counties in the country and the 1-in-40 households sampling rate was first applied. The full implementation of the (household) sampling strategy for ACS entails having the survey mailed to about 250,000 households nationwide every month of every year and was begun in January 2005. In January 2006 sampling of group quarters was added to complete the sample as planned. In any given year about 2.5% (1 in 40) of U.S. households will receive the survey. Over any 5-year period about 1 in 8 households should receive the survey (as compared to about 1 in 6 that received the census long form in the 2000 census). Since receiving the survey is not the same as responding to it, the Bureau has adopted a strategy of sampling for non-response, resulting in something closer to 1 in 11 households actually participating in the survey over any 5-year period. For more information about the American Community Survey visit http://www.census.gov/acs/www.

## Ancestry

Ancestry refers to a person's ethnic origin, heritage, descent, or "roots," which may reflect their place of birth or that of previous generations of their family. Some ethnic identities, such as "Egyptian" or "Polish" can be traced to geographic areas outside the United States, while other ethnicities such as "Pennsylvania German" or "Cajun" evolved in the United States.

The intent of the ancestry question in the ACS was not to measure the degree of attachment the respondent had to a particular ethnicity, but simply to establish that the respondent had a connection to and self-identified with a particular ethnic group. For example, a response of "Irish" might reflect total involvement in an Irish community or only a memory of ancestors several generations removed from the respondent.

The Census Bureau coded the responses into a numeric representation of over 1,000 categories. Responses initially were processed through an automated coding system; then, those that were not automatically assigned a code were coded by individuals trained in coding ancestry responses. The code list reflects the results of the Census Bureau's own research and consultations with many ethnic experts. Many decisions were made to determine the classification of responses. These decisions affected the grouping of the tabulated data. For example, the "Indonesian" category includes the responses of "Indonesian," "Celebesian," "Moluccan," and a number of other responses.

### Ancestries Covered in Profiles of New York State

| | | | |
|---|---|---|---|
| Afghan | Palestinian | French, ex. Basque | Scottish |
| African, Sub-Saharan | Syrian | French Canadian | Serbian |
| African | Other Arab | German | Slavic |
| Cape Verdean | Armenian | German Russian | Slovak |
| Ethiopian | Assyrian/Chaldean/Syriac | Greek | Slovene |
| Ghanaian | Australian | Guyanese | Soviet Union |
| Kenyan | Austrian | Hungarian | Swedish |
| Liberian | Basque | Icelander | Swiss |
| Nigerian | Belgian | Iranian | Turkish |
| Senegalese | Brazilian | Irish | Ukrainian |
| Sierra Leonean | British | Israeli | Welsh |
| Somalian | Bulgarian | Italian | West Indian, ex. |
| South African | Cajun | Latvian | Hispanic |
| Sudanese | Canadian | Lithuanian | Bahamian |
| Ugandan | Carpatho Rusyn | Luxemburger | Barbadian |
| Zimbabwean | Celtic | Macedonian | Belizean |
| Other Sub-Saharan African | Croatian | Maltese | Bermudan |
| Albanian | Cypriot | New Zealander | British West Indian |
| Alsatian | Czech | Northern European | Dutch West Indian |
| American | Czechoslovakian | Norwegian | Haitian |
| Arab | Danish | Pennsylvania German | Jamaican |
| Arab | Dutch | Polish | Trinidadian/ |
| Egyptian | Eastern European | Portuguese | Tobagonian |
| Iraqi | English | Romanian | U.S. Virgin Islander |
| Jordanian | Estonian | Russian | West Indian |
| Lebanese | European | Scandinavian | Other West Indian |
| Moroccan | Finnish | Scotch-Irish | Yugoslavian |

The ancestry question allowed respondents to report one or more ancestry groups. Generally, only the first two responses reported were coded. If a response was in terms of a dual ancestry, for example, "Irish English," the person was assigned two codes, in this case one for Irish and another for English. However, in certain cases, multiple responses such as "French Canadian," "Scotch-Irish," "Greek Cypriot," and "Black Dutch" were assigned a single code reflecting their status as unique groups. If a person reported one of these unique groups in addition to another group, for example, "Scotch-Irish English," resulting in three terms, that person received one code for the unique group (Scotch-Irish) and another one for the remaining group (English). If a person reported "English Irish French," only English and Irish were coded. If there were more than two ancestries listed and one of the ancestries was a part of another, such as "German Bavarian Hawaiian," the responses were coded using the more detailed groups (Bavarian and Hawaiian).

The Census Bureau accepted "American" as a unique ethnicity if it was given alone or with one other ancestry. There were some groups such as "American Indian," "Mexican American," and "African American" that were coded and identified separately.

The ancestry question is asked for every person in the American Community Survey, regardless of age, place of birth, Hispanic origin, or race.

Although some people consider religious affiliation a component of ethnic identity, the ancestry question was not designed to collect any information concerning religion. Thus, if a religion was given as an answer to the ancestry question, it was listed in the "Other groups" category which is not shown in this book.

Ancestry should not be confused with a person's place of birth, although a person's place of birth and ancestry may be the same.

# Hispanic Origin

The data on the Hispanic or Latino population were derived from answers to a Census 2010 question that was asked of all people. The terms "Spanish," "Hispanic origin," and "Latino" are used interchangeably. Some respondents identify with all three terms while others may identify with only one of these three specific terms. Hispanics or Latinos who identify with the terms "Spanish," "Hispanic," or "Latino" are those who classify themselves in one of the specific Spanish, Hispanic, or Latino categories listed on the questionnaire ("Mexican," "Puerto Rican," or "Cuban") as well as those who indicate that they are "other Spanish/Hispanic/Latino." People who do not identify with one of the specific origins listed on the questionnaire but indicate that they are "other Spanish/Hispanic/Latino" are those whose origins are from Spain, the Spanish-speaking countries of Central or South America, the Dominican Republic, or people identifying themselves generally as Spanish, Spanish-American, Hispanic, Hispano, Latino, and so on. All write-in responses to the "other Spanish/Hispanic/Latino" category were coded.

### Hispanic Origins Covered in Profiles of New York State

| | | | |
|---|---|---|---|
| Hispanic or Latino | Salvadoran | Argentinean | Uruguayan |
| Central American, ex. Mexican | Other Central American | Bolivian | Venezuelan |
| Costa Rican | Cuban | Chilean | Other South American |
| Guatemalan | Dominican Republic | Colombian | Other Hispanic or Latino |
| Honduran | Mexican | Ecuadorian | |
| Nicaraguan | Puerto Rican | Paraguayan | |
| Panamanian | South American | Peruvian | |

Origin can be viewed as the heritage, nationality group, lineage, or country of birth of the person or the person's parents or ancestors before their arrival in the United States. People who identify their origin as Hispanic, Latino, or Spanish may be of any race.

# Ethnicities Based on Race

The data on race were derived from answers to the Census 2010 question on race that was asked of individuals in the United States. The Census Bureau collects racial data in accordance with guidelines provided by the U.S. Office of Management and Budget (OMB), and these data are based on self-identification.

The racial categories included in the census questionnaire generally reflect a social definition of race recognized in this country and not an attempt to define race biologically, anthropologically, or genetically. In addition, it is recognized that the categories of the race item include racial and national origin or sociocultural groups. People may choose to report more than one race to indicate their racial mixture, such as "American Indian" and "White." People who identify their origin as Hispanic, Latino, or Spanish may be of any race.

### Racial Groups Covered in Profiles of New York State

| | | | |
|---|---|---|---|
| **African-American/Black** | Crow | Spanish American Indian | Korean |
| *Not Hispanic* | Delaware | Tlingit-Haida *(Alaska Native)* | Laotian |
| *Hispanic* | Hopi | Tohono O'Odham | Malaysian |
| **American Indian/Alaska Native** | Houma | Tsimshian *(Alaska Native)* | Nepalese |
| *Not Hispanic* | Inupiat *(Alaska Native)* | Ute | Pakistani |
| *Hispanic* | Iroquois | Yakama | Sri Lankan |
| Alaska Athabascan *(Ala. Nat.)* | Kiowa | Yaqui | Taiwanese |
| Aleut *(Alaska Native)* | Lumbee | Yuman | Thai |
| Apache | Menominee | Yup'ik *(Alaska Native)* | Vietnamese |
| Arapaho | Mexican American Indian | **Asian** | **Hawaii Native/Pacific Islander** |
| Blackfeet | Navajo | *Not Hispanic* | *Not Hispanic* |
| Canadian/French Am. Indian | Osage | *Hispanic* | *Hispanic* |
| Central American Indian | Ottawa | Bangladeshi | Fijian |
| Cherokee | Paiute | Bhutanese | Guamanian/Chamorro |
| Cheyenne | Pima | Burmese | Marshallese |
| Chickasaw | Potawatomi | Cambodian | Native Hawaiian |
| Chippewa | Pueblo | Chinese, ex. Taiwanese | Samoan |
| Choctaw | Puget Sound Salish | Filipino | Tongan |
| Colville | Seminole | Hmong | **White** |
| Comanche | Shoshone | Indian | *Not Hispanic* |
| Cree | Sioux | Indonesian | *Hispanic* |
| Creek | South American Indian | Japanese | |

**African American or Black:** A person having origins in any of the Black racial groups of Africa. It includes people who indicated their race(s) as "Black, African Am., or Negro" or reported entries such as African American, Kenyan, Nigerian, or Haitian.

**American Indian or Alaska Native:** A person having origins in any of the original peoples of North and South America (including Central America) and who maintains tribal affiliation or community attachment. This category includes people who indicated their race(s) as "American Indian or Alaska Native" or reported their enrolled or principal tribe, such as Navajo, Blackfeet, Inupiat, Yup'ik, or Central American Indian groups or South American Indian groups.

**Asian:** A person having origins in any of the original peoples of the Far East, Southeast Asia, or the Indian subcontinent, including, for example, Cambodia, China, India, Japan, Korea, Malaysia, Pakistan, the Philippine Islands, Thailand, and Vietnam. It includes people who indicated their race(s) as "Asian" or reported entries such as "Asian Indian," "Chinese," "Filipino," "Korean," "Japanese," "Vietnamese," and "Other Asian" or provided other detailed Asian responses.

**Native Hawaiian or Other Pacific Islander:** A person having origins in any of the original peoples of Hawaii, Guam, Samoa, or other Pacific Islands. It includes people who indicated their race(s) as "Pacific Islander" or reported entries such as "Native Hawaiian," "Guamanian or Chamorro," "Samoan," and "Other Pacific Islander" or provided other detailed Pacific Islander responses.

**White:** A person having origins in any of the original peoples of Europe, the Middle East, or North Africa. It includes people who indicated their race(s) as "White" or reported entries such as Irish, German, Italian, Lebanese, Arab, Moroccan, or Caucasian.

## Profiles

Each profile shows the name of the place, the county (if a place spans more than one county, the county that holds the majority of the population is shown), and the 2010 population (based on 100-percent data from Census 2010 Summary File 1). The rest of each profile is comprised of all 218 ethnicities grouped into three sections: ancestry; Hispanic origin; and race.

Column one displays the ancestry/Hispanic origin/race name, column two displays the number of people reporting each ancestry/Hispanic origin/race, and column three is the percent of the total population reporting each ancestry/Hispanic origin/race. The population figure shown is used to calculate the value in the "%" column for ethnicities based on race and Hispanic origin. The 2006-2010 estimated population figure from the American Community Survey (not shown) is used to calculate the value in the "%" column for all other ancestries.

For ethnicities in the ancestries group, the value in the "Number" column includes multiple ancestries reported. For example, if a person reported a multiple ancestry such as "French Danish," that response was counted twice in the tabulations, once in the French category and again in the Danish category. Thus, the sum of the counts is not the total population but the total of all responses. Numbers in parentheses indicate the number of people reporting a single ancestry. People reporting a single ancestry includes all people who reported only one ethnic group such as "German." Also included in this category are people with only a multiple-term response such as "Scotch-Irish" who are assigned a single code because they represent one distinct group. For example, the count for German would be interpreted as "The number of people who reported that German was their only ancestry."

For ethnicities based on Hispanic origin, the value in the "Number" column represents the number of people who reported being Mexican, Puerto Rican, Cuban or other Spanish/Hispanic/ Latino (all written-in responses were coded). All ethnicities based on Hispanic origin can be of any race.

For ethnicities based on race data the value in the "Number" column represents the total number of people who reported each category alone or in combination with one or more other race categories. This number represents the maximum number of people reporting and therefore the individual race categories may add up to more than the total population because people may be included in more than one category. The figures in parentheses show the number of people that reported that particular ethnicity alone, not in combination with any other race. For example, in Alabama, the entry for Korean shows 8,320 in parentheses and 10,624 in the "Number" column. This means that 8,320 people reported being Korean alone and 10,624 people reported being Korean alone or in combination with one or more other races.

# Rankings

In the rankings section, each ethnicity has three tables. The first table shows the top 10 places sorted by ethnic population (based on all places, regardless of total population), the second table shows the top 10 places sorted by percent of the total population (based on all places, regardless of total population), the third table shows the top 10 places sorted by percent of the total population (based on places with total population of 50,000 or more).

Within each table, column one displays the place name, the state, and the county (if a place spans more than one county, the county that holds the majority of the population is shown). Column one in the first table displays the state only. Column two displays the number of people reporting each ancestry (includes people reporting multiple ancestries), Hispanic origin, or race (alone or in combination with any other race). Column three is the percent of the total population reporting each ancestry, Hispanic origin or race. For tables representing ethnicities based on race or Hispanic origin, the 100-percent population figure from SF1 is used to calculate the value in the "%" column. For all other ancestries, the 2006-2010 five-year estimated population figure from the American Community Survey is used to calculate the value in the "%" column.

## Alphabetical Ethnicity Cross-Reference Guide

**Afghan** *see* Ancestry–Afghan
**African** *see* Ancestry–African, Sub-Saharan: African
**African-American** *see* Race–African-American/Black
**African-American: Hispanic** *see* Race–African-American/Black: Hispanic
**African-American: Not Hispanic** *see* Race–African-American/Black: Not Hispanic
**Alaska Athabascan** *see* Race–Alaska Native: Alaska Athabascan
**Alaska Native** *see* Race–American Indian/Alaska Native
**Alaska Native: Hispanic** *see* Race–American Indian/Alaska Native: Hispanic
**Alaska Native: Not Hispanic** *see* Race–American Indian/Alaska Native: Not Hispanic
**Albanian** *see* Ancestry–Albanian
**Aleut** *see* Race–Alaska Native: Aleut
**Alsatian** *see* Ancestry–Alsatian
**American** *see* Ancestry–American
**American Indian** *see* Race–American Indian/Alaska Native
**American Indian: Hispanic** *see* Race–American Indian/Alaska Native: Hispanic
**American Indian: Not Hispanic** *see* Race–American Indian/Alaska Native: Not Hispanic
**Apache** *see* Race–American Indian: Apache
**Arab** *see* Ancestry–Arab: Arab
**Arab: Other** *see* Ancestry–Arab: Other
**Arapaho** *see* Race–American Indian: Arapaho
**Argentinean** *see* Hispanic Origin–South American: Argentinean
**Armenian** *see* Ancestry–Armenian
**Asian** *see* Race–Asian
**Asian Indian** *see* Race–Asian: Indian
**Asian: Hispanic** *see* Race–Asian: Hispanic
**Asian: Not Hispanic** *see* Race–Asian: Not Hispanic
**Assyrian** *see* Ancestry–Assyrian/Chaldean/Syriac
**Australian** *see* Ancestry–Australian
**Austrian** *see* Ancestry–Austrian
**Bahamian** *see* Ancestry–West Indian: Bahamian, except Hispanic
**Bangladeshi** *see* Race–Asian: Bangladeshi
**Barbadian** *see* Ancestry–West Indian: Barbadian, except Hispanic
**Basque** *see* Ancestry–Basque
**Belgian** *see* Ancestry–Belgian
**Belizean** *see* Ancestry–West Indian: Belizean, except Hispanic
**Bermudan** *see* Ancestry–West Indian: Bermudan, except Hispanic
**Bhutanese** *see* Race–Asian: Bhutanese
**Black** *see* Race–African-American/Black
**Black: Hispanic** *see* Race–African-American/Black: Hispanic
**Black: Not Hispanic** *see* Race–African-American/Black: Not Hispanic
**Blackfeet** *see* Race–American Indian: Blackfeet
**Bolivian** *see* Hispanic Origin–South American: Bolivian
**Brazilian** *see* Ancestry–Brazilian
**British** *see* Ancestry–British
**British West Indian** *see* Ancestry–West Indian: British West Indian, except Hispanic

**Bulgarian** *see* Ancestry–Bulgarian
**Burmese** *see* Race–Asian: Burmese
**Cajun** *see* Ancestry–Cajun
**Cambodian** *see* Race–Asian: Cambodian
**Canadian** *see* Ancestry–Canadian
**Canadian/French American Indian** *see* Race–American Indian: Canadian/French American Indian
**Cape Verdean** *see* Ancestry–African, Sub-Saharan: Cape Verdean
**Carpatho Rusyn** *see* Ancestry–Carpatho Rusyn
**Celtic** *see* Ancestry–Celtic
**Central American** *see* Hispanic Origin–Central American, except Mexican
**Central American Indian** *see* Race–American Indian: Central American Indian
**Central American: Other** *see* Hispanic Origin–Central American: Other Central American
**Chaldean** *see* Ancestry–Assyrian/Chaldean/Syriac
**Chamorro** *see* Race–Hawaii Native/Pacific Islander: Guamanian or Chamorro
**Cherokee** *see* Race–American Indian: Cherokee
**Cheyenne** *see* Race–American Indian: Cheyenne
**Chickasaw** *see* Race–American Indian: Chickasaw
**Chilean** *see* Hispanic Origin–South American: Chilean
**Chinese (except Taiwanese)** *see* Race–Asian: Chinese, except Taiwanese
**Chippewa** *see* Race–American Indian: Chippewa
**Choctaw** *see* Race–American Indian: Choctaw
**Colombian** *see* Hispanic Origin–South American: Colombian
**Colville** *see* Race–American Indian: Colville
**Comanche** *see* Race–American Indian: Comanche
**Costa Rican** *see* Hispanic Origin–Central American: Costa Rican
**Cree** *see* Race–American Indian: Cree
**Creek** *see* Race–American Indian: Creek
**Croatian** *see* Ancestry–Croatian
**Crow** *see* Race–American Indian: Crow
**Cuban** *see* Hispanic Origin–Cuban
**Cypriot** *see* Ancestry–Cypriot
**Czech** *see* Ancestry–Czech
**Czechoslovakian** *see* Ancestry–Czechoslovakian
**Danish** *see* Ancestry–Danish
**Delaware** *see* Race–American Indian: Delaware
**Dominican Republic** *see* Hispanic Origin–Dominican Republic
**Dutch** *see* Ancestry–Dutch
**Dutch West Indian** *see* Ancestry–West Indian: Dutch West Indian, except Hispanic
**Eastern European** *see* Ancestry–Eastern European
**Ecuadorian** *see* Hispanic Origin–South American: Ecuadorian
**Egyptian** *see* Ancestry–Arab: Egyptian
**English** *see* Ancestry–English
**Eskimo** *see* Race–Alaska Native: Inupiat
**Estonian** *see* Ancestry–Estonian
**Ethiopian** *see* Ancestry–African, Sub-Saharan: Ethiopian
**European** *see* Ancestry–European
**Fijian** *see* Race–Hawaii Native/Pacific Islander: Fijian
**Filipino** *see* Race–Asian: Filipino
**Finnish** *see* Ancestry–Finnish
**French (except Basque)** *see* Ancestry–French, except Basque
**French Canadian** *see* Ancestry–French Canadian
**German** *see* Ancestry–German
**German Russian** *see* Ancestry–German Russian
**Ghanaian** *see* Ancestry–African, Sub-Saharan: Ghanaian
**Greek** *see* Ancestry–Greek
**Guamanian** *see* Race–Hawaii Native/Pacific Islander: Guamanian or Chamorro
**Guatemalan** *see* Hispanic Origin–Central American: Guatemalan
**Guyanese** *see* Ancestry–Guyanese
**Haitian** *see* Ancestry–West Indian: Haitian, except Hispanic
**Hawaii Native** *see* Race–Hawaii Native/Pacific Islander
**Hawaii Native: Hispanic** *see* Race–Hawaii Native/Pacific Islander: Hispanic
**Hawaii Native: Not Hispanic** *see* Race–Hawaii Native/Pacific Islander: Not Hispanic
**Hispanic or Latino:** *see* Hispanic Origin–Hispanic or Latino (of any race)

**Hispanic or Latino: Other** *see* Hispanic Origin–Other Hispanic or Latino
**Hmong** *see* Race–Asian: Hmong
**Honduran** *see* Hispanic Origin–Central American: Honduran
**Hopi** *see* Race–American Indian: Hopi
**Houma** *see* Race–American Indian: Houma
**Hungarian** *see* Ancestry–Hungarian
**Icelander** *see* Ancestry–Icelander
**Indonesian** *see* Race–Asian: Indonesian
**Inupiat** *see* Race–Alaska Native: Inupiat
**Iranian** *see* Ancestry–Iranian
**Iraqi** *see* Ancestry–Arab: Iraqi
**Irish** *see* Ancestry–Irish
**Iroquois** *see* Race–American Indian: Iroquois
**Israeli** *see* Ancestry–Israeli
**Italian** *see* Ancestry–Italian
**Jamaican** *see* Ancestry–West Indian: Jamaican, except Hispanic
**Japanese** *see* Race–Asian: Japanese
**Jordanian** *see* Ancestry–Arab: Jordanian
**Kenyan** *see* Ancestry–African, Sub-Saharan: Kenyan
**Kiowa** *see* Race–American Indian: Kiowa
**Korean** *see* Race–Asian: Korean
**Laotian** *see* Race–Asian: Laotian
**Latvian** *see* Ancestry–Latvian
**Lebanese** *see* Ancestry–Arab: Lebanese
**Liberian** *see* Ancestry–African, Sub-Saharan: Liberian
**Lithuanian** *see* Ancestry–Lithuanian
**Lumbee** *see* Race–American Indian: Lumbee
**Luxemburger** *see* Ancestry–Luxemburger
**Macedonian** *see* Ancestry–Macedonian
**Malaysian** *see* Race–Asian: Malaysian
**Maltese** *see* Ancestry–Maltese
**Marshallese** *see* Race–Hawaii Native/Pacific Islander: Marshallese
**Menominee** *see* Race–American Indian: Menominee
**Mexican** *see* Hispanic Origin–Mexican
**Mexican American Indian** *see* Race–American Indian: Mexican American Indian
**Moroccan** *see* Ancestry–Arab: Moroccan
**Native Hawaiian** *see* Race–Hawaii Native/Pacific Islander: Native Hawaiian
**Navajo** *see* Race–American Indian: Navajo
**Nepalese** *see* Race–Asian: Nepalese
**New Zealander** *see* Ancestry–New Zealander
**Nicaraguan** *see* Hispanic Origin–Central American: Nicaraguan
**Nigerian** *see* Ancestry–African, Sub-Saharan: Nigerian
**Northern European** *see* Ancestry–Northern European
**Norwegian** *see* Ancestry–Norwegian
**Osage** *see* Race–American Indian: Osage
**Ottawa** *see* Race–American Indian: Ottawa
**Pacific Islander** *see* Race–Hawaii Native/Pacific Islander
**Pacific Islander: Hispanic** *see* Race–Hawaii Native/Pacific Islander: Hispanic
**Pacific Islander: Not Hispanic** *see* Race–Hawaii Native/Pacific Islander: Not Hispanic
**Paiute** *see* Race–American Indian: Paiute
**Pakistani** *see* Race–Asian: Pakistani
**Palestinian** *see* Ancestry–Arab: Palestinian
**Panamanian** *see* Hispanic Origin–Central American: Panamanian
**Paraguayan** *see* Hispanic Origin–South American: Paraguayan
**Pennsylvania German** *see* Ancestry–Pennsylvania German
**Peruvian** *see* Hispanic Origin–South American: Peruvian
**Pima** *see* Race–American Indian: Pima
**Polish** *see* Ancestry–Polish
**Portuguese** *see* Ancestry–Portuguese
**Potawatomi** *see* Race–American Indian: Potawatomi
**Pueblo** *see* Race–American Indian: Pueblo
**Puerto Rican** *see* Hispanic Origin–Puerto Rican
**Puget Sound Salish** *see* Race–American Indian: Puget Sound Salish

**Romanian** *see* Ancestry–Romanian
**Russian** *see* Ancestry–Russian
**Salvadoran** *see* Hispanic Origin–Central American: Salvadoran
**Samoan** *see* Race–Hawaii Native/Pacific Islander: Samoan
**Scandinavian** *see* Ancestry–Scandinavian
**Scotch-Irish** *see* Ancestry–Scotch-Irish
**Scottish** *see* Ancestry–Scottish
**Seminole** *see* Race–American Indian: Seminole
**Senegalese** *see* Ancestry–African, Sub-Saharan: Senegalese
**Serbian** *see* Ancestry–Serbian
**Shoshone** *see* Race–American Indian: Shoshone
**Sierra Leonean** *see* Ancestry–African, Sub-Saharan: Sierra Leonean
**Sioux** *see* Race–American Indian: Sioux
**Slavic** *see* Ancestry–Slavic
**Slovak** *see* Ancestry–Slovak
**Slovene** *see* Ancestry–Slovene
**Somalian** *see* Ancestry–African, Sub-Saharan: Somalian
**South African** *see* Ancestry–African, Sub-Saharan: South African
**South American** *see* Hispanic Origin–South American
**South American Indian** *see* Race–American Indian: South American Indian
**South American: Other** *see* Hispanic Origin–South American: Other South American
**Soviet Union** *see* Ancestry–Soviet Union
**Spanish American Indian** *see* Race–American Indian: Spanish American Indian
**Sri Lankan** *see* Race–Asian: Sri Lankan
**Sub-Saharan African** *see* Ancestry–African, Sub-Saharan
**Sub-Saharan African: Other** *see* Ancestry–African, Sub-Saharan: Other
**Sudanese** *see* Ancestry–African, Sub-Saharan: Sudanese
**Swedish** *see* Ancestry–Swedish
**Swiss** *see* Ancestry–Swiss
**Syriac** *see* Ancestry–Assyrian/Chaldean/Syriac
**Syrian** *see* Ancestry–Arab: Syrian
**Taiwanese** *see* Race–Asian: Taiwanese
**Thai** *see* Race–Asian: Thai
**Tlingit-Haida** *see* Race–Alaska Native: Tlingit-Haida
**Tohono O'Odham** *see* Race–American Indian: Tohono O'Odham
**Tongan** *see* Race–Hawaii Native/Pacific Islander: Tongan
**Trinidadian and Tobagonian** *see* Ancestry–West Indian: Trinidadian and Tobagonian, except Hispanic
**Tsimshian** *see* Race–Alaska Native: Tsimshian
**Turkish** *see* Ancestry–Turkish
**U.S. Virgin Islander** *see* Ancestry–West Indian: U.S. Virgin Islander, except Hispanic
**Ugandan** *see* Ancestry–African, Sub-Saharan: Ugandan
**Ukrainian** *see* Ancestry–Ukrainian
**Uruguayan** *see* Hispanic Origin–South American: Uruguayan
**Ute** *see* Race–American Indian: Ute
**Venezuelan** *see* Hispanic Origin–South American: Venezuelan
**Vietnamese** *see* Race–Asian: Vietnamese
**Welsh** *see* Ancestry–Welsh
**West Indian** *see* Ancestry–West Indian: West Indian, except Hispanic
**West Indian (except Hispanic)** *see* Ancestry–West Indian, except Hispanic
**West Indian: Other** *see* Ancestry–West Indian: Other, except Hispanic
**White** *see* Race–White
**White: Hispanic** *see* Race–White: Hispanic
**White: Not Hispanic** *see* Race–White: Not Hispanic
**Yakama** *see* Race–American Indian: Yakama
**Yaqui** *see* Race–American Indian: Yaqui
**Yugoslavian** *see* Ancestry–Yugoslavian
**Yuman** *see* Race–American Indian: Yuman
**Yup'ik** *see* Race–Alaska Native: Yup'ik
**Zimbabwean** *see* Ancestry–African, Sub-Saharan: Zimbabwean

# User's Guide: Climate

## Sources of the Data

The National Climactic Data Center (NCDC) has two main classes or types of weather stations; first-order stations which are staffed by professional meteorologists and cooperative stations which are staffed by volunteers. All National Weather Service (NWS) stations included in this book are first-order stations.

The data in the climate section of *Profiles of New York State* is compiled from several sources. The majority comes from the original NCDC computer tapes (DSI-3220 Summary of Month Cooperative). This data was used to create the entire table for each cooperative station and part of each National Weather Service station. The remainder of the data for each NWS station comes from the International Station Meteorological Climate Summary, Version 4.0, September 1996, which is also available from the NCDC.

Storm events come from the NCDC Storm Events Database which is accessible over the Internet at http://www4.ncdc.noaa.gov/ cgi-win/wwcgi.dll?wwevent~storms.

## Weather Station Tables

The weather station tables are grouped by type (National Weather Service and Cooperative) and then arranged alphabetically. The station name is almost always a place name, and is shown here just as it appears in NCDC data. The station name is followed by the county in which the station is located (or by county equivalent name), the elevation of the station (at the time beginning of the thirty year period) and the latitude and longitude.

The National Weather Service Station tables contain 32 data elements which were compiled from two different sources, the International Station Meteorological Climate Summary (ISMCS) and NCDC DSI-3220 data tapes. The following 13 elements are from the ISMCS: maximum precipitation, minimum precipitation, maximum snowfall, maximum 24-hour snowfall, thunderstorm days, foggy days, predominant sky cover, relative humidity (morning and afternoon), dewpoint, wind speed and direction, and maximum wind gust. The remaining 19 elements come from the DSI-3220 data tapes. The period of record (POR) for data from the DSI-3220 data tapes is 1980-2009. The POR for ISMCS data varies from station to station and appears in a note below each station.

The Cooperative Station tables contain 19 data elements which were all compiled from the DSI-3220 data tapes with a POR of 1980-2009.

## Weather Elements (NWS and Cooperative Stations)

The following elements were compiled by the editor from the NCDC DSI-3220 data tapes using a period of record of 1980-2009.

The average temperatures (maximum, minimum, and mean) are the average (see Methodology below) of those temperatures for all available values for a given month. For example, for a given station the average maximum temperature for July is the arithmetic average of all available maximum July temperatures for that station. (Maximum means the highest recorded temperature, minimum means the lowest recorded temperature, and mean means an arithmetic average temperature.)

The extreme maximum temperature is the highest temperature recorded in each month over the period 1980-2009. The extreme minimum temperature is the lowest temperature recorded in each month over the same time period. The extreme maximum daily precipitation is the largest amount of precipitation recorded over a 24-hour period in each month from 1980-2009. The maximum snow depth is the maximum snow depth recorded in each month over the period 1980-2009.

The days for maximum temperature and minimum temperature are the average number of days those criteria were met for all available instances. The symbol ≥ means greater than or equal to, the symbol ≤ means less than or equal to. For example, for a given station, the number of days the maximum temperature was greater than or equal to 90°F in July, is just an arithmetic average of the number of days in all the available Julys for that station.

Heating and cooling degree days are based on the median temperature for a given day and its variance from 65°F. For example, for a given station if the day's high temperature was 50°F and the day's low temperature was 30°F, the median (midpoint) temperature was 40°F. 40°F is 25 degrees below 65°F, hence on this day there would be 25 heating degree days. This also applies for cooling degree days. For example, for a given station if the day's high temperature was 80°F and the day's low temperature was 70°F, the median (midpoint) temperature was 75°F. 75°F is 10 degrees above 65°F, hence on this day there would be 10 cooling degree days. All heating and/or cooling degree days in a month are summed for the month giving respective totals for each element for that month. These sums for a given month for a given station over the past thirty years are again summed and then arithmetically averaged. It should be noted that the heating and cooling degree days do not cancel each other out. It is possible to have both for a given station in the same month.

Precipitation data is computed the same as heating and cooling degree days. Mean precipitation and mean snowfall are arithmetic averages of cumulative totals for the month. All available values for the thirty year period for a given month for a given station are summed and then divided by the number of values. The same is true for days of greater than or equal to 0.1", 0.5",and 1.0" of precipitation, and days of greater than or equal to 1.0" of snow depth on the ground. The word trace appears for precipitation and snowfall amounts that are too small to measure.

Finally, remember that all values presented in the tables and the rankings are averages, maximums, or minimums of available data (see Methodology below) for that specific data element for the last thirty years (1980-2009).

## Weather Elements (NWS Stations Only)

The following elements were taken directly from the International Station Meteorological Climate Summary. The periods of records vary per station and are noted at the bottom of each table.

Maximum precipitation, minimum precipitation, maximum snowfall, maximum snow depth, maximum 24-hour snowfall, thunderstorm days, foggy days, relative humidity (morning and afternoon), dewpoint, prevailing wind speed and direction, and maximum wind gust are all self-explanatory.

The word trace appears for precipitation and snowfall amounts that are too small to measure.

Predominant sky cover contains four possible entries: CLR (clear); SCT (scattered); BRK (broken); and OVR (overcast).

## Inclusion Criteria—How Stations Were Selected

The basic criteria is that a station must have data for temperature, precipitation, heating and cooling degree days of sufficient quantity in order to create a meaningful average. More specifically, the definition of sufficiency here has two parts. First, there must be 22 values for a given data element, and second, ten of the nineteen elements included in the table must pass this sufficiency test. For example, in regard to mean maximum temperature (the first element on every data table), a given station needs to have a value for every month of at least 22 of the last thirty years in order to meet the criteria, and, in addition, every station included must have at least ten of the nineteen elements with at least this minimal level of completeness in order to fulfill the criteria. We then removed stations that were geographically close together, giving preference to stations with better data quality.

## Methodology

The following discussion applies only to data compiled from the NCDC DSI-3220 data tapes and excludes weather elements that are extreme maximums or minimums.

The data in *Profiles of New York State* is based on an arithmetic average of all available data for a specific data element at a given station. For example, the average maximum daily high temperature during July for Rochester, New York, was abstracted from NCDC source tapes for the thirty Julys, starting in July, 1980 and ending in July, 2009. These thirty figures were then summed and divided by thirty to produce an arithmetic average. As might be expected, there were not thirty values for every data element on every table. For a variety of reasons, NCDC data is sometimes incomplete. Thus the following standards were established.

For those data elements where there were 26-30 values, the data was taken to be essentially complete and an average was computed. For data elements where there were 22-25 values, the data was taken as being partly complete but still valid enough to use to compute an average. Such averages are shown in **bold italic** type to indicate that there was less than 26 values. For the few data elements where there were not even 22 values, no average was computed and 'na' appears in the space. If any of the twelve months for a given data element reported a value of 'na', no annual average was computed and the annual average was reported as 'na' as well.

Thus the basic computational methodology used in *Profiles of New York State* is designed to provide an arithmetic average. Because of this, such a pure arithmetic average is somewhat different from the special type of average (called a "normal") which NCDC procedures produces and appears in federal publications.

Perhaps the best outline of the contrasting normalization methodology is found in the following paragraph (which appears as part of an NCDC technical document titled, CLIM81 1961-1990 NORMALS TD-9641 prepared by Lewis France of NCDC in May, 1992):

Normals have been defined as the arithmetic mean of a climatological element computed over a long time period. International agreements eventually led to the decision that the appropriate time period would be three consecutive decades (Guttman, 1989). The data record should be consistent (have no changes in location, instruments, observation practices, etc.; these are identified here as "exposure changes") and have no missing values so a normal will reflect the actual average climatic conditions. If any significant exposure changes have occurred, the data record is said to be "inhomogeneous," and the normal may not reflect a true climatic average. Such data need to be adjusted to remove the nonclimatic inhomogeneities. The resulting (adjusted) record is then said to be "homogeneous." If no exposure changes have occurred at a station, the normal is calculated simply by averaging the appropriate 30 values from the 1961-1990 record.

In the main, there are two "inhomogeneities" that NCDC is correcting for with normalization: adjusting for variances in time of day of observation (at the so-called First Order stations data is based on midnight to midnight observation times and this practice is not necessarily followed at cooperative stations which are staffed by volunteers), and second, estimating data that is either missing or incongruent.

The editors had some concerns regarding the comparative results of the two methodologies. Would our methodology produce strikingly different results than NCDC's? To allay concerns, results of the two processes were compared for the time period normalized results are available (1971-2000). In short, what was found was that the answer to this question is no. Never the less, users should be aware that because of both the time period covered (1980-2009) and the methodology used, data in *Profiles of New York State* is not compatible with data from other sources.

## Potential Cautions

First, as with any statistical reference work of this type, users need to be aware of the source of the data. The information here comes from NOAA, and it is the most comprehensive and reliable core data available. Although it is the best, it is not perfect. Most weather stations are staffed by volunteers, times of observation sometimes vary, stations occasionally are moved (especially over a thirty year period), equipment is changed or upgraded, and all of these factors affect the uniformity of the data. The editors do not attempt to correct for these factors, and this data is not intended for either climatologists or atmospheric scientists. Users with concerns about data collection and reporting protocols are both referred to NCDC technical documentation.

Second, users need to be aware of the methodology here which is described above. Although this methodology has produced fully satisfactory results, it is not directly compatible with other methodologies, hence variances in the results published here and those which appear in other publications will doubtlessly arise.

Third, is the trap of that informal logical fallacy known as "hasty generalization," and its corollaries. This may involve presuming the future will be like the past (specifically, next year will be an average year), or it may involve misunderstanding the limitations of an arithmetic average, but more interestingly, it may involve those mistakes made most innocently by generalizing informally on too broad a basis. As weather is highly localized, the data should be taken in that context. A weather station collects data about climatic conditions at that spot, and that spot may or may not be an effective paradigm for an entire town or area.

# Albany County

Located in eastern New York; bounded on the east by the Hudson River; includes the Helderbergs and part of the Catskills. Covers a land area of 523.45 square miles, a water area of 9.76 square miles, and is located in the Eastern Time Zone at 42.66° N. Lat., 73.84° W. Long. The county was founded in 1683. County seat is Albany.

Albany County is part of the Albany-Schenectady-Troy, NY Metropolitan Statistical Area. The entire metro area includes: Albany County, NY; Rensselaer County, NY; Saratoga County, NY; Schenectady County, NY; Schoharie County, NY

Weather Station: Albany County Arpt                    Elevation: 274 feet

|  | Jan | Feb | Mar | Apr | May | Jun | Jul | Aug | Sep | Oct | Nov | Dec |
|---|---|---|---|---|---|---|---|---|---|---|---|---|
| High | 31 | 35 | 44 | 58 | 70 | 78 | 82 | 81 | 72 | 60 | 48 | 36 |
| Low | 14 | 17 | 25 | 37 | 47 | 56 | 61 | 60 | 51 | 39 | 31 | 21 |
| Precip | 2.5 | 2.1 | 3.3 | 3.2 | 3.6 | 3.8 | 4.1 | 3.6 | 3.3 | 3.5 | 3.3 | 2.9 |
| Snow | 17.7 | 11.5 | 11.4 | 2.3 | 0.1 | tr | tr | 0.0 | tr | 0.3 | 3.2 | 13.7 |

*High and Low temperatures in degrees Fahrenheit; Precipitation and Snow in inches*

Weather Station: Alcove Dam                    Elevation: 606 feet

|  | Jan | Feb | Mar | Apr | May | Jun | Jul | Aug | Sep | Oct | Nov | Dec |
|---|---|---|---|---|---|---|---|---|---|---|---|---|
| High | 31 | 35 | 42 | 56 | 68 | 76 | 80 | 79 | 71 | 59 | 47 | 36 |
| Low | 12 | 14 | 22 | 34 | 44 | 53 | 58 | 57 | 49 | 37 | 29 | 19 |
| Precip | 2.4 | 2.1 | 3.5 | 3.8 | 3.5 | 4.5 | 3.8 | 3.5 | 3.7 | 3.5 | 3.5 | 2.8 |
| Snow | na | na | na | 0.4 | tr | 0.0 | 0.0 | 0.0 | 0.0 | 0.1 | 0.4 | na |

*High and Low temperatures in degrees Fahrenheit; Precipitation and Snow in inches*

**Population:** 292,577 (1990); 294,565 (2000); 304,204 (2010); Race: 78.2% White, 12.7% Black, 4.8% Asian, 0.2% American Indian/Alaska Native, 0.0% Native Hawaiian/Other Pacific Islander, 4.1% Other, 4.9% Hispanic of any race (2010); Density: 581.2 persons per square mile (2010); Average household size: 2.27 (2010); Median age: 38.5 (2010); Males per 100 females: 93.6 (2010).
**Religion:** Six largest groups: 28.0% Catholicism, 3.1% Non-Denominational, 2.1% Presbyterian-Reformed, 2.0% Methodist/Pietist, 1.7% Judaism, 1.5% Muslim Estimate (2010)
**Economy:** Unemployment rate: 7.5% (February 2012); Total civilian labor force: 153,597 (February 2012); Leading industries: 18.8% health care and social assistance; 13.0% retail trade; 9.0% professional, scientific & technical services (2009); Farms: 498 totaling 61,030 acres (2007); Companies that employ 500 or more persons: 28 (2009); Companies that employ 100 to 499 persons: 232 (2009); Companies that employ less than 100 persons: 9,143 (2009); Black-owned businesses: n/a (2007); Hispanic-owned businesses: 554 (2007); Asian-owned businesses: n/a (2007); Women-owned businesses: 7,408 (2007); Retail sales per capita: $18,844 (2010). Single-family building permits issued: 186 (2011); Multi-family building permits issued: 174 (2011).
**Income:** Per capita income: $30,863 (2006-2010 5-year est.); Median household income: $56,090 (2006-2010 5-year est.); Average household income: $73,470 (2006-2010 5-year est.); Percent of households with income of $100,000 or more: 24.0% (2006-2010 5-year est.); Poverty rate: 12.6% (2006-2010 5-year est.); Bankruptcy rate: 2.83% (2011).
**Taxes:** Total county taxes per capita: $1,081 (2009); County property taxes per capita: $245 (2009).
**Education:** Percent of population age 25 and over with: High school diploma (including GED) or higher: 90.7% (2006-2010 5-year est.); Bachelor's degree or higher: 37.6% (2006-2010 5-year est.); Master's degree or higher: 17.8% (2006-2010 5-year est.).
**Housing:** Homeownership rate: 57.5% (2010); Median home value: $202,500 (2006-2010 5-year est.); Median contract rent: $713 per month (2006-2010 5-year est.); Median year structure built: 1956 (2006-2010 5-year est.)
**Health:** Birth rate: 100.1 per 10,000 population (2011); Death rate: 84.7 per 10,000 population (2011); Age-adjusted cancer mortality rate: 183.3 deaths per 100,000 population (2009); Number of physicians: 54.0 per 10,000 population (2008); Hospital beds: 63.8 per 10,000 population (2007); Hospital admissions: 2,169.9 per 10,000 population (2007).
**Environment:** Air Quality Index: 84.7% good, 14.5% moderate, 0.8% unhealthy for sensitive individuals, 0.0% unhealthy (percent of days in 2010)
**Elections:** 2008 Presidential election results: 63.8% Obama, 34.4% McCain, 1.1% Nader
**National and State Parks:** Delmar State Game Farm; Thacher State Park
**Additional Information Contacts**

Albany County Government. . . . . . . . . . . . . . . . . . . (518) 447-7300
   http://www.albanycounty.com
Albany-Colonie Regional Chamber of Commerce . . . . . . . . (518) 431-1400
   http://acchamber.org
Albany-Colonie Regional Chamber of Commerce . . . . . . . . (518) 431-1400
   http://www.acchamber.org
Bethlehem Chamber of Commerce . . . . . . . . . . . . . . . (518) 439-0512
   http://www.bethlehemchamber.com
City of Albany . . . . . . . . . . . . . . . . . . . . . . . . . (518) 434-5284
   http://www.albanyny.org
City of Cohoes . . . . . . . . . . . . . . . . . . . . . . . . . (518) 233-2141
   http://www.cohoes.com
City of Watervliet . . . . . . . . . . . . . . . . . . . . . . . . (518) 270-3800
   http://www.watervliet.com
Guilderland Chamber of Commerce . . . . . . . . . . . . . . (518) 456-6611
   http://www.guilderlandchamber.com
Town of Bethlehem . . . . . . . . . . . . . . . . . . . . . . . (518) 439-4955
   http://www.townofbethlehem.org
Town of Coeymans . . . . . . . . . . . . . . . . . . . . . . . (518) 756-6006
   http://www.coeymans.org
Town of Colonie . . . . . . . . . . . . . . . . . . . . . . . . . (518) 783-2700
   http://www.colonie.org
Town of Guilderland . . . . . . . . . . . . . . . . . . . . . . . (518) 356-1980
   http://www.townofguilderland.org
Town of Knox . . . . . . . . . . . . . . . . . . . . . . . . . . (518) 872-2551
   http://www.knoxny.org
Town of New Scotland . . . . . . . . . . . . . . . . . . . . . . (518) 439-4865
   http://www.townofnewscotland.com
Village of Menands . . . . . . . . . . . . . . . . . . . . . . . (518) 434-2922
   http://www.villageofmenands.com

## Albany County Communities

**ALBANY** (city). County seat. Covers a land area of 21.388 square miles and a water area of 0.547 square miles. Located at 42.66° N. Lat; 73.79° W. Long. Elevation is 148 feet.
**History:** Native American trails running in all directions crossed at the site of Albany. Several ship captains, including Henry Hudson, dropped anchor in the shallows near the present city, and made friends with the inhabitants. The next settlers, who came in 1624, were mostly Walloons from Holland. They built a fort and called it Fort Orange. Dutch, Norwegians, Danes, Germans, and Scots all settled on this land. In 1652, Peter Stuyvesant was sent out by the West India Company to set up a court and he laid out space around Fort Orange for a new village called Beverwyck. In 1685, control was relinquished to the English. The town became a mixture of Dutch and British people and cultures. It was chartered as Albany in 1686. Early fur trade made Albany residents wealthy, but wars plagued the area for almost a century. At the end of the wars, Albany found itself at the crossroad of a developing nation, with travelers coming by land, water, and rail. Lumbering and manufacturing also became important in the 19th century.
**Population:** 100,756 (1990); 95,658 (2000); 97,856 (2010); Density: 4,575.2 persons per square mile (2010); Race: 57.0% White, 30.8% Black, 5.0% Asian, 0.3% American Indian/Alaska Native, 0.1% Native Hawaiian/Other Pacific Islander, 6.8% Other, 8.6% Hispanic of any race (2010); Average household size: 2.13 (2010); Median age: 30.3 (2010); Males per 100 females: 93.6 (2010); Marriage status: 56.0% never married, 29.5% now married, 6.0% widowed, 8.4% divorced (2006-2010 5-year est.); Foreign born: 11.6% (2006-2010 5-year est.); Ancestry (includes multiple ancestries): 18.2% Irish, 13.1% Italian, 10.4% German, 5.4% English, 4.6% Polish (2006-2010 5-year est.).
**Economy:** Unemployment rate: 8.2% (February 2012); Total civilian labor force: 46,317 (February 2012); Single-family building permits issued: 17 (2011); Multi-family building permits issued: 6 (2011); Employment by occupation: 11.2% management, 4.7% professional, 12.7% services, 19.2% sales, 5.5% farming, 3.5% construction, 2.3% production (2006-2010 5-year est.).
**Income:** Per capita income: $23,341 (2006-2010 5-year est.); Median household income: $39,158 (2006-2010 5-year est.); Average household income: $53,425 (2006-2010 5-year est.); Percent of households with income of $100,000 or more: 13.8% (2006-2010 5-year est.); Poverty rate: 25.3% (2006-2010 5-year est.).
**Taxes:** Total city taxes per capita: $612 (2009); City property taxes per capita: $530 (2009).
**Education:** Percent of population age 25 and over with: High school diploma (including GED) or higher: 86.0% (2006-2010 5-year est.);

Bachelor's degree or higher: 37.2% (2006-2010 5-year est.); Master's degree or higher: 18.2% (2006-2010 5-year est.).

**School District(s)**

Achievement Academy Charter School (05-08)
  2009-10 Enrollment: 237 . . . . . . . . . . . . . . . . . . . . . . (518) 533-1601
Albany City School District (PK-12)
  2009-10 Enrollment: 8,423 . . . . . . . . . . . . . . . . . . . . (518) 475-6010
Albany Community Charter School (KG-04)
  2009-10 Enrollment: 302 . . . . . . . . . . . . . . . . . . . . . . (518) 433-1500
Albany Preparatory Charter School (05-08)
  2009-10 Enrollment: 193 . . . . . . . . . . . . . . . . . . . . . . (518) 694-5005
Brighter Choice Charter School for Boys (KG-04)
  2009-10 Enrollment: 234 . . . . . . . . . . . . . . . . . . . . . . (518) 694-8200
Brighter Choice School for Girls (KG-04)
  2009-10 Enrollment: 233 . . . . . . . . . . . . . . . . . . . . . . (518) 694-4100
Capital Region Boces
  2009-10 Enrollment: n/a . . . . . . . . . . . . . . . . . . . . . . (518) 862-4900
Green Tech High Charter School (09-10)
  2009-10 Enrollment: 156 . . . . . . . . . . . . . . . . . . . . . . (518) 694-3400
Guilderland Central School District (KG-12)
  2009-10 Enrollment: 5,274 . . . . . . . . . . . . . . . . . . . . (518) 456-6200
Henry Johnson Charter School (KG-03)
  2009-10 Enrollment: 278 . . . . . . . . . . . . . . . . . . . . . . (518) 432-4300
Kipp Tech Valley Charter School (05-08)
  2009-10 Enrollment: 303 . . . . . . . . . . . . . . . . . . . . . . (518) 694-9494
NYS Dept of Corrections (07-11)
  2009-10 Enrollment: n/a . . . . . . . . . . . . . . . . . . . . . . (518) 457-8126
New Covenant Charter School (KG-05)
  2009-10 Enrollment: 653 . . . . . . . . . . . . . . . . . . . . . . (518) 463-3912
New York State OMH (KG-12)
  2009-10 Enrollment: 438 . . . . . . . . . . . . . . . . . . . . . . (518) 999-9999
New York State Office of Mental Retardation (UG-UG)
  2009-10 Enrollment: 18 . . . . . . . . . . . . . . . . . . . . . . . (866) 946-9733
South Colonie Central School District (PK-12)
  2009-10 Enrollment: 5,413 . . . . . . . . . . . . . . . . . . . . (518) 869-3576

**Four-year College(s)**

Albany College of Pharmacy and Health Sciences (Private, Not-for-profit)
  Fall 2010 Enrollment: 1,586 . . . . . . . . . . . . . . . . . . . (518) 694-7200
  2011-12 Tuition: In-state $26,380; Out-of-state $26,380
Albany Law School (Private, Not-for-profit)
  Fall 2010 Enrollment: 945 . . . . . . . . . . . . . . . . . . . . (518) 445-2311
Albany Medical College (Private, Not-for-profit)
  Fall 2010 Enrollment: 1,135 . . . . . . . . . . . . . . . . . . . (518) 262-3125
Excelsior College (Private, Not-for-profit)
  Fall 2010 Enrollment: 12,193 . . . . . . . . . . . . . . . . . . (518) 464-8500
Maria College of Albany (Private, Not-for-profit)
  Fall 2010 Enrollment: 565 . . . . . . . . . . . . . . . . . . . . (518) 438-3111
  2011-12 Tuition: In-state $10,120; Out-of-state $10,120
SUNY at Albany (Public)
  Fall 2010 Enrollment: 15,471 . . . . . . . . . . . . . . . . . . (518) 442-3300
  2011-12 Tuition: In-state $7,172; Out-of-state $15,282
The College of Saint Rose (Private, Not-for-profit)
  Fall 2010 Enrollment: 4,417 . . . . . . . . . . . . . . . . . . . (518) 454-5111
  2011-12 Tuition: In-state $25,464; Out-of-state $25,464

**Two-year College(s)**

Bryant and Stratton College-Albany (Private, For-profit)
  Fall 2010 Enrollment: 903 . . . . . . . . . . . . . . . . . . . . (518) 437-1802
  2011-12 Tuition: In-state $15,605; Out-of-state $15,605
ITT Technical Institute-Albany (Private, For-profit)
  Fall 2010 Enrollment: 429 . . . . . . . . . . . . . . . . . . . . (518) 452-9300
  2011-12 Tuition: In-state $18,048; Out-of-state $18,048
Memorial Hospital School of Nursing (Private, Not-for-profit)
  Fall 2010 Enrollment: 68 . . . . . . . . . . . . . . . . . . . . . (518) 471-3260
  2011-12 Tuition: In-state $9,261; Out-of-state $9,261
Mildred Elley School-Albany Campus (Private, For-profit)
  Fall 2010 Enrollment: 922 . . . . . . . . . . . . . . . . . . . . (518) 786-0855
  2011-12 Tuition: In-state $9,462; Out-of-state $9,462

**Vocational/Technical School(s)**

Albany BOCES-Adult Practical Nursing Program (Public)
  Fall 2010 Enrollment: 171 . . . . . . . . . . . . . . . . . . . . (518) 862-4800
  2011-12 Tuition: $11,305
Austin's School of Spa Technology (Private, For-profit)
  Fall 2010 Enrollment: 310 . . . . . . . . . . . . . . . . . . . . (518) 786-0855
  2011-12 Tuition: $9,415

Branford Hall Career Institute-Albany Campus (Private, For-profit)
  Fall 2010 Enrollment: 298 . . . . . . . . . . . . . . . . . . . . (518) 456-4464
  2011-12 Tuition: $12,200
Center for Natural Wellness School of Massage Therapy (Private, For-profit)
  Fall 2010 Enrollment: 128 . . . . . . . . . . . . . . . . . . . . (518) 489-4026
  2011-12 Tuition: $15,900
New School of Radio and Television (Private, For-profit)
  Fall 2010 Enrollment: 92 . . . . . . . . . . . . . . . . . . . . . (518) 438-7682
  2011-12 Tuition: $10,640
Orlo School of Hair Design and Cosmetology (Private, For-profit)
  Fall 2010 Enrollment: 137 . . . . . . . . . . . . . . . . . . . . (5.1) 846-E+12
  2011-12 Tuition: $9,600

**Housing:** Homeownership rate: 36.6% (2010); Median home value: $177,200 (2006-2010 5-year est.); Median contract rent: $681 per month (2006-2010 5-year est.); Median year structure built: before 1940 (2006-2010 5-year est.).

**Hospitals:** Albany Medical Center Hospital (631 beds); Albany Medical Center/South Clinical Campus (20 beds); Albany Memorial Hospital (165 beds); Albany VA Medical Center: Samuel S Stratton (156 beds); Capital District Psychiatric Center (165 beds); Saint Peter's Hospital (447 beds)

**Safety:** Violent crime rate: 105.8 per 10,000 population; Property crime rate: 500.8 per 10,000 population (2010).

**Newspapers:** At Home - Times Union (Local news; Circulation 100,000); Automotive Weekly (Community news; Circulation 100,000); Business - Times Union (Local news; Circulation 100,000); Community (Local news; Circulation 5,000); Daily Gazette - Albany Bureau (Local news); Daily Gazette - Capitol Bureau (Local news); Democrat and Chronicle - Albany Bureau (Local news); The Evangelist (Regional news; Circulation 50,000); Food - Times Union (Local news; Circulation 100,000); The Legislative Gazette (Regional news; Circulation 19,100); Metroland Magazine (Regional news; Circulation 40,000); New York Daily News - State Capitol Bureau (Regional news); New York Post - State Capitol Bureau (Regional news); The New York Times - State Capitol Bureau (Regional news); Newsday - State Capitol Bureau (Regional news); Preview - Times Union (Local news; Circulation 100,000); Times Union (Local news; Circulation 140,946); capitolwire.com - Albany Bureau (Regional news)

**Transportation:** Commute to work: 69.9% car, 12.9% public transportation, 11.0% walk, 3.7% work from home (2006-2010 5-year est.); Travel time to work: 40.1% less than 15 minutes, 42.5% 15 to 30 minutes, 11.5% 30 to 45 minutes, 3.0% 45 to 60 minutes, 2.9% 60 minutes or more (2006-2010 5-year est.); Amtrak: train service available.

**Airports:** Albany International (primary service/small hub)

**Additional Information Contacts**

Albany-Colonie Regional Chamber of Commerce . . . . . . . (518) 431-1400
  http://www.acchamber.org
City of Albany . . . . . . . . . . . . . . . . . . . . . . . . . . . . . . (518) 434-5284
  http://www.albanyny.org

---

**ALCOVE** (unincorporated postal area)

Zip Code: 12007

Covers a land area of 1.212 square miles and a water area of 0.002 square miles. Located at 42.45° N. Lat; 73.92° W. Long. Elevation is 545 feet. Population: 60 (2010); Density: 49.5 persons per square mile (2010); Race: 96.7% White, 1.7% Black, 0.0% Asian, 1.7% American Indian/Alaska Native, 0.0% Native Hawaiian/Other Pacific Islander, 0.0% Other, 3.3% Hispanic of any race (2010); Average household size: 2.31 (2010); Median age: 47.7 (2010); Males per 100 females: 140.0 (2010); Homeownership rate: 88.5% (2010)

---

**ALTAMONT** (village). Covers a land area of 1.186 square miles and a water area of <.001 square miles. Located at 42.70° N. Lat; 74.03° W. Long. Elevation is 463 feet.

**Population:** 1,638 (1990); 1,737 (2000); 1,720 (2010); Density: 1,449.7 persons per square mile (2010); Race: 96.5% White, 0.7% Black, 1.3% Asian, 0.2% American Indian/Alaska Native, 0.0% Native Hawaiian/Other Pacific Islander, 1.3% Other, 2.2% Hispanic of any race (2010); Average household size: 2.51 (2010); Median age: 44.6 (2010); Males per 100 females: 94.4 (2010); Marriage status: 29.5% never married, 54.4% now married, 8.4% widowed, 7.7% divorced (2006-2010 5-year est.); Foreign born: 1.3% (2006-2010 5-year est.); Ancestry (includes multiple ancestries): 29.0% Irish, 28.6% German, 16.3% English, 14.4% Italian, 12.9% Polish (2006-2010 5-year est.).

**Economy:** Single-family building permits issued: 0 (2011); Multi-family building permits issued: 0 (2011); Employment by occupation: 15.2%

management, 7.5% professional, 7.4% services, 18.6% sales, 4.9% farming, 4.9% construction, 3.8% production (2006-2010 5-year est.).
**Income:** Per capita income: $33,287 (2006-2010 5-year est.); Median household income: $67,440 (2006-2010 5-year est.); Average household income: $80,634 (2006-2010 5-year est.); Percent of households with income of $100,000 or more: 31.1% (2006-2010 5-year est.); Poverty rate: 7.2% (2006-2010 5-year est.).
**Education:** Percent of population age 25 and over with: High school diploma (including GED) or higher: 95.0% (2006-2010 5-year est.); Bachelor's degree or higher: 43.9% (2006-2010 5-year est.); Master's degree or higher: 19.8% (2006-2010 5-year est.).

**School District(s)**
Guilderland Central School District (KG-12)
   2009-10 Enrollment: 5,274 . . . . . . . . . . . . . . . . . . . (518) 456-6200
**Housing:** Homeownership rate: 71.3% (2010); Median home value: $237,600 (2006-2010 5-year est.); Median contract rent: $584 per month (2006-2010 5-year est.); Median year structure built: 1959 (2006-2010 5-year est.).
**Safety:** Violent crime rate: 0.0 per 10,000 population; Property crime rate: 83.5 per 10,000 population (2010).
**Newspapers:** The Altamont Enterprise (Community news; Circulation 7,250)
**Transportation:** Commute to work: 92.2% car, 1.1% public transportation, 0.9% walk, 5.9% work from home (2006-2010 5-year est.); Travel time to work: 19.9% less than 15 minutes, 40.2% 15 to 30 minutes, 27.4% 30 to 45 minutes, 9.4% 45 to 60 minutes, 3.1% 60 minutes or more (2006-2010 5-year est.)

**BERNE** (town). Covers a land area of 64.029 square miles and a water area of 0.704 square miles. Located at 42.60° N. Lat; 74.13° W. Long. Elevation is 971 feet.
**Population:** 3,045 (1990); 2,846 (2000); 2,794 (2010); Density: 43.6 persons per square mile (2010); Race: 97.8% White, 0.7% Black, 0.5% Asian, 0.0% American Indian/Alaska Native, 0.0% Native Hawaiian/Other Pacific Islander, 1.0% Other, 1.3% Hispanic of any race (2010); Average household size: 2.40 (2010); Median age: 46.1 (2010); Males per 100 females: 102.3 (2010); Marriage status: 24.9% never married, 65.4% now married, 4.8% widowed, 4.9% divorced (2006-2010 5-year est.); Foreign born: 5.0% (2006-2010 5-year est.); Ancestry (includes multiple ancestries): 30.9% German, 18.9% Irish, 14.7% English, 10.6% Dutch, 10.4% French (2006-2010 5-year est.).
**Economy:** Single-family building permits issued: 5 (2011); Multi-family building permits issued: 2 (2011); Employment by occupation: 13.9% management, 2.2% professional, 11.1% services, 13.7% sales, 3.8% farming, 11.8% construction, 6.6% production (2006-2010 5-year est.).
**Income:** Per capita income: $28,780 (2006-2010 5-year est.); Median household income: $64,359 (2006-2010 5-year est.); Average household income: $69,778 (2006-2010 5-year est.); Percent of households with income of $100,000 or more: 23.7% (2006-2010 5-year est.); Poverty rate: 2.4% (2006-2010 5-year est.).
**Education:** Percent of population age 25 and over with: High school diploma (including GED) or higher: 92.5% (2006-2010 5-year est.); Bachelor's degree or higher: 31.4% (2006-2010 5-year est.); Master's degree or higher: 16.2% (2006-2010 5-year est.).

**School District(s)**
Berne-Knox-Westerlo Central School District (PK-12)
   2009-10 Enrollment: 991 . . . . . . . . . . . . . . . . . . . . (518) 872-1293
**Housing:** Homeownership rate: 87.9% (2010); Median home value: $177,900 (2006-2010 5-year est.); Median contract rent: $531 per month (2006-2010 5-year est.); Median year structure built: 1962 (2006-2010 5-year est.).
**Transportation:** Commute to work: 92.0% car, 0.0% public transportation, 0.6% walk, 6.7% work from home (2006-2010 5-year est.); Travel time to work: 18.6% less than 15 minutes, 14.5% 15 to 30 minutes, 47.3% 30 to 45 minutes, 16.1% 45 to 60 minutes, 3.4% 60 minutes or more (2006-2010 5-year est.)

**BETHLEHEM** (town). Covers a land area of 49.029 square miles and a water area of 0.833 square miles. Located at 42.58° N. Lat; 73.82° W. Long. Elevation is 210 feet.
**Population:** 27,552 (1990); 31,304 (2000); 33,656 (2010); Density: 686.4 persons per square mile (2010); Race: 91.9% White, 2.6% Black, 3.2% Asian, 0.1% American Indian/Alaska Native, 0.0% Native Hawaiian/Other Pacific Islander, 2.2% Other, 2.7% Hispanic of any race (2010); Average household size: 2.46 (2010); Median age: 43.6 (2010); Males per 100

females: 92.2 (2010); Marriage status: 26.5% never married, 61.5% now married, 5.9% widowed, 6.0% divorced (2006-2010 5-year est.); Foreign born: 6.2% (2006-2010 5-year est.); Ancestry (includes multiple ancestries): 26.0% Irish, 20.1% German, 19.1% Italian, 13.3% English, 6.4% Polish (2006-2010 5-year est.).
**Economy:** Unemployment rate: 5.8% (February 2012); Total civilian labor force: 17,005 (February 2012); Single-family building permits issued: 22 (2011); Multi-family building permits issued: 107 (2011); Employment by occupation: 16.1% management, 7.4% professional, 7.1% services, 13.8% sales, 3.3% farming, 4.4% construction, 2.1% production (2006-2010 5-year est.).
**Income:** Per capita income: $39,867 (2006-2010 5-year est.); Median household income: $87,711 (2006-2010 5-year est.); Average household income: $101,025 (2006-2010 5-year est.); Percent of households with income of $100,000 or more: 41.2% (2006-2010 5-year est.); Poverty rate: 5.1% (2006-2010 5-year est.).
**Taxes:** Total city taxes per capita: $362 (2009); City property taxes per capita: $304 (2009).
**Education:** Percent of population age 25 and over with: High school diploma (including GED) or higher: 95.9% (2006-2010 5-year est.); Bachelor's degree or higher: 54.3% (2006-2010 5-year est.); Master's degree or higher: 29.5% (2006-2010 5-year est.).
**Housing:** Homeownership rate: 75.0% (2010); Median home value: $262,200 (2006-2010 5-year est.); Median contract rent: $885 per month (2006-2010 5-year est.); Median year structure built: 1972 (2006-2010 5-year est.).
**Safety:** Violent crime rate: 6.1 per 10,000 population; Property crime rate: 150.6 per 10,000 population (2010).
**Transportation:** Commute to work: 91.4% car, 1.8% public transportation, 1.3% walk, 4.1% work from home (2006-2010 5-year est.); Travel time to work: 26.8% less than 15 minutes, 52.5% 15 to 30 minutes, 15.3% 30 to 45 minutes, 2.0% 45 to 60 minutes, 3.4% 60 minutes or more (2006-2010 5-year est.)
**Additional Information Contacts**
Town of Bethlehem . . . . . . . . . . . . . . . . . . . . . . . (518) 439-4955
   http://www.townofbethlehem.org

**CLARKSVILLE** (unincorporated postal area)
Zip Code: 12041
   Covers a land area of 1.582 square miles and a water area of 0 square miles. Located at 42.57° N. Lat; 73.95° W. Long. Elevation is 663 feet. Population: 481 (2010); Density: 304.0 persons per square mile (2010); Race: 97.7% White, 0.4% Black, 0.2% Asian, 0.0% American Indian/Alaska Native, 0.0% Native Hawaiian/Other Pacific Islander, 1.7% Other, 1.5% Hispanic of any race (2010); Average household size: 2.57 (2010); Median age: 42.7 (2010); Males per 100 females: 113.8 (2010); Homeownership rate: 74.9% (2010)

**COEYMANS** (town). Covers a land area of 50.128 square miles and a water area of 3.038 square miles. Located at 42.49° N. Lat; 73.87° W. Long. Elevation is 59 feet.
**Population:** 8,158 (1990); 8,151 (2000); 7,418 (2010); Density: 148.0 persons per square mile (2010); Race: 92.9% White, 2.9% Black, 0.8% Asian, 0.2% American Indian/Alaska Native, 0.0% Native Hawaiian/Other Pacific Islander, 3.2% Other, 4.9% Hispanic of any race (2010); Average household size: 2.47 (2010); Median age: 40.5 (2010); Males per 100 females: 99.3 (2010); Marriage status: 28.3% never married, 57.3% now married, 6.9% widowed, 7.5% divorced (2006-2010 5-year est.); Foreign born: 4.6% (2006-2010 5-year est.); Ancestry (includes multiple ancestries): 26.6% German, 23.4% Irish, 18.0% Italian, 8.6% Dutch, 7.8% French (2006-2010 5-year est.).
**Economy:** Single-family building permits issued: 9 (2011); Multi-family building permits issued: 0 (2011); Employment by occupation: 5.8% management, 4.7% professional, 8.7% services, 21.0% sales, 3.4% farming, 14.1% construction, 12.9% production (2006-2010 5-year est.).
**Income:** Per capita income: $27,455 (2006-2010 5-year est.); Median household income: $59,659 (2006-2010 5-year est.); Average household income: $68,730 (2006-2010 5-year est.); Percent of households with income of $100,000 or more: 18.2% (2006-2010 5-year est.); Poverty rate: 4.7% (2006-2010 5-year est.).
**Education:** Percent of population age 25 and over with: High school diploma (including GED) or higher: 91.1% (2006-2010 5-year est.); Bachelor's degree or higher: 15.0% (2006-2010 5-year est.); Master's degree or higher: 7.7% (2006-2010 5-year est.).

**School District(s)**

Ravena-Coeymans-Selkirk Central School District (PK-12)

  2009-10 Enrollment: 2,070 . . . . . . . . . . . . . . . (518) 756-5200

**Housing:** Homeownership rate: 69.9% (2010); Median home value: $163,100 (2006-2010 5-year est.); Median contract rent: $549 per month (2006-2010 5-year est.); Median year structure built: 1969 (2006-2010 5-year est.).

**Safety:** Violent crime rate: 18.9 per 10,000 population; Property crime rate: 60.5 per 10,000 population (2010).

**Transportation:** Commute to work: 94.8% car, 0.0% public transportation, 1.3% walk, 2.2% work from home (2006-2010 5-year est.); Travel time to work: 21.9% less than 15 minutes, 35.1% 15 to 30 minutes, 34.5% 30 to 45 minutes, 5.1% 45 to 60 minutes, 3.4% 60 minutes or more (2006-2010 5-year est.)

**Additional Information Contacts**

Town of Coeymans . . . . . . . . . . . . . . . . . . . . . . . . (518) 756-6006

  http://www.coeymans.org

---

**COEYMANS HOLLOW** (unincorporated postal area)

Zip Code: 12046

Covers a land area of 15.348 square miles and a water area of 2.080 square miles. Located at 42.50° N. Lat; 73.92° W. Long. Elevation is 413 feet. Population: 817 (2010); Density: 53.2 persons per square mile (2010); Race: 97.3% White, 0.5% Black, 0.6% Asian, 0.6% American Indian/Alaska Native, 0.0% Native Hawaiian/Other Pacific Islander, 1.0% Other, 1.7% Hispanic of any race (2010); Average household size: 2.55 (2010); Median age: 43.9 (2010); Males per 100 females: 97.8 (2010); Homeownership rate: 87.3% (2010)

---

**COHOES** (city). Covers a land area of 3.773 square miles and a water area of 0.462 square miles. Located at 42.77° N. Lat; 73.70° W. Long. Elevation is 98 feet.

**History:** The world's first power-operated knitting mill was opened here in 1832. Van Schaick Mansion (1735), now a Museum, was used as headquarters by General Horatio Gates during the American Revolution. Settled by Dutch 1665, Incorporated 1869.

**Population:** 16,825 (1990); 15,521 (2000); 16,168 (2010); Density: 4,284.6 persons per square mile (2010); Race: 90.2% White, 4.7% Black, 0.9% Asian, 0.2% American Indian/Alaska Native, 0.0% Native Hawaiian/Other Pacific Islander, 4.0% Other, 3.7% Hispanic of any race (2010); Average household size: 2.13 (2010); Median age: 39.5 (2010); Males per 100 females: 89.7 (2010); Marriage status: 33.0% never married, 45.5% now married, 8.5% widowed, 12.9% divorced (2006-2010 5-year est.); Foreign born: 6.0% (2006-2010 5-year est.); Ancestry (includes multiple ancestries): 27.2% Irish, 18.7% French, 15.3% Italian, 13.7% German, 11.5% Polish (2006-2010 5-year est.).

**Economy:** Single-family building permits issued: 2 (2011); Multi-family building permits issued: 7 (2011); Employment by occupation: 8.8% management, 5.2% professional, 9.0% services, 23.5% sales, 5.7% farming, 7.2% construction, 5.8% production (2006-2010 5-year est.).

**Income:** Per capita income: $24,815 (2006-2010 5-year est.); Median household income: $41,443 (2006-2010 5-year est.); Average household income: $51,075 (2006-2010 5-year est.); Percent of households with income of $100,000 or more: 11.3% (2006-2010 5-year est.); Poverty rate: 14.6% (2006-2010 5-year est.).

**Education:** Percent of population age 25 and over with: High school diploma (including GED) or higher: 84.7% (2006-2010 5-year est.); Bachelor's degree or higher: 18.1% (2006-2010 5-year est.); Master's degree or higher: 6.2% (2006-2010 5-year est.).

**School District(s)**

Cohoes City School District (KG-12)

  2009-10 Enrollment: 2,024 . . . . . . . . . . . . . . . (518) 237-0100

North Colonie Csd (KG-12)

  2009-10 Enrollment: 5,527 . . . . . . . . . . . . . . . (518) 785-8591

**Housing:** Homeownership rate: 43.3% (2010); Median home value: $145,100 (2006-2010 5-year est.); Median contract rent: $545 per month (2006-2010 5-year est.); Median year structure built: before 1940 (2006-2010 5-year est.).

**Safety:** Violent crime rate: 26.9 per 10,000 population; Property crime rate: 202.9 per 10,000 population (2010).

**Transportation:** Commute to work: 92.9% car, 2.2% public transportation, 2.5% walk, 2.2% work from home (2006-2010 5-year est.); Travel time to work: 26.9% less than 15 minutes, 54.3% 15 to 30 minutes, 13.9% 30 to 45 minutes, 2.6% 45 to 60 minutes, 2.4% 60 minutes or more (2006-2010 5-year est.)

**Additional Information Contacts**

Albany-Colonie Regional Chamber of Commerce . . . . . (518) 431-1400

  http://acchamber.org

City of Cohoes . . . . . . . . . . . . . . . . . . . . . . . . . . (518) 233-2141

  http://www.cohoes.com

---

**COLONIE** (village). Covers a land area of 3.241 square miles and a water area of 0.003 square miles. Located at 42.72° N. Lat; 73.83° W. Long. Elevation is 312 feet.

**Population:** 7,989 (1990); 7,916 (2000); 7,793 (2010); Density: 2,404.1 persons per square mile (2010); Race: 86.7% White, 4.6% Black, 6.5% Asian, 0.1% American Indian/Alaska Native, 0.0% Native Hawaiian/Other Pacific Islander, 2.1% Other, 2.6% Hispanic of any race (2010); Average household size: 2.41 (2010); Median age: 44.2 (2010); Males per 100 females: 91.4 (2010); Marriage status: 28.0% never married, 53.4% now married, 7.9% widowed, 10.7% divorced (2006-2010 5-year est.); Foreign born: 10.1% (2006-2010 5-year est.); Ancestry (includes multiple ancestries): 30.1% Irish, 20.1% Italian, 19.0% German, 10.1% English, 8.5% Polish (2006-2010 5-year est.).

**Economy:** Single-family building permits issued: 0 (2011); Multi-family building permits issued: 20 (2011); Employment by occupation: 14.0% management, 5.6% professional, 6.9% services, 23.7% sales, 5.4% farming, 4.6% construction, 2.7% production (2006-2010 5-year est.).

**Income:** Per capita income: $37,126 (2006-2010 5-year est.); Median household income: $67,755 (2006-2010 5-year est.); Average household income: $88,704 (2006-2010 5-year est.); Percent of households with income of $100,000 or more: 27.4% (2006-2010 5-year est.); Poverty rate: 3.0% (2006-2010 5-year est.).

**Education:** Percent of population age 25 and over with: High school diploma (including GED) or higher: 94.4% (2006-2010 5-year est.); Bachelor's degree or higher: 31.3% (2006-2010 5-year est.); Master's degree or higher: 11.9% (2006-2010 5-year est.).

**Housing:** Homeownership rate: 80.8% (2010); Median home value: $185,200 (2006-2010 5-year est.); Median contract rent: $968 per month (2006-2010 5-year est.); Median year structure built: 1961 (2006-2010 5-year est.).

**Transportation:** Commute to work: 94.4% car, 0.9% public transportation, 0.2% walk, 2.3% work from home (2006-2010 5-year est.); Travel time to work: 34.5% less than 15 minutes, 50.2% 15 to 30 minutes, 11.2% 30 to 45 minutes, 2.0% 45 to 60 minutes, 2.0% 60 minutes or more (2006-2010 5-year est.)

**Additional Information Contacts**

Colonie Chamber of Commerce . . . . . . . . . . . . . . . (518) 785-6995

  http://www.coloniechamber.org

---

**COLONIE** (town). Covers a land area of 55.942 square miles and a water area of 1.899 square miles. Located at 42.74° N. Lat; 73.78° W. Long. Elevation is 312 feet.

**History:** Incorporated 1921.

**Population:** 76,536 (1990); 79,258 (2000); 81,591 (2010); Density: 1,458.5 persons per square mile (2010); Race: 85.2% White, 5.3% Black, 6.6% Asian, 0.1% American Indian/Alaska Native, 0.0% Native Hawaiian/Other Pacific Islander, 2.8% Other, 3.1% Hispanic of any race (2010); Average household size: 2.35 (2010); Median age: 42.6 (2010); Males per 100 females: 92.8 (2010); Marriage status: 33.0% never married, 51.6% now married, 6.5% widowed, 8.9% divorced (2006-2010 5-year est.); Foreign born: 9.1% (2006-2010 5-year est.); Ancestry (includes multiple ancestries): 28.3% Irish, 20.1% Italian, 17.8% German, 10.2% English, 8.5% Polish (2006-2010 5-year est.).

**Economy:** Unemployment rate: 6.8% (February 2012); Total civilian labor force: 42,248 (February 2012); Single-family building permits issued: 72 (2011); Multi-family building permits issued: 28 (2011); Employment by occupation: 13.4% management, 7.1% professional, 7.8% services, 19.6% sales, 5.6% farming, 5.4% construction, 3.1% production (2006-2010 5-year est.).

**Income:** Per capita income: $35,075 (2006-2010 5-year est.); Median household income: $68,134 (2006-2010 5-year est.); Average household income: $86,844 (2006-2010 5-year est.); Percent of households with income of $100,000 or more: 30.3% (2006-2010 5-year est.); Poverty rate: 5.7% (2006-2010 5-year est.).

**Taxes:** Total city taxes per capita: $335 (2009); City property taxes per capita: $295 (2009).

**Education:** Percent of population age 25 and over with: High school diploma (including GED) or higher: 93.0% (2006-2010 5-year est.);

Bachelor's degree or higher: 37.5% (2006-2010 5-year est.); Master's degree or higher: 16.3% (2006-2010 5-year est.).
**Housing:** Homeownership rate: 71.1% (2010); Median home value: $210,700 (2006-2010 5-year est.); Median contract rent: $782 per month (2006-2010 5-year est.); Median year structure built: 1965 (2006-2010 5-year est.).
**Safety:** Violent crime rate: 7.0 per 10,000 population; Property crime rate: 293.1 per 10,000 population (2010).
**Transportation:** Commute to work: 91.9% car, 1.4% public transportation, 1.6% walk, 3.9% work from home (2006-2010 5-year est.); Travel time to work: 35.9% less than 15 minutes, 50.5% 15 to 30 minutes, 10.2% 30 to 45 minutes, 1.8% 45 to 60 minutes, 1.6% 60 minutes or more (2006-2010 5-year est.)
**Additional Information Contacts**
Colonie Chamber of Commerce . . . . . . . . . . . . . . . . . . . . . . (518) 785-6995
   http://www.coloniechamber.org
Town of Colonie . . . . . . . . . . . . . . . . . . . . . . . . . . . . . . . . (518) 783-2700
   http://www.colonie.org

## EAST BERNE (unincorporated postal area)
Zip Code: 12059
   Covers a land area of 25.949 square miles and a water area of 0.698 square miles. Located at 42.61° N. Lat; 74.06° W. Long. Elevation is 1,178 feet. Population: 1,632 (2010); Density: 62.9 persons per square mile (2010); Race: 98.3% White, 0.5% Black, 0.2% Asian, 0.1% American Indian/Alaska Native, 0.0% Native Hawaiian/Other Pacific Islander, 0.9% Other, 0.7% Hispanic of any race (2010); Average household size: 2.43 (2010); Median age: 46.9 (2010); Males per 100 females: 105.5 (2010); Homeownership rate: 85.1% (2010)

## FEURA BUSH (unincorporated postal area)
Zip Code: 12067
   Covers a land area of 21.410 square miles and a water area of 0.196 square miles. Located at 42.55° N. Lat; 73.92° W. Long. Elevation is 262 feet. Population: 1,506 (2010); Density: 70.3 persons per square mile (2010); Race: 95.8% White, 0.9% Black, 1.1% Asian, 0.3% American Indian/Alaska Native, 0.0% Native Hawaiian/Other Pacific Islander, 1.9% Other, 1.9% Hispanic of any race (2010); Average household size: 2.43 (2010); Median age: 47.1 (2010); Males per 100 females: 100.5 (2010); Homeownership rate: 83.7% (2010)

## GLENMONT (unincorporated postal area)
Zip Code: 12077
   Covers a land area of 10.085 square miles and a water area of 0.396 square miles. Located at 42.58° N. Lat; 73.77° W. Long. Elevation is 46 feet. Population: 6,246 (2010); Density: 619.3 persons per square mile (2010); Race: 88.8% White, 5.3% Black, 3.9% Asian, 0.1% American Indian/Alaska Native, 0.0% Native Hawaiian/Other Pacific Islander, 1.9% Other, 3.0% Hispanic of any race (2010); Average household size: 2.53 (2010); Median age: 41.7 (2010); Males per 100 females: 95.4 (2010); Homeownership rate: 77.9% (2010)

## GREEN ISLAND (town and village). Covers a land area of 0.747 square miles and a water area of 0.186 square miles. Located at 42.74° N. Lat; 73.69° W. Long. Elevation is 23 feet.
**History:** Incorporated 1869.
**Population:** 2,490 (1990); 2,278 (2000); 2,620 (2010); Density: 3,506.7 persons per square mile (2010); Race: 89.2% White, 5.0% Black, 1.8% Asian, 0.5% American Indian/Alaska Native, 0.0% Native Hawaiian/Other Pacific Islander, 3.5% Other, 3.3% Hispanic of any race (2010); Average household size: 2.04 (2010); Median age: 38.9 (2010); Males per 100 females: 89.7 (2010); Marriage status: 43.0% never married, 39.5% now married, 8.9% widowed, 8.5% divorced (2006-2010 5-year est.); Foreign born: 3.3% (2006-2010 5-year est.); Ancestry (includes multiple ancestries): 30.6% Irish, 19.9% French, 18.0% Italian, 17.8% German, 7.0% English (2006-2010 5-year est.).
**Economy:** Single-family building permits issued: 3 (2011); Multi-family building permits issued: 0 (2011); Employment by occupation: 11.4% management, 6.2% professional, 8.9% services, 23.2% sales, 10.0% farming, 9.1% construction, 5.0% production (2006-2010 5-year est.).
**Income:** Per capita income: $26,718 (2006-2010 5-year est.); Median household income: $51,417 (2006-2010 5-year est.); Average household income: $57,344 (2006-2010 5-year est.); Percent of households with income of $100,000 or more: 10.9% (2006-2010 5-year est.); Poverty rate: 17.7% (2006-2010 5-year est.).

**Education:** Percent of population age 25 and over with: High school diploma (including GED) or higher: 91.5% (2006-2010 5-year est.); Bachelor's degree or higher: 18.9% (2006-2010 5-year est.); Master's degree or higher: 9.1% (2006-2010 5-year est.).
### School District(s)
Green Island Union Free School District (KG-12)
   2009-10 Enrollment: 323 . . . . . . . . . . . . . . . . . . . . . (518) 273-1422
**Housing:** Homeownership rate: 35.0% (2010); Median home value: $121,200 (2006-2010 5-year est.); Median contract rent: $662 per month (2006-2010 5-year est.); Median year structure built: before 1940 (2006-2010 5-year est.).
**Safety:** Violent crime rate: 23.7 per 10,000 population; Property crime rate: 233.3 per 10,000 population (2010).
**Transportation:** Commute to work: 89.4% car, 1.5% public transportation, 5.7% walk, 2.6% work from home (2006-2010 5-year est.); Travel time to work: 38.7% less than 15 minutes, 38.4% 15 to 30 minutes, 14.0% 30 to 45 minutes, 2.4% 45 to 60 minutes, 6.5% 60 minutes or more (2006-2010 5-year est.)

## GUILDERLAND (town). Covers a land area of 57.902 square miles and a water area of 0.884 square miles. Located at 42.70° N. Lat; 73.96° W. Long. Elevation is 207 feet.
**Population:** 28,877 (1990); 32,688 (2000); 35,303 (2010); Density: 609.7 persons per square mile (2010); Race: 86.2% White, 3.4% Black, 7.5% Asian, 0.2% American Indian/Alaska Native, 0.0% Native Hawaiian/Other Pacific Islander, 2.7% Other, 3.2% Hispanic of any race (2010); Average household size: 2.34 (2010); Median age: 41.5 (2010); Males per 100 females: 94.0 (2010); Marriage status: 30.3% never married, 55.4% now married, 6.3% widowed, 8.0% divorced (2006-2010 5-year est.); Foreign born: 10.8% (2006-2010 5-year est.); Ancestry (includes multiple ancestries): 24.2% Irish, 21.1% Italian, 19.9% German, 12.0% English, 7.8% Polish (2006-2010 5-year est.).
**Economy:** Unemployment rate: 6.0% (February 2012); Total civilian labor force: 19,046 (February 2012); Single-family building permits issued: 36 (2011); Multi-family building permits issued: 0 (2011); Employment by occupation: 16.4% management, 9.1% professional, 6.2% services, 15.8% sales, 3.3% farming, 5.5% construction, 2.8% production (2006-2010 5-year est.).
**Income:** Per capita income: $38,039 (2006-2010 5-year est.); Median household income: $76,741 (2006-2010 5-year est.); Average household income: $92,769 (2006-2010 5-year est.); Percent of households with income of $100,000 or more: 35.9% (2006-2010 5-year est.); Poverty rate: 5.5% (2006-2010 5-year est.).
**Taxes:** Total city taxes per capita: $281 (2009); City property taxes per capita: $231 (2009).
**Education:** Percent of population age 25 and over with: High school diploma (including GED) or higher: 94.3% (2006-2010 5-year est.); Bachelor's degree or higher: 46.7% (2006-2010 5-year est.); Master's degree or higher: 23.1% (2006-2010 5-year est.).
### School District(s)
Guilderland Central School District (KG-12)
   2009-10 Enrollment: 5,274 . . . . . . . . . . . . . . . . . . . (518) 456-6200
**Housing:** Homeownership rate: 67.9% (2010); Median home value: $235,100 (2006-2010 5-year est.); Median contract rent: $875 per month (2006-2010 5-year est.); Median year structure built: 1973 (2006-2010 5-year est.).
**Safety:** Violent crime rate: 3.4 per 10,000 population; Property crime rate: 299.0 per 10,000 population (2010).
**Transportation:** Commute to work: 92.4% car, 1.9% public transportation, 1.6% walk, 3.5% work from home (2006-2010 5-year est.); Travel time to work: 29.1% less than 15 minutes, 47.2% 15 to 30 minutes, 18.1% 30 to 45 minutes, 3.9% 45 to 60 minutes, 1.7% 60 minutes or more (2006-2010 5-year est.)
**Additional Information Contacts**
Guilderland Chamber of Commerce . . . . . . . . . . . . . . . . . . (518) 456-6611
   http://www.guilderlandchamber.com
Town of Guilderland . . . . . . . . . . . . . . . . . . . . . . . . . . . . (518) 356-1980
   http://www.townofguilderland.org

## GUILDERLAND CENTER (unincorporated postal area)
Zip Code: 12085
   Covers a land area of 0.175 square miles and a water area of 0 square miles. Located at 42.70° N. Lat; 73.96° W. Long. Elevation is 318 feet. Population: 479 (2010); Density: 2,728.3 persons per square mile (2010); Race: 82.5% White, 7.9% Black, 5.0% Asian, 0.2% American

Indian/Alaska Native, 0.0% Native Hawaiian/Other Pacific Islander, 4.4% Other, 3.3% Hispanic of any race (2010); Average household size: 1.84 (2010); Median age: 49.5 (2010); Males per 100 females: 59.1 (2010); Homeownership rate: 18.4% (2010)

## KNOX (town).
Covers a land area of 41.762 square miles and a water area of 0.174 square miles. Located at 42.68° N. Lat; 74.10° W. Long. Elevation is 1,234 feet.

**Population:** 2,655 (1990); 2,647 (2000); 2,692 (2010); Density: 64.5 persons per square mile (2010); Race: 98.0% White, 0.4% Black, 0.2% Asian, 0.0% American Indian/Alaska Native, 0.0% Native Hawaiian/Other Pacific Islander, 1.4% Other, 0.7% Hispanic of any race (2010); Average household size: 2.62 (2010); Median age: 43.7 (2010); Males per 100 females: 103.2 (2010); Marriage status: 23.0% never married, 64.6% now married, 3.2% widowed, 9.3% divorced (2006-2010 5-year est.); Foreign born: 2.1% (2006-2010 5-year est.); Ancestry (includes multiple ancestries): 29.8% German, 24.2% Irish, 22.8% English, 15.1% Italian, 10.3% French (2006-2010 5-year est.).

**Economy:** Single-family building permits issued: 5 (2011); Multi-family building permits issued: 0 (2011); Employment by occupation: 14.3% management, 4.1% professional, 5.5% services, 15.7% sales, 4.8% farming, 12.3% construction, 10.7% production (2006-2010 5-year est.).

**Income:** Per capita income: $29,968 (2006-2010 5-year est.); Median household income: $73,500 (2006-2010 5-year est.); Average household income: $82,246 (2006-2010 5-year est.); Percent of households with income of $100,000 or more: 30.7% (2006-2010 5-year est.); Poverty rate: 10.4% (2006-2010 5-year est.).

**Education:** Percent of population age 25 and over with: High school diploma (including GED) or higher: 92.9% (2006-2010 5-year est.); Bachelor's degree or higher: 26.4% (2006-2010 5-year est.); Master's degree or higher: 12.0% (2006-2010 5-year est.).

**Housing:** Homeownership rate: 88.2% (2010); Median home value: $197,900 (2006-2010 5-year est.); Median contract rent: $806 per month (2006-2010 5-year est.); Median year structure built: 1970 (2006-2010 5-year est.).

**Transportation:** Commute to work: 89.2% car, 0.8% public transportation, 1.3% walk, 4.2% work from home (2006-2010 5-year est.); Travel time to work: 16.8% less than 15 minutes, 26.3% 15 to 30 minutes, 38.4% 30 to 45 minutes, 14.0% 45 to 60 minutes, 4.5% 60 minutes or more (2006-2010 5-year est.)

**Additional Information Contacts**
Town of Knox . . . . . . . . . . . . . . . . . . . . . . . . . . . . . . . (518) 872-2551
  http://www.knoxny.org

## LATHAM (unincorporated postal area)
Zip Code: 12110
  Covers a land area of 14.685 square miles and a water area of 0.449 square miles. Located at 42.75° N. Lat; 73.77° W. Long. Elevation is 354 feet. Population: 21,908 (2010); Density: 1,491.8 persons per square mile (2010); Race: 84.3% White, 5.5% Black, 7.1% Asian, 0.2% American Indian/Alaska Native, 0.0% Native Hawaiian/Other Pacific Islander, 2.9% Other, 3.4% Hispanic of any race (2010); Average household size: 2.41 (2010); Median age: 38.9 (2010); Males per 100 females: 94.3 (2010); Homeownership rate: 72.3% (2010)

## MENANDS (village).
Covers a land area of 3.058 square miles and a water area of 0.250 square miles. Located at 42.69° N. Lat; 73.72° W. Long. Elevation is 36 feet.

**History:** Incorporated 1924.

**Population:** 4,326 (1990); 3,910 (2000); 3,990 (2010); Density: 1,304.7 persons per square mile (2010); Race: 70.8% White, 12.2% Black, 13.2% Asian, 0.3% American Indian/Alaska Native, 0.0% Native Hawaiian/Other Pacific Islander, 3.5% Other, 3.8% Hispanic of any race (2010); Average household size: 2.08 (2010); Median age: 41.5 (2010); Males per 100 females: 91.1 (2010); Marriage status: 40.6% never married, 44.3% now married, 5.9% widowed, 9.2% divorced (2006-2010 5-year est.); Foreign born: 15.0% (2006-2010 5-year est.); Ancestry (includes multiple ancestries): 25.1% Irish, 21.3% Italian, 16.8% German, 12.6% English, 5.2% Polish (2006-2010 5-year est.).

**Economy:** Single-family building permits issued: 1 (2011); Multi-family building permits issued: 0 (2011); Employment by occupation: 15.6% management, 12.6% professional, 6.8% services, 13.5% sales, 5.8% farming, 2.7% construction, 1.6% production (2006-2010 5-year est.).

**Income:** Per capita income: $44,310 (2006-2010 5-year est.); Median household income: $64,481 (2006-2010 5-year est.); Average household

income: $94,569 (2006-2010 5-year est.); Percent of households with income of $100,000 or more: 24.5% (2006-2010 5-year est.); Poverty rate: 11.1% (2006-2010 5-year est.).

**Education:** Percent of population age 25 and over with: High school diploma (including GED) or higher: 97.9% (2006-2010 5-year est.); Bachelor's degree or higher: 54.7% (2006-2010 5-year est.); Master's degree or higher: 27.7% (2006-2010 5-year est.).

### School District(s)
Menands Union Free School District (KG-08)
  2009-10 Enrollment: 229 . . . . . . . . . . . . . . . . . . . (518) 465-4561

**Housing:** Homeownership rate: 41.0% (2010); Median home value: $211,100 (2006-2010 5-year est.); Median contract rent: $901 per month (2006-2010 5-year est.); Median year structure built: 1962 (2006-2010 5-year est.).

**Safety:** Violent crime rate: 16.1 per 10,000 population; Property crime rate: 452.6 per 10,000 population (2010).

**Transportation:** Commute to work: 85.0% car, 5.9% public transportation, 5.4% walk, 2.5% work from home (2006-2010 5-year est.); Travel time to work: 42.7% less than 15 minutes, 37.5% 15 to 30 minutes, 13.1% 30 to 45 minutes, 5.5% 45 to 60 minutes, 1.2% 60 minutes or more (2006-2010 5-year est.)

**Additional Information Contacts**
Village of Menands . . . . . . . . . . . . . . . . . . . . . . . . . (518) 434-2922
  http://www.villageofmenands.com

## NEW SCOTLAND (town).
Covers a land area of 57.498 square miles and a water area of 0.470 square miles. Located at 42.60° N. Lat; 73.93° W. Long. Elevation is 282 feet.

**Population:** 9,102 (1990); 8,626 (2000); 8,648 (2010); Density: 150.4 persons per square mile (2010); Race: 96.5% White, 0.6% Black, 1.1% Asian, 0.2% American Indian/Alaska Native, 0.1% Native Hawaiian/Other Pacific Islander, 1.5% Other, 1.7% Hispanic of any race (2010); Average household size: 2.50 (2010); Median age: 45.2 (2010); Males per 100 females: 98.4 (2010); Marriage status: 21.4% never married, 65.6% now married, 5.3% widowed, 7.7% divorced (2006-2010 5-year est.); Foreign born: 4.4% (2006-2010 5-year est.); Ancestry (includes multiple ancestries): 28.7% German, 26.7% Irish, 15.9% English, 12.5% Italian, 6.4% Dutch (2006-2010 5-year est.).

**Economy:** Single-family building permits issued: 4 (2011); Multi-family building permits issued: 0 (2011); Employment by occupation: 16.8% management, 5.0% professional, 5.8% services, 16.2% sales, 2.1% farming, 10.4% construction, 6.2% production (2006-2010 5-year est.).

**Income:** Per capita income: $40,542 (2006-2010 5-year est.); Median household income: $72,660 (2006-2010 5-year est.); Average household income: $101,545 (2006-2010 5-year est.); Percent of households with income of $100,000 or more: 33.1% (2006-2010 5-year est.); Poverty rate: 6.7% (2006-2010 5-year est.).

**Education:** Percent of population age 25 and over with: High school diploma (including GED) or higher: 93.0% (2006-2010 5-year est.); Bachelor's degree or higher: 43.3% (2006-2010 5-year est.); Master's degree or higher: 20.9% (2006-2010 5-year est.).

**Housing:** Homeownership rate: 83.2% (2010); Median home value: $231,000 (2006-2010 5-year est.); Median contract rent: $663 per month (2006-2010 5-year est.); Median year structure built: 1960 (2006-2010 5-year est.).

**Transportation:** Commute to work: 92.9% car, 0.4% public transportation, 2.0% walk, 3.5% work from home (2006-2010 5-year est.); Travel time to work: 19.0% less than 15 minutes, 48.2% 15 to 30 minutes, 25.2% 30 to 45 minutes, 3.4% 45 to 60 minutes, 4.2% 60 minutes or more (2006-2010 5-year est.)

**Additional Information Contacts**
Town of New Scotland . . . . . . . . . . . . . . . . . . . . . . . (518) 439-4865
  http://www.townofnewscotland.com

## PRESTON HOLLOW (unincorporated postal area)
Zip Code: 12469
  Covers a land area of 33.904 square miles and a water area of 0.019 square miles. Located at 42.44° N. Lat; 74.23° W. Long. Elevation is 846 feet. Population: 677 (2010); Density: 20.0 persons per square mile (2010); Race: 97.6% White, 1.0% Black, 0.1% Asian, 0.0% American Indian/Alaska Native, 0.0% Native Hawaiian/Other Pacific Islander, 1.3% Other, 1.6% Hispanic of any race (2010); Average household size: 2.24 (2010); Median age: 48.6 (2010); Males per 100 females: 102.7 (2010); Homeownership rate: 87.8% (2010)

## PRESTON-POTTER HOLLOW (CDP). Covers a land area of 10.134 square miles and a water area of 0 square miles. Located at 42.43° N. Lat; 74.22° W. Long. Elevation is 860 feet.

**Population:** 407 (1990); 374 (2000); 366 (2010); Density: 36.1 persons per square mile (2010); Race: 97.0% White, 1.4% Black, 0.3% Asian, 0.0% American Indian/Alaska Native, 0.0% Native Hawaiian/Other Pacific Islander, 1.3% Other, 0.8% Hispanic of any race (2010); Average household size: 2.47 (2010); Median age: 42.0 (2010); Males per 100 females: 95.7 (2010); Marriage status: 19.8% never married, 53.2% now married, 12.5% widowed, 14.5% divorced (2006-2010 5-year est.); Foreign born: 6.2% (2006-2010 5-year est.); Ancestry (includes multiple ancestries): 26.4% Italian, 22.0% German, 13.9% Irish, 13.6% American, 10.6% French (2006-2010 5-year est.).

**Economy:** Employment by occupation: 19.3% management, 0.0% professional, 6.4% services, 16.5% sales, 0.0% farming, 5.5% construction, 10.1% production (2006-2010 5-year est.).

**Income:** Per capita income: $23,894 (2006-2010 5-year est.); Median household income: $45,556 (2006-2010 5-year est.); Average household income: $46,301 (2006-2010 5-year est.); Percent of households with income of $100,000 or more: 7.2% (2006-2010 5-year est.); Poverty rate: 6.6% (2006-2010 5-year est.).

**Education:** Percent of population age 25 and over with: High school diploma (including GED) or higher: 89.2% (2006-2010 5-year est.); Bachelor's degree or higher: 28.2% (2006-2010 5-year est.); Master's degree or higher: 0.0% (2006-2010 5-year est.).

**Housing:** Homeownership rate: 89.2% (2010); Median home value: $145,000 (2006-2010 5-year est.); Median contract rent: n/a per month (2006-2010 5-year est.); Median year structure built: 1954 (2006-2010 5-year est.).

**Transportation:** Commute to work: 75.2% car, 0.0% public transportation, 0.0% walk, 24.8% work from home (2006-2010 5-year est.); Travel time to work: 19.5% less than 15 minutes, 34.1% 15 to 30 minutes, 41.5% 30 to 45 minutes, 4.9% 45 to 60 minutes, 0.0% 60 minutes or more (2006-2010 5-year est.).

## RAVENA (village). Covers a land area of 1.467 square miles and a water area of 0.005 square miles. Located at 42.47° N. Lat; 73.81° W. Long. Elevation is 230 feet.

**History:** Incorporated 1914.

**Population:** 3,497 (1990); 3,369 (2000); 3,268 (2010); Density: 2,227.6 persons per square mile (2010); Race: 90.2% White, 4.4% Black, 0.9% Asian, 0.2% American Indian/Alaska Native, 0.0% Native Hawaiian/Other Pacific Islander, 4.3% Other, 7.5% Hispanic of any race (2010); Average household size: 2.43 (2010); Median age: 37.7 (2010); Males per 100 females: 94.2 (2010); Marriage status: 20.0% never married, 64.4% now married, 9.0% widowed, 6.6% divorced (2006-2010 5-year est.); Foreign born: 7.5% (2006-2010 5-year est.); Ancestry (includes multiple ancestries): 22.3% German, 22.2% Italian, 16.8% Irish, 7.1% English, 6.6% Dutch (2006-2010 5-year est.).

**Economy:** Single-family building permits issued: 0 (2011); Multi-family building permits issued: 0 (2011); Employment by occupation: 5.4% management, 4.1% professional, 8.8% services, 22.7% sales, 3.7% farming, 9.6% construction, 6.2% production (2006-2010 5-year est.).

**Income:** Per capita income: $25,593 (2006-2010 5-year est.); Median household income: $52,714 (2006-2010 5-year est.); Average household income: $62,653 (2006-2010 5-year est.); Percent of households with income of $100,000 or more: 14.4% (2006-2010 5-year est.); Poverty rate: 3.5% (2006-2010 5-year est.).

**Education:** Percent of population age 25 and over with: High school diploma (including GED) or higher: 93.0% (2006-2010 5-year est.); Bachelor's degree or higher: 13.3% (2006-2010 5-year est.); Master's degree or higher: 7.0% (2006-2010 5-year est.).

### School District(s)
Ravena-Coeymans-Selkirk Central School District (PK-12)
    2009-10 Enrollment: 2,070 . . . . . . . . . . . . . . . . . . . . . . (518) 756-5200

**Housing:** Homeownership rate: 61.1% (2010); Median home value: $160,800 (2006-2010 5-year est.); Median contract rent: $554 per month (2006-2010 5-year est.); Median year structure built: 1967 (2006-2010 5-year est.).

**Newspapers:** Greenville Local (Community news; Circulation 1,050); News-Herald (Local news; Circulation 3,250)

**Transportation:** Commute to work: 95.0% car, 0.0% public transportation, 1.0% walk, 2.1% work from home (2006-2010 5-year est.); Travel time to work: 19.2% less than 15 minutes, 40.7% 15 to 30 minutes, 32.3% 30 to 45

minutes, 4.0% 45 to 60 minutes, 3.9% 60 minutes or more (2006-2010 5-year est.)

## RENSSELAERVILLE (town). Covers a land area of 61.464 square miles and a water area of 0.420 square miles. Located at 42.47° N. Lat; 74.17° W. Long. Elevation is 1,365 feet.

**Population:** 1,981 (1990); 1,915 (2000); 1,843 (2010); Density: 30.0 persons per square mile (2010); Race: 97.7% White, 1.0% Black, 0.2% Asian, 0.0% American Indian/Alaska Native, 0.0% Native Hawaiian/Other Pacific Islander, 1.1% Other, 1.8% Hispanic of any race (2010); Average household size: 2.40 (2010); Median age: 46.2 (2010); Males per 100 females: 103.6 (2010); Marriage status: 28.4% never married, 55.5% now married, 7.4% widowed, 8.7% divorced (2006-2010 5-year est.); Foreign born: 2.4% (2006-2010 5-year est.); Ancestry (includes multiple ancestries): 28.2% German, 25.7% Irish, 16.4% Dutch, 16.0% Italian, 12.8% English (2006-2010 5-year est.).

**Economy:** Single-family building permits issued: 3 (2011); Multi-family building permits issued: 0 (2011); Employment by occupation: 11.1% management, 3.3% professional, 9.9% services, 14.2% sales, 1.2% farming, 16.9% construction, 5.1% production (2006-2010 5-year est.).

**Income:** Per capita income: $27,708 (2006-2010 5-year est.); Median household income: $62,614 (2006-2010 5-year est.); Average household income: $67,899 (2006-2010 5-year est.); Percent of households with income of $100,000 or more: 19.2% (2006-2010 5-year est.); Poverty rate: 14.4% (2006-2010 5-year est.).

**Taxes:** Total city taxes per capita: $624 (2009); City property taxes per capita: $585 (2009).

**Education:** Percent of population age 25 and over with: High school diploma (including GED) or higher: 85.9% (2006-2010 5-year est.); Bachelor's degree or higher: 30.3% (2006-2010 5-year est.); Master's degree or higher: 13.1% (2006-2010 5-year est.).

**Housing:** Homeownership rate: 86.2% (2010); Median home value: $169,600 (2006-2010 5-year est.); Median contract rent: $572 per month (2006-2010 5-year est.); Median year structure built: 1958 (2006-2010 5-year est.).

**Transportation:** Commute to work: 89.5% car, 2.3% public transportation, 1.8% walk, 6.4% work from home (2006-2010 5-year est.); Travel time to work: 20.7% less than 15 minutes, 18.7% 15 to 30 minutes, 35.0% 30 to 45 minutes, 15.7% 45 to 60 minutes, 9.9% 60 minutes or more (2006-2010 5-year est.)

## SELKIRK (unincorporated postal area)
Zip Code: 12158

Covers a land area of 30.594 square miles and a water area of 0.943 square miles. Located at 42.54° N. Lat; 73.82° W. Long. Elevation is 161 feet. Population: 6,309 (2010); Density: 206.2 persons per square mile (2010); Race: 91.7% White, 3.1% Black, 2.2% Asian, 0.2% American Indian/Alaska Native, 0.0% Native Hawaiian/Other Pacific Islander, 2.8% Other, 3.4% Hispanic of any race (2010); Average household size: 2.56 (2010); Median age: 40.4 (2010); Males per 100 females: 98.3 (2010); Homeownership rate: 77.9% (2010)

## SLINGERLANDS (unincorporated postal area)
Zip Code: 12159

Covers a land area of 14.088 square miles and a water area of 0.044 square miles. Located at 42.65° N. Lat; 73.88° W. Long. Elevation is 220 feet. Population: 7,896 (2010); Density: 560.5 persons per square mile (2010); Race: 89.1% White, 2.0% Black, 6.6% Asian, 0.2% American Indian/Alaska Native, 0.0% Native Hawaiian/Other Pacific Islander, 2.1% Other, 2.2% Hispanic of any race (2010); Average household size: 2.38 (2010); Median age: 45.4 (2010); Males per 100 females: 89.1 (2010); Homeownership rate: 69.7% (2010)

## SOUTH BETHLEHEM (unincorporated postal area)
Zip Code: 12161

Covers a land area of 0.409 square miles and a water area of 0.006 square miles. Located at 42.53° N. Lat; 73.85° W. Long. Elevation is 213 feet. Population: 160 (2010); Density: 391.0 persons per square mile (2010); Race: 97.5% White, 0.6% Black, 1.3% Asian, 0.0% American Indian/Alaska Native, 0.0% Native Hawaiian/Other Pacific Islander, 0.6% Other, 1.3% Hispanic of any race (2010); Average household size: 2.54 (2010); Median age: 42.6 (2010); Males per 100 females: 102.5 (2010); Homeownership rate: 82.6% (2010)

**VOORHEESVILLE** (village). Covers a land area of 2.138 square miles and a water area of 0.004 square miles. Located at 42.65° N. Lat; 73.93° W. Long. Elevation is 338 feet.

**Population:** 3,090 (1990); 2,705 (2000); 2,789 (2010); Density: 1,304.0 persons per square mile (2010); Race: 96.5% White, 0.8% Black, 1.5% Asian, 0.2% American Indian/Alaska Native, 0.0% Native Hawaiian/Other Pacific Islander, 1.0% Other, 2.2% Hispanic of any race (2010); Average household size: 2.51 (2010); Median age: 43.7 (2010); Males per 100 females: 94.8 (2010); Marriage status: 21.6% never married, 66.1% now married, 4.1% widowed, 8.2% divorced (2006-2010 5-year est.); Foreign born: 3.5% (2006-2010 5-year est.); Ancestry (includes multiple ancestries): 35.3% Irish, 18.9% Italian, 17.7% German, 17.4% English, 8.9% French (2006-2010 5-year est.).

**Economy:** Single-family building permits issued: 2 (2011); Multi-family building permits issued: 0 (2011); Employment by occupation: 17.2% management, 5.9% professional, 5.5% services, 18.2% sales, 4.5% farming, 9.0% construction, 4.5% production (2006-2010 5-year est.).

**Income:** Per capita income: $35,017 (2006-2010 5-year est.); Median household income: $76,587 (2006-2010 5-year est.); Average household income: $86,868 (2006-2010 5-year est.); Percent of households with income of $100,000 or more: 33.1% (2006-2010 5-year est.); Poverty rate: 7.9% (2006-2010 5-year est.).

**Education:** Percent of population age 25 and over with: High school diploma (including GED) or higher: 94.8% (2006-2010 5-year est.); Bachelor's degree or higher: 46.9% (2006-2010 5-year est.); Master's degree or higher: 22.2% (2006-2010 5-year est.).

### School District(s)
Voorheesville Central School District (KG-12)
    2009-10 Enrollment: 1,192 . . . . . . . . . . . . . . . . . . . . . . . . (518) 765-3313

**Housing:** Homeownership rate: 80.6% (2010); Median home value: $227,600 (2006-2010 5-year est.); Median contract rent: $760 per month (2006-2010 5-year est.); Median year structure built: 1964 (2006-2010 5-year est.).

**Transportation:** Commute to work: 93.9% car, 0.4% public transportation, 2.6% walk, 1.5% work from home (2006-2010 5-year est.); Travel time to work: 15.5% less than 15 minutes, 52.3% 15 to 30 minutes, 29.3% 30 to 45 minutes, 1.9% 45 to 60 minutes, 1.0% 60 minutes or more (2006-2010 5-year est.)

**WATERVLIET** (city). Covers a land area of 1.345 square miles and a water area of 0.129 square miles. Located at 42.72° N. Lat; 73.70° W. Long. Elevation is 30 feet.

**History:** The U.S. Watervliet Arsenal here, which specializes in the production of heavy ordnance, was established 1813. In 1776, Ann Lee founded the first American community of Shakers (United Society of Believers) in Watervliet. Founded by the Dutch 1735, Incorporated as a city 1896.

**Population:** 11,275 (1990); 10,207 (2000); 10,254 (2010); Density: 7,621.0 persons per square mile (2010); Race: 83.5% White, 8.9% Black, 2.5% Asian, 0.4% American Indian/Alaska Native, 0.0% Native Hawaiian/Other Pacific Islander, 4.7% Other, 6.1% Hispanic of any race (2010); Average household size: 2.12 (2010); Median age: 35.2 (2010); Males per 100 females: 92.9 (2010); Marriage status: 42.0% never married, 39.8% now married, 7.2% widowed, 11.0% divorced (2006-2010 5-year est.); Foreign born: 3.6% (2006-2010 5-year est.); Ancestry (includes multiple ancestries): 29.8% Irish, 23.1% Italian, 14.2% German, 10.7% French, 9.3% Polish (2006-2010 5-year est.).

**Economy:** Single-family building permits issued: 1 (2011); Multi-family building permits issued: 4 (2011); Employment by occupation: 9.5% management, 3.2% professional, 10.6% services, 24.3% sales, 5.2% farming, 7.9% construction, 5.9% production (2006-2010 5-year est.).

**Income:** Per capita income: $22,469 (2006-2010 5-year est.); Median household income: $41,375 (2006-2010 5-year est.); Average household income: $47,905 (2006-2010 5-year est.); Percent of households with income of $100,000 or more: 8.8% (2006-2010 5-year est.); Poverty rate: 12.2% (2006-2010 5-year est.).

**Education:** Percent of population age 25 and over with: High school diploma (including GED) or higher: 87.3% (2006-2010 5-year est.); Bachelor's degree or higher: 17.8% (2006-2010 5-year est.); Master's degree or higher: 4.9% (2006-2010 5-year est.).

### School District(s)
North Colonie Csd (KG-12)
    2009-10 Enrollment: 5,527 . . . . . . . . . . . . . . . . . . . . . . . (518) 785-8591
Watervliet City School District (PK-12)
    2009-10 Enrollment: 1,420 . . . . . . . . . . . . . . . . . . . . . . . (518) 629-3201

**Housing:** Homeownership rate: 37.8% (2010); Median home value: $131,800 (2006-2010 5-year est.); Median contract rent: $590 per month (2006-2010 5-year est.); Median year structure built: before 1940 (2006-2010 5-year est.).

**Safety:** Violent crime rate: 24.7 per 10,000 population; Property crime rate: 277.9 per 10,000 population (2010).

**Transportation:** Commute to work: 87.1% car, 6.2% public transportation, 4.9% walk, 1.0% work from home (2006-2010 5-year est.); Travel time to work: 31.4% less than 15 minutes, 49.1% 15 to 30 minutes, 14.7% 30 to 45 minutes, 2.4% 45 to 60 minutes, 2.5% 60 minutes or more (2006-2010 5-year est.)

**Additional Information Contacts**
City of Watervliet . . . . . . . . . . . . . . . . . . . . . . . . . . . . . . (518) 270-3800
    http://www.watervliet.com

**WESTERLO** (town). Covers a land area of 57.791 square miles and a water area of 0.745 square miles. Located at 42.50° N. Lat; 74.05° W. Long. Elevation is 1,165 feet.

**Population:** 3,325 (1990); 3,466 (2000); 3,361 (2010); Density: 58.2 persons per square mile (2010); Race: 97.6% White, 0.3% Black, 0.2% Asian, 0.2% American Indian/Alaska Native, 0.0% Native Hawaiian/Other Pacific Islander, 1.7% Other, 1.5% Hispanic of any race (2010); Average household size: 2.48 (2010); Median age: 44.6 (2010); Males per 100 females: 102.7 (2010); Marriage status: 21.0% never married, 64.6% now married, 6.9% widowed, 7.5% divorced (2006-2010 5-year est.); Foreign born: 2.7% (2006-2010 5-year est.); Ancestry (includes multiple ancestries): 38.9% German, 26.5% Irish, 18.3% Italian, 9.8% Dutch, 8.0% French (2006-2010 5-year est.).

**Economy:** Single-family building permits issued: 4 (2011); Multi-family building permits issued: 0 (2011); Employment by occupation: 11.0% management, 7.5% professional, 4.7% services, 24.8% sales, 3.5% farming, 15.5% construction, 3.6% production (2006-2010 5-year est.).

**Income:** Per capita income: $28,284 (2006-2010 5-year est.); Median household income: $64,805 (2006-2010 5-year est.); Average household income: $71,046 (2006-2010 5-year est.); Percent of households with income of $100,000 or more: 18.6% (2006-2010 5-year est.); Poverty rate: 9.5% (2006-2010 5-year est.).

**Education:** Percent of population age 25 and over with: High school diploma (including GED) or higher: 92.0% (2006-2010 5-year est.); Bachelor's degree or higher: 18.6% (2006-2010 5-year est.); Master's degree or higher: 6.6% (2006-2010 5-year est.).

**Housing:** Homeownership rate: 84.9% (2010); Median home value: $182,800 (2006-2010 5-year est.); Median contract rent: $545 per month (2006-2010 5-year est.); Median year structure built: 1974 (2006-2010 5-year est.).

**Transportation:** Commute to work: 90.8% car, 0.0% public transportation, 3.4% walk, 5.8% work from home (2006-2010 5-year est.); Travel time to work: 20.2% less than 15 minutes, 12.2% 15 to 30 minutes, 45.9% 30 to 45 minutes, 15.7% 45 to 60 minutes, 6.0% 60 minutes or more (2006-2010 5-year est.)

**WESTMERE** (CDP). Covers a land area of 3.171 square miles and a water area of 0.009 square miles. Located at 42.68° N. Lat; 73.87° W. Long. Elevation is 292 feet.

**Population:** 6,750 (1990); 7,188 (2000); 7,284 (2010); Density: 2,297.0 persons per square mile (2010); Race: 82.5% White, 4.0% Black, 10.8% Asian, 0.1% American Indian/Alaska Native, 0.1% Native Hawaiian/Other Pacific Islander, 2.5% Other, 3.1% Hispanic of any race (2010); Average household size: 2.27 (2010); Median age: 41.8 (2010); Males per 100 females: 94.8 (2010); Marriage status: 30.2% never married, 56.7% now married, 5.1% widowed, 8.0% divorced (2006-2010 5-year est.); Foreign born: 14.2% (2006-2010 5-year est.); Ancestry (includes multiple ancestries): 25.0% Irish, 19.8% Italian, 18.4% German, 14.4% English, 9.3% Polish (2006-2010 5-year est.).

**Economy:** Employment by occupation: 16.3% management, 12.2% professional, 8.2% services, 13.9% sales, 3.4% farming, 6.5% construction, 3.1% production (2006-2010 5-year est.).

**Income:** Per capita income: $34,820 (2006-2010 5-year est.); Median household income: $67,529 (2006-2010 5-year est.); Average household income: $80,586 (2006-2010 5-year est.); Percent of households with income of $100,000 or more: 33.6% (2006-2010 5-year est.); Poverty rate: 5.7% (2006-2010 5-year est.).

**Education:** Percent of population age 25 and over with: High school diploma (including GED) or higher: 91.3% (2006-2010 5-year est.);

Bachelor's degree or higher: 45.2% (2006-2010 5-year est.); Master's degree or higher: 21.7% (2006-2010 5-year est.).
**Housing:** Homeownership rate: 57.2% (2010); Median home value: $212,900 (2006-2010 5-year est.); Median contract rent: $908 per month (2006-2010 5-year est.); Median year structure built: 1969 (2006-2010 5-year est.).
**Transportation:** Commute to work: 90.6% car, 3.5% public transportation, 3.2% walk, 1.1% work from home (2006-2010 5-year est.); Travel time to work: 33.5% less than 15 minutes, 51.6% 15 to 30 minutes, 10.3% 30 to 45 minutes, 2.0% 45 to 60 minutes, 2.6% 60 minutes or more (2006-2010 5-year est.)

# Allegany County

Located in western New York; bounded on the south by Pennsylvania. Covers a land area of 1,030.22 square miles, a water area of 4.20 square miles, and is located in the Eastern Time Zone at 42.23° N. Lat., 78.02° W. Long. The county was founded in 1806. County seat is Belmont.

| Weather Station: Alfred | | | | | | | | | | | Elevation: 1,770 feet | |
|---|---|---|---|---|---|---|---|---|---|---|---|---|
| | Jan | Feb | Mar | Apr | May | Jun | Jul | Aug | Sep | Oct | Nov | Dec |
| High | 31 | 35 | 44 | 57 | 68 | 76 | 80 | 79 | 71 | 59 | 47 | 36 |
| Low | 13 | 13 | 20 | 31 | 40 | 50 | 54 | 52 | 46 | 35 | 28 | 19 |
| Precip | 2.2 | 1.7 | 2.7 | 3.0 | 3.3 | 4.3 | 3.9 | 3.6 | 3.7 | 3.3 | 3.3 | 2.6 |
| Snow | 20.8 | 16.7 | 17.1 | 4.0 | 0.3 | 0.0 | 0.0 | 0.0 | 0.0 | 0.5 | 8.6 | 19.6 |

*High and Low temperatures in degrees Fahrenheit; Precipitation and Snow in inches*

| Weather Station: Angelica | | | | | | | | | | | Elevation: 1,444 feet | |
|---|---|---|---|---|---|---|---|---|---|---|---|---|
| | Jan | Feb | Mar | Apr | May | Jun | Jul | Aug | Sep | Oct | Nov | Dec |
| High | 32 | 34 | 43 | 56 | 67 | 75 | 79 | 78 | 71 | 59 | 47 | 36 |
| Low | 13 | 13 | 20 | 31 | 39 | 49 | 53 | 52 | 45 | 35 | 28 | 19 |
| Precip | 2.2 | 1.9 | 2.6 | 3.1 | 3.3 | 4.5 | 3.9 | 4.1 | 3.7 | 3.3 | 3.2 | 2.5 |
| Snow | 15.8 | 11.3 | 11.8 | 3.2 | 0.2 | 0.0 | 0.0 | 0.0 | 0.0 | 0.2 | 7.1 | 14.1 |

*High and Low temperatures in degrees Fahrenheit; Precipitation and Snow in inches*

**Population:** 50,470 (1990); 49,927 (2000); 48,946 (2010); Race: 96.2% White, 1.1% Black, 0.9% Asian, 0.2% American Indian/Alaska Native, 0.0% Native Hawaiian/Other Pacific Islander, 1.6% Other, 1.4% Hispanic of any race (2010); Density: 47.5 persons per square mile (2010); Average household size: 2.44 (2010); Median age: 37.8 (2010); Males per 100 females: 101.8 (2010).
**Religion:** Six largest groups: 8.8% Catholicism, 6.9% Methodist/Pietist, 3.8% Holiness, 2.8% Non-Denominational, 2.6% Baptist, 1.4% European Free-Church (2010)
**Economy:** Unemployment rate: 9.4% (February 2012); Total civilian labor force: 24,044 (February 2012); Leading industries: 24.1% manufacturing; 14.8% health care and social assistance; 10.5% retail trade (2009); Farms: 847 totaling 150,832 acres (2007); Companies that employ 500 or more persons: 4 (2009); Companies that employ 100 to 499 persons: 13 (2009); Companies that employ less than 100 persons: 786 (2009); Black-owned businesses: n/a (2007); Hispanic-owned businesses: n/a (2007); Asian-owned businesses: n/a (2007); Women-owned businesses: 974 (2007); Retail sales per capita: $6,412 (2010). Single-family building permits issued: 50 (2011); Multi-family building permits issued: 0 (2011).
**Income:** Per capita income: $20,058 (2006-2010 5-year est.); Median household income: $41,305 (2006-2010 5-year est.); Average household income: $51,306 (2006-2010 5-year est.); Percent of households with income of $100,000 or more: 9.9% (2006-2010 5-year est.); Poverty rate: 16.5% (2006-2010 5-year est.); Bankruptcy rate: 2.28% (2011).
**Education:** Percent of population age 25 and over with: High school diploma (including GED) or higher: 88.3% (2006-2010 5-year est.); Bachelor's degree or higher: 18.6% (2006-2010 5-year est.); Master's degree or higher: 9.6% (2006-2010 5-year est.).
**Housing:** Homeownership rate: 74.5% (2010); Median home value: $66,100 (2006-2010 5-year est.); Median contract rent: $419 per month (2006-2010 5-year est.); Median year structure built: 1961 (2006-2010 5-year est.)
**Health:** Birth rate: 103.5 per 10,000 population (2011); Death rate: 93.1 per 10,000 population (2011); Age-adjusted cancer mortality rate: 171.9 deaths per 100,000 population (2009); Number of physicians: 8.1 per 10,000 population (2008); Hospital beds: 30.7 per 10,000 population (2007); Hospital admissions: 594.7 per 10,000 population (2007).
**Elections:** 2008 Presidential election results: 38.1% Obama, 59.8% McCain, 1.1% Nader
**Additional Information Contacts**

Allegany County Government . . . . . . . . . . . . . . . . (585) 268-9222
  http://www.alleganyco.com
Town of Hume . . . . . . . . . . . . . . . . . . . . . . . . . (585) 567-2666
  http://www.humetown.org
Village of Alfred . . . . . . . . . . . . . . . . . . . . . . . (607) 587-9188
  http://www.alfredny.org
Wellsville Area Chamber of Commerce . . . . . . . . . . . . (585) 593-5080
  http://www.wellsvilleareachamber.com

## Allegany County Communities

**ALFRED** (village). Covers a land area of 1.189 square miles and a water area of 0 square miles. Located at 42.25° N. Lat; 77.78° W. Long. Elevation is 1,765 feet.
**Population:** 4,559 (1990); 3,954 (2000); 4,174 (2010); Density: 3,508.0 persons per square mile (2010); Race: 84.2% White, 7.1% Black, 4.6% Asian, 0.2% American Indian/Alaska Native, 0.0% Native Hawaiian/Other Pacific Islander, 3.9% Other, 4.4% Hispanic of any race (2010); Average household size: 2.01 (2010); Median age: 20.5 (2010); Males per 100 females: 154.7 (2010); Marriage status: 88.2% never married, 9.9% now married, 1.0% widowed, 0.8% divorced (2006-2010 5-year est.); Foreign born: 5.4% (2006-2010 5-year est.); Ancestry (includes multiple ancestries): 23.5% German, 20.4% Irish, 10.6% English, 10.4% Italian, 8.6% Polish (2006-2010 5-year est.).
**Economy:** Single-family building permits issued: 0 (2011); Multi-family building permits issued: 0 (2011); Employment by occupation: 3.8% management, 5.6% professional, 15.6% services, 15.2% sales, 8.9% farming, 5.8% construction, 3.1% production (2006-2010 5-year est.).
**Income:** Per capita income: $10,143 (2006-2010 5-year est.); Median household income: $35,000 (2006-2010 5-year est.); Average household income: $53,177 (2006-2010 5-year est.); Percent of households with income of $100,000 or more: 18.3% (2006-2010 5-year est.); Poverty rate: 23.3% (2006-2010 5-year est.).
**Education:** Percent of population age 25 and over with: High school diploma (including GED) or higher: 97.4% (2006-2010 5-year est.); Bachelor's degree or higher: 80.2% (2006-2010 5-year est.); Master's degree or higher: 53.8% (2006-2010 5-year est.).

#### Four-year College(s)
Alfred University (Private, Not-for-profit)
  Fall 2010 Enrollment: 2,418 . . . . . . . . . . . . . . . . (607) 871-2111
  2011-12 Tuition: In-state $26,884; Out-of-state $26,884
SUNY College of Technology at Alfred (Public)
  Fall 2010 Enrollment: 3,602 . . . . . . . . . . . . . . . . (800) 425-3733
  2011-12 Tuition: In-state $6,542; Out-of-state $11,012
**Housing:** Homeownership rate: 31.1% (2010); Median home value: $109,500 (2006-2010 5-year est.); Median contract rent: $604 per month (2006-2010 5-year est.); Median year structure built: 1963 (2006-2010 5-year est.).
**Safety:** Violent crime rate: 14.2 per 10,000 population; Property crime rate: 105.4 per 10,000 population (2010).
**Transportation:** Commute to work: 33.6% car, 1.1% public transportation, 55.6% walk, 6.5% work from home (2006-2010 5-year est.); Travel time to work: 76.3% less than 15 minutes, 19.4% 15 to 30 minutes, 1.3% 30 to 45 minutes, 1.5% 45 to 60 minutes, 1.4% 60 minutes or more (2006-2010 5-year est.)
**Additional Information Contacts**
Village of Alfred . . . . . . . . . . . . . . . . . . . . . . . (607) 587-9188
  http://www.alfredny.org

**ALFRED** (town). Covers a land area of 31.476 square miles and a water area of 0.149 square miles. Located at 42.23° N. Lat; 77.79° W. Long. Elevation is 1,765 feet.
**Population:** 5,791 (1990); 5,140 (2000); 5,237 (2010); Density: 166.4 persons per square mile (2010); Race: 86.9% White, 5.7% Black, 4.0% Asian, 0.2% American Indian/Alaska Native, 0.0% Native Hawaiian/Other Pacific Islander, 3.2% Other, 3.7% Hispanic of any race (2010); Average household size: 2.19 (2010); Median age: 20.8 (2010); Males per 100 females: 143.2 (2010); Marriage status: 76.9% never married, 18.9% now married, 2.5% widowed, 1.6% divorced (2006-2010 5-year est.); Foreign born: 5.2% (2006-2010 5-year est.); Ancestry (includes multiple ancestries): 23.2% German, 21.1% Irish, 11.5% English, 10.8% Italian, 8.5% Polish (2006-2010 5-year est.).
**Economy:** Single-family building permits issued: 0 (2011); Multi-family building permits issued: 0 (2011); Employment by occupation: 4.4%

management, 4.8% professional, 15.0% services, 14.5% sales, 7.0% farming, 6.5% construction, 2.8% production (2006-2010 5-year est.). **Income:** Per capita income: $14,375 (2006-2010 5-year est.); Median household income: $47,692 (2006-2010 5-year est.); Average household income: $62,818 (2006-2010 5-year est.); Percent of households with income of $100,000 or more: 21.4% (2006-2010 5-year est.); Poverty rate: 14.9% (2006-2010 5-year est.). **Education:** Percent of population age 25 and over with: High school diploma (including GED) or higher: 97.4% (2006-2010 5-year est.); Bachelor's degree or higher: 67.3% (2006-2010 5-year est.); Master's degree or higher: 47.7% (2006-2010 5-year est.).

### Four-year College(s)
Alfred University (Private, Not-for-profit)
    Fall 2010 Enrollment: 2,418. . . . . . . . . . . . . . . . . . (607) 871-2111
    2011-12 Tuition: In-state $26,884; Out-of-state $26,884
SUNY College of Technology at Alfred (Public)
    Fall 2010 Enrollment: 3,602. . . . . . . . . . . . . . . . . . (800) 425-3733
    2011-12 Tuition: In-state $6,542; Out-of-state $11,012
**Housing:** Homeownership rate: 52.6% (2010); Median home value: $108,200 (2006-2010 5-year est.); Median contract rent: $612 per month (2006-2010 5-year est.); Median year structure built: 1966 (2006-2010 5-year est.). **Transportation:** Commute to work: 46.1% car, 0.8% public transportation, 43.8% walk, 6.1% work from home (2006-2010 5-year est.); Travel time to work: 70.7% less than 15 minutes, 23.1% 15 to 30 minutes, 2.4% 30 to 45 minutes, 1.4% 45 to 60 minutes, 2.3% 60 minutes or more (2006-2010 5-year est.)

**ALFRED STATION** (unincorporated postal area)
Zip Code: 14803
    Covers a land area of 24.923 square miles and a water area of 0.096 square miles. Located at 42.27° N. Lat; 77.74° W. Long. Elevation is 1,644 feet. Population: 1,174 (2010); Density: 47.1 persons per square mile (2010); Race: 97.0% White, 0.3% Black, 1.4% Asian, 0.1% American Indian/Alaska Native, 0.0% Native Hawaiian/Other Pacific Islander, 1.2% Other, 1.0% Hispanic of any race (2010); Average household size: 2.39 (2010); Median age: 42.4 (2010); Males per 100 females: 110.0 (2010); Homeownership rate: 73.1% (2010)

**ALLEN** (town). Covers a land area of 36.377 square miles and a water area of 0.202 square miles. Located at 42.39° N. Lat; 78.00° W. Long. **Population:** 406 (1990); 462 (2000); 448 (2010); Density: 12.3 persons per square mile (2010); Race: 98.2% White, 0.0% Black, 0.2% Asian, 0.0% American Indian/Alaska Native, 1.6% Other, 0.9% Hispanic of any race (2010); Average household size: 2.50 (2010); Median age: 42.8 (2010); Males per 100 females: 111.3 (2010); Marriage status: 23.0% never married, 60.5% now married, 4.1% widowed, 12.4% divorced (2006-2010 5-year est.); Foreign born: 0.0% (2006-2010 5-year est.); Ancestry (includes multiple ancestries): 55.4% German, 16.2% English, 15.2% Irish, 13.2% Italian, 7.7% Polish (2006-2010 5-year est.). **Economy:** Single-family building permits issued: 3 (2011); Multi-family building permits issued: 0 (2011); Employment by occupation: 6.4% management, 1.3% professional, 19.2% services, 12.4% sales, 7.7% farming, 23.9% construction, 18.8% production (2006-2010 5-year est.). **Income:** Per capita income: $21,645 (2006-2010 5-year est.); Median household income: $40,313 (2006-2010 5-year est.); Average household income: $50,224 (2006-2010 5-year est.); Percent of households with income of $100,000 or more: 8.0% (2006-2010 5-year est.); Poverty rate: 12.6% (2006-2010 5-year est.). **Education:** Percent of population age 25 and over with: High school diploma (including GED) or higher: 89.6% (2006-2010 5-year est.); Bachelor's degree or higher: 7.9% (2006-2010 5-year est.); Master's degree or higher: 1.4% (2006-2010 5-year est.). **Housing:** Homeownership rate: 87.1% (2010); Median home value: $70,700 (2006-2010 5-year est.); Median contract rent: $300 per month (2006-2010 5-year est.); Median year structure built: 1972 (2006-2010 5-year est.). **Transportation:** Commute to work: 95.5% car, 0.0% public transportation, 0.0% walk, 2.7% work from home (2006-2010 5-year est.); Travel time to work: 16.4% less than 15 minutes, 34.1% 15 to 30 minutes, 18.7% 30 to 45 minutes, 6.1% 45 to 60 minutes, 24.8% 60 minutes or more (2006-2010 5-year est.)

**ALMA** (town). Covers a land area of 36.215 square miles and a water area of 0.301 square miles. Located at 42.04° N. Lat; 78.01° W. Long. Elevation is 1,542 feet. **Population:** 846 (1990); 847 (2000); 842 (2010); Density: 23.3 persons per square mile (2010); Race: 97.6% White, 0.1% Black, 0.2% Asian, 0.0% American Indian/Alaska Native, 0.1% Native Hawaiian/Other Pacific Islander, 2.0% Other, 0.4% Hispanic of any race (2010); Average household size: 2.52 (2010); Median age: 41.7 (2010); Males per 100 females: 113.7 (2010); Marriage status: 18.2% never married, 66.7% now married, 5.9% widowed, 9.2% divorced (2006-2010 5-year est.); Foreign born: 1.5% (2006-2010 5-year est.); Ancestry (includes multiple ancestries): 43.4% German, 18.2% Irish, 7.9% English, 5.0% Polish, 4.8% French (2006-2010 5-year est.). **Economy:** Single-family building permits issued: 6 (2011); Multi-family building permits issued: 0 (2011); Employment by occupation: 7.8% management, 2.8% professional, 10.0% services, 10.8% sales, 6.5% farming, 17.3% construction, 1.8% production (2006-2010 5-year est.). **Income:** Per capita income: $18,727 (2006-2010 5-year est.); Median household income: $44,792 (2006-2010 5-year est.); Average household income: $50,611 (2006-2010 5-year est.); Percent of households with income of $100,000 or more: 7.5% (2006-2010 5-year est.); Poverty rate: 9.8% (2006-2010 5-year est.). **Education:** Percent of population age 25 and over with: High school diploma (including GED) or higher: 88.8% (2006-2010 5-year est.); Bachelor's degree or higher: 8.5% (2006-2010 5-year est.); Master's degree or higher: 5.5% (2006-2010 5-year est.). **Housing:** Homeownership rate: 86.8% (2010); Median home value: $54,800 (2006-2010 5-year est.); Median contract rent: $332 per month (2006-2010 5-year est.); Median year structure built: 1968 (2006-2010 5-year est.). **Transportation:** Commute to work: 98.0% car, 0.0% public transportation, 0.0% walk, 2.0% work from home (2006-2010 5-year est.); Travel time to work: 21.6% less than 15 minutes, 36.4% 15 to 30 minutes, 27.8% 30 to 45 minutes, 9.1% 45 to 60 minutes, 5.2% 60 minutes or more (2006-2010 5-year est.)

**ALMOND** (village). Covers a land area of 0.564 square miles and a water area of 0 square miles. Located at 42.31° N. Lat; 77.73° W. Long. Elevation is 1,335 feet. **Population:** 458 (1990); 461 (2000); 466 (2010); Density: 825.7 persons per square mile (2010); Race: 97.4% White, 0.0% Black, 0.6% Asian, 0.0% American Indian/Alaska Native, 0.0% Native Hawaiian/Other Pacific Islander, 2.0% Other, 1.5% Hispanic of any race (2010); Average household size: 2.48 (2010); Median age: 39.6 (2010); Males per 100 females: 104.4 (2010); Marriage status: 24.8% never married, 58.0% now married, 4.9% widowed, 12.3% divorced (2006-2010 5-year est.); Foreign born: 3.5% (2006-2010 5-year est.); Ancestry (includes multiple ancestries): 33.9% German, 25.7% Irish, 19.5% English, 12.5% Scottish, 5.1% American (2006-2010 5-year est.). **Economy:** Single-family building permits issued: 0 (2011); Multi-family building permits issued: 0 (2011); Employment by occupation: 11.5% management, 6.3% professional, 1.4% services, 21.2% sales, 4.3% farming, 11.1% construction, 6.3% production (2006-2010 5-year est.). **Income:** Per capita income: $21,183 (2006-2010 5-year est.); Median household income: $42,031 (2006-2010 5-year est.); Average household income: $51,297 (2006-2010 5-year est.); Percent of households with income of $100,000 or more: 10.6% (2006-2010 5-year est.); Poverty rate: 12.7% (2006-2010 5-year est.). **Education:** Percent of population age 25 and over with: High school diploma (including GED) or higher: 96.3% (2006-2010 5-year est.); Bachelor's degree or higher: 28.7% (2006-2010 5-year est.); Master's degree or higher: 8.6% (2006-2010 5-year est.).

### School District(s)
Alfred-Almond Central School District (PK-12)
    2009-10 Enrollment: 635 . . . . . . . . . . . . . . . . . . . . . (607) 276-2981
**Housing:** Homeownership rate: 68.1% (2010); Median home value: $67,500 (2006-2010 5-year est.); Median contract rent: $401 per month (2006-2010 5-year est.); Median year structure built: before 1940 (2006-2010 5-year est.). **Transportation:** Commute to work: 81.7% car, 1.4% public transportation, 10.1% walk, 2.9% work from home (2006-2010 5-year est.); Travel time to work: 57.4% less than 15 minutes, 18.8% 15 to 30 minutes, 12.9% 30 to 45 minutes, 5.9% 45 to 60 minutes, 5.0% 60 minutes or more (2006-2010 5-year est.)

## ALMOND (town)

**ALMOND** (town). Covers a land area of 45.717 square miles and a water area of 0.067 square miles. Located at 42.34° N. Lat; 77.78° W. Long. Elevation is 1,335 feet.

**Population:** 1,640 (1990); 1,604 (2000); 1,633 (2010); Density: 35.7 persons per square mile (2010); Race: 98.0% White, 0.1% Black, 0.5% Asian, 0.1% American Indian/Alaska Native, 0.0% Native Hawaiian/Other Pacific Islander, 1.3% Other, 1.0% Hispanic of any race (2010); Average household size: 2.57 (2010); Median age: 41.1 (2010); Males per 100 females: 99.6 (2010); Marriage status: 19.9% never married, 69.1% now married, 3.6% widowed, 7.4% divorced (2006-2010 5-year est.); Foreign born: 3.4% (2006-2010 5-year est.); Ancestry (includes multiple ancestries): 29.6% German, 22.0% Irish, 19.1% English, 7.7% American, 7.2% Scottish (2006-2010 5-year est.).

**Economy:** Single-family building permits issued: 0 (2011); Multi-family building permits issued: 0 (2011); Employment by occupation: 8.9% management, 5.7% professional, 5.2% services, 14.8% sales, 2.9% farming, 17.4% construction, 8.9% production (2006-2010 5-year est.).

**Income:** Per capita income: $27,116 (2006-2010 5-year est.); Median household income: $57,917 (2006-2010 5-year est.); Average household income: $65,063 (2006-2010 5-year est.); Percent of households with income of $100,000 or more: 18.1% (2006-2010 5-year est.); Poverty rate: 7.9% (2006-2010 5-year est.).

**Education:** Percent of population age 25 and over with: High school diploma (including GED) or higher: 95.7% (2006-2010 5-year est.); Bachelor's degree or higher: 27.1% (2006-2010 5-year est.); Master's degree or higher: 15.3% (2006-2010 5-year est.).

### School District(s)

Alfred-Almond Central School District (PK-12)

   2009-10 Enrollment: 635 . . . . . . . . . . . . . . . . . . . . . . . (607) 276-2981

**Housing:** Homeownership rate: 80.9% (2010); Median home value: $83,800 (2006-2010 5-year est.); Median contract rent: $405 per month (2006-2010 5-year est.); Median year structure built: 1968 (2006-2010 5-year est.).

**Transportation:** Commute to work: 91.0% car, 1.0% public transportation, 4.6% walk, 2.0% work from home (2006-2010 5-year est.); Travel time to work: 45.0% less than 15 minutes, 32.3% 15 to 30 minutes, 9.7% 30 to 45 minutes, 3.6% 45 to 60 minutes, 9.4% 60 minutes or more (2006-2010 5-year est.)

## AMITY (town)

**AMITY** (town). Covers a land area of 34.441 square miles and a water area of 0.122 square miles. Located at 42.22° N. Lat; 78.00° W. Long. Elevation is 1,391 feet.

**Population:** 2,255 (1990); 2,245 (2000); 2,308 (2010); Density: 67.0 persons per square mile (2010); Race: 95.8% White, 1.9% Black, 0.3% Asian, 0.3% American Indian/Alaska Native, 0.0% Native Hawaiian/Other Pacific Islander, 1.7% Other, 1.5% Hispanic of any race (2010); Average household size: 2.37 (2010); Median age: 41.4 (2010); Males per 100 females: 102.6 (2010); Marriage status: 18.1% never married, 61.1% now married, 7.8% widowed, 12.9% divorced (2006-2010 5-year est.); Foreign born: 1.7% (2006-2010 5-year est.); Ancestry (includes multiple ancestries): 27.2% German, 16.5% English, 14.5% Italian, 13.8% Irish, 8.8% American (2006-2010 5-year est.).

**Economy:** Single-family building permits issued: 0 (2011); Multi-family building permits issued: 0 (2011); Employment by occupation: 7.3% management, 1.5% professional, 7.2% services, 13.3% sales, 6.5% farming, 8.0% construction, 1.8% production (2006-2010 5-year est.).

**Income:** Per capita income: $20,820 (2006-2010 5-year est.); Median household income: $40,479 (2006-2010 5-year est.); Average household income: $48,785 (2006-2010 5-year est.); Percent of households with income of $100,000 or more: 11.8% (2006-2010 5-year est.); Poverty rate: 19.5% (2006-2010 5-year est.).

**Education:** Percent of population age 25 and over with: High school diploma (including GED) or higher: 87.1% (2006-2010 5-year est.); Bachelor's degree or higher: 18.6% (2006-2010 5-year est.); Master's degree or higher: 9.0% (2006-2010 5-year est.).

**Housing:** Homeownership rate: 72.0% (2010); Median home value: $62,200 (2006-2010 5-year est.); Median contract rent: $378 per month (2006-2010 5-year est.); Median year structure built: 1957 (2006-2010 5-year est.).

**Transportation:** Commute to work: 91.1% car, 0.6% public transportation, 3.7% walk, 4.2% work from home (2006-2010 5-year est.); Travel time to work: 41.7% less than 15 minutes, 36.1% 15 to 30 minutes, 9.8% 30 to 45 minutes, 2.0% 45 to 60 minutes, 10.4% 60 minutes or more (2006-2010 5-year est.)

## ANDOVER (village)

**ANDOVER** (village). Covers a land area of 1.000 square miles and a water area of 0.015 square miles. Located at 42.15° N. Lat; 77.79° W. Long. Elevation is 1,660 feet.

**Population:** 1,125 (1990); 1,073 (2000); 1,042 (2010); Density: 1,041.0 persons per square mile (2010); Race: 97.7% White, 0.3% Black, 0.1% Asian, 0.1% American Indian/Alaska Native, 0.0% Native Hawaiian/Other Pacific Islander, 1.8% Other, 1.3% Hispanic of any race (2010); Average household size: 2.57 (2010); Median age: 38.1 (2010); Males per 100 females: 91.2 (2010); Marriage status: 25.6% never married, 49.9% now married, 10.4% widowed, 14.1% divorced (2006-2010 5-year est.); Foreign born: 1.1% (2006-2010 5-year est.); Ancestry (includes multiple ancestries): 33.4% Irish, 33.1% German, 16.4% English, 6.4% French, 5.0% American (2006-2010 5-year est.).

**Economy:** Single-family building permits issued: 1 (2011); Multi-family building permits issued: 0 (2011); Employment by occupation: 13.1% management, 0.0% professional, 8.6% services, 14.3% sales, 1.6% farming, 11.3% construction, 6.8% production (2006-2010 5-year est.).

**Income:** Per capita income: $20,470 (2006-2010 5-year est.); Median household income: $41,042 (2006-2010 5-year est.); Average household income: $46,482 (2006-2010 5-year est.); Percent of households with income of $100,000 or more: 7.2% (2006-2010 5-year est.); Poverty rate: 23.8% (2006-2010 5-year est.).

**Education:** Percent of population age 25 and over with: High school diploma (including GED) or higher: 92.2% (2006-2010 5-year est.); Bachelor's degree or higher: 19.4% (2006-2010 5-year est.); Master's degree or higher: 13.7% (2006-2010 5-year est.).

### School District(s)

Andover Central School District (PK-12)

   2009-10 Enrollment: 407 . . . . . . . . . . . . . . . . . . . . . . . (607) 478-8491

**Housing:** Homeownership rate: 73.3% (2010); Median home value: $53,500 (2006-2010 5-year est.); Median contract rent: $425 per month (2006-2010 5-year est.); Median year structure built: before 1940 (2006-2010 5-year est.).

**Transportation:** Commute to work: 87.1% car, 0.0% public transportation, 6.9% walk, 6.0% work from home (2006-2010 5-year est.); Travel time to work: 45.5% less than 15 minutes, 43.5% 15 to 30 minutes, 3.7% 30 to 45 minutes, 1.5% 45 to 60 minutes, 5.9% 60 minutes or more (2006-2010 5-year est.)

## ANDOVER (town)

**ANDOVER** (town). Covers a land area of 39.430 square miles and a water area of 0.066 square miles. Located at 42.15° N. Lat; 77.81° W. Long. Elevation is 1,660 feet.

**History:** Incorporated 1892.

**Population:** 1,981 (1990); 1,945 (2000); 1,830 (2010); Density: 46.4 persons per square mile (2010); Race: 97.6% White, 0.3% Black, 0.2% Asian, 0.1% American Indian/Alaska Native, 0.1% Native Hawaiian/Other Pacific Islander, 1.7% Other, 1.3% Hispanic of any race (2010); Average household size: 2.61 (2010); Median age: 39.5 (2010); Males per 100 females: 96.8 (2010); Marriage status: 24.3% never married, 58.4% now married, 7.6% widowed, 9.7% divorced (2006-2010 5-year est.); Foreign born: 0.6% (2006-2010 5-year est.); Ancestry (includes multiple ancestries): 38.9% German, 27.6% Irish, 18.0% English, 5.6% American, 5.3% Italian (2006-2010 5-year est.).

**Economy:** Single-family building permits issued: 0 (2011); Multi-family building permits issued: 0 (2011); Employment by occupation: 11.1% management, 0.4% professional, 9.5% services, 11.2% sales, 2.9% farming, 13.8% construction, 7.6% production (2006-2010 5-year est.).

**Income:** Per capita income: $19,274 (2006-2010 5-year est.); Median household income: $45,068 (2006-2010 5-year est.); Average household income: $48,993 (2006-2010 5-year est.); Percent of households with income of $100,000 or more: 8.3% (2006-2010 5-year est.); Poverty rate: 21.1% (2006-2010 5-year est.).

**Education:** Percent of population age 25 and over with: High school diploma (including GED) or higher: 85.5% (2006-2010 5-year est.); Bachelor's degree or higher: 16.4% (2006-2010 5-year est.); Master's degree or higher: 10.9% (2006-2010 5-year est.).

### School District(s)

Andover Central School District (PK-12)

   2009-10 Enrollment: 407 . . . . . . . . . . . . . . . . . . . . . . . (607) 478-8491

**Housing:** Homeownership rate: 78.5% (2010); Median home value: $56,800 (2006-2010 5-year est.); Median contract rent: $422 per month (2006-2010 5-year est.); Median year structure built: 1943 (2006-2010 5-year est.).

**Transportation:** Commute to work: 90.9% car, 0.0% public transportation, 3.8% walk, 4.6% work from home (2006-2010 5-year est.); Travel time to

work: 36.3% less than 15 minutes, 49.9% 15 to 30 minutes, 7.8% 30 to 45 minutes, 0.8% 45 to 60 minutes, 5.2% 60 minutes or more (2006-2010 5-year est.)

## ANGELICA (village). Covers a land area of 2.151 square miles and a water area of 0 square miles. Located at 42.30° N. Lat; 78.02° W. Long. Elevation is 1,434 feet.

**Population:** 963 (1990); 903 (2000); 869 (2010); Density: 403.8 persons per square mile (2010); Race: 97.9% White, 0.0% Black, 1.2% Asian, 0.3% American Indian/Alaska Native, 0.0% Native Hawaiian/Other Pacific Islander, 0.6% Other, 0.7% Hispanic of any race (2010); Average household size: 2.46 (2010); Median age: 41.4 (2010); Males per 100 females: 104.5 (2010); Marriage status: 15.0% never married, 66.3% now married, 7.9% widowed, 10.8% divorced (2006-2010 5-year est.); Foreign born: 1.6% (2006-2010 5-year est.); Ancestry (includes multiple ancestries): 27.8% German, 21.7% Irish, 16.8% English, 9.7% Italian, 5.1% Scottish (2006-2010 5-year est.).
**Economy:** Single-family building permits issued: 0 (2011); Multi-family building permits issued: 0 (2011); Employment by occupation: 12.7% management, 2.8% professional, 9.5% services, 8.1% sales, 2.5% farming, 18.2% construction, 5.5% production (2006-2010 5-year est.).
**Income:** Per capita income: $18,335 (2006-2010 5-year est.); Median household income: $37,426 (2006-2010 5-year est.); Average household income: $46,678 (2006-2010 5-year est.); Percent of households with income of $100,000 or more: 6.6% (2006-2010 5-year est.); Poverty rate: 20.0% (2006-2010 5-year est.).
**Education:** Percent of population age 25 and over with: High school diploma (including GED) or higher: 90.0% (2006-2010 5-year est.); Bachelor's degree or higher: 13.3% (2006-2010 5-year est.); Master's degree or higher: 6.7% (2006-2010 5-year est.).
**Housing:** Homeownership rate: 72.5% (2010); Median home value: $69,000 (2006-2010 5-year est.); Median contract rent: $420 per month (2006-2010 5-year est.); Median year structure built: before 1940 (2006-2010 5-year est.).
**Transportation:** Commute to work: 85.8% car, 0.9% public transportation, 1.8% walk, 6.0% work from home (2006-2010 5-year est.); Travel time to work: 42.6% less than 15 minutes, 31.2% 15 to 30 minutes, 13.9% 30 to 45 minutes, 3.8% 45 to 60 minutes, 8.5% 60 minutes or more (2006-2010 5-year est.)

## ANGELICA (town). Covers a land area of 36.394 square miles and a water area of 0.037 square miles. Located at 42.30° N. Lat; 78.01° W. Long. Elevation is 1,434 feet.

**History:** Oldest village in the county; founded in 1800 by Captain Philip Church, nephew of Alexander Hamilton. Church is buried with his wife at Until the Day Dawns Cemetery. Contingent of French royalists settled here in 1806; one of them became the French ambassador to U.S; another was Victor Marie du Pont de Nemours.
**Population:** 1,446 (1990); 1,411 (2000); 1,403 (2010); Density: 38.6 persons per square mile (2010); Race: 97.8% White, 0.1% Black, 1.0% Asian, 0.3% American Indian/Alaska Native, 0.0% Native Hawaiian/Other Pacific Islander, 0.8% Other, 0.6% Hispanic of any race (2010); Average household size: 2.42 (2010); Median age: 42.3 (2010); Males per 100 females: 111.9 (2010); Marriage status: 19.2% never married, 66.6% now married, 6.1% widowed, 8.0% divorced (2006-2010 5-year est.); Foreign born: 1.1% (2006-2010 5-year est.); Ancestry (includes multiple ancestries): 25.2% German, 19.2% English, 17.8% Irish, 7.9% Italian, 4.3% Scottish (2006-2010 5-year est.).
**Economy:** Single-family building permits issued: 5 (2011); Multi-family building permits issued: 0 (2011); Employment by occupation: 11.1% management, 2.4% professional, 8.5% services, 8.2% sales, 1.8% farming, 15.1% construction, 10.7% production (2006-2010 5-year est.).
**Income:** Per capita income: $19,453 (2006-2010 5-year est.); Median household income: $45,676 (2006-2010 5-year est.); Average household income: $49,275 (2006-2010 5-year est.); Percent of households with income of $100,000 or more: 8.1% (2006-2010 5-year est.); Poverty rate: 19.3% (2006-2010 5-year est.).
**Education:** Percent of population age 25 and over with: High school diploma (including GED) or higher: 85.7% (2006-2010 5-year est.); Bachelor's degree or higher: 12.4% (2006-2010 5-year est.); Master's degree or higher: 6.3% (2006-2010 5-year est.).
**Housing:** Homeownership rate: 77.2% (2010); Median home value: $71,300 (2006-2010 5-year est.); Median contract rent: $420 per month (2006-2010 5-year est.); Median year structure built: 1956 (2006-2010 5-year est.).

**Transportation:** Commute to work: 85.2% car, 0.6% public transportation, 2.2% walk, 8.2% work from home (2006-2010 5-year est.); Travel time to work: 45.4% less than 15 minutes, 27.4% 15 to 30 minutes, 15.3% 30 to 45 minutes, 3.9% 45 to 60 minutes, 8.1% 60 minutes or more (2006-2010 5-year est.)

## BELFAST (town). Covers a land area of 36.295 square miles and a water area of 0.248 square miles. Located at 42.29° N. Lat; 78.13° W. Long. Elevation is 1,309 feet.

**Population:** 1,539 (1990); 1,714 (2000); 1,663 (2010); Density: 45.8 persons per square mile (2010); Race: 96.9% White, 0.4% Black, 0.6% Asian, 0.2% American Indian/Alaska Native, 0.0% Native Hawaiian/Other Pacific Islander, 1.9% Other, 1.0% Hispanic of any race (2010); Average household size: 2.54 (2010); Median age: 39.1 (2010); Males per 100 females: 98.0 (2010); Marriage status: 25.0% never married, 55.7% now married, 5.7% widowed, 13.7% divorced (2006-2010 5-year est.); Foreign born: 0.4% (2006-2010 5-year est.); Ancestry (includes multiple ancestries): 27.3% German, 19.1% English, 15.2% Irish, 7.0% Italian, 5.1% French (2006-2010 5-year est.).
**Economy:** Single-family building permits issued: 3 (2011); Multi-family building permits issued: 0 (2011); Employment by occupation: 7.9% management, 1.5% professional, 13.5% services, 14.7% sales, 3.2% farming, 7.9% construction, 4.3% production (2006-2010 5-year est.).
**Income:** Per capita income: $19,825 (2006-2010 5-year est.); Median household income: $43,047 (2006-2010 5-year est.); Average household income: $48,331 (2006-2010 5-year est.); Percent of households with income of $100,000 or more: 6.5% (2006-2010 5-year est.); Poverty rate: 17.4% (2006-2010 5-year est.).
**Education:** Percent of population age 25 and over with: High school diploma (including GED) or higher: 84.3% (2006-2010 5-year est.); Bachelor's degree or higher: 17.4% (2006-2010 5-year est.); Master's degree or higher: 11.1% (2006-2010 5-year est.).

**School District(s)**
Belfast Central School District (PK-12)
   2009-10 Enrollment: 379 . . . . . . . . . . . . . . . . . . . . . . . . . . (585) 365-9940
**Housing:** Homeownership rate: 75.2% (2010); Median home value: $67,700 (2006-2010 5-year est.); Median contract rent: $340 per month (2006-2010 5-year est.); Median year structure built: 1969 (2006-2010 5-year est.).
**Transportation:** Commute to work: 88.3% car, 0.9% public transportation, 8.4% walk, 2.3% work from home (2006-2010 5-year est.); Travel time to work: 36.0% less than 15 minutes, 28.9% 15 to 30 minutes, 22.2% 30 to 45 minutes, 6.2% 45 to 60 minutes, 6.7% 60 minutes or more (2006-2010 5-year est.)

## BELFAST (CDP). Covers a land area of 1.384 square miles and a water area of 0.026 square miles. Located at 42.33° N. Lat; 78.11° W. Long. Elevation is 1,309 feet.

**Population:** n/a (1990); n/a (2000); 837 (2010); Density: 604.3 persons per square mile (2010); Race: 95.9% White, 0.7% Black, 1.1% Asian, 0.2% American Indian/Alaska Native, 0.0% Native Hawaiian/Other Pacific Islander, 2.1% Other, 0.7% Hispanic of any race (2010); Average household size: 2.48 (2010); Median age: 37.9 (2010); Males per 100 females: 87.7 (2010); Marriage status: 30.3% never married, 51.5% now married, 4.4% widowed, 13.7% divorced (2006-2010 5-year est.); Foreign born: 0.8% (2006-2010 5-year est.); Ancestry (includes multiple ancestries): 29.8% German, 20.7% English, 17.9% Irish, 7.7% Welsh, 7.6% French (2006-2010 5-year est.).
**Economy:** Employment by occupation: 13.5% management, 2.6% professional, 15.3% services, 11.7% sales, 5.7% farming, 2.8% construction, 1.3% production (2006-2010 5-year est.).
**Income:** Per capita income: $20,094 (2006-2010 5-year est.); Median household income: $41,016 (2006-2010 5-year est.); Average household income: $48,413 (2006-2010 5-year est.); Percent of households with income of $100,000 or more: 2.7% (2006-2010 5-year est.); Poverty rate: 13.2% (2006-2010 5-year est.).
**Education:** Percent of population age 25 and over with: High school diploma (including GED) or higher: 83.7% (2006-2010 5-year est.); Bachelor's degree or higher: 18.6% (2006-2010 5-year est.); Master's degree or higher: 14.3% (2006-2010 5-year est.).

**School District(s)**
Belfast Central School District (PK-12)
   2009-10 Enrollment: 379 . . . . . . . . . . . . . . . . . . . . . . . . . . (585) 365-9940
**Housing:** Homeownership rate: 64.7% (2010); Median home value: $65,800 (2006-2010 5-year est.); Median contract rent: $342 per month

(2006-2010 5-year est.); Median year structure built: before 1940 (2006-2010 5-year est.).
**Transportation:** Commute to work: 84.9% car, 1.6% public transportation, 10.1% walk, 3.3% work from home (2006-2010 5-year est.); Travel time to work: 42.5% less than 15 minutes, 22.1% 15 to 30 minutes, 25.8% 30 to 45 minutes, 4.0% 45 to 60 minutes, 5.7% 60 minutes or more (2006-2010 5-year est.)

## BELMONT (village). County seat. Covers a land area of 0.995 square miles and a water area of 0.001 square miles. Located at 42.22° N. Lat; 78.03° W. Long. Elevation is 1,391 feet.
**History:** Incorporated 1871.
**Population:** 1,006 (1990); 952 (2000); 969 (2010); Density: 973.1 persons per square mile (2010); Race: 96.8% White, 0.6% Black, 0.1% Asian, 0.5% American Indian/Alaska Native, 0.0% Native Hawaiian/Other Pacific Islander, 2.0% Other, 1.1% Hispanic of any race (2010); Average household size: 2.33 (2010); Median age: 39.8 (2010); Males per 100 females: 94.2 (2010); Marriage status: 24.3% never married, 57.2% now married, 5.0% widowed, 13.5% divorced (2006-2010 5-year est.); Foreign born: 0.6% (2006-2010 5-year est.); Ancestry (includes multiple ancestries): 37.1% German, 18.0% Irish, 16.4% English, 13.3% Italian, 5.7% American (2006-2010 5-year est.).
**Economy:** Single-family building permits issued: 0 (2011); Multi-family building permits issued: 0 (2011); Employment by occupation: 7.3% management, 0.5% professional, 10.4% services, 12.7% sales, 6.0% farming, 6.2% construction, 2.6% production (2006-2010 5-year est.).
**Income:** Per capita income: $18,706 (2006-2010 5-year est.); Median household income: $39,904 (2006-2010 5-year est.); Average household income: $45,180 (2006-2010 5-year est.); Percent of households with income of $100,000 or more: 10.2% (2006-2010 5-year est.); Poverty rate: 18.2% (2006-2010 5-year est.).
**Education:** Percent of population age 25 and over with: High school diploma (including GED) or higher: 91.6% (2006-2010 5-year est.); Bachelor's degree or higher: 16.5% (2006-2010 5-year est.); Master's degree or higher: 6.6% (2006-2010 5-year est.).
### School District(s)
Genesee Valley Central School District at Angelica (PK-12)
   2009-10 Enrollment: 661 . . . . . . . . . . . . . . . . . . . . . . . . . (585) 268-7900
**Housing:** Homeownership rate: 62.9% (2010); Median home value: $65,000 (2006-2010 5-year est.); Median contract rent: $418 per month (2006-2010 5-year est.); Median year structure built: before 1940 (2006-2010 5-year est.).
**Transportation:** Commute to work: 86.4% car, 1.3% public transportation, 6.1% walk, 5.3% work from home (2006-2010 5-year est.); Travel time to work: 50.3% less than 15 minutes, 29.2% 15 to 30 minutes, 10.7% 30 to 45 minutes, 1.7% 45 to 60 minutes, 8.1% 60 minutes or more (2006-2010 5-year est.)

## BIRDSALL (town). Covers a land area of 35.888 square miles and a water area of 0.171 square miles. Located at 42.39° N. Lat; 77.88° W. Long. Elevation is 1,693 feet.
**Population:** 232 (1990); 268 (2000); 221 (2010); Density: 6.2 persons per square mile (2010); Race: 100.0% White, 0.0% Black, 0.0% Asian, 0.0% American Indian/Alaska Native, 0.0% Native Hawaiian/Other Pacific Islander, 0.0% Other, 0.0% Hispanic of any race (2010); Average household size: 2.23 (2010); Median age: 48.9 (2010); Males per 100 females: 104.6 (2010); Marriage status: 28.6% never married, 50.0% now married, 6.8% widowed, 14.7% divorced (2006-2010 5-year est.); Foreign born: 0.7% (2006-2010 5-year est.); Ancestry (includes multiple ancestries): 49.2% German, 18.2% Irish, 16.3% English, 9.4% Italian, 8.1% Scotch-Irish (2006-2010 5-year est.).
**Economy:** Single-family building permits issued: 1 (2011); Multi-family building permits issued: 0 (2011); Employment by occupation: 4.5% management, 0.0% professional, 19.5% services, 2.3% sales, 5.3% farming, 32.3% construction, 19.5% production (2006-2010 5-year est.).
**Income:** Per capita income: $17,885 (2006-2010 5-year est.); Median household income: $40,000 (2006-2010 5-year est.); Average household income: $39,800 (2006-2010 5-year est.); Percent of households with income of $100,000 or more: 0.0% (2006-2010 5-year est.); Poverty rate: 20.0% (2006-2010 5-year est.).
**Education:** Percent of population age 25 and over with: High school diploma (including GED) or higher: 78.4% (2006-2010 5-year est.); Bachelor's degree or higher: 3.6% (2006-2010 5-year est.); Master's degree or higher: 1.0% (2006-2010 5-year est.).

**Housing:** Homeownership rate: 78.8% (2010); Median home value: $62,500 (2006-2010 5-year est.); Median contract rent: $338 per month (2006-2010 5-year est.); Median year structure built: 1975 (2006-2010 5-year est.).
**Transportation:** Commute to work: 97.0% car, 0.0% public transportation, 3.0% walk, 0.0% work from home (2006-2010 5-year est.); Travel time to work: 31.8% less than 15 minutes, 45.5% 15 to 30 minutes, 7.6% 30 to 45 minutes, 2.3% 45 to 60 minutes, 12.9% 60 minutes or more (2006-2010 5-year est.)

## BLACK CREEK (unincorporated postal area)
Zip Code: 14714
   Covers a land area of 18.174 square miles and a water area of 0.080 square miles. Located at 42.29° N. Lat; 78.23° W. Long. Elevation is 1,509 feet. Population: 487 (2010); Density: 26.8 persons per square mile (2010); Race: 97.5% White, 0.4% Black, 0.0% Asian, 0.4% American Indian/Alaska Native, 0.0% Native Hawaiian/Other Pacific Islander, 1.7% Other, 0.4% Hispanic of any race (2010); Average household size: 2.82 (2010); Median age: 35.9 (2010); Males per 100 females: 107.2 (2010); Homeownership rate: 82.7% (2010)

## BOLIVAR (village). Covers a land area of 0.798 square miles and a water area of 0 square miles. Located at 42.06° N. Lat; 78.16° W. Long. Elevation is 1,594 feet.
**Population:** 1,261 (1990); 1,173 (2000); 1,047 (2010); Density: 1,311.4 persons per square mile (2010); Race: 97.6% White, 1.1% Black, 0.3% Asian, 0.4% American Indian/Alaska Native, 0.0% Native Hawaiian/Other Pacific Islander, 0.6% Other, 1.1% Hispanic of any race (2010); Average household size: 2.46 (2010); Median age: 35.7 (2010); Males per 100 females: 96.8 (2010); Marriage status: 25.9% never married, 54.7% now married, 6.5% widowed, 12.8% divorced (2006-2010 5-year est.); Foreign born: 0.9% (2006-2010 5-year est.); Ancestry (includes multiple ancestries): 32.8% German, 20.0% Irish, 16.7% English, 7.5% Italian, 4.7% Scotch-Irish (2006-2010 5-year est.).
**Economy:** Single-family building permits issued: 0 (2011); Multi-family building permits issued: 0 (2011); Employment by occupation: 11.9% management, 1.0% professional, 17.8% services, 9.8% sales, 1.2% farming, 8.4% construction, 2.2% production (2006-2010 5-year est.).
**Income:** Per capita income: $20,014 (2006-2010 5-year est.); Median household income: $40,227 (2006-2010 5-year est.); Average household income: $51,045 (2006-2010 5-year est.); Percent of households with income of $100,000 or more: 11.6% (2006-2010 5-year est.); Poverty rate: 16.4% (2006-2010 5-year est.).
**Education:** Percent of population age 25 and over with: High school diploma (including GED) or higher: 91.4% (2006-2010 5-year est.); Bachelor's degree or higher: 17.9% (2006-2010 5-year est.); Master's degree or higher: 7.6% (2006-2010 5-year est.).
### School District(s)
Bolivar-Richburg Central School District (PK-12)
   2009-10 Enrollment: 874 . . . . . . . . . . . . . . . . . . . . . . . . . (585) 928-2561
**Housing:** Homeownership rate: 67.0% (2010); Median home value: $53,600 (2006-2010 5-year est.); Median contract rent: $338 per month (2006-2010 5-year est.); Median year structure built: before 1940 (2006-2010 5-year est.).
**Safety:** Violent crime rate: 0.0 per 10,000 population; Property crime rate: 65.5 per 10,000 population (2010).
**Newspapers:** Moneysaver Shopping Guide & Shopping News (Community news)
**Transportation:** Commute to work: 80.0% car, 0.0% public transportation, 10.5% walk, 4.6% work from home (2006-2010 5-year est.); Travel time to work: 41.0% less than 15 minutes, 28.3% 15 to 30 minutes, 24.3% 30 to 45 minutes, 3.4% 45 to 60 minutes, 3.0% 60 minutes or more (2006-2010 5-year est.)

## BOLIVAR (town). Covers a land area of 35.862 square miles and a water area of 0.010 square miles. Located at 42.03° N. Lat; 78.13° W. Long. Elevation is 1,594 feet.
**History:** Surrounding region was prominent early petroleum-producing area from late 19th to early 20th century. Incorporated 1882.
**Population:** 2,361 (1990); 2,223 (2000); 2,189 (2010); Density: 61.0 persons per square mile (2010); Race: 98.1% White, 0.6% Black, 0.4% Asian, 0.3% American Indian/Alaska Native, 0.0% Native Hawaiian/Other Pacific Islander, 0.6% Other, 0.7% Hispanic of any race (2010); Average household size: 2.55 (2010); Median age: 38.0 (2010); Males per 100 females: 96.5 (2010); Marriage status: 22.2% never married, 60.6% now

married, 5.6% widowed, 11.7% divorced (2006-2010 5-year est.); Foreign born: 1.0% (2006-2010 5-year est.); Ancestry (includes multiple ancestries): 28.7% German, 19.3% Irish, 16.8% English, 8.4% Italian, 7.5% American (2006-2010 5-year est.).
**Economy:** Single-family building permits issued: 0 (2011); Multi-family building permits issued: 0 (2011); Employment by occupation: 10.4% management, 1.6% professional, 14.9% services, 9.8% sales, 0.6% farming, 10.2% construction, 4.4% production (2006-2010 5-year est.).
**Income:** Per capita income: $19,329 (2006-2010 5-year est.); Median household income: $42,862 (2006-2010 5-year est.); Average household income: $48,563 (2006-2010 5-year est.); Percent of households with income of $100,000 or more: 6.5% (2006-2010 5-year est.); Poverty rate: 13.3% (2006-2010 5-year est.).
**Education:** Percent of population age 25 and over with: High school diploma (including GED) or higher: 87.8% (2006-2010 5-year est.); Bachelor's degree or higher: 14.5% (2006-2010 5-year est.); Master's degree or higher: 6.6% (2006-2010 5-year est.).

**School District(s)**
Bolivar-Richburg Central School District (PK-12)
    2009-10 Enrollment: 874 . . . . . . . . . . . . . . . . . . (585) 928-2561
**Housing:** Homeownership rate: 75.2% (2010); Median home value: $55,300 (2006-2010 5-year est.); Median contract rent: $356 per month (2006-2010 5-year est.); Median year structure built: before 1940 (2006-2010 5-year est.).
**Newspapers:** Moneysaver Shopping Guide & Shopping News (Community news)
**Transportation:** Commute to work: 87.4% car, 0.9% public transportation, 5.8% walk, 3.4% work from home (2006-2010 5-year est.); Travel time to work: 27.8% less than 15 minutes, 34.1% 15 to 30 minutes, 28.2% 30 to 45 minutes, 5.2% 45 to 60 minutes, 4.8% 60 minutes or more (2006-2010 5-year est.)

**BURNS** (town). Covers a land area of 27.220 square miles and a water area of 0.036 square miles. Located at 42.43° N. Lat; 77.78° W. Long. Elevation is 1,198 feet.
**Population:** 1,299 (1990); 1,248 (2000); 1,180 (2010); Density: 43.4 persons per square mile (2010); Race: 98.4% White, 0.1% Black, 0.0% Asian, 0.3% American Indian/Alaska Native, 0.0% Native Hawaiian/Other Pacific Islander, 1.2% Other, 0.6% Hispanic of any race (2010); Average household size: 2.51 (2010); Median age: 41.6 (2010); Males per 100 females: 104.2 (2010); Marriage status: 21.7% never married, 62.5% now married, 5.1% widowed, 10.7% divorced (2006-2010 5-year est.); Foreign born: 1.2% (2006-2010 5-year est.); Ancestry (includes multiple ancestries): 23.1% English, 20.6% German, 18.1% Irish, 7.4% Italian, 4.9% American (2006-2010 5-year est.).
**Economy:** Single-family building permits issued: 0 (2011); Multi-family building permits issued: 0 (2011); Employment by occupation: 11.7% management, 4.6% professional, 10.3% services, 19.8% sales, 1.8% farming, 16.3% construction, 9.1% production (2006-2010 5-year est.).
**Income:** Per capita income: $21,594 (2006-2010 5-year est.); Median household income: $41,696 (2006-2010 5-year est.); Average household income: $54,778 (2006-2010 5-year est.); Percent of households with income of $100,000 or more: 12.9% (2006-2010 5-year est.); Poverty rate: 9.0% (2006-2010 5-year est.).
**Education:** Percent of population age 25 and over with: High school diploma (including GED) or higher: 87.8% (2006-2010 5-year est.); Bachelor's degree or higher: 7.7% (2006-2010 5-year est.); Master's degree or higher: 2.2% (2006-2010 5-year est.).
**Housing:** Homeownership rate: 75.6% (2010); Median home value: $71,700 (2006-2010 5-year est.); Median contract rent: $513 per month (2006-2010 5-year est.); Median year structure built: 1950 (2006-2010 5-year est.).
**Transportation:** Commute to work: 94.2% car, 0.9% public transportation, 1.9% walk, 3.0% work from home (2006-2010 5-year est.); Travel time to work: 33.4% less than 15 minutes, 34.2% 15 to 30 minutes, 12.5% 30 to 45 minutes, 10.2% 45 to 60 minutes, 9.7% 60 minutes or more (2006-2010 5-year est.).

**CANASERAGA** (village). Covers a land area of 1.062 square miles and a water area of 0 square miles. Located at 42.46° N. Lat; 77.77° W. Long. Elevation is 1,250 feet.
**Population:** 684 (1990); 594 (2000); 550 (2010); Density: 517.8 persons per square mile (2010); Race: 97.5% White, 0.2% Black, 0.0% Asian, 0.5% American Indian/Alaska Native, 0.0% Native Hawaiian/Other Pacific Islander, 1.8% Other, 1.3% Hispanic of any race (2010); Average

household size: 2.48 (2010); Median age: 39.0 (2010); Males per 100 females: 101.5 (2010); Marriage status: 25.6% never married, 60.9% now married, 5.2% widowed, 8.4% divorced (2006-2010 5-year est.); Foreign born: 1.7% (2006-2010 5-year est.); Ancestry (includes multiple ancestries): 27.6% English, 18.8% Irish, 17.3% German, 5.1% Greek, 4.9% Italian (2006-2010 5-year est.).
**Economy:** Single-family building permits issued: 0 (2011); Multi-family building permits issued: 0 (2011); Employment by occupation: 13.3% management, 6.0% professional, 12.0% services, 18.5% sales, 0.0% farming, 19.7% construction, 6.0% production (2006-2010 5-year est.).
**Income:** Per capita income: $21,417 (2006-2010 5-year est.); Median household income: $35,924 (2006-2010 5-year est.); Average household income: $50,859 (2006-2010 5-year est.); Percent of households with income of $100,000 or more: 12.5% (2006-2010 5-year est.); Poverty rate: 9.1% (2006-2010 5-year est.).
**Education:** Percent of population age 25 and over with: High school diploma (including GED) or higher: 86.0% (2006-2010 5-year est.); Bachelor's degree or higher: 3.1% (2006-2010 5-year est.); Master's degree or higher: 0.5% (2006-2010 5-year est.).

**School District(s)**
Canaseraga Central School District (PK-12)
    2009-10 Enrollment: 293 . . . . . . . . . . . . . . . . . . (607) 545-6421
**Housing:** Homeownership rate: 66.7% (2010); Median home value: $52,300 (2006-2010 5-year est.); Median contract rent: $521 per month (2006-2010 5-year est.); Median year structure built: before 1940 (2006-2010 5-year est.).
**Transportation:** Commute to work: 97.0% car, 0.0% public transportation, 1.7% walk, 1.3% work from home (2006-2010 5-year est.); Travel time to work: 36.2% less than 15 minutes, 29.7% 15 to 30 minutes, 9.2% 30 to 45 minutes, 16.6% 45 to 60 minutes, 8.3% 60 minutes or more (2006-2010 5-year est.)

**CANEADEA** (town). Covers a land area of 35.648 square miles and a water area of 0.693 square miles. Located at 42.39° N. Lat; 78.13° W. Long. Elevation is 1,253 feet.
**Population:** 2,551 (1990); 2,694 (2000); 2,542 (2010); Density: 71.3 persons per square mile (2010); Race: 93.9% White, 1.5% Black, 3.1% Asian, 0.1% American Indian/Alaska Native, 0.0% Native Hawaiian/Other Pacific Islander, 1.4% Other, 2.1% Hispanic of any race (2010); Average household size: 2.60 (2010); Median age: 22.1 (2010); Males per 100 females: 79.6 (2010); Marriage status: 60.4% never married, 32.2% now married, 4.6% widowed, 2.8% divorced (2006-2010 5-year est.); Foreign born: 4.9% (2006-2010 5-year est.); Ancestry (includes multiple ancestries): 30.7% German, 20.4% English, 18.4% Irish, 7.1% Polish, 5.6% Scottish (2006-2010 5-year est.).
**Economy:** Single-family building permits issued: 3 (2011); Multi-family building permits issued: 0 (2011); Employment by occupation: 3.1% management, 0.6% professional, 22.8% services, 10.8% sales, 5.5% farming, 8.5% construction, 5.7% production (2006-2010 5-year est.).
**Income:** Per capita income: $13,493 (2006-2010 5-year est.); Median household income: $44,766 (2006-2010 5-year est.); Average household income: $52,594 (2006-2010 5-year est.); Percent of households with income of $100,000 or more: 10.0% (2006-2010 5-year est.); Poverty rate: 14.8% (2006-2010 5-year est.).
**Education:** Percent of population age 25 and over with: High school diploma (including GED) or higher: 92.3% (2006-2010 5-year est.); Bachelor's degree or higher: 43.8% (2006-2010 5-year est.); Master's degree or higher: 22.1% (2006-2010 5-year est.).
**Housing:** Homeownership rate: 75.9% (2010); Median home value: $87,100 (2006-2010 5-year est.); Median contract rent: $452 per month (2006-2010 5-year est.); Median year structure built: 1969 (2006-2010 5-year est.).
**Transportation:** Commute to work: 48.1% car, 0.3% public transportation, 46.1% walk, 4.8% work from home (2006-2010 5-year est.); Travel time to work: 70.3% less than 15 minutes, 14.1% 15 to 30 minutes, 8.0% 30 to 45 minutes, 3.1% 45 to 60 minutes, 4.5% 60 minutes or more (2006-2010 5-year est.)

**CENTERVILLE** (town). Covers a land area of 35.435 square miles and a water area of 0.046 square miles. Located at 42.47° N. Lat; 78.26° W. Long. Elevation is 1,759 feet.
**Population:** 678 (1990); 762 (2000); 822 (2010); Density: 23.2 persons per square mile (2010); Race: 97.7% White, 0.1% Black, 0.0% Asian, 0.2% American Indian/Alaska Native, 0.0% Native Hawaiian/Other Pacific Islander, 2.0% Other, 1.2% Hispanic of any race (2010); Average

household size: 2.89 (2010); Median age: 34.5 (2010); Males per 100 females: 98.1 (2010); Marriage status: 21.0% never married, 58.5% now married, 4.1% widowed, 16.3% divorced (2006-2010 5-year est.); Foreign born: 1.6% (2006-2010 5-year est.); Ancestry (includes multiple ancestries): 23.5% German, 15.8% Polish, 15.4% Irish, 14.5% English, 7.3% French Canadian (2006-2010 5-year est.).

**Economy:** Single-family building permits issued: 2 (2011); Multi-family building permits issued: 0 (2011); Employment by occupation: 14.0% management, 0.0% professional, 11.2% services, 10.1% sales, 3.1% farming, 18.5% construction, 10.7% production (2006-2010 5-year est.).

**Income:** Per capita income: $16,152 (2006-2010 5-year est.); Median household income: $44,423 (2006-2010 5-year est.); Average household income: $47,038 (2006-2010 5-year est.); Percent of households with income of $100,000 or more: 3.9% (2006-2010 5-year est.); Poverty rate: 22.5% (2006-2010 5-year est.).

**Education:** Percent of population age 25 and over with: High school diploma (including GED) or higher: 78.9% (2006-2010 5-year est.); Bachelor's degree or higher: 8.4% (2006-2010 5-year est.); Master's degree or higher: 1.5% (2006-2010 5-year est.).

**Housing:** Homeownership rate: 86.6% (2010); Median home value: $80,700 (2006-2010 5-year est.); Median contract rent: $398 per month (2006-2010 5-year est.); Median year structure built: 1980 (2006-2010 5-year est.).

**Transportation:** Commute to work: 89.4% car, 0.0% public transportation, 6.2% walk, 2.6% work from home (2006-2010 5-year est.); Travel time to work: 19.6% less than 15 minutes, 23.9% 15 to 30 minutes, 26.0% 30 to 45 minutes, 11.2% 45 to 60 minutes, 19.3% 60 minutes or more (2006-2010 5-year est.)

## CERES (unincorporated postal area)

Zip Code: 14721

Covers a land area of 3.732 square miles and a water area of 0 square miles. Located at 42.01° N. Lat; 78.26° W. Long. Elevation is 1,447 feet.
Population: 230 (2010); Density: 61.6 persons per square mile (2010); Race: 99.6% White, 0.0% Black, 0.0% Asian, 0.0% American Indian/Alaska Native, 0.0% Native Hawaiian/Other Pacific Islander, 0.4% Other, 0.0% Hispanic of any race (2010); Average household size: 2.45 (2010); Median age: 41.5 (2010); Males per 100 females: 98.3 (2010); Homeownership rate: 87.2% (2010)

## CLARKSVILLE (town). Covers a land area of 36.276 square miles and a water area of 0.020 square miles. Located at 42.14° N. Lat; 78.24° W. Long.

**Population:** 1,041 (1990); 1,146 (2000); 1,161 (2010); Density: 32.0 persons per square mile (2010); Race: 98.2% White, 0.3% Black, 0.0% Asian, 0.0% American Indian/Alaska Native, 0.0% Native Hawaiian/Other Pacific Islander, 1.5% Other, 1.1% Hispanic of any race (2010); Average household size: 2.39 (2010); Median age: 45.1 (2010); Males per 100 females: 101.6 (2010); Marriage status: 19.9% never married, 66.4% now married, 6.8% widowed, 7.0% divorced (2006-2010 5-year est.); Foreign born: 0.6% (2006-2010 5-year est.); Ancestry (includes multiple ancestries): 31.9% German, 26.0% English, 15.9% Irish, 8.0% Italian, 7.5% Polish (2006-2010 5-year est.).

**Economy:** Single-family building permits issued: 0 (2011); Multi-family building permits issued: 0 (2011); Employment by occupation: 4.6% management, 1.3% professional, 7.3% services, 17.7% sales, 0.0% farming, 6.2% construction, 5.2% production (2006-2010 5-year est.).

**Income:** Per capita income: $19,168 (2006-2010 5-year est.); Median household income: $34,375 (2006-2010 5-year est.); Average household income: $45,323 (2006-2010 5-year est.); Percent of households with income of $100,000 or more: 4.9% (2006-2010 5-year est.); Poverty rate: 9.0% (2006-2010 5-year est.).

**Education:** Percent of population age 25 and over with: High school diploma (including GED) or higher: 85.5% (2006-2010 5-year est.); Bachelor's degree or higher: 14.5% (2006-2010 5-year est.); Master's degree or higher: 6.3% (2006-2010 5-year est.).

**Housing:** Homeownership rate: 87.6% (2010); Median home value: $66,300 (2006-2010 5-year est.); Median contract rent: $427 per month (2006-2010 5-year est.); Median year structure built: 1973 (2006-2010 5-year est.).

**Transportation:** Commute to work: 99.0% car, 0.0% public transportation, 0.0% walk, 1.0% work from home (2006-2010 5-year est.); Travel time to work: 18.1% less than 15 minutes, 44.5% 15 to 30 minutes, 23.0% 30 to 45 minutes, 11.0% 45 to 60 minutes, 3.3% 60 minutes or more (2006-2010 5-year est.)

## CUBA (village). Covers a land area of 1.216 square miles and a water area of 0 square miles. Located at 42.21° N. Lat; 78.27° W. Long. Elevation is 1,496 feet.

**Population:** 1,677 (1990); 1,633 (2000); 1,575 (2010); Density: 1,294.7 persons per square mile (2010); Race: 97.4% White, 0.7% Black, 0.3% Asian, 0.3% American Indian/Alaska Native, 0.0% Native Hawaiian/Other Pacific Islander, 1.3% Other, 1.7% Hispanic of any race (2010); Average household size: 2.43 (2010); Median age: 37.8 (2010); Males per 100 females: 85.5 (2010); Marriage status: 30.1% never married, 50.9% now married, 10.4% widowed, 8.7% divorced (2006-2010 5-year est.); Foreign born: 3.0% (2006-2010 5-year est.); Ancestry (includes multiple ancestries): 26.8% German, 24.0% Irish, 19.2% English, 9.7% Italian, 6.2% Polish (2006-2010 5-year est.).

**Economy:** Single-family building permits issued: 1 (2011); Multi-family building permits issued: 0 (2011); Employment by occupation: 9.2% management, 2.6% professional, 14.7% services, 16.1% sales, 3.2% farming, 8.7% construction, 4.2% production (2006-2010 5-year est.).

**Income:** Per capita income: $21,987 (2006-2010 5-year est.); Median household income: $39,167 (2006-2010 5-year est.); Average household income: $53,287 (2006-2010 5-year est.); Percent of households with income of $100,000 or more: 11.3% (2006-2010 5-year est.); Poverty rate: 16.2% (2006-2010 5-year est.).

**Education:** Percent of population age 25 and over with: High school diploma (including GED) or higher: 88.8% (2006-2010 5-year est.); Bachelor's degree or higher: 27.3% (2006-2010 5-year est.); Master's degree or higher: 10.8% (2006-2010 5-year est.).

### School District(s)

Cuba-Rushford Central School District (PK-12)
    2009-10 Enrollment: 952 . . . . . . . . . . . . . . . . . . . . . . . (585) 968-1556

**Housing:** Homeownership rate: 61.5% (2010); Median home value: $67,300 (2006-2010 5-year est.); Median contract rent: $365 per month (2006-2010 5-year est.); Median year structure built: before 1940 (2006-2010 5-year est.).

**Hospitals:** Cuba Memorial Hospital (80 beds)

**Newspapers:** Cuba Pennysaver (Community news; Circulation 6,800); Franklinville Pennysaver (Community news; Circulation 12,150); Patriot & Free Press (Community news; Circulation 6,000)

**Transportation:** Commute to work: 86.8% car, 1.0% public transportation, 5.0% walk, 5.7% work from home (2006-2010 5-year est.); Travel time to work: 31.9% less than 15 minutes, 41.9% 15 to 30 minutes, 20.1% 30 to 45 minutes, 2.4% 45 to 60 minutes, 3.8% 60 minutes or more (2006-2010 5-year est.)

## CUBA (town). Covers a land area of 35.129 square miles and a water area of 0.762 square miles. Located at 42.20° N. Lat; 78.24° W. Long. Elevation is 1,496 feet.

**History:** Seneca Oil Spring, where oil was first noted by Jesuit missionaries in early 17th century, is nearby; the spring was the precursor of the "Pennsylvania field," the first oil field in the U.S. Incorporated 1850.
**Population:** 3,401 (1990); 3,392 (2000); 3,243 (2010); Density: 92.3 persons per square mile (2010); Race: 97.1% White, 0.6% Black, 0.3% Asian, 0.2% American Indian/Alaska Native, 0.0% Native Hawaiian/Other Pacific Islander, 1.8% Other, 1.3% Hispanic of any race (2010); Average household size: 2.37 (2010); Median age: 44.1 (2010); Males per 100 females: 91.7 (2010); Marriage status: 24.1% never married, 61.1% now married, 9.3% widowed, 5.6% divorced (2006-2010 5-year est.); Foreign born: 1.7% (2006-2010 5-year est.); Ancestry (includes multiple ancestries): 27.9% German, 26.3% English, 18.1% Irish, 6.6% Polish, 6.2% Italian (2006-2010 5-year est.).

**Economy:** Single-family building permits issued: 4 (2011); Multi-family building permits issued: 0 (2011); Employment by occupation: 8.2% management, 2.8% professional, 12.2% services, 19.5% sales, 3.5% farming, 7.8% construction, 3.1% production (2006-2010 5-year est.).

**Income:** Per capita income: $24,816 (2006-2010 5-year est.); Median household income: $49,583 (2006-2010 5-year est.); Average household income: $59,310 (2006-2010 5-year est.); Percent of households with income of $100,000 or more: 14.6% (2006-2010 5-year est.); Poverty rate: 10.3% (2006-2010 5-year est.).

**Education:** Percent of population age 25 and over with: High school diploma (including GED) or higher: 89.7% (2006-2010 5-year est.); Bachelor's degree or higher: 20.4% (2006-2010 5-year est.); Master's degree or higher: 9.6% (2006-2010 5-year est.).

### School District(s)

Cuba-Rushford Central School District (PK-12)
    2009-10 Enrollment: 952 . . . . . . . . . . . . . . . . . . . . . . . (585) 968-1556

**Housing:** Homeownership rate: 75.1% (2010); Median home value: $78,400 (2006-2010 5-year est.); Median contract rent: $371 per month (2006-2010 5-year est.); Median year structure built: 1949 (2006-2010 5-year est.).
**Hospitals:** Cuba Memorial Hospital (80 beds)
**Safety:** Violent crime rate: 6.2 per 10,000 population; Property crime rate: 379.2 per 10,000 population (2010).
**Newspapers:** Cuba Pennysaver (Community news; Circulation 6,800); Franklinville Pennysaver (Community news; Circulation 12,150); Patriot & Free Press (Community news; Circulation 6,000)
**Transportation:** Commute to work: 91.9% car, 0.5% public transportation, 2.7% walk, 3.6% work from home (2006-2010 5-year est.); Travel time to work: 40.6% less than 15 minutes, 38.0% 15 to 30 minutes, 14.5% 30 to 45 minutes, 2.9% 45 to 60 minutes, 4.0% 60 minutes or more (2006-2010 5-year est.)

**FILLMORE** (CDP). Covers a land area of 0.815 square miles and a water area of 0 square miles. Located at 42.46° N. Lat; 78.11° W. Long. Elevation is 1,198 feet.
**Population:** n/a (1990); n/a (2000); 603 (2010); Density: 739.2 persons per square mile (2010); Race: 98.7% White, 0.3% Black, 0.0% Asian, 1.0% American Indian/Alaska Native, 0.0% Native Hawaiian/Other Pacific Islander, 0.0% Other, 1.5% Hispanic of any race (2010); Average household size: 2.45 (2010); Median age: 33.8 (2010); Males per 100 females: 91.4 (2010); Marriage status: 18.5% never married, 68.7% now married, 6.8% widowed, 5.9% divorced (2006-2010 5-year est.); Foreign born: 1.3% (2006-2010 5-year est.); Ancestry (includes multiple ancestries): 26.7% German, 23.9% Irish, 17.4% English, 11.7% Italian, 10.4% French (2006-2010 5-year est.).
**Economy:** Employment by occupation: 14.1% management, 0.0% professional, 17.4% services, 6.5% sales, 4.0% farming, 17.4% construction, 12.3% production (2006-2010 5-year est.).
**Income:** Per capita income: $20,744 (2006-2010 5-year est.); Median household income: $47,500 (2006-2010 5-year est.); Average household income: $49,752 (2006-2010 5-year est.); Percent of households with income of $100,000 or more: 11.2% (2006-2010 5-year est.); Poverty rate: 18.9% (2006-2010 5-year est.).
**Education:** Percent of population age 25 and over with: High school diploma (including GED) or higher: 95.5% (2006-2010 5-year est.); Bachelor's degree or higher: 19.6% (2006-2010 5-year est.); Master's degree or higher: 12.1% (2006-2010 5-year est.).

**School District(s)**
Fillmore Central School District (PK-12)
    2009-10 Enrollment: 735 . . . . . . . . . . . . . . . . . . . . . . (585) 567-2251
**Housing:** Homeownership rate: 60.6% (2010); Median home value: $69,000 (2006-2010 5-year est.); Median contract rent: $474 per month (2006-2010 5-year est.); Median year structure built: before 1940 (2006-2010 5-year est.).
**Transportation:** Commute to work: 87.3% car, 0.0% public transportation, 9.8% walk, 1.8% work from home (2006-2010 5-year est.); Travel time to work: 44.6% less than 15 minutes, 18.1% 15 to 30 minutes, 17.0% 30 to 45 minutes, 4.1% 45 to 60 minutes, 16.2% 60 minutes or more (2006-2010 5-year est.)

**FRIENDSHIP** (town). Covers a land area of 36.215 square miles and a water area of 0.013 square miles. Located at 42.21° N. Lat; 78.13° W. Long. Elevation is 1,506 feet.
**History:** Incorporated 1898.
**Population:** 2,185 (1990); 1,927 (2000); 2,004 (2010); Density: 55.3 persons per square mile (2010); Race: 96.9% White, 0.5% Black, 0.1% Asian, 0.4% American Indian/Alaska Native, 0.0% Native Hawaiian/Other Pacific Islander, 2.1% Other, 1.7% Hispanic of any race (2010); Average household size: 2.51 (2010); Median age: 38.0 (2010); Males per 100 females: 99.8 (2010); Marriage status: 25.1% never married, 55.2% now married, 7.8% widowed, 11.9% divorced (2006-2010 5-year est.); Foreign born: 1.0% (2006-2010 5-year est.); Ancestry (includes multiple ancestries): 31.9% German, 17.8% Irish, 16.8% English, 7.0% American, 3.5% Polish (2006-2010 5-year est.).
**Economy:** Single-family building permits issued: 0 (2011); Multi-family building permits issued: 0 (2011); Employment by occupation: 8.3% management, 1.2% professional, 15.7% services, 12.3% sales, 4.5% farming, 15.3% construction, 9.8% production (2006-2010 5-year est.).
**Income:** Per capita income: $17,218 (2006-2010 5-year est.); Median household income: $36,958 (2006-2010 5-year est.); Average household income: $42,966 (2006-2010 5-year est.); Percent of households with

income of $100,000 or more: 5.4% (2006-2010 5-year est.); Poverty rate: 23.5% (2006-2010 5-year est.).
**Education:** Percent of population age 25 and over with: High school diploma (including GED) or higher: 84.6% (2006-2010 5-year est.); Bachelor's degree or higher: 13.0% (2006-2010 5-year est.); Master's degree or higher: 4.6% (2006-2010 5-year est.).
**School District(s)**
Friendship Central School District (PK-12)
    2009-10 Enrollment: 392 . . . . . . . . . . . . . . . . . . . . . . (585) 973-3534
**Housing:** Homeownership rate: 71.8% (2010); Median home value: $53,100 (2006-2010 5-year est.); Median contract rent: $375 per month (2006-2010 5-year est.); Median year structure built: 1953 (2006-2010 5-year est.).
**Safety:** Violent crime rate: 0.0 per 10,000 population; Property crime rate: 67.1 per 10,000 population (2010).
**Transportation:** Commute to work: 91.9% car, 0.9% public transportation, 2.1% walk, 3.7% work from home (2006-2010 5-year est.); Travel time to work: 26.6% less than 15 minutes, 39.0% 15 to 30 minutes, 15.5% 30 to 45 minutes, 8.0% 45 to 60 minutes, 10.9% 60 minutes or more (2006-2010 5-year est.)

**FRIENDSHIP** (CDP). Covers a land area of 2.888 square miles and a water area of 0 square miles. Located at 42.20° N. Lat; 78.14° W. Long. Elevation is 1,506 feet.
**Population:** 1,413 (1990); 1,176 (2000); 1,218 (2010); Density: 421.6 persons per square mile (2010); Race: 97.8% White, 0.6% Black, 0.1% Asian, 0.4% American Indian/Alaska Native, 0.0% Native Hawaiian/Other Pacific Islander, 1.1% Other, 1.8% Hispanic of any race (2010); Average household size: 2.67 (2010); Median age: 34.2 (2010); Males per 100 females: 93.3 (2010); Marriage status: 25.0% never married, 55.1% now married, 7.7% widowed, 12.1% divorced (2006-2010 5-year est.); Foreign born: 1.2% (2006-2010 5-year est.); Ancestry (includes multiple ancestries): 29.8% German, 20.1% Irish, 14.8% English, 6.8% American, 4.5% Scottish (2006-2010 5-year est.).
**Economy:** Employment by occupation: 9.6% management, 0.9% professional, 19.0% services, 10.7% sales, 3.8% farming, 12.8% construction, 8.7% production (2006-2010 5-year est.).
**Income:** Per capita income: $16,453 (2006-2010 5-year est.); Median household income: $35,484 (2006-2010 5-year est.); Average household income: $40,805 (2006-2010 5-year est.); Percent of households with income of $100,000 or more: 5.8% (2006-2010 5-year est.); Poverty rate: 23.6% (2006-2010 5-year est.).
**Education:** Percent of population age 25 and over with: High school diploma (including GED) or higher: 81.3% (2006-2010 5-year est.); Bachelor's degree or higher: 14.3% (2006-2010 5-year est.); Master's degree or higher: 5.8% (2006-2010 5-year est.).
**School District(s)**
Friendship Central School District (PK-12)
    2009-10 Enrollment: 392 . . . . . . . . . . . . . . . . . . . . . . (585) 973-3534
**Housing:** Homeownership rate: 64.1% (2010); Median home value: $53,400 (2006-2010 5-year est.); Median contract rent: $363 per month (2006-2010 5-year est.); Median year structure built: before 1940 (2006-2010 5-year est.).
**Transportation:** Commute to work: 93.7% car, 1.1% public transportation, 3.4% walk, 1.3% work from home (2006-2010 5-year est.); Travel time to work: 26.8% less than 15 minutes, 40.8% 15 to 30 minutes, 15.0% 30 to 45 minutes, 4.8% 45 to 60 minutes, 12.7% 60 minutes or more (2006-2010 5-year est.)

**GENESEE** (town). Covers a land area of 36.238 square miles and a water area of 0.048 square miles. Located at 42.04° N. Lat; 78.24° W. Long.
**Population:** 1,672 (1990); 1,803 (2000); 1,693 (2010); Density: 46.7 persons per square mile (2010); Race: 98.5% White, 0.1% Black, 0.4% Asian, 0.1% American Indian/Alaska Native, 0.0% Native Hawaiian/Other Pacific Islander, 0.9% Other, 0.4% Hispanic of any race (2010); Average household size: 2.57 (2010); Median age: 42.8 (2010); Males per 100 females: 99.6 (2010); Marriage status: 19.6% never married, 65.5% now married, 4.5% widowed, 10.5% divorced (2006-2010 5-year est.); Foreign born: 0.0% (2006-2010 5-year est.); Ancestry (includes multiple ancestries): 36.5% German, 23.6% Irish, 19.9% English, 8.0% Polish, 7.4% Italian (2006-2010 5-year est.).
**Economy:** Single-family building permits issued: 1 (2011); Multi-family building permits issued: 0 (2011); Employment by occupation: 11.1%

management, 2.8% professional, 6.6% services, 14.7% sales, 4.4% farming, 13.8% construction, 12.3% production (2006-2010 5-year est.).
**Income:** Per capita income: $21,489 (2006-2010 5-year est.); Median household income: $42,443 (2006-2010 5-year est.); Average household income: $50,190 (2006-2010 5-year est.); Percent of households with income of $100,000 or more: 8.4% (2006-2010 5-year est.); Poverty rate: 10.1% (2006-2010 5-year est.).
**Education:** Percent of population age 25 and over with: High school diploma (including GED) or higher: 83.0% (2006-2010 5-year est.); Bachelor's degree or higher: 10.1% (2006-2010 5-year est.); Master's degree or higher: 4.4% (2006-2010 5-year est.).
**Housing:** Homeownership rate: 88.1% (2010); Median home value: $59,100 (2006-2010 5-year est.); Median contract rent: $425 per month (2006-2010 5-year est.); Median year structure built: 1975 (2006-2010 5-year est.).
**Transportation:** Commute to work: 95.4% car, 0.3% public transportation, 2.2% walk, 2.1% work from home (2006-2010 5-year est.); Travel time to work: 21.4% less than 15 minutes, 40.1% 15 to 30 minutes, 32.5% 30 to 45 minutes, 2.2% 45 to 60 minutes, 3.9% 60 minutes or more (2006-2010 5-year est.)

## GRANGER (town).
Covers a land area of 31.937 square miles and a water area of 0.100 square miles. Located at 42.47° N. Lat; 78.01° W. Long.
**Population:** 515 (1990); 577 (2000); 538 (2010); Density: 16.8 persons per square mile (2010); Race: 98.3% White, 0.0% Black, 0.0% Asian, 0.2% American Indian/Alaska Native, 0.0% Native Hawaiian/Other Pacific Islander, 1.5% Other, 0.4% Hispanic of any race (2010); Average household size: 2.47 (2010); Median age: 45.0 (2010); Males per 100 females: 116.1 (2010); Marriage status: 25.8% never married, 52.2% now married, 7.5% widowed, 14.4% divorced (2006-2010 5-year est.); Foreign born: 1.6% (2006-2010 5-year est.); Ancestry (includes multiple ancestries): 25.7% English, 24.6% German, 14.1% Irish, 4.9% Polish, 4.2% French (2006-2010 5-year est.).
**Economy:** Single-family building permits issued: 0 (2011); Multi-family building permits issued: 0 (2011); Employment by occupation: 18.2% management, 0.0% professional, 9.3% services, 10.9% sales, 0.0% farming, 25.6% construction, 1.6% production (2006-2010 5-year est.).
**Income:** Per capita income: $20,032 (2006-2010 5-year est.); Median household income: $34,423 (2006-2010 5-year est.); Average household income: $50,003 (2006-2010 5-year est.); Percent of households with income of $100,000 or more: 12.0% (2006-2010 5-year est.); Poverty rate: 24.6% (2006-2010 5-year est.).
**Education:** Percent of population age 25 and over with: High school diploma (including GED) or higher: 86.6% (2006-2010 5-year est.); Bachelor's degree or higher: 9.7% (2006-2010 5-year est.); Master's degree or higher: 3.8% (2006-2010 5-year est.).
**Housing:** Homeownership rate: 87.6% (2010); Median home value: $71,200 (2006-2010 5-year est.); Median contract rent: $470 per month (2006-2010 5-year est.); Median year structure built: 1971 (2006-2010 5-year est.).
**Transportation:** Commute to work: 80.7% car, 0.0% public transportation, 8.3% walk, 11.0% work from home (2006-2010 5-year est.); Travel time to work: 23.5% less than 15 minutes, 42.5% 15 to 30 minutes, 10.2% 30 to 45 minutes, 14.6% 45 to 60 minutes, 9.3% 60 minutes or more (2006-2010 5-year est.)

## GROVE (town).
Covers a land area of 33.365 square miles and a water area of 0.335 square miles. Located at 42.47° N. Lat; 77.89° W. Long. Elevation is 1,627 feet.
**Population:** 479 (1990); 533 (2000); 548 (2010); Density: 16.4 persons per square mile (2010); Race: 98.4% White, 0.2% Black, 0.0% Asian, 0.0% American Indian/Alaska Native, 0.0% Native Hawaiian/Other Pacific Islander, 1.4% Other, 1.3% Hispanic of any race (2010); Average household size: 2.23 (2010); Median age: 46.9 (2010); Males per 100 females: 113.2 (2010); Marriage status: 28.8% never married, 53.2% now married, 7.7% widowed, 10.3% divorced (2006-2010 5-year est.); Foreign born: 0.0% (2006-2010 5-year est.); Ancestry (includes multiple ancestries): 29.7% Irish, 24.9% German, 16.6% English, 6.6% Polish, 6.6% American (2006-2010 5-year est.).
**Economy:** Single-family building permits issued: 1 (2011); Multi-family building permits issued: 0 (2011); Employment by occupation: 17.1% management, 2.9% professional, 14.6% services, 6.7% sales, 1.7% farming, 22.1% construction, 8.3% production (2006-2010 5-year est.).

**Income:** Per capita income: $22,378 (2006-2010 5-year est.); Median household income: $49,000 (2006-2010 5-year est.); Average household income: $54,145 (2006-2010 5-year est.); Percent of households with income of $100,000 or more: 9.8% (2006-2010 5-year est.); Poverty rate: 18.7% (2006-2010 5-year est.).
**Education:** Percent of population age 25 and over with: High school diploma (including GED) or higher: 90.0% (2006-2010 5-year est.); Bachelor's degree or higher: 9.5% (2006-2010 5-year est.); Master's degree or higher: 0.5% (2006-2010 5-year est.).
**Housing:** Homeownership rate: 83.0% (2010); Median home value: $68,300 (2006-2010 5-year est.); Median contract rent: $466 per month (2006-2010 5-year est.); Median year structure built: 1974 (2006-2010 5-year est.).
**Transportation:** Commute to work: 93.7% car, 0.0% public transportation, 6.3% walk, 0.0% work from home (2006-2010 5-year est.); Travel time to work: 19.8% less than 15 minutes, 27.8% 15 to 30 minutes, 19.4% 30 to 45 minutes, 10.1% 45 to 60 minutes, 22.8% 60 minutes or more (2006-2010 5-year est.)

## HOUGHTON (CDP).
Covers a land area of 2.478 square miles and a water area of 0.009 square miles. Located at 42.42° N. Lat; 78.17° W. Long. Elevation is 1,207 feet.
**History:** Seat of Houghton College (1923).
**Population:** 1,740 (1990); 1,748 (2000); 1,693 (2010); Density: 682.9 persons per square mile (2010); Race: 91.4% White, 2.1% Black, 4.5% Asian, 0.2% American Indian/Alaska Native, 0.0% Native Hawaiian/Other Pacific Islander, 1.8% Other, 1.9% Hispanic of any race (2010); Average household size: 2.68 (2010); Median age: 21.1 (2010); Males per 100 females: 67.5 (2010); Marriage status: 73.2% never married, 21.2% now married, 5.5% widowed, 0.1% divorced (2006-2010 5-year est.); Foreign born: 6.9% (2006-2010 5-year est.); Ancestry (includes multiple ancestries): 28.4% German, 22.1% English, 13.9% Irish, 7.7% Polish, 6.7% Scottish (2006-2010 5-year est.).
**Economy:** Employment by occupation: 2.7% management, 0.0% professional, 25.5% services, 11.5% sales, 6.6% farming, 5.7% construction, 4.8% production (2006-2010 5-year est.).
**Income:** Per capita income: $11,191 (2006-2010 5-year est.); Median household income: $50,500 (2006-2010 5-year est.); Average household income: $58,443 (2006-2010 5-year est.); Percent of households with income of $100,000 or more: 17.3% (2006-2010 5-year est.); Poverty rate: 13.7% (2006-2010 5-year est.).
**Education:** Percent of population age 25 and over with: High school diploma (including GED) or higher: 93.9% (2006-2010 5-year est.); Bachelor's degree or higher: 72.9% (2006-2010 5-year est.); Master's degree or higher: 37.0% (2006-2010 5-year est.).

### Four-year College(s)
Houghton College (Private, Not-for-profit, Wesleyan)
    Fall 2010 Enrollment: 1,274. . . . . . . . . . . . . . . . . . . . . . . (585) 567-9200
    2011-12 Tuition: In-state $26,094; Out-of-state $26,094
**Housing:** Homeownership rate: 66.8% (2010); Median home value: $125,000 (2006-2010 5-year est.); Median contract rent: $463 per month (2006-2010 5-year est.); Median year structure built: 1962 (2006-2010 5-year est.).
**Transportation:** Commute to work: 29.0% car, 0.0% public transportation, 64.4% walk, 6.0% work from home (2006-2010 5-year est.); Travel time to work: 86.4% less than 15 minutes, 10.1% 15 to 30 minutes, 1.0% 30 to 45 minutes, 1.5% 45 to 60 minutes, 1.0% 60 minutes or more (2006-2010 5-year est.)

## HUME (town).
Covers a land area of 37.890 square miles and a water area of 0.430 square miles. Located at 42.48° N. Lat; 78.12° W. Long. Elevation is 1,273 feet.
**Population:** 1,970 (1990); 1,987 (2000); 2,071 (2010); Density: 54.7 persons per square mile (2010); Race: 98.5% White, 0.2% Black, 0.0% Asian, 0.7% American Indian/Alaska Native, 0.0% Native Hawaiian/Other Pacific Islander, 0.6% Other, 0.9% Hispanic of any race (2010); Average household size: 2.64 (2010); Median age: 35.5 (2010); Males per 100 females: 100.7 (2010); Marriage status: 16.6% never married, 68.8% now married, 6.3% widowed, 8.3% divorced (2006-2010 5-year est.); Foreign born: 1.4% (2006-2010 5-year est.); Ancestry (includes multiple ancestries): 31.4% German, 18.2% English, 15.3% Irish, 10.7% Pennsylvania German, 6.5% Dutch (2006-2010 5-year est.).
**Economy:** Single-family building permits issued: 2 (2011); Multi-family building permits issued: 0 (2011); Employment by occupation: 13.3%

management, 1.5% professional, 8.8% services, 12.1% sales, 3.3% farming, 15.9% construction, 12.0% production (2006-2010 5-year est.).
**Income:** Per capita income: $19,229 (2006-2010 5-year est.); Median household income: $41,250 (2006-2010 5-year est.); Average household income: $48,844 (2006-2010 5-year est.); Percent of households with income of $100,000 or more: 11.0% (2006-2010 5-year est.); Poverty rate: 23.9% (2006-2010 5-year est.).
**Education:** Percent of population age 25 and over with: High school diploma (including GED) or higher: 85.5% (2006-2010 5-year est.); Bachelor's degree or higher: 19.6% (2006-2010 5-year est.); Master's degree or higher: 8.5% (2006-2010 5-year est.).
**Housing:** Homeownership rate: 71.8% (2010); Median home value: $72,800 (2006-2010 5-year est.); Median contract rent: $463 per month (2006-2010 5-year est.); Median year structure built: 1953 (2006-2010 5-year est.).
**Transportation:** Commute to work: 89.7% car, 0.7% public transportation, 6.7% walk, 2.2% work from home (2006-2010 5-year est.); Travel time to work: 42.5% less than 15 minutes, 21.6% 15 to 30 minutes, 14.1% 30 to 45 minutes, 6.0% 45 to 60 minutes, 15.8% 60 minutes or more (2006-2010 5-year est.)
**Additional Information Contacts**
Town of Hume . . . . . . . . . . . . . . . . . . . . . . . . . . . . . . . . (585) 567-2666
  http://www.humetown.org

**INDEPENDENCE** (town). Covers a land area of 34.484 square miles and a water area of 0.005 square miles. Located at 42.04° N. Lat; 77.79° W. Long. Elevation is 2,057 feet.
**Population:** 1,026 (1990); 1,074 (2000); 1,167 (2010); Density: 33.8 persons per square mile (2010); Race: 98.0% White, 0.4% Black, 0.3% Asian, 0.1% American Indian/Alaska Native, 0.0% Native Hawaiian/Other Pacific Islander, 1.2% Other, 0.8% Hispanic of any race (2010); Average household size: 2.77 (2010); Median age: 37.7 (2010); Males per 100 females: 105.5 (2010); Marriage status: 17.9% never married, 72.4% now married, 4.1% widowed, 5.6% divorced (2006-2010 5-year est.); Foreign born: 0.4% (2006-2010 5-year est.); Ancestry (includes multiple ancestries): 21.0% German, 19.6% English, 16.6% Irish, 6.9% American, 6.2% Dutch (2006-2010 5-year est.).
**Economy:** Single-family building permits issued: 5 (2011); Multi-family building permits issued: 0 (2011); Employment by occupation: 9.8% management, 2.4% professional, 10.8% services, 11.6% sales, 1.8% farming, 20.5% construction, 4.8% production (2006-2010 5-year est.).
**Income:** Per capita income: $21,382 (2006-2010 5-year est.); Median household income: $50,938 (2006-2010 5-year est.); Average household income: $52,708 (2006-2010 5-year est.); Percent of households with income of $100,000 or more: 10.2% (2006-2010 5-year est.); Poverty rate: 8.0% (2006-2010 5-year est.).
**Education:** Percent of population age 25 and over with: High school diploma (including GED) or higher: 85.9% (2006-2010 5-year est.); Bachelor's degree or higher: 11.0% (2006-2010 5-year est.); Master's degree or higher: 4.6% (2006-2010 5-year est.).
**Housing:** Homeownership rate: 82.2% (2010); Median home value: $54,700 (2006-2010 5-year est.); Median contract rent: $354 per month (2006-2010 5-year est.); Median year structure built: before 1940 (2006-2010 5-year est.).
**Safety:** Violent crime rate: 0.0 per 10,000 population; Property crime rate: 39.6 per 10,000 population (2010).
**Transportation:** Commute to work: 93.1% car, 0.0% public transportation, 1.1% walk, 5.9% work from home (2006-2010 5-year est.); Travel time to work: 23.7% less than 15 minutes, 38.3% 15 to 30 minutes, 15.7% 30 to 45 minutes, 9.4% 45 to 60 minutes, 13.0% 60 minutes or more (2006-2010 5-year est.)

**LITTLE GENESEE** (unincorporated postal area)
Zip Code: 14754
  Covers a land area of 16.613 square miles and a water area of 0.013 square miles. Located at 42.02° N. Lat; 78.20° W. Long. Elevation is 1,549 feet. Population: 667 (2010); Density: 40.1 persons per square mile (2010); Race: 98.5% White, 0.1% Black, 0.3% Asian, 0.3% American Indian/Alaska Native, 0.0% Native Hawaiian/Other Pacific Islander, 0.8% Other, 0.4% Hispanic of any race (2010); Average household size: 2.51 (2010); Median age: 43.3 (2010); Males per 100 females: 102.1 (2010); Homeownership rate: 88.0% (2010)

**NEW HUDSON** (town). Covers a land area of 36.194 square miles and a water area of 0.123 square miles. Located at 42.28° N. Lat; 78.25° W. Long.
**Population:** 715 (1990); 736 (2000); 781 (2010); Density: 21.6 persons per square mile (2010); Race: 98.5% White, 0.4% Black, 0.0% Asian, 0.3% American Indian/Alaska Native, 0.0% Native Hawaiian/Other Pacific Islander, 0.8% Other, 1.2% Hispanic of any race (2010); Average household size: 2.74 (2010); Median age: 39.7 (2010); Males per 100 females: 111.1 (2010); Marriage status: 23.5% never married, 66.2% now married, 3.4% widowed, 6.9% divorced (2006-2010 5-year est.); Foreign born: 1.5% (2006-2010 5-year est.); Ancestry (includes multiple ancestries): 36.6% German, 17.2% Irish, 13.4% English, 10.1% Polish, 7.3% French (2006-2010 5-year est.).
**Economy:** Single-family building permits issued: 2 (2011); Multi-family building permits issued: 0 (2011); Employment by occupation: 5.5% management, 0.0% professional, 7.2% services, 12.2% sales, 3.9% farming, 21.6% construction, 18.8% production (2006-2010 5-year est.).
**Income:** Per capita income: $37,266 (2006-2010 5-year est.); Median household income: $46,875 (2006-2010 5-year est.); Average household income: $88,895 (2006-2010 5-year est.); Percent of households with income of $100,000 or more: 17.7% (2006-2010 5-year est.); Poverty rate: 12.1% (2006-2010 5-year est.).
**Education:** Percent of population age 25 and over with: High school diploma (including GED) or higher: 81.3% (2006-2010 5-year est.); Bachelor's degree or higher: 12.2% (2006-2010 5-year est.); Master's degree or higher: 8.8% (2006-2010 5-year est.).
**Housing:** Homeownership rate: 86.0% (2010); Median home value: $79,600 (2006-2010 5-year est.); Median contract rent: $675 per month (2006-2010 5-year est.); Median year structure built: 1974 (2006-2010 5-year est.).
**Transportation:** Commute to work: 82.2% car, 1.7% public transportation, 4.4% walk, 10.5% work from home (2006-2010 5-year est.); Travel time to work: 42.3% less than 15 minutes, 24.8% 15 to 30 minutes, 18.2% 30 to 45 minutes, 6.2% 45 to 60 minutes, 8.5% 60 minutes or more (2006-2010 5-year est.)

**RICHBURG** (village). Covers a land area of 0.900 square miles and a water area of 0 square miles. Located at 42.08° N. Lat; 78.15° W. Long. Elevation is 1,660 feet.
**Population:** 494 (1990); 448 (2000); 450 (2010); Density: 499.9 persons per square mile (2010); Race: 98.9% White, 0.0% Black, 0.7% Asian, 0.0% American Indian/Alaska Native, 0.0% Native Hawaiian/Other Pacific Islander, 0.4% Other, 0.4% Hispanic of any race (2010); Average household size: 2.78 (2010); Median age: 32.9 (2010); Males per 100 females: 89.1 (2010); Marriage status: 35.3% never married, 46.6% now married, 6.9% widowed, 11.3% divorced (2006-2010 5-year est.); Foreign born: 0.0% (2006-2010 5-year est.); Ancestry (includes multiple ancestries): 30.8% German, 20.3% Irish, 18.2% English, 7.1% Italian, 5.5% Dutch (2006-2010 5-year est.).
**Economy:** Single-family building permits issued: 0 (2011); Multi-family building permits issued: 0 (2011); Employment by occupation: 7.3% management, 3.9% professional, 11.2% services, 8.3% sales, 3.9% farming, 13.6% construction, 17.5% production (2006-2010 5-year est.).
**Income:** Per capita income: $18,616 (2006-2010 5-year est.); Median household income: $40,993 (2006-2010 5-year est.); Average household income: $50,222 (2006-2010 5-year est.); Percent of households with income of $100,000 or more: 7.4% (2006-2010 5-year est.); Poverty rate: 29.5% (2006-2010 5-year est.).
**Education:** Percent of population age 25 and over with: High school diploma (including GED) or higher: 90.2% (2006-2010 5-year est.); Bachelor's degree or higher: 6.4% (2006-2010 5-year est.); Master's degree or higher: 0.6% (2006-2010 5-year est.).
**School District(s)**
Bolivar-Richburg Central School District (PK-12)
    2009-10 Enrollment: 874 . . . . . . . . . . . . . . . . . . . (585) 928-2561
**Housing:** Homeownership rate: 69.2% (2010); Median home value: $49,100 (2006-2010 5-year est.); Median contract rent: $380 per month (2006-2010 5-year est.); Median year structure built: 1944 (2006-2010 5-year est.).
**Transportation:** Commute to work: 89.1% car, 0.0% public transportation, 3.5% walk, 7.5% work from home (2006-2010 5-year est.); Travel time to work: 33.9% less than 15 minutes, 35.5% 15 to 30 minutes, 23.1% 30 to 45 minutes, 4.3% 45 to 60 minutes, 3.2% 60 minutes or more (2006-2010 5-year est.)

**RUSHFORD** (town). Covers a land area of 35.294 square miles and a water area of 0.790 square miles. Located at 42.39° N. Lat; 78.25° W. Long. Elevation is 1,499 feet.

**Population:** 1,176 (1990); 1,259 (2000); 1,150 (2010); Density: 32.6 persons per square mile (2010); Race: 98.3% White, 0.3% Black, 0.6% Asian, 0.1% American Indian/Alaska Native, 0.0% Native Hawaiian/Other Pacific Islander, 0.7% Other, 0.7% Hispanic of any race (2010); Average household size: 2.34 (2010); Median age: 48.1 (2010); Males per 100 females: 104.6 (2010); Marriage status: 22.5% never married, 57.9% now married, 11.8% widowed, 7.8% divorced (2006-2010 5-year est.); Foreign born: 0.9% (2006-2010 5-year est.); Ancestry (includes multiple ancestries): 49.0% German, 25.7% Irish, 24.3% English, 8.7% Polish, 5.1% Italian (2006-2010 5-year est.).

**Economy:** Single-family building permits issued: 9 (2011); Multi-family building permits issued: 0 (2011); Employment by occupation: 17.9% management, 0.0% professional, 6.2% services, 9.0% sales, 3.0% farming, 17.0% construction, 10.8% production (2006-2010 5-year est.).

**Income:** Per capita income: $21,197 (2006-2010 5-year est.); Median household income: $32,944 (2006-2010 5-year est.); Average household income: $42,610 (2006-2010 5-year est.); Percent of households with income of $100,000 or more: 7.3% (2006-2010 5-year est.); Poverty rate: 15.5% (2006-2010 5-year est.).

**Education:** Percent of population age 25 and over with: High school diploma (including GED) or higher: 84.6% (2006-2010 5-year est.); Bachelor's degree or higher: 14.4% (2006-2010 5-year est.); Master's degree or higher: 5.6% (2006-2010 5-year est.).

**School District(s)**
Cuba-Rushford Central School District (PK-12)
    2009-10 Enrollment: 952 . . . . . . . . . . . . . . . . . . . . . (585) 968-1556

**Housing:** Homeownership rate: 86.0% (2010); Median home value: $74,700 (2006-2010 5-year est.); Median contract rent: $403 per month (2006-2010 5-year est.); Median year structure built: 1967 (2006-2010 5-year est.).

**Transportation:** Commute to work: 88.3% car, 0.7% public transportation, 0.0% walk, 2.3% work from home (2006-2010 5-year est.); Travel time to work: 33.2% less than 15 minutes, 22.8% 15 to 30 minutes, 19.5% 30 to 45 minutes, 8.7% 45 to 60 minutes, 15.8% 60 minutes or more (2006-2010 5-year est.)

**RUSHFORD** (CDP). Covers a land area of 0.558 square miles and a water area of 0 square miles. Located at 42.38° N. Lat; 78.25° W. Long. Elevation is 1,499 feet.

**Population:** n/a (1990); n/a (2000); 363 (2010); Density: 649.8 persons per square mile (2010); Race: 98.9% White, 0.6% Black, 0.3% Asian, 0.3% American Indian/Alaska Native, 0.0% Native Hawaiian/Other Pacific Islander, 0.0% Other, 1.4% Hispanic of any race (2010); Average household size: 2.50 (2010); Median age: 43.2 (2010); Males per 100 females: 81.5 (2010); Marriage status: 29.1% never married, 32.1% now married, 29.6% widowed, 9.2% divorced (2006-2010 5-year est.); Foreign born: 0.0% (2006-2010 5-year est.); Ancestry (includes multiple ancestries): 44.6% German, 30.7% Irish, 19.3% English, 12.4% American, 11.4% Italian (2006-2010 5-year est.).

**Economy:** Employment by occupation: 8.0% management, 0.0% professional, 5.4% services, 8.9% sales, 0.0% farming, 14.3% construction, 5.4% production (2006-2010 5-year est.).

**Income:** Per capita income: $27,633 (2006-2010 5-year est.); Median household income: $27,885 (2006-2010 5-year est.); Average household income: $39,070 (2006-2010 5-year est.); Percent of households with income of $100,000 or more: 4.2% (2006-2010 5-year est.); Poverty rate: 6.9% (2006-2010 5-year est.).

**Education:** Percent of population age 25 and over with: High school diploma (including GED) or higher: 84.2% (2006-2010 5-year est.); Bachelor's degree or higher: 21.4% (2006-2010 5-year est.); Master's degree or higher: 2.6% (2006-2010 5-year est.).

**School District(s)**
Cuba-Rushford Central School District (PK-12)
    2009-10 Enrollment: 952 . . . . . . . . . . . . . . . . . . . . . (585) 968-1556

**Housing:** Homeownership rate: 83.4% (2010); Median home value: $43,500 (2006-2010 5-year est.); Median contract rent: $315 per month (2006-2010 5-year est.); Median year structure built: before 1940 (2006-2010 5-year est.).

**Transportation:** Commute to work: 95.5% car, 2.7% public transportation, 0.0% walk, 1.8% work from home (2006-2010 5-year est.); Travel time to work: 29.1% less than 15 minutes, 35.5% 15 to 30 minutes, 9.1% 30 to 45

minutes, 2.7% 45 to 60 minutes, 23.6% 60 minutes or more (2006-2010 5-year est.)

**SCIO** (town). Covers a land area of 35.294 square miles and a water area of 0.039 square miles. Located at 42.14° N. Lat; 77.99° W. Long. Elevation is 1,457 feet.

**Population:** 1,965 (1990); 1,914 (2000); 1,833 (2010); Density: 51.9 persons per square mile (2010); Race: 97.4% White, 0.4% Black, 0.6% Asian, 0.4% American Indian/Alaska Native, 0.2% Native Hawaiian/Other Pacific Islander, 1.0% Other, 1.1% Hispanic of any race (2010); Average household size: 2.52 (2010); Median age: 42.5 (2010); Males per 100 females: 103.7 (2010); Marriage status: 22.5% never married, 58.0% now married, 9.6% widowed, 9.9% divorced (2006-2010 5-year est.); Foreign born: 0.3% (2006-2010 5-year est.); Ancestry (includes multiple ancestries): 29.0% German, 20.8% English, 14.5% Irish, 8.7% American, 5.2% Italian (2006-2010 5-year est.).

**Economy:** Single-family building permits issued: 0 (2011); Multi-family building permits issued: 0 (2011); Employment by occupation: 12.3% management, 0.9% professional, 10.7% services, 17.5% sales, 3.9% farming, 14.7% construction, 10.6% production (2006-2010 5-year est.).

**Income:** Per capita income: $20,782 (2006-2010 5-year est.); Median household income: $37,300 (2006-2010 5-year est.); Average household income: $49,134 (2006-2010 5-year est.); Percent of households with income of $100,000 or more: 7.8% (2006-2010 5-year est.); Poverty rate: 16.5% (2006-2010 5-year est.).

**Education:** Percent of population age 25 and over with: High school diploma (including GED) or higher: 89.7% (2006-2010 5-year est.); Bachelor's degree or higher: 11.3% (2006-2010 5-year est.); Master's degree or higher: 4.7% (2006-2010 5-year est.).

**School District(s)**
Scio Central School District (PK-12)
    2009-10 Enrollment: 441 . . . . . . . . . . . . . . . . . . . . . (585) 593-5076

**Housing:** Homeownership rate: 80.5% (2010); Median home value: $57,800 (2006-2010 5-year est.); Median contract rent: $415 per month (2006-2010 5-year est.); Median year structure built: 1960 (2006-2010 5-year est.).

**Transportation:** Commute to work: 92.4% car, 0.9% public transportation, 5.0% walk, 0.9% work from home (2006-2010 5-year est.); Travel time to work: 57.0% less than 15 minutes, 27.7% 15 to 30 minutes, 7.8% 30 to 45 minutes, 2.7% 45 to 60 minutes, 4.8% 60 minutes or more (2006-2010 5-year est.)

**SCIO** (CDP). Covers a land area of 1.352 square miles and a water area of 0 square miles. Located at 42.17° N. Lat; 77.97° W. Long. Elevation is 1,457 feet.

**Population:** n/a (1990); n/a (2000); 609 (2010); Density: 450.4 persons per square mile (2010); Race: 97.4% White, 0.7% Black, 0.3% Asian, 0.0% American Indian/Alaska Native, 0.2% Native Hawaiian/Other Pacific Islander, 1.4% Other, 1.1% Hispanic of any race (2010); Average household size: 2.51 (2010); Median age: 43.4 (2010); Males per 100 females: 102.3 (2010); Marriage status: 16.9% never married, 64.7% now married, 11.0% widowed, 7.4% divorced (2006-2010 5-year est.); Foreign born: 0.4% (2006-2010 5-year est.); Ancestry (includes multiple ancestries): 22.9% German, 20.7% English, 14.3% Irish, 10.3% American, 7.8% Italian (2006-2010 5-year est.).

**Economy:** Employment by occupation: 11.3% management, 2.0% professional, 9.6% services, 18.9% sales, 4.0% farming, 15.3% construction, 13.6% production (2006-2010 5-year est.).

**Income:** Per capita income: $20,789 (2006-2010 5-year est.); Median household income: $48,125 (2006-2010 5-year est.); Average household income: $54,624 (2006-2010 5-year est.); Percent of households with income of $100,000 or more: 12.1% (2006-2010 5-year est.); Poverty rate: 10.0% (2006-2010 5-year est.).

**Education:** Percent of population age 25 and over with: High school diploma (including GED) or higher: 95.0% (2006-2010 5-year est.); Bachelor's degree or higher: 13.4% (2006-2010 5-year est.); Master's degree or higher: 4.5% (2006-2010 5-year est.).

**School District(s)**
Scio Central School District (PK-12)
    2009-10 Enrollment: 441 . . . . . . . . . . . . . . . . . . . . . (585) 593-5076

**Housing:** Homeownership rate: 83.9% (2010); Median home value: $56,000 (2006-2010 5-year est.); Median contract rent: $378 per month (2006-2010 5-year est.); Median year structure built: 1953 (2006-2010 5-year est.)

**Transportation:** Commute to work: 93.7% car, 0.6% public transportation, 4.5% walk, 1.2% work from home (2006-2010 5-year est.); Travel time to work: 57.0% less than 15 minutes, 22.6% 15 to 30 minutes, 9.5% 30 to 45 minutes, 5.5% 45 to 60 minutes, 5.5% 60 minutes or more (2006-2010 5-year est.)

---

**STANNARDS** (CDP). Covers a land area of 2.797 square miles and a water area of 0 square miles. Located at 42.07° N. Lat; 77.91° W. Long. Elevation is 1,549 feet.
**Population:** 1,028 (1990); 868 (2000); 798 (2010); Density: 285.3 persons per square mile (2010); Race: 97.2% White, 0.5% Black, 0.5% Asian, 0.1% American Indian/Alaska Native, 0.0% Native Hawaiian/Other Pacific Islander, 1.7% Other, 1.1% Hispanic of any race (2010); Average household size: 2.19 (2010); Median age: 45.7 (2010); Males per 100 females: 89.5 (2010); Marriage status: 11.5% never married, 66.5% now married, 10.6% widowed, 11.4% divorced (2006-2010 5-year est.); Foreign born: 3.3% (2006-2010 5-year est.); Ancestry (includes multiple ancestries): 25.8% German, 19.1% Irish, 15.9% English, 10.4% Italian, 6.9% American (2006-2010 5-year est.).
**Economy:** Employment by occupation: 5.9% management, 8.6% professional, 14.5% services, 14.5% sales, 6.2% farming, 7.4% construction, 4.6% production (2006-2010 5-year est.).
**Income:** Per capita income: $25,094 (2006-2010 5-year est.); Median household income: $38,625 (2006-2010 5-year est.); Average household income: $54,503 (2006-2010 5-year est.); Percent of households with income of $100,000 or more: 10.8% (2006-2010 5-year est.); Poverty rate: 6.4% (2006-2010 5-year est.).
**Education:** Percent of population age 25 and over with: High school diploma (including GED) or higher: 86.9% (2006-2010 5-year est.); Bachelor's degree or higher: 16.4% (2006-2010 5-year est.); Master's degree or higher: 9.1% (2006-2010 5-year est.).
**Housing:** Homeownership rate: 65.4% (2010); Median home value: $77,000 (2006-2010 5-year est.); Median contract rent: $410 per month (2006-2010 5-year est.); Median year structure built: 1972 (2006-2010 5-year est.).
**Transportation:** Commute to work: 96.3% car, 0.0% public transportation, 0.3% walk, 0.6% work from home (2006-2010 5-year est.); Travel time to work: 50.8% less than 15 minutes, 10.7% 15 to 30 minutes, 22.6% 30 to 45 minutes, 3.1% 45 to 60 minutes, 12.9% 60 minutes or more (2006-2010 5-year est.)

---

**SWAIN** (unincorporated postal area)
Zip Code: 14884
Covers a land area of 19.161 square miles and a water area of 0.324 square miles. Located at 42.47° N. Lat; 77.89° W. Long. Elevation is 1,316 feet. Population: 273 (2010); Density: 14.2 persons per square mile (2010); Race: 97.8% White, 0.4% Black, 0.0% Asian, 0.0% American Indian/Alaska Native, 0.0% Native Hawaiian/Other Pacific Islander, 1.8% Other, 2.2% Hispanic of any race (2010); Average household size: 2.07 (2010); Median age: 49.3 (2010); Males per 100 females: 108.4 (2010); Homeownership rate: 83.4% (2010)

---

**WARD** (town). Covers a land area of 29.174 square miles and a water area of 0.016 square miles. Located at 42.22° N. Lat; 77.90° W. Long.
**Population:** 334 (1990); 390 (2000); 368 (2010); Density: 12.6 persons per square mile (2010); Race: 98.4% White, 0.0% Black, 0.5% Asian, 0.0% American Indian/Alaska Native, 0.0% Native Hawaiian/Other Pacific Islander, 1.1% Other, 2.2% Hispanic of any race (2010); Average household size: 2.63 (2010); Median age: 43.3 (2010); Males per 100 females: 106.7 (2010); Marriage status: 23.6% never married, 64.8% now married, 6.4% widowed, 5.2% divorced (2006-2010 5-year est.); Foreign born: 5.3% (2006-2010 5-year est.); Ancestry (includes multiple ancestries): 29.4% German, 18.4% Irish, 14.5% English, 10.4% Scottish, 7.4% American (2006-2010 5-year est.).
**Economy:** Single-family building permits issued: 1 (2011); Multi-family building permits issued: 0 (2011); Employment by occupation: 7.7% management, 2.6% professional, 1.9% services, 14.7% sales, 7.1% farming, 19.2% construction, 7.1% production (2006-2010 5-year est.).
**Income:** Per capita income: $22,207 (2006-2010 5-year est.); Median household income: $51,250 (2006-2010 5-year est.); Average household income: $65,229 (2006-2010 5-year est.); Percent of households with income of $100,000 or more: 17.0% (2006-2010 5-year est.); Poverty rate: 3.1% (2006-2010 5-year est.).
**Education:** Percent of population age 25 and over with: High school diploma (including GED) or higher: 91.8% (2006-2010 5-year est.);

Bachelor's degree or higher: 22.1% (2006-2010 5-year est.); Master's degree or higher: 14.9% (2006-2010 5-year est.).
**Housing:** Homeownership rate: 87.9% (2010); Median home value: $82,200 (2006-2010 5-year est.); Median contract rent: $650 per month (2006-2010 5-year est.); Median year structure built: 1972 (2006-2010 5-year est.).
**Transportation:** Commute to work: 90.3% car, 1.3% public transportation, 2.6% walk, 5.8% work from home (2006-2010 5-year est.); Travel time to work: 53.8% less than 15 minutes, 22.1% 15 to 30 minutes, 15.9% 30 to 45 minutes, 4.1% 45 to 60 minutes, 4.1% 60 minutes or more (2006-2010 5-year est.)

---

**WELLSVILLE** (village). Covers a land area of 2.424 square miles and a water area of 0 square miles. Located at 42.12° N. Lat; 77.94° W. Long. Elevation is 1,512 feet.
**Population:** 5,423 (1990); 5,171 (2000); 4,679 (2010); Density: 1,930.2 persons per square mile (2010); Race: 96.6% White, 0.6% Black, 0.9% Asian, 0.3% American Indian/Alaska Native, 0.0% Native Hawaiian/Other Pacific Islander, 1.6% Other, 1.1% Hispanic of any race (2010); Average household size: 2.20 (2010); Median age: 41.4 (2010); Males per 100 females: 88.9 (2010); Marriage status: 21.9% never married, 52.9% now married, 10.6% widowed, 14.5% divorced (2006-2010 5-year est.); Foreign born: 1.5% (2006-2010 5-year est.); Ancestry (includes multiple ancestries): 27.7% German, 18.4% English, 18.1% Irish, 8.5% Italian, 6.0% French (2006-2010 5-year est.).
**Economy:** Single-family building permits issued: 0 (2011); Multi-family building permits issued: 0 (2011); Employment by occupation: 8.8% management, 2.7% professional, 8.8% services, 15.5% sales, 2.3% farming, 7.3% construction, 4.7% production (2006-2010 5-year est.).
**Income:** Per capita income: $22,328 (2006-2010 5-year est.); Median household income: $29,177 (2006-2010 5-year est.); Average household income: $46,161 (2006-2010 5-year est.); Percent of households with income of $100,000 or more: 7.6% (2006-2010 5-year est.); Poverty rate: 25.4% (2006-2010 5-year est.).
**Education:** Percent of population age 25 and over with: High school diploma (including GED) or higher: 89.4% (2006-2010 5-year est.); Bachelor's degree or higher: 20.8% (2006-2010 5-year est.); Master's degree or higher: 10.0% (2006-2010 5-year est.).

**School District(s)**
Wellsville Central School District (PK-12)
    2009-10 Enrollment: 1,344 . . . . . . . . . . . . . . . . . . . . . . . (585) 596-2170
**Housing:** Homeownership rate: 55.8% (2010); Median home value: $57,300 (2006-2010 5-year est.); Median contract rent: $434 per month (2006-2010 5-year est.); Median year structure built: 1945 (2006-2010 5-year est.).
**Hospitals:** Jones Memorial Hospital (70 beds)
**Safety:** Violent crime rate: 76.1 per 10,000 population; Property crime rate: 302.5 per 10,000 population (2010).
**Newspapers:** Allegany Pennysaver (Community news); Wellsville Daily Reporter (Local news; Circulation 1,000)
**Transportation:** Commute to work: 82.3% car, 4.6% public transportation, 8.6% walk, 3.0% work from home (2006-2010 5-year est.); Travel time to work: 72.1% less than 15 minutes, 10.9% 15 to 30 minutes, 12.2% 30 to 45 minutes, 3.1% 45 to 60 minutes, 1.7% 60 minutes or more (2006-2010 5-year est.)
**Airports:** Wellsville Municipal Airport, Tarantine Field (general aviation)
**Additional Information Contacts**
Wellsville Area Chamber of Commerce . . . . . . . . . . . . . . . . (585) 593-5080
    http://www.wellsvilleareachamber.com

---

**WELLSVILLE** (town). Covers a land area of 36.645 square miles and a water area of 0.037 square miles. Located at 42.11° N. Lat; 77.92° W. Long. Elevation is 1,512 feet.
**History:** Wellsville was settled in 1795 and named for Gardiner Wells, early settler and chief landowner. Site of David A. Howe Library (1937), with museum and theater. Special museum, Mather Homestead, for visually impaired. Incorporated in 1871.
**Population:** 8,116 (1990); 7,678 (2000); 7,397 (2010); Density: 201.9 persons per square mile (2010); Race: 97.2% White, 0.5% Black, 0.7% Asian, 0.2% American Indian/Alaska Native, 0.0% Native Hawaiian/Other Pacific Islander, 1.4% Other, 0.9% Hispanic of any race (2010); Average household size: 2.21 (2010); Median age: 43.5 (2010); Males per 100 females: 89.8 (2010); Marriage status: 22.2% never married, 55.3% now married, 9.9% widowed, 12.7% divorced (2006-2010 5-year est.); Foreign born: 1.4% (2006-2010 5-year est.); Ancestry (includes multiple

ancestries): 29.2% German, 19.3% Irish, 16.7% English, 6.9% Italian, 6.3% American (2006-2010 5-year est.).

**Economy:** Single-family building permits issued: 0 (2011); Multi-family building permits issued: 0 (2011); Employment by occupation: 8.9% management, 3.9% professional, 8.9% services, 16.1% sales, 1.7% farming, 9.2% construction, 4.6% production (2006-2010 5-year est.).

**Income:** Per capita income: $21,322 (2006-2010 5-year est.); Median household income: $35,525 (2006-2010 5-year est.); Average household income: $46,671 (2006-2010 5-year est.); Percent of households with income of $100,000 or more: 7.2% (2006-2010 5-year est.); Poverty rate: 23.4% (2006-2010 5-year est.).

**Education:** Percent of population age 25 and over with: High school diploma (including GED) or higher: 90.7% (2006-2010 5-year est.); Bachelor's degree or higher: 17.5% (2006-2010 5-year est.); Master's degree or higher: 8.4% (2006-2010 5-year est.).

### School District(s)
Wellsville Central School District (PK-12)
   2009-10 Enrollment: 1,344 . . . . . . . . . . . . . . . . . . . . . . (585) 596-2170

**Housing:** Homeownership rate: 60.9% (2010); Median home value: $56,900 (2006-2010 5-year est.); Median contract rent: $429 per month (2006-2010 5-year est.); Median year structure built: 1952 (2006-2010 5-year est.).

**Hospitals:** Jones Memorial Hospital (70 beds)

**Newspapers:** Allegany Pennysaver (Community news); Wellsville Daily Reporter (Local news; Circulation 1,000)

**Transportation:** Commute to work: 86.5% car, 3.3% public transportation, 6.3% walk, 3.0% work from home (2006-2010 5-year est.); Travel time to work: 69.4% less than 15 minutes, 14.5% 15 to 30 minutes, 11.1% 30 to 45 minutes, 2.8% 45 to 60 minutes, 2.2% 60 minutes or more (2006-2010 5-year est.)

**Airports:** Wellsville Municipal Airport, Tarantine Field (general aviation)

## WEST ALMOND (town).
Covers a land area of 35.995 square miles and a water area of 0.095 square miles. Located at 42.31° N. Lat; 77.90° W. Long. Elevation is 1,854 feet.

**Population:** 277 (1990); 353 (2000); 334 (2010); Density: 9.3 persons per square mile (2010); Race: 90.1% White, 1.8% Black, 3.0% Asian, 0.0% American Indian/Alaska Native, 0.0% Native Hawaiian/Other Pacific Islander, 5.1% Other, 3.6% Hispanic of any race (2010); Average household size: 2.46 (2010); Median age: 45.7 (2010); Males per 100 females: 115.5 (2010); Marriage status: 19.9% never married, 66.9% now married, 8.9% widowed, 4.2% divorced (2006-2010 5-year est.); Foreign born: 1.7% (2006-2010 5-year est.); Ancestry (includes multiple ancestries): 25.7% English, 24.0% German, 16.0% Irish, 8.7% Italian, 8.3% American (2006-2010 5-year est.).

**Economy:** Employment by occupation: 10.6% management, 5.3% professional, 15.9% services, 10.6% sales, 4.4% farming, 13.3% construction, 3.5% production (2006-2010 5-year est.).

**Income:** Per capita income: $18,887 (2006-2010 5-year est.); Median household income: $46,875 (2006-2010 5-year est.); Average household income: $46,910 (2006-2010 5-year est.); Percent of households with income of $100,000 or more: 4.3% (2006-2010 5-year est.); Poverty rate: 6.9% (2006-2010 5-year est.).

**Education:** Percent of population age 25 and over with: High school diploma (including GED) or higher: 93.6% (2006-2010 5-year est.); Bachelor's degree or higher: 17.8% (2006-2010 5-year est.); Master's degree or higher: 7.4% (2006-2010 5-year est.).

**Housing:** Homeownership rate: 85.3% (2010); Median home value: $79,500 (2006-2010 5-year est.); Median contract rent: $817 per month (2006-2010 5-year est.); Median year structure built: 1973 (2006-2010 5-year est.).

**Transportation:** Commute to work: 92.7% car, 0.0% public transportation, 0.0% walk, 7.3% work from home (2006-2010 5-year est.); Travel time to work: 13.9% less than 15 minutes, 40.6% 15 to 30 minutes, 23.8% 30 to 45 minutes, 7.9% 45 to 60 minutes, 13.9% 60 minutes or more (2006-2010 5-year est.)

## WHITESVILLE (unincorporated postal area)
Zip Code: 14897

   Covers a land area of 25.531 square miles and a water area of 0.002 square miles. Located at 42.02° N. Lat; 77.79° W. Long. Elevation is 1,716 feet. Population: 980 (2010); Density: 38.4 persons per square mile (2010); Race: 98.2% White, 0.4% Black, 0.2% Asian, 0.2% American Indian/Alaska Native, 0.0% Native Hawaiian/Other Pacific Islander, 1.0% Other, 0.7% Hispanic of any race (2010); Average

household size: 2.78 (2010); Median age: 37.7 (2010); Males per 100 females: 103.3 (2010); Homeownership rate: 80.4% (2010)

## WILLING (town).
Covers a land area of 36.239 square miles and a water area of 0.030 square miles. Located at 42.03° N. Lat; 77.89° W. Long.

**Population:** 1,428 (1990); 1,371 (2000); 1,228 (2010); Density: 33.9 persons per square mile (2010); Race: 98.0% White, 0.6% Black, 0.3% Asian, 0.5% American Indian/Alaska Native, 0.0% Native Hawaiian/Other Pacific Islander, 0.6% Other, 0.9% Hispanic of any race (2010); Average household size: 2.33 (2010); Median age: 46.9 (2010); Males per 100 females: 99.7 (2010); Marriage status: 17.6% never married, 63.7% now married, 9.5% widowed, 9.2% divorced (2006-2010 5-year est.); Foreign born: 2.1% (2006-2010 5-year est.); Ancestry (includes multiple ancestries): 31.0% German, 26.7% English, 20.7% Irish, 7.9% American, 6.3% Polish (2006-2010 5-year est.).

**Economy:** Single-family building permits issued: 0 (2011); Multi-family building permits issued: 0 (2011); Employment by occupation: 5.1% management, 7.9% professional, 13.3% services, 13.8% sales, 5.3% farming, 14.0% construction, 5.1% production (2006-2010 5-year est.).

**Income:** Per capita income: $24,035 (2006-2010 5-year est.); Median household income: $38,944 (2006-2010 5-year est.); Average household income: $52,436 (2006-2010 5-year est.); Percent of households with income of $100,000 or more: 11.8% (2006-2010 5-year est.); Poverty rate: 7.3% (2006-2010 5-year est.).

**Education:** Percent of population age 25 and over with: High school diploma (including GED) or higher: 89.1% (2006-2010 5-year est.); Bachelor's degree or higher: 11.0% (2006-2010 5-year est.); Master's degree or higher: 4.8% (2006-2010 5-year est.).

**Housing:** Homeownership rate: 84.7% (2010); Median home value: $71,900 (2006-2010 5-year est.); Median contract rent: $415 per month (2006-2010 5-year est.); Median year structure built: 1959 (2006-2010 5-year est.).

**Transportation:** Commute to work: 93.5% car, 0.4% public transportation, 0.2% walk, 3.5% work from home (2006-2010 5-year est.); Travel time to work: 39.8% less than 15 minutes, 25.3% 15 to 30 minutes, 13.6% 30 to 45 minutes, 10.5% 45 to 60 minutes, 10.8% 60 minutes or more (2006-2010 5-year est.)

## WIRT (town).
Covers a land area of 35.938 square miles and a water area of 0.066 square miles. Located at 42.12° N. Lat; 78.13° W. Long. Elevation is 1,877 feet.

**Population:** 1,143 (1990); 1,215 (2000); 1,111 (2010); Density: 30.9 persons per square mile (2010); Race: 97.7% White, 0.5% Black, 0.2% Asian, 0.2% American Indian/Alaska Native, 0.0% Native Hawaiian/Other Pacific Islander, 1.4% Other, 1.6% Hispanic of any race (2010); Average household size: 2.51 (2010); Median age: 40.9 (2010); Males per 100 females: 94.9 (2010); Marriage status: 24.3% never married, 54.9% now married, 5.8% widowed, 15.0% divorced (2006-2010 5-year est.); Foreign born: 1.4% (2006-2010 5-year est.); Ancestry (includes multiple ancestries): 38.0% German, 21.5% Irish, 14.1% English, 9.2% Italian, 4.3% Dutch (2006-2010 5-year est.).

**Economy:** Single-family building permits issued: 0 (2011); Multi-family building permits issued: 0 (2011); Employment by occupation: 9.1% management, 1.2% professional, 11.3% services, 14.7% sales, 2.2% farming, 21.7% construction, 15.7% production (2006-2010 5-year est.).

**Income:** Per capita income: $19,454 (2006-2010 5-year est.); Median household income: $39,850 (2006-2010 5-year est.); Average household income: $50,712 (2006-2010 5-year est.); Percent of households with income of $100,000 or more: 8.0% (2006-2010 5-year est.); Poverty rate: 18.8% (2006-2010 5-year est.).

**Education:** Percent of population age 25 and over with: High school diploma (including GED) or higher: 86.6% (2006-2010 5-year est.); Bachelor's degree or higher: 11.1% (2006-2010 5-year est.); Master's degree or higher: 3.0% (2006-2010 5-year est.).

**Housing:** Homeownership rate: 84.7% (2010); Median home value: $51,700 (2006-2010 5-year est.); Median contract rent: $358 per month (2006-2010 5-year est.); Median year structure built: 1971 (2006-2010 5-year est.).

**Transportation:** Commute to work: 93.1% car, 0.9% public transportation, 1.1% walk, 4.3% work from home (2006-2010 5-year est.); Travel time to work: 25.3% less than 15 minutes, 31.4% 15 to 30 minutes, 27.8% 30 to 45 minutes, 10.3% 45 to 60 minutes, 5.2% 60 minutes or more (2006-2010 5-year est.)

# Bronx County and Borough

*See New York City*

# Brooklyn Borough

*See New York City*

# Broome County

Located in southern New York; bounded on the south by Pennsylvania. Covers a land area of 706.82 square miles, a water area of 8.64 square miles, and is located in the Eastern Time Zone at 42.13° N. Lat., 75.88° W. Long. The county was founded in 1806. County seat is Binghamton.

Broome County is part of the Binghamton, NY Metropolitan Statistical Area. The entire metro area includes: Broome County, NY; Tioga County, NY

| Weather Station: Binghamton Edwin A Link Field | | | | | | | | | Elevation: 1,600 feet | | |
|---|---|---|---|---|---|---|---|---|---|---|---|
|  | Jan | Feb | Mar | Apr | May | Jun | Jul | Aug | Sep | Oct | Nov | Dec |
| High | 29 | 33 | 41 | 55 | 66 | 74 | 78 | 77 | 69 | 57 | 45 | 34 |
| Low | 16 | 17 | 25 | 36 | 46 | 55 | 60 | 58 | 51 | 40 | 31 | 21 |
| Precip | 2.4 | 2.3 | 3.1 | 3.5 | 3.5 | 4.3 | 3.7 | 3.4 | 3.6 | 3.3 | 3.3 | 2.8 |
| Snow | 21.7 | 15.9 | 15.5 | 4.3 | 0.1 | tr | 0.0 | tr | tr | 1.1 | 7.0 | 17.2 |

*High and Low temperatures in degrees Fahrenheit; Precipitation and Snow in inches*

**Population:** 212,160 (1990); 200,536 (2000); 200,600 (2010); Race: 88.0% White, 4.8% Black, 3.5% Asian, 0.2% American Indian/Alaska Native, 0.0% Native Hawaiian/Other Pacific Islander, 3.5% Other, 3.4% Hispanic of any race (2010); Density: 283.8 persons per square mile (2010); Average household size: 2.32 (2010); Median age: 40.2 (2010); Males per 100 females: 96.2 (2010).
**Religion:** Six largest groups: 31.0% Catholicism, 7.1% Methodist/Pietist, 3.0% Non-Denominational, 1.9% Holiness, 1.5% Presbyterian-Reformed, 1.4% Lutheran (2010)
**Economy:** Unemployment rate: 9.4% (February 2012); Total civilian labor force: 93,933 (February 2012); Leading industries: 19.5% health care and social assistance; 16.0% retail trade; 13.1% manufacturing (2009); Farms: 580 totaling 86,613 acres (2007); Companies that employ 500 or more persons: 13 (2009); Companies that employ 100 to 499 persons: 98 (2009); Companies that employ less than 100 persons: 4,176 (2009); Black-owned businesses: 273 (2007); Hispanic-owned businesses: n/a (2007); Asian-owned businesses: n/a (2007); Women-owned businesses: 4,066 (2007); Retail sales per capita: $14,306 (2010). Single-family building permits issued: 41 (2011); Multi-family building permits issued: 4 (2011).
**Income:** Per capita income: $24,314 (2006-2010 5-year est.); Median household income: $44,457 (2006-2010 5-year est.); Average household income: $58,839 (2006-2010 5-year est.); Percent of households with income of $100,000 or more: 15.0% (2006-2010 5-year est.); Poverty rate: 15.5% (2006-2010 5-year est.); Bankruptcy rate: 2.08% (2011).
**Taxes:** Total county taxes per capita: $1,126 (2009); County property taxes per capita: $313 (2009).
**Education:** Percent of population age 25 and over with: High school diploma (including GED) or higher: 88.3% (2006-2010 5-year est.); Bachelor's degree or higher: 25.1% (2006-2010 5-year est.); Master's degree or higher: 11.4% (2006-2010 5-year est.).
**Housing:** Homeownership rate: 64.9% (2010); Median home value: $99,500 (2006-2010 5-year est.); Median contract rent: $503 per month (2006-2010 5-year est.); Median year structure built: 1955 (2006-2010 5-year est.)
**Health:** Birth rate: 101.4 per 10,000 population (2011); Death rate: 104.2 per 10,000 population (2011); Age-adjusted cancer mortality rate: 185.1 deaths per 100,000 population (2009); Number of physicians: 30.3 per 10,000 population (2008); Hospital beds: 41.1 per 10,000 population (2007); Hospital admissions: 1,337.6 per 10,000 population (2007).
**Elections:** 2008 Presidential election results: 53.1% Obama, 45.1% McCain, 0.9% Nader
**National and State Parks:** Broome State Forest; Chenango Valley State Park; Tracy Creek State Forest
**Additional Information Contacts**
Broome County Government . . . . . . . . . . . . . . . . . . . . . (607) 778-2109
  http://www.gobroomecounty.com
City of Binghamton . . . . . . . . . . . . . . . . . . . . . . . . . . . (607) 772-7001
  http://www.cityofbinghamton.com

Greater Binghamton Chamber of Commerce . . . . . . . . . . . (607) 772-8860
  http://www.greaterbinghamtonchamber.com
Town of Union . . . . . . . . . . . . . . . . . . . . . . . . . . . . . . . (607) 786-2900
  http://www.townofunion.com
Town of Vestal . . . . . . . . . . . . . . . . . . . . . . . . . . . . . . . (607) 748-1514
  http://www.vestalny.com
Village of Johnson City . . . . . . . . . . . . . . . . . . . . . . . . . (607) 798-7861
  http://www.villageofjc.com

## *Broome County Communities*

**BARKER** (town). Covers a land area of 41.403 square miles and a water area of 0.376 square miles. Located at 42.26° N. Lat; 75.91° W. Long.
**Population:** 2,714 (1990); 2,738 (2000); 2,732 (2010); Density: 66.0 persons per square mile (2010); Race: 95.7% White, 0.8% Black, 0.6% Asian, 0.1% American Indian/Alaska Native, 0.0% Native Hawaiian/Other Pacific Islander, 2.8% Other, 1.9% Hispanic of any race (2010); Average household size: 2.67 (2010); Median age: 42.4 (2010); Males per 100 females: 104.6 (2010); Marriage status: 22.1% never married, 65.0% now married, 4.6% widowed, 8.2% divorced (2006-2010 5-year est.); Foreign born: 2.5% (2006-2010 5-year est.); Ancestry (includes multiple ancestries): 24.7% Irish, 15.0% German, 11.1% Italian, 10.2% English, 7.6% Scottish (2006-2010 5-year est.).
**Economy:** Single-family building permits issued: 4 (2011); Multi-family building permits issued: 0 (2011); Employment by occupation: 8.1% management, 6.5% professional, 9.3% services, 18.0% sales, 3.1% farming, 9.3% construction, 5.2% production (2006-2010 5-year est.).
**Income:** Per capita income: $23,608 (2006-2010 5-year est.); Median household income: $54,875 (2006-2010 5-year est.); Average household income: $65,756 (2006-2010 5-year est.); Percent of households with income of $100,000 or more: 18.2% (2006-2010 5-year est.); Poverty rate: 10.8% (2006-2010 5-year est.).
**Education:** Percent of population age 25 and over with: High school diploma (including GED) or higher: 89.8% (2006-2010 5-year est.); Bachelor's degree or higher: 18.7% (2006-2010 5-year est.); Master's degree or higher: 9.1% (2006-2010 5-year est.).
**Housing:** Homeownership rate: 86.9% (2010); Median home value: $95,000 (2006-2010 5-year est.); Median contract rent: $393 per month (2006-2010 5-year est.); Median year structure built: 1968 (2006-2010 5-year est.).
**Transportation:** Commute to work: 91.4% car, 0.3% public transportation, 4.3% walk, 4.0% work from home (2006-2010 5-year est.); Travel time to work: 21.7% less than 15 minutes, 47.5% 15 to 30 minutes, 25.6% 30 to 45 minutes, 0.8% 45 to 60 minutes, 4.4% 60 minutes or more (2006-2010 5-year est.)

**BINGHAMTON** (city). County seat. Covers a land area of 10.488 square miles and a water area of 0.646 square miles. Located at 42.10° N. Lat; 75.90° W. Long. Elevation is 866 feet.
**History:** Little is known of the Binghamton area before the Revolution. The site was purchased in 1786 by William Bingham, a Philadelphia merchant. Joseph Leonard, first permanent settler, built his log cabin nearby in 1787 and was soon joined by other pioneers, who called the new settlement Chenango. It was later renamed in honor of Bingham, who made liberal donations of land to the settlement. It was incorporated as a village in 1834 and as a city in 1867.
**Population:** 53,017 (1990); 47,380 (2000); 47,376 (2010); Density: 4,516.8 persons per square mile (2010); Race: 77.6% White, 11.4% Black, 4.2% Asian, 0.3% American Indian/Alaska Native, 0.0% Native Hawaiian/Other Pacific Islander, 6.5% Other, 6.4% Hispanic of any race (2010); Average household size: 2.18 (2010); Median age: 35.8 (2010); Males per 100 females: 96.1 (2010); Marriage status: 40.0% never married, 38.4% now married, 9.2% widowed, 12.3% divorced (2006-2010 5-year est.); Foreign born: 9.7% (2006-2010 5-year est.); Ancestry (includes multiple ancestries): 22.5% Irish, 16.3% German, 13.3% Italian, 9.7% English, 4.9% Polish (2006-2010 5-year est.).
**Economy:** Unemployment rate: 9.4% (February 2012); Total civilian labor force: 20,590 (February 2012); Single-family building permits issued: 0 (2011); Multi-family building permits issued: 0 (2011); Employment by occupation: 6.8% management, 4.1% professional, 13.6% services, 15.9% sales, 4.6% farming, 5.9% construction, 5.2% production (2006-2010 5-year est.).
**Income:** Per capita income: $21,455 (2006-2010 5-year est.); Median household income: $30,702 (2006-2010 5-year est.); Average household

income: $46,513 (2006-2010 5-year est.); Percent of households with income of $100,000 or more: 9.3% (2006-2010 5-year est.); Poverty rate: 27.8% (2006-2010 5-year est.).

**Taxes:** Total city taxes per capita: $623 (2009); City property taxes per capita: $585 (2009).

**Education:** Percent of population age 25 and over with: High school diploma (including GED) or higher: 83.5% (2006-2010 5-year est.); Bachelor's degree or higher: 23.0% (2006-2010 5-year est.); Master's degree or higher: 11.4% (2006-2010 5-year est.).

### School District(s)

Binghamton City School District (PK-12)
  2009-10 Enrollment: 5,911 . . . . . . . . . . . . . . . . . . (607) 762-8100
Broome-Delaware-Tioga Boces
  2009-10 Enrollment: n/a . . . . . . . . . . . . . . . . . . . (607) 766-3802
Chenango Forks Central School District (PK-12)
  2009-10 Enrollment: 1,703 . . . . . . . . . . . . . . . . . . (607) 648-7543
Chenango Valley Central School District (PK-12)
  2009-10 Enrollment: 1,912 . . . . . . . . . . . . . . . . . . (607) 779-4711
Susquehanna Valley Central School District (KG-12)
  2009-10 Enrollment: 1,807 . . . . . . . . . . . . . . . . . . (607) 775-0170

### Two-year College(s)

Broome Community College (Public)
  Fall 2010 Enrollment: 5,162 . . . . . . . . . . . . . . . . . (607) 778-5000
  2011-12 Tuition: In-state $4,139; Out-of-state $7,833

### Vocational/Technical School(s)

Ann Marie's World of Beauty School (Private, For-profit)
  Fall 2010 Enrollment: 16 . . . . . . . . . . . . . . . . . . . (607) 724-1113
  2011-12 Tuition: $12,000
Broome Delaware Tioga BOCES-Practical Nursing Program (Public)
  Fall 2010 Enrollment: 57 . . . . . . . . . . . . . . . . . . . (607) 763-3465
  2011-12 Tuition: $10,194
Ridley-Lowell School of Business (Private, For-profit)
  Fall 2010 Enrollment: 185 . . . . . . . . . . . . . . . . . . (607) 724-2941
  2011-12 Tuition: $10,700

**Housing:** Homeownership rate: 42.5% (2010); Median home value: $82,600 (2006-2010 5-year est.); Median contract rent: $467 per month (2006-2010 5-year est.); Median year structure built: before 1940 (2006-2010 5-year est.).

**Hospitals:** Greater Binghamton Health Center (161 beds)

**Safety:** Violent crime rate: 61.0 per 10,000 population; Property crime rate: 477.9 per 10,000 population (2010).

**Newspapers:** Press & Sun Bulletin (Local news; Circulation 66,059)

**Transportation:** Commute to work: 81.4% car, 6.5% public transportation, 5.3% walk, 2.9% work from home (2006-2010 5-year est.); Travel time to work: 52.6% less than 15 minutes, 37.5% 15 to 30 minutes, 5.3% 30 to 45 minutes, 1.7% 45 to 60 minutes, 3.0% 60 minutes or more (2006-2010 5-year est.)

**Airports:** Greater Binghamton/Edwin A Link Field (primary service)

**Additional Information Contacts**
City of Binghamton. . . . . . . . . . . . . . . . . . . . . . . . (607) 772-7001
  http://www.cityofbinghamton.com
Greater Binghamton Chamber of Commerce . . . . . . . . (607) 772-8860
  http://www.greaterbinghamtonchamber.com

**BINGHAMTON** (town). Covers a land area of 25.250 square miles and a water area of 0.088 square miles. Located at 42.03° N. Lat; 75.90° W. Long. Elevation is 866 feet.

**History:** Grew mainly after the Chenango Canal connected it with Utica in 1837. First railroad service began in 1869. State University of N.Y. at Binghamton in the vicinity. Settled 1787, Incorporated as a city 1867.

**Population:** 4,997 (1990); 4,969 (2000); 4,942 (2010); Density: 195.7 persons per square mile (2010); Race: 95.3% White, 1.4% Black, 1.7% Asian, 0.0% American Indian/Alaska Native, 0.0% Native Hawaiian/Other Pacific Islander, 1.6% Other, 1.2% Hispanic of any race (2010); Average household size: 2.61 (2010); Median age: 44.1 (2010); Males per 100 females: 101.6 (2010); Marriage status: 17.4% never married, 65.8% now married, 7.3% widowed, 9.6% divorced (2006-2010 5-year est.); Foreign born: 3.1% (2006-2010 5-year est.); Ancestry (includes multiple ancestries): 19.4% Irish, 18.7% German, 14.7% Italian, 14.6% English, 6.9% American (2006-2010 5-year est.).

**Economy:** Single-family building permits issued: 0 (2011); Multi-family building permits issued: 0 (2011); Employment by occupation: 13.9% management, 6.2% professional, 5.2% services, 15.9% sales, 4.6% farming, 4.9% construction, 4.8% production (2006-2010 5-year est.).

**Income:** Per capita income: $33,696 (2006-2010 5-year est.); Median household income: $68,029 (2006-2010 5-year est.); Average household income: $91,658 (2006-2010 5-year est.); Percent of households with income of $100,000 or more: 32.8% (2006-2010 5-year est.); Poverty rate: 9.2% (2006-2010 5-year est.).

**Education:** Percent of population age 25 and over with: High school diploma (including GED) or higher: 91.6% (2006-2010 5-year est.); Bachelor's degree or higher: 32.8% (2006-2010 5-year est.); Master's degree or higher: 14.7% (2006-2010 5-year est.).

### School District(s)

Binghamton City School District (PK-12)
  2009-10 Enrollment: 5,911 . . . . . . . . . . . . . . . . . . (607) 762-8100
Broome-Delaware-Tioga Boces
  2009-10 Enrollment: n/a . . . . . . . . . . . . . . . . . . . (607) 766-3802
Chenango Forks Central School District (PK-12)
  2009-10 Enrollment: 1,703 . . . . . . . . . . . . . . . . . . (607) 648-7543
Chenango Valley Central School District (PK-12)
  2009-10 Enrollment: 1,912 . . . . . . . . . . . . . . . . . . (607) 779-4711
Susquehanna Valley Central School District (KG-12)
  2009-10 Enrollment: 1,807 . . . . . . . . . . . . . . . . . . (607) 775-0170

### Two-year College(s)

Broome Community College (Public)
  Fall 2010 Enrollment: 5,162 . . . . . . . . . . . . . . . . . (607) 778-5000
  2011-12 Tuition: In-state $4,139; Out-of-state $7,833

### Vocational/Technical School(s)

Ann Marie's World of Beauty School (Private, For-profit)
  Fall 2010 Enrollment: 16 . . . . . . . . . . . . . . . . . . . (607) 724-1113
  2011-12 Tuition: $12,000
Broome Delaware Tioga BOCES-Practical Nursing Program (Public)
  Fall 2010 Enrollment: 57 . . . . . . . . . . . . . . . . . . . (607) 763-3465
  2011-12 Tuition: $10,194
Ridley-Lowell School of Business (Private, For-profit)
  Fall 2010 Enrollment: 185 . . . . . . . . . . . . . . . . . . (607) 724-2941
  2011-12 Tuition: $10,700

**Housing:** Homeownership rate: 90.8% (2010); Median home value: $131,300 (2006-2010 5-year est.); Median contract rent: $575 per month (2006-2010 5-year est.); Median year structure built: 1970 (2006-2010 5-year est.).

**Hospitals:** Greater Binghamton Health Center (161 beds); Lourdes Hospital (161 beds); Lourdes Hospital (161 beds)

**Newspapers:** Press & Sun Bulletin (Local news; Circulation 66,059)

**Transportation:** Commute to work: 95.1% car, 0.0% public transportation, 0.9% walk, 3.9% work from home (2006-2010 5-year est.); Travel time to work: 30.9% less than 15 minutes, 57.2% 15 to 30 minutes, 7.7% 30 to 45 minutes, 0.9% 45 to 60 minutes, 3.3% 60 minutes or more (2006-2010 5-year est.)

**Airports:** Greater Binghamton/Edwin A Link Field (primary service)

**BINGHAMTON UNIVERSITY** (CDP). Covers a land area of 0.775 square miles and a water area of 0 square miles. Located at 42.08° N. Lat; 75.96° W. Long.

**Population:** n/a (1990); n/a (2000); 6,177 (2010); Density: 7,965.3 persons per square mile (2010); Race: 65.5% White, 7.5% Black, 20.8% Asian, 0.1% American Indian/Alaska Native, 0.0% Native Hawaiian/Other Pacific Islander, 6.1% Other, 8.9% Hispanic of any race (2010); Average household size: 0.00 (2010); Median age: 19.9 (2010); Males per 100 females: 109.1 (2010); Marriage status: 97.5% never married, 2.3% now married, 0.2% widowed, 0.0% divorced (2006-2010 5-year est.); Foreign born: 12.0% (2006-2010 5-year est.); Ancestry (includes multiple ancestries): 11.7% Irish, 7.9% Italian, 7.5% German, 6.6% Russian, 6.6% Polish (2006-2010 5-year est.).

**Economy:** Employment by occupation: 0.7% management, 0.8% professional, 11.2% services, 34.4% sales, 4.7% farming, 2.2% construction, 0.0% production (2006-2010 5-year est.).

**Income:** Per capita income: $2,499 (2006-2010 5-year est.); Median household income: $0 (2006-2010 5-year est.); Average household income: $0 (2006-2010 5-year est.); Percent of households with income of $100,000 or more: 0.0% (2006-2010 5-year est.); Poverty rate: ***.*% (2006-2010 5-year est.).

**Education:** Percent of population age 25 and over with: High school diploma (including GED) or higher: 100.0% (2006-2010 5-year est.); Bachelor's degree or higher: 49.3% (2006-2010 5-year est.); Master's degree or higher: 17.3% (2006-2010 5-year est.).

**Housing:** Homeownership rate: 0.0% (2010); Median home value: n/a (2006-2010 5-year est.); Median contract rent: n/a per month (2006-2010 5-year est.); Median year structure built: n/a (2006-2010 5-year est.).
**Transportation:** Commute to work: 21.9% car, 1.4% public transportation, 37.7% walk, 37.5% work from home (2006-2010 5-year est.); Travel time to work: 84.3% less than 15 minutes, 12.4% 15 to 30 minutes, 3.3% 30 to 45 minutes, 0.0% 45 to 60 minutes, 0.0% 60 minutes or more (2006-2010 5-year est.)

**CASTLE CREEK** (unincorporated postal area)
Zip Code: 13744
Covers a land area of 11.586 square miles and a water area of 0.003 square miles. Located at 42.24° N. Lat; 75.90° W. Long. Elevation is 1,050 feet. Population: 1,137 (2010); Density: 98.1 persons per square mile (2010); Race: 95.7% White, 0.4% Black, 1.4% Asian, 0.2% American Indian/Alaska Native, 0.0% Native Hawaiian/Other Pacific Islander, 2.3% Other, 1.8% Hispanic of any race (2010); Average household size: 2.56 (2010); Median age: 42.0 (2010); Males per 100 females: 105.2 (2010); Homeownership rate: 87.6% (2010)

**CHENANGO** (town). Covers a land area of 33.834 square miles and a water area of 0.433 square miles. Located at 42.21° N. Lat; 75.90° W. Long.
**Population:** 12,280 (1990); 11,454 (2000); 11,252 (2010); Density: 332.6 persons per square mile (2010); Race: 96.1% White, 0.8% Black, 0.8% Asian, 0.2% American Indian/Alaska Native, 0.0% Native Hawaiian/Other Pacific Islander, 2.1% Other, 1.5% Hispanic of any race (2010); Average household size: 2.44 (2010); Median age: 44.9 (2010); Males per 100 females: 96.5 (2010); Marriage status: 23.0% never married, 60.9% now married, 6.4% widowed, 9.7% divorced (2006-2010 5-year est.); Foreign born: 2.6% (2006-2010 5-year est.); Ancestry (includes multiple ancestries): 25.7% Irish, 18.9% German, 15.6% English, 12.6% Italian, 8.6% Polish (2006-2010 5-year est.).
**Economy:** Single-family building permits issued: 3 (2011); Multi-family building permits issued: 0 (2011); Employment by occupation: 13.5% management, 6.8% professional, 7.1% services, 18.8% sales, 4.9% farming, 6.5% construction, 6.6% production (2006-2010 5-year est.).
**Income:** Per capita income: $29,219 (2006-2010 5-year est.); Median household income: $56,643 (2006-2010 5-year est.); Average household income: $70,065 (2006-2010 5-year est.); Percent of households with income of $100,000 or more: 20.8% (2006-2010 5-year est.); Poverty rate: 6.3% (2006-2010 5-year est.).
**Education:** Percent of population age 25 and over with: High school diploma (including GED) or higher: 92.7% (2006-2010 5-year est.); Bachelor's degree or higher: 29.2% (2006-2010 5-year est.); Master's degree or higher: 10.7% (2006-2010 5-year est.).
**Housing:** Homeownership rate: 84.0% (2010); Median home value: $125,200 (2006-2010 5-year est.); Median contract rent: $585 per month (2006-2010 5-year est.); Median year structure built: 1963 (2006-2010 5-year est.).
**Transportation:** Commute to work: 93.6% car, 0.3% public transportation, 1.5% walk, 4.3% work from home (2006-2010 5-year est.); Travel time to work: 32.9% less than 15 minutes, 53.4% 15 to 30 minutes, 9.9% 30 to 45 minutes, 1.4% 45 to 60 minutes, 2.5% 60 minutes or more (2006-2010 5-year est.)

**CHENANGO BRIDGE** (CDP). Covers a land area of 2.448 square miles and a water area of 0.143 square miles. Located at 42.17° N. Lat; 75.85° W. Long. Elevation is 896 feet.
**Population:** n/a (1990); n/a (2000); 2,883 (2010); Density: 1,177.5 persons per square mile (2010); Race: 96.3% White, 0.8% Black, 1.0% Asian, 0.3% American Indian/Alaska Native, 0.0% Native Hawaiian/Other Pacific Islander, 1.6% Other, 1.1% Hispanic of any race (2010); Average household size: 2.40 (2010); Median age: 46.0 (2010); Males per 100 females: 96.0 (2010); Marriage status: 24.4% never married, 62.2% now married, 4.4% widowed, 9.0% divorced (2006-2010 5-year est.); Foreign born: 1.0% (2006-2010 5-year est.); Ancestry (includes multiple ancestries): 28.1% Irish, 21.7% German, 17.5% English, 15.8% Italian, 10.8% Polish (2006-2010 5-year est.).
**Economy:** Employment by occupation: 16.7% management, 5.4% professional, 6.0% services, 14.7% sales, 7.3% farming, 4.8% construction, 8.8% production (2006-2010 5-year est.).
**Income:** Per capita income: $26,274 (2006-2010 5-year est.); Median household income: $56,531 (2006-2010 5-year est.); Average household income: $64,645 (2006-2010 5-year est.); Percent of households with

income of $100,000 or more: 15.7% (2006-2010 5-year est.); Poverty rate: 9.0% (2006-2010 5-year est.).
**Education:** Percent of population age 25 and over with: High school diploma (including GED) or higher: 95.8% (2006-2010 5-year est.); Bachelor's degree or higher: 34.5% (2006-2010 5-year est.); Master's degree or higher: 11.9% (2006-2010 5-year est.).
**Housing:** Homeownership rate: 90.2% (2010); Median home value: $150,100 (2006-2010 5-year est.); Median contract rent: $868 per month (2006-2010 5-year est.); Median year structure built: 1956 (2006-2010 5-year est.).
**Transportation:** Commute to work: 95.0% car, 0.0% public transportation, 0.0% walk, 3.8% work from home (2006-2010 5-year est.); Travel time to work: 39.5% less than 15 minutes, 48.6% 15 to 30 minutes, 8.1% 30 to 45 minutes, 2.4% 45 to 60 minutes, 1.5% 60 minutes or more (2006-2010 5-year est.)

**CHENANGO FORKS** (unincorporated postal area)
Zip Code: 13746
Covers a land area of 27.734 square miles and a water area of 0.482 square miles. Located at 42.26° N. Lat; 75.88° W. Long. Elevation is 915 feet. Population: 2,539 (2010); Density: 91.5 persons per square mile (2010); Race: 95.9% White, 0.7% Black, 0.3% Asian, 0.4% American Indian/Alaska Native, 0.0% Native Hawaiian/Other Pacific Islander, 2.7% Other, 1.6% Hispanic of any race (2010); Average household size: 2.56 (2010); Median age: 45.2 (2010); Males per 100 females: 104.9 (2010); Homeownership rate: 87.5% (2010)

**COLESVILLE** (town). Covers a land area of 78.347 square miles and a water area of 0.823 square miles. Located at 42.17° N. Lat; 75.65° W. Long.
**Population:** 5,590 (1990); 5,441 (2000); 5,232 (2010); Density: 66.8 persons per square mile (2010); Race: 97.2% White, 0.5% Black, 0.4% Asian, 0.2% American Indian/Alaska Native, 0.0% Native Hawaiian/Other Pacific Islander, 1.7% Other, 1.5% Hispanic of any race (2010); Average household size: 2.60 (2010); Median age: 42.4 (2010); Males per 100 females: 107.3 (2010); Marriage status: 25.8% never married, 56.2% now married, 7.0% widowed, 11.0% divorced (2006-2010 5-year est.); Foreign born: 1.4% (2006-2010 5-year est.); Ancestry (includes multiple ancestries): 26.9% German, 21.6% Irish, 16.0% English, 10.9% Italian, 6.9% Scottish (2006-2010 5-year est.).
**Economy:** Single-family building permits issued: 9 (2011); Multi-family building permits issued: 0 (2011); Employment by occupation: 7.3% management, 1.9% professional, 9.7% services, 16.4% sales, 3.4% farming, 11.1% construction, 6.5% production (2006-2010 5-year est.).
**Income:** Per capita income: $18,938 (2006-2010 5-year est.); Median household income: $50,893 (2006-2010 5-year est.); Average household income: $55,373 (2006-2010 5-year est.); Percent of households with income of $100,000 or more: 9.5% (2006-2010 5-year est.); Poverty rate: 13.9% (2006-2010 5-year est.).
**Education:** Percent of population age 25 and over with: High school diploma (including GED) or higher: 88.0% (2006-2010 5-year est.); Bachelor's degree or higher: 11.1% (2006-2010 5-year est.); Master's degree or higher: 4.3% (2006-2010 5-year est.).
**Housing:** Homeownership rate: 82.4% (2010); Median home value: $124,900 (2006-2010 5-year est.); Median contract rent: $440 per month (2006-2010 5-year est.); Median year structure built: 1961 (2006-2010 5-year est.).
**Transportation:** Commute to work: 90.6% car, 1.0% public transportation, 1.8% walk, 4.8% work from home (2006-2010 5-year est.); Travel time to work: 20.4% less than 15 minutes, 34.7% 15 to 30 minutes, 36.9% 30 to 45 minutes, 5.5% 45 to 60 minutes, 2.5% 60 minutes or more (2006-2010 5-year est.)

**CONKLIN** (town). Covers a land area of 24.384 square miles and a water area of 0.503 square miles. Located at 42.04° N. Lat; 75.83° W. Long. Elevation is 869 feet.
**Population:** 6,265 (1990); 5,940 (2000); 5,441 (2010); Density: 223.1 persons per square mile (2010); Race: 96.8% White, 1.0% Black, 0.3% Asian, 0.3% American Indian/Alaska Native, 0.0% Native Hawaiian/Other Pacific Islander, 1.6% Other, 1.4% Hispanic of any race (2010); Average household size: 2.50 (2010); Median age: 44.3 (2010); Males per 100 females: 97.2 (2010); Marriage status: 22.0% never married, 65.3% now married, 4.8% widowed, 7.9% divorced (2006-2010 5-year est.); Foreign born: 2.6% (2006-2010 5-year est.); Ancestry (includes multiple

ancestries): 25.0% Irish, 21.8% German, 16.2% English, 14.2% Italian, 9.2% Polish (2006-2010 5-year est.).
**Economy:** Single-family building permits issued: 0 (2011); Multi-family building permits issued: 0 (2011); Employment by occupation: 15.5% management, 6.1% professional, 11.3% services, 17.4% sales, 2.0% farming, 8.6% construction, 4.5% production (2006-2010 5-year est.).
**Income:** Per capita income: $24,848 (2006-2010 5-year est.); Median household income: $52,546 (2006-2010 5-year est.); Average household income: $61,391 (2006-2010 5-year est.); Percent of households with income of $100,000 or more: 12.2% (2006-2010 5-year est.); Poverty rate: 14.7% (2006-2010 5-year est.).
**Education:** Percent of population age 25 and over with: High school diploma (including GED) or higher: 92.5% (2006-2010 5-year est.); Bachelor's degree or higher: 15.5% (2006-2010 5-year est.); Master's degree or higher: 5.3% (2006-2010 5-year est.).

**School District(s)**
Susquehanna Valley Central School District (KG-12)
    2009-10 Enrollment: 1,807 . . . . . . . . . . . . . . . . . . . . . . (607) 775-0170
**Housing:** Homeownership rate: 84.4% (2010); Median home value: $100,300 (2006-2010 5-year est.); Median contract rent: $470 per month (2006-2010 5-year est.); Median year structure built: 1968 (2006-2010 5-year est.).
**Newspapers:** Country Courier (Local news; Circulation 1,500); Vestal Town Crier (Local news; Circulation 1,400); Windsor Standard (Community news; Circulation 1,400)
**Transportation:** Commute to work: 91.6% car, 0.5% public transportation, 0.6% walk, 6.9% work from home (2006-2010 5-year est.); Travel time to work: 34.0% less than 15 minutes, 44.3% 15 to 30 minutes, 13.5% 30 to 45 minutes, 2.5% 45 to 60 minutes, 5.7% 60 minutes or more (2006-2010 5-year est.)

**DICKINSON** (town). Covers a land area of 4.771 square miles and a water area of 0.104 square miles. Located at 42.13° N. Lat; 75.91° W. Long.
**History:** Incorporated 1876.
**Population:** 5,486 (1990); 5,335 (2000); 5,278 (2010); Density: 1,106.1 persons per square mile (2010); Race: 90.1% White, 6.3% Black, 1.1% Asian, 0.0% American Indian/Alaska Native, 0.0% Native Hawaiian/Other Pacific Islander, 2.5% Other, 2.6% Hispanic of any race (2010); Average household size: 2.17 (2010); Median age: 43.0 (2010); Males per 100 females: 103.8 (2010); Marriage status: 40.8% never married, 43.0% now married, 6.6% widowed, 9.6% divorced (2006-2010 5-year est.); Foreign born: 8.0% (2006-2010 5-year est.); Ancestry (includes multiple ancestries): 15.4% Irish, 14.4% German, 12.3% English, 10.3% Italian, 9.8% Polish (2006-2010 5-year est.).
**Economy:** Single-family building permits issued: 0 (2011); Multi-family building permits issued: 0 (2011); Employment by occupation: 6.9% management, 7.0% professional, 14.4% services, 17.7% sales, 4.4% farming, 9.1% construction, 11.0% production (2006-2010 5-year est.).
**Income:** Per capita income: $19,829 (2006-2010 5-year est.); Median household income: $50,107 (2006-2010 5-year est.); Average household income: $57,089 (2006-2010 5-year est.); Percent of households with income of $100,000 or more: 11.9% (2006-2010 5-year est.); Poverty rate: 20.1% (2006-2010 5-year est.).
**Education:** Percent of population age 25 and over with: High school diploma (including GED) or higher: 80.5% (2006-2010 5-year est.); Bachelor's degree or higher: 18.7% (2006-2010 5-year est.); Master's degree or higher: 8.6% (2006-2010 5-year est.).
**Housing:** Homeownership rate: 68.8% (2010); Median home value: $100,000 (2006-2010 5-year est.); Median contract rent: $544 per month (2006-2010 5-year est.); Median year structure built: 1946 (2006-2010 5-year est.).
**Transportation:** Commute to work: 94.7% car, 1.5% public transportation, 0.0% walk, 1.5% work from home (2006-2010 5-year est.); Travel time to work: 50.4% less than 15 minutes, 37.6% 15 to 30 minutes, 8.5% 30 to 45 minutes, 2.0% 45 to 60 minutes, 1.5% 60 minutes or more (2006-2010 5-year est.)

**ENDICOTT** (village). Covers a land area of 3.193 square miles and a water area of 0.004 square miles. Located at 42.09° N. Lat; 76.06° W. Long. Elevation is 840 feet.
**History:** Settled c.1795; incorporated 1906.
**Population:** 13,531 (1990); 13,038 (2000); 13,392 (2010); Density: 4,193.0 persons per square mile (2010); Race: 86.6% White, 7.0% Black, 1.8% Asian, 0.2% American Indian/Alaska Native, 0.1% Native Hawaiian/Other

Pacific Islander, 4.3% Other, 4.4% Hispanic of any race (2010); Average household size: 2.14 (2010); Median age: 38.2 (2010); Males per 100 females: 93.4 (2010); Marriage status: 37.7% never married, 35.1% now married, 10.6% widowed, 16.6% divorced (2006-2010 5-year est.); Foreign born: 4.0% (2006-2010 5-year est.); Ancestry (includes multiple ancestries): 21.0% Irish, 19.5% Italian, 19.1% German, 11.2% English, 5.8% Polish (2006-2010 5-year est.).
**Economy:** Single-family building permits issued: 0 (2011); Multi-family building permits issued: 2 (2011); Employment by occupation: 7.9% management, 3.8% professional, 13.8% services, 19.5% sales, 3.1% farming, 6.5% construction, 4.9% production (2006-2010 5-year est.).
**Income:** Per capita income: $20,712 (2006-2010 5-year est.); Median household income: $32,772 (2006-2010 5-year est.); Average household income: $42,012 (2006-2010 5-year est.); Percent of households with income of $100,000 or more: 7.3% (2006-2010 5-year est.); Poverty rate: 16.8% (2006-2010 5-year est.).
**Taxes:** Total city taxes per capita: $523 (2009); City property taxes per capita: $501 (2009).
**Education:** Percent of population age 25 and over with: High school diploma (including GED) or higher: 84.0% (2006-2010 5-year est.); Bachelor's degree or higher: 17.6% (2006-2010 5-year est.); Master's degree or higher: 6.8% (2006-2010 5-year est.).

**School District(s)**
Union-Endicott Central School District (KG-12)
    2009-10 Enrollment: 4,092 . . . . . . . . . . . . . . . . . . . . . . (607) 757-2103
**Housing:** Homeownership rate: 41.6% (2010); Median home value: $80,300 (2006-2010 5-year est.); Median contract rent: $501 per month (2006-2010 5-year est.); Median year structure built: 1941 (2006-2010 5-year est.).
**Safety:** Violent crime rate: 35.5 per 10,000 population; Property crime rate: 499.1 per 10,000 population (2010).
**Transportation:** Commute to work: 85.9% car, 2.0% public transportation, 7.7% walk, 3.6% work from home (2006-2010 5-year est.); Travel time to work: 47.8% less than 15 minutes, 43.9% 15 to 30 minutes, 5.8% 30 to 45 minutes, 0.7% 45 to 60 minutes, 1.8% 60 minutes or more (2006-2010 5-year est.)

**ENDWELL** (CDP). Aka Hooper. Covers a land area of 3.743 square miles and a water area of 0.032 square miles. Located at 42.12° N. Lat; 76.02° W. Long. Elevation is 846 feet.
**History:** Also called Hooper.
**Population:** 12,602 (1990); 11,706 (2000); 11,446 (2010); Density: 3,057.5 persons per square mile (2010); Race: 93.1% White, 2.4% Black, 2.0% Asian, 0.2% American Indian/Alaska Native, 0.1% Native Hawaiian/Other Pacific Islander, 2.2% Other, 2.6% Hispanic of any race (2010); Average household size: 2.21 (2010); Median age: 45.2 (2010); Males per 100 females: 91.2 (2010); Marriage status: 25.3% never married, 54.0% now married, 8.9% widowed, 11.8% divorced (2006-2010 5-year est.); Foreign born: 6.6% (2006-2010 5-year est.); Ancestry (includes multiple ancestries): 21.9% Irish, 19.2% German, 19.1% Italian, 15.5% English, 9.5% Polish (2006-2010 5-year est.).
**Economy:** Employment by occupation: 11.4% management, 7.5% professional, 7.9% services, 17.5% sales, 4.7% farming, 3.3% construction, 3.4% production (2006-2010 5-year est.).
**Income:** Per capita income: $30,955 (2006-2010 5-year est.); Median household income: $56,071 (2006-2010 5-year est.); Average household income: $69,218 (2006-2010 5-year est.); Percent of households with income of $100,000 or more: 21.2% (2006-2010 5-year est.); Poverty rate: 7.0% (2006-2010 5-year est.).
**Education:** Percent of population age 25 and over with: High school diploma (including GED) or higher: 92.8% (2006-2010 5-year est.); Bachelor's degree or higher: 39.7% (2006-2010 5-year est.); Master's degree or higher: 19.6% (2006-2010 5-year est.).

**School District(s)**
Maine-Endwell Central School District (PK-12)
    2009-10 Enrollment: 2,594 . . . . . . . . . . . . . . . . . . . . . . (607) 754-1400
**Housing:** Homeownership rate: 72.4% (2010); Median home value: $119,800 (2006-2010 5-year est.); Median contract rent: $520 per month (2006-2010 5-year est.); Median year structure built: 1957 (2006-2010 5-year est.).
**Newspapers:** Owego News (Community news; Circulation 2,500); Vestal News (Local news)
**Transportation:** Commute to work: 91.8% car, 2.7% public transportation, 2.7% walk, 2.6% work from home (2006-2010 5-year est.); Travel time to work: 42.7% less than 15 minutes, 47.2% 15 to 30 minutes, 4.1% 30 to 45

minutes, 1.8% 45 to 60 minutes, 4.2% 60 minutes or more (2006-2010 5-year est.)

**FENTON** (town). Covers a land area of 32.772 square miles and a water area of 0.591 square miles. Located at 42.20° N. Lat; 75.80° W. Long.
**Population:** 7,236 (1990); 6,909 (2000); 6,674 (2010); Density: 203.6 persons per square mile (2010); Race: 96.8% White, 0.8% Black, 0.4% Asian, 0.2% American Indian/Alaska Native, 0.0% Native Hawaiian/Other Pacific Islander, 1.8% Other, 0.9% Hispanic of any race (2010); Average household size: 2.41 (2010); Median age: 45.4 (2010); Males per 100 females: 97.6 (2010); Marriage status: 24.4% never married, 57.4% now married, 5.9% widowed, 12.3% divorced (2006-2010 5-year est.); Foreign born: 1.2% (2006-2010 5-year est.); Ancestry (includes multiple ancestries): 23.1% Irish, 20.3% German, 15.2% English, 14.2% Italian, 7.4% Polish (2006-2010 5-year est.).
**Economy:** Single-family building permits issued: 3 (2011); Multi-family building permits issued: 2 (2011); Employment by occupation: 6.8% management, 4.9% professional, 14.7% services, 18.2% sales, 2.6% farming, 6.1% construction, 5.7% production (2006-2010 5-year est.).
**Income:** Per capita income: $24,705 (2006-2010 5-year est.); Median household income: $50,491 (2006-2010 5-year est.); Average household income: $61,138 (2006-2010 5-year est.); Percent of households with income of $100,000 or more: 18.9% (2006-2010 5-year est.); Poverty rate: 6.9% (2006-2010 5-year est.).
**Education:** Percent of population age 25 and over with: High school diploma (including GED) or higher: 90.2% (2006-2010 5-year est.); Bachelor's degree or higher: 19.1% (2006-2010 5-year est.); Master's degree or higher: 7.8% (2006-2010 5-year est.).
**Housing:** Homeownership rate: 86.0% (2010); Median home value: $90,500 (2006-2010 5-year est.); Median contract rent: $472 per month (2006-2010 5-year est.); Median year structure built: 1964 (2006-2010 5-year est.).
**Transportation:** Commute to work: 92.7% car, 1.5% public transportation, 0.9% walk, 2.2% work from home (2006-2010 5-year est.); Travel time to work: 27.8% less than 15 minutes, 57.0% 15 to 30 minutes, 8.7% 30 to 45 minutes, 2.1% 45 to 60 minutes, 4.5% 60 minutes or more (2006-2010 5-year est.).

**GLEN AUBREY** (CDP). Covers a land area of 0.986 square miles and a water area of 0 square miles. Located at 42.26° N. Lat; 76.00° W. Long. Elevation is 991 feet.
**Population:** n/a (1990); n/a (2000); 485 (2010); Density: 491.7 persons per square mile (2010); Race: 97.3% White, 0.6% Black, 0.0% Asian, 0.0% American Indian/Alaska Native, 0.0% Native Hawaiian/Other Pacific Islander, 2.1% Other, 0.4% Hispanic of any race (2010); Average household size: 2.69 (2010); Median age: 37.1 (2010); Males per 100 females: 84.4 (2010); Marriage status: 24.3% never married, 63.8% now married, 3.8% widowed, 8.1% divorced (2006-2010 5-year est.); Foreign born: 0.0% (2006-2010 5-year est.); Ancestry (includes multiple ancestries): 31.2% Irish, 25.8% German, 24.4% English, 8.7% Polish, 8.0% Italian (2006-2010 5-year est.).
**Economy:** Employment by occupation: 3.9% management, 14.4% professional, 17.8% services, 8.9% sales, 3.3% farming, 13.3% construction, 8.9% production (2006-2010 5-year est.).
**Income:** Per capita income: $20,827 (2006-2010 5-year est.); Median household income: $50,804 (2006-2010 5-year est.); Average household income: $53,825 (2006-2010 5-year est.); Percent of households with income of $100,000 or more: 11.5% (2006-2010 5-year est.); Poverty rate: 16.8% (2006-2010 5-year est.).
**Education:** Percent of population age 25 and over with: High school diploma (including GED) or higher: 81.1% (2006-2010 5-year est.); Bachelor's degree or higher: 9.4% (2006-2010 5-year est.); Master's degree or higher: 1.0% (2006-2010 5-year est.).
**Housing:** Homeownership rate: 81.1% (2010); Median home value: $64,500 (2006-2010 5-year est.); Median contract rent: $428 per month (2006-2010 5-year est.); Median year structure built: 1976 (2006-2010 5-year est.).
**Transportation:** Commute to work: 97.7% car, 0.0% public transportation, 0.0% walk, 2.3% work from home (2006-2010 5-year est.); Travel time to work: 12.7% less than 15 minutes, 39.3% 15 to 30 minutes, 37.6% 30 to 45 minutes, 6.4% 45 to 60 minutes, 4.0% 60 minutes or more (2006-2010 5-year est.).

**HARPURSVILLE** (unincorporated postal area)
Zip Code: 13787
Covers a land area of 63.639 square miles and a water area of 0.464 square miles. Located at 42.21° N. Lat; 75.67° W. Long. Elevation is 1,024 feet. Population: 3,629 (2010); Density: 57.0 persons per square mile (2010); Race: 97.6% White, 0.5% Black, 0.4% Asian, 0.1% American Indian/Alaska Native, 0.0% Native Hawaiian/Other Pacific Islander, 1.4% Other, 1.5% Hispanic of any race (2010); Average household size: 2.62 (2010); Median age: 41.9 (2010); Males per 100 females: 103.9 (2010); Homeownership rate: 82.4% (2010)

**JOHNSON CITY** (village). Covers a land area of 4.536 square miles and a water area of 0.098 square miles. Located at 42.12° N. Lat; 75.96° W. Long. Elevation is 873 feet.
**History:** Originally called Lestershire, the area remained rural until a shoe company built a factory here in 1890. The name was changed in 1916. Incorporated 1892.
**Population:** 16,890 (1990); 15,535 (2000); 15,174 (2010); Density: 3,344.9 persons per square mile (2010); Race: 82.9% White, 6.3% Black, 5.3% Asian, 0.2% American Indian/Alaska Native, 0.1% Native Hawaiian/Other Pacific Islander, 5.2% Other, 4.2% Hispanic of any race (2010); Average household size: 2.19 (2010); Median age: 38.4 (2010); Males per 100 females: 92.1 (2010); Marriage status: 33.7% never married, 44.8% now married, 9.5% widowed, 11.9% divorced (2006-2010 5-year est.); Foreign born: 6.3% (2006-2010 5-year est.); Ancestry (includes multiple ancestries): 24.7% Irish, 15.0% German, 11.5% English, 10.9% Italian, 8.3% Polish (2006-2010 5-year est.).
**Economy:** Single-family building permits issued: 1 (2011); Multi-family building permits issued: 0 (2011); Employment by occupation: 6.4% management, 3.0% professional, 10.5% services, 19.4% sales, 4.8% farming, 6.3% construction, 4.5% production (2006-2010 5-year est.).
**Income:** Per capita income: $21,049 (2006-2010 5-year est.); Median household income: $36,598 (2006-2010 5-year est.); Average household income: $46,214 (2006-2010 5-year est.); Percent of households with income of $100,000 or more: 9.5% (2006-2010 5-year est.); Poverty rate: 20.9% (2006-2010 5-year est.).
**Education:** Percent of population age 25 and over with: High school diploma (including GED) or higher: 85.5% (2006-2010 5-year est.); Bachelor's degree or higher: 21.8% (2006-2010 5-year est.); Master's degree or higher: 10.6% (2006-2010 5-year est.).

**School District(s)**
Johnson City Central School District (KG-12)
    2009-10 Enrollment: 2,578 . . . . . . . . . . . . . . . . . . (607) 763-1230
**Four-year College(s)**
Davis College (Private, Not-for-profit, Baptist)
    Fall 2010 Enrollment: 216 . . . . . . . . . . . . . . . . . . (607) 729-1581
    2011-12 Tuition: In-state $11,990; Out-of-state $11,990
**Housing:** Homeownership rate: 53.2% (2010); Median home value: $81,800 (2006-2010 5-year est.); Median contract rent: $525 per month (2006-2010 5-year est.); Median year structure built: 1944 (2006-2010 5-year est.).
**Hospitals:** United Health Services Hospitals (516 beds)
**Safety:** Violent crime rate: 45.2 per 10,000 population; Property crime rate: 615.3 per 10,000 population (2010).
**Transportation:** Commute to work: 88.7% car, 4.2% public transportation, 3.9% walk, 2.8% work from home (2006-2010 5-year est.); Travel time to work: 58.6% less than 15 minutes, 32.5% 15 to 30 minutes, 3.6% 30 to 45 minutes, 2.7% 45 to 60 minutes, 2.5% 60 minutes or more (2006-2010 5-year est.).
**Additional Information Contacts**
Village of Johnson City . . . . . . . . . . . . . . . . . . . . (607) 798-7861
    http://www.villageofjc.com

**KILLAWOG** (unincorporated postal area)
Zip Code: 13794
Covers a land area of 0.717 square miles and a water area of 0 square miles. Located at 42.39° N. Lat; 76.01° W. Long. Elevation is 1,007 feet. Population: 105 (2010); Density: 146.3 persons per square mile (2010); Race: 99.0% White, 0.0% Black, 0.0% Asian, 0.0% American Indian/Alaska Native, 0.0% Native Hawaiian/Other Pacific Islander, 1.0% Other, 0.0% Hispanic of any race (2010); Average household size: 2.39 (2010); Median age: 43.5 (2010); Males per 100 females: 114.3 (2010); Homeownership rate: 63.6% (2010)

**KIRKWOOD** (town). Covers a land area of 30.794 square miles and a water area of 0.397 square miles. Located at 42.09° N. Lat; 75.79° W. Long. Elevation is 892 feet.
**Population:** 6,096 (1990); 5,651 (2000); 5,857 (2010); Density: 190.2 persons per square mile (2010); Race: 96.2% White, 1.0% Black, 0.8% Asian, 0.1% American Indian/Alaska Native, 0.1% Native Hawaiian/Other Pacific Islander, 1.8% Other, 1.6% Hispanic of any race (2010); Average household size: 2.44 (2010); Median age: 42.5 (2010); Males per 100 females: 97.9 (2010); Marriage status: 29.3% never married, 57.3% now married, 6.3% widowed, 7.1% divorced (2006-2010 5-year est.); Foreign born: 0.4% (2006-2010 5-year est.); Ancestry (includes multiple ancestries): 24.1% Irish, 23.7% German, 21.0% English, 10.6% Italian, 9.9% American (2006-2010 5-year est.).
**Economy:** Single-family building permits issued: 2 (2011); Multi-family building permits issued: 0 (2011); Employment by occupation: 9.4% management, 1.6% professional, 6.3% services, 21.7% sales, 2.9% farming, 6.1% construction, 4.9% production (2006-2010 5-year est.).
**Income:** Per capita income: $24,661 (2006-2010 5-year est.); Median household income: $51,192 (2006-2010 5-year est.); Average household income: $62,484 (2006-2010 5-year est.); Percent of households with income of $100,000 or more: 19.1% (2006-2010 5-year est.); Poverty rate: 11.7% (2006-2010 5-year est.).
**Taxes:** Total city taxes per capita: $222 (2009); City property taxes per capita: $199 (2009).
**Education:** Percent of population age 25 and over with: High school diploma (including GED) or higher: 93.2% (2006-2010 5-year est.); Bachelor's degree or higher: 19.3% (2006-2010 5-year est.); Master's degree or higher: 10.9% (2006-2010 5-year est.).
**School District(s)**
Windsor Central School District (PK-12)
    2009-10 Enrollment: 1,937 . . . . . . . . . . . . . . . . . . . . (607) 655-8216
**Housing:** Homeownership rate: 72.4% (2010); Median home value: $108,700 (2006-2010 5-year est.); Median contract rent: $515 per month (2006-2010 5-year est.); Median year structure built: 1965 (2006-2010 5-year est.).
**Transportation:** Commute to work: 91.6% car, 2.9% public transportation, 2.7% walk, 2.1% work from home (2006-2010 5-year est.); Travel time to work: 45.0% less than 15 minutes, 46.4% 15 to 30 minutes, 3.8% 30 to 45 minutes, 0.0% 45 to 60 minutes, 4.8% 60 minutes or more (2006-2010 5-year est.).

**LISLE** (village). Covers a land area of 0.936 square miles and a water area of 0 square miles. Located at 42.34° N. Lat; 76.00° W. Long. Elevation is 974 feet.
**Population:** 361 (1990); 302 (2000); 320 (2010); Density: 341.7 persons per square mile (2010); Race: 97.8% White, 0.9% Black, 0.0% Asian, 0.6% American Indian/Alaska Native, 0.0% Native Hawaiian/Other Pacific Islander, 0.7% Other, 0.6% Hispanic of any race (2010); Average household size: 2.46 (2010); Median age: 32.8 (2010); Males per 100 females: 93.9 (2010); Marriage status: 30.1% never married, 50.8% now married, 7.4% widowed, 11.7% divorced (2006-2010 5-year est.); Foreign born: 0.0% (2006-2010 5-year est.); Ancestry (includes multiple ancestries): 25.4% English, 18.0% German, 12.4% Irish, 10.8% Polish, 8.7% American (2006-2010 5-year est.).
**Economy:** Single-family building permits issued: 0 (2011); Multi-family building permits issued: 0 (2011); Employment by occupation: 7.6% management, 0.0% professional, 3.4% services, 22.1% sales, 7.6% farming, 6.9% construction, 11.0% production (2006-2010 5-year est.).
**Income:** Per capita income: $23,420 (2006-2010 5-year est.); Median household income: $52,750 (2006-2010 5-year est.); Average household income: $61,696 (2006-2010 5-year est.); Percent of households with income of $100,000 or more: 23.7% (2006-2010 5-year est.); Poverty rate: 6.8% (2006-2010 5-year est.).
**Education:** Percent of population age 25 and over with: High school diploma (including GED) or higher: 93.1% (2006-2010 5-year est.); Bachelor's degree or higher: 9.9% (2006-2010 5-year est.); Master's degree or higher: 3.0% (2006-2010 5-year est.).
**Housing:** Homeownership rate: 72.3% (2010); Median home value: $76,400 (2006-2010 5-year est.); Median contract rent: $392 per month (2006-2010 5-year est.); Median year structure built: before 1940 (2006-2010 5-year est.).
**Transportation:** Commute to work: 97.9% car, 0.0% public transportation, 0.0% walk, 2.1% work from home (2006-2010 5-year est.); Travel time to work: 21.2% less than 15 minutes, 24.8% 15 to 30 minutes, 33.6% 30 to 45 minutes, 13.1% 45 to 60 minutes, 7.3% 60 minutes or more (2006-2010 5-year est.)

**LISLE** (town). Covers a land area of 46.894 square miles and a water area of 0.090 square miles. Located at 42.37° N. Lat; 76.05° W. Long. Elevation is 974 feet.
**Population:** 2,486 (1990); 2,707 (2000); 2,751 (2010); Density: 58.7 persons per square mile (2010); Race: 98.0% White, 0.4% Black, 0.2% Asian, 0.2% American Indian/Alaska Native, 0.0% Native Hawaiian/Other Pacific Islander, 1.2% Other, 1.2% Hispanic of any race (2010); Average household size: 2.58 (2010); Median age: 39.9 (2010); Males per 100 females: 94.6 (2010); Marriage status: 29.1% never married, 60.4% now married, 4.5% widowed, 6.0% divorced (2006-2010 5-year est.); Foreign born: 0.3% (2006-2010 5-year est.); Ancestry (includes multiple ancestries): 14.5% English, 11.6% German, 11.2% Irish, 11.0% Polish, 8.9% American (2006-2010 5-year est.).
**Economy:** Single-family building permits issued: 2 (2011); Multi-family building permits issued: 0 (2011); Employment by occupation: 6.9% management, 1.2% professional, 10.1% services, 17.6% sales, 3.5% farming, 14.5% construction, 9.2% production (2006-2010 5-year est.).
**Income:** Per capita income: $21,595 (2006-2010 5-year est.); Median household income: $46,793 (2006-2010 5-year est.); Average household income: $59,470 (2006-2010 5-year est.); Percent of households with income of $100,000 or more: 17.4% (2006-2010 5-year est.); Poverty rate: 15.6% (2006-2010 5-year est.).
**Education:** Percent of population age 25 and over with: High school diploma (including GED) or higher: 86.7% (2006-2010 5-year est.); Bachelor's degree or higher: 12.3% (2006-2010 5-year est.); Master's degree or higher: 3.1% (2006-2010 5-year est.).
**Housing:** Homeownership rate: 83.3% (2010); Median home value: $85,200 (2006-2010 5-year est.); Median contract rent: $465 per month (2006-2010 5-year est.); Median year structure built: 1976 (2006-2010 5-year est.).
**Transportation:** Commute to work: 94.7% car, 0.0% public transportation, 1.1% walk, 3.5% work from home (2006-2010 5-year est.); Travel time to work: 24.9% less than 15 minutes, 25.2% 15 to 30 minutes, 39.4% 30 to 45 minutes, 8.6% 45 to 60 minutes, 1.9% 60 minutes or more (2006-2010 5-year est.)

**MAINE** (town). Covers a land area of 45.643 square miles and a water area of 0.117 square miles. Located at 42.19° N. Lat; 76.01° W. Long. Elevation is 912 feet.
**Population:** 5,606 (1990); 5,459 (2000); 5,377 (2010); Density: 117.8 persons per square mile (2010); Race: 97.6% White, 0.4% Black, 0.4% Asian, 0.1% American Indian/Alaska Native, 0.0% Native Hawaiian/Other Pacific Islander, 1.5% Other, 0.8% Hispanic of any race (2010); Average household size: 2.55 (2010); Median age: 43.3 (2010); Males per 100 females: 98.0 (2010); Marriage status: 24.9% never married, 58.1% now married, 6.0% widowed, 11.0% divorced (2006-2010 5-year est.); Foreign born: 1.7% (2006-2010 5-year est.); Ancestry (includes multiple ancestries): 26.5% Irish, 18.1% German, 17.9% English, 13.5% Italian, 7.8% Polish (2006-2010 5-year est.).
**Economy:** Single-family building permits issued: 3 (2011); Multi-family building permits issued: 0 (2011); Employment by occupation: 6.5% management, 4.4% professional, 10.4% services, 19.3% sales, 5.1% farming, 9.2% construction, 7.7% production (2006-2010 5-year est.).
**Income:** Per capita income: $22,220 (2006-2010 5-year est.); Median household income: $52,861 (2006-2010 5-year est.); Average household income: $59,981 (2006-2010 5-year est.); Percent of households with income of $100,000 or more: 16.6% (2006-2010 5-year est.); Poverty rate: 16.4% (2006-2010 5-year est.).
**Education:** Percent of population age 25 and over with: High school diploma (including GED) or higher: 90.7% (2006-2010 5-year est.); Bachelor's degree or higher: 14.9% (2006-2010 5-year est.); Master's degree or higher: 5.2% (2006-2010 5-year est.).
**School District(s)**
Maine-Endwell Central School District (PK-12)
    2009-10 Enrollment: 2,594 . . . . . . . . . . . . . . . . . . . . (607) 754-1400
**Housing:** Homeownership rate: 86.4% (2010); Median home value: $98,700 (2006-2010 5-year est.); Median contract rent: $507 per month (2006-2010 5-year est.); Median year structure built: 1970 (2006-2010 5-year est.).
**Transportation:** Commute to work: 95.0% car, 0.0% public transportation, 0.5% walk, 4.6% work from home (2006-2010 5-year est.); Travel time to work: 19.9% less than 15 minutes, 55.8% 15 to 30 minutes, 14.6% 30 to 45

minutes, 1.9% 45 to 60 minutes, 7.8% 60 minutes or more (2006-2010 5-year est.)

**NANTICOKE** (town). Covers a land area of 24.270 square miles and a water area of 0.089 square miles. Located at 42.28° N. Lat; 76.02° W. Long. Elevation is 1,089 feet.
**Population:** 1,846 (1990); 1,790 (2000); 1,672 (2010); Density: 68.9 persons per square mile (2010); Race: 97.5% White, 0.4% Black, 0.1% Asian, 0.2% American Indian/Alaska Native, 0.0% Native Hawaiian/Other Pacific Islander, 1.8% Other, 0.7% Hispanic of any race (2010); Average household size: 2.78 (2010); Median age: 39.8 (2010); Males per 100 females: 102.2 (2010); Marriage status: 24.7% never married, 63.0% now married, 4.3% widowed, 8.0% divorced (2006-2010 5-year est.); Foreign born: 1.0% (2006-2010 5-year est.); Ancestry (includes multiple ancestries): 26.6% Irish, 21.8% English, 19.3% German, 9.9% Polish, 7.3% American (2006-2010 5-year est.).
**Economy:** Single-family building permits issued: 0 (2011); Multi-family building permits issued: 0 (2011); Employment by occupation: 8.9% management, 5.3% professional, 15.4% services, 17.3% sales, 1.6% farming, 13.8% construction, 5.7% production (2006-2010 5-year est.).
**Income:** Per capita income: $20,624 (2006-2010 5-year est.); Median household income: $50,156 (2006-2010 5-year est.); Average household income: $55,869 (2006-2010 5-year est.); Percent of households with income of $100,000 or more: 10.1% (2006-2010 5-year est.); Poverty rate: 14.3% (2006-2010 5-year est.).
**Education:** Percent of population age 25 and over with: High school diploma (including GED) or higher: 85.0% (2006-2010 5-year est.); Bachelor's degree or higher: 9.2% (2006-2010 5-year est.); Master's degree or higher: 2.8% (2006-2010 5-year est.).
**Housing:** Homeownership rate: 84.0% (2010); Median home value: $85,800 (2006-2010 5-year est.); Median contract rent: $438 per month (2006-2010 5-year est.); Median year structure built: 1978 (2006-2010 5-year est.).
**Transportation:** Commute to work: 95.9% car, 0.4% public transportation, 1.3% walk, 2.4% work from home (2006-2010 5-year est.); Travel time to work: 15.9% less than 15 minutes, 42.4% 15 to 30 minutes, 32.2% 30 to 45 minutes, 5.0% 45 to 60 minutes, 4.5% 60 minutes or more (2006-2010 5-year est.)

**NINEVEH** (unincorporated postal area)
Zip Code: 13813
Covers a land area of 27.856 square miles and a water area of 0.664 square miles. Located at 42.16° N. Lat; 75.55° W. Long. Elevation is 965 feet. Population: 977 (2010); Density: 35.1 persons per square mile (2010); Race: 96.1% White, 0.6% Black, 0.1% Asian, 0.3% American Indian/Alaska Native, 0.0% Native Hawaiian/Other Pacific Islander, 2.9% Other, 1.3% Hispanic of any race (2010); Average household size: 2.64 (2010); Median age: 41.7 (2010); Males per 100 females: 105.3 (2010); Homeownership rate: 82.0% (2010)

**OUAQUAGA** (unincorporated postal area)
Zip Code: 13826
Covers a land area of 0.837 square miles and a water area of 0.245 square miles. Located at 42.09° N. Lat; 75.63° W. Long. Elevation is 945 feet. Population: 58 (2010); Density: 69.2 persons per square mile (2010); Race: 100.0% White, 0.0% Black, 0.0% Asian, 0.0% American Indian/Alaska Native, 0.0% Native Hawaiian/Other Pacific Islander, 0.0% Other, 1.7% Hispanic of any race (2010); Average household size: 2.52 (2010); Median age: 50.3 (2010); Males per 100 females: 100.0 (2010); Homeownership rate: 87.0% (2010)

**PORT CRANE** (unincorporated postal area)
Zip Code: 13833
Covers a land area of 35.733 square miles and a water area of 0.150 square miles. Located at 42.19° N. Lat; 75.76° W. Long. Elevation is 889 feet. Population: 4,255 (2010); Density: 119.1 persons per square mile (2010); Race: 96.7% White, 0.3% Black, 0.3% Asian, 0.3% American Indian/Alaska Native, 0.0% Native Hawaiian/Other Pacific Islander, 2.4% Other, 1.4% Hispanic of any race (2010); Average household size: 2.53 (2010); Median age: 43.8 (2010); Males per 100 females: 104.3 (2010); Homeownership rate: 83.6% (2010)

**PORT DICKINSON** (village). Covers a land area of 0.637 square miles and a water area of 0.078 square miles. Located at 42.13° N. Lat; 75.89° W. Long. Elevation is 863 feet.
**Population:** 1,785 (1990); 1,697 (2000); 1,641 (2010); Density: 2,574.2 persons per square mile (2010); Race: 95.1% White, 2.0% Black, 0.6% Asian, 0.0% American Indian/Alaska Native, 0.0% Native Hawaiian/Other Pacific Islander, 2.3% Other, 1.1% Hispanic of any race (2010); Average household size: 2.22 (2010); Median age: 39.8 (2010); Males per 100 females: 83.8 (2010); Marriage status: 35.5% never married, 45.3% now married, 6.4% widowed, 12.9% divorced (2006-2010 5-year est.); Foreign born: 2.4% (2006-2010 5-year est.); Ancestry (includes multiple ancestries): 29.5% Irish, 23.1% German, 20.4% Italian, 19.1% English, 7.7% Slovak (2006-2010 5-year est.).
**Economy:** Single-family building permits issued: 0 (2011); Multi-family building permits issued: 0 (2011); Employment by occupation: 10.1% management, 6.0% professional, 11.2% services, 21.3% sales, 5.0% farming, 8.2% construction, 4.1% production (2006-2010 5-year est.).
**Income:** Per capita income: $23,320 (2006-2010 5-year est.); Median household income: $42,438 (2006-2010 5-year est.); Average household income: $52,549 (2006-2010 5-year est.); Percent of households with income of $100,000 or more: 9.9% (2006-2010 5-year est.); Poverty rate: 13.4% (2006-2010 5-year est.).
**Education:** Percent of population age 25 and over with: High school diploma (including GED) or higher: 93.2% (2006-2010 5-year est.); Bachelor's degree or higher: 27.1% (2006-2010 5-year est.); Master's degree or higher: 12.9% (2006-2010 5-year est.).
**Housing:** Homeownership rate: 60.8% (2010); Median home value: $95,000 (2006-2010 5-year est.); Median contract rent: $492 per month (2006-2010 5-year est.); Median year structure built: before 1940 (2006-2010 5-year est.).
**Safety:** Violent crime rate: 19.3 per 10,000 population; Property crime rate: 83.5 per 10,000 population (2010).
**Transportation:** Commute to work: 90.6% car, 0.6% public transportation, 0.2% walk, 3.2% work from home (2006-2010 5-year est.); Travel time to work: 55.2% less than 15 minutes, 35.2% 15 to 30 minutes, 4.9% 30 to 45 minutes, 1.6% 45 to 60 minutes, 3.0% 60 minutes or more (2006-2010 5-year est.)

**SANFORD** (town). Covers a land area of 90.098 square miles and a water area of 0.923 square miles. Located at 42.09° N. Lat; 75.49° W. Long. Elevation is 1,178 feet.
**Population:** 2,576 (1990); 2,477 (2000); 2,407 (2010); Density: 26.7 persons per square mile (2010); Race: 98.3% White, 0.5% Black, 0.1% Asian, 0.1% American Indian/Alaska Native, 0.0% Native Hawaiian/Other Pacific Islander, 1.0% Other, 1.6% Hispanic of any race (2010); Average household size: 2.48 (2010); Median age: 45.2 (2010); Males per 100 females: 101.1 (2010); Marriage status: 32.0% never married, 52.5% now married, 8.0% widowed, 7.6% divorced (2006-2010 5-year est.); Foreign born: 2.7% (2006-2010 5-year est.); Ancestry (includes multiple ancestries): 33.6% Irish, 27.4% German, 17.7% Italian, 9.5% English, 5.7% American (2006-2010 5-year est.).
**Economy:** Single-family building permits issued: 2 (2011); Multi-family building permits issued: 0 (2011); Employment by occupation: 7.5% management, 1.7% professional, 16.4% services, 19.1% sales, 4.9% farming, 16.0% construction, 10.7% production (2006-2010 5-year est.).
**Income:** Per capita income: $20,007 (2006-2010 5-year est.); Median household income: $40,163 (2006-2010 5-year est.); Average household income: $50,410 (2006-2010 5-year est.); Percent of households with income of $100,000 or more: 8.6% (2006-2010 5-year est.); Poverty rate: 11.6% (2006-2010 5-year est.).
**Education:** Percent of population age 25 and over with: High school diploma (including GED) or higher: 86.6% (2006-2010 5-year est.); Bachelor's degree or higher: 12.8% (2006-2010 5-year est.); Master's degree or higher: 5.6% (2006-2010 5-year est.).
**Housing:** Homeownership rate: 82.2% (2010); Median home value: $98,000 (2006-2010 5-year est.); Median contract rent: $450 per month (2006-2010 5-year est.); Median year structure built: 1962 (2006-2010 5-year est.).
**Transportation:** Commute to work: 85.5% car, 0.7% public transportation, 6.0% walk, 4.7% work from home (2006-2010 5-year est.); Travel time to work: 33.6% less than 15 minutes, 26.9% 15 to 30 minutes, 19.1% 30 to 45 minutes, 13.6% 45 to 60 minutes, 6.7% 60 minutes or more (2006-2010 5-year est.)

**TRIANGLE** (town). Covers a land area of 37.874 square miles and a water area of 1.906 square miles. Located at 42.35° N. Lat; 75.92° W. Long. Elevation is 1,070 feet.
**Population:** 3,006 (1990); 3,032 (2000); 2,946 (2010); Density: 77.8 persons per square mile (2010); Race: 96.9% White, 0.4% Black, 0.4% Asian, 0.1% American Indian/Alaska Native, 0.0% Native Hawaiian/Other Pacific Islander, 2.2% Other, 1.5% Hispanic of any race (2010); Average household size: 2.60 (2010); Median age: 40.2 (2010); Males per 100 females: 96.4 (2010); Marriage status: 25.2% never married, 58.6% now married, 9.7% widowed, 6.6% divorced (2006-2010 5-year est.); Foreign born: 1.1% (2006-2010 5-year est.); Ancestry (includes multiple ancestries): 18.7% English, 12.7% German, 12.1% Irish, 11.0% American, 7.9% Italian (2006-2010 5-year est.).
**Economy:** Single-family building permits issued: 1 (2011); Multi-family building permits issued: 0 (2011); Employment by occupation: 11.0% management, 1.1% professional, 9.5% services, 19.5% sales, 2.3% farming, 12.7% construction, 6.0% production (2006-2010 5-year est.).
**Income:** Per capita income: $22,335 (2006-2010 5-year est.); Median household income: $44,556 (2006-2010 5-year est.); Average household income: $57,481 (2006-2010 5-year est.); Percent of households with income of $100,000 or more: 13.9% (2006-2010 5-year est.); Poverty rate: 9.3% (2006-2010 5-year est.).
**Education:** Percent of population age 25 and over with: High school diploma (including GED) or higher: 86.3% (2006-2010 5-year est.); Bachelor's degree or higher: 15.9% (2006-2010 5-year est.); Master's degree or higher: 8.1% (2006-2010 5-year est.).
**Housing:** Homeownership rate: 76.5% (2010); Median home value: $100,500 (2006-2010 5-year est.); Median contract rent: $436 per month (2006-2010 5-year est.); Median year structure built: 1973 (2006-2010 5-year est.).
**Transportation:** Commute to work: 92.2% car, 0.0% public transportation, 3.1% walk, 4.7% work from home (2006-2010 5-year est.); Travel time to work: 23.3% less than 15 minutes, 25.5% 15 to 30 minutes, 34.5% 30 to 45 minutes, 9.7% 45 to 60 minutes, 7.0% 60 minutes or more (2006-2010 5-year est.)

**UNION** (town). Covers a land area of 35.451 square miles and a water area of 0.537 square miles. Located at 42.12° N. Lat; 76.03° W. Long. Elevation is 846 feet.
**Population:** 59,786 (1990); 56,298 (2000); 56,346 (2010); Density: 1,589.4 persons per square mile (2010); Race: 89.1% White, 4.4% Black, 2.9% Asian, 0.2% American Indian/Alaska Native, 0.1% Native Hawaiian/Other Pacific Islander, 3.3% Other, 3.2% Hispanic of any race (2010); Average household size: 2.21 (2010); Median age: 41.8 (2010); Males per 100 females: 92.3 (2010); Marriage status: 31.7% never married, 46.7% now married, 9.2% widowed, 12.4% divorced (2006-2010 5-year est.); Foreign born: 5.3% (2006-2010 5-year est.); Ancestry (includes multiple ancestries): 21.9% Irish, 18.8% German, 17.2% Italian, 12.6% English, 8.2% Polish (2006-2010 5-year est.).
**Economy:** Unemployment rate: 9.0% (February 2012); Total civilian labor force: 27,634 (February 2012); Single-family building permits issued: 4 (2011); Multi-family building permits issued: 0 (2011); Employment by occupation: 9.8% management, 6.0% professional, 10.3% services, 17.8% sales, 4.5% farming, 5.5% construction, 4.4% production (2006-2010 5-year est.).
**Income:** Per capita income: $25,732 (2006-2010 5-year est.); Median household income: $43,543 (2006-2010 5-year est.); Average household income: $56,634 (2006-2010 5-year est.); Percent of households with income of $100,000 or more: 13.9% (2006-2010 5-year est.); Poverty rate: 13.7% (2006-2010 5-year est.).
**Taxes:** Total city taxes per capita: $171 (2009); City property taxes per capita: $155 (2009).
**Education:** Percent of population age 25 and over with: High school diploma (including GED) or higher: 88.4% (2006-2010 5-year est.); Bachelor's degree or higher: 26.7% (2006-2010 5-year est.); Master's degree or higher: 11.7% (2006-2010 5-year est.).
**Housing:** Homeownership rate: 60.3% (2010); Median home value: $96,500 (2006-2010 5-year est.); Median contract rent: $525 per month (2006-2010 5-year est.); Median year structure built: 1953 (2006-2010 5-year est.).
**Transportation:** Commute to work: 89.6% car, 2.6% public transportation, 4.0% walk, 3.3% work from home (2006-2010 5-year est.); Travel time to work: 47.8% less than 15 minutes, 42.7% 15 to 30 minutes, 4.9% 30 to 45 minutes, 1.6% 45 to 60 minutes, 2.9% 60 minutes or more (2006-2010 5-year est.)

**Additional Information Contacts**
Town of Union . . . . . . . . . . . . . . . . . . . . . . . . . . . . (607) 786-2900
  http://www.townofunion.com

**VESTAL** (town). Covers a land area of 51.742 square miles and a water area of 0.853 square miles. Located at 42.04° N. Lat; 76.01° W. Long. Elevation is 830 feet.
**Population:** 26,733 (1990); 26,535 (2000); 28,043 (2010); Density: 542.0 persons per square mile (2010); Race: 82.9% White, 3.2% Black, 10.8% Asian, 0.2% American Indian/Alaska Native, 0.0% Native Hawaiian/Other Pacific Islander, 2.9% Other, 3.3% Hispanic of any race (2010); Average household size: 2.39 (2010); Median age: 30.7 (2010); Males per 100 females: 96.2 (2010); Marriage status: 44.5% never married, 43.8% now married, 6.3% widowed, 5.4% divorced (2006-2010 5-year est.); Foreign born: 11.1% (2006-2010 5-year est.); Ancestry (includes multiple ancestries): 18.5% Irish, 16.0% German, 12.8% English, 12.1% Italian, 8.3% Polish (2006-2010 5-year est.).
**Economy:** Unemployment rate: 8.3% (February 2012); Total civilian labor force: 12,246 (February 2012); Single-family building permits issued: 1 (2011); Multi-family building permits issued: 0 (2011); Employment by occupation: 11.1% management, 7.6% professional, 8.3% services, 19.6% sales, 3.5% farming, 2.6% construction, 3.1% production (2006-2010 5-year est.).
**Income:** Per capita income: $26,452 (2006-2010 5-year est.); Median household income: $63,433 (2006-2010 5-year est.); Average household income: $81,804 (2006-2010 5-year est.); Percent of households with income of $100,000 or more: 27.7% (2006-2010 5-year est.); Poverty rate: 6.0% (2006-2010 5-year est.).
**Education:** Percent of population age 25 and over with: High school diploma (including GED) or higher: 95.4% (2006-2010 5-year est.); Bachelor's degree or higher: 43.6% (2006-2010 5-year est.); Master's degree or higher: 22.0% (2006-2010 5-year est.).
**School District(s)**
Vestal Central School District (KG-12)
  2009-10 Enrollment: 3,767 . . . . . . . . . . . . . . . . . (607) 757-2241
**Four-year College(s)**
SUNY at Binghamton (Public)
  Fall 2010 Enrollment: 14,533 . . . . . . . . . . . . . . . . (607) 777-2000
  2011-12 Tuition: In-state $7,216; Out-of-state $15,326
**Housing:** Homeownership rate: 77.2% (2010); Median home value: $132,700 (2006-2010 5-year est.); Median contract rent: $661 per month (2006-2010 5-year est.); Median year structure built: 1965 (2006-2010 5-year est.).
**Safety:** Violent crime rate: 5.2 per 10,000 population; Property crime rate: 201.1 per 10,000 population (2010).
**Newspapers:** The Jewish Observer of Central New York (Regional news; Circulation 5,000); The New Jewish Voice (Local news; Circulation 7,000); The Voice of the Dutchess Jewish Community (Local news); The Wyoming Valley Jewish Reporter (Local news)
**Transportation:** Commute to work: 80.7% car, 0.8% public transportation, 6.9% walk, 10.3% work from home (2006-2010 5-year est.); Travel time to work: 48.7% less than 15 minutes, 42.3% 15 to 30 minutes, 4.9% 30 to 45 minutes, 1.3% 45 to 60 minutes, 2.7% 60 minutes or more (2006-2010 5-year est.)
**Additional Information Contacts**
Town of Vestal . . . . . . . . . . . . . . . . . . . . . . . . . . . . (607) 748-1514
  http://www.vestalny.com

**WHITNEY POINT** (village). Covers a land area of 1.042 square miles and a water area of 0.070 square miles. Located at 42.33° N. Lat; 75.97° W. Long. Elevation is 958 feet.
**Population:** 1,007 (1990); 965 (2000); 964 (2010); Density: 924.7 persons per square mile (2010); Race: 95.7% White, 0.4% Black, 0.5% Asian, 0.0% American Indian/Alaska Native, 0.0% Native Hawaiian/Other Pacific Islander, 3.4% Other, 3.1% Hispanic of any race (2010); Average household size: 2.56 (2010); Median age: 35.7 (2010); Males per 100 females: 90.9 (2010); Marriage status: 30.6% never married, 50.8% now married, 9.6% widowed, 9.0% divorced (2006-2010 5-year est.); Foreign born: 1.0% (2006-2010 5-year est.); Ancestry (includes multiple ancestries): 10.6% German, 10.5% English, 10.0% Italian, 9.8% Irish, 5.4% American (2006-2010 5-year est.).
**Economy:** Single-family building permits issued: 0 (2011); Multi-family building permits issued: 0 (2011); Employment by occupation: 16.9% management, 0.7% professional, 5.6% services, 18.9% sales, 2.5% farming, 9.6% construction, 7.4% production (2006-2010 5-year est.).

**Income:** Per capita income: $19,981 (2006-2010 5-year est.); Median household income: $42,566 (2006-2010 5-year est.); Average household income: $50,928 (2006-2010 5-year est.); Percent of households with income of $100,000 or more: 9.8% (2006-2010 5-year est.); Poverty rate: 11.4% (2006-2010 5-year est.).
**Education:** Percent of population age 25 and over with: High school diploma (including GED) or higher: 85.8% (2006-2010 5-year est.); Bachelor's degree or higher: 16.4% (2006-2010 5-year est.); Master's degree or higher: 7.0% (2006-2010 5-year est.).

### School District(s)
Whitney Point Central School District (PK-12)
   2009-10 Enrollment: 1,487 . . . . . . . . . . . . . . . . . . . . . . (607) 692-8202
**Housing:** Homeownership rate: 59.5% (2010); Median home value: $95,800 (2006-2010 5-year est.); Median contract rent: $473 per month (2006-2010 5-year est.); Median year structure built: 1951 (2006-2010 5-year est.).
**Transportation:** Commute to work: 94.3% car, 0.0% public transportation, 5.0% walk, 0.7% work from home (2006-2010 5-year est.); Travel time to work: 28.7% less than 15 minutes, 22.5% 15 to 30 minutes, 32.5% 30 to 45 minutes, 10.5% 45 to 60 minutes, 5.8% 60 minutes or more (2006-2010 5-year est.)

**WINDSOR** (village). Covers a land area of 1.094 square miles and a water area of 0.071 square miles. Located at 42.07° N. Lat; 75.64° W. Long. Elevation is 951 feet.
**Population:** 1,051 (1990); 901 (2000); 916 (2010); Density: 836.6 persons per square mile (2010); Race: 96.7% White, 0.5% Black, 0.5% Asian, 0.3% American Indian/Alaska Native, 0.0% Native Hawaiian/Other Pacific Islander, 2.0% Other, 1.2% Hispanic of any race (2010); Average household size: 2.44 (2010); Median age: 39.1 (2010); Males per 100 females: 92.4 (2010); Marriage status: 27.0% never married, 51.3% now married, 3.9% widowed, 17.8% divorced (2006-2010 5-year est.); Foreign born: 2.1% (2006-2010 5-year est.); Ancestry (includes multiple ancestries): 29.1% Irish, 22.2% German, 9.8% Italian, 9.5% English, 7.0% Polish (2006-2010 5-year est.).
**Economy:** Employment by occupation: 12.0% management, 2.9% professional, 13.6% services, 9.8% sales, 6.0% farming, 9.3% construction, 7.1% production (2006-2010 5-year est.).
**Income:** Per capita income: $21,381 (2006-2010 5-year est.); Median household income: $39,118 (2006-2010 5-year est.); Average household income: $54,030 (2006-2010 5-year est.); Percent of households with income of $100,000 or more: 12.5% (2006-2010 5-year est.); Poverty rate: 15.7% (2006-2010 5-year est.).
**Education:** Percent of population age 25 and over with: High school diploma (including GED) or higher: 88.1% (2006-2010 5-year est.); Bachelor's degree or higher: 14.4% (2006-2010 5-year est.); Master's degree or higher: 4.8% (2006-2010 5-year est.).

### School District(s)
Windsor Central School District (PK-12)
   2009-10 Enrollment: 1,937 . . . . . . . . . . . . . . . . . . . . . . (607) 655-8216
**Housing:** Homeownership rate: 62.2% (2010); Median home value: $95,100 (2006-2010 5-year est.); Median contract rent: $403 per month (2006-2010 5-year est.); Median year structure built: 1942 (2006-2010 5-year est.).
**Transportation:** Commute to work: 95.4% car, 0.0% public transportation, 2.5% walk, 2.1% work from home (2006-2010 5-year est.); Travel time to work: 20.6% less than 15 minutes, 51.1% 15 to 30 minutes, 18.4% 30 to 45 minutes, 5.9% 45 to 60 minutes, 4.0% 60 minutes or more (2006-2010 5-year est.)

**WINDSOR** (town). Covers a land area of 91.742 square miles and a water area of 1.263 square miles. Located at 42.06° N. Lat; 75.67° W. Long. Elevation is 951 feet.
**Population:** 6,440 (1990); 6,421 (2000); 6,274 (2010); Density: 68.4 persons per square mile (2010); Race: 97.2% White, 0.4% Black, 0.4% Asian, 0.1% American Indian/Alaska Native, 0.0% Native Hawaiian/Other Pacific Islander, 1.9% Other, 1.6% Hispanic of any race (2010); Average household size: 2.61 (2010); Median age: 42.5 (2010); Males per 100 females: 102.8 (2010); Marriage status: 24.9% never married, 58.5% now married, 5.7% widowed, 10.8% divorced (2006-2010 5-year est.); Foreign born: 0.8% (2006-2010 5-year est.); Ancestry (includes multiple ancestries): 23.1% Irish, 20.1% German, 14.3% English, 11.8% Italian, 8.0% American (2006-2010 5-year est.).
**Economy:** Single-family building permits issued: 6 (2011); Multi-family building permits issued: 0 (2011); Employment by occupation: 8.5%

management, 3.7% professional, 8.5% services, 15.8% sales, 3.5% farming, 12.8% construction, 11.0% production (2006-2010 5-year est.).
**Income:** Per capita income: $21,418 (2006-2010 5-year est.); Median household income: $47,246 (2006-2010 5-year est.); Average household income: $58,083 (2006-2010 5-year est.); Percent of households with income of $100,000 or more: 9.4% (2006-2010 5-year est.); Poverty rate: 9.0% (2006-2010 5-year est.).
**Education:** Percent of population age 25 and over with: High school diploma (including GED) or higher: 83.5% (2006-2010 5-year est.); Bachelor's degree or higher: 11.6% (2006-2010 5-year est.); Master's degree or higher: 4.8% (2006-2010 5-year est.).

### School District(s)
Windsor Central School District (PK-12)
   2009-10 Enrollment: 1,937 . . . . . . . . . . . . . . . . . . . . . . (607) 655-8216
**Housing:** Homeownership rate: 83.7% (2010); Median home value: $89,400 (2006-2010 5-year est.); Median contract rent: $449 per month (2006-2010 5-year est.); Median year structure built: 1972 (2006-2010 5-year est.).
**Transportation:** Commute to work: 95.4% car, 0.0% public transportation, 1.6% walk, 2.2% work from home (2006-2010 5-year est.); Travel time to work: 17.2% less than 15 minutes, 43.1% 15 to 30 minutes, 28.8% 30 to 45 minutes, 3.1% 45 to 60 minutes, 7.8% 60 minutes or more (2006-2010 5-year est.)

# Cattaraugus County

Located in western New York; bounded on the south by Pennsylvania; crossed by the Allegheny River. Covers a land area of 1,309.85 square miles, a water area of 12.40 square miles, and is located in the Eastern Time Zone at 42.23° N. Lat., 78.63° W. Long. The county was founded in 1808. County seat is Little Valley.

Cattaraugus County is part of the Olean, NY Micropolitan Statistical Area. The entire metro area includes: Cattaraugus County, NY

Weather Station: Allegany State Park         Elevation: 1,500 feet

|  | Jan | Feb | Mar | Apr | May | Jun | Jul | Aug | Sep | Oct | Nov | Dec |
|---|---|---|---|---|---|---|---|---|---|---|---|---|
| High | 30 | 33 | 42 | 55 | 67 | 75 | 78 | 76 | 69 | 57 | 46 | 35 |
| Low | 13 | 14 | 20 | 32 | 41 | 50 | 54 | 53 | 47 | 36 | 29 | 19 |
| Precip | 3.0 | 2.3 | 3.1 | 3.5 | 3.8 | 4.9 | 4.6 | 4.1 | 4.1 | 3.8 | 3.9 | 3.4 |
| Snow | na | na | 10.5 | 2.1 | tr | 0.0 | 0.0 | 0.0 | 0.0 | 0.1 | 4.3 | na |

*High and Low temperatures in degrees Fahrenheit; Precipitation and Snow in inches*

Weather Station: Franklinville         Elevation: 1,549 feet

|  | Jan | Feb | Mar | Apr | May | Jun | Jul | Aug | Sep | Oct | Nov | Dec |
|---|---|---|---|---|---|---|---|---|---|---|---|---|
| High | 30 | 32 | 40 | 54 | 66 | 74 | 78 | 77 | 70 | 58 | 46 | 34 |
| Low | 12 | 12 | 18 | 31 | 39 | 49 | 54 | 53 | 46 | 35 | 28 | 18 |
| Precip | 2.6 | 2.1 | 2.9 | 3.3 | 3.7 | 4.4 | 4.5 | 4.0 | 4.4 | 3.8 | 3.6 | 3.1 |
| Snow | 27.8 | 17.7 | 16.7 | 4.0 | 0.2 | 0.0 | 0.0 | 0.0 | 0.0 | 0.6 | 10.2 | 25.6 |

*High and Low temperatures in degrees Fahrenheit; Precipitation and Snow in inches*

Weather Station: Little Valley         Elevation: 1,625 feet

|  | Jan | Feb | Mar | Apr | May | Jun | Jul | Aug | Sep | Oct | Nov | Dec |
|---|---|---|---|---|---|---|---|---|---|---|---|---|
| High | 30 | 33 | 41 | 54 | 66 | 74 | 78 | 77 | 70 | 58 | 46 | 34 |
| Low | 13 | 14 | 20 | 32 | 41 | 50 | 55 | 54 | 47 | 37 | 30 | 19 |
| Precip | 3.2 | 2.5 | 3.1 | 3.6 | 3.6 | 4.4 | 4.5 | 4.0 | 4.5 | 4.3 | 4.3 | 3.8 |
| Snow | 28.2 | 19.8 | 16.7 | 4.5 | 0.3 | 0.0 | 0.0 | 0.0 | 0.0 | 0.8 | 12.9 | 30.3 |

*High and Low temperatures in degrees Fahrenheit; Precipitation and Snow in inches*

**Population:** 84,234 (1990); 83,955 (2000); 80,317 (2010); Race: 92.9% White, 1.3% Black, 0.7% Asian, 3.0% American Indian/Alaska Native, 0.0% Native Hawaiian/Other Pacific Islander, 2.1% Other, 1.7% Hispanic of any race (2010); Density: 61.3 persons per square mile (2010); Average household size: 2.41 (2010); Median age: 40.7 (2010); Males per 100 females: 97.9 (2010).
**Religion:** Six largest groups: 15.4% Catholicism, 5.4% Methodist/Pietist, 2.5% Lutheran, 2.2% Holiness, 1.9% Non-Denominational, 1.9% Muslim Estimate (2010)
**Economy:** Unemployment rate: 9.7% (February 2012); Total civilian labor force: 41,087 (February 2012); Leading industries: 17.4% retail trade; 17.4% manufacturing; 17.3% accommodation & food services (2009); Farms: 1,122 totaling 183,439 acres (2007); Companies that employ 500 or more persons: 6 (2009); Companies that employ 100 to 499 persons: 25 (2009); Companies that employ less than 100 persons: 1,732 (2009); Black-owned businesses: n/a (2007); Hispanic-owned businesses: n/a (2007); Asian-owned businesses: 75 (2007); Women-owned businesses: 1,494 (2007); Retail sales per capita: $13,848 (2010). Single-family

building permits issued: 85 (2011); Multi-family building permits issued: 0 (2011).

**Income:** Per capita income: $20,824 (2006-2010 5-year est.); Median household income: $42,466 (2006-2010 5-year est.); Average household income: $50,935 (2006-2010 5-year est.); Percent of households with income of $100,000 or more: 9.2% (2006-2010 5-year est.); Poverty rate: 16.0% (2006-2010 5-year est.); Bankruptcy rate: 2.30% (2011).

**Education:** Percent of population age 25 and over with: High school diploma (including GED) or higher: 87.4% (2006-2010 5-year est.); Bachelor's degree or higher: 18.1% (2006-2010 5-year est.); Master's degree or higher: 8.4% (2006-2010 5-year est.).

**Housing:** Homeownership rate: 72.3% (2010); Median home value: $77,000 (2006-2010 5-year est.); Median contract rent: $421 per month (2006-2010 5-year est.); Median year structure built: 1956 (2006-2010 5-year est.)

**Health:** Birth rate: 119.3 per 10,000 population (2011); Death rate: 101.2 per 10,000 population (2011); Age-adjusted cancer mortality rate: 182.1 deaths per 100,000 population (2009); Number of physicians: 13.8 per 10,000 population (2008); Hospital beds: 91.2 per 10,000 population (2007); Hospital admissions: 1,696.9 per 10,000 population (2007).

**Elections:** 2008 Presidential election results: 43.9% Obama, 54.5% McCain, 0.9% Nader

**National and State Parks:** Allegany State Park; Harry E Dobbins Memorial State Forest

**Additional Information Contacts**
Cattaraugus County Government . . . . . . . . . . . . . . . (716) 938-9111
   http://www.cattco.org
City of Olean . . . . . . . . . . . . . . . . . . . . . . . . . . . . (716) 376-5600
   http://www.cityofolean.com
Ellicottville Chamber of Commerce . . . . . . . . . . . . . (716) 699-5046
   http://www.ellicottvilleny.com
Franklinville Area Chamber of Commerce . . . . . . . . (716) 676-5013
   http://franklinvillechamber.org/wordpress
Gowanda Area Chamber of Commerce . . . . . . . . . . (716) 532-2834
   http://gowandachamber.com
Greater Olean Area Chamber of Commerce . . . . . . . (716) 372-4433
   http://oleanny.com
Greater Olean Area Chamber of Commerce . . . . . . . (716) 372-4433
   http://www.oleanny.com
Seneca Salamanca Chamber of Commerce . . . . . . . (716) 945-2034
   http://salamancachamber.org
Town of Allegany . . . . . . . . . . . . . . . . . . . . . . . . . (716) 373-0120
   http://www.allegany.org
Town of Franklinville . . . . . . . . . . . . . . . . . . . . . . . (716) 676-3077
   http://www.franklinvilleny.org
Village of Allegany . . . . . . . . . . . . . . . . . . . . . . . . (716) 373-1460
   http://www.allegany.org
Village of Franklinville . . . . . . . . . . . . . . . . . . . . . . (716) 676-3010
   http://www.franklinvilleny.org

## Cattaraugus County Communities

**ALLEGANY** (village). Covers a land area of 0.705 square miles and a water area of 0.007 square miles. Located at 42.09° N. Lat; 78.49° W. Long. Elevation is 1,421 feet.

**Population:** 2,104 (1990); 1,883 (2000); 1,816 (2010); Density: 2,574.3 persons per square mile (2010); Race: 96.1% White, 0.2% Black, 2.2% Asian, 0.1% American Indian/Alaska Native, 0.0% Native Hawaiian/Other Pacific Islander, 1.4% Other, 2.0% Hispanic of any race (2010); Average household size: 2.37 (2010); Median age: 36.8 (2010); Males per 100 females: 90.8 (2010); Marriage status: 32.0% never married, 50.4% now married, 7.8% widowed, 9.8% divorced (2006-2010 5-year est.); Foreign born: 3.8% (2006-2010 5-year est.); Ancestry (includes multiple ancestries): 30.8% Irish, 28.5% German, 24.9% Italian, 13.0% English, 10.9% Polish (2006-2010 5-year est.).

**Economy:** Single-family building permits issued: 0 (2011); Multi-family building permits issued: 0 (2011); Employment by occupation: 14.6% management, 4.3% professional, 4.7% services, 21.2% sales, 2.9% farming, 3.5% construction, 3.2% production (2006-2010 5-year est.).

**Income:** Per capita income: $24,369 (2006-2010 5-year est.); Median household income: $43,472 (2006-2010 5-year est.); Average household income: $54,959 (2006-2010 5-year est.); Percent of households with income of $100,000 or more: 16.2% (2006-2010 5-year est.); Poverty rate: 15.4% (2006-2010 5-year est.).

**Education:** Percent of population age 25 and over with: High school diploma (including GED) or higher: 95.2% (2006-2010 5-year est.); Bachelor's degree or higher: 33.5% (2006-2010 5-year est.); Master's degree or higher: 16.3% (2006-2010 5-year est.).
**School District(s)**
Allegany-Limestone Central School District (PK-12)
   2009-10 Enrollment: 1,333 . . . . . . . . . . . . . . . . (716) 375-6600

**Housing:** Homeownership rate: 63.2% (2010); Median home value: $97,800 (2006-2010 5-year est.); Median contract rent: $422 per month (2006-2010 5-year est.); Median year structure built: 1950 (2006-2010 5-year est.).

**Safety:** Violent crime rate: 11.7 per 10,000 population; Property crime rate: 99.1 per 10,000 population (2010).

**Transportation:** Commute to work: 91.8% car, 0.0% public transportation, 4.3% walk, 3.1% work from home (2006-2010 5-year est.); Travel time to work: 66.0% less than 15 minutes, 19.0% 15 to 30 minutes, 8.3% 30 to 45 minutes, 1.5% 45 to 60 minutes, 5.1% 60 minutes or more (2006-2010 5-year est.)

**Additional Information Contacts**
Village of Allegany . . . . . . . . . . . . . . . . . . . . . . . . (716) 373-1460
   http://www.allegany.org

**ALLEGANY** (town). Covers a land area of 70.922 square miles and a water area of 0.657 square miles. Located at 42.09° N. Lat; 78.53° W. Long. Elevation is 1,421 feet.

**History:** Incorporated 1906.

**Population:** 8,327 (1990); 8,230 (2000); 8,004 (2010); Density: 112.9 persons per square mile (2010); Race: 94.1% White, 1.9% Black, 1.9% Asian, 0.3% American Indian/Alaska Native, 0.0% Native Hawaiian/Other Pacific Islander, 1.8% Other, 1.9% Hispanic of any race (2010); Average household size: 2.39 (2010); Median age: 34.5 (2010); Males per 100 females: 90.8 (2010); Marriage status: 46.0% never married, 40.7% now married, 5.6% widowed, 7.6% divorced (2006-2010 5-year est.); Foreign born: 3.9% (2006-2010 5-year est.); Ancestry (includes multiple ancestries): 28.8% German, 24.1% Irish, 21.4% Italian, 10.7% Polish, 9.3% English (2006-2010 5-year est.).

**Economy:** Single-family building permits issued: 5 (2011); Multi-family building permits issued: 0 (2011); Employment by occupation: 10.1% management, 1.3% professional, 12.5% services, 19.1% sales, 3.7% farming, 8.3% construction, 5.9% production (2006-2010 5-year est.).

**Income:** Per capita income: $19,675 (2006-2010 5-year est.); Median household income: $48,841 (2006-2010 5-year est.); Average household income: $56,885 (2006-2010 5-year est.); Percent of households with income of $100,000 or more: 13.7% (2006-2010 5-year est.); Poverty rate: 12.7% (2006-2010 5-year est.).

**Education:** Percent of population age 25 and over with: High school diploma (including GED) or higher: 92.4% (2006-2010 5-year est.); Bachelor's degree or higher: 27.0% (2006-2010 5-year est.); Master's degree or higher: 15.2% (2006-2010 5-year est.).
**School District(s)**
Allegany-Limestone Central School District (PK-12)
   2009-10 Enrollment: 1,333 . . . . . . . . . . . . . . . . (716) 375-6600

**Housing:** Homeownership rate: 79.1% (2010); Median home value: $91,500 (2006-2010 5-year est.); Median contract rent: $444 per month (2006-2010 5-year est.); Median year structure built: 1965 (2006-2010 5-year est.).

**Transportation:** Commute to work: 86.8% car, 1.1% public transportation, 9.7% walk, 1.8% work from home (2006-2010 5-year est.); Travel time to work: 60.9% less than 15 minutes, 28.1% 15 to 30 minutes, 6.2% 30 to 45 minutes, 2.0% 45 to 60 minutes, 2.7% 60 minutes or more (2006-2010 5-year est.)

**Additional Information Contacts**
Town of Allegany . . . . . . . . . . . . . . . . . . . . . . . . . (716) 373-0120
   http://www.allegany.org

**ALLEGANY RESERVATION** (Reservation). Covers a land area of 36.288 square miles and a water area of 7.380 square miles. Located at 42.12° N. Lat; 78.67° W. Long.

**Population:** 1,143 (1990); 1,099 (2000); 1,020 (2010); Density: 28.1 persons per square mile (2010); Race: 33.5% White, 0.4% Black, 0.0% Asian, 62.7% American Indian/Alaska Native, 0.0% Native Hawaiian/Other Pacific Islander, 3.4% Other, 3.4% Hispanic of any race (2010); Average household size: 2.62 (2010); Median age: 37.2 (2010); Males per 100 females: 92.8 (2010); Marriage status: 35.9% never married, 40.9% now married, 6.3% widowed, 16.9% divorced (2006-2010 5-year est.); Foreign

born: 9.2% (2006-2010 5-year est.); Ancestry (includes multiple ancestries): 19.1% German, 9.5% Irish, 8.7% English, 6.9% Scottish, 2.2% Polish (2006-2010 5-year est.).
**Economy:** Employment by occupation: 8.2% management, 3.0% professional, 8.0% services, 29.5% sales, 0.0% farming, 21.3% construction, 4.4% production (2006-2010 5-year est.).
**Income:** Per capita income: $15,643 (2006-2010 5-year est.); Median household income: $33,750 (2006-2010 5-year est.); Average household income: $43,747 (2006-2010 5-year est.); Percent of households with income of $100,000 or more: 7.0% (2006-2010 5-year est.); Poverty rate: 26.7% (2006-2010 5-year est.).
**Education:** Percent of population age 25 and over with: High school diploma (including GED) or higher: 86.7% (2006-2010 5-year est.); Bachelor's degree or higher: 6.6% (2006-2010 5-year est.); Master's degree or higher: 2.2% (2006-2010 5-year est.).
**Housing:** Homeownership rate: 71.0% (2010); Median home value: $57,400 (2006-2010 5-year est.); Median contract rent: $263 per month (2006-2010 5-year est.); Median year structure built: 1969 (2006-2010 5-year est.).
**Transportation:** Commute to work: 89.7% car, 0.0% public transportation, 4.8% walk, 4.4% work from home (2006-2010 5-year est.); Travel time to work: 47.4% less than 15 minutes, 35.8% 15 to 30 minutes, 11.8% 30 to 45 minutes, 1.4% 45 to 60 minutes, 3.6% 60 minutes or more (2006-2010 5-year est.)

**ASHFORD** (town). Covers a land area of 51.737 square miles and a water area of 0.164 square miles. Located at 42.44° N. Lat; 78.64° W. Long. Elevation is 1,634 feet.
**Population:** 2,162 (1990); 2,223 (2000); 2,132 (2010); Density: 41.2 persons per square mile (2010); Race: 97.8% White, 1.1% Black, 0.1% Asian, 0.3% American Indian/Alaska Native, 0.0% Native Hawaiian/Other Pacific Islander, 0.7% Other, 0.8% Hispanic of any race (2010); Average household size: 2.41 (2010); Median age: 45.0 (2010); Males per 100 females: 106.4 (2010); Marriage status: 25.4% never married, 56.7% now married, 8.4% widowed, 9.6% divorced (2006-2010 5-year est.); Foreign born: 0.9% (2006-2010 5-year est.); Ancestry (includes multiple ancestries): 46.0% German, 17.7% Irish, 17.1% Polish, 15.8% English, 7.1% Italian (2006-2010 5-year est.).
**Economy:** Single-family building permits issued: 2 (2011); Multi-family building permits issued: 0 (2011); Employment by occupation: 10.9% management, 1.5% professional, 7.7% services, 15.8% sales, 1.0% farming, 15.9% construction, 15.1% production (2006-2010 5-year est.).
**Income:** Per capita income: $21,662 (2006-2010 5-year est.); Median household income: $46,786 (2006-2010 5-year est.); Average household income: $50,713 (2006-2010 5-year est.); Percent of households with income of $100,000 or more: 9.2% (2006-2010 5-year est.); Poverty rate: 11.7% (2006-2010 5-year est.).
**Education:** Percent of population age 25 and over with: High school diploma (including GED) or higher: 86.0% (2006-2010 5-year est.); Bachelor's degree or higher: 17.8% (2006-2010 5-year est.); Master's degree or higher: 6.1% (2006-2010 5-year est.).
**Housing:** Homeownership rate: 82.7% (2010); Median home value: $87,800 (2006-2010 5-year est.); Median contract rent: $420 per month (2006-2010 5-year est.); Median year structure built: 1974 (2006-2010 5-year est.).
**Transportation:** Commute to work: 95.0% car, 0.0% public transportation, 0.0% walk, 3.4% work from home (2006-2010 5-year est.); Travel time to work: 27.2% less than 15 minutes, 32.6% 15 to 30 minutes, 14.2% 30 to 45 minutes, 14.1% 45 to 60 minutes, 11.9% 60 minutes or more (2006-2010 5-year est.)

**CARROLLTON** (town). Covers a land area of 42.298 square miles and a water area of 0.040 square miles. Located at 42.05° N. Lat; 78.63° W. Long. Elevation is 1,398 feet.
**Population:** 1,555 (1990); 1,410 (2000); 1,297 (2010); Density: 30.7 persons per square mile (2010); Race: 97.1% White, 0.5% Black, 0.4% Asian, 1.0% American Indian/Alaska Native, 0.0% Native Hawaiian/Other Pacific Islander, 1.0% Other, 0.4% Hispanic of any race (2010); Average household size: 2.37 (2010); Median age: 43.1 (2010); Males per 100 females: 95.3 (2010); Marriage status: 29.0% never married, 56.1% now married, 8.2% widowed, 6.6% divorced (2006-2010 5-year est.); Foreign born: 0.0% (2006-2010 5-year est.); Ancestry (includes multiple ancestries): 23.6% German, 18.5% Irish, 12.4% Italian, 12.0% English, 5.1% American (2006-2010 5-year est.).

**Economy:** Single-family building permits issued: 0 (2011); Multi-family building permits issued: 0 (2011); Employment by occupation: 6.3% management, 2.8% professional, 13.8% services, 16.6% sales, 3.7% farming, 10.9% construction, 8.8% production (2006-2010 5-year est.).
**Income:** Per capita income: $17,421 (2006-2010 5-year est.); Median household income: $38,846 (2006-2010 5-year est.); Average household income: $45,091 (2006-2010 5-year est.); Percent of households with income of $100,000 or more: 7.5% (2006-2010 5-year est.); Poverty rate: 19.1% (2006-2010 5-year est.).
**Education:** Percent of population age 25 and over with: High school diploma (including GED) or higher: 85.4% (2006-2010 5-year est.); Bachelor's degree or higher: 13.9% (2006-2010 5-year est.); Master's degree or higher: 4.8% (2006-2010 5-year est.).
**Housing:** Homeownership rate: 81.6% (2010); Median home value: $58,700 (2006-2010 5-year est.); Median contract rent: $323 per month (2006-2010 5-year est.); Median year structure built: 1966 (2006-2010 5-year est.).
**Transportation:** Commute to work: 94.3% car, 0.5% public transportation, 0.9% walk, 3.6% work from home (2006-2010 5-year est.); Travel time to work: 28.2% less than 15 minutes, 51.9% 15 to 30 minutes, 7.8% 30 to 45 minutes, 5.3% 45 to 60 minutes, 6.8% 60 minutes or more (2006-2010 5-year est.)

**CATTARAUGUS** (village). Covers a land area of 1.117 square miles and a water area of 0.002 square miles. Located at 42.32° N. Lat; 78.86° W. Long. Elevation is 1,375 feet.
**History:** Settled 1851 during construction of Erie Railroad; incorporated 1882.
**Population:** 1,100 (1990); 1,075 (2000); 1,002 (2010); Density: 896.7 persons per square mile (2010); Race: 98.4% White, 0.3% Black, 0.0% Asian, 0.7% American Indian/Alaska Native, 0.0% Native Hawaiian/Other Pacific Islander, 0.6% Other, 1.9% Hispanic of any race (2010); Average household size: 2.41 (2010); Median age: 40.7 (2010); Males per 100 females: 94.2 (2010); Marriage status: 22.7% never married, 58.1% now married, 10.2% widowed, 9.0% divorced (2006-2010 5-year est.); Foreign born: 0.7% (2006-2010 5-year est.); Ancestry (includes multiple ancestries): 37.6% German, 18.6% English, 17.4% Irish, 11.3% Polish, 6.7% American (2006-2010 5-year est.).
**Economy:** Single-family building permits issued: 0 (2011); Multi-family building permits issued: 0 (2011); Employment by occupation: 11.5% management, 2.6% professional, 15.0% services, 13.9% sales, 2.4% farming, 9.2% construction, 5.7% production (2006-2010 5-year est.).
**Income:** Per capita income: $20,284 (2006-2010 5-year est.); Median household income: $40,250 (2006-2010 5-year est.); Average household income: $48,649 (2006-2010 5-year est.); Percent of households with income of $100,000 or more: 9.4% (2006-2010 5-year est.); Poverty rate: 14.3% (2006-2010 5-year est.).
**Education:** Percent of population age 25 and over with: High school diploma (including GED) or higher: 87.9% (2006-2010 5-year est.); Bachelor's degree or higher: 23.7% (2006-2010 5-year est.); Master's degree or higher: 9.7% (2006-2010 5-year est.).
**School District(s)**
Cattaraugus-Little Valley Central School District (PK-12)
    2009-10 Enrollment: 1,012 . . . . . . . . . . . . . . . . . . . . . . . . . (716) 257-5292
**Housing:** Homeownership rate: 71.5% (2010); Median home value: $56,700 (2006-2010 5-year est.); Median contract rent: $375 per month (2006-2010 5-year est.); Median year structure built: before 1940 (2006-2010 5-year est.).
**Transportation:** Commute to work: 87.7% car, 0.0% public transportation, 8.1% walk, 2.8% work from home (2006-2010 5-year est.); Travel time to work: 39.3% less than 15 minutes, 23.3% 15 to 30 minutes, 21.9% 30 to 45 minutes, 9.3% 45 to 60 minutes, 6.2% 60 minutes or more (2006-2010 5-year est.)

**CATTARAUGUS RESERVATION** (Reservation). Covers a land area of 5.844 square miles and a water area of 0.194 square miles. Located at 42.53° N. Lat; 79.03° W. Long.
**Population:** 359 (1990); 388 (2000); 314 (2010); Density: 53.7 persons per square mile (2010); Race: 6.4% White, 0.0% Black, 0.0% Asian, 90.1% American Indian/Alaska Native, 0.0% Native Hawaiian/Other Pacific Islander, 3.5% Other, 3.5% Hispanic of any race (2010); Average household size: 3.17 (2010); Median age: 30.0 (2010); Males per 100 females: 84.7 (2010); Marriage status: 17.0% never married, 68.0% now married, 5.7% widowed, 9.3% divorced (2006-2010 5-year est.); Foreign

born: 4.1% (2006-2010 5-year est.); Ancestry (includes multiple ancestries): 4.3% American, 2.0% French (2006-2010 5-year est.).
**Economy:** Employment by occupation: 15.9% management, 0.0% professional, 0.0% services, 26.1% sales, 10.1% farming, 20.3% construction, 0.0% production (2006-2010 5-year est.).
**Income:** Per capita income: $12,449 (2006-2010 5-year est.); Median household income: $37,813 (2006-2010 5-year est.); Average household income: $43,915 (2006-2010 5-year est.); Percent of households with income of $100,000 or more: 4.1% (2006-2010 5-year est.); Poverty rate: 54.2% (2006-2010 5-year est.).
**Education:** Percent of population age 25 and over with: High school diploma (including GED) or higher: 100.0% (2006-2010 5-year est.); Bachelor's degree or higher: 10.6% (2006-2010 5-year est.); Master's degree or higher: 0.0% (2006-2010 5-year est.).
**Housing:** Homeownership rate: 80.8% (2010); Median home value: $118,800 (2006-2010 5-year est.); Median contract rent: $234 per month (2006-2010 5-year est.); Median year structure built: 2000 (2006-2010 5-year est.).
**Transportation:** Commute to work: 100.0% car, 0.0% public transportation, 0.0% walk, 0.0% work from home (2006-2010 5-year est.); Travel time to work: 42.0% less than 15 minutes, 0.0% 15 to 30 minutes, 43.5% 30 to 45 minutes, 10.1% 45 to 60 minutes, 4.3% 60 minutes or more (2006-2010 5-year est.)

## COLDSPRING (town).
Covers a land area of 51.464 square miles and a water area of 0.553 square miles. Located at 42.05° N. Lat; 78.84° W. Long. Elevation is 1,407 feet.
**Population:** 732 (1990); 751 (2000); 663 (2010); Density: 12.9 persons per square mile (2010); Race: 96.7% White, 0.3% Black, 0.0% Asian, 2.1% American Indian/Alaska Native, 0.0% Native Hawaiian/Other Pacific Islander, 0.9% Other, 1.1% Hispanic of any race (2010); Average household size: 2.38 (2010); Median age: 44.8 (2010); Males per 100 females: 108.5 (2010); Marriage status: 21.3% never married, 58.3% now married, 5.2% widowed, 15.3% divorced (2006-2010 5-year est.); Foreign born: 1.2% (2006-2010 5-year est.); Ancestry (includes multiple ancestries): 22.6% German, 19.7% English, 18.9% Irish, 9.4% American, 7.0% Swedish (2006-2010 5-year est.).
**Economy:** Single-family building permits issued: 2 (2011); Multi-family building permits issued: 0 (2011); Employment by occupation: 12.6% management, 1.7% professional, 11.8% services, 14.3% sales, 0.8% farming, 5.3% construction, 4.8% production (2006-2010 5-year est.).
**Income:** Per capita income: $21,690 (2006-2010 5-year est.); Median household income: $49,152 (2006-2010 5-year est.); Average household income: $56,451 (2006-2010 5-year est.); Percent of households with income of $100,000 or more: 6.8% (2006-2010 5-year est.); Poverty rate: 11.2% (2006-2010 5-year est.).
**Education:** Percent of population age 25 and over with: High school diploma (including GED) or higher: 87.0% (2006-2010 5-year est.); Bachelor's degree or higher: 8.7% (2006-2010 5-year est.); Master's degree or higher: 4.3% (2006-2010 5-year est.).
**Housing:** Homeownership rate: 84.9% (2010); Median home value: $71,400 (2006-2010 5-year est.); Median contract rent: $375 per month (2006-2010 5-year est.); Median year structure built: 1958 (2006-2010 5-year est.).
**Transportation:** Commute to work: 85.3% car, 0.0% public transportation, 3.1% walk, 11.6% work from home (2006-2010 5-year est.); Travel time to work: 26.6% less than 15 minutes, 32.7% 15 to 30 minutes, 31.1% 30 to 45 minutes, 1.9% 45 to 60 minutes, 7.7% 60 minutes or more (2006-2010 5-year est.)

## CONEWANGO (town).
Covers a land area of 36.114 square miles and a water area of 0.022 square miles. Located at 42.22° N. Lat; 79.00° W. Long. Elevation is 1,293 feet.
**Population:** 1,702 (1990); 1,732 (2000); 1,857 (2010); Density: 51.4 persons per square mile (2010); Race: 98.1% White, 0.3% Black, 0.3% Asian, 0.3% American Indian/Alaska Native, 0.0% Native Hawaiian/Other Pacific Islander, 1.0% Other, 1.0% Hispanic of any race (2010); Average household size: 3.58 (2010); Median age: 23.8 (2010); Males per 100 females: 100.8 (2010); Marriage status: 24.5% never married, 62.1% now married, 4.5% widowed, 8.9% divorced (2006-2010 5-year est.); Foreign born: 0.2% (2006-2010 5-year est.); Ancestry (includes multiple ancestries): 23.6% German, 18.0% Pennsylvania German, 15.4% Irish, 13.4% English, 7.2% Italian (2006-2010 5-year est.).
**Economy:** Single-family building permits issued: 0 (2011); Multi-family building permits issued: 0 (2011); Employment by occupation: 11.2%

management, 2.0% professional, 9.9% services, 13.7% sales, 4.8% farming, 14.7% construction, 6.0% production (2006-2010 5-year est.).
**Income:** Per capita income: $14,203 (2006-2010 5-year est.); Median household income: $43,603 (2006-2010 5-year est.); Average household income: $44,371 (2006-2010 5-year est.); Percent of households with income of $100,000 or more: 3.4% (2006-2010 5-year est.); Poverty rate: 24.0% (2006-2010 5-year est.).
**Education:** Percent of population age 25 and over with: High school diploma (including GED) or higher: 70.6% (2006-2010 5-year est.); Bachelor's degree or higher: 6.2% (2006-2010 5-year est.); Master's degree or higher: 3.1% (2006-2010 5-year est.).
**Housing:** Homeownership rate: 79.7% (2010); Median home value: $70,800 (2006-2010 5-year est.); Median contract rent: $390 per month (2006-2010 5-year est.); Median year structure built: 1967 (2006-2010 5-year est.).
**Transportation:** Commute to work: 78.8% car, 0.0% public transportation, 7.3% walk, 8.4% work from home (2006-2010 5-year est.); Travel time to work: 29.2% less than 15 minutes, 31.5% 15 to 30 minutes, 26.3% 30 to 45 minutes, 8.6% 45 to 60 minutes, 4.4% 60 minutes or more (2006-2010 5-year est.)

## CONEWANGO VALLEY (unincorporated postal area)
Zip Code: 14726
Covers a land area of 40.668 square miles and a water area of <.001 square miles. Located at 42.25° N. Lat; 79.02° W. Long. Population: 2,156 (2010); Density: 53.0 persons per square mile (2010); Race: 98.2% White, 0.3% Black, 0.0% Asian, 0.4% American Indian/Alaska Native, 0.0% Native Hawaiian/Other Pacific Islander, 1.1% Other, 0.8% Hispanic of any race (2010); Average household size: 3.76 (2010); Median age: 22.0 (2010); Males per 100 females: 103.0 (2010); Homeownership rate: 81.5% (2010)

## DAYTON (town).
Covers a land area of 35.527 square miles and a water area of 0.617 square miles. Located at 42.37° N. Lat; 78.99° W. Long. Elevation is 1,339 feet.
**Population:** 1,915 (1990); 1,945 (2000); 1,886 (2010); Density: 53.1 persons per square mile (2010); Race: 96.3% White, 0.7% Black, 0.3% Asian, 0.9% American Indian/Alaska Native, 0.0% Native Hawaiian/Other Pacific Islander, 1.8% Other, 0.6% Hispanic of any race (2010); Average household size: 2.57 (2010); Median age: 40.5 (2010); Males per 100 females: 102.6 (2010); Marriage status: 30.7% never married, 56.4% now married, 6.1% widowed, 6.9% divorced (2006-2010 5-year est.); Foreign born: 1.0% (2006-2010 5-year est.); Ancestry (includes multiple ancestries): 48.5% German, 18.4% Irish, 17.0% English, 11.0% Polish, 8.0% Italian (2006-2010 5-year est.).
**Economy:** Single-family building permits issued: 1 (2011); Multi-family building permits issued: 0 (2011); Employment by occupation: 7.0% management, 0.7% professional, 15.2% services, 19.5% sales, 3.8% farming, 15.1% construction, 12.5% production (2006-2010 5-year est.).
**Income:** Per capita income: $18,866 (2006-2010 5-year est.); Median household income: $50,694 (2006-2010 5-year est.); Average household income: $52,710 (2006-2010 5-year est.); Percent of households with income of $100,000 or more: 5.4% (2006-2010 5-year est.); Poverty rate: 13.6% (2006-2010 5-year est.).
**Education:** Percent of population age 25 and over with: High school diploma (including GED) or higher: 85.8% (2006-2010 5-year est.); Bachelor's degree or higher: 11.1% (2006-2010 5-year est.); Master's degree or higher: 3.1% (2006-2010 5-year est.).
**Housing:** Homeownership rate: 78.7% (2010); Median home value: $63,800 (2006-2010 5-year est.); Median contract rent: $421 per month (2006-2010 5-year est.); Median year structure built: before 1940 (2006-2010 5-year est.).
**Transportation:** Commute to work: 91.5% car, 0.0% public transportation, 2.7% walk, 2.7% work from home (2006-2010 5-year est.); Travel time to work: 24.5% less than 15 minutes, 36.2% 15 to 30 minutes, 23.2% 30 to 45 minutes, 6.2% 45 to 60 minutes, 9.9% 60 minutes or more (2006-2010 5-year est.)

## DELEVAN (village).
Covers a land area of 0.993 square miles and a water area of 0 square miles. Located at 42.49° N. Lat; 78.47° W. Long. Elevation is 1,424 feet.
**Population:** 1,214 (1990); 1,089 (2000); 1,089 (2010); Density: 1,095.6 persons per square mile (2010); Race: 97.5% White, 0.3% Black, 0.9% Asian, 0.4% American Indian/Alaska Native, 0.0% Native Hawaiian/Other Pacific Islander, 0.9% Other, 0.4% Hispanic of any race (2010); Average

household size: 2.46 (2010); Median age: 36.3 (2010); Males per 100 females: 98.7 (2010); Marriage status: 30.3% never married, 50.9% now married, 7.1% widowed, 11.7% divorced (2006-2010 5-year est.); Foreign born: 0.3% (2006-2010 5-year est.); Ancestry (includes multiple ancestries): 35.6% German, 19.9% Polish, 17.8% Irish, 12.7% English, 4.5% Italian (2006-2010 5-year est.).

**Economy:** Single-family building permits issued: 0 (2011); Multi-family building permits issued: 0 (2011); Employment by occupation: 7.1% management, 1.1% professional, 20.8% services, 15.5% sales, 3.2% farming, 9.4% construction, 10.3% production (2006-2010 5-year est.).

**Income:** Per capita income: $16,783 (2006-2010 5-year est.); Median household income: $39,293 (2006-2010 5-year est.); Average household income: $41,695 (2006-2010 5-year est.); Percent of households with income of $100,000 or more: 4.1% (2006-2010 5-year est.); Poverty rate: 20.7% (2006-2010 5-year est.).

**Education:** Percent of population age 25 and over with: High school diploma (including GED) or higher: 82.9% (2006-2010 5-year est.); Bachelor's degree or higher: 11.1% (2006-2010 5-year est.); Master's degree or higher: 4.0% (2006-2010 5-year est.).

### School District(s)
Yorkshire-Pioneer Central School District (PK-12)

   2009-10 Enrollment: 2,515 . . . . . . . . . . . . . . . . . . (716) 492-9304

**Housing:** Homeownership rate: 56.2% (2010); Median home value: $100,400 (2006-2010 5-year est.); Median contract rent: $334 per month (2006-2010 5-year est.); Median year structure built: 1962 (2006-2010 5-year est.).

**Transportation:** Commute to work: 91.3% car, 0.7% public transportation, 3.1% walk, 5.0% work from home (2006-2010 5-year est.); Travel time to work: 42.1% less than 15 minutes, 18.4% 15 to 30 minutes, 15.2% 30 to 45 minutes, 16.8% 45 to 60 minutes, 7.6% 60 minutes or more (2006-2010 5-year est.)

---

**EAST OTTO** (town). Covers a land area of 40.070 square miles and a water area of 0.325 square miles. Located at 42.40° N. Lat; 78.74° W. Long. Elevation is 1,427 feet.

**Population:** 1,003 (1990); 1,105 (2000); 1,062 (2010); Density: 26.5 persons per square mile (2010); Race: 98.0% White, 0.5% Black, 0.3% Asian, 0.3% American Indian/Alaska Native, 0.0% Native Hawaiian/Other Pacific Islander, 0.9% Other, 0.3% Hispanic of any race (2010); Average household size: 2.50 (2010); Median age: 41.5 (2010); Males per 100 females: 113.7 (2010); Marriage status: 28.8% never married, 58.4% now married, 2.0% widowed, 10.8% divorced (2006-2010 5-year est.); Foreign born: 0.5% (2006-2010 5-year est.); Ancestry (includes multiple ancestries): 50.6% German, 13.0% Irish, 12.1% Polish, 10.1% English, 9.0% Italian (2006-2010 5-year est.).

**Economy:** Single-family building permits issued: 2 (2011); Multi-family building permits issued: 0 (2011); Employment by occupation: 7.6% management, 1.7% professional, 11.1% services, 13.5% sales, 2.8% farming, 20.9% construction, 9.8% production (2006-2010 5-year est.).

**Income:** Per capita income: $19,291 (2006-2010 5-year est.); Median household income: $46,923 (2006-2010 5-year est.); Average household income: $50,160 (2006-2010 5-year est.); Percent of households with income of $100,000 or more: 7.0% (2006-2010 5-year est.); Poverty rate: 13.8% (2006-2010 5-year est.).

**Education:** Percent of population age 25 and over with: High school diploma (including GED) or higher: 87.4% (2006-2010 5-year est.); Bachelor's degree or higher: 12.1% (2006-2010 5-year est.); Master's degree or higher: 5.0% (2006-2010 5-year est.).

**Housing:** Homeownership rate: 83.5% (2010); Median home value: $92,800 (2006-2010 5-year est.); Median contract rent: $431 per month (2006-2010 5-year est.); Median year structure built: 1973 (2006-2010 5-year est.).

**Transportation:** Commute to work: 91.0% car, 0.0% public transportation, 3.2% walk, 4.8% work from home (2006-2010 5-year est.); Travel time to work: 16.3% less than 15 minutes, 45.3% 15 to 30 minutes, 14.4% 30 to 45 minutes, 13.4% 45 to 60 minutes, 10.5% 60 minutes or more (2006-2010 5-year est.)

---

**EAST RANDOLPH** (village). Covers a land area of 1.088 square miles and a water area of <.001 square miles. Located at 42.16° N. Lat; 78.95° W. Long. Elevation is 1,325 feet.

**Population:** 629 (1990); 630 (2000); 620 (2010); Density: 569.6 persons per square mile (2010); Race: 94.7% White, 2.9% Black, 0.3% Asian, 0.5% American Indian/Alaska Native, 0.0% Native Hawaiian/Other Pacific Islander, 1.6% Other, 5.6% Hispanic of any race (2010); Average

household size: 2.59 (2010); Median age: 34.4 (2010); Males per 100 females: 112.3 (2010); Marriage status: 33.4% never married, 55.0% now married, 5.0% widowed, 6.5% divorced (2006-2010 5-year est.); Foreign born: 1.0% (2006-2010 5-year est.); Ancestry (includes multiple ancestries): 29.3% German, 23.3% Irish, 15.7% English, 5.8% American, 4.8% Swedish (2006-2010 5-year est.).

**Economy:** Single-family building permits issued: 1 (2011); Multi-family building permits issued: 0 (2011); Employment by occupation: 5.7% management, 2.6% professional, 18.7% services, 11.4% sales, 5.7% farming, 15.5% construction, 5.7% production (2006-2010 5-year est.).

**Income:** Per capita income: $17,108 (2006-2010 5-year est.); Median household income: $45,139 (2006-2010 5-year est.); Average household income: $48,770 (2006-2010 5-year est.); Percent of households with income of $100,000 or more: 8.3% (2006-2010 5-year est.); Poverty rate: 12.7% (2006-2010 5-year est.).

**Education:** Percent of population age 25 and over with: High school diploma (including GED) or higher: 95.5% (2006-2010 5-year est.); Bachelor's degree or higher: 17.3% (2006-2010 5-year est.); Master's degree or higher: 10.0% (2006-2010 5-year est.).

**Housing:** Homeownership rate: 61.9% (2010); Median home value: $82,500 (2006-2010 5-year est.); Median contract rent: $367 per month (2006-2010 5-year est.); Median year structure built: before 1940 (2006-2010 5-year est.).

**Transportation:** Commute to work: 91.4% car, 0.0% public transportation, 3.8% walk, 4.8% work from home (2006-2010 5-year est.); Travel time to work: 41.2% less than 15 minutes, 34.5% 15 to 30 minutes, 14.7% 30 to 45 minutes, 6.8% 45 to 60 minutes, 2.8% 60 minutes or more (2006-2010 5-year est.)

---

**ELLICOTTVILLE** (village). Covers a land area of 0.820 square miles and a water area of 0.013 square miles. Located at 42.27° N. Lat; 78.67° W. Long. Elevation is 1,549 feet.

**Population:** 513 (1990); 472 (2000); 376 (2010); Density: 458.3 persons per square mile (2010); Race: 98.4% White, 0.0% Black, 0.0% Asian, 0.3% American Indian/Alaska Native, 0.0% Native Hawaiian/Other Pacific Islander, 1.3% Other, 0.3% Hispanic of any race (2010); Average household size: 1.79 (2010); Median age: 51.4 (2010); Males per 100 females: 106.6 (2010); Marriage status: 30.4% never married, 56.2% now married, 8.5% widowed, 4.9% divorced (2006-2010 5-year est.); Foreign born: 7.3% (2006-2010 5-year est.); Ancestry (includes multiple ancestries): 42.7% German, 22.8% Irish, 9.6% Polish, 9.6% French, 7.9% Italian (2006-2010 5-year est.).

**Economy:** Single-family building permits issued: 8 (2011); Multi-family building permits issued: 0 (2011); Employment by occupation: 19.3% management, 9.7% professional, 1.4% services, 23.7% sales, 5.3% farming, 0.0% construction, 10.1% production (2006-2010 5-year est.).

**Income:** Per capita income: $35,472 (2006-2010 5-year est.); Median household income: $42,917 (2006-2010 5-year est.); Average household income: $69,349 (2006-2010 5-year est.); Percent of households with income of $100,000 or more: 14.4% (2006-2010 5-year est.); Poverty rate: 2.1% (2006-2010 5-year est.).

**Education:** Percent of population age 25 and over with: High school diploma (including GED) or higher: 97.2% (2006-2010 5-year est.); Bachelor's degree or higher: 29.5% (2006-2010 5-year est.); Master's degree or higher: 19.7% (2006-2010 5-year est.).

### School District(s)
Ellicottville Central School District (PK-12)

   2009-10 Enrollment: 595 . . . . . . . . . . . . . . . . . . . (716) 699-2368

**Housing:** Homeownership rate: 67.1% (2010); Median home value: $222,400 (2006-2010 5-year est.); Median contract rent: $417 per month (2006-2010 5-year est.); Median year structure built: before 1940 (2006-2010 5-year est.).

**Transportation:** Commute to work: 59.9% car, 0.0% public transportation, 32.9% walk, 7.2% work from home (2006-2010 5-year est.); Travel time to work: 57.8% less than 15 minutes, 13.0% 15 to 30 minutes, 12.5% 30 to 45 minutes, 9.9% 45 to 60 minutes, 6.8% 60 minutes or more (2006-2010 5-year est.)

**Additional Information Contacts**
Ellicottville Chamber of Commerce . . . . . . . . . . . . . . . . . . (716) 699-5046
  http://www.ellicottvilleny.com

---

**ELLICOTTVILLE** (town). Covers a land area of 45.095 square miles and a water area of 0.092 square miles. Located at 42.30° N. Lat; 78.64° W. Long. Elevation is 1,549 feet.

**History:** Incorporated 1881.

**Population:** 1,607 (1990); 1,738 (2000); 1,598 (2010); Density: 35.4 persons per square mile (2010); Race: 96.8% White, 0.2% Black, 0.3% Asian, 0.8% American Indian/Alaska Native, 0.1% Native Hawaiian/Other Pacific Islander, 1.8% Other, 1.4% Hispanic of any race (2010); Average household size: 2.10 (2010); Median age: 49.3 (2010); Males per 100 females: 104.9 (2010); Marriage status: 23.9% never married, 53.3% now married, 10.0% widowed, 12.9% divorced (2006-2010 5-year est.); Foreign born: 3.0% (2006-2010 5-year est.); Ancestry (includes multiple ancestries): 40.6% German, 20.2% Irish, 15.7% Polish, 11.1% Italian, 10.3% English (2006-2010 5-year est.).
**Economy:** Single-family building permits issued: 7 (2011); Multi-family building permits issued: 0 (2011); Employment by occupation: 12.7% management, 3.9% professional, 6.2% services, 18.2% sales, 2.9% farming, 8.4% construction, 6.6% production (2006-2010 5-year est.).
**Income:** Per capita income: $24,788 (2006-2010 5-year est.); Median household income: $39,737 (2006-2010 5-year est.); Average household income: $55,540 (2006-2010 5-year est.); Percent of households with income of $100,000 or more: 11.8% (2006-2010 5-year est.); Poverty rate: 8.2% (2006-2010 5-year est.).
**Education:** Percent of population age 25 and over with: High school diploma (including GED) or higher: 93.7% (2006-2010 5-year est.); Bachelor's degree or higher: 31.5% (2006-2010 5-year est.); Master's degree or higher: 14.9% (2006-2010 5-year est.).

**School District(s)**

Ellicottville Central School District (PK-12)
  2009-10 Enrollment: 595 . . . . . . . . . . . . . . . . . . . . . (716) 699-2368
**Housing:** Homeownership rate: 75.6% (2010); Median home value: $174,000 (2006-2010 5-year est.); Median contract rent: $428 per month (2006-2010 5-year est.); Median year structure built: 1981 (2006-2010 5-year est.).
**Safety:** Violent crime rate: 0.0 per 10,000 population; Property crime rate: 2,181.5 per 10,000 population (2010).
**Transportation:** Commute to work: 82.1% car, 0.5% public transportation, 12.0% walk, 5.0% work from home (2006-2010 5-year est.); Travel time to work: 44.4% less than 15 minutes, 21.5% 15 to 30 minutes, 11.0% 30 to 45 minutes, 9.7% 45 to 60 minutes, 13.4% 60 minutes or more (2006-2010 5-year est.)

## FARMERSVILLE (town). Covers a land area of 47.832 square miles and a water area of 0.137 square miles. Located at 42.38° N. Lat; 78.40° W. Long. Elevation is 1,837 feet.
**Population:** 869 (1990); 1,028 (2000); 1,090 (2010); Density: 22.8 persons per square mile (2010); Race: 97.2% White, 0.2% Black, 0.1% Asian, 0.4% American Indian/Alaska Native, 0.0% Native Hawaiian/Other Pacific Islander, 2.1% Other, 1.7% Hispanic of any race (2010); Average household size: 2.45 (2010); Median age: 44.3 (2010); Males per 100 females: 97.5 (2010); Marriage status: 23.0% never married, 58.0% now married, 5.7% widowed, 13.3% divorced (2006-2010 5-year est.); Foreign born: 0.0% (2006-2010 5-year est.); Ancestry (includes multiple ancestries): 34.8% German, 16.9% English, 15.4% Irish, 12.6% Polish, 5.6% Welsh (2006-2010 5-year est.).
**Economy:** Single-family building permits issued: 2 (2011); Multi-family building permits issued: 0 (2011); Employment by occupation: 4.3% management, 0.6% professional, 8.9% services, 14.0% sales, 8.7% farming, 15.9% construction, 9.5% production (2006-2010 5-year est.).
**Income:** Per capita income: $23,568 (2006-2010 5-year est.); Median household income: $41,450 (2006-2010 5-year est.); Average household income: $55,773 (2006-2010 5-year est.); Percent of households with income of $100,000 or more: 7.6% (2006-2010 5-year est.); Poverty rate: 13.7% (2006-2010 5-year est.).
**Education:** Percent of population age 25 and over with: High school diploma (including GED) or higher: 83.9% (2006-2010 5-year est.); Bachelor's degree or higher: 10.1% (2006-2010 5-year est.); Master's degree or higher: 2.3% (2006-2010 5-year est.).
**Housing:** Homeownership rate: 83.9% (2010); Median home value: $77,900 (2006-2010 5-year est.); Median contract rent: $410 per month (2006-2010 5-year est.); Median year structure built: 1980 (2006-2010 5-year est.).
**Transportation:** Commute to work: 91.3% car, 0.0% public transportation, 3.9% walk, 3.5% work from home (2006-2010 5-year est.); Travel time to work: 17.1% less than 15 minutes, 28.8% 15 to 30 minutes, 29.5% 30 to 45 minutes, 4.1% 45 to 60 minutes, 20.5% 60 minutes or more (2006-2010 5-year est.)

## FARMERSVILLE STATION (unincorporated postal area)
Zip Code: 14060
  Covers a land area of 17.740 square miles and a water area of 0.148 square miles. Located at 42.45° N. Lat; 78.29° W. Long. Population: 443 (2010); Density: 25.0 persons per square mile (2010); Race: 98.0% White, 0.2% Black, 0.0% Asian, 0.0% American Indian/Alaska Native, 0.0% Native Hawaiian/Other Pacific Islander, 1.8% Other, 1.8% Hispanic of any race (2010); Average household size: 2.46 (2010); Median age: 44.1 (2010); Males per 100 females: 113.0 (2010); Homeownership rate: 84.5% (2010)

## FRANKLINVILLE (village). Covers a land area of 1.100 square miles and a water area of 0 square miles. Located at 42.33° N. Lat; 78.45° W. Long. Elevation is 1,591 feet.
**Population:** 1,739 (1990); 1,855 (2000); 1,740 (2010); Density: 1,581.8 persons per square mile (2010); Race: 97.0% White, 0.1% Black, 0.9% Asian, 0.3% American Indian/Alaska Native, 0.0% Native Hawaiian/Other Pacific Islander, 1.7% Other, 1.7% Hispanic of any race (2010); Average household size: 2.53 (2010); Median age: 35.4 (2010); Males per 100 females: 95.5 (2010); Marriage status: 25.6% never married, 53.1% now married, 7.2% widowed, 14.2% divorced (2006-2010 5-year est.); Foreign born: 1.3% (2006-2010 5-year est.); Ancestry (includes multiple ancestries): 37.3% German, 14.2% English, 12.5% Irish, 10.6% Polish, 7.5% Italian (2006-2010 5-year est.).
**Economy:** Single-family building permits issued: 0 (2011); Multi-family building permits issued: 0 (2011); Employment by occupation: 2.9% management, 2.5% professional, 7.9% services, 17.2% sales, 1.1% farming, 11.3% construction, 9.7% production (2006-2010 5-year est.).
**Income:** Per capita income: $17,863 (2006-2010 5-year est.); Median household income: $37,222 (2006-2010 5-year est.); Average household income: $44,025 (2006-2010 5-year est.); Percent of households with income of $100,000 or more: 5.9% (2006-2010 5-year est.); Poverty rate: 25.9% (2006-2010 5-year est.).
**Education:** Percent of population age 25 and over with: High school diploma (including GED) or higher: 88.8% (2006-2010 5-year est.); Bachelor's degree or higher: 16.9% (2006-2010 5-year est.); Master's degree or higher: 9.3% (2006-2010 5-year est.).

**School District(s)**

Franklinville Central School District (PK-12)
  2009-10 Enrollment: 777 . . . . . . . . . . . . . . . . . . . . . (716) 676-8029
**Housing:** Homeownership rate: 67.0% (2010); Median home value: $62,100 (2006-2010 5-year est.); Median contract rent: $337 per month (2006-2010 5-year est.); Median year structure built: before 1940 (2006-2010 5-year est.).
**Safety:** Violent crime rate: 6.0 per 10,000 population; Property crime rate: 253.2 per 10,000 population (2010).
**Transportation:** Commute to work: 85.4% car, 0.0% public transportation, 10.2% walk, 2.1% work from home (2006-2010 5-year est.); Travel time to work: 30.8% less than 15 minutes, 26.8% 15 to 30 minutes, 22.5% 30 to 45 minutes, 6.4% 45 to 60 minutes, 13.5% 60 minutes or more (2006-2010 5-year est.)
**Additional Information Contacts**
Franklinville Area Chamber of Commerce . . . . . . . . . . . . . . (716) 676-5013
  http://franklinvillechamber.org/wordpress
Village of Franklinville . . . . . . . . . . . . . . . . . . . . . . . . . . (716) 676-3010
  http://www.franklinvilleny.org

## FRANKLINVILLE (town). Covers a land area of 51.811 square miles and a water area of 0.172 square miles. Located at 42.30° N. Lat; 78.49° W. Long. Elevation is 1,591 feet.
**History:** Settled 1806, incorporated 1874.
**Population:** 2,968 (1990); 3,128 (2000); 2,990 (2010); Density: 57.7 persons per square mile (2010); Race: 96.9% White, 0.2% Black, 0.6% Asian, 0.5% American Indian/Alaska Native, 0.0% Native Hawaiian/Other Pacific Islander, 1.8% Other, 1.7% Hispanic of any race (2010); Average household size: 2.47 (2010); Median age: 39.8 (2010); Males per 100 females: 98.9 (2010); Marriage status: 24.0% never married, 53.5% now married, 7.6% widowed, 14.9% divorced (2006-2010 5-year est.); Foreign born: 1.3% (2006-2010 5-year est.); Ancestry (includes multiple ancestries): 37.7% German, 13.5% Irish, 12.1% Polish, 11.1% English, 6.1% Italian (2006-2010 5-year est.).
**Economy:** Single-family building permits issued: 4 (2011); Multi-family building permits issued: 0 (2011); Employment by occupation: 3.3% management, 2.3% professional, 8.3% services, 17.0% sales, 1.2% farming, 10.6% construction, 12.3% production (2006-2010 5-year est.).

**Income:** Per capita income: $18,299 (2006-2010 5-year est.); Median household income: $38,966 (2006-2010 5-year est.); Average household income: $44,922 (2006-2010 5-year est.); Percent of households with income of $100,000 or more: 5.3% (2006-2010 5-year est.); Poverty rate: 21.1% (2006-2010 5-year est.).

**Education:** Percent of population age 25 and over with: High school diploma (including GED) or higher: 86.7% (2006-2010 5-year est.); Bachelor's degree or higher: 14.5% (2006-2010 5-year est.); Master's degree or higher: 6.8% (2006-2010 5-year est.).

**School District(s)**
Franklinville Central School District (PK-12)
  2009-10 Enrollment: 777 . . . . . . . . . . . . . . . . . . . . (716) 676-8029

**Housing:** Homeownership rate: 74.9% (2010); Median home value: $63,600 (2006-2010 5-year est.); Median contract rent: $354 per month (2006-2010 5-year est.); Median year structure built: 1948 (2006-2010 5-year est.).

**Transportation:** Commute to work: 89.4% car, 0.0% public transportation, 7.2% walk, 1.9% work from home (2006-2010 5-year est.); Travel time to work: 24.3% less than 15 minutes, 31.0% 15 to 30 minutes, 21.7% 30 to 45 minutes, 10.3% 45 to 60 minutes, 12.7% 60 minutes or more (2006-2010 5-year est.)

**Additional Information Contacts**
Franklinville Area Chamber of Commerce . . . . . . . . . . . . . . (716) 676-5013
  http://franklinvillechamber.org/wordpress
Town of Franklinville . . . . . . . . . . . . . . . . . . . . . . . . . . . (716) 676-3077
  http://www.franklinvilleny.org

**FREEDOM** (town). Covers a land area of 40.986 square miles and a water area of 0.328 square miles. Located at 42.47° N. Lat; 78.37° W. Long. Elevation is 1,801 feet.

**Population:** 2,018 (1990); 2,493 (2000); 2,405 (2010); Density: 58.7 persons per square mile (2010); Race: 98.3% White, 0.2% Black, 0.5% Asian, 0.0% American Indian/Alaska Native, 0.0% Native Hawaiian/Other Pacific Islander, 1.0% Other, 1.2% Hispanic of any race (2010); Average household size: 2.66 (2010); Median age: 41.3 (2010); Males per 100 females: 106.1 (2010); Marriage status: 20.8% never married, 65.0% now married, 3.8% widowed, 10.5% divorced (2006-2010 5-year est.); Foreign born: 1.1% (2006-2010 5-year est.); Ancestry (includes multiple ancestries): 29.5% German, 15.4% Irish, 14.8% English, 9.1% Polish, 6.0% American (2006-2010 5-year est.).

**Economy:** Single-family building permits issued: 2 (2011); Multi-family building permits issued: 0 (2011); Employment by occupation: 5.6% management, 2.7% professional, 8.1% services, 15.7% sales, 2.7% farming, 15.0% construction, 15.4% production (2006-2010 5-year est.).

**Income:** Per capita income: $22,183 (2006-2010 5-year est.); Median household income: $51,324 (2006-2010 5-year est.); Average household income: $54,868 (2006-2010 5-year est.); Percent of households with income of $100,000 or more: 12.0% (2006-2010 5-year est.); Poverty rate: 4.4% (2006-2010 5-year est.).

**Education:** Percent of population age 25 and over with: High school diploma (including GED) or higher: 79.9% (2006-2010 5-year est.); Bachelor's degree or higher: 14.6% (2006-2010 5-year est.); Master's degree or higher: 7.6% (2006-2010 5-year est.).

**Housing:** Homeownership rate: 85.5% (2010); Median home value: $87,700 (2006-2010 5-year est.); Median contract rent: $478 per month (2006-2010 5-year est.); Median year structure built: 1976 (2006-2010 5-year est.).

**Transportation:** Commute to work: 92.8% car, 0.0% public transportation, 2.3% walk, 4.9% work from home (2006-2010 5-year est.); Travel time to work: 38.8% less than 15 minutes, 23.1% 15 to 30 minutes, 12.4% 30 to 45 minutes, 13.4% 45 to 60 minutes, 12.3% 60 minutes or more (2006-2010 5-year est.)

**GOWANDA** (village). Covers a land area of 1.593 square miles and a water area of 0.016 square miles. Located at 42.46° N. Lat; 78.93° W. Long. Elevation is 761 feet.

**Population:** 2,901 (1990); 2,842 (2000); 2,709 (2010); Density: 1,700.3 persons per square mile (2010); Race: 90.6% White, 0.7% Black, 0.4% Asian, 5.5% American Indian/Alaska Native, 0.0% Native Hawaiian/Other Pacific Islander, 2.8% Other, 3.0% Hispanic of any race (2010); Average household size: 2.24 (2010); Median age: 42.1 (2010); Males per 100 females: 91.7 (2010); Marriage status: 28.3% never married, 49.0% now married, 9.7% widowed, 13.0% divorced (2006-2010 5-year est.); Foreign born: 2.2% (2006-2010 5-year est.); Ancestry (includes multiple

ancestries): 34.8% German, 19.8% Irish, 15.7% Polish, 13.0% English, 11.8% Italian (2006-2010 5-year est.).

**Economy:** Single-family building permits issued: 0 (2011); Multi-family building permits issued: 0 (2011); Employment by occupation: 5.1% management, 0.4% professional, 18.3% services, 13.7% sales, 1.2% farming, 12.3% construction, 13.3% production (2006-2010 5-year est.).

**Income:** Per capita income: $22,173 (2006-2010 5-year est.); Median household income: $39,884 (2006-2010 5-year est.); Average household income: $49,552 (2006-2010 5-year est.); Percent of households with income of $100,000 or more: 7.4% (2006-2010 5-year est.); Poverty rate: 13.7% (2006-2010 5-year est.).

**Education:** Percent of population age 25 and over with: High school diploma (including GED) or higher: 87.5% (2006-2010 5-year est.); Bachelor's degree or higher: 17.1% (2006-2010 5-year est.); Master's degree or higher: 7.5% (2006-2010 5-year est.).

**School District(s)**
Gowanda Central School District (PK-12)
  2009-10 Enrollment: 1,441 . . . . . . . . . . . . . . . . . . . (716) 532-3325

**Housing:** Homeownership rate: 60.5% (2010); Median home value: $71,100 (2006-2010 5-year est.); Median contract rent: $428 per month (2006-2010 5-year est.); Median year structure built: before 1940 (2006-2010 5-year est.).

**Hospitals:** Tri-County Memorial Hospital (65 beds)

**Newspapers:** Gowanda Pennysaver (Community news; Circulation 11,800)

**Transportation:** Commute to work: 80.8% car, 1.0% public transportation, 10.7% walk, 3.8% work from home (2006-2010 5-year est.); Travel time to work: 50.3% less than 15 minutes, 23.0% 15 to 30 minutes, 13.1% 30 to 45 minutes, 6.5% 45 to 60 minutes, 7.1% 60 minutes or more (2006-2010 5-year est.)

**Additional Information Contacts**
Gowanda Area Chamber of Commerce . . . . . . . . . . . . . . (716) 532-2834
  http://gowandachamber.com

**GREAT VALLEY** (town). Covers a land area of 49.635 square miles and a water area of 0.036 square miles. Located at 42.20° N. Lat; 78.63° W. Long. Elevation is 1,460 feet.

**Population:** 2,090 (1990); 2,145 (2000); 1,974 (2010); Density: 39.8 persons per square mile (2010); Race: 98.3% White, 0.1% Black, 0.2% Asian, 0.6% American Indian/Alaska Native, 0.0% Native Hawaiian/Other Pacific Islander, 0.8% Other, 1.0% Hispanic of any race (2010); Average household size: 2.41 (2010); Median age: 46.6 (2010); Males per 100 females: 97.6 (2010); Marriage status: 21.4% never married, 58.9% now married, 9.5% widowed, 10.3% divorced (2006-2010 5-year est.); Foreign born: 2.4% (2006-2010 5-year est.); Ancestry (includes multiple ancestries): 29.0% Irish, 25.6% German, 14.6% English, 12.6% Polish, 12.2% Italian (2006-2010 5-year est.).

**Economy:** Single-family building permits issued: 5 (2011); Multi-family building permits issued: 0 (2011); Employment by occupation: 15.7% management, 0.8% professional, 8.6% services, 11.0% sales, 0.7% farming, 14.4% construction, 7.6% production (2006-2010 5-year est.).

**Income:** Per capita income: $23,886 (2006-2010 5-year est.); Median household income: $48,490 (2006-2010 5-year est.); Average household income: $54,766 (2006-2010 5-year est.); Percent of households with income of $100,000 or more: 14.0% (2006-2010 5-year est.); Poverty rate: 14.0% (2006-2010 5-year est.).

**Education:** Percent of population age 25 and over with: High school diploma (including GED) or higher: 86.8% (2006-2010 5-year est.); Bachelor's degree or higher: 22.1% (2006-2010 5-year est.); Master's degree or higher: 9.9% (2006-2010 5-year est.).

**Housing:** Homeownership rate: 84.1% (2010); Median home value: $88,300 (2006-2010 5-year est.); Median contract rent: $375 per month (2006-2010 5-year est.); Median year structure built: 1981 (2006-2010 5-year est.).

**Transportation:** Commute to work: 95.3% car, 0.0% public transportation, 0.0% walk, 4.0% work from home (2006-2010 5-year est.); Travel time to work: 49.7% less than 15 minutes, 28.1% 15 to 30 minutes, 15.6% 30 to 45 minutes, 1.2% 45 to 60 minutes, 5.4% 60 minutes or more (2006-2010 5-year est.)

**HINSDALE** (town). Covers a land area of 38.730 square miles and a water area of 0.041 square miles. Located at 42.16° N. Lat; 78.37° W. Long. Elevation is 1,480 feet.

**Population:** 2,095 (1990); 2,270 (2000); 2,168 (2010); Density: 56.0 persons per square mile (2010); Race: 97.3% White, 0.7% Black, 0.4%

Asian, 0.0% American Indian/Alaska Native, 0.0% Native Hawaiian/Other Pacific Islander, 1.6% Other, 0.7% Hispanic of any race (2010); Average household size: 2.43 (2010); Median age: 44.2 (2010); Males per 100 females: 98.2 (2010); Marriage status: 18.5% never married, 65.9% now married, 6.8% widowed, 8.8% divorced (2006-2010 5-year est.); Foreign born: 0.0% (2006-2010 5-year est.); Ancestry (includes multiple ancestries): 40.3% German, 14.0% Irish, 11.8% English, 9.9% Polish, 8.3% Italian (2006-2010 5-year est.).

**Economy:** Single-family building permits issued: 0 (2011); Multi-family building permits issued: 0 (2011); Employment by occupation: 4.3% management, 0.0% professional, 11.5% services, 17.9% sales, 3.6% farming, 12.1% construction, 9.2% production (2006-2010 5-year est.).

**Income:** Per capita income: $19,513 (2006-2010 5-year est.); Median household income: $42,447 (2006-2010 5-year est.); Average household income: $49,158 (2006-2010 5-year est.); Percent of households with income of $100,000 or more: 9.0% (2006-2010 5-year est.); Poverty rate: 18.9% (2006-2010 5-year est.).

**Education:** Percent of population age 25 and over with: High school diploma (including GED) or higher: 89.8% (2006-2010 5-year est.); Bachelor's degree or higher: 10.9% (2006-2010 5-year est.); Master's degree or higher: 2.6% (2006-2010 5-year est.).

**School District(s)**

Hinsdale Central School District (PK-12)

   2009-10 Enrollment: 462 . . . . . . . . . . . . . . . . . . . . . . . . (716) 557-2227

**Housing:** Homeownership rate: 85.1% (2010); Median home value: $63,400 (2006-2010 5-year est.); Median contract rent: $429 per month (2006-2010 5-year est.); Median year structure built: 1976 (2006-2010 5-year est.).

**Transportation:** Commute to work: 99.1% car, 0.9% public transportation, 0.0% walk, 0.0% work from home (2006-2010 5-year est.); Travel time to work: 20.8% less than 15 minutes, 52.5% 15 to 30 minutes, 13.2% 30 to 45 minutes, 6.3% 45 to 60 minutes, 7.3% 60 minutes or more (2006-2010 5-year est.)

---

**HUMPHREY** (town). Covers a land area of 37.136 square miles and a water area of 0.016 square miles. Located at 42.23° N. Lat; 78.49° W. Long. Elevation is 1,617 feet.

**Population:** 580 (1990); 721 (2000); 687 (2010); Density: 18.5 persons per square mile (2010); Race: 99.0% White, 0.0% Black, 0.1% Asian, 0.6% American Indian/Alaska Native, 0.0% Native Hawaiian/Other Pacific Islander, 0.3% Other, 0.6% Hispanic of any race (2010); Average household size: 2.52 (2010); Median age: 42.6 (2010); Males per 100 females: 113.4 (2010); Marriage status: 26.2% never married, 52.9% now married, 5.4% widowed, 15.5% divorced (2006-2010 5-year est.); Foreign born: 0.4% (2006-2010 5-year est.); Ancestry (includes multiple ancestries): 33.0% German, 21.3% Irish, 9.2% English, 8.1% French, 5.1% Polish (2006-2010 5-year est.).

**Economy:** Single-family building permits issued: 3 (2011); Multi-family building permits issued: 0 (2011); Employment by occupation: 8.0% management, 0.0% professional, 11.3% services, 10.4% sales, 8.5% farming, 23.4% construction, 0.8% production (2006-2010 5-year est.).

**Income:** Per capita income: $20,323 (2006-2010 5-year est.); Median household income: $42,500 (2006-2010 5-year est.); Average household income: $48,383 (2006-2010 5-year est.); Percent of households with income of $100,000 or more: 7.0% (2006-2010 5-year est.); Poverty rate: 20.3% (2006-2010 5-year est.).

**Education:** Percent of population age 25 and over with: High school diploma (including GED) or higher: 80.1% (2006-2010 5-year est.); Bachelor's degree or higher: 24.7% (2006-2010 5-year est.); Master's degree or higher: 10.0% (2006-2010 5-year est.).

**Housing:** Homeownership rate: 82.4% (2010); Median home value: $89,800 (2006-2010 5-year est.); Median contract rent: $467 per month (2006-2010 5-year est.); Median year structure built: 1974 (2006-2010 5-year est.).

**Transportation:** Commute to work: 94.6% car, 0.0% public transportation, 0.0% walk, 5.4% work from home (2006-2010 5-year est.); Travel time to work: 20.1% less than 15 minutes, 59.5% 15 to 30 minutes, 11.4% 30 to 45 minutes, 5.4% 45 to 60 minutes, 3.6% 60 minutes or more (2006-2010 5-year est.)

---

**ISCHUA** (town). Covers a land area of 32.377 square miles and a water area of 0.020 square miles. Located at 42.23° N. Lat; 78.38° W. Long. Elevation is 1,542 feet.

**Population:** 847 (1990); 895 (2000); 859 (2010); Density: 26.5 persons per square mile (2010); Race: 97.3% White, 1.4% Black, 0.1% Asian, 0.2%

American Indian/Alaska Native, 0.2% Native Hawaiian/Other Pacific Islander, 0.8% Other, 0.6% Hispanic of any race (2010); Average household size: 2.48 (2010); Median age: 45.0 (2010); Males per 100 females: 116.4 (2010); Marriage status: 21.1% never married, 58.3% now married, 7.5% widowed, 13.2% divorced (2006-2010 5-year est.); Foreign born: 2.1% (2006-2010 5-year est.); Ancestry (includes multiple ancestries): 28.3% German, 15.2% Irish, 14.5% Italian, 13.0% English, 12.3% American (2006-2010 5-year est.).

**Economy:** Single-family building permits issued: 0 (2011); Multi-family building permits issued: 0 (2011); Employment by occupation: 4.6% management, 5.7% professional, 15.9% services, 18.1% sales, 3.0% farming, 14.0% construction, 10.0% production (2006-2010 5-year est.).

**Income:** Per capita income: $19,744 (2006-2010 5-year est.); Median household income: $43,500 (2006-2010 5-year est.); Average household income: $46,116 (2006-2010 5-year est.); Percent of households with income of $100,000 or more: 7.9% (2006-2010 5-year est.); Poverty rate: 8.8% (2006-2010 5-year est.).

**Education:** Percent of population age 25 and over with: High school diploma (including GED) or higher: 86.0% (2006-2010 5-year est.); Bachelor's degree or higher: 11.7% (2006-2010 5-year est.); Master's degree or higher: 4.2% (2006-2010 5-year est.).

**Housing:** Homeownership rate: 87.9% (2010); Median home value: $73,400 (2006-2010 5-year est.); Median contract rent: $318 per month (2006-2010 5-year est.); Median year structure built: 1974 (2006-2010 5-year est.).

**Transportation:** Commute to work: 95.7% car, 0.0% public transportation, 0.8% walk, 3.5% work from home (2006-2010 5-year est.); Travel time to work: 12.1% less than 15 minutes, 54.6% 15 to 30 minutes, 17.2% 30 to 45 minutes, 6.5% 45 to 60 minutes, 9.6% 60 minutes or more (2006-2010 5-year est.)

---

**KILL BUCK** (unincorporated postal area)

Zip Code: 14748

   Covers a land area of 17.902 square miles and a water area of 0.376 square miles. Located at 42.15° N. Lat; 78.64° W. Long. Elevation is 1,407 feet. Population: 746 (2010); Density: 41.7 persons per square mile (2010); Race: 74.5% White, 0.4% Black, 0.3% Asian, 23.2% American Indian/Alaska Native, 0.0% Native Hawaiian/Other Pacific Islander, 1.6% Other, 2.4% Hispanic of any race (2010); Average household size: 2.57 (2010); Median age: 38.3 (2010); Males per 100 females: 95.8 (2010); Homeownership rate: 71.4% (2010)

---

**LEON** (town). Covers a land area of 36.182 square miles and a water area of 0.026 square miles. Located at 42.30° N. Lat; 79.00° W. Long. Elevation is 1,375 feet.

**Population:** 1,245 (1990); 1,380 (2000); 1,365 (2010); Density: 37.7 persons per square mile (2010); Race: 98.5% White, 0.4% Black, 0.1% Asian, 0.3% American Indian/Alaska Native, 0.0% Native Hawaiian/Other Pacific Islander, 0.7% Other, 1.3% Hispanic of any race (2010); Average household size: 3.45 (2010); Median age: 26.1 (2010); Males per 100 females: 103.1 (2010); Marriage status: 33.7% never married, 56.7% now married, 3.9% widowed, 5.6% divorced (2006-2010 5-year est.); Foreign born: 0.6% (2006-2010 5-year est.); Ancestry (includes multiple ancestries): 44.9% German, 10.1% Pennsylvania German, 8.3% English, 7.9% Swiss, 6.2% Polish (2006-2010 5-year est.).

**Economy:** Single-family building permits issued: 1 (2011); Multi-family building permits issued: 0 (2011); Employment by occupation: 14.9% management, 0.6% professional, 12.0% services, 9.0% sales, 4.1% farming, 18.3% construction, 13.8% production (2006-2010 5-year est.).

**Income:** Per capita income: $13,400 (2006-2010 5-year est.); Median household income: $45,333 (2006-2010 5-year est.); Average household income: $54,462 (2006-2010 5-year est.); Percent of households with income of $100,000 or more: 6.6% (2006-2010 5-year est.); Poverty rate: 40.3% (2006-2010 5-year est.).

**Education:** Percent of population age 25 and over with: High school diploma (including GED) or higher: 57.3% (2006-2010 5-year est.); Bachelor's degree or higher: 9.7% (2006-2010 5-year est.); Master's degree or higher: 3.5% (2006-2010 5-year est.).

**Housing:** Homeownership rate: 79.5% (2010); Median home value: $82,200 (2006-2010 5-year est.); Median contract rent: $288 per month (2006-2010 5-year est.); Median year structure built: 1973 (2006-2010 5-year est.).

**Transportation:** Commute to work: 53.1% car, 1.5% public transportation, 34.1% walk, 7.5% work from home (2006-2010 5-year est.); Travel time to work: 50.5% less than 15 minutes, 20.7% 15 to 30 minutes, 16.4% 30 to 45

minutes, 3.7% 45 to 60 minutes, 8.8% 60 minutes or more (2006-2010 5-year est.)

**LIME LAKE** (CDP). Covers a land area of 2.377 square miles and a water area of 0.266 square miles. Located at 42.43° N. Lat; 78.48° W. Long. Elevation is 1,660 feet.
**Population:** n/a (1990); n/a (2000); 867 (2010); Density: 364.6 persons per square mile (2010); Race: 98.4% White, 0.1% Black, 0.1% Asian, 0.2% American Indian/Alaska Native, 0.0% Native Hawaiian/Other Pacific Islander, 1.2% Other, 1.5% Hispanic of any race (2010); Average household size: 2.38 (2010); Median age: 46.4 (2010); Males per 100 females: 91.8 (2010); Marriage status: 30.4% never married, 42.3% now married, 13.5% widowed, 13.8% divorced (2006-2010 5-year est.); Foreign born: 0.0% (2006-2010 5-year est.); Ancestry (includes multiple ancestries): 35.9% German, 20.5% Irish, 11.5% English, 6.1% Polish, 4.4% French (2006-2010 5-year est.).
**Economy:** Employment by occupation: 11.3% management, 1.6% professional, 7.0% services, 11.3% sales, 8.8% farming, 13.1% construction, 7.7% production (2006-2010 5-year est.).
**Income:** Per capita income: $22,873 (2006-2010 5-year est.); Median household income: $49,306 (2006-2010 5-year est.); Average household income: $55,849 (2006-2010 5-year est.); Percent of households with income of $100,000 or more: 11.0% (2006-2010 5-year est.); Poverty rate: 12.3% (2006-2010 5-year est.).
**Education:** Percent of population age 25 and over with: High school diploma (including GED) or higher: 78.5% (2006-2010 5-year est.); Bachelor's degree or higher: 16.8% (2006-2010 5-year est.); Master's degree or higher: 3.0% (2006-2010 5-year est.).
**Housing:** Homeownership rate: 75.7% (2010); Median home value: $85,900 (2006-2010 5-year est.); Median contract rent: $404 per month (2006-2010 5-year est.); Median year structure built: 1950 (2006-2010 5-year est.).
**Transportation:** Commute to work: 82.4% car, 0.0% public transportation, 17.6% walk, 0.0% work from home (2006-2010 5-year est.); Travel time to work: 36.1% less than 15 minutes, 26.6% 15 to 30 minutes, 15.1% 30 to 45 minutes, 14.0% 45 to 60 minutes, 8.1% 60 minutes or more (2006-2010 5-year est.)

**LIMESTONE** (village). Covers a land area of 1.622 square miles and a water area of 0.010 square miles. Located at 42.01° N. Lat; 78.63° W. Long. Elevation is 1,411 feet.
**History:** The field was the first major oil-producing region in the U.S. When the first well was successfully drilled near Titusville, Pennsylvania, in 1859, Allegany, Cattaraugus, and Chautauqua counties all shared in the prosperity.
**Population:** 459 (1990); 411 (2000); 389 (2010); Density: 239.7 persons per square mile (2010); Race: 98.2% White, 0.0% Black, 0.3% Asian, 1.0% American Indian/Alaska Native, 0.0% Native Hawaiian/Other Pacific Islander, 0.5% Other, 0.0% Hispanic of any race (2010); Average household size: 2.40 (2010); Median age: 38.9 (2010); Males per 100 females: 87.9 (2010); Marriage status: 18.8% never married, 50.8% now married, 17.2% widowed, 13.3% divorced (2006-2010 5-year est.); Foreign born: 0.0% (2006-2010 5-year est.); Ancestry (includes multiple ancestries): 24.1% Irish, 23.1% German, 16.1% Italian, 10.1% English, 7.9% Dutch (2006-2010 5-year est.).
**Economy:** Single-family building permits issued: 0 (2011); Multi-family building permits issued: 0 (2011); Employment by occupation: 6.3% management, 0.0% professional, 18.9% services, 14.7% sales, 2.1% farming, 11.2% construction, 9.1% production (2006-2010 5-year est.).
**Income:** Per capita income: $18,666 (2006-2010 5-year est.); Median household income: $34,479 (2006-2010 5-year est.); Average household income: $40,948 (2006-2010 5-year est.); Percent of households with income of $100,000 or more: 4.0% (2006-2010 5-year est.); Poverty rate: 11.7% (2006-2010 5-year est.).
**Education:** Percent of population age 25 and over with: High school diploma (including GED) or higher: 87.9% (2006-2010 5-year est.); Bachelor's degree or higher: 10.4% (2006-2010 5-year est.); Master's degree or higher: 3.0% (2006-2010 5-year est.).
**School District(s)**
Allegany-Limestone Central School District (PK-12)
    2009-10 Enrollment: 1,333 . . . . . . . . . . . . . . . . . . . . . (716) 375-6600
**Housing:** Homeownership rate: 69.7% (2010); Median home value: $61,800 (2006-2010 5-year est.); Median contract rent: $232 per month (2006-2010 5-year est.); Median year structure built: 1964 (2006-2010 5-year est.).

**Transportation:** Commute to work: 92.1% car, 0.0% public transportation, 2.1% walk, 5.7% work from home (2006-2010 5-year est.); Travel time to work: 28.8% less than 15 minutes, 46.2% 15 to 30 minutes, 16.7% 30 to 45 minutes, 6.1% 45 to 60 minutes, 2.3% 60 minutes or more (2006-2010 5-year est.)

**LITTLE VALLEY** (village). County seat. Covers a land area of 1.002 square miles and a water area of 0 square miles. Located at 42.24° N. Lat; 78.79° W. Long. Elevation is 1,598 feet.
**Population:** 1,188 (1990); 1,130 (2000); 1,143 (2010); Density: 1,140.7 persons per square mile (2010); Race: 95.1% White, 2.1% Black, 0.1% Asian, 1.3% American Indian/Alaska Native, 0.0% Native Hawaiian/Other Pacific Islander, 1.4% Other, 1.5% Hispanic of any race (2010); Average household size: 2.35 (2010); Median age: 35.0 (2010); Males per 100 females: 112.8 (2010); Marriage status: 30.9% never married, 45.1% now married, 11.4% widowed, 12.6% divorced (2006-2010 5-year est.); Foreign born: 0.5% (2006-2010 5-year est.); Ancestry (includes multiple ancestries): 31.7% German, 23.6% English, 20.5% Irish, 8.6% Italian, 7.7% American (2006-2010 5-year est.).
**Economy:** Employment by occupation: 6.7% management, 0.0% professional, 16.4% services, 16.2% sales, 3.8% farming, 19.7% construction, 6.4% production (2006-2010 5-year est.).
**Income:** Per capita income: $18,326 (2006-2010 5-year est.); Median household income: $35,156 (2006-2010 5-year est.); Average household income: $41,419 (2006-2010 5-year est.); Percent of households with income of $100,000 or more: 4.3% (2006-2010 5-year est.); Poverty rate: 12.7% (2006-2010 5-year est.).
**Education:** Percent of population age 25 and over with: High school diploma (including GED) or higher: 85.4% (2006-2010 5-year est.); Bachelor's degree or higher: 8.4% (2006-2010 5-year est.); Master's degree or higher: 4.4% (2006-2010 5-year est.).
**School District(s)**
Cattaraugus-Little Valley Central School District (PK-12)
    2009-10 Enrollment: 1,012 . . . . . . . . . . . . . . . . . . . . . (716) 257-5292
**Housing:** Homeownership rate: 58.1% (2010); Median home value: $67,100 (2006-2010 5-year est.); Median contract rent: $372 per month (2006-2010 5-year est.); Median year structure built: before 1940 (2006-2010 5-year est.).
**Transportation:** Commute to work: 90.7% car, 0.0% public transportation, 5.7% walk, 2.7% work from home (2006-2010 5-year est.); Travel time to work: 36.6% less than 15 minutes, 39.4% 15 to 30 minutes, 16.4% 30 to 45 minutes, 1.5% 45 to 60 minutes, 6.1% 60 minutes or more (2006-2010 5-year est.)

**LITTLE VALLEY** (town). Covers a land area of 29.787 square miles and a water area of 0.006 square miles. Located at 42.22° N. Lat; 78.75° W. Long. Elevation is 1,598 feet.
**History:** Incorporated 1876.
**Population:** 1,881 (1990); 1,788 (2000); 1,740 (2010); Density: 58.4 persons per square mile (2010); Race: 95.8% White, 1.7% Black, 0.1% Asian, 1.3% American Indian/Alaska Native, 0.0% Native Hawaiian/Other Pacific Islander, 1.1% Other, 1.3% Hispanic of any race (2010); Average household size: 2.34 (2010); Median age: 40.0 (2010); Males per 100 females: 111.7 (2010); Marriage status: 24.1% never married, 53.7% now married, 10.0% widowed, 12.2% divorced (2006-2010 5-year est.); Foreign born: 1.0% (2006-2010 5-year est.); Ancestry (includes multiple ancestries): 34.0% German, 22.8% English, 18.8% Irish, 7.2% Polish, 6.8% Italian (2006-2010 5-year est.).
**Economy:** Single-family building permits issued: 0 (2011); Multi-family building permits issued: 0 (2011); Employment by occupation: 7.9% management, 0.4% professional, 16.5% services, 18.4% sales, 3.9% farming, 15.0% construction, 5.8% production (2006-2010 5-year est.).
**Income:** Per capita income: $22,294 (2006-2010 5-year est.); Median household income: $41,625 (2006-2010 5-year est.); Average household income: $49,752 (2006-2010 5-year est.); Percent of households with income of $100,000 or more: 9.1% (2006-2010 5-year est.); Poverty rate: 8.7% (2006-2010 5-year est.).
**Education:** Percent of population age 25 and over with: High school diploma (including GED) or higher: 84.8% (2006-2010 5-year est.); Bachelor's degree or higher: 11.1% (2006-2010 5-year est.); Master's degree or higher: 5.5% (2006-2010 5-year est.).
**School District(s)**
Cattaraugus-Little Valley Central School District (PK-12)
    2009-10 Enrollment: 1,012 . . . . . . . . . . . . . . . . . . . . . (716) 257-5292

**Housing:** Homeownership rate: 69.3% (2010); Median home value: $80,700 (2006-2010 5-year est.); Median contract rent: $382 per month (2006-2010 5-year est.); Median year structure built: 1943 (2006-2010 5-year est.).
**Transportation:** Commute to work: 92.2% car, 0.0% public transportation, 4.2% walk, 3.0% work from home (2006-2010 5-year est.); Travel time to work: 42.6% less than 15 minutes, 33.2% 15 to 30 minutes, 15.8% 30 to 45 minutes, 3.0% 45 to 60 minutes, 5.4% 60 minutes or more (2006-2010 5-year est.).

**LYNDON** (town). Covers a land area of 33.231 square miles and a water area of 0.035 square miles. Located at 42.31° N. Lat; 78.37° W. Long. Elevation is 2,064 feet.
**Population:** 503 (1990); 661 (2000); 707 (2010); Density: 21.3 persons per square mile (2010); Race: 98.0% White, 0.6% Black, 0.1% Asian, 0.4% American Indian/Alaska Native, 0.0% Native Hawaiian/Other Pacific Islander, 0.9% Other, 2.8% Hispanic of any race (2010); Average household size: 2.41 (2010); Median age: 46.7 (2010); Males per 100 females: 115.5 (2010); Marriage status: 21.0% never married, 68.6% now married, 2.1% widowed, 8.4% divorced (2006-2010 5-year est.); Foreign born: 5.9% (2006-2010 5-year est.); Ancestry (includes multiple ancestries): 40.3% German, 17.9% Polish, 12.9% Irish, 9.9% English, 9.2% Italian (2006-2010 5-year est.).
**Economy:** Single-family building permits issued: 0 (2011); Multi-family building permits issued: 0 (2011); Employment by occupation: 9.6% management, 1.5% professional, 6.6% services, 17.3% sales, 15.9% farming, 27.3% construction, 6.6% production (2006-2010 5-year est.).
**Income:** Per capita income: $21,288 (2006-2010 5-year est.); Median household income: $47,438 (2006-2010 5-year est.); Average household income: $52,673 (2006-2010 5-year est.); Percent of households with income of $100,000 or more: 14.0% (2006-2010 5-year est.); Poverty rate: 10.0% (2006-2010 5-year est.).
**Education:** Percent of population age 25 and over with: High school diploma (including GED) or higher: 84.6% (2006-2010 5-year est.); Bachelor's degree or higher: 14.1% (2006-2010 5-year est.); Master's degree or higher: 5.7% (2006-2010 5-year est.).
**Housing:** Homeownership rate: 90.1% (2010); Median home value: $84,800 (2006-2010 5-year est.); Median contract rent: $467 per month (2006-2010 5-year est.); Median year structure built: 1982 (2006-2010 5-year est.).
**Transportation:** Commute to work: 70.1% car, 4.4% public transportation, 1.5% walk, 21.8% work from home (2006-2010 5-year est.); Travel time to work: 11.3% less than 15 minutes, 44.3% 15 to 30 minutes, 20.3% 30 to 45 minutes, 6.1% 45 to 60 minutes, 17.9% 60 minutes or more (2006-2010 5-year est.).

**MACHIAS** (town). Covers a land area of 40.428 square miles and a water area of 0.648 square miles. Located at 42.39° N. Lat; 78.50° W. Long. Elevation is 1,680 feet.
**Population:** 2,338 (1990); 2,482 (2000); 2,375 (2010); Density: 58.7 persons per square mile (2010); Race: 97.5% White, 0.6% Black, 0.1% Asian, 0.3% American Indian/Alaska Native, 0.0% Native Hawaiian/Other Pacific Islander, 1.5% Other, 1.3% Hispanic of any race (2010); Average household size: 2.47 (2010); Median age: 43.1 (2010); Males per 100 females: 94.4 (2010); Marriage status: 25.6% never married, 55.7% now married, 7.3% widowed, 11.5% divorced (2006-2010 5-year est.); Foreign born: 0.7% (2006-2010 5-year est.); Ancestry (includes multiple ancestries): 42.6% German, 18.3% Irish, 10.9% Polish, 10.2% English, 5.0% American (2006-2010 5-year est.).
**Economy:** Single-family building permits issued: 4 (2011); Multi-family building permits issued: 0 (2011); Employment by occupation: 9.3% management, 1.0% professional, 11.1% services, 15.3% sales, 4.6% farming, 12.8% construction, 12.6% production (2006-2010 5-year est.).
**Income:** Per capita income: $19,513 (2006-2010 5-year est.); Median household income: $47,108 (2006-2010 5-year est.); Average household income: $51,463 (2006-2010 5-year est.); Percent of households with income of $100,000 or more: 7.6% (2006-2010 5-year est.); Poverty rate: 10.9% (2006-2010 5-year est.).
**Education:** Percent of population age 25 and over with: High school diploma (including GED) or higher: 87.7% (2006-2010 5-year est.); Bachelor's degree or higher: 12.9% (2006-2010 5-year est.); Master's degree or higher: 6.0% (2006-2010 5-year est.).
**Housing:** Homeownership rate: 77.8% (2010); Median home value: $82,800 (2006-2010 5-year est.); Median contract rent: $425 per month

(2006-2010 5-year est.); Median year structure built: 1964 (2006-2010 5-year est.).
**Transportation:** Commute to work: 87.1% car, 0.6% public transportation, 11.0% walk, 1.2% work from home (2006-2010 5-year est.); Travel time to work: 28.0% less than 15 minutes, 29.3% 15 to 30 minutes, 17.9% 30 to 45 minutes, 12.1% 45 to 60 minutes, 12.7% 60 minutes or more (2006-2010 5-year est.)

**MACHIAS** (CDP). Covers a land area of 0.865 square miles and a water area of 0.167 square miles. Located at 42.41° N. Lat; 78.48° W. Long. Elevation is 1,680 feet.
**Population:** n/a (1990); n/a (2000); 471 (2010); Density: 544.3 persons per square mile (2010); Race: 97.0% White, 1.9% Black, 0.0% Asian, 0.2% American Indian/Alaska Native, 0.0% Native Hawaiian/Other Pacific Islander, 0.9% Other, 0.2% Hispanic of any race (2010); Average household size: 2.52 (2010); Median age: 35.9 (2010); Males per 100 females: 89.9 (2010); Marriage status: 24.9% never married, 59.2% now married, 1.1% widowed, 14.8% divorced (2006-2010 5-year est.); Foreign born: 0.8% (2006-2010 5-year est.); Ancestry (includes multiple ancestries): 53.9% German, 21.4% Irish, 13.7% English, 9.5% Polish, 5.1% Canadian (2006-2010 5-year est.).
**Economy:** Employment by occupation: 15.5% management, 0.0% professional, 10.1% services, 18.3% sales, 5.2% farming, 7.5% construction, 8.0% production (2006-2010 5-year est.).
**Income:** Per capita income: $18,725 (2006-2010 5-year est.); Median household income: $51,250 (2006-2010 5-year est.); Average household income: $53,715 (2006-2010 5-year est.); Percent of households with income of $100,000 or more: 13.0% (2006-2010 5-year est.); Poverty rate: 15.4% (2006-2010 5-year est.).
**Education:** Percent of population age 25 and over with: High school diploma (including GED) or higher: 95.8% (2006-2010 5-year est.); Bachelor's degree or higher: 19.2% (2006-2010 5-year est.); Master's degree or higher: 16.5% (2006-2010 5-year est.).
**Housing:** Homeownership rate: 69.5% (2010); Median home value: $72,000 (2006-2010 5-year est.); Median contract rent: $438 per month (2006-2010 5-year est.); Median year structure built: 1954 (2006-2010 5-year est.).
**Transportation:** Commute to work: 90.4% car, 0.0% public transportation, 7.3% walk, 2.3% work from home (2006-2010 5-year est.); Travel time to work: 36.6% less than 15 minutes, 19.9% 15 to 30 minutes, 14.6% 30 to 45 minutes, 7.7% 45 to 60 minutes, 21.1% 60 minutes or more (2006-2010 5-year est.)

**MANSFIELD** (town). Covers a land area of 40.126 square miles and a water area of 0.030 square miles. Located at 42.30° N. Lat; 78.76° W. Long.
**Population:** 724 (1990); 800 (2000); 808 (2010); Density: 20.1 persons per square mile (2010); Race: 98.9% White, 0.2% Black, 0.5% Asian, 0.0% American Indian/Alaska Native, 0.0% Native Hawaiian/Other Pacific Islander, 0.4% Other, 1.2% Hispanic of any race (2010); Average household size: 2.38 (2010); Median age: 46.9 (2010); Males per 100 females: 101.5 (2010); Marriage status: 21.6% never married, 61.7% now married, 4.9% widowed, 11.8% divorced (2006-2010 5-year est.); Foreign born: 1.9% (2006-2010 5-year est.); Ancestry (includes multiple ancestries): 39.4% German, 19.3% English, 18.5% Polish, 15.9% Irish, 11.3% Italian (2006-2010 5-year est.).
**Economy:** Single-family building permits issued: 6 (2011); Multi-family building permits issued: 0 (2011); Employment by occupation: 8.0% management, 0.0% professional, 12.6% services, 22.3% sales, 0.9% farming, 13.1% construction, 5.1% production (2006-2010 5-year est.).
**Income:** Per capita income: $29,641 (2006-2010 5-year est.); Median household income: $51,364 (2006-2010 5-year est.); Average household income: $62,781 (2006-2010 5-year est.); Percent of households with income of $100,000 or more: 17.5% (2006-2010 5-year est.); Poverty rate: 2.8% (2006-2010 5-year est.).
**Education:** Percent of population age 25 and over with: High school diploma (including GED) or higher: 88.8% (2006-2010 5-year est.); Bachelor's degree or higher: 25.0% (2006-2010 5-year est.); Master's degree or higher: 12.7% (2006-2010 5-year est.).
**Housing:** Homeownership rate: 92.0% (2010); Median home value: $113,300 (2006-2010 5-year est.); Median contract rent: $458 per month (2006-2010 5-year est.); Median year structure built: 1974 (2006-2010 5-year est.).
**Transportation:** Commute to work: 91.0% car, 0.0% public transportation, 5.7% walk, 3.3% work from home (2006-2010 5-year est.); Travel time to

work: 28.8% less than 15 minutes, 44.0% 15 to 30 minutes, 13.6% 30 to 45 minutes, 5.3% 45 to 60 minutes, 8.4% 60 minutes or more (2006-2010 5-year est.)

**NAPOLI** (town). Covers a land area of 36.375 square miles and a water area of 0.169 square miles. Located at 42.21° N. Lat; 78.88° W. Long. Elevation is 1,732 feet.
**Population:** 1,102 (1990); 1,159 (2000); 1,248 (2010); Density: 34.3 persons per square mile (2010); Race: 95.4% White, 0.5% Black, 0.5% Asian, 2.0% American Indian/Alaska Native, 0.0% Native Hawaiian/Other Pacific Islander, 1.6% Other, 1.5% Hispanic of any race (2010); Average household size: 3.05 (2010); Median age: 35.9 (2010); Males per 100 females: 112.2 (2010); Marriage status: 30.2% never married, 54.3% now married, 5.2% widowed, 10.3% divorced (2006-2010 5-year est.); Foreign born: 0.4% (2006-2010 5-year est.); Ancestry (includes multiple ancestries): 28.9% German, 11.9% Pennsylvania German, 11.1% English, 11.0% Irish, 9.9% Polish (2006-2010 5-year est.).
**Economy:** Single-family building permits issued: 8 (2011); Multi-family building permits issued: 0 (2011); Employment by occupation: 9.6% management, 1.5% professional, 9.7% services, 13.2% sales, 0.5% farming, 11.5% construction, 10.1% production (2006-2010 5-year est.).
**Income:** Per capita income: $16,553 (2006-2010 5-year est.); Median household income: $44,821 (2006-2010 5-year est.); Average household income: $54,034 (2006-2010 5-year est.); Percent of households with income of $100,000 or more: 12.2% (2006-2010 5-year est.); Poverty rate: 32.8% (2006-2010 5-year est.).
**Education:** Percent of population age 25 and over with: High school diploma (including GED) or higher: 75.2% (2006-2010 5-year est.); Bachelor's degree or higher: 13.6% (2006-2010 5-year est.); Master's degree or higher: 6.1% (2006-2010 5-year est.).
**Housing:** Homeownership rate: 90.1% (2010); Median home value: $68,500 (2006-2010 5-year est.); Median contract rent: $603 per month (2006-2010 5-year est.); Median year structure built: 1973 (2006-2010 5-year est.).
**Transportation:** Commute to work: 85.8% car, 2.4% public transportation, 3.3% walk, 6.3% work from home (2006-2010 5-year est.); Travel time to work: 25.0% less than 15 minutes, 30.8% 15 to 30 minutes, 33.5% 30 to 45 minutes, 8.9% 45 to 60 minutes, 1.8% 60 minutes or more (2006-2010 5-year est.)

**NEW ALBION** (town). Covers a land area of 35.628 square miles and a water area of 0.193 square miles. Located at 42.30° N. Lat; 78.88° W. Long. Elevation is 1,417 feet.
**Population:** 1,978 (1990); 2,068 (2000); 1,972 (2010); Density: 55.3 persons per square mile (2010); Race: 97.9% White, 0.4% Black, 0.1% Asian, 0.9% American Indian/Alaska Native, 0.0% Native Hawaiian/Other Pacific Islander, 0.7% Other, 1.2% Hispanic of any race (2010); Average household size: 2.46 (2010); Median age: 42.9 (2010); Males per 100 females: 98.4 (2010); Marriage status: 22.6% never married, 59.2% now married, 9.8% widowed, 8.4% divorced (2006-2010 5-year est.); Foreign born: 0.4% (2006-2010 5-year est.); Ancestry (includes multiple ancestries): 45.8% German, 21.7% Irish, 19.4% English, 11.0% Polish, 9.3% Italian (2006-2010 5-year est.).
**Economy:** Single-family building permits issued: 2 (2011); Multi-family building permits issued: 0 (2011); Employment by occupation: 7.6% management, 2.0% professional, 15.0% services, 19.1% sales, 1.9% farming, 16.2% construction, 6.7% production (2006-2010 5-year est.).
**Income:** Per capita income: $20,787 (2006-2010 5-year est.); Median household income: $42,283 (2006-2010 5-year est.); Average household income: $48,590 (2006-2010 5-year est.); Percent of households with income of $100,000 or more: 8.8% (2006-2010 5-year est.); Poverty rate: 9.5% (2006-2010 5-year est.).
**Education:** Percent of population age 25 and over with: High school diploma (including GED) or higher: 87.0% (2006-2010 5-year est.); Bachelor's degree or higher: 16.8% (2006-2010 5-year est.); Master's degree or higher: 8.3% (2006-2010 5-year est.).
**Housing:** Homeownership rate: 80.2% (2010); Median home value: $67,100 (2006-2010 5-year est.); Median contract rent: $374 per month (2006-2010 5-year est.); Median year structure built: before 1940 (2006-2010 5-year est.).
**Transportation:** Commute to work: 91.9% car, 0.0% public transportation, 4.8% walk, 2.7% work from home (2006-2010 5-year est.); Travel time to work: 36.0% less than 15 minutes, 22.6% 15 to 30 minutes, 24.0% 30 to 45 minutes, 9.3% 45 to 60 minutes, 8.1% 60 minutes or more (2006-2010 5-year est.)

**OLEAN** (city). Covers a land area of 5.907 square miles and a water area of 0.258 square miles. Located at 42.08° N. Lat; 78.43° W. Long. Elevation is 1,447 feet.
**History:** Olean came to life as a lumber camp. From their lumber, settlers built rafts to sell to emigrants who gathered to await the spring flood which would float them down the Allegheny and Ohio Rivers to the western frontier.
**Population:** 16,946 (1990); 15,347 (2000); 14,452 (2010); Density: 2,446.3 persons per square mile (2010); Race: 90.6% White, 3.7% Black, 1.3% Asian, 0.7% American Indian/Alaska Native, 0.0% Native Hawaiian/Other Pacific Islander, 3.7% Other, 2.3% Hispanic of any race (2010); Average household size: 2.20 (2010); Median age: 38.9 (2010); Males per 100 females: 92.2 (2010); Marriage status: 31.8% never married, 48.0% now married, 8.5% widowed, 11.7% divorced (2006-2010 5-year est.); Foreign born: 1.2% (2006-2010 5-year est.); Ancestry (includes multiple ancestries): 23.7% Irish, 23.5% German, 14.4% Italian, 14.0% Polish, 11.0% English (2006-2010 5-year est.).
**Economy:** Single-family building permits issued: 0 (2011); Multi-family building permits issued: 0 (2011); Employment by occupation: 9.9% management, 3.3% professional, 7.4% services, 17.6% sales, 6.0% farming, 6.3% construction, 5.3% production (2006-2010 5-year est.).
**Income:** Per capita income: $22,601 (2006-2010 5-year est.); Median household income: $37,950 (2006-2010 5-year est.); Average household income: $49,183 (2006-2010 5-year est.); Percent of households with income of $100,000 or more: 10.5% (2006-2010 5-year est.); Poverty rate: 18.9% (2006-2010 5-year est.).
**Education:** Percent of population age 25 and over with: High school diploma (including GED) or higher: 90.0% (2006-2010 5-year est.); Bachelor's degree or higher: 24.4% (2006-2010 5-year est.); Master's degree or higher: 12.6% (2006-2010 5-year est.).

**School District(s)**
Cattaraugus-Allegany-Erie-Wyoming Boces
   2009-10 Enrollment: n/a . . . . . . . . . . . . . . . . . . . . . . . . (716) 376-8246
Olean City School District (PK-12)
   2009-10 Enrollment: 2,501 . . . . . . . . . . . . . . . . . . . . . (716) 375-8055
**Two-year College(s)**
Olean Business Institute (Private, For-profit)
   Fall 2010 Enrollment: 85 . . . . . . . . . . . . . . . . . . . . . . . (716) 372-7978
   2011-12 Tuition: In-state $11,660; Out-of-state $11,660
**Vocational/Technical School(s)**
Cattaraugus Allegany BOCES-Practical Nursing Program (Public)
   Fall 2010 Enrollment: 65 . . . . . . . . . . . . . . . . . . . . . . . (716) 376-8268
Continental School of Beauty Culture-Olean (Private, For-profit)
   Fall 2010 Enrollment: 118 . . . . . . . . . . . . . . . . . . . . . . (716) 372-5095
   2011-12 Tuition: $11,050
**Housing:** Homeownership rate: 54.0% (2010); Median home value: $68,200 (2006-2010 5-year est.); Median contract rent: $456 per month (2006-2010 5-year est.); Median year structure built: before 1940 (2006-2010 5-year est.).
**Hospitals:** Olean General Hospital (209 beds)
**Safety:** Violent crime rate: 53.0 per 10,000 population; Property crime rate: 403.5 per 10,000 population (2010).
**Newspapers:** Olean Times Herald (Local news; Circulation 19,000)
**Transportation:** Commute to work: 86.5% car, 1.3% public transportation, 7.2% walk, 2.2% work from home (2006-2010 5-year est.); Travel time to work: 65.4% less than 15 minutes, 16.9% 15 to 30 minutes, 9.2% 30 to 45 minutes, 4.1% 45 to 60 minutes, 4.4% 60 minutes or more (2006-2010 5-year est.)
**Airports:** Cattaraugus County-Olean (general aviation)
**Additional Information Contacts**
City of Olean . . . . . . . . . . . . . . . . . . . . . . . . . . . . . . (716) 376-5600
   http://www.cityofolean.com
Greater Olean Area Chamber of Commerce . . . . . . . . . . . . (716) 372-4433
   http://oleanny.com
Greater Olean Area Chamber of Commerce . . . . . . . . . . . . (716) 372-4433
   http://www.oleanny.com

**OLEAN** (town). Covers a land area of 29.609 square miles and a water area of 0.127 square miles. Located at 42.06° N. Lat; 78.42° W. Long. Elevation is 1,447 feet.
**History:** Once an oil-based economy emanating from nearby Pennsylvania oil fields. St. Bonaventure University nearby. Major outfitting post for settlers moving west down the Allegheny and Ohio rivers in early 1800s. In 1972 a severe flood associated with Hurricane Agnes flooded large areas and damaged more than 2,900 homes. Settled 1804, Incorporated 1893.

**Population:** 1,999 (1990); 2,029 (2000); 1,963 (2010); Density: 66.3 persons per square mile (2010); Race: 96.8% White, 1.1% Black, 1.0% Asian, 0.2% American Indian/Alaska Native, 0.0% Native Hawaiian/Other Pacific Islander, 0.9% Other, 1.0% Hispanic of any race (2010); Average household size: 2.26 (2010); Median age: 46.6 (2010); Males per 100 females: 103.0 (2010); Marriage status: 29.7% never married, 54.5% now married, 5.2% widowed, 10.7% divorced (2006-2010 5-year est.); Foreign born: 1.2% (2006-2010 5-year est.); Ancestry (includes multiple ancestries): 29.5% German, 23.7% Irish, 20.6% Italian, 10.0% English, 8.7% Polish (2006-2010 5-year est.).
**Economy:** Single-family building permits issued: 2 (2011); Multi-family building permits issued: 0 (2011); Employment by occupation: 6.9% management, 3.4% professional, 8.8% services, 15.5% sales, 4.0% farming, 10.2% construction, 7.5% production (2006-2010 5-year est.).
**Income:** Per capita income: $28,112 (2006-2010 5-year est.); Median household income: $55,735 (2006-2010 5-year est.); Average household income: $63,727 (2006-2010 5-year est.); Percent of households with income of $100,000 or more: 8.3% (2006-2010 5-year est.); Poverty rate: 8.0% (2006-2010 5-year est.).
**Education:** Percent of population age 25 and over with: High school diploma (including GED) or higher: 90.5% (2006-2010 5-year est.); Bachelor's degree or higher: 24.0% (2006-2010 5-year est.); Master's degree or higher: 10.2% (2006-2010 5-year est.).

### School District(s)
Cattaraugus-Allegany-Erie-Wyoming Boces
   2009-10 Enrollment: n/a . . . . . . . . . . . . . . . . . . . . . (716) 376-8246
Olean City School District (PK-12)
   2009-10 Enrollment: 2,501 . . . . . . . . . . . . . . . . . . . . (716) 375-8055
### Two-year College(s)
Olean Business Institute (Private, For-profit)
   Fall 2010 Enrollment: 85 . . . . . . . . . . . . . . . . . . . . (716) 372-7978
   2011-12 Tuition: In-state $11,660; Out-of-state $11,660
### Vocational/Technical School(s)
Cattaraugus Allegany BOCES-Practical Nursing Program (Public)
   Fall 2010 Enrollment: 65 . . . . . . . . . . . . . . . . . . . . (716) 376-8268
Continental School of Beauty Culture-Olean (Private, For-profit)
   Fall 2010 Enrollment: 118 . . . . . . . . . . . . . . . . . . . (716) 372-5095
   2011-12 Tuition: $11,050
**Housing:** Homeownership rate: 80.9% (2010); Median home value: $82,000 (2006-2010 5-year est.); Median contract rent: $401 per month (2006-2010 5-year est.); Median year structure built: 1959 (2006-2010 5-year est.).
**Hospitals:** Olean General Hospital (209 beds)
**Newspapers:** Olean Times Herald (Local news; Circulation 19,000)
**Transportation:** Commute to work: 96.2% car, 1.0% public transportation, 1.5% walk, 0.9% work from home (2006-2010 5-year est.); Travel time to work: 68.8% less than 15 minutes, 20.2% 15 to 30 minutes, 5.2% 30 to 45 minutes, 5.1% 45 to 60 minutes, 0.7% 60 minutes or more (2006-2010 5-year est.)
**Airports:** Cattaraugus County-Olean (general aviation)

**OTTO** (town). Covers a land area of 32.729 square miles and a water area of 0.117 square miles. Located at 42.39° N. Lat; 78.84° W. Long. Elevation is 1,260 feet.
**Population:** 777 (1990); 831 (2000); 808 (2010); Density: 24.7 persons per square mile (2010); Race: 97.3% White, 1.2% Black, 0.0% Asian, 0.6% American Indian/Alaska Native, 0.0% Native Hawaiian/Other Pacific Islander, 0.9% Other, 1.4% Hispanic of any race (2010); Average household size: 2.53 (2010); Median age: 42.9 (2010); Males per 100 females: 106.1 (2010); Marriage status: 17.9% never married, 69.1% now married, 7.2% widowed, 5.9% divorced (2006-2010 5-year est.); Foreign born: 1.6% (2006-2010 5-year est.); Ancestry (includes multiple ancestries): 35.5% German, 16.2% English, 16.2% Irish, 13.4% Polish, 9.2% French (2006-2010 5-year est.).
**Economy:** Single-family building permits issued: 0 (2011); Multi-family building permits issued: 0 (2011); Employment by occupation: 4.5% management, 4.2% professional, 7.0% services, 14.2% sales, 0.0% farming, 20.3% construction, 12.3% production (2006-2010 5-year est.).
**Income:** Per capita income: $19,008 (2006-2010 5-year est.); Median household income: $38,889 (2006-2010 5-year est.); Average household income: $50,407 (2006-2010 5-year est.); Percent of households with income of $100,000 or more: 8.8% (2006-2010 5-year est.); Poverty rate: 16.9% (2006-2010 5-year est.).
**Education:** Percent of population age 25 and over with: High school diploma (including GED) or higher: 86.0% (2006-2010 5-year est.);

Bachelor's degree or higher: 13.3% (2006-2010 5-year est.); Master's degree or higher: 7.1% (2006-2010 5-year est.).
**Housing:** Homeownership rate: 89.9% (2010); Median home value: $79,600 (2006-2010 5-year est.); Median contract rent: $612 per month (2006-2010 5-year est.); Median year structure built: 1971 (2006-2010 5-year est.).
**Transportation:** Commute to work: 94.8% car, 0.0% public transportation, 1.2% walk, 4.0% work from home (2006-2010 5-year est.); Travel time to work: 23.7% less than 15 minutes, 27.3% 15 to 30 minutes, 13.2% 30 to 45 minutes, 9.3% 45 to 60 minutes, 26.4% 60 minutes or more (2006-2010 5-year est.)

**PERRYSBURG** (village). Covers a land area of 0.984 square miles and a water area of 0.002 square miles. Located at 42.45° N. Lat; 79.00° W. Long. Elevation is 1,322 feet.
**Population:** 404 (1990); 408 (2000); 401 (2010); Density: 407.4 persons per square mile (2010); Race: 90.8% White, 1.7% Black, 0.2% Asian, 3.7% American Indian/Alaska Native, 0.0% Native Hawaiian/Other Pacific Islander, 3.6% Other, 1.0% Hispanic of any race (2010); Average household size: 2.50 (2010); Median age: 42.3 (2010); Males per 100 females: 95.6 (2010); Marriage status: 30.8% never married, 48.1% now married, 5.8% widowed, 15.4% divorced (2006-2010 5-year est.); Foreign born: 4.3% (2006-2010 5-year est.); Ancestry (includes multiple ancestries): 34.7% German, 22.3% Irish, 17.5% English, 16.5% Polish, 5.6% French (2006-2010 5-year est.).
**Economy:** Single-family building permits issued: 0 (2011); Multi-family building permits issued: 0 (2011); Employment by occupation: 6.3% management, 0.0% professional, 14.3% services, 16.6% sales, 5.1% farming, 21.1% construction, 8.0% production (2006-2010 5-year est.).
**Income:** Per capita income: $19,632 (2006-2010 5-year est.); Median household income: $48,438 (2006-2010 5-year est.); Average household income: $50,440 (2006-2010 5-year est.); Percent of households with income of $100,000 or more: 5.9% (2006-2010 5-year est.); Poverty rate: 29.9% (2006-2010 5-year est.).
**Education:** Percent of population age 25 and over with: High school diploma (including GED) or higher: 78.5% (2006-2010 5-year est.); Bachelor's degree or higher: 15.7% (2006-2010 5-year est.); Master's degree or higher: 10.9% (2006-2010 5-year est.).
**Housing:** Homeownership rate: 70.7% (2010); Median home value: $75,700 (2006-2010 5-year est.); Median contract rent: $372 per month (2006-2010 5-year est.); Median year structure built: before 1940 (2006-2010 5-year est.).
**Transportation:** Commute to work: 95.8% car, 0.0% public transportation, 4.2% walk, 0.0% work from home (2006-2010 5-year est.); Travel time to work: 59.0% less than 15 minutes, 19.3% 15 to 30 minutes, 3.6% 30 to 45 minutes, 6.0% 45 to 60 minutes, 12.0% 60 minutes or more (2006-2010 5-year est.)

**PERRYSBURG** (town). Covers a land area of 28.421 square miles and a water area of 0.126 square miles. Located at 42.48° N. Lat; 79.01° W. Long. Elevation is 1,322 feet.
**Population:** 1,838 (1990); 1,771 (2000); 1,626 (2010); Density: 57.2 persons per square mile (2010); Race: 93.4% White, 0.7% Black, 0.3% Asian, 4.1% American Indian/Alaska Native, 0.0% Native Hawaiian/Other Pacific Islander, 1.5% Other, 0.7% Hispanic of any race (2010); Average household size: 2.38 (2010); Median age: 44.1 (2010); Males per 100 females: 97.3 (2010); Marriage status: 21.7% never married, 59.2% now married, 7.0% widowed, 12.0% divorced (2006-2010 5-year est.); Foreign born: 3.0% (2006-2010 5-year est.); Ancestry (includes multiple ancestries): 38.1% German, 18.5% English, 15.5% Irish, 12.1% Polish, 9.0% Italian (2006-2010 5-year est.).
**Economy:** Single-family building permits issued: 5 (2011); Multi-family building permits issued: 0 (2011); Employment by occupation: 11.8% management, 1.2% professional, 10.1% services, 18.5% sales, 1.1% farming, 14.4% construction, 5.5% production (2006-2010 5-year est.).
**Income:** Per capita income: $23,529 (2006-2010 5-year est.); Median household income: $51,500 (2006-2010 5-year est.); Average household income: $57,221 (2006-2010 5-year est.); Percent of households with income of $100,000 or more: 8.0% (2006-2010 5-year est.); Poverty rate: 9.7% (2006-2010 5-year est.).
**Education:** Percent of population age 25 and over with: High school diploma (including GED) or higher: 88.3% (2006-2010 5-year est.); Bachelor's degree or higher: 16.1% (2006-2010 5-year est.); Master's degree or higher: 7.5% (2006-2010 5-year est.).

**Housing:** Homeownership rate: 81.5% (2010); Median home value: $93,900 (2006-2010 5-year est.); Median contract rent: $395 per month (2006-2010 5-year est.); Median year structure built: 1953 (2006-2010 5-year est.).
**Transportation:** Commute to work: 94.0% car, 0.0% public transportation, 4.1% walk, 0.8% work from home (2006-2010 5-year est.); Travel time to work: 48.6% less than 15 minutes, 21.3% 15 to 30 minutes, 12.0% 30 to 45 minutes, 8.1% 45 to 60 minutes, 10.1% 60 minutes or more (2006-2010 5-year est.).

**PERSIA** (town). Covers a land area of 20.892 square miles and a water area of 0.096 square miles. Located at 42.41° N. Lat; 78.91° W. Long. Elevation is 1,342 feet.
**Population:** 2,530 (1990); 2,512 (2000); 2,404 (2010); Density: 115.1 persons per square mile (2010); Race: 93.3% White, 0.5% Black, 0.3% Asian, 3.3% American Indian/Alaska Native, 0.0% Native Hawaiian/Other Pacific Islander, 2.6% Other, 3.0% Hispanic of any race (2010); Average household size: 2.33 (2010); Median age: 42.4 (2010); Males per 100 females: 96.1 (2010); Marriage status: 28.2% never married, 50.4% now married, 6.8% widowed, 14.5% divorced (2006-2010 5-year est.); Foreign born: 0.6% (2006-2010 5-year est.); Ancestry (includes multiple ancestries): 35.8% German, 23.1% Irish, 15.1% English, 14.6% Polish, 9.8% Italian (2006-2010 5-year est.).
**Economy:** Single-family building permits issued: 0 (2011); Multi-family building permits issued: 0 (2011); Employment by occupation: 7.1% management, 0.5% professional, 19.5% services, 12.4% sales, 1.7% farming, 16.8% construction, 11.2% production (2006-2010 5-year est.).
**Income:** Per capita income: $22,646 (2006-2010 5-year est.); Median household income: $45,208 (2006-2010 5-year est.); Average household income: $57,285 (2006-2010 5-year est.); Percent of households with income of $100,000 or more: 10.1% (2006-2010 5-year est.); Poverty rate: 13.7% (2006-2010 5-year est.).
**Education:** Percent of population age 25 and over with: High school diploma (including GED) or higher: 87.6% (2006-2010 5-year est.); Bachelor's degree or higher: 18.4% (2006-2010 5-year est.); Master's degree or higher: 7.7% (2006-2010 5-year est.).
**Housing:** Homeownership rate: 67.4% (2010); Median home value: $71,800 (2006-2010 5-year est.); Median contract rent: $435 per month (2006-2010 5-year est.); Median year structure built: 1941 (2006-2010 5-year est.).
**Transportation:** Commute to work: 83.6% car, 1.3% public transportation, 8.3% walk, 3.7% work from home (2006-2010 5-year est.); Travel time to work: 44.0% less than 15 minutes, 27.3% 15 to 30 minutes, 13.6% 30 to 45 minutes, 6.4% 45 to 60 minutes, 8.8% 60 minutes or more (2006-2010 5-year est.).

**PORTVILLE** (village). Covers a land area of 0.802 square miles and a water area of 0 square miles. Located at 42.03° N. Lat; 78.33° W. Long. Elevation is 1,430 feet.
**Population:** 1,233 (1990); 1,024 (2000); 1,014 (2010); Density: 1,264.3 persons per square mile (2010); Race: 96.3% White, 1.2% Black, 0.1% Asian, 0.2% American Indian/Alaska Native, 0.0% Native Hawaiian/Other Pacific Islander, 2.2% Other, 1.4% Hispanic of any race (2010); Average household size: 2.44 (2010); Median age: 37.6 (2010); Males per 100 females: 86.4 (2010); Marriage status: 26.6% never married, 47.8% now married, 9.5% widowed, 16.1% divorced (2006-2010 5-year est.); Foreign born: 1.3% (2006-2010 5-year est.); Ancestry (includes multiple ancestries): 41.7% German, 25.1% Irish, 23.2% English, 10.7% Italian, 8.4% Polish (2006-2010 5-year est.).
**Economy:** Employment by occupation: 2.3% management, 0.9% professional, 6.6% services, 17.0% sales, 1.6% farming, 11.1% construction, 7.0% production (2006-2010 5-year est.).
**Income:** Per capita income: $24,060 (2006-2010 5-year est.); Median household income: $39,663 (2006-2010 5-year est.); Average household income: $59,320 (2006-2010 5-year est.); Percent of households with income of $100,000 or more: 10.3% (2006-2010 5-year est.); Poverty rate: 15.2% (2006-2010 5-year est.).
**Education:** Percent of population age 25 and over with: High school diploma (including GED) or higher: 94.2% (2006-2010 5-year est.); Bachelor's degree or higher: 28.3% (2006-2010 5-year est.); Master's degree or higher: 17.7% (2006-2010 5-year est.).
**School District(s)**
Portville Central School District (PK-12)
   2009-10 Enrollment: 960 . . . . . . . . . . . . . . . . . . . . . . . . . (716) 933-7140

**Housing:** Homeownership rate: 61.2% (2010); Median home value: $71,500 (2006-2010 5-year est.); Median contract rent: $393 per month (2006-2010 5-year est.); Median year structure built: before 1940 (2006-2010 5-year est.).
**Safety:** Violent crime rate: 10.8 per 10,000 population; Property crime rate: 32.4 per 10,000 population (2010).
**Transportation:** Commute to work: 95.4% car, 0.0% public transportation, 3.9% walk, 0.7% work from home (2006-2010 5-year est.); Travel time to work: 43.7% less than 15 minutes, 39.3% 15 to 30 minutes, 7.5% 30 to 45 minutes, 8.4% 45 to 60 minutes, 1.2% 60 minutes or more (2006-2010 5-year est.).

**PORTVILLE** (town). Covers a land area of 35.579 square miles and a water area of 0.447 square miles. Located at 42.05° N. Lat; 78.34° W. Long. Elevation is 1,430 feet.
**History:** Incorporated 1895.
**Population:** 4,397 (1990); 3,952 (2000); 3,730 (2010); Density: 104.8 persons per square mile (2010); Race: 97.2% White, 0.9% Black, 0.2% Asian, 0.3% American Indian/Alaska Native, 0.0% Native Hawaiian/Other Pacific Islander, 1.4% Other, 1.2% Hispanic of any race (2010); Average household size: 2.42 (2010); Median age: 43.1 (2010); Males per 100 females: 94.9 (2010); Marriage status: 20.3% never married, 61.2% now married, 7.0% widowed, 11.4% divorced (2006-2010 5-year est.); Foreign born: 0.4% (2006-2010 5-year est.); Ancestry (includes multiple ancestries): 38.6% German, 25.1% Irish, 19.2% English, 8.8% Italian, 6.5% Polish (2006-2010 5-year est.).
**Economy:** Single-family building permits issued: 2 (2011); Multi-family building permits issued: 0 (2011); Employment by occupation: 5.3% management, 3.5% professional, 6.8% services, 19.4% sales, 4.4% farming, 7.8% construction, 7.9% production (2006-2010 5-year est.).
**Income:** Per capita income: $24,343 (2006-2010 5-year est.); Median household income: $47,423 (2006-2010 5-year est.); Average household income: $55,410 (2006-2010 5-year est.); Percent of households with income of $100,000 or more: 9.2% (2006-2010 5-year est.); Poverty rate: 8.2% (2006-2010 5-year est.).
**Education:** Percent of population age 25 and over with: High school diploma (including GED) or higher: 94.3% (2006-2010 5-year est.); Bachelor's degree or higher: 22.7% (2006-2010 5-year est.); Master's degree or higher: 10.6% (2006-2010 5-year est.).
**School District(s)**
Portville Central School District (PK-12)
   2009-10 Enrollment: 960 . . . . . . . . . . . . . . . . . . . . . . . . . (716) 933-7140

**Housing:** Homeownership rate: 76.7% (2010); Median home value: $69,200 (2006-2010 5-year est.); Median contract rent: $414 per month (2006-2010 5-year est.); Median year structure built: 1955 (2006-2010 5-year est.).
**Transportation:** Commute to work: 96.6% car, 0.0% public transportation, 1.0% walk, 1.8% work from home (2006-2010 5-year est.); Travel time to work: 42.4% less than 15 minutes, 42.7% 15 to 30 minutes, 10.5% 30 to 45 minutes, 2.8% 45 to 60 minutes, 1.5% 60 minutes or more (2006-2010 5-year est.).

**RANDOLPH** (village). Covers a land area of 3.250 square miles and a water area of 0.010 square miles. Located at 42.16° N. Lat; 78.97° W. Long. Elevation is 1,276 feet.
**Population:** 1,298 (1990); 1,316 (2000); 1,286 (2010); Density: 395.6 persons per square mile (2010); Race: 97.3% White, 0.0% Black, 0.1% Asian, 0.4% American Indian/Alaska Native, 0.2% Native Hawaiian/Other Pacific Islander, 2.0% Other, 1.7% Hispanic of any race (2010); Average household size: 2.48 (2010); Median age: 38.9 (2010); Males per 100 females: 91.9 (2010); Marriage status: 27.5% never married, 47.0% now married, 12.1% widowed, 13.4% divorced (2006-2010 5-year est.); Foreign born: 0.8% (2006-2010 5-year est.); Ancestry (includes multiple ancestries): 25.3% German, 22.8% Irish, 20.7% English, 8.7% Polish, 6.6% Italian (2006-2010 5-year est.).
**Economy:** Single-family building permits issued: 3 (2011); Multi-family building permits issued: 0 (2011); Employment by occupation: 3.7% management, 2.7% professional, 10.3% services, 15.0% sales, 2.1% farming, 15.2% construction, 6.4% production (2006-2010 5-year est.).
**Income:** Per capita income: $20,398 (2006-2010 5-year est.); Median household income: $36,136 (2006-2010 5-year est.); Average household income: $44,328 (2006-2010 5-year est.); Percent of households with income of $100,000 or more: 6.1% (2006-2010 5-year est.); Poverty rate: 14.7% (2006-2010 5-year est.).

**Education:** Percent of population age 25 and over with: High school diploma (including GED) or higher: 89.9% (2006-2010 5-year est.); Bachelor's degree or higher: 16.2% (2006-2010 5-year est.); Master's degree or higher: 9.9% (2006-2010 5-year est.).

**School District(s)**

Randolph Academy Union Free School District (03-12)

  2009-10 Enrollment: 98 . . . . . . . . . . . . . . . . . . . . . (716) 358-6866

Randolph Central School District (PK-12)

  2009-10 Enrollment: 967 . . . . . . . . . . . . . . . . . . . . . (716) 358-7005

**Housing:** Homeownership rate: 62.2% (2010); Median home value: $67,200 (2006-2010 5-year est.); Median contract rent: $343 per month (2006-2010 5-year est.); Median year structure built: before 1940 (2006-2010 5-year est.).

**Newspapers:** Randolph Register (Local news; Circulation 1,500)

**Transportation:** Commute to work: 97.6% car, 0.6% public transportation, 1.8% walk, 0.0% work from home (2006-2010 5-year est.); Travel time to work: 32.3% less than 15 minutes, 33.5% 15 to 30 minutes, 19.7% 30 to 45 minutes, 6.6% 45 to 60 minutes, 8.0% 60 minutes or more (2006-2010 5-year est.)

**RANDOLPH** (town). Covers a land area of 36.064 square miles and a water area of 0.223 square miles. Located at 42.13° N. Lat; 78.99° W. Long. Elevation is 1,276 feet.

**Population:** 2,613 (1990); 2,681 (2000); 2,602 (2010); Density: 72.1 persons per square mile (2010); Race: 97.0% White, 0.6% Black, 0.3% Asian, 0.5% American Indian/Alaska Native, 0.1% Native Hawaiian/Other Pacific Islander, 1.5% Other, 2.3% Hispanic of any race (2010); Average household size: 2.51 (2010); Median age: 40.1 (2010); Males per 100 females: 103.6 (2010); Marriage status: 22.2% never married, 57.5% now married, 8.2% widowed, 12.1% divorced (2006-2010 5-year est.); Foreign born: 0.6% (2006-2010 5-year est.); Ancestry (includes multiple ancestries): 27.7% German, 18.1% Irish, 17.3% English, 7.7% Swedish, 6.6% Italian (2006-2010 5-year est.).

**Economy:** Single-family building permits issued: 3 (2011); Multi-family building permits issued: 0 (2011); Employment by occupation: 5.8% management, 3.3% professional, 9.8% services, 13.1% sales, 1.4% farming, 15.5% construction, 8.4% production (2006-2010 5-year est.).

**Income:** Per capita income: $20,698 (2006-2010 5-year est.); Median household income: $41,613 (2006-2010 5-year est.); Average household income: $49,975 (2006-2010 5-year est.); Percent of households with income of $100,000 or more: 7.1% (2006-2010 5-year est.); Poverty rate: 13.5% (2006-2010 5-year est.).

**Education:** Percent of population age 25 and over with: High school diploma (including GED) or higher: 91.8% (2006-2010 5-year est.); Bachelor's degree or higher: 17.2% (2006-2010 5-year est.); Master's degree or higher: 8.6% (2006-2010 5-year est.).

**School District(s)**

Randolph Academy Union Free School District (03-12)

  2009-10 Enrollment: 98 . . . . . . . . . . . . . . . . . . . . . (716) 358-6866

Randolph Central School District (PK-12)

  2009-10 Enrollment: 967 . . . . . . . . . . . . . . . . . . . . . (716) 358-7005

**Housing:** Homeownership rate: 71.2% (2010); Median home value: $77,100 (2006-2010 5-year est.); Median contract rent: $337 per month (2006-2010 5-year est.); Median year structure built: before 1940 (2006-2010 5-year est.).

**Newspapers:** Randolph Register (Local news; Circulation 1,500)

**Transportation:** Commute to work: 94.7% car, 0.3% public transportation, 1.4% walk, 3.7% work from home (2006-2010 5-year est.); Travel time to work: 28.4% less than 15 minutes, 40.5% 15 to 30 minutes, 17.7% 30 to 45 minutes, 8.2% 45 to 60 minutes, 5.2% 60 minutes or more (2006-2010 5-year est.)

**RED HOUSE** (town). Covers a land area of 55.668 square miles and a water area of 0.188 square miles. Located at 42.06° N. Lat; 78.73° W. Long. Elevation is 1,339 feet.

**Population:** 159 (1990); 38 (2000); 38 (2010); Density: 0.7 persons per square mile (2010); Race: 97.4% White, 0.0% Black, 0.0% Asian, 0.0% American Indian/Alaska Native, 0.0% Native Hawaiian/Other Pacific Islander, 2.6% Other, 0.0% Hispanic of any race (2010); Average household size: 2.24 (2010); Median age: 51.0 (2010); Males per 100 females: 123.5 (2010); Marriage status: 12.5% never married, 87.5% now married, 0.0% widowed, 0.0% divorced (2006-2010 5-year est.); Foreign born: 0.0% (2006-2010 5-year est.); Ancestry (includes multiple ancestries): 38.5% German, 23.1% English, 15.4% Irish, 7.7% Swiss, 7.7% Polish (2006-2010 5-year est.).

**Economy:** Single-family building permits issued: 1 (2011); Multi-family building permits issued: 0 (2011); Employment by occupation: 10.0% management, 0.0% professional, 0.0% services, 20.0% sales, 10.0% farming, 10.0% construction, 10.0% production (2006-2010 5-year est.).

**Income:** Per capita income: $32,704 (2006-2010 5-year est.); Median household income: $71,250 (2006-2010 5-year est.); Average household income: $70,425 (2006-2010 5-year est.); Percent of households with income of $100,000 or more: 8.3% (2006-2010 5-year est.); Poverty rate: 0.0% (2006-2010 5-year est.).

**Education:** Percent of population age 25 and over with: High school diploma (including GED) or higher: 100.0% (2006-2010 5-year est.); Bachelor's degree or higher: 26.1% (2006-2010 5-year est.); Master's degree or higher: 4.3% (2006-2010 5-year est.).

**Housing:** Homeownership rate: 47.0% (2010); Median home value: $137,500 (2006-2010 5-year est.); Median contract rent: n/a per month (2006-2010 5-year est.); Median year structure built: before 1940 (2006-2010 5-year est.).

**Transportation:** Commute to work: 80.0% car, 0.0% public transportation, 20.0% walk, 0.0% work from home (2006-2010 5-year est.); Travel time to work: 30.0% less than 15 minutes, 45.0% 15 to 30 minutes, 25.0% 30 to 45 minutes, 0.0% 45 to 60 minutes, 0.0% 60 minutes or more (2006-2010 5-year est.)

**SAINT BONAVENTURE** (CDP). Covers a land area of 1.976 square miles and a water area of 0.152 square miles. Located at 42.07° N. Lat; 78.47° W. Long. Elevation is 1,427 feet.

**Population:** 2,306 (1990); 2,127 (2000); 2,044 (2010); Density: 1,034.3 persons per square mile (2010); Race: 88.3% White, 5.5% Black, 3.3% Asian, 0.2% American Indian/Alaska Native, 0.0% Native Hawaiian/Other Pacific Islander, 2.7% Other, 3.7% Hispanic of any race (2010); Average household size: 1.95 (2010); Median age: 20.9 (2010); Males per 100 females: 85.3 (2010); Marriage status: 84.8% never married, 10.2% now married, 3.1% widowed, 1.9% divorced (2006-2010 5-year est.); Foreign born: 6.6% (2006-2010 5-year est.); Ancestry (includes multiple ancestries): 29.7% Irish, 28.9% German, 25.8% Italian, 10.2% Polish, 8.0% English (2006-2010 5-year est.).

**Economy:** Employment by occupation: 4.8% management, 0.0% professional, 22.8% services, 24.9% sales, 6.5% farming, 4.0% construction, 2.3% production (2006-2010 5-year est.).

**Income:** Per capita income: $6,610 (2006-2010 5-year est.); Median household income: $19,531 (2006-2010 5-year est.); Average household income: $34,661 (2006-2010 5-year est.); Percent of households with income of $100,000 or more: 6.6% (2006-2010 5-year est.); Poverty rate: 25.7% (2006-2010 5-year est.).

**Education:** Percent of population age 25 and over with: High school diploma (including GED) or higher: 79.7% (2006-2010 5-year est.); Bachelor's degree or higher: 30.3% (2006-2010 5-year est.); Master's degree or higher: 22.3% (2006-2010 5-year est.).

**Four-year College(s)**

Saint Bonaventure University (Private, Not-for-profit, Roman Catholic)

  Fall 2010 Enrollment: 2,377 . . . . . . . . . . . . . . . . . . (716) 375-2000

  2011-12 Tuition: In-state $27,890; Out-of-state $27,890

**Housing:** Homeownership rate: 67.5% (2010); Median home value: $86,600 (2006-2010 5-year est.); Median contract rent: $242 per month (2006-2010 5-year est.); Median year structure built: 1959 (2006-2010 5-year est.).

**Transportation:** Commute to work: 56.9% car, 3.8% public transportation, 34.3% walk, 4.1% work from home (2006-2010 5-year est.); Travel time to work: 88.9% less than 15 minutes, 5.6% 15 to 30 minutes, 3.4% 30 to 45 minutes, 1.3% 45 to 60 minutes, 0.8% 60 minutes or more (2006-2010 5-year est.)

**SALAMANCA** (city). Covers a land area of 5.993 square miles and a water area of 0.241 square miles. Located at 42.16° N. Lat; 78.74° W. Long. Elevation is 1,381 feet.

**Population:** 6,566 (1990); 6,097 (2000); 5,815 (2010); Density: 970.2 persons per square mile (2010); Race: 77.0% White, 0.9% Black, 0.5% Asian, 16.9% American Indian/Alaska Native, 0.1% Native Hawaiian/Other Pacific Islander, 4.6% Other, 3.3% Hispanic of any race (2010); Average household size: 2.30 (2010); Median age: 37.9 (2010); Males per 100 females: 91.0 (2010); Marriage status: 29.6% never married, 48.6% now married, 8.5% widowed, 13.3% divorced (2006-2010 5-year est.); Foreign born: 1.9% (2006-2010 5-year est.); Ancestry (includes multiple ancestries): 22.9% German, 20.8% Irish, 11.1% Polish, 9.1% English, 7.4% Italian (2006-2010 5-year est.).

**Economy:** Single-family building permits issued: 0 (2011); Multi-family building permits issued: 0 (2011); Employment by occupation: 6.1% management, 1.4% professional, 13.8% services, 21.6% sales, 3.5% farming, 13.1% construction, 6.8% production (2006-2010 5-year est.).
**Income:** Per capita income: $18,286 (2006-2010 5-year est.); Median household income: $32,741 (2006-2010 5-year est.); Average household income: $41,510 (2006-2010 5-year est.); Percent of households with income of $100,000 or more: 6.1% (2006-2010 5-year est.); Poverty rate: 20.6% (2006-2010 5-year est.).
**Education:** Percent of population age 25 and over with: High school diploma (including GED) or higher: 86.1% (2006-2010 5-year est.); Bachelor's degree or higher: 13.8% (2006-2010 5-year est.); Master's degree or higher: 4.7% (2006-2010 5-year est.).

**School District(s)**
Salamanca City School District (PK-12)
   2009-10 Enrollment: 1,431 . . . . . . . . . . . . . . . . . . . . . (716) 945-2400
**Housing:** Homeownership rate: 54.7% (2010); Median home value: $70,500 (2006-2010 5-year est.); Median contract rent: $400 per month (2006-2010 5-year est.); Median year structure built: before 1940 (2006-2010 5-year est.).
**Safety:** Violent crime rate: 59.8 per 10,000 population; Property crime rate: 441.9 per 10,000 population (2010).
**Newspapers:** Salamanca Pennysaver (Community news; Circulation 2,000); Salamanca Press (Local news; Circulation 2,000)
**Transportation:** Commute to work: 87.2% car, 0.0% public transportation, 9.0% walk, 2.3% work from home (2006-2010 5-year est.); Travel time to work: 59.1% less than 15 minutes, 22.7% 15 to 30 minutes, 12.5% 30 to 45 minutes, 2.8% 45 to 60 minutes, 2.9% 60 minutes or more (2006-2010 5-year est.)
**Additional Information Contacts**
Seneca Salamanca Chamber of Commerce . . . . . . . . . . (716) 945-2034
   http://salamancachamber.org

---

**SALAMANCA** (town). Covers a land area of 18.390 square miles and a water area of <.001 square miles. Located at 42.17° N. Lat; 78.80° W. Long. Elevation is 1,381 feet.
**History:** In Allegany Indian Reservation. Allegany State Park is just S. Furniture, plastic and wood prods; printing. Most of the city is built on land that is leased from the Seneca Nation's Allegany Indian Reservation. Settled in 1860s; inc. as city 1913.
**Population:** 477 (1990); 544 (2000); 481 (2010); Density: 26.2 persons per square mile (2010); Race: 93.3% White, 0.6% Black, 0.6% Asian, 2.5% American Indian/Alaska Native, 0.0% Native Hawaiian/Other Pacific Islander, 3.0% Other, 1.0% Hispanic of any race (2010); Average household size: 2.37 (2010); Median age: 49.3 (2010); Males per 100 females: 114.7 (2010); Marriage status: 14.6% never married, 71.3% now married, 6.5% widowed, 7.7% divorced (2006-2010 5-year est.); Foreign born: 2.6% (2006-2010 5-year est.); Ancestry (includes multiple ancestries): 33.6% German, 24.1% Irish, 17.2% Polish, 15.4% English, 8.1% Italian (2006-2010 5-year est.).
**Economy:** Single-family building permits issued: 0 (2011); Multi-family building permits issued: 0 (2011); Employment by occupation: 11.0% management, 1.6% professional, 5.3% services, 18.4% sales, 4.9% farming, 7.8% construction, 1.6% production (2006-2010 5-year est.).
**Income:** Per capita income: $24,408 (2006-2010 5-year est.); Median household income: $54,091 (2006-2010 5-year est.); Average household income: $59,670 (2006-2010 5-year est.); Percent of households with income of $100,000 or more: 14.6% (2006-2010 5-year est.); Poverty rate: 11.9% (2006-2010 5-year est.).
**Education:** Percent of population age 25 and over with: High school diploma (including GED) or higher: 84.6% (2006-2010 5-year est.); Bachelor's degree or higher: 15.4% (2006-2010 5-year est.); Master's degree or higher: 8.0% (2006-2010 5-year est.).

**School District(s)**
Salamanca City School District (PK-12)
   2009-10 Enrollment: 1,431 . . . . . . . . . . . . . . . . . . . . . (716) 945-2400
**Housing:** Homeownership rate: 93.1% (2010); Median home value: $78,000 (2006-2010 5-year est.); Median contract rent: $463 per month (2006-2010 5-year est.); Median year structure built: 1963 (2006-2010 5-year est.).
**Newspapers:** Salamanca Pennysaver (Community news; Circulation 2,000); Salamanca Press (Local news; Circulation 2,000)
**Transportation:** Commute to work: 96.6% car, 0.0% public transportation, 0.9% walk, 1.3% work from home (2006-2010 5-year est.); Travel time to work: 39.7% less than 15 minutes, 37.1% 15 to 30 minutes, 20.3% 30 to 45

minutes, 1.3% 45 to 60 minutes, 1.7% 60 minutes or more (2006-2010 5-year est.)

---

**SOUTH DAYTON** (village). Covers a land area of 1.005 square miles and a water area of 0 square miles. Located at 42.36° N. Lat; 79.05° W. Long. Elevation is 1,306 feet.
**Population:** 601 (1990); 662 (2000); 620 (2010); Density: 616.5 persons per square mile (2010); Race: 96.8% White, 0.3% Black, 0.3% Asian, 0.5% American Indian/Alaska Native, 0.0% Native Hawaiian/Other Pacific Islander, 2.1% Other, 1.3% Hispanic of any race (2010); Average household size: 2.59 (2010); Median age: 36.0 (2010); Males per 100 females: 94.4 (2010); Marriage status: 30.8% never married, 56.3% now married, 7.1% widowed, 5.7% divorced (2006-2010 5-year est.); Foreign born: 0.4% (2006-2010 5-year est.); Ancestry (includes multiple ancestries): 46.1% German, 27.7% Irish, 12.3% English, 10.8% Italian, 9.1% Polish (2006-2010 5-year est.).
**Economy:** Single-family building permits issued: 0 (2011); Multi-family building permits issued: 0 (2011); Employment by occupation: 5.7% management, 0.0% professional, 14.8% services, 26.7% sales, 6.6% farming, 17.6% construction, 16.4% production (2006-2010 5-year est.).
**Income:** Per capita income: $16,743 (2006-2010 5-year est.); Median household income: $43,563 (2006-2010 5-year est.); Average household income: $46,742 (2006-2010 5-year est.); Percent of households with income of $100,000 or more: 1.2% (2006-2010 5-year est.); Poverty rate: 10.5% (2006-2010 5-year est.).
**Education:** Percent of population age 25 and over with: High school diploma (including GED) or higher: 89.0% (2006-2010 5-year est.); Bachelor's degree or higher: 7.6% (2006-2010 5-year est.); Master's degree or higher: 5.0% (2006-2010 5-year est.).

**School District(s)**
Pine Valley Central School District (south Dayton) (PK-12)
   2009-10 Enrollment: 714 . . . . . . . . . . . . . . . . . . . . . . (716) 988-3293
**Housing:** Homeownership rate: 73.6% (2010); Median home value: $51,900 (2006-2010 5-year est.); Median contract rent: $430 per month (2006-2010 5-year est.); Median year structure built: before 1940 (2006-2010 5-year est.).
**Transportation:** Commute to work: 88.3% car, 0.0% public transportation, 4.2% walk, 3.6% work from home (2006-2010 5-year est.); Travel time to work: 19.8% less than 15 minutes, 35.9% 15 to 30 minutes, 38.3% 30 to 45 minutes, 1.0% 45 to 60 minutes, 5.0% 60 minutes or more (2006-2010 5-year est.)

---

**SOUTH VALLEY** (town). Covers a land area of 36.840 square miles and a water area of 0.246 square miles. Located at 42.04° N. Lat; 79.00° W. Long.
**Population:** 281 (1990); 302 (2000); 264 (2010); Density: 7.2 persons per square mile (2010); Race: 98.5% White, 0.4% Black, 0.0% Asian, 1.1% American Indian/Alaska Native, 0.0% Native Hawaiian/Other Pacific Islander, 0.0% Other, 0.0% Hispanic of any race (2010); Average household size: 1.93 (2010); Median age: 52.8 (2010); Males per 100 females: 123.7 (2010); Marriage status: 13.0% never married, 59.0% now married, 13.0% widowed, 15.0% divorced (2006-2010 5-year est.); Foreign born: 0.0% (2006-2010 5-year est.); Ancestry (includes multiple ancestries): 35.7% German, 18.4% English, 15.0% Irish, 12.1% Polish, 10.1% Italian (2006-2010 5-year est.).
**Economy:** Single-family building permits issued: 3 (2011); Multi-family building permits issued: 0 (2011); Employment by occupation: 10.7% management, 3.6% professional, 9.8% services, 12.5% sales, 3.6% farming, 13.4% construction, 2.7% production (2006-2010 5-year est.).
**Income:** Per capita income: $28,379 (2006-2010 5-year est.); Median household income: $43,056 (2006-2010 5-year est.); Average household income: $47,290 (2006-2010 5-year est.); Percent of households with income of $100,000 or more: 4.8% (2006-2010 5-year est.); Poverty rate: 2.4% (2006-2010 5-year est.).
**Education:** Percent of population age 25 and over with: High school diploma (including GED) or higher: 86.8% (2006-2010 5-year est.); Bachelor's degree or higher: 19.5% (2006-2010 5-year est.); Master's degree or higher: 9.5% (2006-2010 5-year est.).
**Housing:** Homeownership rate: 95.6% (2010); Median home value: $93,100 (2006-2010 5-year est.); Median contract rent: n/a per month (2006-2010 5-year est.); Median year structure built: 1972 (2006-2010 5-year est.).
**Transportation:** Commute to work: 93.8% car, 0.0% public transportation, 3.1% walk, 3.1% work from home (2006-2010 5-year est.); Travel time to work: 19.4% less than 15 minutes, 53.8% 15 to 30 minutes, 24.7% 30 to 45

minutes, 2.2% 45 to 60 minutes, 0.0% 60 minutes or more (2006-2010 5-year est.)

## STEAMBURG (unincorporated postal area)
Zip Code: 14783

Covers a land area of 24.917 square miles and a water area of 6.425 square miles. Located at 42.08° N. Lat; 78.88° W. Long. Elevation is 1,407 feet. Population: 320 (2010); Density: 12.8 persons per square mile (2010); Race: 37.5% White, 0.0% Black, 0.0% Asian, 61.9% American Indian/Alaska Native, 0.0% Native Hawaiian/Other Pacific Islander, 0.6% Other, 0.9% Hispanic of any race (2010); Average household size: 2.46 (2010); Median age: 40.2 (2010); Males per 100 females: 113.3 (2010); Homeownership rate: 75.4% (2010)

## VERSAILLES (unincorporated postal area)
Zip Code: 14168

Covers a land area of 0.039 square miles and a water area of 0 square miles. Located at 42.52° N. Lat; 78.99° W. Long. Elevation is 764 feet. Population: 36 (2010); Density: 908.3 persons per square mile (2010); Race: 61.1% White, 0.0% Black, 0.0% Asian, 38.9% American Indian/Alaska Native, 0.0% Native Hawaiian/Other Pacific Islander, 0.0% Other, 8.3% Hispanic of any race (2010); Average household size: 2.57 (2010); Median age: 49.5 (2010); Males per 100 females: 111.8 (2010); Homeownership rate: 78.6% (2010)

## WEST VALLEY (CDP). Covers a land area of 1.532 square miles and a water area of 0.002 square miles. Located at 42.40° N. Lat; 78.60° W. Long. Elevation is 1,522 feet.

Population: n/a (1990); n/a (2000); 518 (2010); Density: 338.1 persons per square mile (2010); Race: 99.0% White, 0.8% Black, 0.0% Asian, 0.2% American Indian/Alaska Native, 0.0% Native Hawaiian/Other Pacific Islander, 0.0% Other, 0.0% Hispanic of any race (2010); Average household size: 2.43 (2010); Median age: 42.9 (2010); Males per 100 females: 103.9 (2010); Marriage status: 35.5% never married, 52.6% now married, 5.8% widowed, 6.1% divorced (2006-2010 5-year est.); Foreign born: 0.0% (2006-2010 5-year est.); Ancestry (includes multiple ancestries): 34.6% German, 26.1% Irish, 16.3% Polish, 8.9% American, 7.8% English (2006-2010 5-year est.).
Economy: Employment by occupation: 12.5% management, 0.0% professional, 14.7% services, 9.1% sales, 0.0% farming, 17.7% construction, 16.8% production (2006-2010 5-year est.).
Income: Per capita income: $19,788 (2006-2010 5-year est.); Median household income: $47,955 (2006-2010 5-year est.); Average household income: $50,761 (2006-2010 5-year est.); Percent of households with income of $100,000 or more: 11.9% (2006-2010 5-year est.); Poverty rate: 8.3% (2006-2010 5-year est.).
Education: Percent of population age 25 and over with: High school diploma (including GED) or higher: 93.5% (2006-2010 5-year est.); Bachelor's degree or higher: 18.2% (2006-2010 5-year est.); Master's degree or higher: 3.8% (2006-2010 5-year est.).

### School District(s)
West Valley Central School District (PK-12)
    2009-10 Enrollment: 378 . . . . . . . . . . . . . . . . . . . . . . . . (716) 942-3293
Housing: Homeownership rate: 76.6% (2010); Median home value: $87,000 (2006-2010 5-year est.); Median contract rent: $400 per month (2006-2010 5-year est.); Median year structure built: before 1940 (2006-2010 5-year est.).
Transportation: Commute to work: 90.9% car, 0.0% public transportation, 0.0% walk, 2.7% work from home (2006-2010 5-year est.); Travel time to work: 20.2% less than 15 minutes, 41.3% 15 to 30 minutes, 6.6% 30 to 45 minutes, 9.4% 45 to 60 minutes, 22.5% 60 minutes or more (2006-2010 5-year est.)

## WESTON MILLS (CDP). Covers a land area of 6.669 square miles and a water area of 0.073 square miles. Located at 42.07° N. Lat; 78.37° W. Long. Elevation is 1,463 feet.

Population: 1,750 (1990); 1,608 (2000); 1,472 (2010); Density: 220.7 persons per square mile (2010); Race: 96.3% White, 1.6% Black, 0.5% Asian, 0.1% American Indian/Alaska Native, 0.0% Native Hawaiian/Other Pacific Islander, 1.5% Other, 1.7% Hispanic of any race (2010); Average household size: 2.28 (2010); Median age: 46.2 (2010); Males per 100 females: 96.3 (2010); Marriage status: 24.1% never married, 57.3% now married, 9.7% widowed, 8.9% divorced (2006-2010 5-year est.); Foreign born: 0.9% (2006-2010 5-year est.); Ancestry (includes multiple

ancestries): 35.3% German, 19.2% Irish, 17.3% English, 9.8% Italian, 7.5% American (2006-2010 5-year est.).
Economy: Employment by occupation: 5.1% management, 4.7% professional, 7.2% services, 14.3% sales, 5.5% farming, 4.3% construction, 4.0% production (2006-2010 5-year est.).
Income: Per capita income: $31,036 (2006-2010 5-year est.); Median household income: $49,044 (2006-2010 5-year est.); Average household income: $65,966 (2006-2010 5-year est.); Percent of households with income of $100,000 or more: 9.3% (2006-2010 5-year est.); Poverty rate: 8.2% (2006-2010 5-year est.).
Education: Percent of population age 25 and over with: High school diploma (including GED) or higher: 90.5% (2006-2010 5-year est.); Bachelor's degree or higher: 25.9% (2006-2010 5-year est.); Master's degree or higher: 11.6% (2006-2010 5-year est.).
Housing: Homeownership rate: 78.3% (2010); Median home value: $69,700 (2006-2010 5-year est.); Median contract rent: $439 per month (2006-2010 5-year est.); Median year structure built: 1953 (2006-2010 5-year est.).
Transportation: Commute to work: 96.4% car, 0.0% public transportation, 1.4% walk, 2.2% work from home (2006-2010 5-year est.); Travel time to work: 61.5% less than 15 minutes, 23.3% 15 to 30 minutes, 7.0% 30 to 45 minutes, 8.2% 45 to 60 minutes, 0.0% 60 minutes or more (2006-2010 5-year est.)

## WESTONS MILLS (unincorporated postal area)
Zip Code: 14788

Covers a land area of 0.210 square miles and a water area of 0 square miles. Located at 42.06° N. Lat; 78.38° W. Long. Elevation is 1,440 feet. Population: 163 (2010); Density: 774.6 persons per square mile (2010); Race: 93.3% White, 4.9% Black, 0.0% Asian, 0.0% American Indian/Alaska Native, 0.0% Native Hawaiian/Other Pacific Islander, 1.8% Other, 1.8% Hispanic of any race (2010); Average household size: 2.32 (2010); Median age: 43.9 (2010); Males per 100 females: 123.3 (2010); Homeownership rate: 57.1% (2010)

## YORKSHIRE (town). Covers a land area of 36.249 square miles and a water area of 0.144 square miles. Located at 42.47° N. Lat; 78.52° W. Long. Elevation is 1,434 feet.

Population: 3,905 (1990); 4,210 (2000); 3,913 (2010); Density: 107.9 persons per square mile (2010); Race: 97.1% White, 0.3% Black, 0.6% Asian, 0.5% American Indian/Alaska Native, 0.0% Native Hawaiian/Other Pacific Islander, 1.5% Other, 0.9% Hispanic of any race (2010); Average household size: 2.38 (2010); Median age: 40.8 (2010); Males per 100 females: 99.7 (2010); Marriage status: 30.2% never married, 56.0% now married, 6.0% widowed, 7.7% divorced (2006-2010 5-year est.); Foreign born: 1.0% (2006-2010 5-year est.); Ancestry (includes multiple ancestries): 35.1% German, 22.1% Irish, 21.1% Polish, 9.2% English, 8.3% Italian (2006-2010 5-year est.).
Economy: Single-family building permits issued: 2 (2011); Multi-family building permits issued: 0 (2011); Employment by occupation: 9.4% management, 1.7% professional, 10.5% services, 20.3% sales, 1.8% farming, 12.0% construction, 5.5% production (2006-2010 5-year est.).
Income: Per capita income: $18,873 (2006-2010 5-year est.); Median household income: $35,274 (2006-2010 5-year est.); Average household income: $46,556 (2006-2010 5-year est.); Percent of households with income of $100,000 or more: 7.0% (2006-2010 5-year est.); Poverty rate: 19.8% (2006-2010 5-year est.).
Education: Percent of population age 25 and over with: High school diploma (including GED) or higher: 85.6% (2006-2010 5-year est.); Bachelor's degree or higher: 9.6% (2006-2010 5-year est.); Master's degree or higher: 3.3% (2006-2010 5-year est.).

### School District(s)
Yorkshire-Pioneer Central School District (PK-12)
    2009-10 Enrollment: 2,515 . . . . . . . . . . . . . . . . . . . . . . . (716) 492-9304
Housing: Homeownership rate: 72.5% (2010); Median home value: $88,200 (2006-2010 5-year est.); Median contract rent: $417 per month (2006-2010 5-year est.); Median year structure built: 1978 (2006-2010 5-year est.).
Transportation: Commute to work: 91.6% car, 0.2% public transportation, 2.3% walk, 2.7% work from home (2006-2010 5-year est.); Travel time to work: 39.6% less than 15 minutes, 19.8% 15 to 30 minutes, 13.6% 30 to 45 minutes, 16.2% 45 to 60 minutes, 10.7% 60 minutes or more (2006-2010 5-year est.)

**YORKSHIRE** (CDP). Covers a land area of 1.844 square miles and a water area of 0.010 square miles. Located at 42.52° N. Lat; 78.47° W. Long. Elevation is 1,434 feet.

**Population:** 1,340 (1990); 1,403 (2000); 1,180 (2010); Density: 639.6 persons per square mile (2010); Race: 97.5% White, 0.3% Black, 0.2% Asian, 0.4% American Indian/Alaska Native, 0.0% Native Hawaiian/Other Pacific Islander, 1.6% Other, 0.6% Hispanic of any race (2010); Average household size: 2.10 (2010); Median age: 44.3 (2010); Males per 100 females: 85.8 (2010); Marriage status: 41.1% never married, 45.8% now married, 5.2% widowed, 7.9% divorced (2006-2010 5-year est.); Foreign born: 0.9% (2006-2010 5-year est.); Ancestry (includes multiple ancestries): 28.8% German, 24.0% Polish, 15.6% Irish, 12.3% Italian, 7.1% Swedish (2006-2010 5-year est.).

**Economy:** Employment by occupation: 10.2% management, 1.9% professional, 10.2% services, 14.5% sales, 3.0% farming, 13.1% construction, 0.0% production (2006-2010 5-year est.).

**Income:** Per capita income: $17,545 (2006-2010 5-year est.); Median household income: $29,104 (2006-2010 5-year est.); Average household income: $40,746 (2006-2010 5-year est.); Percent of households with income of $100,000 or more: 6.7% (2006-2010 5-year est.); Poverty rate: 12.1% (2006-2010 5-year est.).

**Education:** Percent of population age 25 and over with: High school diploma (including GED) or higher: 81.1% (2006-2010 5-year est.); Bachelor's degree or higher: 14.0% (2006-2010 5-year est.); Master's degree or higher: 1.6% (2006-2010 5-year est.).

### School District(s)

Yorkshire-Pioneer Central School District (PK-12)

    2009-10 Enrollment: 2,515 . . . . . . . . . . . . . . . . . . . . . . (716) 492-9304

**Housing:** Homeownership rate: 72.4% (2010); Median home value: $27,900 (2006-2010 5-year est.); Median contract rent: $491 per month (2006-2010 5-year est.); Median year structure built: 1981 (2006-2010 5-year est.).

**Transportation:** Commute to work: 93.8% car, 0.0% public transportation, 4.6% walk, 0.0% work from home (2006-2010 5-year est.); Travel time to work: 50.0% less than 15 minutes, 15.9% 15 to 30 minutes, 8.5% 30 to 45 minutes, 10.4% 45 to 60 minutes, 15.2% 60 minutes or more (2006-2010 5-year est.)

## Cayuga County

Located in west central New York; bounded on the north by Lake Ontario; drained by the Seneca River. Covers a land area of 693.18 square miles, a water area of 170.46 square miles, and is located in the Eastern Time Zone at 42.93° N. Lat., 76.56° W. Long. The county was founded in 1799. County seat is Auburn.

Cayuga County is part of the Auburn, NY Micropolitan Statistical Area. The entire metro area includes: Cayuga County, NY

Weather Station: Aurora Research Farm            Elevation: 830 feet

|        | Jan  | Feb  | Mar  | Apr | May | Jun | Jul | Aug | Sep | Oct | Nov | Dec  |
|--------|------|------|------|-----|-----|-----|-----|-----|-----|-----|-----|------|
| High   | 32   | 34   | 42   | 56  | 68  | 77  | 81  | 80  | 73  | 60  | 48  | 37   |
| Low    | 17   | 18   | 25   | 36  | 46  | 56  | 61  | 59  | 52  | 41  | 33  | 23   |
| Precip | 1.9  | 1.7  | 2.6  | 3.3 | 3.2 | 3.8 | 3.5 | 3.1 | 4.1 | 3.4 | 3.2 | 2.3  |
| Snow   | 14.5 | 11.8 | 12.1 | 4.0 | 0.2 | 0.0 | 0.0 | 0.0 | 0.0 | 0.2 | 4.9 | 11.3 |

*High and Low temperatures in degrees Fahrenheit; Precipitation and Snow in inches*

**Population:** 82,313 (1990); 81,963 (2000); 80,026 (2010); Race: 92.5% White, 4.0% Black, 0.5% Asian, 0.4% American Indian/Alaska Native, 0.0% Native Hawaiian/Other Pacific Islander, 2.6% Other, 2.4% Hispanic of any race (2010); Density: 115.4 persons per square mile (2010); Average household size: 2.41 (2010); Median age: 41.5 (2010); Males per 100 females: 104.2 (2010).

**Religion:** Six largest groups: 29.9% Catholicism, 4.2% Methodist/Pietist, 2.0% Baptist, 1.6% Presbyterian-Reformed, 1.4% Non-Denominational, 1.0% Holiness (2010)

**Economy:** Unemployment rate: 9.3% (February 2012); Total civilian labor force: 40,018 (February 2012); Leading industries: 20.5% retail trade; 17.1% manufacturing; 16.4% health care and social assistance (2009); Farms: 936 totaling 249,476 acres (2007); Companies that employ 500 or more persons: 1 (2009); Companies that employ 100 to 499 persons: 26 (2009); Companies that employ less than 100 persons: 1,597 (2009); Black-owned businesses: n/a (2007); Hispanic-owned businesses: n/a (2007); Asian-owned businesses: n/a (2007); Women-owned businesses: 1,119 (2007); Retail sales per capita: $12,631 (2010). Single-family

building permits issued: 69 (2011); Multi-family building permits issued: 0 (2011).

**Income:** Per capita income: $22,959 (2006-2010 5-year est.); Median household income: $48,415 (2006-2010 5-year est.); Average household income: $57,809 (2006-2010 5-year est.); Percent of households with income of $100,000 or more: 13.8% (2006-2010 5-year est.); Poverty rate: 12.1% (2006-2010 5-year est.); Bankruptcy rate: 2.57% (2011).

**Education:** Percent of population age 25 and over with: High school diploma (including GED) or higher: 84.8% (2006-2010 5-year est.); Bachelor's degree or higher: 18.4% (2006-2010 5-year est.); Master's degree or higher: 7.2% (2006-2010 5-year est.).

**Housing:** Homeownership rate: 71.1% (2010); Median home value: $98,400 (2006-2010 5-year est.); Median contract rent: $470 per month (2006-2010 5-year est.); Median year structure built: 1952 (2006-2010 5-year est.)

**Health:** Birth rate: 100.3 per 10,000 population (2011); Death rate: 85.7 per 10,000 population (2011); Age-adjusted cancer mortality rate: 142.6 deaths per 100,000 population (2009); Number of physicians: 9.8 per 10,000 population (2008); Hospital beds: 16.4 per 10,000 population (2007); Hospital admissions: 594.3 per 10,000 population (2007).

**Elections:** 2008 Presidential election results: 53.3% Obama, 44.8% McCain, 1.0% Nader

**National and State Parks:** Bear Swamp State Forest; Fair Haven Beach State Park; Fillmore Glen State Park; Long Point State Park; Summer Hill State Forest

**Additional Information Contacts**

Cayuga County Government . . . . . . . . . . . . . . . . . . . . (315) 253-1211
    http://www.co.cayuga.ny.us
Cayuga County Chamber of Commerce . . . . . . . . . . . (315) 252-7291
    http://www.cayugacountychamber.org
City of Auburn . . . . . . . . . . . . . . . . . . . . . . . . . . . . . (315) 255-4100
    http://www.auburnny.gov
Fair Haven Area Chamber of Commerce . . . . . . . . . . (315) 947-6037
    http://www.fairhavenny.com
Moravia-Locke Chamber of Commerce . . . . . . . . . . . (315) 497-1341
    http://www.moravia-locke.com
Town of Aurelius . . . . . . . . . . . . . . . . . . . . . . . . . . . (315) 255-1894
    http://co.cayuga.ny.us/aurelius/index.html
Town of Brutus . . . . . . . . . . . . . . . . . . . . . . . . . . . . (315) 834-9398
    http://www.townofbrutus.org
Town of Conquest . . . . . . . . . . . . . . . . . . . . . . . . . . (315) 776-4539
    http://co.cayuga.ny.us/conquest
Town of Fleming . . . . . . . . . . . . . . . . . . . . . . . . . . . (315) 252-8988
    http://co.cayuga.ny.us/fleming
Town of Genoa . . . . . . . . . . . . . . . . . . . . . . . . . . . . (315) 364-5055
    http://co.cayuga.ny.us/genoa
Town of Ira . . . . . . . . . . . . . . . . . . . . . . . . . . . . . . . (315) 626-6905
    http://co.cayuga.ny.us/ira
Town of Ledyard . . . . . . . . . . . . . . . . . . . . . . . . . . . (315) 364-5707
    http://co.cayuga.ny.us/ledyard
Town of Locke . . . . . . . . . . . . . . . . . . . . . . . . . . . . . (315) 497-9338
    http://co.cayuga.ny.us/locke
Town of Mentz . . . . . . . . . . . . . . . . . . . . . . . . . . . . (315) 776-8692
    http://www.townofmentz.com
Town of Montezuma . . . . . . . . . . . . . . . . . . . . . . . . (315) 776-8844
    http://co.cayuga.ny.us/montezuma
Town of Moravia . . . . . . . . . . . . . . . . . . . . . . . . . . . (315) 497-1972
    http://co.cayuga.ny.us/townofmoravia
Town of Niles . . . . . . . . . . . . . . . . . . . . . . . . . . . . . (315) 497-0066
    http://co.cayuga.ny.us/niles
Town of Owasco . . . . . . . . . . . . . . . . . . . . . . . . . . . (315) 253-9021
    http://co.cayuga.ny.us/owasco
Town of Scipio . . . . . . . . . . . . . . . . . . . . . . . . . . . . (315) 364-5740
    http://co.cayuga.ny.us/scipio
Town of Sempronius . . . . . . . . . . . . . . . . . . . . . . . . (315) 496-2376
    http://co.cayuga.ny.us/sempronius
Town of Sennett . . . . . . . . . . . . . . . . . . . . . . . . . . . (315) 253-3712
    http://co.cayuga.ny.us/sennett
Town of Springport . . . . . . . . . . . . . . . . . . . . . . . . . (315) 889-7717
    http://co.cayuga.ny.us/springport
Town of Sterling . . . . . . . . . . . . . . . . . . . . . . . . . . . (315) 947-5666
    http://co.cayuga.ny.us/sterling
Town of Throop . . . . . . . . . . . . . . . . . . . . . . . . . . . (315) 252-7373
    http://co.cayuga.ny.us/throop
Town of Venice . . . . . . . . . . . . . . . . . . . . . . . . . . . (315) 497-1898
    http://co.cayuga.ny.us/venice

Village of Cayuga . . . . . . . . . . . . . . . . . . . . (315) 252-1707
    http://co.cayuga.ny.us/cayugavil
Village of Fair Haven . . . . . . . . . . . . . . . . (315) 947-5112
    http://co.cayuga.ny.us/fairhaven
Village of Moravia . . . . . . . . . . . . . . . . . . (315) 497-1820
    http://co.cayuga.ny.us/villageofmoravia
Village of Port Byron . . . . . . . . . . . . . . . . (315) 776-4321
    http://www.villageofportbyron.com
Village of Union Springs . . . . . . . . . . . . . . (315) 889-7341
    http://unionspringsny.com
Village of Weedsport . . . . . . . . . . . . . . . . (315) 834-6634
    http://co.cayuga.ny.us/weedsport
Weedsport Area Chamber of Commerce . . . . (315) 834-9263
    http://chamber.weedsport.com

## Cayuga County Communities

**AUBURN** (city). County seat. Covers a land area of 8.336 square miles and a water area of 0.074 square miles. Located at 42.93° N. Lat; 76.56° W. Long. Elevation is 686 feet.

**History:** In 1793, Colonel John Hardenbergh, surveyor and Revolutionary veteran, built the first cabin on the present site of Auburn and a year later erected the first gristmill on the Owasco Outlet. At a meeting in 1805 the present name was taken from Goldsmith's "The Deserted Village." Transportation facilities and abundant water power attracted industry. A scythe factory, a carpet factory, and the D. M. Osborne Company, which was later absorbed by International Harvester, were among its industries. The Auburn Theological Seminary, chartered by the Presbyterian General Assembly in 1819, was merged with the Union Theological Seminary in New York City 120 years later.

**Population:** 31,258 (1990); 28,574 (2000); 27,687 (2010); Density: 3,321.3 persons per square mile (2010); Race: 86.3% White, 8.5% Black, 0.6% Asian, 0.4% American Indian/Alaska Native, 0.0% Native Hawaiian/Other Pacific Islander, 4.2% Other, 3.6% Hispanic of any race (2010); Average household size: 2.17 (2010); Median age: 39.1 (2010); Males per 100 females: 102.9 (2010); Marriage status: 35.3% never married, 42.4% now married, 10.1% widowed, 12.2% divorced (2006-2010 5-year est.); Foreign born: 2.9% (2006-2010 5-year est.); Ancestry (includes multiple ancestries): 25.6% Irish, 19.4% Italian, 15.5% English, 13.7% German, 7.9% Polish (2006-2010 5-year est.).

**Economy:** Unemployment rate: 9.9% (February 2012); Total civilian labor force: 12,870 (February 2012); Single-family building permits issued: 2 (2011); Multi-family building permits issued: 0 (2011); Employment by occupation: 8.4% management, 3.0% professional, 12.1% services, 17.6% sales, 3.6% farming, 7.7% construction, 7.9% production (2006-2010 5-year est.).

**Income:** Per capita income: $20,874 (2006-2010 5-year est.); Median household income: $36,846 (2006-2010 5-year est.); Average household income: $47,421 (2006-2010 5-year est.); Percent of households with income of $100,000 or more: 9.0% (2006-2010 5-year est.); Poverty rate: 18.0% (2006-2010 5-year est.).

**Taxes:** Total city taxes per capita: $439 (2009); City property taxes per capita: $390 (2009).

**Education:** Percent of population age 25 and over with: High school diploma (including GED) or higher: 80.8% (2006-2010 5-year est.); Bachelor's degree or higher: 17.9% (2006-2010 5-year est.); Master's degree or higher: 6.3% (2006-2010 5-year est.).

**School District(s)**
Auburn City School District (KG-12)
    2009-10 Enrollment: 4,378 . . . . . . . . . . . . . (315) 255-8835
Cayuga-Onondaga Boces
    2009-10 Enrollment: n/a . . . . . . . . . . . . . . . (315) 253-0361
**Two-year College(s)**
Cayuga County Community College (Public)
    Fall 2010 Enrollment: 3,501 . . . . . . . . . . . . (315) 255-1743
    2011-12 Tuition: In-state $4,199; Out-of-state $8,019
**Vocational/Technical School(s)**
Cayuga Onondaga BOCES-Practical Nursing Program (Public)
    Fall 2010 Enrollment: 44 . . . . . . . . . . . . . . (315) 253-0361
    2011-12 Tuition: In-state $7,635; Out-of-state $7,635

**Housing:** Homeownership rate: 48.5% (2010); Median home value: $90,500 (2006-2010 5-year est.); Median contract rent: $469 per month (2006-2010 5-year est.); Median year structure built: before 1940 (2006-2010 5-year est.).

**Hospitals:** Auburn Memorial Hospital (226 beds)

**Safety:** Violent crime rate: 36.3 per 10,000 population; Property crime rate: 369.0 per 10,000 population (2010).
**Newspapers:** The Citizen (Local news; Circulation 2,064); The Post-Standard - Cayuga County Bureau (Regional news)
**Transportation:** Commute to work: 87.7% car, 3.3% public transportation, 5.7% walk, 1.8% work from home (2006-2010 5-year est.); Travel time to work: 62.5% less than 15 minutes, 21.1% 15 to 30 minutes, 8.2% 30 to 45 minutes, 5.4% 45 to 60 minutes, 2.9% 60 minutes or more (2006-2010 5-year est.)
**Additional Information Contacts**
Cayuga County Chamber of Commerce . . . . . . . . (315) 252-7291
    http://www.cayugacountychamber.org
City of Auburn . . . . . . . . . . . . . . . . . . . . . (315) 255-4100
    http://www.auburnny.gov

**AURELIUS** (town). Covers a land area of 30.245 square miles and a water area of 1.749 square miles. Located at 42.92° N. Lat; 76.66° W. Long.
**Population:** 2,913 (1990); 2,936 (2000); 2,792 (2010); Density: 92.3 persons per square mile (2010); Race: 97.4% White, 0.5% Black, 0.4% Asian, 0.5% American Indian/Alaska Native, 0.2% Native Hawaiian/Other Pacific Islander, 1.0% Other, 0.7% Hispanic of any race (2010); Average household size: 2.46 (2010); Median age: 45.2 (2010); Males per 100 females: 100.6 (2010); Marriage status: 21.2% never married, 60.6% now married, 4.8% widowed, 13.4% divorced (2006-2010 5-year est.); Foreign born: 1.9% (2006-2010 5-year est.); Ancestry (includes multiple ancestries): 24.7% Irish, 21.5% German, 20.1% English, 17.8% Italian, 7.2% American (2006-2010 5-year est.).
**Economy:** Single-family building permits issued: 2 (2011); Multi-family building permits issued: 0 (2011); Employment by occupation: 7.4% management, 6.4% professional, 6.0% services, 17.4% sales, 3.2% farming, 13.0% construction, 14.9% production (2006-2010 5-year est.).
**Income:** Per capita income: $29,332 (2006-2010 5-year est.); Median household income: $57,739 (2006-2010 5-year est.); Average household income: $68,488 (2006-2010 5-year est.); Percent of households with income of $100,000 or more: 22.1% (2006-2010 5-year est.); Poverty rate: 5.1% (2006-2010 5-year est.).
**Education:** Percent of population age 25 and over with: High school diploma (including GED) or higher: 87.7% (2006-2010 5-year est.); Bachelor's degree or higher: 21.9% (2006-2010 5-year est.); Master's degree or higher: 5.9% (2006-2010 5-year est.).
**Housing:** Homeownership rate: 84.1% (2010); Median home value: $107,900 (2006-2010 5-year est.); Median contract rent: $380 per month (2006-2010 5-year est.); Median year structure built: 1968 (2006-2010 5-year est.).
**Transportation:** Commute to work: 96.4% car, 0.2% public transportation, 0.5% walk, 2.3% work from home (2006-2010 5-year est.); Travel time to work: 47.0% less than 15 minutes, 31.4% 15 to 30 minutes, 5.6% 30 to 45 minutes, 7.3% 45 to 60 minutes, 8.7% 60 minutes or more (2006-2010 5-year est.)
**Additional Information Contacts**
Town of Aurelius . . . . . . . . . . . . . . . . . . . (315) 255-1894
    http://co.cayuga.ny.us/aurelius/index.html

**AURORA** (village). Covers a land area of 0.919 square miles and a water area of <.001 square miles. Located at 42.75° N. Lat; 76.69° W. Long. Elevation is 413 feet.
**History:** Seat of Wells College (1869).
**Population:** 687 (1990); 720 (2000); 724 (2010); Density: 787.7 persons per square mile (2010); Race: 91.0% White, 3.3% Black, 1.8% Asian, 0.1% American Indian/Alaska Native, 0.0% Native Hawaiian/Other Pacific Islander, 3.8% Other, 5.7% Hispanic of any race (2010); Average household size: 2.10 (2010); Median age: 21.3 (2010); Males per 100 females: 60.5 (2010); Marriage status: 84.3% never married, 13.8% now married, 0.7% widowed, 1.2% divorced (2006-2010 5-year est.); Foreign born: 3.0% (2006-2010 5-year est.); Ancestry (includes multiple ancestries): 28.5% German, 21.5% English, 18.9% Italian, 12.2% Irish, 11.9% American (2006-2010 5-year est.).
**Economy:** Single-family building permits issued: 0 (2011); Multi-family building permits issued: 0 (2011); Employment by occupation: 2.8% management, 0.4% professional, 23.8% services, 31.8% sales, 12.7% farming, 1.0% construction, 0.0% production (2006-2010 5-year est.).
**Income:** Per capita income: $11,947 (2006-2010 5-year est.); Median household income: $64,500 (2006-2010 5-year est.); Average household income: $90,945 (2006-2010 5-year est.); Percent of households with

income of $100,000 or more: 27.1% (2006-2010 5-year est.); Poverty rate: 0.4% (2006-2010 5-year est.).

**Education:** Percent of population age 25 and over with: High school diploma (including GED) or higher: 98.6% (2006-2010 5-year est.); Bachelor's degree or higher: 65.4% (2006-2010 5-year est.); Master's degree or higher: 37.0% (2006-2010 5-year est.).

### School District(s)

Southern Cayuga Central School District (PK-12)
   2009-10 Enrollment: 807 . . . . . . . . . . . . . . . . . . . . . . . (315) 364-7211

### Four-year College(s)

Wells College (Private, Not-for-profit)
   Fall 2010 Enrollment: 558 . . . . . . . . . . . . . . . . . . . . . . . (315) 364-3266
   2011-12 Tuition: In-state $33,410; Out-of-state $33,410

**Housing:** Homeownership rate: 59.1% (2010); Median home value: $196,900 (2006-2010 5-year est.); Median contract rent: $520 per month (2006-2010 5-year est.); Median year structure built: before 1940 (2006-2010 5-year est.).

**Transportation:** Commute to work: 19.7% car, 0.0% public transportation, 60.2% walk, 20.0% work from home (2006-2010 5-year est.); Travel time to work: 85.8% less than 15 minutes, 4.3% 15 to 30 minutes, 8.2% 30 to 45 minutes, 0.4% 45 to 60 minutes, 1.4% 60 minutes or more (2006-2010 5-year est.)

**BRUTUS** (town). Covers a land area of 22.106 square miles and a water area of 0.393 square miles. Located at 43.04° N. Lat; 76.54° W. Long.

**Population:** 5,013 (1990); 4,777 (2000); 4,464 (2010); Density: 201.9 persons per square mile (2010); Race: 97.2% White, 0.3% Black, 0.4% Asian, 0.4% American Indian/Alaska Native, 0.0% Native Hawaiian/Other Pacific Islander, 1.7% Other, 1.1% Hispanic of any race (2010); Average household size: 2.50 (2010); Median age: 42.2 (2010); Males per 100 females: 94.6 (2010); Marriage status: 27.8% never married, 60.5% now married, 6.0% widowed, 5.7% divorced (2006-2010 5-year est.); Foreign born: 0.5% (2006-2010 5-year est.); Ancestry (includes multiple ancestries): 24.7% Irish, 21.0% German, 18.9% English, 9.5% Italian, 9.0% American (2006-2010 5-year est.).

**Economy:** Single-family building permits issued: 3 (2011); Multi-family building permits issued: 0 (2011); Employment by occupation: 8.8% management, 2.6% professional, 12.6% services, 19.8% sales, 2.7% farming, 13.1% construction, 12.3% production (2006-2010 5-year est.).

**Income:** Per capita income: $23,567 (2006-2010 5-year est.); Median household income: $48,348 (2006-2010 5-year est.); Average household income: $57,953 (2006-2010 5-year est.); Percent of households with income of $100,000 or more: 12.6% (2006-2010 5-year est.); Poverty rate: 9.2% (2006-2010 5-year est.).

**Education:** Percent of population age 25 and over with: High school diploma (including GED) or higher: 88.4% (2006-2010 5-year est.); Bachelor's degree or higher: 15.7% (2006-2010 5-year est.); Master's degree or higher: 7.2% (2006-2010 5-year est.).

**Housing:** Homeownership rate: 78.5% (2010); Median home value: $85,100 (2006-2010 5-year est.); Median contract rent: $510 per month (2006-2010 5-year est.); Median year structure built: 1972 (2006-2010 5-year est.).

**Transportation:** Commute to work: 94.3% car, 0.3% public transportation, 1.9% walk, 2.2% work from home (2006-2010 5-year est.); Travel time to work: 30.1% less than 15 minutes, 41.9% 15 to 30 minutes, 17.3% 30 to 45 minutes, 5.9% 45 to 60 minutes, 4.9% 60 minutes or more (2006-2010 5-year est.)

**Additional Information Contacts**

Town of Brutus. . . . . . . . . . . . . . . . . . . . . . . . . . . . . . (315) 834-9398
   http://www.townofbrutus.org

**CATO** (village). Covers a land area of 0.988 square miles and a water area of 0.024 square miles. Located at 43.16° N. Lat; 76.56° W. Long. Elevation is 459 feet.

**Population:** 581 (1990); 601 (2000); 532 (2010); Density: 538.2 persons per square mile (2010); Race: 96.4% White, 0.0% Black, 0.0% Asian, 0.2% American Indian/Alaska Native, 0.0% Native Hawaiian/Other Pacific Islander, 3.4% Other, 1.3% Hispanic of any race (2010); Average household size: 2.46 (2010); Median age: 36.2 (2010); Males per 100 females: 90.0 (2010); Marriage status: 30.0% never married, 58.1% now married, 8.3% widowed, 3.6% divorced (2006-2010 5-year est.); Foreign born: 0.4% (2006-2010 5-year est.); Ancestry (includes multiple ancestries): 26.2% German, 22.4% English, 21.7% Irish, 13.8% French, 8.9% French Canadian (2006-2010 5-year est.).

**Economy:** Single-family building permits issued: 0 (2011); Multi-family building permits issued: 0 (2011); Employment by occupation: 9.2% management, 3.5% professional, 12.7% services, 7.3% sales, 0.0% farming, 19.0% construction, 7.9% production (2006-2010 5-year est.).

**Income:** Per capita income: $18,271 (2006-2010 5-year est.); Median household income: $40,288 (2006-2010 5-year est.); Average household income: $56,227 (2006-2010 5-year est.); Percent of households with income of $100,000 or more: 15.3% (2006-2010 5-year est.); Poverty rate: 20.2% (2006-2010 5-year est.).

**Education:** Percent of population age 25 and over with: High school diploma (including GED) or higher: 90.7% (2006-2010 5-year est.); Bachelor's degree or higher: 7.5% (2006-2010 5-year est.); Master's degree or higher: 4.9% (2006-2010 5-year est.).

### School District(s)

Cato-Meridian Central School District (PK-12)
   2009-10 Enrollment: 1,089 . . . . . . . . . . . . . . . . . . . (315) 626-3439

**Housing:** Homeownership rate: 62.5% (2010); Median home value: $97,000 (2006-2010 5-year est.); Median contract rent: $441 per month (2006-2010 5-year est.); Median year structure built: before 1940 (2006-2010 5-year est.).

**Transportation:** Commute to work: 83.5% car, 0.0% public transportation, 1.6% walk, 14.9% work from home (2006-2010 5-year est.); Travel time to work: 14.2% less than 15 minutes, 35.8% 15 to 30 minutes, 33.6% 30 to 45 minutes, 12.7% 45 to 60 minutes, 3.7% 60 minutes or more (2006-2010 5-year est.)

**CATO** (town). Covers a land area of 33.643 square miles and a water area of 2.543 square miles. Located at 43.12° N. Lat; 76.53° W. Long. Elevation is 459 feet.

**Population:** 2,452 (1990); 2,744 (2000); 2,537 (2010); Density: 75.4 persons per square mile (2010); Race: 97.2% White, 0.6% Black, 0.6% Asian, 0.4% American Indian/Alaska Native, 0.0% Native Hawaiian/Other Pacific Islander, 1.2% Other, 0.8% Hispanic of any race (2010); Average household size: 2.62 (2010); Median age: 42.4 (2010); Males per 100 females: 104.3 (2010); Marriage status: 23.7% never married, 60.0% now married, 5.0% widowed, 11.4% divorced (2006-2010 5-year est.); Foreign born: 0.9% (2006-2010 5-year est.); Ancestry (includes multiple ancestries): 25.2% German, 23.5% English, 22.5% Irish, 9.9% Polish, 7.8% French (2006-2010 5-year est.).

**Economy:** Single-family building permits issued: 4 (2011); Multi-family building permits issued: 0 (2011); Employment by occupation: 14.3% management, 3.1% professional, 5.0% services, 11.2% sales, 2.4% farming, 12.7% construction, 14.0% production (2006-2010 5-year est.).

**Income:** Per capita income: $25,950 (2006-2010 5-year est.); Median household income: $56,500 (2006-2010 5-year est.); Average household income: $61,087 (2006-2010 5-year est.); Percent of households with income of $100,000 or more: 15.5% (2006-2010 5-year est.); Poverty rate: 7.0% (2006-2010 5-year est.).

**Education:** Percent of population age 25 and over with: High school diploma (including GED) or higher: 91.2% (2006-2010 5-year est.); Bachelor's degree or higher: 14.9% (2006-2010 5-year est.); Master's degree or higher: 8.2% (2006-2010 5-year est.).

### School District(s)

Cato-Meridian Central School District (PK-12)
   2009-10 Enrollment: 1,089 . . . . . . . . . . . . . . . . . . . (315) 626-3439

**Housing:** Homeownership rate: 86.2% (2010); Median home value: $101,500 (2006-2010 5-year est.); Median contract rent: $498 per month (2006-2010 5-year est.); Median year structure built: 1972 (2006-2010 5-year est.).

**Transportation:** Commute to work: 89.5% car, 0.0% public transportation, 2.7% walk, 7.3% work from home (2006-2010 5-year est.); Travel time to work: 19.4% less than 15 minutes, 23.6% 15 to 30 minutes, 41.8% 30 to 45 minutes, 9.3% 45 to 60 minutes, 6.0% 60 minutes or more (2006-2010 5-year est.)

**CAYUGA** (village). Covers a land area of 0.903 square miles and a water area of 0.461 square miles. Located at 42.91° N. Lat; 76.72° W. Long. Elevation is 482 feet.

**Population:** 677 (1990); 509 (2000); 549 (2010); Density: 607.4 persons per square mile (2010); Race: 97.1% White, 0.9% Black, 0.2% Asian, 0.2% American Indian/Alaska Native, 0.0% Native Hawaiian/Other Pacific Islander, 1.6% Other, 0.2% Hispanic of any race (2010); Average household size: 2.47 (2010); Median age: 40.5 (2010); Males per 100 females: 94.7 (2010); Marriage status: 20.1% never married, 54.3% now married, 8.5% widowed, 17.1% divorced (2006-2010 5-year est.); Foreign

born: 0.9% (2006-2010 5-year est.); Ancestry (includes multiple ancestries): 37.7% Irish, 20.7% German, 16.7% English, 10.1% French, 8.4% Italian (2006-2010 5-year est.).

**Economy:** Single-family building permits issued: 0 (2011); Multi-family building permits issued: 0 (2011); Employment by occupation: 7.6% management, 10.0% professional, 8.8% services, 13.5% sales, 4.0% farming, 12.4% construction, 8.8% production (2006-2010 5-year est.).

**Income:** Per capita income: $26,265 (2006-2010 5-year est.); Median household income: $67,917 (2006-2010 5-year est.); Average household income: $68,418 (2006-2010 5-year est.); Percent of households with income of $100,000 or more: 25.3% (2006-2010 5-year est.); Poverty rate: 2.7% (2006-2010 5-year est.).

**Education:** Percent of population age 25 and over with: High school diploma (including GED) or higher: 95.0% (2006-2010 5-year est.); Bachelor's degree or higher: 24.8% (2006-2010 5-year est.); Master's degree or higher: 5.6% (2006-2010 5-year est.).

**School District(s)**

Union Springs Central School District (KG-12)

   2009-10 Enrollment: 891 . . . . . . . . . . . . . . . . . . . . . . . . (315) 889-4101

**Housing:** Homeownership rate: 74.3% (2010); Median home value: $107,500 (2006-2010 5-year est.); Median contract rent: $650 per month (2006-2010 5-year est.); Median year structure built: 1944 (2006-2010 5-year est.).

**Transportation:** Commute to work: 97.2% car, 0.8% public transportation, 2.0% walk, 0.0% work from home (2006-2010 5-year est.); Travel time to work: 33.7% less than 15 minutes, 39.8% 15 to 30 minutes, 15.4% 30 to 45 minutes, 3.3% 45 to 60 minutes, 7.7% 60 minutes or more (2006-2010 5-year est.)

**Additional Information Contacts**

Village of Cayuga. . . . . . . . . . . . . . . . . . . . . . . . . . . . . . . . (315) 252-1707
   http://co.cayuga.ny.us/cayugavil

**CONQUEST** (town). Covers a land area of 35.221 square miles and a water area of 1.095 square miles. Located at 43.11° N. Lat; 76.65° W. Long. Elevation is 440 feet.

**Population:** 1,859 (1990); 1,925 (2000); 1,819 (2010); Density: 51.6 persons per square mile (2010); Race: 98.5% White, 0.3% Black, 0.0% Asian, 0.2% American Indian/Alaska Native, 0.0% Native Hawaiian/Other Pacific Islander, 1.0% Other, 0.8% Hispanic of any race (2010); Average household size: 2.67 (2010); Median age: 41.8 (2010); Males per 100 females: 106.7 (2010); Marriage status: 24.9% never married, 60.9% now married, 3.8% widowed, 10.4% divorced (2006-2010 5-year est.); Foreign born: 0.0% (2006-2010 5-year est.); Ancestry (includes multiple ancestries): 21.2% Irish, 19.6% German, 16.7% English, 10.1% Italian, 7.8% Dutch (2006-2010 5-year est.).

**Economy:** Single-family building permits issued: 2 (2011); Multi-family building permits issued: 0 (2011); Employment by occupation: 11.5% management, 3.0% professional, 14.3% services, 12.8% sales, 0.6% farming, 19.0% construction, 12.7% production (2006-2010 5-year est.).

**Income:** Per capita income: $24,472 (2006-2010 5-year est.); Median household income: $47,963 (2006-2010 5-year est.); Average household income: $58,073 (2006-2010 5-year est.); Percent of households with income of $100,000 or more: 12.5% (2006-2010 5-year est.); Poverty rate: 11.1% (2006-2010 5-year est.).

**Education:** Percent of population age 25 and over with: High school diploma (including GED) or higher: 83.4% (2006-2010 5-year est.); Bachelor's degree or higher: 8.7% (2006-2010 5-year est.); Master's degree or higher: 2.7% (2006-2010 5-year est.).

**Housing:** Homeownership rate: 89.3% (2010); Median home value: $85,700 (2006-2010 5-year est.); Median contract rent: $525 per month (2006-2010 5-year est.); Median year structure built: 1978 (2006-2010 5-year est.).

**Transportation:** Commute to work: 87.1% car, 0.0% public transportation, 4.6% walk, 6.7% work from home (2006-2010 5-year est.); Travel time to work: 22.2% less than 15 minutes, 32.9% 15 to 30 minutes, 28.9% 30 to 45 minutes, 12.4% 45 to 60 minutes, 3.7% 60 minutes or more (2006-2010 5-year est.)

**Additional Information Contacts**

Town of Conquest . . . . . . . . . . . . . . . . . . . . . . . . . . . . . . (315) 776-4539
   http://co.cayuga.ny.us/conquest

**FAIR HAVEN** (village). Covers a land area of 1.754 square miles and a water area of 1.167 square miles. Located at 43.32° N. Lat; 76.70° W. Long. Elevation is 285 feet.

**Population:** 895 (1990); 884 (2000); 745 (2010); Density: 424.6 persons per square mile (2010); Race: 97.6% White, 0.1% Black, 0.4% Asian, 0.8% American Indian/Alaska Native, 0.0% Native Hawaiian/Other Pacific Islander, 1.1% Other, 1.7% Hispanic of any race (2010); Average household size: 2.21 (2010); Median age: 49.2 (2010); Males per 100 females: 94.0 (2010); Marriage status: 20.1% never married, 56.2% now married, 10.0% widowed, 13.7% divorced (2006-2010 5-year est.); Foreign born: 3.8% (2006-2010 5-year est.); Ancestry (includes multiple ancestries): 21.5% English, 19.1% German, 17.7% Irish, 10.7% Dutch, 6.1% American (2006-2010 5-year est.).

**Economy:** Single-family building permits issued: 4 (2011); Multi-family building permits issued: 0 (2011); Employment by occupation: 5.0% management, 0.6% professional, 6.9% services, 22.7% sales, 0.9% farming, 12.3% construction, 18.0% production (2006-2010 5-year est.).

**Income:** Per capita income: $28,578 (2006-2010 5-year est.); Median household income: $49,271 (2006-2010 5-year est.); Average household income: $59,993 (2006-2010 5-year est.); Percent of households with income of $100,000 or more: 20.5% (2006-2010 5-year est.); Poverty rate: 11.1% (2006-2010 5-year est.).

**Education:** Percent of population age 25 and over with: High school diploma (including GED) or higher: 89.3% (2006-2010 5-year est.); Bachelor's degree or higher: 21.5% (2006-2010 5-year est.); Master's degree or higher: 9.3% (2006-2010 5-year est.).

**Housing:** Homeownership rate: 78.3% (2010); Median home value: $95,900 (2006-2010 5-year est.); Median contract rent: $451 per month (2006-2010 5-year est.); Median year structure built: 1952 (2006-2010 5-year est.).

**Transportation:** Commute to work: 88.8% car, 0.0% public transportation, 10.3% walk, 1.0% work from home (2006-2010 5-year est.); Travel time to work: 30.7% less than 15 minutes, 23.9% 15 to 30 minutes, 14.9% 30 to 45 minutes, 13.3% 45 to 60 minutes, 17.2% 60 minutes or more (2006-2010 5-year est.)

**Additional Information Contacts**

Fair Haven Area Chamber of Commerce . . . . . . . . . . . . . . (315) 947-6037
   http://www.fairhavenny.com

Village of Fair Haven . . . . . . . . . . . . . . . . . . . . . . . . . . . . (315) 947-5112
   http://co.cayuga.ny.us/fairhaven

**FLEMING** (town). Covers a land area of 21.818 square miles and a water area of 2.480 square miles. Located at 42.87° N. Lat; 76.57° W. Long. Elevation is 902 feet.

**Population:** 2,644 (1990); 2,647 (2000); 2,636 (2010); Density: 120.8 persons per square mile (2010); Race: 97.7% White, 0.1% Black, 0.3% Asian, 0.2% American Indian/Alaska Native, 0.0% Native Hawaiian/Other Pacific Islander, 1.7% Other, 1.7% Hispanic of any race (2010); Average household size: 2.43 (2010); Median age: 48.0 (2010); Males per 100 females: 102.6 (2010); Marriage status: 27.6% never married, 61.6% now married, 3.0% widowed, 7.8% divorced (2006-2010 5-year est.); Foreign born: 2.4% (2006-2010 5-year est.); Ancestry (includes multiple ancestries): 34.3% Irish, 23.7% Italian, 18.5% English, 14.3% German, 8.5% Polish (2006-2010 5-year est.).

**Economy:** Single-family building permits issued: 3 (2011); Multi-family building permits issued: 0 (2011); Employment by occupation: 5.8% management, 7.1% professional, 8.9% services, 8.7% sales, 2.4% farming, 14.7% construction, 11.6% production (2006-2010 5-year est.).

**Income:** Per capita income: $31,395 (2006-2010 5-year est.); Median household income: $61,675 (2006-2010 5-year est.); Average household income: $78,920 (2006-2010 5-year est.); Percent of households with income of $100,000 or more: 27.9% (2006-2010 5-year est.); Poverty rate: 3.5% (2006-2010 5-year est.).

**Education:** Percent of population age 25 and over with: High school diploma (including GED) or higher: 91.8% (2006-2010 5-year est.); Bachelor's degree or higher: 21.3% (2006-2010 5-year est.); Master's degree or higher: 9.6% (2006-2010 5-year est.).

**Housing:** Homeownership rate: 89.2% (2010); Median home value: $122,800 (2006-2010 5-year est.); Median contract rent: $655 per month (2006-2010 5-year est.); Median year structure built: 1959 (2006-2010 5-year est.).

**Transportation:** Commute to work: 96.6% car, 0.0% public transportation, 0.0% walk, 3.0% work from home (2006-2010 5-year est.); Travel time to work: 37.5% less than 15 minutes, 37.9% 15 to 30 minutes, 13.0% 30 to 45

minutes, 5.0% 45 to 60 minutes, 6.6% 60 minutes or more (2006-2010 5-year est.)
**Additional Information Contacts**
Town of Fleming . . . . . . . . . . . . . . . . . . . . . . . . . . . . . . . . (315) 252-8988
  http://co.cayuga.ny.us/fleming

**GENOA** (town). Covers a land area of 39.597 square miles and a water area of 3.565 square miles. Located at 42.65° N. Lat; 76.57° W. Long. Elevation is 853 feet.
**Population:** 1,868 (1990); 1,914 (2000); 1,935 (2010); Density: 48.9 persons per square mile (2010); Race: 94.8% White, 0.5% Black, 0.5% Asian, 0.6% American Indian/Alaska Native, 0.3% Native Hawaiian/Other Pacific Islander, 3.3% Other, 3.4% Hispanic of any race (2010); Average household size: 2.55 (2010); Median age: 42.5 (2010); Males per 100 females: 105.6 (2010); Marriage status: 24.9% never married, 60.7% now married, 6.6% widowed, 7.8% divorced (2006-2010 5-year est.); Foreign born: 1.1% (2006-2010 5-year est.); Ancestry (includes multiple ancestries): 18.7% German, 15.3% English, 15.3% Irish, 12.5% American, 9.1% Italian (2006-2010 5-year est.).
**Economy:** Single-family building permits issued: 6 (2011); Multi-family building permits issued: 0 (2011); Employment by occupation: 12.4% management, 3.9% professional, 12.2% services, 12.8% sales, 3.4% farming, 18.5% construction, 8.9% production (2006-2010 5-year est.).
**Income:** Per capita income: $23,917 (2006-2010 5-year est.); Median household income: $51,289 (2006-2010 5-year est.); Average household income: $59,529 (2006-2010 5-year est.); Percent of households with income of $100,000 or more: 10.1% (2006-2010 5-year est.); Poverty rate: 14.5% (2006-2010 5-year est.).
**Education:** Percent of population age 25 and over with: High school diploma (including GED) or higher: 88.1% (2006-2010 5-year est.); Bachelor's degree or higher: 19.6% (2006-2010 5-year est.); Master's degree or higher: 4.7% (2006-2010 5-year est.).
**Housing:** Homeownership rate: 78.9% (2010); Median home value: $105,900 (2006-2010 5-year est.); Median contract rent: $474 per month (2006-2010 5-year est.); Median year structure built: 1964 (2006-2010 5-year est.).
**Transportation:** Commute to work: 87.5% car, 0.8% public transportation, 3.9% walk, 6.8% work from home (2006-2010 5-year est.); Travel time to work: 27.6% less than 15 minutes, 26.9% 15 to 30 minutes, 32.3% 30 to 45 minutes, 8.4% 45 to 60 minutes, 4.8% 60 minutes or more (2006-2010 5-year est.).
**Additional Information Contacts**
Town of Genoa . . . . . . . . . . . . . . . . . . . . . . . . . . . . . . . (315) 364-5055
  http://co.cayuga.ny.us/genoa

**IRA** (town). Covers a land area of 34.795 square miles and a water area of 0.103 square miles. Located at 43.20° N. Lat; 76.53° W. Long. Elevation is 489 feet.
**Population:** 1,990 (1990); 2,426 (2000); 2,206 (2010); Density: 63.4 persons per square mile (2010); Race: 96.5% White, 0.5% Black, 0.1% Asian, 0.5% American Indian/Alaska Native, 0.0% Native Hawaiian/Other Pacific Islander, 2.4% Other, 0.9% Hispanic of any race (2010); Average household size: 2.70 (2010); Median age: 41.0 (2010); Males per 100 females: 103.1 (2010); Marriage status: 24.8% never married, 62.2% now married, 5.5% widowed, 7.6% divorced (2006-2010 5-year est.); Foreign born: 0.9% (2006-2010 5-year est.); Ancestry (includes multiple ancestries): 22.7% Irish, 22.5% German, 17.4% English, 11.5% Italian, 9.9% French (2006-2010 5-year est.).
**Economy:** Single-family building permits issued: 8 (2011); Multi-family building permits issued: 0 (2011); Employment by occupation: 8.3% management, 3.4% professional, 8.4% services, 13.4% sales, 1.3% farming, 18.2% construction, 10.1% production (2006-2010 5-year est.).
**Income:** Per capita income: $23,325 (2006-2010 5-year est.); Median household income: $51,202 (2006-2010 5-year est.); Average household income: $62,208 (2006-2010 5-year est.); Percent of households with income of $100,000 or more: 14.0% (2006-2010 5-year est.); Poverty rate: 9.6% (2006-2010 5-year est.).
**Education:** Percent of population age 25 and over with: High school diploma (including GED) or higher: 89.4% (2006-2010 5-year est.); Bachelor's degree or higher: 14.9% (2006-2010 5-year est.); Master's degree or higher: 7.0% (2006-2010 5-year est.).
**Housing:** Homeownership rate: 86.3% (2010); Median home value: $89,900 (2006-2010 5-year est.); Median contract rent: $410 per month (2006-2010 5-year est.); Median year structure built: 1974 (2006-2010 5-year est.).

**Transportation:** Commute to work: 92.2% car, 0.4% public transportation, 1.5% walk, 5.5% work from home (2006-2010 5-year est.); Travel time to work: 14.0% less than 15 minutes, 40.5% 15 to 30 minutes, 36.1% 30 to 45 minutes, 7.3% 45 to 60 minutes, 2.2% 60 minutes or more (2006-2010 5-year est.)
**Additional Information Contacts**
Town of Ira . . . . . . . . . . . . . . . . . . . . . . . . . . . . . . . . . . (315) 626-6905
  http://co.cayuga.ny.us/ira

**KING FERRY** (unincorporated postal area)
Zip Code: 13081
  Covers a land area of 28.958 square miles and a water area of 0.011 square miles. Located at 42.67° N. Lat; 76.62° W. Long. Elevation is 955 feet. Population: 1,169 (2010); Density: 40.4 persons per square mile (2010); Race: 94.6% White, 0.3% Black, 0.3% Asian, 0.2% American Indian/Alaska Native, 0.4% Native Hawaiian/Other Pacific Islander, 4.2% Other, 4.3% Hispanic of any race (2010); Average household size: 2.54 (2010); Median age: 44.9 (2010); Males per 100 females: 101.6 (2010); Homeownership rate: 81.8% (2010)

**LEDYARD** (town). Covers a land area of 36.111 square miles and a water area of 12.468 square miles. Located at 42.74° N. Lat; 76.67° W. Long. Elevation is 984 feet.
**Population:** 1,737 (1990); 1,832 (2000); 1,886 (2010); Density: 52.2 persons per square mile (2010); Race: 94.9% White, 1.5% Black, 0.8% Asian, 0.2% American Indian/Alaska Native, 0.0% Native Hawaiian/Other Pacific Islander, 2.6% Other, 2.7% Hispanic of any race (2010); Average household size: 2.43 (2010); Median age: 35.5 (2010); Males per 100 females: 84.0 (2010); Marriage status: 55.6% never married, 38.2% now married, 2.6% widowed, 3.6% divorced (2006-2010 5-year est.); Foreign born: 2.1% (2006-2010 5-year est.); Ancestry (includes multiple ancestries): 25.4% English, 25.0% German, 15.6% Irish, 11.0% Italian, 10.4% American (2006-2010 5-year est.).
**Economy:** Single-family building permits issued: 2 (2011); Multi-family building permits issued: 0 (2011); Employment by occupation: 9.6% management, 0.7% professional, 16.3% services, 26.3% sales, 8.6% farming, 5.2% construction, 3.3% production (2006-2010 5-year est.).
**Income:** Per capita income: $18,191 (2006-2010 5-year est.); Median household income: $57,500 (2006-2010 5-year est.); Average household income: $68,867 (2006-2010 5-year est.); Percent of households with income of $100,000 or more: 20.9% (2006-2010 5-year est.); Poverty rate: 7.6% (2006-2010 5-year est.).
**Education:** Percent of population age 25 and over with: High school diploma (including GED) or higher: 89.3% (2006-2010 5-year est.); Bachelor's degree or higher: 43.0% (2006-2010 5-year est.); Master's degree or higher: 21.3% (2006-2010 5-year est.).
**Housing:** Homeownership rate: 79.0% (2010); Median home value: $149,100 (2006-2010 5-year est.); Median contract rent: $509 per month (2006-2010 5-year est.); Median year structure built: 1955 (2006-2010 5-year est.).
**Transportation:** Commute to work: 51.9% car, 0.0% public transportation, 34.6% walk, 13.5% work from home (2006-2010 5-year est.); Travel time to work: 62.0% less than 15 minutes, 18.5% 15 to 30 minutes, 13.4% 30 to 45 minutes, 4.1% 45 to 60 minutes, 2.1% 60 minutes or more (2006-2010 5-year est.)
**Additional Information Contacts**
Town of Ledyard . . . . . . . . . . . . . . . . . . . . . . . . . . . . . . (315) 364-5707
  http://co.cayuga.ny.us/ledyard

**LOCKE** (town). Covers a land area of 24.305 square miles and a water area of 0.104 square miles. Located at 42.65° N. Lat; 76.41° W. Long. Elevation is 791 feet.
**History:** President Millard Fillmore born here.
**Population:** 1,917 (1990); 1,900 (2000); 1,951 (2010); Density: 80.3 persons per square mile (2010); Race: 97.4% White, 0.5% Black, 0.9% Asian, 0.2% American Indian/Alaska Native, 0.1% Native Hawaiian/Other Pacific Islander, 0.9% Other, 1.0% Hispanic of any race (2010); Average household size: 2.64 (2010); Median age: 41.2 (2010); Males per 100 females: 100.5 (2010); Marriage status: 21.9% never married, 57.5% now married, 7.5% widowed, 13.2% divorced (2006-2010 5-year est.); Foreign born: 1.4% (2006-2010 5-year est.); Ancestry (includes multiple ancestries): 21.2% German, 18.7% Irish, 17.5% English, 7.3% American, 6.2% French (2006-2010 5-year est.).
**Economy:** Single-family building permits issued: 2 (2011); Multi-family building permits issued: 0 (2011); Employment by occupation: 8.4%

management, 4.3% professional, 8.9% services, 12.6% sales, 3.0% farming, 13.8% construction, 14.2% production (2006-2010 5-year est.).

**Income:** Per capita income: $24,322 (2006-2010 5-year est.); Median household income: $50,500 (2006-2010 5-year est.); Average household income: $63,907 (2006-2010 5-year est.); Percent of households with income of $100,000 or more: 15.5% (2006-2010 5-year est.); Poverty rate: 15.0% (2006-2010 5-year est.).

**Education:** Percent of population age 25 and over with: High school diploma (including GED) or higher: 85.2% (2006-2010 5-year est.); Bachelor's degree or higher: 15.6% (2006-2010 5-year est.); Master's degree or higher: 5.6% (2006-2010 5-year est.).

**Housing:** Homeownership rate: 82.2% (2010); Median home value: $87,500 (2006-2010 5-year est.); Median contract rent: $431 per month (2006-2010 5-year est.); Median year structure built: 1979 (2006-2010 5-year est.).

**Transportation:** Commute to work: 89.6% car, 0.5% public transportation, 1.3% walk, 7.3% work from home (2006-2010 5-year est.); Travel time to work: 22.7% less than 15 minutes, 34.3% 15 to 30 minutes, 30.2% 30 to 45 minutes, 6.4% 45 to 60 minutes, 6.4% 60 minutes or more (2006-2010 5-year est.)

**Additional Information Contacts**

Moravia-Locke Chamber of Commerce . . . . . . . . . . . . . . . (315) 497-1341
  http://www.moravia-locke.com
Town of Locke . . . . . . . . . . . . . . . . . . . . . . . . . . . . . . . (315) 497-9338
  http://co.cayuga.ny.us/locke

**MARTVILLE** (unincorporated postal area)

Zip Code: 13111

Covers a land area of 26.606 square miles and a water area of 0.090 square miles. Located at 43.25° N. Lat; 76.61° W. Long. Elevation is 354 feet. Population: 1,700 (2010); Density: 63.9 persons per square mile (2010); Race: 96.7% White, 0.5% Black, 0.3% Asian, 0.8% American Indian/Alaska Native, 0.0% Native Hawaiian/Other Pacific Islander, 1.7% Other, 0.7% Hispanic of any race (2010); Average household size: 2.70 (2010); Median age: 38.7 (2010); Males per 100 females: 109.6 (2010); Homeownership rate: 83.8% (2010)

**MELROSE PARK** (CDP). Aka Auburn Southeast. Covers a land area of 3.731 square miles and a water area of 0.584 square miles. Located at 42.90° N. Lat; 76.51° W. Long. Elevation is 732 feet.

**Population:** 2,091 (1990); 2,359 (2000); 2,294 (2010); Density: 614.8 persons per square mile (2010); Race: 98.3% White, 0.0% Black, 0.4% Asian, 0.0% American Indian/Alaska Native, 0.0% Native Hawaiian/Other Pacific Islander, 1.3% Other, 0.9% Hispanic of any race (2010); Average household size: 2.44 (2010); Median age: 46.5 (2010); Males per 100 females: 93.8 (2010); Marriage status: 15.8% never married, 73.3% now married, 5.7% widowed, 5.2% divorced (2006-2010 5-year est.); Foreign born: 4.4% (2006-2010 5-year est.); Ancestry (includes multiple ancestries): 34.0% Irish, 29.5% Italian, 19.6% English, 15.0% German, 6.5% Polish (2006-2010 5-year est.).

**Economy:** Employment by occupation: 12.9% management, 6.7% professional, 2.2% services, 9.7% sales, 3.8% farming, 7.5% construction, 3.1% production (2006-2010 5-year est.).

**Income:** Per capita income: $39,068 (2006-2010 5-year est.); Median household income: $70,156 (2006-2010 5-year est.); Average household income: $91,988 (2006-2010 5-year est.); Percent of households with income of $100,000 or more: 28.1% (2006-2010 5-year est.); Poverty rate: 4.6% (2006-2010 5-year est.).

**Education:** Percent of population age 25 and over with: High school diploma (including GED) or higher: 92.2% (2006-2010 5-year est.); Bachelor's degree or higher: 45.4% (2006-2010 5-year est.); Master's degree or higher: 22.0% (2006-2010 5-year est.).

**Housing:** Homeownership rate: 91.7% (2010); Median home value: $134,200 (2006-2010 5-year est.); Median contract rent: n/a per month (2006-2010 5-year est.); Median year structure built: 1949 (2006-2010 5-year est.).

**Transportation:** Commute to work: 87.2% car, 1.6% public transportation, 0.0% walk, 8.7% work from home (2006-2010 5-year est.); Travel time to work: 43.5% less than 15 minutes, 21.6% 15 to 30 minutes, 19.3% 30 to 45 minutes, 9.5% 45 to 60 minutes, 6.1% 60 minutes or more (2006-2010 5-year est.)

**MENTZ** (town). Covers a land area of 16.921 square miles and a water area of 0.259 square miles. Located at 43.04° N. Lat; 76.63° W. Long.

**Population:** 2,453 (1990); 2,446 (2000); 2,378 (2010); Density: 140.5 persons per square mile (2010); Race: 96.2% White, 1.0% Black, 0.1% Asian, 0.2% American Indian/Alaska Native, 0.0% Native Hawaiian/Other Pacific Islander, 2.5% Other, 1.7% Hispanic of any race (2010); Average household size: 2.53 (2010); Median age: 40.5 (2010); Males per 100 females: 95.6 (2010); Marriage status: 24.3% never married, 56.6% now married, 9.3% widowed, 9.8% divorced (2006-2010 5-year est.); Foreign born: 3.6% (2006-2010 5-year est.); Ancestry (includes multiple ancestries): 24.5% Irish, 22.5% English, 20.5% German, 10.9% Italian, 8.3% Polish (2006-2010 5-year est.).

**Economy:** Single-family building permits issued: 1 (2011); Multi-family building permits issued: 0 (2011); Employment by occupation: 6.8% management, 2.2% professional, 10.3% services, 15.9% sales, 2.1% farming, 19.0% construction, 15.5% production (2006-2010 5-year est.).

**Income:** Per capita income: $19,701 (2006-2010 5-year est.); Median household income: $41,042 (2006-2010 5-year est.); Average household income: $49,814 (2006-2010 5-year est.); Percent of households with income of $100,000 or more: 9.5% (2006-2010 5-year est.); Poverty rate: 14.3% (2006-2010 5-year est.).

**Education:** Percent of population age 25 and over with: High school diploma (including GED) or higher: 77.8% (2006-2010 5-year est.); Bachelor's degree or higher: 7.8% (2006-2010 5-year est.); Master's degree or higher: 2.5% (2006-2010 5-year est.).

**Housing:** Homeownership rate: 75.6% (2010); Median home value: $86,300 (2006-2010 5-year est.); Median contract rent: $476 per month (2006-2010 5-year est.); Median year structure built: 1968 (2006-2010 5-year est.).

**Transportation:** Commute to work: 94.9% car, 0.0% public transportation, 1.2% walk, 3.1% work from home (2006-2010 5-year est.); Travel time to work: 29.6% less than 15 minutes, 50.7% 15 to 30 minutes, 12.7% 30 to 45 minutes, 4.9% 45 to 60 minutes, 2.2% 60 minutes or more (2006-2010 5-year est.)

**Additional Information Contacts**

Town of Mentz . . . . . . . . . . . . . . . . . . . . . . . . . . . . . . . (315) 776-8692
  http://www.townofmentz.com

**MERIDIAN** (village). Covers a land area of 0.690 square miles and a water area of 0 square miles. Located at 43.16° N. Lat; 76.53° W. Long. Elevation is 453 feet.

**Population:** 351 (1990); 350 (2000); 309 (2010); Density: 447.3 persons per square mile (2010); Race: 95.8% White, 0.0% Black, 0.0% Asian, 0.3% American Indian/Alaska Native, 0.0% Native Hawaiian/Other Pacific Islander, 3.9% Other, 2.3% Hispanic of any race (2010); Average household size: 2.97 (2010); Median age: 38.4 (2010); Males per 100 females: 103.3 (2010); Marriage status: 23.1% never married, 51.6% now married, 8.8% widowed, 16.5% divorced (2006-2010 5-year est.); Foreign born: 0.0% (2006-2010 5-year est.); Ancestry (includes multiple ancestries): 26.4% German, 23.6% Irish, 20.0% English, 15.9% Italian, 12.7% French (2006-2010 5-year est.).

**Economy:** Single-family building permits issued: 0 (2011); Multi-family building permits issued: 0 (2011); Employment by occupation: 8.1% management, 10.8% professional, 5.4% services, 26.1% sales, 0.0% farming, 12.6% construction, 6.3% production (2006-2010 5-year est.).

**Income:** Per capita income: $24,594 (2006-2010 5-year est.); Median household income: $57,321 (2006-2010 5-year est.); Average household income: $58,803 (2006-2010 5-year est.); Percent of households with income of $100,000 or more: 7.4% (2006-2010 5-year est.); Poverty rate: 13.6% (2006-2010 5-year est.).

**Education:** Percent of population age 25 and over with: High school diploma (including GED) or higher: 92.8% (2006-2010 5-year est.); Bachelor's degree or higher: 25.5% (2006-2010 5-year est.); Master's degree or higher: 9.2% (2006-2010 5-year est.).

**Housing:** Homeownership rate: 84.6% (2010); Median home value: $97,000 (2006-2010 5-year est.); Median contract rent: $559 per month (2006-2010 5-year est.); Median year structure built: before 1940 (2006-2010 5-year est.).

**Transportation:** Commute to work: 97.1% car, 0.0% public transportation, 0.0% walk, 2.9% work from home (2006-2010 5-year est.); Travel time to work: 14.7% less than 15 minutes, 21.6% 15 to 30 minutes, 54.9% 30 to 45 minutes, 2.0% 45 to 60 minutes, 6.9% 60 minutes or more (2006-2010 5-year est.)

**MONTEZUMA** (town). Covers a land area of 18.241 square miles and a water area of 0.472 square miles. Located at 43.01° N. Lat; 76.69° W. Long. Elevation is 397 feet.
**Population:** 1,280 (1990); 1,431 (2000); 1,277 (2010); Density: 70.0 persons per square mile (2010); Race: 98.4% White, 0.3% Black, 0.2% Asian, 0.2% American Indian/Alaska Native, 0.0% Native Hawaiian/Other Pacific Islander, 0.9% Other, 1.3% Hispanic of any race (2010); Average household size: 2.64 (2010); Median age: 42.3 (2010); Males per 100 females: 102.7 (2010); Marriage status: 22.1% never married, 65.7% now married, 3.2% widowed, 9.0% divorced (2006-2010 5-year est.); Foreign born: 0.2% (2006-2010 5-year est.); Ancestry (includes multiple ancestries): 29.8% Irish, 27.0% English, 23.7% German, 10.2% French, 7.3% Italian (2006-2010 5-year est.).
**Economy:** Single-family building permits issued: 0 (2011); Multi-family building permits issued: 0 (2011); Employment by occupation: 10.7% management, 2.1% professional, 10.6% services, 14.4% sales, 2.1% farming, 9.3% construction, 13.7% production (2006-2010 5-year est.).
**Income:** Per capita income: $20,290 (2006-2010 5-year est.); Median household income: $51,481 (2006-2010 5-year est.); Average household income: $57,067 (2006-2010 5-year est.); Percent of households with income of $100,000 or more: 10.7% (2006-2010 5-year est.); Poverty rate: 7.9% (2006-2010 5-year est.).
**Education:** Percent of population age 25 and over with: High school diploma (including GED) or higher: 80.7% (2006-2010 5-year est.); Bachelor's degree or higher: 11.6% (2006-2010 5-year est.); Master's degree or higher: 4.2% (2006-2010 5-year est.).
**Housing:** Homeownership rate: 84.5% (2010); Median home value: $87,200 (2006-2010 5-year est.); Median contract rent: $469 per month (2006-2010 5-year est.); Median year structure built: 1979 (2006-2010 5-year est.).
**Transportation:** Commute to work: 92.0% car, 0.0% public transportation, 3.1% walk, 4.1% work from home (2006-2010 5-year est.); Travel time to work: 18.7% less than 15 minutes, 49.6% 15 to 30 minutes, 17.8% 30 to 45 minutes, 8.4% 45 to 60 minutes, 5.5% 60 minutes or more (2006-2010 5-year est.)
**Additional Information Contacts**
Town of Montezuma . . . . . . . . . . . . . . . . . . . . . . . . . . . (315) 776-8844
    http://co.cayuga.ny.us/montezuma

**MORAVIA** (village). Covers a land area of 1.703 square miles and a water area of 0.021 square miles. Located at 42.71° N. Lat; 76.42° W. Long. Elevation is 735 feet.
**Population:** 1,559 (1990); 1,363 (2000); 1,282 (2010); Density: 752.7 persons per square mile (2010); Race: 97.8% White, 0.5% Black, 0.0% Asian, 0.3% American Indian/Alaska Native, 0.1% Native Hawaiian/Other Pacific Islander, 1.3% Other, 1.1% Hispanic of any race (2010); Average household size: 2.36 (2010); Median age: 42.6 (2010); Males per 100 females: 92.8 (2010); Marriage status: 29.2% never married, 48.0% now married, 10.0% widowed, 12.7% divorced (2006-2010 5-year est.); Foreign born: 0.1% (2006-2010 5-year est.); Ancestry (includes multiple ancestries): 28.5% English, 16.1% German, 15.2% Irish, 7.0% Italian, 6.5% Dutch (2006-2010 5-year est.).
**Economy:** Single-family building permits issued: 0 (2011); Multi-family building permits issued: 0 (2011); Employment by occupation: 6.1% management, 2.2% professional, 9.1% services, 15.6% sales, 2.4% farming, 8.7% construction, 6.7% production (2006-2010 5-year est.).
**Income:** Per capita income: $25,821 (2006-2010 5-year est.); Median household income: $49,200 (2006-2010 5-year est.); Average household income: $58,110 (2006-2010 5-year est.); Percent of households with income of $100,000 or more: 13.7% (2006-2010 5-year est.); Poverty rate: 7.6% (2006-2010 5-year est.).
**Education:** Percent of population age 25 and over with: High school diploma (including GED) or higher: 88.9% (2006-2010 5-year est.); Bachelor's degree or higher: 19.2% (2006-2010 5-year est.); Master's degree or higher: 9.7% (2006-2010 5-year est.).
**School District(s)**
Moravia Central School District (PK-12)
    2009-10 Enrollment: 1,012 . . . . . . . . . . . . . . . . . . (315) 497-2670
**Housing:** Homeownership rate: 69.1% (2010); Median home value: $88,800 (2006-2010 5-year est.); Median contract rent: $464 per month (2006-2010 5-year est.); Median year structure built: before 1940 (2006-2010 5-year est.).
**Safety:** Violent crime rate: 7.9 per 10,000 population; Property crime rate: 95.0 per 10,000 population (2010).
**Newspapers:** Moravia Republican Register (Local news; Circulation 2,200)

**Transportation:** Commute to work: 91.1% car, 0.0% public transportation, 5.9% walk, 2.7% work from home (2006-2010 5-year est.); Travel time to work: 30.0% less than 15 minutes, 20.7% 15 to 30 minutes, 42.7% 30 to 45 minutes, 3.5% 45 to 60 minutes, 3.1% 60 minutes or more (2006-2010 5-year est.)
**Additional Information Contacts**
Moravia-Locke Chamber of Commerce . . . . . . . . . . . . . (315) 497-1341
    http://www.moravia-locke.com
Village of Moravia . . . . . . . . . . . . . . . . . . . . . . . . . . . (315) 497-1820
    http://co.cayuga.ny.us/villageofmoravia

**MORAVIA** (town). Covers a land area of 28.883 square miles and a water area of 0.753 square miles. Located at 42.73° N. Lat; 76.41° W. Long. Elevation is 735 feet.
**History:** Fillmore Glen State Park and the birthplace of President Millard Fillmore are nearby. Incorporated 1837.
**Population:** 3,871 (1990); 4,040 (2000); 3,626 (2010); Density: 125.5 persons per square mile (2010); Race: 80.7% White, 15.9% Black, 0.3% Asian, 0.7% American Indian/Alaska Native, 0.0% Native Hawaiian/Other Pacific Islander, 2.4% Other, 4.1% Hispanic of any race (2010); Average household size: 2.43 (2010); Median age: 37.9 (2010); Males per 100 females: 173.7 (2010); Marriage status: 45.6% never married, 37.9% now married, 3.6% widowed, 12.9% divorced (2006-2010 5-year est.); Foreign born: 3.6% (2006-2010 5-year est.); Ancestry (includes multiple ancestries): 16.7% German, 14.7% English, 14.0% Irish, 7.6% Italian, 4.2% Dutch (2006-2010 5-year est.).
**Economy:** Single-family building permits issued: 0 (2011); Multi-family building permits issued: 0 (2011); Employment by occupation: 5.2% management, 3.0% professional, 8.0% services, 16.4% sales, 1.3% farming, 13.0% construction, 8.5% production (2006-2010 5-year est.).
**Income:** Per capita income: $14,989 (2006-2010 5-year est.); Median household income: $51,806 (2006-2010 5-year est.); Average household income: $58,609 (2006-2010 5-year est.); Percent of households with income of $100,000 or more: 13.8% (2006-2010 5-year est.); Poverty rate: 6.3% (2006-2010 5-year est.).
**Education:** Percent of population age 25 and over with: High school diploma (including GED) or higher: 75.8% (2006-2010 5-year est.); Bachelor's degree or higher: 10.9% (2006-2010 5-year est.); Master's degree or higher: 5.0% (2006-2010 5-year est.).
**School District(s)**
Moravia Central School District (PK-12)
    2009-10 Enrollment: 1,012 . . . . . . . . . . . . . . . . . . (315) 497-2670
**Housing:** Homeownership rate: 75.3% (2010); Median home value: $100,300 (2006-2010 5-year est.); Median contract rent: $462 per month (2006-2010 5-year est.); Median year structure built: 1952 (2006-2010 5-year est.).
**Newspapers:** Moravia Republican Register (Local news; Circulation 2,200)
**Transportation:** Commute to work: 92.3% car, 0.4% public transportation, 3.7% walk, 3.0% work from home (2006-2010 5-year est.); Travel time to work: 31.3% less than 15 minutes, 25.2% 15 to 30 minutes, 33.6% 30 to 45 minutes, 2.8% 45 to 60 minutes, 7.0% 60 minutes or more (2006-2010 5-year est.)
**Additional Information Contacts**
Town of Moravia . . . . . . . . . . . . . . . . . . . . . . . . . . . . (315) 497-1972
    http://co.cayuga.ny.us/townofmoravia

**NILES** (town). Covers a land area of 38.974 square miles and a water area of 4.376 square miles. Located at 42.81° N. Lat; 76.40° W. Long. Elevation is 915 feet.
**Population:** 1,194 (1990); 1,208 (2000); 1,194 (2010); Density: 30.6 persons per square mile (2010); Race: 97.4% White, 0.8% Black, 0.3% Asian, 0.2% American Indian/Alaska Native, 0.0% Native Hawaiian/Other Pacific Islander, 1.3% Other, 0.6% Hispanic of any race (2010); Average household size: 2.51 (2010); Median age: 45.6 (2010); Males per 100 females: 111.7 (2010); Marriage status: 16.0% never married, 73.3% now married, 5.5% widowed, 5.2% divorced (2006-2010 5-year est.); Foreign born: 3.9% (2006-2010 5-year est.); Ancestry (includes multiple ancestries): 24.6% English, 19.8% German, 19.7% Irish, 8.5% Polish, 7.9% Dutch (2006-2010 5-year est.).
**Economy:** Single-family building permits issued: 1 (2011); Multi-family building permits issued: 0 (2011); Employment by occupation: 13.7% management, 2.2% professional, 8.0% services, 14.1% sales, 4.9% farming, 20.6% construction, 13.1% production (2006-2010 5-year est.).
**Income:** Per capita income: $32,800 (2006-2010 5-year est.); Median household income: $67,875 (2006-2010 5-year est.); Average household

income: $74,970 (2006-2010 5-year est.); Percent of households with income of $100,000 or more: 23.0% (2006-2010 5-year est.); Poverty rate: 5.7% (2006-2010 5-year est.).

**Education:** Percent of population age 25 and over with: High school diploma (including GED) or higher: 91.9% (2006-2010 5-year est.); Bachelor's degree or higher: 22.1% (2006-2010 5-year est.); Master's degree or higher: 9.6% (2006-2010 5-year est.).

**Housing:** Homeownership rate: 87.8% (2010); Median home value: $144,100 (2006-2010 5-year est.); Median contract rent: $657 per month (2006-2010 5-year est.); Median year structure built: 1956 (2006-2010 5-year est.).

**Transportation:** Commute to work: 90.8% car, 0.2% public transportation, 2.9% walk, 6.1% work from home (2006-2010 5-year est.); Travel time to work: 25.4% less than 15 minutes, 29.2% 15 to 30 minutes, 23.0% 30 to 45 minutes, 13.4% 45 to 60 minutes, 8.9% 60 minutes or more (2006-2010 5-year est.)

**Additional Information Contacts**

Town of Niles . . . . . . . . . . . . . . . . . . . . . . . . . . . . . (315) 497-0066
  http://co.cayuga.ny.us/niles

**OWASCO** (town). Covers a land area of 20.881 square miles and a water area of 2.594 square miles. Located at 42.89° N. Lat; 76.49° W. Long. Elevation is 892 feet.

**Population:** 3,490 (1990); 3,755 (2000); 3,793 (2010); Density: 181.6 persons per square mile (2010); Race: 98.4% White, 0.1% Black, 0.4% Asian, 0.0% American Indian/Alaska Native, 0.0% Native Hawaiian/Other Pacific Islander, 1.1% Other, 0.9% Hispanic of any race (2010); Average household size: 2.46 (2010); Median age: 46.8 (2010); Males per 100 females: 97.9 (2010); Marriage status: 17.0% never married, 71.8% now married, 6.7% widowed, 4.5% divorced (2006-2010 5-year est.); Foreign born: 3.6% (2006-2010 5-year est.); Ancestry (includes multiple ancestries): 34.8% Irish, 27.9% Italian, 23.8% English, 14.5% German, 7.2% Polish (2006-2010 5-year est.).

**Economy:** Single-family building permits issued: 4 (2011); Multi-family building permits issued: 0 (2011); Employment by occupation: 10.7% management, 4.7% professional, 4.6% services, 11.4% sales, 3.4% farming, 8.2% construction, 3.8% production (2006-2010 5-year est.).

**Income:** Per capita income: $35,017 (2006-2010 5-year est.); Median household income: $67,768 (2006-2010 5-year est.); Average household income: $83,337 (2006-2010 5-year est.); Percent of households with income of $100,000 or more: 25.7% (2006-2010 5-year est.); Poverty rate: 5.5% (2006-2010 5-year est.).

**Taxes:** Total city taxes per capita: $227 (2009); City property taxes per capita: $202 (2009).

**Education:** Percent of population age 25 and over with: High school diploma (including GED) or higher: 91.6% (2006-2010 5-year est.); Bachelor's degree or higher: 39.3% (2006-2010 5-year est.); Master's degree or higher: 16.2% (2006-2010 5-year est.).

**Housing:** Homeownership rate: 91.2% (2010); Median home value: $147,500 (2006-2010 5-year est.); Median contract rent: n/a per month (2006-2010 5-year est.); Median year structure built: 1950 (2006-2010 5-year est.).

**Transportation:** Commute to work: 92.2% car, 1.0% public transportation, 0.0% walk, 5.3% work from home (2006-2010 5-year est.); Travel time to work: 46.5% less than 15 minutes, 24.6% 15 to 30 minutes, 15.4% 30 to 45 minutes, 10.0% 45 to 60 minutes, 3.6% 60 minutes or more (2006-2010 5-year est.)

**Additional Information Contacts**

Town of Owasco . . . . . . . . . . . . . . . . . . . . . . . . . . . (315) 253-9021
  http://co.cayuga.ny.us/owasco

**PORT BYRON** (village). Covers a land area of 0.978 square miles and a water area of 0.029 square miles. Located at 43.03° N. Lat; 76.62° W. Long. Elevation is 407 feet.

**Population:** 1,359 (1990); 1,297 (2000); 1,290 (2010); Density: 1,317.9 persons per square mile (2010); Race: 95.1% White, 1.4% Black, 0.0% Asian, 0.2% American Indian/Alaska Native, 0.0% Native Hawaiian/Other Pacific Islander, 3.3% Other, 2.9% Hispanic of any race (2010); Average household size: 2.55 (2010); Median age: 38.0 (2010); Males per 100 females: 90.3 (2010); Marriage status: 33.6% never married, 51.4% now married, 8.4% widowed, 6.5% divorced (2006-2010 5-year est.); Foreign born: 0.4% (2006-2010 5-year est.); Ancestry (includes multiple ancestries): 22.1% English, 20.6% Irish, 17.0% German, 11.5% Italian, 10.8% Polish (2006-2010 5-year est.).

**Economy:** Single-family building permits issued: 0 (2011); Multi-family building permits issued: 0 (2011); Employment by occupation: 5.3% management, 2.5% professional, 13.3% services, 16.0% sales, 1.0% farming, 18.2% construction, 17.2% production (2006-2010 5-year est.).

**Income:** Per capita income: $17,953 (2006-2010 5-year est.); Median household income: $39,435 (2006-2010 5-year est.); Average household income: $44,733 (2006-2010 5-year est.); Percent of households with income of $100,000 or more: 5.1% (2006-2010 5-year est.); Poverty rate: 13.7% (2006-2010 5-year est.).

**Education:** Percent of population age 25 and over with: High school diploma (including GED) or higher: 86.2% (2006-2010 5-year est.); Bachelor's degree or higher: 7.4% (2006-2010 5-year est.); Master's degree or higher: 2.5% (2006-2010 5-year est.).

**School District(s)**

Port Byron Central School District (PK-12)
  2009-10 Enrollment: 1,061 . . . . . . . . . . . . . . . . . (315) 776-5728

**Housing:** Homeownership rate: 66.2% (2010); Median home value: $78,600 (2006-2010 5-year est.); Median contract rent: $488 per month (2006-2010 5-year est.); Median year structure built: 1952 (2006-2010 5-year est.).

**Safety:** Violent crime rate: 0.0 per 10,000 population; Property crime rate: 0.0 per 10,000 population (2010).

**Newspapers:** Port Byron Shopping Guide & Press (Community news)

**Transportation:** Commute to work: 96.0% car, 0.0% public transportation, 1.1% walk, 1.5% work from home (2006-2010 5-year est.); Travel time to work: 33.8% less than 15 minutes, 49.0% 15 to 30 minutes, 10.1% 30 to 45 minutes, 6.2% 45 to 60 minutes, 0.9% 60 minutes or more (2006-2010 5-year est.)

**Additional Information Contacts**

Village of Port Byron . . . . . . . . . . . . . . . . . . . . . . . (315) 776-4321
  http://www.villageofportbyron.com

**SCIPIO** (town). Covers a land area of 36.558 square miles and a water area of 2.750 square miles. Located at 42.79° N. Lat; 76.57° W. Long.

**Population:** 1,517 (1990); 1,537 (2000); 1,713 (2010); Density: 46.9 persons per square mile (2010); Race: 95.0% White, 0.5% Black, 0.6% Asian, 0.1% American Indian/Alaska Native, 0.1% Native Hawaiian/Other Pacific Islander, 3.7% Other, 3.7% Hispanic of any race (2010); Average household size: 2.64 (2010); Median age: 40.5 (2010); Males per 100 females: 106.4 (2010); Marriage status: 30.0% never married, 58.6% now married, 5.8% widowed, 5.6% divorced (2006-2010 5-year est.); Foreign born: 2.6% (2006-2010 5-year est.); Ancestry (includes multiple ancestries): 32.6% German, 29.1% Irish, 21.7% English, 9.0% Polish, 8.5% Dutch (2006-2010 5-year est.).

**Economy:** Single-family building permits issued: 0 (2011); Multi-family building permits issued: 0 (2011); Employment by occupation: 9.2% management, 2.3% professional, 11.4% services, 14.1% sales, 5.7% farming, 21.9% construction, 5.8% production (2006-2010 5-year est.).

**Income:** Per capita income: $23,719 (2006-2010 5-year est.); Median household income: $63,824 (2006-2010 5-year est.); Average household income: $66,868 (2006-2010 5-year est.); Percent of households with income of $100,000 or more: 21.7% (2006-2010 5-year est.); Poverty rate: 8.7% (2006-2010 5-year est.).

**Education:** Percent of population age 25 and over with: High school diploma (including GED) or higher: 86.0% (2006-2010 5-year est.); Bachelor's degree or higher: 15.4% (2006-2010 5-year est.); Master's degree or higher: 5.4% (2006-2010 5-year est.).

**Housing:** Homeownership rate: 84.3% (2010); Median home value: $105,300 (2006-2010 5-year est.); Median contract rent: $413 per month (2006-2010 5-year est.); Median year structure built: before 1940 (2006-2010 5-year est.).

**Transportation:** Commute to work: 87.1% car, 0.9% public transportation, 4.9% walk, 7.0% work from home (2006-2010 5-year est.); Travel time to work: 32.0% less than 15 minutes, 44.0% 15 to 30 minutes, 17.6% 30 to 45 minutes, 3.6% 45 to 60 minutes, 2.8% 60 minutes or more (2006-2010 5-year est.)

**Additional Information Contacts**

Town of Scipio . . . . . . . . . . . . . . . . . . . . . . . . . . . . (315) 364-5740
  http://co.cayuga.ny.us/scipio

**SCIPIO CENTER** (unincorporated postal area)

Zip Code: 13147

  Covers a land area of 35.885 square miles and a water area of 0.007 square miles. Located at 42.77° N. Lat; 76.56° W. Long. Elevation is 1,191 feet. Population: 1,281 (2010); Density: 35.7 persons per square mile (2010); Race: 92.8% White, 0.6% Black, 0.2% Asian, 0.1% American Indian/Alaska Native, 0.1% Native Hawaiian/Other Pacific Islander, 6.2% Other, 8.0% Hispanic of any race (2010); Average household size: 2.71 (2010); Median age: 40.7 (2010); Males per 100 females: 113.1 (2010); Homeownership rate: 83.2% (2010)

**SEMPRONIUS** (town). Covers a land area of 29.338 square miles and a water area of 0.379 square miles. Located at 42.74° N. Lat; 76.32° W. Long. Elevation is 1,598 feet.
**Population:** 802 (1990); 893 (2000); 895 (2010); Density: 30.5 persons per square mile (2010); Race: 99.1% White, 0.1% Black, 0.2% Asian, 0.3% American Indian/Alaska Native, 0.0% Native Hawaiian/Other Pacific Islander, 0.3% Other, 0.6% Hispanic of any race (2010); Average household size: 2.58 (2010); Median age: 39.7 (2010); Males per 100 females: 114.6 (2010); Marriage status: 29.8% never married, 58.2% now married, 6.7% widowed, 5.3% divorced (2006-2010 5-year est.); Foreign born: 0.5% (2006-2010 5-year est.); Ancestry (includes multiple ancestries): 33.2% German, 21.7% Irish, 15.4% English, 10.9% Dutch, 5.3% Polish (2006-2010 5-year est.).
**Economy:** Single-family building permits issued: 6 (2011); Multi-family building permits issued: 0 (2011); Employment by occupation: 15.6% management, 1.5% professional, 9.2% services, 10.6% sales, 3.2% farming, 20.8% construction, 11.6% production (2006-2010 5-year est.).
**Income:** Per capita income: $20,946 (2006-2010 5-year est.); Median household income: $51,607 (2006-2010 5-year est.); Average household income: $59,131 (2006-2010 5-year est.); Percent of households with income of $100,000 or more: 14.6% (2006-2010 5-year est.); Poverty rate: 11.8% (2006-2010 5-year est.).
**Education:** Percent of population age 25 and over with: High school diploma (including GED) or higher: 79.4% (2006-2010 5-year est.); Bachelor's degree or higher: 16.1% (2006-2010 5-year est.); Master's degree or higher: 5.7% (2006-2010 5-year est.).
**Housing:** Homeownership rate: 85.3% (2010); Median home value: $89,400 (2006-2010 5-year est.); Median contract rent: $506 per month (2006-2010 5-year est.); Median year structure built: 1972 (2006-2010 5-year est.).
**Transportation:** Commute to work: 86.5% car, 1.2% public transportation, 8.0% walk, 4.2% work from home (2006-2010 5-year est.); Travel time to work: 30.5% less than 15 minutes, 40.6% 15 to 30 minutes, 22.1% 30 to 45 minutes, 4.7% 45 to 60 minutes, 2.1% 60 minutes or more (2006-2010 5-year est.)
**Additional Information Contacts**
Town of Sempronius . . . . . . . . . . . . . . . . . . . . . . . . . . . (315) 496-2376
  http://co.cayuga.ny.us/sempronius

**SENNETT** (town). Covers a land area of 28.819 square miles and a water area of 0.023 square miles. Located at 42.97° N. Lat; 76.51° W. Long. Elevation is 594 feet.
**Population:** 2,913 (1990); 3,244 (2000); 3,595 (2010); Density: 124.7 persons per square mile (2010); Race: 95.3% White, 1.7% Black, 0.9% Asian, 0.3% American Indian/Alaska Native, 0.0% Native Hawaiian/Other Pacific Islander, 1.8% Other, 1.7% Hispanic of any race (2010); Average household size: 2.62 (2010); Median age: 43.7 (2010); Males per 100 females: 102.8 (2010); Marriage status: 25.6% never married, 58.7% now married, 11.8% widowed, 3.8% divorced (2006-2010 5-year est.); Foreign born: 2.4% (2006-2010 5-year est.); Ancestry (includes multiple ancestries): 31.9% Irish, 22.0% Italian, 17.9% English, 15.8% German, 6.5% Polish (2006-2010 5-year est.).
**Economy:** Single-family building permits issued: 7 (2011); Multi-family building permits issued: 0 (2011); Employment by occupation: 11.4% management, 0.9% professional, 8.5% services, 15.9% sales, 3.0% farming, 11.6% construction, 10.4% production (2006-2010 5-year est.).
**Income:** Per capita income: $26,359 (2006-2010 5-year est.); Median household income: $58,000 (2006-2010 5-year est.); Average household income: $79,170 (2006-2010 5-year est.); Percent of households with income of $100,000 or more: 24.1% (2006-2010 5-year est.); Poverty rate: 3.0% (2006-2010 5-year est.).
**Education:** Percent of population age 25 and over with: High school diploma (including GED) or higher: 88.8% (2006-2010 5-year est.); Bachelor's degree or higher: 21.6% (2006-2010 5-year est.); Master's degree or higher: 10.4% (2006-2010 5-year est.).
**Housing:** Homeownership rate: 91.6% (2010); Median home value: $148,600 (2006-2010 5-year est.); Median contract rent: $608 per month (2006-2010 5-year est.); Median year structure built: 1972 (2006-2010 5-year est.).

**Transportation:** Commute to work: 95.5% car, 0.5% public transportation, 1.3% walk, 2.3% work from home (2006-2010 5-year est.); Travel time to work: 61.2% less than 15 minutes, 17.4% 15 to 30 minutes, 13.7% 30 to 45 minutes, 6.7% 45 to 60 minutes, 1.1% 60 minutes or more (2006-2010 5-year est.)
**Additional Information Contacts**
Town of Sennett . . . . . . . . . . . . . . . . . . . . . . . . . . . . . (315) 253-3712
  http://co.cayuga.ny.us/sennett

**SPRINGPORT** (town). Covers a land area of 21.398 square miles and a water area of 5.430 square miles. Located at 42.85° N. Lat; 76.67° W. Long.
**Population:** 2,198 (1990); 2,256 (2000); 2,367 (2010); Density: 110.6 persons per square mile (2010); Race: 96.5% White, 0.8% Black, 0.6% Asian, 0.1% American Indian/Alaska Native, 0.1% Native Hawaiian/Other Pacific Islander, 1.9% Other, 2.5% Hispanic of any race (2010); Average household size: 2.52 (2010); Median age: 43.5 (2010); Males per 100 females: 98.9 (2010); Marriage status: 24.2% never married, 60.6% now married, 5.5% widowed, 9.7% divorced (2006-2010 5-year est.); Foreign born: 1.0% (2006-2010 5-year est.); Ancestry (includes multiple ancestries): 29.0% English, 26.7% Irish, 20.3% German, 9.3% Polish, 9.0% Italian (2006-2010 5-year est.).
**Economy:** Single-family building permits issued: 0 (2011); Multi-family building permits issued: 0 (2011); Employment by occupation: 9.8% management, 2.4% professional, 10.5% services, 14.6% sales, 3.5% farming, 10.9% construction, 11.2% production (2006-2010 5-year est.).
**Income:** Per capita income: $24,383 (2006-2010 5-year est.); Median household income: $50,547 (2006-2010 5-year est.); Average household income: $61,412 (2006-2010 5-year est.); Percent of households with income of $100,000 or more: 17.7% (2006-2010 5-year est.); Poverty rate: 9.4% (2006-2010 5-year est.).
**Education:** Percent of population age 25 and over with: High school diploma (including GED) or higher: 90.5% (2006-2010 5-year est.); Bachelor's degree or higher: 23.4% (2006-2010 5-year est.); Master's degree or higher: 10.0% (2006-2010 5-year est.).
**Housing:** Homeownership rate: 81.3% (2010); Median home value: $107,600 (2006-2010 5-year est.); Median contract rent: $457 per month (2006-2010 5-year est.); Median year structure built: 1964 (2006-2010 5-year est.).
**Transportation:** Commute to work: 89.7% car, 0.0% public transportation, 4.9% walk, 4.0% work from home (2006-2010 5-year est.); Travel time to work: 32.5% less than 15 minutes, 42.5% 15 to 30 minutes, 12.2% 30 to 45 minutes, 6.0% 45 to 60 minutes, 6.9% 60 minutes or more (2006-2010 5-year est.)
**Additional Information Contacts**
Town of Springport . . . . . . . . . . . . . . . . . . . . . . . . . . . (315) 889-7717
  http://co.cayuga.ny.us/springport

**STERLING** (town). Aka Sterling Station. Covers a land area of 45.453 square miles and a water area of 1.661 square miles. Located at 43.31° N. Lat; 76.65° W. Long. Elevation is 315 feet.
**Population:** 3,285 (1990); 3,432 (2000); 3,040 (2010); Density: 66.9 persons per square mile (2010); Race: 98.0% White, 0.3% Black, 0.2% Asian, 0.7% American Indian/Alaska Native, 0.0% Native Hawaiian/Other Pacific Islander, 0.8% Other, 1.1% Hispanic of any race (2010); Average household size: 2.48 (2010); Median age: 44.0 (2010); Males per 100 females: 102.9 (2010); Marriage status: 20.5% never married, 62.3% now married, 4.3% widowed, 12.8% divorced (2006-2010 5-year est.); Foreign born: 0.9% (2006-2010 5-year est.); Ancestry (includes multiple ancestries): 19.6% German, 15.6% Irish, 15.2% English, 14.2% Dutch, 10.0% French (2006-2010 5-year est.).
**Economy:** Single-family building permits issued: 5 (2011); Multi-family building permits issued: 0 (2011); Employment by occupation: 7.3% management, 0.2% professional, 8.4% services, 20.4% sales, 2.6% farming, 21.2% construction, 14.8% production (2006-2010 5-year est.).
**Income:** Per capita income: $19,569 (2006-2010 5-year est.); Median household income: $44,364 (2006-2010 5-year est.); Average household income: $52,904 (2006-2010 5-year est.); Percent of households with income of $100,000 or more: 10.2% (2006-2010 5-year est.); Poverty rate: 17.0% (2006-2010 5-year est.).
**Education:** Percent of population age 25 and over with: High school diploma (including GED) or higher: 88.2% (2006-2010 5-year est.); Bachelor's degree or higher: 14.7% (2006-2010 5-year est.); Master's degree or higher: 5.5% (2006-2010 5-year est.).

**Housing:** Homeownership rate: 84.7% (2010); Median home value: $79,900 (2006-2010 5-year est.); Median contract rent: $415 per month (2006-2010 5-year est.); Median year structure built: 1953 (2006-2010 5-year est.).
**Transportation:** Commute to work: 92.1% car, 0.0% public transportation, 3.2% walk, 4.2% work from home (2006-2010 5-year est.); Travel time to work: 17.5% less than 15 minutes, 30.0% 15 to 30 minutes, 14.2% 30 to 45 minutes, 25.6% 45 to 60 minutes, 12.6% 60 minutes or more (2006-2010 5-year est.)
**Additional Information Contacts**
Town of Sterling . . . . . . . . . . . . . . . . . . . . . . . . . . (315) 947-5666
    http://co.cayuga.ny.us/sterling

**SUMMERHILL** (town). Aka Summer Hill. Covers a land area of 25.861 square miles and a water area of 0.123 square miles. Located at 42.65° N. Lat; 76.32° W. Long.
**Population:** 1,017 (1990); 1,098 (2000); 1,217 (2010); Density: 47.1 persons per square mile (2010); Race: 97.3% White, 0.2% Black, 0.3% Asian, 0.7% American Indian/Alaska Native, 0.1% Native Hawaiian/Other Pacific Islander, 1.4% Other, 1.0% Hispanic of any race (2010); Average household size: 2.79 (2010); Median age: 38.8 (2010); Males per 100 females: 104.2 (2010); Marriage status: 25.2% never married, 67.0% now married, 2.3% widowed, 5.5% divorced (2006-2010 5-year est.); Foreign born: 1.6% (2006-2010 5-year est.); Ancestry (includes multiple ancestries): 17.2% German, 14.5% Irish, 10.1% English, 8.7% Dutch, 8.6% Italian (2006-2010 5-year est.).
**Economy:** Single-family building permits issued: 0 (2011); Multi-family building permits issued: 0 (2011); Employment by occupation: 10.8% management, 1.9% professional, 12.2% services, 12.4% sales, 4.6% farming, 13.7% construction, 17.3% production (2006-2010 5-year est.).
**Income:** Per capita income: $21,396 (2006-2010 5-year est.); Median household income: $56,481 (2006-2010 5-year est.); Average household income: $64,382 (2006-2010 5-year est.); Percent of households with income of $100,000 or more: 16.3% (2006-2010 5-year est.); Poverty rate: 14.2% (2006-2010 5-year est.).
**Education:** Percent of population age 25 and over with: High school diploma (including GED) or higher: 89.2% (2006-2010 5-year est.); Bachelor's degree or higher: 13.9% (2006-2010 5-year est.); Master's degree or higher: 5.9% (2006-2010 5-year est.).
**Housing:** Homeownership rate: 86.0% (2010); Median home value: $91,000 (2006-2010 5-year est.); Median contract rent: $450 per month (2006-2010 5-year est.); Median year structure built: 1979 (2006-2010 5-year est.).
**Transportation:** Commute to work: 87.9% car, 0.0% public transportation, 7.6% walk, 3.1% work from home (2006-2010 5-year est.); Travel time to work: 30.8% less than 15 minutes, 40.5% 15 to 30 minutes, 18.9% 30 to 45 minutes, 7.9% 45 to 60 minutes, 1.9% 60 minutes or more (2006-2010 5-year est.)
**Additional Information Contacts**
Town of Summerhill . . . . . . . . . . . . . . . . . . . . . . . . (315) 497-3494
    http://co.cayuga.ny.us/summerhill

**THROOP** (town). Covers a land area of 18.585 square miles and a water area of 0.111 square miles. Located at 42.98° N. Lat; 76.61° W. Long. Elevation is 548 feet.
**Population:** 1,792 (1990); 1,824 (2000); 1,990 (2010); Density: 107.1 persons per square mile (2010); Race: 98.4% White, 0.5% Black, 0.1% Asian, 0.1% American Indian/Alaska Native, 0.1% Native Hawaiian/Other Pacific Islander, 0.8% Other, 1.4% Hispanic of any race (2010); Average household size: 2.64 (2010); Median age: 44.4 (2010); Males per 100 females: 99.0 (2010); Marriage status: 20.0% never married, 60.8% now married, 8.2% widowed, 11.0% divorced (2006-2010 5-year est.); Foreign born: 1.2% (2006-2010 5-year est.); Ancestry (includes multiple ancestries): 26.5% Irish, 21.0% Italian, 20.8% German, 18.5% English, 11.9% Polish (2006-2010 5-year est.).
**Economy:** Single-family building permits issued: 2 (2011); Multi-family building permits issued: 0 (2011); Employment by occupation: 10.0% management, 2.0% professional, 6.1% services, 17.5% sales, 3.7% farming, 13.0% construction, 11.6% production (2006-2010 5-year est.).
**Income:** Per capita income: $23,463 (2006-2010 5-year est.); Median household income: $54,911 (2006-2010 5-year est.); Average household income: $61,339 (2006-2010 5-year est.); Percent of households with income of $100,000 or more: 13.4% (2006-2010 5-year est.); Poverty rate: 7.2% (2006-2010 5-year est.).

**Education:** Percent of population age 25 and over with: High school diploma (including GED) or higher: 87.1% (2006-2010 5-year est.); Bachelor's degree or higher: 16.8% (2006-2010 5-year est.); Master's degree or higher: 6.9% (2006-2010 5-year est.).
**Housing:** Homeownership rate: 92.5% (2010); Median home value: $111,300 (2006-2010 5-year est.); Median contract rent: $475 per month (2006-2010 5-year est.); Median year structure built: 1965 (2006-2010 5-year est.).
**Transportation:** Commute to work: 96.5% car, 0.0% public transportation, 0.0% walk, 3.5% work from home (2006-2010 5-year est.); Travel time to work: 45.5% less than 15 minutes, 31.2% 15 to 30 minutes, 10.4% 30 to 45 minutes, 8.2% 45 to 60 minutes, 4.7% 60 minutes or more (2006-2010 5-year est.)
**Additional Information Contacts**
Town of Throop . . . . . . . . . . . . . . . . . . . . . . . . . . . (315) 252-7373
    http://co.cayuga.ny.us/throop

**UNION SPRINGS** (village). Covers a land area of 1.737 square miles and a water area of 0.014 square miles. Located at 42.84° N. Lat; 76.68° W. Long. Elevation is 410 feet.
**Population:** 1,118 (1990); 1,074 (2000); 1,197 (2010); Density: 689.0 persons per square mile (2010); Race: 94.3% White, 1.5% Black, 1.2% Asian, 0.1% American Indian/Alaska Native, 0.2% Native Hawaiian/Other Pacific Islander, 2.7% Other, 3.1% Hispanic of any race (2010); Average household size: 2.41 (2010); Median age: 41.7 (2010); Males per 100 females: 97.5 (2010); Marriage status: 24.4% never married, 61.3% now married, 5.5% widowed, 8.8% divorced (2006-2010 5-year est.); Foreign born: 0.6% (2006-2010 5-year est.); Ancestry (includes multiple ancestries): 27.6% Irish, 22.2% English, 19.5% German, 11.4% Polish, 10.8% Italian (2006-2010 5-year est.).
**Economy:** Single-family building permits issued: 2 (2011); Multi-family building permits issued: 0 (2011); Employment by occupation: 7.7% management, 3.4% professional, 9.6% services, 17.3% sales, 3.8% farming, 6.6% construction, 12.8% production (2006-2010 5-year est.).
**Income:** Per capita income: $23,137 (2006-2010 5-year est.); Median household income: $52,292 (2006-2010 5-year est.); Average household income: $62,345 (2006-2010 5-year est.); Percent of households with income of $100,000 or more: 15.4% (2006-2010 5-year est.); Poverty rate: 10.7% (2006-2010 5-year est.).
**Education:** Percent of population age 25 and over with: High school diploma (including GED) or higher: 91.9% (2006-2010 5-year est.); Bachelor's degree or higher: 20.2% (2006-2010 5-year est.); Master's degree or higher: 7.8% (2006-2010 5-year est.).
**School District(s)**
Union Springs Central School District (KG-12)
    2009-10 Enrollment: 891 . . . . . . . . . . . . . . . . . . (315) 889-4101
**Housing:** Homeownership rate: 74.5% (2010); Median home value: $95,200 (2006-2010 5-year est.); Median contract rent: $479 per month (2006-2010 5-year est.); Median year structure built: before 1940 (2006-2010 5-year est.).
**Transportation:** Commute to work: 86.8% car, 0.0% public transportation, 8.5% walk, 2.4% work from home (2006-2010 5-year est.); Travel time to work: 31.3% less than 15 minutes, 42.9% 15 to 30 minutes, 12.7% 30 to 45 minutes, 4.6% 45 to 60 minutes, 8.5% 60 minutes or more (2006-2010 5-year est.)
**Additional Information Contacts**
Village of Union Springs . . . . . . . . . . . . . . . . . . . . . (315) 889-7341
    http://unionspringsny.com

**VENICE** (town). Aka Stewart Corners. Covers a land area of 41.087 square miles and a water area of 0.200 square miles. Located at 42.72° N. Lat; 76.54° W. Long.
**Population:** 1,315 (1990); 1,286 (2000); 1,368 (2010); Density: 33.3 persons per square mile (2010); Race: 95.8% White, 0.1% Black, 0.1% Asian, 0.0% American Indian/Alaska Native, 0.0% Native Hawaiian/Other Pacific Islander, 4.0% Other, 6.0% Hispanic of any race (2010); Average household size: 2.69 (2010); Median age: 41.2 (2010); Males per 100 females: 112.8 (2010); Marriage status: 18.7% never married, 70.9% now married, 3.8% widowed, 6.6% divorced (2006-2010 5-year est.); Foreign born: 1.3% (2006-2010 5-year est.); Ancestry (includes multiple ancestries): 21.7% English, 21.5% Irish, 20.4% German, 13.4% American, 8.6% Polish (2006-2010 5-year est.).
**Economy:** Single-family building permits issued: 3 (2011); Multi-family building permits issued: 0 (2011); Employment by occupation: 14.4%

management, 3.7% professional, 3.7% services, 18.4% sales, 0.5% farming, 16.2% construction, 12.3% production (2006-2010 5-year est.).
**Income:** Per capita income: $24,285 (2006-2010 5-year est.); Median household income: $57,404 (2006-2010 5-year est.); Average household income: $63,763 (2006-2010 5-year est.); Percent of households with income of $100,000 or more: 17.4% (2006-2010 5-year est.); Poverty rate: 7.5% (2006-2010 5-year est.).
**Education:** Percent of population age 25 and over with: High school diploma (including GED) or higher: 87.7% (2006-2010 5-year est.); Bachelor's degree or higher: 18.4% (2006-2010 5-year est.); Master's degree or higher: 5.7% (2006-2010 5-year est.).
**Housing:** Homeownership rate: 83.2% (2010); Median home value: $101,400 (2006-2010 5-year est.); Median contract rent: $433 per month (2006-2010 5-year est.); Median year structure built: before 1940 (2006-2010 5-year est.).
**Transportation:** Commute to work: 84.4% car, 1.1% public transportation, 3.9% walk, 10.1% work from home (2006-2010 5-year est.); Travel time to work: 31.0% less than 15 minutes, 30.3% 15 to 30 minutes, 17.9% 30 to 45 minutes, 10.9% 45 to 60 minutes, 10.0% 60 minutes or more (2006-2010 5-year est.)
**Additional Information Contacts**
Town of Venice . . . . . . . . . . . . . . . . . . . . . . . . . . . . . . (315) 497-1898
  http://co.cayuga.ny.us/venice

**VICTORY** (town). Covers a land area of 34.393 square miles and a water area of 0.058 square miles. Located at 43.21° N. Lat; 76.64° W. Long. Elevation is 423 feet.
**Population:** 1,535 (1990); 1,838 (2000); 1,660 (2010); Density: 48.3 persons per square mile (2010); Race: 95.7% White, 0.5% Black, 1.2% Asian, 0.8% American Indian/Alaska Native, 0.1% Native Hawaiian/Other Pacific Islander, 1.7% Other, 1.0% Hispanic of any race (2010); Average household size: 2.70 (2010); Median age: 41.8 (2010); Males per 100 females: 103.7 (2010); Marriage status: 26.4% never married, 58.0% now married, 5.9% widowed, 9.7% divorced (2006-2010 5-year est.); Foreign born: 0.8% (2006-2010 5-year est.); Ancestry (includes multiple ancestries): 22.1% Irish, 22.0% German, 16.3% English, 12.3% French, 10.5% Italian (2006-2010 5-year est.).
**Economy:** Single-family building permits issued: 0 (2011); Multi-family building permits issued: 0 (2011); Employment by occupation: 12.2% management, 0.0% professional, 8.6% services, 16.5% sales, 1.0% farming, 16.6% construction, 9.5% production (2006-2010 5-year est.).
**Income:** Per capita income: $18,217 (2006-2010 5-year est.); Median household income: $49,904 (2006-2010 5-year est.); Average household income: $49,950 (2006-2010 5-year est.); Percent of households with income of $100,000 or more: 5.1% (2006-2010 5-year est.); Poverty rate: 14.8% (2006-2010 5-year est.).
**Education:** Percent of population age 25 and over with: High school diploma (including GED) or higher: 87.7% (2006-2010 5-year est.); Bachelor's degree or higher: 9.4% (2006-2010 5-year est.); Master's degree or higher: 4.1% (2006-2010 5-year est.).
**Housing:** Homeownership rate: 89.2% (2010); Median home value: $86,800 (2006-2010 5-year est.); Median contract rent: $440 per month (2006-2010 5-year est.); Median year structure built: 1972 (2006-2010 5-year est.).
**Transportation:** Commute to work: 93.4% car, 0.0% public transportation, 3.5% walk, 2.7% work from home (2006-2010 5-year est.); Travel time to work: 20.0% less than 15 minutes, 22.5% 15 to 30 minutes, 30.3% 30 to 45 minutes, 16.8% 45 to 60 minutes, 10.4% 60 minutes or more (2006-2010 5-year est.)

**WEEDSPORT** (village). Covers a land area of 0.975 square miles and a water area of 0 square miles. Located at 43.04° N. Lat; 76.56° W. Long. Elevation is 413 feet.
**History:** Incorporated 1831.
**Population:** 1,996 (1990); 2,017 (2000); 1,815 (2010); Density: 1,860.3 persons per square mile (2010); Race: 98.3% White, 0.3% Black, 0.4% Asian, 0.2% American Indian/Alaska Native, 0.0% Native Hawaiian/Other Pacific Islander, 0.8% Other, 0.9% Hispanic of any race (2010); Average household size: 2.39 (2010); Median age: 42.2 (2010); Males per 100 females: 89.9 (2010); Marriage status: 30.4% never married, 53.2% now married, 8.0% widowed, 8.4% divorced (2006-2010 5-year est.); Foreign born: 0.5% (2006-2010 5-year est.); Ancestry (includes multiple ancestries): 29.9% Irish, 20.5% German, 20.1% English, 15.5% Italian, 7.0% Polish (2006-2010 5-year est.).

**Economy:** Single-family building permits issued: 0 (2011); Multi-family building permits issued: 0 (2011); Employment by occupation: 11.5% management, 1.1% professional, 8.8% services, 17.1% sales, 3.4% farming, 9.6% construction, 6.4% production (2006-2010 5-year est.).
**Income:** Per capita income: $25,461 (2006-2010 5-year est.); Median household income: $50,968 (2006-2010 5-year est.); Average household income: $63,423 (2006-2010 5-year est.); Percent of households with income of $100,000 or more: 17.8% (2006-2010 5-year est.); Poverty rate: 13.0% (2006-2010 5-year est.).
**Education:** Percent of population age 25 and over with: High school diploma (including GED) or higher: 90.1% (2006-2010 5-year est.); Bachelor's degree or higher: 19.5% (2006-2010 5-year est.); Master's degree or higher: 9.4% (2006-2010 5-year est.).
    **School District(s)**
Weedsport Central School District (KG-12)
    2009-10 Enrollment: 877 . . . . . . . . . . . . . . . . . . (315) 834-6637
**Housing:** Homeownership rate: 65.7% (2010); Median home value: $95,700 (2006-2010 5-year est.); Median contract rent: $475 per month (2006-2010 5-year est.); Median year structure built: before 1940 (2006-2010 5-year est.).
**Safety:** Violent crime rate: 0.0 per 10,000 population; Property crime rate: 150.0 per 10,000 population (2010).
**Transportation:** Commute to work: 92.5% car, 0.8% public transportation, 4.5% walk, 1.3% work from home (2006-2010 5-year est.); Travel time to work: 34.8% less than 15 minutes, 38.1% 15 to 30 minutes, 19.9% 30 to 45 minutes, 4.5% 45 to 60 minutes, 2.7% 60 minutes or more (2006-2010 5-year est.)
**Additional Information Contacts**
Village of Weedsport . . . . . . . . . . . . . . . . . . . . . . . . . (315) 834-6634
  http://co.cayuga.ny.us/weedsport
Weedsport Area Chamber of Commerce. . . . . . . . . . . (315) 834-9263
  http://chamber.weedsport.com

# Chautauqua County

Located in western New York; bounded on the northwest by Lake Erie, and on the west and south by Pennsylvania. Covers a land area of 1,062.05 square miles, a water area of 437.97 square miles, and is located in the Eastern Time Zone at 42.24° N. Lat., 79.34° W. Long. The county was founded in 1808. County seat is Mayville.

Chautauqua County is part of the Jamestown-Dunkirk-Fredonia, NY Micropolitan Statistical Area. The entire metro area includes: Chautauqua County, NY

Weather Station: Fredonia                                    Elevation: 759 feet

| | Jan | Feb | Mar | Apr | May | Jun | Jul | Aug | Sep | Oct | Nov | Dec |
|---|---|---|---|---|---|---|---|---|---|---|---|---|
| High | 33 | 36 | 44 | 57 | 68 | 77 | 80 | 79 | 73 | 61 | 50 | 38 |
| Low | 20 | 20 | 27 | 38 | 48 | 58 | 63 | 62 | 55 | 45 | 36 | 26 |
| Precip | 2.6 | 2.1 | 2.7 | 3.3 | 3.5 | 3.7 | 4.1 | 3.7 | 4.6 | 4.3 | 4.0 | 3.4 |
| Snow | 25.4 | 13.3 | 11.1 | 2.7 | 0.3 | 0.0 | 0.0 | 0.0 | 0.0 | 0.2 | 5.9 | 20.3 |

*High and Low temperatures in degrees Fahrenheit; Precipitation and Snow in inches*

Weather Station: Jamestown 4 NE                              Elevation: 1,250 feet

| | Jan | Feb | Mar | Apr | May | Jun | Jul | Aug | Sep | Oct | Nov | Dec |
|---|---|---|---|---|---|---|---|---|---|---|---|---|
| High | 32 | 35 | 43 | 57 | 67 | 76 | 80 | 79 | 72 | 59 | 48 | 36 |
| Low | 15 | 15 | 22 | 33 | 42 | 52 | 56 | 55 | 48 | 37 | 31 | 21 |
| Precip | 3.1 | 2.5 | 3.0 | 3.6 | 3.9 | 4.8 | 4.8 | 4.1 | 4.4 | 3.8 | 4.1 | 3.5 |
| Snow | 24.9 | 15.6 | 13.1 | 2.9 | tr | 0.0 | 0.0 | 0.0 | 0.0 | 0.4 | 8.3 | 21.4 |

*High and Low temperatures in degrees Fahrenheit; Precipitation and Snow in inches*

Weather Station: Westfield 2 SSE                             Elevation: 707 feet

| | Jan | Feb | Mar | Apr | May | Jun | Jul | Aug | Sep | Oct | Nov | Dec |
|---|---|---|---|---|---|---|---|---|---|---|---|---|
| High | 33 | 35 | 43 | 56 | 67 | 76 | 80 | 78 | 71 | 60 | 48 | 37 |
| Low | 20 | 21 | 27 | 38 | 49 | 58 | 63 | 62 | 55 | 45 | 35 | 26 |
| Precip | 2.5 | 2.2 | 2.9 | 3.4 | 3.8 | 4.1 | 4.2 | 4.0 | 4.9 | 4.9 | 4.3 | 3.4 |
| Snow | 21.2 | 14.0 | 12.7 | 2.7 | 0.4 | 0.0 | 0.0 | 0.0 | tr | 0.4 | 8.7 | 24.4 |

*High and Low temperatures in degrees Fahrenheit; Precipitation and Snow in inches*

**Population:** 141,845 (1990); 139,750 (2000); 134,905 (2010); Race: 92.6% White, 2.4% Black, 0.5% Asian, 0.5% American Indian/Alaska Native, 0.0% Native Hawaiian/Other Pacific Islander, 4.0% Other, 6.1% Hispanic of any race (2010); Density: 127.0 persons per square mile (2010); Average household size: 2.37 (2010); Median age: 40.9 (2010); Males per 100 females: 97.2 (2010).

**Religion:** Six largest groups: 15.5% Catholicism, 8.4% Methodist/Pietist, 3.3% Lutheran, 2.2% Presbyterian-Reformed, 2.1% Holiness, 2.1% Non-Denominational (2010)

**Economy:** Unemployment rate: 9.1% (February 2012); Total civilian labor force: 62,431 (February 2012); Leading industries: 23.3% manufacturing; 19.8% health care and social assistance; 15.1% retail trade (2009); Farms: 1,658 totaling 235,858 acres (2007); Companies that employ 500 or more persons: 7 (2009); Companies that employ 100 to 499 persons: 61 (2009); Companies that employ less than 100 persons: 2,924 (2009); Black-owned businesses: 182 (2007); Hispanic-owned businesses: n/a (2007); Asian-owned businesses: n/a (2007); Women-owned businesses: n/a (2007); Retail sales per capita: $10,849 (2010). Single-family building permits issued: 88 (2011); Multi-family building permits issued: 41 (2011).

**Income:** Per capita income: $21,033 (2006-2010 5-year est.); Median household income: $40,639 (2006-2010 5-year est.); Average household income: $50,823 (2006-2010 5-year est.); Percent of households with income of $100,000 or more: 10.4% (2006-2010 5-year est.); Poverty rate: 17.1% (2006-2010 5-year est.); Bankruptcy rate: 2.93% (2011).

**Taxes:** Total county taxes per capita: $870 (2009); County property taxes per capita: $430 (2009).

**Education:** Percent of population age 25 and over with: High school diploma (including GED) or higher: 86.2% (2006-2010 5-year est.); Bachelor's degree or higher: 20.3% (2006-2010 5-year est.); Master's degree or higher: 8.9% (2006-2010 5-year est.).

**Housing:** Homeownership rate: 68.0% (2010); Median home value: $79,600 (2006-2010 5-year est.); Median contract rent: $425 per month (2006-2010 5-year est.); Median year structure built: 1945 (2006-2010 5-year est.)

**Health:** Birth rate: 107.8 per 10,000 population (2011); Death rate: 100.3 per 10,000 population (2011); Age-adjusted cancer mortality rate: 186.7 deaths per 100,000 population (2009); Number of physicians: 13.5 per 10,000 population (2008); Hospital beds: 66.4 per 10,000 population (2007); Hospital admissions: 1,295.6 per 10,000 population (2007).

**Environment:** Air Quality Index: 84.1% good, 14.2% moderate, 1.6% unhealthy for sensitive individuals, 0.0% unhealthy (percent of days in 2010)

**Elections:** 2008 Presidential election results: 49.5% Obama, 48.6% McCain, 1.1% Nader

**National and State Parks:** Lake Erie State Park

**Additional Information Contacts**

Chautauqua County Government . . . . . . . . . . . . . . . . . . . . (716) 753-4211
  http://www.co.chautauqua.ny.us
Chautauqua County Chamber of Commerce. . . . . . . . . . . (716) 366-6200
  http://www.chautauquachamber.org
Chautauqua County Chamber of Commerce. . . . . . . . . . . (716) 484-1101
  http://www.chautauquachamber.org
Chautauqua County Visitor's Bureau. . . . . . . . . . . . . . . (866) 908-4569
  http://www.tourchautauqua.com
Findley Lake Area Chamber of Commerce . . . . . . . . . . . (716) 769-7609
  http://www.findleylakeinfo.org
Fredonia Chamber of Commerce . . . . . . . . . . . . . . . . (716) 679-1565
  http://www.fredoniachamber.org
Town of Busti . . . . . . . . . . . . . . . . . . . . . . . . . . . (716) 763-8561
  http://www.townofbusti.com
Town of Ellicott. . . . . . . . . . . . . . . . . . . . . . . . . . (716) 665-5317
  http://www.townofellicott.com
Town of Portland . . . . . . . . . . . . . . . . . . . . . . . . . (716) 792-9614
  http://www.town.portland.ny.us

## Chautauqua County Communities

**ARKWRIGHT** (town). Covers a land area of 35.669 square miles and a water area of 0.059 square miles. Located at 42.38° N. Lat; 79.24° W. Long. Elevation is 1,634 feet.

**Population:** 1,040 (1990); 1,126 (2000); 1,061 (2010); Density: 29.7 persons per square mile (2010); Race: 98.4% White, 0.4% Black, 0.2% Asian, 0.2% American Indian/Alaska Native, 0.0% Native Hawaiian/Other Pacific Islander, 0.8% Other, 2.5% Hispanic of any race (2010); Average household size: 2.36 (2010); Median age: 47.7 (2010); Males per 100 females: 108.4 (2010); Marriage status: 22.4% never married, 64.4% now married, 3.0% widowed, 10.2% divorced (2006-2010 5-year est.); Foreign born: 2.0% (2006-2010 5-year est.); Ancestry (includes multiple ancestries): 33.4% German, 22.7% English, 20.0% Polish, 13.0% Italian, 12.7% Irish (2006-2010 5-year est.).

**Economy:** Single-family building permits issued: 3 (2011); Multi-family building permits issued: 0 (2011); Employment by occupation: 10.8% management, 3.0% professional, 10.2% services, 10.4% sales, 5.2% farming, 12.3% construction, 4.3% production (2006-2010 5-year est.).

**Income:** Per capita income: $26,947 (2006-2010 5-year est.); Median household income: $62,955 (2006-2010 5-year est.); Average household income: $66,222 (2006-2010 5-year est.); Percent of households with income of $100,000 or more: 18.3% (2006-2010 5-year est.); Poverty rate: 8.4% (2006-2010 5-year est.).

**Education:** Percent of population age 25 and over with: High school diploma (including GED) or higher: 88.3% (2006-2010 5-year est.); Bachelor's degree or higher: 27.1% (2006-2010 5-year est.); Master's degree or higher: 13.4% (2006-2010 5-year est.).

**Housing:** Homeownership rate: 90.0% (2010); Median home value: $86,100 (2006-2010 5-year est.); Median contract rent: $447 per month (2006-2010 5-year est.); Median year structure built: 1974 (2006-2010 5-year est.).

**Transportation:** Commute to work: 95.5% car, 0.0% public transportation, 1.6% walk, 1.6% work from home (2006-2010 5-year est.); Travel time to work: 29.7% less than 15 minutes, 38.6% 15 to 30 minutes, 19.9% 30 to 45 minutes, 3.3% 45 to 60 minutes, 8.5% 60 minutes or more (2006-2010 5-year est.)

**ASHVILLE** (unincorporated postal area)
Zip Code: 14710
  Covers a land area of 48.364 square miles and a water area of 0.056 square miles. Located at 42.08° N. Lat; 79.41° W. Long. Elevation is 1,358 feet. Population: 3,540 (2010); Density: 73.2 persons per square mile (2010); Race: 98.8% White, 0.2% Black, 0.3% Asian, 0.1% American Indian/Alaska Native, 0.0% Native Hawaiian/Other Pacific Islander, 0.6% Other, 0.8% Hispanic of any race (2010); Average household size: 2.49 (2010); Median age: 46.4 (2010); Males per 100 females: 100.0 (2010); Homeownership rate: 86.3% (2010)

**BEMUS POINT** (village). Covers a land area of 0.436 square miles and a water area of 0 square miles. Located at 42.16° N. Lat; 79.38° W. Long. Elevation is 1,322 feet.

**Population:** 383 (1990); 340 (2000); 364 (2010); Density: 834.8 persons per square mile (2010); Race: 96.4% White, 0.0% Black, 2.2% Asian, 0.0% American Indian/Alaska Native, 0.0% Native Hawaiian/Other Pacific Islander, 1.4% Other, 0.3% Hispanic of any race (2010); Average household size: 2.14 (2010); Median age: 50.6 (2010); Males per 100 females: 86.7 (2010); Marriage status: 24.6% never married, 51.6% now married, 15.5% widowed, 8.3% divorced (2006-2010 5-year est.); Foreign born: 1.0% (2006-2010 5-year est.); Ancestry (includes multiple ancestries): 29.1% German, 21.2% English, 19.9% Swedish, 18.2% Irish, 7.5% Scottish (2006-2010 5-year est.).

**Economy:** Single-family building permits issued: 0 (2011); Multi-family building permits issued: 0 (2011); Employment by occupation: 12.4% management, 4.7% professional, 3.9% services, 20.9% sales, 0.0% farming, 5.4% construction, 4.7% production (2006-2010 5-year est.).

**Income:** Per capita income: $29,013 (2006-2010 5-year est.); Median household income: $50,313 (2006-2010 5-year est.); Average household income: $60,036 (2006-2010 5-year est.); Percent of households with income of $100,000 or more: 19.7% (2006-2010 5-year est.); Poverty rate: 4.1% (2006-2010 5-year est.).

**Education:** Percent of population age 25 and over with: High school diploma (including GED) or higher: 92.7% (2006-2010 5-year est.); Bachelor's degree or higher: 45.0% (2006-2010 5-year est.); Master's degree or higher: 25.7% (2006-2010 5-year est.).

**School District(s)**
Bemus Point Central School District (PK-12)
  2009-10 Enrollment: 786 . . . . . . . . . . . . . . . . . . . . (716) 386-2375

**Housing:** Homeownership rate: 64.1% (2010); Median home value: $172,300 (2006-2010 5-year est.); Median contract rent: $345 per month (2006-2010 5-year est.); Median year structure built: before 1940 (2006-2010 5-year est.).

**Transportation:** Commute to work: 93.4% car, 0.0% public transportation, 6.6% walk, 0.0% work from home (2006-2010 5-year est.); Travel time to work: 15.7% less than 15 minutes, 63.6% 15 to 30 minutes, 15.7% 30 to 45 minutes, 3.3% 45 to 60 minutes, 1.7% 60 minutes or more (2006-2010 5-year est.)

**BROCTON** (village). Covers a land area of 1.709 square miles and a water area of 0 square miles. Located at 42.38° N. Lat; 79.44° W. Long. Elevation is 735 feet.

**History:** A short-lived community of the Brotherhood of the New Life was founded here in 1867 by Thomas L. Harris. Incorporated 1894.

**Population:** 1,387 (1990); 1,547 (2000); 1,486 (2010); Density: 869.1 persons per square mile (2010); Race: 96.1% White, 0.2% Black, 0.2% Asian, 0.8% American Indian/Alaska Native, 0.0% Native Hawaiian/Other Pacific Islander, 2.7% Other, 4.8% Hispanic of any race (2010); Average household size: 2.45 (2010); Median age: 37.3 (2010); Males per 100 females: 91.5 (2010); Marriage status: 24.0% never married, 53.4% now married, 9.0% widowed, 13.7% divorced (2006-2010 5-year est.); Foreign born: 0.5% (2006-2010 5-year est.); Ancestry (includes multiple ancestries): 34.3% German, 24.9% English, 18.1% Irish, 15.9% Polish, 14.8% Italian (2006-2010 5-year est.).

**Economy:** Single-family building permits issued: 0 (2011); Multi-family building permits issued: 0 (2011); Employment by occupation: 5.1% management, 2.2% professional, 11.6% services, 15.1% sales, 2.6% farming, 12.3% construction, 5.8% production (2006-2010 5-year est.).

**Income:** Per capita income: $22,313 (2006-2010 5-year est.); Median household income: $34,089 (2006-2010 5-year est.); Average household income: $53,433 (2006-2010 5-year est.); Percent of households with income of $100,000 or more: 6.9% (2006-2010 5-year est.); Poverty rate: 24.0% (2006-2010 5-year est.).

**Taxes:** Total city taxes per capita: $218 (2009); City property taxes per capita: $207 (2009).

**Education:** Percent of population age 25 and over with: High school diploma (including GED) or higher: 83.8% (2006-2010 5-year est.); Bachelor's degree or higher: 15.7% (2006-2010 5-year est.); Master's degree or higher: 8.3% (2006-2010 5-year est.).

###### School District(s)
Brocton Central School District (PK-12)

   2009-10 Enrollment: 624 . . . . . . . . . . . . . . . . . . . . . . (716) 792-2173

**Housing:** Homeownership rate: 63.7% (2010); Median home value: $70,500 (2006-2010 5-year est.); Median contract rent: $388 per month (2006-2010 5-year est.); Median year structure built: before 1940 (2006-2010 5-year est.).

**Transportation:** Commute to work: 95.9% car, 0.0% public transportation, 1.9% walk, 1.0% work from home (2006-2010 5-year est.); Travel time to work: 29.1% less than 15 minutes, 60.2% 15 to 30 minutes, 2.9% 30 to 45 minutes, 3.5% 45 to 60 minutes, 4.3% 60 minutes or more (2006-2010 5-year est.)

**BUSTI** (town). Covers a land area of 47.824 square miles and a water area of 0.014 square miles. Located at 42.05° N. Lat; 79.32° W. Long. Elevation is 1,365 feet.

**Population:** 8,050 (1990); 7,760 (2000); 7,351 (2010); Density: 153.7 persons per square mile (2010); Race: 96.8% White, 0.6% Black, 1.1% Asian, 0.3% American Indian/Alaska Native, 0.0% Native Hawaiian/Other Pacific Islander, 1.2% Other, 1.0% Hispanic of any race (2010); Average household size: 2.29 (2010); Median age: 47.3 (2010); Males per 100 females: 98.4 (2010); Marriage status: 22.4% never married, 60.3% now married, 7.4% widowed, 10.0% divorced (2006-2010 5-year est.); Foreign born: 2.1% (2006-2010 5-year est.); Ancestry (includes multiple ancestries): 30.5% Swedish, 24.0% German, 21.8% English, 16.5% Italian, 15.4% Irish (2006-2010 5-year est.).

**Economy:** Single-family building permits issued: 4 (2011); Multi-family building permits issued: 0 (2011); Employment by occupation: 13.4% management, 3.0% professional, 10.6% services, 13.9% sales, 4.4% farming, 8.3% construction, 7.9% production (2006-2010 5-year est.).

**Income:** Per capita income: $29,141 (2006-2010 5-year est.); Median household income: $47,897 (2006-2010 5-year est.); Average household income: $66,892 (2006-2010 5-year est.); Percent of households with income of $100,000 or more: 18.2% (2006-2010 5-year est.); Poverty rate: 8.2% (2006-2010 5-year est.).

**Education:** Percent of population age 25 and over with: High school diploma (including GED) or higher: 90.2% (2006-2010 5-year est.); Bachelor's degree or higher: 25.7% (2006-2010 5-year est.); Master's degree or higher: 11.3% (2006-2010 5-year est.).

**Housing:** Homeownership rate: 76.0% (2010); Median home value: $91,600 (2006-2010 5-year est.); Median contract rent: $500 per month (2006-2010 5-year est.); Median year structure built: 1956 (2006-2010 5-year est.).

**Transportation:** Commute to work: 93.2% car, 0.0% public transportation, 1.6% walk, 4.4% work from home (2006-2010 5-year est.); Travel time to

work: 46.6% less than 15 minutes, 40.0% 15 to 30 minutes, 5.1% 30 to 45 minutes, 5.5% 45 to 60 minutes, 2.7% 60 minutes or more (2006-2010 5-year est.)

**Additional Information Contacts**

Town of Busti . . . . . . . . . . . . . . . . . . . . . . . . . . . . . . . . . (716) 763-8561
  http://www.townofbusti.com

**BUSTI** (CDP). Covers a land area of 2.263 square miles and a water area of 0 square miles. Located at 42.04° N. Lat; 79.27° W. Long. Elevation is 1,365 feet.

**Population:** n/a (1990); n/a (2000); 391 (2010); Density: 172.7 persons per square mile (2010); Race: 95.4% White, 1.0% Black, 0.8% Asian, 1.3% American Indian/Alaska Native, 0.0% Native Hawaiian/Other Pacific Islander, 1.5% Other, 0.8% Hispanic of any race (2010); Average household size: 2.73 (2010); Median age: 38.8 (2010); Males per 100 females: 100.5 (2010); Marriage status: 36.6% never married, 51.4% now married, 9.8% widowed, 2.2% divorced (2006-2010 5-year est.); Foreign born: 0.0% (2006-2010 5-year est.); Ancestry (includes multiple ancestries): 29.8% Swedish, 18.9% English, 17.7% Italian, 16.2% Irish, 5.5% Norwegian (2006-2010 5-year est.).

**Economy:** Employment by occupation: 0.0% management, 0.0% professional, 11.7% services, 12.1% sales, 0.0% farming, 15.0% construction, 10.7% production (2006-2010 5-year est.).

**Income:** Per capita income: $18,448 (2006-2010 5-year est.); Median household income: $31,250 (2006-2010 5-year est.); Average household income: $54,459 (2006-2010 5-year est.); Percent of households with income of $100,000 or more: 19.2% (2006-2010 5-year est.); Poverty rate: 18.9% (2006-2010 5-year est.).

**Education:** Percent of population age 25 and over with: High school diploma (including GED) or higher: 96.0% (2006-2010 5-year est.); Bachelor's degree or higher: 16.5% (2006-2010 5-year est.); Master's degree or higher: 3.3% (2006-2010 5-year est.).

**Housing:** Homeownership rate: 74.1% (2010); Median home value: $111,800 (2006-2010 5-year est.); Median contract rent: $381 per month (2006-2010 5-year est.); Median year structure built: 1948 (2006-2010 5-year est.).

**Transportation:** Commute to work: 93.7% car, 0.0% public transportation, 6.3% walk, 0.0% work from home (2006-2010 5-year est.); Travel time to work: 40.3% less than 15 minutes, 40.8% 15 to 30 minutes, 6.8% 30 to 45 minutes, 12.1% 45 to 60 minutes, 0.0% 60 minutes or more (2006-2010 5-year est.)

**CARROLL** (town). Covers a land area of 33.320 square miles and a water area of 0.022 square miles. Located at 42.03° N. Lat; 79.09° W. Long.

**Population:** 3,504 (1990); 3,635 (2000); 3,524 (2010); Density: 105.8 persons per square mile (2010); Race: 97.3% White, 0.4% Black, 0.1% Asian, 0.6% American Indian/Alaska Native, 0.0% Native Hawaiian/Other Pacific Islander, 1.6% Other, 1.3% Hispanic of any race (2010); Average household size: 2.41 (2010); Median age: 45.3 (2010); Males per 100 females: 95.5 (2010); Marriage status: 26.1% never married, 56.0% now married, 7.9% widowed, 10.0% divorced (2006-2010 5-year est.); Foreign born: 0.4% (2006-2010 5-year est.); Ancestry (includes multiple ancestries): 26.0% German, 25.7% Swedish, 19.1% English, 13.8% Irish, 11.6% Italian (2006-2010 5-year est.).

**Economy:** Single-family building permits issued: 1 (2011); Multi-family building permits issued: 0 (2011); Employment by occupation: 6.1% management, 0.6% professional, 15.2% services, 11.2% sales, 6.5% farming, 6.2% construction, 3.0% production (2006-2010 5-year est.).

**Income:** Per capita income: $21,715 (2006-2010 5-year est.); Median household income: $48,810 (2006-2010 5-year est.); Average household income: $56,307 (2006-2010 5-year est.); Percent of households with income of $100,000 or more: 9.7% (2006-2010 5-year est.); Poverty rate: 3.0% (2006-2010 5-year est.).

**Education:** Percent of population age 25 and over with: High school diploma (including GED) or higher: 90.4% (2006-2010 5-year est.); Bachelor's degree or higher: 23.8% (2006-2010 5-year est.); Master's degree or higher: 9.8% (2006-2010 5-year est.).

**Housing:** Homeownership rate: 77.4% (2010); Median home value: $77,800 (2006-2010 5-year est.); Median contract rent: $404 per month (2006-2010 5-year est.); Median year structure built: 1957 (2006-2010 5-year est.).

**Safety:** Violent crime rate: 5.9 per 10,000 population; Property crime rate: 23.5 per 10,000 population (2010).

**Transportation:** Commute to work: 93.8% car, 0.0% public transportation, 4.8% walk, 0.4% work from home (2006-2010 5-year est.); Travel time to work: 36.6% less than 15 minutes, 46.0% 15 to 30 minutes, 11.8% 30 to 45 minutes, 2.3% 45 to 60 minutes, 3.3% 60 minutes or more (2006-2010 5-year est.)

## CASSADAGA (village). Covers a land area of 0.838 square miles and a water area of 0.217 square miles. Located at 42.34° N. Lat; 79.31° W. Long. Elevation is 1,339 feet.

**Population:** 768 (1990); 676 (2000); 634 (2010); Density: 756.0 persons per square mile (2010); Race: 98.3% White, 0.2% Black, 0.3% Asian, 0.2% American Indian/Alaska Native, 0.0% Native Hawaiian/Other Pacific Islander, 1.0% Other, 0.8% Hispanic of any race (2010); Average household size: 2.37 (2010); Median age: 46.0 (2010); Males per 100 females: 100.6 (2010); Marriage status: 15.8% never married, 65.9% now married, 11.9% widowed, 6.5% divorced (2006-2010 5-year est.); Foreign born: 0.7% (2006-2010 5-year est.); Ancestry (includes multiple ancestries): 36.0% German, 27.8% English, 16.6% Irish, 14.1% Swedish, 8.5% Italian (2006-2010 5-year est.).
**Economy:** Single-family building permits issued: 0 (2011); Multi-family building permits issued: 0 (2011); Employment by occupation: 6.7% management, 0.0% professional, 4.0% services, 18.7% sales, 3.0% farming, 6.0% construction, 6.7% production (2006-2010 5-year est.).
**Income:** Per capita income: $25,176 (2006-2010 5-year est.); Median household income: $48,750 (2006-2010 5-year est.); Average household income: $59,380 (2006-2010 5-year est.); Percent of households with income of $100,000 or more: 14.2% (2006-2010 5-year est.); Poverty rate: 6.9% (2006-2010 5-year est.).
**Education:** Percent of population age 25 and over with: High school diploma (including GED) or higher: 89.2% (2006-2010 5-year est.); Bachelor's degree or higher: 27.5% (2006-2010 5-year est.); Master's degree or higher: 11.0% (2006-2010 5-year est.).

### School District(s)
Cassadaga Valley Central School District (PK-12)
    2009-10 Enrollment: 1,201 . . . . . . . . . . . . . . . . . . . (716) 962-5155
**Housing:** Homeownership rate: 79.7% (2010); Median home value: $76,900 (2006-2010 5-year est.); Median contract rent: $409 per month (2006-2010 5-year est.); Median year structure built: before 1940 (2006-2010 5-year est.).
**Transportation:** Commute to work: 93.6% car, 1.0% public transportation, 4.0% walk, 1.3% work from home (2006-2010 5-year est.); Travel time to work: 25.9% less than 15 minutes, 44.4% 15 to 30 minutes, 16.4% 30 to 45 minutes, 4.8% 45 to 60 minutes, 8.5% 60 minutes or more (2006-2010 5-year est.)

## CATTARAUGUS RESERVATION (Reservation). Covers a land area of 2.446 square miles and a water area of 0.328 square miles. Located at 42.54° N. Lat; 79.08° W. Long.

**Population:** 30 (1990); 23 (2000); 38 (2010); Density: 15.5 persons per square mile (2010); Race: 23.7% White, 0.0% Black, 0.0% Asian, 68.4% American Indian/Alaska Native, 0.0% Native Hawaiian/Other Pacific Islander, 7.9% Other, 13.2% Hispanic of any race (2010); Average household size: 2.53 (2010); Median age: 32.0 (2010); Males per 100 females: 123.5 (2010); Marriage status: 18.8% never married, 81.3% now married, 0.0% widowed, 0.0% divorced (2006-2010 5-year est.); Foreign born: 50.0% (2006-2010 5-year est.); Ancestry (includes multiple ancestries): 18.8% Dutch (2006-2010 5-year est.).
**Economy:** Employment by occupation: 0.0% management, 0.0% professional, 0.0% services, 100.0% sales, 0.0% farming, 0.0% construction, 0.0% production (2006-2010 5-year est.).
**Income:** Per capita income: $30,681 (2006-2010 5-year est.); Median household income: $44,500 (2006-2010 5-year est.); Average household income: $0 (2006-2010 5-year est.); Percent of households with income of $100,000 or more: 0.0% (2006-2010 5-year est.); Poverty rate: 0.0% (2006-2010 5-year est.).
**Education:** Percent of population age 25 and over with: High school diploma (including GED) or higher: 50.0% (2006-2010 5-year est.); Bachelor's degree or higher: 0.0% (2006-2010 5-year est.); Master's degree or higher: 0.0% (2006-2010 5-year est.).
**Housing:** Homeownership rate: 80.0% (2010); Median home value: n/a (2006-2010 5-year est.); Median contract rent: n/a per month (2006-2010 5-year est.); Median year structure built: 1994 (2006-2010 5-year est.).
**Transportation:** Commute to work: 100.0% car, 0.0% public transportation, 0.0% walk, 0.0% work from home (2006-2010 5-year est.); Travel time to work: 0.0% less than 15 minutes, 0.0% 15 to 30 minutes,

0.0% 30 to 45 minutes, 100.0% 45 to 60 minutes, 0.0% 60 minutes or more (2006-2010 5-year est.)

## CELORON (village). Covers a land area of 0.747 square miles and a water area of <.001 square miles. Located at 42.10° N. Lat; 79.27° W. Long. Elevation is 1,319 feet.

**History:** Incorporated 1896.
**Population:** 1,232 (1990); 1,295 (2000); 1,112 (2010); Density: 1,487.8 persons per square mile (2010); Race: 95.9% White, 0.8% Black, 0.5% Asian, 0.2% American Indian/Alaska Native, 0.0% Native Hawaiian/Other Pacific Islander, 2.6% Other, 2.9% Hispanic of any race (2010); Average household size: 2.29 (2010); Median age: 42.4 (2010); Males per 100 females: 98.6 (2010); Marriage status: 28.9% never married, 47.1% now married, 12.8% widowed, 11.2% divorced (2006-2010 5-year est.); Foreign born: 1.1% (2006-2010 5-year est.); Ancestry (includes multiple ancestries): 30.5% Swedish, 18.5% Italian, 18.5% German, 17.7% English, 14.1% Irish (2006-2010 5-year est.).
**Economy:** Single-family building permits issued: 0 (2011); Multi-family building permits issued: 0 (2011); Employment by occupation: 7.9% management, 0.9% professional, 12.9% services, 19.6% sales, 2.3% farming, 15.0% construction, 11.1% production (2006-2010 5-year est.).
**Income:** Per capita income: $17,561 (2006-2010 5-year est.); Median household income: $35,625 (2006-2010 5-year est.); Average household income: $44,952 (2006-2010 5-year est.); Percent of households with income of $100,000 or more: 6.1% (2006-2010 5-year est.); Poverty rate: 31.1% (2006-2010 5-year est.).
**Education:** Percent of population age 25 and over with: High school diploma (including GED) or higher: 85.1% (2006-2010 5-year est.); Bachelor's degree or higher: 11.7% (2006-2010 5-year est.); Master's degree or higher: 5.6% (2006-2010 5-year est.).
**Housing:** Homeownership rate: 68.1% (2010); Median home value: $54,700 (2006-2010 5-year est.); Median contract rent: $531 per month (2006-2010 5-year est.); Median year structure built: before 1940 (2006-2010 5-year est.).
**Transportation:** Commute to work: 96.2% car, 0.0% public transportation, 2.1% walk, 0.0% work from home (2006-2010 5-year est.); Travel time to work: 45.5% less than 15 minutes, 42.6% 15 to 30 minutes, 7.9% 30 to 45 minutes, 1.4% 45 to 60 minutes, 2.6% 60 minutes or more (2006-2010 5-year est.)

## CHARLOTTE (town). Covers a land area of 36.431 square miles and a water area of 0 square miles. Located at 42.30° N. Lat; 79.23° W. Long. Elevation is 1,532 feet.

**Population:** 1,528 (1990); 1,713 (2000); 1,729 (2010); Density: 47.5 persons per square mile (2010); Race: 97.9% White, 0.2% Black, 0.3% Asian, 0.3% American Indian/Alaska Native, 0.0% Native Hawaiian/Other Pacific Islander, 1.3% Other, 2.0% Hispanic of any race (2010); Average household size: 2.58 (2010); Median age: 40.7 (2010); Males per 100 females: 105.3 (2010); Marriage status: 26.9% never married, 57.5% now married, 5.8% widowed, 9.7% divorced (2006-2010 5-year est.); Foreign born: 0.0% (2006-2010 5-year est.); Ancestry (includes multiple ancestries): 24.8% German, 23.9% Irish, 22.7% English, 14.0% Swedish, 8.8% Italian (2006-2010 5-year est.).
**Economy:** Single-family building permits issued: 4 (2011); Multi-family building permits issued: 0 (2011); Employment by occupation: 8.5% management, 2.9% professional, 19.1% services, 9.5% sales, 0.7% farming, 13.2% construction, 7.2% production (2006-2010 5-year est.).
**Income:** Per capita income: $19,046 (2006-2010 5-year est.); Median household income: $46,289 (2006-2010 5-year est.); Average household income: $50,871 (2006-2010 5-year est.); Percent of households with income of $100,000 or more: 7.2% (2006-2010 5-year est.); Poverty rate: 12.2% (2006-2010 5-year est.).
**Education:** Percent of population age 25 and over with: High school diploma (including GED) or higher: 88.2% (2006-2010 5-year est.); Bachelor's degree or higher: 15.5% (2006-2010 5-year est.); Master's degree or higher: 4.9% (2006-2010 5-year est.).
**Housing:** Homeownership rate: 80.6% (2010); Median home value: $67,100 (2006-2010 5-year est.); Median contract rent: $469 per month (2006-2010 5-year est.); Median year structure built: 1980 (2006-2010 5-year est.).
**Transportation:** Commute to work: 91.7% car, 0.0% public transportation, 0.9% walk, 2.9% work from home (2006-2010 5-year est.); Travel time to work: 23.1% less than 15 minutes, 43.9% 15 to 30 minutes, 24.0% 30 to 45 minutes, 4.0% 45 to 60 minutes, 5.0% 60 minutes or more (2006-2010 5-year est.)

**CHAUTAUQUA** (town). Covers a land area of 67.098 square miles and a water area of 0.093 square miles. Located at 42.24° N. Lat; 79.50° W. Long. Elevation is 1,362 feet.

**History:** Founded as meeting place for Methodist ministers and laity. Chautauqua Institute, founded in 1864, is located here. Famous people connected with the school include U.S. Presidents Garfield, Grant, McKinley, Harding, and both Roosevelts; explorers Admiral Richard Byrd and Amelia Earhart; inventors Henry Ford and Thomas Edison; Senator Robert Kennedy, William Jennings Bryan, Jane Addams, Ida Tarbell and N.Y. governor Al Smith. Village formerly known as Fair Point.

**Population:** 4,554 (1990); 4,666 (2000); 4,464 (2010); Density: 66.5 persons per square mile (2010); Race: 95.9% White, 2.2% Black, 0.2% Asian, 0.2% American Indian/Alaska Native, 0.1% Native Hawaiian/Other Pacific Islander, 1.4% Other, 2.3% Hispanic of any race (2010); Average household size: 2.32 (2010); Median age: 44.7 (2010); Males per 100 females: 108.3 (2010); Marriage status: 22.0% never married, 59.5% now married, 5.1% widowed, 13.3% divorced (2006-2010 5-year est.); Foreign born: 2.6% (2006-2010 5-year est.); Ancestry (includes multiple ancestries): 23.3% English, 23.3% German, 16.3% Irish, 12.2% Swedish, 9.4% Italian (2006-2010 5-year est.).

**Economy:** Single-family building permits issued: 8 (2011); Multi-family building permits issued: 0 (2011); Employment by occupation: 14.8% management, 3.9% professional, 6.7% services, 13.9% sales, 3.7% farming, 15.9% construction, 5.6% production (2006-2010 5-year est.).

**Income:** Per capita income: $22,730 (2006-2010 5-year est.); Median household income: $49,216 (2006-2010 5-year est.); Average household income: $57,305 (2006-2010 5-year est.); Percent of households with income of $100,000 or more: 13.9% (2006-2010 5-year est.); Poverty rate: 10.0% (2006-2010 5-year est.).

**Education:** Percent of population age 25 and over with: High school diploma (including GED) or higher: 85.1% (2006-2010 5-year est.); Bachelor's degree or higher: 30.1% (2006-2010 5-year est.); Master's degree or higher: 12.2% (2006-2010 5-year est.).

**Housing:** Homeownership rate: 76.3% (2010); Median home value: $111,300 (2006-2010 5-year est.); Median contract rent: $415 per month (2006-2010 5-year est.); Median year structure built: 1944 (2006-2010 5-year est.).

**Transportation:** Commute to work: 89.5% car, 0.9% public transportation, 4.8% walk, 3.5% work from home (2006-2010 5-year est.); Travel time to work: 48.4% less than 15 minutes, 28.3% 15 to 30 minutes, 18.5% 30 to 45 minutes, 2.5% 45 to 60 minutes, 2.2% 60 minutes or more (2006-2010 5-year est.)

**CHAUTAUQUA** (CDP). Covers a land area of 0.427 square miles and a water area of 0 square miles. Located at 42.21° N. Lat; 79.46° W. Long. Elevation is 1,362 feet.

**Population:** n/a (1990); n/a (2000); 191 (2010); Density: 447.3 persons per square mile (2010); Race: 99.5% White, 0.0% Black, 0.5% Asian, 0.0% American Indian/Alaska Native, 0.0% Native Hawaiian/Other Pacific Islander, 0.0% Other, 1.0% Hispanic of any race (2010); Average household size: 1.71 (2010); Median age: 67.6 (2010); Males per 100 females: 83.7 (2010); Marriage status: 0.0% never married, 94.0% now married, 6.0% widowed, 0.0% divorced (2006-2010 5-year est.); Foreign born: 0.0% (2006-2010 5-year est.); Ancestry (includes multiple ancestries): 45.1% Swedish, 35.6% Italian, 22.0% Irish, 16.3% German, 11.4% English (2006-2010 5-year est.).

**Economy:** Employment by occupation: 0.0% management, 0.0% professional, 0.0% services, 0.0% sales, 18.6% farming, 0.0% construction, 0.0% production (2006-2010 5-year est.).

**Income:** Per capita income: $23,553 (2006-2010 5-year est.); Median household income: $57,500 (2006-2010 5-year est.); Average household income: $55,312 (2006-2010 5-year est.); Percent of households with income of $100,000 or more: 13.2% (2006-2010 5-year est.); Poverty rate: 5.7% (2006-2010 5-year est.).

**Education:** Percent of population age 25 and over with: High school diploma (including GED) or higher: 100.0% (2006-2010 5-year est.); Bachelor's degree or higher: 80.9% (2006-2010 5-year est.); Master's degree or higher: 51.3% (2006-2010 5-year est.).

**Housing:** Homeownership rate: 86.6% (2010); Median home value: $165,800 (2006-2010 5-year est.); Median contract rent: n/a per month (2006-2010 5-year est.); Median year structure built: before 1940 (2006-2010 5-year est.).

**Transportation:** Commute to work: 81.4% car, 18.6% public transportation, 0.0% walk, 0.0% work from home (2006-2010 5-year est.); Travel time to work: 100.0% less than 15 minutes, 0.0% 15 to 30 minutes, 0.0% 30 to 45 minutes, 0.0% 45 to 60 minutes, 0.0% 60 minutes or more (2006-2010 5-year est.)

**CHERRY CREEK** (village). Covers a land area of 1.362 square miles and a water area of 0 square miles. Located at 42.29° N. Lat; 79.10° W. Long. Elevation is 1,302 feet.

**Population:** 523 (1990); 551 (2000); 461 (2010); Density: 338.4 persons per square mile (2010); Race: 98.3% White, 0.2% Black, 0.4% Asian, 0.0% American Indian/Alaska Native, 0.0% Native Hawaiian/Other Pacific Islander, 1.1% Other, 2.6% Hispanic of any race (2010); Average household size: 2.62 (2010); Median age: 39.3 (2010); Males per 100 females: 97.9 (2010); Marriage status: 37.2% never married, 44.1% now married, 7.0% widowed, 11.8% divorced (2006-2010 5-year est.); Foreign born: 1.1% (2006-2010 5-year est.); Ancestry (includes multiple ancestries): 41.9% German, 22.2% English, 16.7% Irish, 15.9% Polish, 9.1% Italian (2006-2010 5-year est.).

**Economy:** Single-family building permits issued: 0 (2011); Multi-family building permits issued: 0 (2011); Employment by occupation: 3.7% management, 0.0% professional, 8.3% services, 18.9% sales, 1.4% farming, 6.5% construction, 6.5% production (2006-2010 5-year est.).

**Income:** Per capita income: $15,542 (2006-2010 5-year est.); Median household income: $41,053 (2006-2010 5-year est.); Average household income: $46,353 (2006-2010 5-year est.); Percent of households with income of $100,000 or more: 7.6% (2006-2010 5-year est.); Poverty rate: 25.2% (2006-2010 5-year est.).

**Education:** Percent of population age 25 and over with: High school diploma (including GED) or higher: 77.7% (2006-2010 5-year est.); Bachelor's degree or higher: 11.6% (2006-2010 5-year est.); Master's degree or higher: 5.5% (2006-2010 5-year est.).

**Housing:** Homeownership rate: 75.5% (2010); Median home value: $55,000 (2006-2010 5-year est.); Median contract rent: $327 per month (2006-2010 5-year est.); Median year structure built: before 1940 (2006-2010 5-year est.).

**Transportation:** Commute to work: 96.2% car, 0.0% public transportation, 1.0% walk, 1.9% work from home (2006-2010 5-year est.); Travel time to work: 26.5% less than 15 minutes, 16.7% 15 to 30 minutes, 36.3% 30 to 45 minutes, 13.7% 45 to 60 minutes, 6.9% 60 minutes or more (2006-2010 5-year est.)

**CHERRY CREEK** (town). Covers a land area of 36.631 square miles and a water area of 0.013 square miles. Located at 42.30° N. Lat; 79.12° W. Long. Elevation is 1,302 feet.

**Population:** 1,064 (1990); 1,152 (2000); 1,118 (2010); Density: 30.5 persons per square mile (2010); Race: 97.4% White, 0.5% Black, 0.2% Asian, 0.1% American Indian/Alaska Native, 0.0% Native Hawaiian/Other Pacific Islander, 1.8% Other, 2.1% Hispanic of any race (2010); Average household size: 2.64 (2010); Median age: 39.8 (2010); Males per 100 females: 101.8 (2010); Marriage status: 28.0% never married, 53.8% now married, 7.7% widowed, 10.5% divorced (2006-2010 5-year est.); Foreign born: 1.4% (2006-2010 5-year est.); Ancestry (includes multiple ancestries): 32.8% German, 15.2% English, 13.7% Irish, 12.7% Polish, 10.8% Italian (2006-2010 5-year est.).

**Economy:** Single-family building permits issued: 0 (2011); Multi-family building permits issued: 0 (2011); Employment by occupation: 7.4% management, 0.6% professional, 11.1% services, 13.6% sales, 2.3% farming, 14.0% construction, 4.9% production (2006-2010 5-year est.).

**Income:** Per capita income: $17,862 (2006-2010 5-year est.); Median household income: $40,511 (2006-2010 5-year est.); Average household income: $51,861 (2006-2010 5-year est.); Percent of households with income of $100,000 or more: 11.8% (2006-2010 5-year est.); Poverty rate: 21.5% (2006-2010 5-year est.).

**Education:** Percent of population age 25 and over with: High school diploma (including GED) or higher: 77.2% (2006-2010 5-year est.); Bachelor's degree or higher: 13.5% (2006-2010 5-year est.); Master's degree or higher: 5.5% (2006-2010 5-year est.).

**Housing:** Homeownership rate: 82.1% (2010); Median home value: $77,000 (2006-2010 5-year est.); Median contract rent: $339 per month (2006-2010 5-year est.); Median year structure built: 1954 (2006-2010 5-year est.).

**Transportation:** Commute to work: 89.2% car, 0.0% public transportation, 6.4% walk, 2.0% work from home (2006-2010 5-year est.); Travel time to work: 26.8% less than 15 minutes, 25.4% 15 to 30 minutes, 31.1% 30 to 45 minutes, 11.7% 45 to 60 minutes, 5.1% 60 minutes or more (2006-2010 5-year est.)

**CLYMER** (town). Covers a land area of 36.069 square miles and a water area of 0.093 square miles. Located at 42.04° N. Lat; 79.58° W. Long. Elevation is 1,457 feet.
**Population:** 1,445 (1990); 1,501 (2000); 1,698 (2010); Density: 47.1 persons per square mile (2010); Race: 98.4% White, 0.1% Black, 0.1% Asian, 0.1% American Indian/Alaska Native, 0.0% Native Hawaiian/Other Pacific Islander, 1.3% Other, 0.6% Hispanic of any race (2010); Average household size: 3.06 (2010); Median age: 32.5 (2010); Males per 100 females: 100.0 (2010); Marriage status: 19.9% never married, 68.4% now married, 6.6% widowed, 5.1% divorced (2006-2010 5-year est.); Foreign born: 0.0% (2006-2010 5-year est.); Ancestry (includes multiple ancestries): 27.2% German, 24.8% Dutch, 10.0% Irish, 10.0% English, 6.7% American (2006-2010 5-year est.).
**Economy:** Single-family building permits issued: 4 (2011); Multi-family building permits issued: 0 (2011); Employment by occupation: 13.5% management, 2.3% professional, 7.9% services, 8.8% sales, 2.4% farming, 13.1% construction, 8.7% production (2006-2010 5-year est.).
**Income:** Per capita income: $17,447 (2006-2010 5-year est.); Median household income: $43,672 (2006-2010 5-year est.); Average household income: $53,914 (2006-2010 5-year est.); Percent of households with income of $100,000 or more: 8.8% (2006-2010 5-year est.); Poverty rate: 25.2% (2006-2010 5-year est.).
**Education:** Percent of population age 25 and over with: High school diploma (including GED) or higher: 74.9% (2006-2010 5-year est.); Bachelor's degree or higher: 17.9% (2006-2010 5-year est.); Master's degree or higher: 6.1% (2006-2010 5-year est.).
### School District(s)
Clymer Central School District (PK-12)
   2009-10 Enrollment: 452 . . . . . . . . . . . . . . . . . . . . . . . . . (716) 355-4444
**Housing:** Homeownership rate: 82.2% (2010); Median home value: $91,700 (2006-2010 5-year est.); Median contract rent: $396 per month (2006-2010 5-year est.); Median year structure built: 1948 (2006-2010 5-year est.).
**Transportation:** Commute to work: 76.7% car, 0.6% public transportation, 8.3% walk, 12.2% work from home (2006-2010 5-year est.); Travel time to work: 39.2% less than 15 minutes, 26.9% 15 to 30 minutes, 25.5% 30 to 45 minutes, 5.2% 45 to 60 minutes, 3.2% 60 minutes or more (2006-2010 5-year est.)

**DEWITTVILLE** (unincorporated postal area)
Zip Code: 14728
   Covers a land area of 26.795 square miles and a water area of 0.046 square miles. Located at 42.26° N. Lat; 79.42° W. Long. Elevation is 1,325 feet. Population: 1,031 (2010); Density: 38.5 persons per square mile (2010); Race: 97.7% White, 0.1% Black, 0.1% Asian, 0.1% American Indian/Alaska Native, 0.0% Native Hawaiian/Other Pacific Islander, 2.0% Other, 2.5% Hispanic of any race (2010); Average household size: 2.47 (2010); Median age: 46.4 (2010); Males per 100 females: 105.8 (2010); Homeownership rate: 87.8% (2010)

**DUNKIRK** (city). Covers a land area of 4.501 square miles and a water area of 0.050 square miles. Located at 42.48° N. Lat; 79.33° W. Long. Elevation is 617 feet.
**History:** In 1946, it developed a program to help Dunkerque, France (for which it was named), recover from World War II. Other U.S. cities followed, and established a program, called the One World Plan, to aid war-damaged European cities. Founded c.1800, Incorporated as city 1880.
**Population:** 13,989 (1990); 13,131 (2000); 12,563 (2010); Density: 2,790.6 persons per square mile (2010); Race: 77.5% White, 6.1% Black, 0.4% Asian, 1.0% American Indian/Alaska Native, 0.0% Native Hawaiian/Other Pacific Islander, 15.0% Other, 26.4% Hispanic of any race (2010); Average household size: 2.30 (2010); Median age: 38.7 (2010); Males per 100 females: 96.2 (2010); Marriage status: 34.1% never married, 45.3% now married, 8.3% widowed, 12.3% divorced (2006-2010 5-year est.); Foreign born: 3.3% (2006-2010 5-year est.); Ancestry (includes multiple ancestries): 28.6% Polish, 19.0% German, 15.9% Italian, 10.1% Irish, 6.9% English (2006-2010 5-year est.).
**Economy:** Single-family building permits issued: 1 (2011); Multi-family building permits issued: 0 (2011); Employment by occupation: 7.2% management, 1.3% professional, 10.9% services, 12.4% sales, 6.2% farming, 7.9% construction, 9.5% production (2006-2010 5-year est.).
**Income:** Per capita income: $19,373 (2006-2010 5-year est.); Median household income: $33,849 (2006-2010 5-year est.); Average household income: $42,966 (2006-2010 5-year est.); Percent of households with

income of $100,000 or more: 6.2% (2006-2010 5-year est.); Poverty rate: 25.8% (2006-2010 5-year est.).
**Education:** Percent of population age 25 and over with: High school diploma (including GED) or higher: 80.2% (2006-2010 5-year est.); Bachelor's degree or higher: 17.5% (2006-2010 5-year est.); Master's degree or higher: 8.0% (2006-2010 5-year est.).
### School District(s)
Dunkirk City School District (KG-12)
   2009-10 Enrollment: 1,999 . . . . . . . . . . . . . . . . . . . . . (716) 366-9300
**Housing:** Homeownership rate: 58.4% (2010); Median home value: $57,400 (2006-2010 5-year est.); Median contract rent: $432 per month (2006-2010 5-year est.); Median year structure built: before 1940 (2006-2010 5-year est.).
**Hospitals:** Brooks Memorial Hospital (99 beds)
**Safety:** Violent crime rate: 38.1 per 10,000 population; Property crime rate: 299.1 per 10,000 population (2010).
**Newspapers:** Observer (Local news; Circulation 15,000)
**Transportation:** Commute to work: 86.3% car, 0.7% public transportation, 7.0% walk, 1.4% work from home (2006-2010 5-year est.); Travel time to work: 67.6% less than 15 minutes, 19.5% 15 to 30 minutes, 7.0% 30 to 45 minutes, 4.4% 45 to 60 minutes, 1.5% 60 minutes or more (2006-2010 5-year est.); Amtrak: bus service available.
**Additional Information Contacts**
Chautauqua County Chamber of Commerce. . . . . . . . . . . (716) 366-6200
   http://www.chautauquachamber.org

**DUNKIRK** (town). Covers a land area of 6.227 square miles and a water area of 0.053 square miles. Located at 42.46° N. Lat; 79.32° W. Long. Elevation is 617 feet.
**Population:** 1,482 (1990); 1,387 (2000); 1,318 (2010); Density: 211.6 persons per square mile (2010); Race: 91.3% White, 3.0% Black, 0.5% Asian, 0.6% American Indian/Alaska Native, 0.0% Native Hawaiian/Other Pacific Islander, 4.6% Other, 9.0% Hispanic of any race (2010); Average household size: 2.11 (2010); Median age: 55.2 (2010); Males per 100 females: 83.8 (2010); Marriage status: 19.0% never married, 49.5% now married, 23.5% widowed, 8.1% divorced (2006-2010 5-year est.); Foreign born: 3.0% (2006-2010 5-year est.); Ancestry (includes multiple ancestries): 27.4% Polish, 24.2% German, 15.0% Italian, 7.6% English, 7.1% Irish (2006-2010 5-year est.).
**Economy:** Single-family building permits issued: 0 (2011); Multi-family building permits issued: 0 (2011); Employment by occupation: 10.0% management, 3.8% professional, 8.8% services, 21.5% sales, 1.9% farming, 8.3% construction, 7.1% production (2006-2010 5-year est.).
**Income:** Per capita income: $22,270 (2006-2010 5-year est.); Median household income: $39,861 (2006-2010 5-year est.); Average household income: $56,640 (2006-2010 5-year est.); Percent of households with income of $100,000 or more: 13.2% (2006-2010 5-year est.); Poverty rate: 16.5% (2006-2010 5-year est.).
**Education:** Percent of population age 25 and over with: High school diploma (including GED) or higher: 80.7% (2006-2010 5-year est.); Bachelor's degree or higher: 20.6% (2006-2010 5-year est.); Master's degree or higher: 8.6% (2006-2010 5-year est.).
### School District(s)
Dunkirk City School District (KG-12)
   2009-10 Enrollment: 1,999 . . . . . . . . . . . . . . . . . . . . . (716) 366-9300
**Housing:** Homeownership rate: 80.5% (2010); Median home value: $90,000 (2006-2010 5-year est.); Median contract rent: $469 per month (2006-2010 5-year est.); Median year structure built: 1957 (2006-2010 5-year est.).
**Hospitals:** Brooks Memorial Hospital (99 beds)
**Newspapers:** Observer (Local news; Circulation 15,000)
**Transportation:** Commute to work: 97.2% car, 0.0% public transportation, 1.1% walk, 1.3% work from home (2006-2010 5-year est.); Travel time to work: 63.4% less than 15 minutes, 28.3% 15 to 30 minutes, 2.9% 30 to 45 minutes, 2.4% 45 to 60 minutes, 3.1% 60 minutes or more (2006-2010 5-year est.); Amtrak: bus service available.

**ELLERY** (town). Covers a land area of 47.453 square miles and a water area of 0.116 square miles. Located at 42.18° N. Lat; 79.35° W. Long.
**Population:** 4,534 (1990); 4,576 (2000); 4,528 (2010); Density: 95.4 persons per square mile (2010); Race: 97.9% White, 0.5% Black, 0.5% Asian, 0.1% American Indian/Alaska Native, 0.0% Native Hawaiian/Other Pacific Islander, 1.0% Other, 0.6% Hispanic of any race (2010); Average household size: 2.32 (2010); Median age: 49.4 (2010); Males per 100 females: 95.9 (2010); Marriage status: 22.8% never married, 47.2% now

married, 17.8% widowed, 12.3% divorced (2006-2010 5-year est.); Foreign born: 0.3% (2006-2010 5-year est.); Ancestry (includes multiple ancestries): 25.9% German, 22.6% English, 20.5% Swedish, 19.3% Irish, 10.3% Italian (2006-2010 5-year est.).

**Economy:** Single-family building permits issued: 8 (2011); Multi-family building permits issued: 0 (2011); Employment by occupation: 13.5% management, 4.9% professional, 10.9% services, 15.7% sales, 3.1% farming, 7.8% construction, 3.1% production (2006-2010 5-year est.).

**Income:** Per capita income: $23,778 (2006-2010 5-year est.); Median household income: $45,412 (2006-2010 5-year est.); Average household income: $62,760 (2006-2010 5-year est.); Percent of households with income of $100,000 or more: 16.0% (2006-2010 5-year est.); Poverty rate: 7.6% (2006-2010 5-year est.).

**Education:** Percent of population age 25 and over with: High school diploma (including GED) or higher: 91.1% (2006-2010 5-year est.); Bachelor's degree or higher: 31.0% (2006-2010 5-year est.); Master's degree or higher: 11.4% (2006-2010 5-year est.).

**Housing:** Homeownership rate: 84.5% (2010); Median home value: $114,500 (2006-2010 5-year est.); Median contract rent: $475 per month (2006-2010 5-year est.); Median year structure built: 1963 (2006-2010 5-year est.).

**Transportation:** Commute to work: 87.8% car, 1.0% public transportation, 1.3% walk, 10.0% work from home (2006-2010 5-year est.); Travel time to work: 30.2% less than 15 minutes, 54.4% 15 to 30 minutes, 9.7% 30 to 45 minutes, 3.4% 45 to 60 minutes, 2.3% 60 minutes or more (2006-2010 5-year est.)

---

**ELLICOTT** (town). Covers a land area of 30.449 square miles and a water area of 0.023 square miles. Located at 42.13° N. Lat; 79.23° W. Long.

**Population:** 9,447 (1990); 9,280 (2000); 8,714 (2010); Density: 286.2 persons per square mile (2010); Race: 97.4% White, 0.7% Black, 0.6% Asian, 0.1% American Indian/Alaska Native, 0.0% Native Hawaiian/Other Pacific Islander, 1.2% Other, 1.7% Hispanic of any race (2010); Average household size: 2.28 (2010); Median age: 46.5 (2010); Males per 100 females: 94.5 (2010); Marriage status: 23.0% never married, 55.3% now married, 9.3% widowed, 12.4% divorced (2006-2010 5-year est.); Foreign born: 1.0% (2006-2010 5-year est.); Ancestry (includes multiple ancestries): 25.5% Swedish, 21.9% German, 19.7% English, 16.4% Irish, 15.1% Italian (2006-2010 5-year est.).

**Economy:** Single-family building permits issued: 6 (2011); Multi-family building permits issued: 0 (2011); Employment by occupation: 8.3% management, 2.6% professional, 9.2% services, 14.7% sales, 4.4% farming, 7.3% construction, 7.7% production (2006-2010 5-year est.).

**Income:** Per capita income: $23,955 (2006-2010 5-year est.); Median household income: $47,618 (2006-2010 5-year est.); Average household income: $55,454 (2006-2010 5-year est.); Percent of households with income of $100,000 or more: 12.7% (2006-2010 5-year est.); Poverty rate: 14.9% (2006-2010 5-year est.).

**Education:** Percent of population age 25 and over with: High school diploma (including GED) or higher: 92.1% (2006-2010 5-year est.); Bachelor's degree or higher: 20.2% (2006-2010 5-year est.); Master's degree or higher: 9.1% (2006-2010 5-year est.).

**Housing:** Homeownership rate: 73.5% (2010); Median home value: $78,400 (2006-2010 5-year est.); Median contract rent: $495 per month (2006-2010 5-year est.); Median year structure built: 1945 (2006-2010 5-year est.).

**Safety:** Violent crime rate: 23.2 per 10,000 population; Property crime rate: 433.9 per 10,000 population (2010).

**Transportation:** Commute to work: 93.6% car, 0.6% public transportation, 3.7% walk, 1.1% work from home (2006-2010 5-year est.); Travel time to work: 59.1% less than 15 minutes, 26.7% 15 to 30 minutes, 7.8% 30 to 45 minutes, 1.2% 45 to 60 minutes, 5.3% 60 minutes or more (2006-2010 5-year est.)

**Additional Information Contacts**

Town of Ellicott. . . . . . . . . . . . . . . . . . . . . . . . . . . . . (716) 665-5317
    http://www.townofellicott.com

---

**ELLINGTON** (town). Covers a land area of 36.545 square miles and a water area of 0.013 square miles. Located at 42.22° N. Lat; 79.12° W. Long. Elevation is 1,371 feet.

**Population:** 1,615 (1990); 1,639 (2000); 1,643 (2010); Density: 45.0 persons per square mile (2010); Race: 98.2% White, 0.0% Black, 0.1% Asian, 0.2% American Indian/Alaska Native, 0.0% Native Hawaiian/Other Pacific Islander, 1.5% Other, 1.0% Hispanic of any race (2010); Average

household size: 2.72 (2010); Median age: 39.8 (2010); Males per 100 females: 105.6 (2010); Marriage status: 27.9% never married, 56.8% now married, 5.1% widowed, 10.2% divorced (2006-2010 5-year est.); Foreign born: 0.9% (2006-2010 5-year est.); Ancestry (includes multiple ancestries): 27.6% German, 16.4% Swedish, 16.4% English, 14.2% Irish, 8.3% Italian (2006-2010 5-year est.).

**Economy:** Single-family building permits issued: 0 (2011); Multi-family building permits issued: 0 (2011); Employment by occupation: 11.4% management, 1.9% professional, 10.8% services, 12.8% sales, 2.9% farming, 12.6% construction, 8.3% production (2006-2010 5-year est.).

**Income:** Per capita income: $18,427 (2006-2010 5-year est.); Median household income: $43,182 (2006-2010 5-year est.); Average household income: $46,621 (2006-2010 5-year est.); Percent of households with income of $100,000 or more: 4.6% (2006-2010 5-year est.); Poverty rate: 21.1% (2006-2010 5-year est.).

**Education:** Percent of population age 25 and over with: High school diploma (including GED) or higher: 81.6% (2006-2010 5-year est.); Bachelor's degree or higher: 15.7% (2006-2010 5-year est.); Master's degree or higher: 7.0% (2006-2010 5-year est.).

**Housing:** Homeownership rate: 87.6% (2010); Median home value: $72,900 (2006-2010 5-year est.); Median contract rent: $368 per month (2006-2010 5-year est.); Median year structure built: 1971 (2006-2010 5-year est.).

**Transportation:** Commute to work: 87.9% car, 0.0% public transportation, 4.0% walk, 6.9% work from home (2006-2010 5-year est.); Travel time to work: 20.9% less than 15 minutes, 44.0% 15 to 30 minutes, 22.0% 30 to 45 minutes, 5.6% 45 to 60 minutes, 7.5% 60 minutes or more (2006-2010 5-year est.)

---

**FALCONER** (village). Covers a land area of 1.092 square miles and a water area of 0 square miles. Located at 42.11° N. Lat; 79.19° W. Long. Elevation is 1,263 feet.

**History:** Settled 1807, incorporated 1891.

**Population:** 2,623 (1990); 2,540 (2000); 2,420 (2010); Density: 2,214.4 persons per square mile (2010); Race: 97.3% White, 0.6% Black, 0.3% Asian, 0.3% American Indian/Alaska Native, 0.0% Native Hawaiian/Other Pacific Islander, 1.5% Other, 2.2% Hispanic of any race (2010); Average household size: 2.24 (2010); Median age: 41.1 (2010); Males per 100 females: 100.2 (2010); Marriage status: 24.4% never married, 51.1% now married, 8.7% widowed, 15.7% divorced (2006-2010 5-year est.); Foreign born: 1.3% (2006-2010 5-year est.); Ancestry (includes multiple ancestries): 21.5% German, 20.7% English, 18.2% Italian, 18.0% Irish, 17.9% Swedish (2006-2010 5-year est.).

**Economy:** Single-family building permits issued: 0 (2011); Multi-family building permits issued: 0 (2011); Employment by occupation: 1.6% management, 2.3% professional, 15.1% services, 13.9% sales, 4.7% farming, 7.3% construction, 10.1% production (2006-2010 5-year est.).

**Income:** Per capita income: $16,385 (2006-2010 5-year est.); Median household income: $37,425 (2006-2010 5-year est.); Average household income: $41,824 (2006-2010 5-year est.); Percent of households with income of $100,000 or more: 4.0% (2006-2010 5-year est.); Poverty rate: 16.9% (2006-2010 5-year est.).

**Taxes:** Total city taxes per capita: $362 (2009); City property taxes per capita: $350 (2009).

**Education:** Percent of population age 25 and over with: High school diploma (including GED) or higher: 88.9% (2006-2010 5-year est.); Bachelor's degree or higher: 9.0% (2006-2010 5-year est.); Master's degree or higher: 3.7% (2006-2010 5-year est.).

**School District(s)**

Falconer Central School District (PK-12)
    2009-10 Enrollment: 1,299 . . . . . . . . . . . . . . . . . . . . . . (716) 665-6624

**Housing:** Homeownership rate: 60.6% (2010); Median home value: $65,000 (2006-2010 5-year est.); Median contract rent: $428 per month (2006-2010 5-year est.); Median year structure built: before 1940 (2006-2010 5-year est.).

**Transportation:** Commute to work: 88.8% car, 1.0% public transportation, 7.9% walk, 0.5% work from home (2006-2010 5-year est.); Travel time to work: 62.9% less than 15 minutes, 22.8% 15 to 30 minutes, 4.4% 30 to 45 minutes, 3.6% 45 to 60 minutes, 6.3% 60 minutes or more (2006-2010 5-year est.)

---

**FINDLEY LAKE** (unincorporated postal area)

Zip Code: 14736

    Covers a land area of 5.226 square miles and a water area of 0 square miles. Located at 42.14° N. Lat; 79.74° W. Long. Elevation is 1,440 feet.

Population: 282 (2010); Density: 54.0 persons per square mile (2010); Race: 96.8% White, 0.0% Black, 1.4% Asian, 0.0% American Indian/Alaska Native, 0.0% Native Hawaiian/Other Pacific Islander, 1.8% Other, 0.7% Hispanic of any race (2010); Average household size: 2.71 (2010); Median age: 43.0 (2010); Males per 100 females: 100.0 (2010); Homeownership rate: 75.0% (2010)

## FORESTVILLE (village). Covers a land area of 0.979 square miles and a water area of 0 square miles. Located at 42.46° N. Lat; 79.17° W. Long. Elevation is 932 feet.
Population: 738 (1990); 770 (2000); 697 (2010); Density: 711.7 persons per square mile (2010); Race: 96.3% White, 0.7% Black, 0.4% Asian, 1.0% American Indian/Alaska Native, 0.0% Native Hawaiian/Other Pacific Islander, 1.6% Other, 1.7% Hispanic of any race (2010); Average household size: 2.47 (2010); Median age: 39.4 (2010); Males per 100 females: 112.5 (2010); Marriage status: 33.4% never married, 44.4% now married, 12.1% widowed, 10.1% divorced (2006-2010 5-year est.); Foreign born: 3.6% (2006-2010 5-year est.); Ancestry (includes multiple ancestries): 42.9% German, 22.6% Irish, 17.8% English, 13.4% Italian, 7.8% Dutch (2006-2010 5-year est.).
Economy: Single-family building permits issued: 0 (2011); Multi-family building permits issued: 0 (2011); Employment by occupation: 10.2% management, 0.7% professional, 13.6% services, 26.5% sales, 3.7% farming, 6.8% construction, 7.8% production (2006-2010 5-year est.).
Income: Per capita income: $19,773 (2006-2010 5-year est.); Median household income: $39,630 (2006-2010 5-year est.); Average household income: $49,091 (2006-2010 5-year est.); Percent of households with income of $100,000 or more: 9.8% (2006-2010 5-year est.); Poverty rate: 12.8% (2006-2010 5-year est.).
Education: Percent of population age 25 and over with: High school diploma (including GED) or higher: 95.7% (2006-2010 5-year est.); Bachelor's degree or higher: 17.9% (2006-2010 5-year est.); Master's degree or higher: 8.3% (2006-2010 5-year est.).
**School District(s)**
Forestville Central School District (PK-12)
   2009-10 Enrollment: 588 . . . . . . . . . . . . . . . . . . . . . . . (716) 965-2742
Housing: Homeownership rate: 74.2% (2010); Median home value: $80,900 (2006-2010 5-year est.); Median contract rent: $423 per month (2006-2010 5-year est.); Median year structure built: before 1940 (2006-2010 5-year est.).
Transportation: Commute to work: 88.9% car, 0.0% public transportation, 7.6% walk, 3.5% work from home (2006-2010 5-year est.); Travel time to work: 41.9% less than 15 minutes, 35.5% 15 to 30 minutes, 7.9% 30 to 45 minutes, 10.4% 45 to 60 minutes, 4.3% 60 minutes or more (2006-2010 5-year est.)

## FREDONIA (village). Covers a land area of 5.189 square miles and a water area of 0 square miles. Located at 42.44° N. Lat; 79.33° W. Long. Elevation is 722 feet.
History: Incorporated 1829. Was the site of the first gas well in the U.S. The first local unit of the Natioanl Grange (Patrons of Husbandry) Movement was also founded here. State University of N.Y. at Fredonia here.
Population: 10,436 (1990); 10,706 (2000); 11,230 (2010); Density: 2,164.2 persons per square mile (2010); Race: 93.8% White, 1.8% Black, 1.6% Asian, 0.3% American Indian/Alaska Native, 0.0% Native Hawaiian/Other Pacific Islander, 2.5% Other, 3.9% Hispanic of any race (2010); Average household size: 2.24 (2010); Median age: 22.8 (2010); Males per 100 females: 88.1 (2010); Marriage status: 55.5% never married, 31.5% now married, 5.3% widowed, 7.8% divorced (2006-2010 5-year est.); Foreign born: 4.3% (2006-2010 5-year est.); Ancestry (includes multiple ancestries): 29.5% German, 26.9% Italian, 19.9% Polish, 17.5% Irish, 13.5% English (2006-2010 5-year est.).
Economy: Single-family building permits issued: 2 (2011); Multi-family building permits issued: 0 (2011); Employment by occupation: 7.4% management, 1.8% professional, 13.2% services, 18.3% sales, 5.5% farming, 5.3% construction, 2.6% production (2006-2010 5-year est.).
Income: Per capita income: $19,821 (2006-2010 5-year est.); Median household income: $39,838 (2006-2010 5-year est.); Average household income: $51,923 (2006-2010 5-year est.); Percent of households with income of $100,000 or more: 15.5% (2006-2010 5-year est.); Poverty rate: 19.0% (2006-2010 5-year est.).
Taxes: Total city taxes per capita: $256 (2009); City property taxes per capita: $227 (2009).

Education: Percent of population age 25 and over with: High school diploma (including GED) or higher: 94.3% (2006-2010 5-year est.); Bachelor's degree or higher: 39.4% (2006-2010 5-year est.); Master's degree or higher: 20.1% (2006-2010 5-year est.).
**School District(s)**
Fredonia Central School District (PK-12)
   2009-10 Enrollment: 1,650 . . . . . . . . . . . . . . . . . . . (716) 679-1581
**Four-year College(s)**
SUNY at Fredonia (Public)
   Fall 2010 Enrollment: 5,754 . . . . . . . . . . . . . . . . . (716) 673-3111
   2011-12 Tuition: In-state $6,688; Out-of-state $15,738
Housing: Homeownership rate: 50.5% (2010); Median home value: $119,800 (2006-2010 5-year est.); Median contract rent: $470 per month (2006-2010 5-year est.); Median year structure built: 1941 (2006-2010 5-year est.).
Safety: Violent crime rate: 16.4 per 10,000 population; Property crime rate: 281.4 per 10,000 population (2010).
Newspapers: Dunkirk/Fredonia/Westfield Shopping Guide (Community news; Circulation 24,000)
Transportation: Commute to work: 77.4% car, 0.7% public transportation, 15.4% walk, 3.9% work from home (2006-2010 5-year est.); Travel time to work: 67.7% less than 15 minutes, 20.2% 15 to 30 minutes, 4.9% 30 to 45 minutes, 4.3% 45 to 60 minutes, 2.8% 60 minutes or more (2006-2010 5-year est.); Amtrak: train service available.
Additional Information Contacts
Fredonia Chamber of Commerce . . . . . . . . . . . . . . . . . . . (716) 679-1565
   http://www.fredoniachamber.org

## FRENCH CREEK (town). Covers a land area of 36.258 square miles and a water area of 0.020 square miles. Located at 42.04° N. Lat; 79.71° W. Long. Elevation is 1,417 feet.
Population: 916 (1990); 935 (2000); 906 (2010); Density: 25.0 persons per square mile (2010); Race: 98.0% White, 0.2% Black, 0.2% Asian, 0.0% American Indian/Alaska Native, 0.0% Native Hawaiian/Other Pacific Islander, 1.6% Other, 0.9% Hispanic of any race (2010); Average household size: 2.67 (2010); Median age: 38.7 (2010); Males per 100 females: 106.4 (2010); Marriage status: 20.9% never married, 70.2% now married, 3.7% widowed, 5.2% divorced (2006-2010 5-year est.); Foreign born: 0.5% (2006-2010 5-year est.); Ancestry (includes multiple ancestries): 41.5% German, 14.7% English, 14.3% Polish, 13.5% Irish, 6.7% Swedish (2006-2010 5-year est.).
Economy: Single-family building permits issued: 0 (2011); Multi-family building permits issued: 0 (2011); Employment by occupation: 7.2% management, 1.5% professional, 13.9% services, 15.7% sales, 0.0% farming, 19.9% construction, 10.0% production (2006-2010 5-year est.).
Income: Per capita income: $18,554 (2006-2010 5-year est.); Median household income: $42,656 (2006-2010 5-year est.); Average household income: $49,534 (2006-2010 5-year est.); Percent of households with income of $100,000 or more: 5.5% (2006-2010 5-year est.); Poverty rate: 15.5% (2006-2010 5-year est.).
Education: Percent of population age 25 and over with: High school diploma (including GED) or higher: 83.3% (2006-2010 5-year est.); Bachelor's degree or higher: 10.9% (2006-2010 5-year est.); Master's degree or higher: 3.6% (2006-2010 5-year est.).
Housing: Homeownership rate: 80.8% (2010); Median home value: $68,500 (2006-2010 5-year est.); Median contract rent: $317 per month (2006-2010 5-year est.); Median year structure built: 1981 (2006-2010 5-year est.).
Transportation: Commute to work: 85.5% car, 1.0% public transportation, 2.3% walk, 6.0% work from home (2006-2010 5-year est.); Travel time to work: 33.9% less than 15 minutes, 34.7% 15 to 30 minutes, 18.7% 30 to 45 minutes, 6.9% 45 to 60 minutes, 5.9% 60 minutes or more (2006-2010 5-year est.)

## FREWSBURG (CDP). Covers a land area of 3.372 square miles and a water area of 0.014 square miles. Located at 42.05° N. Lat; 79.13° W. Long. Elevation is 1,299 feet.
Population: 1,958 (1990); 1,965 (2000); 1,906 (2010); Density: 565.1 persons per square mile (2010); Race: 97.3% White, 0.5% Black, 0.0% Asian, 0.5% American Indian/Alaska Native, 0.1% Native Hawaiian/Other Pacific Islander, 1.6% Other, 0.9% Hispanic of any race (2010); Average household size: 2.38 (2010); Median age: 44.7 (2010); Males per 100 females: 90.0 (2010); Marriage status: 28.5% never married, 49.5% now married, 7.4% widowed, 14.6% divorced (2006-2010 5-year est.); Foreign born: 0.0% (2006-2010 5-year est.); Ancestry (includes multiple

ancestries): 29.2% German, 26.1% Swedish, 17.5% English, 12.9% Polish, 12.2% Irish (2006-2010 5-year est.).
**Economy:** Employment by occupation: 7.1% management, 0.0% professional, 13.0% services, 11.5% sales, 7.8% farming, 9.9% construction, 2.4% production (2006-2010 5-year est.).
**Income:** Per capita income: $22,453 (2006-2010 5-year est.); Median household income: $52,337 (2006-2010 5-year est.); Average household income: $62,997 (2006-2010 5-year est.); Percent of households with income of $100,000 or more: 18.3% (2006-2010 5-year est.); Poverty rate: 4.1% (2006-2010 5-year est.).
**Education:** Percent of population age 25 and over with: High school diploma (including GED) or higher: 87.8% (2006-2010 5-year est.); Bachelor's degree or higher: 23.3% (2006-2010 5-year est.); Master's degree or higher: 10.4% (2006-2010 5-year est.).

**School District(s)**
Frewsburg Central School District (PK-12)
   2009-10 Enrollment: 925 . . . . . . . . . . . . . . . . . . . . . . . . (716) 569-9241
**Housing:** Homeownership rate: 67.7% (2010); Median home value: $82,700 (2006-2010 5-year est.); Median contract rent: $405 per month (2006-2010 5-year est.); Median year structure built: 1952 (2006-2010 5-year est.).
**Transportation:** Commute to work: 91.7% car, 0.0% public transportation, 7.5% walk, 0.8% work from home (2006-2010 5-year est.); Travel time to work: 44.6% less than 15 minutes, 41.5% 15 to 30 minutes, 9.8% 30 to 45 minutes, 2.8% 45 to 60 minutes, 1.3% 60 minutes or more (2006-2010 5-year est.)

**GERRY** (town). Covers a land area of 36.124 square miles and a water area of 0.017 square miles. Located at 42.21° N. Lat; 79.24° W. Long. Elevation is 1,302 feet.
**Population:** 2,147 (1990); 2,054 (2000); 1,905 (2010); Density: 52.7 persons per square mile (2010); Race: 97.9% White, 0.2% Black, 0.5% Asian, 0.2% American Indian/Alaska Native, 0.0% Native Hawaiian/Other Pacific Islander, 1.2% Other, 1.0% Hispanic of any race (2010); Average household size: 2.47 (2010); Median age: 46.4 (2010); Males per 100 females: 91.8 (2010); Marriage status: 22.0% never married, 62.7% now married, 7.0% widowed, 8.3% divorced (2006-2010 5-year est.); Foreign born: 1.6% (2006-2010 5-year est.); Ancestry (includes multiple ancestries): 22.1% German, 19.8% English, 19.0% Swedish, 15.1% Irish, 8.3% Italian (2006-2010 5-year est.).
**Economy:** Single-family building permits issued: 0 (2011); Multi-family building permits issued: 0 (2011); Employment by occupation: 12.7% management, 2.8% professional, 11.6% services, 19.7% sales, 1.6% farming, 9.8% construction, 7.3% production (2006-2010 5-year est.).
**Income:** Per capita income: $22,195 (2006-2010 5-year est.); Median household income: $41,667 (2006-2010 5-year est.); Average household income: $54,250 (2006-2010 5-year est.); Percent of households with income of $100,000 or more: 13.2% (2006-2010 5-year est.); Poverty rate: 21.4% (2006-2010 5-year est.).
**Education:** Percent of population age 25 and over with: High school diploma (including GED) or higher: 84.4% (2006-2010 5-year est.); Bachelor's degree or higher: 13.4% (2006-2010 5-year est.); Master's degree or higher: 3.0% (2006-2010 5-year est.).
**Housing:** Homeownership rate: 74.5% (2010); Median home value: $73,800 (2006-2010 5-year est.); Median contract rent: $448 per month (2006-2010 5-year est.); Median year structure built: 1975 (2006-2010 5-year est.).
**Transportation:** Commute to work: 90.8% car, 0.2% public transportation, 3.3% walk, 5.3% work from home (2006-2010 5-year est.); Travel time to work: 25.7% less than 15 minutes, 51.7% 15 to 30 minutes, 17.4% 30 to 45 minutes, 2.7% 45 to 60 minutes, 2.5% 60 minutes or more (2006-2010 5-year est.)

**GREENHURST** (unincorporated postal area)
Zip Code: 14742
   Covers a land area of 0.224 square miles and a water area of 0 square miles. Located at 42.12° N. Lat; 79.30° W. Long. Elevation is 1,319 feet.
Population: 314 (2010); Density: 1,398.3 persons per square mile (2010); Race: 98.1% White, 1.3% Black, 0.0% Asian, 0.3% American Indian/Alaska Native, 0.0% Native Hawaiian/Other Pacific Islander, 0.3% Other, 0.0% Hispanic of any race (2010); Average household size: 2.13 (2010); Median age: 66.7 (2010); Males per 100 females: 67.9 (2010); Homeownership rate: 85.9% (2010)

**HANOVER** (town). Covers a land area of 49.177 square miles and a water area of 0.283 square miles. Located at 42.48° N. Lat; 79.12° W. Long.
**Population:** 7,380 (1990); 7,638 (2000); 7,127 (2010); Density: 144.9 persons per square mile (2010); Race: 95.4% White, 0.9% Black, 0.3% Asian, 1.6% American Indian/Alaska Native, 0.0% Native Hawaiian/Other Pacific Islander, 1.8% Other, 2.2% Hispanic of any race (2010); Average household size: 2.42 (2010); Median age: 43.4 (2010); Males per 100 females: 97.3 (2010); Marriage status: 27.7% never married, 51.8% now married, 10.5% widowed, 10.0% divorced (2006-2010 5-year est.); Foreign born: 1.0% (2006-2010 5-year est.); Ancestry (includes multiple ancestries): 38.3% German, 18.2% Italian, 17.9% Irish, 14.8% English, 11.3% Polish (2006-2010 5-year est.).
**Economy:** Single-family building permits issued: 7 (2011); Multi-family building permits issued: 0 (2011); Employment by occupation: 5.8% management, 1.2% professional, 10.0% services, 16.5% sales, 2.8% farming, 11.8% construction, 12.9% production (2006-2010 5-year est.).
**Income:** Per capita income: $21,876 (2006-2010 5-year est.); Median household income: $44,696 (2006-2010 5-year est.); Average household income: $53,609 (2006-2010 5-year est.); Percent of households with income of $100,000 or more: 11.8% (2006-2010 5-year est.); Poverty rate: 14.5% (2006-2010 5-year est.).
**Education:** Percent of population age 25 and over with: High school diploma (including GED) or higher: 85.1% (2006-2010 5-year est.); Bachelor's degree or higher: 15.4% (2006-2010 5-year est.); Master's degree or higher: 8.1% (2006-2010 5-year est.).
**Housing:** Homeownership rate: 78.9% (2010); Median home value: $86,200 (2006-2010 5-year est.); Median contract rent: $433 per month (2006-2010 5-year est.); Median year structure built: 1949 (2006-2010 5-year est.).
**Transportation:** Commute to work: 94.5% car, 0.3% public transportation, 2.7% walk, 2.5% work from home (2006-2010 5-year est.); Travel time to work: 35.7% less than 15 minutes, 39.4% 15 to 30 minutes, 12.0% 30 to 45 minutes, 6.5% 45 to 60 minutes, 6.3% 60 minutes or more (2006-2010 5-year est.)

**HARMONY** (town). Covers a land area of 45.399 square miles and a water area of 0.160 square miles. Located at 42.04° N. Lat; 79.45° W. Long.
**Population:** 2,177 (1990); 2,339 (2000); 2,206 (2010); Density: 48.6 persons per square mile (2010); Race: 98.5% White, 0.3% Black, 0.5% Asian, 0.2% American Indian/Alaska Native, 0.0% Native Hawaiian/Other Pacific Islander, 0.5% Other, 1.6% Hispanic of any race (2010); Average household size: 2.57 (2010); Median age: 43.4 (2010); Males per 100 females: 97.3 (2010); Marriage status: 19.3% never married, 64.4% now married, 6.8% widowed, 9.5% divorced (2006-2010 5-year est.); Foreign born: 0.4% (2006-2010 5-year est.); Ancestry (includes multiple ancestries): 24.2% English, 23.6% German, 14.9% Irish, 12.4% Italian, 12.0% Swedish (2006-2010 5-year est.).
**Economy:** Single-family building permits issued: 1 (2011); Multi-family building permits issued: 0 (2011); Employment by occupation: 10.5% management, 1.7% professional, 9.5% services, 12.0% sales, 2.0% farming, 13.2% construction, 9.7% production (2006-2010 5-year est.).
**Income:** Per capita income: $20,627 (2006-2010 5-year est.); Median household income: $44,457 (2006-2010 5-year est.); Average household income: $51,042 (2006-2010 5-year est.); Percent of households with income of $100,000 or more: 7.9% (2006-2010 5-year est.); Poverty rate: 8.5% (2006-2010 5-year est.).
**Education:** Percent of population age 25 and over with: High school diploma (including GED) or higher: 84.1% (2006-2010 5-year est.); Bachelor's degree or higher: 16.0% (2006-2010 5-year est.); Master's degree or higher: 5.8% (2006-2010 5-year est.).
**Housing:** Homeownership rate: 85.4% (2010); Median home value: $76,400 (2006-2010 5-year est.); Median contract rent: $411 per month (2006-2010 5-year est.); Median year structure built: 1959 (2006-2010 5-year est.).
**Transportation:** Commute to work: 91.5% car, 0.0% public transportation, 2.3% walk, 4.9% work from home (2006-2010 5-year est.); Travel time to work: 25.8% less than 15 minutes, 41.8% 15 to 30 minutes, 26.3% 30 to 45 minutes, 3.4% 45 to 60 minutes, 2.7% 60 minutes or more (2006-2010 5-year est.)

**IRVING** (unincorporated postal area)
Zip Code: 14081

Covers a land area of 35.169 square miles and a water area of 0.905 square miles. Located at 42.56° N. Lat; 79.06° W. Long. Population: 3,095 (2010); Density: 88.0 persons per square mile (2010); Race: 61.2% White, 0.9% Black, 0.3% Asian, 35.7% American Indian/Alaska Native, 0.0% Native Hawaiian/Other Pacific Islander, 1.9% Other, 2.7% Hispanic of any race (2010); Average household size: 2.46 (2010); Median age: 43.3 (2010); Males per 100 females: 92.7 (2010); Homeownership rate: 76.6% (2010).

**JAMESTOWN** (city). Covers a land area of 8.934 square miles and a water area of 0.127 square miles. Located at 42.09° N. Lat; 79.23° W. Long. Elevation is 1,378 feet.

**History:** The founder of the Jamestown settlement was James Prendergast, who purchased 1,000 acres of land his brother had earlier bought from the Holland Land Company. Among the early settlers were a number of skilled woodworkers, who began to make furniture to supply the needs of the pioneers of the region. In 1849, some Swedish immigrants appeared. After the close of the Civil War, many others joined them. Most of them were cabinet makers attracted by the furniture factories. In 1888, two years after Jamestown had become officially a city, construction of metal furniture was begun.

**Population:** 34,689 (1990); 31,730 (2000); 31,146 (2010); Density: 3,486.0 persons per square mile (2010); Race: 88.4% White, 4.1% Black, 0.4% Asian, 0.6% American Indian/Alaska Native, 0.0% Native Hawaiian/Other Pacific Islander, 6.5% Other, 8.8% Hispanic of any race (2010); Average household size: 2.29 (2010); Median age: 36.9 (2010); Males per 100 females: 94.6 (2010); Marriage status: 34.9% never married, 46.2% now married, 6.7% widowed, 12.2% divorced (2006-2010 5-year est.); Foreign born: 1.9% (2006-2010 5-year est.); Ancestry (includes multiple ancestries): 21.7% Italian, 18.8% German, 18.6% Swedish, 14.9% Irish, 14.1% English (2006-2010 5-year est.).

**Economy:** Unemployment rate: 9.8% (February 2012); Total civilian labor force: 14,143 (February 2012); Single-family building permits issued: 1 (2011); Multi-family building permits issued: 35 (2011); Employment by occupation: 8.2% management, 2.9% professional, 15.2% services, 15.8% sales, 5.3% farming, 5.0% construction, 6.6% production (2006-2010 5-year est.).

**Income:** Per capita income: $18,374 (2006-2010 5-year est.); Median household income: $33,092 (2006-2010 5-year est.); Average household income: $42,215 (2006-2010 5-year est.); Percent of households with income of $100,000 or more: 6.6% (2006-2010 5-year est.); Poverty rate: 23.4% (2006-2010 5-year est.).

**Taxes:** Total city taxes per capita: $456 (2009); City property taxes per capita: $431 (2009).

**Education:** Percent of population age 25 and over with: High school diploma (including GED) or higher: 84.3% (2006-2010 5-year est.); Bachelor's degree or higher: 16.7% (2006-2010 5-year est.); Master's degree or higher: 7.0% (2006-2010 5-year est.).

**School District(s)**
Jamestown City School District (PK-12)
    2009-10 Enrollment: 5,168 . . . . . . . . . . . . . . . . . . . . (716) 483-4420
Southwestern Central School District at Jamestown (PK-12)
    2009-10 Enrollment: 1,501 . . . . . . . . . . . . . . . . . . . . (716) 484-1136
**Four-year College(s)**
Jamestown Business College (Private, For-profit)
    Fall 2010 Enrollment: 387 . . . . . . . . . . . . . . . . . . . . (716) 664-5100
    2011-12 Tuition: In-state $11,100; Out-of-state $11,100
**Two-year College(s)**
Jamestown Community College (Public)
    Fall 2010 Enrollment: 3,862 . . . . . . . . . . . . . . . . . . . . (716) 338-1000
    2011-12 Tuition: In-state $4,410; Out-of-state $8,310

**Housing:** Homeownership rate: 49.2% (2010); Median home value: $63,500 (2006-2010 5-year est.); Median contract rent: $402 per month (2006-2010 5-year est.); Median year structure built: before 1940 (2006-2010 5-year est.).

**Hospitals:** WCA Hospital (342 beds)

**Safety:** Violent crime rate: 62.5 per 10,000 population; Property crime rate: 445.0 per 10,000 population (2010).

**Newspapers:** Jamestown Post-Journal (Local news; Circulation 20,500); Southern Tier Pennysaver (Community news; Circulation 45,000)

**Transportation:** Commute to work: 86.1% car, 0.2% public transportation, 9.1% walk, 2.3% work from home (2006-2010 5-year est.); Travel time to work: 56.0% less than 15 minutes, 33.1% 15 to 30 minutes, 6.0% 30 to 45 minutes, 2.3% 45 to 60 minutes, 2.6% 60 minutes or more (2006-2010 5-year est.); Amtrak: bus service available.

**Airports:** Chautauqua County/Jamestown (commercial service)
**Additional Information Contacts**
Chautauqua County Chamber of Commerce. . . . . . . . . . . (716) 484-1101
    http://www.chautauquachamber.org

**JAMESTOWN WEST** (CDP). Aka West Ellicott. Covers a land area of 2.516 square miles and a water area of 0 square miles. Located at 42.08° N. Lat; 79.28° W. Long.
**Population:** 2,625 (1990); 2,535 (2000); 2,408 (2010); Density: 956.8 persons per square mile (2010); Race: 97.5% White, 0.6% Black, 1.3% Asian, 0.0% American Indian/Alaska Native, 0.0% Native Hawaiian/Other Pacific Islander, 0.6% Other, 0.9% Hispanic of any race (2010); Average household size: 2.19 (2010); Median age: 52.2 (2010); Males per 100 females: 86.7 (2010); Marriage status: 18.9% never married, 65.4% now married, 8.6% widowed, 7.1% divorced (2006-2010 5-year est.); Foreign born: 1.3% (2006-2010 5-year est.); Ancestry (includes multiple ancestries): 24.8% Swedish, 22.9% German, 15.5% Italian, 14.4% English, 14.2% Irish (2006-2010 5-year est.).
**Economy:** Employment by occupation: 13.1% management, 2.4% professional, 9.3% services, 10.0% sales, 4.0% farming, 4.5% construction, 6.3% production (2006-2010 5-year est.).
**Income:** Per capita income: $31,998 (2006-2010 5-year est.); Median household income: $57,194 (2006-2010 5-year est.); Average household income: $71,345 (2006-2010 5-year est.); Percent of households with income of $100,000 or more: 22.6% (2006-2010 5-year est.); Poverty rate: 7.0% (2006-2010 5-year est.).
**Education:** Percent of population age 25 and over with: High school diploma (including GED) or higher: 94.1% (2006-2010 5-year est.); Bachelor's degree or higher: 30.9% (2006-2010 5-year est.); Master's degree or higher: 14.0% (2006-2010 5-year est.).
**Housing:** Homeownership rate: 79.3% (2010); Median home value: $83,500 (2006-2010 5-year est.); Median contract rent: $545 per month (2006-2010 5-year est.); Median year structure built: 1954 (2006-2010 5-year est.).
**Transportation:** Commute to work: 94.1% car, 0.0% public transportation, 3.3% walk, 2.7% work from home (2006-2010 5-year est.); Travel time to work: 61.9% less than 15 minutes, 25.0% 15 to 30 minutes, 11.2% 30 to 45 minutes, 0.0% 45 to 60 minutes, 1.9% 60 minutes or more (2006-2010 5-year est.)

**KENNEDY** (CDP). Covers a land area of 2.035 square miles and a water area of 0 square miles. Located at 42.15° N. Lat; 79.09° W. Long. Elevation is 1,266 feet.
**Population:** n/a (1990); n/a (2000); 465 (2010); Density: 228.5 persons per square mile (2010); Race: 99.4% White, 0.0% Black, 0.0% Asian, 0.0% American Indian/Alaska Native, 0.0% Native Hawaiian/Other Pacific Islander, 0.6% Other, 0.6% Hispanic of any race (2010); Average household size: 2.41 (2010); Median age: 42.4 (2010); Males per 100 females: 97.0 (2010); Marriage status: 12.0% never married, 75.8% now married, 4.4% widowed, 7.9% divorced (2006-2010 5-year est.); Foreign born: 0.0% (2006-2010 5-year est.); Ancestry (includes multiple ancestries): 32.7% German, 21.8% Swedish, 19.3% English, 16.2% Italian, 8.0% Dutch (2006-2010 5-year est.).
**Economy:** Employment by occupation: 2.6% management, 0.0% professional, 13.3% services, 19.4% sales, 0.0% farming, 10.2% construction, 11.2% production (2006-2010 5-year est.).
**Income:** Per capita income: $18,483 (2006-2010 5-year est.); Median household income: $38,846 (2006-2010 5-year est.); Average household income: $41,821 (2006-2010 5-year est.); Percent of households with income of $100,000 or more: 2.5% (2006-2010 5-year est.); Poverty rate: 8.0% (2006-2010 5-year est.).
**Education:** Percent of population age 25 and over with: High school diploma (including GED) or higher: 84.4% (2006-2010 5-year est.); Bachelor's degree or higher: 13.5% (2006-2010 5-year est.); Master's degree or higher: 1.8% (2006-2010 5-year est.).
**School District(s)**
Falconer Central School District (PK-12)
    2009-10 Enrollment: 1,299 . . . . . . . . . . . . . . . . . . . . (716) 665-6624
**Housing:** Homeownership rate: 77.7% (2010); Median home value: $54,500 (2006-2010 5-year est.); Median contract rent: $339 per month (2006-2010 5-year est.); Median year structure built: 1945 (2006-2010 5-year est.).
**Transportation:** Commute to work: 87.2% car, 0.0% public transportation, 0.0% walk, 12.8% work from home (2006-2010 5-year est.); Travel time to work: 39.8% less than 15 minutes, 40.4% 15 to 30 minutes, 4.1% 30 to 45

minutes, 0.0% 45 to 60 minutes, 15.8% 60 minutes or more (2006-2010 5-year est.)

**KIANTONE** (town). Covers a land area of 18.397 square miles and a water area of 0.139 square miles. Located at 42.02° N. Lat; 79.19° W. Long. Elevation is 1,506 feet.
**Population:** 1,301 (1990); 1,385 (2000); 1,350 (2010); Density: 73.4 persons per square mile (2010); Race: 98.4% White, 1.0% Black, 0.0% Asian, 0.2% American Indian/Alaska Native, 0.0% Native Hawaiian/Other Pacific Islander, 0.4% Other, 0.5% Hispanic of any race (2010); Average household size: 2.47 (2010); Median age: 46.9 (2010); Males per 100 females: 96.8 (2010); Marriage status: 21.5% never married, 63.1% now married, 5.9% widowed, 9.4% divorced (2006-2010 5-year est.); Foreign born: 2.2% (2006-2010 5-year est.); Ancestry (includes multiple ancestries): 32.4% Swedish, 23.7% Italian, 22.7% German, 14.0% English, 13.3% Irish (2006-2010 5-year est.).
**Economy:** Single-family building permits issued: 1 (2011); Multi-family building permits issued: 0 (2011); Employment by occupation: 7.8% management, 3.0% professional, 10.3% services, 15.6% sales, 5.0% farming, 10.3% construction, 6.6% production (2006-2010 5-year est.).
**Income:** Per capita income: $26,680 (2006-2010 5-year est.); Median household income: $65,417 (2006-2010 5-year est.); Average household income: $67,714 (2006-2010 5-year est.); Percent of households with income of $100,000 or more: 15.2% (2006-2010 5-year est.); Poverty rate: 3.6% (2006-2010 5-year est.).
**Education:** Percent of population age 25 and over with: High school diploma (including GED) or higher: 92.9% (2006-2010 5-year est.); Bachelor's degree or higher: 22.7% (2006-2010 5-year est.); Master's degree or higher: 9.2% (2006-2010 5-year est.).
**Housing:** Homeownership rate: 90.1% (2010); Median home value: $108,700 (2006-2010 5-year est.); Median contract rent: $548 per month (2006-2010 5-year est.); Median year structure built: 1961 (2006-2010 5-year est.).
**Transportation:** Commute to work: 88.2% car, 0.0% public transportation, 0.0% walk, 10.2% work from home (2006-2010 5-year est.); Travel time to work: 43.1% less than 15 minutes, 41.7% 15 to 30 minutes, 7.4% 30 to 45 minutes, 4.2% 45 to 60 minutes, 3.7% 60 minutes or more (2006-2010 5-year est.)

**LAKEWOOD** (village). Covers a land area of 1.976 square miles and a water area of 0 square miles. Located at 42.09° N. Lat; 79.32° W. Long. Elevation is 1,325 feet.
**History:** Settled 1809, incorporated 1893.
**Population:** 3,564 (1990); 3,258 (2000); 3,002 (2010); Density: 1,519.1 persons per square mile (2010); Race: 96.2% White, 0.7% Black, 1.3% Asian, 0.3% American Indian/Alaska Native, 0.0% Native Hawaiian/Other Pacific Islander, 1.5% Other, 1.5% Hispanic of any race (2010); Average household size: 2.13 (2010); Median age: 47.3 (2010); Males per 100 females: 92.4 (2010); Marriage status: 20.5% never married, 55.4% now married, 9.6% widowed, 14.5% divorced (2006-2010 5-year est.); Foreign born: 1.3% (2006-2010 5-year est.); Ancestry (includes multiple ancestries): 25.4% Swedish, 24.4% German, 20.8% English, 18.8% Irish, 18.8% Italian (2006-2010 5-year est.).
**Economy:** Single-family building permits issued: 4 (2011); Multi-family building permits issued: 6 (2011); Employment by occupation: 16.6% management, 4.0% professional, 7.6% services, 11.0% sales, 3.5% farming, 2.0% construction, 5.6% production (2006-2010 5-year est.).
**Income:** Per capita income: $30,926 (2006-2010 5-year est.); Median household income: $42,047 (2006-2010 5-year est.); Average household income: $66,365 (2006-2010 5-year est.); Percent of households with income of $100,000 or more: 16.7% (2006-2010 5-year est.); Poverty rate: 11.3% (2006-2010 5-year est.).
**Education:** Percent of population age 25 and over with: High school diploma (including GED) or higher: 90.4% (2006-2010 5-year est.); Bachelor's degree or higher: 30.7% (2006-2010 5-year est.); Master's degree or higher: 11.8% (2006-2010 5-year est.).
**Housing:** Homeownership rate: 69.0% (2010); Median home value: $88,300 (2006-2010 5-year est.); Median contract rent: $584 per month (2006-2010 5-year est.); Median year structure built: 1954 (2006-2010 5-year est.).
**Transportation:** Commute to work: 91.5% car, 0.0% public transportation, 1.7% walk, 4.9% work from home (2006-2010 5-year est.); Travel time to work: 48.1% less than 15 minutes, 39.8% 15 to 30 minutes, 2.5% 30 to 45 minutes, 6.9% 45 to 60 minutes, 2.6% 60 minutes or more (2006-2010 5-year est.)

**LILY DALE** (unincorporated postal area)
Zip Code: 14752
Covers a land area of 0.250 square miles and a water area of 0 square miles. Located at 42.35° N. Lat; 79.31° W. Long. Elevation is 1,332 feet. Population: 169 (2010); Density: 673.9 persons per square mile (2010); Race: 94.1% White, 0.0% Black, 0.0% Asian, 3.6% American Indian/Alaska Native, 0.0% Native Hawaiian/Other Pacific Islander, 2.3% Other, 1.8% Hispanic of any race (2010); Average household size: 1.69 (2010); Median age: 59.9 (2010); Males per 100 females: 65.7 (2010); Homeownership rate: 93.0% (2010)

**MAPLE SPRINGS** (unincorporated postal area)
Zip Code: 14756
Covers a land area of 0.137 square miles and a water area of 0 square miles. Located at 42.19° N. Lat; 79.42° W. Long. Elevation is 1,312 feet. Population: 110 (2010); Density: 802.2 persons per square mile (2010); Race: 95.5% White, 0.0% Black, 0.0% Asian, 0.9% American Indian/Alaska Native, 0.0% Native Hawaiian/Other Pacific Islander, 3.6% Other, 0.9% Hispanic of any race (2010); Average household size: 2.12 (2010); Median age: 49.3 (2010); Males per 100 females: 89.7 (2010); Homeownership rate: 69.3% (2010)

**MAYVILLE** (village). County seat. Covers a land area of 1.991 square miles and a water area of 0.002 square miles. Located at 42.25° N. Lat; 79.50° W. Long. Elevation is 1,453 feet.
**History:** Incorporated 1830.
**Population:** 1,663 (1990); 1,756 (2000); 1,711 (2010); Density: 859.2 persons per square mile (2010); Race: 93.5% White, 5.1% Black, 0.1% Asian, 0.1% American Indian/Alaska Native, 0.1% Native Hawaiian/Other Pacific Islander, 1.1% Other, 3.2% Hispanic of any race (2010); Average household size: 2.24 (2010); Median age: 40.1 (2010); Males per 100 females: 116.3 (2010); Marriage status: 26.0% never married, 51.1% now married, 7.4% widowed, 15.4% divorced (2006-2010 5-year est.); Foreign born: 2.4% (2006-2010 5-year est.); Ancestry (includes multiple ancestries): 23.0% German, 21.7% English, 20.4% Irish, 10.2% Swedish, 8.5% Italian (2006-2010 5-year est.).
**Economy:** Single-family building permits issued: 1 (2011); Multi-family building permits issued: 0 (2011); Employment by occupation: 15.9% management, 3.4% professional, 10.0% services, 19.5% sales, 2.2% farming, 5.8% construction, 2.8% production (2006-2010 5-year est.).
**Income:** Per capita income: $21,635 (2006-2010 5-year est.); Median household income: $44,438 (2006-2010 5-year est.); Average household income: $55,023 (2006-2010 5-year est.); Percent of households with income of $100,000 or more: 10.4% (2006-2010 5-year est.); Poverty rate: 10.6% (2006-2010 5-year est.).
**Education:** Percent of population age 25 and over with: High school diploma (including GED) or higher: 86.9% (2006-2010 5-year est.); Bachelor's degree or higher: 25.8% (2006-2010 5-year est.); Master's degree or higher: 9.1% (2006-2010 5-year est.).
**School District(s)**
Chautauqua Lake Central School District (PK-12)
    2009-10 Enrollment: 836 . . . . . . . . . . . . . . . . . . (716) 753-5808
**Housing:** Homeownership rate: 62.6% (2010); Median home value: $96,100 (2006-2010 5-year est.); Median contract rent: $414 per month (2006-2010 5-year est.); Median year structure built: 1946 (2006-2010 5-year est.).
**Transportation:** Commute to work: 85.7% car, 0.4% public transportation, 9.2% walk, 2.7% work from home (2006-2010 5-year est.); Travel time to work: 54.8% less than 15 minutes, 24.5% 15 to 30 minutes, 13.2% 30 to 45 minutes, 1.7% 45 to 60 minutes, 5.8% 60 minutes or more (2006-2010 5-year est.)

**MINA** (town). Covers a land area of 35.816 square miles and a water area of 0.511 square miles. Located at 42.12° N. Lat; 79.69° W. Long. Elevation is 1,594 feet.
**Population:** 1,129 (1990); 1,176 (2000); 1,106 (2010); Density: 30.9 persons per square mile (2010); Race: 98.1% White, 0.0% Black, 0.5% Asian, 0.0% American Indian/Alaska Native, 0.0% Native Hawaiian/Other Pacific Islander, 1.4% Other, 0.7% Hispanic of any race (2010); Average household size: 2.68 (2010); Median age: 42.5 (2010); Males per 100 females: 97.9 (2010); Marriage status: 18.9% never married, 68.7% now married, 3.8% widowed, 8.6% divorced (2006-2010 5-year est.); Foreign born: 1.0% (2006-2010 5-year est.); Ancestry (includes multiple ancestries): 32.1% German, 20.2% English, 12.6% Irish, 10.3% Italian, 8.5% Polish (2006-2010 5-year est.).

**Economy:** Single-family building permits issued: 2 (2011); Multi-family building permits issued: 0 (2011); Employment by occupation: 4.0% management, 4.3% professional, 8.1% services, 24.4% sales, 3.8% farming, 14.5% construction, 9.2% production (2006-2010 5-year est.).
**Income:** Per capita income: $21,384 (2006-2010 5-year est.); Median household income: $46,417 (2006-2010 5-year est.); Average household income: $52,031 (2006-2010 5-year est.); Percent of households with income of $100,000 or more: 11.2% (2006-2010 5-year est.); Poverty rate: 12.6% (2006-2010 5-year est.).
**Education:** Percent of population age 25 and over with: High school diploma (including GED) or higher: 86.5% (2006-2010 5-year est.); Bachelor's degree or higher: 16.5% (2006-2010 5-year est.); Master's degree or higher: 7.4% (2006-2010 5-year est.).
**Housing:** Homeownership rate: 83.5% (2010); Median home value: $124,800 (2006-2010 5-year est.); Median contract rent: $505 per month (2006-2010 5-year est.); Median year structure built: 1967 (2006-2010 5-year est.).
**Transportation:** Commute to work: 92.4% car, 0.0% public transportation, 3.7% walk, 2.7% work from home (2006-2010 5-year est.); Travel time to work: 35.9% less than 15 minutes, 33.9% 15 to 30 minutes, 25.8% 30 to 45 minutes, 2.0% 45 to 60 minutes, 2.3% 60 minutes or more (2006-2010 5-year est.)

## NORTH HARMONY (town). Covers a land area of 42.132 square miles and a water area of 0.022 square miles. Located at 42.12° N. Lat; 79.46° W. Long.

**Population:** 2,301 (1990); 2,521 (2000); 2,267 (2010); Density: 53.8 persons per square mile (2010); Race: 99.0% White, 0.1% Black, 0.1% Asian, 0.2% American Indian/Alaska Native, 0.0% Native Hawaiian/Other Pacific Islander, 0.6% Other, 0.5% Hispanic of any race (2010); Average household size: 2.50 (2010); Median age: 46.3 (2010); Males per 100 females: 104.1 (2010); Marriage status: 19.7% never married, 63.3% now married, 5.2% widowed, 11.8% divorced (2006-2010 5-year est.); Foreign born: 0.4% (2006-2010 5-year est.); Ancestry (includes multiple ancestries): 25.7% English, 17.9% German, 17.1% Irish, 11.7% Swedish, 10.4% Italian (2006-2010 5-year est.).
**Economy:** Single-family building permits issued: 6 (2011); Multi-family building permits issued: 0 (2011); Employment by occupation: 18.1% management, 2.9% professional, 11.9% services, 10.0% sales, 2.7% farming, 9.8% construction, 10.6% production (2006-2010 5-year est.).
**Income:** Per capita income: $25,878 (2006-2010 5-year est.); Median household income: $45,238 (2006-2010 5-year est.); Average household income: $60,887 (2006-2010 5-year est.); Percent of households with income of $100,000 or more: 13.6% (2006-2010 5-year est.); Poverty rate: 7.1% (2006-2010 5-year est.).
**Education:** Percent of population age 25 and over with: High school diploma (including GED) or higher: 89.9% (2006-2010 5-year est.); Bachelor's degree or higher: 23.3% (2006-2010 5-year est.); Master's degree or higher: 10.6% (2006-2010 5-year est.).
**Housing:** Homeownership rate: 87.6% (2010); Median home value: $105,800 (2006-2010 5-year est.); Median contract rent: $466 per month (2006-2010 5-year est.); Median year structure built: 1953 (2006-2010 5-year est.).
**Transportation:** Commute to work: 90.6% car, 0.0% public transportation, 3.3% walk, 4.9% work from home (2006-2010 5-year est.); Travel time to work: 36.7% less than 15 minutes, 47.1% 15 to 30 minutes, 9.7% 30 to 45 minutes, 3.8% 45 to 60 minutes, 2.7% 60 minutes or more (2006-2010 5-year est.)

## PANAMA (village). Covers a land area of 2.200 square miles and a water area of 0.005 square miles. Located at 42.06° N. Lat; 79.48° W. Long. Elevation is 1,552 feet.

**History:** Panama Rocks, a 25-acre park with a 60-foot high rock outcropping containing abundant early Paleozoic marine fossils, is 1 mile West Southwest.
**Population:** 468 (1990); 491 (2000); 479 (2010); Density: 217.7 persons per square mile (2010); Race: 97.7% White, 0.2% Black, 0.4% Asian, 0.6% American Indian/Alaska Native, 0.0% Native Hawaiian/Other Pacific Islander, 1.1% Other, 1.9% Hispanic of any race (2010); Average household size: 2.46 (2010); Median age: 40.7 (2010); Males per 100 females: 94.7 (2010); Marriage status: 19.8% never married, 65.0% now married, 9.6% widowed, 5.6% divorced (2006-2010 5-year est.); Foreign born: 0.4% (2006-2010 5-year est.); Ancestry (includes multiple ancestries): 26.2% English, 21.8% Swedish, 18.6% German, 16.7% Irish, 12.6% Italian (2006-2010 5-year est.).

**Economy:** Single-family building permits issued: 0 (2011); Multi-family building permits issued: 0 (2011); Employment by occupation: 8.7% management, 1.0% professional, 13.6% services, 11.7% sales, 6.8% farming, 10.2% construction, 11.7% production (2006-2010 5-year est.).
**Income:** Per capita income: $19,702 (2006-2010 5-year est.); Median household income: $40,000 (2006-2010 5-year est.); Average household income: $48,624 (2006-2010 5-year est.); Percent of households with income of $100,000 or more: 7.7% (2006-2010 5-year est.); Poverty rate: 5.0% (2006-2010 5-year est.).
**Education:** Percent of population age 25 and over with: High school diploma (including GED) or higher: 90.5% (2006-2010 5-year est.); Bachelor's degree or higher: 25.8% (2006-2010 5-year est.); Master's degree or higher: 12.0% (2006-2010 5-year est.).
**School District(s)**
Panama Central School District (KG-12)
   2009-10 Enrollment: 610 . . . . . . . . . . . . . . . . . . . . . . (716) 782-2455
**Housing:** Homeownership rate: 68.2% (2010); Median home value: $75,700 (2006-2010 5-year est.); Median contract rent: $432 per month (2006-2010 5-year est.); Median year structure built: 1955 (2006-2010 5-year est.).
**Transportation:** Commute to work: 91.7% car, 0.0% public transportation, 7.3% walk, 1.0% work from home (2006-2010 5-year est.); Travel time to work: 24.5% less than 15 minutes, 51.5% 15 to 30 minutes, 18.1% 30 to 45 minutes, 2.9% 45 to 60 minutes, 2.9% 60 minutes or more (2006-2010 5-year est.)

## POLAND (town). Covers a land area of 36.616 square miles and a water area of 0.265 square miles. Located at 42.13° N. Lat; 79.12° W. Long.

**Population:** 2,639 (1990); 2,467 (2000); 2,356 (2010); Density: 64.3 persons per square mile (2010); Race: 98.1% White, 0.1% Black, 0.1% Asian, 0.4% American Indian/Alaska Native, 0.0% Native Hawaiian/Other Pacific Islander, 1.3% Other, 1.5% Hispanic of any race (2010); Average household size: 2.49 (2010); Median age: 43.9 (2010); Males per 100 females: 102.6 (2010); Marriage status: 21.0% never married, 66.9% now married, 5.5% widowed, 6.5% divorced (2006-2010 5-year est.); Foreign born: 2.2% (2006-2010 5-year est.); Ancestry (includes multiple ancestries): 27.5% Swedish, 26.1% German, 18.8% English, 14.9% Irish, 10.5% Italian (2006-2010 5-year est.).
**Economy:** Single-family building permits issued: 0 (2011); Multi-family building permits issued: 0 (2011); Employment by occupation: 9.8% management, 1.0% professional, 11.4% services, 14.4% sales, 3.4% farming, 11.3% construction, 7.9% production (2006-2010 5-year est.).
**Income:** Per capita income: $20,877 (2006-2010 5-year est.); Median household income: $46,226 (2006-2010 5-year est.); Average household income: $52,849 (2006-2010 5-year est.); Percent of households with income of $100,000 or more: 8.3% (2006-2010 5-year est.); Poverty rate: 14.3% (2006-2010 5-year est.).
**Education:** Percent of population age 25 and over with: High school diploma (including GED) or higher: 90.0% (2006-2010 5-year est.); Bachelor's degree or higher: 15.9% (2006-2010 5-year est.); Master's degree or higher: 5.6% (2006-2010 5-year est.).
**Housing:** Homeownership rate: 83.5% (2010); Median home value: $71,500 (2006-2010 5-year est.); Median contract rent: $386 per month (2006-2010 5-year est.); Median year structure built: 1961 (2006-2010 5-year est.).
**Transportation:** Commute to work: 91.8% car, 0.6% public transportation, 2.0% walk, 5.6% work from home (2006-2010 5-year est.); Travel time to work: 44.7% less than 15 minutes, 36.4% 15 to 30 minutes, 10.9% 30 to 45 minutes, 1.9% 45 to 60 minutes, 6.1% 60 minutes or more (2006-2010 5-year est.)

## POMFRET (town). Covers a land area of 43.854 square miles and a water area of 0.334 square miles. Located at 42.40° N. Lat; 79.33° W. Long.

**Population:** 14,224 (1990); 14,703 (2000); 14,965 (2010); Density: 341.2 persons per square mile (2010); Race: 93.5% White, 2.3% Black, 1.4% Asian, 0.4% American Indian/Alaska Native, 0.0% Native Hawaiian/Other Pacific Islander, 2.4% Other, 4.1% Hispanic of any race (2010); Average household size: 2.28 (2010); Median age: 25.5 (2010); Males per 100 females: 90.5 (2010); Marriage status: 49.8% never married, 35.3% now married, 5.4% widowed, 9.5% divorced (2006-2010 5-year est.); Foreign born: 3.7% (2006-2010 5-year est.); Ancestry (includes multiple ancestries): 28.2% German, 23.0% Italian, 19.3% Polish, 15.1% Irish, 12.9% English (2006-2010 5-year est.).

**Economy:** Single-family building permits issued: 11 (2011); Multi-family building permits issued: 0 (2011); Employment by occupation: 8.2% management, 1.8% professional, 11.7% services, 17.9% sales, 4.7% farming, 7.4% construction, 5.7% production (2006-2010 5-year est.).
**Income:** Per capita income: $20,404 (2006-2010 5-year est.); Median household income: $41,930 (2006-2010 5-year est.); Average household income: $53,124 (2006-2010 5-year est.); Percent of households with income of $100,000 or more: 15.5% (2006-2010 5-year est.); Poverty rate: 18.1% (2006-2010 5-year est.).
**Education:** Percent of population age 25 and over with: High school diploma (including GED) or higher: 93.8% (2006-2010 5-year est.); Bachelor's degree or higher: 32.6% (2006-2010 5-year est.); Master's degree or higher: 16.7% (2006-2010 5-year est.).
**Housing:** Homeownership rate: 59.9% (2010); Median home value: $116,600 (2006-2010 5-year est.); Median contract rent: $462 per month (2006-2010 5-year est.); Median year structure built: 1948 (2006-2010 5-year est.).
**Transportation:** Commute to work: 80.3% car, 0.9% public transportation, 12.4% walk, 4.1% work from home (2006-2010 5-year est.); Travel time to work: 64.2% less than 15 minutes, 23.4% 15 to 30 minutes, 5.9% 30 to 45 minutes, 4.2% 45 to 60 minutes, 2.3% 60 minutes or more (2006-2010 5-year est.)

## PORTLAND (town). Covers a land area of 34.116 square miles and a water area of 0.064 square miles. Located at 42.37° N. Lat; 79.46° W. Long. Elevation is 761 feet.

**Population:** 4,832 (1990); 5,502 (2000); 4,827 (2010); Density: 141.5 persons per square mile (2010); Race: 88.3% White, 7.6% Black, 0.3% Asian, 0.4% American Indian/Alaska Native, 0.0% Native Hawaiian/Other Pacific Islander, 3.4% Other, 6.0% Hispanic of any race (2010); Average household size: 2.48 (2010); Median age: 36.1 (2010); Males per 100 females: 126.6 (2010); Marriage status: 29.4% never married, 53.5% now married, 5.7% widowed, 11.4% divorced (2006-2010 5-year est.); Foreign born: 3.2% (2006-2010 5-year est.); Ancestry (includes multiple ancestries): 27.9% German, 20.2% English, 14.1% Irish, 13.5% Polish, 10.8% Italian (2006-2010 5-year est.).
**Economy:** Single-family building permits issued: 3 (2011); Multi-family building permits issued: 0 (2011); Employment by occupation: 6.7% management, 1.5% professional, 11.6% services, 14.2% sales, 2.3% farming, 13.7% construction, 9.6% production (2006-2010 5-year est.).
**Income:** Per capita income: $20,985 (2006-2010 5-year est.); Median household income: $39,325 (2006-2010 5-year est.); Average household income: $52,747 (2006-2010 5-year est.); Percent of households with income of $100,000 or more: 9.7% (2006-2010 5-year est.); Poverty rate: 14.8% (2006-2010 5-year est.).
**Taxes:** Total city taxes per capita: $153 (2009); City property taxes per capita: $145 (2009).
**Education:** Percent of population age 25 and over with: High school diploma (including GED) or higher: 80.6% (2006-2010 5-year est.); Bachelor's degree or higher: 14.2% (2006-2010 5-year est.); Master's degree or higher: 7.0% (2006-2010 5-year est.).
**Housing:** Homeownership rate: 76.1% (2010); Median home value: $84,600 (2006-2010 5-year est.); Median contract rent: $368 per month (2006-2010 5-year est.); Median year structure built: 1945 (2006-2010 5-year est.).
**Transportation:** Commute to work: 95.8% car, 0.0% public transportation, 1.6% walk, 1.6% work from home (2006-2010 5-year est.); Travel time to work: 27.5% less than 15 minutes, 58.0% 15 to 30 minutes, 5.7% 30 to 45 minutes, 2.2% 45 to 60 minutes, 6.6% 60 minutes or more (2006-2010 5-year est.)
**Additional Information Contacts**
Town of Portland . . . . . . . . . . . . . . . . . . . . . . . . . . . . . . . . . . (716) 792-9614
  http://www.town.portland.ny.us

## RIPLEY (town). Aka Ripley Center. Covers a land area of 48.762 square miles and a water area of 0.104 square miles. Located at 42.22° N. Lat; 79.69° W. Long. Elevation is 735 feet.

**Population:** 2,967 (1990); 2,636 (2000); 2,415 (2010); Density: 49.5 persons per square mile (2010); Race: 97.7% White, 0.2% Black, 0.0% Asian, 0.2% American Indian/Alaska Native, 0.1% Native Hawaiian/Other Pacific Islander, 1.8% Other, 1.4% Hispanic of any race (2010); Average household size: 2.49 (2010); Median age: 42.7 (2010); Males per 100 females: 101.6 (2010); Marriage status: 21.8% never married, 62.4% now married, 7.5% widowed, 8.3% divorced (2006-2010 5-year est.); Foreign born: 1.0% (2006-2010 5-year est.); Ancestry (includes multiple

ancestries): 26.9% German, 13.8% American, 13.4% Irish, 12.0% English, 11.3% Polish (2006-2010 5-year est.).
**Economy:** Single-family building permits issued: 1 (2011); Multi-family building permits issued: 0 (2011); Employment by occupation: 5.9% management, 3.0% professional, 10.2% services, 14.6% sales, 2.1% farming, 14.7% construction, 11.2% production (2006-2010 5-year est.).
**Income:** Per capita income: $18,877 (2006-2010 5-year est.); Median household income: $41,400 (2006-2010 5-year est.); Average household income: $47,909 (2006-2010 5-year est.); Percent of households with income of $100,000 or more: 6.0% (2006-2010 5-year est.); Poverty rate: 11.0% (2006-2010 5-year est.).
**Education:** Percent of population age 25 and over with: High school diploma (including GED) or higher: 82.9% (2006-2010 5-year est.); Bachelor's degree or higher: 10.8% (2006-2010 5-year est.); Master's degree or higher: 5.7% (2006-2010 5-year est.).
**School District(s)**
Ripley Central School District (PK-12)
  2009-10 Enrollment: 345 . . . . . . . . . . . . . . . . . . . (716) 736-6201
**Housing:** Homeownership rate: 79.9% (2010); Median home value: $69,300 (2006-2010 5-year est.); Median contract rent: $343 per month (2006-2010 5-year est.); Median year structure built: 1952 (2006-2010 5-year est.).
**Transportation:** Commute to work: 92.8% car, 0.9% public transportation, 0.4% walk, 4.7% work from home (2006-2010 5-year est.); Travel time to work: 32.6% less than 15 minutes, 39.1% 15 to 30 minutes, 14.0% 30 to 45 minutes, 10.4% 45 to 60 minutes, 3.8% 60 minutes or more (2006-2010 5-year est.)

## RIPLEY (CDP). Covers a land area of 1.371 square miles and a water area of 0 square miles. Located at 42.26° N. Lat; 79.71° W. Long. Elevation is 735 feet.

**Population:** 1,189 (1990); 1,030 (2000); 872 (2010); Density: 635.6 persons per square mile (2010); Race: 97.0% White, 0.0% Black, 0.0% Asian, 0.3% American Indian/Alaska Native, 0.0% Native Hawaiian/Other Pacific Islander, 2.7% Other, 2.2% Hispanic of any race (2010); Average household size: 2.36 (2010); Median age: 43.0 (2010); Males per 100 females: 95.1 (2010); Marriage status: 27.4% never married, 50.0% now married, 14.3% widowed, 8.3% divorced (2006-2010 5-year est.); Foreign born: 1.3% (2006-2010 5-year est.); Ancestry (includes multiple ancestries): 28.8% German, 20.9% American, 13.9% Irish, 13.3% English, 9.0% French (2006-2010 5-year est.).
**Economy:** Employment by occupation: 0.0% management, 0.0% professional, 15.4% services, 13.0% sales, 2.4% farming, 9.1% construction, 16.3% production (2006-2010 5-year est.).
**Income:** Per capita income: $19,592 (2006-2010 5-year est.); Median household income: $28,250 (2006-2010 5-year est.); Average household income: $39,396 (2006-2010 5-year est.); Percent of households with income of $100,000 or more: 2.7% (2006-2010 5-year est.); Poverty rate: 15.8% (2006-2010 5-year est.).
**Education:** Percent of population age 25 and over with: High school diploma (including GED) or higher: 78.1% (2006-2010 5-year est.); Bachelor's degree or higher: 8.1% (2006-2010 5-year est.); Master's degree or higher: 5.2% (2006-2010 5-year est.).
**School District(s)**
Ripley Central School District (PK-12)
  2009-10 Enrollment: 345 . . . . . . . . . . . . . . . . . . . (716) 736-6201
**Housing:** Homeownership rate: 72.6% (2010); Median home value: $56,000 (2006-2010 5-year est.); Median contract rent: $373 per month (2006-2010 5-year est.); Median year structure built: before 1940 (2006-2010 5-year est.).
**Transportation:** Commute to work: 95.0% car, 0.0% public transportation, 0.0% walk, 5.0% work from home (2006-2010 5-year est.); Travel time to work: 22.4% less than 15 minutes, 46.4% 15 to 30 minutes, 20.8% 30 to 45 minutes, 3.6% 45 to 60 minutes, 6.8% 60 minutes or more (2006-2010 5-year est.)

## SHERIDAN (town). Covers a land area of 37.251 square miles and a water area of 0.050 square miles. Located at 42.48° N. Lat; 79.22° W. Long. Elevation is 748 feet.

**Population:** 2,582 (1990); 2,838 (2000); 2,673 (2010); Density: 71.8 persons per square mile (2010); Race: 96.4% White, 0.4% Black, 0.3% Asian, 0.7% American Indian/Alaska Native, 0.0% Native Hawaiian/Other Pacific Islander, 2.2% Other, 3.6% Hispanic of any race (2010); Average household size: 2.43 (2010); Median age: 47.2 (2010); Males per 100 females: 98.9 (2010); Marriage status: 23.5% never married, 62.8% now

married, 6.6% widowed, 7.2% divorced (2006-2010 5-year est.); Foreign born: 2.8% (2006-2010 5-year est.); Ancestry (includes multiple ancestries): 30.9% German, 24.2% Polish, 20.9% Irish, 16.7% English, 11.9% Italian (2006-2010 5-year est.).

**Economy:** Single-family building permits issued: 2 (2011); Multi-family building permits issued: 0 (2011); Employment by occupation: 13.5% management, 1.6% professional, 9.9% services, 16.4% sales, 2.0% farming, 10.6% construction, 9.5% production (2006-2010 5-year est.).

**Income:** Per capita income: $25,736 (2006-2010 5-year est.); Median household income: $56,887 (2006-2010 5-year est.); Average household income: $61,887 (2006-2010 5-year est.); Percent of households with income of $100,000 or more: 17.4% (2006-2010 5-year est.); Poverty rate: 10.9% (2006-2010 5-year est.).

**Taxes:** Total city taxes per capita: $265 (2009); City property taxes per capita: $249 (2009).

**Education:** Percent of population age 25 and over with: High school diploma (including GED) or higher: 90.5% (2006-2010 5-year est.); Bachelor's degree or higher: 17.8% (2006-2010 5-year est.); Master's degree or higher: 8.7% (2006-2010 5-year est.).

**Housing:** Homeownership rate: 85.3% (2010); Median home value: $117,800 (2006-2010 5-year est.); Median contract rent: $489 per month (2006-2010 5-year est.); Median year structure built: 1954 (2006-2010 5-year est.).

**Transportation:** Commute to work: 94.2% car, 0.8% public transportation, 0.6% walk, 0.5% work from home (2006-2010 5-year est.); Travel time to work: 53.8% less than 15 minutes, 27.9% 15 to 30 minutes, 8.2% 30 to 45 minutes, 4.8% 45 to 60 minutes, 5.2% 60 minutes or more (2006-2010 5-year est.)

**SHERMAN** (village). Covers a land area of 0.853 square miles and a water area of 0 square miles. Located at 42.15° N. Lat; 79.59° W. Long. Elevation is 1,539 feet.

**Population:** 694 (1990); 714 (2000); 730 (2010); Density: 855.1 persons per square mile (2010); Race: 97.8% White, 0.1% Black, 0.0% Asian, 0.0% American Indian/Alaska Native, 0.0% Native Hawaiian/Other Pacific Islander, 2.1% Other, 1.0% Hispanic of any race (2010); Average household size: 2.62 (2010); Median age: 35.0 (2010); Males per 100 females: 97.3 (2010); Marriage status: 19.9% never married, 66.6% now married, 2.8% widowed, 10.7% divorced (2006-2010 5-year est.); Foreign born: 0.8% (2006-2010 5-year est.); Ancestry (includes multiple ancestries): 34.0% German, 22.7% Irish, 16.6% English, 10.7% Dutch, 10.6% Swedish (2006-2010 5-year est.).

**Economy:** Single-family building permits issued: 0 (2011); Multi-family building permits issued: 0 (2011); Employment by occupation: 5.3% management, 0.9% professional, 24.0% services, 10.1% sales, 0.9% farming, 20.8% construction, 20.5% production (2006-2010 5-year est.).

**Income:** Per capita income: $16,108 (2006-2010 5-year est.); Median household income: $34,118 (2006-2010 5-year est.); Average household income: $43,414 (2006-2010 5-year est.); Percent of households with income of $100,000 or more: 2.2% (2006-2010 5-year est.); Poverty rate: 12.7% (2006-2010 5-year est.).

**Education:** Percent of population age 25 and over with: High school diploma (including GED) or higher: 90.2% (2006-2010 5-year est.); Bachelor's degree or higher: 15.1% (2006-2010 5-year est.); Master's degree or higher: 2.5% (2006-2010 5-year est.).

**School District(s)**

Sherman Central School District (PK-12)

    2009-10 Enrollment: 480 . . . . . . . . . . . . . . . . . . . . . . . . . (716) 761-6122

**Housing:** Homeownership rate: 73.9% (2010); Median home value: $58,600 (2006-2010 5-year est.); Median contract rent: $347 per month (2006-2010 5-year est.); Median year structure built: before 1940 (2006-2010 5-year est.).

**Transportation:** Commute to work: 85.4% car, 0.0% public transportation, 10.7% walk, 3.9% work from home (2006-2010 5-year est.); Travel time to work: 24.8% less than 15 minutes, 41.3% 15 to 30 minutes, 30.1% 30 to 45 minutes, 2.8% 45 to 60 minutes, 0.9% 60 minutes or more (2006-2010 5-year est.)

**Airports:** Pratt's Eastern Divide (general aviation)

**SHERMAN** (town). Covers a land area of 36.271 square miles and a water area of 0.129 square miles. Located at 42.13° N. Lat; 79.57° W. Long. Elevation is 1,539 feet.

**Population:** 1,505 (1990); 1,553 (2000); 1,653 (2010); Density: 45.6 persons per square mile (2010); Race: 97.6% White, 0.2% Black, 0.4% Asian, 0.1% American Indian/Alaska Native, 0.0% Native Hawaiian/Other

Pacific Islander, 1.7% Other, 1.6% Hispanic of any race (2010); Average household size: 3.01 (2010); Median age: 32.4 (2010); Males per 100 females: 100.1 (2010); Marriage status: 24.6% never married, 64.9% now married, 3.4% widowed, 7.1% divorced (2006-2010 5-year est.); Foreign born: 1.6% (2006-2010 5-year est.); Ancestry (includes multiple ancestries): 39.9% German, 11.8% Irish, 10.5% English, 9.0% Pennsylvania German, 7.6% Dutch (2006-2010 5-year est.).

**Economy:** Single-family building permits issued: 2 (2011); Multi-family building permits issued: 0 (2011); Employment by occupation: 8.5% management, 0.4% professional, 18.0% services, 9.3% sales, 1.2% farming, 27.7% construction, 12.9% production (2006-2010 5-year est.).

**Income:** Per capita income: $13,256 (2006-2010 5-year est.); Median household income: $34,674 (2006-2010 5-year est.); Average household income: $41,733 (2006-2010 5-year est.); Percent of households with income of $100,000 or more: 3.5% (2006-2010 5-year est.); Poverty rate: 26.5% (2006-2010 5-year est.).

**Education:** Percent of population age 25 and over with: High school diploma (including GED) or higher: 75.6% (2006-2010 5-year est.); Bachelor's degree or higher: 12.4% (2006-2010 5-year est.); Master's degree or higher: 4.2% (2006-2010 5-year est.).

**School District(s)**

Sherman Central School District (PK-12)

    2009-10 Enrollment: 480 . . . . . . . . . . . . . . . . . . . . . . . . . (716) 761-6122

**Housing:** Homeownership rate: 77.5% (2010); Median home value: $70,800 (2006-2010 5-year est.); Median contract rent: $377 per month (2006-2010 5-year est.); Median year structure built: before 1940 (2006-2010 5-year est.).

**Transportation:** Commute to work: 78.9% car, 1.7% public transportation, 11.7% walk, 6.8% work from home (2006-2010 5-year est.); Travel time to work: 31.4% less than 15 minutes, 36.2% 15 to 30 minutes, 24.3% 30 to 45 minutes, 2.8% 45 to 60 minutes, 5.2% 60 minutes or more (2006-2010 5-year est.)

**Airports:** Pratt's Eastern Divide (general aviation)

**SILVER CREEK** (village). Covers a land area of 1.160 square miles and a water area of 0 square miles. Located at 42.54° N. Lat; 79.16° W. Long. Elevation is 587 feet.

**History:** Annual grape festival held here in October. Incorporated 1848.

**Population:** 3,032 (1990); 2,896 (2000); 2,656 (2010); Density: 2,289.3 persons per square mile (2010); Race: 94.2% White, 0.9% Black, 0.5% Asian, 1.8% American Indian/Alaska Native, 0.0% Native Hawaiian/Other Pacific Islander, 2.6% Other, 2.8% Hispanic of any race (2010); Average household size: 2.51 (2010); Median age: 37.7 (2010); Males per 100 females: 95.9 (2010); Marriage status: 29.9% never married, 52.8% now married, 7.9% widowed, 9.4% divorced (2006-2010 5-year est.); Foreign born: 1.2% (2006-2010 5-year est.); Ancestry (includes multiple ancestries): 39.0% German, 20.5% Italian, 19.1% Irish, 13.9% English, 10.9% Polish (2006-2010 5-year est.).

**Economy:** Single-family building permits issued: 0 (2011); Multi-family building permits issued: 0 (2011); Employment by occupation: 8.7% management, 1.1% professional, 11.0% services, 12.9% sales, 0.5% farming, 8.3% construction, 14.1% production (2006-2010 5-year est.).

**Income:** Per capita income: $22,714 (2006-2010 5-year est.); Median household income: $44,911 (2006-2010 5-year est.); Average household income: $54,706 (2006-2010 5-year est.); Percent of households with income of $100,000 or more: 11.7% (2006-2010 5-year est.); Poverty rate: 16.5% (2006-2010 5-year est.).

**Education:** Percent of population age 25 and over with: High school diploma (including GED) or higher: 91.3% (2006-2010 5-year est.); Bachelor's degree or higher: 19.7% (2006-2010 5-year est.); Master's degree or higher: 9.3% (2006-2010 5-year est.).

**School District(s)**

Silver Creek Central School District (PK-12)

    2009-10 Enrollment: 1,114 . . . . . . . . . . . . . . . . . . . . . (716) 934-2603

**Housing:** Homeownership rate: 74.3% (2010); Median home value: $77,700 (2006-2010 5-year est.); Median contract rent: $488 per month (2006-2010 5-year est.); Median year structure built: before 1940 (2006-2010 5-year est.).

**Safety:** Violent crime rate: 21.8 per 10,000 population; Property crime rate: 119.7 per 10,000 population (2010).

**Newspapers:** Lakeshore Pennysaver (Community news; Circulation 5,384)

**Transportation:** Commute to work: 94.1% car, 0.7% public transportation, 4.4% walk, 0.8% work from home (2006-2010 5-year est.); Travel time to work: 36.0% less than 15 minutes, 38.1% 15 to 30 minutes, 14.4% 30 to 45

minutes, 5.5% 45 to 60 minutes, 6.0% 60 minutes or more (2006-2010 5-year est.)

**SINCLAIRVILLE** (village). Covers a land area of 1.612 square miles and a water area of 0 square miles. Located at 42.26° N. Lat; 79.25° W. Long. Elevation is 1,401 feet.
**Population:** 708 (1990); 665 (2000); 588 (2010); Density: 364.8 persons per square mile (2010); Race: 97.3% White, 0.0% Black, 0.5% Asian, 0.3% American Indian/Alaska Native, 0.0% Native Hawaiian/Other Pacific Islander, 1.9% Other, 2.0% Hispanic of any race (2010); Average household size: 2.31 (2010); Median age: 40.6 (2010); Males per 100 females: 102.1 (2010); Marriage status: 24.0% never married, 52.0% now married, 6.1% widowed, 17.9% divorced (2006-2010 5-year est.); Foreign born: 0.0% (2006-2010 5-year est.); Ancestry (includes multiple ancestries): 27.6% German, 25.7% English, 16.2% Irish, 13.8% Swedish, 13.0% Italian (2006-2010 5-year est.).
**Economy:** Single-family building permits issued: 1 (2011); Multi-family building permits issued: 0 (2011); Employment by occupation: 13.1% management, 4.1% professional, 22.1% services, 4.9% sales, 1.2% farming, 6.1% construction, 1.2% production (2006-2010 5-year est.).
**Income:** Per capita income: $18,547 (2006-2010 5-year est.); Median household income: $32,813 (2006-2010 5-year est.); Average household income: $43,112 (2006-2010 5-year est.); Percent of households with income of $100,000 or more: 4.8% (2006-2010 5-year est.); Poverty rate: 7.6% (2006-2010 5-year est.).
**Education:** Percent of population age 25 and over with: High school diploma (including GED) or higher: 90.1% (2006-2010 5-year est.); Bachelor's degree or higher: 16.7% (2006-2010 5-year est.); Master's degree or higher: 1.5% (2006-2010 5-year est.).
**School District(s)**
Cassadaga Valley Central School District (PK-12)
    2009-10 Enrollment: 1,201 . . . . . . . . . . . . . . . . . . . . . . . (716) 962-5155
**Housing:** Homeownership rate: 69.8% (2010); Median home value: $53,800 (2006-2010 5-year est.); Median contract rent: $393 per month (2006-2010 5-year est.); Median year structure built: before 1940 (2006-2010 5-year est.).
**Transportation:** Commute to work: 81.7% car, 0.0% public transportation, 1.7% walk, 4.6% work from home (2006-2010 5-year est.); Travel time to work: 23.0% less than 15 minutes, 49.1% 15 to 30 minutes, 22.2% 30 to 45 minutes, 3.0% 45 to 60 minutes, 2.6% 60 minutes or more (2006-2010 5-year est.)

**STOCKTON** (town). Covers a land area of 47.160 square miles and a water area of 0.488 square miles. Located at 42.29° N. Lat; 79.35° W. Long. Elevation is 1,325 feet.
**Population:** 2,515 (1990); 2,331 (2000); 2,248 (2010); Density: 47.7 persons per square mile (2010); Race: 97.5% White, 0.4% Black, 0.3% Asian, 0.1% American Indian/Alaska Native, 0.0% Native Hawaiian/Other Pacific Islander, 1.7% Other, 1.4% Hispanic of any race (2010); Average household size: 2.51 (2010); Median age: 42.2 (2010); Males per 100 females: 98.4 (2010); Marriage status: 22.3% never married, 64.5% now married, 4.9% widowed, 8.4% divorced (2006-2010 5-year est.); Foreign born: 0.5% (2006-2010 5-year est.); Ancestry (includes multiple ancestries): 29.4% German, 21.8% English, 15.9% Irish, 9.8% Italian, 8.8% Swedish (2006-2010 5-year est.).
**Economy:** Single-family building permits issued: 0 (2011); Multi-family building permits issued: 0 (2011); Employment by occupation: 9.7% management, 0.0% professional, 7.6% services, 17.9% sales, 3.1% farming, 9.5% construction, 5.6% production (2006-2010 5-year est.).
**Income:** Per capita income: $19,412 (2006-2010 5-year est.); Median household income: $43,667 (2006-2010 5-year est.); Average household income: $51,233 (2006-2010 5-year est.); Percent of households with income of $100,000 or more: 11.0% (2006-2010 5-year est.); Poverty rate: 21.7% (2006-2010 5-year est.).
**Education:** Percent of population age 25 and over with: High school diploma (including GED) or higher: 84.6% (2006-2010 5-year est.); Bachelor's degree or higher: 18.0% (2006-2010 5-year est.); Master's degree or higher: 6.7% (2006-2010 5-year est.).
**Housing:** Homeownership rate: 79.2% (2010); Median home value: $71,300 (2006-2010 5-year est.); Median contract rent: $436 per month (2006-2010 5-year est.); Median year structure built: 1957 (2006-2010 5-year est.).
**Transportation:** Commute to work: 92.7% car, 0.3% public transportation, 3.0% walk, 3.3% work from home (2006-2010 5-year est.); Travel time to work: 21.6% less than 15 minutes, 48.3% 15 to 30 minutes, 22.3% 30 to 45

minutes, 3.3% 45 to 60 minutes, 4.4% 60 minutes or more (2006-2010 5-year est.)

**SUNSET BAY** (CDP). Covers a land area of 0.660 square miles and a water area of 0.044 square miles. Located at 42.56° N. Lat; 79.12° W. Long. Elevation is 577 feet.
**Population:** n/a (1990); n/a (2000); 660 (2010); Density: 999.0 persons per square mile (2010); Race: 94.4% White, 2.0% Black, 0.2% Asian, 2.3% American Indian/Alaska Native, 0.0% Native Hawaiian/Other Pacific Islander, 1.1% Other, 1.8% Hispanic of any race (2010); Average household size: 2.13 (2010); Median age: 52.2 (2010); Males per 100 females: 91.9 (2010); Marriage status: 31.7% never married, 37.3% now married, 19.2% widowed, 11.8% divorced (2006-2010 5-year est.); Foreign born: 0.0% (2006-2010 5-year est.); Ancestry (includes multiple ancestries): 19.2% German, 15.9% Irish, 11.5% Italian, 11.2% Polish, 10.7% English (2006-2010 5-year est.).
**Economy:** Employment by occupation: 0.0% management, 0.0% professional, 12.0% services, 0.0% sales, 6.6% farming, 4.9% construction, 10.4% production (2006-2010 5-year est.).
**Income:** Per capita income: $25,540 (2006-2010 5-year est.); Median household income: $61,250 (2006-2010 5-year est.); Average household income: $74,279 (2006-2010 5-year est.); Percent of households with income of $100,000 or more: 23.3% (2006-2010 5-year est.); Poverty rate: 4.3% (2006-2010 5-year est.).
**Education:** Percent of population age 25 and over with: High school diploma (including GED) or higher: 69.3% (2006-2010 5-year est.); Bachelor's degree or higher: 13.4% (2006-2010 5-year est.); Master's degree or higher: 9.5% (2006-2010 5-year est.).
**Housing:** Homeownership rate: 77.8% (2010); Median home value: $110,000 (2006-2010 5-year est.); Median contract rent: n/a per month (2006-2010 5-year est.); Median year structure built: 1959 (2006-2010 5-year est.).
**Transportation:** Commute to work: 95.1% car, 0.0% public transportation, 0.0% walk, 4.9% work from home (2006-2010 5-year est.); Travel time to work: 19.0% less than 15 minutes, 50.0% 15 to 30 minutes, 19.5% 30 to 45 minutes, 0.0% 45 to 60 minutes, 11.5% 60 minutes or more (2006-2010 5-year est.)

**VILLENOVA** (town). Covers a land area of 36.092 square miles and a water area of 0.111 square miles. Located at 42.39° N. Lat; 79.11° W. Long.
**Population:** 1,065 (1990); 1,121 (2000); 1,110 (2010); Density: 30.8 persons per square mile (2010); Race: 96.7% White, 0.5% Black, 0.5% Asian, 1.0% American Indian/Alaska Native, 0.0% Native Hawaiian/Other Pacific Islander, 1.3% Other, 2.4% Hispanic of any race (2010); Average household size: 2.54 (2010); Median age: 42.4 (2010); Males per 100 females: 97.5 (2010); Marriage status: 24.8% never married, 62.6% now married, 5.6% widowed, 7.1% divorced (2006-2010 5-year est.); Foreign born: 0.9% (2006-2010 5-year est.); Ancestry (includes multiple ancestries): 42.7% German, 21.7% English, 14.2% Irish, 12.7% Polish, 11.5% Italian (2006-2010 5-year est.).
**Economy:** Single-family building permits issued: 0 (2011); Multi-family building permits issued: 0 (2011); Employment by occupation: 6.4% management, 2.3% professional, 14.9% services, 13.6% sales, 3.1% farming, 16.7% construction, 8.7% production (2006-2010 5-year est.).
**Income:** Per capita income: $19,970 (2006-2010 5-year est.); Median household income: $43,929 (2006-2010 5-year est.); Average household income: $48,324 (2006-2010 5-year est.); Percent of households with income of $100,000 or more: 8.0% (2006-2010 5-year est.); Poverty rate: 10.5% (2006-2010 5-year est.).
**Education:** Percent of population age 25 and over with: High school diploma (including GED) or higher: 88.4% (2006-2010 5-year est.); Bachelor's degree or higher: 10.2% (2006-2010 5-year est.); Master's degree or higher: 5.6% (2006-2010 5-year est.).
**Housing:** Homeownership rate: 85.2% (2010); Median home value: $80,000 (2006-2010 5-year est.); Median contract rent: $446 per month (2006-2010 5-year est.); Median year structure built: 1964 (2006-2010 5-year est.).
**Transportation:** Commute to work: 90.2% car, 0.4% public transportation, 2.4% walk, 6.4% work from home (2006-2010 5-year est.); Travel time to work: 20.4% less than 15 minutes, 33.9% 15 to 30 minutes, 26.0% 30 to 45 minutes, 8.4% 45 to 60 minutes, 11.4% 60 minutes or more (2006-2010 5-year est.)

**WESTFIELD** (village). Covers a land area of 3.822 square miles and a water area of 0 square miles. Located at 42.32° N. Lat; 79.57° W. Long. Elevation is 745 feet.

**Population:** 3,451 (1990); 3,481 (2000); 3,224 (2010); Density: 843.5 persons per square mile (2010); Race: 96.6% White, 0.5% Black, 0.5% Asian, 0.1% American Indian/Alaska Native, 0.0% Native Hawaiian/Other Pacific Islander, 2.3% Other, 3.9% Hispanic of any race (2010); Average household size: 2.34 (2010); Median age: 45.8 (2010); Males per 100 females: 89.3 (2010); Marriage status: 26.7% never married, 49.8% now married, 12.0% widowed, 11.5% divorced (2006-2010 5-year est.); Foreign born: 1.7% (2006-2010 5-year est.); Ancestry (includes multiple ancestries): 30.9% German, 16.9% English, 14.4% Irish, 13.5% Italian, 7.4% Swedish (2006-2010 5-year est.).

**Economy:** Single-family building permits issued: 0 (2011); Multi-family building permits issued: 0 (2011); Employment by occupation: 6.1% management, 1.0% professional, 11.6% services, 18.3% sales, 5.2% farming, 7.0% construction, 8.3% production (2006-2010 5-year est.).

**Income:** Per capita income: $22,316 (2006-2010 5-year est.); Median household income: $34,854 (2006-2010 5-year est.); Average household income: $48,636 (2006-2010 5-year est.); Percent of households with income of $100,000 or more: 9.3% (2006-2010 5-year est.); Poverty rate: 14.7% (2006-2010 5-year est.).

**Education:** Percent of population age 25 and over with: High school diploma (including GED) or higher: 87.2% (2006-2010 5-year est.); Bachelor's degree or higher: 26.2% (2006-2010 5-year est.); Master's degree or higher: 10.7% (2006-2010 5-year est.).

**School District(s)**
Westfield Central School District (KG-12)
   2009-10 Enrollment: 763 . . . . . . . . . . . . . . . . . . . . . . . . (716) 326-2151

**Housing:** Homeownership rate: 69.2% (2010); Median home value: $81,600 (2006-2010 5-year est.); Median contract rent: $476 per month (2006-2010 5-year est.); Median year structure built: before 1940 (2006-2010 5-year est.).

**Hospitals:** Westfield Memorial Hospital (32 beds)

**Safety:** Violent crime rate: 15.1 per 10,000 population; Property crime rate: 130.2 per 10,000 population (2010).

**Newspapers:** Mayville Sentinel (Community news; Circulation 500); West County Quality Guide (Community news; Circulation 10,100); Westfield Republican (Community news; Circulation 1,455)

**Transportation:** Commute to work: 83.2% car, 0.0% public transportation, 3.8% walk, 12.6% work from home (2006-2010 5-year est.); Travel time to work: 46.2% less than 15 minutes, 33.2% 15 to 30 minutes, 17.0% 30 to 45 minutes, 0.2% 45 to 60 minutes, 3.4% 60 minutes or more (2006-2010 5-year est.)

**Additional Information Contacts**
Chautauqua County Visitor's Bureau . . . . . . . . . . . . . . . . (866) 908-4569
   http://www.tourchautauqua.com

**WESTFIELD** (town). Covers a land area of 47.185 square miles and a water area of 0.065 square miles. Located at 42.26° N. Lat; 79.59° W. Long. Elevation is 745 feet.

**History:** In 1873 Thomas and Charles Bradwell Welch, ardent Prohibitionists, devised method of pressing Concord grapes into unfermented wine. Settled 1800, incorporated 1833.

**Population:** 5,194 (1990); 5,232 (2000); 4,896 (2010); Density: 103.8 persons per square mile (2010); Race: 97.1% White, 0.7% Black, 0.4% Asian, 0.1% American Indian/Alaska Native, 0.0% Native Hawaiian/Other Pacific Islander, 1.7% Other, 3.2% Hispanic of any race (2010); Average household size: 2.34 (2010); Median age: 46.6 (2010); Males per 100 females: 93.8 (2010); Marriage status: 24.2% never married, 54.2% now married, 11.7% widowed, 9.8% divorced (2006-2010 5-year est.); Foreign born: 1.2% (2006-2010 5-year est.); Ancestry (includes multiple ancestries): 35.1% German, 18.2% English, 15.3% Irish, 11.1% Italian, 6.5% Swedish (2006-2010 5-year est.).

**Economy:** Single-family building permits issued: 4 (2011); Multi-family building permits issued: 0 (2011); Employment by occupation: 8.2% management, 0.7% professional, 13.5% services, 19.4% sales, 3.7% farming, 10.6% construction, 9.0% production (2006-2010 5-year est.).

**Income:** Per capita income: $21,506 (2006-2010 5-year est.); Median household income: $34,365 (2006-2010 5-year est.); Average household income: $47,371 (2006-2010 5-year est.); Percent of households with income of $100,000 or more: 8.6% (2006-2010 5-year est.); Poverty rate: 13.3% (2006-2010 5-year est.).

**Education:** Percent of population age 25 and over with: High school diploma (including GED) or higher: 84.7% (2006-2010 5-year est.);

Bachelor's degree or higher: 24.7% (2006-2010 5-year est.); Master's degree or higher: 9.4% (2006-2010 5-year est.).

**School District(s)**
Westfield Central School District (KG-12)
   2009-10 Enrollment: 763 . . . . . . . . . . . . . . . . . . . . . . . . (716) 326-2151

**Housing:** Homeownership rate: 74.0% (2010); Median home value: $84,600 (2006-2010 5-year est.); Median contract rent: $482 per month (2006-2010 5-year est.); Median year structure built: before 1940 (2006-2010 5-year est.).

**Hospitals:** Westfield Memorial Hospital (32 beds)

**Newspapers:** Mayville Sentinel (Community news; Circulation 500); West County Quality Guide (Community news; Circulation 10,100); Westfield Republican (Community news; Circulation 1,455)

**Transportation:** Commute to work: 85.8% car, 0.0% public transportation, 3.7% walk, 10.2% work from home (2006-2010 5-year est.); Travel time to work: 46.6% less than 15 minutes, 29.0% 15 to 30 minutes, 19.9% 30 to 45 minutes, 0.5% 45 to 60 minutes, 4.0% 60 minutes or more (2006-2010 5-year est.).

# Chemung County

Located in southern New York; hilly area bounded on the south by Pennsylvania; cut by the Chemung River Valley. Covers a land area of 408.17 square miles, a water area of 2.62 square miles, and is located in the Eastern Time Zone at 42.12° N. Lat., 76.79° W. Long. The county was founded in 1836. County seat is Elmira.

Chemung County is part of the Elmira, NY Metropolitan Statistical Area. The entire metro area includes: Chemung County, NY

| Weather Station: Elmira | | | | | | | | | | Elevation: 844 feet | |
|---|---|---|---|---|---|---|---|---|---|---|---|
| | Jan | Feb | Mar | Apr | May | Jun | Jul | Aug | Sep | Oct | Nov | Dec |
| High | 33 | 36 | 44 | 58 | 70 | 78 | 82 | 81 | 73 | 61 | 49 | 37 |
| Low | 16 | 17 | 23 | 34 | 44 | 53 | 58 | 57 | 49 | 38 | 31 | 21 |
| Precip | 1.9 | 1.8 | 2.9 | 3.2 | 3.0 | 4.2 | 3.7 | 3.6 | 3.5 | 2.8 | 3.0 | 2.3 |
| Snow | 10.6 | 8.2 | 9.4 | 1.3 | 0.0 | 0.0 | 0.0 | 0.0 | 0.0 | 0.2 | 2.7 | 7.8 |

*High and Low temperatures in degrees Fahrenheit; Precipitation and Snow in inches*

**Population:** 95,195 (1990); 91,070 (2000); 88,830 (2010); Race: 88.7% White, 6.6% Black, 1.2% Asian, 0.3% American Indian/Alaska Native, 0.0% Native Hawaiian/Other Pacific Islander, 3.2% Other, 2.5% Hispanic of any race (2010); Density: 217.6 persons per square mile (2010); Average household size: 2.37 (2010); Median age: 40.9 (2010); Males per 100 females: 98.9 (2010).

**Religion:** Six largest groups: 16.4% Catholicism, 5.3% Methodist/Pietist, 2.4% Non-Denominational, 1.9% Holiness, 1.9% Baptist, 1.9% Muslim Estimate (2010)

**Economy:** Unemployment rate: 9.2% (February 2012); Total civilian labor force: 38,574 (February 2012); Leading industries: 21.7% health care and social assistance; 18.7% manufacturing; 16.8% retail trade (2009); Farms: 373 totaling 65,124 acres (2007); Companies that employ 500 or more persons: 5 (2009); Companies that employ 100 to 499 persons: 43 (2009); Companies that employ less than 100 persons: 1,821 (2009); Black-owned businesses: 196 (2007); Hispanic-owned businesses: n/a (2007); Asian-owned businesses: n/a (2007); Women-owned businesses: 2,033 (2007); Retail sales per capita: $14,719 (2010). Single-family building permits issued: 34 (2011); Multi-family building permits issued: 104 (2011).

**Income:** Per capita income: $23,457 (2006-2010 5-year est.); Median household income: $44,502 (2006-2010 5-year est.); Average household income: $57,869 (2006-2010 5-year est.); Percent of households with income of $100,000 or more: 14.1% (2006-2010 5-year est.); Poverty rate: 15.2% (2006-2010 5-year est.); Bankruptcy rate: 1.63% (2011).

**Taxes:** Total county taxes per capita: $937 (2009); County property taxes per capita: $311 (2009).

**Education:** Percent of population age 25 and over with: High school diploma (including GED) or higher: 87.6% (2006-2010 5-year est.); Bachelor's degree or higher: 20.9% (2006-2010 5-year est.); Master's degree or higher: 9.3% (2006-2010 5-year est.).

**Housing:** Homeownership rate: 67.7% (2010); Median home value: $85,900 (2006-2010 5-year est.); Median contract rent: $503 per month (2006-2010 5-year est.); Median year structure built: 1951 (2006-2010 5-year est.)

**Health:** Birth rate: 109.6 per 10,000 population (2011); Death rate: 106.0 per 10,000 population (2011); Age-adjusted cancer mortality rate: 213.2 deaths per 100,000 population (2009); Number of physicians: 25.4 per

10,000 population (2008); Hospital beds: 66.9 per 10,000 population (2007); Hospital admissions: 1,974.3 per 10,000 population (2007).
**Environment:** Air Quality Index: 93.4% good, 6.3% moderate, 0.3% unhealthy for sensitive individuals, 0.0% unhealthy (percent of days in 2010)
**Elections:** 2008 Presidential election results: 48.8% Obama, 50.0% McCain, 0.6% Nader
**Additional Information Contacts**
Chemung County Government . . . . . . . . . . . . . . . . . . . . . (607) 737-2920
  http://www.chemungcounty.com
Chemung County Chamber of Commerce. . . . . . . . . . . . . (607) 734-5137
  http://www.chemungchamber.org
City of Elmira . . . . . . . . . . . . . . . . . . . . . . . . . . . . . . . . (607) 737-5672
  http://www.cityofelmira.net
Town of Big Flats . . . . . . . . . . . . . . . . . . . . . . . . . . . . . (607) 562-8443
  http://www.bigflatsny.gov/pmwiki.php
Town of Chemung . . . . . . . . . . . . . . . . . . . . . . . . . . . . (607) 529-3532
  http://townofchemung.com
Town of Southport . . . . . . . . . . . . . . . . . . . . . . . . . . . . (607) 734-1548
  http://www.townofsouthport.com
Village of Horseheads . . . . . . . . . . . . . . . . . . . . . . . . . (607) 739-5691
  http://www.horseheads.org

## *Chemung County Communities*

**ASHLAND** (town). Covers a land area of 14.182 square miles and a water area of 0.354 square miles. Located at 42.01° N. Lat; 76.75° W. Long.
**Population:** 1,948 (1990); 1,951 (2000); 1,695 (2010); Density: 119.5 persons per square mile (2010); Race: 96.8% White, 0.6% Black, 0.3% Asian, 0.2% American Indian/Alaska Native, 0.0% Native Hawaiian/Other Pacific Islander, 2.1% Other, 1.4% Hispanic of any race (2010); Average household size: 2.38 (2010); Median age: 45.0 (2010); Males per 100 females: 98.9 (2010); Marriage status: 31.7% never married, 52.9% now married, 3.8% widowed, 11.6% divorced (2006-2010 5-year est.); Foreign born: 0.4% (2006-2010 5-year est.); Ancestry (includes multiple ancestries): 28.2% German, 24.1% Irish, 16.3% English, 11.6% Italian, 11.0% American (2006-2010 5-year est.).
**Economy:** Single-family building permits issued: 0 (2011); Multi-family building permits issued: 0 (2011); Employment by occupation: 7.8% management, 2.0% professional, 7.9% services, 18.6% sales, 2.4% farming, 15.0% construction, 11.7% production (2006-2010 5-year est.).
**Income:** Per capita income: $18,385 (2006-2010 5-year est.); Median household income: $41,125 (2006-2010 5-year est.); Average household income: $50,531 (2006-2010 5-year est.); Percent of households with income of $100,000 or more: 9.3% (2006-2010 5-year est.); Poverty rate: 8.2% (2006-2010 5-year est.).
**Education:** Percent of population age 25 and over with: High school diploma (including GED) or higher: 80.6% (2006-2010 5-year est.); Bachelor's degree or higher: 8.3% (2006-2010 5-year est.); Master's degree or higher: 3.3% (2006-2010 5-year est.).
**Housing:** Homeownership rate: 81.7% (2010); Median home value: $74,700 (2006-2010 5-year est.); Median contract rent: $342 per month (2006-2010 5-year est.); Median year structure built: 1962 (2006-2010 5-year est.).
**Transportation:** Commute to work: 94.1% car, 0.2% public transportation, 2.2% walk, 2.6% work from home (2006-2010 5-year est.); Travel time to work: 23.4% less than 15 minutes, 59.7% 15 to 30 minutes, 9.8% 30 to 45 minutes, 5.1% 45 to 60 minutes, 2.1% 60 minutes or more (2006-2010 5-year est.).

**BALDWIN** (town). Covers a land area of 25.716 square miles and a water area of 0.019 square miles. Located at 42.10° N. Lat; 76.65° W. Long.
**Population:** 829 (1990); 853 (2000); 832 (2010); Density: 32.4 persons per square mile (2010); Race: 95.8% White, 1.6% Black, 0.2% Asian, 0.4% American Indian/Alaska Native, 0.0% Native Hawaiian/Other Pacific Islander, 2.0% Other, 1.0% Hispanic of any race (2010); Average household size: 2.46 (2010); Median age: 44.8 (2010); Males per 100 females: 108.5 (2010); Marriage status: 24.7% never married, 54.9% now married, 6.3% widowed, 14.1% divorced (2006-2010 5-year est.); Foreign born: 3.7% (2006-2010 5-year est.); Ancestry (includes multiple ancestries): 21.0% Irish, 19.3% German, 15.7% English, 11.4% American, 9.5% Italian (2006-2010 5-year est.).

**Economy:** Single-family building permits issued: 0 (2011); Multi-family building permits issued: 0 (2011); Employment by occupation: 12.9% management, 4.3% professional, 10.8% services, 11.7% sales, 3.5% farming, 11.5% construction, 3.9% production (2006-2010 5-year est.).
**Income:** Per capita income: $22,958 (2006-2010 5-year est.); Median household income: $49,125 (2006-2010 5-year est.); Average household income: $57,189 (2006-2010 5-year est.); Percent of households with income of $100,000 or more: 11.3% (2006-2010 5-year est.); Poverty rate: 16.2% (2006-2010 5-year est.).
**Education:** Percent of population age 25 and over with: High school diploma (including GED) or higher: 86.0% (2006-2010 5-year est.); Bachelor's degree or higher: 10.5% (2006-2010 5-year est.); Master's degree or higher: 4.9% (2006-2010 5-year est.).
**Housing:** Homeownership rate: 87.0% (2010); Median home value: $86,400 (2006-2010 5-year est.); Median contract rent: $382 per month (2006-2010 5-year est.); Median year structure built: 1974 (2006-2010 5-year est.).
**Transportation:** Commute to work: 95.1% car, 0.0% public transportation, 1.1% walk, 1.7% work from home (2006-2010 5-year est.); Travel time to work: 13.1% less than 15 minutes, 51.1% 15 to 30 minutes, 25.4% 30 to 45 minutes, 2.6% 45 to 60 minutes, 7.8% 60 minutes or more (2006-2010 5-year est.)

**BIG FLATS** (town). Covers a land area of 44.484 square miles and a water area of 0.581 square miles. Located at 42.13° N. Lat; 76.91° W. Long. Elevation is 902 feet.
**Population:** 7,596 (1990); 7,224 (2000); 7,731 (2010); Density: 173.8 persons per square mile (2010); Race: 94.1% White, 1.7% Black, 2.7% Asian, 0.2% American Indian/Alaska Native, 0.0% Native Hawaiian/Other Pacific Islander, 1.3% Other, 1.3% Hispanic of any race (2010); Average household size: 2.50 (2010); Median age: 44.9 (2010); Males per 100 females: 97.9 (2010); Marriage status: 18.5% never married, 69.9% now married, 4.5% widowed, 7.1% divorced (2006-2010 5-year est.); Foreign born: 3.5% (2006-2010 5-year est.); Ancestry (includes multiple ancestries): 28.5% German, 18.2% Irish, 15.2% Italian, 14.0% English, 7.6% American (2006-2010 5-year est.).
**Economy:** Single-family building permits issued: 6 (2011); Multi-family building permits issued: 0 (2011); Employment by occupation: 16.1% management, 9.2% professional, 4.5% services, 14.4% sales, 4.0% farming, 3.9% construction, 3.7% production (2006-2010 5-year est.).
**Income:** Per capita income: $36,916 (2006-2010 5-year est.); Median household income: $71,291 (2006-2010 5-year est.); Average household income: $92,826 (2006-2010 5-year est.); Percent of households with income of $100,000 or more: 34.3% (2006-2010 5-year est.); Poverty rate: 6.0% (2006-2010 5-year est.).
**Education:** Percent of population age 25 and over with: High school diploma (including GED) or higher: 94.5% (2006-2010 5-year est.); Bachelor's degree or higher: 43.2% (2006-2010 5-year est.); Master's degree or higher: 19.4% (2006-2010 5-year est.).
**School District(s)**
Horseheads Central School District (PK-12)
  2009-10 Enrollment: 4,326 . . . . . . . . . . . . . . . . . . . . . (607) 739-5601
**Housing:** Homeownership rate: 82.8% (2010); Median home value: $137,000 (2006-2010 5-year est.); Median contract rent: $815 per month (2006-2010 5-year est.); Median year structure built: 1970 (2006-2010 5-year est.).
**Transportation:** Commute to work: 97.3% car, 0.0% public transportation, 0.0% walk, 1.2% work from home (2006-2010 5-year est.); Travel time to work: 31.4% less than 15 minutes, 51.1% 15 to 30 minutes, 9.1% 30 to 45 minutes, 2.6% 45 to 60 minutes, 5.7% 60 minutes or more (2006-2010 5-year est.)
**Additional Information Contacts**
Town of Big Flats . . . . . . . . . . . . . . . . . . . . . . . . . . . . . (607) 562-8443
  http://www.bigflatsny.gov/pmwiki.php

**BIG FLATS** (CDP). Covers a land area of 16.300 square miles and a water area of 0.077 square miles. Located at 42.16° N. Lat; 76.90° W. Long. Elevation is 902 feet.
**Population:** 2,658 (1990); 2,482 (2000); 5,277 (2010); Density: 323.7 persons per square mile (2010); Race: 94.1% White, 1.5% Black, 2.9% Asian, 0.2% American Indian/Alaska Native, 0.0% Native Hawaiian/Other Pacific Islander, 1.3% Other, 1.2% Hispanic of any race (2010); Average household size: 2.47 (2010); Median age: 45.7 (2010); Males per 100 females: 97.6 (2010); Marriage status: 17.4% never married, 73.2% now married, 2.9% widowed, 6.5% divorced (2006-2010 5-year est.); Foreign

born: 4.6% (2006-2010 5-year est.); Ancestry (includes multiple ancestries): 27.9% German, 18.5% Irish, 13.2% English, 12.3% Italian, 7.7% American (2006-2010 5-year est.).
**Economy:** Employment by occupation: 17.7% management, 5.8% professional, 4.5% services, 13.9% sales, 4.8% farming, 4.1% construction, 4.7% production (2006-2010 5-year est.).
**Income:** Per capita income: $38,132 (2006-2010 5-year est.); Median household income: $71,821 (2006-2010 5-year est.); Average household income: $98,290 (2006-2010 5-year est.); Percent of households with income of $100,000 or more: 35.4% (2006-2010 5-year est.); Poverty rate: 7.4% (2006-2010 5-year est.).
**Education:** Percent of population age 25 and over with: High school diploma (including GED) or higher: 94.2% (2006-2010 5-year est.); Bachelor's degree or higher: 41.7% (2006-2010 5-year est.); Master's degree or higher: 17.7% (2006-2010 5-year est.).

**School District(s)**
Horseheads Central School District (PK-12)
　2009-10 Enrollment: 4,326 . . . . . . . . . . . . . . . . . . . . (607) 739-5601
**Housing:** Homeownership rate: 81.4% (2010); Median home value: $140,800 (2006-2010 5-year est.); Median contract rent: $929 per month (2006-2010 5-year est.); Median year structure built: 1971 (2006-2010 5-year est.).
**Transportation:** Commute to work: 98.3% car, 0.0% public transportation, 0.0% walk, 1.1% work from home (2006-2010 5-year est.); Travel time to work: 34.4% less than 15 minutes, 47.0% 15 to 30 minutes, 10.5% 30 to 45 minutes, 3.7% 45 to 60 minutes, 4.4% 60 minutes or more (2006-2010 5-year est.)

**BREESPORT** (CDP). Covers a land area of 1.628 square miles and a water area of 0.012 square miles. Located at 42.18° N. Lat; 76.73° W. Long. Elevation is 1,099 feet.
**Population:** n/a (1990); n/a (2000); 626 (2010); Density: 384.4 persons per square mile (2010); Race: 97.3% White, 0.3% Black, 0.5% Asian, 1.0% American Indian/Alaska Native, 0.0% Native Hawaiian/Other Pacific Islander, 0.9% Other, 1.8% Hispanic of any race (2010); Average household size: 2.61 (2010); Median age: 44.7 (2010); Males per 100 females: 108.0 (2010); Marriage status: 21.8% never married, 72.0% now married, 2.4% widowed, 3.8% divorced (2006-2010 5-year est.); Foreign born: 0.0% (2006-2010 5-year est.); Ancestry (includes multiple ancestries): 40.1% German, 13.4% American, 13.4% English, 10.8% Scotch-Irish, 6.0% Polish (2006-2010 5-year est.).
**Economy:** Employment by occupation: 0.0% management, 4.1% professional, 5.9% services, 39.8% sales, 10.5% farming, 13.1% construction, 0.0% production (2006-2010 5-year est.).
**Income:** Per capita income: $25,193 (2006-2010 5-year est.); Median household income: $90,580 (2006-2010 5-year est.); Average household income: $78,209 (2006-2010 5-year est.); Percent of households with income of $100,000 or more: 0.0% (2006-2010 5-year est.); Poverty rate: 3.8% (2006-2010 5-year est.).
**Education:** Percent of population age 25 and over with: High school diploma (including GED) or higher: 95.8% (2006-2010 5-year est.); Bachelor's degree or higher: 3.2% (2006-2010 5-year est.); Master's degree or higher: 0.0% (2006-2010 5-year est.).
**Housing:** Homeownership rate: 89.1% (2010); Median home value: $86,900 (2006-2010 5-year est.); Median contract rent: n/a per month (2006-2010 5-year est.); Median year structure built: 1965 (2006-2010 5-year est.).
**Transportation:** Commute to work: 98.1% car, 0.0% public transportation, 0.0% walk, 0.0% work from home (2006-2010 5-year est.); Travel time to work: 53.4% less than 15 minutes, 14.7% 15 to 30 minutes, 11.0% 30 to 45 minutes, 7.2% 45 to 60 minutes, 13.7% 60 minutes or more (2006-2010 5-year est.)

**CATLIN** (town). Covers a land area of 37.988 square miles and a water area of 0.027 square miles. Located at 42.23° N. Lat; 76.89° W. Long.
**Population:** 2,626 (1990); 2,649 (2000); 2,618 (2010); Density: 68.9 persons per square mile (2010); Race: 97.6% White, 0.5% Black, 0.5% Asian, 0.3% American Indian/Alaska Native, 0.0% Native Hawaiian/Other Pacific Islander, 1.1% Other, 0.8% Hispanic of any race (2010); Average household size: 2.51 (2010); Median age: 41.9 (2010); Males per 100 females: 101.7 (2010); Marriage status: 21.7% never married, 60.8% now married, 5.5% widowed, 11.9% divorced (2006-2010 5-year est.); Foreign born: 0.9% (2006-2010 5-year est.); Ancestry (includes multiple ancestries): 19.9% German, 18.1% Irish, 12.1% English, 11.5% Italian, 10.4% American (2006-2010 5-year est.).

**Economy:** Single-family building permits issued: 2 (2011); Multi-family building permits issued: 0 (2011); Employment by occupation: 6.3% management, 3.7% professional, 12.1% services, 17.3% sales, 2.1% farming, 13.0% construction, 7.3% production (2006-2010 5-year est.).
**Income:** Per capita income: $26,299 (2006-2010 5-year est.); Median household income: $50,577 (2006-2010 5-year est.); Average household income: $65,782 (2006-2010 5-year est.); Percent of households with income of $100,000 or more: 15.0% (2006-2010 5-year est.); Poverty rate: 12.1% (2006-2010 5-year est.).
**Education:** Percent of population age 25 and over with: High school diploma (including GED) or higher: 86.6% (2006-2010 5-year est.); Bachelor's degree or higher: 11.6% (2006-2010 5-year est.); Master's degree or higher: 4.4% (2006-2010 5-year est.).
**Housing:** Homeownership rate: 82.9% (2010); Median home value: $81,300 (2006-2010 5-year est.); Median contract rent: $587 per month (2006-2010 5-year est.); Median year structure built: 1977 (2006-2010 5-year est.).
**Transportation:** Commute to work: 97.0% car, 0.0% public transportation, 0.5% walk, 2.0% work from home (2006-2010 5-year est.); Travel time to work: 22.8% less than 15 minutes, 50.2% 15 to 30 minutes, 19.2% 30 to 45 minutes, 4.2% 45 to 60 minutes, 3.5% 60 minutes or more (2006-2010 5-year est.)

**CHEMUNG** (town). Covers a land area of 49.479 square miles and a water area of 0.561 square miles. Located at 42.05° N. Lat; 76.60° W. Long. Elevation is 846 feet.
**Population:** 2,558 (1990); 2,665 (2000); 2,563 (2010); Density: 51.8 persons per square mile (2010); Race: 97.2% White, 0.4% Black, 0.2% Asian, 0.4% American Indian/Alaska Native, 0.0% Native Hawaiian/Other Pacific Islander, 1.8% Other, 1.7% Hispanic of any race (2010); Average household size: 2.57 (2010); Median age: 42.1 (2010); Males per 100 females: 98.8 (2010); Marriage status: 24.4% never married, 59.0% now married, 7.4% widowed, 9.3% divorced (2006-2010 5-year est.); Foreign born: 1.1% (2006-2010 5-year est.); Ancestry (includes multiple ancestries): 24.1% German, 15.0% Irish, 14.3% English, 11.2% American, 9.3% French (2006-2010 5-year est.).
**Economy:** Single-family building permits issued: 3 (2011); Multi-family building permits issued: 0 (2011); Employment by occupation: 5.8% management, 2.4% professional, 9.4% services, 19.7% sales, 0.4% farming, 19.0% construction, 15.3% production (2006-2010 5-year est.).
**Income:** Per capita income: $20,927 (2006-2010 5-year est.); Median household income: $49,500 (2006-2010 5-year est.); Average household income: $54,405 (2006-2010 5-year est.); Percent of households with income of $100,000 or more: 11.6% (2006-2010 5-year est.); Poverty rate: 16.3% (2006-2010 5-year est.).
**Education:** Percent of population age 25 and over with: High school diploma (including GED) or higher: 79.5% (2006-2010 5-year est.); Bachelor's degree or higher: 11.8% (2006-2010 5-year est.); Master's degree or higher: 5.8% (2006-2010 5-year est.).
**School District(s)**
Waverly Central School District (PK-12)
　2009-10 Enrollment: 1,724 . . . . . . . . . . . . . . . . . . . . (607) 565-2841
**Housing:** Homeownership rate: 83.3% (2010); Median home value: $80,900 (2006-2010 5-year est.); Median contract rent: $443 per month (2006-2010 5-year est.); Median year structure built: 1966 (2006-2010 5-year est.).
**Transportation:** Commute to work: 95.8% car, 0.0% public transportation, 1.3% walk, 2.3% work from home (2006-2010 5-year est.); Travel time to work: 35.1% less than 15 minutes, 39.4% 15 to 30 minutes, 15.6% 30 to 45 minutes, 4.7% 45 to 60 minutes, 5.1% 60 minutes or more (2006-2010 5-year est.)
**Additional Information Contacts**
Town of Chemung . . . . . . . . . . . . . . . . . . . . . . . . . . (607) 529-3532
　http://townofchemung.com

**ELMIRA** (city). County seat. Covers a land area of 7.248 square miles and a water area of 0.326 square miles. Located at 42.09° N. Lat; 76.80° W. Long. Elevation is 853 feet.
**History:** The Sullivan-Clinton Expedition entered the region of Elmira in 1779. Most of the early settlers were emigrants from Wyoming and Wilkes-Barre, Pennsylvania. In 1789 a famine struck the valley as the result of a frost. The only deaths that occurred resulted not from starvation but from overeating when food was finally obtained. The present name was adopted in 1828. According to local tradition, Nathan Teall, an early settler, had a daughter named Elmira, for whom her mother called in a shrill,

far-reaching voice. When it was decided to adopt a new name, several people suggested the one they had heard so often when Elmira was a child.
**Population:** 33,719 (1990); 30,940 (2000); 29,200 (2010); Density: 4,028.2 persons per square mile (2010); Race: 78.3% White, 14.6% Black, 0.6% Asian, 0.4% American Indian/Alaska Native, 0.0% Native Hawaiian/Other Pacific Islander, 6.1% Other, 4.3% Hispanic of any race (2010); Average household size: 2.34 (2010); Median age: 33.9 (2010); Males per 100 females: 102.4 (2010); Marriage status: 40.9% never married, 39.4% now married, 8.0% widowed, 11.7% divorced (2006-2010 5-year est.); Foreign born: 2.9% (2006-2010 5-year est.); Ancestry (includes multiple ancestries): 19.6% Irish, 16.6% German, 11.5% Italian, 9.5% English, 6.8% American (2006-2010 5-year est.).
**Economy:** Unemployment rate: 11.1% (February 2012); Total civilian labor force: 11,235 (February 2012); Single-family building permits issued: 0 (2011); Multi-family building permits issued: 0 (2011); Employment by occupation: 5.6% management, 2.1% professional, 16.0% services, 21.8% sales, 4.1% farming, 7.0% construction, 6.1% production (2006-2010 5-year est.).
**Income:** Per capita income: $17,399 (2006-2010 5-year est.); Median household income: $31,724 (2006-2010 5-year est.); Average household income: $44,261 (2006-2010 5-year est.); Percent of households with income of $100,000 or more: 7.4% (2006-2010 5-year est.); Poverty rate: 25.9% (2006-2010 5-year est.).
**Taxes:** Total city taxes per capita: $398 (2009); City property taxes per capita: $358 (2009).
**Education:** Percent of population age 25 and over with: High school diploma (including GED) or higher: 82.3% (2006-2010 5-year est.); Bachelor's degree or higher: 13.3% (2006-2010 5-year est.); Master's degree or higher: 5.6% (2006-2010 5-year est.).

**School District(s)**

Elmira City School District (PK-12)
    2009-10 Enrollment: 7,086 . . . . . . . . . . . . . . . . . . . . . (607) 735-3010

**Four-year College(s)**

Elmira College (Private, Not-for-profit)
    Fall 2010 Enrollment: 1,632 . . . . . . . . . . . . . . . . . . . (607) 735-1800
    2011-12 Tuition: In-state $36,950; Out-of-state $36,950

**Two-year College(s)**

Arnot Ogden Medical Center (Private, Not-for-profit)
    Fall 2010 Enrollment: 64 . . . . . . . . . . . . . . . . . . . . . (607) 737-4153
Elmira Business Institute (Private, For-profit)
    Fall 2010 Enrollment: 422 . . . . . . . . . . . . . . . . . . . . (607) 733-7177
    2011-12 Tuition: In-state $14,140; Out-of-state $14,140

**Vocational/Technical School(s)**

Schuyler-Steuben-Chemung-Tioga-Allegany BOCES (Public)
    Fall 2010 Enrollment: 119 . . . . . . . . . . . . . . . . . . . . (607) 739-3581
    2011-12 Tuition: $8,495
**Housing:** Homeownership rate: 48.0% (2010); Median home value: $65,300 (2006-2010 5-year est.); Median contract rent: $465 per month (2006-2010 5-year est.); Median year structure built: before 1940 (2006-2010 5-year est.).
**Hospitals:** Arnot Ogden Medical Center (256 beds); Arnot Ogden Medical Center (256 beds)
**Safety:** Violent crime rate: 37.5 per 10,000 population; Property crime rate: 366.7 per 10,000 population (2010).
**Newspapers:** Star-Gazette (Community news; Circulation 28,740)
**Transportation:** Commute to work: 84.3% car, 1.8% public transportation, 7.8% walk, 4.5% work from home (2006-2010 5-year est.); Travel time to work: 52.1% less than 15 minutes, 31.2% 15 to 30 minutes, 9.7% 30 to 45 minutes, 3.6% 45 to 60 minutes, 3.4% 60 minutes or more (2006-2010 5-year est.)
**Airports:** Elmira/Corning Regional (primary service)
**Additional Information Contacts**
Chemung County Chamber of Commerce. . . . . . . . . . . . . (607) 734-5137
    http://www.chemungchamber.org
City of Elmira . . . . . . . . . . . . . . . . . . . . . . . . . . . . . (607) 737-5672
    http://www.cityofelmira.net

**ELMIRA** (town). Covers a land area of 22.212 square miles and a water area of 0.328 square miles. Located at 42.09° N. Lat; 76.77° W. Long. Elevation is 853 feet.
**History:** Formerly Newtown, renamed for Elmira Teall, an innkeeper's daughter. The Treaty of Painted Post, ending warfare between settlers and the Iroquois confederation, was signed here in 1791. Site of a Confederate prison camp in 1864-1865 and 3,000 Confederate prisoners are buried

here. The well-known Elmira Correctional Facility (est. 1876) led the way in prison reform. Mark Twain spent many summers in Elmira and is buried here. Settled 1788, Incorporated 1864.
**Population:** 7,445 (1990); 7,199 (2000); 6,934 (2010); Density: 312.2 persons per square mile (2010); Race: 95.1% White, 1.8% Black, 1.2% Asian, 0.1% American Indian/Alaska Native, 0.0% Native Hawaiian/Other Pacific Islander, 1.8% Other, 1.1% Hispanic of any race (2010); Average household size: 2.31 (2010); Median age: 45.8 (2010); Males per 100 females: 90.0 (2010); Marriage status: 20.1% never married, 57.3% now married, 10.7% widowed, 12.0% divorced (2006-2010 5-year est.); Foreign born: 2.7% (2006-2010 5-year est.); Ancestry (includes multiple ancestries): 25.9% Irish, 23.6% German, 16.8% Italian, 15.7% English, 6.7% Polish (2006-2010 5-year est.).
**Economy:** Single-family building permits issued: 2 (2011); Multi-family building permits issued: 0 (2011); Employment by occupation: 16.3% management, 3.7% professional, 6.3% services, 13.0% sales, 1.7% farming, 4.7% construction, 2.9% production (2006-2010 5-year est.).
**Income:** Per capita income: $32,714 (2006-2010 5-year est.); Median household income: $56,117 (2006-2010 5-year est.); Average household income: $76,422 (2006-2010 5-year est.); Percent of households with income of $100,000 or more: 25.8% (2006-2010 5-year est.); Poverty rate: 10.7% (2006-2010 5-year est.).
**Education:** Percent of population age 25 and over with: High school diploma (including GED) or higher: 97.4% (2006-2010 5-year est.); Bachelor's degree or higher: 39.4% (2006-2010 5-year est.); Master's degree or higher: 20.5% (2006-2010 5-year est.).

**School District(s)**

Elmira City School District (PK-12)
    2009-10 Enrollment: 7,086 . . . . . . . . . . . . . . . . . . . . . (607) 735-3010

**Four-year College(s)**

Elmira College (Private, Not-for-profit)
    Fall 2010 Enrollment: 1,632 . . . . . . . . . . . . . . . . . . . (607) 735-1800
    2011-12 Tuition: In-state $36,950; Out-of-state $36,950

**Two-year College(s)**

Arnot Ogden Medical Center (Private, Not-for-profit)
    Fall 2010 Enrollment: 64 . . . . . . . . . . . . . . . . . . . . . (607) 737-4153
Elmira Business Institute (Private, For-profit)
    Fall 2010 Enrollment: 422 . . . . . . . . . . . . . . . . . . . . (607) 733-7177
    2011-12 Tuition: In-state $14,140; Out-of-state $14,140

**Vocational/Technical School(s)**

Schuyler-Steuben-Chemung-Tioga-Allegany BOCES (Public)
    Fall 2010 Enrollment: 119 . . . . . . . . . . . . . . . . . . . . (607) 739-3581
    2011-12 Tuition: $8,495
**Housing:** Homeownership rate: 83.5% (2010); Median home value: $111,300 (2006-2010 5-year est.); Median contract rent: $660 per month (2006-2010 5-year est.); Median year structure built: 1942 (2006-2010 5-year est.).
**Hospitals:** St. Joseph's Hospital (295 beds); St. Joseph's Hospital (295 beds)
**Safety:** Violent crime rate: 1.7 per 10,000 population; Property crime rate: 6.9 per 10,000 population (2010).
**Newspapers:** Star-Gazette (Community news; Circulation 28,740)
**Transportation:** Commute to work: 91.3% car, 0.8% public transportation, 3.2% walk, 3.0% work from home (2006-2010 5-year est.); Travel time to work: 49.8% less than 15 minutes, 35.0% 15 to 30 minutes, 11.4% 30 to 45 minutes, 0.3% 45 to 60 minutes, 3.5% 60 minutes or more (2006-2010 5-year est.)
**Airports:** Elmira/Corning Regional (primary service)

**ELMIRA HEIGHTS** (village). Covers a land area of 1.146 square miles and a water area of 0 square miles. Located at 42.12° N. Lat; 76.82° W. Long. Elevation is 879 feet.
**Population:** 4,359 (1990); 4,170 (2000); 4,097 (2010); Density: 3,573.7 persons per square mile (2010); Race: 94.1% White, 2.1% Black, 1.0% Asian, 0.2% American Indian/Alaska Native, 0.0% Native Hawaiian/Other Pacific Islander, 2.6% Other, 1.4% Hispanic of any race (2010); Average household size: 2.22 (2010); Median age: 39.6 (2010); Males per 100 females: 93.3 (2010); Marriage status: 33.4% never married, 41.4% now married, 9.4% widowed, 15.8% divorced (2006-2010 5-year est.); Foreign born: 1.7% (2006-2010 5-year est.); Ancestry (includes multiple ancestries): 24.3% Irish, 18.3% Italian, 17.8% German, 13.4% English, 9.7% Polish (2006-2010 5-year est.).
**Economy:** Single-family building permits issued: 0 (2011); Multi-family building permits issued: 0 (2011); Employment by occupation: 5.2%

management, 2.2% professional, 14.5% services, 18.1% sales, 3.1% farming, 4.3% construction, 6.0% production (2006-2010 5-year est.).
**Income:** Per capita income: $18,685 (2006-2010 5-year est.); Median household income: $31,500 (2006-2010 5-year est.); Average household income: $40,798 (2006-2010 5-year est.); Percent of households with income of $100,000 or more: 6.0% (2006-2010 5-year est.); Poverty rate: 19.3% (2006-2010 5-year est.).
**Education:** Percent of population age 25 and over with: High school diploma (including GED) or higher: 91.1% (2006-2010 5-year est.); Bachelor's degree or higher: 12.4% (2006-2010 5-year est.); Master's degree or higher: 4.2% (2006-2010 5-year est.).

**School District(s)**

Elmira Heights Central School District (PK-12)
    2009-10 Enrollment: 1,120 . . . . . . . . . . . . . . . . . . . (607) 734-7114
**Housing:** Homeownership rate: 52.2% (2010); Median home value: $70,900 (2006-2010 5-year est.); Median contract rent: $480 per month (2006-2010 5-year est.); Median year structure built: before 1940 (2006-2010 5-year est.).
**Safety:** Violent crime rate: 18.2 per 10,000 population; Property crime rate: 228.6 per 10,000 population (2010).
**Transportation:** Commute to work: 84.8% car, 5.0% public transportation, 7.7% walk, 2.4% work from home (2006-2010 5-year est.); Travel time to work: 58.8% less than 15 minutes, 29.7% 15 to 30 minutes, 4.6% 30 to 45 minutes, 3.5% 45 to 60 minutes, 3.5% 60 minutes or more (2006-2010 5-year est.)

**ERIN** (town). Covers a land area of 44.247 square miles and a water area of 0.220 square miles. Located at 42.18° N. Lat; 76.67° W. Long. Elevation is 1,263 feet.
**Population:** 2,002 (1990); 2,054 (2000); 1,962 (2010); Density: 44.3 persons per square mile (2010); Race: 96.8% White, 0.3% Black, 0.3% Asian, 0.2% American Indian/Alaska Native, 0.1% Native Hawaiian/Other Pacific Islander, 2.3% Other, 1.3% Hispanic of any race (2010); Average household size: 2.53 (2010); Median age: 43.7 (2010); Males per 100 females: 106.5 (2010); Marriage status: 23.6% never married, 61.1% now married, 5.1% widowed, 10.1% divorced (2006-2010 5-year est.); Foreign born: 0.9% (2006-2010 5-year est.); Ancestry (includes multiple ancestries): 17.3% German, 17.1% American, 14.2% Irish, 12.0% English, 10.6% Italian (2006-2010 5-year est.).
**Economy:** Single-family building permits issued: 4 (2011); Multi-family building permits issued: 0 (2011); Employment by occupation: 6.9% management, 2.5% professional, 8.5% services, 23.5% sales, 4.4% farming, 14.3% construction, 8.1% production (2006-2010 5-year est.).
**Income:** Per capita income: $21,189 (2006-2010 5-year est.); Median household income: $45,347 (2006-2010 5-year est.); Average household income: $53,120 (2006-2010 5-year est.); Percent of households with income of $100,000 or more: 12.2% (2006-2010 5-year est.); Poverty rate: 13.7% (2006-2010 5-year est.).
**Education:** Percent of population age 25 and over with: High school diploma (including GED) or higher: 83.1% (2006-2010 5-year est.); Bachelor's degree or higher: 9.5% (2006-2010 5-year est.); Master's degree or higher: 5.1% (2006-2010 5-year est.).
**Housing:** Homeownership rate: 90.6% (2010); Median home value: $77,000 (2006-2010 5-year est.); Median contract rent: $425 per month (2006-2010 5-year est.); Median year structure built: 1975 (2006-2010 5-year est.).
**Transportation:** Commute to work: 96.0% car, 0.7% public transportation, 0.7% walk, 2.3% work from home (2006-2010 5-year est.); Travel time to work: 12.1% less than 15 minutes, 59.0% 15 to 30 minutes, 18.2% 30 to 45 minutes, 6.0% 45 to 60 minutes, 4.7% 60 minutes or more (2006-2010 5-year est.)

**ERIN** (CDP). Covers a land area of 0.747 square miles and a water area of 0.009 square miles. Located at 42.18° N. Lat; 76.67° W. Long. Elevation is 1,263 feet.
**Population:** n/a (1990); n/a (2000); 483 (2010); Density: 646.3 persons per square mile (2010); Race: 97.3% White, 0.2% Black, 0.2% Asian, 0.2% American Indian/Alaska Native, 0.0% Native Hawaiian/Other Pacific Islander, 2.1% Other, 0.4% Hispanic of any race (2010); Average household size: 2.56 (2010); Median age: 39.5 (2010); Males per 100 females: 104.7 (2010); Marriage status: 34.3% never married, 53.6% now married, 5.8% widowed, 6.4% divorced (2006-2010 5-year est.); Foreign born: 1.3% (2006-2010 5-year est.); Ancestry (includes multiple ancestries): 19.1% German, 17.6% Irish, 14.2% American, 8.2% Italian, 7.7% English (2006-2010 5-year est.).

**Economy:** Employment by occupation: 1.2% management, 0.0% professional, 21.3% services, 19.5% sales, 4.3% farming, 18.9% construction, 10.4% production (2006-2010 5-year est.).
**Income:** Per capita income: $14,121 (2006-2010 5-year est.); Median household income: $34,643 (2006-2010 5-year est.); Average household income: $35,936 (2006-2010 5-year est.); Percent of households with income of $100,000 or more: 3.8% (2006-2010 5-year est.); Poverty rate: 20.2% (2006-2010 5-year est.).
**Education:** Percent of population age 25 and over with: High school diploma (including GED) or higher: 83.5% (2006-2010 5-year est.); Bachelor's degree or higher: 7.4% (2006-2010 5-year est.); Master's degree or higher: 1.1% (2006-2010 5-year est.).
**Housing:** Homeownership rate: 89.4% (2010); Median home value: $27,100 (2006-2010 5-year est.); Median contract rent: $400 per month (2006-2010 5-year est.); Median year structure built: 1978 (2006-2010 5-year est.).
**Transportation:** Commute to work: 100.0% car, 0.0% public transportation, 0.0% walk, 0.0% work from home (2006-2010 5-year est.); Travel time to work: 18.0% less than 15 minutes, 44.1% 15 to 30 minutes, 16.8% 30 to 45 minutes, 12.4% 45 to 60 minutes, 8.7% 60 minutes or more (2006-2010 5-year est.)

**HORSEHEADS** (village). Covers a land area of 3.887 square miles and a water area of 0.014 square miles. Located at 42.16° N. Lat; 76.82° W. Long. Elevation is 896 feet.
**Population:** 6,802 (1990); 6,452 (2000); 6,461 (2010); Density: 1,662.2 persons per square mile (2010); Race: 93.9% White, 1.9% Black, 2.3% Asian, 0.2% American Indian/Alaska Native, 0.0% Native Hawaiian/Other Pacific Islander, 1.7% Other, 1.6% Hispanic of any race (2010); Average household size: 2.08 (2010); Median age: 45.5 (2010); Males per 100 females: 82.8 (2010); Marriage status: 22.4% never married, 52.8% now married, 13.0% widowed, 11.8% divorced (2006-2010 5-year est.); Foreign born: 2.1% (2006-2010 5-year est.); Ancestry (includes multiple ancestries): 23.2% German, 20.2% Irish, 17.3% English, 8.7% Polish, 8.3% American (2006-2010 5-year est.).
**Economy:** Single-family building permits issued: 4 (2011); Multi-family building permits issued: 96 (2011); Employment by occupation: 13.8% management, 5.3% professional, 11.2% services, 19.3% sales, 2.4% farming, 5.6% construction, 6.7% production (2006-2010 5-year est.).
**Income:** Per capita income: $26,552 (2006-2010 5-year est.); Median household income: $41,319 (2006-2010 5-year est.); Average household income: $55,508 (2006-2010 5-year est.); Percent of households with income of $100,000 or more: 9.3% (2006-2010 5-year est.); Poverty rate: 4.5% (2006-2010 5-year est.).
**Education:** Percent of population age 25 and over with: High school diploma (including GED) or higher: 90.8% (2006-2010 5-year est.); Bachelor's degree or higher: 23.8% (2006-2010 5-year est.); Master's degree or higher: 9.1% (2006-2010 5-year est.).

**School District(s)**

Horseheads Central School District (PK-12)
    2009-10 Enrollment: 4,326 . . . . . . . . . . . . . . . . . . . (607) 739-5601
**Housing:** Homeownership rate: 61.0% (2010); Median home value: $88,900 (2006-2010 5-year est.); Median contract rent: $533 per month (2006-2010 5-year est.); Median year structure built: 1955 (2006-2010 5-year est.).
**Safety:** Violent crime rate: 19.4 per 10,000 population; Property crime rate: 234.1 per 10,000 population (2010).
**Newspapers:** Chemung Valley Reporter (Community news; Circulation 1,500)
**Transportation:** Commute to work: 94.6% car, 0.4% public transportation, 2.0% walk, 1.8% work from home (2006-2010 5-year est.); Travel time to work: 54.6% less than 15 minutes, 31.3% 15 to 30 minutes, 5.6% 30 to 45 minutes, 5.1% 45 to 60 minutes, 3.3% 60 minutes or more (2006-2010 5-year est.)

**Additional Information Contacts**

Village of Horseheads . . . . . . . . . . . . . . . . . . . . . . . . (607) 739-5691
http://www.horseheads.org

**HORSEHEADS** (town). Covers a land area of 35.606 square miles and a water area of 0.313 square miles. Located at 42.15° N. Lat; 76.77° W. Long. Elevation is 896 feet.
**History:** Settled 1789, incorporated 1837.
**Population:** 19,926 (1990); 19,561 (2000); 19,485 (2010); Density: 547.2 persons per square mile (2010); Race: 93.4% White, 2.0% Black, 2.5% Asian, 0.2% American Indian/Alaska Native, 0.0% Native Hawaiian/Other

Pacific Islander, 1.9% Other, 1.7% Hispanic of any race (2010); Average household size: 2.29 (2010); Median age: 43.6 (2010); Males per 100 females: 90.3 (2010); Marriage status: 24.2% never married, 55.0% now married, 10.1% widowed, 10.7% divorced (2006-2010 5-year est.); Foreign born: 2.9% (2006-2010 5-year est.); Ancestry (includes multiple ancestries): 22.2% German, 20.2% Irish, 17.1% English, 10.2% Italian, 9.2% Polish (2006-2010 5-year est.).

**Economy:** Single-family building permits issued: 8 (2011); Multi-family building permits issued: 8 (2011); Employment by occupation: 11.8% management, 4.5% professional, 11.6% services, 18.7% sales, 3.7% farming, 4.9% construction, 4.2% production (2006-2010 5-year est.).

**Income:** Per capita income: $25,646 (2006-2010 5-year est.); Median household income: $46,259 (2006-2010 5-year est.); Average household income: $58,568 (2006-2010 5-year est.); Percent of households with income of $100,000 or more: 13.3% (2006-2010 5-year est.); Poverty rate: 11.0% (2006-2010 5-year est.).

**Education:** Percent of population age 25 and over with: High school diploma (including GED) or higher: 91.6% (2006-2010 5-year est.); Bachelor's degree or higher: 24.0% (2006-2010 5-year est.); Master's degree or higher: 8.8% (2006-2010 5-year est.).

**School District(s)**
Horseheads Central School District (PK-12)
    2009-10 Enrollment: 4,326 . . . . . . . . . . . . . . . . . . . . . . . . (607) 739-5601
**Housing:** Homeownership rate: 66.9% (2010); Median home value: $94,600 (2006-2010 5-year est.); Median contract rent: $528 per month (2006-2010 5-year est.); Median year structure built: 1957 (2006-2010 5-year est.).
**Newspapers:** Chemung Valley Reporter (Community news; Circulation 1,500)
**Transportation:** Commute to work: 92.5% car, 1.3% public transportation, 3.0% walk, 2.5% work from home (2006-2010 5-year est.); Travel time to work: 51.6% less than 15 minutes, 30.9% 15 to 30 minutes, 8.8% 30 to 45 minutes, 4.6% 45 to 60 minutes, 4.0% 60 minutes or more (2006-2010 5-year est.)

**HORSEHEADS NORTH** (CDP). Covers a land area of 2.211 square miles and a water area of 0.028 square miles. Located at 42.19° N. Lat; 76.80° W. Long.
**Population:** 3,003 (1990); 2,852 (2000); 2,843 (2010); Density: 1,285.6 persons per square mile (2010); Race: 95.0% White, 1.7% Black, 1.7% Asian, 0.1% American Indian/Alaska Native, 0.0% Native Hawaiian/Other Pacific Islander, 1.5% Other, 1.5% Hispanic of any race (2010); Average household size: 2.50 (2010); Median age: 42.0 (2010); Males per 100 females: 89.3 (2010); Marriage status: 27.0% never married, 60.5% now married, 5.5% widowed, 7.1% divorced (2006-2010 5-year est.); Foreign born: 7.0% (2006-2010 5-year est.); Ancestry (includes multiple ancestries): 22.7% German, 17.9% Polish, 17.1% English, 15.2% Irish, 14.6% Italian (2006-2010 5-year est.).
**Economy:** Employment by occupation: 17.8% management, 5.1% professional, 8.6% services, 13.2% sales, 5.1% farming, 2.0% construction, 1.4% production (2006-2010 5-year est.).
**Income:** Per capita income: $30,440 (2006-2010 5-year est.); Median household income: $69,934 (2006-2010 5-year est.); Average household income: $76,688 (2006-2010 5-year est.); Percent of households with income of $100,000 or more: 24.7% (2006-2010 5-year est.); Poverty rate: 11.1% (2006-2010 5-year est.).
**Education:** Percent of population age 25 and over with: High school diploma (including GED) or higher: 97.3% (2006-2010 5-year est.); Bachelor's degree or higher: 35.5% (2006-2010 5-year est.); Master's degree or higher: 9.9% (2006-2010 5-year est.).
**Housing:** Homeownership rate: 76.0% (2010); Median home value: $129,900 (2006-2010 5-year est.); Median contract rent: $612 per month (2006-2010 5-year est.); Median year structure built: 1967 (2006-2010 5-year est.).
**Transportation:** Commute to work: 93.9% car, 0.0% public transportation, 0.7% walk, 5.4% work from home (2006-2010 5-year est.); Travel time to work: 37.2% less than 15 minutes, 43.1% 15 to 30 minutes, 16.4% 30 to 45 minutes, 2.6% 45 to 60 minutes, 0.7% 60 minutes or more (2006-2010 5-year est.)

**LOWMAN** (unincorporated postal area)
Zip Code: 14861
    Covers a land area of 34.222 square miles and a water area of 0.260 square miles. Located at 42.08° N. Lat; 76.68° W. Long. Elevation is 840 feet. Population: 1,404 (2010); Density: 41.0 persons per square mile

(2010); Race: 97.0% White, 0.8% Black, 0.1% Asian, 0.1% American Indian/Alaska Native, 0.0% Native Hawaiian/Other Pacific Islander, 2.0% Other, 1.1% Hispanic of any race (2010); Average household size: 2.45 (2010); Median age: 44.6 (2010); Males per 100 females: 100.6 (2010); Homeownership rate: 86.3% (2010)

**MILLPORT** (village). Covers a land area of 0.348 square miles and a water area of 0 square miles. Located at 42.26° N. Lat; 76.83° W. Long. Elevation is 719 feet.
**Population:** 342 (1990); 297 (2000); 312 (2010); Density: 896.5 persons per square mile (2010); Race: 96.2% White, 0.3% Black, 0.0% Asian, 1.3% American Indian/Alaska Native, 0.0% Native Hawaiian/Other Pacific Islander, 2.2% Other, 1.0% Hispanic of any race (2010); Average household size: 2.54 (2010); Median age: 39.8 (2010); Males per 100 females: 98.7 (2010); Marriage status: 32.8% never married, 47.8% now married, 2.2% widowed, 17.2% divorced (2006-2010 5-year est.); Foreign born: 0.0% (2006-2010 5-year est.); Ancestry (includes multiple ancestries): 33.7% Irish, 19.0% German, 15.9% American, 14.9% Italian, 13.4% Dutch (2006-2010 5-year est.).
**Economy:** Single-family building permits issued: 0 (2011); Multi-family building permits issued: 0 (2011); Employment by occupation: 9.6% management, 1.8% professional, 14.5% services, 12.0% sales, 5.4% farming, 12.0% construction, 9.6% production (2006-2010 5-year est.).
**Income:** Per capita income: $17,504 (2006-2010 5-year est.); Median household income: $33,750 (2006-2010 5-year est.); Average household income: $41,446 (2006-2010 5-year est.); Percent of households with income of $100,000 or more: 7.2% (2006-2010 5-year est.); Poverty rate: 22.0% (2006-2010 5-year est.).
**Education:** Percent of population age 25 and over with: High school diploma (including GED) or higher: 85.2% (2006-2010 5-year est.); Bachelor's degree or higher: 6.4% (2006-2010 5-year est.); Master's degree or higher: 1.5% (2006-2010 5-year est.).
**Housing:** Homeownership rate: 78.1% (2010); Median home value: $52,500 (2006-2010 5-year est.); Median contract rent: $538 per month (2006-2010 5-year est.); Median year structure built: before 1940 (2006-2010 5-year est.).
**Transportation:** Commute to work: 92.9% car, 0.0% public transportation, 0.0% walk, 7.1% work from home (2006-2010 5-year est.); Travel time to work: 20.8% less than 15 minutes, 56.9% 15 to 30 minutes, 11.1% 30 to 45 minutes, 11.1% 45 to 60 minutes, 0.0% 60 minutes or more (2006-2010 5-year est.)

**PINE CITY** (unincorporated postal area)
Zip Code: 14871
    Covers a land area of 57.174 square miles and a water area of 0.499 square miles. Located at 42.03° N. Lat; 76.91° W. Long. Elevation is 1,001 feet. Population: 5,456 (2010); Density: 95.4 persons per square mile (2010); Race: 85.1% White, 11.7% Black, 0.6% Asian, 0.1% American Indian/Alaska Native, 0.0% Native Hawaiian/Other Pacific Islander, 2.5% Other, 3.8% Hispanic of any race (2010); Average household size: 2.49 (2010); Median age: 43.0 (2010); Males per 100 females: 131.8 (2010); Homeownership rate: 89.2% (2010)

**PINE VALLEY** (CDP). Covers a land area of 1.204 square miles and a water area of 0.013 square miles. Located at 42.23° N. Lat; 76.84° W. Long. Elevation is 932 feet.
**Population:** n/a (1990); n/a (2000); 813 (2010); Density: 675.1 persons per square mile (2010); Race: 96.3% White, 0.6% Black, 0.7% Asian, 0.0% American Indian/Alaska Native, 0.0% Native Hawaiian/Other Pacific Islander, 2.4% Other, 2.0% Hispanic of any race (2010); Average household size: 2.26 (2010); Median age: 42.2 (2010); Males per 100 females: 96.9 (2010); Marriage status: 26.2% never married, 45.9% now married, 8.2% widowed, 19.7% divorced (2006-2010 5-year est.); Foreign born: 2.3% (2006-2010 5-year est.); Ancestry (includes multiple ancestries): 22.7% Irish, 13.4% Italian, 11.6% English, 8.1% German, 6.9% American (2006-2010 5-year est.).
**Economy:** Employment by occupation: 8.0% management, 0.0% professional, 17.2% services, 18.0% sales, 4.3% farming, 4.6% construction, 13.1% production (2006-2010 5-year est.).
**Income:** Per capita income: $19,586 (2006-2010 5-year est.); Median household income: $34,821 (2006-2010 5-year est.); Average household income: $44,211 (2006-2010 5-year est.); Percent of households with income of $100,000 or more: 0.0% (2006-2010 5-year est.); Poverty rate: 14.2% (2006-2010 5-year est.).

**Education:** Percent of population age 25 and over with: High school diploma (including GED) or higher: 79.4% (2006-2010 5-year est.); Bachelor's degree or higher: 10.1% (2006-2010 5-year est.); Master's degree or higher: 2.6% (2006-2010 5-year est.).
**Housing:** Homeownership rate: 71.9% (2010); Median home value: $63,900 (2006-2010 5-year est.); Median contract rent: $528 per month (2006-2010 5-year est.); Median year structure built: 1970 (2006-2010 5-year est.).
**Transportation:** Commute to work: 86.7% car, 0.0% public transportation, 2.0% walk, 9.5% work from home (2006-2010 5-year est.); Travel time to work: 19.4% less than 15 minutes, 36.9% 15 to 30 minutes, 31.5% 30 to 45 minutes, 3.2% 45 to 60 minutes, 8.9% 60 minutes or more (2006-2010 5-year est.)

## SOUTHPORT (town).
Covers a land area of 46.413 square miles and a water area of 0.426 square miles. Located at 42.04° N. Lat; 76.87° W. Long. Elevation is 889 feet.
**Population:** 11,571 (1990); 11,185 (2000); 10,940 (2010); Density: 235.7 persons per square mile (2010); Race: 89.1% White, 7.6% Black, 0.6% Asian, 0.2% American Indian/Alaska Native, 0.0% Native Hawaiian/Other Pacific Islander, 2.5% Other, 2.8% Hispanic of any race (2010); Average household size: 2.34 (2010); Median age: 42.8 (2010); Males per 100 females: 111.5 (2010); Marriage status: 29.5% never married, 54.6% now married, 7.0% widowed, 8.9% divorced (2006-2010 5-year est.); Foreign born: 1.3% (2006-2010 5-year est.); Ancestry (includes multiple ancestries): 20.9% Irish, 20.3% German, 19.6% English, 8.4% American, 7.6% Italian (2006-2010 5-year est.).
**Economy:** Single-family building permits issued: 4 (2011); Multi-family building permits issued: 0 (2011); Employment by occupation: 5.4% management, 2.7% professional, 7.9% services, 23.8% sales, 4.2% farming, 8.5% construction, 5.0% production (2006-2010 5-year est.).
**Income:** Per capita income: $21,353 (2006-2010 5-year est.); Median household income: $43,923 (2006-2010 5-year est.); Average household income: $54,926 (2006-2010 5-year est.); Percent of households with income of $100,000 or more: 13.7% (2006-2010 5-year est.); Poverty rate: 11.3% (2006-2010 5-year est.).
**Education:** Percent of population age 25 and over with: High school diploma (including GED) or higher: 85.6% (2006-2010 5-year est.); Bachelor's degree or higher: 16.4% (2006-2010 5-year est.); Master's degree or higher: 9.2% (2006-2010 5-year est.).
**Housing:** Homeownership rate: 75.3% (2010); Median home value: $80,300 (2006-2010 5-year est.); Median contract rent: $514 per month (2006-2010 5-year est.); Median year structure built: 1950 (2006-2010 5-year est.).
**Transportation:** Commute to work: 90.9% car, 2.3% public transportation, 2.6% walk, 2.4% work from home (2006-2010 5-year est.); Travel time to work: 38.0% less than 15 minutes, 40.7% 15 to 30 minutes, 10.5% 30 to 45 minutes, 3.1% 45 to 60 minutes, 7.7% 60 minutes or more (2006-2010 5-year est.)
**Additional Information Contacts**
Town of Southport . . . . . . . . . . . . . . . . . . . . . . . . . . . . . (607) 734-1548
  http://www.townofsouthport.com

## SOUTHPORT (CDP).
Covers a land area of 6.376 square miles and a water area of 0.238 square miles. Located at 42.06° N. Lat; 76.82° W. Long. Elevation is 889 feet.
**Population:** 7,857 (1990); 7,396 (2000); 7,238 (2010); Density: 1,135.1 persons per square mile (2010); Race: 94.3% White, 2.7% Black, 0.5% Asian, 0.3% American Indian/Alaska Native, 0.0% Native Hawaiian/Other Pacific Islander, 2.2% Other, 1.7% Hispanic of any race (2010); Average household size: 2.27 (2010); Median age: 43.7 (2010); Males per 100 females: 93.4 (2010); Marriage status: 27.8% never married, 54.9% now married, 7.4% widowed, 9.9% divorced (2006-2010 5-year est.); Foreign born: 0.9% (2006-2010 5-year est.); Ancestry (includes multiple ancestries): 23.8% Irish, 22.1% English, 19.8% German, 9.4% American, 8.4% Polish (2006-2010 5-year est.).
**Economy:** Employment by occupation: 3.2% management, 3.5% professional, 8.0% services, 26.1% sales, 3.1% farming, 8.0% construction, 6.0% production (2006-2010 5-year est.).
**Income:** Per capita income: $20,461 (2006-2010 5-year est.); Median household income: $38,852 (2006-2010 5-year est.); Average household income: $48,549 (2006-2010 5-year est.); Percent of households with income of $100,000 or more: 10.1% (2006-2010 5-year est.); Poverty rate: 14.1% (2006-2010 5-year est.).

**Education:** Percent of population age 25 and over with: High school diploma (including GED) or higher: 87.5% (2006-2010 5-year est.); Bachelor's degree or higher: 15.3% (2006-2010 5-year est.); Master's degree or higher: 8.5% (2006-2010 5-year est.).
**Housing:** Homeownership rate: 69.8% (2010); Median home value: $73,200 (2006-2010 5-year est.); Median contract rent: $512 per month (2006-2010 5-year est.); Median year structure built: 1949 (2006-2010 5-year est.).
**Transportation:** Commute to work: 89.7% car, 2.8% public transportation, 2.6% walk, 2.5% work from home (2006-2010 5-year est.); Travel time to work: 40.4% less than 15 minutes, 35.9% 15 to 30 minutes, 11.7% 30 to 45 minutes, 3.6% 45 to 60 minutes, 8.4% 60 minutes or more (2006-2010 5-year est.)

## VAN ETTEN (village).
Covers a land area of 0.869 square miles and a water area of <.001 square miles. Located at 42.19° N. Lat; 76.55° W. Long. Elevation is 1,017 feet.
**Population:** 552 (1990); 581 (2000); 537 (2010); Density: 617.7 persons per square mile (2010); Race: 96.6% White, 0.4% Black, 0.0% Asian, 0.2% American Indian/Alaska Native, 0.0% Native Hawaiian/Other Pacific Islander, 2.8% Other, 1.9% Hispanic of any race (2010); Average household size: 2.47 (2010); Median age: 36.2 (2010); Males per 100 females: 96.7 (2010); Marriage status: 32.9% never married, 38.7% now married, 6.1% widowed, 22.3% divorced (2006-2010 5-year est.); Foreign born: 0.0% (2006-2010 5-year est.); Ancestry (includes multiple ancestries): 25.0% German, 20.5% Irish, 15.4% English, 10.7% Dutch, 8.7% Finnish (2006-2010 5-year est.).
**Economy:** Employment by occupation: 16.6% management, 3.6% professional, 7.6% services, 8.1% sales, 2.7% farming, 8.5% construction, 15.2% production (2006-2010 5-year est.).
**Income:** Per capita income: $23,826 (2006-2010 5-year est.); Median household income: $44,615 (2006-2010 5-year est.); Average household income: $51,800 (2006-2010 5-year est.); Percent of households with income of $100,000 or more: 9.4% (2006-2010 5-year est.); Poverty rate: 17.2% (2006-2010 5-year est.).
**Education:** Percent of population age 25 and over with: High school diploma (including GED) or higher: 86.5% (2006-2010 5-year est.); Bachelor's degree or higher: 19.9% (2006-2010 5-year est.); Master's degree or higher: 6.7% (2006-2010 5-year est.).
**School District(s)**
Spencer-Van Etten Central School District (PK-12)
    2009-10 Enrollment: 1,019 . . . . . . . . . . . . . . . . . . . (607) 589-7100
**Housing:** Homeownership rate: 65.9% (2010); Median home value: $86,000 (2006-2010 5-year est.); Median contract rent: $466 per month (2006-2010 5-year est.); Median year structure built: 1955 (2006-2010 5-year est.).
**Transportation:** Commute to work: 87.9% car, 1.3% public transportation, 8.5% walk, 0.9% work from home (2006-2010 5-year est.); Travel time to work: 27.1% less than 15 minutes, 13.1% 15 to 30 minutes, 38.5% 30 to 45 minutes, 17.6% 45 to 60 minutes, 3.6% 60 minutes or more (2006-2010 5-year est.)

## VAN ETTEN (town).
Covers a land area of 41.445 square miles and a water area of 0.123 square miles. Located at 42.23° N. Lat; 76.57° W. Long. Elevation is 1,017 feet.
**Population:** 1,507 (1990); 1,518 (2000); 1,557 (2010); Density: 37.6 persons per square mile (2010); Race: 96.7% White, 0.4% Black, 0.1% Asian, 0.1% American Indian/Alaska Native, 0.0% Native Hawaiian/Other Pacific Islander, 2.7% Other, 1.8% Hispanic of any race (2010); Average household size: 2.49 (2010); Median age: 41.3 (2010); Males per 100 females: 99.4 (2010); Marriage status: 29.1% never married, 52.5% now married, 4.6% widowed, 13.8% divorced (2006-2010 5-year est.); Foreign born: 1.4% (2006-2010 5-year est.); Ancestry (includes multiple ancestries): 19.8% German, 17.4% Irish, 16.1% English, 11.4% Dutch, 8.8% American (2006-2010 5-year est.).
**Economy:** Single-family building permits issued: 0 (2011); Multi-family building permits issued: 0 (2011); Employment by occupation: 8.8% management, 3.6% professional, 11.3% services, 10.0% sales, 2.9% farming, 17.4% construction, 11.5% production (2006-2010 5-year est.).
**Income:** Per capita income: $20,634 (2006-2010 5-year est.); Median household income: $44,837 (2006-2010 5-year est.); Average household income: $52,694 (2006-2010 5-year est.); Percent of households with income of $100,000 or more: 8.8% (2006-2010 5-year est.); Poverty rate: 18.6% (2006-2010 5-year est.).

**Education:** Percent of population age 25 and over with: High school diploma (including GED) or higher: 82.0% (2006-2010 5-year est.); Bachelor's degree or higher: 16.7% (2006-2010 5-year est.); Master's degree or higher: 5.8% (2006-2010 5-year est.).

**School District(s)**

Spencer-Van Etten Central School District (PK-12)

   2009-10 Enrollment: 1,019 . . . . . . . . . . . . . . . . . (607) 589-7100

**Housing:** Homeownership rate: 76.8% (2010); Median home value: $91,000 (2006-2010 5-year est.); Median contract rent: $471 per month (2006-2010 5-year est.); Median year structure built: 1963 (2006-2010 5-year est.).

**Transportation:** Commute to work: 89.1% car, 1.0% public transportation, 5.0% walk, 3.2% work from home (2006-2010 5-year est.); Travel time to work: 24.2% less than 15 minutes, 23.5% 15 to 30 minutes, 32.9% 30 to 45 minutes, 15.9% 45 to 60 minutes, 3.5% 60 minutes or more (2006-2010 5-year est.).

**VETERAN** (town). Covers a land area of 38.326 square miles and a water area of 0.142 square miles. Located at 42.24° N. Lat; 76.79° W. Long.

**Population:** 3,468 (1990); 3,271 (2000); 3,313 (2010); Density: 86.4 persons per square mile (2010); Race: 97.0% White, 0.6% Black, 0.4% Asian, 0.2% American Indian/Alaska Native, 0.0% Native Hawaiian/Other Pacific Islander, 1.8% Other, 1.0% Hispanic of any race (2010); Average household size: 2.50 (2010); Median age: 45.2 (2010); Males per 100 females: 95.5 (2010); Marriage status: 18.4% never married, 63.3% now married, 6.8% widowed, 11.5% divorced (2006-2010 5-year est.); Foreign born: 2.3% (2006-2010 5-year est.); Ancestry (includes multiple ancestries): 26.8% German, 23.4% Irish, 15.5% English, 11.7% Italian, 8.0% American (2006-2010 5-year est.).

**Economy:** Single-family building permits issued: 1 (2011); Multi-family building permits issued: 0 (2011); Employment by occupation: 6.5% management, 5.8% professional, 13.5% services, 14.4% sales, 3.9% farming, 5.1% construction, 9.2% production (2006-2010 5-year est.).

**Income:** Per capita income: $26,330 (2006-2010 5-year est.); Median household income: $51,037 (2006-2010 5-year est.); Average household income: $60,222 (2006-2010 5-year est.); Percent of households with income of $100,000 or more: 12.6% (2006-2010 5-year est.); Poverty rate: 4.8% (2006-2010 5-year est.).

**Education:** Percent of population age 25 and over with: High school diploma (including GED) or higher: 92.4% (2006-2010 5-year est.); Bachelor's degree or higher: 21.9% (2006-2010 5-year est.); Master's degree or higher: 11.6% (2006-2010 5-year est.).

**Housing:** Homeownership rate: 87.9% (2010); Median home value: $98,000 (2006-2010 5-year est.); Median contract rent: $565 per month (2006-2010 5-year est.); Median year structure built: 1964 (2006-2010 5-year est.).

**Transportation:** Commute to work: 91.2% car, 0.0% public transportation, 3.0% walk, 5.7% work from home (2006-2010 5-year est.); Travel time to work: 17.3% less than 15 minutes, 59.9% 15 to 30 minutes, 14.8% 30 to 45 minutes, 2.0% 45 to 60 minutes, 5.9% 60 minutes or more (2006-2010 5-year est.).

**WELLSBURG** (village). Covers a land area of 0.568 square miles and a water area of 0.008 square miles. Located at 42.01° N. Lat; 76.73° W. Long. Elevation is 827 feet.

**Population:** 617 (1990); 631 (2000); 580 (2010); Density: 1,020.9 persons per square mile (2010); Race: 97.9% White, 0.3% Black, 0.3% Asian, 0.3% American Indian/Alaska Native, 0.0% Native Hawaiian/Other Pacific Islander, 1.2% Other, 0.9% Hispanic of any race (2010); Average household size: 2.51 (2010); Median age: 39.5 (2010); Males per 100 females: 106.4 (2010); Marriage status: 38.5% never married, 53.1% now married, 1.1% widowed, 7.2% divorced (2006-2010 5-year est.); Foreign born: 1.3% (2006-2010 5-year est.); Ancestry (includes multiple ancestries): 27.5% Irish, 26.7% German, 21.1% English, 10.6% Dutch, 5.9% Italian (2006-2010 5-year est.).

**Economy:** Single-family building permits issued: 0 (2011); Multi-family building permits issued: 0 (2011); Employment by occupation: 1.1% management, 4.0% professional, 9.4% services, 18.4% sales, 1.1% farming, 5.4% construction, 10.8% production (2006-2010 5-year est.).

**Income:** Per capita income: $16,459 (2006-2010 5-year est.); Median household income: $38,000 (2006-2010 5-year est.); Average household income: $44,568 (2006-2010 5-year est.); Percent of households with income of $100,000 or more: 6.9% (2006-2010 5-year est.); Poverty rate: 16.9% (2006-2010 5-year est.).

**Taxes:** Total city taxes per capita: $113 (2009); City property taxes per capita: $96 (2009).

**Education:** Percent of population age 25 and over with: High school diploma (including GED) or higher: 91.2% (2006-2010 5-year est.); Bachelor's degree or higher: 6.5% (2006-2010 5-year est.); Master's degree or higher: 0.9% (2006-2010 5-year est.).

**Housing:** Homeownership rate: 76.4% (2010); Median home value: $73,300 (2006-2010 5-year est.); Median contract rent: $462 per month (2006-2010 5-year est.); Median year structure built: before 1940 (2006-2010 5-year est.).

**Transportation:** Commute to work: 86.7% car, 0.8% public transportation, 3.5% walk, 9.0% work from home (2006-2010 5-year est.); Travel time to work: 29.2% less than 15 minutes, 50.6% 15 to 30 minutes, 13.3% 30 to 45 minutes, 3.4% 45 to 60 minutes, 3.4% 60 minutes or more (2006-2010 5-year est.)

**WEST ELMIRA** (CDP). Covers a land area of 3.038 square miles and a water area of 0.116 square miles. Located at 42.08° N. Lat; 76.84° W. Long. Elevation is 886 feet.

**Population:** 5,218 (1990); 5,136 (2000); 4,967 (2010); Density: 1,634.8 persons per square mile (2010); Race: 94.2% White, 2.3% Black, 1.3% Asian, 0.1% American Indian/Alaska Native, 0.1% Native Hawaiian/Other Pacific Islander, 2.0% Other, 1.2% Hispanic of any race (2010); Average household size: 2.30 (2010); Median age: 46.3 (2010); Males per 100 females: 89.4 (2010); Marriage status: 17.3% never married, 58.9% now married, 11.4% widowed, 12.4% divorced (2006-2010 5-year est.); Foreign born: 3.7% (2006-2010 5-year est.); Ancestry (includes multiple ancestries): 24.2% Irish, 22.5% German, 20.1% Italian, 16.3% English, 7.0% Polish (2006-2010 5-year est.).

**Economy:** Employment by occupation: 18.7% management, 4.2% professional, 8.3% services, 13.1% sales, 1.5% farming, 4.5% construction, 1.3% production (2006-2010 5-year est.).

**Income:** Per capita income: $37,339 (2006-2010 5-year est.); Median household income: $61,143 (2006-2010 5-year est.); Average household income: $85,247 (2006-2010 5-year est.); Percent of households with income of $100,000 or more: 32.1% (2006-2010 5-year est.); Poverty rate: 12.1% (2006-2010 5-year est.).

**Education:** Percent of population age 25 and over with: High school diploma (including GED) or higher: 98.9% (2006-2010 5-year est.); Bachelor's degree or higher: 47.3% (2006-2010 5-year est.); Master's degree or higher: 24.0% (2006-2010 5-year est.).

**Housing:** Homeownership rate: 85.9% (2010); Median home value: $122,700 (2006-2010 5-year est.); Median contract rent: $694 per month (2006-2010 5-year est.); Median year structure built: 1943 (2006-2010 5-year est.).

**Transportation:** Commute to work: 92.4% car, 0.0% public transportation, 2.4% walk, 2.7% work from home (2006-2010 5-year est.); Travel time to work: 50.8% less than 15 minutes, 30.1% 15 to 30 minutes, 13.5% 30 to 45 minutes, 0.5% 45 to 60 minutes, 5.1% 60 minutes or more (2006-2010 5-year est.)

# Chenango County

Located in central New York; bounded on the east by the Unadilla River; drained by the Susquehanna, Otselic, and Chenango Rivers. Covers a land area of 894.36 square miles, a water area of 4.34 square miles, and is located in the Eastern Time Zone at 42.48° N. Lat., 75.60° W. Long. The county was founded in 1798. County seat is Norwich.

Weather Station: Norwich                        Elevation: 1,020 feet

| | Jan | Feb | Mar | Apr | May | Jun | Jul | Aug | Sep | Oct | Nov | Dec |
|---|---|---|---|---|---|---|---|---|---|---|---|---|
| High | 32 | 35 | 44 | 57 | 69 | 77 | 81 | 79 | 72 | 60 | 48 | 36 |
| Low | 13 | 14 | 22 | 33 | 43 | 52 | 57 | 56 | 48 | 37 | 29 | 19 |
| Precip | 2.9 | 2.6 | 3.3 | 3.6 | 3.7 | 4.3 | 3.8 | 3.8 | 4.0 | 3.6 | 3.6 | 3.3 |
| Snow | 17.9 | 14.1 | 11.5 | 2.7 | tr | 0.0 | 0.0 | 0.0 | 0.0 | 0.5 | 5.6 | 15.4 |

*High and Low temperatures in degrees Fahrenheit; Precipitation and Snow in inches*

Weather Station: Sherburne 2 S                  Elevation: 1,080 feet

| | Jan | Feb | Mar | Apr | May | Jun | Jul | Aug | Sep | Oct | Nov | Dec |
|---|---|---|---|---|---|---|---|---|---|---|---|---|
| High | 32 | 34 | 42 | 56 | 68 | 77 | 81 | 80 | 72 | 60 | 48 | 36 |
| Low | 13 | 12 | 20 | 32 | 42 | 53 | 56 | 55 | 47 | 37 | 29 | 19 |
| Precip | 2.2 | 2.0 | 2.9 | 3.3 | 3.5 | 4.5 | 3.8 | 3.4 | 3.8 | 3.5 | 3.3 | 2.6 |
| Snow | 16.9 | 14.1 | 13.1 | 2.9 | tr | 0.0 | 0.0 | 0.0 | tr | 0.5 | 6.0 | 14.5 |

*High and Low temperatures in degrees Fahrenheit; Precipitation and Snow in inches*

**Population:** 51,768 (1990); 51,401 (2000); 50,477 (2010); Race: 96.9% White, 0.7% Black, 0.4% Asian, 0.3% American Indian/Alaska Native, 0.0% Native Hawaiian/Other Pacific Islander, 1.7% Other, 1.8% Hispanic of any race (2010); Density: 56.4 persons per square mile (2010); Average household size: 2.43 (2010); Median age: 42.9 (2010); Males per 100 females: 99.2 (2010).

**Religion:** Six largest groups: 11.0% Catholicism, 5.7% Methodist/Pietist, 2.9% Episcopalianism/Anglicanism, 2.1% Baptist, 2.1% Presbyterian-Reformed, 2.0% Non-Denominational (2010)

**Economy:** Unemployment rate: 9.5% (February 2012); Total civilian labor force: 24,687 (February 2012); Leading industries: 22.3% manufacturing; 18.6% retail trade; 15.3% health care and social assistance (2009); Farms: 908 totaling 177,267 acres (2007); Companies that employ 500 or more persons: 0 (2009); Companies that employ 100 to 499 persons: 21 (2009); Companies that employ less than 100 persons: 954 (2009); Black-owned businesses: n/a (2007); Hispanic-owned businesses: n/a (2007); Asian-owned businesses: n/a (2007); Women-owned businesses: 1,155 (2007); Retail sales per capita: $8,984 (2010). Single-family building permits issued: 29 (2011); Multi-family building permits issued: 39 (2011).

**Income:** Per capita income: $22,036 (2006-2010 5-year est.); Median household income: $43,943 (2006-2010 5-year est.); Average household income: $55,277 (2006-2010 5-year est.); Percent of households with income of $100,000 or more: 11.2% (2006-2010 5-year est.); Poverty rate: 13.6% (2006-2010 5-year est.); Bankruptcy rate: 2.92% (2011).

**Education:** Percent of population age 25 and over with: High school diploma (including GED) or higher: 85.0% (2006-2010 5-year est.); Bachelor's degree or higher: 17.0% (2006-2010 5-year est.); Master's degree or higher: 6.7% (2006-2010 5-year est.).

**Housing:** Homeownership rate: 75.0% (2010); Median home value: $88,200 (2006-2010 5-year est.); Median contract rent: $437 per month (2006-2010 5-year est.); Median year structure built: 1958 (2006-2010 5-year est.)

**Health:** Birth rate: 104.2 per 10,000 population (2011); Death rate: 106.5 per 10,000 population (2011); Age-adjusted cancer mortality rate: 185.2 deaths per 100,000 population (2009); Number of physicians: 12.6 per 10,000 population (2008); Hospital beds: 27.0 per 10,000 population (2007); Hospital admissions: 414.8 per 10,000 population (2007).

**Elections:** 2008 Presidential election results: 48.4% Obama, 49.6% McCain, 1.1% Nader

**National and State Parks:** Chenango State Forest

**Additional Information Contacts**

Chenango County Government . . . . . . . . . . . . . . . (607) 337-1470
   http://www.co.chenango.ny.us
Bainbridge Chamber of Commerce . . . . . . . . . . . . (607) 967-8700
   http://www.bainbridgeny.org/chamber.htm
City of Norwich . . . . . . . . . . . . . . . . . . . . . . . . . . (607) 334-1230
   http://www.norwichnewyork.net
Commerce Chenango . . . . . . . . . . . . . . . . . . . . . . (607) 334-1400
   http://www.chenangony.org
Greater Greene Chamber of Commerce . . . . . . . . . (607) 656-8225
   http://www.greenenys.com

## Chenango County Communities

**AFTON** (village). Covers a land area of 1.526 square miles and a water area of 0.073 square miles. Located at 42.22° N. Lat; 75.52° W. Long. Elevation is 1,001 feet.

**Population:** 838 (1990); 836 (2000); 822 (2010); Density: 538.5 persons per square mile (2010); Race: 98.3% White, 0.2% Black, 0.7% Asian, 0.0% American Indian/Alaska Native, 0.0% Native Hawaiian/Other Pacific Islander, 0.8% Other, 3.6% Hispanic of any race (2010); Average household size: 2.14 (2010); Median age: 42.9 (2010); Males per 100 females: 86.4 (2010); Marriage status: 26.6% never married, 46.4% now married, 14.6% widowed, 12.4% divorced (2006-2010 5-year est.); Foreign born: 8.0% (2006-2010 5-year est.); Ancestry (includes multiple ancestries): 19.9% German, 17.8% English, 12.5% Irish, 11.6% Italian, 4.1% French (2006-2010 5-year est.).

**Economy:** Employment by occupation: 11.4% management, 6.8% professional, 12.4% services, 11.2% sales, 1.6% farming, 19.5% construction, 3.0% production (2006-2010 5-year est.).

**Income:** Per capita income: $24,231 (2006-2010 5-year est.); Median household income: $46,667 (2006-2010 5-year est.); Average household income: $53,174 (2006-2010 5-year est.); Percent of households with income of $100,000 or more: 10.8% (2006-2010 5-year est.); Poverty rate: 12.0% (2006-2010 5-year est.).

**Education:** Percent of population age 25 and over with: High school diploma (including GED) or higher: 84.9% (2006-2010 5-year est.); Bachelor's degree or higher: 16.5% (2006-2010 5-year est.); Master's degree or higher: 6.0% (2006-2010 5-year est.).

**School District(s)**

Afton Central School District (PK-12)
   2009-10 Enrollment: 629 . . . . . . . . . . . . . . . . . (607) 639-8229

**Housing:** Homeownership rate: 64.8% (2010); Median home value: $83,100 (2006-2010 5-year est.); Median contract rent: $431 per month (2006-2010 5-year est.); Median year structure built: before 1940 (2006-2010 5-year est.).

**Transportation:** Commute to work: 82.2% car, 0.0% public transportation, 11.1% walk, 6.7% work from home (2006-2010 5-year est.); Travel time to work: 46.1% less than 15 minutes, 32.9% 15 to 30 minutes, 18.5% 30 to 45 minutes, 1.7% 45 to 60 minutes, 0.8% 60 minutes or more (2006-2010 5-year est.)

**AFTON** (town). Covers a land area of 45.835 square miles and a water area of 0.678 square miles. Located at 42.22° N. Lat; 75.52° W. Long. Elevation is 1,001 feet.

**Population:** 2,972 (1990); 2,977 (2000); 2,851 (2010); Density: 62.2 persons per square mile (2010); Race: 97.4% White, 0.5% Black, 0.4% Asian, 0.5% American Indian/Alaska Native, 0.0% Native Hawaiian/Other Pacific Islander, 1.2% Other, 2.0% Hispanic of any race (2010); Average household size: 2.38 (2010); Median age: 44.3 (2010); Males per 100 females: 97.0 (2010); Marriage status: 26.1% never married, 46.9% now married, 9.5% widowed, 17.6% divorced (2006-2010 5-year est.); Foreign born: 3.2% (2006-2010 5-year est.); Ancestry (includes multiple ancestries): 16.5% English, 14.9% Irish, 14.6% Italian, 14.3% German, 6.6% American (2006-2010 5-year est.).

**Economy:** Employment by occupation: 9.1% management, 2.3% professional, 15.7% services, 10.0% sales, 4.0% farming, 11.3% construction, 10.0% production (2006-2010 5-year est.).

**Income:** Per capita income: $23,645 (2006-2010 5-year est.); Median household income: $39,783 (2006-2010 5-year est.); Average household income: $50,923 (2006-2010 5-year est.); Percent of households with income of $100,000 or more: 8.4% (2006-2010 5-year est.); Poverty rate: 18.0% (2006-2010 5-year est.).

**Education:** Percent of population age 25 and over with: High school diploma (including GED) or higher: 81.8% (2006-2010 5-year est.); Bachelor's degree or higher: 13.2% (2006-2010 5-year est.); Master's degree or higher: 4.4% (2006-2010 5-year est.).

**School District(s)**

Afton Central School District (PK-12)
   2009-10 Enrollment: 629 . . . . . . . . . . . . . . . . . (607) 639-8229

**Housing:** Homeownership rate: 78.8% (2010); Median home value: $83,200 (2006-2010 5-year est.); Median contract rent: $410 per month (2006-2010 5-year est.); Median year structure built: 1960 (2006-2010 5-year est.).

**Transportation:** Commute to work: 88.3% car, 1.8% public transportation, 5.0% walk, 4.9% work from home (2006-2010 5-year est.); Travel time to work: 27.9% less than 15 minutes, 35.2% 15 to 30 minutes, 30.9% 30 to 45 minutes, 2.8% 45 to 60 minutes, 3.2% 60 minutes or more (2006-2010 5-year est.)

**BAINBRIDGE** (village). Covers a land area of 1.238 square miles and a water area of 0.034 square miles. Located at 42.30° N. Lat; 75.47° W. Long. Elevation is 994 feet.

**Population:** 1,574 (1990); 1,365 (2000); 1,355 (2010); Density: 1,093.8 persons per square mile (2010); Race: 97.7% White, 0.2% Black, 0.3% Asian, 0.1% American Indian/Alaska Native, 0.0% Native Hawaiian/Other Pacific Islander, 1.7% Other, 2.4% Hispanic of any race (2010); Average household size: 2.30 (2010); Median age: 40.1 (2010); Males per 100 females: 93.3 (2010); Marriage status: 25.3% never married, 56.7% now married, 8.4% widowed, 9.6% divorced (2006-2010 5-year est.); Foreign born: 1.4% (2006-2010 5-year est.); Ancestry (includes multiple ancestries): 23.9% German, 21.5% English, 17.3% Irish, 12.4% Italian, 4.8% American (2006-2010 5-year est.).

**Economy:** Employment by occupation: 4.5% management, 2.5% professional, 8.7% services, 14.0% sales, 2.5% farming, 7.9% construction, 16.6% production (2006-2010 5-year est.).

**Income:** Per capita income: $21,276 (2006-2010 5-year est.); Median household income: $43,281 (2006-2010 5-year est.); Average household income: $50,279 (2006-2010 5-year est.); Percent of households with

income of $100,000 or more: 8.7% (2006-2010 5-year est.); Poverty rate: 15.2% (2006-2010 5-year est.).
**Education:** Percent of population age 25 and over with: High school diploma (including GED) or higher: 90.2% (2006-2010 5-year est.); Bachelor's degree or higher: 18.7% (2006-2010 5-year est.); Master's degree or higher: 10.9% (2006-2010 5-year est.).

**School District(s)**
Bainbridge-Guilford Central School District (PK-12)
　2009-10 Enrollment: 885 . . . . . . . . . . . . . . . . . . . . . . (607) 967-6321
**Housing:** Homeownership rate: 62.8% (2010); Median home value: $86,800 (2006-2010 5-year est.); Median contract rent: $429 per month (2006-2010 5-year est.); Median year structure built: before 1940 (2006-2010 5-year est.).
**Transportation:** Commute to work: 87.0% car, 2.4% public transportation, 6.0% walk, 1.6% work from home (2006-2010 5-year est.); Travel time to work: 54.9% less than 15 minutes, 21.6% 15 to 30 minutes, 16.2% 30 to 45 minutes, 4.2% 45 to 60 minutes, 3.1% 60 minutes or more (2006-2010 5-year est.)
**Additional Information Contacts**
Bainbridge Chamber of Commerce . . . . . . . . . . . . . . . . . . (607) 967-8700
　http://www.bainbridgeny.org/chamber.htm

## BAINBRIDGE (town). Covers a land area of 34.322 square miles and a water area of 0.432 square miles. Located at 42.29° N. Lat; 75.47° W. Long. Elevation is 994 feet.
**History:** Settled before 1790, incorporated 1829.
**Population:** 3,445 (1990); 3,401 (2000); 3,308 (2010); Density: 96.4 persons per square mile (2010); Race: 97.8% White, 0.2% Black, 0.5% Asian, 0.2% American Indian/Alaska Native, 0.0% Native Hawaiian/Other Pacific Islander, 1.3% Other, 1.8% Hispanic of any race (2010); Average household size: 2.37 (2010); Median age: 43.7 (2010); Males per 100 females: 99.6 (2010); Marriage status: 27.2% never married, 56.1% now married, 7.9% widowed, 8.9% divorced (2006-2010 5-year est.); Foreign born: 1.5% (2006-2010 5-year est.); Ancestry (includes multiple ancestries): 19.8% German, 18.9% English, 17.8% Irish, 9.3% Italian, 6.9% Dutch (2006-2010 5-year est.).
**Economy:** Employment by occupation: 6.1% management, 4.0% professional, 9.5% services, 16.9% sales, 2.1% farming, 13.7% construction, 10.8% production (2006-2010 5-year est.).
**Income:** Per capita income: $22,473 (2006-2010 5-year est.); Median household income: $45,582 (2006-2010 5-year est.); Average household income: $53,613 (2006-2010 5-year est.); Percent of households with income of $100,000 or more: 12.4% (2006-2010 5-year est.); Poverty rate: 8.2% (2006-2010 5-year est.).
**Education:** Percent of population age 25 and over with: High school diploma (including GED) or higher: 82.1% (2006-2010 5-year est.); Bachelor's degree or higher: 19.1% (2006-2010 5-year est.); Master's degree or higher: 10.0% (2006-2010 5-year est.).

**School District(s)**
Bainbridge-Guilford Central School District (PK-12)
　2009-10 Enrollment: 885 . . . . . . . . . . . . . . . . . . . . . . (607) 967-6321
**Housing:** Homeownership rate: 77.1% (2010); Median home value: $93,400 (2006-2010 5-year est.); Median contract rent: $447 per month (2006-2010 5-year est.); Median year structure built: before 1940 (2006-2010 5-year est.).
**Transportation:** Commute to work: 89.3% car, 2.1% public transportation, 4.0% walk, 2.3% work from home (2006-2010 5-year est.); Travel time to work: 49.3% less than 15 minutes, 20.5% 15 to 30 minutes, 18.8% 30 to 45 minutes, 5.4% 45 to 60 minutes, 6.0% 60 minutes or more (2006-2010 5-year est.)

## COLUMBUS (town). Covers a land area of 37.368 square miles and a water area of 0.124 square miles. Located at 42.69° N. Lat; 75.36° W. Long. Elevation is 1,296 feet.
**Population:** 869 (1990); 931 (2000); 975 (2010); Density: 26.1 persons per square mile (2010); Race: 97.6% White, 0.2% Black, 0.0% Asian, 0.2% American Indian/Alaska Native, 0.0% Native Hawaiian/Other Pacific Islander, 2.0% Other, 0.7% Hispanic of any race (2010); Average household size: 2.68 (2010); Median age: 42.8 (2010); Males per 100 females: 109.7 (2010); Marriage status: 21.6% never married, 63.6% now married, 7.3% widowed, 7.5% divorced (2006-2010 5-year est.); Foreign born: 2.0% (2006-2010 5-year est.); Ancestry (includes multiple ancestries): 18.0% English, 13.6% German, 9.4% Irish, 8.4% French, 5.0% American (2006-2010 5-year est.).

**Economy:** Employment by occupation: 15.8% management, 0.7% professional, 8.1% services, 10.9% sales, 5.1% farming, 13.0% construction, 9.3% production (2006-2010 5-year est.).
**Income:** Per capita income: $19,858 (2006-2010 5-year est.); Median household income: $38,750 (2006-2010 5-year est.); Average household income: $50,213 (2006-2010 5-year est.); Percent of households with income of $100,000 or more: 14.3% (2006-2010 5-year est.); Poverty rate: 9.8% (2006-2010 5-year est.).
**Education:** Percent of population age 25 and over with: High school diploma (including GED) or higher: 85.1% (2006-2010 5-year est.); Bachelor's degree or higher: 18.0% (2006-2010 5-year est.); Master's degree or higher: 7.5% (2006-2010 5-year est.).
**Housing:** Homeownership rate: 82.2% (2010); Median home value: $97,400 (2006-2010 5-year est.); Median contract rent: $435 per month (2006-2010 5-year est.); Median year structure built: 1973 (2006-2010 5-year est.).
**Transportation:** Commute to work: 83.5% car, 0.0% public transportation, 12.2% walk, 3.7% work from home (2006-2010 5-year est.); Travel time to work: 40.9% less than 15 minutes, 23.1% 15 to 30 minutes, 22.0% 30 to 45 minutes, 7.0% 45 to 60 minutes, 7.0% 60 minutes or more (2006-2010 5-year est.)

## COVENTRY (town). Covers a land area of 48.696 square miles and a water area of 0.166 square miles. Located at 42.29° N. Lat; 75.62° W. Long. Elevation is 1,660 feet.
**Population:** 1,517 (1990); 1,589 (2000); 1,655 (2010); Density: 34.0 persons per square mile (2010); Race: 96.4% White, 0.2% Black, 0.8% Asian, 0.8% American Indian/Alaska Native, 0.1% Native Hawaiian/Other Pacific Islander, 1.7% Other, 1.7% Hispanic of any race (2010); Average household size: 2.65 (2010); Median age: 43.3 (2010); Males per 100 females: 106.6 (2010); Marriage status: 25.7% never married, 59.2% now married, 4.9% widowed, 10.1% divorced (2006-2010 5-year est.); Foreign born: 0.5% (2006-2010 5-year est.); Ancestry (includes multiple ancestries): 25.2% German, 18.6% Irish, 15.4% English, 12.9% American, 9.4% Italian (2006-2010 5-year est.).
**Economy:** Employment by occupation: 12.9% management, 3.0% professional, 8.1% services, 12.2% sales, 2.8% farming, 11.9% construction, 8.1% production (2006-2010 5-year est.).
**Income:** Per capita income: $18,525 (2006-2010 5-year est.); Median household income: $45,185 (2006-2010 5-year est.); Average household income: $50,500 (2006-2010 5-year est.); Percent of households with income of $100,000 or more: 6.7% (2006-2010 5-year est.); Poverty rate: 12.0% (2006-2010 5-year est.).
**Education:** Percent of population age 25 and over with: High school diploma (including GED) or higher: 83.3% (2006-2010 5-year est.); Bachelor's degree or higher: 9.5% (2006-2010 5-year est.); Master's degree or higher: 3.8% (2006-2010 5-year est.).
**Housing:** Homeownership rate: 87.0% (2010); Median home value: $84,900 (2006-2010 5-year est.); Median contract rent: $508 per month (2006-2010 5-year est.); Median year structure built: 1980 (2006-2010 5-year est.).
**Transportation:** Commute to work: 88.4% car, 1.2% public transportation, 3.0% walk, 7.3% work from home (2006-2010 5-year est.); Travel time to work: 27.6% less than 15 minutes, 33.7% 15 to 30 minutes, 26.7% 30 to 45 minutes, 8.3% 45 to 60 minutes, 3.6% 60 minutes or more (2006-2010 5-year est.)

## GERMAN (town). Covers a land area of 28.408 square miles and a water area of 0.030 square miles. Located at 42.50° N. Lat; 75.82° W. Long.
**Population:** 311 (1990); 378 (2000); 370 (2010); Density: 13.0 persons per square mile (2010); Race: 93.5% White, 1.1% Black, 2.2% Asian, 0.0% American Indian/Alaska Native, 0.0% Native Hawaiian/Other Pacific Islander, 3.2% Other, 2.7% Hispanic of any race (2010); Average household size: 2.45 (2010); Median age: 42.2 (2010); Males per 100 females: 105.6 (2010); Marriage status: 34.5% never married, 55.5% now married, 3.4% widowed, 6.7% divorced (2006-2010 5-year est.); Foreign born: 0.6% (2006-2010 5-year est.); Ancestry (includes multiple ancestries): 12.3% American, 11.1% English, 8.9% Irish, 8.2% Italian, 6.3% German (2006-2010 5-year est.).
**Economy:** Employment by occupation: 4.1% management, 0.0% professional, 12.3% services, 16.4% sales, 1.4% farming, 15.1% construction, 20.5% production (2006-2010 5-year est.).
**Income:** Per capita income: $15,826 (2006-2010 5-year est.); Median household income: $36,000 (2006-2010 5-year est.); Average household

income: $46,241 (2006-2010 5-year est.); Percent of households with income of $100,000 or more: 8.5% (2006-2010 5-year est.); Poverty rate: 16.8% (2006-2010 5-year est.).

**Education:** Percent of population age 25 and over with: High school diploma (including GED) or higher: 85.9% (2006-2010 5-year est.); Bachelor's degree or higher: 15.8% (2006-2010 5-year est.); Master's degree or higher: 11.9% (2006-2010 5-year est.).

**Housing:** Homeownership rate: 84.8% (2010); Median home value: $75,700 (2006-2010 5-year est.); Median contract rent: $146 per month (2006-2010 5-year est.); Median year structure built: 1982 (2006-2010 5-year est.).

**Transportation:** Commute to work: 90.3% car, 0.0% public transportation, 0.0% walk, 9.7% work from home (2006-2010 5-year est.); Travel time to work: 3.1% less than 15 minutes, 42.3% 15 to 30 minutes, 30.8% 30 to 45 minutes, 14.6% 45 to 60 minutes, 9.2% 60 minutes or more (2006-2010 5-year est.)

**GREENE** (village). Covers a land area of 1.067 square miles and a water area of 0.037 square miles. Located at 42.33° N. Lat; 75.76° W. Long. Elevation is 919 feet.

**Population:** 1,819 (1990); 1,701 (2000); 1,580 (2010); Density: 1,479.8 persons per square mile (2010); Race: 98.9% White, 0.1% Black, 0.1% Asian, 0.0% American Indian/Alaska Native, 0.0% Native Hawaiian/Other Pacific Islander, 0.9% Other, 0.6% Hispanic of any race (2010); Average household size: 2.13 (2010); Median age: 42.5 (2010); Males per 100 females: 87.4 (2010); Marriage status: 37.8% never married, 41.0% now married, 8.1% widowed, 13.2% divorced (2006-2010 5-year est.); Foreign born: 2.5% (2006-2010 5-year est.); Ancestry (includes multiple ancestries): 23.1% German, 23.0% Irish, 18.6% English, 9.3% Italian, 8.6% Dutch (2006-2010 5-year est.).

**Economy:** Employment by occupation: 7.7% management, 3.4% professional, 11.7% services, 15.0% sales, 1.9% farming, 8.0% construction, 7.8% production (2006-2010 5-year est.).

**Income:** Per capita income: $21,993 (2006-2010 5-year est.); Median household income: $42,012 (2006-2010 5-year est.); Average household income: $50,398 (2006-2010 5-year est.); Percent of households with income of $100,000 or more: 7.8% (2006-2010 5-year est.); Poverty rate: 13.5% (2006-2010 5-year est.).

**Education:** Percent of population age 25 and over with: High school diploma (including GED) or higher: 89.8% (2006-2010 5-year est.); Bachelor's degree or higher: 19.5% (2006-2010 5-year est.); Master's degree or higher: 11.2% (2006-2010 5-year est.).

**School District(s)**
Greene Central School District (PK-12)
  2009-10 Enrollment: 1,183 . . . . . . . . . . . . . . . . . . . . . . (607) 656-4161
**Housing:** Homeownership rate: 49.3% (2010); Median home value: $92,200 (2006-2010 5-year est.); Median contract rent: $453 per month (2006-2010 5-year est.); Median year structure built: before 1940 (2006-2010 5-year est.).

**Safety:** Violent crime rate: 0.0 per 10,000 population; Property crime rate: 0.0 per 10,000 population (2010).

**Newspapers:** Chenango American (Community news); Oxford Review Times (Community news; Circulation 3,500); Whitney Point Reporter (Community news)

**Transportation:** Commute to work: 85.0% car, 0.3% public transportation, 13.0% walk, 1.0% work from home (2006-2010 5-year est.); Travel time to work: 37.5% less than 15 minutes, 22.4% 15 to 30 minutes, 32.0% 30 to 45 minutes, 4.2% 45 to 60 minutes, 3.9% 60 minutes or more (2006-2010 5-year est.)

**Additional Information Contacts**
Greater Greene Chamber of Commerce . . . . . . . . . . . . . . (607) 656-8225
http://www.greenenys.com

**GREENE** (town). Covers a land area of 75.076 square miles and a water area of 0.542 square miles. Located at 42.30° N. Lat; 75.75° W. Long. Elevation is 919 feet.

**History:** Settled 1792, incorporated 1842.

**Population:** 6,053 (1990); 5,729 (2000); 5,604 (2010); Density: 74.6 persons per square mile (2010); Race: 97.5% White, 0.4% Black, 0.3% Asian, 0.3% American Indian/Alaska Native, 0.0% Native Hawaiian/Other Pacific Islander, 1.5% Other, 1.1% Hispanic of any race (2010); Average household size: 2.39 (2010); Median age: 43.6 (2010); Males per 100 females: 98.1 (2010); Marriage status: 30.4% never married, 53.4% now married, 7.1% widowed, 9.0% divorced (2006-2010 5-year est.); Foreign born: 2.3% (2006-2010 5-year est.); Ancestry (includes multiple

ancestries): 23.4% German, 20.7% English, 17.9% Irish, 10.1% Italian, 6.5% Polish (2006-2010 5-year est.).

**Economy:** Single-family building permits issued: 2 (2011); Multi-family building permits issued: 0 (2011); Employment by occupation: 14.6% management, 2.3% professional, 15.8% services, 13.7% sales, 3.5% farming, 9.6% construction, 8.4% production (2006-2010 5-year est.).

**Income:** Per capita income: $22,941 (2006-2010 5-year est.); Median household income: $48,257 (2006-2010 5-year est.); Average household income: $57,319 (2006-2010 5-year est.); Percent of households with income of $100,000 or more: 12.8% (2006-2010 5-year est.); Poverty rate: 6.8% (2006-2010 5-year est.).

**Education:** Percent of population age 25 and over with: High school diploma (including GED) or higher: 88.8% (2006-2010 5-year est.); Bachelor's degree or higher: 21.9% (2006-2010 5-year est.); Master's degree or higher: 12.0% (2006-2010 5-year est.).

**School District(s)**
Greene Central School District (PK-12)
  2009-10 Enrollment: 1,183 . . . . . . . . . . . . . . . . . . . . . . (607) 656-4161
**Housing:** Homeownership rate: 74.3% (2010); Median home value: $99,200 (2006-2010 5-year est.); Median contract rent: $447 per month (2006-2010 5-year est.); Median year structure built: 1961 (2006-2010 5-year est.).

**Newspapers:** Chenango American (Community news); Oxford Review Times (Community news; Circulation 3,500); Whitney Point Reporter (Community news)

**Transportation:** Commute to work: 90.2% car, 0.1% public transportation, 4.6% walk, 4.3% work from home (2006-2010 5-year est.); Travel time to work: 37.4% less than 15 minutes, 20.9% 15 to 30 minutes, 31.9% 30 to 45 minutes, 5.1% 45 to 60 minutes, 4.6% 60 minutes or more (2006-2010 5-year est.)

**GUILFORD** (town). Covers a land area of 61.715 square miles and a water area of 0.243 square miles. Located at 42.40° N. Lat; 75.45° W. Long. Elevation is 1,486 feet.

**Population:** 2,875 (1990); 3,046 (2000); 2,922 (2010); Density: 47.3 persons per square mile (2010); Race: 97.5% White, 0.3% Black, 0.2% Asian, 0.2% American Indian/Alaska Native, 0.0% Native Hawaiian/Other Pacific Islander, 1.8% Other, 2.3% Hispanic of any race (2010); Average household size: 2.42 (2010); Median age: 44.8 (2010); Males per 100 females: 101.5 (2010); Marriage status: 22.6% never married, 59.1% now married, 5.6% widowed, 12.7% divorced (2006-2010 5-year est.); Foreign born: 1.5% (2006-2010 5-year est.); Ancestry (includes multiple ancestries): 22.3% German, 20.3% Irish, 18.1% English, 11.2% American, 9.0% Italian (2006-2010 5-year est.).

**Economy:** Employment by occupation: 16.7% management, 5.6% professional, 10.4% services, 16.1% sales, 2.6% farming, 10.8% construction, 5.1% production (2006-2010 5-year est.).

**Income:** Per capita income: $21,131 (2006-2010 5-year est.); Median household income: $46,589 (2006-2010 5-year est.); Average household income: $52,310 (2006-2010 5-year est.); Percent of households with income of $100,000 or more: 11.8% (2006-2010 5-year est.); Poverty rate: 13.6% (2006-2010 5-year est.).

**Education:** Percent of population age 25 and over with: High school diploma (including GED) or higher: 86.6% (2006-2010 5-year est.); Bachelor's degree or higher: 12.9% (2006-2010 5-year est.); Master's degree or higher: 5.2% (2006-2010 5-year est.).

**School District(s)**
Bainbridge-Guilford Central School District (PK-12)
  2009-10 Enrollment: 885 . . . . . . . . . . . . . . . . . . . . . . . (607) 967-6321
**Housing:** Homeownership rate: 87.2% (2010); Median home value: $84,300 (2006-2010 5-year est.); Median contract rent: $451 per month (2006-2010 5-year est.); Median year structure built: 1965 (2006-2010 5-year est.).

**Transportation:** Commute to work: 84.3% car, 0.8% public transportation, 4.1% walk, 6.6% work from home (2006-2010 5-year est.); Travel time to work: 30.1% less than 15 minutes, 38.2% 15 to 30 minutes, 19.4% 30 to 45 minutes, 5.2% 45 to 60 minutes, 7.0% 60 minutes or more (2006-2010 5-year est.)

**GUILFORD** (CDP). Covers a land area of 1.335 square miles and a water area of 0.118 square miles. Located at 42.40° N. Lat; 75.48° W. Long. Elevation is 1,486 feet.

**Population:** n/a (1990); n/a (2000); 362 (2010); Density: 271.0 persons per square mile (2010); Race: 98.9% White, 0.0% Black, 0.3% Asian, 0.6% American Indian/Alaska Native, 0.0% Native Hawaiian/Other Pacific

Islander, 0.2% Other, 0.6% Hispanic of any race (2010); Average household size: 2.53 (2010); Median age: 42.3 (2010); Males per 100 females: 101.1 (2010); Marriage status: 5.7% never married, 80.6% now married, 0.0% widowed, 13.7% divorced (2006-2010 5-year est.); Foreign born: 0.0% (2006-2010 5-year est.); Ancestry (includes multiple ancestries): 28.1% English, 7.4% Irish, 6.9% Scotch-Irish, 6.5% Scottish, 6.1% French (2006-2010 5-year est.).
**Economy:** Employment by occupation: 0.0% management, 40.0% professional, 0.0% services, 25.5% sales, 0.0% farming, 0.0% construction, 0.0% production (2006-2010 5-year est.).
**Income:** Per capita income: $17,194 (2006-2010 5-year est.); Median household income: $36,515 (2006-2010 5-year est.); Average household income: $43,431 (2006-2010 5-year est.); Percent of households with income of $100,000 or more: 12.5% (2006-2010 5-year est.); Poverty rate: 12.1% (2006-2010 5-year est.).
**Education:** Percent of population age 25 and over with: High school diploma (including GED) or higher: 94.9% (2006-2010 5-year est.); Bachelor's degree or higher: 26.9% (2006-2010 5-year est.); Master's degree or higher: 0.0% (2006-2010 5-year est.).

**School District(s)**
Bainbridge-Guilford Central School District (PK-12)
    2009-10 Enrollment: 885 . . . . . . . . . . . . . . . . . . . . . . . (607) 967-6321
**Housing:** Homeownership rate: 88.2% (2010); Median home value: $102,300 (2006-2010 5-year est.); Median contract rent: n/a per month (2006-2010 5-year est.); Median year structure built: before 1940 (2006-2010 5-year est.).
**Transportation:** Commute to work: 100.0% car, 0.0% public transportation, 0.0% walk, 0.0% work from home (2006-2010 5-year est.); Travel time to work: 0.0% less than 15 minutes, 100.0% 15 to 30 minutes, 0.0% 30 to 45 minutes, 0.0% 45 to 60 minutes, 0.0% 60 minutes or more (2006-2010 5-year est.).

**LINCKLAEN** (town). Covers a land area of 26.263 square miles and a water area of 0.010 square miles. Located at 42.67° N. Lat; 75.84° W. Long. Elevation is 1,191 feet.
**Population:** 486 (1990); 416 (2000); 396 (2010); Density: 15.1 persons per square mile (2010); Race: 98.0% White, 0.0% Black, 0.5% Asian, 0.3% American Indian/Alaska Native, 0.0% Native Hawaiian/Other Pacific Islander, 1.2% Other, 1.8% Hispanic of any race (2010); Average household size: 2.44 (2010); Median age: 42.5 (2010); Males per 100 females: 106.3 (2010); Marriage status: 27.9% never married, 59.4% now married, 4.7% widowed, 8.0% divorced (2006-2010 5-year est.); Foreign born: 0.6% (2006-2010 5-year est.); Ancestry (includes multiple ancestries): 21.3% English, 18.2% Irish, 11.2% German, 5.8% Scottish, 5.2% Dutch (2006-2010 5-year est.).
**Economy:** Employment by occupation: 9.7% management, 0.7% professional, 12.4% services, 11.0% sales, 4.1% farming, 27.6% construction, 6.2% production (2006-2010 5-year est.).
**Income:** Per capita income: $19,425 (2006-2010 5-year est.); Median household income: $36,875 (2006-2010 5-year est.); Average household income: $46,099 (2006-2010 5-year est.); Percent of households with income of $100,000 or more: 8.6% (2006-2010 5-year est.); Poverty rate: 23.5% (2006-2010 5-year est.).
**Education:** Percent of population age 25 and over with: High school diploma (including GED) or higher: 80.8% (2006-2010 5-year est.); Bachelor's degree or higher: 14.5% (2006-2010 5-year est.); Master's degree or higher: 4.7% (2006-2010 5-year est.).
**Housing:** Homeownership rate: 80.3% (2010); Median home value: $83,200 (2006-2010 5-year est.); Median contract rent: $368 per month (2006-2010 5-year est.); Median year structure built: 1974 (2006-2010 5-year est.).
**Transportation:** Commute to work: 81.8% car, 0.0% public transportation, 2.1% walk, 16.1% work from home (2006-2010 5-year est.); Travel time to work: 33.3% less than 15 minutes, 6.7% 15 to 30 minutes, 23.3% 30 to 45 minutes, 25.8% 45 to 60 minutes, 10.8% 60 minutes or more (2006-2010 5-year est.).

**MCDONOUGH** (town). Covers a land area of 39.037 square miles and a water area of 0.592 square miles. Located at 42.50° N. Lat; 75.72° W. Long. Elevation is 1,430 feet.
**Population:** 809 (1990); 870 (2000); 886 (2010); Density: 22.7 persons per square mile (2010); Race: 96.4% White, 0.7% Black, 0.3% Asian, 0.7% American Indian/Alaska Native, 0.0% Native Hawaiian/Other Pacific Islander, 1.9% Other, 3.8% Hispanic of any race (2010); Average household size: 2.38 (2010); Median age: 46.7 (2010); Males per 100

females: 111.5 (2010); Marriage status: 22.3% never married, 66.3% now married, 7.2% widowed, 4.2% divorced (2006-2010 5-year est.); Foreign born: 2.1% (2006-2010 5-year est.); Ancestry (includes multiple ancestries): 15.3% German, 14.5% English, 12.6% Italian, 11.7% Irish, 7.9% American (2006-2010 5-year est.).
**Economy:** Employment by occupation: 15.7% management, 0.0% professional, 10.4% services, 11.4% sales, 2.7% farming, 12.0% construction, 13.3% production (2006-2010 5-year est.).
**Income:** Per capita income: $17,896 (2006-2010 5-year est.); Median household income: $39,524 (2006-2010 5-year est.); Average household income: $47,009 (2006-2010 5-year est.); Percent of households with income of $100,000 or more: 9.0% (2006-2010 5-year est.); Poverty rate: 6.2% (2006-2010 5-year est.).
**Education:** Percent of population age 25 and over with: High school diploma (including GED) or higher: 77.6% (2006-2010 5-year est.); Bachelor's degree or higher: 6.8% (2006-2010 5-year est.); Master's degree or higher: 0.8% (2006-2010 5-year est.).
**Housing:** Homeownership rate: 84.5% (2010); Median home value: $77,900 (2006-2010 5-year est.); Median contract rent: $383 per month (2006-2010 5-year est.); Median year structure built: 1973 (2006-2010 5-year est.).
**Transportation:** Commute to work: 90.2% car, 0.0% public transportation, 4.1% walk, 4.3% work from home (2006-2010 5-year est.); Travel time to work: 14.5% less than 15 minutes, 36.4% 15 to 30 minutes, 28.1% 30 to 45 minutes, 6.3% 45 to 60 minutes, 14.8% 60 minutes or more (2006-2010 5-year est.)

**MOUNT UPTON** (unincorporated postal area)
Zip Code: 13809
    Covers a land area of 30.076 square miles and a water area of 0 square miles. Located at 42.40° N. Lat; 75.39° W. Long. Elevation is 1,030 feet. Population: 1,517 (2010); Density: 50.4 persons per square mile (2010); Race: 98.4% White, 0.5% Black, 0.3% Asian, 0.0% American Indian/Alaska Native, 0.0% Native Hawaiian/Other Pacific Islander, 0.8% Other, 1.5% Hispanic of any race (2010); Average household size: 2.39 (2010); Median age: 44.3 (2010); Males per 100 females: 101.5 (2010); Homeownership rate: 83.8% (2010)

**NEW BERLIN** (village). Covers a land area of 1.065 square miles and a water area of 0 square miles. Located at 42.62° N. Lat; 75.33° W. Long. Elevation is 1,112 feet.
**Population:** 1,220 (1990); 1,129 (2000); 1,028 (2010); Density: 964.8 persons per square mile (2010); Race: 97.0% White, 0.8% Black, 0.3% Asian, 0.2% American Indian/Alaska Native, 0.0% Native Hawaiian/Other Pacific Islander, 1.7% Other, 1.4% Hispanic of any race (2010); Average household size: 2.36 (2010); Median age: 43.4 (2010); Males per 100 females: 85.6 (2010); Marriage status: 26.9% never married, 47.8% now married, 16.1% widowed, 9.3% divorced (2006-2010 5-year est.); Foreign born: 0.3% (2006-2010 5-year est.); Ancestry (includes multiple ancestries): 19.7% English, 19.3% Irish, 17.1% German, 7.2% French, 7.0% American (2006-2010 5-year est.).
**Economy:** Employment by occupation: 9.1% management, 1.7% professional, 7.9% services, 14.7% sales, 6.7% farming, 7.0% construction, 6.0% production (2006-2010 5-year est.).
**Income:** Per capita income: $22,302 (2006-2010 5-year est.); Median household income: $42,179 (2006-2010 5-year est.); Average household income: $54,725 (2006-2010 5-year est.); Percent of households with income of $100,000 or more: 7.0% (2006-2010 5-year est.); Poverty rate: 14.1% (2006-2010 5-year est.).
**Education:** Percent of population age 25 and over with: High school diploma (including GED) or higher: 84.0% (2006-2010 5-year est.); Bachelor's degree or higher: 19.1% (2006-2010 5-year est.); Master's degree or higher: 4.6% (2006-2010 5-year est.).

**School District(s)**
Unadilla Valley Central School District (PK-12)
    2009-10 Enrollment: 905 . . . . . . . . . . . . . . . . . . . . . . . (607) 847-7500
**Housing:** Homeownership rate: 59.2% (2010); Median home value: $81,700 (2006-2010 5-year est.); Median contract rent: $469 per month (2006-2010 5-year est.); Median year structure built: before 1940 (2006-2010 5-year est.).
**Transportation:** Commute to work: 84.7% car, 1.5% public transportation, 9.2% walk, 4.0% work from home (2006-2010 5-year est.); Travel time to work: 53.4% less than 15 minutes, 20.9% 15 to 30 minutes, 18.6% 30 to 45 minutes, 4.1% 45 to 60 minutes, 3.1% 60 minutes or more (2006-2010 5-year est.)

**NEW BERLIN** (town). Covers a land area of 46.133 square miles and a water area of 0.439 square miles. Located at 42.59° N. Lat; 75.38° W. Long. Elevation is 1,112 feet.
**History:** Incorporated 1819.
**Population:** 3,046 (1990); 2,803 (2000); 2,682 (2010); Density: 58.1 persons per square mile (2010); Race: 96.8% White, 0.6% Black, 0.3% Asian, 0.4% American Indian/Alaska Native, 0.0% Native Hawaiian/Other Pacific Islander, 1.9% Other, 1.4% Hispanic of any race (2010); Average household size: 2.43 (2010); Median age: 44.3 (2010); Males per 100 females: 92.5 (2010); Marriage status: 24.1% never married, 60.4% now married, 7.7% widowed, 7.8% divorced (2006-2010 5-year est.); Foreign born: 1.5% (2006-2010 5-year est.); Ancestry (includes multiple ancestries): 23.6% English, 18.5% Irish, 17.9% German, 6.1% Italian, 5.2% American (2006-2010 5-year est.).
**Economy:** Single-family building permits issued: 0 (2011); Multi-family building permits issued: 0 (2011); Employment by occupation: 10.1% management, 3.4% professional, 9.8% services, 14.5% sales, 2.3% farming, 11.1% construction, 8.4% production (2006-2010 5-year est.).
**Income:** Per capita income: $25,485 (2006-2010 5-year est.); Median household income: $46,029 (2006-2010 5-year est.); Average household income: $60,811 (2006-2010 5-year est.); Percent of households with income of $100,000 or more: 11.8% (2006-2010 5-year est.); Poverty rate: 9.7% (2006-2010 5-year est.).
**Education:** Percent of population age 25 and over with: High school diploma (including GED) or higher: 85.3% (2006-2010 5-year est.); Bachelor's degree or higher: 20.3% (2006-2010 5-year est.); Master's degree or higher: 7.0% (2006-2010 5-year est.).

### School District(s)
Unadilla Valley Central School District (PK-12)
    2009-10 Enrollment: 905 . . . . . . . . . . . . . . . . . . . . . (607) 847-7500
**Housing:** Homeownership rate: 73.8% (2010); Median home value: $103,000 (2006-2010 5-year est.); Median contract rent: $457 per month (2006-2010 5-year est.); Median year structure built: 1952 (2006-2010 5-year est.).
**Safety:** Violent crime rate: 17.9 per 10,000 population; Property crime rate: 328.9 per 10,000 population (2010).
**Transportation:** Commute to work: 88.6% car, 0.5% public transportation, 5.6% walk, 3.7% work from home (2006-2010 5-year est.); Travel time to work: 31.5% less than 15 minutes, 35.0% 15 to 30 minutes, 19.1% 30 to 45 minutes, 5.5% 45 to 60 minutes, 9.0% 60 minutes or more (2006-2010 5-year est.)

**NORTH NORWICH** (town). Aka Galena. Covers a land area of 28.142 square miles and a water area of 0.102 square miles. Located at 42.59° N. Lat; 75.50° W. Long. Elevation is 1,037 feet.
**Population:** 1,998 (1990); 1,966 (2000); 1,783 (2010); Density: 63.4 persons per square mile (2010); Race: 97.0% White, 0.6% Black, 0.7% Asian, 0.4% American Indian/Alaska Native, 0.0% Native Hawaiian/Other Pacific Islander, 1.3% Other, 1.2% Hispanic of any race (2010); Average household size: 2.49 (2010); Median age: 42.9 (2010); Males per 100 females: 99.2 (2010); Marriage status: 26.6% never married, 58.1% now married, 6.7% widowed, 8.5% divorced (2006-2010 5-year est.); Foreign born: 1.1% (2006-2010 5-year est.); Ancestry (includes multiple ancestries): 22.0% Irish, 17.6% German, 14.9% English, 14.1% Italian, 5.1% American (2006-2010 5-year est.).
**Economy:** Employment by occupation: 10.0% management, 1.4% professional, 4.8% services, 20.4% sales, 2.5% farming, 13.0% construction, 15.7% production (2006-2010 5-year est.).
**Income:** Per capita income: $21,178 (2006-2010 5-year est.); Median household income: $53,711 (2006-2010 5-year est.); Average household income: $58,715 (2006-2010 5-year est.); Percent of households with income of $100,000 or more: 11.6% (2006-2010 5-year est.); Poverty rate: 11.6% (2006-2010 5-year est.).
**Education:** Percent of population age 25 and over with: High school diploma (including GED) or higher: 87.9% (2006-2010 5-year est.); Bachelor's degree or higher: 13.6% (2006-2010 5-year est.); Master's degree or higher: 5.8% (2006-2010 5-year est.).
**Housing:** Homeownership rate: 85.7% (2010); Median home value: $77,900 (2006-2010 5-year est.); Median contract rent: $436 per month (2006-2010 5-year est.); Median year structure built: 1974 (2006-2010 5-year est.).
**Transportation:** Commute to work: 96.7% car, 0.0% public transportation, 2.6% walk, 0.5% work from home (2006-2010 5-year est.); Travel time to work: 46.6% less than 15 minutes, 32.7% 15 to 30 minutes, 9.0% 30 to 45

**NORTH PITCHER** (unincorporated postal area)
Zip Code: 13124
    Covers a land area of 4.685 square miles and a water area of 0.005 square miles. Located at 42.66° N. Lat; 75.82° W. Long. Elevation is 1,161 feet. Population: 124 (2010); Density: 26.5 persons per square mile (2010); Race: 100.0% White, 0.0% Black, 0.0% Asian, 0.0% American Indian/Alaska Native, 0.0% Native Hawaiian/Other Pacific Islander, 0.0% Other, 1.6% Hispanic of any race (2010); Average household size: 2.30 (2010); Median age: 44.0 (2010); Males per 100 females: 138.5 (2010); Homeownership rate: 87.0% (2010)

**NORWICH** (city). County seat. Covers a land area of 2.124 square miles and a water area of 0 square miles. Located at 42.53° N. Lat; 75.52° W. Long. Elevation is 1,014 feet.
**Population:** 7,753 (1990); 7,355 (2000); 7,190 (2010); Density: 3,384.5 persons per square mile (2010); Race: 94.6% White, 1.8% Black, 0.6% Asian, 0.2% American Indian/Alaska Native, 0.1% Native Hawaiian/Other Pacific Islander, 2.7% Other, 2.9% Hispanic of any race (2010); Average household size: 2.24 (2010); Median age: 38.3 (2010); Males per 100 females: 84.5 (2010); Marriage status: 31.4% never married, 43.6% now married, 13.0% widowed, 12.1% divorced (2006-2010 5-year est.); Foreign born: 4.3% (2006-2010 5-year est.); Ancestry (includes multiple ancestries): 17.5% English, 16.4% Irish, 15.0% German, 13.2% Italian, 5.3% Polish (2006-2010 5-year est.).
**Economy:** Single-family building permits issued: 0 (2011); Multi-family building permits issued: 0 (2011); Employment by occupation: 6.9% management, 6.5% professional, 11.8% services, 19.1% sales, 2.9% farming, 7.1% construction, 6.4% production (2006-2010 5-year est.).
**Income:** Per capita income: $20,117 (2006-2010 5-year est.); Median household income: $31,090 (2006-2010 5-year est.); Average household income: $47,099 (2006-2010 5-year est.); Percent of households with income of $100,000 or more: 9.4% (2006-2010 5-year est.); Poverty rate: 19.5% (2006-2010 5-year est.).
**Taxes:** Total city taxes per capita: $582 (2009); City property taxes per capita: $341 (2009).
**Education:** Percent of population age 25 and over with: High school diploma (including GED) or higher: 84.9% (2006-2010 5-year est.); Bachelor's degree or higher: 25.2% (2006-2010 5-year est.); Master's degree or higher: 8.4% (2006-2010 5-year est.).

### School District(s)
Delaware-Chenango-Madison-Otsego Boces
    2009-10 Enrollment: n/a . . . . . . . . . . . . . . . . . . . . . (607) 335-1233
Norwich City School District (PK-12)
    2009-10 Enrollment: 2,175 . . . . . . . . . . . . . . . . . . . (607) 334-1600
### Vocational/Technical School(s)
Delaware Chenango Madison Ostego BOCES-Practical Nursing (Public)
    Fall 2010 Enrollment: 84 . . . . . . . . . . . . . . . . . . . . . (607) 337-3304
    2011-12 Tuition: $8,105
**Housing:** Homeownership rate: 46.6% (2010); Median home value: $91,200 (2006-2010 5-year est.); Median contract rent: $459 per month (2006-2010 5-year est.); Median year structure built: before 1940 (2006-2010 5-year est.).
**Hospitals:** Chenango Memorial Hospital (139 beds)
**Safety:** Violent crime rate: 13.3 per 10,000 population; Property crime rate: 420.5 per 10,000 population (2010).
**Newspapers:** The Evening Sun (Local news; Circulation 5,800); Gazette (Community news; Circulation 2,500); New Berlin Gazette (Local news); Norwich Evening Sun (Local news; Circulation 5,400); The Norwich Pennysaver (Community news; Circulation 16,937)
**Transportation:** Commute to work: 86.6% car, 0.8% public transportation, 11.0% walk, 0.8% work from home (2006-2010 5-year est.); Travel time to work: 67.8% less than 15 minutes, 14.6% 15 to 30 minutes, 10.1% 30 to 45 minutes, 1.8% 45 to 60 minutes, 5.7% 60 minutes or more (2006-2010 5-year est.)
**Airports:** Lt Warren Eaton (general aviation)
**Additional Information Contacts**
City of Norwich . . . . . . . . . . . . . . . . . . . . . . . . . . . . (607) 334-1230
    http://www.norwichnewyork.net
Commerce Chenango . . . . . . . . . . . . . . . . . . . . . . . . (607) 334-1400
    http://www.chenangony.org

**NORWICH** (town). Covers a land area of 41.963 square miles and a water area of 0.074 square miles. Located at 42.51° N. Lat; 75.48° W. Long. Elevation is 1,014 feet.
**History:** Gail Borden born here. Settled 1788. Incorporated 1915.
**Population:** 3,944 (1990); 3,836 (2000); 3,998 (2010); Density: 95.3 persons per square mile (2010); Race: 96.6% White, 1.1% Black, 0.5% Asian, 0.4% American Indian/Alaska Native, 0.0% Native Hawaiian/Other Pacific Islander, 1.4% Other, 1.3% Hispanic of any race (2010); Average household size: 2.49 (2010); Median age: 42.2 (2010); Males per 100 females: 103.3 (2010); Marriage status: 21.3% never married, 64.7% now married, 6.8% widowed, 7.2% divorced (2006-2010 5-year est.); Foreign born: 2.6% (2006-2010 5-year est.); Ancestry (includes multiple ancestries): 19.5% Irish, 18.8% German, 18.4% English, 17.0% American, 6.5% Italian (2006-2010 5-year est.).
**Economy:** Employment by occupation: 8.0% management, 2.6% professional, 11.0% services, 16.0% sales, 2.3% farming, 6.0% construction, 6.3% production (2006-2010 5-year est.).
**Income:** Per capita income: $25,237 (2006-2010 5-year est.); Median household income: $41,199 (2006-2010 5-year est.); Average household income: $61,189 (2006-2010 5-year est.); Percent of households with income of $100,000 or more: 13.1% (2006-2010 5-year est.); Poverty rate: 12.2% (2006-2010 5-year est.).
**Education:** Percent of population age 25 and over with: High school diploma (including GED) or higher: 89.6% (2006-2010 5-year est.); Bachelor's degree or higher: 17.1% (2006-2010 5-year est.); Master's degree or higher: 4.8% (2006-2010 5-year est.).

**School District(s)**
Delaware-Chenango-Madison-Otsego Boces
   2009-10 Enrollment: n/a . . . . . . . . . . . . . . . . . . . . . . . . (607) 335-1233
Norwich City School District (PK-12)
   2009-10 Enrollment: 2,175 . . . . . . . . . . . . . . . . . . . . (607) 334-1600
**Vocational/Technical School(s)**
Delaware Chenango Madison Ostego BOCES-Practical Nursing (Public)
   Fall 2010 Enrollment: 84 . . . . . . . . . . . . . . . . . . . . . . (607) 337-3304
   2011-12 Tuition: $8,105
**Housing:** Homeownership rate: 84.3% (2010); Median home value: $84,500 (2006-2010 5-year est.); Median contract rent: $490 per month (2006-2010 5-year est.); Median year structure built: 1968 (2006-2010 5-year est.).
**Hospitals:** Chenango Memorial Hospital (139 beds)
**Newspapers:** The Evening Sun (Local news; Circulation 5,800); Gazette (Community news; Circulation 2,500); New Berlin Gazette (Local news); Norwich Evening Sun (Local news; Circulation 5,400); The Norwich Pennysaver (Community news; Circulation 16,937)
**Transportation:** Commute to work: 96.8% car, 0.0% public transportation, 0.6% walk, 1.7% work from home (2006-2010 5-year est.); Travel time to work: 59.5% less than 15 minutes, 29.1% 15 to 30 minutes, 6.8% 30 to 45 minutes, 2.3% 45 to 60 minutes, 2.3% 60 minutes or more (2006-2010 5-year est.)
**Airports:** Lt Warren Eaton (general aviation)

**OTSELIC** (town). Covers a land area of 37.976 square miles and a water area of 0.067 square miles. Located at 42.68° N. Lat; 75.73° W. Long. Elevation is 1,355 feet.
**Population:** 990 (1990); 1,001 (2000); 1,054 (2010); Density: 27.8 persons per square mile (2010); Race: 97.5% White, 0.3% Black, 0.8% Asian, 0.3% American Indian/Alaska Native, 0.0% Native Hawaiian/Other Pacific Islander, 1.1% Other, 2.8% Hispanic of any race (2010); Average household size: 2.77 (2010); Median age: 36.5 (2010); Males per 100 females: 116.0 (2010); Marriage status: 28.3% never married, 56.7% now married, 2.5% widowed, 12.5% divorced (2006-2010 5-year est.); Foreign born: 0.8% (2006-2010 5-year est.); Ancestry (includes multiple ancestries): 17.3% German, 13.0% English, 12.2% Irish, 7.2% American, 4.6% Dutch (2006-2010 5-year est.).
**Economy:** Employment by occupation: 9.2% management, 0.5% professional, 7.9% services, 9.6% sales, 0.5% farming, 13.4% construction, 11.9% production (2006-2010 5-year est.).
**Income:** Per capita income: $17,813 (2006-2010 5-year est.); Median household income: $42,006 (2006-2010 5-year est.); Average household income: $52,141 (2006-2010 5-year est.); Percent of households with income of $100,000 or more: 8.3% (2006-2010 5-year est.); Poverty rate: 18.5% (2006-2010 5-year est.).
**Education:** Percent of population age 25 and over with: High school diploma (including GED) or higher: 79.3% (2006-2010 5-year est.);

Bachelor's degree or higher: 17.9% (2006-2010 5-year est.); Master's degree or higher: 7.6% (2006-2010 5-year est.).
**Housing:** Homeownership rate: 79.5% (2010); Median home value: $78,600 (2006-2010 5-year est.); Median contract rent: $395 per month (2006-2010 5-year est.); Median year structure built: 1941 (2006-2010 5-year est.).
**Transportation:** Commute to work: 91.3% car, 0.0% public transportation, 5.6% walk, 2.5% work from home (2006-2010 5-year est.); Travel time to work: 30.2% less than 15 minutes, 21.6% 15 to 30 minutes, 31.8% 30 to 45 minutes, 5.8% 45 to 60 minutes, 10.6% 60 minutes or more (2006-2010 5-year est.)

**OXFORD** (village). Covers a land area of 1.784 square miles and a water area of 0 square miles. Located at 42.44° N. Lat; 75.59° W. Long. Elevation is 971 feet.
**Population:** 1,738 (1990); 1,584 (2000); 1,450 (2010); Density: 812.4 persons per square mile (2010); Race: 96.8% White, 0.5% Black, 0.2% Asian, 0.1% American Indian/Alaska Native, 0.0% Native Hawaiian/Other Pacific Islander, 2.4% Other, 2.5% Hispanic of any race (2010); Average household size: 2.44 (2010); Median age: 40.3 (2010); Males per 100 females: 90.0 (2010); Marriage status: 36.2% never married, 51.5% now married, 4.1% widowed, 8.3% divorced (2006-2010 5-year est.); Foreign born: 0.2% (2006-2010 5-year est.); Ancestry (includes multiple ancestries): 15.6% English, 11.2% German, 10.5% Irish, 4.9% Italian, 3.9% Polish (2006-2010 5-year est.).
**Economy:** Employment by occupation: 6.1% management, 0.8% professional, 8.1% services, 22.2% sales, 5.1% farming, 8.1% construction, 9.3% production (2006-2010 5-year est.).
**Income:** Per capita income: $20,053 (2006-2010 5-year est.); Median household income: $47,578 (2006-2010 5-year est.); Average household income: $57,084 (2006-2010 5-year est.); Percent of households with income of $100,000 or more: 13.1% (2006-2010 5-year est.); Poverty rate: 22.5% (2006-2010 5-year est.).
**Education:** Percent of population age 25 and over with: High school diploma (including GED) or higher: 85.2% (2006-2010 5-year est.); Bachelor's degree or higher: 20.2% (2006-2010 5-year est.); Master's degree or higher: 8.8% (2006-2010 5-year est.).

**School District(s)**
Oxford Academy and Central School District (PK-12)
   2009-10 Enrollment: 897 . . . . . . . . . . . . . . . . . . . . . (607) 843-2025
**Housing:** Homeownership rate: 68.6% (2010); Median home value: $87,300 (2006-2010 5-year est.); Median contract rent: $465 per month (2006-2010 5-year est.); Median year structure built: before 1940 (2006-2010 5-year est.).
**Safety:** Violent crime rate: 0.0 per 10,000 population; Property crime rate: 26.8 per 10,000 population (2010).
**Transportation:** Commute to work: 92.6% car, 0.0% public transportation, 1.9% walk, 5.5% work from home (2006-2010 5-year est.); Travel time to work: 35.0% less than 15 minutes, 36.1% 15 to 30 minutes, 14.8% 30 to 45 minutes, 7.8% 45 to 60 minutes, 6.3% 60 minutes or more (2006-2010 5-year est.)

**OXFORD** (town). Covers a land area of 60.063 square miles and a water area of 0.351 square miles. Located at 42.39° N. Lat; 75.59° W. Long. Elevation is 971 feet.
**History:** Site of N.Y. State Women's Relief Corps Home built in 1896 and now operated as the N.Y. State Veterans' Home. Settled 1788; incorporated 1808.
**Population:** 4,075 (1990); 3,992 (2000); 3,901 (2010); Density: 64.9 persons per square mile (2010); Race: 97.0% White, 0.5% Black, 0.3% Asian, 0.3% American Indian/Alaska Native, 0.0% Native Hawaiian/Other Pacific Islander, 1.9% Other, 2.2% Hispanic of any race (2010); Average household size: 2.46 (2010); Median age: 46.1 (2010); Males per 100 females: 105.7 (2010); Marriage status: 26.5% never married, 53.4% now married, 9.3% widowed, 10.9% divorced (2006-2010 5-year est.); Foreign born: 1.6% (2006-2010 5-year est.); Ancestry (includes multiple ancestries): 16.2% English, 14.1% German, 11.5% Irish, 5.9% American, 5.6% Dutch (2006-2010 5-year est.).
**Economy:** Employment by occupation: 12.2% management, 1.7% professional, 12.9% services, 18.1% sales, 2.7% farming, 9.8% construction, 9.7% production (2006-2010 5-year est.).
**Income:** Per capita income: $19,421 (2006-2010 5-year est.); Median household income: $47,407 (2006-2010 5-year est.); Average household income: $54,316 (2006-2010 5-year est.); Percent of households with

income of $100,000 or more: 7.8% (2006-2010 5-year est.); Poverty rate: 27.4% (2006-2010 5-year est.).

**Education:** Percent of population age 25 and over with: High school diploma (including GED) or higher: 84.5% (2006-2010 5-year est.); Bachelor's degree or higher: 13.6% (2006-2010 5-year est.); Master's degree or higher: 4.3% (2006-2010 5-year est.).

### School District(s)

Oxford Academy and Central School District (PK-12)

   2009-10 Enrollment: 897 . . . . . . . . . . . . . . . . . . . . . . . . . (607) 843-2025

**Housing:** Homeownership rate: 81.0% (2010); Median home value: $92,900 (2006-2010 5-year est.); Median contract rent: $475 per month (2006-2010 5-year est.); Median year structure built: 1954 (2006-2010 5-year est.).

**Transportation:** Commute to work: 90.0% car, 0.0% public transportation, 2.2% walk, 6.6% work from home (2006-2010 5-year est.); Travel time to work: 27.7% less than 15 minutes, 42.6% 15 to 30 minutes, 16.5% 30 to 45 minutes, 5.1% 45 to 60 minutes, 8.1% 60 minutes or more (2006-2010 5-year est.)

**PHARSALIA** (town). Covers a land area of 38.816 square miles and a water area of 0.291 square miles. Located at 42.59° N. Lat; 75.73° W. Long. Elevation is 1,562 feet.

**Population:** 735 (1990); 542 (2000); 593 (2010); Density: 15.3 persons per square mile (2010); Race: 98.0% White, 0.2% Black, 0.0% Asian, 0.8% American Indian/Alaska Native, 0.0% Native Hawaiian/Other Pacific Islander, 1.0% Other, 1.7% Hispanic of any race (2010); Average household size: 2.47 (2010); Median age: 45.9 (2010); Males per 100 females: 99.7 (2010); Marriage status: 32.8% never married, 53.9% now married, 2.9% widowed, 10.4% divorced (2006-2010 5-year est.); Foreign born: 0.0% (2006-2010 5-year est.); Ancestry (includes multiple ancestries): 16.9% English, 10.8% German, 7.9% Irish, 4.8% Polish, 3.3% Scotch-Irish (2006-2010 5-year est.).

**Economy:** Employment by occupation: 15.9% management, 1.1% professional, 6.2% services, 19.2% sales, 3.3% farming, 10.9% construction, 5.1% production (2006-2010 5-year est.).

**Income:** Per capita income: $17,308 (2006-2010 5-year est.); Median household income: $52,656 (2006-2010 5-year est.); Average household income: $52,345 (2006-2010 5-year est.); Percent of households with income of $100,000 or more: 2.8% (2006-2010 5-year est.); Poverty rate: 10.3% (2006-2010 5-year est.).

**Education:** Percent of population age 25 and over with: High school diploma (including GED) or higher: 78.8% (2006-2010 5-year est.); Bachelor's degree or higher: 15.4% (2006-2010 5-year est.); Master's degree or higher: 6.9% (2006-2010 5-year est.).

**Housing:** Homeownership rate: 88.0% (2010); Median home value: $61,000 (2006-2010 5-year est.); Median contract rent: $247 per month (2006-2010 5-year est.); Median year structure built: 1975 (2006-2010 5-year est.).

**Transportation:** Commute to work: 95.9% car, 0.0% public transportation, 1.1% walk, 1.9% work from home (2006-2010 5-year est.); Travel time to work: 18.3% less than 15 minutes, 52.9% 15 to 30 minutes, 16.3% 30 to 45 minutes, 2.7% 45 to 60 minutes, 9.9% 60 minutes or more (2006-2010 5-year est.)

**PITCHER** (town). Covers a land area of 28.464 square miles and a water area of 0.014 square miles. Located at 42.58° N. Lat; 75.82° W. Long. Elevation is 1,135 feet.

**Population:** 751 (1990); 848 (2000); 803 (2010); Density: 28.2 persons per square mile (2010); Race: 97.1% White, 0.7% Black, 0.0% Asian, 0.2% American Indian/Alaska Native, 0.0% Native Hawaiian/Other Pacific Islander, 2.0% Other, 3.7% Hispanic of any race (2010); Average household size: 2.56 (2010); Median age: 42.0 (2010); Males per 100 females: 111.3 (2010); Marriage status: 16.1% never married, 64.1% now married, 6.1% widowed, 13.7% divorced (2006-2010 5-year est.); Foreign born: 0.0% (2006-2010 5-year est.); Ancestry (includes multiple ancestries): 22.4% English, 14.2% German, 13.7% Irish, 10.0% Italian, 7.1% Norwegian (2006-2010 5-year est.).

**Economy:** Employment by occupation: 12.6% management, 3.4% professional, 9.8% services, 18.4% sales, 4.3% farming, 6.6% construction, 11.5% production (2006-2010 5-year est.).

**Income:** Per capita income: $28,243 (2006-2010 5-year est.); Median household income: $47,000 (2006-2010 5-year est.); Average household income: $61,714 (2006-2010 5-year est.); Percent of households with income of $100,000 or more: 18.1% (2006-2010 5-year est.); Poverty rate: 17.0% (2006-2010 5-year est.).

**Education:** Percent of population age 25 and over with: High school diploma (including GED) or higher: 89.4% (2006-2010 5-year est.); Bachelor's degree or higher: 13.1% (2006-2010 5-year est.); Master's degree or higher: 6.0% (2006-2010 5-year est.).

**Housing:** Homeownership rate: 83.7% (2010); Median home value: $78,000 (2006-2010 5-year est.); Median contract rent: $317 per month (2006-2010 5-year est.); Median year structure built: 1967 (2006-2010 5-year est.).

**Transportation:** Commute to work: 82.1% car, 0.0% public transportation, 1.8% walk, 14.3% work from home (2006-2010 5-year est.); Travel time to work: 23.3% less than 15 minutes, 15.7% 15 to 30 minutes, 39.7% 30 to 45 minutes, 13.2% 45 to 60 minutes, 8.0% 60 minutes or more (2006-2010 5-year est.)

**PLYMOUTH** (town). Covers a land area of 42.177 square miles and a water area of 0.168 square miles. Located at 42.60° N. Lat; 75.60° W. Long. Elevation is 1,243 feet.

**Population:** 1,704 (1990); 2,049 (2000); 1,804 (2010); Density: 42.8 persons per square mile (2010); Race: 97.1% White, 0.5% Black, 0.2% Asian, 0.4% American Indian/Alaska Native, 0.0% Native Hawaiian/Other Pacific Islander, 1.8% Other, 1.7% Hispanic of any race (2010); Average household size: 2.54 (2010); Median age: 44.4 (2010); Males per 100 females: 101.3 (2010); Marriage status: 25.4% never married, 62.1% now married, 4.4% widowed, 8.0% divorced (2006-2010 5-year est.); Foreign born: 0.8% (2006-2010 5-year est.); Ancestry (includes multiple ancestries): 22.3% German, 21.8% Irish, 19.8% English, 7.4% Italian, 6.2% French (2006-2010 5-year est.).

**Economy:** Employment by occupation: 9.2% management, 2.2% professional, 13.8% services, 18.1% sales, 4.0% farming, 16.6% construction, 9.0% production (2006-2010 5-year est.).

**Income:** Per capita income: $23,200 (2006-2010 5-year est.); Median household income: $53,864 (2006-2010 5-year est.); Average household income: $66,087 (2006-2010 5-year est.); Percent of households with income of $100,000 or more: 18.1% (2006-2010 5-year est.); Poverty rate: 9.4% (2006-2010 5-year est.).

**Education:** Percent of population age 25 and over with: High school diploma (including GED) or higher: 81.5% (2006-2010 5-year est.); Bachelor's degree or higher: 15.4% (2006-2010 5-year est.); Master's degree or higher: 8.2% (2006-2010 5-year est.).

**Housing:** Homeownership rate: 84.0% (2010); Median home value: $87,900 (2006-2010 5-year est.); Median contract rent: $443 per month (2006-2010 5-year est.); Median year structure built: 1975 (2006-2010 5-year est.).

**Transportation:** Commute to work: 90.4% car, 0.4% public transportation, 0.3% walk, 8.8% work from home (2006-2010 5-year est.); Travel time to work: 31.8% less than 15 minutes, 42.9% 15 to 30 minutes, 14.4% 30 to 45 minutes, 7.2% 45 to 60 minutes, 3.7% 60 minutes or more (2006-2010 5-year est.)

**PRESTON** (town). Covers a land area of 34.875 square miles and a water area of 0.171 square miles. Located at 42.50° N. Lat; 75.61° W. Long. Elevation is 1,470 feet.

**Population:** 1,100 (1990); 928 (2000); 1,044 (2010); Density: 29.9 persons per square mile (2010); Race: 97.7% White, 0.8% Black, 0.4% Asian, 0.2% American Indian/Alaska Native, 0.0% Native Hawaiian/Other Pacific Islander, 0.9% Other, 1.0% Hispanic of any race (2010); Average household size: 2.49 (2010); Median age: 44.3 (2010); Males per 100 females: 114.4 (2010); Marriage status: 21.5% never married, 56.4% now married, 9.9% widowed, 12.2% divorced (2006-2010 5-year est.); Foreign born: 0.9% (2006-2010 5-year est.); Ancestry (includes multiple ancestries): 19.6% English, 16.8% German, 10.8% Irish, 9.2% Italian, 7.6% American (2006-2010 5-year est.).

**Economy:** Employment by occupation: 8.8% management, 0.0% professional, 9.5% services, 17.1% sales, 3.2% farming, 17.6% construction, 9.8% production (2006-2010 5-year est.).

**Income:** Per capita income: $23,884 (2006-2010 5-year est.); Median household income: $60,179 (2006-2010 5-year est.); Average household income: $64,124 (2006-2010 5-year est.); Percent of households with income of $100,000 or more: 14.7% (2006-2010 5-year est.); Poverty rate: 18.5% (2006-2010 5-year est.).

**Education:** Percent of population age 25 and over with: High school diploma (including GED) or higher: 76.7% (2006-2010 5-year est.); Bachelor's degree or higher: 11.0% (2006-2010 5-year est.); Master's degree or higher: 3.3% (2006-2010 5-year est.).

**Housing:** Homeownership rate: 89.3% (2010); Median home value: $83,700 (2006-2010 5-year est.); Median contract rent: $255 per month (2006-2010 5-year est.); Median year structure built: 1972 (2006-2010 5-year est.).

**Transportation:** Commute to work: 88.5% car, 0.0% public transportation, 0.8% walk, 9.3% work from home (2006-2010 5-year est.); Travel time to work: 27.9% less than 15 minutes, 42.0% 15 to 30 minutes, 16.9% 30 to 45 minutes, 6.4% 45 to 60 minutes, 6.9% 60 minutes or more (2006-2010 5-year est.)

**SHERBURNE** (village). Covers a land area of 1.519 square miles and a water area of 0 square miles. Located at 42.68° N. Lat; 75.49° W. Long. Elevation is 1,047 feet.

**Population:** 1,531 (1990); 1,455 (2000); 1,367 (2010); Density: 899.7 persons per square mile (2010); Race: 97.2% White, 0.8% Black, 0.5% Asian, 0.3% American Indian/Alaska Native, 0.0% Native Hawaiian/Other Pacific Islander, 1.2% Other, 2.1% Hispanic of any race (2010); Average household size: 2.15 (2010); Median age: 42.3 (2010); Males per 100 females: 83.7 (2010); Marriage status: 18.5% never married, 60.2% now married, 8.9% widowed, 12.4% divorced (2006-2010 5-year est.); Foreign born: 1.1% (2006-2010 5-year est.); Ancestry (includes multiple ancestries): 17.4% Irish, 14.8% English, 10.0% German, 7.7% American, 6.4% French (2006-2010 5-year est.).

**Economy:** Employment by occupation: 9.4% management, 3.5% professional, 7.3% services, 17.1% sales, 0.8% farming, 7.2% construction, 6.1% production (2006-2010 5-year est.).

**Income:** Per capita income: $26,975 (2006-2010 5-year est.); Median household income: $44,318 (2006-2010 5-year est.); Average household income: $60,811 (2006-2010 5-year est.); Percent of households with income of $100,000 or more: 15.2% (2006-2010 5-year est.); Poverty rate: 12.0% (2006-2010 5-year est.).

**Taxes:** Total city taxes per capita: $243 (2009); City property taxes per capita: $216 (2009).

**Education:** Percent of population age 25 and over with: High school diploma (including GED) or higher: 88.6% (2006-2010 5-year est.); Bachelor's degree or higher: 18.7% (2006-2010 5-year est.); Master's degree or higher: 9.1% (2006-2010 5-year est.).

**School District(s)**
Sherburne-Earlville Central School District (PK-12)
    2009-10 Enrollment: 1,518 . . . . . . . . . . . . . . . . . . . . . (607) 674-7300

**Housing:** Homeownership rate: 50.5% (2010); Median home value: $108,800 (2006-2010 5-year est.); Median contract rent: $384 per month (2006-2010 5-year est.); Median year structure built: before 1940 (2006-2010 5-year est.).

**Safety:** Violent crime rate: 7.3 per 10,000 population; Property crime rate: 218.3 per 10,000 population (2010).

**Newspapers:** NEWS (Community news; Circulation 2,000)

**Transportation:** Commute to work: 84.4% car, 0.0% public transportation, 11.4% walk, 2.1% work from home (2006-2010 5-year est.); Travel time to work: 43.6% less than 15 minutes, 39.5% 15 to 30 minutes, 8.2% 30 to 45 minutes, 5.1% 45 to 60 minutes, 3.6% 60 minutes or more (2006-2010 5-year est.)

**SHERBURNE** (town). Covers a land area of 43.553 square miles and a water area of 0.019 square miles. Located at 42.69° N. Lat; 75.48° W. Long. Elevation is 1,047 feet.

**History:** Former summer resort. Settled 1793, incorporated 1830.

**Population:** 3,903 (1990); 3,979 (2000); 4,048 (2010); Density: 92.9 persons per square mile (2010); Race: 97.6% White, 0.4% Black, 0.3% Asian, 0.2% American Indian/Alaska Native, 0.0% Native Hawaiian/Other Pacific Islander, 1.5% Other, 1.6% Hispanic of any race (2010); Average household size: 2.43 (2010); Median age: 42.3 (2010); Males per 100 females: 94.0 (2010); Marriage status: 20.7% never married, 63.8% now married, 5.8% widowed, 9.7% divorced (2006-2010 5-year est.); Foreign born: 1.3% (2006-2010 5-year est.); Ancestry (includes multiple ancestries): 17.9% Irish, 16.2% English, 14.8% German, 10.1% Italian, 6.9% American (2006-2010 5-year est.).

**Economy:** Employment by occupation: 17.5% management, 2.2% professional, 7.5% services, 17.8% sales, 1.0% farming, 8.3% construction, 5.4% production (2006-2010 5-year est.).

**Income:** Per capita income: $25,041 (2006-2010 5-year est.); Median household income: $47,868 (2006-2010 5-year est.); Average household income: $64,953 (2006-2010 5-year est.); Percent of households with income of $100,000 or more: 11.3% (2006-2010 5-year est.); Poverty rate: 6.7% (2006-2010 5-year est.).

**Education:** Percent of population age 25 and over with: High school diploma (including GED) or higher: 86.0% (2006-2010 5-year est.); Bachelor's degree or higher: 14.3% (2006-2010 5-year est.); Master's degree or higher: 5.4% (2006-2010 5-year est.).

**School District(s)**
Sherburne-Earlville Central School District (PK-12)
    2009-10 Enrollment: 1,518 . . . . . . . . . . . . . . . . . . . . . (607) 674-7300

**Housing:** Homeownership rate: 69.8% (2010); Median home value: $99,800 (2006-2010 5-year est.); Median contract rent: $390 per month (2006-2010 5-year est.); Median year structure built: 1957 (2006-2010 5-year est.).

**Newspapers:** NEWS (Community news; Circulation 2,000)

**Transportation:** Commute to work: 85.6% car, 0.0% public transportation, 4.8% walk, 8.6% work from home (2006-2010 5-year est.); Travel time to work: 45.2% less than 15 minutes, 38.8% 15 to 30 minutes, 7.7% 30 to 45 minutes, 3.4% 45 to 60 minutes, 5.0% 60 minutes or more (2006-2010 5-year est.)

**SMITHVILLE** (town). Covers a land area of 50.444 square miles and a water area of 0.480 square miles. Located at 42.41° N. Lat; 75.75° W. Long.

**Population:** 1,167 (1990); 1,347 (2000); 1,330 (2010); Density: 26.4 persons per square mile (2010); Race: 97.1% White, 0.8% Black, 0.2% Asian, 0.8% American Indian/Alaska Native, 0.0% Native Hawaiian/Other Pacific Islander, 1.1% Other, 0.8% Hispanic of any race (2010); Average household size: 2.53 (2010); Median age: 44.6 (2010); Males per 100 females: 115.2 (2010); Marriage status: 28.1% never married, 50.7% now married, 9.4% widowed, 11.8% divorced (2006-2010 5-year est.); Foreign born: 3.6% (2006-2010 5-year est.); Ancestry (includes multiple ancestries): 19.3% Irish, 14.4% English, 13.2% German, 8.0% American, 4.0% Italian (2006-2010 5-year est.).

**Economy:** Employment by occupation: 6.4% management, 3.5% professional, 16.9% services, 11.3% sales, 3.0% farming, 15.2% construction, 11.3% production (2006-2010 5-year est.).

**Income:** Per capita income: $21,804 (2006-2010 5-year est.); Median household income: $46,080 (2006-2010 5-year est.); Average household income: $57,576 (2006-2010 5-year est.); Percent of households with income of $100,000 or more: 14.0% (2006-2010 5-year est.); Poverty rate: 15.4% (2006-2010 5-year est.).

**Education:** Percent of population age 25 and over with: High school diploma (including GED) or higher: 85.2% (2006-2010 5-year est.); Bachelor's degree or higher: 11.7% (2006-2010 5-year est.); Master's degree or higher: 5.1% (2006-2010 5-year est.).

**Housing:** Homeownership rate: 84.9% (2010); Median home value: $84,600 (2006-2010 5-year est.); Median contract rent: $324 per month (2006-2010 5-year est.); Median year structure built: 1970 (2006-2010 5-year est.).

**Transportation:** Commute to work: 87.4% car, 0.0% public transportation, 4.5% walk, 7.4% work from home (2006-2010 5-year est.); Travel time to work: 26.9% less than 15 minutes, 24.4% 15 to 30 minutes, 26.5% 30 to 45 minutes, 12.4% 45 to 60 minutes, 9.8% 60 minutes or more (2006-2010 5-year est.)

**SMITHVILLE FLATS** (CDP). Covers a land area of 1.421 square miles and a water area of 0 square miles. Located at 42.39° N. Lat; 75.81° W. Long. Elevation is 1,024 feet.

**Population:** n/a (1990); n/a (2000); 351 (2010); Density: 246.8 persons per square mile (2010); Race: 97.7% White, 0.6% Black, 0.0% Asian, 0.9% American Indian/Alaska Native, 0.0% Native Hawaiian/Other Pacific Islander, 0.8% Other, 0.0% Hispanic of any race (2010); Average household size: 2.42 (2010); Median age: 41.9 (2010); Males per 100 females: 123.6 (2010); Marriage status: 32.7% never married, 35.3% now married, 13.6% widowed, 18.4% divorced (2006-2010 5-year est.); Foreign born: 6.0% (2006-2010 5-year est.); Ancestry (includes multiple ancestries): 34.9% Irish, 16.2% English, 8.1% German, 8.1% Scottish, 8.1% Pennsylvania German (2006-2010 5-year est.).

**Economy:** Employment by occupation: 0.0% management, 0.0% professional, 19.7% services, 16.5% sales, 3.9% farming, 7.9% construction, 10.2% production (2006-2010 5-year est.).

**Income:** Per capita income: $18,440 (2006-2010 5-year est.); Median household income: $38,333 (2006-2010 5-year est.); Average household income: $42,592 (2006-2010 5-year est.); Percent of households with income of $100,000 or more: 6.6% (2006-2010 5-year est.); Poverty rate: 20.1% (2006-2010 5-year est.).

**Education:** Percent of population age 25 and over with: High school diploma (including GED) or higher: 76.7% (2006-2010 5-year est.); Bachelor's degree or higher: 8.1% (2006-2010 5-year est.); Master's degree or higher: 1.8% (2006-2010 5-year est.).
**Housing:** Homeownership rate: 80.7% (2010); Median home value: $81,100 (2006-2010 5-year est.); Median contract rent: $195 per month (2006-2010 5-year est.); Median year structure built: 1956 (2006-2010 5-year est.).
**Transportation:** Commute to work: 97.3% car, 0.0% public transportation, 2.7% walk, 0.0% work from home (2006-2010 5-year est.); Travel time to work: 33.0% less than 15 minutes, 22.3% 15 to 30 minutes, 21.4% 30 to 45 minutes, 20.5% 45 to 60 minutes, 2.7% 60 minutes or more (2006-2010 5-year est.)

**SMYRNA** (village). Covers a land area of 0.244 square miles and a water area of 0 square miles. Located at 42.68° N. Lat; 75.56° W. Long. Elevation is 1,204 feet.
**Population:** 211 (1990); 241 (2000); 213 (2010); Density: 872.4 persons per square mile (2010); Race: 98.1% White, 0.9% Black, 0.0% Asian, 0.0% American Indian/Alaska Native, 0.0% Native Hawaiian/Other Pacific Islander, 1.0% Other, 0.0% Hispanic of any race (2010); Average household size: 2.70 (2010); Median age: 38.8 (2010); Males per 100 females: 95.4 (2010); Marriage status: 24.5% never married, 63.9% now married, 2.6% widowed, 9.0% divorced (2006-2010 5-year est.); Foreign born: 0.0% (2006-2010 5-year est.); Ancestry (includes multiple ancestries): 12.9% Italian, 12.3% English, 9.9% American, 9.4% German, 8.2% Polish (2006-2010 5-year est.).
**Economy:** Employment by occupation: 3.4% management, 0.0% professional, 4.6% services, 21.8% sales, 0.0% farming, 16.1% construction, 0.0% production (2006-2010 5-year est.).
**Income:** Per capita income: $19,850 (2006-2010 5-year est.); Median household income: $41,875 (2006-2010 5-year est.); Average household income: $47,652 (2006-2010 5-year est.); Percent of households with income of $100,000 or more: 7.2% (2006-2010 5-year est.); Poverty rate: 18.1% (2006-2010 5-year est.).
**Education:** Percent of population age 25 and over with: High school diploma (including GED) or higher: 90.0% (2006-2010 5-year est.); Bachelor's degree or higher: 21.5% (2006-2010 5-year est.); Master's degree or higher: 6.9% (2006-2010 5-year est.).
**Housing:** Homeownership rate: 68.4% (2010); Median home value: $77,000 (2006-2010 5-year est.); Median contract rent: $371 per month (2006-2010 5-year est.); Median year structure built: before 1940 (2006-2010 5-year est.).
**Transportation:** Commute to work: 94.3% car, 0.0% public transportation, 3.4% walk, 2.3% work from home (2006-2010 5-year est.); Travel time to work: 48.2% less than 15 minutes, 37.6% 15 to 30 minutes, 14.1% 30 to 45 minutes, 0.0% 45 to 60 minutes, 0.0% 60 minutes or more (2006-2010 5-year est.)

**SMYRNA** (town). Covers a land area of 42.087 square miles and a water area of 0.075 square miles. Located at 42.68° N. Lat; 75.61° W. Long. Elevation is 1,204 feet.
**Population:** 1,265 (1990); 1,418 (2000); 1,280 (2010); Density: 30.4 persons per square mile (2010); Race: 98.0% White, 0.3% Black, 0.2% Asian, 0.5% American Indian/Alaska Native, 0.0% Native Hawaiian/Other Pacific Islander, 1.0% Other, 0.9% Hispanic of any race (2010); Average household size: 2.66 (2010); Median age: 41.8 (2010); Males per 100 females: 113.0 (2010); Marriage status: 26.8% never married, 61.1% now married, 4.3% widowed, 7.8% divorced (2006-2010 5-year est.); Foreign born: 0.9% (2006-2010 5-year est.); Ancestry (includes multiple ancestries): 29.2% English, 14.9% German, 8.2% Irish, 7.9% Italian, 6.8% American (2006-2010 5-year est.).
**Economy:** Employment by occupation: 7.7% management, 4.1% professional, 12.7% services, 13.0% sales, 4.8% farming, 13.0% construction, 11.8% production (2006-2010 5-year est.).
**Income:** Per capita income: $20,506 (2006-2010 5-year est.); Median household income: $42,969 (2006-2010 5-year est.); Average household income: $51,062 (2006-2010 5-year est.); Percent of households with income of $100,000 or more: 9.5% (2006-2010 5-year est.); Poverty rate: 17.2% (2006-2010 5-year est.).
**Education:** Percent of population age 25 and over with: High school diploma (including GED) or higher: 87.2% (2006-2010 5-year est.); Bachelor's degree or higher: 10.7% (2006-2010 5-year est.); Master's degree or higher: 3.8% (2006-2010 5-year est.).

**Housing:** Homeownership rate: 85.0% (2010); Median home value: $79,900 (2006-2010 5-year est.); Median contract rent: $410 per month (2006-2010 5-year est.); Median year structure built: 1973 (2006-2010 5-year est.).
**Transportation:** Commute to work: 84.5% car, 1.7% public transportation, 6.1% walk, 6.6% work from home (2006-2010 5-year est.); Travel time to work: 32.8% less than 15 minutes, 40.9% 15 to 30 minutes, 18.2% 30 to 45 minutes, 3.2% 45 to 60 minutes, 4.9% 60 minutes or more (2006-2010 5-year est.)

**SOUTH NEW BERLIN** (unincorporated postal area)
Zip Code: 13843
Covers a land area of 54.416 square miles and a water area of 0.078 square miles. Located at 42.50° N. Lat; 75.38° W. Long. Elevation is 1,058 feet. Population: 1,888 (2010); Density: 34.7 persons per square mile (2010); Race: 97.4% White, 0.4% Black, 0.2% Asian, 0.2% American Indian/Alaska Native, 0.0% Native Hawaiian/Other Pacific Islander, 1.8% Other, 1.5% Hispanic of any race (2010); Average household size: 2.42 (2010); Median age: 45.0 (2010); Males per 100 females: 102.1 (2010); Homeownership rate: 86.5% (2010)

**SOUTH OTSELIC** (unincorporated postal area)
Zip Code: 13155
Covers a land area of 20.451 square miles and a water area of 0.053 square miles. Located at 42.67° N. Lat; 75.77° W. Long. Elevation is 1,227 feet. Population: 663 (2010); Density: 32.4 persons per square mile (2010); Race: 97.4% White, 0.5% Black, 0.5% Asian, 0.5% American Indian/Alaska Native, 0.0% Native Hawaiian/Other Pacific Islander, 1.1% Other, 2.6% Hispanic of any race (2010); Average household size: 2.67 (2010); Median age: 38.2 (2010); Males per 100 females: 110.5 (2010); Homeownership rate: 77.0% (2010)

**SOUTH PLYMOUTH** (unincorporated postal area)
Zip Code: 13844
Covers a land area of 23.990 square miles and a water area of 0.041 square miles. Located at 42.60° N. Lat; 75.66° W. Long. Elevation is 1,138 feet. Population: 724 (2010); Density: 30.2 persons per square mile (2010); Race: 97.7% White, 0.0% Black, 0.3% Asian, 0.1% American Indian/Alaska Native, 0.0% Native Hawaiian/Other Pacific Islander, 1.9% Other, 2.3% Hispanic of any race (2010); Average household size: 2.54 (2010); Median age: 44.3 (2010); Males per 100 females: 102.2 (2010); Homeownership rate: 85.3% (2010)

# Clinton County

Located in northeastern New York; bounded on the north by the Canadian province of Quebec, and on the east by Lake Champlain and the Vermont border; includes the North Adirondacks. Covers a land area of 1,038.95 square miles, a water area of 78.67 square miles, and is located in the Eastern Time Zone at 44.73° N. Lat., 73.59° W. Long. The county was founded in 1788. County seat is Plattsburgh.

Clinton County is part of the Plattsburgh, NY Micropolitan Statistical Area. The entire metro area includes: Clinton County, NY

| Weather Station: Chazy | | | | | | | | | | Elevation: 169 feet | | |
|---|---|---|---|---|---|---|---|---|---|---|---|---|
| | Jan | Feb | Mar | Apr | May | Jun | Jul | Aug | Sep | Oct | Nov | Dec |
| High | 27 | 30 | 40 | 55 | 68 | 76 | 80 | 79 | 70 | 57 | 45 | 33 |
| Low | 8 | 10 | 20 | 34 | 45 | 54 | 59 | 57 | 49 | 39 | 29 | 16 |
| Precip | 0.8 | na | 0.9 | 2.3 | 2.9 | 3.5 | 3.5 | 3.8 | 3.2 | 3.1 | 2.2 | 0.8 |
| Snow | 13.7 | 12.7 | 11.1 | 2.9 | 0.1 | 0.0 | 0.0 | 0.0 | 0.0 | 0.3 | 4.6 | 11.2 |

*High and Low temperatures in degrees Fahrenheit; Precipitation and Snow in inches*

| Weather Station: Dannemora | | | | | | | | | | Elevation: 1,339 feet | | |
|---|---|---|---|---|---|---|---|---|---|---|---|---|
| | Jan | Feb | Mar | Apr | May | Jun | Jul | Aug | Sep | Oct | Nov | Dec |
| High | 26 | 30 | 38 | 53 | 65 | 74 | 78 | 76 | 68 | 56 | 43 | 31 |
| Low | 8 | 11 | 20 | 33 | 45 | 54 | 58 | 57 | 49 | 38 | 28 | 15 |
| Precip | 2.5 | 2.1 | 2.5 | 3.3 | 3.6 | 4.0 | 4.2 | 4.4 | 3.9 | 3.9 | 3.6 | 2.9 |
| Snow | na | na | na | tr | 0.0 | 0.0 | 0.0 | 0.0 | 0.0 | tr | 1.0 | na |

*High and Low temperatures in degrees Fahrenheit; Precipitation and Snow in inches*

| Weather Station: Peru 2 WSW | | | | | | | | | | Elevation: 509 feet | |
|---|---|---|---|---|---|---|---|---|---|---|---|
| | Jan | Feb | Mar | Apr | May | Jun | Jul | Aug | Sep | Oct | Nov | Dec |
| High | 28 | 32 | 41 | 56 | 68 | 77 | 81 | 79 | 71 | 58 | 45 | 33 |
| Low | 9 | 12 | 21 | 34 | 45 | 54 | 59 | 57 | 49 | 38 | 29 | 17 |
| Precip | 1.4 | 1.3 | 1.7 | 2.6 | 2.7 | 3.6 | 3.5 | 3.5 | 2.8 | 3.0 | 2.7 | 2.0 |
| Snow | 11.3 | 10.4 | 11.1 | 2.9 | 0.0 | 0.0 | 0.0 | 0.0 | 0.0 | 0.5 | 3.2 | 12.6 |

*High and Low temperatures in degrees Fahrenheit; Precipitation and Snow in inches*

**Population:** 85,969 (1990); 79,894 (2000); 82,128 (2010); Race: 92.5% White, 3.9% Black, 1.1% Asian, 0.3% American Indian/Alaska Native, 0.0% Native Hawaiian/Other Pacific Islander, 2.2% Other, 2.5% Hispanic of any race (2010); Density: 79.0 persons per square mile (2010); Average household size: 2.37 (2010); Median age: 39.1 (2010); Males per 100 females: 105.2 (2010).
**Religion:** Six largest groups: 33.7% Catholicism, 2.2% Methodist/Pietist, 1.9% Muslim Estimate, 1.4% Holiness, 0.8% Presbyterian-Reformed, 0.7% Non-Denominational (2010)
**Economy:** Unemployment rate: 10.7% (February 2012); Total civilian labor force: 37,989 (February 2012); Leading industries: 20.1% health care and social assistance; 20.0% retail trade; 13.7% manufacturing (2009); Farms: 590 totaling 149,219 acres (2007); Companies that employ 500 or more persons: 3 (2009); Companies that employ 100 to 499 persons: 31 (2009); Companies that employ less than 100 persons: 1,877 (2009); Black-owned businesses: n/a (2007); Hispanic-owned businesses: n/a (2007); Asian-owned businesses: n/a (2007); Women-owned businesses: 1,269 (2007); Retail sales per capita: $14,347 (2010). Single-family building permits issued: 68 (2011); Multi-family building permits issued: 26 (2011).
**Income:** Per capita income: $22,660 (2006-2010 5-year est.); Median household income: $47,489 (2006-2010 5-year est.); Average household income: $58,803 (2006-2010 5-year est.); Percent of households with income of $100,000 or more: 14.9% (2006-2010 5-year est.); Poverty rate: 13.3% (2006-2010 5-year est.); Bankruptcy rate: 2.34% (2011).
**Education:** Percent of population age 25 and over with: High school diploma (including GED) or higher: 84.2% (2006-2010 5-year est.); Bachelor's degree or higher: 21.7% (2006-2010 5-year est.); Master's degree or higher: 9.5% (2006-2010 5-year est.).
**Housing:** Homeownership rate: 68.3% (2010); Median home value: $117,800 (2006-2010 5-year est.); Median contract rent: $553 per month (2006-2010 5-year est.); Median year structure built: 1968 (2006-2010 5-year est.)
**Health:** Birth rate: 93.7 per 10,000 population (2011); Death rate: 79.2 per 10,000 population (2011); Age-adjusted cancer mortality rate: 159.7 deaths per 100,000 population (2009); Number of physicians: 22.8 per 10,000 population (2008); Hospital beds: 39.3 per 10,000 population (2007); Hospital admissions: 1,286.5 per 10,000 population (2007).
**Elections:** 2008 Presidential election results: 60.6% Obama, 37.7% McCain, 0.9% Nader
**National and State Parks:** Ausable Marsh State Game Management Area; Clinton State Forest; Clinton State Forest Number Eight; Cumberland Bay State Park; King Bay State Wetlands Game Management Area; Lake Alice State Game Management Area; Miner Lake State Park; New York State Game Management Area
**Additional Information Contacts**
Clinton County Government . . . . . . . . . . . . . . . . . . . . . . . (518) 565-4700
  http://www.co.clinton.ny.us
Plattsburgh North Country Chamber of Commerce . . . . . . . (518) 563-1000
  http://www.northcountrychamber.com
Town of Clinton . . . . . . . . . . . . . . . . . . . . . . . . . . . . . . (845) 266-5853
  http://www.townofclinton.com

## Clinton County Communities

**ALTONA** (town). Covers a land area of 100.983 square miles and a water area of 0.356 square miles. Located at 44.84° N. Lat; 73.67° W. Long. Elevation is 636 feet.
**Population:** 2,775 (1990); 3,160 (2000); 2,887 (2010); Density: 28.6 persons per square mile (2010); Race: 88.9% White, 8.5% Black, 0.1% Asian, 0.6% American Indian/Alaska Native, 0.0% Native Hawaiian/Other Pacific Islander, 1.9% Other, 2.8% Hispanic of any race (2010); Average household size: 2.58 (2010); Median age: 38.6 (2010); Males per 100 females: 134.7 (2010); Marriage status: 33.5% never married, 52.8% now married, 5.6% widowed, 8.2% divorced (2006-2010 5-year est.); Foreign born: 2.2% (2006-2010 5-year est.); Ancestry (includes multiple ancestries): 28.9% French, 11.2% Irish, 10.4% English, 9.1% American, 7.7% French Canadian (2006-2010 5-year est.).

**Economy:** Single-family building permits issued: 5 (2011); Multi-family building permits issued: 0 (2011); Employment by occupation: 4.5% management, 0.2% professional, 9.1% services, 12.6% sales, 3.1% farming, 17.4% construction, 10.1% production (2006-2010 5-year est.).
**Income:** Per capita income: $16,986 (2006-2010 5-year est.); Median household income: $40,606 (2006-2010 5-year est.); Average household income: $47,301 (2006-2010 5-year est.); Percent of households with income of $100,000 or more: 6.2% (2006-2010 5-year est.); Poverty rate: 16.4% (2006-2010 5-year est.).
**Education:** Percent of population age 25 and over with: High school diploma (including GED) or higher: 72.9% (2006-2010 5-year est.); Bachelor's degree or higher: 6.4% (2006-2010 5-year est.); Master's degree or higher: 2.7% (2006-2010 5-year est.).
**Housing:** Homeownership rate: 80.9% (2010); Median home value: $87,200 (2006-2010 5-year est.); Median contract rent: $364 per month (2006-2010 5-year est.); Median year structure built: 1983 (2006-2010 5-year est.).
**Transportation:** Commute to work: 93.9% car, 0.7% public transportation, 0.9% walk, 4.5% work from home (2006-2010 5-year est.); Travel time to work: 16.2% less than 15 minutes, 60.0% 15 to 30 minutes, 18.4% 30 to 45 minutes, 3.0% 45 to 60 minutes, 2.5% 60 minutes or more (2006-2010 5-year est.)

**ALTONA** (CDP). Covers a land area of 1.709 square miles and a water area of 0 square miles. Located at 44.89° N. Lat; 73.65° W. Long. Elevation is 636 feet.
**Population:** 1,018 (1990); 1,056 (2000); 730 (2010); Density: 427.1 persons per square mile (2010); Race: 63.4% White, 32.9% Black, 0.4% Asian, 0.5% American Indian/Alaska Native, 0.0% Native Hawaiian/Other Pacific Islander, 2.8% Other, 9.9% Hispanic of any race (2010); Average household size: 2.28 (2010); Median age: 36.3 (2010); Males per 100 females: 371.0 (2010); Marriage status: 49.9% never married, 39.3% now married, 5.4% widowed, 5.4% divorced (2006-2010 5-year est.); Foreign born: 5.0% (2006-2010 5-year est.); Ancestry (includes multiple ancestries): 25.7% French, 9.6% Irish, 5.3% English, 3.0% German, 1.2% Italian (2006-2010 5-year est.).
**Economy:** Employment by occupation: 0.0% management, 0.0% professional, 13.6% services, 30.7% sales, 0.0% farming, 8.0% construction, 0.0% production (2006-2010 5-year est.).
**Income:** Per capita income: $6,612 (2006-2010 5-year est.); Median household income: $38,929 (2006-2010 5-year est.); Average household income: $42,188 (2006-2010 5-year est.); Percent of households with income of $100,000 or more: 6.1% (2006-2010 5-year est.); Poverty rate: 13.7% (2006-2010 5-year est.).
**Education:** Percent of population age 25 and over with: High school diploma (including GED) or higher: 53.3% (2006-2010 5-year est.); Bachelor's degree or higher: 2.0% (2006-2010 5-year est.); Master's degree or higher: 1.1% (2006-2010 5-year est.).
**Housing:** Homeownership rate: 64.5% (2010); Median home value: $92,500 (2006-2010 5-year est.); Median contract rent: $245 per month (2006-2010 5-year est.); Median year structure built: 1956 (2006-2010 5-year est.).
**Transportation:** Commute to work: 86.4% car, 0.0% public transportation, 13.6% walk, 0.0% work from home (2006-2010 5-year est.); Travel time to work: 13.6% less than 15 minutes, 70.4% 15 to 30 minutes, 16.0% 30 to 45 minutes, 0.0% 45 to 60 minutes, 0.0% 60 minutes or more (2006-2010 5-year est.)

**AU SABLE** (town). Covers a land area of 39.109 square miles and a water area of 4.739 square miles. Located at 44.50° N. Lat; 73.53° W. Long.
**Population:** 2,870 (1990); 3,015 (2000); 3,146 (2010); Density: 80.4 persons per square mile (2010); Race: 96.7% White, 0.9% Black, 0.5% Asian, 0.2% American Indian/Alaska Native, 0.0% Native Hawaiian/Other Pacific Islander, 1.7% Other, 1.5% Hispanic of any race (2010); Average household size: 2.41 (2010); Median age: 40.8 (2010); Males per 100 females: 99.9 (2010); Marriage status: 29.5% never married, 56.1% now married, 6.3% widowed, 8.0% divorced (2006-2010 5-year est.); Foreign born: 2.6% (2006-2010 5-year est.); Ancestry (includes multiple ancestries): 29.1% French, 19.2% Irish, 7.9% American, 7.7% English, 7.4% German (2006-2010 5-year est.).
**Economy:** Single-family building permits issued: 5 (2011); Multi-family building permits issued: 0 (2011); Employment by occupation: 7.3% management, 0.5% professional, 13.2% services, 15.5% sales, 6.5% farming, 19.5% construction, 8.4% production (2006-2010 5-year est.).

**Income:** Per capita income: $20,901 (2006-2010 5-year est.); Median household income: $38,688 (2006-2010 5-year est.); Average household income: $49,780 (2006-2010 5-year est.); Percent of households with income of $100,000 or more: 6.4% (2006-2010 5-year est.); Poverty rate: 15.8% (2006-2010 5-year est.).
**Education:** Percent of population age 25 and over with: High school diploma (including GED) or higher: 82.9% (2006-2010 5-year est.); Bachelor's degree or higher: 12.8% (2006-2010 5-year est.); Master's degree or higher: 3.6% (2006-2010 5-year est.).
**Housing:** Homeownership rate: 73.1% (2010); Median home value: $90,600 (2006-2010 5-year est.); Median contract rent: $527 per month (2006-2010 5-year est.); Median year structure built: 1974 (2006-2010 5-year est.).
**Transportation:** Commute to work: 87.2% car, 1.5% public transportation, 2.2% walk, 4.7% work from home (2006-2010 5-year est.); Travel time to work: 19.4% less than 15 minutes, 57.5% 15 to 30 minutes, 14.6% 30 to 45 minutes, 3.4% 45 to 60 minutes, 5.0% 60 minutes or more (2006-2010 5-year est.)

## AU SABLE FORKS (CDP).
Covers a land area of 2.519 square miles and a water area of 0.022 square miles. Located at 44.45° N. Lat; 73.67° W. Long. Elevation is 551 feet.
**Population:** 668 (1990); 670 (2000); 559 (2010); Density: 221.9 persons per square mile (2010); Race: 98.9% White, 0.0% Black, 0.0% Asian, 0.2% American Indian/Alaska Native, 0.0% Native Hawaiian/Other Pacific Islander, 0.9% Other, 0.0% Hispanic of any race (2010); Average household size: 2.37 (2010); Median age: 43.6 (2010); Males per 100 females: 103.3 (2010); Marriage status: 20.2% never married, 57.9% now married, 14.9% widowed, 7.0% divorced (2006-2010 5-year est.); Foreign born: 1.2% (2006-2010 5-year est.); Ancestry (includes multiple ancestries): 23.4% French, 19.9% English, 18.1% Irish, 14.2% American, 10.6% Italian (2006-2010 5-year est.).
**Economy:** Employment by occupation: 6.5% management, 1.2% professional, 10.1% services, 29.4% sales, 2.4% farming, 8.9% construction, 5.6% production (2006-2010 5-year est.).
**Income:** Per capita income: $22,189 (2006-2010 5-year est.); Median household income: $35,714 (2006-2010 5-year est.); Average household income: $46,482 (2006-2010 5-year est.); Percent of households with income of $100,000 or more: 11.2% (2006-2010 5-year est.); Poverty rate: 12.8% (2006-2010 5-year est.).
**Education:** Percent of population age 25 and over with: High school diploma (including GED) or higher: 80.9% (2006-2010 5-year est.); Bachelor's degree or higher: 12.0% (2006-2010 5-year est.); Master's degree or higher: 4.6% (2006-2010 5-year est.).

### School District(s)
Ausable Valley Central School District (KG-12)
   2009-10 Enrollment: 1,239 . . . . . . . . . . . . . . . . . . . . (518) 834-2845
**Housing:** Homeownership rate: 71.6% (2010); Median home value: $95,000 (2006-2010 5-year est.); Median contract rent: $475 per month (2006-2010 5-year est.); Median year structure built: 1956 (2006-2010 5-year est.).
**Transportation:** Commute to work: 97.2% car, 1.2% public transportation, 0.0% walk, 0.0% work from home (2006-2010 5-year est.); Travel time to work: 22.0% less than 15 minutes, 15.4% 15 to 30 minutes, 51.2% 30 to 45 minutes, 9.8% 45 to 60 minutes, 1.6% 60 minutes or more (2006-2010 5-year est.)

## BEEKMANTOWN (town).
Covers a land area of 60.424 square miles and a water area of 9.201 square miles. Located at 44.78° N. Lat; 73.50° W. Long. Elevation is 253 feet.
**Population:** 5,108 (1990); 5,326 (2000); 5,545 (2010); Density: 91.8 persons per square mile (2010); Race: 97.1% White, 1.2% Black, 0.4% Asian, 0.2% American Indian/Alaska Native, 0.0% Native Hawaiian/Other Pacific Islander, 1.1% Other, 1.3% Hispanic of any race (2010); Average household size: 2.49 (2010); Median age: 42.9 (2010); Males per 100 females: 99.5 (2010); Marriage status: 27.1% never married, 61.2% now married, 2.8% widowed, 8.9% divorced (2006-2010 5-year est.); Foreign born: 4.3% (2006-2010 5-year est.); Ancestry (includes multiple ancestries): 26.2% French, 14.8% American, 13.5% English, 11.8% Irish, 8.7% Italian (2006-2010 5-year est.).
**Economy:** Single-family building permits issued: 7 (2011); Multi-family building permits issued: 0 (2011); Employment by occupation: 7.2% management, 1.3% professional, 9.7% services, 18.9% sales, 3.4% farming, 10.5% construction, 5.5% production (2006-2010 5-year est.).

**Income:** Per capita income: $27,800 (2006-2010 5-year est.); Median household income: $70,709 (2006-2010 5-year est.); Average household income: $70,502 (2006-2010 5-year est.); Percent of households with income of $100,000 or more: 19.8% (2006-2010 5-year est.); Poverty rate: 6.3% (2006-2010 5-year est.).
**Education:** Percent of population age 25 and over with: High school diploma (including GED) or higher: 88.5% (2006-2010 5-year est.); Bachelor's degree or higher: 26.5% (2006-2010 5-year est.); Master's degree or higher: 12.5% (2006-2010 5-year est.).
**Housing:** Homeownership rate: 80.7% (2010); Median home value: $130,700 (2006-2010 5-year est.); Median contract rent: $620 per month (2006-2010 5-year est.); Median year structure built: 1976 (2006-2010 5-year est.).
**Transportation:** Commute to work: 93.3% car, 0.8% public transportation, 1.9% walk, 1.7% work from home (2006-2010 5-year est.); Travel time to work: 34.5% less than 15 minutes, 51.8% 15 to 30 minutes, 8.4% 30 to 45 minutes, 1.9% 45 to 60 minutes, 3.4% 60 minutes or more (2006-2010 5-year est.)

## BLACK BROOK (town).
Covers a land area of 129.973 square miles and a water area of 4.360 square miles. Located at 44.52° N. Lat; 73.81° W. Long. Elevation is 974 feet.
**Population:** 1,556 (1990); 1,660 (2000); 1,497 (2010); Density: 11.5 persons per square mile (2010); Race: 97.9% White, 0.2% Black, 0.1% Asian, 0.5% American Indian/Alaska Native, 0.0% Native Hawaiian/Other Pacific Islander, 1.3% Other, 0.8% Hispanic of any race (2010); Average household size: 2.42 (2010); Median age: 44.4 (2010); Males per 100 females: 105.1 (2010); Marriage status: 22.4% never married, 61.7% now married, 9.8% widowed, 6.1% divorced (2006-2010 5-year est.); Foreign born: 1.6% (2006-2010 5-year est.); Ancestry (includes multiple ancestries): 27.9% French, 18.4% Irish, 16.4% English, 8.2% American, 8.2% German (2006-2010 5-year est.).
**Economy:** Single-family building permits issued: 2 (2011); Multi-family building permits issued: 0 (2011); Employment by occupation: 7.3% management, 2.4% professional, 8.4% services, 14.2% sales, 2.8% farming, 14.8% construction, 11.5% production (2006-2010 5-year est.).
**Income:** Per capita income: $23,885 (2006-2010 5-year est.); Median household income: $46,250 (2006-2010 5-year est.); Average household income: $54,336 (2006-2010 5-year est.); Percent of households with income of $100,000 or more: 11.2% (2006-2010 5-year est.); Poverty rate: 8.6% (2006-2010 5-year est.).
**Education:** Percent of population age 25 and over with: High school diploma (including GED) or higher: 84.5% (2006-2010 5-year est.); Bachelor's degree or higher: 17.6% (2006-2010 5-year est.); Master's degree or higher: 4.4% (2006-2010 5-year est.).
**Housing:** Homeownership rate: 81.3% (2010); Median home value: $105,800 (2006-2010 5-year est.); Median contract rent: $500 per month (2006-2010 5-year est.); Median year structure built: 1965 (2006-2010 5-year est.).
**Transportation:** Commute to work: 94.9% car, 0.4% public transportation, 0.0% walk, 2.9% work from home (2006-2010 5-year est.); Travel time to work: 21.5% less than 15 minutes, 17.4% 15 to 30 minutes, 43.6% 30 to 45 minutes, 12.5% 45 to 60 minutes, 5.1% 60 minutes or more (2006-2010 5-year est.)

## CADYVILLE (unincorporated postal area)
Zip Code: 12918
   Covers a land area of 39.293 square miles and a water area of 0.415 square miles. Located at 44.70° N. Lat; 73.67° W. Long. Elevation is 745 feet. Population: 2,381 (2010); Density: 60.6 persons per square mile (2010); Race: 98.5% White, 0.1% Black, 0.2% Asian, 0.4% American Indian/Alaska Native, 0.0% Native Hawaiian/Other Pacific Islander, 0.8% Other, 1.0% Hispanic of any race (2010); Average household size: 2.54 (2010); Median age: 42.4 (2010); Males per 100 females: 96.8 (2010); Homeownership rate: 84.9% (2010)

## CHAMPLAIN (village).
Covers a land area of 1.389 square miles and a water area of 0.038 square miles. Located at 44.98° N. Lat; 73.43° W. Long. Elevation is 105 feet.
**Population:** 1,326 (1990); 1,173 (2000); 1,101 (2010); Density: 792.3 persons per square mile (2010); Race: 96.3% White, 0.2% Black, 1.4% Asian, 0.3% American Indian/Alaska Native, 0.0% Native Hawaiian/Other Pacific Islander, 1.8% Other, 2.5% Hispanic of any race (2010); Average household size: 2.30 (2010); Median age: 40.7 (2010); Males per 100 females: 89.5 (2010); Marriage status: 26.5% never married, 59.4% now

married, 6.0% widowed, 8.0% divorced (2006-2010 5-year est.); Foreign born: 5.3% (2006-2010 5-year est.); Ancestry (includes multiple ancestries): 30.6% French, 19.8% American, 15.5% English, 12.6% French Canadian, 11.9% Irish (2006-2010 5-year est.).

**Economy:** Single-family building permits issued: 0 (2011); Multi-family building permits issued: 0 (2011); Employment by occupation: 11.7% management, 1.3% professional, 8.8% services, 15.2% sales, 6.4% farming, 8.3% construction, 11.2% production (2006-2010 5-year est.).

**Income:** Per capita income: $24,684 (2006-2010 5-year est.); Median household income: $37,292 (2006-2010 5-year est.); Average household income: $52,087 (2006-2010 5-year est.); Percent of households with income of $100,000 or more: 11.9% (2006-2010 5-year est.); Poverty rate: 11.7% (2006-2010 5-year est.).

**Education:** Percent of population age 25 and over with: High school diploma (including GED) or higher: 75.8% (2006-2010 5-year est.); Bachelor's degree or higher: 15.6% (2006-2010 5-year est.); Master's degree or higher: 5.4% (2006-2010 5-year est.).

### School District(s)
Northeastern Clinton Central School District (KG-12)

   2009-10 Enrollment: 1,380 . . . . . . . . . . . . . . . . . . . . (518) 298-8242

**Housing:** Homeownership rate: 63.6% (2010); Median home value: $90,300 (2006-2010 5-year est.); Median contract rent: $443 per month (2006-2010 5-year est.); Median year structure built: before 1940 (2006-2010 5-year est.).

**Transportation:** Commute to work: 83.9% car, 1.1% public transportation, 10.2% walk, 2.5% work from home (2006-2010 5-year est.); Travel time to work: 59.1% less than 15 minutes, 24.4% 15 to 30 minutes, 9.9% 30 to 45 minutes, 5.4% 45 to 60 minutes, 1.1% 60 minutes or more (2006-2010 5-year est.)

**CHAMPLAIN** (town). Covers a land area of 51.231 square miles and a water area of 7.584 square miles. Located at 44.96° N. Lat; 73.43° W. Long. Elevation is 105 feet.

**History:** Settled 1789, incorporated 1873.

**Population:** 5,796 (1990); 5,791 (2000); 5,754 (2010); Density: 112.3 persons per square mile (2010); Race: 96.9% White, 0.4% Black, 1.1% Asian, 0.2% American Indian/Alaska Native, 0.0% Native Hawaiian/Other Pacific Islander, 1.4% Other, 1.4% Hispanic of any race (2010); Average household size: 2.30 (2010); Median age: 42.8 (2010); Males per 100 females: 95.8 (2010); Marriage status: 26.0% never married, 57.4% now married, 6.6% widowed, 10.0% divorced (2006-2010 5-year est.); Foreign born: 5.9% (2006-2010 5-year est.); Ancestry (includes multiple ancestries): 23.0% French, 18.6% French Canadian, 14.4% English, 11.4% Irish, 9.4% American (2006-2010 5-year est.).

**Economy:** Single-family building permits issued: 0 (2011); Multi-family building permits issued: 0 (2011); Employment by occupation: 11.1% management, 3.7% professional, 10.2% services, 19.5% sales, 3.6% farming, 7.8% construction, 9.1% production (2006-2010 5-year est.).

**Income:** Per capita income: $24,191 (2006-2010 5-year est.); Median household income: $50,833 (2006-2010 5-year est.); Average household income: $59,523 (2006-2010 5-year est.); Percent of households with income of $100,000 or more: 14.6% (2006-2010 5-year est.); Poverty rate: 12.0% (2006-2010 5-year est.).

**Education:** Percent of population age 25 and over with: High school diploma (including GED) or higher: 85.6% (2006-2010 5-year est.); Bachelor's degree or higher: 20.7% (2006-2010 5-year est.); Master's degree or higher: 5.9% (2006-2010 5-year est.).

### School District(s)
Northeastern Clinton Central School District (KG-12)

   2009-10 Enrollment: 1,380 . . . . . . . . . . . . . . . . . . . . (518) 298-8242

**Housing:** Homeownership rate: 68.9% (2010); Median home value: $118,900 (2006-2010 5-year est.); Median contract rent: $551 per month (2006-2010 5-year est.); Median year structure built: 1962 (2006-2010 5-year est.).

**Transportation:** Commute to work: 88.3% car, 1.9% public transportation, 4.2% walk, 3.7% work from home (2006-2010 5-year est.); Travel time to work: 60.4% less than 15 minutes, 14.6% 15 to 30 minutes, 16.6% 30 to 45 minutes, 1.5% 45 to 60 minutes, 7.0% 60 minutes or more (2006-2010 5-year est.)

**CHAZY** (town). Covers a land area of 54.153 square miles and a water area of 7.162 square miles. Located at 44.85° N. Lat; 73.46° W. Long. Elevation is 148 feet.

**History:** Miner Institute, agricultural and environmental research center, founded by William Miner, Railroad industrialist and philanthropist, in the 19th century.

**Population:** 3,890 (1990); 4,181 (2000); 4,284 (2010); Density: 79.1 persons per square mile (2010); Race: 97.5% White, 0.7% Black, 0.5% Asian, 0.2% American Indian/Alaska Native, 0.0% Native Hawaiian/Other Pacific Islander, 1.1% Other, 0.8% Hispanic of any race (2010); Average household size: 2.53 (2010); Median age: 40.8 (2010); Males per 100 females: 101.9 (2010); Marriage status: 22.5% never married, 59.2% now married, 5.2% widowed, 13.1% divorced (2006-2010 5-year est.); Foreign born: 2.2% (2006-2010 5-year est.); Ancestry (includes multiple ancestries): 26.5% French, 13.6% English, 12.9% Irish, 12.5% American, 12.0% French Canadian (2006-2010 5-year est.).

**Economy:** Single-family building permits issued: 2 (2011); Multi-family building permits issued: 0 (2011); Employment by occupation: 5.5% management, 1.8% professional, 10.9% services, 16.9% sales, 2.6% farming, 16.1% construction, 12.7% production (2006-2010 5-year est.).

**Income:** Per capita income: $23,500 (2006-2010 5-year est.); Median household income: $55,733 (2006-2010 5-year est.); Average household income: $61,203 (2006-2010 5-year est.); Percent of households with income of $100,000 or more: 15.8% (2006-2010 5-year est.); Poverty rate: 8.3% (2006-2010 5-year est.).

**Education:** Percent of population age 25 and over with: High school diploma (including GED) or higher: 78.2% (2006-2010 5-year est.); Bachelor's degree or higher: 18.9% (2006-2010 5-year est.); Master's degree or higher: 12.1% (2006-2010 5-year est.).

### School District(s)
Chazy Union Free School District (KG-12)

   2009-10 Enrollment: 498 . . . . . . . . . . . . . . . . . . . . . . (518) 846-7135

**Housing:** Homeownership rate: 80.0% (2010); Median home value: $125,900 (2006-2010 5-year est.); Median contract rent: $634 per month (2006-2010 5-year est.); Median year structure built: 1976 (2006-2010 5-year est.).

**Transportation:** Commute to work: 90.6% car, 1.0% public transportation, 0.8% walk, 3.8% work from home (2006-2010 5-year est.); Travel time to work: 26.0% less than 15 minutes, 51.1% 15 to 30 minutes, 18.5% 30 to 45 minutes, 0.0% 45 to 60 minutes, 4.4% 60 minutes or more (2006-2010 5-year est.)

**CHAZY** (CDP). Covers a land area of 1.695 square miles and a water area of 0.017 square miles. Located at 44.89° N. Lat; 73.42° W. Long. Elevation is 148 feet.

**Population:** n/a (1990); n/a (2000); 565 (2010); Density: 333.2 persons per square mile (2010); Race: 96.6% White, 0.9% Black, 0.5% Asian, 0.0% American Indian/Alaska Native, 0.0% Native Hawaiian/Other Pacific Islander, 2.0% Other, 1.1% Hispanic of any race (2010); Average household size: 2.48 (2010); Median age: 38.1 (2010); Males per 100 females: 89.6 (2010); Marriage status: 27.1% never married, 46.9% now married, 9.3% widowed, 16.7% divorced (2006-2010 5-year est.); Foreign born: 13.4% (2006-2010 5-year est.); Ancestry (includes multiple ancestries): 57.8% French, 16.0% Italian, 15.4% Irish, 12.8% English, 9.9% French Canadian (2006-2010 5-year est.).

**Economy:** Employment by occupation: 2.9% management, 3.9% professional, 4.5% services, 19.5% sales, 0.0% farming, 30.5% construction, 28.9% production (2006-2010 5-year est.).

**Income:** Per capita income: $24,764 (2006-2010 5-year est.); Median household income: $56,094 (2006-2010 5-year est.); Average household income: $59,004 (2006-2010 5-year est.); Percent of households with income of $100,000 or more: 12.4% (2006-2010 5-year est.); Poverty rate: 0.0% (2006-2010 5-year est.).

**Education:** Percent of population age 25 and over with: High school diploma (including GED) or higher: 92.4% (2006-2010 5-year est.); Bachelor's degree or higher: 20.5% (2006-2010 5-year est.); Master's degree or higher: 11.7% (2006-2010 5-year est.).

### School District(s)
Chazy Union Free School District (KG-12)

   2009-10 Enrollment: 498 . . . . . . . . . . . . . . . . . . . . . . (518) 846-7135

**Housing:** Homeownership rate: 70.2% (2010); Median home value: $145,100 (2006-2010 5-year est.); Median contract rent: $567 per month (2006-2010 5-year est.); Median year structure built: before 1940 (2006-2010 5-year est.).

**Transportation:** Commute to work: 77.4% car, 0.0% public transportation, 0.0% walk, 12.8% work from home (2006-2010 5-year est.); Travel time to work: 20.8% less than 15 minutes, 62.2% 15 to 30 minutes, 13.9% 30 to 45 minutes, 0.0% 45 to 60 minutes, 3.1% 60 minutes or more (2006-2010 5-year est.)

## CHURUBUSCO (unincorporated postal area)
Zip Code: 12923

Covers a land area of 52.386 square miles and a water area of 0.029 square miles. Located at 44.96° N. Lat; 73.93° W. Long. Elevation is 1,191 feet. Population: 632 (2010); Density: 12.1 persons per square mile (2010); Race: 95.9% White, 0.3% Black, 0.3% Asian, 0.3% American Indian/Alaska Native, 0.0% Native Hawaiian/Other Pacific Islander, 3.2% Other, 0.9% Hispanic of any race (2010); Average household size: 2.48 (2010); Median age: 41.5 (2010); Males per 100 females: 107.2 (2010); Homeownership rate: 81.2% (2010)

## CLINTON (town). Covers a land area of 67.069 square miles and a water area of 0.030 square miles. Located at 44.93° N. Lat; 73.92° W. Long.
**Population:** 663 (1990); 727 (2000); 737 (2010); Density: 11.0 persons per square mile (2010); Race: 96.2% White, 0.3% Black, 0.5% Asian, 0.3% American Indian/Alaska Native, 0.0% Native Hawaiian/Other Pacific Islander, 2.7% Other, 0.8% Hispanic of any race (2010); Average household size: 2.50 (2010); Median age: 41.5 (2010); Males per 100 females: 104.2 (2010); Marriage status: 37.3% never married, 42.8% now married, 12.3% widowed, 7.7% divorced (2006-2010 5-year est.); Foreign born: 0.8% (2006-2010 5-year est.); Ancestry (includes multiple ancestries): 28.1% French, 14.4% French Canadian, 10.8% English, 10.5% Irish, 9.2% American (2006-2010 5-year est.).
**Economy:** Single-family building permits issued: 2 (2011); Multi-family building permits issued: 0 (2011); Employment by occupation: 10.5% management, 0.0% professional, 20.5% services, 8.2% sales, 6.4% farming, 12.0% construction, 4.3% production (2006-2010 5-year est.).
**Income:** Per capita income: $17,578 (2006-2010 5-year est.); Median household income: $41,065 (2006-2010 5-year est.); Average household income: $45,180 (2006-2010 5-year est.); Percent of households with income of $100,000 or more: 4.6% (2006-2010 5-year est.); Poverty rate: 15.8% (2006-2010 5-year est.).
**Education:** Percent of population age 25 and over with: High school diploma (including GED) or higher: 73.7% (2006-2010 5-year est.); Bachelor's degree or higher: 5.6% (2006-2010 5-year est.); Master's degree or higher: 3.6% (2006-2010 5-year est.).
**Housing:** Homeownership rate: 82.4% (2010); Median home value: $77,000 (2006-2010 5-year est.); Median contract rent: $325 per month (2006-2010 5-year est.); Median year structure built: 1959 (2006-2010 5-year est.).
**Transportation:** Commute to work: 78.2% car, 0.0% public transportation, 5.9% walk, 16.0% work from home (2006-2010 5-year est.); Travel time to work: 39.6% less than 15 minutes, 19.0% 15 to 30 minutes, 27.2% 30 to 45 minutes, 12.3% 45 to 60 minutes, 1.9% 60 minutes or more (2006-2010 5-year est.)
**Additional Information Contacts**
Town of Clinton . . . . . . . . . . . . . . . . . . . . . . . . . . . . (845) 266-5853
  http://www.townofclinton.com

## CUMBERLAND HEAD (CDP). Covers a land area of 3.591 square miles and a water area of 0 square miles. Located at 44.71° N. Lat; 73.39° W. Long. Elevation is 144 feet.
**Population:** 1,698 (1990); 1,532 (2000); 1,627 (2010); Density: 453.0 persons per square mile (2010); Race: 96.9% White, 0.4% Black, 0.6% Asian, 0.4% American Indian/Alaska Native, 0.0% Native Hawaiian/Other Pacific Islander, 1.7% Other, 1.7% Hispanic of any race (2010); Average household size: 2.38 (2010); Median age: 45.0 (2010); Males per 100 females: 99.9 (2010); Marriage status: 16.9% never married, 67.6% now married, 6.6% widowed, 8.9% divorced (2006-2010 5-year est.); Foreign born: 8.0% (2006-2010 5-year est.); Ancestry (includes multiple ancestries): 29.5% French, 27.7% Irish, 13.1% German, 11.4% English, 8.0% Italian (2006-2010 5-year est.).
**Economy:** Employment by occupation: 10.9% management, 0.0% professional, 6.2% services, 9.8% sales, 4.9% farming, 8.2% construction, 5.0% production (2006-2010 5-year est.).
**Income:** Per capita income: $37,247 (2006-2010 5-year est.); Median household income: $74,615 (2006-2010 5-year est.); Average household income: $90,767 (2006-2010 5-year est.); Percent of households with

income of $100,000 or more: 35.9% (2006-2010 5-year est.); Poverty rate: 5.5% (2006-2010 5-year est.).
**Education:** Percent of population age 25 and over with: High school diploma (including GED) or higher: 94.2% (2006-2010 5-year est.); Bachelor's degree or higher: 39.7% (2006-2010 5-year est.); Master's degree or higher: 23.3% (2006-2010 5-year est.).
**Housing:** Homeownership rate: 88.3% (2010); Median home value: $196,400 (2006-2010 5-year est.); Median contract rent: $430 per month (2006-2010 5-year est.); Median year structure built: 1959 (2006-2010 5-year est.).
**Transportation:** Commute to work: 95.8% car, 0.0% public transportation, 0.0% walk, 4.2% work from home (2006-2010 5-year est.); Travel time to work: 33.2% less than 15 minutes, 50.8% 15 to 30 minutes, 5.5% 30 to 45 minutes, 5.2% 45 to 60 minutes, 5.2% 60 minutes or more (2006-2010 5-year est.)

## DANNEMORA (village). Covers a land area of 1.147 square miles and a water area of 0 square miles. Located at 44.72° N. Lat; 73.71° W. Long. Elevation is 1,414 feet.
**Population:** 4,005 (1990); 4,129 (2000); 3,936 (2010); Density: 3,429.4 persons per square mile (2010); Race: 52.2% White, 41.9% Black, 0.5% Asian, 0.7% American Indian/Alaska Native, 0.0% Native Hawaiian/Other Pacific Islander, 4.7% Other, 13.3% Hispanic of any race (2010); Average household size: 2.48 (2010); Median age: 37.1 (2010); Males per 100 females: 578.6 (2010); Marriage status: 58.1% never married, 33.1% now married, 3.3% widowed, 5.6% divorced (2006-2010 5-year est.); Foreign born: 8.9% (2006-2010 5-year est.); Ancestry (includes multiple ancestries): 9.7% French, 5.8% Irish, 2.9% English, 1.9% Polish, 1.5% Italian (2006-2010 5-year est.).
**Economy:** Single-family building permits issued: 1 (2011); Multi-family building permits issued: 0 (2011); Employment by occupation: 6.8% management, 0.7% professional, 13.7% services, 13.9% sales, 0.0% farming, 15.7% construction, 7.7% production (2006-2010 5-year est.).
**Income:** Per capita income: $5,639 (2006-2010 5-year est.); Median household income: $48,859 (2006-2010 5-year est.); Average household income: $51,325 (2006-2010 5-year est.); Percent of households with income of $100,000 or more: 8.0% (2006-2010 5-year est.); Poverty rate: 20.1% (2006-2010 5-year est.).
**Education:** Percent of population age 25 and over with: High school diploma (including GED) or higher: 67.6% (2006-2010 5-year est.); Bachelor's degree or higher: 4.5% (2006-2010 5-year est.); Master's degree or higher: 1.1% (2006-2010 5-year est.).
**Housing:** Homeownership rate: 65.5% (2010); Median home value: $97,400 (2006-2010 5-year est.); Median contract rent: $527 per month (2006-2010 5-year est.); Median year structure built: 1940 (2006-2010 5-year est.).
**Transportation:** Commute to work: 84.4% car, 3.4% public transportation, 7.9% walk, 2.6% work from home (2006-2010 5-year est.); Travel time to work: 25.7% less than 15 minutes, 51.6% 15 to 30 minutes, 16.8% 30 to 45 minutes, 2.2% 45 to 60 minutes, 3.7% 60 minutes or more (2006-2010 5-year est.)

## DANNEMORA (town). Covers a land area of 59.079 square miles and a water area of 6.759 square miles. Located at 44.74° N. Lat; 73.81° W. Long. Elevation is 1,414 feet.
**History:** Incorporated 1881.
**Population:** 5,232 (1990); 5,149 (2000); 4,898 (2010); Density: 82.9 persons per square mile (2010); Race: 59.5% White, 35.2% Black, 0.4% Asian, 0.6% American Indian/Alaska Native, 0.0% Native Hawaiian/Other Pacific Islander, 4.3% Other, 11.3% Hispanic of any race (2010); Average household size: 2.38 (2010); Median age: 38.6 (2010); Males per 100 females: 380.2 (2010); Marriage status: 50.3% never married, 39.8% now married, 4.0% widowed, 6.0% divorced (2006-2010 5-year est.); Foreign born: 8.6% (2006-2010 5-year est.); Ancestry (includes multiple ancestries): 10.5% French, 5.3% Irish, 4.9% American, 4.3% English, 3.3% German (2006-2010 5-year est.).
**Economy:** Single-family building permits issued: 1 (2011); Multi-family building permits issued: 0 (2011); Employment by occupation: 7.0% management, 0.0% professional, 14.0% services, 14.1% sales, 0.0% farming, 14.0% construction, 8.1% production (2006-2010 5-year est.).
**Income:** Per capita income: $8,828 (2006-2010 5-year est.); Median household income: $45,938 (2006-2010 5-year est.); Average household income: $50,058 (2006-2010 5-year est.); Percent of households with income of $100,000 or more: 7.9% (2006-2010 5-year est.); Poverty rate: 12.6% (2006-2010 5-year est.).

**Education:** Percent of population age 25 and over with: High school diploma (including GED) or higher: 70.6% (2006-2010 5-year est.); Bachelor's degree or higher: 6.7% (2006-2010 5-year est.); Master's degree or higher: 3.4% (2006-2010 5-year est.).
**Housing:** Homeownership rate: 75.0% (2010); Median home value: $83,200 (2006-2010 5-year est.); Median contract rent: $607 per month (2006-2010 5-year est.); Median year structure built: 1954 (2006-2010 5-year est.).
**Transportation:** Commute to work: 88.7% car, 0.0% public transportation, 4.0% walk, 5.3% work from home (2006-2010 5-year est.); Travel time to work: 23.6% less than 15 minutes, 46.4% 15 to 30 minutes, 22.1% 30 to 45 minutes, 4.0% 45 to 60 minutes, 3.9% 60 minutes or more (2006-2010 5-year est.)

**ELLENBURG** (town). Covers a land area of 106.566 square miles and a water area of 0.889 square miles. Located at 44.81° N. Lat; 73.86° W. Long. Elevation is 961 feet.
**Population:** 1,847 (1990); 1,812 (2000); 1,743 (2010); Density: 16.4 persons per square mile (2010); Race: 98.2% White, 0.1% Black, 0.3% Asian, 0.3% American Indian/Alaska Native, 0.0% Native Hawaiian/Other Pacific Islander, 1.1% Other, 0.7% Hispanic of any race (2010); Average household size: 2.43 (2010); Median age: 42.8 (2010); Males per 100 females: 102.2 (2010); Marriage status: 26.7% never married, 60.6% now married, 6.5% widowed, 6.2% divorced (2006-2010 5-year est.); Foreign born: 3.1% (2006-2010 5-year est.); Ancestry (includes multiple ancestries): 31.5% French, 19.0% Irish, 13.5% American, 12.7% German, 9.9% French Canadian (2006-2010 5-year est.).
**Economy:** Single-family building permits issued: 1 (2011); Multi-family building permits issued: 0 (2011); Employment by occupation: 13.8% management, 0.6% professional, 15.2% services, 14.9% sales, 1.2% farming, 13.9% construction, 7.2% production (2006-2010 5-year est.).
**Income:** Per capita income: $24,256 (2006-2010 5-year est.); Median household income: $47,333 (2006-2010 5-year est.); Average household income: $56,883 (2006-2010 5-year est.); Percent of households with income of $100,000 or more: 12.7% (2006-2010 5-year est.); Poverty rate: 12.7% (2006-2010 5-year est.).
**Education:** Percent of population age 25 and over with: High school diploma (including GED) or higher: 82.1% (2006-2010 5-year est.); Bachelor's degree or higher: 15.2% (2006-2010 5-year est.); Master's degree or higher: 4.1% (2006-2010 5-year est.).
**Housing:** Homeownership rate: 78.0% (2010); Median home value: $86,100 (2006-2010 5-year est.); Median contract rent: $453 per month (2006-2010 5-year est.); Median year structure built: 1969 (2006-2010 5-year est.).
**Transportation:** Commute to work: 89.1% car, 0.0% public transportation, 2.8% walk, 8.1% work from home (2006-2010 5-year est.); Travel time to work: 22.0% less than 15 minutes, 18.7% 15 to 30 minutes, 39.6% 30 to 45 minutes, 12.4% 45 to 60 minutes, 7.3% 60 minutes or more (2006-2010 5-year est.)

**ELLENBURG CENTER** (unincorporated postal area)
Zip Code: 12934
   Covers a land area of 58.851 square miles and a water area of 0.021 square miles. Located at 44.87° N. Lat; 73.87° W. Long. Elevation is 1,220 feet. Population: 1,074 (2010); Density: 18.2 persons per square mile (2010); Race: 98.7% White, 0.2% Black, 0.5% Asian, 0.4% American Indian/Alaska Native, 0.0% Native Hawaiian/Other Pacific Islander, 0.2% Other, 0.9% Hispanic of any race (2010); Average household size: 2.52 (2010); Median age: 40.9 (2010); Males per 100 females: 102.6 (2010); Homeownership rate: 80.3% (2010)

**ELLENBURG DEPOT** (unincorporated postal area)
Zip Code: 12935
   Covers a land area of 98.613 square miles and a water area of 3.513 square miles. Located at 44.84° N. Lat; 73.79° W. Long. Elevation is 873 feet. Population: 1,748 (2010); Density: 17.7 persons per square mile (2010); Race: 93.5% White, 4.2% Black, 0.1% Asian, 0.2% American Indian/Alaska Native, 0.0% Native Hawaiian/Other Pacific Islander, 2.0% Other, 1.4% Hispanic of any race (2010); Average household size: 2.60 (2010); Median age: 41.3 (2010); Males per 100 females: 109.1 (2010); Homeownership rate: 79.4% (2010)

**KEESEVILLE** (village). Covers a land area of 1.173 square miles and a water area of 0.054 square miles. Located at 44.50° N. Lat; 73.48° W. Long. Elevation is 417 feet.
**Population:** 1,854 (1990); 1,850 (2000); 1,815 (2010); Density: 1,546.8 persons per square mile (2010); Race: 96.2% White, 0.9% Black, 0.7% Asian, 0.3% American Indian/Alaska Native, 0.0% Native Hawaiian/Other Pacific Islander, 1.9% Other, 1.4% Hispanic of any race (2010); Average household size: 2.40 (2010); Median age: 40.1 (2010); Males per 100 females: 98.6 (2010); Marriage status: 27.3% never married, 56.7% now married, 6.4% widowed, 9.5% divorced (2006-2010 5-year est.); Foreign born: 1.6% (2006-2010 5-year est.); Ancestry (includes multiple ancestries): 32.2% French, 23.8% Irish, 13.3% English, 11.2% Italian, 7.5% German (2006-2010 5-year est.).
**Economy:** Single-family building permits issued: 0 (2011); Multi-family building permits issued: 0 (2011); Employment by occupation: 4.5% management, 1.3% professional, 14.4% services, 14.9% sales, 5.7% farming, 13.9% construction, 7.8% production (2006-2010 5-year est.).
**Income:** Per capita income: $20,964 (2006-2010 5-year est.); Median household income: $45,203 (2006-2010 5-year est.); Average household income: $52,524 (2006-2010 5-year est.); Percent of households with income of $100,000 or more: 9.4% (2006-2010 5-year est.); Poverty rate: 14.6% (2006-2010 5-year est.).
**Education:** Percent of population age 25 and over with: High school diploma (including GED) or higher: 83.1% (2006-2010 5-year est.); Bachelor's degree or higher: 14.0% (2006-2010 5-year est.); Master's degree or higher: 5.9% (2006-2010 5-year est.).
**School District(s)**
Ausable Valley Central School District (KG-12)
   2009-10 Enrollment: 1,239 . . . . . . . . . . . . . . . . . . . . . (518) 834-2845
**Housing:** Homeownership rate: 63.3% (2010); Median home value: $83,200 (2006-2010 5-year est.); Median contract rent: $567 per month (2006-2010 5-year est.); Median year structure built: before 1940 (2006-2010 5-year est.).
**Transportation:** Commute to work: 92.3% car, 0.8% public transportation, 3.2% walk, 3.2% work from home (2006-2010 5-year est.); Travel time to work: 24.4% less than 15 minutes, 56.4% 15 to 30 minutes, 11.9% 30 to 45 minutes, 2.9% 45 to 60 minutes, 4.5% 60 minutes or more (2006-2010 5-year est.)

**LYON MOUNTAIN** (CDP). Covers a land area of 10.146 square miles and a water area of 0 square miles. Located at 44.72° N. Lat; 73.88° W. Long. Elevation is 1,798 feet.
**Population:** 508 (1990); 458 (2000); 423 (2010); Density: 41.7 persons per square mile (2010); Race: 96.0% White, 1.4% Black, 0.5% Asian, 0.5% American Indian/Alaska Native, 0.0% Native Hawaiian/Other Pacific Islander, 1.6% Other, 1.4% Hispanic of any race (2010); Average household size: 2.10 (2010); Median age: 48.4 (2010); Males per 100 females: 88.0 (2010); Marriage status: 21.7% never married, 53.9% now married, 12.3% widowed, 12.1% divorced (2006-2010 5-year est.); Foreign born: 5.0% (2006-2010 5-year est.); Ancestry (includes multiple ancestries): 20.0% English, 17.1% French, 16.1% Lithuanian, 13.9% Russian, 7.6% American (2006-2010 5-year est.).
**Economy:** Employment by occupation: 13.5% management, 0.0% professional, 17.0% services, 5.7% sales, 0.0% farming, 5.0% construction, 0.0% production (2006-2010 5-year est.).
**Income:** Per capita income: $22,764 (2006-2010 5-year est.); Median household income: $29,938 (2006-2010 5-year est.); Average household income: $42,584 (2006-2010 5-year est.); Percent of households with income of $100,000 or more: 7.8% (2006-2010 5-year est.); Poverty rate: 1.6% (2006-2010 5-year est.).
**Education:** Percent of population age 25 and over with: High school diploma (including GED) or higher: 82.5% (2006-2010 5-year est.); Bachelor's degree or higher: 0.0% (2006-2010 5-year est.); Master's degree or higher: 0.0% (2006-2010 5-year est.).
**Housing:** Homeownership rate: 81.1% (2010); Median home value: $44,800 (2006-2010 5-year est.); Median contract rent: $554 per month (2006-2010 5-year est.); Median year structure built: 1943 (2006-2010 5-year est.).
**Transportation:** Commute to work: 100.0% car, 0.0% public transportation, 0.0% walk, 0.0% work from home (2006-2010 5-year est.); Travel time to work: 16.3% less than 15 minutes, 51.8% 15 to 30 minutes, 21.3% 30 to 45 minutes, 10.6% 45 to 60 minutes, 0.0% 60 minutes or more (2006-2010 5-year est.)

**MOOERS** (CDP). Covers a land area of 1.193 square miles and a water area of 0.037 square miles. Located at 44.96° N. Lat; 73.59° W. Long. Elevation is 282 feet.
**Population:** 481 (1990); 440 (2000); 442 (2010); Density: 370.5 persons per square mile (2010); Race: 99.5% White, 0.2% Black, 0.0% Asian, 0.0% American Indian/Alaska Native, 0.0% Native Hawaiian/Other Pacific Islander, 0.3% Other, 0.7% Hispanic of any race (2010); Average household size: 2.30 (2010); Median age: 43.7 (2010); Males per 100 females: 90.5 (2010); Marriage status: 30.1% never married, 47.3% now married, 15.3% widowed, 7.3% divorced (2006-2010 5-year est.); Foreign born: 0.0% (2006-2010 5-year est.); Ancestry (includes multiple ancestries): 38.9% French, 22.1% French Canadian, 15.3% English, 8.7% American, 4.3% Irish (2006-2010 5-year est.).
**Economy:** Employment by occupation: 30.8% management, 15.0% professional, 0.0% services, 0.0% sales, 9.8% farming, 7.3% construction, 13.7% production (2006-2010 5-year est.).
**Income:** Per capita income: $16,951 (2006-2010 5-year est.); Median household income: $22,778 (2006-2010 5-year est.); Average household income: $32,289 (2006-2010 5-year est.); Percent of households with income of $100,000 or more: 4.4% (2006-2010 5-year est.); Poverty rate: 25.1% (2006-2010 5-year est.).
**Education:** Percent of population age 25 and over with: High school diploma (including GED) or higher: 88.8% (2006-2010 5-year est.); Bachelor's degree or higher: 24.2% (2006-2010 5-year est.); Master's degree or higher: 3.8% (2006-2010 5-year est.).

**School District(s)**
Northeastern Clinton Central School District (KG-12)
    2009-10 Enrollment: 1,380 . . . . . . . . . . . . . . . . . . . . . . (518) 298-8242
**Housing:** Homeownership rate: 68.2% (2010); Median home value: $117,000 (2006-2010 5-year est.); Median contract rent: $360 per month (2006-2010 5-year est.); Median year structure built: 1948 (2006-2010 5-year est.).
**Transportation:** Commute to work: 67.1% car, 0.0% public transportation, 23.9% walk, 0.0% work from home (2006-2010 5-year est.); Travel time to work: 60.7% less than 15 minutes, 39.3% 15 to 30 minutes, 0.0% 30 to 45 minutes, 0.0% 45 to 60 minutes, 0.0% 60 minutes or more (2006-2010 5-year est.)

**MOOERS** (town). Covers a land area of 87.631 square miles and a water area of 0.290 square miles. Located at 44.95° N. Lat; 73.65° W. Long. Elevation is 282 feet.
**Population:** 2,995 (1990); 3,404 (2000); 3,592 (2010); Density: 41.0 persons per square mile (2010); Race: 97.9% White, 0.3% Black, 0.3% Asian, 0.8% American Indian/Alaska Native, 0.0% Native Hawaiian/Other Pacific Islander, 0.7% Other, 0.8% Hispanic of any race (2010); Average household size: 2.57 (2010); Median age: 40.4 (2010); Males per 100 females: 101.5 (2010); Marriage status: 25.3% never married, 58.9% now married, 4.3% widowed, 11.4% divorced (2006-2010 5-year est.); Foreign born: 3.6% (2006-2010 5-year est.); Ancestry (includes multiple ancestries): 20.9% French, 17.2% French Canadian, 14.9% American, 13.4% Irish, 10.1% English (2006-2010 5-year est.).
**Economy:** Single-family building permits issued: 7 (2011); Multi-family building permits issued: 0 (2011); Employment by occupation: 14.0% management, 4.4% professional, 2.5% services, 12.1% sales, 7.4% farming, 12.2% construction, 12.5% production (2006-2010 5-year est.).
**Income:** Per capita income: $19,090 (2006-2010 5-year est.); Median household income: $41,127 (2006-2010 5-year est.); Average household income: $49,375 (2006-2010 5-year est.); Percent of households with income of $100,000 or more: 6.4% (2006-2010 5-year est.); Poverty rate: 10.8% (2006-2010 5-year est.).
**Education:** Percent of population age 25 and over with: High school diploma (including GED) or higher: 83.5% (2006-2010 5-year est.); Bachelor's degree or higher: 19.9% (2006-2010 5-year est.); Master's degree or higher: 5.5% (2006-2010 5-year est.).

**School District(s)**
Northeastern Clinton Central School District (KG-12)
    2009-10 Enrollment: 1,380 . . . . . . . . . . . . . . . . . . . . . . (518) 298-8242
**Housing:** Homeownership rate: 83.5% (2010); Median home value: $97,000 (2006-2010 5-year est.); Median contract rent: $366 per month (2006-2010 5-year est.); Median year structure built: 1975 (2006-2010 5-year est.).
**Transportation:** Commute to work: 90.8% car, 1.4% public transportation, 4.8% walk, 0.0% work from home (2006-2010 5-year est.); Travel time to work: 27.9% less than 15 minutes, 37.5% 15 to 30 minutes, 23.8% 30 to 45 minutes, 7.4% 45 to 60 minutes, 3.5% 60 minutes or more (2006-2010 5-year est.)

**MOOERS FORKS** (unincorporated postal area)
Zip Code: 12959
    Covers a land area of 38.629 square miles and a water area of 0.100 square miles. Located at 44.95° N. Lat; 73.71° W. Long. Elevation is 374 feet. Population: 1,369 (2010); Density: 35.4 persons per square mile (2010); Race: 97.2% White, 0.4% Black, 0.2% Asian, 1.5% American Indian/Alaska Native, 0.1% Native Hawaiian/Other Pacific Islander, 0.6% Other, 0.2% Hispanic of any race (2010); Average household size: 2.55 (2010); Median age: 41.5 (2010); Males per 100 females: 99.9 (2010); Homeownership rate: 83.7% (2010)

**MORRISONVILLE** (CDP). Covers a land area of 2.611 square miles and a water area of 0.090 square miles. Located at 44.69° N. Lat; 73.55° W. Long. Elevation is 361 feet.
**Population:** 1,742 (1990); 1,702 (2000); 1,545 (2010); Density: 591.7 persons per square mile (2010); Race: 97.0% White, 1.1% Black, 0.2% Asian, 0.1% American Indian/Alaska Native, 0.0% Native Hawaiian/Other Pacific Islander, 1.6% Other, 1.6% Hispanic of any race (2010); Average household size: 2.34 (2010); Median age: 43.1 (2010); Males per 100 females: 92.4 (2010); Marriage status: 21.3% never married, 60.1% now married, 6.8% widowed, 11.8% divorced (2006-2010 5-year est.); Foreign born: 1.5% (2006-2010 5-year est.); Ancestry (includes multiple ancestries): 28.2% Irish, 26.9% French, 18.8% English, 11.5% French Canadian, 9.6% American (2006-2010 5-year est.).
**Economy:** Employment by occupation: 10.6% management, 6.5% professional, 2.0% services, 20.4% sales, 5.0% farming, 2.6% construction, 6.3% production (2006-2010 5-year est.).
**Income:** Per capita income: $28,243 (2006-2010 5-year est.); Median household income: $59,267 (2006-2010 5-year est.); Average household income: $74,197 (2006-2010 5-year est.); Percent of households with income of $100,000 or more: 30.8% (2006-2010 5-year est.); Poverty rate: 7.2% (2006-2010 5-year est.).
**Education:** Percent of population age 25 and over with: High school diploma (including GED) or higher: 81.0% (2006-2010 5-year est.); Bachelor's degree or higher: 22.8% (2006-2010 5-year est.); Master's degree or higher: 4.9% (2006-2010 5-year est.).

**School District(s)**
Saranac Central School District (KG-12)
    2009-10 Enrollment: 1,625 . . . . . . . . . . . . . . . . . . . . . . (518) 565-5600
**Housing:** Homeownership rate: 72.1% (2010); Median home value: $146,100 (2006-2010 5-year est.); Median contract rent: $550 per month (2006-2010 5-year est.); Median year structure built: 1958 (2006-2010 5-year est.).
**Transportation:** Commute to work: 95.7% car, 0.0% public transportation, 1.0% walk, 3.3% work from home (2006-2010 5-year est.); Travel time to work: 49.4% less than 15 minutes, 43.9% 15 to 30 minutes, 2.8% 30 to 45 minutes, 1.4% 45 to 60 minutes, 2.5% 60 minutes or more (2006-2010 5-year est.)

**PARC** (CDP). Covers a land area of 1.231 square miles and a water area of 0 square miles. Located at 44.66° N. Lat; 73.45° W. Long. Elevation is 180 feet.
**Population:** 5,560 (1990); 54 (2000); 254 (2010); Density: 206.3 persons per square mile (2010); Race: 72.0% White, 23.2% Black, 0.8% Asian, 1.2% American Indian/Alaska Native, 0.0% Native Hawaiian/Other Pacific Islander, 2.8% Other, 7.5% Hispanic of any race (2010); Average household size: 2.11 (2010); Median age: 19.7 (2010); Males per 100 females: 91.0 (2010); Marriage status: 0.0% never married, 100.0% now married, 0.0% widowed, 0.0% divorced (2006-2010 5-year est.); Foreign born: 100.0% (2006-2010 5-year est.); Ancestry (includes multiple ancestries): 52.4% Welsh, 47.6% Irish (2006-2010 5-year est.).
**Economy:** Employment by occupation: n/a management, n/a professional, n/a services, n/a sales, n/a farming, n/a construction, n/a production (2006-2010 5-year est.).
**Income:** Per capita income: $-1 (2006-2010 5-year est.); Median household income: $0 (2006-2010 5-year est.); Average household income: $0 (2006-2010 5-year est.); Percent of households with income of $100,000 or more: 0.0% (2006-2010 5-year est.); Poverty rate: 0.0% (2006-2010 5-year est.).
**Education:** Percent of population age 25 and over with: High school diploma (including GED) or higher: 100.0% (2006-2010 5-year est.);

Bachelor's degree or higher: 0.0% (2006-2010 5-year est.); Master's degree or higher: 0.0% (2006-2010 5-year est.).
**Housing:** Homeownership rate: 37.0% (2010); Median home value: n/a (2006-2010 5-year est.); Median contract rent: n/a per month (2006-2010 5-year est.); Median year structure built: n/a (2006-2010 5-year est.).
**Transportation:** Commute to work: n/a car, n/a public transportation, n/a walk, n/a work from home (2006-2010 5-year est.); Travel time to work: n/a less than 15 minutes, n/a 15 to 30 minutes, n/a 30 to 45 minutes, n/a 45 to 60 minutes, n/a 60 minutes or more (2006-2010 5-year est.)

**PERU** (town). Covers a land area of 78.887 square miles and a water area of 13.491 square miles. Located at 44.58° N. Lat; 73.56° W. Long. Elevation is 335 feet.
**Population:** 6,254 (1990); 6,370 (2000); 6,998 (2010); Density: 88.7 persons per square mile (2010); Race: 96.5% White, 1.5% Black, 0.5% Asian, 0.2% American Indian/Alaska Native, 0.0% Native Hawaiian/Other Pacific Islander, 1.3% Other, 1.7% Hispanic of any race (2010); Average household size: 2.63 (2010); Median age: 40.9 (2010); Males per 100 females: 100.5 (2010); Marriage status: 15.1% never married, 65.6% now married, 8.3% widowed, 11.0% divorced (2006-2010 5-year est.); Foreign born: 2.3% (2006-2010 5-year est.); Ancestry (includes multiple ancestries): 26.6% French, 20.8% Irish, 15.9% English, 11.8% German, 8.5% American (2006-2010 5-year est.).
**Economy:** Single-family building permits issued: 8 (2011); Multi-family building permits issued: 0 (2011); Employment by occupation: 8.7% management, 2.3% professional, 11.3% services, 13.9% sales, 5.3% farming, 8.6% construction, 9.0% production (2006-2010 5-year est.).
**Income:** Per capita income: $28,174 (2006-2010 5-year est.); Median household income: $54,707 (2006-2010 5-year est.); Average household income: $68,501 (2006-2010 5-year est.); Percent of households with income of $100,000 or more: 21.3% (2006-2010 5-year est.); Poverty rate: 9.8% (2006-2010 5-year est.).
**Education:** Percent of population age 25 and over with: High school diploma (including GED) or higher: 92.7% (2006-2010 5-year est.); Bachelor's degree or higher: 28.8% (2006-2010 5-year est.); Master's degree or higher: 13.8% (2006-2010 5-year est.).

**School District(s)**
Peru Central School District (KG-12)
   2009-10 Enrollment: 2,079 . . . . . . . . . . . . . . . . . . . . (518) 643-6000
**Housing:** Homeownership rate: 81.7% (2010); Median home value: $124,600 (2006-2010 5-year est.); Median contract rent: $392 per month (2006-2010 5-year est.); Median year structure built: 1973 (2006-2010 5-year est.).
**Transportation:** Commute to work: 91.2% car, 0.0% public transportation, 2.3% walk, 4.8% work from home (2006-2010 5-year est.); Travel time to work: 28.7% less than 15 minutes, 51.9% 15 to 30 minutes, 8.7% 30 to 45 minutes, 4.1% 45 to 60 minutes, 6.7% 60 minutes or more (2006-2010 5-year est.)

**PERU** (CDP). Covers a land area of 1.589 square miles and a water area of 0 square miles. Located at 44.57° N. Lat; 73.53° W. Long. Elevation is 335 feet.
**Population:** 1,565 (1990); 1,514 (2000); 1,591 (2010); Density: 1,000.7 persons per square mile (2010); Race: 97.2% White, 0.9% Black, 0.8% Asian, 0.1% American Indian/Alaska Native, 0.0% Native Hawaiian/Other Pacific Islander, 1.0% Other, 2.1% Hispanic of any race (2010); Average household size: 2.57 (2010); Median age: 41.8 (2010); Males per 100 females: 96.9 (2010); Marriage status: 15.3% never married, 65.1% now married, 11.1% widowed, 8.5% divorced (2006-2010 5-year est.); Foreign born: 2.3% (2006-2010 5-year est.); Ancestry (includes multiple ancestries): 30.4% French, 21.7% Irish, 17.9% Italian, 17.2% English, 9.2% German (2006-2010 5-year est.).
**Economy:** Employment by occupation: 0.0% management, 1.9% professional, 12.1% services, 17.3% sales, 6.6% farming, 1.2% construction, 2.8% production (2006-2010 5-year est.).
**Income:** Per capita income: $29,976 (2006-2010 5-year est.); Median household income: $58,056 (2006-2010 5-year est.); Average household income: $67,647 (2006-2010 5-year est.); Percent of households with income of $100,000 or more: 24.6% (2006-2010 5-year est.); Poverty rate: 2.5% (2006-2010 5-year est.).
**Education:** Percent of population age 25 and over with: High school diploma (including GED) or higher: 98.3% (2006-2010 5-year est.); Bachelor's degree or higher: 40.9% (2006-2010 5-year est.); Master's degree or higher: 14.3% (2006-2010 5-year est.).

**School District(s)**
Peru Central School District (KG-12)
   2009-10 Enrollment: 2,079 . . . . . . . . . . . . . . . . . . . . (518) 643-6000
**Housing:** Homeownership rate: 76.4% (2010); Median home value: $115,900 (2006-2010 5-year est.); Median contract rent: $393 per month (2006-2010 5-year est.); Median year structure built: 1957 (2006-2010 5-year est.).
**Transportation:** Commute to work: 89.9% car, 0.0% public transportation, 3.5% walk, 4.4% work from home (2006-2010 5-year est.); Travel time to work: 21.4% less than 15 minutes, 46.5% 15 to 30 minutes, 15.0% 30 to 45 minutes, 8.6% 45 to 60 minutes, 8.5% 60 minutes or more (2006-2010 5-year est.)

**PLATTSBURGH** (city). County seat. Covers a land area of 5.018 square miles and a water area of 1.555 square miles. Located at 44.69° N. Lat; 73.45° W. Long. Elevation is 138 feet.
**History:** Plattsburg was established at the mouth of the Saranac River, which began to provide water power for manufacturing in 1785. The first mills ground corn and cut lumber for the settlers.
**Population:** 21,242 (1990); 18,816 (2000); 19,989 (2010); Density: 3,983.0 persons per square mile (2010); Race: 89.9% White, 3.5% Black, 2.8% Asian, 0.4% American Indian/Alaska Native, 0.0% Native Hawaiian/Other Pacific Islander, 3.4% Other, 3.4% Hispanic of any race (2010); Average household size: 2.06 (2010); Median age: 29.7 (2010); Males per 100 females: 89.1 (2010); Marriage status: 50.1% never married, 32.0% now married, 6.7% widowed, 11.3% divorced (2006-2010 5-year est.); Foreign born: 7.5% (2006-2010 5-year est.); Ancestry (includes multiple ancestries): 20.8% Irish, 20.8% French, 11.7% Italian, 11.3% German, 10.1% English (2006-2010 5-year est.).
**Economy:** Single-family building permits issued: 6 (2011); Multi-family building permits issued: 24 (2011); Employment by occupation: 7.5% management, 3.7% professional, 12.0% services, 19.5% sales, 3.7% farming, 5.6% construction, 4.4% production (2006-2010 5-year est.).
**Income:** Per capita income: $20,842 (2006-2010 5-year est.); Median household income: $37,638 (2006-2010 5-year est.); Average household income: $51,054 (2006-2010 5-year est.); Percent of households with income of $100,000 or more: 13.1% (2006-2010 5-year est.); Poverty rate: 21.0% (2006-2010 5-year est.).
**Education:** Percent of population age 25 and over with: High school diploma (including GED) or higher: 87.6% (2006-2010 5-year est.); Bachelor's degree or higher: 31.5% (2006-2010 5-year est.); Master's degree or higher: 14.6% (2006-2010 5-year est.).

**School District(s)**
Clinton-Essex-Warren-washington Boces
   2009-10 Enrollment: n/a . . . . . . . . . . . . . . . . . . . . (518) 561-0100
Plattsburgh City School District (PK-12)
   2009-10 Enrollment: 1,916 . . . . . . . . . . . . . . . . . . (518) 957-6002
**Four-year College(s)**
SUNY College at Plattsburgh (Public)
   Fall 2010 Enrollment: 6,233 . . . . . . . . . . . . . . . . . . (518) 564-2000
   2011-12 Tuition: In-state $6,502; Out-of-state $15,552
**Two-year College(s)**
CVPH Medical Center School of Radiologic Technology (Private, Not-for-profit)
   Fall 2010 Enrollment: 26 . . . . . . . . . . . . . . . . . . (518) 562-7510
Clinton Community College (Public)
   Fall 2010 Enrollment: 1,631 . . . . . . . . . . . . . . . . . . (518) 562-4200
   2011-12 Tuition: In-state $4,084; Out-of-state $8,964
**Vocational/Technical School(s)**
Clinton Essex Warren Washington BOCES-Practical Nursing Program (Public)
   Fall 2010 Enrollment: 35 . . . . . . . . . . . . . . . . . . (518) 561-0100
   2011-12 Tuition: $9,750
**Housing:** Homeownership rate: 38.5% (2010); Median home value: $142,000 (2006-2010 5-year est.); Median contract rent: $568 per month (2006-2010 5-year est.); Median year structure built: 1954 (2006-2010 5-year est.).
**Hospitals:** Champlain Valley Physicians Hospital (405 beds)
**Safety:** Violent crime rate: 15.6 per 10,000 population; Property crime rate: 312.7 per 10,000 population (2010).
**Newspapers:** Out & About (National news); Press-Republican (Local news; Circulation 20,754)
**Transportation:** Commute to work: 78.7% car, 2.1% public transportation, 10.6% walk, 3.9% work from home (2006-2010 5-year est.); Travel time to work: 74.4% less than 15 minutes, 19.5% 15 to 30 minutes, 3.7% 30 to 45

minutes, 1.0% 45 to 60 minutes, 1.4% 60 minutes or more (2006-2010 5-year est.); Amtrak: train service available.
**Airports:** Clinton County (general aviation); Plattsburgh International (primary service); Plattsburgh International (primary service)
**Additional Information Contacts**
Plattsburgh North Country Chamber of Commerce . . . . . . . (518) 563-1000
  http://www.northcountrychamber.com

**PLATTSBURGH** (town). Covers a land area of 45.920 square miles and a water area of 22.287 square miles. Located at 44.69° N. Lat; 73.51° W. Long. Elevation is 138 feet.
**History:** During the War of 1812 a makeshift American fleet under Thomas Macdonough defeated the British in a pitched battle on Lake Champlain near Plattsburgh, compelling an accompanying land-invasion force under Sir George Prevost to return to Canada. Seat of the State University of N.Y. College at Plattsburgh. Settled 1767, Incorporated 1902.
**Population:** 17,166 (1990); 11,190 (2000); 11,870 (2010); Density: 258.5 persons per square mile (2010); Race: 95.0% White, 1.9% Black, 0.9% Asian, 0.4% American Indian/Alaska Native, 0.0% Native Hawaiian/Other Pacific Islander, 1.8% Other, 1.9% Hispanic of any race (2010); Average household size: 2.41 (2010); Median age: 41.1 (2010); Males per 100 females: 98.6 (2010); Marriage status: 28.8% never married, 53.3% now married, 6.4% widowed, 11.4% divorced (2006-2010 5-year est.); Foreign born: 5.4% (2006-2010 5-year est.); Ancestry (includes multiple ancestries): 26.3% French, 16.2% Irish, 11.6% English, 10.3% French Canadian, 10.2% American (2006-2010 5-year est.).
**Economy:** Single-family building permits issued: 16 (2011); Multi-family building permits issued: 2 (2011); Employment by occupation: 6.9% management, 1.3% professional, 8.8% services, 16.7% sales, 5.4% farming, 9.0% construction, 7.8% production (2006-2010 5-year est.).
**Income:** Per capita income: $26,094 (2006-2010 5-year est.); Median household income: $53,610 (2006-2010 5-year est.); Average household income: $64,801 (2006-2010 5-year est.); Percent of households with income of $100,000 or more: 17.3% (2006-2010 5-year est.); Poverty rate: 13.1% (2006-2010 5-year est.).
**Education:** Percent of population age 25 and over with: High school diploma (including GED) or higher: 82.9% (2006-2010 5-year est.); Bachelor's degree or higher: 21.1% (2006-2010 5-year est.); Master's degree or higher: 9.7% (2006-2010 5-year est.).
**School District(s)**
Clinton-Essex-Warren-washington Boces
  2009-10 Enrollment: n/a . . . . . . . . . . . . . . . . . . . . . (518) 561-0100
Plattsburgh City School District (PK-12)
  2009-10 Enrollment: 1,916 . . . . . . . . . . . . . . . . . . . (518) 957-6002
**Four-year College(s)**
SUNY College at Plattsburgh (Public)
  Fall 2010 Enrollment: 6,233 . . . . . . . . . . . . . . . . . . (518) 564-2000
  2011-12 Tuition: In-state $6,502; Out-of-state $15,552
**Two-year College(s)**
CVPH Medical Center School of Radiologic Technology (Private, Not-for-profit)
  Fall 2010 Enrollment: 26 . . . . . . . . . . . . . . . . . . . . (518) 562-7510
Clinton Community College (Public)
  Fall 2010 Enrollment: 1,631 . . . . . . . . . . . . . . . . . . (518) 562-4200
  2011-12 Tuition: In-state $4,084; Out-of-state $8,964
**Vocational/Technical School(s)**
Clinton Essex Warren Washington BOCES-Practical Nursing Program (Public)
  Fall 2010 Enrollment: 35 . . . . . . . . . . . . . . . . . . . . (518) 561-0100
  2011-12 Tuition: $9,750
**Housing:** Homeownership rate: 77.1% (2010); Median home value: $126,400 (2006-2010 5-year est.); Median contract rent: $562 per month (2006-2010 5-year est.); Median year structure built: 1978 (2006-2010 5-year est.).
**Hospitals:** Champlain Valley Physicians Hospital (405 beds)
**Newspapers:** Out & About (National news); Press-Republican (Local news; Circulation 20,754)
**Transportation:** Commute to work: 93.0% car, 0.0% public transportation, 1.0% walk, 3.0% work from home (2006-2010 5-year est.); Travel time to work: 47.7% less than 15 minutes, 40.5% 15 to 30 minutes, 5.7% 30 to 45 minutes, 2.4% 45 to 60 minutes, 3.7% 60 minutes or more (2006-2010 5-year est.); Amtrak: train service available.
**Airports:** Clinton County (general aviation)

**PLATTSBURGH WEST** (CDP). Covers a land area of 1.773 square miles and a water area of 0.054 square miles. Located at 44.68° N. Lat; 73.50° W. Long.
**Population:** 1,274 (1990); 1,289 (2000); 1,364 (2010); Density: 769.0 persons per square mile (2010); Race: 95.1% White, 1.5% Black, 0.5% Asian, 0.3% American Indian/Alaska Native, 0.0% Native Hawaiian/Other Pacific Islander, 2.6% Other, 1.6% Hispanic of any race (2010); Average household size: 2.49 (2010); Median age: 38.3 (2010); Males per 100 females: 92.7 (2010); Marriage status: 27.4% never married, 49.2% now married, 5.1% widowed, 18.2% divorced (2006-2010 5-year est.); Foreign born: 0.7% (2006-2010 5-year est.); Ancestry (includes multiple ancestries): 23.0% American, 22.4% French, 12.2% French Canadian, 7.4% German, 5.9% Irish (2006-2010 5-year est.).
**Economy:** Employment by occupation: 4.0% management, 0.0% professional, 4.2% services, 22.6% sales, 2.7% farming, 3.5% construction, 10.9% production (2006-2010 5-year est.).
**Income:** Per capita income: $15,907 (2006-2010 5-year est.); Median household income: $34,861 (2006-2010 5-year est.); Average household income: $45,255 (2006-2010 5-year est.); Percent of households with income of $100,000 or more: 6.2% (2006-2010 5-year est.); Poverty rate: 21.3% (2006-2010 5-year est.).
**Education:** Percent of population age 25 and over with: High school diploma (including GED) or higher: 71.7% (2006-2010 5-year est.); Bachelor's degree or higher: 6.7% (2006-2010 5-year est.); Master's degree or higher: 3.2% (2006-2010 5-year est.).
**Housing:** Homeownership rate: 76.6% (2010); Median home value: $32,600 (2006-2010 5-year est.); Median contract rent: $469 per month (2006-2010 5-year est.); Median year structure built: 1986 (2006-2010 5-year est.).
**Transportation:** Commute to work: 92.9% car, 0.0% public transportation, 7.1% walk, 0.0% work from home (2006-2010 5-year est.); Travel time to work: 60.1% less than 15 minutes, 23.3% 15 to 30 minutes, 4.7% 30 to 45 minutes, 0.0% 45 to 60 minutes, 11.9% 60 minutes or more (2006-2010 5-year est.)

**REDFORD** (CDP). Covers a land area of 1.346 square miles and a water area of 0.108 square miles. Located at 44.60° N. Lat; 73.80° W. Long. Elevation is 1,171 feet.
**Population:** 463 (1990); 512 (2000); 477 (2010); Density: 354.1 persons per square mile (2010); Race: 96.4% White, 1.0% Black, 0.0% Asian, 0.0% American Indian/Alaska Native, 0.0% Native Hawaiian/Other Pacific Islander, 2.6% Other, 0.6% Hispanic of any race (2010); Average household size: 2.73 (2010); Median age: 38.3 (2010); Males per 100 females: 107.4 (2010); Marriage status: 29.5% never married, 61.8% now married, 6.5% widowed, 2.2% divorced (2006-2010 5-year est.); Foreign born: 8.4% (2006-2010 5-year est.); Ancestry (includes multiple ancestries): 53.2% French, 22.3% Irish, 15.9% Italian, 11.5% American, 6.5% Estonian (2006-2010 5-year est.).
**Economy:** Employment by occupation: 5.4% management, 0.0% professional, 13.8% services, 16.7% sales, 4.4% farming, 28.6% construction, 8.4% production (2006-2010 5-year est.).
**Income:** Per capita income: $20,432 (2006-2010 5-year est.); Median household income: $67,571 (2006-2010 5-year est.); Average household income: $64,877 (2006-2010 5-year est.); Percent of households with income of $100,000 or more: 17.6% (2006-2010 5-year est.); Poverty rate: 10.9% (2006-2010 5-year est.).
**Education:** Percent of population age 25 and over with: High school diploma (including GED) or higher: 89.6% (2006-2010 5-year est.); Bachelor's degree or higher: 12.5% (2006-2010 5-year est.); Master's degree or higher: 0.0% (2006-2010 5-year est.).
**Housing:** Homeownership rate: 86.8% (2010); Median home value: $107,700 (2006-2010 5-year est.); Median contract rent: n/a per month (2006-2010 5-year est.); Median year structure built: 1959 (2006-2010 5-year est.).
**Transportation:** Commute to work: 85.2% car, 0.0% public transportation, 7.4% walk, 0.0% work from home (2006-2010 5-year est.); Travel time to work: 22.8% less than 15 minutes, 14.3% 15 to 30 minutes, 54.0% 30 to 45 minutes, 9.0% 45 to 60 minutes, 0.0% 60 minutes or more (2006-2010 5-year est.)

**ROUSES POINT** (village). Covers a land area of 1.760 square miles and a water area of 0.725 square miles. Located at 44.99° N. Lat; 73.36° W. Long. Elevation is 112 feet.
**History:** Incorporated 1877.

**Population:** 2,377 (1990); 2,277 (2000); 2,209 (2010); Density: 1,254.5 persons per square mile (2010); Race: 96.2% White, 0.8% Black, 1.4% Asian, 0.2% American Indian/Alaska Native, 0.0% Native Hawaiian/Other Pacific Islander, 1.4% Other, 1.5% Hispanic of any race (2010); Average household size: 2.09 (2010); Median age: 44.2 (2010); Males per 100 females: 92.3 (2010); Marriage status: 28.5% never married, 51.2% now married, 6.5% widowed, 13.9% divorced (2006-2010 5-year est.); Foreign born: 9.0% (2006-2010 5-year est.); Ancestry (includes multiple ancestries): 28.1% French, 22.4% English, 11.8% Irish, 11.0% French Canadian, 8.8% German (2006-2010 5-year est.).
**Economy:** Single-family building permits issued: 1 (2011); Multi-family building permits issued: 0 (2011); Employment by occupation: 12.5% management, 2.8% professional, 6.8% services, 20.8% sales, 3.9% farming, 10.2% construction, 12.1% production (2006-2010 5-year est.).
**Income:** Per capita income: $26,272 (2006-2010 5-year est.); Median household income: $50,362 (2006-2010 5-year est.); Average household income: $61,109 (2006-2010 5-year est.); Percent of households with income of $100,000 or more: 16.6% (2006-2010 5-year est.); Poverty rate: 12.8% (2006-2010 5-year est.).
**Education:** Percent of population age 25 and over with: High school diploma (including GED) or higher: 87.7% (2006-2010 5-year est.); Bachelor's degree or higher: 19.5% (2006-2010 5-year est.); Master's degree or higher: 4.4% (2006-2010 5-year est.).

### School District(s)
Northeastern Clinton Central School District (KG-12)

    2009-10 Enrollment: 1,380 . . . . . . . . . . . . . . . . . . . . . . . (518) 298-8242
**Housing:** Homeownership rate: 57.0% (2010); Median home value: $143,100 (2006-2010 5-year est.); Median contract rent: $577 per month (2006-2010 5-year est.); Median year structure built: 1952 (2006-2010 5-year est.).
**Safety:** Violent crime rate: 0.0 per 10,000 population; Property crime rate: 44.2 per 10,000 population (2010).
**Transportation:** Commute to work: 86.4% car, 2.7% public transportation, 4.5% walk, 2.6% work from home (2006-2010 5-year est.); Travel time to work: 60.0% less than 15 minutes, 18.1% 15 to 30 minutes, 11.9% 30 to 45 minutes, 1.6% 45 to 60 minutes, 8.3% 60 minutes or more (2006-2010 5-year est.); Amtrak: train service available.

**SARANAC** (town). Covers a land area of 115.286 square miles and a water area of 0.660 square miles. Located at 44.65° N. Lat; 73.80° W. Long. Elevation is 797 feet.
**Population:** 3,801 (1990); 4,165 (2000); 4,007 (2010); Density: 34.8 persons per square mile (2010); Race: 97.4% White, 0.2% Black, 0.3% Asian, 0.4% American Indian/Alaska Native, 0.0% Native Hawaiian/Other Pacific Islander, 1.7% Other, 1.1% Hispanic of any race (2010); Average household size: 2.53 (2010); Median age: 43.1 (2010); Males per 100 females: 100.5 (2010); Marriage status: 28.1% never married, 56.7% now married, 7.2% widowed, 8.0% divorced (2006-2010 5-year est.); Foreign born: 2.0% (2006-2010 5-year est.); Ancestry (includes multiple ancestries): 41.7% French, 21.1% Irish, 13.8% American, 7.9% German, 6.3% Italian (2006-2010 5-year est.).
**Economy:** Single-family building permits issued: 0 (2011); Multi-family building permits issued: 0 (2011); Employment by occupation: 9.4% management, 4.9% professional, 12.1% services, 12.3% sales, 2.6% farming, 12.9% construction, 3.5% production (2006-2010 5-year est.).
**Income:** Per capita income: $24,620 (2006-2010 5-year est.); Median household income: $60,942 (2006-2010 5-year est.); Average household income: $66,301 (2006-2010 5-year est.); Percent of households with income of $100,000 or more: 14.2% (2006-2010 5-year est.); Poverty rate: 6.5% (2006-2010 5-year est.).
**Education:** Percent of population age 25 and over with: High school diploma (including GED) or higher: 89.5% (2006-2010 5-year est.); Bachelor's degree or higher: 18.1% (2006-2010 5-year est.); Master's degree or higher: 8.4% (2006-2010 5-year est.).

### School District(s)
Saranac Central School District (KG-12)

    2009-10 Enrollment: 1,625 . . . . . . . . . . . . . . . . . . . . . . . (518) 565-5600
**Housing:** Homeownership rate: 86.2% (2010); Median home value: $114,700 (2006-2010 5-year est.); Median contract rent: $634 per month (2006-2010 5-year est.); Median year structure built: 1978 (2006-2010 5-year est.).
**Transportation:** Commute to work: 90.0% car, 0.8% public transportation, 0.8% walk, 6.9% work from home (2006-2010 5-year est.); Travel time to work: 16.4% less than 15 minutes, 45.1% 15 to 30 minutes, 27.1% 30 to 45

minutes, 5.3% 45 to 60 minutes, 6.1% 60 minutes or more (2006-2010 5-year est.)

**SCHUYLER FALLS** (town). Covers a land area of 36.516 square miles and a water area of 0.302 square miles. Located at 44.65° N. Lat; 73.58° W. Long. Elevation is 430 feet.
**Population:** 4,774 (1990); 5,128 (2000); 5,181 (2010); Density: 141.9 persons per square mile (2010); Race: 97.2% White, 0.7% Black, 0.5% Asian, 0.1% American Indian/Alaska Native, 0.0% Native Hawaiian/Other Pacific Islander, 1.5% Other, 1.1% Hispanic of any race (2010); Average household size: 2.61 (2010); Median age: 40.4 (2010); Males per 100 females: 99.7 (2010); Marriage status: 31.7% never married, 51.0% now married, 5.1% widowed, 12.1% divorced (2006-2010 5-year est.); Foreign born: 3.6% (2006-2010 5-year est.); Ancestry (includes multiple ancestries): 28.9% French, 16.6% Irish, 11.3% American, 10.9% English, 8.5% German (2006-2010 5-year est.).
**Economy:** Single-family building permits issued: 4 (2011); Multi-family building permits issued: 0 (2011); Employment by occupation: 14.5% management, 2.4% professional, 8.8% services, 14.8% sales, 4.8% farming, 9.5% construction, 7.5% production (2006-2010 5-year est.).
**Income:** Per capita income: $25,001 (2006-2010 5-year est.); Median household income: $54,211 (2006-2010 5-year est.); Average household income: $66,203 (2006-2010 5-year est.); Percent of households with income of $100,000 or more: 25.2% (2006-2010 5-year est.); Poverty rate: 13.0% (2006-2010 5-year est.).
**Education:** Percent of population age 25 and over with: High school diploma (including GED) or higher: 85.2% (2006-2010 5-year est.); Bachelor's degree or higher: 22.7% (2006-2010 5-year est.); Master's degree or higher: 7.8% (2006-2010 5-year est.).
**Housing:** Homeownership rate: 81.0% (2010); Median home value: $120,600 (2006-2010 5-year est.); Median contract rent: $577 per month (2006-2010 5-year est.); Median year structure built: 1975 (2006-2010 5-year est.).
**Transportation:** Commute to work: 92.1% car, 0.0% public transportation, 1.6% walk, 3.7% work from home (2006-2010 5-year est.); Travel time to work: 42.7% less than 15 minutes, 47.9% 15 to 30 minutes, 5.6% 30 to 45 minutes, 0.6% 45 to 60 minutes, 3.3% 60 minutes or more (2006-2010 5-year est.)

**WEST CHAZY** (CDP). Covers a land area of 1.877 square miles and a water area of 0 square miles. Located at 44.81° N. Lat; 73.51° W. Long. Elevation is 302 feet.
**Population:** n/a (1990); n/a (2000); 529 (2010); Density: 281.8 persons per square mile (2010); Race: 96.0% White, 0.4% Black, 0.2% Asian, 0.8% American Indian/Alaska Native, 0.4% Native Hawaiian/Other Pacific Islander, 2.2% Other, 0.6% Hispanic of any race (2010); Average household size: 2.68 (2010); Median age: 37.9 (2010); Males per 100 females: 101.9 (2010); Marriage status: 16.2% never married, 74.2% now married, 4.1% widowed, 5.5% divorced (2006-2010 5-year est.); Foreign born: 0.0% (2006-2010 5-year est.); Ancestry (includes multiple ancestries): 35.1% French, 15.3% German, 14.2% Irish, 7.7% Scottish, 6.1% Italian (2006-2010 5-year est.).
**Economy:** Employment by occupation: 3.1% management, 0.0% professional, 18.0% services, 23.5% sales, 0.0% farming, 12.2% construction, 12.2% production (2006-2010 5-year est.).
**Income:** Per capita income: $22,331 (2006-2010 5-year est.); Median household income: $55,774 (2006-2010 5-year est.); Average household income: $62,783 (2006-2010 5-year est.); Percent of households with income of $100,000 or more: 21.8% (2006-2010 5-year est.); Poverty rate: 7.3% (2006-2010 5-year est.).
**Education:** Percent of population age 25 and over with: High school diploma (including GED) or higher: 90.6% (2006-2010 5-year est.); Bachelor's degree or higher: 9.4% (2006-2010 5-year est.); Master's degree or higher: 4.2% (2006-2010 5-year est.).

### School District(s)
Beekmantown Central School District (PK-12)

    2009-10 Enrollment: 2,025 . . . . . . . . . . . . . . . . . . . . . . . (518) 324-2993
**Housing:** Homeownership rate: 77.9% (2010); Median home value: $128,000 (2006-2010 5-year est.); Median contract rent: $605 per month (2006-2010 5-year est.); Median year structure built: 1971 (2006-2010 5-year est.).
**Transportation:** Commute to work: 100.0% car, 0.0% public transportation, 0.0% walk, 0.0% work from home (2006-2010 5-year est.); Travel time to work: 20.3% less than 15 minutes, 65.2% 15 to 30 minutes,

3.6% 30 to 45 minutes, 0.0% 45 to 60 minutes, 10.9% 60 minutes or more (2006-2010 5-year est.)

## Columbia County

Located in southeastern New York; bounded on the east by Massachusetts, and on the west by the Hudson River. Covers a land area of 635.73 square miles, a water area of 12.54 square miles, and is located in the Eastern Time Zone at 42.26° N. Lat., 73.65° W. Long. The county was founded in 1786. County seat is Hudson.

Columbia County is part of the Hudson, NY Micropolitan Statistical Area. The entire metro area includes: Columbia County, NY

Weather Station: Hudson Correctionl Fac                    Elevation: 60 feet

| | Jan | Feb | Mar | Apr | May | Jun | Jul | Aug | Sep | Oct | Nov | Dec |
|---|---|---|---|---|---|---|---|---|---|---|---|---|
| High | 34 | 38 | 48 | 62 | 73 | 81 | 84 | 82 | 74 | 63 | 51 | 39 |
| Low | 16 | 19 | 27 | 37 | 47 | 57 | 61 | 60 | 53 | 41 | 33 | 23 |
| Precip | 2.6 | 2.3 | 3.4 | 3.7 | 3.8 | 4.3 | 3.9 | 3.8 | 4.0 | 4.0 | 3.2 | 3.0 |
| Snow | 11.0 | 7.4 | 4.8 | 1.1 | 0.0 | 0.0 | 0.0 | 0.0 | 0.0 | 0.1 | 1.0 | 6.2 |

*High and Low temperatures in degrees Fahrenheit; Precipitation and Snow in inches*

Weather Station: Valatie 1 N                    Elevation: 299 feet

| | Jan | Feb | Mar | Apr | May | Jun | Jul | Aug | Sep | Oct | Nov | Dec |
|---|---|---|---|---|---|---|---|---|---|---|---|---|
| High | 32 | 36 | 44 | 58 | 69 | 78 | 82 | 81 | 73 | 61 | 49 | 37 |
| Low | 13 | 16 | 24 | 35 | 46 | 55 | 59 | 58 | 50 | 38 | 31 | 19 |
| Precip | 2.1 | 1.9 | 2.8 | 3.7 | 4.1 | 4.5 | 4.1 | 4.1 | 4.0 | 3.9 | 3.3 | 2.6 |
| Snow | 10.8 | 8.1 | 6.4 | 2.2 | 0.0 | 0.0 | 0.0 | 0.0 | 0.0 | 0.3 | 2.4 | 11.1 |

*High and Low temperatures in degrees Fahrenheit; Precipitation and Snow in inches*

**Population:** 62,982 (1990); 63,094 (2000); 63,096 (2010); Race: 90.6% White, 4.5% Black, 1.6% Asian, 0.2% American Indian/Alaska Native, 0.0% Native Hawaiian/Other Pacific Islander, 3.1% Other, 3.9% Hispanic of any race (2010); Density: 99.2 persons per square mile (2010); Average household size: 2.35 (2010); Median age: 45.3 (2010); Males per 100 females: 101.4 (2010).
**Religion:** Six largest groups: 24.4% Catholicism, 3.5% Methodist/Pietist, 3.1% Lutheran, 3.0% Presbyterian-Reformed, 1.3% Episcopalianism/Anglicanism, 1.2% Non-Denominational (2010)
**Economy:** Unemployment rate: 8.4% (February 2012); Total civilian labor force: 29,711 (February 2012); Leading industries: 27.3% health care and social assistance; 16.1% retail trade; 10.1% manufacturing (2009); Farms: 554 totaling 106,574 acres (2007); Companies that employ 500 or more persons: 1 (2009); Companies that employ 100 to 499 persons: 16 (2009); Companies that employ less than 100 persons: 1,707 (2009); Black-owned businesses: n/a (2007); Hispanic-owned businesses: n/a (2007); Asian-owned businesses: n/a (2007); Women-owned businesses: 1,947 (2007); Retail sales per capita: $11,880 (2010). Single-family building permits issued: 59 (2011); Multi-family building permits issued: 3 (2011).
**Income:** Per capita income: $31,844 (2006-2010 5-year est.); Median household income: $55,546 (2006-2010 5-year est.); Average household income: $78,049 (2006-2010 5-year est.); Percent of households with income of $100,000 or more: 23.1% (2006-2010 5-year est.); Poverty rate: 9.5% (2006-2010 5-year est.); Bankruptcy rate: 2.32% (2011).
**Taxes:** Total county taxes per capita: $1,394 (2009); County property taxes per capita: $662 (2009).
**Education:** Percent of population age 25 and over with: High school diploma (including GED) or higher: 87.0% (2006-2010 5-year est.); Bachelor's degree or higher: 28.2% (2006-2010 5-year est.); Master's degree or higher: 12.9% (2006-2010 5-year est.).
**Housing:** Homeownership rate: 71.6% (2010); Median home value: $221,900 (2006-2010 5-year est.); Median contract rent: $609 per month (2006-2010 5-year est.); Median year structure built: 1960 (2006-2010 5-year est.)
**Health:** Birth rate: 84.9 per 10,000 population (2011); Death rate: 98.0 per 10,000 population (2011); Age-adjusted cancer mortality rate: 179.9 deaths per 100,000 population (2009); Number of physicians: 18.1 per 10,000 population (2008); Hospital beds: 37.2 per 10,000 population (2007); Hospital admissions: 983.2 per 10,000 population (2007).
**Elections:** 2008 Presidential election results: 55.9% Obama, 42.4% McCain, 0.8% Nader
**National and State Parks:** Beebe Hill State Forest; Clermont State Park; Lake Taghkanic State Park; Martin Van Buren National Historic Site; Taconic State Park
**Additional Information Contacts**

Columbia County Government. . . . . . . . . . . . . . . (518) 828-3339
http://www.govt.co.columbia.ny.us
Columbia County Chamber of Commerce . . . . . . . . . . (518) 828-4417
http://www.columbiachamber-ny.com

## Columbia County Communities

**ANCRAM** (town). Covers a land area of 42.478 square miles and a water area of 0.259 square miles. Located at 42.03° N. Lat; 73.58° W. Long. Elevation is 518 feet.
**Population:** 1,510 (1990); 1,513 (2000); 1,573 (2010); Density: 37.0 persons per square mile (2010); Race: 96.4% White, 1.4% Black, 0.6% Asian, 0.1% American Indian/Alaska Native, 0.0% Native Hawaiian/Other Pacific Islander, 1.5% Other, 2.6% Hispanic of any race (2010); Average household size: 2.38 (2010); Median age: 48.2 (2010); Males per 100 females: 105.9 (2010); Marriage status: 27.1% never married, 58.0% now married, 4.7% widowed, 10.2% divorced (2006-2010 5-year est.); Foreign born: 5.3% (2006-2010 5-year est.); Ancestry (includes multiple ancestries): 26.9% Irish, 23.3% German, 14.3% English, 8.0% Dutch, 7.9% American (2006-2010 5-year est.).
**Economy:** Single-family building permits issued: 1 (2011); Multi-family building permits issued: 0 (2011); Employment by occupation: 13.9% management, 4.4% professional, 10.9% services, 14.4% sales, 3.7% farming, 12.0% construction, 4.7% production (2006-2010 5-year est.).
**Income:** Per capita income: $37,193 (2006-2010 5-year est.); Median household income: $59,844 (2006-2010 5-year est.); Average household income: $85,130 (2006-2010 5-year est.); Percent of households with income of $100,000 or more: 18.7% (2006-2010 5-year est.); Poverty rate: 9.2% (2006-2010 5-year est.).
**Education:** Percent of population age 25 and over with: High school diploma (including GED) or higher: 83.2% (2006-2010 5-year est.); Bachelor's degree or higher: 23.2% (2006-2010 5-year est.); Master's degree or higher: 10.8% (2006-2010 5-year est.).
**Housing:** Homeownership rate: 79.7% (2010); Median home value: $248,800 (2006-2010 5-year est.); Median contract rent: $772 per month (2006-2010 5-year est.); Median year structure built: 1971 (2006-2010 5-year est.).
**Transportation:** Commute to work: 81.1% car, 4.2% public transportation, 4.2% walk, 9.0% work from home (2006-2010 5-year est.); Travel time to work: 35.8% less than 15 minutes, 25.8% 15 to 30 minutes, 22.1% 30 to 45 minutes, 9.0% 45 to 60 minutes, 7.2% 60 minutes or more (2006-2010 5-year est.)

**ANCRAMDALE** (unincorporated postal area)
Zip Code: 12503
Covers a land area of 21.029 square miles and a water area of 0.157 square miles. Located at 42.03° N. Lat; 73.58° W. Long. Elevation is 548 feet. Population: 775 (2010); Density: 36.9 persons per square mile (2010); Race: 95.9% White, 1.7% Black, 0.4% Asian, 0.3% American Indian/Alaska Native, 0.0% Native Hawaiian/Other Pacific Islander, 1.7% Other, 2.6% Hispanic of any race (2010); Average household size: 2.47 (2010); Median age: 47.3 (2010); Males per 100 females: 107.2 (2010); Homeownership rate: 81.9% (2010)

**AUSTERLITZ** (town). Covers a land area of 48.722 square miles and a water area of 0.091 square miles. Located at 42.31° N. Lat; 73.51° W. Long. Elevation is 1,129 feet.
**Population:** 1,456 (1990); 1,453 (2000); 1,654 (2010); Density: 33.9 persons per square mile (2010); Race: 96.6% White, 0.7% Black, 1.0% Asian, 0.2% American Indian/Alaska Native, 0.0% Native Hawaiian/Other Pacific Islander, 1.5% Other, 1.6% Hispanic of any race (2010); Average household size: 2.28 (2010); Median age: 50.0 (2010); Males per 100 females: 102.4 (2010); Marriage status: 18.6% never married, 74.1% now married, 1.3% widowed, 6.0% divorced (2006-2010 5-year est.); Foreign born: 6.7% (2006-2010 5-year est.); Ancestry (includes multiple ancestries): 22.2% American, 18.3% German, 14.1% Irish, 13.7% Italian, 8.8% English (2006-2010 5-year est.).
**Economy:** Single-family building permits issued: 4 (2011); Multi-family building permits issued: 0 (2011); Employment by occupation: 13.0% management, 4.5% professional, 9.5% services, 11.2% sales, 2.5% farming, 12.1% construction, 4.0% production (2006-2010 5-year est.).
**Income:** Per capita income: $39,321 (2006-2010 5-year est.); Median household income: $66,413 (2006-2010 5-year est.); Average household income: $96,306 (2006-2010 5-year est.); Percent of households with

income of $100,000 or more: 25.3% (2006-2010 5-year est.); Poverty rate: 3.6% (2006-2010 5-year est.).

**Education:** Percent of population age 25 and over with: High school diploma (including GED) or higher: 93.6% (2006-2010 5-year est.); Bachelor's degree or higher: 39.9% (2006-2010 5-year est.); Master's degree or higher: 16.7% (2006-2010 5-year est.).

**Housing:** Homeownership rate: 85.5% (2010); Median home value: $353,900 (2006-2010 5-year est.); Median contract rent: $572 per month (2006-2010 5-year est.); Median year structure built: 1973 (2006-2010 5-year est.).

**Transportation:** Commute to work: 77.2% car, 0.6% public transportation, 6.4% walk, 14.7% work from home (2006-2010 5-year est.); Travel time to work: 29.4% less than 15 minutes, 31.9% 15 to 30 minutes, 23.5% 30 to 45 minutes, 6.8% 45 to 60 minutes, 8.4% 60 minutes or more (2006-2010 5-year est.)

**CANAAN** (town). Covers a land area of 36.676 square miles and a water area of 0.279 square miles. Located at 42.40° N. Lat; 73.46° W. Long. Elevation is 850 feet.

**Population:** 1,773 (1990); 1,820 (2000); 1,710 (2010); Density: 46.6 persons per square mile (2010); Race: 92.6% White, 4.3% Black, 0.8% Asian, 0.1% American Indian/Alaska Native, 0.0% Native Hawaiian/Other Pacific Islander, 2.2% Other, 2.2% Hispanic of any race (2010); Average household size: 2.35 (2010); Median age: 45.6 (2010); Males per 100 females: 110.9 (2010); Marriage status: 62.5% never married, 30.3% now married, 2.7% widowed, 4.4% divorced (2006-2010 5-year est.); Foreign born: 1.5% (2006-2010 5-year est.); Ancestry (includes multiple ancestries): 17.5% American, 14.1% German, 10.6% English, 9.5% Irish, 8.3% Polish (2006-2010 5-year est.).

**Economy:** Single-family building permits issued: 2 (2011); Multi-family building permits issued: 0 (2011); Employment by occupation: 8.9% management, 2.7% professional, 9.4% services, 14.0% sales, 14.1% farming, 13.7% construction, 2.7% production (2006-2010 5-year est.).

**Income:** Per capita income: $23,249 (2006-2010 5-year est.); Median household income: $74,306 (2006-2010 5-year est.); Average household income: $98,704 (2006-2010 5-year est.); Percent of households with income of $100,000 or more: 30.8% (2006-2010 5-year est.); Poverty rate: 3.2% (2006-2010 5-year est.).

**Education:** Percent of population age 25 and over with: High school diploma (including GED) or higher: 96.9% (2006-2010 5-year est.); Bachelor's degree or higher: 43.3% (2006-2010 5-year est.); Master's degree or higher: 21.9% (2006-2010 5-year est.).

School District(s)
Berkshire Union Free School District (07-11)
   2009-10 Enrollment: 76 . . . . . . . . . . . . . . . . . . . . . . . . (518) 781-3500

**Housing:** Homeownership rate: 84.7% (2010); Median home value: $258,700 (2006-2010 5-year est.); Median contract rent: $680 per month (2006-2010 5-year est.); Median year structure built: 1951 (2006-2010 5-year est.).

**Transportation:** Commute to work: 72.1% car, 2.3% public transportation, 3.0% walk, 22.3% work from home (2006-2010 5-year est.); Travel time to work: 28.3% less than 15 minutes, 27.8% 15 to 30 minutes, 26.8% 30 to 45 minutes, 13.9% 45 to 60 minutes, 3.2% 60 minutes or more (2006-2010 5-year est.)

**CHATHAM** (village). Covers a land area of 1.236 square miles and a water area of 0.004 square miles. Located at 42.36° N. Lat; 73.59° W. Long. Elevation is 463 feet.

**Population:** 1,920 (1990); 1,758 (2000); 1,770 (2010); Density: 1,431.0 persons per square mile (2010); Race: 88.8% White, 3.4% Black, 2.0% Asian, 0.3% American Indian/Alaska Native, 0.1% Native Hawaiian/Other Pacific Islander, 5.4% Other, 5.0% Hispanic of any race (2010); Average household size: 2.20 (2010); Median age: 43.4 (2010); Males per 100 females: 96.4 (2010); Marriage status: 30.2% never married, 50.1% now married, 6.1% widowed, 13.7% divorced (2006-2010 5-year est.); Foreign born: 5.0% (2006-2010 5-year est.); Ancestry (includes multiple ancestries): 23.5% Irish, 21.1% German, 15.7% English, 14.2% Italian, 11.0% American (2006-2010 5-year est.).

**Economy:** Single-family building permits issued: 0 (2011); Multi-family building permits issued: 0 (2011); Employment by occupation: 15.7% management, 3.9% professional, 9.5% services, 17.1% sales, 4.4% farming, 6.3% construction, 3.3% production (2006-2010 5-year est.).

**Income:** Per capita income: $26,804 (2006-2010 5-year est.); Median household income: $51,528 (2006-2010 5-year est.); Average household income: $63,206 (2006-2010 5-year est.); Percent of households with

income of $100,000 or more: 17.2% (2006-2010 5-year est.); Poverty rate: 8.5% (2006-2010 5-year est.).

**Education:** Percent of population age 25 and over with: High school diploma (including GED) or higher: 90.7% (2006-2010 5-year est.); Bachelor's degree or higher: 34.2% (2006-2010 5-year est.); Master's degree or higher: 12.9% (2006-2010 5-year est.).

School District(s)
Chatham Central School District (KG-12)
   2009-10 Enrollment: 1,255 . . . . . . . . . . . . . . . . . . . . (518) 392-1501

**Housing:** Homeownership rate: 48.8% (2010); Median home value: $203,800 (2006-2010 5-year est.); Median contract rent: $590 per month (2006-2010 5-year est.); Median year structure built: before 1940 (2006-2010 5-year est.).

**Safety:** Violent crime rate: 91.5 per 10,000 population; Property crime rate: 372.2 per 10,000 population (2010).

**Transportation:** Commute to work: 83.3% car, 1.5% public transportation, 10.0% walk, 3.9% work from home (2006-2010 5-year est.); Travel time to work: 33.2% less than 15 minutes, 30.5% 15 to 30 minutes, 16.7% 30 to 45 minutes, 11.2% 45 to 60 minutes, 8.4% 60 minutes or more (2006-2010 5-year est.)

**CHATHAM** (town). Covers a land area of 53.226 square miles and a water area of 0.316 square miles. Located at 42.42° N. Lat; 73.58° W. Long. Elevation is 463 feet.

**History:** Incorporated 1869.

**Population:** 4,413 (1990); 4,249 (2000); 4,128 (2010); Density: 77.6 persons per square mile (2010); Race: 94.7% White, 1.9% Black, 0.7% Asian, 0.1% American Indian/Alaska Native, 0.0% Native Hawaiian/Other Pacific Islander, 2.6% Other, 2.2% Hispanic of any race (2010); Average household size: 2.30 (2010); Median age: 48.3 (2010); Males per 100 females: 99.7 (2010); Marriage status: 20.9% never married, 64.2% now married, 4.3% widowed, 10.5% divorced (2006-2010 5-year est.); Foreign born: 6.1% (2006-2010 5-year est.); Ancestry (includes multiple ancestries): 25.7% German, 21.3% Italian, 20.8% Irish, 19.6% English, 12.7% American (2006-2010 5-year est.).

**Economy:** Single-family building permits issued: 6 (2011); Multi-family building permits issued: 0 (2011); Employment by occupation: 18.2% management, 5.5% professional, 6.3% services, 12.1% sales, 4.5% farming, 5.7% construction, 2.5% production (2006-2010 5-year est.).

**Income:** Per capita income: $48,976 (2006-2010 5-year est.); Median household income: $75,954 (2006-2010 5-year est.); Average household income: $113,442 (2006-2010 5-year est.); Percent of households with income of $100,000 or more: 37.0% (2006-2010 5-year est.); Poverty rate: 6.9% (2006-2010 5-year est.).

**Education:** Percent of population age 25 and over with: High school diploma (including GED) or higher: 93.2% (2006-2010 5-year est.); Bachelor's degree or higher: 43.5% (2006-2010 5-year est.); Master's degree or higher: 22.1% (2006-2010 5-year est.).

School District(s)
Chatham Central School District (KG-12)
   2009-10 Enrollment: 1,255 . . . . . . . . . . . . . . . . . . . . (518) 392-1501

**Housing:** Homeownership rate: 77.7% (2010); Median home value: $289,500 (2006-2010 5-year est.); Median contract rent: $567 per month (2006-2010 5-year est.); Median year structure built: 1957 (2006-2010 5-year est.).

**Transportation:** Commute to work: 83.8% car, 2.9% public transportation, 4.9% walk, 7.8% work from home (2006-2010 5-year est.); Travel time to work: 24.5% less than 15 minutes, 31.3% 15 to 30 minutes, 31.6% 30 to 45 minutes, 6.5% 45 to 60 minutes, 6.1% 60 minutes or more (2006-2010 5-year est.)

**CLAVERACK** (town). Covers a land area of 47.558 square miles and a water area of 0.389 square miles. Located at 42.21° N. Lat; 73.68° W. Long. Elevation is 203 feet.

**History:** Fine old buildings include Van Rensselaer manor house; former county courthouse (built 1786).

**Population:** 6,414 (1990); 6,401 (2000); 6,021 (2010); Density: 126.6 persons per square mile (2010); Race: 93.4% White, 3.0% Black, 0.7% Asian, 0.1% American Indian/Alaska Native, 0.0% Native Hawaiian/Other Pacific Islander, 2.8% Other, 3.4% Hispanic of any race (2010); Average household size: 2.33 (2010); Median age: 46.2 (2010); Males per 100 females: 99.0 (2010); Marriage status: 28.7% never married, 45.0% now married, 11.6% widowed, 14.7% divorced (2006-2010 5-year est.); Foreign born: 4.4% (2006-2010 5-year est.); Ancestry (includes multiple

ancestries): 25.9% German, 16.3% Irish, 12.7% Italian, 11.6% English, 10.3% Dutch (2006-2010 5-year est.).
**Economy:** Single-family building permits issued: 6 (2011); Multi-family building permits issued: 0 (2011); Employment by occupation: 13.6% management, 3.2% professional, 7.9% services, 13.9% sales, 2.4% farming, 13.5% construction, 7.3% production (2006-2010 5-year est.).
**Income:** Per capita income: $31,965 (2006-2010 5-year est.); Median household income: $52,857 (2006-2010 5-year est.); Average household income: $78,372 (2006-2010 5-year est.); Percent of households with income of $100,000 or more: 18.7% (2006-2010 5-year est.); Poverty rate: 8.5% (2006-2010 5-year est.).
**Education:** Percent of population age 25 and over with: High school diploma (including GED) or higher: 86.1% (2006-2010 5-year est.); Bachelor's degree or higher: 25.3% (2006-2010 5-year est.); Master's degree or higher: 10.6% (2006-2010 5-year est.).
**Housing:** Homeownership rate: 75.2% (2010); Median home value: $177,100 (2006-2010 5-year est.); Median contract rent: $714 per month (2006-2010 5-year est.); Median year structure built: 1956 (2006-2010 5-year est.).
**Transportation:** Commute to work: 85.4% car, 1.7% public transportation, 1.7% walk, 9.8% work from home (2006-2010 5-year est.); Travel time to work: 41.6% less than 15 minutes, 35.6% 15 to 30 minutes, 11.4% 30 to 45 minutes, 6.5% 45 to 60 minutes, 4.9% 60 minutes or more (2006-2010 5-year est.)

### CLAVERACK-RED MILLS (CDP). Covers a land area of 2.978 square miles and a water area of 0.018 square miles. Located at 42.22° N. Lat; 73.72° W. Long.
**Population:** 1,152 (1990); 1,061 (2000); 913 (2010); Density: 306.6 persons per square mile (2010); Race: 95.9% White, 1.9% Black, 0.7% Asian, 0.1% American Indian/Alaska Native, 0.0% Native Hawaiian/Other Pacific Islander, 1.4% Other, 1.4% Hispanic of any race (2010); Average household size: 2.05 (2010); Median age: 52.4 (2010); Males per 100 females: 98.5 (2010); Marriage status: 31.6% never married, 37.6% now married, 11.4% widowed, 19.4% divorced (2006-2010 5-year est.); Foreign born: 2.1% (2006-2010 5-year est.); Ancestry (includes multiple ancestries): 27.1% English, 19.7% Irish, 14.6% German, 13.7% Dutch, 12.8% Scotch-Irish (2006-2010 5-year est.).
**Economy:** Employment by occupation: 18.1% management, 0.0% professional, 11.2% services, 8.6% sales, 0.0% farming, 2.6% construction, 0.0% production (2006-2010 5-year est.).
**Income:** Per capita income: $34,003 (2006-2010 5-year est.); Median household income: $67,061 (2006-2010 5-year est.); Average household income: $62,141 (2006-2010 5-year est.); Percent of households with income of $100,000 or more: 5.2% (2006-2010 5-year est.); Poverty rate: 7.8% (2006-2010 5-year est.).
**Education:** Percent of population age 25 and over with: High school diploma (including GED) or higher: 96.2% (2006-2010 5-year est.); Bachelor's degree or higher: 38.0% (2006-2010 5-year est.); Master's degree or higher: 10.5% (2006-2010 5-year est.).
**Housing:** Homeownership rate: 78.2% (2010); Median home value: $170,300 (2006-2010 5-year est.); Median contract rent: $735 per month (2006-2010 5-year est.); Median year structure built: 1954 (2006-2010 5-year est.).
**Transportation:** Commute to work: 91.2% car, 0.0% public transportation, 0.0% walk, 8.8% work from home (2006-2010 5-year est.); Travel time to work: 51.8% less than 15 minutes, 13.8% 15 to 30 minutes, 4.2% 30 to 45 minutes, 14.3% 45 to 60 minutes, 15.9% 60 minutes or more (2006-2010 5-year est.)
**Safety:** Violent crime rate: 0.0 per 10,000 population; Property

### CLERMONT (town). Covers a land area of 17.996 square miles and a water area of 1.196 square miles. Located at 42.08° N. Lat; 73.85° W. Long. Elevation is 223 feet.
**Population:** 1,443 (1990); 1,726 (2000); 1,965 (2010); Density: 109.2 persons per square mile (2010); Race: 94.4% White, 0.8% Black, 1.2% Asian, 0.3% American Indian/Alaska Native, 0.1% Native Hawaiian/Other Pacific Islander, 3.2% Other, 5.2% Hispanic of any race (2010); Average household size: 2.63 (2010); Median age: 43.8 (2010); Males per 100 females: 103.2 (2010); Marriage status: 29.2% never married, 52.5% now married, 6.6% widowed, 11.7% divorced (2006-2010 5-year est.); Foreign born: 4.3% (2006-2010 5-year est.); Ancestry (includes multiple ancestries): 28.6% German, 27.1% Irish, 18.7% Italian, 9.6% English, 9.2% Dutch (2006-2010 5-year est.).
**Economy:** Single-family building permits issued: 3 (2011); Multi-family building permits issued: 0 (2011); Employment by occupation: 12.8%

management, 4.9% professional, 14.7% services, 11.4% sales, 4.2% farming, 15.5% construction, 5.7% production (2006-2010 5-year est.).
**Income:** Per capita income: $29,615 (2006-2010 5-year est.); Median household income: $65,682 (2006-2010 5-year est.); Average household income: $81,906 (2006-2010 5-year est.); Percent of households with income of $100,000 or more: 25.6% (2006-2010 5-year est.); Poverty rate: 9.2% (2006-2010 5-year est.).
**Education:** Percent of population age 25 and over with: High school diploma (including GED) or higher: 83.1% (2006-2010 5-year est.); Bachelor's degree or higher: 25.4% (2006-2010 5-year est.); Master's degree or higher: 13.0% (2006-2010 5-year est.).
**Housing:** Homeownership rate: 75.6% (2010); Median home value: $279,200 (2006-2010 5-year est.); Median contract rent: $688 per month (2006-2010 5-year est.); Median year structure built: 1978 (2006-2010 5-year est.).
**Transportation:** Commute to work: 83.6% car, 0.5% public transportation, 6.2% walk, 9.3% work from home (2006-2010 5-year est.); Travel time to work: 28.5% less than 15 minutes, 33.5% 15 to 30 minutes, 21.7% 30 to 45 minutes, 7.3% 45 to 60 minutes, 8.9% 60 minutes or more (2006-2010 5-year est.)

### COPAKE (town). Covers a land area of 40.761 square miles and a water area of 1.279 square miles. Located at 42.12° N. Lat; 73.54° W. Long. Elevation is 545 feet.
**Population:** 3,118 (1990); 3,278 (2000); 3,615 (2010); Density: 88.7 persons per square mile (2010); Race: 96.0% White, 0.9% Black, 0.7% Asian, 0.1% American Indian/Alaska Native, 0.1% Native Hawaiian/Other Pacific Islander, 2.2% Other, 3.6% Hispanic of any race (2010); Average household size: 2.37 (2010); Median age: 45.8 (2010); Males per 100 females: 99.2 (2010); Marriage status: 23.9% never married, 64.0% now married, 4.2% widowed, 7.9% divorced (2006-2010 5-year est.); Foreign born: 4.4% (2006-2010 5-year est.); Ancestry (includes multiple ancestries): 21.6% German, 17.6% Italian, 16.2% Irish, 13.1% English, 12.9% American (2006-2010 5-year est.).
**Economy:** Single-family building permits issued: 5 (2011); Multi-family building permits issued: 0 (2011); Employment by occupation: 16.0% management, 4.0% professional, 12.8% services, 15.5% sales, 5.0% farming, 7.6% construction, 1.0% production (2006-2010 5-year est.).
**Income:** Per capita income: $41,046 (2006-2010 5-year est.); Median household income: $68,929 (2006-2010 5-year est.); Average household income: $105,086 (2006-2010 5-year est.); Percent of households with income of $100,000 or more: 32.0% (2006-2010 5-year est.); Poverty rate: 8.3% (2006-2010 5-year est.).
**Education:** Percent of population age 25 and over with: High school diploma (including GED) or higher: 91.7% (2006-2010 5-year est.); Bachelor's degree or higher: 31.0% (2006-2010 5-year est.); Master's degree or higher: 16.6% (2006-2010 5-year est.).
**Housing:** Homeownership rate: 75.2% (2010); Median home value: $215,900 (2006-2010 5-year est.); Median contract rent: $815 per month (2006-2010 5-year est.); Median year structure built: 1967 (2006-2010 5-year est.).
**Safety:** Violent crime rate: 3.1 per 10,000 population; Property crime rate: 78.4 per 10,000 population (2010).
**Transportation:** Commute to work: 82.6% car, 2.5% public transportation, 3.0% walk, 9.1% work from home (2006-2010 5-year est.); Travel time to work: 21.8% less than 15 minutes, 26.7% 15 to 30 minutes, 23.9% 30 to 45 minutes, 11.0% 45 to 60 minutes, 16.6% 60 minutes or more (2006-2010 5-year est.)

### COPAKE FALLS (unincorporated postal area)
Zip Code: 12517
Covers a land area of 10.459 square miles and a water area of 0.015 square miles. Located at 42.11° N. Lat; 73.50° W. Long. Elevation is 643 feet. Population: 509 (2010); Density: 48.7 persons per square mile (2010); Race: 94.7% White, 1.8% Black, 0.4% Asian, 0.0% American Indian/Alaska Native, 0.0% Native Hawaiian/Other Pacific Islander, 3.1% Other, 8.1% Hispanic of any race (2010); Average household size: 2.35 (2010); Median age: 44.3 (2010); Males per 100 females: 104.4 (2010); Homeownership rate: 65.3% (2010)

### COPAKE LAKE (CDP). Covers a land area of 9.509 square miles and a water area of 0.804 square miles. Located at 42.14° N. Lat; 73.59° W. Long. Elevation is 719 feet.
**Population:** 606 (1990); 762 (2000); 823 (2010); Density: 86.5 persons per square mile (2010); Race: 97.6% White, 0.5% Black, 0.4% Asian, 0.4%

American Indian/Alaska Native, 0.0% Native Hawaiian/Other Pacific Islander, 1.1% Other, 2.8% Hispanic of any race (2010); Average household size: 2.49 (2010); Median age: 46.9 (2010); Males per 100 females: 105.2 (2010); Marriage status: 12.3% never married, 80.6% now married, 4.6% widowed, 2.5% divorced (2006-2010 5-year est.); Foreign born: 2.3% (2006-2010 5-year est.); Ancestry (includes multiple ancestries): 33.6% Italian, 21.5% Irish, 18.7% German, 9.7% Polish, 5.1% American (2006-2010 5-year est.).

**Economy:** Employment by occupation: 18.9% management, 11.3% professional, 1.4% services, 18.9% sales, 5.4% farming, 8.7% construction, 0.0% production (2006-2010 5-year est.).

**Income:** Per capita income: $46,348 (2006-2010 5-year est.); Median household income: $96,935 (2006-2010 5-year est.); Average household income: $97,113 (2006-2010 5-year est.); Percent of households with income of $100,000 or more: 48.0% (2006-2010 5-year est.); Poverty rate: 3.0% (2006-2010 5-year est.).

**Education:** Percent of population age 25 and over with: High school diploma (including GED) or higher: 93.5% (2006-2010 5-year est.); Bachelor's degree or higher: 43.3% (2006-2010 5-year est.); Master's degree or higher: 21.8% (2006-2010 5-year est.).

**Housing:** Homeownership rate: 83.9% (2010); Median home value: $270,100 (2006-2010 5-year est.); Median contract rent: $633 per month (2006-2010 5-year est.); Median year structure built: 1965 (2006-2010 5-year est.).

**Transportation:** Commute to work: 82.7% car, 5.4% public transportation, 3.1% walk, 3.5% work from home (2006-2010 5-year est.); Travel time to work: 17.4% less than 15 minutes, 23.8% 15 to 30 minutes, 21.3% 30 to 45 minutes, 5.6% 45 to 60 minutes, 31.9% 60 minutes or more (2006-2010 5-year est.)

### CRARYVILLE (unincorporated postal area)

Zip Code: 12521

Covers a land area of 32.888 square miles and a water area of 0.314 square miles. Located at 42.17° N. Lat; 73.65° W. Long. Elevation is 636 feet. Population: 1,644 (2010); Density: 50.0 persons per square mile (2010); Race: 95.1% White, 0.9% Black, 0.9% Asian, 0.3% American Indian/Alaska Native, 0.0% Native Hawaiian/Other Pacific Islander, 2.8% Other, 3.4% Hispanic of any race (2010); Average household size: 2.39 (2010); Median age: 46.4 (2010); Males per 100 females: 104.7 (2010); Homeownership rate: 82.7% (2010)

### EAST CHATHAM (unincorporated postal area)

Zip Code: 12060

Covers a land area of 34.503 square miles and a water area of 0.132 square miles. Located at 42.41° N. Lat; 73.50° W. Long. Elevation is 702 feet. Population: 1,507 (2010); Density: 43.7 persons per square mile (2010); Race: 97.0% White, 0.8% Black, 0.8% Asian, 0.1% American Indian/Alaska Native, 0.0% Native Hawaiian/Other Pacific Islander, 1.3% Other, 2.5% Hispanic of any race (2010); Average household size: 2.38 (2010); Median age: 47.6 (2010); Males per 100 females: 102.0 (2010); Homeownership rate: 85.8% (2010)

### ELIZAVILLE (unincorporated postal area)

Zip Code: 12523

Covers a land area of 21.889 square miles and a water area of 0.184 square miles. Located at 42.08° N. Lat; 73.75° W. Long. Elevation is 289 feet. Population: 1,798 (2010); Density: 82.1 persons per square mile (2010); Race: 96.3% White, 1.1% Black, 0.8% Asian, 0.3% American Indian/Alaska Native, 0.0% Native Hawaiian/Other Pacific Islander, 1.5% Other, 3.4% Hispanic of any race (2010); Average household size: 2.33 (2010); Median age: 44.6 (2010); Males per 100 females: 100.4 (2010); Homeownership rate: 75.8% (2010)

### GALLATIN (town). Aka Gallatinville. Covers a land area of 39.111 square miles and a water area of 0.520 square miles. Located at 42.06° N. Lat; 73.71° W. Long.

**Population:** 1,658 (1990); 1,499 (2000); 1,668 (2010); Density: 42.6 persons per square mile (2010); Race: 97.2% White, 0.7% Black, 0.4% Asian, 0.2% American Indian/Alaska Native, 0.0% Native Hawaiian/Other Pacific Islander, 1.5% Other, 3.6% Hispanic of any race (2010); Average household size: 2.36 (2010); Median age: 46.1 (2010); Males per 100 females: 105.7 (2010); Marriage status: 30.8% never married, 56.6% now married, 2.8% widowed, 9.8% divorced (2006-2010 5-year est.); Foreign born: 4.6% (2006-2010 5-year est.); Ancestry (includes multiple

ancestries): 27.9% German, 23.9% Italian, 23.4% Irish, 9.4% English, 9.1% French (2006-2010 5-year est.).

**Economy:** Single-family building permits issued: 2 (2011); Multi-family building permits issued: 0 (2011); Employment by occupation: 7.7% management, 1.9% professional, 10.7% services, 12.2% sales, 2.1% farming, 21.4% construction, 8.0% production (2006-2010 5-year est.).

**Income:** Per capita income: $32,145 (2006-2010 5-year est.); Median household income: $65,083 (2006-2010 5-year est.); Average household income: $81,954 (2006-2010 5-year est.); Percent of households with income of $100,000 or more: 24.0% (2006-2010 5-year est.); Poverty rate: 6.2% (2006-2010 5-year est.).

**Education:** Percent of population age 25 and over with: High school diploma (including GED) or higher: 85.8% (2006-2010 5-year est.); Bachelor's degree or higher: 29.3% (2006-2010 5-year est.); Master's degree or higher: 13.5% (2006-2010 5-year est.).

**Housing:** Homeownership rate: 84.7% (2010); Median home value: $240,000 (2006-2010 5-year est.); Median contract rent: $739 per month (2006-2010 5-year est.); Median year structure built: 1966 (2006-2010 5-year est.).

**Transportation:** Commute to work: 84.7% car, 6.2% public transportation, 2.0% walk, 7.1% work from home (2006-2010 5-year est.); Travel time to work: 18.4% less than 15 minutes, 30.0% 15 to 30 minutes, 19.0% 30 to 45 minutes, 11.2% 45 to 60 minutes, 21.3% 60 minutes or more (2006-2010 5-year est.)

### GERMANTOWN (town). Covers a land area of 12.102 square miles and a water area of 1.818 square miles. Located at 42.13° N. Lat; 73.87° W. Long. Elevation is 135 feet.

**Population:** 2,010 (1990); 2,018 (2000); 1,954 (2010); Density: 161.4 persons per square mile (2010); Race: 95.8% White, 0.8% Black, 1.2% Asian, 0.3% American Indian/Alaska Native, 0.0% Native Hawaiian/Other Pacific Islander, 1.9% Other, 3.1% Hispanic of any race (2010); Average household size: 2.30 (2010); Median age: 46.1 (2010); Males per 100 females: 96.8 (2010); Marriage status: 16.1% never married, 61.9% now married, 5.7% widowed, 16.3% divorced (2006-2010 5-year est.); Foreign born: 3.2% (2006-2010 5-year est.); Ancestry (includes multiple ancestries): 25.4% German, 21.3% Italian, 18.7% Irish, 18.0% English, 9.3% Scottish (2006-2010 5-year est.).

**Economy:** Single-family building permits issued: 1 (2011); Multi-family building permits issued: 0 (2011); Employment by occupation: 16.0% management, 3.4% professional, 8.3% services, 20.6% sales, 4.8% farming, 7.8% construction, 3.8% production (2006-2010 5-year est.).

**Income:** Per capita income: $34,456 (2006-2010 5-year est.); Median household income: $53,542 (2006-2010 5-year est.); Average household income: $77,054 (2006-2010 5-year est.); Percent of households with income of $100,000 or more: 20.3% (2006-2010 5-year est.); Poverty rate: 5.6% (2006-2010 5-year est.).

**Education:** Percent of population age 25 and over with: High school diploma (including GED) or higher: 87.4% (2006-2010 5-year est.); Bachelor's degree or higher: 28.6% (2006-2010 5-year est.); Master's degree or higher: 13.9% (2006-2010 5-year est.).

**School District(s)**

Germantown Central School District (KG-12)

    2009-10 Enrollment: 611 . . . . . . . . . . . . . . . . . . . . . . . . (518) 537-6280

**Housing:** Homeownership rate: 73.3% (2010); Median home value: $258,100 (2006-2010 5-year est.); Median contract rent: $636 per month (2006-2010 5-year est.); Median year structure built: 1947 (2006-2010 5-year est.).

**Safety:** Violent crime rate: 0.0 per 10,000 population; Property crime rate: 15.6 per 10,000 population (2010).

**Transportation:** Commute to work: 85.4% car, 5.3% public transportation, 0.6% walk, 7.9% work from home (2006-2010 5-year est.); Travel time to work: 28.0% less than 15 minutes, 32.0% 15 to 30 minutes, 23.1% 30 to 45 minutes, 7.7% 45 to 60 minutes, 9.3% 60 minutes or more (2006-2010 5-year est.)

### GERMANTOWN (CDP). Covers a land area of 2.678 square miles and a water area of 0.015 square miles. Located at 42.13° N. Lat; 73.88° W. Long. Elevation is 135 feet.

**Population:** 820 (1990); 862 (2000); 845 (2010); Density: 315.5 persons per square mile (2010); Race: 94.8% White, 0.6% Black, 1.8% Asian, 0.2% American Indian/Alaska Native, 0.0% Native Hawaiian/Other Pacific Islander, 2.6% Other, 4.3% Hispanic of any race (2010); Average household size: 2.33 (2010); Median age: 45.1 (2010); Males per 100 females: 96.1 (2010); Marriage status: 17.2% never married, 60.2% now

married, 3.0% widowed, 19.5% divorced (2006-2010 5-year est.); Foreign born: 3.1% (2006-2010 5-year est.); Ancestry (includes multiple ancestries): 23.7% German, 20.9% Italian, 16.7% Irish, 13.1% English, 9.1% Scottish (2006-2010 5-year est.).
**Economy:** Employment by occupation: 10.4% management, 5.7% professional, 8.9% services, 20.0% sales, 4.7% farming, 8.9% construction, 8.2% production (2006-2010 5-year est.).
**Income:** Per capita income: $31,327 (2006-2010 5-year est.); Median household income: $53,235 (2006-2010 5-year est.); Average household income: $75,318 (2006-2010 5-year est.); Percent of households with income of $100,000 or more: 14.9% (2006-2010 5-year est.); Poverty rate: 3.0% (2006-2010 5-year est.).
**Education:** Percent of population age 25 and over with: High school diploma (including GED) or higher: 84.3% (2006-2010 5-year est.); Bachelor's degree or higher: 24.0% (2006-2010 5-year est.); Master's degree or higher: 9.7% (2006-2010 5-year est.).

**School District(s)**
Germantown Central School District (KG-12)
   2009-10 Enrollment: 611 . . . . . . . . . . . . . . . . . . . . . . . (518) 537-6280
**Housing:** Homeownership rate: 75.5% (2010); Median home value: $240,200 (2006-2010 5-year est.); Median contract rent: $755 per month (2006-2010 5-year est.); Median year structure built: 1941 (2006-2010 5-year est.).
**Transportation:** Commute to work: 91.5% car, 1.6% public transportation, 1.3% walk, 4.1% work from home (2006-2010 5-year est.); Travel time to work: 18.9% less than 15 minutes, 32.3% 15 to 30 minutes, 37.5% 30 to 45 minutes, 4.3% 45 to 60 minutes, 7.0% 60 minutes or more (2006-2010 5-year est.)

## GHENT (town).
Covers a land area of 45.131 square miles and a water area of 0.268 square miles. Located at 42.31° N. Lat; 73.64° W. Long. Elevation is 407 feet.
**Population:** 4,812 (1990); 5,276 (2000); 5,402 (2010); Density: 119.7 persons per square mile (2010); Race: 94.5% White, 1.6% Black, 0.9% Asian, 0.3% American Indian/Alaska Native, 0.1% Native Hawaiian/Other Pacific Islander, 2.6% Other, 3.8% Hispanic of any race (2010); Average household size: 2.37 (2010); Median age: 46.4 (2010); Males per 100 females: 99.4 (2010); Marriage status: 21.2% never married, 63.1% now married, 5.9% widowed, 9.8% divorced (2006-2010 5-year est.); Foreign born: 3.5% (2006-2010 5-year est.); Ancestry (includes multiple ancestries): 30.3% German, 25.4% Irish, 10.9% Italian, 7.4% English, 7.2% Dutch (2006-2010 5-year est.).
**Economy:** Single-family building permits issued: 5 (2011); Multi-family building permits issued: 0 (2011); Employment by occupation: 16.7% management, 2.8% professional, 6.5% services, 16.7% sales, 3.4% farming, 9.5% construction, 7.4% production (2006-2010 5-year est.).
**Income:** Per capita income: $30,304 (2006-2010 5-year est.); Median household income: $50,106 (2006-2010 5-year est.); Average household income: $73,712 (2006-2010 5-year est.); Percent of households with income of $100,000 or more: 25.9% (2006-2010 5-year est.); Poverty rate: 9.2% (2006-2010 5-year est.).
**Education:** Percent of population age 25 and over with: High school diploma (including GED) or higher: 87.9% (2006-2010 5-year est.); Bachelor's degree or higher: 30.9% (2006-2010 5-year est.); Master's degree or higher: 13.7% (2006-2010 5-year est.).
**Housing:** Homeownership rate: 71.5% (2010); Median home value: $200,200 (2006-2010 5-year est.); Median contract rent: $571 per month (2006-2010 5-year est.); Median year structure built: 1959 (2006-2010 5-year est.).
**Transportation:** Commute to work: 92.2% car, 1.5% public transportation, 1.9% walk, 4.0% work from home (2006-2010 5-year est.); Travel time to work: 35.3% less than 15 minutes, 34.0% 15 to 30 minutes, 16.8% 30 to 45 minutes, 7.2% 45 to 60 minutes, 6.8% 60 minutes or more (2006-2010 5-year est.)

## GHENT (CDP).
Covers a land area of 1.538 square miles and a water area of 0.010 square miles. Located at 42.32° N. Lat; 73.61° W. Long. Elevation is 407 feet.
**Population:** 549 (1990); 586 (2000); 564 (2010); Density: 366.7 persons per square mile (2010); Race: 97.3% White, 0.5% Black, 0.2% Asian, 0.0% American Indian/Alaska Native, 0.0% Native Hawaiian/Other Pacific Islander, 2.0% Other, 4.4% Hispanic of any race (2010); Average household size: 2.41 (2010); Median age: 42.8 (2010); Males per 100 females: 105.8 (2010); Marriage status: 21.3% never married, 68.1% now married, 3.2% widowed, 7.4% divorced (2006-2010 5-year est.); Foreign

born: 2.8% (2006-2010 5-year est.); Ancestry (includes multiple ancestries): 32.3% German, 21.4% Italian, 12.0% Dutch, 11.5% Irish, 11.0% European (2006-2010 5-year est.).
**Economy:** Employment by occupation: 8.2% management, 0.0% professional, 0.0% services, 19.9% sales, 0.0% farming, 8.5% construction, 5.0% production (2006-2010 5-year est.).
**Income:** Per capita income: $36,084 (2006-2010 5-year est.); Median household income: $78,250 (2006-2010 5-year est.); Average household income: $79,082 (2006-2010 5-year est.); Percent of households with income of $100,000 or more: 37.3% (2006-2010 5-year est.); Poverty rate: 0.0% (2006-2010 5-year est.).
**Education:** Percent of population age 25 and over with: High school diploma (including GED) or higher: 97.8% (2006-2010 5-year est.); Bachelor's degree or higher: 34.2% (2006-2010 5-year est.); Master's degree or higher: 9.0% (2006-2010 5-year est.).
**Housing:** Homeownership rate: 79.4% (2010); Median home value: $185,500 (2006-2010 5-year est.); Median contract rent: $345 per month (2006-2010 5-year est.); Median year structure built: 1973 (2006-2010 5-year est.).
**Transportation:** Commute to work: 100.0% car, 0.0% public transportation, 0.0% walk, 0.0% work from home (2006-2010 5-year est.); Travel time to work: 36.6% less than 15 minutes, 33.2% 15 to 30 minutes, 21.8% 30 to 45 minutes, 8.5% 45 to 60 minutes, 0.0% 60 minutes or more (2006-2010 5-year est.)

## GREENPORT (town).
Covers a land area of 18.606 square miles and a water area of 1.880 square miles. Located at 42.23° N. Lat; 73.79° W. Long.
**Population:** 4,101 (1990); 4,180 (2000); 4,165 (2010); Density: 223.8 persons per square mile (2010); Race: 86.1% White, 7.4% Black, 1.9% Asian, 0.1% American Indian/Alaska Native, 0.0% Native Hawaiian/Other Pacific Islander, 4.5% Other, 4.4% Hispanic of any race (2010); Average household size: 2.19 (2010); Median age: 46.6 (2010); Males per 100 females: 101.0 (2010); Marriage status: 24.5% never married, 55.0% now married, 10.8% widowed, 9.7% divorced (2006-2010 5-year est.); Foreign born: 4.6% (2006-2010 5-year est.); Ancestry (includes multiple ancestries): 30.0% Italian, 23.0% Irish, 22.1% German, 12.9% Dutch, 10.4% English (2006-2010 5-year est.).
**Economy:** Single-family building permits issued: 1 (2011); Multi-family building permits issued: 0 (2011); Employment by occupation: 8.6% management, 8.5% professional, 11.3% services, 22.2% sales, 2.3% farming, 5.1% construction, 4.7% production (2006-2010 5-year est.).
**Income:** Per capita income: $28,621 (2006-2010 5-year est.); Median household income: $38,975 (2006-2010 5-year est.); Average household income: $54,639 (2006-2010 5-year est.); Percent of households with income of $100,000 or more: 11.3% (2006-2010 5-year est.); Poverty rate: 11.3% (2006-2010 5-year est.).
**Taxes:** Total city taxes per capita: $578 (2009); City property taxes per capita: $529 (2009).
**Education:** Percent of population age 25 and over with: High school diploma (including GED) or higher: 83.0% (2006-2010 5-year est.); Bachelor's degree or higher: 15.2% (2006-2010 5-year est.); Master's degree or higher: 4.5% (2006-2010 5-year est.).
**Housing:** Homeownership rate: 65.5% (2010); Median home value: $170,700 (2006-2010 5-year est.); Median contract rent: $519 per month (2006-2010 5-year est.); Median year structure built: 1963 (2006-2010 5-year est.).
**Transportation:** Commute to work: 90.9% car, 2.4% public transportation, 5.3% walk, 1.5% work from home (2006-2010 5-year est.); Travel time to work: 52.1% less than 15 minutes, 20.9% 15 to 30 minutes, 12.0% 30 to 45 minutes, 11.4% 45 to 60 minutes, 3.6% 60 minutes or more (2006-2010 5-year est.)

## HILLSDALE (town).
Covers a land area of 47.724 square miles and a water area of 0.163 square miles. Located at 42.22° N. Lat; 73.52° W. Long. Elevation is 709 feet.
**Population:** 1,793 (1990); 1,927 (2000); 1,927 (2010); Density: 40.4 persons per square mile (2010); Race: 96.7% White, 1.1% Black, 0.6% Asian, 0.1% American Indian/Alaska Native, 0.0% Native Hawaiian/Other Pacific Islander, 1.5% Other, 2.8% Hispanic of any race (2010); Average household size: 2.27 (2010); Median age: 49.4 (2010); Males per 100 females: 107.4 (2010); Marriage status: 28.6% never married, 55.5% now married, 3.8% widowed, 12.2% divorced (2006-2010 5-year est.); Foreign born: 3.8% (2006-2010 5-year est.); Ancestry (includes multiple

ancestries): 22.7% German, 21.0% Irish, 15.3% Italian, 12.9% English, 12.7% American (2006-2010 5-year est.).
**Economy:** Single-family building permits issued: 2 (2011); Multi-family building permits issued: 0 (2011); Employment by occupation: 17.5% management, 1.8% professional, 3.9% services, 12.4% sales, 2.8% farming, 14.7% construction, 6.1% production (2006-2010 5-year est.).
**Income:** Per capita income: $38,425 (2006-2010 5-year est.); Median household income: $48,565 (2006-2010 5-year est.); Average household income: $90,041 (2006-2010 5-year est.); Percent of households with income of $100,000 or more: 24.3% (2006-2010 5-year est.); Poverty rate: 15.9% (2006-2010 5-year est.).
**Education:** Percent of population age 25 and over with: High school diploma (including GED) or higher: 88.8% (2006-2010 5-year est.); Bachelor's degree or higher: 37.8% (2006-2010 5-year est.); Master's degree or higher: 19.0% (2006-2010 5-year est.).
**Housing:** Homeownership rate: 75.8% (2010); Median home value: $257,200 (2006-2010 5-year est.); Median contract rent: $691 per month (2006-2010 5-year est.); Median year structure built: 1958 (2006-2010 5-year est.).
**Newspapers:** Independent (Local news; Circulation 20,000); The Independent (Local news)
**Transportation:** Commute to work: 76.1% car, 5.5% public transportation, 6.9% walk, 10.1% work from home (2006-2010 5-year est.); Travel time to work: 25.4% less than 15 minutes, 31.6% 15 to 30 minutes, 28.7% 30 to 45 minutes, 5.7% 45 to 60 minutes, 8.7% 60 minutes or more (2006-2010 5-year est.)

## HOLLOWVILLE (unincorporated postal area)
Zip Code: 12530
Covers a land area of 0.347 square miles and a water area of 0 square miles. Located at 42.20° N. Lat; 73.68° W. Long. Elevation is 325 feet.
Population: 124 (2010); Density: 356.7 persons per square mile (2010); Race: 96.8% White, 0.8% Black, 0.8% Asian, 0.0% American Indian/Alaska Native, 0.0% Native Hawaiian/Other Pacific Islander, 1.6% Other, 4.8% Hispanic of any race (2010); Average household size: 2.30 (2010); Median age: 46.3 (2010); Males per 100 females: 110.2 (2010); Homeownership rate: 62.9% (2010)

## HUDSON (city). County seat. Covers a land area of 2.157 square miles and a water area of 0.171 square miles. Located at 42.25° N. Lat; 73.78° W. Long. Elevation is 82 feet.
**History:** The city was a whaling and trading port until 1812. Its industries included textiles, furniture, cement, and metal products, but these are largely gone. Many colonial and Revolutionary era homes are in the area. Olana, estate of Frederic E. Church, 2.5 miles South of city. Settled c.1622 by the Dutch and later in 1783 by English whalers; incorporated 1785.
**Population:** 8,034 (1990); 7,524 (2000); 6,713 (2010); Density: 3,110.9 persons per square mile (2010); Race: 59.0% White, 25.0% Black, 7.1% Asian, 0.4% American Indian/Alaska Native, 0.1% Native Hawaiian/Other Pacific Islander, 8.4% Other, 8.2% Hispanic of any race (2010); Average household size: 2.24 (2010); Median age: 37.5 (2010); Males per 100 females: 106.7 (2010); Marriage status: 37.4% never married, 39.9% now married, 10.4% widowed, 12.3% divorced (2006-2010 5-year est.); Foreign born: 11.0% (2006-2010 5-year est.); Ancestry (includes multiple ancestries): 13.9% Irish, 13.5% Italian, 12.4% German, 5.8% English, 5.4% American (2006-2010 5-year est.).
**Economy:** Single-family building permits issued: 4 (2011); Multi-family building permits issued: 3 (2011); Employment by occupation: 13.2% management, 4.0% professional, 11.7% services, 13.7% sales, 4.9% farming, 11.3% construction, 4.9% production (2006-2010 5-year est.).
**Income:** Per capita income: $24,628 (2006-2010 5-year est.); Median household income: $40,203 (2006-2010 5-year est.); Average household income: $57,162 (2006-2010 5-year est.); Percent of households with income of $100,000 or more: 17.6% (2006-2010 5-year est.); Poverty rate: 21.8% (2006-2010 5-year est.).
**Taxes:** Total city taxes per capita: $648 (2009); City property taxes per capita: $593 (2009).
**Education:** Percent of population age 25 and over with: High school diploma (including GED) or higher: 77.0% (2006-2010 5-year est.); Bachelor's degree or higher: 23.7% (2006-2010 5-year est.); Master's degree or higher: 9.3% (2006-2010 5-year est.).
**School District(s)**
Hudson City School District (PK-12)
    2009-10 Enrollment: 1,953 . . . . . . . . . . . . . . . . . . (518) 828-4360

Columbia-Greene Community College (Public)
    Fall 2010 Enrollment: 1,409 . . . . . . . . . . . . . . . . (518) 828-4181
    2011-12 Tuition: In-state $3,978; Out-of-state $7,626
**Housing:** Homeownership rate: 35.5% (2010); Median home value: $175,400 (2006-2010 5-year est.); Median contract rent: $567 per month (2006-2010 5-year est.); Median year structure built: before 1940 (2006-2010 5-year est.).
**Hospitals:** Columbia Memorial Hospital (192 beds)
**Safety:** Violent crime rate: 44.8 per 10,000 population; Property crime rate: 391.6 per 10,000 population (2010).
**Newspapers:** Hudson Register-Star (Local news)
**Transportation:** Commute to work: 71.2% car, 8.0% public transportation, 16.6% walk, 1.9% work from home (2006-2010 5-year est.); Travel time to work: 50.5% less than 15 minutes, 27.8% 15 to 30 minutes, 8.2% 30 to 45 minutes, 4.8% 45 to 60 minutes, 8.7% 60 minutes or more (2006-2010 5-year est.); Amtrak: train service available.
**Airports:** Columbia County (general aviation)
**Additional Information Contacts**
Columbia County Chamber of Commerce . . . . . . . . . . . . . . (518) 828-4417
    http://www.columbiachamber-ny.com

## KINDERHOOK (village). Covers a land area of 2.103 square miles and a water area of 0 square miles. Located at 42.39° N. Lat; 73.70° W. Long. Elevation is 253 feet.
**Population:** 1,293 (1990); 1,275 (2000); 1,211 (2010); Density: 575.6 persons per square mile (2010); Race: 96.9% White, 0.2% Black, 0.6% Asian, 0.2% American Indian/Alaska Native, 0.0% Native Hawaiian/Other Pacific Islander, 2.1% Other, 3.8% Hispanic of any race (2010); Average household size: 2.25 (2010); Median age: 50.7 (2010); Males per 100 females: 89.5 (2010); Marriage status: 20.8% never married, 69.6% now married, 3.8% widowed, 5.7% divorced (2006-2010 5-year est.); Foreign born: 7.1% (2006-2010 5-year est.); Ancestry (includes multiple ancestries): 26.9% German, 19.8% Irish, 18.5% Italian, 16.0% American, 10.4% English (2006-2010 5-year est.).
**Economy:** Single-family building permits issued: 1 (2011); Multi-family building permits issued: 0 (2011); Employment by occupation: 17.9% management, 7.7% professional, 5.5% services, 11.6% sales, 2.3% farming, 3.8% construction, 0.9% production (2006-2010 5-year est.).
**Income:** Per capita income: $33,232 (2006-2010 5-year est.); Median household income: $75,769 (2006-2010 5-year est.); Average household income: $84,974 (2006-2010 5-year est.); Percent of households with income of $100,000 or more: 36.2% (2006-2010 5-year est.); Poverty rate: 7.4% (2006-2010 5-year est.).
**Education:** Percent of population age 25 and over with: High school diploma (including GED) or higher: 97.3% (2006-2010 5-year est.); Bachelor's degree or higher: 56.2% (2006-2010 5-year est.); Master's degree or higher: 32.6% (2006-2010 5-year est.).
**School District(s)**
Kinderhook Central School District (KG-12)
    2009-10 Enrollment: 1,987 . . . . . . . . . . . . . . . . . . (518) 758-7575
**Housing:** Homeownership rate: 83.2% (2010); Median home value: $285,400 (2006-2010 5-year est.); Median contract rent: $812 per month (2006-2010 5-year est.); Median year structure built: 1947 (2006-2010 5-year est.).
**Transportation:** Commute to work: 86.6% car, 2.2% public transportation, 5.1% walk, 5.1% work from home (2006-2010 5-year est.); Travel time to work: 30.5% less than 15 minutes, 21.9% 15 to 30 minutes, 31.8% 30 to 45 minutes, 9.5% 45 to 60 minutes, 6.4% 60 minutes or more (2006-2010 5-year est.)

## KINDERHOOK (town). Covers a land area of 31.806 square miles and a water area of 0.606 square miles. Located at 42.41° N. Lat; 73.68° W. Long. Elevation is 253 feet.
**History:** Kinderhook (Dutch for "children's corner") was named by its Dutch settlers. President Martin Van Buren was born and buried in Kinderhook. Settled before the American Revolution. Richard Upjohn designed St. Paul's Church (1851) here. The Van Buren homestead, "Lindenwald," is South of the village. The House of History, maintained by the county historical society, occupies an early-19th-century mansion. Incorporated 1838.
**Population:** 8,112 (1990); 8,296 (2000); 8,498 (2010); Density: 267.2 persons per square mile (2010); Race: 95.5% White, 1.0% Black, 1.0% Asian, 0.2% American Indian/Alaska Native, 0.0% Native Hawaiian/Other Pacific Islander, 2.3% Other, 4.2% Hispanic of any race (2010); Average

household size: 2.46 (2010); Median age: 45.2 (2010); Males per 100 females: 96.6 (2010); Marriage status: 23.7% never married, 60.2% now married, 8.4% widowed, 7.7% divorced (2006-2010 5-year est.); Foreign born: 4.4% (2006-2010 5-year est.); Ancestry (includes multiple ancestries): 23.2% German, 17.8% Irish, 17.2% Italian, 12.7% American, 12.0% English (2006-2010 5-year est.).

**Economy:** Single-family building permits issued: 1 (2011); Multi-family building permits issued: 0 (2011); Employment by occupation: 15.6% management, 6.3% professional, 5.5% services, 17.6% sales, 3.9% farming, 10.7% construction, 7.3% production (2006-2010 5-year est.).

**Income:** Per capita income: $32,133 (2006-2010 5-year est.); Median household income: $69,155 (2006-2010 5-year est.); Average household income: $83,655 (2006-2010 5-year est.); Percent of households with income of $100,000 or more: 31.0% (2006-2010 5-year est.); Poverty rate: 4.7% (2006-2010 5-year est.).

**Education:** Percent of population age 25 and over with: High school diploma (including GED) or higher: 92.3% (2006-2010 5-year est.); Bachelor's degree or higher: 36.1% (2006-2010 5-year est.); Master's degree or higher: 16.8% (2006-2010 5-year est.).

**School District(s)**
Kinderhook Central School District (KG-12)
    2009-10 Enrollment: 1,987 . . . . . . . . . . . . . . . . (518) 758-7575

**Housing:** Homeownership rate: 78.8% (2010); Median home value: $240,900 (2006-2010 5-year est.); Median contract rent: $657 per month (2006-2010 5-year est.); Median year structure built: 1968 (2006-2010 5-year est.).

**Transportation:** Commute to work: 91.5% car, 0.6% public transportation, 2.2% walk, 4.4% work from home (2006-2010 5-year est.); Travel time to work: 27.6% less than 15 minutes, 28.5% 15 to 30 minutes, 31.5% 30 to 45 minutes, 8.0% 45 to 60 minutes, 4.3% 60 minutes or more (2006-2010 5-year est.)

## LIVINGSTON (town). Covers a land area of 38.162 square miles and a water area of 0.784 square miles. Located at 42.13° N. Lat; 73.79° W. Long. Elevation is 200 feet.

**Population:** 3,582 (1990); 3,424 (2000); 3,646 (2010); Density: 95.5 persons per square mile (2010); Race: 95.0% White, 1.8% Black, 0.9% Asian, 0.3% American Indian/Alaska Native, 0.0% Native Hawaiian/Other Pacific Islander, 2.0% Other, 3.0% Hispanic of any race (2010); Average household size: 2.35 (2010); Median age: 45.1 (2010); Males per 100 females: 97.7 (2010); Marriage status: 26.3% never married, 43.4% now married, 18.8% widowed, 11.5% divorced (2006-2010 5-year est.); Foreign born: 8.7% (2006-2010 5-year est.); Ancestry (includes multiple ancestries): 24.0% German, 17.4% Irish, 12.9% Italian, 7.1% English, 6.4% Dutch (2006-2010 5-year est.).

**Economy:** Single-family building permits issued: 4 (2011); Multi-family building permits issued: 0 (2011); Employment by occupation: 9.5% management, 3.2% professional, 4.2% services, 20.2% sales, 3.0% farming, 18.0% construction, 11.6% production (2006-2010 5-year est.).

**Income:** Per capita income: $22,822 (2006-2010 5-year est.); Median household income: $47,375 (2006-2010 5-year est.); Average household income: $61,815 (2006-2010 5-year est.); Percent of households with income of $100,000 or more: 12.8% (2006-2010 5-year est.); Poverty rate: 13.8% (2006-2010 5-year est.).

**Education:** Percent of population age 25 and over with: High school diploma (including GED) or higher: 77.3% (2006-2010 5-year est.); Bachelor's degree or higher: 11.4% (2006-2010 5-year est.); Master's degree or higher: 3.8% (2006-2010 5-year est.).

**Housing:** Homeownership rate: 74.7% (2010); Median home value: $210,100 (2006-2010 5-year est.); Median contract rent: $673 per month (2006-2010 5-year est.); Median year structure built: 1973 (2006-2010 5-year est.).

**Transportation:** Commute to work: 85.8% car, 0.7% public transportation, 3.1% walk, 9.8% work from home (2006-2010 5-year est.); Travel time to work: 33.4% less than 15 minutes, 40.1% 15 to 30 minutes, 11.8% 30 to 45 minutes, 8.0% 45 to 60 minutes, 6.8% 60 minutes or more (2006-2010 5-year est.)

## LORENZ PARK (CDP). Covers a land area of 1.784 square miles and a water area of 0.162 square miles. Located at 42.26° N. Lat; 73.77° W. Long. Elevation is 180 feet.

**Population:** 1,804 (1990); 1,981 (2000); 2,053 (2010); Density: 1,150.6 persons per square mile (2010); Race: 82.2% White, 9.7% Black, 2.6% Asian, 0.1% American Indian/Alaska Native, 0.0% Native Hawaiian/Other Pacific Islander, 5.4% Other, 5.2% Hispanic of any race (2010); Average

household size: 2.22 (2010); Median age: 45.6 (2010); Males per 100 females: 93.0 (2010); Marriage status: 30.4% never married, 45.1% now married, 14.2% widowed, 10.4% divorced (2006-2010 5-year est.); Foreign born: 8.1% (2006-2010 5-year est.); Ancestry (includes multiple ancestries): 31.0% Italian, 28.3% German, 19.0% Irish, 12.3% Dutch, 9.2% Polish (2006-2010 5-year est.).

**Economy:** Employment by occupation: 9.8% management, 7.2% professional, 11.4% services, 27.6% sales, 2.7% farming, 6.1% construction, 5.7% production (2006-2010 5-year est.).

**Income:** Per capita income: $27,321 (2006-2010 5-year est.); Median household income: $40,279 (2006-2010 5-year est.); Average household income: $49,158 (2006-2010 5-year est.); Percent of households with income of $100,000 or more: 11.9% (2006-2010 5-year est.); Poverty rate: 5.8% (2006-2010 5-year est.).

**Education:** Percent of population age 25 and over with: High school diploma (including GED) or higher: 85.1% (2006-2010 5-year est.); Bachelor's degree or higher: 16.8% (2006-2010 5-year est.); Master's degree or higher: 4.0% (2006-2010 5-year est.).

**Housing:** Homeownership rate: 67.5% (2010); Median home value: $152,700 (2006-2010 5-year est.); Median contract rent: $395 per month (2006-2010 5-year est.); Median year structure built: 1974 (2006-2010 5-year est.).

**Transportation:** Commute to work: 93.0% car, 0.0% public transportation, 6.0% walk, 1.0% work from home (2006-2010 5-year est.); Travel time to work: 66.5% less than 15 minutes, 12.9% 15 to 30 minutes, 7.5% 30 to 45 minutes, 6.9% 45 to 60 minutes, 6.2% 60 minutes or more (2006-2010 5-year est.)

## MALDEN BRIDGE (unincorporated postal area)
Zip Code: 12115
    Covers a land area of 5.182 square miles and a water area of 0.034 square miles. Located at 42.47° N. Lat; 73.57° W. Long. Elevation is 387 feet. Population: 189 (2010); Density: 36.5 persons per square mile (2010); Race: 97.4% White, 1.1% Black, 0.0% Asian, 0.0% American Indian/Alaska Native, 0.0% Native Hawaiian/Other Pacific Islander, 1.5% Other, 1.6% Hispanic of any race (2010); Average household size: 2.20 (2010); Median age: 54.9 (2010); Males per 100 females: 90.9 (2010); Homeownership rate: 87.2% (2010)

## NEW LEBANON (town). Covers a land area of 35.857 square miles and a water area of 0.115 square miles. Located at 42.47° N. Lat; 73.44° W. Long. Elevation is 696 feet.

**History:** Samuel Tilden was born here. Site of Roman Catholic Shrine of Our Lady of Lourdes.

**Population:** 2,379 (1990); 2,454 (2000); 2,305 (2010); Density: 64.3 persons per square mile (2010); Race: 96.4% White, 1.3% Black, 1.0% Asian, 0.1% American Indian/Alaska Native, 0.0% Native Hawaiian/Other Pacific Islander, 1.2% Other, 2.1% Hispanic of any race (2010); Average household size: 2.20 (2010); Median age: 46.8 (2010); Males per 100 females: 105.8 (2010); Marriage status: 22.8% never married, 58.5% now married, 2.1% widowed, 16.6% divorced (2006-2010 5-year est.); Foreign born: 8.4% (2006-2010 5-year est.); Ancestry (includes multiple ancestries): 21.2% Irish, 17.4% German, 15.7% Italian, 15.3% English, 12.4% American (2006-2010 5-year est.).

**Economy:** Single-family building permits issued: 1 (2011); Multi-family building permits issued: 0 (2011); Employment by occupation: 6.6% management, 5.8% professional, 13.2% services, 11.4% sales, 4.7% farming, 8.6% construction, 6.7% production (2006-2010 5-year est.).

**Income:** Per capita income: $32,723 (2006-2010 5-year est.); Median household income: $59,688 (2006-2010 5-year est.); Average household income: $74,235 (2006-2010 5-year est.); Percent of households with income of $100,000 or more: 22.2% (2006-2010 5-year est.); Poverty rate: 7.0% (2006-2010 5-year est.).

**Education:** Percent of population age 25 and over with: High school diploma (including GED) or higher: 94.9% (2006-2010 5-year est.); Bachelor's degree or higher: 32.0% (2006-2010 5-year est.); Master's degree or higher: 14.7% (2006-2010 5-year est.).

**School District(s)**
New Lebanon Central School District (KG-12)
    2009-10 Enrollment: 505 . . . . . . . . . . . . . . . . . . (518) 794-9016

**Housing:** Homeownership rate: 72.6% (2010); Median home value: $226,700 (2006-2010 5-year est.); Median contract rent: $581 per month (2006-2010 5-year est.); Median year structure built: 1959 (2006-2010 5-year est.).

**Transportation:** Commute to work: 86.6% car, 1.6% public transportation, 7.5% walk, 4.0% work from home (2006-2010 5-year est.); Travel time to work: 26.8% less than 15 minutes, 32.0% 15 to 30 minutes, 25.8% 30 to 45 minutes, 8.7% 45 to 60 minutes, 6.6% 60 minutes or more (2006-2010 5-year est.)

## NIVERVILLE (CDP).

Covers a land area of 2.874 square miles and a water area of 0.545 square miles. Located at 42.44° N. Lat; 73.64° W. Long. Elevation is 318 feet.
**Population:** 1,809 (1990); 1,737 (2000); 1,662 (2010); Density: 578.2 persons per square mile (2010); Race: 96.3% White, 0.8% Black, 0.6% Asian, 0.1% American Indian/Alaska Native, 0.0% Native Hawaiian/Other Pacific Islander, 2.2% Other, 2.0% Hispanic of any race (2010); Average household size: 2.45 (2010); Median age: 44.7 (2010); Males per 100 females: 104.2 (2010); Marriage status: 27.3% never married, 59.6% now married, 4.9% widowed, 8.2% divorced (2006-2010 5-year est.); Foreign born: 2.1% (2006-2010 5-year est.); Ancestry (includes multiple ancestries): 28.7% German, 25.4% Italian, 18.5% English, 16.8% Irish, 16.1% American (2006-2010 5-year est.).
**Economy:** Employment by occupation: 12.7% management, 7.1% professional, 4.3% services, 30.3% sales, 5.5% farming, 18.0% construction, 6.8% production (2006-2010 5-year est.).
**Income:** Per capita income: $30,060 (2006-2010 5-year est.); Median household income: $62,679 (2006-2010 5-year est.); Average household income: $78,712 (2006-2010 5-year est.); Percent of households with income of $100,000 or more: 23.3% (2006-2010 5-year est.); Poverty rate: 5.4% (2006-2010 5-year est.).
**Education:** Percent of population age 25 and over with: High school diploma (including GED) or higher: 89.8% (2006-2010 5-year est.); Bachelor's degree or higher: 21.2% (2006-2010 5-year est.); Master's degree or higher: 14.1% (2006-2010 5-year est.).
**Housing:** Homeownership rate: 81.2% (2010); Median home value: $212,300 (2006-2010 5-year est.); Median contract rent: $556 per month (2006-2010 5-year est.); Median year structure built: 1963 (2006-2010 5-year est.).
**Transportation:** Commute to work: 98.0% car, 0.0% public transportation, 2.0% walk, 0.0% work from home (2006-2010 5-year est.); Travel time to work: 14.0% less than 15 minutes, 36.3% 15 to 30 minutes, 46.0% 30 to 45 minutes, 3.8% 45 to 60 minutes, 0.0% 60 minutes or more (2006-2010 5-year est.)

## NORTH CHATHAM (unincorporated postal area)
Zip Code: 12132
Covers a land area of 1.859 square miles and a water area of 0 square miles. Located at 42.47° N. Lat; 73.63° W. Long. Elevation is 351 feet. Population: 338 (2010); Density: 181.8 persons per square mile (2010); Race: 95.3% White, 2.7% Black, 2.1% Asian, 0.0% American Indian/Alaska Native, 0.0% Native Hawaiian/Other Pacific Islander, 0.0% Other, 1.8% Hispanic of any race (2010); Average household size: 2.35 (2010); Median age: 47.5 (2010); Males per 100 females: 87.8 (2010); Homeownership rate: 73.0% (2010)

## OLD CHATHAM (unincorporated postal area)
Zip Code: 12136
Covers a land area of 18.150 square miles and a water area of 0.019 square miles. Located at 42.43° N. Lat; 73.55° W. Long. Elevation is 535 feet. Population: 804 (2010); Density: 44.3 persons per square mile (2010); Race: 97.3% White, 0.2% Black, 0.5% Asian, 0.0% American Indian/Alaska Native, 0.1% Native Hawaiian/Other Pacific Islander, 1.9% Other, 2.1% Hispanic of any race (2010); Average household size: 2.30 (2010); Median age: 52.4 (2010); Males per 100 females: 100.0 (2010); Homeownership rate: 88.0% (2010)

## PHILMONT (village).
Covers a land area of 1.187 square miles and a water area of 0.038 square miles. Located at 42.24° N. Lat; 73.64° W. Long. Elevation is 407 feet.
**Population:** 1,623 (1990); 1,480 (2000); 1,379 (2010); Density: 1,161.4 persons per square mile (2010); Race: 92.1% White, 1.9% Black, 0.7% Asian, 0.1% American Indian/Alaska Native, 0.0% Native Hawaiian/Other Pacific Islander, 5.2% Other, 3.1% Hispanic of any race (2010); Average household size: 2.44 (2010); Median age: 39.7 (2010); Males per 100 females: 93.4 (2010); Marriage status: 42.0% never married, 37.3% now married, 5.5% widowed, 15.1% divorced (2006-2010 5-year est.); Foreign born: 2.8% (2006-2010 5-year est.); Ancestry (includes multiple

ancestries): 26.6% German, 23.6% Irish, 17.2% Dutch, 10.6% French, 9.6% English (2006-2010 5-year est.).
**Economy:** Single-family building permits issued: 0 (2011); Multi-family building permits issued: 0 (2011); Employment by occupation: 4.6% management, 2.4% professional, 6.0% services, 18.4% sales, 1.0% farming, 10.4% construction, 5.4% production (2006-2010 5-year est.).
**Income:** Per capita income: $20,478 (2006-2010 5-year est.); Median household income: $31,891 (2006-2010 5-year est.); Average household income: $47,513 (2006-2010 5-year est.); Percent of households with income of $100,000 or more: 11.1% (2006-2010 5-year est.); Poverty rate: 21.0% (2006-2010 5-year est.).
**Education:** Percent of population age 25 and over with: High school diploma (including GED) or higher: 82.1% (2006-2010 5-year est.); Bachelor's degree or higher: 18.8% (2006-2010 5-year est.); Master's degree or higher: 3.6% (2006-2010 5-year est.).
**Housing:** Homeownership rate: 48.9% (2010); Median home value: $138,700 (2006-2010 5-year est.); Median contract rent: $644 per month (2006-2010 5-year est.); Median year structure built: before 1940 (2006-2010 5-year est.).
**Transportation:** Commute to work: 89.4% car, 2.1% public transportation, 3.8% walk, 3.2% work from home (2006-2010 5-year est.); Travel time to work: 29.9% less than 15 minutes, 55.2% 15 to 30 minutes, 4.8% 30 to 45 minutes, 5.5% 45 to 60 minutes, 4.6% 60 minutes or more (2006-2010 5-year est.)

## SPENCERTOWN (unincorporated postal area)
Zip Code: 12165
Covers a land area of 3.227 square miles and a water area of 0.001 square miles. Located at 42.30° N. Lat; 73.51° W. Long. Elevation is 686 feet. Population: 175 (2010); Density: 54.2 persons per square mile (2010); Race: 97.7% White, 0.0% Black, 2.3% Asian, 0.0% American Indian/Alaska Native, 0.0% Native Hawaiian/Other Pacific Islander, 0.0% Other, 0.0% Hispanic of any race (2010); Average household size: 2.16 (2010); Median age: 55.5 (2010); Males per 100 females: 110.8 (2010); Homeownership rate: 82.7% (2010)

## STOCKPORT (town).
Covers a land area of 11.648 square miles and a water area of 1.505 square miles. Located at 42.31° N. Lat; 73.75° W. Long. Elevation is 135 feet.
**Population:** 3,085 (1990); 2,933 (2000); 2,815 (2010); Density: 241.7 persons per square mile (2010); Race: 92.0% White, 4.0% Black, 0.7% Asian, 0.0% American Indian/Alaska Native, 0.0% Native Hawaiian/Other Pacific Islander, 3.3% Other, 3.2% Hispanic of any race (2010); Average household size: 2.60 (2010); Median age: 41.2 (2010); Males per 100 females: 106.2 (2010); Marriage status: 31.6% never married, 52.8% now married, 5.0% widowed, 10.6% divorced (2006-2010 5-year est.); Foreign born: 3.4% (2006-2010 5-year est.); Ancestry (includes multiple ancestries): 29.2% Irish, 25.5% German, 19.2% Italian, 9.5% English, 9.2% Polish (2006-2010 5-year est.).
**Economy:** Single-family building permits issued: 1 (2011); Multi-family building permits issued: 0 (2011); Employment by occupation: 3.9% management, 2.0% professional, 10.8% services, 18.7% sales, 3.7% farming, 13.6% construction, 8.9% production (2006-2010 5-year est.).
**Income:** Per capita income: $25,920 (2006-2010 5-year est.); Median household income: $51,250 (2006-2010 5-year est.); Average household income: $61,285 (2006-2010 5-year est.); Percent of households with income of $100,000 or more: 18.1% (2006-2010 5-year est.); Poverty rate: 10.0% (2006-2010 5-year est.).
**Education:** Percent of population age 25 and over with: High school diploma (including GED) or higher: 85.1% (2006-2010 5-year est.); Bachelor's degree or higher: 13.6% (2006-2010 5-year est.); Master's degree or higher: 7.7% (2006-2010 5-year est.).
**Housing:** Homeownership rate: 73.9% (2010); Median home value: $193,600 (2006-2010 5-year est.); Median contract rent: $621 per month (2006-2010 5-year est.); Median year structure built: 1964 (2006-2010 5-year est.).
**Safety:** Violent crime rate: 0.0 per 10,000 population; Property crime rate: 50.9 per 10,000 population (2010).
**Transportation:** Commute to work: 85.1% car, 1.7% public transportation, 4.4% walk, 6.1% work from home (2006-2010 5-year est.); Travel time to work: 29.9% less than 15 minutes, 47.6% 15 to 30 minutes, 9.9% 30 to 45 minutes, 7.8% 45 to 60 minutes, 4.8% 60 minutes or more (2006-2010 5-year est.)

## STOTTVILLE (CDP).

Covers a land area of 4.179 square miles and a water area of 0.029 square miles. Located at 42.29° N. Lat; 73.76° W. Long. Elevation is 115 feet.

**Population:** 1,360 (1990); 1,355 (2000); 1,375 (2010); Density: 329.0 persons per square mile (2010); Race: 87.3% White, 7.1% Black, 1.4% Asian, 0.1% American Indian/Alaska Native, 0.0% Native Hawaiian/Other Pacific Islander, 4.1% Other, 2.3% Hispanic of any race (2010); Average household size: 2.54 (2010); Median age: 41.4 (2010); Males per 100 females: 100.4 (2010); Marriage status: 29.2% never married, 50.8% now married, 10.1% widowed, 9.9% divorced (2006-2010 5-year est.); Foreign born: 2.6% (2006-2010 5-year est.); Ancestry (includes multiple ancestries): 29.0% Irish, 27.3% Italian, 22.4% German, 13.1% American, 12.0% English (2006-2010 5-year est.).

**Economy:** Employment by occupation: 2.9% management, 1.7% professional, 10.0% services, 16.3% sales, 5.0% farming, 7.9% construction, 6.0% production (2006-2010 5-year est.).

**Income:** Per capita income: $21,906 (2006-2010 5-year est.); Median household income: $32,951 (2006-2010 5-year est.); Average household income: $49,162 (2006-2010 5-year est.); Percent of households with income of $100,000 or more: 15.3% (2006-2010 5-year est.); Poverty rate: 10.6% (2006-2010 5-year est.).

**Education:** Percent of population age 25 and over with: High school diploma (including GED) or higher: 82.7% (2006-2010 5-year est.); Bachelor's degree or higher: 9.6% (2006-2010 5-year est.); Master's degree or higher: 6.0% (2006-2010 5-year est.).

**Housing:** Homeownership rate: 63.1% (2010); Median home value: $202,900 (2006-2010 5-year est.); Median contract rent: $446 per month (2006-2010 5-year est.); Median year structure built: 1961 (2006-2010 5-year est.).

**Transportation:** Commute to work: 79.0% car, 4.6% public transportation, 4.3% walk, 8.3% work from home (2006-2010 5-year est.); Travel time to work: 32.1% less than 15 minutes, 51.6% 15 to 30 minutes, 11.5% 30 to 45 minutes, 4.9% 45 to 60 minutes, 0.0% 60 minutes or more (2006-2010 5-year est.)

## STUYVESANT (town).

Covers a land area of 25.004 square miles and a water area of 1.745 square miles. Located at 42.39° N. Lat; 73.75° W. Long. Elevation is 105 feet.

**Population:** 2,178 (1990); 2,188 (2000); 2,027 (2010); Density: 81.1 persons per square mile (2010); Race: 95.8% White, 0.9% Black, 0.4% Asian, 0.2% American Indian/Alaska Native, 0.0% Native Hawaiian/Other Pacific Islander, 2.7% Other, 3.1% Hispanic of any race (2010); Average household size: 2.56 (2010); Median age: 42.2 (2010); Males per 100 females: 101.1 (2010); Marriage status: 26.7% never married, 53.9% now married, 3.6% widowed, 15.7% divorced (2006-2010 5-year est.); Foreign born: 2.4% (2006-2010 5-year est.); Ancestry (includes multiple ancestries): 29.8% German, 20.1% Irish, 18.2% Dutch, 14.1% American, 11.5% Italian (2006-2010 5-year est.).

**Economy:** Single-family building permits issued: 3 (2011); Multi-family building permits issued: 0 (2011); Employment by occupation: 11.0% management, 2.1% professional, 21.3% services, 10.4% sales, 2.6% farming, 12.6% construction, 6.3% production (2006-2010 5-year est.).

**Income:** Per capita income: $28,106 (2006-2010 5-year est.); Median household income: $53,264 (2006-2010 5-year est.); Average household income: $70,809 (2006-2010 5-year est.); Percent of households with income of $100,000 or more: 16.8% (2006-2010 5-year est.); Poverty rate: 4.2% (2006-2010 5-year est.).

**Education:** Percent of population age 25 and over with: High school diploma (including GED) or higher: 87.6% (2006-2010 5-year est.); Bachelor's degree or higher: 25.7% (2006-2010 5-year est.); Master's degree or higher: 12.1% (2006-2010 5-year est.).

**Housing:** Homeownership rate: 79.3% (2010); Median home value: $184,400 (2006-2010 5-year est.); Median contract rent: $591 per month (2006-2010 5-year est.); Median year structure built: 1953 (2006-2010 5-year est.).

**Transportation:** Commute to work: 92.4% car, 1.4% public transportation, 0.0% walk, 6.1% work from home (2006-2010 5-year est.); Travel time to work: 27.0% less than 15 minutes, 40.4% 15 to 30 minutes, 20.8% 30 to 45 minutes, 7.8% 45 to 60 minutes, 4.0% 60 minutes or more (2006-2010 5-year est.)

## STUYVESANT FALLS (unincorporated postal area)

Zip Code: 12174

Covers a land area of 1.149 square miles and a water area of 0 square miles. Located at 42.35° N. Lat; 73.72° W. Long. Elevation is 210 feet.

Population: 345 (2010); Density: 300.2 persons per square mile (2010); Race: 97.7% White, 0.3% Black, 0.0% Asian, 0.0% American Indian/Alaska Native, 0.0% Native Hawaiian/Other Pacific Islander, 2.0% Other, 3.5% Hispanic of any race (2010); Average household size: 2.74 (2010); Median age: 38.9 (2010); Males per 100 females: 99.4 (2010); Homeownership rate: 69.8% (2010)

## TAGHKANIC (town).

Covers a land area of 39.971 square miles and a water area of 0.166 square miles. Located at 42.13° N. Lat; 73.67° W. Long. Elevation is 725 feet.

**Population:** 1,111 (1990); 1,118 (2000); 1,310 (2010); Density: 32.8 persons per square mile (2010); Race: 95.4% White, 0.8% Black, 1.3% Asian, 0.5% American Indian/Alaska Native, 0.2% Native Hawaiian/Other Pacific Islander, 1.8% Other, 2.7% Hispanic of any race (2010); Average household size: 2.42 (2010); Median age: 48.3 (2010); Males per 100 females: 102.5 (2010); Marriage status: 24.7% never married, 65.4% now married, 4.6% widowed, 5.3% divorced (2006-2010 5-year est.); Foreign born: 5.8% (2006-2010 5-year est.); Ancestry (includes multiple ancestries): 22.6% Irish, 22.3% German, 18.3% English, 17.2% Italian, 14.8% Dutch (2006-2010 5-year est.).

**Economy:** Single-family building permits issued: 8 (2011); Multi-family building permits issued: 0 (2011); Employment by occupation: 9.8% management, 0.9% professional, 8.1% services, 20.9% sales, 0.9% farming, 12.0% construction, 3.6% production (2006-2010 5-year est.).

**Income:** Per capita income: $40,612 (2006-2010 5-year est.); Median household income: $69,167 (2006-2010 5-year est.); Average household income: $95,595 (2006-2010 5-year est.); Percent of households with income of $100,000 or more: 34.8% (2006-2010 5-year est.); Poverty rate: 3.5% (2006-2010 5-year est.).

**Education:** Percent of population age 25 and over with: High school diploma (including GED) or higher: 91.4% (2006-2010 5-year est.); Bachelor's degree or higher: 34.7% (2006-2010 5-year est.); Master's degree or higher: 15.2% (2006-2010 5-year est.).

**Housing:** Homeownership rate: 86.8% (2010); Median home value: $293,900 (2006-2010 5-year est.); Median contract rent: $675 per month (2006-2010 5-year est.); Median year structure built: 1966 (2006-2010 5-year est.).

**Transportation:** Commute to work: 84.6% car, 3.7% public transportation, 3.1% walk, 8.7% work from home (2006-2010 5-year est.); Travel time to work: 16.7% less than 15 minutes, 45.5% 15 to 30 minutes, 17.5% 30 to 45 minutes, 14.4% 45 to 60 minutes, 5.9% 60 minutes or more (2006-2010 5-year est.)

## VALATIE (village).

Covers a land area of 1.254 square miles and a water area of 0.012 square miles. Located at 42.41° N. Lat; 73.67° W. Long. Elevation is 240 feet.

**History:** Incorporated 1856.

**Population:** 1,467 (1990); 1,712 (2000); 1,819 (2010); Density: 1,450.3 persons per square mile (2010); Race: 93.8% White, 1.4% Black, 0.5% Asian, 0.4% American Indian/Alaska Native, 0.0% Native Hawaiian/Other Pacific Islander, 3.9% Other, 10.2% Hispanic of any race (2010); Average household size: 2.60 (2010); Median age: 42.6 (2010); Males per 100 females: 93.1 (2010); Marriage status: 24.7% never married, 42.8% now married, 23.3% widowed, 9.3% divorced (2006-2010 5-year est.); Foreign born: 8.0% (2006-2010 5-year est.); Ancestry (includes multiple ancestries): 18.4% German, 16.0% Irish, 10.1% American, 8.4% English, 8.3% Italian (2006-2010 5-year est.).

**Economy:** Single-family building permits issued: 0 (2011); Multi-family building permits issued: 0 (2011); Employment by occupation: 9.8% management, 4.2% professional, 5.5% services, 16.3% sales, 3.8% farming, 15.0% construction, 10.5% production (2006-2010 5-year est.).

**Income:** Per capita income: $24,036 (2006-2010 5-year est.); Median household income: $60,365 (2006-2010 5-year est.); Average household income: $72,175 (2006-2010 5-year est.); Percent of households with income of $100,000 or more: 22.4% (2006-2010 5-year est.); Poverty rate: 8.7% (2006-2010 5-year est.).

**Education:** Percent of population age 25 and over with: High school diploma (including GED) or higher: 80.7% (2006-2010 5-year est.); Bachelor's degree or higher: 19.8% (2006-2010 5-year est.); Master's degree or higher: 8.8% (2006-2010 5-year est.).

**School District(s)**

Kinderhook Central School District (KG-12)

2009-10 Enrollment: 1,987 . . . . . . . . . . . . . . . . . . . . . . . . . (518) 758-7575

**Housing:** Homeownership rate: 65.6% (2010); Median home value: $211,700 (2006-2010 5-year est.); Median contract rent: $661 per month

(2006-2010 5-year est.); Median year structure built: 1956 (2006-2010 5-year est.).

**Transportation:** Commute to work: 87.7% car, 0.0% public transportation, 3.8% walk, 5.4% work from home (2006-2010 5-year est.); Travel time to work: 33.6% less than 15 minutes, 29.4% 15 to 30 minutes, 28.2% 30 to 45 minutes, 7.0% 45 to 60 minutes, 1.9% 60 minutes or more (2006-2010 5-year est.)

**WEST LEBANON** (unincorporated postal area)
Zip Code: 12195

Covers a land area of 1.955 square miles and a water area of 0 square miles. Located at 42.48° N. Lat; 73.47° W. Long. Elevation is 623 feet.
Population: 154 (2010); Density: 78.8 persons per square mile (2010); Race: 96.8% White, 0.6% Black, 0.6% Asian, 0.6% American Indian/Alaska Native, 0.0% Native Hawaiian/Other Pacific Islander, 1.4% Other, 0.0% Hispanic of any race (2010); Average household size: 2.05 (2010); Median age: 46.1 (2010); Males per 100 females: 97.4 (2010); Homeownership rate: 66.7% (2010)

# Cortland County

Located in central New York; drained by the Tioughnioga River. Covers a land area of 499.65 square miles, a water area of 1.87 square miles, and is located in the Eastern Time Zone at 42.58° N. Lat., 76.10° W. Long. The county was founded in 1808. County seat is Cortland.

Cortland County is part of the Cortland, NY Micropolitan Statistical Area. The entire metro area includes: Cortland County, NY

| Weather Station: Tully Heiberg Forest | | | | | | | | | | Elevation: 1,898 feet | |
|---|---|---|---|---|---|---|---|---|---|---|---|
| | Jan | Feb | Mar | Apr | May | Jun | Jul | Aug | Sep | Oct | Nov | Dec |
| High | 27 | 30 | 37 | 51 | 63 | 72 | 76 | 75 | 67 | 55 | 43 | 32 |
| Low | 12 | 13 | 20 | 32 | 43 | 52 | 57 | 56 | 48 | 37 | 28 | 18 |
| Precip | 2.9 | 2.7 | 3.3 | 4.0 | 4.0 | 4.9 | 4.0 | 4.0 | 4.8 | 4.0 | 4.0 | 3.3 |
| Snow | 26.3 | 23.3 | 21.1 | 7.6 | 0.4 | tr | 0.0 | 0.0 | tr | 1.8 | 11.9 | 23.4 |

*High and Low temperatures in degrees Fahrenheit; Precipitation and Snow in inches*

**Population:** 48,963 (1990); 48,599 (2000); 49,336 (2010); Race: 95.1% White, 1.5% Black, 0.8% Asian, 0.3% American Indian/Alaska Native, 0.0% Native Hawaiian/Other Pacific Islander, 2.3% Other, 2.2% Hispanic of any race (2010); Density: 98.7 persons per square mile (2010); Average household size: 2.45 (2010); Median age: 35.8 (2010); Males per 100 females: 95.4 (2010).
**Religion:** Six largest groups: 12.9% Catholicism, 5.6% Methodist/Pietist, 2.5% Non-Denominational, 2.4% Presbyterian-Reformed, 1.1% Baptist, 0.8% Latter-day Saints (2010)
**Economy:** Unemployment rate: 10.1% (February 2012); Total civilian labor force: 24,574 (February 2012); Leading industries: 21.0% health care and social assistance; 18.7% manufacturing; 15.0% retail trade (2009); Farms: 587 totaling 124,824 acres (2007); Companies that employ 500 or more persons: 4 (2009); Companies that employ 100 to 499 persons: 16 (2009); Companies that employ less than 100 persons: 1,004 (2009); Black-owned businesses: n/a (2007); Hispanic-owned businesses: n/a (2007); Asian-owned businesses: n/a (2007); Women-owned businesses: n/a (2007); Retail sales per capita: $12,329 (2010). Single-family building permits issued: 37 (2011); Multi-family building permits issued: 0 (2011).
**Income:** Per capita income: $22,078 (2006-2010 5-year est.); Median household income: $45,338 (2006-2010 5-year est.); Average household income: $57,489 (2006-2010 5-year est.); Percent of households with income of $100,000 or more: 13.8% (2006-2010 5-year est.); Poverty rate: 14.1% (2006-2010 5-year est.); Bankruptcy rate: 2.16% (2011).
**Taxes:** Total county taxes per capita: $1,027 (2009); County property taxes per capita: $505 (2009).
**Education:** Percent of population age 25 and over with: High school diploma (including GED) or higher: 89.1% (2006-2010 5-year est.); Bachelor's degree or higher: 24.3% (2006-2010 5-year est.); Master's degree or higher: 9.3% (2006-2010 5-year est.).
**Housing:** Homeownership rate: 64.9% (2010); Median home value: $95,100 (2006-2010 5-year est.); Median contract rent: $517 per month (2006-2010 5-year est.); Median year structure built: 1952 (2006-2010 5-year est.)
**Health:** Birth rate: 109.8 per 10,000 population (2011); Death rate: 82.9 per 10,000 population (2011); Age-adjusted cancer mortality rate: 185.4 deaths per 100,000 population (2009); Number of physicians: 11.8 per 10,000 population (2008); Hospital beds: 44.9 per 10,000 population (2007); Hospital admissions: 1,102.6 per 10,000 population (2007).

**Elections:** 2008 Presidential election results: 54.1% Obama, 44.2% McCain, 1.0% Nader
**Additional Information Contacts**
Cortland County Government . . . . . . . . . . . . . . . . . . . . . (607) 753-5021
http://www.cortland-co.org
City of Cortland . . . . . . . . . . . . . . . . . . . . . . . . . . . . . . (607) 756-6521
http://www.cortland.org
Cortland County Chamber of Commerce. . . . . . . . . . . . . . (607) 756-2814
http://www.cortlandareachamber.com
Town of Preble . . . . . . . . . . . . . . . . . . . . . . . . . . . . . . . (607) 749-3199
http://www.preble-ny.org

## *Cortland County Communities*

**BLODGETT MILLS** (CDP). Covers a land area of 2.174 square miles and a water area of 0 square miles. Located at 42.56° N. Lat; 76.13° W. Long. Elevation is 1,102 feet.
**Population:** n/a (1990); n/a (2000); 303 (2010); Density: 139.4 persons per square mile (2010); Race: 99.0% White, 0.0% Black, 0.0% Asian, 0.7% American Indian/Alaska Native, 0.0% Native Hawaiian/Other Pacific Islander, 0.3% Other, 0.7% Hispanic of any race (2010); Average household size: 2.68 (2010); Median age: 40.4 (2010); Males per 100 females: 104.7 (2010); Marriage status: 5.8% never married, 40.8% now married, 22.5% widowed, 30.9% divorced (2006-2010 5-year est.); Foreign born: 0.0% (2006-2010 5-year est.); Ancestry (includes multiple ancestries): 29.2% English, 14.6% German, 13.7% Italian, 5.9% French, 2.3% American (2006-2010 5-year est.).
**Economy:** Employment by occupation: 0.0% management, 0.0% professional, 14.7% services, 0.0% sales, 5.5% farming, 10.1% construction, 31.2% production (2006-2010 5-year est.).
**Income:** Per capita income: $21,382 (2006-2010 5-year est.); Median household income: $34,107 (2006-2010 5-year est.); Average household income: $37,031 (2006-2010 5-year est.); Percent of households with income of $100,000 or more: 0.0% (2006-2010 5-year est.); Poverty rate: 11.0% (2006-2010 5-year est.).
**Education:** Percent of population age 25 and over with: High school diploma (including GED) or higher: 85.6% (2006-2010 5-year est.); Bachelor's degree or higher: 0.0% (2006-2010 5-year est.); Master's degree or higher: 0.0% (2006-2010 5-year est.).
**Housing:** Homeownership rate: 84.0% (2010); Median home value: $64,900 (2006-2010 5-year est.); Median contract rent: $636 per month (2006-2010 5-year est.); Median year structure built: 1951 (2006-2010 5-year est.).
**Transportation:** Commute to work: 89.7% car, 0.0% public transportation, 0.0% walk, 10.3% work from home (2006-2010 5-year est.); Travel time to work: 42.5% less than 15 minutes, 51.7% 15 to 30 minutes, 5.7% 30 to 45 minutes, 0.0% 45 to 60 minutes, 0.0% 60 minutes or more (2006-2010 5-year est.)

**CINCINNATUS** (town). Covers a land area of 25.356 square miles and a water area of 0.129 square miles. Located at 42.53° N. Lat; 75.91° W. Long. Elevation is 1,050 feet.
**Population:** 1,122 (1990); 1,051 (2000); 1,056 (2010); Density: 41.6 persons per square mile (2010); Race: 96.9% White, 0.5% Black, 0.5% Asian, 0.5% American Indian/Alaska Native, 0.0% Native Hawaiian/Other Pacific Islander, 1.6% Other, 2.0% Hispanic of any race (2010); Average household size: 2.53 (2010); Median age: 41.5 (2010); Males per 100 females: 98.9 (2010); Marriage status: 21.5% never married, 63.2% now married, 8.2% widowed, 7.1% divorced (2006-2010 5-year est.); Foreign born: 0.8% (2006-2010 5-year est.); Ancestry (includes multiple ancestries): 20.4% English, 13.2% Irish, 12.7% Dutch, 10.0% German, 8.0% French (2006-2010 5-year est.).
**Economy:** Single-family building permits issued: 1 (2011); Multi-family building permits issued: 0 (2011); Employment by occupation: 5.8% management, 1.6% professional, 12.9% services, 14.0% sales, 1.4% farming, 12.6% construction, 4.4% production (2006-2010 5-year est.).
**Income:** Per capita income: $21,689 (2006-2010 5-year est.); Median household income: $42,813 (2006-2010 5-year est.); Average household income: $51,175 (2006-2010 5-year est.); Percent of households with income of $100,000 or more: 10.6% (2006-2010 5-year est.); Poverty rate: 12.6% (2006-2010 5-year est.).
**Education:** Percent of population age 25 and over with: High school diploma (including GED) or higher: 87.2% (2006-2010 5-year est.); Bachelor's degree or higher: 12.4% (2006-2010 5-year est.); Master's degree or higher: 3.8% (2006-2010 5-year est.).

Cincinnatus Central School District (PK-12)
  2009-10 Enrollment: 658 . . . . . . . . . . . . . . . . . . . . . (607) 863-4069
**Housing:** Homeownership rate: 76.3% (2010); Median home value: $84,900 (2006-2010 5-year est.); Median contract rent: $516 per month (2006-2010 5-year est.); Median year structure built: before 1940 (2006-2010 5-year est.).
**Transportation:** Commute to work: 89.0% car, 0.8% public transportation, 4.2% walk, 3.9% work from home (2006-2010 5-year est.); Travel time to work: 20.8% less than 15 minutes, 25.5% 15 to 30 minutes, 36.4% 30 to 45 minutes, 7.0% 45 to 60 minutes, 10.3% 60 minutes or more (2006-2010 5-year est.)

**CORTLAND** (city). County seat. Covers a land area of 3.893 square miles and a water area of 0.020 square miles. Located at 42.60° N. Lat; 76.17° W. Long. Elevation is 1,129 feet.
**History:** Elmer Ambrose Sperry (1860-1030), inventor, was born in Cortland. Sperry is credited with 400 patents.
**Population:** 19,801 (1990); 18,740 (2000); 19,204 (2010); Density: 4,931.7 persons per square mile (2010); Race: 92.8% White, 2.8% Black, 0.9% Asian, 0.2% American Indian/Alaska Native, 0.0% Native Hawaiian/Other Pacific Islander, 3.3% Other, 3.2% Hispanic of any race (2010); Average household size: 2.30 (2010); Median age: 26.0 (2010); Males per 100 females: 90.7 (2010); Marriage status: 51.2% never married, 34.0% now married, 7.3% widowed, 7.5% divorced (2006-2010 5-year est.); Foreign born: 2.0% (2006-2010 5-year est.); Ancestry (includes multiple ancestries): 19.7% Irish, 14.5% German, 13.3% English, 13.3% Italian, 3.3% American (2006-2010 5-year est.).
**Economy:** Single-family building permits issued: 1 (2011); Multi-family building permits issued: 0 (2011); Employment by occupation: 10.2% management, 2.9% professional, 14.5% services, 18.8% sales, 3.5% farming, 5.7% construction, 5.4% production (2006-2010 5-year est.).
**Income:** Per capita income: $19,111 (2006-2010 5-year est.); Median household income: $36,980 (2006-2010 5-year est.); Average household income: $49,344 (2006-2010 5-year est.); Percent of households with income of $100,000 or more: 10.0% (2006-2010 5-year est.); Poverty rate: 21.1% (2006-2010 5-year est.).
**Education:** Percent of population age 25 and over with: High school diploma (including GED) or higher: 87.6% (2006-2010 5-year est.); Bachelor's degree or higher: 26.9% (2006-2010 5-year est.); Master's degree or higher: 10.8% (2006-2010 5-year est.).
Cortland City School District (KG-12)
  2009-10 Enrollment: 2,709 . . . . . . . . . . . . . . . . . . . . (607) 758-4100
SUNY College at Cortland (Public)
  Fall 2010 Enrollment: 6,946 . . . . . . . . . . . . . . . . . . . (607) 753-2011
  2011-12 Tuition: In-state $6,574; Out-of-state $15,624
**Housing:** Homeownership rate: 43.7% (2010); Median home value: $89,800 (2006-2010 5-year est.); Median contract rent: $519 per month (2006-2010 5-year est.); Median year structure built: before 1940 (2006-2010 5-year est.).
**Hospitals:** Cortland Regional Medical Center (181 beds)
**Safety:** Violent crime rate: 25.1 per 10,000 population; Property crime rate: 199.1 per 10,000 population (2010).
**Newspapers:** Consumer News (Community news; Circulation 11,337); Cortland Standard (Local news; Circulation 11,500)
**Transportation:** Commute to work: 79.8% car, 1.2% public transportation, 11.7% walk, 5.0% work from home (2006-2010 5-year est.); Travel time to work: 58.9% less than 15 minutes, 18.1% 15 to 30 minutes, 12.9% 30 to 45 minutes, 7.5% 45 to 60 minutes, 2.6% 60 minutes or more (2006-2010 5-year est.)
**Airports:** Cortland County-Chase Field (general aviation)
**Additional Information Contacts**
City of Cortland . . . . . . . . . . . . . . . . . . . . . . . . . . . . . . (607) 756-6521
  http://www.cortland.org
Cortland County Chamber of Commerce . . . . . . . . . . . . . (607) 756-2814
  http://www.cortlandareachamber.com

**CORTLAND WEST** (CDP). Covers a land area of 5.165 square miles and a water area of 0 square miles. Located at 42.59° N. Lat; 76.22° W. Long.
**Population:** 1,073 (1990); 1,345 (2000); 1,356 (2010); Density: 262.5 persons per square mile (2010); Race: 95.7% White, 0.4% Black, 1.8% Asian, 0.4% American Indian/Alaska Native, 0.0% Native Hawaiian/Other

Pacific Islander, 1.7% Other, 1.4% Hispanic of any race (2010); Average household size: 2.51 (2010); Median age: 48.1 (2010); Males per 100 females: 95.1 (2010); Marriage status: 21.5% never married, 69.6% now married, 5.6% widowed, 3.3% divorced (2006-2010 5-year est.); Foreign born: 0.0% (2006-2010 5-year est.); Ancestry (includes multiple ancestries): 25.3% Italian, 21.3% German, 20.9% Irish, 20.5% English, 3.5% European (2006-2010 5-year est.).
**Economy:** Employment by occupation: 21.1% management, 7.3% professional, 4.2% services, 17.9% sales, 2.1% farming, 5.8% construction, 3.5% production (2006-2010 5-year est.).
**Income:** Per capita income: $29,620 (2006-2010 5-year est.); Median household income: $74,375 (2006-2010 5-year est.); Average household income: $76,463 (2006-2010 5-year est.); Percent of households with income of $100,000 or more: 26.7% (2006-2010 5-year est.); Poverty rate: 3.3% (2006-2010 5-year est.).
**Education:** Percent of population age 25 and over with: High school diploma (including GED) or higher: 90.8% (2006-2010 5-year est.); Bachelor's degree or higher: 52.1% (2006-2010 5-year est.); Master's degree or higher: 21.7% (2006-2010 5-year est.).
**Housing:** Homeownership rate: 90.7% (2010); Median home value: $177,300 (2006-2010 5-year est.); Median contract rent: $575 per month (2006-2010 5-year est.); Median year structure built: 1972 (2006-2010 5-year est.).
**Transportation:** Commute to work: 91.1% car, 0.0% public transportation, 0.0% walk, 8.9% work from home (2006-2010 5-year est.); Travel time to work: 72.1% less than 15 minutes, 10.7% 15 to 30 minutes, 2.8% 30 to 45 minutes, 11.4% 45 to 60 minutes, 3.0% 60 minutes or more (2006-2010 5-year est.)

**CORTLANDVILLE** (town). Covers a land area of 49.719 square miles and a water area of 0.180 square miles. Located at 42.60° N. Lat; 76.11° W. Long.
**Population:** 8,054 (1990); 7,919 (2000); 8,509 (2010); Density: 171.1 persons per square mile (2010); Race: 94.8% White, 1.3% Black, 1.5% Asian, 0.4% American Indian/Alaska Native, 0.0% Native Hawaiian/Other Pacific Islander, 2.0% Other, 1.5% Hispanic of any race (2010); Average household size: 2.42 (2010); Median age: 41.6 (2010); Males per 100 females: 94.4 (2010); Marriage status: 32.1% never married, 53.6% now married, 7.3% widowed, 7.0% divorced (2006-2010 5-year est.); Foreign born: 1.8% (2006-2010 5-year est.); Ancestry (includes multiple ancestries): 19.4% Irish, 19.3% German, 16.9% English, 16.2% Italian, 4.7% European (2006-2010 5-year est.).
**Economy:** Single-family building permits issued: 6 (2011); Multi-family building permits issued: 0 (2011); Employment by occupation: 10.2% management, 3.6% professional, 7.0% services, 22.8% sales, 2.9% farming, 7.3% construction, 5.2% production (2006-2010 5-year est.).
**Income:** Per capita income: $25,714 (2006-2010 5-year est.); Median household income: $51,382 (2006-2010 5-year est.); Average household income: $63,037 (2006-2010 5-year est.); Percent of households with income of $100,000 or more: 18.7% (2006-2010 5-year est.); Poverty rate: 13.4% (2006-2010 5-year est.).
**Taxes:** Total city taxes per capita: $251 (2009); City property taxes per capita: $211 (2009).
**Education:** Percent of population age 25 and over with: High school diploma (including GED) or higher: 92.2% (2006-2010 5-year est.); Bachelor's degree or higher: 28.9% (2006-2010 5-year est.); Master's degree or higher: 12.0% (2006-2010 5-year est.).
**Housing:** Homeownership rate: 71.4% (2010); Median home value: $112,000 (2006-2010 5-year est.); Median contract rent: $584 per month (2006-2010 5-year est.); Median year structure built: 1966 (2006-2010 5-year est.).
**Transportation:** Commute to work: 94.4% car, 0.3% public transportation, 1.9% walk, 3.4% work from home (2006-2010 5-year est.); Travel time to work: 55.0% less than 15 minutes, 26.7% 15 to 30 minutes, 9.9% 30 to 45 minutes, 6.2% 45 to 60 minutes, 2.2% 60 minutes or more (2006-2010 5-year est.)

**CUYLER** (town). Covers a land area of 43.477 square miles and a water area of 0.031 square miles. Located at 42.72° N. Lat; 75.93° W. Long. Elevation is 1,214 feet.
**Population:** 850 (1990); 1,036 (2000); 980 (2010); Density: 22.5 persons per square mile (2010); Race: 95.8% White, 0.1% Black, 0.7% Asian, 0.4% American Indian/Alaska Native, 0.0% Native Hawaiian/Other Pacific Islander, 3.0% Other, 1.9% Hispanic of any race (2010); Average household size: 2.72 (2010); Median age: 37.8 (2010); Males per 100

females: 105.5 (2010); Marriage status: 24.1% never married, 58.0% now married, 7.7% widowed, 10.1% divorced (2006-2010 5-year est.); Foreign born: 1.0% (2006-2010 5-year est.); Ancestry (includes multiple ancestries): 20.3% English, 14.8% Irish, 11.1% German, 8.8% American, 7.3% Italian (2006-2010 5-year est.).

**Economy:** Single-family building permits issued: 1 (2011); Multi-family building permits issued: 0 (2011); Employment by occupation: 7.8% management, 2.3% professional, 18.6% services, 15.1% sales, 1.4% farming, 8.7% construction, 11.6% production (2006-2010 5-year est.).

**Income:** Per capita income: $16,581 (2006-2010 5-year est.); Median household income: $43,021 (2006-2010 5-year est.); Average household income: $48,265 (2006-2010 5-year est.); Percent of households with income of $100,000 or more: 9.5% (2006-2010 5-year est.); Poverty rate: 14.8% (2006-2010 5-year est.).

**Education:** Percent of population age 25 and over with: High school diploma (including GED) or higher: 78.2% (2006-2010 5-year est.); Bachelor's degree or higher: 4.4% (2006-2010 5-year est.); Master's degree or higher: 1.1% (2006-2010 5-year est.).

**Housing:** Homeownership rate: 75.5% (2010); Median home value: $66,500 (2006-2010 5-year est.); Median contract rent: $446 per month (2006-2010 5-year est.); Median year structure built: 1975 (2006-2010 5-year est.).

**Transportation:** Commute to work: 97.7% car, 0.0% public transportation, 0.9% walk, 1.5% work from home (2006-2010 5-year est.); Travel time to work: 10.1% less than 15 minutes, 42.4% 15 to 30 minutes, 29.7% 30 to 45 minutes, 12.2% 45 to 60 minutes, 5.6% 60 minutes or more (2006-2010 5-year est.)

**FREETOWN** (town). Covers a land area of 25.486 square miles and a water area of 0.141 square miles. Located at 42.52° N. Lat; 76.02° W. Long.

**Population:** 688 (1990); 789 (2000); 757 (2010); Density: 29.7 persons per square mile (2010); Race: 97.6% White, 0.9% Black, 0.3% Asian, 0.3% American Indian/Alaska Native, 0.0% Native Hawaiian/Other Pacific Islander, 0.9% Other, 0.8% Hispanic of any race (2010); Average household size: 2.65 (2010); Median age: 40.3 (2010); Males per 100 females: 96.1 (2010); Marriage status: 17.5% never married, 63.0% now married, 7.0% widowed, 12.5% divorced (2006-2010 5-year est.); Foreign born: 0.0% (2006-2010 5-year est.); Ancestry (includes multiple ancestries): 20.6% English, 17.8% German, 14.1% Irish, 7.9% American, 6.2% Italian (2006-2010 5-year est.).

**Economy:** Single-family building permits issued: 5 (2011); Multi-family building permits issued: 0 (2011); Employment by occupation: 20.6% management, 4.1% professional, 13.2% services, 10.5% sales, 4.1% farming, 11.5% construction, 5.1% production (2006-2010 5-year est.).

**Income:** Per capita income: $19,765 (2006-2010 5-year est.); Median household income: $38,917 (2006-2010 5-year est.); Average household income: $50,936 (2006-2010 5-year est.); Percent of households with income of $100,000 or more: 7.4% (2006-2010 5-year est.); Poverty rate: 19.4% (2006-2010 5-year est.).

**Education:** Percent of population age 25 and over with: High school diploma (including GED) or higher: 84.8% (2006-2010 5-year est.); Bachelor's degree or higher: 15.4% (2006-2010 5-year est.); Master's degree or higher: 3.6% (2006-2010 5-year est.).

**Housing:** Homeownership rate: 83.9% (2010); Median home value: $78,000 (2006-2010 5-year est.); Median contract rent: $408 per month (2006-2010 5-year est.); Median year structure built: 1983 (2006-2010 5-year est.).

**Transportation:** Commute to work: 80.9% car, 0.0% public transportation, 4.3% walk, 14.9% work from home (2006-2010 5-year est.); Travel time to work: 16.3% less than 15 minutes, 40.8% 15 to 30 minutes, 16.7% 30 to 45 minutes, 16.7% 45 to 60 minutes, 9.6% 60 minutes or more (2006-2010 5-year est.)

**HARFORD** (town). Covers a land area of 24.152 square miles and a water area of 0.022 square miles. Located at 42.43° N. Lat; 76.20° W. Long. Elevation is 1,198 feet.

**Population:** 886 (1990); 920 (2000); 943 (2010); Density: 39.0 persons per square mile (2010); Race: 97.9% White, 0.7% Black, 0.2% Asian, 0.1% American Indian/Alaska Native, 0.0% Native Hawaiian/Other Pacific Islander, 1.1% Other, 0.2% Hispanic of any race (2010); Average household size: 2.60 (2010); Median age: 39.3 (2010); Males per 100 females: 107.7 (2010); Marriage status: 17.8% never married, 69.3% now married, 5.6% widowed, 7.3% divorced (2006-2010 5-year est.); Foreign born: 0.3% (2006-2010 5-year est.); Ancestry (includes multiple

ancestries): 20.9% German, 16.7% English, 13.3% Irish, 7.2% American, 4.8% French (2006-2010 5-year est.).

**Economy:** Single-family building permits issued: 2 (2011); Multi-family building permits issued: 0 (2011); Employment by occupation: 14.9% management, 6.9% professional, 9.4% services, 12.2% sales, 1.7% farming, 13.3% construction, 8.8% production (2006-2010 5-year est.).

**Income:** Per capita income: $16,840 (2006-2010 5-year est.); Median household income: $47,813 (2006-2010 5-year est.); Average household income: $46,143 (2006-2010 5-year est.); Percent of households with income of $100,000 or more: 4.8% (2006-2010 5-year est.); Poverty rate: 13.4% (2006-2010 5-year est.).

**Education:** Percent of population age 25 and over with: High school diploma (including GED) or higher: 81.0% (2006-2010 5-year est.); Bachelor's degree or higher: 14.4% (2006-2010 5-year est.); Master's degree or higher: 4.0% (2006-2010 5-year est.).

**Housing:** Homeownership rate: 81.5% (2010); Median home value: $79,000 (2006-2010 5-year est.); Median contract rent: $520 per month (2006-2010 5-year est.); Median year structure built: 1971 (2006-2010 5-year est.).

**Transportation:** Commute to work: 90.8% car, 2.5% public transportation, 1.7% walk, 2.5% work from home (2006-2010 5-year est.); Travel time to work: 21.3% less than 15 minutes, 48.6% 15 to 30 minutes, 20.4% 30 to 45 minutes, 6.0% 45 to 60 minutes, 3.7% 60 minutes or more (2006-2010 5-year est.)

**HOMER** (village). Covers a land area of 1.925 square miles and a water area of 0.012 square miles. Located at 42.63° N. Lat; 76.18° W. Long. Elevation is 1,125 feet.

**Population:** 3,635 (1990); 3,368 (2000); 3,291 (2010); Density: 1,709.2 persons per square mile (2010); Race: 95.7% White, 0.6% Black, 1.2% Asian, 0.2% American Indian/Alaska Native, 0.0% Native Hawaiian/Other Pacific Islander, 2.3% Other, 1.3% Hispanic of any race (2010); Average household size: 2.38 (2010); Median age: 41.7 (2010); Males per 100 females: 86.1 (2010); Marriage status: 27.0% never married, 55.5% now married, 8.2% widowed, 9.4% divorced (2006-2010 5-year est.); Foreign born: 3.4% (2006-2010 5-year est.); Ancestry (includes multiple ancestries): 20.2% English, 19.5% Irish, 19.4% German, 6.2% Italian, 6.2% American (2006-2010 5-year est.).

**Economy:** Single-family building permits issued: 1 (2011); Multi-family building permits issued: 0 (2011); Employment by occupation: 11.2% management, 3.6% professional, 8.7% services, 18.0% sales, 2.1% farming, 9.0% construction, 7.7% production (2006-2010 5-year est.).

**Income:** Per capita income: $28,116 (2006-2010 5-year est.); Median household income: $61,360 (2006-2010 5-year est.); Average household income: $65,626 (2006-2010 5-year est.); Percent of households with income of $100,000 or more: 16.8% (2006-2010 5-year est.); Poverty rate: 8.3% (2006-2010 5-year est.).

**Education:** Percent of population age 25 and over with: High school diploma (including GED) or higher: 92.0% (2006-2010 5-year est.); Bachelor's degree or higher: 34.5% (2006-2010 5-year est.); Master's degree or higher: 11.2% (2006-2010 5-year est.).

**School District(s)**

Homer Central School District (KG-12)
   2009-10 Enrollment: 2,139 . . . . . . . . . . . . . . . . (607) 749-7241

**Housing:** Homeownership rate: 68.1% (2010); Median home value: $99,400 (2006-2010 5-year est.); Median contract rent: $501 per month (2006-2010 5-year est.); Median year structure built: before 1940 (2006-2010 5-year est.).

**Safety:** Violent crime rate: 3.2 per 10,000 population; Property crime rate: 188.2 per 10,000 population (2010).

**Transportation:** Commute to work: 89.6% car, 0.3% public transportation, 4.2% walk, 5.8% work from home (2006-2010 5-year est.); Travel time to work: 40.4% less than 15 minutes, 26.3% 15 to 30 minutes, 19.9% 30 to 45 minutes, 6.4% 45 to 60 minutes, 7.0% 60 minutes or more (2006-2010 5-year est.)

**HOMER** (town). Covers a land area of 50.195 square miles and a water area of 0.460 square miles. Located at 42.66° N. Lat; 76.17° W. Long. Elevation is 1,125 feet.

**History:** Old Homer Village Historic District here. Settled 1791, incorporated 1835.

**Population:** 6,508 (1990); 6,363 (2000); 6,405 (2010); Density: 127.6 persons per square mile (2010); Race: 96.5% White, 0.5% Black, 0.9% Asian, 0.2% American Indian/Alaska Native, 0.0% Native Hawaiian/Other Pacific Islander, 1.9% Other, 1.4% Hispanic of any race (2010); Average

household size: 2.53 (2010); Median age: 41.8 (2010); Males per 100 females: 93.7 (2010); Marriage status: 27.3% never married, 56.7% now married, 6.6% widowed, 9.4% divorced (2006-2010 5-year est.); Foreign born: 5.3% (2006-2010 5-year est.); Ancestry (includes multiple ancestries): 20.5% German, 19.0% English, 18.1% Irish, 7.1% American, 7.1% Italian (2006-2010 5-year est.).

**Economy:** Single-family building permits issued: 6 (2011); Multi-family building permits issued: 0 (2011); Employment by occupation: 10.5% management, 4.0% professional, 12.0% services, 19.1% sales, 2.6% farming, 9.3% construction, 5.5% production (2006-2010 5-year est.).

**Income:** Per capita income: $25,687 (2006-2010 5-year est.); Median household income: $55,136 (2006-2010 5-year est.); Average household income: $66,641 (2006-2010 5-year est.); Percent of households with income of $100,000 or more: 19.2% (2006-2010 5-year est.); Poverty rate: 7.2% (2006-2010 5-year est.).

**Education:** Percent of population age 25 and over with: High school diploma (including GED) or higher: 91.4% (2006-2010 5-year est.); Bachelor's degree or higher: 28.7% (2006-2010 5-year est.); Master's degree or higher: 9.7% (2006-2010 5-year est.).

**School District(s)**

Homer Central School District (KG-12)

   2009-10 Enrollment: 2,139 . . . . . . . . . . . . . . . . . . . (607) 749-7241

**Housing:** Homeownership rate: 76.2% (2010); Median home value: $110,200 (2006-2010 5-year est.); Median contract rent: $498 per month (2006-2010 5-year est.); Median year structure built: 1950 (2006-2010 5-year est.).

**Transportation:** Commute to work: 91.7% car, 0.2% public transportation, 2.3% walk, 5.2% work from home (2006-2010 5-year est.); Travel time to work: 31.8% less than 15 minutes, 37.6% 15 to 30 minutes, 19.0% 30 to 45 minutes, 7.8% 45 to 60 minutes, 3.8% 60 minutes or more (2006-2010 5-year est.)

**LAPEER** (town). Covers a land area of 25.039 square miles and a water area of 0.142 square miles. Located at 42.45° N. Lat; 76.11° W. Long. Elevation is 1,329 feet.

**Population:** 613 (1990); 686 (2000); 767 (2010); Density: 30.6 persons per square mile (2010); Race: 98.8% White, 0.1% Black, 0.3% Asian, 0.0% American Indian/Alaska Native, 0.0% Native Hawaiian/Other Pacific Islander, 0.8% Other, 1.4% Hispanic of any race (2010); Average household size: 2.81 (2010); Median age: 40.5 (2010); Males per 100 females: 100.3 (2010); Marriage status: 22.7% never married, 64.9% now married, 6.6% widowed, 5.8% divorced (2006-2010 5-year est.); Foreign born: 0.5% (2006-2010 5-year est.); Ancestry (includes multiple ancestries): 20.9% Irish, 20.7% English, 19.9% German, 5.7% Polish, 3.4% American (2006-2010 5-year est.).

**Economy:** Single-family building permits issued: 0 (2011); Multi-family building permits issued: 0 (2011); Employment by occupation: 11.1% management, 1.0% professional, 5.2% services, 22.8% sales, 6.5% farming, 6.2% construction, 4.9% production (2006-2010 5-year est.).

**Income:** Per capita income: $18,373 (2006-2010 5-year est.); Median household income: $43,833 (2006-2010 5-year est.); Average household income: $51,799 (2006-2010 5-year est.); Percent of households with income of $100,000 or more: 6.6% (2006-2010 5-year est.); Poverty rate: 7.2% (2006-2010 5-year est.).

**Education:** Percent of population age 25 and over with: High school diploma (including GED) or higher: 91.1% (2006-2010 5-year est.); Bachelor's degree or higher: 7.4% (2006-2010 5-year est.); Master's degree or higher: 4.7% (2006-2010 5-year est.).

**Housing:** Homeownership rate: 85.7% (2010); Median home value: $110,400 (2006-2010 5-year est.); Median contract rent: n/a per month (2006-2010 5-year est.); Median year structure built: 1984 (2006-2010 5-year est.).

**Transportation:** Commute to work: 85.9% car, 0.0% public transportation, 2.3% walk, 10.2% work from home (2006-2010 5-year est.); Travel time to work: 22.0% less than 15 minutes, 29.7% 15 to 30 minutes, 39.2% 30 to 45 minutes, 8.1% 45 to 60 minutes, 1.1% 60 minutes or more (2006-2010 5-year est.)

**LITTLE YORK** (unincorporated postal area)

Zip Code: 13087

   Covers a land area of 0.204 square miles and a water area of 0.168 square miles. Located at 42.70° N. Lat; 76.15° W. Long. Elevation is 1,161 feet. Population: 168 (2010); Density: 822.0 persons per square mile (2010); Race: 98.8% White, 0.6% Black, 0.0% Asian, 0.0% American Indian/Alaska Native, 0.0% Native Hawaiian/Other Pacific

Islander, 0.6% Other, 0.0% Hispanic of any race (2010); Average household size: 2.13 (2010); Median age: 54.1 (2010); Males per 100 females: 90.9 (2010); Homeownership rate: 88.6% (2010)

**MARATHON** (village). Covers a land area of 1.129 square miles and a water area of 0.002 square miles. Located at 42.44° N. Lat; 76.03° W. Long. Elevation is 1,024 feet.

**Population:** 1,171 (1990); 1,063 (2000); 919 (2010); Density: 813.6 persons per square mile (2010); Race: 98.0% White, 0.2% Black, 0.3% Asian, 0.5% American Indian/Alaska Native, 0.0% Native Hawaiian/Other Pacific Islander, 1.0% Other, 1.2% Hispanic of any race (2010); Average household size: 2.36 (2010); Median age: 40.2 (2010); Males per 100 females: 90.7 (2010); Marriage status: 33.1% never married, 52.2% now married, 5.8% widowed, 9.0% divorced (2006-2010 5-year est.); Foreign born: 6.4% (2006-2010 5-year est.); Ancestry (includes multiple ancestries): 17.4% English, 13.8% German, 12.1% Irish, 3.8% Welsh, 2.6% Italian (2006-2010 5-year est.).

**Economy:** Single-family building permits issued: 0 (2011); Multi-family building permits issued: 0 (2011); Employment by occupation: 15.4% management, 2.0% professional, 9.8% services, 21.5% sales, 3.4% farming, 3.8% construction, 5.2% production (2006-2010 5-year est.).

**Income:** Per capita income: $22,633 (2006-2010 5-year est.); Median household income: $51,417 (2006-2010 5-year est.); Average household income: $61,691 (2006-2010 5-year est.); Percent of households with income of $100,000 or more: 15.8% (2006-2010 5-year est.); Poverty rate: 11.1% (2006-2010 5-year est.).

**Education:** Percent of population age 25 and over with: High school diploma (including GED) or higher: 92.7% (2006-2010 5-year est.); Bachelor's degree or higher: 19.3% (2006-2010 5-year est.); Master's degree or higher: 7.1% (2006-2010 5-year est.).

**School District(s)**

Marathon Central School District (PK-12)

   2009-10 Enrollment: 806 . . . . . . . . . . . . . . . . . . . . (607) 849-3251

**Housing:** Homeownership rate: 59.6% (2010); Median home value: $87,300 (2006-2010 5-year est.); Median contract rent: $415 per month (2006-2010 5-year est.); Median year structure built: before 1940 (2006-2010 5-year est.).

**Transportation:** Commute to work: 91.8% car, 1.5% public transportation, 0.0% walk, 6.7% work from home (2006-2010 5-year est.); Travel time to work: 14.7% less than 15 minutes, 39.0% 15 to 30 minutes, 31.5% 30 to 45 minutes, 8.6% 45 to 60 minutes, 6.2% 60 minutes or more (2006-2010 5-year est.)

**MARATHON** (town). Covers a land area of 24.936 square miles and a water area of 0.133 square miles. Located at 42.42° N. Lat; 76.00° W. Long. Elevation is 1,024 feet.

**Population:** 2,019 (1990); 2,189 (2000); 1,967 (2010); Density: 78.9 persons per square mile (2010); Race: 97.9% White, 0.4% Black, 0.3% Asian, 0.3% American Indian/Alaska Native, 0.0% Native Hawaiian/Other Pacific Islander, 1.1% Other, 1.7% Hispanic of any race (2010); Average household size: 2.49 (2010); Median age: 40.8 (2010); Males per 100 females: 102.4 (2010); Marriage status: 31.5% never married, 55.1% now married, 4.2% widowed, 9.2% divorced (2006-2010 5-year est.); Foreign born: 3.7% (2006-2010 5-year est.); Ancestry (includes multiple ancestries): 19.7% German, 19.6% English, 11.4% Irish, 8.1% American, 4.3% Dutch (2006-2010 5-year est.).

**Economy:** Single-family building permits issued: 1 (2011); Multi-family building permits issued: 0 (2011); Employment by occupation: 14.2% management, 2.4% professional, 9.5% services, 19.7% sales, 2.4% farming, 8.5% construction, 3.2% production (2006-2010 5-year est.).

**Income:** Per capita income: $24,739 (2006-2010 5-year est.); Median household income: $51,685 (2006-2010 5-year est.); Average household income: $64,763 (2006-2010 5-year est.); Percent of households with income of $100,000 or more: 10.7% (2006-2010 5-year est.); Poverty rate: 9.6% (2006-2010 5-year est.).

**Education:** Percent of population age 25 and over with: High school diploma (including GED) or higher: 93.7% (2006-2010 5-year est.); Bachelor's degree or higher: 17.4% (2006-2010 5-year est.); Master's degree or higher: 6.1% (2006-2010 5-year est.).

**School District(s)**

Marathon Central School District (PK-12)

   2009-10 Enrollment: 806 . . . . . . . . . . . . . . . . . . . . (607) 849-3251

**Housing:** Homeownership rate: 75.1% (2010); Median home value: $93,000 (2006-2010 5-year est.); Median contract rent: $420 per month

(2006-2010 5-year est.); Median year structure built: 1949 (2006-2010 5-year est.).
**Transportation:** Commute to work: 89.0% car, 0.8% public transportation, 2.7% walk, 7.6% work from home (2006-2010 5-year est.); Travel time to work: 19.9% less than 15 minutes, 35.0% 15 to 30 minutes, 34.6% 30 to 45 minutes, 7.3% 45 to 60 minutes, 3.2% 60 minutes or more (2006-2010 5-year est.)

**MCGRAW** (village). Covers a land area of 0.986 square miles and a water area of 0 square miles. Located at 42.59° N. Lat; 76.09° W. Long. Elevation is 1,158 feet.
**History:** Incorporated 1869.
**Population:** 1,058 (1990); 1,000 (2000); 1,053 (2010); Density: 1,066.9 persons per square mile (2010); Race: 95.5% White, 0.9% Black, 0.3% Asian, 0.8% American Indian/Alaska Native, 0.0% Native Hawaiian/Other Pacific Islander, 2.5% Other, 0.9% Hispanic of any race (2010); Average household size: 2.57 (2010); Median age: 35.7 (2010); Males per 100 females: 98.7 (2010); Marriage status: 18.7% never married, 66.2% now married, 8.8% widowed, 6.3% divorced (2006-2010 5-year est.); Foreign born: 0.6% (2006-2010 5-year est.); Ancestry (includes multiple ancestries): 18.2% English, 17.1% German, 13.4% Irish, 5.9% European, 5.3% French (2006-2010 5-year est.).
**Economy:** Single-family building permits issued: 0 (2011); Multi-family building permits issued: 0 (2011); Employment by occupation: 10.8% management, 2.0% professional, 10.8% services, 20.4% sales, 4.6% farming, 7.1% construction, 5.5% production (2006-2010 5-year est.).
**Income:** Per capita income: $25,818 (2006-2010 5-year est.); Median household income: $55,089 (2006-2010 5-year est.); Average household income: $63,842 (2006-2010 5-year est.); Percent of households with income of $100,000 or more: 12.3% (2006-2010 5-year est.); Poverty rate: 9.7% (2006-2010 5-year est.).
**Education:** Percent of population age 25 and over with: High school diploma (including GED) or higher: 89.4% (2006-2010 5-year est.); Bachelor's degree or higher: 15.3% (2006-2010 5-year est.); Master's degree or higher: 6.2% (2006-2010 5-year est.).

**School District(s)**
Mcgraw Central School District (KG-12)
   2009-10 Enrollment: 577 . . . . . . . . . . . . . . . . . (607) 836-3636
**Housing:** Homeownership rate: 62.6% (2010); Median home value: $77,700 (2006-2010 5-year est.); Median contract rent: $459 per month (2006-2010 5-year est.); Median year structure built: before 1940 (2006-2010 5-year est.).
**Transportation:** Commute to work: 90.9% car, 0.0% public transportation, 1.5% walk, 7.5% work from home (2006-2010 5-year est.); Travel time to work: 25.8% less than 15 minutes, 52.3% 15 to 30 minutes, 8.3% 30 to 45 minutes, 7.3% 45 to 60 minutes, 6.3% 60 minutes or more (2006-2010 5-year est.)

**MUNSONS CORNERS** (CDP). Covers a land area of 2.218 square miles and a water area of 0.009 square miles. Located at 42.57° N. Lat; 76.20° W. Long. Elevation is 1,178 feet.
**Population:** 2,576 (1990); 2,426 (2000); 2,728 (2010); Density: 1,229.4 persons per square mile (2010); Race: 91.1% White, 3.0% Black, 2.5% Asian, 0.5% American Indian/Alaska Native, 0.0% Native Hawaiian/Other Pacific Islander, 2.9% Other, 2.5% Hispanic of any race (2010); Average household size: 2.18 (2010); Median age: 36.0 (2010); Males per 100 females: 87.0 (2010); Marriage status: 46.0% never married, 41.9% now married, 7.9% widowed, 4.2% divorced (2006-2010 5-year est.); Foreign born: 4.6% (2006-2010 5-year est.); Ancestry (includes multiple ancestries): 25.1% Irish, 22.8% German, 21.7% Italian, 11.4% English, 5.7% Polish (2006-2010 5-year est.).
**Economy:** Employment by occupation: 8.0% management, 3.6% professional, 3.7% services, 23.5% sales, 4.3% farming, 8.2% construction, 1.1% production (2006-2010 5-year est.).
**Income:** Per capita income: $22,858 (2006-2010 5-year est.); Median household income: $43,689 (2006-2010 5-year est.); Average household income: $52,795 (2006-2010 5-year est.); Percent of households with income of $100,000 or more: 10.0% (2006-2010 5-year est.); Poverty rate: 19.6% (2006-2010 5-year est.).
**Education:** Percent of population age 25 and over with: High school diploma (including GED) or higher: 91.1% (2006-2010 5-year est.); Bachelor's degree or higher: 24.2% (2006-2010 5-year est.); Master's degree or higher: 11.6% (2006-2010 5-year est.).
**Housing:** Homeownership rate: 51.4% (2010); Median home value: $111,400 (2006-2010 5-year est.); Median contract rent: $615 per month

(2006-2010 5-year est.); Median year structure built: 1970 (2006-2010 5-year est.).
**Transportation:** Commute to work: 94.3% car, 1.0% public transportation, 4.8% walk, 0.0% work from home (2006-2010 5-year est.); Travel time to work: 59.3% less than 15 minutes, 14.9% 15 to 30 minutes, 18.5% 30 to 45 minutes, 4.9% 45 to 60 minutes, 2.4% 60 minutes or more (2006-2010 5-year est.)

**PREBLE** (town). Covers a land area of 26.844 square miles and a water area of 0.714 square miles. Located at 42.74° N. Lat; 76.13° W. Long. Elevation is 1,224 feet.
**Population:** 1,577 (1990); 1,582 (2000); 1,393 (2010); Density: 51.9 persons per square mile (2010); Race: 97.7% White, 0.1% Black, 0.5% Asian, 0.4% American Indian/Alaska Native, 0.0% Native Hawaiian/Other Pacific Islander, 1.3% Other, 2.1% Hispanic of any race (2010); Average household size: 2.38 (2010); Median age: 45.5 (2010); Males per 100 females: 107.0 (2010); Marriage status: 29.8% never married, 54.1% now married, 6.5% widowed, 9.6% divorced (2006-2010 5-year est.); Foreign born: 0.5% (2006-2010 5-year est.); Ancestry (includes multiple ancestries): 18.5% English, 12.3% German, 12.2% Irish, 6.5% American, 6.1% Italian (2006-2010 5-year est.).
**Economy:** Single-family building permits issued: 0 (2011); Multi-family building permits issued: 0 (2011); Employment by occupation: 11.2% management, 5.8% professional, 7.6% services, 13.0% sales, 2.8% farming, 16.6% construction, 7.5% production (2006-2010 5-year est.).
**Income:** Per capita income: $24,657 (2006-2010 5-year est.); Median household income: $48,875 (2006-2010 5-year est.); Average household income: $59,839 (2006-2010 5-year est.); Percent of households with income of $100,000 or more: 11.2% (2006-2010 5-year est.); Poverty rate: 16.7% (2006-2010 5-year est.).
**Education:** Percent of population age 25 and over with: High school diploma (including GED) or higher: 90.2% (2006-2010 5-year est.); Bachelor's degree or higher: 26.0% (2006-2010 5-year est.); Master's degree or higher: 8.1% (2006-2010 5-year est.).
**Housing:** Homeownership rate: 81.9% (2010); Median home value: $97,700 (2006-2010 5-year est.); Median contract rent: $479 per month (2006-2010 5-year est.); Median year structure built: 1965 (2006-2010 5-year est.).
**Transportation:** Commute to work: 89.4% car, 0.3% public transportation, 7.0% walk, 2.4% work from home (2006-2010 5-year est.); Travel time to work: 30.0% less than 15 minutes, 35.4% 15 to 30 minutes, 25.4% 30 to 45 minutes, 6.0% 45 to 60 minutes, 3.2% 60 minutes or more (2006-2010 5-year est.)
**Additional Information Contacts**
Town of Preble . . . . . . . . . . . . . . . . . . . . . . . . . (607) 749-3199
   http://www.preble-ny.org

**SCOTT** (town). Covers a land area of 22.266 square miles and a water area of 0.146 square miles. Located at 42.73° N. Lat; 76.23° W. Long. Elevation is 1,411 feet.
**Population:** 1,167 (1990); 1,193 (2000); 1,176 (2010); Density: 52.8 persons per square mile (2010); Race: 98.4% White, 0.4% Black, 0.4% Asian, 0.1% American Indian/Alaska Native, 0.0% Native Hawaiian/Other Pacific Islander, 0.7% Other, 1.4% Hispanic of any race (2010); Average household size: 2.77 (2010); Median age: 40.8 (2010); Males per 100 females: 108.1 (2010); Marriage status: 26.3% never married, 59.8% now married, 6.8% widowed, 7.0% divorced (2006-2010 5-year est.); Foreign born: 0.2% (2006-2010 5-year est.); Ancestry (includes multiple ancestries): 16.8% German, 16.4% English, 14.4% Irish, 8.5% American, 8.2% Italian (2006-2010 5-year est.).
**Economy:** Single-family building permits issued: 0 (2011); Multi-family building permits issued: 0 (2011); Employment by occupation: 8.7% management, 2.4% professional, 12.3% services, 13.0% sales, 4.3% farming, 11.5% construction, 10.6% production (2006-2010 5-year est.).
**Income:** Per capita income: $23,027 (2006-2010 5-year est.); Median household income: $50,568 (2006-2010 5-year est.); Average household income: $59,968 (2006-2010 5-year est.); Percent of households with income of $100,000 or more: 12.8% (2006-2010 5-year est.); Poverty rate: 6.3% (2006-2010 5-year est.).
**Education:** Percent of population age 25 and over with: High school diploma (including GED) or higher: 81.7% (2006-2010 5-year est.); Bachelor's degree or higher: 17.2% (2006-2010 5-year est.); Master's degree or higher: 7.1% (2006-2010 5-year est.).
**Housing:** Homeownership rate: 87.8% (2010); Median home value: $89,300 (2006-2010 5-year est.); Median contract rent: $566 per month

(2006-2010 5-year est.); Median year structure built: 1973 (2006-2010 5-year est.).

**Transportation:** Commute to work: 96.6% car, 0.0% public transportation, 0.0% walk, 2.3% work from home (2006-2010 5-year est.); Travel time to work: 11.7% less than 15 minutes, 56.4% 15 to 30 minutes, 23.5% 30 to 45 minutes, 7.0% 45 to 60 minutes, 1.3% 60 minutes or more (2006-2010 5-year est.)

**SOLON** (town). Covers a land area of 29.651 square miles and a water area of 0.076 square miles. Located at 42.61° N. Lat; 76.02° W. Long. Elevation is 1,312 feet.

**Population:** 1,008 (1990); 1,108 (2000); 1,079 (2010); Density: 36.4 persons per square mile (2010); Race: 97.8% White, 0.2% Black, 0.1% Asian, 0.3% American Indian/Alaska Native, 0.0% Native Hawaiian/Other Pacific Islander, 1.6% Other, 1.6% Hispanic of any race (2010); Average household size: 2.67 (2010); Median age: 42.6 (2010); Males per 100 females: 100.6 (2010); Marriage status: 27.6% never married, 56.0% now married, 5.1% widowed, 11.3% divorced (2006-2010 5-year est.); Foreign born: 4.2% (2006-2010 5-year est.); Ancestry (includes multiple ancestries): 18.0% German, 11.8% Irish, 8.7% American, 7.7% English, 3.6% French Canadian (2006-2010 5-year est.).

**Economy:** Single-family building permits issued: 4 (2011); Multi-family building permits issued: 0 (2011); Employment by occupation: 10.3% management, 2.6% professional, 11.7% services, 13.0% sales, 2.1% farming, 19.1% construction, 14.0% production (2006-2010 5-year est.).

**Income:** Per capita income: $18,404 (2006-2010 5-year est.); Median household income: $43,875 (2006-2010 5-year est.); Average household income: $52,956 (2006-2010 5-year est.); Percent of households with income of $100,000 or more: 8.3% (2006-2010 5-year est.); Poverty rate: 13.6% (2006-2010 5-year est.).

**Education:** Percent of population age 25 and over with: High school diploma (including GED) or higher: 85.9% (2006-2010 5-year est.); Bachelor's degree or higher: 13.7% (2006-2010 5-year est.); Master's degree or higher: 5.5% (2006-2010 5-year est.).

**Housing:** Homeownership rate: 86.9% (2010); Median home value: $81,000 (2006-2010 5-year est.); Median contract rent: $546 per month (2006-2010 5-year est.); Median year structure built: 1975 (2006-2010 5-year est.).

**Transportation:** Commute to work: 92.5% car, 2.8% public transportation, 0.0% walk, 4.7% work from home (2006-2010 5-year est.); Travel time to work: 14.7% less than 15 minutes, 62.0% 15 to 30 minutes, 14.5% 30 to 45 minutes, 5.6% 45 to 60 minutes, 3.2% 60 minutes or more (2006-2010 5-year est.)

**TAYLOR** (town). Covers a land area of 29.995 square miles and a water area of 0.123 square miles. Located at 42.59° N. Lat; 75.91° W. Long. Elevation is 1,109 feet.

**Population:** 542 (1990); 500 (2000); 523 (2010); Density: 17.4 persons per square mile (2010); Race: 97.7% White, 0.4% Black, 0.4% Asian, 0.0% American Indian/Alaska Native, 0.0% Native Hawaiian/Other Pacific Islander, 1.5% Other, 3.4% Hispanic of any race (2010); Average household size: 2.74 (2010); Median age: 40.7 (2010); Males per 100 females: 99.6 (2010); Marriage status: 32.1% never married, 64.7% now married, 1.5% widowed, 1.7% divorced (2006-2010 5-year est.); Foreign born: 0.7% (2006-2010 5-year est.); Ancestry (includes multiple ancestries): 23.1% German, 16.2% English, 12.6% Irish, 5.9% American, 5.2% Italian (2006-2010 5-year est.).

**Economy:** Single-family building permits issued: 0 (2011); Multi-family building permits issued: 0 (2011); Employment by occupation: 16.2% management, 2.6% professional, 6.2% services, 16.9% sales, 2.2% farming, 14.7% construction, 10.7% production (2006-2010 5-year est.).

**Income:** Per capita income: $24,716 (2006-2010 5-year est.); Median household income: $53,036 (2006-2010 5-year est.); Average household income: $69,792 (2006-2010 5-year est.); Percent of households with income of $100,000 or more: 25.3% (2006-2010 5-year est.); Poverty rate: 17.8% (2006-2010 5-year est.).

**Education:** Percent of population age 25 and over with: High school diploma (including GED) or higher: 84.3% (2006-2010 5-year est.); Bachelor's degree or higher: 13.9% (2006-2010 5-year est.); Master's degree or higher: 4.9% (2006-2010 5-year est.).

**Housing:** Homeownership rate: 79.6% (2010); Median home value: $96,100 (2006-2010 5-year est.); Median contract rent: $508 per month (2006-2010 5-year est.); Median year structure built: 1976 (2006-2010 5-year est.).

**Transportation:** Commute to work: 82.8% car, 0.0% public transportation, 3.1% walk, 14.2% work from home (2006-2010 5-year est.); Travel time to work: 20.1% less than 15 minutes, 22.3% 15 to 30 minutes, 27.7% 30 to 45 minutes, 15.2% 45 to 60 minutes, 14.7% 60 minutes or more (2006-2010 5-year est.)

**TRUXTON** (town). Covers a land area of 44.648 square miles and a water area of 0.077 square miles. Located at 42.71° N. Lat; 76.02° W. Long. Elevation is 1,152 feet.

**Population:** 1,064 (1990); 1,225 (2000); 1,133 (2010); Density: 25.4 persons per square mile (2010); Race: 97.8% White, 0.6% Black, 0.2% Asian, 0.2% American Indian/Alaska Native, 0.0% Native Hawaiian/Other Pacific Islander, 1.2% Other, 2.2% Hispanic of any race (2010); Average household size: 2.58 (2010); Median age: 41.7 (2010); Males per 100 females: 103.4 (2010); Marriage status: 24.3% never married, 62.6% now married, 7.1% widowed, 6.1% divorced (2006-2010 5-year est.); Foreign born: 2.1% (2006-2010 5-year est.); Ancestry (includes multiple ancestries): 21.7% German, 16.8% English, 16.5% Irish, 10.9% American, 5.4% Italian (2006-2010 5-year est.).

**Economy:** Single-family building permits issued: 1 (2011); Multi-family building permits issued: 0 (2011); Employment by occupation: 7.2% management, 5.1% professional, 14.0% services, 14.6% sales, 5.4% farming, 11.7% construction, 9.3% production (2006-2010 5-year est.).

**Income:** Per capita income: $22,907 (2006-2010 5-year est.); Median household income: $51,528 (2006-2010 5-year est.); Average household income: $67,999 (2006-2010 5-year est.); Percent of households with income of $100,000 or more: 18.3% (2006-2010 5-year est.); Poverty rate: 4.9% (2006-2010 5-year est.).

**Education:** Percent of population age 25 and over with: High school diploma (including GED) or higher: 90.4% (2006-2010 5-year est.); Bachelor's degree or higher: 21.4% (2006-2010 5-year est.); Master's degree or higher: 7.2% (2006-2010 5-year est.).

**School District(s)**
Homer Central School District (KG-12)
   2009-10 Enrollment: 2,139 . . . . . . . . . . . . . . . . . . . (607) 749-7241

**Housing:** Homeownership rate: 79.7% (2010); Median home value: $94,500 (2006-2010 5-year est.); Median contract rent: $430 per month (2006-2010 5-year est.); Median year structure built: 1971 (2006-2010 5-year est.).

**Transportation:** Commute to work: 87.7% car, 0.5% public transportation, 4.4% walk, 6.6% work from home (2006-2010 5-year est.); Travel time to work: 17.2% less than 15 minutes, 44.6% 15 to 30 minutes, 25.8% 30 to 45 minutes, 6.7% 45 to 60 minutes, 5.7% 60 minutes or more (2006-2010 5-year est.)

**VIRGIL** (town). Covers a land area of 47.362 square miles and a water area of 0.036 square miles. Located at 42.52° N. Lat; 76.16° W. Long. Elevation is 1,404 feet.

**Population:** 2,172 (1990); 2,287 (2000); 2,401 (2010); Density: 50.7 persons per square mile (2010); Race: 97.0% White, 0.7% Black, 0.5% Asian, 0.5% American Indian/Alaska Native, 0.0% Native Hawaiian/Other Pacific Islander, 1.3% Other, 1.7% Hispanic of any race (2010); Average household size: 2.62 (2010); Median age: 41.5 (2010); Males per 100 females: 103.0 (2010); Marriage status: 28.3% never married, 58.3% now married, 5.2% widowed, 8.2% divorced (2006-2010 5-year est.); Foreign born: 1.2% (2006-2010 5-year est.); Ancestry (includes multiple ancestries): 19.1% English, 18.7% German, 17.9% Irish, 12.1% French, 7.1% Italian (2006-2010 5-year est.).

**Economy:** Single-family building permits issued: 7 (2011); Multi-family building permits issued: 0 (2011); Employment by occupation: 14.2% management, 4.0% professional, 5.8% services, 19.0% sales, 2.1% farming, 9.7% construction, 7.9% production (2006-2010 5-year est.).

**Income:** Per capita income: $27,764 (2006-2010 5-year est.); Median household income: $61,815 (2006-2010 5-year est.); Average household income: $75,490 (2006-2010 5-year est.); Percent of households with income of $100,000 or more: 24.6% (2006-2010 5-year est.); Poverty rate: 3.9% (2006-2010 5-year est.).

**Education:** Percent of population age 25 and over with: High school diploma (including GED) or higher: 92.8% (2006-2010 5-year est.); Bachelor's degree or higher: 23.3% (2006-2010 5-year est.); Master's degree or higher: 9.5% (2006-2010 5-year est.).

**Housing:** Homeownership rate: 85.8% (2010); Median home value: $119,400 (2006-2010 5-year est.); Median contract rent: $564 per month (2006-2010 5-year est.); Median year structure built: 1974 (2006-2010 5-year est.).

**Transportation:** Commute to work: 89.9% car, 2.0% public transportation, 0.8% walk, 6.0% work from home (2006-2010 5-year est.); Travel time to work: 21.9% less than 15 minutes, 48.7% 15 to 30 minutes, 15.6% 30 to 45 minutes, 9.1% 45 to 60 minutes, 4.7% 60 minutes or more (2006-2010 5-year est.)

**WILLET** (town). Covers a land area of 25.733 square miles and a water area of 0.321 square miles. Located at 42.45° N. Lat; 75.92° W. Long. Elevation is 1,040 feet.
**Population:** 892 (1990); 1,011 (2000); 1,043 (2010); Density: 40.5 persons per square mile (2010); Race: 96.5% White, 0.8% Black, 0.1% Asian, 0.6% American Indian/Alaska Native, 0.0% Native Hawaiian/Other Pacific Islander, 2.0% Other, 1.5% Hispanic of any race (2010); Average household size: 2.83 (2010); Median age: 37.2 (2010); Males per 100 females: 106.1 (2010); Marriage status: 22.3% never married, 71.1% now married, 3.0% widowed, 3.6% divorced (2006-2010 5-year est.); Foreign born: 0.3% (2006-2010 5-year est.); Ancestry (includes multiple ancestries): 14.9% Irish, 14.0% German, 11.0% English, 6.0% Dutch, 5.3% American (2006-2010 5-year est.).
**Economy:** Single-family building permits issued: 1 (2011); Multi-family building permits issued: 0 (2011); Employment by occupation: 3.0% management, 0.8% professional, 7.8% services, 14.9% sales, 2.0% farming, 27.8% construction, 9.3% production (2006-2010 5-year est.).
**Income:** Per capita income: $16,727 (2006-2010 5-year est.); Median household income: $43,438 (2006-2010 5-year est.); Average household income: $53,045 (2006-2010 5-year est.); Percent of households with income of $100,000 or more: 9.5% (2006-2010 5-year est.); Poverty rate: 6.6% (2006-2010 5-year est.).
**Education:** Percent of population age 25 and over with: High school diploma (including GED) or higher: 81.3% (2006-2010 5-year est.); Bachelor's degree or higher: 12.0% (2006-2010 5-year est.); Master's degree or higher: 3.4% (2006-2010 5-year est.).
**Housing:** Homeownership rate: 81.1% (2010); Median home value: $77,700 (2006-2010 5-year est.); Median contract rent: $357 per month (2006-2010 5-year est.); Median year structure built: 1971 (2006-2010 5-year est.).
**Transportation:** Commute to work: 94.6% car, 1.8% public transportation, 1.8% walk, 1.0% work from home (2006-2010 5-year est.); Travel time to work: 14.8% less than 15 minutes, 29.8% 15 to 30 minutes, 30.3% 30 to 45 minutes, 10.9% 45 to 60 minutes, 14.2% 60 minutes or more (2006-2010 5-year est.)

## Delaware County

Located in southern New York, in the west Catskills; bounded on the northwest by the Susquehanna River, and on the southwest by the Delaware River and the Pennsylvania border. Covers a land area of 1,446.37 square miles, a water area of 21.67 square miles, and is located in the Eastern Time Zone at 42.21° N. Lat., 75.00° W. Long. The county was founded in 1797. County seat is Delhi.

Weather Station: Delhi 2 SE                                Elevation: 1,439 feet

| | Jan | Feb | Mar | Apr | May | Jun | Jul | Aug | Sep | Oct | Nov | Dec |
|---|---|---|---|---|---|---|---|---|---|---|---|---|
| High | 31 | 34 | 42 | 55 | 67 | 75 | 79 | 78 | 71 | 59 | 47 | 36 |
| Low | 11 | 12 | 20 | 32 | 41 | 50 | 54 | 53 | 46 | 35 | 28 | 18 |
| Precip | 3.2 | 2.5 | 3.5 | 3.9 | 4.2 | 4.6 | 4.6 | 3.6 | 4.4 | 4.0 | 3.9 | 3.5 |
| Snow | 18.2 | 12.4 | 11.2 | 3.8 | 0.1 | 0.0 | 0.0 | 0.0 | 0.0 | 0.6 | 4.3 | 14.8 |

*High and Low temperatures in degrees Fahrenheit; Precipitation and Snow in inches*

Weather Station: Deposit                                   Elevation: 1,000 feet

| | Jan | Feb | Mar | Apr | May | Jun | Jul | Aug | Sep | Oct | Nov | Dec |
|---|---|---|---|---|---|---|---|---|---|---|---|---|
| High | 32 | 36 | 45 | 59 | 70 | 77 | 81 | 80 | 72 | 60 | 48 | 36 |
| Low | 14 | 16 | 23 | 34 | 44 | 53 | 57 | 56 | 50 | 38 | 30 | 20 |
| Precip | 2.8 | 2.5 | 3.2 | 3.9 | 3.9 | 4.2 | 4.1 | 3.8 | 4.0 | 3.7 | 3.8 | 3.1 |
| Snow | na | na | na | 1.7 | 0.0 | 0.0 | 0.0 | 0.0 | 0.0 | tr | 1.7 | na |

*High and Low temperatures in degrees Fahrenheit; Precipitation and Snow in inches*

**Population:** 47,263 (1990); 48,055 (2000); 47,980 (2010); Race: 95.2% White, 1.6% Black, 0.8% Asian, 0.3% American Indian/Alaska Native, 0.0% Native Hawaiian/Other Pacific Islander, 2.1% Other, 3.3% Hispanic of any race (2010); Density: 33.2 persons per square mile (2010); Average household size: 2.29 (2010); Median age: 45.4 (2010); Males per 100 females: 100.9 (2010).
**Religion:** Six largest groups: 17.8% Catholicism, 8.7% Methodist/Pietist, 3.9% Presbyterian-Reformed, 3.5% Holiness, 3.2% Muslim Estimate, 1.3% Episcopalianism/Anglicanism (2010)

**Economy:** Unemployment rate: 9.9% (February 2012); Total civilian labor force: 20,923 (February 2012); Leading industries: 38.3% manufacturing; 16.5% health care and social assistance; 12.9% retail trade (2009); Farms: 747 totaling 165,572 acres (2007); Companies that employ 500 or more persons: 3 (2009); Companies that employ 100 to 499 persons: 14 (2009); Companies that employ less than 100 persons: 1,048 (2009); Black-owned businesses: n/a (2007); Hispanic-owned businesses: 45 (2007); Asian-owned businesses: n/a (2007); Women-owned businesses: 899 (2007); Retail sales per capita: $10,646 (2010). Single-family building permits issued: 60 (2011); Multi-family building permits issued: 0 (2011).
**Income:** Per capita income: $22,928 (2006-2010 5-year est.); Median household income: $42,967 (2006-2010 5-year est.); Average household income: $54,149 (2006-2010 5-year est.); Percent of households with income of $100,000 or more: 11.1% (2006-2010 5-year est.); Poverty rate: 13.3% (2006-2010 5-year est.); Bankruptcy rate: 1.87% (2011).
**Education:** Percent of population age 25 and over with: High school diploma (including GED) or higher: 87.0% (2006-2010 5-year est.); Bachelor's degree or higher: 19.1% (2006-2010 5-year est.); Master's degree or higher: 8.1% (2006-2010 5-year est.).
**Housing:** Homeownership rate: 74.2% (2010); Median home value: $126,700 (2006-2010 5-year est.); Median contract rent: $470 per month (2006-2010 5-year est.); Median year structure built: 1964 (2006-2010 5-year est.).
**Health:** Birth rate: 91.3 per 10,000 population (2011); Death rate: 113.5 per 10,000 population (2011); Age-adjusted cancer mortality rate: 174.0 deaths per 100,000 population (2009); Number of physicians: 8.9 per 10,000 population (2008); Hospital beds: 12.1 per 10,000 population (2007); Hospital admissions: 371.4 per 10,000 population (2007).
**Elections:** 2008 Presidential election results: 46.4% Obama, 51.6% McCain, 1.0% Nader
**National and State Parks:** Delaware State Forest
**Additional Information Contacts**

Delaware County Government . . . . . . . . . . . . . . . . . . . . . . . . (607) 746-2123
  http://www.co.delaware.ny.us
Central Catskills Chamber of Commerce . . . . . . . . . . . . . . . (845) 586-3300
  http://centralcatskills.com
Delaware County Chamber of Commerce . . . . . . . . . . . . . . (607) 746-2281
  http://delawarecounty.org
Deposit Chamber of Commerce . . . . . . . . . . . . . . . . . . . . . (607) 467-4161
  http://www.depositchamber.com
Hancock Area Chamber of Commerce . . . . . . . . . . . . . . . . (607) 637-4756
  http://www.hancockchamber.org
Sidney Chamber of Commerce . . . . . . . . . . . . . . . . . . . . . . (607) 561-2642
  http://www.sidneychamber.org
Town of Franklin . . . . . . . . . . . . . . . . . . . . . . . . . . . . . . . . . (518) 891-2189
  http://townoffranklin.com
Village of Stamford . . . . . . . . . . . . . . . . . . . . . . . . . . . . . . . (607) 652-6671
  http://www.stamfordny.com/villagewebsite/
Walton Chamber of Commerce . . . . . . . . . . . . . . . . . . . . . . (607) 865-6656
  http://www.waltonchamber.com

## Delaware County Communities

**ANDES** (village). Covers a land area of 1.193 square miles and a water area of <.001 square miles. Located at 42.18° N. Lat; 74.78° W. Long. Elevation is 1,598 feet.
**Population:** 292 (1990); 289 (2000); 252 (2010); Density: 211.2 persons per square mile (2010); Race: 96.4% White, 0.8% Black, 0.8% Asian, 0.4% American Indian/Alaska Native, 0.0% Native Hawaiian/Other Pacific Islander, 1.6% Other, 6.0% Hispanic of any race (2010); Average household size: 2.02 (2010); Median age: 53.5 (2010); Males per 100 females: 96.9 (2010); Marriage status: 33.1% never married, 47.8% now married, 6.9% widowed, 12.2% divorced (2006-2010 5-year est.); Foreign born: 5.4% (2006-2010 5-year est.); Ancestry (includes multiple ancestries): 44.2% German, 15.1% Irish, 11.5% Italian, 8.3% English, 7.6% Dutch (2006-2010 5-year est.).
**Economy:** Employment by occupation: 2.6% management, 5.8% professional, 15.2% services, 15.2% sales, 0.0% farming, 21.5% construction, 12.0% production (2006-2010 5-year est.).
**Income:** Per capita income: $47,734 (2006-2010 5-year est.); Median household income: $64,722 (2006-2010 5-year est.); Average household income: $105,916 (2006-2010 5-year est.); Percent of households with income of $100,000 or more: 16.1% (2006-2010 5-year est.); Poverty rate: 12.2% (2006-2010 5-year est.).

**Education:** Percent of population age 25 and over with: High school diploma (including GED) or higher: 89.0% (2006-2010 5-year est.); Bachelor's degree or higher: 26.0% (2006-2010 5-year est.); Master's degree or higher: 11.6% (2006-2010 5-year est.).

**School District(s)**

Andes Central School District (PK-12)

    2009-10 Enrollment: 120 . . . . . . . . . . . . . . . . . . . . . . . . (845) 676-3167

**Housing:** Homeownership rate: 76.0% (2010); Median home value: $165,100 (2006-2010 5-year est.); Median contract rent: $667 per month (2006-2010 5-year est.); Median year structure built: before 1940 (2006-2010 5-year est.).

**Transportation:** Commute to work: 70.7% car, 8.8% public transportation, 17.7% walk, 2.8% work from home (2006-2010 5-year est.); Travel time to work: 39.8% less than 15 minutes, 36.4% 15 to 30 minutes, 15.3% 30 to 45 minutes, 0.0% 45 to 60 minutes, 8.5% 60 minutes or more (2006-2010 5-year est.)

**ANDES** (town). Covers a land area of 108.592 square miles and a water area of 3.693 square miles. Located at 42.12° N. Lat; 74.78° W. Long. Elevation is 1,598 feet.

**Population:** 1,292 (1990); 1,356 (2000); 1,301 (2010); Density: 12.0 persons per square mile (2010); Race: 95.8% White, 0.9% Black, 1.2% Asian, 0.2% American Indian/Alaska Native, 0.0% Native Hawaiian/Other Pacific Islander, 1.9% Other, 2.6% Hispanic of any race (2010); Average household size: 2.06 (2010); Median age: 54.4 (2010); Males per 100 females: 107.8 (2010); Marriage status: 23.2% never married, 50.2% now married, 15.7% widowed, 11.0% divorced (2006-2010 5-year est.); Foreign born: 9.2% (2006-2010 5-year est.); Ancestry (includes multiple ancestries): 34.0% German, 16.5% Irish, 15.6% Scottish, 11.8% English, 10.4% Italian (2006-2010 5-year est.).

**Economy:** Single-family building permits issued: 5 (2011); Multi-family building permits issued: 0 (2011); Employment by occupation: 9.1% management, 3.2% professional, 7.5% services, 11.6% sales, 2.3% farming, 23.5% construction, 10.3% production (2006-2010 5-year est.).

**Income:** Per capita income: $32,656 (2006-2010 5-year est.); Median household income: $39,306 (2006-2010 5-year est.); Average household income: $64,047 (2006-2010 5-year est.); Percent of households with income of $100,000 or more: 14.0% (2006-2010 5-year est.); Poverty rate: 10.4% (2006-2010 5-year est.).

**Education:** Percent of population age 25 and over with: High school diploma (including GED) or higher: 84.3% (2006-2010 5-year est.); Bachelor's degree or higher: 22.8% (2006-2010 5-year est.); Master's degree or higher: 9.3% (2006-2010 5-year est.).

**School District(s)**

Andes Central School District (PK-12)

    2009-10 Enrollment: 120 . . . . . . . . . . . . . . . . . . . . . . . . (845) 676-3167

**Housing:** Homeownership rate: 86.1% (2010); Median home value: $169,900 (2006-2010 5-year est.); Median contract rent: $658 per month (2006-2010 5-year est.); Median year structure built: 1976 (2006-2010 5-year est.).

**Transportation:** Commute to work: 64.8% car, 7.0% public transportation, 18.3% walk, 9.9% work from home (2006-2010 5-year est.); Travel time to work: 34.1% less than 15 minutes, 26.3% 15 to 30 minutes, 21.9% 30 to 45 minutes, 0.8% 45 to 60 minutes, 16.9% 60 minutes or more (2006-2010 5-year est.)

**ARKVILLE** (unincorporated postal area)

Zip Code: 12406

    Covers a land area of 43.231 square miles and a water area of 0.079 square miles. Located at 42.07° N. Lat; 74.52° W. Long. Elevation is 1,373 feet. Population: 823 (2010); Density: 19.0 persons per square mile (2010); Race: 93.9% White, 0.2% Black, 0.4% Asian, 1.8% American Indian/Alaska Native, 0.0% Native Hawaiian/Other Pacific Islander, 3.7% Other, 5.5% Hispanic of any race (2010); Average household size: 2.03 (2010); Median age: 46.9 (2010); Males per 100 females: 94.6 (2010); Homeownership rate: 64.1% (2010)

**BLOOMVILLE** (CDP). Covers a land area of 1.316 square miles and a water area of 0.002 square miles. Located at 42.33° N. Lat; 74.82° W. Long. Elevation is 1,457 feet.

**Population:** n/a (1990); n/a (2000); 213 (2010); Density: 161.8 persons per square mile (2010); Race: 96.2% White, 0.9% Black, 0.5% Asian, 0.5% American Indian/Alaska Native, 0.0% Native Hawaiian/Other Pacific Islander, 1.9% Other, 2.3% Hispanic of any race (2010); Average household size: 2.37 (2010); Median age: 43.5 (2010); Males per 100

females: 104.8 (2010); Marriage status: 26.6% never married, 60.8% now married, 8.0% widowed, 4.6% divorced (2006-2010 5-year est.); Foreign born: 9.6% (2006-2010 5-year est.); Ancestry (includes multiple ancestries): 30.3% German, 21.8% Irish, 18.8% English, 12.6% Dutch, 10.0% Polish (2006-2010 5-year est.).

**Economy:** Employment by occupation: 3.3% management, 0.0% professional, 5.8% services, 21.7% sales, 4.2% farming, 20.8% construction, 26.7% production (2006-2010 5-year est.).

**Income:** Per capita income: $21,507 (2006-2010 5-year est.); Median household income: $46,563 (2006-2010 5-year est.); Average household income: $53,306 (2006-2010 5-year est.); Percent of households with income of $100,000 or more: 10.5% (2006-2010 5-year est.); Poverty rate: 18.8% (2006-2010 5-year est.).

**Education:** Percent of population age 25 and over with: High school diploma (including GED) or higher: 74.5% (2006-2010 5-year est.); Bachelor's degree or higher: 6.4% (2006-2010 5-year est.); Master's degree or higher: 2.1% (2006-2010 5-year est.).

**Housing:** Homeownership rate: 68.9% (2010); Median home value: $95,800 (2006-2010 5-year est.); Median contract rent: $493 per month (2006-2010 5-year est.); Median year structure built: before 1940 (2006-2010 5-year est.).

**Transportation:** Commute to work: 81.3% car, 0.0% public transportation, 0.0% walk, 18.7% work from home (2006-2010 5-year est.); Travel time to work: 31.0% less than 15 minutes, 43.7% 15 to 30 minutes, 19.5% 30 to 45 minutes, 0.0% 45 to 60 minutes, 5.7% 60 minutes or more (2006-2010 5-year est.)

**BOVINA** (town). Covers a land area of 44.263 square miles and a water area of 0.231 square miles. Located at 42.27° N. Lat; 74.75° W. Long. Elevation is 1,844 feet.

**Population:** 549 (1990); 664 (2000); 633 (2010); Density: 14.3 persons per square mile (2010); Race: 95.9% White, 0.8% Black, 1.7% Asian, 0.2% American Indian/Alaska Native, 0.0% Native Hawaiian/Other Pacific Islander, 1.4% Other, 1.9% Hispanic of any race (2010); Average household size: 2.21 (2010); Median age: 52.2 (2010); Males per 100 females: 109.6 (2010); Marriage status: 22.0% never married, 61.1% now married, 6.2% widowed, 10.7% divorced (2006-2010 5-year est.); Foreign born: 9.8% (2006-2010 5-year est.); Ancestry (includes multiple ancestries): 26.1% Irish, 16.9% Italian, 16.1% German, 15.1% English, 5.7% Scottish (2006-2010 5-year est.).

**Economy:** Single-family building permits issued: 0 (2011); Multi-family building permits issued: 0 (2011); Employment by occupation: 5.4% management, 9.0% professional, 9.0% services, 6.3% sales, 8.5% farming, 9.4% construction, 1.8% production (2006-2010 5-year est.).

**Income:** Per capita income: $22,803 (2006-2010 5-year est.); Median household income: $32,750 (2006-2010 5-year est.); Average household income: $52,492 (2006-2010 5-year est.); Percent of households with income of $100,000 or more: 10.2% (2006-2010 5-year est.); Poverty rate: 9.8% (2006-2010 5-year est.).

**Education:** Percent of population age 25 and over with: High school diploma (including GED) or higher: 92.6% (2006-2010 5-year est.); Bachelor's degree or higher: 43.4% (2006-2010 5-year est.); Master's degree or higher: 25.0% (2006-2010 5-year est.).

**Housing:** Homeownership rate: 84.0% (2010); Median home value: $172,500 (2006-2010 5-year est.); Median contract rent: $441 per month (2006-2010 5-year est.); Median year structure built: 1974 (2006-2010 5-year est.).

**Transportation:** Commute to work: 84.4% car, 3.7% public transportation, 2.3% walk, 9.6% work from home (2006-2010 5-year est.); Travel time to work: 34.0% less than 15 minutes, 43.7% 15 to 30 minutes, 7.6% 30 to 45 minutes, 4.1% 45 to 60 minutes, 10.7% 60 minutes or more (2006-2010 5-year est.)

**BOVINA CENTER** (unincorporated postal area)

Zip Code: 13740

    Covers a land area of 39.569 square miles and a water area of 0.049 square miles. Located at 42.27° N. Lat; 74.75° W. Long. Elevation is 1,660 feet. Population: 554 (2010); Density: 14.0 persons per square mile (2010); Race: 95.3% White, 0.9% Black, 2.0% Asian, 0.2% American Indian/Alaska Native, 0.0% Native Hawaiian/Other Pacific Islander, 1.6% Other, 2.0% Hispanic of any race (2010); Average household size: 2.22 (2010); Median age: 52.9 (2010); Males per 100 females: 109.8 (2010); Homeownership rate: 83.6% (2010)

**COLCHESTER** (town). Covers a land area of 136.778 square miles and a water area of 5.397 square miles. Located at 42.03° N. Lat; 74.95° W. Long. Elevation is 1,280 feet.
**Population:** 1,928 (1990); 2,042 (2000); 2,077 (2010); Density: 15.2 persons per square mile (2010); Race: 97.9% White, 0.6% Black, 0.3% Asian, 0.1% American Indian/Alaska Native, 0.0% Native Hawaiian/Other Pacific Islander, 1.1% Other, 1.9% Hispanic of any race (2010); Average household size: 2.22 (2010); Median age: 48.9 (2010); Males per 100 females: 103.6 (2010); Marriage status: 25.6% never married, 55.2% now married, 9.5% widowed, 9.7% divorced (2006-2010 5-year est.); Foreign born: 2.3% (2006-2010 5-year est.); Ancestry (includes multiple ancestries): 28.1% German, 19.6% Italian, 19.1% Irish, 19.0% English, 7.1% Polish (2006-2010 5-year est.).
**Economy:** Single-family building permits issued: 11 (2011); Multi-family building permits issued: 0 (2011); Employment by occupation: 7.2% management, 3.4% professional, 16.3% services, 13.1% sales, 5.3% farming, 13.9% construction, 6.0% production (2006-2010 5-year est.).
**Income:** Per capita income: $21,150 (2006-2010 5-year est.); Median household income: $41,804 (2006-2010 5-year est.); Average household income: $47,225 (2006-2010 5-year est.); Percent of households with income of $100,000 or more: 6.3% (2006-2010 5-year est.); Poverty rate: 10.5% (2006-2010 5-year est.).
**Education:** Percent of population age 25 and over with: High school diploma (including GED) or higher: 87.9% (2006-2010 5-year est.); Bachelor's degree or higher: 16.0% (2006-2010 5-year est.); Master's degree or higher: 5.4% (2006-2010 5-year est.).
**Housing:** Homeownership rate: 80.3% (2010); Median home value: $146,300 (2006-2010 5-year est.); Median contract rent: $430 per month (2006-2010 5-year est.); Median year structure built: 1969 (2006-2010 5-year est.).
**Safety:** Violent crime rate: 0.0 per 10,000 population; Property crime rate: 0.0 per 10,000 population (2010).
**Transportation:** Commute to work: 87.2% car, 0.0% public transportation, 5.0% walk, 6.1% work from home (2006-2010 5-year est.); Travel time to work: 28.4% less than 15 minutes, 35.1% 15 to 30 minutes, 22.5% 30 to 45 minutes, 6.9% 45 to 60 minutes, 7.2% 60 minutes or more (2006-2010 5-year est.)

**DAVENPORT** (town). Covers a land area of 51.562 square miles and a water area of 0.349 square miles. Located at 42.45° N. Lat; 74.90° W. Long. Elevation is 1,306 feet.
**Population:** 2,476 (1990); 2,774 (2000); 2,965 (2010); Density: 57.5 persons per square mile (2010); Race: 97.9% White, 0.6% Black, 0.5% Asian, 0.1% American Indian/Alaska Native, 0.0% Native Hawaiian/Other Pacific Islander, 0.9% Other, 1.9% Hispanic of any race (2010); Average household size: 2.40 (2010); Median age: 44.0 (2010); Males per 100 females: 94.7 (2010); Marriage status: 25.3% never married, 57.3% now married, 8.0% widowed, 9.4% divorced (2006-2010 5-year est.); Foreign born: 1.9% (2006-2010 5-year est.); Ancestry (includes multiple ancestries): 28.2% German, 24.3% Irish, 23.8% English, 9.9% Italian, 8.7% Dutch (2006-2010 5-year est.).
**Economy:** Single-family building permits issued: 3 (2011); Multi-family building permits issued: 0 (2011); Employment by occupation: 5.3% management, 4.0% professional, 13.5% services, 15.7% sales, 3.0% farming, 12.9% construction, 9.1% production (2006-2010 5-year est.).
**Income:** Per capita income: $20,610 (2006-2010 5-year est.); Median household income: $48,063 (2006-2010 5-year est.); Average household income: $50,050 (2006-2010 5-year est.); Percent of households with income of $100,000 or more: 9.4% (2006-2010 5-year est.); Poverty rate: 13.9% (2006-2010 5-year est.).
**Education:** Percent of population age 25 and over with: High school diploma (including GED) or higher: 88.7% (2006-2010 5-year est.); Bachelor's degree or higher: 16.7% (2006-2010 5-year est.); Master's degree or higher: 5.5% (2006-2010 5-year est.).
**School District(s)**
Charlotte Valley Central School District (PK-12)
    2009-10 Enrollment: 416 . . . . . . . . . . . . . . . . . . . . (607) 278-5511
**Housing:** Homeownership rate: 77.3% (2010); Median home value: $77,600 (2006-2010 5-year est.); Median contract rent: $523 per month (2006-2010 5-year est.); Median year structure built: 1978 (2006-2010 5-year est.).
**Transportation:** Commute to work: 94.5% car, 0.6% public transportation, 1.7% walk, 3.2% work from home (2006-2010 5-year est.); Travel time to work: 34.9% less than 15 minutes, 39.8% 15 to 30 minutes, 15.0% 30 to 45

minutes, 6.4% 45 to 60 minutes, 3.8% 60 minutes or more (2006-2010 5-year est.)

**DAVENPORT CENTER** (CDP). Covers a land area of 3.102 square miles and a water area of 0.040 square miles. Located at 42.44° N. Lat; 74.90° W. Long. Elevation is 1,217 feet.
**Population:** n/a (1990); n/a (2000); 349 (2010); Density: 112.5 persons per square mile (2010); Race: 98.9% White, 0.6% Black, 0.0% Asian, 0.0% American Indian/Alaska Native, 0.0% Native Hawaiian/Other Pacific Islander, 0.5% Other, 0.6% Hispanic of any race (2010); Average household size: 2.34 (2010); Median age: 44.3 (2010); Males per 100 females: 90.7 (2010); Marriage status: 15.5% never married, 45.4% now married, 4.2% widowed, 34.9% divorced (2006-2010 5-year est.); Foreign born: 0.0% (2006-2010 5-year est.); Ancestry (includes multiple ancestries): 38.2% English, 34.8% Irish, 19.3% German, 4.7% Portuguese, 4.7% Scottish (2006-2010 5-year est.).
**Economy:** Employment by occupation: 6.3% management, 0.0% professional, 3.9% services, 5.5% sales, 10.2% farming, 17.3% construction, 37.0% production (2006-2010 5-year est.).
**Income:** Per capita income: $31,039 (2006-2010 5-year est.); Median household income: $73,424 (2006-2010 5-year est.); Average household income: $66,457 (2006-2010 5-year est.); Percent of households with income of $100,000 or more: 12.8% (2006-2010 5-year est.); Poverty rate: 3.7% (2006-2010 5-year est.).
**Education:** Percent of population age 25 and over with: High school diploma (including GED) or higher: 96.6% (2006-2010 5-year est.); Bachelor's degree or higher: 17.2% (2006-2010 5-year est.); Master's degree or higher: 3.1% (2006-2010 5-year est.).
**Housing:** Homeownership rate: 74.5% (2010); Median home value: $77,100 (2006-2010 5-year est.); Median contract rent: $266 per month (2006-2010 5-year est.); Median year structure built: 1977 (2006-2010 5-year est.).
**Transportation:** Commute to work: 100.0% car, 0.0% public transportation, 0.0% walk, 0.0% work from home (2006-2010 5-year est.); Travel time to work: 0.0% less than 15 minutes, 100.0% 15 to 30 minutes, 0.0% 30 to 45 minutes, 0.0% 45 to 60 minutes, 0.0% 60 minutes or more (2006-2010 5-year est.)

**DE LANCEY** (unincorporated postal area)
Zip Code: 13752
    Covers a land area of 48.520 square miles and a water area of 1.401 square miles. Located at 42.19° N. Lat; 74.89° W. Long. Elevation is 1,309 feet. Population: 782 (2010); Density: 16.1 persons per square mile (2010); Race: 98.0% White, 0.3% Black, 0.0% Asian, 0.3% American Indian/Alaska Native, 0.0% Native Hawaiian/Other Pacific Islander, 1.4% Other, 3.1% Hispanic of any race (2010); Average household size: 2.18 (2010); Median age: 51.3 (2010); Males per 100 females: 108.5 (2010); Homeownership rate: 86.1% (2010)

**DELHI** (village). County seat. Covers a land area of 3.141 square miles and a water area of 0.050 square miles. Located at 42.27° N. Lat; 74.91° W. Long. Elevation is 1,371 feet.
**Population:** 3,064 (1990); 2,583 (2000); 3,087 (2010); Density: 982.5 persons per square mile (2010); Race: 85.0% White, 8.1% Black, 1.9% Asian, 0.4% American Indian/Alaska Native, 0.0% Native Hawaiian/Other Pacific Islander, 4.6% Other, 7.4% Hispanic of any race (2010); Average household size: 2.13 (2010); Median age: 20.9 (2010); Males per 100 females: 119.1 (2010); Marriage status: 48.3% never married, 32.7% now married, 6.7% widowed, 12.3% divorced (2006-2010 5-year est.); Foreign born: 5.0% (2006-2010 5-year est.); Ancestry (includes multiple ancestries): 18.6% German, 16.3% Irish, 15.6% Italian, 11.5% English, 6.0% Scottish (2006-2010 5-year est.).
**Economy:** Single-family building permits issued: 0 (2011); Multi-family building permits issued: 0 (2011); Employment by occupation: 8.8% management, 4.8% professional, 18.9% services, 14.5% sales, 3.1% farming, 8.4% construction, 3.4% production (2006-2010 5-year est.).
**Income:** Per capita income: $18,529 (2006-2010 5-year est.); Median household income: $37,750 (2006-2010 5-year est.); Average household income: $46,620 (2006-2010 5-year est.); Percent of households with income of $100,000 or more: 10.8% (2006-2010 5-year est.); Poverty rate: 22.6% (2006-2010 5-year est.).
**Education:** Percent of population age 25 and over with: High school diploma (including GED) or higher: 88.3% (2006-2010 5-year est.); Bachelor's degree or higher: 40.3% (2006-2010 5-year est.); Master's degree or higher: 19.2% (2006-2010 5-year est.).

## School District(s)

Delhi Central School District (KG-12)

    2009-10 Enrollment: 801 . . . . . . . . . . . . . . . . . . . . . . (607) 746-1300

### Four-year College(s)

SUNY College of Technology at Delhi (Public)

    Fall 2010 Enrollment: 2,895 . . . . . . . . . . . . . . . . (607) 746-4000

    2011-12 Tuition: In-state $6,780; Out-of-state $11,250

**Housing:** Homeownership rate: 49.9% (2010); Median home value: $153,000 (2006-2010 5-year est.); Median contract rent: $564 per month (2006-2010 5-year est.); Median year structure built: before 1940 (2006-2010 5-year est.).

**Hospitals:** O'Connor Hospital (28 beds)

**Safety:** Violent crime rate: 10.9 per 10,000 population; Property crime rate: 152.8 per 10,000 population (2010).

**Newspapers:** County Shopper (Community news; Circulation 16,400); Delaware County Times (Community news; Circulation 1,500)

**Transportation:** Commute to work: 65.8% car, 1.8% public transportation, 23.4% walk, 8.6% work from home (2006-2010 5-year est.); Travel time to work: 67.7% less than 15 minutes, 17.8% 15 to 30 minutes, 10.4% 30 to 45 minutes, 0.5% 45 to 60 minutes, 3.7% 60 minutes or more (2006-2010 5-year est.)

**Additional Information Contacts**

Delaware County Chamber of Commerce . . . . . . . . . . . . . (607) 746-2281

    http://delawarecounty.org

**DELHI** (town). Covers a land area of 64.197 square miles and a water area of 0.400 square miles. Located at 42.27° N. Lat; 74.90° W. Long. Elevation is 1,371 feet.

**History:** Shortly after the Revolutionary War, Ebenezer Foote was so influential locally and as a member of the state legislature that he was nicknamed "the Great Mogul." At the suggestions of facetious citizens the community was named for Delhi, India, the capital city of the real Great Mogul.

**Population:** 5,015 (1990); 4,629 (2000); 5,117 (2010); Density: 79.7 persons per square mile (2010); Race: 89.4% White, 5.3% Black, 1.5% Asian, 0.2% American Indian/Alaska Native, 0.0% Native Hawaiian/Other Pacific Islander, 3.6% Other, 5.0% Hispanic of any race (2010); Average household size: 2.22 (2010); Median age: 26.4 (2010); Males per 100 females: 109.8 (2010); Marriage status: 37.3% never married, 42.8% now married, 8.5% widowed, 11.5% divorced (2006-2010 5-year est.); Foreign born: 2.7% (2006-2010 5-year est.); Ancestry (includes multiple ancestries): 20.2% German, 17.8% English, 16.1% Italian, 15.8% Irish, 7.2% Scottish (2006-2010 5-year est.).

**Economy:** Single-family building permits issued: 3 (2011); Multi-family building permits issued: 0 (2011); Employment by occupation: 18.1% management, 2.2% professional, 12.7% services, 9.9% sales, 3.5% farming, 11.6% construction, 4.6% production (2006-2010 5-year est.).

**Income:** Per capita income: $24,855 (2006-2010 5-year est.); Median household income: $49,750 (2006-2010 5-year est.); Average household income: $60,473 (2006-2010 5-year est.); Percent of households with income of $100,000 or more: 16.4% (2006-2010 5-year est.); Poverty rate: 12.5% (2006-2010 5-year est.).

**Education:** Percent of population age 25 and over with: High school diploma (including GED) or higher: 89.1% (2006-2010 5-year est.); Bachelor's degree or higher: 34.8% (2006-2010 5-year est.); Master's degree or higher: 14.3% (2006-2010 5-year est.).

### School District(s)

Delhi Central School District (KG-12)

    2009-10 Enrollment: 801 . . . . . . . . . . . . . . . . . . . . (607) 746-1300

### Four-year College(s)

SUNY College of Technology at Delhi (Public)

    Fall 2010 Enrollment: 2,895 . . . . . . . . . . . . . . . . (607) 746-4000

    2011-12 Tuition: In-state $6,780; Out-of-state $11,250

**Housing:** Homeownership rate: 66.2% (2010); Median home value: $165,300 (2006-2010 5-year est.); Median contract rent: $564 per month (2006-2010 5-year est.); Median year structure built: 1950 (2006-2010 5-year est.).

**Hospitals:** O'Connor Hospital (28 beds)

**Newspapers:** County Shopper (Community news; Circulation 16,400); Delaware County Times (Community news; Circulation 1,500)

**Transportation:** Commute to work: 70.6% car, 0.8% public transportation, 13.3% walk, 15.0% work from home (2006-2010 5-year est.); Travel time to work: 58.9% less than 15 minutes, 18.8% 15 to 30 minutes, 16.1% 30 to 45 minutes, 3.8% 45 to 60 minutes, 2.4% 60 minutes or more (2006-2010 5-year est.)

**DENVER** (unincorporated postal area)

Zip Code: 12421

Covers a land area of 19.605 square miles and a water area of 0.008 square miles. Located at 42.25° N. Lat; 74.54° W. Long. Elevation is 1,631 feet. Population: 470 (2010); Density: 24.0 persons per square mile (2010); Race: 98.7% White, 0.9% Black, 0.2% Asian, 0.0% American Indian/Alaska Native, 0.0% Native Hawaiian/Other Pacific Islander, 0.2% Other, 2.6% Hispanic of any race (2010); Average household size: 2.12 (2010); Median age: 52.5 (2010); Males per 100 females: 103.5 (2010); Homeownership rate: 91.9% (2010)

**DEPOSIT** (village). Covers a land area of 1.262 square miles and a water area of 0.053 square miles. Located at 42.06° N. Lat; 75.42° W. Long. Elevation is 1,001 feet.

**Population:** 1,936 (1990); 1,699 (2000); 1,663 (2010); Density: 1,316.8 persons per square mile (2010); Race: 96.6% White, 1.6% Black, 0.1% Asian, 0.2% American Indian/Alaska Native, 0.0% Native Hawaiian/Other Pacific Islander, 1.5% Other, 2.8% Hispanic of any race (2010); Average household size: 2.45 (2010); Median age: 40.0 (2010); Males per 100 females: 87.7 (2010); Marriage status: 33.0% never married, 50.2% now married, 6.7% widowed, 10.1% divorced (2006-2010 5-year est.); Foreign born: 2.5% (2006-2010 5-year est.); Ancestry (includes multiple ancestries): 22.4% Irish, 18.6% German, 13.1% Italian, 12.9% English, 6.7% Polish (2006-2010 5-year est.).

**Economy:** Single-family building permits issued: 0 (2011); Multi-family building permits issued: 0 (2011); Employment by occupation: 7.1% management, 0.4% professional, 15.4% services, 20.1% sales, 4.8% farming, 10.2% construction, 5.4% production (2006-2010 5-year est.).

**Income:** Per capita income: $18,726 (2006-2010 5-year est.); Median household income: $33,218 (2006-2010 5-year est.); Average household income: $45,019 (2006-2010 5-year est.); Percent of households with income of $100,000 or more: 9.8% (2006-2010 5-year est.); Poverty rate: 24.8% (2006-2010 5-year est.).

**Education:** Percent of population age 25 and over with: High school diploma (including GED) or higher: 90.4% (2006-2010 5-year est.); Bachelor's degree or higher: 18.5% (2006-2010 5-year est.); Master's degree or higher: 6.8% (2006-2010 5-year est.).

### School District(s)

Deposit Central School District (PK-12)

    2009-10 Enrollment: 580 . . . . . . . . . . . . . . . . . . . . (607) 467-5380

**Housing:** Homeownership rate: 59.7% (2010); Median home value: $89,300 (2006-2010 5-year est.); Median contract rent: $465 per month (2006-2010 5-year est.); Median year structure built: before 1940 (2006-2010 5-year est.).

**Safety:** Violent crime rate: 0.0 per 10,000 population; Property crime rate: 129.3 per 10,000 population (2010).

**Newspapers:** Deposit Courier (Community news; Circulation 2,250); Towne Crier (Community news; Circulation 7,500)

**Transportation:** Commute to work: 81.9% car, 0.2% public transportation, 12.3% walk, 2.1% work from home (2006-2010 5-year est.); Travel time to work: 46.9% less than 15 minutes, 17.1% 15 to 30 minutes, 21.2% 30 to 45 minutes, 8.2% 45 to 60 minutes, 6.5% 60 minutes or more (2006-2010 5-year est.)

**DEPOSIT** (town). Covers a land area of 43.015 square miles and a water area of 1.564 square miles. Located at 42.09° N. Lat; 75.36° W. Long.

**Population:** 1,824 (1990); 1,687 (2000); 1,712 (2010); Density: 39.8 persons per square mile (2010); Race: 95.6% White, 2.3% Black, 0.2% Asian, 0.3% American Indian/Alaska Native, 0.0% Native Hawaiian/Other Pacific Islander, 1.6% Other, 2.9% Hispanic of any race (2010); Average household size: 2.41 (2010); Median age: 43.4 (2010); Males per 100 females: 91.9 (2010); Marriage status: 28.4% never married, 56.2% now married, 5.9% widowed, 9.6% divorced (2006-2010 5-year est.); Foreign born: 2.2% (2006-2010 5-year est.); Ancestry (includes multiple ancestries): 26.0% German, 22.2% English, 13.0% Irish, 8.7% Italian, 5.6% Dutch (2006-2010 5-year est.).

**Economy:** Single-family building permits issued: 3 (2011); Multi-family building permits issued: 0 (2011); Employment by occupation: 10.4% management, 0.3% professional, 15.4% services, 15.7% sales, 3.9% farming, 14.4% construction, 4.9% production (2006-2010 5-year est.).

**Income:** Per capita income: $18,893 (2006-2010 5-year est.); Median household income: $34,375 (2006-2010 5-year est.); Average household income: $45,997 (2006-2010 5-year est.); Percent of households with

income of $100,000 or more: 6.9% (2006-2010 5-year est.); Poverty rate: 18.8% (2006-2010 5-year est.).

**Education:** Percent of population age 25 and over with: High school diploma (including GED) or higher: 88.9% (2006-2010 5-year est.); Bachelor's degree or higher: 14.8% (2006-2010 5-year est.); Master's degree or higher: 5.5% (2006-2010 5-year est.).

**School District(s)**

Deposit Central School District (PK-12)

2009-10 Enrollment: 580 . . . . . . . . . . . . . . . . . . . . . . . . (607) 467-5380

**Housing:** Homeownership rate: 68.0% (2010); Median home value: $91,400 (2006-2010 5-year est.); Median contract rent: $498 per month (2006-2010 5-year est.); Median year structure built: 1953 (2006-2010 5-year est.).

**Newspapers:** Deposit Courier (Community news; Circulation 2,250); Towne Crier (Community news; Circulation 7,500)

**Transportation:** Commute to work: 89.0% car, 0.2% public transportation, 7.8% walk, 0.3% work from home (2006-2010 5-year est.); Travel time to work: 43.0% less than 15 minutes, 19.7% 15 to 30 minutes, 23.2% 30 to 45 minutes, 9.2% 45 to 60 minutes, 4.9% 60 minutes or more (2006-2010 5-year est.)

**Additional Information Contacts**

Deposit Chamber of Commerce . . . . . . . . . . . . . . . . . . (607) 467-4161
http://www.depositchamber.com

**DOWNSVILLE** (CDP). Covers a land area of 3.953 square miles and a water area of 0.079 square miles. Located at 42.08° N. Lat; 74.99° W. Long. Elevation is 1,125 feet.

**Population:** n/a (1990); n/a (2000); 617 (2010); Density: 156.1 persons per square mile (2010); Race: 97.6% White, 0.5% Black, 0.0% Asian, 0.0% American Indian/Alaska Native, 0.0% Native Hawaiian/Other Pacific Islander, 1.9% Other, 0.6% Hispanic of any race (2010); Average household size: 2.24 (2010); Median age: 43.0 (2010); Males per 100 females: 91.6 (2010); Marriage status: 29.5% never married, 58.5% now married, 6.8% widowed, 5.2% divorced (2006-2010 5-year est.); Foreign born: 0.9% (2006-2010 5-year est.); Ancestry (includes multiple ancestries): 26.1% German, 24.2% Italian, 20.0% English, 13.0% Polish, 12.9% Irish (2006-2010 5-year est.).

**Economy:** Employment by occupation: 12.2% management, 2.2% professional, 16.4% services, 13.9% sales, 4.0% farming, 13.2% construction, 1.7% production (2006-2010 5-year est.).

**Income:** Per capita income: $21,713 (2006-2010 5-year est.); Median household income: $40,893 (2006-2010 5-year est.); Average household income: $50,850 (2006-2010 5-year est.); Percent of households with income of $100,000 or more: 15.1% (2006-2010 5-year est.); Poverty rate: 16.1% (2006-2010 5-year est.).

**Education:** Percent of population age 25 and over with: High school diploma (including GED) or higher: 93.7% (2006-2010 5-year est.); Bachelor's degree or higher: 15.6% (2006-2010 5-year est.); Master's degree or higher: 3.9% (2006-2010 5-year est.).

**School District(s)**

Downsville Central School District (PK-12)

2009-10 Enrollment: 297 . . . . . . . . . . . . . . . . . . . . . . . . (607) 363-2101

**Housing:** Homeownership rate: 65.0% (2010); Median home value: $136,300 (2006-2010 5-year est.); Median contract rent: $429 per month (2006-2010 5-year est.); Median year structure built: 1943 (2006-2010 5-year est.).

**Transportation:** Commute to work: 78.6% car, 0.0% public transportation, 11.2% walk, 7.0% work from home (2006-2010 5-year est.); Travel time to work: 34.2% less than 15 minutes, 32.8% 15 to 30 minutes, 23.8% 30 to 45 minutes, 4.5% 45 to 60 minutes, 4.8% 60 minutes or more (2006-2010 5-year est.)

**EAST BRANCH** (unincorporated postal area)

Zip Code: 13756

Covers a land area of 45.878 square miles and a water area of 0.644 square miles. Located at 42.00° N. Lat; 75.10° W. Long. Elevation is 1,007 feet. Population: 613 (2010); Density: 13.4 persons per square mile (2010); Race: 98.2% White, 0.7% Black, 0.5% Asian, 0.0% American Indian/Alaska Native, 0.0% Native Hawaiian/Other Pacific Islander, 0.6% Other, 0.7% Hispanic of any race (2010); Average household size: 2.46 (2010); Median age: 48.3 (2010); Males per 100 females: 108.5 (2010); Homeownership rate: 82.7% (2010)

**EAST MEREDITH** (unincorporated postal area)

Zip Code: 13757

Covers a land area of 37.198 square miles and a water area of 0.086 square miles. Located at 42.41° N. Lat; 74.89° W. Long. Elevation is 1,401 feet. Population: 1,045 (2010); Density: 28.1 persons per square mile (2010); Race: 97.4% White, 0.9% Black, 0.3% Asian, 0.8% American Indian/Alaska Native, 0.0% Native Hawaiian/Other Pacific Islander, 0.6% Other, 2.5% Hispanic of any race (2010); Average household size: 2.39 (2010); Median age: 44.9 (2010); Males per 100 females: 96.1 (2010); Homeownership rate: 84.9% (2010)

**FISHS EDDY** (unincorporated postal area)

Zip Code: 13774

Covers a land area of 2.844 square miles and a water area of 0.149 square miles. Located at 41.96° N. Lat; 75.14° W. Long. Elevation is 984 feet. Population: 201 (2010); Density: 70.7 persons per square mile (2010); Race: 98.0% White, 1.5% Black, 0.0% Asian, 0.0% American Indian/Alaska Native, 0.0% Native Hawaiian/Other Pacific Islander, 0.5% Other, 1.5% Hispanic of any race (2010); Average household size: 2.31 (2010); Median age: 47.8 (2010); Males per 100 females: 123.3 (2010); Homeownership rate: 83.9% (2010)

**FLEISCHMANNS** (village). Covers a land area of 0.655 square miles and a water area of 0.014 square miles. Located at 42.15° N. Lat; 74.53° W. Long. Elevation is 1,499 feet.

**Population:** 351 (1990); 351 (2000); 351 (2010); Density: 535.8 persons per square mile (2010); Race: 70.1% White, 0.6% Black, 0.9% Asian, 2.3% American Indian/Alaska Native, 0.0% Native Hawaiian/Other Pacific Islander, 26.1% Other, 36.5% Hispanic of any race (2010); Average household size: 2.56 (2010); Median age: 35.7 (2010); Males per 100 females: 102.9 (2010); Marriage status: 34.8% never married, 48.1% now married, 4.4% widowed, 12.7% divorced (2006-2010 5-year est.); Foreign born: 18.0% (2006-2010 5-year est.); Ancestry (includes multiple ancestries): 21.8% Italian, 21.4% German, 13.6% English, 10.2% Irish, 2.9% Yugoslavian (2006-2010 5-year est.).

**Economy:** Single-family building permits issued: 0 (2011); Multi-family building permits issued: 0 (2011); Employment by occupation: 9.8% management, 0.0% professional, 11.0% services, 4.9% sales, 0.0% farming, 7.3% construction, 9.8% production (2006-2010 5-year est.).

**Income:** Per capita income: $14,468 (2006-2010 5-year est.); Median household income: $27,083 (2006-2010 5-year est.); Average household income: $35,590 (2006-2010 5-year est.); Percent of households with income of $100,000 or more: 7.2% (2006-2010 5-year est.); Poverty rate: 30.1% (2006-2010 5-year est.).

**Education:** Percent of population age 25 and over with: High school diploma (including GED) or higher: 72.0% (2006-2010 5-year est.); Bachelor's degree or higher: 21.0% (2006-2010 5-year est.); Master's degree or higher: 7.7% (2006-2010 5-year est.).

**Housing:** Homeownership rate: 56.2% (2010); Median home value: $216,700 (2006-2010 5-year est.); Median contract rent: $575 per month (2006-2010 5-year est.); Median year structure built: before 1940 (2006-2010 5-year est.).

**Transportation:** Commute to work: 87.8% car, 4.9% public transportation, 1.2% walk, 6.1% work from home (2006-2010 5-year est.); Travel time to work: 53.2% less than 15 minutes, 16.9% 15 to 30 minutes, 16.9% 30 to 45 minutes, 5.2% 45 to 60 minutes, 7.8% 60 minutes or more (2006-2010 5-year est.)

**FRANKLIN** (village). Covers a land area of 0.338 square miles and a water area of 0.006 square miles. Located at 42.34° N. Lat; 75.16° W. Long. Elevation is 1,234 feet.

**Population:** 409 (1990); 402 (2000); 374 (2010); Density: 1,103.7 persons per square mile (2010); Race: 96.3% White, 1.1% Black, 0.3% Asian, 0.0% American Indian/Alaska Native, 0.0% Native Hawaiian/Other Pacific Islander, 2.3% Other, 1.6% Hispanic of any race (2010); Average household size: 2.44 (2010); Median age: 42.0 (2010); Males per 100 females: 93.8 (2010); Marriage status: 23.1% never married, 60.7% now married, 6.4% widowed, 9.8% divorced (2006-2010 5-year est.); Foreign born: 6.6% (2006-2010 5-year est.); Ancestry (includes multiple ancestries): 31.6% Irish, 28.1% German, 17.0% English, 9.3% Dutch, 6.0% Polish (2006-2010 5-year est.).

**Economy:** Single-family building permits issued: 0 (2011); Multi-family building permits issued: 0 (2011); Employment by occupation: 10.6% management, 1.9% professional, 13.1% services, 26.9% sales, 0.0% farming, 13.8% construction, 10.0% production (2006-2010 5-year est.).

**Income:** Per capita income: $23,427 (2006-2010 5-year est.); Median household income: $28,125 (2006-2010 5-year est.); Average household

income: $47,357 (2006-2010 5-year est.); Percent of households with income of $100,000 or more: 7.1% (2006-2010 5-year est.); Poverty rate: 33.7% (2006-2010 5-year est.).

**Education:** Percent of population age 25 and over with: High school diploma (including GED) or higher: 94.4% (2006-2010 5-year est.); Bachelor's degree or higher: 27.6% (2006-2010 5-year est.); Master's degree or higher: 11.6% (2006-2010 5-year est.).

**School District(s)**

Franklin Central School District (PK-12)

   2009-10 Enrollment: 271 . . . . . . . . . . . . . . . . . . . . . . (607) 829-3551

**Housing:** Homeownership rate: 66.6% (2010); Median home value: $150,500 (2006-2010 5-year est.); Median contract rent: $436 per month (2006-2010 5-year est.); Median year structure built: before 1940 (2006-2010 5-year est.).

**Transportation:** Commute to work: 63.1% car, 1.9% public transportation, 17.5% walk, 17.5% work from home (2006-2010 5-year est.); Travel time to work: 34.1% less than 15 minutes, 42.4% 15 to 30 minutes, 18.2% 30 to 45 minutes, 1.5% 45 to 60 minutes, 3.8% 60 minutes or more (2006-2010 5-year est.)

**FRANKLIN** (town). Covers a land area of 81.248 square miles and a water area of 0.278 square miles. Located at 42.33° N. Lat; 75.11° W. Long. Elevation is 1,234 feet.

**Population:** 2,471 (1990); 2,621 (2000); 2,411 (2010); Density: 29.7 persons per square mile (2010); Race: 96.0% White, 0.9% Black, 0.6% Asian, 0.2% American Indian/Alaska Native, 0.1% Native Hawaiian/Other Pacific Islander, 2.2% Other, 2.1% Hispanic of any race (2010); Average household size: 2.40 (2010); Median age: 46.7 (2010); Males per 100 females: 102.3 (2010); Marriage status: 23.1% never married, 62.4% now married, 5.4% widowed, 9.2% divorced (2006-2010 5-year est.); Foreign born: 6.3% (2006-2010 5-year est.); Ancestry (includes multiple ancestries): 22.4% German, 17.9% Irish, 13.8% English, 11.7% Italian, 7.5% French (2006-2010 5-year est.).

**Economy:** Employment by occupation: 11.9% management, 3.2% professional, 9.2% services, 19.8% sales, 1.8% farming, 11.9% construction, 5.1% production (2006-2010 5-year est.).

**Income:** Per capita income: $25,100 (2006-2010 5-year est.); Median household income: $50,781 (2006-2010 5-year est.); Average household income: $59,176 (2006-2010 5-year est.); Percent of households with income of $100,000 or more: 16.2% (2006-2010 5-year est.); Poverty rate: 10.9% (2006-2010 5-year est.).

**Education:** Percent of population age 25 and over with: High school diploma (including GED) or higher: 93.3% (2006-2010 5-year est.); Bachelor's degree or higher: 21.8% (2006-2010 5-year est.); Master's degree or higher: 9.5% (2006-2010 5-year est.).

**School District(s)**

Franklin Central School District (PK-12)

   2009-10 Enrollment: 271 . . . . . . . . . . . . . . . . . . . . . . (607) 829-3551

**Housing:** Homeownership rate: 82.5% (2010); Median home value: $141,100 (2006-2010 5-year est.); Median contract rent: $446 per month (2006-2010 5-year est.); Median year structure built: 1965 (2006-2010 5-year est.).

**Transportation:** Commute to work: 78.0% car, 0.6% public transportation, 12.6% walk, 8.3% work from home (2006-2010 5-year est.); Travel time to work: 30.6% less than 15 minutes, 43.0% 15 to 30 minutes, 14.0% 30 to 45 minutes, 2.4% 45 to 60 minutes, 10.0% 60 minutes or more (2006-2010 5-year est.)

**Additional Information Contacts**

Town of Franklin . . . . . . . . . . . . . . . . . . . . . . . . . . . . . (518) 891-2189
   http://townoffranklin.com

**GRAND GORGE** (unincorporated postal area)

Zip Code: 12434

   Covers a land area of 13.768 square miles and a water area of 0.427 square miles. Located at 42.36° N. Lat; 74.50° W. Long. Elevation is 1,401 feet. Population: 751 (2010); Density: 54.5 persons per square mile (2010); Race: 97.1% White, 1.6% Black, 0.3% Asian, 0.1% American Indian/Alaska Native, 0.0% Native Hawaiian/Other Pacific Islander, 0.9% Other, 1.9% Hispanic of any race (2010); Average household size: 2.26 (2010); Median age: 44.6 (2010); Males per 100 females: 96.1 (2010); Homeownership rate: 68.4% (2010)

**HALCOTTSVILLE** (unincorporated postal area)

Zip Code: 12438

Covers a land area of 0.439 square miles and a water area of 0.041 square miles. Located at 42.20° N. Lat; 74.60° W. Long. Elevation is 1,401 feet. Population: 59 (2010); Density: 134.4 persons per square mile (2010); Race: 98.3% White, 1.7% Black, 0.0% Asian, 0.0% American Indian/Alaska Native, 0.0% Native Hawaiian/Other Pacific Islander, 0.0% Other, 3.4% Hispanic of any race (2010); Average household size: 2.27 (2010); Median age: 50.4 (2010); Males per 100 females: 84.4 (2010); Homeownership rate: 88.5% (2010)

**HAMDEN** (town). Covers a land area of 59.930 square miles and a water area of 0.269 square miles. Located at 42.20° N. Lat; 74.98° W. Long. Elevation is 1,286 feet.

**Population:** 1,144 (1990); 1,280 (2000); 1,323 (2010); Density: 22.1 persons per square mile (2010); Race: 97.4% White, 0.5% Black, 0.2% Asian, 0.7% American Indian/Alaska Native, 0.0% Native Hawaiian/Other Pacific Islander, 1.2% Other, 3.7% Hispanic of any race (2010); Average household size: 2.32 (2010); Median age: 47.4 (2010); Males per 100 females: 100.2 (2010); Marriage status: 20.5% never married, 56.7% now married, 8.8% widowed, 14.0% divorced (2006-2010 5-year est.); Foreign born: 3.6% (2006-2010 5-year est.); Ancestry (includes multiple ancestries): 26.0% German, 21.7% Irish, 15.7% English, 10.4% Italian, 7.8% French (2006-2010 5-year est.).

**Economy:** Single-family building permits issued: 1 (2011); Multi-family building permits issued: 0 (2011); Employment by occupation: 9.4% management, 1.3% professional, 7.5% services, 17.8% sales, 2.1% farming, 16.3% construction, 8.6% production (2006-2010 5-year est.).

**Income:** Per capita income: $24,296 (2006-2010 5-year est.); Median household income: $38,125 (2006-2010 5-year est.); Average household income: $51,864 (2006-2010 5-year est.); Percent of households with income of $100,000 or more: 9.7% (2006-2010 5-year est.); Poverty rate: 13.2% (2006-2010 5-year est.).

**Education:** Percent of population age 25 and over with: High school diploma (including GED) or higher: 93.0% (2006-2010 5-year est.); Bachelor's degree or higher: 16.6% (2006-2010 5-year est.); Master's degree or higher: 6.3% (2006-2010 5-year est.).

**Housing:** Homeownership rate: 81.2% (2010); Median home value: $163,300 (2006-2010 5-year est.); Median contract rent: $505 per month (2006-2010 5-year est.); Median year structure built: 1957 (2006-2010 5-year est.).

**Transportation:** Commute to work: 88.3% car, 2.5% public transportation, 3.5% walk, 5.0% work from home (2006-2010 5-year est.); Travel time to work: 40.9% less than 15 minutes, 39.5% 15 to 30 minutes, 11.2% 30 to 45 minutes, 5.1% 45 to 60 minutes, 3.3% 60 minutes or more (2006-2010 5-year est.)

**HANCOCK** (village). Covers a land area of 1.501 square miles and a water area of 0.140 square miles. Located at 41.95° N. Lat; 75.28° W. Long. Elevation is 922 feet.

**Population:** 1,330 (1990); 1,189 (2000); 1,031 (2010); Density: 686.5 persons per square mile (2010); Race: 95.2% White, 0.9% Black, 0.8% Asian, 0.6% American Indian/Alaska Native, 0.0% Native Hawaiian/Other Pacific Islander, 2.5% Other, 5.3% Hispanic of any race (2010); Average household size: 2.19 (2010); Median age: 46.5 (2010); Males per 100 females: 97.5 (2010); Marriage status: 23.7% never married, 54.1% now married, 10.5% widowed, 11.7% divorced (2006-2010 5-year est.); Foreign born: 3.6% (2006-2010 5-year est.); Ancestry (includes multiple ancestries): 26.5% Irish, 22.9% German, 18.9% English, 13.3% Italian, 6.4% French (2006-2010 5-year est.).

**Economy:** Single-family building permits issued: 0 (2011); Multi-family building permits issued: 0 (2011); Employment by occupation: 9.0% management, 0.0% professional, 13.3% services, 18.3% sales, 5.4% farming, 9.0% construction, 5.0% production (2006-2010 5-year est.).

**Income:** Per capita income: $25,191 (2006-2010 5-year est.); Median household income: $33,438 (2006-2010 5-year est.); Average household income: $46,402 (2006-2010 5-year est.); Percent of households with income of $100,000 or more: 15.0% (2006-2010 5-year est.); Poverty rate: 15.1% (2006-2010 5-year est.).

**Education:** Percent of population age 25 and over with: High school diploma (including GED) or higher: 89.3% (2006-2010 5-year est.); Bachelor's degree or higher: 13.1% (2006-2010 5-year est.); Master's degree or higher: 7.9% (2006-2010 5-year est.).

**School District(s)**

Hancock Central School District (PK-12)

   2009-10 Enrollment: 450 . . . . . . . . . . . . . . . . . . . . . . (607) 637-1301

**Housing:** Homeownership rate: 56.0% (2010); Median home value: $123,400 (2006-2010 5-year est.); Median contract rent: $397 per month (2006-2010 5-year est.); Median year structure built: 1943 (2006-2010 5-year est.).

**Safety:** Violent crime rate: 9.5 per 10,000 population; Property crime rate: 38.1 per 10,000 population (2010).

**Newspapers:** Herald (Local news; Circulation 2,300)

**Transportation:** Commute to work: 82.2% car, 0.0% public transportation, 14.2% walk, 3.6% work from home (2006-2010 5-year est.); Travel time to work: 50.1% less than 15 minutes, 25.3% 15 to 30 minutes, 12.6% 30 to 45 minutes, 9.1% 45 to 60 minutes, 2.8% 60 minutes or more (2006-2010 5-year est.)

**Additional Information Contacts**

Hancock Area Chamber of Commerce . . . . . . . . . . . . . . . . (607) 637-4756
  http://www.hancockchamber.org

**HANCOCK** (town). Covers a land area of 158.821 square miles and a water area of 2.994 square miles. Located at 41.95° N. Lat; 75.18° W. Long. Elevation is 922 feet.

**Population:** 3,384 (1990); 3,449 (2000); 3,224 (2010); Density: 20.3 persons per square mile (2010); Race: 96.5% White, 0.8% Black, 0.6% Asian, 0.2% American Indian/Alaska Native, 0.0% Native Hawaiian/Other Pacific Islander, 1.9% Other, 3.4% Hispanic of any race (2010); Average household size: 2.28 (2010); Median age: 46.4 (2010); Males per 100 females: 110.3 (2010); Marriage status: 25.0% never married, 53.9% now married, 9.3% widowed, 11.8% divorced (2006-2010 5-year est.); Foreign born: 2.5% (2006-2010 5-year est.); Ancestry (includes multiple ancestries): 32.6% German, 26.1% Irish, 15.1% Italian, 12.6% English, 8.0% Dutch (2006-2010 5-year est.).

**Economy:** Single-family building permits issued: 3 (2011); Multi-family building permits issued: 0 (2011); Employment by occupation: 8.7% management, 1.0% professional, 15.1% services, 23.8% sales, 1.7% farming, 9.0% construction, 4.9% production (2006-2010 5-year est.).

**Income:** Per capita income: $23,292 (2006-2010 5-year est.); Median household income: $36,743 (2006-2010 5-year est.); Average household income: $51,444 (2006-2010 5-year est.); Percent of households with income of $100,000 or more: 10.8% (2006-2010 5-year est.); Poverty rate: 13.1% (2006-2010 5-year est.).

**Education:** Percent of population age 25 and over with: High school diploma (including GED) or higher: 84.2% (2006-2010 5-year est.); Bachelor's degree or higher: 12.7% (2006-2010 5-year est.); Master's degree or higher: 6.5% (2006-2010 5-year est.).

**School District(s)**

Hancock Central School District (PK-12)

  2009-10 Enrollment: 450 . . . . . . . . . . . . . . . . . . . . . . . . (607) 637-1301

**Housing:** Homeownership rate: 74.4% (2010); Median home value: $143,400 (2006-2010 5-year est.); Median contract rent: $412 per month (2006-2010 5-year est.); Median year structure built: 1966 (2006-2010 5-year est.).

**Newspapers:** Herald (Local news; Circulation 2,300)

**Transportation:** Commute to work: 89.3% car, 0.8% public transportation, 7.1% walk, 2.8% work from home (2006-2010 5-year est.); Travel time to work: 47.3% less than 15 minutes, 27.6% 15 to 30 minutes, 13.1% 30 to 45 minutes, 4.7% 45 to 60 minutes, 7.3% 60 minutes or more (2006-2010 5-year est.)

**HARPERSFIELD** (town). Covers a land area of 42.020 square miles and a water area of 0.267 square miles. Located at 42.44° N. Lat; 74.70° W. Long. Elevation is 1,667 feet.

**Population:** 1,450 (1990); 1,603 (2000); 1,577 (2010); Density: 37.5 persons per square mile (2010); Race: 96.1% White, 1.3% Black, 0.5% Asian, 0.3% American Indian/Alaska Native, 0.0% Native Hawaiian/Other Pacific Islander, 1.8% Other, 3.6% Hispanic of any race (2010); Average household size: 2.40 (2010); Median age: 48.8 (2010); Males per 100 females: 96.4 (2010); Marriage status: 23.4% never married, 47.8% now married, 19.5% widowed, 9.4% divorced (2006-2010 5-year est.); Foreign born: 5.2% (2006-2010 5-year est.); Ancestry (includes multiple ancestries): 33.7% German, 17.7% Irish, 12.1% English, 11.8% Italian, 8.5% Dutch (2006-2010 5-year est.).

**Economy:** Single-family building permits issued: 1 (2011); Multi-family building permits issued: 0 (2011); Employment by occupation: 7.6% management, 2.8% professional, 11.2% services, 12.2% sales, 1.7% farming, 12.4% construction, 8.9% production (2006-2010 5-year est.).

**Income:** Per capita income: $21,844 (2006-2010 5-year est.); Median household income: $50,444 (2006-2010 5-year est.); Average household

income: $56,389 (2006-2010 5-year est.); Percent of households with income of $100,000 or more: 7.9% (2006-2010 5-year est.); Poverty rate: 9.4% (2006-2010 5-year est.).

**Education:** Percent of population age 25 and over with: High school diploma (including GED) or higher: 82.3% (2006-2010 5-year est.); Bachelor's degree or higher: 19.2% (2006-2010 5-year est.); Master's degree or higher: 6.7% (2006-2010 5-year est.).

**Housing:** Homeownership rate: 76.4% (2010); Median home value: $130,400 (2006-2010 5-year est.); Median contract rent: $467 per month (2006-2010 5-year est.); Median year structure built: 1964 (2006-2010 5-year est.).

**Transportation:** Commute to work: 80.8% car, 0.5% public transportation, 7.4% walk, 10.1% work from home (2006-2010 5-year est.); Travel time to work: 37.1% less than 15 minutes, 31.9% 15 to 30 minutes, 22.4% 30 to 45 minutes, 5.7% 45 to 60 minutes, 2.9% 60 minutes or more (2006-2010 5-year est.)

**HOBART** (village). Covers a land area of 0.497 square miles and a water area of 0.006 square miles. Located at 42.37° N. Lat; 74.66° W. Long. Elevation is 1,650 feet.

**Population:** 385 (1990); 390 (2000); 441 (2010); Density: 885.8 persons per square mile (2010); Race: 95.5% White, 2.5% Black, 0.2% Asian, 0.2% American Indian/Alaska Native, 0.0% Native Hawaiian/Other Pacific Islander, 1.6% Other, 2.7% Hispanic of any race (2010); Average household size: 2.41 (2010); Median age: 38.4 (2010); Males per 100 females: 106.1 (2010); Marriage status: 25.9% never married, 62.9% now married, 3.5% widowed, 7.7% divorced (2006-2010 5-year est.); Foreign born: 6.0% (2006-2010 5-year est.); Ancestry (includes multiple ancestries): 31.6% Irish, 27.5% German, 14.0% English, 9.1% Dutch, 8.3% Scottish (2006-2010 5-year est.).

**Economy:** Single-family building permits issued: 0 (2011); Multi-family building permits issued: 0 (2011); Employment by occupation: 7.4% management, 0.0% professional, 12.9% services, 3.9% sales, 0.0% farming, 19.5% construction, 14.1% production (2006-2010 5-year est.).

**Income:** Per capita income: $30,586 (2006-2010 5-year est.); Median household income: $51,705 (2006-2010 5-year est.); Average household income: $71,951 (2006-2010 5-year est.); Percent of households with income of $100,000 or more: 21.5% (2006-2010 5-year est.); Poverty rate: 5.0% (2006-2010 5-year est.).

**Education:** Percent of population age 25 and over with: High school diploma (including GED) or higher: 89.6% (2006-2010 5-year est.); Bachelor's degree or higher: 15.7% (2006-2010 5-year est.); Master's degree or higher: 8.5% (2006-2010 5-year est.).

**Housing:** Homeownership rate: 66.1% (2010); Median home value: $95,600 (2006-2010 5-year est.); Median contract rent: $468 per month (2006-2010 5-year est.); Median year structure built: before 1940 (2006-2010 5-year est.).

**Transportation:** Commute to work: 77.7% car, 2.0% public transportation, 9.4% walk, 10.9% work from home (2006-2010 5-year est.); Travel time to work: 59.6% less than 15 minutes, 18.9% 15 to 30 minutes, 7.0% 30 to 45 minutes, 1.8% 45 to 60 minutes, 12.7% 60 minutes or more (2006-2010 5-year est.)

**KORTRIGHT** (town). Covers a land area of 62.450 square miles and a water area of 0.182 square miles. Located at 42.40° N. Lat; 74.78° W. Long.

**Population:** 1,410 (1990); 1,633 (2000); 1,675 (2010); Density: 26.8 persons per square mile (2010); Race: 93.9% White, 2.6% Black, 0.9% Asian, 0.4% American Indian/Alaska Native, 0.0% Native Hawaiian/Other Pacific Islander, 2.2% Other, 3.9% Hispanic of any race (2010); Average household size: 2.40 (2010); Median age: 45.7 (2010); Males per 100 females: 107.8 (2010); Marriage status: 30.9% never married, 57.3% now married, 5.9% widowed, 5.9% divorced (2006-2010 5-year est.); Foreign born: 8.4% (2006-2010 5-year est.); Ancestry (includes multiple ancestries): 24.0% German, 22.8% English, 22.3% Irish, 9.5% Italian, 5.4% Dutch (2006-2010 5-year est.).

**Economy:** Single-family building permits issued: 7 (2011); Multi-family building permits issued: 0 (2011); Employment by occupation: 10.3% management, 0.5% professional, 8.3% services, 15.1% sales, 7.6% farming, 20.1% construction, 7.8% production (2006-2010 5-year est.).

**Income:** Per capita income: $20,090 (2006-2010 5-year est.); Median household income: $43,906 (2006-2010 5-year est.); Average household income: $50,868 (2006-2010 5-year est.); Percent of households with income of $100,000 or more: 11.3% (2006-2010 5-year est.); Poverty rate: 9.5% (2006-2010 5-year est.).

**Education:** Percent of population age 25 and over with: High school diploma (including GED) or higher: 85.7% (2006-2010 5-year est.); Bachelor's degree or higher: 16.1% (2006-2010 5-year est.); Master's degree or higher: 3.7% (2006-2010 5-year est.).
**Housing:** Homeownership rate: 81.0% (2010); Median home value: $128,000 (2006-2010 5-year est.); Median contract rent: $533 per month (2006-2010 5-year est.); Median year structure built: 1980 (2006-2010 5-year est.).
**Transportation:** Commute to work: 84.5% car, 1.9% public transportation, 5.3% walk, 8.3% work from home (2006-2010 5-year est.); Travel time to work: 33.3% less than 15 minutes, 40.6% 15 to 30 minutes, 21.3% 30 to 45 minutes, 2.6% 45 to 60 minutes, 2.1% 60 minutes or more (2006-2010 5-year est.)

## MARGARETVILLE (village).
Covers a land area of 0.684 square miles and a water area of 0.018 square miles. Located at 42.14° N. Lat; 74.65° W. Long. Elevation is 1,316 feet.
**Population:** 639 (1990); 643 (2000); 596 (2010); Density: 871.0 persons per square mile (2010); Race: 92.3% White, 0.8% Black, 4.7% Asian, 1.2% American Indian/Alaska Native, 0.0% Native Hawaiian/Other Pacific Islander, 1.0% Other, 2.9% Hispanic of any race (2010); Average household size: 1.86 (2010); Median age: 57.7 (2010); Males per 100 females: 86.8 (2010); Marriage status: 34.5% never married, 47.8% now married, 11.7% widowed, 6.0% divorced (2006-2010 5-year est.); Foreign born: 9.1% (2006-2010 5-year est.); Ancestry (includes multiple ancestries): 31.0% German, 25.0% Irish, 13.2% Italian, 10.4% English, 9.8% Norwegian (2006-2010 5-year est.).
**Economy:** Single-family building permits issued: 0 (2011); Multi-family building permits issued: 0 (2011); Employment by occupation: 8.7% management, 0.0% professional, 9.6% services, 10.4% sales, 4.3% farming, 23.0% construction, 4.8% production (2006-2010 5-year est.).
**Income:** Per capita income: $24,723 (2006-2010 5-year est.); Median household income: $45,625 (2006-2010 5-year est.); Average household income: $54,115 (2006-2010 5-year est.); Percent of households with income of $100,000 or more: 8.0% (2006-2010 5-year est.); Poverty rate: 15.7% (2006-2010 5-year est.).
**Education:** Percent of population age 25 and over with: High school diploma (including GED) or higher: 78.1% (2006-2010 5-year est.); Bachelor's degree or higher: 15.7% (2006-2010 5-year est.); Master's degree or higher: 6.4% (2006-2010 5-year est.).

### School District(s)
Margaretville Central School District (PK-12)
    2009-10 Enrollment: 469 . . . . . . . . . . . . . . . . (845) 586-2647
**Housing:** Homeownership rate: 58.7% (2010); Median home value: $161,100 (2006-2010 5-year est.); Median contract rent: $459 per month (2006-2010 5-year est.); Median year structure built: before 1940 (2006-2010 5-year est.).
**Hospitals:** Margaretville Memorial Hospital (15 beds)
**Transportation:** Commute to work: 71.1% car, 0.0% public transportation, 18.4% walk, 8.8% work from home (2006-2010 5-year est.); Travel time to work: 66.3% less than 15 minutes, 18.3% 15 to 30 minutes, 3.4% 30 to 45 minutes, 1.9% 45 to 60 minutes, 10.1% 60 minutes or more (2006-2010 5-year est.)
**Additional Information Contacts**
Central Catskills Chamber of Commerce. . . . . . . . . . . (845) 586-3300
    http://centralcatskills.com

## MASONVILLE (town).
Covers a land area of 54.264 square miles and a water area of 0.179 square miles. Located at 42.22° N. Lat; 75.34° W. Long. Elevation is 1,293 feet.
**Population:** 1,389 (1990); 1,405 (2000); 1,320 (2010); Density: 24.3 persons per square mile (2010); Race: 97.3% White, 0.8% Black, 0.3% Asian, 0.0% American Indian/Alaska Native, 0.0% Native Hawaiian/Other Pacific Islander, 1.6% Other, 1.3% Hispanic of any race (2010); Average household size: 2.40 (2010); Median age: 45.5 (2010); Males per 100 females: 107.9 (2010); Marriage status: 22.6% never married, 62.2% now married, 6.4% widowed, 8.7% divorced (2006-2010 5-year est.); Foreign born: 7.1% (2006-2010 5-year est.); Ancestry (includes multiple ancestries): 22.2% Irish, 21.2% German, 13.9% English, 7.0% Italian, 6.5% Scottish (2006-2010 5-year est.).
**Economy:** Single-family building permits issued: 7 (2011); Multi-family building permits issued: 0 (2011); Employment by occupation: 5.2% management, 1.3% professional, 13.4% services, 9.5% sales, 8.7% farming, 14.4% construction, 8.8% production (2006-2010 5-year est.).

**Income:** Per capita income: $21,458 (2006-2010 5-year est.); Median household income: $48,971 (2006-2010 5-year est.); Average household income: $51,312 (2006-2010 5-year est.); Percent of households with income of $100,000 or more: 10.2% (2006-2010 5-year est.); Poverty rate: 11.8% (2006-2010 5-year est.).
**Education:** Percent of population age 25 and over with: High school diploma (including GED) or higher: 79.9% (2006-2010 5-year est.); Bachelor's degree or higher: 14.9% (2006-2010 5-year est.); Master's degree or higher: 3.9% (2006-2010 5-year est.).
**Housing:** Homeownership rate: 82.9% (2010); Median home value: $92,100 (2006-2010 5-year est.); Median contract rent: $411 per month (2006-2010 5-year est.); Median year structure built: 1970 (2006-2010 5-year est.).
**Transportation:** Commute to work: 92.2% car, 1.7% public transportation, 3.3% walk, 2.8% work from home (2006-2010 5-year est.); Travel time to work: 35.6% less than 15 minutes, 36.1% 15 to 30 minutes, 15.6% 30 to 45 minutes, 4.6% 45 to 60 minutes, 8.0% 60 minutes or more (2006-2010 5-year est.)

## MEREDITH (town).
Covers a land area of 58.101 square miles and a water area of 0.213 square miles. Located at 42.36° N. Lat; 74.93° W. Long. Elevation is 2,169 feet.
**Population:** 1,513 (1990); 1,588 (2000); 1,529 (2010); Density: 26.3 persons per square mile (2010); Race: 95.2% White, 0.7% Black, 1.5% Asian, 0.5% American Indian/Alaska Native, 0.1% Native Hawaiian/Other Pacific Islander, 2.0% Other, 1.9% Hispanic of any race (2010); Average household size: 2.40 (2010); Median age: 46.9 (2010); Males per 100 females: 99.6 (2010); Marriage status: 26.8% never married, 55.4% now married, 8.3% widowed, 9.5% divorced (2006-2010 5-year est.); Foreign born: 7.2% (2006-2010 5-year est.); Ancestry (includes multiple ancestries): 21.4% Irish, 18.9% German, 14.7% English, 10.4% Italian, 6.9% Scottish (2006-2010 5-year est.).
**Economy:** Single-family building permits issued: 0 (2011); Multi-family building permits issued: 0 (2011); Employment by occupation: 15.0% management, 1.7% professional, 4.9% services, 17.2% sales, 0.9% farming, 14.6% construction, 3.7% production (2006-2010 5-year est.).
**Income:** Per capita income: $27,554 (2006-2010 5-year est.); Median household income: $56,250 (2006-2010 5-year est.); Average household income: $66,091 (2006-2010 5-year est.); Percent of households with income of $100,000 or more: 10.8% (2006-2010 5-year est.); Poverty rate: 9.9% (2006-2010 5-year est.).
**Education:** Percent of population age 25 and over with: High school diploma (including GED) or higher: 91.0% (2006-2010 5-year est.); Bachelor's degree or higher: 34.5% (2006-2010 5-year est.); Master's degree or higher: 14.3% (2006-2010 5-year est.).
**Housing:** Homeownership rate: 84.6% (2010); Median home value: $188,500 (2006-2010 5-year est.); Median contract rent: $505 per month (2006-2010 5-year est.); Median year structure built: 1974 (2006-2010 5-year est.).
**Transportation:** Commute to work: 83.7% car, 0.5% public transportation, 2.0% walk, 13.8% work from home (2006-2010 5-year est.); Travel time to work: 27.6% less than 15 minutes, 41.6% 15 to 30 minutes, 22.6% 30 to 45 minutes, 5.0% 45 to 60 minutes, 3.2% 60 minutes or more (2006-2010 5-year est.)

## MERIDALE (unincorporated postal area)
Zip Code: 13806
    Covers a land area of 3.095 square miles and a water area of 0.004 square miles. Located at 42.37° N. Lat; 74.95° W. Long. Elevation is 1,778 feet. Population: 205 (2010); Density: 66.2 persons per square mile (2010); Race: 97.6% White, 0.0% Black, 1.5% Asian, 0.5% American Indian/Alaska Native, 0.5% Native Hawaiian/Other Pacific Islander, 0.0% Other, 1.5% Hispanic of any race (2010); Average household size: 2.63 (2010); Median age: 48.3 (2010); Males per 100 females: 97.1 (2010); Homeownership rate: 78.2% (2010)

## MIDDLETOWN (town).
Covers a land area of 96.674 square miles and a water area of 0.619 square miles. Located at 42.16° N. Lat; 74.62° W. Long.
**Population:** 3,406 (1990); 4,051 (2000); 3,750 (2010); Density: 38.8 persons per square mile (2010); Race: 90.8% White, 0.8% Black, 1.5% Asian, 0.7% American Indian/Alaska Native, 0.1% Native Hawaiian/Other Pacific Islander, 6.1% Other, 8.4% Hispanic of any race (2010); Average household size: 2.15 (2010); Median age: 50.4 (2010); Males per 100 females: 96.7 (2010); Marriage status: 23.3% never married, 63.2% now

married, 4.5% widowed, 8.9% divorced (2006-2010 5-year est.); Foreign born: 9.7% (2006-2010 5-year est.); Ancestry (includes multiple ancestries): 34.4% German, 20.1% Irish, 13.7% English, 10.1% Italian, 7.2% Scottish (2006-2010 5-year est.).

**Economy:** Single-family building permits issued: 2 (2011); Multi-family building permits issued: 0 (2011); Employment by occupation: 13.4% management, 2.6% professional, 14.3% services, 12.9% sales, 2.1% farming, 10.7% construction, 4.4% production (2006-2010 5-year est.).

**Income:** Per capita income: $22,245 (2006-2010 5-year est.); Median household income: $45,461 (2006-2010 5-year est.); Average household income: $53,354 (2006-2010 5-year est.); Percent of households with income of $100,000 or more: 11.3% (2006-2010 5-year est.); Poverty rate: 16.3% (2006-2010 5-year est.).

**Education:** Percent of population age 25 and over with: High school diploma (including GED) or higher: 89.4% (2006-2010 5-year est.); Bachelor's degree or higher: 19.3% (2006-2010 5-year est.); Master's degree or higher: 4.7% (2006-2010 5-year est.).

**Housing:** Homeownership rate: 73.5% (2010); Median home value: $213,200 (2006-2010 5-year est.); Median contract rent: $476 per month (2006-2010 5-year est.); Median year structure built: 1968 (2006-2010 5-year est.).

**Transportation:** Commute to work: 85.1% car, 0.2% public transportation, 4.4% walk, 8.0% work from home (2006-2010 5-year est.); Travel time to work: 60.0% less than 15 minutes, 13.7% 15 to 30 minutes, 15.6% 30 to 45 minutes, 1.7% 45 to 60 minutes, 9.0% 60 minutes or more (2006-2010 5-year est.)

## NEW KINGSTON (unincorporated postal area)
Zip Code: 12459

Covers a land area of 7.608 square miles and a water area of 0.006 square miles. Located at 42.24° N. Lat; 74.67° W. Long. Elevation is 1,686 feet. Population: 161 (2010); Density: 21.2 persons per square mile (2010); Race: 95.7% White, 0.6% Black, 1.2% Asian, 0.0% American Indian/Alaska Native, 0.0% Native Hawaiian/Other Pacific Islander, 2.5% Other, 1.9% Hispanic of any race (2010); Average household size: 1.89 (2010); Median age: 55.7 (2010); Males per 100 females: 103.8 (2010); Homeownership rate: 89.4% (2010)

## ROXBURY (town). Covers a land area of 87.114 square miles and a water area of 0.490 square miles. Located at 42.30° N. Lat; 74.52° W. Long. Elevation is 1,493 feet.

**Population:** 2,388 (1990); 2,509 (2000); 2,502 (2010); Density: 28.7 persons per square mile (2010); Race: 97.8% White, 0.7% Black, 0.2% Asian, 0.2% American Indian/Alaska Native, 0.1% Native Hawaiian/Other Pacific Islander, 1.0% Other, 2.3% Hispanic of any race (2010); Average household size: 2.19 (2010); Median age: 49.3 (2010); Males per 100 females: 98.7 (2010); Marriage status: 24.1% never married, 56.8% now married, 12.0% widowed, 7.1% divorced (2006-2010 5-year est.); Foreign born: 4.8% (2006-2010 5-year est.); Ancestry (includes multiple ancestries): 30.2% German, 25.7% Irish, 18.8% English, 16.0% Italian, 15.3% Dutch (2006-2010 5-year est.).

**Economy:** Single-family building permits issued: 3 (2011); Multi-family building permits issued: 0 (2011); Employment by occupation: 13.9% management, 1.5% professional, 10.7% services, 16.1% sales, 1.0% farming, 15.2% construction, 4.2% production (2006-2010 5-year est.).

**Income:** Per capita income: $24,002 (2006-2010 5-year est.); Median household income: $53,308 (2006-2010 5-year est.); Average household income: $57,691 (2006-2010 5-year est.); Percent of households with income of $100,000 or more: 12.1% (2006-2010 5-year est.); Poverty rate: 4.5% (2006-2010 5-year est.).

**Education:** Percent of population age 25 and over with: High school diploma (including GED) or higher: 84.4% (2006-2010 5-year est.); Bachelor's degree or higher: 20.1% (2006-2010 5-year est.); Master's degree or higher: 10.2% (2006-2010 5-year est.).

**School District(s)**
Roxbury Central School District (PK-12)
    2009-10 Enrollment: 349 . . . . . . . . . . . . . . . . . . . . . (607) 326-4151
**Housing:** Homeownership rate: 77.5% (2010); Median home value: $152,600 (2006-2010 5-year est.); Median contract rent: $397 per month (2006-2010 5-year est.); Median year structure built: 1972 (2006-2010 5-year est.).
**Transportation:** Commute to work: 80.4% car, 0.0% public transportation, 5.7% walk, 13.9% work from home (2006-2010 5-year est.); Travel time to work: 34.4% less than 15 minutes, 26.1% 15 to 30 minutes, 18.3% 30 to 45

minutes, 13.2% 45 to 60 minutes, 7.9% 60 minutes or more (2006-2010 5-year est.)

## SIDNEY (village). Covers a land area of 2.374 square miles and a water area of 0.015 square miles. Located at 42.30° N. Lat; 75.40° W. Long. Elevation is 991 feet.

**Population:** 4,720 (1990); 4,068 (2000); 3,900 (2010); Density: 1,642.6 persons per square mile (2010); Race: 96.1% White, 0.8% Black, 1.1% Asian, 0.1% American Indian/Alaska Native, 0.0% Native Hawaiian/Other Pacific Islander, 1.9% Other, 2.3% Hispanic of any race (2010); Average household size: 2.28 (2010); Median age: 41.5 (2010); Males per 100 females: 88.9 (2010); Marriage status: 26.8% never married, 49.2% now married, 9.6% widowed, 14.4% divorced (2006-2010 5-year est.); Foreign born: 2.6% (2006-2010 5-year est.); Ancestry (includes multiple ancestries): 29.5% German, 26.4% Irish, 15.5% English, 13.9% Italian, 8.0% American (2006-2010 5-year est.).

**Economy:** Single-family building permits issued: 0 (2011); Multi-family building permits issued: 0 (2011); Employment by occupation: 2.9% management, 5.9% professional, 9.0% services, 16.8% sales, 4.7% farming, 7.2% construction, 9.8% production (2006-2010 5-year est.).

**Income:** Per capita income: $24,717 (2006-2010 5-year est.); Median household income: $38,472 (2006-2010 5-year est.); Average household income: $53,513 (2006-2010 5-year est.); Percent of households with income of $100,000 or more: 8.0% (2006-2010 5-year est.); Poverty rate: 17.8% (2006-2010 5-year est.).

**Education:** Percent of population age 25 and over with: High school diploma (including GED) or higher: 91.1% (2006-2010 5-year est.); Bachelor's degree or higher: 26.9% (2006-2010 5-year est.); Master's degree or higher: 14.6% (2006-2010 5-year est.).

**School District(s)**
Sidney Central School District (PK-12)
    2009-10 Enrollment: 1,105 . . . . . . . . . . . . . . . . . . . (607) 563-2135
**Housing:** Homeownership rate: 57.0% (2010); Median home value: $86,500 (2006-2010 5-year est.); Median contract rent: $465 per month (2006-2010 5-year est.); Median year structure built: 1947 (2006-2010 5-year est.).
**Hospitals:** Hospital of Sidney (87 beds)
**Safety:** Violent crime rate: 36.7 per 10,000 population; Property crime rate: 511.2 per 10,000 population (2010).
**Newspapers:** Tri-Town News (Community news; Circulation 5,000)
**Transportation:** Commute to work: 90.0% car, 1.0% public transportation, 7.3% walk, 0.5% work from home (2006-2010 5-year est.); Travel time to work: 49.1% less than 15 minutes, 17.8% 15 to 30 minutes, 15.7% 30 to 45 minutes, 12.3% 45 to 60 minutes, 5.1% 60 minutes or more (2006-2010 5-year est.)
**Airports:** Sidney Municipal (general aviation)
**Additional Information Contacts**
Sidney Chamber of Commerce . . . . . . . . . . . . . . . . . . . . (607) 561-2642
    http://www.sidneychamber.org

## SIDNEY (town). Covers a land area of 49.928 square miles and a water area of 0.674 square miles. Located at 42.30° N. Lat; 75.27° W. Long. Elevation is 991 feet.

**Population:** 6,630 (1990); 6,109 (2000); 5,774 (2010); Density: 115.6 persons per square mile (2010); Race: 96.4% White, 0.9% Black, 0.8% Asian, 0.2% American Indian/Alaska Native, 0.0% Native Hawaiian/Other Pacific Islander, 1.7% Other, 2.0% Hispanic of any race (2010); Average household size: 2.28 (2010); Median age: 44.9 (2010); Males per 100 females: 94.8 (2010); Marriage status: 24.9% never married, 55.6% now married, 9.6% widowed, 9.9% divorced (2006-2010 5-year est.); Foreign born: 1.9% (2006-2010 5-year est.); Ancestry (includes multiple ancestries): 24.6% German, 24.1% Irish, 11.5% English, 11.3% Italian, 6.0% American (2006-2010 5-year est.).

**Economy:** Single-family building permits issued: 3 (2011); Multi-family building permits issued: 0 (2011); Employment by occupation: 5.7% management, 3.6% professional, 11.9% services, 14.6% sales, 3.6% farming, 11.7% construction, 10.6% production (2006-2010 5-year est.).

**Income:** Per capita income: $23,892 (2006-2010 5-year est.); Median household income: $42,097 (2006-2010 5-year est.); Average household income: $56,434 (2006-2010 5-year est.); Percent of households with income of $100,000 or more: 9.7% (2006-2010 5-year est.); Poverty rate: 15.3% (2006-2010 5-year est.).

**Education:** Percent of population age 25 and over with: High school diploma (including GED) or higher: 86.3% (2006-2010 5-year est.);

Bachelor's degree or higher: 19.2% (2006-2010 5-year est.); Master's degree or higher: 9.6% (2006-2010 5-year est.).

### School District(s)
Sidney Central School District (PK-12)

   2009-10 Enrollment: 1,105 . . . . . . . . . . . . . . . . . . . . . . . . (607) 563-2135

**Housing:** Homeownership rate: 67.2% (2010); Median home value: $88,700 (2006-2010 5-year est.); Median contract rent: $469 per month (2006-2010 5-year est.); Median year structure built: 1949 (2006-2010 5-year est.).

**Hospitals:** Hospital of Sidney (87 beds)

**Newspapers:** Tri-Town News (Community news; Circulation 5,000)

**Transportation:** Commute to work: 91.6% car, 0.6% public transportation, 5.4% walk, 1.7% work from home (2006-2010 5-year est.); Travel time to work: 43.3% less than 15 minutes, 27.4% 15 to 30 minutes, 15.1% 30 to 45 minutes, 8.3% 45 to 60 minutes, 5.9% 60 minutes or more (2006-2010 5-year est.)

**Airports:** Sidney Municipal (general aviation)

## SIDNEY CENTER (unincorporated postal area)
Zip Code: 13839

   Covers a land area of 39.753 square miles and a water area of 0.154 square miles. Located at 42.26° N. Lat; 75.25° W. Long. Elevation is 1,299 feet. Population: 1,405 (2010); Density: 35.3 persons per square mile (2010); Race: 96.9% White, 1.3% Black, 0.2% Asian, 0.2% American Indian/Alaska Native, 0.0% Native Hawaiian/Other Pacific Islander, 1.4% Other, 1.5% Hispanic of any race (2010); Average household size: 2.39 (2010); Median age: 46.9 (2010); Males per 100 females: 103.3 (2010); Homeownership rate: 89.1% (2010)

## SOUTH KORTRIGHT (unincorporated postal area)
Zip Code: 13842

   Covers a land area of 12.490 square miles and a water area of 0.129 square miles. Located at 42.37° N. Lat; 74.72° W. Long. Elevation is 1,509 feet. Population: 695 (2010); Density: 55.6 persons per square mile (2010); Race: 81.0% White, 14.0% Black, 0.0% Asian, 0.9% American Indian/Alaska Native, 0.4% Native Hawaiian/Other Pacific Islander, 3.7% Other, 8.9% Hispanic of any race (2010); Average household size: 2.58 (2010); Median age: 39.6 (2010); Males per 100 females: 155.5 (2010); Homeownership rate: 85.9% (2010)

## STAMFORD (village). Covers a land area of 1.332 square miles and a water area of 0.008 square miles. Located at 42.40° N. Lat; 74.61° W. Long. Elevation is 1,818 feet.
**Population:** 1,211 (1990); 1,265 (2000); 1,119 (2010); Density: 839.7 persons per square mile (2010); Race: 96.0% White, 1.3% Black, 0.4% Asian, 0.0% American Indian/Alaska Native, 0.0% Native Hawaiian/Other Pacific Islander, 2.3% Other, 3.9% Hispanic of any race (2010); Average household size: 2.18 (2010); Median age: 41.6 (2010); Males per 100 females: 82.5 (2010); Marriage status: 26.3% never married, 35.4% now married, 26.0% widowed, 12.4% divorced (2006-2010 5-year est.); Foreign born: 5.9% (2006-2010 5-year est.); Ancestry (includes multiple ancestries): 26.1% German, 24.8% Irish, 15.1% English, 9.4% Italian, 6.0% Polish (2006-2010 5-year est.).

**Economy:** Single-family building permits issued: 2 (2011); Multi-family building permits issued: 0 (2011); Employment by occupation: 6.5% management, 2.7% professional, 17.5% services, 13.1% sales, 2.5% farming, 5.3% construction, 6.5% production (2006-2010 5-year est.).

**Income:** Per capita income: $18,293 (2006-2010 5-year est.); Median household income: $31,136 (2006-2010 5-year est.); Average household income: $43,376 (2006-2010 5-year est.); Percent of households with income of $100,000 or more: 5.8% (2006-2010 5-year est.); Poverty rate: 23.1% (2006-2010 5-year est.).

**Education:** Percent of population age 25 and over with: High school diploma (including GED) or higher: 82.0% (2006-2010 5-year est.); Bachelor's degree or higher: 19.5% (2006-2010 5-year est.); Master's degree or higher: 8.5% (2006-2010 5-year est.).

### School District(s)
Otsego-Delaware-Schoharie-Greene Boces

   2009-10 Enrollment: n/a . . . . . . . . . . . . . . . . . . . . . . . . . (607) 652-1209

Stamford Central School District (PK-12)

   2009-10 Enrollment: 391 . . . . . . . . . . . . . . . . . . . . . . . . (607) 652-7301

**Housing:** Homeownership rate: 51.7% (2010); Median home value: $117,500 (2006-2010 5-year est.); Median contract rent: $500 per month (2006-2010 5-year est.); Median year structure built: before 1940 (2006-2010 5-year est.).

**Newspapers:** Mountain Eagle (Community news; Circulation 5,000)

**Transportation:** Commute to work: 85.7% car, 0.6% public transportation, 9.0% walk, 3.9% work from home (2006-2010 5-year est.); Travel time to work: 60.5% less than 15 minutes, 13.6% 15 to 30 minutes, 15.9% 30 to 45 minutes, 4.9% 45 to 60 minutes, 5.1% 60 minutes or more (2006-2010 5-year est.)

**Additional Information Contacts**

Village of Stamford. . . . . . . . . . . . . . . . . . . . . . . . . . . . . (607) 652-6671
   http://www.stamfordny.com/villagewebsite/

## STAMFORD (town). Covers a land area of 48.505 square miles and a water area of 0.105 square miles. Located at 42.33° N. Lat; 74.66° W. Long. Elevation is 1,818 feet.
**Population:** 2,047 (1990); 1,943 (2000); 2,267 (2010); Density: 46.7 persons per square mile (2010); Race: 93.9% White, 3.8% Black, 0.3% Asian, 0.1% American Indian/Alaska Native, 0.1% Native Hawaiian/Other Pacific Islander, 1.8% Other, 3.4% Hispanic of any race (2010); Average household size: 2.29 (2010); Median age: 43.4 (2010); Males per 100 females: 99.9 (2010); Marriage status: 27.3% never married, 55.8% now married, 7.3% widowed, 9.6% divorced (2006-2010 5-year est.); Foreign born: 3.6% (2006-2010 5-year est.); Ancestry (includes multiple ancestries): 32.8% German, 30.1% Irish, 13.1% English, 12.5% Italian, 9.0% French (2006-2010 5-year est.).

**Economy:** Employment by occupation: 8.2% management, 1.0% professional, 12.9% services, 11.3% sales, 3.2% farming, 9.6% construction, 9.5% production (2006-2010 5-year est.).

**Income:** Per capita income: $21,255 (2006-2010 5-year est.); Median household income: $39,688 (2006-2010 5-year est.); Average household income: $53,582 (2006-2010 5-year est.); Percent of households with income of $100,000 or more: 12.7% (2006-2010 5-year est.); Poverty rate: 13.2% (2006-2010 5-year est.).

**Education:** Percent of population age 25 and over with: High school diploma (including GED) or higher: 86.2% (2006-2010 5-year est.); Bachelor's degree or higher: 16.1% (2006-2010 5-year est.); Master's degree or higher: 8.4% (2006-2010 5-year est.).

### School District(s)
Otsego-Delaware-Schoharie-Greene Boces

   2009-10 Enrollment: n/a . . . . . . . . . . . . . . . . . . . . . . . . . (607) 652-1209

Stamford Central School District (PK-12)

   2009-10 Enrollment: 391 . . . . . . . . . . . . . . . . . . . . . . . . (607) 652-7301

**Housing:** Homeownership rate: 66.4% (2010); Median home value: $117,200 (2006-2010 5-year est.); Median contract rent: $463 per month (2006-2010 5-year est.); Median year structure built: 1942 (2006-2010 5-year est.).

**Newspapers:** Mountain Eagle (Community news; Circulation 5,000)

**Transportation:** Commute to work: 82.4% car, 0.5% public transportation, 8.0% walk, 6.0% work from home (2006-2010 5-year est.); Travel time to work: 62.9% less than 15 minutes, 16.3% 15 to 30 minutes, 9.3% 30 to 45 minutes, 5.7% 45 to 60 minutes, 5.7% 60 minutes or more (2006-2010 5-year est.)

## TOMPKINS (town). Covers a land area of 98.132 square miles and a water area of 6.314 square miles. Located at 42.11° N. Lat; 75.27° W. Long.
**Population:** 994 (1990); 1,105 (2000); 1,247 (2010); Density: 12.7 persons per square mile (2010); Race: 94.2% White, 4.2% Black, 0.2% Asian, 0.2% American Indian/Alaska Native, 0.0% Native Hawaiian/Other Pacific Islander, 1.2% Other, 1.9% Hispanic of any race (2010); Average household size: 2.44 (2010); Median age: 44.1 (2010); Males per 100 females: 104.4 (2010); Marriage status: 30.4% never married, 47.4% now married, 8.9% widowed, 13.2% divorced (2006-2010 5-year est.); Foreign born: 2.9% (2006-2010 5-year est.); Ancestry (includes multiple ancestries): 27.0% German, 19.0% Irish, 15.4% Dutch, 12.6% English, 7.7% Italian (2006-2010 5-year est.).

**Economy:** Single-family building permits issued: 0 (2011); Multi-family building permits issued: 0 (2011); Employment by occupation: 5.6% management, 2.3% professional, 20.4% services, 9.1% sales, 0.0% farming, 21.2% construction, 13.0% production (2006-2010 5-year est.).

**Income:** Per capita income: $21,017 (2006-2010 5-year est.); Median household income: $37,470 (2006-2010 5-year est.); Average household income: $47,403 (2006-2010 5-year est.); Percent of households with income of $100,000 or more: 8.7% (2006-2010 5-year est.); Poverty rate: 15.1% (2006-2010 5-year est.).

**Education:** Percent of population age 25 and over with: High school diploma (including GED) or higher: 83.8% (2006-2010 5-year est.);

Bachelor's degree or higher: 9.7% (2006-2010 5-year est.); Master's degree or higher: 3.2% (2006-2010 5-year est.).
**Housing:** Homeownership rate: 86.5% (2010); Median home value: $115,600 (2006-2010 5-year est.); Median contract rent: $392 per month (2006-2010 5-year est.); Median year structure built: 1974 (2006-2010 5-year est.).
**Transportation:** Commute to work: 92.5% car, 0.6% public transportation, 3.2% walk, 3.6% work from home (2006-2010 5-year est.); Travel time to work: 22.6% less than 15 minutes, 41.5% 15 to 30 minutes, 11.5% 30 to 45 minutes, 9.5% 45 to 60 minutes, 14.9% 60 minutes or more (2006-2010 5-year est.)

**TREADWELL** (unincorporated postal area)
Zip Code: 13846
    Covers a land area of 8.130 square miles and a water area of 0.033 square miles. Located at 42.36° N. Lat; 75.05° W. Long. Elevation is 1,529 feet. Population: 305 (2010); Density: 37.5 persons per square mile (2010); Race: 92.5% White, 0.7% Black, 3.0% Asian, 0.3% American Indian/Alaska Native, 0.0% Native Hawaiian/Other Pacific Islander, 3.5% Other, 3.3% Hispanic of any race (2010); Average household size: 2.26 (2010); Median age: 48.8 (2010); Males per 100 females: 90.6 (2010); Homeownership rate: 77.7% (2010)

**TROUT CREEK** (unincorporated postal area)
Zip Code: 13847
    Covers a land area of 3.259 square miles and a water area of 0.022 square miles. Located at 42.18° N. Lat; 75.29° W. Long. Elevation is 1,289 feet. Population: 67 (2010); Density: 20.6 persons per square mile (2010); Race: 97.0% White, 0.0% Black, 0.0% Asian, 0.0% American Indian/Alaska Native, 0.0% Native Hawaiian/Other Pacific Islander, 3.0% Other, 0.0% Hispanic of any race (2010); Average household size: 2.31 (2010); Median age: 41.3 (2010); Males per 100 females: 86.1 (2010); Homeownership rate: 72.4% (2010)

**WALTON** (village). Covers a land area of 1.540 square miles and a water area of 0.059 square miles. Located at 42.16° N. Lat; 75.13° W. Long. Elevation is 1,207 feet.
**Population:** 3,418 (1990); 3,070 (2000); 3,088 (2010); Density: 2,004.0 persons per square mile (2010); Race: 96.0% White, 1.1% Black, 0.7% Asian, 0.5% American Indian/Alaska Native, 0.0% Native Hawaiian/Other Pacific Islander, 1.7% Other, 3.3% Hispanic of any race (2010); Average household size: 2.27 (2010); Median age: 39.9 (2010); Males per 100 females: 92.0 (2010); Marriage status: 28.8% never married, 43.2% now married, 16.1% widowed, 12.0% divorced (2006-2010 5-year est.); Foreign born: 3.1% (2006-2010 5-year est.); Ancestry (includes multiple ancestries): 34.6% German, 21.4% Irish, 20.0% English, 14.1% Scottish, 11.9% Italian (2006-2010 5-year est.).
**Economy:** Single-family building permits issued: 0 (2011); Multi-family building permits issued: 0 (2011); Employment by occupation: 3.8% management, 3.3% professional, 21.3% services, 15.7% sales, 2.1% farming, 5.2% construction, 2.8% production (2006-2010 5-year est.).
**Income:** Per capita income: $23,881 (2006-2010 5-year est.); Median household income: $35,287 (2006-2010 5-year est.); Average household income: $48,628 (2006-2010 5-year est.); Percent of households with income of $100,000 or more: 10.7% (2006-2010 5-year est.); Poverty rate: 14.6% (2006-2010 5-year est.).
**Education:** Percent of population age 25 and over with: High school diploma (including GED) or higher: 87.6% (2006-2010 5-year est.); Bachelor's degree or higher: 14.8% (2006-2010 5-year est.); Master's degree or higher: 8.8% (2006-2010 5-year est.).
                        **School District(s)**
Walton Central School District (PK-12)
    2009-10 Enrollment: 1,085 . . . . . . . . . . . . . . . . . . . . . (607) 865-4116
**Housing:** Homeownership rate: 53.3% (2010); Median home value: $102,500 (2006-2010 5-year est.); Median contract rent: $419 per month (2006-2010 5-year est.); Median year structure built: before 1940 (2006-2010 5-year est.).
**Hospitals:** Delaware Valley Hospital (42 beds)
**Safety:** Violent crime rate: 18.3 per 10,000 population; Property crime rate: 193.5 per 10,000 population (2010).
**Newspapers:** Reporter (Community news; Circulation 7,100); The Walton Reporter (Local news; Circulation 7,100)
**Transportation:** Commute to work: 84.7% car, 4.5% public transportation, 8.1% walk, 2.6% work from home (2006-2010 5-year est.); Travel time to work: 55.2% less than 15 minutes, 21.6% 15 to 30 minutes, 12.4% 30 to 45

minutes, 4.2% 45 to 60 minutes, 6.6% 60 minutes or more (2006-2010 5-year est.)
**Additional Information Contacts**
Walton Chamber of Commerce . . . . . . . . . . . . . . . . . . (607) 865-6656
    http://www.waltonchamber.com

**WALTON** (town). Covers a land area of 96.837 square miles and a water area of 0.779 square miles. Located at 42.17° N. Lat; 75.12° W. Long. Elevation is 1,207 feet.
**Population:** 5,953 (1990); 5,607 (2000); 5,576 (2010); Density: 57.6 persons per square mile (2010); Race: 97.0% White, 0.7% Black, 0.6% Asian, 0.4% American Indian/Alaska Native, 0.0% Native Hawaiian/Other Pacific Islander, 1.3% Other, 2.7% Hispanic of any race (2010); Average household size: 2.31 (2010); Median age: 43.7 (2010); Males per 100 females: 98.2 (2010); Marriage status: 25.9% never married, 53.9% now married, 11.0% widowed, 9.2% divorced (2006-2010 5-year est.); Foreign born: 2.7% (2006-2010 5-year est.); Ancestry (includes multiple ancestries): 29.5% German, 20.2% English, 19.2% Irish, 10.9% Italian, 9.4% American (2006-2010 5-year est.).
**Economy:** Single-family building permits issued: 6 (2011); Multi-family building permits issued: 0 (2011); Employment by occupation: 3.5% management, 2.4% professional, 20.4% services, 18.3% sales, 2.0% farming, 8.9% construction, 7.8% production (2006-2010 5-year est.).
**Income:** Per capita income: $21,881 (2006-2010 5-year est.); Median household income: $39,417 (2006-2010 5-year est.); Average household income: $50,939 (2006-2010 5-year est.); Percent of households with income of $100,000 or more: 10.4% (2006-2010 5-year est.); Poverty rate: 17.4% (2006-2010 5-year est.).
**Education:** Percent of population age 25 and over with: High school diploma (including GED) or higher: 84.6% (2006-2010 5-year est.); Bachelor's degree or higher: 9.8% (2006-2010 5-year est.); Master's degree or higher: 6.3% (2006-2010 5-year est.).
                        **School District(s)**
Walton Central School District (PK-12)
    2009-10 Enrollment: 1,085 . . . . . . . . . . . . . . . . . . . . . (607) 865-4116
**Housing:** Homeownership rate: 67.4% (2010); Median home value: $109,300 (2006-2010 5-year est.); Median contract rent: $440 per month (2006-2010 5-year est.); Median year structure built: 1953 (2006-2010 5-year est.).
**Hospitals:** Delaware Valley Hospital (42 beds)
**Newspapers:** Reporter (Community news; Circulation 7,100); The Walton Reporter (Local news; Circulation 7,100)
**Transportation:** Commute to work: 89.4% car, 2.2% public transportation, 5.0% walk, 3.4% work from home (2006-2010 5-year est.); Travel time to work: 54.1% less than 15 minutes, 16.0% 15 to 30 minutes, 19.0% 30 to 45 minutes, 6.0% 45 to 60 minutes, 4.8% 60 minutes or more (2006-2010 5-year est.)

**WEST DAVENPORT** (unincorporated postal area)
Zip Code: 13860
    Covers a land area of 0.915 square miles and a water area of 0.001 square miles. Located at 42.44° N. Lat; 74.94° W. Long. Elevation is 1,181 feet. Population: 94 (2010); Density: 102.6 persons per square mile (2010); Race: 97.9% White, 0.0% Black, 2.1% Asian, 0.0% American Indian/Alaska Native, 0.0% Native Hawaiian/Other Pacific Islander, 0.0% Other, 13.8% Hispanic of any race (2010); Average household size: 2.54 (2010); Median age: 43.4 (2010); Males per 100 females: 91.8 (2010); Homeownership rate: 75.6% (2010)

# Dutchess County

Located in southeastern New York; bounded on the west by the Hudson River, and on the east by Connecticut; includes part of the Taconic Mountains. Covers a land area of 801.59 square miles, a water area of 23.78 square miles, and is located in the Eastern Time Zone at 41.71° N. Lat., 73.80° W. Long. The county was founded in 1683. County seat is Poughkeepsie.

Dutchess County is part of the Poughkeepsie-Newburgh-Middletown, NY Metropolitan Statistical Area. The entire metro area includes: Dutchess County, NY; Orange County, NY

Weather Station: Poughkeepsie Dutchess Co Arpt      Elevation: 154 feet

| | Jan | Feb | Mar | Apr | May | Jun | Jul | Aug | Sep | Oct | Nov | Dec |
|---|---|---|---|---|---|---|---|---|---|---|---|---|
| High | 35 | 39 | 48 | 60 | 71 | 79 | 84 | 82 | 74 | 62 | 51 | 40 |
| Low | 16 | 19 | 26 | 37 | 47 | 56 | 61 | 60 | 51 | 40 | 31 | 22 |
| Precip | 3.0 | 2.5 | 3.4 | 3.8 | 4.4 | 4.2 | 4.6 | 4.0 | 3.9 | 4.1 | 3.5 | 3.4 |
| Snow | 10.8 | 7.9 | 4.9 | 1.4 | 0.0 | 0.0 | 0.0 | 0.0 | 0.0 | tr | 1.8 | 7.4 |

*High and Low temperatures in degrees Fahrenheit; Precipitation and Snow in inches*

**Population:** 259,462 (1990); 280,150 (2000); 297,488 (2010); Race: 80.1% White, 9.9% Black, 3.5% Asian, 0.3% American Indian/Alaska Native, 0.0% Native Hawaiian/Other Pacific Islander, 6.2% Other, 10.5% Hispanic of any race (2010); Density: 371.1 persons per square mile (2010); Average household size: 2.57 (2010); Median age: 40.2 (2010); Males per 100 females: 99.2 (2010).
**Religion:** Six largest groups: 37.4% Catholicism, 2.6% Methodist/Pietist, 2.4% Muslim Estimate, 1.9% Presbyterian-Reformed, 1.7% Episcopalianism/Anglicanism, 1.6% Non-Denominational (2010).
**Economy:** Unemployment rate: 8.1% (February 2012); Total civilian labor force: 145,159 (February 2012); Leading industries: 19.3% health care and social assistance; 15.1% retail trade; 13.7% manufacturing (2009); Farms: 656 totaling 102,360 acres (2007); Companies that employ 500 or more persons: 12 (2009); Companies that employ 100 to 499 persons: 113 (2009); Companies that employ less than 100 persons: 7,372 (2009); Black-owned businesses: 1,368 (2007); Hispanic-owned businesses: n/a (2007); Asian-owned businesses: n/a (2007); Women-owned businesses: 8,716 (2007); Retail sales per capita: $14,496 (2010). Single-family building permits issued: 266 (2011); Multi-family building permits issued: 31 (2011).
**Income:** Per capita income: $31,642 (2006-2010 5-year est.); Median household income: $69,838 (2006-2010 5-year est.); Average household income: $85,739 (2006-2010 5-year est.); Percent of households with income of $100,000 or more: 30.8% (2006-2010 5-year est.); Poverty rate: 8.4% (2006-2010 5-year est.); Bankruptcy rate: 3.71% (2011).
**Taxes:** Total county taxes per capita: $910 (2009); County property taxes per capita: $352 (2009).
**Education:** Percent of population age 25 and over with: High school diploma (including GED) or higher: 89.1% (2006-2010 5-year est.); Bachelor's degree or higher: 32.0% (2006-2010 5-year est.); Master's degree or higher: 13.9% (2006-2010 5-year est.).
**Housing:** Homeownership rate: 69.5% (2010); Median home value: $323,300 (2006-2010 5-year est.); Median contract rent: $896 per month (2006-2010 5-year est.); Median year structure built: 1968 (2006-2010 5-year est.)
**Health:** Birth rate: 96.6 per 10,000 population (2011); Death rate: 77.5 per 10,000 population (2011); Age-adjusted cancer mortality rate: 181.0 deaths per 100,000 population (2009); Number of physicians: 25.5 per 10,000 population (2008); Hospital beds: 41.3 per 10,000 population (2007); Hospital admissions: 1,153.5 per 10,000 population (2007).
**Environment:** Air Quality Index: 94.5% good, 4.4% moderate, 1.1% unhealthy for sensitive individuals, 0.0% unhealthy (percent of days in 2010)
**Elections:** 2008 Presidential election results: 53.7% Obama, 45.1% McCain, 0.6% Nader
**National and State Parks:** Eleanor Roosevelt National Historic Site; Home of Franklin D Roosevelt National Historic Site; James Baird State Park; Mills Memorial State Park; Norrie State Park; Vanderbilt Mansion National Historic Site
**Additional Information Contacts**
Dutchess County Government . . . . . . . . . . . . . . . . . . . . . . (845) 486-2120
   http://www.dutchessny.gov
City of Beacon . . . . . . . . . . . . . . . . . . . . . . . . . . . . . . . . (845) 838-5000
   http://www.cityofbeacon.org
City of Poughkeepsie . . . . . . . . . . . . . . . . . . . . . . . . . . . (845) 451-4200
   http://www.cityofpoughkeepsie.com
Dover-Wingdale Chamber of Commerce . . . . . . . . . . . . . (845) 877-9800
Dutchess County Regional Chamber of Commerce . . . . . . (845) 454-1700
   http://www.dutchesscountyregionalchamber.org
Hyde Park Chamber of Commerce . . . . . . . . . . . . . . . . . (845) 229-8612
   http://www.hydeparkchamber.org
Pawling Chamber of Commerce . . . . . . . . . . . . . . . . . . . (845) 855-0500
   http://www.pawling.org
Red Hook Area Chamber of Commerce . . . . . . . . . . . . . . (845) 758-0824
   http://www.redhookchamber.org
Rhinebeck Chamber of Commerce . . . . . . . . . . . . . . . . . (845) 876-5904
   http://www.rhinebeckchamber.com

Town of Beekman . . . . . . . . . . . . . . . . . . . . . . . . . . . . . (845) 724-5300
   http://www.townofbeekman.com
Town of East Fishkill . . . . . . . . . . . . . . . . . . . . . . . . . . . (845) 221-4303
   http://www.eastfishkillny.org
Town of Hyde Park . . . . . . . . . . . . . . . . . . . . . . . . . . . . (845) 229-5111
   http://www.hydeparkny.us
Town of La Grange . . . . . . . . . . . . . . . . . . . . . . . . . . . . (845) 452-1830
   http://www.lagrangeny.org
Town of Pine Plains . . . . . . . . . . . . . . . . . . . . . . . . . . . . (518) 398-7155
   http://pineplains-ny.gov/content
Town of Pleasant Valley . . . . . . . . . . . . . . . . . . . . . . . . . (845) 635-3274
   http://pleasantvalley-ny.gov
Town of Red Hook . . . . . . . . . . . . . . . . . . . . . . . . . . . . . (845) 758-4606
   http://www.redhook.org
Town of Union Vale . . . . . . . . . . . . . . . . . . . . . . . . . . . . (845) 724-5600
   http://www2.marist.edu/unionvale

## Dutchess County Communities

**AMENIA** (town). Covers a land area of 43.219 square miles and a water area of 0.395 square miles. Located at 41.82° N. Lat; 73.53° W. Long. Elevation is 568 feet.
**History:** Thomas L. Harris had his Brotherhood of the New Life sect here, 1863—1867.
**Population:** 5,195 (1990); 4,048 (2000); 4,436 (2010); Density: 102.6 persons per square mile (2010); Race: 89.1% White, 4.1% Black, 1.4% Asian, 0.4% American Indian/Alaska Native, 0.0% Native Hawaiian/Other Pacific Islander, 5.0% Other, 8.5% Hispanic of any race (2010); Average household size: 2.37 (2010); Median age: 44.0 (2010); Males per 100 females: 97.9 (2010); Marriage status: 29.6% never married, 55.9% now married, 5.7% widowed, 8.8% divorced (2006-2010 5-year est.); Foreign born: 9.8% (2006-2010 5-year est.); Ancestry (includes multiple ancestries): 29.0% Irish, 18.7% German, 12.9% Italian, 12.7% French, 12.7% English (2006-2010 5-year est.).
**Economy:** Single-family building permits issued: 5 (2011); Multi-family building permits issued: 0 (2011); Employment by occupation: 14.5% management, 0.1% professional, 16.0% services, 12.3% sales, 4.3% farming, 13.6% construction, 7.9% production (2006-2010 5-year est.).
**Income:** Per capita income: $27,536 (2006-2010 5-year est.); Median household income: $45,156 (2006-2010 5-year est.); Average household income: $69,973 (2006-2010 5-year est.); Percent of households with income of $100,000 or more: 15.2% (2006-2010 5-year est.); Poverty rate: 13.8% (2006-2010 5-year est.).
**Education:** Percent of population age 25 and over with: High school diploma (including GED) or higher: 80.4% (2006-2010 5-year est.); Bachelor's degree or higher: 15.1% (2006-2010 5-year est.); Master's degree or higher: 5.5% (2006-2010 5-year est.).
### School District(s)
Northeast Central School District (PK-12)
   2009-10 Enrollment: 826 . . . . . . . . . . . . . . . . . . . . . . (845) 373-4100
**Housing:** Homeownership rate: 66.5% (2010); Median home value: $199,300 (2006-2010 5-year est.); Median contract rent: $791 per month (2006-2010 5-year est.); Median year structure built: 1958 (2006-2010 5-year est.).
**Transportation:** Commute to work: 91.6% car, 1.3% public transportation, 3.7% walk, 3.4% work from home (2006-2010 5-year est.); Travel time to work: 37.8% less than 15 minutes, 31.6% 15 to 30 minutes, 13.8% 30 to 45 minutes, 3.5% 45 to 60 minutes, 13.2% 60 minutes or more (2006-2010 5-year est.)

**AMENIA** (CDP). Covers a land area of 1.217 square miles and a water area of 0.027 square miles. Located at 41.84° N. Lat; 73.55° W. Long. Elevation is 568 feet.
**Population:** 1,057 (1990); 1,115 (2000); 955 (2010); Density: 784.3 persons per square mile (2010); Race: 88.0% White, 3.7% Black, 1.5% Asian, 0.6% American Indian/Alaska Native, 0.0% Native Hawaiian/Other Pacific Islander, 6.2% Other, 13.9% Hispanic of any race (2010); Average household size: 2.40 (2010); Median age: 42.0 (2010); Males per 100 females: 97.3 (2010); Marriage status: 26.4% never married, 68.5% now married, 2.1% widowed, 3.0% divorced (2006-2010 5-year est.); Foreign born: 18.9% (2006-2010 5-year est.); Ancestry (includes multiple ancestries): 31.2% Irish, 20.9% German, 13.3% French, 5.7% Italian, 5.3% English (2006-2010 5-year est.).

**Economy:** Employment by occupation: 8.9% management, 0.0% professional, 13.4% services, 14.1% sales, 2.0% farming, 24.5% construction, 17.3% production (2006-2010 5-year est.).
**Income:** Per capita income: $18,009 (2006-2010 5-year est.); Median household income: $42,614 (2006-2010 5-year est.); Average household income: $55,393 (2006-2010 5-year est.); Percent of households with income of $100,000 or more: 15.5% (2006-2010 5-year est.); Poverty rate: 26.3% (2006-2010 5-year est.).
**Education:** Percent of population age 25 and over with: High school diploma (including GED) or higher: 72.9% (2006-2010 5-year est.); Bachelor's degree or higher: 8.6% (2006-2010 5-year est.); Master's degree or higher: 4.4% (2006-2010 5-year est.).

### School District(s)
Northeast Central School District (PK-12)
   2009-10 Enrollment: 826 . . . . . . . . . . . . . . . . . . . . . . . (845) 373-4100
**Housing:** Homeownership rate: 58.2% (2010); Median home value: $189,500 (2006-2010 5-year est.); Median contract rent: $808 per month (2006-2010 5-year est.); Median year structure built: before 1940 (2006-2010 5-year est.).
**Transportation:** Commute to work: 84.4% car, 0.0% public transportation, 13.6% walk, 1.9% work from home (2006-2010 5-year est.); Travel time to work: 40.4% less than 15 minutes, 26.5% 15 to 30 minutes, 12.8% 30 to 45 minutes, 4.0% 45 to 60 minutes, 16.2% 60 minutes or more (2006-2010 5-year est.)

## ANNANDALE-ON-HUDSON (unincorporated postal area)
Zip Code: 12504

Covers a land area of 1.470 square miles and a water area of 0.813 square miles. Located at 42.03° N. Lat; 73.91° W. Long. Population: 1,395 (2010); Density: 948.4 persons per square mile (2010); Race: 86.3% White, 5.4% Black, 3.3% Asian, 0.5% American Indian/Alaska Native, 0.0% Native Hawaiian/Other Pacific Islander, 4.5% Other, 5.3% Hispanic of any race (2010); Average household size: 2.35 (2010); Median age: 20.1 (2010); Males per 100 females: 76.8 (2010); Homeownership rate: 22.6% (2010)

## ARLINGTON (CDP). Covers a land area of 0.667 square miles and a water area of 0 square miles. Located at 41.69° N. Lat; 73.89° W. Long. Elevation is 187 feet.
**History:** Seat of Vassar College.
**Population:** 11,948 (1990); 12,481 (2000); 4,061 (2010); Density: 6,082.3 persons per square mile (2010); Race: 63.4% White, 16.4% Black, 8.1% Asian, 0.9% American Indian/Alaska Native, 0.0% Native Hawaiian/Other Pacific Islander, 11.2% Other, 14.1% Hispanic of any race (2010); Average household size: 2.43 (2010); Median age: 22.9 (2010); Males per 100 females: 83.3 (2010); Marriage status: 56.3% never married, 35.7% now married, 5.5% widowed, 2.6% divorced (2006-2010 5-year est.); Foreign born: 16.7% (2006-2010 5-year est.); Ancestry (includes multiple ancestries): 21.4% Irish, 15.4% German, 12.3% Italian, 11.8% English, 7.0% Dutch (2006-2010 5-year est.).
**Economy:** Employment by occupation: 4.8% management, 2.7% professional, 11.7% services, 18.3% sales, 3.4% farming, 7.6% construction, 4.9% production (2006-2010 5-year est.).
**Income:** Per capita income: $17,658 (2006-2010 5-year est.); Median household income: $45,417 (2006-2010 5-year est.); Average household income: $57,664 (2006-2010 5-year est.); Percent of households with income of $100,000 or more: 15.1% (2006-2010 5-year est.); Poverty rate: 9.3% (2006-2010 5-year est.).
**Education:** Percent of population age 25 and over with: High school diploma (including GED) or higher: 85.0% (2006-2010 5-year est.); Bachelor's degree or higher: 24.5% (2006-2010 5-year est.); Master's degree or higher: 13.0% (2006-2010 5-year est.).
**Housing:** Homeownership rate: 35.8% (2010); Median home value: $260,900 (2006-2010 5-year est.); Median contract rent: $927 per month (2006-2010 5-year est.); Median year structure built: 1960 (2006-2010 5-year est.).
**Transportation:** Commute to work: 63.9% car, 0.4% public transportation, 25.3% walk, 6.4% work from home (2006-2010 5-year est.); Travel time to work: 52.9% less than 15 minutes, 31.0% 15 to 30 minutes, 5.0% 30 to 45 minutes, 3.9% 45 to 60 minutes, 7.2% 60 minutes or more (2006-2010 5-year est.)

## BARRYTOWN (unincorporated postal area)
Zip Code: 12507

Covers a land area of 1.393 square miles and a water area of 0.118 square miles. Located at 42.00° N. Lat; 73.91° W. Long. Elevation is 121 feet. Population: 167 (2010); Density: 119.8 persons per square mile (2010); Race: 84.4% White, 0.6% Black, 4.2% Asian, 0.0% American Indian/Alaska Native, 0.0% Native Hawaiian/Other Pacific Islander, 10.8% Other, 0.6% Hispanic of any race (2010); Average household size: 2.39 (2010); Median age: 43.4 (2010); Males per 100 females: 111.4 (2010); Homeownership rate: 69.5% (2010)

## BEACON (city). Covers a land area of 4.738 square miles and a water area of 0.136 square miles. Located at 41.50° N. Lat; 73.96° W. Long. Elevation is 138 feet.
**History:** An incline railroad ascends Mt. Beacon, site of a towering monument to American Revolutionary soldiers who built signal fires there to warn of the coming of the British. Beacon's historic buildings include the Madam Brett homestead (1709) and the Van Wyck homestead (1732). Settled 1663, Incorporated as a city in 1913.
**Population:** 13,256 (1990); 13,808 (2000); 15,541 (2010); Density: 3,279.6 persons per square mile (2010); Race: 63.6% White, 23.2% Black, 1.6% Asian, 0.3% American Indian/Alaska Native, 0.0% Native Hawaiian/Other Pacific Islander, 11.3% Other, 20.7% Hispanic of any race (2010); Average household size: 2.47 (2010); Median age: 39.8 (2010); Males per 100 females: 113.5 (2010); Marriage status: 35.6% never married, 47.0% now married, 5.1% widowed, 12.3% divorced (2006-2010 5-year est.); Foreign born: 8.4% (2006-2010 5-year est.); Ancestry (includes multiple ancestries): 20.9% Irish, 15.2% Italian, 10.8% German, 6.7% English, 4.6% Polish (2006-2010 5-year est.).
**Economy:** Single-family building permits issued: 1 (2011); Multi-family building permits issued: 0 (2011); Employment by occupation: 9.7% management, 3.9% professional, 13.0% services, 14.3% sales, 4.6% farming, 8.4% construction, 7.3% production (2006-2010 5-year est.).
**Income:** Per capita income: $27,712 (2006-2010 5-year est.); Median household income: $60,987 (2006-2010 5-year est.); Average household income: $72,336 (2006-2010 5-year est.); Percent of households with income of $100,000 or more: 23.3% (2006-2010 5-year est.); Poverty rate: 15.5% (2006-2010 5-year est.).
**Taxes:** Total city taxes per capita: $542 (2009); City property taxes per capita: $483 (2009).
**Education:** Percent of population age 25 and over with: High school diploma (including GED) or higher: 86.4% (2006-2010 5-year est.); Bachelor's degree or higher: 23.7% (2006-2010 5-year est.); Master's degree or higher: 10.2% (2006-2010 5-year est.).

### School District(s)
Beacon City School District (PK-12)
   2009-10 Enrollment: 3,431 . . . . . . . . . . . . . . . . . . . . (845) 838-6900
**Housing:** Homeownership rate: 56.5% (2010); Median home value: $294,600 (2006-2010 5-year est.); Median contract rent: $814 per month (2006-2010 5-year est.); Median year structure built: 1947 (2006-2010 5-year est.).
**Hospitals:** St. Francis Hospital (100 beds)
**Safety:** Violent crime rate: 43.9 per 10,000 population; Property crime rate: 223.1 per 10,000 population (2010).
**Transportation:** Commute to work: 82.6% car, 9.4% public transportation, 3.8% walk, 2.5% work from home (2006-2010 5-year est.); Travel time to work: 27.7% less than 15 minutes, 26.6% 15 to 30 minutes, 18.4% 30 to 45 minutes, 9.2% 45 to 60 minutes, 18.1% 60 minutes or more (2006-2010 5-year est.)
**Additional Information Contacts**
City of Beacon . . . . . . . . . . . . . . . . . . . . . . . . . . . . . . (845) 838-5000
   http://www.cityofbeacon.org

## BEEKMAN (town). Covers a land area of 29.838 square miles and a water area of 0.516 square miles. Located at 41.60° N. Lat; 73.69° W. Long. Elevation is 377 feet.
**Population:** 10,447 (1990); 11,452 (2000); 14,621 (2010); Density: 490.0 persons per square mile (2010); Race: 81.1% White, 11.8% Black, 2.7% Asian, 0.2% American Indian/Alaska Native, 0.0% Native Hawaiian/Other Pacific Islander, 4.2% Other, 9.1% Hispanic of any race (2010); Average household size: 2.95 (2010); Median age: 40.3 (2010); Males per 100 females: 131.0 (2010); Marriage status: 30.8% never married, 58.6% now married, 3.0% widowed, 7.6% divorced (2006-2010 5-year est.); Foreign born: 9.0% (2006-2010 5-year est.); Ancestry (includes multiple ancestries): 29.6% Italian, 22.6% Irish, 16.5% German, 5.7% English, 5.3% Polish (2006-2010 5-year est.).

**Economy:** Single-family building permits issued: 22 (2011); Multi-family building permits issued: 0 (2011); Employment by occupation: 15.7% management, 5.8% professional, 7.7% services, 17.1% sales, 1.8% farming, 15.1% construction, 8.7% production (2006-2010 5-year est.).
**Income:** Per capita income: $28,591 (2006-2010 5-year est.); Median household income: $88,750 (2006-2010 5-year est.); Average household income: $102,222 (2006-2010 5-year est.); Percent of households with income of $100,000 or more: 42.5% (2006-2010 5-year est.); Poverty rate: 3.1% (2006-2010 5-year est.).
**Education:** Percent of population age 25 and over with: High school diploma (including GED) or higher: 86.8% (2006-2010 5-year est.); Bachelor's degree or higher: 26.6% (2006-2010 5-year est.); Master's degree or higher: 10.5% (2006-2010 5-year est.).
**Housing:** Homeownership rate: 88.1% (2010); Median home value: $361,700 (2006-2010 5-year est.); Median contract rent: $837 per month (2006-2010 5-year est.); Median year structure built: 1983 (2006-2010 5-year est.).
**Transportation:** Commute to work: 90.8% car, 3.3% public transportation, 1.2% walk, 3.8% work from home (2006-2010 5-year est.); Travel time to work: 14.6% less than 15 minutes, 26.3% 15 to 30 minutes, 27.0% 30 to 45 minutes, 11.5% 45 to 60 minutes, 20.5% 60 minutes or more (2006-2010 5-year est.)
**Additional Information Contacts**
Town of Beekman . . . . . . . . . . . . . . . . . . . . . . . . . (845) 724-5300
   http://www.townofbeekman.com

**BRINCKERHOFF** (CDP). Covers a land area of 1.119 square miles and a water area of 0.005 square miles. Located at 41.55° N. Lat; 73.87° W. Long. Elevation is 220 feet.
**Population:** 2,756 (1990); 2,734 (2000); 2,900 (2010); Density: 2,589.4 persons per square mile (2010); Race: 86.5% White, 5.6% Black, 3.9% Asian, 0.1% American Indian/Alaska Native, 0.0% Native Hawaiian/Other Pacific Islander, 3.9% Other, 10.8% Hispanic of any race (2010); Average household size: 2.71 (2010); Median age: 43.5 (2010); Males per 100 females: 93.2 (2010); Marriage status: 27.0% never married, 64.8% now married, 4.4% widowed, 3.8% divorced (2006-2010 5-year est.); Foreign born: 12.2% (2006-2010 5-year est.); Ancestry (includes multiple ancestries): 36.1% Italian, 29.6% Irish, 19.6% German, 7.8% English, 5.1% Polish (2006-2010 5-year est.).
**Economy:** Employment by occupation: 16.1% management, 2.9% professional, 5.7% services, 11.6% sales, 3.4% farming, 11.7% construction, 6.4% production (2006-2010 5-year est.).
**Income:** Per capita income: $32,173 (2006-2010 5-year est.); Median household income: $90,625 (2006-2010 5-year est.); Average household income: $99,530 (2006-2010 5-year est.); Percent of households with income of $100,000 or more: 42.6% (2006-2010 5-year est.); Poverty rate: 4.8% (2006-2010 5-year est.).
**Education:** Percent of population age 25 and over with: High school diploma (including GED) or higher: 93.2% (2006-2010 5-year est.); Bachelor's degree or higher: 26.6% (2006-2010 5-year est.); Master's degree or higher: 11.8% (2006-2010 5-year est.).
**Housing:** Homeownership rate: 85.9% (2010); Median home value: $326,500 (2006-2010 5-year est.); Median contract rent: $1,060 per month (2006-2010 5-year est.); Median year structure built: 1974 (2006-2010 5-year est.).
**Transportation:** Commute to work: 89.7% car, 8.7% public transportation, 0.0% walk, 0.0% work from home (2006-2010 5-year est.); Travel time to work: 29.1% less than 15 minutes, 13.1% 15 to 30 minutes, 14.2% 30 to 45 minutes, 17.2% 45 to 60 minutes, 26.3% 60 minutes or more (2006-2010 5-year est.)

**CHELSEA** (unincorporated postal area)
Zip Code: 12512
   Covers a land area of 0.446 square miles and a water area of <.001 square miles. Located at 41.54° N. Lat; 73.96° W. Long. Elevation is 39 feet. Population: 127 (2010); Density: 284.6 persons per square mile (2010); Race: 85.8% White, 5.5% Black, 0.0% Asian, 0.0% American Indian/Alaska Native, 0.0% Native Hawaiian/Other Pacific Islander, 8.7% Other, 14.2% Hispanic of any race (2010); Average household size: 2.08 (2010); Median age: 49.3 (2010); Males per 100 females: 104.8 (2010); Homeownership rate: 83.6% (2010)

**CLINTON** (town). Covers a land area of 38.143 square miles and a water area of 0.641 square miles. Located at 41.86° N. Lat; 73.81° W. Long.
**Population:** 3,760 (1990); 4,010 (2000); 4,312 (2010); Density: 113.0 persons per square mile (2010); Race: 93.5% White, 2.5% Black, 1.2% Asian, 0.2% American Indian/Alaska Native, 0.0% Native Hawaiian/Other Pacific Islander, 2.6% Other, 3.7% Hispanic of any race (2010); Average household size: 2.58 (2010); Median age: 46.6 (2010); Males per 100 females: 103.2 (2010); Marriage status: 22.9% never married, 64.1% now married, 3.0% widowed, 10.1% divorced (2006-2010 5-year est.); Foreign born: 5.7% (2006-2010 5-year est.); Ancestry (includes multiple ancestries): 27.5% Irish, 22.2% German, 16.7% English, 16.5% Italian, 5.4% Dutch (2006-2010 5-year est.).
**Economy:** Single-family building permits issued: 4 (2011); Multi-family building permits issued: 0 (2011); Employment by occupation: 15.5% management, 6.8% professional, 8.2% services, 8.4% sales, 2.0% farming, 14.8% construction, 8.2% production (2006-2010 5-year est.).
**Income:** Per capita income: $45,769 (2006-2010 5-year est.); Median household income: $89,255 (2006-2010 5-year est.); Average household income: $117,464 (2006-2010 5-year est.); Percent of households with income of $100,000 or more: 42.5% (2006-2010 5-year est.); Poverty rate: 5.9% (2006-2010 5-year est.).
**Education:** Percent of population age 25 and over with: High school diploma (including GED) or higher: 96.4% (2006-2010 5-year est.); Bachelor's degree or higher: 48.0% (2006-2010 5-year est.); Master's degree or higher: 22.8% (2006-2010 5-year est.).
**Housing:** Homeownership rate: 84.4% (2010); Median home value: $381,500 (2006-2010 5-year est.); Median contract rent: $944 per month (2006-2010 5-year est.); Median year structure built: 1971 (2006-2010 5-year est.).
**Transportation:** Commute to work: 78.9% car, 4.2% public transportation, 5.0% walk, 9.9% work from home (2006-2010 5-year est.); Travel time to work: 20.1% less than 15 minutes, 37.2% 15 to 30 minutes, 28.1% 30 to 45 minutes, 6.2% 45 to 60 minutes, 8.5% 60 minutes or more (2006-2010 5-year est.)

**CLINTON CORNERS** (unincorporated postal area)
Zip Code: 12514
   Covers a land area of 26.645 square miles and a water area of 0.275 square miles. Located at 41.87° N. Lat; 73.76° W. Long. Elevation is 302 feet. Population: 2,938 (2010); Density: 110.3 persons per square mile (2010); Race: 94.8% White, 1.2% Black, 0.8% Asian, 0.3% American Indian/Alaska Native, 0.1% Native Hawaiian/Other Pacific Islander, 2.8% Other, 4.4% Hispanic of any race (2010); Average household size: 2.60 (2010); Median age: 45.8 (2010); Males per 100 females: 101.5 (2010); Homeownership rate: 88.6% (2010)

**CROWN HEIGHTS** (CDP). Covers a land area of 0.843 square miles and a water area of 0 square miles. Located at 41.64° N. Lat; 73.92° W. Long. Elevation is 128 feet.
**Population:** 3,200 (1990); 2,992 (2000); 2,840 (2010); Density: 3,366.4 persons per square mile (2010); Race: 77.6% White, 9.5% Black, 5.7% Asian, 0.3% American Indian/Alaska Native, 0.0% Native Hawaiian/Other Pacific Islander, 6.9% Other, 11.0% Hispanic of any race (2010); Average household size: 2.79 (2010); Median age: 41.8 (2010); Males per 100 females: 91.5 (2010); Marriage status: 24.0% never married, 60.6% now married, 8.1% widowed, 7.3% divorced (2006-2010 5-year est.); Foreign born: 11.6% (2006-2010 5-year est.); Ancestry (includes multiple ancestries): 31.5% Italian, 24.2% Irish, 19.9% German, 8.9% English, 5.7% Dutch (2006-2010 5-year est.).
**Economy:** Employment by occupation: 19.1% management, 5.4% professional, 9.3% services, 19.8% sales, 5.4% farming, 4.0% construction, 5.0% production (2006-2010 5-year est.).
**Income:** Per capita income: $30,299 (2006-2010 5-year est.); Median household income: $77,536 (2006-2010 5-year est.); Average household income: $83,410 (2006-2010 5-year est.); Percent of households with income of $100,000 or more: 36.1% (2006-2010 5-year est.); Poverty rate: 9.2% (2006-2010 5-year est.).
**Education:** Percent of population age 25 and over with: High school diploma (including GED) or higher: 84.0% (2006-2010 5-year est.); Bachelor's degree or higher: 32.5% (2006-2010 5-year est.); Master's degree or higher: 13.1% (2006-2010 5-year est.).
**Housing:** Homeownership rate: 83.2% (2010); Median home value: $299,000 (2006-2010 5-year est.); Median contract rent: $917 per month

(2006-2010 5-year est.); Median year structure built: 1964 (2006-2010 5-year est.).
**Transportation:** Commute to work: 94.6% car, 0.5% public transportation, 0.0% walk, 4.9% work from home (2006-2010 5-year est.); Travel time to work: 36.0% less than 15 minutes, 31.4% 15 to 30 minutes, 11.9% 30 to 45 minutes, 8.4% 45 to 60 minutes, 12.4% 60 minutes or more (2006-2010 5-year est.).

**DOVER** (town). Covers a land area of 55.190 square miles and a water area of 1.148 square miles. Located at 41.67° N. Lat; 73.56° W. Long.
**Population:** 7,778 (1990); 8,565 (2000); 8,699 (2010); Density: 157.6 persons per square mile (2010); Race: 86.0% White, 4.9% Black, 1.3% Asian, 0.2% American Indian/Alaska Native, 0.0% Native Hawaiian/Other Pacific Islander, 7.6% Other, 13.8% Hispanic of any race (2010); Average household size: 2.65 (2010); Median age: 40.8 (2010); Males per 100 females: 102.8 (2010); Marriage status: 25.6% never married, 59.2% now married, 2.1% widowed, 13.1% divorced (2006-2010 5-year est.); Foreign born: 9.7% (2006-2010 5-year est.); Ancestry (includes multiple ancestries): 30.2% Irish, 21.7% Italian, 19.7% German, 9.9% English, 6.5% American (2006-2010 5-year est.).
**Economy:** Single-family building permits issued: 0 (2011); Multi-family building permits issued: 0 (2011); Employment by occupation: 9.2% management, 2.9% professional, 11.3% services, 18.1% sales, 2.4% farming, 13.5% construction, 3.5% production (2006-2010 5-year est.).
**Income:** Per capita income: $28,365 (2006-2010 5-year est.); Median household income: $65,115 (2006-2010 5-year est.); Average household income: $74,158 (2006-2010 5-year est.); Percent of households with income of $100,000 or more: 18.6% (2006-2010 5-year est.); Poverty rate: 6.4% (2006-2010 5-year est.).
**Education:** Percent of population age 25 and over with: High school diploma (including GED) or higher: 83.7% (2006-2010 5-year est.); Bachelor's degree or higher: 14.5% (2006-2010 5-year est.); Master's degree or higher: 5.3% (2006-2010 5-year est.).
**Housing:** Homeownership rate: 73.0% (2010); Median home value: $273,400 (2006-2010 5-year est.); Median contract rent: $700 per month (2006-2010 5-year est.); Median year structure built: 1976 (2006-2010 5-year est.).
**Transportation:** Commute to work: 90.4% car, 4.5% public transportation, 0.9% walk, 3.6% work from home (2006-2010 5-year est.); Travel time to work: 22.9% less than 15 minutes, 22.5% 15 to 30 minutes, 19.4% 30 to 45 minutes, 13.5% 45 to 60 minutes, 21.7% 60 minutes or more (2006-2010 5-year est.).

**DOVER PLAINS** (CDP). Covers a land area of 0.676 square miles and a water area of 0.015 square miles. Located at 41.73° N. Lat; 73.57° W. Long. Elevation is 400 feet.
**Population:** 1,847 (1990); 1,996 (2000); 1,323 (2010); Density: 1,954.9 persons per square mile (2010); Race: 82.9% White, 4.8% Black, 0.6% Asian, 0.8% American Indian/Alaska Native, 0.0% Native Hawaiian/Other Pacific Islander, 10.9% Other, 20.2% Hispanic of any race (2010); Average household size: 2.34 (2010); Median age: 41.2 (2010); Males per 100 females: 110.7 (2010); Marriage status: 21.9% never married, 49.4% now married, 1.8% widowed, 26.9% divorced (2006-2010 5-year est.); Foreign born: 9.4% (2006-2010 5-year est.); Ancestry (includes multiple ancestries): 42.5% Irish, 26.5% German, 18.1% Italian, 13.6% English, 7.2% Polish (2006-2010 5-year est.).
**Economy:** Employment by occupation: 4.6% management, 0.0% professional, 14.9% services, 20.2% sales, 0.0% farming, 10.6% construction, 7.7% production (2006-2010 5-year est.).
**Income:** Per capita income: $30,437 (2006-2010 5-year est.); Median household income: $60,387 (2006-2010 5-year est.); Average household income: $64,090 (2006-2010 5-year est.); Percent of households with income of $100,000 or more: 10.3% (2006-2010 5-year est.); Poverty rate: 7.6% (2006-2010 5-year est.).
**Education:** Percent of population age 25 and over with: High school diploma (including GED) or higher: 75.9% (2006-2010 5-year est.); Bachelor's degree or higher: 11.2% (2006-2010 5-year est.); Master's degree or higher: 2.2% (2006-2010 5-year est.).

### School District(s)
Dover Union Free School District (KG-12)
    2009-10 Enrollment: 1,577 . . . . . . . . . . . . . . . . . . . . . . . (845) 832-4500
**Housing:** Homeownership rate: 59.3% (2010); Median home value: $211,100 (2006-2010 5-year est.); Median contract rent: $627 per month (2006-2010 5-year est.); Median year structure built: 1961 (2006-2010 5-year est.).

**Transportation:** Commute to work: 91.8% car, 5.4% public transportation, 1.3% walk, 1.5% work from home (2006-2010 5-year est.); Travel time to work: 26.8% less than 15 minutes, 31.1% 15 to 30 minutes, 16.6% 30 to 45 minutes, 9.1% 45 to 60 minutes, 16.4% 60 minutes or more (2006-2010 5-year est.)
**Additional Information Contacts**
Dover-Wingdale Chamber of Commerce . . . . . . . . . . . . . . . (845) 877-9800

**EAST FISHKILL** (town). Covers a land area of 56.503 square miles and a water area of 0.883 square miles. Located at 41.56° N. Lat; 73.78° W. Long. Elevation is 276 feet.
**Population:** 22,101 (1990); 25,589 (2000); 29,029 (2010); Density: 513.8 persons per square mile (2010); Race: 88.6% White, 3.4% Black, 4.1% Asian, 0.1% American Indian/Alaska Native, 0.0% Native Hawaiian/Other Pacific Islander, 3.8% Other, 7.7% Hispanic of any race (2010); Average household size: 3.05 (2010); Median age: 41.3 (2010); Males per 100 females: 99.9 (2010); Marriage status: 24.3% never married, 65.2% now married, 4.4% widowed, 6.2% divorced (2006-2010 5-year est.); Foreign born: 11.1% (2006-2010 5-year est.); Ancestry (includes multiple ancestries): 34.8% Italian, 30.3% Irish, 17.1% German, 8.5% English, 5.6% Polish (2006-2010 5-year est.).
**Economy:** Unemployment rate: 7.4% (February 2012); Total civilian labor force: 15,052 (February 2012); Single-family building permits issued: 53 (2011); Multi-family building permits issued: 0 (2011); Employment by occupation: 14.9% management, 6.5% professional, 6.9% services, 14.6% sales, 2.8% farming, 11.4% construction, 6.3% production (2006-2010 5-year est.).
**Income:** Per capita income: $37,928 (2006-2010 5-year est.); Median household income: $97,297 (2006-2010 5-year est.); Average household income: $116,119 (2006-2010 5-year est.); Percent of households with income of $100,000 or more: 48.2% (2006-2010 5-year est.); Poverty rate: 3.9% (2006-2010 5-year est.).
**Education:** Percent of population age 25 and over with: High school diploma (including GED) or higher: 93.4% (2006-2010 5-year est.); Bachelor's degree or higher: 39.8% (2006-2010 5-year est.); Master's degree or higher: 17.4% (2006-2010 5-year est.).
**Housing:** Homeownership rate: 90.1% (2010); Median home value: $391,200 (2006-2010 5-year est.); Median contract rent: $885 per month (2006-2010 5-year est.); Median year structure built: 1977 (2006-2010 5-year est.).
**Transportation:** Commute to work: 90.8% car, 2.9% public transportation, 0.5% walk, 4.9% work from home (2006-2010 5-year est.); Travel time to work: 20.6% less than 15 minutes, 27.3% 15 to 30 minutes, 17.9% 30 to 45 minutes, 13.5% 45 to 60 minutes, 20.7% 60 minutes or more (2006-2010 5-year est.).
**Additional Information Contacts**
Town of East Fishkill . . . . . . . . . . . . . . . . . . . . . . . . . . . . (845) 221-4303
    http://www.eastfishkillny.org

**FAIRVIEW** (CDP). Covers a land area of 3.477 square miles and a water area of 0.075 square miles. Located at 41.73° N. Lat; 73.91° W. Long. Elevation is 217 feet.
**Population:** 4,811 (1990); 5,421 (2000); 5,515 (2010); Density: 1,586.1 persons per square mile (2010); Race: 76.8% White, 12.8% Black, 3.4% Asian, 0.1% American Indian/Alaska Native, 0.0% Native Hawaiian/Other Pacific Islander, 6.9% Other, 8.6% Hispanic of any race (2010); Average household size: 2.62 (2010); Median age: 35.1 (2010); Males per 100 females: 102.4 (2010); Marriage status: 36.0% never married, 47.4% now married, 6.7% widowed, 9.9% divorced (2006-2010 5-year est.); Foreign born: 6.9% (2006-2010 5-year est.); Ancestry (includes multiple ancestries): 29.1% Irish, 27.4% German, 18.9% Italian, 10.1% English, 6.9% American (2006-2010 5-year est.).
**Economy:** Employment by occupation: 13.7% management, 5.0% professional, 8.3% services, 18.8% sales, 1.9% farming, 11.8% construction, 6.6% production (2006-2010 5-year est.).
**Income:** Per capita income: $26,152 (2006-2010 5-year est.); Median household income: $60,030 (2006-2010 5-year est.); Average household income: $67,908 (2006-2010 5-year est.); Percent of households with income of $100,000 or more: 26.8% (2006-2010 5-year est.); Poverty rate: 11.5% (2006-2010 5-year est.).
**Education:** Percent of population age 25 and over with: High school diploma (including GED) or higher: 86.6% (2006-2010 5-year est.); Bachelor's degree or higher: 22.1% (2006-2010 5-year est.); Master's degree or higher: 4.9% (2006-2010 5-year est.).

**Housing:** Homeownership rate: 73.5% (2010); Median home value: $231,000 (2006-2010 5-year est.); Median contract rent: $967 per month (2006-2010 5-year est.); Median year structure built: 1956 (2006-2010 5-year est.).

**Transportation:** Commute to work: 93.2% car, 3.0% public transportation, 2.3% walk, 0.0% work from home (2006-2010 5-year est.); Travel time to work: 43.4% less than 15 minutes, 33.6% 15 to 30 minutes, 13.1% 30 to 45 minutes, 3.0% 45 to 60 minutes, 7.0% 60 minutes or more (2006-2010 5-year est.).

**FISHKILL** (village). Covers a land area of 0.820 square miles and a water area of 0.004 square miles. Located at 41.53° N. Lat; 73.89° W. Long. Elevation is 220 feet.

**Population:** 1,957 (1990); 1,735 (2000); 2,171 (2010); Density: 2,646.3 persons per square mile (2010); Race: 73.6% White, 5.5% Black, 15.1% Asian, 0.1% American Indian/Alaska Native, 0.2% Native Hawaiian/Other Pacific Islander, 5.5% Other, 10.9% Hispanic of any race (2010); Average household size: 2.04 (2010); Median age: 39.5 (2010); Males per 100 females: 87.8 (2010); Marriage status: 29.0% never married, 45.4% now married, 11.6% widowed, 14.1% divorced (2006-2010 5-year est.); Foreign born: 21.9% (2006-2010 5-year est.); Ancestry (includes multiple ancestries): 30.9% Italian, 21.0% Irish, 13.5% German, 6.2% English, 5.3% Portuguese (2006-2010 5-year est.).

**Economy:** Single-family building permits issued: 0 (2011); Multi-family building permits issued: 0 (2011); Employment by occupation: 8.2% management, 17.7% professional, 5.6% services, 18.5% sales, 0.5% farming, 6.8% construction, 5.0% production (2006-2010 5-year est.).

**Income:** Per capita income: $40,872 (2006-2010 5-year est.); Median household income: $67,096 (2006-2010 5-year est.); Average household income: $83,103 (2006-2010 5-year est.); Percent of households with income of $100,000 or more: 26.5% (2006-2010 5-year est.); Poverty rate: 4.4% (2006-2010 5-year est.).

**Education:** Percent of population age 25 and over with: High school diploma (including GED) or higher: 92.6% (2006-2010 5-year est.); Bachelor's degree or higher: 38.0% (2006-2010 5-year est.); Master's degree or higher: 17.0% (2006-2010 5-year est.).

**School District(s)**
Beacon City School District (PK-12)
   2009-10 Enrollment: 3,431 . . . . . . . . . . . . . . . . . . (845) 838-6900
Wappingers Central School District (KG-12)
   2009-10 Enrollment: 12,407 . . . . . . . . . . . . . . . . . (845) 298-5000

**Housing:** Homeownership rate: 39.1% (2010); Median home value: $239,500 (2006-2010 5-year est.); Median contract rent: $1,194 per month (2006-2010 5-year est.); Median year structure built: 1973 (2006-2010 5-year est.).

**Safety:** Violent crime rate: 0.0 per 10,000 population; Property crime rate: 180.1 per 10,000 population (2010).

**Transportation:** Commute to work: 85.7% car, 0.9% public transportation, 1.4% walk, 3.2% work from home (2006-2010 5-year est.); Travel time to work: 40.2% less than 15 minutes, 33.6% 15 to 30 minutes, 16.6% 30 to 45 minutes, 4.2% 45 to 60 minutes, 5.4% 60 minutes or more (2006-2010 5-year est.).

**Additional Information Contacts**
Dutchess County Regional Chamber of Commerce . . . . . (845) 454-1700
   http://www.dutchesscountyregionalchamber.org

**FISHKILL** (town). Covers a land area of 27.336 square miles and a water area of 4.654 square miles. Located at 41.51° N. Lat; 73.92° W. Long. Elevation is 220 feet.

**History:** Nearby village of Fishkill Landing joined Matteawan (1913) to form Beacon city.

**Population:** 17,642 (1990); 20,258 (2000); 22,107 (2010); Density: 808.7 persons per square mile (2010); Race: 77.0% White, 10.4% Black, 7.7% Asian, 0.2% American Indian/Alaska Native, 0.1% Native Hawaiian/Other Pacific Islander, 4.6% Other, 10.9% Hispanic of any race (2010); Average household size: 2.36 (2010); Median age: 40.8 (2010); Males per 100 females: 103.5 (2010); Marriage status: 28.3% never married, 51.9% now married, 8.7% widowed, 11.1% divorced (2006-2010 5-year est.); Foreign born: 12.8% (2006-2010 5-year est.); Ancestry (includes multiple ancestries): 28.1% Italian, 22.6% Irish, 16.7% German, 6.7% English, 4.7% Polish (2006-2010 5-year est.).

**Economy:** Single-family building permits issued: 69 (2011); Multi-family building permits issued: 0 (2011); Employment by occupation: 12.6% management, 8.6% professional, 6.8% services, 14.7% sales, 2.5% farming, 8.7% construction, 6.0% production (2006-2010 5-year est.).

**Income:** Per capita income: $33,425 (2006-2010 5-year est.); Median household income: $75,034 (2006-2010 5-year est.); Average household income: $86,035 (2006-2010 5-year est.); Percent of households with income of $100,000 or more: 33.0% (2006-2010 5-year est.); Poverty rate: 3.7% (2006-2010 5-year est.).

**Education:** Percent of population age 25 and over with: High school diploma (including GED) or higher: 89.4% (2006-2010 5-year est.); Bachelor's degree or higher: 31.2% (2006-2010 5-year est.); Master's degree or higher: 11.8% (2006-2010 5-year est.).

**School District(s)**
Beacon City School District (PK-12)
   2009-10 Enrollment: 3,431 . . . . . . . . . . . . . . . . . . (845) 838-6900
Wappingers Central School District (KG-12)
   2009-10 Enrollment: 12,407 . . . . . . . . . . . . . . . . . (845) 298-5000

**Housing:** Homeownership rate: 65.4% (2010); Median home value: $306,200 (2006-2010 5-year est.); Median contract rent: $1,164 per month (2006-2010 5-year est.); Median year structure built: 1978 (2006-2010 5-year est.).

**Safety:** Violent crime rate: 2.5 per 10,000 population; Property crime rate: 136.1 per 10,000 population (2010).

**Transportation:** Commute to work: 89.3% car, 5.9% public transportation, 0.4% walk, 3.0% work from home (2006-2010 5-year est.); Travel time to work: 26.0% less than 15 minutes, 26.3% 15 to 30 minutes, 16.2% 30 to 45 minutes, 11.9% 45 to 60 minutes, 19.7% 60 minutes or more (2006-2010 5-year est.).

**FREEDOM PLAINS** (CDP). Covers a land area of 1.289 square miles and a water area of 0.043 square miles. Located at 41.66° N. Lat; 73.79° W. Long. Elevation is 315 feet.

**Population:** n/a (1990); n/a (2000); 421 (2010); Density: 326.5 persons per square mile (2010); Race: 90.3% White, 1.4% Black, 4.5% Asian, 0.0% American Indian/Alaska Native, 0.0% Native Hawaiian/Other Pacific Islander, 3.8% Other, 5.7% Hispanic of any race (2010); Average household size: 1.93 (2010); Median age: 48.1 (2010); Males per 100 females: 72.5 (2010); Marriage status: 5.9% never married, 69.8% now married, 13.2% widowed, 11.1% divorced (2006-2010 5-year est.); Foreign born: 13.7% (2006-2010 5-year est.); Ancestry (includes multiple ancestries): 19.1% Portuguese, 18.8% Irish, 16.8% English, 15.4% Italian, 13.5% German (2006-2010 5-year est.).

**Economy:** Employment by occupation: 5.3% management, 11.8% professional, 0.0% services, 8.8% sales, 0.0% farming, 20.6% construction, 0.0% production (2006-2010 5-year est.).

**Income:** Per capita income: $29,248 (2006-2010 5-year est.); Median household income: $65,148 (2006-2010 5-year est.); Average household income: $64,538 (2006-2010 5-year est.); Percent of households with income of $100,000 or more: 21.4% (2006-2010 5-year est.); Poverty rate: 15.2% (2006-2010 5-year est.).

**Education:** Percent of population age 25 and over with: High school diploma (including GED) or higher: 91.7% (2006-2010 5-year est.); Bachelor's degree or higher: 25.4% (2006-2010 5-year est.); Master's degree or higher: 6.1% (2006-2010 5-year est.).

**Housing:** Homeownership rate: 75.7% (2010); Median home value: $254,200 (2006-2010 5-year est.); Median contract rent: $1,278 per month (2006-2010 5-year est.); Median year structure built: 1982 (2006-2010 5-year est.).

**Transportation:** Commute to work: 100.0% car, 0.0% public transportation, 0.0% walk, 0.0% work from home (2006-2010 5-year est.); Travel time to work: 7.0% less than 15 minutes, 41.4% 15 to 30 minutes, 7.5% 30 to 45 minutes, 13.4% 45 to 60 minutes, 30.6% 60 minutes or more (2006-2010 5-year est.).

**GLENHAM** (unincorporated postal area)
Zip Code: 12527
   Covers a land area of 0.155 square miles and a water area of 0 square miles. Located at 41.51° N. Lat; 73.93° W. Long. Elevation is 256 feet. Population: 147 (2010); Density: 944.7 persons per square mile (2010); Race: 64.6% White, 13.6% Black, 0.0% Asian, 0.0% American Indian/Alaska Native, 0.0% Native Hawaiian/Other Pacific Islander, 21.8% Other, 27.9% Hispanic of any race (2010); Average household size: 2.67 (2010); Median age: 36.3 (2010); Males per 100 females: 98.6 (2010); Homeownership rate: 56.3% (2010)

## HAVILAND (CDP).
Covers a land area of 3.863 square miles and a water area of 0.035 square miles. Located at 41.76° N. Lat; 73.89° W. Long. Elevation is 233 feet.
**Population:** 3,605 (1990); 3,710 (2000); 3,634 (2010); Density: 940.6 persons per square mile (2010); Race: 87.2% White, 5.7% Black, 2.2% Asian, 0.1% American Indian/Alaska Native, 0.0% Native Hawaiian/Other Pacific Islander, 4.8% Other, 5.5% Hispanic of any race (2010); Average household size: 2.54 (2010); Median age: 43.7 (2010); Males per 100 females: 93.3 (2010); Marriage status: 28.2% never married, 55.7% now married, 5.1% widowed, 11.1% divorced (2006-2010 5-year est.); Foreign born: 7.2% (2006-2010 5-year est.); Ancestry (includes multiple ancestries): 29.7% Irish, 25.9% German, 22.7% Italian, 12.1% Polish, 11.7% English (2006-2010 5-year est.).
**Economy:** Employment by occupation: 3.6% management, 8.1% professional, 8.5% services, 17.9% sales, 4.2% farming, 5.9% construction, 1.8% production (2006-2010 5-year est.).
**Income:** Per capita income: $30,030 (2006-2010 5-year est.); Median household income: $56,835 (2006-2010 5-year est.); Average household income: $74,107 (2006-2010 5-year est.); Percent of households with income of $100,000 or more: 32.8% (2006-2010 5-year est.); Poverty rate: 9.7% (2006-2010 5-year est.).
**Education:** Percent of population age 25 and over with: High school diploma (including GED) or higher: 90.3% (2006-2010 5-year est.); Bachelor's degree or higher: 34.3% (2006-2010 5-year est.); Master's degree or higher: 15.8% (2006-2010 5-year est.).
**Housing:** Homeownership rate: 84.4% (2010); Median home value: $234,900 (2006-2010 5-year est.); Median contract rent: $1,081 per month (2006-2010 5-year est.); Median year structure built: 1970 (2006-2010 5-year est.).
**Transportation:** Commute to work: 88.4% car, 0.0% public transportation, 2.2% walk, 7.3% work from home (2006-2010 5-year est.); Travel time to work: 43.6% less than 15 minutes, 30.0% 15 to 30 minutes, 11.8% 30 to 45 minutes, 10.6% 45 to 60 minutes, 3.9% 60 minutes or more (2006-2010 5-year est.)

## HILLSIDE LAKE (CDP).
Covers a land area of 0.522 square miles and a water area of 0.039 square miles. Located at 41.61° N. Lat; 73.79° W. Long. Elevation is 374 feet.
**Population:** 1,692 (1990); 2,022 (2000); 1,084 (2010); Density: 2,073.5 persons per square mile (2010); Race: 90.4% White, 2.4% Black, 1.9% Asian, 0.2% American Indian/Alaska Native, 0.0% Native Hawaiian/Other Pacific Islander, 5.1% Other, 8.2% Hispanic of any race (2010); Average household size: 2.74 (2010); Median age: 40.8 (2010); Males per 100 females: 89.5 (2010); Marriage status: 22.2% never married, 67.4% now married, 1.7% widowed, 8.7% divorced (2006-2010 5-year est.); Foreign born: 9.2% (2006-2010 5-year est.); Ancestry (includes multiple ancestries): 51.3% Italian, 33.1% Irish, 15.1% Polish, 8.2% English, 7.3% Dutch (2006-2010 5-year est.).
**Economy:** Employment by occupation: 13.6% management, 0.0% professional, 13.6% services, 18.9% sales, 0.0% farming, 15.1% construction, 7.1% production (2006-2010 5-year est.).
**Income:** Per capita income: $34,611 (2006-2010 5-year est.); Median household income: $80,893 (2006-2010 5-year est.); Average household income: $98,591 (2006-2010 5-year est.); Percent of households with income of $100,000 or more: 43.9% (2006-2010 5-year est.); Poverty rate: 1.2% (2006-2010 5-year est.).
**Education:** Percent of population age 25 and over with: High school diploma (including GED) or higher: 94.7% (2006-2010 5-year est.); Bachelor's degree or higher: 25.5% (2006-2010 5-year est.); Master's degree or higher: 6.9% (2006-2010 5-year est.).
**Housing:** Homeownership rate: 86.8% (2010); Median home value: $345,800 (2006-2010 5-year est.); Median contract rent: $973 per month (2006-2010 5-year est.); Median year structure built: 1959 (2006-2010 5-year est.).
**Transportation:** Commute to work: 92.3% car, 7.7% public transportation, 0.0% walk, 0.0% work from home (2006-2010 5-year est.); Travel time to work: 9.2% less than 15 minutes, 34.3% 15 to 30 minutes, 21.9% 30 to 45 minutes, 9.8% 45 to 60 minutes, 24.9% 60 minutes or more (2006-2010 5-year est.)

## HOLMES (unincorporated postal area)
Zip Code: 12531
Covers a land area of 17.494 square miles and a water area of 1.006 square miles. Located at 41.54° N. Lat; 73.67° W. Long. Elevation is 692 feet. Population: 3,601 (2010); Density: 205.8 persons per square mile

(2010); Race: 92.8% White, 2.0% Black, 1.2% Asian, 0.1% American Indian/Alaska Native, 0.0% Native Hawaiian/Other Pacific Islander, 3.9% Other, 6.1% Hispanic of any race (2010); Average household size: 2.85 (2010); Median age: 42.8 (2010); Males per 100 females: 104.4 (2010); Homeownership rate: 82.6% (2010)

## HOPEWELL JUNCTION (CDP). Aka Hopewell.
Covers a land area of 0.473 square miles and a water area of <.001 square miles. Located at 41.57° N. Lat; 73.80° W. Long. Elevation is 246 feet.
**Population:** 1,786 (1990); 2,610 (2000); 376 (2010); Density: 793.9 persons per square mile (2010); Race: 87.2% White, 2.1% Black, 1.6% Asian, 0.0% American Indian/Alaska Native, 0.0% Native Hawaiian/Other Pacific Islander, 9.1% Other, 8.0% Hispanic of any race (2010); Average household size: 2.76 (2010); Median age: 40.0 (2010); Males per 100 females: 100.0 (2010); Marriage status: 32.3% never married, 54.5% now married, 9.3% widowed, 3.8% divorced (2006-2010 5-year est.); Foreign born: 6.8% (2006-2010 5-year est.); Ancestry (includes multiple ancestries): 62.0% Irish, 42.3% Italian, 22.4% German, 8.8% American, 3.6% Polish (2006-2010 5-year est.).
**Economy:** Employment by occupation: 5.9% management, 0.0% professional, 20.2% services, 29.3% sales, 0.0% farming, 26.1% construction, 0.0% production (2006-2010 5-year est.).
**Income:** Per capita income: $30,141 (2006-2010 5-year est.); Median household income: $103,068 (2006-2010 5-year est.); Average household income: $93,497 (2006-2010 5-year est.); Percent of households with income of $100,000 or more: 51.8% (2006-2010 5-year est.); Poverty rate: 0.0% (2006-2010 5-year est.).
**Education:** Percent of population age 25 and over with: High school diploma (including GED) or higher: 69.3% (2006-2010 5-year est.); Bachelor's degree or higher: 25.8% (2006-2010 5-year est.); Master's degree or higher: 9.8% (2006-2010 5-year est.).
**School District(s)**
Wappingers Central School District (KG-12)
    2009-10 Enrollment: 12,407 . . . . . . . . . . . . . . . . . . (845) 298-5000
**Housing:** Homeownership rate: 72.0% (2010); Median home value: $275,000 (2006-2010 5-year est.); Median contract rent: n/a per month (2006-2010 5-year est.); Median year structure built: 1949 (2006-2010 5-year est.).
**Transportation:** Commute to work: 91.0% car, 0.0% public transportation, 0.0% walk, 9.0% work from home (2006-2010 5-year est.); Travel time to work: 24.6% less than 15 minutes, 7.0% 15 to 30 minutes, 16.4% 30 to 45 minutes, 28.7% 45 to 60 minutes, 23.4% 60 minutes or more (2006-2010 5-year est.)

## HYDE PARK (town).
Covers a land area of 36.662 square miles and a water area of 3.195 square miles. Located at 41.81° N. Lat; 73.89° W. Long. Elevation is 187 feet.
**History:** Site of Roosevelt estate, part of FDR National Historic Site where President Franklin D. Roosevelt was born and is buried. Roosevelt Library contains historical material dating from 1910 until Roosevelt's death. Adjacent is the Eleanor Roosevelt National Historic Site (Val-Kill), an estate built for Mrs. Roosevelt by her husband. Frederick W. Vanderbilt mansion also here. All three homes are national historic sites. Seat of Culinary Institute of America. Settled c.1740.
**Population:** 21,230 (1990); 20,851 (2000); 21,571 (2010); Density: 588.4 persons per square mile (2010); Race: 87.1% White, 6.0% Black, 2.5% Asian, 0.2% American Indian/Alaska Native, 0.0% Native Hawaiian/Other Pacific Islander, 4.2% Other, 5.6% Hispanic of any race (2010); Average household size: 2.47 (2010); Median age: 39.8 (2010); Males per 100 females: 98.9 (2010); Marriage status: 35.9% never married, 47.8% now married, 6.5% widowed, 9.8% divorced (2006-2010 5-year est.); Foreign born: 6.8% (2006-2010 5-year est.); Ancestry (includes multiple ancestries): 27.8% Irish, 22.1% Italian, 21.2% German, 13.1% English, 7.9% Polish (2006-2010 5-year est.).
**Economy:** Single-family building permits issued: 0 (2011); Multi-family building permits issued: 0 (2011); Employment by occupation: 9.0% management, 8.1% professional, 11.1% services, 17.6% sales, 3.0% farming, 9.3% construction, 5.5% production (2006-2010 5-year est.).
**Income:** Per capita income: $29,801 (2006-2010 5-year est.); Median household income: $66,993 (2006-2010 5-year est.); Average household income: $80,870 (2006-2010 5-year est.); Percent of households with income of $100,000 or more: 30.5% (2006-2010 5-year est.); Poverty rate: 7.6% (2006-2010 5-year est.).
**Taxes:** Total city taxes per capita: $264 (2009); City property taxes per capita: $213 (2009).

**Education:** Percent of population age 25 and over with: High school diploma (including GED) or higher: 90.7% (2006-2010 5-year est.); Bachelor's degree or higher: 29.2% (2006-2010 5-year est.); Master's degree or higher: 12.3% (2006-2010 5-year est.).

**School District(s)**

Hyde Park Central School District (KG-12)

　　2009-10 Enrollment: 4,116 . . . . . . . . . . . . . . . . . . . . . . . (845) 229-4005

**Four-year College(s)**

Culinary Institute of America (Private, Not-for-profit)

　　Fall 2010 Enrollment: 4,022 . . . . . . . . . . . . . . . . . . . . . (845) 452-9600

　　2011-12 Tuition: In-state $26,180; Out-of-state $26,180

**Housing:** Homeownership rate: 73.5% (2010); Median home value: $262,400 (2006-2010 5-year est.); Median contract rent: $824 per month (2006-2010 5-year est.); Median year structure built: 1968 (2006-2010 5-year est.).

**Safety:** Violent crime rate: 9.0 per 10,000 population; Property crime rate: 105.0 per 10,000 population (2010).

**Transportation:** Commute to work: 87.0% car, 2.8% public transportation, 3.8% walk, 5.4% work from home (2006-2010 5-year est.); Travel time to work: 29.2% less than 15 minutes, 35.5% 15 to 30 minutes, 18.5% 30 to 45 minutes, 6.6% 45 to 60 minutes, 10.1% 60 minutes or more (2006-2010 5-year est.)

**Additional Information Contacts**

Hyde Park Chamber of Commerce . . . . . . . . . . . . . . . . . . (845) 229-8612

　　http://www.hydeparkchamber.org

Town of Hyde Park . . . . . . . . . . . . . . . . . . . . . . . . . . . (845) 229-5111

　　http://www.hydeparkny.us

## HYDE PARK (CDP).

Covers a land area of 1.205 square miles and a water area of 0.001 square miles. Located at 41.78° N. Lat; 73.93° W. Long. Elevation is 187 feet.

**Population:** n/a (1990); n/a (2000); 1,908 (2010); Density: 1,582.6 persons per square mile (2010); Race: 92.2% White, 3.3% Black, 1.7% Asian, 0.1% American Indian/Alaska Native, 0.0% Native Hawaiian/Other Pacific Islander, 2.7% Other, 4.9% Hispanic of any race (2010); Average household size: 2.36 (2010); Median age: 43.3 (2010); Males per 100 females: 95.5 (2010); Marriage status: 25.4% never married, 59.7% now married, 6.7% widowed, 8.2% divorced (2006-2010 5-year est.); Foreign born: 9.5% (2006-2010 5-year est.); Ancestry (includes multiple ancestries): 29.9% German, 29.1% Irish, 17.6% English, 16.1% Italian, 11.1% Polish (2006-2010 5-year est.).

**Economy:** Employment by occupation: 13.3% management, 8.6% professional, 8.1% services, 21.6% sales, 5.6% farming, 10.8% construction, 5.3% production (2006-2010 5-year est.).

**Income:** Per capita income: $30,570 (2006-2010 5-year est.); Median household income: $67,250 (2006-2010 5-year est.); Average household income: $80,086 (2006-2010 5-year est.); Percent of households with income of $100,000 or more: 22.3% (2006-2010 5-year est.); Poverty rate: 0.5% (2006-2010 5-year est.).

**Education:** Percent of population age 25 and over with: High school diploma (including GED) or higher: 92.1% (2006-2010 5-year est.); Bachelor's degree or higher: 30.6% (2006-2010 5-year est.); Master's degree or higher: 15.6% (2006-2010 5-year est.).

**School District(s)**

Hyde Park Central School District (KG-12)

　　2009-10 Enrollment: 4,116 . . . . . . . . . . . . . . . . . . . . . . . (845) 229-4005

**Four-year College(s)**

Culinary Institute of America (Private, Not-for-profit)

　　Fall 2010 Enrollment: 4,022 . . . . . . . . . . . . . . . . . . . . . (845) 452-9600

　　2011-12 Tuition: In-state $26,180; Out-of-state $26,180

**Housing:** Homeownership rate: 73.8% (2010); Median home value: $283,600 (2006-2010 5-year est.); Median contract rent: $915 per month (2006-2010 5-year est.); Median year structure built: 1955 (2006-2010 5-year est.).

**Transportation:** Commute to work: 89.3% car, 2.9% public transportation, 3.8% walk, 4.0% work from home (2006-2010 5-year est.); Travel time to work: 25.9% less than 15 minutes, 36.7% 15 to 30 minutes, 22.5% 30 to 45 minutes, 9.3% 45 to 60 minutes, 5.5% 60 minutes or more (2006-2010 5-year est.)

## LA GRANGE (town).

Covers a land area of 39.879 square miles and a water area of 0.470 square miles. Located at 41.68° N. Lat; 73.79° W. Long.

**Population:** 13,274 (1990); 14,928 (2000); 15,730 (2010); Density: 394.4 persons per square mile (2010); Race: 88.7% White, 3.8% Black, 4.0%

Asian, 0.2% American Indian/Alaska Native, 0.0% Native Hawaiian/Other Pacific Islander, 3.3% Other, 7.1% Hispanic of any race (2010); Average household size: 2.86 (2010); Median age: 42.7 (2010); Males per 100 females: 98.6 (2010); Marriage status: 24.8% never married, 66.2% now married, 3.8% widowed, 5.2% divorced (2006-2010 5-year est.); Foreign born: 7.6% (2006-2010 5-year est.); Ancestry (includes multiple ancestries): 28.4% Irish, 27.6% Italian, 18.3% German, 9.8% English, 5.6% Polish (2006-2010 5-year est.).

**Economy:** Single-family building permits issued: 15 (2011); Multi-family building permits issued: 0 (2011); Employment by occupation: 12.7% management, 7.3% professional, 7.8% services, 14.9% sales, 4.1% farming, 10.3% construction, 3.7% production (2006-2010 5-year est.).

**Income:** Per capita income: $38,374 (2006-2010 5-year est.); Median household income: $97,799 (2006-2010 5-year est.); Average household income: $114,062 (2006-2010 5-year est.); Percent of households with income of $100,000 or more: 47.7% (2006-2010 5-year est.); Poverty rate: 4.5% (2006-2010 5-year est.).

**Education:** Percent of population age 25 and over with: High school diploma (including GED) or higher: 93.9% (2006-2010 5-year est.); Bachelor's degree or higher: 41.1% (2006-2010 5-year est.); Master's degree or higher: 18.0% (2006-2010 5-year est.).

**Housing:** Homeownership rate: 90.7% (2010); Median home value: $361,400 (2006-2010 5-year est.); Median contract rent: $888 per month (2006-2010 5-year est.); Median year structure built: 1972 (2006-2010 5-year est.).

**Transportation:** Commute to work: 89.6% car, 3.5% public transportation, 2.5% walk, 4.0% work from home (2006-2010 5-year est.); Travel time to work: 22.0% less than 15 minutes, 38.4% 15 to 30 minutes, 15.8% 30 to 45 minutes, 7.9% 45 to 60 minutes, 15.8% 60 minutes or more (2006-2010 5-year est.)

**Additional Information Contacts**

Town of La Grange . . . . . . . . . . . . . . . . . . . . . . . . . . . (845) 452-1830

　　http://www.lagrangeny.org

## LAGRANGEVILLE (unincorporated postal area)

Zip Code: 12540

　　Covers a land area of 34.114 square miles and a water area of 0.299 square miles. Located at 41.67° N. Lat; 73.72° W. Long. Elevation is 358 feet. Population: 7,802 (2010); Density: 228.7 persons per square mile (2010); Race: 91.2% White, 1.9% Black, 3.7% Asian, 0.1% American Indian/Alaska Native, 0.1% Native Hawaiian/Other Pacific Islander, 3.0% Other, 5.1% Hispanic of any race (2010); Average household size: 2.97 (2010); Median age: 42.4 (2010); Males per 100 females: 101.0 (2010); Homeownership rate: 90.2% (2010)

## MERRITT PARK (CDP).

Covers a land area of 0.444 square miles and a water area of 0 square miles. Located at 41.53° N. Lat; 73.87° W. Long. Elevation is 220 feet.

**Population:** n/a (1990); n/a (2000); 1,256 (2010); Density: 2,828.0 persons per square mile (2010); Race: 52.2% White, 9.4% Black, 34.2% Asian, 0.2% American Indian/Alaska Native, 0.0% Native Hawaiian/Other Pacific Islander, 4.0% Other, 8.6% Hispanic of any race (2010); Average household size: 2.74 (2010); Median age: 36.5 (2010); Males per 100 females: 90.3 (2010); Marriage status: 10.6% never married, 78.8% now married, 4.3% widowed, 6.3% divorced (2006-2010 5-year est.); Foreign born: 35.2% (2006-2010 5-year est.); Ancestry (includes multiple ancestries): 35.6% Italian, 22.1% German, 8.0% Irish, 7.6% Polish, 3.2% Austrian (2006-2010 5-year est.).

**Economy:** Employment by occupation: 10.1% management, 13.2% professional, 0.0% services, 6.8% sales, 3.7% farming, 8.8% construction, 8.8% production (2006-2010 5-year est.).

**Income:** Per capita income: $52,884 (2006-2010 5-year est.); Median household income: $101,791 (2006-2010 5-year est.); Average household income: $135,057 (2006-2010 5-year est.); Percent of households with income of $100,000 or more: 62.7% (2006-2010 5-year est.); Poverty rate: 0.0% (2006-2010 5-year est.).

**Education:** Percent of population age 25 and over with: High school diploma (including GED) or higher: 87.7% (2006-2010 5-year est.); Bachelor's degree or higher: 76.0% (2006-2010 5-year est.); Master's degree or higher: 41.7% (2006-2010 5-year est.).

**Housing:** Homeownership rate: 92.8% (2010); Median home value: $451,900 (2006-2010 5-year est.); Median contract rent: n/a per month (2006-2010 5-year est.); Median year structure built: 2005 (2006-2010 5-year est.).

**Transportation:** Commute to work: 91.2% car, 8.8% public transportation, 0.0% walk, 0.0% work from home (2006-2010 5-year est.); Travel time to work: 11.1% less than 15 minutes, 8.4% 15 to 30 minutes, 39.2% 30 to 45 minutes, 12.8% 45 to 60 minutes, 28.4% 60 minutes or more (2006-2010 5-year est.)

**MILAN** (town). Covers a land area of 36.108 square miles and a water area of 0.468 square miles. Located at 41.97° N. Lat; 73.78° W. Long. Elevation is 433 feet.
**Population:** 1,895 (1990); 4,559 (2000); 2,370 (2010); Density: 65.6 persons per square mile (2010); Race: 95.3% White, 1.9% Black, 0.5% Asian, 0.5% American Indian/Alaska Native, 0.0% Native Hawaiian/Other Pacific Islander, 1.8% Other, 4.4% Hispanic of any race (2010); Average household size: 2.45 (2010); Median age: 45.6 (2010); Males per 100 females: 106.4 (2010); Marriage status: 25.2% never married, 64.1% now married, 3.8% widowed, 7.0% divorced (2006-2010 5-year est.); Foreign born: 6.2% (2006-2010 5-year est.); Ancestry (includes multiple ancestries): 24.5% German, 23.8% Irish, 17.5% Italian, 12.4% English, 6.2% Dutch (2006-2010 5-year est.).
**Economy:** Single-family building permits issued: 5 (2011); Multi-family building permits issued: 0 (2011); Employment by occupation: 15.5% management, 3.0% professional, 7.0% services, 14.8% sales, 2.3% farming, 14.4% construction, 6.1% production (2006-2010 5-year est.).
**Income:** Per capita income: $31,859 (2006-2010 5-year est.); Median household income: $69,427 (2006-2010 5-year est.); Average household income: $84,356 (2006-2010 5-year est.); Percent of households with income of $100,000 or more: 29.0% (2006-2010 5-year est.); Poverty rate: 2.8% (2006-2010 5-year est.).
**Education:** Percent of population age 25 and over with: High school diploma (including GED) or higher: 84.2% (2006-2010 5-year est.); Bachelor's degree or higher: 35.9% (2006-2010 5-year est.); Master's degree or higher: 14.9% (2006-2010 5-year est.).
**Housing:** Homeownership rate: 81.0% (2010); Median home value: $348,900 (2006-2010 5-year est.); Median contract rent: $736 per month (2006-2010 5-year est.); Median year structure built: 1963 (2006-2010 5-year est.).
**Transportation:** Commute to work: 89.4% car, 2.0% public transportation, 3.5% walk, 5.1% work from home (2006-2010 5-year est.); Travel time to work: 27.9% less than 15 minutes, 36.2% 15 to 30 minutes, 19.0% 30 to 45 minutes, 9.0% 45 to 60 minutes, 7.8% 60 minutes or more (2006-2010 5-year est.)

**MILLBROOK** (village). Covers a land area of 1.930 square miles and a water area of 0.055 square miles. Located at 41.78° N. Lat; 73.69° W. Long. Elevation is 574 feet.
**History:** Seat of Institute of Ecosystem Studies— N.Y. Botanical Gardens; Millbrook Preparatory School. Many estates and second homes for New Yorkers. Noted for polo playing. Incorporated 1896.
**Population:** 1,339 (1990); 1,429 (2000); 1,452 (2010); Density: 752.0 persons per square mile (2010); Race: 92.6% White, 2.0% Black, 1.0% Asian, 0.1% American Indian/Alaska Native, 0.0% Native Hawaiian/Other Pacific Islander, 4.3% Other, 7.3% Hispanic of any race (2010); Average household size: 2.09 (2010); Median age: 46.4 (2010); Males per 100 females: 87.1 (2010); Marriage status: 20.2% never married, 51.1% now married, 14.4% widowed, 14.4% divorced (2006-2010 5-year est.); Foreign born: 9.0% (2006-2010 5-year est.); Ancestry (includes multiple ancestries): 33.0% Italian, 27.9% Irish, 21.3% German, 18.5% English, 5.9% Scottish (2006-2010 5-year est.).
**Economy:** Single-family building permits issued: 0 (2011); Multi-family building permits issued: 0 (2011); Employment by occupation: 19.0% management, 3.3% professional, 13.5% services, 7.0% sales, 2.1% farming, 10.4% construction, 4.0% production (2006-2010 5-year est.).
**Income:** Per capita income: $40,176 (2006-2010 5-year est.); Median household income: $59,219 (2006-2010 5-year est.); Average household income: $85,945 (2006-2010 5-year est.); Percent of households with income of $100,000 or more: 24.8% (2006-2010 5-year est.); Poverty rate: 10.8% (2006-2010 5-year est.).
**Education:** Percent of population age 25 and over with: High school diploma (including GED) or higher: 85.2% (2006-2010 5-year est.); Bachelor's degree or higher: 39.5% (2006-2010 5-year est.); Master's degree or higher: 22.2% (2006-2010 5-year est.).

**School District(s)**
Millbrook Central School District (KG-12)
   2009-10 Enrollment: 1,214 . . . . . . . . . . . . . . . . . . . . . . . (845) 677-4200

**Housing:** Homeownership rate: 50.9% (2010); Median home value: $410,000 (2006-2010 5-year est.); Median contract rent: $854 per month (2006-2010 5-year est.); Median year structure built: 1956 (2006-2010 5-year est.).
**Newspapers:** Harlem Valley Times (Community news; Circulation 6,000); Hyde Park Townsman (Community news; Circulation 2,550); Millbrook Round Table (Community news; Circulation 2,500); Pawling News Chronicle (Community news); Pine Plains Register Herald (Local news; Circulation 20,000); The Register Herald (Community news; Circulation 20,000); Voice-Ledger (Local news; Circulation 2,580)
**Transportation:** Commute to work: 76.2% car, 3.3% public transportation, 12.2% walk, 8.2% work from home (2006-2010 5-year est.); Travel time to work: 38.5% less than 15 minutes, 19.5% 15 to 30 minutes, 18.0% 30 to 45 minutes, 8.4% 45 to 60 minutes, 15.7% 60 minutes or more (2006-2010 5-year est.)
**Airports:** Sky Acres (general aviation)

**MILLERTON** (village). Covers a land area of 0.618 square miles and a water area of 0.003 square miles. Located at 41.95° N. Lat; 73.51° W. Long. Elevation is 709 feet.
**Population:** 884 (1990); 925 (2000); 958 (2010); Density: 1,549.0 persons per square mile (2010); Race: 81.0% White, 5.3% Black, 1.6% Asian, 0.1% American Indian/Alaska Native, 0.0% Native Hawaiian/Other Pacific Islander, 12.0% Other, 13.7% Hispanic of any race (2010); Average household size: 2.39 (2010); Median age: 39.4 (2010); Males per 100 females: 100.4 (2010); Marriage status: 35.0% never married, 50.5% now married, 5.5% widowed, 8.9% divorced (2006-2010 5-year est.); Foreign born: 11.7% (2006-2010 5-year est.); Ancestry (includes multiple ancestries): 25.5% Irish, 19.2% Italian, 12.6% German, 11.9% English, 9.0% French (2006-2010 5-year est.).
**Economy:** Single-family building permits issued: 0 (2011); Multi-family building permits issued: 0 (2011); Employment by occupation: 2.0% management, 0.0% professional, 18.4% services, 9.8% sales, 2.0% farming, 6.9% construction, 7.3% production (2006-2010 5-year est.).
**Income:** Per capita income: $25,278 (2006-2010 5-year est.); Median household income: $55,203 (2006-2010 5-year est.); Average household income: $69,004 (2006-2010 5-year est.); Percent of households with income of $100,000 or more: 15.8% (2006-2010 5-year est.); Poverty rate: 10.1% (2006-2010 5-year est.).
**Education:** Percent of population age 25 and over with: High school diploma (including GED) or higher: 83.8% (2006-2010 5-year est.); Bachelor's degree or higher: 17.9% (2006-2010 5-year est.); Master's degree or higher: 6.9% (2006-2010 5-year est.).

**School District(s)**
Northeast Central School District (PK-12)
   2009-10 Enrollment: 826 . . . . . . . . . . . . . . . . . . . . . . . (845) 373-4100

**Housing:** Homeownership rate: 52.3% (2010); Median home value: $239,500 (2006-2010 5-year est.); Median contract rent: $742 per month (2006-2010 5-year est.); Median year structure built: before 1940 (2006-2010 5-year est.).
**Newspapers:** Millerton News (Community news; Circulation 2,500)
**Transportation:** Commute to work: 80.0% car, 0.9% public transportation, 9.2% walk, 7.3% work from home (2006-2010 5-year est.); Travel time to work: 60.6% less than 15 minutes, 19.8% 15 to 30 minutes, 9.9% 30 to 45 minutes, 3.1% 45 to 60 minutes, 6.6% 60 minutes or more (2006-2010 5-year est.)

**MYERS CORNER** (CDP). Covers a land area of 5.016 square miles and a water area of 0.038 square miles. Located at 41.59° N. Lat; 73.87° W. Long. Elevation is 217 feet.
**Population:** 5,599 (1990); 5,546 (2000); 6,790 (2010); Density: 1,353.4 persons per square mile (2010); Race: 83.4% White, 5.0% Black, 7.1% Asian, 0.2% American Indian/Alaska Native, 0.0% Native Hawaiian/Other Pacific Islander, 4.3% Other, 10.0% Hispanic of any race (2010); Average household size: 2.93 (2010); Median age: 43.6 (2010); Males per 100 females: 96.8 (2010); Marriage status: 20.4% never married, 70.6% now married, 5.1% widowed, 3.9% divorced (2006-2010 5-year est.); Foreign born: 15.1% (2006-2010 5-year est.); Ancestry (includes multiple ancestries): 34.1% Italian, 20.8% Irish, 15.6% German, 7.1% English, 5.6% Dutch (2006-2010 5-year est.).
**Economy:** Employment by occupation: 12.5% management, 7.8% professional, 5.5% services, 20.4% sales, 4.3% farming, 10.8% construction, 8.1% production (2006-2010 5-year est.).
**Income:** Per capita income: $32,447 (2006-2010 5-year est.); Median household income: $84,245 (2006-2010 5-year est.); Average household

income: $95,526 (2006-2010 5-year est.); Percent of households with income of $100,000 or more: 41.8% (2006-2010 5-year est.); Poverty rate: 6.6% (2006-2010 5-year est.).
**Education:** Percent of population age 25 and over with: High school diploma (including GED) or higher: 93.6% (2006-2010 5-year est.); Bachelor's degree or higher: 37.0% (2006-2010 5-year est.); Master's degree or higher: 15.0% (2006-2010 5-year est.).
**Housing:** Homeownership rate: 95.0% (2010); Median home value: $356,600 (2006-2010 5-year est.); Median contract rent: n/a per month (2006-2010 5-year est.); Median year structure built: 1973 (2006-2010 5-year est.).
**Transportation:** Commute to work: 88.5% car, 5.3% public transportation, 0.8% walk, 4.3% work from home (2006-2010 5-year est.); Travel time to work: 16.8% less than 15 minutes, 26.9% 15 to 30 minutes, 22.1% 30 to 45 minutes, 13.3% 45 to 60 minutes, 21.0% 60 minutes or more (2006-2010 5-year est.)

**NORTH EAST** (town). Covers a land area of 43.163 square miles and a water area of 0.559 square miles. Located at 41.94° N. Lat; 73.54° W. Long.
**Population:** 2,918 (1990); 3,002 (2000); 3,031 (2010); Density: 70.2 persons per square mile (2010); Race: 88.7% White, 2.7% Black, 1.1% Asian, 0.3% American Indian/Alaska Native, 0.0% Native Hawaiian/Other Pacific Islander, 7.2% Other, 9.1% Hispanic of any race (2010); Average household size: 2.39 (2010); Median age: 45.2 (2010); Males per 100 females: 103.3 (2010); Marriage status: 27.5% never married, 56.8% now married, 6.9% widowed, 8.8% divorced (2006-2010 5-year est.); Foreign born: 4.7% (2006-2010 5-year est.); Ancestry (includes multiple ancestries): 30.3% Irish, 21.9% English, 20.3% German, 13.0% French, 11.5% Italian (2006-2010 5-year est.).
**Economy:** Single-family building permits issued: 4 (2011); Multi-family building permits issued: 0 (2011); Employment by occupation: 10.3% management, 1.7% professional, 17.4% services, 10.5% sales, 1.1% farming, 10.2% construction, 5.2% production (2006-2010 5-year est.).
**Income:** Per capita income: $26,419 (2006-2010 5-year est.); Median household income: $57,418 (2006-2010 5-year est.); Average household income: $69,237 (2006-2010 5-year est.); Percent of households with income of $100,000 or more: 17.9% (2006-2010 5-year est.); Poverty rate: 7.0% (2006-2010 5-year est.).
**Education:** Percent of population age 25 and over with: High school diploma (including GED) or higher: 86.2% (2006-2010 5-year est.); Bachelor's degree or higher: 29.5% (2006-2010 5-year est.); Master's degree or higher: 11.5% (2006-2010 5-year est.).
**Housing:** Homeownership rate: 66.0% (2010); Median home value: $262,000 (2006-2010 5-year est.); Median contract rent: $823 per month (2006-2010 5-year est.); Median year structure built: 1954 (2006-2010 5-year est.).
**Transportation:** Commute to work: 83.5% car, 0.8% public transportation, 5.9% walk, 7.7% work from home (2006-2010 5-year est.); Travel time to work: 54.5% less than 15 minutes, 21.3% 15 to 30 minutes, 15.1% 30 to 45 minutes, 4.2% 45 to 60 minutes, 5.0% 60 minutes or more (2006-2010 5-year est.)

**PAWLING** (village). Aka Stonehouse. Covers a land area of 1.996 square miles and a water area of <.001 square miles. Located at 41.56° N. Lat; 73.59° W. Long. Elevation is 463 feet.
**Population:** 1,974 (1990); 2,233 (2000); 2,347 (2010); Density: 1,175.5 persons per square mile (2010); Race: 83.6% White, 2.3% Black, 3.7% Asian, 0.8% American Indian/Alaska Native, 0.0% Native Hawaiian/Other Pacific Islander, 9.6% Other, 16.5% Hispanic of any race (2010); Average household size: 2.34 (2010); Median age: 37.9 (2010); Males per 100 females: 119.6 (2010); Marriage status: 33.1% never married, 45.7% now married, 8.9% widowed, 12.3% divorced (2006-2010 5-year est.); Foreign born: 5.4% (2006-2010 5-year est.); Ancestry (includes multiple ancestries): 27.1% Irish, 27.0% Italian, 18.8% German, 9.6% English, 3.6% Polish (2006-2010 5-year est.).
**Economy:** Single-family building permits issued: 2 (2011); Multi-family building permits issued: 7 (2011); Employment by occupation: 10.6% management, 0.9% professional, 11.8% services, 25.3% sales, 4.8% farming, 12.0% construction, 4.9% production (2006-2010 5-year est.).
**Income:** Per capita income: $31,532 (2006-2010 5-year est.); Median household income: $64,135 (2006-2010 5-year est.); Average household income: $77,691 (2006-2010 5-year est.); Percent of households with income of $100,000 or more: 26.6% (2006-2010 5-year est.); Poverty rate: 4.4% (2006-2010 5-year est.).

**Education:** Percent of population age 25 and over with: High school diploma (including GED) or higher: 90.8% (2006-2010 5-year est.); Bachelor's degree or higher: 35.2% (2006-2010 5-year est.); Master's degree or higher: 17.5% (2006-2010 5-year est.).
**School District(s)**
Pawling Central School District (KG-12)
   2009-10 Enrollment: 1,396 . . . . . . . . . . . . . . . . . . . . (845) 855-4600
**Housing:** Homeownership rate: 57.1% (2010); Median home value: $379,800 (2006-2010 5-year est.); Median contract rent: $869 per month (2006-2010 5-year est.); Median year structure built: 1954 (2006-2010 5-year est.).
**Newspapers:** Pawling News Chronicle (Community news; Circulation 2,100)
**Transportation:** Commute to work: 82.1% car, 8.5% public transportation, 5.9% walk, 2.4% work from home (2006-2010 5-year est.); Travel time to work: 32.2% less than 15 minutes, 15.9% 15 to 30 minutes, 21.0% 30 to 45 minutes, 16.8% 45 to 60 minutes, 14.1% 60 minutes or more (2006-2010 5-year est.)
**Additional Information Contacts**
Pawling Chamber of Commerce . . . . . . . . . . . . . . . . . . . . . (845) 855-0500
   http://www.pawling.org

**PAWLING** (town). Aka Stonehouse. Covers a land area of 43.834 square miles and a water area of 1.186 square miles. Located at 41.56° N. Lat; 73.59° W. Long. Elevation is 463 feet.
**History:** In 1937, Thomas E. Dewey, three-term governor and two-time nominee for U.S. president, purchased a 486-acre farm here, although his legal address was the Roosevelt Hotel in N.Y. city. When he returned to legal practice after being governor, he resided at the World Trade Center. He and his wife are buried in Pawling Cemetery. Settled by Quakers c.1740; Incorporated 1893.
**Population:** 5,947 (1990); 7,521 (2000); 8,463 (2010); Density: 193.1 persons per square mile (2010); Race: 88.7% White, 2.8% Black, 2.3% Asian, 0.4% American Indian/Alaska Native, 0.1% Native Hawaiian/Other Pacific Islander, 5.7% Other, 10.2% Hispanic of any race (2010); Average household size: 2.62 (2010); Median age: 42.3 (2010); Males per 100 females: 105.9 (2010); Marriage status: 25.6% never married, 57.6% now married, 6.8% widowed, 10.0% divorced (2006-2010 5-year est.); Foreign born: 7.8% (2006-2010 5-year est.); Ancestry (includes multiple ancestries): 29.2% Irish, 28.7% Italian, 20.5% German, 8.2% English, 4.5% Polish (2006-2010 5-year est.).
**Economy:** Single-family building permits issued: 0 (2011); Multi-family building permits issued: 0 (2011); Employment by occupation: 18.3% management, 2.5% professional, 7.6% services, 19.2% sales, 4.5% farming, 11.1% construction, 3.7% production (2006-2010 5-year est.).
**Income:** Per capita income: $39,982 (2006-2010 5-year est.); Median household income: $77,340 (2006-2010 5-year est.); Average household income: $102,930 (2006-2010 5-year est.); Percent of households with income of $100,000 or more: 37.4% (2006-2010 5-year est.); Poverty rate: 3.3% (2006-2010 5-year est.).
**Taxes:** Total city taxes per capita: $427 (2009); City property taxes per capita: $373 (2009).
**Education:** Percent of population age 25 and over with: High school diploma (including GED) or higher: 93.6% (2006-2010 5-year est.); Bachelor's degree or higher: 38.6% (2006-2010 5-year est.); Master's degree or higher: 14.5% (2006-2010 5-year est.).
**School District(s)**
Pawling Central School District (KG-12)
   2009-10 Enrollment: 1,396 . . . . . . . . . . . . . . . . . . . . (845) 855-4600
**Housing:** Homeownership rate: 77.5% (2010); Median home value: $385,300 (2006-2010 5-year est.); Median contract rent: $940 per month (2006-2010 5-year est.); Median year structure built: 1969 (2006-2010 5-year est.).
**Newspapers:** Pawling News Chronicle (Community news; Circulation 2,100)
**Transportation:** Commute to work: 81.9% car, 8.5% public transportation, 3.6% walk, 5.4% work from home (2006-2010 5-year est.); Travel time to work: 26.1% less than 15 minutes, 18.8% 15 to 30 minutes, 18.7% 30 to 45 minutes, 13.2% 45 to 60 minutes, 23.1% 60 minutes or more (2006-2010 5-year est.)

**PINE PLAINS** (town). Covers a land area of 30.582 square miles and a water area of 0.589 square miles. Located at 41.97° N. Lat; 73.64° W. Long. Elevation is 469 feet.

**Population:** 2,287 (1990); 2,569 (2000); 2,473 (2010); Density: 80.9 persons per square mile (2010); Race: 92.6% White, 1.5% Black, 1.1% Asian, 0.2% American Indian/Alaska Native, 0.2% Native Hawaiian/Other Pacific Islander, 4.4% Other, 7.0% Hispanic of any race (2010); Average household size: 2.44 (2010); Median age: 44.9 (2010); Males per 100 females: 94.7 (2010); Marriage status: 25.4% never married, 59.2% now married, 8.2% widowed, 7.2% divorced (2006-2010 5-year est.); Foreign born: 2.7% (2006-2010 5-year est.); Ancestry (includes multiple ancestries): 24.8% German, 18.7% Irish, 18.0% Italian, 15.9% English, 7.6% French (2006-2010 5-year est.).

**Economy:** Single-family building permits issued: 1 (2011); Multi-family building permits issued: 0 (2011); Employment by occupation: 14.7% management, 1.9% professional, 10.5% services, 18.6% sales, 3.3% farming, 16.2% construction, 7.9% production (2006-2010 5-year est.).

**Income:** Per capita income: $29,083 (2006-2010 5-year est.); Median household income: $60,543 (2006-2010 5-year est.); Average household income: $73,559 (2006-2010 5-year est.); Percent of households with income of $100,000 or more: 21.8% (2006-2010 5-year est.); Poverty rate: 3.7% (2006-2010 5-year est.).

**Education:** Percent of population age 25 and over with: High school diploma (including GED) or higher: 90.6% (2006-2010 5-year est.); Bachelor's degree or higher: 22.7% (2006-2010 5-year est.); Master's degree or higher: 9.8% (2006-2010 5-year est.).

**School District(s)**

Pine Plains Central School District (KG-12)
    2009-10 Enrollment: 1,126 . . . . . . . . . . . . . . . . . . . . . . . . (518) 398-7181

**Housing:** Homeownership rate: 73.1% (2010); Median home value: $273,400 (2006-2010 5-year est.); Median contract rent: $892 per month (2006-2010 5-year est.); Median year structure built: 1953 (2006-2010 5-year est.).

**Safety:** Violent crime rate: 0.0 per 10,000 population; Property crime rate: 52.3 per 10,000 population (2010).

**Transportation:** Commute to work: 89.1% car, 2.2% public transportation, 4.5% walk, 4.1% work from home (2006-2010 5-year est.); Travel time to work: 31.9% less than 15 minutes, 23.9% 15 to 30 minutes, 18.8% 30 to 45 minutes, 15.1% 45 to 60 minutes, 10.3% 60 minutes or more (2006-2010 5-year est.)

**Additional Information Contacts**

Town of Pine Plains . . . . . . . . . . . . . . . . . . . . . . . . . . . . (518) 398-7155
    http://pineplains-ny.gov/content

**PINE PLAINS** (CDP). Covers a land area of 2.078 square miles and a water area of 0.224 square miles. Located at 41.97° N. Lat; 73.65° W. Long. Elevation is 469 feet.

**Population:** 1,312 (1990); 1,412 (2000); 1,353 (2010); Density: 651.0 persons per square mile (2010); Race: 91.6% White, 0.7% Black, 1.1% Asian, 0.2% American Indian/Alaska Native, 0.1% Native Hawaiian/Other Pacific Islander, 6.3% Other, 8.4% Hispanic of any race (2010); Average household size: 2.42 (2010); Median age: 44.3 (2010); Males per 100 females: 92.2 (2010); Marriage status: 27.9% never married, 60.4% now married, 7.6% widowed, 4.1% divorced (2006-2010 5-year est.); Foreign born: 0.9% (2006-2010 5-year est.); Ancestry (includes multiple ancestries): 27.1% Irish, 24.3% German, 23.5% English, 16.4% Italian, 9.2% French (2006-2010 5-year est.).

**Economy:** Employment by occupation: 7.1% management, 4.0% professional, 12.6% services, 16.6% sales, 4.9% farming, 17.9% construction, 10.0% production (2006-2010 5-year est.).

**Income:** Per capita income: $27,299 (2006-2010 5-year est.); Median household income: $54,519 (2006-2010 5-year est.); Average household income: $61,792 (2006-2010 5-year est.); Percent of households with income of $100,000 or more: 13.3% (2006-2010 5-year est.); Poverty rate: 4.9% (2006-2010 5-year est.).

**Education:** Percent of population age 25 and over with: High school diploma (including GED) or higher: 83.2% (2006-2010 5-year est.); Bachelor's degree or higher: 16.5% (2006-2010 5-year est.); Master's degree or higher: 6.0% (2006-2010 5-year est.).

**School District(s)**

Pine Plains Central School District (KG-12)
    2009-10 Enrollment: 1,126 . . . . . . . . . . . . . . . . . . . . . . . . (518) 398-7181

**Housing:** Homeownership rate: 70.0% (2010); Median home value: $225,000 (2006-2010 5-year est.); Median contract rent: $803 per month

(2006-2010 5-year est.); Median year structure built: 1951 (2006-2010 5-year est.).

**Transportation:** Commute to work: 88.1% car, 5.0% public transportation, 5.5% walk, 1.0% work from home (2006-2010 5-year est.); Travel time to work: 26.9% less than 15 minutes, 25.4% 15 to 30 minutes, 21.2% 30 to 45 minutes, 16.3% 45 to 60 minutes, 10.2% 60 minutes or more (2006-2010 5-year est.)

**PLEASANT VALLEY** (town). Covers a land area of 32.576 square miles and a water area of 0.563 square miles. Located at 41.77° N. Lat; 73.80° W. Long. Elevation is 187 feet.

**Population:** 8,063 (1990); 9,066 (2000); 9,672 (2010); Density: 296.9 persons per square mile (2010); Race: 92.6% White, 2.9% Black, 1.1% Asian, 0.2% American Indian/Alaska Native, 0.0% Native Hawaiian/Other Pacific Islander, 3.2% Other, 4.7% Hispanic of any race (2010); Average household size: 2.56 (2010); Median age: 42.3 (2010); Males per 100 females: 95.6 (2010); Marriage status: 27.7% never married, 59.3% now married, 3.2% widowed, 9.8% divorced (2006-2010 5-year est.); Foreign born: 4.3% (2006-2010 5-year est.); Ancestry (includes multiple ancestries): 27.7% Italian, 27.0% Irish, 25.4% German, 10.0% English, 6.3% Polish (2006-2010 5-year est.).

**Economy:** Single-family building permits issued: 4 (2011); Multi-family building permits issued: 12 (2011); Employment by occupation: 10.7% management, 7.7% professional, 12.9% services, 12.8% sales, 5.3% farming, 13.1% construction, 4.9% production (2006-2010 5-year est.).

**Income:** Per capita income: $35,673 (2006-2010 5-year est.); Median household income: $85,117 (2006-2010 5-year est.); Average household income: $94,479 (2006-2010 5-year est.); Percent of households with income of $100,000 or more: 36.9% (2006-2010 5-year est.); Poverty rate: 5.5% (2006-2010 5-year est.).

**Education:** Percent of population age 25 and over with: High school diploma (including GED) or higher: 89.5% (2006-2010 5-year est.); Bachelor's degree or higher: 32.6% (2006-2010 5-year est.); Master's degree or higher: 15.1% (2006-2010 5-year est.).

**School District(s)**

Arlington Central School District (KG-12)
    2009-10 Enrollment: 10,041 . . . . . . . . . . . . . . . . . . . . . . (845) 486-4460

**Housing:** Homeownership rate: 71.3% (2010); Median home value: $332,100 (2006-2010 5-year est.); Median contract rent: $969 per month (2006-2010 5-year est.); Median year structure built: 1979 (2006-2010 5-year est.).

**Transportation:** Commute to work: 89.4% car, 0.8% public transportation, 2.0% walk, 7.3% work from home (2006-2010 5-year est.); Travel time to work: 25.2% less than 15 minutes, 36.0% 15 to 30 minutes, 22.1% 30 to 45 minutes, 6.0% 45 to 60 minutes, 10.7% 60 minutes or more (2006-2010 5-year est.)

**Additional Information Contacts**

Town of Pleasant Valley . . . . . . . . . . . . . . . . . . . . . . . . . (845) 635-3274
    http://pleasantvalley-ny.gov

**PLEASANT VALLEY** (CDP). Covers a land area of 0.934 square miles and a water area of 0.024 square miles. Located at 41.74° N. Lat; 73.82° W. Long. Elevation is 187 feet.

**Population:** 1,688 (1990); 1,839 (2000); 1,145 (2010); Density: 1,225.3 persons per square mile (2010); Race: 94.0% White, 2.5% Black, 1.0% Asian, 0.1% American Indian/Alaska Native, 0.0% Native Hawaiian/Other Pacific Islander, 2.4% Other, 3.8% Hispanic of any race (2010); Average household size: 2.21 (2010); Median age: 44.0 (2010); Males per 100 females: 90.2 (2010); Marriage status: 21.8% never married, 60.3% now married, 4.1% widowed, 13.9% divorced (2006-2010 5-year est.); Foreign born: 5.4% (2006-2010 5-year est.); Ancestry (includes multiple ancestries): 48.5% German, 34.9% Irish, 25.3% Italian, 10.0% Czech, 9.3% Polish (2006-2010 5-year est.).

**Economy:** Employment by occupation: 15.5% management, 1.5% professional, 12.7% services, 11.0% sales, 2.8% farming, 5.3% construction, 1.7% production (2006-2010 5-year est.).

**Income:** Per capita income: $33,279 (2006-2010 5-year est.); Median household income: $61,488 (2006-2010 5-year est.); Average household income: $73,856 (2006-2010 5-year est.); Percent of households with income of $100,000 or more: 23.1% (2006-2010 5-year est.); Poverty rate: 0.0% (2006-2010 5-year est.).

**Education:** Percent of population age 25 and over with: High school diploma (including GED) or higher: 91.3% (2006-2010 5-year est.); Bachelor's degree or higher: 29.0% (2006-2010 5-year est.); Master's degree or higher: 11.3% (2006-2010 5-year est.).

## School District(s)

Arlington Central School District (KG-12)

   2009-10 Enrollment: 10,041 . . . . . . . . . . . . . . . . . . . . (845) 486-4460

**Housing:** Homeownership rate: 41.3% (2010); Median home value: $327,000 (2006-2010 5-year est.); Median contract rent: $1,308 per month (2006-2010 5-year est.); Median year structure built: 1981 (2006-2010 5-year est.).

**Transportation:** Commute to work: 93.4% car, 2.0% public transportation, 1.5% walk, 3.1% work from home (2006-2010 5-year est.); Travel time to work: 30.1% less than 15 minutes, 32.6% 15 to 30 minutes, 23.3% 30 to 45 minutes, 5.0% 45 to 60 minutes, 8.9% 60 minutes or more (2006-2010 5-year est.)

---

**POUGHKEEPSIE** (city). County seat. Covers a land area of 5.143 square miles and a water area of 0.574 square miles. Located at 41.69° N. Lat; 73.91° W. Long. Elevation is 203 feet.

**History:** It became the temporary state capital in 1777, and the U.S. Constitution was ratified (1788) here. Seat of Vassar and Marist Colleges and a community college. Several historic 18th-century buildings still stand. Hyde Park lies just north. Settled 1687 by the Dutch, Incorporated as a city 1854.

**Population:** 28,844 (1990); 29,871 (2000); 32,736 (2010); Density: 6,364.1 persons per square mile (2010); Race: 50.9% White, 33.5% Black, 1.6% Asian, 0.9% American Indian/Alaska Native, 0.1% Native Hawaiian/Other Pacific Islander, 13.0% Other, 19.5% Hispanic of any race (2010); Average household size: 2.41 (2010); Median age: 32.4 (2010); Males per 100 females: 92.4 (2010); Marriage status: 44.0% never married, 39.8% now married, 6.6% widowed, 9.6% divorced (2006-2010 5-year est.); Foreign born: 22.1% (2006-2010 5-year est.); Ancestry (includes multiple ancestries): 12.6% Italian, 11.3% Irish, 9.5% Jamaican, 9.0% German, 5.0% English (2006-2010 5-year est.).

**Economy:** Unemployment rate: 8.7% (February 2012); Total civilian labor force: 14,394 (February 2012); Single-family building permits issued: 4 (2011); Multi-family building permits issued: 12 (2011); Employment by occupation: 8.4% management, 3.4% professional, 18.0% services, 14.3% sales, 3.2% farming, 9.2% construction, 4.4% production (2006-2010 5-year est.).

**Income:** Per capita income: $23,192 (2006-2010 5-year est.); Median household income: $38,406 (2006-2010 5-year est.); Average household income: $54,723 (2006-2010 5-year est.); Percent of households with income of $100,000 or more: 13.6% (2006-2010 5-year est.); Poverty rate: 23.9% (2006-2010 5-year est.).

**Taxes:** Total city taxes per capita: $655 (2009); City property taxes per capita: $592 (2009).

**Education:** Percent of population age 25 and over with: High school diploma (including GED) or higher: 77.5% (2006-2010 5-year est.); Bachelor's degree or higher: 21.9% (2006-2010 5-year est.); Master's degree or higher: 8.9% (2006-2010 5-year est.).

### School District(s)

Arlington Central School District (KG-12)

   2009-10 Enrollment: 10,041 . . . . . . . . . . . . . . . . . . . . (845) 486-4460

Dutchess Boces

   2009-10 Enrollment: n/a . . . . . . . . . . . . . . . . . . . . . . . (845) 486-4800

Hyde Park Central School District (KG-12)

   2009-10 Enrollment: 4,116 . . . . . . . . . . . . . . . . . . . . (845) 229-4005

Poughkeepsie City School District (KG-12)

   2009-10 Enrollment: 4,500 . . . . . . . . . . . . . . . . . . . . (845) 451-4950

Spackenkill Union Free School District (KG-12)

   2009-10 Enrollment: 1,647 . . . . . . . . . . . . . . . . . . . . (845) 463-7800

Wappingers Central School District (KG-12)

   2009-10 Enrollment: 12,407 . . . . . . . . . . . . . . . . . . . (845) 298-5000

### Four-year College(s)

Marist College (Private, Not-for-profit)

   Fall 2010 Enrollment: 5,692 . . . . . . . . . . . . . . . . . . . (845) 575-3000

   2011-12 Tuition: In-state $28,890; Out-of-state $28,890

Vassar College (Private, Not-for-profit)

   Fall 2010 Enrollment: 2,461 . . . . . . . . . . . . . . . . . . . (845) 437-7000

   2011-12 Tuition: In-state $44,705; Out-of-state $44,705

### Two-year College(s)

Dutchess Community College (Public)

   Fall 2010 Enrollment: 6,708 . . . . . . . . . . . . . . . . . . . (845) 431-8000

   2011-12 Tuition: In-state $3,320; Out-of-state $6,220

### Vocational/Technical School(s)

Dutchess BOCES-School of Practical Nursing (Public)

   Fall 2010 Enrollment: 133 . . . . . . . . . . . . . . . . . . . . (845) 486-8001

   2011-12 Tuition: $9,095

Ridley-Lowell School of Business (Private, For-profit)

   Fall 2010 Enrollment: 272 . . . . . . . . . . . . . . . . . . . . (845) 471-0330

   2011-12 Tuition: $13,600

**Housing:** Homeownership rate: 37.3% (2010); Median home value: $263,100 (2006-2010 5-year est.); Median contract rent: $795 per month (2006-2010 5-year est.); Median year structure built: 1944 (2006-2010 5-year est.).

**Hospitals:** Hudson River Psychiatric Center (125 beds); St. Francis Hospital (400 beds); St. Francis Hospital (400 beds); Vassar Brothers Hospital (365 beds); Vassar Brothers Hospital (365 beds)

**Safety:** Violent crime rate: 136.4 per 10,000 population; Property crime rate: 361.6 per 10,000 population (2010).

**Newspapers:** Poughkeepsie Journal (Local news; Circulation 43,463)

**Transportation:** Commute to work: 78.1% car, 8.9% public transportation, 6.2% walk, 3.5% work from home (2006-2010 5-year est.); Travel time to work: 38.0% less than 15 minutes, 35.1% 15 to 30 minutes, 12.1% 30 to 45 minutes, 5.4% 45 to 60 minutes, 9.3% 60 minutes or more (2006-2010 5-year est.); Amtrak: train service available.

**Airports:** Dutchess County (general aviation)

**Additional Information Contacts**

City of Poughkeepsie . . . . . . . . . . . . . . . . . . . . . . . . . . . (845) 451-4200

   http://www.cityofpoughkeepsie.com

Dutchess County Regional Chamber of Commerce . . . . . . (845) 454-1700

   http://www.dutchesscountyregionalchamber.org

---

**POUGHKEEPSIE** (town). Covers a land area of 28.514 square miles and a water area of 2.629 square miles. Located at 41.66° N. Lat; 73.90° W. Long. Elevation is 203 feet.

**History:** The name of Poughkeepsie had its origins in a Native American name, the original probably meaning "reed-covered lodge by the little water place." The first record of European settlement dates from 1683. Growth at first was slow, but in 1777 Poughkeepsie was made the capital of the state. The chief event in the history of the town was the ratification of the Federal Constitution by the State on July 26, 1788. Early in the 19th century, Poughkeepsie became prominent as a river port. With the opening of the Erie Canal in 1825, however, competition caused a decline in the value of Dutchess County produce. Poughkeepsie turned to industry and trade. It also acquired a reputation as an educational center, with the most important advance being the founding of Vassar College in 1861.

**Population:** 40,143 (1990); 42,777 (2000); 43,341 (2010); Density: 1,520.0 persons per square mile (2010); Race: 77.4% White, 9.8% Black, 6.1% Asian, 0.2% American Indian/Alaska Native, 0.0% Native Hawaiian/Other Pacific Islander, 6.5% Other, 9.8% Hispanic of any race (2010); Average household size: 2.55 (2010); Median age: 37.0 (2010); Males per 100 females: 91.4 (2010); Marriage status: 39.4% never married, 47.7% now married, 6.0% widowed, 6.9% divorced (2006-2010 5-year est.); Foreign born: 11.2% (2006-2010 5-year est.); Ancestry (includes multiple ancestries): 23.4% Italian, 22.3% Irish, 18.3% German, 9.6% English, 5.0% Polish (2006-2010 5-year est.).

**Economy:** Unemployment rate: 8.1% (February 2012); Total civilian labor force: 21,283 (February 2012); Single-family building permits issued: 10 (2011); Multi-family building permits issued: 0 (2011); Employment by occupation: 10.7% management, 7.4% professional, 9.6% services, 18.2% sales, 5.1% farming, 6.7% construction, 4.5% production (2006-2010 5-year est.).

**Income:** Per capita income: $29,442 (2006-2010 5-year est.); Median household income: $66,793 (2006-2010 5-year est.); Average household income: $80,922 (2006-2010 5-year est.); Percent of households with income of $100,000 or more: 29.2% (2006-2010 5-year est.); Poverty rate: 8.9% (2006-2010 5-year est.).

**Taxes:** Total city taxes per capita: $539 (2009); City property taxes per capita: $482 (2009).

**Education:** Percent of population age 25 and over with: High school diploma (including GED) or higher: 90.8% (2006-2010 5-year est.); Bachelor's degree or higher: 34.6% (2006-2010 5-year est.); Master's degree or higher: 16.0% (2006-2010 5-year est.).

### School District(s)

Arlington Central School District (KG-12)

   2009-10 Enrollment: 10,041 . . . . . . . . . . . . . . . . . . . (845) 486-4460

Dutchess Boces

   2009-10 Enrollment: n/a . . . . . . . . . . . . . . . . . . . . . . . (845) 486-4800

Hyde Park Central School District (KG-12)
   2009-10 Enrollment: 4,116 .................... (845) 229-4005
Poughkeepsie City School District (KG-12)
   2009-10 Enrollment: 4,500 .................... (845) 451-4950
Spackenkill Union Free School District (KG-12)
   2009-10 Enrollment: 1,647 .................... (845) 463-7800
Wappingers Central School District (KG-12)
   2009-10 Enrollment: 12,407 ................... (845) 298-5000
**Four-year College(s)**
Marist College (Private, Not-for-profit)
   Fall 2010 Enrollment: 5,692 .................. (845) 575-3000
   2011-12 Tuition: In-state $28,890; Out-of-state $28,890
Vassar College (Private, Not-for-profit)
   Fall 2010 Enrollment: 2,461 .................. (845) 437-7000
   2011-12 Tuition: In-state $44,705; Out-of-state $44,705
**Two-year College(s)**
Dutchess Community College (Public)
   Fall 2010 Enrollment: 6,708 .................. (845) 431-8000
   2011-12 Tuition: In-state $3,320; Out-of-state $6,220
**Vocational/Technical School(s)**
Dutchess BOCES-School of Practical Nursing (Public)
   Fall 2010 Enrollment: 133 .................... (845) 486-8001
   2011-12 Tuition: $9,095
Ridley-Lowell School of Business (Private, For-profit)
   Fall 2010 Enrollment: 272 .................... (845) 471-0330
   2011-12 Tuition: $13,600
**Housing:** Homeownership rate: 69.4% (2010); Median home value: $285,400 (2006-2010 5-year est.); Median contract rent: $960 per month (2006-2010 5-year est.); Median year structure built: 1964 (2006-2010 5-year est.).
**Hospitals:** Hudson River Psychiatric Center (125 beds)
**Safety:** Violent crime rate: 9.2 per 10,000 population; Property crime rate: 312.7 per 10,000 population (2010).
**Newspapers:** Poughkeepsie Journal (Local news; Circulation 43,463)
**Transportation:** Commute to work: 84.9% car, 2.3% public transportation, 7.5% walk, 4.2% work from home (2006-2010 5-year est.); Travel time to work: 39.2% less than 15 minutes, 32.8% 15 to 30 minutes, 12.3% 30 to 45 minutes, 4.5% 45 to 60 minutes, 11.2% 60 minutes or more (2006-2010 5-year est.); Amtrak: train service available.
**Airports:** Dutchess County (general aviation)

**POUGHQUAG** (unincorporated postal area)
Zip Code: 12570
   Covers a land area of 21.510 square miles and a water area of 0.266 square miles. Located at 41.62° N. Lat; 73.67° W. Long. Elevation is 436 feet. Population: 7,699 (2010); Density: 357.9 persons per square mile (2010); Race: 91.3% White, 2.7% Black, 3.4% Asian, 0.2% American Indian/Alaska Native, 0.0% Native Hawaiian/Other Pacific Islander, 2.4% Other, 6.0% Hispanic of any race (2010); Average household size: 3.02 (2010); Median age: 40.4 (2010); Males per 100 females: 98.7 (2010); Homeownership rate: 89.7% (2010)

**RED HOOK** (village). Covers a land area of 1.102 square miles and a water area of 0.012 square miles. Located at 41.99° N. Lat; 73.87° W. Long. Elevation is 220 feet.
**Population:** 1,794 (1990); 1,805 (2000); 1,961 (2010); Density: 1,778.9 persons per square mile (2010); Race: 91.4% White, 1.0% Black, 3.5% Asian, 0.3% American Indian/Alaska Native, 0.0% Native Hawaiian/Other Pacific Islander, 3.8% Other, 6.5% Hispanic of any race (2010); Average household size: 2.20 (2010); Median age: 42.7 (2010); Males per 100 females: 87.5 (2010); Marriage status: 22.6% never married, 57.9% now married, 12.6% widowed, 6.9% divorced (2006-2010 5-year est.); Foreign born: 14.9% (2006-2010 5-year est.); Ancestry (includes multiple ancestries): 26.9% Irish, 22.1% German, 19.6% Italian, 11.3% English, 5.5% Polish (2006-2010 5-year est.).
**Economy:** Single-family building permits issued: 1 (2011); Multi-family building permits issued: 0 (2011); Employment by occupation: 14.9% management, 3.9% professional, 10.3% services, 22.3% sales, 1.3% farming, 11.2% construction, 3.1% production (2006-2010 5-year est.).
**Income:** Per capita income: $27,044 (2006-2010 5-year est.); Median household income: $56,131 (2006-2010 5-year est.); Average household income: $62,766 (2006-2010 5-year est.); Percent of households with income of $100,000 or more: 18.0% (2006-2010 5-year est.); Poverty rate: 10.3% (2006-2010 5-year est.).

**Education:** Percent of population age 25 and over with: High school diploma (including GED) or higher: 88.7% (2006-2010 5-year est.); Bachelor's degree or higher: 34.2% (2006-2010 5-year est.); Master's degree or higher: 16.3% (2006-2010 5-year est.).
**School District(s)**
Red Hook Central School District (KG-12)
   2009-10 Enrollment: 2,231 ................... (845) 758-2241
**Housing:** Homeownership rate: 53.9% (2010); Median home value: $257,100 (2006-2010 5-year est.); Median contract rent: $820 per month (2006-2010 5-year est.); Median year structure built: 1951 (2006-2010 5-year est.).
**Safety:** Violent crime rate: 15.1 per 10,000 population; Property crime rate: 266.2 per 10,000 population (2010).
**Transportation:** Commute to work: 80.5% car, 7.5% public transportation, 3.5% walk, 6.6% work from home (2006-2010 5-year est.); Travel time to work: 25.6% less than 15 minutes, 28.8% 15 to 30 minutes, 25.2% 30 to 45 minutes, 6.5% 45 to 60 minutes, 13.9% 60 minutes or more (2006-2010 5-year est.)
**Additional Information Contacts**
Red Hook Area Chamber of Commerce .......... (845) 758-0824
   http://www.redhookchamber.org

**RED HOOK** (town). Covers a land area of 36.168 square miles and a water area of 3.871 square miles. Located at 42.01° N. Lat; 73.88° W. Long. Elevation is 220 feet.
**Population:** 9,565 (1990); 10,408 (2000); 11,319 (2010); Density: 313.0 persons per square mile (2010); Race: 92.0% White, 1.9% Black, 2.4% Asian, 0.2% American Indian/Alaska Native, 0.0% Native Hawaiian/Other Pacific Islander, 3.5% Other, 4.9% Hispanic of any race (2010); Average household size: 2.47 (2010); Median age: 37.1 (2010); Males per 100 females: 94.5 (2010); Marriage status: 39.5% never married, 48.6% now married, 4.9% widowed, 7.0% divorced (2006-2010 5-year est.); Foreign born: 11.8% (2006-2010 5-year est.); Ancestry (includes multiple ancestries): 25.6% Irish, 20.1% German, 16.3% Italian, 14.9% English, 6.1% Dutch (2006-2010 5-year est.).
**Economy:** Single-family building permits issued: 1 (2011); Multi-family building permits issued: 0 (2011); Employment by occupation: 12.5% management, 2.9% professional, 8.3% services, 18.0% sales, 3.6% farming, 9.2% construction, 3.6% production (2006-2010 5-year est.).
**Income:** Per capita income: $28,964 (2006-2010 5-year est.); Median household income: $69,396 (2006-2010 5-year est.); Average household income: $88,324 (2006-2010 5-year est.); Percent of households with income of $100,000 or more: 34.4% (2006-2010 5-year est.); Poverty rate: 5.3% (2006-2010 5-year est.).
**Education:** Percent of population age 25 and over with: High school diploma (including GED) or higher: 93.6% (2006-2010 5-year est.); Bachelor's degree or higher: 44.0% (2006-2010 5-year est.); Master's degree or higher: 22.2% (2006-2010 5-year est.).
**School District(s)**
Red Hook Central School District (KG-12)
   2009-10 Enrollment: 2,231 ................... (845) 758-2241
**Housing:** Homeownership rate: 72.3% (2010); Median home value: $316,000 (2006-2010 5-year est.); Median contract rent: $787 per month (2006-2010 5-year est.); Median year structure built: 1967 (2006-2010 5-year est.).
**Transportation:** Commute to work: 74.1% car, 2.4% public transportation, 15.0% walk, 8.2% work from home (2006-2010 5-year est.); Travel time to work: 40.9% less than 15 minutes, 28.8% 15 to 30 minutes, 13.5% 30 to 45 minutes, 8.0% 45 to 60 minutes, 8.7% 60 minutes or more (2006-2010 5-year est.)
**Additional Information Contacts**
Town of Red Hook ......................... (845) 758-4606
   http://www.redhook.org

**RED OAKS MILL** (CDP). Covers a land area of 2.276 square miles and a water area of 0.030 square miles. Located at 41.65° N. Lat; 73.87° W. Long. Elevation is 167 feet.
**Population:** 4,906 (1990); 4,930 (2000); 3,613 (2010); Density: 1,587.3 persons per square mile (2010); Race: 86.0% White, 6.2% Black, 3.7% Asian, 0.2% American Indian/Alaska Native, 0.0% Native Hawaiian/Other Pacific Islander, 3.9% Other, 7.9% Hispanic of any race (2010); Average household size: 2.75 (2010); Median age: 44.3 (2010); Males per 100 females: 97.4 (2010); Marriage status: 25.4% never married, 66.9% now married, 3.2% widowed, 4.5% divorced (2006-2010 5-year est.); Foreign born: 6.3% (2006-2010 5-year est.); Ancestry (includes multiple

ancestries): 25.5% Irish, 24.5% German, 21.3% Italian, 16.5% English, 4.6% Russian (2006-2010 5-year est.).
**Economy:** Employment by occupation: 13.4% management, 6.3% professional, 6.1% services, 17.5% sales, 2.5% farming, 7.0% construction, 5.6% production (2006-2010 5-year est.).
**Income:** Per capita income: $37,207 (2006-2010 5-year est.); Median household income: $99,259 (2006-2010 5-year est.); Average household income: $98,654 (2006-2010 5-year est.); Percent of households with income of $100,000 or more: 49.4% (2006-2010 5-year est.); Poverty rate: 2.1% (2006-2010 5-year est.).
**Education:** Percent of population age 25 and over with: High school diploma (including GED) or higher: 96.4% (2006-2010 5-year est.); Bachelor's degree or higher: 44.8% (2006-2010 5-year est.); Master's degree or higher: 24.5% (2006-2010 5-year est.).
**Housing:** Homeownership rate: 93.8% (2010); Median home value: $323,500 (2006-2010 5-year est.); Median contract rent: $936 per month (2006-2010 5-year est.); Median year structure built: 1963 (2006-2010 5-year est.).
**Transportation:** Commute to work: 86.8% car, 2.0% public transportation, 5.3% walk, 5.9% work from home (2006-2010 5-year est.); Travel time to work: 32.2% less than 15 minutes, 38.2% 15 to 30 minutes, 10.0% 30 to 45 minutes, 8.2% 45 to 60 minutes, 11.4% 60 minutes or more (2006-2010 5-year est.)

**RHINEBECK** (village). Covers a land area of 1.523 square miles and a water area of 0.020 square miles. Located at 41.92° N. Lat; 73.91° W. Long. Elevation is 200 feet.
**Population:** 3,038 (1990); 3,077 (2000); 2,657 (2010); Density: 1,744.1 persons per square mile (2010); Race: 91.9% White, 1.7% Black, 2.1% Asian, 0.0% American Indian/Alaska Native, 0.0% Native Hawaiian/Other Pacific Islander, 4.3% Other, 6.7% Hispanic of any race (2010); Average household size: 1.92 (2010); Median age: 49.6 (2010); Males per 100 females: 80.5 (2010); Marriage status: 23.0% never married, 55.3% now married, 11.3% widowed, 10.4% divorced (2006-2010 5-year est.); Foreign born: 7.2% (2006-2010 5-year est.); Ancestry (includes multiple ancestries): 35.0% Irish, 27.3% German, 19.6% English, 14.3% Italian, 9.9% Dutch (2006-2010 5-year est.).
**Economy:** Single-family building permits issued: 2 (2011); Multi-family building permits issued: 0 (2011); Employment by occupation: 17.8% management, 4.6% professional, 6.5% services, 13.6% sales, 2.0% farming, 3.3% construction, 3.3% production (2006-2010 5-year est.).
**Income:** Per capita income: $39,109 (2006-2010 5-year est.); Median household income: $61,125 (2006-2010 5-year est.); Average household income: $86,863 (2006-2010 5-year est.); Percent of households with income of $100,000 or more: 29.6% (2006-2010 5-year est.); Poverty rate: 8.3% (2006-2010 5-year est.).
**Education:** Percent of population age 25 and over with: High school diploma (including GED) or higher: 95.1% (2006-2010 5-year est.); Bachelor's degree or higher: 59.0% (2006-2010 5-year est.); Master's degree or higher: 31.8% (2006-2010 5-year est.).
**School District(s)**
Rhinebeck Central School District (KG-12)
    2009-10 Enrollment: 1,189 . . . . . . . . . . . . . . . . . . . . (845) 871-5520
**Housing:** Homeownership rate: 56.7% (2010); Median home value: $362,300 (2006-2010 5-year est.); Median contract rent: $887 per month (2006-2010 5-year est.); Median year structure built: 1960 (2006-2010 5-year est.).
**Hospitals:** Northern Dutchess Hospital (68 beds)
**Safety:** Violent crime rate: 13.4 per 10,000 population; Property crime rate: 147.6 per 10,000 population (2010).
**Newspapers:** Gazette-Advertiser (Local news; Circulation 9,000)
**Transportation:** Commute to work: 76.5% car, 5.3% public transportation, 6.3% walk, 10.8% work from home (2006-2010 5-year est.); Travel time to work: 37.8% less than 15 minutes, 27.8% 15 to 30 minutes, 21.7% 30 to 45 minutes, 4.1% 45 to 60 minutes, 8.7% 60 minutes or more (2006-2010 5-year est.); Amtrak: train service available.
**Additional Information Contacts**
Rhinebeck Chamber of Commerce . . . . . . . . . . . . . . . . . . (845) 876-5904
    http://www.rhinebeckchamber.com

**RHINEBECK** (town). Covers a land area of 35.681 square miles and a water area of 4.067 square miles. Located at 41.92° N. Lat; 73.90° W. Long. Elevation is 200 feet.
**History:** It is the site of Beekman Arms, said to be the oldest hotel in the U.S., and of a pre-Revolutionary Dutch Reformed church and cemetery.

Unique collection of aircraft from before and during World War I at Old Rhinebeck Aerodrome. Settled before 1700, incorporated 1834.
**Population:** 7,558 (1990); 7,762 (2000); 7,548 (2010); Density: 211.5 persons per square mile (2010); Race: 92.4% White, 2.5% Black, 1.8% Asian, 0.1% American Indian/Alaska Native, 0.1% Native Hawaiian/Other Pacific Islander, 3.1% Other, 5.1% Hispanic of any race (2010); Average household size: 2.12 (2010); Median age: 50.4 (2010); Males per 100 females: 83.3 (2010); Marriage status: 25.1% never married, 49.5% now married, 14.3% widowed, 11.1% divorced (2006-2010 5-year est.); Foreign born: 5.8% (2006-2010 5-year est.); Ancestry (includes multiple ancestries): 26.3% Irish, 24.3% German, 14.8% English, 13.6% Italian, 6.3% Dutch (2006-2010 5-year est.).
**Economy:** Single-family building permits issued: 14 (2011); Multi-family building permits issued: 0 (2011); Employment by occupation: 14.3% management, 4.3% professional, 10.8% services, 13.3% sales, 3.0% farming, 6.9% construction, 4.0% production (2006-2010 5-year est.).
**Income:** Per capita income: $37,356 (2006-2010 5-year est.); Median household income: $67,284 (2006-2010 5-year est.); Average household income: $93,620 (2006-2010 5-year est.); Percent of households with income of $100,000 or more: 30.7% (2006-2010 5-year est.); Poverty rate: 7.8% (2006-2010 5-year est.).
**Education:** Percent of population age 25 and over with: High school diploma (including GED) or higher: 90.0% (2006-2010 5-year est.); Bachelor's degree or higher: 42.3% (2006-2010 5-year est.); Master's degree or higher: 21.3% (2006-2010 5-year est.).
**School District(s)**
Rhinebeck Central School District (KG-12)
    2009-10 Enrollment: 1,189 . . . . . . . . . . . . . . . . . . . . (845) 871-5520
**Housing:** Homeownership rate: 67.9% (2010); Median home value: $390,500 (2006-2010 5-year est.); Median contract rent: $889 per month (2006-2010 5-year est.); Median year structure built: 1964 (2006-2010 5-year est.).
**Hospitals:** Northern Dutchess Hospital (68 beds)
**Newspapers:** Gazette-Advertiser (Local news; Circulation 9,000)
**Transportation:** Commute to work: 79.9% car, 5.5% public transportation, 5.1% walk, 9.0% work from home (2006-2010 5-year est.); Travel time to work: 36.0% less than 15 minutes, 31.4% 15 to 30 minutes, 18.4% 30 to 45 minutes, 4.5% 45 to 60 minutes, 9.8% 60 minutes or more (2006-2010 5-year est.); Amtrak: train service available.

**RHINECLIFF** (CDP). Covers a land area of 0.994 square miles and a water area of 0.013 square miles. Located at 41.92° N. Lat; 73.94° W. Long. Elevation is 46 feet.
**Population:** n/a (1990); n/a (2000); 425 (2010); Density: 427.4 persons per square mile (2010); Race: 93.4% White, 2.8% Black, 0.7% Asian, 0.0% American Indian/Alaska Native, 0.0% Native Hawaiian/Other Pacific Islander, 3.1% Other, 1.9% Hispanic of any race (2010); Average household size: 2.11 (2010); Median age: 47.2 (2010); Males per 100 females: 120.2 (2010); Marriage status: 24.3% never married, 52.7% now married, 8.5% widowed, 14.5% divorced (2006-2010 5-year est.); Foreign born: 14.8% (2006-2010 5-year est.); Ancestry (includes multiple ancestries): 34.2% Irish, 29.9% German, 23.2% Scottish, 18.6% Italian, 17.5% Dutch (2006-2010 5-year est.).
**Economy:** Employment by occupation: 0.0% management, 4.5% professional, 31.5% services, 0.0% sales, 10.7% farming, 0.0% construction, 0.0% production (2006-2010 5-year est.).
**Income:** Per capita income: $33,758 (2006-2010 5-year est.); Median household income: $62,813 (2006-2010 5-year est.); Average household income: $66,293 (2006-2010 5-year est.); Percent of households with income of $100,000 or more: 12.1% (2006-2010 5-year est.); Poverty rate: 7.0% (2006-2010 5-year est.).
**Education:** Percent of population age 25 and over with: High school diploma (including GED) or higher: 93.6% (2006-2010 5-year est.); Bachelor's degree or higher: 42.2% (2006-2010 5-year est.); Master's degree or higher: 19.5% (2006-2010 5-year est.).
**Housing:** Homeownership rate: 67.2% (2010); Median home value: $331,900 (2006-2010 5-year est.); Median contract rent: $792 per month (2006-2010 5-year est.); Median year structure built: before 1940 (2006-2010 5-year est.).
**Transportation:** Commute to work: 84.9% car, 8.2% public transportation, 0.0% walk, 6.9% work from home (2006-2010 5-year est.); Travel time to work: 16.2% less than 15 minutes, 24.3% 15 to 30 minutes, 35.8% 30 to 45 minutes, 16.2% 45 to 60 minutes, 7.4% 60 minutes or more (2006-2010 5-year est.)

**SALT POINT** (CDP). Covers a land area of 0.829 square miles and a water area of 0.003 square miles. Located at 41.80° N. Lat; 73.78° W. Long. Elevation is 236 feet.
**Population:** n/a (1990); n/a (2000); 190 (2010); Density: 229.1 persons per square mile (2010); Race: 93.2% White, 3.2% Black, 2.1% Asian, 0.0% American Indian/Alaska Native, 0.0% Native Hawaiian/Other Pacific Islander, 1.5% Other, 1.1% Hispanic of any race (2010); Average household size: 2.60 (2010); Median age: 43.3 (2010); Males per 100 females: 91.9 (2010); Marriage status: 38.9% never married, 61.1% now married, 0.0% widowed, 0.0% divorced (2006-2010 5-year est.); Foreign born: 10.1% (2006-2010 5-year est.); Ancestry (includes multiple ancestries): 30.7% German, 23.3% Irish, 22.1% English, 15.0% American, 14.4% Scottish (2006-2010 5-year est.).
**Economy:** Employment by occupation: 2.5% management, 18.8% professional, 10.6% services, 28.7% sales, 11.3% farming, 10.0% construction, 0.0% production (2006-2010 5-year est.).
**Income:** Per capita income: $34,600 (2006-2010 5-year est.); Median household income: $147,679 (2006-2010 5-year est.); Average household income: $134,896 (2006-2010 5-year est.); Percent of households with income of $100,000 or more: 95.0% (2006-2010 5-year est.); Poverty rate: 0.0% (2006-2010 5-year est.).
**Education:** Percent of population age 25 and over with: High school diploma (including GED) or higher: 82.5% (2006-2010 5-year est.); Bachelor's degree or higher: 24.3% (2006-2010 5-year est.); Master's degree or higher: 15.9% (2006-2010 5-year est.).
**Housing:** Homeownership rate: 75.3% (2010); Median home value: $340,600 (2006-2010 5-year est.); Median contract rent: n/a per month (2006-2010 5-year est.); Median year structure built: 1985 (2006-2010 5-year est.).
**Transportation:** Commute to work: 100.0% car, 0.0% public transportation, 0.0% walk, 0.0% work from home (2006-2010 5-year est.); Travel time to work: 40.6% less than 15 minutes, 40.6% 15 to 30 minutes, 18.8% 30 to 45 minutes, 0.0% 45 to 60 minutes, 0.0% 60 minutes or more (2006-2010 5-year est.)

**SPACKENKILL** (CDP). Covers a land area of 1.774 square miles and a water area of <.001 square miles. Located at 41.65° N. Lat; 73.91° W. Long. Elevation is 164 feet.
**Population:** 4,660 (1990); 4,756 (2000); 4,123 (2010); Density: 2,323.0 persons per square mile (2010); Race: 79.9% White, 4.7% Black, 10.9% Asian, 0.0% American Indian/Alaska Native, 0.1% Native Hawaiian/Other Pacific Islander, 4.4% Other, 7.2% Hispanic of any race (2010); Average household size: 2.87 (2010); Median age: 44.0 (2010); Males per 100 females: 95.5 (2010); Marriage status: 24.3% never married, 66.0% now married, 4.6% widowed, 5.1% divorced (2006-2010 5-year est.); Foreign born: 10.3% (2006-2010 5-year est.); Ancestry (includes multiple ancestries): 24.3% Italian, 20.4% Irish, 16.2% German, 10.4% English, 7.3% Polish (2006-2010 5-year est.).
**Economy:** Employment by occupation: 14.9% management, 12.1% professional, 2.3% services, 14.2% sales, 1.1% farming, 4.7% construction, 3.6% production (2006-2010 5-year est.).
**Income:** Per capita income: $44,219 (2006-2010 5-year est.); Median household income: $104,819 (2006-2010 5-year est.); Average household income: $135,228 (2006-2010 5-year est.); Percent of households with income of $100,000 or more: 53.9% (2006-2010 5-year est.); Poverty rate: 8.4% (2006-2010 5-year est.).
**Education:** Percent of population age 25 and over with: High school diploma (including GED) or higher: 94.3% (2006-2010 5-year est.); Bachelor's degree or higher: 58.5% (2006-2010 5-year est.); Master's degree or higher: 30.4% (2006-2010 5-year est.).
**Housing:** Homeownership rate: 94.7% (2010); Median home value: $360,100 (2006-2010 5-year est.); Median contract rent: $1,652 per month (2006-2010 5-year est.); Median year structure built: 1962 (2006-2010 5-year est.).
**Transportation:** Commute to work: 91.2% car, 2.7% public transportation, 2.1% walk, 4.0% work from home (2006-2010 5-year est.); Travel time to work: 47.6% less than 15 minutes, 32.5% 15 to 30 minutes, 7.1% 30 to 45 minutes, 2.6% 45 to 60 minutes, 10.2% 60 minutes or more (2006-2010 5-year est.)

**STAATSBURG** (CDP). Covers a land area of 1.065 square miles and a water area of 0.001 square miles. Located at 41.85° N. Lat; 73.92° W. Long. Elevation is 30 feet.
**Population:** 975 (1990); 911 (2000); 377 (2010); Density: 353.9 persons per square mile (2010); Race: 96.3% White, 0.3% Black, 1.1% Asian, 0.5%

American Indian/Alaska Native, 0.0% Native Hawaiian/Other Pacific Islander, 1.8% Other, 5.3% Hispanic of any race (2010); Average household size: 2.33 (2010); Median age: 44.1 (2010); Males per 100 females: 99.5 (2010); Marriage status: 11.4% never married, 68.8% now married, 4.3% widowed, 15.5% divorced (2006-2010 5-year est.); Foreign born: 3.4% (2006-2010 5-year est.); Ancestry (includes multiple ancestries): 52.3% Irish, 21.9% English, 20.2% Italian, 14.5% German, 5.5% Scottish (2006-2010 5-year est.).
**Economy:** Employment by occupation: 12.8% management, 4.0% professional, 23.6% services, 12.8% sales, 0.0% farming, 3.4% construction, 1.7% production (2006-2010 5-year est.).
**Income:** Per capita income: $30,895 (2006-2010 5-year est.); Median household income: $63,889 (2006-2010 5-year est.); Average household income: $84,018 (2006-2010 5-year est.); Percent of households with income of $100,000 or more: 27.4% (2006-2010 5-year est.); Poverty rate: 2.8% (2006-2010 5-year est.).
**Education:** Percent of population age 25 and over with: High school diploma (including GED) or higher: 92.3% (2006-2010 5-year est.); Bachelor's degree or higher: 43.3% (2006-2010 5-year est.); Master's degree or higher: 22.7% (2006-2010 5-year est.).
**Housing:** Homeownership rate: 70.4% (2010); Median home value: $224,500 (2006-2010 5-year est.); Median contract rent: $335 per month (2006-2010 5-year est.); Median year structure built: before 1940 (2006-2010 5-year est.).
**Transportation:** Commute to work: 97.0% car, 0.0% public transportation, 0.0% walk, 3.0% work from home (2006-2010 5-year est.); Travel time to work: 4.2% less than 15 minutes, 46.5% 15 to 30 minutes, 36.1% 30 to 45 minutes, 0.0% 45 to 60 minutes, 13.2% 60 minutes or more (2006-2010 5-year est.)

**STANFORD** (town). Covers a land area of 49.637 square miles and a water area of 0.649 square miles. Located at 41.89° N. Lat; 73.67° W. Long.
**Population:** 3,495 (1990); 3,544 (2000); 3,823 (2010); Density: 77.0 persons per square mile (2010); Race: 93.8% White, 1.8% Black, 1.0% Asian, 0.3% American Indian/Alaska Native, 0.1% Native Hawaiian/Other Pacific Islander, 3.0% Other, 5.7% Hispanic of any race (2010); Average household size: 2.38 (2010); Median age: 44.6 (2010); Males per 100 females: 101.0 (2010); Marriage status: 22.9% never married, 61.6% now married, 1.7% widowed, 13.8% divorced (2006-2010 5-year est.); Foreign born: 6.4% (2006-2010 5-year est.); Ancestry (includes multiple ancestries): 27.6% German, 22.4% Irish, 16.5% English, 15.7% Italian, 6.5% Polish (2006-2010 5-year est.).
**Economy:** Single-family building permits issued: 4 (2011); Multi-family building permits issued: 0 (2011); Employment by occupation: 14.6% management, 4.3% professional, 9.3% services, 13.8% sales, 2.5% farming, 12.8% construction, 7.0% production (2006-2010 5-year est.).
**Income:** Per capita income: $37,195 (2006-2010 5-year est.); Median household income: $67,488 (2006-2010 5-year est.); Average household income: $87,370 (2006-2010 5-year est.); Percent of households with income of $100,000 or more: 25.5% (2006-2010 5-year est.); Poverty rate: 4.7% (2006-2010 5-year est.).
**Education:** Percent of population age 25 and over with: High school diploma (including GED) or higher: 94.9% (2006-2010 5-year est.); Bachelor's degree or higher: 32.8% (2006-2010 5-year est.); Master's degree or higher: 14.3% (2006-2010 5-year est.).
**Housing:** Homeownership rate: 74.6% (2010); Median home value: $315,900 (2006-2010 5-year est.); Median contract rent: $966 per month (2006-2010 5-year est.); Median year structure built: 1957 (2006-2010 5-year est.).
**Transportation:** Commute to work: 86.8% car, 3.2% public transportation, 2.5% walk, 6.6% work from home (2006-2010 5-year est.); Travel time to work: 19.6% less than 15 minutes, 31.0% 15 to 30 minutes, 28.9% 30 to 45 minutes, 7.8% 45 to 60 minutes, 12.8% 60 minutes or more (2006-2010 5-year est.)

**STANFORDVILLE** (unincorporated postal area)
Zip Code: 12581
    Covers a land area of 40.431 square miles and a water area of 0.394 square miles. Located at 41.90° N. Lat; 73.70° W. Long. Elevation is 358 feet. Population: 2,246 (2010); Density: 55.6 persons per square mile (2010); Race: 93.1% White, 2.3% Black, 0.9% Asian, 0.4% American Indian/Alaska Native, 0.0% Native Hawaiian/Other Pacific Islander, 3.3% Other, 6.6% Hispanic of any race (2010); Average household size: 2.31

(2010); Median age: 46.2 (2010); Males per 100 females: 98.6 (2010); Homeownership rate: 71.6% (2010)

**STORMVILLE** (unincorporated postal area)
Zip Code: 12582

Covers a land area of 12.782 square miles and a water area of 0.402 square miles. Located at 41.54° N. Lat; 73.73° W. Long. Elevation is 328 feet. Population: 6,191 (2010); Density: 484.3 persons per square mile (2010); Race: 70.7% White, 21.9% Black, 2.0% Asian, 0.3% American Indian/Alaska Native, 0.0% Native Hawaiian/Other Pacific Islander, 5.1% Other, 11.2% Hispanic of any race (2010); Average household size: 3.00 (2010); Median age: 41.6 (2010); Males per 100 females: 209.2 (2010); Homeownership rate: 90.1% (2010)

**TITUSVILLE** (CDP). Covers a land area of 0.690 square miles and a water area of <.001 square miles. Located at 41.66° N. Lat; 73.86° W. Long. Elevation is 154 feet.
**Population:** n/a (1990); n/a (2000); 811 (2010); Density: 1,174.3 persons per square mile (2010); Race: 91.1% White, 4.8% Black, 1.8% Asian, 0.0% American Indian/Alaska Native, 0.0% Native Hawaiian/Other Pacific Islander, 2.3% Other, 7.6% Hispanic of any race (2010); Average household size: 2.74 (2010); Median age: 46.6 (2010); Males per 100 females: 96.8 (2010); Marriage status: 9.0% never married, 76.4% now married, 11.1% widowed, 3.6% divorced (2006-2010 5-year est.); Foreign born: 1.9% (2006-2010 5-year est.); Ancestry (includes multiple ancestries): 28.5% Italian, 21.8% Irish, 20.7% German, 5.9% Russian, 5.0% Dutch (2006-2010 5-year est.).
**Economy:** Employment by occupation: 21.6% management, 9.2% professional, 8.8% services, 14.4% sales, 3.6% farming, 3.6% construction, 3.6% production (2006-2010 5-year est.).
**Income:** Per capita income: $54,774 (2006-2010 5-year est.); Median household income: $104,519 (2006-2010 5-year est.); Average household income: $125,953 (2006-2010 5-year est.); Percent of households with income of $100,000 or more: 59.0% (2006-2010 5-year est.); Poverty rate: 1.7% (2006-2010 5-year est.).
**Education:** Percent of population age 25 and over with: High school diploma (including GED) or higher: 90.7% (2006-2010 5-year est.); Bachelor's degree or higher: 43.0% (2006-2010 5-year est.); Master's degree or higher: 29.5% (2006-2010 5-year est.).
**Housing:** Homeownership rate: 94.9% (2010); Median home value: $365,200 (2006-2010 5-year est.); Median contract rent: n/a per month (2006-2010 5-year est.); Median year structure built: 1957 (2006-2010 5-year est.).
**Transportation:** Commute to work: 96.4% car, 3.6% public transportation, 0.0% walk, 0.0% work from home (2006-2010 5-year est.); Travel time to work: 29.2% less than 15 minutes, 51.6% 15 to 30 minutes, 6.8% 30 to 45 minutes, 0.0% 45 to 60 minutes, 12.4% 60 minutes or more (2006-2010 5-year est.)

**TIVOLI** (village). Covers a land area of 1.610 square miles and a water area of 0.027 square miles. Located at 42.05° N. Lat; 73.91° W. Long. Elevation is 151 feet.
**Population:** 1,035 (1990); 1,163 (2000); 1,118 (2010); Density: 694.4 persons per square mile (2010); Race: 93.5% White, 0.3% Black, 2.1% Asian, 0.1% American Indian/Alaska Native, 0.4% Native Hawaiian/Other Pacific Islander, 3.6% Other, 5.3% Hispanic of any race (2010); Average household size: 2.32 (2010); Median age: 35.0 (2010); Males per 100 females: 89.2 (2010); Marriage status: 33.6% never married, 47.2% now married, 5.4% widowed, 13.8% divorced (2006-2010 5-year est.); Foreign born: 5.7% (2006-2010 5-year est.); Ancestry (includes multiple ancestries): 23.3% German, 21.7% Italian, 19.3% Irish, 18.7% English, 9.5% Scottish (2006-2010 5-year est.).
**Economy:** Single-family building permits issued: 0 (2011); Multi-family building permits issued: 0 (2011); Employment by occupation: 9.3% management, 5.8% professional, 12.2% services, 12.9% sales, 7.1% farming, 14.9% construction, 6.4% production (2006-2010 5-year est.).
**Income:** Per capita income: $31,900 (2006-2010 5-year est.); Median household income: $58,000 (2006-2010 5-year est.); Average household income: $76,743 (2006-2010 5-year est.); Percent of households with income of $100,000 or more: 24.2% (2006-2010 5-year est.); Poverty rate: 16.5% (2006-2010 5-year est.).
**Education:** Percent of population age 25 and over with: High school diploma (including GED) or higher: 97.3% (2006-2010 5-year est.); Bachelor's degree or higher: 41.4% (2006-2010 5-year est.); Master's degree or higher: 19.2% (2006-2010 5-year est.).

**Housing:** Homeownership rate: 56.0% (2010); Median home value: $293,100 (2006-2010 5-year est.); Median contract rent: $911 per month (2006-2010 5-year est.); Median year structure built: 1981 (2006-2010 5-year est.).
**Transportation:** Commute to work: 85.0% car, 2.7% public transportation, 3.4% walk, 9.0% work from home (2006-2010 5-year est.); Travel time to work: 38.3% less than 15 minutes, 21.8% 15 to 30 minutes, 14.4% 30 to 45 minutes, 15.2% 45 to 60 minutes, 10.4% 60 minutes or more (2006-2010 5-year est.)

**UNION VALE** (town). Covers a land area of 37.481 square miles and a water area of 0.323 square miles. Located at 41.69° N. Lat; 73.69° W. Long.
**Population:** 3,577 (1990); 4,546 (2000); 4,877 (2010); Density: 130.1 persons per square mile (2010); Race: 93.4% White, 1.6% Black, 2.4% Asian, 0.0% American Indian/Alaska Native, 0.0% Native Hawaiian/Other Pacific Islander, 2.6% Other, 4.7% Hispanic of any race (2010); Average household size: 2.83 (2010); Median age: 43.6 (2010); Males per 100 females: 98.2 (2010); Marriage status: 26.5% never married, 61.6% now married, 5.2% widowed, 6.7% divorced (2006-2010 5-year est.); Foreign born: 9.7% (2006-2010 5-year est.); Ancestry (includes multiple ancestries): 29.7% Italian, 27.3% Irish, 19.7% German, 11.8% English, 5.2% Scotch-Irish (2006-2010 5-year est.).
**Economy:** Single-family building permits issued: 5 (2011); Multi-family building permits issued: 0 (2011); Employment by occupation: 13.1% management, 5.3% professional, 7.3% services, 10.7% sales, 2.6% farming, 15.6% construction, 6.9% production (2006-2010 5-year est.).
**Income:** Per capita income: $36,173 (2006-2010 5-year est.); Median household income: $82,278 (2006-2010 5-year est.); Average household income: $99,885 (2006-2010 5-year est.); Percent of households with income of $100,000 or more: 37.6% (2006-2010 5-year est.); Poverty rate: 4.4% (2006-2010 5-year est.).
**Education:** Percent of population age 25 and over with: High school diploma (including GED) or higher: 92.3% (2006-2010 5-year est.); Bachelor's degree or higher: 43.3% (2006-2010 5-year est.); Master's degree or higher: 22.2% (2006-2010 5-year est.).
**Housing:** Homeownership rate: 81.9% (2010); Median home value: $397,600 (2006-2010 5-year est.); Median contract rent: $1,102 per month (2006-2010 5-year est.); Median year structure built: 1976 (2006-2010 5-year est.).
**Transportation:** Commute to work: 90.5% car, 0.9% public transportation, 3.9% walk, 4.4% work from home (2006-2010 5-year est.); Travel time to work: 19.0% less than 15 minutes, 31.3% 15 to 30 minutes, 22.2% 30 to 45 minutes, 7.6% 45 to 60 minutes, 19.9% 60 minutes or more (2006-2010 5-year est.)
**Additional Information Contacts**
Town of Union Vale . . . . . . . . . . . . . . . . . . . . . . . . . . . . (845) 724-5600
  http://www2.marist.edu/unionvale

**VERBANK** (unincorporated postal area)
Zip Code: 12585

Covers a land area of 4.922 square miles and a water area of 0.078 square miles. Located at 41.72° N. Lat; 73.69° W. Long. Elevation is 591 feet. Population: 885 (2010); Density: 179.8 persons per square mile (2010); Race: 92.7% White, 3.8% Black, 1.2% Asian, 0.0% American Indian/Alaska Native, 0.0% Native Hawaiian/Other Pacific Islander, 2.3% Other, 4.0% Hispanic of any race (2010); Average household size: 2.82 (2010); Median age: 42.6 (2010); Males per 100 females: 103.9 (2010); Homeownership rate: 84.4% (2010)

**WAPPINGER** (town). Covers a land area of 27.054 square miles and a water area of 1.476 square miles. Located at 41.58° N. Lat; 73.89° W. Long.
**History:** Society of the Cincinnati founded here in 1783. Incorporated 1871.
**Population:** 26,008 (1990); 26,274 (2000); 27,048 (2010); Density: 999.8 persons per square mile (2010); Race: 81.1% White, 6.4% Black, 5.0% Asian, 0.2% American Indian/Alaska Native, 0.0% Native Hawaiian/Other Pacific Islander, 7.3% Other, 14.3% Hispanic of any race (2010); Average household size: 2.61 (2010); Median age: 40.0 (2010); Males per 100 females: 98.0 (2010); Marriage status: 28.7% never married, 58.5% now married, 4.7% widowed, 8.1% divorced (2006-2010 5-year est.); Foreign born: 14.2% (2006-2010 5-year est.); Ancestry (includes multiple ancestries): 29.5% Italian, 23.4% Irish, 14.2% German, 8.2% English, 3.9% Polish (2006-2010 5-year est.).

**Economy:** Unemployment rate: 8.1% (February 2012); Total civilian labor force: 14,553 (February 2012); Single-family building permits issued: 33 (2011); Multi-family building permits issued: 0 (2011); Employment by occupation: 12.2% management, 5.9% professional, 5.8% services, 17.9% sales, 5.5% farming, 9.6% construction, 6.0% production (2006-2010 5-year est.).
**Income:** Per capita income: $31,490 (2006-2010 5-year est.); Median household income: $73,078 (2006-2010 5-year est.); Average household income: $84,638 (2006-2010 5-year est.); Percent of households with income of $100,000 or more: 32.8% (2006-2010 5-year est.); Poverty rate: 5.4% (2006-2010 5-year est.).
**Education:** Percent of population age 25 and over with: High school diploma (including GED) or higher: 92.0% (2006-2010 5-year est.); Bachelor's degree or higher: 31.2% (2006-2010 5-year est.); Master's degree or higher: 12.9% (2006-2010 5-year est.).
**Housing:** Homeownership rate: 68.6% (2010); Median home value: $330,800 (2006-2010 5-year est.); Median contract rent: $981 per month (2006-2010 5-year est.); Median year structure built: 1968 (2006-2010 5-year est.).
**Transportation:** Commute to work: 88.9% car, 6.6% public transportation, 1.4% walk, 2.9% work from home (2006-2010 5-year est.); Travel time to work: 21.1% less than 15 minutes, 32.0% 15 to 30 minutes, 18.9% 30 to 45 minutes, 10.8% 45 to 60 minutes, 17.2% 60 minutes or more (2006-2010 5-year est.)

## WAPPINGERS FALLS (village).
Covers a land area of 1.108 square miles and a water area of 0.076 square miles. Located at 41.59° N. Lat; 73.91° W. Long. Elevation is 154 feet.
**Population:** 4,605 (1990); 4,929 (2000); 5,522 (2010); Density: 4,983.1 persons per square mile (2010); Race: 72.5% White, 7.4% Black, 4.8% Asian, 0.3% American Indian/Alaska Native, 0.0% Native Hawaiian/Other Pacific Islander, 15.0% Other, 26.2% Hispanic of any race (2010); Average household size: 2.43 (2010); Median age: 35.5 (2010); Males per 100 females: 93.6 (2010); Marriage status: 40.7% never married, 42.5% now married, 7.2% widowed, 9.5% divorced (2006-2010 5-year est.); Foreign born: 24.0% (2006-2010 5-year est.); Ancestry (includes multiple ancestries): 32.9% Italian, 22.9% Irish, 9.5% German, 4.5% English, 3.5% Jamaican (2006-2010 5-year est.).
**Economy:** Single-family building permits issued: 0 (2011); Multi-family building permits issued: 0 (2011); Employment by occupation: 5.4% management, 2.1% professional, 6.7% services, 15.8% sales, 9.1% farming, 11.0% construction, 2.8% production (2006-2010 5-year est.).
**Income:** Per capita income: $22,893 (2006-2010 5-year est.); Median household income: $47,659 (2006-2010 5-year est.); Average household income: $53,201 (2006-2010 5-year est.); Percent of households with income of $100,000 or more: 11.1% (2006-2010 5-year est.); Poverty rate: 12.1% (2006-2010 5-year est.).
**Education:** Percent of population age 25 and over with: High school diploma (including GED) or higher: 84.8% (2006-2010 5-year est.); Bachelor's degree or higher: 15.1% (2006-2010 5-year est.); Master's degree or higher: 9.3% (2006-2010 5-year est.).
### School District(s)
Wappingers Central School District (KG-12)
    2009-10 Enrollment: 12,407 . . . . . . . . . . . . . . . . . . . . . . . (845) 298-5000
**Housing:** Homeownership rate: 37.7% (2010); Median home value: $262,200 (2006-2010 5-year est.); Median contract rent: $895 per month (2006-2010 5-year est.); Median year structure built: 1957 (2006-2010 5-year est.).
**Safety:** Violent crime rate: 13.2 per 10,000 population; Property crime rate: 268.4 per 10,000 population (2010).
**Newspapers:** Beacon Free Press (Community news; Circulation 8,300); Southern Dutchess News (Community news; Circulation 12,000)
**Transportation:** Commute to work: 87.3% car, 7.1% public transportation, 5.2% walk, 0.4% work from home (2006-2010 5-year est.); Travel time to work: 26.5% less than 15 minutes, 33.5% 15 to 30 minutes, 20.6% 30 to 45 minutes, 9.8% 45 to 60 minutes, 9.6% 60 minutes or more (2006-2010 5-year est.)

## WASHINGTON (town).
Covers a land area of 58.169 square miles and a water area of 0.713 square miles. Located at 41.79° N. Lat; 73.67° W. Long.
**Population:** 4,479 (1990); 4,742 (2000); 4,741 (2010); Density: 81.5 persons per square mile (2010); Race: 91.8% White, 2.6% Black, 1.3% Asian, 0.2% American Indian/Alaska Native, 0.1% Native Hawaiian/Other Pacific Islander, 4.0% Other, 5.9% Hispanic of any race (2010); Average

household size: 2.33 (2010); Median age: 45.7 (2010); Males per 100 females: 99.4 (2010); Marriage status: 23.3% never married, 58.4% now married, 8.7% widowed, 9.6% divorced (2006-2010 5-year est.); Foreign born: 6.8% (2006-2010 5-year est.); Ancestry (includes multiple ancestries): 29.3% Irish, 26.9% German, 20.2% Italian, 17.1% English, 6.1% Polish (2006-2010 5-year est.).
**Economy:** Single-family building permits issued: 7 (2011); Multi-family building permits issued: 0 (2011); Employment by occupation: 18.2% management, 3.9% professional, 15.9% services, 11.2% sales, 1.2% farming, 6.5% construction, 2.4% production (2006-2010 5-year est.).
**Income:** Per capita income: $39,435 (2006-2010 5-year est.); Median household income: $59,911 (2006-2010 5-year est.); Average household income: $95,074 (2006-2010 5-year est.); Percent of households with income of $100,000 or more: 27.5% (2006-2010 5-year est.); Poverty rate: 7.3% (2006-2010 5-year est.).
**Education:** Percent of population age 25 and over with: High school diploma (including GED) or higher: 89.9% (2006-2010 5-year est.); Bachelor's degree or higher: 41.5% (2006-2010 5-year est.); Master's degree or higher: 16.7% (2006-2010 5-year est.).
**Housing:** Homeownership rate: 64.6% (2010); Median home value: $378,000 (2006-2010 5-year est.); Median contract rent: $871 per month (2006-2010 5-year est.); Median year structure built: 1968 (2006-2010 5-year est.).
**Transportation:** Commute to work: 80.1% car, 6.3% public transportation, 6.3% walk, 5.5% work from home (2006-2010 5-year est.); Travel time to work: 32.2% less than 15 minutes, 24.5% 15 to 30 minutes, 18.1% 30 to 45 minutes, 7.7% 45 to 60 minutes, 17.6% 60 minutes or more (2006-2010 5-year est.)

## WASSAIC (unincorporated postal area)
Zip Code: 12592
    Covers a land area of 18.704 square miles and a water area of 0.231 square miles. Located at 41.80° N. Lat; 73.57° W. Long. Elevation is 456 feet. Population: 1,486 (2010); Density: 79.4 persons per square mile (2010); Race: 89.1% White, 6.4% Black, 0.7% Asian, 0.3% American Indian/Alaska Native, 0.0% Native Hawaiian/Other Pacific Islander, 3.5% Other, 7.5% Hispanic of any race (2010); Average household size: 2.37 (2010); Median age: 45.9 (2010); Males per 100 females: 96.8 (2010); Homeownership rate: 68.2% (2010)

## WINGDALE (unincorporated postal area)
Zip Code: 12594
    Covers a land area of 24.062 square miles and a water area of 0.617 square miles. Located at 41.68° N. Lat; 73.55° W. Long. Elevation is 420 feet. Population: 4,275 (2010); Density: 177.7 persons per square mile (2010); Race: 83.6% White, 6.8% Black, 1.6% Asian, 0.1% American Indian/Alaska Native, 0.0% Native Hawaiian/Other Pacific Islander, 7.9% Other, 14.8% Hispanic of any race (2010); Average household size: 2.81 (2010); Median age: 39.3 (2010); Males per 100 females: 99.4 (2010); Homeownership rate: 74.6% (2010)

# Erie County

Located in western New York; bounded on the west by Lake Erie; drained by the Cattaraugus and Tonawanda Creeks. Covers a land area of 1,044.21 square miles, a water area of 182.68 square miles, and is located in the Eastern Time Zone at 42.86° N. Lat., 78.79° W. Long. The county was founded in 1821. County seat is Buffalo.

Erie County is part of the Buffalo-Niagara Falls, NY Metropolitan Statistical Area. The entire metro area includes: Erie County, NY; Niagara County, NY

Weather Station: Buffalo Greater Buffalo Int'l          Elevation: 705 feet

|  | Jan | Feb | Mar | Apr | May | Jun | Jul | Aug | Sep | Oct | Nov | Dec |
|---|---|---|---|---|---|---|---|---|---|---|---|---|
| High | 32 | 34 | 42 | 55 | 67 | 75 | 80 | 79 | 71 | 59 | 48 | 36 |
| Low | 19 | 19 | 26 | 37 | 47 | 57 | 62 | 61 | 54 | 43 | 34 | 24 |
| Precip | 3.1 | 2.5 | 2.9 | 3.0 | 3.4 | 3.6 | 3.2 | 3.3 | 4.0 | 3.6 | 4.0 | 3.9 |
| Snow | 24.4 | 17.2 | 13.4 | 2.8 | 0.3 | tr | tr | tr | tr | 0.9 | 8.1 | 26.9 |

*High and Low temperatures in degrees Fahrenheit; Precipitation and Snow in inches*

Weather Station: Wales                                        Elevation: 1,089 feet

| | Jan | Feb | Mar | Apr | May | Jun | Jul | Aug | Sep | Oct | Nov | Dec |
|---|---|---|---|---|---|---|---|---|---|---|---|---|
| High | 31 | 32 | 41 | 55 | 65 | 74 | 77 | 76 | 70 | 58 | 47 | 35 |
| Low | 16 | 15 | 22 | 33 | 43 | 54 | 57 | 56 | 49 | 39 | 31 | 21 |
| Precip | 3.5 | 2.6 | 3.0 | 3.4 | 3.4 | 4.2 | 3.9 | 3.7 | 4.3 | 3.7 | 3.7 | 3.8 |
| Snow | 32.8 | 19.0 | 15.9 | 4.8 | 0.3 | 0.0 | 0.0 | 0.0 | 0.0 | 0.3 | 10.1 | 27.7 |

*High and Low temperatures in degrees Fahrenheit; Precipitation and Snow in inches*

**Population:** 968,532 (1990); 950,265 (2000); 919,040 (2010); Race: 80.0% White, 13.5% Black, 2.6% Asian, 0.6% American Indian/Alaska Native, 0.0% Native Hawaiian/Other Pacific Islander, 3.3% Other, 4.5% Hispanic of any race (2010); Density: 880.1 persons per square mile (2010); Average household size: 2.32 (2010); Median age: 40.4 (2010); Males per 100 females: 93.0 (2010).
**Religion:** Six largest groups: 38.4% Catholicism, 3.1% Baptist, 2.7% Lutheran, 2.1% Non-Denominational, 2.0% Methodist/Pietist, 2.0% Presbyterian-Reformed (2010)
**Economy:** Unemployment rate: 8.9% (February 2012); Total civilian labor force: 458,460 (February 2012); Leading industries: 18.1% health care and social assistance; 13.3% retail trade; 11.1% manufacturing (2009); Farms: 1,215 totaling 149,356 acres (2007); Companies that employ 500 or more persons: 73 (2009); Companies that employ 100 to 499 persons: 552 (2009); Companies that employ less than 100 persons: 21,747 (2009); Black-owned businesses: 2,756 (2007); Hispanic-owned businesses: 768 (2007); Asian-owned businesses: 1,771 (2007); Women-owned businesses: 16,104 (2007); Retail sales per capita: $13,578 (2010). Single-family building permits issued: 643 (2011); Multi-family building permits issued: 443 (2011).
**Income:** Per capita income: $26,378 (2006-2010 5-year est.); Median household income: $47,372 (2006-2010 5-year est.); Average household income: $62,893 (2006-2010 5-year est.); Percent of households with income of $100,000 or more: 17.3% (2006-2010 5-year est.); Poverty rate: 14.0% (2006-2010 5-year est.); Bankruptcy rate: 3.08% (2011).
**Taxes:** Total county taxes per capita: $992 (2009); County property taxes per capita: $257 (2009).
**Education:** Percent of population age 25 and over with: High school diploma (including GED) or higher: 88.4% (2006-2010 5-year est.); Bachelor's degree or higher: 29.1% (2006-2010 5-year est.); Master's degree or higher: 12.7% (2006-2010 5-year est.).
**Housing:** Homeownership rate: 64.8% (2010); Median home value: $117,700 (2006-2010 5-year est.); Median contract rent: $520 per month (2006-2010 5-year est.); Median year structure built: 1953 (2006-2010 5-year est.)
**Health:** Birth rate: 104.8 per 10,000 population (2011); Death rate: 102.5 per 10,000 population (2011); Age-adjusted cancer mortality rate: 193.3 deaths per 100,000 population (2009); Number of physicians: 38.1 per 10,000 population (2008); Hospital beds: 52.6 per 10,000 population (2007); Hospital admissions: 1,528.0 per 10,000 population (2007).
**Environment:** Air Quality Index: 75.6% good, 23.6% moderate, 0.8% unhealthy for sensitive individuals, 0.0% unhealthy (percent of days in 2010)
**Elections:** 2008 Presidential election results: 58.0% Obama, 40.5% McCain, 1.0% Nader
**National and State Parks:** Beaver Island State Park; Buckhorn Island State Park; Evangola State Park
**Additional Information Contacts**

Erie County Government . . . . . . . . . . . . . . . . . . . . (716) 858-8865
  http://www.erie.gov
Alden Chamber of Commerce . . . . . . . . . . . . . . . . (716) 937-6177
  http://www.aldenny.org
Amherst Chamber of Commerce . . . . . . . . . . . . . . (716) 632-6905
  http://www.amherst.org
Buffalo Niagara Partnership . . . . . . . . . . . . . . . . . (716) 852-7100
  http://www.thepartnership.org
Cheektowaga Chamber of Commerce . . . . . . . . . . (716) 684-5838
  http://www.cheektowaga.org
City of Buffalo . . . . . . . . . . . . . . . . . . . . . . . . . . . (716) 851-4200
  http://www.ci.buffalo.ny.us
City of Lackawanna . . . . . . . . . . . . . . . . . . . . . . . (716) 827-6452
  http://www.ci.lackawanna.ny.us
City of Tonawanda . . . . . . . . . . . . . . . . . . . . . . . . (716) 695-1800
  http://www.ci.tonawanda.ny.us
Clarence Chamber of Commerce . . . . . . . . . . . . . . (716) 631-3888
  http://www.clarence.org
Eden Chamber of Commerce . . . . . . . . . . . . . . . . (716) 992-4799
  http://www.edenny.org/chamber.html

Evans-Brant Chamber of Commerce . . . . . . . . . . . (716) 549-3221
  http://www.ebccny.org
Grand Island Chamber of Commerce . . . . . . . . . . . (716) 773-3651
  http://www.gichamber.org
Greater East Aurora Chamber of Commerce . . . . . . (716) 652-8444
  http://www.eanycc.com
Hamburg Chamber of Commerce . . . . . . . . . . . . . (716) 649-7917
  http://www.hamburg-chamber.org
Kenmore-Town of Tonawanda Chamber of Commerce . . . (716) 874-1202
  http://www.ken-ton.org
Lackawanna Area Chamber of Commerce . . . . . . . . (716) 823-8841
  http://www.lackawannachamber.com
Lancaster Area Chamber of Commerce . . . . . . . . . (716) 681-9755
  http://www.laccny.org
Orchard Park Chamber of Commerce . . . . . . . . . . . (716) 662-3366
  http://www.orchardparkchamber.com
Springville Chamber of Commerce . . . . . . . . . . . . . (716) 592-4746
  http://www.springvillechamber.com
Town of Amherst . . . . . . . . . . . . . . . . . . . . . . . . . (716) 631-7000
  http://www.amherst.ny.us
Town of Cheektowaga . . . . . . . . . . . . . . . . . . . . . (716) 686-3400
  http://tocny.org
Town of Eden . . . . . . . . . . . . . . . . . . . . . . . . . . . . (716) 992-3408
  http://www.edenny.org
Town of Evans . . . . . . . . . . . . . . . . . . . . . . . . . . . (716) 549-5787
  http://www.townofevans.org
Town of Grand Island . . . . . . . . . . . . . . . . . . . . . . (716) 773-9600
  http://www.gigov.com
Town of Hamburg . . . . . . . . . . . . . . . . . . . . . . . . . (716) 649-6111
  http://www.townofhamburgny.com
Town of Orchard Park . . . . . . . . . . . . . . . . . . . . . . (716) 662-6410
  http://www.orchardparkny.org
Town of Tonawanda . . . . . . . . . . . . . . . . . . . . . . . (716) 877-8800
  http://www.tonawanda.ny.us
Town of West Seneca . . . . . . . . . . . . . . . . . . . . . . (716) 674-5600
  http://www.westseneca.net
Village of Akron . . . . . . . . . . . . . . . . . . . . . . . . . . (716) 542-9636
  http://www.erie.gov/akron
Village of Depew . . . . . . . . . . . . . . . . . . . . . . . . . (716) 683-1400
  http://www.villageofdepew.org
Village of East Aurora . . . . . . . . . . . . . . . . . . . . . (716) 652-6000
  http://www.east-aurora.ny.us
Village of Hamburg . . . . . . . . . . . . . . . . . . . . . . . . (716) 649-0200
  http://www.villagehamburg.com
Village of Kenmore . . . . . . . . . . . . . . . . . . . . . . . . (716) 873-5700
  http://www.vi.kenmore.ny.us
Village of Lancaster . . . . . . . . . . . . . . . . . . . . . . . (716) 684-4891
  http://www.lancastervillage.org
Village of Williamsville . . . . . . . . . . . . . . . . . . . . . (716) 632-4120
  http://village.williamsville.ny.us
West Seneca Chamber of Commerce . . . . . . . . . . . (716) 674-4900
  http://www.westseneca.org

## Erie County Communities

**AKRON** (village). Covers a land area of 1.975 square miles and a water area of 0 square miles. Located at 43.01° N. Lat; 78.49° W. Long. Elevation is 741 feet.
**History:** Nearby is Tonawanda Indian Reservation. Incorporated 1849.
**Population:** 2,942 (1990); 3,085 (2000); 2,868 (2010); Density: 1,451.5 persons per square mile (2010); Race: 96.3% White, 0.5% Black, 0.3% Asian, 1.5% American Indian/Alaska Native, 0.0% Native Hawaiian/Other Pacific Islander, 1.4% Other, 1.3% Hispanic of any race (2010); Average household size: 2.21 (2010); Median age: 42.3 (2010); Males per 100 females: 93.1 (2010); Marriage status: 29.5% never married, 51.3% now married, 7.4% widowed, 11.7% divorced (2006-2010 5-year est.); Foreign born: 1.8% (2006-2010 5-year est.); Ancestry (includes multiple ancestries): 42.3% German, 20.9% Irish, 17.3% English, 15.8% Italian, 10.5% Polish (2006-2010 5-year est.).
**Economy:** Single-family building permits issued: 2 (2011); Multi-family building permits issued: 0 (2011); Employment by occupation: 12.7% management, 2.3% professional, 9.1% services, 18.4% sales, 3.2% farming, 10.1% construction, 6.2% production (2006-2010 5-year est.).
**Income:** Per capita income: $21,972 (2006-2010 5-year est.); Median household income: $49,886 (2006-2010 5-year est.); Average household

income: $53,197 (2006-2010 5-year est.); Percent of households with income of $100,000 or more: 10.6% (2006-2010 5-year est.); Poverty rate: 10.7% (2006-2010 5-year est.).

**Education:** Percent of population age 25 and over with: High school diploma (including GED) or higher: 88.8% (2006-2010 5-year est.); Bachelor's degree or higher: 21.5% (2006-2010 5-year est.); Master's degree or higher: 8.6% (2006-2010 5-year est.).

### School District(s)
Akron Central School District (KG-12)

    2009-10 Enrollment: 1,531 . . . . . . . . . . . . . . . . . . . . . . (716) 542-5010

**Housing:** Homeownership rate: 63.7% (2010); Median home value: $117,800 (2006-2010 5-year est.); Median contract rent: $529 per month (2006-2010 5-year est.); Median year structure built: before 1940 (2006-2010 5-year est.).

**Safety:** Violent crime rate: 6.8 per 10,000 population; Property crime rate: 126.6 per 10,000 population (2010).

**Newspapers:** Akron Bugle (Community news; Circulation 1,800); Clarence News (Local news; Circulation 7,600)

**Transportation:** Commute to work: 91.9% car, 0.0% public transportation, 2.6% walk, 5.5% work from home (2006-2010 5-year est.); Travel time to work: 33.5% less than 15 minutes, 27.6% 15 to 30 minutes, 27.9% 30 to 45 minutes, 11.0% 45 to 60 minutes, 0.0% 60 minutes or more (2006-2010 5-year est.)

**Additional Information Contacts**

Village of Akron . . . . . . . . . . . . . . . . . . . . . . . . . . . . . . (716) 542-9636
   http://www.erie.gov/akron

---

## ALDEN (village).
Covers a land area of 2.718 square miles and a water area of 0 square miles. Located at 42.89° N. Lat; 78.49° W. Long. Elevation is 863 feet.

**Population:** 2,457 (1990); 2,666 (2000); 2,605 (2010); Density: 958.3 persons per square mile (2010); Race: 97.4% White, 0.5% Black, 1.2% Asian, 0.3% American Indian/Alaska Native, 0.0% Native Hawaiian/Other Pacific Islander, 0.6% Other, 0.5% Hispanic of any race (2010); Average household size: 2.38 (2010); Median age: 42.4 (2010); Males per 100 females: 98.4 (2010); Marriage status: 30.4% never married, 50.8% now married, 7.8% widowed, 11.0% divorced (2006-2010 5-year est.); Foreign born: 1.8% (2006-2010 5-year est.); Ancestry (includes multiple ancestries): 46.8% German, 28.8% Polish, 18.8% Irish, 14.3% Italian, 9.3% English (2006-2010 5-year est.).

**Economy:** Single-family building permits issued: 1 (2011); Multi-family building permits issued: 8 (2011); Employment by occupation: 9.3% management, 1.5% professional, 17.1% services, 17.5% sales, 4.8% farming, 7.3% construction, 3.9% production (2006-2010 5-year est.).

**Income:** Per capita income: $24,181 (2006-2010 5-year est.); Median household income: $47,621 (2006-2010 5-year est.); Average household income: $58,342 (2006-2010 5-year est.); Percent of households with income of $100,000 or more: 15.6% (2006-2010 5-year est.); Poverty rate: 7.6% (2006-2010 5-year est.).

**Education:** Percent of population age 25 and over with: High school diploma (including GED) or higher: 90.8% (2006-2010 5-year est.); Bachelor's degree or higher: 19.6% (2006-2010 5-year est.); Master's degree or higher: 6.9% (2006-2010 5-year est.).

### School District(s)
Alden Central School District (PK-12)

    2009-10 Enrollment: 1,865 . . . . . . . . . . . . . . . . . . . . (716) 937-9116

**Housing:** Homeownership rate: 68.6% (2010); Median home value: $120,200 (2006-2010 5-year est.); Median contract rent: $513 per month (2006-2010 5-year est.); Median year structure built: 1957 (2006-2010 5-year est.).

**Newspapers:** Alden Advertiser (Community news; Circulation 3,700)

**Transportation:** Commute to work: 89.8% car, 0.6% public transportation, 4.6% walk, 3.3% work from home (2006-2010 5-year est.); Travel time to work: 23.6% less than 15 minutes, 30.1% 15 to 30 minutes, 30.0% 30 to 45 minutes, 12.3% 45 to 60 minutes, 3.9% 60 minutes or more (2006-2010 5-year est.)

**Additional Information Contacts**

Alden Chamber of Commerce . . . . . . . . . . . . . . . . . . . . (716) 937-6177
   http://www.aldenny.org

---

## ALDEN (town).
Covers a land area of 34.307 square miles and a water area of 0.200 square miles. Located at 42.90° N. Lat; 78.52° W. Long. Elevation is 863 feet.

**History:** Incorporated 1869.

**Population:** 10,372 (1990); 10,470 (2000); 10,865 (2010); Density: 316.7 persons per square mile (2010); Race: 86.8% White, 10.7% Black, 0.4% Asian, 0.3% American Indian/Alaska Native, 0.0% Native Hawaiian/Other Pacific Islander, 1.8% Other, 2.6% Hispanic of any race (2010); Average household size: 2.53 (2010); Median age: 43.2 (2010); Males per 100 females: 135.8 (2010); Marriage status: 30.1% never married, 52.6% now married, 6.7% widowed, 10.6% divorced (2006-2010 5-year est.); Foreign born: 3.3% (2006-2010 5-year est.); Ancestry (includes multiple ancestries): 38.8% German, 29.3% Polish, 13.8% Irish, 11.2% Italian, 7.1% English (2006-2010 5-year est.).

**Economy:** Single-family building permits issued: 9 (2011); Multi-family building permits issued: 0 (2011); Employment by occupation: 10.7% management, 3.3% professional, 12.0% services, 16.7% sales, 3.9% farming, 11.2% construction, 7.9% production (2006-2010 5-year est.).

**Income:** Per capita income: $23,452 (2006-2010 5-year est.); Median household income: $53,272 (2006-2010 5-year est.); Average household income: $67,309 (2006-2010 5-year est.); Percent of households with income of $100,000 or more: 15.3% (2006-2010 5-year est.); Poverty rate: 5.5% (2006-2010 5-year est.).

**Education:** Percent of population age 25 and over with: High school diploma (including GED) or higher: 85.7% (2006-2010 5-year est.); Bachelor's degree or higher: 13.9% (2006-2010 5-year est.); Master's degree or higher: 5.7% (2006-2010 5-year est.).

### School District(s)
Alden Central School District (PK-12)

    2009-10 Enrollment: 1,865 . . . . . . . . . . . . . . . . . . . . (716) 937-9116

**Housing:** Homeownership rate: 83.0% (2010); Median home value: $138,700 (2006-2010 5-year est.); Median contract rent: $549 per month (2006-2010 5-year est.); Median year structure built: 1959 (2006-2010 5-year est.).

**Newspapers:** Alden Advertiser (Community news; Circulation 3,700)

**Transportation:** Commute to work: 94.5% car, 0.5% public transportation, 1.2% walk, 2.1% work from home (2006-2010 5-year est.); Travel time to work: 28.3% less than 15 minutes, 30.3% 15 to 30 minutes, 29.4% 30 to 45 minutes, 8.4% 45 to 60 minutes, 3.6% 60 minutes or more (2006-2010 5-year est.)

---

## AMHERST (town).
Covers a land area of 53.202 square miles and a water area of 0.391 square miles. Located at 43.01° N. Lat; 78.75° W. Long. Elevation is 597 feet.

**Population:** 111,711 (1990); 116,510 (2000); 122,366 (2010); Density: 2,300.0 persons per square mile (2010); Race: 83.8% White, 5.7% Black, 7.9% Asian, 0.2% American Indian/Alaska Native, 0.0% Native Hawaiian/Other Pacific Islander, 2.4% Other, 2.3% Hispanic of any race (2010); Average household size: 2.33 (2010); Median age: 40.2 (2010); Males per 100 females: 89.9 (2010); Marriage status: 32.0% never married, 51.9% now married, 7.8% widowed, 8.3% divorced (2006-2010 5-year est.); Foreign born: 12.1% (2006-2010 5-year est.); Ancestry (includes multiple ancestries): 25.3% German, 19.5% Italian, 18.3% Irish, 14.1% Polish, 9.8% English (2006-2010 5-year est.).

**Economy:** Unemployment rate: 6.6% (February 2012); Total civilian labor force: 62,142 (February 2012); Single-family building permits issued: 65 (2011); Multi-family building permits issued: 233 (2011); Employment by occupation: 14.8% management, 6.4% professional, 7.8% services, 15.9% sales, 3.8% farming, 3.2% construction, 2.8% production (2006-2010 5-year est.).

**Income:** Per capita income: $34,312 (2006-2010 5-year est.); Median household income: $65,439 (2006-2010 5-year est.); Average household income: $84,333 (2006-2010 5-year est.); Percent of households with income of $100,000 or more: 29.3% (2006-2010 5-year est.); Poverty rate: 8.2% (2006-2010 5-year est.).

**Taxes:** Total city taxes per capita: $684 (2009); City property taxes per capita: $634 (2009).

**Education:** Percent of population age 25 and over with: High school diploma (including GED) or higher: 94.4% (2006-2010 5-year est.); Bachelor's degree or higher: 51.6% (2006-2010 5-year est.); Master's degree or higher: 26.6% (2006-2010 5-year est.).

### School District(s)
Amherst Central School District (PK-12)

    2009-10 Enrollment: 2,965 . . . . . . . . . . . . . . . . . . . . (716) 362-3051

Sweet Home Central School District (KG-12)

    2009-10 Enrollment: 3,488 . . . . . . . . . . . . . . . . . . . . (716) 250-1402

### Four-year College(s)

Daemen College (Private, Not-for-profit)
Fall 2010 Enrollment: 2,550 . . . . . . . . . . . . . . . . . . . . . (716) 839-3600
2011-12 Tuition: In-state $22,310; Out-of-state $22,310

**Housing:** Homeownership rate: 71.4% (2010); Median home value: $162,600 (2006-2010 5-year est.); Median contract rent: $731 per month (2006-2010 5-year est.); Median year structure built: 1969 (2006-2010 5-year est.).

**Safety:** Violent crime rate: 10.9 per 10,000 population; Property crime rate: 189.3 per 10,000 population (2010).

**Transportation:** Commute to work: 91.7% car, 2.3% public transportation, 1.9% walk, 3.4% work from home (2006-2010 5-year est.); Travel time to work: 33.2% less than 15 minutes, 46.3% 15 to 30 minutes, 16.9% 30 to 45 minutes, 1.7% 45 to 60 minutes, 2.0% 60 minutes or more (2006-2010 5-year est.).

**Additional Information Contacts**
Amherst Chamber of Commerce . . . . . . . . . . . . . . . . . . . (716) 632-6905
   http://www.amherst.org
Town of Amherst . . . . . . . . . . . . . . . . . . . . . . . . . . . . . . (716) 631-7000
   http://www.amherst.ny.us

## ANGOLA (village).
Covers a land area of 1.416 square miles and a water area of 0 square miles. Located at 42.63° N. Lat; 79.02° W. Long. Elevation is 686 feet.

**History:** Incorporated 1873.

**Population:** 2,231 (1990); 2,266 (2000); 2,127 (2010); Density: 1,501.4 persons per square mile (2010); Race: 95.0% White, 0.6% Black, 0.1% Asian, 2.1% American Indian/Alaska Native, 0.0% Native Hawaiian/Other Pacific Islander, 2.2% Other, 3.0% Hispanic of any race (2010); Average household size: 2.55 (2010); Median age: 39.4 (2010); Males per 100 females: 87.7 (2010); Marriage status: 26.1% never married, 55.7% now married, 9.3% widowed, 9.0% divorced (2006-2010 5-year est.); Foreign born: 2.5% (2006-2010 5-year est.); Ancestry (includes multiple ancestries): 33.7% German, 28.5% Italian, 25.9% Irish, 18.4% Polish, 10.9% English (2006-2010 5-year est.).

**Economy:** Employment by occupation: 5.6% management, 0.8% professional, 13.2% services, 19.3% sales, 4.8% farming, 11.2% construction, 7.7% production (2006-2010 5-year est.).

**Income:** Per capita income: $20,475 (2006-2010 5-year est.); Median household income: $51,548 (2006-2010 5-year est.); Average household income: $53,966 (2006-2010 5-year est.); Percent of households with income of $100,000 or more: 13.6% (2006-2010 5-year est.); Poverty rate: 15.9% (2006-2010 5-year est.).

**Education:** Percent of population age 25 and over with: High school diploma (including GED) or higher: 92.1% (2006-2010 5-year est.); Bachelor's degree or higher: 17.1% (2006-2010 5-year est.); Master's degree or higher: 8.6% (2006-2010 5-year est.).

**School District(s)**
Erie 2-Chautauqua-cattaraugus Boces
2009-10 Enrollment: n/a . . . . . . . . . . . . . . . . . . . . . . . (716) 549-4454
Evans-Brant Central School District (lake Shore) (KG-12)
2009-10 Enrollment: 2,850 . . . . . . . . . . . . . . . . . . . . . (716) 926-2201

**Vocational/Technical School(s)**
Erie 2 Chautauqua Cattaraugus BOCES-Practical Nursing Program (Public)
Fall 2010 Enrollment: 305 . . . . . . . . . . . . . . . . . . . . . . (7.1) 654-9E+1
2011-12 Tuition: $9,000

**Housing:** Homeownership rate: 72.4% (2010); Median home value: $101,900 (2006-2010 5-year est.); Median contract rent: $426 per month (2006-2010 5-year est.); Median year structure built: 1950 (2006-2010 5-year est.).

**Transportation:** Commute to work: 95.4% car, 0.8% public transportation, 2.3% walk, 0.0% work from home (2006-2010 5-year est.); Travel time to work: 29.3% less than 15 minutes, 31.3% 15 to 30 minutes, 24.5% 30 to 45 minutes, 9.6% 45 to 60 minutes, 5.4% 60 minutes or more (2006-2010 5-year est.).

## ANGOLA ON THE LAKE (CDP).
Covers a land area of 2.545 square miles and a water area of 0 square miles. Located at 42.65° N. Lat; 79.05° W. Long. Elevation is 600 feet.

**Population:** 1,719 (1990); 1,771 (2000); 1,675 (2010); Density: 658.0 persons per square mile (2010); Race: 96.9% White, 0.5% Black, 0.1% Asian, 1.4% American Indian/Alaska Native, 0.0% Native Hawaiian/Other Pacific Islander, 1.1% Other, 1.4% Hispanic of any race (2010); Average household size: 2.26 (2010); Median age: 46.4 (2010); Males per 100

females: 93.4 (2010); Marriage status: 20.6% never married, 65.0% now married, 6.1% widowed, 8.3% divorced (2006-2010 5-year est.); Foreign born: 7.1% (2006-2010 5-year est.); Ancestry (includes multiple ancestries): 44.0% German, 24.4% Italian, 22.3% Irish, 10.6% Polish, 6.7% English (2006-2010 5-year est.).

**Economy:** Employment by occupation: 11.8% management, 0.0% professional, 15.1% services, 18.1% sales, 2.0% farming, 4.3% construction, 6.9% production (2006-2010 5-year est.).

**Income:** Per capita income: $27,297 (2006-2010 5-year est.); Median household income: $49,434 (2006-2010 5-year est.); Average household income: $65,029 (2006-2010 5-year est.); Percent of households with income of $100,000 or more: 9.5% (2006-2010 5-year est.); Poverty rate: 8.5% (2006-2010 5-year est.).

**Education:** Percent of population age 25 and over with: High school diploma (including GED) or higher: 89.0% (2006-2010 5-year est.); Bachelor's degree or higher: 17.8% (2006-2010 5-year est.); Master's degree or higher: 5.7% (2006-2010 5-year est.).

**Housing:** Homeownership rate: 81.0% (2010); Median home value: $87,300 (2006-2010 5-year est.); Median contract rent: $392 per month (2006-2010 5-year est.); Median year structure built: 1950 (2006-2010 5-year est.).

**Transportation:** Commute to work: 97.7% car, 0.0% public transportation, 2.3% walk, 0.0% work from home (2006-2010 5-year est.); Travel time to work: 27.1% less than 15 minutes, 20.7% 15 to 30 minutes, 37.8% 30 to 45 minutes, 14.4% 45 to 60 minutes, 0.0% 60 minutes or more (2006-2010 5-year est.).

## AURORA (town).
Covers a land area of 36.392 square miles and a water area of 0.046 square miles. Located at 42.73° N. Lat; 78.63° W. Long.

**History:** Seat of Christ the King Seminary. Site (1895-1939) of the Roycroft Shops, founded by Elbert Hubbard. Restored home of Millard and Abigail Fillmore as a National Historic Landmark. Incorporated 1874.

**Population:** 13,433 (1990); 13,996 (2000); 13,782 (2010); Density: 378.7 persons per square mile (2010); Race: 98.0% White, 0.3% Black, 0.6% Asian, 0.1% American Indian/Alaska Native, 0.0% Native Hawaiian/Other Pacific Islander, 1.0% Other, 1.0% Hispanic of any race (2010); Average household size: 2.44 (2010); Median age: 45.3 (2010); Males per 100 females: 92.7 (2010); Marriage status: 21.3% never married, 62.7% now married, 9.1% widowed, 7.0% divorced (2006-2010 5-year est.); Foreign born: 3.6% (2006-2010 5-year est.); Ancestry (includes multiple ancestries): 40.6% German, 25.1% Irish, 18.7% Polish, 15.7% Italian, 12.9% English (2006-2010 5-year est.).

**Economy:** Single-family building permits issued: 14 (2011); Multi-family building permits issued: 0 (2011); Employment by occupation: 16.7% management, 4.7% professional, 7.4% services, 12.5% sales, 2.3% farming, 7.2% construction, 4.5% production (2006-2010 5-year est.).

**Income:** Per capita income: $38,421 (2006-2010 5-year est.); Median household income: $66,009 (2006-2010 5-year est.); Average household income: $94,689 (2006-2010 5-year est.); Percent of households with income of $100,000 or more: 30.8% (2006-2010 5-year est.); Poverty rate: 3.1% (2006-2010 5-year est.).

**Education:** Percent of population age 25 and over with: High school diploma (including GED) or higher: 93.5% (2006-2010 5-year est.); Bachelor's degree or higher: 42.9% (2006-2010 5-year est.); Master's degree or higher: 18.8% (2006-2010 5-year est.).

**Housing:** Homeownership rate: 80.5% (2010); Median home value: $173,100 (2006-2010 5-year est.); Median contract rent: $533 per month (2006-2010 5-year est.); Median year structure built: 1953 (2006-2010 5-year est.).

**Transportation:** Commute to work: 89.9% car, 0.6% public transportation, 3.3% walk, 5.1% work from home (2006-2010 5-year est.); Travel time to work: 33.6% less than 15 minutes, 29.1% 15 to 30 minutes, 27.9% 30 to 45 minutes, 6.3% 45 to 60 minutes, 3.1% 60 minutes or more (2006-2010 5-year est.).

## BILLINGTON HEIGHTS (CDP).
Covers a land area of 3.192 square miles and a water area of 0.006 square miles. Located at 42.78° N. Lat; 78.62° W. Long. Elevation is 951 feet.

**Population:** 1,729 (1990); 1,691 (2000); 1,685 (2010); Density: 527.7 persons per square mile (2010); Race: 98.2% White, 0.1% Black, 0.6% Asian, 0.1% American Indian/Alaska Native, 0.0% Native Hawaiian/Other Pacific Islander, 1.0% Other, 0.7% Hispanic of any race (2010); Average household size: 2.45 (2010); Median age: 49.1 (2010); Males per 100 females: 95.9 (2010); Marriage status: 20.9% never married, 68.6% now

married, 5.7% widowed, 4.7% divorced (2006-2010 5-year est.); Foreign born: 0.0% (2006-2010 5-year est.); Ancestry (includes multiple ancestries): 31.7% Irish, 30.2% German, 17.9% Italian, 16.3% Polish, 16.1% English (2006-2010 5-year est.).

**Economy:** Employment by occupation: 9.4% management, 2.1% professional, 12.7% services, 8.8% sales, 7.7% farming, 9.7% construction, 8.8% production (2006-2010 5-year est.).

**Income:** Per capita income: $38,922 (2006-2010 5-year est.); Median household income: $72,212 (2006-2010 5-year est.); Average household income: $99,224 (2006-2010 5-year est.); Percent of households with income of $100,000 or more: 36.1% (2006-2010 5-year est.); Poverty rate: 9.5% (2006-2010 5-year est.).

**Education:** Percent of population age 25 and over with: High school diploma (including GED) or higher: 93.9% (2006-2010 5-year est.); Bachelor's degree or higher: 35.7% (2006-2010 5-year est.); Master's degree or higher: 13.6% (2006-2010 5-year est.).

**Housing:** Homeownership rate: 87.6% (2010); Median home value: $223,900 (2006-2010 5-year est.); Median contract rent: $295 per month (2006-2010 5-year est.); Median year structure built: 1963 (2006-2010 5-year est.).

**Transportation:** Commute to work: 95.1% car, 0.0% public transportation, 0.0% walk, 4.9% work from home (2006-2010 5-year est.); Travel time to work: 32.1% less than 15 minutes, 32.9% 15 to 30 minutes, 31.0% 30 to 45 minutes, 4.0% 45 to 60 minutes, 0.0% 60 minutes or more (2006-2010 5-year est.)

**BLASDELL** (village). Covers a land area of 1.122 square miles and a water area of 0 square miles. Located at 42.79° N. Lat; 78.83° W. Long. Elevation is 610 feet.

**History:** Incorporated 1898.

**Population:** 2,900 (1990); 2,718 (2000); 2,553 (2010); Density: 2,274.2 persons per square mile (2010); Race: 95.7% White, 1.4% Black, 0.4% Asian, 0.4% American Indian/Alaska Native, 0.0% Native Hawaiian/Other Pacific Islander, 2.1% Other, 3.7% Hispanic of any race (2010); Average household size: 2.19 (2010); Median age: 38.0 (2010); Males per 100 females: 89.4 (2010); Marriage status: 25.1% never married, 47.7% now married, 9.4% widowed, 17.8% divorced (2006-2010 5-year est.); Foreign born: 3.7% (2006-2010 5-year est.); Ancestry (includes multiple ancestries): 35.6% Irish, 32.6% German, 24.9% Polish, 13.8% English, 12.8% Italian (2006-2010 5-year est.).

**Economy:** Employment by occupation: 6.5% management, 1.2% professional, 14.7% services, 23.7% sales, 4.5% farming, 4.0% construction, 7.8% production (2006-2010 5-year est.).

**Income:** Per capita income: $22,006 (2006-2010 5-year est.); Median household income: $37,813 (2006-2010 5-year est.); Average household income: $46,578 (2006-2010 5-year est.); Percent of households with income of $100,000 or more: 9.4% (2006-2010 5-year est.); Poverty rate: 13.5% (2006-2010 5-year est.).

**Education:** Percent of population age 25 and over with: High school diploma (including GED) or higher: 87.5% (2006-2010 5-year est.); Bachelor's degree or higher: 19.7% (2006-2010 5-year est.); Master's degree or higher: 5.0% (2006-2010 5-year est.).

**School District(s)**

Frontier Central School District (PK-12)

   2009-10 Enrollment: 5,326 . . . . . . . . . . . . . . . . . . . . . . . (716) 926-1711

**Housing:** Homeownership rate: 55.9% (2010); Median home value: $91,500 (2006-2010 5-year est.); Median contract rent: $433 per month (2006-2010 5-year est.); Median year structure built: 1944 (2006-2010 5-year est.).

**Transportation:** Commute to work: 87.7% car, 3.5% public transportation, 3.5% walk, 3.1% work from home (2006-2010 5-year est.); Travel time to work: 35.0% less than 15 minutes, 44.6% 15 to 30 minutes, 16.1% 30 to 45 minutes, 0.8% 45 to 60 minutes, 3.6% 60 minutes or more (2006-2010 5-year est.)

**BOSTON** (town). Covers a land area of 35.819 square miles and a water area of 0 square miles. Located at 42.65° N. Lat; 78.75° W. Long. Elevation is 942 feet.

**Population:** 7,445 (1990); 7,897 (2000); 8,023 (2010); Density: 224.0 persons per square mile (2010); Race: 98.4% White, 0.1% Black, 0.3% Asian, 0.2% American Indian/Alaska Native, 0.0% Native Hawaiian/Other Pacific Islander, 1.0% Other, 1.0% Hispanic of any race (2010); Average household size: 2.49 (2010); Median age: 44.3 (2010); Males per 100 females: 101.0 (2010); Marriage status: 19.5% never married, 61.8% now married, 7.5% widowed, 11.2% divorced (2006-2010 5-year est.); Foreign

born: 1.0% (2006-2010 5-year est.); Ancestry (includes multiple ancestries): 39.9% German, 26.1% Irish, 23.2% Polish, 13.9% English, 12.3% Italian (2006-2010 5-year est.).

**Economy:** Single-family building permits issued: 8 (2011); Multi-family building permits issued: 0 (2011); Employment by occupation: 10.4% management, 2.9% professional, 12.9% services, 17.8% sales, 3.2% farming, 11.7% construction, 8.2% production (2006-2010 5-year est.).

**Income:** Per capita income: $29,537 (2006-2010 5-year est.); Median household income: $62,500 (2006-2010 5-year est.); Average household income: $73,524 (2006-2010 5-year est.); Percent of households with income of $100,000 or more: 23.0% (2006-2010 5-year est.); Poverty rate: 5.8% (2006-2010 5-year est.).

**Education:** Percent of population age 25 and over with: High school diploma (including GED) or higher: 93.5% (2006-2010 5-year est.); Bachelor's degree or higher: 25.1% (2006-2010 5-year est.); Master's degree or higher: 11.0% (2006-2010 5-year est.).

**Housing:** Homeownership rate: 82.6% (2010); Median home value: $155,200 (2006-2010 5-year est.); Median contract rent: $568 per month (2006-2010 5-year est.); Median year structure built: 1966 (2006-2010 5-year est.).

**Transportation:** Commute to work: 95.1% car, 0.7% public transportation, 2.1% walk, 1.6% work from home (2006-2010 5-year est.); Travel time to work: 25.5% less than 15 minutes, 32.5% 15 to 30 minutes, 32.4% 30 to 45 minutes, 7.6% 45 to 60 minutes, 2.0% 60 minutes or more (2006-2010 5-year est.)

**BOWMANSVILLE** (unincorporated postal area)
Zip Code: 14026

   Covers a land area of 0.752 square miles and a water area of 0 square miles. Located at 42.94° N. Lat; 78.68° W. Long. Elevation is 709 feet. Population: 674 (2010); Density: 895.3 persons per square mile (2010); Race: 99.4% White, 0.0% Black, 0.1% Asian, 0.0% American Indian/Alaska Native, 0.0% Native Hawaiian/Other Pacific Islander, 0.5% Other, 2.7% Hispanic of any race (2010); Average household size: 2.48 (2010); Median age: 43.0 (2010); Males per 100 females: 103.0 (2010); Homeownership rate: 81.3% (2010)

**BRANT** (town). Covers a land area of 24.313 square miles and a water area of 0.424 square miles. Located at 42.59° N. Lat; 79.02° W. Long. Elevation is 745 feet.

**Population:** 2,119 (1990); 1,906 (2000); 2,065 (2010); Density: 84.9 persons per square mile (2010); Race: 92.7% White, 1.0% Black, 0.0% Asian, 4.6% American Indian/Alaska Native, 0.0% Native Hawaiian/Other Pacific Islander, 1.7% Other, 2.8% Hispanic of any race (2010); Average household size: 2.51 (2010); Median age: 43.0 (2010); Males per 100 females: 101.5 (2010); Marriage status: 28.8% never married, 55.8% now married, 5.8% widowed, 9.6% divorced (2006-2010 5-year est.); Foreign born: 2.4% (2006-2010 5-year est.); Ancestry (includes multiple ancestries): 36.0% German, 29.4% Italian, 18.8% Irish, 15.1% Polish, 9.3% English (2006-2010 5-year est.).

**Economy:** Single-family building permits issued: 3 (2011); Multi-family building permits issued: 0 (2011); Employment by occupation: 9.8% management, 1.6% professional, 11.8% services, 14.0% sales, 0.6% farming, 11.1% construction, 7.0% production (2006-2010 5-year est.).

**Income:** Per capita income: $24,215 (2006-2010 5-year est.); Median household income: $54,688 (2006-2010 5-year est.); Average household income: $60,773 (2006-2010 5-year est.); Percent of households with income of $100,000 or more: 11.8% (2006-2010 5-year est.); Poverty rate: 7.3% (2006-2010 5-year est.).

**Education:** Percent of population age 25 and over with: High school diploma (including GED) or higher: 84.7% (2006-2010 5-year est.); Bachelor's degree or higher: 14.9% (2006-2010 5-year est.); Master's degree or higher: 7.4% (2006-2010 5-year est.).

**School District(s)**

Evans-Brant Central School District (lake Shore) (KG-12)

   2009-10 Enrollment: 2,850 . . . . . . . . . . . . . . . . . . . . . . . (716) 926-2201

**Housing:** Homeownership rate: 77.0% (2010); Median home value: $97,500 (2006-2010 5-year est.); Median contract rent: $483 per month (2006-2010 5-year est.); Median year structure built: 1949 (2006-2010 5-year est.).

**Safety:** Violent crime rate: 5.6 per 10,000 population; Property crime rate: 188.8 per 10,000 population (2010).

**Transportation:** Commute to work: 93.9% car, 0.3% public transportation, 2.0% walk, 2.9% work from home (2006-2010 5-year est.); Travel time to work: 34.4% less than 15 minutes, 22.9% 15 to 30 minutes, 20.0% 30 to 45

minutes, 11.0% 45 to 60 minutes, 11.8% 60 minutes or more (2006-2010 5-year est.)

**BUFFALO** (city). County seat. Covers a land area of 40.384 square miles and a water area of 12.109 square miles. Located at 42.89° N. Lat; 78.85° W. Long. Elevation is 600 feet.

**History:** Although Joseph Ellicott chose and mapped the site of Buffalo for the Holland Land Company in 1799, it was not until 1804 that he divided the land into lots and offered them for sale. He modeled the city plan after that of Washington, D.C. He called the place New Amsterdam, but settlers preferred to name it after Buffalo Creek. Buffalo was incorporated as a village in 1816. The early welfare of the settlement depended on its function as a trading center. The Erie Canal, opened in 1825, brought trade and prosperity. Buffalo stood at the transportation break in the great east-west route. In 1832, Buffalo was incorporated into a city. Steam engine manufacturers and other industries sprang up. After the Civil War, Buffalo became a railroad center.

**Population:** 328,123 (1990); 292,648 (2000); 261,310 (2010); Density: 6,470.6 persons per square mile (2010); Race: 50.4% White, 38.6% Black, 3.2% Asian, 0.8% American Indian/Alaska Native, 0.0% Native Hawaiian/Other Pacific Islander, 7.0% Other, 10.5% Hispanic of any race (2010); Average household size: 2.24 (2010); Median age: 33.2 (2010); Males per 100 females: 92.0 (2010); Marriage status: 48.9% never married, 32.4% now married, 7.3% widowed, 11.4% divorced (2006-2010 5-year est.); Foreign born: 7.0% (2006-2010 5-year est.); Ancestry (includes multiple ancestries): 13.4% German, 12.8% Irish, 11.5% Italian, 10.6% Polish, 4.2% English (2006-2010 5-year est.).

**Economy:** Unemployment rate: 10.9% (February 2012); Total civilian labor force: 113,951 (February 2012); Single-family building permits issued: 6 (2011); Multi-family building permits issued: 26 (2011); Employment by occupation: 7.1% management, 2.5% professional, 13.4% services, 17.1% sales, 5.6% farming, 5.4% construction, 6.4% production (2006-2010 5-year est.).

**Income:** Per capita income: $19,409 (2006-2010 5-year est.); Median household income: $30,043 (2006-2010 5-year est.); Average household income: $44,120 (2006-2010 5-year est.); Percent of households with income of $100,000 or more: 8.5% (2006-2010 5-year est.); Poverty rate: 29.6% (2006-2010 5-year est.).

**Taxes:** Total city taxes per capita: $588 (2009); City property taxes per capita: $519 (2009).

**Education:** Percent of population age 25 and over with: High school diploma (including GED) or higher: 80.6% (2006-2010 5-year est.); Bachelor's degree or higher: 21.7% (2006-2010 5-year est.); Master's degree or higher: 9.3% (2006-2010 5-year est.).

### School District(s)

Aloma D Johnson Community Charter School (KG-03)
  2009-10 Enrollment: 226 . . . . . . . . . . . . . . . . . . . . . . (716) 856-4390
Buffalo Academy of Science Charter School (07-12)
  2009-10 Enrollment: 387 . . . . . . . . . . . . . . . . . . . . . . (716) 854-2490
Buffalo City School District (PK-12)
  2009-10 Enrollment: 34,526 . . . . . . . . . . . . . . . . . . . (716) 816-3575
Buffalo United Charter School (KG-08)
  2009-10 Enrollment: 643 . . . . . . . . . . . . . . . . . . . . . . (716) 835-9862
Charter School for Applied Technologies (KG-12)
  2009-10 Enrollment: 1,613 . . . . . . . . . . . . . . . . . . . . (716) 876-7505
Cheektowaga Central School District (PK-12)
  2009-10 Enrollment: 2,372 . . . . . . . . . . . . . . . . . . . . (716) 686-3606
Community Charter School (KG-06)
  2009-10 Enrollment: 304 . . . . . . . . . . . . . . . . . . . . . . (716) 833-5967
Elmwood Village Charter School (KG-06)
  2009-10 Enrollment: 173 . . . . . . . . . . . . . . . . . . . . . . (716) 886-4581
Enterprise Charter School (KG-08)
  2009-10 Enrollment: 406 . . . . . . . . . . . . . . . . . . . . . . (716) 855-2114
Kenmore-Tonawanda Union Free School District (PK-12)
  2009-10 Enrollment: 8,128 . . . . . . . . . . . . . . . . . . . . (716) 874-8400
King Center Charter School (KG-04)
  2009-10 Enrollment: 133 . . . . . . . . . . . . . . . . . . . . . . (716) 891-7912
Oracle Charter School (08-12)
  2009-10 Enrollment: 351 . . . . . . . . . . . . . . . . . . . . . . (716) 362-3188
Pinnacle Charter School (KG-08)
  2009-10 Enrollment: 520 . . . . . . . . . . . . . . . . . . . . . . (716) 842-1244
South Buffalo Charter School (KG-08)
  2009-10 Enrollment: 646 . . . . . . . . . . . . . . . . . . . . . . (716) 826-7213
Tapestry Charter School (KG-12)
  2009-10 Enrollment: 502 . . . . . . . . . . . . . . . . . . . . . . (716) 332-0754

Western New York Maritime Charter School (09-12)
  2009-10 Enrollment: 325 . . . . . . . . . . . . . . . . . . . . . . (716) 842-6289
Westminster Community Charter School (KG-08)
  2009-10 Enrollment: 552 . . . . . . . . . . . . . . . . . . . . . . (716) 816-3450

### Four-year College(s)

Bryant and Stratton College-Buffalo (Private, For-profit)
  Fall 2010 Enrollment: 928 . . . . . . . . . . . . . . . . . . . . . (716) 884-9120
  2011-12 Tuition: In-state $15,570; Out-of-state $15,570
Canisius College (Private, Not-for-profit, Roman Catholic)
  Fall 2010 Enrollment: 4,583 . . . . . . . . . . . . . . . . . . . (716) 883-7000
  2011-12 Tuition: In-state $30,713; Out-of-state $30,713
D'Youville College (Private, Not-for-profit)
  Fall 2010 Enrollment: 2,962 . . . . . . . . . . . . . . . . . . . (716) 829-8000
  2011-12 Tuition: In-state $21,760; Out-of-state $21,760
Medaille College (Private, Not-for-profit)
  Fall 2010 Enrollment: 2,958 . . . . . . . . . . . . . . . . . . . (716) 880-2000
  2011-12 Tuition: In-state $21,598; Out-of-state $21,598
SUNY College at Buffalo (Public)
  Fall 2010 Enrollment: 10,573 . . . . . . . . . . . . . . . . . . (716) 878-4000
  2011-12 Tuition: In-state $6,353; Out-of-state $15,313
Trocaire College (Private, Not-for-profit, Roman Catholic)
  Fall 2010 Enrollment: 1,084 . . . . . . . . . . . . . . . . . . . (716) 826-1200
  2011-12 Tuition: In-state $13,900; Out-of-state $13,900
University at Buffalo (Public)
  Fall 2010 Enrollment: 28,894 . . . . . . . . . . . . . . . . . . (716) 645-2000
  2011-12 Tuition: In-state $7,482; Out-of-state $16,932
Villa Maria College (Private, Not-for-profit, Roman Catholic)
  Fall 2010 Enrollment: 401 . . . . . . . . . . . . . . . . . . . . . (716) 896-0700
  2011-12 Tuition: In-state $16,800; Out-of-state $16,800

### Two-year College(s)

Erie Community College (Public)
  Fall 2010 Enrollment: 13,049 . . . . . . . . . . . . . . . . . . (716) 842-2770
  2011-12 Tuition: In-state $4,030; Out-of-state $7,630

### Vocational/Technical School(s)

Continental School of Beauty Culture-Buffalo (Private, For-profit)
  Fall 2010 Enrollment: 99 . . . . . . . . . . . . . . . . . . . . . . (716) 833-5016
  2011-12 Tuition: $11,050
National Tractor Trailer School Inc-Buffalo (Private, For-profit)
  Fall 2010 Enrollment: 114 . . . . . . . . . . . . . . . . . . . . . (716) 849-6887
  2011-12 Tuition: $9,008

**Housing:** Homeownership rate: 40.7% (2010); Median home value: $65,700 (2006-2010 5-year est.); Median contract rent: $464 per month (2006-2010 5-year est.); Median year structure built: before 1940 (2006-2010 5-year est.).

**Hospitals:** Bry Lin Hospitals (88 beds); Buffalo General Hospital; Buffalo Psychiatric Center (240 beds); Department of Veterans Affairs Western New York Healthcare; Erie County Medical Center (550 beds); Mercy Hospital of Buffalo (349 beds); Millard Fillmore Gates Circle Hospital (189 beds); Millard Fillmore Suburban Hospital (189 beds); Roswell Park Cancer Institute (133 beds); Sheehan Memorial Hospital (109 beds); Sisters of Charity Hospital (413 beds); Women & Children's Hospital of Buffalo (160 beds)

**Safety:** Violent crime rate: 135.7 per 10,000 population; Property crime rate: 556.4 per 10,000 population (2010).

**Newspapers:** Buffalo Criterion (Local news; Circulation 10,000); Buffalo Jewish Review (Local news; Circulation 4,800); Buffalo News (Local news; Circulation 271,613); Buffalo Rocket (Community news; Circulation 16,500); Challenger (Regional news; Circulation 10,000); Entertainment - Buffalo News (Local news); Fine Print News (Local news; Circulation 32,000); Gusto - Buffalo News (Local news); La Ultima Hora (Local news; Circulation 20,000); North Buffalo Rocket (Community news; Circulation 25,400); Panorama Hispano (Local news; Circulation 20,000); Riverside Review (Community news; Circulation 14,300); Riverside Times (Local news; Circulation 12,000); West Side Times (Community news; Circulation 13,000)

**Transportation:** Commute to work: 76.3% car, 13.2% public transportation, 6.2% walk, 2.6% work from home (2006-2010 5-year est.); Travel time to work: 31.6% less than 15 minutes, 47.4% 15 to 30 minutes, 13.9% 30 to 45 minutes, 3.3% 45 to 60 minutes, 3.7% 60 minutes or more (2006-2010 5-year est.); Amtrak: train service available.

**Airports:** Buffalo Niagara International (primary service/medium hub)

**Additional Information Contacts**

Buffalo Niagara Partnership . . . . . . . . . . . . . . . . . . . . . (716) 852-7100
  http://www.thepartnership.org

City of Buffalo. . . . . . . . . . . . . . . . . . . . . . . . . . . . . . . . . (716) 851-4200
http://www.ci.buffalo.ny.us

## CATTARAUGUS RESERVATION (Reservation). Covers a land area of 25.262 square miles and a water area of 0.337 square miles. Located at 42.54° N. Lat; 79.00° W. Long.

**Population:** 1,789 (1990); 2,001 (2000); 1,833 (2010); Density: 72.6 persons per square mile (2010); Race: 8.2% White, 0.1% Black, 0.4% Asian, 87.8% American Indian/Alaska Native, 0.0% Native Hawaiian/Other Pacific Islander, 3.5% Other, 3.5% Hispanic of any race (2010); Average household size: 2.72 (2010); Median age: 32.5 (2010); Males per 100 females: 89.6 (2010); Marriage status: 52.6% never married, 31.0% now married, 11.8% widowed, 4.6% divorced (2006-2010 5-year est.); Foreign born: 16.1% (2006-2010 5-year est.); Ancestry (includes multiple ancestries): 5.6% Italian, 3.1% English, 2.1% Haitian, 1.6% German, 1.4% French Canadian (2006-2010 5-year est.).
**Economy:** Employment by occupation: 17.2% management, 1.5% professional, 6.4% services, 14.5% sales, 5.8% farming, 6.6% construction, 3.7% production (2006-2010 5-year est.).
**Income:** Per capita income: $29,549 (2006-2010 5-year est.); Median household income: $41,641 (2006-2010 5-year est.); Average household income: $70,683 (2006-2010 5-year est.); Percent of households with income of $100,000 or more: 18.7% (2006-2010 5-year est.); Poverty rate: 12.9% (2006-2010 5-year est.).
**Education:** Percent of population age 25 and over with: High school diploma (including GED) or higher: 90.6% (2006-2010 5-year est.); Bachelor's degree or higher: 26.2% (2006-2010 5-year est.); Master's degree or higher: 4.0% (2006-2010 5-year est.).
**Housing:** Homeownership rate: 72.6% (2010); Median home value: $80,500 (2006-2010 5-year est.); Median contract rent: $379 per month (2006-2010 5-year est.); Median year structure built: 1974 (2006-2010 5-year est.).
**Transportation:** Commute to work: 90.4% car, 0.0% public transportation, 9.3% walk, 0.0% work from home (2006-2010 5-year est.); Travel time to work: 70.0% less than 15 minutes, 11.6% 15 to 30 minutes, 6.3% 30 to 45 minutes, 4.0% 45 to 60 minutes, 8.1% 60 minutes or more (2006-2010 5-year est.)

## CHAFFEE (unincorporated postal area)
Zip Code: 14030
Covers a land area of 19.865 square miles and a water area of 0.215 square miles. Located at 42.56° N. Lat; 78.50° W. Long. Elevation is 1,460 feet. Population: 1,807 (2010); Density: 91.0 persons per square mile (2010); Race: 96.3% White, 0.3% Black, 1.4% Asian, 0.9% American Indian/Alaska Native, 0.0% Native Hawaiian/Other Pacific Islander, 1.1% Other, 0.9% Hispanic of any race (2010); Average household size: 2.53 (2010); Median age: 42.9 (2010); Males per 100 females: 107.0 (2010); Homeownership rate: 80.4% (2010)

## CHEEKTOWAGA (town). Covers a land area of 29.422 square miles and a water area of 0.062 square miles. Located at 42.91° N. Lat; 78.74° W. Long. Elevation is 650 feet.

**History:** Named for the Indian translation of "place of the crab apple tree". Population grew significantly after World War II. Settled 1809. Incorporated 1834.
**Population:** 99,314 (1990); 94,019 (2000); 88,226 (2010); Density: 2,998.6 persons per square mile (2010); Race: 88.1% White, 8.0% Black, 1.5% Asian, 0.3% American Indian/Alaska Native, 0.0% Native Hawaiian/Other Pacific Islander, 2.1% Other, 2.2% Hispanic of any race (2010); Average household size: 2.22 (2010); Median age: 43.2 (2010); Males per 100 females: 88.9 (2010); Marriage status: 30.7% never married, 50.1% now married, 9.5% widowed, 9.8% divorced (2006-2010 5-year est.); Foreign born: 4.9% (2006-2010 5-year est.); Ancestry (includes multiple ancestries): 35.4% Polish, 29.4% German, 16.5% Italian, 15.0% Irish, 5.4% English (2006-2010 5-year est.).
**Economy:** Unemployment rate: 9.3% (February 2012); Total civilian labor force: 46,920 (February 2012); Single-family building permits issued: 2 (2011); Multi-family building permits issued: 0 (2011); Employment by occupation: 8.0% management, 3.4% professional, 10.5% services, 21.0% sales, 4.2% farming, 6.9% construction, 5.7% production (2006-2010 5-year est.).
**Income:** Per capita income: $23,918 (2006-2010 5-year est.); Median household income: $45,893 (2006-2010 5-year est.); Average household income: $53,966 (2006-2010 5-year est.); Percent of households with

income of $100,000 or more: 10.0% (2006-2010 5-year est.); Poverty rate: 8.9% (2006-2010 5-year est.).
**Taxes:** Total city taxes per capita: $644 (2009); City property taxes per capita: $611 (2009).
**Education:** Percent of population age 25 and over with: High school diploma (including GED) or higher: 86.8% (2006-2010 5-year est.); Bachelor's degree or higher: 18.1% (2006-2010 5-year est.); Master's degree or higher: 6.1% (2006-2010 5-year est.).

**School District(s)**
Cheektowaga Central School District (PK-12)
 2009-10 Enrollment: 2,372 . . . . . . . . . . . . . . . . (716) 686-3606
Cheektowaga-Maryvale Union Free School District (PK-12)
 2009-10 Enrollment: 2,281 . . . . . . . . . . . . . . . . (716) 631-7407
Cheektowaga-Sloan Union Free School District (PK-12)
 2009-10 Enrollment: 1,570 . . . . . . . . . . . . . . . . (716) 891-6402
Cleveland Hill Union Free School District (PK-12)
 2009-10 Enrollment: 1,452 . . . . . . . . . . . . . . . . (716) 836-7200
**Housing:** Homeownership rate: 71.5% (2010); Median home value: $93,200 (2006-2010 5-year est.); Median contract rent: $591 per month (2006-2010 5-year est.); Median year structure built: 1959 (2006-2010 5-year est.).
**Hospitals:** St. Joseph Hospital (208 beds)
**Safety:** Violent crime rate: 20.2 per 10,000 population; Property crime rate: 358.4 per 10,000 population (2010).
**Newspapers:** AM-Pol Eagle (Local news; Circulation 2,400); Cheektowaga Times (Community news; Circulation 5,600); Metro Community News Am-ton (Community news; Circulation 15,493); Metro Community News Amherst/Getzville (Community news; Circulation 17,542); Metro Community News Cheektowaga/Harlem/Genesee (Community news; Circulation 11,396); Metro Community News Cheektowaga/Union/Genesee (Community news; Circulation 9,623); Metro Community News Clarence (Community news; Circulation 8,705); Metro Community News Eggertsville (Community news; Circulation 12,917); Metro Community News Grand Island (Community news; Circulation 6,439); Metro Community News Kenmore/Tonawanda (Community news; Circulation 14,251); Metro Community News Lancaster (Community news; Circulation 11,661); Metro Community News Lewiston/Youngstown (Community news; Circulation 11,614); Metro Community News Lockport Town (Community news; Circulation 10,395); Metro Community News Newfane/Gasport (Community news; Circulation 8,680); Metro Community News Niagara Falls North (Community news; Circulation 8,811); Metro Community News Niagara Falls South (Community news; Circulation 11,680); Metro Community News Niagara Falls/La Salle (Community news; Circulation 11,178); Metro Community News North Tonawanda (Community news; Circulation 14,495); Metro Community News South Buffalo (Community news; Circulation 17,325); Metro Community News South Cheektowaga (Community news; Circulation 17,537); Metro Community News Tonawanda (Community news; Circulation 11,751); Metro Community News Wheatfield (Community news; Circulation 4,486); Metro Community News Williamsville (Community news; Circulation 12,500)
**Transportation:** Commute to work: 94.7% car, 1.3% public transportation, 1.8% walk, 1.6% work from home (2006-2010 5-year est.); Travel time to work: 31.5% less than 15 minutes, 53.1% 15 to 30 minutes, 11.4% 30 to 45 minutes, 1.6% 45 to 60 minutes, 2.5% 60 minutes or more (2006-2010 5-year est.)
**Additional Information Contacts**
Cheektowaga Chamber of Commerce. . . . . . . . . . . . . . . . . (716) 684-5838
 http://www.cheektowaga.org
Town of Cheektowaga . . . . . . . . . . . . . . . . . . . . . . . . . . . (716) 686-3400
 http://tocny.org

## CHEEKTOWAGA (CDP). Covers a land area of 25.343 square miles and a water area of 0.056 square miles. Located at 42.90° N. Lat; 78.75° W. Long. Elevation is 650 feet.

**Population:** 84,387 (1990); 79,988 (2000); 75,178 (2010); Density: 2,966.4 persons per square mile (2010); Race: 86.8% White, 9.2% Black, 1.7% Asian, 0.3% American Indian/Alaska Native, 0.0% Native Hawaiian/Other Pacific Islander, 2.0% Other, 2.2% Hispanic of any race (2010); Average household size: 2.21 (2010); Median age: 43.0 (2010); Males per 100 females: 88.5 (2010); Marriage status: 31.2% never married, 49.6% now married, 9.4% widowed, 9.7% divorced (2006-2010 5-year est.); Foreign born: 4.9% (2006-2010 5-year est.); Ancestry (includes multiple ancestries): 34.6% Polish, 28.8% German, 16.3% Italian, 14.9% Irish, 5.6% English (2006-2010 5-year est.).

**Economy:** Employment by occupation: 8.3% management, 3.3% professional, 10.6% services, 20.7% sales, 4.2% farming, 6.8% construction, 5.4% production (2006-2010 5-year est.).
**Income:** Per capita income: $24,085 (2006-2010 5-year est.); Median household income: $45,998 (2006-2010 5-year est.); Average household income: $54,475 (2006-2010 5-year est.); Percent of households with income of $100,000 or more: 10.3% (2006-2010 5-year est.); Poverty rate: 9.1% (2006-2010 5-year est.).
**Education:** Percent of population age 25 and over with: High school diploma (including GED) or higher: 87.0% (2006-2010 5-year est.); Bachelor's degree or higher: 18.7% (2006-2010 5-year est.); Master's degree or higher: 6.5% (2006-2010 5-year est.).

### School District(s)
Cheektowaga Central School District (PK-12)
   2009-10 Enrollment: 2,372 . . . . . . . . . . . . . . . . . . . . . . . . (716) 686-3606
Cheektowaga-Maryvale Union Free School District (PK-12)
   2009-10 Enrollment: 2,281 . . . . . . . . . . . . . . . . . . . . . . . . (716) 631-7407
Cheektowaga-Sloan Union Free School District (PK-12)
   2009-10 Enrollment: 1,570 . . . . . . . . . . . . . . . . . . . . . . . . (716) 891-6402
Cleveland Hill Union Free School District (PK-12)
   2009-10 Enrollment: 1,452 . . . . . . . . . . . . . . . . . . . . . . . . (716) 836-7200
**Housing:** Homeownership rate: 70.8% (2010); Median home value: $94,000 (2006-2010 5-year est.); Median contract rent: $589 per month (2006-2010 5-year est.); Median year structure built: 1959 (2006-2010 5-year est.).
**Hospitals:** Sisters of Charity Hospital, St. Joseph Campus (123 beds)
**Transportation:** Commute to work: 94.5% car, 1.4% public transportation, 1.7% walk, 1.7% work from home (2006-2010 5-year est.); Travel time to work: 31.0% less than 15 minutes, 53.4% 15 to 30 minutes, 11.5% 30 to 45 minutes, 1.7% 45 to 60 minutes, 2.4% 60 minutes or more (2006-2010 5-year est.)

## CLARENCE (town).
Covers a land area of 53.502 square miles and a water area of 0.131 square miles. Located at 43.02° N. Lat; 78.64° W. Long. Elevation is 738 feet.
**Population:** 20,041 (1990); 26,123 (2000); 30,673 (2010); Density: 573.3 persons per square mile (2010); Race: 93.8% White, 1.1% Black, 3.6% Asian, 0.1% American Indian/Alaska Native, 0.0% Native Hawaiian/Other Pacific Islander, 1.4% Other, 1.4% Hispanic of any race (2010); Average household size: 2.68 (2010); Median age: 43.7 (2010); Males per 100 females: 94.2 (2010); Marriage status: 23.3% never married, 63.9% now married, 6.6% widowed, 6.3% divorced (2006-2010 5-year est.); Foreign born: 7.2% (2006-2010 5-year est.); Ancestry (includes multiple ancestries): 34.9% German, 21.8% Italian, 19.0% Irish, 14.8% Polish, 10.1% English (2006-2010 5-year est.).
**Economy:** Single-family building permits issued: 73 (2011); Multi-family building permits issued: 0 (2011); Employment by occupation: 16.2% management, 5.7% professional, 6.1% services, 16.9% sales, 3.9% farming, 4.6% construction, 3.1% production (2006-2010 5-year est.).
**Income:** Per capita income: $37,745 (2006-2010 5-year est.); Median household income: $81,623 (2006-2010 5-year est.); Average household income: $103,633 (2006-2010 5-year est.); Percent of households with income of $100,000 or more: 38.8% (2006-2010 5-year est.); Poverty rate: 4.1% (2006-2010 5-year est.).
**Taxes:** Total city taxes per capita: $401 (2009); City property taxes per capita: $344 (2009).
**Education:** Percent of population age 25 and over with: High school diploma (including GED) or higher: 95.7% (2006-2010 5-year est.); Bachelor's degree or higher: 50.1% (2006-2010 5-year est.); Master's degree or higher: 24.5% (2006-2010 5-year est.).
**Housing:** Homeownership rate: 84.9% (2010); Median home value: $222,800 (2006-2010 5-year est.); Median contract rent: $748 per month (2006-2010 5-year est.); Median year structure built: 1979 (2006-2010 5-year est.).
**Transportation:** Commute to work: 92.8% car, 0.4% public transportation, 1.1% walk, 4.9% work from home (2006-2010 5-year est.); Travel time to work: 26.1% less than 15 minutes, 41.7% 15 to 30 minutes, 26.7% 30 to 45 minutes, 3.3% 45 to 60 minutes, 2.1% 60 minutes or more (2006-2010 5-year est.)
**Additional Information Contacts**
Clarence Chamber of Commerce . . . . . . . . . . . . . . . . . . (716) 631-3888
   http://www.clarence.org

## CLARENCE (CDP).
Covers a land area of 2.845 square miles and a water area of 0.064 square miles. Located at 42.97° N. Lat; 78.59° W. Long. Elevation is 738 feet.
**Population:** n/a (1990); n/a (2000); 2,646 (2010); Density: 930.0 persons per square mile (2010); Race: 98.0% White, 0.5% Black, 0.8% Asian, 0.2% American Indian/Alaska Native, 0.0% Native Hawaiian/Other Pacific Islander, 0.5% Other, 0.8% Hispanic of any race (2010); Average household size: 2.25 (2010); Median age: 52.2 (2010); Males per 100 females: 79.4 (2010); Marriage status: 24.4% never married, 46.7% now married, 20.6% widowed, 8.3% divorced (2006-2010 5-year est.); Foreign born: 2.6% (2006-2010 5-year est.); Ancestry (includes multiple ancestries): 30.1% German, 23.3% Polish, 19.0% Italian, 14.3% Irish, 5.7% English (2006-2010 5-year est.).
**Economy:** Employment by occupation: 9.2% management, 6.5% professional, 4.4% services, 19.7% sales, 3.2% farming, 3.5% construction, 3.1% production (2006-2010 5-year est.).
**Income:** Per capita income: $30,867 (2006-2010 5-year est.); Median household income: $71,576 (2006-2010 5-year est.); Average household income: $86,981 (2006-2010 5-year est.); Percent of households with income of $100,000 or more: 25.3% (2006-2010 5-year est.); Poverty rate: 14.9% (2006-2010 5-year est.).
**Education:** Percent of population age 25 and over with: High school diploma (including GED) or higher: 91.2% (2006-2010 5-year est.); Bachelor's degree or higher: 36.1% (2006-2010 5-year est.); Master's degree or higher: 19.5% (2006-2010 5-year est.).
**Housing:** Homeownership rate: 68.8% (2010); Median home value: $196,900 (2006-2010 5-year est.); Median contract rent: $419 per month (2006-2010 5-year est.); Median year structure built: 1962 (2006-2010 5-year est.).
**Transportation:** Commute to work: 94.5% car, 0.0% public transportation, 0.0% walk, 5.5% work from home (2006-2010 5-year est.); Travel time to work: 14.5% less than 15 minutes, 43.0% 15 to 30 minutes, 39.2% 30 to 45 minutes, 2.3% 45 to 60 minutes, 1.0% 60 minutes or more (2006-2010 5-year est.)

## CLARENCE CENTER (CDP).
Covers a land area of 2.257 square miles and a water area of 0 square miles. Located at 43.00° N. Lat; 78.63° W. Long. Elevation is 633 feet.
**Population:** 1,376 (1990); 1,747 (2000); 2,257 (2010); Density: 999.6 persons per square mile (2010); Race: 94.6% White, 1.1% Black, 2.4% Asian, 0.1% American Indian/Alaska Native, 0.0% Native Hawaiian/Other Pacific Islander, 1.8% Other, 1.2% Hispanic of any race (2010); Average household size: 2.89 (2010); Median age: 39.7 (2010); Males per 100 females: 96.4 (2010); Marriage status: 25.1% never married, 63.5% now married, 3.7% widowed, 7.7% divorced (2006-2010 5-year est.); Foreign born: 2.0% (2006-2010 5-year est.); Ancestry (includes multiple ancestries): 33.7% German, 21.6% Irish, 20.2% Italian, 17.7% Polish, 11.7% English (2006-2010 5-year est.).
**Economy:** Employment by occupation: 12.1% management, 5.9% professional, 7.9% services, 14.8% sales, 3.4% farming, 10.7% construction, 6.2% production (2006-2010 5-year est.).
**Income:** Per capita income: $35,874 (2006-2010 5-year est.); Median household income: $86,306 (2006-2010 5-year est.); Average household income: $96,518 (2006-2010 5-year est.); Percent of households with income of $100,000 or more: 40.0% (2006-2010 5-year est.); Poverty rate: 2.5% (2006-2010 5-year est.).
**Education:** Percent of population age 25 and over with: High school diploma (including GED) or higher: 99.3% (2006-2010 5-year est.); Bachelor's degree or higher: 51.1% (2006-2010 5-year est.); Master's degree or higher: 25.6% (2006-2010 5-year est.).

### School District(s)
Clarence Central School District (KG-12)
   2009-10 Enrollment: 5,101 . . . . . . . . . . . . . . . . . . . . . . . . (716) 407-9102
**Housing:** Homeownership rate: 89.9% (2010); Median home value: $195,800 (2006-2010 5-year est.); Median contract rent: $408 per month (2006-2010 5-year est.); Median year structure built: 1968 (2006-2010 5-year est.).
**Transportation:** Commute to work: 95.3% car, 0.0% public transportation, 1.8% walk, 2.0% work from home (2006-2010 5-year est.); Travel time to work: 44.6% less than 15 minutes, 26.7% 15 to 30 minutes, 22.5% 30 to 45 minutes, 3.3% 45 to 60 minutes, 3.0% 60 minutes or more (2006-2010 5-year est.)

**COLDEN** (town). Covers a land area of 35.632 square miles and a water area of 0.089 square miles. Located at 42.64° N. Lat; 78.64° W. Long. Elevation is 1,079 feet.
**Population:** 2,899 (1990); 3,323 (2000); 3,265 (2010); Density: 91.6 persons per square mile (2010); Race: 98.6% White, 0.1% Black, 0.4% Asian, 0.2% American Indian/Alaska Native, 0.1% Native Hawaiian/Other Pacific Islander, 0.6% Other, 0.5% Hispanic of any race (2010); Average household size: 2.50 (2010); Median age: 45.2 (2010); Males per 100 females: 98.2 (2010); Marriage status: 14.7% never married, 73.9% now married, 2.9% widowed, 8.6% divorced (2006-2010 5-year est.); Foreign born: 6.0% (2006-2010 5-year est.); Ancestry (includes multiple ancestries): 45.1% German, 19.2% Irish, 17.1% Polish, 12.4% English, 5.7% American (2006-2010 5-year est.).
**Economy:** Single-family building permits issued: 8 (2011); Multi-family building permits issued: 0 (2011); Employment by occupation: 13.1% management, 7.6% professional, 5.9% services, 17.0% sales, 3.2% farming, 9.7% construction, 6.4% production (2006-2010 5-year est.).
**Income:** Per capita income: $34,488 (2006-2010 5-year est.); Median household income: $71,411 (2006-2010 5-year est.); Average household income: $82,121 (2006-2010 5-year est.); Percent of households with income of $100,000 or more: 30.7% (2006-2010 5-year est.); Poverty rate: 6.3% (2006-2010 5-year est.).
**Education:** Percent of population age 25 and over with: High school diploma (including GED) or higher: 96.1% (2006-2010 5-year est.); Bachelor's degree or higher: 36.2% (2006-2010 5-year est.); Master's degree or higher: 16.3% (2006-2010 5-year est.).

### School District(s)
Springville-Griffith Institute Central School Dist (KG-12)
  2009-10 Enrollment: 2,098 . . . . . . . . . . . . . . . . . . . . . . . (716) 592-3230
**Housing:** Homeownership rate: 87.0% (2010); Median home value: $176,600 (2006-2010 5-year est.); Median contract rent: $483 per month (2006-2010 5-year est.); Median year structure built: 1966 (2006-2010 5-year est.).
**Transportation:** Commute to work: 90.0% car, 1.4% public transportation, 0.5% walk, 6.4% work from home (2006-2010 5-year est.); Travel time to work: 13.7% less than 15 minutes, 28.8% 15 to 30 minutes, 32.3% 30 to 45 minutes, 14.4% 45 to 60 minutes, 10.8% 60 minutes or more (2006-2010 5-year est.)

**COLLINS** (town). Covers a land area of 47.965 square miles and a water area of 0.173 square miles. Located at 42.49° N. Lat; 78.86° W. Long. Elevation is 879 feet.
**Population:** 6,020 (1990); 8,307 (2000); 6,601 (2010); Density: 137.6 persons per square mile (2010); Race: 75.9% White, 17.1% Black, 0.2% Asian, 2.9% American Indian/Alaska Native, 0.0% Native Hawaiian/Other Pacific Islander, 3.9% Other, 6.9% Hispanic of any race (2010); Average household size: 2.40 (2010); Median age: 40.1 (2010); Males per 100 females: 228.6 (2010); Marriage status: 38.8% never married, 41.7% now married, 6.0% widowed, 13.5% divorced (2006-2010 5-year est.); Foreign born: 6.4% (2006-2010 5-year est.); Ancestry (includes multiple ancestries): 27.1% German, 15.4% Irish, 10.8% English, 9.7% Italian, 7.8% Polish (2006-2010 5-year est.).
**Economy:** Single-family building permits issued: 2 (2011); Multi-family building permits issued: 0 (2011); Employment by occupation: 4.9% management, 3.7% professional, 9.5% services, 16.3% sales, 1.2% farming, 16.6% construction, 12.7% production (2006-2010 5-year est.).
**Income:** Per capita income: $14,908 (2006-2010 5-year est.); Median household income: $43,934 (2006-2010 5-year est.); Average household income: $49,090 (2006-2010 5-year est.); Percent of households with income of $100,000 or more: 8.2% (2006-2010 5-year est.); Poverty rate: 6.3% (2006-2010 5-year est.).
**Education:** Percent of population age 25 and over with: High school diploma (including GED) or higher: 75.0% (2006-2010 5-year est.); Bachelor's degree or higher: 9.3% (2006-2010 5-year est.); Master's degree or higher: 2.8% (2006-2010 5-year est.).
**Housing:** Homeownership rate: 77.2% (2010); Median home value: $85,400 (2006-2010 5-year est.); Median contract rent: $404 per month (2006-2010 5-year est.); Median year structure built: 1952 (2006-2010 5-year est.).
**Transportation:** Commute to work: 91.9% car, 0.0% public transportation, 5.4% walk, 1.5% work from home (2006-2010 5-year est.); Travel time to work: 40.2% less than 15 minutes, 20.9% 15 to 30 minutes, 15.3% 30 to 45 minutes, 15.2% 45 to 60 minutes, 8.4% 60 minutes or more (2006-2010 5-year est.)

**COLLINS CENTER** (unincorporated postal area)
Zip Code: 14035
  Covers a land area of 0.228 square miles and a water area of 0 square miles. Located at 42.49° N. Lat; 78.84° W. Long. Elevation is 1,102 feet. Population: 125 (2010); Density: 547.2 persons per square mile (2010); Race: 97.6% White, 0.8% Black, 0.0% Asian, 0.0% American Indian/Alaska Native, 0.0% Native Hawaiian/Other Pacific Islander, 1.6% Other, 2.4% Hispanic of any race (2010); Average household size: 2.31 (2010); Median age: 39.3 (2010); Males per 100 females: 98.4 (2010); Homeownership rate: 64.8% (2010)

**CONCORD** (town). Covers a land area of 69.933 square miles and a water area of 0.159 square miles. Located at 42.54° N. Lat; 78.70° W. Long. Elevation is 1,352 feet.
**Population:** 8,387 (1990); 8,526 (2000); 8,494 (2010); Density: 121.5 persons per square mile (2010); Race: 97.3% White, 0.6% Black, 0.4% Asian, 0.5% American Indian/Alaska Native, 0.0% Native Hawaiian/Other Pacific Islander, 1.2% Other, 1.8% Hispanic of any race (2010); Average household size: 2.43 (2010); Median age: 42.9 (2010); Males per 100 females: 98.0 (2010); Marriage status: 25.5% never married, 49.4% now married, 13.9% widowed, 11.3% divorced (2006-2010 5-year est.); Foreign born: 2.9% (2006-2010 5-year est.); Ancestry (includes multiple ancestries): 39.7% German, 18.5% Irish, 16.0% English, 14.3% Polish, 12.4% Italian (2006-2010 5-year est.).
**Economy:** Single-family building permits issued: 8 (2011); Multi-family building permits issued: 0 (2011); Employment by occupation: 12.8% management, 2.8% professional, 10.5% services, 19.3% sales, 4.0% farming, 10.4% construction, 7.3% production (2006-2010 5-year est.).
**Income:** Per capita income: $23,650 (2006-2010 5-year est.); Median household income: $46,977 (2006-2010 5-year est.); Average household income: $56,055 (2006-2010 5-year est.); Percent of households with income of $100,000 or more: 13.1% (2006-2010 5-year est.); Poverty rate: 9.3% (2006-2010 5-year est.).
**Education:** Percent of population age 25 and over with: High school diploma (including GED) or higher: 86.6% (2006-2010 5-year est.); Bachelor's degree or higher: 21.4% (2006-2010 5-year est.); Master's degree or higher: 8.3% (2006-2010 5-year est.).
**Housing:** Homeownership rate: 74.1% (2010); Median home value: $124,800 (2006-2010 5-year est.); Median contract rent: $450 per month (2006-2010 5-year est.); Median year structure built: 1963 (2006-2010 5-year est.).
**Transportation:** Commute to work: 87.6% car, 0.5% public transportation, 6.7% walk, 2.8% work from home (2006-2010 5-year est.); Travel time to work: 36.1% less than 15 minutes, 22.1% 15 to 30 minutes, 20.7% 30 to 45 minutes, 15.3% 45 to 60 minutes, 5.8% 60 minutes or more (2006-2010 5-year est.)

**DEPEW** (village). Covers a land area of 5.073 square miles and a water area of 0 square miles. Located at 42.91° N. Lat; 78.70° W. Long. Elevation is 673 feet.
**History:** Founded in 1892 as a village, it was named for Chauncey M. Depew (1834-1928), a Railroad executive and later a U.S. senator. Incorporated 1894.
**Population:** 17,673 (1990); 16,629 (2000); 15,303 (2010); Density: 3,016.0 persons per square mile (2010); Race: 96.5% White, 1.2% Black, 0.7% Asian, 0.2% American Indian/Alaska Native, 0.0% Native Hawaiian/Other Pacific Islander, 1.4% Other, 1.7% Hispanic of any race (2010); Average household size: 2.28 (2010); Median age: 42.7 (2010); Males per 100 females: 92.8 (2010); Marriage status: 28.0% never married, 53.7% now married, 8.9% widowed, 9.4% divorced (2006-2010 5-year est.); Foreign born: 3.8% (2006-2010 5-year est.); Ancestry (includes multiple ancestries): 38.7% Polish, 35.1% German, 19.0% Italian, 14.9% Irish, 5.3% English (2006-2010 5-year est.).
**Economy:** Single-family building permits issued: 1 (2011); Multi-family building permits issued: 2 (2011); Employment by occupation: 6.8% management, 5.1% professional, 10.8% services, 20.4% sales, 5.3% farming, 7.2% construction, 6.5% production (2006-2010 5-year est.).
**Income:** Per capita income: $23,473 (2006-2010 5-year est.); Median household income: $48,558 (2006-2010 5-year est.); Average household income: $54,804 (2006-2010 5-year est.); Percent of households with income of $100,000 or more: 11.5% (2006-2010 5-year est.); Poverty rate: 8.3% (2006-2010 5-year est.).
**Education:** Percent of population age 25 and over with: High school diploma (including GED) or higher: 88.4% (2006-2010 5-year est.);

Bachelor's degree or higher: 18.7% (2006-2010 5-year est.); Master's degree or higher: 5.6% (2006-2010 5-year est.).

**School District(s)**

Depew Union Free School District (KG-12)
   2009-10 Enrollment: 2,078 . . . . . . . . . . . . . . . . . . . (716) 686-2251
Lancaster Central School District (PK-12)
   2009-10 Enrollment: 6,263 . . . . . . . . . . . . . . . . . . . (716) 686-3201

**Housing:** Homeownership rate: 71.8% (2010); Median home value: $98,600 (2006-2010 5-year est.); Median contract rent: $581 per month (2006-2010 5-year est.); Median year structure built: 1957 (2006-2010 5-year est.).

**Safety:** Violent crime rate: 17.4 per 10,000 population; Property crime rate: 229.9 per 10,000 population (2010).

**Transportation:** Commute to work: 94.2% car, 0.9% public transportation, 3.3% walk, 1.1% work from home (2006-2010 5-year est.); Travel time to work: 30.8% less than 15 minutes, 51.8% 15 to 30 minutes, 13.8% 30 to 45 minutes, 1.1% 45 to 60 minutes, 2.5% 60 minutes or more (2006-2010 5-year est.); Amtrak: train service available.

**Additional Information Contacts**

Village of Depew . . . . . . . . . . . . . . . . . . . . . . . . . . . . . (716) 683-1400
   http://www.villageofdepew.org

## DERBY (unincorporated postal area)

Zip Code: 14047

Covers a land area of 13.137 square miles and a water area of 1.000 square miles. Located at 42.68° N. Lat; 78.98° W. Long. Elevation is 702 feet. Population: 6,440 (2010); Density: 490.2 persons per square mile (2010); Race: 97.1% White, 0.7% Black, 0.3% Asian, 0.9% American Indian/Alaska Native, 0.1% Native Hawaiian/Other Pacific Islander, 0.9% Other, 1.8% Hispanic of any race (2010); Average household size: 2.46 (2010); Median age: 43.5 (2010); Males per 100 females: 98.4 (2010); Homeownership rate: 82.5% (2010).

## EAST AMHERST (unincorporated postal area)

Zip Code: 14051

Covers a land area of 16.336 square miles and a water area of 0.069 square miles. Located at 43.04° N. Lat; 78.69° W. Long. Elevation is 594 feet. Population: 19,533 (2010); Density: 1,195.7 persons per square mile (2010); Race: 88.5% White, 2.2% Black, 7.2% Asian, 0.1% American Indian/Alaska Native, 0.0% Native Hawaiian/Other Pacific Islander, 2.0% Other, 1.8% Hispanic of any race (2010); Average household size: 2.73 (2010); Median age: 43.1 (2010); Males per 100 females: 95.1 (2010); Homeownership rate: 89.3% (2010).

## EAST AURORA (village). Covers a land area of 2.511 square miles and a water area of 0.010 square miles. Located at 42.76° N. Lat; 78.61° W. Long. Elevation is 919 feet.

**Population:** 6,764 (1990); 6,673 (2000); 6,236 (2010); Density: 2,483.0 persons per square mile (2010); Race: 97.8% White, 0.4% Black, 0.5% Asian, 0.1% American Indian/Alaska Native, 0.0% Native Hawaiian/Other Pacific Islander, 1.2% Other, 1.1% Hispanic of any race (2010); Average household size: 2.34 (2010); Median age: 43.8 (2010); Males per 100 females: 85.7 (2010); Marriage status: 17.7% never married, 64.7% now married, 9.2% widowed, 8.4% divorced (2006-2010 5-year est.); Foreign born: 3.2% (2006-2010 5-year est.); Ancestry (includes multiple ancestries): 36.3% German, 30.6% Irish, 14.4% Polish, 14.3% Italian, 13.7% English (2006-2010 5-year est.).

**Economy:** Employment by occupation: 15.4% management, 5.4% professional, 7.1% services, 12.0% sales, 2.4% farming, 4.0% construction, 3.1% production (2006-2010 5-year est.).

**Income:** Per capita income: $34,619 (2006-2010 5-year est.); Median household income: $62,894 (2006-2010 5-year est.); Average household income: $82,783 (2006-2010 5-year est.); Percent of households with income of $100,000 or more: 27.2% (2006-2010 5-year est.); Poverty rate: 3.0% (2006-2010 5-year est.).

**Education:** Percent of population age 25 and over with: High school diploma (including GED) or higher: 95.4% (2006-2010 5-year est.); Bachelor's degree or higher: 49.7% (2006-2010 5-year est.); Master's degree or higher: 22.9% (2006-2010 5-year est.).

**School District(s)**

East Aurora Union Free School District (KG-12)
   2009-10 Enrollment: 1,964 . . . . . . . . . . . . . . . . . . (716) 687-2302
Iroquois Central School District (KG-12)
   2009-10 Enrollment: 2,635 . . . . . . . . . . . . . . . . . . (716) 652-3000

**Four-year College(s)**

Christ the King Seminary (Private, Not-for-profit, Roman Catholic)
   Fall 2010 Enrollment: 31 . . . . . . . . . . . . . . . . . . . . (716) 652-8900

**Housing:** Homeownership rate: 72.0% (2010); Median home value: $165,000 (2006-2010 5-year est.); Median contract rent: $555 per month (2006-2010 5-year est.); Median year structure built: before 1940 (2006-2010 5-year est.).

**Hospitals:** Mercy Diagnostic Center - East Aurora

**Newspapers:** East Aurora Advertiser (Community news; Circulation 4,550); Elma Review (Community news; Circulation 1,200)

**Transportation:** Commute to work: 87.4% car, 0.9% public transportation, 5.3% walk, 4.6% work from home (2006-2010 5-year est.); Travel time to work: 38.6% less than 15 minutes, 25.8% 15 to 30 minutes, 27.6% 30 to 45 minutes, 4.1% 45 to 60 minutes, 4.0% 60 minutes or more (2006-2010 5-year est.)

**Additional Information Contacts**

Greater East Aurora Chamber of Commerce . . . . . . . . . . (716) 652-8444
   http://www.eanycc.com
Village of East Aurora . . . . . . . . . . . . . . . . . . . . . . . . (716) 652-6000
   http://www.east-aurora.ny.us

## EAST CONCORD (unincorporated postal area)

Zip Code: 14055

Covers a land area of 32.336 square miles and a water area of 0.034 square miles. Located at 42.56° N. Lat; 78.60° W. Long. Elevation is 1,457 feet. Population: 1,405 (2010); Density: 43.4 persons per square mile (2010); Race: 98.7% White, 0.2% Black, 0.1% Asian, 0.2% American Indian/Alaska Native, 0.0% Native Hawaiian/Other Pacific Islander, 0.8% Other, 1.1% Hispanic of any race (2010); Average household size: 2.48 (2010); Median age: 47.0 (2010); Males per 100 females: 100.1 (2010); Homeownership rate: 88.5% (2010)

## EDEN (town). Aka Eden Center. Covers a land area of 39.790 square miles and a water area of 0.069 square miles. Located at 42.65° N. Lat; 78.88° W. Long. Elevation is 820 feet.

**History:** The "Original American Kazoo" is still made here, and though the factory itself may no longer be toured, there is still a visitors center that explains modern production methods as well as West African origins of the instrument. Established in 1916, this is now the world's only metal kazoo factory.

**Population:** 7,416 (1990); 8,076 (2000); 7,688 (2010); Density: 193.2 persons per square mile (2010); Race: 98.0% White, 0.4% Black, 0.2% Asian, 0.3% American Indian/Alaska Native, 0.0% Native Hawaiian/Other Pacific Islander, 1.1% Other, 1.8% Hispanic of any race (2010); Average household size: 2.58 (2010); Median age: 44.3 (2010); Males per 100 females: 100.4 (2010); Marriage status: 27.0% never married, 58.6% now married, 6.8% widowed, 7.6% divorced (2006-2010 5-year est.); Foreign born: 2.9% (2006-2010 5-year est.); Ancestry (includes multiple ancestries): 42.8% German, 22.1% Irish, 22.0% Polish, 12.9% English, 10.5% Italian (2006-2010 5-year est.).

**Economy:** Single-family building permits issued: 10 (2011); Multi-family building permits issued: 0 (2011); Employment by occupation: 12.9% management, 3.3% professional, 8.8% services, 12.5% sales, 6.1% farming, 11.7% construction, 8.1% production (2006-2010 5-year est.).

**Income:** Per capita income: $28,379 (2006-2010 5-year est.); Median household income: $61,750 (2006-2010 5-year est.); Average household income: $75,260 (2006-2010 5-year est.); Percent of households with income of $100,000 or more: 26.1% (2006-2010 5-year est.); Poverty rate: 3.1% (2006-2010 5-year est.).

**Education:** Percent of population age 25 and over with: High school diploma (including GED) or higher: 91.2% (2006-2010 5-year est.); Bachelor's degree or higher: 29.9% (2006-2010 5-year est.); Master's degree or higher: 11.2% (2006-2010 5-year est.).

**School District(s)**

Eden Central School District (PK-12)
   2009-10 Enrollment: 1,699 . . . . . . . . . . . . . . . . . . (716) 992-3629

**Housing:** Homeownership rate: 83.7% (2010); Median home value: $148,700 (2006-2010 5-year est.); Median contract rent: $435 per month (2006-2010 5-year est.); Median year structure built: 1958 (2006-2010 5-year est.).

**Safety:** Violent crime rate: 3.9 per 10,000 population; Property crime rate: 55.2 per 10,000 population (2010).

**Transportation:** Commute to work: 91.7% car, 0.9% public transportation, 2.3% walk, 3.5% work from home (2006-2010 5-year est.); Travel time to work: 23.9% less than 15 minutes, 28.5% 15 to 30 minutes, 32.9% 30 to 45

minutes, 9.7% 45 to 60 minutes, 5.1% 60 minutes or more (2006-2010 5-year est.)

**Additional Information Contacts**

Eden Chamber of Commerce . . . . . . . . . . . . . . . . . . . . . . . . . (716) 992-4799
  http://www.edenny.org/chamber.html
Town of Eden. . . . . . . . . . . . . . . . . . . . . . . . . . . . . . . . . . . . (716) 992-3408
  http://www.edenny.org

**EDEN** (CDP). Covers a land area of 5.594 square miles and a water area of 0 square miles. Located at 42.65° N. Lat; 78.90° W. Long. Elevation is 820 feet.
**Population:** 3,250 (1990); 3,579 (2000); 3,516 (2010); Density: 628.5 persons per square mile (2010); Race: 98.0% White, 0.5% Black, 0.3% Asian, 0.3% American Indian/Alaska Native, 0.0% Native Hawaiian/Other Pacific Islander, 0.9% Other, 0.7% Hispanic of any race (2010); Average household size: 2.66 (2010); Median age: 43.2 (2010); Males per 100 females: 100.5 (2010); Marriage status: 27.2% never married, 62.1% now married, 5.2% widowed, 5.4% divorced (2006-2010 5-year est.); Foreign born: 2.4% (2006-2010 5-year est.); Ancestry (includes multiple ancestries): 45.7% German, 19.7% Irish, 16.1% Polish, 13.5% English, 10.6% Italian (2006-2010 5-year est.).
**Economy:** Employment by occupation: 10.3% management, 4.0% professional, 8.8% services, 13.1% sales, 5.3% farming, 10.0% construction, 7.8% production (2006-2010 5-year est.).
**Income:** Per capita income: $25,288 (2006-2010 5-year est.); Median household income: $68,669 (2006-2010 5-year est.); Average household income: $73,858 (2006-2010 5-year est.); Percent of households with income of $100,000 or more: 29.8% (2006-2010 5-year est.); Poverty rate: 1.7% (2006-2010 5-year est.).
**Education:** Percent of population age 25 and over with: High school diploma (including GED) or higher: 92.5% (2006-2010 5-year est.); Bachelor's degree or higher: 29.1% (2006-2010 5-year est.); Master's degree or higher: 9.4% (2006-2010 5-year est.).

**School District(s)**

Eden Central School District (PK-12)
  2009-10 Enrollment: 1,699 . . . . . . . . . . . . . . . . . . . . . . . (716) 992-3629
**Housing:** Homeownership rate: 84.0% (2010); Median home value: $141,700 (2006-2010 5-year est.); Median contract rent: $513 per month (2006-2010 5-year est.); Median year structure built: 1958 (2006-2010 5-year est.).
**Transportation:** Commute to work: 88.9% car, 1.8% public transportation, 4.3% walk, 3.3% work from home (2006-2010 5-year est.); Travel time to work: 24.5% less than 15 minutes, 23.9% 15 to 30 minutes, 36.5% 30 to 45 minutes, 8.3% 45 to 60 minutes, 6.9% 60 minutes or more (2006-2010 5-year est.)

**EGGERTSVILLE** (CDP). Covers a land area of 2.851 square miles and a water area of 0.001 square miles. Located at 42.96° N. Lat; 78.80° W. Long. Elevation is 653 feet.
**Population:** n/a (1990); n/a (2000); 15,019 (2010); Density: 5,267.4 persons per square mile (2010); Race: 77.2% White, 12.2% Black, 7.3% Asian, 0.2% American Indian/Alaska Native, 0.0% Native Hawaiian/Other Pacific Islander, 3.1% Other, 2.9% Hispanic of any race (2010); Average household size: 2.33 (2010); Median age: 38.2 (2010); Males per 100 females: 92.2 (2010); Marriage status: 33.7% never married, 50.4% now married, 6.3% widowed, 9.6% divorced (2006-2010 5-year est.); Foreign born: 14.5% (2006-2010 5-year est.); Ancestry (includes multiple ancestries): 22.7% German, 17.9% Italian, 16.9% Irish, 13.0% Polish, 9.3% English (2006-2010 5-year est.).
**Economy:** Employment by occupation: 10.9% management, 6.8% professional, 9.1% services, 14.5% sales, 4.2% farming, 5.9% construction, 3.5% production (2006-2010 5-year est.).
**Income:** Per capita income: $32,682 (2006-2010 5-year est.); Median household income: $55,935 (2006-2010 5-year est.); Average household income: $76,210 (2006-2010 5-year est.); Percent of households with income of $100,000 or more: 22.8% (2006-2010 5-year est.); Poverty rate: 12.8% (2006-2010 5-year est.).
**Education:** Percent of population age 25 and over with: High school diploma (including GED) or higher: 93.1% (2006-2010 5-year est.); Bachelor's degree or higher: 48.4% (2006-2010 5-year est.); Master's degree or higher: 24.6% (2006-2010 5-year est.).
**Housing:** Homeownership rate: 74.1% (2010); Median home value: $113,500 (2006-2010 5-year est.); Median contract rent: $535 per month (2006-2010 5-year est.); Median year structure built: 1952 (2006-2010 5-year est.).

**Transportation:** Commute to work: 88.3% car, 7.0% public transportation, 0.9% walk, 2.4% work from home (2006-2010 5-year est.); Travel time to work: 28.1% less than 15 minutes, 51.6% 15 to 30 minutes, 17.0% 30 to 45 minutes, 0.9% 45 to 60 minutes, 2.4% 60 minutes or more (2006-2010 5-year est.)

**ELMA** (town). Covers a land area of 34.517 square miles and a water area of 0.010 square miles. Located at 42.82° N. Lat; 78.64° W. Long. Elevation is 712 feet.
**Population:** 10,355 (1990); 11,304 (2000); 11,317 (2010); Density: 327.9 persons per square mile (2010); Race: 98.9% White, 0.2% Black, 0.3% Asian, 0.1% American Indian/Alaska Native, 0.0% Native Hawaiian/Other Pacific Islander, 0.5% Other, 0.6% Hispanic of any race (2010); Average household size: 2.53 (2010); Median age: 47.4 (2010); Males per 100 females: 98.8 (2010); Marriage status: 23.1% never married, 60.9% now married, 7.8% widowed, 8.2% divorced (2006-2010 5-year est.); Foreign born: 3.6% (2006-2010 5-year est.); Ancestry (includes multiple ancestries): 39.5% German, 20.5% Polish, 18.6% Irish, 15.5% Italian, 12.8% English (2006-2010 5-year est.).
**Economy:** Single-family building permits issued: 32 (2011); Multi-family building permits issued: 48 (2011); Employment by occupation: 13.9% management, 6.2% professional, 8.9% services, 18.6% sales, 3.7% farming, 8.4% construction, 8.0% production (2006-2010 5-year est.).
**Income:** Per capita income: $36,237 (2006-2010 5-year est.); Median household income: $74,282 (2006-2010 5-year est.); Average household income: $90,708 (2006-2010 5-year est.); Percent of households with income of $100,000 or more: 31.7% (2006-2010 5-year est.); Poverty rate: 5.2% (2006-2010 5-year est.).
**Taxes:** Total city taxes per capita: $153 (2009); City property taxes per capita: $120 (2009).
**Education:** Percent of population age 25 and over with: High school diploma (including GED) or higher: 93.9% (2006-2010 5-year est.); Bachelor's degree or higher: 32.8% (2006-2010 5-year est.); Master's degree or higher: 13.4% (2006-2010 5-year est.).

**School District(s)**

Iroquois Central School District (KG-12)
  2009-10 Enrollment: 2,635 . . . . . . . . . . . . . . . . . . . . . . . (716) 652-3000
**Housing:** Homeownership rate: 88.8% (2010); Median home value: $193,600 (2006-2010 5-year est.); Median contract rent: $646 per month (2006-2010 5-year est.); Median year structure built: 1965 (2006-2010 5-year est.).
**Transportation:** Commute to work: 93.6% car, 0.4% public transportation, 0.6% walk, 4.2% work from home (2006-2010 5-year est.); Travel time to work: 26.6% less than 15 minutes, 42.2% 15 to 30 minutes, 22.5% 30 to 45 minutes, 6.2% 45 to 60 minutes, 2.6% 60 minutes or more (2006-2010 5-year est.)

**ELMA CENTER** (CDP). Aka Elma. Covers a land area of 6.253 square miles and a water area of 0 square miles. Located at 42.82° N. Lat; 78.63° W. Long. Elevation is 804 feet.
**Population:** 2,354 (1990); 2,491 (2000); 2,571 (2010); Density: 411.1 persons per square mile (2010); Race: 99.2% White, 0.2% Black, 0.3% Asian, 0.2% American Indian/Alaska Native, 0.0% Native Hawaiian/Other Pacific Islander, 0.1% Other, 0.5% Hispanic of any race (2010); Average household size: 2.46 (2010); Median age: 48.4 (2010); Males per 100 females: 93.9 (2010); Marriage status: 21.9% never married, 56.0% now married, 12.1% widowed, 10.0% divorced (2006-2010 5-year est.); Foreign born: 5.4% (2006-2010 5-year est.); Ancestry (includes multiple ancestries): 31.3% German, 20.2% Polish, 19.5% Irish, 19.5% Italian, 12.4% English (2006-2010 5-year est.).
**Economy:** Employment by occupation: 17.1% management, 5.7% professional, 6.0% services, 19.0% sales, 2.6% farming, 6.3% construction, 4.5% production (2006-2010 5-year est.).
**Income:** Per capita income: $35,264 (2006-2010 5-year est.); Median household income: $61,167 (2006-2010 5-year est.); Average household income: $81,531 (2006-2010 5-year est.); Percent of households with income of $100,000 or more: 24.3% (2006-2010 5-year est.); Poverty rate: 7.3% (2006-2010 5-year est.).
**Education:** Percent of population age 25 and over with: High school diploma (including GED) or higher: 93.9% (2006-2010 5-year est.); Bachelor's degree or higher: 33.8% (2006-2010 5-year est.); Master's degree or higher: 17.5% (2006-2010 5-year est.).
**Housing:** Homeownership rate: 90.0% (2010); Median home value: $193,500 (2006-2010 5-year est.); Median contract rent: $754 per month

(2006-2010 5-year est.); Median year structure built: 1968 (2006-2010 5-year est.).
**Transportation:** Commute to work: 91.8% car, 0.0% public transportation, 0.0% walk, 3.8% work from home (2006-2010 5-year est.); Travel time to work: 23.5% less than 15 minutes, 52.5% 15 to 30 minutes, 20.1% 30 to 45 minutes, 2.5% 45 to 60 minutes, 1.3% 60 minutes or more (2006-2010 5-year est.)

## EVANS (town).
Covers a land area of 41.529 square miles and a water area of 0.031 square miles. Located at 42.65° N. Lat; 79.00° W. Long.
**Population:** 17,478 (1990); 17,594 (2000); 16,356 (2010); Density: 393.8 persons per square mile (2010); Race: 96.4% White, 0.7% Black, 0.2% Asian, 1.2% American Indian/Alaska Native, 0.0% Native Hawaiian/Other Pacific Islander, 1.5% Other, 1.8% Hispanic of any race (2010); Average household size: 2.43 (2010); Median age: 43.7 (2010); Males per 100 females: 96.6 (2010); Marriage status: 27.4% never married, 59.5% now married, 5.9% widowed, 7.2% divorced (2006-2010 5-year est.); Foreign born: 2.5% (2006-2010 5-year est.); Ancestry (includes multiple ancestries): 33.8% German, 24.4% Polish, 23.0% Irish, 19.1% Italian, 7.5% English (2006-2010 5-year est.).
**Economy:** Single-family building permits issued: 17 (2011); Multi-family building permits issued: 0 (2011); Employment by occupation: 12.1% management, 1.5% professional, 11.8% services, 20.3% sales, 3.2% farming, 8.2% construction, 7.0% production (2006-2010 5-year est.).
**Income:** Per capita income: $26,968 (2006-2010 5-year est.); Median household income: $58,181 (2006-2010 5-year est.); Average household income: $68,087 (2006-2010 5-year est.); Percent of households with income of $100,000 or more: 18.7% (2006-2010 5-year est.); Poverty rate: 7.6% (2006-2010 5-year est.).
**Education:** Percent of population age 25 and over with: High school diploma (including GED) or higher: 89.2% (2006-2010 5-year est.); Bachelor's degree or higher: 20.5% (2006-2010 5-year est.); Master's degree or higher: 8.6% (2006-2010 5-year est.).
**Housing:** Homeownership rate: 81.3% (2010); Median home value: $103,900 (2006-2010 5-year est.); Median contract rent: $463 per month (2006-2010 5-year est.); Median year structure built: 1955 (2006-2010 5-year est.).
**Safety:** Violent crime rate: 15.1 per 10,000 population; Property crime rate: 198.1 per 10,000 population (2010).
**Transportation:** Commute to work: 95.6% car, 0.8% public transportation, 1.5% walk, 1.4% work from home (2006-2010 5-year est.); Travel time to work: 20.9% less than 15 minutes, 30.8% 15 to 30 minutes, 30.6% 30 to 45 minutes, 10.8% 45 to 60 minutes, 6.9% 60 minutes or more (2006-2010 5-year est.)
**Additional Information Contacts**
Town of Evans . . . . . . . . . . . . . . . . . . . . . . . . . . . . . (716) 549-5787
  http://www.townofevans.org

## FARNHAM (village).
Covers a land area of 1.206 square miles and a water area of 0 square miles. Located at 42.59° N. Lat; 79.08° W. Long. Elevation is 640 feet.
**Population:** 427 (1990); 322 (2000); 382 (2010); Density: 316.5 persons per square mile (2010); Race: 89.0% White, 1.6% Black, 0.0% Asian, 7.3% American Indian/Alaska Native, 0.0% Native Hawaiian/Other Pacific Islander, 2.1% Other, 1.3% Hispanic of any race (2010); Average household size: 2.60 (2010); Median age: 36.8 (2010); Males per 100 females: 94.9 (2010); Marriage status: 28.9% never married, 49.5% now married, 10.8% widowed, 10.8% divorced (2006-2010 5-year est.); Foreign born: 0.0% (2006-2010 5-year est.); Ancestry (includes multiple ancestries): 62.4% German, 29.5% Irish, 21.5% Polish, 16.5% Italian, 14.8% English (2006-2010 5-year est.).
**Economy:** Single-family building permits issued: 0 (2011); Multi-family building permits issued: 0 (2011); Employment by occupation: 5.9% management, 3.0% professional, 13.9% services, 5.9% sales, 3.0% farming, 5.9% construction, 12.9% production (2006-2010 5-year est.).
**Income:** Per capita income: $17,949 (2006-2010 5-year est.); Median household income: $47,083 (2006-2010 5-year est.); Average household income: $47,719 (2006-2010 5-year est.); Percent of households with income of $100,000 or more: 2.2% (2006-2010 5-year est.); Poverty rate: 7.2% (2006-2010 5-year est.).
**Education:** Percent of population age 25 and over with: High school diploma (including GED) or higher: 82.5% (2006-2010 5-year est.); Bachelor's degree or higher: 1.3% (2006-2010 5-year est.); Master's degree or higher: 0.0% (2006-2010 5-year est.).

**Housing:** Homeownership rate: 68.8% (2010); Median home value: $69,500 (2006-2010 5-year est.); Median contract rent: $294 per month (2006-2010 5-year est.); Median year structure built: before 1940 (2006-2010 5-year est.).
**Transportation:** Commute to work: 96.7% car, 0.0% public transportation, 2.2% walk, 1.1% work from home (2006-2010 5-year est.); Travel time to work: 30.8% less than 15 minutes, 33.0% 15 to 30 minutes, 13.2% 30 to 45 minutes, 11.0% 45 to 60 minutes, 12.1% 60 minutes or more (2006-2010 5-year est.)

## GETZVILLE (unincorporated postal area)
Zip Code: 14068
Covers a land area of 3.459 square miles and a water area of 0 square miles. Located at 43.02° N. Lat; 78.75° W. Long. Elevation is 584 feet. Population: 7,150 (2010); Density: 2,066.7 persons per square mile (2010); Race: 88.4% White, 3.3% Black, 6.9% Asian, 0.1% American Indian/Alaska Native, 0.0% Native Hawaiian/Other Pacific Islander, 1.3% Other, 1.3% Hispanic of any race (2010); Average household size: 2.43 (2010); Median age: 45.9 (2010); Males per 100 females: 81.7 (2010); Homeownership rate: 72.9% (2010)

## GLENWOOD (unincorporated postal area)
Zip Code: 14069
Covers a land area of 8.515 square miles and a water area of 0.012 square miles. Located at 42.61° N. Lat; 78.64° W. Long. Elevation is 1,191 feet. Population: 844 (2010); Density: 99.1 persons per square mile (2010); Race: 98.5% White, 0.4% Black, 0.4% Asian, 0.1% American Indian/Alaska Native, 0.0% Native Hawaiian/Other Pacific Islander, 0.6% Other, 0.2% Hispanic of any race (2010); Average household size: 2.28 (2010); Median age: 46.1 (2010); Males per 100 females: 105.9 (2010); Homeownership rate: 83.3% (2010)

## GRAND ISLAND (town).
Covers a land area of 28.273 square miles and a water area of 5.019 square miles. Located at 43.01° N. Lat; 78.96° W. Long.
**Population:** 17,561 (1990); 18,621 (2000); 20,374 (2010); Density: 720.6 persons per square mile (2010); Race: 93.6% White, 2.2% Black, 2.3% Asian, 0.5% American Indian/Alaska Native, 0.0% Native Hawaiian/Other Pacific Islander, 1.4% Other, 1.8% Hispanic of any race (2010); Average household size: 2.55 (2010); Median age: 42.8 (2010); Males per 100 females: 97.3 (2010); Marriage status: 23.1% never married, 63.8% now married, 3.7% widowed, 9.4% divorced (2006-2010 5-year est.); Foreign born: 5.8% (2006-2010 5-year est.); Ancestry (includes multiple ancestries): 31.9% German, 21.4% Italian, 19.2% Irish, 15.5% Polish, 13.0% English (2006-2010 5-year est.).
**Economy:** Single-family building permits issued: 55 (2011); Multi-family building permits issued: 0 (2011); Employment by occupation: 16.0% management, 7.8% professional, 7.8% services, 17.3% sales, 3.0% farming, 7.5% construction, 5.3% production (2006-2010 5-year est.).
**Income:** Per capita income: $33,626 (2006-2010 5-year est.); Median household income: $77,595 (2006-2010 5-year est.); Average household income: $87,394 (2006-2010 5-year est.); Percent of households with income of $100,000 or more: 34.2% (2006-2010 5-year est.); Poverty rate: 4.7% (2006-2010 5-year est.).
**Taxes:** Total city taxes per capita: $472 (2009); City property taxes per capita: $421 (2009).
**Education:** Percent of population age 25 and over with: High school diploma (including GED) or higher: 95.7% (2006-2010 5-year est.); Bachelor's degree or higher: 40.8% (2006-2010 5-year est.); Master's degree or higher: 18.8% (2006-2010 5-year est.).
### School District(s)
Grand Island Central School District (PK-12)
  2009-10 Enrollment: 3,201 . . . . . . . . . . . . . . . . . . (716) 773-8801
**Housing:** Homeownership rate: 81.2% (2010); Median home value: $173,800 (2006-2010 5-year est.); Median contract rent: $759 per month (2006-2010 5-year est.); Median year structure built: 1973 (2006-2010 5-year est.).
**Newspapers:** Grand Island Pennysaver (Community news; Circulation 7,400); Island Dispatch (Community news; Circulation 11,000); Lewiston/Porter Sentinel (Community news; Circulation 10,792); Niagara/Wheatfield Tribune (Community news; Circulation 11,900)
**Transportation:** Commute to work: 94.9% car, 1.3% public transportation, 0.5% walk, 2.7% work from home (2006-2010 5-year est.); Travel time to work: 29.4% less than 15 minutes, 52.4% 15 to 30 minutes, 14.5% 30 to 45

minutes, 2.4% 45 to 60 minutes, 1.4% 60 minutes or more (2006-2010 5-year est.)

**Additional Information Contacts**
Grand Island Chamber of Commerce . . . . . . . . . . . . . . . (716) 773-3651
  http://www.gichamber.org
Town of Grand Island. . . . . . . . . . . . . . . . . . . . . . . . (716) 773-9600
  http://www.gigov.com

## GRANDYLE VILLAGE (CDP). Covers a land area of 1.882 square miles and a water area of 0 square miles. Located at 42.98° N. Lat; 78.95° W. Long. Elevation is 594 feet.

**Population:** n/a (1990); n/a (2000); 4,629 (2010); Density: 2,458.4 persons per square mile (2010); Race: 95.4% White, 1.3% Black, 1.5% Asian, 0.6% American Indian/Alaska Native, 0.0% Native Hawaiian/Other Pacific Islander, 1.2% Other, 2.1% Hispanic of any race (2010); Average household size: 2.52 (2010); Median age: 41.1 (2010); Males per 100 females: 93.7 (2010); Marriage status: 18.7% never married, 66.0% now married, 3.2% widowed, 12.1% divorced (2006-2010 5-year est.); Foreign born: 2.1% (2006-2010 5-year est.); Ancestry (includes multiple ancestries): 39.2% German, 24.8% Italian, 23.5% Irish, 12.3% Polish, 10.4% English (2006-2010 5-year est.).

**Economy:** Employment by occupation: 14.6% management, 7.8% professional, 9.3% services, 16.4% sales, 1.3% farming, 4.8% construction, 6.8% production (2006-2010 5-year est.).

**Income:** Per capita income: $30,973 (2006-2010 5-year est.); Median household income: $73,661 (2006-2010 5-year est.); Average household income: $80,353 (2006-2010 5-year est.); Percent of households with income of $100,000 or more: 35.2% (2006-2010 5-year est.); Poverty rate: 5.4% (2006-2010 5-year est.).

**Education:** Percent of population age 25 and over with: High school diploma (including GED) or higher: 95.6% (2006-2010 5-year est.); Bachelor's degree or higher: 30.5% (2006-2010 5-year est.); Master's degree or higher: 11.9% (2006-2010 5-year est.).

**Housing:** Homeownership rate: 87.5% (2010); Median home value: $142,700 (2006-2010 5-year est.); Median contract rent: $484 per month (2006-2010 5-year est.); Median year structure built: 1960 (2006-2010 5-year est.).

**Transportation:** Commute to work: 94.8% car, 1.5% public transportation, 0.6% walk, 2.0% work from home (2006-2010 5-year est.); Travel time to work: 31.3% less than 15 minutes, 51.2% 15 to 30 minutes, 16.0% 30 to 45 minutes, 1.5% 45 to 60 minutes, 0.0% 60 minutes or more (2006-2010 5-year est.)

## HAMBURG (village). Covers a land area of 2.486 square miles and a water area of 0 square miles. Located at 42.72° N. Lat; 78.83° W. Long. Elevation is 820 feet.

**Population:** 10,442 (1990); 10,116 (2000); 9,409 (2010); Density: 3,784.8 persons per square mile (2010); Race: 98.2% White, 0.4% Black, 0.4% Asian, 0.2% American Indian/Alaska Native, 0.0% Native Hawaiian/Other Pacific Islander, 0.8% Other, 1.4% Hispanic of any race (2010); Average household size: 2.36 (2010); Median age: 41.4 (2010); Males per 100 females: 90.1 (2010); Marriage status: 22.9% never married, 56.8% now married, 7.9% widowed, 12.4% divorced (2006-2010 5-year est.); Foreign born: 3.8% (2006-2010 5-year est.); Ancestry (includes multiple ancestries): 36.1% German, 29.4% Irish, 17.0% Italian, 15.3% Polish, 10.7% English (2006-2010 5-year est.).

**Economy:** Employment by occupation: 9.1% management, 7.1% professional, 5.3% services, 19.7% sales, 6.7% farming, 6.2% construction, 4.5% production (2006-2010 5-year est.).

**Income:** Per capita income: $32,333 (2006-2010 5-year est.); Median household income: $64,063 (2006-2010 5-year est.); Average household income: $76,695 (2006-2010 5-year est.); Percent of households with income of $100,000 or more: 24.2% (2006-2010 5-year est.); Poverty rate: 4.4% (2006-2010 5-year est.).

**Education:** Percent of population age 25 and over with: High school diploma (including GED) or higher: 96.0% (2006-2010 5-year est.); Bachelor's degree or higher: 44.4% (2006-2010 5-year est.); Master's degree or higher: 18.7% (2006-2010 5-year est.).

**School District(s)**
Frontier Central School District (PK-12)
  2009-10 Enrollment: 5,326 . . . . . . . . . . . . . . . . . . (716) 926-1711
Hamburg Central School District (PK-12)
  2009-10 Enrollment: 4,019 . . . . . . . . . . . . . . . . . . (716) 646-3220
Hopevale Union Free School District at Hamburg (07-12)
  2009-10 Enrollment: 139 . . . . . . . . . . . . . . . . . . . . (716) 648-1930

**Four-year College(s)**
Hilbert College (Private, Not-for-profit, Roman Catholic)
  Fall 2010 Enrollment: 918 . . . . . . . . . . . . . . . . (716) 649-7900
  2011-12 Tuition: In-state $18,940; Out-of-state $18,940

**Housing:** Homeownership rate: 71.7% (2010); Median home value: $137,300 (2006-2010 5-year est.); Median contract rent: $586 per month (2006-2010 5-year est.); Median year structure built: 1952 (2006-2010 5-year est.).

**Safety:** Violent crime rate: 5.4 per 10,000 population; Property crime rate: 239.4 per 10,000 population (2010).

**Newspapers:** Blasdell/Lackawanna Pennysaver (Community news; Circulation 13,876); Buffalo News - Southtown Bureau (Local news); Hamburg Pennysaver (Community news; Circulation 25,244); The Sun (Local news)

**Transportation:** Commute to work: 94.3% car, 0.2% public transportation, 1.7% walk, 3.1% work from home (2006-2010 5-year est.); Travel time to work: 27.8% less than 15 minutes, 40.9% 15 to 30 minutes, 23.3% 30 to 45 minutes, 5.2% 45 to 60 minutes, 2.7% 60 minutes or more (2006-2010 5-year est.)

**Additional Information Contacts**
Hamburg Chamber of Commerce . . . . . . . . . . . . . . . . (716) 649-7917
  http://www.hamburg-chamber.org
Village of Hamburg . . . . . . . . . . . . . . . . . . . . . . . . (716) 649-0200
  http://www.villagehamburg.com

## HAMBURG (town). Covers a land area of 41.321 square miles and a water area of 0.027 square miles. Located at 42.73° N. Lat; 78.85° W. Long. Elevation is 820 feet.

**History:** Seat of Hilbert College. Settled c.1808, incorporated 1874.

**Population:** 53,735 (1990); 56,259 (2000); 56,936 (2010); Density: 1,377.9 persons per square mile (2010); Race: 97.0% White, 0.8% Black, 0.6% Asian, 0.3% American Indian/Alaska Native, 0.0% Native Hawaiian/Other Pacific Islander, 1.3% Other, 2.1% Hispanic of any race (2010); Average household size: 2.40 (2010); Median age: 42.2 (2010); Males per 100 females: 92.1 (2010); Marriage status: 26.6% never married, 56.5% now married, 6.8% widowed, 10.1% divorced (2006-2010 5-year est.); Foreign born: 3.4% (2006-2010 5-year est.); Ancestry (includes multiple ancestries): 34.6% German, 27.7% Irish, 23.3% Polish, 18.0% Italian, 9.3% English (2006-2010 5-year est.).

**Economy:** Unemployment rate: 8.3% (February 2012); Total civilian labor force: 31,054 (February 2012); Single-family building permits issued: 108 (2011); Multi-family building permits issued: 124 (2011); Employment by occupation: 10.8% management, 4.0% professional, 9.6% services, 19.7% sales, 4.8% farming, 6.3% construction, 5.0% production (2006-2010 5-year est.).

**Income:** Per capita income: $29,730 (2006-2010 5-year est.); Median household income: $59,477 (2006-2010 5-year est.); Average household income: $71,343 (2006-2010 5-year est.); Percent of households with income of $100,000 or more: 21.4% (2006-2010 5-year est.); Poverty rate: 6.3% (2006-2010 5-year est.).

**Taxes:** Total city taxes per capita: $448 (2009); City property taxes per capita: $406 (2009).

**Education:** Percent of population age 25 and over with: High school diploma (including GED) or higher: 93.0% (2006-2010 5-year est.); Bachelor's degree or higher: 30.0% (2006-2010 5-year est.); Master's degree or higher: 11.9% (2006-2010 5-year est.).

**School District(s)**
Frontier Central School District (PK-12)
  2009-10 Enrollment: 5,326 . . . . . . . . . . . . . . . . . . (716) 926-1711
Hamburg Central School District (PK-12)
  2009-10 Enrollment: 4,019 . . . . . . . . . . . . . . . . . . (716) 646-3220
Hopevale Union Free School District at Hamburg (07-12)
  2009-10 Enrollment: 139 . . . . . . . . . . . . . . . . . . . . (716) 648-1930

**Four-year College(s)**
Hilbert College (Private, Not-for-profit, Roman Catholic)
  Fall 2010 Enrollment: 918 . . . . . . . . . . . . . . . . (716) 649-7900
  2011-12 Tuition: In-state $18,940; Out-of-state $18,940

**Housing:** Homeownership rate: 75.4% (2010); Median home value: $133,300 (2006-2010 5-year est.); Median contract rent: $567 per month (2006-2010 5-year est.); Median year structure built: 1964 (2006-2010 5-year est.).

**Safety:** Violent crime rate: 8.5 per 10,000 population; Property crime rate: 228.7 per 10,000 population (2010).

**Newspapers:** Blasdell/Lackawanna Pennysaver (Community news; Circulation 13,876); Buffalo News - Southtown Bureau (Local news);

Hamburg Pennysaver (Community news; Circulation 25,244); The Sun (Local news)
**Transportation:** Commute to work: 94.7% car, 1.1% public transportation, 1.4% walk, 1.9% work from home (2006-2010 5-year est.); Travel time to work: 29.2% less than 15 minutes, 41.7% 15 to 30 minutes, 21.3% 30 to 45 minutes, 4.7% 45 to 60 minutes, 3.1% 60 minutes or more (2006-2010 5-year est.)
**Additional Information Contacts**
Town of Hamburg . . . . . . . . . . . . . . . . . . . . . . . . . . . . . . . . . . . . (716) 649-6111
    http://www.townofhamburgny.com

## HARRIS HILL (CDP). Covers a land area of 4.040 square miles and a water area of 0 square miles. Located at 42.97° N. Lat; 78.67° W. Long. Elevation is 728 feet.

**Population:** 4,577 (1990); 4,881 (2000); 5,508 (2010); Density: 1,363.2 persons per square mile (2010); Race: 93.1% White, 1.4% Black, 3.9% Asian, 0.1% American Indian/Alaska Native, 0.0% Native Hawaiian/Other Pacific Islander, 1.5% Other, 1.7% Hispanic of any race (2010); Average household size: 2.44 (2010); Median age: 44.2 (2010); Males per 100 females: 93.2 (2010); Marriage status: 23.0% never married, 61.4% now married, 5.3% widowed, 10.2% divorced (2006-2010 5-year est.); Foreign born: 4.8% (2006-2010 5-year est.); Ancestry (includes multiple ancestries): 36.1% German, 23.2% Italian, 21.0% Irish, 17.2% Polish, 10.4% English (2006-2010 5-year est.).
**Economy:** Employment by occupation: 11.0% management, 7.4% professional, 6.6% services, 16.4% sales, 7.6% farming, 5.5% construction, 3.2% production (2006-2010 5-year est.).
**Income:** Per capita income: $33,064 (2006-2010 5-year est.); Median household income: $76,333 (2006-2010 5-year est.); Average household income: $81,998 (2006-2010 5-year est.); Percent of households with income of $100,000 or more: 33.0% (2006-2010 5-year est.); Poverty rate: 3.8% (2006-2010 5-year est.).
**Education:** Percent of population age 25 and over with: High school diploma (including GED) or higher: 96.3% (2006-2010 5-year est.); Bachelor's degree or higher: 48.7% (2006-2010 5-year est.); Master's degree or higher: 23.4% (2006-2010 5-year est.).
**Housing:** Homeownership rate: 79.2% (2010); Median home value: $173,000 (2006-2010 5-year est.); Median contract rent: $1,071 per month (2006-2010 5-year est.); Median year structure built: 1959 (2006-2010 5-year est.).
**Transportation:** Commute to work: 89.7% car, 0.0% public transportation, 0.5% walk, 7.9% work from home (2006-2010 5-year est.); Travel time to work: 32.1% less than 15 minutes, 38.0% 15 to 30 minutes, 26.2% 30 to 45 minutes, 1.9% 45 to 60 minutes, 1.9% 60 minutes or more (2006-2010 5-year est.)

## HOLLAND (town). Covers a land area of 35.789 square miles and a water area of 0.036 square miles. Located at 42.67° N. Lat; 78.52° W. Long. Elevation is 1,106 feet.

**Population:** 3,604 (1990); 3,603 (2000); 3,401 (2010); Density: 95.0 persons per square mile (2010); Race: 97.9% White, 0.5% Black, 0.2% Asian, 0.4% American Indian/Alaska Native, 0.0% Native Hawaiian/Other Pacific Islander, 1.0% Other, 1.1% Hispanic of any race (2010); Average household size: 2.48 (2010); Median age: 42.8 (2010); Males per 100 females: 101.6 (2010); Marriage status: 24.1% never married, 63.7% now married, 4.3% widowed, 7.8% divorced (2006-2010 5-year est.); Foreign born: 0.3% (2006-2010 5-year est.); Ancestry (includes multiple ancestries): 43.9% German, 26.6% Polish, 17.4% English, 10.6% Irish, 5.5% French (2006-2010 5-year est.).
**Economy:** Single-family building permits issued: 1 (2011); Multi-family building permits issued: 0 (2011); Employment by occupation: 14.9% management, 0.5% professional, 7.5% services, 16.1% sales, 1.4% farming, 15.7% construction, 8.4% production (2006-2010 5-year est.).
**Income:** Per capita income: $27,329 (2006-2010 5-year est.); Median household income: $61,759 (2006-2010 5-year est.); Average household income: $66,796 (2006-2010 5-year est.); Percent of households with income of $100,000 or more: 19.9% (2006-2010 5-year est.); Poverty rate: 9.7% (2006-2010 5-year est.).
**Education:** Percent of population age 25 and over with: High school diploma (including GED) or higher: 87.6% (2006-2010 5-year est.); Bachelor's degree or higher: 20.5% (2006-2010 5-year est.); Master's degree or higher: 8.6% (2006-2010 5-year est.).
**School District(s)**
Holland Central School District (PK-12)
    2009-10 Enrollment: 1,038 . . . . . . . . . . . . . . . . . . . . . . (716) 537-8222

**Housing:** Homeownership rate: 79.9% (2010); Median home value: $144,700 (2006-2010 5-year est.); Median contract rent: $436 per month (2006-2010 5-year est.); Median year structure built: 1961 (2006-2010 5-year est.).
**Transportation:** Commute to work: 94.4% car, 0.0% public transportation, 1.8% walk, 1.6% work from home (2006-2010 5-year est.); Travel time to work: 14.0% less than 15 minutes, 35.7% 15 to 30 minutes, 27.0% 30 to 45 minutes, 19.4% 45 to 60 minutes, 3.8% 60 minutes or more (2006-2010 5-year est.)

## HOLLAND (CDP). Covers a land area of 4.004 square miles and a water area of 0 square miles. Located at 42.63° N. Lat; 78.55° W. Long. Elevation is 1,106 feet.

**Population:** 1,288 (1990); 1,261 (2000); 1,206 (2010); Density: 301.2 persons per square mile (2010); Race: 98.2% White, 0.3% Black, 0.0% Asian, 0.6% American Indian/Alaska Native, 0.0% Native Hawaiian/Other Pacific Islander, 0.9% Other, 1.2% Hispanic of any race (2010); Average household size: 2.34 (2010); Median age: 40.7 (2010); Males per 100 females: 95.1 (2010); Marriage status: 39.1% never married, 51.7% now married, 1.8% widowed, 7.4% divorced (2006-2010 5-year est.); Foreign born: 0.0% (2006-2010 5-year est.); Ancestry (includes multiple ancestries): 42.8% German, 23.7% Polish, 18.1% English, 12.6% Irish, 7.4% Dutch (2006-2010 5-year est.).
**Economy:** Employment by occupation: 17.8% management, 1.4% professional, 10.2% services, 16.8% sales, 3.7% farming, 8.0% construction, 1.8% production (2006-2010 5-year est.).
**Income:** Per capita income: $27,718 (2006-2010 5-year est.); Median household income: $58,051 (2006-2010 5-year est.); Average household income: $66,354 (2006-2010 5-year est.); Percent of households with income of $100,000 or more: 21.6% (2006-2010 5-year est.); Poverty rate: 8.4% (2006-2010 5-year est.).
**Education:** Percent of population age 25 and over with: High school diploma (including GED) or higher: 93.3% (2006-2010 5-year est.); Bachelor's degree or higher: 12.2% (2006-2010 5-year est.); Master's degree or higher: 3.6% (2006-2010 5-year est.).
**School District(s)**
Holland Central School District (PK-12)
    2009-10 Enrollment: 1,038 . . . . . . . . . . . . . . . . . . . . . . (716) 537-8222
**Housing:** Homeownership rate: 67.1% (2010); Median home value: $123,200 (2006-2010 5-year est.); Median contract rent: $409 per month (2006-2010 5-year est.); Median year structure built: before 1940 (2006-2010 5-year est.).
**Transportation:** Commute to work: 91.7% car, 0.0% public transportation, 4.8% walk, 1.8% work from home (2006-2010 5-year est.); Travel time to work: 10.3% less than 15 minutes, 48.7% 15 to 30 minutes, 26.2% 30 to 45 minutes, 12.5% 45 to 60 minutes, 2.2% 60 minutes or more (2006-2010 5-year est.)

## KENMORE (village). Covers a land area of 1.435 square miles and a water area of 0 square miles. Located at 42.96° N. Lat; 78.87° W. Long. Elevation is 614 feet.

**History:** Named for a prominent citizen. Incorporated 1899.
**Population:** 17,180 (1990); 16,426 (2000); 15,423 (2010); Density: 10,744.9 persons per square mile (2010); Race: 92.8% White, 3.0% Black, 1.0% Asian, 0.6% American Indian/Alaska Native, 0.0% Native Hawaiian/Other Pacific Islander, 2.6% Other, 3.4% Hispanic of any race (2010); Average household size: 2.19 (2010); Median age: 39.7 (2010); Males per 100 females: 87.4 (2010); Marriage status: 34.8% never married, 48.4% now married, 6.8% widowed, 9.9% divorced (2006-2010 5-year est.); Foreign born: 2.6% (2006-2010 5-year est.); Ancestry (includes multiple ancestries): 31.8% Italian, 30.8% German, 23.8% Irish, 15.9% Polish, 7.2% English (2006-2010 5-year est.).
**Economy:** Single-family building permits issued: 1 (2011); Multi-family building permits issued: 0 (2011); Employment by occupation: 8.7% management, 3.5% professional, 10.4% services, 18.3% sales, 4.1% farming, 6.6% construction, 4.6% production (2006-2010 5-year est.).
**Income:** Per capita income: $25,041 (2006-2010 5-year est.); Median household income: $46,430 (2006-2010 5-year est.); Average household income: $58,389 (2006-2010 5-year est.); Percent of households with income of $100,000 or more: 13.7% (2006-2010 5-year est.); Poverty rate: 8.9% (2006-2010 5-year est.).
**Education:** Percent of population age 25 and over with: High school diploma (including GED) or higher: 93.0% (2006-2010 5-year est.); Bachelor's degree or higher: 33.5% (2006-2010 5-year est.); Master's degree or higher: 12.4% (2006-2010 5-year est.).

**School District(s)**

Kenmore-Tonawanda Union Free School District (PK-12)

    2009-10 Enrollment: 8,128 . . . . . . . . . . . . . . . . . . . . . . (716) 874-8400

**Housing:** Homeownership rate: 66.6% (2010); Median home value: $99,000 (2006-2010 5-year est.); Median contract rent: $529 per month (2006-2010 5-year est.); Median year structure built: before 1940 (2006-2010 5-year est.).

**Hospitals:** Kenmore Mercy Hospital (184 beds)

**Safety:** Violent crime rate: 18.4 per 10,000 population; Property crime rate: 231.4 per 10,000 population (2010).

**Transportation:** Commute to work: 91.0% car, 3.2% public transportation, 2.4% walk, 1.1% work from home (2006-2010 5-year est.); Travel time to work: 33.7% less than 15 minutes, 49.7% 15 to 30 minutes, 11.7% 30 to 45 minutes, 2.3% 45 to 60 minutes, 2.6% 60 minutes or more (2006-2010 5-year est.)

**Additional Information Contacts**

Kenmore-Town of Tonawanda Chamber of Commerce . . . (716) 874-1202

    http://www.ken-ton.org

Village of Kenmore. . . . . . . . . . . . . . . . . . . . . . . . . . . . . . (716) 873-5700

    http://www.vi.kenmore.ny.us

**LACKAWANNA** (city). Covers a land area of 6.571 square miles and a water area of 0.049 square miles. Located at 42.81° N. Lat; 78.83° W. Long. Elevation is 623 feet.

**History:** Named for the Lackawanna Steel Company. Formerly a major steel-making center, Lackawanna experienced the total decline of its foremost industry in the 1970s and 1980s. A distinguished city landmark is the elaborate Basilica of Our Lady of Victory, a Roman Catholic shrine. Incorporated 1909.

**Population:** 20,585 (1990); 19,064 (2000); 18,141 (2010); Density: 2,760.7 persons per square mile (2010); Race: 83.9% White, 9.9% Black, 0.7% Asian, 0.3% American Indian/Alaska Native, 0.0% Native Hawaiian/Other Pacific Islander, 5.2% Other, 7.1% Hispanic of any race (2010); Average household size: 2.17 (2010); Median age: 40.0 (2010); Males per 100 females: 91.8 (2010); Marriage status: 36.3% never married, 40.7% now married, 11.3% widowed, 11.7% divorced (2006-2010 5-year est.); Foreign born: 9.8% (2006-2010 5-year est.); Ancestry (includes multiple ancestries): 25.7% Polish, 19.0% German, 16.5% Italian, 12.6% Irish, 7.3% Arab (2006-2010 5-year est.).

**Economy:** Single-family building permits issued: 3 (2011); Multi-family building permits issued: 0 (2011); Employment by occupation: 6.8% management, 2.2% professional, 12.9% services, 18.6% sales, 4.9% farming, 5.7% construction, 3.6% production (2006-2010 5-year est.).

**Income:** Per capita income: $19,785 (2006-2010 5-year est.); Median household income: $33,544 (2006-2010 5-year est.); Average household income: $42,806 (2006-2010 5-year est.); Percent of households with income of $100,000 or more: 6.4% (2006-2010 5-year est.); Poverty rate: 21.2% (2006-2010 5-year est.).

**Education:** Percent of population age 25 and over with: High school diploma (including GED) or higher: 79.3% (2006-2010 5-year est.); Bachelor's degree or higher: 15.8% (2006-2010 5-year est.); Master's degree or higher: 7.0% (2006-2010 5-year est.).

**School District(s)**

Global Concepts Charter School (KG-08)

    2009-10 Enrollment: 558 . . . . . . . . . . . . . . . . . . . . . . (716) 821-1903

Lackawanna City School District (PK-12)

    2009-10 Enrollment: 1,947 . . . . . . . . . . . . . . . . . . . . (716) 827-6767

**Housing:** Homeownership rate: 52.4% (2010); Median home value: $82,400 (2006-2010 5-year est.); Median contract rent: $417 per month (2006-2010 5-year est.); Median year structure built: 1946 (2006-2010 5-year est.).

**Hospitals:** Our Lady of Victory Hospital (74 beds)

**Safety:** Violent crime rate: 66.9 per 10,000 population; Property crime rate: 272.6 per 10,000 population (2010).

**Newspapers:** Front Page (Community news); South Buffalo News (Community news; Circulation 14,000)

**Transportation:** Commute to work: 91.9% car, 2.5% public transportation, 2.9% walk, 1.6% work from home (2006-2010 5-year est.); Travel time to work: 38.8% less than 15 minutes, 42.4% 15 to 30 minutes, 12.8% 30 to 45 minutes, 3.9% 45 to 60 minutes, 2.2% 60 minutes or more (2006-2010 5-year est.)

**Additional Information Contacts**

City of Lackawanna . . . . . . . . . . . . . . . . . . . . . . . . . . . . . (716) 827-6452

    http://www.ci.lackawanna.ny.us

Lackawanna Area Chamber of Commerce . . . . . . . . . . . (716) 823-8841

    http://www.lackawannachamber.com

**LAKE ERIE BEACH** (CDP). Covers a land area of 3.820 square miles and a water area of 0 square miles. Located at 42.62° N. Lat; 79.07° W. Long. Elevation is 627 feet.

**Population:** 4,509 (1990); 4,499 (2000); 3,872 (2010); Density: 1,013.6 persons per square mile (2010); Race: 96.4% White, 0.5% Black, 0.1% Asian, 1.2% American Indian/Alaska Native, 0.0% Native Hawaiian/Other Pacific Islander, 1.8% Other, 1.4% Hispanic of any race (2010); Average household size: 2.39 (2010); Median age: 44.1 (2010); Males per 100 females: 98.3 (2010); Marriage status: 27.7% never married, 57.4% now married, 5.0% widowed, 9.9% divorced (2006-2010 5-year est.); Foreign born: 0.7% (2006-2010 5-year est.); Ancestry (includes multiple ancestries): 30.5% German, 26.3% Polish, 20.1% Irish, 16.5% Italian, 5.6% Scottish (2006-2010 5-year est.).

**Economy:** Employment by occupation: 8.7% management, 0.7% professional, 11.0% services, 21.8% sales, 5.6% farming, 9.6% construction, 11.7% production (2006-2010 5-year est.).

**Income:** Per capita income: $24,952 (2006-2010 5-year est.); Median household income: $54,645 (2006-2010 5-year est.); Average household income: $60,343 (2006-2010 5-year est.); Percent of households with income of $100,000 or more: 12.7% (2006-2010 5-year est.); Poverty rate: 8.0% (2006-2010 5-year est.).

**Education:** Percent of population age 25 and over with: High school diploma (including GED) or higher: 86.7% (2006-2010 5-year est.); Bachelor's degree or higher: 16.3% (2006-2010 5-year est.); Master's degree or higher: 10.7% (2006-2010 5-year est.).

**Housing:** Homeownership rate: 84.6% (2010); Median home value: $88,900 (2006-2010 5-year est.); Median contract rent: $550 per month (2006-2010 5-year est.); Median year structure built: 1953 (2006-2010 5-year est.).

**Transportation:** Commute to work: 95.5% car, 0.7% public transportation, 0.0% walk, 2.6% work from home (2006-2010 5-year est.); Travel time to work: 21.2% less than 15 minutes, 25.8% 15 to 30 minutes, 25.7% 30 to 45 minutes, 13.3% 45 to 60 minutes, 14.0% 60 minutes or more (2006-2010 5-year est.)

**LAKE VIEW** (unincorporated postal area)

Zip Code: 14085

    Covers a land area of 6.968 square miles and a water area of 0.345 square miles. Located at 42.72° N. Lat; 78.91° W. Long. Elevation is 719 feet. Population: 7,353 (2010); Density: 1,055.2 persons per square mile (2010); Race: 97.9% White, 0.4% Black, 0.5% Asian, 0.4% American Indian/Alaska Native, 0.0% Native Hawaiian/Other Pacific Islander, 0.8% Other, 1.8% Hispanic of any race (2010); Average household size: 2.85 (2010); Median age: 38.0 (2010); Males per 100 females: 101.9 (2010); Homeownership rate: 94.9% (2010)

**LANCASTER** (village). Covers a land area of 2.697 square miles and a water area of 0.033 square miles. Located at 42.90° N. Lat; 78.66° W. Long. Elevation is 669 feet.

**Population:** 11,940 (1990); 11,188 (2000); 10,352 (2010); Density: 3,837.6 persons per square mile (2010); Race: 97.4% White, 0.7% Black, 0.2% Asian, 0.3% American Indian/Alaska Native, 0.0% Native Hawaiian/Other Pacific Islander, 1.4% Other, 1.4% Hispanic of any race (2010); Average household size: 2.24 (2010); Median age: 41.4 (2010); Males per 100 females: 91.5 (2010); Marriage status: 33.4% never married, 45.7% now married, 8.3% widowed, 12.6% divorced (2006-2010 5-year est.); Foreign born: 0.4% (2006-2010 5-year est.); Ancestry (includes multiple ancestries): 43.2% German, 30.0% Polish, 23.1% Irish, 19.3% Italian, 10.3% English (2006-2010 5-year est.).

**Economy:** Single-family building permits issued: 0 (2011); Multi-family building permits issued: 0 (2011); Employment by occupation: 7.9% management, 4.8% professional, 14.1% services, 18.0% sales, 6.6% farming, 8.3% construction, 5.9% production (2006-2010 5-year est.).

**Income:** Per capita income: $24,917 (2006-2010 5-year est.); Median household income: $52,305 (2006-2010 5-year est.); Average household income: $58,438 (2006-2010 5-year est.); Percent of households with income of $100,000 or more: 13.0% (2006-2010 5-year est.); Poverty rate: 8.4% (2006-2010 5-year est.).

**Taxes:** Total city taxes per capita: $400 (2009); City property taxes per capita: $371 (2009).

**Education:** Percent of population age 25 and over with: High school diploma (including GED) or higher: 90.9% (2006-2010 5-year est.); Bachelor's degree or higher: 22.0% (2006-2010 5-year est.); Master's degree or higher: 8.0% (2006-2010 5-year est.).

**School District(s)**

Lancaster Central School District (PK-12)

   2009-10 Enrollment: 6,263 . . . . . . . . . . . . . . . . . . . . (716) 686-3201

**Housing:** Homeownership rate: 68.3% (2010); Median home value: $103,700 (2006-2010 5-year est.); Median contract rent: $483 per month (2006-2010 5-year est.); Median year structure built: 1952 (2006-2010 5-year est.).

**Transportation:** Commute to work: 94.0% car, 0.0% public transportation, 3.2% walk, 0.8% work from home (2006-2010 5-year est.); Travel time to work: 34.3% less than 15 minutes, 46.1% 15 to 30 minutes, 15.3% 30 to 45 minutes, 3.8% 45 to 60 minutes, 0.6% 60 minutes or more (2006-2010 5-year est.).

**Additional Information Contacts**

Lancaster Area Chamber of Commerce . . . . . . . . . . . . . . (716) 681-9755

   http://www.laccny.org

Village of Lancaster . . . . . . . . . . . . . . . . . . . . . . . . . . . . (716) 684-4891

   http://www.lancastervillage.org

**LANCASTER** (town). Covers a land area of 37.702 square miles and a water area of 0.233 square miles. Located at 42.91° N. Lat; 78.63° W. Long. Elevation is 669 feet.

**History:** Incorporated 1849.

**Population:** 32,181 (1990); 39,019 (2000); 41,604 (2010); Density: 1,103.5 persons per square mile (2010); Race: 97.0% White, 1.0% Black, 0.6% Asian, 0.2% American Indian/Alaska Native, 0.0% Native Hawaiian/Other Pacific Islander, 1.2% Other, 1.4% Hispanic of any race (2010); Average household size: 2.47 (2010); Median age: 41.7 (2010); Males per 100 females: 93.8 (2010); Marriage status: 28.4% never married, 55.2% now married, 7.5% widowed, 8.9% divorced (2006-2010 5-year est.); Foreign born: 2.5% (2006-2010 5-year est.); Ancestry (includes multiple ancestries): 36.7% Polish, 34.9% German, 20.3% Italian, 17.6% Irish, 7.3% English (2006-2010 5-year est.).

**Economy:** Unemployment rate: 7.8% (February 2012); Total civilian labor force: 23,407 (February 2012); Single-family building permits issued: 102 (2011); Multi-family building permits issued: 0 (2011); Employment by occupation: 12.3% management, 5.5% professional, 9.0% services, 17.6% sales, 4.8% farming, 7.2% construction, 5.3% production (2006-2010 5-year est.).

**Income:** Per capita income: $28,005 (2006-2010 5-year est.); Median household income: $63,314 (2006-2010 5-year est.); Average household income: $72,141 (2006-2010 5-year est.); Percent of households with income of $100,000 or more: 25.5% (2006-2010 5-year est.); Poverty rate: 7.2% (2006-2010 5-year est.).

**Taxes:** Total city taxes per capita: $469 (2009); City property taxes per capita: $423 (2009).

**Education:** Percent of population age 25 and over with: High school diploma (including GED) or higher: 91.3% (2006-2010 5-year est.); Bachelor's degree or higher: 29.7% (2006-2010 5-year est.); Master's degree or higher: 11.3% (2006-2010 5-year est.).

**School District(s)**

Lancaster Central School District (PK-12)

   2009-10 Enrollment: 6,263 . . . . . . . . . . . . . . . . . . . . (716) 686-3201

**Housing:** Homeownership rate: 77.1% (2010); Median home value: $150,200 (2006-2010 5-year est.); Median contract rent: $542 per month (2006-2010 5-year est.); Median year structure built: 1967 (2006-2010 5-year est.).

**Safety:** Violent crime rate: 9.0 per 10,000 population; Property crime rate: 216.9 per 10,000 population (2010).

**Transportation:** Commute to work: 94.5% car, 0.4% public transportation, 2.0% walk, 1.8% work from home (2006-2010 5-year est.); Travel time to work: 26.4% less than 15 minutes, 48.3% 15 to 30 minutes, 21.2% 30 to 45 minutes, 2.2% 45 to 60 minutes, 1.9% 60 minutes or more (2006-2010 5-year est.).

**LAWTONS** (unincorporated postal area)

Zip Code: 14091

   Covers a land area of 21.261 square miles and a water area of 0.008 square miles. Located at 42.53° N. Lat; 78.89° W. Long. Elevation is 850 feet. Population: 1,079 (2010); Density: 50.7 persons per square mile (2010); Race: 74.3% White, 0.2% Black, 0.0% Asian, 24.2% American Indian/Alaska Native, 0.0% Native Hawaiian/Other Pacific Islander, 1.3% Other, 3.5% Hispanic of any race (2010); Average household size: 2.65 (2010); Median age: 40.8 (2010); Males per 100 females: 105.5 (2010); Homeownership rate: 84.8% (2010)

**MARILLA** (town). Covers a land area of 27.505 square miles and a water area of 0.037 square miles. Located at 42.82° N. Lat; 78.52° W. Long. Elevation is 846 feet.

**Population:** 5,250 (1990); 5,709 (2000); 5,327 (2010); Density: 193.7 persons per square mile (2010); Race: 98.6% White, 0.2% Black, 0.4% Asian, 0.2% American Indian/Alaska Native, 0.0% Native Hawaiian/Other Pacific Islander, 0.6% Other, 0.6% Hispanic of any race (2010); Average household size: 2.57 (2010); Median age: 45.3 (2010); Males per 100 females: 96.6 (2010); Marriage status: 29.0% never married, 62.3% now married, 3.2% widowed, 5.4% divorced (2006-2010 5-year est.); Foreign born: 0.5% (2006-2010 5-year est.); Ancestry (includes multiple ancestries): 43.6% German, 35.1% Polish, 13.7% Irish, 13.3% English, 13.1% Italian (2006-2010 5-year est.).

**Economy:** Single-family building permits issued: 5 (2011); Multi-family building permits issued: 0 (2011); Employment by occupation: 10.3% management, 3.6% professional, 7.2% services, 18.7% sales, 4.0% farming, 15.3% construction, 9.4% production (2006-2010 5-year est.).

**Income:** Per capita income: $28,383 (2006-2010 5-year est.); Median household income: $72,455 (2006-2010 5-year est.); Average household income: $81,597 (2006-2010 5-year est.); Percent of households with income of $100,000 or more: 29.0% (2006-2010 5-year est.); Poverty rate: 2.6% (2006-2010 5-year est.).

**Education:** Percent of population age 25 and over with: High school diploma (including GED) or higher: 94.1% (2006-2010 5-year est.); Bachelor's degree or higher: 21.4% (2006-2010 5-year est.); Master's degree or higher: 7.8% (2006-2010 5-year est.).

**School District(s)**

Iroquois Central School District (KG-12)

   2009-10 Enrollment: 2,635 . . . . . . . . . . . . . . . . . . . . . (716) 652-3000

**Housing:** Homeownership rate: 90.3% (2010); Median home value: $159,600 (2006-2010 5-year est.); Median contract rent: $439 per month (2006-2010 5-year est.); Median year structure built: 1971 (2006-2010 5-year est.).

**Transportation:** Commute to work: 95.9% car, 0.0% public transportation, 0.6% walk, 1.2% work from home (2006-2010 5-year est.); Travel time to work: 15.6% less than 15 minutes, 38.8% 15 to 30 minutes, 37.4% 30 to 45 minutes, 4.8% 45 to 60 minutes, 3.3% 60 minutes or more (2006-2010 5-year est.)

**NEWSTEAD** (town). Covers a land area of 50.758 square miles and a water area of 0.286 square miles. Located at 43.01° N. Lat; 78.52° W. Long.

**Population:** 7,440 (1990); 8,404 (2000); 8,594 (2010); Density: 169.3 persons per square mile (2010); Race: 97.0% White, 0.5% Black, 0.4% Asian, 1.0% American Indian/Alaska Native, 0.0% Native Hawaiian/Other Pacific Islander, 1.1% Other, 1.0% Hispanic of any race (2010); Average household size: 2.39 (2010); Median age: 43.8 (2010); Males per 100 females: 97.4 (2010); Marriage status: 29.3% never married, 55.5% now married, 6.1% widowed, 9.1% divorced (2006-2010 5-year est.); Foreign born: 3.4% (2006-2010 5-year est.); Ancestry (includes multiple ancestries): 40.7% German, 19.8% Irish, 18.8% Polish, 13.5% English, 13.0% Italian (2006-2010 5-year est.).

**Economy:** Single-family building permits issued: 18 (2011); Multi-family building permits issued: 0 (2011); Employment by occupation: 12.4% management, 2.8% professional, 6.9% services, 16.8% sales, 3.2% farming, 16.4% construction, 7.6% production (2006-2010 5-year est.).

**Income:** Per capita income: $24,587 (2006-2010 5-year est.); Median household income: $55,655 (2006-2010 5-year est.); Average household income: $60,707 (2006-2010 5-year est.); Percent of households with income of $100,000 or more: 14.1% (2006-2010 5-year est.); Poverty rate: 8.6% (2006-2010 5-year est.).

**Education:** Percent of population age 25 and over with: High school diploma (including GED) or higher: 89.1% (2006-2010 5-year est.); Bachelor's degree or higher: 22.3% (2006-2010 5-year est.); Master's degree or higher: 8.4% (2006-2010 5-year est.).

**Housing:** Homeownership rate: 78.6% (2010); Median home value: $129,900 (2006-2010 5-year est.); Median contract rent: $486 per month (2006-2010 5-year est.); Median year structure built: 1971 (2006-2010 5-year est.).

**Transportation:** Commute to work: 93.8% car, 0.0% public transportation, 1.2% walk, 2.7% work from home (2006-2010 5-year est.); Travel time to work: 24.7% less than 15 minutes, 32.9% 15 to 30 minutes, 33.6% 30 to 45 minutes, 6.2% 45 to 60 minutes, 2.5% 60 minutes or more (2006-2010 5-year est.)

## NORTH BOSTON (CDP).
Covers a land area of 4.074 square miles and a water area of 0 square miles. Located at 42.67° N. Lat; 78.77° W. Long. Elevation is 823 feet.

**Population:** 2,581 (1990); 2,680 (2000); 2,521 (2010); Density: 618.8 persons per square mile (2010); Race: 98.9% White, 0.1% Black, 0.3% Asian, 0.0% American Indian/Alaska Native, 0.0% Native Hawaiian/Other Pacific Islander, 0.7% Other, 1.0% Hispanic of any race (2010); Average household size: 2.35 (2010); Median age: 45.7 (2010); Males per 100 females: 95.7 (2010); Marriage status: 18.0% never married, 61.5% now married, 10.4% widowed, 10.2% divorced (2006-2010 5-year est.); Foreign born: 0.0% (2006-2010 5-year est.); Ancestry (includes multiple ancestries): 38.6% German, 26.1% Irish, 18.2% Polish, 17.6% English, 12.4% Italian (2006-2010 5-year est.).

**Economy:** Employment by occupation: 8.4% management, 2.9% professional, 6.0% services, 26.3% sales, 3.4% farming, 6.7% construction, 4.2% production (2006-2010 5-year est.).

**Income:** Per capita income: $28,643 (2006-2010 5-year est.); Median household income: $60,054 (2006-2010 5-year est.); Average household income: $65,955 (2006-2010 5-year est.); Percent of households with income of $100,000 or more: 14.1% (2006-2010 5-year est.); Poverty rate: 6.2% (2006-2010 5-year est.).

**Education:** Percent of population age 25 and over with: High school diploma (including GED) or higher: 93.6% (2006-2010 5-year est.); Bachelor's degree or higher: 20.5% (2006-2010 5-year est.); Master's degree or higher: 8.9% (2006-2010 5-year est.).

**Housing:** Homeownership rate: 79.5% (2010); Median home value: $145,600 (2006-2010 5-year est.); Median contract rent: $557 per month (2006-2010 5-year est.); Median year structure built: 1963 (2006-2010 5-year est.).

**Transportation:** Commute to work: 92.5% car, 2.0% public transportation, 4.1% walk, 1.4% work from home (2006-2010 5-year est.); Travel time to work: 31.9% less than 15 minutes, 33.0% 15 to 30 minutes, 24.8% 30 to 45 minutes, 7.9% 45 to 60 minutes, 2.4% 60 minutes or more (2006-2010 5-year est.)

## NORTH COLLINS (village).
Covers a land area of 0.801 square miles and a water area of 0 square miles. Located at 42.59° N. Lat; 78.93° W. Long. Elevation is 827 feet.

**Population:** 1,335 (1990); 1,079 (2000); 1,232 (2010); Density: 1,538.0 persons per square mile (2010); Race: 94.2% White, 0.2% Black, 0.0% Asian, 2.3% American Indian/Alaska Native, 0.0% Native Hawaiian/Other Pacific Islander, 3.3% Other, 3.7% Hispanic of any race (2010); Average household size: 2.51 (2010); Median age: 39.0 (2010); Males per 100 females: 94.6 (2010); Marriage status: 28.4% never married, 52.6% now married, 8.1% widowed, 11.0% divorced (2006-2010 5-year est.); Foreign born: 1.0% (2006-2010 5-year est.); Ancestry (includes multiple ancestries): 42.0% German, 25.8% Polish, 22.5% Italian, 14.3% Irish, 14.2% English (2006-2010 5-year est.).

**Economy:** Single-family building permits issued: 0 (2011); Multi-family building permits issued: 0 (2011); Employment by occupation: 5.8% management, 2.8% professional, 12.0% services, 9.6% sales, 3.8% farming, 10.2% construction, 8.0% production (2006-2010 5-year est.).

**Income:** Per capita income: $21,362 (2006-2010 5-year est.); Median household income: $46,250 (2006-2010 5-year est.); Average household income: $52,220 (2006-2010 5-year est.); Percent of households with income of $100,000 or more: 6.8% (2006-2010 5-year est.); Poverty rate: 14.1% (2006-2010 5-year est.).

**Education:** Percent of population age 25 and over with: High school diploma (including GED) or higher: 91.6% (2006-2010 5-year est.); Bachelor's degree or higher: 15.4% (2006-2010 5-year est.); Master's degree or higher: 5.6% (2006-2010 5-year est.).

**School District(s)**
North Collins Central School District (PK-12)
   2009-10 Enrollment: 658 . . . . . . . . . . . . . . . . . . . . . . (716) 337-0101

**Housing:** Homeownership rate: 66.0% (2010); Median home value: $80,000 (2006-2010 5-year est.); Median contract rent: $555 per month (2006-2010 5-year est.); Median year structure built: before 1940 (2006-2010 5-year est.).

**Transportation:** Commute to work: 90.3% car, 1.0% public transportation, 5.7% walk, 2.5% work from home (2006-2010 5-year est.); Travel time to work: 34.7% less than 15 minutes, 27.6% 15 to 30 minutes, 11.6% 30 to 45 minutes, 21.3% 45 to 60 minutes, 4.8% 60 minutes or more (2006-2010 5-year est.)

## NORTH COLLINS (town).
Covers a land area of 42.853 square miles and a water area of 0.172 square miles. Located at 42.57° N. Lat; 78.85° W. Long. Elevation is 827 feet.

**History:** Settled c.1810, incorporated 1911.

**Population:** 3,502 (1990); 3,376 (2000); 3,523 (2010); Density: 82.2 persons per square mile (2010); Race: 96.5% White, 0.3% Black, 0.0% Asian, 1.3% American Indian/Alaska Native, 0.0% Native Hawaiian/Other Pacific Islander, 1.9% Other, 2.3% Hispanic of any race (2010); Average household size: 2.56 (2010); Median age: 42.1 (2010); Males per 100 females: 98.5 (2010); Marriage status: 27.0% never married, 56.9% now married, 5.8% widowed, 10.2% divorced (2006-2010 5-year est.); Foreign born: 2.8% (2006-2010 5-year est.); Ancestry (includes multiple ancestries): 44.4% German, 22.8% Irish, 15.4% Italian, 14.2% English, 13.7% Polish (2006-2010 5-year est.).

**Economy:** Single-family building permits issued: 1 (2011); Multi-family building permits issued: 0 (2011); Employment by occupation: 10.6% management, 1.5% professional, 10.8% services, 9.7% sales, 4.2% farming, 13.9% construction, 9.5% production (2006-2010 5-year est.).

**Income:** Per capita income: $26,168 (2006-2010 5-year est.); Median household income: $48,456 (2006-2010 5-year est.); Average household income: $67,004 (2006-2010 5-year est.); Percent of households with income of $100,000 or more: 12.5% (2006-2010 5-year est.); Poverty rate: 12.3% (2006-2010 5-year est.).

**Education:** Percent of population age 25 and over with: High school diploma (including GED) or higher: 88.8% (2006-2010 5-year est.); Bachelor's degree or higher: 19.2% (2006-2010 5-year est.); Master's degree or higher: 7.8% (2006-2010 5-year est.).

**School District(s)**
North Collins Central School District (PK-12)
   2009-10 Enrollment: 658 . . . . . . . . . . . . . . . . . . . . . . (716) 337-0101

**Housing:** Homeownership rate: 81.1% (2010); Median home value: $110,100 (2006-2010 5-year est.); Median contract rent: $551 per month (2006-2010 5-year est.); Median year structure built: 1951 (2006-2010 5-year est.).

**Transportation:** Commute to work: 88.6% car, 0.3% public transportation, 3.6% walk, 5.8% work from home (2006-2010 5-year est.); Travel time to work: 21.1% less than 15 minutes, 32.7% 15 to 30 minutes, 20.4% 30 to 45 minutes, 16.2% 45 to 60 minutes, 9.6% 60 minutes or more (2006-2010 5-year est.)

## NORTH EVANS (unincorporated postal area)
Zip Code: 14112

   Covers a land area of 0.039 square miles and a water area of 0 square miles. Located at 42.69° N. Lat; 78.93° W. Long. Elevation is 702 feet. Population: 85 (2010); Density: 2,127.8 persons per square mile (2010); Race: 96.5% White, 0.0% Black, 0.0% Asian, 3.5% American Indian/Alaska Native, 0.0% Native Hawaiian/Other Pacific Islander, 0.0% Other, 4.7% Hispanic of any race (2010); Average household size: 3.11 (2010); Median age: 31.5 (2010); Males per 100 females: 97.7 (2010); Homeownership rate: 81.5% (2010)

## ORCHARD PARK (village).
Covers a land area of 1.346 square miles and a water area of 0.040 square miles. Located at 42.76° N. Lat; 78.74° W. Long. Elevation is 863 feet.

**Population:** 3,280 (1990); 3,294 (2000); 3,246 (2010); Density: 2,411.0 persons per square mile (2010); Race: 96.2% White, 0.9% Black, 1.1% Asian, 0.4% American Indian/Alaska Native, 0.0% Native Hawaiian/Other Pacific Islander, 1.4% Other, 1.8% Hispanic of any race (2010); Average household size: 2.34 (2010); Median age: 42.4 (2010); Males per 100 females: 93.0 (2010); Marriage status: 28.8% never married, 57.4% now married, 6.0% widowed, 7.8% divorced (2006-2010 5-year est.); Foreign born: 2.3% (2006-2010 5-year est.); Ancestry (includes multiple ancestries): 27.2% Irish, 27.0% German, 19.2% Polish, 13.6% Italian, 13.5% English (2006-2010 5-year est.).

**Economy:** Single-family building permits issued: 0 (2011); Multi-family building permits issued: 0 (2011); Employment by occupation: 19.2% management, 4.8% professional, 9.6% services, 19.9% sales, 2.5% farming, 2.8% construction, 2.5% production (2006-2010 5-year est.).

**Income:** Per capita income: $34,701 (2006-2010 5-year est.); Median household income: $73,468 (2006-2010 5-year est.); Average household income: $83,441 (2006-2010 5-year est.); Percent of households with income of $100,000 or more: 32.5% (2006-2010 5-year est.); Poverty rate: 4.2% (2006-2010 5-year est.).

**Education:** Percent of population age 25 and over with: High school diploma (including GED) or higher: 99.6% (2006-2010 5-year est.);

Bachelor's degree or higher: 54.8% (2006-2010 5-year est.); Master's degree or higher: 22.8% (2006-2010 5-year est.).

### School District(s)
Orchard Park Central School District (KG-12)
    2009-10 Enrollment: 5,238 . . . . . . . . . . . . . . . . . . . . . . (716) 209-6280

#### Four-year College(s)
Bryant and Stratton College-Southtowns (Private, For-profit)
    Fall 2010 Enrollment: 2,247 . . . . . . . . . . . . . . . . . . . . . (716) 677-9500
    2011-12 Tuition: In-state $15,570; Out-of-state $15,570

**Housing:** Homeownership rate: 65.0% (2010); Median home value: $188,500 (2006-2010 5-year est.); Median contract rent: $781 per month (2006-2010 5-year est.); Median year structure built: 1957 (2006-2010 5-year est.).

**Newspapers:** Akron/Corfu Pennysaver (Community news; Circulation 7,700); Attica Pennysaver (Community news; Circulation 7,000); East Aurora/Elma Pennysaver (Community news; Circulation 16,200); Orchard Park Pennysaver (Community news; Circulation 12,800); Southtowns Citizen (Local news; Circulation 5,990); West Seneca Pennysaver (Community news; Circulation 19,600)

**Transportation:** Commute to work: 89.6% car, 0.0% public transportation, 5.8% walk, 4.6% work from home (2006-2010 5-year est.); Travel time to work: 22.1% less than 15 minutes, 49.6% 15 to 30 minutes, 20.0% 30 to 45 minutes, 8.3% 45 to 60 minutes, 0.0% 60 minutes or more (2006-2010 5-year est.)

**Additional Information Contacts**
Orchard Park Chamber of Commerce . . . . . . . . . . . . . . . . (716) 662-3366
    http://www.orchardparkchamber.com

## ORCHARD PARK (town). Covers a land area of 38.440 square miles and a water area of 0.079 square miles. Located at 42.75° N. Lat; 78.73° W. Long. Elevation is 863 feet.

**History:** Until 1934, called East Hamburg. Incorporated 1921.
**Population:** 24,632 (1990); 27,637 (2000); 29,054 (2010); Density: 755.8 persons per square mile (2010); Race: 96.7% White, 0.7% Black, 1.3% Asian, 0.2% American Indian/Alaska Native, 0.0% Native Hawaiian/Other Pacific Islander, 1.1% Other, 1.6% Hispanic of any race (2010); Average household size: 2.51 (2010); Median age: 44.4 (2010); Males per 100 females: 92.1 (2010); Marriage status: 25.7% never married, 59.1% now married, 8.6% widowed, 6.6% divorced (2006-2010 5-year est.); Foreign born: 4.2% (2006-2010 5-year est.); Ancestry (includes multiple ancestries): 32.3% German, 24.8% Irish, 20.9% Polish, 18.2% Italian, 10.2% English (2006-2010 5-year est.).
**Economy:** Unemployment rate: 7.3% (February 2012); Total civilian labor force: 15,190 (February 2012); Single-family building permits issued: 25 (2011); Multi-family building permits issued: 0 (2011); Employment by occupation: 15.2% management, 5.2% professional, 5.7% services, 16.0% sales, 3.9% farming, 5.4% construction, 4.3% production (2006-2010 5-year est.).
**Income:** Per capita income: $37,932 (2006-2010 5-year est.); Median household income: $75,158 (2006-2010 5-year est.); Average household income: $95,968 (2006-2010 5-year est.); Percent of households with income of $100,000 or more: 34.7% (2006-2010 5-year est.); Poverty rate: 3.9% (2006-2010 5-year est.).
**Education:** Percent of population age 25 and over with: High school diploma (including GED) or higher: 94.1% (2006-2010 5-year est.); Bachelor's degree or higher: 44.1% (2006-2010 5-year est.); Master's degree or higher: 20.2% (2006-2010 5-year est.).

### School District(s)
Orchard Park Central School District (KG-12)
    2009-10 Enrollment: 5,238 . . . . . . . . . . . . . . . . . . . . . . (716) 209-6280

#### Four-year College(s)
Bryant and Stratton College-Southtowns (Private, For-profit)
    Fall 2010 Enrollment: 2,247 . . . . . . . . . . . . . . . . . . . . . (716) 677-9500
    2011-12 Tuition: In-state $15,570; Out-of-state $15,570

**Housing:** Homeownership rate: 76.3% (2010); Median home value: $187,300 (2006-2010 5-year est.); Median contract rent: $761 per month (2006-2010 5-year est.); Median year structure built: 1972 (2006-2010 5-year est.).
**Safety:** Violent crime rate: 4.9 per 10,000 population; Property crime rate: 130.4 per 10,000 population (2010).
**Newspapers:** Akron/Corfu Pennysaver (Community news; Circulation 7,700); Attica Pennysaver (Community news; Circulation 7,000); East Aurora/Elma Pennysaver (Community news; Circulation 16,200); Orchard Park Pennysaver (Community news; Circulation 12,800); Southtowns

Citizen (Local news; Circulation 5,990); West Seneca Pennysaver (Community news; Circulation 19,600)
**Transportation:** Commute to work: 94.2% car, 0.1% public transportation, 1.3% walk, 3.2% work from home (2006-2010 5-year est.); Travel time to work: 23.8% less than 15 minutes, 47.2% 15 to 30 minutes, 22.5% 30 to 45 minutes, 3.7% 45 to 60 minutes, 2.8% 60 minutes or more (2006-2010 5-year est.)
**Additional Information Contacts**
Town of Orchard Park . . . . . . . . . . . . . . . . . . . . . . . . . . . (716) 662-6410
    http://www.orchardparkny.org

## SARDINIA (town). Covers a land area of 50.175 square miles and a water area of 0.232 square miles. Located at 42.55° N. Lat; 78.53° W. Long. Elevation is 1,394 feet.

**Population:** 2,635 (1990); 2,692 (2000); 2,775 (2010); Density: 55.3 persons per square mile (2010); Race: 97.9% White, 0.2% Black, 0.6% Asian, 0.5% American Indian/Alaska Native, 0.0% Native Hawaiian/Other Pacific Islander, 0.8% Other, 0.6% Hispanic of any race (2010); Average household size: 2.53 (2010); Median age: 44.4 (2010); Males per 100 females: 103.9 (2010); Marriage status: 22.6% never married, 63.9% now married, 4.3% widowed, 9.2% divorced (2006-2010 5-year est.); Foreign born: 1.4% (2006-2010 5-year est.); Ancestry (includes multiple ancestries): 45.3% German, 23.4% Polish, 15.9% Irish, 11.9% Italian, 9.8% English (2006-2010 5-year est.).
**Economy:** Single-family building permits issued: 1 (2011); Multi-family building permits issued: 0 (2011); Employment by occupation: 9.2% management, 3.4% professional, 10.9% services, 17.7% sales, 1.8% farming, 18.7% construction, 10.2% production (2006-2010 5-year est.).
**Income:** Per capita income: $28,104 (2006-2010 5-year est.); Median household income: $56,901 (2006-2010 5-year est.); Average household income: $76,614 (2006-2010 5-year est.); Percent of households with income of $100,000 or more: 21.2% (2006-2010 5-year est.); Poverty rate: 8.6% (2006-2010 5-year est.).
**Taxes:** Total city taxes per capita: $103 (2009); City property taxes per capita: $79 (2009).
**Education:** Percent of population age 25 and over with: High school diploma (including GED) or higher: 90.0% (2006-2010 5-year est.); Bachelor's degree or higher: 15.9% (2006-2010 5-year est.); Master's degree or higher: 5.7% (2006-2010 5-year est.).
**Housing:** Homeownership rate: 87.6% (2010); Median home value: $138,500 (2006-2010 5-year est.); Median contract rent: $473 per month (2006-2010 5-year est.); Median year structure built: 1956 (2006-2010 5-year est.).
**Transportation:** Commute to work: 90.6% car, 0.0% public transportation, 2.2% walk, 6.2% work from home (2006-2010 5-year est.); Travel time to work: 28.2% less than 15 minutes, 22.8% 15 to 30 minutes, 24.7% 30 to 45 minutes, 14.5% 45 to 60 minutes, 9.8% 60 minutes or more (2006-2010 5-year est.)

## SLOAN (village). Covers a land area of 0.786 square miles and a water area of 0.006 square miles. Located at 42.89° N. Lat; 78.79° W. Long. Elevation is 614 feet.

**History:** Incorporated 1896.
**Population:** 3,830 (1990); 3,775 (2000); 3,661 (2010); Density: 4,657.5 persons per square mile (2010); Race: 95.8% White, 1.4% Black, 0.5% Asian, 0.4% American Indian/Alaska Native, 0.0% Native Hawaiian/Other Pacific Islander, 1.9% Other, 2.1% Hispanic of any race (2010); Average household size: 2.19 (2010); Median age: 42.2 (2010); Males per 100 females: 92.4 (2010); Marriage status: 29.9% never married, 50.6% now married, 8.4% widowed, 11.1% divorced (2006-2010 5-year est.); Foreign born: 4.9% (2006-2010 5-year est.); Ancestry (includes multiple ancestries): 49.9% Polish, 27.5% German, 14.3% Irish, 9.7% Italian, 2.4% French (2006-2010 5-year est.).
**Economy:** Single-family building permits issued: 0 (2011); Multi-family building permits issued: 0 (2011); Employment by occupation: 6.3% management, 2.1% professional, 9.9% services, 21.1% sales, 2.7% farming, 10.3% construction, 10.6% production (2006-2010 5-year est.).
**Income:** Per capita income: $20,466 (2006-2010 5-year est.); Median household income: $38,421 (2006-2010 5-year est.); Average household income: $42,554 (2006-2010 5-year est.); Percent of households with income of $100,000 or more: 2.4% (2006-2010 5-year est.); Poverty rate: 16.9% (2006-2010 5-year est.).
**Education:** Percent of population age 25 and over with: High school diploma (including GED) or higher: 76.1% (2006-2010 5-year est.);

Bachelor's degree or higher: 7.9% (2006-2010 5-year est.); Master's degree or higher: 2.1% (2006-2010 5-year est.).

**School District(s)**

Cheektowaga-Sloan Union Free School District (PK-12)
    2009-10 Enrollment: 1,570 . . . . . . . . . . . . . . . . . . . . . . (716) 891-6402

**Housing:** Homeownership rate: 70.4% (2010); Median home value: $73,600 (2006-2010 5-year est.); Median contract rent: $492 per month (2006-2010 5-year est.); Median year structure built: 1944 (2006-2010 5-year est.).

**Transportation:** Commute to work: 92.9% car, 0.5% public transportation, 1.6% walk, 2.1% work from home (2006-2010 5-year est.); Travel time to work: 38.3% less than 15 minutes, 52.5% 15 to 30 minutes, 6.1% 30 to 45 minutes, 0.5% 45 to 60 minutes, 2.6% 60 minutes or more (2006-2010 5-year est.)

## SOUTH WALES (unincorporated postal area)

Zip Code: 14139
    Covers a land area of 23.859 square miles and a water area of 0.031 square miles. Located at 42.71° N. Lat; 78.54° W. Long. Elevation is 932 feet. Population: 2,125 (2010); Density: 89.1 persons per square mile (2010); Race: 97.5% White, 0.3% Black, 0.5% Asian, 0.5% American Indian/Alaska Native, 0.0% Native Hawaiian/Other Pacific Islander, 1.2% Other, 0.9% Hispanic of any race (2010); Average household size: 2.43 (2010); Median age: 45.3 (2010); Males per 100 females: 99.7 (2010); Homeownership rate: 85.0% (2010)

## SPRINGVILLE (village).

Covers a land area of 3.672 square miles and a water area of 0.009 square miles. Located at 42.50° N. Lat; 78.66° W. Long. Elevation is 1,329 feet.

**History:** Settled 1807, incorporated 1834.

**Population:** 4,330 (1990); 4,252 (2000); 4,296 (2010); Density: 1,169.9 persons per square mile (2010); Race: 96.1% White, 1.1% Black, 0.6% Asian, 0.8% American Indian/Alaska Native, 0.0% Native Hawaiian/Other Pacific Islander, 1.4% Other, 2.3% Hispanic of any race (2010); Average household size: 2.37 (2010); Median age: 40.2 (2010); Males per 100 females: 91.6 (2010); Marriage status: 26.6% never married, 42.6% now married, 19.7% widowed, 11.2% divorced (2006-2010 5-year est.); Foreign born: 2.9% (2006-2010 5-year est.); Ancestry (includes multiple ancestries): 37.1% German, 18.9% Irish, 15.8% English, 11.9% Polish, 8.8% Italian (2006-2010 5-year est.).

**Economy:** Single-family building permits issued: 1 (2011); Multi-family building permits issued: 0 (2011); Employment by occupation: 13.4% management, 2.0% professional, 11.1% services, 16.5% sales, 6.4% farming, 7.4% construction, 6.3% production (2006-2010 5-year est.).

**Income:** Per capita income: $22,644 (2006-2010 5-year est.); Median household income: $39,444 (2006-2010 5-year est.); Average household income: $51,030 (2006-2010 5-year est.); Percent of households with income of $100,000 or more: 11.7% (2006-2010 5-year est.); Poverty rate: 10.9% (2006-2010 5-year est.).

**Education:** Percent of population age 25 and over with: High school diploma (including GED) or higher: 83.7% (2006-2010 5-year est.); Bachelor's degree or higher: 23.1% (2006-2010 5-year est.); Master's degree or higher: 8.5% (2006-2010 5-year est.).

**School District(s)**

Springville-Griffith Institute Central School Dist (KG-12)
    2009-10 Enrollment: 2,098 . . . . . . . . . . . . . . . . . . . . . (716) 592-3230

**Housing:** Homeownership rate: 59.7% (2010); Median home value: $113,600 (2006-2010 5-year est.); Median contract rent: $458 per month (2006-2010 5-year est.); Median year structure built: 1945 (2006-2010 5-year est.).

**Hospitals:** Bertrand Chaffee Hospital (49 beds)

**Newspapers:** Springville Journal (Community news; Circulation 4,512)

**Transportation:** Commute to work: 84.0% car, 1.0% public transportation, 13.3% walk, 1.1% work from home (2006-2010 5-year est.); Travel time to work: 43.6% less than 15 minutes, 19.2% 15 to 30 minutes, 16.2% 30 to 45 minutes, 14.7% 45 to 60 minutes, 6.3% 60 minutes or more (2006-2010 5-year est.)

**Additional Information Contacts**

Springville Chamber of Commerce . . . . . . . . . . . . . . . (716) 592-4746
    http://www.springvillechamber.com

## TONAWANDA (city).

Covers a land area of 3.803 square miles and a water area of 0.287 square miles. Located at 43.01° N. Lat; 78.88° W. Long. Elevation is 574 feet.

**Population:** 17,284 (1990); 16,136 (2000); 15,130 (2010); Density: 3,978.1 persons per square mile (2010); Race: 96.6% White, 0.9% Black, 0.6% Asian, 0.5% American Indian/Alaska Native, 0.0% Native Hawaiian/Other Pacific Islander, 1.4% Other, 2.0% Hispanic of any race (2010); Average household size: 2.24 (2010); Median age: 42.7 (2010); Males per 100 females: 94.5 (2010); Marriage status: 30.0% never married, 49.6% now married, 9.3% widowed, 11.0% divorced (2006-2010 5-year est.); Foreign born: 2.7% (2006-2010 5-year est.); Ancestry (includes multiple ancestries): 44.2% German, 20.2% Italian, 20.1% Irish, 16.6% Polish, 9.5% English (2006-2010 5-year est.).

**Economy:** Single-family building permits issued: 2 (2011); Multi-family building permits issued: 0 (2011); Employment by occupation: 9.1% management, 3.5% professional, 9.5% services, 22.0% sales, 6.3% farming, 5.9% construction, 5.7% production (2006-2010 5-year est.).

**Income:** Per capita income: $23,463 (2006-2010 5-year est.); Median household income: $47,105 (2006-2010 5-year est.); Average household income: $53,922 (2006-2010 5-year est.); Percent of households with income of $100,000 or more: 10.6% (2006-2010 5-year est.); Poverty rate: 11.3% (2006-2010 5-year est.).

**Education:** Percent of population age 25 and over with: High school diploma (including GED) or higher: 90.1% (2006-2010 5-year est.); Bachelor's degree or higher: 16.2% (2006-2010 5-year est.); Master's degree or higher: 6.2% (2006-2010 5-year est.).

**School District(s)**

Kenmore-Tonawanda Union Free School District (PK-12)
    2009-10 Enrollment: 8,128 . . . . . . . . . . . . . . . . . . . . . (716) 874-8400
Sweet Home Central School District (KG-12)
    2009-10 Enrollment: 3,488 . . . . . . . . . . . . . . . . . . . . . (716) 250-1402
Tonawanda City School District (PK-12)
    2009-10 Enrollment: 1,998 . . . . . . . . . . . . . . . . . . . . . (716) 694-7784

**Vocational/Technical School(s)**

MarJon School of Beauty Culture Ltd (Private, For-profit)
    Fall 2010 Enrollment: 54 . . . . . . . . . . . . . . . . . . . . . . (716) 836-6240
    2011-12 Tuition: $9,000
The Salon Professional Academy-Tonawanda (Private, For-profit)
    Fall 2010 Enrollment: 94 . . . . . . . . . . . . . . . . . . . . . . (7.1) 683-4E+1
    2011-12 Tuition: $11,600

**Housing:** Homeownership rate: 71.2% (2010); Median home value: $88,400 (2006-2010 5-year est.); Median contract rent: $445 per month (2006-2010 5-year est.); Median year structure built: 1948 (2006-2010 5-year est.).

**Safety:** Violent crime rate: 14.5 per 10,000 population; Property crime rate: 215.5 per 10,000 population (2010).

**Transportation:** Commute to work: 93.2% car, 1.5% public transportation, 2.2% walk, 1.0% work from home (2006-2010 5-year est.); Travel time to work: 33.6% less than 15 minutes, 46.0% 15 to 30 minutes, 15.1% 30 to 45 minutes, 2.2% 45 to 60 minutes, 3.2% 60 minutes or more (2006-2010 5-year est.)

**Additional Information Contacts**

City of Tonawanda . . . . . . . . . . . . . . . . . . . . . . . . . . (716) 695-1800
    http://www.ci.tonawanda.ny.us

## TONAWANDA (town).

Covers a land area of 18.734 square miles and a water area of 1.543 square miles. Located at 42.98° N. Lat; 78.87° W. Long. Elevation is 574 feet.

**History:** Named for the Iroquois translation of "swift water". Incorporated as a village 1854, and as a city in 1903.

**Population:** 82,464 (1990); 78,155 (2000); 73,567 (2010); Density: 3,926.7 persons per square mile (2010); Race: 93.1% White, 3.0% Black, 1.3% Asian, 0.4% American Indian/Alaska Native, 0.0% Native Hawaiian/Other Pacific Islander, 2.2% Other, 2.7% Hispanic of any race (2010); Average household size: 2.21 (2010); Median age: 43.3 (2010); Males per 100 females: 88.8 (2010); Marriage status: 31.8% never married, 50.0% now married, 8.7% widowed, 9.6% divorced (2006-2010 5-year est.); Foreign born: 4.9% (2006-2010 5-year est.); Ancestry (includes multiple ancestries): 32.5% German, 25.9% Italian, 21.2% Irish, 15.5% Polish, 9.8% English (2006-2010 5-year est.).

**Economy:** Unemployment rate: 8.0% (February 2012); Total civilian labor force: 38,324 (February 2012); Single-family building permits issued: 7 (2011); Multi-family building permits issued: 0 (2011); Employment by occupation: 9.4% management, 3.7% professional, 9.8% services, 19.5%

sales, 5.5% farming, 5.7% construction, 4.3% production (2006-2010 5-year est.).

**Income:** Per capita income: $25,999 (2006-2010 5-year est.); Median household income: $47,871 (2006-2010 5-year est.); Average household income: $58,741 (2006-2010 5-year est.); Percent of households with income of $100,000 or more: 13.4% (2006-2010 5-year est.); Poverty rate: 9.6% (2006-2010 5-year est.).

**Taxes:** Total city taxes per capita: $510 (2009); City property taxes per capita: $475 (2009).

**Education:** Percent of population age 25 and over with: High school diploma (including GED) or higher: 91.9% (2006-2010 5-year est.); Bachelor's degree or higher: 30.5% (2006-2010 5-year est.); Master's degree or higher: 11.7% (2006-2010 5-year est.).

**School District(s)**

Kenmore-Tonawanda Union Free School District (PK-12)
   2009-10 Enrollment: 8,128 . . . . . . . . . . . . . . . . . . . . . . (716) 874-8400
Sweet Home Central School District (KG-12)
   2009-10 Enrollment: 3,488 . . . . . . . . . . . . . . . . . . . . . . (716) 250-1402
Tonawanda City School District (PK-12)
   2009-10 Enrollment: 1,998 . . . . . . . . . . . . . . . . . . . . . . (716) 694-7784

**Vocational/Technical School(s)**

MarJon School of Beauty Culture Ltd (Private, For-profit)
   Fall 2010 Enrollment: 54 . . . . . . . . . . . . . . . . . . . . . . . (716) 836-6240
   2011-12 Tuition: $9,000
The Salon Professional Academy-Tonawanda (Private, For-profit)
   Fall 2010 Enrollment: 94 . . . . . . . . . . . . . . . . . . . . . . . (7.1) 683-4E+1
   2011-12 Tuition: $11,600

**Housing:** Homeownership rate: 72.6% (2010); Median home value: $106,300 (2006-2010 5-year est.); Median contract rent: $558 per month (2006-2010 5-year est.); Median year structure built: 1953 (2006-2010 5-year est.).

**Safety:** Violent crime rate: 23.2 per 10,000 population; Property crime rate: 200.2 per 10,000 population (2010).

**Transportation:** Commute to work: 91.4% car, 2.5% public transportation, 2.1% walk, 2.2% work from home (2006-2010 5-year est.); Travel time to work: 35.4% less than 15 minutes, 48.9% 15 to 30 minutes, 11.5% 30 to 45 minutes, 1.6% 45 to 60 minutes, 2.5% 60 minutes or more (2006-2010 5-year est.)

**Additional Information Contacts**

Town of Tonawanda . . . . . . . . . . . . . . . . . . . . . . . . . . . (716) 877-8800
   http://www.tonawanda.ny.us

**TONAWANDA** (CDP). Covers a land area of 17.299 square miles and a water area of 1.336 square miles. Located at 42.98° N. Lat; 78.87° W. Long. Elevation is 574 feet.

**Population:** 65,284 (1990); 61,729 (2000); 58,144 (2010); Density: 3,361.0 persons per square mile (2010); Race: 93.1% White, 3.0% Black, 1.4% Asian, 0.4% American Indian/Alaska Native, 0.0% Native Hawaiian/Other Pacific Islander, 2.1% Other, 2.6% Hispanic of any race (2010); Average household size: 2.22 (2010); Median age: 44.4 (2010); Males per 100 females: 89.1 (2010); Marriage status: 31.0% never married, 50.4% now married, 9.2% widowed, 9.5% divorced (2006-2010 5-year est.); Foreign born: 5.6% (2006-2010 5-year est.); Ancestry (includes multiple ancestries): 33.0% German, 24.4% Italian, 20.5% Irish, 15.4% Polish, 10.4% English (2006-2010 5-year est.).

**Economy:** Employment by occupation: 9.6% management, 3.8% professional, 9.6% services, 19.8% sales, 5.8% farming, 5.5% construction, 4.2% production (2006-2010 5-year est.).

**Income:** Per capita income: $26,253 (2006-2010 5-year est.); Median household income: $48,330 (2006-2010 5-year est.); Average household income: $58,831 (2006-2010 5-year est.); Percent of households with income of $100,000 or more: 13.4% (2006-2010 5-year est.); Poverty rate: 9.8% (2006-2010 5-year est.).

**Education:** Percent of population age 25 and over with: High school diploma (including GED) or higher: 91.6% (2006-2010 5-year est.); Bachelor's degree or higher: 29.8% (2006-2010 5-year est.); Master's degree or higher: 11.6% (2006-2010 5-year est.).

**Housing:** Homeownership rate: 74.2% (2010); Median home value: $108,100 (2006-2010 5-year est.); Median contract rent: $573 per month (2006-2010 5-year est.); Median year structure built: 1954 (2006-2010 5-year est.).

**Transportation:** Commute to work: 91.4% car, 2.4% public transportation, 2.0% walk, 2.5% work from home (2006-2010 5-year est.); Travel time to work: 35.8% less than 15 minutes, 48.7% 15 to 30 minutes, 11.5% 30 to 45

minutes, 1.5% 45 to 60 minutes, 2.5% 60 minutes or more (2006-2010 5-year est.)

**TONAWANDA RESERVATION** (Reservation). Covers a land area of 1.838 square miles and a water area of 0 square miles. Located at 43.07° N. Lat; 78.47° W. Long.

**Population:** 10 (1990); 10 (2000); 34 (2010); Density: 18.5 persons per square mile (2010); Race: 0.0% White, 0.0% Black, 0.0% Asian, 100.0% American Indian/Alaska Native, 0.0% Native Hawaiian/Other Pacific Islander, 0.0% Other, 0.0% Hispanic of any race (2010); Average household size: 3.78 (2010); Median age: 19.5 (2010); Males per 100 females: 78.9 (2010); Marriage status: 0.0% never married, 100.0% now married, 0.0% widowed, 0.0% divorced (2006-2010 5-year est.); Foreign born: 0.0% (2006-2010 5-year est.); Ancestry (includes multiple ancestries): n/a (2006-2010 5-year est.).

**Income:** Per capita income: $0 (2006-2010 5-year est.); Median household income: $2 (2006-2010 5-year est.); Average household income: $0 (2006-2010 5-year est.); Percent of households with income of $100,000 or more: 0.0% (2006-2010 5-year est.); Poverty rate: 100.0% (2006-2010 5-year est.).

**Education:** Percent of population age 25 and over with: High school diploma (including GED) or higher: 0.0% (2006-2010 5-year est.); Bachelor's degree or higher: 0.0% (2006-2010 5-year est.); Master's degree or higher: 0.0% (2006-2010 5-year est.).

**Housing:** Homeownership rate: 55.5% (2010); Median home value: n/a (2006-2010 5-year est.); Median contract rent: n/a per month (2006-2010 5-year est.); Median year structure built: n/a (2006-2010 5-year est.).

**TOWN LINE** (CDP). Covers a land area of 4.621 square miles and a water area of 0.004 square miles. Located at 42.88° N. Lat; 78.56° W. Long. Elevation is 751 feet.

**Population:** 2,721 (1990); 2,521 (2000); 2,367 (2010); Density: 512.2 persons per square mile (2010); Race: 99.0% White, 0.1% Black, 0.1% Asian, 0.1% American Indian/Alaska Native, 0.0% Native Hawaiian/Other Pacific Islander, 0.7% Other, 0.8% Hispanic of any race (2010); Average household size: 2.63 (2010); Median age: 46.0 (2010); Males per 100 females: 98.1 (2010); Marriage status: 21.2% never married, 63.4% now married, 7.8% widowed, 7.6% divorced (2006-2010 5-year est.); Foreign born: 3.7% (2006-2010 5-year est.); Ancestry (includes multiple ancestries): 40.5% German, 29.8% Polish, 13.1% Irish, 12.1% Italian, 8.0% American (2006-2010 5-year est.).

**Economy:** Employment by occupation: 11.8% management, 3.2% professional, 13.9% services, 14.4% sales, 0.0% farming, 14.3% construction, 8.3% production (2006-2010 5-year est.).

**Income:** Per capita income: $26,460 (2006-2010 5-year est.); Median household income: $51,532 (2006-2010 5-year est.); Average household income: $66,504 (2006-2010 5-year est.); Percent of households with income of $100,000 or more: 16.4% (2006-2010 5-year est.); Poverty rate: 4.2% (2006-2010 5-year est.).

**Education:** Percent of population age 25 and over with: High school diploma (including GED) or higher: 92.9% (2006-2010 5-year est.); Bachelor's degree or higher: 17.3% (2006-2010 5-year est.); Master's degree or higher: 6.2% (2006-2010 5-year est.).

**Housing:** Homeownership rate: 93.0% (2010); Median home value: $143,700 (2006-2010 5-year est.); Median contract rent: $582 per month (2006-2010 5-year est.); Median year structure built: 1961 (2006-2010 5-year est.).

**Transportation:** Commute to work: 96.4% car, 0.0% public transportation, 0.0% walk, 2.0% work from home (2006-2010 5-year est.); Travel time to work: 26.2% less than 15 minutes, 33.2% 15 to 30 minutes, 34.2% 30 to 45 minutes, 3.3% 45 to 60 minutes, 3.1% 60 minutes or more (2006-2010 5-year est.)

**UNIVERSITY AT BUFFALO** (CDP). Covers a land area of 1.372 square miles and a water area of 0.089 square miles. Located at 42.99° N. Lat; 78.79° W. Long.

**Population:** n/a (1990); n/a (2000); 6,066 (2010); Density: 4,418.8 persons per square mile (2010); Race: 64.3% White, 8.6% Black, 22.3% Asian, 0.2% American Indian/Alaska Native, 0.0% Native Hawaiian/Other Pacific Islander, 4.6% Other, 5.0% Hispanic of any race (2010); Average household size: 2.40 (2010); Median age: 20.4 (2010); Males per 100 females: 104.1 (2010); Marriage status: 97.3% never married, 2.7% now married, 0.0% widowed, 0.0% divorced (2006-2010 5-year est.); Foreign born: 16.0% (2006-2010 5-year est.); Ancestry (includes multiple

ancestries): 18.5% German, 17.7% Irish, 16.9% Italian, 14.7% Polish, 7.1% English (2006-2010 5-year est.).
**Economy:** Employment by occupation: 2.9% management, 3.6% professional, 13.1% services, 27.1% sales, 8.1% farming, 1.7% construction, 4.2% production (2006-2010 5-year est.).
**Income:** Per capita income: $4,496 (2006-2010 5-year est.); Median household income: $25,134 (2006-2010 5-year est.); Average household income: $36,659 (2006-2010 5-year est.); Percent of households with income of $100,000 or more: 0.0% (2006-2010 5-year est.); Poverty rate: 57.7% (2006-2010 5-year est.).
**Education:** Percent of population age 25 and over with: High school diploma (including GED) or higher: 100.0% (2006-2010 5-year est.); Bachelor's degree or higher: 90.3% (2006-2010 5-year est.); Master's degree or higher: 67.9% (2006-2010 5-year est.).
**Housing:** Homeownership rate: 12.5% (2010); Median home value: n/a (2006-2010 5-year est.); Median contract rent: $916 per month (2006-2010 5-year est.); Median year structure built: 1992 (2006-2010 5-year est.).
**Transportation:** Commute to work: 57.9% car, 10.9% public transportation, 19.0% walk, 10.7% work from home (2006-2010 5-year est.); Travel time to work: 56.6% less than 15 minutes, 34.8% 15 to 30 minutes, 5.6% 30 to 45 minutes, 0.9% 45 to 60 minutes, 2.1% 60 minutes or more (2006-2010 5-year est.)

**WALES** (town). Covers a land area of 35.588 square miles and a water area of 0.050 square miles. Located at 42.73° N. Lat; 78.51° W. Long.
**Population:** 2,917 (1990); 2,960 (2000); 3,005 (2010); Density: 84.4 persons per square mile (2010); Race: 97.3% White, 0.5% Black, 0.4% Asian, 0.5% American Indian/Alaska Native, 0.0% Native Hawaiian/Other Pacific Islander, 1.3% Other, 1.1% Hispanic of any race (2010); Average household size: 2.47 (2010); Median age: 45.0 (2010); Males per 100 females: 98.0 (2010); Marriage status: 28.8% never married, 56.2% now married, 5.7% widowed, 9.2% divorced (2006-2010 5-year est.); Foreign born: 4.5% (2006-2010 5-year est.); Ancestry (includes multiple ancestries): 41.5% German, 19.1% Polish, 14.3% Irish, 10.4% English, 9.1% Italian (2006-2010 5-year est.).
**Economy:** Single-family building permits issued: 7 (2011); Multi-family building permits issued: 0 (2011); Employment by occupation: 15.2% management, 3.9% professional, 15.7% services, 8.7% sales, 2.8% farming, 13.2% construction, 5.0% production (2006-2010 5-year est.).
**Income:** Per capita income: $25,365 (2006-2010 5-year est.); Median household income: $50,064 (2006-2010 5-year est.); Average household income: $63,360 (2006-2010 5-year est.); Percent of households with income of $100,000 or more: 23.9% (2006-2010 5-year est.); Poverty rate: 12.0% (2006-2010 5-year est.).
**Education:** Percent of population age 25 and over with: High school diploma (including GED) or higher: 92.2% (2006-2010 5-year est.); Bachelor's degree or higher: 23.8% (2006-2010 5-year est.); Master's degree or higher: 7.7% (2006-2010 5-year est.).
**Housing:** Homeownership rate: 87.9% (2010); Median home value: $165,500 (2006-2010 5-year est.); Median contract rent: $483 per month (2006-2010 5-year est.); Median year structure built: 1963 (2006-2010 5-year est.).
**Transportation:** Commute to work: 92.5% car, 0.0% public transportation, 2.5% walk, 4.2% work from home (2006-2010 5-year est.); Travel time to work: 22.6% less than 15 minutes, 32.5% 15 to 30 minutes, 24.2% 30 to 45 minutes, 13.7% 45 to 60 minutes, 7.0% 60 minutes or more (2006-2010 5-year est.)

**WALES CENTER** (unincorporated postal area)
Zip Code: 14169
Covers a land area of 0.308 square miles and a water area of 0 square miles. Located at 42.76° N. Lat; 78.52° W. Long. Elevation is 889 feet. Population: 151 (2010); Density: 489.8 persons per square mile (2010); Race: 97.4% White, 0.0% Black, 0.0% Asian, 0.0% American Indian/Alaska Native, 0.0% Native Hawaiian/Other Pacific Islander, 2.6% Other, 0.7% Hispanic of any race (2010); Average household size: 2.25 (2010); Median age: 37.6 (2010); Males per 100 females: 86.4 (2010); Homeownership rate: 65.6% (2010)

**WANAKAH** (CDP). Covers a land area of 1.204 square miles and a water area of 0 square miles. Located at 42.74° N. Lat; 78.90° W. Long. Elevation is 591 feet.
**Population:** n/a (1990); n/a (2000); 3,199 (2010); Density: 2,656.1 persons per square mile (2010); Race: 97.3% White, 0.3% Black, 0.6% Asian, 0.7% American Indian/Alaska Native, 0.0% Native Hawaiian/Other Pacific

Islander, 1.1% Other, 1.7% Hispanic of any race (2010); Average household size: 2.41 (2010); Median age: 46.5 (2010); Males per 100 females: 92.2 (2010); Marriage status: 30.9% never married, 51.9% now married, 5.4% widowed, 11.7% divorced (2006-2010 5-year est.); Foreign born: 0.9% (2006-2010 5-year est.); Ancestry (includes multiple ancestries): 29.3% German, 29.2% Irish, 23.9% Polish, 21.5% Italian, 10.0% English (2006-2010 5-year est.).
**Economy:** Employment by occupation: 6.9% management, 0.9% professional, 6.1% services, 24.7% sales, 9.3% farming, 6.1% construction, 4.9% production (2006-2010 5-year est.).
**Income:** Per capita income: $38,735 (2006-2010 5-year est.); Median household income: $68,393 (2006-2010 5-year est.); Average household income: $90,355 (2006-2010 5-year est.); Percent of households with income of $100,000 or more: 23.7% (2006-2010 5-year est.); Poverty rate: 4.5% (2006-2010 5-year est.).
**Education:** Percent of population age 25 and over with: High school diploma (including GED) or higher: 95.8% (2006-2010 5-year est.); Bachelor's degree or higher: 26.1% (2006-2010 5-year est.); Master's degree or higher: 11.3% (2006-2010 5-year est.).
**Housing:** Homeownership rate: 93.8% (2010); Median home value: $111,000 (2006-2010 5-year est.); Median contract rent: $486 per month (2006-2010 5-year est.); Median year structure built: 1955 (2006-2010 5-year est.).
**Transportation:** Commute to work: 97.9% car, 0.6% public transportation, 0.0% walk, 1.5% work from home (2006-2010 5-year est.); Travel time to work: 21.9% less than 15 minutes, 42.6% 15 to 30 minutes, 29.5% 30 to 45 minutes, 2.0% 45 to 60 minutes, 4.1% 60 minutes or more (2006-2010 5-year est.)

**WEST FALLS** (unincorporated postal area)
Zip Code: 14170
Covers a land area of 12.325 square miles and a water area of 0.054 square miles. Located at 42.70° N. Lat; 78.67° W. Long. Elevation is 925 feet. Population: 2,286 (2010); Density: 185.5 persons per square mile (2010); Race: 98.7% White, 0.3% Black, 0.1% Asian, 0.1% American Indian/Alaska Native, 0.0% Native Hawaiian/Other Pacific Islander, 0.8% Other, 1.7% Hispanic of any race (2010); Average household size: 2.49 (2010); Median age: 45.9 (2010); Males per 100 females: 102.3 (2010); Homeownership rate: 85.8% (2010)

**WEST SENECA** (town and CDP). Covers a land area of 21.357 square miles and a water area of 0.057 square miles. Located at 42.83° N. Lat; 78.75° W. Long. Elevation is 597 feet.
**Population:** 47,830 (1990); 45,920 (2000); 44,711 (2010); Density: 2,093.5 persons per square mile (2010); Race: 97.2% White, 0.9% Black, 0.6% Asian, 0.2% American Indian/Alaska Native, 0.0% Native Hawaiian/Other Pacific Islander, 1.1% Other, 1.7% Hispanic of any race (2010); Average household size: 2.31 (2010); Median age: 44.7 (2010); Males per 100 females: 91.7 (2010); Marriage status: 27.1% never married, 54.8% now married, 9.3% widowed, 8.8% divorced (2006-2010 5-year est.); Foreign born: 3.7% (2006-2010 5-year est.); Ancestry (includes multiple ancestries): 31.0% German, 29.6% Polish, 25.1% Irish, 18.5% Italian, 7.1% English (2006-2010 5-year est.).
**Economy:** Unemployment rate: 8.1% (February 2012); Total civilian labor force: 23,916 (February 2012); Single-family building permits issued: 44 (2011); Multi-family building permits issued: 2 (2011); Employment by occupation: 8.1% management, 4.1% professional, 9.5% services, 19.6% sales, 5.4% farming, 7.7% construction, 5.0% production (2006-2010 5-year est.).
**Income:** Per capita income: $26,728 (2006-2010 5-year est.); Median household income: $52,301 (2006-2010 5-year est.); Average household income: $63,052 (2006-2010 5-year est.); Percent of households with income of $100,000 or more: 17.2% (2006-2010 5-year est.); Poverty rate: 6.3% (2006-2010 5-year est.).
**Taxes:** Total city taxes per capita: $637 (2009); City property taxes per capita: $609 (2009).
**Education:** Percent of population age 25 and over with: High school diploma (including GED) or higher: 92.0% (2006-2010 5-year est.); Bachelor's degree or higher: 23.6% (2006-2010 5-year est.); Master's degree or higher: 9.7% (2006-2010 5-year est.).

### School District(s)
Erie 1 Boces
  2009-10 Enrollment: n/a . . . . . . . . . . . . . . . . . . . . . . . . (716) 821-7001
West Seneca Central School District (PK-12)
  2009-10 Enrollment: 7,198 . . . . . . . . . . . . . . . . . . . . . . . . (716) 677-3101

**Vocational/Technical School(s)**

Continental School of Beauty Culture-West Seneca (Private, For-profit)
Fall 2010 Enrollment: 120 . . . . . . . . . . . . . . . . . . . . . . . (716) 675-8205
2011-12 Tuition: $11,050

Erie 1 BOCES (Public)
Fall 2010 Enrollment: 383 . . . . . . . . . . . . . . . . . . . . . . (716) 822-3333
2011-12 Tuition: $8,800

**Housing:** Homeownership rate: 76.2% (2010); Median home value: $122,900 (2006-2010 5-year est.); Median contract rent: $570 per month (2006-2010 5-year est.); Median year structure built: 1963 (2006-2010 5-year est.).

**Hospitals:** Western New York Children's Psychiatric Center (46 beds)

**Safety:** Violent crime rate: 11.1 per 10,000 population; Property crime rate: 226.7 per 10,000 population (2010).

**Transportation:** Commute to work: 95.6% car, 0.6% public transportation, 1.6% walk, 1.2% work from home (2006-2010 5-year est.); Travel time to work: 30.9% less than 15 minutes, 49.2% 15 to 30 minutes, 14.2% 30 to 45 minutes, 3.3% 45 to 60 minutes, 2.4% 60 minutes or more (2006-2010 5-year est.)

**Additional Information Contacts**

Town of West Seneca . . . . . . . . . . . . . . . . . . . . . . . . . . (716) 674-5600
http://www.westseneca.net
West Seneca Chamber of Commerce . . . . . . . . . . . . . . (716) 674-4900
http://www.westseneca.org

---

**WEST SENECA** (CDP). Covers a land area of 21.357 square miles and a water area of 0.057 square miles. Located at 42.83° N. Lat; 78.75° W. Long. Elevation is 597 feet.

**Population:** 47,866 (1990); 45,943 (2000); 44,711 (2010); Density: 2,093.5 persons per square mile (2010); Race: 97.2% White, 0.9% Black, 0.6% Asian, 0.2% American Indian/Alaska Native, 0.0% Native Hawaiian/Other Pacific Islander, 1.1% Other, 1.7% Hispanic of any race (2010); Average household size: 2.31 (2010); Median age: 44.7 (2010); Males per 100 females: 91.7 (2010); Marriage status: 27.1% never married, 54.8% now married, 9.3% widowed, 8.8% divorced (2006-2010 5-year est.); Foreign born: 3.7% (2006-2010 5-year est.); Ancestry (includes multiple ancestries): 31.0% German, 29.6% Polish, 25.1% Irish, 18.5% Italian, 7.1% English (2006-2010 5-year est.).

**Economy:** Employment by occupation: 8.1% management, 4.1% professional, 9.5% services, 19.6% sales, 5.4% farming, 7.7% construction, 5.0% production (2006-2010 5-year est.).

**Income:** Per capita income: $26,728 (2006-2010 5-year est.); Median household income: $52,301 (2006-2010 5-year est.); Average household income: $63,052 (2006-2010 5-year est.); Percent of households with income of $100,000 or more: 17.2% (2006-2010 5-year est.); Poverty rate: 6.3% (2006-2010 5-year est.).

**Education:** Percent of population age 25 and over with: High school diploma (including GED) or higher: 92.0% (2006-2010 5-year est.); Bachelor's degree or higher: 23.6% (2006-2010 5-year est.); Master's degree or higher: 9.7% (2006-2010 5-year est.).

**School District(s)**

Erie 1 Boces
2009-10 Enrollment: n/a . . . . . . . . . . . . . . . . . . . . . . . . (716) 821-7001
West Seneca Central School District (PK-12)
2009-10 Enrollment: 7,198 . . . . . . . . . . . . . . . . . . . . . (716) 677-3101

**Vocational/Technical School(s)**

Continental School of Beauty Culture-West Seneca (Private, For-profit)
Fall 2010 Enrollment: 120 . . . . . . . . . . . . . . . . . . . . . . . (716) 675-8205
2011-12 Tuition: $11,050
Erie 1 BOCES (Public)
Fall 2010 Enrollment: 383 . . . . . . . . . . . . . . . . . . . . . . (716) 822-3333
2011-12 Tuition: $8,800

**Housing:** Homeownership rate: 76.2% (2010); Median home value: $122,900 (2006-2010 5-year est.); Median contract rent: $570 per month (2006-2010 5-year est.); Median year structure built: 1963 (2006-2010 5-year est.).

**Hospitals:** Western New York Children's Psychiatric Center (46 beds)

**Transportation:** Commute to work: 95.6% car, 0.6% public transportation, 1.6% walk, 1.2% work from home (2006-2010 5-year est.); Travel time to work: 30.9% less than 15 minutes, 49.2% 15 to 30 minutes, 14.2% 30 to 45 minutes, 3.3% 45 to 60 minutes, 2.4% 60 minutes or more (2006-2010 5-year est.)

**WILLIAMSVILLE** (village). Covers a land area of 1.260 square miles and a water area of 0.009 square miles. Located at 42.96° N. Lat; 78.74° W. Long. Elevation is 676 feet.

**History:** Settled c.1800, incorporated 1869.

**Population:** 5,583 (1990); 5,573 (2000); 5,300 (2010); Density: 4,205.8 persons per square mile (2010); Race: 91.6% White, 2.2% Black, 4.2% Asian, 0.1% American Indian/Alaska Native, 0.0% Native Hawaiian/Other Pacific Islander, 1.9% Other, 1.7% Hispanic of any race (2010); Average household size: 2.01 (2010); Median age: 46.4 (2010); Males per 100 females: 77.7 (2010); Marriage status: 30.3% never married, 46.1% now married, 13.1% widowed, 10.5% divorced (2006-2010 5-year est.); Foreign born: 6.6% (2006-2010 5-year est.); Ancestry (includes multiple ancestries): 30.8% German, 24.1% Irish, 19.3% Italian, 15.5% Polish, 13.8% English (2006-2010 5-year est.).

**Economy:** Single-family building permits issued: 1 (2011); Multi-family building permits issued: 0 (2011); Employment by occupation: 15.6% management, 11.9% professional, 7.8% services, 13.2% sales, 2.9% farming, 3.2% construction, 2.0% production (2006-2010 5-year est.).

**Income:** Per capita income: $38,977 (2006-2010 5-year est.); Median household income: $65,381 (2006-2010 5-year est.); Average household income: $83,949 (2006-2010 5-year est.); Percent of households with income of $100,000 or more: 28.7% (2006-2010 5-year est.); Poverty rate: 8.3% (2006-2010 5-year est.).

**Taxes:** Total city taxes per capita: $322 (2009); City property taxes per capita: $268 (2009).

**Education:** Percent of population age 25 and over with: High school diploma (including GED) or higher: 95.8% (2006-2010 5-year est.); Bachelor's degree or higher: 56.6% (2006-2010 5-year est.); Master's degree or higher: 31.5% (2006-2010 5-year est.).

**School District(s)**

Clarence Central School District (KG-12)
2009-10 Enrollment: 5,101 . . . . . . . . . . . . . . . . . . . . . (716) 407-9102
Williamsville Central School District (KG-12)
2009-10 Enrollment: 10,511 . . . . . . . . . . . . . . . . . . . . (716) 626-8000

**Vocational/Technical School(s)**

Leon Studio One School of Hair Design (Private, For-profit)
Fall 2010 Enrollment: 82 . . . . . . . . . . . . . . . . . . . . . . . (716) 631-3878
2011-12 Tuition: $10,000
New York Institute of Massage Inc (Private, For-profit)
Fall 2010 Enrollment: 172 . . . . . . . . . . . . . . . . . . . . . . (716) 633-0355
2011-12 Tuition: $14,600

**Housing:** Homeownership rate: 60.3% (2010); Median home value: $154,600 (2006-2010 5-year est.); Median contract rent: $772 per month (2006-2010 5-year est.); Median year structure built: 1953 (2006-2010 5-year est.).

**Newspapers:** Amherst Bee (Community news; Circulation 11,774); Cheektowaga Bee (Community news; Circulation 1,425); Clarence Bee (Community news; Circulation 4,595); Depew Bee (Community news; Circulation 1,450); East Aurora Bee (Community news; Circulation 1,656); Ken-Ton Bee (Community news; Circulation 1,554); Lancaster Bee (Community news; Circulation 3,547); Orchard Park Bee (Community news; Circulation 2,598); West Seneca Bee (Community news; Circulation 5,962)

**Transportation:** Commute to work: 87.1% car, 2.0% public transportation, 2.6% walk, 5.5% work from home (2006-2010 5-year est.); Travel time to work: 32.9% less than 15 minutes, 42.8% 15 to 30 minutes, 16.0% 30 to 45 minutes, 4.1% 45 to 60 minutes, 4.1% 60 minutes or more (2006-2010 5-year est.)

**Additional Information Contacts**

Amherst Chamber of Commerce . . . . . . . . . . . . . . . . . (716) 632-6905
http://www.amherst.org
Village of Williamsville . . . . . . . . . . . . . . . . . . . . . . . . (716) 632-4120
http://village.williamsville.ny.us

## Essex County

Located in northeastern New York, in the Adirondacks; bounded on the east by Lake Champlain; drained by the Hudson and Ausable Rivers; includes Lake Placid and Saranac Lake, and Mt. Marcy, the highest point in the state (5,344 ft). Covers a land area of 1,796.80 square miles, a water area of 119.70 square miles, and is located in the Eastern Time Zone at 44.16° N. Lat., 73.73° W. Long. The county was founded in 1799. County seat is Elizabethtown.

**Weather Station: Lake Placid 2 S**        Elevation: 1,938 feet

| | Jan | Feb | Mar | Apr | May | Jun | Jul | Aug | Sep | Oct | Nov | Dec |
|---|---|---|---|---|---|---|---|---|---|---|---|---|
| High | 27 | 31 | 40 | 53 | 65 | 73 | 77 | 75 | 68 | 56 | 43 | 32 |
| Low | 6 | 8 | 16 | 29 | 39 | 48 | 53 | 51 | 44 | 34 | 24 | 12 |
| Precip | 2.5 | 2.1 | 2.6 | 2.8 | 3.5 | 4.3 | 4.4 | 4.2 | 3.9 | 3.9 | 3.5 | 3.0 |
| Snow | na | na | 18.8 | 7.2 | 0.3 | 0.0 | 0.0 | 0.0 | tr | 2.5 | 10.8 | 22.7 |

*High and Low temperatures in degrees Fahrenheit; Precipitation and Snow in inches*

**Weather Station: Newcomb**        Elevation: 1,620 feet

| | Jan | Feb | Mar | Apr | May | Jun | Jul | Aug | Sep | Oct | Nov | Dec |
|---|---|---|---|---|---|---|---|---|---|---|---|---|
| High | 25 | 28 | 38 | 51 | 64 | 72 | 76 | 74 | 66 | 55 | 41 | 29 |
| Low | 5 | 4 | 14 | 28 | 39 | 49 | 53 | 52 | 45 | 34 | 25 | 11 |
| Precip | 3.0 | 2.7 | 2.9 | 3.2 | 3.8 | 3.7 | 3.9 | 3.9 | 3.9 | 4.0 | 3.8 | 3.4 |
| Snow | 24.3 | 22.6 | 18.7 | 5.7 | 0.2 | tr | 0.0 | 0.0 | tr | 1.1 | 8.9 | 24.2 |

*High and Low temperatures in degrees Fahrenheit; Precipitation and Snow in inches*

**Weather Station: Ray Brook**        Elevation: 1,620 feet

| | Jan | Feb | Mar | Apr | May | Jun | Jul | Aug | Sep | Oct | Nov | Dec |
|---|---|---|---|---|---|---|---|---|---|---|---|---|
| High | 25 | 29 | 38 | 51 | 64 | 72 | 77 | 75 | 67 | 54 | 41 | 30 |
| Low | 3 | 5 | 14 | 28 | 39 | 48 | 52 | 51 | 43 | 33 | 25 | 12 |
| Precip | na | na | 2.5 | 2.7 | 3.1 | 3.8 | 3.7 | 3.8 | 4.1 | 3.4 | 3.4 | na |
| Snow | 23.5 | 19.6 | 19.9 | 9.2 | 0.8 | tr | 0.0 | tr | 0.1 | 1.6 | 14.6 | 22.4 |

*High and Low temperatures in degrees Fahrenheit; Precipitation and Snow in inches*

**Population:** 37,152 (1990); 38,851 (2000); 39,370 (2010); Race: 94.2% White, 2.7% Black, 0.7% Asian, 0.3% American Indian/Alaska Native, 0.0% Native Hawaiian/Other Pacific Islander, 2.1% Other, 2.5% Hispanic of any race (2010); Density: 21.9 persons per square mile (2010); Average household size: 2.26 (2010); Median age: 44.5 (2010); Males per 100 females: 107.4 (2010).

**Religion:** Six largest groups: 21.5% Catholicism, 5.6% Methodist/Pietist, 2.0% Non-Denominational, 1.3% Presbyterian-Reformed, 1.1% Episcopalianism/Anglicanism, 1.1% Baptist (2010)

**Economy:** Unemployment rate: 11.5% (February 2012); Total civilian labor force: 17,912 (February 2012); Leading industries: 21.8% accommodation & food services; 19.2% health care and social assistance; 18.6% retail trade (2009); Farms: 243 totaling 50,226 acres (2007); Companies that employ 500 or more persons: 1 (2009); Companies that employ 100 to 499 persons: 12 (2009); Companies that employ less than 100 persons: 1,168 (2009); Black-owned businesses: n/a (2007); Hispanic-owned businesses: n/a (2007); Asian-owned businesses: n/a (2007); Women-owned businesses: 1,361 (2007); Retail sales per capita: $12,343 (2010). Single-family building permits issued: 59 (2011); Multi-family building permits issued: 0 (2011).

**Income:** Per capita income: $24,390 (2006-2010 5-year est.); Median household income: $45,216 (2006-2010 5-year est.); Average household income: $58,895 (2006-2010 5-year est.); Percent of households with income of $100,000 or more: 13.3% (2006-2010 5-year est.); Poverty rate: 12.9% (2006-2010 5-year est.); Bankruptcy rate: 1.95% (2011).

**Education:** Percent of population age 25 and over with: High school diploma (including GED) or higher: 88.7% (2006-2010 5-year est.); Bachelor's degree or higher: 25.5% (2006-2010 5-year est.); Master's degree or higher: 10.5% (2006-2010 5-year est.).

**Housing:** Homeownership rate: 73.7% (2010); Median home value: $148,100 (2006-2010 5-year est.); Median contract rent: $545 per month (2006-2010 5-year est.); Median year structure built: 1955 (2006-2010 5-year est.)

**Health:** Birth rate: 87.8 per 10,000 population (2011); Death rate: 100.0 per 10,000 population (2011); Age-adjusted cancer mortality rate: 198.8 deaths per 100,000 population (2009); Number of physicians: 8.2 per 10,000 population (2008); Hospital beds: 7.9 per 10,000 population (2007); Hospital admissions: 221.9 per 10,000 population (2007).

**Environment:** Air Quality Index: 91.0% good, 7.7% moderate, 1.1% unhealthy for sensitive individuals, 0.3% unhealthy (percent of days in 2010)

**Elections:** 2008 Presidential election results: 55.9% Obama, 42.6% McCain, 0.8% Nader

**National and State Parks:** Wickham Marsh State Game Management Area

**Additional Information Contacts**

Essex County Government . . . . . . . . . . . . . . . . . . . . . . (518) 873-3601
    http://www.co.essex.ny.us
Lake Placid/Essex County Convention & Visitors Bureau . . (518) 523-2445
    http://www.lakeplacid.com
Schroon Lake Area Chamber of Commerce . . . . . . . . . . . (518) 532-7675
    http://www.schroonlakeregion.com

Ticonderoga Area Chamber of Commerce . . . . . . . . . . . . (518) 585-6619
    http://www.ticonderogany.com
Town of Newcomb . . . . . . . . . . . . . . . . . . . . . . . . . . . . (518) 582-3211
    http://www.newcombny.com/theHeartoftheAdirondacks
Town of North Elba . . . . . . . . . . . . . . . . . . . . . . . . . . . (518) 523-9516
    http://www.northelba.org
Town of Westport . . . . . . . . . . . . . . . . . . . . . . . . . . . . (518) 962-4419
    http://www.westportny.net
Westport Chamber of Commerce . . . . . . . . . . . . . . . . . . (518) 962-8383
    http://www.westportny.com

## Essex County Communities

### BLOOMINGDALE (unincorporated postal area)

Zip Code: 12913

Covers a land area of 27.122 square miles and a water area of 2.224 square miles. Located at 44.43° N. Lat; 74.00° W. Long. Elevation is 1,572 feet. Population: 1,157 (2010); Density: 42.7 persons per square mile (2010); Race: 97.3% White, 0.0% Black, 0.0% Asian, 0.4% American Indian/Alaska Native, 0.0% Native Hawaiian/Other Pacific Islander, 2.3% Other, 2.2% Hispanic of any race (2010); Average household size: 2.34 (2010); Median age: 41.3 (2010); Males per 100 females: 102.3 (2010); Homeownership rate: 76.9% (2010)

### CHESTERFIELD (town). Covers a land area of 79.035 square miles and a water area of 26.336 square miles. Located at 44.45° N. Lat; 73.44° W. Long.

**Population:** 2,250 (1990); 2,409 (2000); 2,445 (2010); Density: 30.9 persons per square mile (2010); Race: 98.1% White, 0.2% Black, 0.3% Asian, 0.1% American Indian/Alaska Native, 0.0% Native Hawaiian/Other Pacific Islander, 1.3% Other, 0.6% Hispanic of any race (2010); Average household size: 2.38 (2010); Median age: 45.8 (2010); Males per 100 females: 101.7 (2010); Marriage status: 23.6% never married, 58.7% now married, 6.4% widowed, 11.4% divorced (2006-2010 5-year est.); Foreign born: 2.4% (2006-2010 5-year est.); Ancestry (includes multiple ancestries): 21.6% French, 19.9% Irish, 17.3% English, 12.7% German, 8.3% Italian (2006-2010 5-year est.).

**Economy:** Single-family building permits issued: 5 (2011); Multi-family building permits issued: 0 (2011); Employment by occupation: 7.7% management, 4.5% professional, 15.3% services, 16.6% sales, 3.2% farming, 8.7% construction, 3.0% production (2006-2010 5-year est.).

**Income:** Per capita income: $26,486 (2006-2010 5-year est.); Median household income: $49,470 (2006-2010 5-year est.); Average household income: $61,762 (2006-2010 5-year est.); Percent of households with income of $100,000 or more: 16.3% (2006-2010 5-year est.); Poverty rate: 11.7% (2006-2010 5-year est.).

**Education:** Percent of population age 25 and over with: High school diploma (including GED) or higher: 89.2% (2006-2010 5-year est.); Bachelor's degree or higher: 27.2% (2006-2010 5-year est.); Master's degree or higher: 11.3% (2006-2010 5-year est.).

**Housing:** Homeownership rate: 80.3% (2010); Median home value: $128,100 (2006-2010 5-year est.); Median contract rent: $618 per month (2006-2010 5-year est.); Median year structure built: 1961 (2006-2010 5-year est.).

**Transportation:** Commute to work: 89.2% car, 0.4% public transportation, 2.9% walk, 5.8% work from home (2006-2010 5-year est.); Travel time to work: 22.1% less than 15 minutes, 44.0% 15 to 30 minutes, 15.1% 30 to 45 minutes, 4.6% 45 to 60 minutes, 14.2% 60 minutes or more (2006-2010 5-year est.)

### CROWN POINT (town). Covers a land area of 76.120 square miles and a water area of 5.723 square miles. Located at 43.96° N. Lat; 73.58° W. Long. Elevation is 223 feet.

**History:** The French began building Fort St. Frederic in 1731. In the French and Indian Wars the fort resisted early English attacks but was demolished (1759) before the advance of Jeffrey Amherst. The British began building a new fort, Fort Amherst (renamed Crown Point), in 1759. Early in the Revolution, Crown Point was captured by Seth Warner and the Green Mt. Boys. Abandoned (1777) to Gen. John Burgoyne. Crown Point Reservation, with bathing and fishing, a Museum and ruins of colonial forts, is nearby.

**Population:** 2,048 (1990); 2,119 (2000); 2,024 (2010); Density: 26.6 persons per square mile (2010); Race: 97.7% White, 0.1% Black, 0.9% Asian, 0.0% American Indian/Alaska Native, 0.0% Native Hawaiian/Other Pacific Islander, 1.3% Other, 1.1% Hispanic of any race (2010); Average

household size: 2.43 (2010); Median age: 43.5 (2010); Males per 100 females: 104.0 (2010); Marriage status: 18.6% never married, 67.1% now married, 5.5% widowed, 8.8% divorced (2006-2010 5-year est.); Foreign born: 3.2% (2006-2010 5-year est.); Ancestry (includes multiple ancestries): 36.2% French, 20.6% Irish, 10.8% Italian, 10.5% English, 8.7% German (2006-2010 5-year est.).
**Economy:** Single-family building permits issued: 1 (2011); Multi-family building permits issued: 0 (2011); Employment by occupation: 10.8% management, 0.5% professional, 9.0% services, 10.7% sales, 2.2% farming, 21.5% construction, 10.2% production (2006-2010 5-year est.).
**Income:** Per capita income: $23,981 (2006-2010 5-year est.); Median household income: $53,378 (2006-2010 5-year est.); Average household income: $62,560 (2006-2010 5-year est.); Percent of households with income of $100,000 or more: 8.7% (2006-2010 5-year est.); Poverty rate: 6.5% (2006-2010 5-year est.).
**Education:** Percent of population age 25 and over with: High school diploma (including GED) or higher: 93.6% (2006-2010 5-year est.); Bachelor's degree or higher: 15.9% (2006-2010 5-year est.); Master's degree or higher: 6.4% (2006-2010 5-year est.).

#### School District(s)

Crown Point Central School District (PK-12)
     2009-10 Enrollment: 267 . . . . . . . . . . . . . . . . . . . . . . . . . . (518) 597-4200
**Housing:** Homeownership rate: 78.6% (2010); Median home value: $155,100 (2006-2010 5-year est.); Median contract rent: $452 per month (2006-2010 5-year est.); Median year structure built: 1971 (2006-2010 5-year est.).
**Transportation:** Commute to work: 93.1% car, 1.4% public transportation, 0.9% walk, 3.3% work from home (2006-2010 5-year est.); Travel time to work: 28.5% less than 15 minutes, 34.5% 15 to 30 minutes, 16.6% 30 to 45 minutes, 5.4% 45 to 60 minutes, 15.0% 60 minutes or more (2006-2010 5-year est.)

**ELIZABETHTOWN** (town). County seat. Covers a land area of 81.633 square miles and a water area of 1.476 square miles. Located at 44.19° N. Lat; 73.65° W. Long. Elevation is 564 feet.
**Population:** 1,324 (1990); 1,315 (2000); 1,163 (2010); Density: 14.2 persons per square mile (2010); Race: 97.2% White, 0.4% Black, 0.4% Asian, 0.1% American Indian/Alaska Native, 0.3% Native Hawaiian/Other Pacific Islander, 1.6% Other, 0.6% Hispanic of any race (2010); Average household size: 2.08 (2010); Median age: 52.4 (2010); Males per 100 females: 92.9 (2010); Marriage status: 30.8% never married, 45.3% now married, 14.3% widowed, 9.7% divorced (2006-2010 5-year est.); Foreign born: 3.6% (2006-2010 5-year est.); Ancestry (includes multiple ancestries): 28.2% Irish, 22.3% French, 18.3% German, 9.4% English, 7.5% Polish (2006-2010 5-year est.).
**Economy:** Single-family building permits issued: 2 (2011); Multi-family building permits issued: 0 (2011); Employment by occupation: 9.0% management, 3.6% professional, 14.3% services, 14.3% sales, 1.0% farming, 8.7% construction, 3.6% production (2006-2010 5-year est.).
**Income:** Per capita income: $22,723 (2006-2010 5-year est.); Median household income: $54,702 (2006-2010 5-year est.); Average household income: $61,833 (2006-2010 5-year est.); Percent of households with income of $100,000 or more: 15.0% (2006-2010 5-year est.); Poverty rate: 13.0% (2006-2010 5-year est.).
**Education:** Percent of population age 25 and over with: High school diploma (including GED) or higher: 86.0% (2006-2010 5-year est.); Bachelor's degree or higher: 19.9% (2006-2010 5-year est.); Master's degree or higher: 8.3% (2006-2010 5-year est.).

#### School District(s)

Elizabethtown-Lewis Central School District (KG-12)
     2009-10 Enrollment: 310 . . . . . . . . . . . . . . . . . . . . . . . . . . (518) 873-6371
**Housing:** Homeownership rate: 71.2% (2010); Median home value: $147,900 (2006-2010 5-year est.); Median contract rent: $485 per month (2006-2010 5-year est.); Median year structure built: 1949 (2006-2010 5-year est.).
**Hospitals:** Elizabethtown Community Hospital (25 beds)
**Newspapers:** Adirondack Journal (Community news; Circulation 12,600); North Countryman (Community news; Circulation 3,500); Rouses Point North Countryman (Community news; Circulation 3,500); Times Of Ti (Local news; Circulation 11,300); Tri-Lakes Free Trader (Community news; Circulation 14,000); Valley News (Local news; Circulation 3,058)
**Transportation:** Commute to work: 76.7% car, 0.0% public transportation, 8.1% walk, 8.6% work from home (2006-2010 5-year est.); Travel time to work: 62.5% less than 15 minutes, 23.8% 15 to 30 minutes, 5.7% 30 to 45

minutes, 6.8% 45 to 60 minutes, 1.2% 60 minutes or more (2006-2010 5-year est.)

**ELIZABETHTOWN** (CDP). Covers a land area of 3.307 square miles and a water area of 0.004 square miles. Located at 44.22° N. Lat; 73.58° W. Long. Elevation is 564 feet.
**Population:** n/a (1990); n/a (2000); 754 (2010); Density: 228.0 persons per square mile (2010); Race: 96.4% White, 0.5% Black, 0.4% Asian, 0.0% American Indian/Alaska Native, 0.4% Native Hawaiian/Other Pacific Islander, 2.3% Other, 0.3% Hispanic of any race (2010); Average household size: 1.97 (2010); Median age: 54.1 (2010); Males per 100 females: 87.1 (2010); Marriage status: 32.8% never married, 35.2% now married, 18.6% widowed, 13.5% divorced (2006-2010 5-year est.); Foreign born: 2.8% (2006-2010 5-year est.); Ancestry (includes multiple ancestries): 26.1% Irish, 22.8% German, 17.9% French, 9.6% Polish, 7.1% English (2006-2010 5-year est.).
**Economy:** Employment by occupation: 14.6% management, 4.1% professional, 17.4% services, 11.3% sales, 1.9% farming, 7.4% construction, 5.2% production (2006-2010 5-year est.).
**Income:** Per capita income: $19,576 (2006-2010 5-year est.); Median household income: $50,078 (2006-2010 5-year est.); Average household income: $55,142 (2006-2010 5-year est.); Percent of households with income of $100,000 or more: 11.1% (2006-2010 5-year est.); Poverty rate: 16.0% (2006-2010 5-year est.).
**Education:** Percent of population age 25 and over with: High school diploma (including GED) or higher: 87.3% (2006-2010 5-year est.); Bachelor's degree or higher: 19.4% (2006-2010 5-year est.); Master's degree or higher: 7.6% (2006-2010 5-year est.).

#### School District(s)

Elizabethtown-Lewis Central School District (KG-12)
     2009-10 Enrollment: 310 . . . . . . . . . . . . . . . . . . . . . . . . . . (518) 873-6371
**Housing:** Homeownership rate: 63.7% (2010); Median home value: $108,900 (2006-2010 5-year est.); Median contract rent: $458 per month (2006-2010 5-year est.); Median year structure built: before 1940 (2006-2010 5-year est.).
**Transportation:** Commute to work: 72.7% car, 0.0% public transportation, 15.2% walk, 10.3% work from home (2006-2010 5-year est.); Travel time to work: 66.3% less than 15 minutes, 26.1% 15 to 30 minutes, 3.9% 30 to 45 minutes, 3.6% 45 to 60 minutes, 0.0% 60 minutes or more (2006-2010 5-year est.)

**ESSEX** (town). Covers a land area of 31.630 square miles and a water area of 5.969 square miles. Located at 44.28° N. Lat; 73.39° W. Long. Elevation is 125 feet.
**Population:** 702 (1990); 713 (2000); 671 (2010); Density: 21.2 persons per square mile (2010); Race: 98.8% White, 0.0% Black, 0.3% Asian, 0.0% American Indian/Alaska Native, 0.0% Native Hawaiian/Other Pacific Islander, 0.9% Other, 0.7% Hispanic of any race (2010); Average household size: 2.16 (2010); Median age: 49.8 (2010); Males per 100 females: 104.0 (2010); Marriage status: 23.2% never married, 57.1% now married, 10.5% widowed, 9.2% divorced (2006-2010 5-year est.); Foreign born: 2.6% (2006-2010 5-year est.); Ancestry (includes multiple ancestries): 28.9% French, 20.4% German, 17.5% Irish, 17.0% English, 11.9% Italian (2006-2010 5-year est.).
**Economy:** Single-family building permits issued: 0 (2011); Multi-family building permits issued: 0 (2011); Employment by occupation: 15.8% management, 3.9% professional, 15.0% services, 15.0% sales, 6.4% farming, 19.2% construction, 7.5% production (2006-2010 5-year est.).
**Income:** Per capita income: $30,711 (2006-2010 5-year est.); Median household income: $51,563 (2006-2010 5-year est.); Average household income: $64,641 (2006-2010 5-year est.); Percent of households with income of $100,000 or more: 20.3% (2006-2010 5-year est.); Poverty rate: 7.1% (2006-2010 5-year est.).
**Education:** Percent of population age 25 and over with: High school diploma (including GED) or higher: 89.9% (2006-2010 5-year est.); Bachelor's degree or higher: 41.5% (2006-2010 5-year est.); Master's degree or higher: 18.6% (2006-2010 5-year est.).
**Housing:** Homeownership rate: 83.9% (2010); Median home value: $172,000 (2006-2010 5-year est.); Median contract rent: $523 per month (2006-2010 5-year est.); Median year structure built: before 1940 (2006-2010 5-year est.).
**Transportation:** Commute to work: 84.9% car, 0.0% public transportation, 1.1% walk, 6.7% work from home (2006-2010 5-year est.); Travel time to work: 36.6% less than 15 minutes, 31.8% 15 to 30 minutes, 18.0% 30 to 45

minutes, 7.8% 45 to 60 minutes, 5.7% 60 minutes or more (2006-2010 5-year est.).

**JAY** (town). Covers a land area of 67.687 square miles and a water area of 0.421 square miles. Located at 44.37° N. Lat; 73.69° W. Long. Elevation is 709 feet.
**Population:** 2,276 (1990); 2,306 (2000); 2,506 (2010); Density: 37.0 persons per square mile (2010); Race: 97.9% White, 0.5% Black, 0.1% Asian, 0.3% American Indian/Alaska Native, 0.0% Native Hawaiian/Other Pacific Islander, 1.2% Other, 1.2% Hispanic of any race (2010); Average household size: 2.34 (2010); Median age: 45.6 (2010); Males per 100 females: 98.4 (2010); Marriage status: 21.4% never married, 58.4% now married, 7.2% widowed, 13.1% divorced (2006-2010 5-year est.); Foreign born: 1.7% (2006-2010 5-year est.); Ancestry (includes multiple ancestries): 32.5% French, 23.7% Irish, 11.8% German, 10.9% English, 4.0% Scottish (2006-2010 5-year est.).
**Economy:** Single-family building permits issued: 4 (2011); Multi-family building permits issued: 0 (2011); Employment by occupation: 7.4% management, 3.5% professional, 20.9% services, 18.1% sales, 4.2% farming, 15.2% construction, 5.8% production (2006-2010 5-year est.).
**Income:** Per capita income: $31,409 (2006-2010 5-year est.); Median household income: $51,623 (2006-2010 5-year est.); Average household income: $73,494 (2006-2010 5-year est.); Percent of households with income of $100,000 or more: 11.6% (2006-2010 5-year est.); Poverty rate: 6.1% (2006-2010 5-year est.).
**Education:** Percent of population age 25 and over with: High school diploma (including GED) or higher: 91.9% (2006-2010 5-year est.); Bachelor's degree or higher: 28.2% (2006-2010 5-year est.); Master's degree or higher: 9.2% (2006-2010 5-year est.).
**Housing:** Homeownership rate: 80.1% (2010); Median home value: $138,700 (2006-2010 5-year est.); Median contract rent: $494 per month (2006-2010 5-year est.); Median year structure built: 1965 (2006-2010 5-year est.).
**Transportation:** Commute to work: 83.9% car, 0.0% public transportation, 2.2% walk, 12.1% work from home (2006-2010 5-year est.); Travel time to work: 18.1% less than 15 minutes, 25.3% 15 to 30 minutes, 41.0% 30 to 45 minutes, 10.6% 45 to 60 minutes, 5.0% 60 minutes or more (2006-2010 5-year est.).

**KEENE** (town). Covers a land area of 155.940 square miles and a water area of 0.676 square miles. Located at 44.12° N. Lat; 73.88° W. Long. Elevation is 840 feet.
**Population:** 908 (1990); 1,063 (2000); 1,105 (2010); Density: 7.1 persons per square mile (2010); Race: 97.6% White, 0.2% Black, 0.7% Asian, 0.2% American Indian/Alaska Native, 0.0% Native Hawaiian/Other Pacific Islander, 1.3% Other, 0.2% Hispanic of any race (2010); Average household size: 2.10 (2010); Median age: 51.1 (2010); Males per 100 females: 90.8 (2010); Marriage status: 20.7% never married, 62.0% now married, 7.4% widowed, 9.9% divorced (2006-2010 5-year est.); Foreign born: 9.8% (2006-2010 5-year est.); Ancestry (includes multiple ancestries): 26.7% English, 20.5% German, 15.4% French, 11.8% Irish, 7.9% Italian (2006-2010 5-year est.).
**Economy:** Single-family building permits issued: 9 (2011); Multi-family building permits issued: 0 (2011); Employment by occupation: 12.7% management, 2.9% professional, 12.2% services, 12.7% sales, 3.1% farming, 10.0% construction, 2.9% production (2006-2010 5-year est.).
**Income:** Per capita income: $30,391 (2006-2010 5-year est.); Median household income: $46,250 (2006-2010 5-year est.); Average household income: $60,600 (2006-2010 5-year est.); Percent of households with income of $100,000 or more: 18.5% (2006-2010 5-year est.); Poverty rate: 13.2% (2006-2010 5-year est.).
**Education:** Percent of population age 25 and over with: High school diploma (including GED) or higher: 95.7% (2006-2010 5-year est.); Bachelor's degree or higher: 47.6% (2006-2010 5-year est.); Master's degree or higher: 24.5% (2006-2010 5-year est.).
**Housing:** Homeownership rate: 79.6% (2010); Median home value: $298,600 (2006-2010 5-year est.); Median contract rent: $665 per month (2006-2010 5-year est.); Median year structure built: 1954 (2006-2010 5-year est.).
**Transportation:** Commute to work: 72.5% car, 2.5% public transportation, 6.2% walk, 15.2% work from home (2006-2010 5-year est.); Travel time to work: 51.2% less than 15 minutes, 34.1% 15 to 30 minutes, 8.4% 30 to 45 minutes, 0.0% 45 to 60 minutes, 6.3% 60 minutes or more (2006-2010 5-year est.).

**KEENE VALLEY** (unincorporated postal area)
Zip Code: 12943
Covers a land area of 103.005 square miles and a water area of 0.553 square miles. Located at 44.12° N. Lat; 73.88° W. Long. Elevation is 1,024 feet. Population: 459 (2010); Density: 4.5 persons per square mile (2010); Race: 96.7% White, 0.0% Black, 0.9% Asian, 0.0% American Indian/Alaska Native, 0.0% Native Hawaiian/Other Pacific Islander, 2.4% Other, 0.2% Hispanic of any race (2010); Average household size: 2.00 (2010); Median age: 55.1 (2010); Males per 100 females: 92.1 (2010); Homeownership rate: 77.3% (2010)

**LAKE PLACID** (village). Covers a land area of 1.371 square miles and a water area of 0.165 square miles. Located at 44.28° N. Lat; 73.98° W. Long. Elevation is 1,801 feet.
**History:** Winter Olympics (1932, 1980) and the World Bobsled Championships (1969) were held here. The farm and burial place of the abolitionist John Brown are nearby. Terminus of 133-mile Northville—Lake Placid trail connecting Adirondack foothills and High Peaks region. Settled 1850, Incorporated 1900.
**Population:** 2,485 (1990); 2,638 (2000); 2,521 (2010); Density: 1,838.7 persons per square mile (2010); Race: 95.8% White, 0.9% Black, 1.8% Asian, 0.3% American Indian/Alaska Native, 0.1% Native Hawaiian/Other Pacific Islander, 1.1% Other, 1.3% Hispanic of any race (2010); Average household size: 1.91 (2010); Median age: 41.5 (2010); Males per 100 females: 99.6 (2010); Marriage status: 29.1% never married, 39.8% now married, 8.1% widowed, 23.0% divorced (2006-2010 5-year est.); Foreign born: 8.3% (2006-2010 5-year est.); Ancestry (includes multiple ancestries): 15.8% Irish, 13.1% German, 12.0% French, 10.6% American, 9.9% English (2006-2010 5-year est.).
**Economy:** Single-family building permits issued: 1 (2011); Multi-family building permits issued: 0 (2011); Employment by occupation: 12.8% management, 0.8% professional, 14.0% services, 13.5% sales, 2.9% farming, 5.0% construction, 1.2% production (2006-2010 5-year est.).
**Income:** Per capita income: $24,181 (2006-2010 5-year est.); Median household income: $41,569 (2006-2010 5-year est.); Average household income: $48,499 (2006-2010 5-year est.); Percent of households with income of $100,000 or more: 6.1% (2006-2010 5-year est.); Poverty rate: 12.3% (2006-2010 5-year est.).
**Taxes:** Total city taxes per capita: $1,286 (2009); City property taxes per capita: $1,212 (2009).
**Education:** Percent of population age 25 and over with: High school diploma (including GED) or higher: 92.0% (2006-2010 5-year est.); Bachelor's degree or higher: 32.1% (2006-2010 5-year est.); Master's degree or higher: 10.0% (2006-2010 5-year est.).

**School District(s)**
Lake Placid Central School District (KG-12)
    2009-10 Enrollment: 714 . . . . . . . . . . . . . . . . (518) 523-2475
**Housing:** Homeownership rate: 44.1% (2010); Median home value: $238,900 (2006-2010 5-year est.); Median contract rent: $614 per month (2006-2010 5-year est.); Median year structure built: 1943 (2006-2010 5-year est.).
**Safety:** Violent crime rate: 0.0 per 10,000 population; Property crime rate: 263.0 per 10,000 population (2010).
**Newspapers:** Lake Placid News (Community news; Circulation 4,500); Press-Republican - Lake Placid Bureau (Local news)
**Transportation:** Commute to work: 67.4% car, 0.0% public transportation, 25.2% walk, 6.7% work from home (2006-2010 5-year est.); Travel time to work: 75.8% less than 15 minutes, 14.9% 15 to 30 minutes, 8.2% 30 to 45 minutes, 1.1% 45 to 60 minutes, 0.0% 60 minutes or more (2006-2010 5-year est.); Amtrak: bus service available.
**Additional Information Contacts**
Lake Placid/Essex County Convention & Visitors Bureau . . (518) 523-2445
    http://www.lakeplacid.com

**LEWIS** (town). Covers a land area of 84.789 square miles and a water area of 0.210 square miles. Located at 44.31° N. Lat; 73.58° W. Long. Elevation is 666 feet.
**Population:** 1,009 (1990); 1,200 (2000); 1,382 (2010); Density: 16.3 persons per square mile (2010); Race: 96.3% White, 2.3% Black, 0.1% Asian, 0.3% American Indian/Alaska Native, 0.0% Native Hawaiian/Other Pacific Islander, 1.0% Other, 0.9% Hispanic of any race (2010); Average household size: 2.42 (2010); Median age: 44.0 (2010); Males per 100 females: 107.2 (2010); Marriage status: 19.8% never married, 64.8% now married, 5.5% widowed, 9.9% divorced (2006-2010 5-year est.); Foreign born: 1.7% (2006-2010 5-year est.); Ancestry (includes multiple

ancestries): 32.1% Irish, 23.7% English, 18.0% German, 14.0% French, 5.4% Italian (2006-2010 5-year est.).

**Economy:** Single-family building permits issued: 1 (2011); Multi-family building permits issued: 0 (2011); Employment by occupation: 15.6% management, 1.9% professional, 9.8% services, 12.5% sales, 2.4% farming, 22.9% construction, 6.3% production (2006-2010 5-year est.).

**Income:** Per capita income: $24,041 (2006-2010 5-year est.); Median household income: $44,028 (2006-2010 5-year est.); Average household income: $61,915 (2006-2010 5-year est.); Percent of households with income of $100,000 or more: 11.1% (2006-2010 5-year est.); Poverty rate: 14.2% (2006-2010 5-year est.).

**Education:** Percent of population age 25 and over with: High school diploma (including GED) or higher: 82.0% (2006-2010 5-year est.); Bachelor's degree or higher: 15.4% (2006-2010 5-year est.); Master's degree or higher: 5.9% (2006-2010 5-year est.).

**Housing:** Homeownership rate: 80.7% (2010); Median home value: $119,000 (2006-2010 5-year est.); Median contract rent: $575 per month (2006-2010 5-year est.); Median year structure built: 1970 (2006-2010 5-year est.).

**Transportation:** Commute to work: 86.7% car, 0.0% public transportation, 3.9% walk, 4.6% work from home (2006-2010 5-year est.); Travel time to work: 43.8% less than 15 minutes, 25.6% 15 to 30 minutes, 19.7% 30 to 45 minutes, 5.9% 45 to 60 minutes, 5.0% 60 minutes or more (2006-2010 5-year est.)

**MINERVA** (town). Covers a land area of 156.765 square miles and a water area of 3.508 square miles. Located at 43.85° N. Lat; 74.11° W. Long. Elevation is 1,388 feet.

**Population:** 779 (1990); 796 (2000); 809 (2010); Density: 5.2 persons per square mile (2010); Race: 95.9% White, 0.1% Black, 1.1% Asian, 0.2% American Indian/Alaska Native, 0.0% Native Hawaiian/Other Pacific Islander, 2.7% Other, 0.2% Hispanic of any race (2010); Average household size: 2.34 (2010); Median age: 46.1 (2010); Males per 100 females: 104.8 (2010); Marriage status: 16.2% never married, 69.0% now married, 7.1% widowed, 7.7% divorced (2006-2010 5-year est.); Foreign born: 1.2% (2006-2010 5-year est.); Ancestry (includes multiple ancestries): 35.2% Irish, 19.6% English, 19.2% French, 16.3% German, 8.7% Italian (2006-2010 5-year est.).

**Economy:** Single-family building permits issued: 4 (2011); Multi-family building permits issued: 0 (2011); Employment by occupation: 6.9% management, 1.8% professional, 13.8% services, 11.0% sales, 2.8% farming, 23.9% construction, 11.0% production (2006-2010 5-year est.).

**Income:** Per capita income: $22,623 (2006-2010 5-year est.); Median household income: $39,688 (2006-2010 5-year est.); Average household income: $50,852 (2006-2010 5-year est.); Percent of households with income of $100,000 or more: 8.2% (2006-2010 5-year est.); Poverty rate: 14.1% (2006-2010 5-year est.).

**Education:** Percent of population age 25 and over with: High school diploma (including GED) or higher: 87.7% (2006-2010 5-year est.); Bachelor's degree or higher: 15.7% (2006-2010 5-year est.); Master's degree or higher: 6.5% (2006-2010 5-year est.).

**Housing:** Homeownership rate: 86.0% (2010); Median home value: $147,500 (2006-2010 5-year est.); Median contract rent: $600 per month (2006-2010 5-year est.); Median year structure built: 1956 (2006-2010 5-year est.).

**Transportation:** Commute to work: 93.8% car, 0.0% public transportation, 2.9% walk, 3.3% work from home (2006-2010 5-year est.); Travel time to work: 40.1% less than 15 minutes, 20.3% 15 to 30 minutes, 24.3% 30 to 45 minutes, 8.4% 45 to 60 minutes, 6.9% 60 minutes or more (2006-2010 5-year est.)

**MINEVILLE** (CDP). Covers a land area of 3.702 square miles and a water area of 0.006 square miles. Located at 44.09° N. Lat; 73.52° W. Long. Elevation is 1,296 feet.

**Population:** n/a (1990); n/a (2000); 1,269 (2010); Density: 342.8 persons per square mile (2010); Race: 92.4% White, 5.2% Black, 0.3% Asian, 0.2% American Indian/Alaska Native, 0.0% Native Hawaiian/Other Pacific Islander, 1.9% Other, 2.2% Hispanic of any race (2010); Average household size: 2.33 (2010); Median age: 36.9 (2010); Males per 100 females: 111.9 (2010); Marriage status: 39.2% never married, 46.3% now married, 8.5% widowed, 6.0% divorced (2006-2010 5-year est.); Foreign born: 1.9% (2006-2010 5-year est.); Ancestry (includes multiple ancestries): 23.5% Italian, 18.4% Irish, 9.6% French, 9.3% German, 8.9% Swedish (2006-2010 5-year est.).

**Economy:** Employment by occupation: 0.0% management, 0.0% professional, 17.9% services, 13.8% sales, 0.0% farming, 21.2% construction, 10.0% production (2006-2010 5-year est.).

**Income:** Per capita income: $15,674 (2006-2010 5-year est.); Median household income: $38,971 (2006-2010 5-year est.); Average household income: $48,733 (2006-2010 5-year est.); Percent of households with income of $100,000 or more: 8.4% (2006-2010 5-year est.); Poverty rate: 32.8% (2006-2010 5-year est.).

**Education:** Percent of population age 25 and over with: High school diploma (including GED) or higher: 88.1% (2006-2010 5-year est.); Bachelor's degree or higher: 12.3% (2006-2010 5-year est.); Master's degree or higher: 9.1% (2006-2010 5-year est.).

**Housing:** Homeownership rate: 80.1% (2010); Median home value: $81,400 (2006-2010 5-year est.); Median contract rent: $608 per month (2006-2010 5-year est.); Median year structure built: before 1940 (2006-2010 5-year est.).

**Transportation:** Commute to work: 100.0% car, 0.0% public transportation, 0.0% walk, 0.0% work from home (2006-2010 5-year est.); Travel time to work: 22.6% less than 15 minutes, 27.6% 15 to 30 minutes, 42.5% 30 to 45 minutes, 0.0% 45 to 60 minutes, 7.4% 60 minutes or more (2006-2010 5-year est.)

**MORIAH** (town). Covers a land area of 64.490 square miles and a water area of 6.619 square miles. Located at 44.05° N. Lat; 73.53° W. Long. Elevation is 850 feet.

**Population:** 4,808 (1990); 4,879 (2000); 4,798 (2010); Density: 74.4 persons per square mile (2010); Race: 96.4% White, 1.7% Black, 0.3% Asian, 0.2% American Indian/Alaska Native, 0.0% Native Hawaiian/Other Pacific Islander, 1.4% Other, 2.0% Hispanic of any race (2010); Average household size: 2.35 (2010); Median age: 41.7 (2010); Males per 100 females: 105.3 (2010); Marriage status: 26.5% never married, 55.8% now married, 6.7% widowed, 11.1% divorced (2006-2010 5-year est.); Foreign born: 2.7% (2006-2010 5-year est.); Ancestry (includes multiple ancestries): 26.0% French, 23.3% Irish, 15.5% Italian, 10.4% German, 9.7% English (2006-2010 5-year est.).

**Economy:** Single-family building permits issued: 3 (2011); Multi-family building permits issued: 0 (2011); Employment by occupation: 5.4% management, 1.7% professional, 15.9% services, 9.0% sales, 1.0% farming, 14.5% construction, 6.6% production (2006-2010 5-year est.).

**Income:** Per capita income: $21,198 (2006-2010 5-year est.); Median household income: $40,169 (2006-2010 5-year est.); Average household income: $51,922 (2006-2010 5-year est.); Percent of households with income of $100,000 or more: 9.9% (2006-2010 5-year est.); Poverty rate: 12.8% (2006-2010 5-year est.).

**Education:** Percent of population age 25 and over with: High school diploma (including GED) or higher: 89.1% (2006-2010 5-year est.); Bachelor's degree or higher: 15.8% (2006-2010 5-year est.); Master's degree or higher: 8.6% (2006-2010 5-year est.).

**Housing:** Homeownership rate: 77.3% (2010); Median home value: $96,300 (2006-2010 5-year est.); Median contract rent: $584 per month (2006-2010 5-year est.); Median year structure built: 1941 (2006-2010 5-year est.).

**Safety:** Violent crime rate: 14.7 per 10,000 population; Property crime rate: 20.6 per 10,000 population (2010).

**Transportation:** Commute to work: 93.2% car, 0.3% public transportation, 1.0% walk, 2.1% work from home (2006-2010 5-year est.); Travel time to work: 32.4% less than 15 minutes, 21.1% 15 to 30 minutes, 25.6% 30 to 45 minutes, 4.9% 45 to 60 minutes, 15.9% 60 minutes or more (2006-2010 5-year est.)

**MORIAH CENTER** (unincorporated postal area)
Zip Code: 12961

Covers a land area of 4.000 square miles and a water area of 0 square miles. Located at 44.05° N. Lat; 73.54° W. Long. Elevation is 791 feet. Population: 180 (2010); Density: 45.0 persons per square mile (2010); Race: 99.4% White, 0.0% Black, 0.0% Asian, 0.0% American Indian/Alaska Native, 0.0% Native Hawaiian/Other Pacific Islander, 0.6% Other, 2.2% Hispanic of any race (2010); Average household size: 2.54 (2010); Median age: 47.3 (2010); Males per 100 females: 133.8 (2010); Homeownership rate: 91.5% (2010)

**NEW RUSSIA** (unincorporated postal area)
Zip Code: 12964

Covers a land area of 34.498 square miles and a water area of 0.709 square miles. Located at 44.12° N. Lat; 73.62° W. Long. Elevation is 627 feet. Population: 161 (2010); Density: 4.7 persons per square mile (2010); Race: 99.4% White, 0.6% Black, 0.0% Asian, 0.0% American Indian/Alaska Native, 0.0% Native Hawaiian/Other Pacific Islander, 0.0% Other, 0.0% Hispanic of any race (2010); Average household size: 2.37 (2010); Median age: 48.9 (2010); Males per 100 females: 91.7 (2010); Homeownership rate: 80.9% (2010)

## NEWCOMB (town).

**NEWCOMB** (town). Covers a land area of 226.271 square miles and a water area of 6.897 square miles. Located at 44.00° N. Lat; 74.09° W. Long. Elevation is 1,555 feet.
**Population:** 544 (1990); 481 (2000); 436 (2010); Density: 1.9 persons per square mile (2010); Race: 98.6% White, 0.0% Black, 0.5% Asian, 0.2% American Indian/Alaska Native, 0.0% Native Hawaiian/Other Pacific Islander, 0.7% Other, 1.1% Hispanic of any race (2010); Average household size: 2.08 (2010); Median age: 55.3 (2010); Males per 100 females: 102.8 (2010); Marriage status: 14.8% never married, 70.5% now married, 10.0% widowed, 4.6% divorced (2006-2010 5-year est.); Foreign born: 1.4% (2006-2010 5-year est.); Ancestry (includes multiple ancestries): 31.6% Irish, 22.9% English, 14.6% French, 12.3% German, 11.1% Polish (2006-2010 5-year est.).
**Economy:** Single-family building permits issued: 0 (2011); Multi-family building permits issued: 0 (2011); Employment by occupation: 4.9% management, 2.7% professional, 15.2% services, 15.2% sales, 8.1% farming, 7.6% construction, 4.5% production (2006-2010 5-year est.).
**Income:** Per capita income: $24,887 (2006-2010 5-year est.); Median household income: $50,893 (2006-2010 5-year est.); Average household income: $53,584 (2006-2010 5-year est.); Percent of households with income of $100,000 or more: 9.0% (2006-2010 5-year est.); Poverty rate: 6.1% (2006-2010 5-year est.).
**Education:** Percent of population age 25 and over with: High school diploma (including GED) or higher: 85.0% (2006-2010 5-year est.); Bachelor's degree or higher: 26.5% (2006-2010 5-year est.); Master's degree or higher: 15.5% (2006-2010 5-year est.).
### School District(s)
Newcomb Central School District (PK-12)
    2009-10 Enrollment: 82 . . . . . . . . . . . . . . . . . . . . (518) 582-3341
**Housing:** Homeownership rate: 88.4% (2010); Median home value: $148,100 (2006-2010 5-year est.); Median contract rent: $469 per month (2006-2010 5-year est.); Median year structure built: 1961 (2006-2010 5-year est.).
**Transportation:** Commute to work: 93.6% car, 0.0% public transportation, 2.3% walk, 2.3% work from home (2006-2010 5-year est.); Travel time to work: 36.3% less than 15 minutes, 25.6% 15 to 30 minutes, 16.3% 30 to 45 minutes, 8.4% 45 to 60 minutes, 13.5% 60 minutes or more (2006-2010 5-year est.)
**Additional Information Contacts**
Town of Newcomb . . . . . . . . . . . . . . . . . . . . . . . . (518) 582-3211
    http://www.newcombny.com/theHeartoftheAdirondacks

## NORTH ELBA (town).

**NORTH ELBA** (town). Covers a land area of 151.653 square miles and a water area of 4.736 square miles. Located at 44.20° N. Lat; 74.04° W. Long. Elevation is 1,965 feet.
**History:** Here are the farm, home (now a museum), and grave of John Brown.
**Population:** 7,871 (1990); 8,661 (2000); 8,957 (2010); Density: 59.1 persons per square mile (2010); Race: 83.9% White, 9.9% Black, 1.3% Asian, 0.6% American Indian/Alaska Native, 0.1% Native Hawaiian/Other Pacific Islander, 4.2% Other, 7.3% Hispanic of any race (2010); Average household size: 2.05 (2010); Median age: 39.7 (2010); Males per 100 females: 139.9 (2010); Marriage status: 39.4% never married, 43.8% now married, 5.0% widowed, 11.7% divorced (2006-2010 5-year est.); Foreign born: 9.2% (2006-2010 5-year est.); Ancestry (includes multiple ancestries): 19.5% Irish, 12.6% German, 12.4% French, 9.2% English, 7.6% Italian (2006-2010 5-year est.).
**Economy:** Single-family building permits issued: 4 (2011); Multi-family building permits issued: 0 (2011); Employment by occupation: 12.2% management, 1.0% professional, 11.1% services, 14.0% sales, 2.3% farming, 10.3% construction, 5.4% production (2006-2010 5-year est.).
**Income:** Per capita income: $24,121 (2006-2010 5-year est.); Median household income: $47,743 (2006-2010 5-year est.); Average household income: $65,654 (2006-2010 5-year est.); Percent of households with income of $100,000 or more: 16.1% (2006-2010 5-year est.); Poverty rate: 13.2% (2006-2010 5-year est.).
**Education:** Percent of population age 25 and over with: High school diploma (including GED) or higher: 87.7% (2006-2010 5-year est.);

Bachelor's degree or higher: 29.4% (2006-2010 5-year est.); Master's degree or higher: 11.8% (2006-2010 5-year est.).
**Housing:** Homeownership rate: 58.4% (2010); Median home value: $236,500 (2006-2010 5-year est.); Median contract rent: $610 per month (2006-2010 5-year est.); Median year structure built: 1954 (2006-2010 5-year est.).
**Transportation:** Commute to work: 77.0% car, 0.5% public transportation, 12.8% walk, 5.6% work from home (2006-2010 5-year est.); Travel time to work: 68.2% less than 15 minutes, 20.6% 15 to 30 minutes, 9.7% 30 to 45 minutes, 0.7% 45 to 60 minutes, 0.8% 60 minutes or more (2006-2010 5-year est.)
**Additional Information Contacts**
Town of North Elba . . . . . . . . . . . . . . . . . . . . . . . (518) 523-9516
    http://www.northelba.org

## NORTH HUDSON (town).

**NORTH HUDSON** (town). Covers a land area of 181.452 square miles and a water area of 3.217 square miles. Located at 44.02° N. Lat; 73.75° W. Long. Elevation is 883 feet.
**Population:** 256 (1990); 266 (2000); 240 (2010); Density: 1.3 persons per square mile (2010); Race: 99.2% White, 0.0% Black, 0.4% Asian, 0.0% American Indian/Alaska Native, 0.0% Native Hawaiian/Other Pacific Islander, 0.4% Other, 1.3% Hispanic of any race (2010); Average household size: 2.38 (2010); Median age: 48.7 (2010); Males per 100 females: 95.1 (2010); Marriage status: 25.5% never married, 53.9% now married, 13.9% widowed, 6.7% divorced (2006-2010 5-year est.); Foreign born: 2.0% (2006-2010 5-year est.); Ancestry (includes multiple ancestries): 30.4% French, 24.5% Irish, 21.1% English, 15.2% German, 11.8% Italian (2006-2010 5-year est.).
**Economy:** Single-family building permits issued: 2 (2011); Multi-family building permits issued: 0 (2011); Employment by occupation: 13.4% management, 0.0% professional, 2.1% services, 11.3% sales, 0.0% farming, 11.3% construction, 6.2% production (2006-2010 5-year est.).
**Income:** Per capita income: $24,836 (2006-2010 5-year est.); Median household income: $47,292 (2006-2010 5-year est.); Average household income: $57,404 (2006-2010 5-year est.); Percent of households with income of $100,000 or more: 4.4% (2006-2010 5-year est.); Poverty rate: 16.7% (2006-2010 5-year est.).
**Education:** Percent of population age 25 and over with: High school diploma (including GED) or higher: 85.4% (2006-2010 5-year est.); Bachelor's degree or higher: 22.2% (2006-2010 5-year est.); Master's degree or higher: 9.0% (2006-2010 5-year est.).
**Housing:** Homeownership rate: 89.1% (2010); Median home value: $139,800 (2006-2010 5-year est.); Median contract rent: <$101 per month (2006-2010 5-year est.); Median year structure built: 1962 (2006-2010 5-year est.).
**Transportation:** Commute to work: 95.7% car, 0.0% public transportation, 0.0% walk, 0.0% work from home (2006-2010 5-year est.); Travel time to work: 21.3% less than 15 minutes, 37.2% 15 to 30 minutes, 16.0% 30 to 45 minutes, 18.1% 45 to 60 minutes, 7.4% 60 minutes or more (2006-2010 5-year est.)

## OLMSTEDVILLE (unincorporated postal area)

**OLMSTEDVILLE** (unincorporated postal area)
Zip Code: 12857
    Covers a land area of 42.932 square miles and a water area of 0.550 square miles. Located at 43.81° N. Lat; 73.89° W. Long. Elevation is 1,181 feet. Population: 498 (2010); Density: 11.6 persons per square mile (2010); Race: 96.6% White, 0.2% Black, 1.2% Asian, 0.4% American Indian/Alaska Native, 0.0% Native Hawaiian/Other Pacific Islander, 1.6% Other, 0.2% Hispanic of any race (2010); Average household size: 2.28 (2010); Median age: 46.9 (2010); Males per 100 females: 100.8 (2010); Homeownership rate: 89.9% (2010)

## PARADOX (unincorporated postal area)

**PARADOX** (unincorporated postal area)
Zip Code: 12858
    Covers a land area of 9.785 square miles and a water area of 1.447 square miles. Located at 43.90° N. Lat; 73.67° W. Long. Elevation is 873 feet. Population: 59 (2010); Density: 6.0 persons per square mile (2010); Race: 100.0% White, 0.0% Black, 0.0% Asian, 0.0% American Indian/Alaska Native, 0.0% Native Hawaiian/Other Pacific Islander, 0.0% Other, 0.0% Hispanic of any race (2010); Average household size: 2.11 (2010); Median age: 56.8 (2010); Males per 100 females: 73.5 (2010); Homeownership rate: 100.0% (2010)

## PORT HENRY (village).
Covers a land area of 1.176 square miles and a water area of 0.299 square miles. Located at 44.04° N. Lat; 73.46° W. Long. Elevation is 243 feet.

**History:** Incorporated 1869.

**Population:** 1,263 (1990); 1,152 (2000); 1,194 (2010); Density: 1,014.8 persons per square mile (2010); Race: 97.9% White, 0.3% Black, 0.3% Asian, 0.0% American Indian/Alaska Native, 0.0% Native Hawaiian/Other Pacific Islander, 1.5% Other, 2.9% Hispanic of any race (2010); Average household size: 2.22 (2010); Median age: 42.0 (2010); Males per 100 females: 98.7 (2010); Marriage status: 28.5% never married, 53.8% now married, 5.6% widowed, 12.2% divorced (2006-2010 5-year est.); Foreign born: 3.8% (2006-2010 5-year est.); Ancestry (includes multiple ancestries): 20.5% French, 19.4% Irish, 13.2% German, 13.0% Italian, 11.9% English (2006-2010 5-year est.).

**Economy:** Single-family building permits issued: 0 (2011); Multi-family building permits issued: 0 (2011); Employment by occupation: 10.7% management, 3.9% professional, 17.7% services, 9.1% sales, 1.5% farming, 8.6% construction, 5.4% production (2006-2010 5-year est.).

**Income:** Per capita income: $24,232 (2006-2010 5-year est.); Median household income: $54,737 (2006-2010 5-year est.); Average household income: $58,519 (2006-2010 5-year est.); Percent of households with income of $100,000 or more: 13.7% (2006-2010 5-year est.); Poverty rate: 11.2% (2006-2010 5-year est.).

**Education:** Percent of population age 25 and over with: High school diploma (including GED) or higher: 86.8% (2006-2010 5-year est.); Bachelor's degree or higher: 25.1% (2006-2010 5-year est.); Master's degree or higher: 10.3% (2006-2010 5-year est.).

**School District(s)**
Moriah Central School District (PK-12)
    2009-10 Enrollment: 766 . . . . . . . . . . . . . . . . . . . . . . . (518) 546-3301

**Housing:** Homeownership rate: 61.6% (2010); Median home value: $107,000 (2006-2010 5-year est.); Median contract rent: $551 per month (2006-2010 5-year est.); Median year structure built: before 1940 (2006-2010 5-year est.).

**Transportation:** Commute to work: 86.7% car, 0.7% public transportation, 2.1% walk, 3.2% work from home (2006-2010 5-year est.); Travel time to work: 36.0% less than 15 minutes, 19.2% 15 to 30 minutes, 14.5% 30 to 45 minutes, 5.6% 45 to 60 minutes, 24.6% 60 minutes or more (2006-2010 5-year est.); Amtrak: train service available.

## PORT KENT (unincorporated postal area)
Zip Code: 12975
    Covers a land area of 2.851 square miles and a water area of 0 square miles. Located at 44.52° N. Lat; 73.43° W. Long. Elevation is 154 feet. Population: 265 (2010); Density: 92.9 persons per square mile (2010); Race: 98.5% White, 0.0% Black, 1.1% Asian, 0.0% American Indian/Alaska Native, 0.0% Native Hawaiian/Other Pacific Islander, 0.4% Other, 0.0% Hispanic of any race (2010); Average household size: 2.25 (2010); Median age: 47.3 (2010); Males per 100 females: 86.6 (2010); Homeownership rate: 73.8% (2010)

## RAY BROOK (unincorporated postal area)
Zip Code: 12977
    Covers a land area of 8.944 square miles and a water area of 0.112 square miles. Located at 44.27° N. Lat; 74.07° W. Long. Elevation is 1,591 feet. Population: 1,753 (2010); Density: 196.0 persons per square mile (2010); Race: 33.1% White, 47.5% Black, 1.2% Asian, 2.1% American Indian/Alaska Native, 0.2% Native Hawaiian/Other Pacific Islander, 15.9% Other, 32.6% Hispanic of any race (2010); Average household size: 2.37 (2010); Median age: 33.8 (2010); Males per 100 females: ***.* (2010); Homeownership rate: 79.6% (2010)

## SAINT ARMAND (town).
Covers a land area of 56.510 square miles and a water area of 0.934 square miles. Located at 44.37° N. Lat; 74.01° W. Long.

**Population:** 1,317 (1990); 1,321 (2000); 1,548 (2010); Density: 27.4 persons per square mile (2010); Race: 97.5% White, 0.1% Black, 0.1% Asian, 0.6% American Indian/Alaska Native, 0.0% Native Hawaiian/Other Pacific Islander, 1.7% Other, 1.5% Hispanic of any race (2010); Average household size: 2.36 (2010); Median age: 41.3 (2010); Males per 100 females: 96.7 (2010); Marriage status: 22.2% never married, 60.7% now married, 7.7% widowed, 9.4% divorced (2006-2010 5-year est.); Foreign born: 2.1% (2006-2010 5-year est.); Ancestry (includes multiple ancestries): 26.7% Irish, 20.7% French, 18.3% German, 13.8% English, 9.4% Italian (2006-2010 5-year est.).

**Economy:** Single-family building permits issued: 0 (2011); Multi-family building permits issued: 0 (2011); Employment by occupation: 11.1% management, 3.9% professional, 8.8% services, 12.4% sales, 0.9% farming, 6.8% construction, 3.0% production (2006-2010 5-year est.).

**Income:** Per capita income: $28,952 (2006-2010 5-year est.); Median household income: $48,448 (2006-2010 5-year est.); Average household income: $60,382 (2006-2010 5-year est.); Percent of households with income of $100,000 or more: 16.0% (2006-2010 5-year est.); Poverty rate: 5.2% (2006-2010 5-year est.).

**Education:** Percent of population age 25 and over with: High school diploma (including GED) or higher: 93.0% (2006-2010 5-year est.); Bachelor's degree or higher: 43.5% (2006-2010 5-year est.); Master's degree or higher: 16.4% (2006-2010 5-year est.).

**Housing:** Homeownership rate: 74.0% (2010); Median home value: $167,200 (2006-2010 5-year est.); Median contract rent: $559 per month (2006-2010 5-year est.); Median year structure built: 1948 (2006-2010 5-year est.).

**Transportation:** Commute to work: 85.2% car, 0.0% public transportation, 2.2% walk, 11.3% work from home (2006-2010 5-year est.); Travel time to work: 39.9% less than 15 minutes, 43.9% 15 to 30 minutes, 9.8% 30 to 45 minutes, 3.7% 45 to 60 minutes, 2.7% 60 minutes or more (2006-2010 5-year est.)

## SCHROON (town).
Covers a land area of 132.678 square miles and a water area of 8.731 square miles. Located at 43.85° N. Lat; 73.76° W. Long.

**Population:** 1,695 (1990); 1,759 (2000); 1,654 (2010); Density: 12.5 persons per square mile (2010); Race: 96.4% White, 0.3% Black, 0.4% Asian, 0.5% American Indian/Alaska Native, 0.0% Native Hawaiian/Other Pacific Islander, 2.4% Other, 1.4% Hispanic of any race (2010); Average household size: 2.19 (2010); Median age: 49.4 (2010); Males per 100 females: 91.2 (2010); Marriage status: 31.1% never married, 51.7% now married, 8.7% widowed, 8.5% divorced (2006-2010 5-year est.); Foreign born: 3.3% (2006-2010 5-year est.); Ancestry (includes multiple ancestries): 24.5% German, 19.9% Irish, 19.4% French, 19.1% English, 10.1% Dutch (2006-2010 5-year est.).

**Economy:** Single-family building permits issued: 8 (2011); Multi-family building permits issued: 0 (2011); Employment by occupation: 12.1% management, 0.4% professional, 25.2% services, 8.8% sales, 1.5% farming, 12.9% construction, 6.7% production (2006-2010 5-year est.).

**Income:** Per capita income: $20,069 (2006-2010 5-year est.); Median household income: $42,594 (2006-2010 5-year est.); Average household income: $51,014 (2006-2010 5-year est.); Percent of households with income of $100,000 or more: 7.1% (2006-2010 5-year est.); Poverty rate: 19.9% (2006-2010 5-year est.).

**Education:** Percent of population age 25 and over with: High school diploma (including GED) or higher: 89.0% (2006-2010 5-year est.); Bachelor's degree or higher: 18.5% (2006-2010 5-year est.); Master's degree or higher: 5.9% (2006-2010 5-year est.).

**Housing:** Homeownership rate: 76.8% (2010); Median home value: $170,600 (2006-2010 5-year est.); Median contract rent: $401 per month (2006-2010 5-year est.); Median year structure built: 1961 (2006-2010 5-year est.).

**Transportation:** Commute to work: 74.8% car, 0.8% public transportation, 3.3% walk, 21.1% work from home (2006-2010 5-year est.); Travel time to work: 58.7% less than 15 minutes, 12.9% 15 to 30 minutes, 14.2% 30 to 45 minutes, 5.3% 45 to 60 minutes, 9.0% 60 minutes or more (2006-2010 5-year est.)

## SCHROON LAKE (CDP).
Covers a land area of 2.886 square miles and a water area of 0.799 square miles. Located at 43.83° N. Lat; 73.76° W. Long. Elevation is 869 feet.

**Population:** n/a (1990); n/a (2000); 833 (2010); Density: 288.6 persons per square mile (2010); Race: 96.4% White, 0.5% Black, 0.4% Asian, 0.6% American Indian/Alaska Native, 0.0% Native Hawaiian/Other Pacific Islander, 2.1% Other, 1.2% Hispanic of any race (2010); Average household size: 2.13 (2010); Median age: 47.9 (2010); Males per 100 females: 86.8 (2010); Marriage status: 22.7% never married, 51.8% now married, 13.0% widowed, 12.5% divorced (2006-2010 5-year est.); Foreign born: 5.1% (2006-2010 5-year est.); Ancestry (includes multiple ancestries): 24.9% German, 21.0% Irish, 18.7% French, 18.2% English, 9.2% Italian (2006-2010 5-year est.).

**Economy:** Employment by occupation: 17.2% management, 0.9% professional, 12.8% services, 10.4% sales, 2.6% farming, 12.8% construction, 5.4% production (2006-2010 5-year est.).

**Income:** Per capita income: $20,551 (2006-2010 5-year est.); Median household income: $38,125 (2006-2010 5-year est.); Average household income: $45,979 (2006-2010 5-year est.); Percent of households with income of $100,000 or more: 5.3% (2006-2010 5-year est.); Poverty rate: 6.3% (2006-2010 5-year est.).

**Education:** Percent of population age 25 and over with: High school diploma (including GED) or higher: 87.5% (2006-2010 5-year est.); Bachelor's degree or higher: 23.1% (2006-2010 5-year est.); Master's degree or higher: 7.9% (2006-2010 5-year est.).

### School District(s)
Schroon Lake Central School District (KG-12)

   2009-10 Enrollment: 246 . . . . . . . . . . . . . . . . . (518) 532-7164

**Housing:** Homeownership rate: 63.7% (2010); Median home value: $156,700 (2006-2010 5-year est.); Median contract rent: $418 per month (2006-2010 5-year est.); Median year structure built: 1962 (2006-2010 5-year est.).

**Transportation:** Commute to work: 79.0% car, 2.0% public transportation, 7.8% walk, 11.2% work from home (2006-2010 5-year est.); Travel time to work: 63.7% less than 15 minutes, 7.1% 15 to 30 minutes, 17.4% 30 to 45 minutes, 5.5% 45 to 60 minutes, 6.3% 60 minutes or more (2006-2010 5-year est.)

## SEVERANCE (unincorporated postal area)
Zip Code: 12872

   Covers a land area of 0.305 square miles and a water area of 0 square miles. Located at 43.87° N. Lat; 73.73° W. Long. Elevation is 840 feet. Population: 31 (2010); Density: 101.6 persons per square mile (2010); Race: 96.8% White, 0.0% Black, 0.0% Asian, 3.2% American Indian/Alaska Native, 0.0% Native Hawaiian/Other Pacific Islander, 0.0% Other, 0.0% Hispanic of any race (2010); Average household size: 1.72 (2010); Median age: 57.5 (2010); Males per 100 females: 82.4 (2010); Homeownership rate: 83.4% (2010)

## TICONDEROGA (town). Covers a land area of 81.433 square miles and a water area of 7.011 square miles. Located at 43.83° N. Lat; 73.55° W. Long. Elevation is 151 feet.
**History:** Ticonderoga is a variation of the Native American "Cheonderoga," meaning "between two waters." The French built a military road at the site and in 1755 they constructed Fort Carillon, later called Fort Ticonderoga.

**Population:** 5,145 (1990); 5,167 (2000); 5,042 (2010); Density: 61.9 persons per square mile (2010); Race: 97.1% White, 0.4% Black, 0.9% Asian, 0.3% American Indian/Alaska Native, 0.0% Native Hawaiian/Other Pacific Islander, 1.3% Other, 1.0% Hispanic of any race (2010); Average household size: 2.34 (2010); Median age: 44.8 (2010); Males per 100 females: 97.9 (2010); Marriage status: 20.4% never married, 60.1% now married, 11.3% widowed, 8.2% divorced (2006-2010 5-year est.); Foreign born: 1.6% (2006-2010 5-year est.); Ancestry (includes multiple ancestries): 28.2% French, 21.8% Irish, 16.8% English, 12.6% Italian, 10.1% German (2006-2010 5-year est.).

**Economy:** Single-family building permits issued: 6 (2011); Multi-family building permits issued: 0 (2011); Employment by occupation: 5.7% management, 2.3% professional, 15.8% services, 8.0% sales, 3.3% farming, 8.7% construction, 6.0% production (2006-2010 5-year est.).

**Income:** Per capita income: $23,412 (2006-2010 5-year est.); Median household income: $35,608 (2006-2010 5-year est.); Average household income: $50,072 (2006-2010 5-year est.); Percent of households with income of $100,000 or more: 12.3% (2006-2010 5-year est.); Poverty rate: 15.6% (2006-2010 5-year est.).

**Taxes:** Total city taxes per capita: $702 (2009); City property taxes per capita: $658 (2009).

**Education:** Percent of population age 25 and over with: High school diploma (including GED) or higher: 86.8% (2006-2010 5-year est.); Bachelor's degree or higher: 24.0% (2006-2010 5-year est.); Master's degree or higher: 11.1% (2006-2010 5-year est.).

### School District(s)
Ticonderoga Central School District (PK-12)

   2009-10 Enrollment: 886 . . . . . . . . . . . . . . . . . (518) 585-7400

**Housing:** Homeownership rate: 73.5% (2010); Median home value: $133,900 (2006-2010 5-year est.); Median contract rent: $461 per month (2006-2010 5-year est.); Median year structure built: 1942 (2006-2010 5-year est.).

**Hospitals:** Moses-Ludington Hospital (15 beds)

**Safety:** Violent crime rate: 20.6 per 10,000 population; Property crime rate: 138.1 per 10,000 population (2010).

**Transportation:** Commute to work: 90.0% car, 0.0% public transportation, 6.3% walk, 2.3% work from home (2006-2010 5-year est.); Travel time to work: 76.0% less than 15 minutes, 14.0% 15 to 30 minutes, 0.6% 30 to 45 minutes, 3.2% 45 to 60 minutes, 6.2% 60 minutes or more (2006-2010 5-year est.); Amtrak: train service available.

**Additional Information Contacts**
Ticonderoga Area Chamber of Commerce . . . . . . . . . . . . (518) 585-6619
  http://www.ticonderogany.com

## TICONDEROGA (CDP). Covers a land area of 4.272 square miles and a water area of 0.078 square miles. Located at 43.84° N. Lat; 73.42° W. Long. Elevation is 151 feet.
**Population:** n/a (1990); n/a (2000); 3,382 (2010); Density: 791.6 persons per square mile (2010); Race: 96.9% White, 0.2% Black, 1.1% Asian, 0.3% American Indian/Alaska Native, 0.0% Native Hawaiian/Other Pacific Islander, 1.5% Other, 1.1% Hispanic of any race (2010); Average household size: 2.34 (2010); Median age: 43.0 (2010); Males per 100 females: 94.4 (2010); Marriage status: 19.0% never married, 59.3% now married, 14.2% widowed, 7.5% divorced (2006-2010 5-year est.); Foreign born: 1.6% (2006-2010 5-year est.); Ancestry (includes multiple ancestries): 29.1% French, 24.3% Irish, 16.7% English, 12.8% Italian, 11.7% German (2006-2010 5-year est.).

**Economy:** Employment by occupation: 5.9% management, 3.4% professional, 15.4% services, 7.8% sales, 2.0% farming, 6.4% construction, 2.5% production (2006-2010 5-year est.).

**Income:** Per capita income: $24,386 (2006-2010 5-year est.); Median household income: $35,729 (2006-2010 5-year est.); Average household income: $49,738 (2006-2010 5-year est.); Percent of households with income of $100,000 or more: 12.2% (2006-2010 5-year est.); Poverty rate: 16.0% (2006-2010 5-year est.).

**Education:** Percent of population age 25 and over with: High school diploma (including GED) or higher: 85.7% (2006-2010 5-year est.); Bachelor's degree or higher: 24.9% (2006-2010 5-year est.); Master's degree or higher: 9.9% (2006-2010 5-year est.).

### School District(s)
Ticonderoga Central School District (PK-12)

   2009-10 Enrollment: 886 . . . . . . . . . . . . . . . . . (518) 585-7400

**Housing:** Homeownership rate: 68.1% (2010); Median home value: $126,100 (2006-2010 5-year est.); Median contract rent: $447 per month (2006-2010 5-year est.); Median year structure built: before 1940 (2006-2010 5-year est.).

**Transportation:** Commute to work: 90.8% car, 0.0% public transportation, 3.8% walk, 3.4% work from home (2006-2010 5-year est.); Travel time to work: 77.1% less than 15 minutes, 13.4% 15 to 30 minutes, 0.9% 30 to 45 minutes, 2.2% 45 to 60 minutes, 6.5% 60 minutes or more (2006-2010 5-year est.)

## UPPER JAY (unincorporated postal area)
Zip Code: 12987

   Covers a land area of 6.198 square miles and a water area of 0.014 square miles. Located at 44.32° N. Lat; 73.75° W. Long. Elevation is 669 feet. Population: 201 (2010); Density: 32.4 persons per square mile (2010); Race: 94.0% White, 1.0% Black, 0.5% Asian, 0.0% American Indian/Alaska Native, 0.5% Native Hawaiian/Other Pacific Islander, 4.0% Other, 2.0% Hispanic of any race (2010); Average household size: 2.19 (2010); Median age: 49.9 (2010); Males per 100 females: 95.1 (2010); Homeownership rate: 90.0% (2010)

## WESTPORT (town). Covers a land area of 58.170 square miles and a water area of 8.635 square miles. Located at 44.18° N. Lat; 73.44° W. Long. Elevation is 121 feet.
**Population:** 1,446 (1990); 1,362 (2000); 1,312 (2010); Density: 22.6 persons per square mile (2010); Race: 97.1% White, 0.5% Black, 0.7% Asian, 0.1% American Indian/Alaska Native, 0.0% Native Hawaiian/Other Pacific Islander, 1.6% Other, 1.8% Hispanic of any race (2010); Average household size: 2.23 (2010); Median age: 49.0 (2010); Males per 100 females: 92.4 (2010); Marriage status: 18.0% never married, 67.4% now married, 7.3% widowed, 7.2% divorced (2006-2010 5-year est.); Foreign born: 4.7% (2006-2010 5-year est.); Ancestry (includes multiple ancestries): 22.4% German, 19.8% English, 19.0% Irish, 16.1% French, 9.9% American (2006-2010 5-year est.).

**Economy:** Single-family building permits issued: 1 (2011); Multi-family building permits issued: 0 (2011); Employment by occupation: 12.3% management, 6.6% professional, 8.5% services, 11.9% sales, 3.2% farming, 13.0% construction, 1.7% production (2006-2010 5-year est.).

**Income:** Per capita income: $23,243 (2006-2010 5-year est.); Median household income: $41,125 (2006-2010 5-year est.); Average household income: $55,601 (2006-2010 5-year est.); Percent of households with income of $100,000 or more: 15.6% (2006-2010 5-year est.); Poverty rate: 22.9% (2006-2010 5-year est.).

**Education:** Percent of population age 25 and over with: High school diploma (including GED) or higher: 91.2% (2006-2010 5-year est.); Bachelor's degree or higher: 35.6% (2006-2010 5-year est.); Master's degree or higher: 9.3% (2006-2010 5-year est.).

### School District(s)

Westport Central School District (KG-12)

   2009-10 Enrollment: 267 . . . . . . . . . . . . . . . . . (518) 962-8244

**Housing:** Homeownership rate: 75.4% (2010); Median home value: $175,000 (2006-2010 5-year est.); Median contract rent: $525 per month (2006-2010 5-year est.); Median year structure built: before 1940 (2006-2010 5-year est.).

**Transportation:** Commute to work: 83.7% car, 0.0% public transportation, 1.5% walk, 14.8% work from home (2006-2010 5-year est.); Travel time to work: 51.0% less than 15 minutes, 28.5% 15 to 30 minutes, 9.6% 30 to 45 minutes, 10.9% 45 to 60 minutes, 0.0% 60 minutes or more (2006-2010 5-year est.); Amtrak: train service available.

### Additional Information Contacts

Town of Westport . . . . . . . . . . . . . . . . . . . . . . . . (518) 962-4419
  http://www.westportny.net
Westport Chamber of Commerce . . . . . . . . . . . . . (518) 962-8383
  http://www.westportny.com

## WESTPORT (CDP).

Covers a land area of 2.360 square miles and a water area of 0 square miles. Located at 44.18° N. Lat; 73.43° W. Long. Elevation is 121 feet.

**Population:** n/a (1990); n/a (2000); 518 (2010); Density: 219.4 persons per square mile (2010); Race: 96.1% White, 0.6% Black, 1.0% Asian, 0.2% American Indian/Alaska Native, 0.0% Native Hawaiian/Other Pacific Islander, 2.1% Other, 3.9% Hispanic of any race (2010); Average household size: 2.13 (2010); Median age: 47.1 (2010); Males per 100 females: 81.8 (2010); Marriage status: 5.3% never married, 76.6% now married, 10.4% widowed, 7.7% divorced (2006-2010 5-year est.); Foreign born: 0.0% (2006-2010 5-year est.); Ancestry (includes multiple ancestries): 26.2% German, 22.9% French, 18.9% Irish, 16.9% English, 12.4% American (2006-2010 5-year est.).

**Economy:** Employment by occupation: 5.5% management, 14.7% professional, 3.1% services, 17.8% sales, 1.2% farming, 12.3% construction, 0.0% production (2006-2010 5-year est.).

**Income:** Per capita income: $27,314 (2006-2010 5-year est.); Median household income: $40,750 (2006-2010 5-year est.); Average household income: $54,648 (2006-2010 5-year est.); Percent of households with income of $100,000 or more: 14.1% (2006-2010 5-year est.); Poverty rate: 9.1% (2006-2010 5-year est.).

**Education:** Percent of population age 25 and over with: High school diploma (including GED) or higher: 87.6% (2006-2010 5-year est.); Bachelor's degree or higher: 37.7% (2006-2010 5-year est.); Master's degree or higher: 7.5% (2006-2010 5-year est.).

### School District(s)

Westport Central School District (KG-12)

   2009-10 Enrollment: 267 . . . . . . . . . . . . . . . . . (518) 962-8244

**Housing:** Homeownership rate: 66.7% (2010); Median home value: $153,100 (2006-2010 5-year est.); Median contract rent: $536 per month (2006-2010 5-year est.); Median year structure built: before 1940 (2006-2010 5-year est.).

**Transportation:** Commute to work: 80.4% car, 0.0% public transportation, 0.0% walk, 19.6% work from home (2006-2010 5-year est.); Travel time to work: 40.2% less than 15 minutes, 31.5% 15 to 30 minutes, 9.4% 30 to 45 minutes, 18.9% 45 to 60 minutes, 0.0% 60 minutes or more (2006-2010 5-year est.)

## WILLSBORO (town).

Covers a land area of 42.723 square miles and a water area of 30.660 square miles. Located at 44.38° N. Lat; 73.39° W. Long. Elevation is 223 feet.

**Population:** 1,754 (1990); 1,903 (2000); 2,025 (2010); Density: 47.4 persons per square mile (2010); Race: 97.5% White, 0.4% Black, 0.2% Asian, 0.2% American Indian/Alaska Native, 0.0% Native Hawaiian/Other Pacific Islander, 1.7% Other, 0.3% Hispanic of any race (2010); Average household size: 2.32 (2010); Median age: 48.0 (2010); Males per 100 females: 97.4 (2010); Marriage status: 21.4% never married, 61.5% now married, 8.1% widowed, 9.0% divorced (2006-2010 5-year est.); Foreign

born: 4.0% (2006-2010 5-year est.); Ancestry (includes multiple ancestries): 27.5% Irish, 23.0% English, 9.2% French, 7.3% German, 6.6% Dutch (2006-2010 5-year est.).

**Economy:** Single-family building permits issued: 3 (2011); Multi-family building permits issued: 0 (2011); Employment by occupation: 8.1% management, 2.0% professional, 9.6% services, 12.1% sales, 2.3% farming, 24.6% construction, 5.7% production (2006-2010 5-year est.).

**Income:** Per capita income: $25,501 (2006-2010 5-year est.); Median household income: $45,020 (2006-2010 5-year est.); Average household income: $55,315 (2006-2010 5-year est.); Percent of households with income of $100,000 or more: 17.9% (2006-2010 5-year est.); Poverty rate: 12.5% (2006-2010 5-year est.).

**Education:** Percent of population age 25 and over with: High school diploma (including GED) or higher: 85.0% (2006-2010 5-year est.); Bachelor's degree or higher: 21.2% (2006-2010 5-year est.); Master's degree or higher: 8.5% (2006-2010 5-year est.).

### School District(s)

Willsboro Central School District (PK-12)

   2009-10 Enrollment: 326 . . . . . . . . . . . . . . . . . (518) 963-4456

**Housing:** Homeownership rate: 79.5% (2010); Median home value: $99,700 (2006-2010 5-year est.); Median contract rent: $457 per month (2006-2010 5-year est.); Median year structure built: 1959 (2006-2010 5-year est.).

**Transportation:** Commute to work: 89.0% car, 0.0% public transportation, 2.2% walk, 4.3% work from home (2006-2010 5-year est.); Travel time to work: 43.3% less than 15 minutes, 33.8% 15 to 30 minutes, 15.5% 30 to 45 minutes, 3.4% 45 to 60 minutes, 4.0% 60 minutes or more (2006-2010 5-year est.)

## WILLSBORO (CDP).

Covers a land area of 1.923 square miles and a water area of 0.033 square miles. Located at 44.36° N. Lat; 73.39° W. Long. Elevation is 223 feet.

**Population:** n/a (1990); n/a (2000); 753 (2010); Density: 391.4 persons per square mile (2010); Race: 98.1% White, 0.0% Black, 0.0% Asian, 0.1% American Indian/Alaska Native, 0.0% Native Hawaiian/Other Pacific Islander, 1.8% Other, 0.0% Hispanic of any race (2010); Average household size: 2.30 (2010); Median age: 46.3 (2010); Males per 100 females: 98.2 (2010); Marriage status: 14.9% never married, 66.4% now married, 5.6% widowed, 13.1% divorced (2006-2010 5-year est.); Foreign born: 3.4% (2006-2010 5-year est.); Ancestry (includes multiple ancestries): 32.5% English, 32.2% Irish, 17.8% French, 10.4% Dutch, 8.9% German (2006-2010 5-year est.).

**Economy:** Employment by occupation: 14.8% management, 3.0% professional, 10.2% services, 3.4% sales, 1.9% farming, 27.3% construction, 11.4% production (2006-2010 5-year est.).

**Income:** Per capita income: $24,882 (2006-2010 5-year est.); Median household income: $46,512 (2006-2010 5-year est.); Average household income: $52,419 (2006-2010 5-year est.); Percent of households with income of $100,000 or more: 15.9% (2006-2010 5-year est.); Poverty rate: 11.4% (2006-2010 5-year est.).

**Education:** Percent of population age 25 and over with: High school diploma (including GED) or higher: 87.4% (2006-2010 5-year est.); Bachelor's degree or higher: 10.0% (2006-2010 5-year est.); Master's degree or higher: 4.3% (2006-2010 5-year est.).

### School District(s)

Willsboro Central School District (PK-12)

   2009-10 Enrollment: 326 . . . . . . . . . . . . . . . . . (518) 963-4456

**Housing:** Homeownership rate: 71.0% (2010); Median home value: $71,800 (2006-2010 5-year est.); Median contract rent: $606 per month (2006-2010 5-year est.); Median year structure built: 1953 (2006-2010 5-year est.).

**Transportation:** Commute to work: 82.6% car, 0.0% public transportation, 4.2% walk, 0.0% work from home (2006-2010 5-year est.); Travel time to work: 32.6% less than 15 minutes, 30.3% 15 to 30 minutes, 21.6% 30 to 45 minutes, 7.6% 45 to 60 minutes, 8.0% 60 minutes or more (2006-2010 5-year est.)

## WILMINGTON (town).

Covers a land area of 65.240 square miles and a water area of 0.232 square miles. Located at 44.37° N. Lat; 73.89° W. Long. Elevation is 1,014 feet.

**Population:** 1,020 (1990); 1,131 (2000); 1,253 (2010); Density: 19.2 persons per square mile (2010); Race: 98.1% White, 0.4% Black, 0.7% Asian, 0.1% American Indian/Alaska Native, 0.0% Native Hawaiian/Other Pacific Islander, 0.7% Other, 1.1% Hispanic of any race (2010); Average household size: 2.31 (2010); Median age: 43.7 (2010); Males per 100

females: 101.1 (2010); Marriage status: 21.3% never married, 61.6% now married, 6.7% widowed, 10.4% divorced (2006-2010 5-year est.); Foreign born: 10.4% (2006-2010 5-year est.); Ancestry (includes multiple ancestries): 20.1% Irish, 16.4% German, 14.3% English, 13.5% French, 6.1% American (2006-2010 5-year est.).

**Economy:** Single-family building permits issued: 5 (2011); Multi-family building permits issued: 0 (2011); Employment by occupation: 15.0% management, 1.5% professional, 9.7% services, 17.6% sales, 1.3% farming, 14.1% construction, 2.4% production (2006-2010 5-year est.).

**Income:** Per capita income: $24,297 (2006-2010 5-year est.); Median household income: $52,303 (2006-2010 5-year est.); Average household income: $60,266 (2006-2010 5-year est.); Percent of households with income of $100,000 or more: 11.8% (2006-2010 5-year est.); Poverty rate: 16.1% (2006-2010 5-year est.).

**Education:** Percent of population age 25 and over with: High school diploma (including GED) or higher: 93.1% (2006-2010 5-year est.); Bachelor's degree or higher: 33.5% (2006-2010 5-year est.); Master's degree or higher: 13.4% (2006-2010 5-year est.).

**Housing:** Homeownership rate: 75.3% (2010); Median home value: $235,600 (2006-2010 5-year est.); Median contract rent: $495 per month (2006-2010 5-year est.); Median year structure built: 1963 (2006-2010 5-year est.).

**Transportation:** Commute to work: 80.0% car, 0.0% public transportation, 6.9% walk, 13.1% work from home (2006-2010 5-year est.); Travel time to work: 44.7% less than 15 minutes, 27.5% 15 to 30 minutes, 13.1% 30 to 45 minutes, 12.5% 45 to 60 minutes, 2.2% 60 minutes or more (2006-2010 5-year est.).

**WILMINGTON** (CDP). Covers a land area of 8.252 square miles and a water area of 0.087 square miles. Located at 44.38° N. Lat; 73.81° W. Long. Elevation is 1,014 feet.

**Population:** n/a (1990); n/a (2000); 937 (2010); Density: 113.5 persons per square mile (2010); Race: 98.3% White, 0.2% Black, 0.6% Asian, 0.1% American Indian/Alaska Native, 0.0% Native Hawaiian/Other Pacific Islander, 0.8% Other, 1.1% Hispanic of any race (2010); Average household size: 2.29 (2010); Median age: 43.6 (2010); Males per 100 females: 96.0 (2010); Marriage status: 24.5% never married, 57.6% now married, 6.9% widowed, 11.0% divorced (2006-2010 5-year est.); Foreign born: 8.8% (2006-2010 5-year est.); Ancestry (includes multiple ancestries): 15.2% Irish, 14.5% English, 12.4% French, 12.1% German, 8.4% American (2006-2010 5-year est.).

**Economy:** Employment by occupation: 17.4% management, 2.0% professional, 11.8% services, 16.7% sales, 15.2% farming, construction, 1.7% production (2006-2010 5-year est.).

**Income:** Per capita income: $23,861 (2006-2010 5-year est.); Median household income: $45,313 (2006-2010 5-year est.); Average household income: $58,716 (2006-2010 5-year est.); Percent of households with income of $100,000 or more: 10.1% (2006-2010 5-year est.); Poverty rate: 22.4% (2006-2010 5-year est.).

**Education:** Percent of population age 25 and over with: High school diploma (including GED) or higher: 94.1% (2006-2010 5-year est.); Bachelor's degree or higher: 29.3% (2006-2010 5-year est.); Master's degree or higher: 13.0% (2006-2010 5-year est.).

**Housing:** Homeownership rate: 74.3% (2010); Median home value: $237,900 (2006-2010 5-year est.); Median contract rent: $491 per month (2006-2010 5-year est.); Median year structure built: 1962 (2006-2010 5-year est.).

**Transportation:** Commute to work: 79.9% car, 0.0% public transportation, 7.6% walk, 12.5% work from home (2006-2010 5-year est.); Travel time to work: 45.4% less than 15 minutes, 30.8% 15 to 30 minutes, 12.3% 30 to 45 minutes, 9.8% 45 to 60 minutes, 1.7% 60 minutes or more (2006-2010 5-year est.).

**WITHERBEE** (CDP). Covers a land area of 0.734 square miles and a water area of 0 square miles. Located at 44.08° N. Lat; 73.53° W. Long. Elevation is 1,257 feet.

**Population:** n/a (1990); n/a (2000); 347 (2010); Density: 472.7 persons per square mile (2010); Race: 97.1% White, 1.4% Black, 0.0% Asian, 0.9% American Indian/Alaska Native, 0.0% Native Hawaiian/Other Pacific Islander, 0.6% Other, 1.4% Hispanic of any race (2010); Average household size: 2.55 (2010); Median age: 38.2 (2010); Males per 100 females: 94.9 (2010); Marriage status: 12.6% never married, 66.7% now married, 0.0% widowed, 20.8% divorced (2006-2010 5-year est.); Foreign born: 0.0% (2006-2010 5-year est.); Ancestry (includes multiple

ancestries): 70.6% French, 60.1% Italian, 13.3% German, 6.5% Irish (2006-2010 5-year est.).

**Income:** Per capita income: $20,330 (2006-2010 5-year est.); Median household income: $65,719 (2006-2010 5-year est.); Average household income: $61,436 (2006-2010 5-year est.); Percent of households with income of $100,000 or more: 0.0% (2006-2010 5-year est.); Poverty rate: 0.0% (2006-2010 5-year est.).

**Education:** Percent of population age 25 and over with: High school diploma (including GED) or higher: 100.0% (2006-2010 5-year est.); Bachelor's degree or higher: 0.0% (2006-2010 5-year est.); Master's degree or higher: 0.0% (2006-2010 5-year est.).

**Housing:** Homeownership rate: 72.0% (2010); Median home value: n/a (2006-2010 5-year est.); Median contract rent: n/a per month (2006-2010 5-year est.); Median year structure built: 1941 (2006-2010 5-year est.).

**Transportation:** Commute to work: 100.0% car, 0.0% public transportation, 0.0% walk, 0.0% work from home (2006-2010 5-year est.); Travel time to work: 0.0% less than 15 minutes, 0.0% 15 to 30 minutes, 32.7% 30 to 45 minutes, 67.3% 45 to 60 minutes, 0.0% 60 minutes or more (2006-2010 5-year est.)

# Franklin County

Located in northeastern New York, partly in the Adirondacks; bounded on the north by the Canadian province of Quebec; drained by the Saranac, St. Regis, Salmon, Little Salmon, Chateaugay, and Raquette Rivers; includes many lakes, including Saranac La ke and Tupper Lake. Covers a land area of 1,631.49 square miles, a water area of 65.95 square miles, and is located in the Eastern Time Zone at 44.60° N. Lat., 74.30° W. Long. The county was founded in 1808. County seat is Malone.

Franklin County is part of the Malone, NY Micropolitan Statistical Area. The entire metro area includes: Franklin County, NY.

Weather Station: Malone — Elevation: 879 feet

|        | Jan  | Feb  | Mar  | Apr | May | Jun | Jul | Aug | Sep | Oct | Nov | Dec  |
|--------|------|------|------|-----|-----|-----|-----|-----|-----|-----|-----|------|
| High   | 24   | 26   | 35   | 51  | 63  | 72  | 76  | 75  | 67  | 54  | 42  | 30   |
| Low    | 6    | 7    | 17   | 32  | 44  | 54  | 58  | 56  | 48  | 37  | 27  | 13   |
| Precip | 2.3  | 1.8  | 2.2  | 3.0 | 3.2 | 4.0 | 4.3 | 4.3 | 3.8 | 3.8 | 3.3 | 2.7  |
| Snow   | 22.1 | 18.1 | 16.3 | 7.0 | 0.6 | 0.0 | 0.0 | 0.0 | tr  | 2.0 | 9.3 | 20.2 |

*High and Low temperatures in degrees Fahrenheit; Precipitation and Snow in inches*

Weather Station: Tupper Lake Sunmount — Elevation: 1,680 feet

|        | Jan  | Feb  | Mar  | Apr | May | Jun | Jul | Aug | Sep | Oct | Nov | Dec  |
|--------|------|------|------|-----|-----|-----|-----|-----|-----|-----|-----|------|
| High   | 25   | 29   | 36   | 51  | 64  | 72  | 76  | 75  | 68  | 55  | 42  | 30   |
| Low    | 3    | 5    | 13   | 29  | 40  | 49  | 53  | 52  | 44  | 34  | 25  | 11   |
| Precip | 3.1  | 2.6  | 3.0  | 3.3 | 3.7 | 4.0 | 4.6 | 4.6 | 4.1 | 4.0 | 3.9 | 3.3  |
| Snow   | 24.6 | 22.7 | 16.8 | 5.1 | 0.2 | tr  | 0.0 | 0.0 | tr  | 1.1 | 7.9 | 22.6 |

*High and Low temperatures in degrees Fahrenheit; Precipitation and Snow in inches*

**Population:** 46,540 (1990); 51,134 (2000); 51,599 (2010); Race: 84.2% White, 6.1% Black, 0.4% Asian, 7.4% American Indian/Alaska Native, 0.0% Native Hawaiian/Other Pacific Islander, 1.9% Other, 2.9% Hispanic of any race (2010); Density: 31.6 persons per square mile (2010); Average household size: 2.37 (2010); Median age: 39.3 (2010); Males per 100 females: 121.8 (2010).

**Religion:** Six largest groups: 35.7% Catholicism, 3.6% Methodist/Pietist, 1.0% Presbyterian-Reformed, 0.9% Baptist, 0.8% Episcopalianism/Anglicanism, 0.8% Non-Denominational (2010)

**Economy:** Unemployment rate: 10.7% (February 2012); Total civilian labor force: 22,205 (February 2012); Leading industries: 28.8% health care and social assistance; 18.6% retail trade; 10.7% arts, entertainment & recreation (2009); Farms: 604 totaling 130,852 acres (2007); Companies that employ 500 or more persons: 2 (2009); Companies that employ 100 to 499 persons: 10 (2009); Companies that employ less than 100 persons: 1,036 (2009); Black-owned businesses: n/a (2007); Hispanic-owned businesses: n/a (2007); Asian-owned businesses: n/a (2007); Women-owned businesses: n/a (2007); Retail sales per capita: $8,743 (2010). Single-family building permits issued: 57 (2011); Multi-family building permits issued: 0 (2011).

**Income:** Per capita income: $19,807 (2006-2010 5-year est.); Median household income: $42,050 (2006-2010 5-year est.); Average household income: $52,867 (2006-2010 5-year est.); Percent of households with income of $100,000 or more: 12.2% (2006-2010 5-year est.); Poverty rate: 14.4% (2006-2010 5-year est.); Bankruptcy rate: 2.42% (2011).

**Education:** Percent of population age 25 and over with: High school diploma (including GED) or higher: 83.3% (2006-2010 5-year est.);

Bachelor's degree or higher: 17.3% (2006-2010 5-year est.); Master's degree or higher: 7.9% (2006-2010 5-year est.).

**Housing:** Homeownership rate: 71.4% (2010); Median home value: $88,800 (2006-2010 5-year est.); Median contract rent: $484 per month (2006-2010 5-year est.); Median year structure built: 1958 (2006-2010 5-year est.)

**Health:** Birth rate: 99.5 per 10,000 population (2011); Death rate: 85.5 per 10,000 population (2011); Age-adjusted cancer mortality rate: 182.7 deaths per 100,000 population (2009); Number of physicians: 15.9 per 10,000 population (2008); Hospital beds: 77.7 per 10,000 population (2007); Hospital admissions: 1,116.8 per 10,000 population (2007).

**Environment:** Air Quality Index: 99.7% good, 0.3% moderate, 0.0% unhealthy for sensitive individuals, 0.0% unhealthy (percent of days in 2010)

**Elections:** 2008 Presidential election results: 60.3% Obama, 38.1% McCain, 0.8% Nader

**National and State Parks:** Franklin State Forest; Franklin State Forest Number Four; Franklin State Forest Number Nine; Franklin State Forest Number One; Franklin State Forest Number Six; Franklin State Forest Number Three; Franklin State Forest Number Two

**Additional Information Contacts**
Franklin County Government . . . . . . . . . . . . . . . . . . . . . (518) 481-1681
  http://www.franklincony.org
Malone Chamber of Commerce . . . . . . . . . . . . . . . . . . (518) 483-3760
  http://www.malonenychamber.com
Saranac Lake Area Chamber of Commerce . . . . . . . . . . . (518) 891-1990
  http://www.saranaclake.com
Town of Brighton . . . . . . . . . . . . . . . . . . . . . . . . . . . . (585) 784-5250
  http://www.townofbrighton.org
Tupper Lake Chamber Commerce . . . . . . . . . . . . . . . . (518) 359-3328
  http://tupper-lake.com

## Franklin County Communities

**BANGOR** (town). Covers a land area of 43.118 square miles and a water area of 0 square miles. Located at 44.83° N. Lat; 74.43° W. Long. Elevation is 768 feet.

**Population:** 2,080 (1990); 2,147 (2000); 2,224 (2010); Density: 51.6 persons per square mile (2010); Race: 97.4% White, 0.3% Black, 0.1% Asian, 0.5% American Indian/Alaska Native, 0.0% Native Hawaiian/Other Pacific Islander, 1.7% Other, 0.9% Hispanic of any race (2010); Average household size: 2.58 (2010); Median age: 39.8 (2010); Males per 100 females: 102.6 (2010); Marriage status: 20.7% never married, 63.4% now married, 4.2% widowed, 11.6% divorced (2006-2010 5-year est.); Foreign born: 2.9% (2006-2010 5-year est.); Ancestry (includes multiple ancestries): 36.7% French, 23.0% Irish, 12.3% English, 8.8% German, 8.8% American (2006-2010 5-year est.).

**Economy:** Single-family building permits issued: 7 (2011); Multi-family building permits issued: 0 (2011); Employment by occupation: 12.8% management, 0.3% professional, 8.9% services, 11.5% sales, 3.2% farming, 11.8% construction, 8.2% production (2006-2010 5-year est.).

**Income:** Per capita income: $20,972 (2006-2010 5-year est.); Median household income: $48,077 (2006-2010 5-year est.); Average household income: $54,870 (2006-2010 5-year est.); Percent of households with income of $100,000 or more: 16.0% (2006-2010 5-year est.); Poverty rate: 13.4% (2006-2010 5-year est.).

**Education:** Percent of population age 25 and over with: High school diploma (including GED) or higher: 86.6% (2006-2010 5-year est.); Bachelor's degree or higher: 17.3% (2006-2010 5-year est.); Master's degree or higher: 8.6% (2006-2010 5-year est.).

**Housing:** Homeownership rate: 81.2% (2010); Median home value: $77,300 (2006-2010 5-year est.); Median contract rent: $421 per month (2006-2010 5-year est.); Median year structure built: 1965 (2006-2010 5-year est.).

**Transportation:** Commute to work: 83.6% car, 1.1% public transportation, 1.1% walk, 12.0% work from home (2006-2010 5-year est.); Travel time to work: 36.0% less than 15 minutes, 36.2% 15 to 30 minutes, 18.0% 30 to 45 minutes, 4.3% 45 to 60 minutes, 5.4% 60 minutes or more (2006-2010 5-year est.)

**BELLMONT** (town). Covers a land area of 164.141 square miles and a water area of 3.018 square miles. Located at 44.76° N. Lat; 74.13° W. Long.

**Population:** 1,246 (1990); 1,423 (2000); 1,434 (2010); Density: 8.7 persons per square mile (2010); Race: 97.6% White, 0.3% Black, 0.4%

Asian, 0.7% American Indian/Alaska Native, 0.0% Native Hawaiian/Other Pacific Islander, 1.0% Other, 1.0% Hispanic of any race (2010); Average household size: 2.29 (2010); Median age: 46.1 (2010); Males per 100 females: 109.3 (2010); Marriage status: 24.8% never married, 62.5% now married, 4.8% widowed, 7.9% divorced (2006-2010 5-year est.); Foreign born: 4.0% (2006-2010 5-year est.); Ancestry (includes multiple ancestries): 39.8% French, 23.1% Irish, 15.1% English, 12.9% German, 5.5% French Canadian (2006-2010 5-year est.).

**Economy:** Single-family building permits issued: 2 (2011); Multi-family building permits issued: 0 (2011); Employment by occupation: 7.5% management, 1.6% professional, 15.8% services, 17.9% sales, 1.5% farming, 13.8% construction, 5.1% production (2006-2010 5-year est.).

**Income:** Per capita income: $23,945 (2006-2010 5-year est.); Median household income: $48,182 (2006-2010 5-year est.); Average household income: $58,892 (2006-2010 5-year est.); Percent of households with income of $100,000 or more: 16.4% (2006-2010 5-year est.); Poverty rate: 14.2% (2006-2010 5-year est.).

**Education:** Percent of population age 25 and over with: High school diploma (including GED) or higher: 82.9% (2006-2010 5-year est.); Bachelor's degree or higher: 13.0% (2006-2010 5-year est.); Master's degree or higher: 6.7% (2006-2010 5-year est.).

**Housing:** Homeownership rate: 88.3% (2010); Median home value: $83,600 (2006-2010 5-year est.); Median contract rent: $757 per month (2006-2010 5-year est.); Median year structure built: 1971 (2006-2010 5-year est.).

**Transportation:** Commute to work: 90.0% car, 1.5% public transportation, 4.1% walk, 2.9% work from home (2006-2010 5-year est.); Travel time to work: 20.9% less than 15 minutes, 49.8% 15 to 30 minutes, 11.9% 30 to 45 minutes, 8.6% 45 to 60 minutes, 8.9% 60 minutes or more (2006-2010 5-year est.)

**BOMBAY** (town). Covers a land area of 35.743 square miles and a water area of 0.125 square miles. Located at 44.91° N. Lat; 74.58° W. Long. Elevation is 194 feet.

**Population:** 1,158 (1990); 1,192 (2000); 1,357 (2010); Density: 38.0 persons per square mile (2010); Race: 79.6% White, 0.7% Black, 0.8% Asian, 16.9% American Indian/Alaska Native, 0.0% Native Hawaiian/Other Pacific Islander, 2.0% Other, 0.9% Hispanic of any race (2010); Average household size: 2.76 (2010); Median age: 33.6 (2010); Males per 100 females: 99.6 (2010); Marriage status: 29.0% never married, 51.5% now married, 8.1% widowed, 11.3% divorced (2006-2010 5-year est.); Foreign born: 4.3% (2006-2010 5-year est.); Ancestry (includes multiple ancestries): 29.2% French, 13.6% Irish, 8.5% English, 5.5% Scottish, 4.3% French Canadian (2006-2010 5-year est.).

**Economy:** Single-family building permits issued: 0 (2011); Multi-family building permits issued: 0 (2011); Employment by occupation: 3.3% management, 1.0% professional, 12.2% services, 21.1% sales, 2.3% farming, 10.9% construction, 9.5% production (2006-2010 5-year est.).

**Income:** Per capita income: $16,741 (2006-2010 5-year est.); Median household income: $24,926 (2006-2010 5-year est.); Average household income: $39,134 (2006-2010 5-year est.); Percent of households with income of $100,000 or more: 9.4% (2006-2010 5-year est.); Poverty rate: 35.0% (2006-2010 5-year est.).

**Education:** Percent of population age 25 and over with: High school diploma (including GED) or higher: 86.2% (2006-2010 5-year est.); Bachelor's degree or higher: 7.7% (2006-2010 5-year est.); Master's degree or higher: 2.9% (2006-2010 5-year est.).

**Housing:** Homeownership rate: 72.2% (2010); Median home value: $71,500 (2006-2010 5-year est.); Median contract rent: $533 per month (2006-2010 5-year est.); Median year structure built: 1969 (2006-2010 5-year est.).

**Transportation:** Commute to work: 96.2% car, 0.0% public transportation, 2.7% walk, 1.0% work from home (2006-2010 5-year est.); Travel time to work: 27.0% less than 15 minutes, 47.8% 15 to 30 minutes, 15.2% 30 to 45 minutes, 5.9% 45 to 60 minutes, 4.2% 60 minutes or more (2006-2010 5-year est.)

**BRANDON** (town). Covers a land area of 41.255 square miles and a water area of 0.067 square miles. Located at 44.73° N. Lat; 74.41° W. Long.

**Population:** 394 (1990); 542 (2000); 577 (2010); Density: 14.0 persons per square mile (2010); Race: 96.7% White, 0.2% Black, 0.3% Asian, 0.5% American Indian/Alaska Native, 0.0% Native Hawaiian/Other Pacific Islander, 2.3% Other, 1.6% Hispanic of any race (2010); Average household size: 2.60 (2010); Median age: 41.5 (2010); Males per 100 females: 113.7 (2010); Marriage status: 18.1% never married, 66.8% now married, 5.7% widowed, 9.4% divorced (2006-2010 5-year est.); Foreign born: 3.9% (2006-2010 5-year est.); Ancestry (includes multiple ancestries): 24.0% French, 21.4% Irish, 17.2% English, 10.5% American, 5.1% German (2006-2010 5-year est.).

**Economy:** Single-family building permits issued: 0 (2011); Multi-family building permits issued: 0 (2011); Employment by occupation: 8.3% management, 2.1% professional, 15.3% services, 24.2% sales, 0.3% farming, 12.9% construction, 3.1% production (2006-2010 5-year est.).

**Income:** Per capita income: $17,380 (2006-2010 5-year est.); Median household income: $45,329 (2006-2010 5-year est.); Average household income: $53,179 (2006-2010 5-year est.); Percent of households with income of $100,000 or more: 12.4% (2006-2010 5-year est.); Poverty rate: 22.6% (2006-2010 5-year est.).

**Education:** Percent of population age 25 and over with: High school diploma (including GED) or higher: 79.8% (2006-2010 5-year est.); Bachelor's degree or higher: 9.2% (2006-2010 5-year est.); Master's degree or higher: 0.8% (2006-2010 5-year est.).

**Housing:** Homeownership rate: 87.8% (2010); Median home value: $67,900 (2006-2010 5-year est.); Median contract rent: $392 per month (2006-2010 5-year est.); Median year structure built: 1965 (2006-2010 5-year est.).

**Transportation:** Commute to work: 92.9% car, 0.0% public transportation, 0.0% walk, 7.1% work from home (2006-2010 5-year est.); Travel time to work: 40.9% less than 15 minutes, 46.2% 15 to 30 minutes, 7.6% 30 to 45 minutes, 2.6% 45 to 60 minutes, 2.6% 60 minutes or more (2006-2010 5-year est.)

**BRIGHTON** (town). Covers a land area of 77.895 square miles and a water area of 5.100 square miles. Located at 44.46° N. Lat; 74.24° W. Long.

**Population:** 1,511 (1990); 1,682 (2000); 1,435 (2010); Density: 18.4 persons per square mile (2010); Race: 95.3% White, 1.9% Black, 0.8% Asian, 0.4% American Indian/Alaska Native, 0.1% Native Hawaiian/Other Pacific Islander, 1.5% Other, 1.6% Hispanic of any race (2010); Average household size: 2.32 (2010); Median age: 21.4 (2010); Males per 100 females: 146.1 (2010); Marriage status: 76.7% never married, 18.1% now married, 2.3% widowed, 3.0% divorced (2006-2010 5-year est.); Foreign born: 1.1% (2006-2010 5-year est.); Ancestry (includes multiple ancestries): 21.0% Irish, 16.8% French, 15.7% German, 8.9% Italian, 6.8% American (2006-2010 5-year est.).

**Economy:** Unemployment rate: 5.6% (February 2012); Total civilian labor force: 18,290 (February 2012); Single-family building permits issued: 4 (2011); Multi-family building permits issued: 0 (2011); Employment by occupation: 7.7% management, 5.7% professional, 16.6% services, 19.0% sales, 4.8% farming, 7.2% construction, 1.8% production (2006-2010 5-year est.).

**Income:** Per capita income: $11,719 (2006-2010 5-year est.); Median household income: $46,250 (2006-2010 5-year est.); Average household income: $56,601 (2006-2010 5-year est.); Percent of households with income of $100,000 or more: 12.4% (2006-2010 5-year est.); Poverty rate: 9.2% (2006-2010 5-year est.).

**Education:** Percent of population age 25 and over with: High school diploma (including GED) or higher: 87.8% (2006-2010 5-year est.); Bachelor's degree or higher: 18.0% (2006-2010 5-year est.); Master's degree or higher: 5.5% (2006-2010 5-year est.).

**Housing:** Homeownership rate: 78.6% (2010); Median home value: $118,800 (2006-2010 5-year est.); Median contract rent: $719 per month (2006-2010 5-year est.); Median year structure built: 1943 (2006-2010 5-year est.).

**Transportation:** Commute to work: 49.7% car, 0.0% public transportation, 31.9% walk, 18.4% work from home (2006-2010 5-year est.); Travel time to work: 62.0% less than 15 minutes, 25.9% 15 to 30 minutes, 4.9% 30 to 45 minutes, 5.6% 45 to 60 minutes, 1.5% 60 minutes or more (2006-2010 5-year est.)

**Additional Information Contacts**

Town of Brighton . . . . . . . . . . . . . . . . . . . . . . . . . . . . . . . . . (585) 784-5250
    http://www.townofbrighton.org

**BRUSHTON** (village). Covers a land area of 0.276 square miles and a water area of 0 square miles. Located at 44.83° N. Lat; 74.51° W. Long. Elevation is 420 feet.

**Population:** 522 (1990); 479 (2000); 474 (2010); Density: 1,714.9 persons per square mile (2010); Race: 96.8% White, 0.0% Black, 0.0% Asian, 1.5% American Indian/Alaska Native, 0.0% Native Hawaiian/Other Pacific

Islander, 1.7% Other, 0.6% Hispanic of any race (2010); Average household size: 2.24 (2010); Median age: 39.8 (2010); Males per 100 females: 95.9 (2010); Marriage status: 22.6% never married, 58.6% now married, 3.7% widowed, 15.2% divorced (2006-2010 5-year est.); Foreign born: 0.6% (2006-2010 5-year est.); Ancestry (includes multiple ancestries): 31.9% French, 17.1% Irish, 11.1% Dutch, 10.9% English, 3.4% Scottish (2006-2010 5-year est.).

**Economy:** Single-family building permits issued: 0 (2011); Multi-family building permits issued: 0 (2011); Employment by occupation: 2.2% management, 0.0% professional, 9.8% services, 12.4% sales, 0.9% farming, 8.0% construction, 3.6% production (2006-2010 5-year est.).

**Income:** Per capita income: $20,413 (2006-2010 5-year est.); Median household income: $26,250 (2006-2010 5-year est.); Average household income: $43,129 (2006-2010 5-year est.); Percent of households with income of $100,000 or more: 5.1% (2006-2010 5-year est.); Poverty rate: 23.8% (2006-2010 5-year est.).

**Education:** Percent of population age 25 and over with: High school diploma (including GED) or higher: 87.0% (2006-2010 5-year est.); Bachelor's degree or higher: 26.3% (2006-2010 5-year est.); Master's degree or higher: 16.6% (2006-2010 5-year est.).

### School District(s)

Brushton-Moira Central School District (PK-12)
    2009-10 Enrollment: 813 . . . . . . . . . . . . . . . . . . . . . . (518) 529-8948

**Housing:** Homeownership rate: 57.6% (2010); Median home value: $61,000 (2006-2010 5-year est.); Median contract rent: $369 per month (2006-2010 5-year est.); Median year structure built: before 1940 (2006-2010 5-year est.).

**Transportation:** Commute to work: 96.5% car, 0.0% public transportation, 0.0% walk, 3.5% work from home (2006-2010 5-year est.); Travel time to work: 23.2% less than 15 minutes, 40.2% 15 to 30 minutes, 12.4% 30 to 45 minutes, 12.4% 45 to 60 minutes, 11.9% 60 minutes or more (2006-2010 5-year est.)

**BURKE** (village). Covers a land area of 0.289 square miles and a water area of 0 square miles. Located at 44.90° N. Lat; 74.17° W. Long. Elevation is 863 feet.

**Population:** 209 (1990); 213 (2000); 211 (2010); Density: 728.0 persons per square mile (2010); Race: 96.7% White, 0.0% Black, 0.0% Asian, 0.0% American Indian/Alaska Native, 0.0% Native Hawaiian/Other Pacific Islander, 3.3% Other, 3.3% Hispanic of any race (2010); Average household size: 2.57 (2010); Median age: 31.3 (2010); Males per 100 females: 106.9 (2010); Marriage status: 31.0% never married, 58.6% now married, 5.5% widowed, 4.8% divorced (2006-2010 5-year est.); Foreign born: 9.9% (2006-2010 5-year est.); Ancestry (includes multiple ancestries): 31.9% French, 22.5% Irish, 19.8% German, 11.5% English, 11.0% American (2006-2010 5-year est.).

**Economy:** Single-family building permits issued: 0 (2011); Multi-family building permits issued: 0 (2011); Employment by occupation: 5.7% management, 2.3% professional, 8.0% services, 16.1% sales, 2.3% farming, 9.2% construction, 5.7% production (2006-2010 5-year est.).

**Income:** Per capita income: $32,042 (2006-2010 5-year est.); Median household income: $40,417 (2006-2010 5-year est.); Average household income: $67,927 (2006-2010 5-year est.); Percent of households with income of $100,000 or more: 3.5% (2006-2010 5-year est.); Poverty rate: 12.1% (2006-2010 5-year est.).

**Education:** Percent of population age 25 and over with: High school diploma (including GED) or higher: 85.9% (2006-2010 5-year est.); Bachelor's degree or higher: 19.5% (2006-2010 5-year est.); Master's degree or higher: 1.6% (2006-2010 5-year est.).

**Housing:** Homeownership rate: 67.1% (2010); Median home value: $54,400 (2006-2010 5-year est.); Median contract rent: $295 per month (2006-2010 5-year est.); Median year structure built: before 1940 (2006-2010 5-year est.).

**Transportation:** Commute to work: 88.0% car, 0.0% public transportation, 0.0% walk, 4.8% work from home (2006-2010 5-year est.); Travel time to work: 8.9% less than 15 minutes, 68.4% 15 to 30 minutes, 15.2% 30 to 45 minutes, 0.0% 45 to 60 minutes, 7.6% 60 minutes or more (2006-2010 5-year est.)

**BURKE** (town). Covers a land area of 44.405 square miles and a water area of 0 square miles. Located at 44.92° N. Lat; 74.18° W. Long. Elevation is 863 feet.

**Population:** 1,231 (1990); 1,359 (2000); 1,465 (2010); Density: 33.0 persons per square mile (2010); Race: 97.2% White, 0.4% Black, 0.3% Asian, 0.5% American Indian/Alaska Native, 0.0% Native Hawaiian/Other

Pacific Islander, 1.6% Other, 0.8% Hispanic of any race (2010); Average household size: 2.67 (2010); Median age: 38.0 (2010); Males per 100 females: 109.9 (2010); Marriage status: 22.6% never married, 65.7% now married, 6.0% widowed, 5.7% divorced (2006-2010 5-year est.); Foreign born: 7.0% (2006-2010 5-year est.); Ancestry (includes multiple ancestries): 20.4% French, 18.9% Irish, 14.4% German, 12.3% English, 10.0% French Canadian (2006-2010 5-year est.).
**Economy:** Single-family building permits issued: 6 (2011); Multi-family building permits issued: 0 (2011); Employment by occupation: 17.8% management, 2.2% professional, 6.5% services, 13.9% sales, 4.3% farming, 8.7% construction, 3.8% production (2006-2010 5-year est.).
**Income:** Per capita income: $23,852 (2006-2010 5-year est.); Median household income: $42,578 (2006-2010 5-year est.); Average household income: $58,062 (2006-2010 5-year est.); Percent of households with income of $100,000 or more: 11.8% (2006-2010 5-year est.); Poverty rate: 10.2% (2006-2010 5-year est.).
**Education:** Percent of population age 25 and over with: High school diploma (including GED) or higher: 84.6% (2006-2010 5-year est.); Bachelor's degree or higher: 15.2% (2006-2010 5-year est.); Master's degree or higher: 4.7% (2006-2010 5-year est.).
**Housing:** Homeownership rate: 83.6% (2010); Median home value: $95,700 (2006-2010 5-year est.); Median contract rent: $414 per month (2006-2010 5-year est.); Median year structure built: 1971 (2006-2010 5-year est.).
**Transportation:** Commute to work: 82.4% car, 0.0% public transportation, 2.8% walk, 12.8% work from home (2006-2010 5-year est.); Travel time to work: 32.3% less than 15 minutes, 51.3% 15 to 30 minutes, 9.8% 30 to 45 minutes, 1.9% 45 to 60 minutes, 4.7% 60 minutes or more (2006-2010 5-year est.)

**CHATEAUGAY** (village). Covers a land area of 1.083 square miles and a water area of 0 square miles. Located at 44.92° N. Lat; 74.08° W. Long. Elevation is 945 feet.
**Population:** 862 (1990); 798 (2000); 833 (2010); Density: 768.9 persons per square mile (2010); Race: 98.3% White, 0.2% Black, 0.1% Asian, 0.2% American Indian/Alaska Native, 0.7% Native Hawaiian/Other Pacific Islander, 0.5% Other, 0.7% Hispanic of any race (2010); Average household size: 2.32 (2010); Median age: 40.9 (2010); Males per 100 females: 87.2 (2010); Marriage status: 26.4% never married, 58.6% now married, 8.0% widowed, 6.9% divorced (2006-2010 5-year est.); Foreign born: 3.8% (2006-2010 5-year est.); Ancestry (includes multiple ancestries): 28.4% French, 26.6% Irish, 14.8% English, 6.3% Scotch-Irish, 5.5% Canadian (2006-2010 5-year est.).
**Economy:** Employment by occupation: 7.7% management, 0.0% professional, 16.2% services, 22.3% sales, 3.5% farming, 8.5% construction, 1.2% production (2006-2010 5-year est.).
**Income:** Per capita income: $19,232 (2006-2010 5-year est.); Median household income: $31,938 (2006-2010 5-year est.); Average household income: $42,933 (2006-2010 5-year est.); Percent of households with income of $100,000 or more: 6.6% (2006-2010 5-year est.); Poverty rate: 19.1% (2006-2010 5-year est.).
**Education:** Percent of population age 25 and over with: High school diploma (including GED) or higher: 90.6% (2006-2010 5-year est.); Bachelor's degree or higher: 18.0% (2006-2010 5-year est.); Master's degree or higher: 8.1% (2006-2010 5-year est.).
**School District(s)**
Chateaugay Central School District (PK-12)
    2009-10 Enrollment: 566 . . . . . . . . . . . . . . . . . . . . . . (518) 497-6420
**Housing:** Homeownership rate: 63.0% (2010); Median home value: $63,600 (2006-2010 5-year est.); Median contract rent: $394 per month (2006-2010 5-year est.); Median year structure built: before 1940 (2006-2010 5-year est.).
**Transportation:** Commute to work: 89.0% car, 3.7% public transportation, 6.5% walk, 0.8% work from home (2006-2010 5-year est.); Travel time to work: 48.4% less than 15 minutes, 31.1% 15 to 30 minutes, 3.3% 30 to 45 minutes, 4.9% 45 to 60 minutes, 12.3% 60 minutes or more (2006-2010 5-year est.)

**CHATEAUGAY** (town). Covers a land area of 49.788 square miles and a water area of 0.012 square miles. Located at 44.93° N. Lat; 74.07° W. Long. Elevation is 945 feet.
**History:** Settled 1796, incorporated 1869.
**Population:** 1,659 (1990); 2,036 (2000); 2,155 (2010); Density: 43.3 persons per square mile (2010); Race: 92.0% White, 5.7% Black, 0.1% Asian, 0.6% American Indian/Alaska Native, 0.3% Native Hawaiian/Other

Pacific Islander, 1.3% Other, 2.4% Hispanic of any race (2010); Average household size: 2.43 (2010); Median age: 39.4 (2010); Males per 100 females: 116.1 (2010); Marriage status: 35.9% never married, 50.0% now married, 4.7% widowed, 9.4% divorced (2006-2010 5-year est.); Foreign born: 2.8% (2006-2010 5-year est.); Ancestry (includes multiple ancestries): 32.8% French, 21.1% Irish, 8.5% English, 5.9% American, 5.6% French Canadian (2006-2010 5-year est.).
**Economy:** Single-family building permits issued: 1 (2011); Multi-family building permits issued: 0 (2011); Employment by occupation: 10.6% management, 0.5% professional, 14.0% services, 17.1% sales, 2.3% farming, 12.2% construction, 2.5% production (2006-2010 5-year est.).
**Income:** Per capita income: $19,209 (2006-2010 5-year est.); Median household income: $40,625 (2006-2010 5-year est.); Average household income: $51,941 (2006-2010 5-year est.); Percent of households with income of $100,000 or more: 9.7% (2006-2010 5-year est.); Poverty rate: 10.8% (2006-2010 5-year est.).
**Education:** Percent of population age 25 and over with: High school diploma (including GED) or higher: 79.1% (2006-2010 5-year est.); Bachelor's degree or higher: 10.8% (2006-2010 5-year est.); Master's degree or higher: 5.0% (2006-2010 5-year est.).
**School District(s)**
Chateaugay Central School District (PK-12)
    2009-10 Enrollment: 566 . . . . . . . . . . . . . . . . . . . . . . (518) 497-6420
**Housing:** Homeownership rate: 74.7% (2010); Median home value: $76,300 (2006-2010 5-year est.); Median contract rent: $409 per month (2006-2010 5-year est.); Median year structure built: 1959 (2006-2010 5-year est.).
**Transportation:** Commute to work: 88.2% car, 2.5% public transportation, 4.4% walk, 4.7% work from home (2006-2010 5-year est.); Travel time to work: 42.9% less than 15 minutes, 28.4% 15 to 30 minutes, 13.6% 30 to 45 minutes, 9.1% 45 to 60 minutes, 5.9% 60 minutes or more (2006-2010 5-year est.)

**CONSTABLE** (town). Covers a land area of 32.805 square miles and a water area of 0.012 square miles. Located at 44.96° N. Lat; 74.28° W. Long. Elevation is 354 feet.
**Population:** 1,203 (1990); 1,428 (2000); 1,566 (2010); Density: 47.7 persons per square mile (2010); Race: 97.8% White, 0.4% Black, 0.1% Asian, 1.0% American Indian/Alaska Native, 0.1% Native Hawaiian/Other Pacific Islander, 0.6% Other, 1.0% Hispanic of any race (2010); Average household size: 2.52 (2010); Median age: 40.5 (2010); Males per 100 females: 109.1 (2010); Marriage status: 26.0% never married, 58.4% now married, 5.8% widowed, 9.8% divorced (2006-2010 5-year est.); Foreign born: 3.3% (2006-2010 5-year est.); Ancestry (includes multiple ancestries): 27.8% French, 18.4% Irish, 12.3% American, 8.7% German, 7.2% French Canadian (2006-2010 5-year est.).
**Economy:** Single-family building permits issued: 8 (2011); Multi-family building permits issued: 0 (2011); Employment by occupation: 7.1% management, 0.0% professional, 24.3% services, 12.2% sales, 2.9% farming, 10.0% construction, 3.5% production (2006-2010 5-year est.).
**Income:** Per capita income: $19,086 (2006-2010 5-year est.); Median household income: $42,500 (2006-2010 5-year est.); Average household income: $47,072 (2006-2010 5-year est.); Percent of households with income of $100,000 or more: 6.6% (2006-2010 5-year est.); Poverty rate: 11.9% (2006-2010 5-year est.).
**Education:** Percent of population age 25 and over with: High school diploma (including GED) or higher: 82.8% (2006-2010 5-year est.); Bachelor's degree or higher: 9.8% (2006-2010 5-year est.); Master's degree or higher: 3.5% (2006-2010 5-year est.).
**Housing:** Homeownership rate: 81.9% (2010); Median home value: $73,500 (2006-2010 5-year est.); Median contract rent: $419 per month (2006-2010 5-year est.); Median year structure built: 1977 (2006-2010 5-year est.).
**Transportation:** Commute to work: 88.8% car, 1.1% public transportation, 4.5% walk, 4.5% work from home (2006-2010 5-year est.); Travel time to work: 39.7% less than 15 minutes, 40.3% 15 to 30 minutes, 8.2% 30 to 45 minutes, 4.3% 45 to 60 minutes, 7.5% 60 minutes or more (2006-2010 5-year est.)

**DICKINSON** (town). Covers a land area of 44.223 square miles and a water area of 0.089 square miles. Located at 44.72° N. Lat; 74.53° W. Long. Elevation is 722 feet.
**Population:** 751 (1990); 739 (2000); 823 (2010); Density: 18.6 persons per square mile (2010); Race: 97.9% White, 0.2% Black, 0.4% Asian, 0.4% American Indian/Alaska Native, 0.0% Native Hawaiian/Other Pacific

Islander, 1.1% Other, 0.4% Hispanic of any race (2010); Average household size: 2.44 (2010); Median age: 43.9 (2010); Males per 100 females: 103.7 (2010); Marriage status: 30.2% never married, 45.7% now married, 10.6% widowed, 13.6% divorced (2006-2010 5-year est.); Foreign born: 3.0% (2006-2010 5-year est.); Ancestry (includes multiple ancestries): 29.4% Irish, 23.7% French, 15.9% German, 14.8% Italian, 13.9% English (2006-2010 5-year est.).
**Economy:** Single-family building permits issued: 0 (2011); Multi-family building permits issued: 0 (2011); Employment by occupation: 8.0% management, 7.2% professional, 13.6% services, 5.6% sales, 7.2% farming, 30.2% construction, 9.6% production (2006-2010 5-year est.).
**Income:** Per capita income: $15,874 (2006-2010 5-year est.); Median household income: $33,063 (2006-2010 5-year est.); Average household income: $42,201 (2006-2010 5-year est.); Percent of households with income of $100,000 or more: 7.2% (2006-2010 5-year est.); Poverty rate: 30.3% (2006-2010 5-year est.).
**Education:** Percent of population age 25 and over with: High school diploma (including GED) or higher: 83.9% (2006-2010 5-year est.); Bachelor's degree or higher: 14.6% (2006-2010 5-year est.); Master's degree or higher: 5.9% (2006-2010 5-year est.).
**Housing:** Homeownership rate: 89.3% (2010); Median home value: $74,700 (2006-2010 5-year est.); Median contract rent: $397 per month (2006-2010 5-year est.); Median year structure built: 1961 (2006-2010 5-year est.).
**Transportation:** Commute to work: 88.2% car, 0.0% public transportation, 0.8% walk, 11.0% work from home (2006-2010 5-year est.); Travel time to work: 18.5% less than 15 minutes, 29.9% 15 to 30 minutes, 25.3% 30 to 45 minutes, 19.1% 45 to 60 minutes, 7.1% 60 minutes or more (2006-2010 5-year est.)

## DICKINSON CENTER (unincorporated postal area)
Zip Code: 12930

Covers a land area of 36.166 square miles and a water area of 0.075 square miles. Located at 44.72° N. Lat; 74.54° W. Long. Elevation is 955 feet. Population: 634 (2010); Density: 17.5 persons per square mile (2010); Race: 97.5% White, 0.2% Black, 0.5% Asian, 0.5% American Indian/Alaska Native, 0.0% Native Hawaiian/Other Pacific Islander, 1.3% Other, 0.5% Hispanic of any race (2010); Average household size: 2.37 (2010); Median age: 44.0 (2010); Males per 100 females: 103.2 (2010); Homeownership rate: 89.2% (2010)

## DUANE (town). Covers a land area of 74.951 square miles and a water area of 3.031 square miles. Located at 44.60° N. Lat; 74.23° W. Long.
**Population:** 152 (1990); 159 (2000); 174 (2010); Density: 2.3 persons per square mile (2010); Race: 99.4% White, 0.0% Black, 0.0% Asian, 0.0% American Indian/Alaska Native, 0.0% Native Hawaiian/Other Pacific Islander, 0.6% Other, 1.1% Hispanic of any race (2010); Average household size: 1.87 (2010); Median age: 53.7 (2010); Males per 100 females: 123.1 (2010); Marriage status: 7.5% never married, 78.2% now married, 7.5% widowed, 6.9% divorced (2006-2010 5-year est.); Foreign born: 10.2% (2006-2010 5-year est.); Ancestry (includes multiple ancestries): 29.4% French, 26.0% Irish, 19.8% English, 7.9% Dutch, 6.2% Polish (2006-2010 5-year est.).
**Economy:** Single-family building permits issued: 3 (2011); Multi-family building permits issued: 0 (2011); Employment by occupation: 5.3% management, 5.3% professional, 14.0% services, 7.0% sales, 1.8% farming, 3.5% construction, 0.0% production (2006-2010 5-year est.).
**Income:** Per capita income: $27,620 (2006-2010 5-year est.); Median household income: $46,688 (2006-2010 5-year est.); Average household income: $54,792 (2006-2010 5-year est.); Percent of households with income of $100,000 or more: 11.0% (2006-2010 5-year est.); Poverty rate: 7.9% (2006-2010 5-year est.).
**Education:** Percent of population age 25 and over with: High school diploma (including GED) or higher: 88.1% (2006-2010 5-year est.); Bachelor's degree or higher: 22.6% (2006-2010 5-year est.); Master's degree or higher: 14.3% (2006-2010 5-year est.).
**Housing:** Homeownership rate: 87.1% (2010); Median home value: $167,500 (2006-2010 5-year est.); Median contract rent: $183 per month (2006-2010 5-year est.); Median year structure built: 1968 (2006-2010 5-year est.).
**Transportation:** Commute to work: 74.1% car, 0.0% public transportation, 5.6% walk, 20.4% work from home (2006-2010 5-year est.); Travel time to work: 9.3% less than 15 minutes, 37.2% 15 to 30 minutes, 9.3% 30 to 45 minutes, 18.6% 45 to 60 minutes, 25.6% 60 minutes or more (2006-2010 5-year est.)

## FORT COVINGTON (town). Covers a land area of 36.734 square miles and a water area of 0 square miles. Located at 44.95° N. Lat; 74.48° W. Long. Elevation is 180 feet.
**Population:** 1,676 (1990); 1,645 (2000); 1,676 (2010); Density: 45.6 persons per square mile (2010); Race: 84.1% White, 0.5% Black, 0.1% Asian, 11.4% American Indian/Alaska Native, 0.0% Native Hawaiian/Other Pacific Islander, 3.9% Other, 2.8% Hispanic of any race (2010); Average household size: 2.52 (2010); Median age: 42.0 (2010); Males per 100 females: 100.7 (2010); Marriage status: 26.4% never married, 57.7% now married, 7.0% widowed, 9.0% divorced (2006-2010 5-year est.); Foreign born: 4.8% (2006-2010 5-year est.); Ancestry (includes multiple ancestries): 26.7% French, 16.0% Irish, 12.7% English, 7.2% French Canadian, 6.3% German (2006-2010 5-year est.).
**Economy:** Single-family building permits issued: 0 (2011); Multi-family building permits issued: 0 (2011); Employment by occupation: 7.1% management, 0.0% professional, 11.5% services, 13.5% sales, 4.1% farming, 11.2% construction, 7.8% production (2006-2010 5-year est.).
**Income:** Per capita income: $18,926 (2006-2010 5-year est.); Median household income: $41,484 (2006-2010 5-year est.); Average household income: $48,517 (2006-2010 5-year est.); Percent of households with income of $100,000 or more: 11.2% (2006-2010 5-year est.); Poverty rate: 17.1% (2006-2010 5-year est.).
**Education:** Percent of population age 25 and over with: High school diploma (including GED) or higher: 83.1% (2006-2010 5-year est.); Bachelor's degree or higher: 14.9% (2006-2010 5-year est.); Master's degree or higher: 7.0% (2006-2010 5-year est.).

**School District(s)**
Salmon River Central School District (PK-12)
   2009-10 Enrollment: 1,577 . . . . . . . . . . . . . . . . . . . . . . . (518) 358-6610
**Housing:** Homeownership rate: 80.6% (2010); Median home value: $64,600 (2006-2010 5-year est.); Median contract rent: $470 per month (2006-2010 5-year est.); Median year structure built: 1948 (2006-2010 5-year est.).
**Transportation:** Commute to work: 91.4% car, 2.0% public transportation, 0.7% walk, 5.7% work from home (2006-2010 5-year est.); Travel time to work: 33.9% less than 15 minutes, 48.3% 15 to 30 minutes, 13.3% 30 to 45 minutes, 1.2% 45 to 60 minutes, 3.3% 60 minutes or more (2006-2010 5-year est.)

## FORT COVINGTON HAMLET (CDP). Covers a land area of 19.321 square miles and a water area of 0.010 square miles. Located at 44.97° N. Lat; 74.50° W. Long.
**Population:** n/a (1990); n/a (2000); 1,308 (2010); Density: 67.7 persons per square mile (2010); Race: 80.8% White, 0.4% Black, 0.1% Asian, 14.2% American Indian/Alaska Native, 0.0% Native Hawaiian/Other Pacific Islander, 4.5% Other, 3.2% Hispanic of any race (2010); Average household size: 2.51 (2010); Median age: 41.3 (2010); Males per 100 females: 99.4 (2010); Marriage status: 28.5% never married, 58.0% now married, 7.4% widowed, 6.1% divorced (2006-2010 5-year est.); Foreign born: 5.0% (2006-2010 5-year est.); Ancestry (includes multiple ancestries): 29.1% French, 18.5% Irish, 10.3% English, 7.5% French Canadian, 6.0% German (2006-2010 5-year est.).
**Economy:** Employment by occupation: 8.1% management, 0.0% professional, 10.8% services, 12.6% sales, 4.1% farming, 12.2% construction, 9.1% production (2006-2010 5-year est.).
**Income:** Per capita income: $20,120 (2006-2010 5-year est.); Median household income: $45,573 (2006-2010 5-year est.); Average household income: $53,365 (2006-2010 5-year est.); Percent of households with income of $100,000 or more: 14.7% (2006-2010 5-year est.); Poverty rate: 13.3% (2006-2010 5-year est.).
**Education:** Percent of population age 25 and over with: High school diploma (including GED) or higher: 84.8% (2006-2010 5-year est.); Bachelor's degree or higher: 19.0% (2006-2010 5-year est.); Master's degree or higher: 8.7% (2006-2010 5-year est.).
**Housing:** Homeownership rate: 79.7% (2010); Median home value: $66,100 (2006-2010 5-year est.); Median contract rent: $446 per month (2006-2010 5-year est.); Median year structure built: 1944 (2006-2010 5-year est.).
**Transportation:** Commute to work: 90.7% car, 2.5% public transportation, 2.5% walk, 3.9% work from home (2006-2010 5-year est.); Travel time to work: 36.8% less than 15 minutes, 44.9% 15 to 30 minutes, 14.4% 30 to 45 minutes, 0.4% 45 to 60 minutes, 3.4% 60 minutes or more (2006-2010 5-year est.)

**FRANKLIN** (town). Covers a land area of 169.826 square miles and a water area of 5.395 square miles. Located at 44.52° N. Lat; 74.06° W. Long.

**Population:** 1,016 (1990); 1,197 (2000); 1,140 (2010); Density: 6.7 persons per square mile (2010); Race: 97.7% White, 0.0% Black, 0.0% Asian, 0.8% American Indian/Alaska Native, 0.1% Native Hawaiian/Other Pacific Islander, 1.4% Other, 1.1% Hispanic of any race (2010); Average household size: 2.24 (2010); Median age: 48.1 (2010); Males per 100 females: 102.5 (2010); Marriage status: 24.1% never married, 66.9% now married, 4.1% widowed, 4.9% divorced (2006-2010 5-year est.); Foreign born: 0.9% (2006-2010 5-year est.); Ancestry (includes multiple ancestries): 24.1% Irish, 20.6% French, 18.1% German, 8.5% English, 8.2% Italian (2006-2010 5-year est.).

**Economy:** Single-family building permits issued: 4 (2011); Multi-family building permits issued: 0 (2011); Employment by occupation: 5.6% management, 5.8% professional, 10.6% services, 19.7% sales, 3.5% farming, 19.0% construction, 5.1% production (2006-2010 5-year est.).

**Income:** Per capita income: $25,852 (2006-2010 5-year est.); Median household income: $54,630 (2006-2010 5-year est.); Average household income: $59,995 (2006-2010 5-year est.); Percent of households with income of $100,000 or more: 13.1% (2006-2010 5-year est.); Poverty rate: 6.0% (2006-2010 5-year est.).

**Education:** Percent of population age 25 and over with: High school diploma (including GED) or higher: 92.4% (2006-2010 5-year est.); Bachelor's degree or higher: 21.5% (2006-2010 5-year est.); Master's degree or higher: 9.2% (2006-2010 5-year est.).

**Housing:** Homeownership rate: 89.6% (2010); Median home value: $132,100 (2006-2010 5-year est.); Median contract rent: $564 per month (2006-2010 5-year est.); Median year structure built: 1973 (2006-2010 5-year est.).

**Transportation:** Commute to work: 83.0% car, 0.6% public transportation, 1.2% walk, 12.2% work from home (2006-2010 5-year est.); Travel time to work: 9.7% less than 15 minutes, 55.8% 15 to 30 minutes, 22.4% 30 to 45 minutes, 10.6% 45 to 60 minutes, 1.5% 60 minutes or more (2006-2010 5-year est.)

**GABRIELS** (unincorporated postal area)
Zip Code: 12939

Covers a land area of 4.136 square miles and a water area of 0.022 square miles. Located at 44.43° N. Lat; 74.16° W. Long. Elevation is 1,699 feet. Population: 205 (2010); Density: 49.6 persons per square mile (2010); Race: 95.6% White, 0.5% Black, 1.5% Asian, 0.0% American Indian/Alaska Native, 0.0% Native Hawaiian/Other Pacific Islander, 2.4% Other, 1.5% Hispanic of any race (2010); Average household size: 2.38 (2010); Median age: 38.2 (2010); Males per 100 females: 97.1 (2010); Homeownership rate: 75.5% (2010)

**HARRIETSTOWN** (town). Covers a land area of 196.866 square miles and a water area of 16.814 square miles. Located at 44.21° N. Lat; 74.20° W. Long. Elevation is 1,854 feet.

**Population:** 5,621 (1990); 5,575 (2000); 5,709 (2010); Density: 29.0 persons per square mile (2010); Race: 95.4% White, 1.3% Black, 0.8% Asian, 0.6% American Indian/Alaska Native, 0.0% Native Hawaiian/Other Pacific Islander, 1.9% Other, 1.6% Hispanic of any race (2010); Average household size: 2.11 (2010); Median age: 41.2 (2010); Males per 100 females: 103.9 (2010); Marriage status: 26.4% never married, 56.1% now married, 4.6% widowed, 12.9% divorced (2006-2010 5-year est.); Foreign born: 6.8% (2006-2010 5-year est.); Ancestry (includes multiple ancestries): 22.3% Irish, 17.1% French, 16.0% English, 14.4% German, 9.4% Italian (2006-2010 5-year est.).

**Economy:** Single-family building permits issued: 3 (2011); Multi-family building permits issued: 0 (2011); Employment by occupation: 8.5% management, 3.5% professional, 11.7% services, 18.4% sales, 2.6% farming, 10.6% construction, 4.9% production (2006-2010 5-year est.).

**Income:** Per capita income: $25,442 (2006-2010 5-year est.); Median household income: $41,834 (2006-2010 5-year est.); Average household income: $54,745 (2006-2010 5-year est.); Percent of households with income of $100,000 or more: 15.9% (2006-2010 5-year est.); Poverty rate: 10.2% (2006-2010 5-year est.).

**Taxes:** Total city taxes per capita: $310 (2009); City property taxes per capita: $284 (2009).

**Education:** Percent of population age 25 and over with: High school diploma (including GED) or higher: 92.4% (2006-2010 5-year est.); Bachelor's degree or higher: 36.9% (2006-2010 5-year est.); Master's degree or higher: 21.1% (2006-2010 5-year est.).

**Housing:** Homeownership rate: 54.2% (2010); Median home value: $147,900 (2006-2010 5-year est.); Median contract rent: $514 per month (2006-2010 5-year est.); Median year structure built: before 1940 (2006-2010 5-year est.).

**Transportation:** Commute to work: 85.2% car, 0.2% public transportation, 9.7% walk, 4.1% work from home (2006-2010 5-year est.); Travel time to work: 54.6% less than 15 minutes, 35.1% 15 to 30 minutes, 7.2% 30 to 45 minutes, 1.3% 45 to 60 minutes, 1.9% 60 minutes or more (2006-2010 5-year est.)

**HOGANSBURG** (unincorporated postal area)
Zip Code: 13655

Covers a land area of 20.221 square miles and a water area of 2.251 square miles. Located at 44.98° N. Lat; 74.65° W. Long. Elevation is 171 feet. Population: 3,512 (2010); Density: 173.7 persons per square mile (2010); Race: 4.4% White, 0.1% Black, 0.0% Asian, 92.7% American Indian/Alaska Native, 0.0% Native Hawaiian/Other Pacific Islander, 2.8% Other, 0.6% Hispanic of any race (2010); Average household size: 2.73 (2010); Median age: 31.2 (2010); Males per 100 females: 96.4 (2010); Homeownership rate: 74.6% (2010)

**LAKE CLEAR** (unincorporated postal area)
Zip Code: 12945

Covers a land area of 33.207 square miles and a water area of 7.217 square miles. Located at 44.30° N. Lat; 74.24° W. Long. Elevation is 1,640 feet. Population: 638 (2010); Density: 19.2 persons per square mile (2010); Race: 96.6% White, 0.5% Black, 0.3% Asian, 0.3% American Indian/Alaska Native, 0.0% Native Hawaiian/Other Pacific Islander, 2.3% Other, 0.8% Hispanic of any race (2010); Average household size: 2.35 (2010); Median age: 45.6 (2010); Males per 100 females: 98.8 (2010); Homeownership rate: 83.8% (2010)

**MALONE** (village). County seat. Covers a land area of 3.110 square miles and a water area of 0.065 square miles. Located at 44.84° N. Lat; 74.28° W. Long. Elevation is 712 feet.

**History:** Was gathering point for the Fenians, who raided Canada in 1866. Settled c.1800. Incorporated 1833.

**Population:** 6,778 (1990); 6,075 (2000); 5,911 (2010); Density: 1,900.2 persons per square mile (2010); Race: 96.0% White, 0.6% Black, 0.8% Asian, 1.1% American Indian/Alaska Native, 0.0% Native Hawaiian/Other Pacific Islander, 1.5% Other, 1.6% Hispanic of any race (2010); Average household size: 2.21 (2010); Median age: 41.0 (2010); Males per 100 females: 85.0 (2010); Marriage status: 24.4% never married, 56.2% now married, 9.6% widowed, 9.8% divorced (2006-2010 5-year est.); Foreign born: 4.4% (2006-2010 5-year est.); Ancestry (includes multiple ancestries): 23.9% French, 22.6% Irish, 12.3% English, 11.9% American, 10.8% German (2006-2010 5-year est.).

**Economy:** Single-family building permits issued: 0 (2011); Multi-family building permits issued: 0 (2011); Employment by occupation: 6.8% management, 0.9% professional, 14.2% services, 17.5% sales, 2.5% farming, 9.7% construction, 7.3% production (2006-2010 5-year est.).

**Income:** Per capita income: $20,715 (2006-2010 5-year est.); Median household income: $35,482 (2006-2010 5-year est.); Average household income: $46,492 (2006-2010 5-year est.); Percent of households with income of $100,000 or more: 8.2% (2006-2010 5-year est.); Poverty rate: 22.3% (2006-2010 5-year est.).

**Education:** Percent of population age 25 and over with: High school diploma (including GED) or higher: 90.4% (2006-2010 5-year est.); Bachelor's degree or higher: 20.4% (2006-2010 5-year est.); Master's degree or higher: 7.4% (2006-2010 5-year est.).

### School District(s)

Franklin-Essex-Hamilton Boces
  2009-10 Enrollment: n/a . . . . . . . . . . . . . . . . . . . . . . . . . . (518) 483-6420
Malone Central School District (PK-12)
  2009-10 Enrollment: 2,455 . . . . . . . . . . . . . . . . . . . . . (518) 483-7800

**Housing:** Homeownership rate: 50.0% (2010); Median home value: $75,100 (2006-2010 5-year est.); Median contract rent: $485 per month (2006-2010 5-year est.); Median year structure built: before 1940 (2006-2010 5-year est.).

**Hospitals:** Alice Hyde Medical Center (76 beds)

**Safety:** Violent crime rate: 12.4 per 10,000 population; Property crime rate: 463.8 per 10,000 population (2010).

**Newspapers:** Malone Telegram (Local news; Circulation 6,500)

**Transportation:** Commute to work: 82.3% car, 0.5% public transportation, 8.8% walk, 6.0% work from home (2006-2010 5-year est.); Travel time to

work: 64.1% less than 15 minutes, 14.8% 15 to 30 minutes, 5.5% 30 to 45 minutes, 5.5% 45 to 60 minutes, 10.1% 60 minutes or more (2006-2010 5-year est.)

**Additional Information Contacts**

Malone Chamber of Commerce . . . . . . . . . . . . . . . . . . . . (518) 483-3760
  http://www.malonenychamber.com

**MALONE** (town). Covers a land area of 101.519 square miles and a water area of 1.282 square miles. Located at 44.79° N. Lat; 74.28° W. Long. Elevation is 712 feet.

**History:** Malone was settled by Vermonters in 1802. The name was bestowed by William Constable, an early landowner, in honor of his friend, Edmund Malone, Shakespearian scholar.

**Population:** 12,982 (1990); 14,981 (2000); 14,545 (2010); Density: 143.3 persons per square mile (2010); Race: 77.1% White, 18.5% Black, 0.6% Asian, 0.8% American Indian/Alaska Native, 0.0% Native Hawaiian/Other Pacific Islander, 3.0% Other, 7.2% Hispanic of any race (2010); Average household size: 2.31 (2010); Median age: 37.7 (2010); Males per 100 females: 175.8 (2010); Marriage status: 42.5% never married, 44.2% now married, 5.5% widowed, 7.9% divorced (2006-2010 5-year est.); Foreign born: 5.9% (2006-2010 5-year est.); Ancestry (includes multiple ancestries): 15.6% French, 14.6% Irish, 7.3% English, 6.6% German, 6.6% American (2006-2010 5-year est.).

**Economy:** Single-family building permits issued: 9 (2011); Multi-family building permits issued: 0 (2011); Employment by occupation: 7.7% management, 1.2% professional, 13.2% services, 18.5% sales, 3.4% farming, 8.6% construction, 5.2% production (2006-2010 5-year est.).

**Income:** Per capita income: $15,784 (2006-2010 5-year est.); Median household income: $39,266 (2006-2010 5-year est.); Average household income: $53,622 (2006-2010 5-year est.); Percent of households with income of $100,000 or more: 11.0% (2006-2010 5-year est.); Poverty rate: 19.4% (2006-2010 5-year est.).

**Education:** Percent of population age 25 and over with: High school diploma (including GED) or higher: 79.5% (2006-2010 5-year est.); Bachelor's degree or higher: 12.8% (2006-2010 5-year est.); Master's degree or higher: 5.0% (2006-2010 5-year est.).

**School District(s)**

Franklin-Essex-Hamilton Boces

  2009-10 Enrollment: n/a . . . . . . . . . . . . . . . . . . . . . . (518) 483-6420

Malone Central School District (PK-12)

  2009-10 Enrollment: 2,455 . . . . . . . . . . . . . . . . . . . . (518) 483-7800

**Housing:** Homeownership rate: 63.1% (2010); Median home value: $79,900 (2006-2010 5-year est.); Median contract rent: $482 per month (2006-2010 5-year est.); Median year structure built: 1945 (2006-2010 5-year est.).

**Hospitals:** Alice Hyde Medical Center (76 beds)

**Newspapers:** Malone Telegram (Local news; Circulation 6,500)

**Transportation:** Commute to work: 87.6% car, 1.0% public transportation, 5.6% walk, 4.0% work from home (2006-2010 5-year est.); Travel time to work: 64.0% less than 15 minutes, 17.8% 15 to 30 minutes, 4.9% 30 to 45 minutes, 5.5% 45 to 60 minutes, 7.8% 60 minutes or more (2006-2010 5-year est.)

**MOIRA** (town). Covers a land area of 45.227 square miles and a water area of 0 square miles. Located at 44.82° N. Lat; 74.55° W. Long. Elevation is 420 feet.

**Population:** 2,684 (1990); 2,857 (2000); 2,934 (2010); Density: 64.9 persons per square mile (2010); Race: 97.5% White, 0.0% Black, 0.6% Asian, 1.2% American Indian/Alaska Native, 0.0% Native Hawaiian/Other Pacific Islander, 0.7% Other, 0.6% Hispanic of any race (2010); Average household size: 2.45 (2010); Median age: 39.0 (2010); Males per 100 females: 96.5 (2010); Marriage status: 25.1% never married, 54.1% now married, 8.1% widowed, 12.7% divorced (2006-2010 5-year est.); Foreign born: 2.3% (2006-2010 5-year est.); Ancestry (includes multiple ancestries): 31.0% French, 25.4% Irish, 18.5% English, 4.1% German, 3.7% Italian (2006-2010 5-year est.).

**Economy:** Employment by occupation: 5.4% management, 0.0% professional, 16.0% services, 14.2% sales, 2.4% farming, 6.0% construction, 2.4% production (2006-2010 5-year est.).

**Income:** Per capita income: $21,475 (2006-2010 5-year est.); Median household income: $34,031 (2006-2010 5-year est.); Average household income: $47,569 (2006-2010 5-year est.); Percent of households with income of $100,000 or more: 9.6% (2006-2010 5-year est.); Poverty rate: 14.7% (2006-2010 5-year est.).

**Education:** Percent of population age 25 and over with: High school diploma (including GED) or higher: 84.3% (2006-2010 5-year est.); Bachelor's degree or higher: 18.4% (2006-2010 5-year est.); Master's degree or higher: 10.4% (2006-2010 5-year est.).

**Housing:** Homeownership rate: 74.5% (2010); Median home value: $73,200 (2006-2010 5-year est.); Median contract rent: $428 per month (2006-2010 5-year est.); Median year structure built: 1971 (2006-2010 5-year est.).

**Transportation:** Commute to work: 90.4% car, 0.0% public transportation, 4.7% walk, 4.8% work from home (2006-2010 5-year est.); Travel time to work: 26.6% less than 15 minutes, 45.2% 15 to 30 minutes, 15.2% 30 to 45 minutes, 8.5% 45 to 60 minutes, 4.5% 60 minutes or more (2006-2010 5-year est.)

**NORTH BANGOR** (unincorporated postal area)

Zip Code: 12966

  Covers a land area of 86.157 square miles and a water area of 0.067 square miles. Located at 44.79° N. Lat; 74.41° W. Long. Elevation is 666 feet. Population: 2,915 (2010); Density: 33.8 persons per square mile (2010); Race: 97.3% White, 0.4% Black, 0.1% Asian, 0.3% American Indian/Alaska Native, 0.0% Native Hawaiian/Other Pacific Islander, 1.9% Other, 1.0% Hispanic of any race (2010); Average household size: 2.57 (2010); Median age: 40.4 (2010); Males per 100 females: 105.1 (2010); Homeownership rate: 83.6% (2010)

**OWLS HEAD** (unincorporated postal area)

Zip Code: 12969

  Covers a land area of 98.651 square miles and a water area of 1.856 square miles. Located at 44.71° N. Lat; 74.09° W. Long. Elevation is 1,532 feet. Population: 423 (2010); Density: 4.3 persons per square mile (2010); Race: 96.5% White, 0.2% Black, 0.5% Asian, 1.2% American Indian/Alaska Native, 0.0% Native Hawaiian/Other Pacific Islander, 1.6% Other, 1.7% Hispanic of any race (2010); Average household size: 2.17 (2010); Median age: 48.2 (2010); Males per 100 females: 119.2 (2010); Homeownership rate: 93.8% (2010)

**PAUL SMITHS** (CDP). Covers a land area of 0.255 square miles and a water area of 0.135 square miles. Located at 44.43° N. Lat; 74.24° W. Long. Elevation is 1,673 feet.

**Population:** n/a (1990); n/a (2000); 671 (2010); Density: 2,628.9 persons per square mile (2010); Race: 92.8% White, 3.6% Black, 1.0% Asian, 0.7% American Indian/Alaska Native, 0.1% Native Hawaiian/Other Pacific Islander, 1.8% Other, 2.5% Hispanic of any race (2010); Average household size: 1.50 (2010); Median age: 20.0 (2010); Males per 100 females: 238.9 (2010); Marriage status: 98.8% never married, 0.8% now married, 0.0% widowed, 0.4% divorced (2006-2010 5-year est.); Foreign born: 0.0% (2006-2010 5-year est.); Ancestry (includes multiple ancestries): 17.3% German, 16.8% French, 16.4% Irish, 11.9% Italian, 5.9% Scottish (2006-2010 5-year est.).

**Economy:** Employment by occupation: 8.0% management, 8.0% professional, 18.6% services, 21.9% sales, 4.3% farming, 2.9% construction, 2.9% production (2006-2010 5-year est.).

**Income:** Per capita income: $5,765 (2006-2010 5-year est.); Median household income: $82,188 (2006-2010 5-year est.); Average household income: $0 (2006-2010 5-year est.); Percent of households with income of $100,000 or more: 42.9% (2006-2010 5-year est.); Poverty rate: 0.0% (2006-2010 5-year est.).

**Education:** Percent of population age 25 and over with: High school diploma (including GED) or higher: 100.0% (2006-2010 5-year est.); Bachelor's degree or higher: 100.0% (2006-2010 5-year est.); Master's degree or higher: 100.0% (2006-2010 5-year est.).

**Four-year College(s)**

Paul Smiths College of Arts and Science (Private, Not-for-profit)

  Fall 2010 Enrollment: 1,017 . . . . . . . . . . . . . . . . . . . . . . . (518) 327-6000

  2011-12 Tuition: In-state $23,695; Out-of-state $23,695

**Housing:** Homeownership rate: 0.0% (2010); Median home value: n/a (2006-2010 5-year est.); Median contract rent: n/a per month (2006-2010 5-year est.); Median year structure built: before 1940 (2006-2010 5-year est.).

**Transportation:** Commute to work: 27.0% car, 0.0% public transportation, 47.2% walk, 25.8% work from home (2006-2010 5-year est.); Travel time to work: 85.4% less than 15 minutes, 4.9% 15 to 30 minutes, 0.0% 30 to 45 minutes, 9.7% 45 to 60 minutes, 0.0% 60 minutes or more (2006-2010 5-year est.)

## RAINBOW LAKE (unincorporated postal area)

Zip Code: 12976

Covers a land area of 38.370 square miles and a water area of 1.197 square miles. Located at 44.52° N. Lat; 74.21° W. Long. Elevation is 1,690 feet. Population: 260 (2010); Density: 6.8 persons per square mile (2010); Race: 98.8% White, 0.0% Black, 0.0% Asian, 0.0% American Indian/Alaska Native, 0.0% Native Hawaiian/Other Pacific Islander, 1.2% Other, 0.0% Hispanic of any race (2010); Average household size: 2.26 (2010); Median age: 47.0 (2010); Males per 100 females: 100.0 (2010); Homeownership rate: 86.1% (2010).

## SAINT REGIS MOHAWK RESERVATION (Reservation).

Covers a land area of 18.940 square miles and a water area of 2.048 square miles. Located at 44.97° N. Lat; 74.64° W. Long.

Population: 1,978 (1990); 2,699 (2000); 3,228 (2010); Density: 170.4 persons per square mile (2010); Race: 2.9% White, 0.1% Black, 0.0% Asian, 94.5% American Indian/Alaska Native, 0.0% Native Hawaiian/Other Pacific Islander, 2.5% Other, 0.5% Hispanic of any race (2010); Average household size: 2.79 (2010); Median age: 30.9 (2010); Males per 100 females: 94.8 (2010); Marriage status: 38.9% never married, 44.4% now married, 6.4% widowed, 10.3% divorced (2006-2010 5-year est.); Foreign born: 25.3% (2006-2010 5-year est.); Ancestry (includes multiple ancestries): 5.2% Guyanese, 4.3% African, 2.8% French, 2.2% Irish, 2.1% Other Arab (2006-2010 5-year est.).

Economy: Employment by occupation: 12.2% management, 1.1% professional, 20.4% services, 9.7% sales, 0.0% farming, 16.6% construction, 0.6% production (2006-2010 5-year est.).

Income: Per capita income: $18,225 (2006-2010 5-year est.); Median household income: $43,777 (2006-2010 5-year est.); Average household income: $47,623 (2006-2010 5-year est.); Percent of households with income of $100,000 or more: 4.8% (2006-2010 5-year est.); Poverty rate: 12.9% (2006-2010 5-year est.).

Education: Percent of population age 25 and over with: High school diploma (including GED) or higher: 76.9% (2006-2010 5-year est.); Bachelor's degree or higher: 28.5% (2006-2010 5-year est.); Master's degree or higher: 11.0% (2006-2010 5-year est.).

Housing: Homeownership rate: 79.5% (2010); Median home value: $112,500 (2006-2010 5-year est.); Median contract rent: $625 per month (2006-2010 5-year est.); Median year structure built: 1975 (2006-2010 5-year est.).

Transportation: Commute to work: 97.7% car, 0.0% public transportation, 0.0% walk, 2.3% work from home (2006-2010 5-year est.); Travel time to work: 61.2% less than 15 minutes, 29.6% 15 to 30 minutes, 9.2% 30 to 45 minutes, 0.0% 45 to 60 minutes, 0.0% 60 minutes or more (2006-2010 5-year est.)

## SANTA CLARA (town). Covers a land area of 174.417 square miles and a water area of 17.291 square miles. Located at 44.49° N. Lat; 74.36° W. Long. Elevation is 1,339 feet.

Population: 311 (1990); 395 (2000); 345 (2010); Density: 2.0 persons per square mile (2010); Race: 98.3% White, 0.3% Black, 0.0% Asian, 0.9% American Indian/Alaska Native, 0.0% Native Hawaiian/Other Pacific Islander, 0.5% Other, 0.0% Hispanic of any race (2010); Average household size: 2.27 (2010); Median age: 50.4 (2010); Males per 100 females: 113.0 (2010); Marriage status: 15.4% never married, 72.8% now married, 6.6% widowed, 5.2% divorced (2006-2010 5-year est.); Foreign born: 3.0% (2006-2010 5-year est.); Ancestry (includes multiple ancestries): 22.1% Irish, 20.1% French, 18.3% English, 18.0% Italian, 17.0% German (2006-2010 5-year est.).

Economy: Single-family building permits issued: 1 (2011); Multi-family building permits issued: 0 (2011); Employment by occupation: 10.3% management, 0.0% professional, 15.4% services, 25.7% sales, 5.1% farming, 14.9% construction, 6.9% production (2006-2010 5-year est.).

Income: Per capita income: $33,932 (2006-2010 5-year est.); Median household income: $55,227 (2006-2010 5-year est.); Average household income: $69,678 (2006-2010 5-year est.); Percent of households with income of $100,000 or more: 19.5% (2006-2010 5-year est.); Poverty rate: 2.8% (2006-2010 5-year est.).

Education: Percent of population age 25 and over with: High school diploma (including GED) or higher: 99.1% (2006-2010 5-year est.); Bachelor's degree or higher: 35.2% (2006-2010 5-year est.); Master's degree or higher: 16.7% (2006-2010 5-year est.).

Housing: Homeownership rate: 70.2% (2010); Median home value: $268,200 (2006-2010 5-year est.); Median contract rent: $618 per month

(2006-2010 5-year est.); Median year structure built: 1972 (2006-2010 5-year est.).

Transportation: Commute to work: 84.6% car, 0.0% public transportation, 5.7% walk, 8.6% work from home (2006-2010 5-year est.); Travel time to work: 28.1% less than 15 minutes, 25.0% 15 to 30 minutes, 39.4% 30 to 45 minutes, 5.0% 45 to 60 minutes, 2.5% 60 minutes or more (2006-2010 5-year est.)

## SARANAC LAKE (village). Covers a land area of 2.779 square miles and a water area of 0.248 square miles. Located at 44.32° N. Lat; 74.13° W. Long. Elevation is 1,545 feet.

Population: 5,377 (1990); 5,041 (2000); 5,406 (2010); Density: 1,945.3 persons per square mile (2010); Race: 94.9% White, 1.5% Black, 0.9% Asian, 0.7% American Indian/Alaska Native, 0.0% Native Hawaiian/Other Pacific Islander, 2.0% Other, 1.8% Hispanic of any race (2010); Average household size: 1.98 (2010); Median age: 39.6 (2010); Males per 100 females: 98.1 (2010); Marriage status: 32.1% never married, 48.9% now married, 5.6% widowed, 13.4% divorced (2006-2010 5-year est.); Foreign born: 7.3% (2006-2010 5-year est.); Ancestry (includes multiple ancestries): 23.5% Irish, 18.0% French, 13.8% English, 13.3% German, 7.3% Italian (2006-2010 5-year est.).

Economy: Single-family building permits issued: 2 (2011); Multi-family building permits issued: 0 (2011); Employment by occupation: 5.6% management, 2.9% professional, 9.7% services, 18.1% sales, 2.8% farming, 13.5% construction, 5.5% production (2006-2010 5-year est.).

Income: Per capita income: $23,354 (2006-2010 5-year est.); Median household income: $40,104 (2006-2010 5-year est.); Average household income: $50,187 (2006-2010 5-year est.); Percent of households with income of $100,000 or more: 12.7% (2006-2010 5-year est.); Poverty rate: 11.3% (2006-2010 5-year est.).

Education: Percent of population age 25 and over with: High school diploma (including GED) or higher: 93.2% (2006-2010 5-year est.); Bachelor's degree or higher: 34.8% (2006-2010 5-year est.); Master's degree or higher: 17.8% (2006-2010 5-year est.).

### School District(s)

Saranac Lake Central School District (PK-12)

2009-10 Enrollment: 1,426 . . . . . . . . . . . . . . . . . . . . . . . (518) 891-5460

### Two-year College(s)

North Country Community College (Public)

Fall 2010 Enrollment: 1,358 . . . . . . . . . . . . . . . . . . . . . (518) 891-2915

2011-12 Tuition: In-state $4,735; Out-of-state $10,435

Housing: Homeownership rate: 44.0% (2010); Median home value: $141,800 (2006-2010 5-year est.); Median contract rent: $523 per month (2006-2010 5-year est.); Median year structure built: before 1940 (2006-2010 5-year est.).

Hospitals: Adirondack Medical Center (97 beds)

Safety: Violent crime rate: 19.2 per 10,000 population; Property crime rate: 337.0 per 10,000 population (2010).

Newspapers: Adirondack Enterprise (Local news; Circulation 5,000); Adirondack Explorer (Regional news; Circulation 12,000)

Transportation: Commute to work: 85.8% car, 0.2% public transportation, 10.0% walk, 3.3% work from home (2006-2010 5-year est.); Travel time to work: 59.3% less than 15 minutes, 32.5% 15 to 30 minutes, 5.8% 30 to 45 minutes, 1.3% 45 to 60 minutes, 1.2% 60 minutes or more (2006-2010 5-year est.)

Airports: Adirondack Regional (commercial service)

**Additional Information Contacts**

Saranac Lake Area Chamber of Commerce . . . . . . . . . . . . (518) 891-1990

http://www.saranaclake.com

## ST. REGIS FALLS (CDP). Covers a land area of 1.291 square miles and a water area of 0 square miles. Located at 44.67° N. Lat; 74.53° W. Long.

Population: n/a (1990); n/a (2000); 464 (2010); Density: 359.2 persons per square mile (2010); Race: 96.6% White, 0.2% Black, 0.0% Asian, 1.1% American Indian/Alaska Native, 0.0% Native Hawaiian/Other Pacific Islander, 2.1% Other, 2.2% Hispanic of any race (2010); Average household size: 2.33 (2010); Median age: 40.0 (2010); Males per 100 females: 89.4 (2010); Marriage status: 34.4% never married, 42.1% now married, 10.3% widowed, 13.2% divorced (2006-2010 5-year est.); Foreign born: 2.1% (2006-2010 5-year est.); Ancestry (includes multiple ancestries): 17.8% French, 16.5% Irish, 14.7% French Canadian, 9.8% English, 8.5% American (2006-2010 5-year est.).

**Economy:** Employment by occupation: 16.9% management, 0.0% professional, 13.4% services, 11.3% sales, 1.4% farming, 10.6% construction, 4.9% production (2006-2010 5-year est.).
**Income:** Per capita income: $16,903 (2006-2010 5-year est.); Median household income: $33,295 (2006-2010 5-year est.); Average household income: $38,577 (2006-2010 5-year est.); Percent of households with income of $100,000 or more: 2.3% (2006-2010 5-year est.); Poverty rate: 10.3% (2006-2010 5-year est.).
**Education:** Percent of population age 25 and over with: High school diploma (including GED) or higher: 82.2% (2006-2010 5-year est.); Bachelor's degree or higher: 8.1% (2006-2010 5-year est.); Master's degree or higher: 4.9% (2006-2010 5-year est.).
**Housing:** Homeownership rate: 66.8% (2010); Median home value: $58,700 (2006-2010 5-year est.); Median contract rent: $388 per month (2006-2010 5-year est.); Median year structure built: before 1940 (2006-2010 5-year est.).
**Transportation:** Commute to work: 100.0% car, 0.0% public transportation, 0.0% walk, 0.0% work from home (2006-2010 5-year est.); Travel time to work: 13.0% less than 15 minutes, 20.6% 15 to 30 minutes, 28.2% 30 to 45 minutes, 26.7% 45 to 60 minutes, 11.5% 60 minutes or more (2006-2010 5-year est.)

**TUPPER LAKE** (village). Covers a land area of 2.090 square miles and a water area of 0.043 square miles. Located at 44.22° N. Lat; 74.46° W. Long. Elevation is 1,598 feet.
**History:** Settled 1890, incorporated 1902.
**Population:** 4,087 (1990); 3,935 (2000); 3,667 (2010); Density: 1,754.2 persons per square mile (2010); Race: 97.5% White, 0.5% Black, 0.3% Asian, 0.7% American Indian/Alaska Native, 0.0% Native Hawaiian/Other Pacific Islander, 1.0% Other, 0.9% Hispanic of any race (2010); Average household size: 2.22 (2010); Median age: 40.3 (2010); Males per 100 females: 97.7 (2010); Marriage status: 27.6% never married, 54.0% now married, 7.9% widowed, 10.5% divorced (2006-2010 5-year est.); Foreign born: 4.0% (2006-2010 5-year est.); Ancestry (includes multiple ancestries): 25.7% French, 15.1% French Canadian, 13.3% German, 13.3% Irish, 6.8% English (2006-2010 5-year est.).
**Economy:** Single-family building permits issued: 0 (2011); Multi-family building permits issued: 0 (2011); Employment by occupation: 4.2% management, 2.9% professional, 21.9% services, 14.6% sales, 4.0% farming, 16.4% construction, 2.2% production (2006-2010 5-year est.).
**Income:** Per capita income: $21,259 (2006-2010 5-year est.); Median household income: $38,463 (2006-2010 5-year est.); Average household income: $48,631 (2006-2010 5-year est.); Percent of households with income of $100,000 or more: 12.0% (2006-2010 5-year est.); Poverty rate: 12.9% (2006-2010 5-year est.).
**Education:** Percent of population age 25 and over with: High school diploma (including GED) or higher: 82.2% (2006-2010 5-year est.); Bachelor's degree or higher: 13.7% (2006-2010 5-year est.); Master's degree or higher: 3.5% (2006-2010 5-year est.).

**School District(s)**
Tupper Lake Central School District (PK-12)
    2009-10 Enrollment: 925 . . . . . . . . . . . . . . . . . . . . . . (518) 359-3371
**Housing:** Homeownership rate: 62.5% (2010); Median home value: $85,500 (2006-2010 5-year est.); Median contract rent: $487 per month (2006-2010 5-year est.); Median year structure built: 1947 (2006-2010 5-year est.).
**Safety:** Violent crime rate: 10.7 per 10,000 population; Property crime rate: 283.4 per 10,000 population (2010).
**Newspapers:** Tupper Lake Free Press (Community news; Circulation 3,700)
**Transportation:** Commute to work: 89.1% car, 0.0% public transportation, 5.7% walk, 3.5% work from home (2006-2010 5-year est.); Travel time to work: 69.4% less than 15 minutes, 10.2% 15 to 30 minutes, 12.1% 30 to 45 minutes, 4.7% 45 to 60 minutes, 3.7% 60 minutes or more (2006-2010 5-year est.)
**Additional Information Contacts**
Tupper Lake Chamber Commerce . . . . . . . . . . . . . . . . . . (518) 359-3328
http://tupper-lake.com

**TUPPER LAKE** (town). Aka known as Altamont prior to July 2004. Covers a land area of 117.347 square miles and a water area of 12.754 square miles. Located at 44.24° N. Lat; 74.47° W. Long. Elevation is 1,598 feet.
**Population:** 6,199 (1990); 6,137 (2000); 5,971 (2010); Density: 50.9 persons per square mile (2010); Race: 95.8% White, 2.5% Black, 0.3%

Asian, 0.5% American Indian/Alaska Native, 0.0% Native Hawaiian/Other Pacific Islander, 0.9% Other, 1.3% Hispanic of any race (2010); Average household size: 2.25 (2010); Median age: 42.4 (2010); Males per 100 females: 111.2 (2010); Marriage status: 26.4% never married, 55.8% now married, 8.5% widowed, 9.4% divorced (2006-2010 5-year est.); Foreign born: 4.6% (2006-2010 5-year est.); Ancestry (includes multiple ancestries): 27.4% French, 19.0% Irish, 13.1% German, 12.9% French Canadian, 9.6% English (2006-2010 5-year est.).
**Economy:** Employment by occupation: 6.0% management, 3.5% professional, 18.3% services, 16.6% sales, 3.0% farming, 13.5% construction, 4.2% production (2006-2010 5-year est.).
**Income:** Per capita income: $22,939 (2006-2010 5-year est.); Median household income: $46,301 (2006-2010 5-year est.); Average household income: $56,448 (2006-2010 5-year est.); Percent of households with income of $100,000 or more: 17.0% (2006-2010 5-year est.); Poverty rate: 9.1% (2006-2010 5-year est.).
**Education:** Percent of population age 25 and over with: High school diploma (including GED) or higher: 83.0% (2006-2010 5-year est.); Bachelor's degree or higher: 14.0% (2006-2010 5-year est.); Master's degree or higher: 5.5% (2006-2010 5-year est.).
**School District(s)**
Tupper Lake Central School District (PK-12)
    2009-10 Enrollment: 925 . . . . . . . . . . . . . . . . . . . . . . (518) 359-3371
**Housing:** Homeownership rate: 69.3% (2010); Median home value: $104,600 (2006-2010 5-year est.); Median contract rent: $488 per month (2006-2010 5-year est.); Median year structure built: 1958 (2006-2010 5-year est.).
**Transportation:** Commute to work: 90.6% car, 0.4% public transportation, 3.9% walk, 3.4% work from home (2006-2010 5-year est.); Travel time to work: 65.3% less than 15 minutes, 12.6% 15 to 30 minutes, 12.2% 30 to 45 minutes, 4.8% 45 to 60 minutes, 5.1% 60 minutes or more (2006-2010 5-year est.)

**VERMONTVILLE** (unincorporated postal area)
Zip Code: 12989
    Covers a land area of 147.752 square miles and a water area of 2.814 square miles. Located at 44.52° N. Lat; 74.06° W. Long. Elevation is 1,644 feet. Population: 1,010 (2010); Density: 6.8 persons per square mile (2010); Race: 97.8% White, 0.0% Black, 0.0% Asian, 0.8% American Indian/Alaska Native, 0.1% Native Hawaiian/Other Pacific Islander, 1.3% Other, 0.6% Hispanic of any race (2010); Average household size: 2.25 (2010); Median age: 48.2 (2010); Males per 100 females: 103.6 (2010); Homeownership rate: 89.3% (2010)

**WAVERLY** (town). Covers a land area of 125.111 square miles and a water area of 1.294 square miles. Located at 44.52° N. Lat; 74.54° W. Long.
**Population:** 1,068 (1990); 1,118 (2000); 1,022 (2010); Density: 8.2 persons per square mile (2010); Race: 97.6% White, 0.2% Black, 0.1% Asian, 0.8% American Indian/Alaska Native, 0.0% Native Hawaiian/Other Pacific Islander, 1.3% Other, 1.8% Hispanic of any race (2010); Average household size: 2.31 (2010); Median age: 45.1 (2010); Males per 100 females: 92.5 (2010); Marriage status: 24.5% never married, 52.5% now married, 11.3% widowed, 11.7% divorced (2006-2010 5-year est.); Foreign born: 2.1% (2006-2010 5-year est.); Ancestry (includes multiple ancestries): 23.1% French, 16.7% Irish, 15.2% French Canadian, 14.7% German, 9.3% English (2006-2010 5-year est.).
**Economy:** Single-family building permits issued: 2 (2011); Multi-family building permits issued: 0 (2011); Employment by occupation: 8.2% management, 0.0% professional, 16.4% services, 18.7% sales, 4.7% farming, 14.0% construction, 4.4% production (2006-2010 5-year est.).
**Income:** Per capita income: $17,385 (2006-2010 5-year est.); Median household income: $33,000 (2006-2010 5-year est.); Average household income: $37,768 (2006-2010 5-year est.); Percent of households with income of $100,000 or more: 2.5% (2006-2010 5-year est.); Poverty rate: 20.4% (2006-2010 5-year est.).
**Education:** Percent of population age 25 and over with: High school diploma (including GED) or higher: 82.0% (2006-2010 5-year est.); Bachelor's degree or higher: 8.3% (2006-2010 5-year est.); Master's degree or higher: 5.1% (2006-2010 5-year est.).
**Housing:** Homeownership rate: 75.9% (2010); Median home value: $61,100 (2006-2010 5-year est.); Median contract rent: $294 per month (2006-2010 5-year est.); Median year structure built: 1956 (2006-2010 5-year est.).

**Transportation:** Commute to work: 97.9% car, 1.2% public transportation, 0.0% walk, 0.0% work from home (2006-2010 5-year est.); Travel time to work: 13.3% less than 15 minutes, 15.4% 15 to 30 minutes, 39.6% 30 to 45 minutes, 20.2% 45 to 60 minutes, 11.5% 60 minutes or more (2006-2010 5-year est.)

## WESTVILLE (town). Aka West Constable. Covers a land area of 34.797 square miles and a water area of 0.013 square miles. Located at 44.94° N. Lat; 74.38° W. Long. Elevation is 200 feet.

**Population:** 1,620 (1990); 1,823 (2000); 1,819 (2010); Density: 52.3 persons per square mile (2010); Race: 96.2% White, 0.4% Black, 0.3% Asian, 0.6% American Indian/Alaska Native, 0.0% Native Hawaiian/Other Pacific Islander, 2.5% Other, 1.2% Hispanic of any race (2010); Average household size: 2.46 (2010); Median age: 41.0 (2010); Males per 100 females: 106.7 (2010); Marriage status: 28.4% never married, 56.1% now married, 5.1% widowed, 10.4% divorced (2006-2010 5-year est.); Foreign born: 3.1% (2006-2010 5-year est.); Ancestry (includes multiple ancestries): 30.2% French, 20.2% Irish, 12.3% American, 9.7% German, 9.4% English (2006-2010 5-year est.).
**Economy:** Single-family building permits issued: 2 (2011); Multi-family building permits issued: 0 (2011); Employment by occupation: 8.9% management, 0.9% professional, 15.0% services, 13.6% sales, 2.7% farming, 16.8% construction, 7.9% production (2006-2010 5-year est.).
**Income:** Per capita income: $21,847 (2006-2010 5-year est.); Median household income: $42,696 (2006-2010 5-year est.); Average household income: $54,270 (2006-2010 5-year est.); Percent of households with income of $100,000 or more: 11.6% (2006-2010 5-year est.); Poverty rate: 13.5% (2006-2010 5-year est.).
**Education:** Percent of population age 25 and over with: High school diploma (including GED) or higher: 81.2% (2006-2010 5-year est.); Bachelor's degree or higher: 7.7% (2006-2010 5-year est.); Master's degree or higher: 1.6% (2006-2010 5-year est.).
**Housing:** Homeownership rate: 81.1% (2010); Median home value: $67,200 (2006-2010 5-year est.); Median contract rent: $469 per month (2006-2010 5-year est.); Median year structure built: 1978 (2006-2010 5-year est.).
**Transportation:** Commute to work: 89.0% car, 0.3% public transportation, 1.4% walk, 8.4% work from home (2006-2010 5-year est.); Travel time to work: 46.5% less than 15 minutes, 38.6% 15 to 30 minutes, 6.5% 30 to 45 minutes, 4.8% 45 to 60 minutes, 3.5% 60 minutes or more (2006-2010 5-year est.)

# Fulton County

Located in east central New York, in the Adirondacks; drained by East Canada Creek and the Sacandaga River; includes several lakes. Covers a land area of 496.17 square miles, a water area of 36.73 square miles, and is located in the Eastern Time Zone at 43.07° N. Lat., 74.36° W. Long. The county was founded in 1838. County seat is Johnstown.

Fulton County is part of the Gloversville, NY Micropolitan Statistical Area. The entire metro area includes: Fulton County, NY

Weather Station: Gloversville                                Elevation: 898 feet

|        | Jan  | Feb  | Mar  | Apr | May | Jun | Jul | Aug | Sep | Oct | Nov | Dec  |
|--------|------|------|------|-----|-----|-----|-----|-----|-----|-----|-----|------|
| High   | 29   | 32   | 41   | 56  | 68  | 76  | 80  | 79  | 71  | 58  | 46  | 33   |
| Low    | 10   | 12   | 21   | 33  | 44  | 54  | 59  | 57  | 49  | 36  | 29  | 17   |
| Precip | 3.1  | 2.7  | 3.5  | 4.1 | 4.3 | 4.3 | 4.2 | 4.5 | 3.9 | 4.1 | 3.4 | 3.4  |
| Snow   | 20.9 | 14.2 | 14.6 | 1.6 | tr  | 0.0 | 0.0 | 0.0 | 0.0 | 0.1 | 4.3 | 17.0 |

*High and Low temperatures in degrees Fahrenheit; Precipitation and Snow in inches*

**Population:** 54,191 (1990); 55,073 (2000); 55,531 (2010); Race: 95.3% White, 1.9% Black, 0.6% Asian, 0.2% American Indian/Alaska Native, 0.0% Native Hawaiian/Other Pacific Islander, 2.0% Other, 2.3% Hispanic of any race (2010); Density: 111.9 persons per square mile (2010); Average household size: 2.40 (2010); Median age: 41.8 (2010); Males per 100 females: 97.9 (2010).
**Religion:** Six largest groups: 14.3% Catholicism, 5.1% Methodist/Pietist, 1.9% Presbyterian-Reformed, 1.4% Non-Denominational, 0.8% Latter-day Saints, 0.7% Episcopalianism/Anglicanism (2010)
**Economy:** Unemployment rate: 11.4% (February 2012); Total civilian labor force: 26,633 (February 2012); Leading industries: 23.0% health care and social assistance; 16.1% retail trade; 13.9% manufacturing (2009); Farms: 222 totaling 33,851 acres (2007); Companies that employ 500 or more persons: 2 (2009); Companies that employ 100 to 499 persons: 21 (2009); Companies that employ less than 100 persons: 1,209 (2009); Black-owned

businesses: n/a (2007); Hispanic-owned businesses: n/a (2007); Asian-owned businesses: n/a (2007); Women-owned businesses: n/a (2007); Retail sales per capita: $10,994 (2010). Single-family building permits issued: 88 (2011); Multi-family building permits issued: 0 (2011).
**Income:** Per capita income: $23,147 (2006-2010 5-year est.); Median household income: $43,240 (2006-2010 5-year est.); Average household income: $55,790 (2006-2010 5-year est.); Percent of households with income of $100,000 or more: 11.5% (2006-2010 5-year est.); Poverty rate: 17.2% (2006-2010 5-year est.); Bankruptcy rate: 3.52% (2011).
**Education:** Percent of population age 25 and over with: High school diploma (including GED) or higher: 83.2% (2006-2010 5-year est.); Bachelor's degree or higher: 14.3% (2006-2010 5-year est.); Master's degree or higher: 5.6% (2006-2010 5-year est.).
**Housing:** Homeownership rate: 70.9% (2010); Median home value: $95,200 (2006-2010 5-year est.); Median contract rent: $485 per month (2006-2010 5-year est.); Median year structure built: 1951 (2006-2010 5-year est.).
**Health:** Birth rate: 97.9 per 10,000 population (2011); Death rate: 105.5 per 10,000 population (2011); Age-adjusted cancer mortality rate: 197.8 deaths per 100,000 population (2009); Number of physicians: 10.3 per 10,000 population (2008); Hospital beds: 28.7 per 10,000 population (2007); Hospital admissions: 688.3 per 10,000 population (2007).
**Elections:** 2008 Presidential election results: 44.4% Obama, 53.7% McCain, 1.2% Nader
**National and State Parks:** Adirondack State Park; Sir William Johnson State Park
**Additional Information Contacts**
Fulton County Government . . . . . . . . . . . . . . . . . . . . . . (518) 725-0641
  http://www.fultoncountyny.org
City of Gloversville . . . . . . . . . . . . . . . . . . . . . . . . . . . (518) 773-4542
  http://www.cityofgloversville.com
City of Johnstown . . . . . . . . . . . . . . . . . . . . . . . . . . . . (518) 736-4011
  http://www.cityofjohnstown-ny.com
Fulton County Regional Chamber of Commerce & Industry (518) 725-0641
  http://www.fultoncountyny.org

# Fulton County Communities

## BLEECKER (town). Covers a land area of 57.126 square miles and a water area of 2.284 square miles. Located at 43.17° N. Lat; 74.38° W. Long. Elevation is 1,503 feet.

**Population:** 515 (1990); 573 (2000); 533 (2010); Density: 9.3 persons per square mile (2010); Race: 97.7% White, 0.0% Black, 0.2% Asian, 0.2% American Indian/Alaska Native, 0.0% Native Hawaiian/Other Pacific Islander, 1.9% Other, 0.4% Hispanic of any race (2010); Average household size: 2.22 (2010); Median age: 51.7 (2010); Males per 100 females: 109.8 (2010); Marriage status: 16.0% never married, 69.8% now married, 0.8% widowed, 13.4% divorced (2006-2010 5-year est.); Foreign born: 2.0% (2006-2010 5-year est.); Ancestry (includes multiple ancestries): 25.4% German, 20.4% English, 15.2% Irish, 8.8% Dutch, 8.6% Italian (2006-2010 5-year est.).
**Economy:** Single-family building permits issued: 0 (2011); Multi-family building permits issued: 0 (2011); Employment by occupation: 23.4% management, 1.0% professional, 7.1% services, 19.3% sales, 1.0% farming, 9.6% construction, 3.6% production (2006-2010 5-year est.).
**Income:** Per capita income: $28,806 (2006-2010 5-year est.); Median household income: $69,583 (2006-2010 5-year est.); Average household income: $71,444 (2006-2010 5-year est.); Percent of households with income of $100,000 or more: 17.9% (2006-2010 5-year est.); Poverty rate: 13.7% (2006-2010 5-year est.).
**Education:** Percent of population age 25 and over with: High school diploma (including GED) or higher: 87.1% (2006-2010 5-year est.); Bachelor's degree or higher: 31.8% (2006-2010 5-year est.); Master's degree or higher: 12.3% (2006-2010 5-year est.).
**Housing:** Homeownership rate: 96.3% (2010); Median home value: $165,300 (2006-2010 5-year est.); Median contract rent: n/a per month (2006-2010 5-year est.); Median year structure built: 1971 (2006-2010 5-year est.).
**Transportation:** Commute to work: 87.9% car, 0.0% public transportation, 0.0% walk, 9.5% work from home (2006-2010 5-year est.); Travel time to work: 17.4% less than 15 minutes, 49.4% 15 to 30 minutes, 14.5% 30 to 45 minutes, 5.8% 45 to 60 minutes, 12.8% 60 minutes or more (2006-2010 5-year est.)

**BROADALBIN** (village). Covers a land area of 1.121 square miles and a water area of 0.004 square miles. Located at 43.06° N. Lat; 74.19° W. Long. Elevation is 804 feet.
**Population:** 1,397 (1990); 1,411 (2000); 1,327 (2010); Density: 1,183.2 persons per square mile (2010); Race: 95.8% White, 1.5% Black, 0.9% Asian, 0.0% American Indian/Alaska Native, 0.2% Native Hawaiian/Other Pacific Islander, 1.6% Other, 1.9% Hispanic of any race (2010); Average household size: 2.40 (2010); Median age: 40.7 (2010); Males per 100 females: 92.3 (2010); Marriage status: 23.2% never married, 58.9% now married, 10.0% widowed, 7.9% divorced (2006-2010 5-year est.); Foreign born: 4.5% (2006-2010 5-year est.); Ancestry (includes multiple ancestries): 27.7% Irish, 23.8% German, 21.6% English, 16.3% Italian, 15.8% Polish (2006-2010 5-year est.).
**Economy:** Single-family building permits issued: 0 (2011); Multi-family building permits issued: 0 (2011); Employment by occupation: 6.3% management, 2.9% professional, 11.0% services, 13.4% sales, 0.5% farming, 11.5% construction, 5.3% production (2006-2010 5-year est.).
**Income:** Per capita income: $25,222 (2006-2010 5-year est.); Median household income: $45,227 (2006-2010 5-year est.); Average household income: $59,971 (2006-2010 5-year est.); Percent of households with income of $100,000 or more: 16.1% (2006-2010 5-year est.); Poverty rate: 4.0% (2006-2010 5-year est.).
**Education:** Percent of population age 25 and over with: High school diploma (including GED) or higher: 90.6% (2006-2010 5-year est.); Bachelor's degree or higher: 29.3% (2006-2010 5-year est.); Master's degree or higher: 9.5% (2006-2010 5-year est.).
**School District(s)**
Broadalbin-Perth Central School District (PK-12)
   2009-10 Enrollment: 1,960 . . . . . . . . . . . . . . . . . . . . . . . (518) 954-2500
**Housing:** Homeownership rate: 73.4% (2010); Median home value: $130,500 (2006-2010 5-year est.); Median contract rent: $566 per month (2006-2010 5-year est.); Median year structure built: before 1940 (2006-2010 5-year est.).
**Transportation:** Commute to work: 94.8% car, 0.7% public transportation, 1.9% walk, 0.5% work from home (2006-2010 5-year est.); Travel time to work: 30.1% less than 15 minutes, 36.8% 15 to 30 minutes, 14.3% 30 to 45 minutes, 11.7% 45 to 60 minutes, 7.1% 60 minutes or more (2006-2010 5-year est.)

**BROADALBIN** (town). Covers a land area of 31.721 square miles and a water area of 8.058 square miles. Located at 43.07° N. Lat; 74.15° W. Long. Elevation is 804 feet.
**History:** Settled 1770, incorporated 1924.
**Population:** 4,397 (1990); 5,066 (2000); 5,260 (2010); Density: 165.8 persons per square mile (2010); Race: 97.2% White, 0.7% Black, 0.5% Asian, 0.3% American Indian/Alaska Native, 0.0% Native Hawaiian/Other Pacific Islander, 1.3% Other, 1.8% Hispanic of any race (2010); Average household size: 2.49 (2010); Median age: 41.4 (2010); Males per 100 females: 98.1 (2010); Marriage status: 23.8% never married, 57.2% now married, 9.7% widowed, 9.2% divorced (2006-2010 5-year est.); Foreign born: 1.6% (2006-2010 5-year est.); Ancestry (includes multiple ancestries): 24.1% Irish, 24.0% German, 16.7% Italian, 15.3% Polish, 11.8% English (2006-2010 5-year est.).
**Economy:** Single-family building permits issued: 13 (2011); Multi-family building permits issued: 0 (2011); Employment by occupation: 9.6% management, 1.7% professional, 10.4% services, 15.5% sales, 4.8% farming, 8.7% construction, 11.1% production (2006-2010 5-year est.).
**Income:** Per capita income: $33,119 (2006-2010 5-year est.); Median household income: $52,547 (2006-2010 5-year est.); Average household income: $75,780 (2006-2010 5-year est.); Percent of households with income of $100,000 or more: 19.7% (2006-2010 5-year est.); Poverty rate: 4.0% (2006-2010 5-year est.).
**Education:** Percent of population age 25 and over with: High school diploma (including GED) or higher: 89.5% (2006-2010 5-year est.); Bachelor's degree or higher: 15.6% (2006-2010 5-year est.); Master's degree or higher: 4.2% (2006-2010 5-year est.).
**School District(s)**
Broadalbin-Perth Central School District (PK-12)
   2009-10 Enrollment: 1,960 . . . . . . . . . . . . . . . . . . . . . . . (518) 954-2500
**Housing:** Homeownership rate: 82.9% (2010); Median home value: $131,000 (2006-2010 5-year est.); Median contract rent: $560 per month (2006-2010 5-year est.); Median year structure built: 1969 (2006-2010 5-year est.).
**Transportation:** Commute to work: 89.8% car, 0.7% public transportation, 1.2% walk, 5.6% work from home (2006-2010 5-year est.); Travel time to

work: 23.3% less than 15 minutes, 44.1% 15 to 30 minutes, 9.6% 30 to 45 minutes, 11.9% 45 to 60 minutes, 11.1% 60 minutes or more (2006-2010 5-year est.)

**CAROGA** (town). Covers a land area of 50.626 square miles and a water area of 3.650 square miles. Located at 43.12° N. Lat; 74.52° W. Long.
**Population:** 1,337 (1990); 1,407 (2000); 1,205 (2010); Density: 23.8 persons per square mile (2010); Race: 98.3% White, 0.0% Black, 0.0% Asian, 0.1% American Indian/Alaska Native, 0.0% Native Hawaiian/Other Pacific Islander, 1.4% Other, 0.2% Hispanic of any race (2010); Average household size: 2.29 (2010); Median age: 46.9 (2010); Males per 100 females: 113.3 (2010); Marriage status: 18.8% never married, 66.1% now married, 6.0% widowed, 9.1% divorced (2006-2010 5-year est.); Foreign born: 3.7% (2006-2010 5-year est.); Ancestry (includes multiple ancestries): 22.4% German, 20.3% Irish, 16.8% English, 10.7% Dutch, 9.3% Italian (2006-2010 5-year est.).
**Economy:** Single-family building permits issued: 3 (2011); Multi-family building permits issued: 0 (2011); Employment by occupation: 7.8% management, 2.2% professional, 14.5% services, 12.6% sales, 1.6% farming, 7.2% construction, 7.4% production (2006-2010 5-year est.).
**Income:** Per capita income: $24,998 (2006-2010 5-year est.); Median household income: $46,450 (2006-2010 5-year est.); Average household income: $58,768 (2006-2010 5-year est.); Percent of households with income of $100,000 or more: 14.6% (2006-2010 5-year est.); Poverty rate: 17.8% (2006-2010 5-year est.).
**Education:** Percent of population age 25 and over with: High school diploma (including GED) or higher: 85.7% (2006-2010 5-year est.); Bachelor's degree or higher: 22.1% (2006-2010 5-year est.); Master's degree or higher: 9.2% (2006-2010 5-year est.).
**Housing:** Homeownership rate: 89.5% (2010); Median home value: $111,400 (2006-2010 5-year est.); Median contract rent: $417 per month (2006-2010 5-year est.); Median year structure built: 1950 (2006-2010 5-year est.).
**Transportation:** Commute to work: 93.1% car, 0.0% public transportation, 1.6% walk, 4.7% work from home (2006-2010 5-year est.); Travel time to work: 27.5% less than 15 minutes, 39.7% 15 to 30 minutes, 14.7% 30 to 45 minutes, 6.3% 45 to 60 minutes, 11.8% 60 minutes or more (2006-2010 5-year est.)

**CAROGA LAKE** (CDP). Covers a land area of 2.500 square miles and a water area of 0.873 square miles. Located at 43.13° N. Lat; 74.48° W. Long. Elevation is 1,480 feet.
**Population:** n/a (1990); n/a (2000); 518 (2010); Density: 207.2 persons per square mile (2010); Race: 97.9% White, 0.0% Black, 0.4% Asian, 0.2% American Indian/Alaska Native, 0.0% Native Hawaiian/Other Pacific Islander, 1.5% Other, 0.2% Hispanic of any race (2010); Average household size: 2.19 (2010); Median age: 48.4 (2010); Males per 100 females: 112.3 (2010); Marriage status: 18.2% never married, 69.4% now married, 5.1% widowed, 7.4% divorced (2006-2010 5-year est.); Foreign born: 1.3% (2006-2010 5-year est.); Ancestry (includes multiple ancestries): 19.4% English, 17.8% German, 16.3% Irish, 13.2% Dutch, 12.7% French (2006-2010 5-year est.).
**Economy:** Employment by occupation: 8.9% management, 3.4% professional, 13.5% services, 13.5% sales, 3.2% farming, 5.2% construction, 6.0% production (2006-2010 5-year est.).
**Income:** Per capita income: $28,585 (2006-2010 5-year est.); Median household income: $50,673 (2006-2010 5-year est.); Average household income: $61,199 (2006-2010 5-year est.); Percent of households with income of $100,000 or more: 11.4% (2006-2010 5-year est.); Poverty rate: 14.7% (2006-2010 5-year est.).
**Education:** Percent of population age 25 and over with: High school diploma (including GED) or higher: 86.6% (2006-2010 5-year est.); Bachelor's degree or higher: 19.7% (2006-2010 5-year est.); Master's degree or higher: 6.4% (2006-2010 5-year est.).
**School District(s)**
Wheelerville Union Free School District (PK-08)
   2009-10 Enrollment: 144 . . . . . . . . . . . . . . . . . . . . . . . (518) 835-2171
**Housing:** Homeownership rate: 87.7% (2010); Median home value: $108,800 (2006-2010 5-year est.); Median contract rent: $386 per month (2006-2010 5-year est.); Median year structure built: 1947 (2006-2010 5-year est.).
**Transportation:** Commute to work: 92.1% car, 0.0% public transportation, 1.8% walk, 6.1% work from home (2006-2010 5-year est.); Travel time to work: 29.8% less than 15 minutes, 40.5% 15 to 30 minutes, 14.2% 30 to 45

minutes, 3.2% 45 to 60 minutes, 12.3% 60 minutes or more (2006-2010 5-year est.)

## EPHRATAH (town). Covers a land area of 39.170 square miles and a water area of 0.277 square miles. Located at 43.03° N. Lat; 74.56° W. Long. Elevation is 682 feet.

**Population:** 1,556 (1990); 1,693 (2000); 1,682 (2010); Density: 42.9 persons per square mile (2010); Race: 98.6% White, 0.7% Black, 0.1% Asian, 0.0% American Indian/Alaska Native, 0.0% Native Hawaiian/Other Pacific Islander, 0.6% Other, 0.6% Hispanic of any race (2010); Average household size: 2.53 (2010); Median age: 44.2 (2010); Males per 100 females: 108.2 (2010); Marriage status: 23.6% never married, 60.5% now married, 4.3% widowed, 11.6% divorced (2006-2010 5-year est.); Foreign born: 2.6% (2006-2010 5-year est.); Ancestry (includes multiple ancestries): 22.2% American, 19.2% German, 10.9% English, 9.5% Irish, 6.7% Dutch (2006-2010 5-year est.).

**Economy:** Single-family building permits issued: 1 (2011); Multi-family building permits issued: 0 (2011); Employment by occupation: 7.2% management, 0.0% professional, 14.8% services, 15.1% sales, 2.6% farming, 18.6% construction, 12.9% production (2006-2010 5-year est.).

**Income:** Per capita income: $21,511 (2006-2010 5-year est.); Median household income: $52,000 (2006-2010 5-year est.); Average household income: $53,878 (2006-2010 5-year est.); Percent of households with income of $100,000 or more: 10.4% (2006-2010 5-year est.); Poverty rate: 11.9% (2006-2010 5-year est.).

**Education:** Percent of population age 25 and over with: High school diploma (including GED) or higher: 80.4% (2006-2010 5-year est.); Bachelor's degree or higher: 13.1% (2006-2010 5-year est.); Master's degree or higher: 4.3% (2006-2010 5-year est.).

**Housing:** Homeownership rate: 86.7% (2010); Median home value: $68,500 (2006-2010 5-year est.); Median contract rent: $518 per month (2006-2010 5-year est.); Median year structure built: 1973 (2006-2010 5-year est.).

**Transportation:** Commute to work: 91.9% car, 0.0% public transportation, 1.6% walk, 4.3% work from home (2006-2010 5-year est.); Travel time to work: 14.1% less than 15 minutes, 44.3% 15 to 30 minutes, 22.0% 30 to 45 minutes, 7.7% 45 to 60 minutes, 11.9% 60 minutes or more (2006-2010 5-year est.)

## GLOVERSVILLE (city). Covers a land area of 5.139 square miles and a water area of 0.008 square miles. Located at 43.04° N. Lat; 74.34° W. Long. Elevation is 820 feet.

**History:** Gloversville was named for its outstanding industry. The making of fine kid gloves became a Fulton County specialty. The beginnings of the industry in the county have been traced back to the 1760's when Sir William Johnson brought over as settlers a group of glovers from Perthshire, Scotland, who made gloves for local sale.

**Population:** 16,656 (1990); 15,413 (2000); 15,665 (2010); Density: 3,048.1 persons per square mile (2010); Race: 93.4% White, 2.8% Black, 0.5% Asian, 0.3% American Indian/Alaska Native, 0.0% Native Hawaiian/Other Pacific Islander, 3.0% Other, 3.4% Hispanic of any race (2010); Average household size: 2.37 (2010); Median age: 37.1 (2010); Males per 100 females: 92.5 (2010); Marriage status: 32.1% never married, 48.6% now married, 7.0% widowed, 12.4% divorced (2006-2010 5-year est.); Foreign born: 0.6% (2006-2010 5-year est.); Ancestry (includes multiple ancestries): 23.7% German, 20.3% Irish, 16.7% Italian, 10.2% English, 10.1% American (2006-2010 5-year est.).

**Economy:** Single-family building permits issued: 2 (2011); Multi-family building permits issued: 0 (2011); Employment by occupation: 8.1% management, 0.9% professional, 16.2% services, 18.7% sales, 3.0% farming, 7.3% construction, 10.8% production (2006-2010 5-year est.).

**Income:** Per capita income: $17,889 (2006-2010 5-year est.); Median household income: $31,994 (2006-2010 5-year est.); Average household income: $41,690 (2006-2010 5-year est.); Percent of households with income of $100,000 or more: 5.9% (2006-2010 5-year est.); Poverty rate: 27.5% (2006-2010 5-year est.).

**Education:** Percent of population age 25 and over with: High school diploma (including GED) or higher: 80.0% (2006-2010 5-year est.); Bachelor's degree or higher: 10.9% (2006-2010 5-year est.); Master's degree or higher: 3.9% (2006-2010 5-year est.).

### School District(s)

Gloversville City School District (PK-12)
    2009-10 Enrollment: 3,166 . . . . . . . . . . . . . . . . . . . . . (518) 775-5791

**Housing:** Homeownership rate: 51.7% (2010); Median home value: $75,200 (2006-2010 5-year est.); Median contract rent: $470 per month

(2006-2010 5-year est.); Median year structure built: before 1940 (2006-2010 5-year est.).

**Hospitals:** Nathan Littauer Hospital and Nursing Home (208 beds)

**Safety:** Violent crime rate: 55.7 per 10,000 population; Property crime rate: 432.3 per 10,000 population (2010).

**Newspapers:** Daily Gazette - Gloversville Bureau (Local news; Circulation 50,393); Gloversville Leader-Herald (Local news; Circulation 11,508)

**Transportation:** Commute to work: 92.0% car, 0.3% public transportation, 2.6% walk, 3.4% work from home (2006-2010 5-year est.); Travel time to work: 47.6% less than 15 minutes, 32.6% 15 to 30 minutes, 9.7% 30 to 45 minutes, 4.8% 45 to 60 minutes, 5.3% 60 minutes or more (2006-2010 5-year est.)

**Additional Information Contacts**

City of Gloversville . . . . . . . . . . . . . . . . . . . . . . . . (518) 773-4542
    http://www.cityofgloversville.com
Fulton County Regional Chamber of Commerce & Industry (518) 725-0641
    http://www.fultoncountyny.org

## JOHNSTOWN (city). County seat. Covers a land area of 4.875 square miles and a water area of 0.008 square miles. Located at 43.00° N. Lat; 74.37° W. Long. Elevation is 673 feet.

**History:** Its leather-glove industry dates back to 1800. Notable buildings include the county courthouse (1774) and Fort Johnstown (1771) and the county jail. The last American Revolutionary battle in N.Y. state was fought in Johnstown on Oct. 25, 1781. Elizabeth Cady Stanton born here. Founded 1772, Incorporated 1895.

**Population:** 9,059 (1990); 8,511 (2000); 8,743 (2010); Density: 1,793.4 persons per square mile (2010); Race: 95.4% White, 1.0% Black, 1.3% Asian, 0.1% American Indian/Alaska Native, 0.0% Native Hawaiian/Other Pacific Islander, 2.2% Other, 2.4% Hispanic of any race (2010); Average household size: 2.28 (2010); Median age: 40.4 (2010); Males per 100 females: 89.4 (2010); Marriage status: 30.8% never married, 48.9% now married, 9.0% widowed, 11.3% divorced (2006-2010 5-year est.); Foreign born: 2.1% (2006-2010 5-year est.); Ancestry (includes multiple ancestries): 21.8% Italian, 18.4% Irish, 17.9% German, 15.8% English, 8.2% Polish (2006-2010 5-year est.).

**Economy:** Single-family building permits issued: 7 (2011); Multi-family building permits issued: 0 (2011); Employment by occupation: 11.8% management, 2.7% professional, 11.6% services, 17.0% sales, 3.7% farming, 5.8% construction, 8.2% production (2006-2010 5-year est.).

**Income:** Per capita income: $22,424 (2006-2010 5-year est.); Median household income: $44,234 (2006-2010 5-year est.); Average household income: $51,969 (2006-2010 5-year est.); Percent of households with income of $100,000 or more: 11.2% (2006-2010 5-year est.); Poverty rate: 14.5% (2006-2010 5-year est.).

**Education:** Percent of population age 25 and over with: High school diploma (including GED) or higher: 83.9% (2006-2010 5-year est.); Bachelor's degree or higher: 18.3% (2006-2010 5-year est.); Master's degree or higher: 8.8% (2006-2010 5-year est.).

### School District(s)

Hamilton-Fulton-Montgomery Boces
    2009-10 Enrollment: n/a . . . . . . . . . . . . . . . . . . . . (518) 736-4300
Johnstown City School District (PK-12)
    2009-10 Enrollment: 1,911 . . . . . . . . . . . . . . . . . . . (518) 762-4611

### Two-year College(s)

Fulton-Montgomery Community College (Public)
    Fall 2010 Enrollment: 2,192 . . . . . . . . . . . . . . . . . . (518) 762-4651
    2011-12 Tuition: In-state $3,838; Out-of-state $7,232

### Vocational/Technical School(s)

Hamilton Fulton Montgomery BOCES-Practical Nursing Program (Public)
    Fall 2010 Enrollment: 30 . . . . . . . . . . . . . . . . . . . . . (518) 736-4681

**Housing:** Homeownership rate: 58.7% (2010); Median home value: $90,500 (2006-2010 5-year est.); Median contract rent: $490 per month (2006-2010 5-year est.); Median year structure built: before 1940 (2006-2010 5-year est.).

**Safety:** Violent crime rate: 16.8 per 10,000 population; Property crime rate: 360.3 per 10,000 population (2010).

**Transportation:** Commute to work: 88.4% car, 0.5% public transportation, 6.4% walk, 2.9% work from home (2006-2010 5-year est.); Travel time to work: 49.0% less than 15 minutes, 31.5% 15 to 30 minutes, 10.7% 30 to 45 minutes, 4.0% 45 to 60 minutes, 4.8% 60 minutes or more (2006-2010 5-year est.)

**Airports:** Fulton County (general aviation)

**Additional Information Contacts**

City of Johnstown. . . . . . . . . . . . . . . . . . . . . . . . . . (518) 736-4011
http://www.cityofjohnstown-ny.com

**JOHNSTOWN** (town). Covers a land area of 70.214 square miles and a water area of 1.082 square miles. Located at 43.04° N. Lat; 74.39° W. Long. Elevation is 673 feet.
**Population:** 6,417 (1990); 7,166 (2000); 7,098 (2010); Density: 101.1 persons per square mile (2010); Race: 92.4% White, 5.2% Black, 0.5% Asian, 0.1% American Indian/Alaska Native, 0.0% Native Hawaiian/Other Pacific Islander, 1.8% Other, 2.6% Hispanic of any race (2010); Average household size: 2.49 (2010); Median age: 44.7 (2010); Males per 100 females: 111.3 (2010); Marriage status: 24.2% never married, 55.1% now married, 10.1% widowed, 10.6% divorced (2006-2010 5-year est.); Foreign born: 1.1% (2006-2010 5-year est.); Ancestry (includes multiple ancestries): 18.9% German, 17.8% English, 16.6% Italian, 11.6% Irish, 8.4% American (2006-2010 5-year est.).
**Economy:** Single-family building permits issued: 33 (2011); Multi-family building permits issued: 0 (2011); Employment by occupation: 6.4% management, 0.8% professional, 6.1% services, 18.1% sales, 5.7% farming, 14.7% construction, 6.9% production (2006-2010 5-year est.).
**Income:** Per capita income: $27,382 (2006-2010 5-year est.); Median household income: $53,654 (2006-2010 5-year est.); Average household income: $74,590 (2006-2010 5-year est.); Percent of households with income of $100,000 or more: 18.1% (2006-2010 5-year est.); Poverty rate: 8.2% (2006-2010 5-year est.).
**Education:** Percent of population age 25 and over with: High school diploma (including GED) or higher: 78.2% (2006-2010 5-year est.); Bachelor's degree or higher: 13.5% (2006-2010 5-year est.); Master's degree or higher: 6.0% (2006-2010 5-year est.).
**School District(s)**
Hamilton-Fulton-Montgomery Boces
 2009-10 Enrollment: n/a . . . . . . . . . . . . . . . . . . . (518) 736-4300
Johnstown City School District (PK-12)
 2009-10 Enrollment: 1,911 . . . . . . . . . . . . . . . . . . (518) 762-4611
**Two-year College(s)**
Fulton-Montgomery Community College (Public)
 Fall 2010 Enrollment: 2,192 . . . . . . . . . . . . . . . . . (518) 762-4651
 2011-12 Tuition: In-state $3,838; Out-of-state $7,232
**Vocational/Technical School(s)**
Hamilton Fulton Montgomery BOCES-Practical Nursing Program (Public)
 Fall 2010 Enrollment: 30 . . . . . . . . . . . . . . . . . . . (518) 736-4681
**Housing:** Homeownership rate: 89.2% (2010); Median home value: $100,800 (2006-2010 5-year est.); Median contract rent: $561 per month (2006-2010 5-year est.); Median year structure built: 1971 (2006-2010 5-year est.).
**Transportation:** Commute to work: 94.5% car, 0.8% public transportation, 0.0% walk, 3.1% work from home (2006-2010 5-year est.); Travel time to work: 38.9% less than 15 minutes, 37.1% 15 to 30 minutes, 6.2% 30 to 45 minutes, 10.3% 45 to 60 minutes, 7.5% 60 minutes or more (2006-2010 5-year est.)
**Airports:** Fulton County (general aviation)

**MAYFIELD** (village). Covers a land area of 0.906 square miles and a water area of 0.177 square miles. Located at 43.10° N. Lat; 74.26° W. Long. Elevation is 850 feet.
**Population:** 815 (1990); 800 (2000); 832 (2010); Density: 917.5 persons per square mile (2010); Race: 98.0% White, 0.5% Black, 0.6% Asian, 0.2% American Indian/Alaska Native, 0.0% Native Hawaiian/Other Pacific Islander, 0.7% Other, 1.7% Hispanic of any race (2010); Average household size: 2.59 (2010); Median age: 37.5 (2010); Males per 100 females: 90.4 (2010); Marriage status: 20.8% never married, 62.6% now married, 6.9% widowed, 9.8% divorced (2006-2010 5-year est.); Foreign born: 3.8% (2006-2010 5-year est.); Ancestry (includes multiple ancestries): 23.1% Irish, 22.3% German, 15.2% Italian, 14.6% English, 11.2% French (2006-2010 5-year est.).
**Economy:** Single-family building permits issued: 0 (2011); Multi-family building permits issued: 0 (2011); Employment by occupation: 3.8% management, 0.0% professional, 7.4% services, 17.6% sales, 3.8% farming, 16.2% construction, 8.6% production (2006-2010 5-year est.).
**Income:** Per capita income: $20,413 (2006-2010 5-year est.); Median household income: $50,100 (2006-2010 5-year est.); Average household income: $58,174 (2006-2010 5-year est.); Percent of households with income of $100,000 or more: 7.8% (2006-2010 5-year est.); Poverty rate: 3.2% (2006-2010 5-year est.).

**Education:** Percent of population age 25 and over with: High school diploma (including GED) or higher: 91.9% (2006-2010 5-year est.); Bachelor's degree or higher: 9.6% (2006-2010 5-year est.); Master's degree or higher: 3.7% (2006-2010 5-year est.).
**School District(s)**
Mayfield Central School District (PK-12)
 2009-10 Enrollment: 1,042 . . . . . . . . . . . . . . . . . . (518) 661-8207
**Housing:** Homeownership rate: 77.8% (2010); Median home value: $95,800 (2006-2010 5-year est.); Median contract rent: $495 per month (2006-2010 5-year est.); Median year structure built: before 1940 (2006-2010 5-year est.).
**Transportation:** Commute to work: 97.3% car, 0.0% public transportation, 1.2% walk, 1.5% work from home (2006-2010 5-year est.); Travel time to work: 38.0% less than 15 minutes, 42.8% 15 to 30 minutes, 11.1% 30 to 45 minutes, 2.3% 45 to 60 minutes, 5.8% 60 minutes or more (2006-2010 5-year est.)

**MAYFIELD** (town). Covers a land area of 58.384 square miles and a water area of 6.298 square miles. Located at 43.12° N. Lat; 74.26° W. Long. Elevation is 850 feet.
**Population:** 5,738 (1990); 6,432 (2000); 6,495 (2010); Density: 111.2 persons per square mile (2010); Race: 97.8% White, 0.5% Black, 0.5% Asian, 0.2% American Indian/Alaska Native, 0.0% Native Hawaiian/Other Pacific Islander, 1.0% Other, 1.1% Hispanic of any race (2010); Average household size: 2.42 (2010); Median age: 44.8 (2010); Males per 100 females: 98.3 (2010); Marriage status: 19.3% never married, 65.4% now married, 6.9% widowed, 8.4% divorced (2006-2010 5-year est.); Foreign born: 1.5% (2006-2010 5-year est.); Ancestry (includes multiple ancestries): 25.7% German, 19.5% Irish, 16.6% English, 12.0% Italian, 8.9% Polish (2006-2010 5-year est.).
**Economy:** Single-family building permits issued: 8 (2011); Multi-family building permits issued: 0 (2011); Employment by occupation: 9.3% management, 0.8% professional, 9.1% services, 19.8% sales, 2.7% farming, 14.9% construction, 7.4% production (2006-2010 5-year est.).
**Income:** Per capita income: $21,422 (2006-2010 5-year est.); Median household income: $46,690 (2006-2010 5-year est.); Average household income: $53,967 (2006-2010 5-year est.); Percent of households with income of $100,000 or more: 10.6% (2006-2010 5-year est.); Poverty rate: 17.1% (2006-2010 5-year est.).
**Education:** Percent of population age 25 and over with: High school diploma (including GED) or higher: 87.3% (2006-2010 5-year est.); Bachelor's degree or higher: 12.6% (2006-2010 5-year est.); Master's degree or higher: 4.8% (2006-2010 5-year est.).
**School District(s)**
Mayfield Central School District (PK-12)
 2009-10 Enrollment: 1,042 . . . . . . . . . . . . . . . . . . (518) 661-8207
**Housing:** Homeownership rate: 81.0% (2010); Median home value: $110,200 (2006-2010 5-year est.); Median contract rent: $511 per month (2006-2010 5-year est.); Median year structure built: 1972 (2006-2010 5-year est.).
**Transportation:** Commute to work: 95.6% car, 0.0% public transportation, 0.8% walk, 2.8% work from home (2006-2010 5-year est.); Travel time to work: 31.1% less than 15 minutes, 39.8% 15 to 30 minutes, 15.0% 30 to 45 minutes, 4.3% 45 to 60 minutes, 9.8% 60 minutes or more (2006-2010 5-year est.)

**NORTHAMPTON** (town). Covers a land area of 21.116 square miles and a water area of 13.613 square miles. Located at 43.15° N. Lat; 74.17° W. Long.
**Population:** 2,705 (1990); 2,760 (2000); 2,670 (2010); Density: 126.4 persons per square mile (2010); Race: 97.2% White, 0.3% Black, 0.4% Asian, 0.3% American Indian/Alaska Native, 0.2% Native Hawaiian/Other Pacific Islander, 1.6% Other, 1.6% Hispanic of any race (2010); Average household size: 2.31 (2010); Median age: 46.0 (2010); Males per 100 females: 100.6 (2010); Marriage status: 23.0% never married, 60.3% now married, 6.6% widowed, 10.1% divorced (2006-2010 5-year est.); Foreign born: 0.5% (2006-2010 5-year est.); Ancestry (includes multiple ancestries): 23.7% English, 23.3% Irish, 20.7% German, 12.1% Dutch, 11.2% Polish (2006-2010 5-year est.).
**Economy:** Single-family building permits issued: 4 (2011); Multi-family building permits issued: 0 (2011); Employment by occupation: 11.9% management, 2.4% professional, 12.5% services, 16.8% sales, 0.9% farming, 11.5% construction, 7.4% production (2006-2010 5-year est.).
**Income:** Per capita income: $22,221 (2006-2010 5-year est.); Median household income: $45,465 (2006-2010 5-year est.); Average household

income: $52,029 (2006-2010 5-year est.); Percent of households with income of $100,000 or more: 12.2% (2006-2010 5-year est.); Poverty rate: 14.3% (2006-2010 5-year est.).

**Education:** Percent of population age 25 and over with: High school diploma (including GED) or higher: 85.6% (2006-2010 5-year est.); Bachelor's degree or higher: 16.9% (2006-2010 5-year est.); Master's degree or higher: 7.7% (2006-2010 5-year est.).

**Housing:** Homeownership rate: 75.7% (2010); Median home value: $140,700 (2006-2010 5-year est.); Median contract rent: $554 per month (2006-2010 5-year est.); Median year structure built: 1954 (2006-2010 5-year est.).

**Transportation:** Commute to work: 85.9% car, 0.0% public transportation, 10.6% walk, 3.2% work from home (2006-2010 5-year est.); Travel time to work: 28.7% less than 15 minutes, 20.9% 15 to 30 minutes, 16.3% 30 to 45 minutes, 17.8% 45 to 60 minutes, 16.3% 60 minutes or more (2006-2010 5-year est.)

**NORTHVILLE** (village). Covers a land area of 1.038 square miles and a water area of 0.344 square miles. Located at 43.22° N. Lat; 74.16° W. Long. Elevation is 807 feet.

**History:** Incorporated 1873.

**Population:** 1,180 (1990); 1,139 (2000); 1,099 (2010); Density: 1,057.8 persons per square mile (2010); Race: 96.7% White, 0.6% Black, 0.6% Asian, 0.0% American Indian/Alaska Native, 0.1% Native Hawaiian/Other Pacific Islander, 2.0% Other, 1.9% Hispanic of any race (2010); Average household size: 2.29 (2010); Median age: 43.7 (2010); Males per 100 females: 86.0 (2010); Marriage status: 24.6% never married, 54.8% now married, 8.9% widowed, 11.7% divorced (2006-2010 5-year est.); Foreign born: 0.7% (2006-2010 5-year est.); Ancestry (includes multiple ancestries): 29.3% German, 22.3% Irish, 16.3% English, 16.3% Dutch, 11.0% Italian (2006-2010 5-year est.).

**Economy:** Single-family building permits issued: 2 (2011); Multi-family building permits issued: 0 (2011); Employment by occupation: 9.2% management, 0.7% professional, 11.3% services, 19.5% sales, 2.3% farming, 14.8% construction, 6.6% production (2006-2010 5-year est.).

**Income:** Per capita income: $20,784 (2006-2010 5-year est.); Median household income: $33,947 (2006-2010 5-year est.); Average household income: $46,665 (2006-2010 5-year est.); Percent of households with income of $100,000 or more: 9.4% (2006-2010 5-year est.); Poverty rate: 17.6% (2006-2010 5-year est.).

**Education:** Percent of population age 25 and over with: High school diploma (including GED) or higher: 82.5% (2006-2010 5-year est.); Bachelor's degree or higher: 14.1% (2006-2010 5-year est.); Master's degree or higher: 7.8% (2006-2010 5-year est.).

### School District(s)

Northville Central School District (PK-12)

    2009-10 Enrollment: 497 . . . . . . . . . . . . . . . . . . . . . . . . (518) 863-7000

**Housing:** Homeownership rate: 64.2% (2010); Median home value: $132,500 (2006-2010 5-year est.); Median contract rent: $540 per month (2006-2010 5-year est.); Median year structure built: before 1940 (2006-2010 5-year est.).

**Safety:** Violent crime rate: 0.0 per 10,000 population; Property crime rate: 96.0 per 10,000 population (2010).

**Transportation:** Commute to work: 77.2% car, 0.0% public transportation, 19.8% walk, 2.2% work from home (2006-2010 5-year est.); Travel time to work: 32.2% less than 15 minutes, 24.1% 15 to 30 minutes, 25.6% 30 to 45 minutes, 4.8% 45 to 60 minutes, 13.4% 60 minutes or more (2006-2010 5-year est.)

**OPPENHEIM** (town). Covers a land area of 56.134 square miles and a water area of 0.306 square miles. Located at 43.08° N. Lat; 74.67° W. Long. Elevation is 1,096 feet.

**Population:** 1,848 (1990); 1,774 (2000); 1,924 (2010); Density: 34.3 persons per square mile (2010); Race: 97.9% White, 0.7% Black, 0.4% Asian, 0.4% American Indian/Alaska Native, 0.0% Native Hawaiian/Other Pacific Islander, 0.6% Other, 1.4% Hispanic of any race (2010); Average household size: 2.58 (2010); Median age: 41.5 (2010); Males per 100 females: 108.7 (2010); Marriage status: 27.5% never married, 55.1% now married, 5.1% widowed, 12.3% divorced (2006-2010 5-year est.); Foreign born: 1.1% (2006-2010 5-year est.); Ancestry (includes multiple ancestries): 30.0% German, 20.0% Irish, 16.0% American, 14.1% English, 9.0% Dutch (2006-2010 5-year est.).

**Economy:** Single-family building permits issued: 7 (2011); Multi-family building permits issued: 0 (2011); Employment by occupation: 5.4%

management, 0.5% professional, 11.7% services, 16.0% sales, 3.4% farming, 14.6% construction, 9.8% production (2006-2010 5-year est.).

**Income:** Per capita income: $18,034 (2006-2010 5-year est.); Median household income: $36,111 (2006-2010 5-year est.); Average household income: $43,261 (2006-2010 5-year est.); Percent of households with income of $100,000 or more: 5.9% (2006-2010 5-year est.); Poverty rate: 20.3% (2006-2010 5-year est.).

**Education:** Percent of population age 25 and over with: High school diploma (including GED) or higher: 74.9% (2006-2010 5-year est.); Bachelor's degree or higher: 9.7% (2006-2010 5-year est.); Master's degree or higher: 2.7% (2006-2010 5-year est.).

**Housing:** Homeownership rate: 85.6% (2010); Median home value: $70,500 (2006-2010 5-year est.); Median contract rent: $398 per month (2006-2010 5-year est.); Median year structure built: 1976 (2006-2010 5-year est.).

**Transportation:** Commute to work: 90.8% car, 0.5% public transportation, 3.4% walk, 4.9% work from home (2006-2010 5-year est.); Travel time to work: 33.5% less than 15 minutes, 25.3% 15 to 30 minutes, 24.1% 30 to 45 minutes, 4.7% 45 to 60 minutes, 12.4% 60 minutes or more (2006-2010 5-year est.)

**PERTH** (town). Covers a land area of 26.083 square miles and a water area of 0.027 square miles. Located at 43.00° N. Lat; 74.20° W. Long. Elevation is 869 feet.

**Population:** 3,377 (1990); 3,638 (2000); 3,646 (2010); Density: 139.8 persons per square mile (2010); Race: 96.1% White, 1.7% Black, 0.4% Asian, 0.1% American Indian/Alaska Native, 0.0% Native Hawaiian/Other Pacific Islander, 1.7% Other, 1.9% Hispanic of any race (2010); Average household size: 2.45 (2010); Median age: 43.2 (2010); Males per 100 females: 98.3 (2010); Marriage status: 30.7% never married, 54.5% now married, 6.9% widowed, 7.9% divorced (2006-2010 5-year est.); Foreign born: 3.6% (2006-2010 5-year est.); Ancestry (includes multiple ancestries): 20.8% German, 19.4% American, 16.4% Italian, 15.2% Polish, 12.3% English (2006-2010 5-year est.).

**Economy:** Single-family building permits issued: 5 (2011); Multi-family building permits issued: 0 (2011); Employment by occupation: 9.0% management, 1.5% professional, 11.1% services, 12.0% sales, 6.0% farming, 15.4% construction, 6.8% production (2006-2010 5-year est.).

**Income:** Per capita income: $31,232 (2006-2010 5-year est.); Median household income: $54,542 (2006-2010 5-year est.); Average household income: $80,981 (2006-2010 5-year est.); Percent of households with income of $100,000 or more: 16.9% (2006-2010 5-year est.); Poverty rate: 15.2% (2006-2010 5-year est.).

**Education:** Percent of population age 25 and over with: High school diploma (including GED) or higher: 92.6% (2006-2010 5-year est.); Bachelor's degree or higher: 17.6% (2006-2010 5-year est.); Master's degree or higher: 5.8% (2006-2010 5-year est.).

**Housing:** Homeownership rate: 86.9% (2010); Median home value: $134,100 (2006-2010 5-year est.); Median contract rent: $432 per month (2006-2010 5-year est.); Median year structure built: 1977 (2006-2010 5-year est.).

**Transportation:** Commute to work: 90.4% car, 0.0% public transportation, 1.5% walk, 7.6% work from home (2006-2010 5-year est.); Travel time to work: 29.9% less than 15 minutes, 44.6% 15 to 30 minutes, 15.9% 30 to 45 minutes, 6.3% 45 to 60 minutes, 3.4% 60 minutes or more (2006-2010 5-year est.)

**STRATFORD** (town). Covers a land area of 74.876 square miles and a water area of 1.794 square miles. Located at 43.20° N. Lat; 74.61° W. Long. Elevation is 1,066 feet.

**Population:** 586 (1990); 640 (2000); 610 (2010); Density: 8.1 persons per square mile (2010); Race: 98.4% White, 0.0% Black, 0.0% Asian, 0.0% American Indian/Alaska Native, 0.0% Native Hawaiian/Other Pacific Islander, 1.6% Other, 2.6% Hispanic of any race (2010); Average household size: 2.45 (2010); Median age: 46.2 (2010); Males per 100 females: 99.3 (2010); Marriage status: 22.9% never married, 60.0% now married, 8.1% widowed, 9.0% divorced (2006-2010 5-year est.); Foreign born: 0.5% (2006-2010 5-year est.); Ancestry (includes multiple ancestries): 19.6% English, 18.0% German, 15.7% American, 11.4% Irish, 7.1% French (2006-2010 5-year est.).

**Economy:** Single-family building permits issued: 3 (2011); Multi-family building permits issued: 0 (2011); Employment by occupation: 4.5% management, 3.6% professional, 15.9% services, 16.4% sales, 3.2% farming, 16.4% construction, 11.8% production (2006-2010 5-year est.).

**Income:** Per capita income: $18,666 (2006-2010 5-year est.); Median household income: $39,107 (2006-2010 5-year est.); Average household income: $45,899 (2006-2010 5-year est.); Percent of households with income of $100,000 or more: 11.0% (2006-2010 5-year est.); Poverty rate: 16.6% (2006-2010 5-year est.).

**Education:** Percent of population age 25 and over with: High school diploma (including GED) or higher: 80.0% (2006-2010 5-year est.); Bachelor's degree or higher: 8.6% (2006-2010 5-year est.); Master's degree or higher: 0.7% (2006-2010 5-year est.).

**Housing:** Homeownership rate: 89.7% (2010); Median home value: $77,200 (2006-2010 5-year est.); Median contract rent: $504 per month (2006-2010 5-year est.); Median year structure built: 1975 (2006-2010 5-year est.).

**Transportation:** Commute to work: 96.1% car, 0.0% public transportation, 0.0% walk, 3.9% work from home (2006-2010 5-year est.); Travel time to work: 4.6% less than 15 minutes, 35.0% 15 to 30 minutes, 28.4% 30 to 45 minutes, 15.7% 45 to 60 minutes, 16.2% 60 minutes or more (2006-2010 5-year est.)

## Genesee County

Located in western New York; drained by Tonawanda and Oak Orchard Creeks. Covers a land area of 494.11 square miles, a water area of 1.22 square miles, and is located in the Eastern Time Zone at 42.99° N. Lat., 78.17° W. Long. The county was founded in 1802. County seat is Batavia.

Genesee County is part of the Batavia, NY Micropolitan Statistical Area. The entire metro area includes: Genesee County, NY

Weather Station: Batavia                                    Elevation: 899 feet

|        | Jan  | Feb  | Mar  | Apr | May | Jun | Jul | Aug | Sep | Oct | Nov | Dec  |
|--------|------|------|------|-----|-----|-----|-----|-----|-----|-----|-----|------|
| High   | 32   | 35   | 44   | 57  | 69  | 78  | 81  | 80  | 73  | 61  | 49  | 37   |
| Low    | 17   | 18   | 25   | 37  | 47  | 57  | 61  | 60  | 53  | 42  | 33  | 22   |
| Precip | 2.0  | 1.8  | 2.2  | 3.0 | 3.3 | 3.7 | 3.3 | 3.2 | 3.8 | 3.2 | 2.8 | 2.4  |
| Snow   | 19.6 | 13.2 | 11.9 | 2.2 | 0.3 | 0.0 | 0.0 | 0.0 | 0.0 | 0.4 | 5.0 | 16.2 |

*High and Low temperatures in degrees Fahrenheit; Precipitation and Snow in inches*

**Population:** 60,060 (1990); 60,370 (2000); 60,079 (2010); Race: 92.9% White, 2.7% Black, 0.6% Asian, 1.1% American Indian/Alaska Native, 0.0% Native Hawaiian/Other Pacific Islander, 2.7% Other, 2.7% Hispanic of any race (2010); Density: 121.6 persons per square mile (2010); Average household size: 2.45 (2010); Median age: 41.5 (2010); Males per 100 females: 98.1 (2010).

**Religion:** Six largest groups: 25.7% Catholicism, 5.0% Methodist/Pietist, 2.8% Presbyterian-Reformed, 2.6% Holiness, 2.4% Non-Denominational, 2.2% Baptist (2010)

**Economy:** Unemployment rate: 9.3% (February 2012); Total civilian labor force: 31,014 (February 2012); Leading industries: 17.8% retail trade; 17.7% manufacturing; 12.4% health care and social assistance (2009); Farms: 551 totaling 183,539 acres (2007); Companies that employ 500 or more persons: 1 (2009); Companies that employ 100 to 499 persons: 19 (2009); Companies that employ less than 100 persons: 1,306 (2009); Black-owned businesses: n/a (2007); Hispanic-owned businesses: n/a (2007); Asian-owned businesses: n/a (2007); Women-owned businesses: 1,265 (2007); Retail sales per capita: $11,639 (2010). Single-family building permits issued: 19 (2011); Multi-family building permits issued: 0 (2011).

**Income:** Per capita income: $24,323 (2006-2010 5-year est.); Median household income: $49,750 (2006-2010 5-year est.); Average household income: $59,990 (2006-2010 5-year est.); Percent of households with income of $100,000 or more: 13.8% (2006-2010 5-year est.); Poverty rate: 11.7% (2006-2010 5-year est.); Bankruptcy rate: 2.74% (2011).

**Education:** Percent of population age 25 and over with: High school diploma (including GED) or higher: 90.4% (2006-2010 5-year est.); Bachelor's degree or higher: 20.2% (2006-2010 5-year est.); Master's degree or higher: 8.0% (2006-2010 5-year est.).

**Housing:** Homeownership rate: 71.9% (2010); Median home value: $101,400 (2006-2010 5-year est.); Median contract rent: $511 per month (2006-2010 5-year est.); Median year structure built: 1953 (2006-2010 5-year est.)

**Health:** Birth rate: 107.5 per 10,000 population (2011); Death rate: 101.5 per 10,000 population (2011); Age-adjusted cancer mortality rate: 196.3 deaths per 100,000 population (2009); Number of physicians: 10.5 per 10,000 population (2008); Hospital beds: 49.7 per 10,000 population (2007); Hospital admissions: 1,561.6 per 10,000 population (2007).

**Elections:** 2008 Presidential election results: 40.0% Obama, 58.4% McCain, 0.9% Nader

**National and State Parks:** Iroquois National Wildlife Refuge; Oak Orchard Creek State Game Refuge; White Memorial State Game Farm

**Additional Information Contacts**

Genesee County Government . . . . . . . . . . . . . . . . . (585) 344-2550
  http://www.co.genesee.ny.us
City of Batavia . . . . . . . . . . . . . . . . . . . . . . . . . . (585) 345-6305
  http://www.batavianewyork.com
Genesee County Chamber of Commerce . . . . . . . . . (518) 343-7440
  http://www.geneseeny.com
Town of Batavia . . . . . . . . . . . . . . . . . . . . . . . . . (585) 343-1729
  http://www.townofbatavia.com
Village of Oakfield . . . . . . . . . . . . . . . . . . . . . . . . (585) 948-5862
  http://www.oakfield.govoffice.com

## Genesee County Communities

**ALABAMA** (town). Covers a land area of 42.369 square miles and a water area of 0.405 square miles. Located at 43.09° N. Lat; 78.36° W. Long. Elevation is 643 feet.

**Population:** 1,998 (1990); 1,881 (2000); 1,869 (2010); Density: 44.1 persons per square mile (2010); Race: 95.6% White, 0.9% Black, 0.1% Asian, 1.4% American Indian/Alaska Native, 0.0% Native Hawaiian/Other Pacific Islander, 2.0% Other, 1.3% Hispanic of any race (2010); Average household size: 2.63 (2010); Median age: 42.2 (2010); Males per 100 females: 101.4 (2010); Marriage status: 24.3% never married, 63.6% now married, 4.3% widowed, 7.9% divorced (2006-2010 5-year est.); Foreign born: 1.0% (2006-2010 5-year est.); Ancestry (includes multiple ancestries): 43.3% German, 19.1% English, 15.6% Irish, 12.9% Polish, 9.5% Italian (2006-2010 5-year est.).

**Economy:** Single-family building permits issued: 0 (2011); Multi-family building permits issued: 0 (2011); Employment by occupation: 14.5% management, 1.5% professional, 8.7% services, 15.3% sales, 3.5% farming, 14.4% construction, 11.5% production (2006-2010 5-year est.).

**Income:** Per capita income: $22,263 (2006-2010 5-year est.); Median household income: $54,476 (2006-2010 5-year est.); Average household income: $56,724 (2006-2010 5-year est.); Percent of households with income of $100,000 or more: 11.3% (2006-2010 5-year est.); Poverty rate: 6.2% (2006-2010 5-year est.).

**Education:** Percent of population age 25 and over with: High school diploma (including GED) or higher: 88.2% (2006-2010 5-year est.); Bachelor's degree or higher: 12.6% (2006-2010 5-year est.); Master's degree or higher: 4.0% (2006-2010 5-year est.).

**Housing:** Homeownership rate: 82.7% (2010); Median home value: $96,600 (2006-2010 5-year est.); Median contract rent: $445 per month (2006-2010 5-year est.); Median year structure built: before 1940 (2006-2010 5-year est.).

**Transportation:** Commute to work: 92.9% car, 0.0% public transportation, 2.2% walk, 3.9% work from home (2006-2010 5-year est.); Travel time to work: 19.1% less than 15 minutes, 43.1% 15 to 30 minutes, 21.1% 30 to 45 minutes, 10.6% 45 to 60 minutes, 6.2% 60 minutes or more (2006-2010 5-year est.)

**ALEXANDER** (village). Covers a land area of 0.437 square miles and a water area of 0 square miles. Located at 42.90° N. Lat; 78.25° W. Long. Elevation is 932 feet.

**Population:** 445 (1990); 481 (2000); 509 (2010); Density: 1,164.1 persons per square mile (2010); Race: 97.1% White, 0.2% Black, 1.2% Asian, 0.0% American Indian/Alaska Native, 0.0% Native Hawaiian/Other Pacific Islander, 1.5% Other, 1.2% Hispanic of any race (2010); Average household size: 2.86 (2010); Median age: 34.9 (2010); Males per 100 females: 89.2 (2010); Marriage status: 29.6% never married, 58.8% now married, 2.0% widowed, 9.6% divorced (2006-2010 5-year est.); Foreign born: 2.3% (2006-2010 5-year est.); Ancestry (includes multiple ancestries): 53.2% German, 20.5% Irish, 16.9% English, 9.4% Italian, 9.4% Polish (2006-2010 5-year est.).

**Economy:** Single-family building permits issued: 0 (2011); Multi-family building permits issued: 0 (2011); Employment by occupation: 11.1% management, 3.2% professional, 16.1% services, 15.2% sales, 7.9% farming, 9.4% construction, 3.8% production (2006-2010 5-year est.).

**Income:** Per capita income: $21,979 (2006-2010 5-year est.); Median household income: $54,318 (2006-2010 5-year est.); Average household income: $67,057 (2006-2010 5-year est.); Percent of households with

income of $100,000 or more: 16.5% (2006-2010 5-year est.); Poverty rate: 5.6% (2006-2010 5-year est.).

**Education:** Percent of population age 25 and over with: High school diploma (including GED) or higher: 91.1% (2006-2010 5-year est.); Bachelor's degree or higher: 24.2% (2006-2010 5-year est.); Master's degree or higher: 7.1% (2006-2010 5-year est.).

### School District(s)

Alexander Central School District (PK-12)

    2009-10 Enrollment: 926 . . . . . . . . . . . . . . . . . . . . . . (585) 591-1551

**Housing:** Homeownership rate: 73.0% (2010); Median home value: $92,500 (2006-2010 5-year est.); Median contract rent: $564 per month (2006-2010 5-year est.); Median year structure built: before 1940 (2006-2010 5-year est.).

**Transportation:** Commute to work: 88.0% car, 3.1% public transportation, 4.3% walk, 4.0% work from home (2006-2010 5-year est.); Travel time to work: 25.0% less than 15 minutes, 33.7% 15 to 30 minutes, 21.8% 30 to 45 minutes, 10.9% 45 to 60 minutes, 8.7% 60 minutes or more (2006-2010 5-year est.)

**ALEXANDER** (town). Covers a land area of 35.466 square miles and a water area of 0.096 square miles. Located at 42.92° N. Lat; 78.25° W. Long. Elevation is 932 feet.

**Population:** 2,233 (1990); 2,451 (2000); 2,534 (2010); Density: 71.4 persons per square mile (2010); Race: 97.3% White, 0.4% Black, 0.3% Asian, 0.1% American Indian/Alaska Native, 0.0% Native Hawaiian/Other Pacific Islander, 1.9% Other, 1.5% Hispanic of any race (2010); Average household size: 2.70 (2010); Median age: 40.9 (2010); Males per 100 females: 97.2 (2010); Marriage status: 26.5% never married, 61.6% now married, 3.0% widowed, 8.8% divorced (2006-2010 5-year est.); Foreign born: 0.8% (2006-2010 5-year est.); Ancestry (includes multiple ancestries): 50.0% German, 25.4% English, 22.9% Irish, 12.5% Polish, 8.9% Italian (2006-2010 5-year est.).

**Economy:** Single-family building permits issued: 0 (2011); Multi-family building permits issued: 0 (2011); Employment by occupation: 9.6% management, 2.3% professional, 10.0% services, 16.8% sales, 4.5% farming, 15.2% construction, 10.0% production (2006-2010 5-year est.).

**Income:** Per capita income: $23,013 (2006-2010 5-year est.); Median household income: $56,719 (2006-2010 5-year est.); Average household income: $61,685 (2006-2010 5-year est.); Percent of households with income of $100,000 or more: 12.6% (2006-2010 5-year est.); Poverty rate: 6.4% (2006-2010 5-year est.).

**Education:** Percent of population age 25 and over with: High school diploma (including GED) or higher: 91.4% (2006-2010 5-year est.); Bachelor's degree or higher: 12.0% (2006-2010 5-year est.); Master's degree or higher: 4.3% (2006-2010 5-year est.).

### School District(s)

Alexander Central School District (PK-12)

    2009-10 Enrollment: 926 . . . . . . . . . . . . . . . . . . . . . . (585) 591-1551

**Housing:** Homeownership rate: 81.4% (2010); Median home value: $101,700 (2006-2010 5-year est.); Median contract rent: $502 per month (2006-2010 5-year est.); Median year structure built: 1955 (2006-2010 5-year est.).

**Transportation:** Commute to work: 89.6% car, 0.7% public transportation, 4.0% walk, 3.3% work from home (2006-2010 5-year est.); Travel time to work: 35.5% less than 15 minutes, 31.2% 15 to 30 minutes, 17.7% 30 to 45 minutes, 9.4% 45 to 60 minutes, 6.2% 60 minutes or more (2006-2010 5-year est.)

**BASOM** (unincorporated postal area)
Zip Code: 14013

    Covers a land area of 40.496 square miles and a water area of 0.365 square miles. Located at 43.08° N. Lat; 78.39° W. Long. Elevation is 715 feet. Population: 1,751 (2010); Density: 43.2 persons per square mile (2010); Race: 69.3% White, 0.3% Black, 0.1% Asian, 28.6% American Indian/Alaska Native, 0.0% Native Hawaiian/Other Pacific Islander, 1.7% Other, 1.7% Hispanic of any race (2010); Average household size: 2.63 (2010); Median age: 41.3 (2010); Males per 100 females: 99.7 (2010); Homeownership rate: 86.0% (2010)

**BATAVIA** (city). County seat. Covers a land area of 5.195 square miles and a water area of 0.080 square miles. Located at 42.99° N. Lat; 78.18° W. Long. Elevation is 892 feet.

**History:** Batavia is noteworthy as the "capital" of the Holland Land Purchase. In 1801, Joseph Ellicott, surveyor and subagent for the company, built a land office on the site. Ellicott proposed naming the place

Bustia or Bustiville, for Paul Busti, the company's general agent. The latter objected and proposed Batavia, the name of the Dutch republic to which the proprietors belonged.

**Population:** 16,310 (1990); 16,256 (2000); 15,465 (2010); Density: 2,976.4 persons per square mile (2010); Race: 89.4% White, 5.4% Black, 0.8% Asian, 0.4% American Indian/Alaska Native, 0.0% Native Hawaiian/Other Pacific Islander, 4.0% Other, 3.0% Hispanic of any race (2010); Average household size: 2.22 (2010); Median age: 40.4 (2010); Males per 100 females: 89.9 (2010); Marriage status: 31.9% never married, 44.8% now married, 9.4% widowed, 13.8% divorced (2006-2010 5-year est.); Foreign born: 2.6% (2006-2010 5-year est.); Ancestry (includes multiple ancestries): 29.7% German, 21.3% Italian, 18.2% Irish, 16.3% English, 11.1% Polish (2006-2010 5-year est.).

**Economy:** Single-family building permits issued: 1 (2011); Multi-family building permits issued: 0 (2011); Employment by occupation: 8.6% management, 2.1% professional, 16.0% services, 17.1% sales, 3.5% farming, 7.8% construction, 5.8% production (2006-2010 5-year est.).

**Income:** Per capita income: $20,597 (2006-2010 5-year est.); Median household income: $37,522 (2006-2010 5-year est.); Average household income: $48,959 (2006-2010 5-year est.); Percent of households with income of $100,000 or more: 10.3% (2006-2010 5-year est.); Poverty rate: 21.3% (2006-2010 5-year est.).

**Education:** Percent of population age 25 and over with: High school diploma (including GED) or higher: 89.9% (2006-2010 5-year est.); Bachelor's degree or higher: 20.9% (2006-2010 5-year est.); Master's degree or higher: 9.3% (2006-2010 5-year est.).

### School District(s)

Batavia City School District (PK-12)

    2009-10 Enrollment: 2,430 . . . . . . . . . . . . . . . . . . . . (585) 343-2480

New York State School for the Blind (UG-UG)

    2009-10 Enrollment: 52 . . . . . . . . . . . . . . . . . . . . . . (585) 343-5384

### Two-year College(s)

Genesee Community College (Public)

    Fall 2010 Enrollment: 4,620 . . . . . . . . . . . . . . . . . . . (585) 343-0055

    2011-12 Tuition: In-state $3,720; Out-of-state $4,320

### Vocational/Technical School(s)

Continental School of Beauty Culture-Batavia (Private, For-profit)

    Fall 2010 Enrollment: 52 . . . . . . . . . . . . . . . . . . . . . (585) 344-0886

    2011-12 Tuition: $11,050

Genesee Valley BOCES-Practical Nursing Program (Public)

    Fall 2010 Enrollment: 246 . . . . . . . . . . . . . . . . . . . . (585) 344-7788

    2011-12 Tuition: $9,750

**Housing:** Homeownership rate: 52.3% (2010); Median home value: $90,600 (2006-2010 5-year est.); Median contract rent: $518 per month (2006-2010 5-year est.); Median year structure built: before 1940 (2006-2010 5-year est.).

**Hospitals:** United Memorial Medical Center (126 beds)

**Safety:** Violent crime rate: 29.6 per 10,000 population; Property crime rate: 347.0 per 10,000 population (2010).

**Newspapers:** Batavia Daily News (Local news; Circulation 15,452); The Drummer (Community news; Circulation 23,000)

**Transportation:** Commute to work: 90.6% car, 0.7% public transportation, 4.5% walk, 1.6% work from home (2006-2010 5-year est.); Travel time to work: 57.6% less than 15 minutes, 18.2% 15 to 30 minutes, 13.4% 30 to 45 minutes, 8.2% 45 to 60 minutes, 2.6% 60 minutes or more (2006-2010 5-year est.)

**Airports:** Genesee County (general aviation)

**Additional Information Contacts**

City of Batavia . . . . . . . . . . . . . . . . . . . . . . . . . . . . (585) 345-6305

    http://www.batavianewyork.com

Genesee County Chamber of Commerce . . . . . . . . . . . . (518) 343-7440

    http://www.geneseeny.com

**BATAVIA** (town). Covers a land area of 48.186 square miles and a water area of 0.218 square miles. Located at 42.99° N. Lat; 78.22° W. Long. Elevation is 892 feet.

**History:** Laid out in 1801 by Joseph Ellicott, agent for the Holland Land Company, the city was a center of the Anti-Masonic movement in the 19th century. Attica prison, site of the 1971 riots, is nearby. Incorporated 1915.

**Population:** 6,055 (1990); 5,915 (2000); 6,809 (2010); Density: 141.3 persons per square mile (2010); Race: 89.0% White, 6.1% Black, 1.6% Asian, 0.5% American Indian/Alaska Native, 0.0% Native Hawaiian/Other Pacific Islander, 2.8% Other, 3.7% Hispanic of any race (2010); Average household size: 2.39 (2010); Median age: 41.3 (2010); Males per 100 females: 112.0 (2010); Marriage status: 25.0% never married, 54.7% now

married, 7.9% widowed, 12.4% divorced (2006-2010 5-year est.); Foreign born: 4.8% (2006-2010 5-year est.); Ancestry (includes multiple ancestries): 35.4% German, 19.3% Italian, 17.3% Irish, 16.1% English, 10.8% Polish (2006-2010 5-year est.).

**Economy:** Single-family building permits issued: 5 (2011); Multi-family building permits issued: 0 (2011); Employment by occupation: 9.4% management, 0.3% professional, 7.0% services, 17.7% sales, 3.3% farming, 11.5% construction, 9.7% production (2006-2010 5-year est.).

**Income:** Per capita income: $31,729 (2006-2010 5-year est.); Median household income: $48,598 (2006-2010 5-year est.); Average household income: $72,287 (2006-2010 5-year est.); Percent of households with income of $100,000 or more: 14.4% (2006-2010 5-year est.); Poverty rate: 8.9% (2006-2010 5-year est.).

**Education:** Percent of population age 25 and over with: High school diploma (including GED) or higher: 93.6% (2006-2010 5-year est.); Bachelor's degree or higher: 22.1% (2006-2010 5-year est.); Master's degree or higher: 8.1% (2006-2010 5-year est.).

#### School District(s)
Batavia City School District (PK-12)
   2009-10 Enrollment: 2,430 . . . . . . . . . . . . . . . . . . . . . . (585) 343-2480
New York State School for the Blind (UG-UG)
   2009-10 Enrollment: 52 . . . . . . . . . . . . . . . . . . . . . . . . (585) 343-5384

#### Two-year College(s)
Genesee Community College (Public)
   Fall 2010 Enrollment: 4,620 . . . . . . . . . . . . . . . . . . . . (585) 343-0055
   2011-12 Tuition: In-state $3,720; Out-of-state $4,320

#### Vocational/Technical School(s)
Continental School of Beauty Culture-Batavia (Private, For-profit)
   Fall 2010 Enrollment: 52 . . . . . . . . . . . . . . . . . . . . . . (585) 344-0886
   2011-12 Tuition: $11,050
Genesee Valley BOCES-Practical Nursing Program (Public)
   Fall 2010 Enrollment: 246 . . . . . . . . . . . . . . . . . . . . . (585) 344-7788
   2011-12 Tuition: $9,750

**Housing:** Homeownership rate: 81.8% (2010); Median home value: $97,200 (2006-2010 5-year est.); Median contract rent: $482 per month (2006-2010 5-year est.); Median year structure built: 1971 (2006-2010 5-year est.).

**Hospitals:** United Memorial Medical Center (126 beds)

**Newspapers:** Batavia Daily News (Local news; Circulation 15,452); The Drummer (Community news; Circulation 23,000)

**Transportation:** Commute to work: 97.6% car, 0.0% public transportation, 1.1% walk, 1.0% work from home (2006-2010 5-year est.); Travel time to work: 46.9% less than 15 minutes, 23.0% 15 to 30 minutes, 15.4% 30 to 45 minutes, 14.2% 45 to 60 minutes, 0.6% 60 minutes or more (2006-2010 5-year est.).

**Airports:** Genesee County (general aviation)

**Additional Information Contacts**
Town of Batavia . . . . . . . . . . . . . . . . . . . . . . . . . . . . . . . (585) 343-1729
   http://www.townofbatavia.com

**BERGEN** (village). Covers a land area of 0.736 square miles and a water area of 0 square miles. Located at 43.08° N. Lat; 77.94° W. Long. Elevation is 607 feet.

**Population:** 1,111 (1990); 1,240 (2000); 1,176 (2010); Density: 1,596.6 persons per square mile (2010); Race: 96.5% White, 0.3% Black, 0.9% Asian, 0.0% American Indian/Alaska Native, 0.0% Native Hawaiian/Other Pacific Islander, 2.3% Other, 2.2% Hispanic of any race (2010); Average household size: 2.64 (2010); Median age: 39.5 (2010); Males per 100 females: 94.4 (2010); Marriage status: 37.4% never married, 48.7% now married, 4.3% widowed, 9.7% divorced (2006-2010 5-year est.); Foreign born: 2.5% (2006-2010 5-year est.); Ancestry (includes multiple ancestries): 31.8% German, 24.0% English, 21.8% Irish, 10.7% Italian, 7.8% French (2006-2010 5-year est.).

**Economy:** Single-family building permits issued: 0 (2011); Multi-family building permits issued: 0 (2011); Employment by occupation: 8.5% management, 3.6% professional, 9.8% services, 15.7% sales, 8.7% farming, 6.0% construction, 10.4% production (2006-2010 5-year est.).

**Income:** Per capita income: $21,495 (2006-2010 5-year est.); Median household income: $48,833 (2006-2010 5-year est.); Average household income: $52,967 (2006-2010 5-year est.); Percent of households with income of $100,000 or more: 7.5% (2006-2010 5-year est.); Poverty rate: 6.0% (2006-2010 5-year est.).

**Education:** Percent of population age 25 and over with: High school diploma (including GED) or higher: 90.4% (2006-2010 5-year est.);

Bachelor's degree or higher: 17.7% (2006-2010 5-year est.); Master's degree or higher: 5.8% (2006-2010 5-year est.).

#### School District(s)
Byron-Bergen Central School District (PK-12)
   2009-10 Enrollment: 1,106 . . . . . . . . . . . . . . . . . . . . (585) 494-1220

**Housing:** Homeownership rate: 74.2% (2010); Median home value: $96,100 (2006-2010 5-year est.); Median contract rent: $482 per month (2006-2010 5-year est.); Median year structure built: before 1940 (2006-2010 5-year est.).

**Transportation:** Commute to work: 85.9% car, 0.0% public transportation, 8.9% walk, 2.4% work from home (2006-2010 5-year est.); Travel time to work: 25.3% less than 15 minutes, 39.9% 15 to 30 minutes, 30.1% 30 to 45 minutes, 2.4% 45 to 60 minutes, 2.2% 60 minutes or more (2006-2010 5-year est.)

**BERGEN** (town). Covers a land area of 27.559 square miles and a water area of 0.035 square miles. Located at 43.09° N. Lat; 77.95° W. Long. Elevation is 607 feet.

**Population:** 2,794 (1990); 3,182 (2000); 3,120 (2010); Density: 113.2 persons per square mile (2010); Race: 97.2% White, 0.6% Black, 0.6% Asian, 0.1% American Indian/Alaska Native, 0.0% Native Hawaiian/Other Pacific Islander, 1.5% Other, 1.6% Hispanic of any race (2010); Average household size: 2.58 (2010); Median age: 42.8 (2010); Males per 100 females: 98.7 (2010); Marriage status: 28.6% never married, 57.2% now married, 4.4% widowed, 9.9% divorced (2006-2010 5-year est.); Foreign born: 2.6% (2006-2010 5-year est.); Ancestry (includes multiple ancestries): 31.3% German, 28.2% English, 23.6% Irish, 10.8% Italian, 6.8% Polish (2006-2010 5-year est.).

**Economy:** Single-family building permits issued: 0 (2011); Multi-family building permits issued: 0 (2011); Employment by occupation: 13.7% management, 7.9% professional, 10.1% services, 15.2% sales, 5.1% farming, 11.5% construction, 8.5% production (2006-2010 5-year est.).

**Income:** Per capita income: $23,985 (2006-2010 5-year est.); Median household income: $56,854 (2006-2010 5-year est.); Average household income: $60,084 (2006-2010 5-year est.); Percent of households with income of $100,000 or more: 15.9% (2006-2010 5-year est.); Poverty rate: 6.4% (2006-2010 5-year est.).

**Education:** Percent of population age 25 and over with: High school diploma (including GED) or higher: 92.8% (2006-2010 5-year est.); Bachelor's degree or higher: 17.8% (2006-2010 5-year est.); Master's degree or higher: 7.9% (2006-2010 5-year est.).

#### School District(s)
Byron-Bergen Central School District (PK-12)
   2009-10 Enrollment: 1,106 . . . . . . . . . . . . . . . . . . . . (585) 494-1220

**Housing:** Homeownership rate: 80.4% (2010); Median home value: $99,100 (2006-2010 5-year est.); Median contract rent: $481 per month (2006-2010 5-year est.); Median year structure built: 1963 (2006-2010 5-year est.).

**Transportation:** Commute to work: 93.2% car, 0.0% public transportation, 5.0% walk, 0.8% work from home (2006-2010 5-year est.); Travel time to work: 22.9% less than 15 minutes, 38.4% 15 to 30 minutes, 29.0% 30 to 45 minutes, 8.3% 45 to 60 minutes, 1.4% 60 minutes or more (2006-2010 5-year est.)

**BETHANY** (town). Aka Bethany Center. Covers a land area of 36.035 square miles and a water area of 0.034 square miles. Located at 42.91° N. Lat; 78.12° W. Long.

**Population:** 1,808 (1990); 1,760 (2000); 1,765 (2010); Density: 49.0 persons per square mile (2010); Race: 96.1% White, 0.6% Black, 0.7% Asian, 0.1% American Indian/Alaska Native, 0.0% Native Hawaiian/Other Pacific Islander, 2.5% Other, 2.9% Hispanic of any race (2010); Average household size: 2.62 (2010); Median age: 41.9 (2010); Males per 100 females: 103.6 (2010); Marriage status: 22.9% never married, 61.2% now married, 4.6% widowed, 11.3% divorced (2006-2010 5-year est.); Foreign born: 6.8% (2006-2010 5-year est.); Ancestry (includes multiple ancestries): 31.2% German, 21.1% Irish, 17.3% English, 10.2% Italian, 9.3% Polish (2006-2010 5-year est.).

**Economy:** Single-family building permits issued: 2 (2011); Multi-family building permits issued: 0 (2011); Employment by occupation: 8.9% management, 3.0% professional, 9.1% services, 11.8% sales, 5.9% farming, 17.7% construction, 7.6% production (2006-2010 5-year est.).

**Income:** Per capita income: $25,966 (2006-2010 5-year est.); Median household income: $58,214 (2006-2010 5-year est.); Average household income: $66,043 (2006-2010 5-year est.); Percent of households with

income of $100,000 or more: 19.5% (2006-2010 5-year est.); Poverty rate: 13.0% (2006-2010 5-year est.).

**Education:** Percent of population age 25 and over with: High school diploma (including GED) or higher: 86.9% (2006-2010 5-year est.); Bachelor's degree or higher: 15.0% (2006-2010 5-year est.); Master's degree or higher: 6.3% (2006-2010 5-year est.).

**Housing:** Homeownership rate: 82.2% (2010); Median home value: $105,500 (2006-2010 5-year est.); Median contract rent: $525 per month (2006-2010 5-year est.); Median year structure built: 1957 (2006-2010 5-year est.).

**Transportation:** Commute to work: 86.3% car, 0.7% public transportation, 2.6% walk, 10.2% work from home (2006-2010 5-year est.); Travel time to work: 44.6% less than 15 minutes, 27.9% 15 to 30 minutes, 11.3% 30 to 45 minutes, 14.0% 45 to 60 minutes, 2.2% 60 minutes or more (2006-2010 5-year est.)

**BYRON** (town). Covers a land area of 32.211 square miles and a water area of 0.078 square miles. Located at 43.08° N. Lat; 78.06° W. Long. Elevation is 620 feet.

**Population:** 2,345 (1990); 2,493 (2000); 2,369 (2010); Density: 73.5 persons per square mile (2010); Race: 94.4% White, 0.4% Black, 0.3% Asian, 0.4% American Indian/Alaska Native, 0.0% Native Hawaiian/Other Pacific Islander, 4.5% Other, 4.9% Hispanic of any race (2010); Average household size: 2.58 (2010); Median age: 41.5 (2010); Males per 100 females: 104.6 (2010); Marriage status: 27.5% never married, 60.8% now married, 5.5% widowed, 6.2% divorced (2006-2010 5-year est.); Foreign born: 0.3% (2006-2010 5-year est.); Ancestry (includes multiple ancestries): 24.9% German, 24.3% English, 22.7% Irish, 14.7% Italian, 11.9% Polish (2006-2010 5-year est.).

**Economy:** Single-family building permits issued: 1 (2011); Multi-family building permits issued: 0 (2011); Employment by occupation: 11.0% management, 6.8% professional, 5.2% services, 15.1% sales, 3.0% farming, 14.4% construction, 9.6% production (2006-2010 5-year est.).

**Income:** Per capita income: $26,729 (2006-2010 5-year est.); Median household income: $64,516 (2006-2010 5-year est.); Average household income: $71,679 (2006-2010 5-year est.); Percent of households with income of $100,000 or more: 19.4% (2006-2010 5-year est.); Poverty rate: 5.0% (2006-2010 5-year est.).

**Education:** Percent of population age 25 and over with: High school diploma (including GED) or higher: 93.8% (2006-2010 5-year est.); Bachelor's degree or higher: 21.3% (2006-2010 5-year est.); Master's degree or higher: 5.9% (2006-2010 5-year est.).

**Housing:** Homeownership rate: 86.5% (2010); Median home value: $97,800 (2006-2010 5-year est.); Median contract rent: $536 per month (2006-2010 5-year est.); Median year structure built: 1969 (2006-2010 5-year est.).

**Transportation:** Commute to work: 92.8% car, 0.8% public transportation, 2.4% walk, 2.1% work from home (2006-2010 5-year est.); Travel time to work: 29.9% less than 15 minutes, 26.2% 15 to 30 minutes, 31.4% 30 to 45 minutes, 10.7% 45 to 60 minutes, 1.8% 60 minutes or more (2006-2010 5-year est.)

**CORFU** (village). Covers a land area of 0.995 square miles and a water area of 0 square miles. Located at 42.96° N. Lat; 78.40° W. Long. Elevation is 863 feet.

**Population:** 835 (1990); 795 (2000); 709 (2010); Density: 712.5 persons per square mile (2010); Race: 97.5% White, 0.7% Black, 0.3% Asian, 0.0% American Indian/Alaska Native, 0.0% Native Hawaiian/Other Pacific Islander, 1.5% Other, 2.0% Hispanic of any race (2010); Average household size: 2.32 (2010); Median age: 43.2 (2010); Males per 100 females: 92.1 (2010); Marriage status: 25.9% never married, 55.3% now married, 6.1% widowed, 12.8% divorced (2006-2010 5-year est.); Foreign born: 0.9% (2006-2010 5-year est.); Ancestry (includes multiple ancestries): 58.8% German, 23.2% Irish, 19.2% English, 16.8% Polish, 7.4% French (2006-2010 5-year est.).

**Economy:** Single-family building permits issued: 0 (2011); Multi-family building permits issued: 0 (2011); Employment by occupation: 8.8% management, 1.4% professional, 7.4% services, 17.8% sales, 1.6% farming, 8.5% construction, 3.0% production (2006-2010 5-year est.).

**Income:** Per capita income: $22,040 (2006-2010 5-year est.); Median household income: $50,845 (2006-2010 5-year est.); Average household income: $55,122 (2006-2010 5-year est.); Percent of households with income of $100,000 or more: 11.0% (2006-2010 5-year est.); Poverty rate: 11.9% (2006-2010 5-year est.).

**Education:** Percent of population age 25 and over with: High school diploma (including GED) or higher: 91.0% (2006-2010 5-year est.); Bachelor's degree or higher: 21.1% (2006-2010 5-year est.); Master's degree or higher: 8.1% (2006-2010 5-year est.).

**School District(s)**

Pembroke Central School District (PK-12)

   2009-10 Enrollment: 1,101 . . . . . . . . . . . . . . . . . . . . . . . (585) 599-4525

**Housing:** Homeownership rate: 68.6% (2010); Median home value: $93,900 (2006-2010 5-year est.); Median contract rent: $540 per month (2006-2010 5-year est.); Median year structure built: 1943 (2006-2010 5-year est.).

**Transportation:** Commute to work: 94.9% car, 0.0% public transportation, 4.5% walk, 0.6% work from home (2006-2010 5-year est.); Travel time to work: 26.3% less than 15 minutes, 43.4% 15 to 30 minutes, 21.7% 30 to 45 minutes, 7.7% 45 to 60 minutes, 0.9% 60 minutes or more (2006-2010 5-year est.)

**DARIEN** (town). Covers a land area of 47.370 square miles and a water area of 0.218 square miles. Located at 42.90° N. Lat; 78.38° W. Long. Elevation is 1,001 feet.

**Population:** 2,979 (1990); 3,061 (2000); 3,158 (2010); Density: 66.7 persons per square mile (2010); Race: 98.7% White, 0.1% Black, 0.1% Asian, 0.1% American Indian/Alaska Native, 0.0% Native Hawaiian/Other Pacific Islander, 1.0% Other, 1.1% Hispanic of any race (2010); Average household size: 2.65 (2010); Median age: 44.0 (2010); Males per 100 females: 105.7 (2010); Marriage status: 28.9% never married, 59.1% now married, 6.1% widowed, 5.9% divorced (2006-2010 5-year est.); Foreign born: 0.9% (2006-2010 5-year est.); Ancestry (includes multiple ancestries): 40.7% German, 30.3% Polish, 16.9% Irish, 13.1% Italian, 7.7% English (2006-2010 5-year est.).

**Economy:** Single-family building permits issued: 2 (2011); Multi-family building permits issued: 0 (2011); Employment by occupation: 7.8% management, 2.4% professional, 10.5% services, 14.8% sales, 2.3% farming, 18.1% construction, 11.2% production (2006-2010 5-year est.).

**Income:** Per capita income: $23,413 (2006-2010 5-year est.); Median household income: $56,582 (2006-2010 5-year est.); Average household income: $65,356 (2006-2010 5-year est.); Percent of households with income of $100,000 or more: 16.7% (2006-2010 5-year est.); Poverty rate: 2.7% (2006-2010 5-year est.).

**Education:** Percent of population age 25 and over with: High school diploma (including GED) or higher: 87.4% (2006-2010 5-year est.); Bachelor's degree or higher: 15.3% (2006-2010 5-year est.); Master's degree or higher: 5.5% (2006-2010 5-year est.).

**Housing:** Homeownership rate: 86.5% (2010); Median home value: $134,300 (2006-2010 5-year est.); Median contract rent: $658 per month (2006-2010 5-year est.); Median year structure built: 1963 (2006-2010 5-year est.).

**Transportation:** Commute to work: 94.3% car, 0.0% public transportation, 1.4% walk, 3.4% work from home (2006-2010 5-year est.); Travel time to work: 24.4% less than 15 minutes, 35.0% 15 to 30 minutes, 28.2% 30 to 45 minutes, 8.1% 45 to 60 minutes, 4.3% 60 minutes or more (2006-2010 5-year est.)

**DARIEN CENTER** (unincorporated postal area)

Zip Code: 14040

   Covers a land area of 29.227 square miles and a water area of 0.190 square miles. Located at 42.89° N. Lat; 78.37° W. Long. Elevation is 1,017 feet. Population: 2,217 (2010); Density: 75.9 persons per square mile (2010); Race: 99.3% White, 0.1% Black, 0.1% Asian, 0.0% American Indian/Alaska Native, 0.0% Native Hawaiian/Other Pacific Islander, 0.5% Other, 0.9% Hispanic of any race (2010); Average household size: 2.59 (2010); Median age: 44.6 (2010); Males per 100 females: 108.2 (2010); Homeownership rate: 86.7% (2010)

**EAST BETHANY** (unincorporated postal area)

Zip Code: 14054

   Covers a land area of 24.857 square miles and a water area of 0.023 square miles. Located at 42.91° N. Lat; 78.12° W. Long. Elevation is 1,001 feet. Population: 1,344 (2010); Density: 54.1 persons per square mile (2010); Race: 96.3% White, 0.7% Black, 0.7% Asian, 0.1% American Indian/Alaska Native, 0.0% Native Hawaiian/Other Pacific Islander, 2.2% Other, 2.6% Hispanic of any race (2010); Average household size: 2.61 (2010); Median age: 40.1 (2010); Males per 100 females: 103.3 (2010); Homeownership rate: 81.8% (2010)

**ELBA** (village). Covers a land area of 1.016 square miles and a water area of 0 square miles. Located at 43.07° N. Lat; 78.18° W. Long. Elevation is 761 feet.
**Population:** 703 (1990); 696 (2000); 676 (2010); Density: 664.9 persons per square mile (2010); Race: 93.2% White, 1.0% Black, 0.0% Asian, 0.3% American Indian/Alaska Native, 0.0% Native Hawaiian/Other Pacific Islander, 5.5% Other, 10.1% Hispanic of any race (2010); Average household size: 2.67 (2010); Median age: 41.8 (2010); Males per 100 females: 104.2 (2010); Marriage status: 27.8% never married, 61.9% now married, 3.7% widowed, 6.6% divorced (2006-2010 5-year est.); Foreign born: 4.7% (2006-2010 5-year est.); Ancestry (includes multiple ancestries): 28.1% German, 21.0% English, 17.1% Italian, 14.4% Irish, 9.3% Polish (2006-2010 5-year est.).
**Economy:** Single-family building permits issued: 0 (2011); Multi-family building permits issued: 0 (2011); Employment by occupation: 9.6% management, 0.9% professional, 10.5% services, 12.9% sales, 3.3% farming, 14.0% construction, 4.9% production (2006-2010 5-year est.).
**Income:** Per capita income: $24,291 (2006-2010 5-year est.); Median household income: $60,875 (2006-2010 5-year est.); Average household income: $71,195 (2006-2010 5-year est.); Percent of households with income of $100,000 or more: 18.6% (2006-2010 5-year est.); Poverty rate: 14.3% (2006-2010 5-year est.).
**Education:** Percent of population age 25 and over with: High school diploma (including GED) or higher: 83.8% (2006-2010 5-year est.); Bachelor's degree or higher: 15.0% (2006-2010 5-year est.); Master's degree or higher: 4.0% (2006-2010 5-year est.).
**School District(s)**
Elba Central School District (PK-12)
    2009-10 Enrollment: 513 . . . . . . . . . . . . . . . . . . (585) 757-9967
**Housing:** Homeownership rate: 79.9% (2010); Median home value: $103,300 (2006-2010 5-year est.); Median contract rent: $247 per month (2006-2010 5-year est.); Median year structure built: before 1940 (2006-2010 5-year est.).
**Transportation:** Commute to work: 94.8% car, 0.0% public transportation, 2.8% walk, 2.4% work from home (2006-2010 5-year est.); Travel time to work: 39.7% less than 15 minutes, 36.3% 15 to 30 minutes, 12.1% 30 to 45 minutes, 7.7% 45 to 60 minutes, 4.1% 60 minutes or more (2006-2010 5-year est.)

**ELBA** (town). Covers a land area of 35.649 square miles and a water area of 0.042 square miles. Located at 43.09° N. Lat; 78.17° W. Long. Elevation is 761 feet.
**Population:** 2,407 (1990); 2,439 (2000); 2,370 (2010); Density: 66.5 persons per square mile (2010); Race: 90.6% White, 2.1% Black, 0.4% Asian, 0.3% American Indian/Alaska Native, 0.0% Native Hawaiian/Other Pacific Islander, 6.6% Other, 8.9% Hispanic of any race (2010); Average household size: 2.76 (2010); Median age: 40.7 (2010); Males per 100 females: 100.3 (2010); Marriage status: 25.1% never married, 59.6% now married, 4.6% widowed, 10.7% divorced (2006-2010 5-year est.); Foreign born: 8.5% (2006-2010 5-year est.); Ancestry (includes multiple ancestries): 25.9% German, 22.4% Italian, 18.8% English, 13.5% Irish, 6.6% Polish (2006-2010 5-year est.).
**Economy:** Single-family building permits issued: 1 (2011); Multi-family building permits issued: 0 (2011); Employment by occupation: 13.5% management, 2.3% professional, 13.2% services, 13.2% sales, 1.4% farming, 16.7% construction, 6.8% production (2006-2010 5-year est.).
**Income:** Per capita income: $22,396 (2006-2010 5-year est.); Median household income: $57,598 (2006-2010 5-year est.); Average household income: $62,961 (2006-2010 5-year est.); Percent of households with income of $100,000 or more: 11.8% (2006-2010 5-year est.); Poverty rate: 6.5% (2006-2010 5-year est.).
**Education:** Percent of population age 25 and over with: High school diploma (including GED) or higher: 83.8% (2006-2010 5-year est.); Bachelor's degree or higher: 22.6% (2006-2010 5-year est.); Master's degree or higher: 7.5% (2006-2010 5-year est.).
**School District(s)**
Elba Central School District (PK-12)
    2009-10 Enrollment: 513 . . . . . . . . . . . . . . . . . . (585) 757-9967
**Housing:** Homeownership rate: 81.8% (2010); Median home value: $106,600 (2006-2010 5-year est.); Median contract rent: $645 per month (2006-2010 5-year est.); Median year structure built: 1942 (2006-2010 5-year est.).
**Transportation:** Commute to work: 94.7% car, 0.0% public transportation, 1.8% walk, 3.1% work from home (2006-2010 5-year est.); Travel time to work: 39.8% less than 15 minutes, 32.5% 15 to 30 minutes, 11.7% 30 to 45

minutes, 9.9% 45 to 60 minutes, 6.1% 60 minutes or more (2006-2010 5-year est.)

**LE ROY** (village). Covers a land area of 2.688 square miles and a water area of 0.002 square miles. Located at 42.97° N. Lat; 77.99° W. Long. Elevation is 896 feet.
**Population:** 4,974 (1990); 4,462 (2000); 4,391 (2010); Density: 1,633.3 persons per square mile (2010); Race: 94.7% White, 2.5% Black, 0.3% Asian, 0.3% American Indian/Alaska Native, 0.0% Native Hawaiian/Other Pacific Islander, 2.2% Other, 2.3% Hispanic of any race (2010); Average household size: 2.30 (2010); Median age: 39.8 (2010); Males per 100 females: 93.5 (2010); Marriage status: 23.8% never married, 54.7% now married, 11.3% widowed, 10.1% divorced (2006-2010 5-year est.); Foreign born: 2.5% (2006-2010 5-year est.); Ancestry (includes multiple ancestries): 25.1% German, 24.3% Italian, 18.8% Irish, 16.4% English, 8.2% Polish (2006-2010 5-year est.).
**Economy:** Single-family building permits issued: 0 (2011); Multi-family building permits issued: 0 (2011); Employment by occupation: 8.6% management, 2.5% professional, 11.6% services, 11.5% sales, 5.0% farming, 11.5% construction, 10.6% production (2006-2010 5-year est.).
**Income:** Per capita income: $22,977 (2006-2010 5-year est.); Median household income: $44,500 (2006-2010 5-year est.); Average household income: $56,152 (2006-2010 5-year est.); Percent of households with income of $100,000 or more: 13.5% (2006-2010 5-year est.); Poverty rate: 12.0% (2006-2010 5-year est.).
**Education:** Percent of population age 25 and over with: High school diploma (including GED) or higher: 90.9% (2006-2010 5-year est.); Bachelor's degree or higher: 27.7% (2006-2010 5-year est.); Master's degree or higher: 11.2% (2006-2010 5-year est.).
**School District(s)**
Genesee Valley Boces
    2009-10 Enrollment: n/a . . . . . . . . . . . . . . . . . (585) 658-7903
Le Roy Central School District (PK-12)
    2009-10 Enrollment: 1,335 . . . . . . . . . . . . . . . . (585) 768-8133
**Housing:** Homeownership rate: 57.8% (2010); Median home value: $97,200 (2006-2010 5-year est.); Median contract rent: $492 per month (2006-2010 5-year est.); Median year structure built: before 1940 (2006-2010 5-year est.).
**Safety:** Violent crime rate: 29.6 per 10,000 population; Property crime rate: 271.1 per 10,000 population (2010).
**Transportation:** Commute to work: 93.3% car, 0.0% public transportation, 3.0% walk, 2.4% work from home (2006-2010 5-year est.); Travel time to work: 42.3% less than 15 minutes, 30.2% 15 to 30 minutes, 21.0% 30 to 45 minutes, 6.5% 45 to 60 minutes, 0.0% 60 minutes or more (2006-2010 5-year est.)

**LE ROY** (town). Covers a land area of 42.084 square miles and a water area of 0.089 square miles. Located at 42.99° N. Lat; 77.96° W. Long. Elevation is 896 feet.
**History:** In 1897, Pearl Bixby Wait, a local carpenter, perfected the formula for Jello gelatin dessert, then sold it for $450. Until 1964, General Foods had a plant that produced Jello in the village. Jello Museum is housed in the Historical Society Building. Settled 1793, Incorporated 1834.
**Population:** 8,176 (1990); 7,790 (2000); 7,641 (2010); Density: 181.6 persons per square mile (2010); Race: 95.4% White, 1.8% Black, 0.4% Asian, 0.3% American Indian/Alaska Native, 0.0% Native Hawaiian/Other Pacific Islander, 2.1% Other, 2.0% Hispanic of any race (2010); Average household size: 2.42 (2010); Median age: 41.0 (2010); Males per 100 females: 95.6 (2010); Marriage status: 24.7% never married, 55.3% now married, 10.1% widowed, 9.8% divorced (2006-2010 5-year est.); Foreign born: 1.8% (2006-2010 5-year est.); Ancestry (includes multiple ancestries): 29.1% German, 25.6% Italian, 23.3% Irish, 15.1% English, 7.4% Polish (2006-2010 5-year est.).
**Economy:** Single-family building permits issued: 4 (2011); Multi-family building permits issued: 0 (2011); Employment by occupation: 8.1% management, 2.3% professional, 9.9% services, 14.3% sales, 4.8% farming, 10.3% construction, 11.1% production (2006-2010 5-year est.).
**Income:** Per capita income: $25,179 (2006-2010 5-year est.); Median household income: $51,510 (2006-2010 5-year est.); Average household income: $61,974 (2006-2010 5-year est.); Percent of households with income of $100,000 or more: 15.7% (2006-2010 5-year est.); Poverty rate: 8.2% (2006-2010 5-year est.).
**Education:** Percent of population age 25 and over with: High school diploma (including GED) or higher: 91.8% (2006-2010 5-year est.);

Bachelor's degree or higher: 24.5% (2006-2010 5-year est.); Master's degree or higher: 10.1% (2006-2010 5-year est.).

**School District(s)**

Genesee Valley Boces

   2009-10 Enrollment: n/a . . . . . . . . . . . . . . . . . (585) 658-7903

Le Roy Central School District (PK-12)

   2009-10 Enrollment: 1,335 . . . . . . . . . . . . . . (585) 768-8133

**Housing:** Homeownership rate: 69.1% (2010); Median home value: $112,300 (2006-2010 5-year est.); Median contract rent: $498 per month (2006-2010 5-year est.); Median year structure built: 1948 (2006-2010 5-year est.).

**Transportation:** Commute to work: 93.5% car, 0.0% public transportation, 2.1% walk, 2.9% work from home (2006-2010 5-year est.); Travel time to work: 36.0% less than 15 minutes, 30.1% 15 to 30 minutes, 24.8% 30 to 45 minutes, 7.5% 45 to 60 minutes, 1.6% 60 minutes or more (2006-2010 5-year est.)

**OAKFIELD** (village). Covers a land area of 0.660 square miles and a water area of 0 square miles. Located at 43.06° N. Lat; 78.27° W. Long. Elevation is 755 feet.

**Population:** 1,880 (1990); 1,805 (2000); 1,813 (2010); Density: 2,744.9 persons per square mile (2010); Race: 95.3% White, 1.8% Black, 0.3% Asian, 0.5% American Indian/Alaska Native, 0.0% Native Hawaiian/Other Pacific Islander, 2.1% Other, 3.0% Hispanic of any race (2010); Average household size: 2.74 (2010); Median age: 34.1 (2010); Males per 100 females: 90.8 (2010); Marriage status: 37.7% never married, 50.0% now married, 4.5% widowed, 7.8% divorced (2006-2010 5-year est.); Foreign born: 1.0% (2006-2010 5-year est.); Ancestry (includes multiple ancestries): 27.2% German, 21.8% Italian, 13.9% English, 13.0% Irish, 12.8% Polish (2006-2010 5-year est.).

**Economy:** Single-family building permits issued: 0 (2011); Multi-family building permits issued: 0 (2011); Employment by occupation: 8.2% management, 3.4% professional, 13.4% services, 13.0% sales, 2.7% farming, 10.4% construction, 8.2% production (2006-2010 5-year est.).

**Income:** Per capita income: $19,146 (2006-2010 5-year est.); Median household income: $43,688 (2006-2010 5-year est.); Average household income: $53,303 (2006-2010 5-year est.); Percent of households with income of $100,000 or more: 8.7% (2006-2010 5-year est.); Poverty rate: 20.8% (2006-2010 5-year est.).

**Education:** Percent of population age 25 and over with: High school diploma (including GED) or higher: 80.6% (2006-2010 5-year est.); Bachelor's degree or higher: 12.6% (2006-2010 5-year est.); Master's degree or higher: 5.2% (2006-2010 5-year est.).

**School District(s)**

Oakfield-Alabama Central School District (PK-12)

   2009-10 Enrollment: 962 . . . . . . . . . . . . . . . (585) 948-5211

**Housing:** Homeownership rate: 65.0% (2010); Median home value: $83,800 (2006-2010 5-year est.); Median contract rent: $524 per month (2006-2010 5-year est.); Median year structure built: before 1940 (2006-2010 5-year est.).

**Transportation:** Commute to work: 98.2% car, 0.2% public transportation, 0.6% walk, 1.0% work from home (2006-2010 5-year est.); Travel time to work: 37.7% less than 15 minutes, 38.0% 15 to 30 minutes, 13.5% 30 to 45 minutes, 8.6% 45 to 60 minutes, 2.2% 60 minutes or more (2006-2010 5-year est.)

**Additional Information Contacts**

Village of Oakfield . . . . . . . . . . . . . . . . . . . . (585) 948-5862

   http://www.oakfield.govoffice.com

**OAKFIELD** (town). Covers a land area of 23.309 square miles and a water area of 0.623 square miles. Located at 43.08° N. Lat; 78.27° W. Long. Elevation is 755 feet.

**History:** Settled 1850, incorporated 1858.

**Population:** 3,312 (1990); 3,203 (2000); 3,250 (2010); Density: 139.4 persons per square mile (2010); Race: 95.1% White, 1.3% Black, 0.2% Asian, 0.6% American Indian/Alaska Native, 0.0% Native Hawaiian/Other Pacific Islander, 2.8% Other, 3.2% Hispanic of any race (2010); Average household size: 2.70 (2010); Median age: 38.4 (2010); Males per 100 females: 94.6 (2010); Marriage status: 31.7% never married, 56.4% now married, 5.0% widowed, 6.8% divorced (2006-2010 5-year est.); Foreign born: 0.9% (2006-2010 5-year est.); Ancestry (includes multiple ancestries): 30.8% German, 19.5% Italian, 14.4% Irish, 14.4% English, 11.3% Polish (2006-2010 5-year est.).

**Economy:** Single-family building permits issued: 1 (2011); Multi-family building permits issued: 0 (2011); Employment by occupation: 6.7%

management, 4.0% professional, 11.4% services, 14.2% sales, 3.3% farming, 13.6% construction, 10.1% production (2006-2010 5-year est.).

**Income:** Per capita income: $20,666 (2006-2010 5-year est.); Median household income: $44,870 (2006-2010 5-year est.); Average household income: $56,011 (2006-2010 5-year est.); Percent of households with income of $100,000 or more: 12.1% (2006-2010 5-year est.); Poverty rate: 16.2% (2006-2010 5-year est.).

**Education:** Percent of population age 25 and over with: High school diploma (including GED) or higher: 82.5% (2006-2010 5-year est.); Bachelor's degree or higher: 15.5% (2006-2010 5-year est.); Master's degree or higher: 5.9% (2006-2010 5-year est.).

**School District(s)**

Oakfield-Alabama Central School District (PK-12)

   2009-10 Enrollment: 962 . . . . . . . . . . . . . . . (585) 948-5211

**Housing:** Homeownership rate: 73.0% (2010); Median home value: $87,800 (2006-2010 5-year est.); Median contract rent: $532 per month (2006-2010 5-year est.); Median year structure built: before 1940 (2006-2010 5-year est.).

**Transportation:** Commute to work: 98.4% car, 0.6% public transportation, 0.4% walk, 0.6% work from home (2006-2010 5-year est.); Travel time to work: 34.6% less than 15 minutes, 41.3% 15 to 30 minutes, 10.8% 30 to 45 minutes, 7.8% 45 to 60 minutes, 5.5% 60 minutes or more (2006-2010 5-year est.)

**PAVILION** (town). Covers a land area of 35.611 square miles and a water area of 0.107 square miles. Located at 42.90° N. Lat; 78.01° W. Long. Elevation is 955 feet.

**Population:** 2,327 (1990); 2,467 (2000); 2,495 (2010); Density: 70.1 persons per square mile (2010); Race: 97.4% White, 0.8% Black, 0.3% Asian, 0.2% American Indian/Alaska Native, 0.0% Native Hawaiian/Other Pacific Islander, 1.3% Other, 1.0% Hispanic of any race (2010); Average household size: 2.64 (2010); Median age: 41.9 (2010); Males per 100 females: 108.1 (2010); Marriage status: 18.0% never married, 67.7% now married, 7.1% widowed, 7.2% divorced (2006-2010 5-year est.); Foreign born: 2.3% (2006-2010 5-year est.); Ancestry (includes multiple ancestries): 35.0% German, 26.6% Irish, 22.4% English, 16.1% Italian, 5.8% Polish (2006-2010 5-year est.).

**Economy:** Single-family building permits issued: 1 (2011); Multi-family building permits issued: 0 (2011); Employment by occupation: 19.0% management, 4.3% professional, 8.8% services, 11.1% sales, 1.1% farming, 15.3% construction, 7.6% production (2006-2010 5-year est.).

**Income:** Per capita income: $26,862 (2006-2010 5-year est.); Median household income: $62,321 (2006-2010 5-year est.); Average household income: $67,949 (2006-2010 5-year est.); Percent of households with income of $100,000 or more: 22.4% (2006-2010 5-year est.); Poverty rate: 3.9% (2006-2010 5-year est.).

**Education:** Percent of population age 25 and over with: High school diploma (including GED) or higher: 92.0% (2006-2010 5-year est.); Bachelor's degree or higher: 25.1% (2006-2010 5-year est.); Master's degree or higher: 10.7% (2006-2010 5-year est.).

**School District(s)**

Pavilion Central School District (PK-12)

   2009-10 Enrollment: 853 . . . . . . . . . . . . . . . (585) 584-3115

**Housing:** Homeownership rate: 83.5% (2010); Median home value: $115,100 (2006-2010 5-year est.); Median contract rent: $512 per month (2006-2010 5-year est.); Median year structure built: 1969 (2006-2010 5-year est.).

**Transportation:** Commute to work: 93.3% car, 0.0% public transportation, 2.0% walk, 4.0% work from home (2006-2010 5-year est.); Travel time to work: 30.0% less than 15 minutes, 31.3% 15 to 30 minutes, 19.3% 30 to 45 minutes, 10.8% 45 to 60 minutes, 8.6% 60 minutes or more (2006-2010 5-year est.)

**PAVILION** (CDP). Covers a land area of 3.312 square miles and a water area of 0 square miles. Located at 42.87° N. Lat; 78.02° W. Long. Elevation is 955 feet.

**Population:** n/a (1990); n/a (2000); 646 (2010); Density: 195.0 persons per square mile (2010); Race: 98.0% White, 1.2% Black, 0.0% Asian, 0.5% American Indian/Alaska Native, 0.0% Native Hawaiian/Other Pacific Islander, 0.3% Other, 0.5% Hispanic of any race (2010); Average household size: 2.54 (2010); Median age: 41.0 (2010); Males per 100 females: 104.4 (2010); Marriage status: 10.1% never married, 67.2% now married, 14.5% widowed, 8.1% divorced (2006-2010 5-year est.); Foreign born: 0.0% (2006-2010 5-year est.); Ancestry (includes multiple

ancestries): 36.6% German, 31.7% Irish, 20.7% English, 6.2% American, 4.6% Italian (2006-2010 5-year est.).
**Economy:** Employment by occupation: 21.9% management, 0.0% professional, 3.5% services, 10.4% sales, 3.5% farming, 23.4% construction, 10.9% production (2006-2010 5-year est.).
**Income:** Per capita income: $25,580 (2006-2010 5-year est.); Median household income: $44,866 (2006-2010 5-year est.); Average household income: $61,568 (2006-2010 5-year est.); Percent of households with income of $100,000 or more: 24.1% (2006-2010 5-year est.); Poverty rate: 5.0% (2006-2010 5-year est.).
**Education:** Percent of population age 25 and over with: High school diploma (including GED) or higher: 96.6% (2006-2010 5-year est.); Bachelor's degree or higher: 19.6% (2006-2010 5-year est.); Master's degree or higher: 13.4% (2006-2010 5-year est.).

**School District(s)**
Pavilion Central School District (PK-12)
   2009-10 Enrollment: 853 . . . . . . . . . . . . . . . . . (585) 584-3115
**Housing:** Homeownership rate: 74.8% (2010); Median home value: $104,800 (2006-2010 5-year est.); Median contract rent: $410 per month (2006-2010 5-year est.); Median year structure built: before 1940 (2006-2010 5-year est.).
**Transportation:** Commute to work: 87.1% car, 0.0% public transportation, 8.8% walk, 4.1% work from home (2006-2010 5-year est.); Travel time to work: 31.7% less than 15 minutes, 10.8% 15 to 30 minutes, 29.0% 30 to 45 minutes, 11.8% 45 to 60 minutes, 16.7% 60 minutes or more (2006-2010 5-year est.)

**PEMBROKE** (town). Covers a land area of 41.626 square miles and a water area of 0.090 square miles. Located at 43.00° N. Lat; 78.38° W. Long. Elevation is 843 feet.
**Population:** 4,232 (1990); 4,530 (2000); 4,292 (2010); Density: 103.1 persons per square mile (2010); Race: 97.6% White, 0.6% Black, 0.1% Asian, 0.5% American Indian/Alaska Native, 0.0% Native Hawaiian/Other Pacific Islander, 1.2% Other, 1.0% Hispanic of any race (2010); Average household size: 2.50 (2010); Median age: 43.9 (2010); Males per 100 females: 95.4 (2010); Marriage status: 26.7% never married, 56.5% now married, 7.3% widowed, 9.5% divorced (2006-2010 5-year est.); Foreign born: 1.6% (2006-2010 5-year est.); Ancestry (includes multiple ancestries): 38.3% German, 18.9% Irish, 18.4% Italian, 17.2% Polish, 15.9% English (2006-2010 5-year est.).
**Economy:** Single-family building permits issued: 1 (2011); Multi-family building permits issued: 0 (2011); Employment by occupation: 14.9% management, 3.0% professional, 7.2% services, 12.1% sales, 3.3% farming, 6.8% construction, 5.9% production (2006-2010 5-year est.).
**Income:** Per capita income: $25,795 (2006-2010 5-year est.); Median household income: $48,958 (2006-2010 5-year est.); Average household income: $58,093 (2006-2010 5-year est.); Percent of households with income of $100,000 or more: 11.1% (2006-2010 5-year est.); Poverty rate: 13.5% (2006-2010 5-year est.).
**Education:** Percent of population age 25 and over with: High school diploma (including GED) or higher: 92.9% (2006-2010 5-year est.); Bachelor's degree or higher: 19.0% (2006-2010 5-year est.); Master's degree or higher: 6.7% (2006-2010 5-year est.).
**Housing:** Homeownership rate: 80.7% (2010); Median home value: $107,600 (2006-2010 5-year est.); Median contract rent: $509 per month (2006-2010 5-year est.); Median year structure built: 1958 (2006-2010 5-year est.).
**Transportation:** Commute to work: 95.1% car, 0.0% public transportation, 0.7% walk, 0.1% work from home (2006-2010 5-year est.); Travel time to work: 23.5% less than 15 minutes, 40.2% 15 to 30 minutes, 20.8% 30 to 45 minutes, 10.2% 45 to 60 minutes, 5.3% 60 minutes or more (2006-2010 5-year est.)

**STAFFORD** (town). Covers a land area of 31.097 square miles and a water area of 0.179 square miles. Located at 42.99° N. Lat; 78.08° W. Long. Elevation is 892 feet.
**Population:** 2,593 (1990); 2,409 (2000); 2,459 (2010); Density: 79.1 persons per square mile (2010); Race: 97.8% White, 0.7% Black, 0.4% Asian, 0.2% American Indian/Alaska Native, 0.0% Native Hawaiian/Other Pacific Islander, 0.9% Other, 1.1% Hispanic of any race (2010); Average household size: 2.42 (2010); Median age: 45.4 (2010); Males per 100 females: 101.7 (2010); Marriage status: 25.3% never married, 61.8% now married, 6.1% widowed, 6.7% divorced (2006-2010 5-year est.); Foreign born: 2.4% (2006-2010 5-year est.); Ancestry (includes multiple

ancestries): 32.9% German, 23.1% English, 15.2% Irish, 14.2% Italian, 11.3% Polish (2006-2010 5-year est.).
**Economy:** Single-family building permits issued: 0 (2011); Multi-family building permits issued: 0 (2011); Employment by occupation: 13.5% management, 2.2% professional, 6.9% services, 14.1% sales, 4.2% farming, 9.2% construction, 7.1% production (2006-2010 5-year est.).
**Income:** Per capita income: $30,425 (2006-2010 5-year est.); Median household income: $63,229 (2006-2010 5-year est.); Average household income: $73,120 (2006-2010 5-year est.); Percent of households with income of $100,000 or more: 21.2% (2006-2010 5-year est.); Poverty rate: 4.5% (2006-2010 5-year est.).
**Education:** Percent of population age 25 and over with: High school diploma (including GED) or higher: 94.4% (2006-2010 5-year est.); Bachelor's degree or higher: 25.7% (2006-2010 5-year est.); Master's degree or higher: 9.8% (2006-2010 5-year est.).
**Housing:** Homeownership rate: 84.4% (2010); Median home value: $114,300 (2006-2010 5-year est.); Median contract rent: $580 per month (2006-2010 5-year est.); Median year structure built: 1959 (2006-2010 5-year est.).
**Transportation:** Commute to work: 89.9% car, 0.5% public transportation, 3.5% walk, 5.1% work from home (2006-2010 5-year est.); Travel time to work: 45.2% less than 15 minutes, 24.8% 15 to 30 minutes, 18.7% 30 to 45 minutes, 6.0% 45 to 60 minutes, 5.3% 60 minutes or more (2006-2010 5-year est.)

**TONAWANDA RESERVATION** (Reservation). Covers a land area of 9.161 square miles and a water area of 0.069 square miles. Located at 43.06° N. Lat; 78.43° W. Long.
**Population:** 491 (1990); 533 (2000); 483 (2010); Density: 52.7 persons per square mile (2010); Race: 3.3% White, 0.4% Black, 0.2% Asian, 94.4% American Indian/Alaska Native, 0.0% Native Hawaiian/Other Pacific Islander, 1.7% Other, 3.3% Hispanic of any race (2010); Average household size: 2.63 (2010); Median age: 37.6 (2010); Males per 100 females: 92.4 (2010); Marriage status: 45.0% never married, 39.8% now married, 6.9% widowed, 8.3% divorced (2006-2010 5-year est.); Foreign born: 5.8% (2006-2010 5-year est.); Ancestry (includes multiple ancestries): 4.3% German, 1.1% Irish, 0.6% American, 0.6% English (2006-2010 5-year est.).
**Economy:** Employment by occupation: 6.9% management, 0.0% professional, 23.8% services, 8.7% sales, 10.8% farming, 5.2% construction, 19.9% production (2006-2010 5-year est.).
**Income:** Per capita income: $15,258 (2006-2010 5-year est.); Median household income: $28,472 (2006-2010 5-year est.); Average household income: $34,923 (2006-2010 5-year est.); Percent of households with income of $100,000 or more: 3.6% (2006-2010 5-year est.); Poverty rate: 28.9% (2006-2010 5-year est.).
**Education:** Percent of population age 25 and over with: High school diploma (including GED) or higher: 76.0% (2006-2010 5-year est.); Bachelor's degree or higher: 12.0% (2006-2010 5-year est.); Master's degree or higher: 0.5% (2006-2010 5-year est.).
**Housing:** Homeownership rate: 84.8% (2010); Median home value: $44,500 (2006-2010 5-year est.); Median contract rent: n/a per month (2006-2010 5-year est.); Median year structure built: 1957 (2006-2010 5-year est.).
**Transportation:** Commute to work: 94.8% car, 0.0% public transportation, 5.2% walk, 0.0% work from home (2006-2010 5-year est.); Travel time to work: 45.5% less than 15 minutes, 23.4% 15 to 30 minutes, 13.0% 30 to 45 minutes, 13.9% 45 to 60 minutes, 4.3% 60 minutes or more (2006-2010 5-year est.)

# Greene County

Located in southeastern New York, mainly in the Catskills; bounded on the east by the Hudson River; includes many small lakes. Covers a land area of 647.75 square miles, a water area of 10.38 square miles, and is located in the Eastern Time Zone at 42.30° N. Lat., 74.01° W. Long. The county was founded in 1800. County seat is Catskill.

Weather Station: Cairo 4 NW                          Elevation: 490 feet

| | Jan | Feb | Mar | Apr | May | Jun | Jul | Aug | Sep | Oct | Nov | Dec |
|---|---|---|---|---|---|---|---|---|---|---|---|---|
| High | 32 | 36 | 45 | 58 | 69 | 78 | 82 | 81 | 73 | 61 | 49 | 38 |
| Low | 13 | 15 | 24 | 35 | 45 | 54 | 59 | 57 | 49 | 38 | 30 | 20 |
| Precip | 2.8 | 2.4 | 3.6 | 3.8 | 3.4 | 3.9 | 3.3 | 3.0 | 3.9 | 3.8 | 3.8 | 3.1 |
| Snow | 13.3 | 9.8 | 9.9 | 2.0 | 0.0 | 0.0 | 0.0 | 0.0 | 0.0 | 0.1 | 2.2 | 10.7 |

*High and Low temperatures in degrees Fahrenheit; Precipitation and Snow in inches*

**Population:** 44,739 (1990); 48,195 (2000); 49,221 (2010); Race: 90.3% White, 5.7% Black, 0.8% Asian, 0.3% American Indian/Alaska Native, 0.0% Native Hawaiian/Other Pacific Islander, 2.9% Other, 4.9% Hispanic of any race (2010); Density: 76.0 persons per square mile (2010); Average household size: 2.31 (2010); Median age: 44.0 (2010); Males per 100 females: 109.1 (2010).
**Religion:** Six largest groups: 20.2% Catholicism, 7.4% Methodist/Pietist, 2.3% Presbyterian-Reformed, 2.1% Non-Denominational, 2.0% Lutheran, 0.8% Episcopalianism/Anglicanism (2010)
**Economy:** Unemployment rate: 9.8% (February 2012); Total civilian labor force: 24,182 (February 2012); Leading industries: 21.7% accommodation & food services; 20.6% retail trade; 10.2% health care and social assistance (2009); Farms: 286 totaling 44,328 acres (2007); Companies that employ 500 or more persons: 3 (2009); Companies that employ 100 to 499 persons: 11 (2009); Companies that employ less than 100 persons: 1,122 (2009); Black-owned businesses: n/a (2007); Hispanic-owned businesses: 72 (2007); Asian-owned businesses: n/a (2007); Women-owned businesses: 1,448 (2007); Retail sales per capita: $11,533 (2010). Single-family building permits issued: 78 (2011); Multi-family building permits issued: 0 (2011).
**Income:** Per capita income: $23,461 (2006-2010 5-year est.); Median household income: $46,235 (2006-2010 5-year est.); Average household income: $59,436 (2006-2010 5-year est.); Percent of households with income of $100,000 or more: 13.5% (2006-2010 5-year est.); Poverty rate: 13.2% (2006-2010 5-year est.); Bankruptcy rate: 3.40% (2011).
**Education:** Percent of population age 25 and over with: High school diploma (including GED) or higher: 85.7% (2006-2010 5-year est.); Bachelor's degree or higher: 19.2% (2006-2010 5-year est.); Master's degree or higher: 8.4% (2006-2010 5-year est.).
**Housing:** Homeownership rate: 72.5% (2010); Median home value: $180,500 (2006-2010 5-year est.); Median contract rent: $570 per month (2006-2010 5-year est.); Median year structure built: 1966 (2006-2010 5-year est.)
**Health:** Birth rate: 87.8 per 10,000 population (2011); Death rate: 100.5 per 10,000 population (2011); Age-adjusted cancer mortality rate: 208.9 deaths per 100,000 population (2009); Number of physicians: 7.7 per 10,000 population (2008); Hospital beds: 0.0 per 10,000 population (2007); Hospital admissions: 0.0 per 10,000 population (2007).
**Elections:** 2008 Presidential election results: 44.1% Obama, 54.0% McCain, 0.9% Nader
**National and State Parks:** Catskill State Park
**Additional Information Contacts**
Greene County Government . . . . . . . . . . . . . . . . . . . . . . . . (518) 719-3270
  http://www.greenegovernment.com
Coxsackie Regional Chamber of Commerce . . . . . . . . . . . (518) 731-7300
  http://www.coxsackieareachamber.com
Greene County Chamber of Commerce . . . . . . . . . . . . . . (518) 943-4222
  http://www.greenecounty-chamber.com
Hunter Chamber of Commerce . . . . . . . . . . . . . . . . . . (518) 263-4900
  http://www.hunterchamber.org
Town of Catskill . . . . . . . . . . . . . . . . . . . . . . . . . . . . . (518) 943-2141
  http://www.townofcatskillny.gov/Public_Documents/index
Town of Coxsackie . . . . . . . . . . . . . . . . . . . . . . . . . . (518) 731-2727
  http://www.coxsackie.org
Town of Halcott . . . . . . . . . . . . . . . . . . . . . . . . . . . . . (845) 254-6441
  http://halcottcenter.wordpress.com
Village of Catskill . . . . . . . . . . . . . . . . . . . . . . . . . . . . (518) 943-3830
  http://www.villageofcatskill.net

## Greene County Communities

### ACRA (unincorporated postal area)
Zip Code: 12405
  Covers a land area of 7.145 square miles and a water area of 0.029 square miles. Located at 42.31° N. Lat; 74.08° W. Long. Elevation is 653 feet. Population: 780 (2010); Density: 109.2 persons per square mile (2010); Race: 95.1% White, 1.8% Black, 0.5% Asian, 0.3% American Indian/Alaska Native, 0.3% Native Hawaiian/Other Pacific Islander, 2.0% Other, 4.4% Hispanic of any race (2010); Average household size: 2.45 (2010); Median age: 43.7 (2010); Males per 100 females: 94.0 (2010); Homeownership rate: 74.5% (2010)

### ASHLAND (town). Covers a land area of 25.958 square miles and a water area of 0 square miles. Located at 42.32° N. Lat; 74.33° W. Long. Elevation is 1,421 feet.
**Population:** 803 (1990); 752 (2000); 784 (2010); Density: 30.2 persons per square mile (2010); Race: 97.7% White, 0.4% Black, 0.3% Asian, 0.5% American Indian/Alaska Native, 0.0% Native Hawaiian/Other Pacific Islander, 1.1% Other, 3.2% Hispanic of any race (2010); Average household size: 2.32 (2010); Median age: 46.6 (2010); Males per 100 females: 99.0 (2010); Marriage status: 14.6% never married, 65.8% now married, 17.0% widowed, 2.6% divorced (2006-2010 5-year est.); Foreign born: 10.9% (2006-2010 5-year est.); Ancestry (includes multiple ancestries): 29.7% American, 20.4% German, 17.8% Irish, 13.6% Italian, 8.8% English (2006-2010 5-year est.).
**Economy:** Employment by occupation: 21.6% management, 0.0% professional, 11.2% services, 15.2% sales, 2.4% farming, 12.0% construction, 4.0% production (2006-2010 5-year est.).
**Income:** Per capita income: $22,076 (2006-2010 5-year est.); Median household income: $36,250 (2006-2010 5-year est.); Average household income: $43,912 (2006-2010 5-year est.); Percent of households with income of $100,000 or more: 5.2% (2006-2010 5-year est.); Poverty rate: 15.8% (2006-2010 5-year est.).
**Education:** Percent of population age 25 and over with: High school diploma (including GED) or higher: 89.2% (2006-2010 5-year est.); Bachelor's degree or higher: 10.8% (2006-2010 5-year est.); Master's degree or higher: 3.0% (2006-2010 5-year est.).
**Housing:** Homeownership rate: 81.6% (2010); Median home value: $183,900 (2006-2010 5-year est.); Median contract rent: $565 per month (2006-2010 5-year est.); Median year structure built: 1975 (2006-2010 5-year est.).
**Transportation:** Commute to work: 92.0% car, 0.0% public transportation, 0.0% walk, 3.2% work from home (2006-2010 5-year est.); Travel time to work: 57.9% less than 15 minutes, 27.3% 15 to 30 minutes, 5.8% 30 to 45 minutes, 4.1% 45 to 60 minutes, 5.0% 60 minutes or more (2006-2010 5-year est.)

### ATHENS (village). Covers a land area of 3.419 square miles and a water area of 1.184 square miles. Located at 42.27° N. Lat; 73.81° W. Long. Elevation is 26 feet.
**Population:** 1,708 (1990); 1,695 (2000); 1,668 (2010); Density: 487.8 persons per square mile (2010); Race: 95.9% White, 1.9% Black, 0.4% Asian, 0.0% American Indian/Alaska Native, 0.0% Native Hawaiian/Other Pacific Islander, 1.8% Other, 4.0% Hispanic of any race (2010); Average household size: 2.26 (2010); Median age: 45.3 (2010); Males per 100 females: 91.9 (2010); Marriage status: 28.5% never married, 48.5% now married, 12.3% widowed, 10.7% divorced (2006-2010 5-year est.); Foreign born: 3.7% (2006-2010 5-year est.); Ancestry (includes multiple ancestries): 23.3% Italian, 19.4% German, 17.8% Irish, 9.8% English, 8.7% American (2006-2010 5-year est.).
**Economy:** Single-family building permits issued: 2 (2011); Multi-family building permits issued: 0 (2011); Employment by occupation: 8.8% management, 4.0% professional, 6.0% services, 15.9% sales, 2.8% farming, 13.8% construction, 5.9% production (2006-2010 5-year est.).
**Income:** Per capita income: $28,100 (2006-2010 5-year est.); Median household income: $59,063 (2006-2010 5-year est.); Average household income: $64,492 (2006-2010 5-year est.); Percent of households with income of $100,000 or more: 15.8% (2006-2010 5-year est.); Poverty rate: 5.1% (2006-2010 5-year est.).
**Education:** Percent of population age 25 and over with: High school diploma (including GED) or higher: 83.2% (2006-2010 5-year est.); Bachelor's degree or higher: 19.0% (2006-2010 5-year est.); Master's degree or higher: 9.2% (2006-2010 5-year est.).
#### School District(s)
Coxsackie-Athens Central School District (KG-12)
  2009-10 Enrollment: 1,542 . . . . . . . . . . . . . . . . . . . . . (518) 731-1710
**Housing:** Homeownership rate: 67.8% (2010); Median home value: $175,700 (2006-2010 5-year est.); Median contract rent: $607 per month (2006-2010 5-year est.); Median year structure built: 1942 (2006-2010 5-year est.).
**Transportation:** Commute to work: 89.4% car, 1.2% public transportation, 2.7% walk, 5.4% work from home (2006-2010 5-year est.); Travel time to work: 36.7% less than 15 minutes, 34.8% 15 to 30 minutes, 11.7% 30 to 45 minutes, 8.7% 45 to 60 minutes, 8.1% 60 minutes or more (2006-2010 5-year est.)

**ATHENS** (town). Covers a land area of 26.246 square miles and a water area of 2.622 square miles. Located at 42.27° N. Lat; 73.85° W. Long. Elevation is 26 feet.

**History:** Settled 1686, incorporated 1805.

**Population:** 3,561 (1990); 3,991 (2000); 4,089 (2010); Density: 155.8 persons per square mile (2010); Race: 94.8% White, 1.8% Black, 1.1% Asian, 0.1% American Indian/Alaska Native, 0.1% Native Hawaiian/Other Pacific Islander, 2.1% Other, 3.8% Hispanic of any race (2010); Average household size: 2.33 (2010); Median age: 46.4 (2010); Males per 100 females: 97.6 (2010); Marriage status: 24.1% never married, 57.4% now married, 7.8% widowed, 10.6% divorced (2006-2010 5-year est.); Foreign born: 8.1% (2006-2010 5-year est.); Ancestry (includes multiple ancestries): 22.0% Italian, 21.4% Irish, 16.5% German, 7.9% American, 7.8% English (2006-2010 5-year est.).

**Economy:** Single-family building permits issued: 3 (2011); Multi-family building permits issued: 0 (2011); Employment by occupation: 8.7% management, 3.8% professional, 8.6% services, 17.3% sales, 3.0% farming, 9.6% construction, 5.9% production (2006-2010 5-year est.).

**Income:** Per capita income: $28,016 (2006-2010 5-year est.); Median household income: $56,394 (2006-2010 5-year est.); Average household income: $64,257 (2006-2010 5-year est.); Percent of households with income of $100,000 or more: 17.1% (2006-2010 5-year est.); Poverty rate: 8.8% (2006-2010 5-year est.).

**Education:** Percent of population age 25 and over with: High school diploma (including GED) or higher: 88.2% (2006-2010 5-year est.); Bachelor's degree or higher: 22.5% (2006-2010 5-year est.); Master's degree or higher: 9.9% (2006-2010 5-year est.).

### School District(s)

Coxsackie-Athens Central School District (KG-12)

   2009-10 Enrollment: 1,542 . . . . . . . . . . . . . . . . . . . (518) 731-1710

**Housing:** Homeownership rate: 75.7% (2010); Median home value: $191,600 (2006-2010 5-year est.); Median contract rent: $620 per month (2006-2010 5-year est.); Median year structure built: 1973 (2006-2010 5-year est.).

**Transportation:** Commute to work: 91.8% car, 0.5% public transportation, 1.8% walk, 2.9% work from home (2006-2010 5-year est.); Travel time to work: 29.8% less than 15 minutes, 37.6% 15 to 30 minutes, 14.6% 30 to 45 minutes, 12.1% 45 to 60 minutes, 5.9% 60 minutes or more (2006-2010 5-year est.)

**CAIRO** (town). Covers a land area of 59.827 square miles and a water area of 0.253 square miles. Located at 42.29° N. Lat; 74.01° W. Long. Elevation is 374 feet.

**Population:** 5,418 (1990); 6,355 (2000); 6,670 (2010); Density: 111.5 persons per square mile (2010); Race: 94.9% White, 1.3% Black, 0.7% Asian, 0.4% American Indian/Alaska Native, 0.1% Native Hawaiian/Other Pacific Islander, 2.6% Other, 4.4% Hispanic of any race (2010); Average household size: 2.35 (2010); Median age: 44.6 (2010); Males per 100 females: 95.0 (2010); Marriage status: 32.0% never married, 53.2% now married, 6.0% widowed, 8.7% divorced (2006-2010 5-year est.); Foreign born: 3.2% (2006-2010 5-year est.); Ancestry (includes multiple ancestries): 20.7% German, 18.2% Italian, 16.0% Irish, 15.1% American, 7.0% English (2006-2010 5-year est.).

**Economy:** Single-family building permits issued: 10 (2011); Multi-family building permits issued: 0 (2011); Employment by occupation: 7.6% management, 2.6% professional, 9.7% services, 24.7% sales, 5.7% farming, 10.7% construction, 2.9% production (2006-2010 5-year est.).

**Income:** Per capita income: $25,385 (2006-2010 5-year est.); Median household income: $46,310 (2006-2010 5-year est.); Average household income: $58,747 (2006-2010 5-year est.); Percent of households with income of $100,000 or more: 7.8% (2006-2010 5-year est.); Poverty rate: 19.3% (2006-2010 5-year est.).

**Education:** Percent of population age 25 and over with: High school diploma (including GED) or higher: 90.0% (2006-2010 5-year est.); Bachelor's degree or higher: 20.2% (2006-2010 5-year est.); Master's degree or higher: 11.9% (2006-2010 5-year est.).

### School District(s)

Cairo-Durham Central School District (KG-12)

   2009-10 Enrollment: 1,495 . . . . . . . . . . . . . . . . . . . (518) 622-8534

**Housing:** Homeownership rate: 71.9% (2010); Median home value: $182,900 (2006-2010 5-year est.); Median contract rent: $541 per month (2006-2010 5-year est.); Median year structure built: 1956 (2006-2010 5-year est.).

**Safety:** Violent crime rate: 7.8 per 10,000 population; Property crime rate: 45.2 per 10,000 population (2010).

**Transportation:** Commute to work: 92.9% car, 0.6% public transportation, 0.7% walk, 2.3% work from home (2006-2010 5-year est.); Travel time to work: 31.7% less than 15 minutes, 31.2% 15 to 30 minutes, 9.8% 30 to 45 minutes, 16.5% 45 to 60 minutes, 10.7% 60 minutes or more (2006-2010 5-year est.)

**CAIRO** (CDP). Covers a land area of 4.227 square miles and a water area of 0.006 square miles. Located at 42.30° N. Lat; 74.01° W. Long. Elevation is 374 feet.

**Population:** 1,273 (1990); 1,390 (2000); 1,402 (2010); Density: 331.7 persons per square mile (2010); Race: 93.1% White, 1.8% Black, 0.8% Asian, 0.4% American Indian/Alaska Native, 0.3% Native Hawaiian/Other Pacific Islander, 3.6% Other, 6.3% Hispanic of any race (2010); Average household size: 2.24 (2010); Median age: 43.5 (2010); Males per 100 females: 87.9 (2010); Marriage status: 30.7% never married, 45.7% now married, 13.1% widowed, 10.4% divorced (2006-2010 5-year est.); Foreign born: 1.5% (2006-2010 5-year est.); Ancestry (includes multiple ancestries): 26.2% Italian, 21.4% Irish, 19.1% German, 13.7% Dutch, 11.6% American (2006-2010 5-year est.).

**Economy:** Employment by occupation: 4.4% management, 4.6% professional, 9.0% services, 30.5% sales, 5.3% farming, 12.2% construction, 4.0% production (2006-2010 5-year est.).

**Income:** Per capita income: $19,338 (2006-2010 5-year est.); Median household income: $34,375 (2006-2010 5-year est.); Average household income: $43,465 (2006-2010 5-year est.); Percent of households with income of $100,000 or more: 5.8% (2006-2010 5-year est.); Poverty rate: 25.2% (2006-2010 5-year est.).

**Education:** Percent of population age 25 and over with: High school diploma (including GED) or higher: 83.8% (2006-2010 5-year est.); Bachelor's degree or higher: 9.9% (2006-2010 5-year est.); Master's degree or higher: 4.1% (2006-2010 5-year est.).

### School District(s)

Cairo-Durham Central School District (KG-12)

   2009-10 Enrollment: 1,495 . . . . . . . . . . . . . . . . . . . (518) 622-8534

**Housing:** Homeownership rate: 58.6% (2010); Median home value: $184,100 (2006-2010 5-year est.); Median contract rent: $517 per month (2006-2010 5-year est.); Median year structure built: 1946 (2006-2010 5-year est.).

**Transportation:** Commute to work: 92.6% car, 0.0% public transportation, 0.0% walk, 0.0% work from home (2006-2010 5-year est.); Travel time to work: 38.9% less than 15 minutes, 34.9% 15 to 30 minutes, 1.2% 30 to 45 minutes, 15.7% 45 to 60 minutes, 9.3% 60 minutes or more (2006-2010 5-year est.)

**CATSKILL** (village). County seat. Covers a land area of 2.279 square miles and a water area of 0.579 square miles. Located at 42.21° N. Lat; 73.85° W. Long. Elevation is 43 feet.

**Population:** 4,690 (1990); 4,392 (2000); 4,081 (2010); Density: 1,790.3 persons per square mile (2010); Race: 78.6% White, 12.4% Black, 1.3% Asian, 0.6% American Indian/Alaska Native, 0.0% Native Hawaiian/Other Pacific Islander, 7.1% Other, 9.0% Hispanic of any race (2010); Average household size: 2.30 (2010); Median age: 39.7 (2010); Males per 100 females: 98.9 (2010); Marriage status: 36.8% never married, 36.1% now married, 11.8% widowed, 15.3% divorced (2006-2010 5-year est.); Foreign born: 4.1% (2006-2010 5-year est.); Ancestry (includes multiple ancestries): 22.9% Italian, 16.5% German, 10.2% Irish, 8.2% English, 6.6% Polish (2006-2010 5-year est.).

**Economy:** Single-family building permits issued: 0 (2011); Multi-family building permits issued: 0 (2011); Employment by occupation: 8.7% management, 2.7% professional, 11.7% services, 25.8% sales, 3.6% farming, 3.4% construction, 3.8% production (2006-2010 5-year est.).

**Income:** Per capita income: $23,678 (2006-2010 5-year est.); Median household income: $43,864 (2006-2010 5-year est.); Average household income: $63,949 (2006-2010 5-year est.); Percent of households with income of $100,000 or more: 14.1% (2006-2010 5-year est.); Poverty rate: 22.9% (2006-2010 5-year est.).

**Education:** Percent of population age 25 and over with: High school diploma (including GED) or higher: 80.0% (2006-2010 5-year est.); Bachelor's degree or higher: 26.0% (2006-2010 5-year est.); Master's degree or higher: 8.5% (2006-2010 5-year est.).

### School District(s)

Catskill Central School District (PK-12)

   2009-10 Enrollment: 1,796 . . . . . . . . . . . . . . . . . . . (518) 943-4696

**Housing:** Homeownership rate: 50.5% (2010); Median home value: $166,600 (2006-2010 5-year est.); Median contract rent: $674 per month

(2006-2010 5-year est.); Median year structure built: before 1940 (2006-2010 5-year est.).
**Safety:** Violent crime rate: 29.1 per 10,000 population; Property crime rate: 314.9 per 10,000 population (2010).
**Newspapers:** Catskill Daily Mail (Local news; Circulation 6,000); Entertainment - Catskill Daily Mail (Local news); Greene County News (Local news; Circulation 2,700); Mountain Pennysaver (Community news; Circulation 22,000); Seniors - Catskill Daily Mail (Local news); TV Spotlight - Catskill Daily Mail (Local news; Circulation 7,091)
**Transportation:** Commute to work: 77.2% car, 2.3% public transportation, 13.1% walk, 4.1% work from home (2006-2010 5-year est.); Travel time to work: 56.7% less than 15 minutes, 14.9% 15 to 30 minutes, 16.0% 30 to 45 minutes, 6.7% 45 to 60 minutes, 5.7% 60 minutes or more (2006-2010 5-year est.)
**Additional Information Contacts**
Greene County Chamber of Commerce . . . . . . . . . . . . . . (518) 943-4222
  http://www.greenecounty-chamber.com
Village of Catskill . . . . . . . . . . . . . . . . . . . . . . . . . . . (518) 943-3830
  http://www.villageofcatskill.net

**CATSKILL** (town). Covers a land area of 60.438 square miles and a water area of 3.726 square miles. Located at 42.20° N. Lat; 73.93° W. Long. Elevation is 43 feet.
**History:** Originally known as Catskill Landing, the settlement of Catskill was subsidiary to the old Dutch hamlet of Kaatskill, in the hills to the west. Mountains, creeks, and village were named by the Dutch for the wildcats that occasionally came down from the hills, where they roamed in large numbers. In the heyday of turnpike and river transportation, the place bustled with prosperity. Thomas Cole lived and painted in the village. Settled 17th, incorporated in 1806.
**Population:** 11,965 (1990); 11,849 (2000); 11,775 (2010); Density: 194.8 persons per square mile (2010); Race: 87.9% White, 6.1% Black, 1.0% Asian, 0.4% American Indian/Alaska Native, 0.0% Native Hawaiian/Other Pacific Islander, 4.6% Other, 5.9% Hispanic of any race (2010); Average household size: 2.26 (2010); Median age: 44.1 (2010); Males per 100 females: 95.5 (2010); Marriage status: 32.4% never married, 45.8% now married, 11.3% widowed, 10.5% divorced (2006-2010 5-year est.); Foreign born: 4.1% (2006-2010 5-year est.); Ancestry (includes multiple ancestries): 25.4% Italian, 20.0% Irish, 18.2% German, 7.6% English, 7.0% Dutch (2006-2010 5-year est.).
**Economy:** Single-family building permits issued: 20 (2011); Multi-family building permits issued: 0 (2011); Employment by occupation: 7.7% management, 3.0% professional, 15.7% services, 18.7% sales, 6.7% farming, 6.6% construction, 3.9% production (2006-2010 5-year est.).
**Income:** Per capita income: $25,741 (2006-2010 5-year est.); Median household income: $43,960 (2006-2010 5-year est.); Average household income: $61,225 (2006-2010 5-year est.); Percent of households with income of $100,000 or more: 14.1% (2006-2010 5-year est.); Poverty rate: 13.9% (2006-2010 5-year est.).
**Education:** Percent of population age 25 and over with: High school diploma (including GED) or higher: 83.4% (2006-2010 5-year est.); Bachelor's degree or higher: 17.8% (2006-2010 5-year est.); Master's degree or higher: 6.3% (2006-2010 5-year est.).
**School District(s)**
Catskill Central School District (PK-12)
  2009-10 Enrollment: 1,796 . . . . . . . . . . . . . . . . . . . . (518) 943-4696
**Housing:** Homeownership rate: 63.3% (2010); Median home value: $166,600 (2006-2010 5-year est.); Median contract rent: $654 per month (2006-2010 5-year est.); Median year structure built: 1954 (2006-2010 5-year est.).
**Newspapers:** Catskill Daily Mail (Local news; Circulation 6,000); Entertainment - Catskill Daily Mail (Local news); Greene County News (Local news; Circulation 2,700); Mountain Pennysaver (Community news; Circulation 22,000); Seniors - Catskill Daily Mail (Local news); TV Spotlight - Catskill Daily Mail (Local news; Circulation 7,091)
**Transportation:** Commute to work: 86.2% car, 1.1% public transportation, 5.3% walk, 4.9% work from home (2006-2010 5-year est.); Travel time to work: 39.2% less than 15 minutes, 28.4% 15 to 30 minutes, 18.6% 30 to 45 minutes, 4.4% 45 to 60 minutes, 9.4% 60 minutes or more (2006-2010 5-year est.)
**Additional Information Contacts**
Town of Catskill . . . . . . . . . . . . . . . . . . . . . . . . . . . . (518) 943-2141
  http://www.townofcatskillny.gov/Public_Documents/index

**CLIMAX** (unincorporated postal area)
Zip Code: 12042
  Covers a land area of 4.344 square miles and a water area of 0.012 square miles. Located at 42.41° N. Lat; 73.93° W. Long. Elevation is 246 feet. Population: 271 (2010); Density: 62.4 persons per square mile (2010); Race: 95.9% White, 0.7% Black, 0.0% Asian, 0.0% American Indian/Alaska Native, 0.0% Native Hawaiian/Other Pacific Islander, 3.4% Other, 1.8% Hispanic of any race (2010); Average household size: 2.26 (2010); Median age: 46.5 (2010); Males per 100 females: 108.5 (2010); Homeownership rate: 83.4% (2010)

**CORNWALLVILLE** (unincorporated postal area)
Zip Code: 12418
  Covers a land area of 13.815 square miles and a water area of 0 square miles. Located at 42.35° N. Lat; 74.16° W. Long. Elevation is 958 feet. Population: 537 (2010); Density: 38.9 persons per square mile (2010); Race: 98.0% White, 0.0% Black, 0.0% Asian, 0.0% American Indian/Alaska Native, 0.4% Native Hawaiian/Other Pacific Islander, 1.6% Other, 1.5% Hispanic of any race (2010); Average household size: 2.38 (2010); Median age: 47.0 (2010); Males per 100 females: 94.6 (2010); Homeownership rate: 84.5% (2010)

**COXSACKIE** (village). Covers a land area of 2.171 square miles and a water area of 0.423 square miles. Located at 42.35° N. Lat; 73.80° W. Long. Elevation is 141 feet.
**Population:** 2,789 (1990); 2,895 (2000); 2,813 (2010); Density: 1,295.4 persons per square mile (2010); Race: 93.7% White, 2.6% Black, 0.9% Asian, 0.2% American Indian/Alaska Native, 0.1% Native Hawaiian/Other Pacific Islander, 2.5% Other, 4.5% Hispanic of any race (2010); Average household size: 2.30 (2010); Median age: 41.4 (2010); Males per 100 females: 89.9 (2010); Marriage status: 33.8% never married, 49.0% now married, 7.6% widowed, 9.6% divorced (2006-2010 5-year est.); Foreign born: 2.5% (2006-2010 5-year est.); Ancestry (includes multiple ancestries): 21.3% German, 19.7% Irish, 19.1% Italian, 12.1% American, 10.2% English (2006-2010 5-year est.).
**Economy:** Single-family building permits issued: 0 (2011); Multi-family building permits issued: 0 (2011); Employment by occupation: 7.1% management, 6.9% professional, 9.4% services, 16.7% sales, 3.2% farming, 11.5% construction, 3.9% production (2006-2010 5-year est.).
**Income:** Per capita income: $26,655 (2006-2010 5-year est.); Median household income: $58,266 (2006-2010 5-year est.); Average household income: $63,966 (2006-2010 5-year est.); Percent of households with income of $100,000 or more: 20.9% (2006-2010 5-year est.); Poverty rate: 7.8% (2006-2010 5-year est.).
**Education:** Percent of population age 25 and over with: High school diploma (including GED) or higher: 88.9% (2006-2010 5-year est.); Bachelor's degree or higher: 21.1% (2006-2010 5-year est.); Master's degree or higher: 8.4% (2006-2010 5-year est.).
**School District(s)**
Coxsackie-Athens Central School District (KG-12)
  2009-10 Enrollment: 1,542 . . . . . . . . . . . . . . . . . . . . (518) 731-1710
**Housing:** Homeownership rate: 59.8% (2010); Median home value: $170,800 (2006-2010 5-year est.); Median contract rent: $506 per month (2006-2010 5-year est.); Median year structure built: before 1940 (2006-2010 5-year est.).
**Transportation:** Commute to work: 96.7% car, 0.0% public transportation, 1.2% walk, 0.0% work from home (2006-2010 5-year est.); Travel time to work: 39.5% less than 15 minutes, 19.5% 15 to 30 minutes, 26.8% 30 to 45 minutes, 10.7% 45 to 60 minutes, 3.4% 60 minutes or more (2006-2010 5-year est.)
**Additional Information Contacts**
Coxsackie Regional Chamber of Commerce . . . . . . . . . . . (518) 731-7300
  http://www.coxsackieareachamber.com

**COXSACKIE** (town). Covers a land area of 36.865 square miles and a water area of 1.548 square miles. Located at 42.34° N. Lat; 73.86° W. Long. Elevation is 141 feet.
**History:** Franklin air-cooled automobile engine invented here. Settled by the Dutch before 1700; incorporated 1867.
**Population:** 7,633 (1990); 8,884 (2000); 8,918 (2010); Density: 241.9 persons per square mile (2010); Race: 75.6% White, 20.0% Black, 0.8% Asian, 0.4% American Indian/Alaska Native, 0.0% Native Hawaiian/Other Pacific Islander, 3.2% Other, 8.5% Hispanic of any race (2010); Average household size: 2.39 (2010); Median age: 35.2 (2010); Males per 100 females: 184.3 (2010); Marriage status: 51.8% never married, 36.6% now

married, 3.8% widowed, 7.8% divorced (2006-2010 5-year est.); Foreign born: 4.7% (2006-2010 5-year est.); Ancestry (includes multiple ancestries): 14.7% German, 14.4% Italian, 14.4% Irish, 8.9% English, 7.2% American (2006-2010 5-year est.).

**Economy:** Single-family building permits issued: 4 (2011); Multi-family building permits issued: 0 (2011); Employment by occupation: 9.5% management, 4.7% professional, 9.1% services, 17.1% sales, 4.4% farming, 8.4% construction, 3.2% production (2006-2010 5-year est.).

**Income:** Per capita income: $18,146 (2006-2010 5-year est.); Median household income: $52,246 (2006-2010 5-year est.); Average household income: $64,558 (2006-2010 5-year est.); Percent of households with income of $100,000 or more: 21.1% (2006-2010 5-year est.); Poverty rate: 8.8% (2006-2010 5-year est.).

**Education:** Percent of population age 25 and over with: High school diploma (including GED) or higher: 81.1% (2006-2010 5-year est.); Bachelor's degree or higher: 19.2% (2006-2010 5-year est.); Master's degree or higher: 8.6% (2006-2010 5-year est.).

### School District(s)
Coxsackie-Athens Central School District (KG-12)
    2009-10 Enrollment: 1,542 . . . . . . . . . . . . . . . . . . . . . . . (518) 731-1710

**Housing:** Homeownership rate: 70.4% (2010); Median home value: $181,400 (2006-2010 5-year est.); Median contract rent: $518 per month (2006-2010 5-year est.); Median year structure built: 1964 (2006-2010 5-year est.).

**Transportation:** Commute to work: 95.4% car, 0.0% public transportation, 1.1% walk, 1.7% work from home (2006-2010 5-year est.); Travel time to work: 35.2% less than 15 minutes, 23.8% 15 to 30 minutes, 23.7% 30 to 45 minutes, 13.9% 45 to 60 minutes, 3.5% 60 minutes or more (2006-2010 5-year est.)

**Additional Information Contacts**
Town of Coxsackie. . . . . . . . . . . . . . . . . . . . . . . . . . . . . (518) 731-2727
    http://www.coxsackie.org

**DURHAM** (town). Covers a land area of 49.314 square miles and a water area of 0.041 square miles. Located at 42.37° N. Lat; 74.15° W. Long. Elevation is 771 feet.

**Population:** 2,324 (1990); 2,592 (2000); 2,725 (2010); Density: 55.3 persons per square mile (2010); Race: 97.5% White, 0.6% Black, 0.2% Asian, 0.0% American Indian/Alaska Native, 0.1% Native Hawaiian/Other Pacific Islander, 1.6% Other, 2.3% Hispanic of any race (2010); Average household size: 2.37 (2010); Median age: 47.1 (2010); Males per 100 females: 101.9 (2010); Marriage status: 28.8% never married, 54.7% now married, 9.0% widowed, 7.5% divorced (2006-2010 5-year est.); Foreign born: 8.5% (2006-2010 5-year est.); Ancestry (includes multiple ancestries): 30.0% American, 24.1% Irish, 15.2% German, 6.6% Italian, 5.3% English (2006-2010 5-year est.).

**Economy:** Single-family building permits issued: 10 (2011); Multi-family building permits issued: 0 (2011); Employment by occupation: 10.0% management, 0.8% professional, 14.9% services, 12.0% sales, 1.7% farming, 13.4% construction, 10.1% production (2006-2010 5-year est.).

**Income:** Per capita income: $19,302 (2006-2010 5-year est.); Median household income: $49,961 (2006-2010 5-year est.); Average household income: $56,117 (2006-2010 5-year est.); Percent of households with income of $100,000 or more: 8.9% (2006-2010 5-year est.); Poverty rate: 18.8% (2006-2010 5-year est.).

**Education:** Percent of population age 25 and over with: High school diploma (including GED) or higher: 80.2% (2006-2010 5-year est.); Bachelor's degree or higher: 15.6% (2006-2010 5-year est.); Master's degree or higher: 8.7% (2006-2010 5-year est.).

### School District(s)
Cairo-Durham Central School District (KG-12)
    2009-10 Enrollment: 1,495 . . . . . . . . . . . . . . . . . . . . . . . (518) 622-8534

**Housing:** Homeownership rate: 80.9% (2010); Median home value: $155,600 (2006-2010 5-year est.); Median contract rent: $615 per month (2006-2010 5-year est.); Median year structure built: 1970 (2006-2010 5-year est.).

**Safety:** Violent crime rate: 0.0 per 10,000 population; Property crime rate: 37.5 per 10,000 population (2010).

**Transportation:** Commute to work: 84.0% car, 1.0% public transportation, 0.0% walk, 5.2% work from home (2006-2010 5-year est.); Travel time to work: 29.8% less than 15 minutes, 34.2% 15 to 30 minutes, 17.8% 30 to 45 minutes, 12.3% 45 to 60 minutes, 6.0% 60 minutes or more (2006-2010 5-year est.)

**EARLTON** (unincorporated postal area)
Zip Code: 12058

Covers a land area of 19.231 square miles and a water area of 0.306 square miles. Located at 42.34° N. Lat; 73.91° W. Long. Elevation is 417 feet. Population: 1,445 (2010); Density: 75.1 persons per square mile (2010); Race: 96.7% White, 0.6% Black, 0.8% Asian, 0.2% American Indian/Alaska Native, 0.0% Native Hawaiian/Other Pacific Islander, 1.7% Other, 3.0% Hispanic of any race (2010); Average household size: 2.47 (2010); Median age: 43.4 (2010); Males per 100 females: 106.7 (2010); Homeownership rate: 80.3% (2010)

**EAST DURHAM** (unincorporated postal area)
Zip Code: 12423

Covers a land area of 12.715 square miles and a water area of 0 square miles. Located at 42.37° N. Lat; 74.10° W. Long. Elevation is 535 feet. Population: 1,097 (2010); Density: 86.3 persons per square mile (2010); Race: 98.1% White, 0.5% Black, 0.4% Asian, 0.0% American Indian/Alaska Native, 0.0% Native Hawaiian/Other Pacific Islander, 1.0% Other, 1.7% Hispanic of any race (2010); Average household size: 2.30 (2010); Median age: 47.5 (2010); Males per 100 females: 106.6 (2010); Homeownership rate: 78.4% (2010)

**EAST JEWETT** (unincorporated postal area)
Zip Code: 12424

Covers a land area of 17.771 square miles and a water area of 0.114 square miles. Located at 42.24° N. Lat; 74.11° W. Long. Elevation is 1,965 feet. Population: 250 (2010); Density: 14.1 persons per square mile (2010); Race: 97.2% White, 0.0% Black, 1.2% Asian, 0.0% American Indian/Alaska Native, 0.0% Native Hawaiian/Other Pacific Islander, 1.6% Other, 3.2% Hispanic of any race (2010); Average household size: 2.07 (2010); Median age: 54.8 (2010); Males per 100 females: 111.9 (2010); Homeownership rate: 85.9% (2010)

**ELKA PARK** (unincorporated postal area)
Zip Code: 12427

Covers a land area of 40.999 square miles and a water area of 0.036 square miles. Located at 42.13° N. Lat; 74.13° W. Long. Elevation is 2,178 feet. Population: 576 (2010); Density: 14.0 persons per square mile (2010); Race: 88.5% White, 5.7% Black, 1.4% Asian, 0.3% American Indian/Alaska Native, 0.0% Native Hawaiian/Other Pacific Islander, 4.1% Other, 5.2% Hispanic of any race (2010); Average household size: 2.28 (2010); Median age: 37.6 (2010); Males per 100 females: 82.9 (2010); Homeownership rate: 81.9% (2010)

**FREEHOLD** (unincorporated postal area)
Zip Code: 12431

Covers a land area of 15.466 square miles and a water area of 0.026 square miles. Located at 42.36° N. Lat; 74.02° W. Long. Elevation is 423 feet. Population: 1,381 (2010); Density: 89.3 persons per square mile (2010); Race: 98.5% White, 0.4% Black, 0.8% Asian, 0.0% American Indian/Alaska Native, 0.0% Native Hawaiian/Other Pacific Islander, 0.3% Other, 1.5% Hispanic of any race (2010); Average household size: 2.43 (2010); Median age: 44.6 (2010); Males per 100 females: 105.5 (2010); Homeownership rate: 79.9% (2010)

**GREENVILLE** (town). Covers a land area of 38.788 square miles and a water area of 0.295 square miles. Located at 42.39° N. Lat; 74.01° W. Long. Elevation is 709 feet.

**Population:** 3,135 (1990); 3,316 (2000); 3,739 (2010); Density: 96.4 persons per square mile (2010); Race: 96.7% White, 0.9% Black, 0.9% Asian, 0.1% American Indian/Alaska Native, 0.0% Native Hawaiian/Other Pacific Islander, 1.4% Other, 2.5% Hispanic of any race (2010); Average household size: 2.44 (2010); Median age: 44.5 (2010); Males per 100 females: 97.0 (2010); Marriage status: 29.5% never married, 50.8% now married, 11.3% widowed, 8.4% divorced (2006-2010 5-year est.); Foreign born: 3.3% (2006-2010 5-year est.); Ancestry (includes multiple ancestries): 24.0% German, 22.5% Irish, 18.3% Italian, 15.8% American, 7.3% English (2006-2010 5-year est.).

**Economy:** Single-family building permits issued: 3 (2011); Multi-family building permits issued: 0 (2011); Employment by occupation: 7.7% management, 0.8% professional, 13.2% services, 16.8% sales, 1.5% farming, 18.0% construction, 7.7% production (2006-2010 5-year est.).

**Income:** Per capita income: $21,973 (2006-2010 5-year est.); Median household income: $42,790 (2006-2010 5-year est.); Average household income: $53,295 (2006-2010 5-year est.); Percent of households with

income of $100,000 or more: 14.0% (2006-2010 5-year est.); Poverty rate: 12.8% (2006-2010 5-year est.).
**Taxes:** Total city taxes per capita: $449 (2009); City property taxes per capita: $416 (2009).
**Education:** Percent of population age 25 and over with: High school diploma (including GED) or higher: 87.4% (2006-2010 5-year est.); Bachelor's degree or higher: 12.8% (2006-2010 5-year est.); Master's degree or higher: 5.5% (2006-2010 5-year est.).

### School District(s)
Greenville Central School District (KG-12)
    2009-10 Enrollment: 1,253 . . . . . . . . . . . . . . . . . . . . . (518) 966-5070
**Housing:** Homeownership rate: 81.0% (2010); Median home value: $176,700 (2006-2010 5-year est.); Median contract rent: $709 per month (2006-2010 5-year est.); Median year structure built: 1965 (2006-2010 5-year est.).
**Transportation:** Commute to work: 90.9% car, 0.0% public transportation, 0.0% walk, 3.4% work from home (2006-2010 5-year est.); Travel time to work: 27.6% less than 15 minutes, 33.5% 15 to 30 minutes, 15.2% 30 to 45 minutes, 12.5% 45 to 60 minutes, 11.3% 60 minutes or more (2006-2010 5-year est.)

**GREENVILLE** (CDP). Covers a land area of 3.431 square miles and a water area of 0.019 square miles. Located at 42.41° N. Lat; 74.02° W. Long. Elevation is 709 feet.
**Population:** 508 (1990); 493 (2000); 688 (2010); Density: 200.5 persons per square mile (2010); Race: 94.5% White, 1.7% Black, 1.7% Asian, 0.4% American Indian/Alaska Native, 0.0% Native Hawaiian/Other Pacific Islander, 1.7% Other, 2.9% Hispanic of any race (2010); Average household size: 2.14 (2010); Median age: 48.9 (2010); Males per 100 females: 89.5 (2010); Marriage status: 41.9% never married, 39.2% now married, 10.3% widowed, 8.6% divorced (2006-2010 5-year est.); Foreign born: 1.3% (2006-2010 5-year est.); Ancestry (includes multiple ancestries): 35.7% German, 24.8% Irish, 15.7% Italian, 12.2% English, 7.7% Polish (2006-2010 5-year est.).
**Economy:** Employment by occupation: 10.3% management, 0.0% professional, 10.1% services, 17.1% sales, 0.0% farming, 13.3% construction, 6.7% production (2006-2010 5-year est.).
**Income:** Per capita income: $24,294 (2006-2010 5-year est.); Median household income: $42,863 (2006-2010 5-year est.); Average household income: $54,560 (2006-2010 5-year est.); Percent of households with income of $100,000 or more: 17.5% (2006-2010 5-year est.); Poverty rate: 7.1% (2006-2010 5-year est.).
**Education:** Percent of population age 25 and over with: High school diploma (including GED) or higher: 93.6% (2006-2010 5-year est.); Bachelor's degree or higher: 12.0% (2006-2010 5-year est.); Master's degree or higher: 3.7% (2006-2010 5-year est.).

### School District(s)
Greenville Central School District (KG-12)
    2009-10 Enrollment: 1,253 . . . . . . . . . . . . . . . . . . . . . (518) 966-5070
**Housing:** Homeownership rate: 77.3% (2010); Median home value: $172,600 (2006-2010 5-year est.); Median contract rent: $546 per month (2006-2010 5-year est.); Median year structure built: 1946 (2006-2010 5-year est.).
**Transportation:** Commute to work: 88.9% car, 0.0% public transportation, 0.0% walk, 2.8% work from home (2006-2010 5-year est.); Travel time to work: 17.2% less than 15 minutes, 35.3% 15 to 30 minutes, 27.1% 30 to 45 minutes, 9.5% 45 to 60 minutes, 10.9% 60 minutes or more (2006-2010 5-year est.)

**HAINES FALLS** (unincorporated postal area)
Zip Code: 12436
    Covers a land area of 15.352 square miles and a water area of 0.138 square miles. Located at 42.19° N. Lat; 74.07° W. Long. Elevation is 1,903 feet. Population: 417 (2010); Density: 27.2 persons per square mile (2010); Race: 95.9% White, 1.4% Black, 1.0% Asian, 0.0% American Indian/Alaska Native, 0.0% Native Hawaiian/Other Pacific Islander, 1.7% Other, 1.2% Hispanic of any race (2010); Average household size: 2.19 (2010); Median age: 47.8 (2010); Males per 100 females: 99.5 (2010); Homeownership rate: 69.4% (2010)

**HALCOTT** (town). Covers a land area of 23.040 square miles and a water area of 0 square miles. Located at 42.22° N. Lat; 74.47° W. Long.
**Population:** 189 (1990); 193 (2000); 258 (2010); Density: 11.2 persons per square mile (2010); Race: 95.3% White, 0.8% Black, 1.9% Asian, 0.0% American Indian/Alaska Native, 0.0% Native Hawaiian/Other Pacific

Islander, 2.0% Other, 2.3% Hispanic of any race (2010); Average household size: 2.15 (2010); Median age: 55.7 (2010); Males per 100 females: 100.0 (2010); Marriage status: 20.4% never married, 67.0% now married, 7.3% widowed, 5.2% divorced (2006-2010 5-year est.); Foreign born: 2.3% (2006-2010 5-year est.); Ancestry (includes multiple ancestries): 22.9% American, 14.3% German, 13.5% English, 10.5% Italian, 10.5% Russian (2006-2010 5-year est.).
**Economy:** Single-family building permits issued: 4 (2011); Multi-family building permits issued: 0 (2011); Employment by occupation: 9.4% management, 4.3% professional, 11.1% services, 26.5% sales, 2.6% farming, 10.3% construction, 2.6% production (2006-2010 5-year est.).
**Income:** Per capita income: $19,941 (2006-2010 5-year est.); Median household income: $46,563 (2006-2010 5-year est.); Average household income: $56,598 (2006-2010 5-year est.); Percent of households with income of $100,000 or more: 15.4% (2006-2010 5-year est.); Poverty rate: 4.5% (2006-2010 5-year est.).
**Education:** Percent of population age 25 and over with: High school diploma (including GED) or higher: 86.0% (2006-2010 5-year est.); Bachelor's degree or higher: 28.5% (2006-2010 5-year est.); Master's degree or higher: 12.2% (2006-2010 5-year est.).
**Housing:** Homeownership rate: 86.7% (2010); Median home value: $158,300 (2006-2010 5-year est.); Median contract rent: $850 per month (2006-2010 5-year est.); Median year structure built: 1972 (2006-2010 5-year est.).
**Transportation:** Commute to work: 60.2% car, 8.0% public transportation, 0.0% walk, 24.8% work from home (2006-2010 5-year est.); Travel time to work: 20.0% less than 15 minutes, 55.3% 15 to 30 minutes, 12.9% 30 to 45 minutes, 0.0% 45 to 60 minutes, 11.8% 60 minutes or more (2006-2010 5-year est.)
**Additional Information Contacts**
Town of Halcott . . . . . . . . . . . . . . . . . . . . . . . . . . . (845) 254-6441
    http://halcottcenter.wordpress.com

**HANNACROIX** (unincorporated postal area)
Zip Code: 12087
    Covers a land area of 19.688 square miles and a water area of 0.254 square miles. Located at 42.43° N. Lat; 73.89° W. Long. Elevation is 190 feet. Population: 1,073 (2010); Density: 54.5 persons per square mile (2010); Race: 96.7% White, 1.4% Black, 0.6% Asian, 0.1% American Indian/Alaska Native, 0.0% Native Hawaiian/Other Pacific Islander, 1.2% Other, 3.4% Hispanic of any race (2010); Average household size: 2.66 (2010); Median age: 41.8 (2010); Males per 100 females: 105.6 (2010); Homeownership rate: 86.4% (2010)

**HENSONVILLE** (unincorporated postal area)
Zip Code: 12439
    Covers a land area of 7.832 square miles and a water area of 0.022 square miles. Located at 42.27° N. Lat; 74.21° W. Long. Elevation is 1,637 feet. Population: 305 (2010); Density: 38.9 persons per square mile (2010); Race: 98.0% White, 0.3% Black, 0.0% Asian, 1.3% American Indian/Alaska Native, 0.0% Native Hawaiian/Other Pacific Islander, 0.4% Other, 2.6% Hispanic of any race (2010); Average household size: 2.07 (2010); Median age: 47.9 (2010); Males per 100 females: 117.9 (2010); Homeownership rate: 66.7% (2010)

**HUNTER** (village). Covers a land area of 1.735 square miles and a water area of 0.032 square miles. Located at 42.21° N. Lat; 74.21° W. Long. Elevation is 1,588 feet.
**Population:** 458 (1990); 490 (2000); 502 (2010); Density: 289.3 persons per square mile (2010); Race: 93.6% White, 0.4% Black, 2.4% Asian, 0.0% American Indian/Alaska Native, 0.0% Native Hawaiian/Other Pacific Islander, 3.6% Other, 5.4% Hispanic of any race (2010); Average household size: 1.97 (2010); Median age: 51.7 (2010); Males per 100 females: 111.8 (2010); Marriage status: 35.5% never married, 34.0% now married, 17.4% widowed, 13.1% divorced (2006-2010 5-year est.); Foreign born: 7.9% (2006-2010 5-year est.); Ancestry (includes multiple ancestries): 31.0% Italian, 24.9% Irish, 15.2% American, 8.3% English, 8.1% German (2006-2010 5-year est.).
**Economy:** Single-family building permits issued: 1 (2011); Multi-family building permits issued: 0 (2011); Employment by occupation: 15.5% management, 2.7% professional, 7.5% services, 17.6% sales, 3.2% farming, 17.6% construction, 10.2% production (2006-2010 5-year est.).
**Income:** Per capita income: $21,403 (2006-2010 5-year est.); Median household income: $29,583 (2006-2010 5-year est.); Average household income: $38,545 (2006-2010 5-year est.); Percent of households with

income of $100,000 or more: 7.0% (2006-2010 5-year est.); Poverty rate: 15.2% (2006-2010 5-year est.).
**Education:** Percent of population age 25 and over with: High school diploma (including GED) or higher: 73.8% (2006-2010 5-year est.); Bachelor's degree or higher: 33.1% (2006-2010 5-year est.); Master's degree or higher: 9.7% (2006-2010 5-year est.).

**School District(s)**
Hunter-Tannersville Central School District (PK-12)
    2009-10 Enrollment: 437 . . . . . . . . . . . . . . . . . . . (518) 589-5400
**Housing:** Homeownership rate: 65.9% (2010); Median home value: $217,700 (2006-2010 5-year est.); Median contract rent: $478 per month (2006-2010 5-year est.); Median year structure built: 1972 (2006-2010 5-year est.).
**Transportation:** Commute to work: 72.5% car, 0.0% public transportation, 0.0% walk, 0.0% work from home (2006-2010 5-year est.); Travel time to work: 44.0% less than 15 minutes, 17.0% 15 to 30 minutes, 13.7% 30 to 45 minutes, 9.3% 45 to 60 minutes, 15.9% 60 minutes or more (2006-2010 5-year est.)
**Additional Information Contacts**
Hunter Chamber of Commerce . . . . . . . . . . . . . . . . . . (518) 263-4900
    http://www.hunterchamber.org

**HUNTER** (town). Covers a land area of 90.419 square miles and a water area of 0.321 square miles. Located at 42.16° N. Lat; 74.15° W. Long. Elevation is 1,588 feet.
**Population:** 2,116 (1990); 2,721 (2000); 2,732 (2010); Density: 30.2 persons per square mile (2010); Race: 93.3% White, 1.8% Black, 1.3% Asian, 0.3% American Indian/Alaska Native, 0.1% Native Hawaiian/Other Pacific Islander, 3.2% Other, 4.5% Hispanic of any race (2010); Average household size: 2.07 (2010); Median age: 47.2 (2010); Males per 100 females: 102.4 (2010); Marriage status: 35.4% never married, 45.1% now married, 7.3% widowed, 12.3% divorced (2006-2010 5-year est.); Foreign born: 11.7% (2006-2010 5-year est.); Ancestry (includes multiple ancestries): 17.0% Irish, 15.1% English, 14.3% Italian, 12.8% German, 11.2% American (2006-2010 5-year est.).
**Economy:** Single-family building permits issued: 2 (2011); Multi-family building permits issued: 0 (2011); Employment by occupation: 15.5% management, 0.4% professional, 15.8% services, 13.7% sales, 8.7% farming, 7.8% construction, 4.7% production (2006-2010 5-year est.).
**Income:** Per capita income: $20,164 (2006-2010 5-year est.); Median household income: $35,286 (2006-2010 5-year est.); Average household income: $43,167 (2006-2010 5-year est.); Percent of households with income of $100,000 or more: 6.0% (2006-2010 5-year est.); Poverty rate: 18.6% (2006-2010 5-year est.).
**Education:** Percent of population age 25 and over with: High school diploma (including GED) or higher: 88.2% (2006-2010 5-year est.); Bachelor's degree or higher: 27.0% (2006-2010 5-year est.); Master's degree or higher: 8.5% (2006-2010 5-year est.).

**School District(s)**
Hunter-Tannersville Central School District (PK-12)
    2009-10 Enrollment: 437 . . . . . . . . . . . . . . . . . . . (518) 589-5400
**Housing:** Homeownership rate: 63.2% (2010); Median home value: $215,700 (2006-2010 5-year est.); Median contract rent: $527 per month (2006-2010 5-year est.); Median year structure built: 1965 (2006-2010 5-year est.).
**Safety:** Violent crime rate: 11.3 per 10,000 population; Property crime rate: 22.6 per 10,000 population (2010).
**Transportation:** Commute to work: 82.8% car, 0.0% public transportation, 1.3% walk, 8.6% work from home (2006-2010 5-year est.); Travel time to work: 40.9% less than 15 minutes, 28.6% 15 to 30 minutes, 9.6% 30 to 45 minutes, 8.5% 45 to 60 minutes, 12.4% 60 minutes or more (2006-2010 5-year est.)

**JEFFERSON HEIGHTS** (CDP). Aka Jefferson. Covers a land area of 1.476 square miles and a water area of 0.021 square miles. Located at 42.23° N. Lat; 73.88° W. Long. Elevation is 177 feet.
**Population:** 1,055 (1990); 1,104 (2000); 1,094 (2010); Density: 741.2 persons per square mile (2010); Race: 92.2% White, 3.6% Black, 0.6% Asian, 0.0% American Indian/Alaska Native, 0.0% Native Hawaiian/Other Pacific Islander, 3.6% Other, 4.8% Hispanic of any race (2010); Average household size: 2.11 (2010); Median age: 55.8 (2010); Males per 100 females: 73.7 (2010); Marriage status: 24.1% never married, 48.8% now married, 23.2% widowed, 3.9% divorced (2006-2010 5-year est.); Foreign born: 3.2% (2006-2010 5-year est.); Ancestry (includes multiple

ancestries): 35.6% Italian, 20.2% German, 19.6% Irish, 13.1% Dutch, 4.3% Polish (2006-2010 5-year est.).
**Economy:** Employment by occupation: 16.6% management, 3.3% professional, 20.3% services, 13.0% sales, 6.3% farming, 10.7% construction, 0.0% production (2006-2010 5-year est.).
**Income:** Per capita income: $24,255 (2006-2010 5-year est.); Median household income: $48,991 (2006-2010 5-year est.); Average household income: $63,475 (2006-2010 5-year est.); Percent of households with income of $100,000 or more: 10.5% (2006-2010 5-year est.); Poverty rate: 8.1% (2006-2010 5-year est.).
**Education:** Percent of population age 25 and over with: High school diploma (including GED) or higher: 85.3% (2006-2010 5-year est.); Bachelor's degree or higher: 11.7% (2006-2010 5-year est.); Master's degree or higher: 4.1% (2006-2010 5-year est.).
**Housing:** Homeownership rate: 59.7% (2010); Median home value: $229,000 (2006-2010 5-year est.); Median contract rent: $750 per month (2006-2010 5-year est.); Median year structure built: 1962 (2006-2010 5-year est.).
**Transportation:** Commute to work: 84.3% car, 0.0% public transportation, 0.0% walk, 12.8% work from home (2006-2010 5-year est.); Travel time to work: 28.0% less than 15 minutes, 54.6% 15 to 30 minutes, 7.3% 30 to 45 minutes, 1.9% 45 to 60 minutes, 8.3% 60 minutes or more (2006-2010 5-year est.)

**JEWETT** (town). Covers a land area of 50.323 square miles and a water area of 0.198 square miles. Located at 42.23° N. Lat; 74.23° W. Long. Elevation is 1,801 feet.
**Population:** 923 (1990); 970 (2000); 953 (2010); Density: 18.9 persons per square mile (2010); Race: 97.9% White, 0.0% Black, 0.4% Asian, 0.0% American Indian/Alaska Native, 0.0% Native Hawaiian/Other Pacific Islander, 1.7% Other, 3.1% Hispanic of any race (2010); Average household size: 2.08 (2010); Median age: 53.1 (2010); Males per 100 females: 107.6 (2010); Marriage status: 21.7% never married, 57.3% now married, 8.5% widowed, 12.5% divorced (2006-2010 5-year est.); Foreign born: 6.7% (2006-2010 5-year est.); Ancestry (includes multiple ancestries): 22.8% English, 19.7% American, 18.2% Italian, 13.0% Irish, 11.1% German (2006-2010 5-year est.).
**Economy:** Single-family building permits issued: 6 (2011); Multi-family building permits issued: 0 (2011); Employment by occupation: 19.1% management, 0.7% professional, 5.1% services, 18.3% sales, 4.2% farming, 22.5% construction, 6.4% production (2006-2010 5-year est.).
**Income:** Per capita income: $23,607 (2006-2010 5-year est.); Median household income: $46,375 (2006-2010 5-year est.); Average household income: $57,528 (2006-2010 5-year est.); Percent of households with income of $100,000 or more: 12.6% (2006-2010 5-year est.); Poverty rate: 9.8% (2006-2010 5-year est.).
**Education:** Percent of population age 25 and over with: High school diploma (including GED) or higher: 85.1% (2006-2010 5-year est.); Bachelor's degree or higher: 24.4% (2006-2010 5-year est.); Master's degree or higher: 9.9% (2006-2010 5-year est.).
**Housing:** Homeownership rate: 84.3% (2010); Median home value: $248,200 (2006-2010 5-year est.); Median contract rent: $519 per month (2006-2010 5-year est.); Median year structure built: 1979 (2006-2010 5-year est.).
**Transportation:** Commute to work: 85.2% car, 0.0% public transportation, 7.8% walk, 1.1% work from home (2006-2010 5-year est.); Travel time to work: 45.4% less than 15 minutes, 17.7% 15 to 30 minutes, 14.1% 30 to 45 minutes, 7.1% 45 to 60 minutes, 15.8% 60 minutes or more (2006-2010 5-year est.)

**LANESVILLE** (unincorporated postal area)
Zip Code: 12450
    Covers a land area of 9.897 square miles and a water area of 0 square miles. Located at 42.13° N. Lat; 74.24° W. Long. Elevation is 1,280 feet.
Population: 183 (2010); Density: 18.5 persons per square mile (2010); Race: 91.8% White, 1.6% Black, 0.0% Asian, 1.1% American Indian/Alaska Native, 0.0% Native Hawaiian/Other Pacific Islander, 5.5% Other, 7.7% Hispanic of any race (2010); Average household size: 1.95 (2010); Median age: 51.8 (2010); Males per 100 females: 105.6 (2010); Homeownership rate: 64.9% (2010)

**LEEDS** (CDP). Covers a land area of 0.529 square miles and a water area of 0.009 square miles. Located at 42.24° N. Lat; 73.89° W. Long. Elevation is 157 feet.
**Population:** 377 (1990); 369 (2000); 377 (2010); Density: 712.5 persons per square mile (2010); Race: 91.2% White, 3.2% Black, 1.6% Asian, 0.5% American Indian/Alaska Native, 0.0% Native Hawaiian/Other Pacific Islander, 3.5% Other, 6.1% Hispanic of any race (2010); Average household size: 2.05 (2010); Median age: 41.3 (2010); Males per 100 females: 84.8 (2010); Marriage status: 38.6% never married, 38.9% now married, 16.8% widowed, 5.7% divorced (2006-2010 5-year est.); Foreign born: 0.0% (2006-2010 5-year est.); Ancestry (includes multiple ancestries): 47.2% Italian, 33.8% German, 18.4% American, 13.4% Irish, 5.3% French (2006-2010 5-year est.).
**Economy:** Employment by occupation: 5.0% management, 8.5% professional, 4.5% services, 0.0% sales, 8.5% farming, 8.0% construction, 12.9% production (2006-2010 5-year est.).
**Income:** Per capita income: $26,268 (2006-2010 5-year est.); Median household income: $24,922 (2006-2010 5-year est.); Average household income: $59,765 (2006-2010 5-year est.); Percent of households with income of $100,000 or more: 15.0% (2006-2010 5-year est.); Poverty rate: 18.1% (2006-2010 5-year est.).
**Education:** Percent of population age 25 and over with: High school diploma (including GED) or higher: 93.5% (2006-2010 5-year est.); Bachelor's degree or higher: 8.5% (2006-2010 5-year est.); Master's degree or higher: 0.0% (2006-2010 5-year est.).
**Housing:** Homeownership rate: 52.7% (2010); Median home value: $161,100 (2006-2010 5-year est.); Median contract rent: $500 per month (2006-2010 5-year est.); Median year structure built: before 1940 (2006-2010 5-year est.).
**Transportation:** Commute to work: 92.0% car, 0.0% public transportation, 0.0% walk, 8.0% work from home (2006-2010 5-year est.); Travel time to work: 41.1% less than 15 minutes, 8.6% 15 to 30 minutes, 32.4% 30 to 45 minutes, 0.0% 45 to 60 minutes, 17.8% 60 minutes or more (2006-2010 5-year est.)

**LEXINGTON** (town). Covers a land area of 79.685 square miles and a water area of 0.036 square miles. Located at 42.20° N. Lat; 74.33° W. Long. Elevation is 1,322 feet.
**Population:** 845 (1990); 830 (2000); 805 (2010); Density: 10.1 persons per square mile (2010); Race: 97.6% White, 0.6% Black, 0.4% Asian, 0.4% American Indian/Alaska Native, 0.0% Native Hawaiian/Other Pacific Islander, 1.0% Other, 3.0% Hispanic of any race (2010); Average household size: 2.07 (2010); Median age: 53.7 (2010); Males per 100 females: 82.1 (2010); Marriage status: 24.2% never married, 60.8% now married, 5.4% widowed, 9.6% divorced (2006-2010 5-year est.); Foreign born: 6.1% (2006-2010 5-year est.); Ancestry (includes multiple ancestries): 15.1% German, 13.4% Irish, 13.0% American, 11.6% Italian, 11.4% French (2006-2010 5-year est.).
**Economy:** Single-family building permits issued: 2 (2011); Multi-family building permits issued: 0 (2011); Employment by occupation: 11.4% management, 3.0% professional, 16.0% services, 14.2% sales, 0.9% farming, 19.5% construction, 2.3% production (2006-2010 5-year est.).
**Income:** Per capita income: $27,386 (2006-2010 5-year est.); Median household income: $41,413 (2006-2010 5-year est.); Average household income: $58,927 (2006-2010 5-year est.); Percent of households with income of $100,000 or more: 10.4% (2006-2010 5-year est.); Poverty rate: 18.3% (2006-2010 5-year est.).
**Education:** Percent of population age 25 and over with: High school diploma (including GED) or higher: 88.7% (2006-2010 5-year est.); Bachelor's degree or higher: 26.7% (2006-2010 5-year est.); Master's degree or higher: 11.1% (2006-2010 5-year est.).
**Housing:** Homeownership rate: 86.1% (2010); Median home value: $209,500 (2006-2010 5-year est.); Median contract rent: $418 per month (2006-2010 5-year est.); Median year structure built: 1971 (2006-2010 5-year est.).
**Transportation:** Commute to work: 76.1% car, 1.7% public transportation, 2.7% walk, 12.5% work from home (2006-2010 5-year est.); Travel time to work: 25.1% less than 15 minutes, 39.4% 15 to 30 minutes, 16.5% 30 to 45 minutes, 9.6% 45 to 60 minutes, 9.4% 60 minutes or more (2006-2010 5-year est.)

**MAPLECREST** (unincorporated postal area)
Zip Code: 12454
Covers a land area of 11.134 square miles and a water area of 0.044 square miles. Located at 42.28° N. Lat; 74.14° W. Long. Elevation is

1,762 feet. Population: 297 (2010); Density: 26.7 persons per square mile (2010); Race: 99.7% White, 0.0% Black, 0.3% Asian, 0.0% American Indian/Alaska Native, 0.0% Native Hawaiian/Other Pacific Islander, 0.0% Other, 2.4% Hispanic of any race (2010); Average household size: 2.38 (2010); Median age: 48.5 (2010); Males per 100 females: 106.3 (2010); Homeownership rate: 83.2% (2010)

**NEW BALTIMORE** (town). Covers a land area of 41.426 square miles and a water area of 1.600 square miles. Located at 42.42° N. Lat; 73.86° W. Long. Elevation is 82 feet.
**Population:** 3,371 (1990); 3,417 (2000); 3,370 (2010); Density: 81.3 persons per square mile (2010); Race: 96.3% White, 1.4% Black, 0.6% Asian, 0.1% American Indian/Alaska Native, 0.0% Native Hawaiian/Other Pacific Islander, 1.6% Other, 1.9% Hispanic of any race (2010); Average household size: 2.51 (2010); Median age: 45.3 (2010); Males per 100 females: 99.6 (2010); Marriage status: 24.5% never married, 59.8% now married, 5.5% widowed, 10.2% divorced (2006-2010 5-year est.); Foreign born: 0.2% (2006-2010 5-year est.); Ancestry (includes multiple ancestries): 24.2% American, 19.1% German, 18.6% Irish, 12.3% Italian, 9.6% Dutch (2006-2010 5-year est.).
**Economy:** Single-family building permits issued: 2 (2011); Multi-family building permits issued: 0 (2011); Employment by occupation: 9.1% management, 2.5% professional, 11.7% services, 20.4% sales, 5.2% farming, 14.6% construction, 4.7% production (2006-2010 5-year est.).
**Income:** Per capita income: $27,624 (2006-2010 5-year est.); Median household income: $56,094 (2006-2010 5-year est.); Average household income: $69,468 (2006-2010 5-year est.); Percent of households with income of $100,000 or more: 19.5% (2006-2010 5-year est.); Poverty rate: 5.7% (2006-2010 5-year est.).
**Education:** Percent of population age 25 and over with: High school diploma (including GED) or higher: 92.2% (2006-2010 5-year est.); Bachelor's degree or higher: 16.9% (2006-2010 5-year est.); Master's degree or higher: 5.2% (2006-2010 5-year est.).
**Housing:** Homeownership rate: 87.1% (2010); Median home value: $165,400 (2006-2010 5-year est.); Median contract rent: $493 per month (2006-2010 5-year est.); Median year structure built: 1960 (2006-2010 5-year est.).
**Transportation:** Commute to work: 93.5% car, 0.0% public transportation, 0.9% walk, 2.1% work from home (2006-2010 5-year est.); Travel time to work: 31.7% less than 15 minutes, 29.4% 15 to 30 minutes, 26.8% 30 to 45 minutes, 4.7% 45 to 60 minutes, 7.4% 60 minutes or more (2006-2010 5-year est.)

**OAK HILL** (unincorporated postal area)
Zip Code: 12460
Covers a land area of 2.063 square miles and a water area of 0 square miles. Located at 42.41° N. Lat; 74.14° W. Long. Elevation is 643 feet. Population: 277 (2010); Density: 134.2 persons per square mile (2010); Race: 94.6% White, 2.5% Black, 0.0% Asian, 0.0% American Indian/Alaska Native, 0.0% Native Hawaiian/Other Pacific Islander, 2.9% Other, 0.4% Hispanic of any race (2010); Average household size: 2.52 (2010); Median age: 43.9 (2010); Males per 100 females: 97.9 (2010); Homeownership rate: 84.5% (2010)

**PALENVILLE** (CDP). Covers a land area of 3.325 square miles and a water area of 0.009 square miles. Located at 42.18° N. Lat; 74.02° W. Long. Elevation is 568 feet.
**History:** Legendary home of Rip Van Winkle; Sleepy Hollow, where he reputedly slept for 20 years, is nearby.
**Population:** 1,096 (1990); 1,120 (2000); 1,037 (2010); Density: 311.8 persons per square mile (2010); Race: 96.0% White, 0.8% Black, 1.4% Asian, 0.1% American Indian/Alaska Native, 0.0% Native Hawaiian/Other Pacific Islander, 1.7% Other, 3.4% Hispanic of any race (2010); Average household size: 2.32 (2010); Median age: 45.3 (2010); Males per 100 females: 91.3 (2010); Marriage status: 35.7% never married, 33.9% now married, 13.1% widowed, 17.2% divorced (2006-2010 5-year est.); Foreign born: 2.6% (2006-2010 5-year est.); Ancestry (includes multiple ancestries): 51.5% Irish, 24.8% German, 24.5% Italian, 7.6% English, 6.2% Austrian (2006-2010 5-year est.).
**Economy:** Employment by occupation: 2.1% management, 4.5% professional, 11.7% services, 18.8% sales, 7.5% farming, 0.0% construction, 4.1% production (2006-2010 5-year est.).
**Income:** Per capita income: $24,662 (2006-2010 5-year est.); Median household income: $33,333 (2006-2010 5-year est.); Average household income: $49,224 (2006-2010 5-year est.); Percent of households with

income of $100,000 or more: 14.2% (2006-2010 5-year est.); Poverty rate: 10.5% (2006-2010 5-year est.).
**Education:** Percent of population age 25 and over with: High school diploma (including GED) or higher: 89.0% (2006-2010 5-year est.); Bachelor's degree or higher: 10.9% (2006-2010 5-year est.); Master's degree or higher: 5.4% (2006-2010 5-year est.).
**Housing:** Homeownership rate: 73.4% (2010); Median home value: $147,700 (2006-2010 5-year est.); Median contract rent: $543 per month (2006-2010 5-year est.); Median year structure built: 1958 (2006-2010 5-year est.).
**Transportation:** Commute to work: 100.0% car, 0.0% public transportation, 0.0% walk, 0.0% work from home (2006-2010 5-year est.); Travel time to work: 23.8% less than 15 minutes, 33.0% 15 to 30 minutes, 26.4% 30 to 45 minutes, 2.6% 45 to 60 minutes, 14.2% 60 minutes or more (2006-2010 5-year est.)

**PRATTSVILLE** (town). Covers a land area of 19.626 square miles and a water area of 0.106 square miles. Located at 42.31° N. Lat; 74.41° W. Long. Elevation is 1,161 feet.
**Population:** 774 (1990); 665 (2000); 700 (2010); Density: 35.7 persons per square mile (2010); Race: 98.4% White, 0.1% Black, 0.6% Asian, 0.1% American Indian/Alaska Native, 0.0% Native Hawaiian/Other Pacific Islander, 0.8% Other, 1.1% Hispanic of any race (2010); Average household size: 2.33 (2010); Median age: 46.1 (2010); Males per 100 females: 101.7 (2010); Marriage status: 27.8% never married, 57.3% now married, 13.3% widowed, 1.6% divorced (2006-2010 5-year est.); Foreign born: 9.7% (2006-2010 5-year est.); Ancestry (includes multiple ancestries): 24.3% German, 22.3% Irish, 20.3% English, 14.9% Italian, 13.7% American (2006-2010 5-year est.).
**Economy:** Single-family building permits issued: 2 (2011); Multi-family building permits issued: 0 (2011); Employment by occupation: 4.4% management, 0.0% professional, 11.9% services, 14.6% sales, 2.2% farming, 35.1% construction, 9.4% production (2006-2010 5-year est.).
**Income:** Per capita income: $23,907 (2006-2010 5-year est.); Median household income: $40,764 (2006-2010 5-year est.); Average household income: $53,646 (2006-2010 5-year est.); Percent of households with income of $100,000 or more: 12.3% (2006-2010 5-year est.); Poverty rate: 16.4% (2006-2010 5-year est.).
**Education:** Percent of population age 25 and over with: High school diploma (including GED) or higher: 80.2% (2006-2010 5-year est.); Bachelor's degree or higher: 6.3% (2006-2010 5-year est.); Master's degree or higher: 3.8% (2006-2010 5-year est.).
**Housing:** Homeownership rate: 82.0% (2010); Median home value: $155,000 (2006-2010 5-year est.); Median contract rent: $246 per month (2006-2010 5-year est.); Median year structure built: 1960 (2006-2010 5-year est.).
**Transportation:** Commute to work: 90.7% car, 0.0% public transportation, 0.0% walk, 9.3% work from home (2006-2010 5-year est.); Travel time to work: 30.0% less than 15 minutes, 44.7% 15 to 30 minutes, 16.8% 30 to 45 minutes, 4.0% 45 to 60 minutes, 4.4% 60 minutes or more (2006-2010 5-year est.)

**PRATTSVILLE** (CDP). Covers a land area of 4.038 square miles and a water area of 0 square miles. Located at 42.34° N. Lat; 74.42° W. Long. Elevation is 1,161 feet.
**Population:** n/a (1990); n/a (2000); 355 (2010); Density: 87.9 persons per square mile (2010); Race: 98.6% White, 0.0% Black, 0.0% Asian, 0.3% American Indian/Alaska Native, 0.0% Native Hawaiian/Other Pacific Islander, 1.1% Other, 0.6% Hispanic of any race (2010); Average household size: 2.34 (2010); Median age: 42.5 (2010); Males per 100 females: 101.7 (2010); Marriage status: 51.8% never married, 21.3% now married, 23.2% widowed, 3.7% divorced (2006-2010 5-year est.); Foreign born: 2.2% (2006-2010 5-year est.); Ancestry (includes multiple ancestries): 30.1% English, 24.1% German, 19.1% Italian, 16.9% American, 12.9% Hungarian (2006-2010 5-year est.).
**Economy:** Employment by occupation: 4.0% management, 0.0% professional, 10.6% services, 19.2% sales, 0.0% farming, 24.5% construction, 15.2% production (2006-2010 5-year est.).
**Income:** Per capita income: $18,607 (2006-2010 5-year est.); Median household income: $37,917 (2006-2010 5-year est.); Average household income: $35,997 (2006-2010 5-year est.); Percent of households with income of $100,000 or more: 3.2% (2006-2010 5-year est.); Poverty rate: 19.9% (2006-2010 5-year est.).
**Education:** Percent of population age 25 and over with: High school diploma (including GED) or higher: 71.3% (2006-2010 5-year est.);

Bachelor's degree or higher: 5.4% (2006-2010 5-year est.); Master's degree or higher: 5.4% (2006-2010 5-year est.).
**Housing:** Homeownership rate: 72.3% (2010); Median home value: $36,800 (2006-2010 5-year est.); Median contract rent: $216 per month (2006-2010 5-year est.); Median year structure built: 1958 (2006-2010 5-year est.).
**Transportation:** Commute to work: 100.0% car, 0.0% public transportation, 0.0% walk, 0.0% work from home (2006-2010 5-year est.); Travel time to work: 41.1% less than 15 minutes, 32.9% 15 to 30 minutes, 15.8% 30 to 45 minutes, 5.5% 45 to 60 minutes, 4.8% 60 minutes or more (2006-2010 5-year est.)

**PURLING** (unincorporated postal area)
Zip Code: 12470
Covers a land area of 9.785 square miles and a water area of 0.039 square miles. Located at 42.30° N. Lat; 74.09° W. Long. Elevation is 482 feet. Population: 536 (2010); Density: 54.8 persons per square mile (2010); Race: 98.3% White, 0.6% Black, 0.2% Asian, 0.2% American Indian/Alaska Native, 0.0% Native Hawaiian/Other Pacific Islander, 0.7% Other, 2.8% Hispanic of any race (2010); Average household size: 2.39 (2010); Median age: 44.7 (2010); Males per 100 females: 92.8 (2010); Homeownership rate: 67.4% (2010)

**ROUND TOP** (unincorporated postal area)
Zip Code: 12473
Covers a land area of 15.015 square miles and a water area of 0 square miles. Located at 42.25° N. Lat; 74.04° W. Long. Elevation is 604 feet. Population: 861 (2010); Density: 57.3 persons per square mile (2010); Race: 97.1% White, 0.5% Black, 0.8% Asian, 0.0% American Indian/Alaska Native, 0.0% Native Hawaiian/Other Pacific Islander, 1.6% Other, 3.1% Hispanic of any race (2010); Average household size: 2.40 (2010); Median age: 45.5 (2010); Males per 100 females: 97.9 (2010); Homeownership rate: 79.1% (2010)

**SOUTH CAIRO** (unincorporated postal area)
Zip Code: 12482
Covers a land area of 2.211 square miles and a water area of 0 square miles. Located at 42.26° N. Lat; 73.95° W. Long. Elevation is 200 feet. Population: 680 (2010); Density: 307.5 persons per square mile (2010); Race: 91.6% White, 3.5% Black, 1.9% Asian, 0.0% American Indian/Alaska Native, 0.0% Native Hawaiian/Other Pacific Islander, 3.0% Other, 5.0% Hispanic of any race (2010); Average household size: 2.31 (2010); Median age: 42.2 (2010); Males per 100 females: 98.3 (2010); Homeownership rate: 76.2% (2010)

**SURPRISE** (unincorporated postal area)
Zip Code: 12176
Covers a land area of 3.326 square miles and a water area of 0.099 square miles. Located at 42.38° N. Lat; 73.98° W. Long. Elevation is 548 feet. Population: 198 (2010); Density: 59.5 persons per square mile (2010); Race: 93.4% White, 1.5% Black, 3.0% Asian, 0.0% American Indian/Alaska Native, 0.0% Native Hawaiian/Other Pacific Islander, 2.1% Other, 2.0% Hispanic of any race (2010); Average household size: 2.71 (2010); Median age: 42.0 (2010); Males per 100 females: 108.4 (2010); Homeownership rate: 89.0% (2010)

**TANNERSVILLE** (village). Covers a land area of 1.164 square miles and a water area of 0.032 square miles. Located at 42.19° N. Lat; 74.13° W. Long. Elevation is 1,900 feet.
**Population:** 471 (1990); 448 (2000); 539 (2010); Density: 462.9 persons per square mile (2010); Race: 93.3% White, 0.4% Black, 1.3% Asian, 0.2% American Indian/Alaska Native, 0.0% Native Hawaiian/Other Pacific Islander, 4.8% Other, 4.1% Hispanic of any race (2010); Average household size: 2.07 (2010); Median age: 45.5 (2010); Males per 100 females: 117.3 (2010); Marriage status: 30.6% never married, 43.6% now married, 10.8% widowed, 15.0% divorced (2006-2010 5-year est.); Foreign born: 6.9% (2006-2010 5-year est.); Ancestry (includes multiple ancestries): 16.6% German, 15.0% Irish, 14.7% Italian, 14.7% American, 10.4% English (2006-2010 5-year est.).
**Economy:** Single-family building permits issued: 1 (2011); Multi-family building permits issued: 0 (2011); Employment by occupation: 19.1% management, 0.0% professional, 3.5% services, 18.1% sales, 3.5% farming, 11.6% construction, 12.1% production (2006-2010 5-year est.).
**Income:** Per capita income: $20,102 (2006-2010 5-year est.); Median household income: $31,389 (2006-2010 5-year est.); Average household

income: $39,207 (2006-2010 5-year est.); Percent of households with income of $100,000 or more: 9.3% (2006-2010 5-year est.); Poverty rate: 14.5% (2006-2010 5-year est.).

**Education:** Percent of population age 25 and over with: High school diploma (including GED) or higher: 84.5% (2006-2010 5-year est.); Bachelor's degree or higher: 16.1% (2006-2010 5-year est.); Master's degree or higher: 0.0% (2006-2010 5-year est.).

### School District(s)
Hunter-Tannersville Central School District (PK-12)

   2009-10 Enrollment: 437 . . . . . . . . . . . . . . . . . . . . . . . . (518) 589-5400

**Housing:** Homeownership rate: 46.9% (2010); Median home value: $253,200 (2006-2010 5-year est.); Median contract rent: $615 per month (2006-2010 5-year est.); Median year structure built: 1943 (2006-2010 5-year est.).

**Transportation:** Commute to work: 85.8% car, 0.0% public transportation, 0.0% walk, 0.0% work from home (2006-2010 5-year est.); Travel time to work: 41.6% less than 15 minutes, 30.0% 15 to 30 minutes, 14.2% 30 to 45 minutes, 6.3% 45 to 60 minutes, 7.9% 60 minutes or more (2006-2010 5-year est.)

## WEST COXSACKIE (unincorporated postal area)
Zip Code: 12192

   Covers a land area of 17.165 square miles and a water area of 0.042 square miles. Located at 42.40° N. Lat; 73.82° W. Long. Elevation is 131 feet. Population: 1,722 (2010); Density: 100.3 persons per square mile (2010); Race: 96.6% White, 1.2% Black, 0.5% Asian, 0.2% American Indian/Alaska Native, 0.0% Native Hawaiian/Other Pacific Islander, 1.5% Other, 3.2% Hispanic of any race (2010); Average household size: 2.49 (2010); Median age: 45.5 (2010); Males per 100 females: 95.9 (2010); Homeownership rate: 87.0% (2010)

## WEST KILL (unincorporated postal area)
Zip Code: 12492

   Covers a land area of 38.463 square miles and a water area of 0 square miles. Located at 42.18° N. Lat; 74.33° W. Long. Elevation is 1,470 feet. Population: 271 (2010); Density: 7.0 persons per square mile (2010); Race: 97.8% White, 0.0% Black, 0.0% Asian, 0.4% American Indian/Alaska Native, 0.0% Native Hawaiian/Other Pacific Islander, 1.8% Other, 4.1% Hispanic of any race (2010); Average household size: 2.20 (2010); Median age: 51.8 (2010); Males per 100 females: 81.9 (2010); Homeownership rate: 81.3% (2010)

## WINDHAM (town). Covers a land area of 45.199 square miles and a water area of 0.136 square miles. Located at 42.31° N. Lat; 74.21° W. Long. Elevation is 1,516 feet.

**Population:** 1,682 (1990); 1,660 (2000); 1,703 (2010); Density: 37.7 persons per square mile (2010); Race: 97.0% White, 0.5% Black, 0.4% Asian, 0.4% American Indian/Alaska Native, 0.0% Native Hawaiian/Other Pacific Islander, 1.7% Other, 4.6% Hispanic of any race (2010); Average household size: 2.20 (2010); Median age: 48.5 (2010); Males per 100 females: 104.2 (2010); Marriage status: 25.8% never married, 59.1% now married, 4.8% widowed, 10.4% divorced (2006-2010 5-year est.); Foreign born: 1.9% (2006-2010 5-year est.); Ancestry (includes multiple ancestries): 26.7% American, 21.6% Irish, 17.8% Italian, 14.5% German, 9.6% English (2006-2010 5-year est.).

**Economy:** Single-family building permits issued: 6 (2011); Multi-family building permits issued: 0 (2011); Employment by occupation: 14.3% management, 3.0% professional, 7.3% services, 16.1% sales, 1.4% farming, 10.1% construction, 0.5% production (2006-2010 5-year est.).

**Income:** Per capita income: $22,619 (2006-2010 5-year est.); Median household income: $55,285 (2006-2010 5-year est.); Average household income: $58,086 (2006-2010 5-year est.); Percent of households with income of $100,000 or more: 10.8% (2006-2010 5-year est.); Poverty rate: 7.6% (2006-2010 5-year est.).

**Education:** Percent of population age 25 and over with: High school diploma (including GED) or higher: 88.3% (2006-2010 5-year est.); Bachelor's degree or higher: 28.1% (2006-2010 5-year est.); Master's degree or higher: 18.5% (2006-2010 5-year est.).

### School District(s)
Windham-Ashland-Jewett Central School District (KG-12)

   2009-10 Enrollment: 401 . . . . . . . . . . . . . . . . . . . . . . . . (518) 734-3400

**Housing:** Homeownership rate: 70.5% (2010); Median home value: $239,900 (2006-2010 5-year est.); Median contract rent: $601 per month (2006-2010 5-year est.); Median year structure built: 1978 (2006-2010 5-year est.).

**Safety:** Violent crime rate: 0.0 per 10,000 population; Property crime rate: 308.5 per 10,000 population (2010).

**Newspapers:** Windham Journal (Community news; Circulation 2,000)

**Transportation:** Commute to work: 82.6% car, 0.0% public transportation, 3.6% walk, 2.9% work from home (2006-2010 5-year est.); Travel time to work: 40.6% less than 15 minutes, 21.7% 15 to 30 minutes, 22.6% 30 to 45 minutes, 7.9% 45 to 60 minutes, 7.3% 60 minutes or more (2006-2010 5-year est.)

## WINDHAM (CDP). Covers a land area of 1.876 square miles and a water area of 0 square miles. Located at 42.31° N. Lat; 74.24° W. Long. Elevation is 1,516 feet.

**Population:** 367 (1990); 359 (2000); 367 (2010); Density: 195.5 persons per square mile (2010); Race: 92.4% White, 0.3% Black, 1.6% Asian, 0.0% American Indian/Alaska Native, 0.0% Native Hawaiian/Other Pacific Islander, 5.7% Other, 7.9% Hispanic of any race (2010); Average household size: 2.04 (2010); Median age: 47.9 (2010); Males per 100 females: 107.3 (2010); Marriage status: 28.6% never married, 51.4% now married, 9.3% widowed, 10.8% divorced (2006-2010 5-year est.); Foreign born: 2.3% (2006-2010 5-year est.); Ancestry (includes multiple ancestries): 29.5% Irish, 28.1% Italian, 17.7% American, 9.4% Scotch-Irish, 8.5% Danish (2006-2010 5-year est.).

**Economy:** Employment by occupation: 22.0% management, 0.0% professional, 17.0% services, 6.3% sales, 1.9% farming, 0.0% construction, 0.0% production (2006-2010 5-year est.).

**Income:** Per capita income: $26,349 (2006-2010 5-year est.); Median household income: $52,935 (2006-2010 5-year est.); Average household income: $57,270 (2006-2010 5-year est.); Percent of households with income of $100,000 or more: 20.5% (2006-2010 5-year est.); Poverty rate: 14.1% (2006-2010 5-year est.).

**Education:** Percent of population age 25 and over with: High school diploma (including GED) or higher: 95.7% (2006-2010 5-year est.); Bachelor's degree or higher: 13.1% (2006-2010 5-year est.); Master's degree or higher: 10.2% (2006-2010 5-year est.).

### School District(s)
Windham-Ashland-Jewett Central School District (KG-12)

   2009-10 Enrollment: 401 . . . . . . . . . . . . . . . . . . . . . . . . (518) 734-3400

**Housing:** Homeownership rate: 52.2% (2010); Median home value: $240,000 (2006-2010 5-year est.); Median contract rent: $514 per month (2006-2010 5-year est.); Median year structure built: 1961 (2006-2010 5-year est.).

**Transportation:** Commute to work: 86.5% car, 0.0% public transportation, 7.4% walk, 6.1% work from home (2006-2010 5-year est.); Travel time to work: 45.3% less than 15 minutes, 33.8% 15 to 30 minutes, 0.0% 30 to 45 minutes, 5.8% 45 to 60 minutes, 15.1% 60 minutes or more (2006-2010 5-year est.)

# Hamilton County

Located in north central New York, in the Adirondacks; drained by tributaries of the Hudson, and by the Raquette, Black, and Sacandaga Rivers; includes many lakes. Covers a land area of 1,720.39 square miles, a water area of 87.41 square miles, and is located in the Eastern Time Zone at 43.61° N. Lat., 74.50° W. Long. The county was founded in 1816. County seat is Lake Pleasant.

| Weather Station: Indian Lake 2 SW | | | | | | | | | Elevation: 1,660 feet | | |
|---|---|---|---|---|---|---|---|---|---|---|---|
| | Jan | Feb | Mar | Apr | May | Jun | Jul | Aug | Sep | Oct | Nov | Dec |
| High | 25 | 29 | 37 | 50 | 63 | 71 | 74 | 73 | 66 | 54 | 42 | 30 |
| Low | 5 | 6 | 15 | 28 | 39 | 49 | 53 | 52 | 45 | 34 | 25 | 13 |
| Precip | 2.8 | 2.3 | 2.9 | 3.2 | 3.6 | 3.7 | 3.9 | 3.6 | 3.7 | 4.2 | 3.3 | 2.9 |
| Snow | na | na | na | 3.0 | 0.1 | 0.0 | 0.0 | 0.0 | 0.0 | 0.7 | na | na |

*High and Low temperatures in degrees Fahrenheit; Precipitation and Snow in inches*

**Population:** 5,279 (1990); 5,379 (2000); 4,836 (2010); Race: 97.3% White, 0.7% Black, 0.5% Asian, 0.2% American Indian/Alaska Native, 0.1% Native Hawaiian/Other Pacific Islander, 1.2% Other, 1.1% Hispanic of any race (2010); Density: 2.8 persons per square mile (2010); Average household size: 2.10 (2010); Median age: 51.3 (2010); Males per 100 females: 102.3 (2010).

**Religion:** Six largest groups: 33.7% Catholicism, 15.7% Muslim Estimate, 8.0% Methodist/Pietist, 3.3% Presbyterian-Reformed, 2.3% Holiness, 0.8% Episcopalianism/Anglicanism (2010)

**Economy:** Unemployment rate: 11.2% (February 2012); Total civilian labor force: 2,723 (February 2012); Leading industries: 20.5% accommodation & food services; 18.3% retail trade; 12.7% construction (2009); Farms: 20

totaling 450 acres (2007); Companies that employ 500 or more persons: 0 (2009); Companies that employ 100 to 499 persons: 0 (2009); Companies that employ less than 100 persons: 198 (2009); Black-owned businesses: n/a (2007); Hispanic-owned businesses: n/a (2007); Asian-owned businesses: n/a (2007); Women-owned businesses: n/a (2007); Retail sales per capita: $6,741 (2010). Single-family building permits issued: 27 (2011); Multi-family building permits issued: 0 (2011).

**Income:** Per capita income: $29,965 (2006-2010 5-year est.); Median household income: $49,557 (2006-2010 5-year est.); Average household income: $62,903 (2006-2010 5-year est.); Percent of households with income of $100,000 or more: 15.4% (2006-2010 5-year est.); Poverty rate: 9.5% (2006-2010 5-year est.); Bankruptcy rate: 2.68% (2011).

**Education:** Percent of population age 25 and over with: High school diploma (including GED) or higher: 88.6% (2006-2010 5-year est.); Bachelor's degree or higher: 25.9% (2006-2010 5-year est.); Master's degree or higher: 12.0% (2006-2010 5-year est.).

**Housing:** Homeownership rate: 80.7% (2010); Median home value: $172,300 (2006-2010 5-year est.); Median contract rent: $505 per month (2006-2010 5-year est.); Median year structure built: 1963 (2006-2010 5-year est.).

**Health:** Birth rate: 73.0 per 10,000 population (2011); Death rate: 154.4 per 10,000 population (2011); Age-adjusted cancer mortality rate: 279.0 deaths per 100,000 population (2009); Number of physicians: 4.0 per 10,000 population (2008); Hospital beds: 0.0 per 10,000 population (2007); Hospital admissions: 0.0 per 10,000 population (2007).

**Environment:** Air Quality Index: 96.2% good, 3.8% moderate, 0.0% unhealthy for sensitive individuals, 0.0% unhealthy (percent of days in 2010)

**Elections:** 2008 Presidential election results: 35.9% Obama, 62.8% McCain, 0.8% Nader

**Additional Information Contacts**

Hamilton County Government . . . . . . . . . . . . . . . . . . . (518) 548-3076
   http://www.hamiltoncounty.com
Adirondacks Speculator Region Chamber of Commerce . . (518) 548-4521
   http://www.adrkmts.com
Indian Lake Chamber of Commerce . . . . . . . . . . . . . . . . (518) 648-5112
   http://www.indian-lake.com
Inlet Area Business Association. . . . . . . . . . . . . . . . . . . (315) 357-5501
   http://inletny.com

## Hamilton County Communities

**ARIETTA** (town). Covers a land area of 317.177 square miles and a water area of 12.229 square miles. Located at 43.50° N. Lat; 74.57° W. Long. Elevation is 1,693 feet.

**Population:** 300 (1990); 293 (2000); 304 (2010); Density: 1.0 persons per square mile (2010); Race: 98.4% White, 0.0% Black, 1.0% Asian, 0.0% American Indian/Alaska Native, 0.3% Native Hawaiian/Other Pacific Islander, 0.3% Other, 0.3% Hispanic of any race (2010); Average household size: 2.27 (2010); Median age: 50.0 (2010); Males per 100 females: 93.6 (2010); Marriage status: 19.8% never married, 54.3% now married, 13.8% widowed, 12.1% divorced (2006-2010 5-year est.); Foreign born: 2.7% (2006-2010 5-year est.); Ancestry (includes multiple ancestries): 43.2% German, 26.4% English, 23.6% Irish, 12.8% Italian, 7.4% American (2006-2010 5-year est.).

**Economy:** Single-family building permits issued: 3 (2011); Multi-family building permits issued: 0 (2011); Employment by occupation: 7.3% management, 0.0% professional, 4.9% services, 12.2% sales, 3.7% farming, 18.3% construction, 7.3% production (2006-2010 5-year est.).

**Income:** Per capita income: $25,930 (2006-2010 5-year est.); Median household income: $39,485 (2006-2010 5-year est.); Average household income: $59,313 (2006-2010 5-year est.); Percent of households with income of $100,000 or more: 22.7% (2006-2010 5-year est.); Poverty rate: 14.2% (2006-2010 5-year est.).

**Education:** Percent of population age 25 and over with: High school diploma (including GED) or higher: 96.5% (2006-2010 5-year est.); Bachelor's degree or higher: 29.6% (2006-2010 5-year est.); Master's degree or higher: 6.1% (2006-2010 5-year est.).

**Housing:** Homeownership rate: 88.8% (2010); Median home value: $187,500 (2006-2010 5-year est.); Median contract rent: n/a per month (2006-2010 5-year est.); Median year structure built: 1971 (2006-2010 5-year est.).

**Transportation:** Commute to work: 74.4% car, 0.0% public transportation, 6.1% walk, 12.2% work from home (2006-2010 5-year est.); Travel time to work: 50.0% less than 15 minutes, 23.6% 15 to 30 minutes, 9.7% 30 to 45

minutes, 12.5% 45 to 60 minutes, 4.2% 60 minutes or more (2006-2010 5-year est.)

**BENSON** (town). Covers a land area of 82.617 square miles and a water area of 0.580 square miles. Located at 43.29° N. Lat; 74.36° W. Long. Elevation is 1,165 feet.

**Population:** 168 (1990); 201 (2000); 192 (2010); Density: 2.3 persons per square mile (2010); Race: 93.2% White, 0.0% Black, 0.0% Asian, 0.5% American Indian/Alaska Native, 0.0% Native Hawaiian/Other Pacific Islander, 6.3% Other, 0.5% Hispanic of any race (2010); Average household size: 2.21 (2010); Median age: 46.0 (2010); Males per 100 females: 102.1 (2010); Marriage status: 13.3% never married, 80.7% now married, 1.5% widowed, 4.4% divorced (2006-2010 5-year est.); Foreign born: 3.3% (2006-2010 5-year est.); Ancestry (includes multiple ancestries): 27.0% Irish, 25.7% German, 24.3% English, 7.2% Norwegian, 5.9% Russian (2006-2010 5-year est.).

**Economy:** Employment by occupation: 16.7% management, 0.0% professional, 5.6% services, 12.5% sales, 0.0% farming, 6.9% construction, 2.8% production (2006-2010 5-year est.).

**Income:** Per capita income: $29,303 (2006-2010 5-year est.); Median household income: $58,000 (2006-2010 5-year est.); Average household income: $64,959 (2006-2010 5-year est.); Percent of households with income of $100,000 or more: 14.1% (2006-2010 5-year est.); Poverty rate: 3.9% (2006-2010 5-year est.).

**Education:** Percent of population age 25 and over with: High school diploma (including GED) or higher: 88.7% (2006-2010 5-year est.); Bachelor's degree or higher: 29.0% (2006-2010 5-year est.); Master's degree or higher: 12.1% (2006-2010 5-year est.).

**Housing:** Homeownership rate: 87.4% (2010); Median home value: $172,200 (2006-2010 5-year est.); Median contract rent: $950 per month (2006-2010 5-year est.); Median year structure built: 1966 (2006-2010 5-year est.).

**Transportation:** Commute to work: 87.8% car, 0.0% public transportation, 0.0% walk, 12.2% work from home (2006-2010 5-year est.); Travel time to work: 21.5% less than 15 minutes, 18.5% 15 to 30 minutes, 27.7% 30 to 45 minutes, 10.8% 45 to 60 minutes, 21.5% 60 minutes or more (2006-2010 5-year est.)

**BLUE MOUNTAIN LAKE** (unincorporated postal area)

Zip Code: 12812

Covers a land area of 61.949 square miles and a water area of 4.533 square miles. Located at 43.87° N. Lat; 74.38° W. Long. Elevation is 1,824 feet. Population: 150 (2010); Density: 2.4 persons per square mile (2010); Race: 98.7% White, 0.0% Black, 0.0% Asian, 0.0% American Indian/Alaska Native, 0.0% Native Hawaiian/Other Pacific Islander, 1.3% Other, 0.0% Hispanic of any race (2010); Average household size: 1.97 (2010); Median age: 56.0 (2010); Males per 100 females: 80.7 (2010); Homeownership rate: 79.0% (2010)

**HOFFMEISTER** (unincorporated postal area)

Zip Code: 13353

Covers a land area of 197.913 square miles and a water area of 3.716 square miles. Located at 43.44° N. Lat; 74.69° W. Long. Elevation is 1,857 feet. Population: 86 (2010); Density: 0.4 persons per square mile (2010); Race: 98.8% White, 0.0% Black, 0.0% Asian, 0.0% American Indian/Alaska Native, 0.0% Native Hawaiian/Other Pacific Islander, 1.2% Other, 0.0% Hispanic of any race (2010); Average household size: 1.95 (2010); Median age: 53.0 (2010); Males per 100 females: 138.9 (2010); Homeownership rate: 95.5% (2010)

**HOPE** (town). Covers a land area of 40.702 square miles and a water area of 0.932 square miles. Located at 43.32° N. Lat; 74.23° W. Long. Elevation is 810 feet.

**Population:** 358 (1990); 392 (2000); 403 (2010); Density: 9.9 persons per square mile (2010); Race: 98.3% White, 0.2% Black, 0.0% Asian, 0.2% American Indian/Alaska Native, 0.0% Native Hawaiian/Other Pacific Islander, 1.3% Other, 1.0% Hispanic of any race (2010); Average household size: 2.37 (2010); Median age: 46.8 (2010); Males per 100 females: 98.5 (2010); Marriage status: 25.5% never married, 60.9% now married, 4.9% widowed, 8.7% divorced (2006-2010 5-year est.); Foreign born: 2.9% (2006-2010 5-year est.); Ancestry (includes multiple ancestries): 14.1% German, 13.6% Irish, 12.7% English, 8.9% Dutch, 6.5% French (2006-2010 5-year est.).

**Economy:** Single-family building permits issued: 0 (2011); Multi-family building permits issued: 0 (2011); Employment by occupation: 4.1%

management, 0.8% professional, 23.4% services, 8.6% sales, 1.6% farming, 18.9% construction, 4.9% production (2006-2010 5-year est.).
**Income:** Per capita income: $34,339 (2006-2010 5-year est.); Median household income: $45,625 (2006-2010 5-year est.); Average household income: $74,338 (2006-2010 5-year est.); Percent of households with income of $100,000 or more: 24.5% (2006-2010 5-year est.); Poverty rate: 10.0% (2006-2010 5-year est.).
**Education:** Percent of population age 25 and over with: High school diploma (including GED) or higher: 89.4% (2006-2010 5-year est.); Bachelor's degree or higher: 28.0% (2006-2010 5-year est.); Master's degree or higher: 11.8% (2006-2010 5-year est.).
**Housing:** Homeownership rate: 86.5% (2010); Median home value: $118,100 (2006-2010 5-year est.); Median contract rent: $496 per month (2006-2010 5-year est.); Median year structure built: 1970 (2006-2010 5-year est.).
**Transportation:** Commute to work: 96.2% car, 0.0% public transportation, 0.0% walk, 1.3% work from home (2006-2010 5-year est.); Travel time to work: 34.7% less than 15 minutes, 15.7% 15 to 30 minutes, 37.3% 30 to 45 minutes, 1.3% 45 to 60 minutes, 11.0% 60 minutes or more (2006-2010 5-year est.)

## INDIAN LAKE (town). Covers a land area of 251.800 square miles and a water area of 14.438 square miles. Located at 43.80° N. Lat; 74.41° W. Long. Elevation is 1,742 feet.

**History:** Dr. Thomas Durant and William West Durant, father and son, were early promoters of the Indian Lake section of the Adirondacks. The father, financier and railroad builder, constructed a railroad from Saratoga to Blue Mountain Lake, and the son expanded his father's promotional activities by building elaborate camps and selling them to the wealthy.
**Population:** 1,481 (1990); 1,471 (2000); 1,352 (2010); Density: 5.4 persons per square mile (2010); Race: 97.8% White, 0.6% Black, 0.3% Asian, 0.2% American Indian/Alaska Native, 0.0% Native Hawaiian/Other Pacific Islander, 1.1% Other, 1.0% Hispanic of any race (2010); Average household size: 2.01 (2010); Median age: 52.7 (2010); Males per 100 females: 99.7 (2010); Marriage status: 11.4% never married, 65.4% now married, 11.2% widowed, 12.0% divorced (2006-2010 5-year est.); Foreign born: 3.7% (2006-2010 5-year est.); Ancestry (includes multiple ancestries): 23.2% Irish, 21.3% English, 16.4% German, 13.0% French, 8.1% Scottish (2006-2010 5-year est.).
**Economy:** Single-family building permits issued: 3 (2011); Multi-family building permits issued: 0 (2011); Employment by occupation: 8.1% management, 0.0% professional, 13.1% services, 16.8% sales, 0.3% farming, 19.0% construction, 5.9% production (2006-2010 5-year est.).
**Income:** Per capita income: $26,630 (2006-2010 5-year est.); Median household income: $44,135 (2006-2010 5-year est.); Average household income: $54,637 (2006-2010 5-year est.); Percent of households with income of $100,000 or more: 11.3% (2006-2010 5-year est.); Poverty rate: 5.6% (2006-2010 5-year est.).
**Education:** Percent of population age 25 and over with: High school diploma (including GED) or higher: 90.4% (2006-2010 5-year est.); Bachelor's degree or higher: 26.3% (2006-2010 5-year est.); Master's degree or higher: 12.1% (2006-2010 5-year est.).
**School District(s)**
Indian Lake Central School District (PK-12)
   2009-10 Enrollment: 166 . . . . . . . . . . . . . . . . . . . . . (518) 648-5024
**Housing:** Homeownership rate: 78.7% (2010); Median home value: $159,800 (2006-2010 5-year est.); Median contract rent: $511 per month (2006-2010 5-year est.); Median year structure built: 1963 (2006-2010 5-year est.).
**Transportation:** Commute to work: 88.7% car, 0.0% public transportation, 4.7% walk, 4.9% work from home (2006-2010 5-year est.); Travel time to work: 46.4% less than 15 minutes, 25.7% 15 to 30 minutes, 16.6% 30 to 45 minutes, 1.9% 45 to 60 minutes, 9.4% 60 minutes or more (2006-2010 5-year est.)
**Additional Information Contacts**
Indian Lake Chamber of Commerce . . . . . . . . . . . . . . . (518) 648-5112
   http://www.indian-lake.com

## INLET (town). Covers a land area of 62.195 square miles and a water area of 4.176 square miles. Located at 43.72° N. Lat; 74.71° W. Long. Elevation is 1,749 feet.

**Population:** 343 (1990); 406 (2000); 333 (2010); Density: 5.4 persons per square mile (2010); Race: 98.8% White, 0.0% Black, 0.3% Asian, 0.6% American Indian/Alaska Native, 0.0% Native Hawaiian/Other Pacific Islander, 0.3% Other, 0.3% Hispanic of any race (2010); Average

household size: 2.11 (2010); Median age: 46.9 (2010); Males per 100 females: 106.8 (2010); Marriage status: 19.2% never married, 71.6% now married, 4.5% widowed, 4.7% divorced (2006-2010 5-year est.); Foreign born: 0.4% (2006-2010 5-year est.); Ancestry (includes multiple ancestries): 31.6% German, 31.4% English, 27.6% Irish, 14.9% Italian, 13.5% American (2006-2010 5-year est.).
**Economy:** Single-family building permits issued: 5 (2011); Multi-family building permits issued: 0 (2011); Employment by occupation: 23.3% management, 0.0% professional, 18.6% services, 23.3% sales, 6.5% farming, 10.2% construction, 0.0% production (2006-2010 5-year est.).
**Income:** Per capita income: $30,172 (2006-2010 5-year est.); Median household income: $62,083 (2006-2010 5-year est.); Average household income: $63,675 (2006-2010 5-year est.); Percent of households with income of $100,000 or more: 14.8% (2006-2010 5-year est.); Poverty rate: 8.6% (2006-2010 5-year est.).
**Education:** Percent of population age 25 and over with: High school diploma (including GED) or higher: 93.1% (2006-2010 5-year est.); Bachelor's degree or higher: 40.5% (2006-2010 5-year est.); Master's degree or higher: 18.2% (2006-2010 5-year est.).
**School District(s)**
Inlet Common School District (PK-06)
   2009-10 Enrollment: 36 . . . . . . . . . . . . . . . . . . . . . . . (315) 357-3305
**Housing:** Homeownership rate: 71.5% (2010); Median home value: $290,000 (2006-2010 5-year est.); Median contract rent: $389 per month (2006-2010 5-year est.); Median year structure built: 1953 (2006-2010 5-year est.).
**Safety:** Violent crime rate: 0.0 per 10,000 population; Property crime rate: 275.5 per 10,000 population (2010).
**Transportation:** Commute to work: 79.5% car, 0.0% public transportation, 14.0% walk, 6.5% work from home (2006-2010 5-year est.); Travel time to work: 57.2% less than 15 minutes, 34.2% 15 to 30 minutes, 5.3% 30 to 45 minutes, 1.6% 45 to 60 minutes, 1.6% 60 minutes or more (2006-2010 5-year est.)
**Additional Information Contacts**
Inlet Area Business Association . . . . . . . . . . . . . . . . . . (315) 357-5501
   http://inletny.com

## LAKE PLEASANT (town). County seat. Covers a land area of 187.983 square miles and a water area of 9.999 square miles. Located at 43.57° N. Lat; 74.42° W. Long. Elevation is 1,785 feet.

**Population:** 887 (1990); 876 (2000); 781 (2010); Density: 4.2 persons per square mile (2010); Race: 97.4% White, 0.5% Black, 0.8% Asian, 0.4% American Indian/Alaska Native, 0.4% Native Hawaiian/Other Pacific Islander, 0.5% Other, 1.0% Hispanic of any race (2010); Average household size: 2.13 (2010); Median age: 52.8 (2010); Males per 100 females: 98.7 (2010); Marriage status: 17.2% never married, 72.1% now married, 6.4% widowed, 4.3% divorced (2006-2010 5-year est.); Foreign born: 1.3% (2006-2010 5-year est.); Ancestry (includes multiple ancestries): 28.2% German, 25.4% Irish, 16.6% English, 15.1% French, 11.6% Italian (2006-2010 5-year est.).
**Economy:** Single-family building permits issued: 4 (2011); Multi-family building permits issued: 0 (2011); Employment by occupation: 10.9% management, 1.5% professional, 17.0% services, 16.2% sales, 0.3% farming, 36.0% construction, 8.1% production (2006-2010 5-year est.).
**Income:** Per capita income: $35,335 (2006-2010 5-year est.); Median household income: $45,417 (2006-2010 5-year est.); Average household income: $75,159 (2006-2010 5-year est.); Percent of households with income of $100,000 or more: 15.4% (2006-2010 5-year est.); Poverty rate: 12.6% (2006-2010 5-year est.).
**Education:** Percent of population age 25 and over with: High school diploma (including GED) or higher: 83.8% (2006-2010 5-year est.); Bachelor's degree or higher: 15.6% (2006-2010 5-year est.); Master's degree or higher: 9.0% (2006-2010 5-year est.).
**Housing:** Homeownership rate: 76.4% (2010); Median home value: $159,700 (2006-2010 5-year est.); Median contract rent: $556 per month (2006-2010 5-year est.); Median year structure built: 1965 (2006-2010 5-year est.).
**Transportation:** Commute to work: 79.0% car, 0.0% public transportation, 17.8% walk, 2.9% work from home (2006-2010 5-year est.); Travel time to work: 77.6% less than 15 minutes, 10.4% 15 to 30 minutes, 0.0% 30 to 45 minutes, 0.5% 45 to 60 minutes, 11.5% 60 minutes or more (2006-2010 5-year est.)

**LONG LAKE** (town). Covers a land area of 407.032 square miles and a water area of 42.804 square miles. Located at 43.95° N. Lat; 74.64° W. Long. Elevation is 1,673 feet.

**Population:** 930 (1990); 852 (2000); 711 (2010); Density: 1.7 persons per square mile (2010); Race: 96.9% White, 1.5% Black, 0.4% Asian, 0.1% American Indian/Alaska Native, 0.0% Native Hawaiian/Other Pacific Islander, 1.1% Other, 2.1% Hispanic of any race (2010); Average household size: 1.96 (2010); Median age: 53.5 (2010); Males per 100 females: 112.9 (2010); Marriage status: 8.2% never married, 74.3% now married, 7.6% widowed, 9.9% divorced (2006-2010 5-year est.); Foreign born: 4.5% (2006-2010 5-year est.); Ancestry (includes multiple ancestries): 29.2% Irish, 22.8% English, 15.7% German, 11.7% Scottish, 10.4% French (2006-2010 5-year est.).

**Economy:** Single-family building permits issued: 3 (2011); Multi-family building permits issued: 0 (2011); Employment by occupation: 14.6% management, 0.3% professional, 14.0% services, 9.3% sales, 1.1% farming, 11.0% construction, 4.8% production (2006-2010 5-year est.).

**Income:** Per capita income: $33,530 (2006-2010 5-year est.); Median household income: $54,712 (2006-2010 5-year est.); Average household income: $67,946 (2006-2010 5-year est.); Percent of households with income of $100,000 or more: 21.9% (2006-2010 5-year est.); Poverty rate: 2.8% (2006-2010 5-year est.).

**Education:** Percent of population age 25 and over with: High school diploma (including GED) or higher: 97.0% (2006-2010 5-year est.); Bachelor's degree or higher: 39.9% (2006-2010 5-year est.); Master's degree or higher: 21.9% (2006-2010 5-year est.).

### School District(s)
Long Lake Central School District (PK-12)
   2009-10 Enrollment: 64 . . . . . . . . . . . . . . . . . . . . . . . . . . . (518) 624-2147

**Housing:** Homeownership rate: 77.7% (2010); Median home value: $227,700 (2006-2010 5-year est.); Median contract rent: $475 per month (2006-2010 5-year est.); Median year structure built: 1961 (2006-2010 5-year est.).

**Transportation:** Commute to work: 82.6% car, 0.0% public transportation, 13.8% walk, 2.4% work from home (2006-2010 5-year est.); Travel time to work: 72.7% less than 15 minutes, 9.7% 15 to 30 minutes, 14.4% 30 to 45 minutes, 0.3% 45 to 60 minutes, 2.8% 60 minutes or more (2006-2010 5-year est.)

**LONG LAKE** (CDP). Covers a land area of 11.721 square miles and a water area of 2.209 square miles. Located at 43.95° N. Lat; 74.44° W. Long. Elevation is 1,673 feet.

**Population:** n/a (1990); n/a (2000); 547 (2010); Density: 46.7 persons per square mile (2010); Race: 96.5% White, 1.6% Black, 0.4% Asian, 0.2% American Indian/Alaska Native, 0.0% Native Hawaiian/Other Pacific Islander, 1.3% Other, 1.5% Hispanic of any race (2010); Average household size: 1.95 (2010); Median age: 52.3 (2010); Males per 100 females: 109.6 (2010); Marriage status: 9.6% never married, 77.8% now married, 7.3% widowed, 5.2% divorced (2006-2010 5-year est.); Foreign born: 5.2% (2006-2010 5-year est.); Ancestry (includes multiple ancestries): 35.1% Irish, 22.0% English, 18.1% German, 13.8% Scottish, 9.7% French (2006-2010 5-year est.).

**Economy:** Employment by occupation: 16.0% management, 0.4% professional, 18.1% services, 7.6% sales, 0.0% farming, 5.9% construction, 2.1% production (2006-2010 5-year est.).

**Income:** Per capita income: $33,410 (2006-2010 5-year est.); Median household income: $54,615 (2006-2010 5-year est.); Average household income: $70,967 (2006-2010 5-year est.); Percent of households with income of $100,000 or more: 22.1% (2006-2010 5-year est.); Poverty rate: 3.0% (2006-2010 5-year est.).

**Education:** Percent of population age 25 and over with: High school diploma (including GED) or higher: 98.4% (2006-2010 5-year est.); Bachelor's degree or higher: 40.9% (2006-2010 5-year est.); Master's degree or higher: 22.1% (2006-2010 5-year est.).

### School District(s)
Long Lake Central School District (PK-12)
   2009-10 Enrollment: 64 . . . . . . . . . . . . . . . . . . . . . . . . . . . (518) 624-2147

**Housing:** Homeownership rate: 78.3% (2010); Median home value: $223,300 (2006-2010 5-year est.); Median contract rent: $515 per month (2006-2010 5-year est.); Median year structure built: 1957 (2006-2010 5-year est.).

**Transportation:** Commute to work: 84.3% car, 0.0% public transportation, 13.5% walk, 2.2% work from home (2006-2010 5-year est.); Travel time to work: 80.7% less than 15 minutes, 7.8% 15 to 30 minutes, 11.5% 30 to 45

**MOREHOUSE** (town). Covers a land area of 191.063 square miles and a water area of 3.704 square miles. Located at 43.44° N. Lat; 74.69° W. Long.

**Population:** 106 (1990); 151 (2000); 86 (2010); Density: 0.5 persons per square mile (2010); Race: 98.8% White, 0.0% Black, 0.0% Asian, 0.0% American Indian/Alaska Native, 0.0% Native Hawaiian/Other Pacific Islander, 1.2% Other, 0.0% Hispanic of any race (2010); Average household size: 1.95 (2010); Median age: 53.0 (2010); Males per 100 females: 138.9 (2010); Marriage status: 5.2% never married, 53.4% now married, 27.6% widowed, 13.8% divorced (2006-2010 5-year est.); Foreign born: 0.0% (2006-2010 5-year est.); Ancestry (includes multiple ancestries): 18.6% German, 15.7% French, 11.4% Dutch, 8.6% Irish, 4.3% American (2006-2010 5-year est.).

**Economy:** Single-family building permits issued: 0 (2011); Multi-family building permits issued: 0 (2011); Employment by occupation: 19.4% management, 0.0% professional, 8.3% services, 38.9% sales, 0.0% farming, 19.4% construction, 0.0% production (2006-2010 5-year est.).

**Income:** Per capita income: $18,840 (2006-2010 5-year est.); Median household income: $27,222 (2006-2010 5-year est.); Average household income: $38,976 (2006-2010 5-year est.); Percent of households with income of $100,000 or more: 0.0% (2006-2010 5-year est.); Poverty rate: 4.3% (2006-2010 5-year est.).

**Education:** Percent of population age 25 and over with: High school diploma (including GED) or higher: 94.8% (2006-2010 5-year est.); Bachelor's degree or higher: 0.0% (2006-2010 5-year est.); Master's degree or higher: 0.0% (2006-2010 5-year est.).

**Housing:** Homeownership rate: 95.5% (2010); Median home value: $281,300 (2006-2010 5-year est.); Median contract rent: n/a per month (2006-2010 5-year est.); Median year structure built: 1960 (2006-2010 5-year est.).

**Transportation:** Commute to work: 100.0% car, 0.0% public transportation, 0.0% walk, 0.0% work from home (2006-2010 5-year est.); Travel time to work: 19.4% less than 15 minutes, 44.4% 15 to 30 minutes, 25.0% 30 to 45 minutes, 11.1% 45 to 60 minutes, 0.0% 60 minutes or more (2006-2010 5-year est.)

**PISECO** (unincorporated postal area)
Zip Code: 12139
   Covers a land area of 239.084 square miles and a water area of 10.022 square miles. Located at 43.50° N. Lat; 74.57° W. Long. Elevation is 1,677 feet. Population: 295 (2010); Density: 1.2 persons per square mile (2010); Race: 98.3% White, 0.0% Black, 1.0% Asian, 0.0% American Indian/Alaska Native, 0.3% Native Hawaiian/Other Pacific Islander, 0.4% Other, 0.3% Hispanic of any race (2010); Average household size: 2.27 (2010); Median age: 49.8 (2010); Males per 100 females: 94.1 (2010); Homeownership rate: 88.4% (2010)

**RAQUETTE LAKE** (unincorporated postal area)
Zip Code: 13436
   Covers a land area of 38.336 square miles and a water area of 9.611 square miles. Located at 43.81° N. Lat; 74.66° W. Long. Elevation is 1,765 feet. Population: 108 (2010); Density: 2.8 persons per square mile (2010); Race: 100.0% White, 0.0% Black, 0.0% Asian, 0.0% American Indian/Alaska Native, 0.0% Native Hawaiian/Other Pacific Islander, 0.0% Other, 0.0% Hispanic of any race (2010); Average household size: 1.86 (2010); Median age: 55.4 (2010); Males per 100 females: 129.8 (2010); Homeownership rate: 75.8% (2010)

**SABAEL** (unincorporated postal area)
Zip Code: 12864
   Covers a land area of 0.208 square miles and a water area of 0 square miles. Located at 43.72° N. Lat; 74.30° W. Long. Elevation is 1,745 feet. Population: 36 (2010); Density: 172.5 persons per square mile (2010); Race: 97.2% White, 0.0% Black, 0.0% Asian, 0.0% American Indian/Alaska Native, 0.0% Native Hawaiian/Other Pacific Islander, 2.8% Other, 0.0% Hispanic of any race (2010); Average household size: 2.00 (2010); Median age: 56.5 (2010); Males per 100 females: 100.0 (2010); Homeownership rate: 83.3% (2010)

**SPECULATOR** (village). Covers a land area of 44.570 square miles and a water area of 2.594 square miles. Located at 43.58° N. Lat; 74.35° W. Long. Elevation is 1,739 feet.
**Population:** 400 (1990); 348 (2000); 324 (2010); Density: 7.3 persons per square mile (2010); Race: 95.7% White, 0.9% Black, 1.9% Asian, 0.6% American Indian/Alaska Native, 0.9% Native Hawaiian/Other Pacific Islander, 0.0% Other, 0.9% Hispanic of any race (2010); Average household size: 2.09 (2010); Median age: 53.0 (2010); Males per 100 females: 97.6 (2010); Marriage status: 23.7% never married, 60.9% now married, 7.5% widowed, 7.9% divorced (2006-2010 5-year est.); Foreign born: 2.9% (2006-2010 5-year est.); Ancestry (includes multiple ancestries): 24.4% English, 22.8% German, 22.1% Irish, 21.2% French, 9.9% Polish (2006-2010 5-year est.).
**Economy:** Single-family building permits issued: 3 (2011); Multi-family building permits issued: 0 (2011); Employment by occupation: 15.5% management, 3.6% professional, 16.1% services, 24.4% sales, 0.6% farming, 19.0% construction, 4.2% production (2006-2010 5-year est.).
**Income:** Per capita income: $50,912 (2006-2010 5-year est.); Median household income: $54,583 (2006-2010 5-year est.); Average household income: $110,399 (2006-2010 5-year est.); Percent of households with income of $100,000 or more: 22.9% (2006-2010 5-year est.); Poverty rate: 3.2% (2006-2010 5-year est.).
**Education:** Percent of population age 25 and over with: High school diploma (including GED) or higher: 89.2% (2006-2010 5-year est.); Bachelor's degree or higher: 28.6% (2006-2010 5-year est.); Master's degree or higher: 18.2% (2006-2010 5-year est.).

### School District(s)
Lake Pleasant Central School District (PK-09)
  2009-10 Enrollment: 99 . . . . . . . . . . . . . . . . . . . . . . . . (518) 548-7571
**Housing:** Homeownership rate: 68.5% (2010); Median home value: $155,600 (2006-2010 5-year est.); Median contract rent: $511 per month (2006-2010 5-year est.); Median year structure built: 1959 (2006-2010 5-year est.).
**Newspapers:** Hamilton County News (Community news; Circulation 3,699)
**Transportation:** Commute to work: 83.9% car, 0.0% public transportation, 15.5% walk, 0.0% work from home (2006-2010 5-year est.); Travel time to work: 67.9% less than 15 minutes, 14.9% 15 to 30 minutes, 0.0% 30 to 45 minutes, 1.2% 45 to 60 minutes, 16.1% 60 minutes or more (2006-2010 5-year est.).
**Additional Information Contacts**
Adirondacks Speculator Region Chamber of Commerce . . (518) 548-4521
  http://www.adrkmts.com

**WELLS** (town). Covers a land area of 176.799 square miles and a water area of 1.564 square miles. Located at 43.47° N. Lat; 74.28° W. Long. Elevation is 1,010 feet.
**Population:** 706 (1990); 737 (2000); 674 (2010); Density: 3.8 persons per square mile (2010); Race: 95.7% White, 1.6% Black, 1.0% Asian, 0.0% American Indian/Alaska Native, 0.0% Native Hawaiian/Other Pacific Islander, 1.7% Other, 1.2% Hispanic of any race (2010); Average household size: 2.21 (2010); Median age: 49.2 (2010); Males per 100 females: 101.8 (2010); Marriage status: 30.1% never married, 56.2% now married, 5.6% widowed, 8.1% divorced (2006-2010 5-year est.); Foreign born: 3.5% (2006-2010 5-year est.); Ancestry (includes multiple ancestries): 22.8% German, 18.6% English, 16.2% Irish, 9.5% Italian, 8.8% French (2006-2010 5-year est.).
**Economy:** Single-family building permits issued: 6 (2011); Multi-family building permits issued: 0 (2011); Employment by occupation: 6.5% management, 1.7% professional, 20.1% services, 26.4% sales, 4.4% farming, 14.8% construction, 11.6% production (2006-2010 5-year est.).
**Income:** Per capita income: $26,972 (2006-2010 5-year est.); Median household income: $47,788 (2006-2010 5-year est.); Average household income: $56,301 (2006-2010 5-year est.); Percent of households with income of $100,000 or more: 11.5% (2006-2010 5-year est.); Poverty rate: 19.6% (2006-2010 5-year est.).
**Education:** Percent of population age 25 and over with: High school diploma (including GED) or higher: 76.5% (2006-2010 5-year est.); Bachelor's degree or higher: 11.6% (2006-2010 5-year est.); Master's degree or higher: 3.7% (2006-2010 5-year est.).

### School District(s)
Wells Central School District (PK-12)
  2009-10 Enrollment: 188 . . . . . . . . . . . . . . . . . . . . . . (518) 924-6000
**Housing:** Homeownership rate: 87.8% (2010); Median home value: $169,500 (2006-2010 5-year est.); Median contract rent: $525 per month

(2006-2010 5-year est.); Median year structure built: 1966 (2006-2010 5-year est.).
**Transportation:** Commute to work: 92.4% car, 0.0% public transportation, 4.7% walk, 2.9% work from home (2006-2010 5-year est.); Travel time to work: 21.5% less than 15 minutes, 29.1% 15 to 30 minutes, 24.3% 30 to 45 minutes, 16.5% 45 to 60 minutes, 8.6% 60 minutes or more (2006-2010 5-year est.)

# Herkimer County

Located in central and north central New York, extending north into the Adirondacks and south into the Mohawk Valley; drained by the Mohawk, Unadilla, Black, and Moose Rivers. Covers a land area of 1,411.25 square miles, a water area of 47.10 square miles, and is located in the Eastern Time Zone at 43.18° N. Lat., 74.97° W. Long. The county was founded in 1791. County seat is Herkimer.

Herkimer County is part of the Utica-Rome, NY Metropolitan Statistical Area. The entire metro area includes: Herkimer County, NY; Oneida County, NY

Weather Station: Old Forge                     Elevation: 1,720 feet

| | Jan | Feb | Mar | Apr | May | Jun | Jul | Aug | Sep | Oct | Nov | Dec |
|---|---|---|---|---|---|---|---|---|---|---|---|---|
| High | 25 | 29 | 37 | 50 | 63 | 71 | 75 | 74 | 66 | 54 | 41 | 30 |
| Low | 3 | 6 | 15 | 28 | 39 | 49 | 53 | 52 | 44 | 33 | 24 | 11 |
| Precip | 3.9 | 2.9 | 3.4 | 3.7 | 4.2 | 4.1 | 4.4 | 4.4 | 4.7 | 4.7 | 4.6 | 4.3 |
| Snow | 48.4 | 31.6 | 27.4 | 9.2 | 0.8 | tr | 0.0 | 0.0 | tr | 3.1 | 19.3 | 41.4 |

*High and Low temperatures in degrees Fahrenheit; Precipitation and Snow in inches*

**Population:** 65,797 (1990); 64,427 (2000); 64,519 (2010); Race: 96.6% White, 1.1% Black, 0.5% Asian, 0.2% American Indian/Alaska Native, 0.0% Native Hawaiian/Other Pacific Islander, 1.6% Other, 1.6% Hispanic of any race (2010); Density: 45.7 persons per square mile (2010); Average household size: 2.40 (2010); Median age: 42.1 (2010); Males per 100 females: 95.9 (2010).
**Religion:** Six largest groups: 23.9% Catholicism, 4.5% Methodist/Pietist, 2.0% Baptist, 1.9% Presbyterian-Reformed, 1.6% Lutheran, 1.1% Episcopalianism/Anglicanism (2010)
**Economy:** Unemployment rate: 10.4% (February 2012); Total civilian labor force: 31,265 (February 2012); Leading industries: 23.4% manufacturing; 19.7% health care and social assistance; 18.4% retail trade (2009); Farms: 672 totaling 140,017 acres (2007); Companies that employ 500 or more persons: 1 (2009); Companies that employ 100 to 499 persons: 14 (2009); Companies that employ less than 100 persons: 1,155 (2009); Black-owned businesses: n/a (2007); Hispanic-owned businesses: n/a (2007); Asian-owned businesses: n/a (2007); Women-owned businesses: 1,133 (2007); Retail sales per capita: $8,153 (2010). Single-family building permits issued: 81 (2011); Multi-family building permits issued: 0 (2011).
**Income:** Per capita income: $21,908 (2006-2010 5-year est.); Median household income: $42,318 (2006-2010 5-year est.); Average household income: $52,516 (2006-2010 5-year est.); Percent of households with income of $100,000 or more: 10.5% (2006-2010 5-year est.); Poverty rate: 12.8% (2006-2010 5-year est.); Bankruptcy rate: 3.07% (2011).
**Taxes:** Total county taxes per capita: $839 (2009); County property taxes per capita: $397 (2009).
**Education:** Percent of population age 25 and over with: High school diploma (including GED) or higher: 86.4% (2006-2010 5-year est.); Bachelor's degree or higher: 18.2% (2006-2010 5-year est.); Master's degree or higher: 7.4% (2006-2010 5-year est.).
**Housing:** Homeownership rate: 71.3% (2010); Median home value: $87,600 (2006-2010 5-year est.); Median contract rent: $448 per month (2006-2010 5-year est.); Median year structure built: 1952 (2006-2010 5-year est.).
**Health:** Birth rate: 101.6 per 10,000 population (2011); Death rate: 102.7 per 10,000 population (2011); Age-adjusted cancer mortality rate: 157.3 deaths per 100,000 population (2009); Number of physicians: 6.7 per 10,000 population (2008); Hospital beds: 43.7 per 10,000 population (2007); Hospital admissions: 705.7 per 10,000 population (2007).
**Environment:** Air Quality Index: 97.3% good, 2.7% moderate, 0.0% unhealthy for sensitive individuals, 0.0% unhealthy (percent of days in 2010)
**Elections:** 2008 Presidential election results: 44.5% Obama, 53.8% McCain, 1.1% Nader
**National and State Parks:** Black Creek State Forest
**Additional Information Contacts**

Herkimer County Government . . . . . . . . . . . . . . . . . . . . . . . (315) 867-1129
    http://www.herkimercounty.org
Herkimer County Chamber of Commerce . . . . . . . . . . . . . . (315) 866-7820
    http://www.herkimercountychamber.com
Town of Danube . . . . . . . . . . . . . . . . . . . . . . . . . . . . . . . . (315) 823-3400
    http://town.danube.ny.us
Town of Schuyler . . . . . . . . . . . . . . . . . . . . . . . . . . . . . . . (315) 733-7458
    http://townofschuyler.com
Village of Ilion . . . . . . . . . . . . . . . . . . . . . . . . . . . . . . . . . (315) 895-7449
    http://www.ilionny.com

## Herkimer County Communities

### COLD BROOK (village). Covers a land area of 0.439 square miles and a water area of 0 square miles. Located at 43.23° N. Lat; 75.03° W. Long. Elevation is 945 feet.

**Population:** 310 (1990); 336 (2000); 329 (2010); Density: 749.1 persons per square mile (2010); Race: 99.1% White, 0.0% Black, 0.0% Asian, 0.0% American Indian/Alaska Native, 0.0% Native Hawaiian/Other Pacific Islander, 0.9% Other, 0.6% Hispanic of any race (2010); Average household size: 2.63 (2010); Median age: 33.8 (2010); Males per 100 females: 105.6 (2010); Marriage status: 40.6% never married, 44.2% now married, 6.3% widowed, 8.9% divorced (2006-2010 5-year est.); Foreign born: 0.0% (2006-2010 5-year est.); Ancestry (includes multiple ancestries): 23.8% Irish, 18.5% English, 18.3% German, 11.1% Welsh, 9.0% French (2006-2010 5-year est.).
**Economy:** Single-family building permits issued: 0 (2011); Multi-family building permits issued: 0 (2011); Employment by occupation: 9.4% management, 0.0% professional, 21.9% services, 15.6% sales, 0.0% farming, 5.6% construction, 2.5% production (2006-2010 5-year est.).
**Income:** Per capita income: $16,018 (2006-2010 5-year est.); Median household income: $38,000 (2006-2010 5-year est.); Average household income: $43,600 (2006-2010 5-year est.); Percent of households with income of $100,000 or more: 3.6% (2006-2010 5-year est.); Poverty rate: 5.6% (2006-2010 5-year est.).
**Education:** Percent of population age 25 and over with: High school diploma (including GED) or higher: 88.5% (2006-2010 5-year est.); Bachelor's degree or higher: 9.7% (2006-2010 5-year est.); Master's degree or higher: 4.0% (2006-2010 5-year est.).
**Housing:** Homeownership rate: 72.0% (2010); Median home value: $68,800 (2006-2010 5-year est.); Median contract rent: $506 per month (2006-2010 5-year est.); Median year structure built: before 1940 (2006-2010 5-year est.).
**Transportation:** Commute to work: 100.0% car, 0.0% public transportation, 0.0% walk, 0.0% work from home (2006-2010 5-year est.); Travel time to work: 22.9% less than 15 minutes, 31.2% 15 to 30 minutes, 36.9% 30 to 45 minutes, 1.9% 45 to 60 minutes, 7.0% 60 minutes or more (2006-2010 5-year est.)

### COLUMBIA (town). Covers a land area of 35.072 square miles and a water area of 0.030 square miles. Located at 42.92° N. Lat; 75.04° W. Long.

**Population:** 1,587 (1990); 1,630 (2000); 1,580 (2010); Density: 45.0 persons per square mile (2010); Race: 97.0% White, 0.6% Black, 0.3% Asian, 0.3% American Indian/Alaska Native, 0.0% Native Hawaiian/Other Pacific Islander, 1.8% Other, 1.3% Hispanic of any race (2010); Average household size: 2.59 (2010); Median age: 43.7 (2010); Males per 100 females: 107.1 (2010); Marriage status: 22.4% never married, 66.1% now married, 4.0% widowed, 7.5% divorced (2006-2010 5-year est.); Foreign born: 1.7% (2006-2010 5-year est.); Ancestry (includes multiple ancestries): 29.1% German, 18.5% Irish, 17.8% English, 11.4% Polish, 9.0% French (2006-2010 5-year est.).
**Economy:** Single-family building permits issued: 5 (2011); Multi-family building permits issued: 0 (2011); Employment by occupation: 11.5% management, 2.8% professional, 12.1% services, 11.2% sales, 3.1% farming, 15.6% construction, 7.0% production (2006-2010 5-year est.).
**Income:** Per capita income: $22,485 (2006-2010 5-year est.); Median household income: $57,163 (2006-2010 5-year est.); Average household income: $61,557 (2006-2010 5-year est.); Percent of households with income of $100,000 or more: 14.5% (2006-2010 5-year est.); Poverty rate: 7.5% (2006-2010 5-year est.).
**Education:** Percent of population age 25 and over with: High school diploma (including GED) or higher: 84.3% (2006-2010 5-year est.); Bachelor's degree or higher: 15.6% (2006-2010 5-year est.); Master's degree or higher: 6.6% (2006-2010 5-year est.).

**Housing:** Homeownership rate: 87.6% (2010); Median home value: $98,800 (2006-2010 5-year est.); Median contract rent: $531 per month (2006-2010 5-year est.); Median year structure built: 1973 (2006-2010 5-year est.).
**Transportation:** Commute to work: 86.9% car, 0.0% public transportation, 2.8% walk, 7.3% work from home (2006-2010 5-year est.); Travel time to work: 19.0% less than 15 minutes, 37.8% 15 to 30 minutes, 26.7% 30 to 45 minutes, 9.2% 45 to 60 minutes, 7.3% 60 minutes or more (2006-2010 5-year est.)

### DANUBE (town). Covers a land area of 29.353 square miles and a water area of 0.258 square miles. Located at 42.98° N. Lat; 74.79° W. Long.

**Population:** 1,099 (1990); 1,098 (2000); 1,039 (2010); Density: 35.4 persons per square mile (2010); Race: 98.5% White, 0.1% Black, 0.5% Asian, 0.2% American Indian/Alaska Native, 0.0% Native Hawaiian/Other Pacific Islander, 0.7% Other, 0.5% Hispanic of any race (2010); Average household size: 2.55 (2010); Median age: 41.9 (2010); Males per 100 females: 115.6 (2010); Marriage status: 25.1% never married, 62.7% now married, 3.1% widowed, 9.1% divorced (2006-2010 5-year est.); Foreign born: 1.5% (2006-2010 5-year est.); Ancestry (includes multiple ancestries): 26.9% German, 24.0% Irish, 11.9% Italian, 8.6% English, 7.6% Polish (2006-2010 5-year est.).
**Economy:** Single-family building permits issued: 0 (2011); Multi-family building permits issued: 0 (2011); Employment by occupation: 11.1% management, 2.7% professional, 5.7% services, 25.4% sales, 3.9% farming, 13.1% construction, 7.0% production (2006-2010 5-year est.).
**Income:** Per capita income: $17,714 (2006-2010 5-year est.); Median household income: $38,382 (2006-2010 5-year est.); Average household income: $48,887 (2006-2010 5-year est.); Percent of households with income of $100,000 or more: 11.0% (2006-2010 5-year est.); Poverty rate: 30.8% (2006-2010 5-year est.).
**Education:** Percent of population age 25 and over with: High school diploma (including GED) or higher: 77.2% (2006-2010 5-year est.); Bachelor's degree or higher: 10.8% (2006-2010 5-year est.); Master's degree or higher: 4.5% (2006-2010 5-year est.).
**Housing:** Homeownership rate: 83.6% (2010); Median home value: $70,000 (2006-2010 5-year est.); Median contract rent: $559 per month (2006-2010 5-year est.); Median year structure built: 1971 (2006-2010 5-year est.).
**Transportation:** Commute to work: 88.3% car, 0.0% public transportation, 8.1% walk, 2.3% work from home (2006-2010 5-year est.); Travel time to work: 27.5% less than 15 minutes, 35.4% 15 to 30 minutes, 17.3% 30 to 45 minutes, 10.9% 45 to 60 minutes, 8.9% 60 minutes or more (2006-2010 5-year est.)
**Additional Information Contacts**
Town of Danube . . . . . . . . . . . . . . . . . . . . . . . . . . . . . . . (315) 823-3400
    http://town.danube.ny.us

### DOLGEVILLE (village). Covers a land area of 1.790 square miles and a water area of 0.043 square miles. Located at 43.10° N. Lat; 74.77° W. Long. Elevation is 791 feet.

**History:** Incorporated 1891.
**Population:** 2,452 (1990); 2,166 (2000); 2,206 (2010); Density: 1,232.1 persons per square mile (2010); Race: 96.9% White, 0.3% Black, 0.6% Asian, 0.4% American Indian/Alaska Native, 0.0% Native Hawaiian/Other Pacific Islander, 1.8% Other, 1.8% Hispanic of any race (2010); Average household size: 2.32 (2010); Median age: 39.8 (2010); Males per 100 females: 91.8 (2010); Marriage status: 32.5% never married, 49.5% now married, 9.7% widowed, 8.3% divorced (2006-2010 5-year est.); Foreign born: 2.0% (2006-2010 5-year est.); Ancestry (includes multiple ancestries): 31.4% German, 23.6% Irish, 12.2% English, 11.2% Italian, 8.6% French (2006-2010 5-year est.).
**Economy:** Single-family building permits issued: 0 (2011); Multi-family building permits issued: 0 (2011); Employment by occupation: 7.5% management, 1.9% professional, 6.3% services, 16.3% sales, 7.1% farming, 9.9% construction, 10.2% production (2006-2010 5-year est.).
**Income:** Per capita income: $22,530 (2006-2010 5-year est.); Median household income: $38,456 (2006-2010 5-year est.); Average household income: $47,260 (2006-2010 5-year est.); Percent of households with income of $100,000 or more: 6.7% (2006-2010 5-year est.); Poverty rate: 9.6% (2006-2010 5-year est.).
**Education:** Percent of population age 25 and over with: High school diploma (including GED) or higher: 88.2% (2006-2010 5-year est.);

Bachelor's degree or higher: 18.6% (2006-2010 5-year est.); Master's degree or higher: 7.3% (2006-2010 5-year est.).

**School District(s)**
Dolgeville Central School District (KG-12)
    2009-10 Enrollment: 902 . . . . . . . . . . . . . . . . (315) 429-3155
**Housing:** Homeownership rate: 63.1% (2010); Median home value: $75,500 (2006-2010 5-year est.); Median contract rent: $410 per month (2006-2010 5-year est.); Median year structure built: before 1940 (2006-2010 5-year est.).
**Safety:** Violent crime rate: 15.2 per 10,000 population; Property crime rate: 299.0 per 10,000 population (2010).
**Transportation:** Commute to work: 90.2% car, 1.8% public transportation, 5.7% walk, 2.3% work from home (2006-2010 5-year est.); Travel time to work: 43.8% less than 15 minutes, 24.9% 15 to 30 minutes, 13.3% 30 to 45 minutes, 13.2% 45 to 60 minutes, 4.8% 60 minutes or more (2006-2010 5-year est.)

## EAGLE BAY (unincorporated postal area)
Zip Code: 13331
    Covers a land area of 80.667 square miles and a water area of 4.673 square miles. Located at 43.86° N. Lat; 74.88° W. Long. Elevation is 1,778 feet. Population: 189 (2010); Density: 2.3 persons per square mile (2010); Race: 99.5% White, 0.0% Black, 0.0% Asian, 0.0% American Indian/Alaska Native, 0.0% Native Hawaiian/Other Pacific Islander, 0.5% Other, 0.0% Hispanic of any race (2010); Average household size: 1.87 (2010); Median age: 55.6 (2010); Males per 100 females: 110.0 (2010); Homeownership rate: 88.1% (2010)

## FAIRFIELD (town). Covers a land area of 41.295 square miles and a water area of 0.161 square miles. Located at 43.13° N. Lat; 74.93° W. Long. Elevation is 1,266 feet.
**Population:** 1,442 (1990); 1,607 (2000); 1,627 (2010); Density: 39.4 persons per square mile (2010); Race: 98.3% White, 0.4% Black, 0.1% Asian, 0.2% American Indian/Alaska Native, 0.0% Native Hawaiian/Other Pacific Islander, 1.0% Other, 0.9% Hispanic of any race (2010); Average household size: 2.65 (2010); Median age: 42.1 (2010); Males per 100 females: 102.6 (2010); Marriage status: 23.8% never married, 57.9% now married, 5.6% widowed, 12.7% divorced (2006-2010 5-year est.); Foreign born: 5.0% (2006-2010 5-year est.); Ancestry (includes multiple ancestries): 31.5% German, 21.1% Irish, 13.9% English, 9.1% American, 8.4% Polish (2006-2010 5-year est.).
**Economy:** Single-family building permits issued: 0 (2011); Multi-family building permits issued: 0 (2011); Employment by occupation: 8.1% management, 1.9% professional, 5.3% services, 21.6% sales, 5.4% farming, 12.0% construction, 7.8% production (2006-2010 5-year est.).
**Income:** Per capita income: $23,944 (2006-2010 5-year est.); Median household income: $50,121 (2006-2010 5-year est.); Average household income: $59,272 (2006-2010 5-year est.); Percent of households with income of $100,000 or more: 8.9% (2006-2010 5-year est.); Poverty rate: 6.8% (2006-2010 5-year est.).
**Education:** Percent of population age 25 and over with: High school diploma (including GED) or higher: 89.7% (2006-2010 5-year est.); Bachelor's degree or higher: 15.3% (2006-2010 5-year est.); Master's degree or higher: 4.0% (2006-2010 5-year est.).
**Housing:** Homeownership rate: 82.9% (2010); Median home value: $81,300 (2006-2010 5-year est.); Median contract rent: $515 per month (2006-2010 5-year est.); Median year structure built: 1957 (2006-2010 5-year est.).
**Transportation:** Commute to work: 90.0% car, 0.0% public transportation, 3.6% walk, 5.4% work from home (2006-2010 5-year est.); Travel time to work: 19.6% less than 15 minutes, 35.2% 15 to 30 minutes, 31.8% 30 to 45 minutes, 5.7% 45 to 60 minutes, 7.7% 60 minutes or more (2006-2010 5-year est.)

## FRANKFORT (village). Covers a land area of 1.013 square miles and a water area of 0.017 square miles. Located at 43.03° N. Lat; 75.07° W. Long. Elevation is 407 feet.
**Population:** 2,693 (1990); 2,537 (2000); 2,598 (2010); Density: 2,562.8 persons per square mile (2010); Race: 97.0% White, 0.7% Black, 0.3% Asian, 0.2% American Indian/Alaska Native, 0.0% Native Hawaiian/Other Pacific Islander, 1.8% Other, 1.5% Hispanic of any race (2010); Average household size: 2.40 (2010); Median age: 38.5 (2010); Males per 100 females: 91.5 (2010); Marriage status: 31.6% never married, 47.5% now married, 6.3% widowed, 14.6% divorced (2006-2010 5-year est.); Foreign born: 3.3% (2006-2010 5-year est.); Ancestry (includes multiple

ancestries): 50.2% Italian, 13.6% Irish, 12.1% German, 9.9% English, 5.8% French (2006-2010 5-year est.).
**Economy:** Single-family building permits issued: 0 (2011); Multi-family building permits issued: 0 (2011); Employment by occupation: 10.5% management, 2.8% professional, 6.4% services, 21.7% sales, 1.5% farming, 12.6% construction, 9.0% production (2006-2010 5-year est.).
**Income:** Per capita income: $19,425 (2006-2010 5-year est.); Median household income: $35,039 (2006-2010 5-year est.); Average household income: $46,969 (2006-2010 5-year est.); Percent of households with income of $100,000 or more: 7.9% (2006-2010 5-year est.); Poverty rate: 17.7% (2006-2010 5-year est.).
**Education:** Percent of population age 25 and over with: High school diploma (including GED) or higher: 85.4% (2006-2010 5-year est.); Bachelor's degree or higher: 8.8% (2006-2010 5-year est.); Master's degree or higher: 4.0% (2006-2010 5-year est.).

**School District(s)**
Frankfort-Schuyler Central School District (KG-12)
    2009-10 Enrollment: 1,209 . . . . . . . . . . . . . . (315) 894-5083
**Housing:** Homeownership rate: 60.0% (2010); Median home value: $79,000 (2006-2010 5-year est.); Median contract rent: $479 per month (2006-2010 5-year est.); Median year structure built: before 1940 (2006-2010 5-year est.).
**Transportation:** Commute to work: 90.6% car, 0.0% public transportation, 5.6% walk, 3.1% work from home (2006-2010 5-year est.); Travel time to work: 33.5% less than 15 minutes, 43.6% 15 to 30 minutes, 14.0% 30 to 45 minutes, 3.7% 45 to 60 minutes, 5.1% 60 minutes or more (2006-2010 5-year est.)

## FRANKFORT (town). Covers a land area of 36.421 square miles and a water area of 0.106 square miles. Located at 43.04° N. Lat; 75.13° W. Long. Elevation is 407 feet.
**History:** Settled 1723, incorporated 1863.
**Population:** 7,494 (1990); 7,478 (2000); 7,636 (2010); Density: 209.7 persons per square mile (2010); Race: 97.1% White, 0.7% Black, 0.4% Asian, 0.1% American Indian/Alaska Native, 0.0% Native Hawaiian/Other Pacific Islander, 1.7% Other, 1.3% Hispanic of any race (2010); Average household size: 2.48 (2010); Median age: 42.7 (2010); Males per 100 females: 94.1 (2010); Marriage status: 24.8% never married, 60.8% now married, 5.8% widowed, 8.6% divorced (2006-2010 5-year est.); Foreign born: 4.7% (2006-2010 5-year est.); Ancestry (includes multiple ancestries): 37.3% Italian, 17.0% Irish, 15.4% German, 11.2% English, 7.8% Polish (2006-2010 5-year est.).
**Economy:** Single-family building permits issued: 7 (2011); Multi-family building permits issued: 0 (2011); Employment by occupation: 7.3% management, 4.6% professional, 10.2% services, 16.1% sales, 5.2% farming, 10.2% construction, 10.3% production (2006-2010 5-year est.).
**Income:** Per capita income: $22,609 (2006-2010 5-year est.); Median household income: $44,472 (2006-2010 5-year est.); Average household income: $53,282 (2006-2010 5-year est.); Percent of households with income of $100,000 or more: 11.4% (2006-2010 5-year est.); Poverty rate: 12.2% (2006-2010 5-year est.).
**Education:** Percent of population age 25 and over with: High school diploma (including GED) or higher: 83.3% (2006-2010 5-year est.); Bachelor's degree or higher: 16.2% (2006-2010 5-year est.); Master's degree or higher: 7.0% (2006-2010 5-year est.).

**School District(s)**
Frankfort-Schuyler Central School District (KG-12)
    2009-10 Enrollment: 1,209 . . . . . . . . . . . . . . (315) 894-5083
**Housing:** Homeownership rate: 76.3% (2010); Median home value: $98,900 (2006-2010 5-year est.); Median contract rent: $507 per month (2006-2010 5-year est.); Median year structure built: 1949 (2006-2010 5-year est.).
**Safety:** Violent crime rate: 8.5 per 10,000 population; Property crime rate: 116.9 per 10,000 population (2010).
**Transportation:** Commute to work: 94.8% car, 0.0% public transportation, 2.0% walk, 3.0% work from home (2006-2010 5-year est.); Travel time to work: 31.4% less than 15 minutes, 45.7% 15 to 30 minutes, 14.3% 30 to 45 minutes, 3.4% 45 to 60 minutes, 5.1% 60 minutes or more (2006-2010 5-year est.)

## GERMAN FLATTS (town). Covers a land area of 33.695 square miles and a water area of 0.498 square miles. Located at 42.98° N. Lat; 74.98° W. Long.
**Population:** 14,345 (1990); 13,629 (2000); 13,258 (2010); Density: 393.5 persons per square mile (2010); Race: 96.2% White, 1.2% Black, 0.5%

Asian, 0.3% American Indian/Alaska Native, 0.0% Native Hawaiian/Other Pacific Islander, 1.8% Other, 2.0% Hispanic of any race (2010); Average household size: 2.37 (2010); Median age: 39.8 (2010); Males per 100 females: 93.2 (2010); Marriage status: 27.9% never married, 51.1% now married, 9.4% widowed, 11.6% divorced (2006-2010 5-year est.); Foreign born: 0.9% (2006-2010 5-year est.); Ancestry (includes multiple ancestries): 25.5% Irish, 23.2% German, 16.1% Italian, 15.7% English, 7.7% French (2006-2010 5-year est.).

**Economy:** Single-family building permits issued: 2 (2011); Multi-family building permits issued: 0 (2011); Employment by occupation: 6.8% management, 2.4% professional, 10.7% services, 18.2% sales, 6.4% farming, 7.2% construction, 6.5% production (2006-2010 5-year est.).

**Income:** Per capita income: $21,360 (2006-2010 5-year est.); Median household income: $41,348 (2006-2010 5-year est.); Average household income: $50,907 (2006-2010 5-year est.); Percent of households with income of $100,000 or more: 9.2% (2006-2010 5-year est.); Poverty rate: 13.2% (2006-2010 5-year est.).

**Education:** Percent of population age 25 and over with: High school diploma (including GED) or higher: 88.3% (2006-2010 5-year est.); Bachelor's degree or higher: 18.2% (2006-2010 5-year est.); Master's degree or higher: 6.2% (2006-2010 5-year est.).

**Housing:** Homeownership rate: 64.7% (2010); Median home value: $82,700 (2006-2010 5-year est.); Median contract rent: $436 per month (2006-2010 5-year est.); Median year structure built: before 1940 (2006-2010 5-year est.).

**Transportation:** Commute to work: 92.2% car, 0.4% public transportation, 2.2% walk, 4.4% work from home (2006-2010 5-year est.); Travel time to work: 39.9% less than 15 minutes, 31.1% 15 to 30 minutes, 20.0% 30 to 45 minutes, 3.5% 45 to 60 minutes, 5.5% 60 minutes or more (2006-2010 5-year est.)

**HERKIMER** (village). County seat. Covers a land area of 2.588 square miles and a water area of 0.115 square miles. Located at 43.02° N. Lat; 74.99° W. Long. Elevation is 384 feet.

**History:** Formerly shipping, commercial and trade center for surrounding Mohawk valley Agriculture and industrial area that stretched west through village of Mohawk to Ilion and Frankfort. Herkimer County Historical Society has important documents and exhibits here. World-renowned Herkimer diamonds (actually a clear quartz) are to be found along West Canada Creek Valley north of the village. Settled c.1725, Incorporated 1807.

**Population:** 7,945 (1990); 7,498 (2000); 7,743 (2010); Density: 2,991.4 persons per square mile (2010); Race: 91.5% White, 4.5% Black, 1.1% Asian, 0.3% American Indian/Alaska Native, 0.1% Native Hawaiian/Other Pacific Islander, 2.5% Other, 3.3% Hispanic of any race (2010); Average household size: 2.15 (2010); Median age: 37.0 (2010); Males per 100 females: 88.6 (2010); Marriage status: 33.3% never married, 41.0% now married, 17.0% widowed, 8.7% divorced (2006-2010 5-year est.); Foreign born: 1.9% (2006-2010 5-year est.); Ancestry (includes multiple ancestries): 23.4% Irish, 20.7% Italian, 17.7% German, 10.0% Polish, 8.7% English (2006-2010 5-year est.).

**Economy:** Single-family building permits issued: 0 (2011); Multi-family building permits issued: 0 (2011); Employment by occupation: 5.3% management, 1.1% professional, 18.3% services, 17.5% sales, 7.2% farming, 5.3% construction, 3.9% production (2006-2010 5-year est.).

**Income:** Per capita income: $16,271 (2006-2010 5-year est.); Median household income: $25,778 (2006-2010 5-year est.); Average household income: $35,832 (2006-2010 5-year est.); Percent of households with income of $100,000 or more: 5.0% (2006-2010 5-year est.); Poverty rate: 24.8% (2006-2010 5-year est.).

**Education:** Percent of population age 25 and over with: High school diploma (including GED) or higher: 81.3% (2006-2010 5-year est.); Bachelor's degree or higher: 14.9% (2006-2010 5-year est.); Master's degree or higher: 8.3% (2006-2010 5-year est.).

**School District(s)**
Herkimer Central School District (PK-12)
    2009-10 Enrollment: 1,228 . . . . . . . . . . . . . . . . . . . (315) 866-2230
Herkimer-Fulton-Hamilton-Otsego Boces
    2009-10 Enrollment: n/a . . . . . . . . . . . . . . . . . . . . . (315) 867-2023
**Two-year College(s)**
Herkimer County Community College (Public)
    Fall 2010 Enrollment: 3,084 . . . . . . . . . . . . . . . . . . (315) 866-0300
    2011-12 Tuition: In-state $4,140; Out-of-state $6,400
**Housing:** Homeownership rate: 47.6% (2010); Median home value: $74,900 (2006-2010 5-year est.); Median contract rent: $459 per month

(2006-2010 5-year est.); Median year structure built: before 1940 (2006-2010 5-year est.).

**Safety:** Violent crime rate: 108.4 per 10,000 population; Property crime rate: 518.8 per 10,000 population (2010).

**Newspapers:** Herkimer Evening Telegram (Local news; Circulation 7,095); Images (Community news; Circulation 8,500); Mohawk Valley Pennysaver (Community news; Circulation 17,300); The Observer-Dispatch - Valley Bureau (Local news)

**Transportation:** Commute to work: 85.5% car, 1.4% public transportation, 6.0% walk, 6.1% work from home (2006-2010 5-year est.); Travel time to work: 48.3% less than 15 minutes, 32.5% 15 to 30 minutes, 12.8% 30 to 45 minutes, 4.7% 45 to 60 minutes, 1.7% 60 minutes or more (2006-2010 5-year est.)

**Additional Information Contacts**
Herkimer County Chamber of Commerce . . . . . . . . . . . . . (315) 866-7820
    http://www.herkimercountychamber.com

**HERKIMER** (town). Covers a land area of 31.661 square miles and a water area of 0.566 square miles. Located at 43.06° N. Lat; 75.00° W. Long. Elevation is 384 feet.

**History:** Herkimer was settled by a group of Palatines in 1725 and was long known as German Flats. In 1776 Fort Dayton, a wooden structure surrounded by a stockade, was built on a plot now at the center of town. From that fort on August 4, 1777, General Nicholas Herkimer marched to the Battle of Oriskany. The town was named for him.

**Population:** 10,401 (1990); 9,962 (2000); 10,175 (2010); Density: 321.4 persons per square mile (2010); Race: 93.2% White, 3.5% Black, 0.9% Asian, 0.3% American Indian/Alaska Native, 0.0% Native Hawaiian/Other Pacific Islander, 2.1% Other, 2.7% Hispanic of any race (2010); Average household size: 2.22 (2010); Median age: 40.8 (2010); Males per 100 females: 90.5 (2010); Marriage status: 30.8% never married, 45.8% now married, 14.8% widowed, 8.6% divorced (2006-2010 5-year est.); Foreign born: 2.2% (2006-2010 5-year est.); Ancestry (includes multiple ancestries): 21.7% Irish, 20.3% German, 19.9% Italian, 9.6% English, 8.9% Polish (2006-2010 5-year est.).

**Economy:** Single-family building permits issued: 3 (2011); Multi-family building permits issued: 0 (2011); Employment by occupation: 6.8% management, 1.7% professional, 16.8% services, 16.3% sales, 6.2% farming, 5.8% construction, 4.5% production (2006-2010 5-year est.).

**Income:** Per capita income: $18,478 (2006-2010 5-year est.); Median household income: $31,141 (2006-2010 5-year est.); Average household income: $43,016 (2006-2010 5-year est.); Percent of households with income of $100,000 or more: 6.9% (2006-2010 5-year est.); Poverty rate: 20.0% (2006-2010 5-year est.).

**Education:** Percent of population age 25 and over with: High school diploma (including GED) or higher: 83.1% (2006-2010 5-year est.); Bachelor's degree or higher: 16.7% (2006-2010 5-year est.); Master's degree or higher: 8.1% (2006-2010 5-year est.).

**School District(s)**
Herkimer Central School District (PK-12)
    2009-10 Enrollment: 1,228 . . . . . . . . . . . . . . . . . . . (315) 866-2230
Herkimer-Fulton-Hamilton-Otsego Boces
    2009-10 Enrollment: n/a . . . . . . . . . . . . . . . . . . . . . (315) 867-2023
**Two-year College(s)**
Herkimer County Community College (Public)
    Fall 2010 Enrollment: 3,084 . . . . . . . . . . . . . . . . . . (315) 866-0300
    2011-12 Tuition: In-state $4,140; Out-of-state $6,400
**Housing:** Homeownership rate: 56.6% (2010); Median home value: $80,900 (2006-2010 5-year est.); Median contract rent: $459 per month (2006-2010 5-year est.); Median year structure built: 1941 (2006-2010 5-year est.).

**Newspapers:** Herkimer Evening Telegram (Local news; Circulation 7,095); Images (Community news; Circulation 8,500); Mohawk Valley Pennysaver (Community news; Circulation 17,300); The Observer-Dispatch - Valley Bureau (Local news)

**Transportation:** Commute to work: 88.7% car, 1.1% public transportation, 4.6% walk, 5.0% work from home (2006-2010 5-year est.); Travel time to work: 48.5% less than 15 minutes, 32.0% 15 to 30 minutes, 12.5% 30 to 45 minutes, 3.7% 45 to 60 minutes, 3.3% 60 minutes or more (2006-2010 5-year est.)

**Additional Information Contacts**
Herkimer County Chamber of Commerce . . . . . . . . . . . . . (315) 866-7820
    http://www.herkimercountychamber.com

**ILION** (village). Covers a land area of 2.492 square miles and a water area of 0.059 square miles. Located at 43.01° N. Lat; 75.03° W. Long. Elevation is 407 feet.
**History:** Part of the former Herkimer (village). Remington Arms Museum. Incorporated 1852.
**Population:** 8,911 (1990); 8,610 (2000); 8,053 (2010); Density: 3,230.4 persons per square mile (2010); Race: 96.0% White, 1.2% Black, 0.5% Asian, 0.3% American Indian/Alaska Native, 0.0% Native Hawaiian/Other Pacific Islander, 2.0% Other, 2.4% Hispanic of any race (2010); Average household size: 2.38 (2010); Median age: 38.4 (2010); Males per 100 females: 91.8 (2010); Marriage status: 30.2% never married, 48.4% now married, 9.8% widowed, 11.7% divorced (2006-2010 5-year est.); Foreign born: 1.3% (2006-2010 5-year est.); Ancestry (includes multiple ancestries): 26.7% Irish, 21.4% German, 16.2% English, 14.8% Italian, 8.3% French (2006-2010 5-year est.).
**Economy:** Single-family building permits issued: 0 (2011); Multi-family building permits issued: 0 (2011); Employment by occupation: 6.2% management, 2.9% professional, 7.7% services, 20.1% sales, 7.7% farming, 7.9% construction, 6.5% production (2006-2010 5-year est.).
**Income:** Per capita income: $20,798 (2006-2010 5-year est.); Median household income: $41,583 (2006-2010 5-year est.); Average household income: $50,486 (2006-2010 5-year est.); Percent of households with income of $100,000 or more: 8.5% (2006-2010 5-year est.); Poverty rate: 13.4% (2006-2010 5-year est.).
**Education:** Percent of population age 25 and over with: High school diploma (including GED) or higher: 89.5% (2006-2010 5-year est.); Bachelor's degree or higher: 16.0% (2006-2010 5-year est.); Master's degree or higher: 4.9% (2006-2010 5-year est.).

### School District(s)
Ilion Central School District (PK-12)
    2009-10 Enrollment: 1,652 . . . . . . . . . . . . . . . . . . . . . . . (315) 894-9934
### Vocational/Technical School(s)
Herkimer County BOCES-Practical Nursing Program (Public)
    Fall 2010 Enrollment: 106 . . . . . . . . . . . . . . . . . . . . . . . (315) 895-2210
    2011-12 Tuition: $8,450
**Housing:** Homeownership rate: 60.9% (2010); Median home value: $82,200 (2006-2010 5-year est.); Median contract rent: $445 per month (2006-2010 5-year est.); Median year structure built: before 1940 (2006-2010 5-year est.).
**Safety:** Violent crime rate: 17.8 per 10,000 population; Property crime rate: 295.8 per 10,000 population (2010).
**Transportation:** Commute to work: 93.2% car, 0.4% public transportation, 2.1% walk, 3.3% work from home (2006-2010 5-year est.); Travel time to work: 41.5% less than 15 minutes, 30.5% 15 to 30 minutes, 18.9% 30 to 45 minutes, 3.8% 45 to 60 minutes, 5.4% 60 minutes or more (2006-2010 5-year est.)
**Additional Information Contacts**
Village of Ilion. . . . . . . . . . . . . . . . . . . . . . . . . . . . . . . . . . (315) 895-7449
    http://www.ilionny.com

**JORDANVILLE** (unincorporated postal area)
Zip Code: 13361
    Covers a land area of 28.324 square miles and a water area of 0.002 square miles. Located at 42.90° N. Lat; 74.86° W. Long. Elevation is 1,499 feet. Population: 824 (2010); Density: 29.1 persons per square mile (2010); Race: 97.9% White, 1.5% Black, 0.4% Asian, 0.0% American Indian/Alaska Native, 0.0% Native Hawaiian/Other Pacific Islander, 0.2% Other, 0.2% Hispanic of any race (2010); Average household size: 2.81 (2010); Median age: 39.5 (2010); Males per 100 females: 119.1 (2010); Homeownership rate: 82.3% (2010)

**LITCHFIELD** (town). Covers a land area of 29.992 square miles and a water area of 0.060 square miles. Located at 42.96° N. Lat; 75.16° W. Long. Elevation is 1,506 feet.
**Population:** 1,414 (1990); 1,453 (2000); 1,513 (2010); Density: 50.4 persons per square mile (2010); Race: 98.1% White, 0.4% Black, 0.1% Asian, 0.0% American Indian/Alaska Native, 0.0% Native Hawaiian/Other Pacific Islander, 1.4% Other, 1.1% Hispanic of any race (2010); Average household size: 2.67 (2010); Median age: 42.2 (2010); Males per 100 females: 105.0 (2010); Marriage status: 25.1% never married, 62.4% now married, 2.4% widowed, 10.1% divorced (2006-2010 5-year est.); Foreign born: 0.9% (2006-2010 5-year est.); Ancestry (includes multiple ancestries): 28.0% Irish, 23.0% German, 15.1% English, 14.5% Italian, 10.4% Polish (2006-2010 5-year est.).

**Economy:** Single-family building permits issued: 11 (2011); Multi-family building permits issued: 0 (2011); Employment by occupation: 12.1% management, 1.5% professional, 8.7% services, 17.6% sales, 3.0% farming, 14.5% construction, 6.5% production (2006-2010 5-year est.).
**Income:** Per capita income: $23,623 (2006-2010 5-year est.); Median household income: $57,250 (2006-2010 5-year est.); Average household income: $62,539 (2006-2010 5-year est.); Percent of households with income of $100,000 or more: 13.3% (2006-2010 5-year est.); Poverty rate: 5.7% (2006-2010 5-year est.).
**Education:** Percent of population age 25 and over with: High school diploma (including GED) or higher: 90.0% (2006-2010 5-year est.); Bachelor's degree or higher: 19.9% (2006-2010 5-year est.); Master's degree or higher: 9.0% (2006-2010 5-year est.).
**Housing:** Homeownership rate: 87.0% (2010); Median home value: $94,800 (2006-2010 5-year est.); Median contract rent: $525 per month (2006-2010 5-year est.); Median year structure built: 1973 (2006-2010 5-year est.).
**Transportation:** Commute to work: 89.8% car, 0.0% public transportation, 1.6% walk, 7.9% work from home (2006-2010 5-year est.); Travel time to work: 19.0% less than 15 minutes, 59.4% 15 to 30 minutes, 14.4% 30 to 45 minutes, 4.2% 45 to 60 minutes, 2.9% 60 minutes or more (2006-2010 5-year est.)

**LITTLE FALLS** (city). Covers a land area of 3.838 square miles and a water area of 0.151 square miles. Located at 43.04° N. Lat; 74.85° W. Long. Elevation is 420 feet.
**Population:** 5,829 (1990); 5,188 (2000); 4,946 (2010); Density: 1,288.6 persons per square mile (2010); Race: 96.8% White, 0.6% Black, 0.5% Asian, 0.1% American Indian/Alaska Native, 0.0% Native Hawaiian/Other Pacific Islander, 2.0% Other, 1.4% Hispanic of any race (2010); Average household size: 2.20 (2010); Median age: 41.1 (2010); Males per 100 females: 88.3 (2010); Marriage status: 27.6% never married, 46.9% now married, 10.1% widowed, 15.4% divorced (2006-2010 5-year est.); Foreign born: 2.1% (2006-2010 5-year est.); Ancestry (includes multiple ancestries): 24.6% Irish, 22.0% German, 19.6% Italian, 13.8% English, 10.0% Polish (2006-2010 5-year est.).
**Economy:** Single-family building permits issued: 0 (2011); Multi-family building permits issued: 0 (2011); Employment by occupation: 7.2% management, 1.2% professional, 13.1% services, 21.3% sales, 1.6% farming, 4.1% construction, 4.0% production (2006-2010 5-year est.).
**Income:** Per capita income: $23,860 (2006-2010 5-year est.); Median household income: $34,473 (2006-2010 5-year est.); Average household income: $51,107 (2006-2010 5-year est.); Percent of households with income of $100,000 or more: 9.6% (2006-2010 5-year est.); Poverty rate: 18.2% (2006-2010 5-year est.).
**Education:** Percent of population age 25 and over with: High school diploma (including GED) or higher: 88.2% (2006-2010 5-year est.); Bachelor's degree or higher: 23.6% (2006-2010 5-year est.); Master's degree or higher: 7.9% (2006-2010 5-year est.).
### School District(s)
Little Falls City School District (KG-12)
    2009-10 Enrollment: 1,162 . . . . . . . . . . . . . . . . . . . . . . (315) 823-1470
**Housing:** Homeownership rate: 53.9% (2010); Median home value: $66,900 (2006-2010 5-year est.); Median contract rent: $423 per month (2006-2010 5-year est.); Median year structure built: before 1940 (2006-2010 5-year est.).
**Hospitals:** Little Falls Hospital (25 beds)
**Safety:** Violent crime rate: 63.1 per 10,000 population; Property crime rate: 317.8 per 10,000 population (2010).
**Newspapers:** The Evening Times (Local news; Circulation 5,023)
**Transportation:** Commute to work: 91.8% car, 2.5% public transportation, 4.1% walk, 1.6% work from home (2006-2010 5-year est.); Travel time to work: 44.0% less than 15 minutes, 31.5% 15 to 30 minutes, 12.6% 30 to 45 minutes, 4.8% 45 to 60 minutes, 7.2% 60 minutes or more (2006-2010 5-year est.)

**LITTLE FALLS** (town). Covers a land area of 22.339 square miles and a water area of 0.163 square miles. Located at 43.01° N. Lat; 74.89° W. Long. Elevation is 420 feet.
**History:** Home of Gen. Nicholas Herkimer, hero of Battle of Oriskany. Settled c.1725; incorporated as city 1895.
**Population:** 1,642 (1990); 1,544 (2000); 1,587 (2010); Density: 71.0 persons per square mile (2010); Race: 97.5% White, 0.4% Black, 0.5% Asian, 0.2% American Indian/Alaska Native, 0.1% Native Hawaiian/Other Pacific Islander, 1.3% Other, 0.9% Hispanic of any race (2010); Average

household size: 2.58 (2010); Median age: 45.0 (2010); Males per 100 females: 109.1 (2010); Marriage status: 23.1% never married, 56.8% now married, 7.3% widowed, 12.8% divorced (2006-2010 5-year est.); Foreign born: 2.5% (2006-2010 5-year est.); Ancestry (includes multiple ancestries): 23.3% Irish, 18.0% German, 17.2% Italian, 10.8% English, 10.4% Polish (2006-2010 5-year est.).

**Economy:** Single-family building permits issued: 1 (2011); Multi-family building permits issued: 0 (2011); Employment by occupation: 11.0% management, 2.2% professional, 7.9% services, 16.7% sales, 2.4% farming, 13.2% construction, 8.1% production (2006-2010 5-year est.).

**Income:** Per capita income: $27,351 (2006-2010 5-year est.); Median household income: $55,972 (2006-2010 5-year est.); Average household income: $67,288 (2006-2010 5-year est.); Percent of households with income of $100,000 or more: 16.0% (2006-2010 5-year est.); Poverty rate: 9.6% (2006-2010 5-year est.).

**Education:** Percent of population age 25 and over with: High school diploma (including GED) or higher: 89.2% (2006-2010 5-year est.); Bachelor's degree or higher: 15.9% (2006-2010 5-year est.); Master's degree or higher: 7.3% (2006-2010 5-year est.).

### School District(s)
Little Falls City School District (KG-12)
    2009-10 Enrollment: 1,162 . . . . . . . . . . . . . . . . . . . . . . . (315) 823-1470

**Housing:** Homeownership rate: 87.0% (2010); Median home value: $99,500 (2006-2010 5-year est.); Median contract rent: $431 per month (2006-2010 5-year est.); Median year structure built: 1973 (2006-2010 5-year est.).

**Hospitals:** Little Falls Hospital (25 beds)

**Newspapers:** The Evening Times (Local news; Circulation 5,023)

**Transportation:** Commute to work: 96.1% car, 0.0% public transportation, 2.0% walk, 1.4% work from home (2006-2010 5-year est.); Travel time to work: 43.8% less than 15 minutes, 29.4% 15 to 30 minutes, 15.3% 30 to 45 minutes, 5.7% 45 to 60 minutes, 5.9% 60 minutes or more (2006-2010 5-year est.)

## MANHEIM (town). Covers a land area of 29.136 square miles and a water area of 0.556 square miles. Located at 43.05° N. Lat; 74.79° W. Long.

**Population:** 3,527 (1990); 3,171 (2000); 3,334 (2010); Density: 114.4 persons per square mile (2010); Race: 97.5% White, 0.4% Black, 0.6% Asian, 0.2% American Indian/Alaska Native, 0.0% Native Hawaiian/Other Pacific Islander, 1.3% Other, 1.1% Hispanic of any race (2010); Average household size: 2.46 (2010); Median age: 40.3 (2010); Males per 100 females: 96.5 (2010); Marriage status: 27.5% never married, 55.1% now married, 7.8% widowed, 9.6% divorced (2006-2010 5-year est.); Foreign born: 1.2% (2006-2010 5-year est.); Ancestry (includes multiple ancestries): 27.3% German, 23.1% Irish, 15.8% English, 10.3% Italian, 9.9% American (2006-2010 5-year est.).

**Economy:** Single-family building permits issued: 4 (2011); Multi-family building permits issued: 0 (2011); Employment by occupation: 11.9% management, 2.2% professional, 6.3% services, 18.9% sales, 7.6% farming, 9.8% construction, 7.0% production (2006-2010 5-year est.).

**Income:** Per capita income: $23,860 (2006-2010 5-year est.); Median household income: $45,969 (2006-2010 5-year est.); Average household income: $53,835 (2006-2010 5-year est.); Percent of households with income of $100,000 or more: 9.4% (2006-2010 5-year est.); Poverty rate: 7.3% (2006-2010 5-year est.).

**Education:** Percent of population age 25 and over with: High school diploma (including GED) or higher: 86.0% (2006-2010 5-year est.); Bachelor's degree or higher: 16.7% (2006-2010 5-year est.); Master's degree or higher: 5.7% (2006-2010 5-year est.).

**Housing:** Homeownership rate: 71.1% (2010); Median home value: $81,400 (2006-2010 5-year est.); Median contract rent: $419 per month (2006-2010 5-year est.); Median year structure built: 1940 (2006-2010 5-year est.).

**Transportation:** Commute to work: 89.4% car, 1.3% public transportation, 4.9% walk, 4.5% work from home (2006-2010 5-year est.); Travel time to work: 37.5% less than 15 minutes, 31.0% 15 to 30 minutes, 11.7% 30 to 45 minutes, 13.2% 45 to 60 minutes, 6.6% 60 minutes or more (2006-2010 5-year est.)

## MIDDLEVILLE (village). Covers a land area of 0.765 square miles and a water area of 0.049 square miles. Located at 43.13° N. Lat; 74.97° W. Long. Elevation is 597 feet.

**Population:** 624 (1990); 550 (2000); 512 (2010); Density: 669.3 persons per square mile (2010); Race: 97.7% White, 0.0% Black, 0.4% Asian, 0.0%

American Indian/Alaska Native, 0.0% Native Hawaiian/Other Pacific Islander, 1.9% Other, 0.2% Hispanic of any race (2010); Average household size: 2.38 (2010); Median age: 40.6 (2010); Males per 100 females: 91.8 (2010); Marriage status: 32.1% never married, 49.6% now married, 5.4% widowed, 12.9% divorced (2006-2010 5-year est.); Foreign born: 6.6% (2006-2010 5-year est.); Ancestry (includes multiple ancestries): 46.8% German, 32.8% Irish, 16.8% English, 9.5% Polish, 6.2% American (2006-2010 5-year est.).

**Economy:** Single-family building permits issued: 0 (2011); Multi-family building permits issued: 0 (2011); Employment by occupation: 10.1% management, 0.0% professional, 5.2% services, 27.0% sales, 12.0% farming, 5.6% construction, 1.1% production (2006-2010 5-year est.).

**Income:** Per capita income: $18,836 (2006-2010 5-year est.); Median household income: $41,731 (2006-2010 5-year est.); Average household income: $46,036 (2006-2010 5-year est.); Percent of households with income of $100,000 or more: 6.4% (2006-2010 5-year est.); Poverty rate: 10.2% (2006-2010 5-year est.).

**Education:** Percent of population age 25 and over with: High school diploma (including GED) or higher: 89.5% (2006-2010 5-year est.); Bachelor's degree or higher: 15.7% (2006-2010 5-year est.); Master's degree or higher: 2.9% (2006-2010 5-year est.).

**Housing:** Homeownership rate: 69.3% (2010); Median home value: $76,500 (2006-2010 5-year est.); Median contract rent: $430 per month (2006-2010 5-year est.); Median year structure built: before 1940 (2006-2010 5-year est.).

**Transportation:** Commute to work: 96.9% car, 0.0% public transportation, 1.6% walk, 1.6% work from home (2006-2010 5-year est.); Travel time to work: 13.0% less than 15 minutes, 35.6% 15 to 30 minutes, 36.0% 30 to 45 minutes, 9.9% 45 to 60 minutes, 5.5% 60 minutes or more (2006-2010 5-year est.)

## MOHAWK (village). Covers a land area of 0.875 square miles and a water area of 0.026 square miles. Located at 43.00° N. Lat; 75.00° W. Long. Elevation is 410 feet.

**History:** Settled 1826, incorporated 1844.

**Population:** 2,986 (1990); 2,660 (2000); 2,731 (2010); Density: 3,118.0 persons per square mile (2010); Race: 96.7% White, 1.1% Black, 0.6% Asian, 0.2% American Indian/Alaska Native, 0.0% Native Hawaiian/Other Pacific Islander, 1.4% Other, 1.5% Hispanic of any race (2010); Average household size: 2.25 (2010); Median age: 40.9 (2010); Males per 100 females: 91.0 (2010); Marriage status: 31.1% never married, 44.1% now married, 10.2% widowed, 14.5% divorced (2006-2010 5-year est.); Foreign born: 0.2% (2006-2010 5-year est.); Ancestry (includes multiple ancestries): 25.9% German, 23.0% Italian, 22.9% Irish, 15.1% English, 8.1% Dutch (2006-2010 5-year est.).

**Economy:** Single-family building permits issued: 0 (2011); Multi-family building permits issued: 0 (2011); Employment by occupation: 8.3% management, 2.4% professional, 13.0% services, 19.7% sales, 4.9% farming, 3.1% construction, 5.9% production (2006-2010 5-year est.).

**Income:** Per capita income: $19,076 (2006-2010 5-year est.); Median household income: $35,656 (2006-2010 5-year est.); Average household income: $43,466 (2006-2010 5-year est.); Percent of households with income of $100,000 or more: 6.2% (2006-2010 5-year est.); Poverty rate: 14.5% (2006-2010 5-year est.).

**Education:** Percent of population age 25 and over with: High school diploma (including GED) or higher: 89.8% (2006-2010 5-year est.); Bachelor's degree or higher: 20.0% (2006-2010 5-year est.); Master's degree or higher: 5.7% (2006-2010 5-year est.).

### School District(s)
Mohawk Central School District (PK-12)
    2009-10 Enrollment: 902 . . . . . . . . . . . . . . . . . . . . . . . (315) 867-2904

**Housing:** Homeownership rate: 60.7% (2010); Median home value: $78,900 (2006-2010 5-year est.); Median contract rent: $426 per month (2006-2010 5-year est.); Median year structure built: before 1940 (2006-2010 5-year est.).

**Transportation:** Commute to work: 91.6% car, 0.9% public transportation, 4.4% walk, 2.8% work from home (2006-2010 5-year est.); Travel time to work: 40.6% less than 15 minutes, 31.5% 15 to 30 minutes, 20.5% 30 to 45 minutes, 1.8% 45 to 60 minutes, 5.6% 60 minutes or more (2006-2010 5-year est.)

**Additional Information Contacts**
Herkimer County Chamber of Commerce . . . . . . . . . . . . . . (315) 866-7820
    http://www.herkimercountychamber.com

**NEWPORT** (village). Covers a land area of 0.525 square miles and a water area of 0.064 square miles. Located at 43.18° N. Lat; 75.01° W. Long. Elevation is 663 feet.

**Population:** 676 (1990); 640 (2000); 640 (2010); Density: 1,217.0 persons per square mile (2010); Race: 97.8% White, 1.1% Black, 0.3% Asian, 0.0% American Indian/Alaska Native, 0.2% Native Hawaiian/Other Pacific Islander, 0.6% Other, 0.9% Hispanic of any race (2010); Average household size: 2.34 (2010); Median age: 38.5 (2010); Males per 100 females: 91.6 (2010); Marriage status: 29.6% never married, 38.5% now married, 20.8% widowed, 11.1% divorced (2006-2010 5-year est.); Foreign born: 7.0% (2006-2010 5-year est.); Ancestry (includes multiple ancestries): 21.1% Irish, 17.4% German, 14.1% English, 11.2% French, 8.4% Italian (2006-2010 5-year est.).

**Economy:** Single-family building permits issued: 0 (2011); Multi-family building permits issued: 0 (2011); Employment by occupation: 0.0% management, 0.0% professional, 0.0% services, 20.2% sales, 2.8% farming, 20.2% construction, 0.0% production (2006-2010 5-year est.).

**Income:** Per capita income: $18,376 (2006-2010 5-year est.); Median household income: $23,500 (2006-2010 5-year est.); Average household income: $33,492 (2006-2010 5-year est.); Percent of households with income of $100,000 or more: 2.8% (2006-2010 5-year est.); Poverty rate: 2.5% (2006-2010 5-year est.).

**Education:** Percent of population age 25 and over with: High school diploma (including GED) or higher: 91.1% (2006-2010 5-year est.); Bachelor's degree or higher: 20.8% (2006-2010 5-year est.); Master's degree or higher: 14.9% (2006-2010 5-year est.).

**School District(s)**

West Canada Valley Central School District (PK-12)

   2009-10 Enrollment: 820 . . . . . . . . . . . . . . . . . . . . . . . . (315) 845-6800

**Housing:** Homeownership rate: 58.9% (2010); Median home value: $77,600 (2006-2010 5-year est.); Median contract rent: $281 per month (2006-2010 5-year est.); Median year structure built: 1958 (2006-2010 5-year est.).

**Transportation:** Commute to work: 91.5% car, 4.7% public transportation, 0.0% walk, 3.8% work from home (2006-2010 5-year est.); Travel time to work: 17.1% less than 15 minutes, 34.1% 15 to 30 minutes, 41.5% 30 to 45 minutes, 0.0% 45 to 60 minutes, 7.3% 60 minutes or more (2006-2010 5-year est.)

**NEWPORT** (town). Covers a land area of 32.008 square miles and a water area of 0.443 square miles. Located at 43.17° N. Lat; 75.03° W. Long. Elevation is 663 feet.

**Population:** 2,148 (1990); 2,192 (2000); 2,302 (2010); Density: 71.9 persons per square mile (2010); Race: 97.7% White, 0.6% Black, 0.2% Asian, 0.0% American Indian/Alaska Native, 0.0% Native Hawaiian/Other Pacific Islander, 1.5% Other, 0.8% Hispanic of any race (2010); Average household size: 2.61 (2010); Median age: 40.8 (2010); Males per 100 females: 94.6 (2010); Marriage status: 23.6% never married, 58.2% now married, 9.8% widowed, 8.4% divorced (2006-2010 5-year est.); Foreign born: 4.8% (2006-2010 5-year est.); Ancestry (includes multiple ancestries): 22.1% German, 19.6% Irish, 13.6% English, 13.5% Italian, 11.6% American (2006-2010 5-year est.).

**Economy:** Single-family building permits issued: 2 (2011); Multi-family building permits issued: 0 (2011); Employment by occupation: 6.6% management, 1.8% professional, 7.3% services, 24.1% sales, 4.0% farming, 16.0% construction, 8.0% production (2006-2010 5-year est.).

**Income:** Per capita income: $21,350 (2006-2010 5-year est.); Median household income: $45,375 (2006-2010 5-year est.); Average household income: $53,608 (2006-2010 5-year est.); Percent of households with income of $100,000 or more: 12.0% (2006-2010 5-year est.); Poverty rate: 10.9% (2006-2010 5-year est.).

**Education:** Percent of population age 25 and over with: High school diploma (including GED) or higher: 84.8% (2006-2010 5-year est.); Bachelor's degree or higher: 17.7% (2006-2010 5-year est.); Master's degree or higher: 7.8% (2006-2010 5-year est.).

**School District(s)**

West Canada Valley Central School District (PK-12)

   2009-10 Enrollment: 820 . . . . . . . . . . . . . . . . . . . . . . . . (315) 845-6800

**Housing:** Homeownership rate: 78.6% (2010); Median home value: $108,200 (2006-2010 5-year est.); Median contract rent: $318 per month (2006-2010 5-year est.); Median year structure built: 1975 (2006-2010 5-year est.).

**Transportation:** Commute to work: 89.7% car, 1.0% public transportation, 1.3% walk, 5.4% work from home (2006-2010 5-year est.); Travel time to work: 27.2% less than 15 minutes, 33.1% 15 to 30 minutes, 28.1% 30 to 45

minutes, 3.9% 45 to 60 minutes, 7.8% 60 minutes or more (2006-2010 5-year est.)

**NORWAY** (town). Covers a land area of 35.559 square miles and a water area of 0.273 square miles. Located at 43.23° N. Lat; 74.95° W. Long. Elevation is 1,332 feet.

**Population:** 663 (1990); 711 (2000); 762 (2010); Density: 21.4 persons per square mile (2010); Race: 99.3% White, 0.1% Black, 0.1% Asian, 0.0% American Indian/Alaska Native, 0.0% Native Hawaiian/Other Pacific Islander, 0.5% Other, 2.0% Hispanic of any race (2010); Average household size: 2.53 (2010); Median age: 41.3 (2010); Males per 100 females: 101.6 (2010); Marriage status: 21.2% never married, 58.2% now married, 5.5% widowed, 15.0% divorced (2006-2010 5-year est.); Foreign born: 0.3% (2006-2010 5-year est.); Ancestry (includes multiple ancestries): 24.8% German, 15.6% Irish, 12.5% American, 10.4% Italian, 9.1% French Canadian (2006-2010 5-year est.).

**Economy:** Single-family building permits issued: 4 (2011); Multi-family building permits issued: 0 (2011); Employment by occupation: 18.1% management, 3.4% professional, 16.9% services, 8.8% sales, 7.1% farming, 14.5% construction, 10.3% production (2006-2010 5-year est.).

**Income:** Per capita income: $23,603 (2006-2010 5-year est.); Median household income: $49,271 (2006-2010 5-year est.); Average household income: $62,279 (2006-2010 5-year est.); Percent of households with income of $100,000 or more: 22.8% (2006-2010 5-year est.); Poverty rate: 4.9% (2006-2010 5-year est.).

**Education:** Percent of population age 25 and over with: High school diploma (including GED) or higher: 93.2% (2006-2010 5-year est.); Bachelor's degree or higher: 13.5% (2006-2010 5-year est.); Master's degree or higher: 3.2% (2006-2010 5-year est.).

**Housing:** Homeownership rate: 87.1% (2010); Median home value: $88,500 (2006-2010 5-year est.); Median contract rent: $386 per month (2006-2010 5-year est.); Median year structure built: 1982 (2006-2010 5-year est.).

**Transportation:** Commute to work: 86.7% car, 0.0% public transportation, 1.0% walk, 11.3% work from home (2006-2010 5-year est.); Travel time to work: 13.3% less than 15 minutes, 22.0% 15 to 30 minutes, 52.3% 30 to 45 minutes, 11.6% 45 to 60 minutes, 0.9% 60 minutes or more (2006-2010 5-year est.)

**OHIO** (town). Covers a land area of 301.344 square miles and a water area of 6.226 square miles. Located at 43.46° N. Lat; 74.89° W. Long. Elevation is 1,371 feet.

**Population:** 880 (1990); 922 (2000); 1,002 (2010); Density: 3.3 persons per square mile (2010); Race: 97.8% White, 0.2% Black, 0.6% Asian, 0.6% American Indian/Alaska Native, 0.0% Native Hawaiian/Other Pacific Islander, 0.8% Other, 0.7% Hispanic of any race (2010); Average household size: 2.37 (2010); Median age: 46.9 (2010); Males per 100 females: 104.1 (2010); Marriage status: 18.7% never married, 61.0% now married, 4.2% widowed, 16.2% divorced (2006-2010 5-year est.); Foreign born: 2.8% (2006-2010 5-year est.); Ancestry (includes multiple ancestries): 22.5% German, 17.7% Irish, 14.2% American, 11.1% Polish, 10.5% English (2006-2010 5-year est.).

**Economy:** Single-family building permits issued: 2 (2011); Multi-family building permits issued: 0 (2011); Employment by occupation: 6.3% management, 3.6% professional, 9.9% services, 17.8% sales, 1.3% farming, 21.1% construction, 5.3% production (2006-2010 5-year est.).

**Income:** Per capita income: $21,811 (2006-2010 5-year est.); Median household income: $38,603 (2006-2010 5-year est.); Average household income: $47,539 (2006-2010 5-year est.); Percent of households with income of $100,000 or more: 8.0% (2006-2010 5-year est.); Poverty rate: 16.3% (2006-2010 5-year est.).

**Education:** Percent of population age 25 and over with: High school diploma (including GED) or higher: 85.7% (2006-2010 5-year est.); Bachelor's degree or higher: 14.0% (2006-2010 5-year est.); Master's degree or higher: 7.3% (2006-2010 5-year est.).

**Housing:** Homeownership rate: 87.4% (2010); Median home value: $86,900 (2006-2010 5-year est.); Median contract rent: $533 per month (2006-2010 5-year est.); Median year structure built: 1966 (2006-2010 5-year est.).

**Transportation:** Commute to work: 94.1% car, 1.0% public transportation, 0.8% walk, 4.1% work from home (2006-2010 5-year est.); Travel time to work: 9.2% less than 15 minutes, 14.3% 15 to 30 minutes, 44.2% 30 to 45 minutes, 22.6% 45 to 60 minutes, 9.7% 60 minutes or more (2006-2010 5-year est.)

**OLD FORGE** (CDP). Covers a land area of 1.786 square miles and a water area of 0.177 square miles. Located at 43.70° N. Lat; 74.96° W. Long. Elevation is 1,736 feet.
**Population:** n/a (1990); n/a (2000); 756 (2010); Density: 423.2 persons per square mile (2010); Race: 97.0% White, 0.4% Black, 0.3% Asian, 0.7% American Indian/Alaska Native, 0.0% Native Hawaiian/Other Pacific Islander, 1.6% Other, 1.2% Hispanic of any race (2010); Average household size: 2.04 (2010); Median age: 47.9 (2010); Males per 100 females: 95.3 (2010); Marriage status: 23.6% never married, 64.9% now married, 11.5% widowed, 0.0% divorced (2006-2010 5-year est.); Foreign born: 4.3% (2006-2010 5-year est.); Ancestry (includes multiple ancestries): 24.1% English, 15.0% German, 12.6% Irish, 10.9% Dutch, 9.7% Italian (2006-2010 5-year est.).
**Economy:** Employment by occupation: 16.8% management, 0.0% professional, 7.5% services, 25.9% sales, 4.4% farming, 19.9% construction, 0.0% production (2006-2010 5-year est.).
**Income:** Per capita income: $29,105 (2006-2010 5-year est.); Median household income: $39,563 (2006-2010 5-year est.); Average household income: $50,169 (2006-2010 5-year est.); Percent of households with income of $100,000 or more: 9.4% (2006-2010 5-year est.); Poverty rate: 0.0% (2006-2010 5-year est.).
**Education:** Percent of population age 25 and over with: High school diploma (including GED) or higher: 90.8% (2006-2010 5-year est.); Bachelor's degree or higher: 28.9% (2006-2010 5-year est.); Master's degree or higher: 5.6% (2006-2010 5-year est.).
**School District(s)**
Town of Webb Union Free School District (KG-12)
    2009-10 Enrollment: 294 . . . . . . . . . . . . . . . . . . . . . (315) 369-3222
**Housing:** Homeownership rate: 62.3% (2010); Median home value: $209,900 (2006-2010 5-year est.); Median contract rent: $567 per month (2006-2010 5-year est.); Median year structure built: 1963 (2006-2010 5-year est.).
**Transportation:** Commute to work: 74.3% car, 0.0% public transportation, 25.7% walk, 0.0% work from home (2006-2010 5-year est.); Travel time to work: 60.6% less than 15 minutes, 24.4% 15 to 30 minutes, 6.3% 30 to 45 minutes, 6.3% 45 to 60 minutes, 2.2% 60 minutes or more (2006-2010 5-year est.).

**POLAND** (village). Covers a land area of 0.542 square miles and a water area of 0.006 square miles. Located at 43.22° N. Lat; 75.06° W. Long. Elevation is 709 feet.
**Population:** 420 (1990); 451 (2000); 508 (2010); Density: 935.7 persons per square mile (2010); Race: 98.4% White, 0.4% Black, 0.0% Asian, 0.6% American Indian/Alaska Native, 0.0% Native Hawaiian/Other Pacific Islander, 0.6% Other, 1.0% Hispanic of any race (2010); Average household size: 2.58 (2010); Median age: 40.0 (2010); Males per 100 females: 89.6 (2010); Marriage status: 31.9% never married, 55.0% now married, 3.5% widowed, 9.5% divorced (2006-2010 5-year est.); Foreign born: 3.7% (2006-2010 5-year est.); Ancestry (includes multiple ancestries): 39.7% German, 28.5% Irish, 12.0% English, 12.0% Polish, 7.2% Italian (2006-2010 5-year est.).
**Economy:** Single-family building permits issued: 0 (2011); Multi-family building permits issued: 0 (2011); Employment by occupation: 2.3% management, 5.6% professional, 6.0% services, 12.1% sales, 5.1% farming, 9.8% construction, 6.0% production (2006-2010 5-year est.).
**Income:** Per capita income: $26,186 (2006-2010 5-year est.); Median household income: $60,083 (2006-2010 5-year est.); Average household income: $76,209 (2006-2010 5-year est.); Percent of households with income of $100,000 or more: 22.7% (2006-2010 5-year est.); Poverty rate: 6.6% (2006-2010 5-year est.).
**Education:** Percent of population age 25 and over with: High school diploma (including GED) or higher: 94.8% (2006-2010 5-year est.); Bachelor's degree or higher: 29.8% (2006-2010 5-year est.); Master's degree or higher: 11.4% (2006-2010 5-year est.).
**School District(s)**
Poland Central School District (PK-12)
    2009-10 Enrollment: 679 . . . . . . . . . . . . . . . . . . . . . (315) 826-0203
**Housing:** Homeownership rate: 74.5% (2010); Median home value: $107,100 (2006-2010 5-year est.); Median contract rent: $429 per month (2006-2010 5-year est.); Median year structure built: before 1940 (2006-2010 5-year est.).
**Transportation:** Commute to work: 79.1% car, 0.0% public transportation, 6.2% walk, 10.9% work from home (2006-2010 5-year est.); Travel time to work: 23.9% less than 15 minutes, 45.2% 15 to 30 minutes, 23.9% 30 to 45

minutes, 1.1% 45 to 60 minutes, 5.9% 60 minutes or more (2006-2010 5-year est.).

**RUSSIA** (town). Covers a land area of 56.961 square miles and a water area of 3.456 square miles. Located at 43.30° N. Lat; 75.06° W. Long. Elevation is 1,129 feet.
**Population:** 2,294 (1990); 2,487 (2000); 2,587 (2010); Density: 45.4 persons per square mile (2010); Race: 98.4% White, 0.1% Black, 0.3% Asian, 0.5% American Indian/Alaska Native, 0.0% Native Hawaiian/Other Pacific Islander, 0.7% Other, 1.0% Hispanic of any race (2010); Average household size: 2.45 (2010); Median age: 44.3 (2010); Males per 100 females: 103.4 (2010); Marriage status: 28.7% never married, 53.1% now married, 6.3% widowed, 11.9% divorced (2006-2010 5-year est.); Foreign born: 0.4% (2006-2010 5-year est.); Ancestry (includes multiple ancestries): 27.6% German, 20.5% Irish, 15.0% English, 12.5% Polish, 9.7% American (2006-2010 5-year est.).
**Economy:** Single-family building permits issued: 0 (2011); Multi-family building permits issued: 0 (2011); Employment by occupation: 8.7% management, 3.0% professional, 9.1% services, 16.3% sales, 4.6% farming, 13.2% construction, 9.0% production (2006-2010 5-year est.).
**Income:** Per capita income: $23,567 (2006-2010 5-year est.); Median household income: $49,853 (2006-2010 5-year est.); Average household income: $58,743 (2006-2010 5-year est.); Percent of households with income of $100,000 or more: 12.6% (2006-2010 5-year est.); Poverty rate: 9.5% (2006-2010 5-year est.).
**Education:** Percent of population age 25 and over with: High school diploma (including GED) or higher: 91.7% (2006-2010 5-year est.); Bachelor's degree or higher: 20.6% (2006-2010 5-year est.); Master's degree or higher: 9.5% (2006-2010 5-year est.).
**Housing:** Homeownership rate: 85.0% (2010); Median home value: $97,200 (2006-2010 5-year est.); Median contract rent: $437 per month (2006-2010 5-year est.); Median year structure built: 1964 (2006-2010 5-year est.).
**Transportation:** Commute to work: 90.5% car, 0.3% public transportation, 4.9% walk, 2.8% work from home (2006-2010 5-year est.); Travel time to work: 18.6% less than 15 minutes, 40.4% 15 to 30 minutes, 31.5% 30 to 45 minutes, 6.9% 45 to 60 minutes, 2.6% 60 minutes or more (2006-2010 5-year est.).

**SALISBURY** (town). Covers a land area of 107.366 square miles and a water area of 0.835 square miles. Located at 43.22° N. Lat; 74.80° W. Long. Elevation is 1,220 feet.
**Population:** 1,934 (1990); 1,953 (2000); 1,958 (2010); Density: 18.2 persons per square mile (2010); Race: 97.9% White, 0.2% Black, 0.3% Asian, 0.3% American Indian/Alaska Native, 0.0% Native Hawaiian/Other Pacific Islander, 1.4% Other, 1.9% Hispanic of any race (2010); Average household size: 2.66 (2010); Median age: 39.3 (2010); Males per 100 females: 102.1 (2010); Marriage status: 21.3% never married, 64.2% now married, 5.1% widowed, 9.5% divorced (2006-2010 5-year est.); Foreign born: 2.5% (2006-2010 5-year est.); Ancestry (includes multiple ancestries): 27.5% German, 17.6% Irish, 13.8% English, 11.0% Dutch, 9.8% American (2006-2010 5-year est.).
**Economy:** Single-family building permits issued: 0 (2011); Multi-family building permits issued: 0 (2011); Employment by occupation: 9.4% management, 0.6% professional, 11.1% services, 12.6% sales, 5.2% farming, 16.1% construction, 8.3% production (2006-2010 5-year est.).
**Income:** Per capita income: $18,618 (2006-2010 5-year est.); Median household income: $40,694 (2006-2010 5-year est.); Average household income: $49,024 (2006-2010 5-year est.); Percent of households with income of $100,000 or more: 7.7% (2006-2010 5-year est.); Poverty rate: 14.4% (2006-2010 5-year est.).
**Education:** Percent of population age 25 and over with: High school diploma (including GED) or higher: 78.8% (2006-2010 5-year est.); Bachelor's degree or higher: 10.5% (2006-2010 5-year est.); Master's degree or higher: 4.2% (2006-2010 5-year est.).
**Housing:** Homeownership rate: 85.9% (2010); Median home value: $80,800 (2006-2010 5-year est.); Median contract rent: $510 per month (2006-2010 5-year est.); Median year structure built: 1972 (2006-2010 5-year est.).
**Transportation:** Commute to work: 92.1% car, 0.7% public transportation, 4.3% walk, 2.9% work from home (2006-2010 5-year est.); Travel time to work: 22.4% less than 15 minutes, 25.9% 15 to 30 minutes, 26.1% 30 to 45 minutes, 11.5% 45 to 60 minutes, 14.1% 60 minutes or more (2006-2010 5-year est.).

## SALISBURY CENTER (unincorporated postal area)
Zip Code: 13454

Covers a land area of 43.049 square miles and a water area of 0.283 square miles. Located at 43.21° N. Lat; 74.75° W. Long. Elevation is 1,073 feet. Population: 826 (2010); Density: 19.2 persons per square mile (2010); Race: 97.1% White, 0.2% Black, 0.4% Asian, 0.0% American Indian/Alaska Native, 0.0% Native Hawaiian/Other Pacific Islander, 2.3% Other, 2.7% Hispanic of any race (2010); Average household size: 2.66 (2010); Median age: 38.2 (2010); Males per 100 females: 99.0 (2010); Homeownership rate: 82.5% (2010)

## SCHUYLER (town). Covers a land area of 39.874 square miles and a water area of 0.357 square miles. Located at 43.11° N. Lat; 75.09° W. Long.
**Population:** 3,508 (1990); 3,385 (2000); 3,420 (2010); Density: 85.8 persons per square mile (2010); Race: 97.8% White, 0.4% Black, 0.6% Asian, 0.2% American Indian/Alaska Native, 0.0% Native Hawaiian/Other Pacific Islander, 1.0% Other, 1.4% Hispanic of any race (2010); Average household size: 2.32 (2010); Median age: 45.6 (2010); Males per 100 females: 94.6 (2010); Marriage status: 23.5% never married, 54.2% now married, 10.1% widowed, 12.2% divorced (2006-2010 5-year est.); Foreign born: 13.9% (2006-2010 5-year est.); Ancestry (includes multiple ancestries): 22.0% German, 21.9% Italian, 18.7% Irish, 13.2% English, 9.5% Ukrainian (2006-2010 5-year est.).
**Economy:** Single-family building permits issued: 12 (2011); Multi-family building permits issued: 0 (2011); Employment by occupation: 11.8% management, 1.5% professional, 10.1% services, 13.6% sales, 3.0% farming, 6.9% construction, 5.9% production (2006-2010 5-year est.).
**Income:** Per capita income: $21,772 (2006-2010 5-year est.); Median household income: $48,172 (2006-2010 5-year est.); Average household income: $53,699 (2006-2010 5-year est.); Percent of households with income of $100,000 or more: 12.1% (2006-2010 5-year est.); Poverty rate: 5.9% (2006-2010 5-year est.).
**Education:** Percent of population age 25 and over with: High school diploma (including GED) or higher: 87.4% (2006-2010 5-year est.); Bachelor's degree or higher: 23.1% (2006-2010 5-year est.); Master's degree or higher: 11.1% (2006-2010 5-year est.).
**Housing:** Homeownership rate: 82.7% (2010); Median home value: $89,000 (2006-2010 5-year est.); Median contract rent: $528 per month (2006-2010 5-year est.); Median year structure built: 1981 (2006-2010 5-year est.).
**Transportation:** Commute to work: 90.6% car, 0.0% public transportation, 2.6% walk, 6.8% work from home (2006-2010 5-year est.); Travel time to work: 23.7% less than 15 minutes, 57.3% 15 to 30 minutes, 13.4% 30 to 45 minutes, 2.6% 45 to 60 minutes, 3.0% 60 minutes or more (2006-2010 5-year est.)
**Additional Information Contacts**
Town of Schuyler . . . . . . . . . . . . . . . . . . . . . . . . . . . . . . . (315) 733-7458
  http://townofschuyler.com

## STARK (town). Covers a land area of 31.833 square miles and a water area of 0.002 square miles. Located at 42.92° N. Lat; 74.82° W. Long.
**Population:** 730 (1990); 767 (2000); 757 (2010); Density: 23.8 persons per square mile (2010); Race: 96.6% White, 0.8% Black, 0.1% Asian, 1.1% American Indian/Alaska Native, 0.0% Native Hawaiian/Other Pacific Islander, 1.4% Other, 1.6% Hispanic of any race (2010); Average household size: 2.73 (2010); Median age: 41.4 (2010); Males per 100 females: 112.6 (2010); Marriage status: 29.0% never married, 55.8% now married, 5.9% widowed, 9.3% divorced (2006-2010 5-year est.); Foreign born: 1.9% (2006-2010 5-year est.); Ancestry (includes multiple ancestries): 27.8% German, 12.2% Dutch, 11.3% Polish, 10.3% English, 9.1% American (2006-2010 5-year est.).
**Economy:** Single-family building permits issued: 0 (2011); Multi-family building permits issued: 0 (2011); Employment by occupation: 15.7% management, 0.0% professional, 13.5% services, 11.6% sales, 0.0% farming, 14.1% construction, 5.7% production (2006-2010 5-year est.).
**Income:** Per capita income: $19,844 (2006-2010 5-year est.); Median household income: $39,938 (2006-2010 5-year est.); Average household income: $51,131 (2006-2010 5-year est.); Percent of households with income of $100,000 or more: 10.5% (2006-2010 5-year est.); Poverty rate: 2.7% (2006-2010 5-year est.).
**Education:** Percent of population age 25 and over with: High school diploma (including GED) or higher: 89.8% (2006-2010 5-year est.); Bachelor's degree or higher: 16.8% (2006-2010 5-year est.); Master's degree or higher: 6.2% (2006-2010 5-year est.).

**Housing:** Homeownership rate: 83.4% (2010); Median home value: $98,800 (2006-2010 5-year est.); Median contract rent: $469 per month (2006-2010 5-year est.); Median year structure built: 1963 (2006-2010 5-year est.).
**Transportation:** Commute to work: 76.4% car, 0.0% public transportation, 4.3% walk, 18.4% work from home (2006-2010 5-year est.); Travel time to work: 20.3% less than 15 minutes, 36.2% 15 to 30 minutes, 21.3% 30 to 45 minutes, 9.0% 45 to 60 minutes, 13.3% 60 minutes or more (2006-2010 5-year est.).

## THENDARA (unincorporated postal area)
Zip Code: 13472

Covers a land area of 14.444 square miles and a water area of 0.424 square miles. Located at 43.69° N. Lat; 75.06° W. Long. Elevation is 1,706 feet. Population: 310 (2010); Density: 21.5 persons per square mile (2010); Race: 97.4% White, 0.6% Black, 0.3% Asian, 0.0% American Indian/Alaska Native, 0.0% Native Hawaiian/Other Pacific Islander, 1.7% Other, 1.3% Hispanic of any race (2010); Average household size: 2.18 (2010); Median age: 51.3 (2010); Males per 100 females: 110.9 (2010); Homeownership rate: 80.9% (2010)

## VAN HORNESVILLE (unincorporated postal area)
Zip Code: 13475

Covers a land area of 0.015 square miles and a water area of 0 square miles. Located at 42.89° N. Lat; 74.83° W. Long. Elevation is 1,152 feet. Population: 28 (2010); Density: 1,853.1 persons per square mile (2010); Race: 100.0% White, 0.0% Black, 0.0% Asian, 0.0% American Indian/Alaska Native, 0.0% Native Hawaiian/Other Pacific Islander, 0.0% Other, 0.0% Hispanic of any race (2010); Average household size: 2.33 (2010); Median age: 51.5 (2010); Males per 100 females: 100.0 (2010); Homeownership rate: 66.6% (2010)

## WARREN (town). Covers a land area of 37.791 square miles and a water area of 0.319 square miles. Located at 42.89° N. Lat; 74.93° W. Long. Elevation is 1,371 feet.
**Population:** 1,077 (1990); 1,136 (2000); 1,143 (2010); Density: 30.2 persons per square mile (2010); Race: 97.9% White, 0.3% Black, 0.4% Asian, 0.0% American Indian/Alaska Native, 0.0% Native Hawaiian/Other Pacific Islander, 1.4% Other, 0.3% Hispanic of any race (2010); Average household size: 2.79 (2010); Median age: 42.3 (2010); Males per 100 females: 102.3 (2010); Marriage status: 25.9% never married, 60.5% now married, 6.8% widowed, 6.9% divorced (2006-2010 5-year est.); Foreign born: 6.8% (2006-2010 5-year est.); Ancestry (includes multiple ancestries): 30.9% Irish, 25.7% German, 11.3% English, 10.0% Italian, 9.1% Polish (2006-2010 5-year est.).
**Economy:** Single-family building permits issued: 0 (2011); Multi-family building permits issued: 0 (2011); Employment by occupation: 14.8% management, 2.1% professional, 11.8% services, 10.4% sales, 6.1% farming, 9.8% construction, 5.0% production (2006-2010 5-year est.).
**Income:** Per capita income: $19,395 (2006-2010 5-year est.); Median household income: $43,750 (2006-2010 5-year est.); Average household income: $50,045 (2006-2010 5-year est.); Percent of households with income of $100,000 or more: 8.9% (2006-2010 5-year est.); Poverty rate: 12.6% (2006-2010 5-year est.).
**Education:** Percent of population age 25 and over with: High school diploma (including GED) or higher: 83.8% (2006-2010 5-year est.); Bachelor's degree or higher: 14.9% (2006-2010 5-year est.); Master's degree or higher: 8.3% (2006-2010 5-year est.).
**Housing:** Homeownership rate: 82.5% (2010); Median home value: $87,800 (2006-2010 5-year est.); Median contract rent: $554 per month (2006-2010 5-year est.); Median year structure built: 1959 (2006-2010 5-year est.).
**Transportation:** Commute to work: 85.1% car, 0.0% public transportation, 6.2% walk, 7.1% work from home (2006-2010 5-year est.); Travel time to work: 21.9% less than 15 minutes, 31.1% 15 to 30 minutes, 27.2% 30 to 45 minutes, 11.2% 45 to 60 minutes, 8.6% 60 minutes or more (2006-2010 5-year est.).

## WEBB (town). Covers a land area of 452.284 square miles and a water area of 32.007 square miles. Located at 43.82° N. Lat; 75.03° W. Long.
**Population:** 1,637 (1990); 1,912 (2000); 1,807 (2010); Density: 4.0 persons per square mile (2010); Race: 97.6% White, 0.5% Black, 0.2% Asian, 0.3% American Indian/Alaska Native, 0.0% Native Hawaiian/Other Pacific Islander, 1.4% Other, 1.1% Hispanic of any race (2010); Average household size: 2.06 (2010); Median age: 51.8 (2010); Males per 100

females: 101.2 (2010); Marriage status: 27.1% never married, 61.9% now married, 8.0% widowed, 3.1% divorced (2006-2010 5-year est.); Foreign born: 1.4% (2006-2010 5-year est.); Ancestry (includes multiple ancestries): 22.3% German, 20.3% Irish, 16.3% English, 12.7% French Canadian, 10.0% American (2006-2010 5-year est.).
**Economy:** Single-family building permits issued: 26 (2011); Multi-family building permits issued: 0 (2011); Employment by occupation: 25.3% management, 0.0% professional, 11.6% services, 18.3% sales, 1.6% farming, 8.8% construction, 0.0% production (2006-2010 5-year est.).
**Income:** Per capita income: $29,153 (2006-2010 5-year est.); Median household income: $50,083 (2006-2010 5-year est.); Average household income: $60,974 (2006-2010 5-year est.); Percent of households with income of $100,000 or more: 16.8% (2006-2010 5-year est.); Poverty rate: 2.8% (2006-2010 5-year est.).
**Education:** Percent of population age 25 and over with: High school diploma (including GED) or higher: 93.1% (2006-2010 5-year est.); Bachelor's degree or higher: 35.0% (2006-2010 5-year est.); Master's degree or higher: 13.6% (2006-2010 5-year est.).
**Housing:** Homeownership rate: 77.3% (2010); Median home value: $309,500 (2006-2010 5-year est.); Median contract rent: $567 per month (2006-2010 5-year est.); Median year structure built: 1961 (2006-2010 5-year est.).
**Transportation:** Commute to work: 80.5% car, 0.0% public transportation, 14.1% walk, 5.3% work from home (2006-2010 5-year est.); Travel time to work: 51.6% less than 15 minutes, 32.5% 15 to 30 minutes, 6.8% 30 to 45 minutes, 2.5% 45 to 60 minutes, 6.6% 60 minutes or more (2006-2010 5-year est.)

**WEST WINFIELD** (village). Covers a land area of 0.911 square miles and a water area of 0 square miles. Located at 42.88° N. Lat; 75.19° W. Long. Elevation is 1,191 feet.
**Population:** 871 (1990); 862 (2000); 826 (2010); Density: 906.5 persons per square mile (2010); Race: 96.7% White, 0.0% Black, 0.4% Asian, 0.7% American Indian/Alaska Native, 0.0% Native Hawaiian/Other Pacific Islander, 2.2% Other, 2.1% Hispanic of any race (2010); Average household size: 2.29 (2010); Median age: 44.1 (2010); Males per 100 females: 84.0 (2010); Marriage status: 20.4% never married, 56.0% now married, 16.2% widowed, 7.4% divorced (2006-2010 5-year est.); Foreign born: 1.4% (2006-2010 5-year est.); Ancestry (includes multiple ancestries): 25.1% Irish, 21.5% German, 19.5% English, 14.4% Polish, 14.1% Welsh (2006-2010 5-year est.).
**Economy:** Single-family building permits issued: 0 (2011); Multi-family building permits issued: 0 (2011); Employment by occupation: 5.8% management, 6.4% professional, 9.0% services, 25.0% sales, 1.0% farming, 16.7% construction, 7.4% production (2006-2010 5-year est.).
**Income:** Per capita income: $23,939 (2006-2010 5-year est.); Median household income: $42,292 (2006-2010 5-year est.); Average household income: $58,196 (2006-2010 5-year est.); Percent of households with income of $100,000 or more: 16.2% (2006-2010 5-year est.); Poverty rate: 13.5% (2006-2010 5-year est.).
**Education:** Percent of population age 25 and over with: High school diploma (including GED) or higher: 93.1% (2006-2010 5-year est.); Bachelor's degree or higher: 25.9% (2006-2010 5-year est.); Master's degree or higher: 11.5% (2006-2010 5-year est.).

**School District(s)**
Mount Markham Central School District (PK-12)
    2009-10 Enrollment: 1,269 . . . . . . . . . . . . . . . . . . . (315) 822-2824
**Housing:** Homeownership rate: 71.4% (2010); Median home value: $94,400 (2006-2010 5-year est.); Median contract rent: $198 per month (2006-2010 5-year est.); Median year structure built: before 1940 (2006-2010 5-year est.).
**Newspapers:** West Winfield Star (Local news; Circulation 1,100)
**Transportation:** Commute to work: 81.1% car, 0.0% public transportation, 10.1% walk, 5.2% work from home (2006-2010 5-year est.); Travel time to work: 39.1% less than 15 minutes, 33.2% 15 to 30 minutes, 23.2% 30 to 45 minutes, 3.0% 45 to 60 minutes, 1.5% 60 minutes or more (2006-2010 5-year est.)

**WINFIELD** (town). Covers a land area of 23.639 square miles and a water area of 0.011 square miles. Located at 42.89° N. Lat; 75.16° W. Long.
**Population:** 2,146 (1990); 2,202 (2000); 2,086 (2010); Density: 88.2 persons per square mile (2010); Race: 97.4% White, 0.0% Black, 0.5% Asian, 0.3% American Indian/Alaska Native, 0.0% Native Hawaiian/Other Pacific Islander, 1.8% Other, 1.3% Hispanic of any race (2010); Average

household size: 2.52 (2010); Median age: 42.4 (2010); Males per 100 females: 96.2 (2010); Marriage status: 22.8% never married, 60.2% now married, 10.0% widowed, 7.0% divorced (2006-2010 5-year est.); Foreign born: 1.5% (2006-2010 5-year est.); Ancestry (includes multiple ancestries): 23.9% Irish, 22.4% English, 21.7% German, 14.0% Welsh, 7.3% Italian (2006-2010 5-year est.).
**Economy:** Single-family building permits issued: 2 (2011); Multi-family building permits issued: 0 (2011); Employment by occupation: 13.1% management, 3.5% professional, 7.9% services, 16.5% sales, 1.7% farming, 18.7% construction, 6.1% production (2006-2010 5-year est.).
**Income:** Per capita income: $25,249 (2006-2010 5-year est.); Median household income: $51,146 (2006-2010 5-year est.); Average household income: $65,547 (2006-2010 5-year est.); Percent of households with income of $100,000 or more: 19.7% (2006-2010 5-year est.); Poverty rate: 12.0% (2006-2010 5-year est.).
**Education:** Percent of population age 25 and over with: High school diploma (including GED) or higher: 89.6% (2006-2010 5-year est.); Bachelor's degree or higher: 19.8% (2006-2010 5-year est.); Master's degree or higher: 8.1% (2006-2010 5-year est.).
**Housing:** Homeownership rate: 78.9% (2010); Median home value: $91,600 (2006-2010 5-year est.); Median contract rent: $405 per month (2006-2010 5-year est.); Median year structure built: 1955 (2006-2010 5-year est.).
**Transportation:** Commute to work: 84.3% car, 0.0% public transportation, 4.4% walk, 10.2% work from home (2006-2010 5-year est.); Travel time to work: 29.9% less than 15 minutes, 38.8% 15 to 30 minutes, 23.3% 30 to 45 minutes, 4.7% 45 to 60 minutes, 3.3% 60 minutes or more (2006-2010 5-year est.)

# Jefferson County

Located in northern New York; bounded on the west by Lake Ontario, and on the northwest by the St. Lawrence River; drained by the Black and Indian Rivers. Covers a land area of 1,272.20 square miles, a water area of 584.88 square miles, and is located in the Eastern Time Zone at 44.03° N. Lat., 75.94° W. Long. The county was founded in 1805. County seat is Watertown.

Jefferson County is part of the Watertown-Fort Drum, NY Micropolitan Statistical Area. The entire metro area includes: Jefferson County, NY

Weather Station: Watertown                                        Elevation: 497 feet

|        | Jan  | Feb  | Mar  | Apr | May | Jun | Jul | Aug | Sep | Oct | Nov | Dec  |
|--------|------|------|------|-----|-----|-----|-----|-----|-----|-----|-----|------|
| High   | 29   | 31   | 40   | 54  | 66  | 75  | 80  | 79  | 71  | 58  | 46  | 35   |
| Low    | 10   | 12   | 22   | 35  | 47  | 56  | 61  | 60  | 52  | 40  | 31  | 18   |
| Precip | 3.3  | 2.7  | 2.7  | 3.2 | 3.6 | 3.3 | 3.4 | 4.0 | 4.3 | 4.2 | 4.6 | 3.7  |
| Snow   | 31.0 | 25.4 | 13.0 | 3.4 | tr  | 0.0 | 0.0 | 0.0 | 0.0 | 0.6 | 7.3 | 31.3 |

*High and Low temperatures in degrees Fahrenheit; Precipitation and Snow in inches*

Weather Station: Watertown Arpt                                   Elevation: 317 feet

|        | Jan  | Feb  | Mar  | Apr | May | Jun | Jul | Aug | Sep | Oct | Nov | Dec  |
|--------|------|------|------|-----|-----|-----|-----|-----|-----|-----|-----|------|
| High   | 29   | 31   | 40   | 54  | 66  | 74  | 79  | 78  | 70  | 58  | 47  | 35   |
| Low    | 10   | 11   | 20   | 33  | 44  | 53  | 58  | 56  | 48  | 38  | 30  | 17   |
| Precip | 2.6  | 2.2  | 2.3  | 3.0 | 3.0 | 2.8 | 2.7 | 3.1 | 3.7 | 3.7 | 3.8 | 3.1  |
| Snow   | na   | na   | na   | na  | na  | na  | na  | na  | na  | na  | na  | na   |

*High and Low temperatures in degrees Fahrenheit; Precipitation and Snow in inches*

**Population:** 110,943 (1990); 111,738 (2000); 116,229 (2010); Race: 88.7% White, 5.1% Black, 1.3% Asian, 0.5% American Indian/Alaska Native, 0.3% Native Hawaiian/Other Pacific Islander, 4.1% Other, 5.3% Hispanic of any race (2010); Density: 91.4 persons per square mile (2010); Average household size: 2.53 (2010); Median age: 32.6 (2010); Males per 100 females: 103.8 (2010).
**Religion:** Six largest groups: 18.2% Catholicism, 4.1% Methodist/Pietist, 2.1% Presbyterian-Reformed, 1.7% Baptist, 1.3% Muslim Estimate, 1.3% Holiness (2010)
**Economy:** Unemployment rate: 11.7% (February 2012); Total civilian labor force: 48,236 (February 2012); Leading industries: 22.9% retail trade; 19.3% health care and social assistance; 10.9% accommodation & food services (2009); Farms: 885 totaling 262,331 acres (2007); Companies that employ 500 or more persons: 4 (2009); Companies that employ 100 to 499 persons: 28 (2009); Companies that employ less than 100 persons: 2,392 (2009); Black-owned businesses: n/a (2007); Hispanic-owned businesses: n/a (2007); Asian-owned businesses: 134 (2007); Women-owned businesses: 2,294 (2007); Retail sales per capita: $14,590 (2010).

Single-family building permits issued: 209 (2011); Multi-family building permits issued: 84 (2011).
**Income:** Per capita income: $21,823 (2006-2010 5-year est.); Median household income: $43,410 (2006-2010 5-year est.); Average household income: $54,737 (2006-2010 5-year est.); Percent of households with income of $100,000 or more: 12.0% (2006-2010 5-year est.); Poverty rate: 14.4% (2006-2010 5-year est.); Bankruptcy rate: 2.59% (2011).
**Taxes:** Total county taxes per capita: $931 (2009); County property taxes per capita: $379 (2009).
**Education:** Percent of population age 25 and over with: High school diploma (including GED) or higher: 87.8% (2006-2010 5-year est.); Bachelor's degree or higher: 20.2% (2006-2010 5-year est.); Master's degree or higher: 8.5% (2006-2010 5-year est.).
**Housing:** Homeownership rate: 58.1% (2010); Median home value: $116,800 (2006-2010 5-year est.); Median contract rent: $596 per month (2006-2010 5-year est.); Median year structure built: 1960 (2006-2010 5-year est.).
**Health:** Birth rate: 170.8 per 10,000 population (2011); Death rate: 77.2 per 10,000 population (2011); Age-adjusted cancer mortality rate: 174.0 deaths per 100,000 population (2009); Number of physicians: 17.0 per 10,000 population (2008); Hospital beds: 30.3 per 10,000 population (2007); Hospital admissions: 817.0 per 10,000 population (2007).
**Environment:** Air Quality Index: 92.2% good, 6.1% moderate, 1.7% unhealthy for sensitive individuals, 0.0% unhealthy (percent of days in 2010)
**Elections:** 2008 Presidential election results: 46.7% Obama, 52.0% McCain, 0.7% Nader
**National and State Parks:** Brownville State Game Farm; Burnham Point State Park; Canoe Point And Picnic Point State Park; Cedar Point State Park; Grass Point State Park; Keewaydin Point State Park; Kring Point State Park; Long Point State Park; Mary Island State Park; Perch River State Game Management Area; Sackets Harbor Battlefield State Park; Southwich Beach State Park; Wellesley Island State Park; Westcott Beach State Park
**Additional Information Contacts**
Jefferson County Government . . . . . . . . . . . . . . . . (315) 785-3200
   http://www.co.jefferson.ny.us
Alexandria Bay Chamber of Commerce . . . . . . . . . . . . (315) 482-9531
   http://www.visitalexbay.org
Cape Vincent Chamber of Commerce . . . . . . . . . . . (315) 654-2481
   http://www.capevincent.org
Carthage Area Chamber of Commerce . . . . . . . . . . (315) 493-3590
   http://carthageny.com
Chaumont-Three Mile Bay Chamber of Commerce . . . . . (315) 649-3404
   http://www.chaumontchamber.com
City of Watertown . . . . . . . . . . . . . . . . . . . . . (315) 785-7780
   http://www.citywatertown.org
Clayton Chamber of Commerce . . . . . . . . . . . . . . (315) 686-3771
   http://www.1000islands-clayton.com
Greater Watertown-North Country Chamber of Commerce. (315) 788-4400
   http://www.watertownny.com
Henderson Harbor Area Chamber of Commerce . . . . . . . (315) 938-5568
   http://www.hendersonharborny.com
Sackets Harbor Chamber of Commerce . . . . . . . . . . (315) 646-1700
   http://www.sacketsharborchamberofcommerce.com
South Jefferson Chamber of Commerce . . . . . . . . . . . (315) 232-4215
   http://www.southjeffchamber.org
Town of Champion . . . . . . . . . . . . . . . . . . . . . (315) 493-3240
   http://www.racog.org/Champion/Championhomepage.php
Village of West Carthage . . . . . . . . . . . . . . . . . (315) 493-2552
   http://villageofwestcarthage.org

## Jefferson County Communities

**ADAMS** (village). Covers a land area of 1.446 square miles and a water area of 0 square miles. Located at 43.81° N. Lat; 76.02° W. Long. Elevation is 614 feet.
**Population:** 1,931 (1990); 1,624 (2000); 1,775 (2010); Density: 1,226.7 persons per square mile (2010); Race: 97.4% White, 0.7% Black, 0.5% Asian, 0.1% American Indian/Alaska Native, 0.0% Native Hawaiian/Other Pacific Islander, 1.3% Other, 0.7% Hispanic of any race (2010); Average household size: 2.40 (2010); Median age: 35.6 (2010); Males per 100 females: 88.8 (2010); Marriage status: 23.8% never married, 56.3% now married, 7.5% widowed, 12.5% divorced (2006-2010 5-year est.); Foreign born: 2.6% (2006-2010 5-year est.); Ancestry (includes multiple

ancestries): 20.0% English, 19.2% Irish, 14.6% Italian, 13.4% German, 9.3% French (2006-2010 5-year est.).
**Economy:** Employment by occupation: 12.7% management, 1.6% professional, 8.3% services, 23.4% sales, 3.4% farming, 11.1% construction, 2.8% production (2006-2010 5-year est.).
**Income:** Per capita income: $21,228 (2006-2010 5-year est.); Median household income: $43,405 (2006-2010 5-year est.); Average household income: $49,684 (2006-2010 5-year est.); Percent of households with income of $100,000 or more: 8.1% (2006-2010 5-year est.); Poverty rate: 13.9% (2006-2010 5-year est.).
**Education:** Percent of population age 25 and over with: High school diploma (including GED) or higher: 85.8% (2006-2010 5-year est.); Bachelor's degree or higher: 20.4% (2006-2010 5-year est.); Master's degree or higher: 9.4% (2006-2010 5-year est.).
**School District(s)**
South Jefferson Central School District (PK-12)
   2009-10 Enrollment: 2,036 . . . . . . . . . . . . . . . . . (315) 583-6104
**Housing:** Homeownership rate: 55.9% (2010); Median home value: $111,100 (2006-2010 5-year est.); Median contract rent: $445 per month (2006-2010 5-year est.); Median year structure built: before 1940 (2006-2010 5-year est.).
**Safety:** Violent crime rate: 6.0 per 10,000 population; Property crime rate: 102.2 per 10,000 population (2010).
**Newspapers:** Lure of the Lake (Local news; Circulation 5,000)
**Transportation:** Commute to work: 93.6% car, 0.0% public transportation, 2.8% walk, 2.2% work from home (2006-2010 5-year est.); Travel time to work: 35.1% less than 15 minutes, 47.8% 15 to 30 minutes, 9.3% 30 to 45 minutes, 5.8% 45 to 60 minutes, 2.0% 60 minutes or more (2006-2010 5-year est.)
**Additional Information Contacts**
South Jefferson Chamber of Commerce . . . . . . . . . . . (315) 232-4215
   http://www.southjeffchamber.org

**ADAMS** (town). Covers a land area of 42.270 square miles and a water area of 0.152 square miles. Located at 43.84° N. Lat; 76.05° W. Long. Elevation is 614 feet.
**History:** Incorporated 1851.
**Population:** 5,006 (1990); 4,782 (2000); 5,143 (2010); Density: 121.7 persons per square mile (2010); Race: 97.2% White, 0.8% Black, 0.4% Asian, 0.2% American Indian/Alaska Native, 0.1% Native Hawaiian/Other Pacific Islander, 1.3% Other, 0.9% Hispanic of any race (2010); Average household size: 2.58 (2010); Median age: 38.5 (2010); Males per 100 females: 93.9 (2010); Marriage status: 24.7% never married, 58.1% now married, 7.2% widowed, 9.9% divorced (2006-2010 5-year est.); Foreign born: 1.0% (2006-2010 5-year est.); Ancestry (includes multiple ancestries): 23.2% Irish, 18.4% English, 17.9% German, 11.5% French, 9.0% Italian (2006-2010 5-year est.).
**Economy:** Employment by occupation: 10.6% management, 2.3% professional, 8.4% services, 15.7% sales, 3.2% farming, 13.9% construction, 4.5% production (2006-2010 5-year est.).
**Income:** Per capita income: $24,398 (2006-2010 5-year est.); Median household income: $53,988 (2006-2010 5-year est.); Average household income: $61,621 (2006-2010 5-year est.); Percent of households with income of $100,000 or more: 15.1% (2006-2010 5-year est.); Poverty rate: 7.1% (2006-2010 5-year est.).
**Education:** Percent of population age 25 and over with: High school diploma (including GED) or higher: 88.9% (2006-2010 5-year est.); Bachelor's degree or higher: 19.8% (2006-2010 5-year est.); Master's degree or higher: 11.4% (2006-2010 5-year est.).
**School District(s)**
South Jefferson Central School District (PK-12)
   2009-10 Enrollment: 2,036 . . . . . . . . . . . . . . . . . (315) 583-6104
**Housing:** Homeownership rate: 73.4% (2010); Median home value: $116,600 (2006-2010 5-year est.); Median contract rent: $503 per month (2006-2010 5-year est.); Median year structure built: 1952 (2006-2010 5-year est.).
**Newspapers:** Lure of the Lake (Local news; Circulation 5,000)
**Transportation:** Commute to work: 93.4% car, 0.0% public transportation, 2.8% walk, 2.9% work from home (2006-2010 5-year est.); Travel time to work: 33.4% less than 15 minutes, 44.6% 15 to 30 minutes, 15.6% 30 to 45 minutes, 2.6% 45 to 60 minutes, 3.8% 60 minutes or more (2006-2010 5-year est.)

**ADAMS CENTER** (CDP). Covers a land area of 4.855 square miles and a water area of 0.135 square miles. Located at 43.86° N. Lat; 75.98° W. Long. Elevation is 640 feet.
**Population:** 1,675 (1990); 1,500 (2000); 1,568 (2010); Density: 322.9 persons per square mile (2010); Race: 95.5% White, 1.5% Black, 0.4% Asian, 0.1% American Indian/Alaska Native, 0.3% Native Hawaiian/Other Pacific Islander, 2.2% Other, 1.3% Hispanic of any race (2010); Average household size: 2.64 (2010); Median age: 38.2 (2010); Males per 100 females: 91.7 (2010); Marriage status: 29.6% never married, 48.9% now married, 7.3% widowed, 14.2% divorced (2006-2010 5-year est.); Foreign born: 0.0% (2006-2010 5-year est.); Ancestry (includes multiple ancestries): 30.9% Irish, 23.8% German, 12.2% French, 11.3% English, 10.4% European (2006-2010 5-year est.).
**Economy:** Employment by occupation: 9.9% management, 0.0% professional, 9.2% services, 9.6% sales, 5.4% farming, 23.0% construction, 8.1% production (2006-2010 5-year est.).
**Income:** Per capita income: $26,794 (2006-2010 5-year est.); Median household income: $58,945 (2006-2010 5-year est.); Average household income: $66,844 (2006-2010 5-year est.); Percent of households with income of $100,000 or more: 14.9% (2006-2010 5-year est.); Poverty rate: 3.2% (2006-2010 5-year est.).
**Education:** Percent of population age 25 and over with: High school diploma (including GED) or higher: 89.9% (2006-2010 5-year est.); Bachelor's degree or higher: 16.5% (2006-2010 5-year est.); Master's degree or higher: 8.1% (2006-2010 5-year est.).
**School District(s)**
South Jefferson Central School District (PK-12)
   2009-10 Enrollment: 2,036 . . . . . . . . . . . . . . . . . . . . . . . . (315) 583-6104
**Housing:** Homeownership rate: 79.8% (2010); Median home value: $123,200 (2006-2010 5-year est.); Median contract rent: $627 per month (2006-2010 5-year est.); Median year structure built: 1972 (2006-2010 5-year est.).
**Transportation:** Commute to work: 94.2% car, 0.0% public transportation, 5.0% walk, 0.8% work from home (2006-2010 5-year est.); Travel time to work: 39.4% less than 15 minutes, 27.0% 15 to 30 minutes, 26.2% 30 to 45 minutes, 0.0% 45 to 60 minutes, 7.3% 60 minutes or more (2006-2010 5-year est.)

**ALEXANDRIA** (town). Covers a land area of 72.657 square miles and a water area of 11.900 square miles. Located at 44.31° N. Lat; 75.87° W. Long.
**History:** Incorporated 1878.
**Population:** 3,956 (1990); 4,097 (2000); 4,061 (2010); Density: 55.9 persons per square mile (2010); Race: 97.8% White, 0.6% Black, 0.2% Asian, 0.2% American Indian/Alaska Native, 0.0% Native Hawaiian/Other Pacific Islander, 1.2% Other, 1.6% Hispanic of any race (2010); Average household size: 2.39 (2010); Median age: 42.8 (2010); Males per 100 females: 100.3 (2010); Marriage status: 19.0% never married, 63.1% now married, 5.5% widowed, 12.3% divorced (2006-2010 5-year est.); Foreign born: 3.2% (2006-2010 5-year est.); Ancestry (includes multiple ancestries): 19.6% German, 17.6% English, 15.2% Irish, 11.6% French, 8.6% Italian (2006-2010 5-year est.).
**Economy:** Employment by occupation: 9.0% management, 1.1% professional, 15.9% services, 15.8% sales, 2.4% farming, 17.4% construction, 8.1% production (2006-2010 5-year est.).
**Income:** Per capita income: $22,112 (2006-2010 5-year est.); Median household income: $38,750 (2006-2010 5-year est.); Average household income: $51,597 (2006-2010 5-year est.); Percent of households with income of $100,000 or more: 11.4% (2006-2010 5-year est.); Poverty rate: 20.6% (2006-2010 5-year est.).
**Education:** Percent of population age 25 and over with: High school diploma (including GED) or higher: 89.8% (2006-2010 5-year est.); Bachelor's degree or higher: 17.6% (2006-2010 5-year est.); Master's degree or higher: 7.6% (2006-2010 5-year est.).
**Housing:** Homeownership rate: 72.6% (2010); Median home value: $113,400 (2006-2010 5-year est.); Median contract rent: $542 per month (2006-2010 5-year est.); Median year structure built: 1966 (2006-2010 5-year est.).
**Transportation:** Commute to work: 83.3% car, 0.0% public transportation, 6.9% walk, 8.8% work from home (2006-2010 5-year est.); Travel time to work: 44.1% less than 15 minutes, 29.7% 15 to 30 minutes, 22.9% 30 to 45 minutes, 1.9% 45 to 60 minutes, 1.4% 60 minutes or more (2006-2010 5-year est.)

**ALEXANDRIA BAY** (village). Covers a land area of 0.766 square miles and a water area of 0.759 square miles. Located at 44.34° N. Lat; 75.92° W. Long. Elevation is 269 feet.
**Population:** 1,194 (1990); 1,088 (2000); 1,078 (2010); Density: 1,407.1 persons per square mile (2010); Race: 96.7% White, 0.9% Black, 0.6% Asian, 0.2% American Indian/Alaska Native, 0.0% Native Hawaiian/Other Pacific Islander, 1.6% Other, 2.8% Hispanic of any race (2010); Average household size: 2.02 (2010); Median age: 42.6 (2010); Males per 100 females: 94.6 (2010); Marriage status: 19.7% never married, 56.1% now married, 6.0% widowed, 18.2% divorced (2006-2010 5-year est.); Foreign born: 1.8% (2006-2010 5-year est.); Ancestry (includes multiple ancestries): 26.1% German, 21.1% Irish, 14.7% English, 9.3% French, 9.3% Italian (2006-2010 5-year est.).
**Economy:** Employment by occupation: 11.7% management, 1.3% professional, 14.3% services, 17.0% sales, 6.6% farming, 11.7% construction, 2.9% production (2006-2010 5-year est.).
**Income:** Per capita income: $21,165 (2006-2010 5-year est.); Median household income: $31,538 (2006-2010 5-year est.); Average household income: $42,017 (2006-2010 5-year est.); Percent of households with income of $100,000 or more: 7.2% (2006-2010 5-year est.); Poverty rate: 14.3% (2006-2010 5-year est.).
**Education:** Percent of population age 25 and over with: High school diploma (including GED) or higher: 90.3% (2006-2010 5-year est.); Bachelor's degree or higher: 20.5% (2006-2010 5-year est.); Master's degree or higher: 7.3% (2006-2010 5-year est.).
**School District(s)**
Alexandria Central School District (PK-12)
   2009-10 Enrollment: 664 . . . . . . . . . . . . . . . . . . . . . . . (315) 482-9971
**Housing:** Homeownership rate: 52.3% (2010); Median home value: $91,600 (2006-2010 5-year est.); Median contract rent: $493 per month (2006-2010 5-year est.); Median year structure built: before 1940 (2006-2010 5-year est.).
**Hospitals:** EJ Noble Hospital/Samaritan (52 beds)
**Safety:** Violent crime rate: 9.0 per 10,000 population; Property crime rate: 188.5 per 10,000 population (2010).
**Newspapers:** Thousand Islands Sun (Community news; Circulation 6,379)
**Transportation:** Commute to work: 85.5% car, 0.0% public transportation, 7.9% walk, 5.2% work from home (2006-2010 5-year est.); Travel time to work: 47.1% less than 15 minutes, 25.1% 15 to 30 minutes, 24.3% 30 to 45 minutes, 2.9% 45 to 60 minutes, 0.6% 60 minutes or more (2006-2010 5-year est.)
**Additional Information Contacts**
Alexandria Bay Chamber of Commerce . . . . . . . . . . . . . . . (315) 482-9531
   http://www.visitalexbay.org

**ANTWERP** (village). Covers a land area of 1.034 square miles and a water area of 0.032 square miles. Located at 44.20° N. Lat; 75.60° W. Long. Elevation is 512 feet.
**Population:** 739 (1990); 716 (2000); 686 (2010); Density: 663.0 persons per square mile (2010); Race: 94.6% White, 1.7% Black, 0.0% Asian, 0.3% American Indian/Alaska Native, 0.0% Native Hawaiian/Other Pacific Islander, 3.4% Other, 3.1% Hispanic of any race (2010); Average household size: 2.71 (2010); Median age: 35.2 (2010); Males per 100 females: 100.6 (2010); Marriage status: 27.8% never married, 60.6% now married, 2.6% widowed, 9.1% divorced (2006-2010 5-year est.); Foreign born: 1.3% (2006-2010 5-year est.); Ancestry (includes multiple ancestries): 19.8% English, 19.7% German, 18.9% Irish, 12.5% French, 10.6% Italian (2006-2010 5-year est.).
**Economy:** Employment by occupation: 9.1% management, 2.7% professional, 9.5% services, 15.5% sales, 9.1% farming, 16.7% construction, 4.5% production (2006-2010 5-year est.).
**Income:** Per capita income: $19,028 (2006-2010 5-year est.); Median household income: $51,875 (2006-2010 5-year est.); Average household income: $54,427 (2006-2010 5-year est.); Percent of households with income of $100,000 or more: 4.5% (2006-2010 5-year est.); Poverty rate: 10.9% (2006-2010 5-year est.).
**Education:** Percent of population age 25 and over with: High school diploma (including GED) or higher: 88.5% (2006-2010 5-year est.); Bachelor's degree or higher: 11.5% (2006-2010 5-year est.); Master's degree or higher: 4.4% (2006-2010 5-year est.).
**School District(s)**
Indian River Central School District (PK-12)
   2009-10 Enrollment: 3,767 . . . . . . . . . . . . . . . . . . . . . . (315) 642-3441
**Housing:** Homeownership rate: 70.4% (2010); Median home value: $91,200 (2006-2010 5-year est.); Median contract rent: $414 per month

(2006-2010 5-year est.); Median year structure built: before 1940 (2006-2010 5-year est.).
**Transportation:** Commute to work: 92.9% car, 1.1% public transportation, 3.4% walk, 2.6% work from home (2006-2010 5-year est.); Travel time to work: 13.1% less than 15 minutes, 36.2% 15 to 30 minutes, 30.4% 30 to 45 minutes, 13.1% 45 to 60 minutes, 7.3% 60 minutes or more (2006-2010 5-year est.).

## ANTWERP (town).
Covers a land area of 106.042 square miles and a water area of 2.377 square miles. Located at 44.22° N. Lat; 75.60° W. Long. Elevation is 512 feet.
**Population:** 1,856 (1990); 1,793 (2000); 1,846 (2010); Density: 17.4 persons per square mile (2010); Race: 97.0% White, 0.8% Black, 0.1% Asian, 0.1% American Indian/Alaska Native, 0.0% Native Hawaiian/Other Pacific Islander, 2.0% Other, 1.7% Hispanic of any race (2010); Average household size: 2.78 (2010); Median age: 36.3 (2010); Males per 100 females: 101.7 (2010); Marriage status: 27.6% never married, 63.0% now married, 2.1% widowed, 7.3% divorced (2006-2010 5-year est.); Foreign born: 0.7% (2006-2010 5-year est.); Ancestry (includes multiple ancestries): 16.6% German, 14.8% Irish, 13.4% English, 12.0% American, 10.2% French (2006-2010 5-year est.).
**Economy:** Employment by occupation: 11.1% management, 3.0% professional, 13.2% services, 15.2% sales, 6.4% farming, 15.5% construction, 7.6% production (2006-2010 5-year est.).
**Income:** Per capita income: $19,235 (2006-2010 5-year est.); Median household income: $49,833 (2006-2010 5-year est.); Average household income: $53,522 (2006-2010 5-year est.); Percent of households with income of $100,000 or more: 8.3% (2006-2010 5-year est.); Poverty rate: 17.8% (2006-2010 5-year est.).
**Education:** Percent of population age 25 and over with: High school diploma (including GED) or higher: 88.7% (2006-2010 5-year est.); Bachelor's degree or higher: 10.0% (2006-2010 5-year est.); Master's degree or higher: 3.7% (2006-2010 5-year est.).

**School District(s)**
Indian River Central School District (PK-12)
   2009-10 Enrollment: 3,767 . . . . . . . . . . . . . . . . . . . . . . (315) 642-3441
**Housing:** Homeownership rate: 79.0% (2010); Median home value: $96,300 (2006-2010 5-year est.); Median contract rent: $430 per month (2006-2010 5-year est.); Median year structure built: 1971 (2006-2010 5-year est.).
**Transportation:** Commute to work: 92.7% car, 0.4% public transportation, 2.8% walk, 4.1% work from home (2006-2010 5-year est.); Travel time to work: 11.8% less than 15 minutes, 39.9% 15 to 30 minutes, 31.2% 30 to 45 minutes, 12.0% 45 to 60 minutes, 5.1% 60 minutes or more (2006-2010 5-year est.).

## BELLEVILLE (CDP).
Covers a land area of 0.264 square miles and a water area of 0 square miles. Located at 43.78° N. Lat; 76.11° W. Long. Elevation is 459 feet.
**Population:** n/a (1990); n/a (2000); 226 (2010); Density: 854.5 persons per square mile (2010); Race: 99.1% White, 0.0% Black, 0.4% Asian, 0.0% American Indian/Alaska Native, 0.0% Native Hawaiian/Other Pacific Islander, 0.5% Other, 1.8% Hispanic of any race (2010); Average household size: 2.97 (2010); Median age: 36.0 (2010); Males per 100 females: 93.2 (2010); Marriage status: 60.4% never married, 39.6% now married, 0.0% widowed, 0.0% divorced (2006-2010 5-year est.); Foreign born: 0.0% (2006-2010 5-year est.); Ancestry (includes multiple ancestries): 67.5% Swiss, 66.7% German, 24.8% English (2006-2010 5-year est.).
**Economy:** Employment by occupation: 0.0% management, 0.0% professional, 0.0% services, 18.8% sales, 0.0% farming, 0.0% construction, 0.0% production (2006-2010 5-year est.).
**Income:** Per capita income: $22,086 (2006-2010 5-year est.); Median household income: $29,181 (2006-2010 5-year est.); Average household income: $0 (2006-2010 5-year est.); Percent of households with income of $100,000 or more: 25.6% (2006-2010 5-year est.); Poverty rate: 0.0% (2006-2010 5-year est.).
**Education:** Percent of population age 25 and over with: High school diploma (including GED) or higher: 60.4% (2006-2010 5-year est.); Bachelor's degree or higher: 0.0% (2006-2010 5-year est.); Master's degree or higher: 0.0% (2006-2010 5-year est.).

**School District(s)**
Belleville Henderson Central School District (PK-12)
   2009-10 Enrollment: 532 . . . . . . . . . . . . . . . . . . . . . . (315) 846-5826

**Housing:** Homeownership rate: 80.3% (2010); Median home value: $216,400 (2006-2010 5-year est.); Median contract rent: n/a per month (2006-2010 5-year est.); Median year structure built: before 1940 (2006-2010 5-year est.).
**Transportation:** Commute to work: 60.4% car, 0.0% public transportation, 0.0% walk, 39.6% work from home (2006-2010 5-year est.); Travel time to work: 0.0% less than 15 minutes, 100.0% 15 to 30 minutes, 0.0% 30 to 45 minutes, 0.0% 45 to 60 minutes, 0.0% 60 minutes or more (2006-2010 5-year est.).

## BLACK RIVER (village).
Covers a land area of 1.791 square miles and a water area of 0.053 square miles. Located at 44.00° N. Lat; 75.79° W. Long. Elevation is 571 feet.
**Population:** 1,349 (1990); 1,285 (2000); 1,348 (2010); Density: 752.5 persons per square mile (2010); Race: 89.6% White, 4.4% Black, 1.9% Asian, 0.2% American Indian/Alaska Native, 0.1% Native Hawaiian/Other Pacific Islander, 3.8% Other, 3.5% Hispanic of any race (2010); Average household size: 2.46 (2010); Median age: 38.9 (2010); Males per 100 females: 94.5 (2010); Marriage status: 26.5% never married, 59.9% now married, 4.5% widowed, 9.1% divorced (2006-2010 5-year est.); Foreign born: 8.7% (2006-2010 5-year est.); Ancestry (includes multiple ancestries): 20.4% German, 20.1% Irish, 13.3% English, 11.2% French, 10.8% Italian (2006-2010 5-year est.).
**Economy:** Single-family building permits issued: 2 (2011); Multi-family building permits issued: 0 (2011); Employment by occupation: 7.1% management, 2.4% professional, 8.4% services, 14.0% sales, 6.2% farming, 12.1% construction, 6.5% production (2006-2010 5-year est.).
**Income:** Per capita income: $26,442 (2006-2010 5-year est.); Median household income: $57,857 (2006-2010 5-year est.); Average household income: $63,574 (2006-2010 5-year est.); Percent of households with income of $100,000 or more: 18.1% (2006-2010 5-year est.); Poverty rate: 9.0% (2006-2010 5-year est.).
**Education:** Percent of population age 25 and over with: High school diploma (including GED) or higher: 92.1% (2006-2010 5-year est.); Bachelor's degree or higher: 21.2% (2006-2010 5-year est.); Master's degree or higher: 10.6% (2006-2010 5-year est.).

**School District(s)**
Carthage Central School District (KG-12)
   2009-10 Enrollment: 3,437 . . . . . . . . . . . . . . . . . . . . . (315) 493-5120
**Housing:** Homeownership rate: 66.5% (2010); Median home value: $151,000 (2006-2010 5-year est.); Median contract rent: $611 per month (2006-2010 5-year est.); Median year structure built: before 1940 (2006-2010 5-year est.).
**Transportation:** Commute to work: 94.4% car, 0.0% public transportation, 0.6% walk, 4.3% work from home (2006-2010 5-year est.); Travel time to work: 50.3% less than 15 minutes, 42.7% 15 to 30 minutes, 3.4% 30 to 45 minutes, 0.9% 45 to 60 minutes, 2.8% 60 minutes or more (2006-2010 5-year est.).

## BROWNVILLE (village).
Covers a land area of 0.672 square miles and a water area of 0.003 square miles. Located at 44.00° N. Lat; 75.98° W. Long. Elevation is 348 feet.
**Population:** 1,138 (1990); 1,022 (2000); 1,119 (2010); Density: 1,662.7 persons per square mile (2010); Race: 97.6% White, 0.4% Black, 0.7% Asian, 0.3% American Indian/Alaska Native, 0.0% Native Hawaiian/Other Pacific Islander, 1.0% Other, 1.3% Hispanic of any race (2010); Average household size: 2.55 (2010); Median age: 36.9 (2010); Males per 100 females: 89.3 (2010); Marriage status: 27.4% never married, 53.0% now married, 11.3% widowed, 8.3% divorced (2006-2010 5-year est.); Foreign born: 1.5% (2006-2010 5-year est.); Ancestry (includes multiple ancestries): 37.8% German, 30.9% Irish, 20.0% English, 19.0% French, 7.5% Italian (2006-2010 5-year est.).
**Economy:** Employment by occupation: 3.5% management, 9.7% professional, 10.6% services, 18.0% sales, 2.3% farming, 8.3% construction, 3.0% production (2006-2010 5-year est.).
**Income:** Per capita income: $21,580 (2006-2010 5-year est.); Median household income: $55,417 (2006-2010 5-year est.); Average household income: $57,492 (2006-2010 5-year est.); Percent of households with income of $100,000 or more: 17.4% (2006-2010 5-year est.); Poverty rate: 13.7% (2006-2010 5-year est.).
**Education:** Percent of population age 25 and over with: High school diploma (including GED) or higher: 92.8% (2006-2010 5-year est.); Bachelor's degree or higher: 26.1% (2006-2010 5-year est.); Master's degree or higher: 5.2% (2006-2010 5-year est.).

General Brown Central School District (PK-12)

   2009-10 Enrollment: 1,538 . . . . . . . . . . . . . . . . . . . . (315) 639-5100

**Housing:** Homeownership rate: 67.7% (2010); Median home value: $117,000 (2006-2010 5-year est.); Median contract rent: $515 per month (2006-2010 5-year est.); Median year structure built: before 1940 (2006-2010 5-year est.).

**Safety:** Violent crime rate: 0.0 per 10,000 population; Property crime rate: 85.6 per 10,000 population (2010).

**Transportation:** Commute to work: 97.9% car, 0.0% public transportation, 0.7% walk, 1.4% work from home (2006-2010 5-year est.); Travel time to work: 58.1% less than 15 minutes, 28.7% 15 to 30 minutes, 4.6% 30 to 45 minutes, 0.5% 45 to 60 minutes, 8.2% 60 minutes or more (2006-2010 5-year est.)

**BROWNVILLE** (town). Covers a land area of 59.131 square miles and a water area of 7.319 square miles. Located at 44.02° N. Lat; 76.08° W. Long. Elevation is 348 feet.

**Population:** 5,604 (1990); 5,843 (2000); 6,263 (2010); Density: 105.9 persons per square mile (2010); Race: 96.8% White, 0.7% Black, 0.6% Asian, 0.3% American Indian/Alaska Native, 0.1% Native Hawaiian/Other Pacific Islander, 1.5% Other, 1.4% Hispanic of any race (2010); Average household size: 2.60 (2010); Median age: 40.1 (2010); Males per 100 females: 97.3 (2010); Marriage status: 24.4% never married, 59.0% now married, 6.4% widowed, 10.2% divorced (2006-2010 5-year est.); Foreign born: 2.9% (2006-2010 5-year est.); Ancestry (includes multiple ancestries): 27.2% Irish, 21.4% German, 20.4% English, 17.1% French, 7.2% Italian (2006-2010 5-year est.).

**Economy:** Employment by occupation: 6.3% management, 5.8% professional, 9.1% services, 19.2% sales, 3.7% farming, 13.1% construction, 9.3% production (2006-2010 5-year est.).

**Income:** Per capita income: $22,664 (2006-2010 5-year est.); Median household income: $52,028 (2006-2010 5-year est.); Average household income: $57,678 (2006-2010 5-year est.); Percent of households with income of $100,000 or more: 12.5% (2006-2010 5-year est.); Poverty rate: 7.4% (2006-2010 5-year est.).

**Education:** Percent of population age 25 and over with: High school diploma (including GED) or higher: 90.1% (2006-2010 5-year est.); Bachelor's degree or higher: 19.3% (2006-2010 5-year est.); Master's degree or higher: 5.4% (2006-2010 5-year est.).

General Brown Central School District (PK-12)

   2009-10 Enrollment: 1,538 . . . . . . . . . . . . . . . . . . . . (315) 639-5100

**Housing:** Homeownership rate: 80.3% (2010); Median home value: $116,100 (2006-2010 5-year est.); Median contract rent: $421 per month (2006-2010 5-year est.); Median year structure built: 1962 (2006-2010 5-year est.).

**Transportation:** Commute to work: 97.6% car, 0.0% public transportation, 0.7% walk, 1.3% work from home (2006-2010 5-year est.); Travel time to work: 25.4% less than 15 minutes, 50.7% 15 to 30 minutes, 19.0% 30 to 45 minutes, 0.9% 45 to 60 minutes, 4.0% 60 minutes or more (2006-2010 5-year est.)

**CALCIUM** (CDP). Covers a land area of 5.544 square miles and a water area of 0.001 square miles. Located at 44.05° N. Lat; 75.84° W. Long. Elevation is 469 feet.

**Population:** 2,465 (1990); 3,346 (2000); 3,491 (2010); Density: 629.7 persons per square mile (2010); Race: 73.0% White, 13.9% Black, 2.1% Asian, 0.7% American Indian/Alaska Native, 0.3% Native Hawaiian/Other Pacific Islander, 10.0% Other, 13.9% Hispanic of any race (2010); Average household size: 2.57 (2010); Median age: 24.8 (2010); Males per 100 females: 102.5 (2010); Marriage status: 19.5% never married, 68.7% now married, 3.0% widowed, 8.8% divorced (2006-2010 5-year est.); Foreign born: 6.5% (2006-2010 5-year est.); Ancestry (includes multiple ancestries): 17.5% German, 8.6% Italian, 7.4% Irish, 5.8% French, 4.6% English (2006-2010 5-year est.).

**Economy:** Employment by occupation: 7.0% management, 2.6% professional, 7.0% services, 12.6% sales, 4.1% farming, 7.6% construction, 10.5% production (2006-2010 5-year est.).

**Income:** Per capita income: $19,525 (2006-2010 5-year est.); Median household income: $40,745 (2006-2010 5-year est.); Average household income: $52,304 (2006-2010 5-year est.); Percent of households with income of $100,000 or more: 10.2% (2006-2010 5-year est.); Poverty rate: 19.5% (2006-2010 5-year est.).

**Education:** Percent of population age 25 and over with: High school diploma (including GED) or higher: 89.8% (2006-2010 5-year est.); Bachelor's degree or higher: 28.3% (2006-2010 5-year est.); Master's degree or higher: 16.5% (2006-2010 5-year est.).

Indian River Central School District (PK-12)

   2009-10 Enrollment: 3,767 . . . . . . . . . . . . . . . . . . . . . . (315) 642-3441

**Housing:** Homeownership rate: 16.2% (2010); Median home value: $106,600 (2006-2010 5-year est.); Median contract rent: $907 per month (2006-2010 5-year est.); Median year structure built: 1983 (2006-2010 5-year est.).

**Transportation:** Commute to work: 84.3% car, 0.0% public transportation, 3.2% walk, 0.0% work from home (2006-2010 5-year est.); Travel time to work: 43.9% less than 15 minutes, 54.9% 15 to 30 minutes, 1.3% 30 to 45 minutes, 0.0% 45 to 60 minutes, 0.0% 60 minutes or more (2006-2010 5-year est.)

**CAPE VINCENT** (village). Covers a land area of 0.723 square miles and a water area of 0.024 square miles. Located at 44.12° N. Lat; 76.33° W. Long. Elevation is 262 feet.

**Population:** 700 (1990); 760 (2000); 726 (2010); Density: 1,003.4 persons per square mile (2010); Race: 97.4% White, 0.4% Black, 0.0% Asian, 0.0% American Indian/Alaska Native, 0.1% Native Hawaiian/Other Pacific Islander, 2.1% Other, 2.3% Hispanic of any race (2010); Average household size: 2.09 (2010); Median age: 47.9 (2010); Males per 100 females: 92.6 (2010); Marriage status: 22.6% never married, 58.7% now married, 12.8% widowed, 6.0% divorced (2006-2010 5-year est.); Foreign born: 5.3% (2006-2010 5-year est.); Ancestry (includes multiple ancestries): 24.6% Irish, 15.5% German, 10.9% Italian, 10.3% English, 10.0% French (2006-2010 5-year est.).

**Economy:** Employment by occupation: 14.6% management, 4.0% professional, 17.0% services, 15.5% sales, 0.0% farming, 9.0% construction, 4.3% production (2006-2010 5-year est.).

**Income:** Per capita income: $32,089 (2006-2010 5-year est.); Median household income: $44,286 (2006-2010 5-year est.); Average household income: $61,803 (2006-2010 5-year est.); Percent of households with income of $100,000 or more: 10.0% (2006-2010 5-year est.); Poverty rate: 14.8% (2006-2010 5-year est.).

**Taxes:** Total city taxes per capita: $364 (2009); City property taxes per capita: $356 (2009).

**Education:** Percent of population age 25 and over with: High school diploma (including GED) or higher: 95.8% (2006-2010 5-year est.); Bachelor's degree or higher: 34.7% (2006-2010 5-year est.); Master's degree or higher: 19.5% (2006-2010 5-year est.).

Thousand Islands Central School District (KG-12)

   2009-10 Enrollment: 1,076 . . . . . . . . . . . . . . . . . . . . . (315) 686-5594

**Housing:** Homeownership rate: 68.4% (2010); Median home value: $155,900 (2006-2010 5-year est.); Median contract rent: $277 per month (2006-2010 5-year est.); Median year structure built: 1954 (2006-2010 5-year est.).

**Safety:** Violent crime rate: 0.0 per 10,000 population; Property crime rate: 89.2 per 10,000 population (2010).

**Transportation:** Commute to work: 79.8% car, 0.0% public transportation, 8.6% walk, 8.9% work from home (2006-2010 5-year est.); Travel time to work: 41.5% less than 15 minutes, 20.0% 15 to 30 minutes, 14.5% 30 to 45 minutes, 12.7% 45 to 60 minutes, 11.3% 60 minutes or more (2006-2010 5-year est.)

**Additional Information Contacts**

Cape Vincent Chamber of Commerce . . . . . . . . . . . . . . . . . (315) 654-2481

   http://www.capevincent.org

**CAPE VINCENT** (town). Covers a land area of 56.353 square miles and a water area of 33.498 square miles. Located at 44.11° N. Lat; 76.29° W. Long. Elevation is 262 feet.

**Population:** 2,768 (1990); 3,345 (2000); 2,777 (2010); Density: 49.3 persons per square mile (2010); Race: 77.0% White, 17.3% Black, 0.2% Asian, 0.2% American Indian/Alaska Native, 0.1% Native Hawaiian/Other Pacific Islander, 5.2% Other, 8.9% Hispanic of any race (2010); Average household size: 2.25 (2010); Median age: 41.8 (2010); Males per 100 females: 177.1 (2010); Marriage status: 34.4% never married, 50.7% now married, 7.5% widowed, 7.4% divorced (2006-2010 5-year est.); Foreign born: 5.4% (2006-2010 5-year est.); Ancestry (includes multiple ancestries): 17.5% Irish, 14.3% German, 11.5% English, 9.2% French, 7.0% Italian (2006-2010 5-year est.).

**Economy:** Employment by occupation: 16.8% management, 2.6% professional, 13.5% services, 14.4% sales, 3.8% farming, 10.7% construction, 5.2% production (2006-2010 5-year est.).
**Income:** Per capita income: $27,784 (2006-2010 5-year est.); Median household income: $60,978 (2006-2010 5-year est.); Average household income: $76,047 (2006-2010 5-year est.); Percent of households with income of $100,000 or more: 20.9% (2006-2010 5-year est.); Poverty rate: 13.4% (2006-2010 5-year est.).
**Education:** Percent of population age 25 and over with: High school diploma (including GED) or higher: 82.0% (2006-2010 5-year est.); Bachelor's degree or higher: 17.1% (2006-2010 5-year est.); Master's degree or higher: 9.8% (2006-2010 5-year est.).

### School District(s)
Thousand Islands Central School District (KG-12)
    2009-10 Enrollment: 1,076 . . . . . . . . . . . . . . . . . . . . . . . . . (315) 686-5594
**Housing:** Homeownership rate: 81.1% (2010); Median home value: $144,200 (2006-2010 5-year est.); Median contract rent: $357 per month (2006-2010 5-year est.); Median year structure built: 1972 (2006-2010 5-year est.).
**Transportation:** Commute to work: 79.8% car, 0.0% public transportation, 3.5% walk, 12.3% work from home (2006-2010 5-year est.); Travel time to work: 31.4% less than 15 minutes, 18.9% 15 to 30 minutes, 33.0% 30 to 45 minutes, 11.1% 45 to 60 minutes, 5.6% 60 minutes or more (2006-2010 5-year est.)

## CARTHAGE (village). Covers a land area of 2.507 square miles and a water area of 0.170 square miles. Located at 43.98° N. Lat; 75.60° W. Long. Elevation is 768 feet.
**History:** Settled before 1801, incorporated 1841.
**Population:** 4,344 (1990); 3,721 (2000); 3,747 (2010); Density: 1,494.3 persons per square mile (2010); Race: 90.0% White, 3.8% Black, 1.6% Asian, 0.5% American Indian/Alaska Native, 0.2% Native Hawaiian/Other Pacific Islander, 3.9% Other, 4.6% Hispanic of any race (2010); Average household size: 2.44 (2010); Median age: 31.3 (2010); Males per 100 females: 89.3 (2010); Marriage status: 27.8% never married, 52.3% now married, 12.7% widowed, 7.1% divorced (2006-2010 5-year est.); Foreign born: 4.2% (2006-2010 5-year est.); Ancestry (includes multiple ancestries): 28.9% German, 18.3% Irish, 17.2% French, 15.2% English, 8.3% Italian (2006-2010 5-year est.).
**Economy:** Single-family building permits issued: 0 (2011); Multi-family building permits issued: 0 (2011); Employment by occupation: 3.9% management, 3.9% professional, 11.4% services, 14.1% sales, 1.6% farming, 6.9% construction, 5.6% production (2006-2010 5-year est.).
**Income:** Per capita income: $21,836 (2006-2010 5-year est.); Median household income: $39,872 (2006-2010 5-year est.); Average household income: $53,080 (2006-2010 5-year est.); Percent of households with income of $100,000 or more: 12.2% (2006-2010 5-year est.); Poverty rate: 15.3% (2006-2010 5-year est.).
**Education:** Percent of population age 25 and over with: High school diploma (including GED) or higher: 84.4% (2006-2010 5-year est.); Bachelor's degree or higher: 23.5% (2006-2010 5-year est.); Master's degree or higher: 10.8% (2006-2010 5-year est.).

### School District(s)
Carthage Central School District (KG-12)
    2009-10 Enrollment: 3,437 . . . . . . . . . . . . . . . . . . . . . . . . . (315) 493-5120
**Housing:** Homeownership rate: 43.7% (2010); Median home value: $98,100 (2006-2010 5-year est.); Median contract rent: $498 per month (2006-2010 5-year est.); Median year structure built: before 1940 (2006-2010 5-year est.).
**Hospitals:** Carthage Area Hospital (78 beds)
**Safety:** Violent crime rate: 8.0 per 10,000 population; Property crime rate: 270.5 per 10,000 population (2010).
**Newspapers:** Carthage Republican Tribune (Community news; Circulation 3,000)
**Transportation:** Commute to work: 95.1% car, 0.0% public transportation, 2.1% walk, 1.4% work from home (2006-2010 5-year est.); Travel time to work: 22.8% less than 15 minutes, 48.0% 15 to 30 minutes, 21.9% 30 to 45 minutes, 7.3% 45 to 60 minutes, 0.0% 60 minutes or more (2006-2010 5-year est.)
**Additional Information Contacts**
Carthage Area Chamber of Commerce . . . . . . . . . . . . . . . (315) 493-3590
    http://carthageny.com

## CHAMPION (town). Covers a land area of 44.184 square miles and a water area of 0.889 square miles. Located at 43.97° N. Lat; 75.70° W. Long. Elevation is 997 feet.
**Population:** 4,574 (1990); 4,361 (2000); 4,494 (2010); Density: 101.7 persons per square mile (2010); Race: 92.3% White, 2.8% Black, 1.4% Asian, 0.4% American Indian/Alaska Native, 0.1% Native Hawaiian/Other Pacific Islander, 3.0% Other, 3.2% Hispanic of any race (2010); Average household size: 2.55 (2010); Median age: 35.3 (2010); Males per 100 females: 100.2 (2010); Marriage status: 23.2% never married, 65.0% now married, 3.6% widowed, 8.2% divorced (2006-2010 5-year est.); Foreign born: 4.2% (2006-2010 5-year est.); Ancestry (includes multiple ancestries): 27.0% German, 18.0% Irish, 11.3% English, 11.2% Italian, 11.1% French (2006-2010 5-year est.).
**Economy:** Employment by occupation: 6.7% management, 2.3% professional, 14.3% services, 11.7% sales, 7.8% farming, 14.3% construction, 8.7% production (2006-2010 5-year est.).
**Income:** Per capita income: $21,795 (2006-2010 5-year est.); Median household income: $45,511 (2006-2010 5-year est.); Average household income: $54,910 (2006-2010 5-year est.); Percent of households with income of $100,000 or more: 12.9% (2006-2010 5-year est.); Poverty rate: 9.5% (2006-2010 5-year est.).
**Education:** Percent of population age 25 and over with: High school diploma (including GED) or higher: 87.0% (2006-2010 5-year est.); Bachelor's degree or higher: 19.0% (2006-2010 5-year est.); Master's degree or higher: 7.2% (2006-2010 5-year est.).
**Housing:** Homeownership rate: 64.8% (2010); Median home value: $110,000 (2006-2010 5-year est.); Median contract rent: $590 per month (2006-2010 5-year est.); Median year structure built: 1954 (2006-2010 5-year est.).
**Transportation:** Commute to work: 94.1% car, 0.5% public transportation, 1.9% walk, 3.5% work from home (2006-2010 5-year est.); Travel time to work: 35.1% less than 15 minutes, 39.0% 15 to 30 minutes, 21.7% 30 to 45 minutes, 1.5% 45 to 60 minutes, 2.8% 60 minutes or more (2006-2010 5-year est.)
**Additional Information Contacts**
Town of Champion. . . . . . . . . . . . . . . . . . . . . . . . . . . . . . (315) 493-3240
    http://www.racog.org/Champion/Championhomepage.php

## CHAUMONT (village). Covers a land area of 0.970 square miles and a water area of 0.093 square miles. Located at 44.06° N. Lat; 76.13° W. Long. Elevation is 289 feet.
**Population:** 613 (1990); 592 (2000); 624 (2010); Density: 642.7 persons per square mile (2010); Race: 96.8% White, 0.5% Black, 0.5% Asian, 0.0% American Indian/Alaska Native, 0.0% Native Hawaiian/Other Pacific Islander, 2.2% Other, 1.1% Hispanic of any race (2010); Average household size: 2.40 (2010); Median age: 40.2 (2010); Males per 100 females: 90.8 (2010); Marriage status: 21.4% never married, 61.9% now married, 7.7% widowed, 9.0% divorced (2006-2010 5-year est.); Foreign born: 5.9% (2006-2010 5-year est.); Ancestry (includes multiple ancestries): 25.2% English, 21.2% German, 18.1% Irish, 11.0% French, 8.8% Italian (2006-2010 5-year est.).
**Economy:** Single-family building permits issued: 0 (2011); Multi-family building permits issued: 0 (2011); Employment by occupation: 12.0% management, 1.6% professional, 12.0% services, 17.1% sales, 1.2% farming, 13.9% construction, 9.2% production (2006-2010 5-year est.).
**Income:** Per capita income: $21,880 (2006-2010 5-year est.); Median household income: $39,167 (2006-2010 5-year est.); Average household income: $51,356 (2006-2010 5-year est.); Percent of households with income of $100,000 or more: 10.5% (2006-2010 5-year est.); Poverty rate: 9.0% (2006-2010 5-year est.).
**Education:** Percent of population age 25 and over with: High school diploma (including GED) or higher: 86.0% (2006-2010 5-year est.); Bachelor's degree or higher: 24.5% (2006-2010 5-year est.); Master's degree or higher: 12.4% (2006-2010 5-year est.).

### School District(s)
Lyme Central School District (PK-12)
    2009-10 Enrollment: 336 . . . . . . . . . . . . . . . . . . . . . . . . . (315) 649-2417
**Housing:** Homeownership rate: 69.1% (2010); Median home value: $134,400 (2006-2010 5-year est.); Median contract rent: $288 per month (2006-2010 5-year est.); Median year structure built: before 1940 (2006-2010 5-year est.).
**Transportation:** Commute to work: 84.5% car, 0.0% public transportation, 9.6% walk, 6.0% work from home (2006-2010 5-year est.); Travel time to work: 22.9% less than 15 minutes, 61.0% 15 to 30 minutes, 11.4% 30 to 45

minutes, 0.0% 45 to 60 minutes, 4.7% 60 minutes or more (2006-2010 5-year est.).

**Additional Information Contacts**
Chaumont-Three Mile Bay Chamber of Commerce........ (315) 649-3404
http://www.chaumontchamber.com

**CLAYTON** (village). Covers a land area of 1.613 square miles and a water area of 0.972 square miles. Located at 44.23° N. Lat; 76.08° W. Long. Elevation is 276 feet.
**Population:** 2,160 (1990); 1,821 (2000); 1,978 (2010); Density: 1,226.3 persons per square mile (2010); Race: 95.6% White, 1.7% Black, 0.3% Asian, 0.5% American Indian/Alaska Native, 0.0% Native Hawaiian/Other Pacific Islander, 1.9% Other, 2.9% Hispanic of any race (2010); Average household size: 2.22 (2010); Median age: 38.1 (2010); Males per 100 females: 84.5 (2010); Marriage status: 23.8% never married, 52.8% now married, 10.4% widowed, 13.0% divorced (2006-2010 5-year est.); Foreign born: 6.5% (2006-2010 5-year est.); Ancestry (includes multiple ancestries): 32.2% Irish, 29.1% German, 15.6% English, 10.3% Polish, 9.3% French (2006-2010 5-year est.).
**Economy:** Employment by occupation: 7.5% management, 0.6% professional, 18.1% services, 18.5% sales, 3.6% farming, 10.2% construction, 7.2% production (2006-2010 5-year est.).
**Income:** Per capita income: $25,520 (2006-2010 5-year est.); Median household income: $43,594 (2006-2010 5-year est.); Average household income: $55,992 (2006-2010 5-year est.); Percent of households with income of $100,000 or more: 16.8% (2006-2010 5-year est.); Poverty rate: 11.9% (2006-2010 5-year est.).
**Education:** Percent of population age 25 and over with: High school diploma (including GED) or higher: 89.5% (2006-2010 5-year est.); Bachelor's degree or higher: 28.0% (2006-2010 5-year est.); Master's degree or higher: 9.1% (2006-2010 5-year est.).
**School District(s)**
Thousand Islands Central School District (KG-12)
    2009-10 Enrollment: 1,076 ...................... (315) 686-5594
**Housing:** Homeownership rate: 48.6% (2010); Median home value: $128,200 (2006-2010 5-year est.); Median contract rent: $590 per month (2006-2010 5-year est.); Median year structure built: 1942 (2006-2010 5-year est.).
**Transportation:** Commute to work: 87.5% car, 0.0% public transportation, 7.6% walk, 1.5% work from home (2006-2010 5-year est.); Travel time to work: 40.1% less than 15 minutes, 24.2% 15 to 30 minutes, 29.8% 30 to 45 minutes, 3.1% 45 to 60 minutes, 2.7% 60 minutes or more (2006-2010 5-year est.).
**Additional Information Contacts**
Clayton Chamber of Commerce ..................... (315) 686-3771
http://www.1000islands-clayton.com

**CLAYTON** (town). Covers a land area of 82.360 square miles and a water area of 21.671 square miles. Located at 44.20° N. Lat; 76.07° W. Long. Elevation is 276 feet.
**History:** North American freshwater craft at Antique Boat Museum, similar to one at Mystic, Connecticut; Thousand Islands Museum; Clayton Historic District. Incorporated 1872.
**Population:** 4,629 (1990); 4,817 (2000); 5,153 (2010); Density: 62.6 persons per square mile (2010); Race: 96.8% White, 1.0% Black, 0.2% Asian, 0.2% American Indian/Alaska Native, 0.1% Native Hawaiian/Other Pacific Islander, 1.7% Other, 2.0% Hispanic of any race (2010); Average household size: 2.47 (2010); Median age: 40.5 (2010); Males per 100 females: 92.7 (2010); Marriage status: 20.7% never married, 60.2% now married, 7.5% widowed, 11.5% divorced (2006-2010 5-year est.); Foreign born: 4.0% (2006-2010 5-year est.); Ancestry (includes multiple ancestries): 26.3% Irish, 19.8% German, 11.6% English, 11.3% French, 7.0% Italian (2006-2010 5-year est.).
**Economy:** Single-family building permits issued: 0 (2011); Multi-family building permits issued: 0 (2011); Employment by occupation: 11.0% management, 0.8% professional, 12.7% services, 19.6% sales, 2.9% farming, 14.4% construction, 9.2% production (2006-2010 5-year est.).
**Income:** Per capita income: $25,568 (2006-2010 5-year est.); Median household income: $45,990 (2006-2010 5-year est.); Average household income: $59,720 (2006-2010 5-year est.); Percent of households with income of $100,000 or more: 18.7% (2006-2010 5-year est.); Poverty rate: 14.8% (2006-2010 5-year est.).
**Education:** Percent of population age 25 and over with: High school diploma (including GED) or higher: 88.3% (2006-2010 5-year est.);

Bachelor's degree or higher: 24.8% (2006-2010 5-year est.); Master's degree or higher: 11.3% (2006-2010 5-year est.).
**School District(s)**
Thousand Islands Central School District (KG-12)
    2009-10 Enrollment: 1,076 ...................... (315) 686-5594
**Housing:** Homeownership rate: 70.9% (2010); Median home value: $145,600 (2006-2010 5-year est.); Median contract rent: $603 per month (2006-2010 5-year est.); Median year structure built: 1961 (2006-2010 5-year est.).
**Transportation:** Commute to work: 88.1% car, 0.4% public transportation, 3.9% walk, 4.6% work from home (2006-2010 5-year est.); Travel time to work: 30.9% less than 15 minutes, 32.9% 15 to 30 minutes, 28.3% 30 to 45 minutes, 5.4% 45 to 60 minutes, 2.5% 60 minutes or more (2006-2010 5-year est.).

**DEFERIET** (village). Covers a land area of 0.649 square miles and a water area of 0.082 square miles. Located at 44.03° N. Lat; 75.68° W. Long. Elevation is 659 feet.
**Population:** 293 (1990); 309 (2000); 294 (2010); Density: 452.4 persons per square mile (2010); Race: 92.5% White, 3.1% Black, 1.0% Asian, 1.0% American Indian/Alaska Native, 0.0% Native Hawaiian/Other Pacific Islander, 2.4% Other, 1.7% Hispanic of any race (2010); Average household size: 2.33 (2010); Median age: 37.0 (2010); Males per 100 females: 82.6 (2010); Marriage status: 45.7% never married, 46.5% now married, 6.3% widowed, 1.5% divorced (2006-2010 5-year est.); Foreign born: 10.2% (2006-2010 5-year est.); Ancestry (includes multiple ancestries): 25.3% German, 19.1% Italian, 12.1% English, 10.6% French, 8.1% Haitian (2006-2010 5-year est.).
**Economy:** Employment by occupation: 5.5% management, 1.7% professional, 13.9% services, 11.4% sales, 6.3% farming, 10.1% construction, 10.1% production (2006-2010 5-year est.).
**Income:** Per capita income: $22,336 (2006-2010 5-year est.); Median household income: $49,375 (2006-2010 5-year est.); Average household income: $56,348 (2006-2010 5-year est.); Percent of households with income of $100,000 or more: 14.8% (2006-2010 5-year est.); Poverty rate: 15.5% (2006-2010 5-year est.).
**Education:** Percent of population age 25 and over with: High school diploma (including GED) or higher: 94.4% (2006-2010 5-year est.); Bachelor's degree or higher: 14.8% (2006-2010 5-year est.); Master's degree or higher: 7.2% (2006-2010 5-year est.).
**Housing:** Homeownership rate: 71.4% (2010); Median home value: $107,000 (2006-2010 5-year est.); Median contract rent: $489 per month (2006-2010 5-year est.); Median year structure built: before 1940 (2006-2010 5-year est.).
**Transportation:** Commute to work: 94.3% car, 0.0% public transportation, 4.5% walk, 0.0% work from home (2006-2010 5-year est.); Travel time to work: 44.3% less than 15 minutes, 37.9% 15 to 30 minutes, 12.9% 30 to 45 minutes, 3.8% 45 to 60 minutes, 1.1% 60 minutes or more (2006-2010 5-year est.).

**DEPAUVILLE** (CDP). Covers a land area of 9.822 square miles and a water area of 0 square miles. Located at 44.14° N. Lat; 76.04° W. Long. Elevation is 305 feet.
**Population:** 474 (1990); 512 (2000); 577 (2010); Density: 58.7 persons per square mile (2010); Race: 97.7% White, 0.0% Black, 0.2% Asian, 0.3% American Indian/Alaska Native, 0.0% Native Hawaiian/Other Pacific Islander, 1.8% Other, 0.7% Hispanic of any race (2010); Average household size: 2.96 (2010); Median age: 37.9 (2010); Males per 100 females: 103.2 (2010); Marriage status: 29.4% never married, 49.3% now married, 0.0% widowed, 21.2% divorced (2006-2010 5-year est.); Foreign born: 0.0% (2006-2010 5-year est.); Ancestry (includes multiple ancestries): 13.5% German, 13.3% Italian, 9.0% French, 6.3% Scottish, 4.5% Hungarian (2006-2010 5-year est.).
**Economy:** Employment by occupation: 0.0% management, 0.0% professional, 7.0% services, 26.3% sales, 0.0% farming, 28.5% construction, 19.7% production (2006-2010 5-year est.).
**Income:** Per capita income: $20,431 (2006-2010 5-year est.); Median household income: $54,615 (2006-2010 5-year est.); Average household income: $51,857 (2006-2010 5-year est.); Percent of households with income of $100,000 or more: 11.9% (2006-2010 5-year est.); Poverty rate: 16.4% (2006-2010 5-year est.).
**Education:** Percent of population age 25 and over with: High school diploma (including GED) or higher: 79.3% (2006-2010 5-year est.); Bachelor's degree or higher: 4.5% (2006-2010 5-year est.); Master's degree or higher: 0.0% (2006-2010 5-year est.).

**Housing:** Homeownership rate: 87.6% (2010); Median home value: $94,800 (2006-2010 5-year est.); Median contract rent: $431 per month (2006-2010 5-year est.); Median year structure built: 1980 (2006-2010 5-year est.).
**Transportation:** Commute to work: 88.1% car, 0.0% public transportation, 0.0% walk, 5.3% work from home (2006-2010 5-year est.); Travel time to work: 24.3% less than 15 minutes, 63.5% 15 to 30 minutes, 12.2% 30 to 45 minutes, 0.0% 45 to 60 minutes, 0.0% 60 minutes or more (2006-2010 5-year est.)

**DEXTER** (village). Covers a land area of 0.691 square miles and a water area of 0.063 square miles. Located at 44.01° N. Lat; 76.04° W. Long. Elevation is 282 feet.
**History:** Incorporated 1855.
**Population:** 1,101 (1990); 1,120 (2000); 1,052 (2010); Density: 1,521.2 persons per square mile (2010); Race: 95.8% White, 1.7% Black, 0.3% Asian, 0.6% American Indian/Alaska Native, 0.3% Native Hawaiian/Other Pacific Islander, 1.3% Other, 1.9% Hispanic of any race (2010); Average household size: 2.37 (2010); Median age: 40.1 (2010); Males per 100 females: 91.6 (2010); Marriage status: 24.1% never married, 58.4% now married, 8.5% widowed, 9.0% divorced (2006-2010 5-year est.); Foreign born: 2.2% (2006-2010 5-year est.); Ancestry (includes multiple ancestries): 32.5% French, 25.6% Irish, 20.6% German, 19.7% English, 4.4% Scottish (2006-2010 5-year est.).
**Economy:** Single-family building permits issued: 7 (2011); Multi-family building permits issued: 0 (2011); Employment by occupation: 7.6% management, 4.4% professional, 16.1% services, 20.3% sales, 2.6% farming, 9.2% construction, 7.6% production (2006-2010 5-year est.).
**Income:** Per capita income: $19,186 (2006-2010 5-year est.); Median household income: $38,333 (2006-2010 5-year est.); Average household income: $47,038 (2006-2010 5-year est.); Percent of households with income of $100,000 or more: 6.8% (2006-2010 5-year est.); Poverty rate: 12.2% (2006-2010 5-year est.).
**Education:** Percent of population age 25 and over with: High school diploma (including GED) or higher: 84.6% (2006-2010 5-year est.); Bachelor's degree or higher: 14.3% (2006-2010 5-year est.); Master's degree or higher: 4.9% (2006-2010 5-year est.).
**School District(s)**
General Brown Central School District (PK-12)
   2009-10 Enrollment: 1,538 . . . . . . . . . . . . . . . . . (315) 639-5100
**Housing:** Homeownership rate: 60.4% (2010); Median home value: $103,300 (2006-2010 5-year est.); Median contract rent: $375 per month (2006-2010 5-year est.); Median year structure built: before 1940 (2006-2010 5-year est.).
**Safety:** Violent crime rate: 0.0 per 10,000 population; Property crime rate: 8.4 per 10,000 population (2010).
**Transportation:** Commute to work: 96.1% car, 0.0% public transportation, 3.2% walk, 0.7% work from home (2006-2010 5-year est.); Travel time to work: 30.2% less than 15 minutes, 47.3% 15 to 30 minutes, 16.1% 30 to 45 minutes, 1.3% 45 to 60 minutes, 5.1% 60 minutes or more (2006-2010 5-year est.)

**ELLISBURG** (village). Covers a land area of 1.014 square miles and a water area of 0 square miles. Located at 43.73° N. Lat; 76.13° W. Long. Elevation is 328 feet.
**Population:** 246 (1990); 269 (2000); 244 (2010); Density: 240.5 persons per square mile (2010); Race: 93.9% White, 0.8% Black, 2.0% Asian, 0.0% American Indian/Alaska Native, 0.0% Native Hawaiian/Other Pacific Islander, 3.3% Other, 0.4% Hispanic of any race (2010); Average household size: 2.77 (2010); Median age: 37.0 (2010); Males per 100 females: 108.5 (2010); Marriage status: 46.6% never married, 41.8% now married, 2.6% widowed, 9.0% divorced (2006-2010 5-year est.); Foreign born: 0.0% (2006-2010 5-year est.); Ancestry (includes multiple ancestries): 29.4% Irish, 25.0% English, 21.0% German, 12.3% Italian, 10.7% Swedish (2006-2010 5-year est.).
**Economy:** Employment by occupation: 18.1% management, 0.0% professional, 1.7% services, 12.1% sales, 5.2% farming, 32.8% construction, 8.6% production (2006-2010 5-year est.).
**Income:** Per capita income: $20,381 (2006-2010 5-year est.); Median household income: $36,250 (2006-2010 5-year est.); Average household income: $52,129 (2006-2010 5-year est.); Percent of households with income of $100,000 or more: 13.8% (2006-2010 5-year est.); Poverty rate: 10.3% (2006-2010 5-year est.).
**Education:** Percent of population age 25 and over with: High school diploma (including GED) or higher: 84.0% (2006-2010 5-year est.);

Bachelor's degree or higher: 21.3% (2006-2010 5-year est.); Master's degree or higher: 9.3% (2006-2010 5-year est.).
**Housing:** Homeownership rate: 77.2% (2010); Median home value: $139,300 (2006-2010 5-year est.); Median contract rent: $291 per month (2006-2010 5-year est.); Median year structure built: before 1940 (2006-2010 5-year est.).
**Transportation:** Commute to work: 91.0% car, 0.0% public transportation, 4.5% walk, 2.7% work from home (2006-2010 5-year est.); Travel time to work: 35.2% less than 15 minutes, 33.3% 15 to 30 minutes, 16.7% 30 to 45 minutes, 1.9% 45 to 60 minutes, 13.0% 60 minutes or more (2006-2010 5-year est.)

**ELLISBURG** (town). Covers a land area of 85.145 square miles and a water area of 1.418 square miles. Located at 43.74° N. Lat; 76.11° W. Long. Elevation is 328 feet.
**Population:** 3,386 (1990); 3,541 (2000); 3,474 (2010); Density: 40.8 persons per square mile (2010); Race: 97.0% White, 0.3% Black, 0.4% Asian, 0.1% American Indian/Alaska Native, 0.0% Native Hawaiian/Other Pacific Islander, 2.2% Other, 2.6% Hispanic of any race (2010); Average household size: 2.77 (2010); Median age: 38.8 (2010); Males per 100 females: 101.4 (2010); Marriage status: 30.0% never married, 58.1% now married, 3.5% widowed, 8.4% divorced (2006-2010 5-year est.); Foreign born: 0.3% (2006-2010 5-year est.); Ancestry (includes multiple ancestries): 21.6% English, 20.9% German, 19.0% Irish, 14.1% Italian, 9.8% French (2006-2010 5-year est.).
**Economy:** Employment by occupation: 11.4% management, 3.2% professional, 8.1% services, 19.5% sales, 7.0% farming, 13.4% construction, 6.1% production (2006-2010 5-year est.).
**Income:** Per capita income: $19,239 (2006-2010 5-year est.); Median household income: $35,778 (2006-2010 5-year est.); Average household income: $50,681 (2006-2010 5-year est.); Percent of households with income of $100,000 or more: 10.1% (2006-2010 5-year est.); Poverty rate: 20.5% (2006-2010 5-year est.).
**Education:** Percent of population age 25 and over with: High school diploma (including GED) or higher: 85.7% (2006-2010 5-year est.); Bachelor's degree or higher: 14.3% (2006-2010 5-year est.); Master's degree or higher: 7.0% (2006-2010 5-year est.).
**Housing:** Homeownership rate: 82.1% (2010); Median home value: $99,100 (2006-2010 5-year est.); Median contract rent: $540 per month (2006-2010 5-year est.); Median year structure built: before 1940 (2006-2010 5-year est.).
**Transportation:** Commute to work: 91.7% car, 0.0% public transportation, 3.4% walk, 4.6% work from home (2006-2010 5-year est.); Travel time to work: 27.1% less than 15 minutes, 36.1% 15 to 30 minutes, 20.3% 30 to 45 minutes, 7.4% 45 to 60 minutes, 9.1% 60 minutes or more (2006-2010 5-year est.)

**EVANS MILLS** (village). Covers a land area of 0.829 square miles and a water area of 0 square miles. Located at 44.08° N. Lat; 75.80° W. Long. Elevation is 423 feet.
**Population:** 661 (1990); 605 (2000); 621 (2010); Density: 749.0 persons per square mile (2010); Race: 88.9% White, 2.4% Black, 2.3% Asian, 0.0% American Indian/Alaska Native, 0.0% Native Hawaiian/Other Pacific Islander, 6.4% Other, 5.2% Hispanic of any race (2010); Average household size: 2.35 (2010); Median age: 38.3 (2010); Males per 100 females: 103.6 (2010); Marriage status: 26.1% never married, 58.7% now married, 8.5% widowed, 6.7% divorced (2006-2010 5-year est.); Foreign born: 6.6% (2006-2010 5-year est.); Ancestry (includes multiple ancestries): 19.1% Irish, 14.8% English, 13.5% German, 10.7% Italian, 8.3% French (2006-2010 5-year est.).
**Economy:** Single-family building permits issued: 1 (2011); Multi-family building permits issued: 0 (2011); Employment by occupation: 4.7% management, 1.3% professional, 16.7% services, 23.4% sales, 7.0% farming, 11.7% construction, 1.7% production (2006-2010 5-year est.).
**Income:** Per capita income: $21,930 (2006-2010 5-year est.); Median household income: $41,944 (2006-2010 5-year est.); Average household income: $52,423 (2006-2010 5-year est.); Percent of households with income of $100,000 or more: 11.8% (2006-2010 5-year est.); Poverty rate: 17.4% (2006-2010 5-year est.).
**Education:** Percent of population age 25 and over with: High school diploma (including GED) or higher: 91.0% (2006-2010 5-year est.); Bachelor's degree or higher: 21.1% (2006-2010 5-year est.); Master's degree or higher: 6.0% (2006-2010 5-year est.).

**School District(s)**
Indian River Central School District (PK-12)

2009-10 Enrollment: 3,767 . . . . . . . . . . . . . . . . . . . . . . . (315) 642-3441

**Housing:** Homeownership rate: 58.5% (2010); Median home value: $121,400 (2006-2010 5-year est.); Median contract rent: $349 per month (2006-2010 5-year est.); Median year structure built: 1953 (2006-2010 5-year est.).

**Transportation:** Commute to work: 91.6% car, 0.0% public transportation, 7.8% walk, 0.7% work from home (2006-2010 5-year est.); Travel time to work: 36.4% less than 15 minutes, 56.1% 15 to 30 minutes, 4.8% 30 to 45 minutes, 1.4% 45 to 60 minutes, 1.4% 60 minutes or more (2006-2010 5-year est.)

## FELTS MILLS (CDP). Covers a land area of 0.328 square miles and a water area of 0 square miles. Located at 44.01° N. Lat; 75.75° W. Long. Elevation is 584 feet.

**Population:** n/a (1990); n/a (2000); 372 (2010); Density: 1,131.5 persons per square mile (2010); Race: 83.3% White, 5.9% Black, 2.4% Asian, 0.0% American Indian/Alaska Native, 0.0% Native Hawaiian/Other Pacific Islander, 8.4% Other, 3.2% Hispanic of any race (2010); Average household size: 2.74 (2010); Median age: 33.0 (2010); Males per 100 females: 95.8 (2010); Marriage status: 14.4% never married, 60.5% now married, 6.1% widowed, 19.0% divorced (2006-2010 5-year est.); Foreign born: 9.0% (2006-2010 5-year est.); Ancestry (includes multiple ancestries): 18.3% Irish, 13.8% German, 11.1% French, 9.8% Italian, 8.5% English (2006-2010 5-year est.).

**Economy:** Employment by occupation: 0.0% management, 4.4% professional, 0.0% services, 45.1% sales, 0.0% farming, 0.0% construction, 5.3% production (2006-2010 5-year est.).

**Income:** Per capita income: $18,480 (2006-2010 5-year est.); Median household income: $43,456 (2006-2010 5-year est.); Average household income: $48,487 (2006-2010 5-year est.); Percent of households with income of $100,000 or more: 6.9% (2006-2010 5-year est.); Poverty rate: 0.0% (2006-2010 5-year est.).

**Education:** Percent of population age 25 and over with: High school diploma (including GED) or higher: 79.3% (2006-2010 5-year est.); Bachelor's degree or higher: 13.3% (2006-2010 5-year est.); Master's degree or higher: 2.0% (2006-2010 5-year est.).

**Housing:** Homeownership rate: 75.0% (2010); Median home value: $89,300 (2006-2010 5-year est.); Median contract rent: $588 per month (2006-2010 5-year est.); Median year structure built: before 1940 (2006-2010 5-year est.).

**Transportation:** Commute to work: 88.0% car, 0.0% public transportation, 12.0% walk, 0.0% work from home (2006-2010 5-year est.); Travel time to work: 59.9% less than 15 minutes, 27.5% 15 to 30 minutes, 12.7% 30 to 45 minutes, 0.0% 45 to 60 minutes, 0.0% 60 minutes or more (2006-2010 5-year est.)

## FISHERS LANDING (CDP). Covers a land area of 0.222 square miles and a water area of 0.001 square miles. Located at 44.27° N. Lat; 76.00° W. Long. Elevation is 262 feet.

**Population:** n/a (1990); n/a (2000); 89 (2010); Density: 400.1 persons per square mile (2010); Race: 94.4% White, 1.1% Black, 1.1% Asian, 0.0% American Indian/Alaska Native, 0.0% Native Hawaiian/Other Pacific Islander, 3.4% Other, 2.2% Hispanic of any race (2010); Average household size: 2.17 (2010); Median age: 54.5 (2010); Males per 100 females: 102.3 (2010); Marriage status: 0.0% never married, 77.4% now married, 22.6% widowed, 0.0% divorced (2006-2010 5-year est.); Foreign born: 0.0% (2006-2010 5-year est.); Ancestry (includes multiple ancestries): 30.2% German, 22.6% Irish, 18.9% Canadian, 18.9% American, 13.2% Polish (2006-2010 5-year est.).

**Economy:** Employment by occupation: 0.0% management, 0.0% professional, 0.0% services, 40.0% sales, 0.0% farming, 0.0% construction, 0.0% production (2006-2010 5-year est.).

**Income:** Per capita income: $25,502 (2006-2010 5-year est.); Median household income: $34,063 (2006-2010 5-year est.); Average household income: $34,918 (2006-2010 5-year est.); Percent of households with income of $100,000 or more: 0.0% (2006-2010 5-year est.); Poverty rate: 0.0% (2006-2010 5-year est.).

**Education:** Percent of population age 25 and over with: High school diploma (including GED) or higher: 86.8% (2006-2010 5-year est.); Bachelor's degree or higher: 0.0% (2006-2010 5-year est.); Master's degree or higher: 0.0% (2006-2010 5-year est.).

**Housing:** Homeownership rate: 82.9% (2010); Median home value: $34,600 (2006-2010 5-year est.); Median contract rent: n/a per month

(2006-2010 5-year est.); Median year structure built: 1975 (2006-2010 5-year est.).

**Transportation:** Commute to work: 100.0% car, 0.0% public transportation, 0.0% walk, 0.0% work from home (2006-2010 5-year est.); Travel time to work: 80.0% less than 15 minutes, 20.0% 15 to 30 minutes, 0.0% 30 to 45 minutes, 0.0% 45 to 60 minutes, 0.0% 60 minutes or more (2006-2010 5-year est.)

## FORT DRUM (CDP). Covers a land area of 14.328 square miles and a water area of 0.093 square miles. Located at 44.04° N. Lat; 75.78° W. Long.

**Population:** 11,586 (1990); 12,123 (2000); 12,955 (2010); Density: 904.1 persons per square mile (2010); Race: 72.4% White, 13.0% Black, 2.7% Asian, 1.0% American Indian/Alaska Native, 1.2% Native Hawaiian/Other Pacific Islander, 9.7% Other, 15.5% Hispanic of any race (2010); Average household size: 3.22 (2010); Median age: 22.4 (2010); Males per 100 females: 135.5 (2010); Marriage status: 20.6% never married, 76.7% now married, 0.0% widowed, 2.8% divorced (2006-2010 5-year est.); Foreign born: 10.7% (2006-2010 5-year est.); Ancestry (includes multiple ancestries): 22.8% German, 19.0% Irish, 7.8% Italian, 6.9% English, 3.8% French (2006-2010 5-year est.).

**Economy:** Employment by occupation: 5.0% management, 0.2% professional, 15.5% services, 26.4% sales, 1.7% farming, 9.3% construction, 4.8% production (2006-2010 5-year est.).

**Income:** Per capita income: $14,307 (2006-2010 5-year est.); Median household income: $35,945 (2006-2010 5-year est.); Average household income: $39,364 (2006-2010 5-year est.); Percent of households with income of $100,000 or more: 3.0% (2006-2010 5-year est.); Poverty rate: 18.5% (2006-2010 5-year est.).

**Education:** Percent of population age 25 and over with: High school diploma (including GED) or higher: 93.0% (2006-2010 5-year est.); Bachelor's degree or higher: 17.3% (2006-2010 5-year est.); Master's degree or higher: 5.5% (2006-2010 5-year est.).

**Housing:** Homeownership rate: 0.7% (2010); Median home value: $170,600 (2006-2010 5-year est.); Median contract rent: $1,226 per month (2006-2010 5-year est.); Median year structure built: 1988 (2006-2010 5-year est.).

**Hospitals:** Guthrie Ambulatory Health Care Clinic

**Newspapers:** Fort Drum Blizzard (Local news; Circulation 36,000)

**Transportation:** Commute to work: 88.0% car, 0.9% public transportation, 7.0% walk, 2.8% work from home (2006-2010 5-year est.); Travel time to work: 68.8% less than 15 minutes, 26.7% 15 to 30 minutes, 3.7% 30 to 45 minutes, 0.0% 45 to 60 minutes, 0.7% 60 minutes or more (2006-2010 5-year est.)

**Airports:** Wheeler-Sack AAF (general aviation)

## GLEN PARK (village). Covers a land area of 0.708 square miles and a water area of 0.024 square miles. Located at 44.00° N. Lat; 75.95° W. Long. Elevation is 341 feet.

**Population:** 527 (1990); 487 (2000); 502 (2010); Density: 708.9 persons per square mile (2010); Race: 96.8% White, 1.0% Black, 0.2% Asian, 0.0% American Indian/Alaska Native, 0.0% Native Hawaiian/Other Pacific Islander, 2.0% Other, 1.0% Hispanic of any race (2010); Average household size: 2.63 (2010); Median age: 35.0 (2010); Males per 100 females: 107.4 (2010); Marriage status: 28.8% never married, 55.9% now married, 3.8% widowed, 11.5% divorced (2006-2010 5-year est.); Foreign born: 3.2% (2006-2010 5-year est.); Ancestry (includes multiple ancestries): 27.5% Irish, 17.2% German, 11.6% Italian, 11.1% English, 10.3% French Canadian (2006-2010 5-year est.).

**Economy:** Employment by occupation: 11.3% management, 6.7% professional, 7.9% services, 12.1% sales, 10.4% farming, 5.8% construction, 3.8% production (2006-2010 5-year est.).

**Income:** Per capita income: $22,649 (2006-2010 5-year est.); Median household income: $53,125 (2006-2010 5-year est.); Average household income: $62,028 (2006-2010 5-year est.); Percent of households with income of $100,000 or more: 10.2% (2006-2010 5-year est.); Poverty rate: 10.9% (2006-2010 5-year est.).

**Education:** Percent of population age 25 and over with: High school diploma (including GED) or higher: 81.9% (2006-2010 5-year est.); Bachelor's degree or higher: 20.3% (2006-2010 5-year est.); Master's degree or higher: 3.2% (2006-2010 5-year est.).

**Housing:** Homeownership rate: 74.3% (2010); Median home value: $108,800 (2006-2010 5-year est.); Median contract rent: $535 per month (2006-2010 5-year est.); Median year structure built: before 1940 (2006-2010 5-year est.).

**Safety:** Violent crime rate: 0.0 per 10,000 population; Property crime rate: 99.8 per 10,000 population (2010).

**Transportation:** Commute to work: 95.0% car, 0.0% public transportation, 0.0% walk, 4.2% work from home (2006-2010 5-year est.); Travel time to work: 47.2% less than 15 minutes, 44.1% 15 to 30 minutes, 5.2% 30 to 45 minutes, 0.9% 45 to 60 minutes, 2.6% 60 minutes or more (2006-2010 5-year est.)

## GREAT BEND (CDP).

Covers a land area of 5.787 square miles and a water area of 0.056 square miles. Located at 44.01° N. Lat; 75.70° W. Long. Elevation is 663 feet.

**Population:** 829 (1990); 801 (2000); 843 (2010); Density: 145.6 persons per square mile (2010); Race: 91.9% White, 2.1% Black, 1.8% Asian, 0.6% American Indian/Alaska Native, 0.1% Native Hawaiian/Other Pacific Islander, 3.5% Other, 3.0% Hispanic of any race (2010); Average household size: 2.63 (2010); Median age: 35.8 (2010); Males per 100 females: 112.3 (2010); Marriage status: 24.5% never married, 59.3% now married, 1.4% widowed, 14.7% divorced (2006-2010 5-year est.); Foreign born: 2.0% (2006-2010 5-year est.); Ancestry (includes multiple ancestries): 25.0% German, 21.5% Irish, 14.9% Italian, 9.5% Norwegian, 9.1% English (2006-2010 5-year est.).

**Economy:** Employment by occupation: 1.7% management, 0.0% professional, 20.9% services, 9.8% sales, 20.1% farming, 11.8% construction, 11.8% production (2006-2010 5-year est.).

**Income:** Per capita income: $26,042 (2006-2010 5-year est.); Median household income: $49,448 (2006-2010 5-year est.); Average household income: $61,254 (2006-2010 5-year est.); Percent of households with income of $100,000 or more: 8.7% (2006-2010 5-year est.); Poverty rate: 3.5% (2006-2010 5-year est.).

**Education:** Percent of population age 25 and over with: High school diploma (including GED) or higher: 98.0% (2006-2010 5-year est.); Bachelor's degree or higher: 31.6% (2006-2010 5-year est.); Master's degree or higher: 10.6% (2006-2010 5-year est.).

**Housing:** Homeownership rate: 76.3% (2010); Median home value: $96,900 (2006-2010 5-year est.); Median contract rent: $1,110 per month (2006-2010 5-year est.); Median year structure built: 1942 (2006-2010 5-year est.).

**Transportation:** Commute to work: 93.9% car, 2.2% public transportation, 0.0% walk, 3.9% work from home (2006-2010 5-year est.); Travel time to work: 43.6% less than 15 minutes, 31.1% 15 to 30 minutes, 22.1% 30 to 45 minutes, 0.0% 45 to 60 minutes, 3.3% 60 minutes or more (2006-2010 5-year est.)

## HENDERSON (town).

Covers a land area of 41.180 square miles and a water area of 11.755 square miles. Located at 43.85° N. Lat; 76.18° W. Long. Elevation is 348 feet.

**Population:** 1,268 (1990); 1,377 (2000); 1,360 (2010); Density: 33.0 persons per square mile (2010); Race: 95.9% White, 0.6% Black, 0.2% Asian, 0.1% American Indian/Alaska Native, 0.1% Native Hawaiian/Other Pacific Islander, 3.1% Other, 2.3% Hispanic of any race (2010); Average household size: 2.35 (2010); Median age: 47.0 (2010); Males per 100 females: 102.4 (2010); Marriage status: 22.7% never married, 61.8% now married, 4.8% widowed, 10.7% divorced (2006-2010 5-year est.); Foreign born: 1.7% (2006-2010 5-year est.); Ancestry (includes multiple ancestries): 20.7% German, 20.7% English, 19.5% Irish, 16.3% Italian, 10.8% French (2006-2010 5-year est.).

**Economy:** Employment by occupation: 15.3% management, 3.1% professional, 6.7% services, 15.4% sales, 0.7% farming, 16.0% construction, 8.9% production (2006-2010 5-year est.).

**Income:** Per capita income: $28,305 (2006-2010 5-year est.); Median household income: $59,750 (2006-2010 5-year est.); Average household income: $69,652 (2006-2010 5-year est.); Percent of households with income of $100,000 or more: 18.8% (2006-2010 5-year est.); Poverty rate: 6.0% (2006-2010 5-year est.).

**Education:** Percent of population age 25 and over with: High school diploma (including GED) or higher: 90.4% (2006-2010 5-year est.); Bachelor's degree or higher: 25.3% (2006-2010 5-year est.); Master's degree or higher: 8.6% (2006-2010 5-year est.).

**Housing:** Homeownership rate: 81.1% (2010); Median home value: $151,300 (2006-2010 5-year est.); Median contract rent: $297 per month (2006-2010 5-year est.); Median year structure built: 1961 (2006-2010 5-year est.).

**Transportation:** Commute to work: 93.4% car, 1.5% public transportation, 0.6% walk, 3.7% work from home (2006-2010 5-year est.); Travel time to work: 12.5% less than 15 minutes, 39.3% 15 to 30 minutes, 32.2% 30 to 45

minutes, 4.2% 45 to 60 minutes, 11.8% 60 minutes or more (2006-2010 5-year est.)

**Additional Information Contacts**
Henderson Harbor Area Chamber of Commerce . . . . . . . . (315) 938-5568
   http://www.hendersonharborny.com

## HENDERSON (CDP).

Covers a land area of 0.505 square miles and a water area of 0 square miles. Located at 43.84° N. Lat; 76.18° W. Long. Elevation is 348 feet.

**Population:** n/a (1990); n/a (2000); 224 (2010); Density: 442.8 persons per square mile (2010); Race: 96.4% White, 0.0% Black, 0.0% Asian, 0.0% American Indian/Alaska Native, 0.0% Native Hawaiian/Other Pacific Islander, 3.6% Other, 0.9% Hispanic of any race (2010); Average household size: 2.24 (2010); Median age: 41.8 (2010); Males per 100 females: 88.2 (2010); Marriage status: 30.8% never married, 55.5% now married, 5.7% widowed, 8.0% divorced (2006-2010 5-year est.); Foreign born: 0.0% (2006-2010 5-year est.); Ancestry (includes multiple ancestries): 35.2% Irish, 29.4% German, 16.1% English, 8.3% French, 7.5% Scotch-Irish (2006-2010 5-year est.).

**Economy:** Employment by occupation: 10.3% management, 3.2% professional, 4.0% services, 20.6% sales, 2.4% farming, 19.0% construction, 1.6% production (2006-2010 5-year est.).

**Income:** Per capita income: $16,992 (2006-2010 5-year est.); Median household income: $53,333 (2006-2010 5-year est.); Average household income: $55,649 (2006-2010 5-year est.); Percent of households with income of $100,000 or more: 4.6% (2006-2010 5-year est.); Poverty rate: 7.2% (2006-2010 5-year est.).

**Education:** Percent of population age 25 and over with: High school diploma (including GED) or higher: 87.9% (2006-2010 5-year est.); Bachelor's degree or higher: 11.6% (2006-2010 5-year est.); Master's degree or higher: 1.5% (2006-2010 5-year est.).

**Housing:** Homeownership rate: 65.0% (2010); Median home value: $93,100 (2006-2010 5-year est.); Median contract rent: $188 per month (2006-2010 5-year est.); Median year structure built: before 1940 (2006-2010 5-year est.).

**Transportation:** Commute to work: 97.6% car, 0.0% public transportation, 0.0% walk, 0.0% work from home (2006-2010 5-year est.); Travel time to work: 22.8% less than 15 minutes, 37.4% 15 to 30 minutes, 22.8% 30 to 45 minutes, 0.0% 45 to 60 minutes, 17.1% 60 minutes or more (2006-2010 5-year est.)

## HENDERSON HARBOR (unincorporated postal area)

Zip Code: 13651

Covers a land area of 2.449 square miles and a water area of 0.202 square miles. Located at 43.86° N. Lat; 76.17° W. Long. Elevation is 246 feet. Population: 127 (2010); Density: 51.9 persons per square mile (2010); Race: 92.9% White, 2.4% Black, 0.0% Asian, 0.8% American Indian/Alaska Native, 0.0% Native Hawaiian/Other Pacific Islander, 3.9% Other, 6.3% Hispanic of any race (2010); Average household size: 2.15 (2010); Median age: 55.5 (2010); Males per 100 females: 101.6 (2010); Homeownership rate: 86.5% (2010)

## HERRINGS (village).

Covers a land area of 0.281 square miles and a water area of 0.048 square miles. Located at 44.02° N. Lat; 75.65° W. Long. Elevation is 689 feet.

**Population:** 140 (1990); 129 (2000); 90 (2010); Density: 319.9 persons per square mile (2010); Race: 86.7% White, 0.0% Black, 1.1% Asian, 0.0% American Indian/Alaska Native, 0.0% Native Hawaiian/Other Pacific Islander, 12.2% Other, 3.3% Hispanic of any race (2010); Average household size: 2.73 (2010); Median age: 47.3 (2010); Males per 100 females: 95.7 (2010); Marriage status: 37.6% never married, 53.8% now married, 5.1% widowed, 3.4% divorced (2006-2010 5-year est.); Foreign born: 1.3% (2006-2010 5-year est.); Ancestry (includes multiple ancestries): 41.8% German, 39.2% Irish, 7.6% French Canadian, 4.4% Italian, 3.2% Polish (2006-2010 5-year est.).

**Economy:** Employment by occupation: 0.0% management, 0.0% professional, 11.5% services, 6.6% sales, 9.8% farming, 19.7% construction, 0.0% production (2006-2010 5-year est.).

**Income:** Per capita income: $14,255 (2006-2010 5-year est.); Median household income: $36,250 (2006-2010 5-year est.); Average household income: $45,423 (2006-2010 5-year est.); Percent of households with income of $100,000 or more: 19.1% (2006-2010 5-year est.); Poverty rate: 42.4% (2006-2010 5-year est.).

**Education:** Percent of population age 25 and over with: High school diploma (including GED) or higher: 87.0% (2006-2010 5-year est.);

Bachelor's degree or higher: 17.4% (2006-2010 5-year est.); Master's degree or higher: 2.9% (2006-2010 5-year est.).
**Housing:** Homeownership rate: 94.0% (2010); Median home value: $78,800 (2006-2010 5-year est.); Median contract rent: $513 per month (2006-2010 5-year est.); Median year structure built: before 1940 (2006-2010 5-year est.).
**Transportation:** Commute to work: 100.0% car, 0.0% public transportation, 0.0% walk, 0.0% work from home (2006-2010 5-year est.); Travel time to work: 11.5% less than 15 minutes, 42.6% 15 to 30 minutes, 41.0% 30 to 45 minutes, 0.0% 45 to 60 minutes, 4.9% 60 minutes or more (2006-2010 5-year est.).

**HOUNSFIELD** (town). Covers a land area of 48.914 square miles and a water area of 71.487 square miles. Located at 43.90° N. Lat; 76.30° W. Long.
**Population:** 3,089 (1990); 3,323 (2000); 3,466 (2010); Density: 70.9 persons per square mile (2010); Race: 95.7% White, 1.6% Black, 0.5% Asian, 0.4% American Indian/Alaska Native, 0.2% Native Hawaiian/Other Pacific Islander, 1.6% Other, 2.4% Hispanic of any race (2010); Average household size: 2.39 (2010); Median age: 40.3 (2010); Males per 100 females: 96.5 (2010); Marriage status: 32.2% never married, 51.6% now married, 8.1% widowed, 8.1% divorced (2006-2010 5-year est.); Foreign born: 3.3% (2006-2010 5-year est.); Ancestry (includes multiple ancestries): 21.0% Irish, 16.1% English, 15.0% German, 11.1% French, 7.9% Scottish (2006-2010 5-year est.).
**Economy:** Employment by occupation: 6.8% management, 1.4% professional, 13.8% services, 9.2% sales, 5.0% farming, 7.9% construction, 5.7% production (2006-2010 5-year est.).
**Income:** Per capita income: $28,733 (2006-2010 5-year est.); Median household income: $56,935 (2006-2010 5-year est.); Average household income: $66,023 (2006-2010 5-year est.); Percent of households with income of $100,000 or more: 16.2% (2006-2010 5-year est.); Poverty rate: 7.2% (2006-2010 5-year est.).
**Education:** Percent of population age 25 and over with: High school diploma (including GED) or higher: 91.6% (2006-2010 5-year est.); Bachelor's degree or higher: 36.0% (2006-2010 5-year est.); Master's degree or higher: 14.4% (2006-2010 5-year est.).
**Housing:** Homeownership rate: 66.7% (2010); Median home value: $123,100 (2006-2010 5-year est.); Median contract rent: $772 per month (2006-2010 5-year est.); Median year structure built: 1961 (2006-2010 5-year est.).
**Transportation:** Commute to work: 86.7% car, 0.9% public transportation, 5.8% walk, 6.6% work from home (2006-2010 5-year est.); Travel time to work: 30.7% less than 15 minutes, 48.1% 15 to 30 minutes, 12.9% 30 to 45 minutes, 2.2% 45 to 60 minutes, 6.1% 60 minutes or more (2006-2010 5-year est.).

**LA FARGEVILLE** (CDP). Covers a land area of 3.318 square miles and a water area of 0.054 square miles. Located at 44.19° N. Lat; 75.96° W. Long. Elevation is 377 feet.
**Population:** 490 (1990); 588 (2000); 608 (2010); Density: 183.2 persons per square mile (2010); Race: 92.9% White, 0.3% Black, 0.3% Asian, 0.5% American Indian/Alaska Native, 0.8% Native Hawaiian/Other Pacific Islander, 5.2% Other, 2.5% Hispanic of any race (2010); Average household size: 2.66 (2010); Median age: 35.9 (2010); Males per 100 females: 91.8 (2010); Marriage status: 32.1% never married, 54.5% now married, 7.0% widowed, 6.4% divorced (2006-2010 5-year est.); Foreign born: 5.0% (2006-2010 5-year est.); Ancestry (includes multiple ancestries): 25.3% English, 22.7% Italian, 21.7% French, 14.1% Canadian, 14.0% German (2006-2010 5-year est.).
**Economy:** Employment by occupation: 24.6% management, 0.0% professional, 18.2% services, 4.5% sales, 0.0% farming, 25.2% construction, 5.8% production (2006-2010 5-year est.).
**Income:** Per capita income: $20,348 (2006-2010 5-year est.); Median household income: $50,000 (2006-2010 5-year est.); Average household income: $68,432 (2006-2010 5-year est.); Percent of households with income of $100,000 or more: 26.0% (2006-2010 5-year est.); Poverty rate: 5.1% (2006-2010 5-year est.).
**Education:** Percent of population age 25 and over with: High school diploma (including GED) or higher: 86.0% (2006-2010 5-year est.); Bachelor's degree or higher: 12.5% (2006-2010 5-year est.); Master's degree or higher: 12.5% (2006-2010 5-year est.).
**School District(s)**
La Fargeville Central School District (PK-12)
2009-10 Enrollment: 599 . . . . . . . . . . . . . . . . . . . . . . (315) 658-2241

**Housing:** Homeownership rate: 66.8% (2010); Median home value: $111,500 (2006-2010 5-year est.); Median contract rent: $493 per month (2006-2010 5-year est.); Median year structure built: before 1940 (2006-2010 5-year est.).
**Transportation:** Commute to work: 95.6% car, 0.0% public transportation, 4.4% walk, 0.0% work from home (2006-2010 5-year est.); Travel time to work: 14.9% less than 15 minutes, 11.5% 15 to 30 minutes, 69.2% 30 to 45 minutes, 0.0% 45 to 60 minutes, 4.4% 60 minutes or more (2006-2010 5-year est.)

**LE RAY** (town). Covers a land area of 73.643 square miles and a water area of 0.361 square miles. Located at 44.07° N. Lat; 75.79° W. Long.
**Population:** 17,973 (1990); 19,836 (2000); 21,782 (2010); Density: 295.8 persons per square mile (2010); Race: 75.8% White, 11.4% Black, 2.5% Asian, 0.8% American Indian/Alaska Native, 0.9% Native Hawaiian/Other Pacific Islander, 8.6% Other, 12.8% Hispanic of any race (2010); Average household size: 2.89 (2010); Median age: 23.8 (2010); Males per 100 females: 123.5 (2010); Marriage status: 22.7% never married, 70.8% now married, 1.7% widowed, 4.9% divorced (2006-2010 5-year est.); Foreign born: 9.3% (2006-2010 5-year est.); Ancestry (includes multiple ancestries): 21.4% German, 15.2% Irish, 8.8% Italian, 8.6% English, 5.6% French (2006-2010 5-year est.).
**Economy:** Employment by occupation: 7.5% management, 1.0% professional, 10.6% services, 19.7% sales, 3.0% farming, 9.4% construction, 6.6% production (2006-2010 5-year est.).
**Income:** Per capita income: $17,940 (2006-2010 5-year est.); Median household income: $37,378 (2006-2010 5-year est.); Average household income: $48,128 (2006-2010 5-year est.); Percent of households with income of $100,000 or more: 8.1% (2006-2010 5-year est.); Poverty rate: 16.5% (2006-2010 5-year est.).
**Education:** Percent of population age 25 and over with: High school diploma (including GED) or higher: 91.3% (2006-2010 5-year est.); Bachelor's degree or higher: 22.0% (2006-2010 5-year est.); Master's degree or higher: 9.3% (2006-2010 5-year est.).
**Housing:** Homeownership rate: 23.8% (2010); Median home value: $155,000 (2006-2010 5-year est.); Median contract rent: $949 per month (2006-2010 5-year est.); Median year structure built: 1983 (2006-2010 5-year est.).
**Transportation:** Commute to work: 89.4% car, 0.5% public transportation, 5.0% walk, 2.2% work from home (2006-2010 5-year est.); Travel time to work: 57.7% less than 15 minutes, 36.5% 15 to 30 minutes, 4.8% 30 to 45 minutes, 0.4% 45 to 60 minutes, 0.6% 60 minutes or more (2006-2010 5-year est.)

**LORRAINE** (town). Covers a land area of 38.978 square miles and a water area of 0.018 square miles. Located at 43.74° N. Lat; 75.97° W. Long. Elevation is 1,001 feet.
**Population:** 737 (1990); 930 (2000); 1,037 (2010); Density: 26.6 persons per square mile (2010); Race: 98.0% White, 0.2% Black, 0.2% Asian, 0.2% American Indian/Alaska Native, 0.2% Native Hawaiian/Other Pacific Islander, 1.2% Other, 0.7% Hispanic of any race (2010); Average household size: 2.71 (2010); Median age: 40.0 (2010); Males per 100 females: 103.7 (2010); Marriage status: 27.4% never married, 61.0% now married, 4.1% widowed, 7.5% divorced (2006-2010 5-year est.); Foreign born: 0.3% (2006-2010 5-year est.); Ancestry (includes multiple ancestries): 17.2% English, 15.2% German, 13.5% French, 12.9% American, 5.9% Irish (2006-2010 5-year est.).
**Economy:** Employment by occupation: 7.3% management, 1.3% professional, 13.2% services, 21.6% sales, 3.1% farming, 18.3% construction, 7.9% production (2006-2010 5-year est.).
**Income:** Per capita income: $19,117 (2006-2010 5-year est.); Median household income: $43,894 (2006-2010 5-year est.); Average household income: $50,340 (2006-2010 5-year est.); Percent of households with income of $100,000 or more: 7.7% (2006-2010 5-year est.); Poverty rate: 22.8% (2006-2010 5-year est.).
**Education:** Percent of population age 25 and over with: High school diploma (including GED) or higher: 82.7% (2006-2010 5-year est.); Bachelor's degree or higher: 11.6% (2006-2010 5-year est.); Master's degree or higher: 2.0% (2006-2010 5-year est.).
**Housing:** Homeownership rate: 87.7% (2010); Median home value: $81,700 (2006-2010 5-year est.); Median contract rent: $475 per month (2006-2010 5-year est.); Median year structure built: 1981 (2006-2010 5-year est.).
**Transportation:** Commute to work: 94.0% car, 0.0% public transportation, 3.8% walk, 1.5% work from home (2006-2010 5-year est.); Travel time to

work: 22.2% less than 15 minutes, 29.9% 15 to 30 minutes, 36.2% 30 to 45 minutes, 5.8% 45 to 60 minutes, 5.8% 60 minutes or more (2006-2010 5-year est.)

**LORRAINE** (CDP). Covers a land area of 0.482 square miles and a water area of 0 square miles. Located at 43.76° N. Lat; 75.95° W. Long. Elevation is 1,001 feet.
**Population:** n/a (1990); n/a (2000); 174 (2010); Density: 360.4 persons per square mile (2010); Race: 97.1% White, 0.6% Black, 1.1% Asian, 0.6% American Indian/Alaska Native, 0.0% Native Hawaiian/Other Pacific Islander, 0.6% Other, 1.1% Hispanic of any race (2010); Average household size: 2.85 (2010); Median age: 41.4 (2010); Males per 100 females: 102.3 (2010); Marriage status: 26.2% never married, 61.0% now married, 4.9% widowed, 7.9% divorced (2006-2010 5-year est.); Foreign born: 0.0% (2006-2010 5-year est.); Ancestry (includes multiple ancestries): 19.1% German, 14.4% American, 10.2% English, 7.9% Dutch, 7.0% French (2006-2010 5-year est.).
**Economy:** Employment by occupation: 3.4% management, 0.0% professional, 9.0% services, 34.8% sales, 0.0% farming, 18.0% construction, 0.0% production (2006-2010 5-year est.).
**Income:** Per capita income: $16,269 (2006-2010 5-year est.); Median household income: $30,250 (2006-2010 5-year est.); Average household income: $37,708 (2006-2010 5-year est.); Percent of households with income of $100,000 or more: 8.6% (2006-2010 5-year est.); Poverty rate: 42.8% (2006-2010 5-year est.).
**Education:** Percent of population age 25 and over with: High school diploma (including GED) or higher: 80.7% (2006-2010 5-year est.); Bachelor's degree or higher: 16.3% (2006-2010 5-year est.); Master's degree or higher: 0.0% (2006-2010 5-year est.).
**Housing:** Homeownership rate: 93.4% (2010); Median home value: $67,400 (2006-2010 5-year est.); Median contract rent: n/a per month (2006-2010 5-year est.); Median year structure built: 1979 (2006-2010 5-year est.).
**Transportation:** Commute to work: 92.1% car, 0.0% public transportation, 0.0% walk, 7.9% work from home (2006-2010 5-year est.); Travel time to work: 11.0% less than 15 minutes, 15.9% 15 to 30 minutes, 42.7% 30 to 45 minutes, 23.2% 45 to 60 minutes, 7.3% 60 minutes or more (2006-2010 5-year est.)

**LYME** (town). Covers a land area of 55.813 square miles and a water area of 51.178 square miles. Located at 44.02° N. Lat; 76.22° W. Long.
**Population:** 1,701 (1990); 2,015 (2000); 2,185 (2010); Density: 39.1 persons per square mile (2010); Race: 97.2% White, 0.6% Black, 0.3% Asian, 0.1% American Indian/Alaska Native, 0.0% Native Hawaiian/Other Pacific Islander, 1.8% Other, 1.5% Hispanic of any race (2010); Average household size: 2.42 (2010); Median age: 46.9 (2010); Males per 100 females: 101.9 (2010); Marriage status: 14.1% never married, 72.1% now married, 7.7% widowed, 6.1% divorced (2006-2010 5-year est.); Foreign born: 5.1% (2006-2010 5-year est.); Ancestry (includes multiple ancestries): 25.9% English, 22.9% Irish, 19.4% German, 13.3% French, 6.2% Italian (2006-2010 5-year est.).
**Economy:** Employment by occupation: 10.7% management, 2.0% professional, 10.3% services, 20.4% sales, 2.4% farming, 12.8% construction, 10.2% production (2006-2010 5-year est.).
**Income:** Per capita income: $25,782 (2006-2010 5-year est.); Median household income: $48,182 (2006-2010 5-year est.); Average household income: $58,868 (2006-2010 5-year est.); Percent of households with income of $100,000 or more: 13.5% (2006-2010 5-year est.); Poverty rate: 11.0% (2006-2010 5-year est.).
**Education:** Percent of population age 25 and over with: High school diploma (including GED) or higher: 89.5% (2006-2010 5-year est.); Bachelor's degree or higher: 22.1% (2006-2010 5-year est.); Master's degree or higher: 7.7% (2006-2010 5-year est.).
**Housing:** Homeownership rate: 84.0% (2010); Median home value: $141,700 (2006-2010 5-year est.); Median contract rent: $390 per month (2006-2010 5-year est.); Median year structure built: 1967 (2006-2010 5-year est.).
**Transportation:** Commute to work: 86.0% car, 0.0% public transportation, 5.4% walk, 8.0% work from home (2006-2010 5-year est.); Travel time to work: 17.7% less than 15 minutes, 46.3% 15 to 30 minutes, 26.5% 30 to 45 minutes, 4.2% 45 to 60 minutes, 5.3% 60 minutes or more (2006-2010 5-year est.)

**MANNSVILLE** (village). Covers a land area of 0.897 square miles and a water area of 0.032 square miles. Located at 43.71° N. Lat; 76.06° W. Long. Elevation is 620 feet.
**Population:** 444 (1990); 400 (2000); 354 (2010); Density: 394.6 persons per square mile (2010); Race: 97.5% White, 0.0% Black, 0.8% Asian, 0.0% American Indian/Alaska Native, 0.0% Native Hawaiian/Other Pacific Islander, 1.7% Other, 1.4% Hispanic of any race (2010); Average household size: 2.64 (2010); Median age: 37.5 (2010); Males per 100 females: 91.4 (2010); Marriage status: 23.0% never married, 53.3% now married, 5.5% widowed, 18.2% divorced (2006-2010 5-year est.); Foreign born: 0.0% (2006-2010 5-year est.); Ancestry (includes multiple ancestries): 15.8% English, 13.4% Irish, 12.6% German, 9.9% American, 7.7% French (2006-2010 5-year est.).
**Economy:** Employment by occupation: 6.9% management, 5.4% professional, 5.9% services, 20.6% sales, 4.4% farming, 14.2% construction, 13.7% production (2006-2010 5-year est.).
**Income:** Per capita income: $22,623 (2006-2010 5-year est.); Median household income: $52,639 (2006-2010 5-year est.); Average household income: $54,896 (2006-2010 5-year est.); Percent of households with income of $100,000 or more: 9.6% (2006-2010 5-year est.); Poverty rate: 5.5% (2006-2010 5-year est.).
**Education:** Percent of population age 25 and over with: High school diploma (including GED) or higher: 89.3% (2006-2010 5-year est.); Bachelor's degree or higher: 8.3% (2006-2010 5-year est.); Master's degree or higher: 4.8% (2006-2010 5-year est.).
**School District(s)**
South Jefferson Central School District (PK-12)
   2009-10 Enrollment: 2,036 . . . . . . . . . . . . . . . . . . . . . (315) 583-6104
**Housing:** Homeownership rate: 85.1% (2010); Median home value: $79,800 (2006-2010 5-year est.); Median contract rent: $525 per month (2006-2010 5-year est.); Median year structure built: before 1940 (2006-2010 5-year est.).
**Transportation:** Commute to work: 97.1% car, 0.0% public transportation, 1.0% walk, 1.0% work from home (2006-2010 5-year est.); Travel time to work: 30.2% less than 15 minutes, 36.6% 15 to 30 minutes, 18.8% 30 to 45 minutes, 5.4% 45 to 60 minutes, 8.9% 60 minutes or more (2006-2010 5-year est.)

**NATURAL BRIDGE** (CDP). Covers a land area of 1.389 square miles and a water area of 0 square miles. Located at 44.07° N. Lat; 75.49° W. Long. Elevation is 817 feet.
**Population:** 425 (1990); 392 (2000); 365 (2010); Density: 262.7 persons per square mile (2010); Race: 94.8% White, 1.1% Black, 0.3% Asian, 2.2% American Indian/Alaska Native, 0.0% Native Hawaiian/Other Pacific Islander, 1.6% Other, 2.2% Hispanic of any race (2010); Average household size: 2.63 (2010); Median age: 39.4 (2010); Males per 100 females: 95.2 (2010); Marriage status: 39.8% never married, 31.3% now married, 0.0% widowed, 28.9% divorced (2006-2010 5-year est.); Foreign born: 0.0% (2006-2010 5-year est.); Ancestry (includes multiple ancestries): 33.9% Hungarian, 29.5% French, 24.8% American, 14.4% German, 14.4% Canadian (2006-2010 5-year est.).
**Economy:** Employment by occupation: 37.9% management, 0.0% professional, 0.0% services, 12.1% sales, 6.5% farming, 0.0% construction, 11.3% production (2006-2010 5-year est.).
**Income:** Per capita income: $15,976 (2006-2010 5-year est.); Median household income: $37,438 (2006-2010 5-year est.); Average household income: $44,069 (2006-2010 5-year est.); Percent of households with income of $100,000 or more: 0.0% (2006-2010 5-year est.); Poverty rate: 10.4% (2006-2010 5-year est.).
**Education:** Percent of population age 25 and over with: High school diploma (including GED) or higher: 71.3% (2006-2010 5-year est.); Bachelor's degree or higher: 0.0% (2006-2010 5-year est.); Master's degree or higher: 0.0% (2006-2010 5-year est.).
**Housing:** Homeownership rate: 71.2% (2010); Median home value: $108,500 (2006-2010 5-year est.); Median contract rent: n/a per month (2006-2010 5-year est.); Median year structure built: 1965 (2006-2010 5-year est.).
**Transportation:** Commute to work: 90.3% car, 0.0% public transportation, 0.0% walk, 0.0% work from home (2006-2010 5-year est.); Travel time to work: 21.5% less than 15 minutes, 59.0% 15 to 30 minutes, 19.4% 30 to 45 minutes, 0.0% 45 to 60 minutes, 0.0% 60 minutes or more (2006-2010 5-year est.)

**ORLEANS** (town). Covers a land area of 71.422 square miles and a water area of 6.620 square miles. Located at 44.22° N. Lat; 75.95° W. Long.
**Population:** 2,248 (1990); 2,465 (2000); 2,789 (2010); Density: 39.0 persons per square mile (2010); Race: 95.6% White, 0.8% Black, 0.5% Asian, 0.6% American Indian/Alaska Native, 0.2% Native Hawaiian/Other Pacific Islander, 2.3% Other, 1.1% Hispanic of any race (2010); Average household size: 2.77 (2010); Median age: 38.3 (2010); Males per 100 females: 101.5 (2010); Marriage status: 25.8% never married, 61.4% now married, 6.2% widowed, 6.6% divorced (2006-2010 5-year est.); Foreign born: 1.7% (2006-2010 5-year est.); Ancestry (includes multiple ancestries): 22.3% Irish, 19.9% German, 19.0% English, 18.5% French, 13.4% Italian (2006-2010 5-year est.).
**Economy:** Employment by occupation: 10.8% management, 0.9% professional, 12.1% services, 13.9% sales, 6.1% farming, 17.8% construction, 5.1% production (2006-2010 5-year est.).
**Income:** Per capita income: $21,556 (2006-2010 5-year est.); Median household income: $49,583 (2006-2010 5-year est.); Average household income: $60,643 (2006-2010 5-year est.); Percent of households with income of $100,000 or more: 17.8% (2006-2010 5-year est.); Poverty rate: 11.4% (2006-2010 5-year est.).
**Taxes:** Total city taxes per capita: $97 (2009); City property taxes per capita: $66 (2009).
**Education:** Percent of population age 25 and over with: High school diploma (including GED) or higher: 87.3% (2006-2010 5-year est.); Bachelor's degree or higher: 20.0% (2006-2010 5-year est.); Master's degree or higher: 11.7% (2006-2010 5-year est.).
**Housing:** Homeownership rate: 79.4% (2010); Median home value: $128,300 (2006-2010 5-year est.); Median contract rent: $624 per month (2006-2010 5-year est.); Median year structure built: 1972 (2006-2010 5-year est.).
**Transportation:** Commute to work: 81.7% car, 0.0% public transportation, 4.8% walk, 9.6% work from home (2006-2010 5-year est.); Travel time to work: 27.4% less than 15 minutes, 26.6% 15 to 30 minutes, 38.8% 30 to 45 minutes, 1.7% 45 to 60 minutes, 5.5% 60 minutes or more (2006-2010 5-year est.)

**OXBOW** (CDP). Covers a land area of 0.202 square miles and a water area of 0 square miles. Located at 44.28° N. Lat; 75.62° W. Long. Elevation is 354 feet.
**Population:** n/a (1990); n/a (2000); 108 (2010); Density: 533.8 persons per square mile (2010); Race: 98.1% White, 0.0% Black, 0.0% Asian, 0.0% American Indian/Alaska Native, 0.0% Native Hawaiian/Other Pacific Islander, 1.9% Other, 0.0% Hispanic of any race (2010); Average household size: 3.00 (2010); Median age: 43.0 (2010); Males per 100 females: 92.9 (2010); Marriage status: 40.0% never married, 56.9% now married, 3.1% widowed, 0.0% divorced (2006-2010 5-year est.); Foreign born: 0.0% (2006-2010 5-year est.); Ancestry (includes multiple ancestries): 34.7% French, 13.9% French Canadian, 12.5% Scotch-Irish, 9.7% German, 2.8% European (2006-2010 5-year est.).
**Economy:** Employment by occupation: 8.3% management, 0.0% professional, 27.1% services, 12.5% sales, 0.0% farming, 4.2% construction, 8.3% production (2006-2010 5-year est.).
**Income:** Per capita income: $17,658 (2006-2010 5-year est.); Median household income: $39,063 (2006-2010 5-year est.); Average household income: $50,687 (2006-2010 5-year est.); Percent of households with income of $100,000 or more: 13.0% (2006-2010 5-year est.); Poverty rate: 2.8% (2006-2010 5-year est.).
**Education:** Percent of population age 25 and over with: High school diploma (including GED) or higher: 89.4% (2006-2010 5-year est.); Bachelor's degree or higher: 27.7% (2006-2010 5-year est.); Master's degree or higher: 0.0% (2006-2010 5-year est.).
**Housing:** Homeownership rate: 88.9% (2010); Median home value: $45,000 (2006-2010 5-year est.); Median contract rent: $1,000 per month (2006-2010 5-year est.); Median year structure built: 1970 (2006-2010 5-year est.).
**Transportation:** Commute to work: 100.0% car, 0.0% public transportation, 0.0% walk, 0.0% work from home (2006-2010 5-year est.); Travel time to work: 12.5% less than 15 minutes, 6.3% 15 to 30 minutes, 52.1% 30 to 45 minutes, 29.2% 45 to 60 minutes, 0.0% 60 minutes or more (2006-2010 5-year est.)

**PAMELIA** (town). Covers a land area of 33.840 square miles and a water area of 1.369 square miles. Located at 44.05° N. Lat; 75.90° W. Long.
**Population:** 2,811 (1990); 2,897 (2000); 3,160 (2010); Density: 93.4 persons per square mile (2010); Race: 91.9% White, 2.9% Black, 2.0% Asian, 0.5% American Indian/Alaska Native, 0.1% Native Hawaiian/Other Pacific Islander, 2.6% Other, 3.0% Hispanic of any race (2010); Average household size: 2.63 (2010); Median age: 39.5 (2010); Males per 100 females: 108.3 (2010); Marriage status: 31.8% never married, 58.9% now married, 4.2% widowed, 5.2% divorced (2006-2010 5-year est.); Foreign born: 2.9% (2006-2010 5-year est.); Ancestry (includes multiple ancestries): 28.4% Irish, 16.3% German, 14.4% French, 10.4% Italian, 8.3% English (2006-2010 5-year est.).
**Economy:** Single-family building permits issued: 1 (2011); Multi-family building permits issued: 0 (2011); Employment by occupation: 10.0% management, 1.4% professional, 12.4% services, 16.3% sales, 8.3% farming, 12.6% construction, 5.4% production (2006-2010 5-year est.).
**Income:** Per capita income: $22,344 (2006-2010 5-year est.); Median household income: $60,117 (2006-2010 5-year est.); Average household income: $63,479 (2006-2010 5-year est.); Percent of households with income of $100,000 or more: 15.0% (2006-2010 5-year est.); Poverty rate: 7.2% (2006-2010 5-year est.).
**Education:** Percent of population age 25 and over with: High school diploma (including GED) or higher: 85.6% (2006-2010 5-year est.); Bachelor's degree or higher: 15.7% (2006-2010 5-year est.); Master's degree or higher: 4.6% (2006-2010 5-year est.).
**Housing:** Homeownership rate: 77.0% (2010); Median home value: $142,600 (2006-2010 5-year est.); Median contract rent: $567 per month (2006-2010 5-year est.); Median year structure built: 1981 (2006-2010 5-year est.).
**Transportation:** Commute to work: 90.7% car, 0.0% public transportation, 0.3% walk, 5.2% work from home (2006-2010 5-year est.); Travel time to work: 54.9% less than 15 minutes, 36.9% 15 to 30 minutes, 3.5% 30 to 45 minutes, 2.3% 45 to 60 minutes, 2.4% 60 minutes or more (2006-2010 5-year est.).

**PAMELIA CENTER** (CDP). Covers a land area of 1.041 square miles and a water area of 0 square miles. Located at 44.04° N. Lat; 75.90° W. Long.
**Population:** n/a (1990); n/a (2000); 264 (2010); Density: 253.6 persons per square mile (2010); Race: 90.2% White, 1.5% Black, 5.7% Asian, 0.8% American Indian/Alaska Native, 0.0% Native Hawaiian/Other Pacific Islander, 1.8% Other, 1.1% Hispanic of any race (2010); Average household size: 2.56 (2010); Median age: 40.6 (2010); Males per 100 females: 107.9 (2010); Marriage status: 15.9% never married, 73.1% now married, 11.0% widowed, 0.0% divorced (2006-2010 5-year est.); Foreign born: 6.0% (2006-2010 5-year est.); Ancestry (includes multiple ancestries): 41.4% Irish, 14.9% Italian, 14.5% Polish, 9.2% French, 9.2% English (2006-2010 5-year est.).
**Economy:** Employment by occupation: 7.7% management, 3.5% professional, 0.0% services, 27.3% sales, 7.7% farming, 4.2% construction, 4.2% production (2006-2010 5-year est.).
**Income:** Per capita income: $26,907 (2006-2010 5-year est.); Median household income: $48,854 (2006-2010 5-year est.); Average household income: $66,658 (2006-2010 5-year est.); Percent of households with income of $100,000 or more: 17.2% (2006-2010 5-year est.); Poverty rate: 0.0% (2006-2010 5-year est.).
**Education:** Percent of population age 25 and over with: High school diploma (including GED) or higher: 86.9% (2006-2010 5-year est.); Bachelor's degree or higher: 19.6% (2006-2010 5-year est.); Master's degree or higher: 7.2% (2006-2010 5-year est.).
**Housing:** Homeownership rate: 87.4% (2010); Median home value: $161,400 (2006-2010 5-year est.); Median contract rent: $509 per month (2006-2010 5-year est.); Median year structure built: 1977 (2006-2010 5-year est.).
**Transportation:** Commute to work: 100.0% car, 0.0% public transportation, 0.0% walk, 0.0% work from home (2006-2010 5-year est.); Travel time to work: 67.1% less than 15 minutes, 32.9% 15 to 30 minutes, 0.0% 30 to 45 minutes, 0.0% 45 to 60 minutes, 0.0% 60 minutes or more (2006-2010 5-year est.)

**PHILADELPHIA** (village). Covers a land area of 0.904 square miles and a water area of 0 square miles. Located at 44.15° N. Lat; 75.70° W. Long. Elevation is 486 feet.
**Population:** 1,478 (1990); 1,519 (2000); 1,252 (2010); Density: 1,384.6 persons per square mile (2010); Race: 84.2% White, 6.5% Black, 1.5% Asian, 0.4% American Indian/Alaska Native, 0.9% Native Hawaiian/Other Pacific Islander, 6.5% Other, 6.2% Hispanic of any race (2010); Average household size: 2.54 (2010); Median age: 27.9 (2010); Males per 100 females: 87.7 (2010); Marriage status: 23.6% never married, 68.0% now married, 3.4% widowed, 4.9% divorced (2006-2010 5-year est.); Foreign born: 1.0% (2006-2010 5-year est.); Ancestry (includes multiple ancestries): 19.9% German, 15.8% Irish, 10.0% French, 8.5% English, 5.7% Italian (2006-2010 5-year est.).
**Economy:** Single-family building permits issued: 1 (2011); Multi-family building permits issued: 0 (2011); Employment by occupation: 13.4% management, 0.0% professional, 10.6% services, 21.4% sales, 3.5% farming, 13.0% construction, 9.7% production (2006-2010 5-year est.).
**Income:** Per capita income: $20,443 (2006-2010 5-year est.); Median household income: $40,000 (2006-2010 5-year est.); Average household income: $51,314 (2006-2010 5-year est.); Percent of households with income of $100,000 or more: 8.0% (2006-2010 5-year est.); Poverty rate: 10.5% (2006-2010 5-year est.).
**Education:** Percent of population age 25 and over with: High school diploma (including GED) or higher: 94.2% (2006-2010 5-year est.); Bachelor's degree or higher: 15.0% (2006-2010 5-year est.); Master's degree or higher: 6.5% (2006-2010 5-year est.).
### School District(s)
Indian River Central School District (PK-12)
    2009-10 Enrollment: 3,767 . . . . . . . . . . . . . . . . . . . . . . . (315) 642-3441
**Housing:** Homeownership rate: 38.5% (2010); Median home value: $109,400 (2006-2010 5-year est.); Median contract rent: $594 per month (2006-2010 5-year est.); Median year structure built: 1978 (2006-2010 5-year est.).
**Transportation:** Commute to work: 91.3% car, 0.0% public transportation, 1.8% walk, 1.0% work from home (2006-2010 5-year est.); Travel time to work: 25.5% less than 15 minutes, 41.4% 15 to 30 minutes, 23.9% 30 to 45 minutes, 5.2% 45 to 60 minutes, 4.1% 60 minutes or more (2006-2010 5-year est.).

**PHILADELPHIA** (town). Covers a land area of 37.592 square miles and a water area of 0.020 square miles. Located at 44.14° N. Lat; 75.70° W. Long. Elevation is 486 feet.
**Population:** 2,136 (1990); 2,140 (2000); 1,947 (2010); Density: 51.8 persons per square mile (2010); Race: 87.7% White, 4.7% Black, 1.2% Asian, 0.8% American Indian/Alaska Native, 0.6% Native Hawaiian/Other Pacific Islander, 5.0% Other, 4.9% Hispanic of any race (2010); Average household size: 2.60 (2010); Median age: 30.7 (2010); Males per 100 females: 89.4 (2010); Marriage status: 26.3% never married, 65.2% now married, 3.5% widowed, 4.9% divorced (2006-2010 5-year est.); Foreign born: 0.7% (2006-2010 5-year est.); Ancestry (includes multiple ancestries): 21.7% German, 19.7% Irish, 11.2% French, 11.2% English, 4.9% Italian (2006-2010 5-year est.).
**Economy:** Single-family building permits issued: 2 (2011); Multi-family building permits issued: 0 (2011); Employment by occupation: 15.4% management, 0.4% professional, 8.8% services, 19.8% sales, 3.6% farming, 13.0% construction, 5.9% production (2006-2010 5-year est.).
**Income:** Per capita income: $21,584 (2006-2010 5-year est.); Median household income: $43,021 (2006-2010 5-year est.); Average household income: $54,448 (2006-2010 5-year est.); Percent of households with income of $100,000 or more: 10.6% (2006-2010 5-year est.); Poverty rate: 10.4% (2006-2010 5-year est.).
**Education:** Percent of population age 25 and over with: High school diploma (including GED) or higher: 93.7% (2006-2010 5-year est.); Bachelor's degree or higher: 14.3% (2006-2010 5-year est.); Master's degree or higher: 6.4% (2006-2010 5-year est.).
### School District(s)
Indian River Central School District (PK-12)
    2009-10 Enrollment: 3,767 . . . . . . . . . . . . . . . . . . . . . . . (315) 642-3441
**Housing:** Homeownership rate: 54.1% (2010); Median home value: $112,500 (2006-2010 5-year est.); Median contract rent: $546 per month (2006-2010 5-year est.); Median year structure built: 1980 (2006-2010 5-year est.).
**Transportation:** Commute to work: 91.7% car, 0.0% public transportation, 1.6% walk, 2.3% work from home (2006-2010 5-year est.); Travel time to work: 25.4% less than 15 minutes, 45.4% 15 to 30 minutes, 21.5% 30 to 45

minutes, 3.9% 45 to 60 minutes, 3.7% 60 minutes or more (2006-2010 5-year est.)

**PIERREPONT MANOR** (CDP). Covers a land area of 0.684 square miles and a water area of 0.003 square miles. Located at 43.73° N. Lat; 76.06° W. Long. Elevation is 623 feet.
**Population:** n/a (1990); n/a (2000); 228 (2010); Density: 333.1 persons per square mile (2010); Race: 100.0% White, 0.0% Black, 0.0% Asian, 0.0% American Indian/Alaska Native, 0.0% Native Hawaiian/Other Pacific Islander, 0.0% Other, 1.3% Hispanic of any race (2010); Average household size: 2.68 (2010); Median age: 39.0 (2010); Males per 100 females: 90.0 (2010); Marriage status: 23.0% never married, 68.9% now married, 0.0% widowed, 8.2% divorced (2006-2010 5-year est.); Foreign born: 0.0% (2006-2010 5-year est.); Ancestry (includes multiple ancestries): 25.4% English, 23.0% British, 22.1% Italian, 22.1% Dutch, 21.3% German (2006-2010 5-year est.).
**Economy:** Employment by occupation: 0.0% management, 0.0% professional, 0.0% services, 0.0% sales, 0.0% farming, 0.0% construction, 100.0% production (2006-2010 5-year est.).
**Income:** Per capita income: $29,183 (2006-2010 5-year est.); Median household income: $26,652 (2006-2010 5-year est.); Average household income: $44,859 (2006-2010 5-year est.); Percent of households with income of $100,000 or more: 0.0% (2006-2010 5-year est.); Poverty rate: 0.0% (2006-2010 5-year est.).
**Education:** Percent of population age 25 and over with: High school diploma (including GED) or higher: 92.6% (2006-2010 5-year est.); Bachelor's degree or higher: 70.5% (2006-2010 5-year est.); Master's degree or higher: 48.4% (2006-2010 5-year est.).
**Housing:** Homeownership rate: 82.4% (2010); Median home value: $58,800 (2006-2010 5-year est.); Median contract rent: n/a per month (2006-2010 5-year est.); Median year structure built: before 1940 (2006-2010 5-year est.).
**Transportation:** Commute to work: 100.0% car, 0.0% public transportation, 0.0% walk, 0.0% work from home (2006-2010 5-year est.); Travel time to work: 0.0% less than 15 minutes, 0.0% 15 to 30 minutes, 0.0% 30 to 45 minutes, 100.0% 45 to 60 minutes, 0.0% 60 minutes or more (2006-2010 5-year est.)

**PLESSIS** (CDP). Covers a land area of 0.345 square miles and a water area of 0 square miles. Located at 44.27° N. Lat; 75.85° W. Long. Elevation is 404 feet.
**Population:** n/a (1990); n/a (2000); 164 (2010); Density: 474.3 persons per square mile (2010); Race: 97.6% White, 0.6% Black, 0.0% Asian, 0.6% American Indian/Alaska Native, 0.0% Native Hawaiian/Other Pacific Islander, 1.2% Other, 3.7% Hispanic of any race (2010); Average household size: 2.78 (2010); Median age: 36.8 (2010); Males per 100 females: 113.0 (2010); Marriage status: 0.0% never married, 0.0% now married, 0.0% widowed, 0.0% divorced (2006-2010 5-year est.); Foreign born: 0.0% (2006-2010 5-year est.); Ancestry (includes multiple ancestries): n/a (2006-2010 5-year est.).
**Income:** Per capita income: $0 (2006-2010 5-year est.); Median household income: $0 (2006-2010 5-year est.); Average household income: $0 (2006-2010 5-year est.); Percent of households with income of $100,000 or more: 0.0% (2006-2010 5-year est.); Poverty rate: 0.0% (2006-2010 5-year est.).
**Education:** Percent of population age 25 and over with: High school diploma (including GED) or higher: 0.0% (2006-2010 5-year est.); Bachelor's degree or higher: 0.0% (2006-2010 5-year est.); Master's degree or higher: 0.0% (2006-2010 5-year est.).
**Housing:** Homeownership rate: 81.4% (2010); Median home value: n/a (2006-2010 5-year est.); Median contract rent: n/a per month (2006-2010 5-year est.); Median year structure built: before 1940 (2006-2010 5-year est.).

**REDWOOD** (CDP). Covers a land area of 2.020 square miles and a water area of 0.533 square miles. Located at 44.29° N. Lat; 75.80° W. Long. Elevation is 367 feet.
**Population:** 530 (1990); 584 (2000); 605 (2010); Density: 299.4 persons per square mile (2010); Race: 97.7% White, 0.5% Black, 0.2% Asian, 0.3% American Indian/Alaska Native, 0.0% Native Hawaiian/Other Pacific Islander, 1.3% Other, 2.0% Hispanic of any race (2010); Average household size: 2.78 (2010); Median age: 35.9 (2010); Males per 100 females: 100.3 (2010); Marriage status: 5.2% never married, 77.4% now married, 11.3% widowed, 6.1% divorced (2006-2010 5-year est.); Foreign born: 0.0% (2006-2010 5-year est.); Ancestry (includes multiple

ancestries): 51.1% French, 49.2% English, 19.1% Italian, 9.7% Ukrainian, 8.4% American (2006-2010 5-year est.).

**Economy:** Employment by occupation: 0.0% management, 0.0% professional, 18.1% services, 20.5% sales, 0.0% farming, 16.3% construction, 0.0% production (2006-2010 5-year est.).

**Income:** Per capita income: $27,759 (2006-2010 5-year est.); Median household income: $61,250 (2006-2010 5-year est.); Average household income: $70,577 (2006-2010 5-year est.); Percent of households with income of $100,000 or more: 36.1% (2006-2010 5-year est.); Poverty rate: 29.1% (2006-2010 5-year est.).

**Education:** Percent of population age 25 and over with: High school diploma (including GED) or higher: 100.0% (2006-2010 5-year est.); Bachelor's degree or higher: 0.0% (2006-2010 5-year est.); Master's degree or higher: 0.0% (2006-2010 5-year est.).

**Housing:** Homeownership rate: 75.7% (2010); Median home value: $81,000 (2006-2010 5-year est.); Median contract rent: $832 per month (2006-2010 5-year est.); Median year structure built: before 1940 (2006-2010 5-year est.).

**Transportation:** Commute to work: 72.9% car, 0.0% public transportation, 20.0% walk, 7.1% work from home (2006-2010 5-year est.); Travel time to work: 42.4% less than 15 minutes, 18.1% 15 to 30 minutes, 39.6% 30 to 45 minutes, 0.0% 45 to 60 minutes, 0.0% 60 minutes or more (2006-2010 5-year est.)

**RODMAN** (town). Covers a land area of 42.226 square miles and a water area of 0.053 square miles. Located at 43.84° N. Lat; 75.90° W. Long. Elevation is 725 feet.

**Population:** 1,016 (1990); 1,147 (2000); 1,176 (2010); Density: 27.8 persons per square mile (2010); Race: 96.8% White, 0.2% Black, 1.0% Asian, 0.3% American Indian/Alaska Native, 0.1% Native Hawaiian/Other Pacific Islander, 1.6% Other, 1.5% Hispanic of any race (2010); Average household size: 2.81 (2010); Median age: 39.5 (2010); Males per 100 females: 104.5 (2010); Marriage status: 29.4% never married, 60.5% now married, 3.7% widowed, 6.4% divorced (2006-2010 5-year est.); Foreign born: 0.9% (2006-2010 5-year est.); Ancestry (includes multiple ancestries): 21.2% Irish, 19.3% German, 17.8% English, 13.1% Italian, 7.3% French (2006-2010 5-year est.).

**Economy:** Employment by occupation: 12.5% management, 0.4% professional, 10.4% services, 16.3% sales, 5.8% farming, 18.4% construction, 6.5% production (2006-2010 5-year est.).

**Income:** Per capita income: $29,742 (2006-2010 5-year est.); Median household income: $64,917 (2006-2010 5-year est.); Average household income: $86,738 (2006-2010 5-year est.); Percent of households with income of $100,000 or more: 26.6% (2006-2010 5-year est.); Poverty rate: 10.6% (2006-2010 5-year est.).

**Education:** Percent of population age 25 and over with: High school diploma (including GED) or higher: 87.6% (2006-2010 5-year est.); Bachelor's degree or higher: 17.2% (2006-2010 5-year est.); Master's degree or higher: 8.1% (2006-2010 5-year est.).

**Housing:** Homeownership rate: 86.2% (2010); Median home value: $147,600 (2006-2010 5-year est.); Median contract rent: $757 per month (2006-2010 5-year est.); Median year structure built: 1978 (2006-2010 5-year est.).

**Transportation:** Commute to work: 90.0% car, 0.4% public transportation, 4.1% walk, 4.8% work from home (2006-2010 5-year est.); Travel time to work: 33.6% less than 15 minutes, 43.9% 15 to 30 minutes, 20.1% 30 to 45 minutes, 0.9% 45 to 60 minutes, 1.5% 60 minutes or more (2006-2010 5-year est.)

**RODMAN** (CDP). Covers a land area of 0.115 square miles and a water area of 0 square miles. Located at 43.85° N. Lat; 75.94° W. Long. Elevation is 725 feet.

**Population:** n/a (1990); n/a (2000); 153 (2010); Density: 1,319.9 persons per square mile (2010); Race: 96.7% White, 0.0% Black, 1.3% Asian, 0.7% American Indian/Alaska Native, 0.0% Native Hawaiian/Other Pacific Islander, 1.3% Other, 0.0% Hispanic of any race (2010); Average household size: 2.68 (2010); Median age: 36.8 (2010); Males per 100 females: 112.5 (2010); Marriage status: 34.0% never married, 46.2% now married, 1.9% widowed, 17.9% divorced (2006-2010 5-year est.); Foreign born: 0.0% (2006-2010 5-year est.); Ancestry (includes multiple ancestries): 25.8% German, 14.6% English, 13.2% Scottish, 6.6% Irish, 6.6% French (2006-2010 5-year est.).

**Economy:** Employment by occupation: 7.6% management, 0.0% professional, 4.5% services, 31.8% sales, 0.0% farming, 42.4% construction, 15.2% production (2006-2010 5-year est.).

**Income:** Per capita income: $43,400 (2006-2010 5-year est.); Median household income: $88,077 (2006-2010 5-year est.); Average household income: $137,056 (2006-2010 5-year est.); Percent of households with income of $100,000 or more: 23.0% (2006-2010 5-year est.); Poverty rate: 0.0% (2006-2010 5-year est.).

**Education:** Percent of population age 25 and over with: High school diploma (including GED) or higher: 94.1% (2006-2010 5-year est.); Bachelor's degree or higher: 18.8% (2006-2010 5-year est.); Master's degree or higher: 5.9% (2006-2010 5-year est.).

**Housing:** Homeownership rate: 91.3% (2010); Median home value: $89,000 (2006-2010 5-year est.); Median contract rent: n/a per month (2006-2010 5-year est.); Median year structure built: before 1940 (2006-2010 5-year est.).

**Transportation:** Commute to work: 81.8% car, 0.0% public transportation, 0.0% walk, 18.2% work from home (2006-2010 5-year est.); Travel time to work: 29.6% less than 15 minutes, 57.4% 15 to 30 minutes, 13.0% 30 to 45 minutes, 0.0% 45 to 60 minutes, 0.0% 60 minutes or more (2006-2010 5-year est.)

**RUTLAND** (town). Covers a land area of 45.102 square miles and a water area of 0.275 square miles. Located at 43.94° N. Lat; 75.78° W. Long.

**Population:** 3,023 (1990); 2,959 (2000); 3,060 (2010); Density: 67.8 persons per square mile (2010); Race: 93.3% White, 2.3% Black, 1.1% Asian, 0.1% American Indian/Alaska Native, 0.1% Native Hawaiian/Other Pacific Islander, 3.1% Other, 2.9% Hispanic of any race (2010); Average household size: 2.61 (2010); Median age: 38.9 (2010); Males per 100 females: 98.8 (2010); Marriage status: 24.2% never married, 61.5% now married, 4.6% widowed, 9.7% divorced (2006-2010 5-year est.); Foreign born: 4.9% (2006-2010 5-year est.); Ancestry (includes multiple ancestries): 27.1% Irish, 21.1% German, 15.2% French, 13.2% English, 10.9% Italian (2006-2010 5-year est.).

**Economy:** Employment by occupation: 4.5% management, 2.5% professional, 8.2% services, 17.1% sales, 5.0% farming, 16.1% construction, 9.9% production (2006-2010 5-year est.).

**Income:** Per capita income: $22,677 (2006-2010 5-year est.); Median household income: $53,817 (2006-2010 5-year est.); Average household income: $60,371 (2006-2010 5-year est.); Percent of households with income of $100,000 or more: 15.4% (2006-2010 5-year est.); Poverty rate: 8.1% (2006-2010 5-year est.).

**Education:** Percent of population age 25 and over with: High school diploma (including GED) or higher: 88.2% (2006-2010 5-year est.); Bachelor's degree or higher: 16.3% (2006-2010 5-year est.); Master's degree or higher: 5.9% (2006-2010 5-year est.).

**Housing:** Homeownership rate: 74.7% (2010); Median home value: $108,200 (2006-2010 5-year est.); Median contract rent: $610 per month (2006-2010 5-year est.); Median year structure built: 1965 (2006-2010 5-year est.).

**Transportation:** Commute to work: 94.8% car, 0.3% public transportation, 1.7% walk, 3.1% work from home (2006-2010 5-year est.); Travel time to work: 33.1% less than 15 minutes, 47.6% 15 to 30 minutes, 14.3% 30 to 45 minutes, 0.7% 45 to 60 minutes, 4.2% 60 minutes or more (2006-2010 5-year est.)

**SACKETS HARBOR** (village). Covers a land area of 2.204 square miles and a water area of 0.005 square miles. Located at 43.93° N. Lat; 76.11° W. Long. Elevation is 282 feet.

**History:** In 1809 infantry was stationed here to enforce the Embargo Act and control smuggling. Following the outbreak of the War of 1812, it became the center of U.S. naval and military activity for Upper St. Lawrence Valley and Lake Ontario. Further expansion occurred during the 1830s and 1840s due to the Patriots War in Canada. Its growth led to the development of Pine Camp (Fort Drum) near Watertown. Zebulon Pike is buried here. Settled c.1801, Incorporated 1814.

**Population:** 1,313 (1990); 1,386 (2000); 1,450 (2010); Density: 657.7 persons per square mile (2010); Race: 94.6% White, 1.8% Black, 0.7% Asian, 0.6% American Indian/Alaska Native, 0.1% Native Hawaiian/Other Pacific Islander, 2.2% Other, 3.2% Hispanic of any race (2010); Average household size: 2.10 (2010); Median age: 38.2 (2010); Males per 100 females: 98.4 (2010); Marriage status: 36.8% never married, 46.0% now married, 5.8% widowed, 11.4% divorced (2006-2010 5-year est.); Foreign born: 3.6% (2006-2010 5-year est.); Ancestry (includes multiple ancestries): 24.3% Irish, 22.7% German, 16.9% English, 12.8% French, 9.7% Italian (2006-2010 5-year est.).

**Economy:** Employment by occupation: 14.1% management, 1.9% professional, 6.7% services, 11.0% sales, 3.0% farming, 5.9% construction, 0.8% production (2006-2010 5-year est.).

**Income:** Per capita income: $36,746 (2006-2010 5-year est.); Median household income: $64,583 (2006-2010 5-year est.); Average household income: $72,061 (2006-2010 5-year est.); Percent of households with income of $100,000 or more: 19.3% (2006-2010 5-year est.); Poverty rate: 5.8% (2006-2010 5-year est.).

**Education:** Percent of population age 25 and over with: High school diploma (including GED) or higher: 94.0% (2006-2010 5-year est.); Bachelor's degree or higher: 38.1% (2006-2010 5-year est.); Master's degree or higher: 15.8% (2006-2010 5-year est.).

### School District(s)

Sackets Harbor Central School District (KG-12)

   2009-10 Enrollment: 475 . . . . . . . . . . . . . . . . . . . . . . . (315) 646-3575

**Housing:** Homeownership rate: 46.6% (2010); Median home value: $165,500 (2006-2010 5-year est.); Median contract rent: $782 per month (2006-2010 5-year est.); Median year structure built: 1950 (2006-2010 5-year est.).

**Transportation:** Commute to work: 87.5% car, 1.8% public transportation, 6.4% walk, 4.3% work from home (2006-2010 5-year est.); Travel time to work: 22.8% less than 15 minutes, 42.1% 15 to 30 minutes, 23.2% 30 to 45 minutes, 4.6% 45 to 60 minutes, 7.2% 60 minutes or more (2006-2010 5-year est.)

**Additional Information Contacts**

Sackets Harbor Chamber of Commerce . . . . . . . . . . (315) 646-1700
   http://www.sacketsharborchamberofcommerce.com

---

**THERESA** (village). Covers a land area of 1.251 square miles and a water area of 0.060 square miles. Located at 44.21° N. Lat; 75.79° W. Long. Elevation is 407 feet.

**Population:** 889 (1990); 812 (2000); 863 (2010); Density: 689.4 persons per square mile (2010); Race: 94.1% White, 1.9% Black, 0.5% Asian, 0.8% American Indian/Alaska Native, 0.0% Native Hawaiian/Other Pacific Islander, 2.7% Other, 1.7% Hispanic of any race (2010); Average household size: 2.64 (2010); Median age: 36.7 (2010); Males per 100 females: 103.5 (2010); Marriage status: 35.8% never married, 51.2% now married, 6.3% widowed, 6.6% divorced (2006-2010 5-year est.); Foreign born: 2.7% (2006-2010 5-year est.); Ancestry (includes multiple ancestries): 22.2% Irish, 21.9% German, 12.8% American, 10.8% English, 10.8% Dutch (2006-2010 5-year est.).

**Economy:** Single-family building permits issued: 0 (2011); Multi-family building permits issued: 0 (2011); Employment by occupation: 8.0% management, 1.7% professional, 6.6% services, 20.2% sales, 12.8% farming, 13.1% construction, 5.4% production (2006-2010 5-year est.).

**Income:** Per capita income: $21,270 (2006-2010 5-year est.); Median household income: $37,344 (2006-2010 5-year est.); Average household income: $52,919 (2006-2010 5-year est.); Percent of households with income of $100,000 or more: 11.0% (2006-2010 5-year est.); Poverty rate: 11.9% (2006-2010 5-year est.).

**Education:** Percent of population age 25 and over with: High school diploma (including GED) or higher: 86.6% (2006-2010 5-year est.); Bachelor's degree or higher: 16.3% (2006-2010 5-year est.); Master's degree or higher: 8.2% (2006-2010 5-year est.).

### School District(s)

Indian River Central School District (PK-12)

   2009-10 Enrollment: 3,767 . . . . . . . . . . . . . . . . . . . . . (315) 642-3441

**Housing:** Homeownership rate: 74.3% (2010); Median home value: $95,000 (2006-2010 5-year est.); Median contract rent: $493 per month (2006-2010 5-year est.); Median year structure built: before 1940 (2006-2010 5-year est.).

**Transportation:** Commute to work: 91.3% car, 0.0% public transportation, 3.7% walk, 2.6% work from home (2006-2010 5-year est.); Travel time to work: 18.2% less than 15 minutes, 53.9% 15 to 30 minutes, 19.0% 30 to 45 minutes, 2.7% 45 to 60 minutes, 6.2% 60 minutes or more (2006-2010 5-year est.)

---

**THERESA** (town). Covers a land area of 64.942 square miles and a water area of 4.788 square miles. Located at 44.26° N. Lat; 75.77° W. Long. Elevation is 407 feet.

**Population:** 2,274 (1990); 2,414 (2000); 2,905 (2010); Density: 44.7 persons per square mile (2010); Race: 94.6% White, 1.5% Black, 0.2% Asian, 0.6% American Indian/Alaska Native, 0.0% Native Hawaiian/Other Pacific Islander, 3.1% Other, 2.0% Hispanic of any race (2010); Average household size: 2.69 (2010); Median age: 37.1 (2010); Males per 100

females: 105.9 (2010); Marriage status: 30.0% never married, 56.9% now married, 6.5% widowed, 6.5% divorced (2006-2010 5-year est.); Foreign born: 1.3% (2006-2010 5-year est.); Ancestry (includes multiple ancestries): 22.3% German, 20.9% Irish, 9.9% Dutch, 9.5% French, 9.2% English (2006-2010 5-year est.).

**Economy:** Single-family building permits issued: 6 (2011); Multi-family building permits issued: 0 (2011); Employment by occupation: 8.0% management, 2.8% professional, 10.0% services, 17.0% sales, 6.4% farming, 16.8% construction, 7.0% production (2006-2010 5-year est.).

**Income:** Per capita income: $23,168 (2006-2010 5-year est.); Median household income: $44,583 (2006-2010 5-year est.); Average household income: $55,253 (2006-2010 5-year est.); Percent of households with income of $100,000 or more: 15.0% (2006-2010 5-year est.); Poverty rate: 14.3% (2006-2010 5-year est.).

**Education:** Percent of population age 25 and over with: High school diploma (including GED) or higher: 81.3% (2006-2010 5-year est.); Bachelor's degree or higher: 15.9% (2006-2010 5-year est.); Master's degree or higher: 7.7% (2006-2010 5-year est.).

### School District(s)

Indian River Central School District (PK-12)

   2009-10 Enrollment: 3,767 . . . . . . . . . . . . . . . . . . . . . (315) 642-3441

**Housing:** Homeownership rate: 80.3% (2010); Median home value: $93,300 (2006-2010 5-year est.); Median contract rent: $472 per month (2006-2010 5-year est.); Median year structure built: 1967 (2006-2010 5-year est.).

**Transportation:** Commute to work: 92.7% car, 0.0% public transportation, 2.4% walk, 1.5% work from home (2006-2010 5-year est.); Travel time to work: 20.1% less than 15 minutes, 50.5% 15 to 30 minutes, 20.2% 30 to 45 minutes, 3.3% 45 to 60 minutes, 5.9% 60 minutes or more (2006-2010 5-year est.)

---

**THOUSAND ISLAND PARK** (CDP). Covers a land area of 0.292 square miles and a water area of 0 square miles. Located at 44.28° N. Lat; 76.02° W. Long. Elevation is 276 feet.

**Population:** n/a (1990); n/a (2000); 31 (2010); Density: 105.8 persons per square mile (2010); Race: 100.0% White, 0.0% Black, 0.0% Asian, 0.0% American Indian/Alaska Native, 0.0% Native Hawaiian/Other Pacific Islander, 0.0% Other, 0.0% Hispanic of any race (2010); Average household size: 1.82 (2010); Median age: 67.5 (2010); Males per 100 females: 106.7 (2010); Marriage status: 0.0% never married, 100.0% now married, 0.0% widowed, 0.0% divorced (2006-2010 5-year est.); Foreign born: 0.0% (2006-2010 5-year est.); Ancestry (includes multiple ancestries): 52.3% English, 29.7% German, 14.4% Danish, 14.4% Scottish, 11.7% Italian (2006-2010 5-year est.).

**Economy:** Employment by occupation: 59.1% management, 0.0% professional, 0.0% services, 0.0% sales, 22.7% farming, 0.0% construction, 0.0% production (2006-2010 5-year est.).

**Income:** Per capita income: $33,047 (2006-2010 5-year est.); Median household income: $72,344 (2006-2010 5-year est.); Average household income: $65,864 (2006-2010 5-year est.); Percent of households with income of $100,000 or more: 0.0% (2006-2010 5-year est.); Poverty rate: 0.0% (2006-2010 5-year est.).

**Education:** Percent of population age 25 and over with: High school diploma (including GED) or higher: 100.0% (2006-2010 5-year est.); Bachelor's degree or higher: 80.2% (2006-2010 5-year est.); Master's degree or higher: 47.7% (2006-2010 5-year est.).

**Housing:** Homeownership rate: 100.0% (2010); Median home value: $350,000 (2006-2010 5-year est.); Median contract rent: n/a per month (2006-2010 5-year est.); Median year structure built: before 1940 (2006-2010 5-year est.).

**Transportation:** Commute to work: 55.6% car, 0.0% public transportation, 44.4% walk, 0.0% work from home (2006-2010 5-year est.); Travel time to work: 44.4% less than 15 minutes, 55.6% 15 to 30 minutes, 0.0% 30 to 45 minutes, 0.0% 45 to 60 minutes, 0.0% 60 minutes or more (2006-2010 5-year est.)

---

**THREE MILE BAY** (CDP). Covers a land area of 0.257 square miles and a water area of 0 square miles. Located at 44.08° N. Lat; 76.19° W. Long. Elevation is 259 feet.

**Population:** n/a (1990); n/a (2000); 227 (2010); Density: 881.6 persons per square mile (2010); Race: 97.4% White, 0.4% Black, 0.0% Asian, 0.0% American Indian/Alaska Native, 0.0% Native Hawaiian/Other Pacific Islander, 2.2% Other, 0.0% Hispanic of any race (2010); Average household size: 2.47 (2010); Median age: 36.5 (2010); Males per 100 females: 95.7 (2010); Marriage status: 28.4% never married, 67.4% now married, 4.3% widowed, 0.0% divorced (2006-2010 5-year est.); Foreign born: 18.5% (2006-2010 5-year est.); Ancestry (includes multiple ancestries): 37.9% French, 22.3% English, 17.5% German, 10.0% Brazilian, 8.5% Dutch (2006-2010 5-year est.).

**Economy:** Employment by occupation: 0.0% management, 0.0% professional, 31.3% services, 22.5% sales, 0.0% farming, 8.8% construction, 27.5% production (2006-2010 5-year est.).

**Income:** Per capita income: $21,598 (2006-2010 5-year est.); Median household income: $32,083 (2006-2010 5-year est.); Average household income: $62,648 (2006-2010 5-year est.); Percent of households with income of $100,000 or more: 37.0% (2006-2010 5-year est.); Poverty rate: 2.8% (2006-2010 5-year est.).

**Education:** Percent of population age 25 and over with: High school diploma (including GED) or higher: 95.0% (2006-2010 5-year est.); Bachelor's degree or higher: 0.0% (2006-2010 5-year est.); Master's degree or higher: 0.0% (2006-2010 5-year est.).

**Housing:** Homeownership rate: 80.4% (2010); Median home value: $134,600 (2006-2010 5-year est.); Median contract rent: n/a per month (2006-2010 5-year est.); Median year structure built: before 1940 (2006-2010 5-year est.).

**Transportation:** Commute to work: 85.1% car, 0.0% public transportation, 0.0% walk, 14.9% work from home (2006-2010 5-year est.); Travel time to work: 29.1% less than 15 minutes, 29.1% 15 to 30 minutes, 41.9% 30 to 45 minutes, 0.0% 45 to 60 minutes, 0.0% 60 minutes or more (2006-2010 5-year est.)

## WATERTOWN (city). County seat. Covers a land area of 9.019 square miles and a water area of 0.344 square miles. Located at 43.97° N. Lat; 75.91° W. Long. Elevation is 466 feet.

**History:** In 1800, five New Englanders hacked their way up from the Mohawk Valley, stopped at the rocky Black River Falls, and named the site Watertown. They built sawmills and gristmills along the river, and burned piles of lumber for potash. The five and ten cent store originated in Watertown during county fair week in 1878. Frank W. Woolworth (1852-1910), a clerk in Moore & Smith's general store, piled leftover odds and ends on a table and put up a sign: "Any Article 5 cents." The entire stock was sold out in a few hours. Inspired by this success, Woolworth opened his first store in Utica the following year.

**Population:** 29,437 (1990); 26,705 (2000); 27,023 (2010); Density: 2,996.0 persons per square mile (2010); Race: 86.2% White, 6.0% Black, 1.8% Asian, 0.6% American Indian/Alaska Native, 0.2% Native Hawaiian/Other Pacific Islander, 5.2% Other, 5.6% Hispanic of any race (2010); Average household size: 2.29 (2010); Median age: 32.1 (2010); Males per 100 females: 91.7 (2010); Marriage status: 31.3% never married, 49.8% now married, 6.6% widowed, 12.3% divorced (2006-2010 5-year est.); Foreign born: 4.5% (2006-2010 5-year est.); Ancestry (includes multiple ancestries): 20.7% Irish, 15.4% Italian, 15.4% German, 11.8% French, 11.0% English (2006-2010 5-year est.).

**Economy:** Unemployment rate: 9.5% (February 2012); Total civilian labor force: 11,279 (February 2012); Single-family building permits issued: 107 (2011); Multi-family building permits issued: 0 (2011); Employment by occupation: 10.0% management, 2.8% professional, 13.6% services, 18.6% sales, 6.1% farming, 7.6% construction, 3.4% production (2006-2010 5-year est.).

**Income:** Per capita income: $20,939 (2006-2010 5-year est.); Median household income: $36,998 (2006-2010 5-year est.); Average household income: $48,356 (2006-2010 5-year est.); Percent of households with income of $100,000 or more: 9.4% (2006-2010 5-year est.); Poverty rate: 19.5% (2006-2010 5-year est.).

**Taxes:** Total city taxes per capita: $319 (2009); City property taxes per capita: $263 (2009).

**Education:** Percent of population age 25 and over with: High school diploma (including GED) or higher: 86.7% (2006-2010 5-year est.); Bachelor's degree or higher: 21.1% (2006-2010 5-year est.); Master's degree or higher: 8.0% (2006-2010 5-year est.).

### School District(s)

Jefferson-Lewis-Hamilton-herkimer-Oneida Boces
  2009-10 Enrollment: n/a . . . . . . . . . . . . . . . . . . . . . . . (315) 779-7010
Watertown City School District (KG-12)
  2009-10 Enrollment: 4,167 . . . . . . . . . . . . . . . . . . . . . (315) 785-3700

### Two-year College(s)

Jefferson Community College (Public)
  Fall 2010 Enrollment: 2,782 . . . . . . . . . . . . . . . . . . . . (315) 786-2200
  2011-12 Tuition: In-state $4,119; Out-of-state $6,279

### Vocational/Technical School(s)

Jefferson Lewis BOCES-Practical Nursing Program (Public)
  Fall 2010 Enrollment: 87 . . . . . . . . . . . . . . . . . . . . . . . (3.1) 578-E+13
  2011-12 Tuition: In-state $7,900; Out-of-state $7,900

**Housing:** Homeownership rate: 41.4% (2010); Median home value: $112,600 (2006-2010 5-year est.); Median contract rent: $533 per month (2006-2010 5-year est.); Median year structure built: before 1940 (2006-2010 5-year est.).

**Hospitals:** Mercy Northern of New York (300 beds); Samaritan Medical Center (287 beds); Samaritan Medical Center (287 beds)

**Safety:** Violent crime rate: 43.3 per 10,000 population; Property crime rate: 427.6 per 10,000 population (2010).

**Newspapers:** Watertown Daily Times (Local news; Circulation 31,959)

**Transportation:** Commute to work: 89.4% car, 2.5% public transportation, 4.2% walk, 2.3% work from home (2006-2010 5-year est.); Travel time to work: 56.4% less than 15 minutes, 31.6% 15 to 30 minutes, 7.7% 30 to 45 minutes, 1.5% 45 to 60 minutes, 2.8% 60 minutes or more (2006-2010 5-year est.)

**Airports:** Watertown International (general aviation)

**Additional Information Contacts**

City of Watertown. . . . . . . . . . . . . . . . . . . . . . . . . . . . . (315) 785-7780
  http://www.citywatertown.org
Greater Watertown-North Country Chamber of Commerce. (315) 788-4400
  http://www.watertownny.com

## WATERTOWN (town). Covers a land area of 35.925 square miles and a water area of 0.101 square miles. Located at 43.93° N. Lat; 75.91° W. Long. Elevation is 466 feet.

**History:** Public Square Historic District in the city. Settled c.1800,Incorporated as a city 1869.

**Population:** 4,333 (1990); 4,482 (2000); 4,470 (2010); Density: 124.4 persons per square mile (2010); Race: 87.2% White, 8.3% Black, 1.0% Asian, 0.7% American Indian/Alaska Native, 0.0% Native Hawaiian/Other Pacific Islander, 2.8% Other, 5.3% Hispanic of any race (2010); Average household size: 2.55 (2010); Median age: 41.3 (2010); Males per 100 females: 128.4 (2010); Marriage status: 35.7% never married, 54.7% now married, 3.0% widowed, 6.5% divorced (2006-2010 5-year est.); Foreign born: 4.1% (2006-2010 5-year est.); Ancestry (includes multiple ancestries): 25.7% Irish, 16.3% Italian, 15.5% French, 12.5% German, 9.4% English (2006-2010 5-year est.).

**Economy:** Employment by occupation: 12.3% management, 2.6% professional, 9.7% services, 11.4% sales, 1.5% farming, 5.4% construction, 7.2% production (2006-2010 5-year est.).

**Income:** Per capita income: $25,159 (2006-2010 5-year est.); Median household income: $66,331 (2006-2010 5-year est.); Average household income: $74,342 (2006-2010 5-year est.); Percent of households with income of $100,000 or more: 17.6% (2006-2010 5-year est.); Poverty rate: 8.3% (2006-2010 5-year est.).

**Education:** Percent of population age 25 and over with: High school diploma (including GED) or higher: 85.5% (2006-2010 5-year est.); Bachelor's degree or higher: 20.9% (2006-2010 5-year est.); Master's degree or higher: 11.4% (2006-2010 5-year est.).

### School District(s)

Jefferson-Lewis-Hamilton-herkimer-Oneida Boces
  2009-10 Enrollment: n/a . . . . . . . . . . . . . . . . . . . . . . . (315) 779-7010
Watertown City School District (KG-12)
  2009-10 Enrollment: 4,167 . . . . . . . . . . . . . . . . . . . . . (315) 785-3700

### Two-year College(s)

Jefferson Community College (Public)
  Fall 2010 Enrollment: 2,782 . . . . . . . . . . . . . . . . . . . . (315) 786-2200
  2011-12 Tuition: In-state $4,119; Out-of-state $6,279

### Vocational/Technical School(s)

Jefferson Lewis BOCES-Practical Nursing Program (Public)
  Fall 2010 Enrollment: 87 . . . . . . . . . . . . . . . . . . . . . . . (3.1) 578-E+13
  2011-12 Tuition: In-state $7,900; Out-of-state $7,900

**Housing:** Homeownership rate: 85.8% (2010); Median home value: $144,200 (2006-2010 5-year est.); Median contract rent: $518 per month (2006-2010 5-year est.); Median year structure built: 1976 (2006-2010 5-year est.).

**Hospitals:** Mercy Northern of New York (300 beds)

**Newspapers:** Watertown Daily Times (Local news; Circulation 31,959)

**Transportation:** Commute to work: 93.5% car, 0.0% public transportation, 0.5% walk, 4.6% work from home (2006-2010 5-year est.); Travel time to work: 41.4% less than 15 minutes, 44.5% 15 to 30 minutes, 11.3% 30 to 45

minutes, 0.6% 45 to 60 minutes, 2.2% 60 minutes or more (2006-2010 5-year est.)
**Airports:** Watertown International (general aviation)

## WELLESLEY ISLAND (unincorporated postal area)
Zip Code: 13640

Covers a land area of 12.359 square miles and a water area of 0.256 square miles. Located at 44.30° N. Lat; 76.02° W. Long. Population: 271 (2010); Density: 21.9 persons per square mile (2010); Race: 97.8% White, 0.7% Black, 0.0% Asian, 0.0% American Indian/Alaska Native, 0.0% Native Hawaiian/Other Pacific Islander, 1.5% Other, 0.4% Hispanic of any race (2010); Average household size: 1.99 (2010); Median age: 59.4 (2010); Males per 100 females: 103.8 (2010); Homeownership rate: 88.2% (2010).

## WEST CARTHAGE (village). Covers a land area of 1.296 square miles and a water area of 0.097 square miles. Located at 43.97° N. Lat; 75.62° W. Long. Elevation is 778 feet.
**History:** Incorporated 1888.
**Population:** 2,185 (1990); 2,102 (2000); 2,012 (2010); Density: 1,551.9 persons per square mile (2010); Race: 90.2% White, 4.2% Black, 1.5% Asian, 0.3% American Indian/Alaska Native, 0.0% Native Hawaiian/Other Pacific Islander, 3.8% Other, 4.1% Hispanic of any race (2010); Average household size: 2.37 (2010); Median age: 31.7 (2010); Males per 100 females: 90.2 (2010); Marriage status: 25.0% never married, 60.8% now married, 5.7% widowed, 8.4% divorced (2006-2010 5-year est.); Foreign born: 6.7% (2006-2010 5-year est.); Ancestry (includes multiple ancestries): 27.1% German, 19.4% Irish, 13.3% Italian, 12.2% French, 10.1% English (2006-2010 5-year est.).
**Economy:** Employment by occupation: 4.8% management, 3.9% professional, 17.7% services, 13.2% sales, 5.8% farming, 14.4% construction, 9.0% production (2006-2010 5-year est.).
**Income:** Per capita income: $18,770 (2006-2010 5-year est.); Median household income: $37,875 (2006-2010 5-year est.); Average household income: $46,252 (2006-2010 5-year est.); Percent of households with income of $100,000 or more: 9.2% (2006-2010 5-year est.); Poverty rate: 16.0% (2006-2010 5-year est.).
**Education:** Percent of population age 25 and over with: High school diploma (including GED) or higher: 85.6% (2006-2010 5-year est.); Bachelor's degree or higher: 12.9% (2006-2010 5-year est.); Master's degree or higher: 4.3% (2006-2010 5-year est.).
**Housing:** Homeownership rate: 45.4% (2010); Median home value: $108,600 (2006-2010 5-year est.); Median contract rent: $539 per month (2006-2010 5-year est.); Median year structure built: 1941 (2006-2010 5-year est.).
**Safety:** Violent crime rate: 9.2 per 10,000 population; Property crime rate: 82.8 per 10,000 population (2010).
**Transportation:** Commute to work: 92.9% car, 0.0% public transportation, 2.3% walk, 4.8% work from home (2006-2010 5-year est.); Travel time to work: 34.2% less than 15 minutes, 39.8% 15 to 30 minutes, 20.8% 30 to 45 minutes, 2.6% 45 to 60 minutes, 2.6% 60 minutes or more (2006-2010 5-year est.)
**Additional Information Contacts**
Village of West Carthage . . . . . . . . . . . . . . . . . . . . . . . . (315) 493-2552
   http://villageofwestcarthage.org

## WILNA (town). Covers a land area of 78.622 square miles and a water area of 0.878 square miles. Located at 44.05° N. Lat; 75.58° W. Long.
**Population:** 6,899 (1990); 6,235 (2000); 6,427 (2010); Density: 81.7 persons per square mile (2010); Race: 91.1% White, 3.2% Black, 1.4% Asian, 0.7% American Indian/Alaska Native, 0.2% Native Hawaiian/Other Pacific Islander, 3.4% Other, 3.7% Hispanic of any race (2010); Average household size: 2.50 (2010); Median age: 33.0 (2010); Males per 100 females: 98.8 (2010); Marriage status: 31.0% never married, 50.7% now married, 9.8% widowed, 8.5% divorced (2006-2010 5-year est.); Foreign born: 3.5% (2006-2010 5-year est.); Ancestry (includes multiple ancestries): 28.2% German, 16.9% Irish, 15.7% French, 12.9% English, 7.3% Italian (2006-2010 5-year est.).
**Economy:** Single-family building permits issued: 1 (2011); Multi-family building permits issued: 0 (2011); Employment by occupation: 7.9% management, 2.6% professional, 11.7% services, 12.0% sales, 3.2% farming, 9.0% construction, 8.4% production (2006-2010 5-year est.).
**Income:** Per capita income: $20,994 (2006-2010 5-year est.); Median household income: $39,787 (2006-2010 5-year est.); Average household income: $51,594 (2006-2010 5-year est.); Percent of households with

income of $100,000 or more: 11.0% (2006-2010 5-year est.); Poverty rate: 14.1% (2006-2010 5-year est.).
**Education:** Percent of population age 25 and over with: High school diploma (including GED) or higher: 84.6% (2006-2010 5-year est.); Bachelor's degree or higher: 17.3% (2006-2010 5-year est.); Master's degree or higher: 7.5% (2006-2010 5-year est.).
**Housing:** Homeownership rate: 57.9% (2010); Median home value: $95,500 (2006-2010 5-year est.); Median contract rent: $522 per month (2006-2010 5-year est.); Median year structure built: before 1940 (2006-2010 5-year est.).
**Transportation:** Commute to work: 96.0% car, 0.0% public transportation, 1.6% walk, 1.1% work from home (2006-2010 5-year est.); Travel time to work: 23.9% less than 15 minutes, 49.7% 15 to 30 minutes, 18.5% 30 to 45 minutes, 6.3% 45 to 60 minutes, 1.7% 60 minutes or more (2006-2010 5-year est.)

## WORTH (town). Covers a land area of 43.217 square miles and a water area of 0.085 square miles. Located at 43.74° N. Lat; 75.84° W. Long. Elevation is 1,237 feet.
**Population:** 219 (1990); 234 (2000); 231 (2010); Density: 5.3 persons per square mile (2010); Race: 97.0% White, 0.4% Black, 0.9% Asian, 0.0% American Indian/Alaska Native, 0.0% Native Hawaiian/Other Pacific Islander, 1.7% Other, 0.0% Hispanic of any race (2010); Average household size: 2.51 (2010); Median age: 42.3 (2010); Males per 100 females: 99.1 (2010); Marriage status: 20.3% never married, 59.5% now married, 11.4% widowed, 8.9% divorced (2006-2010 5-year est.); Foreign born: 0.0% (2006-2010 5-year est.); Ancestry (includes multiple ancestries): 34.2% English, 28.4% Irish, 27.9% German, 8.4% Italian, 6.3% Dutch (2006-2010 5-year est.).
**Economy:** Employment by occupation: 4.3% management, 5.3% professional, 2.1% services, 19.1% sales, 2.1% farming, 33.0% construction, 23.4% production (2006-2010 5-year est.).
**Income:** Per capita income: $21,260 (2006-2010 5-year est.); Median household income: $55,250 (2006-2010 5-year est.); Average household income: $57,739 (2006-2010 5-year est.); Percent of households with income of $100,000 or more: 6.0% (2006-2010 5-year est.); Poverty rate: 8.9% (2006-2010 5-year est.).
**Education:** Percent of population age 25 and over with: High school diploma (including GED) or higher: 71.6% (2006-2010 5-year est.); Bachelor's degree or higher: 15.6% (2006-2010 5-year est.); Master's degree or higher: 9.9% (2006-2010 5-year est.).
**Housing:** Homeownership rate: 90.2% (2010); Median home value: $80,000 (2006-2010 5-year est.); Median contract rent: n/a per month (2006-2010 5-year est.); Median year structure built: 1971 (2006-2010 5-year est.).
**Transportation:** Commute to work: 97.8% car, 0.0% public transportation, 0.0% walk, 2.2% work from home (2006-2010 5-year est.); Travel time to work: 17.0% less than 15 minutes, 58.0% 15 to 30 minutes, 22.7% 30 to 45 minutes, 2.3% 45 to 60 minutes, 0.0% 60 minutes or more (2006-2010 5-year est.)

# Kings County

*See New York City*

# Lewis County

Located in north central New York; includes the foothills of the Adirondacks in the east; drained by the Black River. Covers a land area of 1,275.42 square miles, a water area of 14.47 square miles, and is located in the Eastern Time Zone at 43.76° N. Lat., 75.45° W. Long. The county was founded in 1805. County seat is Lowville.

| Weather Station: Lowville | | | | | | | | | | Elevation: 859 feet | | |
|---|---|---|---|---|---|---|---|---|---|---|---|---|
| | Jan | Feb | Mar | Apr | May | Jun | Jul | Aug | Sep | Oct | Nov | Dec |
| High | 26 | 29 | 37 | 52 | 65 | 74 | 78 | 77 | 69 | 56 | 44 | 32 |
| Low | 7 | 9 | 19 | 32 | 43 | 52 | 56 | 55 | 47 | 36 | 28 | 15 |
| Precip | 3.2 | 2.5 | 2.7 | 3.2 | 3.3 | 3.4 | 3.6 | 3.7 | 4.0 | 4.1 | 3.9 | 3.6 |
| Snow | 33.0 | 25.7 | 14.9 | 4.7 | 0.1 | 0.0 | 0.0 | 0.0 | tr | 0.8 | 9.3 | 32.9 |

*High and Low temperatures in degrees Fahrenheit; Precipitation and Snow in inches*

**Population:** 26,796 (1990); 26,944 (2000); 27,087 (2010); Race: 97.7% White, 0.7% Black, 0.3% Asian, 0.2% American Indian/Alaska Native, 0.1% Native Hawaiian/Other Pacific Islander, 1.0% Other, 1.3% Hispanic of any race (2010); Density: 21.2 persons per square mile (2010); Average household size: 2.55 (2010); Median age: 40.2 (2010); Males per 100 females: 101.1 (2010).

**Religion:** Six largest groups: 23.8% Catholicism, 7.5% European Free-Church, 4.6% Methodist/Pietist, 1.8% Presbyterian-Reformed, 1.4% Non-Denominational, 1.2% Baptist (2010)

**Economy:** Unemployment rate: 11.9% (February 2012); Total civilian labor force: 12,459 (February 2012); Leading industries: 28.3% manufacturing; 18.9% health care and social assistance; 17.0% retail trade (2009); Farms: 616 totaling 167,249 acres (2007); Companies that employ 500 or more persons: 0 (2009); Companies that employ 100 to 499 persons: 7 (2009); Companies that employ less than 100 persons: 511 (2009); Black-owned businesses: n/a (2007); Hispanic-owned businesses: n/a (2007); Asian-owned businesses: n/a (2007); Women-owned businesses: 415 (2007); Retail sales per capita: $7,458 (2010). Single-family building permits issued: 84 (2011); Multi-family building permits issued: 0 (2011).

**Income:** Per capita income: $20,970 (2006-2010 5-year est.); Median household income: $42,846 (2006-2010 5-year est.); Average household income: $52,818 (2006-2010 5-year est.); Percent of households with income of $100,000 or more: 10.0% (2006-2010 5-year est.); Poverty rate: 14.6% (2006-2010 5-year est.); Bankruptcy rate: 1.54% (2011).

**Taxes:** Total county taxes per capita: $835 (2009); County property taxes per capita: $452 (2009).

**Education:** Percent of population age 25 and over with: High school diploma (including GED) or higher: 86.0% (2006-2010 5-year est.); Bachelor's degree or higher: 14.4% (2006-2010 5-year est.); Master's degree or higher: 6.0% (2006-2010 5-year est.).

**Housing:** Homeownership rate: 77.0% (2010); Median home value: $100,700 (2006-2010 5-year est.); Median contract rent: $461 per month (2006-2010 5-year est.); Median year structure built: 1963 (2006-2010 5-year est.).

**Health:** Birth rate: 131.9 per 10,000 population (2011); Death rate: 94.9 per 10,000 population (2011); Age-adjusted cancer mortality rate: 212.0 deaths per 100,000 population (2009); Number of physicians: 9.6 per 10,000 population (2008); Hospital beds: 0.0 per 10,000 population (2007); Hospital admissions: 0.0 per 10,000 population (2007).

**Elections:** 2008 Presidential election results: 44.8% Obama, 53.6% McCain, 0.8% Nader

**National and State Parks:** Sand Flats State Park; Whetstone Gulf State Park

**Additional Information Contacts**

Lewis County Government. . . . . . . . . . . . . . . . . . . . . . . . . . . (315) 376-5355
 http://www.lewiscountyny.org
Lewis County Chamber of Commerce . . . . . . . . . . . . . . . . (315) 376-2213
 http://www.lewiscountychamber.org
Town of Harrisburg . . . . . . . . . . . . . . . . . . . . . . . . . . . . . . (315) 688-4193
 http://www.tughillcouncil.com/Harrisburg.htm

# Lewis County Communities

## BEAVER FALLS (unincorporated postal area)
Zip Code: 13305

Covers a land area of 0.959 square miles and a water area of 0 square miles. Located at 43.89° N. Lat; 75.42° W. Long. Elevation is 807 feet. Population: 293 (2010); Density: 305.4 persons per square mile (2010); Race: 98.0% White, 0.7% Black, 0.7% Asian, 0.0% American Indian/Alaska Native, 0.0% Native Hawaiian/Other Pacific Islander, 0.6% Other, 3.8% Hispanic of any race (2010); Average household size: 2.79 (2010); Median age: 34.8 (2010); Males per 100 females: 99.3 (2010); Homeownership rate: 75.3% (2010)

## BRANTINGHAM (unincorporated postal area)
Zip Code: 13312

Covers a land area of 63.744 square miles and a water area of 1.013 square miles. Located at 43.69° N. Lat; 75.19° W. Long. Elevation is 1,253 feet. Population: 331 (2010); Density: 5.2 persons per square mile (2010); Race: 100.0% White, 0.0% Black, 0.0% Asian, 0.0% American Indian/Alaska Native, 0.0% Native Hawaiian/Other Pacific Islander, 0.0% Other, 0.0% Hispanic of any race (2010); Average household size: 2.01 (2010); Median age: 53.9 (2010); Males per 100 females: 106.9 (2010); Homeownership rate: 80.7% (2010)

## CASTORLAND (village). Covers a land area of 0.321 square miles and a water area of 0 square miles. Located at 43.88° N. Lat; 75.51° W. Long. Elevation is 741 feet.

**Population:** 292 (1990); 306 (2000); 351 (2010); Density: 1,093.3 persons per square mile (2010); Race: 98.0% White, 0.6% Black, 0.3% Asian, 0.0% American Indian/Alaska Native, 0.0% Native Hawaiian/Other Pacific Islander, 1.1% Other, 2.8% Hispanic of any race (2010); Average household size: 2.57 (2010); Median age: 36.9 (2010); Males per 100 females: 83.8 (2010); Marriage status: 53.2% never married, 37.8% now married, 4.2% widowed, 4.8% divorced (2006-2010 5-year est.); Foreign born: 7.0% (2006-2010 5-year est.); Ancestry (includes multiple ancestries): 34.7% German, 14.0% French, 12.7% Irish, 8.8% Swiss, 5.4% Croatian (2006-2010 5-year est.).

**Economy:** Employment by occupation: 10.4% management, 3.1% professional, 15.6% services, 12.5% sales, 0.0% farming, 15.6% construction, 7.3% production (2006-2010 5-year est.).

**Income:** Per capita income: $20,521 (2006-2010 5-year est.); Median household income: $34,063 (2006-2010 5-year est.); Average household income: $64,553 (2006-2010 5-year est.); Percent of households with income of $100,000 or more: 11.7% (2006-2010 5-year est.); Poverty rate: 32.9% (2006-2010 5-year est.).

**Education:** Percent of population age 25 and over with: High school diploma (including GED) or higher: 51.7% (2006-2010 5-year est.); Bachelor's degree or higher: 10.5% (2006-2010 5-year est.); Master's degree or higher: 8.5% (2006-2010 5-year est.).

**Housing:** Homeownership rate: 56.7% (2010); Median home value: $109,400 (2006-2010 5-year est.); Median contract rent: $317 per month (2006-2010 5-year est.); Median year structure built: before 1940 (2006-2010 5-year est.).

**Transportation:** Commute to work: 84.2% car, 0.0% public transportation, 3.0% walk, 10.9% work from home (2006-2010 5-year est.); Travel time to work: 40.0% less than 15 minutes, 44.4% 15 to 30 minutes, 3.3% 30 to 45 minutes, 8.9% 45 to 60 minutes, 3.3% 60 minutes or more (2006-2010 5-year est.)

## CONSTABLEVILLE (village). Covers a land area of 1.118 square miles and a water area of 0 square miles. Located at 43.56° N. Lat; 75.42° W. Long. Elevation is 1,263 feet.

**Population:** 307 (1990); 305 (2000); 242 (2010); Density: 216.4 persons per square mile (2010); Race: 98.8% White, 0.0% Black, 0.0% Asian, 0.4% American Indian/Alaska Native, 0.0% Native Hawaiian/Other Pacific Islander, 0.8% Other, 0.4% Hispanic of any race (2010); Average household size: 2.26 (2010); Median age: 41.7 (2010); Males per 100 females: 98.4 (2010); Marriage status: 26.6% never married, 45.9% now married, 4.3% widowed, 23.2% divorced (2006-2010 5-year est.); Foreign born: 0.0% (2006-2010 5-year est.); Ancestry (includes multiple ancestries): 41.4% German, 19.1% Irish, 11.7% Swiss, 11.3% Polish, 8.4% French (2006-2010 5-year est.).

**Economy:** Employment by occupation: 7.3% management, 0.0% professional, 13.1% services, 10.9% sales, 2.2% farming, 21.2% construction, 2.9% production (2006-2010 5-year est.).

**Income:** Per capita income: $22,324 (2006-2010 5-year est.); Median household income: $55,694 (2006-2010 5-year est.); Average household income: $56,371 (2006-2010 5-year est.); Percent of households with income of $100,000 or more: 11.0% (2006-2010 5-year est.); Poverty rate: 10.3% (2006-2010 5-year est.).

**Education:** Percent of population age 25 and over with: High school diploma (including GED) or higher: 89.5% (2006-2010 5-year est.); Bachelor's degree or higher: 13.9% (2006-2010 5-year est.); Master's degree or higher: 11.0% (2006-2010 5-year est.).

**School District(s)**

South Lewis Central School District (PK-12)
 2009-10 Enrollment: 1,058 . . . . . . . . . . . . . . . . . . . . . . (315) 348-2500

**Housing:** Homeownership rate: 78.5% (2010); Median home value: $70,000 (2006-2010 5-year est.); Median contract rent: $588 per month (2006-2010 5-year est.); Median year structure built: before 1940 (2006-2010 5-year est.).

**Transportation:** Commute to work: 89.1% car, 0.0% public transportation, 10.9% walk, 0.0% work from home (2006-2010 5-year est.); Travel time to work: 42.2% less than 15 minutes, 18.0% 15 to 30 minutes, 8.6% 30 to 45 minutes, 18.8% 45 to 60 minutes, 12.5% 60 minutes or more (2006-2010 5-year est.)

**COPENHAGEN** (village). Covers a land area of 1.175 square miles and a water area of 0 square miles. Located at 43.89° N. Lat; 75.67° W. Long. Elevation is 1,165 feet.

**Population:** 876 (1990); 865 (2000); 801 (2010); Density: 681.4 persons per square mile (2010); Race: 96.4% White, 0.9% Black, 0.9% Asian, 0.2% American Indian/Alaska Native, 0.0% Native Hawaiian/Other Pacific Islander, 1.6% Other, 2.2% Hispanic of any race (2010); Average household size: 2.50 (2010); Median age: 30.2 (2010); Males per 100 females: 103.8 (2010); Marriage status: 20.8% never married, 66.3% now married, 4.9% widowed, 8.1% divorced (2006-2010 5-year est.); Foreign born: 2.2% (2006-2010 5-year est.); Ancestry (includes multiple ancestries): 31.0% German, 19.1% Irish, 13.3% French, 10.1% English, 9.0% Italian (2006-2010 5-year est.).

**Economy:** Employment by occupation: 2.3% management, 5.1% professional, 2.8% services, 23.3% sales, 7.0% farming, 21.4% construction, 15.8% production (2006-2010 5-year est.).

**Income:** Per capita income: $20,595 (2006-2010 5-year est.); Median household income: $43,977 (2006-2010 5-year est.); Average household income: $49,716 (2006-2010 5-year est.); Percent of households with income of $100,000 or more: 5.8% (2006-2010 5-year est.); Poverty rate: 9.7% (2006-2010 5-year est.).

**Education:** Percent of population age 25 and over with: High school diploma (including GED) or higher: 91.6% (2006-2010 5-year est.); Bachelor's degree or higher: 13.8% (2006-2010 5-year est.); Master's degree or higher: 4.5% (2006-2010 5-year est.).

**School District(s)**
Copenhagen Central School District (PK-12)
    2009-10 Enrollment: 531 . . . . . . . . . . . . . . . . . . . . . . (315) 688-4411

**Housing:** Homeownership rate: 51.0% (2010); Median home value: $95,700 (2006-2010 5-year est.); Median contract rent: $679 per month (2006-2010 5-year est.); Median year structure built: before 1940 (2006-2010 5-year est.).

**Transportation:** Commute to work: 95.6% car, 0.0% public transportation, 1.1% walk, 1.5% work from home (2006-2010 5-year est.); Travel time to work: 27.3% less than 15 minutes, 43.9% 15 to 30 minutes, 24.7% 30 to 45 minutes, 1.1% 45 to 60 minutes, 3.0% 60 minutes or more (2006-2010 5-year est.)

**CROGHAN** (village). Covers a land area of 0.433 square miles and a water area of 0 square miles. Located at 43.89° N. Lat; 75.39° W. Long. Elevation is 827 feet.

**Population:** 664 (1990); 665 (2000); 618 (2010); Density: 1,424.4 persons per square mile (2010); Race: 97.2% White, 1.0% Black, 0.6% Asian, 0.0% American Indian/Alaska Native, 0.2% Native Hawaiian/Other Pacific Islander, 1.0% Other, 0.3% Hispanic of any race (2010); Average household size: 2.15 (2010); Median age: 42.8 (2010); Males per 100 females: 89.0 (2010); Marriage status: 33.1% never married, 41.8% now married, 10.8% widowed, 14.3% divorced (2006-2010 5-year est.); Foreign born: 0.0% (2006-2010 5-year est.); Ancestry (includes multiple ancestries): 47.1% German, 28.1% French, 19.7% Irish, 10.8% Italian, 6.7% English (2006-2010 5-year est.).

**Economy:** Employment by occupation: 13.5% management, 0.0% professional, 13.2% services, 2.6% sales, 2.9% farming, 10.0% construction, 1.9% production (2006-2010 5-year est.).

**Income:** Per capita income: $22,840 (2006-2010 5-year est.); Median household income: $31,964 (2006-2010 5-year est.); Average household income: $41,534 (2006-2010 5-year est.); Percent of households with income of $100,000 or more: 7.6% (2006-2010 5-year est.); Poverty rate: 14.7% (2006-2010 5-year est.).

**Education:** Percent of population age 25 and over with: High school diploma (including GED) or higher: 88.4% (2006-2010 5-year est.); Bachelor's degree or higher: 14.8% (2006-2010 5-year est.); Master's degree or higher: 7.9% (2006-2010 5-year est.).

**Housing:** Homeownership rate: 60.1% (2010); Median home value: $97,900 (2006-2010 5-year est.); Median contract rent: $395 per month (2006-2010 5-year est.); Median year structure built: before 1940 (2006-2010 5-year est.).

**Transportation:** Commute to work: 86.3% car, 0.0% public transportation, 5.1% walk, 6.1% work from home (2006-2010 5-year est.); Travel time to work: 24.4% less than 15 minutes, 40.4% 15 to 30 minutes, 13.8% 30 to 45 minutes, 3.6% 45 to 60 minutes, 17.8% 60 minutes or more (2006-2010 5-year est.)

**CROGHAN** (town). Covers a land area of 179.182 square miles and a water area of 2.848 square miles. Located at 43.96° N. Lat; 75.35° W. Long. Elevation is 827 feet.

**History:** American Maple Museum.

**Population:** 3,071 (1990); 3,161 (2000); 3,093 (2010); Density: 17.3 persons per square mile (2010); Race: 97.9% White, 0.5% Black, 0.3% Asian, 0.0% American Indian/Alaska Native, 0.0% Native Hawaiian/Other Pacific Islander, 1.3% Other, 0.9% Hispanic of any race (2010); Average household size: 2.64 (2010); Median age: 39.3 (2010); Males per 100 females: 105.4 (2010); Marriage status: 26.3% never married, 58.1% now married, 6.4% widowed, 9.2% divorced (2006-2010 5-year est.); Foreign born: 0.2% (2006-2010 5-year est.); Ancestry (includes multiple ancestries): 44.1% German, 17.1% Irish, 12.9% French, 9.8% English, 5.8% French Canadian (2006-2010 5-year est.).

**Economy:** Employment by occupation: 7.7% management, 0.4% professional, 17.0% services, 9.1% sales, 4.2% farming, 18.4% construction, 13.5% production (2006-2010 5-year est.).

**Income:** Per capita income: $21,230 (2006-2010 5-year est.); Median household income: $40,899 (2006-2010 5-year est.); Average household income: $51,847 (2006-2010 5-year est.); Percent of households with income of $100,000 or more: 8.6% (2006-2010 5-year est.); Poverty rate: 12.6% (2006-2010 5-year est.).

**Education:** Percent of population age 25 and over with: High school diploma (including GED) or higher: 85.1% (2006-2010 5-year est.); Bachelor's degree or higher: 11.5% (2006-2010 5-year est.); Master's degree or higher: 4.0% (2006-2010 5-year est.).

**Housing:** Homeownership rate: 79.7% (2010); Median home value: $106,000 (2006-2010 5-year est.); Median contract rent: $456 per month (2006-2010 5-year est.); Median year structure built: 1962 (2006-2010 5-year est.).

**Transportation:** Commute to work: 89.2% car, 0.0% public transportation, 3.7% walk, 6.7% work from home (2006-2010 5-year est.); Travel time to work: 20.3% less than 15 minutes, 50.5% 15 to 30 minutes, 12.6% 30 to 45 minutes, 9.1% 45 to 60 minutes, 7.5% 60 minutes or more (2006-2010 5-year est.).

**DENMARK** (town). Covers a land area of 50.601 square miles and a water area of 0.445 square miles. Located at 43.89° N. Lat; 75.63° W. Long. Elevation is 971 feet.

**Population:** 2,718 (1990); 2,747 (2000); 2,860 (2010); Density: 56.5 persons per square mile (2010); Race: 96.8% White, 0.7% Black, 0.5% Asian, 0.3% American Indian/Alaska Native, 0.2% Native Hawaiian/Other Pacific Islander, 1.5% Other, 2.1% Hispanic of any race (2010); Average household size: 2.73 (2010); Median age: 35.8 (2010); Males per 100 females: 101.8 (2010); Marriage status: 20.5% never married, 69.7% now married, 3.2% widowed, 6.6% divorced (2006-2010 5-year est.); Foreign born: 1.5% (2006-2010 5-year est.); Ancestry (includes multiple ancestries): 31.0% German, 15.7% Irish, 13.7% French, 7.9% Italian, 5.8% French Canadian (2006-2010 5-year est.).

**Economy:** Employment by occupation: 13.0% management, 4.4% professional, 11.2% services, 13.8% sales, 2.0% farming, 17.3% construction, 8.2% production (2006-2010 5-year est.).

**Income:** Per capita income: $20,917 (2006-2010 5-year est.); Median household income: $45,417 (2006-2010 5-year est.); Average household income: $57,881 (2006-2010 5-year est.); Percent of households with income of $100,000 or more: 13.6% (2006-2010 5-year est.); Poverty rate: 15.4% (2006-2010 5-year est.).

**Education:** Percent of population age 25 and over with: High school diploma (including GED) or higher: 83.2% (2006-2010 5-year est.); Bachelor's degree or higher: 18.2% (2006-2010 5-year est.); Master's degree or higher: 7.2% (2006-2010 5-year est.).

**Housing:** Homeownership rate: 71.3% (2010); Median home value: $121,600 (2006-2010 5-year est.); Median contract rent: $498 per month (2006-2010 5-year est.); Median year structure built: 1969 (2006-2010 5-year est.).

**Transportation:** Commute to work: 87.6% car, 0.0% public transportation, 6.9% walk, 4.9% work from home (2006-2010 5-year est.); Travel time to work: 47.4% less than 15 minutes, 30.6% 15 to 30 minutes, 17.6% 30 to 45 minutes, 2.1% 45 to 60 minutes, 2.2% 60 minutes or more (2006-2010 5-year est.).

**DIANA** (town). Covers a land area of 137.094 square miles and a water area of 3.737 square miles. Located at 44.10° N. Lat; 75.37° W. Long.

**Population:** 1,743 (1990); 1,661 (2000); 1,709 (2010); Density: 12.5 persons per square mile (2010); Race: 97.1% White, 0.1% Black, 0.4%

Asian, 0.8% American Indian/Alaska Native, 0.1% Native Hawaiian/Other Pacific Islander, 1.5% Other, 1.0% Hispanic of any race (2010); Average household size: 2.51 (2010); Median age: 42.8 (2010); Males per 100 females: 95.8 (2010); Marriage status: 22.6% never married, 63.0% now married, 5.9% widowed, 8.5% divorced (2006-2010 5-year est.); Foreign born: 1.1% (2006-2010 5-year est.); Ancestry (includes multiple ancestries): 20.3% German, 17.7% French, 16.9% Irish, 15.9% English, 10.5% Italian (2006-2010 5-year est.).
**Economy:** Employment by occupation: 15.4% management, 0.8% professional, 7.8% services, 18.8% sales, 1.9% farming, 16.3% construction, 9.1% production (2006-2010 5-year est.).
**Income:** Per capita income: $21,149 (2006-2010 5-year est.); Median household income: $42,664 (2006-2010 5-year est.); Average household income: $50,912 (2006-2010 5-year est.); Percent of households with income of $100,000 or more: 8.9% (2006-2010 5-year est.); Poverty rate: 13.4% (2006-2010 5-year est.).
**Education:** Percent of population age 25 and over with: High school diploma (including GED) or higher: 85.2% (2006-2010 5-year est.); Bachelor's degree or higher: 15.4% (2006-2010 5-year est.); Master's degree or higher: 4.7% (2006-2010 5-year est.).
**Housing:** Homeownership rate: 80.7% (2010); Median home value: $89,100 (2006-2010 5-year est.); Median contract rent: $409 per month (2006-2010 5-year est.); Median year structure built: 1957 (2006-2010 5-year est.).
**Transportation:** Commute to work: 93.2% car, 0.0% public transportation, 4.8% walk, 1.8% work from home (2006-2010 5-year est.); Travel time to work: 22.9% less than 15 minutes, 20.6% 15 to 30 minutes, 31.2% 30 to 45 minutes, 17.5% 45 to 60 minutes, 7.7% 60 minutes or more (2006-2010 5-year est.)

**GLENFIELD** (unincorporated postal area)
Zip Code: 13343
Covers a land area of 56.180 square miles and a water area of 0.954 square miles. Located at 43.75° N. Lat; 75.31° W. Long. Elevation is 768 feet. Population: 1,658 (2010); Density: 29.5 persons per square mile (2010); Race: 98.5% White, 0.2% Black, 0.5% Asian, 0.1% American Indian/Alaska Native, 0.0% Native Hawaiian/Other Pacific Islander, 0.7% Other, 0.3% Hispanic of any race (2010); Average household size: 2.46 (2010); Median age: 42.2 (2010); Males per 100 females: 105.2 (2010); Homeownership rate: 82.6% (2010)

**GREIG** (town). Covers a land area of 93.010 square miles and a water area of 1.354 square miles. Located at 43.69° N. Lat; 75.19° W. Long. Elevation is 807 feet.
**Population:** 1,323 (1990); 1,365 (2000); 1,199 (2010); Density: 12.9 persons per square mile (2010); Race: 98.7% White, 0.2% Black, 0.7% Asian, 0.0% American Indian/Alaska Native, 0.0% Native Hawaiian/Other Pacific Islander, 0.4% Other, 0.2% Hispanic of any race (2010); Average household size: 2.35 (2010); Median age: 45.4 (2010); Males per 100 females: 106.4 (2010); Marriage status: 27.7% never married, 57.3% now married, 6.4% widowed, 8.6% divorced (2006-2010 5-year est.); Foreign born: 2.9% (2006-2010 5-year est.); Ancestry (includes multiple ancestries): 30.4% German, 21.2% Irish, 19.5% English, 12.4% French, 9.2% Italian (2006-2010 5-year est.).
**Economy:** Single-family building permits issued: 8 (2011); Multi-family building permits issued: 0 (2011); Employment by occupation: 14.6% management, 0.7% professional, 9.2% services, 18.1% sales, 3.3% farming, 17.4% construction, 6.5% production (2006-2010 5-year est.).
**Income:** Per capita income: $20,359 (2006-2010 5-year est.); Median household income: $35,125 (2006-2010 5-year est.); Average household income: $48,183 (2006-2010 5-year est.); Percent of households with income of $100,000 or more: 11.2% (2006-2010 5-year est.); Poverty rate: 21.1% (2006-2010 5-year est.).
**Education:** Percent of population age 25 and over with: High school diploma (including GED) or higher: 88.5% (2006-2010 5-year est.); Bachelor's degree or higher: 19.9% (2006-2010 5-year est.); Master's degree or higher: 7.0% (2006-2010 5-year est.).
**Housing:** Homeownership rate: 83.4% (2010); Median home value: $115,700 (2006-2010 5-year est.); Median contract rent: $358 per month (2006-2010 5-year est.); Median year structure built: 1975 (2006-2010 5-year est.).
**Transportation:** Commute to work: 88.0% car, 1.3% public transportation, 5.1% walk, 5.6% work from home (2006-2010 5-year est.); Travel time to work: 32.2% less than 15 minutes, 42.6% 15 to 30 minutes, 6.1% 30 to 45

minutes, 6.4% 45 to 60 minutes, 12.7% 60 minutes or more (2006-2010 5-year est.)

**HARRISBURG** (town). Covers a land area of 39.881 square miles and a water area of 0.028 square miles. Located at 43.83° N. Lat; 75.66° W. Long. Elevation is 1,362 feet.
**Population:** 425 (1990); 423 (2000); 437 (2010); Density: 11.0 persons per square mile (2010); Race: 98.9% White, 0.0% Black, 0.7% Asian, 0.0% American Indian/Alaska Native, 0.0% Native Hawaiian/Other Pacific Islander, 0.4% Other, 0.9% Hispanic of any race (2010); Average household size: 2.73 (2010); Median age: 43.3 (2010); Males per 100 females: 117.4 (2010); Marriage status: 25.9% never married, 63.8% now married, 2.5% widowed, 7.8% divorced (2006-2010 5-year est.); Foreign born: 0.7% (2006-2010 5-year est.); Ancestry (includes multiple ancestries): 27.4% German, 20.9% French, 15.2% Irish, 12.2% English, 6.8% Scottish (2006-2010 5-year est.).
**Economy:** Employment by occupation: 10.2% management, 0.6% professional, 7.9% services, 14.7% sales, 1.1% farming, 27.1% construction, 8.5% production (2006-2010 5-year est.).
**Income:** Per capita income: $23,857 (2006-2010 5-year est.); Median household income: $55,893 (2006-2010 5-year est.); Average household income: $61,738 (2006-2010 5-year est.); Percent of households with income of $100,000 or more: 19.3% (2006-2010 5-year est.); Poverty rate: 4.7% (2006-2010 5-year est.).
**Education:** Percent of population age 25 and over with: High school diploma (including GED) or higher: 84.7% (2006-2010 5-year est.); Bachelor's degree or higher: 8.3% (2006-2010 5-year est.); Master's degree or higher: 5.6% (2006-2010 5-year est.).
**Housing:** Homeownership rate: 89.4% (2010); Median home value: $122,500 (2006-2010 5-year est.); Median contract rent: n/a per month (2006-2010 5-year est.); Median year structure built: 1979 (2006-2010 5-year est.).
**Transportation:** Commute to work: 88.8% car, 0.0% public transportation, 8.8% walk, 2.4% work from home (2006-2010 5-year est.); Travel time to work: 28.3% less than 15 minutes, 42.2% 15 to 30 minutes, 20.5% 30 to 45 minutes, 5.4% 45 to 60 minutes, 3.6% 60 minutes or more (2006-2010 5-year est.)
**Additional Information Contacts**
Town of Harrisburg . . . . . . . . . . . . . . . . . . . . . . . . . . . . . . . (315) 688-4193
http://www.tughillcouncil.com/Harrisburg.htm

**HARRISVILLE** (village). Covers a land area of 0.737 square miles and a water area of 0.046 square miles. Located at 44.15° N. Lat; 75.32° W. Long. Elevation is 807 feet.
**Population:** 703 (1990); 653 (2000); 628 (2010); Density: 851.6 persons per square mile (2010); Race: 98.2% White, 0.2% Black, 0.0% Asian, 0.2% American Indian/Alaska Native, 0.0% Native Hawaiian/Other Pacific Islander, 1.4% Other, 1.0% Hispanic of any race (2010); Average household size: 2.46 (2010); Median age: 38.5 (2010); Males per 100 females: 84.7 (2010); Marriage status: 28.0% never married, 49.7% now married, 10.0% widowed, 12.3% divorced (2006-2010 5-year est.); Foreign born: 2.6% (2006-2010 5-year est.); Ancestry (includes multiple ancestries): 24.8% Irish, 24.4% French, 19.3% German, 18.9% English, 6.6% Italian (2006-2010 5-year est.).
**Economy:** Employment by occupation: 22.7% management, 1.3% professional, 4.6% services, 20.2% sales, 3.4% farming, 13.9% construction, 7.1% production (2006-2010 5-year est.).
**Income:** Per capita income: $20,296 (2006-2010 5-year est.); Median household income: $36,019 (2006-2010 5-year est.); Average household income: $46,499 (2006-2010 5-year est.); Percent of households with income of $100,000 or more: 7.2% (2006-2010 5-year est.); Poverty rate: 12.0% (2006-2010 5-year est.).
**Education:** Percent of population age 25 and over with: High school diploma (including GED) or higher: 88.1% (2006-2010 5-year est.); Bachelor's degree or higher: 18.0% (2006-2010 5-year est.); Master's degree or higher: 5.4% (2006-2010 5-year est.).
**School District(s)**
Harrisville Central School District (PK-12)
2009-10 Enrollment: 424 . . . . . . . . . . . . . . . . . . . . . . . . . (315) 543-2707
**Housing:** Homeownership rate: 69.4% (2010); Median home value: $69,500 (2006-2010 5-year est.); Median contract rent: $405 per month (2006-2010 5-year est.); Median year structure built: before 1940 (2006-2010 5-year est.).
**Transportation:** Commute to work: 88.8% car, 0.0% public transportation, 10.3% walk, 0.0% work from home (2006-2010 5-year est.); Travel time to

work: 36.5% less than 15 minutes, 9.4% 15 to 30 minutes, 30.0% 30 to 45 minutes, 15.0% 45 to 60 minutes, 9.0% 60 minutes or more (2006-2010 5-year est.)

**LEWIS** (town). Covers a land area of 64.607 square miles and a water area of 0.542 square miles. Located at 43.49° N. Lat; 75.55° W. Long.
**Population:** 858 (1990); 857 (2000); 854 (2010); Density: 13.2 persons per square mile (2010); Race: 98.7% White, 0.0% Black, 0.0% Asian, 0.1% American Indian/Alaska Native, 0.1% Native Hawaiian/Other Pacific Islander, 1.1% Other, 0.8% Hispanic of any race (2010); Average household size: 2.60 (2010); Median age: 39.9 (2010); Males per 100 females: 109.3 (2010); Marriage status: 32.0% never married, 51.0% now married, 8.6% widowed, 8.4% divorced (2006-2010 5-year est.); Foreign born: 0.3% (2006-2010 5-year est.); Ancestry (includes multiple ancestries): 26.7% German, 21.9% Irish, 13.0% English, 11.7% Polish, 9.3% French (2006-2010 5-year est.).
**Economy:** Single-family building permits issued: 0 (2011); Multi-family building permits issued: 0 (2011); Employment by occupation: 16.9% management, 0.0% professional, 12.8% services, 15.4% sales, 2.3% farming, 14.0% construction, 9.6% production (2006-2010 5-year est.).
**Income:** Per capita income: $20,531 (2006-2010 5-year est.); Median household income: $39,038 (2006-2010 5-year est.); Average household income: $55,026 (2006-2010 5-year est.); Percent of households with income of $100,000 or more: 11.4% (2006-2010 5-year est.); Poverty rate: 12.6% (2006-2010 5-year est.).
**Education:** Percent of population age 25 and over with: High school diploma (including GED) or higher: 84.9% (2006-2010 5-year est.); Bachelor's degree or higher: 15.3% (2006-2010 5-year est.); Master's degree or higher: 10.1% (2006-2010 5-year est.).
**Housing:** Homeownership rate: 85.7% (2010); Median home value: $95,000 (2006-2010 5-year est.); Median contract rent: $308 per month (2006-2010 5-year est.); Median year structure built: 1956 (2006-2010 5-year est.).
**Transportation:** Commute to work: 93.8% car, 0.0% public transportation, 3.1% walk, 3.1% work from home (2006-2010 5-year est.); Travel time to work: 20.3% less than 15 minutes, 34.2% 15 to 30 minutes, 28.1% 30 to 45 minutes, 11.0% 45 to 60 minutes, 6.5% 60 minutes or more (2006-2010 5-year est.)

**LEYDEN** (town). Covers a land area of 33.329 square miles and a water area of 0.222 square miles. Located at 43.53° N. Lat; 75.38° W. Long.
**History:** Originally known as Kelsey's Mills, it was renamed in 1839 in anticipation of becoming a thriving port upon completion of the Black River Canal.
**Population:** 1,796 (1990); 1,792 (2000); 1,785 (2010); Density: 53.6 persons per square mile (2010); Race: 98.9% White, 0.4% Black, 0.0% Asian, 0.0% American Indian/Alaska Native, 0.0% Native Hawaiian/Other Pacific Islander, 0.7% Other, 0.7% Hispanic of any race (2010); Average household size: 2.51 (2010); Median age: 39.8 (2010); Males per 100 females: 97.7 (2010); Marriage status: 31.7% never married, 53.0% now married, 7.1% widowed, 8.3% divorced (2006-2010 5-year est.); Foreign born: 1.0% (2006-2010 5-year est.); Ancestry (includes multiple ancestries): 26.2% German, 17.8% French, 17.2% Irish, 12.5% Polish, 8.3% Dutch (2006-2010 5-year est.).
**Economy:** Single-family building permits issued: 4 (2011); Multi-family building permits issued: 0 (2011); Employment by occupation: 12.3% management, 0.6% professional, 16.1% services, 10.0% sales, 3.8% farming, 21.0% construction, 8.1% production (2006-2010 5-year est.).
**Income:** Per capita income: $18,821 (2006-2010 5-year est.); Median household income: $40,234 (2006-2010 5-year est.); Average household income: $47,339 (2006-2010 5-year est.); Percent of households with income of $100,000 or more: 4.9% (2006-2010 5-year est.); Poverty rate: 21.6% (2006-2010 5-year est.).
**Education:** Percent of population age 25 and over with: High school diploma (including GED) or higher: 82.0% (2006-2010 5-year est.); Bachelor's degree or higher: 6.6% (2006-2010 5-year est.); Master's degree or higher: 2.4% (2006-2010 5-year est.).
**Housing:** Homeownership rate: 76.8% (2010); Median home value: $90,000 (2006-2010 5-year est.); Median contract rent: $402 per month (2006-2010 5-year est.); Median year structure built: 1962 (2006-2010 5-year est.).
**Transportation:** Commute to work: 85.6% car, 0.0% public transportation, 4.8% walk, 6.7% work from home (2006-2010 5-year est.); Travel time to work: 55.3% less than 15 minutes, 20.2% 15 to 30 minutes, 12.4% 30 to 45

minutes, 8.2% 45 to 60 minutes, 3.9% 60 minutes or more (2006-2010 5-year est.)

**LOWVILLE** (village). County seat. Covers a land area of 1.911 square miles and a water area of 0 square miles. Located at 43.78° N. Lat; 75.48° W. Long. Elevation is 883 feet.
**Population:** 3,617 (1990); 3,476 (2000); 3,470 (2010); Density: 1,815.7 persons per square mile (2010); Race: 96.5% White, 1.4% Black, 0.5% Asian, 0.3% American Indian/Alaska Native, 0.2% Native Hawaiian/Other Pacific Islander, 1.1% Other, 1.7% Hispanic of any race (2010); Average household size: 2.30 (2010); Median age: 39.7 (2010); Males per 100 females: 90.2 (2010); Marriage status: 22.8% never married, 60.0% now married, 9.3% widowed, 7.9% divorced (2006-2010 5-year est.); Foreign born: 4.0% (2006-2010 5-year est.); Ancestry (includes multiple ancestries): 26.2% German, 16.9% Irish, 12.8% English, 8.3% French, 6.5% Italian (2006-2010 5-year est.).
**Economy:** Employment by occupation: 9.6% management, 6.7% professional, 12.9% services, 14.2% sales, 1.1% farming, 4.6% construction, 4.6% production (2006-2010 5-year est.).
**Income:** Per capita income: $20,518 (2006-2010 5-year est.); Median household income: $40,872 (2006-2010 5-year est.); Average household income: $50,749 (2006-2010 5-year est.); Percent of households with income of $100,000 or more: 10.3% (2006-2010 5-year est.); Poverty rate: 17.8% (2006-2010 5-year est.).
**Education:** Percent of population age 25 and over with: High school diploma (including GED) or higher: 85.3% (2006-2010 5-year est.); Bachelor's degree or higher: 18.8% (2006-2010 5-year est.); Master's degree or higher: 8.6% (2006-2010 5-year est.).
**School District(s)**
Lowville Academy & Central School District (PK-12)
   2009-10 Enrollment: 1,449 . . . . . . . . . . . . . . (315) 376-9000
**Housing:** Homeownership rate: 56.3% (2010); Median home value: $112,600 (2006-2010 5-year est.); Median contract rent: $473 per month (2006-2010 5-year est.); Median year structure built: before 1940 (2006-2010 5-year est.).
**Hospitals:** Lewis County General Hospital (54 beds)
**Safety:** Violent crime rate: 16.3 per 10,000 population; Property crime rate: 289.2 per 10,000 population (2010).
**Newspapers:** Journal & Republican (Local news; Circulation 5,280)
**Transportation:** Commute to work: 85.8% car, 0.0% public transportation, 7.0% walk, 7.2% work from home (2006-2010 5-year est.); Travel time to work: 58.3% less than 15 minutes, 17.8% 15 to 30 minutes, 16.0% 30 to 45 minutes, 5.9% 45 to 60 minutes, 1.9% 60 minutes or more (2006-2010 5-year est.)
**Additional Information Contacts**
Lewis County Chamber of Commerce . . . . . . . . . . . . . . (315) 376-2213
   http://www.lewiscountychamber.org

**LOWVILLE** (town). Covers a land area of 37.834 square miles and a water area of 0.291 square miles. Located at 43.81° N. Lat; 75.51° W. Long. Elevation is 883 feet.
**History:** Lowville was the home of Dr. Franklin B. Hough (1822-1885), called the "father of American forestry" for his conservation activities. Settled 1798, incorporated in 1854.
**Population:** 4,849 (1990); 4,548 (2000); 4,982 (2010); Density: 131.7 persons per square mile (2010); Race: 97.1% White, 1.2% Black, 0.4% Asian, 0.3% American Indian/Alaska Native, 0.1% Native Hawaiian/Other Pacific Islander, 0.9% Other, 1.5% Hispanic of any race (2010); Average household size: 2.42 (2010); Median age: 40.8 (2010); Males per 100 females: 91.1 (2010); Marriage status: 22.3% never married, 59.5% now married, 9.4% widowed, 8.8% divorced (2006-2010 5-year est.); Foreign born: 3.7% (2006-2010 5-year est.); Ancestry (includes multiple ancestries): 25.5% German, 16.1% Irish, 12.3% English, 8.9% French, 6.2% Italian (2006-2010 5-year est.).
**Economy:** Single-family building permits issued: 7 (2011); Multi-family building permits issued: 0 (2011); Employment by occupation: 9.0% management, 6.0% professional, 13.5% services, 13.0% sales, 1.5% farming, 7.5% construction, 7.5% production (2006-2010 5-year est.).
**Income:** Per capita income: $21,815 (2006-2010 5-year est.); Median household income: $41,453 (2006-2010 5-year est.); Average household income: $52,817 (2006-2010 5-year est.); Percent of households with income of $100,000 or more: 11.0% (2006-2010 5-year est.); Poverty rate: 16.1% (2006-2010 5-year est.).
**Education:** Percent of population age 25 and over with: High school diploma (including GED) or higher: 85.5% (2006-2010 5-year est.);

Bachelor's degree or higher: 17.6% (2006-2010 5-year est.); Master's degree or higher: 9.0% (2006-2010 5-year est.).

### School District(s)

Lowville Academy & Central School District (PK-12)
    2009-10 Enrollment: 1,449 . . . . . . . . . . . . . . . . . . . . . (315) 376-9000

**Housing:** Homeownership rate: 62.0% (2010); Median home value: $115,700 (2006-2010 5-year est.); Median contract rent: $479 per month (2006-2010 5-year est.); Median year structure built: 1941 (2006-2010 5-year est.).

**Hospitals:** Lewis County General Hospital (54 beds)

**Newspapers:** Journal & Republican (Local news; Circulation 5,280)

**Transportation:** Commute to work: 88.0% car, 0.0% public transportation, 6.3% walk, 5.7% work from home (2006-2010 5-year est.); Travel time to work: 60.3% less than 15 minutes, 17.1% 15 to 30 minutes, 15.7% 30 to 45 minutes, 4.6% 45 to 60 minutes, 2.2% 60 minutes or more (2006-2010 5-year est.)

## LYONS FALLS (village). Covers a land area of 0.970 square miles and a water area of 0.092 square miles. Located at 43.61° N. Lat; 75.36° W. Long. Elevation is 830 feet.

**History:** Black River Canal, begun in 1838, completed in 1858, ceased operation in 1922. Never successfully competed with railroad. Completely abandoned in 1926 when its final function as a feeder of water to the New York State Barge Canal was assumed by Delta Lake (northeast of Rome) and Hinckley Reservoir, north of Utica.

**Population:** 698 (1990); 591 (2000); 566 (2010); Density: 582.9 persons per square mile (2010); Race: 97.3% White, 1.2% Black, 0.4% Asian, 0.0% American Indian/Alaska Native, 0.0% Native Hawaiian/Other Pacific Islander, 1.1% Other, 1.9% Hispanic of any race (2010); Average household size: 2.42 (2010); Median age: 39.3 (2010); Males per 100 females: 102.9 (2010); Marriage status: 27.6% never married, 54.9% now married, 4.1% widowed, 13.4% divorced (2006-2010 5-year est.); Foreign born: 2.4% (2006-2010 5-year est.); Ancestry (includes multiple ancestries): 24.5% German, 21.7% Italian, 18.6% Irish, 16.8% Polish, 8.7% English (2006-2010 5-year est.).

**Economy:** Employment by occupation: 6.6% management, 0.0% professional, 7.8% services, 11.6% sales, 4.1% farming, 17.8% construction, 13.4% production (2006-2010 5-year est.).

**Income:** Per capita income: $21,897 (2006-2010 5-year est.); Median household income: $41,250 (2006-2010 5-year est.); Average household income: $47,830 (2006-2010 5-year est.); Percent of households with income of $100,000 or more: 8.4% (2006-2010 5-year est.); Poverty rate: 6.8% (2006-2010 5-year est.).

**Education:** Percent of population age 25 and over with: High school diploma (including GED) or higher: 93.1% (2006-2010 5-year est.); Bachelor's degree or higher: 13.2% (2006-2010 5-year est.); Master's degree or higher: 4.8% (2006-2010 5-year est.).

**Housing:** Homeownership rate: 71.0% (2010); Median home value: $69,400 (2006-2010 5-year est.); Median contract rent: $512 per month (2006-2010 5-year est.); Median year structure built: before 1940 (2006-2010 5-year est.).

**Transportation:** Commute to work: 98.7% car, 0.0% public transportation, 0.0% walk, 0.0% work from home (2006-2010 5-year est.); Travel time to work: 39.6% less than 15 minutes, 24.4% 15 to 30 minutes, 8.3% 30 to 45 minutes, 8.3% 45 to 60 minutes, 19.5% 60 minutes or more (2006-2010 5-year est.)

## LYONSDALE (town). Covers a land area of 68.742 square miles and a water area of 1.361 square miles. Located at 43.58° N. Lat; 75.24° W. Long. Elevation is 1,066 feet.

**Population:** 1,281 (1990); 1,273 (2000); 1,227 (2010); Density: 17.8 persons per square mile (2010); Race: 96.9% White, 1.5% Black, 0.0% Asian, 0.0% American Indian/Alaska Native, 0.0% Native Hawaiian/Other Pacific Islander, 1.6% Other, 0.1% Hispanic of any race (2010); Average household size: 2.51 (2010); Median age: 40.5 (2010); Males per 100 females: 99.5 (2010); Marriage status: 32.5% never married, 52.5% now married, 4.6% widowed, 10.3% divorced (2006-2010 5-year est.); Foreign born: 3.5% (2006-2010 5-year est.); Ancestry (includes multiple ancestries): 19.9% German, 15.8% Irish, 11.4% French, 9.2% Italian, 5.6% French Canadian (2006-2010 5-year est.).

**Economy:** Single-family building permits issued: 5 (2011); Multi-family building permits issued: 0 (2011); Employment by occupation: 3.9% management, 3.1% professional, 16.4% services, 9.2% sales, 2.7% farming, 21.8% construction, 14.6% production (2006-2010 5-year est.).

**Income:** Per capita income: $16,100 (2006-2010 5-year est.); Median household income: $38,482 (2006-2010 5-year est.); Average household income: $45,873 (2006-2010 5-year est.); Percent of households with income of $100,000 or more: 8.7% (2006-2010 5-year est.); Poverty rate: 20.4% (2006-2010 5-year est.).

**Education:** Percent of population age 25 and over with: High school diploma (including GED) or higher: 83.2% (2006-2010 5-year est.); Bachelor's degree or higher: 11.2% (2006-2010 5-year est.); Master's degree or higher: 3.4% (2006-2010 5-year est.).

**Housing:** Homeownership rate: 78.2% (2010); Median home value: $78,100 (2006-2010 5-year est.); Median contract rent: $429 per month (2006-2010 5-year est.); Median year structure built: 1969 (2006-2010 5-year est.).

**Transportation:** Commute to work: 91.8% car, 0.0% public transportation, 3.0% walk, 4.4% work from home (2006-2010 5-year est.); Travel time to work: 32.5% less than 15 minutes, 25.4% 15 to 30 minutes, 24.3% 30 to 45 minutes, 8.2% 45 to 60 minutes, 9.6% 60 minutes or more (2006-2010 5-year est.)

## MARTINSBURG (town). Covers a land area of 75.683 square miles and a water area of 0.350 square miles. Located at 43.72° N. Lat; 75.54° W. Long. Elevation is 1,263 feet.

**Population:** 1,358 (1990); 1,249 (2000); 1,433 (2010); Density: 18.9 persons per square mile (2010); Race: 96.8% White, 1.0% Black, 0.0% Asian, 0.3% American Indian/Alaska Native, 0.0% Native Hawaiian/Other Pacific Islander, 1.9% Other, 6.1% Hispanic of any race (2010); Average household size: 2.67 (2010); Median age: 37.2 (2010); Males per 100 females: 114.8 (2010); Marriage status: 34.3% never married, 54.9% now married, 3.3% widowed, 7.5% divorced (2006-2010 5-year est.); Foreign born: 1.8% (2006-2010 5-year est.); Ancestry (includes multiple ancestries): 18.7% German, 13.9% Irish, 12.6% French, 8.2% Italian, 7.3% American (2006-2010 5-year est.).

**Economy:** Employment by occupation: 11.0% management, 0.6% professional, 8.1% services, 12.4% sales, 3.4% farming, 28.6% construction, 8.7% production (2006-2010 5-year est.).

**Income:** Per capita income: $21,866 (2006-2010 5-year est.); Median household income: $46,447 (2006-2010 5-year est.); Average household income: $53,154 (2006-2010 5-year est.); Percent of households with income of $100,000 or more: 7.8% (2006-2010 5-year est.); Poverty rate: 18.5% (2006-2010 5-year est.).

**Education:** Percent of population age 25 and over with: High school diploma (including GED) or higher: 91.9% (2006-2010 5-year est.); Bachelor's degree or higher: 11.6% (2006-2010 5-year est.); Master's degree or higher: 5.1% (2006-2010 5-year est.).

**Housing:** Homeownership rate: 76.3% (2010); Median home value: $89,400 (2006-2010 5-year est.); Median contract rent: $632 per month (2006-2010 5-year est.); Median year structure built: 1952 (2006-2010 5-year est.).

**Transportation:** Commute to work: 86.1% car, 0.0% public transportation, 7.3% walk, 6.6% work from home (2006-2010 5-year est.); Travel time to work: 41.8% less than 15 minutes, 25.0% 15 to 30 minutes, 12.3% 30 to 45 minutes, 14.1% 45 to 60 minutes, 6.9% 60 minutes or more (2006-2010 5-year est.)

## MONTAGUE (town). Covers a land area of 65.173 square miles and a water area of 0.162 square miles. Located at 43.71° N. Lat; 75.71° W. Long.

**Population:** 47 (1990); 108 (2000); 78 (2010); Density: 1.2 persons per square mile (2010); Race: 98.7% White, 0.0% Black, 1.3% Asian, 0.0% American Indian/Alaska Native, 0.0% Native Hawaiian/Other Pacific Islander, 0.0% Other, 3.8% Hispanic of any race (2010); Average household size: 2.79 (2010); Median age: 39.5 (2010); Males per 100 females: 85.7 (2010); Marriage status: 21.5% never married, 61.5% now married, 3.1% widowed, 13.8% divorced (2006-2010 5-year est.); Foreign born: 0.0% (2006-2010 5-year est.); Ancestry (includes multiple ancestries): 21.4% Polish, 18.4% French, 17.3% Irish, 14.3% English, 13.3% German (2006-2010 5-year est.).

**Economy:** Employment by occupation: 11.8% management, 0.0% professional, 5.9% services, 5.9% sales, 0.0% farming, 35.3% construction, 0.0% production (2006-2010 5-year est.).

**Income:** Per capita income: $22,900 (2006-2010 5-year est.); Median household income: $62,222 (2006-2010 5-year est.); Average household income: $86,668 (2006-2010 5-year est.); Percent of households with income of $100,000 or more: 35.7% (2006-2010 5-year est.); Poverty rate: 15.3% (2006-2010 5-year est.).

**Education:** Percent of population age 25 and over with: High school diploma (including GED) or higher: 100.0% (2006-2010 5-year est.); Bachelor's degree or higher: 23.5% (2006-2010 5-year est.); Master's degree or higher: 15.7% (2006-2010 5-year est.).

**Housing:** Homeownership rate: 82.2% (2010); Median home value: $131,900 (2006-2010 5-year est.); Median contract rent: n/a per month (2006-2010 5-year est.); Median year structure built: 1973 (2006-2010 5-year est.).

**Transportation:** Commute to work: 100.0% car, 0.0% public transportation, 0.0% walk, 0.0% work from home (2006-2010 5-year est.); Travel time to work: 29.6% less than 15 minutes, 14.8% 15 to 30 minutes, 37.0% 30 to 45 minutes, 18.5% 45 to 60 minutes, 0.0% 60 minutes or more (2006-2010 5-year est.)

**NEW BREMEN** (town). Covers a land area of 55.588 square miles and a water area of 0.200 square miles. Located at 43.85° N. Lat; 75.36° W. Long. Elevation is 771 feet.

**Population:** 2,526 (1990); 2,722 (2000); 2,706 (2010); Density: 48.7 persons per square mile (2010); Race: 97.6% White, 0.8% Black, 0.3% Asian, 0.3% American Indian/Alaska Native, 0.0% Native Hawaiian/Other Pacific Islander, 1.0% Other, 0.6% Hispanic of any race (2010); Average household size: 2.67 (2010); Median age: 40.4 (2010); Males per 100 females: 98.7 (2010); Marriage status: 21.9% never married, 67.1% now married, 3.9% widowed, 7.1% divorced (2006-2010 5-year est.); Foreign born: 0.4% (2006-2010 5-year est.); Ancestry (includes multiple ancestries): 51.5% German, 24.1% French, 14.7% Irish, 9.8% English, 4.7% American (2006-2010 5-year est.).

**Economy:** Employment by occupation: 11.2% management, 0.0% professional, 11.1% services, 8.7% sales, 2.7% farming, 17.3% construction, 6.8% production (2006-2010 5-year est.).

**Income:** Per capita income: $20,577 (2006-2010 5-year est.); Median household income: $49,156 (2006-2010 5-year est.); Average household income: $56,117 (2006-2010 5-year est.); Percent of households with income of $100,000 or more: 9.2% (2006-2010 5-year est.); Poverty rate: 7.6% (2006-2010 5-year est.).

**Education:** Percent of population age 25 and over with: High school diploma (including GED) or higher: 92.0% (2006-2010 5-year est.); Bachelor's degree or higher: 14.2% (2006-2010 5-year est.); Master's degree or higher: 5.7% (2006-2010 5-year est.).

**Housing:** Homeownership rate: 84.0% (2010); Median home value: $104,600 (2006-2010 5-year est.); Median contract rent: $426 per month (2006-2010 5-year est.); Median year structure built: 1971 (2006-2010 5-year est.).

**Transportation:** Commute to work: 93.7% car, 1.2% public transportation, 1.6% walk, 2.9% work from home (2006-2010 5-year est.); Travel time to work: 39.4% less than 15 minutes, 34.4% 15 to 30 minutes, 8.6% 30 to 45 minutes, 8.0% 45 to 60 minutes, 9.6% 60 minutes or more (2006-2010 5-year est.)

**OSCEOLA** (town). Covers a land area of 87.006 square miles and a water area of 0.089 square miles. Located at 43.56° N. Lat; 75.68° W. Long. Elevation is 1,030 feet.

**Population:** 239 (1990); 265 (2000); 229 (2010); Density: 2.6 persons per square mile (2010); Race: 99.6% White, 0.0% Black, 0.0% Asian, 0.0% American Indian/Alaska Native, 0.0% Native Hawaiian/Other Pacific Islander, 0.4% Other, 0.0% Hispanic of any race (2010); Average household size: 2.22 (2010); Median age: 48.8 (2010); Males per 100 females: 106.3 (2010); Marriage status: 32.6% never married, 50.6% now married, 6.4% widowed, 10.5% divorced (2006-2010 5-year est.); Foreign born: 1.6% (2006-2010 5-year est.); Ancestry (includes multiple ancestries): 33.0% Irish, 26.6% German, 17.0% English, 11.7% French Canadian, 9.6% Scottish (2006-2010 5-year est.).

**Economy:** Employment by occupation: 9.2% management, 3.4% professional, 13.8% services, 14.9% sales, 5.7% farming, 18.4% construction, 0.0% production (2006-2010 5-year est.).

**Income:** Per capita income: $26,049 (2006-2010 5-year est.); Median household income: $44,500 (2006-2010 5-year est.); Average household income: $50,835 (2006-2010 5-year est.); Percent of households with income of $100,000 or more: 8.5% (2006-2010 5-year est.); Poverty rate: 16.5% (2006-2010 5-year est.).

**Education:** Percent of population age 25 and over with: High school diploma (including GED) or higher: 95.0% (2006-2010 5-year est.); Bachelor's degree or higher: 12.1% (2006-2010 5-year est.); Master's degree or higher: 6.4% (2006-2010 5-year est.).

**Housing:** Homeownership rate: 93.2% (2010); Median home value: $88,500 (2006-2010 5-year est.); Median contract rent: $350 per month (2006-2010 5-year est.); Median year structure built: 1970 (2006-2010 5-year est.).

**Transportation:** Commute to work: 87.4% car, 0.0% public transportation, 0.0% walk, 12.6% work from home (2006-2010 5-year est.); Travel time to work: 2.6% less than 15 minutes, 30.3% 15 to 30 minutes, 19.7% 30 to 45 minutes, 21.1% 45 to 60 minutes, 26.3% 60 minutes or more (2006-2010 5-year est.)

**PINCKNEY** (town). Covers a land area of 40.973 square miles and a water area of 0.142 square miles. Located at 43.83° N. Lat; 75.78° W. Long.

**Population:** 323 (1990); 319 (2000); 329 (2010); Density: 8.0 persons per square mile (2010); Race: 98.8% White, 0.0% Black, 0.0% Asian, 0.0% American Indian/Alaska Native, 0.0% Native Hawaiian/Other Pacific Islander, 1.2% Other, 0.6% Hispanic of any race (2010); Average household size: 2.40 (2010); Median age: 43.3 (2010); Males per 100 females: 135.0 (2010); Marriage status: 31.5% never married, 58.2% now married, 1.6% widowed, 8.7% divorced (2006-2010 5-year est.); Foreign born: 3.4% (2006-2010 5-year est.); Ancestry (includes multiple ancestries): 23.6% Irish, 18.6% German, 16.9% French, 14.3% English, 11.0% Polish (2006-2010 5-year est.).

**Economy:** Employment by occupation: 5.8% management, 0.0% professional, 5.1% services, 8.0% sales, 5.1% farming, 27.0% construction, 19.0% production (2006-2010 5-year est.).

**Income:** Per capita income: $17,562 (2006-2010 5-year est.); Median household income: $54,091 (2006-2010 5-year est.); Average household income: $54,070 (2006-2010 5-year est.); Percent of households with income of $100,000 or more: 5.4% (2006-2010 5-year est.); Poverty rate: 6.8% (2006-2010 5-year est.).

**Education:** Percent of population age 25 and over with: High school diploma (including GED) or higher: 95.2% (2006-2010 5-year est.); Bachelor's degree or higher: 6.8% (2006-2010 5-year est.); Master's degree or higher: 2.7% (2006-2010 5-year est.).

**Housing:** Homeownership rate: 78.1% (2010); Median home value: $80,000 (2006-2010 5-year est.); Median contract rent: $386 per month (2006-2010 5-year est.); Median year structure built: 1956 (2006-2010 5-year est.).

**Transportation:** Commute to work: 94.7% car, 0.0% public transportation, 5.3% walk, 0.0% work from home (2006-2010 5-year est.); Travel time to work: 23.7% less than 15 minutes, 45.8% 15 to 30 minutes, 27.5% 30 to 45 minutes, 3.1% 45 to 60 minutes, 0.0% 60 minutes or more (2006-2010 5-year est.)

**PORT LEYDEN** (village). Covers a land area of 0.614 square miles and a water area of 0.041 square miles. Located at 43.58° N. Lat; 75.34° W. Long. Elevation is 892 feet.

**Population:** 723 (1990); 665 (2000); 672 (2010); Density: 1,092.7 persons per square mile (2010); Race: 98.2% White, 1.0% Black, 0.0% Asian, 0.0% American Indian/Alaska Native, 0.0% Native Hawaiian/Other Pacific Islander, 0.8% Other, 0.3% Hispanic of any race (2010); Average household size: 2.44 (2010); Median age: 37.3 (2010); Males per 100 females: 92.0 (2010); Marriage status: 36.1% never married, 39.6% now married, 10.2% widowed, 14.1% divorced (2006-2010 5-year est.); Foreign born: 2.4% (2006-2010 5-year est.); Ancestry (includes multiple ancestries): 21.5% Irish, 19.9% German, 13.2% Dutch, 12.7% French, 5.2% Eastern European (2006-2010 5-year est.).

**Economy:** Employment by occupation: 5.0% management, 2.7% professional, 19.0% services, 21.3% sales, 0.0% farming, 15.4% construction, 0.9% production (2006-2010 5-year est.).

**Income:** Per capita income: $15,154 (2006-2010 5-year est.); Median household income: $31,417 (2006-2010 5-year est.); Average household income: $38,254 (2006-2010 5-year est.); Percent of households with income of $100,000 or more: 3.1% (2006-2010 5-year est.); Poverty rate: 21.4% (2006-2010 5-year est.).

**Education:** Percent of population age 25 and over with: High school diploma (including GED) or higher: 86.4% (2006-2010 5-year est.); Bachelor's degree or higher: 13.3% (2006-2010 5-year est.); Master's degree or higher: 2.4% (2006-2010 5-year est.).

**School District(s)**

South Lewis Central School District (PK-12)
    2009-10 Enrollment: 1,058 . . . . . . . . . . . . . . . (315) 348-2500

**Housing:** Homeownership rate: 62.0% (2010); Median home value: $64,700 (2006-2010 5-year est.); Median contract rent: $426 per month

(2006-2010 5-year est.); Median year structure built: before 1940 (2006-2010 5-year est.).

**Transportation:** Commute to work: 89.6% car, 0.0% public transportation, 9.5% walk, 0.0% work from home (2006-2010 5-year est.); Travel time to work: 54.8% less than 15 minutes, 13.1% 15 to 30 minutes, 12.2% 30 to 45 minutes, 14.5% 45 to 60 minutes, 5.4% 60 minutes or more (2006-2010 5-year est.)

**TURIN** (village). Covers a land area of 1.026 square miles and a water area of 0 square miles. Located at 43.62° N. Lat; 75.41° W. Long. Elevation is 1,263 feet.

**Population:** 295 (1990); 263 (2000); 232 (2010); Density: 226.1 persons per square mile (2010); Race: 99.1% White, 0.9% Black, 0.0% Asian, 0.0% American Indian/Alaska Native, 0.0% Native Hawaiian/Other Pacific Islander, 0.0% Other, 1.7% Hispanic of any race (2010); Average household size: 2.32 (2010); Median age: 43.0 (2010); Males per 100 females: 110.9 (2010); Marriage status: 22.5% never married, 40.8% now married, 14.2% widowed, 22.5% divorced (2006-2010 5-year est.); Foreign born: 2.4% (2006-2010 5-year est.); Ancestry (includes multiple ancestries): 22.0% Irish, 17.9% German, 17.1% English, 15.4% French, 11.4% Italian (2006-2010 5-year est.).

**Economy:** Employment by occupation: 9.5% management, 0.0% professional, 11.9% services, 11.9% sales, 4.8% farming, 14.3% construction, 7.1% production (2006-2010 5-year est.).

**Income:** Per capita income: $22,281 (2006-2010 5-year est.); Median household income: $37,614 (2006-2010 5-year est.); Average household income: $37,272 (2006-2010 5-year est.); Percent of households with income of $100,000 or more: 2.5% (2006-2010 5-year est.); Poverty rate: 2.4% (2006-2010 5-year est.).

**Education:** Percent of population age 25 and over with: High school diploma (including GED) or higher: 86.6% (2006-2010 5-year est.); Bachelor's degree or higher: 17.9% (2006-2010 5-year est.); Master's degree or higher: 8.9% (2006-2010 5-year est.).

#### School District(s)

South Lewis Central School District (PK-12)
    2009-10 Enrollment: 1,058 . . . . . . . . . . . . . . . . . . . (315) 348-2500

**Housing:** Homeownership rate: 83.0% (2010); Median home value: $73,900 (2006-2010 5-year est.); Median contract rent: $460 per month (2006-2010 5-year est.); Median year structure built: before 1940 (2006-2010 5-year est.).

**Transportation:** Commute to work: 87.5% car, 0.0% public transportation, 0.0% walk, 12.5% work from home (2006-2010 5-year est.); Travel time to work: 37.1% less than 15 minutes, 28.6% 15 to 30 minutes, 5.7% 30 to 45 minutes, 5.7% 45 to 60 minutes, 22.9% 60 minutes or more (2006-2010 5-year est.)

**TURIN** (town). Covers a land area of 31.176 square miles and a water area of 0.203 square miles. Located at 43.66° N. Lat; 75.42° W. Long. Elevation is 1,263 feet.

**Population:** 873 (1990); 793 (2000); 761 (2010); Density: 24.4 persons per square mile (2010); Race: 98.2% White, 0.8% Black, 0.0% Asian, 0.0% American Indian/Alaska Native, 0.0% Native Hawaiian/Other Pacific Islander, 1.0% Other, 2.0% Hispanic of any race (2010); Average household size: 2.53 (2010); Median age: 40.9 (2010); Males per 100 females: 113.2 (2010); Marriage status: 23.3% never married, 59.5% now married, 9.0% widowed, 8.2% divorced (2006-2010 5-year est.); Foreign born: 1.3% (2006-2010 5-year est.); Ancestry (includes multiple ancestries): 23.4% Irish, 19.0% German, 13.9% English, 13.0% Italian, 10.4% Polish (2006-2010 5-year est.).

**Economy:** Employment by occupation: 21.6% management, 0.0% professional, 5.9% services, 13.8% sales, 1.9% farming, 16.0% construction, 4.5% production (2006-2010 5-year est.).

**Income:** Per capita income: $25,255 (2006-2010 5-year est.); Median household income: $42,955 (2006-2010 5-year est.); Average household income: $52,665 (2006-2010 5-year est.); Percent of households with income of $100,000 or more: 15.2% (2006-2010 5-year est.); Poverty rate: 10.1% (2006-2010 5-year est.).

**Education:** Percent of population age 25 and over with: High school diploma (including GED) or higher: 86.4% (2006-2010 5-year est.); Bachelor's degree or higher: 7.5% (2006-2010 5-year est.); Master's degree or higher: 4.5% (2006-2010 5-year est.).

#### School District(s)

South Lewis Central School District (PK-12)
    2009-10 Enrollment: 1,058 . . . . . . . . . . . . . . . . . . . (315) 348-2500

**Housing:** Homeownership rate: 85.6% (2010); Median home value: $100,700 (2006-2010 5-year est.); Median contract rent: $428 per month (2006-2010 5-year est.); Median year structure built: 1961 (2006-2010 5-year est.).

**Transportation:** Commute to work: 91.0% car, 0.0% public transportation, 7.1% walk, 1.9% work from home (2006-2010 5-year est.); Travel time to work: 49.2% less than 15 minutes, 17.6% 15 to 30 minutes, 0.8% 30 to 45 minutes, 18.3% 45 to 60 minutes, 14.1% 60 minutes or more (2006-2010 5-year est.)

**WATSON** (town). Covers a land area of 112.737 square miles and a water area of 2.959 square miles. Located at 43.82° N. Lat; 75.23° W. Long. Elevation is 748 feet.

**Population:** 1,613 (1990); 1,987 (2000); 1,881 (2010); Density: 16.7 persons per square mile (2010); Race: 98.6% White, 0.5% Black, 0.2% Asian, 0.0% American Indian/Alaska Native, 0.0% Native Hawaiian/Other Pacific Islander, 0.7% Other, 0.6% Hispanic of any race (2010); Average household size: 2.54 (2010); Median age: 40.4 (2010); Males per 100 females: 103.6 (2010); Marriage status: 24.7% never married, 60.5% now married, 5.0% widowed, 9.7% divorced (2006-2010 5-year est.); Foreign born: 0.9% (2006-2010 5-year est.); Ancestry (includes multiple ancestries): 34.1% German, 14.2% Irish, 9.7% Italian, 9.4% French, 9.2% English (2006-2010 5-year est.).

**Economy:** Single-family building permits issued: 6 (2011); Multi-family building permits issued: 0 (2011); Employment by occupation: 10.7% management, 2.1% professional, 15.6% services, 14.8% sales, 4.7% farming, 17.0% construction, 8.2% production (2006-2010 5-year est.).

**Income:** Per capita income: $23,067 (2006-2010 5-year est.); Median household income: $38,944 (2006-2010 5-year est.); Average household income: $58,192 (2006-2010 5-year est.); Percent of households with income of $100,000 or more: 15.0% (2006-2010 5-year est.); Poverty rate: 12.9% (2006-2010 5-year est.).

**Education:** Percent of population age 25 and over with: High school diploma (including GED) or higher: 82.8% (2006-2010 5-year est.); Bachelor's degree or higher: 17.1% (2006-2010 5-year est.); Master's degree or higher: 5.7% (2006-2010 5-year est.).

**Housing:** Homeownership rate: 86.8% (2010); Median home value: $89,600 (2006-2010 5-year est.); Median contract rent: $468 per month (2006-2010 5-year est.); Median year structure built: 1974 (2006-2010 5-year est.).

**Transportation:** Commute to work: 89.3% car, 2.2% public transportation, 2.5% walk, 4.2% work from home (2006-2010 5-year est.); Travel time to work: 30.6% less than 15 minutes, 44.6% 15 to 30 minutes, 8.2% 30 to 45 minutes, 3.3% 45 to 60 minutes, 13.2% 60 minutes or more (2006-2010 5-year est.)

**WEST LEYDEN** (unincorporated postal area)
Zip Code: 13489

Covers a land area of 42.699 square miles and a water area of 0.503 square miles. Located at 43.46° N. Lat; 75.55° W. Long. Elevation is 1,489 feet. Population: 658 (2010); Density: 15.4 persons per square mile (2010); Race: 99.1% White, 0.0% Black, 0.0% Asian, 0.2% American Indian/Alaska Native, 0.0% Native Hawaiian/Other Pacific Islander, 0.7% Other, 0.3% Hispanic of any race (2010); Average household size: 2.54 (2010); Median age: 41.1 (2010); Males per 100 females: 106.3 (2010); Homeownership rate: 85.3% (2010)

**WEST TURIN** (town). Covers a land area of 102.053 square miles and a water area of 0.342 square miles. Located at 43.59° N. Lat; 75.50° W. Long.

**Population:** 1,753 (1990); 1,674 (2000); 1,524 (2010); Density: 14.9 persons per square mile (2010); Race: 98.5% White, 0.4% Black, 0.3% Asian, 0.1% American Indian/Alaska Native, 0.0% Native Hawaiian/Other Pacific Islander, 0.7% Other, 1.0% Hispanic of any race (2010); Average household size: 2.46 (2010); Median age: 41.6 (2010); Males per 100 females: 102.4 (2010); Marriage status: 28.4% never married, 53.6% now married, 2.8% widowed, 15.2% divorced (2006-2010 5-year est.); Foreign born: 0.6% (2006-2010 5-year est.); Ancestry (includes multiple ancestries): 34.5% German, 19.5% Irish, 14.7% Polish, 10.1% French, 9.1% Italian (2006-2010 5-year est.).

**Economy:** Employment by occupation: 22.0% management, 1.0% professional, 6.8% services, 13.6% sales, 2.0% farming, 20.4% construction, 4.3% production (2006-2010 5-year est.).

**Income:** Per capita income: $20,256 (2006-2010 5-year est.); Median household income: $42,442 (2006-2010 5-year est.); Average household

income: $49,267 (2006-2010 5-year est.); Percent of households with income of $100,000 or more: 6.6% (2006-2010 5-year est.); Poverty rate: 12.1% (2006-2010 5-year est.).
**Education:** Percent of population age 25 and over with: High school diploma (including GED) or higher: 88.0% (2006-2010 5-year est.); Bachelor's degree or higher: 13.1% (2006-2010 5-year est.); Master's degree or higher: 6.1% (2006-2010 5-year est.).
**Housing:** Homeownership rate: 81.1% (2010); Median home value: $82,600 (2006-2010 5-year est.); Median contract rent: $516 per month (2006-2010 5-year est.); Median year structure built: before 1940 (2006-2010 5-year est.).
**Transportation:** Commute to work: 84.3% car, 1.2% public transportation, 10.9% walk, 2.4% work from home (2006-2010 5-year est.); Travel time to work: 46.6% less than 15 minutes, 21.3% 15 to 30 minutes, 9.6% 30 to 45 minutes, 10.7% 45 to 60 minutes, 11.9% 60 minutes or more (2006-2010 5-year est.)

## Livingston County

Located in west central New York, in the Finger Lakes area; drained by the Genesee River; includes Conesus and Hemlock Lakes. Covers a land area of 632.13 square miles, a water area of 8.32 square miles, and is located in the Eastern Time Zone at 42.72° N. Lat., 77.77° W. Long. The county was founded in 1821. County seat is Geneseo.

Livingston County is part of the Rochester, NY Metropolitan Statistical Area. The entire metro area includes: Livingston County, NY; Monroe County, NY; Ontario County, NY; Orleans County, NY; Wayne County, NY

Weather Station: Avon                                Elevation: 544 feet

|        | Jan  | Feb  | Mar  | Apr | May | Jun | Jul | Aug | Sep | Oct | Nov | Dec  |
|--------|------|------|------|-----|-----|-----|-----|-----|-----|-----|-----|------|
| High   | 32   | 35   | 43   | 56  | 68  | 77  | 81  | 80  | 73  | 61  | 49  | 37   |
| Low    | 17   | 17   | 24   | 35  | 45  | 55  | 59  | 58  | 50  | 40  | 32  | 23   |
| Precip | 1.8  | 1.6  | 2.4  | 2.7 | 2.8 | 3.3 | 3.3 | 3.4 | 3.4 | 2.7 | 2.7 | 2.1  |
| Snow   | 13.3 | 10.5 | 10.7 | 2.1 | 0.2 | 0.0 | 0.0 | 0.0 | 0.0 | tr  | 3.7 | 11.4 |

*High and Low temperatures in degrees Fahrenheit; Precipitation and Snow in inches*

Weather Station: Dansville                           Elevation: 660 feet

|        | Jan | Feb | Mar | Apr | May | Jun | Jul | Aug | Sep | Oct | Nov | Dec |
|--------|-----|-----|-----|-----|-----|-----|-----|-----|-----|-----|-----|-----|
| High   | 33  | 36  | 44  | 58  | 69  | 78  | 82  | 81  | 74  | 62  | 49  | 38  |
| Low    | 16  | 17  | 24  | 35  | 45  | 54  | 59  | 57  | 50  | 39  | 32  | 22  |
| Precip | 1.5 | 1.2 | 1.9 | 2.5 | 2.9 | 3.4 | 3.6 | 3.4 | 3.4 | 2.7 | 2.5 | 1.9 |
| Snow   | 8.4 | 6.2 | 5.6 | 1.0 | 0.1 | 0.0 | 0.0 | 0.0 | 0.0 | tr  | 1.9 | 6.2 |

*High and Low temperatures in degrees Fahrenheit; Precipitation and Snow in inches*

Weather Station: Hemlock                             Elevation: 901 feet

|        | Jan | Feb | Mar | Apr | May | Jun | Jul | Aug | Sep | Oct | Nov | Dec |
|--------|-----|-----|-----|-----|-----|-----|-----|-----|-----|-----|-----|-----|
| High   | 32  | 34  | 43  | 56  | 68  | 76  | 80  | 79  | 71  | 59  | 48  | 37  |
| Low    | 16  | 16  | 23  | 35  | 45  | 55  | 59  | 58  | 52  | 41  | 32  | 22  |
| Precip | 1.9 | 1.5 | 2.6 | 3.0 | 3.2 | 3.7 | 3.7 | 3.5 | 3.6 | 3.2 | 3.0 | 2.2 |
| Snow   | na  | na  | na  | 0.0 | 0.0 | 0.0 | 0.0 | 0.0 | 0.0 | 0.0 | na  | na  |

*High and Low temperatures in degrees Fahrenheit; Precipitation and Snow in inches*

**Population:** 62,372 (1990); 64,328 (2000); 65,393 (2010); Race: 93.8% White, 2.4% Black, 1.2% Asian, 0.3% American Indian/Alaska Native, 0.0% Native Hawaiian/Other Pacific Islander, 2.3% Other, 2.8% Hispanic of any race (2010); Density: 103.4 persons per square mile (2010); Average household size: 2.44 (2010); Median age: 39.8 (2010); Males per 100 females: 100.7 (2010).
**Religion:** Six largest groups: 22.8% Catholicism, 4.9% Methodist/Pietist, 4.6% Non-Denominational, 3.1% Presbyterian-Reformed, 1.1% Holiness, 0.8% Lutheran (2010)
**Economy:** Unemployment rate: 9.7% (February 2012); Total civilian labor force: 32,568 (February 2012); Leading industries: 20.8% retail trade; 17.8% manufacturing; 16.1% health care and social assistance (2009); Farms: 792 totaling 222,415 acres (2007); Companies that employ 500 or more persons: 2 (2009); Companies that employ 100 to 499 persons: 12 (2009); Companies that employ less than 100 persons: 1,250 (2009); Black-owned businesses: n/a (2007); Hispanic-owned businesses: n/a (2007); Asian-owned businesses: n/a (2007); Women-owned businesses: 1,179 (2007); Retail sales per capita: $10,955 (2010). Single-family building permits issued: 54 (2011); Multi-family building permits issued: 67 (2011).
**Income:** Per capita income: $22,923 (2006-2010 5-year est.); Median household income: $51,690 (2006-2010 5-year est.); Average household income: $61,114 (2006-2010 5-year est.); Percent of households with

income of $100,000 or more: 15.9% (2006-2010 5-year est.); Poverty rate: 11.9% (2006-2010 5-year est.); Bankruptcy rate: 1.66% (2011).
**Education:** Percent of population age 25 and over with: High school diploma (including GED) or higher: 88.7% (2006-2010 5-year est.); Bachelor's degree or higher: 23.4% (2006-2010 5-year est.); Master's degree or higher: 9.9% (2006-2010 5-year est.).
**Housing:** Homeownership rate: 73.1% (2010); Median home value: $112,300 (2006-2010 5-year est.); Median contract rent: $526 per month (2006-2010 5-year est.); Median year structure built: 1964 (2006-2010 5-year est.)
**Health:** Birth rate: 85.6 per 10,000 population (2011); Death rate: 75.3 per 10,000 population (2011); Age-adjusted cancer mortality rate: 173.6 deaths per 100,000 population (2009); Number of physicians: 9.8 per 10,000 population (2008); Hospital beds: 8.6 per 10,000 population (2007); Hospital admissions: 441.2 per 10,000 population (2007).
**Elections:** 2008 Presidential election results: 45.3% Obama, 53.2% McCain, 0.7% Nader
**National and State Parks:** Boyd-Parker State Park; Rattlesnake Hill State Wildlife Management Area
**Additional Information Contacts**

| | |
|---|---|
| Livingston County Government | (585) 243-7010 |
| http://www.co.livingston.state.ny.us | |
| Livingston County Chamber of Commerce | (585) 243-2222 |
| http://www.livingstoncountychamber.com | |
| Town of Geneseo | (585) 991-5000 |
| http://www.geneseony.org | |
| Village of Dansville | (585) 335-5330 |
| http://dansvilleny.us | |
| Village of Geneseo | (585) 243-1177 |
| http://www.geneseony.org | |
| Village of Mount Morris | (585) 658-4160 |
| http://www.mountmorrisny.com/government/village.asp | |

## Livingston County Communities

**AVON** (village). Covers a land area of 3.098 square miles and a water area of 0 square miles. Located at 42.91° N. Lat; 77.74° W. Long. Elevation is 650 feet.
**Population:** 3,001 (1990); 2,977 (2000); 3,394 (2010); Density: 1,095.4 persons per square mile (2010); Race: 95.5% White, 1.3% Black, 0.8% Asian, 0.3% American Indian/Alaska Native, 0.0% Native Hawaiian/Other Pacific Islander, 2.1% Other, 2.1% Hispanic of any race (2010); Average household size: 2.31 (2010); Median age: 42.3 (2010); Males per 100 females: 90.7 (2010); Marriage status: 27.6% never married, 57.0% now married, 5.1% widowed, 10.3% divorced (2006-2010 5-year est.); Foreign born: 2.0% (2006-2010 5-year est.); Ancestry (includes multiple ancestries): 31.7% German, 24.8% Irish, 18.4% Italian, 15.0% English, 7.2% Scotch-Irish (2006-2010 5-year est.).
**Economy:** Single-family building permits issued: 3 (2011); Multi-family building permits issued: 0 (2011); Employment by occupation: 11.5% management, 1.6% professional, 10.8% services, 17.1% sales, 2.3% farming, 10.2% construction, 6.1% production (2006-2010 5-year est.).
**Income:** Per capita income: $25,324 (2006-2010 5-year est.); Median household income: $53,287 (2006-2010 5-year est.); Average household income: $63,794 (2006-2010 5-year est.); Percent of households with income of $100,000 or more: 17.3% (2006-2010 5-year est.); Poverty rate: 4.6% (2006-2010 5-year est.).
**Education:** Percent of population age 25 and over with: High school diploma (including GED) or higher: 94.2% (2006-2010 5-year est.); Bachelor's degree or higher: 40.3% (2006-2010 5-year est.); Master's degree or higher: 18.1% (2006-2010 5-year est.).
**School District(s)**
Avon Central School District (KG-12)
    2009-10 Enrollment: 1,013 . . . . . . . . . . . . . . . . . (585) 226-2455
**Housing:** Homeownership rate: 60.7% (2010); Median home value: $135,400 (2006-2010 5-year est.); Median contract rent: $608 per month (2006-2010 5-year est.); Median year structure built: 1956 (2006-2010 5-year est.).
**Safety:** Violent crime rate: 14.0 per 10,000 population; Property crime rate: 105.3 per 10,000 population (2010).
**Transportation:** Commute to work: 91.6% car, 0.0% public transportation, 4.3% walk, 2.2% work from home (2006-2010 5-year est.); Travel time to work: 34.7% less than 15 minutes, 31.2% 15 to 30 minutes, 25.3% 30 to 45 minutes, 6.4% 45 to 60 minutes, 2.4% 60 minutes or more (2006-2010 5-year est.)

**AVON** (town). Covers a land area of 41.203 square miles and a water area of 0.055 square miles. Located at 42.89° N. Lat; 77.72° W. Long. Elevation is 650 feet.

**History:** Incorporated 1867.

**Population:** 6,283 (1990); 6,443 (2000); 7,164 (2010); Density: 173.9 persons per square mile (2010); Race: 95.3% White, 1.0% Black, 1.0% Asian, 0.3% American Indian/Alaska Native, 0.0% Native Hawaiian/Other Pacific Islander, 2.4% Other, 2.5% Hispanic of any race (2010); Average household size: 2.38 (2010); Median age: 42.6 (2010); Males per 100 females: 96.9 (2010); Marriage status: 24.5% never married, 62.0% now married, 4.6% widowed, 8.9% divorced (2006-2010 5-year est.); Foreign born: 1.0% (2006-2010 5-year est.); Ancestry (includes multiple ancestries): 32.4% German, 25.3% Irish, 18.6% English, 13.0% Italian, 7.1% Polish (2006-2010 5-year est.).

**Economy:** Single-family building permits issued: 1 (2011); Multi-family building permits issued: 0 (2011); Employment by occupation: 8.6% management, 3.2% professional, 10.1% services, 16.8% sales, 3.8% farming, 11.7% construction, 10.4% production (2006-2010 5-year est.).

**Income:** Per capita income: $25,479 (2006-2010 5-year est.); Median household income: $59,306 (2006-2010 5-year est.); Average household income: $65,615 (2006-2010 5-year est.); Percent of households with income of $100,000 or more: 16.9% (2006-2010 5-year est.); Poverty rate: 4.1% (2006-2010 5-year est.).

**Education:** Percent of population age 25 and over with: High school diploma (including GED) or higher: 92.4% (2006-2010 5-year est.); Bachelor's degree or higher: 32.9% (2006-2010 5-year est.); Master's degree or higher: 14.1% (2006-2010 5-year est.).

#### School District(s)

Avon Central School District (KG-12)

   2009-10 Enrollment: 1,013 . . . . . . . . . . . . . . . . . . . . . . . (585) 226-2455

**Housing:** Homeownership rate: 73.0% (2010); Median home value: $131,400 (2006-2010 5-year est.); Median contract rent: $608 per month (2006-2010 5-year est.); Median year structure built: 1967 (2006-2010 5-year est.).

**Transportation:** Commute to work: 91.3% car, 0.4% public transportation, 2.0% walk, 3.1% work from home (2006-2010 5-year est.); Travel time to work: 28.2% less than 15 minutes, 30.3% 15 to 30 minutes, 36.1% 30 to 45 minutes, 3.9% 45 to 60 minutes, 1.5% 60 minutes or more (2006-2010 5-year est.)

**BYERSVILLE** (CDP). Covers a land area of 0.510 square miles and a water area of 0 square miles. Located at 42.58° N. Lat; 77.79° W. Long. Elevation is 1,358 feet.

**Population:** n/a (1990); n/a (2000); 47 (2010); Density: 92.1 persons per square mile (2010); Race: 93.6% White, 2.1% Black, 0.0% Asian, 0.0% American Indian/Alaska Native, 0.0% Native Hawaiian/Other Pacific Islander, 4.3% Other, 0.0% Hispanic of any race (2010); Average household size: 2.47 (2010); Median age: 48.5 (2010); Males per 100 females: 88.0 (2010); Marriage status: 25.0% never married, 69.6% now married, 5.4% widowed, 0.0% divorced (2006-2010 5-year est.); Foreign born: 0.0% (2006-2010 5-year est.); Ancestry (includes multiple ancestries): 37.7% French, 14.8% German, 11.5% English, 8.2% Pennsylvania German, 4.9% European (2006-2010 5-year est.).

**Economy:** Employment by occupation: 0.0% management, 0.0% professional, 16.7% services, 20.8% sales, 0.0% farming, 16.7% construction, 20.8% production (2006-2010 5-year est.).

**Income:** Per capita income: $27,579 (2006-2010 5-year est.); Median household income: $41,667 (2006-2010 5-year est.); Average household income: $66,393 (2006-2010 5-year est.); Percent of households with income of $100,000 or more: 10.7% (2006-2010 5-year est.); Poverty rate: 4.9% (2006-2010 5-year est.).

**Education:** Percent of population age 25 and over with: High school diploma (including GED) or higher: 87.8% (2006-2010 5-year est.); Bachelor's degree or higher: 12.2% (2006-2010 5-year est.); Master's degree or higher: 6.1% (2006-2010 5-year est.).

**Housing:** Homeownership rate: 94.7% (2010); Median home value: $75,000 (2006-2010 5-year est.); Median contract rent: n/a per month (2006-2010 5-year est.); Median year structure built: before 1940 (2006-2010 5-year est.).

**Transportation:** Commute to work: 100.0% car, 0.0% public transportation, 0.0% walk, 0.0% work from home (2006-2010 5-year est.); Travel time to work: 25.0% less than 15 minutes, 25.0% 15 to 30 minutes, 29.2% 30 to 45 minutes, 20.8% 45 to 60 minutes, 0.0% 60 minutes or more (2006-2010 5-year est.)

**CALEDONIA** (village). Covers a land area of 2.097 square miles and a water area of 0 square miles. Located at 42.97° N. Lat; 77.85° W. Long. Elevation is 659 feet.

**Population:** 2,262 (1990); 2,327 (2000); 2,201 (2010); Density: 1,049.5 persons per square mile (2010); Race: 94.1% White, 3.4% Black, 0.7% Asian, 0.0% American Indian/Alaska Native, 0.0% Native Hawaiian/Other Pacific Islander, 1.8% Other, 1.4% Hispanic of any race (2010); Average household size: 2.40 (2010); Median age: 42.5 (2010); Males per 100 females: 94.6 (2010); Marriage status: 26.0% never married, 58.3% now married, 3.5% widowed, 12.2% divorced (2006-2010 5-year est.); Foreign born: 1.8% (2006-2010 5-year est.); Ancestry (includes multiple ancestries): 27.8% Irish, 21.6% German, 20.2% Italian, 19.8% English, 6.2% Scottish (2006-2010 5-year est.).

**Economy:** Single-family building permits issued: 0 (2011); Multi-family building permits issued: 0 (2011); Employment by occupation: 12.4% management, 6.3% professional, 8.5% services, 12.9% sales, 7.7% farming, 8.2% construction, 7.7% production (2006-2010 5-year est.).

**Income:** Per capita income: $25,931 (2006-2010 5-year est.); Median household income: $53,149 (2006-2010 5-year est.); Average household income: $60,911 (2006-2010 5-year est.); Percent of households with income of $100,000 or more: 15.3% (2006-2010 5-year est.); Poverty rate: 7.2% (2006-2010 5-year est.).

**Education:** Percent of population age 25 and over with: High school diploma (including GED) or higher: 89.3% (2006-2010 5-year est.); Bachelor's degree or higher: 21.5% (2006-2010 5-year est.); Master's degree or higher: 6.1% (2006-2010 5-year est.).

#### School District(s)

Caledonia-Mumford Central School District (PK-12)

   2009-10 Enrollment: 965 . . . . . . . . . . . . . . . . . . . . . . . (585) 538-3400

**Housing:** Homeownership rate: 69.4% (2010); Median home value: $106,200 (2006-2010 5-year est.); Median contract rent: $561 per month (2006-2010 5-year est.); Median year structure built: 1952 (2006-2010 5-year est.).

**Transportation:** Commute to work: 91.2% car, 0.7% public transportation, 4.7% walk, 2.5% work from home (2006-2010 5-year est.); Travel time to work: 34.7% less than 15 minutes, 26.3% 15 to 30 minutes, 29.6% 30 to 45 minutes, 5.3% 45 to 60 minutes, 4.1% 60 minutes or more (2006-2010 5-year est.)

**CALEDONIA** (town). Covers a land area of 43.874 square miles and a water area of 0.250 square miles. Located at 42.95° N. Lat; 77.82° W. Long. Elevation is 659 feet.

**History:** Incorporated 1887.

**Population:** 4,441 (1990); 4,567 (2000); 4,255 (2010); Density: 97.0 persons per square mile (2010); Race: 95.0% White, 2.6% Black, 0.6% Asian, 0.0% American Indian/Alaska Native, 0.0% Native Hawaiian/Other Pacific Islander, 1.8% Other, 1.8% Hispanic of any race (2010); Average household size: 2.48 (2010); Median age: 43.9 (2010); Males per 100 females: 98.5 (2010); Marriage status: 24.8% never married, 61.5% now married, 4.6% widowed, 9.2% divorced (2006-2010 5-year est.); Foreign born: 1.6% (2006-2010 5-year est.); Ancestry (includes multiple ancestries): 28.9% Irish, 22.2% German, 18.8% English, 17.3% Italian, 6.1% American (2006-2010 5-year est.).

**Economy:** Single-family building permits issued: 2 (2011); Multi-family building permits issued: 0 (2011); Employment by occupation: 12.4% management, 7.5% professional, 8.3% services, 12.7% sales, 4.7% farming, 9.1% construction, 9.1% production (2006-2010 5-year est.).

**Income:** Per capita income: $25,486 (2006-2010 5-year est.); Median household income: $52,933 (2006-2010 5-year est.); Average household income: $61,144 (2006-2010 5-year est.); Percent of households with income of $100,000 or more: 18.2% (2006-2010 5-year est.); Poverty rate: 7.7% (2006-2010 5-year est.).

**Education:** Percent of population age 25 and over with: High school diploma (including GED) or higher: 93.0% (2006-2010 5-year est.); Bachelor's degree or higher: 22.2% (2006-2010 5-year est.); Master's degree or higher: 6.6% (2006-2010 5-year est.).

#### School District(s)

Caledonia-Mumford Central School District (PK-12)

   2009-10 Enrollment: 965 . . . . . . . . . . . . . . . . . . . . . . . (585) 538-3400

**Housing:** Homeownership rate: 77.9% (2010); Median home value: $125,100 (2006-2010 5-year est.); Median contract rent: $563 per month (2006-2010 5-year est.); Median year structure built: 1965 (2006-2010 5-year est.).

**Transportation:** Commute to work: 90.9% car, 1.0% public transportation, 3.0% walk, 3.5% work from home (2006-2010 5-year est.); Travel time to

work: 31.0% less than 15 minutes, 28.2% 15 to 30 minutes, 32.0% 30 to 45 minutes, 5.8% 45 to 60 minutes, 3.0% 60 minutes or more (2006-2010 5-year est.)

## CONESUS (town).
Covers a land area of 32.890 square miles and a water area of 2.980 square miles. Located at 42.70° N. Lat; 77.64° W. Long. Elevation is 1,198 feet.
**Population:** 2,196 (1990); 2,353 (2000); 2,473 (2010); Density: 75.2 persons per square mile (2010); Race: 97.9% White, 0.4% Black, 0.2% Asian, 0.4% American Indian/Alaska Native, 0.1% Native Hawaiian/Other Pacific Islander, 1.0% Other, 0.5% Hispanic of any race (2010); Average household size: 2.48 (2010); Median age: 44.6 (2010); Males per 100 females: 102.4 (2010); Marriage status: 18.6% never married, 70.9% now married, 3.0% widowed, 7.6% divorced (2006-2010 5-year est.); Foreign born: 3.1% (2006-2010 5-year est.); Ancestry (includes multiple ancestries): 26.8% German, 17.6% English, 15.6% Irish, 12.0% Italian, 7.1% French (2006-2010 5-year est.).
**Economy:** Single-family building permits issued: 5 (2011); Multi-family building permits issued: 0 (2011); Employment by occupation: 14.1% management, 4.8% professional, 7.5% services, 14.4% sales, 2.4% farming, 13.8% construction, 10.9% production (2006-2010 5-year est.).
**Income:** Per capita income: $29,509 (2006-2010 5-year est.); Median household income: $67,717 (2006-2010 5-year est.); Average household income: $75,644 (2006-2010 5-year est.); Percent of households with income of $100,000 or more: 23.5% (2006-2010 5-year est.); Poverty rate: 6.5% (2006-2010 5-year est.).
**Education:** Percent of population age 25 and over with: High school diploma (including GED) or higher: 90.7% (2006-2010 5-year est.); Bachelor's degree or higher: 27.1% (2006-2010 5-year est.); Master's degree or higher: 12.6% (2006-2010 5-year est.).
**Housing:** Homeownership rate: 89.0% (2010); Median home value: $122,700 (2006-2010 5-year est.); Median contract rent: $513 per month (2006-2010 5-year est.); Median year structure built: 1975 (2006-2010 5-year est.).
**Transportation:** Commute to work: 94.9% car, 0.9% public transportation, 0.0% walk, 3.4% work from home (2006-2010 5-year est.); Travel time to work: 12.0% less than 15 minutes, 26.6% 15 to 30 minutes, 28.9% 30 to 45 minutes, 21.4% 45 to 60 minutes, 11.1% 60 minutes or more (2006-2010 5-year est.)

## CONESUS HAMLET (CDP).
Covers a land area of 1.058 square miles and a water area of 0 square miles. Located at 42.72° N. Lat; 77.66° W. Long. Elevation is 1,207 feet.
**Population:** n/a (1990); n/a (2000); 308 (2010); Density: 290.9 persons per square mile (2010); Race: 95.8% White, 1.9% Black, 0.3% Asian, 0.0% American Indian/Alaska Native, 0.0% Native Hawaiian/Other Pacific Islander, 2.0% Other, 1.9% Hispanic of any race (2010); Average household size: 2.70 (2010); Median age: 37.3 (2010); Males per 100 females: 91.3 (2010); Marriage status: 24.7% never married, 43.5% now married, 7.8% widowed, 24.0% divorced (2006-2010 5-year est.); Foreign born: 3.0% (2006-2010 5-year est.); Ancestry (includes multiple ancestries): 23.7% German, 21.2% Irish, 18.2% English, 12.1% Dutch, 3.0% Polish (2006-2010 5-year est.).
**Economy:** Employment by occupation: 13.9% management, 5.9% professional, 9.9% services, 0.0% sales, 0.0% farming, 7.9% construction, 26.7% production (2006-2010 5-year est.).
**Income:** Per capita income: $21,687 (2006-2010 5-year est.); Median household income: $44,205 (2006-2010 5-year est.); Average household income: $50,782 (2006-2010 5-year est.); Percent of households with income of $100,000 or more: 7.1% (2006-2010 5-year est.); Poverty rate: 16.2% (2006-2010 5-year est.).
**Education:** Percent of population age 25 and over with: High school diploma (including GED) or higher: 85.7% (2006-2010 5-year est.); Bachelor's degree or higher: 33.8% (2006-2010 5-year est.); Master's degree or higher: 8.3% (2006-2010 5-year est.).
**Housing:** Homeownership rate: 84.2% (2010); Median home value: $88,000 (2006-2010 5-year est.); Median contract rent: n/a per month (2006-2010 5-year est.); Median year structure built: before 1940 (2006-2010 5-year est.).
**Transportation:** Commute to work: 100.0% car, 0.0% public transportation, 0.0% walk, 0.0% work from home (2006-2010 5-year est.); Travel time to work: 20.4% less than 15 minutes, 46.2% 15 to 30 minutes, 8.6% 30 to 45 minutes, 18.3% 45 to 60 minutes, 6.5% 60 minutes or more (2006-2010 5-year est.)

## CONESUS LAKE (CDP).
Covers a land area of 4.361 square miles and a water area of 5.049 square miles. Located at 42.80° N. Lat; 77.70° W. Long. Elevation is 840 feet.
**Population:** n/a (1990); n/a (2000); 2,584 (2010); Density: 592.5 persons per square mile (2010); Race: 97.3% White, 0.4% Black, 0.9% Asian, 0.4% American Indian/Alaska Native, 0.1% Native Hawaiian/Other Pacific Islander, 0.9% Other, 0.8% Hispanic of any race (2010); Average household size: 2.12 (2010); Median age: 51.6 (2010); Males per 100 females: 105.2 (2010); Marriage status: 23.4% never married, 62.0% now married, 4.6% widowed, 10.0% divorced (2006-2010 5-year est.); Foreign born: 3.3% (2006-2010 5-year est.); Ancestry (includes multiple ancestries): 33.1% German, 19.8% Irish, 18.7% English, 13.4% Italian, 12.1% American (2006-2010 5-year est.).
**Economy:** Employment by occupation: 15.1% management, 7.4% professional, 7.2% services, 12.5% sales, 3.4% farming, 11.3% construction, 8.2% production (2006-2010 5-year est.).
**Income:** Per capita income: $40,946 (2006-2010 5-year est.); Median household income: $76,161 (2006-2010 5-year est.); Average household income: $87,734 (2006-2010 5-year est.); Percent of households with income of $100,000 or more: 28.2% (2006-2010 5-year est.); Poverty rate: 2.1% (2006-2010 5-year est.).
**Education:** Percent of population age 25 and over with: High school diploma (including GED) or higher: 96.8% (2006-2010 5-year est.); Bachelor's degree or higher: 35.1% (2006-2010 5-year est.); Master's degree or higher: 15.3% (2006-2010 5-year est.).
**Housing:** Homeownership rate: 80.6% (2010); Median home value: $168,800 (2006-2010 5-year est.); Median contract rent: $666 per month (2006-2010 5-year est.); Median year structure built: 1960 (2006-2010 5-year est.).
**Transportation:** Commute to work: 95.3% car, 0.0% public transportation, 0.2% walk, 4.3% work from home (2006-2010 5-year est.); Travel time to work: 18.8% less than 15 minutes, 23.3% 15 to 30 minutes, 38.4% 30 to 45 minutes, 18.2% 45 to 60 minutes, 1.3% 60 minutes or more (2006-2010 5-year est.)

## CUMMINSVILLE (CDP).
Covers a land area of 0.130 square miles and a water area of 0 square miles. Located at 42.57° N. Lat; 77.71° W. Long. Elevation is 640 feet.
**Population:** n/a (1990); n/a (2000); 183 (2010); Density: 1,397.0 persons per square mile (2010); Race: 97.3% White, 0.0% Black, 0.5% Asian, 0.0% American Indian/Alaska Native, 0.0% Native Hawaiian/Other Pacific Islander, 2.2% Other, 0.0% Hispanic of any race (2010); Average household size: 2.03 (2010); Median age: 56.8 (2010); Males per 100 females: 77.7 (2010); Marriage status: 14.7% never married, 69.8% now married, 7.8% widowed, 7.8% divorced (2006-2010 5-year est.); Foreign born: 0.0% (2006-2010 5-year est.); Ancestry (includes multiple ancestries): 50.9% American, 31.0% German, 21.6% Irish, 12.1% French Canadian, 10.3% English (2006-2010 5-year est.).
**Economy:** Employment by occupation: 0.0% management, 0.0% professional, 0.0% services, 25.5% sales, 0.0% farming, 0.0% construction, 0.0% production (2006-2010 5-year est.).
**Income:** Per capita income: $24,202 (2006-2010 5-year est.); Median household income: $50,144 (2006-2010 5-year est.); Average household income: $41,921 (2006-2010 5-year est.); Percent of households with income of $100,000 or more: 0.0% (2006-2010 5-year est.); Poverty rate: 7.8% (2006-2010 5-year est.).
**Education:** Percent of population age 25 and over with: High school diploma (including GED) or higher: 81.9% (2006-2010 5-year est.); Bachelor's degree or higher: 7.8% (2006-2010 5-year est.); Master's degree or higher: 0.0% (2006-2010 5-year est.).
**Housing:** Homeownership rate: 74.5% (2010); Median home value: $31,700 (2006-2010 5-year est.); Median contract rent: n/a per month (2006-2010 5-year est.); Median year structure built: 1988 (2006-2010 5-year est.).
**Transportation:** Commute to work: 100.0% car, 0.0% public transportation, 0.0% walk, 0.0% work from home (2006-2010 5-year est.); Travel time to work: 63.8% less than 15 minutes, 36.2% 15 to 30 minutes, 0.0% 30 to 45 minutes, 0.0% 45 to 60 minutes, 0.0% 60 minutes or more (2006-2010 5-year est.)

## CUYLERVILLE (CDP).
Covers a land area of 0.421 square miles and a water area of 0 square miles. Located at 42.77° N. Lat; 77.87° W. Long. Elevation is 571 feet.
**Population:** n/a (1990); n/a (2000); 297 (2010); Density: 704.8 persons per square mile (2010); Race: 96.6% White, 0.0% Black, 1.3% Asian, 0.3%

American Indian/Alaska Native, 0.0% Native Hawaiian/Other Pacific Islander, 1.8% Other, 3.4% Hispanic of any race (2010); Average household size: 2.32 (2010); Median age: 38.5 (2010); Males per 100 females: 104.8 (2010); Marriage status: 24.8% never married, 59.7% now married, 1.6% widowed, 13.9% divorced (2006-2010 5-year est.); Foreign born: 0.0% (2006-2010 5-year est.); Ancestry (includes multiple ancestries): 51.2% German, 11.8% Italian, 6.0% English, 5.8% Austrian, 4.4% American (2006-2010 5-year est.).
**Economy:** Employment by occupation: 4.9% management, 2.7% professional, 10.3% services, 23.7% sales, 8.9% farming, 8.0% construction, 5.4% production (2006-2010 5-year est.).
**Income:** Per capita income: $20,297 (2006-2010 5-year est.); Median household income: $69,250 (2006-2010 5-year est.); Average household income: $70,088 (2006-2010 5-year est.); Percent of households with income of $100,000 or more: 8.7% (2006-2010 5-year est.); Poverty rate: 0.0% (2006-2010 5-year est.).
**Education:** Percent of population age 25 and over with: High school diploma (including GED) or higher: 87.1% (2006-2010 5-year est.); Bachelor's degree or higher: 19.9% (2006-2010 5-year est.); Master's degree or higher: 9.0% (2006-2010 5-year est.).
**Housing:** Homeownership rate: 68.8% (2010); Median home value: $115,200 (2006-2010 5-year est.); Median contract rent: $588 per month (2006-2010 5-year est.); Median year structure built: before 1940 (2006-2010 5-year est.).
**Transportation:** Commute to work: 95.5% car, 0.0% public transportation, 0.0% walk, 4.5% work from home (2006-2010 5-year est.); Travel time to work: 59.8% less than 15 minutes, 18.2% 15 to 30 minutes, 7.0% 30 to 45 minutes, 7.5% 45 to 60 minutes, 7.5% 60 minutes or more (2006-2010 5-year est.)

**DALTON** (CDP). Covers a land area of 0.754 square miles and a water area of 0 square miles. Located at 42.54° N. Lat; 77.95° W. Long. Elevation is 1,342 feet.
**Population:** n/a (1990); n/a (2000); 362 (2010); Density: 479.6 persons per square mile (2010); Race: 97.8% White, 0.6% Black, 0.0% Asian, 0.0% American Indian/Alaska Native, 0.0% Native Hawaiian/Other Pacific Islander, 1.6% Other, 1.1% Hispanic of any race (2010); Average household size: 2.40 (2010); Median age: 43.3 (2010); Males per 100 females: 102.2 (2010); Marriage status: 16.5% never married, 57.1% now married, 22.8% widowed, 3.5% divorced (2006-2010 5-year est.); Foreign born: 1.6% (2006-2010 5-year est.); Ancestry (includes multiple ancestries): 51.2% English, 39.8% German, 14.3% Irish, 6.8% Dutch, 6.8% Italian (2006-2010 5-year est.).
**Economy:** Employment by occupation: 17.1% management, 0.0% professional, 10.3% services, 0.0% sales, 0.0% farming, 15.4% construction, 2.6% production (2006-2010 5-year est.).
**Income:** Per capita income: $23,138 (2006-2010 5-year est.); Median household income: $47,981 (2006-2010 5-year est.); Average household income: $53,074 (2006-2010 5-year est.); Percent of households with income of $100,000 or more: 7.9% (2006-2010 5-year est.); Poverty rate: 6.3% (2006-2010 5-year est.).
**Education:** Percent of population age 25 and over with: High school diploma (including GED) or higher: 82.6% (2006-2010 5-year est.); Bachelor's degree or higher: 17.4% (2006-2010 5-year est.); Master's degree or higher: 5.5% (2006-2010 5-year est.).
**Housing:** Homeownership rate: 84.8% (2010); Median home value: $69,500 (2006-2010 5-year est.); Median contract rent: $520 per month (2006-2010 5-year est.); Median year structure built: before 1940 (2006-2010 5-year est.).
**Transportation:** Commute to work: 92.3% car, 0.0% public transportation, 7.7% walk, 0.0% work from home (2006-2010 5-year est.); Travel time to work: 43.6% less than 15 minutes, 28.2% 15 to 30 minutes, 4.3% 30 to 45 minutes, 4.3% 45 to 60 minutes, 19.7% 60 minutes or more (2006-2010 5-year est.)

**DANSVILLE** (village). Covers a land area of 2.607 square miles and a water area of 0 square miles. Located at 42.56° N. Lat; 77.69° W. Long. Elevation is 705 feet.
**History:** Clara Barton founded (1881) first local chapter of the American Red Cross here. Settled 1795, incorporated 1845.
**Population:** 5,039 (1990); 4,832 (2000); 4,719 (2010); Density: 1,809.7 persons per square mile (2010); Race: 95.8% White, 1.0% Black, 0.8% Asian, 0.3% American Indian/Alaska Native, 0.0% Native Hawaiian/Other Pacific Islander, 2.1% Other, 2.2% Hispanic of any race (2010); Average household size: 2.34 (2010); Median age: 40.1 (2010); Males per 100

females: 89.2 (2010); Marriage status: 36.0% never married, 46.1% now married, 6.3% widowed, 11.6% divorced (2006-2010 5-year est.); Foreign born: 1.8% (2006-2010 5-year est.); Ancestry (includes multiple ancestries): 37.5% German, 20.9% Irish, 13.7% English, 9.1% Dutch, 7.7% Italian (2006-2010 5-year est.).
**Economy:** Single-family building permits issued: 0 (2011); Multi-family building permits issued: 0 (2011); Employment by occupation: 10.5% management, 0.8% professional, 10.6% services, 15.7% sales, 10.2% farming, 9.4% construction, 8.4% production (2006-2010 5-year est.).
**Income:** Per capita income: $19,777 (2006-2010 5-year est.); Median household income: $33,750 (2006-2010 5-year est.); Average household income: $44,594 (2006-2010 5-year est.); Percent of households with income of $100,000 or more: 8.4% (2006-2010 5-year est.); Poverty rate: 20.4% (2006-2010 5-year est.).
**Education:** Percent of population age 25 and over with: High school diploma (including GED) or higher: 85.5% (2006-2010 5-year est.); Bachelor's degree or higher: 18.0% (2006-2010 5-year est.); Master's degree or higher: 6.0% (2006-2010 5-year est.).
### School District(s)
Dansville Central School District (PK-12)
   2009-10 Enrollment: 1,739 . . . . . . . . . . . . . . . . . (585) 335-4000
**Housing:** Homeownership rate: 60.9% (2010); Median home value: $81,900 (2006-2010 5-year est.); Median contract rent: $486 per month (2006-2010 5-year est.); Median year structure built: before 1940 (2006-2010 5-year est.).
**Hospitals:** Nicholas H. Noyes Memorial Hospital (72 beds)
**Safety:** Violent crime rate: 25.2 per 10,000 population; Property crime rate: 261.3 per 10,000 population (2010).
**Newspapers:** Genesee Country Express (Local news; Circulation 3,000); Genesee Way Shopper (Community news; Circulation 3,000)
**Transportation:** Commute to work: 87.4% car, 0.0% public transportation, 11.4% walk, 0.8% work from home (2006-2010 5-year est.); Travel time to work: 56.9% less than 15 minutes, 15.6% 15 to 30 minutes, 14.5% 30 to 45 minutes, 6.9% 45 to 60 minutes, 6.1% 60 minutes or more (2006-2010 5-year est.)
**Airports:** Dansville Municipal (general aviation)
**Additional Information Contacts**
Village of Dansville. . . . . . . . . . . . . . . . . . . . . . . . . . . . . (585) 335-5330
   http://dansvilleny.us

**EAST AVON** (CDP). Covers a land area of 1.309 square miles and a water area of 0 square miles. Located at 42.91° N. Lat; 77.70° W. Long. Elevation is 820 feet.
**Population:** n/a (1990); n/a (2000); 608 (2010); Density: 464.2 persons per square mile (2010); Race: 94.2% White, 0.2% Black, 1.8% Asian, 0.2% American Indian/Alaska Native, 0.2% Native Hawaiian/Other Pacific Islander, 3.4% Other, 2.3% Hispanic of any race (2010); Average household size: 2.55 (2010); Median age: 35.3 (2010); Males per 100 females: 102.0 (2010); Marriage status: 11.9% never married, 81.3% now married, 3.8% widowed, 3.0% divorced (2006-2010 5-year est.); Foreign born: 0.0% (2006-2010 5-year est.); Ancestry (includes multiple ancestries): 41.2% German, 36.9% Irish, 8.5% Hungarian, 5.9% English, 5.2% Italian (2006-2010 5-year est.).
**Economy:** Employment by occupation: 7.8% management, 9.2% professional, 3.1% services, 29.3% sales, 0.0% farming, 8.8% construction, 8.8% production (2006-2010 5-year est.).
**Income:** Per capita income: $19,834 (2006-2010 5-year est.); Median household income: $67,321 (2006-2010 5-year est.); Average household income: $64,936 (2006-2010 5-year est.); Percent of households with income of $100,000 or more: 14.4% (2006-2010 5-year est.); Poverty rate: 0.0% (2006-2010 5-year est.).
**Education:** Percent of population age 25 and over with: High school diploma (including GED) or higher: 87.7% (2006-2010 5-year est.); Bachelor's degree or higher: 35.2% (2006-2010 5-year est.); Master's degree or higher: 0.0% (2006-2010 5-year est.).
**Housing:** Homeownership rate: 82.7% (2010); Median home value: $126,000 (2006-2010 5-year est.); Median contract rent: n/a per month (2006-2010 5-year est.); Median year structure built: before 1940 (2006-2010 5-year est.).
**Transportation:** Commute to work: 97.1% car, 0.0% public transportation, 0.0% walk, 2.9% work from home (2006-2010 5-year est.); Travel time to work: 7.7% less than 15 minutes, 27.1% 15 to 30 minutes, 65.2% 30 to 45 minutes, 0.0% 45 to 60 minutes, 0.0% 60 minutes or more (2006-2010 5-year est.)

## FOWLERVILLE (CDP). Covers a land area of 0.901 square miles and a water area of 0 square miles. Located at 42.89° N. Lat; 77.84° W. Long. Elevation is 636 feet.

**Population:** n/a (1990); n/a (2000); 227 (2010); Density: 251.9 persons per square mile (2010); Race: 93.8% White, 1.3% Black, 3.1% Asian, 0.0% American Indian/Alaska Native, 0.0% Native Hawaiian/Other Pacific Islander, 1.8% Other, 2.2% Hispanic of any race (2010); Average household size: 2.70 (2010); Median age: 40.5 (2010); Males per 100 females: 110.2 (2010); Marriage status: 44.2% never married, 51.3% now married, 0.0% widowed, 4.5% divorced (2006-2010 5-year est.); Foreign born: 0.0% (2006-2010 5-year est.); Ancestry (includes multiple ancestries): 47.0% Italian, 28.7% Irish, 17.8% German, 17.0% Slovak, 13.0% Polish (2006-2010 5-year est.).
**Economy:** Employment by occupation: 17.4% management, 9.6% professional, 16.5% services, 16.5% sales, 0.0% farming, 0.0% construction, 0.0% production (2006-2010 5-year est.).
**Income:** Per capita income: $20,266 (2006-2010 5-year est.); Median household income: $81,354 (2006-2010 5-year est.); Average household income: $69,087 (2006-2010 5-year est.); Percent of households with income of $100,000 or more: 26.1% (2006-2010 5-year est.); Poverty rate: 4.5% (2006-2010 5-year est.).
**Education:** Percent of population age 25 and over with: High school diploma (including GED) or higher: 100.0% (2006-2010 5-year est.); Bachelor's degree or higher: 39.8% (2006-2010 5-year est.); Master's degree or higher: 33.8% (2006-2010 5-year est.).
**Housing:** Homeownership rate: 77.4% (2010); Median home value: $112,500 (2006-2010 5-year est.); Median contract rent: n/a per month (2006-2010 5-year est.); Median year structure built: before 1940 (2006-2010 5-year est.).
**Transportation:** Commute to work: 82.6% car, 0.0% public transportation, 17.4% walk, 0.0% work from home (2006-2010 5-year est.); Travel time to work: 33.9% less than 15 minutes, 47.0% 15 to 30 minutes, 19.1% 30 to 45 minutes, 0.0% 45 to 60 minutes, 0.0% 60 minutes or more (2006-2010 5-year est.)

## GENESEO (village). County seat. Covers a land area of 2.838 square miles and a water area of 0 square miles. Located at 42.79° N. Lat; 77.80° W. Long. Elevation is 771 feet.

**History:** Major salt mine cave-in and diversion of surface drainage into subterranean channels occurred in 1995. Estates of the Wadsworth family, northeast and south of village. English-style Genesee Valley Hunt each fall. Seat of State University of N.Y. College at Geneseo. Settled c.1790, Incorporated 1832.
**Population:** 7,225 (1990); 7,579 (2000); 8,031 (2010); Density: 2,828.9 persons per square mile (2010); Race: 88.8% White, 2.3% Black, 5.3% Asian, 0.2% American Indian/Alaska Native, 0.0% Native Hawaiian/Other Pacific Islander, 3.4% Other, 3.9% Hispanic of any race (2010); Average household size: 2.50 (2010); Median age: 21.1 (2010); Males per 100 females: 81.5 (2010); Marriage status: 70.6% never married, 19.2% now married, 5.1% widowed, 5.0% divorced (2006-2010 5-year est.); Foreign born: 4.6% (2006-2010 5-year est.); Ancestry (includes multiple ancestries): 24.4% Irish, 20.3% German, 19.8% Italian, 14.3% English, 5.9% Polish (2006-2010 5-year est.).
**Economy:** Single-family building permits issued: 1 (2011); Multi-family building permits issued: 4 (2011); Employment by occupation: 8.2% management, 2.4% professional, 18.2% services, 22.2% sales, 6.3% farming, 3.3% construction, 0.0% production (2006-2010 5-year est.).
**Income:** Per capita income: $13,689 (2006-2010 5-year est.); Median household income: $34,387 (2006-2010 5-year est.); Average household income: $49,761 (2006-2010 5-year est.); Percent of households with income of $100,000 or more: 13.9% (2006-2010 5-year est.); Poverty rate: 44.2% (2006-2010 5-year est.).
**Education:** Percent of population age 25 and over with: High school diploma (including GED) or higher: 87.9% (2006-2010 5-year est.); Bachelor's degree or higher: 44.9% (2006-2010 5-year est.); Master's degree or higher: 22.3% (2006-2010 5-year est.).

### School District(s)
Geneseo Central School District (KG-12)
    2009-10 Enrollment: 910 . . . . . . . . . . . . . . . . . . . . . . (585) 243-3450

### Four-year College(s)
SUNY at Geneseo (Public)
    Fall 2010 Enrollment: 5,625 . . . . . . . . . . . . . . . . . . (585) 245-5211
    2011-12 Tuition: In-state $6,758; Out-of-state $15,808
**Housing:** Homeownership rate: 39.2% (2010); Median home value: $149,300 (2006-2010 5-year est.); Median contract rent: $585 per month

(2006-2010 5-year est.); Median year structure built: 1968 (2006-2010 5-year est.).
**Safety:** Violent crime rate: 0.0 per 10,000 population; Property crime rate: 165.4 per 10,000 population (2010).
**Newspapers:** Clarion (Local news; Circulation 2,500); Livingston County News (Community news; Circulation 6,200)
**Transportation:** Commute to work: 65.7% car, 0.0% public transportation, 31.9% walk, 1.9% work from home (2006-2010 5-year est.); Travel time to work: 55.0% less than 15 minutes, 21.3% 15 to 30 minutes, 17.7% 30 to 45 minutes, 5.2% 45 to 60 minutes, 0.7% 60 minutes or more (2006-2010 5-year est.)

### Additional Information Contacts
Livingston County Chamber of Commerce . . . . . . . . . . . . (585) 243-2222
    http://www.livingstoncountychamber.com
Village of Geneseo. . . . . . . . . . . . . . . . . . . . . . . . . . . . . (585) 243-1177
    http://www.geneseony.org

## GENESEO (town). Covers a land area of 43.944 square miles and a water area of 1.197 square miles. Located at 42.80° N. Lat; 77.77° W. Long. Elevation is 771 feet.

**History:** Geneseo is best known for its association with the Wadsworth family. They became the squires of the middle Genesee in 1790. Members of the family served as legislators at the state and national levels.
**Population:** 9,178 (1990); 9,654 (2000); 10,483 (2010); Density: 238.6 persons per square mile (2010); Race: 90.5% White, 2.0% Black, 4.3% Asian, 0.2% American Indian/Alaska Native, 0.0% Native Hawaiian/Other Pacific Islander, 3.0% Other, 3.4% Hispanic of any race (2010); Average household size: 2.41 (2010); Median age: 21.7 (2010); Males per 100 females: 84.0 (2010); Marriage status: 59.6% never married, 28.5% now married, 5.7% widowed, 6.2% divorced (2006-2010 5-year est.); Foreign born: 4.6% (2006-2010 5-year est.); Ancestry (includes multiple ancestries): 25.2% Irish, 21.6% German, 19.3% Italian, 16.9% English, 6.1% Polish (2006-2010 5-year est.).
**Economy:** Single-family building permits issued: 11 (2011); Multi-family building permits issued: 53 (2011); Employment by occupation: 10.4% management, 3.4% professional, 14.9% services, 20.7% sales, 4.6% farming, 5.5% construction, 2.9% production (2006-2010 5-year est.).
**Income:** Per capita income: $18,657 (2006-2010 5-year est.); Median household income: $43,258 (2006-2010 5-year est.); Average household income: $61,030 (2006-2010 5-year est.); Percent of households with income of $100,000 or more: 19.4% (2006-2010 5-year est.); Poverty rate: 30.1% (2006-2010 5-year est.).
**Education:** Percent of population age 25 and over with: High school diploma (including GED) or higher: 91.5% (2006-2010 5-year est.); Bachelor's degree or higher: 41.7% (2006-2010 5-year est.); Master's degree or higher: 19.0% (2006-2010 5-year est.).

### School District(s)
Geneseo Central School District (KG-12)
    2009-10 Enrollment: 910 . . . . . . . . . . . . . . . . . . . . . . (585) 243-3450

### Four-year College(s)
SUNY at Geneseo (Public)
    Fall 2010 Enrollment: 5,625 . . . . . . . . . . . . . . . . . . (585) 245-5211
    2011-12 Tuition: In-state $6,758; Out-of-state $15,808
**Housing:** Homeownership rate: 50.6% (2010); Median home value: $156,100 (2006-2010 5-year est.); Median contract rent: $604 per month (2006-2010 5-year est.); Median year structure built: 1966 (2006-2010 5-year est.).
**Newspapers:** Clarion (Local news; Circulation 2,500); Livingston County News (Community news; Circulation 6,200)
**Transportation:** Commute to work: 73.6% car, 0.0% public transportation, 23.2% walk, 2.8% work from home (2006-2010 5-year est.); Travel time to work: 48.9% less than 15 minutes, 21.4% 15 to 30 minutes, 22.6% 30 to 45 minutes, 5.9% 45 to 60 minutes, 1.2% 60 minutes or more (2006-2010 5-year est.)

### Additional Information Contacts
Town of Geneseo. . . . . . . . . . . . . . . . . . . . . . . . . . . . . . (585) 991-5000
    http://www.geneseony.org

## GREIGSVILLE (CDP). Covers a land area of 0.710 square miles and a water area of 0 square miles. Located at 42.83° N. Lat; 77.90° W. Long. Elevation is 751 feet.

**Population:** n/a (1990); n/a (2000); 209 (2010); Density: 294.2 persons per square mile (2010); Race: 96.7% White, 1.4% Black, 0.0% Asian, 0.0% American Indian/Alaska Native, 0.0% Native Hawaiian/Other Pacific Islander, 1.9% Other, 3.3% Hispanic of any race (2010); Average household size: 2.58 (2010); Median age: 35.3 (2010); Males per 100 females: 104.9 (2010); Marriage status: 18.8% never married, 0.0% now married, 27.1% widowed, 54.2% divorced (2006-2010 5-year est.); Foreign born: 0.0% (2006-2010 5-year est.); Ancestry (includes multiple ancestries): 23.2% Italian, 16.1% German, 16.1% English (2006-2010 5-year est.).

**Economy:** Employment by occupation: 0.0% management, 0.0% professional, 0.0% services, 22.9% sales, 0.0% farming, 25.7% construction, 0.0% production (2006-2010 5-year est.).

**Income:** Per capita income: $36,588 (2006-2010 5-year est.); Median household income: $58,056 (2006-2010 5-year est.); Average household income: $66,103 (2006-2010 5-year est.); Percent of households with income of $100,000 or more: 26.7% (2006-2010 5-year est.); Poverty rate: 0.0% (2006-2010 5-year est.).

**Education:** Percent of population age 25 and over with: High school diploma (including GED) or higher: 100.0% (2006-2010 5-year est.); Bachelor's degree or higher: 0.0% (2006-2010 5-year est.); Master's degree or higher: 0.0% (2006-2010 5-year est.).

**Housing:** Homeownership rate: 69.1% (2010); Median home value: $76,800 (2006-2010 5-year est.); Median contract rent: n/a per month (2006-2010 5-year est.); Median year structure built: before 1940 (2006-2010 5-year est.).

**Transportation:** Commute to work: 77.1% car, 0.0% public transportation, 0.0% walk, 22.9% work from home (2006-2010 5-year est.); Travel time to work: 33.3% less than 15 minutes, 33.3% 15 to 30 minutes, 0.0% 30 to 45 minutes, 33.3% 45 to 60 minutes, 0.0% 60 minutes or more (2006-2010 5-year est.)

## GROVELAND (town). Covers a land area of 39.128 square miles and a water area of 0.724 square miles. Located at 42.70° N. Lat; 77.76° W. Long. Elevation is 614 feet.

**Population:** 3,190 (1990); 3,853 (2000); 3,249 (2010); Density: 83.0 persons per square mile (2010); Race: 67.5% White, 27.5% Black, 0.6% Asian, 0.6% American Indian/Alaska Native, 0.2% Native Hawaiian/Other Pacific Islander, 3.6% Other, 9.5% Hispanic of any race (2010); Average household size: 2.42 (2010); Median age: 39.9 (2010); Males per 100 females: 334.9 (2010); Marriage status: 49.9% never married, 34.7% now married, 2.7% widowed, 12.7% divorced (2006-2010 5-year est.); Foreign born: 5.2% (2006-2010 5-year est.); Ancestry (includes multiple ancestries): 16.4% German, 15.9% Irish, 8.7% Italian, 8.1% English, 3.9% African (2006-2010 5-year est.).

**Economy:** Single-family building permits issued: 1 (2011); Multi-family building permits issued: 0 (2011); Employment by occupation: 14.1% management, 1.0% professional, 9.7% services, 14.7% sales, 6.6% farming, 14.1% construction, 6.1% production (2006-2010 5-year est.).

**Income:** Per capita income: $12,923 (2006-2010 5-year est.); Median household income: $61,397 (2006-2010 5-year est.); Average household income: $79,737 (2006-2010 5-year est.); Percent of households with income of $100,000 or more: 22.8% (2006-2010 5-year est.); Poverty rate: 9.6% (2006-2010 5-year est.).

**Education:** Percent of population age 25 and over with: High school diploma (including GED) or higher: 75.7% (2006-2010 5-year est.); Bachelor's degree or higher: 14.0% (2006-2010 5-year est.); Master's degree or higher: 5.0% (2006-2010 5-year est.).

**Housing:** Homeownership rate: 73.8% (2010); Median home value: $149,400 (2006-2010 5-year est.); Median contract rent: $522 per month (2006-2010 5-year est.); Median year structure built: 1963 (2006-2010 5-year est.).

**Transportation:** Commute to work: 93.0% car, 0.0% public transportation, 3.6% walk, 2.6% work from home (2006-2010 5-year est.); Travel time to work: 19.3% less than 15 minutes, 39.1% 15 to 30 minutes, 18.9% 30 to 45 minutes, 18.7% 45 to 60 minutes, 3.9% 60 minutes or more (2006-2010 5-year est.)

## GROVELAND STATION (CDP). Covers a land area of 0.586 square miles and a water area of 0 square miles. Located at 42.66° N. Lat; 77.76° W. Long. Elevation is 614 feet.

**Population:** n/a (1990); n/a (2000); 281 (2010); Density: 479.2 persons per square mile (2010); Race: 95.4% White, 0.0% Black, 2.5% Asian, 0.7% American Indian/Alaska Native, 0.0% Native Hawaiian/Other Pacific Islander, 1.4% Other, 1.4% Hispanic of any race (2010); Average household size: 2.65 (2010); Median age: 40.9 (2010); Males per 100 females: 109.7 (2010); Marriage status: 24.0% never married, 62.0% now married, 3.0% widowed, 11.0% divorced (2006-2010 5-year est.); Foreign born: 0.0% (2006-2010 5-year est.); Ancestry (includes multiple

ancestries): 38.5% Irish, 23.5% German, 11.5% Italian, 11.5% English, 10.7% American (2006-2010 5-year est.).

**Economy:** Employment by occupation: 13.5% management, 0.0% professional, 6.3% services, 18.3% sales, 8.7% farming, 7.9% construction, 13.5% production (2006-2010 5-year est.).

**Income:** Per capita income: $20,519 (2006-2010 5-year est.); Median household income: $49,792 (2006-2010 5-year est.); Average household income: $51,126 (2006-2010 5-year est.); Percent of households with income of $100,000 or more: 0.0% (2006-2010 5-year est.); Poverty rate: 1.7% (2006-2010 5-year est.).

**Education:** Percent of population age 25 and over with: High school diploma (including GED) or higher: 87.5% (2006-2010 5-year est.); Bachelor's degree or higher: 21.4% (2006-2010 5-year est.); Master's degree or higher: 1.8% (2006-2010 5-year est.).

**Housing:** Homeownership rate: 81.1% (2010); Median home value: $87,100 (2006-2010 5-year est.); Median contract rent: $475 per month (2006-2010 5-year est.); Median year structure built: before 1940 (2006-2010 5-year est.).

**Transportation:** Commute to work: 100.0% car, 0.0% public transportation, 0.0% walk, 0.0% work from home (2006-2010 5-year est.); Travel time to work: 7.4% less than 15 minutes, 54.9% 15 to 30 minutes, 10.7% 30 to 45 minutes, 18.9% 45 to 60 minutes, 8.2% 60 minutes or more (2006-2010 5-year est.)

## HEMLOCK (CDP). Covers a land area of 1.862 square miles and a water area of 0 square miles. Located at 42.79° N. Lat; 77.60° W. Long. Elevation is 909 feet.

**Population:** n/a (1990); n/a (2000); 557 (2010); Density: 299.0 persons per square mile (2010); Race: 94.8% White, 0.9% Black, 0.4% Asian, 0.2% American Indian/Alaska Native, 0.2% Native Hawaiian/Other Pacific Islander, 3.5% Other, 1.1% Hispanic of any race (2010); Average household size: 2.67 (2010); Median age: 38.0 (2010); Males per 100 females: 106.3 (2010); Marriage status: 10.8% never married, 58.2% now married, 23.7% widowed, 7.3% divorced (2006-2010 5-year est.); Foreign born: 0.0% (2006-2010 5-year est.); Ancestry (includes multiple ancestries): 16.2% German, 15.8% English, 8.3% American, 6.7% Scottish, 4.7% Irish (2006-2010 5-year est.).

**Economy:** Employment by occupation: 8.3% management, 0.0% professional, 4.9% services, 0.0% sales, 14.1% farming, 19.4% construction, 6.8% production (2006-2010 5-year est.).

**Income:** Per capita income: $35,414 (2006-2010 5-year est.); Median household income: $44,833 (2006-2010 5-year est.); Average household income: $64,891 (2006-2010 5-year est.); Percent of households with income of $100,000 or more: 15.4% (2006-2010 5-year est.); Poverty rate: 0.0% (2006-2010 5-year est.).

**Education:** Percent of population age 25 and over with: High school diploma (including GED) or higher: 93.1% (2006-2010 5-year est.); Bachelor's degree or higher: 30.3% (2006-2010 5-year est.); Master's degree or higher: 30.3% (2006-2010 5-year est.).

**Housing:** Homeownership rate: 80.3% (2010); Median home value: $88,000 (2006-2010 5-year est.); Median contract rent: n/a per month (2006-2010 5-year est.); Median year structure built: 1946 (2006-2010 5-year est.).

**Transportation:** Commute to work: 66.1% car, 7.7% public transportation, 26.2% walk, 0.0% work from home (2006-2010 5-year est.); Travel time to work: 64.5% less than 15 minutes, 27.9% 15 to 30 minutes, 0.0% 30 to 45 minutes, 0.0% 45 to 60 minutes, 7.7% 60 minutes or more (2006-2010 5-year est.)

## HUNT (CDP). Covers a land area of 0.119 square miles and a water area of 0 square miles. Located at 42.54° N. Lat; 77.99° W. Long. Elevation is 1,342 feet.

**Population:** n/a (1990); n/a (2000); 78 (2010); Density: 655.0 persons per square mile (2010); Race: 94.9% White, 3.8% Black, 0.0% Asian, 0.0% American Indian/Alaska Native, 0.0% Native Hawaiian/Other Pacific Islander, 1.3% Other, 2.6% Hispanic of any race (2010); Average household size: 2.60 (2010); Median age: 42.7 (2010); Males per 100 females: 85.7 (2010); Marriage status: 25.0% never married, 44.2% now married, 5.8% widowed, 25.0% divorced (2006-2010 5-year est.); Foreign born: 0.0% (2006-2010 5-year est.); Ancestry (includes multiple ancestries): 26.8% German, 12.5% Polish, 10.7% Irish, 7.1% Italian, 7.1% Scottish (2006-2010 5-year est.).

**Economy:** Employment by occupation: 0.0% management, 0.0% professional, 44.0% services, 0.0% sales, 0.0% farming, 40.0% construction, 12.0% production (2006-2010 5-year est.).

**Income:** Per capita income: $18,959 (2006-2010 5-year est.); Median household income: $44,375 (2006-2010 5-year est.); Average household income: $45,196 (2006-2010 5-year est.); Percent of households with income of $100,000 or more: 0.0% (2006-2010 5-year est.); Poverty rate: 7.1% (2006-2010 5-year est.).
**Education:** Percent of population age 25 and over with: High school diploma (including GED) or higher: 89.7% (2006-2010 5-year est.); Bachelor's degree or higher: 0.0% (2006-2010 5-year est.); Master's degree or higher: 0.0% (2006-2010 5-year est.).
**Housing:** Homeownership rate: 80.0% (2010); Median home value: $67,500 (2006-2010 5-year est.); Median contract rent: n/a per month (2006-2010 5-year est.); Median year structure built: before 1940 (2006-2010 5-year est.).
**Transportation:** Commute to work: 72.0% car, 12.0% public transportation, 0.0% walk, 16.0% work from home (2006-2010 5-year est.); Travel time to work: 19.0% less than 15 minutes, 33.3% 15 to 30 minutes, 14.3% 30 to 45 minutes, 0.0% 45 to 60 minutes, 33.3% 60 minutes or more (2006-2010 5-year est.)

**KYSORVILLE** (CDP). Covers a land area of 0.826 square miles and a water area of 0 square miles. Located at 42.65° N. Lat; 77.79° W. Long. Elevation is 623 feet.
**Population:** n/a (1990); n/a (2000); 110 (2010); Density: 133.1 persons per square mile (2010); Race: 95.5% White, 4.5% Black, 0.0% Asian, 0.0% American Indian/Alaska Native, 0.0% Native Hawaiian/Other Pacific Islander, 0.0% Other, 0.0% Hispanic of any race (2010); Average household size: 2.56 (2010); Median age: 34.0 (2010); Males per 100 females: 96.4 (2010); Marriage status: 30.4% never married, 60.8% now married, 0.0% widowed, 8.9% divorced (2006-2010 5-year est.); Foreign born: 5.2% (2006-2010 5-year est.); Ancestry (includes multiple ancestries): 49.0% German, 16.7% American, 14.6% Irish, 8.3% English, 6.3% Italian (2006-2010 5-year est.).
**Economy:** Employment by occupation: 8.5% management, 13.6% professional, 8.5% services, 25.4% sales, 3.4% farming, 6.8% construction, 0.0% production (2006-2010 5-year est.).
**Income:** Per capita income: $23,774 (2006-2010 5-year est.); Median household income: $57,813 (2006-2010 5-year est.); Average household income: $54,160 (2006-2010 5-year est.); Percent of households with income of $100,000 or more: 7.0% (2006-2010 5-year est.); Poverty rate: 21.9% (2006-2010 5-year est.).
**Education:** Percent of population age 25 and over with: High school diploma (including GED) or higher: 83.8% (2006-2010 5-year est.); Bachelor's degree or higher: 11.8% (2006-2010 5-year est.); Master's degree or higher: 7.4% (2006-2010 5-year est.).
**Housing:** Homeownership rate: 74.4% (2010); Median home value: $77,700 (2006-2010 5-year est.); Median contract rent: $505 per month (2006-2010 5-year est.); Median year structure built: 1977 (2006-2010 5-year est.).
**Transportation:** Commute to work: 100.0% car, 0.0% public transportation, 0.0% walk, 0.0% work from home (2006-2010 5-year est.); Travel time to work: 25.4% less than 15 minutes, 33.9% 15 to 30 minutes, 18.6% 30 to 45 minutes, 0.0% 45 to 60 minutes, 22.0% 60 minutes or more (2006-2010 5-year est.)

**LAKEVILLE** (CDP). Covers a land area of 0.667 square miles and a water area of 0 square miles. Located at 42.83° N. Lat; 77.70° W. Long. Elevation is 823 feet.
**Population:** n/a (1990); n/a (2000); 756 (2010); Density: 1,132.8 persons per square mile (2010); Race: 91.9% White, 0.3% Black, 2.4% Asian, 1.1% American Indian/Alaska Native, 0.0% Native Hawaiian/Other Pacific Islander, 4.3% Other, 0.9% Hispanic of any race (2010); Average household size: 2.44 (2010); Median age: 35.8 (2010); Males per 100 females: 84.8 (2010); Marriage status: 19.9% never married, 64.5% now married, 9.8% widowed, 5.8% divorced (2006-2010 5-year est.); Foreign born: 0.0% (2006-2010 5-year est.); Ancestry (includes multiple ancestries): 38.4% German, 35.9% Irish, 12.5% Polish, 12.0% American, 8.8% French (2006-2010 5-year est.).
**Economy:** Employment by occupation: 0.0% management, 5.2% professional, 7.0% services, 29.3% sales, 7.9% farming, 29.3% construction, 10.5% production (2006-2010 5-year est.).
**Income:** Per capita income: $18,916 (2006-2010 5-year est.); Median household income: $48,200 (2006-2010 5-year est.); Average household income: $56,843 (2006-2010 5-year est.); Percent of households with income of $100,000 or more: 30.2% (2006-2010 5-year est.); Poverty rate: 8.1% (2006-2010 5-year est.).

**Education:** Percent of population age 25 and over with: High school diploma (including GED) or higher: 87.2% (2006-2010 5-year est.); Bachelor's degree or higher: 11.3% (2006-2010 5-year est.); Master's degree or higher: 11.3% (2006-2010 5-year est.).
**Housing:** Homeownership rate: 52.8% (2010); Median home value: $111,500 (2006-2010 5-year est.); Median contract rent: $219 per month (2006-2010 5-year est.); Median year structure built: 1985 (2006-2010 5-year est.).
**Transportation:** Commute to work: 92.1% car, 0.0% public transportation, 0.0% walk, 7.9% work from home (2006-2010 5-year est.); Travel time to work: 32.2% less than 15 minutes, 19.4% 15 to 30 minutes, 48.3% 30 to 45 minutes, 0.0% 45 to 60 minutes, 0.0% 60 minutes or more (2006-2010 5-year est.)

**LEICESTER** (village). Covers a land area of 0.367 square miles and a water area of 0 square miles. Located at 42.77° N. Lat; 77.89° W. Long. Elevation is 650 feet.
**Population:** 502 (1990); 469 (2000); 468 (2010); Density: 1,274.4 persons per square mile (2010); Race: 97.0% White, 0.2% Black, 1.3% Asian, 0.0% American Indian/Alaska Native, 0.0% Native Hawaiian/Other Pacific Islander, 1.5% Other, 0.4% Hispanic of any race (2010); Average household size: 2.42 (2010); Median age: 41.9 (2010); Males per 100 females: 89.5 (2010); Marriage status: 21.6% never married, 62.9% now married, 7.1% widowed, 8.4% divorced (2006-2010 5-year est.); Foreign born: 3.4% (2006-2010 5-year est.); Ancestry (includes multiple ancestries): 26.7% Italian, 23.6% German, 18.2% English, 14.4% Irish, 7.4% Scottish (2006-2010 5-year est.).
**Economy:** Single-family building permits issued: 2 (2011); Multi-family building permits issued: 0 (2011); Employment by occupation: 4.8% management, 3.0% professional, 10.4% services, 15.7% sales, 3.9% farming, 11.3% construction, 9.1% production (2006-2010 5-year est.).
**Income:** Per capita income: $24,155 (2006-2010 5-year est.); Median household income: $55,278 (2006-2010 5-year est.); Average household income: $59,871 (2006-2010 5-year est.); Percent of households with income of $100,000 or more: 15.3% (2006-2010 5-year est.); Poverty rate: 10.0% (2006-2010 5-year est.).
**Education:** Percent of population age 25 and over with: High school diploma (including GED) or higher: 88.6% (2006-2010 5-year est.); Bachelor's degree or higher: 14.9% (2006-2010 5-year est.); Master's degree or higher: 8.2% (2006-2010 5-year est.).
**Housing:** Homeownership rate: 75.1% (2010); Median home value: $103,500 (2006-2010 5-year est.); Median contract rent: $564 per month (2006-2010 5-year est.); Median year structure built: 1962 (2006-2010 5-year est.).
**Transportation:** Commute to work: 99.1% car, 0.0% public transportation, 0.0% walk, 0.9% work from home (2006-2010 5-year est.); Travel time to work: 31.1% less than 15 minutes, 31.5% 15 to 30 minutes, 26.0% 30 to 45 minutes, 10.0% 45 to 60 minutes, 1.4% 60 minutes or more (2006-2010 5-year est.)

**LEICESTER** (town). Covers a land area of 33.929 square miles and a water area of 0.004 square miles. Located at 42.76° N. Lat; 77.90° W. Long. Elevation is 650 feet.
**Population:** 2,223 (1990); 2,287 (2000); 2,200 (2010); Density: 64.8 persons per square mile (2010); Race: 96.9% White, 0.4% Black, 0.7% Asian, 0.2% American Indian/Alaska Native, 0.0% Native Hawaiian/Other Pacific Islander, 1.8% Other, 2.0% Hispanic of any race (2010); Average household size: 2.42 (2010); Median age: 43.1 (2010); Males per 100 females: 98.9 (2010); Marriage status: 26.6% never married, 56.5% now married, 4.1% widowed, 12.8% divorced (2006-2010 5-year est.); Foreign born: 1.0% (2006-2010 5-year est.); Ancestry (includes multiple ancestries): 31.3% German, 22.5% Irish, 18.7% Italian, 16.6% English, 6.3% American (2006-2010 5-year est.).
**Economy:** Single-family building permits issued: 1 (2011); Multi-family building permits issued: 0 (2011); Employment by occupation: 9.6% management, 2.7% professional, 10.1% services, 16.9% sales, 5.0% farming, 18.2% construction, 9.7% production (2006-2010 5-year est.).
**Income:** Per capita income: $23,709 (2006-2010 5-year est.); Median household income: $55,400 (2006-2010 5-year est.); Average household income: $59,806 (2006-2010 5-year est.); Percent of households with income of $100,000 or more: 15.1% (2006-2010 5-year est.); Poverty rate: 9.4% (2006-2010 5-year est.).
**Education:** Percent of population age 25 and over with: High school diploma (including GED) or higher: 88.4% (2006-2010 5-year est.);

Bachelor's degree or higher: 18.2% (2006-2010 5-year est.); Master's degree or higher: 9.0% (2006-2010 5-year est.).
**Housing:** Homeownership rate: 80.9% (2010); Median home value: $106,300 (2006-2010 5-year est.); Median contract rent: $520 per month (2006-2010 5-year est.); Median year structure built: 1970 (2006-2010 5-year est.).
**Transportation:** Commute to work: 92.6% car, 0.0% public transportation, 1.0% walk, 4.1% work from home (2006-2010 5-year est.); Travel time to work: 44.7% less than 15 minutes, 27.6% 15 to 30 minutes, 13.1% 30 to 45 minutes, 8.8% 45 to 60 minutes, 5.8% 60 minutes or more (2006-2010 5-year est.).

**LIMA** (village). Covers a land area of 1.345 square miles and a water area of 0 square miles. Located at 42.90° N. Lat; 77.61° W. Long. Elevation is 827 feet.
**Population:** 2,165 (1990); 2,459 (2000); 2,139 (2010); Density: 1,589.4 persons per square mile (2010); Race: 95.7% White, 0.6% Black, 1.6% Asian, 0.3% American Indian/Alaska Native, 0.0% Native Hawaiian/Other Pacific Islander, 1.8% Other, 2.5% Hispanic of any race (2010); Average household size: 2.49 (2010); Median age: 38.3 (2010); Males per 100 females: 93.1 (2010); Marriage status: 35.2% never married, 56.6% now married, 1.6% widowed, 6.5% divorced (2006-2010 5-year est.); Foreign born: 3.8% (2006-2010 5-year est.); Ancestry (includes multiple ancestries): 28.1% German, 26.0% Irish, 19.3% English, 10.3% Italian, 6.1% Polish (2006-2010 5-year est.).
**Economy:** Single-family building permits issued: 4 (2011); Multi-family building permits issued: 0 (2011); Employment by occupation: 4.0% management, 4.1% professional, 11.0% services, 21.7% sales, 1.9% farming, 6.8% construction, 6.7% production (2006-2010 5-year est.).
**Income:** Per capita income: $21,254 (2006-2010 5-year est.); Median household income: $47,120 (2006-2010 5-year est.); Average household income: $57,731 (2006-2010 5-year est.); Percent of households with income of $100,000 or more: 14.7% (2006-2010 5-year est.); Poverty rate: 9.5% (2006-2010 5-year est.).
**Education:** Percent of population age 25 and over with: High school diploma (including GED) or higher: 86.7% (2006-2010 5-year est.); Bachelor's degree or higher: 23.8% (2006-2010 5-year est.); Master's degree or higher: 8.3% (2006-2010 5-year est.).
**School District(s)**
Honeoye Falls-Lima Central School District (KG-12)
    2009-10 Enrollment: 2,582 . . . . . . . . . . . . . . . . . . . . (585) 624-7010
**Housing:** Homeownership rate: 66.6% (2010); Median home value: $131,200 (2006-2010 5-year est.); Median contract rent: $515 per month (2006-2010 5-year est.); Median year structure built: 1961 (2006-2010 5-year est.).
**Transportation:** Commute to work: 82.1% car, 0.0% public transportation, 13.5% walk, 4.5% work from home (2006-2010 5-year est.); Travel time to work: 35.9% less than 15 minutes, 34.6% 15 to 30 minutes, 23.3% 30 to 45 minutes, 5.4% 45 to 60 minutes, 0.7% 60 minutes or more (2006-2010 5-year est.).

**LIMA** (town). Covers a land area of 31.890 square miles and a water area of 0.052 square miles. Located at 42.89° N. Lat; 77.60° W. Long. Elevation is 827 feet.
**Population:** 4,187 (1990); 4,541 (2000); 4,305 (2010); Density: 135.0 persons per square mile (2010); Race: 96.8% White, 0.6% Black, 1.0% Asian, 0.3% American Indian/Alaska Native, 0.0% Native Hawaiian/Other Pacific Islander, 1.3% Other, 1.7% Hispanic of any race (2010); Average household size: 2.48 (2010); Median age: 41.9 (2010); Males per 100 females: 97.6 (2010); Marriage status: 30.5% never married, 59.3% now married, 3.3% widowed, 6.9% divorced (2006-2010 5-year est.); Foreign born: 3.2% (2006-2010 5-year est.); Ancestry (includes multiple ancestries): 29.8% German, 25.0% Irish, 19.1% English, 8.7% Italian, 5.0% Polish (2006-2010 5-year est.).
**Economy:** Single-family building permits issued: 4 (2011); Multi-family building permits issued: 0 (2011); Employment by occupation: 9.1% management, 3.2% professional, 7.8% services, 19.2% sales, 0.9% farming, 11.5% construction, 8.5% production (2006-2010 5-year est.).
**Income:** Per capita income: $24,727 (2006-2010 5-year est.); Median household income: $55,500 (2006-2010 5-year est.); Average household income: $64,035 (2006-2010 5-year est.); Percent of households with income of $100,000 or more: 19.2% (2006-2010 5-year est.); Poverty rate: 6.2% (2006-2010 5-year est.).
**Education:** Percent of population age 25 and over with: High school diploma (including GED) or higher: 90.0% (2006-2010 5-year est.);

Bachelor's degree or higher: 24.2% (2006-2010 5-year est.); Master's degree or higher: 7.4% (2006-2010 5-year est.).
**School District(s)**
Honeoye Falls-Lima Central School District (KG-12)
    2009-10 Enrollment: 2,582 . . . . . . . . . . . . . . . . . . . . (585) 624-7010
**Housing:** Homeownership rate: 74.9% (2010); Median home value: $137,700 (2006-2010 5-year est.); Median contract rent: $514 per month (2006-2010 5-year est.); Median year structure built: 1969 (2006-2010 5-year est.).
**Transportation:** Commute to work: 89.6% car, 0.4% public transportation, 6.6% walk, 3.4% work from home (2006-2010 5-year est.); Travel time to work: 38.8% less than 15 minutes, 30.3% 15 to 30 minutes, 24.2% 30 to 45 minutes, 6.3% 45 to 60 minutes, 0.4% 60 minutes or more (2006-2010 5-year est.)

**LINWOOD** (CDP). Covers a land area of 0.928 square miles and a water area of 0 square miles. Located at 42.89° N. Lat; 77.94° W. Long. Elevation is 938 feet.
**Population:** n/a (1990); n/a (2000); 74 (2010); Density: 79.7 persons per square mile (2010); Race: 100.0% White, 0.0% Black, 0.0% Asian, 0.0% American Indian/Alaska Native, 0.0% Native Hawaiian/Other Pacific Islander, 0.0% Other, 0.0% Hispanic of any race (2010); Average household size: 2.74 (2010); Median age: 37.5 (2010); Males per 100 females: 100.0 (2010); Marriage status: 34.4% never married, 54.2% now married, 0.0% widowed, 11.5% divorced (2006-2010 5-year est.); Foreign born: 48.9% (2006-2010 5-year est.); Ancestry (includes multiple ancestries): 48.9% South African, 17.6% French, 12.2% English, 11.5% German, 6.1% Irish (2006-2010 5-year est.).
**Economy:** Employment by occupation: 18.3% management, 0.0% professional, 29.8% services, 22.9% sales, 0.0% farming, 8.4% construction, 0.0% production (2006-2010 5-year est.).
**Income:** Per capita income: $26,864 (2006-2010 5-year est.); Median household income: $90,250 (2006-2010 5-year est.); Average household income: $69,424 (2006-2010 5-year est.); Percent of households with income of $100,000 or more: 22.4% (2006-2010 5-year est.); Poverty rate: 0.0% (2006-2010 5-year est.).
**Education:** Percent of population age 25 and over with: High school diploma (including GED) or higher: 87.2% (2006-2010 5-year est.); Bachelor's degree or higher: 36.0% (2006-2010 5-year est.); Master's degree or higher: 0.0% (2006-2010 5-year est.).
**Housing:** Homeownership rate: 81.5% (2010); Median home value: $129,500 (2006-2010 5-year est.); Median contract rent: n/a per month (2006-2010 5-year est.); Median year structure built: before 1940 (2006-2010 5-year est.).
**Transportation:** Commute to work: 100.0% car, 0.0% public transportation, 0.0% walk, 0.0% work from home (2006-2010 5-year est.); Travel time to work: 9.2% less than 15 minutes, 70.2% 15 to 30 minutes, 12.2% 30 to 45 minutes, 8.4% 45 to 60 minutes, 0.0% 60 minutes or more (2006-2010 5-year est.)

**LIVONIA** (village). Covers a land area of 1.007 square miles and a water area of 0 square miles. Located at 42.82° N. Lat; 77.66° W. Long. Elevation is 1,033 feet.
**Population:** 1,434 (1990); 1,373 (2000); 1,409 (2010); Density: 1,399.2 persons per square mile (2010); Race: 99.1% White, 0.1% Black, 0.2% Asian, 0.1% American Indian/Alaska Native, 0.0% Native Hawaiian/Other Pacific Islander, 0.5% Other, 1.3% Hispanic of any race (2010); Average household size: 2.46 (2010); Median age: 37.8 (2010); Males per 100 females: 92.0 (2010); Marriage status: 28.7% never married, 52.3% now married, 5.0% widowed, 14.0% divorced (2006-2010 5-year est.); Foreign born: 1.4% (2006-2010 5-year est.); Ancestry (includes multiple ancestries): 32.5% Irish, 32.2% German, 18.1% English, 11.6% Italian, 8.9% American (2006-2010 5-year est.).
**Economy:** Single-family building permits issued: 0 (2011); Multi-family building permits issued: 10 (2011); Employment by occupation: 11.3% management, 6.3% professional, 6.4% services, 14.0% sales, 3.4% farming, 5.2% construction, 3.1% production (2006-2010 5-year est.).
**Income:** Per capita income: $23,937 (2006-2010 5-year est.); Median household income: $53,977 (2006-2010 5-year est.); Average household income: $61,657 (2006-2010 5-year est.); Percent of households with income of $100,000 or more: 15.6% (2006-2010 5-year est.); Poverty rate: 10.5% (2006-2010 5-year est.).
**Education:** Percent of population age 25 and over with: High school diploma (including GED) or higher: 94.8% (2006-2010 5-year est.);

Bachelor's degree or higher: 27.2% (2006-2010 5-year est.); Master's degree or higher: 12.8% (2006-2010 5-year est.).

**School District(s)**

Livonia Central School District (PK-12)

   2009-10 Enrollment: 1,915 . . . . . . . . . . . . . . . . . (585) 346-4000

**Housing:** Homeownership rate: 66.3% (2010); Median home value: $122,500 (2006-2010 5-year est.); Median contract rent: $534 per month (2006-2010 5-year est.); Median year structure built: 1949 (2006-2010 5-year est.).

**Transportation:** Commute to work: 90.6% car, 0.4% public transportation, 2.9% walk, 4.7% work from home (2006-2010 5-year est.); Travel time to work: 19.7% less than 15 minutes, 35.4% 15 to 30 minutes, 33.3% 30 to 45 minutes, 7.6% 45 to 60 minutes, 4.0% 60 minutes or more (2006-2010 5-year est.)

**LIVONIA** (town). Covers a land area of 38.261 square miles and a water area of 2.812 square miles. Located at 42.80° N. Lat; 77.65° W. Long. Elevation is 1,033 feet.

**Population:** 6,804 (1990); 7,286 (2000); 7,809 (2010); Density: 204.1 persons per square mile (2010); Race: 97.3% White, 0.6% Black, 0.5% Asian, 0.2% American Indian/Alaska Native, 0.0% Native Hawaiian/Other Pacific Islander, 1.4% Other, 0.9% Hispanic of any race (2010); Average household size: 2.53 (2010); Median age: 41.7 (2010); Males per 100 females: 95.4 (2010); Marriage status: 27.2% never married, 57.8% now married, 6.5% widowed, 8.5% divorced (2006-2010 5-year est.); Foreign born: 1.0% (2006-2010 5-year est.); Ancestry (includes multiple ancestries): 34.2% German, 27.9% Irish, 17.4% English, 13.8% Italian, 10.1% American (2006-2010 5-year est.).

**Economy:** Single-family building permits issued: 8 (2011); Multi-family building permits issued: 0 (2011); Employment by occupation: 9.5% management, 5.5% professional, 7.7% services, 17.6% sales, 5.0% farming, 12.2% construction, 7.0% production (2006-2010 5-year est.).

**Income:** Per capita income: $28,218 (2006-2010 5-year est.); Median household income: $59,568 (2006-2010 5-year est.); Average household income: $69,219 (2006-2010 5-year est.); Percent of households with income of $100,000 or more: 20.6% (2006-2010 5-year est.); Poverty rate: 5.2% (2006-2010 5-year est.).

**Education:** Percent of population age 25 and over with: High school diploma (including GED) or higher: 94.9% (2006-2010 5-year est.); Bachelor's degree or higher: 26.6% (2006-2010 5-year est.); Master's degree or higher: 14.1% (2006-2010 5-year est.).

**School District(s)**

Livonia Central School District (PK-12)

   2009-10 Enrollment: 1,915 . . . . . . . . . . . . . . . . . (585) 346-4000

**Housing:** Homeownership rate: 79.9% (2010); Median home value: $133,000 (2006-2010 5-year est.); Median contract rent: $630 per month (2006-2010 5-year est.); Median year structure built: 1973 (2006-2010 5-year est.).

**Transportation:** Commute to work: 91.9% car, 0.9% public transportation, 2.2% walk, 4.7% work from home (2006-2010 5-year est.); Travel time to work: 25.8% less than 15 minutes, 29.0% 15 to 30 minutes, 30.4% 30 to 45 minutes, 11.9% 45 to 60 minutes, 2.9% 60 minutes or more (2006-2010 5-year est.)

**LIVONIA CENTER** (CDP). Covers a land area of 0.816 square miles and a water area of 0 square miles. Located at 42.82° N. Lat; 77.64° W. Long. Elevation is 1,086 feet.

**Population:** n/a (1990); n/a (2000); 421 (2010); Density: 515.5 persons per square mile (2010); Race: 98.6% White, 1.0% Black, 0.0% Asian, 0.0% American Indian/Alaska Native, 0.0% Native Hawaiian/Other Pacific Islander, 0.4% Other, 0.5% Hispanic of any race (2010); Average household size: 2.45 (2010); Median age: 41.3 (2010); Males per 100 females: 94.9 (2010); Marriage status: 30.9% never married, 48.3% now married, 13.7% widowed, 7.1% divorced (2006-2010 5-year est.); Foreign born: 0.0% (2006-2010 5-year est.); Ancestry (includes multiple ancestries): 56.6% German, 39.8% Irish, 28.9% Dutch, 21.1% English, 19.3% Italian (2006-2010 5-year est.).

**Economy:** Employment by occupation: 0.0% management, 0.0% professional, 0.0% services, 47.7% sales, 0.0% farming, 18.1% construction, 4.9% production (2006-2010 5-year est.).

**Income:** Per capita income: $24,804 (2006-2010 5-year est.); Median household income: $44,949 (2006-2010 5-year est.); Average household income: $67,444 (2006-2010 5-year est.); Percent of households with income of $100,000 or more: 20.6% (2006-2010 5-year est.); Poverty rate: 0.0% (2006-2010 5-year est.).

**Education:** Percent of population age 25 and over with: High school diploma (including GED) or higher: 100.0% (2006-2010 5-year est.); Bachelor's degree or higher: 5.8% (2006-2010 5-year est.); Master's degree or higher: 0.0% (2006-2010 5-year est.).

**Housing:** Homeownership rate: 80.3% (2010); Median home value: $95,600 (2006-2010 5-year est.); Median contract rent: n/a per month (2006-2010 5-year est.); Median year structure built: before 1940 (2006-2010 5-year est.).

**Transportation:** Commute to work: 100.0% car, 0.0% public transportation, 0.0% walk, 0.0% work from home (2006-2010 5-year est.); Travel time to work: 19.4% less than 15 minutes, 11.3% 15 to 30 minutes, 26.6% 30 to 45 minutes, 26.6% 45 to 60 minutes, 16.1% 60 minutes or more (2006-2010 5-year est.)

**MOUNT MORRIS** (village). Covers a land area of 2.047 square miles and a water area of 0 square miles. Located at 42.72° N. Lat; 77.87° W. Long. Elevation is 630 feet.

**Population:** 3,102 (1990); 3,266 (2000); 2,986 (2010); Density: 1,458.3 persons per square mile (2010); Race: 92.5% White, 2.1% Black, 0.6% Asian, 0.6% American Indian/Alaska Native, 0.0% Native Hawaiian/Other Pacific Islander, 4.2% Other, 9.3% Hispanic of any race (2010); Average household size: 2.30 (2010); Median age: 39.2 (2010); Males per 100 females: 98.7 (2010); Marriage status: 22.9% never married, 45.6% now married, 13.7% widowed, 17.8% divorced (2006-2010 5-year est.); Foreign born: 1.1% (2006-2010 5-year est.); Ancestry (includes multiple ancestries): 38.8% German, 22.8% Italian, 17.4% Irish, 13.4% English, 5.4% Dutch (2006-2010 5-year est.).

**Economy:** Single-family building permits issued: 0 (2011); Multi-family building permits issued: 0 (2011); Employment by occupation: 11.6% management, 0.0% professional, 14.8% services, 15.7% sales, 2.6% farming, 18.8% construction, 12.9% production (2006-2010 5-year est.).

**Income:** Per capita income: $18,573 (2006-2010 5-year est.); Median household income: $42,813 (2006-2010 5-year est.); Average household income: $48,325 (2006-2010 5-year est.); Percent of households with income of $100,000 or more: 8.3% (2006-2010 5-year est.); Poverty rate: 24.2% (2006-2010 5-year est.).

**Education:** Percent of population age 25 and over with: High school diploma (including GED) or higher: 79.6% (2006-2010 5-year est.); Bachelor's degree or higher: 16.5% (2006-2010 5-year est.); Master's degree or higher: 6.6% (2006-2010 5-year est.).

**School District(s)**

Mount Morris Central School District (KG-12)

   2009-10 Enrollment: 492 . . . . . . . . . . . . . . . . . . (585) 658-2568

**Housing:** Homeownership rate: 57.6% (2010); Median home value: $71,100 (2006-2010 5-year est.); Median contract rent: $424 per month (2006-2010 5-year est.); Median year structure built: 1949 (2006-2010 5-year est.).

**Safety:** Violent crime rate: 17.8 per 10,000 population; Property crime rate: 363.8 per 10,000 population (2010).

**Transportation:** Commute to work: 91.4% car, 0.0% public transportation, 5.8% walk, 2.8% work from home (2006-2010 5-year est.); Travel time to work: 47.5% less than 15 minutes, 28.2% 15 to 30 minutes, 11.4% 30 to 45 minutes, 5.4% 45 to 60 minutes, 7.4% 60 minutes or more (2006-2010 5-year est.)

**Additional Information Contacts**

Village of Mount Morris . . . . . . . . . . . . . . . . . . (585) 658-4160

   http://www.mountmorrisny.com/government/village.asp

**MOUNT MORRIS** (town). Covers a land area of 50.205 square miles and a water area of 0.106 square miles. Located at 42.66° N. Lat; 77.90° W. Long. Elevation is 630 feet.

**Population:** 4,633 (1990); 4,567 (2000); 4,465 (2010); Density: 88.9 persons per square mile (2010); Race: 93.5% White, 1.8% Black, 0.5% Asian, 0.6% American Indian/Alaska Native, 0.0% Native Hawaiian/Other Pacific Islander, 3.6% Other, 8.0% Hispanic of any race (2010); Average household size: 2.33 (2010); Median age: 43.5 (2010); Males per 100 females: 95.7 (2010); Marriage status: 20.9% never married, 51.3% now married, 12.1% widowed, 15.7% divorced (2006-2010 5-year est.); Foreign born: 0.9% (2006-2010 5-year est.); Ancestry (includes multiple ancestries): 35.3% German, 22.7% Italian, 16.6% Irish, 16.4% English, 6.3% Dutch (2006-2010 5-year est.).

**Economy:** Single-family building permits issued: 3 (2011); Multi-family building permits issued: 0 (2011); Employment by occupation: 11.9% management, 0.0% professional, 13.6% services, 13.3% sales, 2.4% farming, 19.4% construction, 14.3% production (2006-2010 5-year est.).

**Income:** Per capita income: $20,296 (2006-2010 5-year est.); Median household income: $48,333 (2006-2010 5-year est.); Average household income: $52,343 (2006-2010 5-year est.); Percent of households with income of $100,000 or more: 10.5% (2006-2010 5-year est.); Poverty rate: 20.5% (2006-2010 5-year est.).

**Education:** Percent of population age 25 and over with: High school diploma (including GED) or higher: 82.1% (2006-2010 5-year est.); Bachelor's degree or higher: 16.4% (2006-2010 5-year est.); Master's degree or higher: 6.2% (2006-2010 5-year est.).

**School District(s)**

Mount Morris Central School District (KG-12)

2009-10 Enrollment: 492 . . . . . . . . . . . . . . . . . . (585) 658-2568

**Housing:** Homeownership rate: 65.1% (2010); Median home value: $73,200 (2006-2010 5-year est.); Median contract rent: $430 per month (2006-2010 5-year est.); Median year structure built: 1951 (2006-2010 5-year est.).

**Transportation:** Commute to work: 89.9% car, 0.0% public transportation, 5.3% walk, 4.8% work from home (2006-2010 5-year est.); Travel time to work: 43.5% less than 15 minutes, 28.1% 15 to 30 minutes, 13.0% 30 to 45 minutes, 6.5% 45 to 60 minutes, 8.9% 60 minutes or more (2006-2010 5-year est.)

## NORTH DANSVILLE (town). Covers a land area of 9.859 square miles and a water area of 0 square miles. Located at 42.55° N. Lat; 77.69° W. Long. Elevation is 705 feet.

**Population:** 5,783 (1990); 5,738 (2000); 5,538 (2010); Density: 561.7 persons per square mile (2010); Race: 96.0% White, 0.9% Black, 0.8% Asian, 0.3% American Indian/Alaska Native, 0.0% Native Hawaiian/Other Pacific Islander, 2.0% Other, 2.0% Hispanic of any race (2010); Average household size: 2.30 (2010); Median age: 42.1 (2010); Males per 100 females: 89.5 (2010); Marriage status: 31.6% never married, 50.0% now married, 6.7% widowed, 11.6% divorced (2006-2010 5-year est.); Foreign born: 1.9% (2006-2010 5-year est.); Ancestry (includes multiple ancestries): 35.4% German, 20.5% Irish, 15.1% English, 7.9% Dutch, 7.0% American (2006-2010 5-year est.).

**Economy:** Single-family building permits issued: 0 (2011); Multi-family building permits issued: 0 (2011); Employment by occupation: 9.0% management, 0.7% professional, 11.6% services, 15.6% sales, 9.3% farming, 8.4% construction, 7.6% production (2006-2010 5-year est.).

**Income:** Per capita income: $20,317 (2006-2010 5-year est.); Median household income: $34,400 (2006-2010 5-year est.); Average household income: $44,537 (2006-2010 5-year est.); Percent of households with income of $100,000 or more: 8.2% (2006-2010 5-year est.); Poverty rate: 18.2% (2006-2010 5-year est.).

**Education:** Percent of population age 25 and over with: High school diploma (including GED) or higher: 86.5% (2006-2010 5-year est.); Bachelor's degree or higher: 18.0% (2006-2010 5-year est.); Master's degree or higher: 6.5% (2006-2010 5-year est.).

**Housing:** Homeownership rate: 63.5% (2010); Median home value: $79,500 (2006-2010 5-year est.); Median contract rent: $479 per month (2006-2010 5-year est.); Median year structure built: before 1940 (2006-2010 5-year est.).

**Transportation:** Commute to work: 87.8% car, 0.6% public transportation, 10.5% walk, 0.7% work from home (2006-2010 5-year est.); Travel time to work: 55.4% less than 15 minutes, 14.9% 15 to 30 minutes, 16.2% 30 to 45 minutes, 5.9% 45 to 60 minutes, 7.6% 60 minutes or more (2006-2010 5-year est.)

**Airports:** Dansville Municipal (general aviation)

## NUNDA (village). Covers a land area of 0.993 square miles and a water area of 0 square miles. Located at 42.58° N. Lat; 77.93° W. Long. Elevation is 942 feet.

**Population:** 1,379 (1990); 1,330 (2000); 1,377 (2010); Density: 1,386.1 persons per square mile (2010); Race: 96.7% White, 0.9% Black, 0.3% Asian, 0.2% American Indian/Alaska Native, 0.0% Native Hawaiian/Other Pacific Islander, 1.9% Other, 1.7% Hispanic of any race (2010); Average household size: 2.39 (2010); Median age: 40.4 (2010); Males per 100 females: 85.3 (2010); Marriage status: 43.0% never married, 39.4% now married, 6.8% widowed, 10.8% divorced (2006-2010 5-year est.); Foreign born: 0.0% (2006-2010 5-year est.); Ancestry (includes multiple ancestries): 32.9% German, 25.1% English, 22.7% Irish, 8.4% Italian, 6.7% Dutch (2006-2010 5-year est.).

**Economy:** Single-family building permits issued: 0 (2011); Multi-family building permits issued: 0 (2011); Employment by occupation: 8.6%

management, 1.2% professional, 15.0% services, 18.6% sales, 2.1% farming, 15.3% construction, 9.9% production (2006-2010 5-year est.).

**Income:** Per capita income: $16,905 (2006-2010 5-year est.); Median household income: $40,329 (2006-2010 5-year est.); Average household income: $46,671 (2006-2010 5-year est.); Percent of households with income of $100,000 or more: 8.3% (2006-2010 5-year est.); Poverty rate: 23.2% (2006-2010 5-year est.).

**Education:** Percent of population age 25 and over with: High school diploma (including GED) or higher: 81.2% (2006-2010 5-year est.); Bachelor's degree or higher: 10.5% (2006-2010 5-year est.); Master's degree or higher: 5.0% (2006-2010 5-year est.).

**School District(s)**

Dalton-Nunda Central School District (keshequa) (PK-12)

2009-10 Enrollment: 830 . . . . . . . . . . . . . . . . . . . . . . (585) 468-2541

**Housing:** Homeownership rate: 58.0% (2010); Median home value: $79,900 (2006-2010 5-year est.); Median contract rent: $417 per month (2006-2010 5-year est.); Median year structure built: before 1940 (2006-2010 5-year est.).

**Transportation:** Commute to work: 88.4% car, 0.5% public transportation, 6.8% walk, 4.3% work from home (2006-2010 5-year est.); Travel time to work: 37.7% less than 15 minutes, 32.2% 15 to 30 minutes, 15.4% 30 to 45 minutes, 4.3% 45 to 60 minutes, 10.4% 60 minutes or more (2006-2010 5-year est.)

## NUNDA (town). Covers a land area of 37.094 square miles and a water area of 0.026 square miles. Located at 42.57° N. Lat; 77.88° W. Long. Elevation is 942 feet.

**History:** Incorporated 1839.

**Population:** 2,931 (1990); 3,017 (2000); 3,064 (2010); Density: 82.6 persons per square mile (2010); Race: 97.7% White, 0.6% Black, 0.3% Asian, 0.1% American Indian/Alaska Native, 0.1% Native Hawaiian/Other Pacific Islander, 1.2% Other, 1.4% Hispanic of any race (2010); Average household size: 2.45 (2010); Median age: 42.6 (2010); Males per 100 females: 96.4 (2010); Marriage status: 34.5% never married, 51.2% now married, 6.1% widowed, 8.2% divorced (2006-2010 5-year est.); Foreign born: 3.1% (2006-2010 5-year est.); Ancestry (includes multiple ancestries): 33.1% German, 25.8% English, 21.2% Irish, 8.9% Dutch, 6.7% Italian (2006-2010 5-year est.).

**Economy:** Single-family building permits issued: 2 (2011); Multi-family building permits issued: 0 (2011); Employment by occupation: 7.4% management, 1.9% professional, 9.8% services, 15.3% sales, 2.1% farming, 21.6% construction, 9.0% production (2006-2010 5-year est.).

**Income:** Per capita income: $20,618 (2006-2010 5-year est.); Median household income: $43,856 (2006-2010 5-year est.); Average household income: $52,754 (2006-2010 5-year est.); Percent of households with income of $100,000 or more: 11.3% (2006-2010 5-year est.); Poverty rate: 12.9% (2006-2010 5-year est.).

**Education:** Percent of population age 25 and over with: High school diploma (including GED) or higher: 82.2% (2006-2010 5-year est.); Bachelor's degree or higher: 14.9% (2006-2010 5-year est.); Master's degree or higher: 5.8% (2006-2010 5-year est.).

**School District(s)**

Dalton-Nunda Central School District (keshequa) (PK-12)

2009-10 Enrollment: 830 . . . . . . . . . . . . . . . . . . . . . . (585) 468-2541

**Housing:** Homeownership rate: 74.9% (2010); Median home value: $80,400 (2006-2010 5-year est.); Median contract rent: $428 per month (2006-2010 5-year est.); Median year structure built: 1957 (2006-2010 5-year est.).

**Safety:** Violent crime rate: 0.0 per 10,000 population; Property crime rate: 51.9 per 10,000 population (2010).

**Transportation:** Commute to work: 86.3% car, 0.2% public transportation, 10.7% walk, 2.3% work from home (2006-2010 5-year est.); Travel time to work: 41.7% less than 15 minutes, 28.4% 15 to 30 minutes, 9.9% 30 to 45 minutes, 6.0% 45 to 60 minutes, 14.1% 60 minutes or more (2006-2010 5-year est.)

## OSSIAN (town). Covers a land area of 39.634 square miles and a water area of 0.027 square miles. Located at 42.51° N. Lat; 77.77° W. Long. Elevation is 1,342 feet.

**Population:** 797 (1990); 751 (2000); 789 (2010); Density: 19.9 persons per square mile (2010); Race: 97.0% White, 0.6% Black, 0.0% Asian, 0.5% American Indian/Alaska Native, 0.0% Native Hawaiian/Other Pacific Islander, 1.9% Other, 2.2% Hispanic of any race (2010); Average household size: 2.64 (2010); Median age: 41.0 (2010); Males per 100 females: 112.1 (2010); Marriage status: 22.1% never married, 65.7% now

married, 5.6% widowed, 6.6% divorced (2006-2010 5-year est.); Foreign born: 0.0% (2006-2010 5-year est.); Ancestry (includes multiple ancestries): 30.6% German, 19.4% Irish, 18.2% English, 11.3% Italian, 7.2% American (2006-2010 5-year est.).
**Economy:** Single-family building permits issued: 0 (2011); Multi-family building permits issued: 0 (2011); Employment by occupation: 10.4% management, 2.4% professional, 11.3% services, 20.8% sales, 3.1% farming, 9.8% construction, 4.3% production (2006-2010 5-year est.).
**Income:** Per capita income: $30,295 (2006-2010 5-year est.); Median household income: $55,446 (2006-2010 5-year est.); Average household income: $72,417 (2006-2010 5-year est.); Percent of households with income of $100,000 or more: 13.4% (2006-2010 5-year est.); Poverty rate: 9.4% (2006-2010 5-year est.).
**Education:** Percent of population age 25 and over with: High school diploma (including GED) or higher: 85.9% (2006-2010 5-year est.); Bachelor's degree or higher: 12.7% (2006-2010 5-year est.); Master's degree or higher: 6.2% (2006-2010 5-year est.).
**Housing:** Homeownership rate: 87.6% (2010); Median home value: $113,400 (2006-2010 5-year est.); Median contract rent: $398 per month (2006-2010 5-year est.); Median year structure built: 1973 (2006-2010 5-year est.).
**Transportation:** Commute to work: 92.7% car, 0.0% public transportation, 1.8% walk, 5.5% work from home (2006-2010 5-year est.); Travel time to work: 37.2% less than 15 minutes, 25.9% 15 to 30 minutes, 12.9% 30 to 45 minutes, 8.1% 45 to 60 minutes, 15.9% 60 minutes or more (2006-2010 5-year est.).

**PIFFARD** (CDP). Covers a land area of 0.933 square miles and a water area of 0 square miles. Located at 42.83° N. Lat; 77.85° W. Long. Elevation is 568 feet.
**Population:** n/a (1990); n/a (2000); 220 (2010); Density: 235.6 persons per square mile (2010); Race: 91.4% White, 3.2% Black, 0.0% Asian, 0.9% American Indian/Alaska Native, 0.0% Native Hawaiian/Other Pacific Islander, 4.5% Other, 2.7% Hispanic of any race (2010); Average household size: 2.44 (2010); Median age: 47.2 (2010); Males per 100 females: 113.6 (2010); Marriage status: 40.0% never married, 60.0% now married, 0.0% widowed, 0.0% divorced (2006-2010 5-year est.); Foreign born: 0.0% (2006-2010 5-year est.); Ancestry (includes multiple ancestries): 36.7% Russian, 36.7% Polish, 35.0% English, 15.0% American, 13.3% German (2006-2010 5-year est.).
**Economy:** Employment by occupation: 17.0% management, 0.0% professional, 22.6% services, 0.0% sales, 0.0% farming, 26.4% construction, 0.0% production (2006-2010 5-year est.).
**Income:** Per capita income: $24,850 (2006-2010 5-year est.); Median household income: $36,964 (2006-2010 5-year est.); Average household income: $48,415 (2006-2010 5-year est.); Percent of households with income of $100,000 or more: 0.0% (2006-2010 5-year est.); Poverty rate: 0.0% (2006-2010 5-year est.).
**Education:** Percent of population age 25 and over with: High school diploma (including GED) or higher: 100.0% (2006-2010 5-year est.); Bachelor's degree or higher: 0.0% (2006-2010 5-year est.); Master's degree or higher: 0.0% (2006-2010 5-year est.).
**Housing:** Homeownership rate: 80.0% (2010); Median home value: $105,200 (2006-2010 5-year est.); Median contract rent: n/a per month (2006-2010 5-year est.); Median year structure built: before 1940 (2006-2010 5-year est.).
**Transportation:** Commute to work: 100.0% car, 0.0% public transportation, 0.0% walk, 0.0% work from home (2006-2010 5-year est.); Travel time to work: 37.7% less than 15 minutes, 0.0% 15 to 30 minutes, 62.3% 30 to 45 minutes, 0.0% 45 to 60 minutes, 0.0% 60 minutes or more (2006-2010 5-year est.).

**PORTAGE** (town). Covers a land area of 26.399 square miles and a water area of 0.236 square miles. Located at 42.55° N. Lat; 77.99° W. Long. Elevation is 1,342 feet.
**Population:** 893 (1990); 859 (2000); 884 (2010); Density: 33.5 persons per square mile (2010); Race: 97.3% White, 0.3% Black, 0.1% Asian, 0.6% American Indian/Alaska Native, 0.0% Native Hawaiian/Other Pacific Islander, 1.7% Other, 0.8% Hispanic of any race (2010); Average household size: 2.51 (2010); Median age: 42.1 (2010); Males per 100 females: 92.2 (2010); Marriage status: 22.9% never married, 54.3% now married, 9.5% widowed, 13.3% divorced (2006-2010 5-year est.); Foreign born: 0.4% (2006-2010 5-year est.); Ancestry (includes multiple ancestries): 31.7% German, 27.8% English, 26.2% Irish, 9.8% Italian, 5.6% French (2006-2010 5-year est.).

**Economy:** Single-family building permits issued: 0 (2011); Multi-family building permits issued: 0 (2011); Employment by occupation: 15.6% management, 1.2% professional, 8.4% services, 12.6% sales, 1.2% farming, 26.0% construction, 15.3% production (2006-2010 5-year est.).
**Income:** Per capita income: $21,214 (2006-2010 5-year est.); Median household income: $40,208 (2006-2010 5-year est.); Average household income: $51,680 (2006-2010 5-year est.); Percent of households with income of $100,000 or more: 10.9% (2006-2010 5-year est.); Poverty rate: 7.9% (2006-2010 5-year est.).
**Education:** Percent of population age 25 and over with: High school diploma (including GED) or higher: 85.9% (2006-2010 5-year est.); Bachelor's degree or higher: 7.9% (2006-2010 5-year est.); Master's degree or higher: 2.8% (2006-2010 5-year est.).
**Housing:** Homeownership rate: 80.7% (2010); Median home value: $76,300 (2006-2010 5-year est.); Median contract rent: $514 per month (2006-2010 5-year est.); Median year structure built: 1951 (2006-2010 5-year est.).
**Transportation:** Commute to work: 86.2% car, 1.8% public transportation, 4.6% walk, 4.9% work from home (2006-2010 5-year est.); Travel time to work: 35.8% less than 15 minutes, 25.8% 15 to 30 minutes, 18.1% 30 to 45 minutes, 14.5% 45 to 60 minutes, 5.8% 60 minutes or more (2006-2010 5-year est.)

**RETSOF** (CDP). Covers a land area of 0.450 square miles and a water area of 0 square miles. Located at 42.83° N. Lat; 77.87° W. Long. Elevation is 728 feet.
**Population:** n/a (1990); n/a (2000); 340 (2010); Density: 754.6 persons per square mile (2010); Race: 95.9% White, 1.2% Black, 0.0% Asian, 0.0% American Indian/Alaska Native, 0.0% Native Hawaiian/Other Pacific Islander, 2.9% Other, 1.2% Hispanic of any race (2010); Average household size: 2.63 (2010); Median age: 41.3 (2010); Males per 100 females: 86.8 (2010); Marriage status: 21.5% never married, 75.1% now married, 3.4% widowed, 0.0% divorced (2006-2010 5-year est.); Foreign born: 0.0% (2006-2010 5-year est.); Ancestry (includes multiple ancestries): 29.7% Italian, 26.8% Irish, 24.9% German, 17.6% English, 11.8% Swedish (2006-2010 5-year est.).
**Economy:** Employment by occupation: 9.5% management, 0.0% professional, 0.0% services, 31.2% sales, 12.2% farming, 6.3% construction, 13.8% production (2006-2010 5-year est.).
**Income:** Per capita income: $23,880 (2006-2010 5-year est.); Median household income: $76,711 (2006-2010 5-year est.); Average household income: $75,978 (2006-2010 5-year est.); Percent of households with income of $100,000 or more: 30.3% (2006-2010 5-year est.); Poverty rate: 0.0% (2006-2010 5-year est.).
**Education:** Percent of population age 25 and over with: High school diploma (including GED) or higher: 93.4% (2006-2010 5-year est.); Bachelor's degree or higher: 22.7% (2006-2010 5-year est.); Master's degree or higher: 9.2% (2006-2010 5-year est.).

**School District(s)**
York Central School District (KG-12)
   2009-10 Enrollment: 818 . . . . . . . . . . . . . . . . . . . . . . . (585) 243-1730
**Housing:** Homeownership rate: 86.6% (2010); Median home value: $109,400 (2006-2010 5-year est.); Median contract rent: $373 per month (2006-2010 5-year est.); Median year structure built: 1966 (2006-2010 5-year est.).
**Transportation:** Commute to work: 100.0% car, 0.0% public transportation, 0.0% walk, 0.0% work from home (2006-2010 5-year est.); Travel time to work: 35.4% less than 15 minutes, 27.0% 15 to 30 minutes, 14.8% 30 to 45 minutes, 22.8% 45 to 60 minutes, 0.0% 60 minutes or more (2006-2010 5-year est.)

**SCOTTSBURG** (CDP). Covers a land area of 0.164 square miles and a water area of 0 square miles. Located at 42.66° N. Lat; 77.71° W. Long. Elevation is 925 feet.
**Population:** n/a (1990); n/a (2000); 117 (2010); Density: 711.3 persons per square mile (2010); Race: 98.3% White, 0.0% Black, 1.7% Asian, 0.0% American Indian/Alaska Native, 0.0% Native Hawaiian/Other Pacific Islander, 0.0% Other, 0.0% Hispanic of any race (2010); Average household size: 2.54 (2010); Median age: 38.8 (2010); Males per 100 females: 112.7 (2010); Marriage status: 15.0% never married, 78.0% now married, 4.0% widowed, 3.0% divorced (2006-2010 5-year est.); Foreign born: 0.0% (2006-2010 5-year est.); Ancestry (includes multiple ancestries): 29.6% German, 19.2% American, 14.4% Irish, 8.8% Dutch, 7.2% Italian (2006-2010 5-year est.).

**Economy:** Employment by occupation: 0.0% management, 0.0% professional, 4.5% services, 4.5% sales, 0.0% farming, 9.0% construction, 17.9% production (2006-2010 5-year est.).
**Income:** Per capita income: $24,267 (2006-2010 5-year est.); Median household income: $68,125 (2006-2010 5-year est.); Average household income: $65,117 (2006-2010 5-year est.); Percent of households with income of $100,000 or more: 23.4% (2006-2010 5-year est.); Poverty rate: 12.0% (2006-2010 5-year est.).
**Education:** Percent of population age 25 and over with: High school diploma (including GED) or higher: 89.2% (2006-2010 5-year est.); Bachelor's degree or higher: 21.5% (2006-2010 5-year est.); Master's degree or higher: 3.2% (2006-2010 5-year est.).
**Housing:** Homeownership rate: 91.3% (2010); Median home value: $65,000 (2006-2010 5-year est.); Median contract rent: n/a per month (2006-2010 5-year est.); Median year structure built: before 1940 (2006-2010 5-year est.).
**Transportation:** Commute to work: 100.0% car, 0.0% public transportation, 0.0% walk, 0.0% work from home (2006-2010 5-year est.); Travel time to work: 4.5% less than 15 minutes, 46.3% 15 to 30 minutes, 26.9% 30 to 45 minutes, 19.4% 45 to 60 minutes, 3.0% 60 minutes or more (2006-2010 5-year est.).

**SOUTH LIMA** (CDP). Covers a land area of 0.882 square miles and a water area of 0 square miles. Located at 42.85° N. Lat; 77.67° W. Long. Elevation is 889 feet.
**Population:** n/a (1990); n/a (2000); 240 (2010); Density: 271.8 persons per square mile (2010); Race: 96.7% White, 0.4% Black, 0.8% Asian, 0.0% American Indian/Alaska Native, 0.0% Native Hawaiian/Other Pacific Islander, 2.1% Other, 2.9% Hispanic of any race (2010); Average household size: 2.67 (2010); Median age: 39.3 (2010); Males per 100 females: 105.1 (2010); Marriage status: 23.9% never married, 71.0% now married, 5.2% widowed, 0.0% divorced (2006-2010 5-year est.); Foreign born: 0.0% (2006-2010 5-year est.); Ancestry (includes multiple ancestries): 65.0% German, 35.5% Hungarian, 22.7% Irish, 14.8% Italian (2006-2010 5-year est.).
**Economy:** Employment by occupation: 0.0% management, 0.0% professional, 0.0% services, 0.0% sales, 15.6% farming, 27.1% construction, 69.8% production (2006-2010 5-year est.).
**Income:** Per capita income: $23,738 (2006-2010 5-year est.); Median household income: $68,317 (2006-2010 5-year est.); Average household income: $74,249 (2006-2010 5-year est.); Percent of households with income of $100,000 or more: 22.2% (2006-2010 5-year est.); Poverty rate: 0.0% (2006-2010 5-year est.).
**Education:** Percent of population age 25 and over with: High school diploma (including GED) or higher: 100.0% (2006-2010 5-year est.); Bachelor's degree or higher: 0.0% (2006-2010 5-year est.); Master's degree or higher: 0.0% (2006-2010 5-year est.).
**Housing:** Homeownership rate: 80.0% (2010); Median home value: $99,000 (2006-2010 5-year est.); Median contract rent: n/a per month (2006-2010 5-year est.); Median year structure built: before 1940 (2006-2010 5-year est.).
**Transportation:** Commute to work: 100.0% car, 0.0% public transportation, 0.0% walk, 0.0% work from home (2006-2010 5-year est.); Travel time to work: 40.6% less than 15 minutes, 27.1% 15 to 30 minutes, 14.6% 30 to 45 minutes, 17.7% 45 to 60 minutes, 0.0% 60 minutes or more (2006-2010 5-year est.).

**SPARTA** (town). Covers a land area of 27.790 square miles and a water area of 0 square miles. Located at 42.62° N. Lat; 77.69° W. Long.
**Population:** 1,578 (1990); 1,627 (2000); 1,624 (2010); Density: 58.4 persons per square mile (2010); Race: 97.4% White, 0.5% Black, 0.3% Asian, 0.4% American Indian/Alaska Native, 0.1% Native Hawaiian/Other Pacific Islander, 1.3% Other, 0.9% Hispanic of any race (2010); Average household size: 2.67 (2010); Median age: 43.7 (2010); Males per 100 females: 101.2 (2010); Marriage status: 24.7% never married, 61.9% now married, 4.1% widowed, 9.3% divorced (2006-2010 5-year est.); Foreign born: 3.2% (2006-2010 5-year est.); Ancestry (includes multiple ancestries): 30.7% German, 18.7% Irish, 15.8% English, 10.8% American, 7.3% Italian (2006-2010 5-year est.).
**Economy:** Single-family building permits issued: 0 (2011); Multi-family building permits issued: 0 (2011); Employment by occupation: 10.2% management, 1.6% professional, 12.0% services, 15.8% sales, 1.6% farming, 12.3% construction, 10.6% production (2006-2010 5-year est.).
**Income:** Per capita income: $23,061 (2006-2010 5-year est.); Median household income: $54,871 (2006-2010 5-year est.); Average household

income: $62,561 (2006-2010 5-year est.); Percent of households with income of $100,000 or more: 14.0% (2006-2010 5-year est.); Poverty rate: 9.9% (2006-2010 5-year est.).
**Education:** Percent of population age 25 and over with: High school diploma (including GED) or higher: 91.3% (2006-2010 5-year est.); Bachelor's degree or higher: 22.0% (2006-2010 5-year est.); Master's degree or higher: 9.0% (2006-2010 5-year est.).
**Housing:** Homeownership rate: 92.8% (2010); Median home value: $99,500 (2006-2010 5-year est.); Median contract rent: $473 per month (2006-2010 5-year est.); Median year structure built: 1972 (2006-2010 5-year est.).
**Transportation:** Commute to work: 95.8% car, 0.0% public transportation, 0.4% walk, 3.4% work from home (2006-2010 5-year est.); Travel time to work: 17.1% less than 15 minutes, 36.5% 15 to 30 minutes, 20.4% 30 to 45 minutes, 16.5% 45 to 60 minutes, 9.5% 60 minutes or more (2006-2010 5-year est.).

**SPRINGWATER** (town). Covers a land area of 53.105 square miles and a water area of 0.013 square miles. Located at 42.62° N. Lat; 77.57° W. Long. Elevation is 971 feet.
**Population:** 2,407 (1990); 2,322 (2000); 2,439 (2010); Density: 45.9 persons per square mile (2010); Race: 97.8% White, 0.3% Black, 0.3% Asian, 0.4% American Indian/Alaska Native, 0.0% Native Hawaiian/Other Pacific Islander, 1.2% Other, 1.0% Hispanic of any race (2010); Average household size: 2.41 (2010); Median age: 44.1 (2010); Males per 100 females: 105.3 (2010); Marriage status: 22.7% never married, 62.9% now married, 4.2% widowed, 10.2% divorced (2006-2010 5-year est.); Foreign born: 0.1% (2006-2010 5-year est.); Ancestry (includes multiple ancestries): 46.1% German, 22.2% Irish, 19.8% English, 6.4% Italian, 6.3% French (2006-2010 5-year est.).
**Economy:** Single-family building permits issued: 4 (2011); Multi-family building permits issued: 0 (2011); Employment by occupation: 6.3% management, 3.9% professional, 14.1% services, 13.6% sales, 4.7% farming, 12.8% construction, 8.7% production (2006-2010 5-year est.).
**Income:** Per capita income: $24,510 (2006-2010 5-year est.); Median household income: $50,792 (2006-2010 5-year est.); Average household income: $60,121 (2006-2010 5-year est.); Percent of households with income of $100,000 or more: 12.6% (2006-2010 5-year est.); Poverty rate: 7.4% (2006-2010 5-year est.).
**Education:** Percent of population age 25 and over with: High school diploma (including GED) or higher: 88.7% (2006-2010 5-year est.); Bachelor's degree or higher: 15.4% (2006-2010 5-year est.); Master's degree or higher: 6.6% (2006-2010 5-year est.).
**Housing:** Homeownership rate: 85.6% (2010); Median home value: $86,300 (2006-2010 5-year est.); Median contract rent: $489 per month (2006-2010 5-year est.); Median year structure built: 1960 (2006-2010 5-year est.).
**Transportation:** Commute to work: 94.0% car, 0.0% public transportation, 1.8% walk, 3.1% work from home (2006-2010 5-year est.); Travel time to work: 18.2% less than 15 minutes, 18.8% 15 to 30 minutes, 26.9% 30 to 45 minutes, 18.7% 45 to 60 minutes, 17.4% 60 minutes or more (2006-2010 5-year est.).

**SPRINGWATER HAMLET** (CDP). Covers a land area of 1.330 square miles and a water area of 0 square miles. Located at 42.63° N. Lat; 77.59° W. Long.
**Population:** n/a (1990); n/a (2000); 549 (2010); Density: 412.5 persons per square mile (2010); Race: 96.9% White, 1.3% Black, 0.4% Asian, 0.4% American Indian/Alaska Native, 0.0% Native Hawaiian/Other Pacific Islander, 1.0% Other, 0.0% Hispanic of any race (2010); Average household size: 2.48 (2010); Median age: 36.8 (2010); Males per 100 females: 107.2 (2010); Marriage status: 19.8% never married, 60.8% now married, 5.8% widowed, 13.7% divorced (2006-2010 5-year est.); Foreign born: 0.0% (2006-2010 5-year est.); Ancestry (includes multiple ancestries): 27.8% German, 20.0% Irish, 13.2% English, 8.5% Italian, 6.6% American (2006-2010 5-year est.).
**Economy:** Employment by occupation: 0.0% management, 0.0% professional, 11.4% services, 13.4% sales, 11.9% farming, 16.9% construction, 12.4% production (2006-2010 5-year est.).
**Income:** Per capita income: $30,070 (2006-2010 5-year est.); Median household income: $51,429 (2006-2010 5-year est.); Average household income: $70,190 (2006-2010 5-year est.); Percent of households with income of $100,000 or more: 11.2% (2006-2010 5-year est.); Poverty rate: 12.2% (2006-2010 5-year est.).

**Education:** Percent of population age 25 and over with: High school diploma (including GED) or higher: 87.7% (2006-2010 5-year est.); Bachelor's degree or higher: 5.3% (2006-2010 5-year est.); Master's degree or higher: 0.0% (2006-2010 5-year est.).
**Housing:** Homeownership rate: 66.5% (2010); Median home value: $92,600 (2006-2010 5-year est.); Median contract rent: $497 per month (2006-2010 5-year est.); Median year structure built: before 1940 (2006-2010 5-year est.).
**Transportation:** Commute to work: 82.1% car, 0.0% public transportation, 9.0% walk, 4.5% work from home (2006-2010 5-year est.); Travel time to work: 28.6% less than 15 minutes, 17.2% 15 to 30 minutes, 20.3% 30 to 45 minutes, 18.2% 45 to 60 minutes, 15.6% 60 minutes or more (2006-2010 5-year est.)

**TUSCARORA** (CDP). Covers a land area of 0.093 square miles and a water area of 0 square miles. Located at 42.63° N. Lat; 77.86° W. Long. Elevation is 764 feet.
**Population:** n/a (1990); n/a (2000); 74 (2010); Density: 795.2 persons per square mile (2010); Race: 100.0% White, 0.0% Black, 0.0% Asian, 0.0% American Indian/Alaska Native, 0.0% Native Hawaiian/Other Pacific Islander, 0.0% Other, 0.0% Hispanic of any race (2010); Average household size: 2.55 (2010); Median age: 37.5 (2010); Males per 100 females: 131.3 (2010); Marriage status: 0.0% never married, 88.3% now married, 11.7% widowed, 0.0% divorced (2006-2010 5-year est.); Foreign born: 0.0% (2006-2010 5-year est.); Ancestry (includes multiple ancestries): 46.8% Dutch, 41.6% German, 35.1% Irish, 15.6% Scottish, 14.3% Polish (2006-2010 5-year est.).
**Income:** Per capita income: $39,166 (2006-2010 5-year est.); Median household income: $46,759 (2006-2010 5-year est.); Average household income: $53,284 (2006-2010 5-year est.); Percent of households with income of $100,000 or more: 0.0% (2006-2010 5-year est.); Poverty rate: 0.0% (2006-2010 5-year est.).
**Education:** Percent of population age 25 and over with: High school diploma (including GED) or higher: 88.3% (2006-2010 5-year est.); Bachelor's degree or higher: 0.0% (2006-2010 5-year est.); Master's degree or higher: 0.0% (2006-2010 5-year est.).
**Housing:** Homeownership rate: 75.8% (2010); Median home value: $75,000 (2006-2010 5-year est.); Median contract rent: n/a per month (2006-2010 5-year est.); Median year structure built: before 1940 (2006-2010 5-year est.).
**Transportation:** Commute to work: 100.0% car, 0.0% public transportation, 0.0% walk, 0.0% work from home (2006-2010 5-year est.); Travel time to work: 0.0% less than 15 minutes, 25.0% 15 to 30 minutes, 75.0% 30 to 45 minutes, 0.0% 45 to 60 minutes, 0.0% 60 minutes or more (2006-2010 5-year est.)

**WADSWORTH** (CDP). Covers a land area of 0.511 square miles and a water area of 0 square miles. Located at 42.82° N. Lat; 77.89° W. Long. Elevation is 741 feet.
**Population:** n/a (1990); n/a (2000); 190 (2010); Density: 371.3 persons per square mile (2010); Race: 97.4% White, 0.5% Black, 0.0% Asian, 0.0% American Indian/Alaska Native, 0.0% Native Hawaiian/Other Pacific Islander, 2.1% Other, 2.1% Hispanic of any race (2010); Average household size: 2.47 (2010); Median age: 43.3 (2010); Males per 100 females: 106.5 (2010); Marriage status: 13.6% never married, 80.2% now married, 0.0% widowed, 6.2% divorced (2006-2010 5-year est.); Foreign born: 0.0% (2006-2010 5-year est.); Ancestry (includes multiple ancestries): 30.5% Italian, 26.9% Irish, 26.5% German, 17.9% Polish, 10.3% Scottish (2006-2010 5-year est.).
**Economy:** Employment by occupation: 16.3% management, 0.0% professional, 0.0% services, 34.7% sales, 11.2% farming, 29.6% construction, 0.0% production (2006-2010 5-year est.).
**Income:** Per capita income: $23,253 (2006-2010 5-year est.); Median household income: $51,932 (2006-2010 5-year est.); Average household income: $60,502 (2006-2010 5-year est.); Percent of households with income of $100,000 or more: 9.9% (2006-2010 5-year est.); Poverty rate: 0.0% (2006-2010 5-year est.).
**Education:** Percent of population age 25 and over with: High school diploma (including GED) or higher: 85.0% (2006-2010 5-year est.); Bachelor's degree or higher: 13.1% (2006-2010 5-year est.); Master's degree or higher: 0.0% (2006-2010 5-year est.).
**Housing:** Homeownership rate: 83.1% (2010); Median home value: $108,000 (2006-2010 5-year est.); Median contract rent: n/a per month (2006-2010 5-year est.); Median year structure built: 1955 (2006-2010 5-year est.).

**Transportation:** Commute to work: 100.0% car, 0.0% public transportation, 0.0% walk, 0.0% work from home (2006-2010 5-year est.); Travel time to work: 18.4% less than 15 minutes, 44.9% 15 to 30 minutes, 28.6% 30 to 45 minutes, 8.2% 45 to 60 minutes, 0.0% 60 minutes or more (2006-2010 5-year est.)

**WEBSTERS CROSSING** (CDP). Covers a land area of 0.110 square miles and a water area of 0 square miles. Located at 42.66° N. Lat; 77.63° W. Long. Elevation is 1,339 feet.
**Population:** n/a (1990); n/a (2000); 69 (2010); Density: 625.8 persons per square mile (2010); Race: 95.7% White, 0.0% Black, 1.4% Asian, 0.0% American Indian/Alaska Native, 0.0% Native Hawaiian/Other Pacific Islander, 2.9% Other, 4.3% Hispanic of any race (2010); Average household size: 2.23 (2010); Median age: 50.5 (2010); Males per 100 females: 97.1 (2010); Marriage status: 44.1% never married, 0.0% now married, 20.6% widowed, 35.3% divorced (2006-2010 5-year est.); Foreign born: 0.0% (2006-2010 5-year est.); Ancestry (includes multiple ancestries): 100.0% German, 38.1% Italian, 16.7% Dutch, 14.3% English (2006-2010 5-year est.).
**Economy:** Employment by occupation: 0.0% management, 0.0% professional, 28.6% services, 38.1% sales, 0.0% farming, 0.0% construction, 0.0% production (2006-2010 5-year est.).
**Income:** Per capita income: $22,945 (2006-2010 5-year est.); Median household income: $37,656 (2006-2010 5-year est.); Average household income: $35,011 (2006-2010 5-year est.); Percent of households with income of $100,000 or more: 0.0% (2006-2010 5-year est.); Poverty rate: 0.0% (2006-2010 5-year est.).
**Education:** Percent of population age 25 and over with: High school diploma (including GED) or higher: 74.1% (2006-2010 5-year est.); Bachelor's degree or higher: 0.0% (2006-2010 5-year est.); Master's degree or higher: 0.0% (2006-2010 5-year est.).
**Housing:** Homeownership rate: 87.1% (2010); Median home value: $45,400 (2006-2010 5-year est.); Median contract rent: n/a per month (2006-2010 5-year est.); Median year structure built: before 1940 (2006-2010 5-year est.).
**Transportation:** Commute to work: 100.0% car, 0.0% public transportation, 0.0% walk, 0.0% work from home (2006-2010 5-year est.); Travel time to work: 0.0% less than 15 minutes, 0.0% 15 to 30 minutes, 28.6% 30 to 45 minutes, 38.1% 45 to 60 minutes, 33.3% 60 minutes or more (2006-2010 5-year est.)

**WEST SPARTA** (town). Covers a land area of 33.450 square miles and a water area of 0 square miles. Located at 42.61° N. Lat; 77.78° W. Long. Elevation is 617 feet.
**Population:** 1,335 (1990); 1,244 (2000); 1,255 (2010); Density: 37.5 persons per square mile (2010); Race: 94.7% White, 0.8% Black, 0.6% Asian, 0.4% American Indian/Alaska Native, 0.0% Native Hawaiian/Other Pacific Islander, 3.5% Other, 1.8% Hispanic of any race (2010); Average household size: 2.48 (2010); Median age: 43.8 (2010); Males per 100 females: 101.8 (2010); Marriage status: 19.4% never married, 60.0% now married, 5.8% widowed, 14.8% divorced (2006-2010 5-year est.); Foreign born: 0.9% (2006-2010 5-year est.); Ancestry (includes multiple ancestries): 38.5% German, 18.5% Irish, 14.1% English, 10.8% Italian, 6.6% American (2006-2010 5-year est.).
**Economy:** Single-family building permits issued: 1 (2011); Multi-family building permits issued: 0 (2011); Employment by occupation: 8.9% management, 3.5% professional, 10.4% services, 20.3% sales, 2.9% farming, 18.2% construction, 11.0% production (2006-2010 5-year est.).
**Income:** Per capita income: $23,522 (2006-2010 5-year est.); Median household income: $56,445 (2006-2010 5-year est.); Average household income: $57,356 (2006-2010 5-year est.); Percent of households with income of $100,000 or more: 7.5% (2006-2010 5-year est.); Poverty rate: 11.3% (2006-2010 5-year est.).
**Education:** Percent of population age 25 and over with: High school diploma (including GED) or higher: 86.1% (2006-2010 5-year est.); Bachelor's degree or higher: 13.5% (2006-2010 5-year est.); Master's degree or higher: 3.5% (2006-2010 5-year est.).
**Housing:** Homeownership rate: 84.9% (2010); Median home value: $93,300 (2006-2010 5-year est.); Median contract rent: $521 per month (2006-2010 5-year est.); Median year structure built: 1980 (2006-2010 5-year est.).
**Transportation:** Commute to work: 95.7% car, 0.0% public transportation, 0.6% walk, 3.7% work from home (2006-2010 5-year est.); Travel time to work: 20.3% less than 15 minutes, 27.0% 15 to 30 minutes, 18.0% 30 to 45

minutes, 16.4% 45 to 60 minutes, 18.3% 60 minutes or more (2006-2010 5-year est.)

**WOODSVILLE** (CDP). Covers a land area of 0.317 square miles and a water area of 0 square miles. Located at 42.57° N. Lat; 77.73° W. Long. Elevation is 646 feet.
**Population:** n/a (1990); n/a (2000); 80 (2010); Density: 252.2 persons per square mile (2010); Race: 100.0% White, 0.0% Black, 0.0% Asian, 0.0% American Indian/Alaska Native, 0.0% Native Hawaiian/Other Pacific Islander, 0.0% Other, 0.0% Hispanic of any race (2010); Average household size: 2.35 (2010); Median age: 44.0 (2010); Males per 100 females: 116.2 (2010); Marriage status: 3.8% never married, 67.9% now married, 5.7% widowed, 22.6% divorced (2006-2010 5-year est.); Foreign born: 0.0% (2006-2010 5-year est.); Ancestry (includes multiple ancestries): 30.0% German, 11.3% Italian, 7.5% Irish, 3.8% English (2006-2010 5-year est.).
**Economy:** Employment by occupation: 0.0% management, 0.0% professional, 12.8% services, 0.0% sales, 0.0% farming, 23.1% construction, 35.9% production (2006-2010 5-year est.).
**Income:** Per capita income: $15,436 (2006-2010 5-year est.); Median household income: $36,250 (2006-2010 5-year est.); Average household income: $41,997 (2006-2010 5-year est.); Percent of households with income of $100,000 or more: 0.0% (2006-2010 5-year est.); Poverty rate: 45.0% (2006-2010 5-year est.).
**Education:** Percent of population age 25 and over with: High school diploma (including GED) or higher: 58.5% (2006-2010 5-year est.); Bachelor's degree or higher: 11.3% (2006-2010 5-year est.); Master's degree or higher: 11.3% (2006-2010 5-year est.).
**Housing:** Homeownership rate: 88.2% (2010); Median home value: $56,700 (2006-2010 5-year est.); Median contract rent: $583 per month (2006-2010 5-year est.); Median year structure built: 1973 (2006-2010 5-year est.).
**Transportation:** Commute to work: 100.0% car, 0.0% public transportation, 0.0% walk, 0.0% work from home (2006-2010 5-year est.); Travel time to work: 35.9% less than 15 minutes, 20.5% 15 to 30 minutes, 17.9% 30 to 45 minutes, 7.7% 45 to 60 minutes, 17.9% 60 minutes or more (2006-2010 5-year est.)

**YORK** (town). Covers a land area of 49.099 square miles and a water area of 0.007 square miles. Located at 42.86° N. Lat; 77.88° W. Long. Elevation is 784 feet.
**Population:** 3,513 (1990); 3,219 (2000); 3,397 (2010); Density: 69.2 persons per square mile (2010); Race: 95.2% White, 1.4% Black, 0.8% Asian, 0.2% American Indian/Alaska Native, 0.0% Native Hawaiian/Other Pacific Islander, 2.4% Other, 2.4% Hispanic of any race (2010); Average household size: 2.60 (2010); Median age: 41.5 (2010); Males per 100 females: 107.9 (2010); Marriage status: 28.5% never married, 56.4% now married, 7.5% widowed, 7.7% divorced (2006-2010 5-year est.); Foreign born: 2.6% (2006-2010 5-year est.); Ancestry (includes multiple ancestries): 22.0% German, 20.7% Irish, 18.7% English, 16.2% Italian, 5.7% Polish (2006-2010 5-year est.).
**Economy:** Single-family building permits issued: 1 (2011); Multi-family building permits issued: 0 (2011); Employment by occupation: 12.7% management, 1.2% professional, 13.9% services, 21.0% sales, 1.9% farming, 11.7% construction, 6.0% production (2006-2010 5-year est.).
**Income:** Per capita income: $25,162 (2006-2010 5-year est.); Median household income: $60,000 (2006-2010 5-year est.); Average household income: $64,583 (2006-2010 5-year est.); Percent of households with income of $100,000 or more: 15.1% (2006-2010 5-year est.); Poverty rate: 6.5% (2006-2010 5-year est.).
**Taxes:** Total city taxes per capita: $423 (2009); City property taxes per capita: $400 (2009).
**Education:** Percent of population age 25 and over with: High school diploma (including GED) or higher: 87.7% (2006-2010 5-year est.); Bachelor's degree or higher: 19.8% (2006-2010 5-year est.); Master's degree or higher: 10.4% (2006-2010 5-year est.).
**Housing:** Homeownership rate: 81.0% (2010); Median home value: $106,700 (2006-2010 5-year est.); Median contract rent: $480 per month (2006-2010 5-year est.); Median year structure built: 1963 (2006-2010 5-year est.).
**Transportation:** Commute to work: 92.9% car, 0.0% public transportation, 4.3% walk, 1.3% work from home (2006-2010 5-year est.); Travel time to work: 34.5% less than 15 minutes, 34.6% 15 to 30 minutes, 20.4% 30 to 45 minutes, 7.3% 45 to 60 minutes, 3.3% 60 minutes or more (2006-2010 5-year est.)

**YORK HAMLET** (CDP). Covers a land area of 2.754 square miles and a water area of 0 square miles. Located at 42.86° N. Lat; 77.88° W. Long. Elevation is 784 feet.
**Population:** n/a (1990); n/a (2000); 544 (2010); Density: 197.5 persons per square mile (2010); Race: 95.4% White, 0.2% Black, 1.5% Asian, 0.0% American Indian/Alaska Native, 0.0% Native Hawaiian/Other Pacific Islander, 2.9% Other, 0.9% Hispanic of any race (2010); Average household size: 2.58 (2010); Median age: 41.7 (2010); Males per 100 females: 103.7 (2010); Marriage status: 33.4% never married, 45.5% now married, 4.7% widowed, 16.4% divorced (2006-2010 5-year est.); Foreign born: 1.6% (2006-2010 5-year est.); Ancestry (includes multiple ancestries): 29.8% Irish, 18.8% German, 18.4% English, 8.0% Polish, 6.9% Scottish (2006-2010 5-year est.).
**Economy:** Employment by occupation: 11.5% management, 0.0% professional, 22.3% services, 13.0% sales, 0.0% farming, 2.2% construction, 2.2% production (2006-2010 5-year est.).
**Income:** Per capita income: $25,414 (2006-2010 5-year est.); Median household income: $66,705 (2006-2010 5-year est.); Average household income: $73,393 (2006-2010 5-year est.); Percent of households with income of $100,000 or more: 25.4% (2006-2010 5-year est.); Poverty rate: 6.8% (2006-2010 5-year est.).
**Education:** Percent of population age 25 and over with: High school diploma (including GED) or higher: 84.2% (2006-2010 5-year est.); Bachelor's degree or higher: 31.9% (2006-2010 5-year est.); Master's degree or higher: 14.5% (2006-2010 5-year est.).
**Housing:** Homeownership rate: 82.0% (2010); Median home value: $114,400 (2006-2010 5-year est.); Median contract rent: $653 per month (2006-2010 5-year est.); Median year structure built: 1966 (2006-2010 5-year est.).
**Transportation:** Commute to work: 90.1% car, 0.0% public transportation, 4.8% walk, 0.0% work from home (2006-2010 5-year est.); Travel time to work: 23.1% less than 15 minutes, 33.3% 15 to 30 minutes, 32.1% 30 to 45 minutes, 5.1% 45 to 60 minutes, 6.4% 60 minutes or more (2006-2010 5-year est.).

## Madison County

Located in central New York; drained by the Chenango and Unadilla Rivers; includes Cazenovia Lake, part of Oneida Lake, and other lakes. Covers a land area of 655.86 square miles, a water area of 5.69 square miles, and is located in the Eastern Time Zone at 42.94° N. Lat., 75.68° W. Long. The county was founded in 1806. County seat is Wampsville.

Madison County is part of the Syracuse, NY Metropolitan Statistical Area. The entire metro area includes: Madison County, NY; Onondaga County, NY; Oswego County, NY

Weather Station: Morrisville 5 SW | | | | | | | | Elevation: 1,299 feet

| | Jan | Feb | Mar | Apr | May | Jun | Jul | Aug | Sep | Oct | Nov | Dec |
|---|---|---|---|---|---|---|---|---|---|---|---|---|
| High | 29 | 32 | 40 | 54 | 66 | 74 | 78 | 76 | 69 | 57 | 45 | 34 |
| Low | 11 | 13 | 20 | 33 | 43 | 52 | 56 | 55 | 49 | 37 | 29 | 19 |
| Precip | 3.2 | 3.0 | 3.4 | 3.7 | 4.1 | 4.5 | 4.0 | 3.6 | 4.3 | 4.1 | 3.9 | 3.9 |
| Snow | 30.5 | 25.7 | 21.1 | 5.6 | 0.2 | 0.0 | 0.0 | 0.0 | tr | 1.5 | 12.0 | 27.5 |

*High and Low temperatures in degrees Fahrenheit; Precipitation and Snow in inches*

**Population:** 69,120 (1990); 69,441 (2000); 73,442 (2010); Race: 95.0% White, 1.8% Black, 0.8% Asian, 0.7% American Indian/Alaska Native, 0.0% Native Hawaiian/Other Pacific Islander, 1.7% Other, 1.8% Hispanic of any race (2010); Density: 112.0 persons per square mile (2010); Average household size: 2.46 (2010); Median age: 39.5 (2010); Males per 100 females: 96.5 (2010).
**Religion:** Six largest groups: 14.7% Catholicism, 5.8% Methodist/Pietist, 2.1% Baptist, 1.9% Presbyterian-Reformed, 1.3% Non-Denominational, 1.3% Episcopalianism/Anglicanism (2010)
**Economy:** Unemployment rate: 9.9% (February 2012); Total civilian labor force: 36,003 (February 2012); Leading industries: 16.9% health care and social assistance; 15.4% retail trade; 14.4% manufacturing (2009); Farms: 744 totaling 188,320 acres (2007); Companies that employ 500 or more persons: 3 (2009); Companies that employ 100 to 499 persons: 20 (2009); Companies that employ less than 100 persons: 1,403 (2009); Black-owned businesses: n/a (2007); Hispanic-owned businesses: n/a (2007); Asian-owned businesses: n/a (2007); Women-owned businesses: 1,371 (2007); Retail sales per capita: $11,132 (2010). Single-family building permits issued: 63 (2011); Multi-family building permits issued: 2 (2011).
**Income:** Per capita income: $24,311 (2006-2010 5-year est.); Median household income: $53,345 (2006-2010 5-year est.); Average household

income: $64,364 (2006-2010 5-year est.); Percent of households with income of $100,000 or more: 17.1% (2006-2010 5-year est.); Poverty rate: 9.8% (2006-2010 5-year est.); Bankruptcy rate: 2.54% (2011).

**Taxes**: Total county taxes per capita: $652 (2009); County property taxes per capita: $414 (2009).

**Education**: Percent of population age 25 and over with: High school diploma (including GED) or higher: 88.5% (2006-2010 5-year est.); Bachelor's degree or higher: 23.7% (2006-2010 5-year est.); Master's degree or higher: 9.9% (2006-2010 5-year est.).

**Housing**: Homeownership rate: 73.7% (2010); Median home value: $111,700 (2006-2010 5-year est.); Median contract rent: $539 per month (2006-2010 5-year est.); Median year structure built: 1960 (2006-2010 5-year est.)

**Health**: Birth rate: 92.7 per 10,000 population (2011); Death rate: 74.7 per 10,000 population (2011); Age-adjusted cancer mortality rate: 193.3 deaths per 100,000 population (2009); Number of physicians: 16.1 per 10,000 population (2008); Hospital beds: 45.8 per 10,000 population (2007); Hospital admissions: 840.3 per 10,000 population (2007).

**Environment**: Air Quality Index: 94.0% good, 5.8% moderate, 0.3% unhealthy for sensitive individuals, 0.0% unhealthy (percent of days in 2010)

**Elections**: 2008 Presidential election results: 49.3% Obama, 48.4% McCain, 1.1% Nader

**National and State Parks**: Chittenango Falls State Park

**Additional Information Contacts**

Madison County Government . . . . . . . . . . . . . . . . . (315) 366-2261
  http://www.madisoncounty.org
Canastota Chamber of Commerce . . . . . . . . . . . . . . (315) 697-3677
  http://canastota.org
City of Oneida . . . . . . . . . . . . . . . . . . . . . . . . (315) 363-7378
  http://www.oneidacity.com
Greater Cazenovia Area Chamber of Commerce . . . . . . . (315) 655-9243
  http://www.cazenoviachamber.com
Greater Oneida Chamber of Commerce . . . . . . . . . . . (315) 363-4300
  http://oneidachamberny.org
Hamilton Business Alliance . . . . . . . . . . . . . . . . . (315) 824-3903
  http://www.visithamiltonny.com/thrive
Village of Canastota . . . . . . . . . . . . . . . . . . . . (315) 697-7559
  http://www.canastota.com
Village of Chittenango . . . . . . . . . . . . . . . . . . . (315) 687-3936
  http://chittenango.org

## Madison County Communities

### BOUCKVILLE (unincorporated postal area)

Zip Code: 13310

Covers a land area of 7.575 square miles and a water area of 0.092 square miles. Located at 42.88° N. Lat; 75.57° W. Long. Elevation is 1,142 feet. Population: 624 (2010); Density: 82.4 persons per square mile (2010); Race: 98.1% White, 1.0% Black, 0.2% Asian, 0.5% American Indian/Alaska Native, 0.0% Native Hawaiian/Other Pacific Islander, 0.2% Other, 1.1% Hispanic of any race (2010); Average household size: 2.54 (2010); Median age: 39.2 (2010); Males per 100 females: 85.7 (2010); Homeownership rate: 76.4% (2010)

### BROOKFIELD (town). Covers a land area of 77.821 square miles and a water area of 0.196 square miles. Located at 42.80° N. Lat; 75.34° W. Long. Elevation is 1,381 feet.

**Population**: 2,225 (1990); 2,403 (2000); 2,545 (2010); Density: 32.7 persons per square mile (2010); Race: 97.5% White, 0.2% Black, 0.5% Asian, 0.5% American Indian/Alaska Native, 0.0% Native Hawaiian/Other Pacific Islander, 1.3% Other, 0.9% Hispanic of any race (2010); Average household size: 2.62 (2010); Median age: 39.9 (2010); Males per 100 females: 97.0 (2010); Marriage status: 25.9% never married, 57.4% now married, 7.2% widowed, 9.5% divorced (2006-2010 5-year est.); Foreign born: 3.4% (2006-2010 5-year est.); Ancestry (includes multiple ancestries): 22.8% German, 17.6% English, 13.6% Irish, 10.0% American, 7.9% Welsh (2006-2010 5-year est.).

**Economy**: Single-family building permits issued: 0 (2011); Multi-family building permits issued: 0 (2011); Employment by occupation: 9.6% management, 4.7% professional, 12.5% services, 12.0% sales, 1.5% farming, 14.7% construction, 8.4% production (2006-2010 5-year est.).

**Income**: Per capita income: $20,344 (2006-2010 5-year est.); Median household income: $40,588 (2006-2010 5-year est.); Average household income: $51,114 (2006-2010 5-year est.); Percent of households with

income of $100,000 or more: 10.9% (2006-2010 5-year est.); Poverty rate: 16.0% (2006-2010 5-year est.).

**Education**: Percent of population age 25 and over with: High school diploma (including GED) or higher: 85.4% (2006-2010 5-year est.); Bachelor's degree or higher: 17.7% (2006-2010 5-year est.); Master's degree or higher: 7.2% (2006-2010 5-year est.).

**School District(s)**

Brookfield Central School District (PK-12)
  2009-10 Enrollment: 249 . . . . . . . . . . . . . . . . . (315) 899-3323

**Housing**: Homeownership rate: 82.6% (2010); Median home value: $70,300 (2006-2010 5-year est.); Median contract rent: $454 per month (2006-2010 5-year est.); Median year structure built: 1973 (2006-2010 5-year est.).

**Transportation**: Commute to work: 88.0% car, 0.0% public transportation, 3.6% walk, 6.2% work from home (2006-2010 5-year est.); Travel time to work: 18.1% less than 15 minutes, 25.3% 15 to 30 minutes, 41.9% 30 to 45 minutes, 10.5% 45 to 60 minutes, 4.1% 60 minutes or more (2006-2010 5-year est.)

### CANASTOTA (village). Covers a land area of 3.350 square miles and a water area of 0.004 square miles. Located at 43.08° N. Lat; 75.75° W. Long. Elevation is 430 feet.

**History**: International Boxing Hall of Fame is here. Incorporated 1835.

**Population**: 4,673 (1990); 4,425 (2000); 4,804 (2010); Density: 1,433.7 persons per square mile (2010); Race: 95.9% White, 1.0% Black, 0.5% Asian, 0.5% American Indian/Alaska Native, 0.0% Native Hawaiian/Other Pacific Islander, 2.1% Other, 2.0% Hispanic of any race (2010); Average household size: 2.44 (2010); Median age: 37.2 (2010); Males per 100 females: 92.0 (2010); Marriage status: 31.2% never married, 49.7% now married, 9.3% widowed, 9.8% divorced (2006-2010 5-year est.); Foreign born: 2.1% (2006-2010 5-year est.); Ancestry (includes multiple ancestries): 24.4% Italian, 16.9% English, 16.3% German, 15.4% Irish, 11.7% American (2006-2010 5-year est.).

**Economy**: Single-family building permits issued: 1 (2011); Multi-family building permits issued: 0 (2011); Employment by occupation: 7.7% management, 3.3% professional, 8.8% services, 26.5% sales, 3.8% farming, 7.2% construction, 3.6% production (2006-2010 5-year est.).

**Income**: Per capita income: $22,906 (2006-2010 5-year est.); Median household income: $41,910 (2006-2010 5-year est.); Average household income: $54,922 (2006-2010 5-year est.); Percent of households with income of $100,000 or more: 11.6% (2006-2010 5-year est.); Poverty rate: 9.0% (2006-2010 5-year est.).

**Education**: Percent of population age 25 and over with: High school diploma (including GED) or higher: 86.5% (2006-2010 5-year est.); Bachelor's degree or higher: 22.2% (2006-2010 5-year est.); Master's degree or higher: 7.6% (2006-2010 5-year est.).

**School District(s)**

Canastota Central School District (KG-12)
  2009-10 Enrollment: 1,542 . . . . . . . . . . . . . . . . (315) 697-2025

**Housing**: Homeownership rate: 57.2% (2010); Median home value: $89,300 (2006-2010 5-year est.); Median contract rent: $504 per month (2006-2010 5-year est.); Median year structure built: 1955 (2006-2010 5-year est.).

**Newspapers**: Bee-Journal (Community news; Circulation 2,050); Indian Country Today (National news; Circulation 17,000)

**Transportation**: Commute to work: 93.9% car, 0.0% public transportation, 4.9% walk, 1.2% work from home (2006-2010 5-year est.); Travel time to work: 31.0% less than 15 minutes, 37.7% 15 to 30 minutes, 22.7% 30 to 45 minutes, 5.4% 45 to 60 minutes, 3.1% 60 minutes or more (2006-2010 5-year est.)

**Additional Information Contacts**

Canastota Chamber of Commerce . . . . . . . . . . . . . . (315) 697-3677
  http://canastota.org
Village of Canastota . . . . . . . . . . . . . . . . . . . . (315) 697-7559
  http://www.canastota.com

### CAZENOVIA (village). Covers a land area of 1.873 square miles and a water area of 0 square miles. Located at 42.92° N. Lat; 75.85° W. Long. Elevation is 1,224 feet.

**Population**: 3,050 (1990); 2,614 (2000); 2,835 (2010); Density: 1,513.4 persons per square mile (2010); Race: 94.8% White, 1.9% Black, 1.1% Asian, 0.3% American Indian/Alaska Native, 0.0% Native Hawaiian/Other Pacific Islander, 1.9% Other, 3.0% Hispanic of any race (2010); Average household size: 2.09 (2010); Median age: 26.1 (2010); Males per 100 females: 67.4 (2010); Marriage status: 39.0% never married, 42.4% now

married, 9.6% widowed, 9.0% divorced (2006-2010 5-year est.); Foreign born: 1.8% (2006-2010 5-year est.); Ancestry (includes multiple ancestries): 27.4% Irish, 21.2% German, 18.0% English, 10.2% Polish, 9.1% Italian (2006-2010 5-year est.).
**Economy:** Single-family building permits issued: 1 (2011); Multi-family building permits issued: 0 (2011); Employment by occupation: 10.1% management, 5.5% professional, 7.7% services, 12.6% sales, 4.3% farming, 4.0% construction, 3.4% production (2006-2010 5-year est.).
**Income:** Per capita income: $33,334 (2006-2010 5-year est.); Median household income: $60,817 (2006-2010 5-year est.); Average household income: $82,877 (2006-2010 5-year est.); Percent of households with income of $100,000 or more: 28.0% (2006-2010 5-year est.); Poverty rate: 13.2% (2006-2010 5-year est.).
**Education:** Percent of population age 25 and over with: High school diploma (including GED) or higher: 93.0% (2006-2010 5-year est.); Bachelor's degree or higher: 53.9% (2006-2010 5-year est.); Master's degree or higher: 22.7% (2006-2010 5-year est.).

### School District(s)
Cazenovia Central School District (KG-12)
    2009-10 Enrollment: 1,670 . . . . . . . . . . . . . . . . . . (315) 655-1317
### Four-year College(s)
Cazenovia College (Private, Not-for-profit)
    Fall 2010 Enrollment: 1,082 . . . . . . . . . . . . . . . . . (800) 654-3210
    2011-12 Tuition: In-state $26,736; Out-of-state $26,736
**Housing:** Homeownership rate: 59.1% (2010); Median home value: $185,100 (2006-2010 5-year est.); Median contract rent: $634 per month (2006-2010 5-year est.); Median year structure built: 1951 (2006-2010 5-year est.).
**Safety:** Violent crime rate: 3.4 per 10,000 population; Property crime rate: 219.9 per 10,000 population (2010).
**Newspapers:** Hi Neighbor (Community news; Circulation 13,000); Town & Country Shopper (Community news; Circulation 5,050)
**Transportation:** Commute to work: 85.0% car, 0.0% public transportation, 6.7% walk, 7.8% work from home (2006-2010 5-year est.); Travel time to work: 32.0% less than 15 minutes, 23.1% 15 to 30 minutes, 33.6% 30 to 45 minutes, 6.1% 45 to 60 minutes, 5.2% 60 minutes or more (2006-2010 5-year est.)
**Additional Information Contacts**
Greater Cazenovia Area Chamber of Commerce . . . . . . . . (315) 655-9243
    http://www.cazenoviachamber.com

**CAZENOVIA** (town). Covers a land area of 49.870 square miles and a water area of 1.844 square miles. Located at 42.91° N. Lat; 75.86° W. Long. Elevation is 1,224 feet.
**History:** Seat of Cazenovia College. Settled 1793, incorporated 1810.
**Population:** 6,514 (1990); 6,481 (2000); 7,086 (2010); Density: 142.1 persons per square mile (2010); Race: 96.8% White, 0.9% Black, 0.7% Asian, 0.2% American Indian/Alaska Native, 0.1% Native Hawaiian/Other Pacific Islander, 1.3% Other, 2.2% Hispanic of any race (2010); Average household size: 2.45 (2010); Median age: 41.2 (2010); Males per 100 females: 85.9 (2010); Marriage status: 25.5% never married, 60.8% now married, 6.1% widowed, 7.6% divorced (2006-2010 5-year est.); Foreign born: 1.7% (2006-2010 5-year est.); Ancestry (includes multiple ancestries): 24.7% Irish, 23.5% German, 18.3% English, 12.2% Italian, 6.6% American (2006-2010 5-year est.).
**Economy:** Single-family building permits issued: 5 (2011); Multi-family building permits issued: 0 (2011); Employment by occupation: 18.4% management, 3.9% professional, 7.7% services, 10.0% sales, 3.9% farming, 4.3% construction, 1.8% production (2006-2010 5-year est.).
**Income:** Per capita income: $39,056 (2006-2010 5-year est.); Median household income: $72,969 (2006-2010 5-year est.); Average household income: $100,835 (2006-2010 5-year est.); Percent of households with income of $100,000 or more: 33.2% (2006-2010 5-year est.); Poverty rate: 6.1% (2006-2010 5-year est.).
**Education:** Percent of population age 25 and over with: High school diploma (including GED) or higher: 95.0% (2006-2010 5-year est.); Bachelor's degree or higher: 56.7% (2006-2010 5-year est.); Master's degree or higher: 26.2% (2006-2010 5-year est.).

### School District(s)
Cazenovia Central School District (KG-12)
    2009-10 Enrollment: 1,670 . . . . . . . . . . . . . . . . . . (315) 655-1317
### Four-year College(s)
Cazenovia College (Private, Not-for-profit)
    Fall 2010 Enrollment: 1,082 . . . . . . . . . . . . . . . . . (800) 654-3210
    2011-12 Tuition: In-state $26,736; Out-of-state $26,736

**Housing:** Homeownership rate: 77.6% (2010); Median home value: $225,400 (2006-2010 5-year est.); Median contract rent: $692 per month (2006-2010 5-year est.); Median year structure built: 1961 (2006-2010 5-year est.).
**Newspapers:** Hi Neighbor (Community news; Circulation 13,000); Town & Country Shopper (Community news; Circulation 5,050)
**Transportation:** Commute to work: 86.3% car, 0.0% public transportation, 3.6% walk, 9.6% work from home (2006-2010 5-year est.); Travel time to work: 33.9% less than 15 minutes, 18.3% 15 to 30 minutes, 37.3% 30 to 45 minutes, 6.1% 45 to 60 minutes, 4.4% 60 minutes or more (2006-2010 5-year est.)

**CHITTENANGO** (village). Covers a land area of 2.441 square miles and a water area of 0 square miles. Located at 43.04° N. Lat; 75.87° W. Long. Elevation is 453 feet.
**Population:** 4,792 (1990); 4,855 (2000); 5,081 (2010); Density: 2,081.4 persons per square mile (2010); Race: 96.2% White, 1.1% Black, 0.5% Asian, 0.7% American Indian/Alaska Native, 0.0% Native Hawaiian/Other Pacific Islander, 1.5% Other, 1.8% Hispanic of any race (2010); Average household size: 2.51 (2010); Median age: 39.8 (2010); Males per 100 females: 89.0 (2010); Marriage status: 22.1% never married, 60.2% now married, 7.2% widowed, 10.4% divorced (2006-2010 5-year est.); Foreign born: 0.7% (2006-2010 5-year est.); Ancestry (includes multiple ancestries): 24.2% German, 17.1% Irish, 15.7% English, 15.5% American, 14.3% Italian (2006-2010 5-year est.).
**Economy:** Single-family building permits issued: 1 (2011); Multi-family building permits issued: 0 (2011); Employment by occupation: 5.5% management, 4.8% professional, 11.6% services, 19.0% sales, 7.3% farming, 7.3% construction, 5.8% production (2006-2010 5-year est.).
**Income:** Per capita income: $25,356 (2006-2010 5-year est.); Median household income: $56,967 (2006-2010 5-year est.); Average household income: $63,202 (2006-2010 5-year est.); Percent of households with income of $100,000 or more: 17.4% (2006-2010 5-year est.); Poverty rate: 9.9% (2006-2010 5-year est.).
**Education:** Percent of population age 25 and over with: High school diploma (including GED) or higher: 89.9% (2006-2010 5-year est.); Bachelor's degree or higher: 21.8% (2006-2010 5-year est.); Master's degree or higher: 8.0% (2006-2010 5-year est.).

### School District(s)
Chittenango Central School District (KG-12)
    2009-10 Enrollment: 2,228 . . . . . . . . . . . . . . . . . . (315) 687-2840
**Housing:** Homeownership rate: 72.5% (2010); Median home value: $109,000 (2006-2010 5-year est.); Median contract rent: $504 per month (2006-2010 5-year est.); Median year structure built: 1972 (2006-2010 5-year est.).
**Safety:** Violent crime rate: 6.2 per 10,000 population; Property crime rate: 149.7 per 10,000 population (2010).
**Transportation:** Commute to work: 91.7% car, 1.9% public transportation, 1.5% walk, 3.2% work from home (2006-2010 5-year est.); Travel time to work: 18.6% less than 15 minutes, 41.2% 15 to 30 minutes, 31.2% 30 to 45 minutes, 4.8% 45 to 60 minutes, 4.2% 60 minutes or more (2006-2010 5-year est.)
**Additional Information Contacts**
Village of Chittenango . . . . . . . . . . . . . . . . . . . . . . . . . (315) 687-3936
    http://chittenango.org

**DE RUYTER** (village). Covers a land area of 0.343 square miles and a water area of 0 square miles. Located at 42.75° N. Lat; 75.88° W. Long. Elevation is 1,286 feet.
**Population:** 568 (1990); 531 (2000); 558 (2010); Density: 1,622.2 persons per square mile (2010); Race: 97.7% White, 0.5% Black, 0.5% Asian, 0.2% American Indian/Alaska Native, 0.0% Native Hawaiian/Other Pacific Islander, 1.1% Other, 0.4% Hispanic of any race (2010); Average household size: 2.45 (2010); Median age: 43.0 (2010); Males per 100 females: 79.4 (2010); Marriage status: 21.6% never married, 56.0% now married, 9.2% widowed, 13.2% divorced (2006-2010 5-year est.); Foreign born: 4.4% (2006-2010 5-year est.); Ancestry (includes multiple ancestries): 22.3% English, 21.1% American, 15.0% German, 12.6% Irish, 6.5% French Canadian (2006-2010 5-year est.).
**Economy:** Single-family building permits issued: 0 (2011); Multi-family building permits issued: 0 (2011); Employment by occupation: 14.7% management, 2.7% professional, 18.0% services, 14.0% sales, 2.7% farming, 17.3% construction, 13.3% production (2006-2010 5-year est.).
**Income:** Per capita income: $20,872 (2006-2010 5-year est.); Median household income: $48,438 (2006-2010 5-year est.); Average household

income: $51,275 (2006-2010 5-year est.); Percent of households with income of $100,000 or more: 9.6% (2006-2010 5-year est.); Poverty rate: 9.1% (2006-2010 5-year est.).

**Education:** Percent of population age 25 and over with: High school diploma (including GED) or higher: 91.8% (2006-2010 5-year est.); Bachelor's degree or higher: 14.5% (2006-2010 5-year est.); Master's degree or higher: 5.0% (2006-2010 5-year est.).

**Housing:** Homeownership rate: 62.3% (2010); Median home value: $81,100 (2006-2010 5-year est.); Median contract rent: $313 per month (2006-2010 5-year est.); Median year structure built: before 1940 (2006-2010 5-year est.).

**Transportation:** Commute to work: 87.9% car, 0.0% public transportation, 7.9% walk, 4.3% work from home (2006-2010 5-year est.); Travel time to work: 29.9% less than 15 minutes, 17.9% 15 to 30 minutes, 28.4% 30 to 45 minutes, 17.9% 45 to 60 minutes, 6.0% 60 minutes or more (2006-2010 5-year est.)

**DE RUYTER** (town). Covers a land area of 30.439 square miles and a water area of 0.832 square miles. Located at 42.76° N. Lat; 75.84° W. Long.

**Population:** 1,458 (1990); 1,532 (2000); 1,589 (2010); Density: 52.2 persons per square mile (2010); Race: 98.6% White, 0.3% Black, 0.2% Asian, 0.3% American Indian/Alaska Native, 0.0% Native Hawaiian/Other Pacific Islander, 0.6% Other, 0.4% Hispanic of any race (2010); Average household size: 2.50 (2010); Median age: 42.8 (2010); Males per 100 females: 94.0 (2010); Marriage status: 25.7% never married, 54.3% now married, 6.4% widowed, 13.6% divorced (2006-2010 5-year est.); Foreign born: 5.5% (2006-2010 5-year est.); Ancestry (includes multiple ancestries): 19.1% American, 17.0% German, 16.7% English, 15.4% Irish, 5.7% Dutch (2006-2010 5-year est.).

**Economy:** Single-family building permits issued: 2 (2011); Multi-family building permits issued: 0 (2011); Employment by occupation: 9.0% management, 1.0% professional, 12.6% services, 17.6% sales, 3.8% farming, 17.0% construction, 10.6% production (2006-2010 5-year est.).

**Income:** Per capita income: $23,293 (2006-2010 5-year est.); Median household income: $49,113 (2006-2010 5-year est.); Average household income: $59,347 (2006-2010 5-year est.); Percent of households with income of $100,000 or more: 12.8% (2006-2010 5-year est.); Poverty rate: 12.9% (2006-2010 5-year est.).

**Education:** Percent of population age 25 and over with: High school diploma (including GED) or higher: 91.1% (2006-2010 5-year est.); Bachelor's degree or higher: 16.3% (2006-2010 5-year est.); Master's degree or higher: 5.6% (2006-2010 5-year est.).

**Housing:** Homeownership rate: 79.3% (2010); Median home value: $91,100 (2006-2010 5-year est.); Median contract rent: $415 per month (2006-2010 5-year est.); Median year structure built: 1960 (2006-2010 5-year est.).

**Transportation:** Commute to work: 87.4% car, 0.0% public transportation, 5.9% walk, 2.9% work from home (2006-2010 5-year est.); Travel time to work: 27.4% less than 15 minutes, 17.5% 15 to 30 minutes, 36.5% 30 to 45 minutes, 14.1% 45 to 60 minutes, 4.5% 60 minutes or more (2006-2010 5-year est.)

**EARLVILLE** (village). Covers a land area of 1.079 square miles and a water area of 0 square miles. Located at 42.74° N. Lat; 75.54° W. Long. Elevation is 1,099 feet.

**Population:** 883 (1990); 791 (2000); 872 (2010); Density: 807.8 persons per square mile (2010); Race: 98.3% White, 0.6% Black, 0.0% Asian, 0.2% American Indian/Alaska Native, 0.0% Native Hawaiian/Other Pacific Islander, 0.9% Other, 1.5% Hispanic of any race (2010); Average household size: 2.45 (2010); Median age: 40.6 (2010); Males per 100 females: 98.6 (2010); Marriage status: 25.9% never married, 52.0% now married, 8.5% widowed, 13.6% divorced (2006-2010 5-year est.); Foreign born: 0.3% (2006-2010 5-year est.); Ancestry (includes multiple ancestries): 23.2% English, 16.6% German, 11.7% Irish, 8.1% American, 7.1% French (2006-2010 5-year est.).

**Economy:** Single-family building permits issued: 0 (2011); Multi-family building permits issued: 0 (2011); Employment by occupation: 11.8% management, 2.4% professional, 15.8% services, 18.5% sales, 0.7% farming, 14.9% construction, 5.3% production (2006-2010 5-year est.).

**Income:** Per capita income: $25,495 (2006-2010 5-year est.); Median household income: $55,962 (2006-2010 5-year est.); Average household income: $67,255 (2006-2010 5-year est.); Percent of households with income of $100,000 or more: 17.2% (2006-2010 5-year est.); Poverty rate: 8.8% (2006-2010 5-year est.).

**Education:** Percent of population age 25 and over with: High school diploma (including GED) or higher: 92.3% (2006-2010 5-year est.); Bachelor's degree or higher: 22.5% (2006-2010 5-year est.); Master's degree or higher: 7.0% (2006-2010 5-year est.).

**Housing:** Homeownership rate: 70.6% (2010); Median home value: $73,500 (2006-2010 5-year est.); Median contract rent: $540 per month (2006-2010 5-year est.); Median year structure built: before 1940 (2006-2010 5-year est.).

**Transportation:** Commute to work: 92.7% car, 0.0% public transportation, 2.9% walk, 4.4% work from home (2006-2010 5-year est.); Travel time to work: 51.5% less than 15 minutes, 29.2% 15 to 30 minutes, 9.2% 30 to 45 minutes, 5.3% 45 to 60 minutes, 4.8% 60 minutes or more (2006-2010 5-year est.)

**EATON** (town). Covers a land area of 44.621 square miles and a water area of 0.948 square miles. Located at 42.89° N. Lat; 75.63° W. Long. Elevation is 1,204 feet.

**Population:** 5,362 (1990); 4,826 (2000); 5,255 (2010); Density: 117.8 persons per square mile (2010); Race: 85.3% White, 10.6% Black, 0.8% Asian, 0.6% American Indian/Alaska Native, 0.0% Native Hawaiian/Other Pacific Islander, 2.7% Other, 3.6% Hispanic of any race (2010); Average household size: 2.48 (2010); Median age: 23.2 (2010); Males per 100 females: 102.5 (2010); Marriage status: 56.9% never married, 34.8% now married, 3.3% widowed, 4.9% divorced (2006-2010 5-year est.); Foreign born: 4.4% (2006-2010 5-year est.); Ancestry (includes multiple ancestries): 20.0% Irish, 19.0% American, 14.3% German, 12.8% English, 8.1% Italian (2006-2010 5-year est.).

**Economy:** Single-family building permits issued: 4 (2011); Multi-family building permits issued: 0 (2011); Employment by occupation: 11.1% management, 1.7% professional, 10.7% services, 16.6% sales, 3.5% farming, 12.7% construction, 6.9% production (2006-2010 5-year est.).

**Income:** Per capita income: $13,946 (2006-2010 5-year est.); Median household income: $47,864 (2006-2010 5-year est.); Average household income: $56,269 (2006-2010 5-year est.); Percent of households with income of $100,000 or more: 13.6% (2006-2010 5-year est.); Poverty rate: 14.7% (2006-2010 5-year est.).

**Education:** Percent of population age 25 and over with: High school diploma (including GED) or higher: 80.9% (2006-2010 5-year est.); Bachelor's degree or higher: 17.8% (2006-2010 5-year est.); Master's degree or higher: 9.5% (2006-2010 5-year est.).

**Housing:** Homeownership rate: 70.2% (2010); Median home value: $113,900 (2006-2010 5-year est.); Median contract rent: $444 per month (2006-2010 5-year est.); Median year structure built: 1965 (2006-2010 5-year est.).

**Transportation:** Commute to work: 75.6% car, 0.5% public transportation, 13.9% walk, 9.9% work from home (2006-2010 5-year est.); Travel time to work: 44.4% less than 15 minutes, 24.8% 15 to 30 minutes, 16.7% 30 to 45 minutes, 11.9% 45 to 60 minutes, 2.1% 60 minutes or more (2006-2010 5-year est.)

**ERIEVILLE** (unincorporated postal area)
Zip Code: 13061

Covers a land area of 25.987 square miles and a water area of 0.976 square miles. Located at 42.87° N. Lat; 75.76° W. Long. Elevation is 1,545 feet. Population: 1,040 (2010); Density: 40.0 persons per square mile (2010); Race: 98.4% White, 0.1% Black, 0.0% Asian, 0.4% American Indian/Alaska Native, 0.1% Native Hawaiian/Other Pacific Islander, 1.0% Other, 1.2% Hispanic of any race (2010); Average household size: 2.35 (2010); Median age: 45.3 (2010); Males per 100 females: 116.7 (2010); Homeownership rate: 86.5% (2010)

**FENNER** (town). Covers a land area of 31.073 square miles and a water area of 0.047 square miles. Located at 42.97° N. Lat; 75.77° W. Long. Elevation is 1,552 feet.

**Population:** 1,694 (1990); 1,680 (2000); 1,726 (2010); Density: 55.5 persons per square mile (2010); Race: 97.2% White, 0.9% Black, 0.1% Asian, 0.5% American Indian/Alaska Native, 0.0% Native Hawaiian/Other Pacific Islander, 1.3% Other, 0.8% Hispanic of any race (2010); Average household size: 2.58 (2010); Median age: 43.4 (2010); Males per 100 females: 107.2 (2010); Marriage status: 24.7% never married, 65.9% now married, 4.3% widowed, 5.1% divorced (2006-2010 5-year est.); Foreign born: 0.6% (2006-2010 5-year est.); Ancestry (includes multiple ancestries): 21.0% German, 21.0% Irish, 17.5% English, 14.4% American, 8.4% Polish (2006-2010 5-year est.).

**Economy:** Single-family building permits issued: 4 (2011); Multi-family building permits issued: 0 (2011); Employment by occupation: 14.8% management, 6.5% professional, 9.9% services, 16.7% sales, 4.2% farming, 10.0% construction, 7.6% production (2006-2010 5-year est.).
**Income:** Per capita income: $22,276 (2006-2010 5-year est.); Median household income: $51,951 (2006-2010 5-year est.); Average household income: $62,408 (2006-2010 5-year est.); Percent of households with income of $100,000 or more: 21.0% (2006-2010 5-year est.); Poverty rate: 9.0% (2006-2010 5-year est.).
**Education:** Percent of population age 25 and over with: High school diploma (including GED) or higher: 91.0% (2006-2010 5-year est.); Bachelor's degree or higher: 20.9% (2006-2010 5-year est.); Master's degree or higher: 6.8% (2006-2010 5-year est.).
**Housing:** Homeownership rate: 82.5% (2010); Median home value: $100,700 (2006-2010 5-year est.); Median contract rent: $510 per month (2006-2010 5-year est.); Median year structure built: 1975 (2006-2010 5-year est.).
**Transportation:** Commute to work: 91.4% car, 0.0% public transportation, 2.2% walk, 5.2% work from home (2006-2010 5-year est.); Travel time to work: 27.0% less than 15 minutes, 36.2% 15 to 30 minutes, 29.9% 30 to 45 minutes, 4.0% 45 to 60 minutes, 3.0% 60 minutes or more (2006-2010 5-year est.)

**GEORGETOWN** (town). Covers a land area of 40.077 square miles and a water area of 0.098 square miles. Located at 42.78° N. Lat; 75.74° W. Long. Elevation is 1,411 feet.
**Population:** 932 (1990); 946 (2000); 974 (2010); Density: 24.3 persons per square mile (2010); Race: 87.3% White, 10.7% Black, 0.4% Asian, 0.5% American Indian/Alaska Native, 0.0% Native Hawaiian/Other Pacific Islander, 1.1% Other, 3.4% Hispanic of any race (2010); Average household size: 2.72 (2010); Median age: 39.2 (2010); Males per 100 females: 142.3 (2010); Marriage status: 43.6% never married, 47.7% now married, 3.4% widowed, 5.3% divorced (2006-2010 5-year est.); Foreign born: 0.7% (2006-2010 5-year est.); Ancestry (includes multiple ancestries): 17.2% American, 10.8% German, 9.6% Irish, 6.3% English, 3.8% French (2006-2010 5-year est.).
**Economy:** Single-family building permits issued: 2 (2011); Multi-family building permits issued: 0 (2011); Employment by occupation: 7.9% management, 3.2% professional, 12.6% services, 16.6% sales, 1.2% farming, 15.4% construction, 14.6% production (2006-2010 5-year est.).
**Income:** Per capita income: $16,257 (2006-2010 5-year est.); Median household income: $46,875 (2006-2010 5-year est.); Average household income: $55,214 (2006-2010 5-year est.); Percent of households with income of $100,000 or more: 8.3% (2006-2010 5-year est.); Poverty rate: 10.0% (2006-2010 5-year est.).
**Education:** Percent of population age 25 and over with: High school diploma (including GED) or higher: 75.3% (2006-2010 5-year est.); Bachelor's degree or higher: 6.4% (2006-2010 5-year est.); Master's degree or higher: 3.8% (2006-2010 5-year est.).

School District(s)

Georgetown-South Otselic Central School District (KG-12)
   2009-10 Enrollment: 388 . . . . . . . . . . . . . . . . . . . . . . . (315) 653-7218
**Housing:** Homeownership rate: 84.5% (2010); Median home value: $85,500 (2006-2010 5-year est.); Median contract rent: $492 per month (2006-2010 5-year est.); Median year structure built: 1963 (2006-2010 5-year est.).
**Transportation:** Commute to work: 92.3% car, 0.0% public transportation, 2.8% walk, 1.2% work from home (2006-2010 5-year est.); Travel time to work: 16.0% less than 15 minutes, 24.2% 15 to 30 minutes, 33.2% 30 to 45 minutes, 20.5% 45 to 60 minutes, 6.1% 60 minutes or more (2006-2010 5-year est.)

**HAMILTON** (village). Covers a land area of 2.486 square miles and a water area of 0.192 square miles. Located at 42.82° N. Lat; 75.55° W. Long. Elevation is 1,122 feet.
**Population:** 3,828 (1990); 3,509 (2000); 4,239 (2010); Density: 1,704.9 persons per square mile (2010); Race: 85.6% White, 5.0% Black, 5.5% Asian, 0.1% American Indian/Alaska Native, 0.0% Native Hawaiian/Other Pacific Islander, 3.8% Other, 4.6% Hispanic of any race (2010); Average household size: 2.27 (2010); Median age: 21.3 (2010); Males per 100 females: 83.7 (2010); Marriage status: 76.5% never married, 16.7% now married, 2.9% widowed, 3.9% divorced (2006-2010 5-year est.); Foreign born: 6.1% (2006-2010 5-year est.); Ancestry (includes multiple ancestries): 15.9% German, 15.0% Irish, 14.7% English, 10.4% Italian, 9.7% American (2006-2010 5-year est.).

**Economy:** Single-family building permits issued: 0 (2011); Multi-family building permits issued: 0 (2011); Employment by occupation: 7.6% management, 2.9% professional, 9.4% services, 19.4% sales, 1.2% farming, 3.4% construction, 3.0% production (2006-2010 5-year est.).
**Income:** Per capita income: $16,216 (2006-2010 5-year est.); Median household income: $48,036 (2006-2010 5-year est.); Average household income: $75,165 (2006-2010 5-year est.); Percent of households with income of $100,000 or more: 26.3% (2006-2010 5-year est.); Poverty rate: 15.1% (2006-2010 5-year est.).
**Taxes:** Total city taxes per capita: $375 (2009); City property taxes per capita: $354 (2009).
**Education:** Percent of population age 25 and over with: High school diploma (including GED) or higher: 96.7% (2006-2010 5-year est.); Bachelor's degree or higher: 56.8% (2006-2010 5-year est.); Master's degree or higher: 40.5% (2006-2010 5-year est.).

School District(s)

Hamilton Central School District (PK-12)
   2009-10 Enrollment: 610 . . . . . . . . . . . . . . . . . . . . . . . (315) 824-6310

Four-year College(s)

Colgate University (Private, Not-for-profit)
   Fall 2010 Enrollment: 2,887 . . . . . . . . . . . . . . . . . (315) 228-1000
   2011-12 Tuition: In-state $42,920; Out-of-state $42,920
**Housing:** Homeownership rate: 42.7% (2010); Median home value: $196,900 (2006-2010 5-year est.); Median contract rent: $600 per month (2006-2010 5-year est.); Median year structure built: before 1940 (2006-2010 5-year est.).
**Hospitals:** Community Memorial Hospital (88 beds)
**Transportation:** Commute to work: 42.2% car, 0.9% public transportation, 46.0% walk, 7.3% work from home (2006-2010 5-year est.); Travel time to work: 81.0% less than 15 minutes, 12.2% 15 to 30 minutes, 4.5% 30 to 45 minutes, 1.0% 45 to 60 minutes, 1.3% 60 minutes or more (2006-2010 5-year est.).
**Airports:** Hamilton Municipal (general aviation)
**Additional Information Contacts**
Hamilton Business Alliance . . . . . . . . . . . . . . . . . . . (315) 824-3903
   http://www.visithamiltonny.com/thrive

**HAMILTON** (town). Covers a land area of 41.339 square miles and a water area of 0.115 square miles. Located at 42.79° N. Lat; 75.48° W. Long. Elevation is 1,122 feet.
**History:** Seat of Colgate University. Settled 1795, incorporated 1816.
**Population:** 6,221 (1990); 5,733 (2000); 6,690 (2010); Density: 161.8 persons per square mile (2010); Race: 89.6% White, 3.6% Black, 3.7% Asian, 0.1% American Indian/Alaska Native, 0.0% Native Hawaiian/Other Pacific Islander, 3.0% Other, 3.6% Hispanic of any race (2010); Average household size: 2.40 (2010); Median age: 22.1 (2010); Males per 100 females: 90.0 (2010); Marriage status: 54.7% never married, 33.7% now married, 4.3% widowed, 7.3% divorced (2006-2010 5-year est.); Foreign born: 4.2% (2006-2010 5-year est.); Ancestry (includes multiple ancestries): 19.7% German, 15.1% Irish, 14.9% English, 12.3% American, 7.3% Italian (2006-2010 5-year est.).
**Economy:** Single-family building permits issued: 1 (2011); Multi-family building permits issued: 0 (2011); Employment by occupation: 9.7% management, 3.2% professional, 9.8% services, 14.1% sales, 2.0% farming, 8.7% construction, 4.6% production (2006-2010 5-year est.).
**Income:** Per capita income: $20,203 (2006-2010 5-year est.); Median household income: $52,899 (2006-2010 5-year est.); Average household income: $66,851 (2006-2010 5-year est.); Percent of households with income of $100,000 or more: 18.9% (2006-2010 5-year est.); Poverty rate: 7.9% (2006-2010 5-year est.).
**Education:** Percent of population age 25 and over with: High school diploma (including GED) or higher: 95.0% (2006-2010 5-year est.); Bachelor's degree or higher: 38.6% (2006-2010 5-year est.); Master's degree or higher: 23.4% (2006-2010 5-year est.).

School District(s)

Hamilton Central School District (PK-12)
   2009-10 Enrollment: 610 . . . . . . . . . . . . . . . . . . . . . . . (315) 824-6310

Four-year College(s)

Colgate University (Private, Not-for-profit)
   Fall 2010 Enrollment: 2,887 . . . . . . . . . . . . . . . . . (315) 228-1000
   2011-12 Tuition: In-state $42,920; Out-of-state $42,920
**Housing:** Homeownership rate: 61.5% (2010); Median home value: $126,900 (2006-2010 5-year est.); Median contract rent: $581 per month (2006-2010 5-year est.); Median year structure built: before 1940 (2006-2010 5-year est.).

**Hospitals:** Community Memorial Hospital (88 beds)
**Transportation:** Commute to work: 62.2% car, 0.5% public transportation, 25.8% walk, 8.5% work from home (2006-2010 5-year est.); Travel time to work: 64.0% less than 15 minutes, 23.7% 15 to 30 minutes, 9.3% 30 to 45 minutes, 1.1% 45 to 60 minutes, 1.8% 60 minutes or more (2006-2010 5-year est.)
**Airports:** Hamilton Municipal (general aviation)

## HUBBARDSVILLE (unincorporated postal area)
Zip Code: 13355

Covers a land area of 29.107 square miles and a water area of 0.013 square miles. Located at 42.80° N. Lat; 75.43° W. Long. Elevation is 1,214 feet. Population: 905 (2010); Density: 31.1 persons per square mile (2010); Race: 96.4% White, 0.9% Black, 0.1% Asian, 0.4% American Indian/Alaska Native, 0.0% Native Hawaiian/Other Pacific Islander, 2.2% Other, 1.1% Hispanic of any race (2010); Average household size: 2.85 (2010); Median age: 38.0 (2010); Males per 100 females: 107.1 (2010); Homeownership rate: 84.9% (2010)

## LEBANON (town).
Covers a land area of 43.344 square miles and a water area of 0.335 square miles. Located at 42.78° N. Lat; 75.62° W. Long. Elevation is 1,345 feet.
**Population:** 1,265 (1990); 1,329 (2000); 1,332 (2010); Density: 30.7 persons per square mile (2010); Race: 98.2% White, 0.2% Black, 0.1% Asian, 0.5% American Indian/Alaska Native, 0.1% Native Hawaiian/Other Pacific Islander, 0.9% Other, 2.2% Hispanic of any race (2010); Average household size: 2.51 (2010); Median age: 43.2 (2010); Males per 100 females: 105.9 (2010); Marriage status: 21.9% never married, 55.8% now married, 5.8% widowed, 16.4% divorced (2006-2010 5-year est.); Foreign born: 0.5% (2006-2010 5-year est.); Ancestry (includes multiple ancestries): 17.8% German, 16.9% English, 15.4% American, 12.6% Irish, 9.9% Polish (2006-2010 5-year est.).
**Economy:** Single-family building permits issued: 2 (2011); Multi-family building permits issued: 0 (2011); Employment by occupation: 9.4% management, 2.2% professional, 10.1% services, 20.1% sales, 1.5% farming, 13.7% construction, 10.0% production (2006-2010 5-year est.).
**Income:** Per capita income: $23,035 (2006-2010 5-year est.); Median household income: $42,500 (2006-2010 5-year est.); Average household income: $52,680 (2006-2010 5-year est.); Percent of households with income of $100,000 or more: 11.6% (2006-2010 5-year est.); Poverty rate: 9.1% (2006-2010 5-year est.).
**Education:** Percent of population age 25 and over with: High school diploma (including GED) or higher: 87.8% (2006-2010 5-year est.); Bachelor's degree or higher: 19.1% (2006-2010 5-year est.); Master's degree or higher: 8.6% (2006-2010 5-year est.).
**Housing:** Homeownership rate: 82.9% (2010); Median home value: $91,800 (2006-2010 5-year est.); Median contract rent: $499 per month (2006-2010 5-year est.); Median year structure built: 1962 (2006-2010 5-year est.).
**Transportation:** Commute to work: 85.4% car, 0.0% public transportation, 6.9% walk, 4.0% work from home (2006-2010 5-year est.); Travel time to work: 36.6% less than 15 minutes, 35.6% 15 to 30 minutes, 17.7% 30 to 45 minutes, 3.4% 45 to 60 minutes, 6.7% 60 minutes or more (2006-2010 5-year est.)

## LENOX (town).
Covers a land area of 36.242 square miles and a water area of 0.023 square miles. Located at 43.11° N. Lat; 75.75° W. Long. Elevation is 528 feet.
**Population:** 8,621 (1990); 8,665 (2000); 9,122 (2010); Density: 251.7 persons per square mile (2010); Race: 96.2% White, 1.0% Black, 0.4% Asian, 0.6% American Indian/Alaska Native, 0.0% Native Hawaiian/Other Pacific Islander, 1.8% Other, 1.6% Hispanic of any race (2010); Average household size: 2.44 (2010); Median age: 40.9 (2010); Males per 100 females: 94.5 (2010); Marriage status: 28.4% never married, 52.4% now married, 7.5% widowed, 11.8% divorced (2006-2010 5-year est.); Foreign born: 1.6% (2006-2010 5-year est.); Ancestry (includes multiple ancestries): 19.5% Italian, 19.0% German, 16.0% English, 15.7% American, 13.2% Irish (2006-2010 5-year est.).
**Economy:** Single-family building permits issued: 3 (2011); Multi-family building permits issued: 0 (2011); Employment by occupation: 8.0% management, 3.4% professional, 10.1% services, 22.9% sales, 2.7% farming, 9.5% construction, 7.9% production (2006-2010 5-year est.).
**Income:** Per capita income: $22,970 (2006-2010 5-year est.); Median household income: $48,780 (2006-2010 5-year est.); Average household income: $56,729 (2006-2010 5-year est.); Percent of households with

income of $100,000 or more: 12.9% (2006-2010 5-year est.); Poverty rate: 7.2% (2006-2010 5-year est.).
**Education:** Percent of population age 25 and over with: High school diploma (including GED) or higher: 87.4% (2006-2010 5-year est.); Bachelor's degree or higher: 18.3% (2006-2010 5-year est.); Master's degree or higher: 6.6% (2006-2010 5-year est.).
**Housing:** Homeownership rate: 69.0% (2010); Median home value: $95,800 (2006-2010 5-year est.); Median contract rent: $549 per month (2006-2010 5-year est.); Median year structure built: 1958 (2006-2010 5-year est.).
**Transportation:** Commute to work: 93.2% car, 0.9% public transportation, 2.9% walk, 1.9% work from home (2006-2010 5-year est.); Travel time to work: 28.1% less than 15 minutes, 36.5% 15 to 30 minutes, 24.2% 30 to 45 minutes, 6.3% 45 to 60 minutes, 4.9% 60 minutes or more (2006-2010 5-year est.)

## LEONARDSVILLE (unincorporated postal area)
Zip Code: 13364

Covers a land area of 2.956 square miles and a water area of 0 square miles. Located at 42.80° N. Lat; 75.26° W. Long. Elevation is 1,168 feet. Population: 243 (2010); Density: 82.2 persons per square mile (2010); Race: 99.2% White, 0.4% Black, 0.4% Asian, 0.0% American Indian/Alaska Native, 0.0% Native Hawaiian/Other Pacific Islander, 0.0% Other, 1.2% Hispanic of any race (2010); Average household size: 2.64 (2010); Median age: 40.8 (2010); Males per 100 females: 84.1 (2010); Homeownership rate: 84.8% (2010)

## LINCOLN (town).
Covers a land area of 24.999 square miles and a water area of 0.058 square miles. Located at 43.03° N. Lat; 75.73° W. Long. Elevation is 689 feet.
**Population:** 1,669 (1990); 1,818 (2000); 2,012 (2010); Density: 80.5 persons per square mile (2010); Race: 96.6% White, 0.4% Black, 0.4% Asian, 1.5% American Indian/Alaska Native, 0.0% Native Hawaiian/Other Pacific Islander, 1.1% Other, 1.4% Hispanic of any race (2010); Average household size: 2.65 (2010); Median age: 41.6 (2010); Males per 100 females: 113.6 (2010); Marriage status: 20.9% never married, 60.7% now married, 3.8% widowed, 14.6% divorced (2006-2010 5-year est.); Foreign born: 1.2% (2006-2010 5-year est.); Ancestry (includes multiple ancestries): 20.8% American, 18.3% English, 17.3% Italian, 13.9% Irish, 9.4% German (2006-2010 5-year est.).
**Economy:** Single-family building permits issued: 4 (2011); Multi-family building permits issued: 0 (2011); Employment by occupation: 8.0% management, 5.4% professional, 7.3% services, 15.6% sales, 2.9% farming, 14.6% construction, 10.4% production (2006-2010 5-year est.).
**Income:** Per capita income: $30,055 (2006-2010 5-year est.); Median household income: $62,143 (2006-2010 5-year est.); Average household income: $74,885 (2006-2010 5-year est.); Percent of households with income of $100,000 or more: 22.9% (2006-2010 5-year est.); Poverty rate: 4.3% (2006-2010 5-year est.).
**Education:** Percent of population age 25 and over with: High school diploma (including GED) or higher: 86.3% (2006-2010 5-year est.); Bachelor's degree or higher: 19.6% (2006-2010 5-year est.); Master's degree or higher: 6.1% (2006-2010 5-year est.).
**Housing:** Homeownership rate: 88.0% (2010); Median home value: $103,100 (2006-2010 5-year est.); Median contract rent: $554 per month (2006-2010 5-year est.); Median year structure built: 1978 (2006-2010 5-year est.).
**Transportation:** Commute to work: 87.7% car, 0.0% public transportation, 2.4% walk, 7.9% work from home (2006-2010 5-year est.); Travel time to work: 31.7% less than 15 minutes, 35.2% 15 to 30 minutes, 24.2% 30 to 45 minutes, 5.5% 45 to 60 minutes, 3.3% 60 minutes or more (2006-2010 5-year est.)

## MADISON (village).
Covers a land area of 0.502 square miles and a water area of 0 square miles. Located at 42.89° N. Lat; 75.51° W. Long. Elevation is 1,204 feet.
**Population:** 316 (1990); 315 (2000); 305 (2010); Density: 607.6 persons per square mile (2010); Race: 99.7% White, 0.0% Black, 0.0% Asian, 0.0% American Indian/Alaska Native, 0.0% Native Hawaiian/Other Pacific Islander, 0.3% Other, 0.3% Hispanic of any race (2010); Average household size: 2.27 (2010); Median age: 38.9 (2010); Males per 100 females: 89.4 (2010); Marriage status: 31.8% never married, 47.1% now married, 6.7% widowed, 14.3% divorced (2006-2010 5-year est.); Foreign born: 1.5% (2006-2010 5-year est.); Ancestry (includes multiple

ancestries): 19.3% Irish, 18.6% English, 17.6% American, 16.0% German, 12.5% Welsh (2006-2010 5-year est.).
**Economy:** Single-family building permits issued: 0 (2011); Multi-family building permits issued: 0 (2011); Employment by occupation: 8.1% management, 4.1% professional, 17.4% services, 11.0% sales, 15.1% farming, 8.7% construction, 2.3% production (2006-2010 5-year est.).
**Income:** Per capita income: $17,919 (2006-2010 5-year est.); Median household income: $31,429 (2006-2010 5-year est.); Average household income: $40,130 (2006-2010 5-year est.); Percent of households with income of $100,000 or more: 8.3% (2006-2010 5-year est.); Poverty rate: 21.9% (2006-2010 5-year est.).
**Education:** Percent of population age 25 and over with: High school diploma (including GED) or higher: 94.6% (2006-2010 5-year est.); Bachelor's degree or higher: 18.8% (2006-2010 5-year est.); Master's degree or higher: 12.6% (2006-2010 5-year est.).

### School District(s)

Madison Central School District (PK-12)
    2009-10 Enrollment: 507 . . . . . . . . . . . . . . . . . . . . . . . (315) 893-1878
**Housing:** Homeownership rate: 63.4% (2010); Median home value: $90,000 (2006-2010 5-year est.); Median contract rent: $575 per month (2006-2010 5-year est.); Median year structure built: before 1940 (2006-2010 5-year est.).
**Transportation:** Commute to work: 89.8% car, 0.0% public transportation, 1.1% walk, 4.5% work from home (2006-2010 5-year est.); Travel time to work: 37.5% less than 15 minutes, 31.5% 15 to 30 minutes, 25.0% 30 to 45 minutes, 2.4% 45 to 60 minutes, 3.6% 60 minutes or more (2006-2010 5-year est.)

**MADISON** (town). Covers a land area of 40.812 square miles and a water area of 0.576 square miles. Located at 42.89° N. Lat; 75.50° W. Long. Elevation is 1,204 feet.
**Population:** 2,774 (1990); 2,801 (2000); 3,008 (2010); Density: 73.7 persons per square mile (2010); Race: 98.7% White, 0.4% Black, 0.3% Asian, 0.2% American Indian/Alaska Native, 0.0% Native Hawaiian/Other Pacific Islander, 0.4% Other, 1.3% Hispanic of any race (2010); Average household size: 2.37 (2010); Median age: 44.3 (2010); Males per 100 females: 99.9 (2010); Marriage status: 22.5% never married, 58.3% now married, 6.9% widowed, 12.3% divorced (2006-2010 5-year est.); Foreign born: 1.7% (2006-2010 5-year est.); Ancestry (includes multiple ancestries): 22.7% German, 22.0% Irish, 21.2% English, 8.5% American, 7.1% French (2006-2010 5-year est.).
**Economy:** Single-family building permits issued: 2 (2011); Multi-family building permits issued: 0 (2011); Employment by occupation: 14.5% management, 1.9% professional, 12.5% services, 15.4% sales, 3.2% farming, 14.6% construction, 2.9% production (2006-2010 5-year est.).
**Income:** Per capita income: $26,747 (2006-2010 5-year est.); Median household income: $43,913 (2006-2010 5-year est.); Average household income: $59,583 (2006-2010 5-year est.); Percent of households with income of $100,000 or more: 14.6% (2006-2010 5-year est.); Poverty rate: 10.0% (2006-2010 5-year est.).
**Education:** Percent of population age 25 and over with: High school diploma (including GED) or higher: 87.7% (2006-2010 5-year est.); Bachelor's degree or higher: 24.2% (2006-2010 5-year est.); Master's degree or higher: 11.9% (2006-2010 5-year est.).

### School District(s)

Madison Central School District (PK-12)
    2009-10 Enrollment: 507 . . . . . . . . . . . . . . . . . . . . . . . (315) 893-1878
**Housing:** Homeownership rate: 79.7% (2010); Median home value: $122,600 (2006-2010 5-year est.); Median contract rent: $549 per month (2006-2010 5-year est.); Median year structure built: 1968 (2006-2010 5-year est.).
**Transportation:** Commute to work: 83.9% car, 0.7% public transportation, 3.4% walk, 10.0% work from home (2006-2010 5-year est.); Travel time to work: 44.1% less than 15 minutes, 28.8% 15 to 30 minutes, 14.3% 30 to 45 minutes, 6.1% 45 to 60 minutes, 6.7% 60 minutes or more (2006-2010 5-year est.)

**MORRISVILLE** (village). Covers a land area of 1.152 square miles and a water area of 0 square miles. Located at 42.89° N. Lat; 75.64° W. Long. Elevation is 1,348 feet.
**Population:** 2,732 (1990); 2,148 (2000); 2,199 (2010); Density: 1,908.0 persons per square mile (2010); Race: 73.0% White, 20.4% Black, 1.4% Asian, 0.4% American Indian/Alaska Native, 0.0% Native Hawaiian/Other Pacific Islander, 4.8% Other, 6.7% Hispanic of any race (2010); Average household size: 2.26 (2010); Median age: 20.7 (2010); Males per 100

females: 106.1 (2010); Marriage status: 82.6% never married, 10.9% now married, 3.5% widowed, 3.0% divorced (2006-2010 5-year est.); Foreign born: 8.7% (2006-2010 5-year est.); Ancestry (includes multiple ancestries): 17.3% Irish, 15.0% American, 12.4% German, 8.8% English, 7.9% Italian (2006-2010 5-year est.).
**Economy:** Single-family building permits issued: 0 (2011); Multi-family building permits issued: 0 (2011); Employment by occupation: 4.9% management, 0.4% professional, 14.9% services, 22.1% sales, 5.1% farming, 8.3% construction, 4.1% production (2006-2010 5-year est.).
**Income:** Per capita income: $7,794 (2006-2010 5-year est.); Median household income: $49,896 (2006-2010 5-year est.); Average household income: $53,200 (2006-2010 5-year est.); Percent of households with income of $100,000 or more: 8.5% (2006-2010 5-year est.); Poverty rate: 18.6% (2006-2010 5-year est.).
**Education:** Percent of population age 25 and over with: High school diploma (including GED) or higher: 85.2% (2006-2010 5-year est.); Bachelor's degree or higher: 23.7% (2006-2010 5-year est.); Master's degree or higher: 12.8% (2006-2010 5-year est.).

### School District(s)

Morrisville-Eaton Central School District (PK-12)
    2009-10 Enrollment: 784 . . . . . . . . . . . . . . . . . . . . . . . (315) 684-9300

### Four-year College(s)

Morrisville State College (Public)
    Fall 2010 Enrollment: 3,098 . . . . . . . . . . . . . . . . . . . (315) 684-6000
    2011-12 Tuition: In-state $7,520; Out-of-state $11,540
**Housing:** Homeownership rate: 47.2% (2010); Median home value: $114,200 (2006-2010 5-year est.); Median contract rent: $523 per month (2006-2010 5-year est.); Median year structure built: before 1940 (2006-2010 5-year est.).
**Transportation:** Commute to work: 52.5% car, 1.3% public transportation, 32.0% walk, 13.9% work from home (2006-2010 5-year est.); Travel time to work: 57.7% less than 15 minutes, 24.7% 15 to 30 minutes, 10.0% 30 to 45 minutes, 6.6% 45 to 60 minutes, 1.0% 60 minutes or more (2006-2010 5-year est.)

**MUNNSVILLE** (village). Covers a land area of 0.849 square miles and a water area of 0 square miles. Located at 42.97° N. Lat; 75.58° W. Long. Elevation is 659 feet.
**Population:** 438 (1990); 437 (2000); 474 (2010); Density: 558.0 persons per square mile (2010); Race: 96.8% White, 0.6% Black, 0.4% Asian, 1.3% American Indian/Alaska Native, 0.0% Native Hawaiian/Other Pacific Islander, 0.9% Other, 0.6% Hispanic of any race (2010); Average household size: 2.60 (2010); Median age: 32.7 (2010); Males per 100 females: 95.1 (2010); Marriage status: 32.7% never married, 41.3% now married, 6.7% widowed, 19.3% divorced (2006-2010 5-year est.); Foreign born: 0.0% (2006-2010 5-year est.); Ancestry (includes multiple ancestries): 22.3% Irish, 19.0% English, 15.0% German, 10.4% Italian, 8.6% American (2006-2010 5-year est.).
**Economy:** Single-family building permits issued: 0 (2011); Multi-family building permits issued: 0 (2011); Employment by occupation: 10.3% management, 0.6% professional, 9.1% services, 10.3% sales, 1.8% farming, 18.8% construction, 7.3% production (2006-2010 5-year est.).
**Income:** Per capita income: $22,046 (2006-2010 5-year est.); Median household income: $46,250 (2006-2010 5-year est.); Average household income: $48,189 (2006-2010 5-year est.); Percent of households with income of $100,000 or more: 11.3% (2006-2010 5-year est.); Poverty rate: 12.9% (2006-2010 5-year est.).
**Education:** Percent of population age 25 and over with: High school diploma (including GED) or higher: 85.3% (2006-2010 5-year est.); Bachelor's degree or higher: 15.6% (2006-2010 5-year est.); Master's degree or higher: 10.7% (2006-2010 5-year est.).

### School District(s)

Stockbridge Valley Central School District (PK-12)
    2009-10 Enrollment: 498 . . . . . . . . . . . . . . . . . . . . . . . (315) 495-4400
**Housing:** Homeownership rate: 67.0% (2010); Median home value: $87,800 (2006-2010 5-year est.); Median contract rent: $400 per month (2006-2010 5-year est.); Median year structure built: before 1940 (2006-2010 5-year est.).
**Transportation:** Commute to work: 90.0% car, 0.0% public transportation, 1.9% walk, 5.0% work from home (2006-2010 5-year est.); Travel time to work: 40.8% less than 15 minutes, 21.7% 15 to 30 minutes, 24.3% 30 to 45 minutes, 10.5% 45 to 60 minutes, 2.6% 60 minutes or more (2006-2010 5-year est.)

**NELSON** (town). Covers a land area of 43.060 square miles and a water area of 0.995 square miles. Located at 42.88° N. Lat; 75.74° W. Long. Elevation is 1,437 feet.
**Population:** 1,892 (1990); 1,964 (2000); 1,980 (2010); Density: 46.0 persons per square mile (2010); Race: 97.8% White, 0.3% Black, 0.3% Asian, 0.2% American Indian/Alaska Native, 0.1% Native Hawaiian/Other Pacific Islander, 1.3% Other, 1.3% Hispanic of any race (2010); Average household size: 2.45 (2010); Median age: 44.5 (2010); Males per 100 females: 104.3 (2010); Marriage status: 27.3% never married, 56.9% now married, 6.4% widowed, 9.4% divorced (2006-2010 5-year est.); Foreign born: 2.5% (2006-2010 5-year est.); Ancestry (includes multiple ancestries): 27.0% German, 19.6% American, 19.3% English, 18.6% Irish, 9.5% French (2006-2010 5-year est.).
**Economy:** Single-family building permits issued: 3 (2011); Multi-family building permits issued: 0 (2011); Employment by occupation: 12.0% management, 9.2% professional, 8.0% services, 12.4% sales, 2.7% farming, 11.7% construction, 7.1% production (2006-2010 5-year est.).
**Income:** Per capita income: $29,863 (2006-2010 5-year est.); Median household income: $69,732 (2006-2010 5-year est.); Average household income: $80,744 (2006-2010 5-year est.); Percent of households with income of $100,000 or more: 27.5% (2006-2010 5-year est.); Poverty rate: 5.4% (2006-2010 5-year est.).
**Education:** Percent of population age 25 and over with: High school diploma (including GED) or higher: 93.7% (2006-2010 5-year est.); Bachelor's degree or higher: 29.5% (2006-2010 5-year est.); Master's degree or higher: 10.8% (2006-2010 5-year est.).
**Housing:** Homeownership rate: 85.7% (2010); Median home value: $156,100 (2006-2010 5-year est.); Median contract rent: $625 per month (2006-2010 5-year est.); Median year structure built: 1966 (2006-2010 5-year est.).
**Transportation:** Commute to work: 88.8% car, 0.0% public transportation, 1.9% walk, 7.6% work from home (2006-2010 5-year est.); Travel time to work: 22.0% less than 15 minutes, 18.1% 15 to 30 minutes, 32.4% 30 to 45 minutes, 13.1% 45 to 60 minutes, 14.4% 60 minutes or more (2006-2010 5-year est.)

**NEW WOODSTOCK** (unincorporated postal area)
Zip Code: 13122
   Covers a land area of 18.699 square miles and a water area of 0.015 square miles. Located at 42.84° N. Lat; 75.85° W. Long. Elevation is 1,306 feet. Population: 1,174 (2010); Density: 62.8 persons per square mile (2010); Race: 97.8% White, 0.4% Black, 0.3% Asian, 0.3% American Indian/Alaska Native, 0.5% Native Hawaiian/Other Pacific Islander, 0.7% Other, 2.2% Hispanic of any race (2010); Average household size: 2.82 (2010); Median age: 39.1 (2010); Males per 100 females: 93.1 (2010); Homeownership rate: 79.1% (2010)

**NORTH BROOKFIELD** (unincorporated postal area)
Zip Code: 13418
   Covers a land area of 5.216 square miles and a water area of <.001 square miles. Located at 42.84° N. Lat; 75.38° W. Long. Elevation is 1,299 feet. Population: 255 (2010); Density: 48.9 persons per square mile (2010); Race: 96.5% White, 0.4% Black, 0.0% Asian, 0.0% American Indian/Alaska Native, 0.0% Native Hawaiian/Other Pacific Islander, 3.1% Other, 1.2% Hispanic of any race (2010); Average household size: 2.74 (2010); Median age: 36.6 (2010); Males per 100 females: 109.0 (2010); Homeownership rate: 85.0% (2010)

**ONEIDA** (city). Aka East. Covers a land area of 22.047 square miles and a water area of 0.081 square miles. Located at 43.07° N. Lat; 75.67° W. Long. Elevation is 430 feet.
**History:** The establishment and early growth of Oneida resulted from a shrewd bargain made by Sands Higinbotham, owner of the city site, with the railroad. The railroad received free right of way across his land, plus ample ground for a station, on the condition that it stop every passenger train at the depot for ten minutes for refreshments. Higinbotham then built the Railroad House to serve meals to passengers.
**Population:** 10,850 (1990); 10,987 (2000); 11,393 (2010); Density: 516.8 persons per square mile (2010); Race: 94.1% White, 1.2% Black, 0.8% Asian, 2.1% American Indian/Alaska Native, 0.0% Native Hawaiian/Other Pacific Islander, 1.8% Other, 1.4% Hispanic of any race (2010); Average household size: 2.34 (2010); Median age: 40.4 (2010); Males per 100 females: 93.7 (2010); Marriage status: 28.9% never married, 52.0% now married, 8.2% widowed, 10.8% divorced (2006-2010 5-year est.); Foreign born: 2.2% (2006-2010 5-year est.); Ancestry (includes multiple

ancestries): 26.9% German, 24.4% Irish, 16.7% English, 11.7% Italian, 10.8% American (2006-2010 5-year est.).
**Economy:** Single-family building permits issued: 1 (2011); Multi-family building permits issued: 2 (2011); Employment by occupation: 10.8% management, 2.6% professional, 11.3% services, 16.5% sales, 4.2% farming, 6.5% construction, 7.1% production (2006-2010 5-year est.).
**Income:** Per capita income: $23,553 (2006-2010 5-year est.); Median household income: $46,351 (2006-2010 5-year est.); Average household income: $57,081 (2006-2010 5-year est.); Percent of households with income of $100,000 or more: 13.2% (2006-2010 5-year est.); Poverty rate: 10.6% (2006-2010 5-year est.).
**Education:** Percent of population age 25 and over with: High school diploma (including GED) or higher: 88.3% (2006-2010 5-year est.); Bachelor's degree or higher: 19.7% (2006-2010 5-year est.); Master's degree or higher: 7.5% (2006-2010 5-year est.).

**School District(s)**
Oneida City School District (PK-12)
   2009-10 Enrollment: 2,430 . . . . . . . . . . . . . . . . . . . (315) 363-2550
**Housing:** Homeownership rate: 57.3% (2010); Median home value: $96,000 (2006-2010 5-year est.); Median contract rent: $524 per month (2006-2010 5-year est.); Median year structure built: 1940 (2006-2010 5-year est.).
**Hospitals:** Oneida Healthcare Center (101 beds)
**Safety:** Violent crime rate: 12.4 per 10,000 population; Property crime rate: 439.7 per 10,000 population (2010).
**Newspapers:** Chittenango/Bridgeport Pennysaver (Community news; Circulation 24,200); Oneida Daily Dispatch (Local news; Circulation 7,500); Oneida Indian Nation (Local news); Oneida/Canastota/VVS Pennysaver (Community news; Circulation 27,000)
**Transportation:** Commute to work: 90.5% car, 0.2% public transportation, 2.8% walk, 1.8% work from home (2006-2010 5-year est.); Travel time to work: 49.1% less than 15 minutes, 24.9% 15 to 30 minutes, 18.0% 30 to 45 minutes, 4.1% 45 to 60 minutes, 3.9% 60 minutes or more (2006-2010 5-year est.)
**Additional Information Contacts**
City of Oneida . . . . . . . . . . . . . . . . . . . . . . . . . . . . . . (315) 363-7378
   http://www.oneidacity.com
Greater Oneida Chamber of Commerce . . . . . . . . . . . . . . (315) 363-4300
   http://oneidachamberny.org

**PETERBORO** (unincorporated postal area)
Zip Code: 13134
   Covers a land area of 0.082 square miles and a water area of 0 square miles. Located at 42.96° N. Lat; 75.68° W. Long. Elevation is 1,296 feet. Population: 119 (2010); Density: 1,441.6 persons per square mile (2010); Race: 89.9% White, 6.7% Black, 0.0% Asian, 0.0% American Indian/Alaska Native, 0.0% Native Hawaiian/Other Pacific Islander, 3.4% Other, 2.5% Hispanic of any race (2010); Average household size: 2.70 (2010); Median age: 38.8 (2010); Males per 100 females: 70.0 (2010); Homeownership rate: 68.2% (2010)

**SMITHFIELD** (town). Covers a land area of 24.273 square miles and a water area of 0.085 square miles. Located at 42.96° N. Lat; 75.66° W. Long.
**Population:** 1,053 (1990); 1,205 (2000); 1,288 (2010); Density: 53.1 persons per square mile (2010); Race: 96.3% White, 0.9% Black, 1.0% Asian, 0.2% American Indian/Alaska Native, 0.0% Native Hawaiian/Other Pacific Islander, 1.6% Other, 1.2% Hispanic of any race (2010); Average household size: 2.71 (2010); Median age: 40.2 (2010); Males per 100 females: 101.6 (2010); Marriage status: 42.1% never married, 48.2% now married, 4.1% widowed, 5.6% divorced (2006-2010 5-year est.); Foreign born: 0.0% (2006-2010 5-year est.); Ancestry (includes multiple ancestries): 24.9% American, 16.7% German, 12.3% Irish, 11.0% English, 9.2% Italian (2006-2010 5-year est.).
**Economy:** Single-family building permits issued: 0 (2011); Multi-family building permits issued: 0 (2011); Employment by occupation: 13.3% management, 0.0% professional, 8.5% services, 17.4% sales, 1.2% farming, 15.3% construction, 16.7% production (2006-2010 5-year est.).
**Income:** Per capita income: $19,704 (2006-2010 5-year est.); Median household income: $52,500 (2006-2010 5-year est.); Average household income: $62,641 (2006-2010 5-year est.); Percent of households with income of $100,000 or more: 16.3% (2006-2010 5-year est.); Poverty rate: 13.3% (2006-2010 5-year est.).
**Education:** Percent of population age 25 and over with: High school diploma (including GED) or higher: 80.1% (2006-2010 5-year est.);

Bachelor's degree or higher: 11.0% (2006-2010 5-year est.); Master's degree or higher: 4.3% (2006-2010 5-year est.).
**Housing:** Homeownership rate: 87.2% (2010); Median home value: $80,300 (2006-2010 5-year est.); Median contract rent: $413 per month (2006-2010 5-year est.); Median year structure built: 1974 (2006-2010 5-year est.).
**Transportation:** Commute to work: 82.4% car, 5.9% public transportation, 4.0% walk, 4.3% work from home (2006-2010 5-year est.); Travel time to work: 30.7% less than 15 minutes, 35.0% 15 to 30 minutes, 24.0% 30 to 45 minutes, 8.1% 45 to 60 minutes, 2.2% 60 minutes or more (2006-2010 5-year est.)

**STOCKBRIDGE** (town). Covers a land area of 31.655 square miles and a water area of 0 square miles. Located at 42.98° N. Lat; 75.59° W. Long. Elevation is 669 feet.
**Population:** 1,968 (1990); 2,080 (2000); 2,103 (2010); Density: 66.4 persons per square mile (2010); Race: 96.4% White, 0.2% Black, 0.3% Asian, 1.8% American Indian/Alaska Native, 0.0% Native Hawaiian/Other Pacific Islander, 1.3% Other, 0.8% Hispanic of any race (2010); Average household size: 2.63 (2010); Median age: 38.3 (2010); Males per 100 females: 102.8 (2010); Marriage status: 26.8% never married, 59.0% now married, 2.0% widowed, 12.2% divorced (2006-2010 5-year est.); Foreign born: 0.7% (2006-2010 5-year est.); Ancestry (includes multiple ancestries): 18.7% Irish, 17.1% German, 17.0% English, 12.6% American, 7.6% Italian (2006-2010 5-year est.).
**Economy:** Single-family building permits issued: 2 (2011); Multi-family building permits issued: 0 (2011); Employment by occupation: 9.8% management, 2.3% professional, 8.7% services, 12.9% sales, 3.7% farming, 13.5% construction, 6.6% production (2006-2010 5-year est.).
**Income:** Per capita income: $19,449 (2006-2010 5-year est.); Median household income: $45,489 (2006-2010 5-year est.); Average household income: $49,589 (2006-2010 5-year est.); Percent of households with income of $100,000 or more: 8.8% (2006-2010 5-year est.); Poverty rate: 17.6% (2006-2010 5-year est.).
**Education:** Percent of population age 25 and over with: High school diploma (including GED) or higher: 85.4% (2006-2010 5-year est.); Bachelor's degree or higher: 13.6% (2006-2010 5-year est.); Master's degree or higher: 6.5% (2006-2010 5-year est.).
**Housing:** Homeownership rate: 80.5% (2010); Median home value: $81,900 (2006-2010 5-year est.); Median contract rent: $480 per month (2006-2010 5-year est.); Median year structure built: 1954 (2006-2010 5-year est.).
**Transportation:** Commute to work: 90.9% car, 0.0% public transportation, 2.6% walk, 5.8% work from home (2006-2010 5-year est.); Travel time to work: 39.0% less than 15 minutes, 32.3% 15 to 30 minutes, 19.1% 30 to 45 minutes, 7.0% 45 to 60 minutes, 2.7% 60 minutes or more (2006-2010 5-year est.)

**SULLIVAN** (town). Covers a land area of 73.162 square miles and a water area of 0.199 square miles. Located at 43.09° N. Lat; 75.88° W. Long. Elevation is 456 feet.
**Population:** 14,622 (1990); 14,991 (2000); 15,339 (2010); Density: 209.7 persons per square mile (2010); Race: 97.2% White, 0.6% Black, 0.4% Asian, 0.4% American Indian/Alaska Native, 0.0% Native Hawaiian/Other Pacific Islander, 1.4% Other, 1.2% Hispanic of any race (2010); Average household size: 2.48 (2010); Median age: 43.5 (2010); Males per 100 females: 96.8 (2010); Marriage status: 24.9% never married, 58.7% now married, 5.7% widowed, 10.7% divorced (2006-2010 5-year est.); Foreign born: 1.2% (2006-2010 5-year est.); Ancestry (includes multiple ancestries): 25.5% German, 19.8% Irish, 15.1% American, 15.0% English, 13.3% Italian (2006-2010 5-year est.).
**Economy:** Single-family building permits issued: 25 (2011); Multi-family building permits issued: 0 (2011); Employment by occupation: 8.7% management, 4.4% professional, 8.8% services, 21.3% sales, 5.5% farming, 11.5% construction, 8.5% production (2006-2010 5-year est.).
**Income:** Per capita income: $24,982 (2006-2010 5-year est.); Median household income: $56,596 (2006-2010 5-year est.); Average household income: $63,135 (2006-2010 5-year est.); Percent of households with income of $100,000 or more: 17.1% (2006-2010 5-year est.); Poverty rate: 10.5% (2006-2010 5-year est.).
**Education:** Percent of population age 25 and over with: High school diploma (including GED) or higher: 87.9% (2006-2010 5-year est.); Bachelor's degree or higher: 18.2% (2006-2010 5-year est.); Master's degree or higher: 5.6% (2006-2010 5-year est.).

**Housing:** Homeownership rate: 81.7% (2010); Median home value: $110,800 (2006-2010 5-year est.); Median contract rent: $551 per month (2006-2010 5-year est.); Median year structure built: 1969 (2006-2010 5-year est.).
**Transportation:** Commute to work: 93.6% car, 0.7% public transportation, 0.9% walk, 3.1% work from home (2006-2010 5-year est.); Travel time to work: 16.0% less than 15 minutes, 46.1% 15 to 30 minutes, 28.6% 30 to 45 minutes, 5.2% 45 to 60 minutes, 4.0% 60 minutes or more (2006-2010 5-year est.)

**WAMPSVILLE** (village). County seat. Covers a land area of 1.008 square miles and a water area of 0.007 square miles. Located at 43.07° N. Lat; 75.71° W. Long. Elevation is 482 feet.
**Population:** 501 (1990); 561 (2000); 543 (2010); Density: 538.2 persons per square mile (2010); Race: 94.8% White, 1.5% Black, 0.7% Asian, 0.6% American Indian/Alaska Native, 0.0% Native Hawaiian/Other Pacific Islander, 2.4% Other, 0.9% Hispanic of any race (2010); Average household size: 2.61 (2010); Median age: 43.4 (2010); Males per 100 females: 93.9 (2010); Marriage status: 20.4% never married, 67.6% now married, 5.7% widowed, 6.3% divorced (2006-2010 5-year est.); Foreign born: 4.2% (2006-2010 5-year est.); Ancestry (includes multiple ancestries): 29.8% German, 19.8% English, 18.7% Italian, 15.8% Irish, 11.1% American (2006-2010 5-year est.).
**Economy:** Single-family building permits issued: 0 (2011); Multi-family building permits issued: 0 (2011); Employment by occupation: 8.2% management, 3.6% professional, 13.3% services, 12.8% sales, 6.2% farming, 7.2% construction, 4.1% production (2006-2010 5-year est.).
**Income:** Per capita income: $26,573 (2006-2010 5-year est.); Median household income: $57,000 (2006-2010 5-year est.); Average household income: $64,501 (2006-2010 5-year est.); Percent of households with income of $100,000 or more: 24.6% (2006-2010 5-year est.); Poverty rate: 5.0% (2006-2010 5-year est.).
**Education:** Percent of population age 25 and over with: High school diploma (including GED) or higher: 85.2% (2006-2010 5-year est.); Bachelor's degree or higher: 10.4% (2006-2010 5-year est.); Master's degree or higher: 5.7% (2006-2010 5-year est.).

**School District(s)**
Oneida City School District (PK-12)
   2009-10 Enrollment: 2,430 . . . . . . . . . . . . . . . . . . . . . . . (315) 363-2550
**Housing:** Homeownership rate: 82.7% (2010); Median home value: $89,300 (2006-2010 5-year est.); Median contract rent: $500 per month (2006-2010 5-year est.); Median year structure built: 1945 (2006-2010 5-year est.).
**Transportation:** Commute to work: 90.8% car, 0.0% public transportation, 5.8% walk, 1.7% work from home (2006-2010 5-year est.); Travel time to work: 37.1% less than 15 minutes, 24.7% 15 to 30 minutes, 35.9% 30 to 45 minutes, 2.4% 45 to 60 minutes, 0.0% 60 minutes or more (2006-2010 5-year est.)

**WEST EATON** (unincorporated postal area)
Zip Code: 13484
   Covers a land area of 2.550 square miles and a water area of 0 square miles. Located at 42.86° N. Lat; 75.65° W. Long. Elevation is 1,358 feet.
Population: 176 (2010); Density: 69.0 persons per square mile (2010); Race: 94.3% White, 2.3% Black, 0.0% Asian, 0.0% American Indian/Alaska Native, 0.0% Native Hawaiian/Other Pacific Islander, 3.4% Other, 2.3% Hispanic of any race (2010); Average household size: 2.63 (2010); Median age: 37.5 (2010); Males per 100 females: 102.3 (2010); Homeownership rate: 85.0% (2010)

# Manhattan Borough

*See New York City*

# Monroe County

Located in western New York; bounded on the north by Lake Ontario; drained by the Genesee River. Covers a land area of 659.29 square miles, a water area of 706.31 square miles, and is located in the Eastern Time Zone at 43.16° N. Lat., 77.63° W. Long. The county was founded in 1821. County seat is Rochester.

Monroe County is part of the Rochester, NY Metropolitan Statistical Area. The entire metro area includes: Livingston County, NY; Monroe County, NY; Ontario County, NY; Orleans County, NY; Wayne County, NY

Weather Station: Rochester Intl Arpt      Elevation: 600 feet

| | Jan | Feb | Mar | Apr | May | Jun | Jul | Aug | Sep | Oct | Nov | Dec |
|---|---|---|---|---|---|---|---|---|---|---|---|---|
| High | 32 | 34 | 43 | 56 | 68 | 77 | 81 | 79 | 72 | 60 | 48 | 37 |
| Low | 18 | 19 | 26 | 37 | 47 | 56 | 61 | 60 | 52 | 42 | 33 | 23 |
| Precip | 2.4 | 1.9 | 2.6 | 2.8 | 2.8 | 3.4 | 3.2 | 3.5 | 3.4 | 2.7 | 2.9 | 2.6 |
| Snow | 27.0 | 21.3 | 17.0 | 3.9 | 0.4 | tr | tr | 0.0 | tr | 0.1 | 7.6 | 22.1 |

*High and Low temperatures in degrees Fahrenheit; Precipitation and Snow in inches*

**Population:** 713,968 (1990); 735,343 (2000); 744,344 (2010); Race: 76.1% White, 15.2% Black, 3.3% Asian, 0.3% American Indian/Alaska Native, 0.0% Native Hawaiian/Other Pacific Islander, 5.1% Other, 7.3% Hispanic of any race (2010); Density: 1,129.0 persons per square mile (2010); Average household size: 2.39 (2010); Median age: 38.5 (2010); Males per 100 females: 93.2 (2010).
**Religion:** Six largest groups: 25.7% Catholicism, 4.8% Non-Denominational, 2.8% Baptist, 2.3% Methodist/Pietist, 2.1% Lutheran, 2.0% Presbyterian-Reformed (2010)
**Economy:** Unemployment rate: 8.1% (February 2012); Total civilian labor force: 366,740 (February 2012); Leading industries: 17.0% health care and social assistance; 12.3% manufacturing; 12.0% retail trade (2009); Farms: 585 totaling 133,041 acres (2007); Companies that employ 500 or more persons: 67 (2009); Companies that employ 100 to 499 persons: 431 (2009); Companies that employ less than 100 persons: 16,492 (2009); Black-owned businesses: 3,479 (2007); Hispanic-owned businesses: 1,490 (2007); Asian-owned businesses: 1,916 (2007); Women-owned businesses: 17,112 (2007); Retail sales per capita: $12,235 (2010). Single-family building permits issued: 634 (2011); Multi-family building permits issued: 348 (2011).
**Income:** Per capita income: $26,999 (2006-2010 5-year est.); Median household income: $51,303 (2006-2010 5-year est.); Average household income: $66,954 (2006-2010 5-year est.); Percent of households with income of $100,000 or more: 19.5% (2006-2010 5-year est.); Poverty rate: 13.7% (2006-2010 5-year est.); Bankruptcy rate: 2.09% (2011).
**Taxes:** Total county taxes per capita: $958 (2009); County property taxes per capita: $391 (2009).
**Education:** Percent of population age 25 and over with: High school diploma (including GED) or higher: 88.4% (2006-2010 5-year est.); Bachelor's degree or higher: 34.8% (2006-2010 5-year est.); Master's degree or higher: 15.1% (2006-2010 5-year est.).
**Housing:** Homeownership rate: 64.3% (2010); Median home value: $130,400 (2006-2010 5-year est.); Median contract rent: $647 per month (2006-2010 5-year est.); Median year structure built: 1961 (2006-2010 5-year est.)
**Health:** Birth rate: 113.2 per 10,000 population (2011); Death rate: 83.1 per 10,000 population (2011); Age-adjusted cancer mortality rate: 179.6 deaths per 100,000 population (2009); Number of physicians: 47.5 per 10,000 population (2008); Hospital beds: 31.4 per 10,000 population (2007); Hospital admissions: 1,305.5 per 10,000 population (2007).
**Environment:** Air Quality Index: 87.7% good, 12.3% moderate, 0.0% unhealthy for sensitive individuals, 0.0% unhealthy (percent of days in 2010)
**Elections:** 2008 Presidential election results: 58.2% Obama, 40.5% McCain, 0.6% Nader
**National and State Parks:** Braddock Bay State Park; Hamlin Beach State Park
**Additional Information Contacts**

Monroe County Government . . . . . . . . . . . . . . . . . . . . . . . (585) 428-5301
    http://www.monroecounty.gov
City of Rochester . . . . . . . . . . . . . . . . . . . . . . . . . . . . . . (585) 428-5990
    http://www.cityofrochester.gov
Greater Brockport Chamber of Commerce . . . . . . . . . . . . (585) 234-1512
    http://brockportchamber.org
Greece Chamber of Commerce . . . . . . . . . . . . . . . . . . . . (585) 227-7272
    http://www.greecechamber.org
Rochester Business Alliance . . . . . . . . . . . . . . . . . . . . . . (585) 244-1800
    http://www.rochesterbusinessalliance.com
Town of Chili . . . . . . . . . . . . . . . . . . . . . . . . . . . . . . . . . (585) 889-3550
    http://www.townofchili.org
Town of Clarkson . . . . . . . . . . . . . . . . . . . . . . . . . . . . . . (585) 637-1130
    http://www.clarksonny.org
Town of Gates . . . . . . . . . . . . . . . . . . . . . . . . . . . . . . . . (585) 247-6100
    http://www.townofgates.org
Town of Greece . . . . . . . . . . . . . . . . . . . . . . . . . . . . . . . (585) 225-2000
    http://greeceny.gov
Town of Hamlin . . . . . . . . . . . . . . . . . . . . . . . . . . . . . . . (585) 964-2421
    http://www.hamlinny.org

Town of Henrietta . . . . . . . . . . . . . . . . . . . . . . . . . . . . . . (585) 334-7700
    http://www.henrietta.org
Town of Irondequoit . . . . . . . . . . . . . . . . . . . . . . . . . . . . (585) 467-8840
    http://www.irondequoit.org
Town of Mendon . . . . . . . . . . . . . . . . . . . . . . . . . . . . . . (585) 624-6060
    http://www.townofmendon.org
Town of Parma . . . . . . . . . . . . . . . . . . . . . . . . . . . . . . . (585) 392-9461
    http://www.parmany.org
Town of Penfield . . . . . . . . . . . . . . . . . . . . . . . . . . . . . . (585) 340-8629
    http://www.penfield.org
Town of Perinton . . . . . . . . . . . . . . . . . . . . . . . . . . . . . . (585) 223-0770
    http://www.perinton.org
Town of Pittsford . . . . . . . . . . . . . . . . . . . . . . . . . . . . . . (585) 248-6210
    http://townofpittsford.org
Town of Riga . . . . . . . . . . . . . . . . . . . . . . . . . . . . . . . . . (585) 293-3880
    http://www.townofriga.org
Town of Rush . . . . . . . . . . . . . . . . . . . . . . . . . . . . . . . . (585) 533-1312
    http://townofrush.com
Town of Webster . . . . . . . . . . . . . . . . . . . . . . . . . . . . . . (585) 872-1000
    http://www.ci.webster.ny.us
Town of Wheatland . . . . . . . . . . . . . . . . . . . . . . . . . . . . (585) 889-1553
    http://www.townofwheatland.org
Village of Brockport . . . . . . . . . . . . . . . . . . . . . . . . . . . . (585) 637-5300
    http://brockportny.org
Village of Churchville . . . . . . . . . . . . . . . . . . . . . . . . . . . (585) 293-3720
    http://www.churchville.net
Village of Hilton . . . . . . . . . . . . . . . . . . . . . . . . . . . . . . . (585) 392-4144
    http://www.hiltonny.org
Webster Chamber of Commerce . . . . . . . . . . . . . . . . . . . (585) 265-3960
    http://www.websterchamber.com

## Monroe County Communities

**BRIGHTON** (town and CDP). Covers a land area of 15.415 square miles and a water area of 0.167 square miles. Located at 43.11° N. Lat; 77.58° W. Long. Elevation is 446 feet.
**Population:** 34,458 (1990); 35,588 (2000); 36,609 (2010); Density: 2,374.8 persons per square mile (2010); Race: 79.8% White, 5.1% Black, 11.8% Asian, 0.1% American Indian/Alaska Native, 0.0% Native Hawaiian/Other Pacific Islander, 3.2% Other, 3.3% Hispanic of any race (2010); Average household size: 2.16 (2010); Median age: 39.5 (2010); Males per 100 females: 89.3 (2010); Marriage status: 32.4% never married, 52.3% now married, 8.5% widowed, 6.8% divorced (2006-2010 5-year est.); Foreign born: 17.9% (2006-2010 5-year est.); Ancestry (includes multiple ancestries): 17.9% German, 17.7% Irish, 14.7% English, 13.1% Italian, 6.3% Polish (2006-2010 5-year est.).
**Economy:** Unemployment rate: 5.6% (February 2012); Total civilian labor force: 18,290 (February 2012); Single-family building permits issued: 56 (2011); Multi-family building permits issued: 0 (2011); Employment by occupation: 15.4% management, 10.8% professional, 6.2% services, 11.0% sales, 2.8% farming, 2.5% construction, 2.6% production (2006-2010 5-year est.)
**Income:** Per capita income: $37,610 (2006-2010 5-year est.); Median household income: $61,381 (2006-2010 5-year est.); Average household income: $83,702 (2006-2010 5-year est.); Percent of households with income of $100,000 or more: 25.7% (2006-2010 5-year est.); Poverty rate: 9.5% (2006-2010 5-year est.).
**Education:** Percent of population age 25 and over with: High school diploma (including GED) or higher: 94.0% (2006-2010 5-year est.); Bachelor's degree or higher: 62.2% (2006-2010 5-year est.); Master's degree or higher: 33.0% (2006-2010 5-year est.).
**Housing:** Homeownership rate: 56.7% (2010); Median home value: $165,300 (2006-2010 5-year est.); Median contract rent: $797 per month (2006-2010 5-year est.); Median year structure built: 1961 (2006-2010 5-year est.).
**Safety:** Violent crime rate: 13.4 per 10,000 population; Property crime rate: 311.9 per 10,000 population (2010).
**Transportation:** Commute to work: 88.8% car, 2.5% public transportation, 1.5% walk, 5.4% work from home (2006-2010 5-year est.); Travel time to work: 43.1% less than 15 minutes, 49.0% 15 to 30 minutes, 5.0% 30 to 45 minutes, 1.2% 45 to 60 minutes, 1.6% 60 minutes or more (2006-2010 5-year est.)

**BROCKPORT** (village). Covers a land area of 2.161 square miles and a water area of 0.047 square miles. Located at 43.21° N. Lat; 77.94° W. Long. Elevation is 518 feet.

**History:** Seat of State University of N.Y. College at Brockport. Incorporated 1829.

**Population:** 8,799 (1990); 8,103 (2000); 8,366 (2010); Density: 3,870.5 persons per square mile (2010); Race: 91.7% White, 3.8% Black, 1.3% Asian, 0.3% American Indian/Alaska Native, 0.1% Native Hawaiian/Other Pacific Islander, 2.8% Other, 3.8% Hispanic of any race (2010); Average household size: 2.25 (2010); Median age: 22.0 (2010); Males per 100 females: 88.3 (2010); Marriage status: 62.0% never married, 29.0% now married, 2.7% widowed, 6.2% divorced (2006-2010 5-year est.); Foreign born: 5.7% (2006-2010 5-year est.); Ancestry (includes multiple ancestries): 24.3% German, 20.9% Irish, 20.3% Italian, 14.8% English, 7.1% Polish (2006-2010 5-year est.).

**Economy:** Single-family building permits issued: 2 (2011); Multi-family building permits issued: 0 (2011); Employment by occupation: 6.8% management, 4.3% professional, 13.3% services, 23.1% sales, 4.3% farming, 7.6% construction, 5.1% production (2006-2010 5-year est.).

**Income:** Per capita income: $16,702 (2006-2010 5-year est.); Median household income: $42,907 (2006-2010 5-year est.); Average household income: $53,796 (2006-2010 5-year est.); Percent of households with income of $100,000 or more: 11.0% (2006-2010 5-year est.); Poverty rate: 23.0% (2006-2010 5-year est.).

**Education:** Percent of population age 25 and over with: High school diploma (including GED) or higher: 89.1% (2006-2010 5-year est.); Bachelor's degree or higher: 36.4% (2006-2010 5-year est.); Master's degree or higher: 18.2% (2006-2010 5-year est.).

### School District(s)

Brockport Central School District (PK-12)

   2009-10 Enrollment: 4,005 . . . . . . . . . . . . . . . . . . . . . . (585) 637-1810

### Four-year College(s)

SUNY College at Brockport (Public)

   Fall 2010 Enrollment: 7,549. . . . . . . . . . . . . . . . . . . (585) 395-2211

   2011-12 Tuition: In-state $6,508; Out-of-state $15,558

**Housing:** Homeownership rate: 43.4% (2010); Median home value: $108,400 (2006-2010 5-year est.); Median contract rent: $603 per month (2006-2010 5-year est.); Median year structure built: 1962 (2006-2010 5-year est.).

**Hospitals:** Lakeside Memorial Hospital (61 beds)

**Safety:** Violent crime rate: 19.3 per 10,000 population; Property crime rate: 222.5 per 10,000 population (2010).

**Newspapers:** Tri-County Advertiser (Community news; Circulation 16,000)

**Transportation:** Commute to work: 74.0% car, 0.0% public transportation, 23.3% walk, 1.7% work from home (2006-2010 5-year est.); Travel time to work: 47.1% less than 15 minutes, 27.5% 15 to 30 minutes, 21.1% 30 to 45 minutes, 2.0% 45 to 60 minutes, 2.3% 60 minutes or more (2006-2010 5-year est.)

**Airports:** Ledgedale Airpark (general aviation)

**Additional Information Contacts**

Greater Brockport Chamber of Commerce . . . . . . . . . . . . (585) 234-1512

   http://brockportchamber.org

Village of Brockport . . . . . . . . . . . . . . . . . . . . . . . . . (585) 637-5300

   http://brockportny.org

**CHILI** (town). Covers a land area of 39.499 square miles and a water area of 0.368 square miles. Located at 43.08° N. Lat; 77.74° W. Long.

**Population:** 25,178 (1990); 27,638 (2000); 28,625 (2010); Density: 724.7 persons per square mile (2010); Race: 87.6% White, 7.6% Black, 2.1% Asian, 0.2% American Indian/Alaska Native, 0.0% Native Hawaiian/Other Pacific Islander, 2.5% Other, 2.8% Hispanic of any race (2010); Average household size: 2.50 (2010); Median age: 40.8 (2010); Males per 100 females: 93.5 (2010); Marriage status: 28.0% never married, 58.1% now married, 6.1% widowed, 7.8% divorced (2006-2010 5-year est.); Foreign born: 5.7% (2006-2010 5-year est.); Ancestry (includes multiple ancestries): 28.7% German, 22.4% Italian, 20.7% Irish, 14.4% English, 5.0% Polish (2006-2010 5-year est.).

**Economy:** Unemployment rate: 7.3% (February 2012); Total civilian labor force: 14,997 (February 2012); Single-family building permits issued: 32 (2011); Multi-family building permits issued: 0 (2011); Employment by occupation: 12.7% management, 6.7% professional, 8.1% services, 17.8% sales, 3.8% farming, 7.7% construction, 6.4% production (2006-2010 5-year est.).

**Income:** Per capita income: $28,219 (2006-2010 5-year est.); Median household income: $63,937 (2006-2010 5-year est.); Average household

income: $72,710 (2006-2010 5-year est.); Percent of households with income of $100,000 or more: 24.3% (2006-2010 5-year est.); Poverty rate: 4.1% (2006-2010 5-year est.).

**Taxes:** Total city taxes per capita: $305 (2009); City property taxes per capita: $257 (2009).

**Education:** Percent of population age 25 and over with: High school diploma (including GED) or higher: 91.8% (2006-2010 5-year est.); Bachelor's degree or higher: 35.2% (2006-2010 5-year est.); Master's degree or higher: 13.4% (2006-2010 5-year est.).

**Housing:** Homeownership rate: 78.1% (2010); Median home value: $135,100 (2006-2010 5-year est.); Median contract rent: $701 per month (2006-2010 5-year est.); Median year structure built: 1976 (2006-2010 5-year est.).

**Transportation:** Commute to work: 94.1% car, 0.8% public transportation, 2.0% walk, 2.4% work from home (2006-2010 5-year est.); Travel time to work: 31.0% less than 15 minutes, 53.0% 15 to 30 minutes, 12.0% 30 to 45 minutes, 1.9% 45 to 60 minutes, 2.1% 60 minutes or more (2006-2010 5-year est.)

**Additional Information Contacts**

Town of Chili . . . . . . . . . . . . . . . . . . . . . . . . . . . . . . (585) 889-3550

   http://www.townofchili.org

**CHURCHVILLE** (village). Covers a land area of 1.153 square miles and a water area of 0.017 square miles. Located at 43.10° N. Lat; 77.88° W. Long. Elevation is 584 feet.

**History:** Frances E. Willard born here.

**Population:** 1,717 (1990); 1,887 (2000); 1,961 (2010); Density: 1,700.3 persons per square mile (2010); Race: 95.7% White, 1.3% Black, 1.1% Asian, 0.2% American Indian/Alaska Native, 0.0% Native Hawaiian/Other Pacific Islander, 1.7% Other, 1.7% Hispanic of any race (2010); Average household size: 2.38 (2010); Median age: 42.3 (2010); Males per 100 females: 85.5 (2010); Marriage status: 27.8% never married, 56.6% now married, 7.4% widowed, 8.2% divorced (2006-2010 5-year est.); Foreign born: 2.4% (2006-2010 5-year est.); Ancestry (includes multiple ancestries): 27.4% Irish, 26.6% German, 22.2% Italian, 21.3% English, 9.1% Dutch (2006-2010 5-year est.).

**Economy:** Single-family building permits issued: 2 (2011); Multi-family building permits issued: 0 (2011); Employment by occupation: 10.8% management, 4.6% professional, 9.3% services, 19.0% sales, 5.9% farming, 7.0% construction, 6.3% production (2006-2010 5-year est.).

**Income:** Per capita income: $27,336 (2006-2010 5-year est.); Median household income: $57,188 (2006-2010 5-year est.); Average household income: $64,412 (2006-2010 5-year est.); Percent of households with income of $100,000 or more: 18.0% (2006-2010 5-year est.); Poverty rate: 5.3% (2006-2010 5-year est.).

**Education:** Percent of population age 25 and over with: High school diploma (including GED) or higher: 92.8% (2006-2010 5-year est.); Bachelor's degree or higher: 38.1% (2006-2010 5-year est.); Master's degree or higher: 16.3% (2006-2010 5-year est.).

### School District(s)

Churchville-Chili Central School District (KG-12)

   2009-10 Enrollment: 4,156 . . . . . . . . . . . . . . . . . . . (585) 293-1800

**Housing:** Homeownership rate: 83.9% (2010); Median home value: $118,500 (2006-2010 5-year est.); Median contract rent: $593 per month (2006-2010 5-year est.); Median year structure built: 1975 (2006-2010 5-year est.).

**Transportation:** Commute to work: 95.0% car, 0.5% public transportation, 3.0% walk, 0.9% work from home (2006-2010 5-year est.); Travel time to work: 24.3% less than 15 minutes, 45.8% 15 to 30 minutes, 22.8% 30 to 45 minutes, 3.2% 45 to 60 minutes, 3.8% 60 minutes or more (2006-2010 5-year est.)

**Additional Information Contacts**

Village of Churchville . . . . . . . . . . . . . . . . . . . . . . . . (585) 293-3720

   http://www.churchville.net

**CLARKSON** (town). Covers a land area of 33.183 square miles and a water area of 0.004 square miles. Located at 43.24° N. Lat; 77.93° W. Long. Elevation is 427 feet.

**Population:** 4,517 (1990); 6,072 (2000); 6,736 (2010); Density: 203.0 persons per square mile (2010); Race: 93.4% White, 2.1% Black, 1.0% Asian, 0.4% American Indian/Alaska Native, 0.1% Native Hawaiian/Other Pacific Islander, 3.0% Other, 3.5% Hispanic of any race (2010); Average household size: 2.71 (2010); Median age: 40.7 (2010); Males per 100 females: 97.2 (2010); Marriage status: 24.8% never married, 59.3% now married, 6.6% widowed, 9.2% divorced (2006-2010 5-year est.); Foreign

born: 3.8% (2006-2010 5-year est.); Ancestry (includes multiple ancestries): 27.1% German, 19.7% Irish, 19.6% English, 13.6% Italian, 8.7% Polish (2006-2010 5-year est.).

**Economy:** Single-family building permits issued: 1 (2011); Multi-family building permits issued: 0 (2011); Employment by occupation: 8.0% management, 5.2% professional, 10.3% services, 20.0% sales, 4.0% farming, 7.8% construction, 5.9% production (2006-2010 5-year est.).

**Income:** Per capita income: $26,106 (2006-2010 5-year est.); Median household income: $62,324 (2006-2010 5-year est.); Average household income: $71,636 (2006-2010 5-year est.); Percent of households with income of $100,000 or more: 19.6% (2006-2010 5-year est.); Poverty rate: 5.7% (2006-2010 5-year est.).

**Education:** Percent of population age 25 and over with: High school diploma (including GED) or higher: 90.6% (2006-2010 5-year est.); Bachelor's degree or higher: 31.8% (2006-2010 5-year est.); Master's degree or higher: 12.9% (2006-2010 5-year est.).

**Housing:** Homeownership rate: 78.6% (2010); Median home value: $130,600 (2006-2010 5-year est.); Median contract rent: $496 per month (2006-2010 5-year est.); Median year structure built: 1977 (2006-2010 5-year est.).

**Transportation:** Commute to work: 96.6% car, 0.0% public transportation, 0.0% walk, 3.0% work from home (2006-2010 5-year est.); Travel time to work: 26.7% less than 15 minutes, 36.8% 15 to 30 minutes, 30.1% 30 to 45 minutes, 4.9% 45 to 60 minutes, 1.5% 60 minutes or more (2006-2010 5-year est.)

**Additional Information Contacts**

Town of Clarkson . . . . . . . . . . . . . . . . . . . . . . . . . . . . . . (585) 637-1130
  http://www.clarksonny.org

**CLARKSON** (CDP). Covers a land area of 9.110 square miles and a water area of 0 square miles. Located at 43.23° N. Lat; 77.91° W. Long. Elevation is 427 feet.

**Population:** n/a (1990); n/a (2000); 4,358 (2010); Density: 478.3 persons per square mile (2010); Race: 92.8% White, 2.4% Black, 1.4% Asian, 0.4% American Indian/Alaska Native, 0.0% Native Hawaiian/Other Pacific Islander, 3.0% Other, 3.0% Hispanic of any race (2010); Average household size: 2.63 (2010); Median age: 39.5 (2010); Males per 100 females: 93.2 (2010); Marriage status: 23.8% never married, 62.6% now married, 4.5% widowed, 9.1% divorced (2006-2010 5-year est.); Foreign born: 4.6% (2006-2010 5-year est.); Ancestry (includes multiple ancestries): 26.6% German, 21.6% Irish, 12.5% English, 12.2% Italian, 11.8% Polish (2006-2010 5-year est.).

**Economy:** Employment by occupation: 8.6% management, 2.2% professional, 9.2% services, 18.1% sales, 5.3% farming, 7.6% construction, 5.4% production (2006-2010 5-year est.).

**Income:** Per capita income: $23,448 (2006-2010 5-year est.); Median household income: $59,643 (2006-2010 5-year est.); Average household income: $64,681 (2006-2010 5-year est.); Percent of households with income of $100,000 or more: 18.1% (2006-2010 5-year est.); Poverty rate: 5.9% (2006-2010 5-year est.).

**Education:** Percent of population age 25 and over with: High school diploma (including GED) or higher: 91.5% (2006-2010 5-year est.); Bachelor's degree or higher: 29.1% (2006-2010 5-year est.); Master's degree or higher: 9.4% (2006-2010 5-year est.).

**Housing:** Homeownership rate: 74.0% (2010); Median home value: $129,100 (2006-2010 5-year est.); Median contract rent: $287 per month (2006-2010 5-year est.); Median year structure built: 1979 (2006-2010 5-year est.).

**Transportation:** Commute to work: 96.5% car, 0.0% public transportation, 0.0% walk, 2.8% work from home (2006-2010 5-year est.); Travel time to work: 27.4% less than 15 minutes, 41.9% 15 to 30 minutes, 26.8% 30 to 45 minutes, 4.0% 45 to 60 minutes, 0.0% 60 minutes or more (2006-2010 5-year est.)

**EAST ROCHESTER** (town and village). Covers a land area of 1.324 square miles and a water area of 0.003 square miles. Located at 43.11° N. Lat; 77.48° W. Long. Elevation is 420 feet.

**Population:** 6,932 (1990); 6,650 (2000); 6,587 (2010); Density: 4,972.6 persons per square mile (2010); Race: 91.8% White, 3.2% Black, 0.9% Asian, 0.2% American Indian/Alaska Native, 0.0% Native Hawaiian/Other Pacific Islander, 3.9% Other, 5.1% Hispanic of any race (2010); Average household size: 2.29 (2010); Median age: 36.8 (2010); Males per 100 females: 96.6 (2010); Marriage status: 42.0% never married, 37.5% now married, 6.1% widowed, 14.3% divorced (2006-2010 5-year est.); Foreign born: 5.2% (2006-2010 5-year est.); Ancestry (includes multiple

ancestries): 28.2% Italian, 24.6% German, 20.1% Irish, 15.3% English, 5.6% Dutch (2006-2010 5-year est.).

**Economy:** Single-family building permits issued: 0 (2011); Multi-family building permits issued: 4 (2011); Employment by occupation: 11.3% management, 3.5% professional, 14.6% services, 15.7% sales, 2.8% farming, 6.9% construction, 4.8% production (2006-2010 5-year est.).

**Income:** Per capita income: $21,961 (2006-2010 5-year est.); Median household income: $45,374 (2006-2010 5-year est.); Average household income: $51,057 (2006-2010 5-year est.); Percent of households with income of $100,000 or more: 7.2% (2006-2010 5-year est.); Poverty rate: 15.4% (2006-2010 5-year est.).

**Education:** Percent of population age 25 and over with: High school diploma (including GED) or higher: 90.2% (2006-2010 5-year est.); Bachelor's degree or higher: 22.1% (2006-2010 5-year est.); Master's degree or higher: 8.4% (2006-2010 5-year est.).

**School District(s)**

East Rochester Union Free School District (PK-12)
  2009-10 Enrollment: 1,182 . . . . . . . . . . . . . . . . . . . . . (585) 248-6302

**Housing:** Homeownership rate: 62.2% (2010); Median home value: $92,400 (2006-2010 5-year est.); Median contract rent: $606 per month (2006-2010 5-year est.); Median year structure built: 1943 (2006-2010 5-year est.).

**Safety:** Violent crime rate: 14.6 per 10,000 population; Property crime rate: 212.9 per 10,000 population (2010).

**Newspapers:** The Shopping Bag & Advertiser (Community news; Circulation 251,426)

**Transportation:** Commute to work: 87.5% car, 0.8% public transportation, 8.7% walk, 1.3% work from home (2006-2010 5-year est.); Travel time to work: 42.8% less than 15 minutes, 43.3% 15 to 30 minutes, 11.4% 30 to 45 minutes, 1.4% 45 to 60 minutes, 1.2% 60 minutes or more (2006-2010 5-year est.)

**FAIRPORT** (village). Covers a land area of 1.588 square miles and a water area of 0.033 square miles. Located at 43.09° N. Lat; 77.44° W. Long. Elevation is 492 feet.

**History:** Incorporated 1867.

**Population:** 5,943 (1990); 5,740 (2000); 5,353 (2010); Density: 3,369.2 persons per square mile (2010); Race: 95.3% White, 1.4% Black, 1.2% Asian, 0.3% American Indian/Alaska Native, 0.1% Native Hawaiian/Other Pacific Islander, 1.7% Other, 2.1% Hispanic of any race (2010); Average household size: 2.25 (2010); Median age: 43.0 (2010); Males per 100 females: 93.0 (2010); Marriage status: 23.8% never married, 58.7% now married, 6.7% widowed, 10.8% divorced (2006-2010 5-year est.); Foreign born: 5.2% (2006-2010 5-year est.); Ancestry (includes multiple ancestries): 25.5% German, 24.1% English, 22.2% Italian, 19.6% Irish, 6.7% Dutch (2006-2010 5-year est.).

**Economy:** Single-family building permits issued: 0 (2011); Multi-family building permits issued: 0 (2011); Employment by occupation: 16.1% management, 10.1% professional, 9.3% services, 16.8% sales, 0.5% farming, 6.8% construction, 4.6% production (2006-2010 5-year est.).

**Income:** Per capita income: $34,884 (2006-2010 5-year est.); Median household income: $61,660 (2006-2010 5-year est.); Average household income: $77,475 (2006-2010 5-year est.); Percent of households with income of $100,000 or more: 28.9% (2006-2010 5-year est.); Poverty rate: 6.3% (2006-2010 5-year est.).

**Education:** Percent of population age 25 and over with: High school diploma (including GED) or higher: 93.8% (2006-2010 5-year est.); Bachelor's degree or higher: 48.0% (2006-2010 5-year est.); Master's degree or higher: 21.9% (2006-2010 5-year est.).

**School District(s)**

Fairport Central School District (KG-12)
  2009-10 Enrollment: 6,635 . . . . . . . . . . . . . . . . . . . . . (585) 421-2004
Monroe 1 Boces
  2009-10 Enrollment: n/a . . . . . . . . . . . . . . . . . . . . . . . (585) 383-2200

**Housing:** Homeownership rate: 70.7% (2010); Median home value: $163,100 (2006-2010 5-year est.); Median contract rent: $626 per month (2006-2010 5-year est.); Median year structure built: 1949 (2006-2010 5-year est.).

**Safety:** Violent crime rate: 1.9 per 10,000 population; Property crime rate: 74.3 per 10,000 population (2010).

**Transportation:** Commute to work: 91.0% car, 1.3% public transportation, 1.9% walk, 5.2% work from home (2006-2010 5-year est.); Travel time to work: 40.8% less than 15 minutes, 46.3% 15 to 30 minutes, 8.5% 30 to 45 minutes, 2.1% 45 to 60 minutes, 2.3% 60 minutes or more (2006-2010 5-year est.)

## GATES (town).

**GATES** (town). Covers a land area of 15.200 square miles and a water area of 0.081 square miles. Located at 43.15° N. Lat; 77.71° W. Long.
**Population:** 28,583 (1990); 29,275 (2000); 28,400 (2010); Density: 1,868.4 persons per square mile (2010); Race: 83.0% White, 9.9% Black, 3.2% Asian, 0.3% American Indian/Alaska Native, 0.0% Native Hawaiian/Other Pacific Islander, 3.6% Other, 5.2% Hispanic of any race (2010); Average household size: 2.36 (2010); Median age: 42.8 (2010); Males per 100 females: 91.1 (2010); Marriage status: 29.5% never married, 51.7% now married, 8.4% widowed, 10.3% divorced (2006-2010 5-year est.); Foreign born: 11.7% (2006-2010 5-year est.); Ancestry (includes multiple ancestries): 32.2% Italian, 23.2% German, 17.4% Irish, 9.6% English, 5.3% Polish (2006-2010 5-year est.).
**Economy:** Unemployment rate: 8.9% (February 2012); Total civilian labor force: 14,156 (February 2012); Single-family building permits issued: 8 (2011); Multi-family building permits issued: 4 (2011); Employment by occupation: 8.0% management, 6.1% professional, 9.5% services, 19.0% sales, 5.3% farming, 7.7% construction, 8.4% production (2006-2010 5-year est.).
**Income:** Per capita income: $24,279 (2006-2010 5-year est.); Median household income: $50,677 (2006-2010 5-year est.); Average household income: $58,084 (2006-2010 5-year est.); Percent of households with income of $100,000 or more: 13.2% (2006-2010 5-year est.); Poverty rate: 6.6% (2006-2010 5-year est.).
**Education:** Percent of population age 25 and over with: High school diploma (including GED) or higher: 85.3% (2006-2010 5-year est.); Bachelor's degree or higher: 21.1% (2006-2010 5-year est.); Master's degree or higher: 6.2% (2006-2010 5-year est.).
**Housing:** Homeownership rate: 75.5% (2010); Median home value: $108,700 (2006-2010 5-year est.); Median contract rent: $644 per month (2006-2010 5-year est.); Median year structure built: 1968 (2006-2010 5-year est.).
**Safety:** Violent crime rate: 15.5 per 10,000 population; Property crime rate: 330.8 per 10,000 population (2010).
**Transportation:** Commute to work: 96.3% car, 0.7% public transportation, 0.6% walk, 1.7% work from home (2006-2010 5-year est.); Travel time to work: 35.4% less than 15 minutes, 53.9% 15 to 30 minutes, 7.9% 30 to 45 minutes, 1.0% 45 to 60 minutes, 1.8% 60 minutes or more (2006-2010 5-year est.)
**Additional Information Contacts**
Town of Gates . . . . . . . . . . . . . . . . . . . . . . . . . . . . . . . . (585) 247-6100
  http://www.townofgates.org

**GATES** (CDP). Covers a land area of 1.978 square miles and a water area of 0.011 square miles. Located at 43.15° N. Lat; 77.70° W. Long.
**Population:** n/a (1990); n/a (2000); 4,910 (2010); Density: 2,481.1 persons per square mile (2010); Race: 84.6% White, 8.7% Black, 2.9% Asian, 0.2% American Indian/Alaska Native, 0.0% Native Hawaiian/Other Pacific Islander, 3.6% Other, 4.8% Hispanic of any race (2010); Average household size: 2.45 (2010); Median age: 44.6 (2010); Males per 100 females: 90.9 (2010); Marriage status: 27.5% never married, 55.8% now married, 9.6% widowed, 7.1% divorced (2006-2010 5-year est.); Foreign born: 20.2% (2006-2010 5-year est.); Ancestry (includes multiple ancestries): 33.6% Italian, 17.3% German, 11.5% Irish, 5.8% English, 5.0% Jamaican (2006-2010 5-year est.).
**Economy:** Employment by occupation: 6.4% management, 5.2% professional, 8.4% services, 16.4% sales, 5.5% farming, 10.8% construction, 8.8% production (2006-2010 5-year est.).
**Income:** Per capita income: $23,459 (2006-2010 5-year est.); Median household income: $50,271 (2006-2010 5-year est.); Average household income: $62,533 (2006-2010 5-year est.); Percent of households with income of $100,000 or more: 15.5% (2006-2010 5-year est.); Poverty rate: 5.8% (2006-2010 5-year est.).
**Education:** Percent of population age 25 and over with: High school diploma (including GED) or higher: 80.2% (2006-2010 5-year est.); Bachelor's degree or higher: 16.5% (2006-2010 5-year est.); Master's degree or higher: 3.2% (2006-2010 5-year est.).
**Housing:** Homeownership rate: 91.3% (2010); Median home value: $110,200 (2006-2010 5-year est.); Median contract rent: $636 per month (2006-2010 5-year est.); Median year structure built: 1966 (2006-2010 5-year est.).
**Transportation:** Commute to work: 97.7% car, 1.1% public transportation, 0.0% walk, 0.6% work from home (2006-2010 5-year est.); Travel time to work: 48.6% less than 15 minutes, 42.9% 15 to 30 minutes, 4.5% 30 to 45 minutes, 1.1% 45 to 60 minutes, 3.0% 60 minutes or more (2006-2010 5-year est.)

**GREECE** (town). Covers a land area of 47.518 square miles and a water area of 3.874 square miles. Located at 43.25° N. Lat; 77.70° W. Long. Elevation is 430 feet.
**Population:** 90,106 (1990); 94,141 (2000); 96,095 (2010); Density: 2,022.3 persons per square mile (2010); Race: 88.7% White, 6.0% Black, 1.7% Asian, 0.3% American Indian/Alaska Native, 0.0% Native Hawaiian/Other Pacific Islander, 3.3% Other, 4.8% Hispanic of any race (2010); Average household size: 2.41 (2010); Median age: 42.2 (2010); Males per 100 females: 90.4 (2010); Marriage status: 27.6% never married, 54.5% now married, 8.1% widowed, 9.8% divorced (2006-2010 5-year est.); Foreign born: 7.5% (2006-2010 5-year est.); Ancestry (includes multiple ancestries): 27.4% Italian, 26.9% German, 19.9% Irish, 13.2% English, 6.2% Polish (2006-2010 5-year est.).
**Economy:** Unemployment rate: 8.0% (February 2012); Total civilian labor force: 49,208 (February 2012); Single-family building permits issued: 75 (2011); Multi-family building permits issued: 70 (2011); Employment by occupation: 10.9% management, 5.7% professional, 9.0% services, 18.4% sales, 4.7% farming, 7.1% construction, 6.1% production (2006-2010 5-year est.).
**Income:** Per capita income: $26,439 (2006-2010 5-year est.); Median household income: $53,894 (2006-2010 5-year est.); Average household income: $64,661 (2006-2010 5-year est.); Percent of households with income of $100,000 or more: 18.1% (2006-2010 5-year est.); Poverty rate: 7.5% (2006-2010 5-year est.).
**Taxes:** Total city taxes per capita: $413 (2009); City property taxes per capita: $370 (2009).
**Education:** Percent of population age 25 and over with: High school diploma (including GED) or higher: 90.0% (2006-2010 5-year est.); Bachelor's degree or higher: 25.2% (2006-2010 5-year est.); Master's degree or higher: 10.1% (2006-2010 5-year est.).
**Housing:** Homeownership rate: 73.3% (2010); Median home value: $123,700 (2006-2010 5-year est.); Median contract rent: $699 per month (2006-2010 5-year est.); Median year structure built: 1969 (2006-2010 5-year est.).
**Safety:** Violent crime rate: 12.9 per 10,000 population; Property crime rate: 276.5 per 10,000 population (2010).
**Transportation:** Commute to work: 95.0% car, 0.4% public transportation, 1.1% walk, 2.5% work from home (2006-2010 5-year est.); Travel time to work: 27.6% less than 15 minutes, 54.2% 15 to 30 minutes, 14.7% 30 to 45 minutes, 1.5% 45 to 60 minutes, 2.0% 60 minutes or more (2006-2010 5-year est.)
**Additional Information Contacts**
Greece Chamber of Commerce . . . . . . . . . . . . . . . . . . (585) 227-7272
  http://www.greecechamber.org
Town of Greece . . . . . . . . . . . . . . . . . . . . . . . . . . . . . . (585) 225-2000
  http://greeceny.gov

**GREECE** (CDP). Covers a land area of 4.374 square miles and a water area of 0 square miles. Located at 43.20° N. Lat; 77.70° W. Long. Elevation is 430 feet.
**Population:** 15,556 (1990); 14,614 (2000); 14,519 (2010); Density: 3,318.8 persons per square mile (2010); Race: 88.2% White, 5.4% Black, 2.4% Asian, 0.3% American Indian/Alaska Native, 0.0% Native Hawaiian/Other Pacific Islander, 3.7% Other, 5.4% Hispanic of any race (2010); Average household size: 2.32 (2010); Median age: 43.7 (2010); Males per 100 females: 88.8 (2010); Marriage status: 23.0% never married, 55.1% now married, 10.5% widowed, 11.5% divorced (2006-2010 5-year est.); Foreign born: 8.8% (2006-2010 5-year est.); Ancestry (includes multiple ancestries): 28.8% German, 28.4% Italian, 22.2% Irish, 12.6% English, 5.2% Polish (2006-2010 5-year est.).
**Economy:** Employment by occupation: 11.3% management, 4.1% professional, 9.7% services, 19.0% sales, 4.7% farming, 7.6% construction, 8.1% production (2006-2010 5-year est.).
**Income:** Per capita income: $25,424 (2006-2010 5-year est.); Median household income: $50,073 (2006-2010 5-year est.); Average household income: $59,201 (2006-2010 5-year est.); Percent of households with income of $100,000 or more: 14.1% (2006-2010 5-year est.); Poverty rate: 6.1% (2006-2010 5-year est.).
**Education:** Percent of population age 25 and over with: High school diploma (including GED) or higher: 87.5% (2006-2010 5-year est.); Bachelor's degree or higher: 20.6% (2006-2010 5-year est.); Master's degree or higher: 9.2% (2006-2010 5-year est.).
**Housing:** Homeownership rate: 73.0% (2010); Median home value: $115,900 (2006-2010 5-year est.); Median contract rent: $646 per month

(2006-2010 5-year est.); Median year structure built: 1964 (2006-2010 5-year est.).
**Transportation:** Commute to work: 95.8% car, 0.3% public transportation, 0.7% walk, 2.1% work from home (2006-2010 5-year est.); Travel time to work: 38.3% less than 15 minutes, 47.2% 15 to 30 minutes, 10.9% 30 to 45 minutes, 1.4% 45 to 60 minutes, 2.2% 60 minutes or more (2006-2010 5-year est.)

## HAMLIN (town). Covers a land area of 43.468 square miles and a water area of 1.122 square miles. Located at 43.32° N. Lat; 77.91° W. Long. Elevation is 312 feet.

**Population:** 9,203 (1990); 9,355 (2000); 9,045 (2010); Density: 208.1 persons per square mile (2010); Race: 95.6% White, 1.0% Black, 0.4% Asian, 0.5% American Indian/Alaska Native, 0.0% Native Hawaiian/Other Pacific Islander, 2.5% Other, 2.6% Hispanic of any race (2010); Average household size: 2.67 (2010); Median age: 39.9 (2010); Males per 100 females: 98.7 (2010); Marriage status: 31.2% never married, 58.1% now married, 3.1% widowed, 7.6% divorced (2006-2010 5-year est.); Foreign born: 4.9% (2006-2010 5-year est.); Ancestry (includes multiple ancestries): 32.4% German, 22.6% Irish, 18.2% English, 15.7% Italian, 6.0% Polish (2006-2010 5-year est.).
**Economy:** Single-family building permits issued: 5 (2011); Multi-family building permits issued: 4 (2011); Employment by occupation: 6.9% management, 5.0% professional, 11.7% services, 17.8% sales, 3.5% farming, 13.9% construction, 7.2% production (2006-2010 5-year est.).
**Income:** Per capita income: $23,748 (2006-2010 5-year est.); Median household income: $59,286 (2006-2010 5-year est.); Average household income: $64,285 (2006-2010 5-year est.); Percent of households with income of $100,000 or more: 18.8% (2006-2010 5-year est.); Poverty rate: 11.2% (2006-2010 5-year est.).
**Education:** Percent of population age 25 and over with: High school diploma (including GED) or higher: 87.5% (2006-2010 5-year est.); Bachelor's degree or higher: 21.2% (2006-2010 5-year est.); Master's degree or higher: 7.5% (2006-2010 5-year est.).
**Housing:** Homeownership rate: 84.4% (2010); Median home value: $117,000 (2006-2010 5-year est.); Median contract rent: $612 per month (2006-2010 5-year est.); Median year structure built: 1976 (2006-2010 5-year est.).
**Transportation:** Commute to work: 96.1% car, 0.0% public transportation, 1.6% walk, 1.9% work from home (2006-2010 5-year est.); Travel time to work: 12.6% less than 15 minutes, 31.4% 15 to 30 minutes, 39.5% 30 to 45 minutes, 11.5% 45 to 60 minutes, 5.0% 60 minutes or more (2006-2010 5-year est.)
**Additional Information Contacts**
Town of Hamlin . . . . . . . . . . . . . . . . . . . . . . . . . . . . . . . . . (585) 964-2421
  http://www.hamlinny.org

## HAMLIN (CDP). Covers a land area of 7.710 square miles and a water area of 0 square miles. Located at 43.30° N. Lat; 77.92° W. Long. Elevation is 312 feet.

**Population:** n/a (1990); n/a (2000); 5,521 (2010); Density: 716.1 persons per square mile (2010); Race: 94.9% White, 1.2% Black, 0.4% Asian, 0.5% American Indian/Alaska Native, 0.0% Native Hawaiian/Other Pacific Islander, 3.0% Other, 3.2% Hispanic of any race (2010); Average household size: 2.67 (2010); Median age: 37.1 (2010); Males per 100 females: 97.5 (2010); Marriage status: 34.9% never married, 52.1% now married, 3.6% widowed, 9.4% divorced (2006-2010 5-year est.); Foreign born: 4.0% (2006-2010 5-year est.); Ancestry (includes multiple ancestries): 35.8% German, 24.8% Irish, 17.4% English, 16.5% Italian, 6.7% Polish (2006-2010 5-year est.).
**Economy:** Employment by occupation: 8.1% management, 4.1% professional, 11.5% services, 16.8% sales, 2.6% farming, 14.3% construction, 8.0% production (2006-2010 5-year est.).
**Income:** Per capita income: $20,600 (2006-2010 5-year est.); Median household income: $51,944 (2006-2010 5-year est.); Average household income: $58,222 (2006-2010 5-year est.); Percent of households with income of $100,000 or more: 15.2% (2006-2010 5-year est.); Poverty rate: 14.0% (2006-2010 5-year est.).
**Education:** Percent of population age 25 and over with: High school diploma (including GED) or higher: 84.0% (2006-2010 5-year est.); Bachelor's degree or higher: 19.1% (2006-2010 5-year est.); Master's degree or higher: 7.2% (2006-2010 5-year est.).
**Housing:** Homeownership rate: 81.1% (2010); Median home value: $98,400 (2006-2010 5-year est.); Median contract rent: $603 per month

(2006-2010 5-year est.); Median year structure built: 1980 (2006-2010 5-year est.).
**Transportation:** Commute to work: 98.2% car, 0.0% public transportation, 0.8% walk, 0.9% work from home (2006-2010 5-year est.); Travel time to work: 15.1% less than 15 minutes, 25.1% 15 to 30 minutes, 40.4% 30 to 45 minutes, 14.3% 45 to 60 minutes, 5.0% 60 minutes or more (2006-2010 5-year est.)

## HENRIETTA (town). Covers a land area of 35.350 square miles and a water area of 0.296 square miles. Located at 43.05° N. Lat; 77.64° W. Long. Elevation is 600 feet.

**Population:** 36,376 (1990); 39,028 (2000); 42,581 (2010); Density: 1,204.5 persons per square mile (2010); Race: 80.2% White, 8.5% Black, 7.2% Asian, 0.2% American Indian/Alaska Native, 0.0% Native Hawaiian/Other Pacific Islander, 3.9% Other, 4.3% Hispanic of any race (2010); Average household size: 2.51 (2010); Median age: 30.7 (2010); Males per 100 females: 110.7 (2010); Marriage status: 47.2% never married, 43.3% now married, 4.4% widowed, 5.1% divorced (2006-2010 5-year est.); Foreign born: 9.7% (2006-2010 5-year est.); Ancestry (includes multiple ancestries): 22.3% German, 19.7% Irish, 15.6% Italian, 14.2% English, 6.5% Polish (2006-2010 5-year est.).
**Economy:** Unemployment rate: 7.5% (February 2012); Total civilian labor force: 22,438 (February 2012); Single-family building permits issued: 100 (2011); Multi-family building permits issued: 0 (2011); Employment by occupation: 10.3% management, 10.4% professional, 7.7% services, 17.0% sales, 5.7% farming, 5.5% construction, 5.3% production (2006-2010 5-year est.).
**Income:** Per capita income: $22,778 (2006-2010 5-year est.); Median household income: $58,750 (2006-2010 5-year est.); Average household income: $67,241 (2006-2010 5-year est.); Percent of households with income of $100,000 or more: 20.2% (2006-2010 5-year est.); Poverty rate: 11.2% (2006-2010 5-year est.).
**Education:** Percent of population age 25 and over with: High school diploma (including GED) or higher: 92.4% (2006-2010 5-year est.); Bachelor's degree or higher: 34.6% (2006-2010 5-year est.); Master's degree or higher: 12.5% (2006-2010 5-year est.).
**School District(s)**
Rush-Henrietta Central School District (KG-12)
  2009-10 Enrollment: 5,596 . . . . . . . . . . . . . . . . . (585) 359-5012
**Housing:** Homeownership rate: 68.5% (2010); Median home value: $131,500 (2006-2010 5-year est.); Median contract rent: $732 per month (2006-2010 5-year est.); Median year structure built: 1969 (2006-2010 5-year est.).
**Transportation:** Commute to work: 86.3% car, 1.0% public transportation, 8.5% walk, 2.2% work from home (2006-2010 5-year est.); Travel time to work: 40.3% less than 15 minutes, 47.3% 15 to 30 minutes, 9.8% 30 to 45 minutes, 1.5% 45 to 60 minutes, 1.1% 60 minutes or more (2006-2010 5-year est.)
**Additional Information Contacts**
Town of Henrietta. . . . . . . . . . . . . . . . . . . . . . . . . . . . . . . . (585) 334-7700
  http://www.henrietta.org

## HILTON (village). Covers a land area of 1.779 square miles and a water area of 0 square miles. Located at 43.28° N. Lat; 77.79° W. Long. Elevation is 279 feet.

**Population:** 5,237 (1990); 5,856 (2000); 5,886 (2010); Density: 3,307.1 persons per square mile (2010); Race: 96.5% White, 1.5% Black, 0.3% Asian, 0.2% American Indian/Alaska Native, 0.0% Native Hawaiian/Other Pacific Islander, 1.5% Other, 2.3% Hispanic of any race (2010); Average household size: 2.50 (2010); Median age: 38.6 (2010); Males per 100 females: 91.2 (2010); Marriage status: 27.3% never married, 51.6% now married, 10.1% widowed, 11.0% divorced (2006-2010 5-year est.); Foreign born: 8.2% (2006-2010 5-year est.); Ancestry (includes multiple ancestries): 33.8% German, 26.8% English, 19.5% Irish, 16.8% Italian, 10.1% Polish (2006-2010 5-year est.).
**Economy:** Single-family building permits issued: 8 (2011); Multi-family building permits issued: 0 (2011); Employment by occupation: 10.4% management, 2.2% professional, 9.1% services, 20.1% sales, 7.3% farming, 7.9% construction, 5.8% production (2006-2010 5-year est.).
**Income:** Per capita income: $22,736 (2006-2010 5-year est.); Median household income: $53,105 (2006-2010 5-year est.); Average household income: $58,440 (2006-2010 5-year est.); Percent of households with income of $100,000 or more: 10.1% (2006-2010 5-year est.); Poverty rate: 7.6% (2006-2010 5-year est.).

**Education:** Percent of population age 25 and over with: High school diploma (including GED) or higher: 94.1% (2006-2010 5-year est.); Bachelor's degree or higher: 24.3% (2006-2010 5-year est.); Master's degree or higher: 8.9% (2006-2010 5-year est.).

### School District(s)
Hilton Central School District (PK-12)

    2009-10 Enrollment: 4,559 . . . . . . . . . . . . . . . . . . . . . . (585) 392-1000

**Housing:** Homeownership rate: 66.0% (2010); Median home value: $114,500 (2006-2010 5-year est.); Median contract rent: $740 per month (2006-2010 5-year est.); Median year structure built: 1975 (2006-2010 5-year est.).

**Transportation:** Commute to work: 94.6% car, 0.4% public transportation, 0.4% walk, 2.5% work from home (2006-2010 5-year est.); Travel time to work: 16.8% less than 15 minutes, 40.6% 15 to 30 minutes, 38.5% 30 to 45 minutes, 2.0% 45 to 60 minutes, 2.0% 60 minutes or more (2006-2010 5-year est.).

**Additional Information Contacts**

Village of Hilton . . . . . . . . . . . . . . . . . . . . . . . . . . . . . (585) 392-4144
    http://www.hiltonny.org

## HONEOYE FALLS (village). Covers a land area of 2.543 square miles and a water area of 0.051 square miles. Located at 42.95° N. Lat; 77.59° W. Long. Elevation is 656 feet.

**History:** Incorporated 1838.

**Population:** 2,340 (1990); 2,595 (2000); 2,674 (2010); Density: 1,051.5 persons per square mile (2010); Race: 96.4% White, 0.7% Black, 0.6% Asian, 0.2% American Indian/Alaska Native, 0.0% Native Hawaiian/Other Pacific Islander, 2.1% Other, 1.8% Hispanic of any race (2010); Average household size: 2.25 (2010); Median age: 41.9 (2010); Males per 100 females: 88.6 (2010); Marriage status: 28.9% never married, 53.6% now married, 7.4% widowed, 10.2% divorced (2006-2010 5-year est.); Foreign born: 1.2% (2006-2010 5-year est.); Ancestry (includes multiple ancestries): 36.9% German, 23.2% Irish, 19.6% English, 15.9% Italian, 7.1% American (2006-2010 5-year est.).

**Economy:** Single-family building permits issued: 9 (2011); Multi-family building permits issued: 0 (2011); Employment by occupation: 13.8% management, 10.1% professional, 5.9% services, 13.4% sales, 2.5% farming, 4.2% construction, 5.7% production (2006-2010 5-year est.).

**Income:** Per capita income: $32,767 (2006-2010 5-year est.); Median household income: $58,125 (2006-2010 5-year est.); Average household income: $72,414 (2006-2010 5-year est.); Percent of households with income of $100,000 or more: 22.8% (2006-2010 5-year est.); Poverty rate: 8.0% (2006-2010 5-year est.).

**Education:** Percent of population age 25 and over with: High school diploma (including GED) or higher: 96.1% (2006-2010 5-year est.); Bachelor's degree or higher: 46.0% (2006-2010 5-year est.); Master's degree or higher: 20.5% (2006-2010 5-year est.).

### School District(s)
Honeoye Falls-Lima Central School District (KG-12)

    2009-10 Enrollment: 2,582 . . . . . . . . . . . . . . . . . . . . . . (585) 624-7010

**Housing:** Homeownership rate: 61.3% (2010); Median home value: $170,400 (2006-2010 5-year est.); Median contract rent: $601 per month (2006-2010 5-year est.); Median year structure built: 1959 (2006-2010 5-year est.).

**Transportation:** Commute to work: 90.7% car, 0.0% public transportation, 6.2% walk, 2.7% work from home (2006-2010 5-year est.); Travel time to work: 24.5% less than 15 minutes, 42.5% 15 to 30 minutes, 29.1% 30 to 45 minutes, 1.9% 45 to 60 minutes, 2.1% 60 minutes or more (2006-2010 5-year est.)

## IRONDEQUOIT (town and CDP). Covers a land area of 15.001 square miles and a water area of 1.833 square miles. Located at 43.20° N. Lat; 77.57° W. Long. Elevation is 381 feet.

**History:** Named for the Iroquoian translation of "bay". Settled 1791, organized 1839.

**Population:** 52,371 (1990); 52,354 (2000); 51,692 (2010); Density: 3,445.9 persons per square mile (2010); Race: 86.8% White, 7.7% Black, 1.3% Asian, 0.2% American Indian/Alaska Native, 0.0% Native Hawaiian/Other Pacific Islander, 4.0% Other, 6.2% Hispanic of any race (2010); Average household size: 2.26 (2010); Median age: 44.1 (2010); Males per 100 females: 86.6 (2010); Marriage status: 29.2% never married, 52.9% now married, 7.9% widowed, 10.0% divorced (2006-2010 5-year est.); Foreign born: 8.6% (2006-2010 5-year est.); Ancestry (includes multiple ancestries): 28.2% Italian, 22.9% German, 17.6% Irish, 14.0% English, 7.4% Polish (2006-2010 5-year est.).

**Economy:** Unemployment rate: 8.1% (February 2012); Total civilian labor force: 24,648 (February 2012); Single-family building permits issued: 2 (2011); Multi-family building permits issued: 0 (2011); Employment by occupation: 10.1% management, 5.3% professional, 9.5% services, 18.3% sales, 5.1% farming, 6.0% construction, 4.7% production (2006-2010 5-year est.).

**Income:** Per capita income: $27,341 (2006-2010 5-year est.); Median household income: $51,683 (2006-2010 5-year est.); Average household income: $63,192 (2006-2010 5-year est.); Percent of households with income of $100,000 or more: 15.5% (2006-2010 5-year est.); Poverty rate: 10.0% (2006-2010 5-year est.).

**Taxes:** Total city taxes per capita: $419 (2009); City property taxes per capita: $385 (2009).

**Education:** Percent of population age 25 and over with: High school diploma (including GED) or higher: 87.7% (2006-2010 5-year est.); Bachelor's degree or higher: 31.9% (2006-2010 5-year est.); Master's degree or higher: 13.4% (2006-2010 5-year est.).

**Housing:** Homeownership rate: 78.1% (2010); Median home value: $111,800 (2006-2010 5-year est.); Median contract rent: $675 per month (2006-2010 5-year est.); Median year structure built: 1954 (2006-2010 5-year est.).

**Safety:** Violent crime rate: 18.9 per 10,000 population; Property crime rate: 301.8 per 10,000 population (2010).

**Transportation:** Commute to work: 92.7% car, 1.8% public transportation, 1.9% walk, 3.1% work from home (2006-2010 5-year est.); Travel time to work: 30.1% less than 15 minutes, 53.1% 15 to 30 minutes, 13.1% 30 to 45 minutes, 1.7% 45 to 60 minutes, 2.0% 60 minutes or more (2006-2010 5-year est.)

**Additional Information Contacts**

Town of Irondequoit . . . . . . . . . . . . . . . . . . . . . . . . . . . (585) 467-8840
    http://www.irondequoit.org

## MENDON (town). Covers a land area of 39.471 square miles and a water area of 0.514 square miles. Located at 42.98° N. Lat; 77.55° W. Long. Elevation is 561 feet.

**Population:** 6,845 (1990); 8,370 (2000); 9,152 (2010); Density: 231.9 persons per square mile (2010); Race: 96.5% White, 0.5% Black, 1.5% Asian, 0.2% American Indian/Alaska Native, 0.0% Native Hawaiian/Other Pacific Islander, 1.3% Other, 1.7% Hispanic of any race (2010); Average household size: 2.64 (2010); Median age: 43.6 (2010); Males per 100 females: 97.0 (2010); Marriage status: 23.2% never married, 63.7% now married, 4.6% widowed, 8.5% divorced (2006-2010 5-year est.); Foreign born: 3.9% (2006-2010 5-year est.); Ancestry (includes multiple ancestries): 32.4% German, 23.5% Irish, 20.8% English, 17.8% Italian, 5.3% American (2006-2010 5-year est.).

**Economy:** Single-family building permits issued: 8 (2011); Multi-family building permits issued: 0 (2011); Employment by occupation: 21.6% management, 10.3% professional, 7.4% services, 9.1% sales, 3.5% farming, 2.5% construction, 2.2% production (2006-2010 5-year est.).

**Income:** Per capita income: $43,537 (2006-2010 5-year est.); Median household income: $90,326 (2006-2010 5-year est.); Average household income: $114,913 (2006-2010 5-year est.); Percent of households with income of $100,000 or more: 45.1% (2006-2010 5-year est.); Poverty rate: 3.0% (2006-2010 5-year est.).

**Education:** Percent of population age 25 and over with: High school diploma (including GED) or higher: 98.1% (2006-2010 5-year est.); Bachelor's degree or higher: 61.5% (2006-2010 5-year est.); Master's degree or higher: 27.4% (2006-2010 5-year est.).

**Housing:** Homeownership rate: 83.7% (2010); Median home value: $243,500 (2006-2010 5-year est.); Median contract rent: $606 per month (2006-2010 5-year est.); Median year structure built: 1976 (2006-2010 5-year est.).

**Transportation:** Commute to work: 91.3% car, 0.3% public transportation, 2.1% walk, 5.7% work from home (2006-2010 5-year est.); Travel time to work: 21.6% less than 15 minutes, 39.6% 15 to 30 minutes, 31.4% 30 to 45 minutes, 4.9% 45 to 60 minutes, 2.5% 60 minutes or more (2006-2010 5-year est.)

**Additional Information Contacts**

Town of Mendon . . . . . . . . . . . . . . . . . . . . . . . . . . . . . (585) 624-6060
    http://www.townofmendon.org

## MUMFORD (unincorporated postal area)
Zip Code: 14511

    Covers a land area of 2.309 square miles and a water area of 0.041 square miles. Located at 42.99° N. Lat; 77.89° W. Long. Elevation is 617 feet. Population: 497 (2010); Density: 215.2 persons per square mile (2010); Race: 94.8% White, 2.4% Black, 1.0% Asian, 0.0% American Indian/Alaska Native, 0.0% Native Hawaiian/Other Pacific Islander, 1.8% Other, 0.8% Hispanic of any race (2010); Average household size: 2.30 (2010); Median age: 45.5 (2010); Males per 100 females: 87.5 (2010); Homeownership rate: 84.2% (2010)

## NORTH CHILI (unincorporated postal area)
Zip Code: 14514

Covers a land area of 3.746 square miles and a water area of 0.012 square miles. Located at 43.10° N. Lat; 77.81° W. Long. Elevation is 584 feet. Population: 6,389 (2010); Density: 1,705.4 persons per square mile (2010); Race: 87.8% White, 6.0% Black, 2.6% Asian, 0.1% American Indian/Alaska Native, 0.0% Native Hawaiian/Other Pacific Islander, 3.5% Other, 3.6% Hispanic of any race (2010); Average household size: 2.55 (2010); Median age: 38.1 (2010); Males per 100 females: 89.8 (2010); Homeownership rate: 70.2% (2010)

## NORTH GATES (CDP). Covers a land area of 2.662 square miles and a water area of 0.025 square miles. Located at 43.17° N. Lat; 77.70° W. Long. Elevation is 525 feet.
**Population:** n/a (1990); n/a (2000); 9,512 (2010); Density: 3,572.8 persons per square mile (2010); Race: 80.8% White, 10.3% Black, 4.4% Asian, 0.3% American Indian/Alaska Native, 0.0% Native Hawaiian/Other Pacific Islander, 4.2% Other, 6.6% Hispanic of any race (2010); Average household size: 2.22 (2010); Median age: 42.3 (2010); Males per 100 females: 90.9 (2010); Marriage status: 31.2% never married, 48.9% now married, 6.0% widowed, 13.9% divorced (2006-2010 5-year est.); Foreign born: 10.5% (2006-2010 5-year est.); Ancestry (includes multiple ancestries): 35.4% Italian, 18.9% German, 15.0% Irish, 10.4% English, 6.3% Polish (2006-2010 5-year est.).
**Economy:** Employment by occupation: 6.1% management, 6.3% professional, 12.4% services, 19.3% sales, 4.4% farming, 7.0% construction, 9.0% production (2006-2010 5-year est.).
**Income:** Per capita income: $22,605 (2006-2010 5-year est.); Median household income: $43,062 (2006-2010 5-year est.); Average household income: $50,205 (2006-2010 5-year est.); Percent of households with income of $100,000 or more: 9.0% (2006-2010 5-year est.); Poverty rate: 6.7% (2006-2010 5-year est.).
**Education:** Percent of population age 25 and over with: High school diploma (including GED) or higher: 82.0% (2006-2010 5-year est.); Bachelor's degree or higher: 16.5% (2006-2010 5-year est.); Master's degree or higher: 2.2% (2006-2010 5-year est.).
**Housing:** Homeownership rate: 62.0% (2010); Median home value: $102,700 (2006-2010 5-year est.); Median contract rent: $610 per month (2006-2010 5-year est.); Median year structure built: 1969 (2006-2010 5-year est.).
**Transportation:** Commute to work: 96.4% car, 0.7% public transportation, 0.5% walk, 2.0% work from home (2006-2010 5-year est.); Travel time to work: 31.9% less than 15 minutes, 56.0% 15 to 30 minutes, 8.1% 30 to 45 minutes, 1.9% 45 to 60 minutes, 2.1% 60 minutes or more (2006-2010 5-year est.)

## OGDEN (town). Covers a land area of 36.476 square miles and a water area of 0.256 square miles. Located at 43.17° N. Lat; 77.81° W. Long.
**Population:** 16,912 (1990); 18,492 (2000); 19,856 (2010); Density: 544.4 persons per square mile (2010); Race: 94.5% White, 2.3% Black, 0.8% Asian, 0.2% American Indian/Alaska Native, 0.0% Native Hawaiian/Other Pacific Islander, 2.2% Other, 2.8% Hispanic of any race (2010); Average household size: 2.62 (2010); Median age: 40.6 (2010); Males per 100 females: 94.0 (2010); Marriage status: 29.4% never married, 58.6% now married, 4.2% widowed, 7.8% divorced (2006-2010 5-year est.); Foreign born: 4.2% (2006-2010 5-year est.); Ancestry (includes multiple ancestries): 31.7% German, 25.2% Italian, 23.4% Irish, 16.0% English, 5.3% Polish (2006-2010 5-year est.).
**Economy:** Single-family building permits issued: 16 (2011); Multi-family building permits issued: 0 (2011); Employment by occupation: 11.6% management, 5.9% professional, 11.1% services, 15.5% sales, 3.5% farming, 6.5% construction, 4.1% production (2006-2010 5-year est.).
**Income:** Per capita income: $28,971 (2006-2010 5-year est.); Median household income: $67,973 (2006-2010 5-year est.); Average household income: $79,610 (2006-2010 5-year est.); Percent of households with income of $100,000 or more: 25.3% (2006-2010 5-year est.); Poverty rate: 5.4% (2006-2010 5-year est.).

**Education:** Percent of population age 25 and over with: High school diploma (including GED) or higher: 93.7% (2006-2010 5-year est.); Bachelor's degree or higher: 36.1% (2006-2010 5-year est.); Master's degree or higher: 14.9% (2006-2010 5-year est.).
**Housing:** Homeownership rate: 78.4% (2010); Median home value: $141,000 (2006-2010 5-year est.); Median contract rent: $747 per month (2006-2010 5-year est.); Median year structure built: 1973 (2006-2010 5-year est.).
**Safety:** Violent crime rate: 9.4 per 10,000 population; Property crime rate: 198.2 per 10,000 population (2010).
**Transportation:** Commute to work: 94.5% car, 0.7% public transportation, 1.1% walk, 3.2% work from home (2006-2010 5-year est.); Travel time to work: 27.5% less than 15 minutes, 54.3% 15 to 30 minutes, 16.3% 30 to 45 minutes, 1.6% 45 to 60 minutes, 0.3% 60 minutes or more (2006-2010 5-year est.)
**Additional Information Contacts**
Town of Ogden . . . . . . . . . . . . . . . . . . . . . . . . . . . . . (585) 617-6100
   http://www.ogdenny.com

## PARMA (town). Covers a land area of 42.023 square miles and a water area of 0.959 square miles. Located at 43.26° N. Lat; 77.79° W. Long.
**Population:** 13,873 (1990); 14,822 (2000); 15,633 (2010); Density: 372.0 persons per square mile (2010); Race: 96.6% White, 1.2% Black, 0.5% Asian, 0.2% American Indian/Alaska Native, 0.0% Native Hawaiian/Other Pacific Islander, 1.5% Other, 2.0% Hispanic of any race (2010); Average household size: 2.60 (2010); Median age: 41.7 (2010); Males per 100 females: 98.7 (2010); Marriage status: 24.3% never married, 60.4% now married, 6.6% widowed, 8.7% divorced (2006-2010 5-year est.); Foreign born: 6.8% (2006-2010 5-year est.); Ancestry (includes multiple ancestries): 31.1% German, 22.1% Italian, 21.2% English, 19.9% Irish, 6.6% French (2006-2010 5-year est.).
**Economy:** Single-family building permits issued: 16 (2011); Multi-family building permits issued: 0 (2011); Employment by occupation: 9.8% management, 3.5% professional, 8.8% services, 18.0% sales, 6.4% farming, 11.3% construction, 8.1% production (2006-2010 5-year est.).
**Income:** Per capita income: $27,414 (2006-2010 5-year est.); Median household income: $63,607 (2006-2010 5-year est.); Average household income: $73,368 (2006-2010 5-year est.); Percent of households with income of $100,000 or more: 20.3% (2006-2010 5-year est.); Poverty rate: 7.6% (2006-2010 5-year est.).
**Education:** Percent of population age 25 and over with: High school diploma (including GED) or higher: 92.0% (2006-2010 5-year est.); Bachelor's degree or higher: 24.1% (2006-2010 5-year est.); Master's degree or higher: 7.8% (2006-2010 5-year est.).
**Housing:** Homeownership rate: 81.0% (2010); Median home value: $130,400 (2006-2010 5-year est.); Median contract rent: $725 per month (2006-2010 5-year est.); Median year structure built: 1971 (2006-2010 5-year est.).
**Transportation:** Commute to work: 92.5% car, 0.6% public transportation, 0.5% walk, 4.0% work from home (2006-2010 5-year est.); Travel time to work: 17.5% less than 15 minutes, 46.2% 15 to 30 minutes, 30.8% 30 to 45 minutes, 3.0% 45 to 60 minutes, 2.5% 60 minutes or more (2006-2010 5-year est.)
**Additional Information Contacts**
Town of Parma . . . . . . . . . . . . . . . . . . . . . . . . . . . . . (585) 392-9461
   http://www.parmany.org

## PENFIELD (town). Covers a land area of 37.210 square miles and a water area of 0.633 square miles. Located at 43.15° N. Lat; 77.44° W. Long. Elevation is 423 feet.
**Population:** 30,216 (1990); 34,645 (2000); 36,242 (2010); Density: 974.0 persons per square mile (2010); Race: 92.6% White, 2.1% Black, 3.1% Asian, 0.1% American Indian/Alaska Native, 0.0% Native Hawaiian/Other Pacific Islander, 2.1% Other, 2.5% Hispanic of any race (2010); Average household size: 2.44 (2010); Median age: 44.7 (2010); Males per 100 females: 93.0 (2010); Marriage status: 24.1% never married, 59.0% now married, 8.1% widowed, 8.8% divorced (2006-2010 5-year est.); Foreign born: 8.4% (2006-2010 5-year est.); Ancestry (includes multiple ancestries): 25.8% German, 24.3% Italian, 18.9% Irish, 16.3% English, 7.9% Polish (2006-2010 5-year est.).
**Economy:** Unemployment rate: 6.6% (February 2012); Total civilian labor force: 18,617 (February 2012); Single-family building permits issued: 121 (2011); Multi-family building permits issued: 0 (2011); Employment by occupation: 17.2% management, 9.3% professional, 5.9% services, 14.9%

sales, 3.7% farming, 4.2% construction, 4.4% production (2006-2010 5-year est.).

**Income:** Per capita income: $34,767 (2006-2010 5-year est.); Median household income: $71,550 (2006-2010 5-year est.); Average household income: $87,882 (2006-2010 5-year est.); Percent of households with income of $100,000 or more: 34.4% (2006-2010 5-year est.); Poverty rate: 3.7% (2006-2010 5-year est.).

**Education:** Percent of population age 25 and over with: High school diploma (including GED) or higher: 93.6% (2006-2010 5-year est.); Bachelor's degree or higher: 47.9% (2006-2010 5-year est.); Master's degree or higher: 21.4% (2006-2010 5-year est.).

**School District(s)**

Penfield Central School District (KG-12)

   2009-10 Enrollment: 4,612 . . . . . . . . . . . . . . . (585) 249-5700

**Housing:** Homeownership rate: 82.4% (2010); Median home value: $172,300 (2006-2010 5-year est.); Median contract rent: $762 per month (2006-2010 5-year est.); Median year structure built: 1975 (2006-2010 5-year est.).

**Transportation:** Commute to work: 94.3% car, 0.2% public transportation, 1.2% walk, 3.5% work from home (2006-2010 5-year est.); Travel time to work: 27.4% less than 15 minutes, 58.1% 15 to 30 minutes, 11.7% 30 to 45 minutes, 1.2% 45 to 60 minutes, 1.6% 60 minutes or more (2006-2010 5-year est.).

**Additional Information Contacts**

Town of Penfield . . . . . . . . . . . . . . . . . . . . . . . . . (585) 340-8629
  http://www.penfield.org

**PERINTON** (town). Covers a land area of 34.186 square miles and a water area of 0.359 square miles. Located at 43.07° N. Lat; 77.42° W. Long.

**Population:** 43,015 (1990); 46,090 (2000); 46,462 (2010); Density: 1,359.1 persons per square mile (2010); Race: 93.0% White, 2.0% Black, 2.9% Asian, 0.1% American Indian/Alaska Native, 0.0% Native Hawaiian/Other Pacific Islander, 2.0% Other, 2.1% Hispanic of any race (2010); Average household size: 2.44 (2010); Median age: 44.2 (2010); Males per 100 females: 92.6 (2010); Marriage status: 21.5% never married, 62.2% now married, 6.3% widowed, 9.9% divorced (2006-2010 5-year est.); Foreign born: 6.2% (2006-2010 5-year est.); Ancestry (includes multiple ancestries): 25.5% German, 22.4% Italian, 21.3% Irish, 17.9% English, 6.5% Polish (2006-2010 5-year est.).

**Economy:** Unemployment rate: 6.1% (February 2012); Total civilian labor force: 24,861 (February 2012); Single-family building permits issued: 22 (2011); Multi-family building permits issued: 0 (2011); Employment by occupation: 17.6% management, 8.0% professional, 6.5% services, 15.3% sales, 2.8% farming, 3.9% construction, 3.3% production (2006-2010 5-year est.).

**Income:** Per capita income: $38,306 (2006-2010 5-year est.); Median household income: $74,497 (2006-2010 5-year est.); Average household income: $93,429 (2006-2010 5-year est.); Percent of households with income of $100,000 or more: 36.5% (2006-2010 5-year est.); Poverty rate: 4.9% (2006-2010 5-year est.).

**Education:** Percent of population age 25 and over with: High school diploma (including GED) or higher: 96.1% (2006-2010 5-year est.); Bachelor's degree or higher: 54.1% (2006-2010 5-year est.); Master's degree or higher: 24.1% (2006-2010 5-year est.).

**Housing:** Homeownership rate: 79.7% (2010); Median home value: $183,100 (2006-2010 5-year est.); Median contract rent: $789 per month (2006-2010 5-year est.); Median year structure built: 1973 (2006-2010 5-year est.).

**Transportation:** Commute to work: 92.0% car, 0.7% public transportation, 1.3% walk, 5.0% work from home (2006-2010 5-year est.); Travel time to work: 31.2% less than 15 minutes, 49.3% 15 to 30 minutes, 15.8% 30 to 45 minutes, 1.8% 45 to 60 minutes, 1.9% 60 minutes or more (2006-2010 5-year est.).

**Additional Information Contacts**

Town of Perinton . . . . . . . . . . . . . . . . . . . . . . . . . (585) 223-0770
  http://www.perinton.org

**PITTSFORD** (village). Covers a land area of 0.672 square miles and a water area of 0.019 square miles. Located at 43.09° N. Lat; 77.51° W. Long. Elevation is 492 feet.

**Population:** 1,488 (1990); 1,418 (2000); 1,355 (2010); Density: 2,013.7 persons per square mile (2010); Race: 96.9% White, 0.7% Black, 1.2% Asian, 0.1% American Indian/Alaska Native, 0.0% Native Hawaiian/Other Pacific Islander, 1.1% Other, 2.4% Hispanic of any race (2010); Average

household size: 2.20 (2010); Median age: 44.2 (2010); Males per 100 females: 86.1 (2010); Marriage status: 21.9% never married, 62.5% now married, 7.1% widowed, 8.5% divorced (2006-2010 5-year est.); Foreign born: 4.4% (2006-2010 5-year est.); Ancestry (includes multiple ancestries): 31.6% Irish, 30.2% German, 21.5% English, 15.1% Italian, 5.3% Polish (2006-2010 5-year est.).

**Economy:** Single-family building permits issued: 0 (2011); Multi-family building permits issued: 0 (2011); Employment by occupation: 18.5% management, 9.0% professional, 5.4% services, 8.1% sales, 1.1% farming, 5.5% construction, 1.8% production (2006-2010 5-year est.).

**Income:** Per capita income: $46,981 (2006-2010 5-year est.); Median household income: $84,013 (2006-2010 5-year est.); Average household income: $109,445 (2006-2010 5-year est.); Percent of households with income of $100,000 or more: 38.1% (2006-2010 5-year est.); Poverty rate: 1.1% (2006-2010 5-year est.).

**Education:** Percent of population age 25 and over with: High school diploma (including GED) or higher: 97.9% (2006-2010 5-year est.); Bachelor's degree or higher: 69.6% (2006-2010 5-year est.); Master's degree or higher: 39.7% (2006-2010 5-year est.).

**School District(s)**

Pittsford Central School District (KG-12)

   2009-10 Enrollment: 5,969 . . . . . . . . . . . . . . . (585) 267-1004

**Housing:** Homeownership rate: 70.0% (2010); Median home value: $219,300 (2006-2010 5-year est.); Median contract rent: $950 per month (2006-2010 5-year est.); Median year structure built: before 1940 (2006-2010 5-year est.).

**Newspapers:** Brighton-Pittsford Post (Local news; Circulation 9,930); Brockport Post (Community news; Circulation 2,109); Henrietta Post (Community news); Penfield Post (Local news; Circulation 3,652); Perinton-Fairport Post (Community news; Circulation 5,164); Webster Post (Community news; Circulation 4,025)

**Transportation:** Commute to work: 91.6% car, 0.5% public transportation, 1.9% walk, 3.6% work from home (2006-2010 5-year est.); Travel time to work: 36.8% less than 15 minutes, 51.6% 15 to 30 minutes, 9.7% 30 to 45 minutes, 0.8% 45 to 60 minutes, 1.1% 60 minutes or more (2006-2010 5-year est.)

**PITTSFORD** (town). Covers a land area of 23.180 square miles and a water area of 0.208 square miles. Located at 43.07° N. Lat; 77.52° W. Long. Elevation is 492 feet.

**History:** Incorporated 1827.

**Population:** 24,497 (1990); 27,219 (2000); 29,405 (2010); Density: 1,268.5 persons per square mile (2010); Race: 89.3% White, 1.7% Black, 6.8% Asian, 0.1% American Indian/Alaska Native, 0.0% Native Hawaiian/Other Pacific Islander, 2.1% Other, 2.3% Hispanic of any race (2010); Average household size: 2.57 (2010); Median age: 42.9 (2010); Males per 100 females: 86.7 (2010); Marriage status: 27.0% never married, 62.0% now married, 4.5% widowed, 6.5% divorced (2006-2010 5-year est.); Foreign born: 11.2% (2006-2010 5-year est.); Ancestry (includes multiple ancestries): 22.6% Irish, 20.1% German, 17.1% English, 15.3% Italian, 7.0% Polish (2006-2010 5-year est.).

**Economy:** Unemployment rate: 5.7% (February 2012); Total civilian labor force: 14,141 (February 2012); Single-family building permits issued: 33 (2011); Multi-family building permits issued: 0 (2011); Employment by occupation: 22.1% management, 7.6% professional, 5.4% services, 11.5% sales, 2.8% farming, 3.0% construction, 2.1% production (2006-2010 5-year est.).

**Income:** Per capita income: $50,484 (2006-2010 5-year est.); Median household income: $102,355 (2006-2010 5-year est.); Average household income: $143,505 (2006-2010 5-year est.); Percent of households with income of $100,000 or more: 51.0% (2006-2010 5-year est.); Poverty rate: 3.9% (2006-2010 5-year est.).

**Education:** Percent of population age 25 and over with: High school diploma (including GED) or higher: 98.1% (2006-2010 5-year est.); Bachelor's degree or higher: 70.4% (2006-2010 5-year est.); Master's degree or higher: 37.7% (2006-2010 5-year est.).

**School District(s)**

Pittsford Central School District (KG-12)

   2009-10 Enrollment: 5,969 . . . . . . . . . . . . . . . (585) 267-1004

**Housing:** Homeownership rate: 85.3% (2010); Median home value: $246,900 (2006-2010 5-year est.); Median contract rent: $917 per month (2006-2010 5-year est.); Median year structure built: 1969 (2006-2010 5-year est.).

**Newspapers:** Brighton-Pittsford Post (Local news; Circulation 9,930); Brockport Post (Community news; Circulation 2,109); Henrietta Post

(Community news); Penfield Post (Local news; Circulation 3,652); Perinton-Fairport Post (Community news; Circulation 5,164); Webster Post (Community news; Circulation 4,025)

**Transportation:** Commute to work: 87.6% car, 0.5% public transportation, 4.2% walk, 6.5% work from home (2006-2010 5-year est.); Travel time to work: 35.2% less than 15 minutes, 50.5% 15 to 30 minutes, 10.9% 30 to 45 minutes, 1.8% 45 to 60 minutes, 1.5% 60 minutes or more (2006-2010 5-year est.)

**Additional Information Contacts**

Town of Pittsford . . . . . . . . . . . . . . . . . . . . . . . . . . . . . . . . (585) 248-6210
  http://townofpittsford.org

---

**RIGA** (town). Covers a land area of 34.961 square miles and a water area of 0.266 square miles. Located at 43.07° N. Lat; 77.87° W. Long. Elevation is 636 feet.

**Population:** 5,114 (1990); 5,437 (2000); 5,590 (2010); Density: 159.9 persons per square mile (2010); Race: 95.9% White, 1.3% Black, 0.8% Asian, 0.2% American Indian/Alaska Native, 0.1% Native Hawaiian/Other Pacific Islander, 1.7% Other, 2.2% Hispanic of any race (2010); Average household size: 2.59 (2010); Median age: 43.7 (2010); Males per 100 females: 98.6 (2010); Marriage status: 28.9% never married, 58.2% now married, 4.7% widowed, 8.2% divorced (2006-2010 5-year est.); Foreign born: 2.2% (2006-2010 5-year est.); Ancestry (includes multiple ancestries): 29.1% German, 22.9% English, 20.5% Irish, 17.4% Italian, 6.3% Dutch (2006-2010 5-year est.).

**Economy:** Single-family building permits issued: 3 (2011); Multi-family building permits issued: 0 (2011); Employment by occupation: 9.1% management, 5.6% professional, 8.7% services, 21.2% sales, 2.5% farming, 9.7% construction, 7.0% production (2006-2010 5-year est.).

**Income:** Per capita income: $27,010 (2006-2010 5-year est.); Median household income: $64,846 (2006-2010 5-year est.); Average household income: $69,778 (2006-2010 5-year est.); Percent of households with income of $100,000 or more: 23.3% (2006-2010 5-year est.); Poverty rate: 8.0% (2006-2010 5-year est.).

**Education:** Percent of population age 25 and over with: High school diploma (including GED) or higher: 94.4% (2006-2010 5-year est.); Bachelor's degree or higher: 28.5% (2006-2010 5-year est.); Master's degree or higher: 12.1% (2006-2010 5-year est.).

**Housing:** Homeownership rate: 87.7% (2010); Median home value: $132,900 (2006-2010 5-year est.); Median contract rent: $607 per month (2006-2010 5-year est.); Median year structure built: 1977 (2006-2010 5-year est.).

**Transportation:** Commute to work: 93.0% car, 0.2% public transportation, 1.5% walk, 3.3% work from home (2006-2010 5-year est.); Travel time to work: 21.5% less than 15 minutes, 49.0% 15 to 30 minutes, 21.3% 30 to 45 minutes, 2.9% 45 to 60 minutes, 5.3% 60 minutes or more (2006-2010 5-year est.)

**Additional Information Contacts**

Town of Riga . . . . . . . . . . . . . . . . . . . . . . . . . . . . . . . . . . . (585) 293-3880
  http://www.townofriga.org

---

**ROCHESTER** (city). County seat. Covers a land area of 35.780 square miles and a water area of 1.373 square miles. Located at 43.16° N. Lat; 77.61° W. Long. Elevation is 505 feet.

**History:** The first settler on the site of Rochester was Ebenezer "Indian" Allen, who was granted a 100-acre tract at the falls of the Genesee River on the condition that he erect a mill for use by the Native Americans. Allen built his mill in 1789. After changing hands several times, the area was finally purchased in 1803 by Colonel William Fitzhugh, Major Charles Carroll, and Colonel Nathaniel Rochester, all from Maryland. The village was incorporated as Rochesterville in 1817. The construction of the Erie Canal through Rochester assured the town supremacy over its neighbors. Rochester was the home of George Eastman, who invented and manufactured films for cameras. In 1888 the first Kodak camera was put on the market. The Eastman School of Music was later named for him. In 1840, the University of Rochester was founded by a convention of Baptists.

**Population:** 231,642 (1990); 219,773 (2000); 210,565 (2010); Density: 5,884.9 persons per square mile (2010); Race: 43.7% White, 41.7% Black, 3.1% Asian, 0.5% American Indian/Alaska Native, 0.0% Native Hawaiian/Other Pacific Islander, 11.0% Other, 16.4% Hispanic of any race (2010); Average household size: 2.30 (2010); Median age: 30.8 (2010); Males per 100 females: 93.4 (2010); Marriage status: 51.4% never married, 31.1% now married, 5.9% widowed, 11.6% divorced (2006-2010 5-year est.); Foreign born: 8.2% (2006-2010 5-year est.); Ancestry (includes

multiple ancestries): 10.8% German, 9.3% Italian, 9.2% Irish, 6.4% English, 2.7% African (2006-2010 5-year est.).

**Economy:** Unemployment rate: 10.8% (February 2012); Total civilian labor force: 93,136 (February 2012); Single-family building permits issued: 46 (2011); Multi-family building permits issued: 160 (2011); Employment by occupation: 6.7% management, 4.1% professional, 13.2% services, 16.9% sales, 5.0% farming, 5.8% construction, 6.6% production (2006-2010 5-year est.).

**Income:** Per capita income: $17,865 (2006-2010 5-year est.); Median household income: $30,138 (2006-2010 5-year est.); Average household income: $42,129 (2006-2010 5-year est.); Percent of households with income of $100,000 or more: 7.4% (2006-2010 5-year est.); Poverty rate: 30.4% (2006-2010 5-year est.).

**Taxes:** Total city taxes per capita: $805 (2009); City property taxes per capita: $735 (2009).

**Education:** Percent of population age 25 and over with: High school diploma (including GED) or higher: 78.2% (2006-2010 5-year est.); Bachelor's degree or higher: 24.1% (2006-2010 5-year est.); Master's degree or higher: 10.2% (2006-2010 5-year est.).

### School District(s)

Brighton Central School District (KG-12)
  2009-10 Enrollment: 3,477 . . . . . . . . . . . . . . . . . . . . . (585) 242-5080
Churchville-Chili Central School District (KG-12)
  2009-10 Enrollment: 4,156 . . . . . . . . . . . . . . . . . . . . . (585) 293-1800
East Irondequoit Central School District (KG-12)
  2009-10 Enrollment: 3,153 . . . . . . . . . . . . . . . . . . . . . (585) 339-1210
Eugenio Maria De Hostos Charter School (KG-06)
  2009-10 Enrollment: 324 . . . . . . . . . . . . . . . . . . . . . . (585) 544-6170
Gates-Chili Central School District (KG-12)
  2009-10 Enrollment: 4,547 . . . . . . . . . . . . . . . . . . . . . (585) 247-5050
Genesee Community Charter School at the Rochester (KG-06)
  2009-10 Enrollment: 210 . . . . . . . . . . . . . . . . . . . . . . (585) 697-1960
Greece Central School District (PK-12)
  2009-10 Enrollment: 12,513 . . . . . . . . . . . . . . . . . . . . (585) 621-1000
Penfield Central School District (KG-12)
  2009-10 Enrollment: 4,612 . . . . . . . . . . . . . . . . . . . . . (585) 249-5700
Pittsford Central School District (KG-12)
  2009-10 Enrollment: 5,969 . . . . . . . . . . . . . . . . . . . . . (585) 267-1004
Rochester Academy Charter School (07-10)
  2009-10 Enrollment: 206 . . . . . . . . . . . . . . . . . . . . . . (585) 235-4141
Rochester City School District (PK-12)
  2009-10 Enrollment: 32,516 . . . . . . . . . . . . . . . . . . . . (585) 262-8378
Rush-Henrietta Central School District (KG-12)
  2009-10 Enrollment: 5,596 . . . . . . . . . . . . . . . . . . . . . (585) 359-5012
True North Rochester Preparatory Charter School (t (05-08)
  2009-10 Enrollment: 275 . . . . . . . . . . . . . . . . . . . . . . (585) 436-8629
Urban Choice Charter School (KG-08)
  2009-10 Enrollment: 390 . . . . . . . . . . . . . . . . . . . . . . (585) 288-5702
West Irondequoit Central School District (KG-12)
  2009-10 Enrollment: 3,818 . . . . . . . . . . . . . . . . . . . . . (585) 336-2983

### Four-year College(s)

Colgate Rochester Crozer Divinity School (Private, Not-for-profit)
  Fall 2010 Enrollment: 63 . . . . . . . . . . . . . . . . . . . . . . (585) 271-1320
Nazareth College (Private, Not-for-profit)
  Fall 2010 Enrollment: 3,047 . . . . . . . . . . . . . . . . . . . . (585) 389-2525
  2011-12 Tuition: In-state $27,422; Out-of-state $27,422
Northeastern Seminary (Private, Not-for-profit, Interdenominational)
  Fall 2010 Enrollment: 95 . . . . . . . . . . . . . . . . . . . . . . (585) 594-6000
Roberts Wesleyan College (Private, Not-for-profit, Free Methodist)
  Fall 2010 Enrollment: 1,720 . . . . . . . . . . . . . . . . . . . . (585) 594-6000
  2011-12 Tuition: In-state $25,322; Out-of-state $25,322
Rochester Institute of Technology (Private, Not-for-profit)
  Fall 2010 Enrollment: 13,778 . . . . . . . . . . . . . . . . . . . (585) 475-2411
  2011-12 Tuition: In-state $32,037; Out-of-state $32,037
Saint John Fisher College (Private, Not-for-profit, Roman Catholic)
  Fall 2010 Enrollment: 3,834 . . . . . . . . . . . . . . . . . . . . (585) 385-8000
  2011-12 Tuition: In-state $26,260; Out-of-state $26,260
St Bernard's School of Theology and Ministry (Private, Not-for-profit, Roman Catholic)
  Fall 2010 Enrollment: 52 . . . . . . . . . . . . . . . . . . . . . . (585) 271-3657
Talmudical Institute of Upstate New York (Private, Not-for-profit)
  Fall 2010 Enrollment: 30 . . . . . . . . . . . . . . . . . . . . . . (716) 473-2810
  2011-12 Tuition: In-state $5,000; Out-of-state $5,000

University of Rochester (Private, Not-for-profit)
  Fall 2010 Enrollment: 9,832. . . . . . . . . . . . . . . . . . . . . . (888) 822-2256
  2011-12 Tuition: In-state $41,826; Out-of-state $41,826
**Two-year College(s)**
Bryant and Stratton College-Greece (Private, For-profit)
  Fall 2010 Enrollment: 244 . . . . . . . . . . . . . . . . . . . . . . . (585) 720-0660
  2011-12 Tuition: In-state $15,605; Out-of-state $15,605
Bryant and Stratton College-Henrietta (Private, For-profit)
  Fall 2010 Enrollment: 215 . . . . . . . . . . . . . . . . . . . . . . . (585) 292-5627
  2011-12 Tuition: In-state $15,605; Out-of-state $15,605
Everest Institute-Rochester (Private, For-profit)
  Fall 2010 Enrollment: 1,411. . . . . . . . . . . . . . . . . . . . . . (585) 266-0430
  2011-12 Tuition: In-state $12,744; Out-of-state $12,744
Monroe Community College (Public)
  Fall 2010 Enrollment: 15,977. . . . . . . . . . . . . . . . . . . . . (585) 292-2000
  2011-12 Tuition: In-state $3,689; Out-of-state $6,749
**Vocational/Technical School(s)**
Continental School of Beauty Culture-Rochester (Private, For-profit)
  Fall 2010 Enrollment: 330 . . . . . . . . . . . . . . . . . . . . . . . (585) 272-8060
  2011-12 Tuition: $11,050
Isabella G Hart School of Practical Nursing (Private, Not-for-profit)
  Fall 2010 Enrollment: 81 . . . . . . . . . . . . . . . . . . . . . . . . (585) 922-1400
Monroe 2-Orleans BOCES Center for Workforce Development (Public)
  Fall 2010 Enrollment: 116 . . . . . . . . . . . . . . . . . . . . . . . (585) 349-9100
  2011-12 Tuition: $6,200
Onondaga School of Therapeutic Massage-Rochester (Private, For-profit)
  Fall 2010 Enrollment: 60 . . . . . . . . . . . . . . . . . . . . . . . . (585) 241-0070
  2011-12 Tuition: $14,000
Rochester General Hospital School of Medical Technology (Private, Not-for-profit)
  Fall 2010 Enrollment: 15 . . . . . . . . . . . . . . . . . . . . . . . . (585) 922-4274
Shear Ego International School of Hair Design (Private, For-profit)
  Fall 2010 Enrollment: 112 . . . . . . . . . . . . . . . . . . . . . . . (585) 342-0070
  2011-12 Tuition: $10,726
**Housing:** Homeownership rate: 37.6% (2010); Median home value: $73,600 (2006-2010 5-year est.); Median contract rent: $583 per month (2006-2010 5-year est.); Median year structure built: before 1940 (2006-2010 5-year est.).
**Hospitals:** Highland Hospital/University of Rochester Medical Center (272 beds); Monroe Community Hospital (566 beds); Rochester General Hospital (528 beds); Rochester Psychiatric Center (180 beds); Strong Memorial Hospital, University of Rochester (750 beds); Unity Health Systems St. Mary's Hospital (215 beds); Unity Hospital (681 beds)
**Safety:** Violent crime rate: 109.4 per 10,000 population; Property crime rate: 580.0 per 10,000 population (2010).
**Newspapers:** Adnet Community News(Gates-Chili Ed) (Community news; Circulation 16,000); Adnet Community News(Greece Ed.) (Community news; Circulation 30,000); Catholic Courier (Regional news; Circulation 46,147); City Newspaper (Local news; Circulation 40,000); Democrat and Chronicle (Local news; Circulation 147,331); Empty Closet (Community news; Circulation 5,000); Gates-Chili News (Local news; Circulation 9,800); Greece Post (Community news; Circulation 7,993); Ink-Slinger Press (Local news); Insider; Irondequoit Press (Community news; Circulation 4,000); Jewish Ledger (Local news; Circulation 6,000); Rochester Daily Record (Local news; Circulation 15,000)
**Transportation:** Commute to work: 80.2% car, 8.4% public transportation, 6.2% walk, 2.9% work from home (2006-2010 5-year est.); Travel time to work: 37.8% less than 15 minutes, 45.5% 15 to 30 minutes, 10.7% 30 to 45 minutes, 2.7% 45 to 60 minutes, 3.3% 60 minutes or more (2006-2010 5-year est.); Amtrak: train service available.
**Airports:** Greater Rochester International (primary service/small hub)
**Additional Information Contacts**
City of Rochester . . . . . . . . . . . . . . . . . . . . . . . . . . . . . . (585) 428-5990
  http://www.cityofrochester.gov
Rochester Business Alliance . . . . . . . . . . . . . . . . . . . . . (585) 244-1800
  http://www.rochesterbusinessalliance.com

**RUSH** (town). Covers a land area of 30.331 square miles and a water area of 0.373 square miles. Located at 42.97° N. Lat; 77.67° W. Long. Elevation is 551 feet.
**Population:** 3,217 (1990); 3,603 (2000); 3,478 (2010); Density: 114.7 persons per square mile (2010); Race: 95.1% White, 2.7% Black, 1.0% Asian, 0.2% American Indian/Alaska Native, 0.0% Native Hawaiian/Other Pacific Islander, 1.0% Other, 1.4% Hispanic of any race (2010); Average household size: 2.46 (2010); Median age: 47.5 (2010); Males per 100

females: 103.0 (2010); Marriage status: 24.5% never married, 62.5% now married, 7.4% widowed, 5.6% divorced (2006-2010 5-year est.); Foreign born: 9.8% (2006-2010 5-year est.); Ancestry (includes multiple ancestries): 31.7% German, 19.6% Irish, 18.3% English, 12.0% Italian, 5.5% French (2006-2010 5-year est.).
**Economy:** Single-family building permits issued: 3 (2011); Multi-family building permits issued: 0 (2011); Employment by occupation: 14.0% management, 10.2% professional, 5.0% services, 15.4% sales, 3.4% farming, 8.0% construction, 6.8% production (2006-2010 5-year est.).
**Income:** Per capita income: $37,080 (2006-2010 5-year est.); Median household income: $81,184 (2006-2010 5-year est.); Average household income: $94,331 (2006-2010 5-year est.); Percent of households with income of $100,000 or more: 36.8% (2006-2010 5-year est.); Poverty rate: 3.0% (2006-2010 5-year est.).
**Taxes:** Total city taxes per capita: $369 (2009); City property taxes per capita: $342 (2009).
**Education:** Percent of population age 25 and over with: High school diploma (including GED) or higher: 92.9% (2006-2010 5-year est.); Bachelor's degree or higher: 43.0% (2006-2010 5-year est.); Master's degree or higher: 15.6% (2006-2010 5-year est.).
**School District(s)**
Rush-Henrietta Central School District (KG-12)
  2009-10 Enrollment: 5,596 . . . . . . . . . . . . . . . . . . . . . . (585) 359-5012
**Housing:** Homeownership rate: 91.0% (2010); Median home value: $185,700 (2006-2010 5-year est.); Median contract rent: $763 per month (2006-2010 5-year est.); Median year structure built: 1973 (2006-2010 5-year est.).
**Transportation:** Commute to work: 94.0% car, 0.0% public transportation, 1.1% walk, 4.3% work from home (2006-2010 5-year est.); Travel time to work: 25.1% less than 15 minutes, 48.8% 15 to 30 minutes, 18.8% 30 to 45 minutes, 4.0% 45 to 60 minutes, 3.3% 60 minutes or more (2006-2010 5-year est.)
**Additional Information Contacts**
Town of Rush . . . . . . . . . . . . . . . . . . . . . . . . . . . . . . . . . (585) 533-1312
  http://townofrush.com

**SCOTTSVILLE** (village). Covers a land area of 1.082 square miles and a water area of 0.005 square miles. Located at 43.02° N. Lat; 77.75° W. Long. Elevation is 607 feet.
**Population:** 1,912 (1990); 2,128 (2000); 2,001 (2010); Density: 1,849.0 persons per square mile (2010); Race: 88.9% White, 6.2% Black, 0.8% Asian, 0.3% American Indian/Alaska Native, 0.1% Native Hawaiian/Other Pacific Islander, 3.7% Other, 3.7% Hispanic of any race (2010); Average household size: 2.37 (2010); Median age: 41.8 (2010); Males per 100 females: 97.9 (2010); Marriage status: 24.1% never married, 63.8% now married, 2.3% widowed, 9.8% divorced (2006-2010 5-year est.); Foreign born: 4.9% (2006-2010 5-year est.); Ancestry (includes multiple ancestries): 21.9% German, 19.6% Italian, 19.3% Irish, 15.9% English, 5.5% Dutch (2006-2010 5-year est.).
**Economy:** Single-family building permits issued: 0 (2011); Multi-family building permits issued: 0 (2011); Employment by occupation: 12.4% management, 4.6% professional, 5.1% services, 14.5% sales, 4.6% farming, 9.7% construction, 6.4% production (2006-2010 5-year est.).
**Income:** Per capita income: $28,483 (2006-2010 5-year est.); Median household income: $60,192 (2006-2010 5-year est.); Average household income: $71,464 (2006-2010 5-year est.); Percent of households with income of $100,000 or more: 20.2% (2006-2010 5-year est.); Poverty rate: 10.5% (2006-2010 5-year est.).
**Education:** Percent of population age 25 and over with: High school diploma (including GED) or higher: 92.7% (2006-2010 5-year est.); Bachelor's degree or higher: 36.2% (2006-2010 5-year est.); Master's degree or higher: 13.7% (2006-2010 5-year est.).
**School District(s)**
Wheatland-Chili Central School District (KG-12)
  2009-10 Enrollment: 700 . . . . . . . . . . . . . . . . . . . . . . . . (585) 889-6246
**Housing:** Homeownership rate: 74.2% (2010); Median home value: $114,000 (2006-2010 5-year est.); Median contract rent: $660 per month (2006-2010 5-year est.); Median year structure built: 1957 (2006-2010 5-year est.).
**Transportation:** Commute to work: 92.6% car, 0.4% public transportation, 4.1% walk, 2.6% work from home (2006-2010 5-year est.); Travel time to work: 30.8% less than 15 minutes, 49.4% 15 to 30 minutes, 16.9% 30 to 45 minutes, 0.7% 45 to 60 minutes, 2.2% 60 minutes or more (2006-2010 5-year est.)

**SPENCERPORT** (village). Covers a land area of 1.337 square miles and a water area of 0.032 square miles. Located at 43.18° N. Lat; 77.80° W. Long. Elevation is 554 feet.

**History:** Site of John T. Trowbridge's boyhood home. Incorporated 1867.

**Population:** 3,622 (1990); 3,559 (2000); 3,601 (2010); Density: 2,692.7 persons per square mile (2010); Race: 95.3% White, 1.7% Black, 0.6% Asian, 0.3% American Indian/Alaska Native, 0.0% Native Hawaiian/Other Pacific Islander, 2.1% Other, 3.0% Hispanic of any race (2010); Average household size: 2.41 (2010); Median age: 41.0 (2010); Males per 100 females: 91.0 (2010); Marriage status: 24.6% never married, 55.3% now married, 5.5% widowed, 14.6% divorced (2006-2010 5-year est.); Foreign born: 2.5% (2006-2010 5-year est.); Ancestry (includes multiple ancestries): 29.5% German, 26.8% Irish, 21.6% English, 20.2% Italian, 5.2% Dutch (2006-2010 5-year est.).

**Economy:** Single-family building permits issued: 0 (2011); Multi-family building permits issued: 0 (2011); Employment by occupation: 12.5% management, 4.9% professional, 14.6% services, 17.9% sales, 2.9% farming, 5.7% construction, 4.3% production (2006-2010 5-year est.).

**Income:** Per capita income: $28,642 (2006-2010 5-year est.); Median household income: $60,158 (2006-2010 5-year est.); Average household income: $67,186 (2006-2010 5-year est.); Percent of households with income of $100,000 or more: 20.7% (2006-2010 5-year est.); Poverty rate: 4.9% (2006-2010 5-year est.).

**Education:** Percent of population age 25 and over with: High school diploma (including GED) or higher: 94.6% (2006-2010 5-year est.); Bachelor's degree or higher: 34.8% (2006-2010 5-year est.); Master's degree or higher: 13.2% (2006-2010 5-year est.).

**School District(s)**

Monroe 2-Orleans Boces
   2009-10 Enrollment: n/a . . . . . . . . . . . . . . . . . . . . . . . . (585) 352-2410
Spencerport Central School District (KG-12)
   2009-10 Enrollment: 4,018 . . . . . . . . . . . . . . . . . . . . . (585) 349-5102

**Housing:** Homeownership rate: 69.9% (2010); Median home value: $131,500 (2006-2010 5-year est.); Median contract rent: $698 per month (2006-2010 5-year est.); Median year structure built: 1963 (2006-2010 5-year est.).

**Newspapers:** Hamlin-Clarkson Herald (Local news; Circulation 6,006); Suburban News West Edition (Local news; Circulation 32,000)

**Transportation:** Commute to work: 91.5% car, 2.8% public transportation, 2.1% walk, 2.7% work from home (2006-2010 5-year est.); Travel time to work: 23.8% less than 15 minutes, 48.3% 15 to 30 minutes, 26.2% 30 to 45 minutes, 1.7% 45 to 60 minutes, 0.0% 60 minutes or more (2006-2010 5-year est.).

**SWEDEN** (town). Covers a land area of 33.678 square miles and a water area of 0.152 square miles. Located at 43.17° N. Lat; 77.92° W. Long.

**Population:** 14,181 (1990); 13,716 (2000); 14,175 (2010); Density: 420.9 persons per square mile (2010); Race: 92.5% White, 3.2% Black, 1.4% Asian, 0.2% American Indian/Alaska Native, 0.0% Native Hawaiian/Other Pacific Islander, 2.7% Other, 3.5% Hispanic of any race (2010); Average household size: 2.36 (2010); Median age: 24.4 (2010); Males per 100 females: 92.6 (2010); Marriage status: 48.2% never married, 41.6% now married, 2.4% widowed, 7.7% divorced (2006-2010 5-year est.); Foreign born: 5.5% (2006-2010 5-year est.); Ancestry (includes multiple ancestries): 27.6% German, 19.5% Italian, 18.8% Irish, 15.4% English, 7.6% Polish (2006-2010 5-year est.).

**Economy:** Single-family building permits issued: 7 (2011); Multi-family building permits issued: 0 (2011); Employment by occupation: 9.3% management, 4.0% professional, 11.2% services, 20.9% sales, 4.4% farming, 7.8% construction, 4.0% production (2006-2010 5-year est.).

**Income:** Per capita income: $22,808 (2006-2010 5-year est.); Median household income: $52,623 (2006-2010 5-year est.); Average household income: $64,476 (2006-2010 5-year est.); Percent of households with income of $100,000 or more: 18.4% (2006-2010 5-year est.); Poverty rate: 15.0% (2006-2010 5-year est.).

**Education:** Percent of population age 25 and over with: High school diploma (including GED) or higher: 92.3% (2006-2010 5-year est.); Bachelor's degree or higher: 37.6% (2006-2010 5-year est.); Master's degree or higher: 18.7% (2006-2010 5-year est.).

**Housing:** Homeownership rate: 56.6% (2010); Median home value: $122,900 (2006-2010 5-year est.); Median contract rent: $622 per month (2006-2010 5-year est.); Median year structure built: 1967 (2006-2010 5-year est.).

**Transportation:** Commute to work: 83.8% car, 0.2% public transportation, 13.4% walk, 1.7% work from home (2006-2010 5-year est.); Travel time to work: 39.3% less than 15 minutes, 33.7% 15 to 30 minutes, 21.9% 30 to 45 minutes, 2.8% 45 to 60 minutes, 2.3% 60 minutes or more (2006-2010 5-year est.)

**WEBSTER** (village). Covers a land area of 2.202 square miles and a water area of <.001 square miles. Located at 43.21° N. Lat; 77.42° W. Long. Elevation is 446 feet.

**Population:** 5,505 (1990); 5,216 (2000); 5,399 (2010); Density: 2,451.6 persons per square mile (2010); Race: 83.4% White, 5.2% Black, 5.7% Asian, 0.3% American Indian/Alaska Native, 0.1% Native Hawaiian/Other Pacific Islander, 5.3% Other, 5.2% Hispanic of any race (2010); Average household size: 2.27 (2010); Median age: 37.1 (2010); Males per 100 females: 89.4 (2010); Marriage status: 33.6% never married, 46.4% now married, 7.0% widowed, 13.0% divorced (2006-2010 5-year est.); Foreign born: 16.7% (2006-2010 5-year est.); Ancestry (includes multiple ancestries): 21.3% Italian, 18.7% German, 18.0% English, 11.0% Irish, 9.9% Ukrainian (2006-2010 5-year est.).

**Economy:** Single-family building permits issued: 20 (2011); Multi-family building permits issued: 28 (2011); Employment by occupation: 5.4% management, 4.0% professional, 10.1% services, 24.3% sales, 4.8% farming, 9.9% construction, 7.7% production (2006-2010 5-year est.).

**Income:** Per capita income: $23,024 (2006-2010 5-year est.); Median household income: $37,252 (2006-2010 5-year est.); Average household income: $49,156 (2006-2010 5-year est.); Percent of households with income of $100,000 or more: 11.1% (2006-2010 5-year est.); Poverty rate: 15.0% (2006-2010 5-year est.).

**Education:** Percent of population age 25 and over with: High school diploma (including GED) or higher: 90.8% (2006-2010 5-year est.); Bachelor's degree or higher: 28.7% (2006-2010 5-year est.); Master's degree or higher: 9.4% (2006-2010 5-year est.).

**School District(s)**

Webster Central School District (KG-12)
   2009-10 Enrollment: 8,732 . . . . . . . . . . . . . . . . . . . . . (585) 265-3600

**Housing:** Homeownership rate: 42.6% (2010); Median home value: $127,100 (2006-2010 5-year est.); Median contract rent: $658 per month (2006-2010 5-year est.); Median year structure built: 1963 (2006-2010 5-year est.).

**Newspapers:** Wayne County Mail (Community news; Circulation 3,800); Webster Herald (Community news; Circulation 4,332); Webster/Ontario/Walworth Pennysaver (Community news; Circulation 19,900)

**Transportation:** Commute to work: 89.5% car, 6.3% public transportation, 1.9% walk, 0.3% work from home (2006-2010 5-year est.); Travel time to work: 33.0% less than 15 minutes, 39.0% 15 to 30 minutes, 16.6% 30 to 45 minutes, 8.0% 45 to 60 minutes, 3.3% 60 minutes or more (2006-2010 5-year est.)

**Additional Information Contacts**

Webster Chamber of Commerce . . . . . . . . . . . . . . . . . . . (585) 265-3960
   http://www.websterchamber.com

**WEBSTER** (town). Covers a land area of 33.531 square miles and a water area of 1.706 square miles. Located at 43.23° N. Lat; 77.44° W. Long. Elevation is 446 feet.

**History:** Incorporated 1905.

**Population:** 31,639 (1990); 37,926 (2000); 42,641 (2010); Density: 1,271.7 persons per square mile (2010); Race: 92.8% White, 2.0% Black, 2.8% Asian, 0.2% American Indian/Alaska Native, 0.0% Native Hawaiian/Other Pacific Islander, 2.2% Other, 2.9% Hispanic of any race (2010); Average household size: 2.47 (2010); Median age: 42.9 (2010); Males per 100 females: 93.7 (2010); Marriage status: 24.3% never married, 61.1% now married, 6.9% widowed, 7.8% divorced (2006-2010 5-year est.); Foreign born: 9.0% (2006-2010 5-year est.); Ancestry (includes multiple ancestries): 26.6% German, 25.7% Italian, 16.1% Irish, 15.6% English, 8.0% Polish (2006-2010 5-year est.).

**Economy:** Unemployment rate: 6.4% (February 2012); Total civilian labor force: 22,171 (February 2012); Single-family building permits issued: 38 (2011); Multi-family building permits issued: 78 (2011); Employment by occupation: 12.9% management, 7.5% professional, 7.4% services, 17.0% sales, 3.3% farming, 5.9% construction, 5.0% production (2006-2010 5-year est.).

**Income:** Per capita income: $32,270 (2006-2010 5-year est.); Median household income: $66,727 (2006-2010 5-year est.); Average household income: $80,707 (2006-2010 5-year est.); Percent of households with

income of $100,000 or more: 26.8% (2006-2010 5-year est.); Poverty rate: 4.8% (2006-2010 5-year est.).
**Education:** Percent of population age 25 and over with: High school diploma (including GED) or higher: 94.2% (2006-2010 5-year est.); Bachelor's degree or higher: 39.2% (2006-2010 5-year est.); Master's degree or higher: 16.8% (2006-2010 5-year est.).

### School District(s)
Webster Central School District (KG-12)
    2009-10 Enrollment: 8,732 . . . . . . . . . . . . . . . . . . (585) 265-3600
**Housing:** Homeownership rate: 76.8% (2010); Median home value: $166,500 (2006-2010 5-year est.); Median contract rent: $756 per month (2006-2010 5-year est.); Median year structure built: 1978 (2006-2010 5-year est.).
**Safety:** Violent crime rate: 4.5 per 10,000 population; Property crime rate: 126.9 per 10,000 population (2010).
**Newspapers:** Wayne County Mail (Community news; Circulation 3,800); Webster Herald (Community news; Circulation 4,332); Webster/Ontario/Walworth Pennysaver (Community news; Circulation 19,900)
**Transportation:** Commute to work: 94.6% car, 1.1% public transportation, 0.6% walk, 2.8% work from home (2006-2010 5-year est.); Travel time to work: 31.5% less than 15 minutes, 46.9% 15 to 30 minutes, 17.1% 30 to 45 minutes, 2.4% 45 to 60 minutes, 2.1% 60 minutes or more (2006-2010 5-year est.)
**Additional Information Contacts**
Town of Webster . . . . . . . . . . . . . . . . . . . . . . . . . . (585) 872-1000
   http://www.ci.webster.ny.us

## WEST HENRIETTA (unincorporated postal area)
Zip Code: 14586
   Covers a land area of 11.145 square miles and a water area of 0.193 square miles. Located at 43.04° N. Lat; 77.68° W. Long. Elevation is 604 feet. Population: 10,256 (2010); Density: 920.2 persons per square mile (2010); Race: 77.1% White, 9.9% Black, 9.0% Asian, 0.1% American Indian/Alaska Native, 0.0% Native Hawaiian/Other Pacific Islander, 3.9% Other, 4.0% Hispanic of any race (2010); Average household size: 2.64 (2010); Median age: 32.7 (2010); Males per 100 females: 104.3 (2010); Homeownership rate: 73.0% (2010)

## WHEATLAND (town). Covers a land area of 30.410 square miles and a water area of 0.261 square miles. Located at 43.00° N. Lat; 77.81° W. Long. Elevation is 604 feet.
**Population:** 5,093 (1990); 5,149 (2000); 4,775 (2010); Density: 157.0 persons per square mile (2010); Race: 91.3% White, 4.8% Black, 0.8% Asian, 0.3% American Indian/Alaska Native, 0.1% Native Hawaiian/Other Pacific Islander, 2.7% Other, 2.3% Hispanic of any race (2010); Average household size: 2.38 (2010); Median age: 42.6 (2010); Males per 100 females: 100.4 (2010); Marriage status: 30.4% never married, 59.6% now married, 3.6% widowed, 6.4% divorced (2006-2010 5-year est.); Foreign born: 3.6% (2006-2010 5-year est.); Ancestry (includes multiple ancestries): 22.7% German, 21.9% Irish, 18.5% Italian, 14.9% English, 5.8% Dutch (2006-2010 5-year est.).
**Economy:** Single-family building permits issued: 1 (2011); Multi-family building permits issued: 0 (2011); Employment by occupation: 13.4% management, 7.2% professional, 6.4% services, 17.3% sales, 5.9% farming, 7.6% construction, 5.8% production (2006-2010 5-year est.).
**Income:** Per capita income: $27,470 (2006-2010 5-year est.); Median household income: $61,462 (2006-2010 5-year est.); Average household income: $68,537 (2006-2010 5-year est.); Percent of households with income of $100,000 or more: 18.3% (2006-2010 5-year est.); Poverty rate: 8.0% (2006-2010 5-year est.).
**Education:** Percent of population age 25 and over with: High school diploma (including GED) or higher: 93.4% (2006-2010 5-year est.); Bachelor's degree or higher: 37.2% (2006-2010 5-year est.); Master's degree or higher: 14.7% (2006-2010 5-year est.).
**Housing:** Homeownership rate: 71.1% (2010); Median home value: $125,600 (2006-2010 5-year est.); Median contract rent: $753 per month (2006-2010 5-year est.); Median year structure built: 1966 (2006-2010 5-year est.).
**Transportation:** Commute to work: 94.4% car, 0.2% public transportation, 3.2% walk, 2.1% work from home (2006-2010 5-year est.); Travel time to work: 23.3% less than 15 minutes, 51.2% 15 to 30 minutes, 23.0% 30 to 45 minutes, 0.8% 45 to 60 minutes, 1.8% 60 minutes or more (2006-2010 5-year est.)
**Additional Information Contacts**

Town of Wheatland . . . . . . . . . . . . . . . . . . . . . . . . (585) 889-1553
   http://www.townofwheatland.org

# Montgomery County

Located in east central New York, in the Mohawk River Valley; crossed by the Barge Canal; drained by Schoharie Creek. Covers a land area of 404.82 square miles, a water area of 5.51 square miles, and is located in the Eastern Time Zone at 42.91° N. Lat., 74.39° W. Long. The county was founded in 1772. County seat is Fonda.

Montgomery County is part of the Amsterdam, NY Micropolitan Statistical Area. The entire metro area includes: Montgomery County, NY

**Population:** 51,981 (1990); 49,708 (2000); 50,219 (2010); Race: 90.6% White, 1.9% Black, 0.7% Asian, 0.3% American Indian/Alaska Native, 0.0% Native Hawaiian/Other Pacific Islander, 6.5% Other, 11.3% Hispanic of any race (2010); Density: 124.1 persons per square mile (2010); Average household size: 2.43 (2010); Median age: 40.8 (2010); Males per 100 females: 94.9 (2010).
**Religion:** Six largest groups: 27.8% Catholicism, 4.4% Lutheran, 3.6% Presbyterian-Reformed, 2.6% Methodist/Pietist, 2.1% Non-Denominational, 1.0% Baptist (2010)
**Economy:** Unemployment rate: 11.6% (February 2012); Total civilian labor force: 23,566 (February 2012); Leading industries: 27.3% health care and social assistance; 21.2% manufacturing; 15.8% retail trade (2009); Farms: 604 totaling 124,556 acres (2007); Companies that employ 500 or more persons: 5 (2009); Companies that employ 100 to 499 persons: 19 (2009); Companies that employ less than 100 persons: 1,085 (2009); Black-owned businesses: 110 (2007); Hispanic-owned businesses: n/a (2007); Asian-owned businesses: n/a (2007); Women-owned businesses: 1,122 (2007); Retail sales per capita: $15,380 (2010). Single-family building permits issued: 37 (2011); Multi-family building permits issued: 86 (2011).
**Income:** Per capita income: $22,347 (2006-2010 5-year est.); Median household income: $42,603 (2006-2010 5-year est.); Average household income: $54,449 (2006-2010 5-year est.); Percent of households with income of $100,000 or more: 12.2% (2006-2010 5-year est.); Poverty rate: 14.9% (2006-2010 5-year est.); Bankruptcy rate: 2.68% (2011).
**Education:** Percent of population age 25 and over with: High school diploma (including GED) or higher: 82.7% (2006-2010 5-year est.); Bachelor's degree or higher: 15.9% (2006-2010 5-year est.); Master's degree or higher: 7.0% (2006-2010 5-year est.).
**Housing:** Homeownership rate: 67.0% (2010); Median home value: $95,000 (2006-2010 5-year est.); Median contract rent: $477 per month (2006-2010 5-year est.); Median year structure built: 1942 (2006-2010 5-year est.).
**Health:** Birth rate: 122.4 per 10,000 population (2011); Death rate: 115.4 per 10,000 population (2011); Age-adjusted cancer mortality rate: 166.7 deaths per 100,000 population (2009); Number of physicians: 16.0 per 10,000 population (2008); Hospital beds: 70.4 per 10,000 population (2007); Hospital admissions: 1,472.2 per 10,000 population (2007).
**Elections:** 2008 Presidential election results: 45.0% Obama, 53.1% McCain, 1.2% Nader
**Additional Information Contacts**
Montgomery County Government . . . . . . . . . . . . . . . (518) 853-8111
   http://www.co.montgomery.ny.us
Montgomery County Chamber of Commerce . . . . . . . (518) 842-8200
   http://www.montgomerycountyny.com

## Montgomery County Communities

## AMES (village). Covers a land area of 0.130 square miles and a water area of 0 square miles. Located at 42.83° N. Lat; 74.60° W. Long. Elevation is 705 feet.
**Population:** 166 (1990); 173 (2000); 145 (2010); Density: 1,109.6 persons per square mile (2010); Race: 99.3% White, 0.0% Black, 0.0% Asian, 0.0% American Indian/Alaska Native, 0.0% Native Hawaiian/Other Pacific Islander, 0.7% Other, 1.4% Hispanic of any race (2010); Average household size: 2.38 (2010); Median age: 46.3 (2010); Males per 100 females: 107.1 (2010); Marriage status: 16.2% never married, 57.4% now married, 11.0% widowed, 15.4% divorced (2006-2010 5-year est.); Foreign born: 1.2% (2006-2010 5-year est.); Ancestry (includes multiple ancestries): 37.3% German, 18.0% Irish, 14.3% English, 13.0% Scottish, 11.2% Dutch (2006-2010 5-year est.).

**Economy:** Single-family building permits issued: 0 (2011); Multi-family building permits issued: 0 (2011); Employment by occupation: 12.3% management, 0.0% professional, 3.7% services, 7.4% sales, 2.5% farming, 32.1% construction, 17.3% production (2006-2010 5-year est.).
**Income:** Per capita income: $27,281 (2006-2010 5-year est.); Median household income: $65,000 (2006-2010 5-year est.); Average household income: $67,577 (2006-2010 5-year est.); Percent of households with income of $100,000 or more: 18.2% (2006-2010 5-year est.); Poverty rate: 5.6% (2006-2010 5-year est.).
**Education:** Percent of population age 25 and over with: High school diploma (including GED) or higher: 89.7% (2006-2010 5-year est.); Bachelor's degree or higher: 23.9% (2006-2010 5-year est.); Master's degree or higher: 8.5% (2006-2010 5-year est.).
**Housing:** Homeownership rate: 83.6% (2010); Median home value: $98,600 (2006-2010 5-year est.); Median contract rent: $413 per month (2006-2010 5-year est.); Median year structure built: before 1940 (2006-2010 5-year est.).
**Transportation:** Commute to work: 97.5% car, 0.0% public transportation, 0.0% walk, 2.5% work from home (2006-2010 5-year est.); Travel time to work: 21.5% less than 15 minutes, 48.1% 15 to 30 minutes, 15.2% 30 to 45 minutes, 7.6% 45 to 60 minutes, 7.6% 60 minutes or more (2006-2010 5-year est.)

**AMSTERDAM** (city). Covers a land area of 5.862 square miles and a water area of 0.391 square miles. Located at 42.94° N. Lat; 74.19° W. Long. Elevation is 361 feet.
**History:** Amsterdam was first settled by Albert Veeder, who came from Schenectady in 1783. The village of Amsterdam was so named in 1804. It began to grow in size and industrial importance after the Erie Canal was opened in 1825 and the Utica & Schenectady Railroad was constructed through it in 1836. The local carpet industry traces its beginnings to 1838, when William E. Greene established a carpet mill. The knitting industry was started by Greene in 1856.
**Population:** 20,693 (1990); 18,355 (2000); 18,620 (2010); Density: 3,176.3 persons per square mile (2010); Race: 80.4% White, 3.8% Black, 0.9% Asian, 0.6% American Indian/Alaska Native, 0.0% Native Hawaiian/Other Pacific Islander, 14.3% Other, 26.2% Hispanic of any race (2010); Average household size: 2.34 (2010); Median age: 37.4 (2010); Males per 100 females: 90.0 (2010); Marriage status: 35.4% never married, 44.2% now married, 8.7% widowed, 11.7% divorced (2006-2010 5-year est.); Foreign born: 7.0% (2006-2010 5-year est.); Ancestry (includes multiple ancestries): 20.5% Italian, 14.5% Polish, 14.0% Irish, 11.3% German, 9.1% English (2006-2010 5-year est.).
**Economy:** Single-family building permits issued: 0 (2011); Multi-family building permits issued: 0 (2011); Employment by occupation: 8.4% management, 3.2% professional, 10.0% services, 15.1% sales, 5.7% farming, 9.1% construction, 9.7% production (2006-2010 5-year est.).
**Income:** Per capita income: $22,355 (2006-2010 5-year est.); Median household income: $37,295 (2006-2010 5-year est.); Average household income: $49,380 (2006-2010 5-year est.); Percent of households with income of $100,000 or more: 10.3% (2006-2010 5-year est.); Poverty rate: 18.0% (2006-2010 5-year est.).
**Education:** Percent of population age 25 and over with: High school diploma (including GED) or higher: 82.1% (2006-2010 5-year est.); Bachelor's degree or higher: 17.5% (2006-2010 5-year est.); Master's degree or higher: 7.8% (2006-2010 5-year est.).
**School District(s)**
Amsterdam City School District (PK-12)
   2009-10 Enrollment: 3,767 . . . . . . . . . . . . . . . . . . . . . (518) 843-5217
Broadalbin-Perth Central School District (PK-12)
   2009-10 Enrollment: 1,960 . . . . . . . . . . . . . . . . . . . . . (518) 954-2500
**Housing:** Homeownership rate: 48.8% (2010); Median home value: $91,600 (2006-2010 5-year est.); Median contract rent: $490 per month (2006-2010 5-year est.); Median year structure built: before 1940 (2006-2010 5-year est.).
**Safety:** Violent crime rate: 26.2 per 10,000 population; Property crime rate: 329.3 per 10,000 population (2010).
**Newspapers:** Amsterdam Evening Recorder (Community news; Circulation 9,506); Daily Gazette - Amsterdam Bureau (Local news); Outlook - The Recorder; The Recorder (Local news)
**Transportation:** Commute to work: 88.5% car, 1.7% public transportation, 3.0% walk, 2.5% work from home (2006-2010 5-year est.); Travel time to work: 45.0% less than 15 minutes, 23.7% 15 to 30 minutes, 16.0% 30 to 45 minutes, 10.5% 45 to 60 minutes, 4.8% 60 minutes or more (2006-2010 5-year est.); Amtrak: train service available.

**Additional Information Contacts**
Montgomery County Chamber of Commerce . . . . . . . . . . (518) 842-8200
http://www.montgomerycountyny.com

**AMSTERDAM** (town). Covers a land area of 29.701 square miles and a water area of 0.733 square miles. Located at 42.95° N. Lat; 74.16° W. Long. Elevation is 361 feet.
**History:** Historically famous for carpet manufacturing. The area was settled in 1783 and was named Amsterdam for its many early settlers from the Netherlands. Nearby stands Fort Johnson, home of the British colonial leader Sir William Johnson. Incorporated 1885.
**Population:** 5,983 (1990); 5,820 (2000); 5,566 (2010); Density: 187.4 persons per square mile (2010); Race: 96.1% White, 0.9% Black, 0.8% Asian, 0.2% American Indian/Alaska Native, 0.0% Native Hawaiian/Other Pacific Islander, 2.0% Other, 3.8% Hispanic of any race (2010); Average household size: 2.30 (2010); Median age: 49.2 (2010); Males per 100 females: 92.0 (2010); Marriage status: 25.6% never married, 51.4% now married, 9.4% widowed, 13.6% divorced (2006-2010 5-year est.); Foreign born: 2.0% (2006-2010 5-year est.); Ancestry (includes multiple ancestries): 23.3% Italian, 15.8% Polish, 15.6% German, 15.6% Irish, 14.7% English (2006-2010 5-year est.).
**Economy:** Single-family building permits issued: 4 (2011); Multi-family building permits issued: 86 (2011); Employment by occupation: 11.3% management, 1.0% professional, 13.5% services, 20.2% sales, 7.1% farming, 12.1% construction, 9.5% production (2006-2010 5-year est.).
**Income:** Per capita income: $25,950 (2006-2010 5-year est.); Median household income: $55,185 (2006-2010 5-year est.); Average household income: $63,042 (2006-2010 5-year est.); Percent of households with income of $100,000 or more: 20.1% (2006-2010 5-year est.); Poverty rate: 8.0% (2006-2010 5-year est.).
**Education:** Percent of population age 25 and over with: High school diploma (including GED) or higher: 86.5% (2006-2010 5-year est.); Bachelor's degree or higher: 16.8% (2006-2010 5-year est.); Master's degree or higher: 6.0% (2006-2010 5-year est.).
**School District(s)**
Amsterdam City School District (PK-12)
   2009-10 Enrollment: 3,767 . . . . . . . . . . . . . . . . . . . . . (518) 843-5217
Broadalbin-Perth Central School District (PK-12)
   2009-10 Enrollment: 1,960 . . . . . . . . . . . . . . . . . . . . . (518) 954-2500
**Housing:** Homeownership rate: 83.8% (2010); Median home value: $113,800 (2006-2010 5-year est.); Median contract rent: $543 per month (2006-2010 5-year est.); Median year structure built: 1951 (2006-2010 5-year est.).
**Hospitals:** Amsterdam Memorial Hospital (39 beds); Amsterdam Memorial Hospital (39 beds); St. Mary's Hospital (143 beds); St. Mary's Hospital (143 beds)
**Newspapers:** Amsterdam Evening Recorder (Community news; Circulation 9,506); Daily Gazette - Amsterdam Bureau (Local news); Outlook - The Recorder; The Recorder (Local news)
**Transportation:** Commute to work: 94.5% car, 0.0% public transportation, 2.0% walk, 3.4% work from home (2006-2010 5-year est.); Travel time to work: 35.9% less than 15 minutes, 33.0% 15 to 30 minutes, 15.2% 30 to 45 minutes, 14.0% 45 to 60 minutes, 1.8% 60 minutes or more (2006-2010 5-year est.); Amtrak: train service available.

**CANAJOHARIE** (village). Covers a land area of 1.329 square miles and a water area of 0.068 square miles. Located at 42.89° N. Lat; 74.56° W. Long. Elevation is 305 feet.
**Population:** 2,364 (1990); 2,257 (2000); 2,229 (2010); Density: 1,676.0 persons per square mile (2010); Race: 95.0% White, 2.2% Black, 0.6% Asian, 0.4% American Indian/Alaska Native, 0.0% Native Hawaiian/Other Pacific Islander, 1.8% Other, 2.3% Hispanic of any race (2010); Average household size: 2.37 (2010); Median age: 38.5 (2010); Males per 100 females: 90.7 (2010); Marriage status: 28.3% never married, 57.1% now married, 4.8% widowed, 9.8% divorced (2006-2010 5-year est.); Foreign born: 1.4% (2006-2010 5-year est.); Ancestry (includes multiple ancestries): 29.1% German, 23.0% Italian, 19.3% Irish, 18.8% English, 8.5% Dutch (2006-2010 5-year est.).
**Economy:** Single-family building permits issued: 0 (2011); Multi-family building permits issued: 0 (2011); Employment by occupation: 13.5% management, 2.7% professional, 13.6% services, 12.0% sales, 3.1% farming, 9.7% construction, 5.1% production (2006-2010 5-year est.).
**Income:** Per capita income: $20,481 (2006-2010 5-year est.); Median household income: $48,971 (2006-2010 5-year est.); Average household income: $53,497 (2006-2010 5-year est.); Percent of households with

income of $100,000 or more: 12.2% (2006-2010 5-year est.); Poverty rate: 18.5% (2006-2010 5-year est.).

**Education:** Percent of population age 25 and over with: High school diploma (including GED) or higher: 81.2% (2006-2010 5-year est.); Bachelor's degree or higher: 25.0% (2006-2010 5-year est.); Master's degree or higher: 12.7% (2006-2010 5-year est.).

**School District(s)**

Canajoharie Central School District (PK-12)

    2009-10 Enrollment: 1,070 . . . . . . . . . . . . . . . . . . . . (518) 673-6302

**Housing:** Homeownership rate: 58.3% (2010); Median home value: $94,600 (2006-2010 5-year est.); Median contract rent: $490 per month (2006-2010 5-year est.); Median year structure built: before 1940 (2006-2010 5-year est.).

**Transportation:** Commute to work: 90.7% car, 0.8% public transportation, 4.9% walk, 3.6% work from home (2006-2010 5-year est.); Travel time to work: 42.8% less than 15 minutes, 14.4% 15 to 30 minutes, 23.7% 30 to 45 minutes, 8.3% 45 to 60 minutes, 10.8% 60 minutes or more (2006-2010 5-year est.)

**CANAJOHARIE** (town). Covers a land area of 42.632 square miles and a water area of 0.500 square miles. Located at 42.86° N. Lat; 74.61° W. Long. Elevation is 305 feet.

**History:** Here are Van Alstyne House (1749), with historical collections, and a library and art gallery. Settled c.1730 by Dutch and Germans; incorporated 1829.

**Population:** 3,909 (1990); 3,797 (2000); 3,730 (2010); Density: 87.5 persons per square mile (2010); Race: 95.7% White, 1.5% Black, 0.5% Asian, 0.3% American Indian/Alaska Native, 0.1% Native Hawaiian/Other Pacific Islander, 1.9% Other, 1.8% Hispanic of any race (2010); Average household size: 2.44 (2010); Median age: 41.4 (2010); Males per 100 females: 95.1 (2010); Marriage status: 28.8% never married, 55.6% now married, 6.0% widowed, 9.6% divorced (2006-2010 5-year est.); Foreign born: 1.8% (2006-2010 5-year est.); Ancestry (includes multiple ancestries): 28.4% German, 21.6% English, 18.8% Italian, 17.6% Irish, 8.1% American (2006-2010 5-year est.).

**Economy:** Single-family building permits issued: 0 (2011); Multi-family building permits issued: 0 (2011); Employment by occupation: 10.8% management, 2.0% professional, 10.0% services, 15.9% sales, 4.5% farming, 14.6% construction, 7.6% production (2006-2010 5-year est.).

**Income:** Per capita income: $22,109 (2006-2010 5-year est.); Median household income: $48,938 (2006-2010 5-year est.); Average household income: $54,560 (2006-2010 5-year est.); Percent of households with income of $100,000 or more: 10.8% (2006-2010 5-year est.); Poverty rate: 13.1% (2006-2010 5-year est.).

**Education:** Percent of population age 25 and over with: High school diploma (including GED) or higher: 84.9% (2006-2010 5-year est.); Bachelor's degree or higher: 19.6% (2006-2010 5-year est.); Master's degree or higher: 9.9% (2006-2010 5-year est.).

**School District(s)**

Canajoharie Central School District (PK-12)

    2009-10 Enrollment: 1,070 . . . . . . . . . . . . . . . . . . . . (518) 673-6302

**Housing:** Homeownership rate: 69.9% (2010); Median home value: $90,000 (2006-2010 5-year est.); Median contract rent: $503 per month (2006-2010 5-year est.); Median year structure built: before 1940 (2006-2010 5-year est.).

**Transportation:** Commute to work: 91.4% car, 0.4% public transportation, 4.3% walk, 3.9% work from home (2006-2010 5-year est.); Travel time to work: 42.3% less than 15 minutes, 21.3% 15 to 30 minutes, 20.4% 30 to 45 minutes, 6.1% 45 to 60 minutes, 9.9% 60 minutes or more (2006-2010 5-year est.)

**CHARLESTON** (town). Covers a land area of 41.889 square miles and a water area of 0.973 square miles. Located at 42.82° N. Lat; 74.35° W. Long. Elevation is 1,138 feet.

**Population:** 1,107 (1990); 1,292 (2000); 1,373 (2010); Density: 32.8 persons per square mile (2010); Race: 97.2% White, 0.4% Black, 0.7% Asian, 0.1% American Indian/Alaska Native, 0.1% Native Hawaiian/Other Pacific Islander, 1.5% Other, 1.8% Hispanic of any race (2010); Average household size: 2.58 (2010); Median age: 41.0 (2010); Males per 100 females: 102.8 (2010); Marriage status: 25.8% never married, 57.2% now married, 5.7% widowed, 11.3% divorced (2006-2010 5-year est.); Foreign born: 5.3% (2006-2010 5-year est.); Ancestry (includes multiple ancestries): 30.5% German, 16.4% Irish, 16.4% English, 15.2% Italian, 9.0% Polish (2006-2010 5-year est.).

**Economy:** Single-family building permits issued: 1 (2011); Multi-family building permits issued: 0 (2011); Employment by occupation: 7.7% management, 1.7% professional, 9.4% services, 16.1% sales, 4.0% farming, 13.1% construction, 13.1% production (2006-2010 5-year est.).

**Income:** Per capita income: $22,838 (2006-2010 5-year est.); Median household income: $53,333 (2006-2010 5-year est.); Average household income: $62,279 (2006-2010 5-year est.); Percent of households with income of $100,000 or more: 13.0% (2006-2010 5-year est.); Poverty rate: 8.1% (2006-2010 5-year est.).

**Education:** Percent of population age 25 and over with: High school diploma (including GED) or higher: 83.5% (2006-2010 5-year est.); Bachelor's degree or higher: 14.5% (2006-2010 5-year est.); Master's degree or higher: 7.6% (2006-2010 5-year est.).

**Housing:** Homeownership rate: 90.0% (2010); Median home value: $117,100 (2006-2010 5-year est.); Median contract rent: $486 per month (2006-2010 5-year est.); Median year structure built: 1977 (2006-2010 5-year est.).

**Transportation:** Commute to work: 95.1% car, 0.0% public transportation, 0.7% walk, 4.2% work from home (2006-2010 5-year est.); Travel time to work: 14.1% less than 15 minutes, 25.2% 15 to 30 minutes, 31.2% 30 to 45 minutes, 13.8% 45 to 60 minutes, 15.7% 60 minutes or more (2006-2010 5-year est.)

**FLORIDA** (town). Covers a land area of 50.131 square miles and a water area of 1.273 square miles. Located at 42.89° N. Lat; 74.20° W. Long.

**Population:** 2,637 (1990); 2,731 (2000); 2,696 (2010); Density: 53.8 persons per square mile (2010); Race: 95.5% White, 0.8% Black, 1.1% Asian, 0.1% American Indian/Alaska Native, 0.0% Native Hawaiian/Other Pacific Islander, 2.5% Other, 3.1% Hispanic of any race (2010); Average household size: 2.45 (2010); Median age: 44.8 (2010); Males per 100 females: 101.6 (2010); Marriage status: 26.0% never married, 57.7% now married, 6.6% widowed, 9.7% divorced (2006-2010 5-year est.); Foreign born: 5.5% (2006-2010 5-year est.); Ancestry (includes multiple ancestries): 18.2% Polish, 17.6% Italian, 15.8% German, 15.7% Irish, 12.7% American (2006-2010 5-year est.).

**Economy:** Single-family building permits issued: 8 (2011); Multi-family building permits issued: 0 (2011); Employment by occupation: 9.9% management, 2.5% professional, 5.8% services, 13.8% sales, 5.8% farming, 19.0% construction, 8.1% production (2006-2010 5-year est.).

**Income:** Per capita income: $24,550 (2006-2010 5-year est.); Median household income: $53,988 (2006-2010 5-year est.); Average household income: $63,741 (2006-2010 5-year est.); Percent of households with income of $100,000 or more: 19.1% (2006-2010 5-year est.); Poverty rate: 8.2% (2006-2010 5-year est.).

**Education:** Percent of population age 25 and over with: High school diploma (including GED) or higher: 82.8% (2006-2010 5-year est.); Bachelor's degree or higher: 12.6% (2006-2010 5-year est.); Master's degree or higher: 7.0% (2006-2010 5-year est.).

**Housing:** Homeownership rate: 87.8% (2010); Median home value: $117,100 (2006-2010 5-year est.); Median contract rent: $530 per month (2006-2010 5-year est.); Median year structure built: 1965 (2006-2010 5-year est.).

**Transportation:** Commute to work: 90.7% car, 1.4% public transportation, 4.2% walk, 3.3% work from home (2006-2010 5-year est.); Travel time to work: 27.6% less than 15 minutes, 30.1% 15 to 30 minutes, 19.9% 30 to 45 minutes, 10.2% 45 to 60 minutes, 12.1% 60 minutes or more (2006-2010 5-year est.)

**FONDA** (village). County seat. Covers a land area of 0.538 square miles and a water area of 0.069 square miles. Located at 42.95° N. Lat; 74.37° W. Long. Elevation is 295 feet.

**History:** Formally a freight transfer point on the N.Y. Central railroad. Incorporated 1850.

**Population:** 1,072 (1990); 810 (2000); 795 (2010); Density: 1,476.0 persons per square mile (2010); Race: 97.6% White, 0.4% Black, 0.5% Asian, 0.0% American Indian/Alaska Native, 0.0% Native Hawaiian/Other Pacific Islander, 1.5% Other, 2.9% Hispanic of any race (2010); Average household size: 2.27 (2010); Median age: 38.3 (2010); Males per 100 females: 96.3 (2010); Marriage status: 30.9% never married, 43.8% now married, 11.4% widowed, 13.9% divorced (2006-2010 5-year est.); Foreign born: 5.6% (2006-2010 5-year est.); Ancestry (includes multiple ancestries): 14.9% Irish, 14.6% Italian, 14.0% German, 12.9% American, 9.7% English (2006-2010 5-year est.).

**Economy:** Single-family building permits issued: 0 (2011); Multi-family building permits issued: 0 (2011); Employment by occupation: 2.3% management, 0.0% professional, 22.6% services, 8.7% sales, 1.1% farming, 6.0% construction, 7.9% production (2006-2010 5-year est.).
**Income:** Per capita income: $16,775 (2006-2010 5-year est.); Median household income: $40,395 (2006-2010 5-year est.); Average household income: $41,077 (2006-2010 5-year est.); Percent of households with income of $100,000 or more: 5.3% (2006-2010 5-year est.); Poverty rate: 19.6% (2006-2010 5-year est.).
**Education:** Percent of population age 25 and over with: High school diploma (including GED) or higher: 85.5% (2006-2010 5-year est.); Bachelor's degree or higher: 3.5% (2006-2010 5-year est.); Master's degree or higher: 1.3% (2006-2010 5-year est.).

**School District(s)**
Fonda-Fultonville Central School District (PK-12)
    2009-10 Enrollment: 1,461 . . . . . . . . . . . . . . . . . . (518) 853-4415
**Housing:** Homeownership rate: 54.4% (2010); Median home value: $69,000 (2006-2010 5-year est.); Median contract rent: $489 per month (2006-2010 5-year est.); Median year structure built: before 1940 (2006-2010 5-year est.).
**Transportation:** Commute to work: 85.7% car, 0.0% public transportation, 12.4% walk, 0.8% work from home (2006-2010 5-year est.); Travel time to work: 50.2% less than 15 minutes, 32.7% 15 to 30 minutes, 8.9% 30 to 45 minutes, 4.7% 45 to 60 minutes, 3.5% 60 minutes or more (2006-2010 5-year est.)

**FORT HUNTER** (unincorporated postal area)
Zip Code: 12069
    Covers a land area of 0.573 square miles and a water area of 0.118 square miles. Located at 42.94° N. Lat; 74.27° W. Long. Elevation is 292 feet. Population: 256 (2010); Density: 446.6 persons per square mile (2010); Race: 93.0% White, 0.0% Black, 2.3% Asian, 0.4% American Indian/Alaska Native, 0.0% Native Hawaiian/Other Pacific Islander, 4.3% Other, 3.1% Hispanic of any race (2010); Average household size: 2.72 (2010); Median age: 37.8 (2010); Males per 100 females: 111.6 (2010); Homeownership rate: 74.5% (2010)

**FORT JOHNSON** (village). Covers a land area of 0.736 square miles and a water area of 0.108 square miles. Located at 42.95° N. Lat; 74.23° W. Long. Elevation is 308 feet.
**History:** Fort Johnson (1749), once home of Sir William Johnson, is now a museum.
**Population:** 615 (1990); 491 (2000); 490 (2010); Density: 665.1 persons per square mile (2010); Race: 95.7% White, 0.6% Black, 0.8% Asian, 0.2% American Indian/Alaska Native, 0.0% Native Hawaiian/Other Pacific Islander, 2.7% Other, 2.2% Hispanic of any race (2010); Average household size: 2.40 (2010); Median age: 41.8 (2010); Males per 100 females: 86.3 (2010); Marriage status: 42.7% never married, 42.0% now married, 4.2% widowed, 11.1% divorced (2006-2010 5-year est.); Foreign born: 2.7% (2006-2010 5-year est.); Ancestry (includes multiple ancestries): 28.1% Italian, 27.8% Irish, 21.9% English, 12.0% Polish, 11.0% German (2006-2010 5-year est.).
**Economy:** Single-family building permits issued: 0 (2011); Multi-family building permits issued: 0 (2011); Employment by occupation: 5.2% management, 5.6% professional, 17.4% services, 18.5% sales, 10.5% farming, 11.8% construction, 7.3% production (2006-2010 5-year est.).
**Income:** Per capita income: $23,613 (2006-2010 5-year est.); Median household income: $45,074 (2006-2010 5-year est.); Average household income: $59,526 (2006-2010 5-year est.); Percent of households with income of $100,000 or more: 14.7% (2006-2010 5-year est.); Poverty rate: 8.5% (2006-2010 5-year est.).
**Education:** Percent of population age 25 and over with: High school diploma (including GED) or higher: 93.8% (2006-2010 5-year est.); Bachelor's degree or higher: 15.5% (2006-2010 5-year est.); Master's degree or higher: 3.6% (2006-2010 5-year est.).
**Housing:** Homeownership rate: 82.8% (2010); Median home value: $88,300 (2006-2010 5-year est.); Median contract rent: $525 per month (2006-2010 5-year est.); Median year structure built: 1941 (2006-2010 5-year est.).
**Transportation:** Commute to work: 97.1% car, 0.0% public transportation, 0.0% walk, 1.4% work from home (2006-2010 5-year est.); Travel time to work: 52.6% less than 15 minutes, 13.1% 15 to 30 minutes, 27.4% 30 to 45 minutes, 2.2% 45 to 60 minutes, 4.7% 60 minutes or more (2006-2010 5-year est.)

**FORT PLAIN** (village). Aka South Fort Plain. Covers a land area of 1.346 square miles and a water area of 0.056 square miles. Located at 42.93° N. Lat; 74.62° W. Long. Elevation is 305 feet.
**History:** Settled 1723, incorporated 1832.
**Population:** 2,416 (1990); 2,288 (2000); 2,322 (2010); Density: 1,725.0 persons per square mile (2010); Race: 96.9% White, 0.5% Black, 0.2% Asian, 0.3% American Indian/Alaska Native, 0.1% Native Hawaiian/Other Pacific Islander, 2.0% Other, 2.5% Hispanic of any race (2010); Average household size: 2.44 (2010); Median age: 37.6 (2010); Males per 100 females: 89.7 (2010); Marriage status: 27.0% never married, 54.0% now married, 8.1% widowed, 10.9% divorced (2006-2010 5-year est.); Foreign born: 3.6% (2006-2010 5-year est.); Ancestry (includes multiple ancestries): 26.6% German, 14.7% Irish, 11.3% English, 11.2% Italian, 10.0% Dutch (2006-2010 5-year est.).
**Economy:** Single-family building permits issued: 0 (2011); Multi-family building permits issued: 0 (2011); Employment by occupation: 5.3% management, 2.3% professional, 11.8% services, 12.5% sales, 8.6% farming, 9.6% construction, 13.0% production (2006-2010 5-year est.).
**Income:** Per capita income: $20,002 (2006-2010 5-year est.); Median household income: $38,980 (2006-2010 5-year est.); Average household income: $53,748 (2006-2010 5-year est.); Percent of households with income of $100,000 or more: 7.5% (2006-2010 5-year est.); Poverty rate: 28.4% (2006-2010 5-year est.).
**Education:** Percent of population age 25 and over with: High school diploma (including GED) or higher: 82.4% (2006-2010 5-year est.); Bachelor's degree or higher: 19.2% (2006-2010 5-year est.); Master's degree or higher: 7.0% (2006-2010 5-year est.).

**School District(s)**
Fort Plain Central School District (PK-12)
    2009-10 Enrollment: 872 . . . . . . . . . . . . . . . . . . . . (518) 993-4000
**Housing:** Homeownership rate: 57.0% (2010); Median home value: $67,200 (2006-2010 5-year est.); Median contract rent: $438 per month (2006-2010 5-year est.); Median year structure built: before 1940 (2006-2010 5-year est.).
**Safety:** Violent crime rate: 28.0 per 10,000 population; Property crime rate: 349.8 per 10,000 population (2010).
**Newspapers:** Courier-Standard-Enterprise (Community news; Circulation 5,000)
**Transportation:** Commute to work: 89.8% car, 0.6% public transportation, 6.3% walk, 2.0% work from home (2006-2010 5-year est.); Travel time to work: 31.0% less than 15 minutes, 25.7% 15 to 30 minutes, 25.1% 30 to 45 minutes, 11.1% 45 to 60 minutes, 7.2% 60 minutes or more (2006-2010 5-year est.)

**FULTONVILLE** (village). Covers a land area of 0.477 square miles and a water area of 0.042 square miles. Located at 42.94° N. Lat; 74.36° W. Long. Elevation is 289 feet.
**Population:** 748 (1990); 710 (2000); 784 (2010); Density: 1,642.9 persons per square mile (2010); Race: 96.9% White, 0.5% Black, 2.0% Asian, 0.0% American Indian/Alaska Native, 0.0% Native Hawaiian/Other Pacific Islander, 0.6% Other, 1.7% Hispanic of any race (2010); Average household size: 2.70 (2010); Median age: 34.9 (2010); Males per 100 females: 92.6 (2010); Marriage status: 23.6% never married, 55.6% now married, 8.8% widowed, 12.0% divorced (2006-2010 5-year est.); Foreign born: 0.4% (2006-2010 5-year est.); Ancestry (includes multiple ancestries): 23.1% German, 17.2% English, 16.3% Irish, 15.1% Italian, 13.9% American (2006-2010 5-year est.).
**Economy:** Single-family building permits issued: 4 (2011); Multi-family building permits issued: 0 (2011); Employment by occupation: 9.5% management, 5.6% professional, 4.9% services, 17.8% sales, 6.4% farming, 13.7% construction, 7.6% production (2006-2010 5-year est.).
**Income:** Per capita income: $22,744 (2006-2010 5-year est.); Median household income: $54,333 (2006-2010 5-year est.); Average household income: $60,368 (2006-2010 5-year est.); Percent of households with income of $100,000 or more: 14.8% (2006-2010 5-year est.); Poverty rate: 6.2% (2006-2010 5-year est.).
**Education:** Percent of population age 25 and over with: High school diploma (including GED) or higher: 90.7% (2006-2010 5-year est.); Bachelor's degree or higher: 15.4% (2006-2010 5-year est.); Master's degree or higher: 5.3% (2006-2010 5-year est.).
**Housing:** Homeownership rate: 72.4% (2010); Median home value: $90,900 (2006-2010 5-year est.); Median contract rent: $489 per month (2006-2010 5-year est.); Median year structure built: before 1940 (2006-2010 5-year est.).

**Transportation:** Commute to work: 92.7% car, 0.0% public transportation, 2.2% walk, 0.7% work from home (2006-2010 5-year est.); Travel time to work: 53.0% less than 15 minutes, 27.8% 15 to 30 minutes, 7.4% 30 to 45 minutes, 7.6% 45 to 60 minutes, 4.2% 60 minutes or more (2006-2010 5-year est.)

**GLEN** (town). Covers a land area of 38.620 square miles and a water area of 0.705 square miles. Located at 42.90° N. Lat; 74.35° W. Long. Elevation is 686 feet.
**Population:** 1,950 (1990); 2,222 (2000); 2,507 (2010); Density: 64.9 persons per square mile (2010); Race: 95.3% White, 1.7% Black, 1.2% Asian, 0.2% American Indian/Alaska Native, 0.1% Native Hawaiian/Other Pacific Islander, 1.5% Other, 3.9% Hispanic of any race (2010); Average household size: 2.77 (2010); Median age: 36.5 (2010); Males per 100 females: 110.7 (2010); Marriage status: 32.1% never married, 52.6% now married, 6.0% widowed, 9.3% divorced (2006-2010 5-year est.); Foreign born: 0.7% (2006-2010 5-year est.); Ancestry (includes multiple ancestries): 24.2% German, 17.4% English, 17.3% Italian, 15.1% Irish, 10.0% Polish (2006-2010 5-year est.).
**Economy:** Single-family building permits issued: 1 (2011); Multi-family building permits issued: 0 (2011); Employment by occupation: 13.1% management, 1.8% professional, 10.4% services, 16.1% sales, 5.3% farming, 15.8% construction, 4.0% production (2006-2010 5-year est.).
**Income:** Per capita income: $23,784 (2006-2010 5-year est.); Median household income: $58,631 (2006-2010 5-year est.); Average household income: $72,141 (2006-2010 5-year est.); Percent of households with income of $100,000 or more: 18.2% (2006-2010 5-year est.); Poverty rate: 4.8% (2006-2010 5-year est.).
**Education:** Percent of population age 25 and over with: High school diploma (including GED) or higher: 89.8% (2006-2010 5-year est.); Bachelor's degree or higher: 17.9% (2006-2010 5-year est.); Master's degree or higher: 9.2% (2006-2010 5-year est.).
**Housing:** Homeownership rate: 82.5% (2010); Median home value: $104,500 (2006-2010 5-year est.); Median contract rent: $496 per month (2006-2010 5-year est.); Median year structure built: 1973 (2006-2010 5-year est.).
**Transportation:** Commute to work: 81.3% car, 1.4% public transportation, 1.8% walk, 11.8% work from home (2006-2010 5-year est.); Travel time to work: 37.5% less than 15 minutes, 28.2% 15 to 30 minutes, 13.8% 30 to 45 minutes, 12.4% 45 to 60 minutes, 8.1% 60 minutes or more (2006-2010 5-year est.)

**HAGAMAN** (village). Covers a land area of 1.497 square miles and a water area of 0.046 square miles. Located at 42.97° N. Lat; 74.15° W. Long. Elevation is 719 feet.
**Population:** 1,377 (1990); 1,357 (2000); 1,292 (2010); Density: 862.7 persons per square mile (2010); Race: 96.1% White, 0.9% Black, 0.1% Asian, 0.3% American Indian/Alaska Native, 0.0% Native Hawaiian/Other Pacific Islander, 2.6% Other, 3.6% Hispanic of any race (2010); Average household size: 2.38 (2010); Median age: 46.0 (2010); Males per 100 females: 100.6 (2010); Marriage status: 24.7% never married, 51.7% now married, 12.0% widowed, 11.6% divorced (2006-2010 5-year est.); Foreign born: 2.0% (2006-2010 5-year est.); Ancestry (includes multiple ancestries): 22.1% German, 20.7% Irish, 20.0% Italian, 17.3% Polish, 7.5% English (2006-2010 5-year est.).
**Economy:** Single-family building permits issued: 5 (2011); Multi-family building permits issued: 0 (2011); Employment by occupation: 11.3% management, 2.0% professional, 12.8% services, 19.4% sales, 8.7% farming, 8.3% construction, 3.8% production (2006-2010 5-year est.).
**Income:** Per capita income: $25,844 (2006-2010 5-year est.); Median household income: $44,083 (2006-2010 5-year est.); Average household income: $54,655 (2006-2010 5-year est.); Percent of households with income of $100,000 or more: 14.9% (2006-2010 5-year est.); Poverty rate: 9.3% (2006-2010 5-year est.).
**Education:** Percent of population age 25 and over with: High school diploma (including GED) or higher: 90.4% (2006-2010 5-year est.); Bachelor's degree or higher: 18.4% (2006-2010 5-year est.); Master's degree or higher: 5.7% (2006-2010 5-year est.).
**Housing:** Homeownership rate: 81.1% (2010); Median home value: $120,400 (2006-2010 5-year est.); Median contract rent: $565 per month (2006-2010 5-year est.); Median year structure built: 1947 (2006-2010 5-year est.).
**Transportation:** Commute to work: 91.7% car, 0.0% public transportation, 1.1% walk, 7.2% work from home (2006-2010 5-year est.); Travel time to work: 34.5% less than 15 minutes, 30.1% 15 to 30 minutes, 17.4% 30 to 45

minutes, 16.0% 45 to 60 minutes, 2.1% 60 minutes or more (2006-2010 5-year est.)

**MINDEN** (town). Covers a land area of 50.987 square miles and a water area of 0.449 square miles. Located at 42.93° N. Lat; 74.69° W. Long.
**Population:** 4,474 (1990); 4,202 (2000); 4,297 (2010); Density: 84.3 persons per square mile (2010); Race: 97.1% White, 0.5% Black, 0.5% Asian, 0.2% American Indian/Alaska Native, 0.1% Native Hawaiian/Other Pacific Islander, 1.6% Other, 1.9% Hispanic of any race (2010); Average household size: 2.54 (2010); Median age: 38.4 (2010); Males per 100 females: 98.6 (2010); Marriage status: 23.5% never married, 61.1% now married, 7.1% widowed, 8.3% divorced (2006-2010 5-year est.); Foreign born: 2.3% (2006-2010 5-year est.); Ancestry (includes multiple ancestries): 22.5% German, 15.5% English, 15.0% Irish, 13.6% American, 10.2% Italian (2006-2010 5-year est.).
**Economy:** Single-family building permits issued: 0 (2011); Multi-family building permits issued: 0 (2011); Employment by occupation: 7.5% management, 2.8% professional, 12.8% services, 15.5% sales, 5.7% farming, 15.1% construction, 11.6% production (2006-2010 5-year est.).
**Income:** Per capita income: $20,320 (2006-2010 5-year est.); Median household income: $40,804 (2006-2010 5-year est.); Average household income: $54,314 (2006-2010 5-year est.); Percent of households with income of $100,000 or more: 7.5% (2006-2010 5-year est.); Poverty rate: 20.3% (2006-2010 5-year est.).
**Education:** Percent of population age 25 and over with: High school diploma (including GED) or higher: 82.2% (2006-2010 5-year est.); Bachelor's degree or higher: 13.8% (2006-2010 5-year est.); Master's degree or higher: 5.0% (2006-2010 5-year est.).
**Housing:** Homeownership rate: 69.1% (2010); Median home value: $73,800 (2006-2010 5-year est.); Median contract rent: $435 per month (2006-2010 5-year est.); Median year structure built: before 1940 (2006-2010 5-year est.).
**Transportation:** Commute to work: 84.6% car, 0.3% public transportation, 7.5% walk, 5.8% work from home (2006-2010 5-year est.); Travel time to work: 35.5% less than 15 minutes, 29.6% 15 to 30 minutes, 18.4% 30 to 45 minutes, 8.2% 45 to 60 minutes, 8.2% 60 minutes or more (2006-2010 5-year est.)

**MOHAWK** (town). Covers a land area of 34.680 square miles and a water area of 0.712 square miles. Located at 42.95° N. Lat; 74.40° W. Long.
**Population:** 3,976 (1990); 3,902 (2000); 3,844 (2010); Density: 110.8 persons per square mile (2010); Race: 97.7% White, 0.4% Black, 0.5% Asian, 0.2% American Indian/Alaska Native, 0.0% Native Hawaiian/Other Pacific Islander, 1.2% Other, 2.2% Hispanic of any race (2010); Average household size: 2.49 (2010); Median age: 42.2 (2010); Males per 100 females: 97.9 (2010); Marriage status: 23.8% never married, 60.1% now married, 5.2% widowed, 10.9% divorced (2006-2010 5-year est.); Foreign born: 1.9% (2006-2010 5-year est.); Ancestry (includes multiple ancestries): 25.1% Irish, 22.7% Italian, 18.9% English, 14.7% German, 11.3% American (2006-2010 5-year est.).
**Economy:** Single-family building permits issued: 3 (2011); Multi-family building permits issued: 0 (2011); Employment by occupation: 14.0% management, 2.9% professional, 13.7% services, 13.8% sales, 4.0% farming, 7.6% construction, 6.9% production (2006-2010 5-year est.).
**Income:** Per capita income: $22,843 (2006-2010 5-year est.); Median household income: $50,304 (2006-2010 5-year est.); Average household income: $61,636 (2006-2010 5-year est.); Percent of households with income of $100,000 or more: 18.6% (2006-2010 5-year est.); Poverty rate: 8.7% (2006-2010 5-year est.).
**Education:** Percent of population age 25 and over with: High school diploma (including GED) or higher: 87.2% (2006-2010 5-year est.); Bachelor's degree or higher: 17.2% (2006-2010 5-year est.); Master's degree or higher: 8.9% (2006-2010 5-year est.).
**Housing:** Homeownership rate: 79.8% (2010); Median home value: $109,100 (2006-2010 5-year est.); Median contract rent: $493 per month (2006-2010 5-year est.); Median year structure built: 1962 (2006-2010 5-year est.).
**Transportation:** Commute to work: 91.5% car, 0.0% public transportation, 3.3% walk, 5.0% work from home (2006-2010 5-year est.); Travel time to work: 47.5% less than 15 minutes, 32.9% 15 to 30 minutes, 9.1% 30 to 45 minutes, 6.3% 45 to 60 minutes, 4.3% 60 minutes or more (2006-2010 5-year est.)

**NELLISTON** (village). Covers a land area of 1.104 square miles and a water area of 0.090 square miles. Located at 42.93° N. Lat; 74.60° W. Long. Elevation is 367 feet.
**Population:** 569 (1990); 622 (2000); 596 (2010); Density: 539.5 persons per square mile (2010); Race: 96.5% White, 0.0% Black, 0.2% Asian, 0.3% American Indian/Alaska Native, 0.0% Native Hawaiian/Other Pacific Islander, 3.0% Other, 2.2% Hispanic of any race (2010); Average household size: 2.47 (2010); Median age: 40.0 (2010); Males per 100 females: 104.8 (2010); Marriage status: 19.1% never married, 58.7% now married, 13.0% widowed, 9.2% divorced (2006-2010 5-year est.); Foreign born: 3.7% (2006-2010 5-year est.); Ancestry (includes multiple ancestries): 24.8% Irish, 19.8% American, 16.5% English, 15.9% German, 11.2% Dutch (2006-2010 5-year est.).
**Economy:** Single-family building permits issued: 0 (2011); Multi-family building permits issued: 0 (2011); Employment by occupation: 5.7% management, 0.0% professional, 14.9% services, 14.9% sales, 5.3% farming, 10.5% construction, 6.1% production (2006-2010 5-year est.).
**Income:** Per capita income: $19,546 (2006-2010 5-year est.); Median household income: $38,750 (2006-2010 5-year est.); Average household income: $43,341 (2006-2010 5-year est.); Percent of households with income of $100,000 or more: 6.6% (2006-2010 5-year est.); Poverty rate: 2.2% (2006-2010 5-year est.).
**Education:** Percent of population age 25 and over with: High school diploma (including GED) or higher: 71.0% (2006-2010 5-year est.); Bachelor's degree or higher: 7.1% (2006-2010 5-year est.); Master's degree or higher: 2.9% (2006-2010 5-year est.).
**Housing:** Homeownership rate: 75.1% (2010); Median home value: $73,300 (2006-2010 5-year est.); Median contract rent: $436 per month (2006-2010 5-year est.); Median year structure built: before 1940 (2006-2010 5-year est.).
**Newspapers:** My Shopper/Mohawk Valley Edition (Community news; Circulation 11,935)
**Transportation:** Commute to work: 98.2% car, 0.0% public transportation, 0.0% walk, 1.8% work from home (2006-2010 5-year est.); Travel time to work: 26.8% less than 15 minutes, 15.6% 15 to 30 minutes, 19.6% 30 to 45 minutes, 12.9% 45 to 60 minutes, 25.0% 60 minutes or more (2006-2010 5-year est.)

**PALATINE** (town). Covers a land area of 41.071 square miles and a water area of 0.629 square miles. Located at 42.95° N. Lat; 74.53° W. Long. Elevation is 830 feet.
**Population:** 2,787 (1990); 3,070 (2000); 3,240 (2010); Density: 78.9 persons per square mile (2010); Race: 97.9% White, 0.2% Black, 0.6% Asian, 0.3% American Indian/Alaska Native, 0.0% Native Hawaiian/Other Pacific Islander, 1.0% Other, 1.4% Hispanic of any race (2010); Average household size: 2.69 (2010); Median age: 40.5 (2010); Males per 100 females: 101.2 (2010); Marriage status: 21.8% never married, 60.1% now married, 11.6% widowed, 6.5% divorced (2006-2010 5-year est.); Foreign born: 2.5% (2006-2010 5-year est.); Ancestry (includes multiple ancestries): 31.1% German, 21.8% Irish, 16.9% Dutch, 13.4% Italian, 9.2% English (2006-2010 5-year est.).
**Economy:** Single-family building permits issued: 4 (2011); Multi-family building permits issued: 0 (2011); Employment by occupation: 9.5% management, 0.4% professional, 12.0% services, 14.7% sales, 8.0% farming, 10.4% construction, 4.5% production (2006-2010 5-year est.).
**Income:** Per capita income: $19,146 (2006-2010 5-year est.); Median household income: $40,929 (2006-2010 5-year est.); Average household income: $50,324 (2006-2010 5-year est.); Percent of households with income of $100,000 or more: 8.8% (2006-2010 5-year est.); Poverty rate: 16.9% (2006-2010 5-year est.).
**Education:** Percent of population age 25 and over with: High school diploma (including GED) or higher: 70.4% (2006-2010 5-year est.); Bachelor's degree or higher: 12.5% (2006-2010 5-year est.); Master's degree or higher: 5.1% (2006-2010 5-year est.).
**Housing:** Homeownership rate: 79.4% (2010); Median home value: $87,900 (2006-2010 5-year est.); Median contract rent: $373 per month (2006-2010 5-year est.); Median year structure built: 1960 (2006-2010 5-year est.).
**Transportation:** Commute to work: 84.7% car, 0.2% public transportation, 2.5% walk, 10.6% work from home (2006-2010 5-year est.); Travel time to work: 34.1% less than 15 minutes, 23.6% 15 to 30 minutes, 19.8% 30 to 45 minutes, 9.0% 45 to 60 minutes, 13.6% 60 minutes or more (2006-2010 5-year est.)

**PALATINE BRIDGE** (village). Covers a land area of 0.882 square miles and a water area of 0.066 square miles. Located at 42.91° N. Lat; 74.57° W. Long. Elevation is 344 feet.
**Population:** 668 (1990); 706 (2000); 737 (2010); Density: 834.7 persons per square mile (2010); Race: 98.0% White, 0.1% Black, 0.5% Asian, 0.1% American Indian/Alaska Native, 0.0% Native Hawaiian/Other Pacific Islander, 1.3% Other, 1.6% Hispanic of any race (2010); Average household size: 2.13 (2010); Median age: 52.7 (2010); Males per 100 females: 89.0 (2010); Marriage status: 14.7% never married, 52.6% now married, 23.3% widowed, 9.4% divorced (2006-2010 5-year est.); Foreign born: 3.1% (2006-2010 5-year est.); Ancestry (includes multiple ancestries): 30.8% German, 29.2% Irish, 17.1% Italian, 12.2% French, 11.8% Dutch (2006-2010 5-year est.).
**Economy:** Single-family building permits issued: 0 (2011); Multi-family building permits issued: 0 (2011); Employment by occupation: 12.9% management, 0.0% professional, 4.9% services, 11.4% sales, 5.7% farming, 7.6% construction, 9.1% production (2006-2010 5-year est.).
**Income:** Per capita income: $24,359 (2006-2010 5-year est.); Median household income: $35,893 (2006-2010 5-year est.); Average household income: $51,154 (2006-2010 5-year est.); Percent of households with income of $100,000 or more: 12.0% (2006-2010 5-year est.); Poverty rate: 13.6% (2006-2010 5-year est.).
**Education:** Percent of population age 25 and over with: High school diploma (including GED) or higher: 68.2% (2006-2010 5-year est.); Bachelor's degree or higher: 19.7% (2006-2010 5-year est.); Master's degree or higher: 7.5% (2006-2010 5-year est.).
**Housing:** Homeownership rate: 65.3% (2010); Median home value: $89,000 (2006-2010 5-year est.); Median contract rent: $372 per month (2006-2010 5-year est.); Median year structure built: 1955 (2006-2010 5-year est.).
**Newspapers:** Country Folks (Regional news; Circulation 40,482)
**Transportation:** Commute to work: 85.9% car, 1.2% public transportation, 2.7% walk, 7.0% work from home (2006-2010 5-year est.); Travel time to work: 44.5% less than 15 minutes, 11.8% 15 to 30 minutes, 30.3% 30 to 45 minutes, 6.7% 45 to 60 minutes, 6.7% 60 minutes or more (2006-2010 5-year est.)

**ROOT** (town). Covers a land area of 50.623 square miles and a water area of 0.425 square miles. Located at 42.84° N. Lat; 74.48° W. Long.
**Population:** 1,692 (1990); 1,752 (2000); 1,715 (2010); Density: 33.9 persons per square mile (2010); Race: 97.4% White, 0.5% Black, 0.4% Asian, 0.2% American Indian/Alaska Native, 0.0% Native Hawaiian/Other Pacific Islander, 1.5% Other, 2.3% Hispanic of any race (2010); Average household size: 2.53 (2010); Median age: 44.5 (2010); Males per 100 females: 100.4 (2010); Marriage status: 21.3% never married, 61.5% now married, 8.5% widowed, 8.7% divorced (2006-2010 5-year est.); Foreign born: 1.1% (2006-2010 5-year est.); Ancestry (includes multiple ancestries): 23.7% German, 18.9% Italian, 14.2% English, 12.2% Irish, 11.8% American (2006-2010 5-year est.).
**Economy:** Single-family building permits issued: 7 (2011); Multi-family building permits issued: 0 (2011); Employment by occupation: 5.9% management, 1.8% professional, 11.8% services, 13.3% sales, 3.5% farming, 20.5% construction, 11.9% production (2006-2010 5-year est.).
**Income:** Per capita income: $23,568 (2006-2010 5-year est.); Median household income: $48,715 (2006-2010 5-year est.); Average household income: $58,640 (2006-2010 5-year est.); Percent of households with income of $100,000 or more: 6.1% (2006-2010 5-year est.); Poverty rate: 10.1% (2006-2010 5-year est.).
**Education:** Percent of population age 25 and over with: High school diploma (including GED) or higher: 79.2% (2006-2010 5-year est.); Bachelor's degree or higher: 10.0% (2006-2010 5-year est.); Master's degree or higher: 1.8% (2006-2010 5-year est.).
**Housing:** Homeownership rate: 89.1% (2010); Median home value: $92,200 (2006-2010 5-year est.); Median contract rent: $442 per month (2006-2010 5-year est.); Median year structure built: 1974 (2006-2010 5-year est.).
**Transportation:** Commute to work: 91.9% car, 0.3% public transportation, 2.9% walk, 4.7% work from home (2006-2010 5-year est.); Travel time to work: 15.5% less than 15 minutes, 40.0% 15 to 30 minutes, 16.9% 30 to 45 minutes, 10.8% 45 to 60 minutes, 16.8% 60 minutes or more (2006-2010 5-year est.)

**SAINT JOHNSVILLE** (village). Covers a land area of 0.877 square miles and a water area of 0.001 square miles. Located at 43.00° N. Lat; 74.67° W. Long. Elevation is 328 feet.

**Population:** 1,918 (1990); 1,685 (2000); 1,732 (2010); Density: 1,973.7 persons per square mile (2010); Race: 97.7% White, 0.8% Black, 0.2% Asian, 0.2% American Indian/Alaska Native, 0.0% Native Hawaiian/Other Pacific Islander, 1.1% Other, 2.0% Hispanic of any race (2010); Average household size: 2.34 (2010); Median age: 41.6 (2010); Males per 100 females: 85.8 (2010); Marriage status: 21.5% never married, 50.5% now married, 14.2% widowed, 13.9% divorced (2006-2010 5-year est.); Foreign born: 1.3% (2006-2010 5-year est.); Ancestry (includes multiple ancestries): 22.2% German, 20.4% Irish, 13.3% Italian, 13.1% English, 11.3% American (2006-2010 5-year est.).

**Economy:** Single-family building permits issued: 0 (2011); Multi-family building permits issued: 0 (2011); Employment by occupation: 6.6% management, 3.6% professional, 18.3% services, 19.0% sales, 2.7% farming, 5.6% construction, 3.7% production (2006-2010 5-year est.).

**Income:** Per capita income: $17,719 (2006-2010 5-year est.); Median household income: $34,375 (2006-2010 5-year est.); Average household income: $41,749 (2006-2010 5-year est.); Percent of households with income of $100,000 or more: 6.0% (2006-2010 5-year est.); Poverty rate: 22.0% (2006-2010 5-year est.).

**Education:** Percent of population age 25 and over with: High school diploma (including GED) or higher: 82.9% (2006-2010 5-year est.); Bachelor's degree or higher: 10.1% (2006-2010 5-year est.); Master's degree or higher: 3.7% (2006-2010 5-year est.).

### School District(s)

Oppenheim-Ephratah Central School District (PK-12)
    2009-10 Enrollment: 375 . . . . . . . . . . . . . . . . . . . . . . . . (518) 568-2014
Saint Johnsville Central School District (PK-12)
    2009-10 Enrollment: 474 . . . . . . . . . . . . . . . . . . . . . . . . (518) 568-7023

**Housing:** Homeownership rate: 57.3% (2010); Median home value: $69,500 (2006-2010 5-year est.); Median contract rent: $391 per month (2006-2010 5-year est.); Median year structure built: before 1940 (2006-2010 5-year est.).

**Safety:** Violent crime rate: 0.0 per 10,000 population; Property crime rate: 44.5 per 10,000 population (2010).

**Transportation:** Commute to work: 87.0% car, 0.0% public transportation, 9.5% walk, 3.0% work from home (2006-2010 5-year est.); Travel time to work: 33.9% less than 15 minutes, 31.9% 15 to 30 minutes, 17.7% 30 to 45 minutes, 6.3% 45 to 60 minutes, 10.1% 60 minutes or more (2006-2010 5-year est.)

**SAINT JOHNSVILLE** (town). Covers a land area of 16.841 square miles and a water area of 0.518 square miles. Located at 43.00° N. Lat; 74.68° W. Long. Elevation is 328 feet.

**Population:** 2,773 (1990); 2,565 (2000); 2,631 (2010); Density: 156.2 persons per square mile (2010); Race: 97.7% White, 0.5% Black, 0.2% Asian, 0.2% American Indian/Alaska Native, 0.0% Native Hawaiian/Other Pacific Islander, 1.4% Other, 1.8% Hispanic of any race (2010); Average household size: 2.40 (2010); Median age: 41.9 (2010); Males per 100 females: 89.8 (2010); Marriage status: 24.4% never married, 52.6% now married, 10.8% widowed, 12.1% divorced (2006-2010 5-year est.); Foreign born: 1.6% (2006-2010 5-year est.); Ancestry (includes multiple ancestries): 20.1% German, 15.0% Irish, 13.4% American, 10.6% Italian, 9.4% English (2006-2010 5-year est.).

**Economy:** Single-family building permits issued: 0 (2011); Multi-family building permits issued: 0 (2011); Employment by occupation: 9.9% management, 2.1% professional, 15.0% services, 17.1% sales, 3.7% farming, 10.0% construction, 7.9% production (2006-2010 5-year est.).

**Income:** Per capita income: $16,767 (2006-2010 5-year est.); Median household income: $34,338 (2006-2010 5-year est.); Average household income: $41,723 (2006-2010 5-year est.); Percent of households with income of $100,000 or more: 5.9% (2006-2010 5-year est.); Poverty rate: 29.5% (2006-2010 5-year est.).

**Education:** Percent of population age 25 and over with: High school diploma (including GED) or higher: 78.8% (2006-2010 5-year est.); Bachelor's degree or higher: 8.8% (2006-2010 5-year est.); Master's degree or higher: 3.0% (2006-2010 5-year est.).

### School District(s)

Oppenheim-Ephratah Central School District (PK-12)
    2009-10 Enrollment: 375 . . . . . . . . . . . . . . . . . . . . . . . . (518) 568-2014
Saint Johnsville Central School District (PK-12)
    2009-10 Enrollment: 474 . . . . . . . . . . . . . . . . . . . . . . . . (518) 568-7023

**Housing:** Homeownership rate: 66.4% (2010); Median home value: $82,000 (2006-2010 5-year est.); Median contract rent: $391 per month (2006-2010 5-year est.); Median year structure built: before 1940 (2006-2010 5-year est.).

**Transportation:** Commute to work: 86.6% car, 0.0% public transportation, 6.2% walk, 5.7% work from home (2006-2010 5-year est.); Travel time to work: 31.3% less than 15 minutes, 30.3% 15 to 30 minutes, 23.2% 30 to 45 minutes, 6.4% 45 to 60 minutes, 8.8% 60 minutes or more (2006-2010 5-year est.)

**SPRAKERS** (unincorporated postal area)

Zip Code: 12166

Covers a land area of 43.814 square miles and a water area of 0.302 square miles. Located at 42.83° N. Lat; 74.44° W. Long. Elevation is 302 feet. Population: 1,363 (2010); Density: 31.1 persons per square mile (2010); Race: 97.2% White, 0.2% Black, 0.7% Asian, 0.3% American Indian/Alaska Native, 0.0% Native Hawaiian/Other Pacific Islander, 1.6% Other, 2.2% Hispanic of any race (2010); Average household size: 2.53 (2010); Median age: 45.4 (2010); Males per 100 females: 107.1 (2010); Homeownership rate: 89.2% (2010)

**TRIBES HILL** (CDP). Covers a land area of 2.276 square miles and a water area of 0.135 square miles. Located at 42.94° N. Lat; 74.29° W. Long. Elevation is 420 feet.

**Population:** 1,060 (1990); 1,024 (2000); 1,003 (2010); Density: 440.7 persons per square mile (2010); Race: 96.4% White, 0.5% Black, 1.4% Asian, 0.3% American Indian/Alaska Native, 0.0% Native Hawaiian/Other Pacific Islander, 1.4% Other, 1.7% Hispanic of any race (2010); Average household size: 2.31 (2010); Median age: 46.3 (2010); Males per 100 females: 93.6 (2010); Marriage status: 20.6% never married, 56.5% now married, 3.8% widowed, 19.1% divorced (2006-2010 5-year est.); Foreign born: 1.0% (2006-2010 5-year est.); Ancestry (includes multiple ancestries): 38.2% Italian, 25.8% Irish, 16.4% American, 16.0% German, 9.6% English (2006-2010 5-year est.).

**Economy:** Employment by occupation: 18.5% management, 4.5% professional, 19.2% services, 14.2% sales, 10.0% farming, 5.6% construction, 3.0% production (2006-2010 5-year est.).

**Income:** Per capita income: $31,954 (2006-2010 5-year est.); Median household income: $73,009 (2006-2010 5-year est.); Average household income: $72,110 (2006-2010 5-year est.); Percent of households with income of $100,000 or more: 31.5% (2006-2010 5-year est.); Poverty rate: 2.7% (2006-2010 5-year est.).

**Education:** Percent of population age 25 and over with: High school diploma (including GED) or higher: 97.9% (2006-2010 5-year est.); Bachelor's degree or higher: 21.1% (2006-2010 5-year est.); Master's degree or higher: 13.1% (2006-2010 5-year est.).

**Housing:** Homeownership rate: 86.5% (2010); Median home value: $115,800 (2006-2010 5-year est.); Median contract rent: $348 per month (2006-2010 5-year est.); Median year structure built: before 1940 (2006-2010 5-year est.).

**Transportation:** Commute to work: 95.2% car, 0.0% public transportation, 3.5% walk, 1.3% work from home (2006-2010 5-year est.); Travel time to work: 52.1% less than 15 minutes, 35.2% 15 to 30 minutes, 5.4% 30 to 45 minutes, 6.0% 45 to 60 minutes, 1.2% 60 minutes or more (2006-2010 5-year est.)

# Nassau County

Located in southeastern New York, on western Long Island; bounded on the west by Queens borough of New York city, on the south by the Atlantic Ocean, and on the north by Long Island Sound. Covers a land area of 286.69 square miles, a water area of 166.39 square miles, and is located in the Eastern Time Zone at 40.71° N. Lat., 73.60° W. Long. The county was founded in 1899. County seat is Mineola.

Nassau County is part of the New York-Northern New Jersey-Long Island, NY-NJ-PA Metropolitan Statistical Area. The entire metro area includes: Edison-New Brunswick, NJ Metropolitan Division (Middlesex County, NJ; Monmouth County, NJ; Ocean County, NJ; Somerset County, NJ); Nassau-Suffolk, NY Metropolitan Division (Nassau County, NY; Suffolk County, NY); New York-White Plains-Wayne, NY-NJ Metropolitan Division (Bergen County, NJ; Hudson County, NJ; Passaic County, NJ; Bronx County, NY; Kings County, NY; New York County, NY; Putnam County, NY; Queens County, NY; Richmond County, NY; Rockland County, NY; Westchester County, NY); Newark-Union, NJ-PA Metropolitan Division

(Essex County, NJ; Hunterdon County, NJ; Morris County, NJ; Sussex County, NJ; Union County, NJ; Pike County, PA)

**Weather Station: Mineola**                     Elevation: 96 feet

|       | Jan | Feb | Mar | Apr | May | Jun | Jul | Aug | Sep | Oct | Nov | Dec |
|-------|-----|-----|-----|-----|-----|-----|-----|-----|-----|-----|-----|-----|
| High  | 39  | 42  | 49  | 59  | 69  | 79  | 84  | 82  | 75  | 64  | 55  | 44  |
| Low   | 26  | 27  | 33  | 42  | 50  | 60  | 66  | 65  | 58  | 47  | 40  | 31  |
| Precip| 3.5 | 2.7 | 4.3 | 4.4 | 4.0 | 3.9 | 4.4 | 3.7 | 3.8 | 4.0 | 3.8 | 3.7 |
| Snow  | 4.9 | 6.4 | 3.6 | 0.6 | 0.0 | 0.0 | 0.0 | 0.0 | 0.0 | 0.0 | 0.1 | 4.2 |

*High and Low temperatures in degrees Fahrenheit; Precipitation and Snow in inches*

**Weather Station: Wantagh Cedar Creek**          Elevation: 9 feet

|       | Jan | Feb | Mar | Apr | May | Jun | Jul | Aug | Sep | Oct | Nov | Dec |
|-------|-----|-----|-----|-----|-----|-----|-----|-----|-----|-----|-----|-----|
| High  | 38  | 40  | 47  | 56  | 66  | 76  | 81  | 81  | 74  | 64  | 54  | 43  |
| Low   | 26  | 27  | 33  | 42  | 51  | 61  | 67  | 66  | 59  | 49  | 40  | 31  |
| Precip| 3.3 | 2.6 | 4.0 | 4.2 | 3.6 | 3.6 | 3.6 | 3.3 | 3.5 | 3.7 | 3.5 | 3.6 |
| Snow  | na  | na  | na  | 0.0 | 0.0 | 0.0 | 0.0 | 0.0 | 0.0 | 0.0 | 0.0 | na  |

*High and Low temperatures in degrees Fahrenheit; Precipitation and Snow in inches*

**Population:** 1,287,844 (1990); 1,334,544 (2000); 1,339,532 (2010); Race: 73.0% White, 11.1% Black, 7.6% Asian, 0.2% American Indian/Alaska Native, 0.0% Native Hawaiian/Other Pacific Islander, 8.1% Other, 14.6% Hispanic of any race (2010); Density: 4,672.4 persons per square mile (2010); Average household size: 2.94 (2010); Median age: 41.1 (2010); Males per 100 females: 93.7 (2010).

**Religion:** Six largest groups: 50.6% Catholicism, 6.0% Judaism, 1.4% Lutheran, 1.3% Eastern Liturgical (Orthodox), 1.2% Methodist/Pietist, 1.2% Muslim Estimate (2010)

**Economy:** Unemployment rate: 7.2% (February 2012); Total civilian labor force: 674,315 (February 2012); Leading industries: 19.1% health care and social assistance; 14.8% retail trade; 7.7% professional, scientific & technical services (2009); Farms: 59 totaling 1,288 acres (2007); Companies that employ 500 or more persons: 59 (2009); Companies that employ 100 to 499 persons: 655 (2009); Companies that employ less than 100 persons: 46,373 (2009); Black-owned businesses: 10,812 (2007); Hispanic-owned businesses: 11,994 (2007); Asian-owned businesses: 13,388 (2007); Women-owned businesses: 43,488 (2007); Retail sales per capita: $21,047 (2010). Single-family building permits issued: 311 (2011); Multi-family building permits issued: 542 (2011).

**Income:** Per capita income: $41,387 (2006-2010 5-year est.); Median household income: $93,613 (2006-2010 5-year est.); Average household income: $121,567 (2006-2010 5-year est.); Percent of households with income of $100,000 or more: 46.9% (2006-2010 5-year est.); Poverty rate: 5.0% (2006-2010 5-year est.); Bankruptcy rate: 2.40% (2011).

**Taxes:** Total county taxes per capita: $1,490 (2009); County property taxes per capita: $695 (2009).

**Education:** Percent of population age 25 and over with: High school diploma (including GED) or higher: 89.7% (2006-2010 5-year est.); Bachelor's degree or higher: 40.9% (2006-2010 5-year est.); Master's degree or higher: 18.2% (2006-2010 5-year est.).

**Housing:** Homeownership rate: 79.9% (2010); Median home value: $487,900 (2006-2010 5-year est.); Median contract rent: $1,288 per month (2006-2010 5-year est.); Median year structure built: 1954 (2006-2010 5-year est.).

**Health:** Birth rate: 107.3 per 10,000 population (2011); Death rate: 78.1 per 10,000 population (2011); Age-adjusted cancer mortality rate: 150.1 deaths per 100,000 population (2009); Number of physicians: 65.6 per 10,000 population (2008); Hospital beds: 37.7 per 10,000 population (2007); Hospital admissions: 1,836.7 per 10,000 population (2007).

**Environment:** Air Quality Index: 83.6% good, 16.4% moderate, 0.0% unhealthy for sensitive individuals, 0.0% unhealthy (percent of days in 2010)

**Elections:** 2008 Presidential election results: 53.8% Obama, 45.4% McCain, 0.4% Nader

**National and State Parks:** Bethpage State Park; Hempstead Lake State Park; Jones Beach State Park; Oyster Bay National Wildlife Refuge; Sagamore Hill National Historical Site; Valley Stream State Park

**Additional Information Contacts**

Nassau County Government . . . . . . . . . . . . . . . . (516) 571-2664
    http://www.nassaucountyny.gov
Baldwin Chamber of Commerce . . . . . . . . . . . . . (516) 223-8080
    http://www.baldwinchamber.com
Bethpage Chamber of Commerce . . . . . . . . . . . . (516) 433-0010
    http://www.bethpagecommunity.com/community/chamber_of_commer
Chamber of Commerce of the Bellmores . . . . . . . . . . . . (516) 679-1875
    http://www.bellmorechamber.com

Chamber of Commerce of the Willistons . . . . . . . . . . . . (516) 739-1943
    http://www.chamberofthewillistons.org
City of Glen Cove . . . . . . . . . . . . . . . . . . . . . (516) 676-3345
    http://www.glencove-li.com
City of Long Beach . . . . . . . . . . . . . . . . . . . . (516) 431-1000
    http://www.longbeachny.org
East Meadow Chamber of Commerce . . . . . . . . . . . (516) 794-3727
    http://www.eastmeadowchamber.com
Franklin Square Chamber of Commerce . . . . . . . . . (516) 775-0001
Garden City Chamber of Commerce . . . . . . . . . . . (516) 746-7724
    http://www.gardencitychamber.org
Glen Cove Chamber of Commerce . . . . . . . . . . . . (516) 676-6666
    http://www.glencovechamber.org
Great Neck Chamber of Commerce . . . . . . . . . . . (516) 487-2000
    http://www.greatneckchamber.org
Greater New Hyde Park Chamber of Commerce . . . . . . . . (888) 400-0311
    http://www.nhpchamber.org
Hempstead Chamber of Commerce . . . . . . . . . . . (516) 476-2901
    http://hempsteadchamber.com
Hicksville Chamber of Commerce . . . . . . . . . . . . (516) 931-7170
    http://www.hicksvillechamber.com
Locust Valley Chamber of Commerce . . . . . . . . . . (516) 637-8496
    http://www.locustvalleychamber.com
Long Beach Chamber of Commerce . . . . . . . . . . . (516) 432-6000
    http://www.longislandnet.com/longbeach
Lynbrook Chamber of Commerce . . . . . . . . . . . . (516) 599-3436
    http://www.lynbrookusa.com
Manhasset Chamber of Commerce . . . . . . . . . . . (516) 641-1932
    http://manhassetny.org
Massapequa Chamber of Commerce . . . . . . . . . . . (516) 541-1443
    http://www.massapequachamber.com
Merrick Chamber of Commerce . . . . . . . . . . . . . (516) 771-1171
    http://www.merrickchamber.org
Mineola Chamber of Commerce . . . . . . . . . . . . . (516) 408-3554
    http://www.mineolachamber.com
Nassau Council of Chambers of Commerce . . . . . . . . (516) 248-1112
    http://www.ncchambers.org
Oceanside Chamber of Commerce . . . . . . . . . . . (516) 763-9177
    http://www.oceansidechamber.org
Oyster Bay Chamber of Commerce . . . . . . . . . . . (516) 922-6464
    http://www.visitoysterbay.com
Plainview-Old Bethpage Chamber of Commerce . . . . . . (516) 937-5646
    http://pobcoc.com/new_in_town.cfm
Port Washington Chamber of Commerce . . . . . . . . . (516) 883-6566
    http://www.portwashington.org
Rockville Centre Chamber of Commerce . . . . . . . . . (516) 766-0666
    http://rvcchamber.com
Syosset Chamber of Commerce . . . . . . . . . . . . . (516) 364-7150
    http://www.syossetchamber.com
Town of Hempstead . . . . . . . . . . . . . . . . . . . (516) 489-5000
    http://www.townofhempstead.org
Town of North Hempstead . . . . . . . . . . . . . . . . (516) 869-7646
    http://www.northhempsteadny.gov
Town of Oyster Bay . . . . . . . . . . . . . . . . . . . (516) 624-6332
    http://www.oysterbaytown.com
Valley Stream Chamber of Commerce . . . . . . . . . . (516) 825-1741
    http://www.valleystreamchamber.org
Village of Cedarhurst . . . . . . . . . . . . . . . . . . (516) 295-5770
    http://www.cedarhurst.gov
Village of East Hills . . . . . . . . . . . . . . . . . . . (516) 621-5600
    http://www.villageofeasthills.org
Village of East Rockaway . . . . . . . . . . . . . . . . (516) 887-6300
    http://www.villageofeastrockaway.org
Village of East Williston . . . . . . . . . . . . . . . . . (516) 746-0782
    http://eastwilliston.org
Village of Farmingdale . . . . . . . . . . . . . . . . . . (516) 249-0093
    http://www.farmingdalevillage.com
Village of Floral Park . . . . . . . . . . . . . . . . . . (516) 326-6300
    http://www.fpvillage.org
Village of Flower Hill . . . . . . . . . . . . . . . . . . . (516) 627-5000
    http://www.villageflowerhill.org
Village of Freeport . . . . . . . . . . . . . . . . . . . . (516) 377-2300
    http://www.freeportny.com
Village of Garden City . . . . . . . . . . . . . . . . . . (516) 465-4000
    http://www.gardencityny.net

Village of Great Neck................................(516) 482-0019
    http://www.greatneckvillage.org
Village of Great Neck Plaza.........................(516) 482-4500
    http://www.greatneckplaza.net
Village of Hempstead................................(516) 489-3400
    http://www.villageofhempstead.org
Village of Lawrence.................................(516) 239-4600
    http://www.villageoflawrence.org
Village of Massapequa Park..........................(516) 798-0244
    http://www.masspk.com
Village of Matinecock...............................(516) 671-7790
    http://www.matinecockvillage.org
Village of New Hyde Park............................(516) 354-0022
    http://www.vnhp.org
Village of Rockville Centre.........................(516) 678-9300
    http://www.rvcny.us
Village of Saddle Rock..............................(516) 482-9400
    http://www.saddlerock.org
Village of Sands Point..............................(516) 883-3044
    http://www.sandspoint.org
Village of Westbury.................................(516) 334-1700
    http://www.villageofwestbury.org
Wantagh Chamber of Commerce.........................(516) 679-0100
    http://www.wcc.li
Westbury-Carle Place Chamber of Commerce............(516) 997-3966
    http://wcpchamber.com

## Nassau County Communities

**ALBERTSON** (CDP). Covers a land area of 0.679 square miles and a water area of 0 square miles. Located at 40.77° N. Lat; 73.64° W. Long. Elevation is 128 feet.
**Population:** 5,166 (1990); 5,200 (2000); 5,182 (2010); Density: 7,625.5 persons per square mile (2010); Race: 70.4% White, 0.3% Black, 24.3% Asian, 0.1% American Indian/Alaska Native, 0.0% Native Hawaiian/Other Pacific Islander, 4.9% Other, 7.3% Hispanic of any race (2010); Average household size: 2.89 (2010); Median age: 44.3 (2010); Males per 100 females: 94.6 (2010); Marriage status: 28.3% never married, 57.8% now married, 8.0% widowed, 5.9% divorced (2006-2010 5-year est.); Foreign born: 33.7% (2006-2010 5-year est.); Ancestry (includes multiple ancestries): 23.5% Italian, 11.6% Irish, 10.2% German, 5.0% Polish, 4.5% Iranian (2006-2010 5-year est.).
**Economy:** Employment by occupation: 14.4% management, 3.2% professional, 6.5% services, 14.9% sales, 0.9% farming, 2.5% construction, 4.4% production (2006-2010 5-year est.).
**Income:** Per capita income: $34,188 (2006-2010 5-year est.); Median household income: $79,583 (2006-2010 5-year est.); Average household income: $102,786 (2006-2010 5-year est.); Percent of households with income of $100,000 or more: 37.8% (2006-2010 5-year est.); Poverty rate: 2.4% (2006-2010 5-year est.).
**Education:** Percent of population age 25 and over with: High school diploma (including GED) or higher: 90.9% (2006-2010 5-year est.); Bachelor's degree or higher: 43.3% (2006-2010 5-year est.); Master's degree or higher: 19.3% (2006-2010 5-year est.).

##### School District(s)
Herricks Union Free School District (KG-12)
    2009-10 Enrollment: 4,044.......................(516) 305-8901
Mineola Union Free School District (PK-12)
    2009-10 Enrollment: 2,716.......................(516) 237-2001
**Housing:** Homeownership rate: 92.0% (2010); Median home value: $599,100 (2006-2010 5-year est.); Median contract rent: $1,795 per month (2006-2010 5-year est.); Median year structure built: 1954 (2006-2010 5-year est.).
**Transportation:** Commute to work: 73.5% car, 18.0% public transportation, 4.0% walk, 4.5% work from home (2006-2010 5-year est.); Travel time to work: 19.8% less than 15 minutes, 30.0% 15 to 30 minutes, 25.0% 30 to 45 minutes, 3.3% 45 to 60 minutes, 21.9% 60 minutes or more (2006-2010 5-year est.)

**ATLANTIC BEACH** (village). Covers a land area of 0.438 square miles and a water area of 0.600 square miles. Located at 40.58° N. Lat; 73.72° W. Long. Elevation is 16 feet.
**Population:** 1,933 (1990); 1,986 (2000); 1,891 (2010); Density: 4,309.8 persons per square mile (2010); Race: 96.6% White, 0.6% Black, 1.0% Asian, 0.0% American Indian/Alaska Native, 0.0% Native Hawaiian/Other

Pacific Islander, 1.8% Other, 3.9% Hispanic of any race (2010); Average household size: 2.21 (2010); Median age: 53.5 (2010); Males per 100 females: 91.0 (2010); Marriage status: 21.0% never married, 63.6% now married, 6.8% widowed, 8.6% divorced (2006-2010 5-year est.); Foreign born: 9.5% (2006-2010 5-year est.); Ancestry (includes multiple ancestries): 16.5% Italian, 15.9% Irish, 12.4% Russian, 9.6% German, 8.2% American (2006-2010 5-year est.).
**Economy:** Employment by occupation: 18.7% management, 4.9% professional, 1.1% services, 15.8% sales, 5.1% farming, 5.3% construction, 4.5% production (2006-2010 5-year est.).
**Income:** Per capita income: $72,154 (2006-2010 5-year est.); Median household income: $102,188 (2006-2010 5-year est.); Average household income: $168,029 (2006-2010 5-year est.); Percent of households with income of $100,000 or more: 50.4% (2006-2010 5-year est.); Poverty rate: 5.1% (2006-2010 5-year est.).
**Education:** Percent of population age 25 and over with: High school diploma (including GED) or higher: 96.5% (2006-2010 5-year est.); Bachelor's degree or higher: 54.2% (2006-2010 5-year est.); Master's degree or higher: 23.7% (2006-2010 5-year est.).
**Housing:** Homeownership rate: 76.2% (2010); Median home value: $796,400 (2006-2010 5-year est.); Median contract rent: $1,570 per month (2006-2010 5-year est.); Median year structure built: 1955 (2006-2010 5-year est.).
**Transportation:** Commute to work: 61.6% car, 21.0% public transportation, 2.4% walk, 12.6% work from home (2006-2010 5-year est.); Travel time to work: 16.8% less than 15 minutes, 13.2% 15 to 30 minutes, 25.1% 30 to 45 minutes, 13.3% 45 to 60 minutes, 31.7% 60 minutes or more (2006-2010 5-year est.)

**BALDWIN** (CDP). Covers a land area of 2.963 square miles and a water area of 0.024 square miles. Located at 40.66° N. Lat; 73.61° W. Long. Elevation is 23 feet.
**History:** Named for F.W. Baldwin, an early settler. Settled 1640s.
**Population:** 22,719 (1990); 23,455 (2000); 24,033 (2010); Density: 8,110.6 persons per square mile (2010); Race: 48.8% White, 34.6% Black, 4.2% Asian, 0.4% American Indian/Alaska Native, 0.0% Native Hawaiian/Other Pacific Islander, 12.0% Other, 20.2% Hispanic of any race (2010); Average household size: 3.09 (2010); Median age: 39.5 (2010); Males per 100 females: 90.7 (2010); Marriage status: 33.8% never married, 53.5% now married, 4.9% widowed, 7.8% divorced (2006-2010 5-year est.); Foreign born: 27.7% (2006-2010 5-year est.); Ancestry (includes multiple ancestries): 16.8% Italian, 15.3% Irish, 9.7% German, 6.5% Jamaican, 5.6% Haitian (2006-2010 5-year est.).
**Economy:** Employment by occupation: 13.1% management, 2.9% professional, 8.7% services, 15.8% sales, 4.9% farming, 4.9% construction, 4.7% production (2006-2010 5-year est.).
**Income:** Per capita income: $35,788 (2006-2010 5-year est.); Median household income: $99,872 (2006-2010 5-year est.); Average household income: $108,501 (2006-2010 5-year est.); Percent of households with income of $100,000 or more: 49.9% (2006-2010 5-year est.); Poverty rate: 3.5% (2006-2010 5-year est.).
**Education:** Percent of population age 25 and over with: High school diploma (including GED) or higher: 91.7% (2006-2010 5-year est.); Bachelor's degree or higher: 44.6% (2006-2010 5-year est.); Master's degree or higher: 18.3% (2006-2010 5-year est.).

##### School District(s)
Baldwin Union Free School District (KG-12)
    2009-10 Enrollment: 5,244.......................(516) 377-9271
**Housing:** Homeownership rate: 83.2% (2010); Median home value: $418,300 (2006-2010 5-year est.); Median contract rent: $1,270 per month (2006-2010 5-year est.); Median year structure built: 1943 (2006-2010 5-year est.).
**Newspapers:** Noticia Hispanoamericana (National news; Circulation 40,000); Polish American World (Local news; Circulation 9,000)
**Transportation:** Commute to work: 78.9% car, 14.4% public transportation, 2.6% walk, 2.5% work from home (2006-2010 5-year est.); Travel time to work: 22.1% less than 15 minutes, 24.1% 15 to 30 minutes, 26.7% 30 to 45 minutes, 10.6% 45 to 60 minutes, 16.6% 60 minutes or more (2006-2010 5-year est.)
**Additional Information Contacts**
Baldwin Chamber of Commerce........................(516) 223-8080
    http://www.baldwinchamber.com

## BALDWIN HARBOR (CDP). Covers a land area of 1.205 square miles and a water area of 0.521 square miles. Located at 40.62° N. Lat; 73.60° W. Long. Elevation is 10 feet.

**Population:** 7,899 (1990); 8,147 (2000); 8,102 (2010); Density: 6,721.2 persons per square mile (2010); Race: 61.3% White, 26.6% Black, 4.9% Asian, 0.1% American Indian/Alaska Native, 0.0% Native Hawaiian/Other Pacific Islander, 7.1% Other, 11.8% Hispanic of any race (2010); Average household size: 3.01 (2010); Median age: 42.5 (2010); Males per 100 females: 93.1 (2010); Marriage status: 29.5% never married, 55.9% now married, 7.0% widowed, 7.6% divorced (2006-2010 5-year est.); Foreign born: 21.6% (2006-2010 5-year est.); Ancestry (includes multiple ancestries): 15.4% Italian, 14.0% Irish, 10.4% German, 7.0% Polish, 5.4% Haitian (2006-2010 5-year est.).

**Economy:** Employment by occupation: 16.1% management, 3.1% professional, 4.8% services, 19.5% sales, 3.8% farming, 3.1% construction, 2.4% production (2006-2010 5-year est.).

**Income:** Per capita income: $36,543 (2006-2010 5-year est.); Median household income: $95,673 (2006-2010 5-year est.); Average household income: $113,950 (2006-2010 5-year est.); Percent of households with income of $100,000 or more: 49.7% (2006-2010 5-year est.); Poverty rate: 7.1% (2006-2010 5-year est.).

**Education:** Percent of population age 25 and over with: High school diploma (including GED) or higher: 93.6% (2006-2010 5-year est.); Bachelor's degree or higher: 41.3% (2006-2010 5-year est.); Master's degree or higher: 15.1% (2006-2010 5-year est.).

**Housing:** Homeownership rate: 92.5% (2010); Median home value: $461,600 (2006-2010 5-year est.); Median contract rent: $1,689 per month (2006-2010 5-year est.); Median year structure built: 1956 (2006-2010 5-year est.).

**Transportation:** Commute to work: 77.9% car, 18.1% public transportation, 0.5% walk, 2.3% work from home (2006-2010 5-year est.); Travel time to work: 15.1% less than 15 minutes, 25.0% 15 to 30 minutes, 25.2% 30 to 45 minutes, 12.8% 45 to 60 minutes, 21.9% 60 minutes or more (2006-2010 5-year est.)

## BARNUM ISLAND (CDP). Aka North Long Beach. Covers a land area of 0.879 square miles and a water area of 0.387 square miles. Located at 40.60° N. Lat; 73.64° W. Long.

**Population:** 2,624 (1990); 2,487 (2000); 2,414 (2010); Density: 2,745.2 persons per square mile (2010); Race: 87.0% White, 1.7% Black, 2.7% Asian, 0.2% American Indian/Alaska Native, 0.1% Native Hawaiian/Other Pacific Islander, 8.3% Other, 15.6% Hispanic of any race (2010); Average household size: 2.77 (2010); Median age: 47.0 (2010); Males per 100 females: 97.5 (2010); Marriage status: 29.1% never married, 55.8% now married, 7.9% widowed, 7.3% divorced (2006-2010 5-year est.); Foreign born: 16.6% (2006-2010 5-year est.); Ancestry (includes multiple ancestries): 32.4% Italian, 21.0% Irish, 6.0% German, 4.6% American, 4.4% Scottish (2006-2010 5-year est.).

**Economy:** Employment by occupation: 5.8% management, 0.5% professional, 12.5% services, 20.1% sales, 6.1% farming, 13.1% construction, 4.1% production (2006-2010 5-year est.).

**Income:** Per capita income: $40,888 (2006-2010 5-year est.); Median household income: $85,759 (2006-2010 5-year est.); Average household income: $118,180 (2006-2010 5-year est.); Percent of households with income of $100,000 or more: 45.3% (2006-2010 5-year est.); Poverty rate: 9.2% (2006-2010 5-year est.).

**Education:** Percent of population age 25 and over with: High school diploma (including GED) or higher: 91.0% (2006-2010 5-year est.); Bachelor's degree or higher: 28.1% (2006-2010 5-year est.); Master's degree or higher: 8.4% (2006-2010 5-year est.).

**Housing:** Homeownership rate: 86.3% (2010); Median home value: $537,100 (2006-2010 5-year est.); Median contract rent: $1,838 per month (2006-2010 5-year est.); Median year structure built: 1963 (2006-2010 5-year est.).

**Transportation:** Commute to work: 76.0% car, 21.9% public transportation, 0.8% walk, 0.6% work from home (2006-2010 5-year est.); Travel time to work: 29.7% less than 15 minutes, 24.0% 15 to 30 minutes, 19.8% 30 to 45 minutes, 6.0% 45 to 60 minutes, 20.5% 60 minutes or more (2006-2010 5-year est.)

## BAXTER ESTATES (village). Covers a land area of 0.182 square miles and a water area of 0 square miles. Located at 40.83° N. Lat; 73.69° W. Long. Elevation is 39 feet.

**Population:** 1,113 (1990); 1,006 (2000); 999 (2010); Density: 5,474.5 persons per square mile (2010); Race: 81.1% White, 1.3% Black, 6.0%

Asian, 0.5% American Indian/Alaska Native, 0.0% Native Hawaiian/Other Pacific Islander, 11.1% Other, 16.8% Hispanic of any race (2010); Average household size: 2.62 (2010); Median age: 42.8 (2010); Males per 100 females: 105.6 (2010); Marriage status: 24.2% never married, 60.2% now married, 6.6% widowed, 9.0% divorced (2006-2010 5-year est.); Foreign born: 26.2% (2006-2010 5-year est.); Ancestry (includes multiple ancestries): 23.8% Irish, 12.3% Italian, 10.2% English, 9.2% Russian, 8.6% German (2006-2010 5-year est.).

**Economy:** Single-family building permits issued: 0 (2011); Multi-family building permits issued: 0 (2011); Employment by occupation: 22.4% management, 3.2% professional, 1.5% services, 13.3% sales, 1.1% farming, 5.7% construction, 2.3% production (2006-2010 5-year est.).

**Income:** Per capita income: $63,058 (2006-2010 5-year est.); Median household income: $102,000 (2006-2010 5-year est.); Average household income: $168,803 (2006-2010 5-year est.); Percent of households with income of $100,000 or more: 52.2% (2006-2010 5-year est.); Poverty rate: 1.8% (2006-2010 5-year est.).

**Education:** Percent of population age 25 and over with: High school diploma (including GED) or higher: 95.1% (2006-2010 5-year est.); Bachelor's degree or higher: 66.3% (2006-2010 5-year est.); Master's degree or higher: 32.1% (2006-2010 5-year est.).

**Housing:** Homeownership rate: 68.6% (2010); Median home value: $845,000 (2006-2010 5-year est.); Median contract rent: $1,322 per month (2006-2010 5-year est.); Median year structure built: before 1940 (2006-2010 5-year est.).

**Transportation:** Commute to work: 60.0% car, 25.9% public transportation, 4.3% walk, 8.1% work from home (2006-2010 5-year est.); Travel time to work: 19.1% less than 15 minutes, 21.9% 15 to 30 minutes, 9.8% 30 to 45 minutes, 17.2% 45 to 60 minutes, 31.9% 60 minutes or more (2006-2010 5-year est.)

## BAY PARK (CDP). Covers a land area of 0.500 square miles and a water area of 0.101 square miles. Located at 40.62° N. Lat; 73.66° W. Long. Elevation is 10 feet.

**Population:** 2,280 (1990); 2,300 (2000); 2,212 (2010); Density: 4,419.9 persons per square mile (2010); Race: 96.2% White, 0.3% Black, 1.7% Asian, 0.0% American Indian/Alaska Native, 0.0% Native Hawaiian/Other Pacific Islander, 1.8% Other, 6.4% Hispanic of any race (2010); Average household size: 2.55 (2010); Median age: 43.2 (2010); Males per 100 females: 91.8 (2010); Marriage status: 33.4% never married, 54.4% now married, 5.8% widowed, 6.4% divorced (2006-2010 5-year est.); Foreign born: 5.6% (2006-2010 5-year est.); Ancestry (includes multiple ancestries): 32.7% Italian, 29.2% Irish, 20.5% German, 10.6% English, 4.7% Polish (2006-2010 5-year est.).

**Economy:** Employment by occupation: 5.2% management, 5.4% professional, 1.4% services, 19.7% sales, 3.5% farming, 3.7% construction, 0.0% production (2006-2010 5-year est.).

**Income:** Per capita income: $38,740 (2006-2010 5-year est.); Median household income: $87,012 (2006-2010 5-year est.); Average household income: $94,364 (2006-2010 5-year est.); Percent of households with income of $100,000 or more: 30.7% (2006-2010 5-year est.); Poverty rate: 3.5% (2006-2010 5-year est.).

**Education:** Percent of population age 25 and over with: High school diploma (including GED) or higher: 94.6% (2006-2010 5-year est.); Bachelor's degree or higher: 21.3% (2006-2010 5-year est.); Master's degree or higher: 9.2% (2006-2010 5-year est.).

**Housing:** Homeownership rate: 85.6% (2010); Median home value: $405,200 (2006-2010 5-year est.); Median contract rent: $1,687 per month (2006-2010 5-year est.); Median year structure built: 1950 (2006-2010 5-year est.).

**Transportation:** Commute to work: 72.2% car, 21.8% public transportation, 0.0% walk, 1.9% work from home (2006-2010 5-year est.); Travel time to work: 21.7% less than 15 minutes, 22.7% 15 to 30 minutes, 34.6% 30 to 45 minutes, 2.5% 45 to 60 minutes, 18.4% 60 minutes or more (2006-2010 5-year est.)

## BAYVILLE (village). Covers a land area of 1.449 square miles and a water area of 0.100 square miles. Located at 40.90° N. Lat; 73.56° W. Long. Elevation is 39 feet.

**History:** Incorporated 1919.

**Population:** 7,193 (1990); 7,135 (2000); 6,669 (2010); Density: 4,599.5 persons per square mile (2010); Race: 95.0% White, 0.3% Black, 1.7% Asian, 0.4% American Indian/Alaska Native, 0.0% Native Hawaiian/Other Pacific Islander, 2.6% Other, 6.5% Hispanic of any race (2010); Average household size: 2.67 (2010); Median age: 45.6 (2010); Males per 100

females: 93.6 (2010); Marriage status: 28.1% never married, 54.6% now married, 9.5% widowed, 7.8% divorced (2006-2010 5-year est.); Foreign born: 6.8% (2006-2010 5-year est.); Ancestry (includes multiple ancestries): 37.1% Italian, 29.2% Irish, 16.8% German, 8.9% English, 4.6% American (2006-2010 5-year est.).

**Economy:** Single-family building permits issued: 2 (2011); Multi-family building permits issued: 0 (2011); Employment by occupation: 17.7% management, 3.6% professional, 6.5% services, 12.8% sales, 3.7% farming, 7.4% construction, 4.7% production (2006-2010 5-year est.).

**Income:** Per capita income: $37,958 (2006-2010 5-year est.); Median household income: $81,888 (2006-2010 5-year est.); Average household income: $101,546 (2006-2010 5-year est.); Percent of households with income of $100,000 or more: 38.2% (2006-2010 5-year est.); Poverty rate: 3.8% (2006-2010 5-year est.).

**Taxes:** Total city taxes per capita: $587 (2009); City property taxes per capita: $528 (2009).

**Education:** Percent of population age 25 and over with: High school diploma (including GED) or higher: 94.8% (2006-2010 5-year est.); Bachelor's degree or higher: 39.9% (2006-2010 5-year est.); Master's degree or higher: 20.3% (2006-2010 5-year est.).

###### School District(s)
Locust Valley Central School District (KG-12)
   2009-10 Enrollment: 2,211 . . . . . . . . . . . . . . . . . . . . . . . . (516) 674-6310

**Housing:** Homeownership rate: 78.9% (2010); Median home value: $605,900 (2006-2010 5-year est.); Median contract rent: $1,511 per month (2006-2010 5-year est.); Median year structure built: 1957 (2006-2010 5-year est.).

**Transportation:** Commute to work: 85.9% car, 6.6% public transportation, 2.5% walk, 5.1% work from home (2006-2010 5-year est.); Travel time to work: 22.0% less than 15 minutes, 22.4% 15 to 30 minutes, 31.0% 30 to 45 minutes, 8.9% 45 to 60 minutes, 15.6% 60 minutes or more (2006-2010 5-year est.)

## BELLEROSE (village).
Covers a land area of 0.125 square miles and a water area of 0 square miles. Located at 40.72° N. Lat; 73.71° W. Long. Elevation is 85 feet.

**History:** Settled 1908, incorporated 1924.

**Population:** 1,101 (1990); 1,173 (2000); 1,193 (2010); Density: 9,525.5 persons per square mile (2010); Race: 87.1% White, 3.5% Black, 4.4% Asian, 0.3% American Indian/Alaska Native, 0.0% Native Hawaiian/Other Pacific Islander, 4.7% Other, 9.5% Hispanic of any race (2010); Average household size: 3.18 (2010); Median age: 40.9 (2010); Males per 100 females: 96.9 (2010); Marriage status: 22.6% never married, 70.5% now married, 4.1% widowed, 2.8% divorced (2006-2010 5-year est.); Foreign born: 2.4% (2006-2010 5-year est.); Ancestry (includes multiple ancestries): 52.1% Irish, 28.2% Italian, 27.6% German, 6.8% Greek, 4.7% Polish (2006-2010 5-year est.).

**Economy:** Single-family building permits issued: 0 (2011); Multi-family building permits issued: 0 (2011); Employment by occupation: 22.4% management, 2.1% professional, 3.2% services, 11.0% sales, 5.2% farming, 5.4% construction, 1.5% production (2006-2010 5-year est.).

**Income:** Per capita income: $59,857 (2006-2010 5-year est.); Median household income: $171,771 (2006-2010 5-year est.); Average household income: $184,329 (2006-2010 5-year est.); Percent of households with income of $100,000 or more: 67.1% (2006-2010 5-year est.); Poverty rate: 0.6% (2006-2010 5-year est.).

**Education:** Percent of population age 25 and over with: High school diploma (including GED) or higher: 98.6% (2006-2010 5-year est.); Bachelor's degree or higher: 62.7% (2006-2010 5-year est.); Master's degree or higher: 34.7% (2006-2010 5-year est.).

**Housing:** Homeownership rate: 95.0% (2010); Median home value: $620,800 (2006-2010 5-year est.); Median contract rent: $744 per month (2006-2010 5-year est.); Median year structure built: before 1940 (2006-2010 5-year est.).

**Transportation:** Commute to work: 59.0% car, 33.3% public transportation, 1.9% walk, 4.3% work from home (2006-2010 5-year est.); Travel time to work: 12.7% less than 15 minutes, 21.1% 15 to 30 minutes, 21.7% 30 to 45 minutes, 9.4% 45 to 60 minutes, 35.1% 60 minutes or more (2006-2010 5-year est.)

## BELLEROSE TERRACE (CDP).
Covers a land area of 0.124 square miles and a water area of 0 square miles. Located at 40.72° N. Lat; 73.72° W. Long. Elevation is 75 feet.

**Population:** 2,014 (1990); 2,157 (2000); 2,198 (2010); Density: 17,637.2 persons per square mile (2010); Race: 49.5% White, 8.4% Black, 28.1%

Asian, 0.1% American Indian/Alaska Native, 0.0% Native Hawaiian/Other Pacific Islander, 13.9% Other, 25.8% Hispanic of any race (2010); Average household size: 3.47 (2010); Median age: 37.0 (2010); Males per 100 females: 98.2 (2010); Marriage status: 27.4% never married, 65.9% now married, 4.2% widowed, 2.5% divorced (2006-2010 5-year est.); Foreign born: 43.0% (2006-2010 5-year est.); Ancestry (includes multiple ancestries): 12.8% Italian, 11.4% German, 10.5% Irish, 4.0% Polish, 4.0% Haitian (2006-2010 5-year est.).

**Economy:** Employment by occupation: 4.1% management, 8.9% professional, 10.1% services, 18.7% sales, 1.4% farming, 7.4% construction, 7.1% production (2006-2010 5-year est.).

**Income:** Per capita income: $32,718 (2006-2010 5-year est.); Median household income: $83,864 (2006-2010 5-year est.); Average household income: $103,229 (2006-2010 5-year est.); Percent of households with income of $100,000 or more: 37.8% (2006-2010 5-year est.); Poverty rate: 2.3% (2006-2010 5-year est.).

**Education:** Percent of population age 25 and over with: High school diploma (including GED) or higher: 88.7% (2006-2010 5-year est.); Bachelor's degree or higher: 36.6% (2006-2010 5-year est.); Master's degree or higher: 11.2% (2006-2010 5-year est.).

**Housing:** Homeownership rate: 82.3% (2010); Median home value: $415,500 (2006-2010 5-year est.); Median contract rent: $1,665 per month (2006-2010 5-year est.); Median year structure built: before 1940 (2006-2010 5-year est.).

**Transportation:** Commute to work: 70.5% car, 25.8% public transportation, 0.0% walk, 2.2% work from home (2006-2010 5-year est.); Travel time to work: 12.2% less than 15 minutes, 27.1% 15 to 30 minutes, 24.9% 30 to 45 minutes, 11.7% 45 to 60 minutes, 24.0% 60 minutes or more (2006-2010 5-year est.)

## BELLMORE (CDP).
Covers a land area of 2.358 square miles and a water area of 0.615 square miles. Located at 40.65° N. Lat; 73.52° W. Long. Elevation is 16 feet.

**Population:** 16,438 (1990); 16,441 (2000); 16,218 (2010); Density: 6,876.3 persons per square mile (2010); Race: 93.4% White, 1.0% Black, 3.0% Asian, 0.1% American Indian/Alaska Native, 0.0% Native Hawaiian/Other Pacific Islander, 2.5% Other, 5.7% Hispanic of any race (2010); Average household size: 2.85 (2010); Median age: 42.4 (2010); Males per 100 females: 94.8 (2010); Marriage status: 23.8% never married, 64.4% now married, 6.8% widowed, 4.9% divorced (2006-2010 5-year est.); Foreign born: 8.5% (2006-2010 5-year est.); Ancestry (includes multiple ancestries): 30.5% Italian, 22.0% Irish, 16.5% German, 7.8% Polish, 6.3% Russian (2006-2010 5-year est.).

**Economy:** Employment by occupation: 13.9% management, 1.7% professional, 4.7% services, 16.9% sales, 5.0% farming, 6.6% construction, 2.7% production (2006-2010 5-year est.).

**Income:** Per capita income: $44,972 (2006-2010 5-year est.); Median household income: $109,268 (2006-2010 5-year est.); Average household income: $128,392 (2006-2010 5-year est.); Percent of households with income of $100,000 or more: 54.9% (2006-2010 5-year est.); Poverty rate: 1.1% (2006-2010 5-year est.).

**Education:** Percent of population age 25 and over with: High school diploma (including GED) or higher: 93.8% (2006-2010 5-year est.); Bachelor's degree or higher: 42.1% (2006-2010 5-year est.); Master's degree or higher: 18.5% (2006-2010 5-year est.).

###### School District(s)
Bellmore Union Free School District (PK-06)
   2009-10 Enrollment: 1,148 . . . . . . . . . . . . . . . . . . . . . . . (516) 679-2909
Bellmore-Merrick Central High School District (07-12)
   2009-10 Enrollment: 6,086 . . . . . . . . . . . . . . . . . . . . . . . (516) 992-1001
North Bellmore Union Free School District (PK-06)
   2009-10 Enrollment: 2,148 . . . . . . . . . . . . . . . . . . . . . . . (516) 992-3000

**Housing:** Homeownership rate: 87.2% (2010); Median home value: $501,200 (2006-2010 5-year est.); Median contract rent: $1,259 per month (2006-2010 5-year est.); Median year structure built: 1955 (2006-2010 5-year est.).

**Newspapers:** Seaford/Wantagh Observer (Community news; Circulation 5,000)

**Transportation:** Commute to work: 77.7% car, 16.5% public transportation, 2.1% walk, 3.3% work from home (2006-2010 5-year est.); Travel time to work: 19.2% less than 15 minutes, 30.3% 15 to 30 minutes, 17.8% 30 to 45 minutes, 11.5% 45 to 60 minutes, 21.2% 60 minutes or more (2006-2010 5-year est.)

**Additional Information Contacts**

Chamber of Commerce of the Bellmores. . . . . . . . . . . (516) 679-1875
http://www.bellmorechamber.com

## BETHPAGE (CDP).
Covers a land area of 3.575 square miles and a water area of 0 square miles. Located at 40.74° N. Lat; 73.48° W. Long. Elevation is 105 feet.

**History:** Named for the biblical village of Bethpage, between Bethany and the Mount of Olives. A village restoration in Old Bethpage features 20 pre-Civil War buildings.

**Population:** 15,761 (1990); 16,543 (2000); 16,429 (2010); Density: 4,594.4 persons per square mile (2010); Race: 90.8% White, 0.6% Black, 5.5% Asian, 0.1% American Indian/Alaska Native, 0.0% Native Hawaiian/Other Pacific Islander, 3.0% Other, 7.0% Hispanic of any race (2010); Average household size: 2.79 (2010); Median age: 44.1 (2010); Males per 100 females: 89.5 (2010); Marriage status: 22.6% never married, 61.5% now married, 10.2% widowed, 5.8% divorced (2006-2010 5-year est.); Foreign born: 14.2% (2006-2010 5-year est.); Ancestry (includes multiple ancestries): 35.2% Italian, 26.4% Irish, 20.1% German, 5.3% Polish, 3.5% Greek (2006-2010 5-year est.).

**Economy:** Employment by occupation: 12.3% management, 4.5% professional, 5.8% services, 21.9% sales, 4.1% farming, 8.9% construction, 7.1% production (2006-2010 5-year est.).

**Income:** Per capita income: $38,549 (2006-2010 5-year est.); Median household income: $86,946 (2006-2010 5-year est.); Average household income: $107,959 (2006-2010 5-year est.); Percent of households with income of $100,000 or more: 42.9% (2006-2010 5-year est.); Poverty rate: 2.1% (2006-2010 5-year est.).

**Education:** Percent of population age 25 and over with: High school diploma (including GED) or higher: 89.8% (2006-2010 5-year est.); Bachelor's degree or higher: 32.8% (2006-2010 5-year est.); Master's degree or higher: 10.8% (2006-2010 5-year est.).

**School District(s)**
Bethpage Union Free School District (KG-12)
  2009-10 Enrollment: 3,072 . . . . . . . . . . . . . . . (516) 644-4001
Plainedge Union Free School District (KG-12)
  2009-10 Enrollment: 3,437 . . . . . . . . . . . . . . . (516) 992-7455

**Four-year College(s)**
Briarcliffe College (Private, For-profit)
  Fall 2010 Enrollment: 2,074. . . . . . . . . . . . . . . (516) 918-3600
  2011-12 Tuition: In-state $18,360; Out-of-state $18,360

**Housing:** Homeownership rate: 87.5% (2010); Median home value: $469,900 (2006-2010 5-year est.); Median contract rent: $1,648 per month (2006-2010 5-year est.); Median year structure built: 1957 (2006-2010 5-year est.).

**Hospitals:** New Island Hospital (223 beds)

**Newspapers:** Bethpage Tribune (Community news)

**Transportation:** Commute to work: 79.7% car, 14.6% public transportation, 0.8% walk, 4.0% work from home (2006-2010 5-year est.); Travel time to work: 24.6% less than 15 minutes, 31.7% 15 to 30 minutes, 18.1% 30 to 45 minutes, 5.7% 45 to 60 minutes, 19.9% 60 minutes or more (2006-2010 5-year est.)

**Additional Information Contacts**
Bethpage Chamber of Commerce . . . . . . . . . . . . . . (516) 433-0010
  http://www.bethpagecommunity.com/community/chamber_of_commer

## BROOKVILLE (village).
Covers a land area of 3.937 square miles and a water area of 0.011 square miles. Located at 40.81° N. Lat; 73.57° W. Long. Elevation is 236 feet.

**Population:** 4,468 (1990); 2,126 (2000); 3,465 (2010); Density: 880.1 persons per square mile (2010); Race: 75.6% White, 11.5% Black, 10.3% Asian, 0.2% American Indian/Alaska Native, 0.0% Native Hawaiian/Other Pacific Islander, 2.4% Other, 6.3% Hispanic of any race (2010); Average household size: 3.25 (2010); Median age: 21.6 (2010); Males per 100 females: 84.1 (2010); Marriage status: 57.2% never married, 40.2% now married, 1.4% widowed, 1.3% divorced (2006-2010 5-year est.); Foreign born: 14.3% (2006-2010 5-year est.); Ancestry (includes multiple ancestries): 21.2% Italian, 8.6% German, 8.3% Irish, 7.6% Russian, 5.4% Eastern European (2006-2010 5-year est.).

**Economy:** Single-family building permits issued: 0 (2011); Multi-family building permits issued: 0 (2011); Employment by occupation: 18.7% management, 1.2% professional, 8.8% services, 27.4% sales, 1.5% farming, 2.8% construction, 1.3% production (2006-2010 5-year est.).

**Income:** Per capita income: $73,312 (2006-2010 5-year est.); Median household income: $250 (2006-2010 5-year est.); Average household income: $400,113 (2006-2010 5-year est.); Percent of households with income of $100,000 or more: 79.8% (2006-2010 5-year est.); Poverty rate: 1.3% (2006-2010 5-year est.).

**Education:** Percent of population age 25 and over with: High school diploma (including GED) or higher: 98.3% (2006-2010 5-year est.); Bachelor's degree or higher: 78.2% (2006-2010 5-year est.); Master's degree or higher: 37.1% (2006-2010 5-year est.).

**Four-year College(s)**
Long Island University-C W Post Campus (Private, Not-for-profit)
  Fall 2010 Enrollment: 7,038. . . . . . . . . . . . . . . (516) 299-2900
  2011-12 Tuition: In-state $31,646; Out-of-state $31,646

**Housing:** Homeownership rate: 93.8% (2010); Median home value: $1 (2006-2010 5-year est.); Median contract rent: $1,708 per month (2006-2010 5-year est.); Median year structure built: 1968 (2006-2010 5-year est.).

**Transportation:** Commute to work: 62.5% car, 8.0% public transportation, 16.1% walk, 12.4% work from home (2006-2010 5-year est.); Travel time to work: 27.8% less than 15 minutes, 26.4% 15 to 30 minutes, 21.2% 30 to 45 minutes, 4.5% 45 to 60 minutes, 20.1% 60 minutes or more (2006-2010 5-year est.)

## CARLE PLACE (CDP).
Covers a land area of 0.934 square miles and a water area of 0 square miles. Located at 40.75° N. Lat; 73.61° W. Long. Elevation is 102 feet.

**Population:** 5,107 (1990); 5,247 (2000); 4,981 (2010); Density: 5,327.7 persons per square mile (2010); Race: 84.2% White, 2.1% Black, 7.9% Asian, 0.1% American Indian/Alaska Native, 0.0% Native Hawaiian/Other Pacific Islander, 5.7% Other, 11.1% Hispanic of any race (2010); Average household size: 2.67 (2010); Median age: 41.6 (2010); Males per 100 females: 96.5 (2010); Marriage status: 28.0% never married, 61.7% now married, 6.8% widowed, 3.5% divorced (2006-2010 5-year est.); Foreign born: 15.2% (2006-2010 5-year est.); Ancestry (includes multiple ancestries): 34.6% Italian, 19.5% Irish, 15.1% German, 5.7% Portuguese, 3.1% Polish (2006-2010 5-year est.).

**Economy:** Employment by occupation: 15.1% management, 2.2% professional, 7.6% services, 19.7% sales, 2.3% farming, 8.3% construction, 6.4% production (2006-2010 5-year est.).

**Income:** Per capita income: $32,910 (2006-2010 5-year est.); Median household income: $84,511 (2006-2010 5-year est.); Average household income: $93,244 (2006-2010 5-year est.); Percent of households with income of $100,000 or more: 39.0% (2006-2010 5-year est.); Poverty rate: 4.5% (2006-2010 5-year est.).

**Education:** Percent of population age 25 and over with: High school diploma (including GED) or higher: 92.6% (2006-2010 5-year est.); Bachelor's degree or higher: 38.2% (2006-2010 5-year est.); Master's degree or higher: 15.6% (2006-2010 5-year est.).

**School District(s)**
Carle Place Union Free School District (KG-12)
  2009-10 Enrollment: 1,462 . . . . . . . . . . . . . . . (516) 622-6442

**Housing:** Homeownership rate: 71.6% (2010); Median home value: $504,300 (2006-2010 5-year est.); Median contract rent: $1,334 per month (2006-2010 5-year est.); Median year structure built: 1951 (2006-2010 5-year est.).

**Transportation:** Commute to work: 79.9% car, 11.8% public transportation, 0.6% walk, 3.3% work from home (2006-2010 5-year est.); Travel time to work: 27.6% less than 15 minutes, 34.3% 15 to 30 minutes, 14.7% 30 to 45 minutes, 7.6% 45 to 60 minutes, 15.7% 60 minutes or more (2006-2010 5-year est.)

**Additional Information Contacts**
Greater Mahopac-Carmel Chamber of Commerce . . . . . . . . (845) 628-5553
  http://www.mahopaccarmelonline.com

## CEDARHURST (village).
Covers a land area of 0.674 square miles and a water area of 0 square miles. Located at 40.62° N. Lat; 73.72° W. Long. Elevation is 26 feet.

**History:** Incorporated 1910.

**Population:** 5,716 (1990); 6,164 (2000); 6,592 (2010); Density: 9,766.6 persons per square mile (2010); Race: 87.8% White, 2.2% Black, 3.6% Asian, 0.0% American Indian/Alaska Native, 0.0% Native Hawaiian/Other Pacific Islander, 6.4% Other, 10.7% Hispanic of any race (2010); Average household size: 2.94 (2010); Median age: 35.8 (2010); Males per 100 females: 93.8 (2010); Marriage status: 28.6% never married, 54.6% now married, 7.6% widowed, 9.2% divorced (2006-2010 5-year est.); Foreign born: 19.7% (2006-2010 5-year est.); Ancestry (includes multiple ancestries): 13.0% Polish, 10.8% American, 10.2% Italian, 9.0% Russian, 4.9% German (2006-2010 5-year est.).

**Economy:** Single-family building permits issued: 0 (2011); Multi-family building permits issued: 0 (2011); Employment by occupation: 13.8% management, 3.0% professional, 9.7% services, 10.2% sales, 3.1% farming, 3.3% construction, 1.7% production (2006-2010 5-year est.).
**Income:** Per capita income: $37,866 (2006-2010 5-year est.); Median household income: $88,043 (2006-2010 5-year est.); Average household income: $114,750 (2006-2010 5-year est.); Percent of households with income of $100,000 or more: 40.9% (2006-2010 5-year est.); Poverty rate: 4.0% (2006-2010 5-year est.).
**Education:** Percent of population age 25 and over with: High school diploma (including GED) or higher: 92.6% (2006-2010 5-year est.); Bachelor's degree or higher: 51.2% (2006-2010 5-year est.); Master's degree or higher: 23.8% (2006-2010 5-year est.).

**School District(s)**
Lawrence Union Free School District (PK-12)
    2009-10 Enrollment: 3,092 ...................... (516) 295-7030
**Housing:** Homeownership rate: 67.7% (2010); Median home value: $582,300 (2006-2010 5-year est.); Median contract rent: $1,299 per month (2006-2010 5-year est.); Median year structure built: 1941 (2006-2010 5-year est.).
**Transportation:** Commute to work: 73.7% car, 19.1% public transportation, 4.7% walk, 2.5% work from home (2006-2010 5-year est.); Travel time to work: 21.1% less than 15 minutes, 18.6% 15 to 30 minutes, 14.0% 30 to 45 minutes, 19.3% 45 to 60 minutes, 26.9% 60 minutes or more (2006-2010 5-year est.)
**Additional Information Contacts**
Village of Cedarhurst .......................... (516) 295-5770
    http://www.cedarhurst.gov

## CENTRE ISLAND (village). Covers a land area of 1.090 square miles and a water area of 0.001 square miles. Located at 40.89° N. Lat; 73.52° W. Long. Elevation is 33 feet.

**Population:** 439 (1990); 444 (2000); 410 (2010); Density: 376.1 persons per square mile (2010); Race: 93.9% White, 0.0% Black, 3.7% Asian, 0.0% American Indian/Alaska Native, 0.0% Native Hawaiian/Other Pacific Islander, 2.4% Other, 7.3% Hispanic of any race (2010); Average household size: 2.44 (2010); Median age: 51.7 (2010); Males per 100 females: 104.0 (2010); Marriage status: 19.6% never married, 65.7% now married, 7.1% widowed, 7.7% divorced (2006-2010 5-year est.); Foreign born: 13.8% (2006-2010 5-year est.); Ancestry (includes multiple ancestries): 18.0% Italian, 17.2% Irish, 13.3% English, 12.5% German, 7.8% French (2006-2010 5-year est.).
**Economy:** Single-family building permits issued: 0 (2011); Multi-family building permits issued: 0 (2011); Employment by occupation: 37.4% management, 2.6% professional, 1.9% services, 8.4% sales, 1.3% farming, 2.6% construction, 0.0% production (2006-2010 5-year est.).
**Income:** Per capita income: $145,194 (2006-2010 5-year est.); Median household income: $146,250 (2006-2010 5-year est.); Average household income: $361,754 (2006-2010 5-year est.); Percent of households with income of $100,000 or more: 68.8% (2006-2010 5-year est.); Poverty rate: 2.6% (2006-2010 5-year est.).
**Education:** Percent of population age 25 and over with: High school diploma (including GED) or higher: 89.0% (2006-2010 5-year est.); Bachelor's degree or higher: 65.7% (2006-2010 5-year est.); Master's degree or higher: 27.9% (2006-2010 5-year est.).
**Housing:** Homeownership rate: 85.1% (2010); Median home value: $1 (2006-2010 5-year est.); Median contract rent: n/a per month (2006-2010 5-year est.); Median year structure built: 1958 (2006-2010 5-year est.).
**Safety:** Violent crime rate: 0.0 per 10,000 population; Property crime rate: 90.7 per 10,000 population (2010).
**Transportation:** Commute to work: 54.8% car, 11.6% public transportation, 1.3% walk, 30.3% work from home (2006-2010 5-year est.); Travel time to work: 5.6% less than 15 minutes, 31.5% 15 to 30 minutes, 24.1% 30 to 45 minutes, 7.4% 45 to 60 minutes, 31.5% 60 minutes or more (2006-2010 5-year est.)

## COVE NECK (village). Covers a land area of 1.284 square miles and a water area of 0.279 square miles. Located at 40.88° N. Lat; 73.49° W. Long. Elevation is 23 feet.

**History:** "Sagamore Hill," home of Theodore Roosevelt, is here.
**Population:** 332 (1990); 300 (2000); 286 (2010); Density: 222.7 persons per square mile (2010); Race: 96.2% White, 0.3% Black, 1.4% Asian, 0.0% American Indian/Alaska Native, 0.0% Native Hawaiian/Other Pacific Islander, 2.1% Other, 4.9% Hispanic of any race (2010); Average household size: 2.75 (2010); Median age: 46.3 (2010); Males per 100

females: 115.0 (2010); Marriage status: 22.1% never married, 65.3% now married, 7.9% widowed, 4.7% divorced (2006-2010 5-year est.); Foreign born: 7.3% (2006-2010 5-year est.); Ancestry (includes multiple ancestries): 21.5% American, 17.2% Italian, 15.0% German, 11.6% Irish, 11.6% English (2006-2010 5-year est.).
**Economy:** Single-family building permits issued: 0 (2011); Multi-family building permits issued: 0 (2011); Employment by occupation: 27.2% management, 2.2% professional, 2.2% services, 12.0% sales, 3.3% farming, 8.7% construction, 0.0% production (2006-2010 5-year est.).
**Income:** Per capita income: $117,185 (2006-2010 5-year est.); Median household income: $146,250 (2006-2010 5-year est.); Average household income: $300,240 (2006-2010 5-year est.); Percent of households with income of $100,000 or more: 70.4% (2006-2010 5-year est.); Poverty rate: 0.0% (2006-2010 5-year est.).
**Education:** Percent of population age 25 and over with: High school diploma (including GED) or higher: 98.8% (2006-2010 5-year est.); Bachelor's degree or higher: 66.9% (2006-2010 5-year est.); Master's degree or higher: 26.4% (2006-2010 5-year est.).
**Housing:** Homeownership rate: 82.7% (2010); Median home value: $1 (2006-2010 5-year est.); Median contract rent: $850 per month (2006-2010 5-year est.); Median year structure built: 1955 (2006-2010 5-year est.).
**Transportation:** Commute to work: 55.6% car, 25.6% public transportation, 5.6% walk, 13.3% work from home (2006-2010 5-year est.); Travel time to work: 21.8% less than 15 minutes, 28.2% 15 to 30 minutes, 10.3% 30 to 45 minutes, 3.8% 45 to 60 minutes, 35.9% 60 minutes or more (2006-2010 5-year est.)

## EAST ATLANTIC BEACH (CDP). Covers a land area of 0.315 square miles and a water area of 0.368 square miles. Located at 40.58° N. Lat; 73.71° W. Long. Elevation is 69 feet.

**Population:** 2,168 (1990); 2,257 (2000); 2,049 (2010); Density: 6,503.0 persons per square mile (2010); Race: 96.0% White, 0.7% Black, 1.1% Asian, 0.0% American Indian/Alaska Native, 0.0% Native Hawaiian/Other Pacific Islander, 2.2% Other, 5.3% Hispanic of any race (2010); Average household size: 2.41 (2010); Median age: 46.5 (2010); Males per 100 females: 101.1 (2010); Marriage status: 33.8% never married, 50.4% now married, 5.9% widowed, 9.9% divorced (2006-2010 5-year est.); Foreign born: 4.9% (2006-2010 5-year est.); Ancestry (includes multiple ancestries): 30.5% Irish, 24.0% Italian, 13.0% Russian, 10.4% American, 9.1% German (2006-2010 5-year est.).
**Economy:** Employment by occupation: 12.1% management, 3.8% professional, 2.9% services, 17.0% sales, 1.0% farming, 6.7% construction, 3.3% production (2006-2010 5-year est.).
**Income:** Per capita income: $59,724 (2006-2010 5-year est.); Median household income: $108,571 (2006-2010 5-year est.); Average household income: $132,299 (2006-2010 5-year est.); Percent of households with income of $100,000 or more: 58.5% (2006-2010 5-year est.); Poverty rate: 4.1% (2006-2010 5-year est.).
**Education:** Percent of population age 25 and over with: High school diploma (including GED) or higher: 99.4% (2006-2010 5-year est.); Bachelor's degree or higher: 56.9% (2006-2010 5-year est.); Master's degree or higher: 26.6% (2006-2010 5-year est.).
**Housing:** Homeownership rate: 69.4% (2010); Median home value: $715,700 (2006-2010 5-year est.); Median contract rent: $1,780 per month (2006-2010 5-year est.); Median year structure built: 1948 (2006-2010 5-year est.).
**Transportation:** Commute to work: 74.7% car, 17.5% public transportation, 0.0% walk, 7.8% work from home (2006-2010 5-year est.); Travel time to work: 20.2% less than 15 minutes, 8.8% 15 to 30 minutes, 29.3% 30 to 45 minutes, 16.7% 45 to 60 minutes, 24.9% 60 minutes or more (2006-2010 5-year est.)

## EAST GARDEN CITY (CDP). Covers a land area of 2.995 square miles and a water area of 0.007 square miles. Located at 40.73° N. Lat; 73.59° W. Long. Elevation is 95 feet.

**Population:** 1,098 (1990); 979 (2000); 6,208 (2010); Density: 2,072.1 persons per square mile (2010); Race: 72.1% White, 17.5% Black, 4.5% Asian, 0.1% American Indian/Alaska Native, 0.1% Native Hawaiian/Other Pacific Islander, 5.7% Other, 9.0% Hispanic of any race (2010); Average household size: 2.08 (2010); Median age: 21.6 (2010); Males per 100 females: 82.3 (2010); Marriage status: 83.8% never married, 11.7% now married, 2.7% widowed, 1.8% divorced (2006-2010 5-year est.); Foreign born: 6.5% (2006-2010 5-year est.); Ancestry (includes multiple ancestries): 18.1% Italian, 15.3% Irish, 10.2% German, 5.6% Polish, 5.4% Russian (2006-2010 5-year est.).

**Economy:** Employment by occupation: 6.4% management, 4.0% professional, 20.6% services, 29.1% sales, 6.2% farming, 2.1% construction, 2.4% production (2006-2010 5-year est.).
**Income:** Per capita income: $15,607 (2006-2010 5-year est.); Median household income: $76,000 (2006-2010 5-year est.); Average household income: $97,698 (2006-2010 5-year est.); Percent of households with income of $100,000 or more: 33.4% (2006-2010 5-year est.); Poverty rate: 16.2% (2006-2010 5-year est.).
**Education:** Percent of population age 25 and over with: High school diploma (including GED) or higher: 98.8% (2006-2010 5-year est.); Bachelor's degree or higher: 55.1% (2006-2010 5-year est.); Master's degree or higher: 21.8% (2006-2010 5-year est.).
**Housing:** Homeownership rate: 59.8% (2010); Median home value: $580,900 (2006-2010 5-year est.); Median contract rent: n/a per month (2006-2010 5-year est.); Median year structure built: 2002 (2006-2010 5-year est.).
**Transportation:** Commute to work: 41.7% car, 6.3% public transportation, 45.3% walk, 5.9% work from home (2006-2010 5-year est.); Travel time to work: 59.7% less than 15 minutes, 22.7% 15 to 30 minutes, 10.0% 30 to 45 minutes, 2.0% 45 to 60 minutes, 5.7% 60 minutes or more (2006-2010 5-year est.)

## EAST HILLS (village). Covers a land area of 2.272 square miles and a water area of 0 square miles. Located at 40.79° N. Lat; 73.62° W. Long. Elevation is 187 feet.

**History:** Incorporated 1931.
**Population:** 6,746 (1990); 6,842 (2000); 6,955 (2010); Density: 3,060.4 persons per square mile (2010); Race: 89.8% White, 0.9% Black, 7.4% Asian, 0.0% American Indian/Alaska Native, 0.0% Native Hawaiian/Other Pacific Islander, 1.9% Other, 2.2% Hispanic of any race (2010); Average household size: 3.09 (2010); Median age: 43.6 (2010); Males per 100 females: 96.6 (2010); Marriage status: 18.5% never married, 74.4% now married, 3.3% widowed, 3.8% divorced (2006-2010 5-year est.); Foreign born: 12.5% (2006-2010 5-year est.); Ancestry (includes multiple ancestries): 20.2% Russian, 9.1% Polish, 8.1% American, 7.6% Eastern European, 6.8% Italian (2006-2010 5-year est.).
**Economy:** Single-family building permits issued: 9 (2011); Multi-family building permits issued: 0 (2011); Employment by occupation: 19.4% management, 5.3% professional, 3.4% services, 11.8% sales, 2.2% farming, 1.0% construction, 0.3% production (2006-2010 5-year est.).
**Income:** Per capita income: $88,827 (2006-2010 5-year est.); Median household income: $201,974 (2006-2010 5-year est.); Average household income: $276,443 (2006-2010 5-year est.); Percent of households with income of $100,000 or more: 77.4% (2006-2010 5-year est.); Poverty rate: 1.6% (2006-2010 5-year est.).
**Education:** Percent of population age 25 and over with: High school diploma (including GED) or higher: 98.8% (2006-2010 5-year est.); Bachelor's degree or higher: 82.8% (2006-2010 5-year est.); Master's degree or higher: 48.1% (2006-2010 5-year est.).
**Housing:** Homeownership rate: 98.2% (2010); Median home value: $947,400 (2006-2010 5-year est.); Median contract rent: n/a per month (2006-2010 5-year est.); Median year structure built: 1956 (2006-2010 5-year est.).
**Transportation:** Commute to work: 81.5% car, 12.9% public transportation, 2.2% walk, 3.5% work from home (2006-2010 5-year est.); Travel time to work: 16.2% less than 15 minutes, 37.5% 15 to 30 minutes, 17.6% 30 to 45 minutes, 8.7% 45 to 60 minutes, 19.9% 60 minutes or more (2006-2010 5-year est.)

**Additional Information Contacts**
Village of East Hills . . . . . . . . . . . . . . . . . . . . . . . . . . . (516) 621-5600
  http://www.villageofeasthills.org

## EAST MASSAPEQUA (CDP). Covers a land area of 3.439 square miles and a water area of 0.113 square miles. Located at 40.67° N. Lat; 73.43° W. Long. Elevation is 13 feet.

**Population:** 19,782 (1990); 19,565 (2000); 19,069 (2010); Density: 5,543.7 persons per square mile (2010); Race: 80.1% White, 12.7% Black, 2.1% Asian, 0.3% American Indian/Alaska Native, 0.0% Native Hawaiian/Other Pacific Islander, 4.8% Other, 10.1% Hispanic of any race (2010); Average household size: 2.86 (2010); Median age: 42.4 (2010); Males per 100 females: 94.4 (2010); Marriage status: 27.8% never married, 57.9% now married, 7.7% widowed, 6.6% divorced (2006-2010 5-year est.); Foreign born: 12.5% (2006-2010 5-year est.); Ancestry (includes multiple ancestries): 31.1% Italian, 28.2% Irish, 20.9% German, 5.4% English, 5.3% Polish (2006-2010 5-year est.).

**Economy:** Employment by occupation: 13.8% management, 4.4% professional, 7.5% services, 17.9% sales, 4.6% farming, 6.4% construction, 3.4% production (2006-2010 5-year est.).
**Income:** Per capita income: $40,799 (2006-2010 5-year est.); Median household income: $96,500 (2006-2010 5-year est.); Average household income: $112,397 (2006-2010 5-year est.); Percent of households with income of $100,000 or more: 48.0% (2006-2010 5-year est.); Poverty rate: 3.4% (2006-2010 5-year est.).
**Education:** Percent of population age 25 and over with: High school diploma (including GED) or higher: 93.0% (2006-2010 5-year est.); Bachelor's degree or higher: 35.4% (2006-2010 5-year est.); Master's degree or higher: 14.0% (2006-2010 5-year est.).
**Housing:** Homeownership rate: 85.2% (2010); Median home value: $463,800 (2006-2010 5-year est.); Median contract rent: $1,123 per month (2006-2010 5-year est.); Median year structure built: 1957 (2006-2010 5-year est.).
**Transportation:** Commute to work: 80.4% car, 16.1% public transportation, 1.6% walk, 1.4% work from home (2006-2010 5-year est.); Travel time to work: 16.5% less than 15 minutes, 28.9% 15 to 30 minutes, 24.5% 30 to 45 minutes, 7.6% 45 to 60 minutes, 22.6% 60 minutes or more (2006-2010 5-year est.)

## EAST MEADOW (CDP). Covers a land area of 6.303 square miles and a water area of 0.023 square miles. Located at 40.72° N. Lat; 73.55° W. Long. Elevation is 72 feet.

**Population:** 36,909 (1990); 37,461 (2000); 38,132 (2010); Density: 6,048.9 persons per square mile (2010); Race: 77.3% White, 5.2% Black, 11.6% Asian, 0.1% American Indian/Alaska Native, 0.0% Native Hawaiian/Other Pacific Islander, 5.8% Other, 12.2% Hispanic of any race (2010); Average household size: 2.91 (2010); Median age: 41.9 (2010); Males per 100 females: 98.2 (2010); Marriage status: 29.1% never married, 57.6% now married, 7.9% widowed, 5.5% divorced (2006-2010 5-year est.); Foreign born: 17.9% (2006-2010 5-year est.); Ancestry (includes multiple ancestries): 24.3% Italian, 16.9% Irish, 10.2% German, 6.7% Polish, 4.2% Russian (2006-2010 5-year est.).
**Economy:** Employment by occupation: 13.2% management, 4.2% professional, 5.8% services, 20.5% sales, 3.0% farming, 7.8% construction, 3.8% production (2006-2010 5-year est.).
**Income:** Per capita income: $33,772 (2006-2010 5-year est.); Median household income: $89,176 (2006-2010 5-year est.); Average household income: $101,556 (2006-2010 5-year est.); Percent of households with income of $100,000 or more: 43.7% (2006-2010 5-year est.); Poverty rate: 2.4% (2006-2010 5-year est.).
**Education:** Percent of population age 25 and over with: High school diploma (including GED) or higher: 89.6% (2006-2010 5-year est.); Bachelor's degree or higher: 33.3% (2006-2010 5-year est.); Master's degree or higher: 14.8% (2006-2010 5-year est.).

**School District(s)**
East Meadow Union Free School District (KG-12)
  2009-10 Enrollment: 7,372 . . . . . . . . . . . . . . . . . . . . (516) 478-5776
**Housing:** Homeownership rate: 86.3% (2010); Median home value: $444,400 (2006-2010 5-year est.); Median contract rent: $1,120 per month (2006-2010 5-year est.); Median year structure built: 1956 (2006-2010 5-year est.).
**Hospitals:** Nassau University Medical Center (1500 beds)
**Transportation:** Commute to work: 83.8% car, 10.3% public transportation, 1.9% walk, 3.2% work from home (2006-2010 5-year est.); Travel time to work: 21.3% less than 15 minutes, 36.7% 15 to 30 minutes, 18.6% 30 to 45 minutes, 6.7% 45 to 60 minutes, 16.6% 60 minutes or more (2006-2010 5-year est.)

**Additional Information Contacts**
East Meadow Chamber of Commerce. . . . . . . . . . . . . . . . (516) 794-3727
  http://www.eastmeadowchamber.com
Nassau Council of Chambers of Commerce . . . . . . . . . . . (516) 248-1112
  http://www.ncchambers.org

## EAST NORWICH (CDP). Covers a land area of 1.047 square miles and a water area of 0 square miles. Located at 40.84° N. Lat; 73.52° W. Long. Elevation is 200 feet.

**Population:** 2,698 (1990); 2,675 (2000); 2,709 (2010); Density: 2,586.8 persons per square mile (2010); Race: 93.5% White, 0.8% Black, 3.5% Asian, 0.0% American Indian/Alaska Native, 0.0% Native Hawaiian/Other Pacific Islander, 2.2% Other, 4.4% Hispanic of any race (2010); Average household size: 2.85 (2010); Median age: 43.5 (2010); Males per 100 females: 91.6 (2010); Marriage status: 15.6% never married, 65.8% now

married, 8.9% widowed, 9.7% divorced (2006-2010 5-year est.); Foreign born: 6.4% (2006-2010 5-year est.); Ancestry (includes multiple ancestries): 38.9% Italian, 30.3% Irish, 14.2% German, 9.6% Polish, 6.1% Russian (2006-2010 5-year est.).
**Economy:** Employment by occupation: 17.9% management, 2.7% professional, 2.1% services, 19.3% sales, 4.4% farming, 6.2% construction, 2.7% production (2006-2010 5-year est.).
**Income:** Per capita income: $54,102 (2006-2010 5-year est.); Median household income: $131,115 (2006-2010 5-year est.); Average household income: $151,023 (2006-2010 5-year est.); Percent of households with income of $100,000 or more: 60.2% (2006-2010 5-year est.); Poverty rate: 0.5% (2006-2010 5-year est.).
**Education:** Percent of population age 25 and over with: High school diploma (including GED) or higher: 96.0% (2006-2010 5-year est.); Bachelor's degree or higher: 56.7% (2006-2010 5-year est.); Master's degree or higher: 30.4% (2006-2010 5-year est.).

**School District(s)**
Oyster Bay-East Norwich Central School District (PK-12)
    2009-10 Enrollment: 1,662 . . . . . . . . . . . . . . . . . . . . . (516) 624-6505
**Housing:** Homeownership rate: 93.9% (2010); Median home value: $627,700 (2006-2010 5-year est.); Median contract rent: n/a per month (2006-2010 5-year est.); Median year structure built: 1956 (2006-2010 5-year est.).
**Transportation:** Commute to work: 89.4% car, 4.8% public transportation, 0.0% walk, 5.2% work from home (2006-2010 5-year est.); Travel time to work: 22.5% less than 15 minutes, 33.2% 15 to 30 minutes, 23.7% 30 to 45 minutes, 8.6% 45 to 60 minutes, 12.0% 60 minutes or more (2006-2010 5-year est.)

**EAST ROCKAWAY** (village). Covers a land area of 1.016 square miles and a water area of 0.014 square miles. Located at 40.64° N. Lat; 73.66° W. Long. Elevation is 10 feet.
**History:** Named for the Algonquian translation of "sand place". Settled c.1688. Incorporated 1900.
**Population:** 10,152 (1990); 10,414 (2000); 9,818 (2010); Density: 9,658.3 persons per square mile (2010); Race: 93.2% White, 1.4% Black, 2.1% Asian, 0.1% American Indian/Alaska Native, 0.0% Native Hawaiian/Other Pacific Islander, 3.2% Other, 8.0% Hispanic of any race (2010); Average household size: 2.54 (2010); Median age: 43.4 (2010); Males per 100 females: 89.3 (2010); Marriage status: 32.5% never married, 51.9% now married, 6.6% widowed, 9.0% divorced (2006-2010 5-year est.); Foreign born: 11.4% (2006-2010 5-year est.); Ancestry (includes multiple ancestries): 34.3% Italian, 26.5% Irish, 11.2% German, 8.2% American, 6.0% Polish (2006-2010 5-year est.).
**Economy:** Single-family building permits issued: 0 (2011); Multi-family building permits issued: 0 (2011); Employment by occupation: 14.7% management, 2.5% professional, 8.4% services, 19.9% sales, 6.7% farming, 7.7% construction, 2.9% production (2006-2010 5-year est.).
**Income:** Per capita income: $39,734 (2006-2010 5-year est.); Median household income: $89,653 (2006-2010 5-year est.); Average household income: $105,276 (2006-2010 5-year est.); Percent of households with income of $100,000 or more: 46.2% (2006-2010 5-year est.); Poverty rate: 6.0% (2006-2010 5-year est.).
**Education:** Percent of population age 25 and over with: High school diploma (including GED) or higher: 87.6% (2006-2010 5-year est.); Bachelor's degree or higher: 33.6% (2006-2010 5-year est.); Master's degree or higher: 17.2% (2006-2010 5-year est.).

**School District(s)**
East Rockaway Union Free School District (KG-12)
    2009-10 Enrollment: 1,270 . . . . . . . . . . . . . . . . . . . . . (516) 887-8300
Lynbrook Union Free School District (KG-12)
    2009-10 Enrollment: 2,949 . . . . . . . . . . . . . . . . . . . . . (516) 887-0253
**Housing:** Homeownership rate: 73.0% (2010); Median home value: $504,000 (2006-2010 5-year est.); Median contract rent: $1,395 per month (2006-2010 5-year est.); Median year structure built: 1941 (2006-2010 5-year est.).
**Transportation:** Commute to work: 71.7% car, 19.0% public transportation, 2.8% walk, 3.7% work from home (2006-2010 5-year est.); Travel time to work: 25.2% less than 15 minutes, 27.1% 15 to 30 minutes, 19.9% 30 to 45 minutes, 10.6% 45 to 60 minutes, 17.3% 60 minutes or more (2006-2010 5-year est.).
**Additional Information Contacts**
East Rockaway Chamber of Commerce . . . . . . . . . . (516) 887-3131
    http://www.eastrockawaychamber.com

Village of East Rockaway . . . . . . . . . . . . . . . . . . . . . (516) 887-6300
http://www.villageofeastrockaway.org

**EAST WILLISTON** (village). Covers a land area of 0.568 square miles and a water area of 0 square miles. Located at 40.76° N. Lat; 73.63° W. Long. Elevation is 118 feet.
**History:** Incorporated 1926.
**Population:** 2,515 (1990); 2,503 (2000); 2,556 (2010); Density: 4,494.7 persons per square mile (2010); Race: 94.3% White, 0.4% Black, 4.0% Asian, 0.0% American Indian/Alaska Native, 0.0% Native Hawaiian/Other Pacific Islander, 1.3% Other, 4.3% Hispanic of any race (2010); Average household size: 3.04 (2010); Median age: 43.6 (2010); Males per 100 females: 97.8 (2010); Marriage status: 20.8% never married, 71.9% now married, 3.9% widowed, 3.3% divorced (2006-2010 5-year est.); Foreign born: 6.9% (2006-2010 5-year est.); Ancestry (includes multiple ancestries): 37.2% Italian, 31.9% Irish, 15.0% German, 6.9% Polish, 5.1% Russian (2006-2010 5-year est.).
**Economy:** Single-family building permits issued: 0 (2011); Multi-family building permits issued: 0 (2011); Employment by occupation: 18.1% management, 4.2% professional, 2.2% services, 17.9% sales, 4.0% farming, 2.9% construction, 2.0% production (2006-2010 5-year est.).
**Income:** Per capita income: $65,485 (2006-2010 5-year est.); Median household income: $146,477 (2006-2010 5-year est.); Average household income: $193,781 (2006-2010 5-year est.); Percent of households with income of $100,000 or more: 63.8% (2006-2010 5-year est.); Poverty rate: 0.9% (2006-2010 5-year est.).
**Education:** Percent of population age 25 and over with: High school diploma (including GED) or higher: 98.7% (2006-2010 5-year est.); Bachelor's degree or higher: 66.3% (2006-2010 5-year est.); Master's degree or higher: 35.4% (2006-2010 5-year est.).

**School District(s)**
East Williston Union Free School District (KG-12)
    2009-10 Enrollment: 1,798 . . . . . . . . . . . . . . . . . . . . . (516) 333-3758
**Housing:** Homeownership rate: 97.6% (2010); Median home value: $829,800 (2006-2010 5-year est.); Median contract rent: n/a per month (2006-2010 5-year est.); Median year structure built: 1950 (2006-2010 5-year est.).
**Transportation:** Commute to work: 72.8% car, 18.4% public transportation, 2.1% walk, 5.9% work from home (2006-2010 5-year est.); Travel time to work: 25.3% less than 15 minutes, 37.9% 15 to 30 minutes, 11.5% 30 to 45 minutes, 6.0% 45 to 60 minutes, 19.3% 60 minutes or more (2006-2010 5-year est.)
**Additional Information Contacts**
Village of East Williston . . . . . . . . . . . . . . . . . . . . . (516) 746-0782
    http://eastwilliston.org

**ELMONT** (CDP). Covers a land area of 3.368 square miles and a water area of 0.011 square miles. Located at 40.69° N. Lat; 73.70° W. Long. Elevation is 39 feet.
**Population:** 28,612 (1990); 32,657 (2000); 33,198 (2010); Density: 9,854.8 persons per square mile (2010); Race: 28.5% White, 45.5% Black, 10.9% Asian, 0.5% American Indian/Alaska Native, 0.0% Native Hawaiian/Other Pacific Islander, 14.6% Other, 21.8% Hispanic of any race (2010); Average household size: 3.37 (2010); Median age: 37.1 (2010); Males per 100 females: 92.9 (2010); Marriage status: 36.2% never married, 50.1% now married, 6.3% widowed, 7.4% divorced (2006-2010 5-year est.); Foreign born: 42.1% (2006-2010 5-year est.); Ancestry (includes multiple ancestries): 16.2% Haitian, 11.3% Italian, 8.6% Jamaican, 5.1% Irish, 3.8% German (2006-2010 5-year est.).
**Economy:** Employment by occupation: 7.1% management, 2.4% professional, 13.0% services, 17.8% sales, 5.9% farming, 7.2% construction, 5.8% production (2006-2010 5-year est.).
**Income:** Per capita income: $25,961 (2006-2010 5-year est.); Median household income: $80,356 (2006-2010 5-year est.); Average household income: $90,111 (2006-2010 5-year est.); Percent of households with income of $100,000 or more: 38.3% (2006-2010 5-year est.); Poverty rate: 5.4% (2006-2010 5-year est.).
**Education:** Percent of population age 25 and over with: High school diploma (including GED) or higher: 85.1% (2006-2010 5-year est.); Bachelor's degree or higher: 29.0% (2006-2010 5-year est.); Master's degree or higher: 9.3% (2006-2010 5-year est.).

**School District(s)**
Elmont Union Free School District (PK-06)
    2009-10 Enrollment: 3,987 . . . . . . . . . . . . . . . . . . . . . (516) 326-5500

Sewanhaka Central High School District (07-12)
2009-10 Enrollment: 8,449 . . . . . . . . . . . . . . . . . . . . . (516) 488-9800
**Housing:** Homeownership rate: 72.3% (2010); Median home value: $420,000 (2006-2010 5-year est.); Median contract rent: $1,233 per month (2006-2010 5-year est.); Median year structure built: 1952 (2006-2010 5-year est.).
**Newspapers:** Elmont Herald (Community news; Circulation 5,400)
**Transportation:** Commute to work: 75.2% car, 18.1% public transportation, 2.8% walk, 1.8% work from home (2006-2010 5-year est.); Travel time to work: 12.2% less than 15 minutes, 27.7% 15 to 30 minutes, 25.1% 30 to 45 minutes, 13.1% 45 to 60 minutes, 21.8% 60 minutes or more (2006-2010 5-year est.)
**Airports:** Belmont Park (general aviation)

## FARMINGDALE (village). Covers a land area of 1.120 square miles and a water area of 0 square miles. Located at 40.73° N. Lat; 73.44° W. Long. Elevation is 69 feet.
**History:** Seat of State University of N.Y. at Farmingdale Settled 1695, incorporated 1904.
**Population:** 8,134 (1990); 8,399 (2000); 8,189 (2010); Density: 7,307.1 persons per square mile (2010); Race: 85.2% White, 2.6% Black, 5.5% Asian, 0.4% American Indian/Alaska Native, 0.0% Native Hawaiian/Other Pacific Islander, 6.3% Other, 13.7% Hispanic of any race (2010); Average household size: 2.41 (2010); Median age: 43.2 (2010); Males per 100 females: 91.9 (2010); Marriage status: 32.6% never married, 48.3% now married, 9.7% widowed, 9.5% divorced (2006-2010 5-year est.); Foreign born: 15.5% (2006-2010 5-year est.); Ancestry (includes multiple ancestries): 33.7% Italian, 23.2% Irish, 18.5% German, 7.1% English, 5.6% Polish (2006-2010 5-year est.).
**Economy:** Single-family building permits issued: 0 (2011); Multi-family building permits issued: 0 (2011); Employment by occupation: 15.6% management, 5.0% professional, 8.7% services, 15.9% sales, 4.3% farming, 6.9% construction, 3.6% production (2006-2010 5-year est.).
**Income:** Per capita income: $38,049 (2006-2010 5-year est.); Median household income: $76,617 (2006-2010 5-year est.); Average household income: $99,253 (2006-2010 5-year est.); Percent of households with income of $100,000 or more: 38.8% (2006-2010 5-year est.); Poverty rate: 6.5% (2006-2010 5-year est.).
**Education:** Percent of population age 25 and over with: High school diploma (including GED) or higher: 86.8% (2006-2010 5-year est.); Bachelor's degree or higher: 30.1% (2006-2010 5-year est.); Master's degree or higher: 11.2% (2006-2010 5-year est.).

### School District(s)
Farmingdale Union Free School District (KG-12)
2009-10 Enrollment: 6,100 . . . . . . . . . . . . . . . . . . . . . (516) 752-6510

### Four-year College(s)
Farmingdale State College (Public)
Fall 2010 Enrollment: 6,144 . . . . . . . . . . . . . . . . . . . (516) 420-2000
2011-12 Tuition: In-state $6,444; Out-of-state $15,494
**Housing:** Homeownership rate: 65.3% (2010); Median home value: $408,500 (2006-2010 5-year est.); Median contract rent: $1,205 per month (2006-2010 5-year est.); Median year structure built: 1957 (2006-2010 5-year est.).
**Newspapers:** Deer Park South Bay (Community news; Circulation 103,000); South Bay's Newspaper (Community news; Circulation 103,000)
**Transportation:** Commute to work: 84.4% car, 8.1% public transportation, 3.9% walk, 1.9% work from home (2006-2010 5-year est.); Travel time to work: 29.3% less than 15 minutes, 34.4% 15 to 30 minutes, 17.9% 30 to 45 minutes, 4.8% 45 to 60 minutes, 13.6% 60 minutes or more (2006-2010 5-year est.)
**Additional Information Contacts**
Village of Farmingdale . . . . . . . . . . . . . . . . . . . . . . . . (516) 249-0093
http://www.farmingdalevillage.com

## FLORAL PARK (village). Covers a land area of 1.417 square miles and a water area of 0.013 square miles. Located at 40.72° N. Lat; 73.70° W. Long. Elevation is 89 feet.
**History:** Named to promote the beauty of the town. Incorporated 1908.
**Population:** 15,947 (1990); 15,967 (2000); 15,863 (2010); Density: 11,192.0 persons per square mile (2010); Race: 87.0% White, 1.3% Black, 6.9% Asian, 0.1% American Indian/Alaska Native, 0.0% Native Hawaiian/Other Pacific Islander, 4.7% Other, 8.8% Hispanic of any race (2010); Average household size: 2.79 (2010); Median age: 42.3 (2010); Males per 100 females: 95.1 (2010); Marriage status: 29.9% never married, 59.8% now married, 5.1% widowed, 5.2% divorced (2006-2010 5-year

est.); Foreign born: 11.4% (2006-2010 5-year est.); Ancestry (includes multiple ancestries): 37.0% Irish, 29.9% Italian, 20.2% German, 7.7% Polish, 4.4% English (2006-2010 5-year est.).
**Economy:** Single-family building permits issued: 0 (2011); Multi-family building permits issued: 0 (2011); Employment by occupation: 16.4% management, 4.9% professional, 5.7% services, 16.7% sales, 4.4% farming, 8.2% construction, 4.4% production (2006-2010 5-year est.).
**Income:** Per capita income: $41,540 (2006-2010 5-year est.); Median household income: $109,079 (2006-2010 5-year est.); Average household income: $115,904 (2006-2010 5-year est.); Percent of households with income of $100,000 or more: 55.0% (2006-2010 5-year est.); Poverty rate: 2.2% (2006-2010 5-year est.).
**Education:** Percent of population age 25 and over with: High school diploma (including GED) or higher: 92.7% (2006-2010 5-year est.); Bachelor's degree or higher: 43.0% (2006-2010 5-year est.); Master's degree or higher: 19.8% (2006-2010 5-year est.).

### School District(s)
Floral Park-Bellerose Union Free School District (PK-06)
2009-10 Enrollment: 1,608 . . . . . . . . . . . . . . . . . . . . . (516) 327-9300
Sewanhaka Central High School District (07-12)
2009-10 Enrollment: 8,449 . . . . . . . . . . . . . . . . . . . . . (516) 488-9800
**Housing:** Homeownership rate: 80.6% (2010); Median home value: $552,500 (2006-2010 5-year est.); Median contract rent: $1,170 per month (2006-2010 5-year est.); Median year structure built: before 1940 (2006-2010 5-year est.).
**Safety:** Violent crime rate: 10.2 per 10,000 population; Property crime rate: 50.3 per 10,000 population (2010).
**Newspapers:** Floral Park Bulletin (Community news; Circulation 8,000); Franklin Square Bulletin (Community news; Circulation 8,500); The Gateway (Community news; Circulation 12,000)
**Transportation:** Commute to work: 72.0% car, 20.2% public transportation, 3.9% walk, 3.9% work from home (2006-2010 5-year est.); Travel time to work: 19.0% less than 15 minutes, 27.4% 15 to 30 minutes, 23.2% 30 to 45 minutes, 10.9% 45 to 60 minutes, 19.5% 60 minutes or more (2006-2010 5-year est.)
**Additional Information Contacts**
Village of Floral Park . . . . . . . . . . . . . . . . . . . . . . . . (516) 326-6300
http://www.fpvillage.org

## FLOWER HILL (village). Covers a land area of 1.618 square miles and a water area of 0 square miles. Located at 40.80° N. Lat; 73.67° W. Long. Elevation is 167 feet.
**History:** Incorporated 1931.
**Population:** 4,490 (1990); 4,508 (2000); 4,665 (2010); Density: 2,882.7 persons per square mile (2010); Race: 82.8% White, 0.7% Black, 12.7% Asian, 0.0% American Indian/Alaska Native, 0.0% Native Hawaiian/Other Pacific Islander, 3.8% Other, 5.8% Hispanic of any race (2010); Average household size: 3.15 (2010); Median age: 42.5 (2010); Males per 100 females: 95.7 (2010); Marriage status: 16.7% never married, 74.6% now married, 5.0% widowed, 3.7% divorced (2006-2010 5-year est.); Foreign born: 23.8% (2006-2010 5-year est.); Ancestry (includes multiple ancestries): 24.4% Italian, 20.6% Irish, 8.3% German, 8.1% Russian, 6.4% Iranian (2006-2010 5-year est.).
**Economy:** Single-family building permits issued: 6 (2011); Multi-family building permits issued: 0 (2011); Employment by occupation: 30.8% management, 3.8% professional, 1.8% services, 8.3% sales, 1.3% farming, 0.0% construction, 0.0% production (2006-2010 5-year est.).
**Income:** Per capita income: $83,958 (2006-2010 5-year est.); Median household income: $195,833 (2006-2010 5-year est.); Average household income: $265,425 (2006-2010 5-year est.); Percent of households with income of $100,000 or more: 74.2% (2006-2010 5-year est.); Poverty rate: 2.4% (2006-2010 5-year est.).
**Education:** Percent of population age 25 and over with: High school diploma (including GED) or higher: 97.3% (2006-2010 5-year est.); Bachelor's degree or higher: 79.0% (2006-2010 5-year est.); Master's degree or higher: 42.0% (2006-2010 5-year est.).
**Housing:** Homeownership rate: 93.3% (2010); Median home value: $1 (2006-2010 5-year est.); Median contract rent: n/a per month (2006-2010 5-year est.); Median year structure built: 1956 (2006-2010 5-year est.).
**Transportation:** Commute to work: 72.0% car, 22.5% public transportation, 1.0% walk, 4.1% work from home (2006-2010 5-year est.); Travel time to work: 16.9% less than 15 minutes, 21.6% 15 to 30 minutes, 17.0% 30 to 45 minutes, 10.1% 45 to 60 minutes, 34.4% 60 minutes or more (2006-2010 5-year est.)
**Additional Information Contacts**

Village of Flower Hill . . . . . . . . . . . . . . . . . . . . . . . . . . . . (516) 627-5000
http://www.villageflowerhill.org

## FRANKLIN SQUARE (CDP).

Covers a land area of 2.877 square miles and a water area of 0 square miles. Located at 40.70° N. Lat; 73.67° W. Long. Elevation is 66 feet.

**Population:** 28,205 (1990); 29,342 (2000); 29,320 (2010); Density: 10,188.8 persons per square mile (2010); Race: 83.3% White, 3.2% Black, 7.2% Asian, 0.3% American Indian/Alaska Native, 0.0% Native Hawaiian/Other Pacific Islander, 6.0% Other, 13.3% Hispanic of any race (2010); Average household size: 2.92 (2010); Median age: 42.4 (2010); Males per 100 females: 91.1 (2010); Marriage status: 27.0% never married, 57.6% now married, 9.0% widowed, 6.3% divorced (2006-2010 5-year est.); Foreign born: 21.9% (2006-2010 5-year est.); Ancestry (includes multiple ancestries): 45.5% Italian, 15.9% Irish, 10.7% German, 4.3% Polish, 2.7% Greek (2006-2010 5-year est.).

**Economy:** Employment by occupation: 13.4% management, 2.6% professional, 9.0% services, 19.0% sales, 5.2% farming, 11.3% construction, 5.6% production (2006-2010 5-year est.).

**Income:** Per capita income: $32,569 (2006-2010 5-year est.); Median household income: $80,200 (2006-2010 5-year est.); Average household income: $93,680 (2006-2010 5-year est.); Percent of households with income of $100,000 or more: 38.0% (2006-2010 5-year est.); Poverty rate: 3.3% (2006-2010 5-year est.).

**Education:** Percent of population age 25 and over with: High school diploma (including GED) or higher: 85.3% (2006-2010 5-year est.); Bachelor's degree or higher: 28.5% (2006-2010 5-year est.); Master's degree or higher: 10.2% (2006-2010 5-year est.).

### School District(s)
Franklin Square Union Free School District (KG-06)
    2009-10 Enrollment: 1,958 . . . . . . . . . . . . . . . . . . (516) 505-6975
Sewanhaka Central High School District (07-12)
    2009-10 Enrollment: 8,449 . . . . . . . . . . . . . . . . . . (516) 488-9800
Valley Stream 13 Union Free School District (KG-06)
    2009-10 Enrollment: 2,156 . . . . . . . . . . . . . . . . . . (516) 568-6100
Valley Stream Central High School District (07-12)
    2009-10 Enrollment: 4,602 . . . . . . . . . . . . . . . . . . (516) 872-5601

**Housing:** Homeownership rate: 81.0% (2010); Median home value: $464,100 (2006-2010 5-year est.); Median contract rent: $1,103 per month (2006-2010 5-year est.); Median year structure built: 1952 (2006-2010 5-year est.).

**Transportation:** Commute to work: 83.6% car, 12.3% public transportation, 2.0% walk, 1.7% work from home (2006-2010 5-year est.); Travel time to work: 21.3% less than 15 minutes, 29.1% 15 to 30 minutes, 24.1% 30 to 45 minutes, 8.1% 45 to 60 minutes, 17.4% 60 minutes or more (2006-2010 5-year est.)

**Additional Information Contacts**
Franklin Square Chamber of Commerce . . . . . . . . . . . . (516) 775-0001

## FREEPORT (village).

Covers a land area of 4.628 square miles and a water area of 0.240 square miles. Located at 40.65° N. Lat; 73.58° W. Long. Elevation is 20 feet.

**History:** Named for its port, used in colonial days by cargo ships to avoid British taxes. Settled as a village c.1650. Incorporated 1892.

**Population:** 39,894 (1990); 43,783 (2000); 42,860 (2010); Density: 9,260.5 persons per square mile (2010); Race: 40.5% White, 33.3% Black, 1.6% Asian, 0.8% American Indian/Alaska Native, 0.1% Native Hawaiian/Other Pacific Islander, 23.7% Other, 41.7% Hispanic of any race (2010); Average household size: 3.18 (2010); Median age: 37.2 (2010); Males per 100 females: 94.9 (2010); Marriage status: 35.5% never married, 46.9% now married, 6.7% widowed, 10.8% divorced (2006-2010 5-year est.); Foreign born: 34.3% (2006-2010 5-year est.); Ancestry (includes multiple ancestries): 8.4% Italian, 7.3% Irish, 6.6% German, 4.3% Jamaican, 2.4% English (2006-2010 5-year est.).

**Economy:** Unemployment rate: 9.4% (February 2012); Total civilian labor force: 21,937 (February 2012); Single-family building permits issued: 1 (2011); Multi-family building permits issued: 2 (2011); Employment by occupation: 9.8% management, 2.2% professional, 12.6% services, 17.2% sales, 4.7% farming, 9.1% construction, 6.8% production (2006-2010 5-year est.).

**Income:** Per capita income: $29,930 (2006-2010 5-year est.); Median household income: $69,081 (2006-2010 5-year est.); Average household income: $86,662 (2006-2010 5-year est.); Percent of households with income of $100,000 or more: 32.6% (2006-2010 5-year est.); Poverty rate: 11.3% (2006-2010 5-year est.).

**Taxes:** Total city taxes per capita: $904 (2009); City property taxes per capita: $854 (2009).

**Education:** Percent of population age 25 and over with: High school diploma (including GED) or higher: 78.2% (2006-2010 5-year est.); Bachelor's degree or higher: 25.1% (2006-2010 5-year est.); Master's degree or higher: 10.7% (2006-2010 5-year est.).

### School District(s)
Freeport Union Free School District (PK-12)
    2009-10 Enrollment: 6,532 . . . . . . . . . . . . . . . . . . (516) 867-5205

**Housing:** Homeownership rate: 67.0% (2010); Median home value: $382,100 (2006-2010 5-year est.); Median contract rent: $1,111 per month (2006-2010 5-year est.); Median year structure built: 1952 (2006-2010 5-year est.).

**Safety:** Violent crime rate: 49.0 per 10,000 population; Property crime rate: 236.1 per 10,000 population (2010).

**Newspapers:** Freie Zeitung (Local news; Circulation 6,000); Mundo Hispano News (Regional news; Circulation 10,000)

**Transportation:** Commute to work: 75.2% car, 17.0% public transportation, 4.7% walk, 1.4% work from home (2006-2010 5-year est.); Travel time to work: 23.5% less than 15 minutes, 30.7% 15 to 30 minutes, 21.7% 30 to 45 minutes, 7.0% 45 to 60 minutes, 17.1% 60 minutes or more (2006-2010 5-year est.)

**Additional Information Contacts**
Village of Freeport . . . . . . . . . . . . . . . . . . . . . . . . . . (516) 377-2300
http://www.freeportny.com

## GARDEN CITY (village).

Covers a land area of 5.330 square miles and a water area of 0.024 square miles. Located at 40.72° N. Lat; 73.64° W. Long. Elevation is 89 feet.

**History:** Named to promote the city as a beautiful place. Was founded in 1869 and planned by the merchant Alexander Stewart. In 1927, Charles Lindbergh began his historic transatlantic flight from nearby Roosevelt Field. Adelphi University is here. Incorporated 1919.

**Population:** 21,674 (1990); 21,672 (2000); 22,371 (2010); Density: 4,197.2 persons per square mile (2010); Race: 93.0% White, 1.4% Black, 3.6% Asian, 0.1% American Indian/Alaska Native, 0.0% Native Hawaiian/Other Pacific Islander, 1.9% Other, 4.5% Hispanic of any race (2010); Average household size: 2.87 (2010); Median age: 42.2 (2010); Males per 100 females: 90.1 (2010); Marriage status: 28.0% never married, 62.1% now married, 6.8% widowed, 3.1% divorced (2006-2010 5-year est.); Foreign born: 8.3% (2006-2010 5-year est.); Ancestry (includes multiple ancestries): 36.5% Irish, 29.2% Italian, 14.9% German, 7.5% English, 5.4% Polish (2006-2010 5-year est.).

**Economy:** Single-family building permits issued: 2 (2011); Multi-family building permits issued: 0 (2011); Employment by occupation: 24.1% management, 3.2% professional, 6.1% services, 16.0% sales, 2.9% farming, 1.7% construction, 1.0% production (2006-2010 5-year est.).

**Income:** Per capita income: $65,147 (2006-2010 5-year est.); Median household income: $139,956 (2006-2010 5-year est.); Average household income: $202,963 (2006-2010 5-year est.); Percent of households with income of $100,000 or more: 62.9% (2006-2010 5-year est.); Poverty rate: 3.6% (2006-2010 5-year est.).

**Education:** Percent of population age 25 and over with: High school diploma (including GED) or higher: 97.5% (2006-2010 5-year est.); Bachelor's degree or higher: 66.2% (2006-2010 5-year est.); Master's degree or higher: 33.0% (2006-2010 5-year est.).

### School District(s)
Garden City Union Free School District (KG-12)
    2009-10 Enrollment: 4,175 . . . . . . . . . . . . . . . . . . (516) 478-1010
Nassau Boces
    2009-10 Enrollment: n/a . . . . . . . . . . . . . . . . . . . . (516) 396-2200

### Four-year College(s)
Adelphi University (Private, Not-for-profit)
    Fall 2010 Enrollment: 7,333 . . . . . . . . . . . . . . . . . . (516) 877-3000
    2011-12 Tuition: In-state $28,460; Out-of-state $28,460

### Two-year College(s)
Nassau Community College (Public)
    Fall 2010 Enrollment: 19,296 . . . . . . . . . . . . . . . . . (516) 572-7501
    2011-12 Tuition: In-state $4,495; Out-of-state $8,485
Sanford-Brown Institute-Garden City (Private, For-profit)
    Fall 2010 Enrollment: 1,411 . . . . . . . . . . . . . . . . . . (516) 247-2900

### Vocational/Technical School(s)
Career Institute of Health & Technology (Private, For-profit)
    Fall 2010 Enrollment: 913 . . . . . . . . . . . . . . . . . . . (516) 877-1225
    2011-12 Tuition: $19,120

**Housing:** Homeownership rate: 93.9% (2010); Median home value: $835,400 (2006-2010 5-year est.); Median contract rent: $1,696 per month (2006-2010 5-year est.); Median year structure built: 1950 (2006-2010 5-year est.).

**Safety:** Violent crime rate: 4.0 per 10,000 population; Property crime rate: 158.6 per 10,000 population (2010).

**Newspapers:** Garden City News (Community news; Circulation 8,130); Jewish Star (Regional news; Circulation 7,500); Merrick Herald (Community news); New York Daily News - Long Island Bureau (Local news)

**Transportation:** Commute to work: 68.8% car, 23.1% public transportation, 3.2% walk, 4.6% work from home (2006-2010 5-year est.); Travel time to work: 28.0% less than 15 minutes, 19.8% 15 to 30 minutes, 14.3% 30 to 45 minutes, 10.1% 45 to 60 minutes, 27.7% 60 minutes or more (2006-2010 5-year est.)

**Additional Information Contacts**

Garden City Chamber of Commerce . . . . . . . . . . . . . . . . . (516) 746-7724
   http://www.gardencitychamber.org
Village of Garden City . . . . . . . . . . . . . . . . . . . . . . . . (516) 465-4000
   http://www.gardencityny.net

## GARDEN CITY PARK (CDP). Covers a land area of 0.984 square miles and a water area of 0.006 square miles. Located at 40.74° N. Lat; 73.66° W. Long. Elevation is 105 feet.

**Population:** 7,437 (1990); 7,554 (2000); 7,806 (2010); Density: 7,929.3 persons per square mile (2010); Race: 56.4% White, 3.8% Black, 33.1% Asian, 0.3% American Indian/Alaska Native, 0.0% Native Hawaiian/Other Pacific Islander, 6.4% Other, 12.1% Hispanic of any race (2010); Average household size: 3.08 (2010); Median age: 43.2 (2010); Males per 100 females: 93.8 (2010); Marriage status: 27.0% never married, 58.6% now married, 9.3% widowed, 5.2% divorced (2006-2010 5-year est.); Foreign born: 34.4% (2006-2010 5-year est.); Ancestry (includes multiple ancestries): 16.1% Italian, 11.0% Irish, 9.6% German, 5.7% Polish, 3.7% Greek (2006-2010 5-year est.).

**Economy:** Employment by occupation: 15.4% management, 8.2% professional, 4.8% services, 19.4% sales, 4.8% farming, 7.3% construction, 5.1% production (2006-2010 5-year est.).

**Income:** Per capita income: $39,232 (2006-2010 5-year est.); Median household income: $99,583 (2006-2010 5-year est.); Average household income: $119,086 (2006-2010 5-year est.); Percent of households with income of $100,000 or more: 49.7% (2006-2010 5-year est.); Poverty rate: 3.3% (2006-2010 5-year est.).

**Education:** Percent of population age 25 and over with: High school diploma (including GED) or higher: 93.0% (2006-2010 5-year est.); Bachelor's degree or higher: 42.5% (2006-2010 5-year est.); Master's degree or higher: 18.2% (2006-2010 5-year est.).

### School District(s)

Mineola Union Free School District (PK-12)
   2009-10 Enrollment: 2,716 . . . . . . . . . . . . . . . . . (516) 237-2001
New Hyde Park-Garden City Park Union Free School D (KG-06)
   2009-10 Enrollment: 1,621 . . . . . . . . . . . . . . . . . (516) 352-6257

**Housing:** Homeownership rate: 81.8% (2010); Median home value: $566,300 (2006-2010 5-year est.); Median contract rent: $868 per month (2006-2010 5-year est.); Median year structure built: 1953 (2006-2010 5-year est.).

**Newspapers:** The New York Times - Long Island Bureau (Regional news)

**Transportation:** Commute to work: 72.6% car, 22.5% public transportation, 1.5% walk, 2.9% work from home (2006-2010 5-year est.); Travel time to work: 18.2% less than 15 minutes, 27.6% 15 to 30 minutes, 17.0% 30 to 45 minutes, 10.0% 45 to 60 minutes, 27.2% 60 minutes or more (2006-2010 5-year est.)

## GARDEN CITY SOUTH (CDP). Covers a land area of 0.404 square miles and a water area of 0 square miles. Located at 40.71° N. Lat; 73.66° W. Long. Elevation is 69 feet.

**Population:** 4,073 (1990); 3,974 (2000); 4,024 (2010); Density: 9,954.3 persons per square mile (2010); Race: 89.6% White, 1.0% Black, 5.7% Asian, 0.2% American Indian/Alaska Native, 0.2% Native Hawaiian/Other Pacific Islander, 3.3% Other, 7.9% Hispanic of any race (2010); Average household size: 2.90 (2010); Median age: 41.9 (2010); Males per 100 females: 91.1 (2010); Marriage status: 22.0% never married, 56.9% now married, 12.1% widowed, 9.0% divorced (2006-2010 5-year est.); Foreign born: 9.5% (2006-2010 5-year est.); Ancestry (includes multiple ancestries): 39.9% Italian, 27.1% Irish, 15.8% German, 4.1% American, 3.0% European (2006-2010 5-year est.).

**Economy:** Employment by occupation: 14.9% management, 3.7% professional, 8.7% services, 15.5% sales, 3.8% farming, 9.9% construction, 6.3% production (2006-2010 5-year est.).

**Income:** Per capita income: $38,777 (2006-2010 5-year est.); Median household income: $92,076 (2006-2010 5-year est.); Average household income: $109,052 (2006-2010 5-year est.); Percent of households with income of $100,000 or more: 46.3% (2006-2010 5-year est.); Poverty rate: 1.3% (2006-2010 5-year est.).

**Education:** Percent of population age 25 and over with: High school diploma (including GED) or higher: 92.1% (2006-2010 5-year est.); Bachelor's degree or higher: 39.5% (2006-2010 5-year est.); Master's degree or higher: 19.0% (2006-2010 5-year est.).

**Housing:** Homeownership rate: 86.3% (2010); Median home value: $477,700 (2006-2010 5-year est.); Median contract rent: $1,294 per month (2006-2010 5-year est.); Median year structure built: 1948 (2006-2010 5-year est.).

**Transportation:** Commute to work: 87.1% car, 9.2% public transportation, 0.9% walk, 2.8% work from home (2006-2010 5-year est.); Travel time to work: 24.1% less than 15 minutes, 31.3% 15 to 30 minutes, 20.0% 30 to 45 minutes, 6.6% 45 to 60 minutes, 18.1% 60 minutes or more (2006-2010 5-year est.)

## GLEN COVE (city). Covers a land area of 6.654 square miles and a water area of 12.589 square miles. Located at 40.88° N. Lat; 73.64° W. Long. Elevation is 23 feet.

**History:** Settled 1668, attracted affluent class after Civil War. In 1920s it became core of the Gold Coast as mansions were built, including waterfront community on East Island at north end (once known as Morgans Island when owned by J.P. Morgan). In 19th century it attracted industry, including one of the world's largest starch factories. Incorporated as a city 1918.

**Population:** 24,149 (1990); 26,622 (2000); 26,964 (2010); Density: 4,051.7 persons per square mile (2010); Race: 74.2% White, 7.2% Black, 4.6% Asian, 0.4% American Indian/Alaska Native, 0.1% Native Hawaiian/Other Pacific Islander, 13.5% Other, 27.9% Hispanic of any race (2010); Average household size: 2.69 (2010); Median age: 40.6 (2010); Males per 100 females: 94.9 (2010); Marriage status: 35.4% never married, 48.5% now married, 7.9% widowed, 8.2% divorced (2006-2010 5-year est.); Foreign born: 26.9% (2006-2010 5-year est.); Ancestry (includes multiple ancestries): 24.2% Italian, 15.7% Irish, 8.7% German, 6.1% Polish, 5.0% English (2006-2010 5-year est.).

**Economy:** Unemployment rate: 9.1% (February 2012); Total civilian labor force: 13,315 (February 2012); Single-family building permits issued: 2 (2011); Multi-family building permits issued: 0 (2011); Employment by occupation: 12.6% management, 2.3% professional, 11.3% services, 16.5% sales, 3.4% farming, 7.3% construction, 4.4% production (2006-2010 5-year est.).

**Income:** Per capita income: $36,233 (2006-2010 5-year est.); Median household income: $73,624 (2006-2010 5-year est.); Average household income: $99,204 (2006-2010 5-year est.); Percent of households with income of $100,000 or more: 36.6% (2006-2010 5-year est.); Poverty rate: 13.1% (2006-2010 5-year est.).

**Taxes:** Total city taxes per capita: $1,018 (2009); City property taxes per capita: $937 (2009).

**Education:** Percent of population age 25 and over with: High school diploma (including GED) or higher: 84.7% (2006-2010 5-year est.); Bachelor's degree or higher: 38.2% (2006-2010 5-year est.); Master's degree or higher: 16.1% (2006-2010 5-year est.).

### School District(s)

Glen Cove City School District (PK-12)
   2009-10 Enrollment: 3,039 . . . . . . . . . . . . . . . . . (516) 801-7010

### Four-year College(s)

Webb Institute (Private, Not-for-profit)
   Fall 2010 Enrollment: 94 . . . . . . . . . . . . . . . . . (516) 671-2213

**Housing:** Homeownership rate: 56.1% (2010); Median home value: $560,900 (2006-2010 5-year est.); Median contract rent: $1,320 per month (2006-2010 5-year est.); Median year structure built: 1955 (2006-2010 5-year est.).

**Hospitals:** Glen Cove Hospital (265 beds)

**Safety:** Violent crime rate: 8.6 per 10,000 population; Property crime rate: 85.1 per 10,000 population (2010).

**Newspapers:** Gold Coast Gazette (Community news; Circulation 4,000)

**Transportation:** Commute to work: 79.2% car, 7.2% public transportation, 7.7% walk, 4.9% work from home (2006-2010 5-year est.); Travel time to work: 43.1% less than 15 minutes, 21.0% 15 to 30 minutes, 18.2% 30 to 45

minutes, 5.7% 45 to 60 minutes, 11.9% 60 minutes or more (2006-2010 5-year est.)
**Additional Information Contacts**
City of Glen Cove . . . . . . . . . . . . . . . . . . . . . . . . . . (516) 676-3345
  http://www.glencove-li.com
Glen Cove Chamber of Commerce . . . . . . . . . . . . (516) 676-6666
  http://www.glencovechamber.org

**GLEN HEAD** (CDP). Covers a land area of 1.638 square miles and a water area of 0 square miles. Located at 40.84° N. Lat; 73.61° W. Long. Elevation is 115 feet.
**Population:** 4,488 (1990); 4,625 (2000); 4,697 (2010); Density: 2,866.3 persons per square mile (2010); Race: 91.8% White, 0.9% Black, 3.4% Asian, 0.1% American Indian/Alaska Native, 0.0% Native Hawaiian/Other Pacific Islander, 3.8% Other, 8.1% Hispanic of any race (2010); Average household size: 2.72 (2010); Median age: 44.6 (2010); Males per 100 females: 92.1 (2010); Marriage status: 23.6% never married, 61.1% now married, 6.7% widowed, 8.6% divorced (2006-2010 5-year est.); Foreign born: 14.6% (2006-2010 5-year est.); Ancestry (includes multiple ancestries): 33.8% Italian, 19.6% Irish, 15.1% German, 7.3% Polish, 5.6% English (2006-2010 5-year est.).
**Economy:** Employment by occupation: 19.9% management, 1.0% professional, 7.7% services, 18.4% sales, 3.4% farming, 5.7% construction, 1.8% production (2006-2010 5-year est.).
**Income:** Per capita income: $50,669 (2006-2010 5-year est.); Median household income: $106,985 (2006-2010 5-year est.); Average household income: $142,133 (2006-2010 5-year est.); Percent of households with income of $100,000 or more: 52.8% (2006-2010 5-year est.); Poverty rate: 4.1% (2006-2010 5-year est.).
**Education:** Percent of population age 25 and over with: High school diploma (including GED) or higher: 94.5% (2006-2010 5-year est.); Bachelor's degree or higher: 50.4% (2006-2010 5-year est.); Master's degree or higher: 24.1% (2006-2010 5-year est.).
**School District(s)**
North Shore Central School District (KG-12)
  2009-10 Enrollment: 2,866 . . . . . . . . . . . . . . . . . (516) 277-7801
**Housing:** Homeownership rate: 86.2% (2010); Median home value: $659,700 (2006-2010 5-year est.); Median contract rent: $1,398 per month (2006-2010 5-year est.); Median year structure built: 1954 (2006-2010 5-year est.).
**Transportation:** Commute to work: 73.3% car, 14.1% public transportation, 2.1% walk, 4.0% work from home (2006-2010 5-year est.); Travel time to work: 20.8% less than 15 minutes, 30.8% 15 to 30 minutes, 15.1% 30 to 45 minutes, 12.5% 45 to 60 minutes, 20.8% 60 minutes or more (2006-2010 5-year est.)

**GLENWOOD LANDING** (CDP). Covers a land area of 0.971 square miles and a water area of 0 square miles. Located at 40.82° N. Lat; 73.63° W. Long. Elevation is 98 feet.
**Population:** 3,407 (1990); 3,541 (2000); 3,779 (2010); Density: 3,889.5 persons per square mile (2010); Race: 92.9% White, 0.8% Black, 3.7% Asian, 0.1% American Indian/Alaska Native, 0.0% Native Hawaiian/Other Pacific Islander, 2.5% Other, 6.1% Hispanic of any race (2010); Average household size: 2.83 (2010); Median age: 44.2 (2010); Males per 100 females: 89.1 (2010); Marriage status: 20.3% never married, 72.9% now married, 3.6% widowed, 3.2% divorced (2006-2010 5-year est.); Foreign born: 10.9% (2006-2010 5-year est.); Ancestry (includes multiple ancestries): 33.4% Irish, 25.9% Italian, 18.8% German, 7.3% Polish, 5.8% American (2006-2010 5-year est.).
**Economy:** Employment by occupation: 18.9% management, 5.8% professional, 5.5% services, 14.8% sales, 2.2% farming, 5.2% construction, 1.9% production (2006-2010 5-year est.).
**Income:** Per capita income: $45,652 (2006-2010 5-year est.); Median household income: $103,864 (2006-2010 5-year est.); Average household income: $126,739 (2006-2010 5-year est.); Percent of households with income of $100,000 or more: 52.6% (2006-2010 5-year est.); Poverty rate: 5.3% (2006-2010 5-year est.).
**Education:** Percent of population age 25 and over with: High school diploma (including GED) or higher: 94.2% (2006-2010 5-year est.); Bachelor's degree or higher: 54.1% (2006-2010 5-year est.); Master's degree or higher: 21.2% (2006-2010 5-year est.).
**Housing:** Homeownership rate: 88.4% (2010); Median home value: $653,800 (2006-2010 5-year est.); Median contract rent: $1,239 per month (2006-2010 5-year est.); Median year structure built: 1953 (2006-2010 5-year est.).

**Transportation:** Commute to work: 80.9% car, 10.1% public transportation, 2.1% walk, 6.3% work from home (2006-2010 5-year est.); Travel time to work: 20.3% less than 15 minutes, 40.2% 15 to 30 minutes, 17.8% 30 to 45 minutes, 3.5% 45 to 60 minutes, 18.2% 60 minutes or more (2006-2010 5-year est.)

**GREAT NECK** (village). Aka Great Neck Plaza. Covers a land area of 1.328 square miles and a water area of 0.027 square miles. Located at 40.80° N. Lat; 73.73° W. Long. Elevation is 108 feet.
**History:** Great Neck, originally called "Madnan's Neck", was settled in the late 17th century, not long after settlers landed on Plymouth Rock. The area had previously been inhabited by the Mattinecock Native Americans.
**Population:** 8,806 (1990); 9,538 (2000); 9,989 (2010); Density: 7,516.4 persons per square mile (2010); Race: 82.8% White, 2.0% Black, 7.2% Asian, 0.2% American Indian/Alaska Native, 0.0% Native Hawaiian/Other Pacific Islander, 7.8% Other, 10.2% Hispanic of any race (2010); Average household size: 2.87 (2010); Median age: 41.2 (2010); Males per 100 females: 96.5 (2010); Marriage status: 25.6% never married, 59.5% now married, 9.0% widowed, 5.9% divorced (2006-2010 5-year est.); Foreign born: 33.8% (2006-2010 5-year est.); Ancestry (includes multiple ancestries): 24.2% Iranian, 13.9% Russian, 12.1% Polish, 5.2% Italian, 4.9% American (2006-2010 5-year est.).
**Economy:** Single-family building permits issued: 5 (2011); Multi-family building permits issued: 0 (2011); Employment by occupation: 20.2% management, 1.9% professional, 4.3% services, 15.6% sales, 2.7% farming, 2.8% construction, 1.4% production (2006-2010 5-year est.).
**Income:** Per capita income: $43,080 (2006-2010 5-year est.); Median household income: $78,736 (2006-2010 5-year est.); Average household income: $114,664 (2006-2010 5-year est.); Percent of households with income of $100,000 or more: 39.3% (2006-2010 5-year est.); Poverty rate: 5.7% (2006-2010 5-year est.).
**Education:** Percent of population age 25 and over with: High school diploma (including GED) or higher: 90.8% (2006-2010 5-year est.); Bachelor's degree or higher: 55.4% (2006-2010 5-year est.); Master's degree or higher: 28.7% (2006-2010 5-year est.).
**School District(s)**
Great Neck Union Free School District (PK-12)
  2009-10 Enrollment: 6,526 . . . . . . . . . . . . . . . . . (516) 441-4001
**Housing:** Homeownership rate: 71.4% (2010); Median home value: $768,000 (2006-2010 5-year est.); Median contract rent: $1,185 per month (2006-2010 5-year est.); Median year structure built: 1949 (2006-2010 5-year est.).
**Newspapers:** Jewish Sentinel (Local news; Circulation 40,000); Jewish Tribune (Local news; Circulation 10,000); Long Island Jewish World (Regional news; Circulation 26,000)
**Transportation:** Commute to work: 61.6% car, 23.6% public transportation, 6.7% walk, 6.5% work from home (2006-2010 5-year est.); Travel time to work: 27.3% less than 15 minutes, 12.8% 15 to 30 minutes, 22.6% 30 to 45 minutes, 15.9% 45 to 60 minutes, 21.3% 60 minutes or more (2006-2010 5-year est.)
**Additional Information Contacts**
Great Neck Chamber of Commerce . . . . . . . . . . . . (516) 487-2000
  http://www.greatneckchamber.org
Village of Great Neck . . . . . . . . . . . . . . . . . . . . . . (516) 482-0019
  http://www.greatneckvillage.org

**GREAT NECK ESTATES** (village). Covers a land area of 0.756 square miles and a water area of 0.044 square miles. Located at 40.78° N. Lat; 73.74° W. Long. Elevation is 82 feet.
**History:** Incorporated 1911.
**Population:** 2,652 (1990); 2,756 (2000); 2,761 (2010); Density: 3,648.4 persons per square mile (2010); Race: 86.4% White, 0.8% Black, 10.2% Asian, 0.1% American Indian/Alaska Native, 0.0% Native Hawaiian/Other Pacific Islander, 2.5% Other, 2.9% Hispanic of any race (2010); Average household size: 3.06 (2010); Median age: 45.8 (2010); Males per 100 females: 90.4 (2010); Marriage status: 18.7% never married, 70.5% now married, 7.9% widowed, 2.9% divorced (2006-2010 5-year est.); Foreign born: 32.0% (2006-2010 5-year est.); Ancestry (includes multiple ancestries): 20.7% Iranian, 17.4% Russian, 11.4% Polish, 6.6% American, 5.7% Eastern European (2006-2010 5-year est.).
**Economy:** Single-family building permits issued: 3 (2011); Multi-family building permits issued: 0 (2011); Employment by occupation: 17.2% management, 2.5% professional, 4.0% services, 9.3% sales, 0.6% farming, 1.9% construction, 0.6% production (2006-2010 5-year est.).

**Income:** Per capita income: $82,238 (2006-2010 5-year est.); Median household income: $135,104 (2006-2010 5-year est.); Average household income: $227,260 (2006-2010 5-year est.); Percent of households with income of $100,000 or more: 63.4% (2006-2010 5-year est.); Poverty rate: 2.0% (2006-2010 5-year est.).
**Education:** Percent of population age 25 and over with: High school diploma (including GED) or higher: 95.4% (2006-2010 5-year est.); Bachelor's degree or higher: 75.8% (2006-2010 5-year est.); Master's degree or higher: 46.1% (2006-2010 5-year est.).
**Housing:** Homeownership rate: 93.1% (2010); Median home value: $1 (2006-2010 5-year est.); Median contract rent: $1,912 per month (2006-2010 5-year est.); Median year structure built: before 1940 (2006-2010 5-year est.).
**Safety:** Violent crime rate: 0.0 per 10,000 population; Property crime rate: 18.1 per 10,000 population (2010).
**Transportation:** Commute to work: 65.2% car, 18.7% public transportation, 1.4% walk, 14.7% work from home (2006-2010 5-year est.); Travel time to work: 23.9% less than 15 minutes, 16.6% 15 to 30 minutes, 20.3% 30 to 45 minutes, 11.3% 45 to 60 minutes, 27.9% 60 minutes or more (2006-2010 5-year est.).

**GREAT NECK GARDENS** (CDP). Covers a land area of 0.170 square miles and a water area of 0 square miles. Located at 40.79° N. Lat; 73.72° W. Long. Elevation is 184 feet.
**Population:** 1,004 (1990); 1,089 (2000); 1,186 (2010); Density: 6,949.7 persons per square mile (2010); Race: 83.1% White, 0.8% Black, 12.1% Asian, 0.1% American Indian/Alaska Native, 0.0% Native Hawaiian/Other Pacific Islander, 3.9% Other, 1.7% Hispanic of any race (2010); Average household size: 3.02 (2010); Median age: 44.4 (2010); Males per 100 females: 99.7 (2010); Marriage status: 15.9% never married, 75.6% now married, 6.6% widowed, 1.9% divorced (2006-2010 5-year est.); Foreign born: 23.3% (2006-2010 5-year est.); Ancestry (includes multiple ancestries): 28.4% Russian, 11.9% Polish, 11.7% Eastern European, 7.0% Austrian, 6.4% Hungarian (2006-2010 5-year est.).
**Economy:** Employment by occupation: 6.2% management, 8.8% professional, 0.0% services, 7.4% sales, 0.0% farming, 0.0% construction, 0.0% production (2006-2010 5-year est.).
**Income:** Per capita income: $72,469 (2006-2010 5-year est.); Median household income: $126,053 (2006-2010 5-year est.); Average household income: $194,336 (2006-2010 5-year est.); Percent of households with income of $100,000 or more: 64.1% (2006-2010 5-year est.); Poverty rate: 2.8% (2006-2010 5-year est.).
**Education:** Percent of population age 25 and over with: High school diploma (including GED) or higher: 100.0% (2006-2010 5-year est.); Bachelor's degree or higher: 88.0% (2006-2010 5-year est.); Master's degree or higher: 68.1% (2006-2010 5-year est.).
**Housing:** Homeownership rate: 95.2% (2010); Median home value: $879,100 (2006-2010 5-year est.); Median contract rent: n/a per month (2006-2010 5-year est.); Median year structure built: 1945 (2006-2010 5-year est.).
**Transportation:** Commute to work: 61.1% car, 31.8% public transportation, 0.0% walk, 7.1% work from home (2006-2010 5-year est.); Travel time to work: 12.5% less than 15 minutes, 32.6% 15 to 30 minutes, 5.1% 30 to 45 minutes, 19.2% 45 to 60 minutes, 30.7% 60 minutes or more (2006-2010 5-year est.)

**GREAT NECK PLAZA** (village). Aka Great Neck. Covers a land area of 0.312 square miles and a water area of 0 square miles. Located at 40.78° N. Lat; 73.72° W. Long. Elevation is 92 feet.
**Population:** 6,053 (1990); 6,433 (2000); 6,707 (2010); Density: 21,485.0 persons per square mile (2010); Race: 82.2% White, 1.5% Black, 11.6% Asian, 0.0% American Indian/Alaska Native, 0.1% Native Hawaiian/Other Pacific Islander, 4.6% Other, 7.8% Hispanic of any race (2010); Average household size: 1.77 (2010); Median age: 48.7 (2010); Males per 100 females: 75.4 (2010); Marriage status: 20.8% never married, 52.0% now married, 15.0% widowed, 12.2% divorced (2006-2010 5-year est.); Foreign born: 27.4% (2006-2010 5-year est.); Ancestry (includes multiple ancestries): 15.6% Russian, 13.7% Polish, 10.2% Iranian, 6.5% Hungarian, 5.8% Italian (2006-2010 5-year est.).
**Economy:** Single-family building permits issued: 0 (2011); Multi-family building permits issued: 93 (2011); Employment by occupation: 16.6% management, 2.7% professional, 4.3% services, 15.3% sales, 4.2% farming, 3.8% construction, 1.7% production (2006-2010 5-year est.).
**Income:** Per capita income: $55,359 (2006-2010 5-year est.); Median household income: $58,472 (2006-2010 5-year est.); Average household

income: $97,420 (2006-2010 5-year est.); Percent of households with income of $100,000 or more: 34.9% (2006-2010 5-year est.); Poverty rate: 7.4% (2006-2010 5-year est.).
**Education:** Percent of population age 25 and over with: High school diploma (including GED) or higher: 95.1% (2006-2010 5-year est.); Bachelor's degree or higher: 57.8% (2006-2010 5-year est.); Master's degree or higher: 26.3% (2006-2010 5-year est.).
**Housing:** Homeownership rate: 55.0% (2010); Median home value: $380,300 (2006-2010 5-year est.); Median contract rent: $1,523 per month (2006-2010 5-year est.); Median year structure built: 1958 (2006-2010 5-year est.).
**Transportation:** Commute to work: 58.0% car, 27.4% public transportation, 7.1% walk, 6.2% work from home (2006-2010 5-year est.); Travel time to work: 20.2% less than 15 minutes, 29.1% 15 to 30 minutes, 22.4% 30 to 45 minutes, 12.6% 45 to 60 minutes, 15.7% 60 minutes or more (2006-2010 5-year est.).
**Additional Information Contacts**
Village of Great Neck Plaza . . . . . . . . . . . . . . . . . . . . . . . . (516) 482-4500
  http://www.greatneckplaza.net

**GREENVALE** (CDP). Aka North Roslyn. Covers a land area of 0.252 square miles and a water area of 0 square miles. Located at 40.81° N. Lat; 73.62° W. Long. Elevation is 187 feet.
**History:** C.W. Post campus of Long Island University.
**Population:** 965 (1990); 2,231 (2000); 1,094 (2010); Density: 4,338.6 persons per square mile (2010); Race: 69.7% White, 1.9% Black, 18.8% Asian, 0.3% American Indian/Alaska Native, 0.0% Native Hawaiian/Other Pacific Islander, 9.3% Other, 13.6% Hispanic of any race (2010); Average household size: 3.06 (2010); Median age: 41.1 (2010); Males per 100 females: 100.0 (2010); Marriage status: 18.4% never married, 63.1% now married, 12.9% widowed, 5.6% divorced (2006-2010 5-year est.); Foreign born: 22.5% (2006-2010 5-year est.); Ancestry (includes multiple ancestries): 14.5% Italian, 14.3% Polish, 13.8% Irish, 11.8% Russian, 7.3% Eastern European (2006-2010 5-year est.).
**Economy:** Employment by occupation: 22.1% management, 13.9% professional, 5.3% services, 8.7% sales, 0.0% farming, 6.7% construction, 0.0% production (2006-2010 5-year est.).
**Income:** Per capita income: $66,304 (2006-2010 5-year est.); Median household income: $154,500 (2006-2010 5-year est.); Average household income: $162,353 (2006-2010 5-year est.); Percent of households with income of $100,000 or more: 62.6% (2006-2010 5-year est.); Poverty rate: 0.0% (2006-2010 5-year est.).
**Education:** Percent of population age 25 and over with: High school diploma (including GED) or higher: 97.1% (2006-2010 5-year est.); Bachelor's degree or higher: 67.2% (2006-2010 5-year est.); Master's degree or higher: 31.2% (2006-2010 5-year est.).
**School District(s)**
Roslyn Union Free School District (PK-12)
    2009-10 Enrollment: 3,403 . . . . . . . . . . . . . . . . . . . . . . (516) 801-5001
**Housing:** Homeownership rate: 75.5% (2010); Median home value: $760,200 (2006-2010 5-year est.); Median contract rent: $1,583 per month (2006-2010 5-year est.); Median year structure built: 1953 (2006-2010 5-year est.).
**Transportation:** Commute to work: 70.2% car, 22.6% public transportation, 0.0% walk, 1.9% work from home (2006-2010 5-year est.); Travel time to work: 16.2% less than 15 minutes, 33.8% 15 to 30 minutes, 1.5% 30 to 45 minutes, 24.0% 45 to 60 minutes, 24.5% 60 minutes or more (2006-2010 5-year est.)

**HARBOR HILLS** (CDP). Covers a land area of 0.118 square miles and a water area of 0.059 square miles. Located at 40.78° N. Lat; 73.74° W. Long. Elevation is 72 feet.
**Population:** 568 (1990); 563 (2000); 575 (2010); Density: 4,857.1 persons per square mile (2010); Race: 93.6% White, 0.3% Black, 5.2% Asian, 0.0% American Indian/Alaska Native, 0.0% Native Hawaiian/Other Pacific Islander, 0.9% Other, 1.9% Hispanic of any race (2010); Average household size: 3.19 (2010); Median age: 40.7 (2010); Males per 100 females: 89.1 (2010); Marriage status: 31.6% never married, 50.6% now married, 9.0% widowed, 8.8% divorced (2006-2010 5-year est.); Foreign born: 27.1% (2006-2010 5-year est.); Ancestry (includes multiple ancestries): 19.0% Greek, 13.5% Armenian, 11.9% Russian, 10.1% Austrian, 8.9% Eastern European (2006-2010 5-year est.).
**Economy:** Employment by occupation: 40.1% management, 0.0% professional, 0.0% services, 26.2% sales, 5.9% farming, 5.4% construction, 0.0% production (2006-2010 5-year est.).

**Income:** Per capita income: $77,707 (2006-2010 5-year est.); Median household income: $154,167 (2006-2010 5-year est.); Average household income: $246,806 (2006-2010 5-year est.); Percent of households with income of $100,000 or more: 87.4% (2006-2010 5-year est.); Poverty rate: 0.0% (2006-2010 5-year est.).

**Education:** Percent of population age 25 and over with: High school diploma (including GED) or higher: 96.2% (2006-2010 5-year est.); Bachelor's degree or higher: 82.1% (2006-2010 5-year est.); Master's degree or higher: 45.0% (2006-2010 5-year est.).

**Housing:** Homeownership rate: 95.0% (2010); Median home value: $1 (2006-2010 5-year est.); Median contract rent: n/a per month (2006-2010 5-year est.); Median year structure built: 1948 (2006-2010 5-year est.).

**Transportation:** Commute to work: 81.3% car, 18.7% public transportation, 0.0% walk, 0.0% work from home (2006-2010 5-year est.); Travel time to work: 0.0% less than 15 minutes, 21.1% 15 to 30 minutes, 33.9% 30 to 45 minutes, 21.1% 45 to 60 minutes, 24.0% 60 minutes or more (2006-2010 5-year est.)

**HARBOR ISLE** (CDP). Covers a land area of 0.173 square miles and a water area of 0.055 square miles. Located at 40.60° N. Lat; 73.66° W. Long.

**Population:** 1,373 (1990); 1,334 (2000); 1,301 (2010); Density: 7,517.1 persons per square mile (2010); Race: 94.8% White, 0.8% Black, 1.8% Asian, 0.0% American Indian/Alaska Native, 0.0% Native Hawaiian/Other Pacific Islander, 2.6% Other, 5.9% Hispanic of any race (2010); Average household size: 2.77 (2010); Median age: 47.0 (2010); Males per 100 females: 96.5 (2010); Marriage status: 20.6% never married, 69.6% now married, 5.5% widowed, 4.3% divorced (2006-2010 5-year est.); Foreign born: 3.1% (2006-2010 5-year est.); Ancestry (includes multiple ancestries): 31.2% Italian, 24.1% Irish, 8.8% German, 8.6% Russian, 5.3% Polish (2006-2010 5-year est.).

**Economy:** Employment by occupation: 9.9% management, 0.0% professional, 1.3% services, 26.5% sales, 7.2% farming, 8.5% construction, 2.4% production (2006-2010 5-year est.).

**Income:** Per capita income: $48,216 (2006-2010 5-year est.); Median household income: $135,341 (2006-2010 5-year est.); Average household income: $133,139 (2006-2010 5-year est.); Percent of households with income of $100,000 or more: 58.9% (2006-2010 5-year est.); Poverty rate: 5.2% (2006-2010 5-year est.).

**Education:** Percent of population age 25 and over with: High school diploma (including GED) or higher: 97.9% (2006-2010 5-year est.); Bachelor's degree or higher: 43.3% (2006-2010 5-year est.); Master's degree or higher: 17.8% (2006-2010 5-year est.).

**Housing:** Homeownership rate: 96.0% (2010); Median home value: $511,100 (2006-2010 5-year est.); Median contract rent: n/a per month (2006-2010 5-year est.); Median year structure built: 1956 (2006-2010 5-year est.).

**Transportation:** Commute to work: 72.8% car, 15.1% public transportation, 0.0% walk, 12.1% work from home (2006-2010 5-year est.); Travel time to work: 8.6% less than 15 minutes, 12.1% 15 to 30 minutes, 37.7% 30 to 45 minutes, 10.8% 45 to 60 minutes, 30.8% 60 minutes or more (2006-2010 5-year est.)

**HEMPSTEAD** (village). Covers a land area of 3.682 square miles and a water area of 0.004 square miles. Located at 40.70° N. Lat; 73.61° W. Long. Elevation is 56 feet.

**History:** The town grew significantly in the 1970s with the construction of nearby freeways, large retail outlets and the expansion of regional suburban industries. Settled in 1644 by English colonists who named it for their old home in England, Hemel-Hempstead. Seat of Hofstra University. Has many colonial houses and monuments. Founded as a village. Incorporated 1853.

**Population:** 49,435 (1990); 56,554 (2000); 53,891 (2010); Density: 14,636.2 persons per square mile (2010); Race: 21.9% White, 48.3% Black, 1.4% Asian, 0.6% American Indian/Alaska Native, 0.0% Native Hawaiian/Other Pacific Islander, 27.8% Other, 44.2% Hispanic of any race (2010); Average household size: 3.45 (2010); Median age: 32.5 (2010); Males per 100 females: 97.1 (2010); Marriage status: 47.4% never married, 38.3% now married, 6.2% widowed, 8.1% divorced (2006-2010 5-year est.); Foreign born: 39.2% (2006-2010 5-year est.); Ancestry (includes multiple ancestries): 5.3% Jamaican, 3.9% Haitian, 1.6% African, 1.5% West Indian, 1.2% Irish (2006-2010 5-year est.).

**Economy:** Unemployment rate: 10.9% (February 2012); Total civilian labor force: 25,983 (February 2012); Single-family building permits issued: 1 (2011); Multi-family building permits issued: 232 (2011); Employment by

occupation: 5.5% management, 2.0% professional, 18.2% services, 14.7% sales, 4.0% farming, 11.0% construction, 7.6% production (2006-2010 5-year est.).

**Income:** Per capita income: $20,713 (2006-2010 5-year est.); Median household income: $53,333 (2006-2010 5-year est.); Average household income: $64,221 (2006-2010 5-year est.); Percent of households with income of $100,000 or more: 20.3% (2006-2010 5-year est.); Poverty rate: 14.8% (2006-2010 5-year est.).

**Taxes:** Total city taxes per capita: $1,074 (2009); City property taxes per capita: $1,030 (2009).

**Education:** Percent of population age 25 and over with: High school diploma (including GED) or higher: 68.4% (2006-2010 5-year est.); Bachelor's degree or higher: 16.7% (2006-2010 5-year est.); Master's degree or higher: 6.2% (2006-2010 5-year est.).

### School District(s)

Academy Charter School (KG-02)
  2009-10 Enrollment: 166 . . . . . . . . . . . . . . . . . . . . . . (516) 408-2200
Evergreen Charter School (KG-01)
  2009-10 Enrollment: 96 . . . . . . . . . . . . . . . . . . . . . . . (516) 431-1135
Hempstead Union Free School District (PK-12)
  2009-10 Enrollment: 6,037 . . . . . . . . . . . . . . . . . . . . (516) 292-7001
Uniondale Union Free School District (KG-12)
  2009-10 Enrollment: 6,358 . . . . . . . . . . . . . . . . . . . . (516) 560-8824

### Four-year College(s)

Hofstra University (Private, Not-for-profit)
  Fall 2010 Enrollment: 11,156 . . . . . . . . . . . . . . . . . . (516) 463-6600
  2011-12 Tuition: In-state $34,150; Out-of-state $34,150

### Vocational/Technical School(s)

Franklin Career Institute (Private, Not-for-profit)
  Fall 2010 Enrollment: 674 . . . . . . . . . . . . . . . . . . . . . (516) 481-4444
  2011-12 Tuition: $19,400
Long Island Beauty School-Hempstead (Private, For-profit)
  Fall 2010 Enrollment: 173 . . . . . . . . . . . . . . . . . . . . . (516) 483-6259
  2011-12 Tuition: $12,200
Suburban Technical School (Private, For-profit)
  Fall 2010 Enrollment: 411 . . . . . . . . . . . . . . . . . . . . . (516) 481-6660
  2011-12 Tuition: $10,350

**Housing:** Homeownership rate: 42.1% (2010); Median home value: $365,000 (2006-2010 5-year est.); Median contract rent: $1,087 per month (2006-2010 5-year est.); Median year structure built: 1952 (2006-2010 5-year est.).

**Safety:** Violent crime rate: 84.6 per 10,000 population; Property crime rate: 196.7 per 10,000 population (2010).

**Newspapers:** East Meadow Beacon (Community news; Circulation 5,600); Economic Forum (National news; Circulation 10,000); Hempstead Beacon (Local news; Circulation 5,100); La Tribuna Hispana (Local news; Circulation 50,000); La Tribuna Hispana USA (Local news; Circulation 102,670); Merrick Beacon (Local news; Circulation 4,100); Uniondale Beacon (Local news; Circulation 5,300); West Hempstead Beacon (Local news; Circulation 5,400)

**Transportation:** Commute to work: 66.2% car, 23.4% public transportation, 5.3% walk, 1.5% work from home (2006-2010 5-year est.); Travel time to work: 18.3% less than 15 minutes, 31.2% 15 to 30 minutes, 26.6% 30 to 45 minutes, 8.0% 45 to 60 minutes, 15.9% 60 minutes or more (2006-2010 5-year est.)

**Additional Information Contacts**
Hempstead Chamber of Commerce . . . . . . . . . . . . . (516) 476-2901
  http://hempsteadchamber.com
Village of Hempstead. . . . . . . . . . . . . . . . . . . . . . . (516) 489-3400
  http://www.villageofhempstead.org

**HEMPSTEAD** (town). Covers a land area of 118.587 square miles and a water area of 72.999 square miles. Located at 40.63° N. Lat; 73.60° W. Long. Elevation is 56 feet.

**History:** In 1644, the first settlers of Hempstead found a well-watered grassy plain on which their cattle grew fat. The virgin soil was excellent for timothy, rye, wheat, and maize. The score or more families who made up the settlement prospered. Not before 1801, however, did the village begin to grow appreciably.

**Population:** 725,630 (1990); 755,924 (2000); 759,757 (2010); Density: 6,406.7 persons per square mile (2010); Race: 68.3% White, 16.5% Black, 5.2% Asian, 0.3% American Indian/Alaska Native, 0.0% Native Hawaiian/Other Pacific Islander, 9.7% Other, 17.4% Hispanic of any race (2010); Average household size: 3.03 (2010); Median age: 40.0 (2010); Males per 100 females: 93.3 (2010); Marriage status: 31.8% never married,

54.8% now married, 6.8% widowed, 6.6% divorced (2006-2010 5-year est.); Foreign born: 21.2% (2006-2010 5-year est.); Ancestry (includes multiple ancestries): 21.8% Italian, 16.7% Irish, 10.4% German, 4.7% Polish, 3.5% Russian (2006-2010 5-year est.).

**Economy:** Unemployment rate: 7.6% (February 2012); Total civilian labor force: 382,210 (February 2012); Single-family building permits issued: 72 (2011); Multi-family building permits issued: 215 (2011); Employment by occupation: 12.9% management, 3.1% professional, 8.8% services, 17.1% sales, 4.5% farming, 7.5% construction, 4.6% production (2006-2010 5-year est.).

**Income:** Per capita income: $36,416 (2006-2010 5-year est.); Median household income: $89,722 (2006-2010 5-year est.); Average household income: $109,854 (2006-2010 5-year est.); Percent of households with income of $100,000 or more: 44.7% (2006-2010 5-year est.); Poverty rate: 5.3% (2006-2010 5-year est.).

**Taxes:** Total city taxes per capita: $366 (2009); City property taxes per capita: $313 (2009).

**Education:** Percent of population age 25 and over with: High school diploma (including GED) or higher: 88.3% (2006-2010 5-year est.); Bachelor's degree or higher: 36.3% (2006-2010 5-year est.); Master's degree or higher: 15.7% (2006-2010 5-year est.).

### School District(s)
Academy Charter School (KG-02)
  2009-10 Enrollment: 166 . . . . . . . . . . . . . . . . . . . . . (516) 408-2200
Evergreen Charter School (KG-01)
  2009-10 Enrollment: 96 . . . . . . . . . . . . . . . . . . . . . . (516) 431-1135
Hempstead Union Free School District (PK-12)
  2009-10 Enrollment: 6,037 . . . . . . . . . . . . . . . . . . . (516) 292-7001
Uniondale Union Free School District (KG-12)
  2009-10 Enrollment: 6,358 . . . . . . . . . . . . . . . . . . . (516) 560-8824

### Four-year College(s)
Hofstra University (Private, Not-for-profit)
  Fall 2010 Enrollment: 11,156. . . . . . . . . . . . . . . . . . (516) 463-6600
  2011-12 Tuition: In-state $34,150; Out-of-state $34,150

### Vocational/Technical School(s)
Franklin Career Institute (Private, Not-for-profit)
  Fall 2010 Enrollment: 674 . . . . . . . . . . . . . . . . . . . . (516) 481-4444
  2011-12 Tuition: $19,400
Long Island Beauty School-Hempstead (Private, For-profit)
  Fall 2010 Enrollment: 173 . . . . . . . . . . . . . . . . . . . . (516) 483-6259
  2011-12 Tuition: $12,200
Suburban Technical School (Private, For-profit)
  Fall 2010 Enrollment: 411 . . . . . . . . . . . . . . . . . . . . (516) 481-6660
  2011-12 Tuition: $10,350

**Housing:** Homeownership rate: 80.0% (2010); Median home value: $456,700 (2006-2010 5-year est.); Median contract rent: $1,221 per month (2006-2010 5-year est.); Median year structure built: 1952 (2006-2010 5-year est.).

**Newspapers:** East Meadow Beacon (Community news; Circulation 5,600); Economic Forum (National news; Circulation 10,000); Hempstead Beacon (Local news; Circulation 5,100); La Tribuna Hispana (Local news; Circulation 50,000); La Tribuna Hispana USA (Local news; Circulation 102,670); Merrick Beacon (Local news; Circulation 4,100); Uniondale Beacon (Local news; Circulation 5,300); West Hempstead Beacon (Local news; Circulation 5,400)

**Transportation:** Commute to work: 77.0% car, 16.3% public transportation, 2.7% walk, 2.8% work from home (2006-2010 5-year est.); Travel time to work: 20.3% less than 15 minutes, 29.7% 15 to 30 minutes, 21.3% 30 to 45 minutes, 9.1% 45 to 60 minutes, 19.6% 60 minutes or more (2006-2010 5-year est.)

**Additional Information Contacts**
Town of Hempstead . . . . . . . . . . . . . . . . . . . . . . . . . (516) 489-5000
  http://www.townofhempstead.org

## HERRICKS (CDP).
Covers a land area of 0.573 square miles and a water area of 0 square miles. Located at 40.75° N. Lat; 73.66° W. Long. Elevation is 115 feet.

**History:** Named for Capt. James M. Herrick, it is an unincorporated entity, governed under the jurisdiction of the Town of North Hempstead. Mail delivery is provided by the New Hyde Park Post Office utilizing the 11040 Zip Code.

**Population:** 4,097 (1990); 4,076 (2000); 4,295 (2010); Density: 7,490.4 persons per square mile (2010); Race: 52.6% White, 0.5% Black, 43.2% Asian, 0.1% American Indian/Alaska Native, 0.1% Native Hawaiian/Other Pacific Islander, 3.5% Other, 3.9% Hispanic of any race (2010); Average

household size: 3.20 (2010); Median age: 43.5 (2010); Males per 100 females: 93.1 (2010); Marriage status: 24.4% never married, 62.3% now married, 9.6% widowed, 3.8% divorced (2006-2010 5-year est.); Foreign born: 37.2% (2006-2010 5-year est.); Ancestry (includes multiple ancestries): 18.5% Italian, 13.7% Irish, 4.9% Russian, 4.5% German, 3.2% Croatian (2006-2010 5-year est.).

**Economy:** Employment by occupation: 18.3% management, 3.7% professional, 5.3% services, 19.6% sales, 5.0% farming, 7.1% construction, 0.8% production (2006-2010 5-year est.).

**Income:** Per capita income: $42,939 (2006-2010 5-year est.); Median household income: $100,603 (2006-2010 5-year est.); Average household income: $128,105 (2006-2010 5-year est.); Percent of households with income of $100,000 or more: 50.6% (2006-2010 5-year est.); Poverty rate: 2.5% (2006-2010 5-year est.).

**Education:** Percent of population age 25 and over with: High school diploma (including GED) or higher: 91.2% (2006-2010 5-year est.); Bachelor's degree or higher: 52.1% (2006-2010 5-year est.); Master's degree or higher: 22.8% (2006-2010 5-year est.).

**Housing:** Homeownership rate: 95.3% (2010); Median home value: $613,400 (2006-2010 5-year est.); Median contract rent: n/a per month (2006-2010 5-year est.); Median year structure built: 1952 (2006-2010 5-year est.).

**Transportation:** Commute to work: 80.5% car, 16.3% public transportation, 0.5% walk, 2.8% work from home (2006-2010 5-year est.); Travel time to work: 17.3% less than 15 minutes, 27.9% 15 to 30 minutes, 12.6% 30 to 45 minutes, 8.6% 45 to 60 minutes, 33.6% 60 minutes or more (2006-2010 5-year est.)

## HEWLETT (CDP).
Covers a land area of 0.881 square miles and a water area of 0.017 square miles. Located at 40.64° N. Lat; 73.69° W. Long. Elevation is 20 feet.

**Population:** 6,620 (1990); 7,060 (2000); 6,819 (2010); Density: 7,738.8 persons per square mile (2010); Race: 85.0% White, 2.3% Black, 7.1% Asian, 0.0% American Indian/Alaska Native, 0.0% Native Hawaiian/Other Pacific Islander, 5.6% Other, 10.7% Hispanic of any race (2010); Average household size: 2.67 (2010); Median age: 44.2 (2010); Males per 100 females: 92.5 (2010); Marriage status: 18.9% never married, 62.6% now married, 9.9% widowed, 8.6% divorced (2006-2010 5-year est.); Foreign born: 19.3% (2006-2010 5-year est.); Ancestry (includes multiple ancestries): 14.5% Italian, 12.2% Irish, 8.5% Russian, 6.8% Polish, 5.7% German (2006-2010 5-year est.).

**Economy:** Employment by occupation: 17.7% management, 2.4% professional, 8.0% services, 14.0% sales, 3.0% farming, 6.3% construction, 3.9% production (2006-2010 5-year est.).

**Income:** Per capita income: $42,526 (2006-2010 5-year est.); Median household income: $83,600 (2006-2010 5-year est.); Average household income: $107,666 (2006-2010 5-year est.); Percent of households with income of $100,000 or more: 41.1% (2006-2010 5-year est.); Poverty rate: 5.3% (2006-2010 5-year est.).

**Education:** Percent of population age 25 and over with: High school diploma (including GED) or higher: 92.1% (2006-2010 5-year est.); Bachelor's degree or higher: 51.1% (2006-2010 5-year est.); Master's degree or higher: 25.4% (2006-2010 5-year est.).

### School District(s)
Hewlett-Woodmere Union Free School District (PK-12)
  2009-10 Enrollment: 3,075 . . . . . . . . . . . . . . . . . . . (516) 374-8100

**Housing:** Homeownership rate: 79.5% (2010); Median home value: $510,000 (2006-2010 5-year est.); Median contract rent: $1,377 per month (2006-2010 5-year est.); Median year structure built: 1953 (2006-2010 5-year est.).

**Transportation:** Commute to work: 80.5% car, 13.0% public transportation, 3.4% walk, 3.1% work from home (2006-2010 5-year est.); Travel time to work: 28.4% less than 15 minutes, 25.1% 15 to 30 minutes, 15.1% 30 to 45 minutes, 8.0% 45 to 60 minutes, 23.3% 60 minutes or more (2006-2010 5-year est.)

## HEWLETT BAY PARK (village).
Covers a land area of 0.336 square miles and a water area of 0.022 square miles. Located at 40.63° N. Lat; 73.69° W. Long. Elevation is 10 feet.

**Population:** 440 (1990); 484 (2000); 404 (2010); Density: 1,199.3 persons per square mile (2010); Race: 92.6% White, 0.0% Black, 5.7% Asian, 0.0% American Indian/Alaska Native, 0.0% Native Hawaiian/Other Pacific Islander, 1.7% Other, 5.4% Hispanic of any race (2010); Average household size: 3.08 (2010); Median age: 47.0 (2010); Males per 100 females: 106.1 (2010); Marriage status: 24.0% never married, 68.6% now married, 3.9% widowed, 3.4% divorced (2006-2010 5-year est.); Foreign born: 19.1% (2006-2010 5-year est.); Ancestry (includes multiple ancestries): 29.9% Russian, 16.0% American, 8.3% Polish, 6.2% Italian, 5.4% European (2006-2010 5-year est.).

**Economy:** Single-family building permits issued: 0 (2011); Multi-family building permits issued: 0 (2011); Employment by occupation: 26.5% management, 0.0% professional, 3.3% services, 14.3% sales, 6.1% farming, 0.0% construction, 0.0% production (2006-2010 5-year est.).

**Income:** Per capita income: $117,593 (2006-2010 5-year est.); Median household income: $250 (2006-2010 5-year est.); Average household income: $361,626 (2006-2010 5-year est.); Percent of households with income of $100,000 or more: 80.1% (2006-2010 5-year est.); Poverty rate: 1.3% (2006-2010 5-year est.).

**Education:** Percent of population age 25 and over with: High school diploma (including GED) or higher: 99.4% (2006-2010 5-year est.); Bachelor's degree or higher: 77.2% (2006-2010 5-year est.); Master's degree or higher: 35.8% (2006-2010 5-year est.).

**Housing:** Homeownership rate: 96.2% (2010); Median home value: $1 (2006-2010 5-year est.); Median contract rent: n/a per month (2006-2010 5-year est.); Median year structure built: before 1940 (2006-2010 5-year est.).

**Transportation:** Commute to work: 84.5% car, 6.9% public transportation, 0.9% walk, 7.7% work from home (2006-2010 5-year est.); Travel time to work: 33.0% less than 15 minutes, 11.6% 15 to 30 minutes, 21.9% 30 to 45 minutes, 2.3% 45 to 60 minutes, 31.2% 60 minutes or more (2006-2010 5-year est.)

## HEWLETT HARBOR (village).

Covers a land area of 0.726 square miles and a water area of 0.103 square miles. Located at 40.63° N. Lat; 73.68° W. Long. Elevation is 10 feet.

**Population:** 1,193 (1990); 1,271 (2000); 1,263 (2010); Density: 1,739.0 persons per square mile (2010); Race: 93.7% White, 0.8% Black, 3.9% Asian, 0.0% American Indian/Alaska Native, 0.0% Native Hawaiian/Other Pacific Islander, 1.6% Other, 2.4% Hispanic of any race (2010); Average household size: 3.02 (2010); Median age: 46.5 (2010); Males per 100 females: 97.0 (2010); Marriage status: 15.5% never married, 77.1% now married, 4.8% widowed, 2.7% divorced (2006-2010 5-year est.); Foreign born: 16.6% (2006-2010 5-year est.); Ancestry (includes multiple ancestries): 28.2% Russian, 9.3% Eastern European, 8.5% Italian, 7.2% American, 4.5% Polish (2006-2010 5-year est.).

**Economy:** Single-family building permits issued: 0 (2011); Multi-family building permits issued: 0 (2011); Employment by occupation: 27.5% management, 2.6% professional, 1.5% services, 13.6% sales, 2.2% farming, 2.4% construction, 1.3% production (2006-2010 5-year est.).

**Income:** Per capita income: $92,241 (2006-2010 5-year est.); Median household income: $218,750 (2006-2010 5-year est.); Average household income: $289,286 (2006-2010 5-year est.); Percent of households with income of $100,000 or more: 77.2% (2006-2010 5-year est.); Poverty rate: 0.0% (2006-2010 5-year est.).

**Education:** Percent of population age 25 and over with: High school diploma (including GED) or higher: 97.3% (2006-2010 5-year est.); Bachelor's degree or higher: 72.9% (2006-2010 5-year est.); Master's degree or higher: 44.4% (2006-2010 5-year est.).

**Housing:** Homeownership rate: 97.6% (2010); Median home value: $1 (2006-2010 5-year est.); Median contract rent: $1,188 per month (2006-2010 5-year est.); Median year structure built: 1955 (2006-2010 5-year est.).

**Transportation:** Commute to work: 75.0% car, 15.0% public transportation, 0.0% walk, 6.9% work from home (2006-2010 5-year est.); Travel time to work: 30.1% less than 15 minutes, 16.3% 15 to 30 minutes, 17.1% 30 to 45 minutes, 8.0% 45 to 60 minutes, 28.5% 60 minutes or more (2006-2010 5-year est.)

## HEWLETT NECK (village).

Covers a land area of 0.192 square miles and a water area of 0.020 square miles. Located at 40.62° N. Lat; 73.69° W. Long. Elevation is 7 feet.

**Population:** 547 (1990); 504 (2000); 445 (2010); Density: 2,310.5 persons per square mile (2010); Race: 93.5% White, 3.8% Black, 2.0% Asian, 0.0% American Indian/Alaska Native, 0.0% Native Hawaiian/Other Pacific Islander, 0.7% Other, 2.0% Hispanic of any race (2010); Average household size: 3.07 (2010); Median age: 45.6 (2010); Males per 100 females: 96.0 (2010); Marriage status: 20.7% never married, 72.6% now married, 3.5% widowed, 3.2% divorced (2006-2010 5-year est.); Foreign born: 13.5% (2006-2010 5-year est.); Ancestry (includes multiple

ancestries): 20.7% Russian, 18.2% American, 17.1% Polish, 7.3% Eastern European, 3.0% Hungarian (2006-2010 5-year est.).

**Economy:** Single-family building permits issued: 1 (2011); Multi-family building permits issued: 0 (2011); Employment by occupation: 21.5% management, 0.0% professional, 0.0% services, 7.0% sales, 1.0% farming, 3.5% construction, 3.5% production (2006-2010 5-year est.).

**Income:** Per capita income: $91,046 (2006-2010 5-year est.); Median household income: $235,000 (2006-2010 5-year est.); Average household income: $299,344 (2006-2010 5-year est.); Percent of households with income of $100,000 or more: 82.3% (2006-2010 5-year est.); Poverty rate: 0.4% (2006-2010 5-year est.).

**Education:** Percent of population age 25 and over with: High school diploma (including GED) or higher: 98.0% (2006-2010 5-year est.); Bachelor's degree or higher: 76.8% (2006-2010 5-year est.); Master's degree or higher: 39.3% (2006-2010 5-year est.).

**Housing:** Homeownership rate: 97.2% (2010); Median home value: $1 (2006-2010 5-year est.); Median contract rent: n/a per month (2006-2010 5-year est.); Median year structure built: 1949 (2006-2010 5-year est.).

**Transportation:** Commute to work: 85.1% car, 8.2% public transportation, 0.0% walk, 6.7% work from home (2006-2010 5-year est.); Travel time to work: 18.2% less than 15 minutes, 19.9% 15 to 30 minutes, 16.0% 30 to 45 minutes, 11.6% 45 to 60 minutes, 34.3% 60 minutes or more (2006-2010 5-year est.)

## HICKSVILLE (CDP).

Covers a land area of 6.790 square miles and a water area of 0.015 square miles. Located at 40.76° N. Lat; 73.52° W. Long. Elevation is 148 feet.

**History:** Named for Charles Hicks, a Quaker reformer. Founded 1648.

**Population:** 40,174 (1990); 41,260 (2000); 41,547 (2010); Density: 6,118.0 persons per square mile (2010); Race: 70.3% White, 2.3% Black, 19.7% Asian, 0.3% American Indian/Alaska Native, 0.0% Native Hawaiian/Other Pacific Islander, 7.4% Other, 14.5% Hispanic of any race (2010); Average household size: 3.09 (2010); Median age: 41.4 (2010); Males per 100 females: 96.2 (2010); Marriage status: 28.3% never married, 59.4% now married, 6.8% widowed, 5.5% divorced (2006-2010 5-year est.); Foreign born: 26.9% (2006-2010 5-year est.); Ancestry (includes multiple ancestries): 23.3% Italian, 18.3% Irish, 11.3% German, 5.7% Polish, 3.1% English (2006-2010 5-year est.).

**Economy:** Employment by occupation: 14.0% management, 5.3% professional, 7.8% services, 18.1% sales, 5.1% farming, 7.4% construction, 5.5% production (2006-2010 5-year est.).

**Income:** Per capita income: $34,431 (2006-2010 5-year est.); Median household income: $85,397 (2006-2010 5-year est.); Average household income: $103,560 (2006-2010 5-year est.); Percent of households with income of $100,000 or more: 44.3% (2006-2010 5-year est.); Poverty rate: 4.7% (2006-2010 5-year est.).

**Education:** Percent of population age 25 and over with: High school diploma (including GED) or higher: 89.5% (2006-2010 5-year est.); Bachelor's degree or higher: 33.5% (2006-2010 5-year est.); Master's degree or higher: 12.9% (2006-2010 5-year est.).

### School District(s)

Hicksville Union Free School District (PK-12)

    2009-10 Enrollment: 5,465 . . . . . . . . . . . . . . . . . . . . . . . . . . (516) 733-6600

**Housing:** Homeownership rate: 84.8% (2010); Median home value: $438,300 (2006-2010 5-year est.); Median contract rent: $1,324 per month (2006-2010 5-year est.); Median year structure built: 1954 (2006-2010 5-year est.).

**Newspapers:** Pennysaver - Central Huntington/Cold Spring Harbor Edition (Local news; Circulation 16,662); The Pennysaver - Commack (Community news; Circulation 11,977); The Pennysaver - East Northport (Community news; Circulation 10,400); The Pennysaver - Glen Cove (Community news); The Pennysaver - Glen Head (Community news; Circulation 7,790); The Pennysaver - Kings Park (Community news; Circulation 6,486); The Pennysaver - Northport (Community news; Circulation 8,339); The Pennysaver - Oyster Bay/East Norwich (Community news; Circulation 11,256); The Pennysaver - Smithtown/Saint James (Local news; Circulation 14,111); The Shopper's Guide - Great Neck (Community news; Circulation 15,163); Shoppers Guide - Cedarhurst/Lawrence Edition (Community news; Circulation 11,016); Shoppers Guide - Douglaston/Little Neck Edition (Community news; Circulation 9,562); Shoppers Guide - Floral Park/Bellerose South Edition (Community news; Circulation 9,428); Shoppers Guide - Franklin Square Edition (Community news; Circulation 8,815); Shoppers Guide - Freeport Edition (Community news; Circulation 14,521); Shoppers Guide - Garden City Edition (Community news; Circulation 9,000); Shoppers Guide - Hewlett Edition (Community news;

Circulation 15,535); Shoppers Guide - Lynbrook Edition (Community news; Circulation 16,669); Shoppers Guide - Merrick/Bellmore South Edition (Community news; Circulation 13,547); Shoppers Guide - Mineola/Carle Place Edition (Community news; Circulation 11,697); Shoppers Guide - Oceanside Edition (Community news; Circulation 14,607); Shoppers Guide - Port Washington Edition (Community news; Circulation 11,369); Shoppers Guide - Queens Village Edition (Community news; Circulation 13,392); Shoppers Guide - Rockville Centre Edition (Community news; Circulation 10,936); Shoppers Guide - Rosedale Edition (Community news; Circulation 7,452); Shoppers Guide - Uniondale Edition (Community news; Circulation 10,149); Shoppers Guide - Valley Stream Edition (Community news; Circulation 12,794); Shoppers Guide - West Hempstead Edition (Community news; Circulation 10,297); Shoppers Guide - Westbury Edition (Community news; Circulation 13,116); This Week - Centereach Edition (Local news; Circulation 11,825); This Week - Deer Park Edition (Local news; Circulation 14,466); This Week - Farmingdale/Bethpage Edition (Local news; Circulation 16,862); This Week - Moriches/North Mastic/North Shirley Edition (Local news; Circulation 14,199); This Week - Patchogue Edition (Local news; Circulation 19,549); This Week - Plainview/Old Bethpage Editiion (Local news; Circulation 11,699); This Week - Port Jefferson Edition (Local news; Circulation 19,036); This Week - Riverhead Edition (Local news; Circulation 11,166); This Week - Rocky Point Edition (Local news; Circulation 18,413); This Week - Ronkonkoma Edition (Local news; Circulation 15,956); This Week - South Brentwood Edition (Local news; Circulation 12,964); This Week - Syosset/Woodbury Edition (Local news; Circulation 12,373); This Week - West Babylon Edition (Local news; Circulation 15,386)

**Transportation:** Commute to work: 81.2% car, 12.5% public transportation, 1.5% walk, 3.4% work from home (2006-2010 5-year est.); Travel time to work: 23.8% less than 15 minutes, 34.2% 15 to 30 minutes, 17.4% 30 to 45 minutes, 6.7% 45 to 60 minutes, 17.9% 60 minutes or more (2006-2010 5-year est.)

**Additional Information Contacts**

Hicksville Chamber of Commerce . . . . . . . . . . . . . . . . . . (516) 931-7170
http://www.hicksvillechamber.com

**INWOOD** (CDP). Covers a land area of 1.581 square miles and a water area of 0.482 square miles. Located at 40.62° N. Lat; 73.74° W. Long. Elevation is 10 feet.

**Population:** 7,767 (1990); 9,325 (2000); 9,792 (2010); Density: 6,191.6 persons per square mile (2010); Race: 48.0% White, 24.2% Black, 3.3% Asian, 0.7% American Indian/Alaska Native, 0.2% Native Hawaiian/Other Pacific Islander, 23.6% Other, 42.8% Hispanic of any race (2010); Average household size: 3.30 (2010); Median age: 34.7 (2010); Males per 100 females: 94.2 (2010); Marriage status: 44.7% never married, 43.2% now married, 5.8% widowed, 6.4% divorced (2006-2010 5-year est.); Foreign born: 31.4% (2006-2010 5-year est.); Ancestry (includes multiple ancestries): 15.2% Italian, 9.3% Irish, 3.7% German, 2.7% American, 2.1% English (2006-2010 5-year est.).

**Economy:** Employment by occupation: 6.5% management, 1.3% professional, 20.8% services, 17.5% sales, 5.1% farming, 8.7% construction, 5.3% production (2006-2010 5-year est.).

**Income:** Per capita income: $20,908 (2006-2010 5-year est.); Median household income: $52,122 (2006-2010 5-year est.); Average household income: $69,232 (2006-2010 5-year est.); Percent of households with income of $100,000 or more: 25.9% (2006-2010 5-year est.); Poverty rate: 16.7% (2006-2010 5-year est.).

**Education:** Percent of population age 25 and over with: High school diploma (including GED) or higher: 73.2% (2006-2010 5-year est.); Bachelor's degree or higher: 16.1% (2006-2010 5-year est.); Master's degree or higher: 5.9% (2006-2010 5-year est.).

**School District(s)**

Lawrence Union Free School District (PK-12)
    2009-10 Enrollment: 3,092 . . . . . . . . . . . . . . . . (516) 295-7030

**Housing:** Homeownership rate: 44.1% (2010); Median home value: $415,200 (2006-2010 5-year est.); Median contract rent: $1,119 per month (2006-2010 5-year est.); Median year structure built: 1941 (2006-2010 5-year est.).

**Transportation:** Commute to work: 72.4% car, 17.5% public transportation, 6.5% walk, 1.0% work from home (2006-2010 5-year est.); Travel time to work: 33.8% less than 15 minutes, 22.7% 15 to 30 minutes, 19.5% 30 to 45 minutes, 7.7% 45 to 60 minutes, 16.4% 60 minutes or more (2006-2010 5-year est.)

**ISLAND PARK** (village). Covers a land area of 0.445 square miles and a water area of 0 square miles. Located at 40.60° N. Lat; 73.65° W. Long. Elevation is 7 feet.

**History:** Incorporated 1926.

**Population:** 4,860 (1990); 4,732 (2000); 4,655 (2010); Density: 10,460.3 persons per square mile (2010); Race: 83.4% White, 1.9% Black, 2.5% Asian, 0.2% American Indian/Alaska Native, 0.0% Native Hawaiian/Other Pacific Islander, 12.0% Other, 26.5% Hispanic of any race (2010); Average household size: 2.78 (2010); Median age: 40.8 (2010); Males per 100 females: 95.6 (2010); Marriage status: 32.9% never married, 53.5% now married, 6.1% widowed, 7.5% divorced (2006-2010 5-year est.); Foreign born: 17.5% (2006-2010 5-year est.); Ancestry (includes multiple ancestries): 24.6% Irish, 21.7% Italian, 15.5% German, 5.1% Polish, 3.4% English (2006-2010 5-year est.).

**Economy:** Single-family building permits issued: 0 (2011); Multi-family building permits issued: 0 (2011); Employment by occupation: 9.3% management, 2.2% professional, 12.9% services, 18.4% sales, 4.1% farming, 13.2% construction, 7.7% production (2006-2010 5-year est.).

**Income:** Per capita income: $27,797 (2006-2010 5-year est.); Median household income: $74,005 (2006-2010 5-year est.); Average household income: $82,780 (2006-2010 5-year est.); Percent of households with income of $100,000 or more: 31.4% (2006-2010 5-year est.); Poverty rate: 8.3% (2006-2010 5-year est.).

**Education:** Percent of population age 25 and over with: High school diploma (including GED) or higher: 87.5% (2006-2010 5-year est.); Bachelor's degree or higher: 25.7% (2006-2010 5-year est.); Master's degree or higher: 14.2% (2006-2010 5-year est.).

**School District(s)**

Island Park Union Free School District (KG-08)
    2009-10 Enrollment: 681 . . . . . . . . . . . . . . . . . . (516) 431-8100

**Housing:** Homeownership rate: 59.5% (2010); Median home value: $461,500 (2006-2010 5-year est.); Median contract rent: $1,483 per month (2006-2010 5-year est.); Median year structure built: 1953 (2006-2010 5-year est.).

**Newspapers:** Baldwin-Freeport Tribune (Local news; Circulation 9,700); Five Towns Tribune (Community news; Circulation 2,800); Freeport Tribune (Community news; Circulation 18,050); Garden City Tribune (Community news; Circulation 2,800); Hicksville-Levittown Tribune (Community news; Circulation 3,800); Island Park Tribune (Community news; Circulation 10,000); Long Beach Tribune (Community news; Circulation 17,500); Manhattan Tribune (Community news; Circulation 10,000); Merrick-Bellmore-Central Nassau Trib (Local news; Circulation 10,000); Oceanside/Rvc/East Rockaway Tribune (Local news; Circulation 26,059); Valley Stream/Lynbrook/Malverne Trib (Local news; Circulation 36,500)

**Transportation:** Commute to work: 77.3% car, 18.9% public transportation, 1.3% walk, 2.1% work from home (2006-2010 5-year est.); Travel time to work: 26.8% less than 15 minutes, 27.9% 15 to 30 minutes, 18.0% 30 to 45 minutes, 10.4% 45 to 60 minutes, 16.9% 60 minutes or more (2006-2010 5-year est.)

**JERICHO** (CDP). Covers a land area of 3.943 square miles and a water area of 0.015 square miles. Located at 40.78° N. Lat; 73.54° W. Long. Elevation is 197 feet.

**History:** The English families who settled in Jericho were, or soon became, Quakers, members of the Society of Friends. Many fled from persecution in England and in the New England Colonies. They sought a peaceful existence as farmers. The name of the area was changed in 1692 from Lusum to Jericho after the town in the Middle East near the Jordan River mentioned in the Bible as part of the Promised Land.

**Population:** 13,141 (1990); 13,045 (2000); 13,567 (2010); Density: 3,440.8 persons per square mile (2010); Race: 70.8% White, 1.9% Black, 25.4% Asian, 0.1% American Indian/Alaska Native, 0.0% Native Hawaiian/Other Pacific Islander, 1.8% Other, 3.0% Hispanic of any race (2010); Average household size: 2.86 (2010); Median age: 45.1 (2010); Males per 100 females: 93.8 (2010); Marriage status: 21.8% never married, 67.5% now married, 7.1% widowed, 3.6% divorced (2006-2010 5-year est.); Foreign born: 20.1% (2006-2010 5-year est.); Ancestry (includes multiple ancestries): 11.3% Italian, 11.2% Russian, 7.9% Polish, 7.5% Irish, 7.3% American (2006-2010 5-year est.).

**Economy:** Employment by occupation: 22.5% management, 7.2% professional, 2.7% services, 16.8% sales, 2.0% farming, 1.7% construction, 1.5% production (2006-2010 5-year est.).

**Income:** Per capita income: $59,995 (2006-2010 5-year est.); Median household income: $134,265 (2006-2010 5-year est.); Average household

income: $175,118 (2006-2010 5-year est.); Percent of households with income of $100,000 or more: 65.4% (2006-2010 5-year est.); Poverty rate: 2.5% (2006-2010 5-year est.).

**Education:** Percent of population age 25 and over with: High school diploma (including GED) or higher: 96.6% (2006-2010 5-year est.); Bachelor's degree or higher: 64.3% (2006-2010 5-year est.); Master's degree or higher: 33.2% (2006-2010 5-year est.).

### School District(s)

Jericho Union Free School District (KG-12)

   2009-10 Enrollment: 3,094 . . . . . . . . . . . . . . . . . . . (516) 203-3600

**Housing:** Homeownership rate: 84.4% (2010); Median home value: $696,900 (2006-2010 5-year est.); Median contract rent: $1,752 per month (2006-2010 5-year est.); Median year structure built: 1959 (2006-2010 5-year est.).

**Transportation:** Commute to work: 78.2% car, 16.3% public transportation, 0.0% walk, 4.3% work from home (2006-2010 5-year est.); Travel time to work: 19.3% less than 15 minutes, 30.9% 15 to 30 minutes, 14.7% 30 to 45 minutes, 8.3% 45 to 60 minutes, 26.8% 60 minutes or more (2006-2010 5-year est.)

## KENSINGTON (village). Covers a land area of 0.254 square miles and a water area of 0 square miles. Located at 40.79° N. Lat; 73.72° W. Long. Elevation is 128 feet.

**Population:** 1,104 (1990); 1,209 (2000); 1,161 (2010); Density: 4,567.1 persons per square mile (2010); Race: 87.2% White, 0.7% Black, 8.7% Asian, 0.1% American Indian/Alaska Native, 0.0% Native Hawaiian/Other Pacific Islander, 3.3% Other, 2.2% Hispanic of any race (2010); Average household size: 2.82 (2010); Median age: 47.1 (2010); Males per 100 females: 91.3 (2010); Marriage status: 21.4% never married, 68.1% now married, 8.6% widowed, 1.9% divorced (2006-2010 5-year est.); Foreign born: 25.1% (2006-2010 5-year est.); Ancestry (includes multiple ancestries): 17.9% Polish, 17.8% Russian, 14.9% Iranian, 5.5% American, 5.1% Eastern European (2006-2010 5-year est.).

**Economy:** Single-family building permits issued: 0 (2011); Multi-family building permits issued: 0 (2011); Employment by occupation: 30.7% management, 6.1% professional, 2.7% services, 11.9% sales, 1.0% farming, 1.3% construction, 0.6% production (2006-2010 5-year est.).

**Income:** Per capita income: $93,745 (2006-2010 5-year est.); Median household income: $166,071 (2006-2010 5-year est.); Average household income: $265,157 (2006-2010 5-year est.); Percent of households with income of $100,000 or more: 69.8% (2006-2010 5-year est.); Poverty rate: 0.6% (2006-2010 5-year est.).

**Education:** Percent of population age 25 and over with: High school diploma (including GED) or higher: 98.2% (2006-2010 5-year est.); Bachelor's degree or higher: 69.7% (2006-2010 5-year est.); Master's degree or higher: 38.0% (2006-2010 5-year est.).

**Housing:** Homeownership rate: 94.4% (2010); Median home value: $1 (2006-2010 5-year est.); Median contract rent: $825 per month (2006-2010 5-year est.); Median year structure built: 1952 (2006-2010 5-year est.).

**Safety:** Violent crime rate: 16.8 per 10,000 population; Property crime rate: 16.8 per 10,000 population (2010).

**Transportation:** Commute to work: 59.6% car, 30.0% public transportation, 2.7% walk, 7.6% work from home (2006-2010 5-year est.); Travel time to work: 13.9% less than 15 minutes, 29.3% 15 to 30 minutes, 18.8% 30 to 45 minutes, 14.6% 45 to 60 minutes, 23.4% 60 minutes or more (2006-2010 5-year est.)

## KINGS POINT (village). Covers a land area of 3.355 square miles and a water area of 0.642 square miles. Located at 40.81° N. Lat; 73.73° W. Long. Elevation is 26 feet.

**History:** Seat of U.S. Merchant Marine Academy (established 1942). Incorporated 1924.

**Population:** 4,843 (1990); 5,076 (2000); 5,005 (2010); Density: 1,491.6 persons per square mile (2010); Race: 91.4% White, 0.8% Black, 3.4% Asian, 0.0% American Indian/Alaska Native, 0.0% Native Hawaiian/Other Pacific Islander, 4.4% Other, 1.7% Hispanic of any race (2010); Average household size: 3.33 (2010); Median age: 33.7 (2010); Males per 100 females: 123.9 (2010); Marriage status: 45.0% never married, 51.6% now married, 2.4% widowed, 1.0% divorced (2006-2010 5-year est.); Foreign born: 32.7% (2006-2010 5-year est.); Ancestry (includes multiple ancestries): 41.6% Iranian, 8.0% Irish, 7.9% German, 7.2% Italian, 4.9% Russian (2006-2010 5-year est.).

**Economy:** Single-family building permits issued: 4 (2011); Multi-family building permits issued: 0 (2011); Employment by occupation: 29.4%

management, 1.9% professional, 1.9% services, 18.4% sales, 3.4% farming, 1.5% construction, 0.0% production (2006-2010 5-year est.).

**Income:** Per capita income: $57,287 (2006-2010 5-year est.); Median household income: $151,010 (2006-2010 5-year est.); Average household income: $244,214 (2006-2010 5-year est.); Percent of households with income of $100,000 or more: 66.7% (2006-2010 5-year est.); Poverty rate: 4.6% (2006-2010 5-year est.).

**Taxes:** Total city taxes per capita: $2,200 (2009); City property taxes per capita: $2,024 (2009).

**Education:** Percent of population age 25 and over with: High school diploma (including GED) or higher: 90.5% (2006-2010 5-year est.); Bachelor's degree or higher: 59.5% (2006-2010 5-year est.); Master's degree or higher: 24.1% (2006-2010 5-year est.).

### Four-year College(s)

United States Merchant Marine Academy (Public)

   Fall 2010 Enrollment: 1,523 . . . . . . . . . . . . . . . . . (516) 773-5000

**Housing:** Homeownership rate: 93.5% (2010); Median home value: $1 (2006-2010 5-year est.); Median contract rent: $1,159 per month (2006-2010 5-year est.); Median year structure built: 1956 (2006-2010 5-year est.).

**Safety:** Violent crime rate: 1.9 per 10,000 population; Property crime rate: 33.6 per 10,000 population (2010).

**Transportation:** Commute to work: 66.0% car, 24.7% public transportation, 0.0% walk, 9.4% work from home (2006-2010 5-year est.); Travel time to work: 19.1% less than 15 minutes, 12.1% 15 to 30 minutes, 16.6% 30 to 45 minutes, 12.8% 45 to 60 minutes, 39.5% 60 minutes or more (2006-2010 5-year est.)

## LAKE SUCCESS (village). Covers a land area of 1.845 square miles and a water area of 0.049 square miles. Located at 40.76° N. Lat; 73.71° W. Long. Elevation is 203 feet.

**History:** Lake Success was the temporary home of the UN from 1946 to 1950. Settled c.1730, incorporated 1926.

**Population:** 2,484 (1990); 2,797 (2000); 2,934 (2010); Density: 1,590.0 persons per square mile (2010); Race: 67.2% White, 3.4% Black, 27.0% Asian, 0.1% American Indian/Alaska Native, 0.0% Native Hawaiian/Other Pacific Islander, 2.3% Other, 2.8% Hispanic of any race (2010); Average household size: 3.02 (2010); Median age: 52.7 (2010); Males per 100 females: 78.8 (2010); Marriage status: 18.1% never married, 62.9% now married, 13.6% widowed, 5.4% divorced (2006-2010 5-year est.); Foreign born: 26.2% (2006-2010 5-year est.); Ancestry (includes multiple ancestries): 12.1% Russian, 9.0% Polish, 6.2% Italian, 5.9% Israeli, 5.8% German (2006-2010 5-year est.).

**Economy:** Single-family building permits issued: 10 (2011); Multi-family building permits issued: 0 (2011); Employment by occupation: 24.2% management, 1.6% professional, 1.9% services, 15.4% sales, 0.0% farming, 0.0% construction, 0.0% production (2006-2010 5-year est.).

**Income:** Per capita income: $74,555 (2006-2010 5-year est.); Median household income: $202,708 (2006-2010 5-year est.); Average household income: $263,202 (2006-2010 5-year est.); Percent of households with income of $100,000 or more: 73.6% (2006-2010 5-year est.); Poverty rate: 0.3% (2006-2010 5-year est.).

**Education:** Percent of population age 25 and over with: High school diploma (including GED) or higher: 91.4% (2006-2010 5-year est.); Bachelor's degree or higher: 63.6% (2006-2010 5-year est.); Master's degree or higher: 36.3% (2006-2010 5-year est.).

**Housing:** Homeownership rate: 97.2% (2010); Median home value: $1 (2006-2010 5-year est.); Median contract rent: n/a per month (2006-2010 5-year est.); Median year structure built: 1954 (2006-2010 5-year est.).

**Safety:** Violent crime rate: 10.5 per 10,000 population; Property crime rate: 146.4 per 10,000 population (2010).

**Transportation:** Commute to work: 67.2% car, 20.4% public transportation, 0.6% walk, 11.3% work from home (2006-2010 5-year est.); Travel time to work: 25.4% less than 15 minutes, 18.3% 15 to 30 minutes, 15.3% 30 to 45 minutes, 17.6% 45 to 60 minutes, 23.3% 60 minutes or more (2006-2010 5-year est.)

## LAKEVIEW (CDP). Aka Lake View. Covers a land area of 0.999 square miles and a water area of 0.195 square miles. Located at 40.67° N. Lat; 73.64° W. Long. Elevation is 39 feet.

**Population:** 5,476 (1990); 5,607 (2000); 5,615 (2010); Density: 5,615.4 persons per square mile (2010); Race: 5.8% White, 81.4% Black, 0.8% Asian, 0.7% American Indian/Alaska Native, 0.1% Native Hawaiian/Other Pacific Islander, 11.2% Other, 15.2% Hispanic of any race (2010); Average household size: 3.73 (2010); Median age: 36.4 (2010); Males per 100

females: 87.0 (2010); Marriage status: 40.7% never married, 45.2% now married, 4.4% widowed, 9.7% divorced (2006-2010 5-year est.); Foreign born: 22.2% (2006-2010 5-year est.); Ancestry (includes multiple ancestries): 14.2% Jamaican, 3.0% Ghanian, 2.5% German, 2.3% Irish, 1.8% West Indian (2006-2010 5-year est.).

**Economy:** Employment by occupation: 6.6% management, 0.7% professional, 16.2% services, 22.4% sales, 6.7% farming, 7.8% construction, 10.2% production (2006-2010 5-year est.).

**Income:** Per capita income: $28,369 (2006-2010 5-year est.); Median household income: $83,836 (2006-2010 5-year est.); Average household income: $95,378 (2006-2010 5-year est.); Percent of households with income of $100,000 or more: 38.8% (2006-2010 5-year est.); Poverty rate: 3.7% (2006-2010 5-year est.).

**Education:** Percent of population age 25 and over with: High school diploma (including GED) or higher: 90.2% (2006-2010 5-year est.); Bachelor's degree or higher: 25.1% (2006-2010 5-year est.); Master's degree or higher: 9.2% (2006-2010 5-year est.).

**Housing:** Homeownership rate: 88.1% (2010); Median home value: $391,900 (2006-2010 5-year est.); Median contract rent: $1,661 per month (2006-2010 5-year est.); Median year structure built: 1955 (2006-2010 5-year est.).

**Transportation:** Commute to work: 77.2% car, 18.5% public transportation, 1.3% walk, 0.0% work from home (2006-2010 5-year est.); Travel time to work: 18.3% less than 15 minutes, 37.6% 15 to 30 minutes, 17.1% 30 to 45 minutes, 12.4% 45 to 60 minutes, 14.6% 60 minutes or more (2006-2010 5-year est.)

**LATTINGTOWN** (village). Covers a land area of 3.755 square miles and a water area of 0.076 square miles. Located at 40.89° N. Lat; 73.59° W. Long. Elevation is 62 feet.

**Population:** 1,859 (1990); 1,860 (2000); 1,739 (2010); Density: 463.1 persons per square mile (2010); Race: 95.1% White, 0.5% Black, 2.7% Asian, 0.0% American Indian/Alaska Native, 0.0% Native Hawaiian/Other Pacific Islander, 1.7% Other, 2.4% Hispanic of any race (2010); Average household size: 2.82 (2010); Median age: 48.0 (2010); Males per 100 females: 96.3 (2010); Marriage status: 28.6% never married, 61.4% now married, 6.3% widowed, 3.6% divorced (2006-2010 5-year est.); Foreign born: 15.0% (2006-2010 5-year est.); Ancestry (includes multiple ancestries): 28.2% Italian, 18.2% Irish, 15.3% German, 9.7% English, 4.4% Polish (2006-2010 5-year est.).

**Economy:** Single-family building permits issued: 0 (2011); Multi-family building permits issued: 0 (2011); Employment by occupation: 21.5% management, 4.4% professional, 4.1% services, 19.6% sales, 2.5% farming, 4.5% construction, 2.8% production (2006-2010 5-year est.).

**Income:** Per capita income: $83,794 (2006-2010 5-year est.); Median household income: $128,125 (2006-2010 5-year est.); Average household income: $261,276 (2006-2010 5-year est.); Percent of households with income of $100,000 or more: 59.7% (2006-2010 5-year est.); Poverty rate: 9.4% (2006-2010 5-year est.).

**Education:** Percent of population age 25 and over with: High school diploma (including GED) or higher: 93.9% (2006-2010 5-year est.); Bachelor's degree or higher: 64.5% (2006-2010 5-year est.); Master's degree or higher: 28.2% (2006-2010 5-year est.).

**Housing:** Homeownership rate: 88.2% (2010); Median home value: $1 (2006-2010 5-year est.); Median contract rent: $1,847 per month (2006-2010 5-year est.); Median year structure built: 1958 (2006-2010 5-year est.).

**Transportation:** Commute to work: 72.7% car, 15.6% public transportation, 2.5% walk, 8.5% work from home (2006-2010 5-year est.); Travel time to work: 27.9% less than 15 minutes, 20.2% 15 to 30 minutes, 21.1% 30 to 45 minutes, 6.3% 45 to 60 minutes, 24.6% 60 minutes or more (2006-2010 5-year est.)

**LAUREL HOLLOW** (village). Covers a land area of 2.958 square miles and a water area of 0.203 square miles. Located at 40.85° N. Lat; 73.47° W. Long. Elevation is 92 feet.

**History:** Until 1935, called Laurelton.

**Population:** 1,748 (1990); 1,930 (2000); 1,952 (2010); Density: 659.9 persons per square mile (2010); Race: 89.4% White, 1.5% Black, 7.7% Asian, 0.2% American Indian/Alaska Native, 0.0% Native Hawaiian/Other Pacific Islander, 1.2% Other, 2.3% Hispanic of any race (2010); Average household size: 3.13 (2010); Median age: 44.7 (2010); Males per 100 females: 93.8 (2010); Marriage status: 21.1% never married, 72.8% now married, 3.5% widowed, 2.6% divorced (2006-2010 5-year est.); Foreign born: 9.3% (2006-2010 5-year est.); Ancestry (includes multiple

ancestries): 28.1% Italian, 24.4% Irish, 15.0% German, 7.5% English, 6.8% French (2006-2010 5-year est.).

**Economy:** Single-family building permits issued: 3 (2011); Multi-family building permits issued: 0 (2011); Employment by occupation: 26.0% management, 2.6% professional, 5.0% services, 13.4% sales, 4.4% farming, 0.0% construction, 0.0% production (2006-2010 5-year est.).

**Income:** Per capita income: $96,681 (2006-2010 5-year est.); Median household income: $192,917 (2006-2010 5-year est.); Average household income: $306,297 (2006-2010 5-year est.); Percent of households with income of $100,000 or more: 77.2% (2006-2010 5-year est.); Poverty rate: 0.7% (2006-2010 5-year est.).

**Taxes:** Total city taxes per capita: $1,384 (2009); City property taxes per capita: $1,215 (2009).

**Education:** Percent of population age 25 and over with: High school diploma (including GED) or higher: 98.6% (2006-2010 5-year est.); Bachelor's degree or higher: 70.4% (2006-2010 5-year est.); Master's degree or higher: 37.5% (2006-2010 5-year est.).

**Housing:** Homeownership rate: 94.7% (2010); Median home value: $1 (2006-2010 5-year est.); Median contract rent: n/a per month (2006-2010 5-year est.); Median year structure built: 1965 (2006-2010 5-year est.).

**Transportation:** Commute to work: 64.5% car, 19.0% public transportation, 3.3% walk, 12.7% work from home (2006-2010 5-year est.); Travel time to work: 21.2% less than 15 minutes, 25.3% 15 to 30 minutes, 17.8% 30 to 45 minutes, 5.7% 45 to 60 minutes, 29.9% 60 minutes or more (2006-2010 5-year est.)

**LAWRENCE** (village). Covers a land area of 3.718 square miles and a water area of 0.911 square miles. Located at 40.60° N. Lat; 73.71° W. Long. Elevation is 20 feet.

**History:** Incorporated 1897.

**Population:** 6,513 (1990); 6,522 (2000); 6,483 (2010); Density: 1,743.4 persons per square mile (2010); Race: 95.6% White, 1.3% Black, 1.7% Asian, 0.0% American Indian/Alaska Native, 0.0% Native Hawaiian/Other Pacific Islander, 1.4% Other, 2.9% Hispanic of any race (2010); Average household size: 3.17 (2010); Median age: 37.3 (2010); Males per 100 females: 92.2 (2010); Marriage status: 27.3% never married, 59.3% now married, 7.6% widowed, 5.9% divorced (2006-2010 5-year est.); Foreign born: 15.2% (2006-2010 5-year est.); Ancestry (includes multiple ancestries): 13.7% American, 12.6% Polish, 11.6% Hungarian, 6.5% European, 6.1% Italian (2006-2010 5-year est.).

**Economy:** Single-family building permits issued: 5 (2011); Multi-family building permits issued: 0 (2011); Employment by occupation: 22.5% management, 2.5% professional, 2.4% services, 8.0% sales, 2.5% farming, 4.1% construction, 2.7% production (2006-2010 5-year est.).

**Income:** Per capita income: $54,424 (2006-2010 5-year est.); Median household income: $123,482 (2006-2010 5-year est.); Average household income: $169,490 (2006-2010 5-year est.); Percent of households with income of $100,000 or more: 62.5% (2006-2010 5-year est.); Poverty rate: 0.8% (2006-2010 5-year est.).

**Education:** Percent of population age 25 and over with: High school diploma (including GED) or higher: 95.8% (2006-2010 5-year est.); Bachelor's degree or higher: 67.2% (2006-2010 5-year est.); Master's degree or higher: 36.6% (2006-2010 5-year est.).

**School District(s)**

Lawrence Union Free School District (PK-12)
    2009-10 Enrollment: 3,092 . . . . . . . . . . . . . . . . . . . . . . (516) 295-7030

**Four-year College(s)**

Sh'or Yoshuv Rabbinical College (Private, Not-for-profit, Jewish)
    Fall 2010 Enrollment: 224 . . . . . . . . . . . . . . . . (5.1) 624-E+12
    2011-12 Tuition: In-state $9,000; Out-of-state $9,000

**Housing:** Homeownership rate: 84.0% (2010); Median home value: $881,100 (2006-2010 5-year est.); Median contract rent: $1,231 per month (2006-2010 5-year est.); Median year structure built: 1951 (2006-2010 5-year est.).

**Newspapers:** Baldwin Herald (Community news; Circulation 3,500); Long Beach Herald (Community news; Circulation 6,210); Long Island Graphic (Community news; Circulation 1,300); Meadowbrook Times (Community news; Circulation 2,000); Nassau Herald (Community news; Circulation 12,650); Oceanside Island Park Herald (Local news; Circulation 5,250); Rockville Centre Herald (Community news; Circulation 5,386); Valley Stream Herald (Community news; Circulation 9,000); Village Herald (Community news; Circulation 5,271)

**Transportation:** Commute to work: 70.3% car, 22.0% public transportation, 0.9% walk, 6.9% work from home (2006-2010 5-year est.); Travel time to work: 19.4% less than 15 minutes, 19.4% 15 to 30 minutes,

14.8% 30 to 45 minutes, 12.0% 45 to 60 minutes, 34.4% 60 minutes or more (2006-2010 5-year est.)
**Additional Information Contacts**
Village of Lawrence . . . . . . . . . . . . . . . . . . . . . . . . . (516) 239-4600
  http://www.villageoflawrence.org

## LEVITTOWN (CDP). Covers a land area of 6.811 square miles and a water area of 0.024 square miles. Located at 40.72° N. Lat; 73.51° W. Long. Elevation is 82 feet.
**History:** Named for William Levitt, developer of model surburban communities. It was originally developed by Levitt and Sons, Inc. a as mass-produced area of private, low-cost housing, and became the propotype for many postwar housing developments throughout the country. Founded 1947.
**Population:** 53,296 (1990); 53,067 (2000); 51,881 (2010); Density: 7,617.2 persons per square mile (2010); Race: 88.9% White, 0.9% Black, 5.7% Asian, 0.1% American Indian/Alaska Native, 0.0% Native Hawaiian/Other Pacific Islander, 4.4% Other, 11.5% Hispanic of any race (2010); Average household size: 3.05 (2010); Median age: 41.0 (2010); Males per 100 females: 94.7 (2010); Marriage status: 29.4% never married, 57.4% now married, 7.1% widowed, 6.1% divorced (2006-2010 5-year est.); Foreign born: 12.5% (2006-2010 5-year est.); Ancestry (includes multiple ancestries): 32.6% Italian, 27.8% Irish, 17.2% German, 5.0% Polish, 3.9% English (2006-2010 5-year est.).
**Economy:** Employment by occupation: 12.4% management, 4.5% professional, 8.9% services, 18.9% sales, 5.2% farming, 8.5% construction, 4.7% production (2006-2010 5-year est.).
**Income:** Per capita income: $34,485 (2006-2010 5-year est.); Median household income: $91,814 (2006-2010 5-year est.); Average household income: $104,910 (2006-2010 5-year est.); Percent of households with income of $100,000 or more: 44.5% (2006-2010 5-year est.); Poverty rate: 2.5% (2006-2010 5-year est.).
**Education:** Percent of population age 25 and over with: High school diploma (including GED) or higher: 91.6% (2006-2010 5-year est.); Bachelor's degree or higher: 28.7% (2006-2010 5-year est.); Master's degree or higher: 11.4% (2006-2010 5-year est.).
### School District(s)
Island Trees Union Free School District (KG-12)
  2009-10 Enrollment: 2,574 . . . . . . . . . . . . . . . . . (516) 520-2100
Levittown Union Free School District (KG-12)
  2009-10 Enrollment: 7,625 . . . . . . . . . . . . . . . . . (516) 520-8300
### Two-year College(s)
Hunter Business School (Private, For-profit)
  Fall 2010 Enrollment: 1,058 . . . . . . . . . . . . . . . . (516) 796-1000
### Vocational/Technical School(s)
Brittany Beauty School (Private, For-profit)
  Fall 2010 Enrollment: 174 . . . . . . . . . . . . . . . . . (516) 731-8300
  2011-12 Tuition: $12,600
Long Island Nail & Skin Care Institute (Private, For-profit)
  Fall 2010 Enrollment: 91 . . . . . . . . . . . . . . . . . . (516) 520-4800
  2011-12 Tuition: $7,995
**Housing:** Homeownership rate: 89.7% (2010); Median home value: $400,300 (2006-2010 5-year est.); Median contract rent: $1,524 per month (2006-2010 5-year est.); Median year structure built: 1952 (2006-2010 5-year est.).
**Transportation:** Commute to work: 87.4% car, 8.9% public transportation, 0.6% walk, 2.4% work from home (2006-2010 5-year est.); Travel time to work: 20.8% less than 15 minutes, 37.4% 15 to 30 minutes, 19.9% 30 to 45 minutes, 5.3% 45 to 60 minutes, 16.6% 60 minutes or more (2006-2010 5-year est.)

## LIDO BEACH (CDP). Covers a land area of 1.738 square miles and a water area of 2.486 square miles. Located at 40.58° N. Lat; 73.60° W. Long. Elevation is 8 feet.
**Population:** 2,795 (1990); 2,825 (2000); 2,897 (2010); Density: 1,666.0 persons per square mile (2010); Race: 96.0% White, 0.7% Black, 1.8% Asian, 0.0% American Indian/Alaska Native, 0.0% Native Hawaiian/Other Pacific Islander, 1.5% Other, 3.6% Hispanic of any race (2010); Average household size: 2.41 (2010); Median age: 50.5 (2010); Males per 100 females: 95.0 (2010); Marriage status: 16.5% never married, 69.5% now married, 9.1% widowed, 5.0% divorced (2006-2010 5-year est.); Foreign born: 7.9% (2006-2010 5-year est.); Ancestry (includes multiple ancestries): 17.9% Irish, 16.0% Italian, 11.5% Russian, 10.1% American, 8.3% German (2006-2010 5-year est.).

**Economy:** Employment by occupation: 27.9% management, 0.0% professional, 4.9% services, 14.0% sales, 2.9% farming, 6.9% construction, 2.0% production (2006-2010 5-year est.).
**Income:** Per capita income: $62,798 (2006-2010 5-year est.); Median household income: $113,438 (2006-2010 5-year est.); Average household income: $153,518 (2006-2010 5-year est.); Percent of households with income of $100,000 or more: 55.9% (2006-2010 5-year est.); Poverty rate: 5.7% (2006-2010 5-year est.).
**Education:** Percent of population age 25 and over with: High school diploma (including GED) or higher: 95.2% (2006-2010 5-year est.); Bachelor's degree or higher: 57.6% (2006-2010 5-year est.); Master's degree or higher: 28.4% (2006-2010 5-year est.).
### School District(s)
Long Beach City School District (PK-12)
  2009-10 Enrollment: 4,005 . . . . . . . . . . . . . . . . . (516) 897-2104
**Housing:** Homeownership rate: 90.0% (2010); Median home value: $774,800 (2006-2010 5-year est.); Median contract rent: $1,068 per month (2006-2010 5-year est.); Median year structure built: 1962 (2006-2010 5-year est.).
**Transportation:** Commute to work: 78.1% car, 15.9% public transportation, 0.0% walk, 5.1% work from home (2006-2010 5-year est.); Travel time to work: 23.8% less than 15 minutes, 17.3% 15 to 30 minutes, 20.7% 30 to 45 minutes, 8.3% 45 to 60 minutes, 29.9% 60 minutes or more (2006-2010 5-year est.)

## LOCUST VALLEY (CDP). Covers a land area of 0.913 square miles and a water area of 0.023 square miles. Located at 40.87° N. Lat; 73.58° W. Long. Elevation is 128 feet.
**Population:** 3,490 (1990); 3,521 (2000); 3,406 (2010); Density: 3,728.1 persons per square mile (2010); Race: 85.5% White, 3.3% Black, 2.4% Asian, 0.1% American Indian/Alaska Native, 0.0% Native Hawaiian/Other Pacific Islander, 8.7% Other, 17.6% Hispanic of any race (2010); Average household size: 2.80 (2010); Median age: 40.0 (2010); Males per 100 females: 92.6 (2010); Marriage status: 34.2% never married, 47.4% now married, 7.7% widowed, 10.7% divorced (2006-2010 5-year est.); Foreign born: 18.0% (2006-2010 5-year est.); Ancestry (includes multiple ancestries): 36.8% Italian, 22.9% Irish, 14.2% German, 8.3% English, 5.1% Polish (2006-2010 5-year est.).
**Economy:** Employment by occupation: 12.9% management, 3.5% professional, 7.8% services, 21.8% sales, 3.9% farming, 12.2% construction, 3.0% production (2006-2010 5-year est.).
**Income:** Per capita income: $42,468 (2006-2010 5-year est.); Median household income: $81,889 (2006-2010 5-year est.); Average household income: $110,743 (2006-2010 5-year est.); Percent of households with income of $100,000 or more: 37.7% (2006-2010 5-year est.); Poverty rate: 4.5% (2006-2010 5-year est.).
**Education:** Percent of population age 25 and over with: High school diploma (including GED) or higher: 98.1% (2006-2010 5-year est.); Bachelor's degree or higher: 49.9% (2006-2010 5-year est.); Master's degree or higher: 15.5% (2006-2010 5-year est.).
### School District(s)
Locust Valley Central School District (KG-12)
  2009-10 Enrollment: 2,211 . . . . . . . . . . . . . . . . . (516) 674-6310
**Housing:** Homeownership rate: 73.6% (2010); Median home value: $639,200 (2006-2010 5-year est.); Median contract rent: $1,836 per month (2006-2010 5-year est.); Median year structure built: before 1940 (2006-2010 5-year est.).
**Newspapers:** Leader (Community news; Circulation 1,200)
**Transportation:** Commute to work: 76.7% car, 14.0% public transportation, 2.0% walk, 7.3% work from home (2006-2010 5-year est.); Travel time to work: 27.9% less than 15 minutes, 25.8% 15 to 30 minutes, 21.7% 30 to 45 minutes, 6.8% 45 to 60 minutes, 17.8% 60 minutes or more (2006-2010 5-year est.)
**Additional Information Contacts**
Locust Valley Chamber of Commerce . . . . . . . . . . . . (516) 637-8496
  http://www.locustvalleychamber.com

## LONG BEACH (city). Covers a land area of 2.214 square miles and a water area of 1.679 square miles. Located at 40.58° N. Lat; 73.66° W. Long. Elevation is 9 feet.
**History:** Named for its beach on the Atlantic shore of Long Island. Incorporated 1922.
**Population:** 33,510 (1990); 35,462 (2000); 33,275 (2010); Density: 15,024.8 persons per square mile (2010); Race: 83.2% White, 6.4% Black, 2.7% Asian, 0.3% American Indian/Alaska Native, 0.0% Native

Hawaiian/Other Pacific Islander, 7.4% Other, 14.1% Hispanic of any race (2010); Average household size: 2.17 (2010); Median age: 42.5 (2010); Males per 100 females: 93.3 (2010); Marriage status: 36.5% never married, 45.7% now married, 8.1% widowed, 9.7% divorced (2006-2010 5-year est.); Foreign born: 14.9% (2006-2010 5-year est.); Ancestry (includes multiple ancestries): 22.8% Irish, 17.8% Italian, 9.1% German, 7.0% Russian, 5.7% Polish (2006-2010 5-year est.).

**Economy:** Unemployment rate: 7.2% (February 2012); Total civilian labor force: 17,944 (February 2012); Single-family building permits issued: 9 (2011); Multi-family building permits issued: 0 (2011); Employment by occupation: 14.7% management, 1.7% professional, 5.6% services, 15.5% sales, 2.6% farming, 5.7% construction, 3.2% production (2006-2010 5-year est.).

**Income:** Per capita income: $43,377 (2006-2010 5-year est.); Median household income: $77,673 (2006-2010 5-year est.); Average household income: $96,946 (2006-2010 5-year est.); Percent of households with income of $100,000 or more: 38.3% (2006-2010 5-year est.); Poverty rate: 8.9% (2006-2010 5-year est.).

**Taxes:** Total city taxes per capita: $995 (2009); City property taxes per capita: $819 (2009).

**Education:** Percent of population age 25 and over with: High school diploma (including GED) or higher: 92.3% (2006-2010 5-year est.); Bachelor's degree or higher: 45.7% (2006-2010 5-year est.); Master's degree or higher: 20.6% (2006-2010 5-year est.).

**School District(s)**

Long Beach City School District (PK-12)
  2009-10 Enrollment: 4,005 . . . . . . . . . . . . . . . . . . . . (516) 897-2104

**Four-year College(s)**

Rabbinical College of Long Island (Private, Not-for-profit)
  Fall 2010 Enrollment: 124 . . . . . . . . . . . . . . . . . . . . (516) 431-7414
  2011-12 Tuition: In-state $8,800; Out-of-state $8,800

**Housing:** Homeownership rate: 55.7% (2010); Median home value: $523,900 (2006-2010 5-year est.); Median contract rent: $1,473 per month (2006-2010 5-year est.); Median year structure built: 1956 (2006-2010 5-year est.).

**Hospitals:** Long Beach Medical Center (203 beds)

**Transportation:** Commute to work: 69.2% car, 19.9% public transportation, 4.9% walk, 4.6% work from home (2006-2010 5-year est.); Travel time to work: 18.5% less than 15 minutes, 18.6% 15 to 30 minutes, 21.8% 30 to 45 minutes, 11.7% 45 to 60 minutes, 29.5% 60 minutes or more (2006-2010 5-year est.)

**Additional Information Contacts**

City of Long Beach . . . . . . . . . . . . . . . . . . . . . . . . (516) 431-1000
  http://www.longbeachny.org
Long Beach Chamber of Commerce . . . . . . . . . . . . . . . . (516) 432-6000
  http://www.longislandnet.com/longbeach

## LYNBROOK (village).

Covers a land area of 2.013 square miles and a water area of 0 square miles. Located at 40.65° N. Lat; 73.67° W. Long. Elevation is 20 feet.

**History:** Old Church dates from 1800. The area was settled in 1785 and was called Bloomfield. The name *Lynbrook* (formed by reversing the syllables in *Brooklyn*) was adopted in 1895. Incorporated 1911.

**Population:** 19,208 (1990); 19,911 (2000); 19,427 (2010); Density: 9,647.0 persons per square mile (2010); Race: 85.3% White, 3.7% Black, 4.5% Asian, 0.1% American Indian/Alaska Native, 0.0% Native Hawaiian/Other Pacific Islander, 6.4% Other, 13.0% Hispanic of any race (2010); Average household size: 2.58 (2010); Median age: 42.2 (2010); Males per 100 females: 90.2 (2010); Marriage status: 27.6% never married, 57.3% now married, 8.1% widowed, 7.0% divorced (2006-2010 5-year est.); Foreign born: 17.1% (2006-2010 5-year est.); Ancestry (includes multiple ancestries): 35.2% Italian, 26.1% Irish, 14.2% German, 4.8% American, 4.0% Polish (2006-2010 5-year est.).

**Economy:** Single-family building permits issued: 2 (2011); Multi-family building permits issued: 0 (2011); Employment by occupation: 15.6% management, 3.1% professional, 4.9% services, 20.5% sales, 3.4% farming, 6.7% construction, 4.3% production (2006-2010 5-year est.).

**Income:** Per capita income: $36,229 (2006-2010 5-year est.); Median household income: $86,787 (2006-2010 5-year est.); Average household income: $97,780 (2006-2010 5-year est.); Percent of households with income of $100,000 or more: 44.5% (2006-2010 5-year est.); Poverty rate: 3.6% (2006-2010 5-year est.).

**Education:** Percent of population age 25 and over with: High school diploma (including GED) or higher: 91.7% (2006-2010 5-year est.);

Bachelor's degree or higher: 33.8% (2006-2010 5-year est.); Master's degree or higher: 12.0% (2006-2010 5-year est.).

**School District(s)**

Lynbrook Union Free School District (KG-12)
  2009-10 Enrollment: 2,949 . . . . . . . . . . . . . . . . . . . . (516) 887-0253
Malverne Union Free School District (KG-12)
  2009-10 Enrollment: 1,700 . . . . . . . . . . . . . . . . . . . . (516) 887-6405

**Housing:** Homeownership rate: 71.5% (2010); Median home value: $448,400 (2006-2010 5-year est.); Median contract rent: $1,348 per month (2006-2010 5-year est.); Median year structure built: 1943 (2006-2010 5-year est.).

**Safety:** Violent crime rate: 13.2 per 10,000 population; Property crime rate: 83.4 per 10,000 population (2010).

**Transportation:** Commute to work: 76.1% car, 17.4% public transportation, 3.0% walk, 3.1% work from home (2006-2010 5-year est.); Travel time to work: 17.3% less than 15 minutes, 29.6% 15 to 30 minutes, 24.8% 30 to 45 minutes, 8.3% 45 to 60 minutes, 19.9% 60 minutes or more (2006-2010 5-year est.)

**Additional Information Contacts**

Lynbrook Chamber of Commerce . . . . . . . . . . . . . . . . (516) 599-3436
  http://www.lynbrookusa.com

## MALVERNE (village).

Covers a land area of 1.057 square miles and a water area of 0 square miles. Located at 40.67° N. Lat; 73.67° W. Long. Elevation is 36 feet.

**History:** Settled in the early 1800s, incorporated 1921.

**Population:** 9,054 (1990); 8,934 (2000); 8,514 (2010); Density: 8,048.7 persons per square mile (2010); Race: 88.4% White, 3.3% Black, 4.2% Asian, 0.0% American Indian/Alaska Native, 0.0% Native Hawaiian/Other Pacific Islander, 4.1% Other, 8.6% Hispanic of any race (2010); Average household size: 2.77 (2010); Median age: 45.6 (2010); Males per 100 females: 92.8 (2010); Marriage status: 28.8% never married, 60.8% now married, 4.9% widowed, 5.5% divorced (2006-2010 5-year est.); Foreign born: 9.7% (2006-2010 5-year est.); Ancestry (includes multiple ancestries): 40.2% Italian, 25.3% Irish, 21.5% German, 6.3% English, 5.2% Polish (2006-2010 5-year est.).

**Economy:** Single-family building permits issued: 0 (2011); Multi-family building permits issued: 0 (2011); Employment by occupation: 16.0% management, 2.3% professional, 4.0% services, 14.8% sales, 2.6% farming, 6.9% construction, 5.5% production (2006-2010 5-year est.).

**Income:** Per capita income: $44,425 (2006-2010 5-year est.); Median household income: $112,007 (2006-2010 5-year est.); Average household income: $124,544 (2006-2010 5-year est.); Percent of households with income of $100,000 or more: 60.3% (2006-2010 5-year est.); Poverty rate: 1.1% (2006-2010 5-year est.).

**Education:** Percent of population age 25 and over with: High school diploma (including GED) or higher: 94.4% (2006-2010 5-year est.); Bachelor's degree or higher: 41.5% (2006-2010 5-year est.); Master's degree or higher: 16.8% (2006-2010 5-year est.).

**School District(s)**

Malverne Union Free School District (KG-12)
  2009-10 Enrollment: 1,700 . . . . . . . . . . . . . . . . . . . . (516) 887-6405

**Housing:** Homeownership rate: 93.1% (2010); Median home value: $465,700 (2006-2010 5-year est.); Median contract rent: $1,168 per month (2006-2010 5-year est.); Median year structure built: 1944 (2006-2010 5-year est.).

**Safety:** Violent crime rate: 2.3 per 10,000 population; Property crime rate: 53.5 per 10,000 population (2010).

**Transportation:** Commute to work: 78.8% car, 16.4% public transportation, 0.8% walk, 4.0% work from home (2006-2010 5-year est.); Travel time to work: 17.6% less than 15 minutes, 28.6% 15 to 30 minutes, 21.5% 30 to 45 minutes, 12.7% 45 to 60 minutes, 19.5% 60 minutes or more (2006-2010 5-year est.)

## MALVERNE PARK OAKS (CDP).

Covers a land area of 0.130 square miles and a water area of 0 square miles. Located at 40.68° N. Lat; 73.66° W. Long. Elevation is 10 feet.

**Population:** 488 (1990); 470 (2000); 505 (2010); Density: 3,878.1 persons per square mile (2010); Race: 86.1% White, 5.7% Black, 3.8% Asian, 0.0% American Indian/Alaska Native, 0.0% Native Hawaiian/Other Pacific Islander, 4.4% Other, 8.7% Hispanic of any race (2010); Average household size: 2.76 (2010); Median age: 47.9 (2010); Males per 100 females: 89.1 (2010); Marriage status: 26.4% never married, 65.1% now married, 5.8% widowed, 2.7% divorced (2006-2010 5-year est.); Foreign born: 16.7% (2006-2010 5-year est.); Ancestry (includes multiple

ancestries): 42.9% Italian, 8.0% Scottish, 7.8% Irish, 2.9% German, 2.7% British (2006-2010 5-year est.).
**Economy:** Employment by occupation: 16.5% management, 0.0% professional, 0.0% services, 3.0% sales, 29.7% farming, 0.0% construction, 0.0% production (2006-2010 5-year est.).
**Income:** Per capita income: $83,904 (2006-2010 5-year est.); Median household income: $235,035 (2006-2010 5-year est.); Average household income: $191,229 (2006-2010 5-year est.); Percent of households with income of $100,000 or more: 71.8% (2006-2010 5-year est.); Poverty rate: 2.9% (2006-2010 5-year est.).
**Education:** Percent of population age 25 and over with: High school diploma (including GED) or higher: 100.0% (2006-2010 5-year est.); Bachelor's degree or higher: 74.0% (2006-2010 5-year est.); Master's degree or higher: 28.9% (2006-2010 5-year est.).
**Housing:** Homeownership rate: 96.7% (2010); Median home value: $485,900 (2006-2010 5-year est.); Median contract rent: n/a per month (2006-2010 5-year est.); Median year structure built: 1943 (2006-2010 5-year est.).
**Transportation:** Commute to work: 91.0% car, 9.0% public transportation, 0.0% walk, 0.0% work from home (2006-2010 5-year est.); Travel time to work: 61.3% less than 15 minutes, 10.2% 15 to 30 minutes, 0.0% 30 to 45 minutes, 16.5% 45 to 60 minutes, 12.0% 60 minutes or more (2006-2010 5-year est.)

**MANHASSET** (CDP). Covers a land area of 2.381 square miles and a water area of 0.034 square miles. Located at 40.78° N. Lat; 73.69° W. Long. Elevation is 95 feet.
**History:** Manhasset is a Native American term that translates to "the island neighborhood." In 2005, a Wall Street Journal article ranked Manhasset as the best town for raising a family in the New York metropolitan area.
**Population:** 7,718 (1990); 8,362 (2000); 8,080 (2010); Density: 3,392.5 persons per square mile (2010); Race: 75.9% White, 9.4% Black, 10.9% Asian, 0.2% American Indian/Alaska Native, 0.0% Native Hawaiian/Other Pacific Islander, 3.6% Other, 8.8% Hispanic of any race (2010); Average household size: 2.80 (2010); Median age: 43.1 (2010); Males per 100 females: 89.0 (2010); Marriage status: 24.5% never married, 62.9% now married, 7.1% widowed, 5.5% divorced (2006-2010 5-year est.); Foreign born: 22.0% (2006-2010 5-year est.); Ancestry (includes multiple ancestries): 27.5% Italian, 18.8% Irish, 11.2% German, 4.0% Greek, 3.4% Russian (2006-2010 5-year est.).
**Economy:** Employment by occupation: 23.1% management, 3.8% professional, 5.0% services, 12.7% sales, 2.6% farming, 2.3% construction, 1.4% production (2006-2010 5-year est.).
**Income:** Per capita income: $54,430 (2006-2010 5-year est.); Median household income: $108,449 (2006-2010 5-year est.); Average household income: $161,364 (2006-2010 5-year est.); Percent of households with income of $100,000 or more: 54.5% (2006-2010 5-year est.); Poverty rate: 8.0% (2006-2010 5-year est.).
**Education:** Percent of population age 25 and over with: High school diploma (including GED) or higher: 87.9% (2006-2010 5-year est.); Bachelor's degree or higher: 59.8% (2006-2010 5-year est.); Master's degree or higher: 32.0% (2006-2010 5-year est.).

**School District(s)**
Manhasset Union Free School District (KG-12)
    2009-10 Enrollment: 3,105 . . . . . . . . . . . . . . . . . . . (516) 267-7705
**Housing:** Homeownership rate: 75.6% (2010); Median home value: $945,300 (2006-2010 5-year est.); Median contract rent: $823 per month (2006-2010 5-year est.); Median year structure built: 1941 (2006-2010 5-year est.).
**Hospitals:** North Shore University Hospital (900 beds)
**Transportation:** Commute to work: 57.9% car, 31.2% public transportation, 5.3% walk, 4.4% work from home (2006-2010 5-year est.); Travel time to work: 21.9% less than 15 minutes, 19.5% 15 to 30 minutes, 15.1% 30 to 45 minutes, 12.9% 45 to 60 minutes, 30.7% 60 minutes or more (2006-2010 5-year est.)
**Airports:** North Shore University Hospital Nr 2 (general aviation)
**Additional Information Contacts**
Manhasset Chamber of Commerce . . . . . . . . . . . . . . . . . . (516) 641-1932
    http://manhassetny.org

**MANHASSET HILLS** (CDP). Covers a land area of 0.591 square miles and a water area of 0 square miles. Located at 40.75° N. Lat; 73.68° W. Long. Elevation is 125 feet.
**History:** Manhasset is a Native American term that translates to "the island neighborhood. The Valley School, serving Manhasset's African American community, was closed in the 1960s by a desegregation lawsuit.
**Population:** 3,722 (1990); 3,661 (2000); 3,592 (2010); Density: 6,075.6 persons per square mile (2010); Race: 55.8% White, 0.7% Black, 39.5% Asian, 0.1% American Indian/Alaska Native, 0.0% Native Hawaiian/Other Pacific Islander, 3.9% Other, 5.8% Hispanic of any race (2010); Average household size: 3.03 (2010); Median age: 46.6 (2010); Males per 100 females: 91.4 (2010); Marriage status: 18.0% never married, 73.9% now married, 7.2% widowed, 0.9% divorced (2006-2010 5-year est.); Foreign born: 28.8% (2006-2010 5-year est.); Ancestry (includes multiple ancestries): 18.9% Italian, 13.9% Polish, 8.9% Greek, 6.6% American, 4.3% German (2006-2010 5-year est.).
**Economy:** Employment by occupation: 19.1% management, 3.5% professional, 1.9% services, 15.4% sales, 4.0% farming, 8.8% construction, 3.9% production (2006-2010 5-year est.).
**Income:** Per capita income: $49,522 (2006-2010 5-year est.); Median household income: $115,217 (2006-2010 5-year est.); Average household income: $142,088 (2006-2010 5-year est.); Percent of households with income of $100,000 or more: 58.9% (2006-2010 5-year est.); Poverty rate: 4.3% (2006-2010 5-year est.).
**Education:** Percent of population age 25 and over with: High school diploma (including GED) or higher: 94.8% (2006-2010 5-year est.); Bachelor's degree or higher: 59.6% (2006-2010 5-year est.); Master's degree or higher: 25.3% (2006-2010 5-year est.).
**Housing:** Homeownership rate: 92.4% (2010); Median home value: $803,500 (2006-2010 5-year est.); Median contract rent: $1,094 per month (2006-2010 5-year est.); Median year structure built: 1961 (2006-2010 5-year est.).
**Transportation:** Commute to work: 75.2% car, 19.6% public transportation, 0.0% walk, 5.1% work from home (2006-2010 5-year est.); Travel time to work: 17.7% less than 15 minutes, 23.3% 15 to 30 minutes, 18.1% 30 to 45 minutes, 10.4% 45 to 60 minutes, 30.5% 60 minutes or more (2006-2010 5-year est.)

**MANORHAVEN** (village). Covers a land area of 0.464 square miles and a water area of 0.166 square miles. Located at 40.83° N. Lat; 73.71° W. Long. Elevation is 16 feet.
**History:** Incorporated 1930.
**Population:** 5,672 (1990); 6,138 (2000); 6,556 (2010); Density: 14,103.7 persons per square mile (2010); Race: 67.3% White, 1.4% Black, 17.7% Asian, 0.3% American Indian/Alaska Native, 0.0% Native Hawaiian/Other Pacific Islander, 13.3% Other, 27.1% Hispanic of any race (2010); Average household size: 2.68 (2010); Median age: 38.8 (2010); Males per 100 females: 96.9 (2010); Marriage status: 25.9% never married, 56.6% now married, 5.7% widowed, 11.8% divorced (2006-2010 5-year est.); Foreign born: 37.1% (2006-2010 5-year est.); Ancestry (includes multiple ancestries): 24.0% Italian, 8.4% German, 8.2% Irish, 5.4% Russian, 4.2% English (2006-2010 5-year est.).
**Economy:** Single-family building permits issued: 2 (2011); Multi-family building permits issued: 0 (2011); Employment by occupation: 15.9% management, 4.6% professional, 9.7% services, 12.7% sales, 2.3% farming, 6.7% construction, 4.1% production (2006-2010 5-year est.).
**Income:** Per capita income: $38,913 (2006-2010 5-year est.); Median household income: $75,744 (2006-2010 5-year est.); Average household income: $95,233 (2006-2010 5-year est.); Percent of households with income of $100,000 or more: 37.0% (2006-2010 5-year est.); Poverty rate: 6.9% (2006-2010 5-year est.).
**Education:** Percent of population age 25 and over with: High school diploma (including GED) or higher: 86.5% (2006-2010 5-year est.); Bachelor's degree or higher: 44.1% (2006-2010 5-year est.); Master's degree or higher: 21.3% (2006-2010 5-year est.).
**Housing:** Homeownership rate: 37.6% (2010); Median home value: $587,400 (2006-2010 5-year est.); Median contract rent: $1,794 per month (2006-2010 5-year est.); Median year structure built: 1960 (2006-2010 5-year est.).
**Transportation:** Commute to work: 77.0% car, 17.2% public transportation, 4.6% walk, 1.1% work from home (2006-2010 5-year est.); Travel time to work: 22.9% less than 15 minutes, 29.1% 15 to 30 minutes, 20.4% 30 to 45 minutes, 8.5% 45 to 60 minutes, 19.1% 60 minutes or more (2006-2010 5-year est.)

## MASSAPEQUA

**MASSAPEQUA** (CDP). Covers a land area of 3.557 square miles and a water area of 0.435 square miles. Located at 40.66° N. Lat; 73.47° W. Long. Elevation is 26 feet.

**History:** Named for the Masapequa Indians. It is chiefly residential. Pop. figure also includes Arlyn Oaks, Crown Village, and Nassau Shores.

**Population:** 22,018 (1990); 22,652 (2000); 21,685 (2010); Density: 6,095.2 persons per square mile (2010); Race: 96.6% White, 0.4% Black, 1.6% Asian, 0.1% American Indian/Alaska Native, 0.0% Native Hawaiian/Other Pacific Islander, 1.3% Other, 4.2% Hispanic of any race (2010); Average household size: 3.00 (2010); Median age: 43.1 (2010); Males per 100 females: 95.3 (2010); Marriage status: 24.3% never married, 62.9% now married, 6.9% widowed, 5.9% divorced (2006-2010 5-year est.); Foreign born: 5.8% (2006-2010 5-year est.); Ancestry (includes multiple ancestries): 43.5% Italian, 30.3% Irish, 22.3% German, 5.3% Polish, 5.2% English (2006-2010 5-year est.).

**Economy:** Employment by occupation: 16.5% management, 3.4% professional, 4.5% services, 18.7% sales, 4.2% farming, 5.4% construction, 2.8% production (2006-2010 5-year est.).

**Income:** Per capita income: $45,062 (2006-2010 5-year est.); Median household income: $114,975 (2006-2010 5-year est.); Average household income: $136,947 (2006-2010 5-year est.); Percent of households with income of $100,000 or more: 56.8% (2006-2010 5-year est.); Poverty rate: 2.9% (2006-2010 5-year est.).

**Education:** Percent of population age 25 and over with: High school diploma (including GED) or higher: 95.0% (2006-2010 5-year est.); Bachelor's degree or higher: 43.7% (2006-2010 5-year est.); Master's degree or higher: 16.7% (2006-2010 5-year est.).

### School District(s)
Massapequa Union Free School District (KG-12)
    2009-10 Enrollment: 8,132 . . . . . . . . . . . . . . . . . . . . (516) 308-5000
Plainedge Union Free School District (KG-12)
    2009-10 Enrollment: 3,437 . . . . . . . . . . . . . . . . . . . . (516) 992-7455

**Housing:** Homeownership rate: 93.5% (2010); Median home value: $557,000 (2006-2010 5-year est.); Median contract rent: $1,726 per month (2006-2010 5-year est.); Median year structure built: 1956 (2006-2010 5-year est.).

**Newspapers:** Bellmore-Merrick Observer (Community news; Circulation 4,900)

**Transportation:** Commute to work: 80.7% car, 15.3% public transportation, 0.5% walk, 3.1% work from home (2006-2010 5-year est.); Travel time to work: 19.7% less than 15 minutes, 30.8% 15 to 30 minutes, 18.6% 30 to 45 minutes, 7.9% 45 to 60 minutes, 23.0% 60 minutes or more (2006-2010 5-year est.)

**Additional Information Contacts**
Massapequa Chamber of Commerce . . . . . . . . . . . . . . . . (516) 541-1443
    http://www.massapequachamber.com

## MASSAPEQUA PARK

**MASSAPEQUA PARK** (village). Covers a land area of 2.209 square miles and a water area of 0.042 square miles. Located at 40.68° N. Lat; 73.44° W. Long. Elevation is 23 feet.

**History:** Named for the Masapequa Indians. Incorporated 1931.

**Population:** 18,044 (1990); 17,499 (2000); 17,008 (2010); Density: 7,696.5 persons per square mile (2010); Race: 96.9% White, 0.3% Black, 1.5% Asian, 0.0% American Indian/Alaska Native, 0.0% Native Hawaiian/Other Pacific Islander, 1.3% Other, 4.5% Hispanic of any race (2010); Average household size: 2.97 (2010); Median age: 42.5 (2010); Males per 100 females: 94.1 (2010); Marriage status: 23.8% never married, 63.8% now married, 8.6% widowed, 3.9% divorced (2006-2010 5-year est.); Foreign born: 5.3% (2006-2010 5-year est.); Ancestry (includes multiple ancestries): 42.0% Italian, 32.6% Irish, 17.4% German, 5.9% Polish, 5.0% English (2006-2010 5-year est.).

**Economy:** Single-family building permits issued: 2 (2011); Multi-family building permits issued: 0 (2011); Employment by occupation: 16.0% management, 4.6% professional, 5.7% services, 21.5% sales, 4.0% farming, 6.9% construction, 4.6% production (2006-2010 5-year est.).

**Income:** Per capita income: $41,235 (2006-2010 5-year est.); Median household income: $103,789 (2006-2010 5-year est.); Average household income: $123,737 (2006-2010 5-year est.); Percent of households with income of $100,000 or more: 51.9% (2006-2010 5-year est.); Poverty rate: 2.0% (2006-2010 5-year est.).

**Taxes:** Total city taxes per capita: $243 (2009); City property taxes per capita: $197 (2009).

**Education:** Percent of population age 25 and over with: High school diploma (including GED) or higher: 94.8% (2006-2010 5-year est.); Bachelor's degree or higher: 37.2% (2006-2010 5-year est.); Master's degree or higher: 15.2% (2006-2010 5-year est.).

### School District(s)
Massapequa Union Free School District (KG-12)
    2009-10 Enrollment: 8,132 . . . . . . . . . . . . . . . . . . . . (516) 308-5000

**Housing:** Homeownership rate: 96.1% (2010); Median home value: $472,300 (2006-2010 5-year est.); Median contract rent: $850 per month (2006-2010 5-year est.); Median year structure built: 1956 (2006-2010 5-year est.).

**Newspapers:** Massapequa Post (Community news; Circulation 4,700); The Massapequa Post (Local news; Circulation 4,700)

**Transportation:** Commute to work: 83.7% car, 11.7% public transportation, 1.3% walk, 2.8% work from home (2006-2010 5-year est.); Travel time to work: 18.4% less than 15 minutes, 35.6% 15 to 30 minutes, 18.7% 30 to 45 minutes, 8.2% 45 to 60 minutes, 19.0% 60 minutes or more (2006-2010 5-year est.)

**Additional Information Contacts**
Village of Massapequa Park . . . . . . . . . . . . . . . . . . . . . (516) 798-0244
    http://www.masspk.com

## MATINECOCK

**MATINECOCK** (village). Covers a land area of 2.657 square miles and a water area of 0.004 square miles. Located at 40.85° N. Lat; 73.58° W. Long. Elevation is 89 feet.

**Population:** 872 (1990); 836 (2000); 810 (2010); Density: 304.8 persons per square mile (2010); Race: 94.7% White, 1.9% Black, 2.0% Asian, 0.0% American Indian/Alaska Native, 0.0% Native Hawaiian/Other Pacific Islander, 1.4% Other, 6.2% Hispanic of any race (2010); Average household size: 2.98 (2010); Median age: 45.5 (2010); Males per 100 females: 101.0 (2010); Marriage status: 20.4% never married, 72.1% now married, 4.6% widowed, 2.9% divorced (2006-2010 5-year est.); Foreign born: 9.1% (2006-2010 5-year est.); Ancestry (includes multiple ancestries): 29.2% Italian, 20.9% English, 11.6% Irish, 11.1% German, 7.2% French (2006-2010 5-year est.).

**Economy:** Single-family building permits issued: 0 (2011); Multi-family building permits issued: 0 (2011); Employment by occupation: 30.3% management, 3.4% professional, 4.0% services, 13.0% sales, 1.9% farming, 1.9% construction, 4.3% production (2006-2010 5-year est.).

**Income:** Per capita income: $108,118 (2006-2010 5-year est.); Median household income: $170,833 (2006-2010 5-year est.); Average household income: $309,598 (2006-2010 5-year est.); Percent of households with income of $100,000 or more: 62.9% (2006-2010 5-year est.); Poverty rate: 1.8% (2006-2010 5-year est.).

**Education:** Percent of population age 25 and over with: High school diploma (including GED) or higher: 97.1% (2006-2010 5-year est.); Bachelor's degree or higher: 65.6% (2006-2010 5-year est.); Master's degree or higher: 25.7% (2006-2010 5-year est.).

**Housing:** Homeownership rate: 84.2% (2010); Median home value: $1 (2006-2010 5-year est.); Median contract rent: $1,156 per month (2006-2010 5-year est.); Median year structure built: 1953 (2006-2010 5-year est.).

**Transportation:** Commute to work: 83.0% car, 13.0% public transportation, 0.9% walk, 3.1% work from home (2006-2010 5-year est.); Travel time to work: 39.0% less than 15 minutes, 20.8% 15 to 30 minutes, 12.1% 30 to 45 minutes, 2.6% 45 to 60 minutes, 25.6% 60 minutes or more (2006-2010 5-year est.)

**Additional Information Contacts**
Village of Matinecock . . . . . . . . . . . . . . . . . . . . . . . . . (516) 671-7790
    http://www.matinecockvillage.org

## MERRICK

**MERRICK** (CDP). Covers a land area of 4.019 square miles and a water area of 1.133 square miles. Located at 40.65° N. Lat; 73.55° W. Long. Elevation is 13 feet.

**History:** The name Merrick is taken from "Meroke", the name (meaning peaceful) of the Algonquin tribe formerly indigenous to the area. It is served by the Merrick station on the Long Island Rail Road.

**Population:** 23,042 (1990); 22,764 (2000); 22,097 (2010); Density: 5,497.6 persons per square mile (2010); Race: 93.4% White, 1.2% Black, 2.8% Asian, 0.1% American Indian/Alaska Native, 0.0% Native Hawaiian/Other Pacific Islander, 2.5% Other, 5.9% Hispanic of any race (2010); Average household size: 2.96 (2010); Median age: 43.3 (2010); Males per 100 females: 93.3 (2010); Marriage status: 24.5% never married, 64.8% now married, 5.7% widowed, 5.0% divorced (2006-2010 5-year est.); Foreign born: 8.4% (2006-2010 5-year est.); Ancestry (includes multiple ancestries): 24.0% Italian, 18.2% Irish, 11.5% German, 10.2% Russian, 9.9% Polish (2006-2010 5-year est.).

**Economy:** Employment by occupation: 18.8% management, 3.1% professional, 2.2% services, 16.9% sales, 4.2% farming, 5.0% construction, 2.9% production (2006-2010 5-year est.).

**Income:** Per capita income: $48,768 (2006-2010 5-year est.); Median household income: $122,105 (2006-2010 5-year est.); Average household income: $143,344 (2006-2010 5-year est.); Percent of households with income of $100,000 or more: 61.8% (2006-2010 5-year est.); Poverty rate: 2.3% (2006-2010 5-year est.).

**Education:** Percent of population age 25 and over with: High school diploma (including GED) or higher: 97.0% (2006-2010 5-year est.); Bachelor's degree or higher: 54.9% (2006-2010 5-year est.); Master's degree or higher: 28.5% (2006-2010 5-year est.).

**School District(s)**

Bellmore-Merrick Central High School District (07-12)

    2009-10 Enrollment: 6,086 . . . . . . . . . . . . . . . . . . . . (516) 992-1001

Merrick Union Free School District (KG-06)

    2009-10 Enrollment: 1,726 . . . . . . . . . . . . . . . . . . . . (516) 992-7240

North Merrick Union Free School District (KG-06)

    2009-10 Enrollment: 1,314 . . . . . . . . . . . . . . . . . . . . (516) 292-3694

**Housing:** Homeownership rate: 93.5% (2010); Median home value: $556,000 (2006-2010 5-year est.); Median contract rent: $1,517 per month (2006-2010 5-year est.); Median year structure built: 1956 (2006-2010 5-year est.).

**Newspapers:** Bellmore Life (Community news; Circulation 4,062); Freeport-Baldwin Leader (Local news; Circulation 1,903); Merrick Life (Community news; Circulation 6,252); Wantagh/Seaford Citizen (Local news; Circulation 2,850)

**Transportation:** Commute to work: 74.2% car, 20.8% public transportation, 1.2% walk, 3.4% work from home (2006-2010 5-year est.); Travel time to work: 18.7% less than 15 minutes, 30.7% 15 to 30 minutes, 17.2% 30 to 45 minutes, 7.6% 45 to 60 minutes, 25.8% 60 minutes or more (2006-2010 5-year est.)

**Additional Information Contacts**

Merrick Chamber of Commerce. . . . . . . . . . . . . . . . . . . . . (516) 771-1171

    http://www.merrickchamber.org

**MILL NECK** (village). Covers a land area of 2.609 square miles and a water area of 0.320 square miles. Located at 40.88° N. Lat; 73.55° W. Long. Elevation is 141 feet.

**Population:** 977 (1990); 825 (2000); 997 (2010); Density: 382.1 persons per square mile (2010); Race: 89.7% White, 1.2% Black, 6.2% Asian, 0.0% American Indian/Alaska Native, 0.0% Native Hawaiian/Other Pacific Islander, 2.9% Other, 5.7% Hispanic of any race (2010); Average household size: 2.63 (2010); Median age: 50.6 (2010); Males per 100 females: 89.9 (2010); Marriage status: 15.4% never married, 68.7% now married, 9.9% widowed, 5.9% divorced (2006-2010 5-year est.); Foreign born: 14.4% (2006-2010 5-year est.); Ancestry (includes multiple ancestries): 24.8% Italian, 23.4% Irish, 16.3% German, 15.8% English, 13.9% Polish (2006-2010 5-year est.).

**Economy:** Single-family building permits issued: 0 (2011); Multi-family building permits issued: 0 (2011); Employment by occupation: 33.0% management, 2.7% professional, 2.7% services, 8.0% sales, 2.1% farming, 3.0% construction, 3.6% production (2006-2010 5-year est.).

**Income:** Per capita income: $131,103 (2006-2010 5-year est.); Median household income: $120,250 (2006-2010 5-year est.); Average household income: $314,149 (2006-2010 5-year est.); Percent of households with income of $100,000 or more: 60.5% (2006-2010 5-year est.); Poverty rate: 8.4% (2006-2010 5-year est.).

**Education:** Percent of population age 25 and over with: High school diploma (including GED) or higher: 97.7% (2006-2010 5-year est.); Bachelor's degree or higher: 56.3% (2006-2010 5-year est.); Master's degree or higher: 27.4% (2006-2010 5-year est.).

**Housing:** Homeownership rate: 87.0% (2010); Median home value: $1 (2006-2010 5-year est.); Median contract rent: n/a per month (2006-2010 5-year est.); Median year structure built: 1960 (2006-2010 5-year est.).

**Transportation:** Commute to work: 79.9% car, 5.8% public transportation, 1.2% walk, 13.1% work from home (2006-2010 5-year est.); Travel time to work: 34.7% less than 15 minutes, 26.7% 15 to 30 minutes, 17.5% 30 to 45 minutes, 2.8% 45 to 60 minutes, 18.2% 60 minutes or more (2006-2010 5-year est.)

**MINEOLA** (village). County seat. Covers a land area of 1.879 square miles and a water area of 0 square miles. Located at 40.74° N. Lat; 73.63° W. Long. Elevation is 108 feet.

**History:** Named for the Algonquian translation of "pleasant village". Incorporated 1906.

**Population:** 19,006 (1990); 19,234 (2000); 18,799 (2010); Density: 10,002.0 persons per square mile (2010); Race: 81.7% White, 2.0% Black, 8.5% Asian, 0.2% American Indian/Alaska Native, 0.0% Native Hawaiian/Other Pacific Islander, 7.6% Other, 16.4% Hispanic of any race (2010); Average household size: 2.54 (2010); Median age: 40.3 (2010); Males per 100 females: 96.2 (2010); Marriage status: 29.8% never married, 56.8% now married, 6.7% widowed, 6.7% divorced (2006-2010 5-year est.); Foreign born: 28.7% (2006-2010 5-year est.); Ancestry (includes multiple ancestries): 21.6% Italian, 18.0% Irish, 12.7% Portuguese, 11.7% German, 5.0% English (2006-2010 5-year est.).

**Economy:** Single-family building permits issued: 2 (2011); Multi-family building permits issued: 0 (2011); Employment by occupation: 10.1% management, 4.5% professional, 9.1% services, 17.1% sales, 3.3% farming, 10.6% construction, 4.1% production (2006-2010 5-year est.).

**Income:** Per capita income: $35,294 (2006-2010 5-year est.); Median household income: $75,221 (2006-2010 5-year est.); Average household income: $90,171 (2006-2010 5-year est.); Percent of households with income of $100,000 or more: 34.4% (2006-2010 5-year est.); Poverty rate: 3.7% (2006-2010 5-year est.).

**Education:** Percent of population age 25 and over with: High school diploma (including GED) or higher: 87.8% (2006-2010 5-year est.); Bachelor's degree or higher: 35.4% (2006-2010 5-year est.); Master's degree or higher: 15.1% (2006-2010 5-year est.).

**School District(s)**

Mineola Union Free School District (PK-12)

    2009-10 Enrollment: 2,716 . . . . . . . . . . . . . . . . . . . . (516) 237-2001

**Four-year College(s)**

New York College of Traditional Chinese Medicine (Private, Not-for-profit)

    Fall 2010 Enrollment: 218 . . . . . . . . . . . . . . . . . . . . (516) 739-1545

**Housing:** Homeownership rate: 64.3% (2010); Median home value: $470,700 (2006-2010 5-year est.); Median contract rent: $1,293 per month (2006-2010 5-year est.); Median year structure built: 1951 (2006-2010 5-year est.).

**Hospitals:** Winthrop University Hospital (591 beds)

**Newspapers:** Farmingdale Observer (Community news; Circulation 3,120); Floral Park Dispatch (Community news; Circulation 1,320); Garden City Life (Community news; Circulation 2,922); Glen Cove Record-Pilot (Local news; Circulation 5,673); Great Neck Record (Community news; Circulation 5,793); Hicksville Illustrated News (Community news; Circulation 5,162); Levittown Tribune (Community news; Circulation 3,864); Manhasset Press (Community news; Circulation 4,085); Massapequan Observer (Community news; Circulation 2,324); Mineola American (Community news; Circulation 4,007); New Hyde Park Illustrated (Community news; Circulation 3,345); New Hyde Park Illustrated News (Community news; Circulation 3,345); Oyster Bay Enterprise Pilot (Community news; Circulation 2,200); Plainview/Old Bethpage Herald (Community news; Circulation 2,347); Port Washington News (Community news; Circulation 6,729); Roslyn News (Community news; Circulation 3,100); Syosset/Jericho Tribune (Community news; Circulation 3,233); Three Village Times (Community news; Circulation 2,048); Westbury Times (Community news; Circulation 3,148)

**Transportation:** Commute to work: 75.3% car, 17.8% public transportation, 5.8% walk, 0.2% work from home (2006-2010 5-year est.); Travel time to work: 25.8% less than 15 minutes, 29.4% 15 to 30 minutes, 19.4% 30 to 45 minutes, 6.4% 45 to 60 minutes, 9.0% 60 minutes or more (2006-2010 5-year est.)

**Additional Information Contacts**

Mineola Chamber of Commerce . . . . . . . . . . . . . . . . . . . . (516) 408-3554

    http://www.mineolachamber.com

**MUNSEY PARK** (village). Covers a land area of 0.518 square miles and a water area of 0 square miles. Located at 40.79° N. Lat; 73.67° W. Long. Elevation is 157 feet.

**Population:** 2,692 (1990); 2,632 (2000); 2,693 (2010); Density: 5,195.8 persons per square mile (2010); Race: 91.2% White, 0.4% Black, 6.5% Asian, 0.0% American Indian/Alaska Native, 0.0% Native Hawaiian/Other Pacific Islander, 1.9% Other, 3.2% Hispanic of any race (2010); Average household size: 3.29 (2010); Median age: 41.2 (2010); Males per 100 females: 102.0 (2010); Marriage status: 22.6% never married, 70.1% now married, 3.3% widowed, 4.0% divorced (2006-2010 5-year est.); Foreign

born: 9.2% (2006-2010 5-year est.); Ancestry (includes multiple ancestries): 37.6% Italian, 35.8% Irish, 21.4% German, 7.7% English, 3.9% Armenian (2006-2010 5-year est.).

**Economy:** Single-family building permits issued: 0 (2011); Multi-family building permits issued: 0 (2011); Employment by occupation: 23.6% management, 4.2% professional, 2.4% services, 7.4% sales, 3.7% farming, 0.0% construction, 0.9% production (2006-2010 5-year est.).

**Income:** Per capita income: $99,851 (2006-2010 5-year est.); Median household income: $227,716 (2006-2010 5-year est.); Average household income: $352,510 (2006-2010 5-year est.); Percent of households with income of $100,000 or more: 81.7% (2006-2010 5-year est.); Poverty rate: 0.8% (2006-2010 5-year est.).

**Education:** Percent of population age 25 and over with: High school diploma (including GED) or higher: 98.5% (2006-2010 5-year est.); Bachelor's degree or higher: 82.4% (2006-2010 5-year est.); Master's degree or higher: 42.2% (2006-2010 5-year est.).

**Housing:** Homeownership rate: 98.4% (2010); Median home value: $1 (2006-2010 5-year est.); Median contract rent: n/a per month (2006-2010 5-year est.); Median year structure built: 1944 (2006-2010 5-year est.).

**Transportation:** Commute to work: 61.7% car, 28.7% public transportation, 3.7% walk, 5.9% work from home (2006-2010 5-year est.); Travel time to work: 15.3% less than 15 minutes, 21.7% 15 to 30 minutes, 15.1% 30 to 45 minutes, 14.2% 45 to 60 minutes, 33.7% 60 minutes or more (2006-2010 5-year est.)

## MUTTONTOWN

(village). Covers a land area of 6.062 square miles and a water area of 0 square miles. Located at 40.82° N. Lat; 73.53° W. Long. Elevation is 285 feet.

**History:** During colonial times the area was used to raise sheep for wool and meat, thus giving the town its name "mutton". The village was incorporated in 1931.

**Population:** 3,024 (1990); 3,412 (2000); 3,497 (2010); Density: 576.8 persons per square mile (2010); Race: 73.3% White, 1.6% Black, 22.7% Asian, 0.1% American Indian/Alaska Native, 0.0% Native Hawaiian/Other Pacific Islander, 2.3% Other, 3.4% Hispanic of any race (2010); Average household size: 3.27 (2010); Median age: 44.8 (2010); Males per 100 females: 99.8 (2010); Marriage status: 35.3% never married, 58.8% now married, 3.2% widowed, 2.6% divorced (2006-2010 5-year est.); Foreign born: 23.4% (2006-2010 5-year est.); Ancestry (includes multiple ancestries): 23.5% Italian, 9.1% Russian, 5.7% German, 5.6% Polish, 5.3% Irish (2006-2010 5-year est.).

**Economy:** Single-family building permits issued: 15 (2011); Multi-family building permits issued: 0 (2011); Employment by occupation: 21.0% management, 3.6% professional, 4.2% services, 17.9% sales, 1.6% farming, 2.1% construction, 0.0% production (2006-2010 5-year est.).

**Income:** Per capita income: $92,592 (2006-2010 5-year est.); Median household income: $225,417 (2006-2010 5-year est.); Average household income: $361,732 (2006-2010 5-year est.); Percent of households with income of $100,000 or more: 79.7% (2006-2010 5-year est.); Poverty rate: 2.6% (2006-2010 5-year est.).

**Education:** Percent of population age 25 and over with: High school diploma (including GED) or higher: 94.7% (2006-2010 5-year est.); Bachelor's degree or higher: 73.3% (2006-2010 5-year est.); Master's degree or higher: 36.2% (2006-2010 5-year est.).

**Housing:** Homeownership rate: 96.0% (2010); Median home value: $1 (2006-2010 5-year est.); Median contract rent: $1,667 per month (2006-2010 5-year est.); Median year structure built: 1970 (2006-2010 5-year est.).

**Transportation:** Commute to work: 76.5% car, 9.2% public transportation, 7.2% walk, 6.4% work from home (2006-2010 5-year est.); Travel time to work: 25.3% less than 15 minutes, 27.9% 15 to 30 minutes, 22.6% 30 to 45 minutes, 6.2% 45 to 60 minutes, 18.0% 60 minutes or more (2006-2010 5-year est.)

## NEW CASSEL

(CDP). Covers a land area of 1.479 square miles and a water area of 0 square miles. Located at 40.76° N. Lat; 73.56° W. Long. Elevation is 121 feet.

**Population:** 10,257 (1990); 13,298 (2000); 14,059 (2010); Density: 9,504.8 persons per square mile (2010); Race: 26.0% White, 38.2% Black, 1.4% Asian, 0.8% American Indian/Alaska Native, 0.0% Native Hawaiian/Other Pacific Islander, 33.6% Other, 53.9% Hispanic of any race (2010); Average household size: 4.72 (2010); Median age: 30.9 (2010); Males per 100 females: 103.5 (2010); Marriage status: 45.6% never married, 43.0% now married, 5.0% widowed, 6.4% divorced (2006-2010 5-year est.); Foreign born: 48.3% (2006-2010 5-year est.); Ancestry (includes multiple

ancestries): 8.4% Haitian, 2.7% Jamaican, 2.1% Italian, 1.4% African, 1.0% Nigerian (2006-2010 5-year est.).

**Economy:** Employment by occupation: 3.2% management, 0.4% professional, 11.6% services, 14.1% sales, 6.4% farming, 9.4% construction, 12.6% production (2006-2010 5-year est.).

**Income:** Per capita income: $21,482 (2006-2010 5-year est.); Median household income: $69,952 (2006-2010 5-year est.); Average household income: $82,711 (2006-2010 5-year est.); Percent of households with income of $100,000 or more: 31.9% (2006-2010 5-year est.); Poverty rate: 16.6% (2006-2010 5-year est.).

**Education:** Percent of population age 25 and over with: High school diploma (including GED) or higher: 65.1% (2006-2010 5-year est.); Bachelor's degree or higher: 15.2% (2006-2010 5-year est.); Master's degree or higher: 4.3% (2006-2010 5-year est.).

**Housing:** Homeownership rate: 61.6% (2010); Median home value: $378,000 (2006-2010 5-year est.); Median contract rent: $1,056 per month (2006-2010 5-year est.); Median year structure built: 1958 (2006-2010 5-year est.).

**Transportation:** Commute to work: 80.5% car, 11.4% public transportation, 2.5% walk, 2.8% work from home (2006-2010 5-year est.); Travel time to work: 31.8% less than 15 minutes, 30.4% 15 to 30 minutes, 26.7% 30 to 45 minutes, 2.0% 45 to 60 minutes, 9.0% 60 minutes or more (2006-2010 5-year est.)

## NEW HYDE PARK

(village). Covers a land area of 0.859 square miles and a water area of 0 square miles. Located at 40.73° N. Lat; 73.68° W. Long. Elevation is 105 feet.

**History:** Incorporated 1927.

**Population:** 9,728 (1990); 9,523 (2000); 9,712 (2010); Density: 11,298.2 persons per square mile (2010); Race: 65.9% White, 1.3% Black, 26.0% Asian, 0.3% American Indian/Alaska Native, 0.0% Native Hawaiian/Other Pacific Islander, 6.5% Other, 12.2% Hispanic of any race (2010); Average household size: 2.97 (2010); Median age: 42.3 (2010); Males per 100 females: 94.0 (2010); Marriage status: 27.7% never married, 58.6% now married, 8.4% widowed, 5.3% divorced (2006-2010 5-year est.); Foreign born: 29.6% (2006-2010 5-year est.); Ancestry (includes multiple ancestries): 25.6% Italian, 16.0% Irish, 9.3% German, 4.2% Polish, 3.1% English (2006-2010 5-year est.).

**Economy:** Single-family building permits issued: 1 (2011); Multi-family building permits issued: 0 (2011); Employment by occupation: 13.9% management, 4.6% professional, 5.9% services, 18.2% sales, 5.4% farming, 9.4% construction, 5.5% production (2006-2010 5-year est.).

**Income:** Per capita income: $36,152 (2006-2010 5-year est.); Median household income: $89,524 (2006-2010 5-year est.); Average household income: $104,460 (2006-2010 5-year est.); Percent of households with income of $100,000 or more: 42.7% (2006-2010 5-year est.); Poverty rate: 2.4% (2006-2010 5-year est.).

**Education:** Percent of population age 25 and over with: High school diploma (including GED) or higher: 86.9% (2006-2010 5-year est.); Bachelor's degree or higher: 33.2% (2006-2010 5-year est.); Master's degree or higher: 11.8% (2006-2010 5-year est.).

### School District(s)

Great Neck Union Free School District (PK-12)
   2009-10 Enrollment: 6,526 . . . . . . . . . . . . . . . . . . . . (516) 441-4001
Herricks Union Free School District (KG-12)
   2009-10 Enrollment: 4,044 . . . . . . . . . . . . . . . . . . . . (516) 305-8901
New Hyde Park-Garden City Park Union Free School D (KG-06)
   2009-10 Enrollment: 1,621 . . . . . . . . . . . . . . . . . . . . (516) 352-6257
Sewanhaka Central High School District (07-12)
   2009-10 Enrollment: 8,449 . . . . . . . . . . . . . . . . . . . . (516) 488-9800

**Housing:** Homeownership rate: 82.7% (2010); Median home value: $489,100 (2006-2010 5-year est.); Median contract rent: $1,189 per month (2006-2010 5-year est.); Median year structure built: 1950 (2006-2010 5-year est.).

**Hospitals:** Long Island Jewish Medical Center (452 beds); Schneider Children's Hospital (154 beds)

**Transportation:** Commute to work: 74.4% car, 17.8% public transportation, 1.2% walk, 4.1% work from home (2006-2010 5-year est.); Travel time to work: 20.4% less than 15 minutes, 26.1% 15 to 30 minutes, 22.9% 30 to 45 minutes, 10.9% 45 to 60 minutes, 19.7% 60 minutes or more (2006-2010 5-year est.)

**Additional Information Contacts**
Greater New Hyde Park Chamber of Commerce . . . . . . . . (888) 400-0311
   http://www.nhpchamber.org

Village of New Hyde Park . . . . . . . . . . . . . . . . . . . . (516) 354-0022
    http://www.vnhp.org

## NORTH BELLMORE (CDP). Covers a land area of 2.620 square
miles and a water area of 0 square miles. Located at 40.69° N. Lat; 73.53°
W. Long. Elevation is 46 feet.
**Population:** 19,713 (1990); 20,079 (2000); 19,941 (2010); Density: 7,610.4
persons per square mile (2010); Race: 89.5% White, 2.6% Black, 4.6%
Asian, 0.1% American Indian/Alaska Native, 0.0% Native Hawaiian/Other
Pacific Islander, 3.2% Other, 7.7% Hispanic of any race (2010); Average
household size: 2.98 (2010); Median age: 41.6 (2010); Males per 100
females: 93.8 (2010); Marriage status: 26.5% never married, 61.7% now
married, 6.2% widowed, 5.5% divorced (2006-2010 5-year est.); Foreign
born: 10.0% (2006-2010 5-year est.); Ancestry (includes multiple
ancestries): 32.2% Italian, 22.8% Irish, 17.7% German, 7.4% Polish, 5.4%
Russian (2006-2010 5-year est.).
**Economy:** Employment by occupation: 16.6% management, 4.9%
professional, 5.7% services, 15.6% sales, 6.0% farming, 4.6%
construction, 3.5% production (2006-2010 5-year est.).
**Income:** Per capita income: $38,135 (2006-2010 5-year est.); Median
household income: $103,750 (2006-2010 5-year est.); Average household
income: $115,222 (2006-2010 5-year est.); Percent of households with
income of $100,000 or more: 51.7% (2006-2010 5-year est.); Poverty rate:
2.9% (2006-2010 5-year est.).
**Education:** Percent of population age 25 and over with: High school
diploma (including GED) or higher: 91.6% (2006-2010 5-year est.);
Bachelor's degree or higher: 36.7% (2006-2010 5-year est.); Master's
degree or higher: 16.5% (2006-2010 5-year est.).

### School District(s)
North Bellmore Union Free School District (PK-06)
    2009-10 Enrollment: 2,148 . . . . . . . . . . . . . . . . . (516) 992-3000
**Housing:** Homeownership rate: 88.1% (2010); Median home value:
$459,900 (2006-2010 5-year est.); Median contract rent: $1,639 per month
(2006-2010 5-year est.); Median year structure built: 1956 (2006-2010
5-year est.).
**Transportation:** Commute to work: 81.2% car, 12.4% public
transportation, 2.9% walk, 3.1% work from home (2006-2010 5-year est.);
Travel time to work: 21.8% less than 15 minutes, 38.8% 15 to 30 minutes,
16.5% 30 to 45 minutes, 4.6% 45 to 60 minutes, 18.4% 60 minutes or more
(2006-2010 5-year est.)

## NORTH HEMPSTEAD (town). Covers a land area of 53.512 square
miles and a water area of 15.597 square miles. Located at 40.80° N. Lat;
73.67° W. Long. Elevation is 157 feet.
**Population:** 211,355 (1990); 222,611 (2000); 226,322 (2010); Density:
4,229.3 persons per square mile (2010); Race: 71.6% White, 5.6% Black,
15.0% Asian, 0.2% American Indian/Alaska Native, 0.0% Native
Hawaiian/Other Pacific Islander, 7.6% Other, 12.8% Hispanic of any race
(2010); Average household size: 2.87 (2010); Median age: 42.4 (2010);
Males per 100 females: 94.5 (2010); Marriage status: 26.9% never married,
60.3% now married, 7.1% widowed, 5.8% divorced (2006-2010 5-year
est.); Foreign born: 27.3% (2006-2010 5-year est.); Ancestry (includes
multiple ancestries): 18.0% Italian, 12.2% Irish, 8.2% German, 6.6%
Russian, 6.0% Polish (2006-2010 5-year est.).
**Economy:** Unemployment rate: 6.4% (February 2012); Total civilian labor
force: 112,195 (February 2012); Single-family building permits issued: 28
(2011); Multi-family building permits issued: 0 (2011); Employment by
occupation: 17.3% management, 3.8% professional, 5.6% services, 14.9%
sales, 3.4% farming, 5.2% construction, 3.5% production (2006-2010
5-year est.).
**Income:** Per capita income: $51,663 (2006-2010 5-year est.); Median
household income: $100,760 (2006-2010 5-year est.); Average household
income: $147,254 (2006-2010 5-year est.); Percent of households with
income of $100,000 or more: 50.5% (2006-2010 5-year est.); Poverty rate:
4.7% (2006-2010 5-year est.).
**Taxes:** Total city taxes per capita: $567 (2009); City property taxes per
capita: $507 (2009).
**Education:** Percent of population age 25 and over with: High school
diploma (including GED) or higher: 90.2% (2006-2010 5-year est.);
Bachelor's degree or higher: 51.5% (2006-2010 5-year est.); Master's
degree or higher: 25.1% (2006-2010 5-year est.).
**Housing:** Homeownership rate: 78.1% (2010); Median home value:
$659,200 (2006-2010 5-year est.); Median contract rent: $1,378 per month
(2006-2010 5-year est.); Median year structure built: 1953 (2006-2010
5-year est.).

**Transportation:** Commute to work: 72.2% car, 19.5% public
transportation, 3.2% walk, 4.1% work from home (2006-2010 5-year est.);
Travel time to work: 23.1% less than 15 minutes, 26.6% 15 to 30 minutes,
19.7% 30 to 45 minutes, 8.8% 45 to 60 minutes, 21.7% 60 minutes or more
(2006-2010 5-year est.)
**Additional Information Contacts**
Town of North Hempstead . . . . . . . . . . . . . . . . . (516) 869-7646
    http://www.northhempsteadny.gov

## NORTH HILLS (village). Covers a land area of 2.759 square miles
and a water area of 0 square miles. Located at 40.77° N. Lat; 73.67° W.
Long. Elevation is 217 feet.
**Population:** 3,453 (1990); 4,301 (2000); 5,075 (2010); Density: 1,839.4
persons per square mile (2010); Race: 71.1% White, 1.2% Black, 25.3%
Asian, 0.0% American Indian/Alaska Native, 0.0% Native Hawaiian/Other
Pacific Islander, 2.4% Other, 2.2% Hispanic of any race (2010); Average
household size: 2.23 (2010); Median age: 58.7 (2010); Males per 100
females: 87.6 (2010); Marriage status: 15.5% never married, 64.9% now
married, 10.5% widowed, 9.0% divorced (2006-2010 5-year est.); Foreign
born: 22.2% (2006-2010 5-year est.); Ancestry (includes multiple
ancestries): 16.5% Russian, 12.4% Italian, 6.8% Polish, 6.4% Iranian, 5.7%
German (2006-2010 5-year est.).
**Economy:** Single-family building permits issued: 6 (2011); Multi-family
building permits issued: 0 (2011); Employment by occupation: 24.3%
management, 0.9% professional, 1.9% services, 17.0% sales, 2.0%
farming, 1.3% construction, 3.2% production (2006-2010 5-year est.).
**Income:** Per capita income: $94,960 (2006-2010 5-year est.); Median
household income: $128,967 (2006-2010 5-year est.); Average household
income: $208,186 (2006-2010 5-year est.); Percent of households with
income of $100,000 or more: 63.7% (2006-2010 5-year est.); Poverty rate:
2.4% (2006-2010 5-year est.).
**Education:** Percent of population age 25 and over with: High school
diploma (including GED) or higher: 98.5% (2006-2010 5-year est.);
Bachelor's degree or higher: 55.9% (2006-2010 5-year est.); Master's
degree or higher: 24.4% (2006-2010 5-year est.).
**Housing:** Homeownership rate: 89.1% (2010); Median home value:
$972,800 (2006-2010 5-year est.); Median contract rent: n/a per month
(2006-2010 5-year est.); Median year structure built: 1985 (2006-2010
5-year est.).
**Transportation:** Commute to work: 85.5% car, 9.6% public transportation,
1.4% walk, 3.4% work from home (2006-2010 5-year est.); Travel time to
work: 18.5% less than 15 minutes, 28.8% 15 to 30 minutes, 23.5% 30 to 45
minutes, 10.3% 45 to 60 minutes, 19.0% 60 minutes or more (2006-2010
5-year est.)

## NORTH LYNBROOK (CDP). Covers a land area of 0.086 square
miles and a water area of 0 square miles. Located at 40.66° N. Lat; 73.67°
W. Long.
**Population:** 689 (1990); 742 (2000); 793 (2010); Density: 9,165.0 persons
per square mile (2010); Race: 81.6% White, 3.4% Black, 5.7% Asian, 0.0%
American Indian/Alaska Native, 0.0% Native Hawaiian/Other Pacific
Islander, 9.3% Other, 15.0% Hispanic of any race (2010); Average
household size: 2.98 (2010); Median age: 50.0 (2010); Males per 100
females: 91.5 (2010); Marriage status: 15.6% never married, 54.5% now
married, 18.2% widowed, 11.7% divorced (2006-2010 5-year est.); Foreign
born: 29.2% (2006-2010 5-year est.); Ancestry (includes multiple
ancestries): 36.9% Irish, 36.5% Italian, 11.9% German, 4.0% Croatian,
3.0% English (2006-2010 5-year est.).
**Economy:** Employment by occupation: 5.5% management, 0.0%
professional, 8.8% services, 7.4% sales, 10.0% farming, 8.1%
construction, 0.0% production (2006-2010 5-year est.).
**Income:** Per capita income: $39,518 (2006-2010 5-year est.); Median
household income: $89,250 (2006-2010 5-year est.); Average household
income: $95,580 (2006-2010 5-year est.); Percent of households with
income of $100,000 or more: 47.0% (2006-2010 5-year est.); Poverty rate:
1.3% (2006-2010 5-year est.).
**Education:** Percent of population age 25 and over with: High school
diploma (including GED) or higher: 88.6% (2006-2010 5-year est.);
Bachelor's degree or higher: 24.3% (2006-2010 5-year est.); Master's
degree or higher: 12.8% (2006-2010 5-year est.).
**Housing:** Homeownership rate: 88.8% (2010); Median home value:
$476,000 (2006-2010 5-year est.); Median contract rent: n/a per month
(2006-2010 5-year est.); Median year structure built: 1943 (2006-2010
5-year est.).

**Transportation:** Commute to work: 81.1% car, 0.0% public transportation, 9.5% walk, 6.4% work from home (2006-2010 5-year est.); Travel time to work: 37.0% less than 15 minutes, 20.2% 15 to 30 minutes, 25.0% 30 to 45 minutes, 17.9% 45 to 60 minutes, 0.0% 60 minutes or more (2006-2010 5-year est.)

## NORTH MASSAPEQUA (CDP). Covers a land area of 2.995 square miles and a water area of 0.005 square miles. Located at 40.70° N. Lat; 73.46° W. Long. Elevation is 46 feet.

**Population:** 19,397 (1990); 19,152 (2000); 17,886 (2010); Density: 5,971.3 persons per square mile (2010); Race: 96.0% White, 0.4% Black, 1.8% Asian, 0.0% American Indian/Alaska Native, 0.0% Native Hawaiian/Other Pacific Islander, 1.8% Other, 5.4% Hispanic of any race (2010); Average household size: 2.94 (2010); Median age: 42.6 (2010); Males per 100 females: 93.1 (2010); Marriage status: 25.1% never married, 62.8% now married, 7.9% widowed, 4.1% divorced (2006-2010 5-year est.); Foreign born: 8.7% (2006-2010 5-year est.); Ancestry (includes multiple ancestries): 50.3% Italian, 24.8% Irish, 15.6% German, 6.4% Polish, 4.2% Greek (2006-2010 5-year est.).
**Economy:** Employment by occupation: 14.4% management, 3.3% professional, 5.9% services, 19.1% sales, 5.9% farming, 9.0% construction, 5.2% production (2006-2010 5-year est.).
**Income:** Per capita income: $35,733 (2006-2010 5-year est.); Median household income: $99,931 (2006-2010 5-year est.); Average household income: $106,363 (2006-2010 5-year est.); Percent of households with income of $100,000 or more: 49.9% (2006-2010 5-year est.); Poverty rate: 2.6% (2006-2010 5-year est.).
**Education:** Percent of population age 25 and over with: High school diploma (including GED) or higher: 91.6% (2006-2010 5-year est.); Bachelor's degree or higher: 28.5% (2006-2010 5-year est.); Master's degree or higher: 11.4% (2006-2010 5-year est.).
### School District(s)
Farmingdale Union Free School District (KG-12)
   2009-10 Enrollment: 6,100 . . . . . . . . . . . . . . . . . . . (516) 752-6510
Plainedge Union Free School District (KG-12)
   2009-10 Enrollment: 3,437 . . . . . . . . . . . . . . . . . . . (516) 992-7455
**Housing:** Homeownership rate: 92.1% (2010); Median home value: $458,300 (2006-2010 5-year est.); Median contract rent: $1,183 per month (2006-2010 5-year est.); Median year structure built: 1956 (2006-2010 5-year est.).
**Transportation:** Commute to work: 84.5% car, 11.4% public transportation, 1.0% walk, 2.8% work from home (2006-2010 5-year est.); Travel time to work: 24.5% less than 15 minutes, 31.5% 15 to 30 minutes, 19.7% 30 to 45 minutes, 7.3% 45 to 60 minutes, 17.0% 60 minutes or more (2006-2010 5-year est.)

## NORTH MERRICK (CDP). Covers a land area of 1.718 square miles and a water area of 0.007 square miles. Located at 40.68° N. Lat; 73.56° W. Long. Elevation is 46 feet.

**Population:** 12,107 (1990); 11,844 (2000); 12,272 (2010); Density: 7,139.6 persons per square mile (2010); Race: 90.6% White, 1.5% Black, 4.7% Asian, 0.1% American Indian/Alaska Native, 0.0% Native Hawaiian/Other Pacific Islander, 3.1% Other, 7.1% Hispanic of any race (2010); Average household size: 3.03 (2010); Median age: 41.3 (2010); Males per 100 females: 95.6 (2010); Marriage status: 20.8% never married, 67.5% now married, 7.4% widowed, 4.3% divorced (2006-2010 5-year est.); Foreign born: 8.8% (2006-2010 5-year est.); Ancestry (includes multiple ancestries): 36.1% Italian, 27.4% Irish, 18.9% German, 5.8% Polish, 5.1% English (2006-2010 5-year est.).
**Economy:** Employment by occupation: 17.3% management, 2.3% professional, 3.5% services, 17.8% sales, 6.0% farming, 8.1% construction, 3.9% production (2006-2010 5-year est.).
**Income:** Per capita income: $40,825 (2006-2010 5-year est.); Median household income: $113,264 (2006-2010 5-year est.); Average household income: $126,020 (2006-2010 5-year est.); Percent of households with income of $100,000 or more: 54.3% (2006-2010 5-year est.); Poverty rate: 0.9% (2006-2010 5-year est.).
**Education:** Percent of population age 25 and over with: High school diploma (including GED) or higher: 96.1% (2006-2010 5-year est.); Bachelor's degree or higher: 39.7% (2006-2010 5-year est.); Master's degree or higher: 17.5% (2006-2010 5-year est.).
### School District(s)
North Bellmore Union Free School District (PK-06)
   2009-10 Enrollment: 2,148 . . . . . . . . . . . . . . . . . . . (516) 992-3000

North Merrick Union Free School District (KG-06)
   2009-10 Enrollment: 1,314 . . . . . . . . . . . . . . . . . . . (516) 292-3694
**Housing:** Homeownership rate: 93.2% (2010); Median home value: $478,600 (2006-2010 5-year est.); Median contract rent: n/a per month (2006-2010 5-year est.); Median year structure built: 1954 (2006-2010 5-year est.).
**Transportation:** Commute to work: 82.7% car, 14.2% public transportation, 0.5% walk, 2.6% work from home (2006-2010 5-year est.); Travel time to work: 21.9% less than 15 minutes, 33.7% 15 to 30 minutes, 17.6% 30 to 45 minutes, 8.8% 45 to 60 minutes, 18.0% 60 minutes or more (2006-2010 5-year est.)

## NORTH NEW HYDE PARK (CDP). Covers a land area of 1.972 square miles and a water area of 0.021 square miles. Located at 40.74° N. Lat; 73.68° W. Long. Elevation is 115 feet.

**Population:** 14,475 (1990); 14,542 (2000); 14,899 (2010); Density: 7,552.7 persons per square mile (2010); Race: 65.7% White, 0.7% Black, 29.1% Asian, 0.3% American Indian/Alaska Native, 0.0% Native Hawaiian/Other Pacific Islander, 4.2% Other, 7.2% Hispanic of any race (2010); Average household size: 3.05 (2010); Median age: 44.3 (2010); Males per 100 females: 93.2 (2010); Marriage status: 27.5% never married, 62.1% now married, 6.7% widowed, 3.7% divorced (2006-2010 5-year est.); Foreign born: 28.1% (2006-2010 5-year est.); Ancestry (includes multiple ancestries): 25.2% Italian, 16.8% Irish, 8.8% German, 6.3% Polish, 4.8% American (2006-2010 5-year est.).
**Economy:** Employment by occupation: 16.1% management, 7.3% professional, 5.0% services, 16.3% sales, 6.3% farming, 4.6% construction, 1.6% production (2006-2010 5-year est.).
**Income:** Per capita income: $38,193 (2006-2010 5-year est.); Median household income: $97,308 (2006-2010 5-year est.); Average household income: $115,857 (2006-2010 5-year est.); Percent of households with income of $100,000 or more: 48.5% (2006-2010 5-year est.); Poverty rate: 3.6% (2006-2010 5-year est.).
**Education:** Percent of population age 25 and over with: High school diploma (including GED) or higher: 89.3% (2006-2010 5-year est.); Bachelor's degree or higher: 43.1% (2006-2010 5-year est.); Master's degree or higher: 18.2% (2006-2010 5-year est.).
**Housing:** Homeownership rate: 93.3% (2010); Median home value: $569,800 (2006-2010 5-year est.); Median contract rent: n/a per month (2006-2010 5-year est.); Median year structure built: 1948 (2006-2010 5-year est.).
**Transportation:** Commute to work: 75.3% car, 18.1% public transportation, 3.0% walk, 2.7% work from home (2006-2010 5-year est.); Travel time to work: 21.1% less than 15 minutes, 29.8% 15 to 30 minutes, 21.7% 30 to 45 minutes, 5.4% 45 to 60 minutes, 22.0% 60 minutes or more (2006-2010 5-year est.)

## NORTH VALLEY STREAM (CDP). Covers a land area of 1.864 square miles and a water area of 0.032 square miles. Located at 40.68° N. Lat; 73.70° W. Long. Elevation is 36 feet.

**Population:** 14,574 (1990); 15,789 (2000); 16,628 (2010); Density: 8,918.6 persons per square mile (2010); Race: 28.8% White, 48.1% Black, 12.9% Asian, 0.5% American Indian/Alaska Native, 0.0% Native Hawaiian/Other Pacific Islander, 9.7% Other, 14.5% Hispanic of any race (2010); Average household size: 3.24 (2010); Median age: 39.9 (2010); Males per 100 females: 87.6 (2010); Marriage status: 37.5% never married, 49.7% now married, 6.4% widowed, 6.4% divorced (2006-2010 5-year est.); Foreign born: 32.7% (2006-2010 5-year est.); Ancestry (includes multiple ancestries): 11.1% Haitian, 9.7% Italian, 7.6% Jamaican, 5.5% Irish, 4.7% German (2006-2010 5-year est.).
**Economy:** Employment by occupation: 10.3% management, 4.1% professional, 10.6% services, 14.3% sales, 6.3% farming, 5.6% construction, 4.8% production (2006-2010 5-year est.).
**Income:** Per capita income: $32,928 (2006-2010 5-year est.); Median household income: $93,199 (2006-2010 5-year est.); Average household income: $104,058 (2006-2010 5-year est.); Percent of households with income of $100,000 or more: 45.6% (2006-2010 5-year est.); Poverty rate: 3.4% (2006-2010 5-year est.).
**Education:** Percent of population age 25 and over with: High school diploma (including GED) or higher: 92.2% (2006-2010 5-year est.); Bachelor's degree or higher: 36.5% (2006-2010 5-year est.); Master's degree or higher: 14.7% (2006-2010 5-year est.).
**Housing:** Homeownership rate: 90.8% (2010); Median home value: $428,600 (2006-2010 5-year est.); Median contract rent: $1,414 per month

(2006-2010 5-year est.); Median year structure built: 1952 (2006-2010 5-year est.).
**Transportation:** Commute to work: 73.4% car, 22.7% public transportation, 1.1% walk, 2.4% work from home (2006-2010 5-year est.); Travel time to work: 12.1% less than 15 minutes, 23.0% 15 to 30 minutes, 24.5% 30 to 45 minutes, 11.9% 45 to 60 minutes, 28.5% 60 minutes or more (2006-2010 5-year est.).

## NORTH WANTAGH (CDP). Covers a land area of 1.902 square miles and a water area of 0.009 square miles. Located at 40.69° N. Lat; 73.51° W. Long. Elevation is 33 feet.
**Population:** 12,261 (1990); 12,156 (2000); 11,960 (2010); Density: 6,287.5 persons per square mile (2010); Race: 94.1% White, 0.8% Black, 2.5% Asian, 0.1% American Indian/Alaska Native, 0.0% Native Hawaiian/Other Pacific Islander, 2.5% Other, 7.5% Hispanic of any race (2010); Average household size: 2.82 (2010); Median age: 43.3 (2010); Males per 100 females: 91.5 (2010); Marriage status: 21.9% never married, 64.2% now married, 8.8% widowed, 5.1% divorced (2006-2010 5-year est.); Foreign born: 7.1% (2006-2010 5-year est.); Ancestry (includes multiple ancestries): 38.6% Italian, 27.4% Irish, 19.6% German, 6.9% Polish, 5.0% English (2006-2010 5-year est.).
**Economy:** Employment by occupation: 17.1% management, 4.8% professional, 4.7% services, 18.6% sales, 5.3% farming, 5.3% construction, 4.6% production (2006-2010 5-year est.).
**Income:** Per capita income: $38,648 (2006-2010 5-year est.); Median household income: $94,801 (2006-2010 5-year est.); Average household income: $106,722 (2006-2010 5-year est.); Percent of households with income of $100,000 or more: 47.1% (2006-2010 5-year est.); Poverty rate: 2.4% (2006-2010 5-year est.).
**Education:** Percent of population age 25 and over with: High school diploma (including GED) or higher: 93.5% (2006-2010 5-year est.); Bachelor's degree or higher: 35.0% (2006-2010 5-year est.); Master's degree or higher: 14.4% (2006-2010 5-year est.).
**Housing:** Homeownership rate: 91.3% (2010); Median home value: $433,500 (2006-2010 5-year est.); Median contract rent: $936 per month (2006-2010 5-year est.); Median year structure built: 1955 (2006-2010 5-year est.).
**Transportation:** Commute to work: 87.6% car, 7.7% public transportation, 0.2% walk, 4.5% work from home (2006-2010 5-year est.); Travel time to work: 20.1% less than 15 minutes, 37.1% 15 to 30 minutes, 21.3% 30 to 45 minutes, 6.0% 45 to 60 minutes, 15.5% 60 minutes or more (2006-2010 5-year est.)

## OCEANSIDE (CDP). Covers a land area of 4.943 square miles and a water area of 0.473 square miles. Located at 40.63° N. Lat; 73.63° W. Long. Elevation is 10 feet.
**Population:** 32,423 (1990); 32,733 (2000); 32,109 (2010); Density: 6,495.0 persons per square mile (2010); Race: 92.2% White, 1.3% Black, 2.7% Asian, 0.1% American Indian/Alaska Native, 0.0% Native Hawaiian/Other Pacific Islander, 3.7% Other, 9.2% Hispanic of any race (2010); Average household size: 2.84 (2010); Median age: 43.5 (2010); Males per 100 females: 92.8 (2010); Marriage status: 27.2% never married, 58.8% now married, 7.6% widowed, 6.3% divorced (2006-2010 5-year est.); Foreign born: 11.9% (2006-2010 5-year est.); Ancestry (includes multiple ancestries): 29.3% Italian, 19.5% Irish, 11.0% German, 8.1% Russian, 6.8% Polish (2006-2010 5-year est.).
**Economy:** Employment by occupation: 14.5% management, 2.9% professional, 6.9% services, 17.2% sales, 4.1% farming, 7.6% construction, 3.3% production (2006-2010 5-year est.).
**Income:** Per capita income: $40,109 (2006-2010 5-year est.); Median household income: $101,521 (2006-2010 5-year est.); Average household income: $112,053 (2006-2010 5-year est.); Percent of households with income of $100,000 or more: 51.2% (2006-2010 5-year est.); Poverty rate: 3.1% (2006-2010 5-year est.).
**Education:** Percent of population age 25 and over with: High school diploma (including GED) or higher: 92.5% (2006-2010 5-year est.); Bachelor's degree or higher: 42.0% (2006-2010 5-year est.); Master's degree or higher: 19.6% (2006-2010 5-year est.).
### School District(s)
Oceanside Union Free School District (KG-12)
   2009-10 Enrollment: 6,052 . . . . . . . . . . . . . . . . . . . (516) 678-1215
**Housing:** Homeownership rate: 88.0% (2010); Median home value: $476,900 (2006-2010 5-year est.); Median contract rent: $1,301 per month (2006-2010 5-year est.); Median year structure built: 1955 (2006-2010 5-year est.).

**Hospitals:** South Nassau Communities Hospital (435 beds)
**Transportation:** Commute to work: 77.7% car, 15.7% public transportation, 2.3% walk, 3.6% work from home (2006-2010 5-year est.); Travel time to work: 22.5% less than 15 minutes, 23.8% 15 to 30 minutes, 20.5% 30 to 45 minutes, 10.8% 45 to 60 minutes, 22.3% 60 minutes or more (2006-2010 5-year est.)
**Additional Information Contacts**
Oceanside Chamber of Commerce . . . . . . . . . . . . . . . . (516) 763-9177
http://www.oceansidechamber.org

## OLD BETHPAGE (CDP). Covers a land area of 4.182 square miles and a water area of 0.003 square miles. Located at 40.75° N. Lat; 73.45° W. Long. Elevation is 174 feet.
**History:** In 1695, Thomas Powell bought about 10,000 acres (40 sq. km.) from local Indian tribes, including the Marsapeque, Matinecoc, and Sacatogue, for 140 English pounds. Powell called his land Bethphage, because it was situated between two other places on Long Island, Jericho and Jerusalem, just as the biblical town of Bethphage (meaning "house of figs") was situated between Jericho and Jerusalem in Israel.
**Population:** 5,610 (1990); 5,400 (2000); 5,523 (2010); Density: 1,320.6 persons per square mile (2010); Race: 92.1% White, 0.2% Black, 6.2% Asian, 0.0% American Indian/Alaska Native, 0.0% Native Hawaiian/Other Pacific Islander, 1.5% Other, 3.4% Hispanic of any race (2010); Average household size: 2.90 (2010); Median age: 43.6 (2010); Males per 100 females: 93.2 (2010); Marriage status: 25.2% never married, 66.6% now married, 4.5% widowed, 3.7% divorced (2006-2010 5-year est.); Foreign born: 10.6% (2006-2010 5-year est.); Ancestry (includes multiple ancestries): 26.3% Italian, 14.0% Polish, 11.8% Irish, 8.3% Russian, 8.0% German (2006-2010 5-year est.).
**Economy:** Employment by occupation: 21.7% management, 2.2% professional, 4.9% services, 16.6% sales, 3.0% farming, 1.9% construction, 1.1% production (2006-2010 5-year est.).
**Income:** Per capita income: $44,445 (2006-2010 5-year est.); Median household income: $109,050 (2006-2010 5-year est.); Average household income: $133,623 (2006-2010 5-year est.); Percent of households with income of $100,000 or more: 51.8% (2006-2010 5-year est.); Poverty rate: 3.4% (2006-2010 5-year est.).
**Education:** Percent of population age 25 and over with: High school diploma (including GED) or higher: 95.2% (2006-2010 5-year est.); Bachelor's degree or higher: 58.1% (2006-2010 5-year est.); Master's degree or higher: 28.9% (2006-2010 5-year est.).
### School District(s)
Plainview-Old Bethpage Central School District (KG-12)
   2009-10 Enrollment: 5,097 . . . . . . . . . . . . . . . . . . . (516) 937-6301
**Housing:** Homeownership rate: 89.8% (2010); Median home value: $556,800 (2006-2010 5-year est.); Median contract rent: $286 per month (2006-2010 5-year est.); Median year structure built: 1959 (2006-2010 5-year est.).
**Transportation:** Commute to work: 76.9% car, 17.2% public transportation, 0.6% walk, 4.2% work from home (2006-2010 5-year est.); Travel time to work: 23.3% less than 15 minutes, 23.2% 15 to 30 minutes, 21.8% 30 to 45 minutes, 4.8% 45 to 60 minutes, 26.9% 60 minutes or more (2006-2010 5-year est.)

## OLD BROOKVILLE (village). Covers a land area of 3.998 square miles and a water area of 0.001 square miles. Located at 40.83° N. Lat; 73.60° W. Long. Elevation is 95 feet.
**Population:** 1,823 (1990); 2,167 (2000); 2,134 (2010); Density: 533.7 persons per square mile (2010); Race: 82.9% White, 2.0% Black, 11.2% Asian, 0.0% American Indian/Alaska Native, 0.0% Native Hawaiian/Other Pacific Islander, 3.9% Other, 5.7% Hispanic of any race (2010); Average household size: 3.19 (2010); Median age: 45.2 (2010); Males per 100 females: 102.5 (2010); Marriage status: 23.0% never married, 70.2% now married, 5.7% widowed, 1.0% divorced (2006-2010 5-year est.); Foreign born: 18.4% (2006-2010 5-year est.); Ancestry (includes multiple ancestries): 30.8% Italian, 15.2% Irish, 8.5% Greek, 7.8% German, 5.8% American (2006-2010 5-year est.).
**Economy:** Single-family building permits issued: 2 (2011); Multi-family building permits issued: 0 (2011); Employment by occupation: 34.1% management, 2.7% professional, 2.5% services, 14.2% sales, 1.8% farming, 3.4% construction, 0.3% production (2006-2010 5-year est.).
**Income:** Per capita income: $76,355 (2006-2010 5-year est.); Median household income: $127,750 (2006-2010 5-year est.); Average household income: $245,726 (2006-2010 5-year est.); Percent of households with

income of $100,000 or more: 62.6% (2006-2010 5-year est.); Poverty rate: 8.8% (2006-2010 5-year est.).

**Education:** Percent of population age 25 and over with: High school diploma (including GED) or higher: 92.2% (2006-2010 5-year est.); Bachelor's degree or higher: 64.0% (2006-2010 5-year est.); Master's degree or higher: 30.5% (2006-2010 5-year est.).

**Housing:** Homeownership rate: 92.0% (2010); Median home value: $1 (2006-2010 5-year est.); Median contract rent: $2,000 per month (2006-2010 5-year est.); Median year structure built: 1968 (2006-2010 5-year est.).

**Safety:** Violent crime rate: 0.0 per 10,000 population; Property crime rate: 311.7 per 10,000 population (2010).

**Transportation:** Commute to work: 81.7% car, 6.4% public transportation, 3.9% walk, 7.7% work from home (2006-2010 5-year est.); Travel time to work: 20.0% less than 15 minutes, 24.4% 15 to 30 minutes, 16.3% 30 to 45 minutes, 12.3% 45 to 60 minutes, 26.9% 60 minutes or more (2006-2010 5-year est.)

**OLD WESTBURY** (village). Covers a land area of 8.572 square miles and a water area of 0 square miles. Located at 40.78° N. Lat; 73.59° W. Long. Elevation is 164 feet.

**History:** Westbury was named by Henry Willis, one of the first English settlers after a town in his home county of Wiltshire, England. Westbury had been a Quaker community of isolated farms until the railroad came in 1836.

**Population:** 3,257 (1990); 4,228 (2000); 4,671 (2010); Density: 544.9 persons per square mile (2010); Race: 65.6% White, 16.0% Black, 12.3% Asian, 0.3% American Indian/Alaska Native, 0.0% Native Hawaiian/Other Pacific Islander, 5.8% Other, 6.8% Hispanic of any race (2010); Average household size: 3.02 (2010); Median age: 24.4 (2010); Males per 100 females: 94.5 (2010); Marriage status: 42.0% never married, 50.4% now married, 3.9% widowed, 3.7% divorced (2006-2010 5-year est.); Foreign born: 24.5% (2006-2010 5-year est.); Ancestry (includes multiple ancestries): 13.4% Italian, 10.3% Russian, 7.5% Eastern European, 5.6% German, 5.4% Polish (2006-2010 5-year est.).

**Economy:** Single-family building permits issued: 9 (2011); Multi-family building permits issued: 0 (2011); Employment by occupation: 25.1% management, 2.4% professional, 6.0% services, 16.8% sales, 2.3% farming, 0.3% construction, 0.3% production (2006-2010 5-year est.).

**Income:** Per capita income: $86,408 (2006-2010 5-year est.); Median household income: $203,125 (2006-2010 5-year est.); Average household income: $342,551 (2006-2010 5-year est.); Percent of households with income of $100,000 or more: 77.6% (2006-2010 5-year est.); Poverty rate: 0.3% (2006-2010 5-year est.).

**Education:** Percent of population age 25 and over with: High school diploma (including GED) or higher: 94.9% (2006-2010 5-year est.); Bachelor's degree or higher: 75.4% (2006-2010 5-year est.); Master's degree or higher: 40.7% (2006-2010 5-year est.).

**School District(s)**

East Williston Union Free School District (KG-12)
    2009-10 Enrollment: 1,798 . . . . . . . . . . . . . . . . . . (516) 333-3758
Westbury Union Free School District (PK-12)
    2009-10 Enrollment: 4,314 . . . . . . . . . . . . . . . . . . (516) 876-5016

**Four-year College(s)**

New York Institute of Technology (Private, Not-for-profit)
    Fall 2010 Enrollment: 8,703 . . . . . . . . . . . . . . . . . (516) 686-7516
    2011-12 Tuition: In-state $27,290; Out-of-state $27,290
SUNY College at Old Westbury (Public)
    Fall 2010 Enrollment: 4,080 . . . . . . . . . . . . . . . . . (516) 876-3000
    2011-12 Tuition: In-state $6,324; Out-of-state $16,214

**Housing:** Homeownership rate: 91.2% (2010); Median home value: $1 (2006-2010 5-year est.); Median contract rent: n/a per month (2006-2010 5-year est.); Median year structure built: 1976 (2006-2010 5-year est.).

**Safety:** Violent crime rate: 3.8 per 10,000 population; Property crime rate: 46.9 per 10,000 population (2010).

**Transportation:** Commute to work: 76.8% car, 6.4% public transportation, 6.7% walk, 8.5% work from home (2006-2010 5-year est.); Travel time to work: 25.1% less than 15 minutes, 32.9% 15 to 30 minutes, 15.7% 30 to 45 minutes, 12.6% 45 to 60 minutes, 13.7% 60 minutes or more (2006-2010 5-year est.)

**OYSTER BAY** (town). Covers a land area of 103.746 square miles and a water area of 65.651 square miles. Located at 40.79° N. Lat; 73.51° W. Long. Elevation is 46 feet.

**History:** Nearby is Theodore Roosevelt's estate, Sagamore Hill, which was made a national shrine in 1953 and a National Historic Site in 1963. Also of interest in Oyster Bay are several 18th-century houses, the Theodore Roosevelt Memorial Bird Sanctuary, a 12-acre wildlife sanctuary owned by the National Audubon Society, which adjoins Roosevelt's grave and the Oyster Bay National Wildlife Refuge. Settled 1653.

**Population:** 293,200 (1990); 293,925 (2000); 293,214 (2010); Density: 2,826.2 persons per square mile (2010); Race: 85.0% White, 2.3% Black, 9.1% Asian, 0.2% American Indian/Alaska Native, 0.0% Native Hawaiian/Other Pacific Islander, 3.4% Other, 7.5% Hispanic of any race (2010); Average household size: 2.89 (2010); Median age: 43.1 (2010); Males per 100 females: 94.0 (2010); Marriage status: 25.8% never married, 61.3% now married, 7.5% widowed, 5.4% divorced (2006-2010 5-year est.); Foreign born: 14.3% (2006-2010 5-year est.); Ancestry (includes multiple ancestries): 30.4% Italian, 20.5% Irish, 14.2% German, 6.7% Polish, 5.0% Russian (2006-2010 5-year est.).

**Economy:** Unemployment rate: 6.6% (February 2012); Total civilian labor force: 148,644 (February 2012); Single-family building permits issued: 72 (2011); Multi-family building permits issued: 0 (2011); Employment by occupation: 17.4% management, 4.6% professional, 5.7% services, 18.0% sales, 3.8% farming, 5.9% construction, 3.7% production (2006-2010 5-year est.).

**Income:** Per capita income: $46,598 (2006-2010 5-year est.); Median household income: $104,453 (2006-2010 5-year est.); Average household income: $136,353 (2006-2010 5-year est.); Percent of households with income of $100,000 or more: 52.0% (2006-2010 5-year est.); Poverty rate: 3.2% (2006-2010 5-year est.).

**Taxes:** Total city taxes per capita: $677 (2009); City property taxes per capita: $605 (2009).

**Education:** Percent of population age 25 and over with: High school diploma (including GED) or higher: 93.2% (2006-2010 5-year est.); Bachelor's degree or higher: 44.1% (2006-2010 5-year est.); Master's degree or higher: 19.2% (2006-2010 5-year est.).

**School District(s)**

Oyster Bay-East Norwich Central School District (PK-12)
    2009-10 Enrollment: 1,662 . . . . . . . . . . . . . . . . . . (516) 624-6505

**Housing:** Homeownership rate: 86.9% (2010); Median home value: $517,100 (2006-2010 5-year est.); Median contract rent: $1,426 per month (2006-2010 5-year est.); Median year structure built: 1956 (2006-2010 5-year est.).

**Newspapers:** Oyster Bay Guardian (Community news; Circulation 4,000)

**Transportation:** Commute to work: 80.3% car, 13.1% public transportation, 1.5% walk, 4.2% work from home (2006-2010 5-year est.); Travel time to work: 22.4% less than 15 minutes, 30.9% 15 to 30 minutes, 18.8% 30 to 45 minutes, 7.0% 45 to 60 minutes, 20.8% 60 minutes or more (2006-2010 5-year est.)

**Additional Information Contacts**

Oyster Bay Chamber of Commerce . . . . . . . . . . . . . . . . . . (516) 922-6464
    http://www.visitoysterbay.com
Town of Oyster Bay . . . . . . . . . . . . . . . . . . . . . . . . . . (516) 624-6332
    http://www.oysterbaytown.com

**OYSTER BAY** (CDP). Covers a land area of 1.233 square miles and a water area of 0.369 square miles. Located at 40.86° N. Lat; 73.53° W. Long. Elevation is 46 feet.

**Population:** 6,687 (1990); 6,826 (2000); 6,707 (2010); Density: 5,437.6 persons per square mile (2010); Race: 85.0% White, 3.3% Black, 2.9% Asian, 0.3% American Indian/Alaska Native, 0.0% Native Hawaiian/Other Pacific Islander, 8.5% Other, 16.7% Hispanic of any race (2010); Average household size: 2.43 (2010); Median age: 42.6 (2010); Males per 100 females: 93.4 (2010); Marriage status: 28.4% never married, 56.5% now married, 6.4% widowed, 8.6% divorced (2006-2010 5-year est.); Foreign born: 12.8% (2006-2010 5-year est.); Ancestry (includes multiple ancestries): 36.4% Italian, 19.4% Irish, 13.9% German, 6.1% Polish, 5.2% English (2006-2010 5-year est.).

**Economy:** Employment by occupation: 21.0% management, 6.4% professional, 7.6% services, 14.7% sales, 1.3% farming, 4.3% construction, 2.6% production (2006-2010 5-year est.).

**Income:** Per capita income: $49,374 (2006-2010 5-year est.); Median household income: $79,427 (2006-2010 5-year est.); Average household income: $106,077 (2006-2010 5-year est.); Percent of households with

income of $100,000 or more: 35.4% (2006-2010 5-year est.); Poverty rate: 3.2% (2006-2010 5-year est.).
**Education:** Percent of population age 25 and over with: High school diploma (including GED) or higher: 94.4% (2006-2010 5-year est.); Bachelor's degree or higher: 48.1% (2006-2010 5-year est.); Master's degree or higher: 19.5% (2006-2010 5-year est.).

### School District(s)
Oyster Bay-East Norwich Central School District (PK-12)
    2009-10 Enrollment: 1,662 . . . . . . . . . . . . . . . . . . . . . . (516) 624-6505
**Housing:** Homeownership rate: 55.7% (2010); Median home value: $635,600 (2006-2010 5-year est.); Median contract rent: $1,571 per month (2006-2010 5-year est.); Median year structure built: 1958 (2006-2010 5-year est.).
**Transportation:** Commute to work: 80.5% car, 6.5% public transportation, 5.0% walk, 4.1% work from home (2006-2010 5-year est.); Travel time to work: 24.8% less than 15 minutes, 36.6% 15 to 30 minutes, 19.1% 30 to 45 minutes, 6.0% 45 to 60 minutes, 13.6% 60 minutes or more (2006-2010 5-year est.)

## OYSTER BAY COVE (village).
Covers a land area of 4.186 square miles and a water area of 0.069 square miles. Located at 40.86° N. Lat; 73.50° W. Long. Elevation is 59 feet.
**Population:** 2,109 (1990); 2,262 (2000); 2,197 (2010); Density: 524.8 persons per square mile (2010); Race: 88.8% White, 1.6% Black, 8.5% Asian, 0.0% American Indian/Alaska Native, 0.0% Native Hawaiian/Other Pacific Islander, 1.1% Other, 2.2% Hispanic of any race (2010); Average household size: 3.10 (2010); Median age: 45.1 (2010); Males per 100 females: 94.6 (2010); Marriage status: 25.9% never married, 67.2% now married, 2.7% widowed, 4.2% divorced (2006-2010 5-year est.); Foreign born: 13.2% (2006-2010 5-year est.); Ancestry (includes multiple ancestries): 21.5% Italian, 18.9% Irish, 10.0% Russian, 9.8% English, 8.0% German (2006-2010 5-year est.).
**Economy:** Single-family building permits issued: 1 (2011); Multi-family building permits issued: 0 (2011); Employment by occupation: 29.8% management, 3.9% professional, 5.3% services, 7.9% sales, 4.1% farming, 2.7% construction, 0.3% production (2006-2010 5-year est.).
**Income:** Per capita income: $112,762 (2006-2010 5-year est.); Median household income: $246,875 (2006-2010 5-year est.); Average household income: $385,230 (2006-2010 5-year est.); Percent of households with income of $100,000 or more: 81.8% (2006-2010 5-year est.); Poverty rate: 0.2% (2006-2010 5-year est.).
**Education:** Percent of population age 25 and over with: High school diploma (including GED) or higher: 97.0% (2006-2010 5-year est.); Bachelor's degree or higher: 69.9% (2006-2010 5-year est.); Master's degree or higher: 36.2% (2006-2010 5-year est.).
**Housing:** Homeownership rate: 92.5% (2010); Median home value: $1 (2006-2010 5-year est.); Median contract rent: $975 per month (2006-2010 5-year est.); Median year structure built: 1972 (2006-2010 5-year est.).
**Safety:** Violent crime rate: 0.0 per 10,000 population; Property crime rate: 34.9 per 10,000 population (2010).
**Transportation:** Commute to work: 75.6% car, 12.7% public transportation, 2.1% walk, 7.7% work from home (2006-2010 5-year est.); Travel time to work: 18.9% less than 15 minutes, 29.9% 15 to 30 minutes, 21.8% 30 to 45 minutes, 7.0% 45 to 60 minutes, 22.4% 60 minutes or more (2006-2010 5-year est.)

## PLAINEDGE (CDP).
Covers a land area of 1.404 square miles and a water area of 0 square miles. Located at 40.72° N. Lat; 73.47° W. Long. Elevation is 66 feet.
**Population:** 8,712 (1990); 9,195 (2000); 8,817 (2010); Density: 6,279.5 persons per square mile (2010); Race: 92.0% White, 0.8% Black, 4.5% Asian, 0.2% American Indian/Alaska Native, 0.0% Native Hawaiian/Other Pacific Islander, 2.5% Other, 7.8% Hispanic of any race (2010); Average household size: 3.06 (2010); Median age: 41.2 (2010); Males per 100 females: 94.2 (2010); Marriage status: 27.9% never married, 60.2% now married, 7.4% widowed, 4.5% divorced (2006-2010 5-year est.); Foreign born: 11.7% (2006-2010 5-year est.); Ancestry (includes multiple ancestries): 37.7% Italian, 26.6% Irish, 19.7% German, 6.7% Polish, 3.6% English (2006-2010 5-year est.).
**Economy:** Employment by occupation: 11.4% management, 4.9% professional, 6.5% services, 18.3% sales, 4.6% farming, 7.7% construction, 6.0% production (2006-2010 5-year est.).
**Income:** Per capita income: $36,027 (2006-2010 5-year est.); Median household income: $98,837 (2006-2010 5-year est.); Average household income: $114,121 (2006-2010 5-year est.); Percent of households with

income of $100,000 or more: 48.4% (2006-2010 5-year est.); Poverty rate: 2.8% (2006-2010 5-year est.).
**Education:** Percent of population age 25 and over with: High school diploma (including GED) or higher: 91.5% (2006-2010 5-year est.); Bachelor's degree or higher: 30.1% (2006-2010 5-year est.); Master's degree or higher: 10.3% (2006-2010 5-year est.).
**Housing:** Homeownership rate: 91.2% (2010); Median home value: $441,700 (2006-2010 5-year est.); Median contract rent: $733 per month (2006-2010 5-year est.); Median year structure built: n/a (2006-2010 5-year est.).
**Transportation:** Commute to work: 88.2% car, 9.6% public transportation, 0.0% walk, 2.1% work from home (2006-2010 5-year est.); Travel time to work: 21.3% less than 15 minutes, 39.9% 15 to 30 minutes, 16.4% 30 to 45 minutes, 4.0% 45 to 60 minutes, 18.3% 60 minutes or more (2006-2010 5-year est.)

## PLAINVIEW (CDP).
Covers a land area of 5.732 square miles and a water area of 0.010 square miles. Located at 40.78° N. Lat; 73.47° W. Long. Elevation is 151 feet.
**Population:** 26,207 (1990); 25,637 (2000); 26,217 (2010); Density: 4,573.1 persons per square mile (2010); Race: 86.6% White, 0.5% Black, 10.7% Asian, 0.1% American Indian/Alaska Native, 0.0% Native Hawaiian/Other Pacific Islander, 2.1% Other, 4.0% Hispanic of any race (2010); Average household size: 2.86 (2010); Median age: 44.4 (2010); Males per 100 females: 93.3 (2010); Marriage status: 21.7% never married, 66.3% now married, 7.4% widowed, 4.6% divorced (2006-2010 5-year est.); Foreign born: 12.5% (2006-2010 5-year est.); Ancestry (includes multiple ancestries): 19.6% Italian, 12.4% Russian, 12.0% Polish, 9.0% Irish, 7.3% German (2006-2010 5-year est.).
**Economy:** Employment by occupation: 20.1% management, 5.4% professional, 3.1% services, 16.5% sales, 3.1% farming, 3.8% construction, 2.7% production (2006-2010 5-year est.).
**Income:** Per capita income: $49,119 (2006-2010 5-year est.); Median household income: $117,891 (2006-2010 5-year est.); Average household income: $139,180 (2006-2010 5-year est.); Percent of households with income of $100,000 or more: 59.2% (2006-2010 5-year est.); Poverty rate: 2.2% (2006-2010 5-year est.).
**Education:** Percent of population age 25 and over with: High school diploma (including GED) or higher: 94.9% (2006-2010 5-year est.); Bachelor's degree or higher: 56.0% (2006-2010 5-year est.); Master's degree or higher: 27.5% (2006-2010 5-year est.).

### School District(s)
Bethpage Union Free School District (KG-12)
    2009-10 Enrollment: 3,072 . . . . . . . . . . . . . . . . . . . . . (516) 644-4001
Plainview-Old Bethpage Central School District (KG-12)
    2009-10 Enrollment: 5,097 . . . . . . . . . . . . . . . . . . . . . (516) 937-6301
Syosset Central School District (KG-12)
    2009-10 Enrollment: 6,666 . . . . . . . . . . . . . . . . . . . . . (516) 364-5605
**Housing:** Homeownership rate: 91.0% (2010); Median home value: $562,500 (2006-2010 5-year est.); Median contract rent: $983 per month (2006-2010 5-year est.); Median year structure built: 1957 (2006-2010 5-year est.).
**Hospitals:** Plainview Hospital (239 beds)
**Newspapers:** Babylon/West Islip Town Crier (Community news); Bellmore/Merrick Town Crier (Community news); Deer Park/North Babylon Town Crier (Community news); East Meadow Town Crier (Community news); Farmingdale/Bethpage Pennysaver (Community news; Circulation 20,781); Hicksville Town Crier (Community news; Circulation 14,456); Levittown Town Crier (Community news; Circulation 14,250); Lyndenhurst/Amityville/Copiague Town Crier (Community news); Massapequa/Massapequa Park Town Crier (Community news; Circulation 26,475); Mineola/Carle Place/Williston Town Crier (Community news); Plainview/Jericho Pennysaver (Community news; Circulation 16,865); Syosset/Woodbury Pennysaver (Community news; Circulation 12,214); Wantagh/Seaford Town Crier (Community news; Circulation 18,020); Westbury/Old Westbury/Salisbury Town Crier (Community news)
**Transportation:** Commute to work: 78.5% car, 15.0% public transportation, 0.9% walk, 4.9% work from home (2006-2010 5-year est.); Travel time to work: 25.3% less than 15 minutes, 26.2% 15 to 30 minutes, 17.3% 30 to 45 minutes, 7.1% 45 to 60 minutes, 24.1% 60 minutes or more (2006-2010 5-year est.)
**Additional Information Contacts**
Plainview-Old Bethpage Chamber of Commerce . . . . . . . . (516) 937-5646
   http://pobcoc.com/new_in_town.cfm

**PLANDOME** (village). Covers a land area of 0.494 square miles and a water area of 0.009 square miles. Located at 40.80° N. Lat; 73.70° W. Long. Elevation is 72 feet.

**Population:** 1,347 (1990); 1,272 (2000); 1,349 (2010); Density: 2,726.6 persons per square mile (2010); Race: 94.7% White, 0.8% Black, 3.6% Asian, 0.1% American Indian/Alaska Native, 0.0% Native Hawaiian/Other Pacific Islander, 0.8% Other, 2.2% Hispanic of any race (2010); Average household size: 3.24 (2010); Median age: 42.4 (2010); Males per 100 females: 94.1 (2010); Marriage status: 23.5% never married, 69.7% now married, 4.5% widowed, 2.4% divorced (2006-2010 5-year est.); Foreign born: 5.5% (2006-2010 5-year est.); Ancestry (includes multiple ancestries): 42.2% Irish, 25.9% Italian, 18.2% German, 8.6% Russian, 5.2% English (2006-2010 5-year est.).

**Economy:** Single-family building permits issued: 2 (2011); Multi-family building permits issued: 0 (2011); Employment by occupation: 31.2% management, 1.9% professional, 2.9% services, 14.6% sales, 1.8% farming, 2.5% construction, 2.3% production (2006-2010 5-year est.).

**Income:** Per capita income: $105,468 (2006-2010 5-year est.); Median household income: $248,036 (2006-2010 5-year est.); Average household income: $369,328 (2006-2010 5-year est.); Percent of households with income of $100,000 or more: 84.9% (2006-2010 5-year est.); Poverty rate: 0.9% (2006-2010 5-year est.).

**Education:** Percent of population age 25 and over with: High school diploma (including GED) or higher: 99.2% (2006-2010 5-year est.); Bachelor's degree or higher: 85.0% (2006-2010 5-year est.); Master's degree or higher: 41.9% (2006-2010 5-year est.).

**Housing:** Homeownership rate: 97.2% (2010); Median home value: $1 (2006-2010 5-year est.); Median contract rent: $1,938 per month (2006-2010 5-year est.); Median year structure built: before 1940 (2006-2010 5-year est.).

**Transportation:** Commute to work: 57.4% car, 33.7% public transportation, 0.4% walk, 7.7% work from home (2006-2010 5-year est.); Travel time to work: 20.2% less than 15 minutes, 14.9% 15 to 30 minutes, 22.6% 30 to 45 minutes, 13.8% 45 to 60 minutes, 28.4% 60 minutes or more (2006-2010 5-year est.)

**PLANDOME HEIGHTS** (village). Covers a land area of 0.180 square miles and a water area of 0.006 square miles. Located at 40.80° N. Lat; 73.70° W. Long. Elevation is 89 feet.

**Population:** 852 (1990); 971 (2000); 1,005 (2010); Density: 5,556.3 persons per square mile (2010); Race: 89.2% White, 0.2% Black, 8.6% Asian, 0.2% American Indian/Alaska Native, 0.0% Native Hawaiian/Other Pacific Islander, 1.8% Other, 4.5% Hispanic of any race (2010); Average household size: 3.11 (2010); Median age: 42.9 (2010); Males per 100 females: 92.5 (2010); Marriage status: 19.7% never married, 67.1% now married, 5.4% widowed, 7.8% divorced (2006-2010 5-year est.); Foreign born: 12.6% (2006-2010 5-year est.); Ancestry (includes multiple ancestries): 34.5% Italian, 27.2% Irish, 12.3% German, 9.7% Polish, 7.6% English (2006-2010 5-year est.).

**Economy:** Single-family building permits issued: 0 (2011); Multi-family building permits issued: 0 (2011); Employment by occupation: 25.9% management, 3.9% professional, 0.7% services, 6.5% sales, 0.5% farming, 1.2% construction, 0.0% production (2006-2010 5-year est.).

**Income:** Per capita income: $85,425 (2006-2010 5-year est.); Median household income: $200,833 (2006-2010 5-year est.); Average household income: $273,298 (2006-2010 5-year est.); Percent of households with income of $100,000 or more: 77.6% (2006-2010 5-year est.); Poverty rate: 0.0% (2006-2010 5-year est.).

**Education:** Percent of population age 25 and over with: High school diploma (including GED) or higher: 99.1% (2006-2010 5-year est.); Bachelor's degree or higher: 82.3% (2006-2010 5-year est.); Master's degree or higher: 49.1% (2006-2010 5-year est.).

**Housing:** Homeownership rate: 95.3% (2010); Median home value: $1 (2006-2010 5-year est.); Median contract rent: $738 per month (2006-2010 5-year est.); Median year structure built: 1943 (2006-2010 5-year est.).

**Transportation:** Commute to work: 54.0% car, 30.9% public transportation, 1.9% walk, 12.6% work from home (2006-2010 5-year est.); Travel time to work: 17.6% less than 15 minutes, 16.2% 15 to 30 minutes, 13.6% 30 to 45 minutes, 17.8% 45 to 60 minutes, 34.8% 60 minutes or more (2006-2010 5-year est.)

**PLANDOME MANOR** (village). Covers a land area of 0.484 square miles and a water area of 0.021 square miles. Located at 40.81° N. Lat; 73.69° W. Long. Elevation is 36 feet.

**Population:** 790 (1990); 838 (2000); 872 (2010); Density: 1,800.2 persons per square mile (2010); Race: 91.5% White, 0.1% Black, 6.1% Asian, 0.0% American Indian/Alaska Native, 0.0% Native Hawaiian/Other Pacific Islander, 2.3% Other, 2.5% Hispanic of any race (2010); Average household size: 3.11 (2010); Median age: 45.2 (2010); Males per 100 females: 92.1 (2010); Marriage status: 21.9% never married, 65.5% now married, 7.0% widowed, 5.6% divorced (2006-2010 5-year est.); Foreign born: 14.8% (2006-2010 5-year est.); Ancestry (includes multiple ancestries): 32.8% Italian, 16.3% Irish, 15.1% German, 11.0% Greek, 8.6% Polish (2006-2010 5-year est.).

**Economy:** Single-family building permits issued: 0 (2011); Multi-family building permits issued: 0 (2011); Employment by occupation: 26.3% management, 3.2% professional, 2.7% services, 11.3% sales, 5.4% farming, 3.5% construction, 3.5% production (2006-2010 5-year est.).

**Income:** Per capita income: $100,636 (2006-2010 5-year est.); Median household income: $212,917 (2006-2010 5-year est.); Average household income: $302,943 (2006-2010 5-year est.); Percent of households with income of $100,000 or more: 70.6% (2006-2010 5-year est.); Poverty rate: 2.8% (2006-2010 5-year est.).

**Education:** Percent of population age 25 and over with: High school diploma (including GED) or higher: 96.2% (2006-2010 5-year est.); Bachelor's degree or higher: 78.4% (2006-2010 5-year est.); Master's degree or higher: 42.6% (2006-2010 5-year est.).

**Housing:** Homeownership rate: 94.3% (2010); Median home value: $1 (2006-2010 5-year est.); Median contract rent: n/a per month (2006-2010 5-year est.); Median year structure built: 1956 (2006-2010 5-year est.).

**Transportation:** Commute to work: 67.4% car, 26.2% public transportation, 0.6% walk, 5.3% work from home (2006-2010 5-year est.); Travel time to work: 12.6% less than 15 minutes, 29.1% 15 to 30 minutes, 14.7% 30 to 45 minutes, 19.4% 45 to 60 minutes, 24.1% 60 minutes or more (2006-2010 5-year est.)

**POINT LOOKOUT** (CDP). Covers a land area of 0.226 square miles and a water area of 0 square miles. Located at 40.59° N. Lat; 73.57° W. Long. Elevation is 3 feet.

**Population:** 1,510 (1990); 1,472 (2000); 1,219 (2010); Density: 5,393.4 persons per square mile (2010); Race: 97.8% White, 0.5% Black, 1.0% Asian, 0.0% American Indian/Alaska Native, 0.0% Native Hawaiian/Other Pacific Islander, 0.7% Other, 3.2% Hispanic of any race (2010); Average household size: 2.44 (2010); Median age: 50.7 (2010); Males per 100 females: 93.2 (2010); Marriage status: 21.7% never married, 56.7% now married, 10.6% widowed, 11.0% divorced (2006-2010 5-year est.); Foreign born: 0.0% (2006-2010 5-year est.); Ancestry (includes multiple ancestries): 60.0% Irish, 21.5% English, 19.2% Italian, 13.0% German, 9.0% American (2006-2010 5-year est.).

**Economy:** Employment by occupation: 25.8% management, 2.8% professional, 6.7% services, 11.3% sales, 2.8% farming, 4.6% construction, 8.9% production (2006-2010 5-year est.).

**Income:** Per capita income: $76,311 (2006-2010 5-year est.); Median household income: $103,611 (2006-2010 5-year est.); Average household income: $173,093 (2006-2010 5-year est.); Percent of households with income of $100,000 or more: 57.4% (2006-2010 5-year est.); Poverty rate: 4.2% (2006-2010 5-year est.).

**Education:** Percent of population age 25 and over with: High school diploma (including GED) or higher: 100.0% (2006-2010 5-year est.); Bachelor's degree or higher: 59.3% (2006-2010 5-year est.); Master's degree or higher: 32.0% (2006-2010 5-year est.).

**Housing:** Homeownership rate: 79.2% (2010); Median home value: $709,700 (2006-2010 5-year est.); Median contract rent: $1,854 per month (2006-2010 5-year est.); Median year structure built: before 1940 (2006-2010 5-year est.).

**Transportation:** Commute to work: 76.3% car, 16.8% public transportation, 5.6% walk, 0.0% work from home (2006-2010 5-year est.); Travel time to work: 18.0% less than 15 minutes, 38.7% 15 to 30 minutes, 10.1% 30 to 45 minutes, 9.5% 45 to 60 minutes, 23.7% 60 minutes or more (2006-2010 5-year est.)

**PORT WASHINGTON** (CDP). Covers a land area of 4.184 square miles and a water area of 1.429 square miles. Located at 40.82° N. Lat; 73.68° W. Long. Elevation is 98 feet.

**History:** Named for George Washington, first President of the U.S. Initially important for extensive sand pits; center for seaplanes 1900-1920; early College of Long Island, 1920-1930s.

**Population:** 15,235 (1990); 15,215 (2000); 15,846 (2010); Density: 3,786.4 persons per square mile (2010); Race: 82.2% White, 2.4% Black, 8.0% Asian, 0.2% American Indian/Alaska Native, 0.0% Native Hawaiian/Other Pacific Islander, 7.2% Other, 13.4% Hispanic of any race (2010); Average household size: 2.74 (2010); Median age: 43.1 (2010); Males per 100 females: 92.0 (2010); Marriage status: 25.4% never married, 59.8% now married, 7.6% widowed, 7.1% divorced (2006-2010 5-year est.); Foreign born: 23.2% (2006-2010 5-year est.); Ancestry (includes multiple ancestries): 19.0% Italian, 18.5% Irish, 10.9% German, 6.1% Russian, 5.9% Polish (2006-2010 5-year est.).

**Economy:** Employment by occupation: 20.1% management, 2.9% professional, 5.2% services, 9.6% sales, 2.6% farming, 4.5% construction, 3.1% production (2006-2010 5-year est.).

**Income:** Per capita income: $56,860 (2006-2010 5-year est.); Median household income: $115,612 (2006-2010 5-year est.); Average household income: $155,366 (2006-2010 5-year est.); Percent of households with income of $100,000 or more: 54.9% (2006-2010 5-year est.); Poverty rate: 5.3% (2006-2010 5-year est.).

**Education:** Percent of population age 25 and over with: High school diploma (including GED) or higher: 90.2% (2006-2010 5-year est.); Bachelor's degree or higher: 59.0% (2006-2010 5-year est.); Master's degree or higher: 30.7% (2006-2010 5-year est.).

**School District(s)**
Port Washington Union Free School District (KG-12)
    2009-10 Enrollment: 4,974 . . . . . . . . . . . . . . . . . (516) 767-5005

**Housing:** Homeownership rate: 76.2% (2010); Median home value: $737,800 (2006-2010 5-year est.); Median contract rent: $1,471 per month (2006-2010 5-year est.); Median year structure built: 1949 (2006-2010 5-year est.).

**Safety:** Violent crime rate: 1.1 per 10,000 population; Property crime rate: 64.3 per 10,000 population (2010).

**Transportation:** Commute to work: 59.5% car, 29.6% public transportation, 4.7% walk, 5.5% work from home (2006-2010 5-year est.); Travel time to work: 24.8% less than 15 minutes, 21.6% 15 to 30 minutes, 16.8% 30 to 45 minutes, 10.1% 45 to 60 minutes, 26.7% 60 minutes or more (2006-2010 5-year est.)

**Additional Information Contacts**
Port Washington Chamber of Commerce . . . . . . . . . . . . . . (516) 883-6566
    http://www.portwashington.org

**PORT WASHINGTON NORTH** (village). Covers a land area of 0.477 square miles and a water area of 0.018 square miles. Located at 40.84° N. Lat; 73.69° W. Long. Elevation is 26 feet.

**Population:** 2,736 (1990); 2,700 (2000); 3,154 (2010); Density: 6,604.4 persons per square mile (2010); Race: 86.4% White, 1.6% Black, 8.3% Asian, 0.1% American Indian/Alaska Native, 0.0% Native Hawaiian/Other Pacific Islander, 3.6% Other, 6.3% Hispanic of any race (2010); Average household size: 2.42 (2010); Median age: 47.5 (2010); Males per 100 females: 91.0 (2010); Marriage status: 21.9% never married, 65.2% now married, 8.8% widowed, 4.0% divorced (2006-2010 5-year est.); Foreign born: 17.8% (2006-2010 5-year est.); Ancestry (includes multiple ancestries): 26.7% Italian, 10.1% Irish, 8.3% Russian, 7.4% German, 5.7% Polish (2006-2010 5-year est.).

**Economy:** Single-family building permits issued: 6 (2011); Multi-family building permits issued: 0 (2011); Employment by occupation: 23.3% management, 2.9% professional, 4.0% services, 17.1% sales, 1.7% farming, 2.2% construction, 1.2% production (2006-2010 5-year est.).

**Income:** Per capita income: $53,749 (2006-2010 5-year est.); Median household income: $93,393 (2006-2010 5-year est.); Average household income: $139,667 (2006-2010 5-year est.); Percent of households with income of $100,000 or more: 49.2% (2006-2010 5-year est.); Poverty rate: 7.1% (2006-2010 5-year est.).

**Education:** Percent of population age 25 and over with: High school diploma (including GED) or higher: 96.2% (2006-2010 5-year est.); Bachelor's degree or higher: 58.9% (2006-2010 5-year est.); Master's degree or higher: 33.0% (2006-2010 5-year est.).

**Housing:** Homeownership rate: 67.2% (2010); Median home value: $779,200 (2006-2010 5-year est.); Median contract rent: $1,557 per month

(2006-2010 5-year est.); Median year structure built: 1968 (2006-2010 5-year est.).

**Transportation:** Commute to work: 64.7% car, 23.6% public transportation, 4.5% walk, 4.7% work from home (2006-2010 5-year est.); Travel time to work: 16.9% less than 15 minutes, 29.6% 15 to 30 minutes, 18.0% 30 to 45 minutes, 10.2% 45 to 60 minutes, 25.3% 60 minutes or more (2006-2010 5-year est.)

**ROCKVILLE CENTRE** (village). Covers a land area of 3.247 square miles and a water area of 0.085 square miles. Located at 40.66° N. Lat; 73.63° W. Long. Elevation is 30 feet.

**History:** Named for Reverend Mordecai "Rock" Smith. Seat of Molloy Catholic College for Women. Incorporated 1893.

**Population:** 24,727 (1990); 24,568 (2000); 24,023 (2010); Density: 7,398.0 persons per square mile (2010); Race: 88.7% White, 4.6% Black, 2.1% Asian, 0.1% American Indian/Alaska Native, 0.0% Native Hawaiian/Other Pacific Islander, 4.5% Other, 9.0% Hispanic of any race (2010); Average household size: 2.57 (2010); Median age: 43.8 (2010); Males per 100 females: 88.2 (2010); Marriage status: 29.8% never married, 58.0% now married, 7.6% widowed, 4.7% divorced (2006-2010 5-year est.); Foreign born: 9.7% (2006-2010 5-year est.); Ancestry (includes multiple ancestries): 34.5% Irish, 25.9% Italian, 14.9% German, 5.9% Polish, 5.5% English (2006-2010 5-year est.).

**Economy:** Unemployment rate: 6.1% (February 2012); Total civilian labor force: 12,412 (February 2012); Single-family building permits issued: 1 (2011); Multi-family building permits issued: 0 (2011); Employment by occupation: 15.7% management, 2.6% professional, 5.5% services, 15.1% sales, 2.8% farming, 3.8% construction, 2.4% production (2006-2010 5-year est.).

**Income:** Per capita income: $53,417 (2006-2010 5-year est.); Median household income: $104,023 (2006-2010 5-year est.); Average household income: $140,430 (2006-2010 5-year est.); Percent of households with income of $100,000 or more: 51.4% (2006-2010 5-year est.); Poverty rate: 5.2% (2006-2010 5-year est.).

**Taxes:** Total city taxes per capita: $971 (2009); City property taxes per capita: $884 (2009).

**Education:** Percent of population age 25 and over with: High school diploma (including GED) or higher: 93.4% (2006-2010 5-year est.); Bachelor's degree or higher: 57.4% (2006-2010 5-year est.); Master's degree or higher: 27.4% (2006-2010 5-year est.).

**School District(s)**
Rockville Centre Union Free School District (KG-12)
    2009-10 Enrollment: 3,545 . . . . . . . . . . . . . . . . . . (516) 255-8920
**Four-year College(s)**
Molloy College (Private, Not-for-profit)
    Fall 2010 Enrollment: 3,774. . . . . . . . . . . . . . . . . . (516) 678-5000
    2011-12 Tuition: In-state $23,300; Out-of-state $23,300

**Housing:** Homeownership rate: 73.2% (2010); Median home value: $628,000 (2006-2010 5-year est.); Median contract rent: $1,076 per month (2006-2010 5-year est.); Median year structure built: 1945 (2006-2010 5-year est.).

**Hospitals:** Mercy Medical Center (375 beds)

**Safety:** Violent crime rate: 12.8 per 10,000 population; Property crime rate: 120.3 per 10,000 population (2010).

**Transportation:** Commute to work: 71.6% car, 22.3% public transportation, 1.7% walk, 4.2% work from home (2006-2010 5-year est.); Travel time to work: 19.6% less than 15 minutes, 25.4% 15 to 30 minutes, 19.6% 30 to 45 minutes, 11.5% 45 to 60 minutes, 23.8% 60 minutes or more (2006-2010 5-year est.)

**Additional Information Contacts**
Rockville Centre Chamber of Commerce . . . . . . . . . . . . . (516) 766-0666
    http://rvcchamber.com
Village of Rockville Centre. . . . . . . . . . . . . . . . . . . . . . . . (516) 678-9300
    http://www.rvcny.us

**ROOSEVELT** (CDP). Covers a land area of 1.770 square miles and a water area of 0.010 square miles. Located at 40.67° N. Lat; 73.58° W. Long. Elevation is 39 feet.

**History:** Named for Franklin Delano Roosevelt, 32nd President of the U.S. Troubled school district was taken over by the State Department of Education in mid-1990s for restructuring and improvement.

**Population:** 15,030 (1990); 15,854 (2000); 16,258 (2010); Density: 9,183.3 persons per square mile (2010); Race: 13.9% White, 63.1% Black, 0.6% Asian, 0.8% American Indian/Alaska Native, 0.1% Native Hawaiian/Other Pacific Islander, 21.5% Other, 34.1% Hispanic of any race (2010); Average

household size: 4.00 (2010); Median age: 33.0 (2010); Males per 100 females: 93.0 (2010); Marriage status: 47.2% never married, 39.8% now married, 4.4% widowed, 8.6% divorced (2006-2010 5-year est.); Foreign born: 28.7% (2006-2010 5-year est.); Ancestry (includes multiple ancestries): 6.0% Jamaican, 2.3% West Indian, 1.3% American, 1.0% African, 0.9% Haitian (2006-2010 5-year est.).

**Economy:** Employment by occupation: 4.8% management, 1.2% professional, 16.2% services, 14.0% sales, 5.3% farming, 16.2% construction, 7.6% production (2006-2010 5-year est.).

**Income:** Per capita income: $22,969 (2006-2010 5-year est.); Median household income: $69,429 (2006-2010 5-year est.); Average household income: $78,509 (2006-2010 5-year est.); Percent of households with income of $100,000 or more: 27.2% (2006-2010 5-year est.); Poverty rate: 11.9% (2006-2010 5-year est.).

**Education:** Percent of population age 25 and over with: High school diploma (including GED) or higher: 75.4% (2006-2010 5-year est.); Bachelor's degree or higher: 21.0% (2006-2010 5-year est.); Master's degree or higher: 6.1% (2006-2010 5-year est.).

**School District(s)**

Roosevelt Children's Academy Charter School (KG-08)

    2009-10 Enrollment: 521 . . . . . . . . . . . . . . . . . . (516) 867-3890

Roosevelt Union Free School District (PK-12)

    2009-10 Enrollment: 2,766 . . . . . . . . . . . . . . . . (516) 345-7001

**Housing:** Homeownership rate: 70.0% (2010); Median home value: $355,700 (2006-2010 5-year est.); Median contract rent: $1,583 per month (2006-2010 5-year est.); Median year structure built: 1954 (2006-2010 5-year est.).

**Newspapers:** The Long Island Catholic (Regional news; Circulation 112,000).

**Transportation:** Commute to work: 76.1% car, 15.8% public transportation, 3.3% walk, 2.6% work from home (2006-2010 5-year est.); Travel time to work: 16.7% less than 15 minutes, 34.1% 15 to 30 minutes, 26.3% 30 to 45 minutes, 8.0% 45 to 60 minutes, 15.0% 60 minutes or more (2006-2010 5-year est.)

**ROSLYN** (village). Covers a land area of 0.645 square miles and a water area of 0.011 square miles. Located at 40.79° N. Lat; 73.64° W. Long. Elevation is 46 feet.

**History:** Cedarmere, home of William Cullen Bryant, is here. Incorporated 1932.

**Population:** 1,965 (1990); 2,570 (2000); 2,770 (2010); Density: 4,294.1 persons per square mile (2010); Race: 84.1% White, 2.2% Black, 8.8% Asian, 0.2% American Indian/Alaska Native, 0.0% Native Hawaiian/Other Pacific Islander, 4.7% Other, 11.2% Hispanic of any race (2010); Average household size: 2.11 (2010); Median age: 46.9 (2010); Males per 100 females: 82.7 (2010); Marriage status: 25.5% never married, 51.1% now married, 12.5% widowed, 10.9% divorced (2006-2010 5-year est.); Foreign born: 20.8% (2006-2010 5-year est.); Ancestry (includes multiple ancestries): 16.8% Italian, 10.9% German, 8.1% Polish, 8.0% Irish, 6.2% Iranian (2006-2010 5-year est.).

**Economy:** Single-family building permits issued: 0 (2011); Multi-family building permits issued: 0 (2011); Employment by occupation: 14.4% management, 3.5% professional, 2.5% services, 17.4% sales, 2.3% farming, 4.4% construction, 5.4% production (2006-2010 5-year est.).

**Income:** Per capita income: $54,184 (2006-2010 5-year est.); Median household income: $85,469 (2006-2010 5-year est.); Average household income: $125,574 (2006-2010 5-year est.); Percent of households with income of $100,000 or more: 42.0% (2006-2010 5-year est.); Poverty rate: 5.1% (2006-2010 5-year est.).

**Taxes:** Total city taxes per capita: $1,099 (2009); City property taxes per capita: $991 (2009).

**Education:** Percent of population age 25 and over with: High school diploma (including GED) or higher: 90.2% (2006-2010 5-year est.); Bachelor's degree or higher: 59.7% (2006-2010 5-year est.); Master's degree or higher: 28.9% (2006-2010 5-year est.).

**Housing:** Homeownership rate: 65.7% (2010); Median home value: $276,200 (2006-2010 5-year est.); Median contract rent: n/a per month (2006-2010 5-year est.); Median year structure built: 1957 (2006-2010 5-year est.).

**Hospitals:** St. Francis Hospital-Heart Center (279 beds)

**Transportation:** Commute to work: 77.7% car, 10.5% public transportation, 3.9% walk, 7.3% work from home (2006-2010 5-year est.); Travel time to work: 28.2% less than 15 minutes, 31.6% 15 to 30 minutes, 12.0% 30 to 45 minutes, 5.3% 45 to 60 minutes, 22.9% 60 minutes or more (2006-2010 5-year est.)

**ROSLYN ESTATES** (village). Covers a land area of 0.437 square miles and a water area of 0 square miles. Located at 40.79° N. Lat; 73.66° W. Long. Elevation is 174 feet.

**Population:** 1,184 (1990); 1,210 (2000); 1,251 (2010); Density: 2,858.8 persons per square mile (2010); Race: 90.2% White, 0.4% Black, 8.2% Asian, 0.0% American Indian/Alaska Native, 0.0% Native Hawaiian/Other Pacific Islander, 1.2% Other, 1.4% Hispanic of any race (2010); Average household size: 3.01 (2010); Median age: 44.5 (2010); Males per 100 females: 96.7 (2010); Marriage status: 17.2% never married, 76.1% now married, 3.6% widowed, 3.1% divorced (2006-2010 5-year est.); Foreign born: 8.7% (2006-2010 5-year est.); Ancestry (includes multiple ancestries): 26.5% Russian, 11.3% Polish, 9.6% Italian, 7.4% American, 7.0% German (2006-2010 5-year est.).

**Economy:** Single-family building permits issued: 1 (2011); Multi-family building permits issued: 0 (2011); Employment by occupation: 26.2% management, 1.6% professional, 1.4% services, 10.7% sales, 2.7% farming, 1.4% construction, 1.4% production (2006-2010 5-year est.).

**Income:** Per capita income: $86,564 (2006-2010 5-year est.); Median household income: $180,000 (2006-2010 5-year est.); Average household income: $276,188 (2006-2010 5-year est.); Percent of households with income of $100,000 or more: 76.2% (2006-2010 5-year est.); Poverty rate: 0.8% (2006-2010 5-year est.).

**Education:** Percent of population age 25 and over with: High school diploma (including GED) or higher: 99.1% (2006-2010 5-year est.); Bachelor's degree or higher: 82.9% (2006-2010 5-year est.); Master's degree or higher: 46.6% (2006-2010 5-year est.).

**Housing:** Homeownership rate: 96.4% (2010); Median home value: $1 (2006-2010 5-year est.); Median contract rent: $1,563 per month (2006-2010 5-year est.); Median year structure built: 1952 (2006-2010 5-year est.).

**Transportation:** Commute to work: 78.3% car, 12.9% public transportation, 0.8% walk, 8.0% work from home (2006-2010 5-year est.); Travel time to work: 24.4% less than 15 minutes, 16.4% 15 to 30 minutes, 16.7% 30 to 45 minutes, 9.8% 45 to 60 minutes, 32.7% 60 minutes or more (2006-2010 5-year est.)

**ROSLYN HARBOR** (village). Covers a land area of 1.185 square miles and a water area of 0.001 square miles. Located at 40.81° N. Lat; 73.64° W. Long. Elevation is 108 feet.

**Population:** 1,114 (1990); 1,023 (2000); 1,051 (2010); Density: 886.4 persons per square mile (2010); Race: 83.6% White, 1.4% Black, 11.8% Asian, 0.1% American Indian/Alaska Native, 0.0% Native Hawaiian/Other Pacific Islander, 3.1% Other, 5.3% Hispanic of any race (2010); Average household size: 2.91 (2010); Median age: 48.2 (2010); Males per 100 females: 90.4 (2010); Marriage status: 15.7% never married, 75.6% now married, 5.5% widowed, 3.2% divorced (2006-2010 5-year est.); Foreign born: 16.7% (2006-2010 5-year est.); Ancestry (includes multiple ancestries): 17.0% Italian, 12.5% Polish, 11.7% Russian, 10.2% German, 4.3% Irish (2006-2010 5-year est.).

**Economy:** Single-family building permits issued: 0 (2011); Multi-family building permits issued: 0 (2011); Employment by occupation: 22.5% management, 3.4% professional, 2.7% services, 13.4% sales, 1.4% farming, 2.0% construction, 0.5% production (2006-2010 5-year est.).

**Income:** Per capita income: $105,374 (2006-2010 5-year est.); Median household income: $201,985 (2006-2010 5-year est.); Average household income: $302,140 (2006-2010 5-year est.); Percent of households with income of $100,000 or more: 75.4% (2006-2010 5-year est.); Poverty rate: 1.0% (2006-2010 5-year est.).

**Education:** Percent of population age 25 and over with: High school diploma (including GED) or higher: 97.5% (2006-2010 5-year est.); Bachelor's degree or higher: 71.5% (2006-2010 5-year est.); Master's degree or higher: 42.2% (2006-2010 5-year est.).

**Housing:** Homeownership rate: 95.8% (2010); Median home value: $1 (2006-2010 5-year est.); Median contract rent: $1,594 per month (2006-2010 5-year est.); Median year structure built: 1958 (2006-2010 5-year est.).

**Transportation:** Commute to work: 88.7% car, 7.6% public transportation, 0.0% walk, 3.7% work from home (2006-2010 5-year est.); Travel time to work: 14.9% less than 15 minutes, 27.8% 15 to 30 minutes, 24.3% 30 to 45 minutes, 10.6% 45 to 60 minutes, 22.4% 60 minutes or more (2006-2010 5-year est.)

## ROSLYN HEIGHTS (CDP). Covers a land area of 1.475 square miles and a water area of 0 square miles. Located at 40.77° N. Lat; 73.63° W. Long. Elevation is 174 feet.

**History:** Ebenezer Close, stated that the rules [of the Post Office in setting up new names] specified a short, pleasant-sounding name which had not been chosen for any Post Office in the United States. Of the names proposed, only ten fitted the rules. Of these ten, the name Roslyn, said to have been proposed by Mr. Cairns because our valley reminded him of Roslin, Scotland, received the most votes and was subsequently approved by all.

**Population:** 6,405 (1990); 6,295 (2000); 6,577 (2010); Density: 4,456.6 persons per square mile (2010); Race: 66.0% White, 6.4% Black, 20.7% Asian, 0.2% American Indian/Alaska Native, 0.0% Native Hawaiian/Other Pacific Islander, 6.7% Other, 8.5% Hispanic of any race (2010); Average household size: 3.04 (2010); Median age: 40.6 (2010); Males per 100 females: 94.4 (2010); Marriage status: 26.7% never married, 63.6% now married, 5.7% widowed, 4.0% divorced (2006-2010 5-year est.); Foreign born: 26.2% (2006-2010 5-year est.); Ancestry (includes multiple ancestries): 15.2% Italian, 11.0% Russian, 9.8% Polish, 7.0% Iranian, 5.3% German (2006-2010 5-year est.).

**Economy:** Employment by occupation: 16.6% management, 4.2% professional, 5.2% services, 13.4% sales, 1.0% farming, 2.4% construction, 0.3% production (2006-2010 5-year est.).

**Income:** Per capita income: $47,736 (2006-2010 5-year est.); Median household income: $113,125 (2006-2010 5-year est.); Average household income: $148,561 (2006-2010 5-year est.); Percent of households with income of $100,000 or more: 57.4% (2006-2010 5-year est.); Poverty rate: 5.3% (2006-2010 5-year est.).

**Education:** Percent of population age 25 and over with: High school diploma (including GED) or higher: 91.3% (2006-2010 5-year est.); Bachelor's degree or higher: 55.1% (2006-2010 5-year est.); Master's degree or higher: 25.2% (2006-2010 5-year est.).

#### School District(s)

East Williston Union Free School District (KG-12)

    2009-10 Enrollment: 1,798 . . . . . . . . . . . . . . . . . (516) 333-3758

Roslyn Union Free School District (PK-12)

    2009-10 Enrollment: 3,403 . . . . . . . . . . . . . . . . . (516) 801-5001

**Housing:** Homeownership rate: 82.3% (2010); Median home value: $688,100 (2006-2010 5-year est.); Median contract rent: $1,277 per month (2006-2010 5-year est.); Median year structure built: 1953 (2006-2010 5-year est.).

**Transportation:** Commute to work: 77.0% car, 16.5% public transportation, 1.6% walk, 3.7% work from home (2006-2010 5-year est.); Travel time to work: 16.3% less than 15 minutes, 29.0% 15 to 30 minutes, 26.9% 30 to 45 minutes, 9.2% 45 to 60 minutes, 18.5% 60 minutes or more (2006-2010 5-year est.)

## RUSSELL GARDENS (village). Covers a land area of 0.173 square miles and a water area of 0 square miles. Located at 40.78° N. Lat; 73.72° W. Long. Elevation is 131 feet.

**Population:** 1,027 (1990); 1,074 (2000); 945 (2010); Density: 5,442.7 persons per square mile (2010); Race: 76.5% White, 0.3% Black, 20.5% Asian, 0.0% American Indian/Alaska Native, 0.0% Native Hawaiian/Other Pacific Islander, 2.7% Other, 3.9% Hispanic of any race (2010); Average household size: 2.72 (2010); Median age: 46.1 (2010); Males per 100 females: 94.0 (2010); Marriage status: 32.8% never married, 58.9% now married, 5.6% widowed, 2.7% divorced (2006-2010 5-year est.); Foreign born: 19.0% (2006-2010 5-year est.); Ancestry (includes multiple ancestries): 20.7% Russian, 11.6% American, 10.8% Polish, 9.3% German, 6.0% Irish (2006-2010 5-year est.).

**Economy:** Single-family building permits issued: 0 (2011); Multi-family building permits issued: 0 (2011); Employment by occupation: 17.7% management, 5.3% professional, 3.1% services, 17.9% sales, 4.0% farming, 0.0% construction, 0.7% production (2006-2010 5-year est.).

**Income:** Per capita income: $57,515 (2006-2010 5-year est.); Median household income: $117,500 (2006-2010 5-year est.); Average household income: $169,612 (2006-2010 5-year est.); Percent of households with income of $100,000 or more: 59.4% (2006-2010 5-year est.); Poverty rate: 15.2% (2006-2010 5-year est.).

**Education:** Percent of population age 25 and over with: High school diploma (including GED) or higher: 89.2% (2006-2010 5-year est.); Bachelor's degree or higher: 62.2% (2006-2010 5-year est.); Master's degree or higher: 40.3% (2006-2010 5-year est.).

**Housing:** Homeownership rate: 76.1% (2010); Median home value: $1 (2006-2010 5-year est.); Median contract rent: $1,211 per month

(2006-2010 5-year est.); Median year structure built: 1941 (2006-2010 5-year est.).

**Transportation:** Commute to work: 52.3% car, 33.9% public transportation, 6.1% walk, 7.0% work from home (2006-2010 5-year est.); Travel time to work: 20.0% less than 15 minutes, 14.2% 15 to 30 minutes, 17.4% 30 to 45 minutes, 15.9% 45 to 60 minutes, 32.5% 60 minutes or more (2006-2010 5-year est.)

## SADDLE ROCK (village). Covers a land area of 0.246 square miles and a water area of 0.021 square miles. Located at 40.79° N. Lat; 73.74° W. Long. Elevation is 79 feet.

**Population:** 832 (1990); 791 (2000); 830 (2010); Density: 3,372.2 persons per square mile (2010); Race: 90.0% White, 0.4% Black, 6.5% Asian, 0.0% American Indian/Alaska Native, 0.0% Native Hawaiian/Other Pacific Islander, 3.1% Other, 1.7% Hispanic of any race (2010); Average household size: 3.11 (2010); Median age: 45.4 (2010); Males per 100 females: 103.9 (2010); Marriage status: 25.6% never married, 65.4% now married, 6.0% widowed, 3.0% divorced (2006-2010 5-year est.); Foreign born: 39.1% (2006-2010 5-year est.); Ancestry (includes multiple ancestries): 36.3% Iranian, 14.6% Israeli, 5.6% French, 5.1% Russian, 4.4% Iraqi (2006-2010 5-year est.).

**Economy:** Single-family building permits issued: 2 (2011); Multi-family building permits issued: 0 (2011); Employment by occupation: 22.8% management, 0.0% professional, 4.2% services, 23.6% sales, 0.7% farming, 0.0% construction, 0.0% production (2006-2010 5-year est.).

**Income:** Per capita income: $60,761 (2006-2010 5-year est.); Median household income: $132,857 (2006-2010 5-year est.); Average household income: $208,702 (2006-2010 5-year est.); Percent of households with income of $100,000 or more: 61.3% (2006-2010 5-year est.); Poverty rate: 2.3% (2006-2010 5-year est.).

**Education:** Percent of population age 25 and over with: High school diploma (including GED) or higher: 94.3% (2006-2010 5-year est.); Bachelor's degree or higher: 61.6% (2006-2010 5-year est.); Master's degree or higher: 32.1% (2006-2010 5-year est.).

**Housing:** Homeownership rate: 94.8% (2010); Median home value: $1 (2006-2010 5-year est.); Median contract rent: n/a per month (2006-2010 5-year est.); Median year structure built: 1954 (2006-2010 5-year est.).

**Transportation:** Commute to work: 62.9% car, 30.2% public transportation, 0.0% walk, 7.0% work from home (2006-2010 5-year est.); Travel time to work: 19.1% less than 15 minutes, 22.2% 15 to 30 minutes, 18.0% 30 to 45 minutes, 14.4% 45 to 60 minutes, 26.3% 60 minutes or more (2006-2010 5-year est.)

**Additional Information Contacts**

Village of Saddle Rock. . . . . . . . . . . . . . . . . . . . . (516) 482-9400

  http://www.saddlerock.org

## SADDLE ROCK ESTATES (CDP). Covers a land area of 0.077 square miles and a water area of 0 square miles. Located at 40.79° N. Lat; 73.74° W. Long. Elevation is 26 feet.

**Population:** 420 (1990); 424 (2000); 466 (2010); Density: 6,010.8 persons per square mile (2010); Race: 95.3% White, 0.0% Black, 2.4% Asian, 0.0% American Indian/Alaska Native, 0.0% Native Hawaiian/Other Pacific Islander, 2.3% Other, 0.4% Hispanic of any race (2010); Average household size: 3.33 (2010); Median age: 38.4 (2010); Males per 100 females: 99.1 (2010); Marriage status: 21.4% never married, 74.2% now married, 0.0% widowed, 4.4% divorced (2006-2010 5-year est.); Foreign born: 24.6% (2006-2010 5-year est.); Ancestry (includes multiple ancestries): 17.2% Iranian, 11.5% Eastern European, 9.2% Hungarian, 8.0% American, 6.3% Brazilian (2006-2010 5-year est.).

**Economy:** Employment by occupation: 12.7% management, 2.2% professional, 0.0% services, 10.5% sales, 2.8% farming, 2.8% construction, 0.0% production (2006-2010 5-year est.).

**Income:** Per capita income: $58,746 (2006-2010 5-year est.); Median household income: $128,750 (2006-2010 5-year est.); Average household income: $191,393 (2006-2010 5-year est.); Percent of households with income of $100,000 or more: 80.1% (2006-2010 5-year est.); Poverty rate: 0.0% (2006-2010 5-year est.).

**Education:** Percent of population age 25 and over with: High school diploma (including GED) or higher: 100.0% (2006-2010 5-year est.); Bachelor's degree or higher: 78.5% (2006-2010 5-year est.); Master's degree or higher: 46.6% (2006-2010 5-year est.).

**Housing:** Homeownership rate: 95.0% (2010); Median home value: $995,400 (2006-2010 5-year est.); Median contract rent: n/a per month (2006-2010 5-year est.); Median year structure built: before 1940 (2006-2010 5-year est.).

**Transportation:** Commute to work: 64.8% car, 33.0% public transportation, 2.2% walk, 0.0% work from home (2006-2010 5-year est.); Travel time to work: 34.6% less than 15 minutes, 6.8% 15 to 30 minutes, 30.9% 30 to 45 minutes, 6.8% 45 to 60 minutes, 21.0% 60 minutes or more (2006-2010 5-year est.)

**SALISBURY** (CDP). Covers a land area of 1.736 square miles and a water area of 0.024 square miles. Located at 40.74° N. Lat; 73.56° W. Long. Elevation is 108 feet.

**Population:** 12,226 (1990); 12,341 (2000); 12,093 (2010); Density: 6,962.5 persons per square mile (2010); Race: 78.8% White, 2.0% Black, 12.6% Asian, 0.1% American Indian/Alaska Native, 0.0% Native Hawaiian/Other Pacific Islander, 6.5% Other, 14.7% Hispanic of any race (2010); Average household size: 3.01 (2010); Median age: 42.4 (2010); Males per 100 females: 92.3 (2010); Marriage status: 25.3% never married, 62.0% now married, 7.5% widowed, 5.2% divorced (2006-2010 5-year est.); Foreign born: 20.9% (2006-2010 5-year est.); Ancestry (includes multiple ancestries): 28.2% Italian, 17.1% Irish, 13.6% German, 4.9% Polish, 4.0% Russian (2006-2010 5-year est.).

**Economy:** Employment by occupation: 14.0% management, 3.7% professional, 7.2% services, 17.1% sales, 4.1% farming, 7.6% construction, 5.7% production (2006-2010 5-year est.).

**Income:** Per capita income: $37,619 (2006-2010 5-year est.); Median household income: $98,553 (2006-2010 5-year est.); Average household income: $109,898 (2006-2010 5-year est.); Percent of households with income of $100,000 or more: 49.2% (2006-2010 5-year est.); Poverty rate: 1.9% (2006-2010 5-year est.).

**Education:** Percent of population age 25 and over with: High school diploma (including GED) or higher: 92.9% (2006-2010 5-year est.); Bachelor's degree or higher: 38.3% (2006-2010 5-year est.); Master's degree or higher: 16.2% (2006-2010 5-year est.).

**Housing:** Homeownership rate: 90.1% (2010); Median home value: $467,700 (2006-2010 5-year est.); Median contract rent: $1,565 per month (2006-2010 5-year est.); Median year structure built: 1954 (2006-2010 5-year est.).

**Transportation:** Commute to work: 84.6% car, 8.7% public transportation, 0.7% walk, 4.7% work from home (2006-2010 5-year est.); Travel time to work: 24.0% less than 15 minutes, 29.8% 15 to 30 minutes, 20.9% 30 to 45 minutes, 9.4% 45 to 60 minutes, 15.9% 60 minutes or more (2006-2010 5-year est.)

**SANDS POINT** (village). Covers a land area of 4.230 square miles and a water area of 1.378 square miles. Located at 40.85° N. Lat; 73.70° W. Long. Elevation is 43 feet.

**History:** Sands Point promontory (lighthouse) is at tip of Manhasset Neck, Northwest of village.

**Population:** 2,477 (1990); 2,786 (2000); 2,675 (2010); Density: 632.3 persons per square mile (2010); Race: 88.6% White, 0.8% Black, 8.2% Asian, 0.0% American Indian/Alaska Native, 0.0% Native Hawaiian/Other Pacific Islander, 2.4% Other, 4.7% Hispanic of any race (2010); Average household size: 3.03 (2010); Median age: 46.5 (2010); Males per 100 females: 95.7 (2010); Marriage status: 16.4% never married, 77.2% now married, 2.9% widowed, 3.5% divorced (2006-2010 5-year est.); Foreign born: 16.2% (2006-2010 5-year est.); Ancestry (includes multiple ancestries): 17.9% Russian, 13.3% Italian, 10.3% German, 9.6% Irish, 7.7% Polish (2006-2010 5-year est.).

**Economy:** Single-family building permits issued: 3 (2011); Multi-family building permits issued: 0 (2011); Employment by occupation: 27.7% management, 2.4% professional, 4.5% services, 16.7% sales, 0.3% farming, 3.8% construction, 2.1% production (2006-2010 5-year est.).

**Income:** Per capita income: $141,337 (2006-2010 5-year est.); Median household income: $226,250 (2006-2010 5-year est.); Average household income: $404,670 (2006-2010 5-year est.); Percent of households with income of $100,000 or more: 77.4% (2006-2010 5-year est.); Poverty rate: 2.9% (2006-2010 5-year est.).

**Education:** Percent of population age 25 and over with: High school diploma (including GED) or higher: 95.2% (2006-2010 5-year est.); Bachelor's degree or higher: 69.9% (2006-2010 5-year est.); Master's degree or higher: 34.0% (2006-2010 5-year est.).

**Housing:** Homeownership rate: 96.2% (2010); Median home value: $1 (2006-2010 5-year est.); Median contract rent: n/a per month (2006-2010 5-year est.); Median year structure built: 1957 (2006-2010 5-year est.).

**Safety:** Violent crime rate: 0.0 per 10,000 population; Property crime rate: 45.6 per 10,000 population (2010).

**Transportation:** Commute to work: 65.7% car, 23.2% public transportation, 2.0% walk, 9.1% work from home (2006-2010 5-year est.); Travel time to work: 11.3% less than 15 minutes, 15.6% 15 to 30 minutes, 23.1% 30 to 45 minutes, 12.1% 45 to 60 minutes, 38.0% 60 minutes or more (2006-2010 5-year est.)

**Additional Information Contacts**
Village of Sands Point . . . . . . . . . . . . . . . . . . . . . (516) 883-3044
  http://www.sandspoint.org

**SEA CLIFF** (village). Covers a land area of 1.114 square miles and a water area of 0.846 square miles. Located at 40.84° N. Lat; 73.65° W. Long. Elevation is 187 feet.

**History:** Incorporated 1883.

**Population:** 5,054 (1990); 5,066 (2000); 4,995 (2010); Density: 4,480.5 persons per square mile (2010); Race: 92.8% White, 2.4% Black, 1.9% Asian, 0.1% American Indian/Alaska Native, 0.0% Native Hawaiian/Other Pacific Islander, 2.8% Other, 6.8% Hispanic of any race (2010); Average household size: 2.50 (2010); Median age: 44.6 (2010); Males per 100 females: 94.0 (2010); Marriage status: 30.8% never married, 51.2% now married, 8.4% widowed, 9.6% divorced (2006-2010 5-year est.); Foreign born: 9.0% (2006-2010 5-year est.); Ancestry (includes multiple ancestries): 26.6% Italian, 24.3% Irish, 20.3% German, 6.8% English, 6.8% Polish (2006-2010 5-year est.).

**Economy:** Single-family building permits issued: 0 (2011); Multi-family building permits issued: 0 (2011); Employment by occupation: 18.0% management, 4.7% professional, 6.7% services, 20.5% sales, 2.4% farming, 4.8% construction, 0.0% production (2006-2010 5-year est.).

**Income:** Per capita income: $50,219 (2006-2010 5-year est.); Median household income: $98,984 (2006-2010 5-year est.); Average household income: $127,007 (2006-2010 5-year est.); Percent of households with income of $100,000 or more: 49.4% (2006-2010 5-year est.); Poverty rate: 3.7% (2006-2010 5-year est.).

**Education:** Percent of population age 25 and over with: High school diploma (including GED) or higher: 94.4% (2006-2010 5-year est.); Bachelor's degree or higher: 58.1% (2006-2010 5-year est.); Master's degree or higher: 25.8% (2006-2010 5-year est.).

**School District(s)**
North Shore Central School District (KG-12)
  2009-10 Enrollment: 2,866 . . . . . . . . . . . . . . . . (516) 277-7801

**Housing:** Homeownership rate: 74.5% (2010); Median home value: $644,300 (2006-2010 5-year est.); Median contract rent: $1,488 per month (2006-2010 5-year est.); Median year structure built: before 1940 (2006-2010 5-year est.).

**Transportation:** Commute to work: 70.7% car, 12.2% public transportation, 5.0% walk, 10.6% work from home (2006-2010 5-year est.); Travel time to work: 25.1% less than 15 minutes, 25.9% 15 to 30 minutes, 19.4% 30 to 45 minutes, 7.4% 45 to 60 minutes, 22.2% 60 minutes or more (2006-2010 5-year est.)

**SEAFORD** (CDP). Covers a land area of 2.610 square miles and a water area of 0.054 square miles. Located at 40.66° N. Lat; 73.49° W. Long. Elevation is 10 feet.

**History:** The county Museum of Natural History is here. Settled 1643.

**Population:** 15,597 (1990); 15,791 (2000); 15,294 (2010); Density: 5,858.5 persons per square mile (2010); Race: 95.4% White, 0.5% Black, 2.2% Asian, 0.1% American Indian/Alaska Native, 0.0% Native Hawaiian/Other Pacific Islander, 1.8% Other, 5.0% Hispanic of any race (2010); Average household size: 2.89 (2010); Median age: 42.5 (2010); Males per 100 females: 94.9 (2010); Marriage status: 27.7% never married, 58.3% now married, 7.1% widowed, 7.0% divorced (2006-2010 5-year est.); Foreign born: 6.3% (2006-2010 5-year est.); Ancestry (includes multiple ancestries): 40.7% Italian, 30.6% Irish, 20.0% German, 10.2% Polish, 6.0% Russian (2006-2010 5-year est.).

**Economy:** Employment by occupation: 13.2% management, 3.9% professional, 5.2% services, 20.8% sales, 2.5% farming, 6.1% construction, 3.0% production (2006-2010 5-year est.).

**Income:** Per capita income: $40,378 (2006-2010 5-year est.); Median household income: $107,340 (2006-2010 5-year est.); Average household income: $118,765 (2006-2010 5-year est.); Percent of households with income of $100,000 or more: 55.4% (2006-2010 5-year est.); Poverty rate: 2.0% (2006-2010 5-year est.).

**Education:** Percent of population age 25 and over with: High school diploma (including GED) or higher: 94.0% (2006-2010 5-year est.); Bachelor's degree or higher: 36.9% (2006-2010 5-year est.); Master's degree or higher: 13.9% (2006-2010 5-year est.).

**School District(s)**
Levittown Union Free School District (KG-12)
   2009-10 Enrollment: 7,625 . . . . . . . . . . . . . . . . . . . . . . . . (516) 520-8300
Seaford Union Free School District (KG-12)
   2009-10 Enrollment: 2,567 . . . . . . . . . . . . . . . . . . . . . . . (516) 592-4002
**Housing:** Homeownership rate: 89.4% (2010); Median home value:
$477,000 (2006-2010 5-year est.); Median contract rent: $1,641 per month
(2006-2010 5-year est.); Median year structure built: 1955 (2006-2010
5-year est.).
**Transportation:** Commute to work: 83.4% car, 12.5% public
transportation, 1.6% walk, 1.8% work from home (2006-2010 5-year est.);
Travel time to work: 17.7% less than 15 minutes, 35.7% 15 to 30 minutes,
19.9% 30 to 45 minutes, 8.8% 45 to 60 minutes, 17.9% 60 minutes or more
(2006-2010 5-year est.)

## SEARINGTOWN (CDP). Covers a land area of 0.928 square miles
and a water area of 0 square miles. Located at 40.77° N. Lat; 73.66° W.
Long. Elevation is 128 feet.
**History:** The hamlet derives its name from the Searing family, once
numerous in the area and among the first parishioners at the Methodist
church that was erected in 1788.
**Population:** 5,020 (1990); 5,034 (2000); 4,915 (2010); Density: 5,292.9
persons per square mile (2010); Race: 56.7% White, 1.0% Black, 39.0%
Asian, 0.1% American Indian/Alaska Native, 0.0% Native Hawaiian/Other
Pacific Islander, 3.2% Other, 3.6% Hispanic of any race (2010); Average
household size: 3.14 (2010); Median age: 45.8 (2010); Males per 100
females: 95.4 (2010); Marriage status: 24.0% never married, 70.0% now
married, 2.6% widowed, 3.4% divorced (2006-2010 5-year est.); Foreign
born: 37.0% (2006-2010 5-year est.); Ancestry (includes multiple
ancestries): 15.0% Italian, 8.2% Russian, 6.5% Polish, 3.2% Israeli, 3.0%
German (2006-2010 5-year est.).
**Economy:** Employment by occupation: 21.6% management, 2.1%
professional, 4.3% services, 13.6% sales, 2.6% farming, 1.0%
construction, 1.3% production (2006-2010 5-year est.).
**Income:** Per capita income: $58,192 (2006-2010 5-year est.); Median
household income: $128,285 (2006-2010 5-year est.); Average household
income: $179,693 (2006-2010 5-year est.); Percent of households with
income of $100,000 or more: 67.1% (2006-2010 5-year est.); Poverty rate:
0.7% (2006-2010 5-year est.).
**Education:** Percent of population age 25 and over with: High school
diploma (including GED) or higher: 94.2% (2006-2010 5-year est.);
Bachelor's degree or higher: 62.7% (2006-2010 5-year est.); Master's
degree or higher: 32.8% (2006-2010 5-year est.).
**Housing:** Homeownership rate: 96.9% (2010); Median home value:
$808,800 (2006-2010 5-year est.); Median contract rent: $1,225 per month
(2006-2010 5-year est.); Median year structure built: 1960 (2006-2010
5-year est.).
**Transportation:** Commute to work: 85.0% car, 9.8% public transportation,
0.0% walk, 5.1% work from home (2006-2010 5-year est.); Travel time to
work: 12.4% less than 15 minutes, 34.8% 15 to 30 minutes, 25.1% 30 to 45
minutes, 9.0% 45 to 60 minutes, 18.8% 60 minutes or more (2006-2010
5-year est.)

## SOUTH FARMINGDALE (CDP). Covers a land area of 2.217
square miles and a water area of 0.004 square miles. Located at 40.71° N.
Lat; 73.44° W. Long. Elevation is 59 feet.
**Population:** 15,567 (1990); 15,061 (2000); 14,486 (2010); Density: 6,532.2
persons per square mile (2010); Race: 90.1% White, 1.4% Black, 4.5%
Asian, 0.1% American Indian/Alaska Native, 0.0% Native Hawaiian/Other
Pacific Islander, 3.9% Other, 10.0% Hispanic of any race (2010); Average
household size: 3.02 (2010); Median age: 41.7 (2010); Males per 100
females: 95.7 (2010); Marriage status: 25.0% never married, 62.7% now
married, 7.4% widowed, 4.9% divorced (2006-2010 5-year est.); Foreign
born: 10.8% (2006-2010 5-year est.); Ancestry (includes multiple
ancestries): 39.3% Italian, 27.3% Irish, 19.9% German, 7.0% English, 5.3%
Polish (2006-2010 5-year est.).
**Economy:** Employment by occupation: 16.3% management, 3.6%
professional, 6.6% services, 20.7% sales, 4.7% farming, 8.3%
construction, 6.0% production (2006-2010 5-year est.).
**Income:** Per capita income: $36,005 (2006-2010 5-year est.); Median
household income: $92,439 (2006-2010 5-year est.); Average household
income: $105,833 (2006-2010 5-year est.); Percent of households with
income of $100,000 or more: 46.2% (2006-2010 5-year est.); Poverty rate:
3.2% (2006-2010 5-year est.).
**Education:** Percent of population age 25 and over with: High school
diploma (including GED) or higher: 94.0% (2006-2010 5-year est.);

Bachelor's degree or higher: 30.5% (2006-2010 5-year est.); Master's
degree or higher: 12.1% (2006-2010 5-year est.).
**Housing:** Homeownership rate: 90.7% (2010); Median home value:
$436,600 (2006-2010 5-year est.); Median contract rent: $1,047 per month
(2006-2010 5-year est.); Median year structure built: 1955 (2006-2010
5-year est.).
**Transportation:** Commute to work: 85.8% car, 11.1% public
transportation, 0.1% walk, 2.7% work from home (2006-2010 5-year est.);
Travel time to work: 22.9% less than 15 minutes, 29.2% 15 to 30 minutes,
21.2% 30 to 45 minutes, 8.0% 45 to 60 minutes, 18.7% 60 minutes or more
(2006-2010 5-year est.)

## SOUTH FLORAL PARK (village). Aka Jamaica Square. Covers a
land area of 0.095 square miles and a water area of 0 square miles.
Located at 40.71° N. Lat; 73.70° W. Long. Elevation is 69 feet.
**History:** Until 1931 called Jamaica Square.
**Population:** 1,478 (1990); 1,578 (2000); 1,764 (2010); Density: 18,379.4
persons per square mile (2010); Race: 22.2% White, 57.5% Black, 7.9%
Asian, 1.0% American Indian/Alaska Native, 0.0% Native Hawaiian/Other
Pacific Islander, 11.4% Other, 17.9% Hispanic of any race (2010); Average
household size: 3.33 (2010); Median age: 37.3 (2010); Males per 100
females: 87.1 (2010); Marriage status: 30.9% never married, 48.5% now
married, 9.1% widowed, 11.5% divorced (2006-2010 5-year est.); Foreign
born: 33.5% (2006-2010 5-year est.); Ancestry (includes multiple
ancestries): 9.0% Jamaican, 7.5% Irish, 4.5% Italian, 3.8% German, 3.4%
Trinidadian and Tobagonian (2006-2010 5-year est.).
**Economy:** Single-family building permits issued: 0 (2011); Multi-family
building permits issued: 0 (2011); Employment by occupation: 11.2%
management, 3.4% professional, 15.6% services, 21.6% sales, 6.6%
farming, 6.8% construction, 5.1% production (2006-2010 5-year est.).
**Income:** Per capita income: $29,912 (2006-2010 5-year est.); Median
household income: $85,469 (2006-2010 5-year est.); Average household
income: $91,789 (2006-2010 5-year est.); Percent of households with
income of $100,000 or more: 36.1% (2006-2010 5-year est.); Poverty rate:
3.7% (2006-2010 5-year est.).
**Education:** Percent of population age 25 and over with: High school
diploma (including GED) or higher: 90.3% (2006-2010 5-year est.);
Bachelor's degree or higher: 27.8% (2006-2010 5-year est.); Master's
degree or higher: 7.5% (2006-2010 5-year est.).
**Housing:** Homeownership rate: 74.9% (2010); Median home value:
$425,500 (2006-2010 5-year est.); Median contract rent: $1,607 per month
(2006-2010 5-year est.); Median year structure built: 1957 (2006-2010
5-year est.).
**Transportation:** Commute to work: 70.7% car, 23.7% public
transportation, 4.1% walk, 1.4% work from home (2006-2010 5-year est.);
Travel time to work: 16.3% less than 15 minutes, 13.4% 15 to 30 minutes,
37.7% 30 to 45 minutes, 11.8% 45 to 60 minutes, 20.8% 60 minutes or
more (2006-2010 5-year est.)

## SOUTH HEMPSTEAD (CDP). Covers a land area of 0.578 square
miles and a water area of 0 square miles. Located at 40.68° N. Lat; 73.62°
W. Long. Elevation is 43 feet.
**Population:** 3,014 (1990); 3,188 (2000); 3,243 (2010); Density: 5,607.3
persons per square mile (2010); Race: 73.0% White, 14.0% Black, 2.4%
Asian, 0.3% American Indian/Alaska Native, 0.0% Native Hawaiian/Other
Pacific Islander, 10.3% Other, 18.5% Hispanic of any race (2010); Average
household size: 3.10 (2010); Median age: 39.9 (2010); Males per 100
females: 93.3 (2010); Marriage status: 29.3% never married, 58.1% now
married, 4.7% widowed, 7.9% divorced (2006-2010 5-year est.); Foreign
born: 14.1% (2006-2010 5-year est.); Ancestry (includes multiple
ancestries): 21.2% Irish, 18.1% Italian, 13.6% German, 5.4% Polish, 5.2%
American (2006-2010 5-year est.).
**Economy:** Employment by occupation: 15.2% management, 0.5%
professional, 9.7% services, 20.5% sales, 6.5% farming, 11.3%
construction, 4.0% production (2006-2010 5-year est.).
**Income:** Per capita income: $39,211 (2006-2010 5-year est.); Median
household income: $104,545 (2006-2010 5-year est.); Average household
income: $127,068 (2006-2010 5-year est.); Percent of households with
income of $100,000 or more: 52.8% (2006-2010 5-year est.); Poverty rate:
1.5% (2006-2010 5-year est.).
**Education:** Percent of population age 25 and over with: High school
diploma (including GED) or higher: 90.2% (2006-2010 5-year est.);
Bachelor's degree or higher: 47.0% (2006-2010 5-year est.); Master's
degree or higher: 16.7% (2006-2010 5-year est.).

School District(s)
Rockville Centre Union Free School District (KG-12)
    2009-10 Enrollment: 3,545 . . . . . . . . . . . . . . . . . . . (516) 255-8920
**Housing:** Homeownership rate: 89.7% (2010); Median home value:
$444,200 (2006-2010 5-year est.); Median contract rent: n/a per month
(2006-2010 5-year est.); Median year structure built: 1952 (2006-2010
5-year est.).
**Transportation:** Commute to work: 80.3% car, 15.4% public
transportation, 1.7% walk, 2.6% work from home (2006-2010 5-year est.);
Travel time to work: 21.0% less than 15 minutes, 31.2% 15 to 30 minutes,
14.2% 30 to 45 minutes, 9.1% 45 to 60 minutes, 24.5% 60 minutes or more
(2006-2010 5-year est.)

## SOUTH VALLEY STREAM (CDP). Covers a land area of 0.872
square miles and a water area of 0 square miles. Located at 40.65° N. Lat;
73.71° W. Long. Elevation is 7 feet.
**Population:** 5,328 (1990); 5,638 (2000); 5,962 (2010); Density: 6,830.6
persons per square mile (2010); Race: 51.9% White, 23.1% Black, 18.1%
Asian, 0.3% American Indian/Alaska Native, 0.0% Native Hawaiian/Other
Pacific Islander, 6.6% Other, 9.8% Hispanic of any race (2010); Average
household size: 3.02 (2010); Median age: 42.5 (2010); Males per 100
females: 92.1 (2010); Marriage status: 24.0% never married, 59.6% now
married, 11.0% widowed, 5.4% divorced (2006-2010 5-year est.); Foreign
born: 27.8% (2006-2010 5-year est.); Ancestry (includes multiple
ancestries): 9.0% Italian, 8.8% Russian, 5.1% Israeli, 4.6% American, 3.7%
Jamaican (2006-2010 5-year est.).
**Economy:** Employment by occupation: 18.5% management, 3.9%
professional, 6.1% services, 26.5% sales, 2.7% farming, 4.2%
construction, 2.0% production (2006-2010 5-year est.).
**Income:** Per capita income: $38,143 (2006-2010 5-year est.); Median
household income: $101,179 (2006-2010 5-year est.); Average household
income: $105,370 (2006-2010 5-year est.); Percent of households with
income of $100,000 or more: 52.2% (2006-2010 5-year est.); Poverty rate:
12.1% (2006-2010 5-year est.).
**Education:** Percent of population age 25 and over with: High school
diploma (including GED) or higher: 91.0% (2006-2010 5-year est.);
Bachelor's degree or higher: 47.0% (2006-2010 5-year est.); Master's
degree or higher: 18.2% (2006-2010 5-year est.).
**Housing:** Homeownership rate: 78.2% (2010); Median home value:
$487,500 (2006-2010 5-year est.); Median contract rent: $1,254 per month
(2006-2010 5-year est.); Median year structure built: 1954 (2006-2010
5-year est.).
**Transportation:** Commute to work: 62.7% car, 20.8% public
transportation, 9.2% walk, 6.6% work from home (2006-2010 5-year est.);
Travel time to work: 19.1% less than 15 minutes, 20.1% 15 to 30 minutes,
21.0% 30 to 45 minutes, 15.5% 45 to 60 minutes, 24.3% 60 minutes or
more (2006-2010 5-year est.)

## STEWART MANOR (village). Covers a land area of 0.209 square
miles and a water area of 0 square miles. Located at 40.72° N. Lat; 73.68°
W. Long. Elevation is 85 feet.
**History:** Laid out 1926, incorporated 1927.
**Population:** 2,002 (1990); 1,935 (2000); 1,896 (2010); Density: 9,041.8
persons per square mile (2010); Race: 90.5% White, 2.5% Black, 4.8%
Asian, 0.0% American Indian/Alaska Native, 0.2% Native Hawaiian/Other
Pacific Islander, 2.0% Other, 5.0% Hispanic of any race (2010); Average
household size: 2.71 (2010); Median age: 44.8 (2010); Males per 100
females: 88.3 (2010); Marriage status: 25.6% never married, 59.9% now
married, 8.6% widowed, 5.9% divorced (2006-2010 5-year est.); Foreign
born: 12.7% (2006-2010 5-year est.); Ancestry (includes multiple
ancestries): 39.7% Irish, 28.4% Italian, 16.2% German, 5.0% English, 4.9%
Polish (2006-2010 5-year est.).
**Economy:** Single-family building permits issued: 0 (2011); Multi-family
building permits issued: 0 (2011); Employment by occupation: 14.1%
management, 4.5% professional, 5.4% services, 15.9% sales, 3.8%
farming, 3.0% construction, 1.1% production (2006-2010 5-year est.).
**Income:** Per capita income: $43,850 (2006-2010 5-year est.); Median
household income: $107,321 (2006-2010 5-year est.); Average household
income: $129,395 (2006-2010 5-year est.); Percent of households with
income of $100,000 or more: 54.2% (2006-2010 5-year est.); Poverty rate:
3.8% (2006-2010 5-year est.).
**Education:** Percent of population age 25 and over with: High school
diploma (including GED) or higher: 95.3% (2006-2010 5-year est.);
Bachelor's degree or higher: 56.1% (2006-2010 5-year est.); Master's
degree or higher: 24.0% (2006-2010 5-year est.).

School District(s)
Elmont Union Free School District (PK-06)
    2009-10 Enrollment: 3,987 . . . . . . . . . . . . . . . . . . . (516) 326-5500
**Housing:** Homeownership rate: 89.8% (2010); Median home value:
$561,300 (2006-2010 5-year est.); Median contract rent: $1,497 per month
(2006-2010 5-year est.); Median year structure built: before 1940
(2006-2010 5-year est.).
**Transportation:** Commute to work: 70.6% car, 21.4% public
transportation, 3.2% walk, 3.2% work from home (2006-2010 5-year est.);
Travel time to work: 21.1% less than 15 minutes, 26.4% 15 to 30 minutes,
20.8% 30 to 45 minutes, 7.9% 45 to 60 minutes, 23.8% 60 minutes or more
(2006-2010 5-year est.)

## SYOSSET (CDP). Covers a land area of 4.973 square miles and a
water area of 0 square miles. Located at 40.81° N. Lat; 73.50° W. Long.
Elevation is 217 feet.
**History:** Syosset was established in 1846. Booming businesses in the area
during this era included horse and livestock sales, cider milling, a pickle
factory, and entrepreneur enterprises such as DV Horton's "Medicinal Root
Beer".
**Population:** 18,967 (1990); 18,544 (2000); 18,829 (2010); Density: 3,785.8
persons per square mile (2010); Race: 74.4% White, 0.8% Black, 22.2%
Asian, 0.1% American Indian/Alaska Native, 0.0% Native Hawaiian/Other
Pacific Islander, 2.5% Other, 4.1% Hispanic of any race (2010); Average
household size: 3.00 (2010); Median age: 43.0 (2010); Males per 100
females: 98.3 (2010); Marriage status: 23.2% never married, 66.0% now
married, 6.1% widowed, 4.7% divorced (2006-2010 5-year est.); Foreign
born: 17.8% (2006-2010 5-year est.); Ancestry (includes multiple
ancestries): 22.5% Italian, 12.5% Irish, 8.7% German, 6.3% Russian, 6.2%
Polish (2006-2010 5-year est.).
**Economy:** Employment by occupation: 21.3% management, 6.3%
professional, 3.8% services, 16.2% sales, 1.9% farming, 4.5%
construction, 1.7% production (2006-2010 5-year est.).
**Income:** Per capita income: $49,713 (2006-2010 5-year est.); Median
household income: $130,257 (2006-2010 5-year est.); Average household
income: $151,497 (2006-2010 5-year est.); Percent of households with
income of $100,000 or more: 59.5% (2006-2010 5-year est.); Poverty rate:
2.6% (2006-2010 5-year est.).
**Education:** Percent of population age 25 and over with: High school
diploma (including GED) or higher: 95.2% (2006-2010 5-year est.);
Bachelor's degree or higher: 61.6% (2006-2010 5-year est.); Master's
degree or higher: 29.0% (2006-2010 5-year est.).
School District(s)
Cold Spring Harbor Central School District (KG-12)
    2009-10 Enrollment: 2,018 . . . . . . . . . . . . . . . . . . . (631) 367-5931
Nyc Special Schools - District 75 (PK-12)
    2009-10 Enrollment: 21,871 . . . . . . . . . . . . . . . . . . (212) 802-1617
Syosset Central School District (KG-12)
    2009-10 Enrollment: 6,666 . . . . . . . . . . . . . . . . . . . (516) 364-5605
**Four-year College(s)**
New York College of Health Professions (Private, Not-for-profit)
    Fall 2010 Enrollment: 743 . . . . . . . . . . . . . . . . . . . (5.1) 636-4E+1
    2011-12 Tuition: In-state $12,066; Out-of-state $12,066
**Vocational/Technical School(s)**
Star Career Academy-Syosset (Private, For-profit)
    Fall 2010 Enrollment: 372 . . . . . . . . . . . . . . . . . . . (5.1) 636-4E+1
    2011-12 Tuition: $13,957
**Housing:** Homeownership rate: 91.6% (2010); Median home value:
$633,800 (2006-2010 5-year est.); Median contract rent: $1,686 per month
(2006-2010 5-year est.); Median year structure built: 1956 (2006-2010
5-year est.).
**Hospitals:** Northshore University Hospital at Syosset (204 beds)
**Newspapers:** Long Island Press (Local news)
**Transportation:** Commute to work: 75.7% car, 17.9% public
transportation, 0.7% walk, 5.1% work from home (2006-2010 5-year est.);
Travel time to work: 20.1% less than 15 minutes, 28.6% 15 to 30 minutes,
16.2% 30 to 45 minutes, 6.1% 45 to 60 minutes, 28.9% 60 minutes or more
(2006-2010 5-year est.)
**Additional Information Contacts**
Syosset Chamber of Commerce . . . . . . . . . . . . . . . . . . . (516) 364-7150
    http://www.syossetchamber.com

**THOMASTON** (village). Covers a land area of 0.407 square miles and a water area of 0 square miles. Located at 40.78° N. Lat; 73.71° W. Long. Elevation is 197 feet.

**Population:** 2,594 (1990); 2,607 (2000); 2,617 (2010); Density: 6,421.4 persons per square mile (2010); Race: 66.8% White, 1.1% Black, 28.0% Asian, 0.1% American Indian/Alaska Native, 0.0% Native Hawaiian/Other Pacific Islander, 4.0% Other, 5.2% Hispanic of any race (2010); Average household size: 2.73 (2010); Median age: 43.5 (2010); Males per 100 females: 89.9 (2010); Marriage status: 25.4% never married, 59.9% now married, 4.0% widowed, 10.6% divorced (2006-2010 5-year est.); Foreign born: 28.7% (2006-2010 5-year est.); Ancestry (includes multiple ancestries): 18.5% Russian, 10.2% Italian, 10.0% Polish, 5.2% Eastern European, 4.1% Iranian (2006-2010 5-year est.).

**Economy:** Single-family building permits issued: 2 (2011); Multi-family building permits issued: 0 (2011); Employment by occupation: 22.3% management, 9.8% professional, 4.9% services, 10.9% sales, 3.4% farming, 0.9% construction, 0.9% production (2006-2010 5-year est.).

**Income:** Per capita income: $59,504 (2006-2010 5-year est.); Median household income: $126,098 (2006-2010 5-year est.); Average household income: $151,569 (2006-2010 5-year est.); Percent of households with income of $100,000 or more: 62.9% (2006-2010 5-year est.); Poverty rate: 7.1% (2006-2010 5-year est.).

**Education:** Percent of population age 25 and over with: High school diploma (including GED) or higher: 96.0% (2006-2010 5-year est.); Bachelor's degree or higher: 69.1% (2006-2010 5-year est.); Master's degree or higher: 42.1% (2006-2010 5-year est.).

**Housing:** Homeownership rate: 80.8% (2010); Median home value: $760,200 (2006-2010 5-year est.); Median contract rent: n/a per month (2006-2010 5-year est.); Median year structure built: 1948 (2006-2010 5-year est.).

**Transportation:** Commute to work: 67.8% car, 25.3% public transportation, 0.9% walk, 6.1% work from home (2006-2010 5-year est.); Travel time to work: 21.4% less than 15 minutes, 22.7% 15 to 30 minutes, 20.6% 30 to 45 minutes, 11.8% 45 to 60 minutes, 23.5% 60 minutes or more (2006-2010 5-year est.)

**UNIONDALE** (CDP). Covers a land area of 2.706 square miles and a water area of 0 square miles. Located at 40.70° N. Lat; 73.59° W. Long. Elevation is 52 feet.

**History:** Named for the American union of states. Downtown suburban growth since the 1970s.

**Population:** 20,328 (1990); 23,011 (2000); 24,759 (2010); Density: 9,147.8 persons per square mile (2010); Race: 24.4% White, 48.5% Black, 2.0% Asian, 0.6% American Indian/Alaska Native, 0.1% Native Hawaiian/Other Pacific Islander, 24.4% Other, 38.8% Hispanic of any race (2010); Average household size: 3.96 (2010); Median age: 34.6 (2010); Males per 100 females: 93.6 (2010); Marriage status: 42.1% never married, 43.6% now married, 6.5% widowed, 7.8% divorced (2006-2010 5-year est.); Foreign born: 40.6% (2006-2010 5-year est.); Ancestry (includes multiple ancestries): 7.9% Haitian, 7.8% Jamaican, 3.3% Italian, 2.9% Irish, 2.3% West Indian (2006-2010 5-year est.).

**Economy:** Employment by occupation: 4.6% management, 2.0% professional, 13.4% services, 14.6% sales, 5.6% farming, 10.0% construction, 6.8% production (2006-2010 5-year est.).

**Income:** Per capita income: $21,848 (2006-2010 5-year est.); Median household income: $71,839 (2006-2010 5-year est.); Average household income: $81,357 (2006-2010 5-year est.); Percent of households with income of $100,000 or more: 33.1% (2006-2010 5-year est.); Poverty rate: 7.9% (2006-2010 5-year est.).

**Education:** Percent of population age 25 and over with: High school diploma (including GED) or higher: 73.7% (2006-2010 5-year est.); Bachelor's degree or higher: 18.3% (2006-2010 5-year est.); Master's degree or higher: 5.4% (2006-2010 5-year est.).

### School District(s)
Uniondale Union Free School District (KG-12)
    2009-10 Enrollment: 6,358 . . . . . . . . . . . . . . . . . . . . (516) 560-8824

### Vocational/Technical School(s)
Veeb Nassau County School of Practical Nursing (Public)
    Fall 2010 Enrollment: 247 . . . . . . . . . . . . . . . . . . . . (516) 572-1704
    2011-12 Tuition: In-state $13,500; Out-of-state $14,000

**Housing:** Homeownership rate: 74.4% (2010); Median home value: $370,600 (2006-2010 5-year est.); Median contract rent: $1,267 per month (2006-2010 5-year est.); Median year structure built: 1953 (2006-2010 5-year est.).

**Transportation:** Commute to work: 80.9% car, 15.3% public transportation, 0.8% walk, 1.2% work from home (2006-2010 5-year est.); Travel time to work: 17.4% less than 15 minutes, 36.2% 15 to 30 minutes, 25.9% 30 to 45 minutes, 7.1% 45 to 60 minutes, 13.3% 60 minutes or more (2006-2010 5-year est.)

**UNIVERSITY GARDENS** (CDP). Covers a land area of 0.533 square miles and a water area of 0 square miles. Located at 40.77° N. Lat; 73.72° W. Long. Elevation is 148 feet.

**History:** Occupying the northern portion of Lake Success, this area was the temporary headquarters of the United Nations while its headquarters building in New York City was built. It borders the New York City borough of Queens.

**Population:** 4,381 (1990); 4,138 (2000); 4,226 (2010); Density: 7,925.7 persons per square mile (2010); Race: 63.3% White, 1.8% Black, 29.5% Asian, 0.2% American Indian/Alaska Native, 0.0% Native Hawaiian/Other Pacific Islander, 5.2% Other, 7.5% Hispanic of any race (2010); Average household size: 2.57 (2010); Median age: 44.2 (2010); Males per 100 females: 92.6 (2010); Marriage status: 24.5% never married, 57.7% now married, 6.5% widowed, 11.3% divorced (2006-2010 5-year est.); Foreign born: 28.5% (2006-2010 5-year est.); Ancestry (includes multiple ancestries): 17.1% Italian, 13.1% Russian, 10.4% Polish, 5.4% Romanian, 5.4% Irish (2006-2010 5-year est.).

**Economy:** Employment by occupation: 19.0% management, 6.2% professional, 1.1% services, 10.6% sales, 3.3% farming, 8.3% construction, 3.7% production (2006-2010 5-year est.).

**Income:** Per capita income: $52,718 (2006-2010 5-year est.); Median household income: $106,012 (2006-2010 5-year est.); Average household income: $131,526 (2006-2010 5-year est.); Percent of households with income of $100,000 or more: 51.5% (2006-2010 5-year est.); Poverty rate: 0.4% (2006-2010 5-year est.).

**Education:** Percent of population age 25 and over with: High school diploma (including GED) or higher: 96.6% (2006-2010 5-year est.); Bachelor's degree or higher: 63.4% (2006-2010 5-year est.); Master's degree or higher: 31.9% (2006-2010 5-year est.).

**Housing:** Homeownership rate: 84.0% (2010); Median home value: $616,900 (2006-2010 5-year est.); Median contract rent: $895 per month (2006-2010 5-year est.); Median year structure built: 1947 (2006-2010 5-year est.).

**Transportation:** Commute to work: 71.5% car, 23.0% public transportation, 1.4% walk, 4.0% work from home (2006-2010 5-year est.); Travel time to work: 29.0% less than 15 minutes, 25.6% 15 to 30 minutes, 17.2% 30 to 45 minutes, 10.9% 45 to 60 minutes, 17.2% 60 minutes or more (2006-2010 5-year est.)

**UPPER BROOKVILLE** (village). Covers a land area of 4.318 square miles and a water area of 0 square miles. Located at 40.84° N. Lat; 73.56° W. Long. Elevation is 157 feet.

**Population:** 1,453 (1990); 1,801 (2000); 1,698 (2010); Density: 393.2 persons per square mile (2010); Race: 86.8% White, 0.9% Black, 9.5% Asian, 0.1% American Indian/Alaska Native, 0.1% Native Hawaiian/Other Pacific Islander, 2.6% Other, 4.7% Hispanic of any race (2010); Average household size: 2.98 (2010); Median age: 47.6 (2010); Males per 100 females: 94.3 (2010); Marriage status: 24.9% never married, 61.8% now married, 8.4% widowed, 4.9% divorced (2006-2010 5-year est.); Foreign born: 20.1% (2006-2010 5-year est.); Ancestry (includes multiple ancestries): 24.4% Italian, 10.4% German, 9.7% Irish, 6.2% Greek, 5.4% Polish (2006-2010 5-year est.).

**Economy:** Single-family building permits issued: 3 (2011); Multi-family building permits issued: 0 (2011); Employment by occupation: 32.0% management, 2.2% professional, 2.2% services, 18.3% sales, 1.4% farming, 4.1% construction, 5.1% production (2006-2010 5-year est.).

**Income:** Per capita income: $91,910 (2006-2010 5-year est.); Median household income: $170,625 (2006-2010 5-year est.); Average household income: $269,627 (2006-2010 5-year est.); Percent of households with income of $100,000 or more: 67.4% (2006-2010 5-year est.); Poverty rate: 8.7% (2006-2010 5-year est.).

**Education:** Percent of population age 25 and over with: High school diploma (including GED) or higher: 96.0% (2006-2010 5-year est.); Bachelor's degree or higher: 56.8% (2006-2010 5-year est.); Master's degree or higher: 27.8% (2006-2010 5-year est.).

**Housing:** Homeownership rate: 91.2% (2010); Median home value: $1 (2006-2010 5-year est.); Median contract rent: $681 per month (2006-2010 5-year est.); Median year structure built: 1965 (2006-2010 5-year est.).

**Transportation:** Commute to work: 82.4% car, 5.7% public transportation, 0.0% walk, 11.9% work from home (2006-2010 5-year est.); Travel time to work: 9.5% less than 15 minutes, 35.4% 15 to 30 minutes, 23.2% 30 to 45 minutes, 7.0% 45 to 60 minutes, 25.0% 60 minutes or more (2006-2010 5-year est.)

## VALLEY STREAM (village).

Covers a land area of 3.482 square miles and a water area of 0.017 square miles. Located at 40.66° N. Lat; 73.70° W. Long. Elevation is 16 feet.

**Population:** 33,962 (1990); 36,368 (2000); 37,511 (2010); Density: 10,772.4 persons per square mile (2010); Race: 57.2% White, 18.6% Black, 11.4% Asian, 0.3% American Indian/Alaska Native, 0.1% Native Hawaiian/Other Pacific Islander, 12.4% Other, 22.2% Hispanic of any race (2010); Average household size: 3.07 (2010); Median age: 39.7 (2010); Males per 100 females: 92.6 (2010); Marriage status: 32.4% never married, 54.9% now married, 5.7% widowed, 7.0% divorced (2006-2010 5-year est.); Foreign born: 33.0% (2006-2010 5-year est.); Ancestry (includes multiple ancestries): 21.6% Italian, 11.4% Irish, 8.6% German, 4.7% Haitian, 3.4% Jamaican (2006-2010 5-year est.).
**Economy:** Unemployment rate: 7.3% (February 2012); Total civilian labor force: 19,287 (February 2012); Single-family building permits issued: 1 (2011); Multi-family building permits issued: 0 (2011); Employment by occupation: 12.1% management, 3.0% professional, 9.5% services, 15.9% sales, 6.0% farming, 8.3% construction, 5.0% production (2006-2010 5-year est.).
**Income:** Per capita income: $30,608 (2006-2010 5-year est.); Median household income: $82,279 (2006-2010 5-year est.); Average household income: $94,369 (2006-2010 5-year est.); Percent of households with income of $100,000 or more: 39.5% (2006-2010 5-year est.); Poverty rate: 4.5% (2006-2010 5-year est.).
**Education:** Percent of population age 25 and over with: High school diploma (including GED) or higher: 89.2% (2006-2010 5-year est.); Bachelor's degree or higher: 33.0% (2006-2010 5-year est.); Master's degree or higher: 12.9% (2006-2010 5-year est.).

### School District(s)
Elmont Union Free School District (PK-06)
   2009-10 Enrollment: 3,987 . . . . . . . . . . . . . . . . . (516) 326-5500
Hewlett-Woodmere Union Free School District (PK-12)
   2009-10 Enrollment: 3,075 . . . . . . . . . . . . . . . . . (516) 374-8100
Valley Stream 13 Union Free School District (KG-06)
   2009-10 Enrollment: 2,156 . . . . . . . . . . . . . . . . . (516) 568-6100
Valley Stream 24 Union Free School District (KG-06)
   2009-10 Enrollment: 1,079 . . . . . . . . . . . . . . . . . (516) 256-0153
Valley Stream 30 Union Free School District (KG-06)
   2009-10 Enrollment: 1,423 . . . . . . . . . . . . . . . . . (516) 285-9881
Valley Stream Central High School District (07-12)
   2009-10 Enrollment: 4,602 . . . . . . . . . . . . . . . . . (516) 872-5601

### Two-year College(s)
Business Informatics Center Inc (Private, For-profit)
   Fall 2010 Enrollment: 94 . . . . . . . . . . . . . . . . . . . (516) 561-0050
   2011-12 Tuition: In-state $12,880; Out-of-state $12,880
**Housing:** Homeownership rate: 79.2% (2010); Median home value: $429,900 (2006-2010 5-year est.); Median contract rent: $1,205 per month (2006-2010 5-year est.); Median year structure built: 1949 (2006-2010 5-year est.).
**Hospitals:** Franklin Hospital Medical Center (305 beds)
**Transportation:** Commute to work: 75.1% car, 18.2% public transportation, 3.0% walk, 1.5% work from home (2006-2010 5-year est.); Travel time to work: 16.5% less than 15 minutes, 27.5% 15 to 30 minutes, 23.0% 30 to 45 minutes, 11.3% 45 to 60 minutes, 21.7% 60 minutes or more (2006-2010 5-year est.)
**Additional Information Contacts**
Valley Stream Chamber of Commerce . . . . . . . . . . . . . . (516) 825-1741
   http://www.valleystreamchamber.org

## WANTAGH (CDP).

Covers a land area of 3.830 square miles and a water area of 0.296 square miles. Located at 40.66° N. Lat; 73.51° W. Long. Elevation is 23 feet.

**Population:** 18,567 (1990); 18,971 (2000); 18,871 (2010); Density: 4,926.7 persons per square mile (2010); Race: 96.0% White, 0.3% Black, 2.0% Asian, 0.1% American Indian/Alaska Native, 0.0% Native Hawaiian/Other Pacific Islander, 1.6% Other, 4.7% Hispanic of any race (2010); Average household size: 3.07 (2010); Median age: 41.4 (2010); Males per 100 females: 93.5 (2010); Marriage status: 23.3% never married, 64.8% now married, 7.5% widowed, 4.3% divorced (2006-2010 5-year est.); Foreign

born: 8.1% (2006-2010 5-year est.); Ancestry (includes multiple ancestries): 36.6% Italian, 30.5% Irish, 20.0% German, 6.0% Russian, 5.9% Polish (2006-2010 5-year est.).
**Economy:** Employment by occupation: 14.9% management, 3.5% professional, 5.3% services, 17.8% sales, 3.6% farming, 6.6% construction, 3.8% production (2006-2010 5-year est.).
**Income:** Per capita income: $44,263 (2006-2010 5-year est.); Median household income: $111,004 (2006-2010 5-year est.); Average household income: $130,414 (2006-2010 5-year est.); Percent of households with income of $100,000 or more: 56.1% (2006-2010 5-year est.); Poverty rate: 2.0% (2006-2010 5-year est.).
**Education:** Percent of population age 25 and over with: High school diploma (including GED) or higher: 94.2% (2006-2010 5-year est.); Bachelor's degree or higher: 39.1% (2006-2010 5-year est.); Master's degree or higher: 18.1% (2006-2010 5-year est.).

### School District(s)
Levittown Union Free School District (KG-12)
   2009-10 Enrollment: 7,625 . . . . . . . . . . . . . . . . . (516) 520-8300
Wantagh Union Free School District (KG-12)
   2009-10 Enrollment: 3,602 . . . . . . . . . . . . . . . . . (516) 679-6300
**Housing:** Homeownership rate: 93.2% (2010); Median home value: $500,400 (2006-2010 5-year est.); Median contract rent: $1,688 per month (2006-2010 5-year est.); Median year structure built: 1955 (2006-2010 5-year est.).
**Newspapers:** The Mortgage Press (Local news)
**Transportation:** Commute to work: 82.0% car, 12.9% public transportation, 1.8% walk, 2.3% work from home (2006-2010 5-year est.); Travel time to work: 17.0% less than 15 minutes, 39.6% 15 to 30 minutes, 19.4% 30 to 45 minutes, 7.0% 45 to 60 minutes, 16.9% 60 minutes or more (2006-2010 5-year est.)
**Additional Information Contacts**
Wantagh Chamber of Commerce . . . . . . . . . . . . . . . . . (516) 679-0100
   http://www.wcc.li

## WEST HEMPSTEAD (CDP).

Covers a land area of 2.655 square miles and a water area of 0.070 square miles. Located at 40.69° N. Lat; 73.65° W. Long. Elevation is 66 feet.

**Population:** 17,707 (1990); 18,713 (2000); 18,862 (2010); Density: 7,102.9 persons per square mile (2010); Race: 74.0% White, 10.2% Black, 6.1% Asian, 0.1% American Indian/Alaska Native, 0.0% Native Hawaiian/Other Pacific Islander, 9.6% Other, 16.4% Hispanic of any race (2010); Average household size: 3.17 (2010); Median age: 39.9 (2010); Males per 100 females: 96.4 (2010); Marriage status: 29.1% never married, 57.8% now married, 6.3% widowed, 6.7% divorced (2006-2010 5-year est.); Foreign born: 22.6% (2006-2010 5-year est.); Ancestry (includes multiple ancestries): 24.0% Italian, 13.7% Irish, 10.6% German, 5.6% Polish, 3.4% Russian (2006-2010 5-year est.).
**Economy:** Employment by occupation: 15.7% management, 4.5% professional, 6.5% services, 16.8% sales, 3.1% farming, 6.1% construction, 4.5% production (2006-2010 5-year est.).
**Income:** Per capita income: $37,062 (2006-2010 5-year est.); Median household income: $94,348 (2006-2010 5-year est.); Average household income: $113,135 (2006-2010 5-year est.); Percent of households with income of $100,000 or more: 46.9% (2006-2010 5-year est.); Poverty rate: 6.4% (2006-2010 5-year est.).
**Education:** Percent of population age 25 and over with: High school diploma (including GED) or higher: 90.1% (2006-2010 5-year est.); Bachelor's degree or higher: 42.0% (2006-2010 5-year est.); Master's degree or higher: 19.3% (2006-2010 5-year est.).

### School District(s)
West Hempstead Union Free School District (KG-12)
   2009-10 Enrollment: 2,285 . . . . . . . . . . . . . . . . . (516) 390-3107
**Housing:** Homeownership rate: 87.4% (2010); Median home value: $458,700 (2006-2010 5-year est.); Median contract rent: $1,304 per month (2006-2010 5-year est.); Median year structure built: 1951 (2006-2010 5-year est.).
**Transportation:** Commute to work: 78.2% car, 15.2% public transportation, 1.7% walk, 4.0% work from home (2006-2010 5-year est.); Travel time to work: 20.0% less than 15 minutes, 30.1% 15 to 30 minutes, 18.4% 30 to 45 minutes, 7.9% 45 to 60 minutes, 23.5% 60 minutes or more (2006-2010 5-year est.)

**WESTBURY** (village). Covers a land area of 2.373 square miles and a water area of 0 square miles. Located at 40.76° N. Lat; 73.58° W. Long. Elevation is 102 feet.

**History:** Named for Westbury, England. Old Westbury Gardens and manor of former Phipps estate rivals formal gardens of Europe. Seat of N.Y. Institute of Technology's central campus; State University of N.Y. College at Old Westbury. Incorporated 1924.

**Population:** 12,948 (1990); 14,263 (2000); 15,146 (2010); Density: 6,380.2 persons per square mile (2010); Race: 55.0% White, 21.8% Black, 6.0% Asian, 0.4% American Indian/Alaska Native, 0.1% Native Hawaiian/Other Pacific Islander, 16.7% Other, 27.3% Hispanic of any race (2010); Average household size: 2.97 (2010); Median age: 39.2 (2010); Males per 100 females: 96.2 (2010); Marriage status: 35.4% never married, 52.6% now married, 6.9% widowed, 5.1% divorced (2006-2010 5-year est.); Foreign born: 33.1% (2006-2010 5-year est.); Ancestry (includes multiple ancestries): 20.3% Italian, 10.1% Irish, 7.9% German, 7.0% Haitian, 2.1% English (2006-2010 5-year est.).

**Economy:** Single-family building permits issued: 12 (2011); Multi-family building permits issued: 0 (2011); Employment by occupation: 15.4% management, 2.0% professional, 8.0% services, 16.2% sales, 4.3% farming, 7.8% construction, 6.3% production (2006-2010 5-year est.).

**Income:** Per capita income: $33,637 (2006-2010 5-year est.); Median household income: $80,081 (2006-2010 5-year est.); Average household income: $98,377 (2006-2010 5-year est.); Percent of households with income of $100,000 or more: 40.3% (2006-2010 5-year est.); Poverty rate: 6.2% (2006-2010 5-year est.).

**Education:** Percent of population age 25 and over with: High school diploma (including GED) or higher: 82.3% (2006-2010 5-year est.); Bachelor's degree or higher: 37.2% (2006-2010 5-year est.); Master's degree or higher: 14.5% (2006-2010 5-year est.).

### School District(s)

East Meadow Union Free School District (KG-12)

    2009-10 Enrollment: 7,372 . . . . . . . . . . . . . . . . . . . . . . . (516) 478-5776

Westbury Union Free School District (PK-12)

    2009-10 Enrollment: 4,314 . . . . . . . . . . . . . . . . . . . . . . . (516) 876-5016

**Housing:** Homeownership rate: 71.9% (2010); Median home value: $464,300 (2006-2010 5-year est.); Median contract rent: $1,401 per month (2006-2010 5-year est.); Median year structure built: 1955 (2006-2010 5-year est.).

**Transportation:** Commute to work: 76.6% car, 15.6% public transportation, 2.4% walk, 3.1% work from home (2006-2010 5-year est.); Travel time to work: 30.7% less than 15 minutes, 29.6% 15 to 30 minutes, 16.5% 30 to 45 minutes, 6.1% 45 to 60 minutes, 17.1% 60 minutes or more (2006-2010 5-year est.)

**Additional Information Contacts**

Village of Westbury . . . . . . . . . . . . . . . . . . . . . . . . . . . . (516) 334-1700

    http://www.villageofwestbury.org

Westbury-Carle Place Chamber of Commerce . . . . . . . . . . (516) 997-3966

    http://wcpchamber.com

**WILLISTON PARK** (village). Covers a land area of 0.625 square miles and a water area of 0 square miles. Located at 40.75° N. Lat; 73.64° W. Long. Elevation is 121 feet.

**History:** Incorporated 1926.

**Population:** 7,516 (1990); 7,261 (2000); 7,287 (2010); Density: 11,648.7 persons per square mile (2010); Race: 84.2% White, 0.9% Black, 11.8% Asian, 0.1% American Indian/Alaska Native, 0.0% Native Hawaiian/Other Pacific Islander, 3.0% Other, 6.1% Hispanic of any race (2010); Average household size: 2.73 (2010); Median age: 42.9 (2010); Males per 100 females: 92.4 (2010); Marriage status: 24.4% never married, 60.1% now married, 9.4% widowed, 6.0% divorced (2006-2010 5-year est.); Foreign born: 12.0% (2006-2010 5-year est.); Ancestry (includes multiple ancestries): 38.8% Irish, 27.5% Italian, 14.9% German, 4.9% English, 3.9% Polish (2006-2010 5-year est.).

**Economy:** Single-family building permits issued: 1 (2011); Multi-family building permits issued: 0 (2011); Employment by occupation: 18.6% management, 3.9% professional, 4.9% services, 19.4% sales, 3.7% farming, 4.9% construction, 2.6% production (2006-2010 5-year est.).

**Income:** Per capita income: $40,592 (2006-2010 5-year est.); Median household income: $97,602 (2006-2010 5-year est.); Average household income: $112,562 (2006-2010 5-year est.); Percent of households with income of $100,000 or more: 48.2% (2006-2010 5-year est.); Poverty rate: 2.3% (2006-2010 5-year est.).

**Education:** Percent of population age 25 and over with: High school diploma (including GED) or higher: 96.3% (2006-2010 5-year est.);

Bachelor's degree or higher: 41.8% (2006-2010 5-year est.); Master's degree or higher: 19.5% (2006-2010 5-year est.).

### School District(s)

Herricks Union Free School District (KG-12)

    2009-10 Enrollment: 4,044 . . . . . . . . . . . . . . . . . . . . . . . (516) 305-8901

Mineola Union Free School District (PK-12)

    2009-10 Enrollment: 2,716 . . . . . . . . . . . . . . . . . . . . . . . (516) 237-2001

**Housing:** Homeownership rate: 76.0% (2010); Median home value: $544,200 (2006-2010 5-year est.); Median contract rent: $1,411 per month (2006-2010 5-year est.); Median year structure built: before 1940 (2006-2010 5-year est.).

**Newspapers:** New Hyde Park Herald Courier (Community news; Circulation 5,000); Williston Times (Community news; Circulation 5,000)

**Transportation:** Commute to work: 76.5% car, 16.0% public transportation, 3.5% walk, 2.6% work from home (2006-2010 5-year est.); Travel time to work: 30.3% less than 15 minutes, 26.0% 15 to 30 minutes, 17.7% 30 to 45 minutes, 6.9% 45 to 60 minutes, 19.1% 60 minutes or more (2006-2010 5-year est.)

**Additional Information Contacts**

Chamber of Commerce of the Willistons . . . . . . . . . . . . . . (516) 739-1943

    http://www.chamberofthewillistons.org

**WOODBURY** (CDP). Covers a land area of 5.008 square miles and a water area of 0.015 square miles. Located at 40.82° N. Lat; 73.47° W. Long. Elevation is 177 feet.

**History:** Woodbury was originally a part of New Amsterdam. It was a Dutch colony until taken over by the British in the mid 1600s. According to records, one of the early names of this community was East Woods. Poet Walt Whitman and industrialist Andrew Mellon each once resided in Woodbury Hills.

**Population:** 8,008 (1990); 9,010 (2000); 8,907 (2010); Density: 1,778.3 persons per square mile (2010); Race: 87.0% White, 1.4% Black, 10.3% Asian, 0.0% American Indian/Alaska Native, 0.0% Native Hawaiian/Other Pacific Islander, 1.3% Other, 2.2% Hispanic of any race (2010); Average household size: 2.65 (2010); Median age: 49.0 (2010); Males per 100 females: 87.4 (2010); Marriage status: 16.8% never married, 63.0% now married, 14.7% widowed, 5.5% divorced (2006-2010 5-year est.); Foreign born: 14.2% (2006-2010 5-year est.); Ancestry (includes multiple ancestries): 12.5% Italian, 10.2% Russian, 8.2% American, 7.4% Polish, 6.0% German (2006-2010 5-year est.).

**Economy:** Employment by occupation: 25.6% management, 4.9% professional, 2.0% services, 14.0% sales, 1.5% farming, 1.1% construction, 0.4% production (2006-2010 5-year est.).

**Income:** Per capita income: $67,688 (2006-2010 5-year est.); Median household income: $147,026 (2006-2010 5-year est.); Average household income: $191,955 (2006-2010 5-year est.); Percent of households with income of $100,000 or more: 63.6% (2006-2010 5-year est.); Poverty rate: 1.2% (2006-2010 5-year est.).

**Education:** Percent of population age 25 and over with: High school diploma (including GED) or higher: 92.7% (2006-2010 5-year est.); Bachelor's degree or higher: 55.7% (2006-2010 5-year est.); Master's degree or higher: 27.3% (2006-2010 5-year est.).

### School District(s)

Syosset Central School District (KG-12)

    2009-10 Enrollment: 6,666 . . . . . . . . . . . . . . . . . . . . . . . (516) 364-5605

**Housing:** Homeownership rate: 85.2% (2010); Median home value: $808,100 (2006-2010 5-year est.); Median contract rent: $1,841 per month (2006-2010 5-year est.); Median year structure built: 1979 (2006-2010 5-year est.).

**Transportation:** Commute to work: 76.5% car, 14.5% public transportation, 0.7% walk, 7.5% work from home (2006-2010 5-year est.); Travel time to work: 21.2% less than 15 minutes, 31.8% 15 to 30 minutes, 16.2% 30 to 45 minutes, 5.2% 45 to 60 minutes, 25.6% 60 minutes or more (2006-2010 5-year est.)

**WOODMERE** (CDP). Covers a land area of 2.550 square miles and a water area of 0.267 square miles. Located at 40.63° N. Lat; 73.72° W. Long. Elevation is 23 feet.

**History:** Woodmere is one of the Long Island communities known as the "Five Towns", which is usually said to comprise the villages of Lawrence and Cedarhurst, the hamlets of Woodmere and Inwood, and "The Hewletts." It gets its name from Samuel Wood, who opened a hotel there that flopped.

**Population:** 15,562 (1990); 16,447 (2000); 17,121 (2010); Density: 6,712.7 persons per square mile (2010); Race: 89.3% White, 4.1% Black, 4.6%

Asian, 0.0% American Indian/Alaska Native, 0.0% Native Hawaiian/Other Pacific Islander, 2.0% Other, 4.6% Hispanic of any race (2010); Average household size: 3.14 (2010); Median age: 39.5 (2010); Males per 100 females: 96.0 (2010); Marriage status: 24.4% never married, 64.2% now married, 7.0% widowed, 4.4% divorced (2006-2010 5-year est.); Foreign born: 18.1% (2006-2010 5-year est.); Ancestry (includes multiple ancestries): 11.5% American, 11.2% Polish, 9.9% Russian, 6.1% Italian, 5.1% Eastern European (2006-2010 5-year est.).
**Economy:** Employment by occupation: 21.4% management, 4.7% professional, 3.2% services, 10.5% sales, 1.9% farming, 3.5% construction, 1.2% production (2006-2010 5-year est.).
**Income:** Per capita income: $50,364 (2006-2010 5-year est.); Median household income: $121,543 (2006-2010 5-year est.); Average household income: $162,708 (2006-2010 5-year est.); Percent of households with income of $100,000 or more: 58.8% (2006-2010 5-year est.); Poverty rate: 4.2% (2006-2010 5-year est.).
**Education:** Percent of population age 25 and over with: High school diploma (including GED) or higher: 93.8% (2006-2010 5-year est.); Bachelor's degree or higher: 63.6% (2006-2010 5-year est.); Master's degree or higher: 34.7% (2006-2010 5-year est.).
**Housing:** Homeownership rate: 89.0% (2010); Median home value: $640,000 (2006-2010 5-year est.); Median contract rent: $1,162 per month (2006-2010 5-year est.); Median year structure built: 1955 (2006-2010 5-year est.).
**Transportation:** Commute to work: 69.2% car, 21.1% public transportation, 2.6% walk, 5.2% work from home (2006-2010 5-year est.); Travel time to work: 24.3% less than 15 minutes, 14.0% 15 to 30 minutes, 18.4% 30 to 45 minutes, 16.2% 45 to 60 minutes, 27.0% 60 minutes or more (2006-2010 5-year est.)

**WOODSBURGH** (village). Covers a land area of 0.340 square miles and a water area of 0.043 square miles. Located at 40.62° N. Lat; 73.70° W. Long. Elevation is 7 feet.
**Population:** 1,225 (1990); 831 (2000); 778 (2010); Density: 2,285.2 persons per square mile (2010); Race: 94.5% White, 0.9% Black, 2.8% Asian, 0.1% American Indian/Alaska Native, 0.0% Native Hawaiian/Other Pacific Islander, 1.7% Other, 3.0% Hispanic of any race (2010); Average household size: 2.91 (2010); Median age: 48.1 (2010); Males per 100 females: 95.0 (2010); Marriage status: 21.3% never married, 68.0% now married, 8.6% widowed, 2.0% divorced (2006-2010 5-year est.); Foreign born: 10.5% (2006-2010 5-year est.); Ancestry (includes multiple ancestries): 23.9% Russian, 16.6% Polish, 8.5% American, 5.9% Italian, 3.1% German (2006-2010 5-year est.).
**Economy:** Single-family building permits issued: 0 (2011); Multi-family building permits issued: 0 (2011); Employment by occupation: 21.2% management, 1.6% professional, 7.6% services, 18.0% sales, 1.9% farming, 2.5% construction, 0.0% production (2006-2010 5-year est.).
**Income:** Per capita income: $93,962 (2006-2010 5-year est.); Median household income: $153,750 (2006-2010 5-year est.); Average household income: $257,635 (2006-2010 5-year est.); Percent of households with income of $100,000 or more: 69.3% (2006-2010 5-year est.); Poverty rate: 7.0% (2006-2010 5-year est.).
**Education:** Percent of population age 25 and over with: High school diploma (including GED) or higher: 98.4% (2006-2010 5-year est.); Bachelor's degree or higher: 75.9% (2006-2010 5-year est.); Master's degree or higher: 48.0% (2006-2010 5-year est.).
**Housing:** Homeownership rate: 95.9% (2010); Median home value: $1 (2006-2010 5-year est.); Median contract rent: $1,469 per month (2006-2010 5-year est.); Median year structure built: before 1940 (2006-2010 5-year est.).
**Transportation:** Commute to work: 80.7% car, 12.6% public transportation, 0.0% walk, 6.6% work from home (2006-2010 5-year est.); Travel time to work: 27.0% less than 15 minutes, 3.9% 15 to 30 minutes, 26.0% 30 to 45 minutes, 15.7% 45 to 60 minutes, 27.4% 60 minutes or more (2006-2010 5-year est.)

# New York City

Covers a land area of 302.643 square miles and a water area of 165.841 square miles. Located at 40.66° N. Lat; 73.93° W. Long. Elevation is 33 feet.
**History:** Adrien Block erected four trading houses in New York in 1613, prompting permanent settlement. In 1633, the first church was built, and that was soon followed by the establishment of Fort Amsterdam. After the battle of Long Island in 1776, when Sir William Howe's British forces

defeated the forces of General George Washington, the city passed into English hands and remained in their control until 1783. Congress met in New York from 1785-1790, and it was here that George Washington was inaugurated as president.
**Population:** 7,322,552 (1990); 8,008,278 (2000); 8,175,133 (2010); Density: 27,012.4 persons per square mile (2010); Race: 44.0% White, 25.5% Black, 12.7% Asian, 0.7% American Indian/Alaska Native, 0.1% Native Hawaiian/Other Pacific Islander, 17.0% Other, 28.6% Hispanic of any race (2010); Average household size: 2.57 (2010); Median age: 35.5 (2010); Males per 100 females: 90.4 (2010); Marriage status: 42.6% never married, 43.6% now married, 6.0% widowed, 7.8% divorced (2006-2010 5-year est.); Foreign born: 36.8% (2006-2010 5-year est.); Ancestry (includes multiple ancestries): 7.7% Italian, 5.1% Irish, 3.4% German, 3.0% Russian, 2.7% Polish (2006-2010 5-year est.).
**Economy:** Unemployment rate: 10.1% (February 2012); Total civilian labor force: 3,968,110 (February 2012); Single-family building permits issued: 264 (2011); Multi-family building permits issued: 8,672 (2011); Employment by occupation: 11.4% management, 3.2% professional, 12.4% services, 15.7% sales, 4.7% farming, 6.4% construction, 3.8% production (2006-2010 5-year est.).
**Income:** Per capita income: $30,498 (2006-2010 5-year est.); Median household income: $50,285 (2006-2010 5-year est.); Average household income: $77,897 (2006-2010 5-year est.); Percent of households with income of $100,000 or more: 22.8% (2006-2010 5-year est.); Poverty rate: 19.1% (2006-2010 5-year est.).
**Taxes:** Total city taxes per capita: $4,372 (2009); City property taxes per capita: $1,758 (2009).
**Education:** Percent of population age 25 and over with: High school diploma (including GED) or higher: 79.0% (2006-2010 5-year est.); Bachelor's degree or higher: 33.3% (2006-2010 5-year est.); Master's degree or higher: 13.5% (2006-2010 5-year est.).
**Housing:** Homeownership rate: 31.0% (2010); Median home value: $513,900 (2006-2010 5-year est.); Median contract rent: $960 per month (2006-2010 5-year est.); Median year structure built: 1947 (2006-2010 5-year est.).
**Safety:** Violent crime rate: 58.2 per 10,000 population; Property crime rate: 167.5 per 10,000 population (2010).
**Transportation:** Commute to work: 28.4% car, 55.2% public transportation, 10.2% walk, 3.8% work from home (2006-2010 5-year est.); Travel time to work: 11.2% less than 15 minutes, 22.3% 15 to 30 minutes, 26.3% 30 to 45 minutes, 15.1% 45 to 60 minutes, 25.0% 60 minutes or more (2006-2010 5-year est.); Amtrak: train and bus service available.
**Airports:** Downtown Manhattan/Wall Street (general aviation); East 34th Street (commercial service); John F Kennedy International (primary service/large hub); La Guardia (primary service/large hub); New York Skyports (general aviation); Newark Liberty International (primary service/large hub); West 30th Street (general aviation)
**Additional Information Contacts**

Bronx Chamber of Commerce . . . . . . . . . . . . . . . . . . (718) 828-3900
  http://www.bronxchamber.org
Brooklyn Chamber of Commerce . . . . . . . . . . . . . . . . (718) 875-1000
  http://www.ibrooklyn.com
City of New York . . . . . . . . . . . . . . . . . . . . . . . . . . . (212) 669-2400
  http://nyc.gov
Greater Harlem Chamber of Commerce . . . . . . . . . . . (212) 862-7200
  http://greaterharlemchamber.com
Greater New York Chamber of Commerce . . . . . . . . . (212) 686-7220
  http://www.ny-chamber.com
Greenwich Village-Chelsea Chamber of Commerce . . . . . . (646) 470-1773
  http://www.villagechelsea.com
Manhattan Chamber of Commerce . . . . . . . . . . . . . . . (212) 479-7772
  http://www.manhattancc.org
New York Women's Chamber of Commerce . . . . . . . . . (212) 491-9640
  http://www.nywcc.org
Queens Chamber of Commerce . . . . . . . . . . . . . . . . . (718) 898-8500
  http://www.queenschamber.org
Rockaway Chamber of Commerce . . . . . . . . . . . . . . . (718) 979-7030
  http://www.rockawaychamberofcommerce.com
Staten Island Chamber of Commerce . . . . . . . . . . . . . (718) 727-1900
  http://www.sichamber.com

## Five Boroughs of New York City

**BRONX** (borough). Aka Bronx County. Located in southeastern New York State; the northernmost borough of New York city, situated between

Manhattan and the Westchester County line; bounded on the west by the Hudson River, on the southwest by Spuyten Duyvil Creek and the Harlem River, on the south by the East River, and on the east by Long Island Sound. Covers a land area of 42.03 square miles, a water area of 15.40 square miles, and is located in the Eastern Time Zone at 40.84° N. Lat., 73.87° W. Long.

Bronx County is part of the New York-Northern New Jersey-Long Island, NY-NJ-PA Metropolitan Statistical Area. The entire metro area includes: Edison-New Brunswick, NJ Metropolitan Division (Middlesex County, NJ; Monmouth County, NJ; Ocean County, NJ; Somerset County, NJ); Nassau-Suffolk, NY Metropolitan Division (Nassau County, NY; Suffolk County, NY); New York-White Plains-Wayne, NY-NJ Metropolitan Division (Bergen County, NJ; Hudson County, NJ; Passaic County, NJ; Bronx County, NY; Kings County, NY; New York County, NY; Putnam County, NY; Queens County, NY; Richmond County, NY; Rockland County, NY; Westchester County, NY); Newark-Union, NJ-PA Metropolitan Division (Essex County, NJ; Hunterdon County, NJ; Morris County, NJ; Sussex County, NJ; Union County, NJ; Pike County, PA)

**Population:** 1,203,745 (1990); 1,332,650 (2000); 1,385,108 (2010); Race: 27.9% White, 36.5% Black, 3.6% Asian, 1.3% American Indian/Alaska Native, 0.1% Native Hawaiian/Other Pacific Islander, 30.6% Other, 53.5% Hispanic of any race (2010); Density: 32,957.5 persons per square mile (2010); Average household size: 2.77 (2010); Median age: 32.8 (2010); Males per 100 females: 88.3 (2010).

**Religion:** Six largest groups: 25.5% Catholicism, 2.8% Muslim Estimate, 1.8% Non-Denominational, 1.7% Baptist, 1.2% Pentecostal, 1.0% Judaism (2010)

**Economy:** Unemployment rate: 14.0% (February 2012); Total civilian labor force: 552,324 (February 2012); Leading industries: 40.7% health care and social assistance; 10.7% retail trade; 7.9% educational services (2009); Farms: 1 totaling n/a acres (2007); Companies that employ 500 or more persons: 40 (2009); Companies that employ 100 to 499 persons: 253 (2009); Companies that employ less than 100 persons: 15,722 (2009); Black-owned businesses: 38,726 (2007); Hispanic-owned businesses: 41,808 (2007); Asian-owned businesses: 8,297 (2007); Women-owned businesses: 44,939 (2007); Retail sales per capita: $4,600 (2010). Single-family building permits issued: 1 (2011); Multi-family building permits issued: 1,115 (2011).

**Income:** Per capita income: $17,575 (2006-2010 5-year est.); Median household income: $34,264 (2006-2010 5-year est.); Average household income: $47,325 (2006-2010 5-year est.); Percent of households with income of $100,000 or more: 10.5% (2006-2010 5-year est.); Poverty rate: 28.4% (2006-2010 5-year est.); Bankruptcy rate: 2.21% (2011).

**Education:** Percent of population age 25 and over with: High school diploma (including GED) or higher: 68.8% (2006-2010 5-year est.); Bachelor's degree or higher: 17.6% (2006-2010 5-year est.); Master's degree or higher: 6.5% (2006-2010 5-year est.).

**Housing:** Homeownership rate: 19.3% (2010); Median home value: $386,200 (2006-2010 5-year est.); Median contract rent: $814 per month (2006-2010 5-year est.); Median year structure built: 1951 (2006-2010 5-year est.)

**Health:** Birth rate: 163.0 per 10,000 population (2011); Death rate: 67.1 per 10,000 population (2011); Age-adjusted cancer mortality rate: 169.6 deaths per 100,000 population (2009); Number of physicians: 25.0 per 10,000 population (2008); Hospital beds: 37.0 per 10,000 population (2007); Hospital admissions: 1,462.0 per 10,000 population (2007).

**Environment:** Air Quality Index: 68.5% good, 31.0% moderate, 0.5% unhealthy for sensitive individuals, 0.0% unhealthy (percent of days in 2010)

**Elections:** 2008 Presidential election results: 88.7% Obama, 10.9% McCain, 0.1% Nader

### School District(s)

Bronx Academy of Promise Charter School (KG-03)
  2009-10 Enrollment: 249 . . . . . . . . . . . . . . . . . . . . . . (718) 681-8275
Bronx Charter School for Better Learning (KG-05)
  2009-10 Enrollment: 354 . . . . . . . . . . . . . . . . . . . . . . (718) 655-6660
Bronx Charter School for Children (KG-05)
  2009-10 Enrollment: 395 . . . . . . . . . . . . . . . . . . . . . . (718) 402-3300
Bronx Charter School for Excellence (KG-05)
  2009-10 Enrollment: 324 . . . . . . . . . . . . . . . . . . . . . . (718) 828-7301
Bronx Charter School for the Arts (KG-06)
  2009-10 Enrollment: 293 . . . . . . . . . . . . . . . . . . . . . . (718) 893-1042
Bronx Community Charter School (KG-02)
  2009-10 Enrollment: 149 . . . . . . . . . . . . . . . . . . . . . . (347) 668-5229

Bronx Global Learning Institute for Girls Charter (KG-02)
  2009-10 Enrollment: 151 . . . . . . . . . . . . . . . . . . . . . . (718) 993-1740
Bronx Lighthouse Charter School (KG-07)
  2009-10 Enrollment: 422 . . . . . . . . . . . . . . . . . . . . . . (646) 915-0025
Bronx Preparatory Charter School (05-12)
  2009-10 Enrollment: 680 . . . . . . . . . . . . . . . . . . . . . . (718) 294-0841
Equality Charter School (06-07)
  2009-10 Enrollment: 135 . . . . . . . . . . . . . . . . . . . . . . (718) 320-3032
Family Life Academy Charter School (KG-06)
  2009-10 Enrollment: 332 . . . . . . . . . . . . . . . . . . . . . . (718) 410-8100
Girls Prep Charter School of East Harlem (KG-01)
  2009-10 Enrollment: 132 . . . . . . . . . . . . . . . . . . . . . . (718) 292-2113
Grand Concourse Academy Charter School (KG-05)
  2009-10 Enrollment: 401 . . . . . . . . . . . . . . . . . . . . . . (718) 590-1300
Green Dot Ny Charter School (09-10)
  2009-10 Enrollment: 216 . . . . . . . . . . . . . . . . . . . . . . (718) 585-0560
Harriet Tubman Charter School (KG-08)
  2009-10 Enrollment: 427 . . . . . . . . . . . . . . . . . . . . . . (718) 537-9912
Hyde Leadership Charter School (KG-09)
  2009-10 Enrollment: 589 . . . . . . . . . . . . . . . . . . . . . . (718) 991-5500
Icahn Charter School 1 (KG-08)
  2009-10 Enrollment: 328 . . . . . . . . . . . . . . . . . . . . . . (718) 716-8105
Icahn Charter School 2 (KG-04)
  2009-10 Enrollment: 178 . . . . . . . . . . . . . . . . . . . . . . (718) 861-4606
Icahn Charter School 3 (KG-03)
  2009-10 Enrollment: 146 . . . . . . . . . . . . . . . . . . . . . . (718) 991-5157
International Leadership Charter School (09-12)
  2009-10 Enrollment: 322 . . . . . . . . . . . . . . . . . . . . . . (212) 437-8361
Kipp Academy Charter School (05-09)
  2009-10 Enrollment: 393 . . . . . . . . . . . . . . . . . . . . . . (718) 665-3555
Mott Haven Academy Charter School (KG-02)
  2009-10 Enrollment: 130 . . . . . . . . . . . . . . . . . . . . . . (718) 292-7015
New York City Geographic District # 7 (PK-12)
  2009-10 Enrollment: 19,136 . . . . . . . . . . . . . . . . . . . . (718) 742-6500
New York City Geographic District # 8 (PK-12)
  2009-10 Enrollment: 32,753 . . . . . . . . . . . . . . . . . . . . (718) 828-5435
New York City Geographic District # 9 (PK-12)
  2009-10 Enrollment: 35,155 . . . . . . . . . . . . . . . . . . . . (718) 842-0138
New York City Geographic District #10 (PK-12)
  2009-10 Enrollment: 56,222 . . . . . . . . . . . . . . . . . . . . (718) 741-5852
New York City Geographic District #11 (PK-12)
  2009-10 Enrollment: 38,520 . . . . . . . . . . . . . . . . . . . . (718) 519-2620
New York City Geographic District #12 (PK-12)
  2009-10 Enrollment: 22,825 . . . . . . . . . . . . . . . . . . . . (718) 328-2310
NYC Charter Hs-Architecture Engineering Constructi (09-10)
  2009-10 Enrollment: 241 . . . . . . . . . . . . . . . . . . . . . . (646) 400-5561
NYC Special Schools - District 75 (PK-12)
  2009-10 Enrollment: 21,871 . . . . . . . . . . . . . . . . . . . . (212) 802-1617
South Bronx Charter School-Inter Cultures and Arts (KG-05)
  2009-10 Enrollment: 360 . . . . . . . . . . . . . . . . . . . . . . (718) 401-9216
South Bronx Classical Charter School (KG-04)
  2009-10 Enrollment: 274 . . . . . . . . . . . . . . . . . . . . . . (718) 860-4340

### Four-year College(s)

CUNY Lehman College (Public)
  Fall 2010 Enrollment: 9,315 . . . . . . . . . . . . . . . . . . . . (718) 960-8000
  2011-12 Tuition: In-state $5,508; Out-of-state $11,418
College of Mount Saint Vincent (Private, Not-for-profit, Roman Catholic)
  Fall 2010 Enrollment: 1,597 . . . . . . . . . . . . . . . . . . . . (718) 405-3200
  2011-12 Tuition: In-state $27,810; Out-of-state $27,810
Fordham University (Private, Not-for-profit, Roman Catholic)
  Fall 2010 Enrollment: 14,689 . . . . . . . . . . . . . . . . . . . (718) 817-1000
  2011-12 Tuition: In-state $40,292; Out-of-state $40,292
Manhattan College (Riverdale) (Private, Not-for-profit, Roman Catholic)
  Fall 2010 Enrollment: 3,186 . . . . . . . . . . . . . . . . . . . . (718) 862-8000
  2011-12 Tuition: In-state $29,700; Out-of-state $29,700
Monroe College-Main Campus (Private, For-profit)
  Fall 2010 Enrollment: 6,799 . . . . . . . . . . . . . . . . . . . . (718) 933-6700
  2011-12 Tuition: In-state $12,440; Out-of-state $12,440
SUNY Maritime College (Throggs Neck) (Public)
  Fall 2010 Enrollment: 2,168 . . . . . . . . . . . . . . . . . . . . (718) 409-7200
  2011-12 Tuition: In-state $6,457; Out-of-state $15,507
Yeshiva of the Telshe Alumni (Riverdale) (Private, Not-for-profit)
  Fall 2010 Enrollment: 87 . . . . . . . . . . . . . . . . . . . . . . (718) 601-3523
  2011-12 Tuition: In-state $7,900; Out-of-state $7,900

## Two-year College(s)

CUNY Bronx Community College (Public)
    Fall 2010 Enrollment: 8,214 . . . . . . . . . . . . . . . . . (718) 289-5100
    2011-12 Tuition: In-state $3,954; Out-of-state $6,114
CUNY Hostos Community College (Public)
    Fall 2010 Enrollment: 5,005 . . . . . . . . . . . . . . . . . (718) 518-4444
    2011-12 Tuition: In-state $3,955; Out-of-state $6,115
School of Professional Horticulture at the New York Botanical Garden (Private, Not-for-profit)
    Fall 2010 Enrollment: 28 . . . . . . . . . . . . . . . . . . . (718) 817-8797
    2011-12 Tuition: In-state $6,000; Out-of-state $6,000

## Vocational/Technical School(s)

American Beauty School (Private, For-profit)
    Fall 2010 Enrollment: 321 . . . . . . . . . . . . . . . . . . (718) 931-7400
    2011-12 Tuition: $7,490
Brittany Beauty School (Private, For-profit)
    Fall 2010 Enrollment: 218 . . . . . . . . . . . . . . . . . . (718) 220-0400
    2011-12 Tuition: $12,600

**Hospitals:** Bronx Childrens Psychiatric Center (78 beds); Bronx Psychiatric Center (360 beds); Bronx-Lebanon Hospital Center (847 beds); Calvary Hospital (225 beds); Hebrew Hospital Home (480 beds); Jacobi Medical Center (527 beds); Lincoln Medical and Mental Health Center (595 beds); Montefiore Medical Center (1062 beds); North Central Bronx Hospital (202 beds); Our Lady of Mercy Medical Center (345 beds); St. Barnabas Hospital (461 beds); Union Community Health Center (201 beds); Veterans Affairs Medical Center (459 beds); Weiler Hospital; Westchester Square Medical Center (205 beds)

**Newspapers:** Bronx Press Newspaper Group (Local news; Circulation 40,000); Bronx Times Reporter (Local news; Circulation 26,000); Bronx Times Reporter - Bronx North Edition (Community news); Bronx Times Reporter - Castle Hill Edition (Community news; Circulation 29,000); Bronx Times Reporter - Fordham North Edition (Community news); Bronx Times Reporter - Fordham South Edition (Community news); Bronx Times Reporter - Morris Park Edition (Community news); Bronx Times Reporter - Throggs Neck Edition (Community news); The Caribbean Voice (Local news); Co-Op City Times (Community news; Circulation 18,000); Island Current (Local news; Circulation 2,000); Manhattan Times (Local news); New York Daily News - Bronx Bureau (Local news); The New York Times - Bronx Bureau (Regional news); The Riverdale Press (Local news); Riverdale Review (Community news; Circulation 20,000)

**Additional Information Contacts**

Bronx County Government . . . . . . . . . . . . . . . . . . . . . . . (718) 590-3557
    http://bronxboropres.nyc.gov
Bronx Chamber of Commerce . . . . . . . . . . . . . . . . . . . . . (718) 828-3900
    http://www.bronxchamber.org

## BROOKLYN (borough). Aka Kings County. Located in southeastern New York State. One of the five counties/boroughs of New York City. Covers a land area of 70.61 square miles, a water area of 26.29 square miles, and is located in the Eastern Time Zone at 40.65° N. Lat., 73.95° W. Long.

Kings County is part of the New York-Northern New Jersey-Long Island, NY-NJ-PA Metropolitan Statistical Area. The entire metro area includes: Edison-New Brunswick, NJ Metropolitan Division (Middlesex County, NJ; Monmouth County, NJ; Ocean County, NJ; Somerset County, NJ); Nassau-Suffolk, NY Metropolitan Division (Nassau County, NY; Suffolk County, NY); New York-White Plains-Wayne, NY-NJ Metropolitan Division (Bergen County, NJ; Hudson County, NJ; Passaic County, NJ; Bronx County, NY; Kings County, NY; New York County, NY; Putnam County, NY; Queens County, NY; Richmond County, NY; Rockland County, NY; Westchester County, NY); Newark-Union, NJ-PA Metropolitan Division (Essex County, NJ; Hunterdon County, NJ; Morris County, NJ; Sussex County, NJ; Union County, NJ; Pike County, PA)

Weather Station: New York Ave V Brooklyn            Elevation: 20 feet

| | Jan | Feb | Mar | Apr | May | Jun | Jul | Aug | Sep | Oct | Nov | Dec |
|---|---|---|---|---|---|---|---|---|---|---|---|---|
| High | 39 | 42 | 50 | 60 | 70 | 79 | 84 | 83 | 76 | 65 | 55 | 44 |
| Low | 27 | 29 | 35 | 45 | 54 | 64 | 70 | 69 | 62 | 50 | 42 | 32 |
| Precip | 3.5 | 2.7 | 4.2 | 4.4 | 4.2 | 3.9 | 4.8 | 3.7 | 3.7 | 3.7 | 3.8 | 3.3 |
| Snow | 6.6 | 7.3 | 3.9 | 0.7 | 0.0 | 0.0 | 0.0 | 0.0 | 0.0 | tr | 0.3 | 3.5 |

*High and Low temperatures in degrees Fahrenheit; Precipitation and Snow in inches*

**Population:** 2,300,664 (1990); 2,465,326 (2000); 2,504,700 (2010); Race: 42.8% White, 34.3% Black, 10.5% Asian, 0.5% American Indian/Alaska Native, 0.0% Native Hawaiian/Other Pacific Islander, 11.9% Other, 19.8%

Hispanic of any race (2010); Density: 35,474.3 persons per square mile (2010); Average household size: 2.69 (2010); Median age: 34.1 (2010); Males per 100 females: 89.3 (2010).

**Religion:** Six largest groups: 24.9% Catholicism, 11.5% Judaism, 3.8% Muslim Estimate, 3.2% Baptist, 2.4% Non-Denominational, 1.1% Pentecostal (2010)

**Economy:** Unemployment rate: 10.8% (February 2012); Total civilian labor force: 1,125,150 (February 2012); Leading industries: 34.2% health care and social assistance; 11.8% retail trade; 5.8% educational services (2009); Farms: 1 totaling n/a acres (2007); Companies that employ 500 or more persons: 94 (2009); Companies that employ 100 to 499 persons: 492 (2009); Companies that employ less than 100 persons: 45,859 (2009); Black-owned businesses: 52,705 (2007); Hispanic-owned businesses: 27,382 (2007); Asian-owned businesses: 36,765 (2007); Women-owned businesses: 85,164 (2007); Retail sales per capita: $5,785 (2010). Single-family building permits issued: 0 (2011); Multi-family building permits issued: 1,522 (2011).

**Income:** Per capita income: $23,605 (2006-2010 5-year est.); Median household income: $43,567 (2006-2010 5-year est.); Average household income: $62,656 (2006-2010 5-year est.); Percent of households with income of $100,000 or more: 18.0% (2006-2010 5-year est.); Poverty rate: 22.0% (2006-2010 5-year est.); Bankruptcy rate: 1.67% (2011).

**Education:** Percent of population age 25 and over with: High school diploma (including GED) or higher: 77.8% (2006-2010 5-year est.); Bachelor's degree or higher: 28.8% (2006-2010 5-year est.); Master's degree or higher: 10.8% (2006-2010 5-year est.).

**Housing:** Homeownership rate: 27.7% (2010); Median home value: $562,400 (2006-2010 5-year est.); Median contract rent: $916 per month (2006-2010 5-year est.); Median year structure built: before 1940 (2006-2010 5-year est.)

**Health:** Birth rate: 164.1 per 10,000 population (2011); Death rate: 62.2 per 10,000 population (2011); Age-adjusted cancer mortality rate: 146.2 deaths per 100,000 population (2009); Number of physicians: 29.9 per 10,000 population (2008); Hospital beds: 31.3 per 10,000 population (2007); Hospital admissions: 1,192.3 per 10,000 population (2007).

**Environment:** Air Quality Index: 80.8% good, 19.2% moderate, 0.0% unhealthy for sensitive individuals, 0.0% unhealthy (percent of days in 2010)

**Elections:** 2008 Presidential election results: 79.4% Obama, 20.0% McCain, 0.2% Nader

## School District(s)

Achievement First Brownsville Charter School (KG-02)
    2009-10 Enrollment: 248 . . . . . . . . . . . . . . . . . . (718) 342-4302
Achievement First Bushwick Charter School (KG-07)
    2009-10 Enrollment: 657 . . . . . . . . . . . . . . . . . . (718) 453-0425
Achievement First Crown Heights Charter School (KG-09)
    2009-10 Enrollment: 826 . . . . . . . . . . . . . . . . . . (718) 774-0762
Achievement First East New York Charter School (KG-05)
    2009-10 Enrollment: 507 . . . . . . . . . . . . . . . . . . (718) 485-4924
Achievement First Endeavor Charter School
    2009-10 Enrollment: n/a . . . . . . . . . . . . . . . . . . . (718) 622-4786
Bedford Stuyvesant Collegiate Charter School (05-06)
    2009-10 Enrollment: 139 . . . . . . . . . . . . . . . . . . (718) 669-7460
Beginning with Children Charter School (KG-08)
    2009-10 Enrollment: 447 . . . . . . . . . . . . . . . . . . (718) 388-8847
Believe Northside Charter High School
    2009-10 Enrollment: n/a . . . . . . . . . . . . . . . . . . . (718) 782-9830
Believe Southside Charter High School
    2009-10 Enrollment: n/a . . . . . . . . . . . . . . . . . . . (718) 782-9830
Brooklyn Ascend Charter School (KG-03)
    2009-10 Enrollment: 249 . . . . . . . . . . . . . . . . . . (718) 240-9162
Brooklyn Charter School (the) (KG-05)
    2009-10 Enrollment: 225 . . . . . . . . . . . . . . . . . . (718) 302-2085
Brooklyn Excelsior Charter School (KG-08)
    2009-10 Enrollment: 728 . . . . . . . . . . . . . . . . . . (718) 246-5681
Brooklyn Prospect Charter School (06-06)
    2009-10 Enrollment: 100 . . . . . . . . . . . . . . . . . . (718) 965-7950
Brooklyn Scholars Charter School (KG-04)
    2009-10 Enrollment: 195 . . . . . . . . . . . . . . . . . . (718) 348-9360
Brownsville Ascend Charter School (KG-01)
    2009-10 Enrollment: 174 . . . . . . . . . . . . . . . . . . (617) 388-5474
Community Partnership Charter School (KG-05)
    2009-10 Enrollment: 298 . . . . . . . . . . . . . . . . . . (718) 399-1495
Community Roots Charter School (KG-04)
    2009-10 Enrollment: 250 . . . . . . . . . . . . . . . . . . (718) 858-1629

Coney Island Preparatory Public Charter School (05-05)
2009-10 Enrollment: 90 . . . . . . . . . . . . . . . . . . . . . . . . . . (718) 513-6951
East New York Preparatory Charter School (01-04)
2009-10 Enrollment: 158 . . . . . . . . . . . . . . . . . . . . . . . . . (718) 485-8591
Excellence Charter School of Bedford Stuyvesant (KG-06)
2009-10 Enrollment: 360 . . . . . . . . . . . . . . . . . . . . . . . . . (718) 638-1830
Excellence Girls Charter School (KG-01)
2009-10 Enrollment: 145 . . . . . . . . . . . . . . . . . . . . . . . . . (718) 638-1875
Explore Charter School (KG-08)
2009-10 Enrollment: 466 . . . . . . . . . . . . . . . . . . . . . . . . . (718) 703-4484
Explore Empower Charter School (KG-02)
2009-10 Enrollment: 156 . . . . . . . . . . . . . . . . . . . . . . . . . (347) 661-3543
Fahari Academy Charter School (05-05)
2009-10 Enrollment: 91 . . . . . . . . . . . . . . . . . . . . . . . . . . (718) 282-5139
Flatbush Collegiate Charter School (05-06)
2009-10 Enrollment: 103 . . . . . . . . . . . . . . . . . . . . . . . . . (718) 636-0370
Hebrew Language Academy (KG-01)
2009-10 Enrollment: 159 . . . . . . . . . . . . . . . . . . . . . . . . . (212) 792-6295
Hellenic Classical Charter School (KG-08)
2009-10 Enrollment: 357 . . . . . . . . . . . . . . . . . . . . . . . . . (718) 499-0957
Kings Collegiate Charter School (05-07)
2009-10 Enrollment: 206 . . . . . . . . . . . . . . . . . . . . . . . . . (718) 342-6047
Kipp Amp Charter School (05-09)
2009-10 Enrollment: 298 . . . . . . . . . . . . . . . . . . . . . . . . . (718) 943-3710
La Cima Charter School (KG-02)
2009-10 Enrollment: 194 . . . . . . . . . . . . . . . . . . . . . . . . . (718) 443-2136
Leadership Preparatory Brownsville Charter School (KG-01)
2009-10 Enrollment: 119 . . . . . . . . . . . . . . . . . . . . . . . . . (718) 669-7461
Leadership Preparatory Charter School (KG-04)
2009-10 Enrollment: 329 . . . . . . . . . . . . . . . . . . . . . . . . . (718) 636-0360
New York City Geographic District #13 (PK-12)
2009-10 Enrollment: 25,451 . . . . . . . . . . . . . . . . . . . . . . . (718) 636-3204
New York City Geographic District #14 (PK-12)
2009-10 Enrollment: 20,174 . . . . . . . . . . . . . . . . . . . . . . . (718) 302-7600
New York City Geographic District #15 (PK-12)
2009-10 Enrollment: 26,304 . . . . . . . . . . . . . . . . . . . . . . . (718) 642-5868
New York City Geographic District #16 (PK-12)
2009-10 Enrollment: 10,305 . . . . . . . . . . . . . . . . . . . . . . . (718) 935-3900
New York City Geographic District #17 (PK-12)
2009-10 Enrollment: 27,445 . . . . . . . . . . . . . . . . . . . . . . . (718) 221-4372
New York City Geographic District #18 (PK-12)
2009-10 Enrollment: 18,746 . . . . . . . . . . . . . . . . . . . . . . . (718) 566-6008
New York City Geographic District #19 (PK-12)
2009-10 Enrollment: 26,355 . . . . . . . . . . . . . . . . . . . . . . . (718) 342-3625
New York City Geographic District #20 (PK-12)
2009-10 Enrollment: 46,477 . . . . . . . . . . . . . . . . . . . . . . . (718) 759-4912
New York City Geographic District #21 (PK-12)
2009-10 Enrollment: 37,779 . . . . . . . . . . . . . . . . . . . . . . . (718) 714-2502
New York City Geographic District #22 (PK-12)
2009-10 Enrollment: 38,405 . . . . . . . . . . . . . . . . . . . . . . . (718) 968-6117
New York City Geographic District #23 (PK-12)
2009-10 Enrollment: 12,253 . . . . . . . . . . . . . . . . . . . . . . . (718) 240-3677
New York City Geographic District #32 (PK-12)
2009-10 Enrollment: 16,195 . . . . . . . . . . . . . . . . . . . . . . . (718) 574-1100
Pave Academy Charter School (KG-02)
2009-10 Enrollment: 139 . . . . . . . . . . . . . . . . . . . . . . . . . (718) 858-7813
Summit Academy Charter School
2009-10 Enrollment: 92 . . . . . . . . . . . . . . . . . . . . . . . . . . (718) 875-1403
The Ethical Community Charter School (KG-01)
2009-10 Enrollment: 114 . . . . . . . . . . . . . . . . . . . . . . . . . (718) 599-2176
Uft Charter School (KG-09)
2009-10 Enrollment: 802 . . . . . . . . . . . . . . . . . . . . . . . . . (718) 649-0650
Williamsburg Charter High School (09-12)
2009-10 Enrollment: 646 . . . . . . . . . . . . . . . . . . . . . . . . . (718) 782-9830
Williamsburg Collegiate Charter School (05-09)
2009-10 Enrollment: 302 . . . . . . . . . . . . . . . . . . . . . . . . . (718) 302-4018

**Four-year College(s)**
Beth Hamedrash Shaarei Yosher Institute (Private, Not-for-profit)
Fall 2010 Enrollment: 47 . . . . . . . . . . . . . . . . . . . . . . . . . (718) 854-2290
2011-12 Tuition: In-state $6,600; Out-of-state $6,600
Beth Hatalmud Rabbinical College (Private, Not-for-profit)
Fall 2010 Enrollment: 64 . . . . . . . . . . . . . . . . . . . . . . . . . (718) 259-2525
2011-12 Tuition: In-state $6,700; Out-of-state $6,700
Brooklyn Law School (Private, Not-for-profit)
Fall 2010 Enrollment: 1,713 . . . . . . . . . . . . . . . . . . . . . . . (718) 625-2200

CUNY Brooklyn College (Public)
Fall 2010 Enrollment: 13,606 . . . . . . . . . . . . . . . . . . . . . . (718) 951-5000
2011-12 Tuition: In-state $5,584; Out-of-state $11,494
CUNY Medgar Evers College (Public)
Fall 2010 Enrollment: 5,577 . . . . . . . . . . . . . . . . . . . . . . . (718) 270-4900
2011-12 Tuition: In-state $5,432; Out-of-state $11,342
CUNY New York City College of Technology (Public)
Fall 2010 Enrollment: 11,747 . . . . . . . . . . . . . . . . . . . . . . (718) 260-5500
2011-12 Tuition: In-state $5,469; Out-of-state $11,379
Central Yeshiva Tomchei Tmimim Lubavitz (Private, Not-for-profit)
Fall 2010 Enrollment: 733 . . . . . . . . . . . . . . . . . . . . . . . . (718) 774-3430
2011-12 Tuition: In-state $6,200; Out-of-state $6,200
Darkei Noam Rabbinical College (Private, Not-for-profit)
Fall 2010 Enrollment: 20 . . . . . . . . . . . . . . . . . . . . . . . . . (718) 338-9444
Long Island University-Brooklyn Campus (Private, Not-for-profit)
Fall 2010 Enrollment: 7,293 . . . . . . . . . . . . . . . . . . . . . . . (718) 488-1000
2011-12 Tuition: In-state $31,606; Out-of-state $31,606
Machzikei Hadath Rabbinical College (Private, Not-for-profit)
Fall 2010 Enrollment: 91 . . . . . . . . . . . . . . . . . . . . . . . . . (718) 854-8791
2011-12 Tuition: In-state $8,400; Out-of-state $8,400
Mesivta Torah Vodaath Rabbinical Seminary (Private, Not-for-profit, Jewish)
Fall 2010 Enrollment: 245 . . . . . . . . . . . . . . . . . . . . . . . . (718) 621-3651
2011-12 Tuition: In-state $9,050; Out-of-state $9,050
Mesivta of Eastern Parkway-Yeshiva Zichron Meilech (Private, Not-for-profit)
Fall 2010 Enrollment: 47 . . . . . . . . . . . . . . . . . . . . . . . . . (718) 438-1002
2011-12 Tuition: In-state $8,600; Out-of-state $8,600
Mirrer Yeshiva Cent Institute (Private, Not-for-profit, Jewish)
Fall 2010 Enrollment: 277 . . . . . . . . . . . . . . . . . . . . . . . . (718) 645-0536
2011-12 Tuition: In-state $4,700; Out-of-state $4,700
Polytechnic Institute of New York University (Private, Not-for-profit)
Fall 2010 Enrollment: 3,544 . . . . . . . . . . . . . . . . . . . . . . . (718) 260-3100
2011-12 Tuition: In-state $37,882; Out-of-state $37,882
Pratt Institute-Main (Private, Not-for-profit)
Fall 2010 Enrollment: 4,570 . . . . . . . . . . . . . . . . . . . . . . . (718) 636-3600
2011-12 Tuition: In-state $38,980; Out-of-state $38,980
Rabbinical Academy Mesivta Rabbi Chaim Berlin (Private, Not-for-profit)
Fall 2010 Enrollment: 228 . . . . . . . . . . . . . . . . . . . . . . . . (718) 377-0777
2011-12 Tuition: In-state $10,850; Out-of-state $10,850
Rabbinical College Bobover Yeshiva Bnei Zion (Private, Not-for-profit, Jewish)
Fall 2010 Enrollment: 319 . . . . . . . . . . . . . . . . . . . . . . . . (718) 438-2018
2011-12 Tuition: In-state $8,960; Out-of-state $8,960
Rabbinical College of Ch'san Sofer New York (Private, Not-for-profit, Jewish)
Fall 2010 Enrollment: 47 . . . . . . . . . . . . . . . . . . . . . . . . . (718) 236-1171
2011-12 Tuition: In-state $8,000; Out-of-state $8,000
Rabbinical College of Ohr Shimon Yisroel (Private, Not-for-profit, Jewish)
Fall 2010 Enrollment: 177 . . . . . . . . . . . . . . . . . . . . . . . . (718) 855-4092
2011-12 Tuition: In-state $9,000; Out-of-state $9,000
Rabbinical Seminary M'kor Chaim (Private, Not-for-profit)
Fall 2010 Enrollment: 49 . . . . . . . . . . . . . . . . . . . . . . . . . (718) 851-0183
2011-12 Tuition: In-state $6,200; Out-of-state $6,200
SUNY Health Science Center at Brooklyn (Public)
Fall 2010 Enrollment: 1,856 . . . . . . . . . . . . . . . . . . . . . . . (718) 270-1000
Saint Joseph's College-New York (Private, Not-for-profit)
Fall 2010 Enrollment: 4,869 . . . . . . . . . . . . . . . . . . . . . . . (718) 940-5300
2011-12 Tuition: In-state $18,425; Out-of-state $18,425
St. Francis College (Private, Not-for-profit)
Fall 2010 Enrollment: 2,381 . . . . . . . . . . . . . . . . . . . . . . . (718) 522-2300
2011-12 Tuition: In-state $18,100; Out-of-state $18,100
Talmudical Seminary Oholei Torah (Private, Not-for-profit)
Fall 2010 Enrollment: 338 . . . . . . . . . . . . . . . . . . . . . . . . (718) 774-5050
2011-12 Tuition: In-state $7,400; Out-of-state $7,400
Talmudical Seminary of Bobov (Private, Not-for-profit, Jewish)
Fall 2010 Enrollment: 233 . . . . . . . . . . . . . . . . . . . . . . . . (7.1) 843-6E+1
2011-12 Tuition: In-state $6,200; Out-of-state $6,200
Torah Temimah Talmudical Seminary (Private, Not-for-profit)
Fall 2010 Enrollment: 229 . . . . . . . . . . . . . . . . . . . . . . . . (718) 853-8500
2011-12 Tuition: In-state $9,550; Out-of-state $9,550
United Talmudical Seminary (Private, Not-for-profit, Jewish)
Fall 2010 Enrollment: 1,367 . . . . . . . . . . . . . . . . . . . . . . . (718) 963-9770
2011-12 Tuition: In-state $9,000; Out-of-state $9,000

Yeshiva Derech Chaim (Private, Not-for-profit)
  Fall 2010 Enrollment: 178 . . . . . . . . . . . . . . . . . . . . . . . . . (718) 438-5476
  2011-12 Tuition: In-state $9,400; Out-of-state $9,400
Yeshiva Gedolah Imrei Yosef D'spinka (Private, Not-for-profit, Jewish)
  Fall 2010 Enrollment: 116 . . . . . . . . . . . . . . . . . . . . . . . (7.1) 885-2E+1
  2011-12 Tuition: In-state $7,200; Out-of-state $7,200
Yeshiva Karlin Stolin (Private, Not-for-profit)
  Fall 2010 Enrollment: 82 . . . . . . . . . . . . . . . . . . . . . . . . . (718) 232-7800
  2011-12 Tuition: In-state $6,900; Out-of-state $6,900
Yeshiva and Kollel Harbotzas Torah (Private, Not-for-profit)
  Fall 2010 Enrollment: 45 . . . . . . . . . . . . . . . . . . . . . . . . . (718) 692-0208
Yeshiva of Machzikai Hadas (Private, Not-for-profit)
  Fall 2010 Enrollment: 257 . . . . . . . . . . . . . . . . . . . . . . . . (718) 853-2442
  2011-12 Tuition: In-state $6,200; Out-of-state $6,200
Yeshivas Novominsk (Private, Not-for-profit)
  Fall 2010 Enrollment: 153 . . . . . . . . . . . . . . . . . . . . . . . . (718) 438-2727
  2011-12 Tuition: In-state $9,000; Out-of-state $9,000
Yeshivat Mikdash Melech (Private, Not-for-profit)
  Fall 2010 Enrollment: 100 . . . . . . . . . . . . . . . . . . . . . . . . (718) 339-1090
  2011-12 Tuition: In-state $7,500; Out-of-state $7,500

### Two-year College(s)

ASA Institute of Business and Computer Technology (Private, For-profit)
  Fall 2010 Enrollment: 7,835. . . . . . . . . . . . . . . . . . . . . . . (718) 522-9073
  2011-12 Tuition: In-state $12,094; Out-of-state $12,094
Associated Beth Rivkah Schools (Private, Not-for-profit)
  Fall 2010 Enrollment: 82 . . . . . . . . . . . . . . . . . . . . . . . . . (718) 735-0400
  2011-12 Tuition: In-state $6,600; Out-of-state $6,600
CUNY Kingsborough Community College (Public)
  Fall 2010 Enrollment: 13,992. . . . . . . . . . . . . . . . . . . . . . (718) 265-5343
  2011-12 Tuition: In-state $3,950; Out-of-state $6,110
Institute of Design and Construction (Private, Not-for-profit)
  Fall 2010 Enrollment: 87 . . . . . . . . . . . . . . . . . . . . . . . . . (718) 855-3661
  2011-12 Tuition: In-state $8,230; Out-of-state $8,230
Long Island College Hospital School of Radiologic Sciences (Private, Not-for-profit)
  Fall 2010 Enrollment: 68 . . . . . . . . . . . . . . . . . . . . . . . . . (718) 780-1681
Long Island College Hospital of Brooklyn School of Nursing (Private, Not-for-profit)
  Fall 2010 Enrollment: 202 . . . . . . . . . . . . . . . . . . . . . . . . (718) 780-1953
Merkaz Bnos-Business School (Private, Not-for-profit, Jewish)
  Fall 2010 Enrollment: 324 . . . . . . . . . . . . . . . . . . . . . . . . (718) 234-4000
New York Methodist Hospital Center for Allied Health Education (Private, Not-for-profit)
  Fall 2010 Enrollment: 246 . . . . . . . . . . . . . . . . . . . . . . . . (718) 645-3500
  2011-12 Tuition: In-state $16,325; Out-of-state $16,325

### Vocational/Technical School(s)

Allen School-Brooklyn (Private, For-profit)
  Fall 2010 Enrollment: 849 . . . . . . . . . . . . . . . . . . . . . . . . (718) 243-1700
  2011-12 Tuition: $16,080
Career Institute of Health and Technology (Private, For-profit)
  Fall 2010 Enrollment: 365 . . . . . . . . . . . . . . . . . . . . . . . . (718) 422-1212
  2011-12 Tuition: $12,770
Charles Stuart School of Diamond Setting (Private, For-profit)
  Fall 2010 Enrollment: 41 . . . . . . . . . . . . . . . . . . . . . . . . . (718) 339-2640
  2011-12 Tuition: $10,930
EDP School of Computer Programming (Private, Not-for-profit)
  Fall 2010 Enrollment: 74 . . . . . . . . . . . . . . . . . . . . . . . . . (718) 332-6469
  2011-12 Tuition: In-state $4,250; Out-of-state $4,250
Elite Academy of Beauty Arts (Private, For-profit)
  Fall 2010 Enrollment: 111 . . . . . . . . . . . . . . . . . . . . . . . . (718) 998-8182
  2011-12 Tuition: $10,300
Empire Beauty School-Brooklyn (Private, For-profit)
  Fall 2010 Enrollment: 236 . . . . . . . . . . . . . . . . . . . . . . (800) 920-4593
  2011-12 Tuition: $12,000
Hair Design Institute at Fifth Avenue-Brooklyn (Private, For-profit)
  Fall 2010 Enrollment: 125 . . . . . . . . . . . . . . . . . . . . . . (7.1) 874-5E+1
  2011-12 Tuition: $12,200
Manhattan School of Computer Technology (Private, Not-for-profit)
  Fall 2010 Enrollment: 728 . . . . . . . . . . . . . . . . . . . . . . . . (212) 349-9768
  2011-12 Tuition: $3,600
Seminar L'moros Bais Yaakov (Private, Not-for-profit)
  Fall 2010 Enrollment: 397 . . . . . . . . . . . . . . . . . . . . . . . . (718) 851-2900
  2011-12 Tuition: In-state $7,935; Out-of-state $7,935

**Hospitals:** Beth Israel Medical Center-Kings Highway Division (212 beds); Brookdale University Hospital and Medical Center (529 beds); Brooklyn Hospital Center (416 beds); Caledonian Hospital; Coney Island Hospital (387 beds); Interfaith Medical Center (277 beds); Kings County Hospital Center (627 beds); Kingsboro Psychiatric Center (305 beds); Kingsbrook Jewish Medical Center (864 beds); Long Island College Hospital (506 beds); Lutheran Medical Center (476 beds); Maimonides Medical Center (705 beds); NY Community Hospital of Brooklyn (134 beds); New York Methodist Hospital (576 beds); SUNY Downstate Medical Center (376 beds); St. Mary's Hospital (285 beds); VA New York Harbor Healthcare System (942 beds); Victory Memorial Hospital (346 beds); Woodhull Medical & Mental Health Center; Wyckoff Heights Medical Center (305 beds)

**Newspapers:** Afro Times (Local news; Circulation 55,502); Bay News (Community news); Bay Ridge Courier (Community news; Circulation 120,000); Bay Ridge Paper (Community news; Circulation 27,300); Bensonhurst Paper (Community news; Circulation 5,000); Black Reign News (Local news; Circulation 10,000); Brooklyn Arts & Entertainment Journal (Community news; Circulation 50,000); Brooklyn Eagle (Local news; Circulation 100,000); Brooklyn Graphic (Community news); Brooklyn Heights Courier (Community news); Brooklyn Heights Paper (Community news; Circulation 7,100); Brooklyn Heights Press (Community news; Circulation 19,500); Brooklyn Paper Of Carroll Gardens (Local news; Circulation 7,100); Brooklyn Record (Local news; Circulation 2,000); Brooklyn Spectator (Community news; Circulation 8,950); Canarsie Courier (Community news; Circulation 10,000); Canarsie Digest (Community news; Circulation 12,000); Caribbean Life (Local news; Caribbean Life - Bronx Edition (Community news); Caribbean Life - Brooklyn Edition (Community news); Caribbean Life - Queens Edition (Community news; Circulation 41,666); Carroll Gardens-Cobble Hill Courier (Community news; Circulation 120,000); Cobble Hill News (Local news; Circulation 15,000); Cumhuriyet - Bizim Gazet - United Nations Bureau (National news); Daily Challenge (Local news; Circulation 80,000); Darbininkas (Local news; Circulation 3,000); Der Yid (Local news; Circulation 49,000); Downtown News (Community news; Circulation 7,100); Eltingville-Annadale American (Local news; Circulation 28,000); The Everybody Magazine (Local news); Flatbush Life (Community news; Circulation 120,000); Fort Green-Clint Hill Paper (Local news; Circulation 120,000); Great Kills Village Reporter (Local news; Circulation 28,000); Greenpoint Gazette-Advertiser (Local news; Circulation 5,000); Haiti Observateur (Community news; Circulation 75,000); The Haitian Times (National news; Circulation 15,000); Hamodia (Regional news); Harbor Watch (Community news; Circulation 120,000); Home Reporter & Sunset News (Community news; Circulation 9,850); Iltalehti (Local news); Jewish Herald (Local news; Circulation 312,000); The Jewish Press (Local news; Circulation 85,000); Kensington Paper (Community news; Circulation 10,000); Kings Courier (Community news); Kurier Newspaper (Russian Weekly) (Local news; Circulation 40,000); Kurier Russian American Weekly Newspaper (Local news; Circulation 40,000); Manhattan Journal (Local news); Mid-Island Star (Local news; Circulation 22,000); Midwood Paper (Local news; Circulation 2,000); The New American (Local news; Circulation 54,355); New York Daily News - Brooklyn Bureau (Local news); New York Metro News (Community news); New York World (Local news; Circulation 35,000); North Shore Star (Local news; Circulation 28,000); Park Slope Courier (Community news; Circulation 27,000); Park Slope Paper (Community news; Circulation 8,400); South Shore Star (Local news; Circulation 28,000); Spring Creek Sun (Community news; Circulation 8,500); Staten Island Star (Local news; Circulation 28,000); Sunset Park Paper (Local news; Circulation 8,400); The Tablet (Regional news; Circulation 74,000); Willowbrook Star (Local news; Circulation 22,000); Windsor Terrace Paper (Local news; Circulation 3,000)

**Additional Information Contacts**
Kings County Government. . . . . . . . . . . . . . . . . . . . . . . . . (718) 802-3700
  http://www.brooklyn-usa.org
Brooklyn Chamber of Commerce. . . . . . . . . . . . . . . . . . . (718) 875-1000
  http://www.ibrooklyn.com

**MANHATTAN** (borough). Aka New York County. Located in southeastern New York State. One of the five counties/boroughs New York City. Covers a land area of 22.96 square miles, a water area of 10.81 square miles, and is located in the Eastern Time Zone at 40.77° N. Lat., 73.97° W. Long. County seat is New York.

New York County is part of the New York-Northern New Jersey-Long Island, NY-NJ-PA Metropolitan Statistical Area. The entire metro area includes: Edison-New Brunswick, NJ Metropolitan Division (Middlesex County, NJ; Monmouth County, NJ; Ocean County, NJ; Somerset County, NJ); Nassau-Suffolk, NY Metropolitan Division (Nassau County, NY;

Suffolk County, NY); New York-White Plains-Wayne, NY-NJ Metropolitan Division (Bergen County, NJ; Hudson County, NJ; Passaic County, NJ; Bronx County, NY; Kings County, NY; New York County, NY; Putnam County, NY; Queens County, NY; Richmond County, NY; Rockland County, NY; Westchester County, NY); Newark-Union, NJ-PA Metropolitan Division (Essex County, NJ; Hunterdon County, NJ; Morris County, NJ; Sussex County, NJ; Union County, NJ; Pike County, PA)

Weather Station: New York Central Park Observ          Elevation: 131 feet

|        | Jan | Feb | Mar | Apr | May | Jun | Jul | Aug | Sep | Oct | Nov | Dec |
|--------|-----|-----|-----|-----|-----|-----|-----|-----|-----|-----|-----|-----|
| High   | 39  | 42  | 50  | 62  | 72  | 80  | 85  | 84  | 76  | 65  | 55  | 44  |
| Low    | 27  | 29  | 35  | 45  | 54  | 63  | 69  | 68  | 61  | 50  | 41  | 32  |
| Precip | 3.6 | 2.9 | 4.1 | 4.4 | 4.2 | 4.5 | 4.7 | 4.2 | 4.2 | 4.4 | 4.0 | 3.9 |
| Snow   | 7.0 | 7.6 | 3.8 | 0.6 | tr  | 0.0 | tr  | 0.0 | 0.0 | tr  | 0.3 | 4.3 |

*High and Low temperatures in degrees Fahrenheit; Precipitation and Snow in inches*

**Population:** 1,487,530 (1990); 1,537,195 (2000); 1,585,873 (2010); Race: 57.4% White, 15.6% Black, 11.3% Asian, 0.5% American Indian/Alaska Native, 0.1% Native Hawaiian/Other Pacific Islander, 15.1% Other, 25.4% Hispanic of any race (2010); Density: 69,059.8 persons per square mile (2010); Average household size: 1.99 (2010); Median age: 36.4 (2010); Males per 100 females: 88.5 (2010).

**Religion:** Six largest groups: 20.4% Catholicism, 6.2% Judaism, 2.7% Muslim Estimate, 2.7% Non-Denominational, 2.4% Baptist, 1.7% Presbyterian-Reformed (2010)

**Economy:** Unemployment rate: 8.5% (February 2012); Total civilian labor force: 925,509 (February 2012); Leading industries: 14.8% finance & insurance; 14.0% professional, scientific & technical services; 11.7% health care and social assistance (2009); Farms: 0 totaling 0 acres (2007); Companies that employ 500 or more persons: 448 (2009); Companies that employ 100 to 499 persons: 2,584 (2009); Companies that employ less than 100 persons: 100,496 (2009); Black-owned businesses: 26,628 (2007); Hispanic-owned businesses: 32,365 (2007); Asian-owned businesses: 36,440 (2007); Women-owned businesses: 93,986 (2007); Retail sales per capita: $22,935 (2010). Single-family building permits issued: 1 (2011); Multi-family building permits issued: 2,534 (2011).

**Income:** Per capita income: $59,149 (2006-2010 5-year est.); Median household income: $64,971 (2006-2010 5-year est.); Average household income: $122,620 (2006-2010 5-year est.); Percent of households with income of $100,000 or more: 35.3% (2006-2010 5-year est.); Poverty rate: 17.8% (2006-2010 5-year est.); Bankruptcy rate: 1.78% (2011).

**Education:** Percent of population age 25 and over with: High school diploma (including GED) or higher: 84.6% (2006-2010 5-year est.); Bachelor's degree or higher: 57.0% (2006-2010 5-year est.); Master's degree or higher: 27.2% (2006-2010 5-year est.).

**Housing:** Homeownership rate: 22.8% (2010); Median home value: $825,200 (2006-2010 5-year est.); Median contract rent: $1,150 per month (2006-2010 5-year est.); Median year structure built: 1944 (2006-2010 5-year est.)

**Health:** Birth rate: 123.7 per 10,000 population (2011); Death rate: 63.4 per 10,000 population (2011); Age-adjusted cancer mortality rate: 161.3 deaths per 100,000 population (2009); Number of physicians: 118.4 per 10,000 population (2008); Hospital beds: 78.1 per 10,000 population (2007); Hospital admissions: 2,867.3 per 10,000 population (2007).

**Environment:** Air Quality Index: 65.8% good, 33.7% moderate, 0.5% unhealthy for sensitive individuals, 0.0% unhealthy (percent of days in 2010)

**Elections:** 2008 Presidential election results: 85.7% Obama, 13.5% McCain, 0.3% Nader

**National and State Parks:** Castle Clinton National Monument; Statue of Liberty National Monument

**School District(s)**

Amber Charter School (KG-05)
  2009-10 Enrollment: 399 . . . . . . . . . . . . . . . . . . . (212) 534-9667
Carl C Icahn Charter School 4 (KG-02)
  2009-10 Enrollment: 110 . . . . . . . . . . . . . . . . . . . (212) 702-4353
Democracy Preparatory Charter School (06-09)
  2009-10 Enrollment: 403 . . . . . . . . . . . . . . . . . . . (212) 281-1248
Dream Charter School (KG-02)
  2009-10 Enrollment: 147 . . . . . . . . . . . . . . . . . . . (212) 722-0232
Future Leaders Institute Charter School (KG-08)
  2009-10 Enrollment: 335 . . . . . . . . . . . . . . . . . . . (212) 678-2868
Girls Preparatory Charter School of New York (KG-05)
  2009-10 Enrollment: 261 . . . . . . . . . . . . . . . . . . . (212) 388-0241
Growing Up Green Charter School (KG-01)
  2009-10 Enrollment: 148 . . . . . . . . . . . . . . . . . . . (917) 319-0462

Harbor Science and Arts Charter School (01-08)
  2009-10 Enrollment: 216 . . . . . . . . . . . . . . . . . . . (212) 427-2244
Harlem Children's Zone Promise Academy Charter Sch (KG-10)
  2009-10 Enrollment: 781 . . . . . . . . . . . . . . . . . . . (212) 360-3255
Harlem Children's Zone Promise Academy Ii Charter (KG-05)
  2009-10 Enrollment: 409 . . . . . . . . . . . . . . . . . . . (917) 492-1481
Harlem Day Charter School (KG-05)
  2009-10 Enrollment: 241 . . . . . . . . . . . . . . . . . . . (212) 876-9953
Harlem Link Charter School (KG-05)
  2009-10 Enrollment: 306 . . . . . . . . . . . . . . . . . . . (212) 289-3249
Harlem Success Academy Charter School (KG-04)
  2009-10 Enrollment: 524 . . . . . . . . . . . . . . . . . . . (646) 277-7170
Harlem Success Academy Charter School 2 (KG-02)
  2009-10 Enrollment: 363 . . . . . . . . . . . . . . . . . . . (646) 442-6600
Harlem Success Academy Charter School 3 (KG-02)
  2009-10 Enrollment: 249 . . . . . . . . . . . . . . . . . . . (646) 747-6700
Harlem Success Academy Charter School 4 (KG-02)
  2009-10 Enrollment: 248 . . . . . . . . . . . . . . . . . . . (646) 227-7170
Harlem Village Academy Charter School Ehvacs (05-11)
  2009-10 Enrollment: 334 . . . . . . . . . . . . . . . . . . . (646) 812-9399
Harlem Village Academy Leadership (05-09)
  2009-10 Enrollment: 289 . . . . . . . . . . . . . . . . . . . (646) 812-9400
John V Lindsay Wildcat Academy Charter School (09-12)
  2009-10 Enrollment: 411 . . . . . . . . . . . . . . . . . . . (212) 209-6036
Kipp Infinity Charter School (05-09)
  2009-10 Enrollment: 338 . . . . . . . . . . . . . . . . . . . (212) 991-2600
Kipp Success Through Teamwork Achieve & Respon Col (05-09)
  2009-10 Enrollment: 299 . . . . . . . . . . . . . . . . . . . (212) 991-2650
Manhattan Charter School (KG-05)
  2009-10 Enrollment: 234 . . . . . . . . . . . . . . . . . . . (212) 533-2743
New Heights Academy Charter School (05-12)
  2009-10 Enrollment: 750 . . . . . . . . . . . . . . . . . . . (212) 283-5400
New York Center for Autism Charter School (UG-UG)
  2009-10 Enrollment: 28 . . . . . . . . . . . . . . . . . . . (212) 860-2580
New York City Geographic District # 1 (PK-12)
  2009-10 Enrollment: 12,056 . . . . . . . . . . . . . . . . . (212) 356-3740
New York City Geographic District # 2 (PK-12)
  2009-10 Enrollment: 60,687 . . . . . . . . . . . . . . . . . (212) 356-3815
New York City Geographic District # 3 (PK-12)
  2009-10 Enrollment: 22,856 . . . . . . . . . . . . . . . . . (212) 678-5857
New York City Geographic District # 4 (PK-12)
  2009-10 Enrollment: 14,501 . . . . . . . . . . . . . . . . . (212) 831-4981
New York City Geographic District # 5 (PK-12)
  2009-10 Enrollment: 13,391 . . . . . . . . . . . . . . . . . (212) 769-7500
New York City Geographic District # 6 (PK-12)
  2009-10 Enrollment: 25,280 . . . . . . . . . . . . . . . . . (212) 521-3757
Opportunity Charter School (06-12)
  2009-10 Enrollment: 409 . . . . . . . . . . . . . . . . . . . (212) 866-6137
Ross Global Academy Charter School (KG-08)
  2009-10 Enrollment: 413 . . . . . . . . . . . . . . . . . . . (212) 374-3884
Sisulu-Walker Charter School of Harlem (KG-05)
  2009-10 Enrollment: 270 . . . . . . . . . . . . . . . . . . . (212) 663-8216
St Hope Leadership Academy Charter School (05-08)
  2009-10 Enrollment: 207 . . . . . . . . . . . . . . . . . . . (212) 283-1204
The Equity Project Charter School
  2009-10 Enrollment: n/a . . . . . . . . . . . . . . . . . . . (646) 254-6451

**Four-year College(s)**

American Musical and Dramatic Academy (Private, Not-for-profit)
  Fall 2010 Enrollment: 1,460 . . . . . . . . . . . . . . (2.1) 278-8E+1
  2011-12 Tuition: In-state $30,260; Out-of-state $30,260
Bank Street College of Education (Private, Not-for-profit)
  Fall 2010 Enrollment: 734 . . . . . . . . . . . . . . . . . (212) 875-4400
Barnard College (Private, Not-for-profit)
  Fall 2010 Enrollment: 2,325 . . . . . . . . . . . . . . . . (212) 854-5262
  2011-12 Tuition: In-state $42,184; Out-of-state $42,184
Berkeley College-New York (Private, For-profit)
  Fall 2010 Enrollment: 5,653 . . . . . . . . . . . . . . . . (212) 986-4343
  2011-12 Tuition: In-state $21,750; Out-of-state $21,750
Boricua College (Private, Not-for-profit)
  Fall 2010 Enrollment: 1,475 . . . . . . . . . . . . . . . . (212) 694-1000
  2011-12 Tuition: In-state $11,025; Out-of-state $11,025
CUNY Bernard M Baruch College (Public)
  Fall 2010 Enrollment: 15,122 . . . . . . . . . . . . . . . (646) 312-1000
  2011-12 Tuition: In-state $5,550; Out-of-state $11,460

CUNY City College (Public)
Fall 2010 Enrollment: 12,326. . . . . . . . . . . . . . . . . . . . (212) 650-7000
2011-12 Tuition: In-state $5,459; Out-of-state $11,369
CUNY Graduate School and University Center (Public)
Fall 2010 Enrollment: 3,016. . . . . . . . . . . . . . . . . . . . . (212) 817-7000
2011-12 Tuition: In-state $5,360; Out-of-state $11,270
CUNY Hunter College (Public)
Fall 2010 Enrollment: 17,768. . . . . . . . . . . . . . . . . . . . (212) 772-4000
2011-12 Tuition: In-state $5,529; Out-of-state $11,439
CUNY John Jay College of Criminal Justice (Public)
Fall 2010 Enrollment: 12,121. . . . . . . . . . . . . . . . . . . . (212) 237-8000
2011-12 Tuition: In-state $5,459; Out-of-state $11,369
Columbia University in the City of New York (Private, Not-for-profit)
Fall 2010 Enrollment: 24,412. . . . . . . . . . . . . . . . . . . . (212) 854-1754
2011-12 Tuition: In-state $45,290; Out-of-state $45,290
Cooper Union for the Advancement of Science and Art (Private, Not-for-profit)
Fall 2010 Enrollment: 1,118. . . . . . . . . . . . . . . . . . . . . (212) 353-4100
2011-12 Tuition: In-state $39,150; Out-of-state $39,150
DeVry College of New York (Private, For-profit)
Fall 2010 Enrollment: 1,619. . . . . . . . . . . . . . . . . . . . . (212) 312-4300
2011-12 Tuition: In-state $15,188; Out-of-state $15,188
DeVry College of New York's Keller Graduate School of Management (Private, For-profit)
Fall 2010 Enrollment: 674. . . . . . . . . . . . . . . . . . . . . . (212) 312-4300
Fashion Institute of Technology (Public)
Fall 2010 Enrollment: 9,062. . . . . . . . . . . . . . . . . . . . . (212) 217-7999
2011-12 Tuition: In-state $4,459; Out-of-state $12,407
Gerstner Sloan-Kettering Graduate School of Biomedical Sciences at Memorial (Private, Not-for-profit)
Fall 2010 Enrollment: 27. . . . . . . . . . . . . . . . . . . . . . . (646) 888-6639
Globe Institute of Technology (Private, For-profit)
Fall 2010 Enrollment: 783. . . . . . . . . . . . . . . . . . . . . . (212) 624-1613
2011-12 Tuition: In-state $11,120; Out-of-state $11,120
Hebrew Union College-Jewish Institute of Religion-New York (Private, Not-for-profit, Jewish)
Fall 2010 Enrollment: 383. . . . . . . . . . . . . . . . . . . . . . (212) 674-5300
Jewish Theological Seminary of America (Private, Not-for-profit, Jewish)
Fall 2010 Enrollment: 347. . . . . . . . . . . . . . . . . . . . . . (212) 678-8000
2011-12 Tuition: In-state $16,690; Out-of-state $16,690
LIM College (Private, For-profit)
Fall 2010 Enrollment: 1,677. . . . . . . . . . . . . . . . . . . . . (212) 752-1530
2011-12 Tuition: In-state $22,225; Out-of-state $22,225
Manhattan School of Music (Private, Not-for-profit)
Fall 2010 Enrollment: 920. . . . . . . . . . . . . . . . . . . . . . (212) 749-2802
2011-12 Tuition: In-state $33,835; Out-of-state $33,835
Marymount Manhattan College (Private, Not-for-profit)
Fall 2010 Enrollment: 1,838. . . . . . . . . . . . . . . . . . . . . (212) 517-0400
2011-12 Tuition: In-state $24,708; Out-of-state $24,708
Mesivtha Tifereth Jerusalem of America (Private, Not-for-profit, Jewish)
Fall 2010 Enrollment: 86. . . . . . . . . . . . . . . . . . . . . . . (212) 964-2830
2011-12 Tuition: In-state $8,900; Out-of-state $8,900
Metropolitan College of New York (Private, Not-for-profit)
Fall 2010 Enrollment: 1,680. . . . . . . . . . . . . . . . . . . . (8.0) 033-8E+1
2011-12 Tuition: In-state $16,720; Out-of-state $16,720
Mount Sinai School of Medicine (Private, Not-for-profit)
Fall 2010 Enrollment: 992. . . . . . . . . . . . . . . . . . . . . . (212) 241-8716
New York Academy of Art (Private, Not-for-profit)
Fall 2010 Enrollment: 138. . . . . . . . . . . . . . . . . . . . . . (212) 966-0300
New York College of Podiatric Medicine (Private, Not-for-profit)
Fall 2010 Enrollment: 708. . . . . . . . . . . . . . . . . . . . . . (212) 410-8000
New York Film Academy (Private, For-profit)
Fall 2010 Enrollment: 1,150. . . . . . . . . . . . . . . . . . . . . (212) 674-4300
New York Law School (Private, Not-for-profit)
Fall 2010 Enrollment: 1,810. . . . . . . . . . . . . . . . . . . . . (212) 431-2100
New York School of Interior Design (Private, Not-for-profit)
Fall 2010 Enrollment: 469. . . . . . . . . . . . . . . . . . . . . . (212) 472-1500
2011-12 Tuition: In-state $19,774; Out-of-state $19,774
New York Theological Seminary (Private, Not-for-profit, Interdenominational)
Fall 2010 Enrollment: 214. . . . . . . . . . . . . . . . . . . . . . (212) 870-1211
New York University (Private, Not-for-profit)
Fall 2010 Enrollment: 45,353. . . . . . . . . . . . . . . . . . . . (212) 998-1212
2011-12 Tuition: In-state $41,606; Out-of-state $41,606

Pace University-New York (Private, Not-for-profit)
Fall 2010 Enrollment: 11,549. . . . . . . . . . . . . . . . . . . . (212) 346-1200
2011-12 Tuition: In-state $35,032; Out-of-state $35,032
Pacific College of Oriental Medicine-New York (Private, For-profit)
Fall 2010 Enrollment: 751. . . . . . . . . . . . . . . . . . . . . . (212) 982-3456
2011-12 Tuition: In-state $20,488; Out-of-state $20,488
Relay Graduate School of Education (Private, Not-for-profit)
Fall 2010 Enrollment: n/a. . . . . . . . . . . . . . . . . . . . . . (212) 228-1888
Rockefeller University (Private, Not-for-profit)
Fall 2010 Enrollment: 48. . . . . . . . . . . . . . . . . . . . . . . (212) 327-8000
SUNY College of Optometry (Public)
Fall 2010 Enrollment: 300. . . . . . . . . . . . . . . . . . . . . . (212) 938-4000
School of Visual Arts (Private, For-profit)
Fall 2010 Enrollment: 4,030. . . . . . . . . . . . . . . . . . . . . (212) 592-2000
2011-12 Tuition: In-state $29,500; Out-of-state $29,500
Teachers College at Columbia University (Private, Not-for-profit)
Fall 2010 Enrollment: 3,822. . . . . . . . . . . . . . . . . . . . . (212) 678-3000
The General Theological Seminary (Private, Not-for-profit, Protestant Episcopal)
Fall 2010 Enrollment: 141. . . . . . . . . . . . . . . . . . . . . (2.1) 224-4E+1
The Juilliard School (Private, Not-for-profit)
Fall 2010 Enrollment: 1,045. . . . . . . . . . . . . . . . . . . . . (212) 799-5000
2011-12 Tuition: In-state $33,630; Out-of-state $33,630
The Kingâ?(tm)s College (Private, Not-for-profit, Interdenominational)
Fall 2010 Enrollment: 370. . . . . . . . . . . . . . . . . . . . . . (212) 659-7200
2011-12 Tuition: In-state $29,240; Out-of-state $29,240
The New School (Private, Not-for-profit)
Fall 2010 Enrollment: 10,083. . . . . . . . . . . . . . . . . . . . (212) 229-5600
2011-12 Tuition: In-state $38,198; Out-of-state $38,198
Touro College (Private, Not-for-profit)
Fall 2010 Enrollment: 16,319. . . . . . . . . . . . . . . . . . . . (212) 463-0400
2011-12 Tuition: In-state $14,550; Out-of-state $14,550
Tri-State College of Acupuncture (Private, For-profit)
Fall 2010 Enrollment: 249. . . . . . . . . . . . . . . . . . . . . . (212) 242-2255
Union Theological Seminary (Private, Not-for-profit)
Fall 2010 Enrollment: 230. . . . . . . . . . . . . . . . . . . . . . (212) 662-7100
Weill Cornell Medical College (Private, Not-for-profit)
Fall 2010 Enrollment: 1,463. . . . . . . . . . . . . . . . . . . . . (212) 746-1050
Yeshiva University (Private, Not-for-profit)
Fall 2010 Enrollment: 6,312. . . . . . . . . . . . . . . . . . . . . (212) 960-5400
2011-12 Tuition: In-state $35,200; Out-of-state $35,200

### Two-year College(s)

American Academy McAllister Institute of Funeral Service (Private, Not-for-profit)
Fall 2010 Enrollment: 342. . . . . . . . . . . . . . . . . . . . . . (212) 757-1190
2011-12 Tuition: In-state $11,740; Out-of-state $11,740
American Academy of Dramatic Arts-New York (Private, Not-for-profit)
Fall 2010 Enrollment: 250. . . . . . . . . . . . . . . . . . . . . . (212) 686-9244
2011-12 Tuition: In-state $30,500; Out-of-state $30,500
CUNY Borough of Manhattan Community College (Public)
Fall 2010 Enrollment: 18,169. . . . . . . . . . . . . . . . . . . . (212) 220-8000
2011-12 Tuition: In-state $3,918; Out-of-state $6,078
Circle in the Square Theater School (Private, Not-for-profit)
Fall 2010 Enrollment: 104. . . . . . . . . . . . . . . . . . . . . . (212) 307-0388
2011-12 Tuition: In-state $11,525; Out-of-state $11,525
Dance Theatre of Harlem Inc (Private, Not-for-profit)
Fall 2010 Enrollment: 12. . . . . . . . . . . . . . . . . . . . . . . (212) 690-2800
2011-12 Tuition: In-state $7,390; Out-of-state $7,390
Global Business Institute (Private, Not-for-profit)
Fall 2010 Enrollment: 876. . . . . . . . . . . . . . . . . . . . . . (212) 663-1500
2011-12 Tuition: In-state $14,200; Out-of-state $14,200
Helene Fuld College of Nursing (Private, Not-for-profit)
Fall 2010 Enrollment: 369. . . . . . . . . . . . . . . . . . . . . . (212) 616-7200
Joffrey Ballet School-American Ballet Center (Private, For-profit)
Fall 2010 Enrollment: 148. . . . . . . . . . . . . . . . . . . . . . (212) 254-8520
2011-12 Tuition: In-state $12,999; Out-of-state $12,999
Mandl The College of Allied Health (Private, For-profit)
Fall 2010 Enrollment: 1,311. . . . . . . . . . . . . . . . . . . . . (212) 247-3434
2011-12 Tuition: In-state $14,295; Out-of-state $14,295
Memorial Hospital School of Radiation Therapy Technology (Private, Not-for-profit)
Fall 2010 Enrollment: 18. . . . . . . . . . . . . . . . . . . . . . . (212) 639-6835
Neighborhood Playhouse School of the Theater (Private, Not-for-profit)
Fall 2010 Enrollment: 102. . . . . . . . . . . . . . . . . . . . . (2.1) 268-8E+1

New York Career Institute (Private, For-profit)
Fall 2010 Enrollment: 692 . . . . . . . . . . . . . . . . . . (212) 962-0002
2011-12 Tuition: In-state $12,600; Out-of-state $12,600
New York Conservatory for Dramatic Arts (Private, For-profit)
Fall 2010 Enrollment: 351 . . . . . . . . . . . . . . . . . . (212) 645-0030
2011-12 Tuition: In-state $29,050; Out-of-state $29,050
New York Institute of English and Business (Private, Not-for-profit)
Fall 2010 Enrollment: 1,555 . . . . . . . . . . . . . . . . . (212) 725-9400
2011-12 Tuition: In-state $14,774; Out-of-state $14,774
Phillips Beth Israel School of Nursing (Private, Not-for-profit)
Fall 2010 Enrollment: 168 . . . . . . . . . . . . . . . . . . (212) 614-6114
2011-12 Tuition: In-state $19,550; Out-of-state $19,550
Professional Business College (Private, Not-for-profit)
Fall 2010 Enrollment: 771 . . . . . . . . . . . . . . . . . . (212) 226-7300
2011-12 Tuition: In-state $9,805; Out-of-state $9,805
Sanford-Brown Institute-New York (Private, For-profit)
Fall 2010 Enrollment: 2,360 . . . . . . . . . . . . . . . . . (646) 313-4510
Swedish Institute a College of Health Sciences (Private, For-profit)
Fall 2010 Enrollment: 691 . . . . . . . . . . . . . . . . . . (2.1) 292-5E+1
2011-12 Tuition: In-state $11,905; Out-of-state $11,905
Technical Career Institutes (Private, For-profit)
Fall 2010 Enrollment: 5,135 . . . . . . . . . . . . . . . . . (2.1) 259-4E+1
2011-12 Tuition: In-state $12,550; Out-of-state $12,550
The Ailey School (Private, Not-for-profit)
Fall 2010 Enrollment: 96 . . . . . . . . . . . . . . . . . . . (212) 405-9008
2011-12 Tuition: In-state $10,545; Out-of-state $10,545
The Art Institute of New York City (Private, For-profit)
Fall 2010 Enrollment: 1,466 . . . . . . . . . . . . . . . . . (212) 226-5500
2011-12 Tuition: In-state $19,656; Out-of-state $19,656
The Collective School Of Music (Private, For-profit)
Fall 2010 Enrollment: 45 . . . . . . . . . . . . . . . . . . . (212) 741-0091
2011-12 Tuition: In-state $30,250; Out-of-state $30,250
Wood Tobe-Coburn School (Private, For-profit)
Fall 2010 Enrollment: 697 . . . . . . . . . . . . . . . . . . (212) 686-9040
2011-12 Tuition: In-state $16,640; Out-of-state $16,640

**Vocational/Technical School(s)**

A.B.I. School of Barbering & Cosmetology of Chelsea Inc. (Private, For-profit)
Fall 2010 Enrollment: 102 . . . . . . . . . . . . . . . . . . (212) 290-2289
2011-12 Tuition: $4,625
A.B.I. School of Barbering & Cosmetology of Tribeca Inc. (Private, For-profit)
Fall 2010 Enrollment: 51 . . . . . . . . . . . . . . . . . . . (212) 227-6353
2011-12 Tuition: $2,625
Anthem Institute-Manhattan (Private, For-profit)
Fall 2010 Enrollment: 1,300 . . . . . . . . . . . . . . . . . (212) 659-2116
2011-12 Tuition: $14,401
Apex Technical School (Private, For-profit)
Fall 2010 Enrollment: 1,761 . . . . . . . . . . . . . . . . . (212) 645-3300
2011-12 Tuition: $16,487
Atelier Esthetique Institute of Esthetics (Private, For-profit)
Fall 2010 Enrollment: 88 . . . . . . . . . . . . . . . . . . . (212) 725-6130
2011-12 Tuition: $8,600
Aveda Institute-New York (Private, For-profit)
Fall 2010 Enrollment: 251 . . . . . . . . . . . . . . . . . . (212) 807-1492
2011-12 Tuition: $15,080
Carsten Aveda Institute of New York (Private, For-profit)
Fall 2010 Enrollment: 148 . . . . . . . . . . . . . . . . . . (212) 675-4884
2011-12 Tuition: $12,816
Empire Beauty School-Manhattan (Private, For-profit)
Fall 2010 Enrollment: 1,201 . . . . . . . . . . . . . . . . . (800) 920-4593
2011-12 Tuition: $12,000
French Culinary Institute (Private, For-profit)
Fall 2010 Enrollment: 598 . . . . . . . . . . . . . . . . . . (212) 219-8890
2011-12 Tuition: $45,790
Gemological Institute of America-New York (Private, Not-for-profit)
Fall 2010 Enrollment: 149 . . . . . . . . . . . . . . . . . . (2.1) 294-5E+1
2011-12 Tuition: $17,400
Hair Design Institute at Fifth Avenue-New York (Private, For-profit)
Fall 2010 Enrollment: 286 . . . . . . . . . . . . . . . . . . (212) 868-7171
2011-12 Tuition: $12,200
Institute of Allied Medical Professions-New York (Private, Not-for-profit)
Fall 2010 Enrollment: 172 . . . . . . . . . . . . . . . . . . (212) 847-7490

Institute of Audio Research (Private, For-profit)
Fall 2010 Enrollment: 527 . . . . . . . . . . . . . . . . . . (212) 677-7580
2011-12 Tuition: $16,015
Institute of Culinary Education (Private, For-profit)
Fall 2010 Enrollment: 411 . . . . . . . . . . . . . . . . . . (212) 847-0700
Lia Schorr Institute of Cosmetic Skin Care Training (Private, For-profit)
Fall 2010 Enrollment: 61 . . . . . . . . . . . . . . . . . . . (212) 486-9541
2011-12 Tuition: $7,500
Manhattan Institute (The) (Private, For-profit)
Fall 2010 Enrollment: 131 . . . . . . . . . . . . . . . . . . (212) 564-1234
2011-12 Tuition: $11,224
Micropower Career Institute (Private, For-profit)
Fall 2010 Enrollment: 445 . . . . . . . . . . . . . . . . . . (212) 279-2550
2011-12 Tuition: $13,100
Mildred Elley (Private, For-profit)
Fall 2010 Enrollment: 573 . . . . . . . . . . . . . . . . . . (212) 380-9004
2011-12 Tuition: In-state $12,246; Out-of-state $12,246
New Age Training (Private, For-profit)
Fall 2010 Enrollment: 73 . . . . . . . . . . . . . . . . . . . (212) 947-7940
2011-12 Tuition: In-state $5,575; Out-of-state $5,575
SAE Institute of Technology-New York (Private, For-profit)
Fall 2010 Enrollment: 331 . . . . . . . . . . . . . . . . . . (212) 944-9121
2011-12 Tuition: $20,400
Spanish-American Institute (Private, Not-for-profit)
Fall 2010 Enrollment: 21 . . . . . . . . . . . . . . . . . . . (212) 840-7111
2011-12 Tuition: $9,700
Star Career Academy-New York (Private, For-profit)
Fall 2010 Enrollment: 781 . . . . . . . . . . . . . . . . . . (212) 675-6655
2011-12 Tuition: $15,175
Studio Jewelers (Private, For-profit)
Fall 2010 Enrollment: 41 . . . . . . . . . . . . . . . . . . . (212) 686-1944
2011-12 Tuition: $7,800
USA Beauty School International (Private, For-profit)
Fall 2010 Enrollment: n/a . . . . . . . . . . . . . . . . . . (212) 431-0505

**Hospitals:** Bellevue Hospital Center (809 beds); Beth Israel Medical Center (1368 beds); Cabrini Medical Center (493 beds); Cornerstone of Medical Arts Center Hospital (100 beds); Department of Veteran Affairs NY Harbor Health System (350 beds); Gracie Square Hospital (157 beds); Harlem Hospital Center (272 beds); Hospital for Special Surgery (160 beds); Lenox Hill Hospital (652 beds); Manhattan Eye, Ear & Throat Hospital (150 beds); Manhattan Psychiatric Center; Memorial Sloan-Kettering Cancer Center (437 beds); Metropolitan Hospital Center (341 beds); Mount Sinai Medical Center (1171 beds); NYU Hospital for Joint Diseases (216 beds); NYU Langone Medical Center (724 beds); New York - Presbyterian Hospital (2344 beds); New York Downtown Hospital (155 beds); New York Eye and Ear Infirmary (103 beds); New York State Psychiatric Institute (70 beds); North General Hospital (152 beds); Rockefeller University Hospital (20 beds); SVCMC-Saint Vincent's Centers NY & West Branches (756 beds); St. Luke's Roosevelt Hospital Center (1046 beds); St. Vincent's Hospital & Medical Center of NY (727 beds); St. Vincent's Midtown Hospital (150 beds)

**Newspapers:** ABC, Spain - United Nations Bureau (International news); The Advertiser (National news; Circulation 33,000); Aftenposten - UN Bureau (International news); American Chinese Herald (Community news; Circulation 30,000); The Architects Newspaper; Armenian Church (Local news; Circulation 48,000); Asahi Shimbun (International news; Circulation 8,000,000); Asahi Shinbun (Local news); Australian - New York Bureau (Regional news); Automobiles - The New York Times (National news); The Bond Buyer - Washington Bureau (Local news); The Bronx Beat (Local news; Circulation 6,000); Business Day - The New York Times (Local news); CNET - New York Bureau (National news); Catholic New York (Regional news; Circulation 140,000); Chelsea Clinton News (Community news; Circulation 15,000); Chicago Tribune - New York Bureau (Local news); China Press (Local news; Circulation 10,000); Chinese Commercial Journal (Community news; Circulation 15,000); The Christian Science Monitor - New York Bureau (National news); The Christophers (Local news); The Columbia Daily Spectator (Local news; Circulation 10,000); Committed - United Feature Syndicate (Local news); Communications Daily - New York Bureau (National news); Corriere Della Sera - New York Bureau (International news); The Daily Deal (National news; Circulation 40,000); Daily Journal (Local news); Daily Racing Form (National news; Circulation 14,631); Daily Report (Local news; Circulation 2,089); Daily Telegraph (Local news); Dawn - UN Bureau (International news; Circulation 15,000); The Deal (National news; Circulation 40,000); Die Zeit - New York Bureau (International news); Dining In, Dining Out - The New York Times (Local news); Downtown Express (Local news; Circulation

40,000); Downtown Resident (Community news; Circulation 50,000); ENR Magazine (Community news; Circulation 1,500); El Diario - La Prensa (Regional news; Circulation 50,076); El Periodico - UN Bureau (International news); The Epoch Times (International news); Expresso - United Nations Bureau; Filipino Reporter (Local news; Circulation 50,000); Financial Times - New York Bureau (National news; Circulation 133,000); Food - New York Post (Local news); The Forward (Local news); Gay City News (Local news; Circulation 35,000); Greenwich Village Gazette (Community news; Circulation 40,000); Gujarat Times (National news; Circulation 15,000); HFN - Home Furnishings News (National news; Circulation 21,261); Handelsblatt (International news); The Harlem Times (Local news); Hellenic Times (Local news; Circulation 15,000); Hora Hispana - New York Daily News (Local news; Circulation 200,000); Hoy - New York Edition (Local news; Circulation 50,000); Hurriyet (Local news; Circulation 10,000); IDG News Service - New York Bureau (National news); Il Sole-24 Ore/Emc (Local news; Circulation 43,500); Impacto Latin News (National news; Circulation 57,000); The Independent - United Nations Bureau (National news); India Abroad (International news; Circulation 65,117); International Businessman News Bureau - Living Well (Local news); Investor's Business Daily - New York Bureau (National news); Italy Daily (Local news); JTA Daily News Bulletin (Local news; Circulation 12,000); Jerusalem Post (Local news); The Jewish Post (National news; Circulation 19,300); The Jewish Week (Local news; Circulation 97,600); Korea Herald (Local news; Circulation 30,000); La Voz Hispana (Local news; Circulation 68,000); Le Parisien - New York Bureau (Local news); Les Echos - New York Bureau (Local news); London Daily Mail - New York Bureau (International news); Long Island Weekly - The New York Times (Local news); Los Angeles Times - New York Bureau (Local news); Los Angeles Times - UN Bureau (National news); Luann - United Feature Syndicate (Local news); Metro New York (Local news; Circulation 300,000); Mi Zona Hispana; Militant (Local news; Circulation 9,000); Milliyet - United Nations Bureau (International news); Murray Hill News (Local news; Circulation 15,000); National Post - United Nations Bureau (International news); New Jersey China Times (Community news; Circulation 20,000); New Jersey Weekly - The New York Times (Local news); New York Beacon (National news; Circulation 53,000); New York Blade News (Community news; Circulation 50,000); New York Daily News (Local news; Circulation 735,536); New York Daily News - City Hall Bureau (Local news); New York Daily News - Manhattan Supreme Court Bureau (Local news); New York Daily News - Police Bureau (Local news); New York Law Journal (National news; Circulation 12,682); The New York Observer (Local news; Circulation 160,000); New York Post (National news; Circulation 724,748); New York Press (National news; Circulation 115,000); New York Resident (Community news; Circulation 165,000); New York Staats Zeitung und Herold (Community news; Circulation 20,000); The New York Sun (Local news; Circulation 26,263); The New York Times - City Hall Bureau (Local news); The New York Times Sunday Magazine (International news); The New York Times (National news; Circulation 1,142,464); Newsday - City Hall Bureau (Local news); Newsday - New York City Bureau (Regional news); Newsday - Police Bureau (Local news); The Nikkei Weekly - New York Bureau (International news; Circulation 344,321); Nordstjernan (Local news; Circulation 7,400); Novoye Russkoye Slovo (Local news; Circulation 55,000); Nowy Dziennik - Polish Daily News (Local news; Circulation 10,000); Oil Daily (National news); The Onion (Regional news; Circulation 100,000); Our Town (Community news; Circulation 3,650); Pain Medicine News (National news; Circulation 46,556); Papermag.com (Community news; Circulation 2,000); People's Daily - UN Bureau (International news); Przeglad Polski-Polish Daily News (Local news; Circulation 20,000); Public Relations Tactics (National news; Circulation 100,000); Queens Resident (Local news); The Refugio County Press (Community news); Salon.com - New York Bureau (National news); Science Times - The New York Times (National news); Sing Tao Daily (National news; Circulation 50,000); Sing Tao Jih Pao (Local news; Circulation 50,000); Syndicated Features London - United Nations Bureau (International news); TWICE Magazine - This Week In Consumer Electronics (National news; Circulation 20,001); Time Out - Greenville News (Community news); Travel (Local news); The Tribeca Trib (Community news); The Trusted Professional (Regional news; Circulation 34,000); US News & World Report - New York Bureau (National news); USA Today - New York Bureau (National news); Vaba Eesti Sona (Local news; Circulation 2,500); The Village Voice (Local news; Circulation 230,000); The Villager (Community news; Circulation 45,400); The Wall Street Journal Sunday (National news; Circulation 10,100,000); The Wall Street Journal (National news; Circulation 2,062,312); The Washington Post - New York Bureau (National news); Weekend Journal - The Wall Street Journal (National news); West Side Spirit (Community news; Circulation

20,000); Westchester Weekly - The New York Times (Local news); Woodside Herald (Community news; Circulation 14,000); Yomiuri Shimbun - New York Bureau (Local news); ZDNet News - New York Bureau (National news); amNew York (Local news)

**Additional Information Contacts**

City of New York . . . . . . . . . . . . . . . . . . . . . . (212) 669-2400
  http://nyc.gov
Greater Harlem Chamber of Commerce . . . . . . . . . . . . . (212) 862-7200
  http://greaterharlemchamber.com
Greater New York Chamber of Commerce . . . . . . . . . . . (212) 686-7220
  http://www.ny-chamber.com
Greenwich Village-Chelsea Chamber of Commerce . . . . . . (646) 470-1773
  http://www.villagechelsea.com
Manhattan Chamber of Commerce . . . . . . . . . . . . . . (212) 479-7772
  http://www.manhattancc.org
New York Women's Chamber of Commerce . . . . . . . . . . (212) 491-9640
  http://www.nywcc.org

**QUEENS** (borough). Aka Queens County. Located in southeastern southeastern New York State, on Long Island; one of the five counties/boroughs New York City; bounded on the west and north by the East River. Covers a land area of 109.24 square miles, a water area of 69.04 square miles, and is located in the Eastern Time Zone at 40.71° N. Lat.; 73.82° W. Long. The county was founded in 1683. County seat is Jamaica.

Queens County is part of the New York-Northern New Jersey-Long Island, NY-NJ-PA Metropolitan Statistical Area. The entire metro area includes: Edison-New Brunswick, NJ Metropolitan Division (Middlesex County, NJ; Monmouth County, NJ; Ocean County, NJ; Somerset County, NJ); Nassau-Suffolk, NY Metropolitan Division (Nassau County, NY; Suffolk County, NY); New York-White Plains-Wayne, NY-NJ Metropolitan Division (Bergen County, NJ; Hudson County, NJ; Passaic County, NJ; Bronx County, NY; Kings County, NY; New York County, NY; Putnam County, NY; Queens County, NY; Richmond County, NY; Rockland County, NY; Westchester County, NY); Newark-Union, NJ-PA Metropolitan Division (Essex County, NJ; Hunterdon County, NJ; Morris County, NJ; Sussex County, NJ; Union County, NJ; Pike County, PA)

Weather Station: New York J F Kennedy Int'l Arpt · Elevation: 16 feet

|        | Jan | Feb | Mar | Apr | May | Jun | Jul | Aug | Sep | Oct | Nov | Dec |
|--------|-----|-----|-----|-----|-----|-----|-----|-----|-----|-----|-----|-----|
| High   | 39  | 42  | 49  | 59  | 68  | 78  | 83  | 82  | 75  | 64  | 54  | 44  |
| Low    | 26  | 28  | 34  | 44  | 53  | 63  | 69  | 68  | 61  | 50  | 41  | 32  |
| Precip | 3.2 | 2.4 | 3.8 | 4.0 | 4.0 | 3.9 | 4.1 | 3.6 | 3.4 | 3.6 | 3.4 | 3.3 |
| Snow   | 6.4 | 7.4 | 3.6 | 0.8 | tr  | 0.0 | tr  | 0.0 | 0.0 | tr  | 0.3 | 4.2 |

*High and Low temperatures in degrees Fahrenheit; Precipitation and Snow in inches*

Weather Station: New York Laguardia Arpt · Elevation: 11 feet

|        | Jan | Feb | Mar | Apr | May | Jun | Jul | Aug | Sep | Oct | Nov | Dec |
|--------|-----|-----|-----|-----|-----|-----|-----|-----|-----|-----|-----|-----|
| High   | 39  | 42  | 49  | 61  | 71  | 80  | 85  | 84  | 76  | 65  | 54  | 44  |
| Low    | 27  | 29  | 35  | 45  | 55  | 64  | 70  | 70  | 63  | 52  | 42  | 33  |
| Precip | 3.2 | 2.6 | 3.9 | 4.1 | 3.8 | 4.0 | 4.6 | 4.1 | 3.7 | 3.7 | 3.5 | 3.5 |
| Snow   | 7.5 | 8.2 | 4.5 | 0.6 | tr  | 0.0 | tr  | tr  | 0.0 | tr  | 0.3 | 4.8 |

*High and Low temperatures in degrees Fahrenheit; Precipitation and Snow in inches*

**Population:** 1,951,636 (1990); 2,229,379 (2000); 2,230,722 (2010); Race: 39.7% White, 19.1% Black, 22.9% Asian, 0.7% American Indian/Alaska Native, 0.1% Native Hawaiian/Other Pacific Islander, 17.5% Other, 27.5% Hispanic of any race (2010); Density: 20,421.3 persons per square mile (2010); Average household size: 2.82 (2010); Median age: 37.2 (2010); Males per 100 females: 93.8 (2010).
**Religion:** Six largest groups: 30.4% Catholicism, 3.9% Judaism, 3.7% Muslim Estimate, 1.7% Methodist/Pietist, 1.6% Eastern Liturgical (Orthodox), 1.5% Non-Denominational (2010)
**Economy:** Unemployment rate: 9.2% (February 2012); Total civilian labor force: 1,123,574 (February 2012); Leading industries: 23.6% health care and social assistance; 11.9% transportation & warehousing; 11.1% retail trade (2009); Farms: 4 totaling n/a acres (2007); Companies that employ 500 or more persons: 85 (2009); Companies that employ 100 to 499 persons: 555 (2009); Companies that employ less than 100 persons: 41,780 (2009); Black-owned businesses: 34,096 (2007); Hispanic-owned businesses: 38,689 (2007); Asian-owned businesses: 68,605 (2007); Women-owned businesses: 70,202 (2007); Retail sales per capita: $6,578 (2010). Single-family building permits issued: 83 (2011); Multi-family building permits issued: 3,099 (2011).
**Income:** Per capita income: $25,553 (2006-2010 5-year est.); Median household income: $55,291 (2006-2010 5-year est.); Average household

income: $70,208 (2006-2010 5-year est.); Percent of households with income of $100,000 or more: 22.2% (2006-2010 5-year est.); Poverty rate: 13.0% (2006-2010 5-year est.); Bankruptcy rate: 2.43% (2011).
**Education:** Percent of population age 25 and over with: High school diploma (including GED) or higher: 80.0% (2006-2010 5-year est.); Bachelor's degree or higher: 29.5% (2006-2010 5-year est.); Master's degree or higher: 10.3% (2006-2010 5-year est.).
**Housing:** Homeownership rate: 43.0% (2010); Median home value: $479,300 (2006-2010 5-year est.); Median contract rent: $1,086 per month (2006-2010 5-year est.); Median year structure built: 1950 (2006-2010 5-year est.)
**Health:** Birth rate: 134.3 per 10,000 population (2011); Death rate: 62.5 per 10,000 population (2011); Age-adjusted cancer mortality rate: 135.0 deaths per 100,000 population (2009); Number of physicians: 25.9 per 10,000 population (2008); Hospital beds: 17.9 per 10,000 population (2007); Hospital admissions: 781.2 per 10,000 population (2007).
**Environment:** Air Quality Index: 73.7% good, 24.9% moderate, 1.4% unhealthy for sensitive individuals, 0.0% unhealthy (percent of days in 2010)
**Elections:** 2008 Presidential election results: 74.9% Obama, 24.4% McCain, 0.3% Nader

### School District(s)
Merrick Academy-Queens Public Charter School (KG-06)
    2009-10 Enrollment: 494 . . . . . . . . . . . . . . . . . . . (718) 479-3753
NYC Special Schools - District 75 (PK-12)
    2009-10 Enrollment: 21,871 . . . . . . . . . . . . . . . . . (212) 802-1617
New York City Geographic District #24 (PK-12)
    2009-10 Enrollment: 51,213 . . . . . . . . . . . . . . . . . (718) 592-3357
New York City Geographic District #25 (PK-12)
    2009-10 Enrollment: 32,937 . . . . . . . . . . . . . . . . . (718) 281-7605
New York City Geographic District #26 (PK-12)
    2009-10 Enrollment: 37,049 . . . . . . . . . . . . . . . . . (718) 631-6982
New York City Geographic District #27 (PK-12)
    2009-10 Enrollment: 45,929 . . . . . . . . . . . . . . . . . (718) 642-5861
New York City Geographic District #28 (PK-12)
    2009-10 Enrollment: 35,907 . . . . . . . . . . . . . . . . . (718) 557-2622
New York City Geographic District #29 (PK-12)
    2009-10 Enrollment: 27,631 . . . . . . . . . . . . . . . . . (718) 264-3146
New York City Geographic District #30 (PK-12)
    2009-10 Enrollment: 39,122 . . . . . . . . . . . . . . . . . (718) 391-8323
Our World Neighborhood Charter School (KG-08)
    2009-10 Enrollment: 707 . . . . . . . . . . . . . . . . . . . (718) 392-3405
Peninsula Preparatory Academy Charter School (KG-05)
    2009-10 Enrollment: 300 . . . . . . . . . . . . . . . . . . . (347) 403-9234
Renaissance Charter School (KG-12)
    2009-10 Enrollment: 536 . . . . . . . . . . . . . . . . . . . (718) 803-0060
Voice Charter School of New York (KG-02)
    2009-10 Enrollment: 144 . . . . . . . . . . . . . . . . . . . (646) 537-1703

### Four-year College(s)
Beis Medrash Heichal Dovid (Private, Not-for-profit, Jewish)
    Fall 2010 Enrollment: 136 . . . . . . . . . . . . . . . (7.1) 886-8E+1
    2011-12 Tuition: In-state $8,970; Out-of-state $8,970
CUNY Queens College (Public)
    Fall 2010 Enrollment: 16,662. . . . . . . . . . . . . . (718) 997-5000
    2011-12 Tuition: In-state $5,607; Out-of-state $11,517
CUNY School of Law at Queens College (Public)
    Fall 2010 Enrollment: 547 . . . . . . . . . . . . . . . (718) 340-4200
CUNY York College (Public)
    Fall 2010 Enrollment: 5,816. . . . . . . . . . . . . . . (718) 262-2000
    2011-12 Tuition: In-state $5,496; Out-of-state $11,406
Plaza College (Private, For-profit)
    Fall 2010 Enrollment: 1,131. . . . . . . . . . . . . . . (718) 779-1430
    2011-12 Tuition: In-state $11,350; Out-of-state $11,350
Rabbinical Seminary of America (Private, Not-for-profit, Jewish)
    Fall 2010 Enrollment: 551 . . . . . . . . . . . . . . . (718) 268-4700
    2011-12 Tuition: In-state $8,000; Out-of-state $8,000
St John's University-New York (Private, Not-for-profit, Roman Catholic)
    Fall 2010 Enrollment: 17,672. . . . . . . . . . . . . . (718) 990-6161
    2011-12 Tuition: In-state $33,875; Out-of-state $33,875
St. Francis College (Private, Not-for-profit)
    Fall 2010 Enrollment: 2,381. . . . . . . . . . . . . . . (718) 522-2300
    2011-12 Tuition: In-state $18,100; Out-of-state $18,100
Vaughn College of Aeronautics and Technology (Private, Not-for-profit)
    Fall 2010 Enrollment: 1,460. . . . . . . . . . . . . . . (718) 429-6600
    2011-12 Tuition: In-state $18,400; Out-of-state $18,400

Yeshiva Shaar Hatorah (Private, Not-for-profit, Jewish)
    Fall 2010 Enrollment: 88 . . . . . . . . . . . . . . . (7.1) 884-6E+1
    2011-12 Tuition: In-state $13,650; Out-of-state $13,650

### Two-year College(s)
Bramson ORT College (Private, Not-for-profit)
    Fall 2010 Enrollment: 1,086. . . . . . . . . . . . . . . (718) 261-5800
    2011-12 Tuition: In-state $10,970; Out-of-state $10,970
CUNY LaGuardia Community College (Public)
    Fall 2010 Enrollment: 13,260. . . . . . . . . . . . . . (718) 482-7200
    2011-12 Tuition: In-state $3,942; Out-of-state $6,102
CUNY Queensborough Community College (Public)
    Fall 2010 Enrollment: 11,567. . . . . . . . . . . . . . (718) 631-6262
    2011-12 Tuition: In-state $3,940; Out-of-state $6,100
Global Business Institute (Private, Not-for-profit)
    Fall 2010 Enrollment: 340 . . . . . . . . . . . . . . . (7.1) 832-7E+1
    2011-12 Tuition: In-state $14,200; Out-of-state $14,200
Long Island Business Institute (Private, For-profit)
    Fall 2010 Enrollment: 1,433. . . . . . . . . . . . . . . (718) 939-5100
    2011-12 Tuition: In-state $14,124; Out-of-state $14,124
New York Automotive and Diesel Institute (Private, For-profit)
    Fall 2010 Enrollment: 417 . . . . . . . . . . . . . . . (718) 658-0006
St Paul's School of Nursing-Queens (Private, For-profit)
    Fall 2010 Enrollment: 320 . . . . . . . . . . . . . . . (718) 357-0500
    2011-12 Tuition: In-state $19,583; Out-of-state $19,583

### Vocational/Technical School(s)
Ace Computer Training Center (Private, For-profit)
    Fall 2010 Enrollment: 31 . . . . . . . . . . . . . . . . (718) 575-3223
Allen School-Jamaica (Private, For-profit)
    Fall 2010 Enrollment: 701 . . . . . . . . . . . . . . . (718) 291-2200
    2011-12 Tuition: $16,080
Berk Trade and Business School (Private, For-profit)
    Fall 2010 Enrollment: 115 . . . . . . . . . . . . . . . (718) 729-0909
    2011-12 Tuition: $9,675
Empire Beauty School-Queens (Private, For-profit)
    Fall 2010 Enrollment: 372 . . . . . . . . . . . . . . . (800) 920-4593
    2011-12 Tuition: $12,000
Lincoln Technical Institute-Whitestone (Private, For-profit)
    Fall 2010 Enrollment: 1,086. . . . . . . . . . . . . . . (718) 640-9800
    2011-12 Tuition: $28,347
Manhattan School of Computer Technology (Private, Not-for-profit)
    Fall 2010 Enrollment: 728 . . . . . . . . . . . . . . . (212) 349-9768
    2011-12 Tuition: $3,600
Metropolitan Learning Institute (Private, Not-for-profit)
    Fall 2010 Enrollment: 1,246. . . . . . . . . . . . . . . (718) 897-0482
    2011-12 Tuition: $16,500
Midway Paris Beauty School (Private, For-profit)
    Fall 2010 Enrollment: 115 . . . . . . . . . . . . . . . (718) 418-2790
    2011-12 Tuition: $12,500
New Life Business Institute (Private, For-profit)
    Fall 2010 Enrollment: 86 . . . . . . . . . . . . . . . . (718) 737-6524
    2011-12 Tuition: $4,189
New York Medical Career Training Center (Private, For-profit)
    Fall 2010 Enrollment: 318 . . . . . . . . . . . . . . . (718) 460-1717
    2011-12 Tuition: $10,000
New York School for Medical and Dental Assistants (Private, For-profit)
    Fall 2010 Enrollment: 324 . . . . . . . . . . . . . . . (718) 793-2330
    2011-12 Tuition: $14,250
**Hospitals:** Coler-Goldwater Specialty Hospital and Nursing Facility (2014 beds); Creedmoor Psychiatric Center (452 beds); Elmhurst Hospital Center (525 beds); Flushing Hospital Medical Center (293 beds); Forest Hills Hospital (222 beds); Forest Hills Hospital (312 beds); Hillside Hospital (223 beds); Holliswood Hospital (110 beds); Jamaica Hospital Medical Center (387 beds); New York Hospital Queens (439 beds); Peninsula Hospital Center (272 beds); Queens Childrens Psychiatric Center (86 beds); Queens Hospital Center (408 beds); St. John's Episcopal Hospital, South Shore (332 beds); St. Mary's Hospital for Children (95 beds); **Newspapers:** Bayside Times (Community news); Campana (Local news; Circulation 9,500); Chosun Ilbo (Local news); De Norte A Sur -Edicion de Nueva York y Nueva Jersey (Regional news; Circulation 30,000); De Norte a Sur-Uruguay (National news); El Tiempo De Nueva York (Local news; Circulation 38,000); Forest Hills Courier (Community news); Forest Hills Ledger (Community news); Forest Hills Tribune (Community news; Circulation 18,000); Forest Hills/Rego Park Times (Community news; Circulation 30,000); Fresh Meadows Times (Local news); Glen Oaks Ledger (Community news); Glendale Register (Community news;

Circulation 120,000); Greek American (Local news; Circulation 20,000); Greek News (International news; Circulation 15,000); Jackson Heights News (Community news; Circulation 50,000); Jamaica Times (Community news); Korea Central Daily News (Local news; Circulation 10,000); Korea Times (International news; Circulation 45,000); Korea Times - Washington Bureau (International news; Circulation 45,000); Laurelton Times (Local news); Leader Observer (Community news; Circulation 8,000); The Liberty Times, USA (Regional news; Circulation 30,000); Little Neck Ledger (Community news); Long Island City Journal (Community news; Circulation 50,000); The National Herald (National news; Circulation 50,000); The New Voice of New York (International news; Circulation 90,000); New York Daily News - Forest Hills Bureau (Local news); New York Daily News - Queens Bureau (Local news); New York Post - Queens Bureau (Local news); Newsday - Queens Bureau (Local news); Primetimes (Community news; Circulation 160,000); Queens Chronicle (Community news; Circulation 160,000); Queens Examiner (Local news); Queens Ledger (Community news; Circulation 28,500); Queens Tribune (Community news; Circulation 146,000); Queens Village Times (Community news); Resumen (Local news; Circulation 22,000); Richmond Hill Times (Community news); Ridgewood Ledger (Community news); Southeast Queens Courier (Local news; Circulation 10,000); Times Newsweekly (Community news; Circulation 23,075); The Western Queens Gazette (Local news); Western Queens Tribune (Local news; Circulation 18,000); Whitestone Times (Community news); World Journal (National news; Circulation 215,000); World Journal Weekly (National news)

**Additional Information Contacts**
Queens County Government . . . . . . . . . . . . . . . . . . . (718) 286-3000
  http://www.queensbp.org
Queens Chamber of Commerce . . . . . . . . . . . . . . . (718) 898-8500
  http://www.queenschamber.org
Rockaway Chamber of Commerce . . . . . . . . . . . . . . (718) 979-7030
  http://www.rockawaychamberofcommerce.com

## *Neighborhoods in Queens*

**ARVERNE** (unincorporated postal area)
Zip Code: 11692
  Covers a land area of 0.998 square miles and a water area of 0.069 square miles. Located at 40.59° N. Lat; 73.79° W. Long. Elevation is 7 feet. Population: 18,540 (2010); Density: 18,565.5 persons per square mile (2010); Race: 16.4% White, 66.4% Black, 2.8% Asian, 0.6% American Indian/Alaska Native, 0.0% Native Hawaiian/Other Pacific Islander, 13.8% Other, 22.0% Hispanic of any race (2010); Average household size: 2.84 (2010); Median age: 32.5 (2010); Males per 100 females: 84.0 (2010); Homeownership rate: 28.6% (2010)

**ASTORIA** (unincorporated postal area)
Zip Code: 11102
  Covers a land area of 0.807 square miles and a water area of 0.002 square miles. Located at 40.77° N. Lat; 73.92° W. Long. Elevation is 23 feet. Population: 34,133 (2010); Density: 42,254.9 persons per square mile (2010); Race: 55.7% White, 9.8% Black, 15.3% Asian, 0.9% American Indian/Alaska Native, 0.1% Native Hawaiian/Other Pacific Islander, 18.2% Other, 30.3% Hispanic of any race (2010); Average household size: 2.40 (2010); Median age: 33.2 (2010); Males per 100 females: 99.7 (2010); Homeownership rate: 14.6% (2010)
Zip Code: 11103
  Covers a land area of 0.711 square miles and a water area of 0 square miles. Located at 40.76° N. Lat; 73.91° W. Long. Elevation is 23 feet. Population: 38,780 (2010); Density: 54,537.1 persons per square mile (2010); Race: 67.9% White, 1.9% Black, 14.2% Asian, 0.6% American Indian/Alaska Native, 0.1% Native Hawaiian/Other Pacific Islander, 15.3% Other, 24.7% Hispanic of any race (2010); Average household size: 2.29 (2010); Median age: 33.8 (2010); Males per 100 females: 99.8 (2010); Homeownership rate: 15.0% (2010)
Zip Code: 11105
  Covers a land area of 1.631 square miles and a water area of 0 square miles. Located at 40.77° N. Lat; 73.90° W. Long. Elevation is 23 feet. Population: 36,688 (2010); Density: 22,481.1 persons per square mile (2010); Race: 75.5% White, 2.2% Black, 11.2% Asian, 0.3% American Indian/Alaska Native, 0.1% Native Hawaiian/Other Pacific Islander, 10.7% Other, 19.7% Hispanic of any race (2010); Average household size: 2.27 (2010); Median age: 35.5 (2010); Males per 100 females: 95.1 (2010); Homeownership rate: 25.9% (2010)
Zip Code: 11106

Covers a land area of 0.857 square miles and a water area of 0.014 square miles. Located at 40.76° N. Lat; 73.93° W. Long. Elevation is 23 feet. Population: 38,875 (2010); Density: 45,358.6 persons per square mile (2010); Race: 54.5% White, 8.9% Black, 19.2% Asian, 0.6% American Indian/Alaska Native, 0.0% Native Hawaiian/Other Pacific Islander, 16.8% Other, 28.8% Hispanic of any race (2010); Average household size: 2.26 (2010); Median age: 34.7 (2010); Males per 100 females: 94.7 (2010); Homeownership rate: 16.8% (2010)

**BAYSIDE** (unincorporated postal area)
Zip Code: 11360
  Covers a land area of 1.425 square miles and a water area of 0 square miles. Located at 40.78° N. Lat; 73.78° W. Long. Elevation is 79 feet. Population: 18,884 (2010); Density: 13,250.7 persons per square mile (2010); Race: 71.0% White, 1.5% Black, 23.6% Asian, 0.1% American Indian/Alaska Native, 0.0% Native Hawaiian/Other Pacific Islander, 3.8% Other, 8.0% Hispanic of any race (2010); Average household size: 2.15 (2010); Median age: 50.2 (2010); Males per 100 females: 83.3 (2010); Homeownership rate: 71.0% (2010)
Zip Code: 11361
  Covers a land area of 1.758 square miles and a water area of 0.019 square miles. Located at 40.76° N. Lat; 73.77° W. Long. Elevation is 79 feet. Population: 28,606 (2010); Density: 16,269.2 persons per square mile (2010); Race: 54.4% White, 3.9% Black, 35.4% Asian, 0.1% American Indian/Alaska Native, 0.0% Native Hawaiian/Other Pacific Islander, 6.2% Other, 12.8% Hispanic of any race (2010); Average household size: 2.64 (2010); Median age: 40.9 (2010); Males per 100 females: 91.7 (2010); Homeownership rate: 55.8% (2010)

**BREEZY POINT** (unincorporated postal area)
Zip Code: 11697
  Covers a land area of 2.219 square miles and a water area of <.001 square miles. Located at 40.55° N. Lat; 73.92° W. Long. Elevation is 7 feet. Population: 4,079 (2010); Density: 1,837.5 persons per square mile (2010); Race: 98.2% White, 0.1% Black, 0.6% Asian, 0.1% American Indian/Alaska Native, 0.0% Native Hawaiian/Other Pacific Islander, 1.0% Other, 2.2% Hispanic of any race (2010); Average household size: 2.35 (2010); Median age: 49.4 (2010); Males per 100 females: 86.0 (2010); Homeownership rate: 98.0% (2010)

**CAMBRIA HEIGHTS** (unincorporated postal area)
Zip Code: 11411
  Covers a land area of 1.168 square miles and a water area of 0 square miles. Located at 40.69° N. Lat; 73.73° W. Long. Elevation is 49 feet. Population: 18,556 (2010); Density: 15,874.8 persons per square mile (2010); Race: 2.1% White, 93.3% Black, 0.7% Asian, 0.3% American Indian/Alaska Native, 0.0% Native Hawaiian/Other Pacific Islander, 3.6% Other, 5.3% Hispanic of any race (2010); Average household size: 3.15 (2010); Median age: 41.8 (2010); Males per 100 females: 81.1 (2010); Homeownership rate: 81.9% (2010)

**COLLEGE POINT** (unincorporated postal area)
Zip Code: 11356
  Covers a land area of 1.571 square miles and a water area of 0 square miles. Located at 40.78° N. Lat; 73.84° W. Long. Elevation is 69 feet. Population: 23,438 (2010); Density: 14,915.5 persons per square mile (2010); Race: 50.9% White, 2.6% Black, 27.3% Asian, 0.4% American Indian/Alaska Native, 0.0% Native Hawaiian/Other Pacific Islander, 18.8% Other, 36.0% Hispanic of any race (2010); Average household size: 3.02 (2010); Median age: 36.3 (2010); Males per 100 females: 95.1 (2010); Homeownership rate: 47.6% (2010)

**CORONA** (unincorporated postal area)
Zip Code: 11368
  Covers a land area of 2.631 square miles and a water area of 0.036 square miles. Located at 40.74° N. Lat; 73.85° W. Long. Elevation is 43 feet. Population: 109,931 (2010); Density: 41,768.0 persons per square mile (2010); Race: 32.0% White, 11.6% Black, 10.0% Asian, 1.5% American Indian/Alaska Native, 0.0% Native Hawaiian/Other Pacific Islander, 44.9% Other, 73.8% Hispanic of any race (2010); Average household size: 3.77 (2010); Median age: 30.8 (2010); Males per 100 females: 113.4 (2010); Homeownership rate: 20.3% (2010)

**EAST ELMHURST** (unincorporated postal area)
Zip Code: 11369

Covers a land area of 1.067 square miles and a water area of 0 square miles. Located at 40.76° N. Lat; 73.87° W. Long. Elevation is 75 feet. Population: 38,615 (2010); Density: 36,169.7 persons per square mile (2010); Race: 34.4% White, 19.8% Black, 8.8% Asian, 1.1% American Indian/Alaska Native, 0.1% Native Hawaiian/Other Pacific Islander, 35.8% Other, 64.7% Hispanic of any race (2010); Average household size: 3.36 (2010); Median age: 34.3 (2010); Males per 100 females: 99.8 (2010); Homeownership rate: 46.8% (2010)

Zip Code: 11370

Covers a land area of 1.422 square miles and a water area of 0 square miles. Located at 40.76° N. Lat; 73.89° W. Long. Elevation is 75 feet. Population: 39,688 (2010); Density: 27,899.3 persons per square mile (2010); Race: 41.7% White, 17.7% Black, 16.9% Asian, 0.7% American Indian/Alaska Native, 0.1% Native Hawaiian/Other Pacific Islander, 22.9% Other, 41.5% Hispanic of any race (2010); Average household size: 3.03 (2010); Median age: 34.8 (2010); Males per 100 females: 162.0 (2010); Homeownership rate: 45.4% (2010)

## ELMHURST (unincorporated postal area)

Zip Code: 11373

Covers a land area of 1.527 square miles and a water area of 0 square miles. Located at 40.73° N. Lat; 73.87° W. Long. Elevation is 26 feet. Population: 100,820 (2010); Density: 66,006.6 persons per square mile (2010); Race: 26.7% White, 2.1% Black, 47.1% Asian, 0.8% American Indian/Alaska Native, 0.1% Native Hawaiian/Other Pacific Islander, 23.2% Other, 42.4% Hispanic of any race (2010); Average household size: 3.21 (2010); Median age: 35.3 (2010); Males per 100 females: 103.1 (2010); Homeownership rate: 26.7% (2010)

## FAR ROCKAWAY (unincorporated postal area)

Zip Code: 11691

Covers a land area of 2.833 square miles and a water area of 0.033 square miles. Located at 40.60° N. Lat; 73.76° W. Long. Elevation is 16 feet. Population: 60,035 (2010); Density: 21,185.5 persons per square mile (2010); Race: 31.0% White, 50.1% Black, 2.0% Asian, 0.8% American Indian/Alaska Native, 0.1% Native Hawaiian/Other Pacific Islander, 16.0% Other, 25.2% Hispanic of any race (2010); Average household size: 2.93 (2010); Median age: 32.1 (2010); Males per 100 females: 88.3 (2010); Homeownership rate: 23.5% (2010)

Zip Code: 11693

Covers a land area of 0.997 square miles and a water area of 0 square miles. Located at 40.59° N. Lat; 73.80° W. Long. Elevation is 16 feet. Population: 11,916 (2010); Density: 11,950.1 persons per square mile (2010); Race: 55.4% White, 30.8% Black, 3.1% Asian, 0.5% American Indian/Alaska Native, 0.0% Native Hawaiian/Other Pacific Islander, 10.2% Other, 19.1% Hispanic of any race (2010); Average household size: 2.48 (2010); Median age: 38.4 (2010); Males per 100 females: 86.9 (2010); Homeownership rate: 45.1% (2010)

## FLUSHING (unincorporated postal area)

Zip Code: 11354

Covers a land area of 2.167 square miles and a water area of 0.032 square miles. Located at 40.76° N. Lat; 73.82° W. Long. Elevation is 85 feet. Population: 54,878 (2010); Density: 25,323.7 persons per square mile (2010); Race: 28.0% White, 3.8% Black, 58.7% Asian, 0.2% American Indian/Alaska Native, 0.1% Native Hawaiian/Other Pacific Islander, 9.2% Other, 16.2% Hispanic of any race (2010); Average household size: 2.64 (2010); Median age: 43.5 (2010); Males per 100 females: 87.8 (2010); Homeownership rate: 40.6% (2010)

Zip Code: 11355

Covers a land area of 1.735 square miles and a water area of 0 square miles. Located at 40.75° N. Lat; 73.82° W. Long. Elevation is 85 feet. Population: 85,871 (2010); Density: 49,492.4 persons per square mile (2010); Race: 16.5% White, 3.3% Black, 70.9% Asian, 0.3% American Indian/Alaska Native, 0.0% Native Hawaiian/Other Pacific Islander, 9.0% Other, 15.1% Hispanic of any race (2010); Average household size: 2.96 (2010); Median age: 40.5 (2010); Males per 100 females: 93.2 (2010); Homeownership rate: 32.1% (2010)

Zip Code: 11358

Covers a land area of 1.949 square miles and a water area of 0 square miles. Located at 40.76° N. Lat; 73.79° W. Long. Elevation is 85 feet. Population: 37,546 (2010); Density: 19,260.2 persons per square mile (2010); Race: 50.2% White, 1.1% Black, 40.1% Asian, 0.1% American Indian/Alaska Native, 0.0% Native Hawaiian/Other Pacific Islander, 8.5% Other, 16.1% Hispanic of any race (2010); Average household size: 2.80

(2010); Median age: 41.0 (2010); Males per 100 females: 94.3 (2010); Homeownership rate: 56.3% (2010)

Zip Code: 11367

Covers a land area of 2.379 square miles and a water area of 0.186 square miles. Located at 40.73° N. Lat; 73.82° W. Long. Elevation is 85 feet. Population: 41,047 (2010); Density: 17,252.3 persons per square mile (2010); Race: 59.4% White, 10.0% Black, 20.9% Asian, 0.3% American Indian/Alaska Native, 0.0% Native Hawaiian/Other Pacific Islander, 9.4% Other, 15.8% Hispanic of any race (2010); Average household size: 2.68 (2010); Median age: 34.2 (2010); Males per 100 females: 91.0 (2010); Homeownership rate: 49.0% (2010)

## FOREST HILLS (unincorporated postal area)

Zip Code: 11375

Covers a land area of 1.980 square miles and a water area of 0 square miles. Located at 40.72° N. Lat; 73.84° W. Long. Elevation is 59 feet. Population: 68,733 (2010); Density: 34,707.0 persons per square mile (2010); Race: 65.4% White, 2.9% Black, 25.3% Asian, 0.2% American Indian/Alaska Native, 0.0% Native Hawaiian/Other Pacific Islander, 6.2% Other, 12.1% Hispanic of any race (2010); Average household size: 2.10 (2010); Median age: 42.4 (2010); Males per 100 females: 85.7 (2010); Homeownership rate: 49.7% (2010)

## FRESH MEADOWS (unincorporated postal area)

Zip Code: 11365

Covers a land area of 2.496 square miles and a water area of 0.017 square miles. Located at 40.73° N. Lat; 73.79° W. Long. Elevation is 36 feet. Population: 42,252 (2010); Density: 16,923.4 persons per square mile (2010); Race: 40.7% White, 8.8% Black, 41.7% Asian, 0.3% American Indian/Alaska Native, 0.0% Native Hawaiian/Other Pacific Islander, 8.5% Other, 14.4% Hispanic of any race (2010); Average household size: 2.72 (2010); Median age: 40.3 (2010); Males per 100 females: 89.2 (2010); Homeownership rate: 43.4% (2010)

Zip Code: 11366

Covers a land area of 1.094 square miles and a water area of 0 square miles. Located at 40.72° N. Lat; 73.78° W. Long. Elevation is 36 feet. Population: 13,532 (2010); Density: 12,362.4 persons per square mile (2010); Race: 46.0% White, 6.3% Black, 40.4% Asian, 0.3% American Indian/Alaska Native, 0.1% Native Hawaiian/Other Pacific Islander, 6.9% Other, 11.4% Hispanic of any race (2010); Average household size: 2.96 (2010); Median age: 40.7 (2010); Males per 100 females: 93.1 (2010); Homeownership rate: 70.4% (2010)

## GLEN OAKS (unincorporated postal area)

Zip Code: 11004

Covers a land area of 0.950 square miles and a water area of 0 square miles. Located at 40.74° N. Lat; 73.71° W. Long. Elevation is 118 feet. Population: 14,016 (2010); Density: 14,751.9 persons per square mile (2010); Race: 50.0% White, 6.3% Black, 36.5% Asian, 0.4% American Indian/Alaska Native, 0.0% Native Hawaiian/Other Pacific Islander, 6.8% Other, 10.4% Hispanic of any race (2010); Average household size: 2.58 (2010); Median age: 45.9 (2010); Males per 100 females: 87.4 (2010); Homeownership rate: 73.1% (2010)

## HOLLIS (unincorporated postal area)

Zip Code: 11423

Covers a land area of 1.410 square miles and a water area of 0 square miles. Located at 40.71° N. Lat; 73.76° W. Long. Elevation is 59 feet. Population: 29,987 (2010); Density: 21,253.7 persons per square mile (2010); Race: 15.3% White, 42.4% Black, 19.7% Asian, 1.2% American Indian/Alaska Native, 0.2% Native Hawaiian/Other Pacific Islander, 21.2% Other, 16.7% Hispanic of any race (2010); Average household size: 3.10 (2010); Median age: 38.8 (2010); Males per 100 females: 89.5 (2010); Homeownership rate: 56.1% (2010)

## HOWARD BEACH (unincorporated postal area)

Zip Code: 11414

Covers a land area of 2.299 square miles and a water area of 0.086 square miles. Located at 40.65° N. Lat; 73.84° W. Long. Elevation is 3 feet. Population: 26,148 (2010); Density: 11,370.4 persons per square mile (2010); Race: 87.0% White, 2.0% Black, 3.6% Asian, 0.2% American Indian/Alaska Native, 0.0% Native Hawaiian/Other Pacific Islander, 7.2% Other, 16.8% Hispanic of any race (2010); Average household size: 2.44 (2010); Median age: 45.2 (2010); Males per 100 females: 88.8 (2010); Homeownership rate: 72.0% (2010)

## JACKSON HEIGHTS (unincorporated postal area)

Zip Code: 11372

Covers a land area of 0.737 square miles and a water area of 0 square miles. Located at 40.75° N. Lat; 73.88° W. Long. Elevation is 79 feet. Population: 66,636 (2010); Density: 90,359.7 persons per square mile (2010); Race: 45.8% White, 3.1% Black, 20.5% Asian, 0.8% American Indian/Alaska Native, 0.0% Native Hawaiian/Other Pacific Islander, 29.8% Other, 57.2% Hispanic of any race (2010); Average household size: 2.77 (2010); Median age: 37.5 (2010); Males per 100 females: 102.2 (2010); Homeownership rate: 34.1% (2010)

## JAMAICA (unincorporated postal area)

Zip Code: 11430

Covers a land area of 7.117 square miles and a water area of 0.256 square miles. Located at 40.64° N. Lat; 73.78° W. Long. Elevation is 43 feet. Population: 184 (2010); Density: 25.9 persons per square mile (2010); Race: 10.9% White, 68.5% Black, 4.3% Asian, 0.0% American Indian/Alaska Native, 0.0% Native Hawaiian/Other Pacific Islander, 16.3% Other, 28.3% Hispanic of any race (2010); Average household size: 0.00 (2010); Median age: 23.3 (2010); Males per 100 females: 58.6 (2010); Homeownership rate: 0.0% (2010)

Zip Code: 11432

Covers a land area of 2.149 square miles and a water area of 0 square miles. Located at 40.71° N. Lat; 73.79° W. Long. Elevation is 43 feet. Population: 60,809 (2010); Density: 28,294.7 persons per square mile (2010); Race: 23.8% White, 19.8% Black, 35.5% Asian, 0.1% American Indian/Alaska Native, 0.1% Native Hawaiian/Other Pacific Islander, 19.8% Other, 24.9% Hispanic of any race (2010); Average household size: 3.06 (2010); Median age: 35.5 (2010); Males per 100 females: 97.3 (2010); Homeownership rate: 36.7% (2010)

Zip Code: 11433

Covers a land area of 1.551 square miles and a water area of 0 square miles. Located at 40.69° N. Lat; 73.78° W. Long. Elevation is 43 feet. Population: 32,687 (2010); Density: 21,061.8 persons per square mile (2010); Race: 5.3% White, 75.3% Black, 5.0% Asian, 1.2% American Indian/Alaska Native, 0.1% Native Hawaiian/Other Pacific Islander, 13.1% Other, 16.2% Hispanic of any race (2010); Average household size: 3.12 (2010); Median age: 33.7 (2010); Males per 100 females: 82.9 (2010); Homeownership rate: 41.6% (2010)

Zip Code: 11434

Covers a land area of 3.238 square miles and a water area of 0.066 square miles. Located at 40.67° N. Lat; 73.77° W. Long. Elevation is 43 feet. Population: 59,129 (2010); Density: 18,256.4 persons per square mile (2010); Race: 2.9% White, 88.4% Black, 1.5% Asian, 0.5% American Indian/Alaska Native, 0.0% Native Hawaiian/Other Pacific Islander, 6.7% Other, 8.2% Hispanic of any race (2010); Average household size: 2.84 (2010); Median age: 37.4 (2010); Males per 100 females: 77.6 (2010); Homeownership rate: 46.9% (2010)

Zip Code: 11435

Covers a land area of 1.514 square miles and a water area of 0 square miles. Located at 40.70° N. Lat; 73.80° W. Long. Elevation is 43 feet. Population: 53,687 (2010); Density: 35,446.7 persons per square mile (2010); Race: 26.4% White, 27.7% Black, 19.7% Asian, 1.2% American Indian/Alaska Native, 0.2% Native Hawaiian/Other Pacific Islander, 24.8% Other, 32.6% Hispanic of any race (2010); Average household size: 2.97 (2010); Median age: 34.6 (2010); Males per 100 females: 96.4 (2010); Homeownership rate: 35.9% (2010)

Zip Code: 11436

Covers a land area of 0.787 square miles and a water area of 0 square miles. Located at 40.67° N. Lat; 73.79° W. Long. Elevation is 43 feet. Population: 17,949 (2010); Density: 22,782.7 persons per square mile (2010); Race: 3.9% White, 75.7% Black, 6.5% Asian, 1.2% American Indian/Alaska Native, 0.1% Native Hawaiian/Other Pacific Islander, 12.6% Other, 12.0% Hispanic of any race (2010); Average household size: 3.32 (2010); Median age: 35.1 (2010); Males per 100 females: 87.6 (2010); Homeownership rate: 65.2% (2010)

## KEW GARDENS (unincorporated postal area)

Zip Code: 11415

Covers a land area of 0.568 square miles and a water area of 0 square miles. Located at 40.70° N. Lat; 73.82° W. Long. Elevation is 92 feet. Population: 19,341 (2010); Density: 34,042.1 persons per square mile (2010); Race: 62.3% White, 7.3% Black, 16.8% Asian, 0.3% American Indian/Alaska Native, 0.1% Native Hawaiian/Other Pacific Islander, 13.2% Other, 23.2% Hispanic of any race (2010); Average household

size: 2.24 (2010); Median age: 38.5 (2010); Males per 100 females: 91.8 (2010); Homeownership rate: 33.2% (2010)

## LITTLE NECK (unincorporated postal area)

Zip Code: 11362

Covers a land area of 2.516 square miles and a water area of 0.041 square miles. Located at 40.75° N. Lat; 73.73° W. Long. Elevation is 98 feet. Population: 17,823 (2010); Density: 7,081.4 persons per square mile (2010); Race: 56.9% White, 1.6% Black, 37.4% Asian, 0.1% American Indian/Alaska Native, 0.0% Native Hawaiian/Other Pacific Islander, 4.0% Other, 8.0% Hispanic of any race (2010); Average household size: 2.51 (2010); Median age: 45.6 (2010); Males per 100 females: 90.2 (2010); Homeownership rate: 81.0% (2010)

Zip Code: 11363

Covers a land area of 0.868 square miles and a water area of 0 square miles. Located at 40.77° N. Lat; 73.74° W. Long. Elevation is 98 feet. Population: 6,988 (2010); Density: 8,045.4 persons per square mile (2010); Race: 63.2% White, 1.1% Black, 31.3% Asian, 0.1% American Indian/Alaska Native, 0.0% Native Hawaiian/Other Pacific Islander, 4.3% Other, 8.6% Hispanic of any race (2010); Average household size: 2.62 (2010); Median age: 45.7 (2010); Males per 100 females: 90.6 (2010); Homeownership rate: 71.3% (2010)

## LONG ISLAND CITY (unincorporated postal area)

Zip Code: 11101

Covers a land area of 2.615 square miles and a water area of 0.116 square miles. Located at 40.74° N. Lat; 73.93° W. Long. Elevation is 13 feet. Population: 25,484 (2010); Density: 9,743.8 persons per square mile (2010); Race: 42.5% White, 20.8% Black, 16.0% Asian, 0.7% American Indian/Alaska Native, 0.1% Native Hawaiian/Other Pacific Islander, 19.9% Other, 34.5% Hispanic of any race (2010); Average household size: 2.38 (2010); Median age: 34.0 (2010); Males per 100 females: 100.0 (2010); Homeownership rate: 15.1% (2010)

Zip Code: 11109

Covers a land area of 0.040 square miles and a water area of 0.009 square miles. Located at 40.74° N. Lat; 73.95° W. Long. Elevation is 13 feet. Population: 3,523 (2010); Density: 87,800.6 persons per square mile (2010); Race: 66.7% White, 4.4% Black, 21.8% Asian, 0.1% American Indian/Alaska Native, 0.1% Native Hawaiian/Other Pacific Islander, 6.9% Other, 9.1% Hispanic of any race (2010); Average household size: 1.78 (2010); Median age: 31.6 (2010); Males per 100 females: 122.4 (2010); Homeownership rate: 20.1% (2010)

## MASPETH (unincorporated postal area)

Zip Code: 11378

Covers a land area of 2.553 square miles and a water area of 0.056 square miles. Located at 40.72° N. Lat; 73.90° W. Long. Elevation is 30 feet. Population: 34,981 (2010); Density: 13,697.0 persons per square mile (2010); Race: 73.5% White, 1.6% Black, 10.4% Asian, 0.4% American Indian/Alaska Native, 0.0% Native Hawaiian/Other Pacific Islander, 14.1% Other, 27.5% Hispanic of any race (2010); Average household size: 2.72 (2010); Median age: 37.7 (2010); Males per 100 females: 95.9 (2010); Homeownership rate: 49.2% (2010)

## MIDDLE VILLAGE (unincorporated postal area)

Zip Code: 11379

Covers a land area of 2.074 square miles and a water area of 0 square miles. Located at 40.71° N. Lat; 73.87° W. Long. Elevation is 98 feet. Population: 34,821 (2010); Density: 16,785.2 persons per square mile (2010); Race: 83.1% White, 1.0% Black, 8.2% Asian, 0.2% American Indian/Alaska Native, 0.0% Native Hawaiian/Other Pacific Islander, 7.5% Other, 16.4% Hispanic of any race (2010); Average household size: 2.48 (2010); Median age: 42.4 (2010); Males per 100 females: 90.4 (2010); Homeownership rate: 55.8% (2010)

## OAKLAND GARDENS (unincorporated postal area)

Zip Code: 11364

Covers a land area of 2.466 square miles and a water area of 0 square miles. Located at 40.74° N. Lat; 73.76° W. Long. Elevation is 79 feet. Population: 34,555 (2010); Density: 14,012.5 persons per square mile (2010); Race: 46.2% White, 2.3% Black, 47.0% Asian, 0.1% American Indian/Alaska Native, 0.0% Native Hawaiian/Other Pacific Islander, 4.4% Other, 8.4% Hispanic of any race (2010); Average household size: 2.60 (2010); Median age: 43.7 (2010); Males per 100 females: 89.6 (2010); Homeownership rate: 73.1% (2010)

## OZONE PARK (unincorporated postal area)

Zip Code: 11416

Covers a land area of 0.665 square miles and a water area of 0 square miles. Located at 40.68° N. Lat; 73.84° W. Long. Elevation is 33 feet. Population: 24,861 (2010); Density: 37,347.4 persons per square mile (2010); Race: 31.8% White, 11.3% Black, 23.0% Asian, 1.5% American Indian/Alaska Native, 0.1% Native Hawaiian/Other Pacific Islander, 32.3% Other, 44.0% Hispanic of any race (2010); Average household size: 3.43 (2010); Median age: 33.0 (2010); Males per 100 females: 99.0 (2010); Homeownership rate: 39.4% (2010)

Zip Code: 11417

Covers a land area of 1.119 square miles and a water area of 0 square miles. Located at 40.67° N. Lat; 73.84° W. Long. Elevation is 33 feet. Population: 28,967 (2010); Density: 25,885.7 persons per square mile (2010); Race: 41.0% White, 8.9% Black, 20.3% Asian, 1.4% American Indian/Alaska Native, 0.1% Native Hawaiian/Other Pacific Islander, 28.3% Other, 35.5% Hispanic of any race (2010); Average household size: 3.14 (2010); Median age: 36.3 (2010); Males per 100 females: 93.6 (2010); Homeownership rate: 52.4% (2010)

## QUEENS VILLAGE (unincorporated postal area)

Zip Code: 11427

Covers a land area of 1.576 square miles and a water area of 0 square miles. Located at 40.73° N. Lat; 73.74° W. Long. Elevation is 89 feet. Population: 23,593 (2010); Density: 14,967.3 persons per square mile (2010); Race: 28.1% White, 24.0% Black, 32.2% Asian, 0.6% American Indian/Alaska Native, 0.2% Native Hawaiian/Other Pacific Islander, 14.9% Other, 16.9% Hispanic of any race (2010); Average household size: 2.96 (2010); Median age: 40.7 (2010); Males per 100 females: 93.8 (2010); Homeownership rate: 59.4% (2010)

Zip Code: 11428

Covers a land area of 0.832 square miles and a water area of 0 square miles. Located at 40.72° N. Lat; 73.74° W. Long. Elevation is 89 feet. Population: 19,168 (2010); Density: 23,021.3 persons per square mile (2010); Race: 22.8% White, 24.4% Black, 26.7% Asian, 0.9% American Indian/Alaska Native, 0.2% Native Hawaiian/Other Pacific Islander, 25.0% Other, 25.2% Hispanic of any race (2010); Average household size: 3.46 (2010); Median age: 37.3 (2010); Males per 100 females: 94.0 (2010); Homeownership rate: 67.3% (2010)

Zip Code: 11429

Covers a land area of 1.301 square miles and a water area of 0 square miles. Located at 40.70° N. Lat; 73.73° W. Long. Elevation is 89 feet. Population: 25,105 (2010); Density: 19,295.6 persons per square mile (2010); Race: 6.1% White, 80.8% Black, 3.3% Asian, 0.6% American Indian/Alaska Native, 0.1% Native Hawaiian/Other Pacific Islander, 9.1% Other, 12.6% Hispanic of any race (2010); Average household size: 3.42 (2010); Median age: 37.9 (2010); Males per 100 females: 85.2 (2010); Homeownership rate: 67.3% (2010)

## REGO PARK (unincorporated postal area)

Zip Code: 11374

Covers a land area of 0.934 square miles and a water area of 0 square miles. Located at 40.72° N. Lat; 73.86° W. Long. Elevation is 92 feet. Population: 43,600 (2010); Density: 46,663.9 persons per square mile (2010); Race: 61.6% White, 3.0% Black, 26.7% Asian, 0.3% American Indian/Alaska Native, 0.0% Native Hawaiian/Other Pacific Islander, 8.4% Other, 16.1% Hispanic of any race (2010); Average household size: 2.26 (2010); Median age: 41.9 (2010); Males per 100 females: 88.5 (2010); Homeownership rate: 40.7% (2010)

## RICHMOND HILL (unincorporated postal area)

Zip Code: 11418

Covers a land area of 1.633 square miles and a water area of 0 square miles. Located at 40.70° N. Lat; 73.83° W. Long. Elevation is 59 feet. Population: 36,256 (2010); Density: 22,201.4 persons per square mile (2010); Race: 37.0% White, 10.9% Black, 20.8% Asian, 1.2% American Indian/Alaska Native, 0.2% Native Hawaiian/Other Pacific Islander, 29.9% Other, 42.7% Hispanic of any race (2010); Average household size: 3.25 (2010); Median age: 34.5 (2010); Males per 100 females: 100.5 (2010); Homeownership rate: 41.0% (2010)

## RIDGEWOOD (unincorporated postal area)

Zip Code: 11385

Covers a land area of 3.612 square miles and a water area of 0.032 square miles. Located at 40.70° N. Lat; 73.88° W. Long. Elevation is 75

feet. Population: 98,592 (2010); Density: 27,289.9 persons per square mile (2010); Race: 65.5% White, 3.4% Black, 6.5% Asian, 0.7% American Indian/Alaska Native, 0.1% Native Hawaiian/Other Pacific Islander, 23.8% Other, 43.8% Hispanic of any race (2010); Average household size: 2.83 (2010); Median age: 34.6 (2010); Males per 100 females: 96.9 (2010); Homeownership rate: 29.3% (2010)

## ROCKAWAY PARK (unincorporated postal area)

Zip Code: 11694

Covers a land area of 1.365 square miles and a water area of <.001 square miles. Located at 40.57° N. Lat; 73.84° W. Long. Elevation is 7 feet. Population: 20,408 (2010); Density: 14,943.9 persons per square mile (2010); Race: 82.5% White, 9.2% Black, 2.5% Asian, 0.2% American Indian/Alaska Native, 0.0% Native Hawaiian/Other Pacific Islander, 5.6% Other, 12.3% Hispanic of any race (2010); Average household size: 2.31 (2010); Median age: 44.8 (2010); Males per 100 females: 95.4 (2010); Homeownership rate: 48.6% (2010)

## ROSEDALE (unincorporated postal area)

Zip Code: 11422

Covers a land area of 1.968 square miles and a water area of 0.079 square miles. Located at 40.66° N. Lat; 73.73° W. Long. Elevation is 16 feet. Population: 30,425 (2010); Density: 15,455.8 persons per square mile (2010); Race: 7.3% White, 83.7% Black, 2.1% Asian, 0.4% American Indian/Alaska Native, 0.0% Native Hawaiian/Other Pacific Islander, 6.5% Other, 8.7% Hispanic of any race (2010); Average household size: 3.23 (2010); Median age: 36.2 (2010); Males per 100 females: 83.2 (2010); Homeownership rate: 65.0% (2010)

## SAINT ALBANS (unincorporated postal area)

Zip Code: 11412

Covers a land area of 1.646 square miles and a water area of 0 square miles. Located at 40.69° N. Lat; 73.75° W. Long. Elevation is 49 feet. Population: 34,882 (2010); Density: 21,186.0 persons per square mile (2010); Race: 1.4% White, 92.0% Black, 1.0% Asian, 0.4% American Indian/Alaska Native, 0.0% Native Hawaiian/Other Pacific Islander, 5.2% Other, 5.9% Hispanic of any race (2010); Average household size: 3.25 (2010); Median age: 38.0 (2010); Males per 100 females: 80.8 (2010); Homeownership rate: 68.6% (2010)

## SOUTH OZONE PARK (unincorporated postal area)

Zip Code: 11420

Covers a land area of 2.078 square miles and a water area of 0 square miles. Located at 40.67° N. Lat; 73.81° W. Long. Elevation is 26 feet. Population: 44,354 (2010); Density: 21,344.5 persons per square mile (2010); Race: 15.6% White, 32.6% Black, 20.1% Asian, 1.7% American Indian/Alaska Native, 0.2% Native Hawaiian/Other Pacific Islander, 29.8% Other, 22.2% Hispanic of any race (2010); Average household size: 3.43 (2010); Median age: 36.0 (2010); Males per 100 females: 93.7 (2010); Homeownership rate: 61.4% (2010)

## SOUTH RICHMOND HILL (unincorporated postal area)

Zip Code: 11419

Covers a land area of 1.129 square miles and a water area of 0 square miles. Located at 40.68° N. Lat; 73.82° W. Long. Elevation is 46 feet. Population: 47,211 (2010); Density: 41,805.2 persons per square mile (2010); Race: 12.3% White, 18.2% Black, 33.2% Asian, 1.9% American Indian/Alaska Native, 0.2% Native Hawaiian/Other Pacific Islander, 34.2% Other, 20.3% Hispanic of any race (2010); Average household size: 3.72 (2010); Median age: 35.2 (2010); Males per 100 females: 99.6 (2010); Homeownership rate: 49.3% (2010)

## SPRINGFIELD GARDENS (unincorporated postal area)

Zip Code: 11413

Covers a land area of 3.099 square miles and a water area of 0.033 square miles. Located at 40.67° N. Lat; 73.75° W. Long. Elevation is 30 feet. Population: 38,912 (2010); Density: 12,553.3 persons per square mile (2010); Race: 2.3% White, 91.8% Black, 0.9% Asian, 0.4% American Indian/Alaska Native, 0.0% Native Hawaiian/Other Pacific Islander, 4.6% Other, 6.3% Hispanic of any race (2010); Average household size: 3.16 (2010); Median age: 38.7 (2010); Males per 100 females: 83.2 (2010); Homeownership rate: 68.7% (2010)

## SUNNYSIDE (unincorporated postal area)

Zip Code: 11104

Covers a land area of 0.389 square miles and a water area of 0 square miles. Located at 40.74° N. Lat; 73.92° W. Long. Elevation is 16 feet. Population: 27,232 (2010); Density: 69,825.8 persons per square mile (2010); Race: 54.2% White, 2.2% Black, 26.0% Asian, 0.7% American Indian/Alaska Native, 0.0% Native Hawaiian/Other Pacific Islander, 16.9% Other, 29.4% Hispanic of any race (2010); Average household size: 2.30 (2010); Median age: 36.8 (2010); Males per 100 females: 94.7 (2010); Homeownership rate: 16.8% (2010)

## WHITESTONE (unincorporated postal area)
Zip Code: 11357

Covers a land area of 2.801 square miles and a water area of 0 square miles. Located at 40.78° N. Lat; 73.81° W. Long. Elevation is 49 feet. Population: 39,150 (2010); Density: 13,972.9 persons per square mile (2010); Race: 76.2% White, 1.0% Black, 18.3% Asian, 0.1% American Indian/Alaska Native, 0.0% Native Hawaiian/Other Pacific Islander, 4.4% Other, 11.1% Hispanic of any race (2010); Average household size: 2.56 (2010); Median age: 44.9 (2010); Males per 100 females: 90.3 (2010); Homeownership rate: 74.8% (2010)

## WOODHAVEN (unincorporated postal area)
Zip Code: 11421

Covers a land area of 1.288 square miles and a water area of 0 square miles. Located at 40.69° N. Lat; 73.85° W. Long. Elevation is 43 feet. Population: 39,127 (2010); Density: 30,376.5 persons per square mile (2010); Race: 43.2% White, 7.8% Black, 15.7% Asian, 1.3% American Indian/Alaska Native, 0.1% Native Hawaiian/Other Pacific Islander, 31.9% Other, 56.1% Hispanic of any race (2010); Average household size: 3.30 (2010); Median age: 35.2 (2010); Males per 100 females: 97.5 (2010); Homeownership rate: 49.8% (2010)

## WOODSIDE (unincorporated postal area)
Zip Code: 11377

Covers a land area of 2.546 square miles and a water area of 0 square miles. Located at 40.74° N. Lat; 73.90° W. Long. Elevation is 59 feet. Population: 89,830 (2010); Density: 35,274.3 persons per square mile (2010); Race: 37.9% White, 3.4% Black, 36.6% Asian, 0.9% American Indian/Alaska Native, 0.0% Native Hawaiian/Other Pacific Islander, 21.2% Other, 37.6% Hispanic of any race (2010); Average household size: 2.85 (2010); Median age: 35.7 (2010); Males per 100 females: 101.4 (2010); Homeownership rate: 29.6% (2010)

### *End of Neighborhoods in Queens*

## STATEN ISLAND (borough). Aka Richmond County. Located in southeastern New York State. One of the five counties/boroughs of New York City. Covers a land area of 58.48 square miles, a water area of 44.02 square miles, and is located in the Eastern Time Zone at 40.58° N. Lat., 74.14° W. Long. County seat is Saint George.

Richmond County is part of the New York-Northern New Jersey-Long Island, NY-NJ-PA Metropolitan Statistical Area. The entire metro area includes: Edison-New Brunswick, NJ Metropolitan Division (Middlesex County, NJ; Monmouth County, NJ; Ocean County, NJ; Somerset County, NJ); Nassau-Suffolk, NY Metropolitan Division (Nassau County, NY; Suffolk County, NY); New York-White Plains-Wayne, NY-NJ Metropolitan Division (Bergen County, NJ; Hudson County, NJ; Passaic County, NJ; Bronx County, NY; Kings County, NY; New York County, NY; Putnam County, NY; Queens County, NY; Richmond County, NY; Rockland County, NY; Westchester County, NY); Newark-Union, NJ-PA Metropolitan Division (Essex County, NJ; Hunterdon County, NJ; Morris County, NJ; Sussex County, NJ; Union County, NJ; Pike County, PA)

**Population:** 378,977 (1990); 443,728 (2000); 468,730 (2010); Race: 72.9% White, 10.6% Black, 7.5% Asian, 0.4% American Indian/Alaska Native, 0.0% Native Hawaiian/Other Pacific Islander, 8.6% Other, 17.3% Hispanic of any race (2010); Density: 8,015.4 persons per square mile (2010); Average household size: 2.78 (2010); Median age: 38.4 (2010); Males per 100 females: 94.1 (2010).
**Religion:** Six largest groups: 54.2% Catholicism, 1.7% Muslim Estimate, 1.6% Eastern Liturgical (Orthodox), 1.5% Judaism, 1.3% Non-Denominational, 1.1% Pentecostal (2010)
**Economy:** Unemployment rate: 9.1% (February 2012); Total civilian labor force: 241,552 (February 2012); Leading industries: 31.4% health care and social assistance; 16.4% retail trade; 8.0% accommodation & food services (2009); Farms: 14 totaling n/a acres (2007); Companies that employ 500 or

more persons: 14 (2009); Companies that employ 100 to 499 persons: 106 (2009); Companies that employ less than 100 persons: 8,201 (2009); Black-owned businesses: 2,762 (2007); Hispanic-owned businesses: n/a (2007); Asian-owned businesses: n/a (2007); Women-owned businesses: 10,991 (2007); Retail sales per capita: $8,582 (2010). Single-family building permits issued: 179 (2011); Multi-family building permits issued: 402 (2011).
**Income:** Per capita income: $30,843 (2006-2010 5-year est.); Median household income: $71,084 (2006-2010 5-year est.); Average household income: $86,604 (2006-2010 5-year est.); Percent of households with income of $100,000 or more: 33.0% (2006-2010 5-year est.); Poverty rate: 10.3% (2006-2010 5-year est.); Bankruptcy rate: 2.73% (2011).
**Education:** Percent of population age 25 and over with: High school diploma (including GED) or higher: 87.5% (2006-2010 5-year est.); Bachelor's degree or higher: 28.5% (2006-2010 5-year est.); Master's degree or higher: 11.3% (2006-2010 5-year est.).
**Housing:** Homeownership rate: 64.1% (2010); Median home value: $461,700 (2006-2010 5-year est.); Median contract rent: $953 per month (2006-2010 5-year est.); Median year structure built: 1971 (2006-2010 5-year est.)
**Health:** Birth rate: 119.9 per 10,000 population (2011); Death rate: 74.2 per 10,000 population (2011); Age-adjusted cancer mortality rate: 160.3 deaths per 100,000 population (2009); Number of physicians: 37.5 per 10,000 population (2008); Hospital beds: 30.3 per 10,000 population (2007); Hospital admissions: 1,359.4 per 10,000 population (2007).
**Environment:** Air Quality Index: 76.7% good, 20.0% moderate, 3.0% unhealthy for sensitive individuals, 0.3% unhealthy (percent of days in 2010)
**Elections:** 2008 Presidential election results: 47.6% Obama, 51.7% McCain, 0.4% Nader
**National and State Parks:** Gateway National Recreation Area

### School District(s)
Hawthorne-Cedar Knolls Union Free School District (04-12)
   2009-10 Enrollment: 414 . . . . . . . . . . . . . . . . . . . . . . . . . . . (914) 749-2903
John W Lavelle Preparatory Charter School (06-06)
   2009-10 Enrollment: 79 . . . . . . . . . . . . . . . . . . . . . . . . . . . (718) 697-4250
New York City Geographic District #31 (PK-12)
   2009-10 Enrollment: 63,090 . . . . . . . . . . . . . . . . . . . . . . . (718) 420-5667

### Four-year College(s)
CUNY College of Staten Island (Public)
   Fall 2010 Enrollment: 11,313 . . . . . . . . . . . . . . . . . . . . . . (718) 982-2000
   2011-12 Tuition: In-state $5,508; Out-of-state $11,418
Wagner College (Private, Not-for-profit, Lutheran Church in America)
   Fall 2010 Enrollment: 2,014 . . . . . . . . . . . . . . . . . . . . . . . (718) 390-3100
   2011-12 Tuition: In-state $35,820; Out-of-state $35,820

### Two-year College(s)
St Paul's School of Nursing-Staten Island (Private, For-profit)
   Fall 2010 Enrollment: 251 . . . . . . . . . . . . . . . . . . . . . . . . (718) 517-7700
   2011-12 Tuition: In-state $19,615; Out-of-state $19,615

### Vocational/Technical School(s)
Academy of Cosmetology and Esthetics NYC (Private, For-profit)
   Fall 2010 Enrollment: 143 . . . . . . . . . . . . . . . . . . . . . . . . (718) 979-9001
   2011-12 Tuition: $14,500
Career School of NY (Private, Not-for-profit)
   Fall 2010 Enrollment: 76 . . . . . . . . . . . . . . . . . . . . . . . . . (718) 420-6440
   2011-12 Tuition: $9,395
**Housing:** Homeownership rate: 31.0% (2010); Median home value: $513,900 (2006-2010 5-year est.); Median contract rent: $960 per month (2006-2010 5-year est.); Median year structure built: 1947 (2006-2010 5-year est.).
**Hospitals:** Richmond University Medical Center; South Beach Psychiatric Center (322 beds); St. Vincent's Staten Island/Bayley Seton Campuses (198 beds); Staten Island University Hospital (813 beds)
**Safety:** Violent crime rate: 58.2 per 10,000 population; Property crime rate: 167.5 per 10,000 population (2010).
**Newspapers:** The Marketeer Islander (Community news; Circulation 479,000); Staten Island Advance (Local news; Circulation 59,461); Staten Island Pennysaver (Community news; Circulation 75,000); Your Home - Staten Island Advance (Local news)
**Transportation:** Commute to work: 28.4% car, 55.2% public transportation, 10.2% walk, 3.8% work from home (2006-2010 5-year est.); Travel time to work: 11.2% less than 15 minutes, 22.3% 15 to 30 minutes, 26.3% 30 to 45 minutes, 15.1% 45 to 60 minutes, 25.0% 60 minutes or more (2006-2010 5-year est.); Amtrak: train and bus service available.
**Additional Information Contacts**

Richmond County Government . . . . . . . . . . . . . . . . . . . . . (718) 816-8200
  http://statenislandusa.com
Staten Island Chamber of Commerce . . . . . . . . . . . . . . (718) 727-1900
  http://www.sichamber.com

# New York County

*See New York City*

# Niagara County

Located in western New York; bounded on the west by the Niagara River and Lake Erie, and on the north by Lake Ontario; drained by Tonawanda Creek; includes Niagara Falls. Covers a land area of 522.95 square miles, a water area of 616.89 square miles, and is located in the Eastern Time Zone at 43.14° N. Lat., 78.84° W. Long. The county was founded in 1808. County seat is Lockport.

Niagara County is part of the Buffalo-Niagara Falls, NY Metropolitan Statistical Area. The entire metro area includes: Erie County, NY; Niagara County, NY

**Population:** 220,756 (1990); 219,846 (2000); 216,469 (2010); Race: 88.5% White, 6.9% Black, 0.8% Asian, 1.1% American Indian/Alaska Native, 0.0% Native Hawaiian/Other Pacific Islander, 2.7% Other, 2.2% Hispanic of any race (2010); Density: 413.9 persons per square mile (2010); Average household size: 2.34 (2010); Median age: 41.9 (2010); Males per 100 females: 94.2 (2010).
**Religion:** Six largest groups: 24.0% Catholicism, 5.9% Lutheran, 4.1% Methodist/Pietist, 2.0% Presbyterian-Reformed, 1.9% Non-Denominational, 1.3% Baptist (2010)
**Economy:** Unemployment rate: 10.0% (February 2012); Total civilian labor force: 110,480 (February 2012); Leading industries: 17.0% retail trade; 16.6% health care and social assistance; 15.1% manufacturing (2009); Farms: 865 totaling 142,636 acres (2007); Companies that employ 500 or more persons: 6 (2009); Companies that employ 100 to 499 persons: 70 (2009); Companies that employ less than 100 persons: 4,391 (2009); Black-owned businesses: n/a (2007); Hispanic-owned businesses: n/a (2007); Asian-owned businesses: 194 (2007); Women-owned businesses: 3,489 (2007); Retail sales per capita: $10,826 (2010). Single-family building permits issued: 147 (2011); Multi-family building permits issued: 82 (2011).
**Income:** Per capita income: $24,224 (2006-2010 5-year est.); Median household income: $45,964 (2006-2010 5-year est.); Average household income: $58,150 (2006-2010 5-year est.); Percent of households with income of $100,000 or more: 14.8% (2006-2010 5-year est.); Poverty rate: 12.8% (2006-2010 5-year est.); Bankruptcy rate: 3.16% (2011).
**Taxes:** Total county taxes per capita: $859 (2009); County property taxes per capita: $393 (2009).
**Education:** Percent of population age 25 and over with: High school diploma (including GED) or higher: 88.4% (2006-2010 5-year est.); Bachelor's degree or higher: 19.6% (2006-2010 5-year est.); Master's degree or higher: 8.4% (2006-2010 5-year est.).
**Housing:** Homeownership rate: 69.2% (2010); Median home value: $97,600 (2006-2010 5-year est.); Median contract rent: $468 per month (2006-2010 5-year est.); Median year structure built: 1954 (2006-2010 5-year est.)
**Health:** Birth rate: 103.8 per 10,000 population (2011); Death rate: 105.8 per 10,000 population (2011); Age-adjusted cancer mortality rate: 177.6 deaths per 100,000 population (2009); Number of physicians: 12.0 per 10,000 population (2008); Hospital beds: 38.8 per 10,000 population (2007); Hospital admissions: 1,073.7 per 10,000 population (2007).
**Environment:** Air Quality Index: 85.5% good, 14.5% moderate, 0.0% unhealthy for sensitive individuals, 0.0% unhealthy (percent of days in 2010)
**Elections:** 2008 Presidential election results: 49.7% Obama, 48.6% McCain, 1.1% Nader
**National and State Parks:** Brydges State Park; Devils Hole State Park; Fort Niagara State Park; Fourmile Creek State Park; Joseph Davis State Park; Lower Niagara River State Park; New York State Reservation; Whirlpool State Park
**Additional Information Contacts**
Niagara County Government . . . . . . . . . . . . . . . . . . . . . (716) 439-7025
  http://www.niagaracounty.com

Chamber of Commerce of the Tonawandas . . . . . . . . . (716) 692-5120
  http://www.the-tonawandas.com
City of Lockport . . . . . . . . . . . . . . . . . . . . . . . . . . . . . (716) 439-6676
  http://www.elockport.com
City of Niagara Falls . . . . . . . . . . . . . . . . . . . . . . . . . . (716) 286-4393
  http://www.niagarafallsusa.org
City of North Tonawanda . . . . . . . . . . . . . . . . . . . . . . . (716) 695-8555
  http://www.northtonawanda.org
Niagara USA Chamber . . . . . . . . . . . . . . . . . . . . . . . . . (716) 285-9141
  http://www.niagarachamber.org
Town of Cambria . . . . . . . . . . . . . . . . . . . . . . . . . . . . . (716) 433-7664
  http://www.townofcambria.com
Town of Lockport . . . . . . . . . . . . . . . . . . . . . . . . . . . . . (716) 439-9524
  http://www.elockport.com
Town of Niagara . . . . . . . . . . . . . . . . . . . . . . . . . . . . . . (716) 297-2150
  http://www.townofniagara.com
Town of Wheatfield . . . . . . . . . . . . . . . . . . . . . . . . . . . (716) 694-6440
  http://wheatfield.ny.us
Town of Wilson . . . . . . . . . . . . . . . . . . . . . . . . . . . . . . (716) 751-6704
  http://www.wilsonnewyork.com
Village of Wilson . . . . . . . . . . . . . . . . . . . . . . . . . . . . . (716) 751-6704
  http://www.wilsonnewyork.com

## *Niagara County Communities*

**APPLETON** (unincorporated postal area)
Zip Code: 14008
  Covers a land area of 24.451 square miles and a water area of 0.857 square miles. Located at 43.31° N. Lat; 78.62° W. Long. Elevation is 338 feet. Population: 1,467 (2010); Density: 60.0 persons per square mile (2010); Race: 95.2% White, 1.2% Black, 0.1% Asian, 0.9% American Indian/Alaska Native, 0.0% Native Hawaiian/Other Pacific Islander, 2.6% Other, 4.0% Hispanic of any race (2010); Average household size: 2.78 (2010); Median age: 41.6 (2010); Males per 100 females: 102.1 (2010); Homeownership rate: 80.3% (2010)

**BARKER** (village). Covers a land area of 0.419 square miles and a water area of 0 square miles. Located at 43.32° N. Lat; 78.55° W. Long. Elevation is 328 feet.
**Population:** 569 (1990); 577 (2000); 533 (2010); Density: 1,269.6 persons per square mile (2010); Race: 97.2% White, 0.2% Black, 0.0% Asian, 0.9% American Indian/Alaska Native, 0.0% Native Hawaiian/Other Pacific Islander, 1.7% Other, 7.1% Hispanic of any race (2010); Average household size: 2.54 (2010); Median age: 39.9 (2010); Males per 100 females: 88.3 (2010); Marriage status: 22.3% never married, 66.0% now married, 5.0% widowed, 6.7% divorced (2006-2010 5-year est.); Foreign born: 3.6% (2006-2010 5-year est.); Ancestry (includes multiple ancestries): 34.9% German, 20.3% Irish, 20.2% English, 12.1% Italian, 10.7% Polish (2006-2010 5-year est.).
**Economy:** Single-family building permits issued: 0 (2011); Multi-family building permits issued: 0 (2011); Employment by occupation: 9.6% management, 1.1% professional, 4.6% services, 20.6% sales, 5.3% farming, 14.6% construction, 8.2% production (2006-2010 5-year est.).
**Income:** Per capita income: $19,351 (2006-2010 5-year est.); Median household income: $48,309 (2006-2010 5-year est.); Average household income: $53,683 (2006-2010 5-year est.); Percent of households with income of $100,000 or more: 10.0% (2006-2010 5-year est.); Poverty rate: 18.9% (2006-2010 5-year est.).
**Education:** Percent of population age 25 and over with: High school diploma (including GED) or higher: 91.6% (2006-2010 5-year est.); Bachelor's degree or higher: 12.6% (2006-2010 5-year est.); Master's degree or higher: 2.2% (2006-2010 5-year est.).
**School District(s)**
Barker Central School District (PK-12)
  2009-10 Enrollment: 997 . . . . . . . . . . . . . . . . . . . . (716) 795-3832
**Housing:** Homeownership rate: 67.6% (2010); Median home value: $91,000 (2006-2010 5-year est.); Median contract rent: $461 per month (2006-2010 5-year est.); Median year structure built: before 1940 (2006-2010 5-year est.).
**Transportation:** Commute to work: 88.6% car, 0.0% public transportation, 7.0% walk, 2.2% work from home (2006-2010 5-year est.); Travel time to work: 23.8% less than 15 minutes, 30.9% 15 to 30 minutes, 25.7% 30 to 45 minutes, 13.6% 45 to 60 minutes, 6.0% 60 minutes or more (2006-2010 5-year est.)

**BURT** (unincorporated postal area)

Zip Code: 14028

Covers a land area of 13.536 square miles and a water area of 0.511 square miles. Located at 43.31° N. Lat; 78.71° W. Long. Elevation is 315 feet. Population: 1,595 (2010); Density: 117.8 persons per square mile (2010); Race: 96.3% White, 0.4% Black, 0.8% Asian, 0.5% American Indian/Alaska Native, 0.3% Native Hawaiian/Other Pacific Islander, 1.7% Other, 1.9% Hispanic of any race (2010); Average household size: 2.54 (2010); Median age: 43.5 (2010); Males per 100 females: 104.7 (2010); Homeownership rate: 85.5% (2010)

**CAMBRIA** (town). Covers a land area of 39.709 square miles and a water area of 0 square miles. Located at 43.17° N. Lat; 78.82° W. Long. Elevation is 476 feet.

**Population:** 4,779 (1990); 5,393 (2000); 5,839 (2010); Density: 147.0 persons per square mile (2010); Race: 96.1% White, 1.5% Black, 0.2% Asian, 0.8% American Indian/Alaska Native, 0.1% Native Hawaiian/Other Pacific Islander, 1.3% Other, 1.3% Hispanic of any race (2010); Average household size: 2.55 (2010); Median age: 42.3 (2010); Males per 100 females: 101.3 (2010); Marriage status: 26.3% never married, 58.9% now married, 8.5% widowed, 6.3% divorced (2006-2010 5-year est.); Foreign born: 3.0% (2006-2010 5-year est.); Ancestry (includes multiple ancestries): 37.6% German, 22.3% Irish, 19.1% English, 10.0% Polish, 9.8% Italian (2006-2010 5-year est.).
**Economy:** Single-family building permits issued: 5 (2011); Multi-family building permits issued: 0 (2011); Employment by occupation: 14.2% management, 3.4% professional, 6.2% services, 17.2% sales, 8.3% farming, 10.3% construction, 4.8% production (2006-2010 5-year est.).
**Income:** Per capita income: $26,540 (2006-2010 5-year est.); Median household income: $69,306 (2006-2010 5-year est.); Average household income: $70,432 (2006-2010 5-year est.); Percent of households with income of $100,000 or more: 27.5% (2006-2010 5-year est.); Poverty rate: 4.4% (2006-2010 5-year est.).
**Education:** Percent of population age 25 and over with: High school diploma (including GED) or higher: 91.9% (2006-2010 5-year est.); Bachelor's degree or higher: 21.9% (2006-2010 5-year est.); Master's degree or higher: 9.1% (2006-2010 5-year est.).
**Housing:** Homeownership rate: 83.1% (2010); Median home value: $132,400 (2006-2010 5-year est.); Median contract rent: $608 per month (2006-2010 5-year est.); Median year structure built: 1969 (2006-2010 5-year est.).
**Transportation:** Commute to work: 95.8% car, 0.0% public transportation, 0.5% walk, 3.7% work from home (2006-2010 5-year est.); Travel time to work: 31.7% less than 15 minutes, 39.6% 15 to 30 minutes, 22.5% 30 to 45 minutes, 4.9% 45 to 60 minutes, 1.3% 60 minutes or more (2006-2010 5-year est.)
**Additional Information Contacts**
Town of Cambria . . . . . . . . . . . . . . . . . . . . . . . . . . . (716) 433-7664
http://www.townofcambria.com

**GASPORT** (CDP). Covers a land area of 2.869 square miles and a water area of 0.050 square miles. Located at 43.19° N. Lat; 78.57° W. Long. Elevation is 515 feet.

**Population:** 1,336 (1990); 1,248 (2000); 1,248 (2010); Density: 435.0 persons per square mile (2010); Race: 96.6% White, 0.6% Black, 0.3% Asian, 0.6% American Indian/Alaska Native, 0.0% Native Hawaiian/Other Pacific Islander, 1.9% Other, 1.3% Hispanic of any race (2010); Average household size: 2.46 (2010); Median age: 43.2 (2010); Males per 100 females: 89.7 (2010); Marriage status: 27.6% never married, 58.8% now married, 2.7% widowed, 10.9% divorced (2006-2010 5-year est.); Foreign born: 0.0% (2006-2010 5-year est.); Ancestry (includes multiple ancestries): 43.0% German, 31.2% Irish, 25.8% Italian, 12.1% English, 4.8% French Canadian (2006-2010 5-year est.).
**Economy:** Employment by occupation: 2.5% management, 0.0% professional, 4.4% services, 23.1% sales, 8.2% farming, 16.7% construction, 13.9% production (2006-2010 5-year est.).
**Income:** Per capita income: $22,618 (2006-2010 5-year est.); Median household income: $63,412 (2006-2010 5-year est.); Average household income: $68,993 (2006-2010 5-year est.); Percent of households with income of $100,000 or more: 14.5% (2006-2010 5-year est.); Poverty rate: 1.9% (2006-2010 5-year est.).
**Education:** Percent of population age 25 and over with: High school diploma (including GED) or higher: 93.2% (2006-2010 5-year est.); Bachelor's degree or higher: 12.2% (2006-2010 5-year est.); Master's degree or higher: 7.9% (2006-2010 5-year est.).

**School District(s)**
Royalton-Hartland Central School District (PK-12)
    2009-10 Enrollment: 1,576 . . . . . . . . . . . . . . . . . (716) 735-2000
**Housing:** Homeownership rate: 77.2% (2010); Median home value: $119,100 (2006-2010 5-year est.); Median contract rent: $564 per month (2006-2010 5-year est.); Median year structure built: 1952 (2006-2010 5-year est.).
**Transportation:** Commute to work: 96.3% car, 3.7% public transportation, 0.0% walk, 0.0% work from home (2006-2010 5-year est.); Travel time to work: 17.9% less than 15 minutes, 45.3% 15 to 30 minutes, 25.4% 30 to 45 minutes, 8.7% 45 to 60 minutes, 2.6% 60 minutes or more (2006-2010 5-year est.)

**HARTLAND** (town). Covers a land area of 52.377 square miles and a water area of 0.037 square miles. Located at 43.25° N. Lat; 78.55° W. Long. Elevation is 404 feet.

**Population:** 3,911 (1990); 4,165 (2000); 4,117 (2010); Density: 78.6 persons per square mile (2010); Race: 97.1% White, 0.3% Black, 0.3% Asian, 0.7% American Indian/Alaska Native, 0.0% Native Hawaiian/Other Pacific Islander, 1.6% Other, 1.8% Hispanic of any race (2010); Average household size: 2.64 (2010); Median age: 42.4 (2010); Males per 100 females: 103.7 (2010); Marriage status: 27.2% never married, 59.6% now married, 5.6% widowed, 7.6% divorced (2006-2010 5-year est.); Foreign born: 1.2% (2006-2010 5-year est.); Ancestry (includes multiple ancestries): 35.8% German, 22.3% English, 19.7% Irish, 13.0% Italian, 9.0% Polish (2006-2010 5-year est.).
**Economy:** Single-family building permits issued: 5 (2011); Multi-family building permits issued: 0 (2011); Employment by occupation: 6.5% management, 3.9% professional, 8.2% services, 14.4% sales, 4.0% farming, 12.8% construction, 10.3% production (2006-2010 5-year est.).
**Income:** Per capita income: $23,731 (2006-2010 5-year est.); Median household income: $48,987 (2006-2010 5-year est.); Average household income: $65,078 (2006-2010 5-year est.); Percent of households with income of $100,000 or more: 14.4% (2006-2010 5-year est.); Poverty rate: 12.6% (2006-2010 5-year est.).
**Education:** Percent of population age 25 and over with: High school diploma (including GED) or higher: 84.5% (2006-2010 5-year est.); Bachelor's degree or higher: 13.3% (2006-2010 5-year est.); Master's degree or higher: 3.4% (2006-2010 5-year est.).
**Housing:** Homeownership rate: 86.6% (2010); Median home value: $98,200 (2006-2010 5-year est.); Median contract rent: $454 per month (2006-2010 5-year est.); Median year structure built: 1953 (2006-2010 5-year est.).
**Transportation:** Commute to work: 96.2% car, 0.0% public transportation, 0.0% walk, 3.8% work from home (2006-2010 5-year est.); Travel time to work: 21.8% less than 15 minutes, 42.5% 15 to 30 minutes, 15.5% 30 to 45 minutes, 13.1% 45 to 60 minutes, 7.2% 60 minutes or more (2006-2010 5-year est.)

**LEWISTON** (village). Covers a land area of 1.096 square miles and a water area of 0.139 square miles. Located at 43.17° N. Lat; 79.03° W. Long. Elevation is 381 feet.

**Population:** 3,048 (1990); 2,781 (2000); 2,701 (2010); Density: 2,463.0 persons per square mile (2010); Race: 95.8% White, 1.4% Black, 1.1% Asian, 0.7% American Indian/Alaska Native, 0.0% Native Hawaiian/Other Pacific Islander, 1.0% Other, 1.4% Hispanic of any race (2010); Average household size: 2.01 (2010); Median age: 48.3 (2010); Males per 100 females: 80.5 (2010); Marriage status: 26.1% never married, 49.5% now married, 11.3% widowed, 13.1% divorced (2006-2010 5-year est.); Foreign born: 5.9% (2006-2010 5-year est.); Ancestry (includes multiple ancestries): 20.7% English, 19.6% German, 19.6% Irish, 19.0% Italian, 17.7% Polish (2006-2010 5-year est.).
**Economy:** Single-family building permits issued: 6 (2011); Multi-family building permits issued: 0 (2011); Employment by occupation: 18.8% management, 3.6% professional, 10.0% services, 21.7% sales, 2.4% farming, 7.2% construction, 2.5% production (2006-2010 5-year est.).
**Income:** Per capita income: $27,063 (2006-2010 5-year est.); Median household income: $55,429 (2006-2010 5-year est.); Average household income: $58,410 (2006-2010 5-year est.); Percent of households with income of $100,000 or more: 8.8% (2006-2010 5-year est.); Poverty rate: 3.3% (2006-2010 5-year est.).
**Education:** Percent of population age 25 and over with: High school diploma (including GED) or higher: 91.1% (2006-2010 5-year est.); Bachelor's degree or higher: 29.1% (2006-2010 5-year est.); Master's degree or higher: 15.2% (2006-2010 5-year est.).

**School District(s)**
Niagara-Wheatfield Central School District (PK-12)
    2009-10 Enrollment: 4,050 . . . . . . . . . . . . . . . . . . . . . . . (716) 215-3003
**Housing:** Homeownership rate: 62.7% (2010); Median home value: $135,100 (2006-2010 5-year est.); Median contract rent: $642 per month (2006-2010 5-year est.); Median year structure built: 1958 (2006-2010 5-year est.).
**Hospitals:** Mount St. Mary's Hospital and Health Center (179 beds)
**Transportation:** Commute to work: 91.1% car, 0.0% public transportation, 3.3% walk, 5.5% work from home (2006-2010 5-year est.); Travel time to work: 34.6% less than 15 minutes, 46.9% 15 to 30 minutes, 12.5% 30 to 45 minutes, 4.7% 45 to 60 minutes, 1.2% 60 minutes or more (2006-2010 5-year est.)

**LEWISTON** (town). Covers a land area of 37.121 square miles and a water area of 4.010 square miles. Located at 43.18° N. Lat; 78.95° W. Long. Elevation is 381 feet.
**History:** As with Lewis county, named after Governor Morgan Lewis. Settled c.1796, incorporated 1822.
**Population:** 15,500 (1990); 16,257 (2000); 16,262 (2010); Density: 438.1 persons per square mile (2010); Race: 95.6% White, 1.2% Black, 0.8% Asian, 1.0% American Indian/Alaska Native, 0.0% Native Hawaiian/Other Pacific Islander, 1.4% Other, 1.6% Hispanic of any race (2010); Average household size: 2.33 (2010); Median age: 45.2 (2010); Males per 100 females: 88.7 (2010); Marriage status: 31.6% never married, 52.5% now married, 8.0% widowed, 7.9% divorced (2006-2010 5-year est.); Foreign born: 5.5% (2006-2010 5-year est.); Ancestry (includes multiple ancestries): 24.3% Italian, 23.1% German, 21.9% Irish, 14.8% English, 12.8% Polish (2006-2010 5-year est.).
**Economy:** Single-family building permits issued: 7 (2011); Multi-family building permits issued: 0 (2011); Employment by occupation: 9.6% management, 3.8% professional, 9.1% services, 22.2% sales, 3.4% farming, 9.8% construction, 5.2% production (2006-2010 5-year est.).
**Income:** Per capita income: $29,053 (2006-2010 5-year est.); Median household income: $57,936 (2006-2010 5-year est.); Average household income: $76,370 (2006-2010 5-year est.); Percent of households with income of $100,000 or more: 21.9% (2006-2010 5-year est.); Poverty rate: 5.0% (2006-2010 5-year est.).
**Education:** Percent of population age 25 and over with: High school diploma (including GED) or higher: 92.8% (2006-2010 5-year est.); Bachelor's degree or higher: 29.5% (2006-2010 5-year est.); Master's degree or higher: 14.6% (2006-2010 5-year est.).
**School District(s)**
Niagara-Wheatfield Central School District (PK-12)
    2009-10 Enrollment: 4,050 . . . . . . . . . . . . . . . . . . . . . . . (716) 215-3003
**Housing:** Homeownership rate: 79.1% (2010); Median home value: $143,200 (2006-2010 5-year est.); Median contract rent: $621 per month (2006-2010 5-year est.); Median year structure built: 1962 (2006-2010 5-year est.).
**Hospitals:** Mount St. Mary's Hospital and Health Center (179 beds)
**Safety:** Violent crime rate: 2.4 per 10,000 population; Property crime rate: 122.9 per 10,000 population (2010).
**Transportation:** Commute to work: 91.6% car, 0.2% public transportation, 4.9% walk, 3.1% work from home (2006-2010 5-year est.); Travel time to work: 35.2% less than 15 minutes, 41.8% 15 to 30 minutes, 18.2% 30 to 45 minutes, 3.2% 45 to 60 minutes, 1.6% 60 minutes or more (2006-2010 5-year est.)

**LOCKPORT** (city). County seat. Covers a land area of 8.399 square miles and a water area of 0.045 square miles. Located at 43.16° N. Lat; 78.69° W. Long. Elevation is 614 feet.
**Population:** 24,299 (1990); 22,279 (2000); 21,165 (2010); Density: 2,519.7 persons per square mile (2010); Race: 87.5% White, 7.2% Black, 0.5% Asian, 0.5% American Indian/Alaska Native, 0.0% Native Hawaiian/Other Pacific Islander, 4.3% Other, 3.2% Hispanic of any race (2010); Average household size: 2.26 (2010); Median age: 38.1 (2010); Males per 100 females: 91.3 (2010); Marriage status: 35.3% never married, 44.3% now married, 7.5% widowed, 12.8% divorced (2006-2010 5-year est.); Foreign born: 2.6% (2006-2010 5-year est.); Ancestry (includes multiple ancestries): 34.2% German, 22.1% Irish, 15.8% Italian, 11.0% English, 7.5% Polish (2006-2010 5-year est.).
**Economy:** Unemployment rate: 10.4% (February 2012); Total civilian labor force: 10,767 (February 2012); Single-family building permits issued: 1 (2011); Multi-family building permits issued: 26 (2011); Employment by occupation: 8.1% management, 1.8% professional, 11.9% services, 19.9%

sales, 4.0% farming, 8.1% construction, 7.4% production (2006-2010 5-year est.).
**Income:** Per capita income: $21,124 (2006-2010 5-year est.); Median household income: $37,378 (2006-2010 5-year est.); Average household income: $47,556 (2006-2010 5-year est.); Percent of households with income of $100,000 or more: 8.9% (2006-2010 5-year est.); Poverty rate: 19.5% (2006-2010 5-year est.).
**Education:** Percent of population age 25 and over with: High school diploma (including GED) or higher: 84.6% (2006-2010 5-year est.); Bachelor's degree or higher: 17.0% (2006-2010 5-year est.); Master's degree or higher: 8.0% (2006-2010 5-year est.).
**School District(s)**
Lockport City School District (PK-12)
    2009-10 Enrollment: 5,264 . . . . . . . . . . . . . . . . . . . . . . . (716) 478-4835
Starpoint Central School District (KG-12)
    2009-10 Enrollment: 2,757 . . . . . . . . . . . . . . . . . . . . . . . (716) 210-2352
**Vocational/Technical School(s)**
MarJon School of Beauty Culture (Private, For-profit)
    Fall 2010 Enrollment: n/a . . . . . . . . . . . . . . . . . . . . . . . (716) 433-1028
    2011-12 Tuition: $7,000
**Housing:** Homeownership rate: 55.7% (2010); Median home value: $78,500 (2006-2010 5-year est.); Median contract rent: $472 per month (2006-2010 5-year est.); Median year structure built: before 1940 (2006-2010 5-year est.).
**Hospitals:** Lockport Memorial Hospital (134 beds)
**Safety:** Violent crime rate: 30.2 per 10,000 population; Property crime rate: 377.2 per 10,000 population (2010).
**Newspapers:** The Retailer (Community news; Circulation 28,400); Tri-County News (Community news; Circulation 17,000); Union-Sun & Journal (Local news; Circulation 17,500)
**Transportation:** Commute to work: 90.3% car, 1.9% public transportation, 4.9% walk, 1.3% work from home (2006-2010 5-year est.); Travel time to work: 42.7% less than 15 minutes, 24.0% 15 to 30 minutes, 23.4% 30 to 45 minutes, 6.0% 45 to 60 minutes, 3.9% 60 minutes or more (2006-2010 5-year est.)
**Additional Information Contacts**
City of Lockport . . . . . . . . . . . . . . . . . . . . . . . . . . . . . . (716) 439-6676
    http://www.elockport.com

**LOCKPORT** (town). Covers a land area of 44.843 square miles and a water area of 0.051 square miles. Located at 43.14° N. Lat; 78.68° W. Long. Elevation is 614 feet.
**History:** Built around a series of locks on the old Erie Canal. Settled 1821, incorporated 1865.
**Population:** 16,723 (1990); 19,653 (2000); 20,529 (2010); Density: 457.8 persons per square mile (2010); Race: 91.1% White, 4.8% Black, 1.0% Asian, 0.4% American Indian/Alaska Native, 0.0% Native Hawaiian/Other Pacific Islander, 2.7% Other, 2.6% Hispanic of any race (2010); Average household size: 2.40 (2010); Median age: 40.2 (2010); Males per 100 females: 98.9 (2010); Marriage status: 28.5% never married, 55.3% now married, 6.6% widowed, 9.6% divorced (2006-2010 5-year est.); Foreign born: 2.8% (2006-2010 5-year est.); Ancestry (includes multiple ancestries): 38.0% German, 21.1% Irish, 18.4% Italian, 15.3% English, 10.7% Polish (2006-2010 5-year est.).
**Economy:** Single-family building permits issued: 19 (2011); Multi-family building permits issued: 0 (2011); Employment by occupation: 9.9% management, 4.9% professional, 10.0% services, 19.8% sales, 4.3% farming, 8.3% construction, 5.8% production (2006-2010 5-year est.).
**Income:** Per capita income: $26,012 (2006-2010 5-year est.); Median household income: $55,581 (2006-2010 5-year est.); Average household income: $66,130 (2006-2010 5-year est.); Percent of households with income of $100,000 or more: 19.0% (2006-2010 5-year est.); Poverty rate: 9.9% (2006-2010 5-year est.).
**Education:** Percent of population age 25 and over with: High school diploma (including GED) or higher: 89.6% (2006-2010 5-year est.); Bachelor's degree or higher: 24.4% (2006-2010 5-year est.); Master's degree or higher: 10.3% (2006-2010 5-year est.).
**School District(s)**
Lockport City School District (PK-12)
    2009-10 Enrollment: 5,264 . . . . . . . . . . . . . . . . . . . . . . . (716) 478-4835
Starpoint Central School District (KG-12)
    2009-10 Enrollment: 2,757 . . . . . . . . . . . . . . . . . . . . . . . (716) 210-2352

### Vocational/Technical School(s)

MarJon School of Beauty Culture (Private, For-profit)
Fall 2010 Enrollment: n/a. . . . . . . . . . . . . . . . . . . . . . . . (716) 433-1028
2011-12 Tuition: $7,000

**Housing:** Homeownership rate: 76.9% (2010); Median home value: $111,300 (2006-2010 5-year est.); Median contract rent: $435 per month (2006-2010 5-year est.); Median year structure built: 1980 (2006-2010 5-year est.).

**Hospitals:** Lockport Memorial Hospital (134 beds)

**Newspapers:** The Retailer (Community news; Circulation 28,400); Tri-County News (Community news; Circulation 17,000); Union-Sun & Journal (Local news; Circulation 17,500)

**Transportation:** Commute to work: 94.3% car, 0.3% public transportation, 1.3% walk, 3.3% work from home (2006-2010 5-year est.); Travel time to work: 32.3% less than 15 minutes, 33.8% 15 to 30 minutes, 26.8% 30 to 45 minutes, 4.4% 45 to 60 minutes, 2.8% 60 minutes or more (2006-2010 5-year est.)

**Additional Information Contacts**

Town of Lockport . . . . . . . . . . . . . . . . . . . . . . . . . . . . . . . (716) 439-9524
http://www.elockport.com

**MIDDLEPORT** (village). Covers a land area of 0.871 square miles and a water area of 0 square miles. Located at 43.21° N. Lat; 78.47° W. Long. Elevation is 515 feet.

**History:** Grew after completion of Erie Canal (1825). Settled 1812, incorporated 1859.

**Population:** 1,876 (1990); 1,917 (2000); 1,840 (2010); Density: 2,110.3 persons per square mile (2010); Race: 94.9% White, 0.5% Black, 0.4% Asian, 1.0% American Indian/Alaska Native, 0.0% Native Hawaiian/Other Pacific Islander, 3.2% Other, 2.6% Hispanic of any race (2010); Average household size: 2.48 (2010); Median age: 37.9 (2010); Males per 100 females: 91.1 (2010); Marriage status: 30.3% never married, 53.3% now married, 7.1% widowed, 9.3% divorced (2006-2010 5-year est.); Foreign born: 2.1% (2006-2010 5-year est.); Ancestry (includes multiple ancestries): 39.5% German, 25.4% Irish, 19.5% English, 12.0% Italian, 9.4% Polish (2006-2010 5-year est.).

**Economy:** Single-family building permits issued: 0 (2011); Multi-family building permits issued: 0 (2011); Employment by occupation: 9.9% management, 1.1% professional, 9.8% services, 16.0% sales, 4.1% farming, 10.8% construction, 6.2% production (2006-2010 5-year est.).

**Income:** Per capita income: $19,107 (2006-2010 5-year est.); Median household income: $39,896 (2006-2010 5-year est.); Average household income: $48,866 (2006-2010 5-year est.); Percent of households with income of $100,000 or more: 6.7% (2006-2010 5-year est.); Poverty rate: 12.3% (2006-2010 5-year est.).

**Education:** Percent of population age 25 and over with: High school diploma (including GED) or higher: 86.4% (2006-2010 5-year est.); Bachelor's degree or higher: 15.5% (2006-2010 5-year est.); Master's degree or higher: 5.6% (2006-2010 5-year est.).

### School District(s)

Royalton-Hartland Central School District (PK-12)
2009-10 Enrollment: 1,576 . . . . . . . . . . . . . . . . . . . . . (716) 735-2000

**Housing:** Homeownership rate: 67.5% (2010); Median home value: $78,600 (2006-2010 5-year est.); Median contract rent: $427 per month (2006-2010 5-year est.); Median year structure built: before 1940 (2006-2010 5-year est.).

**Safety:** Violent crime rate: 0.0 per 10,000 population; Property crime rate: 206.2 per 10,000 population (2010).

**Transportation:** Commute to work: 91.4% car, 0.0% public transportation, 2.2% walk, 2.7% work from home (2006-2010 5-year est.); Travel time to work: 34.8% less than 15 minutes, 31.3% 15 to 30 minutes, 18.7% 30 to 45 minutes, 9.7% 45 to 60 minutes, 5.5% 60 minutes or more (2006-2010 5-year est.)

**NEWFANE** (town). Covers a land area of 51.823 square miles and a water area of 1.657 square miles. Located at 43.29° N. Lat; 78.69° W. Long. Elevation is 344 feet.

**Population:** 8,996 (1990); 9,657 (2000); 9,666 (2010); Density: 186.5 persons per square mile (2010); Race: 96.3% White, 0.8% Black, 0.4% Asian, 0.5% American Indian/Alaska Native, 0.1% Native Hawaiian/Other Pacific Islander, 1.9% Other, 1.7% Hispanic of any race (2010); Average household size: 2.50 (2010); Median age: 43.3 (2010); Males per 100 females: 96.4 (2010); Marriage status: 24.5% never married, 57.8% now married, 7.7% widowed, 10.0% divorced (2006-2010 5-year est.); Foreign born: 1.5% (2006-2010 5-year est.); Ancestry (includes multiple

ancestries): 35.3% German, 22.0% English, 20.7% Irish, 9.7% Italian, 8.4% Polish (2006-2010 5-year est.).

**Economy:** Single-family building permits issued: 5 (2011); Multi-family building permits issued: 0 (2011); Employment by occupation: 7.5% management, 3.1% professional, 10.0% services, 17.7% sales, 3.2% farming, 14.6% construction, 9.2% production (2006-2010 5-year est.).

**Income:** Per capita income: $23,744 (2006-2010 5-year est.); Median household income: $49,956 (2006-2010 5-year est.); Average household income: $61,078 (2006-2010 5-year est.); Percent of households with income of $100,000 or more: 15.3% (2006-2010 5-year est.); Poverty rate: 12.1% (2006-2010 5-year est.).

**Education:** Percent of population age 25 and over with: High school diploma (including GED) or higher: 90.0% (2006-2010 5-year est.); Bachelor's degree or higher: 16.7% (2006-2010 5-year est.); Master's degree or higher: 6.6% (2006-2010 5-year est.).

### School District(s)

Newfane Central School District (PK-12)
2009-10 Enrollment: 1,911 . . . . . . . . . . . . . . . . . . . . . (716) 778-6850

**Housing:** Homeownership rate: 81.7% (2010); Median home value: $99,500 (2006-2010 5-year est.); Median contract rent: $531 per month (2006-2010 5-year est.); Median year structure built: 1956 (2006-2010 5-year est.).

**Hospitals:** Inter-Community Memorial Hospital (71 beds)

**Transportation:** Commute to work: 95.4% car, 0.0% public transportation, 2.4% walk, 2.2% work from home (2006-2010 5-year est.); Travel time to work: 33.3% less than 15 minutes, 35.7% 15 to 30 minutes, 19.3% 30 to 45 minutes, 9.9% 45 to 60 minutes, 1.8% 60 minutes or more (2006-2010 5-year est.)

**NEWFANE** (CDP). Covers a land area of 5.303 square miles and a water area of 0 square miles. Located at 43.28° N. Lat; 78.69° W. Long. Elevation is 344 feet.

**Population:** 3,001 (1990); 3,129 (2000); 3,822 (2010); Density: 720.7 persons per square mile (2010); Race: 96.3% White, 0.8% Black, 0.5% Asian, 0.4% American Indian/Alaska Native, 0.0% Native Hawaiian/Other Pacific Islander, 2.0% Other, 1.2% Hispanic of any race (2010); Average household size: 2.50 (2010); Median age: 41.5 (2010); Males per 100 females: 89.6 (2010); Marriage status: 22.5% never married, 57.0% now married, 9.6% widowed, 11.0% divorced (2006-2010 5-year est.); Foreign born: 2.5% (2006-2010 5-year est.); Ancestry (includes multiple ancestries): 31.1% German, 19.2% English, 17.8% Irish, 8.0% Polish, 7.7% Italian (2006-2010 5-year est.).

**Economy:** Employment by occupation: 6.0% management, 2.7% professional, 8.2% services, 17.7% sales, 5.8% farming, 18.7% construction, 8.6% production (2006-2010 5-year est.).

**Income:** Per capita income: $25,520 (2006-2010 5-year est.); Median household income: $50,714 (2006-2010 5-year est.); Average household income: $59,494 (2006-2010 5-year est.); Percent of households with income of $100,000 or more: 12.6% (2006-2010 5-year est.); Poverty rate: 3.5% (2006-2010 5-year est.).

**Education:** Percent of population age 25 and over with: High school diploma (including GED) or higher: 87.1% (2006-2010 5-year est.); Bachelor's degree or higher: 16.9% (2006-2010 5-year est.); Master's degree or higher: 6.4% (2006-2010 5-year est.).

### School District(s)

Newfane Central School District (PK-12)
2009-10 Enrollment: 1,911 . . . . . . . . . . . . . . . . . . . . . (716) 778-6850

**Housing:** Homeownership rate: 80.4% (2010); Median home value: $83,700 (2006-2010 5-year est.); Median contract rent: $462 per month (2006-2010 5-year est.); Median year structure built: 1953 (2006-2010 5-year est.).

**Hospitals:** Inter-Community Memorial Hospital (71 beds)

**Transportation:** Commute to work: 99.3% car, 0.0% public transportation, 0.7% walk, 0.0% work from home (2006-2010 5-year est.); Travel time to work: 32.7% less than 15 minutes, 38.2% 15 to 30 minutes, 16.9% 30 to 45 minutes, 12.2% 45 to 60 minutes, 0.0% 60 minutes or more (2006-2010 5-year est.)

**NIAGARA** (town). Covers a land area of 9.483 square miles and a water area of 0 square miles. Located at 43.11° N. Lat; 78.98° W. Long.

**Population:** 9,880 (1990); 8,978 (2000); 8,378 (2010); Density: 883.4 persons per square mile (2010); Race: 91.8% White, 3.4% Black, 0.9% Asian, 1.9% American Indian/Alaska Native, 0.0% Native Hawaiian/Other Pacific Islander, 2.0% Other, 1.7% Hispanic of any race (2010); Average household size: 2.32 (2010); Median age: 43.4 (2010); Males per 100

females: 92.1 (2010); Marriage status: 29.2% never married, 53.2% now married, 6.9% widowed, 10.6% divorced (2006-2010 5-year est.); Foreign born: 8.6% (2006-2010 5-year est.); Ancestry (includes multiple ancestries): 23.8% Italian, 20.1% German, 12.7% Irish, 11.2% Polish, 8.6% English (2006-2010 5-year est.).

**Economy:** Single-family building permits issued: 0 (2011); Multi-family building permits issued: 0 (2011); Employment by occupation: 10.8% management, 2.9% professional, 11.2% services, 26.4% sales, 3.5% farming, 8.0% construction, 6.8% production (2006-2010 5-year est.).

**Income:** Per capita income: $23,156 (2006-2010 5-year est.); Median household income: $40,761 (2006-2010 5-year est.); Average household income: $52,395 (2006-2010 5-year est.); Percent of households with income of $100,000 or more: 11.0% (2006-2010 5-year est.); Poverty rate: 12.4% (2006-2010 5-year est.).

**Education:** Percent of population age 25 and over with: High school diploma (including GED) or higher: 87.1% (2006-2010 5-year est.); Bachelor's degree or higher: 10.3% (2006-2010 5-year est.); Master's degree or higher: 2.7% (2006-2010 5-year est.).

**Housing:** Homeownership rate: 76.2% (2010); Median home value: $85,500 (2006-2010 5-year est.); Median contract rent: $444 per month (2006-2010 5-year est.); Median year structure built: 1968 (2006-2010 5-year est.).

**Transportation:** Commute to work: 94.7% car, 0.8% public transportation, 2.8% walk, 1.4% work from home (2006-2010 5-year est.); Travel time to work: 42.2% less than 15 minutes, 34.9% 15 to 30 minutes, 17.0% 30 to 45 minutes, 4.8% 45 to 60 minutes, 1.2% 60 minutes or more (2006-2010 5-year est.).

**Additional Information Contacts**
Town of Niagara . . . . . . . . . . . . . . . . . . . . . . . . . . . . . . . . (716) 297-2150
  http://www.townofniagara.com

## NIAGARA FALLS (city). Covers a land area of 14.085 square miles and a water area of 2.741 square miles. Located at 43.09° N. Lat; 79.01° W. Long. Elevation is 614 feet.

**History:** Named for the Iroquois Indian translation of "at the neck". The first published view of Niagara Falls, reproduced in a volume in 1697, was a sketch made by Father Louis Hennepin, who visited the falls in 1678. In 1745 and 1750 the French built two forts near the falls to supplement Fort Niagara at the mouth of the river and to guard the upper end of the portage. Before the approach of the British in 1759, Chabert Joncaire, French master of the portage, burned the forts and retreated across the river. Under British occupation, Fort Schlosser was erected. Augustus Porter purchased the land immediately surrounding the falls in 1805 or 1806, and became master of the portage. Visioning a manufacturing center that would rival the English city, Porter named the settlement Manchester. The settlement and fort were burned in the War of 1812. The Niagara water power turned the first generator in 1881, and the falls continued to be a source of power for the surrounding area. The falls have been a tourist attraction since at least the early 19th century.

**Population:** 61,840 (1990); 55,593 (2000); 50,193 (2010); Density: 3,563.3 persons per square mile (2010); Race: 70.5% White, 21.6% Black, 1.2% Asian, 1.9% American Indian/Alaska Native, 0.0% Native Hawaiian/Other Pacific Islander, 4.8% Other, 3.0% Hispanic of any race (2010); Average household size: 2.20 (2010); Median age: 39.8 (2010); Males per 100 females: 91.2 (2010); Marriage status: 37.7% never married, 40.4% now married, 8.4% widowed, 13.4% divorced (2006-2010 5-year est.); Foreign born: 4.4% (2006-2010 5-year est.); Ancestry (includes multiple ancestries): 22.6% Italian, 17.0% German, 13.8% Irish, 11.9% English, 9.8% Polish (2006-2010 5-year est.).

**Economy:** Unemployment rate: 12.6% (February 2012); Total civilian labor force: 22,946 (February 2012); Single-family building permits issued: 8 (2011); Multi-family building permits issued: 52 (2011); Employment by occupation: 7.7% management, 2.4% professional, 16.7% services, 20.3% sales, 4.8% farming, 7.1% construction, 7.2% production (2006-2010 5-year est.).

**Income:** Per capita income: $19,720 (2006-2010 5-year est.); Median household income: $31,452 (2006-2010 5-year est.); Average household income: $43,578 (2006-2010 5-year est.); Percent of households with income of $100,000 or more: 7.7% (2006-2010 5-year est.); Poverty rate: 21.8% (2006-2010 5-year est.).

**Taxes:** Total city taxes per capita: $711 (2009); City property taxes per capita: $522 (2009).

**Education:** Percent of population age 25 and over with: High school diploma (including GED) or higher: 84.5% (2006-2010 5-year est.);

Bachelor's degree or higher: 12.9% (2006-2010 5-year est.); Master's degree or higher: 5.7% (2006-2010 5-year est.).

### School District(s)
Niagara Charter School (KG-06)
  2009-10 Enrollment: 350 . . . . . . . . . . . . . . . . . . . . . . (716) 297-4520
Niagara Falls City School District (PK-12)
  2009-10 Enrollment: 7,263 . . . . . . . . . . . . . . . . . . . . (716) 286-4205
Niagara-Wheatfield Central School District (PK-12)
  2009-10 Enrollment: 4,050 . . . . . . . . . . . . . . . . . . . . (716) 215-3003

### Vocational/Technical School(s)
Cheryl Fells School of Business (Private, For-profit)
  Fall 2010 Enrollment: 85 . . . . . . . . . . . . . . . . . . . . . . (716) 297-2750
  2011-12 Tuition: $12,600

**Housing:** Homeownership rate: 55.1% (2010); Median home value: $65,400 (2006-2010 5-year est.); Median contract rent: $427 per month (2006-2010 5-year est.); Median year structure built: 1941 (2006-2010 5-year est.).

**Hospitals:** Niagara Falls Memorial Medical Center

**Safety:** Violent crime rate: 121.2 per 10,000 population; Property crime rate: 581.1 per 10,000 population (2010).

**Newspapers:** Buffalo News - Niagara Falls Bureau (Local news); Niagara Gazette (Local news; Circulation 26,200)

**Transportation:** Commute to work: 88.0% car, 2.8% public transportation, 5.7% walk, 0.8% work from home (2006-2010 5-year est.); Travel time to work: 51.3% less than 15 minutes, 33.0% 15 to 30 minutes, 11.5% 30 to 45 minutes, 2.8% 45 to 60 minutes, 1.3% 60 minutes or more (2006-2010 5-year est.); Amtrak: train service available.

**Airports:** Niagara Falls International (general aviation)

**Additional Information Contacts**
City of Niagara Falls . . . . . . . . . . . . . . . . . . . . . . . . . . . (716) 286-4393
  http://www.niagarafallsusa.org
Niagara USA Chamber . . . . . . . . . . . . . . . . . . . . . . . . . (716) 285-9141
  http://www.niagarachamber.org

## NIAGARA UNIVERSITY (unincorporated postal area)
Zip Code: 14109
  Covers a land area of 0.473 square miles and a water area of 0 square miles. Located at 43.13° N. Lat; 79.03° W. Long. Population: 1,117 (2010); Density: 2,358.7 persons per square mile (2010); Race: 87.9% White, 6.6% Black, 1.2% Asian, 0.3% American Indian/Alaska Native, 0.0% Native Hawaiian/Other Pacific Islander, 4.0% Other, 3.8% Hispanic of any race (2010); Average household size: 5.00 (2010); Median age: 19.7 (2010); Males per 100 females: 76.2 (2010); Homeownership rate: 100.0% (2010)

## NORTH TONAWANDA (city). Covers a land area of 10.100 square miles and a water area of 0.802 square miles. Located at 43.04° N. Lat; 78.87° W. Long. Elevation is 574 feet.

**History:** Named for its location north of Tonawanda. Settled c.1802. Incorporated as a city 1897.

**Population:** 34,989 (1990); 33,262 (2000); 31,568 (2010); Density: 3,125.4 persons per square mile (2010); Race: 96.5% White, 0.8% Black, 0.7% Asian, 0.4% American Indian/Alaska Native, 0.0% Native Hawaiian/Other Pacific Islander, 1.6% Other, 1.7% Hispanic of any race (2010); Average household size: 2.24 (2010); Median age: 42.4 (2010); Males per 100 females: 95.3 (2010); Marriage status: 27.4% never married, 53.6% now married, 7.1% widowed, 11.8% divorced (2006-2010 5-year est.); Foreign born: 3.8% (2006-2010 5-year est.); Ancestry (includes multiple ancestries): 35.0% German, 20.5% Polish, 17.9% Irish, 17.4% Italian, 10.3% English (2006-2010 5-year est.).

**Economy:** Unemployment rate: 8.4% (February 2012); Total civilian labor force: 17,155 (February 2012); Single-family building permits issued: 13 (2011); Multi-family building permits issued: 0 (2011); Employment by occupation: 7.4% management, 3.8% professional, 8.4% services, 20.2% sales, 5.3% farming, 7.2% construction, 6.8% production (2006-2010 5-year est.).

**Income:** Per capita income: $24,957 (2006-2010 5-year est.); Median household income: $45,278 (2006-2010 5-year est.); Average household income: $55,819 (2006-2010 5-year est.); Percent of households with income of $100,000 or more: 12.8% (2006-2010 5-year est.); Poverty rate: 9.2% (2006-2010 5-year est.).

**Education:** Percent of population age 25 and over with: High school diploma (including GED) or higher: 89.6% (2006-2010 5-year est.); Bachelor's degree or higher: 20.0% (2006-2010 5-year est.); Master's degree or higher: 8.5% (2006-2010 5-year est.).

**School District(s)**
Niagara-Wheatfield Central School District (PK-12)
2009-10 Enrollment: 4,050 . . . . . . . . . . . . . . . . . (716) 215-3003
North Tonawanda City School District (PK-12)
2009-10 Enrollment: 4,041 . . . . . . . . . . . . . . . . . (716) 807-3500
**Housing:** Homeownership rate: 66.8% (2010); Median home value: $95,000 (2006-2010 5-year est.); Median contract rent: $494 per month (2006-2010 5-year est.); Median year structure built: 1952 (2006-2010 5-year est.).
**Hospitals:** DeGraff Memorial Hospital (70 beds)
**Safety:** Violent crime rate: 17.7 per 10,000 population; Property crime rate: 190.7 per 10,000 population (2010).
**Newspapers:** Grand Island Record (Local news; Circulation 8,000); Kenmore Record-Advertiser (Local news; Circulation 31,300); Tonawanda News (Local news; Circulation 10,696); Tonawanda News Extra (Community news; Circulation 13,500)
**Transportation:** Commute to work: 94.7% car, 1.1% public transportation, 1.6% walk, 1.8% work from home (2006-2010 5-year est.); Travel time to work: 30.6% less than 15 minutes, 46.0% 15 to 30 minutes, 18.6% 30 to 45 minutes, 2.8% 45 to 60 minutes, 1.9% 60 minutes or more (2006-2010 5-year est.)
**Additional Information Contacts**
Chamber of Commerce of the Tonawandas . . . . . . . . . . . (716) 692-5120
http://www.the-tonawandas.com
City of North Tonawanda . . . . . . . . . . . . . . . . . . (716) 695-8555
http://www.northtonawanda.org

**OLCOTT** (CDP). Covers a land area of 4.546 square miles and a water area of 0.744 square miles. Located at 43.33° N. Lat; 78.70° W. Long. Elevation is 272 feet.
**Population:** 1,432 (1990); 1,156 (2000); 1,241 (2010); Density: 272.9 persons per square mile (2010); Race: 96.9% White, 0.4% Black, 0.3% Asian, 0.3% American Indian/Alaska Native, 0.0% Native Hawaiian/Other Pacific Islander, 2.1% Other, 2.3% Hispanic of any race (2010); Average household size: 2.27 (2010); Median age: 45.8 (2010); Males per 100 females: 100.2 (2010); Marriage status: 18.1% never married, 73.9% now married, 4.3% widowed, 3.7% divorced (2006-2010 5-year est.); Foreign born: 0.0% (2006-2010 5-year est.); Ancestry (includes multiple ancestries): 39.1% German, 34.1% English, 28.6% Irish, 10.1% Italian, 7.0% Scotch-Irish (2006-2010 5-year est.).
**Economy:** Employment by occupation: 8.7% management, 3.2% professional, 10.7% services, 21.8% sales, 0.0% farming, 2.4% construction, 2.3% production (2006-2010 5-year est.).
**Income:** Per capita income: $26,678 (2006-2010 5-year est.); Median household income: $49,792 (2006-2010 5-year est.); Average household income: $71,156 (2006-2010 5-year est.); Percent of households with income of $100,000 or more: 17.2% (2006-2010 5-year est.); Poverty rate: 4.5% (2006-2010 5-year est.).
**Education:** Percent of population age 25 and over with: High school diploma (including GED) or higher: 97.6% (2006-2010 5-year est.); Bachelor's degree or higher: 25.8% (2006-2010 5-year est.); Master's degree or higher: 9.0% (2006-2010 5-year est.).
**Housing:** Homeownership rate: 77.6% (2010); Median home value: $128,800 (2006-2010 5-year est.); Median contract rent: $600 per month (2006-2010 5-year est.); Median year structure built: 1951 (2006-2010 5-year est.).
**Transportation:** Commute to work: 91.1% car, 0.0% public transportation, 0.0% walk, 8.9% work from home (2006-2010 5-year est.); Travel time to work: 29.4% less than 15 minutes, 46.2% 15 to 30 minutes, 16.4% 30 to 45 minutes, 8.1% 45 to 60 minutes, 0.0% 60 minutes or more (2006-2010 5-year est.)

**PENDLETON** (town). Covers a land area of 27.086 square miles and a water area of 0.270 square miles. Located at 43.10° N. Lat; 78.76° W. Long. Elevation is 581 feet.
**Population:** 5,010 (1990); 6,050 (2000); 6,397 (2010); Density: 236.2 persons per square mile (2010); Race: 97.6% White, 0.6% Black, 0.6% Asian, 0.2% American Indian/Alaska Native, 0.0% Native Hawaiian/Other Pacific Islander, 1.0% Other, 0.9% Hispanic of any race (2010); Average household size: 2.72 (2010); Median age: 44.5 (2010); Males per 100 females: 98.7 (2010); Marriage status: 27.6% never married, 61.8% now married, 6.3% widowed, 4.3% divorced (2006-2010 5-year est.); Foreign born: 2.7% (2006-2010 5-year est.); Ancestry (includes multiple ancestries): 36.9% German, 20.9% Irish, 17.5% Polish, 17.1% Italian, 13.7% English (2006-2010 5-year est.).

**Economy:** Single-family building permits issued: 16 (2011); Multi-family building permits issued: 0 (2011); Employment by occupation: 11.5% management, 4.2% professional, 8.9% services, 13.9% sales, 2.5% farming, 10.9% construction, 9.8% production (2006-2010 5-year est.).
**Income:** Per capita income: $32,819 (2006-2010 5-year est.); Median household income: $81,446 (2006-2010 5-year est.); Average household income: $94,812 (2006-2010 5-year est.); Percent of households with income of $100,000 or more: 37.4% (2006-2010 5-year est.); Poverty rate: 4.1% (2006-2010 5-year est.).
**Education:** Percent of population age 25 and over with: High school diploma (including GED) or higher: 95.4% (2006-2010 5-year est.); Bachelor's degree or higher: 32.0% (2006-2010 5-year est.); Master's degree or higher: 14.6% (2006-2010 5-year est.).
**Housing:** Homeownership rate: 91.9% (2010); Median home value: $152,100 (2006-2010 5-year est.); Median contract rent: $347 per month (2006-2010 5-year est.); Median year structure built: 1971 (2006-2010 5-year est.).
**Transportation:** Commute to work: 96.5% car, 0.0% public transportation, 0.5% walk, 2.6% work from home (2006-2010 5-year est.); Travel time to work: 22.1% less than 15 minutes, 43.5% 15 to 30 minutes, 27.1% 30 to 45 minutes, 4.0% 45 to 60 minutes, 3.3% 60 minutes or more (2006-2010 5-year est.)

**PORTER** (town). Covers a land area of 33.054 square miles and a water area of 4.658 square miles. Located at 43.25° N. Lat; 78.97° W. Long.
**Population:** 7,110 (1990); 6,920 (2000); 6,771 (2010); Density: 204.8 persons per square mile (2010); Race: 96.9% White, 0.4% Black, 0.5% Asian, 0.6% American Indian/Alaska Native, 0.0% Native Hawaiian/Other Pacific Islander, 1.6% Other, 1.7% Hispanic of any race (2010); Average household size: 2.43 (2010); Median age: 45.9 (2010); Males per 100 females: 100.3 (2010); Marriage status: 23.7% never married, 61.3% now married, 6.8% widowed, 8.1% divorced (2006-2010 5-year est.); Foreign born: 6.1% (2006-2010 5-year est.); Ancestry (includes multiple ancestries): 29.5% German, 21.2% Italian, 21.2% Irish, 14.0% English, 11.6% Polish (2006-2010 5-year est.).
**Economy:** Single-family building permits issued: 0 (2011); Multi-family building permits issued: 0 (2011); Employment by occupation: 13.7% management, 3.1% professional, 9.8% services, 16.9% sales, 1.3% farming, 15.7% construction, 4.6% production (2006-2010 5-year est.).
**Income:** Per capita income: $30,329 (2006-2010 5-year est.); Median household income: $60,387 (2006-2010 5-year est.); Average household income: $75,814 (2006-2010 5-year est.); Percent of households with income of $100,000 or more: 21.6% (2006-2010 5-year est.); Poverty rate: 7.1% (2006-2010 5-year est.).
**Education:** Percent of population age 25 and over with: High school diploma (including GED) or higher: 88.6% (2006-2010 5-year est.); Bachelor's degree or higher: 25.8% (2006-2010 5-year est.); Master's degree or higher: 13.7% (2006-2010 5-year est.).
**Housing:** Homeownership rate: 80.1% (2010); Median home value: $127,700 (2006-2010 5-year est.); Median contract rent: $568 per month (2006-2010 5-year est.); Median year structure built: 1954 (2006-2010 5-year est.).
**Transportation:** Commute to work: 96.6% car, 0.0% public transportation, 0.2% walk, 3.0% work from home (2006-2010 5-year est.); Travel time to work: 22.8% less than 15 minutes, 44.7% 15 to 30 minutes, 22.0% 30 to 45 minutes, 7.2% 45 to 60 minutes, 3.3% 60 minutes or more (2006-2010 5-year est.)

**RANSOMVILLE** (CDP). Covers a land area of 6.242 square miles and a water area of 0 square miles. Located at 43.23° N. Lat; 78.91° W. Long. Elevation is 325 feet.
**Population:** 1,542 (1990); 1,488 (2000); 1,419 (2010); Density: 227.3 persons per square mile (2010); Race: 96.1% White, 1.1% Black, 0.2% Asian, 0.8% American Indian/Alaska Native, 0.0% Native Hawaiian/Other Pacific Islander, 1.8% Other, 1.8% Hispanic of any race (2010); Average household size: 2.47 (2010); Median age: 42.2 (2010); Males per 100 females: 103.3 (2010); Marriage status: 25.3% never married, 60.0% now married, 5.6% widowed, 9.1% divorced (2006-2010 5-year est.); Foreign born: 6.4% (2006-2010 5-year est.); Ancestry (includes multiple ancestries): 28.5% German, 18.5% English, 16.4% Italian, 15.6% Irish, 12.5% Polish (2006-2010 5-year est.).
**Economy:** Employment by occupation: 6.5% management, 6.1% professional, 16.9% services, 11.2% sales, 2.3% farming, 19.8% construction, 5.2% production (2006-2010 5-year est.).

**Income:** Per capita income: $20,114 (2006-2010 5-year est.); Median household income: $50,323 (2006-2010 5-year est.); Average household income: $57,508 (2006-2010 5-year est.); Percent of households with income of $100,000 or more: 19.5% (2006-2010 5-year est.); Poverty rate: 15.3% (2006-2010 5-year est.).

**Education:** Percent of population age 25 and over with: High school diploma (including GED) or higher: 79.6% (2006-2010 5-year est.); Bachelor's degree or higher: 5.2% (2006-2010 5-year est.); Master's degree or higher: 3.1% (2006-2010 5-year est.).

### School District(s)

Wilson Central School District (PK-12)

   2009-10 Enrollment: 1,418 . . . . . . . . . . . . . . . . . . . . . . (716) 751-9341

**Housing:** Homeownership rate: 70.4% (2010); Median home value: $117,000 (2006-2010 5-year est.); Median contract rent: $542 per month (2006-2010 5-year est.); Median year structure built: 1951 (2006-2010 5-year est.).

**Transportation:** Commute to work: 99.1% car, 0.0% public transportation, 0.0% walk, 0.0% work from home (2006-2010 5-year est.); Travel time to work: 16.9% less than 15 minutes, 47.3% 15 to 30 minutes, 32.6% 30 to 45 minutes, 3.2% 45 to 60 minutes, 0.0% 60 minutes or more (2006-2010 5-year est.)

**RAPIDS** (CDP). Covers a land area of 3.643 square miles and a water area of 0 square miles. Located at 43.09° N. Lat; 78.64° W. Long. Elevation is 591 feet.

**Population:** 1,152 (1990); 1,356 (2000); 1,636 (2010); Density: 449.0 persons per square mile (2010); Race: 95.5% White, 1.7% Black, 1.1% Asian, 0.1% American Indian/Alaska Native, 0.3% Native Hawaiian/Other Pacific Islander, 1.3% Other, 1.2% Hispanic of any race (2010); Average household size: 2.64 (2010); Median age: 37.1 (2010); Males per 100 females: 99.3 (2010); Marriage status: 31.5% never married, 53.9% now married, 4.5% widowed, 10.1% divorced (2006-2010 5-year est.); Foreign born: 1.7% (2006-2010 5-year est.); Ancestry (includes multiple ancestries): 44.6% German, 12.0% Polish, 11.4% Italian, 8.3% Irish, 8.0% French (2006-2010 5-year est.).

**Economy:** Employment by occupation: 11.6% management, 7.7% professional, 16.0% services, 11.0% sales, 1.6% farming, 4.5% construction, 6.2% production (2006-2010 5-year est.).

**Income:** Per capita income: $32,523 (2006-2010 5-year est.); Median household income: $70,969 (2006-2010 5-year est.); Average household income: $77,167 (2006-2010 5-year est.); Percent of households with income of $100,000 or more: 30.8% (2006-2010 5-year est.); Poverty rate: 13.7% (2006-2010 5-year est.).

**Education:** Percent of population age 25 and over with: High school diploma (including GED) or higher: 90.5% (2006-2010 5-year est.); Bachelor's degree or higher: 38.4% (2006-2010 5-year est.); Master's degree or higher: 12.8% (2006-2010 5-year est.).

**Housing:** Homeownership rate: 90.7% (2010); Median home value: $125,300 (2006-2010 5-year est.); Median contract rent: $775 per month (2006-2010 5-year est.); Median year structure built: 1989 (2006-2010 5-year est.).

**Transportation:** Commute to work: 94.0% car, 0.0% public transportation, 2.7% walk, 3.3% work from home (2006-2010 5-year est.); Travel time to work: 14.0% less than 15 minutes, 39.2% 15 to 30 minutes, 37.3% 30 to 45 minutes, 1.7% 45 to 60 minutes, 7.8% 60 minutes or more (2006-2010 5-year est.)

**ROYALTON** (town). Aka Royalton Center. Covers a land area of 69.965 square miles and a water area of 0.310 square miles. Located at 43.15° N. Lat; 78.55° W. Long.

**Population:** 7,453 (1990); 7,710 (2000); 7,660 (2010); Density: 109.5 persons per square mile (2010); Race: 96.4% White, 0.7% Black, 0.3% Asian, 0.7% American Indian/Alaska Native, 0.0% Native Hawaiian/Other Pacific Islander, 1.9% Other, 1.2% Hispanic of any race (2010); Average household size: 2.57 (2010); Median age: 42.1 (2010); Males per 100 females: 96.6 (2010); Marriage status: 25.4% never married, 60.7% now married, 6.8% widowed, 7.2% divorced (2006-2010 5-year est.); Foreign born: 1.2% (2006-2010 5-year est.); Ancestry (includes multiple ancestries): 34.8% German, 23.2% Irish, 19.4% English, 12.1% Italian, 8.9% Polish (2006-2010 5-year est.).

**Economy:** Single-family building permits issued: 7 (2011); Multi-family building permits issued: 0 (2011); Employment by occupation: 13.2% management, 0.3% professional, 8.8% services, 17.9% sales, 4.5% farming, 9.8% construction, 8.3% production (2006-2010 5-year est.).

**Income:** Per capita income: $24,274 (2006-2010 5-year est.); Median household income: $51,105 (2006-2010 5-year est.); Average household income: $64,932 (2006-2010 5-year est.); Percent of households with income of $100,000 or more: 17.4% (2006-2010 5-year est.); Poverty rate: 8.0% (2006-2010 5-year est.).

**Education:** Percent of population age 25 and over with: High school diploma (including GED) or higher: 89.4% (2006-2010 5-year est.); Bachelor's degree or higher: 16.6% (2006-2010 5-year est.); Master's degree or higher: 7.9% (2006-2010 5-year est.).

**Housing:** Homeownership rate: 81.7% (2010); Median home value: $115,900 (2006-2010 5-year est.); Median contract rent: $478 per month (2006-2010 5-year est.); Median year structure built: 1947 (2006-2010 5-year est.).

**Transportation:** Commute to work: 92.4% car, 0.6% public transportation, 0.5% walk, 5.2% work from home (2006-2010 5-year est.); Travel time to work: 27.5% less than 15 minutes, 33.4% 15 to 30 minutes, 28.5% 30 to 45 minutes, 5.5% 45 to 60 minutes, 5.1% 60 minutes or more (2006-2010 5-year est.).

**SANBORN** (CDP). Covers a land area of 2.633 square miles and a water area of 0 square miles. Located at 43.14° N. Lat; 78.87° W. Long. Elevation is 633 feet.

**Population:** n/a (1990); n/a (2000); 1,645 (2010); Density: 624.7 persons per square mile (2010); Race: 91.7% White, 4.4% Black, 0.3% Asian, 1.6% American Indian/Alaska Native, 0.0% Native Hawaiian/Other Pacific Islander, 2.0% Other, 1.6% Hispanic of any race (2010); Average household size: 2.37 (2010); Median age: 33.2 (2010); Males per 100 females: 92.6 (2010); Marriage status: 33.0% never married, 47.2% now married, 10.7% widowed, 9.0% divorced (2006-2010 5-year est.); Foreign born: 5.0% (2006-2010 5-year est.); Ancestry (includes multiple ancestries): 37.0% German, 14.2% Irish, 10.7% English, 7.2% Italian, 6.9% French (2006-2010 5-year est.).

**Economy:** Employment by occupation: 6.1% management, 0.0% professional, 10.8% services, 30.5% sales, 5.4% farming, 13.4% construction, 5.4% production (2006-2010 5-year est.).

**Income:** Per capita income: $26,778 (2006-2010 5-year est.); Median household income: $41,857 (2006-2010 5-year est.); Average household income: $60,812 (2006-2010 5-year est.); Percent of households with income of $100,000 or more: 21.3% (2006-2010 5-year est.); Poverty rate: 8.5% (2006-2010 5-year est.).

**Education:** Percent of population age 25 and over with: High school diploma (including GED) or higher: 86.6% (2006-2010 5-year est.); Bachelor's degree or higher: 10.2% (2006-2010 5-year est.); Master's degree or higher: 3.3% (2006-2010 5-year est.).

### School District(s)

Niagara-Wheatfield Central School District (PK-12)

   2009-10 Enrollment: 4,050 . . . . . . . . . . . . . . . . . . (716) 215-3003

### Two-year College(s)

Niagara County Community College (Public)

   Fall 2010 Enrollment: 5,269 . . . . . . . . . . . . . . . . . . (716) 614-6222

   2011-12 Tuition: In-state $3,958; Out-of-state $7,582

### Vocational/Technical School(s)

Orleans Niagara BOCES-Practical Nursing Program (Public)

   Fall 2010 Enrollment: 48 . . . . . . . . . . . . . . . . . . . (8.0) 083-7E+1

   2011-12 Tuition: $9,900

**Housing:** Homeownership rate: 67.2% (2010); Median home value: $99,300 (2006-2010 5-year est.); Median contract rent: $624 per month (2006-2010 5-year est.); Median year structure built: 1961 (2006-2010 5-year est.).

**Transportation:** Commute to work: 100.0% car, 0.0% public transportation, 0.0% walk, 0.0% work from home (2006-2010 5-year est.); Travel time to work: 27.2% less than 15 minutes, 49.0% 15 to 30 minutes, 22.1% 30 to 45 minutes, 1.7% 45 to 60 minutes, 0.0% 60 minutes or more (2006-2010 5-year est.)

**SOMERSET** (town). Covers a land area of 37.108 square miles and a water area of 0.063 square miles. Located at 43.33° N. Lat; 78.54° W. Long. Elevation is 305 feet.

**Population:** 2,655 (1990); 2,865 (2000); 2,662 (2010); Density: 71.7 persons per square mile (2010); Race: 97.1% White, 0.7% Black, 0.3% Asian, 0.6% American Indian/Alaska Native, 0.0% Native Hawaiian/Other Pacific Islander, 1.3% Other, 3.2% Hispanic of any race (2010); Average household size: 2.68 (2010); Median age: 41.5 (2010); Males per 100 females: 101.1 (2010); Marriage status: 21.6% never married, 65.3% now married, 6.5% widowed, 6.7% divorced (2006-2010 5-year est.); Foreign

born: 1.8% (2006-2010 5-year est.); Ancestry (includes multiple ancestries): 39.7% German, 26.2% English, 18.8% Irish, 12.7% Polish, 6.6% Italian (2006-2010 5-year est.).

**Economy:** Single-family building permits issued: 0 (2011); Multi-family building permits issued: 0 (2011); Employment by occupation: 10.4% management, 2.9% professional, 7.9% services, 13.7% sales, 3.1% farming, 12.0% construction, 15.1% production (2006-2010 5-year est.).

**Income:** Per capita income: $19,534 (2006-2010 5-year est.); Median household income: $47,868 (2006-2010 5-year est.); Average household income: $54,452 (2006-2010 5-year est.); Percent of households with income of $100,000 or more: 12.8% (2006-2010 5-year est.); Poverty rate: 16.1% (2006-2010 5-year est.).

**Education:** Percent of population age 25 and over with: High school diploma (including GED) or higher: 89.7% (2006-2010 5-year est.); Bachelor's degree or higher: 16.1% (2006-2010 5-year est.); Master's degree or higher: 4.7% (2006-2010 5-year est.).

**Housing:** Homeownership rate: 82.2% (2010); Median home value: $100,200 (2006-2010 5-year est.); Median contract rent: $440 per month (2006-2010 5-year est.); Median year structure built: 1950 (2006-2010 5-year est.).

**Transportation:** Commute to work: 93.8% car, 0.0% public transportation, 1.8% walk, 3.2% work from home (2006-2010 5-year est.); Travel time to work: 25.3% less than 15 minutes, 27.4% 15 to 30 minutes, 22.1% 30 to 45 minutes, 14.0% 45 to 60 minutes, 11.2% 60 minutes or more (2006-2010 5-year est.).

## SOUTH LOCKPORT (CDP).

Covers a land area of 5.713 square miles and a water area of 0.013 square miles. Located at 43.13° N. Lat; 78.68° W. Long. Elevation is 633 feet.

**Population:** 7,112 (1990); 8,552 (2000); 8,324 (2010); Density: 1,456.8 persons per square mile (2010); Race: 89.0% White, 5.3% Black, 1.1% Asian, 0.5% American Indian/Alaska Native, 0.0% Native Hawaiian/Other Pacific Islander, 4.1% Other, 4.1% Hispanic of any race (2010); Average household size: 2.27 (2010); Median age: 39.4 (2010); Males per 100 females: 90.7 (2010); Marriage status: 27.7% never married, 55.2% now married, 7.2% widowed, 9.8% divorced (2006-2010 5-year est.); Foreign born: 3.3% (2006-2010 5-year est.); Ancestry (includes multiple ancestries): 39.7% German, 23.7% Irish, 16.5% English, 14.9% Italian, 10.2% Polish (2006-2010 5-year est.).

**Economy:** Employment by occupation: 6.4% management, 4.1% professional, 8.2% services, 21.8% sales, 6.4% farming, 8.6% construction, 4.9% production (2006-2010 5-year est.).

**Income:** Per capita income: $22,698 (2006-2010 5-year est.); Median household income: $44,419 (2006-2010 5-year est.); Average household income: $54,888 (2006-2010 5-year est.); Percent of households with income of $100,000 or more: 10.7% (2006-2010 5-year est.); Poverty rate: 13.5% (2006-2010 5-year est.).

**Education:** Percent of population age 25 and over with: High school diploma (including GED) or higher: 87.1% (2006-2010 5-year est.); Bachelor's degree or higher: 20.6% (2006-2010 5-year est.); Master's degree or higher: 8.9% (2006-2010 5-year est.).

**Housing:** Homeownership rate: 67.8% (2010); Median home value: $69,700 (2006-2010 5-year est.); Median contract rent: $433 per month (2006-2010 5-year est.); Median year structure built: 1982 (2006-2010 5-year est.).

**Transportation:** Commute to work: 93.0% car, 0.0% public transportation, 2.0% walk, 3.8% work from home (2006-2010 5-year est.); Travel time to work: 31.9% less than 15 minutes, 36.2% 15 to 30 minutes, 25.5% 30 to 45 minutes, 4.8% 45 to 60 minutes, 1.6% 60 minutes or more (2006-2010 5-year est.).

## TUSCARORA RESERVATION (Reservation).

Covers a land area of 9.082 square miles and a water area of 0 square miles. Located at 43.16° N. Lat; 78.95° W. Long.

**Population:** 725 (1990); 1,138 (2000); 1,152 (2010); Density: 126.8 persons per square mile (2010); Race: 62.5% White, 1.2% Black, 1.0% Asian, 27.4% American Indian/Alaska Native, 0.0% Native Hawaiian/Other Pacific Islander, 7.9% Other, 3.6% Hispanic of any race (2010); Average household size: 2.53 (2010); Median age: 33.0 (2010); Males per 100 females: 100.0 (2010); Marriage status: 32.4% never married, 49.3% now married, 9.5% widowed, 8.8% divorced (2006-2010 5-year est.); Foreign born: 5.2% (2006-2010 5-year est.); Ancestry (includes multiple ancestries): 6.2% German, 5.2% Italian, 2.7% Belgian, 1.7% Polish, 0.9% American (2006-2010 5-year est.).

**Economy:** Employment by occupation: 11.3% management, 0.0% professional, 12.3% services, 22.0% sales, 12.3% farming, 16.4% construction, 2.8% production (2006-2010 5-year est.).

**Income:** Per capita income: $15,407 (2006-2010 5-year est.); Median household income: $45,489 (2006-2010 5-year est.); Average household income: $46,710 (2006-2010 5-year est.); Percent of households with income of $100,000 or more: 5.2% (2006-2010 5-year est.); Poverty rate: 17.9% (2006-2010 5-year est.).

**Education:** Percent of population age 25 and over with: High school diploma (including GED) or higher: 85.1% (2006-2010 5-year est.); Bachelor's degree or higher: 13.1% (2006-2010 5-year est.); Master's degree or higher: 6.0% (2006-2010 5-year est.).

**Housing:** Homeownership rate: 79.3% (2010); Median home value: $75,300 (2006-2010 5-year est.); Median contract rent: $135 per month (2006-2010 5-year est.); Median year structure built: 1974 (2006-2010 5-year est.).

**Transportation:** Commute to work: 86.8% car, 5.3% public transportation, 0.0% walk, 2.5% work from home (2006-2010 5-year est.); Travel time to work: 48.4% less than 15 minutes, 31.9% 15 to 30 minutes, 11.0% 30 to 45 minutes, 0.0% 45 to 60 minutes, 8.7% 60 minutes or more (2006-2010 5-year est.).

## WHEATFIELD (town).

Covers a land area of 27.911 square miles and a water area of 0.680 square miles. Located at 43.09° N. Lat; 78.88° W. Long.

**Population:** 11,125 (1990); 14,086 (2000); 18,117 (2010); Density: 649.1 persons per square mile (2010); Race: 94.7% White, 2.2% Black, 1.5% Asian, 0.6% American Indian/Alaska Native, 0.0% Native Hawaiian/Other Pacific Islander, 1.0% Other, 1.4% Hispanic of any race (2010); Average household size: 2.47 (2010); Median age: 44.2 (2010); Males per 100 females: 92.0 (2010); Marriage status: 23.1% never married, 61.1% now married, 9.0% widowed, 6.9% divorced (2006-2010 5-year est.); Foreign born: 5.6% (2006-2010 5-year est.); Ancestry (includes multiple ancestries): 28.4% German, 26.5% Italian, 17.8% Polish, 17.8% Irish, 9.9% English (2006-2010 5-year est.).

**Economy:** Single-family building permits issued: 40 (2011); Multi-family building permits issued: 4 (2011); Employment by occupation: 12.0% management, 4.8% professional, 6.8% services, 20.4% sales, 3.3% farming, 7.5% construction, 3.4% production (2006-2010 5-year est.).

**Income:** Per capita income: $28,328 (2006-2010 5-year est.); Median household income: $62,841 (2006-2010 5-year est.); Average household income: $72,594 (2006-2010 5-year est.); Percent of households with income of $100,000 or more: 25.0% (2006-2010 5-year est.); Poverty rate: 4.9% (2006-2010 5-year est.).

**Education:** Percent of population age 25 and over with: High school diploma (including GED) or higher: 91.6% (2006-2010 5-year est.); Bachelor's degree or higher: 28.9% (2006-2010 5-year est.); Master's degree or higher: 10.6% (2006-2010 5-year est.).

**Housing:** Homeownership rate: 75.4% (2010); Median home value: $158,600 (2006-2010 5-year est.); Median contract rent: $554 per month (2006-2010 5-year est.); Median year structure built: 1984 (2006-2010 5-year est.).

**Transportation:** Commute to work: 95.9% car, 0.2% public transportation, 1.2% walk, 2.5% work from home (2006-2010 5-year est.); Travel time to work: 24.1% less than 15 minutes, 49.8% 15 to 30 minutes, 19.0% 30 to 45 minutes, 3.8% 45 to 60 minutes, 3.4% 60 minutes or more (2006-2010 5-year est.).

**Additional Information Contacts**

Town of Wheatfield . . . . . . . . . . . . . . . . . . . . . . . . . . . . . . (716) 694-6440
   http://wheatfield.ny.us

## WILSON (village).

Covers a land area of 0.813 square miles and a water area of 0.190 square miles. Located at 43.31° N. Lat; 78.82° W. Long. Elevation is 279 feet.

**Population:** 1,307 (1990); 1,213 (2000); 1,264 (2010); Density: 1,554.6 persons per square mile (2010); Race: 97.0% White, 0.6% Black, 0.1% Asian, 0.9% American Indian/Alaska Native, 0.0% Native Hawaiian/Other Pacific Islander, 1.4% Other, 1.7% Hispanic of any race (2010); Average household size: 2.39 (2010); Median age: 43.4 (2010); Males per 100 females: 92.7 (2010); Marriage status: 15.6% never married, 60.6% now married, 8.8% widowed, 15.0% divorced (2006-2010 5-year est.); Foreign born: 1.0% (2006-2010 5-year est.); Ancestry (includes multiple ancestries): 41.4% German, 29.3% English, 14.8% Italian, 14.3% Irish, 8.5% Polish (2006-2010 5-year est.).

**Economy:** Single-family building permits issued: 4 (2011); Multi-family building permits issued: 0 (2011); Employment by occupation: 14.3% management, 0.5% professional, 5.7% services, 13.6% sales, 0.9% farming, 9.0% construction, 7.0% production (2006-2010 5-year est.).
**Income:** Per capita income: $31,454 (2006-2010 5-year est.); Median household income: $52,273 (2006-2010 5-year est.); Average household income: $76,914 (2006-2010 5-year est.); Percent of households with income of $100,000 or more: 18.9% (2006-2010 5-year est.); Poverty rate: 16.4% (2006-2010 5-year est.).
**Education:** Percent of population age 25 and over with: High school diploma (including GED) or higher: 94.8% (2006-2010 5-year est.); Bachelor's degree or higher: 26.8% (2006-2010 5-year est.); Master's degree or higher: 11.3% (2006-2010 5-year est.).

**School District(s)**
Wilson Central School District (PK-12)
   2009-10 Enrollment: 1,418 . . . . . . . . . . . . . . . . . . . (716) 751-9341
**Housing:** Homeownership rate: 70.3% (2010); Median home value: $98,500 (2006-2010 5-year est.); Median contract rent: $430 per month (2006-2010 5-year est.); Median year structure built: 1952 (2006-2010 5-year est.).
**Transportation:** Commute to work: 89.9% car, 0.0% public transportation, 0.8% walk, 6.0% work from home (2006-2010 5-year est.); Travel time to work: 24.7% less than 15 minutes, 25.1% 15 to 30 minutes, 29.3% 30 to 45 minutes, 14.8% 45 to 60 minutes, 6.1% 60 minutes or more (2006-2010 5-year est.)

**Additional Information Contacts**
Village of Wilson . . . . . . . . . . . . . . . . . . . . . . . . . . . (716) 751-6704
   http://www.wilsonnewyork.com

**WILSON** (town). Covers a land area of 49.404 square miles and a water area of 2.057 square miles. Located at 43.27° N. Lat; 78.81° W. Long. Elevation is 279 feet.
**History:** Incorporated 1858.
**Population:** 5,761 (1990); 5,840 (2000); 5,993 (2010); Density: 121.3 persons per square mile (2010); Race: 96.6% White, 0.6% Black, 0.3% Asian, 0.8% American Indian/Alaska Native, 0.1% Native Hawaiian/Other Pacific Islander, 1.6% Other, 1.4% Hispanic of any race (2010); Average household size: 2.49 (2010); Median age: 44.3 (2010); Males per 100 females: 99.1 (2010); Marriage status: 22.3% never married, 64.2% now married, 5.4% widowed, 8.2% divorced (2006-2010 5-year est.); Foreign born: 2.4% (2006-2010 5-year est.); Ancestry (includes multiple ancestries): 36.6% German, 21.3% English, 16.1% Irish, 12.0% Italian, 11.3% Polish (2006-2010 5-year est.).
**Economy:** Single-family building permits issued: 11 (2011); Multi-family building permits issued: 0 (2011); Employment by occupation: 10.9% management, 2.3% professional, 8.6% services, 18.9% sales, 4.5% farming, 9.1% construction, 6.6% production (2006-2010 5-year est.).
**Income:** Per capita income: $26,772 (2006-2010 5-year est.); Median household income: $55,159 (2006-2010 5-year est.); Average household income: $70,007 (2006-2010 5-year est.); Percent of households with income of $100,000 or more: 20.5% (2006-2010 5-year est.); Poverty rate: 10.8% (2006-2010 5-year est.).
**Education:** Percent of population age 25 and over with: High school diploma (including GED) or higher: 91.2% (2006-2010 5-year est.); Bachelor's degree or higher: 20.4% (2006-2010 5-year est.); Master's degree or higher: 7.2% (2006-2010 5-year est.).

**School District(s)**
Wilson Central School District (PK-12)
   2009-10 Enrollment: 1,418 . . . . . . . . . . . . . . . . . . . (716) 751-9341
**Housing:** Homeownership rate: 82.8% (2010); Median home value: $109,700 (2006-2010 5-year est.); Median contract rent: $465 per month (2006-2010 5-year est.); Median year structure built: 1964 (2006-2010 5-year est.).
**Transportation:** Commute to work: 95.3% car, 0.4% public transportation, 0.9% walk, 2.7% work from home (2006-2010 5-year est.); Travel time to work: 18.7% less than 15 minutes, 35.9% 15 to 30 minutes, 26.3% 30 to 45 minutes, 13.9% 45 to 60 minutes, 5.2% 60 minutes or more (2006-2010 5-year est.)

**Additional Information Contacts**
Town of Wilson . . . . . . . . . . . . . . . . . . . . . . . . . . . (716) 751-6704
   http://www.wilsonnewyork.com

**YOUNGSTOWN** (village). Covers a land area of 1.096 square miles and a water area of 0.265 square miles. Located at 43.24° N. Lat; 79.04° W. Long. Elevation is 295 feet.
**History:** Just North is Fort Niagara, which has been restored.
**Population:** 2,075 (1990); 1,957 (2000); 1,935 (2010); Density: 1,764.0 persons per square mile (2010); Race: 97.5% White, 0.4% Black, 0.3% Asian, 0.4% American Indian/Alaska Native, 0.0% Native Hawaiian/Other Pacific Islander, 1.4% Other, 1.7% Hispanic of any race (2010); Average household size: 2.42 (2010); Median age: 45.1 (2010); Males per 100 females: 96.2 (2010); Marriage status: 25.5% never married, 55.9% now married, 9.5% widowed, 9.1% divorced (2006-2010 5-year est.); Foreign born: 5.3% (2006-2010 5-year est.); Ancestry (includes multiple ancestries): 25.3% Irish, 23.5% German, 20.7% Italian, 15.7% English, 10.5% Polish (2006-2010 5-year est.).
**Economy:** Single-family building permits issued: 0 (2011); Multi-family building permits issued: 0 (2011); Employment by occupation: 15.1% management, 5.0% professional, 6.3% services, 27.5% sales, 0.5% farming, 6.1% construction, 3.0% production (2006-2010 5-year est.).
**Income:** Per capita income: $28,766 (2006-2010 5-year est.); Median household income: $59,615 (2006-2010 5-year est.); Average household income: $69,967 (2006-2010 5-year est.); Percent of households with income of $100,000 or more: 17.4% (2006-2010 5-year est.); Poverty rate: 5.9% (2006-2010 5-year est.).
**Education:** Percent of population age 25 and over with: High school diploma (including GED) or higher: 94.3% (2006-2010 5-year est.); Bachelor's degree or higher: 34.8% (2006-2010 5-year est.); Master's degree or higher: 15.2% (2006-2010 5-year est.).

**School District(s)**
Lewiston-Porter Central School District (PK-12)
   2009-10 Enrollment: 2,309 . . . . . . . . . . . . . . . . . . (716) 286-7241
**Housing:** Homeownership rate: 75.4% (2010); Median home value: $137,500 (2006-2010 5-year est.); Median contract rent: $516 per month (2006-2010 5-year est.); Median year structure built: 1957 (2006-2010 5-year est.).
**Safety:** Violent crime rate: 0.0 per 10,000 population; Property crime rate: 27.3 per 10,000 population (2010).
**Transportation:** Commute to work: 97.9% car, 0.0% public transportation, 0.8% walk, 1.3% work from home (2006-2010 5-year est.); Travel time to work: 30.0% less than 15 minutes, 38.7% 15 to 30 minutes, 18.5% 30 to 45 minutes, 8.8% 45 to 60 minutes, 4.0% 60 minutes or more (2006-2010 5-year est.)

# Oneida County

Located in central New York; bounded partly on the west by Oneida Lake, rising to the Adirondacks in the east and northeast; drained by the Mohawk and Black Rivers; includes several lakes. Covers a land area of 1,212.70 square miles, a water area of 44.41 square miles, and is located in the Eastern Time Zone at 43.18° N. Lat., 75.39° W. Long. The county was founded in 1798. County seat is Utica.

Oneida County is part of the Utica-Rome, NY Metropolitan Statistical Area. The entire metro area includes: Herkimer County, NY; Oneida County, NY

| Weather Station: Boonville 2 SSW | | | | | | | | | Elevation: 1,580 feet | | |
| --- | --- | --- | --- | --- | --- | --- | --- | --- | --- | --- | --- |
|  | Jan | Feb | Mar | Apr | May | Jun | Jul | Aug | Sep | Oct | Nov | Dec |
| High | 25 | 28 | 36 | 51 | 63 | 71 | 75 | 74 | 66 | 54 | 41 | 30 |
| Low | 8 | 10 | 19 | 32 | 43 | 52 | 57 | 55 | 48 | 37 | 27 | 15 |
| Precip | 5.0 | 4.0 | 4.5 | 4.5 | 4.5 | 4.7 | 4.4 | 4.7 | 5.5 | 5.6 | 5.4 | 5.5 |
| Snow | 52.9 | 39.8 | 31.4 | 8.6 | 0.2 | tr | 0.0 | 0.0 | tr | 2.2 | 17.8 | 44.7 |

*High and Low temperatures in degrees Fahrenheit; Precipitation and Snow in inches*

| Weather Station: Utica Oneida County Arpt | | | | | | | | | Elevation: 711 feet | | |
| --- | --- | --- | --- | --- | --- | --- | --- | --- | --- | --- | --- |
|  | Jan | Feb | Mar | Apr | May | Jun | Jul | Aug | Sep | Oct | Nov | Dec |
| High | 29 | 32 | 41 | 55 | 68 | 76 | 80 | 79 | 71 | 58 | 46 | 34 |
| Low | 14 | 16 | 24 | 36 | 46 | 55 | 60 | 58 | 51 | 40 | 31 | 20 |
| Precip | 2.9 | 2.4 | 3.2 | 3.5 | 3.9 | 4.3 | 3.9 | 3.9 | 4.1 | 3.7 | 3.9 | 3.4 |
| Snow | na | na | na | na | na | na | na | na | na | na | na | na |

*High and Low temperatures in degrees Fahrenheit; Precipitation and Snow in inches*

**Population:** 250,836 (1990); 235,469 (2000); 234,878 (2010); Race: 87.1% White, 6.3% Black, 2.8% Asian, 0.3% American Indian/Alaska Native, 0.0% Native Hawaiian/Other Pacific Islander, 3.5% Other, 4.6% Hispanic of any race (2010); Density: 193.7 persons per square mile (2010); Average household size: 2.38 (2010); Median age: 40.8 (2010); Males per 100 females: 99.3 (2010).

**Religion:** Six largest groups: 36.9% Catholicism, 3.6% Methodist/Pietist, 1.9% Non-Denominational, 1.6% Presbyterian-Reformed, 1.4% Baptist, 1.3% Lutheran (2010)

**Economy:** Unemployment rate: 9.1% (February 2012); Total civilian labor force: 107,879 (February 2012); Leading industries: 22.7% health care and social assistance; 13.3% retail trade; 12.0% accommodation & food services (2009); Farms: 1,013 totaling 192,232 acres (2007); Companies that employ 500 or more persons: 22 (2009); Companies that employ 100 to 499 persons: 99 (2009); Companies that employ less than 100 persons: 4,784 (2009); Black-owned businesses: 351 (2007); Hispanic-owned businesses: n/a (2007); Asian-owned businesses: 383 (2007); Women-owned businesses: 4,009 (2007); Retail sales per capita: $12,445 (2010). Single-family building permits issued: 155 (2011); Multi-family building permits issued: 18 (2011).

**Income:** Per capita income: $23,458 (2006-2010 5-year est.); Median household income: $46,708 (2006-2010 5-year est.); Average household income: $58,906 (2006-2010 5-year est.); Percent of households with income of $100,000 or more: 15.2% (2006-2010 5-year est.); Poverty rate: 14.9% (2006-2010 5-year est.); Bankruptcy rate: 2.79% (2011).

**Taxes:** Total county taxes per capita: $764 (2009); County property taxes per capita: $259 (2009).

**Education:** Percent of population age 25 and over with: High school diploma (including GED) or higher: 86.0% (2006-2010 5-year est.); Bachelor's degree or higher: 21.5% (2006-2010 5-year est.); Master's degree or higher: 8.6% (2006-2010 5-year est.).

**Housing:** Homeownership rate: 66.6% (2010); Median home value: $101,900 (2006-2010 5-year est.); Median contract rent: $483 per month (2006-2010 5-year est.); Median year structure built: 1953 (2006-2010 5-year est.)

**Health:** Birth rate: 109.4 per 10,000 population (2011); Death rate: 103.3 per 10,000 population (2011); Age-adjusted cancer mortality rate: 183.3 deaths per 100,000 population (2009); Number of physicians: 23.7 per 10,000 population (2008); Hospital beds: 66.0 per 10,000 population (2007); Hospital admissions: 1,503.4 per 10,000 population (2007).

**Environment:** Air Quality Index: 89.6% good, 10.4% moderate, 0.0% unhealthy for sensitive individuals, 0.0% unhealthy (percent of days in 2010)

**Elections:** 2008 Presidential election results: 46.1% Obama, 52.2% McCain, 0.9% Nader

**National and State Parks:** Boonville Gorge State Park; Fort Stanwix National Monument; Verona Beach State Park

**Additional Information Contacts**

| | |
|---|---|
| Oneida County Government | (315) 798-5794 |
| http://www.oneidacounty.org | |
| Boonville Area Chamber of Commerce | (315) 942-5112 |
| http://www.boonvillechamber.com | |
| City of Rome | (315) 336-6000 |
| http://www.romenewyork.com | |
| City of Sherrill | (315) 363-2440 |
| http://www.sherrillny.org | |
| City of Utica | (315) 792-0113 |
| http://www.cityofutica.com | |
| Clinton Chamber of Commerce | (315) 853-1735 |
| http://www.clintonnychamber.org | |
| Marcy Chamber of Commerce | (315) 327-8709 |
| http://www.marcychamber.com | |
| Mohawk Valley Chamber of Commerce | (315) 724-3151 |
| http://www.mvchamber.org | |
| Rome Area Chamber of Commerce | (315) 337-1700 |
| http://www.romechamber.com | |
| Town of Floyd | (315) 865-4256 |
| http://town.floyd.ny.us | |
| Town of New Hartford | (315) 733-7500 |
| http://www.newhartfordtown.com | |
| Town of Paris | (315) 839-5400 |
| http://town.paris.ny.us/content | |
| Town of Westmoreland | (315) 853-8001 |
| http://town.westmoreland.ny.us/content | |
| Town of Whitestown | (315) 736-4224 |
| http://town.whitestown.ny.us/content | |
| Village of Boonville | (315) 943-2061 |
| http://village.boonville.ny.us/content | |
| Village of Holland Patent | (315) 865-4853 |
| http://village.holland-patent.ny.us/content | |
| Village of Whitesboro | (315) 736-1613 |
| http://village.whitesboro.ny.us/content | |

# Oneida County Communities

**ALDER CREEK** (unincorporated postal area)

Zip Code: 13301

Covers a land area of 2.443 square miles and a water area of 0.163 square miles. Located at 43.41° N. Lat; 75.21° W. Long. Elevation is 1,194 feet. Population: 98 (2010); Density: 40.1 persons per square mile (2010); Race: 98.0% White, 0.0% Black, 1.0% Asian, 0.0% American Indian/Alaska Native, 0.0% Native Hawaiian/Other Pacific Islander, 1.0% Other, 0.0% Hispanic of any race (2010); Average household size: 1.81 (2010); Median age: 52.0 (2010); Males per 100 females: 139.0 (2010); Homeownership rate: 87.0% (2010)

**ANNSVILLE** (town). Covers a land area of 60.167 square miles and a water area of 0.307 square miles. Located at 43.34° N. Lat; 75.61° W. Long.

**Population:** 2,786 (1990); 2,956 (2000); 3,012 (2010); Density: 50.1 persons per square mile (2010); Race: 96.7% White, 1.1% Black, 0.6% Asian, 0.3% American Indian/Alaska Native, 0.0% Native Hawaiian/Other Pacific Islander, 1.3% Other, 1.1% Hispanic of any race (2010); Average household size: 2.72 (2010); Median age: 39.3 (2010); Males per 100 females: 102.4 (2010); Marriage status: 31.8% never married, 54.1% now married, 2.3% widowed, 11.8% divorced (2006-2010 5-year est.); Foreign born: 1.6% (2006-2010 5-year est.); Ancestry (includes multiple ancestries): 27.6% Irish, 20.4% German, 15.7% English, 13.8% Polish, 11.2% Italian (2006-2010 5-year est.).

**Economy:** Single-family building permits issued: 2 (2011); Multi-family building permits issued: 0 (2011); Employment by occupation: 6.6% management, 4.0% professional, 7.1% services, 17.4% sales, 4.2% farming, 11.8% construction, 9.6% production (2006-2010 5-year est.).

**Income:** Per capita income: $20,616 (2006-2010 5-year est.); Median household income: $41,397 (2006-2010 5-year est.); Average household income: $50,781 (2006-2010 5-year est.); Percent of households with income of $100,000 or more: 8.9% (2006-2010 5-year est.); Poverty rate: 16.9% (2006-2010 5-year est.).

**Education:** Percent of population age 25 and over with: High school diploma (including GED) or higher: 78.9% (2006-2010 5-year est.); Bachelor's degree or higher: 10.1% (2006-2010 5-year est.); Master's degree or higher: 3.5% (2006-2010 5-year est.).

**Housing:** Homeownership rate: 80.4% (2010); Median home value: $67,600 (2006-2010 5-year est.); Median contract rent: $501 per month (2006-2010 5-year est.); Median year structure built: 1980 (2006-2010 5-year est.).

**Transportation:** Commute to work: 95.2% car, 0.0% public transportation, 0.8% walk, 2.4% work from home (2006-2010 5-year est.); Travel time to work: 16.0% less than 15 minutes, 45.9% 15 to 30 minutes, 24.5% 30 to 45 minutes, 5.4% 45 to 60 minutes, 8.2% 60 minutes or more (2006-2010 5-year est.)

**AUGUSTA** (town). Covers a land area of 27.727 square miles and a water area of 0 square miles. Located at 42.97° N. Lat; 75.50° W. Long. Elevation is 955 feet.

**Population:** 2,070 (1990); 1,966 (2000); 2,020 (2010); Density: 72.9 persons per square mile (2010); Race: 97.2% White, 0.9% Black, 0.4% Asian, 0.0% American Indian/Alaska Native, 0.1% Native Hawaiian/Other Pacific Islander, 1.4% Other, 0.4% Hispanic of any race (2010); Average household size: 2.51 (2010); Median age: 39.7 (2010); Males per 100 females: 100.0 (2010); Marriage status: 28.1% never married, 56.0% now married, 5.1% widowed, 10.8% divorced (2006-2010 5-year est.); Foreign born: 1.1% (2006-2010 5-year est.); Ancestry (includes multiple ancestries): 24.6% Irish, 24.4% German, 17.0% English, 12.9% Italian, 12.4% American (2006-2010 5-year est.).

**Economy:** Single-family building permits issued: 10 (2011); Multi-family building permits issued: 0 (2011); Employment by occupation: 6.1% management, 1.1% professional, 10.5% services, 15.1% sales, 6.0% farming, 18.3% construction, 9.3% production (2006-2010 5-year est.).

**Income:** Per capita income: $21,270 (2006-2010 5-year est.); Median household income: $43,365 (2006-2010 5-year est.); Average household income: $52,263 (2006-2010 5-year est.); Percent of households with income of $100,000 or more: 11.7% (2006-2010 5-year est.); Poverty rate: 6.2% (2006-2010 5-year est.).

**Education:** Percent of population age 25 and over with: High school diploma (including GED) or higher: 85.2% (2006-2010 5-year est.); Bachelor's degree or higher: 11.3% (2006-2010 5-year est.); Master's degree or higher: 4.8% (2006-2010 5-year est.).

**Housing:** Homeownership rate: 77.1% (2010); Median home value: $89,300 (2006-2010 5-year est.); Median contract rent: $415 per month (2006-2010 5-year est.); Median year structure built: before 1940 (2006-2010 5-year est.).
**Transportation:** Commute to work: 92.7% car, 0.0% public transportation, 3.1% walk, 2.8% work from home (2006-2010 5-year est.); Travel time to work: 17.8% less than 15 minutes, 48.8% 15 to 30 minutes, 24.1% 30 to 45 minutes, 2.6% 45 to 60 minutes, 6.7% 60 minutes or more (2006-2010 5-year est.)

**AVA** (town). Covers a land area of 37.666 square miles and a water area of 0.038 square miles. Located at 43.41° N. Lat; 75.44° W. Long. Elevation is 1,371 feet.
**Population:** 792 (1990); 725 (2000); 676 (2010); Density: 17.9 persons per square mile (2010); Race: 98.8% White, 0.1% Black, 0.1% Asian, 0.4% American Indian/Alaska Native, 0.0% Native Hawaiian/Other Pacific Islander, 0.6% Other, 0.3% Hispanic of any race (2010); Average household size: 2.66 (2010); Median age: 39.5 (2010); Males per 100 females: 104.2 (2010); Marriage status: 30.7% never married, 52.7% now married, 4.9% widowed, 11.7% divorced (2006-2010 5-year est.); Foreign born: 0.3% (2006-2010 5-year est.); Ancestry (includes multiple ancestries): 30.6% German, 25.1% Irish, 17.3% Polish, 13.5% French, 11.1% English (2006-2010 5-year est.).
**Economy:** Single-family building permits issued: 4 (2011); Multi-family building permits issued: 0 (2011); Employment by occupation: 13.0% management, 0.0% professional, 9.9% services, 14.6% sales, 1.7% farming, 10.7% construction, 9.3% production (2006-2010 5-year est.).
**Income:** Per capita income: $21,531 (2006-2010 5-year est.); Median household income: $59,875 (2006-2010 5-year est.); Average household income: $64,557 (2006-2010 5-year est.); Percent of households with income of $100,000 or more: 21.2% (2006-2010 5-year est.); Poverty rate: 7.2% (2006-2010 5-year est.).
**Education:** Percent of population age 25 and over with: High school diploma (including GED) or higher: 82.3% (2006-2010 5-year est.); Bachelor's degree or higher: 2.5% (2006-2010 5-year est.); Master's degree or higher: 0.4% (2006-2010 5-year est.).
**Housing:** Homeownership rate: 83.8% (2010); Median home value: $94,200 (2006-2010 5-year est.); Median contract rent: $460 per month (2006-2010 5-year est.); Median year structure built: 1983 (2006-2010 5-year est.).
**Transportation:** Commute to work: 93.2% car, 0.0% public transportation, 0.0% walk, 5.8% work from home (2006-2010 5-year est.); Travel time to work: 14.7% less than 15 minutes, 21.8% 15 to 30 minutes, 26.3% 30 to 45 minutes, 29.7% 45 to 60 minutes, 7.5% 60 minutes or more (2006-2010 5-year est.)

**BARNEVELD** (village). Aka Trenton. Covers a land area of 0.192 square miles and a water area of 0 square miles. Located at 43.27° N. Lat; 75.18° W. Long. Elevation is 801 feet.
**History:** Nearby, in Steuben Memorial Park, is the reconstructed log cabin and the grave of Baron von Steuben.
**Population:** 324 (1990); 332 (2000); 284 (2010); Density: 1,477.8 persons per square mile (2010); Race: 97.9% White, 0.4% Black, 0.4% Asian, 1.1% American Indian/Alaska Native, 0.0% Native Hawaiian/Other Pacific Islander, 0.2% Other, 2.5% Hispanic of any race (2010); Average household size: 2.47 (2010); Median age: 42.5 (2010); Males per 100 females: 104.3 (2010); Marriage status: 30.5% never married, 52.7% now married, 8.8% widowed, 8.0% divorced (2006-2010 5-year est.); Foreign born: 2.0% (2006-2010 5-year est.); Ancestry (includes multiple ancestries): 30.9% German, 25.7% English, 24.1% Welsh, 14.3% Polish, 12.1% Irish (2006-2010 5-year est.).
**Economy:** Employment by occupation: 18.1% management, 5.7% professional, 17.1% services, 14.5% sales, 2.6% farming, 0.0% construction, 0.0% production (2006-2010 5-year est.).
**Income:** Per capita income: $29,181 (2006-2010 5-year est.); Median household income: $58,750 (2006-2010 5-year est.); Average household income: $69,598 (2006-2010 5-year est.); Percent of households with income of $100,000 or more: 16.9% (2006-2010 5-year est.); Poverty rate: 1.6% (2006-2010 5-year est.).
**Education:** Percent of population age 25 and over with: High school diploma (including GED) or higher: 97.5% (2006-2010 5-year est.); Bachelor's degree or higher: 46.8% (2006-2010 5-year est.); Master's degree or higher: 17.7% (2006-2010 5-year est.).
**Housing:** Homeownership rate: 66.1% (2010); Median home value: $133,300 (2006-2010 5-year est.); Median contract rent: $342 per month

(2006-2010 5-year est.); Median year structure built: before 1940 (2006-2010 5-year est.).
**Transportation:** Commute to work: 83.1% car, 0.0% public transportation, 5.6% walk, 10.2% work from home (2006-2010 5-year est.); Travel time to work: 18.2% less than 15 minutes, 55.3% 15 to 30 minutes, 15.7% 30 to 45 minutes, 1.9% 45 to 60 minutes, 8.8% 60 minutes or more (2006-2010 5-year est.)

**BLOSSVALE** (unincorporated postal area)
Zip Code: 13308
Covers a land area of 38.654 square miles and a water area of 0.662 square miles. Located at 43.25° N. Lat; 75.65° W. Long. Elevation is 420 feet. Population: 3,625 (2010); Density: 93.8 persons per square mile (2010); Race: 97.6% White, 0.4% Black, 0.4% Asian, 0.4% American Indian/Alaska Native, 0.0% Native Hawaiian/Other Pacific Islander, 1.2% Other, 0.8% Hispanic of any race (2010); Average household size: 2.57 (2010); Median age: 41.0 (2010); Males per 100 females: 99.1 (2010); Homeownership rate: 82.1% (2010)

**BOONVILLE** (village). Covers a land area of 1.729 square miles and a water area of 0.004 square miles. Located at 43.48° N. Lat; 75.32° W. Long. Elevation is 1,148 feet.
**Population:** 2,220 (1990); 2,138 (2000); 2,072 (2010); Density: 1,198.1 persons per square mile (2010); Race: 99.2% White, 0.0% Black, 0.0% Asian, 0.3% American Indian/Alaska Native, 0.0% Native Hawaiian/Other Pacific Islander, 0.5% Other, 0.9% Hispanic of any race (2010); Average household size: 2.15 (2010); Median age: 45.3 (2010); Males per 100 females: 91.0 (2010); Marriage status: 25.8% never married, 37.8% now married, 20.6% widowed, 15.8% divorced (2006-2010 5-year est.); Foreign born: 0.7% (2006-2010 5-year est.); Ancestry (includes multiple ancestries): 29.4% German, 21.7% Irish, 13.3% English, 10.4% French, 8.7% American (2006-2010 5-year est.).
**Economy:** Single-family building permits issued: 0 (2011); Multi-family building permits issued: 0 (2011); Employment by occupation: 9.4% management, 1.7% professional, 13.3% services, 18.3% sales, 5.9% farming, 10.1% construction, 1.1% production (2006-2010 5-year est.).
**Income:** Per capita income: $20,266 (2006-2010 5-year est.); Median household income: $28,963 (2006-2010 5-year est.); Average household income: $42,277 (2006-2010 5-year est.); Percent of households with income of $100,000 or more: 6.5% (2006-2010 5-year est.); Poverty rate: 14.8% (2006-2010 5-year est.).
**Education:** Percent of population age 25 and over with: High school diploma (including GED) or higher: 73.2% (2006-2010 5-year est.); Bachelor's degree or higher: 11.6% (2006-2010 5-year est.); Master's degree or higher: 5.1% (2006-2010 5-year est.).

**School District(s)**
Adirondack Central School District (PK-12)
   2009-10 Enrollment: 1,395 . . . . . . . . . . . . . . . . . . . . (315) 942-9200
**Housing:** Homeownership rate: 57.1% (2010); Median home value: $89,300 (2006-2010 5-year est.); Median contract rent: $404 per month (2006-2010 5-year est.); Median year structure built: before 1940 (2006-2010 5-year est.).
**Safety:** Violent crime rate: 0.0 per 10,000 population; Property crime rate: 35.1 per 10,000 population (2010).
**Newspapers:** Boonville Herald & Adirondack Tourist (Community news)
**Transportation:** Commute to work: 86.1% car, 0.0% public transportation, 10.5% walk, 0.7% work from home (2006-2010 5-year est.); Travel time to work: 46.4% less than 15 minutes, 6.4% 15 to 30 minutes, 26.1% 30 to 45 minutes, 10.9% 45 to 60 minutes, 10.1% 60 minutes or more (2006-2010 5-year est.)
**Additional Information Contacts**
Boonville Area Chamber of Commerce . . . . . . . . . . . . . . (315) 942-5112
  http://www.boonvillechamber.com
Village of Boonville. . . . . . . . . . . . . . . . . . . . . . . . . . . . (315) 943-2061
  http://village.boonville.ny.us/content

**BOONVILLE** (town). Covers a land area of 71.878 square miles and a water area of 0.697 square miles. Located at 43.45° N. Lat; 75.28° W. Long. Elevation is 1,148 feet.
**History:** Author and critic Walter D. Edmonds born here and lived in nearby Talcottville. Settled c.1791, incorporated 1855.
**Population:** 4,225 (1990); 4,572 (2000); 4,555 (2010); Density: 63.4 persons per square mile (2010); Race: 98.6% White, 0.2% Black, 0.3% Asian, 0.2% American Indian/Alaska Native, 0.0% Native Hawaiian/Other Pacific Islander, 0.7% Other, 0.6% Hispanic of any race (2010); Average

household size: 2.35 (2010); Median age: 44.1 (2010); Males per 100 females: 96.3 (2010); Marriage status: 25.9% never married, 51.2% now married, 11.8% widowed, 11.2% divorced (2006-2010 5-year est.); Foreign born: 0.8% (2006-2010 5-year est.); Ancestry (includes multiple ancestries): 31.6% German, 20.1% Irish, 10.1% Polish, 9.7% English, 8.4% French (2006-2010 5-year est.).

**Economy:** Single-family building permits issued: 4 (2011); Multi-family building permits issued: 0 (2011); Employment by occupation: 6.9% management, 1.8% professional, 11.7% services, 18.9% sales, 5.2% farming, 10.3% construction, 2.8% production (2006-2010 5-year est.).

**Income:** Per capita income: $22,472 (2006-2010 5-year est.); Median household income: $45,453 (2006-2010 5-year est.); Average household income: $55,534 (2006-2010 5-year est.); Percent of households with income of $100,000 or more: 12.7% (2006-2010 5-year est.); Poverty rate: 10.9% (2006-2010 5-year est.).

**Education:** Percent of population age 25 and over with: High school diploma (including GED) or higher: 81.9% (2006-2010 5-year est.); Bachelor's degree or higher: 11.0% (2006-2010 5-year est.); Master's degree or higher: 5.5% (2006-2010 5-year est.).

**School District(s)**
Adirondack Central School District (PK-12)
    2009-10 Enrollment: 1,395 . . . . . . . . . . . . . . . . . . . . . . . . (315) 942-9200

**Housing:** Homeownership rate: 72.0% (2010); Median home value: $110,600 (2006-2010 5-year est.); Median contract rent: $398 per month (2006-2010 5-year est.); Median year structure built: 1959 (2006-2010 5-year est.).

**Newspapers:** Boonville Herald & Adirondack Tourist (Community news)

**Transportation:** Commute to work: 91.0% car, 0.0% public transportation, 3.5% walk, 4.6% work from home (2006-2010 5-year est.); Travel time to work: 45.2% less than 15 minutes, 6.9% 15 to 30 minutes, 31.7% 30 to 45 minutes, 8.5% 45 to 60 minutes, 7.8% 60 minutes or more (2006-2010 5-year est.)

**BRIDGEWATER** (village). Covers a land area of 0.606 square miles and a water area of 0 square miles. Located at 42.87° N. Lat; 75.25° W. Long. Elevation is 1,211 feet.

**Population:** 537 (1990); 579 (2000); 470 (2010); Density: 774.8 persons per square mile (2010); Race: 96.8% White, 0.2% Black, 0.6% Asian, 0.2% American Indian/Alaska Native, 0.0% Native Hawaiian/Other Pacific Islander, 2.2% Other, 3.0% Hispanic of any race (2010); Average household size: 2.57 (2010); Median age: 35.7 (2010); Males per 100 females: 99.2 (2010); Marriage status: 26.3% never married, 60.0% now married, 4.5% widowed, 9.2% divorced (2006-2010 5-year est.); Foreign born: 0.0% (2006-2010 5-year est.); Ancestry (includes multiple ancestries): 17.1% Irish, 16.4% German, 12.6% English, 11.3% American, 9.6% Welsh (2006-2010 5-year est.).

**Economy:** Single-family building permits issued: 0 (2011); Multi-family building permits issued: 0 (2011); Employment by occupation: 0.9% management, 0.0% professional, 22.2% services, 19.9% sales, 0.0% farming, 10.0% construction, 11.8% production (2006-2010 5-year est.).

**Income:** Per capita income: $14,177 (2006-2010 5-year est.); Median household income: $34,444 (2006-2010 5-year est.); Average household income: $37,963 (2006-2010 5-year est.); Percent of households with income of $100,000 or more: 5.6% (2006-2010 5-year est.); Poverty rate: 31.2% (2006-2010 5-year est.).

**Education:** Percent of population age 25 and over with: High school diploma (including GED) or higher: 75.6% (2006-2010 5-year est.); Bachelor's degree or higher: 4.6% (2006-2010 5-year est.); Master's degree or higher: 2.3% (2006-2010 5-year est.).

**Housing:** Homeownership rate: 76.5% (2010); Median home value: $13,500 (2006-2010 5-year est.); Median contract rent: $430 per month (2006-2010 5-year est.); Median year structure built: 1975 (2006-2010 5-year est.).

**Transportation:** Commute to work: 90.0% car, 5.0% public transportation, 1.8% walk, 0.0% work from home (2006-2010 5-year est.); Travel time to work: 15.8% less than 15 minutes, 48.9% 15 to 30 minutes, 23.5% 30 to 45 minutes, 5.4% 45 to 60 minutes, 6.3% 60 minutes or more (2006-2010 5-year est.)

**BRIDGEWATER** (town). Covers a land area of 23.844 square miles and a water area of 0.011 square miles. Located at 42.90° N. Lat; 75.26° W. Long. Elevation is 1,211 feet.

**Population:** 1,591 (1990); 1,671 (2000); 1,522 (2010); Density: 63.8 persons per square mile (2010); Race: 96.6% White, 1.1% Black, 0.5% Asian, 0.1% American Indian/Alaska Native, 0.0% Native Hawaiian/Other

Pacific Islander, 1.7% Other, 3.0% Hispanic of any race (2010); Average household size: 2.59 (2010); Median age: 40.8 (2010); Males per 100 females: 104.6 (2010); Marriage status: 26.8% never married, 55.6% now married, 5.5% widowed, 12.1% divorced (2006-2010 5-year est.); Foreign born: 1.5% (2006-2010 5-year est.); Ancestry (includes multiple ancestries): 20.5% Irish, 17.6% German, 15.8% English, 10.8% Polish, 9.0% Welsh (2006-2010 5-year est.).

**Economy:** Single-family building permits issued: 4 (2011); Multi-family building permits issued: 0 (2011); Employment by occupation: 7.5% management, 2.9% professional, 13.0% services, 19.4% sales, 0.7% farming, 12.9% construction, 7.2% production (2006-2010 5-year est.).

**Income:** Per capita income: $20,417 (2006-2010 5-year est.); Median household income: $42,760 (2006-2010 5-year est.); Average household income: $52,064 (2006-2010 5-year est.); Percent of households with income of $100,000 or more: 10.0% (2006-2010 5-year est.); Poverty rate: 18.6% (2006-2010 5-year est.).

**Education:** Percent of population age 25 and over with: High school diploma (including GED) or higher: 83.4% (2006-2010 5-year est.); Bachelor's degree or higher: 13.8% (2006-2010 5-year est.); Master's degree or higher: 5.8% (2006-2010 5-year est.).

**Housing:** Homeownership rate: 82.9% (2010); Median home value: $66,100 (2006-2010 5-year est.); Median contract rent: $426 per month (2006-2010 5-year est.); Median year structure built: 1981 (2006-2010 5-year est.).

**Transportation:** Commute to work: 93.6% car, 1.6% public transportation, 1.0% walk, 2.8% work from home (2006-2010 5-year est.); Travel time to work: 17.0% less than 15 minutes, 52.1% 15 to 30 minutes, 23.2% 30 to 45 minutes, 2.9% 45 to 60 minutes, 4.8% 60 minutes or more (2006-2010 5-year est.)

**CAMDEN** (village). Covers a land area of 2.436 square miles and a water area of 0 square miles. Located at 43.33° N. Lat; 75.74° W. Long. Elevation is 502 feet.

**Population:** 2,552 (1990); 2,330 (2000); 2,231 (2010); Density: 915.8 persons per square mile (2010); Race: 97.8% White, 0.4% Black, 0.3% Asian, 0.3% American Indian/Alaska Native, 0.0% Native Hawaiian/Other Pacific Islander, 1.2% Other, 0.7% Hispanic of any race (2010); Average household size: 2.30 (2010); Median age: 40.5 (2010); Males per 100 females: 93.8 (2010); Marriage status: 30.0% never married, 47.2% now married, 10.6% widowed, 12.2% divorced (2006-2010 5-year est.); Foreign born: 0.0% (2006-2010 5-year est.); Ancestry (includes multiple ancestries): 24.0% English, 22.1% Irish, 17.0% German, 12.7% French, 9.5% Polish (2006-2010 5-year est.).

**Economy:** Single-family building permits issued: 0 (2011); Multi-family building permits issued: 0 (2011); Employment by occupation: 10.6% management, 1.5% professional, 9.3% services, 17.8% sales, 2.3% farming, 6.2% construction, 3.4% production (2006-2010 5-year est.).

**Income:** Per capita income: $20,948 (2006-2010 5-year est.); Median household income: $38,214 (2006-2010 5-year est.); Average household income: $49,909 (2006-2010 5-year est.); Percent of households with income of $100,000 or more: 11.2% (2006-2010 5-year est.); Poverty rate: 12.1% (2006-2010 5-year est.).

**Education:** Percent of population age 25 and over with: High school diploma (including GED) or higher: 81.7% (2006-2010 5-year est.); Bachelor's degree or higher: 14.7% (2006-2010 5-year est.); Master's degree or higher: 7.8% (2006-2010 5-year est.).

**School District(s)**
Camden Central School District (PK-12)
    2009-10 Enrollment: 2,485 . . . . . . . . . . . . . . . . . . . . . . . . (315) 245-4075

**Housing:** Homeownership rate: 54.4% (2010); Median home value: $83,900 (2006-2010 5-year est.); Median contract rent: $506 per month (2006-2010 5-year est.); Median year structure built: before 1940 (2006-2010 5-year est.).

**Safety:** Violent crime rate: 4.5 per 10,000 population; Property crime rate: 383.1 per 10,000 population (2010).

**Newspapers:** Queen Central News (Community news; Circulation 52)

**Transportation:** Commute to work: 83.3% car, 0.0% public transportation, 6.8% walk, 8.0% work from home (2006-2010 5-year est.); Travel time to work: 40.4% less than 15 minutes, 11.4% 15 to 30 minutes, 33.9% 30 to 45 minutes, 7.1% 45 to 60 minutes, 7.1% 60 minutes or more (2006-2010 5-year est.)

**CAMDEN** (town). Covers a land area of 54.013 square miles and a water area of 0.140 square miles. Located at 43.34° N. Lat; 75.77° W. Long. Elevation is 502 feet.
**History:** Incorporated 1834.
**Population:** 5,134 (1990); 5,028 (2000); 4,934 (2010); Density: 91.3 persons per square mile (2010); Race: 98.0% White, 0.7% Black, 0.2% Asian, 0.2% American Indian/Alaska Native, 0.0% Native Hawaiian/Other Pacific Islander, 0.9% Other, 1.0% Hispanic of any race (2010); Average household size: 2.50 (2010); Median age: 41.4 (2010); Males per 100 females: 97.8 (2010); Marriage status: 25.6% never married, 58.1% now married, 7.0% widowed, 9.2% divorced (2006-2010 5-year est.); Foreign born: 1.1% (2006-2010 5-year est.); Ancestry (includes multiple ancestries): 21.1% English, 21.1% Irish, 16.4% German, 10.7% French, 9.0% American (2006-2010 5-year est.).
**Economy:** Single-family building permits issued: 5 (2011); Multi-family building permits issued: 0 (2011); Employment by occupation: 9.6% management, 1.5% professional, 9.2% services, 18.7% sales, 2.6% farming, 9.3% construction, 5.4% production (2006-2010 5-year est.).
**Income:** Per capita income: $23,005 (2006-2010 5-year est.); Median household income: $50,350 (2006-2010 5-year est.); Average household income: $56,805 (2006-2010 5-year est.); Percent of households with income of $100,000 or more: 11.8% (2006-2010 5-year est.); Poverty rate: 8.4% (2006-2010 5-year est.).
**Education:** Percent of population age 25 and over with: High school diploma (including GED) or higher: 84.7% (2006-2010 5-year est.); Bachelor's degree or higher: 16.5% (2006-2010 5-year est.); Master's degree or higher: 6.7% (2006-2010 5-year est.).

**School District(s)**
Camden Central School District (PK-12)
    2009-10 Enrollment: 2,485 . . . . . . . . . . . . . . . . . . . . . . (315) 245-4075
**Housing:** Homeownership rate: 71.0% (2010); Median home value: $91,600 (2006-2010 5-year est.); Median contract rent: $503 per month (2006-2010 5-year est.); Median year structure built: 1951 (2006-2010 5-year est.).
**Newspapers:** Queen Central News (Community news; Circulation 52)
**Transportation:** Commute to work: 91.1% car, 1.3% public transportation, 3.5% walk, 3.4% work from home (2006-2010 5-year est.); Travel time to work: 40.6% less than 15 minutes, 16.0% 15 to 30 minutes, 25.9% 30 to 45 minutes, 9.8% 45 to 60 minutes, 7.8% 60 minutes or more (2006-2010 5-year est.)

**CASSVILLE** (unincorporated postal area)
Zip Code: 13318
    Covers a land area of 25.382 square miles and a water area of 0.011 square miles. Located at 42.92° N. Lat; 75.26° W. Long. Elevation is 1,240 feet. Population: 1,325 (2010); Density: 52.2 persons per square mile (2010); Race: 96.8% White, 1.0% Black, 0.8% Asian, 0.1% American Indian/Alaska Native, 0.0% Native Hawaiian/Other Pacific Islander, 1.3% Other, 2.3% Hispanic of any race (2010); Average household size: 2.67 (2010); Median age: 43.3 (2010); Males per 100 females: 104.8 (2010); Homeownership rate: 87.1% (2010)

**CHADWICKS** (CDP). Covers a land area of 1.327 square miles and a water area of 0 square miles. Located at 43.02° N. Lat; 75.27° W. Long. Elevation is 709 feet.
**Population:** n/a (1990); n/a (2000); 1,506 (2010); Density: 1,134.7 persons per square mile (2010); Race: 96.9% White, 0.9% Black, 0.6% Asian, 0.3% American Indian/Alaska Native, 0.0% Native Hawaiian/Other Pacific Islander, 1.3% Other, 3.7% Hispanic of any race (2010); Average household size: 2.46 (2010); Median age: 37.3 (2010); Males per 100 females: 92.8 (2010); Marriage status: 43.8% never married, 30.1% now married, 10.7% widowed, 15.3% divorced (2006-2010 5-year est.); Foreign born: 0.0% (2006-2010 5-year est.); Ancestry (includes multiple ancestries): 32.4% German, 25.8% Irish, 24.5% Italian, 18.8% Polish, 7.9% English (2006-2010 5-year est.).
**Economy:** Employment by occupation: 5.8% management, 0.0% professional, 13.0% services, 28.3% sales, 6.3% farming, 6.9% construction, 8.6% production (2006-2010 5-year est.).
**Income:** Per capita income: $33,483 (2006-2010 5-year est.); Median household income: $36,538 (2006-2010 5-year est.); Average household income: $68,416 (2006-2010 5-year est.); Percent of households with income of $100,000 or more: 16.9% (2006-2010 5-year est.); Poverty rate: 12.4% (2006-2010 5-year est.).
**Education:** Percent of population age 25 and over with: High school diploma (including GED) or higher: 85.2% (2006-2010 5-year est.);

Bachelor's degree or higher: 23.6% (2006-2010 5-year est.); Master's degree or higher: 12.0% (2006-2010 5-year est.).
**Housing:** Homeownership rate: 63.0% (2010); Median home value: $86,200 (2006-2010 5-year est.); Median contract rent: $501 per month (2006-2010 5-year est.); Median year structure built: 1963 (2006-2010 5-year est.).
**Transportation:** Commute to work: 91.8% car, 2.4% public transportation, 1.9% walk, 2.0% work from home (2006-2010 5-year est.); Travel time to work: 53.7% less than 15 minutes, 36.4% 15 to 30 minutes, 7.7% 30 to 45 minutes, 2.2% 45 to 60 minutes, 0.0% 60 minutes or more (2006-2010 5-year est.)

**CLARK MILLS** (CDP). Covers a land area of 1.492 square miles and a water area of 0.018 square miles. Located at 43.09° N. Lat; 75.37° W. Long. Elevation is 515 feet.
**Population:** 1,303 (1990); 1,424 (2000); 1,905 (2010); Density: 1,276.6 persons per square mile (2010); Race: 94.7% White, 1.0% Black, 1.5% Asian, 0.3% American Indian/Alaska Native, 0.0% Native Hawaiian/Other Pacific Islander, 2.5% Other, 1.8% Hispanic of any race (2010); Average household size: 2.15 (2010); Median age: 44.5 (2010); Males per 100 females: 95.0 (2010); Marriage status: 33.3% never married, 38.4% now married, 11.8% widowed, 16.5% divorced (2006-2010 5-year est.); Foreign born: 1.2% (2006-2010 5-year est.); Ancestry (includes multiple ancestries): 21.9% German, 18.7% English, 18.1% Irish, 17.2% Italian, 16.0% Polish (2006-2010 5-year est.).
**Economy:** Employment by occupation: 8.2% management, 2.1% professional, 14.2% services, 20.2% sales, 4.0% farming, 14.2% construction, 5.2% production (2006-2010 5-year est.).
**Income:** Per capita income: $29,892 (2006-2010 5-year est.); Median household income: $43,694 (2006-2010 5-year est.); Average household income: $53,932 (2006-2010 5-year est.); Percent of households with income of $100,000 or more: 8.8% (2006-2010 5-year est.); Poverty rate: 5.5% (2006-2010 5-year est.).
**Education:** Percent of population age 25 and over with: High school diploma (including GED) or higher: 92.7% (2006-2010 5-year est.); Bachelor's degree or higher: 22.1% (2006-2010 5-year est.); Master's degree or higher: 10.9% (2006-2010 5-year est.).
**Housing:** Homeownership rate: 60.4% (2010); Median home value: $81,300 (2006-2010 5-year est.); Median contract rent: $581 per month (2006-2010 5-year est.); Median year structure built: 1977 (2006-2010 5-year est.).
**Transportation:** Commute to work: 96.1% car, 0.0% public transportation, 0.0% walk, 3.9% work from home (2006-2010 5-year est.); Travel time to work: 43.4% less than 15 minutes, 46.4% 15 to 30 minutes, 4.2% 30 to 45 minutes, 3.7% 45 to 60 minutes, 2.2% 60 minutes or more (2006-2010 5-year est.)

**CLAYVILLE** (village). Covers a land area of 0.439 square miles and a water area of 0.003 square miles. Located at 42.97° N. Lat; 75.24° W. Long. Elevation is 961 feet.
**Population:** 463 (1990); 445 (2000); 350 (2010); Density: 797.0 persons per square mile (2010); Race: 96.9% White, 1.7% Black, 0.3% Asian, 0.0% American Indian/Alaska Native, 0.0% Native Hawaiian/Other Pacific Islander, 1.1% Other, 0.6% Hispanic of any race (2010); Average household size: 2.41 (2010); Median age: 39.6 (2010); Males per 100 females: 113.4 (2010); Marriage status: 37.0% never married, 43.6% now married, 7.7% widowed, 11.8% divorced (2006-2010 5-year est.); Foreign born: 0.0% (2006-2010 5-year est.); Ancestry (includes multiple ancestries): 32.9% Irish, 19.8% English, 14.1% German, 12.7% Italian, 6.1% Polish (2006-2010 5-year est.).
**Economy:** Single-family building permits issued: 0 (2011); Multi-family building permits issued: 0 (2011); Employment by occupation: 7.5% management, 0.0% professional, 10.8% services, 22.2% sales, 10.4% farming, 5.7% construction, 2.8% production (2006-2010 5-year est.).
**Income:** Per capita income: $20,259 (2006-2010 5-year est.); Median household income: $47,500 (2006-2010 5-year est.); Average household income: $49,049 (2006-2010 5-year est.); Percent of households with income of $100,000 or more: 6.9% (2006-2010 5-year est.); Poverty rate: 10.8% (2006-2010 5-year est.).
**Education:** Percent of population age 25 and over with: High school diploma (including GED) or higher: 85.7% (2006-2010 5-year est.); Bachelor's degree or higher: 8.3% (2006-2010 5-year est.); Master's degree or higher: 1.3% (2006-2010 5-year est.).
**Housing:** Homeownership rate: 63.5% (2010); Median home value: $67,900 (2006-2010 5-year est.); Median contract rent: $468 per month

(2006-2010 5-year est.); Median year structure built: before 1940 (2006-2010 5-year est.).

**Transportation:** Commute to work: 96.9% car, 1.5% public transportation, 0.0% walk, 1.5% work from home (2006-2010 5-year est.); Travel time to work: 17.3% less than 15 minutes, 53.9% 15 to 30 minutes, 19.4% 30 to 45 minutes, 2.6% 45 to 60 minutes, 6.8% 60 minutes or more (2006-2010 5-year est.)

## CLINTON (village).
Covers a land area of 0.625 square miles and a water area of 0 square miles. Located at 43.04° N. Lat; 75.37° W. Long. Elevation is 604 feet.

**History:** Seat of Hamilton College. Elihu Root was born here. Clinton Village Historic District. Incorporated 1843.

**Population:** 2,238 (1990); 1,952 (2000); 1,942 (2010); Density: 3,102.9 persons per square mile (2010); Race: 95.4% White, 0.9% Black, 2.1% Asian, 0.2% American Indian/Alaska Native, 0.0% Native Hawaiian/Other Pacific Islander, 1.4% Other, 1.6% Hispanic of any race (2010); Average household size: 2.03 (2010); Median age: 46.1 (2010); Males per 100 females: 90.2 (2010); Marriage status: 28.0% never married, 57.7% now married, 5.1% widowed, 9.1% divorced (2006-2010 5-year est.); Foreign born: 2.4% (2006-2010 5-year est.); Ancestry (includes multiple ancestries): 27.1% German, 16.5% Irish, 14.4% Italian, 13.1% English, 8.1% French (2006-2010 5-year est.).

**Economy:** Single-family building permits issued: 0 (2011); Multi-family building permits issued: 0 (2011); Employment by occupation: 12.2% management, 4.9% professional, 4.1% services, 15.3% sales, 1.4% farming, 5.0% construction, 3.2% production (2006-2010 5-year est.).

**Income:** Per capita income: $35,024 (2006-2010 5-year est.); Median household income: $58,309 (2006-2010 5-year est.); Average household income: $76,817 (2006-2010 5-year est.); Percent of households with income of $100,000 or more: 24.6% (2006-2010 5-year est.); Poverty rate: 6.3% (2006-2010 5-year est.).

**Education:** Percent of population age 25 and over with: High school diploma (including GED) or higher: 94.4% (2006-2010 5-year est.); Bachelor's degree or higher: 46.6% (2006-2010 5-year est.); Master's degree or higher: 25.1% (2006-2010 5-year est.).

### School District(s)
Clinton Central School District (KG-12)
    2009-10 Enrollment: 1,452 . . . . . . . . . . . . . . . . . . . . . . . . (315) 557-2253

### Four-year College(s)
Hamilton College (Private, Not-for-profit)
    Fall 2010 Enrollment: 1,825 . . . . . . . . . . . . . . . . . . . . . . (315) 859-4011
    2011-12 Tuition: In-state $42,640; Out-of-state $42,640

**Housing:** Homeownership rate: 54.1% (2010); Median home value: $160,000 (2006-2010 5-year est.); Median contract rent: $574 per month (2006-2010 5-year est.); Median year structure built: 1943 (2006-2010 5-year est.).

**Transportation:** Commute to work: 88.8% car, 0.4% public transportation, 5.4% walk, 4.7% work from home (2006-2010 5-year est.); Travel time to work: 49.0% less than 15 minutes, 39.6% 15 to 30 minutes, 2.8% 30 to 45 minutes, 3.8% 45 to 60 minutes, 4.8% 60 minutes or more (2006-2010 5-year est.)

**Additional Information Contacts**
Clinton Chamber of Commerce . . . . . . . . . . . . . . . . . . . (315) 853-1735
    http://www.clintonnychamber.org

## DEANSBORO (unincorporated postal area)
Zip Code: 13328
    Covers a land area of 15.863 square miles and a water area of 0 square miles. Located at 42.98° N. Lat; 75.42° W. Long. Elevation is 817 feet.
    Population: 1,267 (2010); Density: 79.9 persons per square mile (2010); Race: 98.0% White, 0.3% Black, 0.7% Asian, 0.1% American Indian/Alaska Native, 0.0% Native Hawaiian/Other Pacific Islander, 0.9% Other, 1.4% Hispanic of any race (2010); Average household size: 2.46 (2010); Median age: 43.6 (2010); Males per 100 females: 107.0 (2010); Homeownership rate: 81.2% (2010)

## DEERFIELD (town).
Covers a land area of 32.941 square miles and a water area of 0.106 square miles. Located at 43.18° N. Lat; 75.15° W. Long. Elevation is 443 feet.

**Population:** 3,942 (1990); 3,906 (2000); 4,273 (2010); Density: 129.7 persons per square mile (2010); Race: 97.6% White, 0.5% Black, 1.0% Asian, 0.0% American Indian/Alaska Native, 0.0% Native Hawaiian/Other Pacific Islander, 0.9% Other, 1.1% Hispanic of any race (2010); Average household size: 2.59 (2010); Median age: 43.9 (2010); Males per 100

females: 98.7 (2010); Marriage status: 25.1% never married, 58.7% now married, 9.1% widowed, 7.1% divorced (2006-2010 5-year est.); Foreign born: 4.1% (2006-2010 5-year est.); Ancestry (includes multiple ancestries): 29.7% Italian, 21.5% German, 21.0% Irish, 18.3% Polish, 8.5% English (2006-2010 5-year est.).

**Economy:** Single-family building permits issued: 5 (2011); Multi-family building permits issued: 0 (2011); Employment by occupation: 12.6% management, 4.7% professional, 6.2% services, 16.5% sales, 2.8% farming, 10.9% construction, 5.8% production (2006-2010 5-year est.).

**Income:** Per capita income: $26,507 (2006-2010 5-year est.); Median household income: $61,971 (2006-2010 5-year est.); Average household income: $68,220 (2006-2010 5-year est.); Percent of households with income of $100,000 or more: 18.0% (2006-2010 5-year est.); Poverty rate: 4.5% (2006-2010 5-year est.).

**Education:** Percent of population age 25 and over with: High school diploma (including GED) or higher: 96.4% (2006-2010 5-year est.); Bachelor's degree or higher: 25.3% (2006-2010 5-year est.); Master's degree or higher: 11.7% (2006-2010 5-year est.).

**Housing:** Homeownership rate: 93.5% (2010); Median home value: $123,100 (2006-2010 5-year est.); Median contract rent: $331 per month (2006-2010 5-year est.); Median year structure built: 1959 (2006-2010 5-year est.).

**Transportation:** Commute to work: 95.7% car, 0.0% public transportation, 1.1% walk, 2.5% work from home (2006-2010 5-year est.); Travel time to work: 36.1% less than 15 minutes, 50.2% 15 to 30 minutes, 3.7% 30 to 45 minutes, 2.2% 45 to 60 minutes, 7.7% 60 minutes or more (2006-2010 5-year est.)

## DURHAMVILLE (CDP).
Covers a land area of 1.372 square miles and a water area of 0 square miles. Located at 43.12° N. Lat; 75.66° W. Long. Elevation is 433 feet.

**Population:** n/a (1990); n/a (2000); 584 (2010); Density: 425.6 persons per square mile (2010); Race: 97.4% White, 0.0% Black, 0.0% Asian, 0.9% American Indian/Alaska Native, 0.0% Native Hawaiian/Other Pacific Islander, 1.7% Other, 0.3% Hispanic of any race (2010); Average household size: 2.72 (2010); Median age: 36.3 (2010); Males per 100 females: 115.5 (2010); Marriage status: 21.8% never married, 53.3% now married, 9.0% widowed, 15.9% divorced (2006-2010 5-year est.); Foreign born: 0.0% (2006-2010 5-year est.); Ancestry (includes multiple ancestries): 37.2% German, 16.9% Polish, 15.5% French, 13.4% Italian, 12.9% English (2006-2010 5-year est.).

**Economy:** Employment by occupation: 3.1% management, 4.2% professional, 29.1% services, 9.2% sales, 19.2% farming, 13.0% construction, 13.0% production (2006-2010 5-year est.).

**Income:** Per capita income: $16,189 (2006-2010 5-year est.); Median household income: $32,941 (2006-2010 5-year est.); Average household income: $42,497 (2006-2010 5-year est.); Percent of households with income of $100,000 or more: 9.8% (2006-2010 5-year est.); Poverty rate: 23.8% (2006-2010 5-year est.).

**Education:** Percent of population age 25 and over with: High school diploma (including GED) or higher: 92.7% (2006-2010 5-year est.); Bachelor's degree or higher: 19.1% (2006-2010 5-year est.); Master's degree or higher: 0.0% (2006-2010 5-year est.).

### School District(s)
Oneida City School District (PK-12)
    2009-10 Enrollment: 2,430 . . . . . . . . . . . . . . . . . . . . . . (315) 363-2550

**Housing:** Homeownership rate: 83.7% (2010); Median home value: $86,300 (2006-2010 5-year est.); Median contract rent: $523 per month (2006-2010 5-year est.); Median year structure built: before 1940 (2006-2010 5-year est.).

**Transportation:** Commute to work: 80.1% car, 0.0% public transportation, 0.0% walk, 19.9% work from home (2006-2010 5-year est.); Travel time to work: 41.1% less than 15 minutes, 42.1% 15 to 30 minutes, 16.7% 30 to 45 minutes, 0.0% 45 to 60 minutes, 0.0% 60 minutes or more (2006-2010 5-year est.)

## FLORENCE (town).
Covers a land area of 54.922 square miles and a water area of 0.094 square miles. Located at 43.41° N. Lat; 75.73° W. Long. Elevation is 978 feet.

**Population:** 852 (1990); 1,086 (2000); 1,025 (2010); Density: 18.7 persons per square mile (2010); Race: 98.3% White, 0.2% Black, 0.3% Asian, 0.7% American Indian/Alaska Native, 0.0% Native Hawaiian/Other Pacific Islander, 0.5% Other, 0.4% Hispanic of any race (2010); Average household size: 2.82 (2010); Median age: 40.7 (2010); Males per 100 females: 102.2 (2010); Marriage status: 25.2% never married, 63.3% now married, 4.7% widowed, 6.7% divorced (2006-2010 5-year est.); Foreign born: 0.6% (2006-2010 5-year est.); Ancestry (includes multiple ancestries): 26.1% Irish, 22.4% German, 14.1% English, 13.7% American, 12.1% French (2006-2010 5-year est.).

**Economy:** Single-family building permits issued: 2 (2011); Multi-family building permits issued: 0 (2011); Employment by occupation: 6.9% management, 5.9% professional, 11.4% services, 11.2% sales, 2.3% farming, 14.5% construction, 14.1% production (2006-2010 5-year est.).

**Income:** Per capita income: $17,141 (2006-2010 5-year est.); Median household income: $38,950 (2006-2010 5-year est.); Average household income: $49,082 (2006-2010 5-year est.); Percent of households with income of $100,000 or more: 10.4% (2006-2010 5-year est.); Poverty rate: 21.0% (2006-2010 5-year est.).

**Education:** Percent of population age 25 and over with: High school diploma (including GED) or higher: 80.8% (2006-2010 5-year est.); Bachelor's degree or higher: 8.3% (2006-2010 5-year est.); Master's degree or higher: 4.6% (2006-2010 5-year est.).

**Housing:** Homeownership rate: 87.9% (2010); Median home value: $79,000 (2006-2010 5-year est.); Median contract rent: $481 per month (2006-2010 5-year est.); Median year structure built: 1976 (2006-2010 5-year est.).

**Transportation:** Commute to work: 97.3% car, 0.0% public transportation, 0.0% walk, 2.7% work from home (2006-2010 5-year est.); Travel time to work: 24.3% less than 15 minutes, 24.9% 15 to 30 minutes, 16.5% 30 to 45 minutes, 16.0% 45 to 60 minutes, 18.3% 60 minutes or more (2006-2010 5-year est.)

**FLOYD** (town). Covers a land area of 34.616 square miles and a water area of 0.175 square miles. Located at 43.23° N. Lat; 75.32° W. Long. Elevation is 561 feet.

**Population:** 3,856 (1990); 3,869 (2000); 3,819 (2010); Density: 110.3 persons per square mile (2010); Race: 97.6% White, 0.3% Black, 0.8% Asian, 0.1% American Indian/Alaska Native, 0.0% Native Hawaiian/Other Pacific Islander, 1.2% Other, 1.1% Hispanic of any race (2010); Average household size: 2.61 (2010); Median age: 42.0 (2010); Males per 100 females: 102.6 (2010); Marriage status: 29.8% never married, 55.5% now married, 5.0% widowed, 9.7% divorced (2006-2010 5-year est.); Foreign born: 1.7% (2006-2010 5-year est.); Ancestry (includes multiple ancestries): 35.6% German, 18.7% Italian, 17.6% Irish, 17.2% Polish, 11.6% English (2006-2010 5-year est.).

**Economy:** Single-family building permits issued: 5 (2011); Multi-family building permits issued: 0 (2011); Employment by occupation: 6.9% management, 5.9% professional, 6.4% services, 20.3% sales, 3.5% farming, 9.9% construction, 4.1% production (2006-2010 5-year est.).

**Income:** Per capita income: $23,647 (2006-2010 5-year est.); Median household income: $57,484 (2006-2010 5-year est.); Average household income: $63,788 (2006-2010 5-year est.); Percent of households with income of $100,000 or more: 19.1% (2006-2010 5-year est.); Poverty rate: 6.1% (2006-2010 5-year est.).

**Education:** Percent of population age 25 and over with: High school diploma (including GED) or higher: 93.1% (2006-2010 5-year est.); Bachelor's degree or higher: 20.3% (2006-2010 5-year est.); Master's degree or higher: 7.6% (2006-2010 5-year est.).

**Housing:** Homeownership rate: 87.6% (2010); Median home value: $117,300 (2006-2010 5-year est.); Median contract rent: $446 per month (2006-2010 5-year est.); Median year structure built: 1967 (2006-2010 5-year est.).

**Transportation:** Commute to work: 91.5% car, 0.6% public transportation, 0.4% walk, 6.8% work from home (2006-2010 5-year est.); Travel time to work: 32.6% less than 15 minutes, 50.7% 15 to 30 minutes, 9.0% 30 to 45 minutes, 2.3% 45 to 60 minutes, 5.4% 60 minutes or more (2006-2010 5-year est.).

**Additional Information Contacts**

Town of Floyd . . . . . . . . . . . . . . . . . . . . . . . . . . . . . . . . . (315) 865-4256
  http://town.floyd.ny.us

**FORESTPORT** (town). Covers a land area of 76.915 square miles and a water area of 1.984 square miles. Located at 43.49° N. Lat; 75.14° W. Long. Elevation is 1,122 feet.

**Population:** 1,548 (1990); 1,692 (2000); 1,535 (2010); Density: 20.0 persons per square mile (2010); Race: 97.9% White, 0.2% Black, 0.1% Asian, 0.3% American Indian/Alaska Native, 0.0% Native Hawaiian/Other Pacific Islander, 1.5% Other, 0.6% Hispanic of any race (2010); Average household size: 2.23 (2010); Median age: 48.5 (2010); Males per 100 females: 105.8 (2010); Marriage status: 19.8% never married, 59.8% now

married, 3.5% widowed, 17.0% divorced (2006-2010 5-year est.); Foreign born: 3.6% (2006-2010 5-year est.); Ancestry (includes multiple ancestries): 23.8% German, 19.3% Irish, 14.3% English, 10.1% French, 8.9% American (2006-2010 5-year est.).

**Economy:** Single-family building permits issued: 12 (2011); Multi-family building permits issued: 0 (2011); Employment by occupation: 9.4% management, 0.0% professional, 12.8% services, 11.5% sales, 3.4% farming, 9.6% construction, 10.5% production (2006-2010 5-year est.).

**Income:** Per capita income: $22,062 (2006-2010 5-year est.); Median household income: $46,250 (2006-2010 5-year est.); Average household income: $49,446 (2006-2010 5-year est.); Percent of households with income of $100,000 or more: 8.5% (2006-2010 5-year est.); Poverty rate: 15.9% (2006-2010 5-year est.).

**Education:** Percent of population age 25 and over with: High school diploma (including GED) or higher: 93.3% (2006-2010 5-year est.); Bachelor's degree or higher: 16.5% (2006-2010 5-year est.); Master's degree or higher: 5.9% (2006-2010 5-year est.).

**School District(s)**

Adirondack Central School District (PK-12)
  2009-10 Enrollment: 1,395 . . . . . . . . . . . . . . . . . . . . . (315) 942-9200

**Housing:** Homeownership rate: 87.1% (2010); Median home value: $122,100 (2006-2010 5-year est.); Median contract rent: $425 per month (2006-2010 5-year est.); Median year structure built: 1959 (2006-2010 5-year est.).

**Transportation:** Commute to work: 91.8% car, 0.0% public transportation, 4.1% walk, 4.1% work from home (2006-2010 5-year est.); Travel time to work: 21.2% less than 15 minutes, 26.3% 15 to 30 minutes, 26.1% 30 to 45 minutes, 20.6% 45 to 60 minutes, 5.7% 60 minutes or more (2006-2010 5-year est.)

**FRANKLIN SPRINGS** (unincorporated postal area)

Zip Code: 13341

Covers a land area of 0.184 square miles and a water area of 0 square miles. Located at 43.03° N. Lat; 75.39° W. Long. Elevation is 630 feet. Population: 102 (2010); Density: 553.9 persons per square mile (2010); Race: 95.1% White, 0.0% Black, 1.0% Asian, 0.0% American Indian/Alaska Native, 0.0% Native Hawaiian/Other Pacific Islander, 3.9% Other, 0.0% Hispanic of any race (2010); Average household size: 2.62 (2010); Median age: 44.0 (2010); Males per 100 females: 82.1 (2010); Homeownership rate: 94.8% (2010)

**HINCKLEY** (unincorporated postal area)

Zip Code: 13352

Covers a land area of 0.167 square miles and a water area of 0.016 square miles. Located at 43.31° N. Lat; 75.11° W. Long. Elevation is 1,198 feet. Population: 65 (2010); Density: 387.5 persons per square mile (2010); Race: 89.2% White, 0.0% Black, 1.5% Asian, 1.5% American Indian/Alaska Native, 0.0% Native Hawaiian/Other Pacific Islander, 7.8% Other, 0.0% Hispanic of any race (2010); Average household size: 2.24 (2010); Median age: 48.5 (2010); Males per 100 females: 71.1 (2010); Homeownership rate: 89.6% (2010)

**HOLLAND PATENT** (village). Covers a land area of 0.505 square miles and a water area of 0.002 square miles. Located at 43.24° N. Lat; 75.25° W. Long. Elevation is 640 feet.

**Population:** 411 (1990); 461 (2000); 458 (2010); Density: 906.0 persons per square mile (2010); Race: 99.3% White, 0.2% Black, 0.0% Asian, 0.0% American Indian/Alaska Native, 0.0% Native Hawaiian/Other Pacific Islander, 0.5% Other, 1.7% Hispanic of any race (2010); Average household size: 2.27 (2010); Median age: 44.4 (2010); Males per 100 females: 96.6 (2010); Marriage status: 25.1% never married, 57.8% now married, 6.8% widowed, 10.3% divorced (2006-2010 5-year est.); Foreign born: 3.2% (2006-2010 5-year est.); Ancestry (includes multiple ancestries): 44.0% Irish, 27.8% German, 15.7% English, 13.5% Welsh, 10.1% Polish (2006-2010 5-year est.).

**Economy:** Employment by occupation: 9.2% management, 3.3% professional, 2.6% services, 21.4% sales, 9.2% farming, 6.6% construction, 7.4% production (2006-2010 5-year est.).

**Income:** Per capita income: $24,640 (2006-2010 5-year est.); Median household income: $59,375 (2006-2010 5-year est.); Average household income: $66,865 (2006-2010 5-year est.); Percent of households with income of $100,000 or more: 16.7% (2006-2010 5-year est.); Poverty rate: 17.7% (2006-2010 5-year est.).

**Education:** Percent of population age 25 and over with: High school diploma (including GED) or higher: 94.5% (2006-2010 5-year est.);

Bachelor's degree or higher: 31.4% (2006-2010 5-year est.); Master's degree or higher: 15.1% (2006-2010 5-year est.).

### School District(s)

Holland Patent Central School District (PK-12)

    2009-10 Enrollment: 1,647 . . . . . . . . . . . . . . . . . . . . . . (315) 865-7221

**Housing:** Homeownership rate: 63.9% (2010); Median home value: $116,100 (2006-2010 5-year est.); Median contract rent: $534 per month (2006-2010 5-year est.); Median year structure built: before 1940 (2006-2010 5-year est.).

**Newspapers:** Utica Area Home News (Community news; Circulation 13,000); Valley Home News (Community news; Circulation 21,000)

**Transportation:** Commute to work: 91.8% car, 0.0% public transportation, 4.8% walk, 3.3% work from home (2006-2010 5-year est.); Travel time to work: 30.4% less than 15 minutes, 50.4% 15 to 30 minutes, 15.0% 30 to 45 minutes, 4.2% 45 to 60 minutes, 0.0% 60 minutes or more (2006-2010 5-year est.)

**Additional Information Contacts**

Village of Holland Patent . . . . . . . . . . . . . . . . . . . . . . . . (315) 865-4853
    http://village.holland-patent.ny.us/content

**KIRKLAND** (town). Covers a land area of 33.782 square miles and a water area of 0.051 square miles. Located at 43.03° N. Lat; 75.38° W. Long. Elevation is 528 feet.

**Population:** 10,153 (1990); 10,138 (2000); 10,315 (2010); Density: 305.3 persons per square mile (2010); Race: 93.6% White, 1.3% Black, 2.6% Asian, 0.2% American Indian/Alaska Native, 0.0% Native Hawaiian/Other Pacific Islander, 2.3% Other, 2.4% Hispanic of any race (2010); Average household size: 2.23 (2010); Median age: 39.1 (2010); Males per 100 females: 90.5 (2010); Marriage status: 45.6% never married, 41.0% now married, 6.5% widowed, 6.9% divorced (2006-2010 5-year est.); Foreign born: 3.9% (2006-2010 5-year est.); Ancestry (includes multiple ancestries): 22.8% Irish, 22.2% German, 17.7% English, 16.1% Italian, 10.9% Polish (2006-2010 5-year est.).

**Economy:** Single-family building permits issued: 4 (2011); Multi-family building permits issued: 0 (2011); Employment by occupation: 10.5% management, 6.3% professional, 6.8% services, 16.7% sales, 4.7% farming, 5.2% construction, 2.9% production (2006-2010 5-year est.).

**Income:** Per capita income: $27,665 (2006-2010 5-year est.); Median household income: $58,167 (2006-2010 5-year est.); Average household income: $81,296 (2006-2010 5-year est.); Percent of households with income of $100,000 or more: 25.3% (2006-2010 5-year est.); Poverty rate: 4.6% (2006-2010 5-year est.).

**Education:** Percent of population age 25 and over with: High school diploma (including GED) or higher: 93.7% (2006-2010 5-year est.); Bachelor's degree or higher: 41.4% (2006-2010 5-year est.); Master's degree or higher: 21.5% (2006-2010 5-year est.).

**Housing:** Homeownership rate: 63.8% (2010); Median home value: $162,000 (2006-2010 5-year est.); Median contract rent: $601 per month (2006-2010 5-year est.); Median year structure built: 1954 (2006-2010 5-year est.).

**Transportation:** Commute to work: 75.2% car, 0.1% public transportation, 13.5% walk, 10.9% work from home (2006-2010 5-year est.); Travel time to work: 52.1% less than 15 minutes, 40.2% 15 to 30 minutes, 2.9% 30 to 45 minutes, 2.2% 45 to 60 minutes, 2.7% 60 minutes or more (2006-2010 5-year est.)

**KNOXBORO** (unincorporated postal area)

Zip Code: 13362

    Covers a land area of 0.276 square miles and a water area of 0 square miles. Located at 42.98° N. Lat; 75.52° W. Long. Elevation is 1,096 feet. Population: 60 (2010); Density: 217.4 persons per square mile (2010); Race: 100.0% White, 0.0% Black, 0.0% Asian, 0.0% American Indian/Alaska Native, 0.0% Native Hawaiian/Other Pacific Islander, 0.0% Other, 0.0% Hispanic of any race (2010); Average household size: 2.86 (2010); Median age: 35.0 (2010); Males per 100 females: 93.5 (2010); Homeownership rate: 90.5% (2010)

**LEE** (town). Covers a land area of 45.106 square miles and a water area of 0.446 square miles. Located at 43.32° N. Lat; 75.51° W. Long. Elevation is 505 feet.

**Population:** 7,115 (1990); 6,875 (2000); 6,486 (2010); Density: 143.8 persons per square mile (2010); Race: 97.1% White, 0.9% Black, 0.6% Asian, 0.2% American Indian/Alaska Native, 0.0% Native Hawaiian/Other Pacific Islander, 1.2% Other, 1.2% Hispanic of any race (2010); Average household size: 2.52 (2010); Median age: 44.4 (2010); Males per 100

females: 97.7 (2010); Marriage status: 23.1% never married, 62.2% now married, 6.2% widowed, 8.6% divorced (2006-2010 5-year est.); Foreign born: 3.7% (2006-2010 5-year est.); Ancestry (includes multiple ancestries): 30.0% German, 20.3% Italian, 17.7% Irish, 10.9% English, 10.1% French (2006-2010 5-year est.).

**Economy:** Single-family building permits issued: 5 (2011); Multi-family building permits issued: 0 (2011); Employment by occupation: 10.6% management, 7.5% professional, 7.5% services, 16.1% sales, 2.0% farming, 7.3% construction, 7.6% production (2006-2010 5-year est.).

**Income:** Per capita income: $24,121 (2006-2010 5-year est.); Median household income: $59,675 (2006-2010 5-year est.); Average household income: $64,611 (2006-2010 5-year est.); Percent of households with income of $100,000 or more: 19.6% (2006-2010 5-year est.); Poverty rate: 12.5% (2006-2010 5-year est.).

**Education:** Percent of population age 25 and over with: High school diploma (including GED) or higher: 89.0% (2006-2010 5-year est.); Bachelor's degree or higher: 23.2% (2006-2010 5-year est.); Master's degree or higher: 6.8% (2006-2010 5-year est.).

**Housing:** Homeownership rate: 86.8% (2010); Median home value: $106,900 (2006-2010 5-year est.); Median contract rent: $493 per month (2006-2010 5-year est.); Median year structure built: 1965 (2006-2010 5-year est.).

**Transportation:** Commute to work: 95.2% car, 0.3% public transportation, 1.4% walk, 2.8% work from home (2006-2010 5-year est.); Travel time to work: 22.3% less than 15 minutes, 47.9% 15 to 30 minutes, 18.4% 30 to 45 minutes, 6.6% 45 to 60 minutes, 4.9% 60 minutes or more (2006-2010 5-year est.)

**LEE CENTER** (unincorporated postal area)

Zip Code: 13363

    Covers a land area of 21.187 square miles and a water area of 0.045 square miles. Located at 43.32° N. Lat; 75.51° W. Long. Elevation is 617 feet. Population: 2,315 (2010); Density: 109.3 persons per square mile (2010); Race: 98.2% White, 0.6% Black, 0.1% Asian, 0.0% American Indian/Alaska Native, 0.1% Native Hawaiian/Other Pacific Islander, 1.0% Other, 1.0% Hispanic of any race (2010); Average household size: 2.55 (2010); Median age: 42.5 (2010); Males per 100 females: 98.7 (2010); Homeownership rate: 84.3% (2010)

**MARCY** (town). Covers a land area of 32.890 square miles and a water area of 0.428 square miles. Located at 43.17° N. Lat; 75.26° W. Long. Elevation is 604 feet.

**Population:** 8,685 (1990); 9,469 (2000); 8,982 (2010); Density: 273.1 persons per square mile (2010); Race: 78.6% White, 17.5% Black, 0.6% Asian, 0.4% American Indian/Alaska Native, 0.0% Native Hawaiian/Other Pacific Islander, 2.9% Other, 7.2% Hispanic of any race (2010); Average household size: 2.51 (2010); Median age: 39.9 (2010); Males per 100 females: 208.9 (2010); Marriage status: 38.2% never married, 48.1% now married, 3.7% widowed, 10.0% divorced (2006-2010 5-year est.); Foreign born: 6.6% (2006-2010 5-year est.); Ancestry (includes multiple ancestries): 18.7% Italian, 16.5% Irish, 15.0% German, 11.9% Polish, 7.0% English (2006-2010 5-year est.).

**Economy:** Single-family building permits issued: 4 (2011); Multi-family building permits issued: 0 (2011); Employment by occupation: 13.4% management, 2.4% professional, 7.1% services, 15.9% sales, 5.3% farming, 10.0% construction, 7.6% production (2006-2010 5-year est.).

**Income:** Per capita income: $18,842 (2006-2010 5-year est.); Median household income: $64,494 (2006-2010 5-year est.); Average household income: $74,105 (2006-2010 5-year est.); Percent of households with income of $100,000 or more: 26.0% (2006-2010 5-year est.); Poverty rate: 5.4% (2006-2010 5-year est.).

**Taxes:** Total city taxes per capita: $190 (2009); City property taxes per capita: $168 (2009).

**Education:** Percent of population age 25 and over with: High school diploma (including GED) or higher: 76.1% (2006-2010 5-year est.); Bachelor's degree or higher: 13.1% (2006-2010 5-year est.); Master's degree or higher: 5.5% (2006-2010 5-year est.).

### School District(s)

Whitesboro Central School District (KG-12)

    2009-10 Enrollment: 3,531 . . . . . . . . . . . . . . . . . . . . . . (315) 266-3303

**Housing:** Homeownership rate: 83.8% (2010); Median home value: $154,800 (2006-2010 5-year est.); Median contract rent: $544 per month (2006-2010 5-year est.); Median year structure built: 1967 (2006-2010 5-year est.).

**Transportation:** Commute to work: 91.7% car, 1.1% public transportation, 1.5% walk, 5.2% work from home (2006-2010 5-year est.); Travel time to work: 35.5% less than 15 minutes, 49.5% 15 to 30 minutes, 10.4% 30 to 45 minutes, 1.4% 45 to 60 minutes, 3.2% 60 minutes or more (2006-2010 5-year est.)

**Additional Information Contacts**
Marcy Chamber of Commerce. . . . . . . . . . . . . . . . . . . (315) 327-8709
http://www.marcychamber.com

## MARSHALL (town).
Covers a land area of 32.801 square miles and a water area of 0 square miles. Located at 42.96° N. Lat; 75.38° W. Long. Elevation is 1,365 feet.

**Population:** 2,125 (1990); 2,127 (2000); 2,131 (2010); Density: 65.0 persons per square mile (2010); Race: 98.2% White, 0.3% Black, 0.4% Asian, 0.1% American Indian/Alaska Native, 0.0% Native Hawaiian/Other Pacific Islander, 1.0% Other, 1.0% Hispanic of any race (2010); Average household size: 2.56 (2010); Median age: 41.5 (2010); Males per 100 females: 105.5 (2010); Marriage status: 22.5% never married, 65.7% now married, 5.8% widowed, 6.1% divorced (2006-2010 5-year est.); Foreign born: 2.6% (2006-2010 5-year est.); Ancestry (includes multiple ancestries): 25.6% Irish, 21.1% German, 17.6% English, 9.5% French, 7.5% Italian (2006-2010 5-year est.).

**Economy:** Single-family building permits issued: 3 (2011); Multi-family building permits issued: 0 (2011); Employment by occupation: 13.6% management, 0.3% professional, 8.1% services, 14.5% sales, 2.7% farming, 17.7% construction, 7.9% production (2006-2010 5-year est.).

**Income:** Per capita income: $27,719 (2006-2010 5-year est.); Median household income: $66,094 (2006-2010 5-year est.); Average household income: $73,679 (2006-2010 5-year est.); Percent of households with income of $100,000 or more: 25.5% (2006-2010 5-year est.); Poverty rate: 8.6% (2006-2010 5-year est.).

**Education:** Percent of population age 25 and over with: High school diploma (including GED) or higher: 93.0% (2006-2010 5-year est.); Bachelor's degree or higher: 28.8% (2006-2010 5-year est.); Master's degree or higher: 10.9% (2006-2010 5-year est.).

**Housing:** Homeownership rate: 83.3% (2010); Median home value: $128,700 (2006-2010 5-year est.); Median contract rent: $592 per month (2006-2010 5-year est.); Median year structure built: 1952 (2006-2010 5-year est.).

**Transportation:** Commute to work: 95.5% car, 0.0% public transportation, 1.8% walk, 2.8% work from home (2006-2010 5-year est.); Travel time to work: 34.6% less than 15 minutes, 40.8% 15 to 30 minutes, 19.9% 30 to 45 minutes, 1.7% 45 to 60 minutes, 3.0% 60 minutes or more (2006-2010 5-year est.)

## NEW HARTFORD (village).
Covers a land area of 0.616 square miles and a water area of 0 square miles. Located at 43.07° N. Lat; 75.28° W. Long. Elevation is 541 feet.

**Population:** 2,111 (1990); 1,886 (2000); 1,847 (2010); Density: 2,994.7 persons per square mile (2010); Race: 95.6% White, 1.2% Black, 0.9% Asian, 0.1% American Indian/Alaska Native, 0.0% Native Hawaiian/Other Pacific Islander, 2.2% Other, 2.3% Hispanic of any race (2010); Average household size: 2.09 (2010); Median age: 45.8 (2010); Males per 100 females: 82.5 (2010); Marriage status: 27.0% never married, 51.6% now married, 11.1% widowed, 10.3% divorced (2006-2010 5-year est.); Foreign born: 6.6% (2006-2010 5-year est.); Ancestry (includes multiple ancestries): 22.0% German, 21.2% Irish, 18.5% English, 18.0% Italian, 12.9% Polish (2006-2010 5-year est.).

**Economy:** Employment by occupation: 14.9% management, 3.2% professional, 9.3% services, 13.6% sales, 0.5% farming, 6.4% construction, 4.6% production (2006-2010 5-year est.).

**Income:** Per capita income: $32,766 (2006-2010 5-year est.); Median household income: $52,938 (2006-2010 5-year est.); Average household income: $73,788 (2006-2010 5-year est.); Percent of households with income of $100,000 or more: 21.8% (2006-2010 5-year est.); Poverty rate: 3.3% (2006-2010 5-year est.).

**Education:** Percent of population age 25 and over with: High school diploma (including GED) or higher: 95.5% (2006-2010 5-year est.); Bachelor's degree or higher: 43.1% (2006-2010 5-year est.); Master's degree or higher: 24.7% (2006-2010 5-year est.).

**School District(s)**
New Hartford Central School District (KG-12)
   2009-10 Enrollment: 2,622 . . . . . . . . . . . . . . . . . (315) 624-1218
Oneida-Herkimer-Madison Boces
   2009-10 Enrollment: n/a . . . . . . . . . . . . . . . . . . . (315) 793-8561

**Housing:** Homeownership rate: 61.4% (2010); Median home value: $150,700 (2006-2010 5-year est.); Median contract rent: $708 per month (2006-2010 5-year est.); Median year structure built: 1942 (2006-2010 5-year est.).

**Transportation:** Commute to work: 90.0% car, 0.0% public transportation, 2.7% walk, 6.5% work from home (2006-2010 5-year est.); Travel time to work: 58.5% less than 15 minutes, 27.4% 15 to 30 minutes, 9.5% 30 to 45 minutes, 4.1% 45 to 60 minutes, 0.6% 60 minutes or more (2006-2010 5-year est.)

## NEW HARTFORD (town).
Covers a land area of 25.356 square miles and a water area of 0.118 square miles. Located at 43.05° N. Lat; 75.28° W. Long. Elevation is 541 feet.

**History:** Settled c.1787, incorporated 1870.

**Population:** 21,640 (1990); 21,172 (2000); 22,166 (2010); Density: 874.2 persons per square mile (2010); Race: 93.9% White, 1.3% Black, 3.1% Asian, 0.1% American Indian/Alaska Native, 0.0% Native Hawaiian/Other Pacific Islander, 1.6% Other, 2.0% Hispanic of any race (2010); Average household size: 2.23 (2010); Median age: 47.6 (2010); Males per 100 females: 86.6 (2010); Marriage status: 25.4% never married, 54.7% now married, 11.0% widowed, 8.8% divorced (2006-2010 5-year est.); Foreign born: 7.1% (2006-2010 5-year est.); Ancestry (includes multiple ancestries): 27.3% Italian, 20.1% Irish, 17.8% German, 15.0% Polish, 10.3% English (2006-2010 5-year est.).

**Economy:** Single-family building permits issued: 7 (2011); Multi-family building permits issued: 0 (2011); Employment by occupation: 13.3% management, 5.3% professional, 7.0% services, 17.5% sales, 2.5% farming, 5.9% construction, 3.6% production (2006-2010 5-year est.).

**Income:** Per capita income: $33,819 (2006-2010 5-year est.); Median household income: $54,282 (2006-2010 5-year est.); Average household income: $77,502 (2006-2010 5-year est.); Percent of households with income of $100,000 or more: 23.6% (2006-2010 5-year est.); Poverty rate: 8.5% (2006-2010 5-year est.).

**Education:** Percent of population age 25 and over with: High school diploma (including GED) or higher: 91.4% (2006-2010 5-year est.); Bachelor's degree or higher: 39.4% (2006-2010 5-year est.); Master's degree or higher: 19.8% (2006-2010 5-year est.).

**School District(s)**
New Hartford Central School District (KG-12)
   2009-10 Enrollment: 2,622 . . . . . . . . . . . . . . . . . (315) 624-1218
Oneida-Herkimer-Madison Boces
   2009-10 Enrollment: n/a . . . . . . . . . . . . . . . . . . . (315) 793-8561

**Housing:** Homeownership rate: 73.3% (2010); Median home value: $132,600 (2006-2010 5-year est.); Median contract rent: $619 per month (2006-2010 5-year est.); Median year structure built: 1960 (2006-2010 5-year est.).

**Safety:** Violent crime rate: 6.4 per 10,000 population; Property crime rate: 379.3 per 10,000 population (2010).

**Transportation:** Commute to work: 93.9% car, 0.6% public transportation, 1.6% walk, 3.2% work from home (2006-2010 5-year est.); Travel time to work: 53.1% less than 15 minutes, 36.8% 15 to 30 minutes, 6.4% 30 to 45 minutes, 1.7% 45 to 60 minutes, 2.0% 60 minutes or more (2006-2010 5-year est.)

**Additional Information Contacts**
Town of New Hartford . . . . . . . . . . . . . . . . . . . . . . . (315) 733-7500
http://www.newhartfordtown.com

## NEW YORK MILLS (village).
Covers a land area of 1.179 square miles and a water area of 0 square miles. Located at 43.10° N. Lat; 75.29° W. Long. Elevation is 466 feet.

**History:** Incorporated 1922.

**Population:** 3,534 (1990); 3,191 (2000); 3,327 (2010); Density: 2,819.6 persons per square mile (2010); Race: 95.6% White, 1.4% Black, 1.6% Asian, 0.2% American Indian/Alaska Native, 0.0% Native Hawaiian/Other Pacific Islander, 1.2% Other, 2.3% Hispanic of any race (2010); Average household size: 1.96 (2010); Median age: 42.3 (2010); Males per 100 females: 92.1 (2010); Marriage status: 36.1% never married, 41.7% now married, 13.6% widowed, 8.6% divorced (2006-2010 5-year est.); Foreign born: 6.5% (2006-2010 5-year est.); Ancestry (includes multiple ancestries): 24.8% Italian, 23.7% Polish, 16.0% Irish, 12.2% German, 9.2% English (2006-2010 5-year est.).

**Economy:** Single-family building permits issued: 1 (2011); Multi-family building permits issued: 0 (2011); Employment by occupation: 6.5% management, 4.2% professional, 11.5% services, 14.9% sales, 4.9% farming, 9.3% construction, 3.6% production (2006-2010 5-year est.).

**Income:** Per capita income: $25,875 (2006-2010 5-year est.); Median household income: $37,938 (2006-2010 5-year est.); Average household income: $46,405 (2006-2010 5-year est.); Percent of households with income of $100,000 or more: 7.3% (2006-2010 5-year est.); Poverty rate: 7.1% (2006-2010 5-year est.).

**Education:** Percent of population age 25 and over with: High school diploma (including GED) or higher: 91.1% (2006-2010 5-year est.); Bachelor's degree or higher: 25.2% (2006-2010 5-year est.); Master's degree or higher: 9.2% (2006-2010 5-year est.).

### School District(s)

New York Mills Union Free School District (KG-12)
> 2009-10 Enrollment: 574 . . . . . . . . . . . . . . . . . . . . (315) 768-8127

**Housing:** Homeownership rate: 44.9% (2010); Median home value: $94,700 (2006-2010 5-year est.); Median contract rent: $535 per month (2006-2010 5-year est.); Median year structure built: 1955 (2006-2010 5-year est.).

**Safety:** Violent crime rate: 9.2 per 10,000 population; Property crime rate: 154.1 per 10,000 population (2010).

**Transportation:** Commute to work: 95.1% car, 0.8% public transportation, 1.4% walk, 1.4% work from home (2006-2010 5-year est.); Travel time to work: 50.8% less than 15 minutes, 37.8% 15 to 30 minutes, 8.8% 30 to 45 minutes, 1.6% 45 to 60 minutes, 1.0% 60 minutes or more (2006-2010 5-year est.).

## NORTH BAY (unincorporated postal area)

Zip Code: 13123

Covers a land area of 2.366 square miles and a water area of 0 square miles. Located at 43.23° N. Lat; 75.76° W. Long. Elevation is 476 feet.
Population: 314 (2010); Density: 132.7 persons per square mile (2010); Race: 97.8% White, 0.0% Black, 0.6% Asian, 1.3% American Indian/Alaska Native, 0.0% Native Hawaiian/Other Pacific Islander, 0.3% Other, 0.6% Hispanic of any race (2010); Average household size: 2.47 (2010); Median age: 45.7 (2010); Males per 100 females: 101.3 (2010); Homeownership rate: 89.7% (2010)

## ONEIDA CASTLE (village).

Covers a land area of 0.513 square miles and a water area of 0 square miles. Located at 43.08° N. Lat; 75.63° W. Long. Elevation is 449 feet.

**History:** Center of Oneida Territory, site of chief settlement of Oneida people.

**Population:** 671 (1990); 627 (2000); 625 (2010); Density: 1,216.1 persons per square mile (2010); Race: 94.9% White, 0.3% Black, 0.8% Asian, 1.4% American Indian/Alaska Native, 0.0% Native Hawaiian/Other Pacific Islander, 2.6% Other, 0.5% Hispanic of any race (2010); Average household size: 2.21 (2010); Median age: 44.3 (2010); Males per 100 females: 88.3 (2010); Marriage status: 33.1% never married, 48.8% now married, 6.3% widowed, 11.8% divorced (2006-2010 5-year est.); Foreign born: 3.8% (2006-2010 5-year est.); Ancestry (includes multiple ancestries): 27.8% German, 19.0% Irish, 18.2% English, 12.6% American, 11.5% Italian (2006-2010 5-year est.).

**Economy:** Single-family building permits issued: 0 (2011); Multi-family building permits issued: 0 (2011); Employment by occupation: 6.0% management, 0.0% professional, 23.3% services, 6.4% sales, 12.4% farming, 4.5% construction, 5.6% production (2006-2010 5-year est.).

**Income:** Per capita income: $21,598 (2006-2010 5-year est.); Median household income: $35,833 (2006-2010 5-year est.); Average household income: $49,560 (2006-2010 5-year est.); Percent of households with income of $100,000 or more: 10.5% (2006-2010 5-year est.); Poverty rate: 5.7% (2006-2010 5-year est.).

**Education:** Percent of population age 25 and over with: High school diploma (including GED) or higher: 95.3% (2006-2010 5-year est.); Bachelor's degree or higher: 21.8% (2006-2010 5-year est.); Master's degree or higher: 6.2% (2006-2010 5-year est.).

**Housing:** Homeownership rate: 70.3% (2010); Median home value: $113,200 (2006-2010 5-year est.); Median contract rent: $515 per month (2006-2010 5-year est.); Median year structure built: before 1940 (2006-2010 5-year est.).

**Transportation:** Commute to work: 98.1% car, 0.0% public transportation, 0.0% walk, 1.9% work from home (2006-2010 5-year est.); Travel time to work: 63.5% less than 15 minutes, 20.6% 15 to 30 minutes, 9.5% 30 to 45 minutes, 5.2% 45 to 60 minutes, 1.2% 60 minutes or more (2006-2010 5-year est.)

## ORISKANY (village).

Covers a land area of 0.791 square miles and a water area of 0 square miles. Located at 43.15° N. Lat; 75.33° W. Long. Elevation is 430 feet.

**History:** Obelisk at Oriskany Battlefield (Northwest) marks site of an engagement (Aug. 6, 1777) of the Saratoga campaign, one of the bloodiest battles of the American Revolution. Incorporated 1914.

**Population:** 1,573 (1990); 1,459 (2000); 1,400 (2010); Density: 1,768.6 persons per square mile (2010); Race: 97.9% White, 0.6% Black, 0.0% Asian, 0.1% American Indian/Alaska Native, 0.2% Native Hawaiian/Other Pacific Islander, 1.2% Other, 0.9% Hispanic of any race (2010); Average household size: 2.43 (2010); Median age: 42.5 (2010); Males per 100 females: 85.4 (2010); Marriage status: 24.2% never married, 65.8% now married, 5.7% widowed, 4.3% divorced (2006-2010 5-year est.); Foreign born: 2.3% (2006-2010 5-year est.); Ancestry (includes multiple ancestries): 32.2% German, 31.3% Irish, 18.5% Italian, 18.5% Polish, 8.3% English (2006-2010 5-year est.).

**Economy:** Single-family building permits issued: 0 (2011); Multi-family building permits issued: 0 (2011); Employment by occupation: 5.8% management, 1.8% professional, 12.4% services, 19.7% sales, 5.8% farming, 5.7% construction, 3.0% production (2006-2010 5-year est.).

**Income:** Per capita income: $27,251 (2006-2010 5-year est.); Median household income: $58,250 (2006-2010 5-year est.); Average household income: $69,213 (2006-2010 5-year est.); Percent of households with income of $100,000 or more: 17.3% (2006-2010 5-year est.); Poverty rate: 8.3% (2006-2010 5-year est.).

**Education:** Percent of population age 25 and over with: High school diploma (including GED) or higher: 93.6% (2006-2010 5-year est.); Bachelor's degree or higher: 23.0% (2006-2010 5-year est.); Master's degree or higher: 7.8% (2006-2010 5-year est.).

### School District(s)

Oriskany Central School District (PK-12)
> 2009-10 Enrollment: 742 . . . . . . . . . . . . . . . . . . . . (315) 768-2058

**Housing:** Homeownership rate: 70.5% (2010); Median home value: $96,800 (2006-2010 5-year est.); Median contract rent: $503 per month (2006-2010 5-year est.); Median year structure built: 1944 (2006-2010 5-year est.).

**Safety:** Violent crime rate: 0.0 per 10,000 population; Property crime rate: 160.2 per 10,000 population (2010).

**Transportation:** Commute to work: 91.0% car, 1.7% public transportation, 3.1% walk, 3.1% work from home (2006-2010 5-year est.); Travel time to work: 45.0% less than 15 minutes, 45.4% 15 to 30 minutes, 4.8% 30 to 45 minutes, 0.9% 45 to 60 minutes, 4.0% 60 minutes or more (2006-2010 5-year est.)

## ORISKANY FALLS (village).

Covers a land area of 0.506 square miles and a water area of 0 square miles. Located at 42.93° N. Lat; 75.46° W. Long. Elevation is 974 feet.

**Population:** 795 (1990); 698 (2000); 732 (2010); Density: 1,446.0 persons per square mile (2010); Race: 96.4% White, 0.5% Black, 1.0% Asian, 0.0% American Indian/Alaska Native, 0.0% Native Hawaiian/Other Pacific Islander, 2.1% Other, 0.5% Hispanic of any race (2010); Average household size: 2.38 (2010); Median age: 36.8 (2010); Males per 100 females: 99.5 (2010); Marriage status: 32.3% never married, 50.1% now married, 8.9% widowed, 8.7% divorced (2006-2010 5-year est.); Foreign born: 1.6% (2006-2010 5-year est.); Ancestry (includes multiple ancestries): 26.4% German, 24.6% Irish, 16.6% American, 14.2% Italian, 10.3% English (2006-2010 5-year est.).

**Economy:** Single-family building permits issued: 0 (2011); Multi-family building permits issued: 0 (2011); Employment by occupation: 1.9% management, 1.9% professional, 15.0% services, 9.7% sales, 3.9% farming, 10.8% construction, 7.2% production (2006-2010 5-year est.).

**Income:** Per capita income: $19,530 (2006-2010 5-year est.); Median household income: $43,295 (2006-2010 5-year est.); Average household income: $48,022 (2006-2010 5-year est.); Percent of households with income of $100,000 or more: 9.1% (2006-2010 5-year est.); Poverty rate: 7.2% (2006-2010 5-year est.).

**Education:** Percent of population age 25 and over with: High school diploma (including GED) or higher: 74.1% (2006-2010 5-year est.); Bachelor's degree or higher: 5.0% (2006-2010 5-year est.); Master's degree or higher: 0.9% (2006-2010 5-year est.).

**Housing:** Homeownership rate: 58.7% (2010); Median home value: $72,700 (2006-2010 5-year est.); Median contract rent: $383 per month (2006-2010 5-year est.); Median year structure built: before 1940 (2006-2010 5-year est.).

**Transportation:** Commute to work: 88.1% car, 0.0% public transportation, 8.5% walk, 1.1% work from home (2006-2010 5-year est.); Travel time to work: 28.1% less than 15 minutes, 33.5% 15 to 30 minutes, 32.1% 30 to 45 minutes, 1.4% 45 to 60 minutes, 4.9% 60 minutes or more (2006-2010 5-year est.)

**PARIS** (town). Covers a land area of 31.476 square miles and a water area of 0.015 square miles. Located at 42.97° N. Lat; 75.26° W. Long. Elevation is 1,489 feet.
**Population:** 4,414 (1990); 4,609 (2000); 4,411 (2010); Density: 140.1 persons per square mile (2010); Race: 98.3% White, 0.3% Black, 0.5% Asian, 0.1% American Indian/Alaska Native, 0.0% Native Hawaiian/Other Pacific Islander, 0.8% Other, 1.1% Hispanic of any race (2010); Average household size: 2.50 (2010); Median age: 43.6 (2010); Males per 100 females: 97.7 (2010); Marriage status: 22.7% never married, 61.2% now married, 5.2% widowed, 10.8% divorced (2006-2010 5-year est.); Foreign born: 1.7% (2006-2010 5-year est.); Ancestry (includes multiple ancestries): 30.4% German, 19.8% Italian, 19.8% English, 19.4% Irish, 14.3% Polish (2006-2010 5-year est.).
**Economy:** Single-family building permits issued: 0 (2011); Multi-family building permits issued: 0 (2011); Employment by occupation: 13.8% management, 2.4% professional, 9.4% services, 12.1% sales, 6.1% farming, 9.8% construction, 4.3% production (2006-2010 5-year est.).
**Income:** Per capita income: $28,617 (2006-2010 5-year est.); Median household income: $58,750 (2006-2010 5-year est.); Average household income: $68,809 (2006-2010 5-year est.); Percent of households with income of $100,000 or more: 20.9% (2006-2010 5-year est.); Poverty rate: 6.4% (2006-2010 5-year est.).
**Education:** Percent of population age 25 and over with: High school diploma (including GED) or higher: 93.0% (2006-2010 5-year est.); Bachelor's degree or higher: 25.3% (2006-2010 5-year est.); Master's degree or higher: 9.7% (2006-2010 5-year est.).
**Housing:** Homeownership rate: 81.3% (2010); Median home value: $117,700 (2006-2010 5-year est.); Median contract rent: $520 per month (2006-2010 5-year est.); Median year structure built: 1960 (2006-2010 5-year est.).
**Transportation:** Commute to work: 94.1% car, 0.1% public transportation, 0.4% walk, 5.2% work from home (2006-2010 5-year est.); Travel time to work: 33.5% less than 15 minutes, 53.3% 15 to 30 minutes, 6.9% 30 to 45 minutes, 1.6% 45 to 60 minutes, 4.6% 60 minutes or more (2006-2010 5-year est.)
**Additional Information Contacts**
Town of Paris . . . . . . . . . . . . . . . . . . . . . . . . . . . . . . . . . . (315) 839-5400
   http://town.paris.ny.us/content

**PROSPECT** (village). Covers a land area of 0.207 square miles and a water area of 0 square miles. Located at 43.30° N. Lat; 75.15° W. Long. Elevation is 1,184 feet.
**Population:** 312 (1990); 330 (2000); 291 (2010); Density: 1,399.9 persons per square mile (2010); Race: 98.6% White, 0.0% Black, 1.4% Asian, 0.0% American Indian/Alaska Native, 0.0% Native Hawaiian/Other Pacific Islander, 0.0% Other, 0.0% Hispanic of any race (2010); Average household size: 2.47 (2010); Median age: 42.3 (2010); Males per 100 females: 99.3 (2010); Marriage status: 12.7% never married, 77.4% now married, 5.0% widowed, 5.0% divorced (2006-2010 5-year est.); Foreign born: 3.1% (2006-2010 5-year est.); Ancestry (includes multiple ancestries): 36.2% Italian, 27.5% German, 20.9% Irish, 15.0% Polish, 9.1% Welsh (2006-2010 5-year est.).
**Economy:** Employment by occupation: 1.3% management, 6.6% professional, 17.1% services, 9.2% sales, 3.3% farming, 16.4% construction, 9.2% production (2006-2010 5-year est.).
**Income:** Per capita income: $28,202 (2006-2010 5-year est.); Median household income: $68,375 (2006-2010 5-year est.); Average household income: $73,975 (2006-2010 5-year est.); Percent of households with income of $100,000 or more: 18.7% (2006-2010 5-year est.); Poverty rate: 2.1% (2006-2010 5-year est.).
**Education:** Percent of population age 25 and over with: High school diploma (including GED) or higher: 95.4% (2006-2010 5-year est.); Bachelor's degree or higher: 33.0% (2006-2010 5-year est.); Master's degree or higher: 18.3% (2006-2010 5-year est.).
**Housing:** Homeownership rate: 83.9% (2010); Median home value: $86,900 (2006-2010 5-year est.); Median contract rent: $638 per month (2006-2010 5-year est.); Median year structure built: before 1940 (2006-2010 5-year est.).

**Transportation:** Commute to work: 97.3% car, 0.0% public transportation, 0.0% walk, 2.7% work from home (2006-2010 5-year est.); Travel time to work: 22.8% less than 15 minutes, 34.5% 15 to 30 minutes, 41.4% 30 to 45 minutes, 0.0% 45 to 60 minutes, 1.4% 60 minutes or more (2006-2010 5-year est.)

**REMSEN** (village). Covers a land area of 0.372 square miles and a water area of 0 square miles. Located at 43.32° N. Lat; 75.18° W. Long. Elevation is 1,184 feet.
**Population:** 518 (1990); 531 (2000); 508 (2010); Density: 1,364.4 persons per square mile (2010); Race: 98.0% White, 0.6% Black, 0.2% Asian, 0.0% American Indian/Alaska Native, 0.0% Native Hawaiian/Other Pacific Islander, 1.2% Other, 0.6% Hispanic of any race (2010); Average household size: 2.45 (2010); Median age: 34.5 (2010); Males per 100 females: 85.4 (2010); Marriage status: 29.2% never married, 61.2% now married, 5.5% widowed, 4.1% divorced (2006-2010 5-year est.); Foreign born: 2.4% (2006-2010 5-year est.); Ancestry (includes multiple ancestries): 30.7% Italian, 20.3% German, 13.9% Welsh, 9.3% Polish, 8.8% English (2006-2010 5-year est.).
**Economy:** Single-family building permits issued: 0 (2011); Multi-family building permits issued: 0 (2011); Employment by occupation: 4.7% management, 0.0% professional, 15.0% services, 16.6% sales, 7.3% farming, 11.9% construction, 4.1% production (2006-2010 5-year est.).
**Income:** Per capita income: $14,954 (2006-2010 5-year est.); Median household income: $38,194 (2006-2010 5-year est.); Average household income: $45,256 (2006-2010 5-year est.); Percent of households with income of $100,000 or more: 3.9% (2006-2010 5-year est.); Poverty rate: 19.2% (2006-2010 5-year est.).
**Education:** Percent of population age 25 and over with: High school diploma (including GED) or higher: 87.4% (2006-2010 5-year est.); Bachelor's degree or higher: 8.1% (2006-2010 5-year est.); Master's degree or higher: 0.0% (2006-2010 5-year est.).
**School District(s)**
Remsen Central School District (PK-12)
   2009-10 Enrollment: 498 . . . . . . . . . . . . . . . . . . . . . . . . (315) 831-3797
**Housing:** Homeownership rate: 55.1% (2010); Median home value: $83,200 (2006-2010 5-year est.); Median contract rent: $442 per month (2006-2010 5-year est.); Median year structure built: before 1940 (2006-2010 5-year est.).
**Transportation:** Commute to work: 87.5% car, 0.0% public transportation, 2.3% walk, 10.2% work from home (2006-2010 5-year est.); Travel time to work: 30.4% less than 15 minutes, 29.1% 15 to 30 minutes, 32.9% 30 to 45 minutes, 7.6% 45 to 60 minutes, 0.0% 60 minutes or more (2006-2010 5-year est.)

**REMSEN** (town). Covers a land area of 35.464 square miles and a water area of 1.490 square miles. Located at 43.36° N. Lat; 75.14° W. Long. Elevation is 1,184 feet.
**History:** Reconstructed log cabin of Baron von Steuben, drillmaster to Continental Army, state historic site, 2 miles West.
**Population:** 1,768 (1990); 1,958 (2000); 1,929 (2010); Density: 54.4 persons per square mile (2010); Race: 98.7% White, 0.4% Black, 0.2% Asian, 0.1% American Indian/Alaska Native, 0.0% Native Hawaiian/Other Pacific Islander, 0.6% Other, 1.3% Hispanic of any race (2010); Average household size: 2.50 (2010); Median age: 40.4 (2010); Males per 100 females: 99.7 (2010); Marriage status: 26.6% never married, 58.4% now married, 6.6% widowed, 8.4% divorced (2006-2010 5-year est.); Foreign born: 1.4% (2006-2010 5-year est.); Ancestry (includes multiple ancestries): 24.5% German, 21.9% Irish, 17.4% Italian, 14.1% Welsh, 13.4% English (2006-2010 5-year est.).
**Economy:** Single-family building permits issued: 4 (2011); Multi-family building permits issued: 0 (2011); Employment by occupation: 7.8% management, 4.7% professional, 9.9% services, 15.6% sales, 0.9% farming, 10.6% construction, 8.5% production (2006-2010 5-year est.).
**Income:** Per capita income: $22,664 (2006-2010 5-year est.); Median household income: $48,077 (2006-2010 5-year est.); Average household income: $58,807 (2006-2010 5-year est.); Percent of households with income of $100,000 or more: 13.1% (2006-2010 5-year est.); Poverty rate: 14.9% (2006-2010 5-year est.).
**Education:** Percent of population age 25 and over with: High school diploma (including GED) or higher: 91.8% (2006-2010 5-year est.); Bachelor's degree or higher: 21.4% (2006-2010 5-year est.); Master's degree or higher: 6.3% (2006-2010 5-year est.).

**School District(s)**

Remsen Central School District (PK-12)

　2009-10 Enrollment: 498 . . . . . . . . . . . . . . . . . . . . . . . (315) 831-3797

**Housing:** Homeownership rate: 79.2% (2010); Median home value: $104,400 (2006-2010 5-year est.); Median contract rent: $429 per month (2006-2010 5-year est.); Median year structure built: 1964 (2006-2010 5-year est.).

**Transportation:** Commute to work: 89.4% car, 0.0% public transportation, 2.9% walk, 5.9% work from home (2006-2010 5-year est.); Travel time to work: 27.7% less than 15 minutes, 26.8% 15 to 30 minutes, 35.2% 30 to 45 minutes, 5.7% 45 to 60 minutes, 4.7% 60 minutes or more (2006-2010 5-year est.)

**ROME** (city). Covers a land area of 74.790 square miles and a water area of 0.811 square miles. Located at 43.22° N. Lat; 75.49° W. Long. Elevation is 456 feet.

**History:** Laid out c.1786 on the site of Fort Stanwix. The city was a busy portage point, and had great strategic importance during the French and Indian War and in the American Revolution. The Six Nation Treaty of 1768 was concluded here. Site of the Battle of Oriskany, one of the Revolution's bloodiest battles. Construction on the Erie Canal began (1817) in Rome. Incorporated as a city 1870.

**Population:** 44,350 (1990); 34,950 (2000); 33,725 (2010); Density: 450.9 persons per square mile (2010); Race: 87.4% White, 7.1% Black, 1.1% Asian, 0.3% American Indian/Alaska Native, 0.0% Native Hawaiian/Other Pacific Islander, 4.1% Other, 5.3% Hispanic of any race (2010); Average household size: 2.28 (2010); Median age: 40.2 (2010); Males per 100 females: 105.6 (2010); Marriage status: 33.3% never married, 45.4% now married, 8.8% widowed, 12.5% divorced (2006-2010 5-year est.); Foreign born: 4.4% (2006-2010 5-year est.); Ancestry (includes multiple ancestries): 24.6% Italian, 18.4% Irish, 17.5% German, 11.1% English, 7.9% Polish (2006-2010 5-year est.).

**Economy:** Unemployment rate: 9.2% (February 2012); Total civilian labor force: 14,240 (February 2012); Single-family building permits issued: 2 (2011); Multi-family building permits issued: 18 (2011); Employment by occupation: 8.0% management, 2.3% professional, 11.7% services, 17.1% sales, 4.6% farming, 6.5% construction, 5.0% production (2006-2010 5-year est.).

**Income:** Per capita income: $21,989 (2006-2010 5-year est.); Median household income: $42,779 (2006-2010 5-year est.); Average household income: $52,507 (2006-2010 5-year est.); Percent of households with income of $100,000 or more: 10.0% (2006-2010 5-year est.); Poverty rate: 15.3% (2006-2010 5-year est.).

**Taxes:** Total city taxes per capita: $698 (2009); City property taxes per capita: $413 (2009).

**Education:** Percent of population age 25 and over with: High school diploma (including GED) or higher: 83.0% (2006-2010 5-year est.); Bachelor's degree or higher: 16.9% (2006-2010 5-year est.); Master's degree or higher: 6.6% (2006-2010 5-year est.).

**School District(s)**

New York State School for the Deaf (01-12)

　2009-10 Enrollment: 59 . . . . . . . . . . . . . . . . . . . . . . . . (315) 337-8400

Rome City School District (PK-12)

　2009-10 Enrollment: 5,569 . . . . . . . . . . . . . . . . . . . . . (315) 338-6521

**Housing:** Homeownership rate: 57.4% (2010); Median home value: $85,200 (2006-2010 5-year est.); Median contract rent: $456 per month (2006-2010 5-year est.); Median year structure built: 1951 (2006-2010 5-year est.).

**Hospitals:** Central New York Disabilities Services Office (844 beds); Rome Memorial Hospital (129 beds)

**Safety:** Violent crime rate: 12.1 per 10,000 population; Property crime rate: 196.8 per 10,000 population (2010).

**Newspapers:** Daily Sentinel (Rome, NY) (Local news; Circulation 15,000); The Observer-Dispatch - Rome Bureau (Local news); Rome Observer (Community news; Circulation 11,000)

**Transportation:** Commute to work: 91.9% car, 1.9% public transportation, 2.3% walk, 2.4% work from home (2006-2010 5-year est.); Travel time to work: 48.7% less than 15 minutes, 34.4% 15 to 30 minutes, 12.3% 30 to 45 minutes, 1.9% 45 to 60 minutes, 2.7% 60 minutes or more (2006-2010 5-year est.); Amtrak: train service available.

**Airports:** Griffiss International (general aviation)

**Additional Information Contacts**

City of Rome . . . . . . . . . . . . . . . . . . . . . . . . . . . . . (315) 336-6000
　http://www.romenewyork.com

Rome Area Chamber of Commerce . . . . . . . . . . . . . . (315) 337-1700
　http://www.romechamber.com

**SANGERFIELD** (town). Covers a land area of 30.801 square miles and a water area of 0.179 square miles. Located at 42.89° N. Lat; 75.38° W. Long. Elevation is 1,247 feet.

**Population:** 2,460 (1990); 2,610 (2000); 2,561 (2010); Density: 83.1 persons per square mile (2010); Race: 97.0% White, 0.5% Black, 0.3% Asian, 0.1% American Indian/Alaska Native, 0.4% Native Hawaiian/Other Pacific Islander, 1.7% Other, 0.9% Hispanic of any race (2010); Average household size: 2.47 (2010); Median age: 41.9 (2010); Males per 100 females: 96.2 (2010); Marriage status: 25.7% never married, 60.7% now married, 6.4% widowed, 7.2% divorced (2006-2010 5-year est.); Foreign born: 0.6% (2006-2010 5-year est.); Ancestry (includes multiple ancestries): 24.5% Irish, 23.6% German, 16.5% English, 7.2% American, 7.0% Polish (2006-2010 5-year est.).

**Economy:** Single-family building permits issued: 0 (2011); Multi-family building permits issued: 0 (2011); Employment by occupation: 8.7% management, 4.7% professional, 8.6% services, 13.4% sales, 4.2% farming, 13.6% construction, 5.4% production (2006-2010 5-year est.).

**Income:** Per capita income: $23,384 (2006-2010 5-year est.); Median household income: $49,853 (2006-2010 5-year est.); Average household income: $59,275 (2006-2010 5-year est.); Percent of households with income of $100,000 or more: 13.5% (2006-2010 5-year est.); Poverty rate: 11.7% (2006-2010 5-year est.).

**Education:** Percent of population age 25 and over with: High school diploma (including GED) or higher: 90.2% (2006-2010 5-year est.); Bachelor's degree or higher: 14.4% (2006-2010 5-year est.); Master's degree or higher: 5.2% (2006-2010 5-year est.).

**Housing:** Homeownership rate: 66.6% (2010); Median home value: $100,300 (2006-2010 5-year est.); Median contract rent: $472 per month (2006-2010 5-year est.); Median year structure built: before 1940 (2006-2010 5-year est.).

**Transportation:** Commute to work: 91.7% car, 0.0% public transportation, 3.2% walk, 3.0% work from home (2006-2010 5-year est.); Travel time to work: 37.9% less than 15 minutes, 30.4% 15 to 30 minutes, 22.2% 30 to 45 minutes, 4.3% 45 to 60 minutes, 5.1% 60 minutes or more (2006-2010 5-year est.)

**SAUQUOIT** (unincorporated postal area)

Zip Code: 13456

Covers a land area of 28.072 square miles and a water area of 0 square miles. Located at 43.00° N. Lat; 75.25° W. Long. Elevation is 866 feet. Population: 4,164 (2010); Density: 148.3 persons per square mile (2010); Race: 98.3% White, 0.4% Black, 0.2% Asian, 0.1% American Indian/Alaska Native, 0.0% Native Hawaiian/Other Pacific Islander, 1.0% Other, 1.1% Hispanic of any race (2010); Average household size: 2.51 (2010); Median age: 44.1 (2010); Males per 100 females: 94.2 (2010); Homeownership rate: 83.4% (2010)

**SHERRILL** (city). Covers a land area of 2.311 square miles and a water area of 0 square miles. Located at 43.07° N. Lat; 75.59° W. Long. Elevation is 499 feet.

**History:** Incorporated 1916.

**Population:** 2,869 (1990); 3,147 (2000); 3,071 (2010); Density: 1,328.6 persons per square mile (2010); Race: 97.9% White, 0.3% Black, 0.9% Asian, 0.2% American Indian/Alaska Native, 0.0% Native Hawaiian/Other Pacific Islander, 0.7% Other, 1.1% Hispanic of any race (2010); Average household size: 2.31 (2010); Median age: 45.0 (2010); Males per 100 females: 93.5 (2010); Marriage status: 23.7% never married, 58.3% now married, 8.2% widowed, 9.9% divorced (2006-2010 5-year est.); Foreign born: 1.3% (2006-2010 5-year est.); Ancestry (includes multiple ancestries): 29.2% English, 27.8% Irish, 18.1% German, 17.1% Italian, 11.7% French (2006-2010 5-year est.).

**Economy:** Single-family building permits issued: 0 (2011); Multi-family building permits issued: 0 (2011); Employment by occupation: 15.7% management, 4.4% professional, 5.3% services, 19.1% sales, 2.0% farming, 8.9% construction, 4.2% production (2006-2010 5-year est.).

**Income:** Per capita income: $28,678 (2006-2010 5-year est.); Median household income: $61,680 (2006-2010 5-year est.); Average household income: $65,738 (2006-2010 5-year est.); Percent of households with income of $100,000 or more: 22.0% (2006-2010 5-year est.); Poverty rate: 2.5% (2006-2010 5-year est.).

**Education:** Percent of population age 25 and over with: High school diploma (including GED) or higher: 92.1% (2006-2010 5-year est.); Bachelor's degree or higher: 25.0% (2006-2010 5-year est.); Master's degree or higher: 8.9% (2006-2010 5-year est.).

Sherrill City School District (PK-12)
    2009-10 Enrollment: 2,184 . . . . . . . . . . . . . . . . . . (315) 829-2520
**Housing:** Homeownership rate: 75.3% (2010); Median home value: $133,100 (2006-2010 5-year est.); Median contract rent: $566 per month (2006-2010 5-year est.); Median year structure built: 1954 (2006-2010 5-year est.).
**Safety:** Violent crime rate: 0.0 per 10,000 population; Property crime rate: 68.2 per 10,000 population (2010).
**Transportation:** Commute to work: 94.5% car, 0.0% public transportation, 0.0% walk, 4.2% work from home (2006-2010 5-year est.); Travel time to work: 45.9% less than 15 minutes, 25.3% 15 to 30 minutes, 19.7% 30 to 45 minutes, 8.4% 45 to 60 minutes, 0.6% 60 minutes or more (2006-2010 5-year est.)
**Additional Information Contacts**
City of Sherrill . . . . . . . . . . . . . . . . . . . . . . . . . . . . . . (315) 363-2440
    http://www.sherrillny.org

**STEUBEN** (town). Covers a land area of 42.653 square miles and a water area of 0.047 square miles. Located at 43.35° N. Lat; 75.26° W. Long. Elevation is 928 feet.
**Population:** 1,006 (1990); 1,172 (2000); 1,100 (2010); Density: 25.8 persons per square mile (2010); Race: 98.9% White, 0.1% Black, 0.3% Asian, 0.0% American Indian/Alaska Native, 0.0% Native Hawaiian/Other Pacific Islander, 0.7% Other, 0.4% Hispanic of any race (2010); Average household size: 2.49 (2010); Median age: 45.2 (2010); Males per 100 females: 107.9 (2010); Marriage status: 26.9% never married, 60.0% now married, 3.4% widowed, 9.7% divorced (2006-2010 5-year est.); Foreign born: 1.5% (2006-2010 5-year est.); Ancestry (includes multiple ancestries): 32.8% German, 14.5% Irish, 12.0% English, 9.5% Welsh, 9.3% Italian (2006-2010 5-year est.).
**Economy:** Single-family building permits issued: 3 (2011); Multi-family building permits issued: 0 (2011); Employment by occupation: 12.3% management, 0.9% professional, 11.0% services, 11.0% sales, 1.5% farming, 13.3% construction, 8.6% production (2006-2010 5-year est.).
**Income:** Per capita income: $26,929 (2006-2010 5-year est.); Median household income: $55,750 (2006-2010 5-year est.); Average household income: $63,107 (2006-2010 5-year est.); Percent of households with income of $100,000 or more: 15.7% (2006-2010 5-year est.); Poverty rate: 8.9% (2006-2010 5-year est.).
**Education:** Percent of population age 25 and over with: High school diploma (including GED) or higher: 89.9% (2006-2010 5-year est.); Bachelor's degree or higher: 14.0% (2006-2010 5-year est.); Master's degree or higher: 5.9% (2006-2010 5-year est.).
**Housing:** Homeownership rate: 86.4% (2010); Median home value: $100,000 (2006-2010 5-year est.); Median contract rent: $617 per month (2006-2010 5-year est.); Median year structure built: 1975 (2006-2010 5-year est.).
**Transportation:** Commute to work: 91.8% car, 0.0% public transportation, 4.1% walk, 3.4% work from home (2006-2010 5-year est.); Travel time to work: 21.2% less than 15 minutes, 31.7% 15 to 30 minutes, 39.1% 30 to 45 minutes, 2.0% 45 to 60 minutes, 6.0% 60 minutes or more (2006-2010 5-year est.)

**STITTVILLE** (unincorporated postal area). Zip Code: 13469
    Covers a land area of 4.016 square miles and a water area of 0.073 square miles. Located at 43.21° N. Lat; 75.30° W. Long. Elevation is 538 feet. Population: 847 (2010); Density: 210.9 persons per square mile (2010); Race: 97.9% White, 0.2% Black, 0.6% Asian, 0.1% American Indian/Alaska Native, 0.0% Native Hawaiian/Other Pacific Islander, 1.2% Other, 1.1% Hispanic of any race (2010); Average household size: 2.61 (2010); Median age: 40.7 (2010); Males per 100 females: 101.2 (2010); Homeownership rate: 80.4% (2010)

**SYLVAN BEACH** (village). Covers a land area of 0.686 square miles and a water area of 0.021 square miles. Located at 43.20° N. Lat; 75.72° W. Long. Elevation is 374 feet.
**Population:** 1,170 (1990); 1,071 (2000); 897 (2010); Density: 1,306.6 persons per square mile (2010); Race: 98.1% White, 0.7% Black, 0.2% Asian, 0.4% American Indian/Alaska Native, 0.0% Native Hawaiian/Other Pacific Islander, 0.6% Other, 0.8% Hispanic of any race (2010); Average household size: 2.01 (2010); Median age: 49.9 (2010); Males per 100 females: 98.0 (2010); Marriage status: 20.3% never married, 57.9% now married, 9.4% widowed, 12.5% divorced (2006-2010 5-year est.); Foreign born: 1.7% (2006-2010 5-year est.); Ancestry (includes multiple

ancestries): 34.5% German, 30.0% Irish, 14.3% Italian, 10.6% English, 9.8% Dutch (2006-2010 5-year est.).
**Economy:** Single-family building permits issued: 1 (2011); Multi-family building permits issued: 0 (2011); Employment by occupation: 12.9% management, 0.0% professional, 22.0% services, 9.8% sales, 3.8% farming, 10.6% construction, 8.4% production (2006-2010 5-year est.).
**Income:** Per capita income: $22,378 (2006-2010 5-year est.); Median household income: $43,850 (2006-2010 5-year est.); Average household income: $47,566 (2006-2010 5-year est.); Percent of households with income of $100,000 or more: 5.7% (2006-2010 5-year est.); Poverty rate: 8.3% (2006-2010 5-year est.).
**Education:** Percent of population age 25 and over with: High school diploma (including GED) or higher: 83.0% (2006-2010 5-year est.); Bachelor's degree or higher: 14.5% (2006-2010 5-year est.); Master's degree or higher: 5.8% (2006-2010 5-year est.).
**Housing:** Homeownership rate: 73.2% (2010); Median home value: $82,600 (2006-2010 5-year est.); Median contract rent: $531 per month (2006-2010 5-year est.); Median year structure built: 1965 (2006-2010 5-year est.).
**Transportation:** Commute to work: 95.8% car, 1.1% public transportation, 2.0% walk, 1.1% work from home (2006-2010 5-year est.); Travel time to work: 21.3% less than 15 minutes, 38.8% 15 to 30 minutes, 25.3% 30 to 45 minutes, 12.6% 45 to 60 minutes, 2.0% 60 minutes or more (2006-2010 5-year est.)

**TABERG** (unincorporated postal area). Zip Code: 13471
    Covers a land area of 93.841 square miles and a water area of 0.368 square miles. Located at 43.35° N. Lat; 75.57° W. Long. Elevation is 518 feet. Population: 3,540 (2010); Density: 37.7 persons per square mile (2010); Race: 97.2% White, 1.0% Black, 0.5% Asian, 0.3% American Indian/Alaska Native, 0.0% Native Hawaiian/Other Pacific Islander, 1.0% Other, 1.0% Hispanic of any race (2010); Average household size: 2.72 (2010); Median age: 39.6 (2010); Males per 100 females: 101.7 (2010); Homeownership rate: 81.8% (2010)

**TRENTON** (town). Aka Barneveld. Covers a land area of 43.376 square miles and a water area of 0.341 square miles. Located at 43.26° N. Lat; 75.20° W. Long.
**Population:** 4,682 (1990); 4,670 (2000); 4,498 (2010); Density: 103.7 persons per square mile (2010); Race: 97.5% White, 0.4% Black, 0.8% Asian, 0.3% American Indian/Alaska Native, 0.1% Native Hawaiian/Other Pacific Islander, 0.9% Other, 1.0% Hispanic of any race (2010); Average household size: 2.49 (2010); Median age: 44.5 (2010); Males per 100 females: 100.3 (2010); Marriage status: 20.2% never married, 66.0% now married, 7.0% widowed, 6.8% divorced (2006-2010 5-year est.); Foreign born: 5.1% (2006-2010 5-year est.); Ancestry (includes multiple ancestries): 28.7% German, 24.9% Irish, 16.7% Italian, 14.5% Polish, 10.6% English (2006-2010 5-year est.).
**Economy:** Single-family building permits issued: 3 (2011); Multi-family building permits issued: 0 (2011); Employment by occupation: 11.4% management, 6.2% professional, 8.2% services, 13.3% sales, 3.6% farming, 10.6% construction, 7.7% production (2006-2010 5-year est.).
**Income:** Per capita income: $29,860 (2006-2010 5-year est.); Median household income: $68,897 (2006-2010 5-year est.); Average household income: $77,396 (2006-2010 5-year est.); Percent of households with income of $100,000 or more: 21.7% (2006-2010 5-year est.); Poverty rate: 6.0% (2006-2010 5-year est.).
**Education:** Percent of population age 25 and over with: High school diploma (including GED) or higher: 93.2% (2006-2010 5-year est.); Bachelor's degree or higher: 29.9% (2006-2010 5-year est.); Master's degree or higher: 14.6% (2006-2010 5-year est.).
**Housing:** Homeownership rate: 84.0% (2010); Median home value: $128,000 (2006-2010 5-year est.); Median contract rent: $539 per month (2006-2010 5-year est.); Median year structure built: 1951 (2006-2010 5-year est.).
**Transportation:** Commute to work: 93.5% car, 0.2% public transportation, 2.7% walk, 3.5% work from home (2006-2010 5-year est.); Travel time to work: 17.2% less than 15 minutes, 53.6% 15 to 30 minutes, 21.8% 30 to 45 minutes, 1.2% 45 to 60 minutes, 6.3% 60 minutes or more (2006-2010 5-year est.)

**UTICA** (city). County seat. Covers a land area of 16.758 square miles and a water area of 0.255 square miles. Located at 43.09° N. Lat; 75.22° W. Long. Elevation is 456 feet.

**History:** The area around Utica was called "Yah-nun-da-da-sis," meaning "around the hill," by the Oneida people, in reference to the way their trails circled the nearby hills. The site was included in Cosby's Manor, a grant of 22,000 acres made by George II to William Cosby, governor of the Province of New York, and others in 1734. In 1758 the British erected Fort Schuyler. It was abandoned in the early 1760's. In 1798 the settlement was incorporated as a village, and the present name was determined by a chance selection from a hatful of paper slips. The Erie Canal brought new prosperity and the city was chartered in 1832. The textile industry, the backbone of Utica's economic structure, began with the opening of the woolen and cotton mills in the mid-1840's.

**Population:** 68,637 (1990); 60,651 (2000); 62,235 (2010); Density: 3,713.6 persons per square mile (2010); Race: 69.0% White, 15.3% Black, 7.4% Asian, 0.3% American Indian/Alaska Native, 0.1% Native Hawaiian/Other Pacific Islander, 7.9% Other, 10.5% Hispanic of any race (2010); Average household size: 2.38 (2010); Median age: 34.8 (2010); Males per 100 females: 92.6 (2010); Marriage status: 40.1% never married, 41.7% now married, 8.2% widowed, 10.0% divorced (2006-2010 5-year est.); Foreign born: 14.8% (2006-2010 5-year est.); Ancestry (includes multiple ancestries): 22.9% Italian, 15.2% Irish, 11.9% German, 8.7% Polish, 5.2% Yugoslavian (2006-2010 5-year est.).

**Economy:** Unemployment rate: 9.7% (February 2012); Total civilian labor force: 26,496 (February 2012); Single-family building permits issued: 10 (2011); Multi-family building permits issued: 0 (2011); Employment by occupation: 7.7% management, 2.0% professional, 13.2% services, 18.5% sales, 4.8% farming, 6.2% construction, 6.9% production (2006-2010 5-year est.).

**Income:** Per capita income: $17,754 (2006-2010 5-year est.); Median household income: $31,381 (2006-2010 5-year est.); Average household income: $43,669 (2006-2010 5-year est.); Percent of households with income of $100,000 or more: 7.9% (2006-2010 5-year est.); Poverty rate: 29.0% (2006-2010 5-year est.).

**Taxes:** Total city taxes per capita: $576 (2009); City property taxes per capita: $338 (2009).

**Education:** Percent of population age 25 and over with: High school diploma (including GED) or higher: 80.4% (2006-2010 5-year est.); Bachelor's degree or higher: 16.4% (2006-2010 5-year est.); Master's degree or higher: 6.0% (2006-2010 5-year est.).

### School District(s)

Utica City School District (KG-12)
    2009-10 Enrollment: 9,390 . . . . . . . . . . . . . . . . . . . . . . . (315) 792-2222

Whitesboro Central School District (KG-12)
    2009-10 Enrollment: 3,531 . . . . . . . . . . . . . . . . . . . . . . . (315) 266-3303

### Four-year College(s)

SUNY Institute of Technology at Utica-Rome (Public)
    Fall 2010 Enrollment: 2,088 . . . . . . . . . . . . . . . . . . . . . (315) 792-7100
    2011-12 Tuition: In-state $6,439; Out-of-state $15,489

Utica College (Private, Not-for-profit)
    Fall 2010 Enrollment: 3,005 . . . . . . . . . . . . . . . . . . . . . (315) 792-3111
    2011-12 Tuition: In-state $29,996; Out-of-state $29,996

### Two-year College(s)

Faxton-St Luke's Healthcare School of Radiologic Technology (Private, Not-for-profit)
    Fall 2010 Enrollment: 44 . . . . . . . . . . . . . . . . . . . . . . . (315) 624-9260

Mohawk Valley Community College-Utica Branch (Public)
    Fall 2010 Enrollment: 5,677 . . . . . . . . . . . . . . . . . . . . . (315) 792-5400
    2011-12 Tuition: In-state $4,010; Out-of-state $7,490

Saint Elizabeth College of Nursing (Private, Not-for-profit, Roman Catholic)
    Fall 2010 Enrollment: 167 . . . . . . . . . . . . . . . . . . . . . . (315) 798-8144
    2011-12 Tuition: In-state $13,750; Out-of-state $20,200

Saint Elizabeth Medical Center School of Radiography (Private, Not-for-profit, Roman Catholic)
    Fall 2010 Enrollment: 30 . . . . . . . . . . . . . . . . . . . . . . . (315) 798-8386

Utica School of Commerce (Private, For-profit)
    Fall 2010 Enrollment: 473 . . . . . . . . . . . . . . . . . . . . . . (315) 733-2307
    2011-12 Tuition: In-state $12,470; Out-of-state $12,470

**Housing:** Homeownership rate: 47.6% (2010); Median home value: $85,300 (2006-2010 5-year est.); Median contract rent: $456 per month (2006-2010 5-year est.); Median year structure built: before 1940 (2006-2010 5-year est.).

**Hospitals:** Faxton - St. Luke's Healthcare (432 beds); Faxton-Saint Luke's Healthcare; St. Elizabeth Medical Center (201 beds)

**Safety:** Violent crime rate: 72.8 per 10,000 population; Property crime rate: 475.4 per 10,000 population (2010).

**Newspapers:** Farm & Home Pennysaver (Community news; Circulation 8,900); The Mid-York Weekly (Community news; Circulation 100,000); North Country Paper (Community news; Circulation 9,309); The Observer-Dispatch (Local news; Circulation 48,416); Rome Pennysaver (Community news; Circulation 14,044); Town & Country Weekly (Community news; Circulation 18,007); Utica Pennysaver (Community news; Circulation 13,500); Weekend Plus - Observer-Dispatch (Local news)

**Transportation:** Commute to work: 86.5% car, 3.6% public transportation, 6.3% walk, 2.1% work from home (2006-2010 5-year est.); Travel time to work: 49.2% less than 15 minutes, 37.4% 15 to 30 minutes, 7.6% 30 to 45 minutes, 1.7% 45 to 60 minutes, 4.1% 60 minutes or more (2006-2010 5-year est.); Amtrak: train service available.

**Additional Information Contacts**
City of Utica . . . . . . . . . . . . . . . . . . . . . . . . . . . . . (315) 792-0113
    http://www.cityofutica.com
Mohawk Valley Chamber of Commerce . . . . . . . . . . . . . . (315) 724-3151
    http://www.mvchamber.org

**VERNON** (village). Covers a land area of 0.945 square miles and a water area of 0.003 square miles. Located at 43.07° N. Lat; 75.53° W. Long. Elevation is 633 feet.

**Population:** 1,288 (1990); 1,155 (2000); 1,172 (2010); Density: 1,239.0 persons per square mile (2010); Race: 96.7% White, 0.9% Black, 0.6% Asian, 0.3% American Indian/Alaska Native, 0.0% Native Hawaiian/Other Pacific Islander, 1.5% Other, 1.6% Hispanic of any race (2010); Average household size: 2.23 (2010); Median age: 40.3 (2010); Males per 100 females: 99.7 (2010); Marriage status: 30.5% never married, 48.3% now married, 5.7% widowed, 15.4% divorced (2006-2010 5-year est.); Foreign born: 1.4% (2006-2010 5-year est.); Ancestry (includes multiple ancestries): 21.5% German, 19.9% Irish, 17.0% English, 15.4% Italian, 8.9% Polish (2006-2010 5-year est.).

**Economy:** Single-family building permits issued: 0 (2011); Multi-family building permits issued: 0 (2011); Employment by occupation: 5.6% management, 2.0% professional, 11.9% services, 19.5% sales, 5.6% farming, 9.0% construction, 2.7% production (2006-2010 5-year est.).

**Income:** Per capita income: $24,583 (2006-2010 5-year est.); Median household income: $43,646 (2006-2010 5-year est.); Average household income: $56,676 (2006-2010 5-year est.); Percent of households with income of $100,000 or more: 14.6% (2006-2010 5-year est.); Poverty rate: 12.0% (2006-2010 5-year est.).

**Education:** Percent of population age 25 and over with: High school diploma (including GED) or higher: 87.4% (2006-2010 5-year est.); Bachelor's degree or higher: 24.5% (2006-2010 5-year est.); Master's degree or higher: 8.8% (2006-2010 5-year est.).

### School District(s)

Sherrill City School District (PK-12)
    2009-10 Enrollment: 2,184 . . . . . . . . . . . . . . . . . . . . . (315) 829-2520

**Housing:** Homeownership rate: 52.3% (2010); Median home value: $107,800 (2006-2010 5-year est.); Median contract rent: $463 per month (2006-2010 5-year est.); Median year structure built: before 1940 (2006-2010 5-year est.).

**Safety:** Violent crime rate: 0.0 per 10,000 population; Property crime rate: 168.9 per 10,000 population (2010).

**Transportation:** Commute to work: 91.3% car, 0.0% public transportation, 2.5% walk, 6.2% work from home (2006-2010 5-year est.); Travel time to work: 42.3% less than 15 minutes, 42.8% 15 to 30 minutes, 11.4% 30 to 45 minutes, 1.5% 45 to 60 minutes, 1.9% 60 minutes or more (2006-2010 5-year est.)

**VERNON** (town). Covers a land area of 37.826 square miles and a water area of 0.010 square miles. Located at 43.06° N. Lat; 75.52° W. Long. Elevation is 633 feet.

**Population:** 5,333 (1990); 5,335 (2000); 5,408 (2010); Density: 143.0 persons per square mile (2010); Race: 96.8% White, 0.4% Black, 0.4% Asian, 0.8% American Indian/Alaska Native, 0.0% Native Hawaiian/Other Pacific Islander, 1.6% Other, 1.1% Hispanic of any race (2010); Average household size: 2.39 (2010); Median age: 42.8 (2010); Males per 100 females: 98.0 (2010); Marriage status: 29.4% never married, 54.3% now married, 5.6% widowed, 10.7% divorced (2006-2010 5-year est.); Foreign born: 1.5% (2006-2010 5-year est.); Ancestry (includes multiple ancestries): 25.5% German, 21.3% Irish, 18.0% English, 15.1% Italian, 10.1% Polish (2006-2010 5-year est.).

**Economy:** Single-family building permits issued: 12 (2011); Multi-family building permits issued: 0 (2011); Employment by occupation: 7.8% management, 2.4% professional, 12.2% services, 16.8% sales, 7.0% farming, 9.9% construction, 5.9% production (2006-2010 5-year est.).
**Income:** Per capita income: $24,579 (2006-2010 5-year est.); Median household income: $51,607 (2006-2010 5-year est.); Average household income: $64,014 (2006-2010 5-year est.); Percent of households with income of $100,000 or more: 19.9% (2006-2010 5-year est.); Poverty rate: 11.7% (2006-2010 5-year est.).
**Education:** Percent of population age 25 and over with: High school diploma (including GED) or higher: 90.1% (2006-2010 5-year est.); Bachelor's degree or higher: 20.0% (2006-2010 5-year est.); Master's degree or higher: 6.0% (2006-2010 5-year est.).

### School District(s)
Sherrill City School District (PK-12)
   2009-10 Enrollment: 2,184 . . . . . . . . . . . . . . . . . . . . . (315) 829-2520
**Housing:** Homeownership rate: 74.3% (2010); Median home value: $126,300 (2006-2010 5-year est.); Median contract rent: $479 per month (2006-2010 5-year est.); Median year structure built: 1954 (2006-2010 5-year est.).
**Transportation:** Commute to work: 91.9% car, 0.0% public transportation, 2.8% walk, 4.3% work from home (2006-2010 5-year est.); Travel time to work: 39.0% less than 15 minutes, 43.1% 15 to 30 minutes, 8.4% 30 to 45 minutes, 5.9% 45 to 60 minutes, 3.7% 60 minutes or more (2006-2010 5-year est.)

## VERNON CENTER (unincorporated postal area)
Zip Code: 13477
   Covers a land area of 20.250 square miles and a water area of 0 square miles. Located at 43.03° N. Lat; 75.51° W. Long. Elevation is 801 feet.
   Population: 1,452 (2010); Density: 71.7 persons per square mile (2010); Race: 97.2% White, 1.0% Black, 0.1% Asian, 0.3% American Indian/Alaska Native, 0.0% Native Hawaiian/Other Pacific Islander, 1.4% Other, 1.3% Hispanic of any race (2010); Average household size: 2.54 (2010); Median age: 40.3 (2010); Males per 100 females: 98.9 (2010); Homeownership rate: 85.5% (2010)

## VERONA (town). Covers a land area of 69.230 square miles and a water area of 0.365 square miles. Located at 43.15° N. Lat; 75.62° W. Long. Elevation is 495 feet.
**History:** Site of Oneida Nation's Turning Stone Casino (68,000 square foot ; opened in 1990), first legal gambling casino in N.Y. state in over a century. Costing $10 million, it is one of the largest table game operations in the U.S. Owned and operated by the Oneida, one of 70 tribes across the U.S. who are allowed to offer gambling under the Indian Gaming Act of 1988, which was designed to generate wealth on impoverished reservations.
**Population:** 6,460 (1990); 6,425 (2000); 6,293 (2010); Density: 90.9 persons per square mile (2010); Race: 96.3% White, 0.5% Black, 0.7% Asian, 0.7% American Indian/Alaska Native, 0.0% Native Hawaiian/Other Pacific Islander, 1.8% Other, 1.0% Hispanic of any race (2010); Average household size: 2.60 (2010); Median age: 42.3 (2010); Males per 100 females: 102.4 (2010); Marriage status: 19.0% never married, 65.3% now married, 4.9% widowed, 10.8% divorced (2006-2010 5-year est.); Foreign born: 1.5% (2006-2010 5-year est.); Ancestry (includes multiple ancestries): 28.5% German, 23.1% Irish, 19.3% Italian, 17.0% English, 9.9% Polish (2006-2010 5-year est.).
**Economy:** Single-family building permits issued: 7 (2011); Multi-family building permits issued: 0 (2011); Employment by occupation: 7.6% management, 5.8% professional, 11.0% services, 19.1% sales, 4.5% farming, 10.6% construction, 7.3% production (2006-2010 5-year est.).
**Income:** Per capita income: $22,642 (2006-2010 5-year est.); Median household income: $52,631 (2006-2010 5-year est.); Average household income: $61,232 (2006-2010 5-year est.); Percent of households with income of $100,000 or more: 18.7% (2006-2010 5-year est.); Poverty rate: 8.5% (2006-2010 5-year est.).
**Education:** Percent of population age 25 and over with: High school diploma (including GED) or higher: 90.4% (2006-2010 5-year est.); Bachelor's degree or higher: 16.6% (2006-2010 5-year est.); Master's degree or higher: 4.7% (2006-2010 5-year est.).

### School District(s)
Madison-Oneida Boces
   2009-10 Enrollment: n/a . . . . . . . . . . . . . . . . . . . . . . . (315) 361-5510
Sherrill City School District (PK-12)
   2009-10 Enrollment: 2,184 . . . . . . . . . . . . . . . . . . . . . (315) 829-2520

### Vocational/Technical School(s)
Madison Oneida BOCES - Practical Nursing Program (Public)
   Fall 2010 Enrollment: 85 . . . . . . . . . . . . . . . . . . . . . . . (315) 361-5800
   2011-12 Tuition: $6,700
**Housing:** Homeownership rate: 84.9% (2010); Median home value: $96,100 (2006-2010 5-year est.); Median contract rent: $537 per month (2006-2010 5-year est.); Median year structure built: 1962 (2006-2010 5-year est.).
**Transportation:** Commute to work: 93.4% car, 0.0% public transportation, 0.0% walk, 5.4% work from home (2006-2010 5-year est.); Travel time to work: 31.0% less than 15 minutes, 38.2% 15 to 30 minutes, 21.3% 30 to 45 minutes, 6.8% 45 to 60 minutes, 2.7% 60 minutes or more (2006-2010 5-year est.)

## VERONA (CDP). Covers a land area of 1.877 square miles and a water area of 0 square miles. Located at 43.13° N. Lat; 75.57° W. Long. Elevation is 495 feet.
**Population:** n/a (1990); n/a (2000); 852 (2010); Density: 453.7 persons per square mile (2010); Race: 95.3% White, 0.7% Black, 1.4% Asian, 0.2% American Indian/Alaska Native, 0.0% Native Hawaiian/Other Pacific Islander, 2.4% Other, 2.0% Hispanic of any race (2010); Average household size: 2.43 (2010); Median age: 43.6 (2010); Males per 100 females: 95.0 (2010); Marriage status: 7.9% never married, 79.8% now married, 5.0% widowed, 7.3% divorced (2006-2010 5-year est.); Foreign born: 1.5% (2006-2010 5-year est.); Ancestry (includes multiple ancestries): 36.2% German, 28.2% Irish, 22.7% English, 20.6% Italian, 8.5% Dutch (2006-2010 5-year est.).
**Economy:** Employment by occupation: 7.7% management, 6.2% professional, 4.0% services, 17.7% sales, 3.2% farming, 9.2% construction, 9.2% production (2006-2010 5-year est.).
**Income:** Per capita income: $22,815 (2006-2010 5-year est.); Median household income: $51,618 (2006-2010 5-year est.); Average household income: $56,500 (2006-2010 5-year est.); Percent of households with income of $100,000 or more: 8.2% (2006-2010 5-year est.); Poverty rate: 0.0% (2006-2010 5-year est.).
**Education:** Percent of population age 25 and over with: High school diploma (including GED) or higher: 91.5% (2006-2010 5-year est.); Bachelor's degree or higher: 24.3% (2006-2010 5-year est.); Master's degree or higher: 8.7% (2006-2010 5-year est.).

### School District(s)
Madison-Oneida Boces
   2009-10 Enrollment: n/a . . . . . . . . . . . . . . . . . . . . . . . (315) 361-5510
Sherrill City School District (PK-12)
   2009-10 Enrollment: 2,184 . . . . . . . . . . . . . . . . . . . . . (315) 829-2520

### Vocational/Technical School(s)
Madison Oneida BOCES - Practical Nursing Program (Public)
   Fall 2010 Enrollment: 85 . . . . . . . . . . . . . . . . . . . . . . . (315) 361-5800
   2011-12 Tuition: $6,700
**Housing:** Homeownership rate: 83.1% (2010); Median home value: $85,400 (2006-2010 5-year est.); Median contract rent: n/a per month (2006-2010 5-year est.); Median year structure built: 1959 (2006-2010 5-year est.).
**Transportation:** Commute to work: 94.7% car, 0.0% public transportation, 0.0% walk, 5.3% work from home (2006-2010 5-year est.); Travel time to work: 42.9% less than 15 minutes, 29.9% 15 to 30 minutes, 18.2% 30 to 45 minutes, 0.0% 45 to 60 minutes, 9.0% 60 minutes or more (2006-2010 5-year est.)

## VERONA BEACH (unincorporated postal area)
Zip Code: 13162
   Covers a land area of 1.757 square miles and a water area of 0.022 square miles. Located at 43.18° N. Lat; 75.71° W. Long. Elevation is 374 feet. Population: 385 (2010); Density: 219.0 persons per square mile (2010); Race: 97.1% White, 1.0% Black, 0.3% Asian, 0.3% American Indian/Alaska Native, 0.0% Native Hawaiian/Other Pacific Islander, 1.3% Other, 0.8% Hispanic of any race (2010); Average household size: 2.13 (2010); Median age: 52.2 (2010); Males per 100 females: 98.5 (2010); Homeownership rate: 81.7% (2010)

## VIENNA (town). Covers a land area of 61.447 square miles and a water area of 33.627 square miles. Located at 43.23° N. Lat; 75.77° W. Long. Elevation is 463 feet.
**Population:** 5,564 (1990); 5,819 (2000); 5,440 (2010); Density: 88.5 persons per square mile (2010); Race: 97.7% White, 0.5% Black, 0.3% Asian, 0.5% American Indian/Alaska Native, 0.0% Native Hawaiian/Other

Pacific Islander, 1.0% Other, 0.6% Hispanic of any race (2010); Average household size: 2.45 (2010); Median age: 44.1 (2010); Males per 100 females: 102.0 (2010); Marriage status: 24.3% never married, 58.0% now married, 7.6% widowed, 10.1% divorced (2006-2010 5-year est.); Foreign born: 1.2% (2006-2010 5-year est.); Ancestry (includes multiple ancestries): 23.5% German, 21.5% Irish, 14.8% English, 12.9% Italian, 9.8% French (2006-2010 5-year est.).
**Economy:** Single-family building permits issued: 21 (2011); Multi-family building permits issued: 0 (2011); Employment by occupation: 12.3% management, 1.6% professional, 10.3% services, 13.9% sales, 2.9% farming, 14.7% construction, 11.7% production (2006-2010 5-year est.).
**Income:** Per capita income: $22,896 (2006-2010 5-year est.); Median household income: $52,761 (2006-2010 5-year est.); Average household income: $59,595 (2006-2010 5-year est.); Percent of households with income of $100,000 or more: 17.6% (2006-2010 5-year est.); Poverty rate: 7.1% (2006-2010 5-year est.).
**Education:** Percent of population age 25 and over with: High school diploma (including GED) or higher: 80.2% (2006-2010 5-year est.); Bachelor's degree or higher: 14.8% (2006-2010 5-year est.); Master's degree or higher: 3.4% (2006-2010 5-year est.).
**Housing:** Homeownership rate: 82.6% (2010); Median home value: $87,300 (2006-2010 5-year est.); Median contract rent: $541 per month (2006-2010 5-year est.); Median year structure built: 1979 (2006-2010 5-year est.).
**Transportation:** Commute to work: 94.1% car, 0.2% public transportation, 1.5% walk, 1.5% work from home (2006-2010 5-year est.); Travel time to work: 28.2% less than 15 minutes, 23.9% 15 to 30 minutes, 27.9% 30 to 45 minutes, 15.8% 45 to 60 minutes, 4.1% 60 minutes or more (2006-2010 5-year est.)

**WASHINGTON MILLS** (CDP). Covers a land area of 0.669 square miles and a water area of 0 square miles. Located at 43.04° N. Lat; 75.28° W. Long. Elevation is 620 feet.
**Population:** n/a (1990); n/a (2000); 1,183 (2010); Density: 1,766.2 persons per square mile (2010); Race: 92.3% White, 2.2% Black, 1.8% Asian, 0.0% American Indian/Alaska Native, 0.0% Native Hawaiian/Other Pacific Islander, 3.7% Other, 3.0% Hispanic of any race (2010); Average household size: 2.34 (2010); Median age: 40.7 (2010); Males per 100 females: 92.7 (2010); Marriage status: 32.0% never married, 45.5% now married, 10.4% widowed, 12.1% divorced (2006-2010 5-year est.); Foreign born: 29.7% (2006-2010 5-year est.); Ancestry (includes multiple ancestries): 18.3% German, 17.3% Ukrainian, 16.6% English, 15.2% Italian, 13.6% Irish (2006-2010 5-year est.).
**Economy:** Employment by occupation: 7.2% management, 6.6% professional, 3.5% services, 19.7% sales, 2.9% farming, 2.5% construction, 3.1% production (2006-2010 5-year est.).
**Income:** Per capita income: $30,782 (2006-2010 5-year est.); Median household income: $46,905 (2006-2010 5-year est.); Average household income: $59,843 (2006-2010 5-year est.); Percent of households with income of $100,000 or more: 18.6% (2006-2010 5-year est.); Poverty rate: 17.3% (2006-2010 5-year est.).
**Education:** Percent of population age 25 and over with: High school diploma (including GED) or higher: 97.3% (2006-2010 5-year est.); Bachelor's degree or higher: 48.1% (2006-2010 5-year est.); Master's degree or higher: 33.1% (2006-2010 5-year est.).
**Housing:** Homeownership rate: 53.2% (2010); Median home value: $138,800 (2006-2010 5-year est.); Median contract rent: $702 per month (2006-2010 5-year est.); Median year structure built: 1966 (2006-2010 5-year est.).
**Transportation:** Commute to work: 95.3% car, 0.0% public transportation, 1.2% walk, 3.5% work from home (2006-2010 5-year est.); Travel time to work: 28.5% less than 15 minutes, 59.8% 15 to 30 minutes, 9.8% 30 to 45 minutes, 0.0% 45 to 60 minutes, 1.9% 60 minutes or more (2006-2010 5-year est.)

**WATERVILLE** (village). Covers a land area of 1.415 square miles and a water area of 0 square miles. Located at 42.93° N. Lat; 75.38° W. Long. Elevation is 1,201 feet.
**History:** George Eastman born here. Incorporated 1871.
**Population:** 1,664 (1990); 1,721 (2000); 1,583 (2010); Density: 1,118.0 persons per square mile (2010); Race: 97.0% White, 0.3% Black, 0.4% Asian, 0.2% American Indian/Alaska Native, 0.6% Native Hawaiian/Other Pacific Islander, 1.5% Other, 1.0% Hispanic of any race (2010); Average household size: 2.38 (2010); Median age: 42.6 (2010); Males per 100 females: 91.2 (2010); Marriage status: 24.2% never married, 60.1% now

married, 9.4% widowed, 6.3% divorced (2006-2010 5-year est.); Foreign born: 0.8% (2006-2010 5-year est.); Ancestry (includes multiple ancestries): 29.6% Irish, 21.5% German, 18.8% English, 9.0% Italian, 7.8% Welsh (2006-2010 5-year est.).
**Economy:** Single-family building permits issued: 0 (2011); Multi-family building permits issued: 0 (2011); Employment by occupation: 9.8% management, 3.5% professional, 11.1% services, 15.1% sales, 3.9% farming, 11.2% construction, 4.1% production (2006-2010 5-year est.).
**Income:** Per capita income: $26,002 (2006-2010 5-year est.); Median household income: $54,659 (2006-2010 5-year est.); Average household income: $68,206 (2006-2010 5-year est.); Percent of households with income of $100,000 or more: 17.8% (2006-2010 5-year est.); Poverty rate: 12.3% (2006-2010 5-year est.).
**Education:** Percent of population age 25 and over with: High school diploma (including GED) or higher: 90.7% (2006-2010 5-year est.); Bachelor's degree or higher: 20.2% (2006-2010 5-year est.); Master's degree or higher: 8.6% (2006-2010 5-year est.).
#### School District(s)
Waterville Central School District (PK-12)
    2009-10 Enrollment: 910 . . . . . . . . . . . . . . . . . . . (315) 841-3900
**Housing:** Homeownership rate: 59.1% (2010); Median home value: $96,900 (2006-2010 5-year est.); Median contract rent: $460 per month (2006-2010 5-year est.); Median year structure built: before 1940 (2006-2010 5-year est.).
**Newspapers:** Waterville Times (Local news; Circulation 2,700)
**Transportation:** Commute to work: 89.9% car, 0.0% public transportation, 6.2% walk, 2.5% work from home (2006-2010 5-year est.); Travel time to work: 40.3% less than 15 minutes, 32.0% 15 to 30 minutes, 19.3% 30 to 45 minutes, 4.3% 45 to 60 minutes, 4.1% 60 minutes or more (2006-2010 5-year est.)

**WESTDALE** (unincorporated postal area)
Zip Code: 13483
    Covers a land area of 6.919 square miles and a water area of 0.082 square miles. Located at 43.39° N. Lat; 75.82° W. Long. Elevation is 551 feet. Population: 256 (2010); Density: 37.0 persons per square mile (2010); Race: 96.5% White, 0.0% Black, 0.8% Asian, 2.3% American Indian/Alaska Native, 0.0% Native Hawaiian/Other Pacific Islander, 0.4% Other, 0.0% Hispanic of any race (2010); Average household size: 2.88 (2010); Median age: 35.8 (2010); Males per 100 females: 82.9 (2010); Homeownership rate: 78.7% (2010)

**WESTERN** (town). Covers a land area of 51.205 square miles and a water area of 3.465 square miles. Located at 43.35° N. Lat; 75.41° W. Long.
**Population:** 2,057 (1990); 2,029 (2000); 1,951 (2010); Density: 38.1 persons per square mile (2010); Race: 98.2% White, 0.6% Black, 0.7% Asian, 0.0% American Indian/Alaska Native, 0.0% Native Hawaiian/Other Pacific Islander, 0.5% Other, 1.7% Hispanic of any race (2010); Average household size: 2.45 (2010); Median age: 43.9 (2010); Males per 100 females: 104.9 (2010); Marriage status: 23.7% never married, 56.8% now married, 4.0% widowed, 15.4% divorced (2006-2010 5-year est.); Foreign born: 2.7% (2006-2010 5-year est.); Ancestry (includes multiple ancestries): 25.9% German, 23.1% Irish, 15.6% Italian, 14.0% English, 13.0% Polish (2006-2010 5-year est.).
**Economy:** Single-family building permits issued: 6 (2011); Multi-family building permits issued: 0 (2011); Employment by occupation: 13.8% management, 4.0% professional, 6.7% services, 9.8% sales, 0.9% farming, 11.0% construction, 9.5% production (2006-2010 5-year est.).
**Income:** Per capita income: $30,185 (2006-2010 5-year est.); Median household income: $58,625 (2006-2010 5-year est.); Average household income: $70,991 (2006-2010 5-year est.); Percent of households with income of $100,000 or more: 26.9% (2006-2010 5-year est.); Poverty rate: 8.6% (2006-2010 5-year est.).
**Education:** Percent of population age 25 and over with: High school diploma (including GED) or higher: 88.9% (2006-2010 5-year est.); Bachelor's degree or higher: 28.7% (2006-2010 5-year est.); Master's degree or higher: 13.5% (2006-2010 5-year est.).
**Housing:** Homeownership rate: 82.4% (2010); Median home value: $133,400 (2006-2010 5-year est.); Median contract rent: $487 per month (2006-2010 5-year est.); Median year structure built: 1959 (2006-2010 5-year est.).
**Transportation:** Commute to work: 93.4% car, 0.0% public transportation, 0.7% walk, 5.0% work from home (2006-2010 5-year est.); Travel time to work: 14.9% less than 15 minutes, 49.5% 15 to 30 minutes, 24.3% 30 to 45

minutes, 6.0% 45 to 60 minutes, 5.2% 60 minutes or more (2006-2010 5-year est.)

## WESTERNVILLE (unincorporated postal area)
Zip Code: 13486
Covers a land area of 29.449 square miles and a water area of 3.465 square miles. Located at 43.34° N. Lat; 75.34° W. Long. Elevation is 561 feet. Population: 815 (2010); Density: 27.7 persons per square mile (2010); Race: 98.7% White, 0.6% Black, 0.4% Asian, 0.0% American Indian/Alaska Native, 0.0% Native Hawaiian/Other Pacific Islander, 0.3% Other, 2.3% Hispanic of any race (2010); Average household size: 2.43 (2010); Median age: 42.3 (2010); Males per 100 females: 99.3 (2010); Homeownership rate: 82.7% (2010)

## WESTMORELAND (town). Covers a land area of 43.135 square miles and a water area of 0.014 square miles. Located at 43.12° N. Lat; 75.44° W. Long. Elevation is 522 feet.
Population: 5,737 (1990); 6,207 (2000); 6,138 (2010); Density: 142.3 persons per square mile (2010); Race: 97.5% White, 0.9% Black, 0.5% Asian, 0.1% American Indian/Alaska Native, 0.0% Native Hawaiian/Other Pacific Islander, 1.0% Other, 1.2% Hispanic of any race (2010); Average household size: 2.57 (2010); Median age: 44.3 (2010); Males per 100 females: 100.4 (2010); Marriage status: 20.0% never married, 66.0% now married, 7.6% widowed, 6.4% divorced (2006-2010 5-year est.); Foreign born: 2.1% (2006-2010 5-year est.); Ancestry (includes multiple ancestries): 27.8% German, 21.2% Irish, 19.8% English, 17.7% Polish, 14.1% Italian (2006-2010 5-year est.).
Economy: Single-family building permits issued: 4 (2011); Multi-family building permits issued: 0 (2011); Employment by occupation: 9.5% management, 7.6% professional, 8.2% services, 17.2% sales, 3.4% farming, 10.2% construction, 7.9% production (2006-2010 5-year est.).
Income: Per capita income: $28,847 (2006-2010 5-year est.); Median household income: $64,625 (2006-2010 5-year est.); Average household income: $73,595 (2006-2010 5-year est.); Percent of households with income of $100,000 or more: 24.3% (2006-2010 5-year est.); Poverty rate: 2.5% (2006-2010 5-year est.).
Education: Percent of population age 25 and over with: High school diploma (including GED) or higher: 93.0% (2006-2010 5-year est.); Bachelor's degree or higher: 24.4% (2006-2010 5-year est.); Master's degree or higher: 6.3% (2006-2010 5-year est.).
### School District(s)
Westmoreland Central School District (KG-12)
   2009-10 Enrollment: 999 . . . . . . . . . . . . . . . . . . . . . . . . . (315) 557-2614
Housing: Homeownership rate: 89.5% (2010); Median home value: $104,700 (2006-2010 5-year est.); Median contract rent: $579 per month (2006-2010 5-year est.); Median year structure built: 1970 (2006-2010 5-year est.).
Transportation: Commute to work: 95.0% car, 0.0% public transportation, 1.6% walk, 2.4% work from home (2006-2010 5-year est.); Travel time to work: 32.4% less than 15 minutes, 52.8% 15 to 30 minutes, 11.0% 30 to 45 minutes, 2.9% 45 to 60 minutes, 0.9% 60 minutes or more (2006-2010 5-year est.)
Additional Information Contacts
Town of Westmoreland . . . . . . . . . . . . . . . . . . . . . . . . . . (315) 853-8001
   http://town.westmoreland.ny.us/content

## WESTMORELAND (CDP). Covers a land area of 0.686 square miles and a water area of 0 square miles. Located at 43.11° N. Lat; 75.40° W. Long. Elevation is 522 feet.
Population: n/a (1990); n/a (2000); 427 (2010); Density: 621.7 persons per square mile (2010); Race: 94.1% White, 2.6% Black, 1.2% Asian, 0.2% American Indian/Alaska Native, 0.0% Native Hawaiian/Other Pacific Islander, 1.9% Other, 1.2% Hispanic of any race (2010); Average household size: 2.75 (2010); Median age: 37.6 (2010); Males per 100 females: 95.9 (2010); Marriage status: 17.5% never married, 82.5% now married, 0.0% widowed, 0.0% divorced (2006-2010 5-year est.); Foreign born: 2.9% (2006-2010 5-year est.); Ancestry (includes multiple ancestries): 46.5% German, 15.2% Polish, 14.7% Irish, 14.5% English, 4.1% Italian (2006-2010 5-year est.).
Economy: Employment by occupation: 0.0% management, 0.0% professional, 8.6% services, 42.2% sales, 0.0% farming, 0.0% construction, 8.6% production (2006-2010 5-year est.).
Income: Per capita income: $15,729 (2006-2010 5-year est.); Median household income: $31,985 (2006-2010 5-year est.); Average household income: $43,066 (2006-2010 5-year est.); Percent of households with

income of $100,000 or more: 0.0% (2006-2010 5-year est.); Poverty rate: 19.0% (2006-2010 5-year est.).
Education: Percent of population age 25 and over with: High school diploma (including GED) or higher: 93.8% (2006-2010 5-year est.); Bachelor's degree or higher: 23.1% (2006-2010 5-year est.); Master's degree or higher: 0.0% (2006-2010 5-year est.).
### School District(s)
Westmoreland Central School District (KG-12)
   2009-10 Enrollment: 999 . . . . . . . . . . . . . . . . . . . . . . . . . (315) 557-2614
Housing: Homeownership rate: 72.3% (2010); Median home value: $82,600 (2006-2010 5-year est.); Median contract rent: n/a per month (2006-2010 5-year est.); Median year structure built: 1956 (2006-2010 5-year est.).
Transportation: Commute to work: 90.5% car, 0.0% public transportation, 0.0% walk, 9.5% work from home (2006-2010 5-year est.); Travel time to work: 28.8% less than 15 minutes, 49.7% 15 to 30 minutes, 10.5% 30 to 45 minutes, 11.1% 45 to 60 minutes, 0.0% 60 minutes or more (2006-2010 5-year est.)

## WHITESBORO (village). Covers a land area of 1.049 square miles and a water area of 0 square miles. Located at 43.12° N. Lat; 75.29° W. Long. Elevation is 423 feet.
History: Settled 1784, incorporated 1813.
Population: 4,195 (1990); 3,943 (2000); 3,772 (2010); Density: 3,593.7 persons per square mile (2010); Race: 95.7% White, 1.7% Black, 0.6% Asian, 0.2% American Indian/Alaska Native, 0.0% Native Hawaiian/Other Pacific Islander, 1.8% Other, 2.2% Hispanic of any race (2010); Average household size: 2.08 (2010); Median age: 38.8 (2010); Males per 100 females: 86.7 (2010); Marriage status: 31.2% never married, 46.6% now married, 7.6% widowed, 14.5% divorced (2006-2010 5-year est.); Foreign born: 2.9% (2006-2010 5-year est.); Ancestry (includes multiple ancestries): 26.8% Irish, 25.8% Italian, 17.1% German, 12.1% English, 11.9% Polish (2006-2010 5-year est.).
Economy: Single-family building permits issued: 0 (2011); Multi-family building permits issued: 0 (2011); Employment by occupation: 7.1% management, 5.3% professional, 12.8% services, 20.3% sales, 10.5% farming, 6.9% construction, 8.1% production (2006-2010 5-year est.).
Income: Per capita income: $22,173 (2006-2010 5-year est.); Median household income: $41,082 (2006-2010 5-year est.); Average household income: $47,840 (2006-2010 5-year est.); Percent of households with income of $100,000 or more: 9.4% (2006-2010 5-year est.); Poverty rate: 12.7% (2006-2010 5-year est.).
Education: Percent of population age 25 and over with: High school diploma (including GED) or higher: 89.2% (2006-2010 5-year est.); Bachelor's degree or higher: 21.4% (2006-2010 5-year est.); Master's degree or higher: 5.9% (2006-2010 5-year est.).
### School District(s)
Whitesboro Central School District (KG-12)
   2009-10 Enrollment: 3,531 . . . . . . . . . . . . . . . . . . . . . . . (315) 266-3303
Housing: Homeownership rate: 53.3% (2010); Median home value: $95,000 (2006-2010 5-year est.); Median contract rent: $482 per month (2006-2010 5-year est.); Median year structure built: before 1940 (2006-2010 5-year est.).
Safety: Violent crime rate: 16.4 per 10,000 population; Property crime rate: 95.6 per 10,000 population (2010).
Transportation: Commute to work: 92.3% car, 2.0% public transportation, 0.8% walk, 4.1% work from home (2006-2010 5-year est.); Travel time to work: 55.2% less than 15 minutes, 38.3% 15 to 30 minutes, 2.1% 30 to 45 minutes, 0.8% 45 to 60 minutes, 3.7% 60 minutes or more (2006-2010 5-year est.)
Additional Information Contacts
Village of Whitesboro . . . . . . . . . . . . . . . . . . . . . . . . . . . (315) 736-1613
   http://village.whitesboro.ny.us/content

## WHITESTOWN (town). Covers a land area of 27.318 square miles and a water area of 0.001 square miles. Located at 43.13° N. Lat; 75.33° W. Long.
Population: 18,985 (1990); 18,635 (2000); 18,667 (2010); Density: 683.3 persons per square mile (2010); Race: 95.7% White, 2.0% Black, 0.8% Asian, 0.2% American Indian/Alaska Native, 0.0% Native Hawaiian/Other Pacific Islander, 1.3% Other, 1.8% Hispanic of any race (2010); Average household size: 2.30 (2010); Median age: 41.8 (2010); Males per 100 females: 96.0 (2010); Marriage status: 29.0% never married, 54.5% now married, 8.4% widowed, 8.1% divorced (2006-2010 5-year est.); Foreign born: 4.3% (2006-2010 5-year est.); Ancestry (includes multiple

ancestries): 25.5% Irish, 21.6% Italian, 19.7% German, 18.6% Polish, 12.1% English (2006-2010 5-year est.).
**Economy:** Single-family building permits issued: 5 (2011); Multi-family building permits issued: 0 (2011); Employment by occupation: 11.6% management, 4.5% professional, 9.5% services, 18.3% sales, 6.4% farming, 6.7% construction, 4.3% production (2006-2010 5-year est.).
**Income:** Per capita income: $27,192 (2006-2010 5-year est.); Median household income: $52,655 (2006-2010 5-year est.); Average household income: $64,908 (2006-2010 5-year est.); Percent of households with income of $100,000 or more: 18.4% (2006-2010 5-year est.); Poverty rate: 9.2% (2006-2010 5-year est.).
**Taxes:** Total city taxes per capita: $166 (2009); City property taxes per capita: $148 (2009).
**Education:** Percent of population age 25 and over with: High school diploma (including GED) or higher: 91.3% (2006-2010 5-year est.); Bachelor's degree or higher: 26.3% (2006-2010 5-year est.); Master's degree or higher: 8.6% (2006-2010 5-year est.).
**Housing:** Homeownership rate: 71.9% (2010); Median home value: $113,700 (2006-2010 5-year est.); Median contract rent: $511 per month (2006-2010 5-year est.); Median year structure built: 1955 (2006-2010 5-year est.).
**Safety:** Violent crime rate: 4.4 per 10,000 population; Property crime rate: 84.7 per 10,000 population (2010).
**Transportation:** Commute to work: 95.1% car, 1.0% public transportation, 1.0% walk, 2.0% work from home (2006-2010 5-year est.); Travel time to work: 52.0% less than 15 minutes, 36.4% 15 to 30 minutes, 6.4% 30 to 45 minutes, 1.9% 45 to 60 minutes, 3.4% 60 minutes or more (2006-2010 5-year est.)

**Additional Information Contacts**
Town of Whitestown . . . . . . . . . . . . . . . . . . . . . . . . . . . (315) 736-4224
    http://town.whitestown.ny.us/content

## WOODGATE (unincorporated postal area)
Zip Code: 13494
    Covers a land area of 17.509 square miles and a water area of 0.408 square miles. Located at 43.53° N. Lat; 75.14° W. Long. Elevation is 1,480 feet. Population: 314 (2010); Density: 17.9 persons per square mile (2010); Race: 98.1% White, 0.0% Black, 0.0% Asian, 1.0% American Indian/Alaska Native, 0.0% Native Hawaiian/Other Pacific Islander, 0.9% Other, 0.0% Hispanic of any race (2010); Average household size: 2.15 (2010); Median age: 49.0 (2010); Males per 100 females: 107.9 (2010); Homeownership rate: 89.1% (2010)

## YORKVILLE (village).
Covers a land area of 0.671 square miles and a water area of 0 square miles. Located at 43.11° N. Lat; 75.27° W. Long. Elevation is 433 feet.
**History:** Henry Inman, one of the most prominent and versatile of the first generation of American-trained artists, was born here in 1801.
**Population:** 3,042 (1990); 2,675 (2000); 2,689 (2010); Density: 4,005.4 persons per square mile (2010); Race: 94.4% White, 2.1% Black, 0.8% Asian, 0.1% American Indian/Alaska Native, 0.0% Native Hawaiian/Other Pacific Islander, 2.6% Other, 3.2% Hispanic of any race (2010); Average household size: 2.24 (2010); Median age: 37.6 (2010); Males per 100 females: 95.4 (2010); Marriage status: 38.6% never married, 43.7% now married, 8.9% widowed, 8.8% divorced (2006-2010 5-year est.); Foreign born: 2.5% (2006-2010 5-year est.); Ancestry (includes multiple ancestries): 24.9% Irish, 22.1% Polish, 22.0% Italian, 18.9% German, 10.3% English (2006-2010 5-year est.).
**Economy:** Single-family building permits issued: 0 (2011); Multi-family building permits issued: 0 (2011); Employment by occupation: 7.0% management, 1.2% professional, 11.2% services, 24.4% sales, 6.7% farming, 4.2% construction, 6.9% production (2006-2010 5-year est.).
**Income:** Per capita income: $19,499 (2006-2010 5-year est.); Median household income: $37,500 (2006-2010 5-year est.); Average household income: $46,476 (2006-2010 5-year est.); Percent of households with income of $100,000 or more: 8.0% (2006-2010 5-year est.); Poverty rate: 24.2% (2006-2010 5-year est.).
**Education:** Percent of population age 25 and over with: High school diploma (including GED) or higher: 85.6% (2006-2010 5-year est.); Bachelor's degree or higher: 12.9% (2006-2010 5-year est.); Master's degree or higher: 1.9% (2006-2010 5-year est.).
**Housing:** Homeownership rate: 64.7% (2010); Median home value: $81,400 (2006-2010 5-year est.); Median contract rent: $512 per month (2006-2010 5-year est.); Median year structure built: 1943 (2006-2010 5-year est.).

**Safety:** Violent crime rate: 20.0 per 10,000 population; Property crime rate: 203.8 per 10,000 population (2010).
**Transportation:** Commute to work: 93.9% car, 2.0% public transportation, 1.6% walk, 0.9% work from home (2006-2010 5-year est.); Travel time to work: 55.1% less than 15 minutes, 29.5% 15 to 30 minutes, 12.1% 30 to 45 minutes, 1.4% 45 to 60 minutes, 2.0% 60 minutes or more (2006-2010 5-year est.)

# Onondaga County

Located in central New York, in the Finger Lakes area; drained by the Seneca and Oswego Rivers; includes Oneida and Skaneateles Lakes. Covers a land area of 780.29 square miles, a water area of 25.40 square miles, and is located in the Eastern Time Zone at 43.04° N. Lat., 76.17° W. Long. The county was founded in 1794. County seat is Syracuse.

Onondaga County is part of the Syracuse, NY Metropolitan Statistical Area. The entire metro area includes: Madison County, NY; Onondaga County, NY; Oswego County, NY

Weather Station: Syracuse Hancock Int'l Arpt                Elevation: 410 feet

|        | Jan  | Feb  | Mar  | Apr | May | Jun | Jul | Aug | Sep | Oct | Nov | Dec  |
|--------|------|------|------|-----|-----|-----|-----|-----|-----|-----|-----|------|
| High   | 32   | 34   | 43   | 57  | 69  | 77  | 82  | 80  | 72  | 60  | 48  | 37   |
| Low    | 16   | 17   | 25   | 36  | 46  | 56  | 61  | 60  | 52  | 41  | 33  | 22   |
| Precip | 2.5  | 2.0  | 3.0  | 3.3 | 3.2 | 3.2 | 3.7 | 3.4 | 3.6 | 3.4 | 3.5 | 3.1  |
| Snow   | 34.9 | 26.2 | 18.7 | 3.8 | 0.1 | tr  | tr  | tr  | tr  | 0.4 | 9.7 | 30.7 |

*High and Low temperatures in degrees Fahrenheit; Precipitation and Snow in inches*

**Population:** 468,973 (1990); 458,336 (2000); 467,026 (2010); Race: 81.1% White, 11.0% Black, 3.1% Asian, 0.8% American Indian/Alaska Native, 0.0% Native Hawaiian/Other Pacific Islander, 4.0% Other, 4.0% Hispanic of any race (2010); Density: 598.5 persons per square mile (2010); Average household size: 2.40 (2010); Median age: 38.6 (2010); Males per 100 females: 92.9 (2010).
**Religion:** Six largest groups: 35.0% Catholicism, 4.4% Methodist/Pietist, 2.4% Baptist, 2.1% Non-Denominational, 1.7% Lutheran, 1.5% Pentecostal (2010)
**Economy:** Unemployment rate: 8.6% (February 2012); Total civilian labor force: 225,594 (February 2012); Leading industries: 16.7% health care and social assistance; 13.0% retail trade; 10.1% manufacturing (2009); Farms: 692 totaling 150,499 acres (2007); Companies that employ 500 or more persons: 41 (2009); Companies that employ 100 to 499 persons: 270 (2009); Companies that employ less than 100 persons: 11,468 (2009); Black-owned businesses: 1,497 (2007); Hispanic-owned businesses: 725 (2007); Asian-owned businesses: 1,195 (2007); Women-owned businesses: 10,524 (2007); Retail sales per capita: $15,318 (2010). Single-family building permits issued: 475 (2011); Multi-family building permits issued: 465 (2011).
**Income:** Per capita income: $27,037 (2006-2010 5-year est.); Median household income: $50,676 (2006-2010 5-year est.); Average household income: $66,443 (2006-2010 5-year est.); Percent of households with income of $100,000 or more: 19.7% (2006-2010 5-year est.); Poverty rate: 13.6% (2006-2010 5-year est.); Bankruptcy rate: 3.14% (2011).
**Taxes:** Total county taxes per capita: $964 (2009); County property taxes per capita: $304 (2009).
**Education:** Percent of population age 25 and over with: High school diploma (including GED) or higher: 89.3% (2006-2010 5-year est.); Bachelor's degree or higher: 32.0% (2006-2010 5-year est.); Master's degree or higher: 13.8% (2006-2010 5-year est.).
**Housing:** Homeownership rate: 64.7% (2010); Median home value: $124,400 (2006-2010 5-year est.); Median contract rent: $587 per month (2006-2010 5-year est.); Median year structure built: 1959 (2006-2010 5-year est.)
**Health:** Birth rate: 115.2 per 10,000 population (2011); Death rate: 84.1 per 10,000 population (2011); Age-adjusted cancer mortality rate: 190.5 deaths per 100,000 population (2009); Number of physicians: 47.7 per 10,000 population (2008); Hospital beds: 37.7 per 10,000 population (2007); Hospital admissions: 1,606.2 per 10,000 population (2007).
**Environment:** Air Quality Index: 94.0% good, 5.2% moderate, 0.8% unhealthy for sensitive individuals, 0.0% unhealthy (percent of days in 2010)
**Elections:** 2008 Presidential election results: 59.3% Obama, 38.9% McCain, 0.9% Nader
**National and State Parks:** Cicero State Game Management Area; Clark Reservation State Park; Erie Canal State Park; Green Lakes State Park; Three Rivers State Game Management Area

**Additional Information Contacts**

Onondaga County Government . . . . . . . . . . . . . . . . . . . . (315) 435-2229
  http://www.ongov.net
CenterState Chamber of Commerce . . . . . . . . . . . . . . . (315) 470-1800
  http://www.centerstateceo.com
City of Syracuse . . . . . . . . . . . . . . . . . . . . . . . . . . . . . . (315) 448-8005
  http://www.syracuse.ny.us
Greater Baldwinsville Chamber of Commerce . . . . . . . . . . (315) 638-0550
  http://www.b-ville.com
Greater Cicero Chamber of Commerce . . . . . . . . . . . . . . . (315) 699-1358
  http://www.cicerochamber.com
Greater Liverpool Chamber of Commerce . . . . . . . . . . . . . (315) 457-3895
  http://www.liverpoolchamber.com
Greater Manlius Chamber of Commerce . . . . . . . . . . . . . . (315) 637-4760
  http://www.manliuschamber.com
Skaneateles Area Chamber of Commerce . . . . . . . . . . . . (315) 685-0552
  http://www.skaneateles.com
Town of Camillus . . . . . . . . . . . . . . . . . . . . . . . . . . . . . . (315) 488-1335
  http://www.townofcamillus.com
Town of Clay . . . . . . . . . . . . . . . . . . . . . . . . . . . . . . . . . (315) 652-3800
  http://www.townofclay.org
Town of Elbridge . . . . . . . . . . . . . . . . . . . . . . . . . . . . . . (315) 689-9031
  http://www.townofelbridge.com
Town of Geddes . . . . . . . . . . . . . . . . . . . . . . . . . . . . . . . (315) 468-2528
  http://www.townofgeddes.com
Town of Lysander . . . . . . . . . . . . . . . . . . . . . . . . . . . . . . (315) 638-0224
  http://www.townoflysander.org
Town of Manlius . . . . . . . . . . . . . . . . . . . . . . . . . . . . . . . (315) 637-3521
  http://www.townofmanlius.org
Town of Marcellus . . . . . . . . . . . . . . . . . . . . . . . . . . . . . (315) 673-3269
  http://town.marcellusny.com
Town of Salina . . . . . . . . . . . . . . . . . . . . . . . . . . . . . . . . (315) 457-2710
  http://www.salina.ny.us
Town of Skaneateles . . . . . . . . . . . . . . . . . . . . . . . . . . . (315) 685-3473
  http://www.townofskaneateles.com
Town of Van Buren . . . . . . . . . . . . . . . . . . . . . . . . . . . . . (315) 635-3010
  http://www.b-ville.com/content/about-van-buren-ny
Village of Liverpool . . . . . . . . . . . . . . . . . . . . . . . . . . . . (315) 457-3441
  http://www.villageofliverpool.org
Village of Marcellus . . . . . . . . . . . . . . . . . . . . . . . . . . . . (315) 673-3112
  http://villageofmarcellus.com
Village of North Syracuse . . . . . . . . . . . . . . . . . . . . . . . (315) 458-0900
  http://northsyracuseny.org

## Onondaga County Communities

**APULIA STATION** (unincorporated postal area)
Zip Code: 13020
  Covers a land area of 0.467 square miles and a water area of 0 square
  miles. Located at 42.81° N. Lat; 76.07° W. Long. Elevation is 1,243 feet.
  Population: 150 (2010); Density: 320.7 persons per square mile (2010);
  Race: 92.0% White, 0.7% Black, 0.7% Asian, 0.0% American
  Indian/Alaska Native, 0.0% Native Hawaiian/Other Pacific Islander, 6.6%
  Other, 3.3% Hispanic of any race (2010); Average household size: 2.83
  (2010); Median age: 37.3 (2010); Males per 100 females: 120.6 (2010);
  Homeownership rate: 86.8% (2010)

**BALDWINSVILLE** (village). Covers a land area of 3.092 square
miles and a water area of 0.180 square miles. Located at 43.15° N. Lat;
76.33° W. Long. Elevation is 381 feet.
**History:** Settled 1796, incorporated 1847.
**Population:** 6,604 (1990); 7,053 (2000); 7,378 (2010); Density: 2,385.8
persons per square mile (2010); Race: 95.9% White, 0.9% Black, 0.9%
Asian, 0.5% American Indian/Alaska Native, 0.0% Native Hawaiian/Other
Pacific Islander, 1.8% Other, 1.8% Hispanic of any race (2010); Average
household size: 2.34 (2010); Median age: 41.4 (2010); Males per 100
females: 89.8 (2010); Marriage status: 22.8% never married, 53.2% now
married, 11.5% widowed, 12.5% divorced (2006-2010 5-year est.); Foreign
born: 3.7% (2006-2010 5-year est.); Ancestry (includes multiple
ancestries): 25.8% Irish, 23.2% German, 18.2% Italian, 14.6% English,
10.3% French (2006-2010 5-year est.).
**Economy:** Single-family building permits issued: 5 (2011); Multi-family
building permits issued: 48 (2011); Employment by occupation: 12.5%
management, 4.4% professional, 13.8% services, 21.7% sales, 2.7%
farming, 5.9% construction, 2.9% production (2006-2010 5-year est.).

**Income:** Per capita income: $25,364 (2006-2010 5-year est.); Median
household income: $45,949 (2006-2010 5-year est.); Average household
income: $56,787 (2006-2010 5-year est.); Percent of households with
income of $100,000 or more: 17.3% (2006-2010 5-year est.); Poverty rate:
14.4% (2006-2010 5-year est.).
**Education:** Percent of population age 25 and over with: High school
diploma (including GED) or higher: 90.5% (2006-2010 5-year est.);
Bachelor's degree or higher: 29.6% (2006-2010 5-year est.); Master's
degree or higher: 11.6% (2006-2010 5-year est.).

**School District(s)**
Baldwinsville Central School District (KG-12)
  2009-10 Enrollment: 5,815 . . . . . . . . . . . . . . . . . . . (315) 638-6043
**Housing:** Homeownership rate: 61.0% (2010); Median home value:
$118,400 (2006-2010 5-year est.); Median contract rent: $528 per month
(2006-2010 5-year est.); Median year structure built: 1960 (2006-2010
5-year est.).
**Safety:** Violent crime rate: 6.9 per 10,000 population; Property crime rate:
194.4 per 10,000 population (2010).
**Newspapers:** Baldwinsville Messenger (Community news; Circulation
39,927); The Post-Standard - Baldwinsville Bureau (Local news)
**Transportation:** Commute to work: 92.1% car, 2.6% public transportation,
2.9% walk, 2.4% work from home (2006-2010 5-year est.); Travel time to
work: 22.8% less than 15 minutes, 47.3% 15 to 30 minutes, 21.9% 30 to 45
minutes, 4.9% 45 to 60 minutes, 3.2% 60 minutes or more (2006-2010
5-year est.).
**Additional Information Contacts**
Greater Baldwinsville Chamber of Commerce . . . . . . . . . . (315) 638-0550
  http://www.b-ville.com

**BREWERTON** (CDP). Covers a land area of 3.166 square miles and
a water area of 0.172 square miles. Located at 43.23° N. Lat; 76.14° W.
Long. Elevation is 384 feet.
**History:** Here are remains of Fort Brewerton (1759), now in state
reservation.
**Population:** 2,954 (1990); 3,453 (2000); 4,029 (2010); Density: 1,272.4
persons per square mile (2010); Race: 95.3% White, 1.3% Black, 0.8%
Asian, 0.6% American Indian/Alaska Native, 0.0% Native Hawaiian/Other
Pacific Islander, 2.0% Other, 1.5% Hispanic of any race (2010); Average
household size: 2.45 (2010); Median age: 36.9 (2010); Males per 100
females: 96.6 (2010); Marriage status: 38.8% never married, 44.2% now
married, 4.6% widowed, 12.4% divorced (2006-2010 5-year est.); Foreign
born: 1.8% (2006-2010 5-year est.); Ancestry (includes multiple
ancestries): 25.1% German, 24.3% Irish, 20.0% Italian, 14.9% English,
10.6% French (2006-2010 5-year est.).
**Economy:** Employment by occupation: 11.4% management, 2.9%
professional, 8.1% services, 21.9% sales, 5.2% farming, 11.7%
construction, 6.9% production (2006-2010 5-year est.).
**Income:** Per capita income: $22,790 (2006-2010 5-year est.); Median
household income: $47,461 (2006-2010 5-year est.); Average household
income: $57,635 (2006-2010 5-year est.); Percent of households with
income of $100,000 or more: 16.3% (2006-2010 5-year est.); Poverty rate:
8.8% (2006-2010 5-year est.).
**Education:** Percent of population age 25 and over with: High school
diploma (including GED) or higher: 90.0% (2006-2010 5-year est.);
Bachelor's degree or higher: 15.6% (2006-2010 5-year est.); Master's
degree or higher: 6.0% (2006-2010 5-year est.).

**School District(s)**
Central Square Central School District (PK-12)
  2009-10 Enrollment: 4,634 . . . . . . . . . . . . . . . . . . . (315) 668-4220
**Housing:** Homeownership rate: 66.6% (2010); Median home value:
$133,200 (2006-2010 5-year est.); Median contract rent: $480 per month
(2006-2010 5-year est.); Median year structure built: 1975 (2006-2010
5-year est.).
**Transportation:** Commute to work: 91.2% car, 0.0% public transportation,
0.0% walk, 4.1% work from home (2006-2010 5-year est.); Travel time to
work: 11.3% less than 15 minutes, 70.1% 15 to 30 minutes, 14.0% 30 to 45
minutes, 2.7% 45 to 60 minutes, 2.0% 60 minutes or more (2006-2010
5-year est.)

**BRIDGEPORT** (CDP). Covers a land area of 1.723 square miles and
a water area of 0.015 square miles. Located at 43.14° N. Lat; 75.98° W.
Long. Elevation is 390 feet.
**Population:** 1,950 (1990); 1,665 (2000); 1,490 (2010); Density: 864.5
persons per square mile (2010); Race: 95.3% White, 1.3% Black, 0.8%
Asian, 0.7% American Indian/Alaska Native, 0.0% Native Hawaiian/Other

Pacific Islander, 1.9% Other, 1.1% Hispanic of any race (2010); Average household size: 2.28 (2010); Median age: 43.4 (2010); Males per 100 females: 93.8 (2010); Marriage status: 25.4% never married, 52.9% now married, 9.0% widowed, 12.8% divorced (2006-2010 5-year est.); Foreign born: 1.1% (2006-2010 5-year est.); Ancestry (includes multiple ancestries): 36.9% German, 33.8% Irish, 21.8% English, 12.6% Italian, 11.4% French (2006-2010 5-year est.).
**Economy:** Employment by occupation: 10.5% management, 0.0% professional, 4.7% services, 19.2% sales, 8.7% farming, 9.6% construction, 11.5% production (2006-2010 5-year est.).
**Income:** Per capita income: $25,983 (2006-2010 5-year est.); Median household income: $45,326 (2006-2010 5-year est.); Average household income: $55,178 (2006-2010 5-year est.); Percent of households with income of $100,000 or more: 7.0% (2006-2010 5-year est.); Poverty rate: 3.0% (2006-2010 5-year est.).
**Education:** Percent of population age 25 and over with: High school diploma (including GED) or higher: 83.4% (2006-2010 5-year est.); Bachelor's degree or higher: 7.8% (2006-2010 5-year est.); Master's degree or higher: 2.3% (2006-2010 5-year est.).
### School District(s)
Chittenango Central School District (KG-12)
 2009-10 Enrollment: 2,228 . . . . . . . . . . . . . . . . . . . . . . . (315) 687-2840
**Housing:** Homeownership rate: 73.9% (2010); Median home value: $79,200 (2006-2010 5-year est.); Median contract rent: $342 per month (2006-2010 5-year est.); Median year structure built: 1962 (2006-2010 5-year est.).
**Transportation:** Commute to work: 95.6% car, 0.0% public transportation, 0.0% walk, 0.0% work from home (2006-2010 5-year est.); Travel time to work: 17.6% less than 15 minutes, 61.8% 15 to 30 minutes, 6.3% 30 to 45 minutes, 7.9% 45 to 60 minutes, 6.4% 60 minutes or more (2006-2010 5-year est.)

**CAMILLUS** (village). Covers a land area of 0.390 square miles and a water area of 0 square miles. Located at 43.03° N. Lat; 76.30° W. Long. Elevation is 433 feet.
**Population:** 1,264 (1990); 1,249 (2000); 1,213 (2010); Density: 3,107.8 persons per square mile (2010); Race: 94.2% White, 3.5% Black, 0.2% Asian, 0.4% American Indian/Alaska Native, 0.0% Native Hawaiian/Other Pacific Islander, 1.7% Other, 1.8% Hispanic of any race (2010); Average household size: 2.12 (2010); Median age: 40.1 (2010); Males per 100 females: 93.2 (2010); Marriage status: 31.8% never married, 39.7% now married, 9.2% widowed, 19.2% divorced (2006-2010 5-year est.); Foreign born: 1.1% (2006-2010 5-year est.); Ancestry (includes multiple ancestries): 21.9% Irish, 19.5% German, 18.8% Italian, 14.5% Polish, 14.4% English (2006-2010 5-year est.).
**Economy:** Single-family building permits issued: 0 (2011); Multi-family building permits issued: 0 (2011); Employment by occupation: 7.7% management, 3.9% professional, 12.1% services, 23.3% sales, 6.7% farming, 3.7% construction, 6.0% production (2006-2010 5-year est.).
**Income:** Per capita income: $23,927 (2006-2010 5-year est.); Median household income: $43,393 (2006-2010 5-year est.); Average household income: $51,540 (2006-2010 5-year est.); Percent of households with income of $100,000 or more: 7.5% (2006-2010 5-year est.); Poverty rate: 19.0% (2006-2010 5-year est.).
**Education:** Percent of population age 25 and over with: High school diploma (including GED) or higher: 90.8% (2006-2010 5-year est.); Bachelor's degree or higher: 30.0% (2006-2010 5-year est.); Master's degree or higher: 10.3% (2006-2010 5-year est.).
### School District(s)
West Genesee Central School District (KG-12)
 2009-10 Enrollment: 5,017 . . . . . . . . . . . . . . . . . . . . . . . (315) 487-4562
**Housing:** Homeownership rate: 54.1% (2010); Median home value: $105,500 (2006-2010 5-year est.); Median contract rent: $564 per month (2006-2010 5-year est.); Median year structure built: before 1940 (2006-2010 5-year est.).
**Newspapers:** The Post-Standard - Camillus Bureau (Regional news)
**Transportation:** Commute to work: 88.3% car, 5.1% public transportation, 5.1% walk, 0.7% work from home (2006-2010 5-year est.); Travel time to work: 32.3% less than 15 minutes, 54.9% 15 to 30 minutes, 9.6% 30 to 45 minutes, 1.9% 45 to 60 minutes, 1.4% 60 minutes or more (2006-2010 5-year est.)

**CAMILLUS** (town). Covers a land area of 34.424 square miles and a water area of 0.016 square miles. Located at 43.06° N. Lat; 76.31° W. Long. Elevation is 433 feet.
**History:** Once a major cutlery manufacturing center. Incorporated 1852.
**Population:** 23,625 (1990); 23,152 (2000); 24,167 (2010); Density: 702.0 persons per square mile (2010); Race: 94.4% White, 1.8% Black, 1.4% Asian, 0.5% American Indian/Alaska Native, 0.0% Native Hawaiian/Other Pacific Islander, 1.9% Other, 1.8% Hispanic of any race (2010); Average household size: 2.38 (2010); Median age: 43.7 (2010); Males per 100 females: 91.6 (2010); Marriage status: 26.3% never married, 55.9% now married, 8.5% widowed, 9.3% divorced (2006-2010 5-year est.); Foreign born: 6.2% (2006-2010 5-year est.); Ancestry (includes multiple ancestries): 33.4% Irish, 21.5% German, 21.1% Italian, 12.9% English, 10.6% Polish (2006-2010 5-year est.).
**Economy:** Single-family building permits issued: 45 (2011); Multi-family building permits issued: 0 (2011); Employment by occupation: 12.0% management, 4.2% professional, 7.3% services, 17.5% sales, 4.8% farming, 5.8% construction, 3.6% production (2006-2010 5-year est.).
**Income:** Per capita income: $29,981 (2006-2010 5-year est.); Median household income: $60,082 (2006-2010 5-year est.); Average household income: $72,314 (2006-2010 5-year est.); Percent of households with income of $100,000 or more: 22.9% (2006-2010 5-year est.); Poverty rate: 8.1% (2006-2010 5-year est.).
**Education:** Percent of population age 25 and over with: High school diploma (including GED) or higher: 92.7% (2006-2010 5-year est.); Bachelor's degree or higher: 34.7% (2006-2010 5-year est.); Master's degree or higher: 14.3% (2006-2010 5-year est.).
### School District(s)
West Genesee Central School District (KG-12)
 2009-10 Enrollment: 5,017 . . . . . . . . . . . . . . . . . . . . . . . (315) 487-4562
**Housing:** Homeownership rate: 79.6% (2010); Median home value: $132,200 (2006-2010 5-year est.); Median contract rent: $683 per month (2006-2010 5-year est.); Median year structure built: 1964 (2006-2010 5-year est.).
**Safety:** Violent crime rate: 6.0 per 10,000 population; Property crime rate: 130.4 per 10,000 population (2010).
**Newspapers:** The Post-Standard - Camillus Bureau (Regional news)
**Transportation:** Commute to work: 94.5% car, 1.2% public transportation, 1.8% walk, 1.9% work from home (2006-2010 5-year est.); Travel time to work: 29.6% less than 15 minutes, 54.7% 15 to 30 minutes, 11.4% 30 to 45 minutes, 1.6% 45 to 60 minutes, 2.7% 60 minutes or more (2006-2010 5-year est.)
**Additional Information Contacts**
Town of Camillus . . . . . . . . . . . . . . . . . . . . . . . . . . . . . (315) 488-1335
 http://www.townofcamillus.com

**CICERO** (town). Covers a land area of 48.274 square miles and a water area of 0.190 square miles. Located at 43.17° N. Lat; 76.05° W. Long. Elevation is 394 feet.
**Population:** 25,560 (1990); 27,982 (2000); 31,632 (2010); Density: 655.3 persons per square mile (2010); Race: 95.2% White, 1.7% Black, 1.0% Asian, 0.3% American Indian/Alaska Native, 0.0% Native Hawaiian/Other Pacific Islander, 1.8% Other, 1.6% Hispanic of any race (2010); Average household size: 2.55 (2010); Median age: 39.9 (2010); Males per 100 females: 96.1 (2010); Marriage status: 24.7% never married, 59.5% now married, 5.1% widowed, 10.7% divorced (2006-2010 5-year est.); Foreign born: 3.8% (2006-2010 5-year est.); Ancestry (includes multiple ancestries): 26.6% Irish, 24.4% German, 20.7% Italian, 16.2% English, 11.3% Polish (2006-2010 5-year est.).
**Economy:** Unemployment rate: 8.2% (February 2012); Total civilian labor force: 16,571 (February 2012); Single-family building permits issued: 38 (2011); Multi-family building permits issued: 0 (2011); Employment by occupation: 11.8% management, 4.8% professional, 7.5% services, 20.0% sales, 4.1% farming, 7.9% construction, 5.7% production (2006-2010 5-year est.).
**Income:** Per capita income: $29,393 (2006-2010 5-year est.); Median household income: $65,226 (2006-2010 5-year est.); Average household income: $73,241 (2006-2010 5-year est.); Percent of households with income of $100,000 or more: 25.1% (2006-2010 5-year est.); Poverty rate: 6.3% (2006-2010 5-year est.).
**Education:** Percent of population age 25 and over with: High school diploma (including GED) or higher: 91.2% (2006-2010 5-year est.); Bachelor's degree or higher: 28.0% (2006-2010 5-year est.); Master's degree or higher: 11.1% (2006-2010 5-year est.).

North Syracuse Central School District (PK-12)
    2009-10 Enrollment: 9,741 . . . . . . . . . . . . . . . . . . . . . . (315) 218-2151
**Housing:** Homeownership rate: 81.0% (2010); Median home value:
$141,200 (2006-2010 5-year est.); Median contract rent: $584 per month
(2006-2010 5-year est.); Median year structure built: 1975 (2006-2010
5-year est.).
**Safety:** Violent crime rate: 4.6 per 10,000 population; Property crime rate:
183.1 per 10,000 population (2010).
**Newspapers:** National Parts Peddler Newspaper (National news)
**Transportation:** Commute to work: 94.8% car, 0.2% public transportation,
0.7% walk, 3.4% work from home (2006-2010 5-year est.); Travel time to
work: 22.5% less than 15 minutes, 61.6% 15 to 30 minutes, 11.0% 30 to 45
minutes, 1.9% 45 to 60 minutes, 3.0% 60 minutes or more (2006-2010
5-year est.).
**Additional Information Contacts**
Greater Cicero Chamber of Commerce . . . . . . . . . . . . . . . (315) 699-1358
    http://www.cicerochamber.com

**CLAY** (town). Covers a land area of 47.958 square miles and a water
area of 0.901 square miles. Located at 43.17° N. Lat; 76.19° W. Long.
Elevation is 394 feet.
**Population:** 59,749 (1990); 58,805 (2000); 58,206 (2010); Density: 1,213.7
persons per square mile (2010); Race: 89.9% White, 4.3% Black, 2.5%
Asian, 0.5% American Indian/Alaska Native, 0.0% Native Hawaiian/Other
Pacific Islander, 2.8% Other, 2.5% Hispanic of any race (2010); Average
household size: 2.50 (2010); Median age: 38.9 (2010); Males per 100
females: 93.9 (2010); Marriage status: 29.6% never married, 55.3% now
married, 5.3% widowed, 9.8% divorced (2006-2010 5-year est.); Foreign
born: 5.1% (2006-2010 5-year est.); Ancestry (includes multiple
ancestries): 24.5% German, 24.4% Irish, 22.8% Italian, 14.2% English,
8.1% Polish (2006-2010 5-year est.).
**Economy:** Unemployment rate: 7.5% (February 2012); Total civilian labor
force: 31,298 (February 2012); Single-family building permits issued: 83
(2011); Multi-family building permits issued: 58 (2011); Employment by
occupation: 11.2% management, 6.1% professional, 8.3% services, 19.1%
sales, 5.4% farming, 7.1% construction, 5.6% production (2006-2010
5-year est.).
**Income:** Per capita income: $28,637 (2006-2010 5-year est.); Median
household income: $62,193 (2006-2010 5-year est.); Average household
income: $72,093 (2006-2010 5-year est.); Percent of households with
income of $100,000 or more: 22.7% (2006-2010 5-year est.); Poverty rate:
4.7% (2006-2010 5-year est.).
**Taxes:** Total city taxes per capita: $310 (2009); City property taxes per
capita: $276 (2009).
**Education:** Percent of population age 25 and over with: High school
diploma (including GED) or higher: 93.0% (2006-2010 5-year est.);
Bachelor's degree or higher: 30.5% (2006-2010 5-year est.); Master's
degree or higher: 11.2% (2006-2010 5-year est.).
**Housing:** Homeownership rate: 74.3% (2010); Median home value:
$131,200 (2006-2010 5-year est.); Median contract rent: $689 per month
(2006-2010 5-year est.); Median year structure built: 1975 (2006-2010
5-year est.).
**Transportation:** Commute to work: 94.1% car, 1.2% public transportation,
1.2% walk, 2.5% work from home (2006-2010 5-year est.); Travel time to
work: 28.3% less than 15 minutes, 55.0% 15 to 30 minutes, 11.5% 30 to 45
minutes, 2.2% 45 to 60 minutes, 3.1% 60 minutes or more (2006-2010
5-year est.).
**Additional Information Contacts**
Town of Clay . . . . . . . . . . . . . . . . . . . . . . . . . . . . . . . . . . (315) 652-3800
    http://www.townofclay.org

**DE WITT** (town). Covers a land area of 33.773 square miles and a
water area of 0.091 square miles. Located at 43.05° N. Lat; 76.07° W.
Long. Elevation is 564 feet.
**Population:** 25,366 (1990); 24,071 (2000); 25,838 (2010); Density: 765.0
persons per square mile (2010); Race: 86.4% White, 5.9% Black, 4.1%
Asian, 0.6% American Indian/Alaska Native, 0.0% Native Hawaiian/Other
Pacific Islander, 3.0% Other, 2.9% Hispanic of any race (2010); Average
household size: 2.34 (2010); Median age: 42.5 (2010); Males per 100
females: 94.5 (2010); Marriage status: 29.1% never married, 55.9% now
married, 6.3% widowed, 8.8% divorced (2006-2010 5-year est.); Foreign
born: 10.2% (2006-2010 5-year est.); Ancestry (includes multiple
ancestries): 22.1% Irish, 19.2% German, 18.9% Italian, 12.4% English,
7.5% Polish (2006-2010 5-year est.).

**Economy:** Unemployment rate: 8.1% (February 2012); Total civilian labor
force: 12,474 (February 2012); Single-family building permits issued: 11
(2011); Multi-family building permits issued: 0 (2011); Employment by
occupation: 12.3% management, 3.5% professional, 7.8% services, 15.3%
sales, 4.0% farming, 4.9% construction, 3.8% production (2006-2010
5-year est.).
**Income:** Per capita income: $36,542 (2006-2010 5-year est.); Median
household income: $55,349 (2006-2010 5-year est.); Average household
income: $87,702 (2006-2010 5-year est.); Percent of households with
income of $100,000 or more: 27.9% (2006-2010 5-year est.); Poverty rate:
7.9% (2006-2010 5-year est.).
**Education:** Percent of population age 25 and over with: High school
diploma (including GED) or higher: 92.6% (2006-2010 5-year est.);
Bachelor's degree or higher: 43.3% (2006-2010 5-year est.); Master's
degree or higher: 23.5% (2006-2010 5-year est.).
Jamesville-Dewitt Central School District (KG-12)
    2009-10 Enrollment: 2,868 . . . . . . . . . . . . . . . . . . . . (315) 445-8304
**Housing:** Homeownership rate: 72.8% (2010); Median home value:
$155,900 (2006-2010 5-year est.); Median contract rent: $577 per month
(2006-2010 5-year est.); Median year structure built: 1962 (2006-2010
5-year est.).
**Safety:** Violent crime rate: 17.5 per 10,000 population; Property crime rate:
279.2 per 10,000 population (2010).
**Transportation:** Commute to work: 89.0% car, 1.3% public transportation,
4.5% walk, 3.9% work from home (2006-2010 5-year est.); Travel time to
work: 47.0% less than 15 minutes, 43.6% 15 to 30 minutes, 5.5% 30 to 45
minutes, 1.9% 45 to 60 minutes, 2.0% 60 minutes or more (2006-2010
5-year est.).

**DELPHI FALLS** (unincorporated postal area)
Zip Code: 13051
    Covers a land area of 0.235 square miles and a water area of 0 square
    miles. Located at 42.87° N. Lat; 75.90° W. Long. Elevation is 948 feet.
    Population: 153 (2010); Density: 649.1 persons per square mile (2010);
    Race: 92.8% White, 1.3% Black, 1.3% Asian, 0.0% American
    Indian/Alaska Native, 0.0% Native Hawaiian/Other Pacific Islander, 4.6%
    Other, 3.9% Hispanic of any race (2010); Average household size: 2.25
    (2010); Median age: 41.4 (2010); Males per 100 females: 112.5 (2010);
    Homeownership rate: 75.0% (2010)

**EAST SYRACUSE** (village). Covers a land area of 1.622 square
miles and a water area of 0 square miles. Located at 43.06° N. Lat; 76.06°
W. Long. Elevation is 433 feet.
**Population:** 3,343 (1990); 3,178 (2000); 3,084 (2010); Density: 1,901.2
persons per square mile (2010); Race: 90.6% White, 3.0% Black, 0.7%
Asian, 1.0% American Indian/Alaska Native, 0.1% Native Hawaiian/Other
Pacific Islander, 4.6% Other, 2.6% Hispanic of any race (2010); Average
household size: 2.26 (2010); Median age: 37.1 (2010); Males per 100
females: 99.7 (2010); Marriage status: 36.1% never married, 42.1% now
married, 7.5% widowed, 14.4% divorced (2006-2010 5-year est.); Foreign
born: 3.4% (2006-2010 5-year est.); Ancestry (includes multiple
ancestries): 28.3% German, 27.2% Irish, 15.3% Italian, 12.0% English,
6.7% French Canadian (2006-2010 5-year est.).
**Economy:** Single-family building permits issued: 0 (2011); Multi-family
building permits issued: 0 (2011); Employment by occupation: 5.2%
management, 3.2% professional, 9.7% services, 22.8% sales, 3.5%
farming, 10.2% construction, 5.6% production (2006-2010 5-year est.).
**Income:** Per capita income: $20,859 (2006-2010 5-year est.); Median
household income: $35,947 (2006-2010 5-year est.); Average household
income: $43,946 (2006-2010 5-year est.); Percent of households with
income of $100,000 or more: 13.1% (2006-2010 5-year est.); Poverty rate:
19.1% (2006-2010 5-year est.).
**Education:** Percent of population age 25 and over with: High school
diploma (including GED) or higher: 83.3% (2006-2010 5-year est.);
Bachelor's degree or higher: 12.2% (2006-2010 5-year est.); Master's
degree or higher: 4.2% (2006-2010 5-year est.).
East Syracuse-Minoa Central School District (PK-12)
    2009-10 Enrollment: 3,524 . . . . . . . . . . . . . . . . . . . . . . (315) 434-3012
**Housing:** Homeownership rate: 46.5% (2010); Median home value:
$89,100 (2006-2010 5-year est.); Median contract rent: $433 per month
(2006-2010 5-year est.); Median year structure built: 1941 (2006-2010
5-year est.).

**Safety:** Violent crime rate: 30.8 per 10,000 population; Property crime rate: 564.3 per 10,000 population (2010).
**Transportation:** Commute to work: 94.4% car, 2.3% public transportation, 1.6% walk, 0.5% work from home (2006-2010 5-year est.); Travel time to work: 41.6% less than 15 minutes, 49.7% 15 to 30 minutes, 5.2% 30 to 45 minutes, 2.8% 45 to 60 minutes, 0.7% 60 minutes or more (2006-2010 5-year est.)

**ELBRIDGE** (village). Covers a land area of 1.125 square miles and a water area of 0 square miles. Located at 43.03° N. Lat; 76.44° W. Long. Elevation is 545 feet.
**Population:** 1,219 (1990); 1,103 (2000); 1,058 (2010); Density: 939.9 persons per square mile (2010); Race: 96.8% White, 0.3% Black, 0.3% Asian, 0.5% American Indian/Alaska Native, 0.1% Native Hawaiian/Other Pacific Islander, 2.0% Other, 3.0% Hispanic of any race (2010); Average household size: 2.51 (2010); Median age: 44.5 (2010); Males per 100 females: 94.8 (2010); Marriage status: 25.9% never married, 60.6% now married, 6.2% widowed, 7.4% divorced (2006-2010 5-year est.); Foreign born: 2.2% (2006-2010 5-year est.); Ancestry (includes multiple ancestries): 33.9% Irish, 24.4% English, 19.0% German, 13.5% Italian, 7.3% American (2006-2010 5-year est.).
**Economy:** Single-family building permits issued: 0 (2011); Multi-family building permits issued: 0 (2011); Employment by occupation: 9.4% management, 2.8% professional, 12.5% services, 17.6% sales, 2.8% farming, 10.5% construction, 11.0% production (2006-2010 5-year est.).
**Income:** Per capita income: $27,105 (2006-2010 5-year est.); Median household income: $57,813 (2006-2010 5-year est.); Average household income: $67,520 (2006-2010 5-year est.); Percent of households with income of $100,000 or more: 15.0% (2006-2010 5-year est.); Poverty rate: 5.4% (2006-2010 5-year est.).
**Education:** Percent of population age 25 and over with: High school diploma (including GED) or higher: 95.7% (2006-2010 5-year est.); Bachelor's degree or higher: 27.4% (2006-2010 5-year est.); Master's degree or higher: 5.6% (2006-2010 5-year est.).

**School District(s)**
Jordan-Elbridge Central School District (PK-12)
    2009-10 Enrollment: 1,554 . . . . . . . . . . . . . . . . . . (315) 689-8500
**Housing:** Homeownership rate: 79.7% (2010); Median home value: $130,700 (2006-2010 5-year est.); Median contract rent: $522 per month (2006-2010 5-year est.); Median year structure built: 1956 (2006-2010 5-year est.).
**Transportation:** Commute to work: 91.3% car, 0.5% public transportation, 3.9% walk, 3.2% work from home (2006-2010 5-year est.); Travel time to work: 33.1% less than 15 minutes, 33.5% 15 to 30 minutes, 27.4% 30 to 45 minutes, 3.1% 45 to 60 minutes, 2.8% 60 minutes or more (2006-2010 5-year est.)

**ELBRIDGE** (town). Covers a land area of 37.538 square miles and a water area of 0.756 square miles. Located at 43.05° N. Lat; 76.43° W. Long. Elevation is 545 feet.
**Population:** 6,192 (1990); 6,091 (2000); 5,922 (2010); Density: 157.8 persons per square mile (2010); Race: 97.0% White, 0.2% Black, 0.3% Asian, 0.4% American Indian/Alaska Native, 0.0% Native Hawaiian/Other Pacific Islander, 2.1% Other, 2.1% Hispanic of any race (2010); Average household size: 2.52 (2010); Median age: 42.9 (2010); Males per 100 females: 100.9 (2010); Marriage status: 24.2% never married, 59.3% now married, 4.5% widowed, 11.9% divorced (2006-2010 5-year est.); Foreign born: 1.3% (2006-2010 5-year est.); Ancestry (includes multiple ancestries): 25.2% Irish, 22.7% German, 22.7% English, 13.5% Italian, 7.4% French (2006-2010 5-year est.).
**Economy:** Single-family building permits issued: 4 (2011); Multi-family building permits issued: 0 (2011); Employment by occupation: 7.8% management, 4.3% professional, 9.9% services, 18.7% sales, 2.6% farming, 11.1% construction, 9.2% production (2006-2010 5-year est.).
**Income:** Per capita income: $25,385 (2006-2010 5-year est.); Median household income: $65,170 (2006-2010 5-year est.); Average household income: $67,855 (2006-2010 5-year est.); Percent of households with income of $100,000 or more: 21.8% (2006-2010 5-year est.); Poverty rate: 6.5% (2006-2010 5-year est.).
**Education:** Percent of population age 25 and over with: High school diploma (including GED) or higher: 93.5% (2006-2010 5-year est.); Bachelor's degree or higher: 20.9% (2006-2010 5-year est.); Master's degree or higher: 6.4% (2006-2010 5-year est.).

**School District(s)**
Jordan-Elbridge Central School District (PK-12)
    2009-10 Enrollment: 1,554 . . . . . . . . . . . . . . . . . . (315) 689-8500
**Housing:** Homeownership rate: 81.5% (2010); Median home value: $101,300 (2006-2010 5-year est.); Median contract rent: $467 per month (2006-2010 5-year est.); Median year structure built: 1969 (2006-2010 5-year est.).
**Transportation:** Commute to work: 95.5% car, 0.4% public transportation, 3.1% walk, 0.8% work from home (2006-2010 5-year est.); Travel time to work: 29.1% less than 15 minutes, 34.0% 15 to 30 minutes, 28.8% 30 to 45 minutes, 4.4% 45 to 60 minutes, 3.7% 60 minutes or more (2006-2010 5-year est.)
**Additional Information Contacts**
Town of Elbridge . . . . . . . . . . . . . . . . . . . . . . . . . . (315) 689-9031
    http://www.townofelbridge.com

**FABIUS** (village). Covers a land area of 0.397 square miles and a water area of 0 square miles. Located at 42.83° N. Lat; 75.98° W. Long. Elevation is 1,266 feet.
**Population:** 310 (1990); 355 (2000); 352 (2010); Density: 884.7 persons per square mile (2010); Race: 98.0% White, 0.0% Black, 0.0% Asian, 1.7% American Indian/Alaska Native, 0.0% Native Hawaiian/Other Pacific Islander, 0.3% Other, 4.0% Hispanic of any race (2010); Average household size: 2.61 (2010); Median age: 42.3 (2010); Males per 100 females: 89.2 (2010); Marriage status: 34.3% never married, 58.8% now married, 4.0% widowed, 2.9% divorced (2006-2010 5-year est.); Foreign born: 0.4% (2006-2010 5-year est.); Ancestry (includes multiple ancestries): 23.4% English, 20.8% Irish, 16.2% German, 5.5% Polish, 4.8% Swedish (2006-2010 5-year est.).
**Economy:** Single-family building permits issued: 0 (2011); Multi-family building permits issued: 0 (2011); Employment by occupation: 11.2% management, 2.0% professional, 12.7% services, 21.9% sales, 0.0% farming, 7.6% construction, 6.8% production (2006-2010 5-year est.).
**Income:** Per capita income: $24,343 (2006-2010 5-year est.); Median household income: $52,656 (2006-2010 5-year est.); Average household income: $63,100 (2006-2010 5-year est.); Percent of households with income of $100,000 or more: 18.5% (2006-2010 5-year est.); Poverty rate: 6.2% (2006-2010 5-year est.).
**Education:** Percent of population age 25 and over with: High school diploma (including GED) or higher: 89.3% (2006-2010 5-year est.); Bachelor's degree or higher: 31.9% (2006-2010 5-year est.); Master's degree or higher: 16.3% (2006-2010 5-year est.).

**School District(s)**
Fabius-Pompey Central School District (KG-12)
    2009-10 Enrollment: 838 . . . . . . . . . . . . . . . . . . (315) 683-5301
**Housing:** Homeownership rate: 74.1% (2010); Median home value: $101,300 (2006-2010 5-year est.); Median contract rent: $461 per month (2006-2010 5-year est.); Median year structure built: before 1940 (2006-2010 5-year est.).
**Transportation:** Commute to work: 93.8% car, 0.0% public transportation, 4.9% walk, 1.2% work from home (2006-2010 5-year est.); Travel time to work: 31.7% less than 15 minutes, 32.5% 15 to 30 minutes, 24.6% 30 to 45 minutes, 8.8% 45 to 60 minutes, 2.5% 60 minutes or more (2006-2010 5-year est.)

**FABIUS** (town). Covers a land area of 46.497 square miles and a water area of 0.275 square miles. Located at 42.81° N. Lat; 75.98° W. Long. Elevation is 1,266 feet.
**Population:** 1,760 (1990); 1,974 (2000); 1,964 (2010); Density: 42.2 persons per square mile (2010); Race: 96.4% White, 0.2% Black, 0.4% Asian, 0.9% American Indian/Alaska Native, 0.1% Native Hawaiian/Other Pacific Islander, 2.0% Other, 3.7% Hispanic of any race (2010); Average household size: 2.70 (2010); Median age: 42.6 (2010); Males per 100 females: 104.2 (2010); Marriage status: 21.9% never married, 68.4% now married, 4.3% widowed, 5.4% divorced (2006-2010 5-year est.); Foreign born: 2.2% (2006-2010 5-year est.); Ancestry (includes multiple ancestries): 24.7% Irish, 21.6% German, 21.2% English, 9.7% American, 9.2% Italian (2006-2010 5-year est.).
**Economy:** Single-family building permits issued: 3 (2011); Multi-family building permits issued: 0 (2011); Employment by occupation: 9.6% management, 2.7% professional, 8.3% services, 13.1% sales, 1.4% farming, 16.3% construction, 5.3% production (2006-2010 5-year est.).
**Income:** Per capita income: $30,757 (2006-2010 5-year est.); Median household income: $68,947 (2006-2010 5-year est.); Average household income: $81,348 (2006-2010 5-year est.); Percent of households with

income of $100,000 or more: 30.0% (2006-2010 5-year est.); Poverty rate: 4.9% (2006-2010 5-year est.).

**Education:** Percent of population age 25 and over with: High school diploma (including GED) or higher: 92.7% (2006-2010 5-year est.); Bachelor's degree or higher: 32.7% (2006-2010 5-year est.); Master's degree or higher: 18.7% (2006-2010 5-year est.).

### School District(s)
Fabius-Pompey Central School District (KG-12)

  2009-10 Enrollment: 838 . . . . . . . . . . . . . . . . . . (315) 683-5301

**Housing:** Homeownership rate: 82.9% (2010); Median home value: $136,200 (2006-2010 5-year est.); Median contract rent: $497 per month (2006-2010 5-year est.); Median year structure built: 1952 (2006-2010 5-year est.).

**Transportation:** Commute to work: 91.7% car, 0.0% public transportation, 1.8% walk, 5.6% work from home (2006-2010 5-year est.); Travel time to work: 21.8% less than 15 minutes, 33.8% 15 to 30 minutes, 35.2% 30 to 45 minutes, 4.3% 45 to 60 minutes, 4.8% 60 minutes or more (2006-2010 5-year est.)

---

**FAIRMOUNT** (CDP). Covers a land area of 3.333 square miles and a water area of 0 square miles. Located at 43.04° N. Lat; 76.24° W. Long. Elevation is 492 feet.

**Population:** 11,322 (1990); 10,795 (2000); 10,224 (2010); Density: 3,066.8 persons per square mile (2010); Race: 93.2% White, 2.2% Black, 1.7% Asian, 0.6% American Indian/Alaska Native, 0.1% Native Hawaiian/Other Pacific Islander, 2.2% Other, 2.0% Hispanic of any race (2010); Average household size: 2.32 (2010); Median age: 43.9 (2010); Males per 100 females: 88.5 (2010); Marriage status: 27.7% never married, 55.0% now married, 8.4% widowed, 8.9% divorced (2006-2010 5-year est.); Foreign born: 8.2% (2006-2010 5-year est.); Ancestry (includes multiple ancestries): 29.9% Irish, 22.1% Italian, 20.7% German, 10.2% English, 9.3% Polish (2006-2010 5-year est.).

**Economy:** Employment by occupation: 11.8% management, 2.6% professional, 7.0% services, 18.1% sales, 4.8% farming, 3.9% construction, 4.0% production (2006-2010 5-year est.).

**Income:** Per capita income: $28,035 (2006-2010 5-year est.); Median household income: $54,450 (2006-2010 5-year est.); Average household income: $65,475 (2006-2010 5-year est.); Percent of households with income of $100,000 or more: 17.6% (2006-2010 5-year est.); Poverty rate: 7.7% (2006-2010 5-year est.).

**Education:** Percent of population age 25 and over with: High school diploma (including GED) or higher: 92.1% (2006-2010 5-year est.); Bachelor's degree or higher: 32.8% (2006-2010 5-year est.); Master's degree or higher: 11.9% (2006-2010 5-year est.).

**Housing:** Homeownership rate: 79.4% (2010); Median home value: $115,500 (2006-2010 5-year est.); Median contract rent: $717 per month (2006-2010 5-year est.); Median year structure built: 1960 (2006-2010 5-year est.).

**Transportation:** Commute to work: 95.1% car, 1.5% public transportation, 2.3% walk, 0.7% work from home (2006-2010 5-year est.); Travel time to work: 35.3% less than 15 minutes, 51.0% 15 to 30 minutes, 10.6% 30 to 45 minutes, 1.6% 45 to 60 minutes, 1.5% 60 minutes or more (2006-2010 5-year est.)

---

**FAYETTEVILLE** (village). Covers a land area of 1.746 square miles and a water area of 0 square miles. Located at 43.03° N. Lat; 75.99° W. Long. Elevation is 535 feet.

**History:** Incorporated 1844.

**Population:** 4,340 (1990); 4,190 (2000); 4,373 (2010); Density: 2,504.1 persons per square mile (2010); Race: 93.8% White, 1.4% Black, 3.0% Asian, 0.2% American Indian/Alaska Native, 0.0% Native Hawaiian/Other Pacific Islander, 1.6% Other, 2.1% Hispanic of any race (2010); Average household size: 2.28 (2010); Median age: 44.4 (2010); Males per 100 females: 91.2 (2010); Marriage status: 21.4% never married, 61.1% now married, 8.1% widowed, 9.5% divorced (2006-2010 5-year est.); Foreign born: 6.5% (2006-2010 5-year est.); Ancestry (includes multiple ancestries): 28.0% Irish, 22.3% German, 16.9% English, 13.1% Italian, 9.3% Polish (2006-2010 5-year est.).

**Economy:** Single-family building permits issued: 5 (2011); Multi-family building permits issued: 0 (2011); Employment by occupation: 16.8% management, 3.2% professional, 5.3% services, 15.6% sales, 4.0% farming, 3.9% construction, 5.1% production (2006-2010 5-year est.).

**Income:** Per capita income: $41,473 (2006-2010 5-year est.); Median household income: $73,156 (2006-2010 5-year est.); Average household income: $89,453 (2006-2010 5-year est.); Percent of households with

income of $100,000 or more: 37.2% (2006-2010 5-year est.); Poverty rate: 3.1% (2006-2010 5-year est.).

**Education:** Percent of population age 25 and over with: High school diploma (including GED) or higher: 97.6% (2006-2010 5-year est.); Bachelor's degree or higher: 63.5% (2006-2010 5-year est.); Master's degree or higher: 29.4% (2006-2010 5-year est.).

### School District(s)
Fayetteville-Manlius Central School District (KG-12)

  2009-10 Enrollment: 4,588 . . . . . . . . . . . . . . . . (315) 692-1200

**Housing:** Homeownership rate: 75.6% (2010); Median home value: $167,700 (2006-2010 5-year est.); Median contract rent: $642 per month (2006-2010 5-year est.); Median year structure built: 1958 (2006-2010 5-year est.).

**Transportation:** Commute to work: 84.4% car, 1.7% public transportation, 3.2% walk, 7.8% work from home (2006-2010 5-year est.); Travel time to work: 28.8% less than 15 minutes, 56.2% 15 to 30 minutes, 9.6% 30 to 45 minutes, 2.9% 45 to 60 minutes, 2.5% 60 minutes or more (2006-2010 5-year est.)

**Additional Information Contacts**
Greater Manlius Chamber of Commerce . . . . . . . . . . (315) 637-4760
  http://www.manliuschamber.com

---

**GALEVILLE** (CDP). Covers a land area of 1.152 square miles and a water area of 0.006 square miles. Located at 43.08° N. Lat; 76.18° W. Long. Elevation is 423 feet.

**Population:** 4,423 (1990); 4,476 (2000); 4,617 (2010); Density: 4,007.8 persons per square mile (2010); Race: 88.4% White, 4.8% Black, 2.7% Asian, 0.6% American Indian/Alaska Native, 0.0% Native Hawaiian/Other Pacific Islander, 3.5% Other, 3.3% Hispanic of any race (2010); Average household size: 2.15 (2010); Median age: 45.4 (2010); Males per 100 females: 82.4 (2010); Marriage status: 32.6% never married, 41.1% now married, 14.3% widowed, 12.0% divorced (2006-2010 5-year est.); Foreign born: 5.3% (2006-2010 5-year est.); Ancestry (includes multiple ancestries): 31.1% Italian, 26.4% German, 22.0% Irish, 10.3% Polish, 8.7% English (2006-2010 5-year est.).

**Economy:** Employment by occupation: 7.8% management, 3.2% professional, 13.1% services, 24.2% sales, 3.1% farming, 7.1% construction, 4.2% production (2006-2010 5-year est.).

**Income:** Per capita income: $22,816 (2006-2010 5-year est.); Median household income: $42,230 (2006-2010 5-year est.); Average household income: $49,008 (2006-2010 5-year est.); Percent of households with income of $100,000 or more: 6.1% (2006-2010 5-year est.); Poverty rate: 8.4% (2006-2010 5-year est.).

**Education:** Percent of population age 25 and over with: High school diploma (including GED) or higher: 86.5% (2006-2010 5-year est.); Bachelor's degree or higher: 19.4% (2006-2010 5-year est.); Master's degree or higher: 8.0% (2006-2010 5-year est.).

**Housing:** Homeownership rate: 63.9% (2010); Median home value: $88,800 (2006-2010 5-year est.); Median contract rent: $676 per month (2006-2010 5-year est.); Median year structure built: 1955 (2006-2010 5-year est.).

**Transportation:** Commute to work: 93.6% car, 0.6% public transportation, 2.8% walk, 3.0% work from home (2006-2010 5-year est.); Travel time to work: 45.4% less than 15 minutes, 41.3% 15 to 30 minutes, 7.4% 30 to 45 minutes, 3.9% 45 to 60 minutes, 2.0% 60 minutes or more (2006-2010 5-year est.)

---

**GEDDES** (town). Covers a land area of 9.156 square miles and a water area of 3.104 square miles. Located at 43.07° N. Lat; 76.22° W. Long.

**Population:** 17,677 (1990); 17,740 (2000); 17,118 (2010); Density: 1,869.5 persons per square mile (2010); Race: 95.1% White, 1.2% Black, 0.6% Asian, 0.8% American Indian/Alaska Native, 0.0% Native Hawaiian/Other Pacific Islander, 2.3% Other, 2.8% Hispanic of any race (2010); Average household size: 2.31 (2010); Median age: 44.3 (2010); Males per 100 females: 87.4 (2010); Marriage status: 29.4% never married, 49.8% now married, 9.9% widowed, 10.8% divorced (2006-2010 5-year est.); Foreign born: 5.5% (2006-2010 5-year est.); Ancestry (includes multiple ancestries): 29.8% Italian, 29.1% Irish, 21.1% German, 13.6% Polish, 11.1% English (2006-2010 5-year est.).

**Economy:** Single-family building permits issued: 6 (2011); Multi-family building permits issued: 0 (2011); Employment by occupation: 9.4% management, 3.8% professional, 9.2% services, 19.7% sales, 5.8% farming, 6.1% construction, 4.5% production (2006-2010 5-year est.).

**Income:** Per capita income: $26,513 (2006-2010 5-year est.); Median household income: $51,230 (2006-2010 5-year est.); Average household

income: $61,833 (2006-2010 5-year est.); Percent of households with income of $100,000 or more: 17.2% (2006-2010 5-year est.); Poverty rate: 8.9% (2006-2010 5-year est.).

**Education:** Percent of population age 25 and over with: High school diploma (including GED) or higher: 89.5% (2006-2010 5-year est.); Bachelor's degree or higher: 26.4% (2006-2010 5-year est.); Master's degree or higher: 9.9% (2006-2010 5-year est.).

**Housing:** Homeownership rate: 75.2% (2010); Median home value: $120,100 (2006-2010 5-year est.); Median contract rent: $547 per month (2006-2010 5-year est.); Median year structure built: 1954 (2006-2010 5-year est.).

**Safety:** Violent crime rate: 6.8 per 10,000 population; Property crime rate: 220.1 per 10,000 population (2010).

**Transportation:** Commute to work: 92.8% car, 3.2% public transportation, 2.1% walk, 1.4% work from home (2006-2010 5-year est.); Travel time to work: 36.3% less than 15 minutes, 51.9% 15 to 30 minutes, 7.1% 30 to 45 minutes, 2.3% 45 to 60 minutes, 2.4% 60 minutes or more (2006-2010 5-year est.)

**Additional Information Contacts**

Town of Geddes. . . . . . . . . . . . . . . . . . . . . . . . . . . . . (315) 468-2528
http://www.townofgeddes.com

## JAMESVILLE (unincorporated postal area)

Zip Code: 13078

Covers a land area of 38.920 square miles and a water area of 0.463 square miles. Located at 42.95° N. Lat; 76.06° W. Long. Elevation is 607 feet. Population: 9,866 (2010); Density: 253.5 persons per square mile (2010); Race: 86.9% White, 4.2% Black, 5.9% Asian, 0.8% American Indian/Alaska Native, 0.0% Native Hawaiian/Other Pacific Islander, 2.2% Other, 2.4% Hispanic of any race (2010); Average household size: 2.58 (2010); Median age: 44.1 (2010); Males per 100 females: 101.8 (2010); Homeownership rate: 82.2% (2010)

## JORDAN (village). Covers a land area of 1.145 square miles and a water area of 0 square miles. Located at 43.06° N. Long; 76.47° W. Long. Elevation is 413 feet.

**History:** Incorporated 1835.

**Population:** 1,439 (1990); 1,314 (2000); 1,368 (2010); Density: 1,194.1 persons per square mile (2010); Race: 97.7% White, 0.2% Black, 0.4% Asian, 0.5% American Indian/Alaska Native, 0.0% Native Hawaiian/Other Pacific Islander, 1.2% Other, 1.3% Hispanic of any race (2010); Average household size: 2.46 (2010); Median age: 40.3 (2010); Males per 100 females: 102.1 (2010); Marriage status: 27.7% never married, 56.2% now married, 5.6% widowed, 10.5% divorced (2006-2010 5-year est.); Foreign born: 1.2% (2006-2010 5-year est.); Ancestry (includes multiple ancestries): 24.9% German, 22.7% Irish, 21.0% English, 10.8% Italian, 10.3% French (2006-2010 5-year est.).

**Economy:** Single-family building permits issued: 0 (2011); Multi-family building permits issued: 0 (2011); Employment by occupation: 6.3% management, 3.1% professional, 8.1% services, 16.2% sales, 4.2% farming, 5.0% construction, 7.8% production (2006-2010 5-year est.).

**Income:** Per capita income: $21,599 (2006-2010 5-year est.); Median household income: $49,375 (2006-2010 5-year est.); Average household income: $59,801 (2006-2010 5-year est.); Percent of households with income of $100,000 or more: 19.5% (2006-2010 5-year est.); Poverty rate: 12.7% (2006-2010 5-year est.).

**Education:** Percent of population age 25 and over with: High school diploma (including GED) or higher: 89.7% (2006-2010 5-year est.); Bachelor's degree or higher: 18.8% (2006-2010 5-year est.); Master's degree or higher: 6.5% (2006-2010 5-year est.).

**School District(s)**

Jordan-Elbridge Central School District (PK-12)

2009-10 Enrollment: 1,554 . . . . . . . . . . . . . . . . . . . . . . (315) 689-8500

**Housing:** Homeownership rate: 63.2% (2010); Median home value: $100,800 (2006-2010 5-year est.); Median contract rent: $446 per month (2006-2010 5-year est.); Median year structure built: before 1940 (2006-2010 5-year est.).

**Safety:** Violent crime rate: 0.0 per 10,000 population; Property crime rate: 23.1 per 10,000 population (2010).

**Transportation:** Commute to work: 90.8% car, 1.3% public transportation, 6.7% walk, 1.1% work from home (2006-2010 5-year est.); Travel time to work: 34.2% less than 15 minutes, 29.9% 15 to 30 minutes, 22.3% 30 to 45 minutes, 8.8% 45 to 60 minutes, 4.8% 60 minutes or more (2006-2010 5-year est.)

## KIRKVILLE (unincorporated postal area)

Zip Code: 13082

Covers a land area of 23.570 square miles and a water area of 0.413 square miles. Located at 43.10° N. Lat; 75.95° W. Long. Population: 4,871 (2010); Density: 206.7 persons per square mile (2010); Race: 97.6% White, 0.4% Black, 0.2% Asian, 0.4% American Indian/Alaska Native, 0.1% Native Hawaiian/Other Pacific Islander, 1.3% Other, 1.0% Hispanic of any race (2010); Average household size: 2.44 (2010); Median age: 45.4 (2010); Males per 100 females: 93.8 (2010); Homeownership rate: 84.3% (2010)

## LA FAYETTE (town). Covers a land area of 39.232 square miles and a water area of 0.412 square miles. Located at 42.90° N. Lat; 76.10° W. Long.

**Population:** 4,937 (1990); 4,833 (2000); 4,952 (2010); Density: 126.2 persons per square mile (2010); Race: 94.5% White, 0.5% Black, 0.7% Asian, 2.1% American Indian/Alaska Native, 0.1% Native Hawaiian/Other Pacific Islander, 2.1% Other, 0.9% Hispanic of any race (2010); Average household size: 2.48 (2010); Median age: 45.2 (2010); Males per 100 females: 99.4 (2010); Marriage status: 26.0% never married, 59.3% now married, 5.8% widowed, 8.9% divorced (2006-2010 5-year est.); Foreign born: 3.1% (2006-2010 5-year est.); Ancestry (includes multiple ancestries): 31.9% Irish, 25.4% German, 15.4% English, 8.9% Italian, 7.3% French (2006-2010 5-year est.).

**Economy:** Single-family building permits issued: 5 (2011); Multi-family building permits issued: 0 (2011); Employment by occupation: 6.8% management, 5.5% professional, 7.6% services, 17.2% sales, 3.6% farming, 15.3% construction, 5.9% production (2006-2010 5-year est.).

**Income:** Per capita income: $28,304 (2006-2010 5-year est.); Median household income: $65,490 (2006-2010 5-year est.); Average household income: $72,408 (2006-2010 5-year est.); Percent of households with income of $100,000 or more: 26.9% (2006-2010 5-year est.); Poverty rate: 2.9% (2006-2010 5-year est.).

**Education:** Percent of population age 25 and over with: High school diploma (including GED) or higher: 90.1% (2006-2010 5-year est.); Bachelor's degree or higher: 28.5% (2006-2010 5-year est.); Master's degree or higher: 11.1% (2006-2010 5-year est.).

**School District(s)**

Lafayette Central School District (PK-12)

2009-10 Enrollment: 892 . . . . . . . . . . . . . . . . . . . . . . (315) 677-9728

**Housing:** Homeownership rate: 82.0% (2010); Median home value: $154,700 (2006-2010 5-year est.); Median contract rent: $571 per month (2006-2010 5-year est.); Median year structure built: 1970 (2006-2010 5-year est.).

**Transportation:** Commute to work: 94.1% car, 0.0% public transportation, 1.2% walk, 4.7% work from home (2006-2010 5-year est.); Travel time to work: 17.7% less than 15 minutes, 68.8% 15 to 30 minutes, 12.4% 30 to 45 minutes, 0.4% 45 to 60 minutes, 0.8% 60 minutes or more (2006-2010 5-year est.)

## LA FAYETTE (unincorporated postal area)

Zip Code: 13084

Covers a land area of 43.005 square miles and a water area of 0.011 square miles. Located at 42.88° N. Lat; 76.12° W. Long. Population: 4,409 (2010); Density: 102.5 persons per square mile (2010); Race: 93.4% White, 0.7% Black, 0.7% Asian, 2.9% American Indian/Alaska Native, 0.1% Native Hawaiian/Other Pacific Islander, 2.2% Other, 1.3% Hispanic of any race (2010); Average household size: 2.48 (2010); Median age: 43.6 (2010); Males per 100 females: 97.4 (2010); Homeownership rate: 78.8% (2010)

## LAKELAND (CDP). Covers a land area of 1.483 square miles and a water area of 0 square miles. Located at 43.09° N. Lat; 76.24° W. Long. Elevation is 479 feet.

**Population:** 2,822 (1990); 2,852 (2000); 2,786 (2010); Density: 1,878.1 persons per square mile (2010); Race: 97.7% White, 0.4% Black, 0.3% Asian, 0.3% American Indian/Alaska Native, 0.0% Native Hawaiian/Other Pacific Islander, 1.3% Other, 1.3% Hispanic of any race (2010); Average household size: 2.48 (2010); Median age: 46.0 (2010); Males per 100 females: 92.1 (2010); Marriage status: 25.2% never married, 50.5% now married, 9.9% widowed, 14.3% divorced (2006-2010 5-year est.); Foreign born: 8.1% (2006-2010 5-year est.); Ancestry (includes multiple ancestries): 27.8% Italian, 22.1% German, 18.4% Polish, 18.3% Irish, 12.1% English (2006-2010 5-year est.).

**Economy:** Employment by occupation: 11.4% management, 3.0% professional, 7.9% services, 20.7% sales, 4.3% farming, 9.3% construction, 5.7% production (2006-2010 5-year est.).

**Income:** Per capita income: $23,805 (2006-2010 5-year est.); Median household income: $49,893 (2006-2010 5-year est.); Average household income: $57,103 (2006-2010 5-year est.); Percent of households with income of $100,000 or more: 15.4% (2006-2010 5-year est.); Poverty rate: 5.2% (2006-2010 5-year est.).

**Education:** Percent of population age 25 and over with: High school diploma (including GED) or higher: 92.7% (2006-2010 5-year est.); Bachelor's degree or higher: 14.0% (2006-2010 5-year est.); Master's degree or higher: 5.5% (2006-2010 5-year est.).

**Housing:** Homeownership rate: 82.6% (2010); Median home value: $119,700 (2006-2010 5-year est.); Median contract rent: $681 per month (2006-2010 5-year est.); Median year structure built: 1964 (2006-2010 5-year est.).

**Transportation:** Commute to work: 95.4% car, 3.2% public transportation, 0.0% walk, 1.4% work from home (2006-2010 5-year est.); Travel time to work: 32.0% less than 15 minutes, 57.5% 15 to 30 minutes, 4.6% 30 to 45 minutes, 3.1% 45 to 60 minutes, 2.8% 60 minutes or more (2006-2010 5-year est.)

**LIVERPOOL** (village). Covers a land area of 0.757 square miles and a water area of 0 square miles. Located at 43.10° N. Lat; 76.20° W. Long. Elevation is 420 feet.

**History:** Incorporated 1830.

**Population:** 2,624 (1990); 2,505 (2000); 2,347 (2010); Density: 3,100.0 persons per square mile (2010); Race: 94.9% White, 2.1% Black, 0.6% Asian, 0.3% American Indian/Alaska Native, 0.0% Native Hawaiian/Other Pacific Islander, 2.1% Other, 2.4% Hispanic of any race (2010); Average household size: 2.08 (2010); Median age: 44.8 (2010); Males per 100 females: 88.5 (2010); Marriage status: 34.7% never married, 49.6% now married, 5.6% widowed, 10.1% divorced (2006-2010 5-year est.); Foreign born: 2.5% (2006-2010 5-year est.); Ancestry (includes multiple ancestries): 25.1% Irish, 22.7% German, 21.1% Italian, 17.4% English, 6.4% French (2006-2010 5-year est.).

**Economy:** Single-family building permits issued: 0 (2011); Multi-family building permits issued: 0 (2011); Employment by occupation: 14.5% management, 7.4% professional, 8.1% services, 17.9% sales, 2.3% farming, 4.5% construction, 2.6% production (2006-2010 5-year est.).

**Income:** Per capita income: $33,547 (2006-2010 5-year est.); Median household income: $52,188 (2006-2010 5-year est.); Average household income: $69,702 (2006-2010 5-year est.); Percent of households with income of $100,000 or more: 17.7% (2006-2010 5-year est.); Poverty rate: 10.7% (2006-2010 5-year est.).

**Education:** Percent of population age 25 and over with: High school diploma (including GED) or higher: 92.7% (2006-2010 5-year est.); Bachelor's degree or higher: 39.1% (2006-2010 5-year est.); Master's degree or higher: 16.4% (2006-2010 5-year est.).

### School District(s)

Liverpool Central School District (PK-12)
    2009-10 Enrollment: 7,669 ...................... (315) 622-7125

### Two-year College(s)

Bryant and Stratton College-Syracuse North (Private, For-profit)
    Fall 2010 Enrollment: 659 ...................... (315) 652-6500
    2011-12 Tuition: In-state $15,705; Out-of-state $15,705
ITT Technical Institute-Liverpool (Private, For-profit)
    Fall 2010 Enrollment: 362 ...................... (315) 461-8000
    2011-12 Tuition: In-state $18,048; Out-of-state $18,048

### Vocational/Technical School(s)

National Tractor Trailer School Inc-Liverpool (Private, For-profit)
    Fall 2010 Enrollment: 220 ...................... (315) 451-2430
    2011-12 Tuition: $9,008
Onondaga Cortland Madison BOCES (Public)
    Fall 2010 Enrollment: 918 ...................... (315) 453-4455
    2011-12 Tuition: $7,700

**Housing:** Homeownership rate: 64.9% (2010); Median home value: $117,300 (2006-2010 5-year est.); Median contract rent: $591 per month (2006-2010 5-year est.); Median year structure built: 1943 (2006-2010 5-year est.).

**Safety:** Violent crime rate: 0.0 per 10,000 population; Property crime rate: 143.2 per 10,000 population (2010).

**Transportation:** Commute to work: 91.0% car, 0.0% public transportation, 5.6% walk, 1.9% work from home (2006-2010 5-year est.); Travel time to work: 36.9% less than 15 minutes, 51.9% 15 to 30 minutes, 5.6% 30 to 45

minutes, 2.8% 45 to 60 minutes, 2.8% 60 minutes or more (2006-2010 5-year est.)

**Additional Information Contacts**

Greater Liverpool Chamber of Commerce .............. (315) 457-3895
    http://www.liverpoolchamber.com
Village of Liverpool. ...................... (315) 457-3441
    http://www.villageofliverpool.org

**LYNCOURT** (CDP). Covers a land area of 1.243 square miles and a water area of 0 square miles. Located at 43.08° N. Lat; 76.12° W. Long. Elevation is 446 feet.

**Population:** 4,696 (1990); 4,268 (2000); 4,250 (2010); Density: 3,419.0 persons per square mile (2010); Race: 88.3% White, 6.1% Black, 1.7% Asian, 0.5% American Indian/Alaska Native, 0.0% Native Hawaiian/Other Pacific Islander, 3.4% Other, 3.5% Hispanic of any race (2010); Average household size: 2.22 (2010); Median age: 41.9 (2010); Males per 100 females: 90.6 (2010); Marriage status: 33.4% never married, 45.9% now married, 8.8% widowed, 11.9% divorced (2006-2010 5-year est.); Foreign born: 5.6% (2006-2010 5-year est.); Ancestry (includes multiple ancestries): 38.6% Italian, 29.7% German, 25.8% Irish, 7.4% English, 6.5% Polish (2006-2010 5-year est.).

**Economy:** Employment by occupation: 6.7% management, 1.4% professional, 12.3% services, 22.2% sales, 1.6% farming, 6.5% construction, 5.3% production (2006-2010 5-year est.).

**Income:** Per capita income: $21,472 (2006-2010 5-year est.); Median household income: $39,579 (2006-2010 5-year est.); Average household income: $46,470 (2006-2010 5-year est.); Percent of households with income of $100,000 or more: 6.7% (2006-2010 5-year est.); Poverty rate: 5.3% (2006-2010 5-year est.).

**Education:** Percent of population age 25 and over with: High school diploma (including GED) or higher: 86.6% (2006-2010 5-year est.); Bachelor's degree or higher: 17.9% (2006-2010 5-year est.); Master's degree or higher: 6.8% (2006-2010 5-year est.).

**Housing:** Homeownership rate: 70.5% (2010); Median home value: $87,400 (2006-2010 5-year est.); Median contract rent: $567 per month (2006-2010 5-year est.); Median year structure built: 1950 (2006-2010 5-year est.).

**Transportation:** Commute to work: 91.7% car, 1.4% public transportation, 5.7% walk, 1.2% work from home (2006-2010 5-year est.); Travel time to work: 42.3% less than 15 minutes, 50.8% 15 to 30 minutes, 1.8% 30 to 45 minutes, 1.6% 45 to 60 minutes, 3.6% 60 minutes or more (2006-2010 5-year est.)

**LYSANDER** (town). Covers a land area of 61.714 square miles and a water area of 2.894 square miles. Located at 43.18° N. Lat; 76.37° W. Long. Elevation is 413 feet.

**Population:** 16,346 (1990); 19,285 (2000); 21,759 (2010); Density: 352.6 persons per square mile (2010); Race: 95.8% White, 0.8% Black, 1.1% Asian, 0.4% American Indian/Alaska Native, 0.0% Native Hawaiian/Other Pacific Islander, 1.9% Other, 1.6% Hispanic of any race (2010); Average household size: 2.58 (2010); Median age: 41.7 (2010); Males per 100 females: 95.4 (2010); Marriage status: 22.9% never married, 62.9% now married, 4.4% widowed, 9.7% divorced (2006-2010 5-year est.); Foreign born: 4.1% (2006-2010 5-year est.); Ancestry (includes multiple ancestries): 27.6% Irish, 24.9% German, 20.3% English, 17.6% Italian, 7.9% Polish (2006-2010 5-year est.).

**Economy:** Single-family building permits issued: 25 (2011); Multi-family building permits issued: 80 (2011); Employment by occupation: 16.9% management, 6.2% professional, 7.1% services, 18.2% sales, 2.4% farming, 6.4% construction, 4.4% production (2006-2010 5-year est.).

**Income:** Per capita income: $36,019 (2006-2010 5-year est.); Median household income: $73,608 (2006-2010 5-year est.); Average household income: $92,799 (2006-2010 5-year est.); Percent of households with income of $100,000 or more: 35.2% (2006-2010 5-year est.); Poverty rate: 5.6% (2006-2010 5-year est.).

**Education:** Percent of population age 25 and over with: High school diploma (including GED) or higher: 93.4% (2006-2010 5-year est.); Bachelor's degree or higher: 41.2% (2006-2010 5-year est.); Master's degree or higher: 16.7% (2006-2010 5-year est.).

**Housing:** Homeownership rate: 80.1% (2010); Median home value: $161,900 (2006-2010 5-year est.); Median contract rent: $603 per month (2006-2010 5-year est.); Median year structure built: 1979 (2006-2010 5-year est.).

**Transportation:** Commute to work: 95.1% car, 0.7% public transportation, 0.6% walk, 3.4% work from home (2006-2010 5-year est.); Travel time to

work: 20.8% less than 15 minutes, 50.1% 15 to 30 minutes, 23.4% 30 to 45 minutes, 2.8% 45 to 60 minutes, 2.9% 60 minutes or more (2006-2010 5-year est.)

**Additional Information Contacts**
Town of Lysander . . . . . . . . . . . . . . . . . . . . . . . (315) 638-0224
  http://www.townoflysander.org

**MANLIUS** (village). Covers a land area of 1.785 square miles and a water area of 0.001 square miles. Located at 43.00° N. Lat; 75.98° W. Long. Elevation is 591 feet.
**Population:** 4,945 (1990); 4,819 (2000); 4,704 (2010); Density: 2,634.9 persons per square mile (2010); Race: 90.8% White, 1.8% Black, 5.5% Asian, 0.2% American Indian/Alaska Native, 0.0% Native Hawaiian/Other Pacific Islander, 1.7% Other, 1.8% Hispanic of any race (2010); Average household size: 2.31 (2010); Median age: 42.3 (2010); Males per 100 females: 87.4 (2010); Marriage status: 25.1% never married, 57.3% now married, 6.7% widowed, 11.0% divorced (2006-2010 5-year est.); Foreign born: 7.5% (2006-2010 5-year est.); Ancestry (includes multiple ancestries): 23.8% Irish, 18.9% English, 18.7% German, 17.2% Italian, 8.2% French (2006-2010 5-year est.).
**Economy:** Single-family building permits issued: 5 (2011); Multi-family building permits issued: 0 (2011); Employment by occupation: 10.9% management, 4.4% professional, 9.6% services, 14.9% sales, 5.8% farming, 6.2% construction, 3.1% production (2006-2010 5-year est.).
**Income:** Per capita income: $30,302 (2006-2010 5-year est.); Median household income: $56,625 (2006-2010 5-year est.); Average household income: $70,245 (2006-2010 5-year est.); Percent of households with income of $100,000 or more: 25.6% (2006-2010 5-year est.); Poverty rate: 8.2% (2006-2010 5-year est.).
**Education:** Percent of population age 25 and over with: High school diploma (including GED) or higher: 96.8% (2006-2010 5-year est.); Bachelor's degree or higher: 46.5% (2006-2010 5-year est.); Master's degree or higher: 20.9% (2006-2010 5-year est.).
**School District(s)**
Fayetteville-Manlius Central School District (KG-12)
  2009-10 Enrollment: 4,588 . . . . . . . . . . . . . . . (315) 692-1200
**Housing:** Homeownership rate: 57.9% (2010); Median home value: $183,900 (2006-2010 5-year est.); Median contract rent: $659 per month (2006-2010 5-year est.); Median year structure built: 1968 (2006-2010 5-year est.).
**Transportation:** Commute to work: 88.5% car, 1.3% public transportation, 6.1% walk, 3.2% work from home (2006-2010 5-year est.); Travel time to work: 35.5% less than 15 minutes, 44.6% 15 to 30 minutes, 18.6% 30 to 45 minutes, 1.4% 45 to 60 minutes, 0.0% 60 minutes or more (2006-2010 5-year est.)
**Additional Information Contacts**
Greater Manlius Chamber of Commerce . . . . . . . . . . . (315) 637-4760
  http://www.manliuschamber.com

**MANLIUS** (town). Covers a land area of 49.218 square miles and a water area of 0.735 square miles. Located at 43.05° N. Lat; 75.98° W. Long. Elevation is 591 feet.
**History:** Settled 1789 incorporated 1842.
**Population:** 30,656 (1990); 31,872 (2000); 32,370 (2010); Density: 657.7 persons per square mile (2010); Race: 92.9% White, 1.4% Black, 3.7% Asian, 0.3% American Indian/Alaska Native, 0.0% Native Hawaiian/Other Pacific Islander, 1.7% Other, 1.5% Hispanic of any race (2010); Average household size: 2.40 (2010); Median age: 44.9 (2010); Males per 100 females: 91.2 (2010); Marriage status: 24.5% never married, 60.0% now married, 7.5% widowed, 8.0% divorced (2006-2010 5-year est.); Foreign born: 6.5% (2006-2010 5-year est.); Ancestry (includes multiple ancestries): 28.0% Irish, 24.3% German, 15.8% Italian, 15.3% English, 8.3% Polish (2006-2010 5-year est.).
**Economy:** Unemployment rate: 6.8% (February 2012); Total civilian labor force: 15,902 (February 2012); Single-family building permits issued: 30 (2011); Multi-family building permits issued: 0 (2011); Employment by occupation: 14.3% management, 5.9% professional, 6.3% services, 15.0% sales, 3.6% farming, 4.7% construction, 4.0% production (2006-2010 5-year est.).
**Income:** Per capita income: $38,170 (2006-2010 5-year est.); Median household income: $72,428 (2006-2010 5-year est.); Average household income: $93,916 (2006-2010 5-year est.); Percent of households with income of $100,000 or more: 33.5% (2006-2010 5-year est.); Poverty rate: 4.2% (2006-2010 5-year est.).

**Education:** Percent of population age 25 and over with: High school diploma (including GED) or higher: 96.0% (2006-2010 5-year est.); Bachelor's degree or higher: 52.6% (2006-2010 5-year est.); Master's degree or higher: 26.0% (2006-2010 5-year est.).
**School District(s)**
Fayetteville-Manlius Central School District (KG-12)
  2009-10 Enrollment: 4,588 . . . . . . . . . . . . . . . (315) 692-1200
**Housing:** Homeownership rate: 78.2% (2010); Median home value: $169,900 (2006-2010 5-year est.); Median contract rent: $713 per month (2006-2010 5-year est.); Median year structure built: 1970 (2006-2010 5-year est.).
**Safety:** Violent crime rate: 6.5 per 10,000 population; Property crime rate: 180.5 per 10,000 population (2010).
**Transportation:** Commute to work: 92.0% car, 0.5% public transportation, 2.1% walk, 3.9% work from home (2006-2010 5-year est.); Travel time to work: 26.6% less than 15 minutes, 58.0% 15 to 30 minutes, 11.6% 30 to 45 minutes, 2.4% 45 to 60 minutes, 1.3% 60 minutes or more (2006-2010 5-year est.)
**Additional Information Contacts**
Town of Manlius . . . . . . . . . . . . . . . . . . . . . . . . (315) 637-3521
  http://www.townofmanlius.org

**MARCELLUS** (village). Covers a land area of 0.621 square miles and a water area of 0 square miles. Located at 42.98° N. Lat; 76.34° W. Long. Elevation is 682 feet.
**Population:** 1,840 (1990); 1,826 (2000); 1,813 (2010); Density: 2,915.5 persons per square mile (2010); Race: 96.6% White, 0.3% Black, 0.7% Asian, 0.3% American Indian/Alaska Native, 0.0% Native Hawaiian/Other Pacific Islander, 2.1% Other, 1.4% Hispanic of any race (2010); Average household size: 2.24 (2010); Median age: 40.7 (2010); Males per 100 females: 86.5 (2010); Marriage status: 35.5% never married, 47.2% now married, 7.2% widowed, 10.1% divorced (2006-2010 5-year est.); Foreign born: 0.8% (2006-2010 5-year est.); Ancestry (includes multiple ancestries): 35.2% Irish, 29.4% English, 27.4% German, 12.0% Italian, 11.1% Polish (2006-2010 5-year est.).
**Economy:** Single-family building permits issued: 0 (2011); Multi-family building permits issued: 0 (2011); Employment by occupation: 10.9% management, 2.7% professional, 13.4% services, 14.7% sales, 1.7% farming, 9.4% construction, 4.4% production (2006-2010 5-year est.).
**Income:** Per capita income: $28,302 (2006-2010 5-year est.); Median household income: $45,455 (2006-2010 5-year est.); Average household income: $61,657 (2006-2010 5-year est.); Percent of households with income of $100,000 or more: 17.0% (2006-2010 5-year est.); Poverty rate: 4.1% (2006-2010 5-year est.).
**Education:** Percent of population age 25 and over with: High school diploma (including GED) or higher: 94.0% (2006-2010 5-year est.); Bachelor's degree or higher: 32.5% (2006-2010 5-year est.); Master's degree or higher: 9.1% (2006-2010 5-year est.).
**School District(s)**
Marcellus Central School District (KG-12)
  2009-10 Enrollment: 1,988 . . . . . . . . . . . . . . . (315) 673-0201
**Housing:** Homeownership rate: 55.5% (2010); Median home value: $151,600 (2006-2010 5-year est.); Median contract rent: $543 per month (2006-2010 5-year est.); Median year structure built: 1951 (2006-2010 5-year est.).
**Safety:** Violent crime rate: 0.0 per 10,000 population; Property crime rate: 61.4 per 10,000 population (2010).
**Transportation:** Commute to work: 91.1% car, 3.2% public transportation, 3.2% walk, 1.8% work from home (2006-2010 5-year est.); Travel time to work: 19.3% less than 15 minutes, 41.4% 15 to 30 minutes, 30.9% 30 to 45 minutes, 3.7% 45 to 60 minutes, 4.7% 60 minutes or more (2006-2010 5-year est.)
**Additional Information Contacts**
Village of Marcellus . . . . . . . . . . . . . . . . . . . . . (315) 673-3112
  http://villageofmarcellus.com

**MARCELLUS** (town). Covers a land area of 32.445 square miles and a water area of 0.139 square miles. Located at 42.94° N. Lat; 76.32° W. Long. Elevation is 682 feet.
**History:** Incorporated 1846.
**Population:** 6,465 (1990); 6,319 (2000); 6,210 (2010); Density: 191.4 persons per square mile (2010); Race: 97.9% White, 0.3% Black, 0.6% Asian, 0.2% American Indian/Alaska Native, 0.0% Native Hawaiian/Other Pacific Islander, 1.0% Other, 1.0% Hispanic of any race (2010); Average household size: 2.52 (2010); Median age: 44.1 (2010); Males per 100

females: 97.7 (2010); Marriage status: 28.6% never married, 61.0% now married, 3.7% widowed, 6.7% divorced (2006-2010 5-year est.); Foreign born: 0.6% (2006-2010 5-year est.); Ancestry (includes multiple ancestries): 30.7% Irish, 24.0% German, 23.1% English, 18.9% Italian, 8.6% Polish (2006-2010 5-year est.).

**Economy:** Single-family building permits issued: 7 (2011); Multi-family building permits issued: 0 (2011); Employment by occupation: 10.9% management, 6.0% professional, 10.2% services, 14.9% sales, 4.4% farming, 9.5% construction, 6.1% production (2006-2010 5-year est.).

**Income:** Per capita income: $27,699 (2006-2010 5-year est.); Median household income: $62,260 (2006-2010 5-year est.); Average household income: $73,257 (2006-2010 5-year est.); Percent of households with income of $100,000 or more: 26.4% (2006-2010 5-year est.); Poverty rate: 8.9% (2006-2010 5-year est.).

**Education:** Percent of population age 25 and over with: High school diploma (including GED) or higher: 94.4% (2006-2010 5-year est.); Bachelor's degree or higher: 36.3% (2006-2010 5-year est.); Master's degree or higher: 13.6% (2006-2010 5-year est.).

### School District(s)
Marcellus Central School District (KG-12)
  2009-10 Enrollment: 1,988 . . . . . . . . . . . . . . . . . . . . . (315) 673-0201

**Housing:** Homeownership rate: 81.0% (2010); Median home value: $154,700 (2006-2010 5-year est.); Median contract rent: $609 per month (2006-2010 5-year est.); Median year structure built: 1963 (2006-2010 5-year est.).

**Transportation:** Commute to work: 93.6% car, 0.9% public transportation, 1.5% walk, 3.2% work from home (2006-2010 5-year est.); Travel time to work: 19.5% less than 15 minutes, 45.0% 15 to 30 minutes, 29.0% 30 to 45 minutes, 2.4% 45 to 60 minutes, 4.2% 60 minutes or more (2006-2010 5-year est.)

**Additional Information Contacts**
Town of Marcellus . . . . . . . . . . . . . . . . . . . . . . . . . . (315) 673-3269
  http://town.marcellusny.com

## MARIETTA (unincorporated postal area)
Zip Code: 13110
  Covers a land area of 24.573 square miles and a water area of 0.010 square miles. Located at 42.89° N. Lat; 76.28° W. Long. Elevation is 797 feet. Population: 2,338 (2010); Density: 95.1 persons per square mile (2010); Race: 97.6% White, 0.3% Black, 0.4% Asian, 0.8% American Indian/Alaska Native, 0.0% Native Hawaiian/Other Pacific Islander, 0.9% Other, 0.7% Hispanic of any race (2010); Average household size: 2.49 (2010); Median age: 45.9 (2010); Males per 100 females: 106.9 (2010); Homeownership rate: 88.0% (2010)

## MATTYDALE (CDP). Covers a land area of 1.920 square miles and a water area of 0 square miles. Located at 43.09° N. Lat; 76.13° W. Long. Elevation is 404 feet.
**Population:** 6,790 (1990); 6,367 (2000); 6,446 (2010); Density: 3,356.4 persons per square mile (2010); Race: 89.7% White, 4.6% Black, 0.8% Asian, 0.9% American Indian/Alaska Native, 0.0% Native Hawaiian/Other Pacific Islander, 4.0% Other, 3.5% Hispanic of any race (2010); Average household size: 2.43 (2010); Median age: 37.9 (2010); Males per 100 females: 91.5 (2010); Marriage status: 32.5% never married, 40.4% now married, 12.8% widowed, 14.3% divorced (2006-2010 5-year est.); Foreign born: 1.6% (2006-2010 5-year est.); Ancestry (includes multiple ancestries): 24.4% Irish, 22.5% Italian, 18.2% German, 15.5% English, 10.0% French (2006-2010 5-year est.).

**Economy:** Employment by occupation: 6.5% management, 1.5% professional, 15.1% services, 24.2% sales, 4.3% farming, 8.8% construction, 10.7% production (2006-2010 5-year est.).

**Income:** Per capita income: $22,164 (2006-2010 5-year est.); Median household income: $42,972 (2006-2010 5-year est.); Average household income: $51,862 (2006-2010 5-year est.); Percent of households with income of $100,000 or more: 9.1% (2006-2010 5-year est.); Poverty rate: 8.7% (2006-2010 5-year est.).

**Education:** Percent of population age 25 and over with: High school diploma (including GED) or higher: 87.5% (2006-2010 5-year est.); Bachelor's degree or higher: 12.6% (2006-2010 5-year est.); Master's degree or higher: 1.9% (2006-2010 5-year est.).

### Vocational/Technical School(s)
Continental School of Beauty Culture (Private, For-profit)
  Fall 2010 Enrollment: 238 . . . . . . . . . . . . . . . . . . . . . (585) 272-8060
  2011-12 Tuition: $11,505

**Housing:** Homeownership rate: 69.3% (2010); Median home value: $80,600 (2006-2010 5-year est.); Median contract rent: $656 per month (2006-2010 5-year est.); Median year structure built: 1953 (2006-2010 5-year est.).

**Transportation:** Commute to work: 94.4% car, 1.2% public transportation, 2.1% walk, 1.7% work from home (2006-2010 5-year est.); Travel time to work: 42.9% less than 15 minutes, 47.8% 15 to 30 minutes, 6.7% 30 to 45 minutes, 0.7% 45 to 60 minutes, 1.9% 60 minutes or more (2006-2010 5-year est.)

## MEMPHIS (unincorporated postal area)
Zip Code: 13112
  Covers a land area of 20.253 square miles and a water area of 1.328 square miles. Located at 43.10° N. Lat; 76.41° W. Long. Elevation is 433 feet. Population: 1,973 (2010); Density: 97.4 persons per square mile (2010); Race: 97.7% White, 0.5% Black, 0.1% Asian, 0.2% American Indian/Alaska Native, 0.1% Native Hawaiian/Other Pacific Islander, 1.4% Other, 1.6% Hispanic of any race (2010); Average household size: 2.67 (2010); Median age: 43.4 (2010); Males per 100 females: 106.2 (2010); Homeownership rate: 92.5% (2010)

## MINOA (village). Covers a land area of 1.273 square miles and a water area of 0 square miles. Located at 43.07° N. Lat; 76.00° W. Long. Elevation is 413 feet.
**Population:** 3,752 (1990); 3,348 (2000); 3,449 (2010); Density: 2,708.9 persons per square mile (2010); Race: 95.4% White, 0.7% Black, 2.0% Asian, 0.7% American Indian/Alaska Native, 0.0% Native Hawaiian/Other Pacific Islander, 1.2% Other, 0.8% Hispanic of any race (2010); Average household size: 2.41 (2010); Median age: 41.9 (2010); Males per 100 females: 88.0 (2010); Marriage status: 27.5% never married, 55.4% now married, 11.9% widowed, 5.2% divorced (2006-2010 5-year est.); Foreign born: 1.5% (2006-2010 5-year est.); Ancestry (includes multiple ancestries): 28.0% German, 25.5% Irish, 17.3% Italian, 12.7% Polish, 10.0% English (2006-2010 5-year est.).

**Economy:** Single-family building permits issued: 13 (2011); Multi-family building permits issued: 0 (2011); Employment by occupation: 10.1% management, 6.4% professional, 8.8% services, 13.5% sales, 3.6% farming, 4.8% construction, 5.4% production (2006-2010 5-year est.).

**Income:** Per capita income: $25,769 (2006-2010 5-year est.); Median household income: $57,857 (2006-2010 5-year est.); Average household income: $63,553 (2006-2010 5-year est.); Percent of households with income of $100,000 or more: 17.9% (2006-2010 5-year est.); Poverty rate: 3.6% (2006-2010 5-year est.).

**Education:** Percent of population age 25 and over with: High school diploma (including GED) or higher: 92.1% (2006-2010 5-year est.); Bachelor's degree or higher: 31.8% (2006-2010 5-year est.); Master's degree or higher: 13.3% (2006-2010 5-year est.).

### School District(s)
East Syracuse-Minoa Central School District (PK-12)
  2009-10 Enrollment: 3,524 . . . . . . . . . . . . . . . . . . . . . (315) 434-3012

**Housing:** Homeownership rate: 73.5% (2010); Median home value: $116,300 (2006-2010 5-year est.); Median contract rent: $668 per month (2006-2010 5-year est.); Median year structure built: 1973 (2006-2010 5-year est.).

**Transportation:** Commute to work: 93.4% car, 0.0% public transportation, 1.8% walk, 3.7% work from home (2006-2010 5-year est.); Travel time to work: 30.8% less than 15 minutes, 57.9% 15 to 30 minutes, 10.4% 30 to 45 minutes, 0.0% 45 to 60 minutes, 0.9% 60 minutes or more (2006-2010 5-year est.)

## NEDROW (CDP). Covers a land area of 0.959 square miles and a water area of 0 square miles. Located at 42.97° N. Lat; 76.14° W. Long. Elevation is 472 feet.
**Population:** 2,307 (1990); 2,265 (2000); 2,244 (2010); Density: 2,339.0 persons per square mile (2010); Race: 78.2% White, 9.5% Black, 0.6% Asian, 7.6% American Indian/Alaska Native, 0.1% Native Hawaiian/Other Pacific Islander, 4.0% Other, 2.9% Hispanic of any race (2010); Average household size: 2.54 (2010); Median age: 39.5 (2010); Males per 100 females: 91.6 (2010); Marriage status: 27.1% never married, 56.6% now married, 5.8% widowed, 10.6% divorced (2006-2010 5-year est.); Foreign born: 0.7% (2006-2010 5-year est.); Ancestry (includes multiple ancestries): 19.1% Irish, 17.6% German, 17.5% Italian, 12.8% Polish, 10.9% English (2006-2010 5-year est.).

**Economy:** Employment by occupation: 4.7% management, 0.0% professional, 14.2% services, 25.0% sales, 8.7% farming, 12.1% construction, 5.1% production (2006-2010 5-year est.).
**Income:** Per capita income: $19,653 (2006-2010 5-year est.); Median household income: $44,500 (2006-2010 5-year est.); Average household income: $49,123 (2006-2010 5-year est.); Percent of households with income of $100,000 or more: 5.9% (2006-2010 5-year est.); Poverty rate: 13.3% (2006-2010 5-year est.).
**Education:** Percent of population age 25 and over with: High school diploma (including GED) or higher: 91.4% (2006-2010 5-year est.); Bachelor's degree or higher: 10.8% (2006-2010 5-year est.); Master's degree or higher: 1.8% (2006-2010 5-year est.).

### School District(s)

Lafayette Central School District (PK-12)
    2009-10 Enrollment: 892 . . . . . . . . . . . . . . . . . . . . . (315) 677-9728
Onondaga Central School District (PK-12)
    2009-10 Enrollment: 973 . . . . . . . . . . . . . . . . . . . . . (315) 552-5000
**Housing:** Homeownership rate: 86.2% (2010); Median home value: $71,300 (2006-2010 5-year est.); Median contract rent: $574 per month (2006-2010 5-year est.); Median year structure built: 1948 (2006-2010 5-year est.).
**Transportation:** Commute to work: 97.2% car, 0.0% public transportation, 2.8% walk, 0.0% work from home (2006-2010 5-year est.); Travel time to work: 22.3% less than 15 minutes, 60.2% 15 to 30 minutes, 13.3% 30 to 45 minutes, 3.1% 45 to 60 minutes, 1.1% 60 minutes or more (2006-2010 5-year est.)

## NORTH SYRACUSE (village). Covers a land area of 1.957 square miles and a water area of 0 square miles. Located at 43.13° N. Lat; 76.13° W. Long. Elevation is 420 feet.

**History:** Incorporated 1925.
**Population:** 7,363 (1990); 6,862 (2000); 6,800 (2010); Density: 3,473.4 persons per square mile (2010); Race: 93.7% White, 2.3% Black, 0.7% Asian, 0.8% American Indian/Alaska Native, 0.0% Native Hawaiian/Other Pacific Islander, 2.5% Other, 2.6% Hispanic of any race (2010); Average household size: 2.21 (2010); Median age: 41.2 (2010); Males per 100 females: 93.3 (2010); Marriage status: 30.3% never married, 46.0% now married, 8.1% widowed, 15.7% divorced (2006-2010 5-year est.); Foreign born: 3.1% (2006-2010 5-year est.); Ancestry (includes multiple ancestries): 25.1% Irish, 22.4% German, 13.7% Italian, 12.6% English, 11.3% Polish (2006-2010 5-year est.).
**Economy:** Single-family building permits issued: 0 (2011); Multi-family building permits issued: 0 (2011); Employment by occupation: 8.5% management, 4.0% professional, 7.4% services, 25.5% sales, 3.5% farming, 10.2% construction, 8.9% production (2006-2010 5-year est.).
**Income:** Per capita income: $25,741 (2006-2010 5-year est.); Median household income: $49,764 (2006-2010 5-year est.); Average household income: $53,228 (2006-2010 5-year est.); Percent of households with income of $100,000 or more: 10.2% (2006-2010 5-year est.); Poverty rate: 11.1% (2006-2010 5-year est.).
**Education:** Percent of population age 25 and over with: High school diploma (including GED) or higher: 86.3% (2006-2010 5-year est.); Bachelor's degree or higher: 17.1% (2006-2010 5-year est.); Master's degree or higher: 5.2% (2006-2010 5-year est.).

### School District(s)

North Syracuse Central School District (PK-12)
    2009-10 Enrollment: 9,741 . . . . . . . . . . . . . . . . . . . . . (315) 218-2151
**Housing:** Homeownership rate: 62.9% (2010); Median home value: $93,300 (2006-2010 5-year est.); Median contract rent: $592 per month (2006-2010 5-year est.); Median year structure built: 1957 (2006-2010 5-year est.).
**Safety:** Violent crime rate: 9.3 per 10,000 population; Property crime rate: 122.0 per 10,000 population (2010).
**Transportation:** Commute to work: 95.7% car, 0.8% public transportation, 1.4% walk, 1.3% work from home (2006-2010 5-year est.); Travel time to work: 38.3% less than 15 minutes, 50.8% 15 to 30 minutes, 5.9% 30 to 45 minutes, 2.4% 45 to 60 minutes, 2.5% 60 minutes or more (2006-2010 5-year est.)

**Additional Information Contacts**
Village of North Syracuse . . . . . . . . . . . . . . . . . . . . . (315) 458-0900
    http://northsyracuseny.org

## ONONDAGA (town). Aka Onondaga Hill. Covers a land area of 57.740 square miles and a water area of 0.096 square miles. Located at 42.98° N. Lat; 76.22° W. Long.

**Population:** 18,396 (1990); 21,063 (2000); 23,101 (2010); Density: 400.1 persons per square mile (2010); Race: 90.4% White, 3.8% Black, 2.2% Asian, 1.5% American Indian/Alaska Native, 0.0% Native Hawaiian/Other Pacific Islander, 2.1% Other, 2.2% Hispanic of any race (2010); Average household size: 2.56 (2010); Median age: 42.2 (2010); Males per 100 females: 92.8 (2010); Marriage status: 24.2% never married, 59.9% now married, 7.8% widowed, 8.0% divorced (2006-2010 5-year est.); Foreign born: 4.7% (2006-2010 5-year est.); Ancestry (includes multiple ancestries): 30.3% Irish, 18.4% Italian, 17.1% English, 16.8% German, 9.3% Polish (2006-2010 5-year est.).
**Economy:** Single-family building permits issued: 37 (2011); Multi-family building permits issued: 0 (2011); Employment by occupation: 13.0% management, 3.4% professional, 7.6% services, 17.9% sales, 5.1% farming, 6.6% construction, 4.2% production (2006-2010 5-year est.).
**Income:** Per capita income: $30,751 (2006-2010 5-year est.); Median household income: $63,336 (2006-2010 5-year est.); Average household income: $80,462 (2006-2010 5-year est.); Percent of households with income of $100,000 or more: 28.6% (2006-2010 5-year est.); Poverty rate: 5.3% (2006-2010 5-year est.).
**Education:** Percent of population age 25 and over with: High school diploma (including GED) or higher: 93.5% (2006-2010 5-year est.); Bachelor's degree or higher: 32.9% (2006-2010 5-year est.); Master's degree or higher: 14.9% (2006-2010 5-year est.).
**Housing:** Homeownership rate: 78.9% (2010); Median home value: $152,700 (2006-2010 5-year est.); Median contract rent: $652 per month (2006-2010 5-year est.); Median year structure built: 1967 (2006-2010 5-year est.).
**Transportation:** Commute to work: 94.8% car, 0.2% public transportation, 0.6% walk, 4.0% work from home (2006-2010 5-year est.); Travel time to work: 25.8% less than 15 minutes, 57.7% 15 to 30 minutes, 13.0% 30 to 45 minutes, 2.0% 45 to 60 minutes, 1.5% 60 minutes or more (2006-2010 5-year est.)

## ONONDAGA RESERVATION (Reservation). Covers a land area of 9.247 square miles and a water area of 0.046 square miles. Located at 42.92° N. Lat; 76.15° W. Long.

**Population:** 771 (1990); 1,473 (2000); 468 (2010); Density: 50.6 persons per square mile (2010); Race: 1.5% White, 0.2% Black, 0.0% Asian, 97.6% American Indian/Alaska Native, 0.0% Native Hawaiian/Other Pacific Islander, 0.7% Other, 2.1% Hispanic of any race (2010); Average household size: 1.44 (2010); Median age: 52.5 (2010); Males per 100 females: 87.2 (2010); Marriage status: 0.0% never married, 100.0% now married, 0.0% widowed, 0.0% divorced (2006-2010 5-year est.); Foreign born: 0.0% (2006-2010 5-year est.); Ancestry (includes multiple ancestries): 53.3% Scotch-Irish, 46.7% Irish (2006-2010 5-year est.).
**Economy:** Employment by occupation: n/a management, n/a professional, n/a services, n/a sales, n/a farming, n/a construction, n/a production (2006-2010 5-year est.).
**Income:** Per capita income: $-1 (2006-2010 5-year est.); Median household income: $0 (2006-2010 5-year est.); Average household income: $0 (2006-2010 5-year est.); Percent of households with income of $100,000 or more: 0.0% (2006-2010 5-year est.); Poverty rate: 0.0% (2006-2010 5-year est.).
**Education:** Percent of population age 25 and over with: High school diploma (including GED) or higher: 100.0% (2006-2010 5-year est.); Bachelor's degree or higher: 0.0% (2006-2010 5-year est.); Master's degree or higher: 0.0% (2006-2010 5-year est.).
**Housing:** Homeownership rate: 7.1% (2010); Median home value: n/a (2006-2010 5-year est.); Median contract rent: n/a per month (2006-2010 5-year est.); Median year structure built: 1974 (2006-2010 5-year est.).
**Transportation:** Commute to work: n/a car, n/a public transportation, n/a walk, n/a work from home (2006-2010 5-year est.); Travel time to work: n/a less than 15 minutes, n/a 15 to 30 minutes, n/a 30 to 45 minutes, n/a 45 to 60 minutes, n/a 60 minutes or more (2006-2010 5-year est.)

## OTISCO (town). Covers a land area of 29.531 square miles and a water area of 1.628 square miles. Located at 42.86° N. Lat; 76.22° W. Long. Elevation is 1,480 feet.

**Population:** 2,255 (1990); 2,561 (2000); 2,541 (2010); Density: 86.0 persons per square mile (2010); Race: 95.9% White, 1.3% Black, 0.9% Asian, 0.9% American Indian/Alaska Native, 0.0% Native Hawaiian/Other Pacific Islander, 1.0% Other, 1.3% Hispanic of any race (2010); Average

household size: 2.64 (2010); Median age: 42.2 (2010); Males per 100 females: 105.7 (2010); Marriage status: 24.3% never married, 57.6% now married, 5.5% widowed, 12.5% divorced (2006-2010 5-year est.); Foreign born: 0.2% (2006-2010 5-year est.); Ancestry (includes multiple ancestries): 30.5% German, 21.2% English, 17.4% Irish, 13.4% Italian, 6.7% American (2006-2010 5-year est.).

**Economy:** Single-family building permits issued: 6 (2011); Multi-family building permits issued: 0 (2011); Employment by occupation: 10.6% management, 2.9% professional, 9.4% services, 15.4% sales, 2.4% farming, 21.4% construction, 10.8% production (2006-2010 5-year est.).

**Income:** Per capita income: $25,699 (2006-2010 5-year est.); Median household income: $61,898 (2006-2010 5-year est.); Average household income: $68,479 (2006-2010 5-year est.); Percent of households with income of $100,000 or more: 19.6% (2006-2010 5-year est.); Poverty rate: 4.1% (2006-2010 5-year est.).

**Education:** Percent of population age 25 and over with: High school diploma (including GED) or higher: 91.5% (2006-2010 5-year est.); Bachelor's degree or higher: 16.1% (2006-2010 5-year est.); Master's degree or higher: 4.9% (2006-2010 5-year est.).

**Housing:** Homeownership rate: 84.0% (2010); Median home value: $143,200 (2006-2010 5-year est.); Median contract rent: $497 per month (2006-2010 5-year est.); Median year structure built: 1967 (2006-2010 5-year est.).

**Transportation:** Commute to work: 95.3% car, 0.5% public transportation, 1.2% walk, 3.0% work from home (2006-2010 5-year est.); Travel time to work: 13.3% less than 15 minutes, 28.9% 15 to 30 minutes, 44.4% 30 to 45 minutes, 7.7% 45 to 60 minutes, 5.7% 60 minutes or more (2006-2010 5-year est.)

**POMPEY** (town). Covers a land area of 66.378 square miles and a water area of 0.096 square miles. Located at 42.92° N. Lat; 75.98° W. Long. Elevation is 1,673 feet.

**Population:** 5,267 (1990); 6,159 (2000); 7,080 (2010); Density: 106.7 persons per square mile (2010); Race: 94.4% White, 0.8% Black, 2.8% Asian, 0.3% American Indian/Alaska Native, 0.1% Native Hawaiian/Other Pacific Islander, 1.6% Other, 1.5% Hispanic of any race (2010); Average household size: 2.81 (2010); Median age: 43.2 (2010); Males per 100 females: 101.9 (2010); Marriage status: 20.9% never married, 68.3% now married, 4.8% widowed, 6.0% divorced (2006-2010 5-year est.); Foreign born: 5.2% (2006-2010 5-year est.); Ancestry (includes multiple ancestries): 25.9% German, 23.1% Irish, 21.2% English, 18.1% Italian, 6.5% French (2006-2010 5-year est.).

**Economy:** Single-family building permits issued: 28 (2011); Multi-family building permits issued: 0 (2011); Employment by occupation: 16.7% management, 6.7% professional, 5.3% services, 12.8% sales, 3.2% farming, 8.9% construction, 3.6% production (2006-2010 5-year est.).

**Income:** Per capita income: $37,053 (2006-2010 5-year est.); Median household income: $88,438 (2006-2010 5-year est.); Average household income: $106,387 (2006-2010 5-year est.); Percent of households with income of $100,000 or more: 41.7% (2006-2010 5-year est.); Poverty rate: 3.7% (2006-2010 5-year est.).

**Education:** Percent of population age 25 and over with: High school diploma (including GED) or higher: 96.1% (2006-2010 5-year est.); Bachelor's degree or higher: 55.1% (2006-2010 5-year est.); Master's degree or higher: 24.4% (2006-2010 5-year est.).

**Housing:** Homeownership rate: 92.5% (2010); Median home value: $210,800 (2006-2010 5-year est.); Median contract rent: $557 per month (2006-2010 5-year est.); Median year structure built: 1977 (2006-2010 5-year est.).

**Transportation:** Commute to work: 85.8% car, 1.9% public transportation, 1.6% walk, 8.1% work from home (2006-2010 5-year est.); Travel time to work: 12.7% less than 15 minutes, 53.9% 15 to 30 minutes, 25.2% 30 to 45 minutes, 3.0% 45 to 60 minutes, 5.2% 60 minutes or more (2006-2010 5-year est.)

**SALINA** (town). Covers a land area of 13.749 square miles and a water area of 1.311 square miles. Located at 43.10° N. Lat; 76.17° W. Long.

**Population:** 35,145 (1990); 33,290 (2000); 33,710 (2010); Density: 2,451.6 persons per square mile (2010); Race: 90.2% White, 4.0% Black, 2.2% Asian, 0.6% American Indian/Alaska Native, 0.0% Native Hawaiian/Other Pacific Islander, 3.0% Other, 2.8% Hispanic of any race (2010); Average household size: 2.23 (2010); Median age: 41.9 (2010); Males per 100 females: 90.4 (2010); Marriage status: 31.3% never married, 48.2% now married, 9.3% widowed, 11.2% divorced (2006-2010 5-year est.); Foreign born: 5.3% (2006-2010 5-year est.); Ancestry (includes multiple

ancestries): 25.8% Italian, 24.6% Irish, 23.9% German, 13.0% English, 7.4% Polish (2006-2010 5-year est.).

**Economy:** Unemployment rate: 8.1% (February 2012); Total civilian labor force: 17,429 (February 2012); Single-family building permits issued: 0 (2011); Multi-family building permits issued: 0 (2011); Employment by occupation: 8.4% management, 4.1% professional, 10.7% services, 22.1% sales, 4.1% farming, 6.9% construction, 6.5% production (2006-2010 5-year est.).

**Income:** Per capita income: $25,864 (2006-2010 5-year est.); Median household income: $49,124 (2006-2010 5-year est.); Average household income: $57,544 (2006-2010 5-year est.); Percent of households with income of $100,000 or more: 12.4% (2006-2010 5-year est.); Poverty rate: 7.4% (2006-2010 5-year est.).

**Taxes:** Total city taxes per capita: $356 (2009); City property taxes per capita: $322 (2009).

**Education:** Percent of population age 25 and over with: High school diploma (including GED) or higher: 89.9% (2006-2010 5-year est.); Bachelor's degree or higher: 24.5% (2006-2010 5-year est.); Master's degree or higher: 9.7% (2006-2010 5-year est.).

**Housing:** Homeownership rate: 66.9% (2010); Median home value: $99,500 (2006-2010 5-year est.); Median contract rent: $666 per month (2006-2010 5-year est.); Median year structure built: 1958 (2006-2010 5-year est.).

**Transportation:** Commute to work: 93.6% car, 0.6% public transportation, 2.6% walk, 2.1% work from home (2006-2010 5-year est.); Travel time to work: 40.1% less than 15 minutes, 50.5% 15 to 30 minutes, 4.9% 30 to 45 minutes, 1.8% 45 to 60 minutes, 2.7% 60 minutes or more (2006-2010 5-year est.)

**Additional Information Contacts**

Town of Salina . . . . . . . . . . . . . . . . . . . . . . . . . . . . . . (315) 457-2710
http://www.salina.ny.us

**SENECA KNOLLS** (CDP). Covers a land area of 1.248 square miles and a water area of 0 square miles. Located at 43.11° N. Lat; 76.28° W. Long. Elevation is 407 feet.

**Population:** 2,383 (1990); 2,138 (2000); 2,011 (2010); Density: 1,610.8 persons per square mile (2010); Race: 95.8% White, 1.0% Black, 0.2% Asian, 0.9% American Indian/Alaska Native, 0.0% Native Hawaiian/Other Pacific Islander, 2.1% Other, 1.6% Hispanic of any race (2010); Average household size: 2.37 (2010); Median age: 44.0 (2010); Males per 100 females: 94.5 (2010); Marriage status: 27.6% never married, 44.0% now married, 7.5% widowed, 20.9% divorced (2006-2010 5-year est.); Foreign born: 0.0% (2006-2010 5-year est.); Ancestry (includes multiple ancestries): 23.6% German, 23.4% Irish, 16.2% English, 8.6% French, 8.2% Polish (2006-2010 5-year est.).

**Economy:** Employment by occupation: 3.1% management, 4.1% professional, 3.8% services, 16.0% sales, 4.1% farming, 13.6% construction, 6.1% production (2006-2010 5-year est.).

**Income:** Per capita income: $24,510 (2006-2010 5-year est.); Median household income: $44,429 (2006-2010 5-year est.); Average household income: $51,500 (2006-2010 5-year est.); Percent of households with income of $100,000 or more: 7.1% (2006-2010 5-year est.); Poverty rate: 2.9% (2006-2010 5-year est.).

**Education:** Percent of population age 25 and over with: High school diploma (including GED) or higher: 86.3% (2006-2010 5-year est.); Bachelor's degree or higher: 12.2% (2006-2010 5-year est.); Master's degree or higher: 3.2% (2006-2010 5-year est.).

**Housing:** Homeownership rate: 86.2% (2010); Median home value: $76,700 (2006-2010 5-year est.); Median contract rent: $627 per month (2006-2010 5-year est.); Median year structure built: 1959 (2006-2010 5-year est.).

**Transportation:** Commute to work: 95.3% car, 1.2% public transportation, 1.5% walk, 0.0% work from home (2006-2010 5-year est.); Travel time to work: 32.3% less than 15 minutes, 61.7% 15 to 30 minutes, 1.7% 30 to 45 minutes, 1.4% 45 to 60 minutes, 2.8% 60 minutes or more (2006-2010 5-year est.)

**SKANEATELES** (village). Covers a land area of 1.413 square miles and a water area of 0.306 square miles. Located at 42.94° N. Lat; 76.42° W. Long. Elevation is 873 feet.

**Population:** 2,809 (1990); 2,616 (2000); 2,450 (2010); Density: 1,733.2 persons per square mile (2010); Race: 97.8% White, 0.1% Black, 0.8% Asian, 0.1% American Indian/Alaska Native, 0.0% Native Hawaiian/Other Pacific Islander, 1.2% Other, 1.1% Hispanic of any race (2010); Average household size: 2.22 (2010); Median age: 50.0 (2010); Males per 100

females: 81.9 (2010); Marriage status: 17.7% never married, 57.7% now married, 10.5% widowed, 14.1% divorced (2006-2010 5-year est.); Foreign born: 2.9% (2006-2010 5-year est.); Ancestry (includes multiple ancestries): 33.3% Irish, 25.4% English, 25.1% German, 13.8% Italian, 6.6% Polish (2006-2010 5-year est.).

**Economy:** Single-family building permits issued: 0 (2011); Multi-family building permits issued: 0 (2011); Employment by occupation: 16.9% management, 9.5% professional, 4.8% services, 18.7% sales, 1.1% farming, 1.9% construction, 0.7% production (2006-2010 5-year est.).

**Income:** Per capita income: $46,202 (2006-2010 5-year est.); Median household income: $71,324 (2006-2010 5-year est.); Average household income: $98,760 (2006-2010 5-year est.); Percent of households with income of $100,000 or more: 35.0% (2006-2010 5-year est.); Poverty rate: 7.4% (2006-2010 5-year est.).

**Education:** Percent of population age 25 and over with: High school diploma (including GED) or higher: 98.0% (2006-2010 5-year est.); Bachelor's degree or higher: 60.7% (2006-2010 5-year est.); Master's degree or higher: 29.0% (2006-2010 5-year est.).

### School District(s)
Skaneateles Central School District (KG-12)
    2009-10 Enrollment: 1,664 . . . . . . . . . . . . . . . (315) 291-2221

**Housing:** Homeownership rate: 71.1% (2010); Median home value: $318,500 (2006-2010 5-year est.); Median contract rent: $622 per month (2006-2010 5-year est.); Median year structure built: before 1940 (2006-2010 5-year est.).

**Safety:** Violent crime rate: 7.9 per 10,000 population; Property crime rate: 11.8 per 10,000 population (2010).

**Newspapers:** Moravia Pennysaver (Community news; Circulation 9,245); Pennywise Shopper (Community news; Circulation 11,500)

**Transportation:** Commute to work: 83.5% car, 1.3% public transportation, 7.4% walk, 6.0% work from home (2006-2010 5-year est.); Travel time to work: 29.5% less than 15 minutes, 19.1% 15 to 30 minutes, 37.8% 30 to 45 minutes, 7.5% 45 to 60 minutes, 6.1% 60 minutes or more (2006-2010 5-year est.)

**Airports:** Skaneateles Aero Drome (general aviation)

**Additional Information Contacts**
Skaneateles Area Chamber of Commerce . . . . . . . . . . . (315) 685-0552
   http://www.skaneateles.com

## SKANEATELES (town). Covers a land area of 42.605 square miles and a water area of 6.220 square miles. Located at 42.88° N. Lat; 76.41° W. Long. Elevation is 873 feet.

**History:** Village in a Historic District. Settled before 1800, incorporated 1833.

**Population:** 7,526 (1990); 7,323 (2000); 7,209 (2010); Density: 169.2 persons per square mile (2010); Race: 97.8% White, 0.2% Black, 0.7% Asian, 0.3% American Indian/Alaska Native, 0.1% Native Hawaiian/Other Pacific Islander, 0.9% Other, 1.2% Hispanic of any race (2010); Average household size: 2.45 (2010); Median age: 47.3 (2010); Males per 100 females: 94.2 (2010); Marriage status: 23.0% never married, 61.2% now married, 8.0% widowed, 7.8% divorced (2006-2010 5-year est.); Foreign born: 5.1% (2006-2010 5-year est.); Ancestry (includes multiple ancestries): 30.7% Irish, 25.5% English, 25.2% German, 10.9% Italian, 7.7% Polish (2006-2010 5-year est.).

**Economy:** Single-family building permits issued: 8 (2011); Multi-family building permits issued: 4 (2011); Employment by occupation: 16.5% management, 6.7% professional, 5.8% services, 14.7% sales, 0.9% farming, 12.0% construction, 4.5% production (2006-2010 5-year est.).

**Income:** Per capita income: $47,154 (2006-2010 5-year est.); Median household income: $75,548 (2006-2010 5-year est.); Average household income: $118,408 (2006-2010 5-year est.); Percent of households with income of $100,000 or more: 35.8% (2006-2010 5-year est.); Poverty rate: 5.2% (2006-2010 5-year est.).

**Education:** Percent of population age 25 and over with: High school diploma (including GED) or higher: 94.4% (2006-2010 5-year est.); Bachelor's degree or higher: 52.4% (2006-2010 5-year est.); Master's degree or higher: 22.0% (2006-2010 5-year est.).

### School District(s)
Skaneateles Central School District (KG-12)
    2009-10 Enrollment: 1,664 . . . . . . . . . . . . . . . (315) 291-2221

**Housing:** Homeownership rate: 81.5% (2010); Median home value: $261,400 (2006-2010 5-year est.); Median contract rent: $639 per month (2006-2010 5-year est.); Median year structure built: 1951 (2006-2010 5-year est.).

**Newspapers:** Moravia Pennysaver (Community news; Circulation 9,245); Pennywise Shopper (Community news; Circulation 11,500)

**Transportation:** Commute to work: 83.8% car, 0.4% public transportation, 2.9% walk, 6.6% work from home (2006-2010 5-year est.); Travel time to work: 36.0% less than 15 minutes, 20.0% 15 to 30 minutes, 32.3% 30 to 45 minutes, 5.2% 45 to 60 minutes, 6.5% 60 minutes or more (2006-2010 5-year est.)

**Airports:** Skaneateles Aero Drome (general aviation)

**Additional Information Contacts**
Town of Skaneateles . . . . . . . . . . . . . . . . . . . . . . . (315) 685-3473
   http://www.townofskaneateles.com

## SKANEATELES FALLS (unincorporated postal area)
Zip Code: 13153

Covers a land area of 0.894 square miles and a water area of 0 square miles. Located at 42.99° N. Lat; 76.45° W. Long. Elevation is 705 feet. Population: 399 (2010); Density: 446.2 persons per square mile (2010); Race: 96.2% White, 1.0% Black, 0.8% Asian, 0.3% American Indian/Alaska Native, 0.0% Native Hawaiian/Other Pacific Islander, 1.7% Other, 2.3% Hispanic of any race (2010); Average household size: 2.57 (2010); Median age: 39.8 (2010); Males per 100 females: 111.1 (2010); Homeownership rate: 78.0% (2010)

## SOLVAY (village). Covers a land area of 1.653 square miles and a water area of 0 square miles. Located at 43.05° N. Lat; 76.21° W. Long. Elevation is 499 feet.

**History:** In the 20th century, after earlier exploited salt springs had lost their deposits, brine wells provided basis for manufacturing of chlorines, caustic soda, and bicarbonate of soda. Former heavy-manufacturing and chemical-manufacturing have disappeared, mainly due to stricter environmental-quality standards. Incorporated 1894.

**Population:** 6,717 (1990); 6,845 (2000); 6,584 (2010); Density: 3,981.8 persons per square mile (2010); Race: 91.6% White, 2.0% Black, 0.8% Asian, 1.5% American Indian/Alaska Native, 0.1% Native Hawaiian/Other Pacific Islander, 4.0% Other, 4.8% Hispanic of any race (2010); Average household size: 2.22 (2010); Median age: 38.6 (2010); Males per 100 females: 92.0 (2010); Marriage status: 36.9% never married, 43.0% now married, 7.1% widowed, 12.9% divorced (2006-2010 5-year est.); Foreign born: 7.8% (2006-2010 5-year est.); Ancestry (includes multiple ancestries): 34.6% Italian, 24.3% Irish, 14.4% German, 10.0% Polish, 9.4% English (2006-2010 5-year est.).

**Economy:** Single-family building permits issued: 0 (2011); Multi-family building permits issued: 0 (2011); Employment by occupation: 7.0% management, 1.1% professional, 10.5% services, 19.2% sales, 8.3% farming, 7.0% construction, 5.4% production (2006-2010 5-year est.).

**Income:** Per capita income: $24,945 (2006-2010 5-year est.); Median household income: $42,024 (2006-2010 5-year est.); Average household income: $53,322 (2006-2010 5-year est.); Percent of households with income of $100,000 or more: 9.1% (2006-2010 5-year est.); Poverty rate: 13.3% (2006-2010 5-year est.).

**Education:** Percent of population age 25 and over with: High school diploma (including GED) or higher: 85.2% (2006-2010 5-year est.); Bachelor's degree or higher: 21.6% (2006-2010 5-year est.); Master's degree or higher: 7.2% (2006-2010 5-year est.).

### School District(s)
Solvay Union Free School District (KG-12)
    2009-10 Enrollment: 1,571 . . . . . . . . . . . . . . . (315) 468-1111

**Housing:** Homeownership rate: 53.3% (2010); Median home value: $91,400 (2006-2010 5-year est.); Median contract rent: $540 per month (2006-2010 5-year est.); Median year structure built: 1948 (2006-2010 5-year est.).

**Safety:** Violent crime rate: 33.2 per 10,000 population; Property crime rate: 311.8 per 10,000 population (2010).

**Transportation:** Commute to work: 93.4% car, 3.1% public transportation, 2.4% walk, 1.1% work from home (2006-2010 5-year est.); Travel time to work: 37.4% less than 15 minutes, 51.1% 15 to 30 minutes, 7.4% 30 to 45 minutes, 2.0% 45 to 60 minutes, 2.0% 60 minutes or more (2006-2010 5-year est.)

## SPAFFORD (town). Covers a land area of 32.697 square miles and a water area of 6.517 square miles. Located at 42.82° N. Lat; 76.28° W. Long. Elevation is 1,686 feet.

**Population:** 1,675 (1990); 1,661 (2000); 1,686 (2010); Density: 51.6 persons per square mile (2010); Race: 98.3% White, 0.3% Black, 0.4% Asian, 0.2% American Indian/Alaska Native, 0.4% Native Hawaiian/Other

Pacific Islander, 0.4% Other, 1.2% Hispanic of any race (2010); Average household size: 2.52 (2010); Median age: 48.1 (2010); Males per 100 females: 98.6 (2010); Marriage status: 21.7% never married, 67.0% now married, 4.9% widowed, 6.5% divorced (2006-2010 5-year est.); Foreign born: 2.4% (2006-2010 5-year est.); Ancestry (includes multiple ancestries): 26.7% German, 25.6% Irish, 24.1% English, 10.4% Italian, 5.7% Polish (2006-2010 5-year est.).

**Economy:** Single-family building permits issued: 2 (2011); Multi-family building permits issued: 0 (2011); Employment by occupation: 17.1% management, 3.8% professional, 7.6% services, 14.1% sales, 3.1% farming, 6.4% construction, 5.4% production (2006-2010 5-year est.).

**Income:** Per capita income: $37,661 (2006-2010 5-year est.); Median household income: $71,908 (2006-2010 5-year est.); Average household income: $95,254 (2006-2010 5-year est.); Percent of households with income of $100,000 or more: 31.8% (2006-2010 5-year est.); Poverty rate: 2.8% (2006-2010 5-year est.).

**Education:** Percent of population age 25 and over with: High school diploma (including GED) or higher: 94.2% (2006-2010 5-year est.); Bachelor's degree or higher: 44.9% (2006-2010 5-year est.); Master's degree or higher: 18.7% (2006-2010 5-year est.).

**Housing:** Homeownership rate: 91.8% (2010); Median home value: $199,800 (2006-2010 5-year est.); Median contract rent: $517 per month (2006-2010 5-year est.); Median year structure built: 1965 (2006-2010 5-year est.).

**Transportation:** Commute to work: 93.6% car, 0.0% public transportation, 1.4% walk, 5.0% work from home (2006-2010 5-year est.); Travel time to work: 16.0% less than 15 minutes, 35.6% 15 to 30 minutes, 24.2% 30 to 45 minutes, 19.3% 45 to 60 minutes, 4.9% 60 minutes or more (2006-2010 5-year est.)

**SYRACUSE** (city). County seat. Covers a land area of 25.043 square miles and a water area of 0.564 square miles. Located at 43.04° N. Lat; 76.14° W. Long. Elevation is 397 feet.

**History:** The beginnings and early growth of Syracuse are identified with salt. What the French soldiers and Jesuits saw in 1654 was a swamp. The salt springs were discovered by Father Simon LeMoyne. The first settler was Ephraim Webster, who arrived in 1786 and opened a trading station. Syracuse was incorporated as a village in 1825. The name was suggested by John Wilkinson, the first postmaster, who had read a poem describing the ancient Greek city in Sicily, which had also grown around a marsh and salt springs. In 1848, the villages of Syracuse and Salina, together with Lodi, were joined and incorporated as the city of Syracuse in 1881.

**Population:** 163,860 (1990); 147,306 (2000); 145,170 (2010); Density: 5,796.7 persons per square mile (2010); Race: 56.0% White, 29.5% Black, 5.5% Asian, 1.1% American Indian/Alaska Native, 0.0% Native Hawaiian/Other Pacific Islander, 7.9% Other, 8.3% Hispanic of any race (2010); Average household size: 2.31 (2010); Median age: 29.6 (2010); Males per 100 females: 91.0 (2010); Marriage status: 51.4% never married, 31.8% now married, 6.0% widowed, 10.8% divorced (2006-2010 5-year est.); Foreign born: 10.3% (2006-2010 5-year est.); Ancestry (includes multiple ancestries): 15.5% Irish, 12.8% Italian, 11.8% German, 7.0% English, 5.0% Polish (2006-2010 5-year est.).

**Economy:** Unemployment rate: 10.1% (February 2012); Total civilian labor force: 62,393 (February 2012); Single-family building permits issued: 61 (2011); Multi-family building permits issued: 275 (2011); Employment by occupation: 7.5% management, 3.3% professional, 14.5% services, 16.4% sales, 5.0% farming, 6.3% construction, 5.3% production (2006-2010 5-year est.).

**Income:** Per capita income: $17,866 (2006-2010 5-year est.); Median household income: $30,891 (2006-2010 5-year est.); Average household income: $43,385 (2006-2010 5-year est.); Percent of households with income of $100,000 or more: 8.4% (2006-2010 5-year est.); Poverty rate: 31.1% (2006-2010 5-year est.).

**Taxes:** Total city taxes per capita: $631 (2009); City property taxes per capita: $582 (2009).

**Education:** Percent of population age 25 and over with: High school diploma (including GED) or higher: 80.6% (2006-2010 5-year est.); Bachelor's degree or higher: 25.6% (2006-2010 5-year est.); Master's degree or higher: 11.1% (2006-2010 5-year est.).

### School District(s)
Lyncourt Union Free School District (PK-08)
2009-10 Enrollment: 326 . . . . . . . . . . . . . . . . . (315) 455-7571
North Syracuse Central School District (PK-12)
2009-10 Enrollment: 9,741 . . . . . . . . . . . . . . . . (315) 218-2151

Onondaga-Cortland-Madison Boces
2009-10 Enrollment: n/a . . . . . . . . . . . . . . . . . (315) 433-2602
Solvay Union Free School District (KG-12)
2009-10 Enrollment: 1,571 . . . . . . . . . . . . . . . . (315) 468-1111
Southside Academy Charter School (KG-08)
2009-10 Enrollment: 625 . . . . . . . . . . . . . . . . . (315) 476-3019
Syracuse Academy of Science Charter School (07-12)
2009-10 Enrollment: 341 . . . . . . . . . . . . . . . . . (315) 428-8997
Syracuse City School District (PK-12)
2009-10 Enrollment: 21,320 . . . . . . . . . . . . . . . (315) 435-4161
West Genesee Central School District (KG-12)
2009-10 Enrollment: 5,017 . . . . . . . . . . . . . . . . (315) 487-4562
Westhill Central School District (KG-12)
2009-10 Enrollment: 1,884 . . . . . . . . . . . . . . . . (315) 426-3218

#### Four-year College(s)
Le Moyne College (Private, Not-for-profit, Roman Catholic)
Fall 2010 Enrollment: 3,170 . . . . . . . . . . . . . . (315) 445-4100
2011-12 Tuition: In-state $28,380; Out-of-state $28,380
SUNY College of Environmental Science and Forestry (Public)
Fall 2010 Enrollment: 2,066 . . . . . . . . . . . . . . (315) 470-6500
2011-12 Tuition: In-state $6,269; Out-of-state $15,141
Syracuse University (Private, Not-for-profit)
Fall 2010 Enrollment: 20,453 . . . . . . . . . . . . . (315) 443-1870
2011-12 Tuition: In-state $37,668; Out-of-state $37,668
Upstate Medical University (Public)
Fall 2010 Enrollment: 1,951 . . . . . . . . . . . . . . (315) 464-5540

#### Two-year College(s)
Bryant and Stratton College-Main Syracuse (Private, For-profit)
Fall 2010 Enrollment: 787 . . . . . . . . . . . . . . . (315) 472-6603
2011-12 Tuition: In-state $15,705; Out-of-state $15,705
Crouse Hospital College of Nursing (Private, Not-for-profit)
Fall 2010 Enrollment: 176 . . . . . . . . . . . . . . . (315) 470-7481
2011-12 Tuition: In-state $9,366; Out-of-state $15,288
Onondaga Community College (Public)
Fall 2010 Enrollment: 8,399 . . . . . . . . . . . . . . (315) 498-2622
2011-12 Tuition: In-state $8,414; Out-of-state $8,414
Simmons Institute of Funeral Service Inc (Private, For-profit)
Fall 2010 Enrollment: 22 . . . . . . . . . . . . . . . . (315) 475-5142
2011-12 Tuition: In-state $10,600; Out-of-state $10,600
St Joseph's College of Nursing at St Joseph's Hospital Health Center (Private, Not-for-profit, Roman Catholic)
Fall 2010 Enrollment: 296 . . . . . . . . . . . . . . . (315) 448-5040
2011-12 Tuition: In-state $16,210; Out-of-state $16,210

#### Vocational/Technical School(s)
Onondaga School of Therapeutic Massage-Syracuse (Private, For-profit)
Fall 2010 Enrollment: 85 . . . . . . . . . . . . . . . . (315) 424-1159
2011-12 Tuition: $14,000
Phillips Hairstyling Institute (Private, For-profit)
Fall 2010 Enrollment: 119 . . . . . . . . . . . . . . . (3.1) 542-3E+1
2011-12 Tuition: $8,225
Syracuse City Schools Practical Nursing Program (Public)
Fall 2010 Enrollment: 41 . . . . . . . . . . . . . . . . (315) 435-4150
2011-12 Tuition: $8,350

**Housing:** Homeownership rate: 38.6% (2010); Median home value: $83,400 (2006-2010 5-year est.); Median contract rent: $539 per month (2006-2010 5-year est.); Median year structure built: before 1940 (2006-2010 5-year est.).

**Hospitals:** Community General Hospital of Greater Syracuse (356 beds); Crouse Hospital (566 beds); Richard H Hutchings Psychiatric Center (105 beds); SUNY Upstate Medical University (356 beds); St. Joseph's Hospital Health Center (431 beds); Syracuse Veterans Affairs Medical Center (164 beds)

**Safety:** Violent crime rate: 94.7 per 10,000 population; Property crime rate: 418.8 per 10,000 population (2010).

**Newspapers:** The Advocate (Community news; Circulation 3,783); Auburn Pennysaver (Community news; Circulation 19,587); Baldwinsville Pennysaver (Community news; Circulation 11,598); Bellevue-Geddes Pennysaver (Community news; Circulation 11,551); Catholic Sun (Local news; Circulation 32,000); Cazenovia Republican (Community news; Circulation 3,744); Chittenango-Bridgeport Times (Community news; Circulation 1,600); Cicero-North Syracuse Star News (Community news; Circulation 7,200); City Edition Shoppers Guide (Local news; Circulation 5,365); Court-Butternut Pennysaver (Local news; Circulation 10,495); DeWitt Times (Local news; Circulation 1,984); Eagle-Bulletin (Community news; Circulation 7,032); East Syracuse/Minoa/Bridgeport/ Kirkville

Shoppers Guide (Community news; Circulation 10,996); Eastwood Pennysaver (Community news; Circulation 8,490); Fayetteville/Manlius/Dewitt/ Jamesville Shoppers Guide (Community news; Circulation 17,002); Fulton Pennysaver (Community news; Circulation 16,195); Geneva Pennysaver (Community news; Circulation 11,114); Hamilton-Morrisville Tribune (Community news; Circulation 1,600); Liverpool Pennysaver (Community news; Circulation 20,229); Lyncourt Pennysaver (Community news; Circulation 6,375); Marcellus Observer (Community news; Circulation 1,400); Mattydale-North Syracuse Pennysaver (Local news; Circulation 21,847); North Area Pennysaver (Community news; Circulation 8,338); North Syracuse/Cicero Pennysaver (Community news; Circulation 21,922); Oneida Press (Community news); Onondaga Valley News (Community news; Circulation 7,903); Pennywise Pennysaver (Local news; Circulation 9,378); The Post-Standard (Local news; Circulation 167,609); Review (Local news; Circulation 4,775); Seneca Falls/Waterloo Pennysaver (Community news; Circulation 13,000); Skaneateles Press (Community news; Circulation 3,500); Solvay-Camillus Pennysaver (Community news; Circulation 19,065); Solvay-Geddes Express (Community news; Circulation 2,900); The Star News (Local news; Circulation 7,200); Strathmore/Onondaga Hill Pennysaver (Community news; Circulation 4,499); Syracuse East Area Shoppers Guide (Local news; Circulation 9,610); Town & Country Pennysaver (Community news; Circulation 15,460)

**Transportation:** Commute to work: 76.4% car, 7.6% public transportation, 10.7% walk, 3.0% work from home (2006-2010 5-year est.); Travel time to work: 43.8% less than 15 minutes, 43.2% 15 to 30 minutes, 7.6% 30 to 45 minutes, 2.7% 45 to 60 minutes, 2.7% 60 minutes or more (2006-2010 5-year est.); Amtrak: train service available.

**Airports:** Syracuse Hancock International (primary service/small hub)

**Additional Information Contacts**

CenterState Chamber of Commerce . . . . . . . . . . . . . . . . (315) 470-1800
   http://www.centerstateceo.com

City of Syracuse. . . . . . . . . . . . . . . . . . . . . . . . . . . . . (315) 448-8005
   http://www.syracuse.ny.us

---

**TULLY** (village). Covers a land area of 0.717 square miles and a water area of 0 square miles. Located at 42.79° N. Lat; 76.11° W. Long. Elevation is 1,250 feet.

**Population:** 983 (1990); 924 (2000); 873 (2010); Density: 1,216.8 persons per square mile (2010); Race: 94.2% White, 1.8% Black, 1.5% Asian, 0.1% American Indian/Alaska Native, 0.0% Native Hawaiian/Other Pacific Islander, 2.4% Other, 0.9% Hispanic of any race (2010); Average household size: 2.15 (2010); Median age: 40.2 (2010); Males per 100 females: 87.3 (2010); Marriage status: 32.7% never married, 42.5% now married, 10.6% widowed, 14.2% divorced (2006-2010 5-year est.); Foreign born: 5.7% (2006-2010 5-year est.); Ancestry (includes multiple ancestries): 28.2% German, 26.9% Irish, 22.0% English, 7.5% Italian, 4.1% Ukrainian (2006-2010 5-year est.).

**Economy:** Single-family building permits issued: 0 (2011); Multi-family building permits issued: 0 (2011); Employment by occupation: 6.2% management, 3.5% professional, 8.0% services, 13.4% sales, 6.2% farming, 11.9% construction, 7.7% production (2006-2010 5-year est.).

**Income:** Per capita income: $21,538 (2006-2010 5-year est.); Median household income: $41,500 (2006-2010 5-year est.); Average household income: $49,593 (2006-2010 5-year est.); Percent of households with income of $100,000 or more: 11.6% (2006-2010 5-year est.); Poverty rate: 21.7% (2006-2010 5-year est.).

**Education:** Percent of population age 25 and over with: High school diploma (including GED) or higher: 87.3% (2006-2010 5-year est.); Bachelor's degree or higher: 27.9% (2006-2010 5-year est.); Master's degree or higher: 12.5% (2006-2010 5-year est.).

**School District(s)**

Tully Central School District (KG-12)
   2009-10 Enrollment: 1,109 . . . . . . . . . . . . . . . . . . . . . (315) 696-6204

**Housing:** Homeownership rate: 50.3% (2010); Median home value: $110,200 (2006-2010 5-year est.); Median contract rent: $586 per month (2006-2010 5-year est.); Median year structure built: before 1940 (2006-2010 5-year est.).

**Transportation:** Commute to work: 85.0% car, 0.0% public transportation, 14.2% walk, 0.8% work from home (2006-2010 5-year est.); Travel time to work: 36.3% less than 15 minutes, 23.9% 15 to 30 minutes, 31.8% 30 to 45 minutes, 4.5% 45 to 60 minutes, 3.4% 60 minutes or more (2006-2010 5-year est.)

---

**TULLY** (town). Covers a land area of 25.753 square miles and a water area of 0.524 square miles. Located at 42.80° N. Lat; 76.13° W. Long. Elevation is 1,250 feet.

**History:** One of many former Finger Lake valleys, with rich agricultural soils.

**Population:** 2,378 (1990); 2,709 (2000); 2,738 (2010); Density: 106.3 persons per square mile (2010); Race: 96.7% White, 0.9% Black, 0.9% Asian, 0.1% American Indian/Alaska Native, 0.0% Native Hawaiian/Other Pacific Islander, 1.4% Other, 1.5% Hispanic of any race (2010); Average household size: 2.55 (2010); Median age: 42.9 (2010); Males per 100 females: 95.6 (2010); Marriage status: 25.8% never married, 59.9% now married, 5.5% widowed, 8.9% divorced (2006-2010 5-year est.); Foreign born: 4.1% (2006-2010 5-year est.); Ancestry (includes multiple ancestries): 27.0% Irish, 25.9% German, 22.9% English, 13.5% Italian, 6.8% Polish (2006-2010 5-year est.).

**Economy:** Single-family building permits issued: 3 (2011); Multi-family building permits issued: 0 (2011); Employment by occupation: 13.4% management, 4.3% professional, 3.8% services, 14.2% sales, 3.1% farming, 8.0% construction, 4.5% production (2006-2010 5-year est.).

**Income:** Per capita income: $36,094 (2006-2010 5-year est.); Median household income: $71,509 (2006-2010 5-year est.); Average household income: $92,636 (2006-2010 5-year est.); Percent of households with income of $100,000 or more: 35.0% (2006-2010 5-year est.); Poverty rate: 6.8% (2006-2010 5-year est.).

**Education:** Percent of population age 25 and over with: High school diploma (including GED) or higher: 94.1% (2006-2010 5-year est.); Bachelor's degree or higher: 46.6% (2006-2010 5-year est.); Master's degree or higher: 18.8% (2006-2010 5-year est.).

**School District(s)**

Tully Central School District (KG-12)
   2009-10 Enrollment: 1,109 . . . . . . . . . . . . . . . . . . . . . (315) 696-6204

**Housing:** Homeownership rate: 76.9% (2010); Median home value: $190,300 (2006-2010 5-year est.); Median contract rent: $580 per month (2006-2010 5-year est.); Median year structure built: 1974 (2006-2010 5-year est.).

**Transportation:** Commute to work: 89.5% car, 0.0% public transportation, 5.2% walk, 5.3% work from home (2006-2010 5-year est.); Travel time to work: 25.4% less than 15 minutes, 40.0% 15 to 30 minutes, 25.4% 30 to 45 minutes, 6.1% 45 to 60 minutes, 3.2% 60 minutes or more (2006-2010 5-year est.)

---

**VAN BUREN** (town). Covers a land area of 35.407 square miles and a water area of 0.703 square miles. Located at 43.11° N. Lat; 76.35° W. Long. Elevation is 499 feet.

**Population:** 13,367 (1990); 12,667 (2000); 13,185 (2010); Density: 372.4 persons per square mile (2010); Race: 95.7% White, 1.2% Black, 0.7% Asian, 0.4% American Indian/Alaska Native, 0.0% Native Hawaiian/Other Pacific Islander, 2.0% Other, 1.8% Hispanic of any race (2010); Average household size: 2.28 (2010); Median age: 43.6 (2010); Males per 100 females: 94.9 (2010); Marriage status: 26.4% never married, 51.5% now married, 7.8% widowed, 14.4% divorced (2006-2010 5-year est.); Foreign born: 2.5% (2006-2010 5-year est.); Ancestry (includes multiple ancestries): 26.1% Irish, 25.0% German, 16.5% English, 15.7% Italian, 11.9% Polish (2006-2010 5-year est.).

**Economy:** Single-family building permits issued: 45 (2011); Multi-family building permits issued: 0 (2011); Employment by occupation: 9.4% management, 3.0% professional, 11.5% services, 17.4% sales, 2.8% farming, 8.8% construction, 2.9% production (2006-2010 5-year est.).

**Income:** Per capita income: $26,913 (2006-2010 5-year est.); Median household income: $47,762 (2006-2010 5-year est.); Average household income: $59,065 (2006-2010 5-year est.); Percent of households with income of $100,000 or more: 15.5% (2006-2010 5-year est.); Poverty rate: 10.9% (2006-2010 5-year est.).

**Education:** Percent of population age 25 and over with: High school diploma (including GED) or higher: 90.6% (2006-2010 5-year est.); Bachelor's degree or higher: 21.3% (2006-2010 5-year est.); Master's degree or higher: 8.9% (2006-2010 5-year est.).

**Housing:** Homeownership rate: 68.1% (2010); Median home value: $100,000 (2006-2010 5-year est.); Median contract rent: $617 per month (2006-2010 5-year est.); Median year structure built: 1968 (2006-2010 5-year est.).

**Transportation:** Commute to work: 95.5% car, 1.0% public transportation, 1.6% walk, 1.0% work from home (2006-2010 5-year est.); Travel time to work: 24.1% less than 15 minutes, 53.9% 15 to 30 minutes, 15.0% 30 to 45

minutes, 4.1% 45 to 60 minutes, 2.9% 60 minutes or more (2006-2010 5-year est.)
**Additional Information Contacts**
Greater Baldwinsville Chamber of Commerce . . . . . . . . . . (315) 638-0550
http://www.b-ville.com
Town of Van Buren . . . . . . . . . . . . . . . . . . . . . . . . . . . (315) 635-3010
http://www.b-ville.com/content/about-van-buren-ny

**VILLAGE GREEN** (CDP). Covers a land area of 1.153 square miles and a water area of 0.007 square miles. Located at 43.13° N. Lat; 76.31° W. Long. Elevation is 440 feet.
**Population:** 4,198 (1990); 3,945 (2000); 3,891 (2010); Density: 3,371.9 persons per square mile (2010); Race: 93.9% White, 2.2% Black, 1.2% Asian, 0.4% American Indian/Alaska Native, 0.0% Native Hawaiian/Other Pacific Islander, 2.3% Other, 2.2% Hispanic of any race (2010); Average household size: 2.00 (2010); Median age: 41.7 (2010); Males per 100 females: 91.4 (2010); Marriage status: 34.4% never married, 46.0% now married, 2.8% widowed, 16.8% divorced (2006-2010 5-year est.); Foreign born: 2.3% (2006-2010 5-year est.); Ancestry (includes multiple ancestries): 30.6% German, 28.8% Irish, 19.1% Italian, 18.8% English, 16.2% Polish (2006-2010 5-year est.).
**Economy:** Employment by occupation: 11.4% management, 3.6% professional, 13.7% services, 17.1% sales, 3.1% farming, 8.2% construction, 2.1% production (2006-2010 5-year est.).
**Income:** Per capita income: $30,589 (2006-2010 5-year est.); Median household income: $45,594 (2006-2010 5-year est.); Average household income: $61,409 (2006-2010 5-year est.); Percent of households with income of $100,000 or more: 14.2% (2006-2010 5-year est.); Poverty rate: 12.3% (2006-2010 5-year est.).
**Education:** Percent of population age 25 and over with: High school diploma (including GED) or higher: 94.9% (2006-2010 5-year est.); Bachelor's degree or higher: 24.4% (2006-2010 5-year est.); Master's degree or higher: 9.0% (2006-2010 5-year est.).
**Housing:** Homeownership rate: 56.0% (2010); Median home value: $96,600 (2006-2010 5-year est.); Median contract rent: $683 per month (2006-2010 5-year est.); Median year structure built: 1974 (2006-2010 5-year est.).
**Transportation:** Commute to work: 94.4% car, 1.8% public transportation, 1.1% walk, 1.5% work from home (2006-2010 5-year est.); Travel time to work: 23.3% less than 15 minutes, 52.5% 15 to 30 minutes, 16.6% 30 to 45 minutes, 4.0% 45 to 60 minutes, 3.6% 60 minutes or more (2006-2010 5-year est.).

**WARNERS** (unincorporated postal area)
Zip Code: 13164
Covers a land area of 10.725 square miles and a water area of 0.008 square miles. Located at 43.09° N. Lat; 76.31° W. Long. Elevation is 430 feet. Population: 2,338 (2010); Density: 218.0 persons per square mile (2010); Race: 95.8% White, 1.2% Black, 0.7% Asian, 0.6% American Indian/Alaska Native, 0.0% Native Hawaiian/Other Pacific Islander, 1.7% Other, 2.3% Hispanic of any race (2010); Average household size: 2.89 (2010); Median age: 37.4 (2010); Males per 100 females: 105.6 (2010); Homeownership rate: 87.4% (2010).

**WESTVALE** (CDP). Covers a land area of 1.364 square miles and a water area of 0 square miles. Located at 43.03° N. Lat; 76.21° W. Long. Elevation is 505 feet.
**Population:** 5,434 (1990); 5,166 (2000); 4,963 (2010); Density: 3,637.7 persons per square mile (2010); Race: 97.7% White, 0.4% Black, 0.6% Asian, 0.3% American Indian/Alaska Native, 0.0% Native Hawaiian/Other Pacific Islander, 1.0% Other, 1.7% Hispanic of any race (2010); Average household size: 2.40 (2010); Median age: 46.8 (2010); Males per 100 females: 85.8 (2010); Marriage status: 21.3% never married, 57.4% now married, 12.0% widowed, 9.2% divorced (2006-2010 5-year est.); Foreign born: 3.2% (2006-2010 5-year est.); Ancestry (includes multiple ancestries): 37.9% Irish, 28.2% Italian, 27.1% German, 14.8% Polish, 13.0% English (2006-2010 5-year est.).
**Economy:** Employment by occupation: 11.1% management, 7.2% professional, 7.6% services, 21.6% sales, 3.7% farming, 2.4% construction, 1.7% production (2006-2010 5-year est.).
**Income:** Per capita income: $30,934 (2006-2010 5-year est.); Median household income: $67,823 (2006-2010 5-year est.); Average household income: $76,222 (2006-2010 5-year est.); Percent of households with income of $100,000 or more: 30.1% (2006-2010 5-year est.); Poverty rate: 5.5% (2006-2010 5-year est.).

**Education:** Percent of population age 25 and over with: High school diploma (including GED) or higher: 92.3% (2006-2010 5-year est.); Bachelor's degree or higher: 41.2% (2006-2010 5-year est.); Master's degree or higher: 16.2% (2006-2010 5-year est.).
**Housing:** Homeownership rate: 96.5% (2010); Median home value: $138,500 (2006-2010 5-year est.); Median contract rent: $522 per month (2006-2010 5-year est.); Median year structure built: 1953 (2006-2010 5-year est.).
**Transportation:** Commute to work: 94.3% car, 2.5% public transportation, 0.7% walk, 2.5% work from home (2006-2010 5-year est.); Travel time to work: 38.3% less than 15 minutes, 52.5% 15 to 30 minutes, 4.8% 30 to 45 minutes, 2.8% 45 to 60 minutes, 1.7% 60 minutes or more (2006-2010 5-year est.).

# Ontario County

Located in west central New York, in the Finger Lakes area; bounded partly on the east by Seneca Lake; drained by Honeoye, Mud, and Flint Creeks; includes Canandaigua, Honeoye, and Canadice Lakes. Covers a land area of 644.38 square miles, a water area of 18.05 square miles, and is located in the Eastern Time Zone at 42.87° N. Lat., 77.26° W. Long. The county was founded in 1789. County seat is Canandaigua.

Ontario County is part of the Rochester, NY Metropolitan Statistical Area. The entire metro area includes: Livingston County, NY; Monroe County, NY; Ontario County, NY; Orleans County, NY; Wayne County, NY

Weather Station: Canandaigua 3 S — Elevation: 720 feet

| | Jan | Feb | Mar | Apr | May | Jun | Jul | Aug | Sep | Oct | Nov | Dec |
|---|---|---|---|---|---|---|---|---|---|---|---|---|
| High | 33 | 35 | 42 | 55 | 67 | 77 | 81 | 79 | 72 | 60 | 49 | 38 |
| Low | 18 | 19 | 25 | 36 | 46 | 57 | 62 | 60 | 54 | 42 | 34 | 24 |
| Precip | 1.8 | 1.6 | 2.6 | 3.2 | 3.0 | 3.6 | 3.6 | 3.2 | 3.5 | 2.9 | 2.9 | 2.2 |
| Snow | na | na | na | 0.0 | 0.0 | 0.0 | 0.0 | 0.0 | 0.0 | tr | tr | na |

*High and Low temperatures in degrees Fahrenheit; Precipitation and Snow in inches*

Weather Station: Geneva Research Farm — Elevation: 717 feet

| | Jan | Feb | Mar | Apr | May | Jun | Jul | Aug | Sep | Oct | Nov | Dec |
|---|---|---|---|---|---|---|---|---|---|---|---|---|
| High | 31 | 33 | 41 | 55 | 67 | 76 | 80 | 79 | 71 | 59 | 47 | 36 |
| Low | 16 | 17 | 25 | 36 | 47 | 56 | 61 | 59 | 52 | 41 | 33 | 22 |
| Precip | 1.7 | 1.5 | 2.4 | 2.9 | 3.0 | 3.6 | 3.4 | 3.0 | 3.6 | 3.2 | 2.8 | 2.2 |
| Snow | 13.7 | 11.6 | 11.3 | 2.3 | tr | 0.0 | 0.0 | 0.0 | 0.0 | 0.1 | 4.1 | 11.3 |

*High and Low temperatures in degrees Fahrenheit; Precipitation and Snow in inches*

**Population:** 95,101 (1990); 100,224 (2000); 107,931 (2010); Race: 93.7% White, 2.3% Black, 1.0% Asian, 0.3% American Indian/Alaska Native, 0.0% Native Hawaiian/Other Pacific Islander, 2.7% Other, 3.4% Hispanic of any race (2010); Density: 167.5 persons per square mile (2010); Average household size: 2.43 (2010); Median age: 42.1 (2010); Males per 100 females: 95.6 (2010).
**Religion:** Six largest groups: 23.6% Catholicism, 5.8% Methodist/Pietist, 3.4% Presbyterian-Reformed, 2.0% Holiness, 1.9% Baptist, 1.4% Lutheran (2010)
**Economy:** Unemployment rate: 8.9% (February 2012); Total civilian labor force: 56,845 (February 2012); Leading industries: 21.1% retail trade; 16.9% health care and social assistance; 15.7% manufacturing (2009); Farms: 859 totaling 198,937 acres (2007); Companies that employ 500 or more persons: 9 (2009); Companies that employ 100 to 499 persons: 56 (2009); Companies that employ less than 100 persons: 2,736 (2009); Black-owned businesses: n/a (2007); Hispanic-owned businesses: 123 (2007); Asian-owned businesses: 204 (2007); Women-owned businesses: 2,681 (2007); Retail sales per capita: $17,074 (2010). Single-family building permits issued: 256 (2011); Multi-family building permits issued: 49 (2011).
**Income:** Per capita income: $28,950 (2006-2010 5-year est.); Median household income: $56,468 (2006-2010 5-year est.); Average household income: $71,272 (2006-2010 5-year est.); Percent of households with income of $100,000 or more: 20.3% (2006-2010 5-year est.); Poverty rate: 8.7% (2006-2010 5-year est.); Bankruptcy rate: 2.03% (2011).
**Taxes:** Total county taxes per capita: $1,080 (2009); County property taxes per capita: $434 (2009).
**Education:** Percent of population age 25 and over with: High school diploma (including GED) or higher: 91.5% (2006-2010 5-year est.); Bachelor's degree or higher: 31.0% (2006-2010 5-year est.); Master's degree or higher: 12.6% (2006-2010 5-year est.).
**Housing:** Homeownership rate: 73.1% (2010); Median home value: $129,600 (2006-2010 5-year est.); Median contract rent: $601 per month

(2006-2010 5-year est.); Median year structure built: 1970 (2006-2010 5-year est.)
**Health:** Birth rate: 94.0 per 10,000 population (2011); Death rate: 89.7 per 10,000 population (2011); Age-adjusted cancer mortality rate: 175.8 deaths per 100,000 population (2009); Number of physicians: 23.9 per 10,000 population (2008); Hospital beds: 82.0 per 10,000 population (2007); Hospital admissions: 1,309.1 per 10,000 population (2007).
**Elections:** 2008 Presidential election results: 49.2% Obama, 49.3% McCain, 0.7% Nader
**Additional Information Contacts**
Ontario County Government . . . . . . . . . . . . . . . . . . . (585) 396-4447
  http://www.co.ontario.ny.us
Canandaigua Chamber of Commerce . . . . . . . . . . . . (585) 394-4400
  http://www.canandaiguachamber.com
City of Canandaigua . . . . . . . . . . . . . . . . . . . . . . . (585) 396-5000
  http://canandaigua.govoffice.com
City of Geneva . . . . . . . . . . . . . . . . . . . . . . . . . . . (315) 789-2603
  http://www.geneva.ny.us
Clifton Springs Area Chamber of Commerce . . . . . . . . . (315) 462-8200
  http://www.cliftonspringschamber.com
Geneva Area Chamber of Commerce . . . . . . . . . . . . (315) 789-1776
  http://www.genevany.com
Honeoye Lake Area Chamber of Commerce . . . . . . . . . (585) 721-5169
  http://honeoyelakechamber.org
Phelps Chamber of Commerce . . . . . . . . . . . . . . . . (315) 548-5481
  http://www.phelpsny.com/chamber-of-commerce
Town of Bristol . . . . . . . . . . . . . . . . . . . . . . . . . . . (585) 229-2400
  http://www.townofbristol.org
Town of Canandaigua . . . . . . . . . . . . . . . . . . . . . . (585) 394-1120
  http://www.townofcanandaigua.org
Town of Victor . . . . . . . . . . . . . . . . . . . . . . . . . . . (585) 742-5080
  http://www.victorny.org
Victor Chamber of Commerce . . . . . . . . . . . . . . . . . (585) 742-1476
  http://www.victorchamber.com
Village of Bloomfield . . . . . . . . . . . . . . . . . . . . . . . (585) 657-7554
  http://www.bloomfieldny.org
Village of Phelps . . . . . . . . . . . . . . . . . . . . . . . . . . (315) 548-3861
  http://www.phelpsny.com/village

## Ontario County Communities

**BLOOMFIELD** (village). Covers a land area of 1.396 square miles and a water area of 0 square miles. Located at 42.89° N. Lat; 77.42° W. Long. Elevation is 876 feet.
**Population:** 1,452 (1990); 1,267 (2000); 1,361 (2010); Density: 974.3 persons per square mile (2010); Race: 95.6% White, 1.0% Black, 0.2% Asian, 1.0% American Indian/Alaska Native, 0.0% Native Hawaiian/Other Pacific Islander, 2.2% Other, 2.1% Hispanic of any race (2010); Average household size: 2.44 (2010); Median age: 40.3 (2010); Males per 100 females: 89.0 (2010); Marriage status: 23.3% never married, 61.2% now married, 3.2% widowed, 12.3% divorced (2006-2010 5-year est.); Foreign born: 4.5% (2006-2010 5-year est.); Ancestry (includes multiple ancestries): 35.0% German, 31.6% English, 22.0% Irish, 14.2% Italian, 6.9% French (2006-2010 5-year est.).
**Economy:** Single-family building permits issued: 0 (2011); Multi-family building permits issued: 0 (2011); Employment by occupation: 8.5% management, 4.9% professional, 7.7% services, 22.7% sales, 4.0% farming, 8.5% construction, 6.1% production (2006-2010 5-year est.).
**Income:** Per capita income: $26,116 (2006-2010 5-year est.); Median household income: $54,091 (2006-2010 5-year est.); Average household income: $63,578 (2006-2010 5-year est.); Percent of households with income of $100,000 or more: 15.1% (2006-2010 5-year est.); Poverty rate: 7.3% (2006-2010 5-year est.).
**Taxes:** Total city taxes per capita: $128 (2009); City property taxes per capita: $106 (2009).
**Education:** Percent of population age 25 and over with: High school diploma (including GED) or higher: 90.1% (2006-2010 5-year est.); Bachelor's degree or higher: 27.8% (2006-2010 5-year est.); Master's degree or higher: 12.3% (2006-2010 5-year est.).
**School District(s)**
East Bloomfield Central School District (PK-12)
  2009-10 Enrollment: 1,041 . . . . . . . . . . . . . . . (585) 657-6121
**Housing:** Homeownership rate: 62.7% (2010); Median home value: $129,400 (2006-2010 5-year est.); Median contract rent: $632 per month

(2006-2010 5-year est.); Median year structure built: 1956 (2006-2010 5-year est.).
**Transportation:** Commute to work: 90.8% car, 0.0% public transportation, 3.0% walk, 5.0% work from home (2006-2010 5-year est.); Travel time to work: 32.5% less than 15 minutes, 35.6% 15 to 30 minutes, 23.9% 30 to 45 minutes, 4.0% 45 to 60 minutes, 4.0% 60 minutes or more (2006-2010 5-year est.)
**Additional Information Contacts**
Village of Bloomfield . . . . . . . . . . . . . . . . . . . . . . . (585) 657-7554
  http://www.bloomfieldny.org

**BRISTOL** (town). Covers a land area of 36.694 square miles and a water area of 0.014 square miles. Located at 42.80° N. Lat; 77.42° W. Long. Elevation is 1,165 feet.
**Population:** 2,071 (1990); 2,421 (2000); 2,315 (2010); Density: 63.1 persons per square mile (2010); Race: 97.9% White, 0.8% Black, 0.3% Asian, 0.4% American Indian/Alaska Native, 0.0% Native Hawaiian/Other Pacific Islander, 0.6% Other, 0.6% Hispanic of any race (2010); Average household size: 2.48 (2010); Median age: 46.0 (2010); Males per 100 females: 102.4 (2010); Marriage status: 19.0% never married, 65.3% now married, 5.3% widowed, 10.3% divorced (2006-2010 5-year est.); Foreign born: 1.4% (2006-2010 5-year est.); Ancestry (includes multiple ancestries): 33.5% German, 31.4% English, 20.4% Irish, 11.4% Italian, 7.9% Dutch (2006-2010 5-year est.).
**Economy:** Single-family building permits issued: 2 (2011); Multi-family building permits issued: 0 (2011); Employment by occupation: 7.7% management, 3.2% professional, 9.0% services, 19.2% sales, 4.2% farming, 14.5% construction, 8.1% production (2006-2010 5-year est.).
**Income:** Per capita income: $26,665 (2006-2010 5-year est.); Median household income: $55,625 (2006-2010 5-year est.); Average household income: $62,839 (2006-2010 5-year est.); Percent of households with income of $100,000 or more: 15.4% (2006-2010 5-year est.); Poverty rate: 7.9% (2006-2010 5-year est.).
**Education:** Percent of population age 25 and over with: High school diploma (including GED) or higher: 93.5% (2006-2010 5-year est.); Bachelor's degree or higher: 28.7% (2006-2010 5-year est.); Master's degree or higher: 11.0% (2006-2010 5-year est.).
**Housing:** Homeownership rate: 90.9% (2010); Median home value: $133,900 (2006-2010 5-year est.); Median contract rent: $620 per month (2006-2010 5-year est.); Median year structure built: 1977 (2006-2010 5-year est.).
**Transportation:** Commute to work: 93.3% car, 0.0% public transportation, 1.1% walk, 5.2% work from home (2006-2010 5-year est.); Travel time to work: 17.2% less than 15 minutes, 32.5% 15 to 30 minutes, 31.6% 30 to 45 minutes, 14.6% 45 to 60 minutes, 4.2% 60 minutes or more (2006-2010 5-year est.)
**Additional Information Contacts**
Town of Bristol . . . . . . . . . . . . . . . . . . . . . . . . . . . (585) 229-2400
  http://www.townofbristol.org

**CANADICE** (town). Covers a land area of 29.851 square miles and a water area of 2.585 square miles. Located at 42.71° N. Lat; 77.55° W. Long. Elevation is 1,565 feet.
**Population:** 1,857 (1990); 1,846 (2000); 1,664 (2010); Density: 55.7 persons per square mile (2010); Race: 98.5% White, 0.2% Black, 0.2% Asian, 0.3% American Indian/Alaska Native, 0.0% Native Hawaiian/Other Pacific Islander, 0.8% Other, 0.5% Hispanic of any race (2010); Average household size: 2.28 (2010); Median age: 48.4 (2010); Males per 100 females: 103.7 (2010); Marriage status: 21.8% never married, 63.2% now married, 7.1% widowed, 7.9% divorced (2006-2010 5-year est.); Foreign born: 1.3% (2006-2010 5-year est.); Ancestry (includes multiple ancestries): 37.8% German, 25.4% English, 18.4% Irish, 9.7% Italian, 8.0% Polish (2006-2010 5-year est.).
**Economy:** Single-family building permits issued: 2 (2011); Multi-family building permits issued: 0 (2011); Employment by occupation: 9.3% management, 2.8% professional, 13.0% services, 14.1% sales, 4.5% farming, 13.9% construction, 7.9% production (2006-2010 5-year est.).
**Income:** Per capita income: $28,946 (2006-2010 5-year est.); Median household income: $44,878 (2006-2010 5-year est.); Average household income: $64,559 (2006-2010 5-year est.); Percent of households with income of $100,000 or more: 16.3% (2006-2010 5-year est.); Poverty rate: 8.7% (2006-2010 5-year est.).
**Education:** Percent of population age 25 and over with: High school diploma (including GED) or higher: 86.2% (2006-2010 5-year est.);

Bachelor's degree or higher: 16.8% (2006-2010 5-year est.); Master's degree or higher: 7.7% (2006-2010 5-year est.).
**Housing:** Homeownership rate: 85.1% (2010); Median home value: $135,900 (2006-2010 5-year est.); Median contract rent: $466 per month (2006-2010 5-year est.); Median year structure built: 1969 (2006-2010 5-year est.).
**Transportation:** Commute to work: 90.6% car, 1.3% public transportation, 0.9% walk, 6.1% work from home (2006-2010 5-year est.); Travel time to work: 19.4% less than 15 minutes, 32.4% 15 to 30 minutes, 17.9% 30 to 45 minutes, 18.0% 45 to 60 minutes, 12.3% 60 minutes or more (2006-2010 5-year est.)

**CANANDAIGUA** (city). County seat. Covers a land area of 4.594 square miles and a water area of 0.252 square miles. Located at 42.88° N. Lat; 77.28° W. Long. Elevation is 787 feet.
**Population:** 10,725 (1990); 11,264 (2000); 10,545 (2010); Density: 2,295.2 persons per square mile (2010); Race: 95.1% White, 1.8% Black, 0.7% Asian, 0.3% American Indian/Alaska Native, 0.0% Native Hawaiian/Other Pacific Islander, 2.1% Other, 2.0% Hispanic of any race (2010); Average household size: 2.14 (2010); Median age: 42.5 (2010); Males per 100 females: 88.8 (2010); Marriage status: 31.7% never married, 45.0% now married, 10.4% widowed, 12.9% divorced (2006-2010 5-year est.); Foreign born: 2.5% (2006-2010 5-year est.); Ancestry (includes multiple ancestries): 25.1% German, 22.6% Irish, 20.8% English, 14.5% Italian, 6.7% Dutch (2006-2010 5-year est.).
**Economy:** Single-family building permits issued: 10 (2011); Multi-family building permits issued: 0 (2011); Employment by occupation: 11.3% management, 5.1% professional, 13.0% services, 16.7% sales, 2.4% farming, 2.8% construction, 3.3% production (2006-2010 5-year est.).
**Income:** Per capita income: $27,098 (2006-2010 5-year est.); Median household income: $43,776 (2006-2010 5-year est.); Average household income: $58,380 (2006-2010 5-year est.); Percent of households with income of $100,000 or more: 14.8% (2006-2010 5-year est.); Poverty rate: 13.5% (2006-2010 5-year est.).
**Education:** Percent of population age 25 and over with: High school diploma (including GED) or higher: 92.3% (2006-2010 5-year est.); Bachelor's degree or higher: 34.4% (2006-2010 5-year est.); Master's degree or higher: 16.4% (2006-2010 5-year est.).
### School District(s)
Canandaigua City School District (PK-12)
  2009-10 Enrollment: 3,969 . . . . . . . . . . . . . . . . . . (585) 396-3700
### Two-year College(s)
Finger Lakes Community College (Public)
  Fall 2010 Enrollment: 4,899. . . . . . . . . . . . . . . . . . (585) 394-3500
  2011-12 Tuition: In-state $3,894; Out-of-state $7,378
**Housing:** Homeownership rate: 51.5% (2010); Median home value: $135,900 (2006-2010 5-year est.); Median contract rent: $606 per month (2006-2010 5-year est.); Median year structure built: 1954 (2006-2010 5-year est.).
**Hospitals:** FF Thompson Hospital (113 beds)
**Safety:** Violent crime rate: 18.1 per 10,000 population; Property crime rate: 327.5 per 10,000 population (2010).
**Newspapers:** Ad-Net Community News - Canandaigua Edition (Community news; Circulation 16,251); Ad-Net Community News - Naples Edition (Community news; Circulation 10,700); Ad-Net Community News - Victor/Farmington Edition (Community news; Circulation 9,300); Daily Messenger (Local news; Circulation 15,180); East Rochester Post (Community news; Circulation 6,000); Irondequoit Post-Press (Local news); Messenger Post (Local news; Circulation 4,000); Sunday Messenger (Community news)
**Transportation:** Commute to work: 92.2% car, 0.5% public transportation, 4.6% walk, 2.3% work from home (2006-2010 5-year est.); Travel time to work: 45.9% less than 15 minutes, 27.6% 15 to 30 minutes, 16.3% 30 to 45 minutes, 6.7% 45 to 60 minutes, 3.5% 60 minutes or more (2006-2010 5-year est.)
**Airports:** Canandaigua (general aviation)
**Additional Information Contacts**
Canandaigua Chamber of Commerce . . . . . . . . . . . . . (585) 394-4400
  http://www.canandaiguachamber.com
City of Canandaigua . . . . . . . . . . . . . . . . . . . . . . . . (585) 396-5000
  http://canandaigua.govoffice.com

**CANANDAIGUA** (town). Covers a land area of 56.795 square miles and a water area of 5.734 square miles. Located at 42.86° N. Lat; 77.31° W. Long. Elevation is 787 feet.
**Population:** 7,160 (1990); 7,649 (2000); 10,020 (2010); Density: 176.4 persons per square mile (2010); Race: 96.1% White, 1.0% Black, 1.2% Asian, 0.2% American Indian/Alaska Native, 0.0% Native Hawaiian/Other Pacific Islander, 1.5% Other, 1.9% Hispanic of any race (2010); Average household size: 2.44 (2010); Median age: 45.1 (2010); Males per 100 females: 95.6 (2010); Marriage status: 24.1% never married, 62.1% now married, 6.5% widowed, 7.3% divorced (2006-2010 5-year est.); Foreign born: 3.0% (2006-2010 5-year est.); Ancestry (includes multiple ancestries): 29.3% German, 23.9% Irish, 22.6% English, 13.1% Italian, 6.2% Polish (2006-2010 5-year est.).
**Economy:** Single-family building permits issued: 43 (2011); Multi-family building permits issued: 0 (2011); Employment by occupation: 12.9% management, 4.2% professional, 6.7% services, 18.8% sales, 3.7% farming, 5.2% construction, 3.3% production (2006-2010 5-year est.).
**Income:** Per capita income: $34,895 (2006-2010 5-year est.); Median household income: $62,581 (2006-2010 5-year est.); Average household income: $83,127 (2006-2010 5-year est.); Percent of households with income of $100,000 or more: 26.3% (2006-2010 5-year est.); Poverty rate: 7.8% (2006-2010 5-year est.).
**Education:** Percent of population age 25 and over with: High school diploma (including GED) or higher: 94.5% (2006-2010 5-year est.); Bachelor's degree or higher: 41.4% (2006-2010 5-year est.); Master's degree or higher: 19.6% (2006-2010 5-year est.).
### School District(s)
Canandaigua City School District (PK-12)
  2009-10 Enrollment: 3,969 . . . . . . . . . . . . . . . . . . (585) 396-3700
### Two-year College(s)
Finger Lakes Community College (Public)
  Fall 2010 Enrollment: 4,899. . . . . . . . . . . . . . . . . . (585) 394-3500
  2011-12 Tuition: In-state $3,894; Out-of-state $7,378
**Housing:** Homeownership rate: 72.3% (2010); Median home value: $196,700 (2006-2010 5-year est.); Median contract rent: $681 per month (2006-2010 5-year est.); Median year structure built: 1983 (2006-2010 5-year est.).
**Hospitals:** FF Thompson Hospital (113 beds); Veterans Affairs Medical Center (251 beds); Veterans Affairs Medical Center (251 beds)
**Newspapers:** Ad-Net Community News - Canandaigua Edition (Community news; Circulation 16,251); Ad-Net Community News - Naples Edition (Community news; Circulation 10,700); Ad-Net Community News - Victor/Farmington Edition (Community news; Circulation 9,300); Daily Messenger (Local news; Circulation 15,180); East Rochester Post (Community news; Circulation 6,000); Irondequoit Post-Press (Local news); Messenger Post (Local news; Circulation 4,000); Sunday Messenger (Community news)
**Transportation:** Commute to work: 89.9% car, 0.0% public transportation, 3.1% walk, 6.4% work from home (2006-2010 5-year est.); Travel time to work: 33.0% less than 15 minutes, 38.6% 15 to 30 minutes, 16.6% 30 to 45 minutes, 7.9% 45 to 60 minutes, 4.0% 60 minutes or more (2006-2010 5-year est.)
**Airports:** Canandaigua (general aviation)
**Additional Information Contacts**
Town of Canandaigua . . . . . . . . . . . . . . . . . . . . . . . (585) 394-1120
  http://www.townofcanandaigua.org

**CLIFTON SPRINGS** (village). Covers a land area of 1.519 square miles and a water area of 0 square miles. Located at 42.96° N. Lat; 77.13° W. Long. Elevation is 577 feet.
**Population:** 2,218 (1990); 2,223 (2000); 2,127 (2010); Density: 1,400.2 persons per square mile (2010); Race: 96.3% White, 0.9% Black, 1.0% Asian, 0.0% American Indian/Alaska Native, 0.0% Native Hawaiian/Other Pacific Islander, 1.8% Other, 2.4% Hispanic of any race (2010); Average household size: 2.27 (2010); Median age: 44.5 (2010); Males per 100 females: 80.7 (2010); Marriage status: 20.9% never married, 50.3% now married, 16.2% widowed, 12.6% divorced (2006-2010 5-year est.); Foreign born: 3.3% (2006-2010 5-year est.); Ancestry (includes multiple ancestries): 32.7% German, 24.4% Irish, 24.1% English, 11.5% Italian, 10.3% Dutch (2006-2010 5-year est.).
**Economy:** Single-family building permits issued: 2 (2011); Multi-family building permits issued: 0 (2011); Employment by occupation: 10.2% management, 4.3% professional, 10.0% services, 15.0% sales, 4.7% farming, 6.9% construction, 5.3% production (2006-2010 5-year est.).

**Income:** Per capita income: $23,188 (2006-2010 5-year est.); Median household income: $45,208 (2006-2010 5-year est.); Average household income: $55,883 (2006-2010 5-year est.); Percent of households with income of $100,000 or more: 14.8% (2006-2010 5-year est.); Poverty rate: 7.0% (2006-2010 5-year est.).

**Education:** Percent of population age 25 and over with: High school diploma (including GED) or higher: 86.6% (2006-2010 5-year est.); Bachelor's degree or higher: 26.6% (2006-2010 5-year est.); Master's degree or higher: 7.8% (2006-2010 5-year est.).

**School District(s)**
Phelps-Clifton Springs Central School District (KG-12)
    2009-10 Enrollment: 1,833 . . . . . . . . . . . . . . . . . . . . (315) 548-6420
**Housing:** Homeownership rate: 58.0% (2010); Median home value: $110,900 (2006-2010 5-year est.); Median contract rent: $522 per month (2006-2010 5-year est.); Median year structure built: before 1940 (2006-2010 5-year est.).
**Hospitals:** Clifton Springs Hospital & Clinic (262 beds)
**Safety:** Violent crime rate: 0.0 per 10,000 population; Property crime rate: 75.6 per 10,000 population (2010).
**Newspapers:** Merchandiser (Community news; Circulation 8,200)
**Transportation:** Commute to work: 90.0% car, 0.0% public transportation, 8.1% walk, 1.9% work from home (2006-2010 5-year est.); Travel time to work: 33.3% less than 15 minutes, 33.4% 15 to 30 minutes, 21.7% 30 to 45 minutes, 8.9% 45 to 60 minutes, 2.7% 60 minutes or more (2006-2010 5-year est.)

**Additional Information Contacts**
Clifton Springs Area Chamber of Commerce. . . . . . . . . . . (315) 462-8200
    http://www.cliftonspringschamber.com

**CRYSTAL BEACH** (CDP). Covers a land area of 0.681 square miles and a water area of 0.203 square miles. Located at 42.80° N. Lat; 77.25° W. Long. Elevation is 699 feet.
**Population:** n/a (1990); n/a (2000); 644 (2010); Density: 944.9 persons per square mile (2010); Race: 97.0% White, 1.2% Black, 0.8% Asian, 0.2% American Indian/Alaska Native, 0.0% Native Hawaiian/Other Pacific Islander, 0.8% Other, 4.3% Hispanic of any race (2010); Average household size: 2.18 (2010); Median age: 47.3 (2010); Males per 100 females: 100.0 (2010); Marriage status: 19.1% never married, 36.4% now married, 6.6% widowed, 38.0% divorced (2006-2010 5-year est.); Foreign born: 0.0% (2006-2010 5-year est.); Ancestry (includes multiple ancestries): 20.8% German, 17.1% Irish, 10.8% English, 10.4% Italian, 8.1% French (2006-2010 5-year est.).
**Economy:** Employment by occupation: 14.3% management, 0.0% professional, 9.5% services, 0.0% sales, 0.0% farming, 10.0% construction, 31.4% production (2006-2010 5-year est.).
**Income:** Per capita income: $31,961 (2006-2010 5-year est.); Median household income: $35,114 (2006-2010 5-year est.); Average household income: $58,553 (2006-2010 5-year est.); Percent of households with income of $100,000 or more: 10.9% (2006-2010 5-year est.); Poverty rate: 24.6% (2006-2010 5-year est.).
**Education:** Percent of population age 25 and over with: High school diploma (including GED) or higher: 91.1% (2006-2010 5-year est.); Bachelor's degree or higher: 20.7% (2006-2010 5-year est.); Master's degree or higher: 10.6% (2006-2010 5-year est.).
**Housing:** Homeownership rate: 77.6% (2010); Median home value: $123,000 (2006-2010 5-year est.); Median contract rent: $498 per month (2006-2010 5-year est.); Median year structure built: 1940 (2006-2010 5-year est.).
**Transportation:** Commute to work: 100.0% car, 0.0% public transportation, 0.0% walk, 0.0% work from home (2006-2010 5-year est.); Travel time to work: 23.8% less than 15 minutes, 46.7% 15 to 30 minutes, 29.5% 30 to 45 minutes, 0.0% 45 to 60 minutes, 0.0% 60 minutes or more (2006-2010 5-year est.)

**EAST BLOOMFIELD** (town). Covers a land area of 33.194 square miles and a water area of 0.139 square miles. Located at 42.89° N. Lat; 77.42° W. Long. Elevation is 1,070 feet.
**Population:** 3,258 (1990); 3,361 (2000); 3,634 (2010); Density: 109.5 persons per square mile (2010); Race: 96.8% White, 0.6% Black, 0.2% Asian, 0.6% American Indian/Alaska Native, 0.0% Native Hawaiian/Other Pacific Islander, 1.8% Other, 1.8% Hispanic of any race (2010); Average household size: 2.59 (2010); Median age: 42.6 (2010); Males per 100 females: 99.1 (2010); Marriage status: 19.8% never married, 69.2% now married, 3.0% widowed, 7.9% divorced (2006-2010 5-year est.); Foreign born: 2.4% (2006-2010 5-year est.); Ancestry (includes multiple

ancestries): 29.6% German, 28.2% English, 20.8% Irish, 18.0% Italian, 10.0% French (2006-2010 5-year est.).
**Economy:** Single-family building permits issued: 3 (2011); Multi-family building permits issued: 0 (2011); Employment by occupation: 10.8% management, 6.8% professional, 7.0% services, 16.3% sales, 1.4% farming, 11.4% construction, 6.5% production (2006-2010 5-year est.).
**Income:** Per capita income: $33,239 (2006-2010 5-year est.); Median household income: $68,387 (2006-2010 5-year est.); Average household income: $89,503 (2006-2010 5-year est.); Percent of households with income of $100,000 or more: 25.3% (2006-2010 5-year est.); Poverty rate: 4.1% (2006-2010 5-year est.).
**Education:** Percent of population age 25 and over with: High school diploma (including GED) or higher: 93.4% (2006-2010 5-year est.); Bachelor's degree or higher: 34.1% (2006-2010 5-year est.); Master's degree or higher: 14.5% (2006-2010 5-year est.).
**Housing:** Homeownership rate: 77.1% (2010); Median home value: $161,200 (2006-2010 5-year est.); Median contract rent: $628 per month (2006-2010 5-year est.); Median year structure built: 1969 (2006-2010 5-year est.).
**Transportation:** Commute to work: 91.5% car, 0.0% public transportation, 1.0% walk, 7.0% work from home (2006-2010 5-year est.); Travel time to work: 28.4% less than 15 minutes, 35.3% 15 to 30 minutes, 25.5% 30 to 45 minutes, 5.0% 45 to 60 minutes, 5.7% 60 minutes or more (2006-2010 5-year est.)

**FARMINGTON** (town). Covers a land area of 39.430 square miles and a water area of 0 square miles. Located at 42.98° N. Lat; 77.30° W. Long. Elevation is 561 feet.
**Population:** 10,381 (1990); 10,585 (2000); 11,825 (2010); Density: 299.9 persons per square mile (2010); Race: 94.7% White, 1.6% Black, 1.3% Asian, 0.3% American Indian/Alaska Native, 0.0% Native Hawaiian/Other Pacific Islander, 2.1% Other, 3.1% Hispanic of any race (2010); Average household size: 2.63 (2010); Median age: 37.2 (2010); Males per 100 females: 95.8 (2010); Marriage status: 25.3% never married, 60.2% now married, 2.6% widowed, 11.9% divorced (2006-2010 5-year est.); Foreign born: 8.0% (2006-2010 5-year est.); Ancestry (includes multiple ancestries): 30.0% German, 20.1% Irish, 19.8% English, 11.4% Italian, 6.1% Dutch (2006-2010 5-year est.).
**Economy:** Single-family building permits issued: 85 (2011); Multi-family building permits issued: 34 (2011); Employment by occupation: 7.7% management, 8.1% professional, 10.0% services, 18.1% sales, 5.4% farming, 8.2% construction, 5.9% production (2006-2010 5-year est.).
**Income:** Per capita income: $25,276 (2006-2010 5-year est.); Median household income: $58,833 (2006-2010 5-year est.); Average household income: $66,244 (2006-2010 5-year est.); Percent of households with income of $100,000 or more: 16.9% (2006-2010 5-year est.); Poverty rate: 7.0% (2006-2010 5-year est.).
**Education:** Percent of population age 25 and over with: High school diploma (including GED) or higher: 91.6% (2006-2010 5-year est.); Bachelor's degree or higher: 25.1% (2006-2010 5-year est.); Master's degree or higher: 7.0% (2006-2010 5-year est.).
**Housing:** Homeownership rate: 76.5% (2010); Median home value: $126,800 (2006-2010 5-year est.); Median contract rent: $842 per month (2006-2010 5-year est.); Median year structure built: 1978 (2006-2010 5-year est.).
**Transportation:** Commute to work: 92.9% car, 0.3% public transportation, 0.5% walk, 5.3% work from home (2006-2010 5-year est.); Travel time to work: 26.3% less than 15 minutes, 41.4% 15 to 30 minutes, 26.1% 30 to 45 minutes, 3.0% 45 to 60 minutes, 3.2% 60 minutes or more (2006-2010 5-year est.)

**GENEVA** (city). Covers a land area of 4.210 square miles and a water area of 1.631 square miles. Located at 42.86° N. Lat; 76.98° W. Long. Elevation is 443 feet.
**History:** Named for Geneva, Switzerland, by Swiss settlers. The area of the city of Geneva includes the site of the Native American settlement of Kanadesaga. After the Revolution, other settlers began to arrive. Captain Charles Williamson, agent for the Pulteney Estate, recognized the superb advantages of the site and laid out Main Street on the terrace overlooking the lake.
**Population:** 14,236 (1990); 13,617 (2000); 13,261 (2010); Density: 3,149.8 persons per square mile (2010); Race: 77.3% White, 10.5% Black, 1.7% Asian, 0.3% American Indian/Alaska Native, 0.0% Native Hawaiian/Other Pacific Islander, 10.2% Other, 13.2% Hispanic of any race (2010); Average household size: 2.29 (2010); Median age: 31.7 (2010); Males per 100

females: 87.8 (2010); Marriage status: 46.2% never married, 36.7% now married, 8.6% widowed, 8.6% divorced (2006-2010 5-year est.); Foreign born: 5.2% (2006-2010 5-year est.); Ancestry (includes multiple ancestries): 26.6% Italian, 22.1% Irish, 14.2% German, 12.0% English, 3.3% Polish (2006-2010 5-year est.).

**Economy:** Single-family building permits issued: 1 (2011); Multi-family building permits issued: 15 (2011); Employment by occupation: 10.3% management, 3.1% professional, 11.4% services, 13.6% sales, 2.2% farming, 9.9% construction, 7.1% production (2006-2010 5-year est.).

**Income:** Per capita income: $20,911 (2006-2010 5-year est.); Median household income: $37,292 (2006-2010 5-year est.); Average household income: $52,472 (2006-2010 5-year est.); Percent of households with income of $100,000 or more: 12.2% (2006-2010 5-year est.); Poverty rate: 19.0% (2006-2010 5-year est.).

**Taxes:** Total city taxes per capita: $780 (2009); City property taxes per capita: $484 (2009).

**Education:** Percent of population age 25 and over with: High school diploma (including GED) or higher: 84.1% (2006-2010 5-year est.); Bachelor's degree or higher: 24.8% (2006-2010 5-year est.); Master's degree or higher: 8.3% (2006-2010 5-year est.).

**School District(s)**
Geneva City School District (KG-12)
 2009-10 Enrollment: 2,210 . . . . . . . . . . . . . . . . . . . . . . (315) 781-0276

**Four-year College(s)**
Hobart William Smith Colleges (Private, Not-for-profit)
 Fall 2010 Enrollment: 2,121 . . . . . . . . . . . . . . . . . . . . (315) 781-3000
 2011-12 Tuition: In-state $42,915; Out-of-state $42,915

**Vocational/Technical School(s)**
Marion S Whelan School of Nursing of Geneva General Hospital (Private, Not-for-profit)
 Fall 2010 Enrollment: 42 . . . . . . . . . . . . . . . . . . . . . . (315) 787-4005
 2011-12 Tuition: In-state $9,720; Out-of-state $9,720

**Housing:** Homeownership rate: 52.3% (2010); Median home value: $84,900 (2006-2010 5-year est.); Median contract rent: $556 per month (2006-2010 5-year est.); Median year structure built: before 1940 (2006-2010 5-year est.).

**Hospitals:** Geneva General Hospital (136 beds)

**Safety:** Violent crime rate: 25.2 per 10,000 population; Property crime rate: 247.5 per 10,000 population (2010).

**Newspapers:** The Finger Lakes Times (Local news; Circulation 15,607)

**Transportation:** Commute to work: 77.1% car, 1.3% public transportation, 17.4% walk, 2.8% work from home (2006-2010 5-year est.); Travel time to work: 59.8% less than 15 minutes, 23.1% 15 to 30 minutes, 8.6% 30 to 45 minutes, 5.6% 45 to 60 minutes, 3.0% 60 minutes or more (2006-2010 5-year est.)

**Additional Information Contacts**
City of Geneva . . . . . . . . . . . . . . . . . . . . . . . . . . . . (315) 789-2603
 http://www.geneva.ny.us
Geneva Area Chamber of Commerce . . . . . . . . . . . . . . . (315) 789-1776
 http://www.genevany.com

**GENEVA** (town). Covers a land area of 19.091 square miles and a water area of 0.006 square miles. Located at 42.83° N. Lat; 77.00° W. Long. Elevation is 443 feet.

**History:** Hobart College and William Smith College are in the city. Settled 1788; Incorporated as village in 1812, as city in 1897.

**Population:** 2,874 (1990); 3,289 (2000); 3,291 (2010); Density: 172.4 persons per square mile (2010); Race: 92.9% White, 2.8% Black, 2.3% Asian, 0.1% American Indian/Alaska Native, 0.0% Native Hawaiian/Other Pacific Islander, 1.9% Other, 2.4% Hispanic of any race (2010); Average household size: 2.23 (2010); Median age: 49.1 (2010); Males per 100 females: 91.7 (2010); Marriage status: 20.1% never married, 60.8% now married, 7.4% widowed, 11.6% divorced (2006-2010 5-year est.); Foreign born: 4.6% (2006-2010 5-year est.); Ancestry (includes multiple ancestries): 26.5% Italian, 25.5% Irish, 23.1% English, 20.0% German, 4.9% Dutch (2006-2010 5-year est.).

**Economy:** Single-family building permits issued: 1 (2011); Multi-family building permits issued: 0 (2011); Employment by occupation: 16.1% management, 2.4% professional, 5.4% services, 12.7% sales, 3.3% farming, 9.8% construction, 8.9% production (2006-2010 5-year est.).

**Income:** Per capita income: $32,972 (2006-2010 5-year est.); Median household income: $63,571 (2006-2010 5-year est.); Average household income: $77,063 (2006-2010 5-year est.); Percent of households with income of $100,000 or more: 25.9% (2006-2010 5-year est.); Poverty rate: 5.1% (2006-2010 5-year est.).

**Education:** Percent of population age 25 and over with: High school diploma (including GED) or higher: 94.2% (2006-2010 5-year est.); Bachelor's degree or higher: 40.4% (2006-2010 5-year est.); Master's degree or higher: 20.1% (2006-2010 5-year est.).

**School District(s)**
Geneva City School District (KG-12)
 2009-10 Enrollment: 2,210 . . . . . . . . . . . . . . . . . . . . . . (315) 781-0276

**Four-year College(s)**
Hobart William Smith Colleges (Private, Not-for-profit)
 Fall 2010 Enrollment: 2,121 . . . . . . . . . . . . . . . . . . . . (315) 781-3000
 2011-12 Tuition: In-state $42,915; Out-of-state $42,915

**Vocational/Technical School(s)**
Marion S Whelan School of Nursing of Geneva General Hospital (Private, Not-for-profit)
 Fall 2010 Enrollment: 42 . . . . . . . . . . . . . . . . . . . . . . (315) 787-4005
 2011-12 Tuition: In-state $9,720; Out-of-state $9,720

**Housing:** Homeownership rate: 71.2% (2010); Median home value: $157,600 (2006-2010 5-year est.); Median contract rent: $633 per month (2006-2010 5-year est.); Median year structure built: 1969 (2006-2010 5-year est.).

**Hospitals:** Geneva General Hospital (136 beds)

**Newspapers:** The Finger Lakes Times (Local news; Circulation 15,607)

**Transportation:** Commute to work: 91.9% car, 0.0% public transportation, 0.7% walk, 5.2% work from home (2006-2010 5-year est.); Travel time to work: 37.8% less than 15 minutes, 44.0% 15 to 30 minutes, 10.7% 30 to 45 minutes, 1.1% 45 to 60 minutes, 6.3% 60 minutes or more (2006-2010 5-year est.)

**GORHAM** (town). Covers a land area of 48.854 square miles and a water area of 4.314 square miles. Located at 42.79° N. Lat; 77.19° W. Long. Elevation is 889 feet.

**Population:** 3,497 (1990); 3,776 (2000); 4,247 (2010); Density: 86.9 persons per square mile (2010); Race: 97.7% White, 0.6% Black, 0.5% Asian, 0.0% American Indian/Alaska Native, 0.0% Native Hawaiian/Other Pacific Islander, 1.2% Other, 1.7% Hispanic of any race (2010); Average household size: 2.53 (2010); Median age: 44.7 (2010); Males per 100 females: 96.9 (2010); Marriage status: 27.0% never married, 56.4% now married, 4.2% widowed, 12.4% divorced (2006-2010 5-year est.); Foreign born: 0.7% (2006-2010 5-year est.); Ancestry (includes multiple ancestries): 34.9% German, 22.7% Irish, 20.7% English, 10.0% Italian, 6.3% American (2006-2010 5-year est.).

**Economy:** Single-family building permits issued: 8 (2011); Multi-family building permits issued: 0 (2011); Employment by occupation: 12.1% management, 2.4% professional, 9.8% services, 7.8% sales, 2.3% farming, 17.0% construction, 7.9% production (2006-2010 5-year est.).

**Income:** Per capita income: $28,769 (2006-2010 5-year est.); Median household income: $58,295 (2006-2010 5-year est.); Average household income: $68,125 (2006-2010 5-year est.); Percent of households with income of $100,000 or more: 18.5% (2006-2010 5-year est.); Poverty rate: 10.7% (2006-2010 5-year est.).

**Education:** Percent of population age 25 and over with: High school diploma (including GED) or higher: 91.2% (2006-2010 5-year est.); Bachelor's degree or higher: 28.0% (2006-2010 5-year est.); Master's degree or higher: 14.5% (2006-2010 5-year est.).

**School District(s)**
Gorham-Middlesex Central School District (marcus W (PK-12)
 2009-10 Enrollment: 1,395 . . . . . . . . . . . . . . . . . . . . (585) 554-4848

**Housing:** Homeownership rate: 84.0% (2010); Median home value: $132,800 (2006-2010 5-year est.); Median contract rent: $505 per month (2006-2010 5-year est.); Median year structure built: 1947 (2006-2010 5-year est.).

**Transportation:** Commute to work: 95.2% car, 0.0% public transportation, 0.0% walk, 4.8% work from home (2006-2010 5-year est.); Travel time to work: 27.0% less than 15 minutes, 43.0% 15 to 30 minutes, 20.0% 30 to 45 minutes, 6.1% 45 to 60 minutes, 3.8% 60 minutes or more (2006-2010 5-year est.)

**GORHAM** (CDP). Covers a land area of 1.897 square miles and a water area of 0 square miles. Located at 42.79° N. Lat; 77.13° W. Long. Elevation is 889 feet.

**Population:** n/a (1990); n/a (2000); 617 (2010); Density: 325.2 persons per square mile (2010); Race: 96.9% White, 1.0% Black, 0.2% Asian, 0.2% American Indian/Alaska Native, 0.0% Native Hawaiian/Other Pacific Islander, 1.7% Other, 1.8% Hispanic of any race (2010); Average household size: 2.60 (2010); Median age: 42.8 (2010); Males per 100 females: 86.4 (2010); Marriage status: 32.8% never married, 53.8% now married, 10.0% widowed, 3.3% divorced (2006-2010 5-year est.); Foreign born: 0.0% (2006-2010 5-year est.); Ancestry (includes multiple ancestries): 49.8% German, 29.4% English, 26.6% Irish, 11.0% Dutch, 8.1% British (2006-2010 5-year est.).

**Economy:** Employment by occupation: 7.8% management, 3.4% professional, 13.7% services, 3.8% sales, 0.0% farming, 15.7% construction, 8.2% production (2006-2010 5-year est.).

**Income:** Per capita income: $28,706 (2006-2010 5-year est.); Median household income: $47,875 (2006-2010 5-year est.); Average household income: $69,334 (2006-2010 5-year est.); Percent of households with income of $100,000 or more: 33.9% (2006-2010 5-year est.); Poverty rate: 5.5% (2006-2010 5-year est.).

**Education:** Percent of population age 25 and over with: High school diploma (including GED) or higher: 96.3% (2006-2010 5-year est.); Bachelor's degree or higher: 36.6% (2006-2010 5-year est.); Master's degree or higher: 11.7% (2006-2010 5-year est.).

**School District(s)**
Gorham-Middlesex Central School District (marcus W (PK-12)
    2009-10 Enrollment: 1,395 . . . . . . . . . . . . . . . (585) 554-4848

**Housing:** Homeownership rate: 82.7% (2010); Median home value: $98,400 (2006-2010 5-year est.); Median contract rent: $425 per month (2006-2010 5-year est.); Median year structure built: before 1940 (2006-2010 5-year est.).

**Transportation:** Commute to work: 90.8% car, 0.0% public transportation, 0.0% walk, 9.2% work from home (2006-2010 5-year est.); Travel time to work: 26.7% less than 15 minutes, 60.2% 15 to 30 minutes, 0.0% 30 to 45 minutes, 9.0% 45 to 60 minutes, 4.1% 60 minutes or more (2006-2010 5-year est.)

**HALL** (CDP). Covers a land area of 1.022 square miles and a water area of 0 square miles. Located at 42.79° N. Lat; 77.06° W. Long. Elevation is 935 feet.

**Population:** n/a (1990); n/a (2000); 216 (2010); Density: 211.2 persons per square mile (2010); Race: 99.5% White, 0.0% Black, 0.5% Asian, 0.0% American Indian/Alaska Native, 0.0% Native Hawaiian/Other Pacific Islander, 0.0% Other, 0.0% Hispanic of any race (2010); Average household size: 2.54 (2010); Median age: 42.4 (2010); Males per 100 females: 101.9 (2010); Marriage status: 11.3% never married, 77.3% now married, 11.3% widowed, 0.0% divorced (2006-2010 5-year est.); Foreign born: 4.7% (2006-2010 5-year est.); Ancestry (includes multiple ancestries): 37.3% German, 32.6% Irish, 30.6% English, 28.5% Dutch, 9.3% Italian (2006-2010 5-year est.).

**Economy:** Employment by occupation: 13.2% management, 14.7% professional, 0.0% services, 5.9% sales, 0.0% farming, 0.0% construction, 4.4% production (2006-2010 5-year est.).

**Income:** Per capita income: $21,494 (2006-2010 5-year est.); Median household income: $66,000 (2006-2010 5-year est.); Average household income: $57,794 (2006-2010 5-year est.); Percent of households with income of $100,000 or more: 8.3% (2006-2010 5-year est.); Poverty rate: 0.0% (2006-2010 5-year est.).

**Education:** Percent of population age 25 and over with: High school diploma (including GED) or higher: 91.2% (2006-2010 5-year est.); Bachelor's degree or higher: 17.6% (2006-2010 5-year est.); Master's degree or higher: 0.0% (2006-2010 5-year est.).

**Housing:** Homeownership rate: 84.7% (2010); Median home value: $108,200 (2006-2010 5-year est.); Median contract rent: n/a per month (2006-2010 5-year est.); Median year structure built: before 1940 (2006-2010 5-year est.).

**Transportation:** Commute to work: 91.8% car, 0.0% public transportation, 0.0% walk, 0.0% work from home (2006-2010 5-year est.); Travel time to work: 19.2% less than 15 minutes, 49.3% 15 to 30 minutes, 31.5% 30 to 45 minutes, 0.0% 45 to 60 minutes, 0.0% 60 minutes or more (2006-2010 5-year est.)

**HONEOYE** (CDP). Covers a land area of 0.920 square miles and a water area of 0 square miles. Located at 42.79° N. Lat; 77.51° W. Long. Elevation is 814 feet.

**Population:** n/a (1990); n/a (2000); 579 (2010); Density: 628.7 persons per square mile (2010); Race: 97.6% White, 0.2% Black, 0.5% Asian, 0.2% American Indian/Alaska Native, 0.0% Native Hawaiian/Other Pacific Islander, 1.5% Other, 0.7% Hispanic of any race (2010); Average household size: 2.30 (2010); Median age: 41.8 (2010); Males per 100 females: 107.5 (2010); Marriage status: 38.4% never married, 44.7% now married, 11.5% widowed, 5.4% divorced (2006-2010 5-year est.); Foreign

born: 0.0% (2006-2010 5-year est.); Ancestry (includes multiple ancestries): 46.5% German, 37.6% English, 19.2% Irish, 10.3% Polish, 7.4% American (2006-2010 5-year est.).

**Economy:** Employment by occupation: 4.9% management, 3.0% professional, 27.7% services, 19.3% sales, 4.2% farming, 24.0% construction, 0.0% production (2006-2010 5-year est.).

**Income:** Per capita income: $16,528 (2006-2010 5-year est.); Median household income: $40,688 (2006-2010 5-year est.); Average household income: $46,487 (2006-2010 5-year est.); Percent of households with income of $100,000 or more: 11.1% (2006-2010 5-year est.); Poverty rate: 53.3% (2006-2010 5-year est.).

**Education:** Percent of population age 25 and over with: High school diploma (including GED) or higher: 91.2% (2006-2010 5-year est.); Bachelor's degree or higher: 14.7% (2006-2010 5-year est.); Master's degree or higher: 3.7% (2006-2010 5-year est.).

**School District(s)**
Honeoye Central School District (KG-12)
    2009-10 Enrollment: 800 . . . . . . . . . . . . . . . (585) 229-4125

**Housing:** Homeownership rate: 56.7% (2010); Median home value: $108,800 (2006-2010 5-year est.); Median contract rent: $587 per month (2006-2010 5-year est.); Median year structure built: before 1940 (2006-2010 5-year est.).

**Transportation:** Commute to work: 100.0% car, 0.0% public transportation, 0.0% walk, 0.0% work from home (2006-2010 5-year est.); Travel time to work: 37.0% less than 15 minutes, 17.7% 15 to 30 minutes, 22.6% 30 to 45 minutes, 5.6% 45 to 60 minutes, 17.2% 60 minutes or more (2006-2010 5-year est.)

**HOPEWELL** (town). Covers a land area of 35.676 square miles and a water area of 0.019 square miles. Located at 42.89° N. Lat; 77.19° W. Long.

**Population:** 3,016 (1990); 3,346 (2000); 3,747 (2010); Density: 105.0 persons per square mile (2010); Race: 95.4% White, 2.7% Black, 0.2% Asian, 0.2% American Indian/Alaska Native, 0.0% Native Hawaiian/Other Pacific Islander, 1.5% Other, 2.4% Hispanic of any race (2010); Average household size: 2.45 (2010); Median age: 41.9 (2010); Males per 100 females: 112.8 (2010); Marriage status: 22.6% never married, 55.0% now married, 8.8% widowed, 13.6% divorced (2006-2010 5-year est.); Foreign born: 3.5% (2006-2010 5-year est.); Ancestry (includes multiple ancestries): 23.5% German, 19.2% English, 17.5% Irish, 13.4% Italian, 11.1% Dutch (2006-2010 5-year est.).

**Economy:** Single-family building permits issued: 3 (2011); Multi-family building permits issued: 0 (2011); Employment by occupation: 6.0% management, 3.3% professional, 13.8% services, 13.3% sales, 2.1% farming, 16.0% construction, 7.3% production (2006-2010 5-year est.).

**Income:** Per capita income: $23,239 (2006-2010 5-year est.); Median household income: $57,961 (2006-2010 5-year est.); Average household income: $60,529 (2006-2010 5-year est.); Percent of households with income of $100,000 or more: 18.1% (2006-2010 5-year est.); Poverty rate: 11.9% (2006-2010 5-year est.).

**Education:** Percent of population age 25 and over with: High school diploma (including GED) or higher: 86.0% (2006-2010 5-year est.); Bachelor's degree or higher: 17.2% (2006-2010 5-year est.); Master's degree or higher: 4.9% (2006-2010 5-year est.).

**Housing:** Homeownership rate: 78.8% (2010); Median home value: $104,000 (2006-2010 5-year est.); Median contract rent: $603 per month (2006-2010 5-year est.); Median year structure built: 1980 (2006-2010 5-year est.).

**Transportation:** Commute to work: 96.3% car, 0.0% public transportation, 0.0% walk, 2.2% work from home (2006-2010 5-year est.); Travel time to work: 38.0% less than 15 minutes, 38.2% 15 to 30 minutes, 9.8% 30 to 45 minutes, 11.0% 45 to 60 minutes, 3.0% 60 minutes or more (2006-2010 5-year est.)

**IONIA** (unincorporated postal area)
Zip Code: 14475
    Covers a land area of 1.525 square miles and a water area of 0 square miles. Located at 42.93° N. Lat; 77.49° W. Long. Elevation is 889 feet.
    Population: 234 (2010); Density: 153.4 persons per square mile (2010); Race: 97.4% White, 0.9% Black, 0.9% Asian, 0.4% American Indian/Alaska Native, 0.0% Native Hawaiian/Other Pacific Islander, 0.4% Other, 3.0% Hispanic of any race (2010); Average household size: 2.66 (2010); Median age: 44.8 (2010); Males per 100 females: 93.4 (2010); Homeownership rate: 89.7% (2010)

**MANCHESTER** (village). Covers a land area of 1.176 square miles and a water area of 0 square miles. Located at 42.96° N. Lat; 77.23° W. Long. Elevation is 591 feet.

**Population:** 1,598 (1990); 1,475 (2000); 1,709 (2010); Density: 1,452.9 persons per square mile (2010); Race: 96.7% White, 0.7% Black, 0.4% Asian, 0.4% American Indian/Alaska Native, 0.0% Native Hawaiian/Other Pacific Islander, 1.8% Other, 2.4% Hispanic of any race (2010); Average household size: 2.30 (2010); Median age: 42.2 (2010); Males per 100 females: 91.4 (2010); Marriage status: 22.8% never married, 53.5% now married, 10.5% widowed, 13.1% divorced (2006-2010 5-year est.); Foreign born: 1.7% (2006-2010 5-year est.); Ancestry (includes multiple ancestries): 27.0% German, 21.4% Italian, 19.6% Irish, 17.3% English, 10.1% Dutch (2006-2010 5-year est.).

**Economy:** Single-family building permits issued: 2 (2011); Multi-family building permits issued: 0 (2011); Employment by occupation: 5.8% management, 3.9% professional, 10.0% services, 20.5% sales, 4.8% farming, 15.0% construction, 4.6% production (2006-2010 5-year est.).

**Income:** Per capita income: $23,787 (2006-2010 5-year est.); Median household income: $47,500 (2006-2010 5-year est.); Average household income: $54,466 (2006-2010 5-year est.); Percent of households with income of $100,000 or more: 11.0% (2006-2010 5-year est.); Poverty rate: 7.3% (2006-2010 5-year est.).

**Education:** Percent of population age 25 and over with: High school diploma (including GED) or higher: 88.9% (2006-2010 5-year est.); Bachelor's degree or higher: 11.2% (2006-2010 5-year est.); Master's degree or higher: 4.2% (2006-2010 5-year est.).

**Housing:** Homeownership rate: 76.3% (2010); Median home value: $83,800 (2006-2010 5-year est.); Median contract rent: $517 per month (2006-2010 5-year est.); Median year structure built: 1952 (2006-2010 5-year est.).

**Safety:** Violent crime rate: 0.0 per 10,000 population; Property crime rate: 0.0 per 10,000 population (2010).

**Transportation:** Commute to work: 95.0% car, 0.6% public transportation, 2.1% walk, 1.6% work from home (2006-2010 5-year est.); Travel time to work: 32.7% less than 15 minutes, 44.7% 15 to 30 minutes, 19.1% 30 to 45 minutes, 2.9% 45 to 60 minutes, 0.5% 60 minutes or more (2006-2010 5-year est.)

**MANCHESTER** (town). Covers a land area of 37.818 square miles and a water area of 0.032 square miles. Located at 42.98° N. Lat; 77.19° W. Long. Elevation is 591 feet.

**History:** Incorporated 1892.

**Population:** 9,351 (1990); 9,258 (2000); 9,395 (2010); Density: 248.4 persons per square mile (2010); Race: 96.2% White, 1.1% Black, 0.5% Asian, 0.3% American Indian/Alaska Native, 0.0% Native Hawaiian/Other Pacific Islander, 1.9% Other, 2.4% Hispanic of any race (2010); Average household size: 2.44 (2010); Median age: 42.6 (2010); Males per 100 females: 94.2 (2010); Marriage status: 23.6% never married, 55.1% now married, 11.3% widowed, 9.9% divorced (2006-2010 5-year est.); Foreign born: 1.9% (2006-2010 5-year est.); Ancestry (includes multiple ancestries): 33.7% German, 20.4% Irish, 19.2% English, 13.3% Italian, 11.8% Dutch (2006-2010 5-year est.).

**Economy:** Single-family building permits issued: 14 (2011); Multi-family building permits issued: 0 (2011); Employment by occupation: 8.2% management, 3.2% professional, 11.5% services, 15.0% sales, 3.9% farming, 11.2% construction, 6.8% production (2006-2010 5-year est.).

**Income:** Per capita income: $22,147 (2006-2010 5-year est.); Median household income: $48,207 (2006-2010 5-year est.); Average household income: $55,606 (2006-2010 5-year est.); Percent of households with income of $100,000 or more: 10.7% (2006-2010 5-year est.); Poverty rate: 7.8% (2006-2010 5-year est.).

**Education:** Percent of population age 25 and over with: High school diploma (including GED) or higher: 85.4% (2006-2010 5-year est.); Bachelor's degree or higher: 14.8% (2006-2010 5-year est.); Master's degree or higher: 3.1% (2006-2010 5-year est.).

**Housing:** Homeownership rate: 76.3% (2010); Median home value: $90,400 (2006-2010 5-year est.); Median contract rent: $544 per month (2006-2010 5-year est.); Median year structure built: 1957 (2006-2010 5-year est.).

**Transportation:** Commute to work: 92.5% car, 0.4% public transportation, 3.2% walk, 3.6% work from home (2006-2010 5-year est.); Travel time to work: 30.0% less than 15 minutes, 43.3% 15 to 30 minutes, 19.0% 30 to 45 minutes, 5.8% 45 to 60 minutes, 1.8% 60 minutes or more (2006-2010 5-year est.)

**NAPLES** (village). Covers a land area of 0.984 square miles and a water area of 0 square miles. Located at 42.61° N. Lat; 77.40° W. Long. Elevation is 804 feet.

**Population:** 1,237 (1990); 1,072 (2000); 1,041 (2010); Density: 1,057.4 persons per square mile (2010); Race: 96.7% White, 1.0% Black, 0.3% Asian, 0.4% American Indian/Alaska Native, 0.0% Native Hawaiian/Other Pacific Islander, 1.6% Other, 0.8% Hispanic of any race (2010); Average household size: 2.32 (2010); Median age: 40.3 (2010); Males per 100 females: 86.6 (2010); Marriage status: 29.8% never married, 50.1% now married, 7.2% widowed, 12.9% divorced (2006-2010 5-year est.); Foreign born: 2.9% (2006-2010 5-year est.); Ancestry (includes multiple ancestries): 39.4% German, 23.3% Irish, 23.1% English, 8.6% Dutch, 6.5% Italian (2006-2010 5-year est.).

**Economy:** Single-family building permits issued: 0 (2011); Multi-family building permits issued: 0 (2011); Employment by occupation: 10.5% management, 2.5% professional, 9.1% services, 15.8% sales, 2.3% farming, 8.4% construction, 6.4% production (2006-2010 5-year est.).

**Income:** Per capita income: $20,595 (2006-2010 5-year est.); Median household income: $40,054 (2006-2010 5-year est.); Average household income: $52,693 (2006-2010 5-year est.); Percent of households with income of $100,000 or more: 10.8% (2006-2010 5-year est.); Poverty rate: 16.8% (2006-2010 5-year est.).

**Education:** Percent of population age 25 and over with: High school diploma (including GED) or higher: 92.6% (2006-2010 5-year est.); Bachelor's degree or higher: 26.1% (2006-2010 5-year est.); Master's degree or higher: 13.1% (2006-2010 5-year est.).

**School District(s)**

Naples Central School District (PK-12)

    2009-10 Enrollment: 876 . . . . . . . . . . . . . . . . . . . . . . . . . (585) 374-7901

**Housing:** Homeownership rate: 62.4% (2010); Median home value: $104,200 (2006-2010 5-year est.); Median contract rent: $482 per month (2006-2010 5-year est.); Median year structure built: before 1940 (2006-2010 5-year est.).

**Newspapers:** Naples Record (Local news; Circulation 2,000)

**Transportation:** Commute to work: 81.3% car, 1.6% public transportation, 9.6% walk, 7.5% work from home (2006-2010 5-year est.); Travel time to work: 33.8% less than 15 minutes, 15.2% 15 to 30 minutes, 28.5% 30 to 45 minutes, 15.2% 45 to 60 minutes, 7.3% 60 minutes or more (2006-2010 5-year est.)

**NAPLES** (town). Covers a land area of 39.684 square miles and a water area of <.001 square miles. Located at 42.62° N. Lat; 77.43° W. Long. Elevation is 804 feet.

**History:** Incorporated 1894.

**Population:** 2,559 (1990); 2,441 (2000); 2,502 (2010); Density: 63.0 persons per square mile (2010); Race: 97.0% White, 0.6% Black, 0.4% Asian, 0.2% American Indian/Alaska Native, 0.0% Native Hawaiian/Other Pacific Islander, 1.8% Other, 1.0% Hispanic of any race (2010); Average household size: 2.41 (2010); Median age: 43.9 (2010); Males per 100 females: 93.5 (2010); Marriage status: 20.1% never married, 59.6% now married, 6.5% widowed, 13.7% divorced (2006-2010 5-year est.); Foreign born: 1.4% (2006-2010 5-year est.); Ancestry (includes multiple ancestries): 34.3% German, 23.9% English, 19.8% Irish, 8.1% Dutch, 5.8% Italian (2006-2010 5-year est.).

**Economy:** Single-family building permits issued: 5 (2011); Multi-family building permits issued: 0 (2011); Employment by occupation: 10.6% management, 3.4% professional, 8.5% services, 14.7% sales, 2.9% farming, 9.2% construction, 2.8% production (2006-2010 5-year est.).

**Income:** Per capita income: $22,353 (2006-2010 5-year est.); Median household income: $45,000 (2006-2010 5-year est.); Average household income: $57,027 (2006-2010 5-year est.); Percent of households with income of $100,000 or more: 12.7% (2006-2010 5-year est.); Poverty rate: 11.7% (2006-2010 5-year est.).

**Education:** Percent of population age 25 and over with: High school diploma (including GED) or higher: 90.8% (2006-2010 5-year est.); Bachelor's degree or higher: 32.1% (2006-2010 5-year est.); Master's degree or higher: 11.5% (2006-2010 5-year est.).

**School District(s)**

Naples Central School District (PK-12)

    2009-10 Enrollment: 876 . . . . . . . . . . . . . . . . . . . . . . . . . (585) 374-7901

**Housing:** Homeownership rate: 78.6% (2010); Median home value: $111,900 (2006-2010 5-year est.); Median contract rent: $483 per month (2006-2010 5-year est.); Median year structure built: before 1940 (2006-2010 5-year est.).

**Newspapers:** Naples Record (Local news; Circulation 2,000)

**Transportation:** Commute to work: 80.7% car, 0.7% public transportation, 9.1% walk, 8.4% work from home (2006-2010 5-year est.); Travel time to work: 31.6% less than 15 minutes, 15.8% 15 to 30 minutes, 20.3% 30 to 45 minutes, 19.3% 45 to 60 minutes, 13.0% 60 minutes or more (2006-2010 5-year est.)

## PHELPS (village). Covers a land area of 1.172 square miles and a water area of 0 square miles. Located at 42.95° N. Lat; 77.06° W. Long. Elevation is 522 feet.

**Population:** 1,978 (1990); 1,969 (2000); 1,989 (2010); Density: 1,696.5 persons per square mile (2010); Race: 96.5% White, 0.4% Black, 0.4% Asian, 0.4% American Indian/Alaska Native, 0.0% Native Hawaiian/Other Pacific Islander, 2.3% Other, 2.4% Hispanic of any race (2010); Average household size: 2.33 (2010); Median age: 40.1 (2010); Males per 100 females: 93.5 (2010); Marriage status: 27.2% never married, 43.3% now married, 10.8% widowed, 18.6% divorced (2006-2010 5-year est.); Foreign born: 3.9% (2006-2010 5-year est.); Ancestry (includes multiple ancestries): 25.4% English, 22.5% German, 18.4% Irish, 13.9% Dutch, 8.6% Italian (2006-2010 5-year est.).

**Economy:** Single-family building permits issued: 0 (2011); Multi-family building permits issued: 0 (2011); Employment by occupation: 8.8% management, 3.0% professional, 13.2% services, 14.5% sales, 2.2% farming, 3.1% construction, 3.1% production (2006-2010 5-year est.).

**Income:** Per capita income: $23,136 (2006-2010 5-year est.); Median household income: $42,381 (2006-2010 5-year est.); Average household income: $52,320 (2006-2010 5-year est.); Percent of households with income of $100,000 or more: 8.7% (2006-2010 5-year est.); Poverty rate: 3.8% (2006-2010 5-year est.).

**Education:** Percent of population age 25 and over with: High school diploma (including GED) or higher: 91.4% (2006-2010 5-year est.); Bachelor's degree or higher: 16.7% (2006-2010 5-year est.); Master's degree or higher: 4.9% (2006-2010 5-year est.).

**Housing:** Homeownership rate: 63.9% (2010); Median home value: $111,200 (2006-2010 5-year est.); Median contract rent: $525 per month (2006-2010 5-year est.); Median year structure built: 1948 (2006-2010 5-year est.).

**Safety:** Violent crime rate: 0.0 per 10,000 population; Property crime rate: 5.3 per 10,000 population (2010).

**Transportation:** Commute to work: 95.2% car, 2.9% public transportation, 1.2% walk, 0.7% work from home (2006-2010 5-year est.); Travel time to work: 36.3% less than 15 minutes, 40.7% 15 to 30 minutes, 14.7% 30 to 45 minutes, 4.1% 45 to 60 minutes, 4.1% 60 minutes or more (2006-2010 5-year est.)

**Additional Information Contacts**

Phelps Chamber of Commerce . . . . . . . . . . . . . . . . . . . . . . (315) 548-5481
   http://www.phelpsny.com/chamber-of-commerce
Village of Phelps . . . . . . . . . . . . . . . . . . . . . . . . . . . . . . (315) 548-3861
   http://www.phelpsny.com/village

## PHELPS (town). Covers a land area of 64.951 square miles and a water area of 0.293 square miles. Located at 42.95° N. Lat; 77.04° W. Long. Elevation is 522 feet.

**Population:** 6,749 (1990); 7,017 (2000); 7,072 (2010); Density: 108.9 persons per square mile (2010); Race: 97.1% White, 0.6% Black, 0.4% Asian, 0.3% American Indian/Alaska Native, 0.0% Native Hawaiian/Other Pacific Islander, 1.6% Other, 1.8% Hispanic of any race (2010); Average household size: 2.52 (2010); Median age: 42.9 (2010); Males per 100 females: 98.1 (2010); Marriage status: 26.2% never married, 55.4% now married, 6.8% widowed, 11.6% divorced (2006-2010 5-year est.); Foreign born: 1.9% (2006-2010 5-year est.); Ancestry (includes multiple ancestries): 25.5% German, 21.6% English, 20.1% Irish, 14.1% Dutch, 10.7% Italian (2006-2010 5-year est.).

**Economy:** Single-family building permits issued: 3 (2011); Multi-family building permits issued: 0 (2011); Employment by occupation: 11.1% management, 4.1% professional, 7.2% services, 22.4% sales, 3.2% farming, 14.3% construction, 8.0% production (2006-2010 5-year est.).

**Income:** Per capita income: $29,042 (2006-2010 5-year est.); Median household income: $65,484 (2006-2010 5-year est.); Average household income: $73,604 (2006-2010 5-year est.); Percent of households with income of $100,000 or more: 21.1% (2006-2010 5-year est.); Poverty rate: 4.0% (2006-2010 5-year est.).

**Education:** Percent of population age 25 and over with: High school diploma (including GED) or higher: 90.8% (2006-2010 5-year est.); Bachelor's degree or higher: 19.1% (2006-2010 5-year est.); Master's degree or higher: 6.0% (2006-2010 5-year est.).

**Housing:** Homeownership rate: 79.6% (2010); Median home value: $113,700 (2006-2010 5-year est.); Median contract rent: $526 per month (2006-2010 5-year est.); Median year structure built: 1965 (2006-2010 5-year est.).

**Transportation:** Commute to work: 95.5% car, 0.7% public transportation, 1.2% walk, 0.9% work from home (2006-2010 5-year est.); Travel time to work: 37.8% less than 15 minutes, 37.2% 15 to 30 minutes, 10.6% 30 to 45 minutes, 6.3% 45 to 60 minutes, 8.1% 60 minutes or more (2006-2010 5-year est.)

## PORT GIBSON (CDP). Covers a land area of 1.171 square miles and a water area of 0.032 square miles. Located at 43.03° N. Lat; 77.15° W. Long. Elevation is 476 feet.

**Population:** n/a (1990); n/a (2000); 453 (2010); Density: 386.7 persons per square mile (2010); Race: 95.1% White, 2.6% Black, 0.0% Asian, 0.4% American Indian/Alaska Native, 0.2% Native Hawaiian/Other Pacific Islander, 1.7% Other, 1.5% Hispanic of any race (2010); Average household size: 2.48 (2010); Median age: 44.2 (2010); Males per 100 females: 106.8 (2010); Marriage status: 31.9% never married, 60.1% now married, 8.0% widowed, 0.0% divorced (2006-2010 5-year est.); Foreign born: 0.0% (2006-2010 5-year est.); Ancestry (includes multiple ancestries): 18.2% German, 15.0% Scotch-Irish, 14.8% Polish, 10.3% Italian, 9.0% English (2006-2010 5-year est.).

**Economy:** Employment by occupation: 10.7% management, 0.0% professional, 12.0% services, 11.2% sales, 0.0% farming, 20.2% construction, 24.0% production (2006-2010 5-year est.).

**Income:** Per capita income: $15,619 (2006-2010 5-year est.); Median household income: $35,977 (2006-2010 5-year est.); Average household income: $45,047 (2006-2010 5-year est.); Percent of households with income of $100,000 or more: 0.0% (2006-2010 5-year est.); Poverty rate: 10.9% (2006-2010 5-year est.).

**Education:** Percent of population age 25 and over with: High school diploma (including GED) or higher: 59.0% (2006-2010 5-year est.); Bachelor's degree or higher: 4.3% (2006-2010 5-year est.); Master's degree or higher: 0.0% (2006-2010 5-year est.).

**Housing:** Homeownership rate: 82.7% (2010); Median home value: $82,800 (2006-2010 5-year est.); Median contract rent: n/a per month (2006-2010 5-year est.); Median year structure built: before 1940 (2006-2010 5-year est.).

**Transportation:** Commute to work: 95.8% car, 0.0% public transportation, 0.0% walk, 4.2% work from home (2006-2010 5-year est.); Travel time to work: 37.7% less than 15 minutes, 37.2% 15 to 30 minutes, 16.4% 30 to 45 minutes, 3.9% 45 to 60 minutes, 4.8% 60 minutes or more (2006-2010 5-year est.)

## RICHMOND (town). Covers a land area of 42.432 square miles and a water area of 1.960 square miles. Located at 42.79° N. Lat; 77.52° W. Long. Elevation is 814 feet.

**Population:** 3,230 (1990); 3,452 (2000); 3,361 (2010); Density: 79.2 persons per square mile (2010); Race: 98.1% White, 0.2% Black, 0.6% Asian, 0.0% American Indian/Alaska Native, 0.0% Native Hawaiian/Other Pacific Islander, 1.1% Other, 0.8% Hispanic of any race (2010); Average household size: 2.37 (2010); Median age: 47.3 (2010); Males per 100 females: 105.1 (2010); Marriage status: 21.0% never married, 63.0% now married, 5.5% widowed, 10.4% divorced (2006-2010 5-year est.); Foreign born: 0.8% (2006-2010 5-year est.); Ancestry (includes multiple ancestries): 39.4% German, 28.6% English, 18.2% Irish, 12.0% Italian, 8.2% French (2006-2010 5-year est.).

**Economy:** Single-family building permits issued: 10 (2011); Multi-family building permits issued: 0 (2011); Employment by occupation: 4.6% management, 5.5% professional, 11.0% services, 20.8% sales, 1.7% farming, 16.6% construction, 6.7% production (2006-2010 5-year est.).

**Income:** Per capita income: $24,410 (2006-2010 5-year est.); Median household income: $45,781 (2006-2010 5-year est.); Average household income: $59,894 (2006-2010 5-year est.); Percent of households with income of $100,000 or more: 15.0% (2006-2010 5-year est.); Poverty rate: 15.9% (2006-2010 5-year est.).

**Education:** Percent of population age 25 and over with: High school diploma (including GED) or higher: 97.1% (2006-2010 5-year est.); Bachelor's degree or higher: 29.4% (2006-2010 5-year est.); Master's degree or higher: 11.2% (2006-2010 5-year est.).

**Housing:** Homeownership rate: 83.6% (2010); Median home value: $123,500 (2006-2010 5-year est.); Median contract rent: $582 per month (2006-2010 5-year est.); Median year structure built: 1954 (2006-2010 5-year est.).

**Transportation:** Commute to work: 95.7% car, 0.0% public transportation, 0.5% walk, 3.8% work from home (2006-2010 5-year est.); Travel time to work: 27.3% less than 15 minutes, 24.4% 15 to 30 minutes, 20.5% 30 to 45 minutes, 15.4% 45 to 60 minutes, 12.4% 60 minutes or more (2006-2010 5-year est.)

**SENECA** (town). Covers a land area of 50.450 square miles and a water area of 0 square miles. Located at 42.83° N. Lat; 77.07° W. Long.
**Population:** 2,747 (1990); 2,731 (2000); 2,721 (2010); Density: 53.9 persons per square mile (2010); Race: 95.8% White, 0.5% Black, 0.2% Asian, 0.1% American Indian/Alaska Native, 0.0% Native Hawaiian/Other Pacific Islander, 3.4% Other, 4.3% Hispanic of any race (2010); Average household size: 2.67 (2010); Median age: 43.9 (2010); Males per 100 females: 110.1 (2010); Marriage status: 23.0% never married, 63.1% now married, 4.6% widowed, 9.3% divorced (2006-2010 5-year est.); Foreign born: 0.5% (2006-2010 5-year est.); Ancestry (includes multiple ancestries): 34.3% English, 32.4% German, 16.3% Irish, 9.2% Italian, 9.0% Dutch (2006-2010 5-year est.).
**Economy:** Single-family building permits issued: 4 (2011); Multi-family building permits issued: 0 (2011); Employment by occupation: 15.7% management, 2.5% professional, 9.5% services, 20.6% sales, 1.7% farming, 6.6% construction, 2.3% production (2006-2010 5-year est.).
**Income:** Per capita income: $24,199 (2006-2010 5-year est.); Median household income: $56,462 (2006-2010 5-year est.); Average household income: $65,769 (2006-2010 5-year est.); Percent of households with income of $100,000 or more: 17.2% (2006-2010 5-year est.); Poverty rate: 5.7% (2006-2010 5-year est.).
**Education:** Percent of population age 25 and over with: High school diploma (including GED) or higher: 92.9% (2006-2010 5-year est.); Bachelor's degree or higher: 25.8% (2006-2010 5-year est.); Master's degree or higher: 7.6% (2006-2010 5-year est.).
**Housing:** Homeownership rate: 84.2% (2010); Median home value: $113,900 (2006-2010 5-year est.); Median contract rent: $489 per month (2006-2010 5-year est.); Median year structure built: before 1940 (2006-2010 5-year est.).
**Transportation:** Commute to work: 83.3% car, 1.2% public transportation, 1.1% walk, 13.9% work from home (2006-2010 5-year est.); Travel time to work: 34.8% less than 15 minutes, 44.4% 15 to 30 minutes, 11.8% 30 to 45 minutes, 6.4% 45 to 60 minutes, 2.5% 60 minutes or more (2006-2010 5-year est.)

**SHORTSVILLE** (village). Covers a land area of 0.667 square miles and a water area of 0 square miles. Located at 42.95° N. Lat; 77.22° W. Long. Elevation is 620 feet.
**Population:** 1,510 (1990); 1,320 (2000); 1,439 (2010); Density: 2,155.5 persons per square mile (2010); Race: 97.5% White, 0.6% Black, 0.4% Asian, 0.5% American Indian/Alaska Native, 0.0% Native Hawaiian/Other Pacific Islander, 1.0% Other, 1.6% Hispanic of any race (2010); Average household size: 2.51 (2010); Median age: 42.0 (2010); Males per 100 females: 96.3 (2010); Marriage status: 24.9% never married, 57.0% now married, 8.4% widowed, 9.7% divorced (2006-2010 5-year est.); Foreign born: 2.0% (2006-2010 5-year est.); Ancestry (includes multiple ancestries): 22.3% Irish, 19.4% German, 18.5% English, 13.0% Italian, 13.0% Dutch (2006-2010 5-year est.).
**Economy:** Single-family building permits issued: 6 (2011); Multi-family building permits issued: 0 (2011); Employment by occupation: 10.2% management, 2.9% professional, 9.7% services, 8.8% sales, 2.2% farming, 8.6% construction, 6.2% production (2006-2010 5-year est.).
**Income:** Per capita income: $24,676 (2006-2010 5-year est.); Median household income: $54,375 (2006-2010 5-year est.); Average household income: $60,812 (2006-2010 5-year est.); Percent of households with income of $100,000 or more: 12.5% (2006-2010 5-year est.); Poverty rate: 7.0% (2006-2010 5-year est.).
**Education:** Percent of population age 25 and over with: High school diploma (including GED) or higher: 87.9% (2006-2010 5-year est.); Bachelor's degree or higher: 21.3% (2006-2010 5-year est.); Master's degree or higher: 2.8% (2006-2010 5-year est.).
**School District(s)**
Manchester-Shortsville Central School District (re (PK-12)
    2009-10 Enrollment: 893 . . . . . . . . . . . . . . . . . . . . . . . . . (585) 289-3964
**Housing:** Homeownership rate: 78.6% (2010); Median home value: $99,000 (2006-2010 5-year est.); Median contract rent: $538 per month (2006-2010 5-year est.); Median year structure built: before 1940 (2006-2010 5-year est.).

**Safety:** Violent crime rate: 0.0 per 10,000 population; Property crime rate: 0.0 per 10,000 population (2010).
**Transportation:** Commute to work: 96.1% car, 0.0% public transportation, 1.1% walk, 2.4% work from home (2006-2010 5-year est.); Travel time to work: 28.8% less than 15 minutes, 42.3% 15 to 30 minutes, 23.3% 30 to 45 minutes, 5.1% 45 to 60 minutes, 0.5% 60 minutes or more (2006-2010 5-year est.)

**SOUTH BRISTOL** (town). Covers a land area of 38.972 square miles and a water area of 3.050 square miles. Located at 42.69° N. Lat; 77.40° W. Long. Elevation is 1,086 feet.
**Population:** 1,663 (1990); 1,645 (2000); 1,590 (2010); Density: 40.8 persons per square mile (2010); Race: 97.9% White, 0.2% Black, 0.3% Asian, 0.0% American Indian/Alaska Native, 0.1% Native Hawaiian/Other Pacific Islander, 1.5% Other, 1.5% Hispanic of any race (2010); Average household size: 2.24 (2010); Median age: 51.2 (2010); Males per 100 females: 100.3 (2010); Marriage status: 19.2% never married, 60.9% now married, 3.5% widowed, 16.4% divorced (2006-2010 5-year est.); Foreign born: 2.1% (2006-2010 5-year est.); Ancestry (includes multiple ancestries): 33.1% German, 23.8% English, 20.4% Irish, 12.6% Italian, 10.2% Polish (2006-2010 5-year est.).
**Economy:** Single-family building permits issued: 6 (2011); Multi-family building permits issued: 0 (2011); Employment by occupation: 16.5% management, 1.7% professional, 3.4% services, 12.7% sales, 3.9% farming, 13.0% construction, 3.0% production (2006-2010 5-year est.).
**Income:** Per capita income: $42,752 (2006-2010 5-year est.); Median household income: $55,852 (2006-2010 5-year est.); Average household income: $92,327 (2006-2010 5-year est.); Percent of households with income of $100,000 or more: 23.9% (2006-2010 5-year est.); Poverty rate: 4.0% (2006-2010 5-year est.).
**Education:** Percent of population age 25 and over with: High school diploma (including GED) or higher: 96.7% (2006-2010 5-year est.); Bachelor's degree or higher: 41.6% (2006-2010 5-year est.); Master's degree or higher: 20.3% (2006-2010 5-year est.).
**Housing:** Homeownership rate: 90.4% (2010); Median home value: $185,000 (2006-2010 5-year est.); Median contract rent: $738 per month (2006-2010 5-year est.); Median year structure built: 1975 (2006-2010 5-year est.).
**Transportation:** Commute to work: 87.3% car, 1.4% public transportation, 4.0% walk, 6.5% work from home (2006-2010 5-year est.); Travel time to work: 22.1% less than 15 minutes, 25.6% 15 to 30 minutes, 24.1% 30 to 45 minutes, 16.0% 45 to 60 minutes, 12.2% 60 minutes or more (2006-2010 5-year est.)

**STANLEY** (unincorporated postal area)
Zip Code: 14561
    Covers a land area of 51.876 square miles and a water area of 0 square miles. Located at 42.82° N. Lat; 77.13° W. Long. Elevation is 889 feet.
    Population: 3,086 (2010); Density: 59.5 persons per square mile (2010); Race: 97.0% White, 0.5% Black, 0.3% Asian, 0.1% American Indian/Alaska Native, 0.0% Native Hawaiian/Other Pacific Islander, 2.1% Other, 3.4% Hispanic of any race (2010); Average household size: 2.82 (2010); Median age: 40.4 (2010); Males per 100 females: 104.6 (2010); Homeownership rate: 85.5% (2010)

**VICTOR** (village). Covers a land area of 1.372 square miles and a water area of 0 square miles. Located at 42.98° N. Lat; 77.40° W. Long. Elevation is 577 feet.
**Population:** 2,254 (1990); 2,433 (2000); 2,696 (2010); Density: 1,964.0 persons per square mile (2010); Race: 96.4% White, 0.3% Black, 0.9% Asian, 0.3% American Indian/Alaska Native, 0.0% Native Hawaiian/Other Pacific Islander, 2.1% Other, 1.9% Hispanic of any race (2010); Average household size: 2.47 (2010); Median age: 39.9 (2010); Males per 100 females: 96.4 (2010); Marriage status: 24.9% never married, 60.0% now married, 5.7% widowed, 9.4% divorced (2006-2010 5-year est.); Foreign born: 1.8% (2006-2010 5-year est.); Ancestry (includes multiple ancestries): 33.9% German, 22.0% Irish, 18.0% English, 13.4% Polish, 11.6% Italian (2006-2010 5-year est.).
**Economy:** Employment by occupation: 12.1% management, 7.9% professional, 11.6% services, 10.8% sales, 2.2% farming, 5.3% construction, 1.4% production (2006-2010 5-year est.).
**Income:** Per capita income: $31,577 (2006-2010 5-year est.); Median household income: $65,299 (2006-2010 5-year est.); Average household income: $77,539 (2006-2010 5-year est.); Percent of households with

income of $100,000 or more: 27.4% (2006-2010 5-year est.); Poverty rate: 4.0% (2006-2010 5-year est.).

**Education:** Percent of population age 25 and over with: High school diploma (including GED) or higher: 98.6% (2006-2010 5-year est.); Bachelor's degree or higher: 47.3% (2006-2010 5-year est.); Master's degree or higher: 20.9% (2006-2010 5-year est.).

### School District(s)

Victor Central School District (PK-12)

    2009-10 Enrollment: 4,309 . . . . . . . . . . . . . . . . (585) 924-3252

**Housing:** Homeownership rate: 71.8% (2010); Median home value: $154,700 (2006-2010 5-year est.); Median contract rent: $617 per month (2006-2010 5-year est.); Median year structure built: 1969 (2006-2010 5-year est.).

**Transportation:** Commute to work: 92.6% car, 0.5% public transportation, 1.6% walk, 4.6% work from home (2006-2010 5-year est.); Travel time to work: 27.2% less than 15 minutes, 35.1% 15 to 30 minutes, 32.7% 30 to 45 minutes, 3.8% 45 to 60 minutes, 1.2% 60 minutes or more (2006-2010 5-year est.)

**Additional Information Contacts**

Victor Chamber of Commerce . . . . . . . . . . . . . . . . . . (585) 742-1476
  http://www.victorchamber.com

---

**VICTOR** (town). Covers a land area of 35.917 square miles and a water area of 0.012 square miles. Located at 42.98° N. Lat; 77.42° W. Long. Elevation is 577 feet.

**History:** Incorporated 1879.

**Population:** 7,191 (1990); 9,977 (2000); 14,275 (2010); Density: 397.4 persons per square mile (2010); Race: 95.1% White, 0.8% Black, 2.3% Asian, 0.2% American Indian/Alaska Native, 0.0% Native Hawaiian/Other Pacific Islander, 1.6% Other, 1.9% Hispanic of any race (2010); Average household size: 2.60 (2010); Median age: 42.3 (2010); Males per 100 females: 95.5 (2010); Marriage status: 21.7% never married, 65.7% now married, 4.7% widowed, 7.9% divorced (2006-2010 5-year est.); Foreign born: 2.9% (2006-2010 5-year est.); Ancestry (includes multiple ancestries): 29.1% German, 20.8% English, 18.3% Irish, 17.5% Italian, 8.1% Polish (2006-2010 5-year est.).

**Economy:** Single-family building permits issued: 43 (2011); Multi-family building permits issued: 0 (2011); Employment by occupation: 19.3% management, 5.5% professional, 6.5% services, 14.3% sales, 2.3% farming, 5.1% construction, 2.6% production (2006-2010 5-year est.).

**Income:** Per capita income: $42,401 (2006-2010 5-year est.); Median household income: $85,392 (2006-2010 5-year est.); Average household income: $109,563 (2006-2010 5-year est.); Percent of households with income of $100,000 or more: 41.6% (2006-2010 5-year est.); Poverty rate: 1.7% (2006-2010 5-year est.).

**Education:** Percent of population age 25 and over with: High school diploma (including GED) or higher: 98.4% (2006-2010 5-year est.); Bachelor's degree or higher: 52.4% (2006-2010 5-year est.); Master's degree or higher: 24.4% (2006-2010 5-year est.).

### School District(s)

Victor Central School District (PK-12)

    2009-10 Enrollment: 4,309 . . . . . . . . . . . . . . . . (585) 924-3252

**Housing:** Homeownership rate: 82.5% (2010); Median home value: $214,000 (2006-2010 5-year est.); Median contract rent: $686 per month (2006-2010 5-year est.); Median year structure built: 1991 (2006-2010 5-year est.).

**Transportation:** Commute to work: 93.7% car, 0.1% public transportation, 1.0% walk, 5.1% work from home (2006-2010 5-year est.); Travel time to work: 33.5% less than 15 minutes, 39.2% 15 to 30 minutes, 22.1% 30 to 45 minutes, 2.9% 45 to 60 minutes, 2.3% 60 minutes or more (2006-2010 5-year est.)

**Additional Information Contacts**

Town of Victor . . . . . . . . . . . . . . . . . . . . . . . . . . . (585) 742-5080
  http://www.victorny.org

---

**WEST BLOOMFIELD** (town). Covers a land area of 25.461 square miles and a water area of 0.038 square miles. Located at 42.89° N. Lat; 77.50° W. Long. Elevation is 948 feet.

**Population:** 2,536 (1990); 2,549 (2000); 2,466 (2010); Density: 96.9 persons per square mile (2010); Race: 97.7% White, 0.3% Black, 0.4% Asian, 0.4% American Indian/Alaska Native, 0.0% Native Hawaiian/Other Pacific Islander, 1.2% Other, 0.9% Hispanic of any race (2010); Average household size: 2.36 (2010); Median age: 46.9 (2010); Males per 100 females: 100.8 (2010); Marriage status: 26.1% never married, 53.1% now married, 7.3% widowed, 13.5% divorced (2006-2010 5-year est.); Foreign

born: 5.2% (2006-2010 5-year est.); Ancestry (includes multiple ancestries): 36.1% German, 25.2% Irish, 21.8% English, 9.9% Italian, 8.0% Dutch (2006-2010 5-year est.).

**Economy:** Single-family building permits issued: 3 (2011); Multi-family building permits issued: 0 (2011); Employment by occupation: 14.4% management, 5.1% professional, 7.3% services, 14.4% sales, 2.4% farming, 11.5% construction, 6.8% production (2006-2010 5-year est.).

**Income:** Per capita income: $35,067 (2006-2010 5-year est.); Median household income: $47,778 (2006-2010 5-year est.); Average household income: $76,405 (2006-2010 5-year est.); Percent of households with income of $100,000 or more: 22.0% (2006-2010 5-year est.); Poverty rate: 7.7% (2006-2010 5-year est.).

**Education:** Percent of population age 25 and over with: High school diploma (including GED) or higher: 88.7% (2006-2010 5-year est.); Bachelor's degree or higher: 30.0% (2006-2010 5-year est.); Master's degree or higher: 9.3% (2006-2010 5-year est.).

**Housing:** Homeownership rate: 87.6% (2010); Median home value: $134,600 (2006-2010 5-year est.); Median contract rent: $615 per month (2006-2010 5-year est.); Median year structure built: 1973 (2006-2010 5-year est.).

**Transportation:** Commute to work: 89.0% car, 1.3% public transportation, 3.5% walk, 3.1% work from home (2006-2010 5-year est.); Travel time to work: 25.2% less than 15 minutes, 31.4% 15 to 30 minutes, 32.6% 30 to 45 minutes, 6.1% 45 to 60 minutes, 4.7% 60 minutes or more (2006-2010 5-year est.)

# Orange County

Located in southeastern New York; bounded on the east by the Hudson River, and on the southwest by the Delaware River and the New Jersey and Pennsylvania borders; includes parts of the Hudson highlands, the Ramapos, and the Shawangunk Range. Covers a land area of 816.34 square miles, a water area of 22.21 square miles, and is located in the Eastern Time Zone at 41.40° N. Lat., 74.27° W. Long. The county was founded in 1683. County seat is Goshen.

Orange County is part of the Poughkeepsie-Newburgh-Middletown, NY Metropolitan Statistical Area. The entire metro area includes: Dutchess County, NY; Orange County, NY

| Weather Station: Middletown 2 NW | | | | | | | | | | Elevation: 700 feet | | |
|---|---|---|---|---|---|---|---|---|---|---|---|---|
| | Jan | Feb | Mar | Apr | May | Jun | Jul | Aug | Sep | Oct | Nov | Dec |
| High | 35 | 39 | 48 | 61 | 72 | 79 | 83 | 82 | 75 | 63 | 51 | 40 |
| Low | 19 | 20 | 28 | 39 | 49 | 58 | 63 | 62 | 54 | 43 | 34 | 25 |
| Precip | 2.7 | 2.3 | 3.1 | 4.0 | 4.1 | 4.5 | 4.0 | 4.0 | 4.2 | 3.8 | 3.6 | 3.1 |
| Snow | na | na | na | tr | 0.0 | 0.0 | 0.0 | 0.0 | 0.0 | 0.0 | 0.2 | na |

*High and Low temperatures in degrees Fahrenheit; Precipitation and Snow in inches*

| Weather Station: Port Jervis | | | | | | | | | | Elevation: 470 feet | | |
|---|---|---|---|---|---|---|---|---|---|---|---|---|
| | Jan | Feb | Mar | Apr | May | Jun | Jul | Aug | Sep | Oct | Nov | Dec |
| High | 35 | 39 | 48 | 62 | 73 | 80 | 84 | 82 | 74 | 62 | 51 | 39 |
| Low | 17 | 19 | 26 | 37 | 47 | 56 | 61 | 60 | 52 | 40 | 32 | 22 |
| Precip | 3.0 | 2.7 | 3.7 | 4.0 | 4.0 | 4.3 | 4.0 | 3.8 | 4.5 | 4.2 | 3.6 | 3.6 |
| Snow | 12.2 | 9.4 | 7.1 | 1.7 | 0.0 | 0.0 | 0.0 | 0.0 | 0.0 | tr | 2.0 | 9.3 |

*High and Low temperatures in degrees Fahrenheit; Precipitation and Snow in inches*

| Weather Station: Walden 1 ESE | | | | | | | | | | Elevation: 379 feet | | |
|---|---|---|---|---|---|---|---|---|---|---|---|---|
| | Jan | Feb | Mar | Apr | May | Jun | Jul | Aug | Sep | Oct | Nov | Dec |
| High | 34 | 38 | 46 | 59 | 70 | 78 | 83 | 81 | 74 | 62 | 51 | 39 |
| Low | 14 | 17 | 25 | 36 | 46 | 55 | 60 | 58 | 50 | 38 | 30 | 21 |
| Precip | 2.9 | 2.5 | 3.6 | 3.9 | 4.1 | 4.4 | 4.0 | 3.8 | 4.1 | 4.0 | 3.6 | 3.4 |
| Snow | 12.6 | 9.0 | 8.2 | 1.3 | 0.0 | 0.0 | 0.0 | 0.0 | 0.0 | tr | 1.5 | 8.6 |

*High and Low temperatures in degrees Fahrenheit; Precipitation and Snow in inches*

| Weather Station: West Point | | | | | | | | | | Elevation: 319 feet | | |
|---|---|---|---|---|---|---|---|---|---|---|---|---|
| | Jan | Feb | Mar | Apr | May | Jun | Jul | Aug | Sep | Oct | Nov | Dec |
| High | 36 | 39 | 48 | 61 | 72 | 80 | 85 | 83 | 75 | 63 | 52 | 40 |
| Low | 21 | 23 | 30 | 40 | 50 | 59 | 64 | 63 | 55 | 45 | 36 | 26 |
| Precip | 3.6 | 2.8 | 3.9 | 4.2 | 4.1 | 4.6 | 4.5 | 4.4 | 4.5 | 4.8 | 4.4 | 4.1 |
| Snow | 11.5 | 9.4 | 5.8 | 0.0 | 0.0 | 0.0 | 0.0 | 0.0 | 0.0 | tr | 0.8 | 5.7 |

*High and Low temperatures in degrees Fahrenheit; Precipitation and Snow in inches*

**Population:** 307,647 (1990); 341,367 (2000); 372,813 (2010); Race: 77.2% White, 10.2% Black, 2.4% Asian, 0.5% American Indian/Alaska Native, 0.0% Native Hawaiian/Other Pacific Islander, 9.7% Other, 18.0% Hispanic of any race (2010); Density: 456.7 persons per square mile

(2010); Average household size: 2.86 (2010); Median age: 36.6 (2010); Males per 100 females: 99.9 (2010).

**Religion:** Six largest groups: 35.2% Catholicism, 6.5% Judaism, 2.1% Methodist/Pietist, 1.9% Presbyterian-Reformed, 1.2% Lutheran, 1.1% Pentecostal (2010)

**Economy:** Unemployment rate: 8.5% (February 2012); Total civilian labor force: 173,914 (February 2012); Leading industries: 21.2% retail trade; 18.9% health care and social assistance; 8.1% accommodation & food services (2009); Farms: 642 totaling 80,990 acres (2007); Companies that employ 500 or more persons: 9 (2009); Companies that employ 100 to 499 persons: 134 (2009); Companies that employ less than 100 persons: 9,094 (2009); Black-owned businesses: 2,358 (2007); Hispanic-owned businesses: 2,282 (2007); Asian-owned businesses: 1,150 (2007); Women-owned businesses: 9,374 (2007); Retail sales per capita: $14,581 (2010). Single-family building permits issued: 381 (2011); Multi-family building permits issued: 512 (2011).

**Income:** Per capita income: $28,944 (2006-2010 5-year est.); Median household income: $69,523 (2006-2010 5-year est.); Average household income: $83,948 (2006-2010 5-year est.); Percent of households with income of $100,000 or more: 31.9% (2006-2010 5-year est.); Poverty rate: 11.1% (2006-2010 5-year est.); Bankruptcy rate: 3.58% (2011).

**Taxes:** Total county taxes per capita: $970 (2009); County property taxes per capita: $369 (2009).

**Education:** Percent of population age 25 and over with: High school diploma (including GED) or higher: 86.7% (2006-2010 5-year est.); Bachelor's degree or higher: 27.7% (2006-2010 5-year est.); Master's degree or higher: 11.7% (2006-2010 5-year est.).

**Housing:** Homeownership rate: 68.9% (2010); Median home value: $312,100 (2006-2010 5-year est.); Median contract rent: $877 per month (2006-2010 5-year est.); Median year structure built: 1969 (2006-2010 5-year est.)

**Health:** Birth rate: 136.0 per 10,000 population (2011); Death rate: 66.1 per 10,000 population (2011); Age-adjusted cancer mortality rate: 190.5 deaths per 100,000 population (2009); Number of physicians: 21.6 per 10,000 population (2008); Hospital beds: 31.2 per 10,000 population (2007); Hospital admissions: 1,141.9 per 10,000 population (2007).

**Environment:** Air Quality Index: 84.8% good, 14.6% moderate, 0.6% unhealthy for sensitive individuals, 0.0% unhealthy (percent of days in 2010)

**Elections:** 2008 Presidential election results: 51.5% Obama, 47.4% McCain, 0.5% Nader

**National and State Parks:** Hudson Highlands State Park; Storm King State Park

**Additional Information Contacts**

| | |
|---|---|
| Orange County Government | (845) 291-2690 |
| http://www.co.orange.ny.us | |
| City of Middletown | (845) 346-4166 |
| http://www.middletown-ny.com | |
| City of Newburgh | (845) 569-7311 |
| http://www.cityofnewburgh-ny.gov | |
| City of Port Jervis | (845) 858-4014 |
| http://portjervisny.org | |
| Goshen Chamber of Commerce | (845) 294-7741 |
| http://www.goshennychamber.com | |
| Orange County Chamber of Commerce | (845) 457-9700 |
| http://www.orangeny.org | |
| Town of Cornwall | (845) 534-9100 |
| http://www.cornwallny.com | |
| Town of Crawford | (845) 744-2029 |
| http://townofcrawford.org | |
| Town of Goshen | (845) 294-6250 |
| http://www.townofgoshen.org | |
| Town of Hamptonburgh | (845) 427-2424 |
| http://townofhamptonburgh.org/content | |
| Town of Monroe | (845) 783-1900 |
| http://www.monroeny.org | |
| Town of New Windsor | (845) 563-4611 |
| http://town.new-windsor.ny.us | |
| Town of Tuxedo | (845) 351-4411 |
| http://www.tuxedogov.org | |
| Town of Wallkill | (845) 692-7800 |
| http://www.townofwallkill.com | |
| Tri-State Chamber of Commerce | (845) 856-6694 |
| http://www.tristatechamber.org | |
| Village of Maybrook | (845) 427-2717 |
| http://www.villageofmaybrook.com | |
| Village of Otisville | (845) 386-5172 |
| http://villageofotisville.com | |
| Village of Washingtonville | (845) 496-3221 |
| Warwick Valley Chamber of Commerce | (845) 986-2720 |
| http://www.warwickcc.org | |
| Warwick Valley Chamber of Commerce | (845) 986-2720 |
| http://www.warwickcc.org/category/greenwood-lake | |

## Orange County Communities

**ARDEN** (unincorporated postal area)
Zip Code: 10910

Covers a land area of 2.080 square miles and a water area of 0.042 square miles. Located at 41.28° N. Lat; 74.13° W. Long. Elevation is 512 feet. Population: 21 (2010); Density: 10.1 persons per square mile (2010); Race: 76.2% White, 0.0% Black, 23.8% Asian, 0.0% American Indian/Alaska Native, 0.0% Native Hawaiian/Other Pacific Islander, 0.0% Other, 0.0% Hispanic of any race (2010); Average household size: 2.33 (2010); Median age: 42.5 (2010); Males per 100 females: 133.3 (2010); Homeownership rate: 0.0% (2010)

**BALMVILLE** (CDP). Covers a land area of 2.117 square miles and a water area of 0.004 square miles. Located at 41.52° N. Lat; 74.02° W. Long. Elevation is 217 feet.

**Population:** 2,977 (1990); 3,339 (2000); 3,178 (2010); Density: 1,500.9 persons per square mile (2010); Race: 73.1% White, 15.9% Black, 2.6% Asian, 0.3% American Indian/Alaska Native, 0.0% Native Hawaiian/Other Pacific Islander, 8.1% Other, 14.4% Hispanic of any race (2010); Average household size: 2.65 (2010); Median age: 42.7 (2010); Males per 100 females: 96.5 (2010); Marriage status: 21.1% never married, 60.2% now married, 7.4% widowed, 11.2% divorced (2006-2010 5-year est.); Foreign born: 8.5% (2006-2010 5-year est.); Ancestry (includes multiple ancestries): 20.8% Italian, 19.0% Irish, 17.6% German, 11.1% English, 8.5% Polish (2006-2010 5-year est.).

**Economy:** Employment by occupation: 14.0% management, 5.7% professional, 11.0% services, 21.7% sales, 1.9% farming, 4.0% construction, 5.7% production (2006-2010 5-year est.).

**Income:** Per capita income: $37,607 (2006-2010 5-year est.); Median household income: $78,324 (2006-2010 5-year est.); Average household income: $97,591 (2006-2010 5-year est.); Percent of households with income of $100,000 or more: 39.2% (2006-2010 5-year est.); Poverty rate: 6.6% (2006-2010 5-year est.).

**Education:** Percent of population age 25 and over with: High school diploma (including GED) or higher: 92.5% (2006-2010 5-year est.); Bachelor's degree or higher: 35.6% (2006-2010 5-year est.); Master's degree or higher: 19.4% (2006-2010 5-year est.).

**Housing:** Homeownership rate: 79.5% (2010); Median home value: $334,300 (2006-2010 5-year est.); Median contract rent: $924 per month (2006-2010 5-year est.); Median year structure built: 1963 (2006-2010 5-year est.).

**Transportation:** Commute to work: 81.3% car, 10.3% public transportation, 0.0% walk, 6.3% work from home (2006-2010 5-year est.); Travel time to work: 46.4% less than 15 minutes, 17.7% 15 to 30 minutes, 4.8% 30 to 45 minutes, 3.7% 45 to 60 minutes, 27.4% 60 minutes or more (2006-2010 5-year est.)

**BEAVERDAM LAKE-SALISBURY MILLS** (CDP). Covers a land area of 1.811 square miles and a water area of 0.297 square miles. Located at 41.44° N. Lat; 74.11° W. Long.

**Population:** 2,354 (1990); 2,779 (2000); 2,242 (2010); Density: 1,237.5 persons per square mile (2010); Race: 91.3% White, 3.2% Black, 1.5% Asian, 0.3% American Indian/Alaska Native, 0.0% Native Hawaiian/Other Pacific Islander, 3.7% Other, 11.2% Hispanic of any race (2010); Average household size: 3.00 (2010); Median age: 42.4 (2010); Males per 100 females: 95.0 (2010); Marriage status: 19.5% never married, 69.5% now married, 5.4% widowed, 5.5% divorced (2006-2010 5-year est.); Foreign born: 6.9% (2006-2010 5-year est.); Ancestry (includes multiple ancestries): 22.5% Italian, 19.9% Irish, 19.4% German, 15.9% Polish, 4.6% European (2006-2010 5-year est.).

**Economy:** Employment by occupation: 16.9% management, 2.2% professional, 7.7% services, 15.4% sales, 1.2% farming, 18.2% construction, 12.8% production (2006-2010 5-year est.).

**Income:** Per capita income: $30,986 (2006-2010 5-year est.); Median household income: $87,426 (2006-2010 5-year est.); Average household income: $94,160 (2006-2010 5-year est.); Percent of households with

income of $100,000 or more: 42.7% (2006-2010 5-year est.); Poverty rate: 2.3% (2006-2010 5-year est.).

**Education:** Percent of population age 25 and over with: High school diploma (including GED) or higher: 95.5% (2006-2010 5-year est.); Bachelor's degree or higher: 30.1% (2006-2010 5-year est.); Master's degree or higher: 12.4% (2006-2010 5-year est.).

**Housing:** Homeownership rate: 91.1% (2010); Median home value: $347,100 (2006-2010 5-year est.); Median contract rent: $1,654 per month (2006-2010 5-year est.); Median year structure built: 1968 (2006-2010 5-year est.).

**Transportation:** Commute to work: 98.8% car, 1.2% public transportation, 0.0% walk, 0.0% work from home (2006-2010 5-year est.); Travel time to work: 24.2% less than 15 minutes, 23.5% 15 to 30 minutes, 14.3% 30 to 45 minutes, 23.7% 45 to 60 minutes, 14.4% 60 minutes or more (2006-2010 5-year est.)

**BLOOMING GROVE** (town). Covers a land area of 34.736 square miles and a water area of 0.616 square miles. Located at 41.39° N. Lat; 74.18° W. Long. Elevation is 358 feet.

**Population:** 16,651 (1990); 17,351 (2000); 18,028 (2010); Density: 519.0 persons per square mile (2010); Race: 84.5% White, 6.2% Black, 2.2% Asian, 0.5% American Indian/Alaska Native, 0.0% Native Hawaiian/Other Pacific Islander, 6.6% Other, 15.0% Hispanic of any race (2010); Average household size: 2.86 (2010); Median age: 40.8 (2010); Males per 100 females: 97.1 (2010); Marriage status: 26.4% never married, 58.8% now married, 5.1% widowed, 9.7% divorced (2006-2010 5-year est.); Foreign born: 7.3% (2006-2010 5-year est.); Ancestry (includes multiple ancestries): 26.6% Irish, 21.7% Italian, 16.1% German, 6.5% American, 6.4% English (2006-2010 5-year est.).

**Economy:** Single-family building permits issued: 5 (2011); Multi-family building permits issued: 0 (2011); Employment by occupation: 11.8% management, 3.8% professional, 3.5% services, 20.4% sales, 5.0% farming, 9.0% construction, 4.1% production (2006-2010 5-year est.).

**Income:** Per capita income: $31,930 (2006-2010 5-year est.); Median household income: $85,967 (2006-2010 5-year est.); Average household income: $90,991 (2006-2010 5-year est.); Percent of households with income of $100,000 or more: 39.3% (2006-2010 5-year est.); Poverty rate: 6.4% (2006-2010 5-year est.).

**Education:** Percent of population age 25 and over with: High school diploma (including GED) or higher: 91.4% (2006-2010 5-year est.); Bachelor's degree or higher: 25.6% (2006-2010 5-year est.); Master's degree or higher: 10.1% (2006-2010 5-year est.).

**Housing:** Homeownership rate: 84.2% (2010); Median home value: $332,500 (2006-2010 5-year est.); Median contract rent: $867 per month (2006-2010 5-year est.); Median year structure built: 1973 (2006-2010 5-year est.).

**Transportation:** Commute to work: 91.7% car, 3.7% public transportation, 0.1% walk, 3.4% work from home (2006-2010 5-year est.); Travel time to work: 15.5% less than 15 minutes, 22.9% 15 to 30 minutes, 18.6% 30 to 45 minutes, 13.3% 45 to 60 minutes, 29.7% 60 minutes or more (2006-2010 5-year est.)

**BULLVILLE** (unincorporated postal area)

Zip Code: 10915

Covers a land area of 0.144 square miles and a water area of 0 square miles. Located at 41.54° N. Lat; 74.35° W. Long. Elevation is 515 feet. Population: 119 (2010); Density: 824.3 persons per square mile (2010); Race: 89.1% White, 5.9% Black, 0.0% Asian, 0.0% American Indian/Alaska Native, 0.0% Native Hawaiian/Other Pacific Islander, 5.0% Other, 7.6% Hispanic of any race (2010); Average household size: 2.57 (2010); Median age: 39.8 (2010); Males per 100 females: 124.5 (2010); Homeownership rate: 63.6% (2010)

**CAMPBELL HALL** (unincorporated postal area)

Zip Code: 10916

Covers a land area of 20.200 square miles and a water area of 0.090 square miles. Located at 41.44° N. Lat; 74.25° W. Long. Elevation is 400 feet. Population: 4,540 (2010); Density: 224.7 persons per square mile (2010); Race: 90.4% White, 3.6% Black, 2.0% Asian, 0.3% American Indian/Alaska Native, 0.0% Native Hawaiian/Other Pacific Islander, 3.7% Other, 8.5% Hispanic of any race (2010); Average household size: 3.07 (2010); Median age: 41.6 (2010); Males per 100 females: 97.8 (2010); Homeownership rate: 90.3% (2010)

**CHESTER** (village). Covers a land area of 2.148 square miles and a water area of 0 square miles. Located at 41.35° N. Lat; 74.27° W. Long. Elevation is 479 feet.

**Population:** 3,270 (1990); 3,445 (2000); 3,969 (2010); Density: 1,847.6 persons per square mile (2010); Race: 69.8% White, 11.8% Black, 6.2% Asian, 0.6% American Indian/Alaska Native, 0.0% Native Hawaiian/Other Pacific Islander, 11.6% Other, 17.6% Hispanic of any race (2010); Average household size: 2.52 (2010); Median age: 37.9 (2010); Males per 100 females: 94.6 (2010); Marriage status: 24.9% never married, 58.6% now married, 2.7% widowed, 13.8% divorced (2006-2010 5-year est.); Foreign born: 14.3% (2006-2010 5-year est.); Ancestry (includes multiple ancestries): 23.6% Irish, 18.2% Italian, 12.7% German, 5.9% Polish, 4.1% Haitian (2006-2010 5-year est.).

**Economy:** Single-family building permits issued: 0 (2011); Multi-family building permits issued: 0 (2011); Employment by occupation: 12.0% management, 5.9% professional, 7.8% services, 15.3% sales, 5.5% farming, 7.5% construction, 3.7% production (2006-2010 5-year est.).

**Income:** Per capita income: $34,143 (2006-2010 5-year est.); Median household income: $75,856 (2006-2010 5-year est.); Average household income: $81,343 (2006-2010 5-year est.); Percent of households with income of $100,000 or more: 25.7% (2006-2010 5-year est.); Poverty rate: 3.0% (2006-2010 5-year est.).

**Education:** Percent of population age 25 and over with: High school diploma (including GED) or higher: 86.2% (2006-2010 5-year est.); Bachelor's degree or higher: 30.3% (2006-2010 5-year est.); Master's degree or higher: 15.2% (2006-2010 5-year est.).

**School District(s)**

Chester Union Free School District (KG-12)

    2009-10 Enrollment: 1,036 . . . . . . . . . . . . . . . . . . . . . . . (845) 469-5052

**Housing:** Homeownership rate: 66.4% (2010); Median home value: $265,700 (2006-2010 5-year est.); Median contract rent: $963 per month (2006-2010 5-year est.); Median year structure built: 1982 (2006-2010 5-year est.).

**Safety:** Violent crime rate: 11.3 per 10,000 population; Property crime rate: 417.1 per 10,000 population (2010).

**Transportation:** Commute to work: 88.7% car, 6.4% public transportation, 1.9% walk, 2.6% work from home (2006-2010 5-year est.); Travel time to work: 21.0% less than 15 minutes, 24.1% 15 to 30 minutes, 19.7% 30 to 45 minutes, 9.4% 45 to 60 minutes, 25.8% 60 minutes or more (2006-2010 5-year est.)

**CHESTER** (town). Covers a land area of 25.049 square miles and a water area of 0.150 square miles. Located at 41.33° N. Lat; 74.27° W. Long. Elevation is 479 feet.

**History:** Hambletonian, famous trotter, foaled and buried here. Incorporated 1892.

**Population:** 9,138 (1990); 12,140 (2000); 11,981 (2010); Density: 478.3 persons per square mile (2010); Race: 80.6% White, 7.6% Black, 4.1% Asian, 0.4% American Indian/Alaska Native, 0.0% Native Hawaiian/Other Pacific Islander, 7.3% Other, 13.9% Hispanic of any race (2010); Average household size: 2.85 (2010); Median age: 39.8 (2010); Males per 100 females: 94.7 (2010); Marriage status: 24.6% never married, 61.8% now married, 3.8% widowed, 9.8% divorced (2006-2010 5-year est.); Foreign born: 9.7% (2006-2010 5-year est.); Ancestry (includes multiple ancestries): 26.9% Italian, 26.2% Irish, 16.4% German, 7.0% Polish, 5.0% English (2006-2010 5-year est.).

**Economy:** Single-family building permits issued: 1 (2011); Multi-family building permits issued: 0 (2011); Employment by occupation: 16.3% management, 6.1% professional, 6.6% services, 18.0% sales, 5.4% farming, 6.3% construction, 3.3% production (2006-2010 5-year est.).

**Income:** Per capita income: $38,236 (2006-2010 5-year est.); Median household income: $90,915 (2006-2010 5-year est.); Average household income: $103,100 (2006-2010 5-year est.); Percent of households with income of $100,000 or more: 44.1% (2006-2010 5-year est.); Poverty rate: 2.8% (2006-2010 5-year est.).

**Education:** Percent of population age 25 and over with: High school diploma (including GED) or higher: 91.6% (2006-2010 5-year est.); Bachelor's degree or higher: 36.0% (2006-2010 5-year est.); Master's degree or higher: 13.2% (2006-2010 5-year est.).

**School District(s)**

Chester Union Free School District (KG-12)

    2009-10 Enrollment: 1,036 . . . . . . . . . . . . . . . . . . . . . . . (845) 469-5052

**Housing:** Homeownership rate: 83.2% (2010); Median home value: $325,500 (2006-2010 5-year est.); Median contract rent: $1,016 per month

(2006-2010 5-year est.); Median year structure built: 1982 (2006-2010 5-year est.).
**Safety:** Violent crime rate: 0.0 per 10,000 population; Property crime rate: 61.2 per 10,000 population (2010).
**Transportation:** Commute to work: 81.3% car, 10.2% public transportation, 2.2% walk, 6.0% work from home (2006-2010 5-year est.); Travel time to work: 18.8% less than 15 minutes, 22.9% 15 to 30 minutes, 17.4% 30 to 45 minutes, 9.2% 45 to 60 minutes, 31.8% 60 minutes or more (2006-2010 5-year est.)

## CIRCLEVILLE (unincorporated postal area)
Zip Code: 10919
Covers a land area of 4.116 square miles and a water area of 0.019 square miles. Located at 41.52° N. Lat; 74.38° W. Long. Elevation is 617 feet. Population: 1,040 (2010); Density: 252.6 persons per square mile (2010); Race: 85.7% White, 4.1% Black, 2.7% Asian, 0.7% American Indian/Alaska Native, 0.0% Native Hawaiian/Other Pacific Islander, 6.8% Other, 15.3% Hispanic of any race (2010); Average household size: 2.87 (2010); Median age: 40.7 (2010); Males per 100 females: 103.1 (2010); Homeownership rate: 83.6% (2010)

## CORNWALL (town). Aka Cornwall-on-Hudson. Covers a land area of 26.652 square miles and a water area of 1.479 square miles. Located at 41.41° N. Lat; 74.06° W. Long.
**History:** Seat of N.Y. Military Academy and private schools. Incorporated 1884.
**Population:** 11,270 (1990); 12,307 (2000); 12,646 (2010); Density: 474.5 persons per square mile (2010); Race: 92.0% White, 2.0% Black, 1.7% Asian, 0.3% American Indian/Alaska Native, 0.1% Native Hawaiian/Other Pacific Islander, 3.9% Other, 8.3% Hispanic of any race (2010); Average household size: 2.64 (2010); Median age: 41.7 (2010); Males per 100 females: 95.2 (2010); Marriage status: 27.1% never married, 57.0% now married, 7.2% widowed, 8.7% divorced (2006-2010 5-year est.); Foreign born: 6.6% (2006-2010 5-year est.); Ancestry (includes multiple ancestries): 33.4% Irish, 26.5% Italian, 16.4% German, 11.8% American, 8.5% English (2006-2010 5-year est.).
**Economy:** Single-family building permits issued: 4 (2011); Multi-family building permits issued: 0 (2011); Employment by occupation: 12.3% management, 6.5% professional, 7.1% services, 14.2% sales, 3.2% farming, 8.2% construction, 5.6% production (2006-2010 5-year est.).
**Income:** Per capita income: $36,658 (2006-2010 5-year est.); Median household income: $76,495 (2006-2010 5-year est.); Average household income: $97,256 (2006-2010 5-year est.); Percent of households with income of $100,000 or more: 35.7% (2006-2010 5-year est.); Poverty rate: 4.1% (2006-2010 5-year est.).
**Education:** Percent of population age 25 and over with: High school diploma (including GED) or higher: 92.7% (2006-2010 5-year est.); Bachelor's degree or higher: 42.9% (2006-2010 5-year est.); Master's degree or higher: 21.4% (2006-2010 5-year est.).
### School District(s)
Cornwall Central School District (KG-12)
2009-10 Enrollment: 3,434 . . . . . . . . . . . . . . . . . . . . (845) 534-8009
**Housing:** Homeownership rate: 72.3% (2010); Median home value: $348,100 (2006-2010 5-year est.); Median contract rent: $926 per month (2006-2010 5-year est.); Median year structure built: 1960 (2006-2010 5-year est.).
**Hospitals:** Saint Luke's Cornwall Hospital - Cornwall Campus (216 beds)
**Safety:** Violent crime rate: 0.0 per 10,000 population; Property crime rate: n/a per 10,000 population (2010).
**Newspapers:** Cornwall Local (Local news; Circulation 3,500)
**Transportation:** Commute to work: 88.3% car, 3.0% public transportation, 2.2% walk, 5.6% work from home (2006-2010 5-year est.); Travel time to work: 22.9% less than 15 minutes, 26.5% 15 to 30 minutes, 18.0% 30 to 45 minutes, 11.6% 45 to 60 minutes, 21.0% 60 minutes or more (2006-2010 5-year est.)
**Additional Information Contacts**
Town of Cornwall . . . . . . . . . . . . . . . . . . . . . . . . . . . . . (845) 534-9100
http://www.cornwallny.com

## CORNWALL ON HUDSON (village). Covers a land area of 1.986 square miles and a water area of 0.104 square miles. Located at 41.43° N. Lat; 74.01° W. Long. Elevation is 167 feet.
**Population:** 3,143 (1990); 3,058 (2000); 3,018 (2010); Density: 1,518.9 persons per square mile (2010); Race: 94.2% White, 1.1% Black, 1.7% Asian, 0.1% American Indian/Alaska Native, 0.0% Native Hawaiian/Other

Pacific Islander, 2.9% Other, 5.7% Hispanic of any race (2010); Average household size: 2.51 (2010); Median age: 42.8 (2010); Males per 100 females: 97.0 (2010); Marriage status: 28.6% never married, 61.8% now married, 2.7% widowed, 7.0% divorced (2006-2010 5-year est.); Foreign born: 2.2% (2006-2010 5-year est.); Ancestry (includes multiple ancestries): 28.8% Irish, 19.1% Italian, 15.5% German, 15.4% American, 11.4% English (2006-2010 5-year est.).
**Economy:** Single-family building permits issued: 1 (2011); Multi-family building permits issued: 0 (2011); Employment by occupation: 15.5% management, 4.7% professional, 8.6% services, 13.1% sales, 3.0% farming, 4.1% construction, 1.8% production (2006-2010 5-year est.).
**Income:** Per capita income: $42,524 (2006-2010 5-year est.); Median household income: $80,972 (2006-2010 5-year est.); Average household income: $105,768 (2006-2010 5-year est.); Percent of households with income of $100,000 or more: 35.1% (2006-2010 5-year est.); Poverty rate: 9.0% (2006-2010 5-year est.).
**Education:** Percent of population age 25 and over with: High school diploma (including GED) or higher: 97.6% (2006-2010 5-year est.); Bachelor's degree or higher: 59.6% (2006-2010 5-year est.); Master's degree or higher: 33.1% (2006-2010 5-year est.).
### School District(s)
Cornwall Central School District (KG-12)
2009-10 Enrollment: 3,434 . . . . . . . . . . . . . . . . . . . . (845) 534-8009
**Housing:** Homeownership rate: 71.3% (2010); Median home value: $359,300 (2006-2010 5-year est.); Median contract rent: $916 per month (2006-2010 5-year est.); Median year structure built: before 1940 (2006-2010 5-year est.).
**Transportation:** Commute to work: 77.0% car, 7.4% public transportation, 3.9% walk, 10.7% work from home (2006-2010 5-year est.); Travel time to work: 28.6% less than 15 minutes, 21.4% 15 to 30 minutes, 16.3% 30 to 45 minutes, 9.2% 45 to 60 minutes, 24.6% 60 minutes or more (2006-2010 5-year est.)

## CRAWFORD (town). Covers a land area of 40.030 square miles and a water area of 0.084 square miles. Located at 41.57° N. Lat; 74.31° W. Long.
**Population:** 6,400 (1990); 7,875 (2000); 9,316 (2010); Density: 232.7 persons per square mile (2010); Race: 89.3% White, 3.9% Black, 1.6% Asian, 0.2% American Indian/Alaska Native, 0.1% Native Hawaiian/Other Pacific Islander, 4.9% Other, 9.9% Hispanic of any race (2010); Average household size: 2.82 (2010); Median age: 40.8 (2010); Males per 100 females: 99.3 (2010); Marriage status: 20.8% never married, 68.7% now married, 4.4% widowed, 6.1% divorced (2006-2010 5-year est.); Foreign born: 5.0% (2006-2010 5-year est.); Ancestry (includes multiple ancestries): 27.4% Irish, 20.6% German, 19.5% Italian, 12.7% American, 8.7% English (2006-2010 5-year est.).
**Economy:** Single-family building permits issued: 3 (2011); Multi-family building permits issued: 0 (2011); Employment by occupation: 11.5% management, 2.6% professional, 4.2% services, 17.0% sales, 2.8% farming, 16.4% construction, 6.7% production (2006-2010 5-year est.).
**Income:** Per capita income: $31,192 (2006-2010 5-year est.); Median household income: $79,512 (2006-2010 5-year est.); Average household income: $85,822 (2006-2010 5-year est.); Percent of households with income of $100,000 or more: 34.5% (2006-2010 5-year est.); Poverty rate: 2.8% (2006-2010 5-year est.).
**Taxes:** Total city taxes per capita: $450 (2009); City property taxes per capita: $396 (2009).
**Education:** Percent of population age 25 and over with: High school diploma (including GED) or higher: 89.5% (2006-2010 5-year est.); Bachelor's degree or higher: 28.6% (2006-2010 5-year est.); Master's degree or higher: 14.5% (2006-2010 5-year est.).
**Housing:** Homeownership rate: 77.3% (2010); Median home value: $342,400 (2006-2010 5-year est.); Median contract rent: $780 per month (2006-2010 5-year est.); Median year structure built: 1976 (2006-2010 5-year est.).
**Safety:** Violent crime rate: 11.6 per 10,000 population; Property crime rate: 70.6 per 10,000 population (2010).
**Transportation:** Commute to work: 89.3% car, 2.5% public transportation, 1.1% walk, 6.3% work from home (2006-2010 5-year est.); Travel time to work: 21.3% less than 15 minutes, 30.1% 15 to 30 minutes, 24.9% 30 to 45 minutes, 7.7% 45 to 60 minutes, 16.0% 60 minutes or more (2006-2010 5-year est.)
**Additional Information Contacts**
Town of Crawford . . . . . . . . . . . . . . . . . . . . . . . . . . . . . (845) 744-2029
http://townofcrawford.org

## CUDDEBACKVILLE (unincorporated postal area)

Zip Code: 12729

Covers a land area of 22.195 square miles and a water area of 0.345 square miles. Located at 41.47° N. Lat; 74.62° W. Long. Elevation is 535 feet. Population: 1,874 (2010); Density: 84.4 persons per square mile (2010); Race: 89.2% White, 2.8% Black, 1.4% Asian, 1.0% American Indian/Alaska Native, 0.1% Native Hawaiian/Other Pacific Islander, 5.5% Other, 7.2% Hispanic of any race (2010); Average household size: 2.68 (2010); Median age: 40.6 (2010); Males per 100 females: 108.2 (2010); Homeownership rate: 73.0% (2010)

## DEERPARK (town). Covers a land area of 66.501 square miles and a water area of 1.451 square miles. Located at 41.44° N. Lat; 74.65° W. Long.

Population: 7,832 (1990); 7,858 (2000); 7,901 (2010); Density: 118.8 persons per square mile (2010); Race: 91.6% White, 2.5% Black, 1.2% Asian, 0.5% American Indian/Alaska Native, 0.0% Native Hawaiian/Other Pacific Islander, 4.2% Other, 6.9% Hispanic of any race (2010); Average household size: 2.63 (2010); Median age: 41.9 (2010); Males per 100 females: 100.1 (2010); Marriage status: 23.8% never married, 56.1% now married, 8.8% widowed, 11.3% divorced (2006-2010 5-year est.); Foreign born: 5.1% (2006-2010 5-year est.); Ancestry (includes multiple ancestries): 27.1% German, 22.7% Irish, 17.6% Italian, 8.6% English, 7.5% Polish (2006-2010 5-year est.).
Economy: Single-family building permits issued: 8 (2011); Multi-family building permits issued: 0 (2011); Employment by occupation: 17.2% management, 0.2% professional, 12.2% services, 16.2% sales, 5.7% farming, 14.1% construction, 8.0% production (2006-2010 5-year est.).
Income: Per capita income: $24,763 (2006-2010 5-year est.); Median household income: $46,760 (2006-2010 5-year est.); Average household income: $61,241 (2006-2010 5-year est.); Percent of households with income of $100,000 or more: 18.3% (2006-2010 5-year est.); Poverty rate: 10.8% (2006-2010 5-year est.).
Education: Percent of population age 25 and over with: High school diploma (including GED) or higher: 84.7% (2006-2010 5-year est.); Bachelor's degree or higher: 14.3% (2006-2010 5-year est.); Master's degree or higher: 7.1% (2006-2010 5-year est.).
Housing: Homeownership rate: 81.7% (2010); Median home value: $200,300 (2006-2010 5-year est.); Median contract rent: $821 per month (2006-2010 5-year est.); Median year structure built: 1978 (2006-2010 5-year est.).
Safety: Violent crime rate: 9.4 per 10,000 population; Property crime rate: 167.2 per 10,000 population (2010).
Transportation: Commute to work: 90.6% car, 2.1% public transportation, 0.4% walk, 6.6% work from home (2006-2010 5-year est.); Travel time to work: 26.0% less than 15 minutes, 27.2% 15 to 30 minutes, 19.4% 30 to 45 minutes, 7.5% 45 to 60 minutes, 19.9% 60 minutes or more (2006-2010 5-year est.)

## FIRTHCLIFFE (CDP). Aka Cornwall. Covers a land area of 2.964 square miles and a water area of 0.035 square miles. Located at 41.44° N. Lat; 74.03° W. Long. Elevation is 299 feet.

Population: 4,377 (1990); 4,970 (2000); 4,949 (2010); Density: 1,669.2 persons per square mile (2010); Race: 91.4% White, 2.6% Black, 1.0% Asian, 0.4% American Indian/Alaska Native, 0.1% Native Hawaiian/Other Pacific Islander, 4.5% Other, 9.6% Hispanic of any race (2010); Average household size: 2.51 (2010); Median age: 40.6 (2010); Males per 100 females: 87.4 (2010); Marriage status: 28.3% never married, 54.8% now married, 8.9% widowed, 8.0% divorced (2006-2010 5-year est.); Foreign born: 10.2% (2006-2010 5-year est.); Ancestry (includes multiple ancestries): 38.9% Irish, 30.2% Italian, 15.0% German, 6.4% American, 6.3% English (2006-2010 5-year est.).
Economy: Employment by occupation: 13.3% management, 6.3% professional, 5.8% services, 18.5% sales, 4.5% farming, 4.7% construction, 4.4% production (2006-2010 5-year est.).
Income: Per capita income: $34,274 (2006-2010 5-year est.); Median household income: $79,550 (2006-2010 5-year est.); Average household income: $90,459 (2006-2010 5-year est.); Percent of households with income of $100,000 or more: 35.1% (2006-2010 5-year est.); Poverty rate: 1.7% (2006-2010 5-year est.).
Education: Percent of population age 25 and over with: High school diploma (including GED) or higher: 89.3% (2006-2010 5-year est.); Bachelor's degree or higher: 36.9% (2006-2010 5-year est.); Master's degree or higher: 17.8% (2006-2010 5-year est.).

Housing: Homeownership rate: 62.7% (2010); Median home value: $309,200 (2006-2010 5-year est.); Median contract rent: $965 per month (2006-2010 5-year est.); Median year structure built: 1967 (2006-2010 5-year est.).
Transportation: Commute to work: 91.3% car, 2.3% public transportation, 1.3% walk, 4.4% work from home (2006-2010 5-year est.); Travel time to work: 24.6% less than 15 minutes, 28.2% 15 to 30 minutes, 19.3% 30 to 45 minutes, 11.3% 45 to 60 minutes, 16.5% 60 minutes or more (2006-2010 5-year est.)

## FLORIDA (village). Covers a land area of 2.251 square miles and a water area of 0.004 square miles. Located at 41.33° N. Lat; 74.35° W. Long. Elevation is 446 feet.

History: William H. Seward was born here.
Population: 2,497 (1990); 2,571 (2000); 2,833 (2010); Density: 1,258.3 persons per square mile (2010); Race: 86.3% White, 5.7% Black, 2.3% Asian, 0.3% American Indian/Alaska Native, 0.0% Native Hawaiian/Other Pacific Islander, 5.4% Other, 14.2% Hispanic of any race (2010); Average household size: 2.75 (2010); Median age: 40.3 (2010); Males per 100 females: 91.0 (2010); Marriage status: 20.9% never married, 58.7% now married, 10.6% widowed, 9.8% divorced (2006-2010 5-year est.); Foreign born: 10.7% (2006-2010 5-year est.); Ancestry (includes multiple ancestries): 21.2% Irish, 20.0% German, 18.8% Italian, 17.3% Polish, 7.9% American (2006-2010 5-year est.).
Economy: Single-family building permits issued: 14 (2011); Multi-family building permits issued: 0 (2011); Employment by occupation: 16.3% management, 3.7% professional, 8.5% services, 26.4% sales, 2.6% farming, 6.2% construction, 2.3% production (2006-2010 5-year est.).
Income: Per capita income: $36,067 (2006-2010 5-year est.); Median household income: $67,115 (2006-2010 5-year est.); Average household income: $85,845 (2006-2010 5-year est.); Percent of households with income of $100,000 or more: 33.9% (2006-2010 5-year est.); Poverty rate: 3.8% (2006-2010 5-year est.).
Education: Percent of population age 25 and over with: High school diploma (including GED) or higher: 91.5% (2006-2010 5-year est.); Bachelor's degree or higher: 26.0% (2006-2010 5-year est.); Master's degree or higher: 9.5% (2006-2010 5-year est.).

**School District(s)**
Florida Union Free School District (KG-12)
   2009-10 Enrollment: 844 . . . . . . . . . . . . . . . . . . . . . . (845) 651-3095
Housing: Homeownership rate: 83.3% (2010); Median home value: $297,400 (2006-2010 5-year est.); Median contract rent: $964 per month (2006-2010 5-year est.); Median year structure built: 1967 (2006-2010 5-year est.).
Transportation: Commute to work: 88.8% car, 3.0% public transportation, 4.7% walk, 1.7% work from home (2006-2010 5-year est.); Travel time to work: 35.7% less than 15 minutes, 29.6% 15 to 30 minutes, 9.2% 30 to 45 minutes, 12.4% 45 to 60 minutes, 13.1% 60 minutes or more (2006-2010 5-year est.)

## FORT MONTGOMERY (CDP). Covers a land area of 1.483 square miles and a water area of 0.030 square miles. Located at 41.34° N. Lat; 73.98° W. Long. Elevation is 161 feet.

Population: 1,586 (1990); 1,418 (2000); 1,571 (2010); Density: 1,058.9 persons per square mile (2010); Race: 86.1% White, 3.6% Black, 1.2% Asian, 0.8% American Indian/Alaska Native, 0.0% Native Hawaiian/Other Pacific Islander, 8.3% Other, 10.9% Hispanic of any race (2010); Average household size: 2.47 (2010); Median age: 43.0 (2010); Males per 100 females: 104.6 (2010); Marriage status: 23.2% never married, 66.0% now married, 6.8% widowed, 4.0% divorced (2006-2010 5-year est.); Foreign born: 8.4% (2006-2010 5-year est.); Ancestry (includes multiple ancestries): 29.7% Irish, 25.4% Italian, 24.8% German, 14.3% Polish, 8.7% English (2006-2010 5-year est.).
Economy: Employment by occupation: 2.6% management, 5.6% professional, 15.5% services, 22.1% sales, 6.0% farming, 8.8% construction, 6.9% production (2006-2010 5-year est.).
Income: Per capita income: $32,922 (2006-2010 5-year est.); Median household income: $75,234 (2006-2010 5-year est.); Average household income: $81,398 (2006-2010 5-year est.); Percent of households with income of $100,000 or more: 29.8% (2006-2010 5-year est.); Poverty rate: 0.9% (2006-2010 5-year est.).
Education: Percent of population age 25 and over with: High school diploma (including GED) or higher: 97.4% (2006-2010 5-year est.); Bachelor's degree or higher: 29.0% (2006-2010 5-year est.); Master's degree or higher: 7.8% (2006-2010 5-year est.).

Highland Falls Central School District (PK-12)
  2009-10 Enrollment: 1,111 ........................ (845) 446-9575
**Housing:** Homeownership rate: 71.1% (2010); Median home value: $232,300 (2006-2010 5-year est.); Median contract rent: $1,125 per month (2006-2010 5-year est.); Median year structure built: 1962 (2006-2010 5-year est.).
**Transportation:** Commute to work: 93.6% car, 5.5% public transportation, 0.9% walk, 0.0% work from home (2006-2010 5-year est.); Travel time to work: 20.3% less than 15 minutes, 25.4% 15 to 30 minutes, 35.1% 30 to 45 minutes, 8.4% 45 to 60 minutes, 10.8% 60 minutes or more (2006-2010 5-year est.)

**GARDNERTOWN** (CDP). Covers a land area of 4.825 square miles and a water area of 0.016 square miles. Located at 41.53° N. Lat; 74.05° W. Long. Elevation is 410 feet.
**Population:** 4,209 (1990); 4,533 (2000); 4,373 (2010); Density: 906.2 persons per square mile (2010); Race: 77.7% White, 9.9% Black, 1.9% Asian, 0.4% American Indian/Alaska Native, 0.0% Native Hawaiian/Other Pacific Islander, 10.1% Other, 16.9% Hispanic of any race (2010); Average household size: 2.76 (2010); Median age: 40.9 (2010); Males per 100 females: 96.9 (2010); Marriage status: 30.7% never married, 52.2% now married, 7.8% widowed, 9.3% divorced (2006-2010 5-year est.); Foreign born: 8.4% (2006-2010 5-year est.); Ancestry (includes multiple ancestries): 19.9% Irish, 17.3% Italian, 12.8% German, 10.9% American, 6.5% English (2006-2010 5-year est.).
**Economy:** Employment by occupation: 15.4% management, 2.1% professional, 6.3% services, 17.5% sales, 4.2% farming, 13.0% construction, 11.9% production (2006-2010 5-year est.).
**Income:** Per capita income: $29,823 (2006-2010 5-year est.); Median household income: $70,406 (2006-2010 5-year est.); Average household income: $80,755 (2006-2010 5-year est.); Percent of households with income of $100,000 or more: 26.5% (2006-2010 5-year est.); Poverty rate: 3.9% (2006-2010 5-year est.).
**Education:** Percent of population age 25 and over with: High school diploma (including GED) or higher: 91.0% (2006-2010 5-year est.); Bachelor's degree or higher: 24.1% (2006-2010 5-year est.); Master's degree or higher: 9.1% (2006-2010 5-year est.).
**Housing:** Homeownership rate: 83.4% (2010); Median home value: $281,800 (2006-2010 5-year est.); Median contract rent: $912 per month (2006-2010 5-year est.); Median year structure built: 1954 (2006-2010 5-year est.).
**Transportation:** Commute to work: 93.9% car, 2.4% public transportation, 0.0% walk, 3.8% work from home (2006-2010 5-year est.); Travel time to work: 37.6% less than 15 minutes, 27.5% 15 to 30 minutes, 12.1% 30 to 45 minutes, 10.4% 45 to 60 minutes, 12.4% 60 minutes or more (2006-2010 5-year est.)

**GOSHEN** (village). County seat. Covers a land area of 3.329 square miles and a water area of 0 square miles. Located at 41.40° N. Lat; 74.32° W. Long. Elevation is 436 feet.
**Population:** 5,255 (1990); 5,676 (2000); 5,454 (2010); Density: 1,637.9 persons per square mile (2010); Race: 84.5% White, 3.7% Black, 2.3% Asian, 0.4% American Indian/Alaska Native, 0.1% Native Hawaiian/Other Pacific Islander, 9.0% Other, 15.3% Hispanic of any race (2010); Average household size: 2.40 (2010); Median age: 41.8 (2010); Males per 100 females: 87.6 (2010); Marriage status: 34.6% never married, 46.4% now married, 7.4% widowed, 11.7% divorced (2006-2010 5-year est.); Foreign born: 11.8% (2006-2010 5-year est.); Ancestry (includes multiple ancestries): 20.3% Italian, 18.2% Irish, 12.3% German, 8.3% English, 4.7% Polish (2006-2010 5-year est.).
**Economy:** Single-family building permits issued: 3 (2011); Multi-family building permits issued: 0 (2011); Employment by occupation: 17.8% management, 5.4% professional, 6.9% services, 15.2% sales, 2.1% farming, 8.0% construction, 3.9% production (2006-2010 5-year est.).
**Income:** Per capita income: $30,362 (2006-2010 5-year est.); Median household income: $77,422 (2006-2010 5-year est.); Average household income: $87,061 (2006-2010 5-year est.); Percent of households with income of $100,000 or more: 36.9% (2006-2010 5-year est.); Poverty rate: 4.0% (2006-2010 5-year est.).
**Taxes:** Total city taxes per capita: $781 (2009); City property taxes per capita: $722 (2009).
**Education:** Percent of population age 25 and over with: High school diploma (including GED) or higher: 87.2% (2006-2010 5-year est.); Bachelor's degree or higher: 30.7% (2006-2010 5-year est.); Master's degree or higher: 15.3% (2006-2010 5-year est.).

Goshen Central School District (KG-12)
  2009-10 Enrollment: 2,973 ........................ (845) 615-6720
Orange-Ulster Boces
  2009-10 Enrollment: n/a ........................ (845) 290-0110
**Vocational/Technical School(s)**
Orange-Ulster BOCES-School of Practical Nursing (Public)
  Fall 2010 Enrollment: 70 ........................ (845) 291-0100
  2011-12 Tuition: $11,202
**Housing:** Homeownership rate: 57.7% (2010); Median home value: $343,400 (2006-2010 5-year est.); Median contract rent: $1,048 per month (2006-2010 5-year est.); Median year structure built: 1955 (2006-2010 5-year est.).
**Hospitals:** Orange Regional Medical Center Arden Hill Campus (174 beds)
**Safety:** Violent crime rate: 5.4 per 10,000 population; Property crime rate: 140.5 per 10,000 population (2010).
**Newspapers:** Independent Republican (Community news; Circulation 3,800)
**Transportation:** Commute to work: 89.1% car, 3.2% public transportation, 3.1% walk, 4.2% work from home (2006-2010 5-year est.); Travel time to work: 40.5% less than 15 minutes, 27.8% 15 to 30 minutes, 8.6% 30 to 45 minutes, 7.9% 45 to 60 minutes, 15.2% 60 minutes or more (2006-2010 5-year est.)
**Additional Information Contacts**
Goshen Chamber of Commerce ........................ (845) 294-7741
  http://www.goshennychamber.com
Orange County Chamber of Commerce ........................ (845) 457-9700
  http://www.orangeny.org

**GOSHEN** (town). Covers a land area of 43.641 square miles and a water area of 0.290 square miles. Located at 41.38° N. Lat; 74.35° W. Long. Elevation is 436 feet.
**History:** Good Time and Historic (or Harriman) harness-racing tracks are here; and the Hambletonian race is held here. Settled during 18th century; incorporated 1809.
**Population:** 11,510 (1990); 12,913 (2000); 13,687 (2010); Density: 313.6 persons per square mile (2010); Race: 82.4% White, 7.1% Black, 2.6% Asian, 0.4% American Indian/Alaska Native, 0.1% Native Hawaiian/Other Pacific Islander, 7.4% Other, 13.6% Hispanic of any race (2010); Average household size: 2.68 (2010); Median age: 41.7 (2010); Males per 100 females: 102.2 (2010); Marriage status: 31.6% never married, 50.2% now married, 7.5% widowed, 10.7% divorced (2006-2010 5-year est.); Foreign born: 11.9% (2006-2010 5-year est.); Ancestry (includes multiple ancestries): 19.5% Irish, 17.6% Italian, 15.6% German, 8.4% English, 6.5% Polish (2006-2010 5-year est.).
**Economy:** Single-family building permits issued: 16 (2011); Multi-family building permits issued: 0 (2011); Employment by occupation: 18.6% management, 4.3% professional, 8.0% services, 16.1% sales, 3.2% farming, 9.9% construction, 3.5% production (2006-2010 5-year est.).
**Income:** Per capita income: $31,485 (2006-2010 5-year est.); Median household income: $86,940 (2006-2010 5-year est.); Average household income: $98,236 (2006-2010 5-year est.); Percent of households with income of $100,000 or more: 43.1% (2006-2010 5-year est.); Poverty rate: 5.4% (2006-2010 5-year est.).
**Education:** Percent of population age 25 and over with: High school diploma (including GED) or higher: 84.4% (2006-2010 5-year est.); Bachelor's degree or higher: 30.9% (2006-2010 5-year est.); Master's degree or higher: 14.1% (2006-2010 5-year est.).
**School District(s)**
Goshen Central School District (KG-12)
  2009-10 Enrollment: 2,973 ........................ (845) 615-6720
Orange-Ulster Boces
  2009-10 Enrollment: n/a ........................ (845) 290-0110
**Vocational/Technical School(s)**
Orange-Ulster BOCES-School of Practical Nursing (Public)
  Fall 2010 Enrollment: 70 ........................ (845) 291-0100
  2011-12 Tuition: $11,202
**Housing:** Homeownership rate: 70.8% (2010); Median home value: $372,500 (2006-2010 5-year est.); Median contract rent: $1,007 per month (2006-2010 5-year est.); Median year structure built: 1967 (2006-2010 5-year est.).
**Hospitals:** Orange Regional Medical Center Arden Hill Campus (174 beds)
**Safety:** Violent crime rate: 4.8 per 10,000 population; Property crime rate: 60.6 per 10,000 population (2010).

**Newspapers:** Independent Republican (Community news; Circulation 3,800)

**Transportation:** Commute to work: 82.0% car, 5.0% public transportation, 1.8% walk, 10.4% work from home (2006-2010 5-year est.); Travel time to work: 33.5% less than 15 minutes, 25.4% 15 to 30 minutes, 12.7% 30 to 45 minutes, 8.5% 45 to 60 minutes, 20.0% 60 minutes or more (2006-2010 5-year est.)

**Additional Information Contacts**

Town of Goshen. . . . . . . . . . . . . . . . . . . . . . . . . . . . . (845) 294-6250
    http://www.townofgoshen.org

**GREENVILLE** (town). Covers a land area of 30.014 square miles and a water area of 0.484 square miles. Located at 41.37° N. Lat; 74.59° W. Long. Elevation is 1,037 feet.

**Population:** 3,145 (1990); 3,800 (2000); 4,616 (2010); Density: 153.8 persons per square mile (2010); Race: 90.6% White, 2.7% Black, 1.5% Asian, 0.3% American Indian/Alaska Native, 0.0% Native Hawaiian/Other Pacific Islander, 4.9% Other, 9.2% Hispanic of any race (2010); Average household size: 3.04 (2010); Median age: 39.4 (2010); Males per 100 females: 103.1 (2010); Marriage status: 24.5% never married, 62.0% now married, 6.1% widowed, 7.4% divorced (2006-2010 5-year est.); Foreign born: 6.0% (2006-2010 5-year est.); Ancestry (includes multiple ancestries): 22.6% Italian, 19.0% Irish, 14.7% German, 11.1% Polish, 6.2% Dutch (2006-2010 5-year est.).

**Economy:** Single-family building permits issued: 10 (2011); Multi-family building permits issued: 0 (2011); Employment by occupation: 8.3% management, 0.0% professional, 9.5% services, 17.8% sales, 4.7% farming, 11.7% construction, 10.2% production (2006-2010 5-year est.).

**Income:** Per capita income: $31,716 (2006-2010 5-year est.); Median household income: $90,396 (2006-2010 5-year est.); Average household income: $97,196 (2006-2010 5-year est.); Percent of households with income of $100,000 or more: 42.2% (2006-2010 5-year est.); Poverty rate: 4.3% (2006-2010 5-year est.).

**Education:** Percent of population age 25 and over with: High school diploma (including GED) or higher: 89.7% (2006-2010 5-year est.); Bachelor's degree or higher: 26.4% (2006-2010 5-year est.); Master's degree or higher: 9.7% (2006-2010 5-year est.).

**Housing:** Homeownership rate: 88.4% (2010); Median home value: $295,900 (2006-2010 5-year est.); Median contract rent: $1,178 per month (2006-2010 5-year est.); Median year structure built: 1983 (2006-2010 5-year est.).

**Transportation:** Commute to work: 94.4% car, 1.6% public transportation, 1.8% walk, 2.2% work from home (2006-2010 5-year est.); Travel time to work: 7.7% less than 15 minutes, 39.5% 15 to 30 minutes, 21.6% 30 to 45 minutes, 8.3% 45 to 60 minutes, 22.8% 60 minutes or more (2006-2010 5-year est.)

**GREENWOOD LAKE** (village). Covers a land area of 2.048 square miles and a water area of 0.424 square miles. Located at 41.22° N. Lat; 74.29° W. Long. Elevation is 630 feet.

**Population:** 3,161 (1990); 3,411 (2000); 3,154 (2010); Density: 1,539.9 persons per square mile (2010); Race: 89.8% White, 2.5% Black, 2.3% Asian, 0.7% American Indian/Alaska Native, 0.0% Native Hawaiian/Other Pacific Islander, 4.7% Other, 12.4% Hispanic of any race (2010); Average household size: 2.46 (2010); Median age: 42.8 (2010); Males per 100 females: 98.4 (2010); Marriage status: 35.9% never married, 51.3% now married, 2.0% widowed, 10.9% divorced (2006-2010 5-year est.); Foreign born: 9.0% (2006-2010 5-year est.); Ancestry (includes multiple ancestries): 34.1% Irish, 21.0% German, 16.1% Italian, 6.3% English, 5.9% Russian (2006-2010 5-year est.).

**Economy:** Single-family building permits issued: 3 (2011); Multi-family building permits issued: 0 (2011); Employment by occupation: 11.4% management, 3.8% professional, 8.8% services, 20.7% sales, 2.8% farming, 8.7% construction, 6.6% production (2006-2010 5-year est.).

**Income:** Per capita income: $33,586 (2006-2010 5-year est.); Median household income: $69,508 (2006-2010 5-year est.); Average household income: $88,458 (2006-2010 5-year est.); Percent of households with income of $100,000 or more: 34.0% (2006-2010 5-year est.); Poverty rate: 11.2% (2006-2010 5-year est.).

**Education:** Percent of population age 25 and over with: High school diploma (including GED) or higher: 91.7% (2006-2010 5-year est.); Bachelor's degree or higher: 20.9% (2006-2010 5-year est.); Master's degree or higher: 4.7% (2006-2010 5-year est.).

**School District(s)**

Greenwood Lake Union Free School District (KG-08)
    2009-10 Enrollment: 596 . . . . . . . . . . . . . . . . . (845) 782-8678

**Housing:** Homeownership rate: 71.0% (2010); Median home value: $301,700 (2006-2010 5-year est.); Median contract rent: $923 per month (2006-2010 5-year est.); Median year structure built: 1948 (2006-2010 5-year est.).

**Safety:** Violent crime rate: 11.8 per 10,000 population; Property crime rate: 150.8 per 10,000 population (2010).

**Newspapers:** Greenwood Lake News/West Milford News (Local news; Circulation 4,000)

**Transportation:** Commute to work: 89.7% car, 3.6% public transportation, 0.0% walk, 6.8% work from home (2006-2010 5-year est.); Travel time to work: 14.8% less than 15 minutes, 19.7% 15 to 30 minutes, 25.0% 30 to 45 minutes, 21.0% 45 to 60 minutes, 19.5% 60 minutes or more (2006-2010 5-year est.)

**Additional Information Contacts**

Warwick Valley Chamber of Commerce . . . . . . . . . . . . . (845) 986-2720
    http://www.warwickcc.org/category/greenwood-lake

**HAMPTONBURGH** (town). Covers a land area of 26.758 square miles and a water area of 0.210 square miles. Located at 41.44° N. Lat; 74.24° W. Long. Elevation is 446 feet.

**Population:** 3,922 (1990); 4,686 (2000); 5,561 (2010); Density: 207.8 persons per square mile (2010); Race: 89.1% White, 3.8% Black, 3.0% Asian, 0.3% American Indian/Alaska Native, 0.0% Native Hawaiian/Other Pacific Islander, 3.8% Other, 8.7% Hispanic of any race (2010); Average household size: 3.12 (2010); Median age: 41.1 (2010); Males per 100 females: 97.5 (2010); Marriage status: 29.7% never married, 62.1% now married, 3.2% widowed, 5.1% divorced (2006-2010 5-year est.); Foreign born: 5.3% (2006-2010 5-year est.); Ancestry (includes multiple ancestries): 27.4% Irish, 25.0% Italian, 18.4% German, 8.0% English, 8.0% Polish (2006-2010 5-year est.).

**Economy:** Single-family building permits issued: 2 (2011); Multi-family building permits issued: 0 (2011); Employment by occupation: 10.6% management, 1.5% professional, 6.3% services, 17.6% sales, 3.9% farming, 14.8% construction, 12.1% production (2006-2010 5-year est.).

**Income:** Per capita income: $35,249 (2006-2010 5-year est.); Median household income: $106,146 (2006-2010 5-year est.); Average household income: $117,305 (2006-2010 5-year est.); Percent of households with income of $100,000 or more: 55.6% (2006-2010 5-year est.); Poverty rate: 3.2% (2006-2010 5-year est.).

**Education:** Percent of population age 25 and over with: High school diploma (including GED) or higher: 94.3% (2006-2010 5-year est.); Bachelor's degree or higher: 35.0% (2006-2010 5-year est.); Master's degree or higher: 16.6% (2006-2010 5-year est.).

**Housing:** Homeownership rate: 89.5% (2010); Median home value: $397,400 (2006-2010 5-year est.); Median contract rent: $876 per month (2006-2010 5-year est.); Median year structure built: 1982 (2006-2010 5-year est.).

**Transportation:** Commute to work: 82.3% car, 10.3% public transportation, 0.9% walk, 6.5% work from home (2006-2010 5-year est.); Travel time to work: 23.5% less than 15 minutes, 29.6% 15 to 30 minutes, 11.6% 30 to 45 minutes, 11.7% 45 to 60 minutes, 23.5% 60 minutes or more (2006-2010 5-year est.)

**Additional Information Contacts**

Town of Hamptonburgh. . . . . . . . . . . . . . . . . . . . . . . . (845) 427-2424
    http://townofhamptonburgh.org/content

**HARRIMAN** (village). Covers a land area of 1.004 square miles and a water area of 0.017 square miles. Located at 41.30° N. Lat; 74.14° W. Long. Elevation is 538 feet.

**Population:** 2,288 (1990); 2,252 (2000); 2,424 (2010); Density: 2,413.8 persons per square mile (2010); Race: 66.9% White, 13.4% Black, 10.4% Asian, 0.7% American Indian/Alaska Native, 0.0% Native Hawaiian/Other Pacific Islander, 8.6% Other, 18.1% Hispanic of any race (2010); Average household size: 2.45 (2010); Median age: 37.1 (2010); Males per 100 females: 94.4 (2010); Marriage status: 25.1% never married, 53.1% now married, 1.7% widowed, 20.2% divorced (2006-2010 5-year est.); Foreign born: 21.6% (2006-2010 5-year est.); Ancestry (includes multiple ancestries): 17.2% Irish, 14.7% Italian, 10.4% German, 9.1% Polish, 7.6% English (2006-2010 5-year est.).

**Economy:** Single-family building permits issued: 0 (2011); Multi-family building permits issued: 18 (2011); Employment by occupation: 9.9% management, 7.0% professional, 7.7% services, 18.2% sales, 2.8% farming, 9.2% construction, 4.6% production (2006-2010 5-year est.).

**Income:** Per capita income: $38,518 (2006-2010 5-year est.); Median household income: $70,000 (2006-2010 5-year est.); Average household income: $83,716 (2006-2010 5-year est.); Percent of households with income of $100,000 or more: 31.2% (2006-2010 5-year est.); Poverty rate: 1.2% (2006-2010 5-year est.).

**Education:** Percent of population age 25 and over with: High school diploma (including GED) or higher: 95.2% (2006-2010 5-year est.); Bachelor's degree or higher: 34.0% (2006-2010 5-year est.); Master's degree or higher: 17.7% (2006-2010 5-year est.).

**School District(s)**

Monroe-Woodbury Central School District (KG-12)

    2009-10 Enrollment: 7,400 . . . . . . . . . . . . . . . . . . . . . . (845) 460-6200

**Housing:** Homeownership rate: 61.7% (2010); Median home value: $275,500 (2006-2010 5-year est.); Median contract rent: $1,125 per month (2006-2010 5-year est.); Median year structure built: 1984 (2006-2010 5-year est.).

**Safety:** Violent crime rate: 4.3 per 10,000 population; Property crime rate: 51.9 per 10,000 population (2010).

**Transportation:** Commute to work: 90.0% car, 7.1% public transportation, 0.6% walk, 2.3% work from home (2006-2010 5-year est.); Travel time to work: 23.2% less than 15 minutes, 16.2% 15 to 30 minutes, 22.1% 30 to 45 minutes, 14.4% 45 to 60 minutes, 24.1% 60 minutes or more (2006-2010 5-year est.)

**HIGHLAND FALLS** (village). Covers a land area of 1.090 square miles and a water area of 0.009 square miles. Located at 41.36° N. Lat; 73.96° W. Long. Elevation is 144 feet.

**Population:** 3,937 (1990); 3,678 (2000); 3,900 (2010); Density: 3,576.7 persons per square mile (2010); Race: 70.4% White, 13.0% Black, 2.3% Asian, 0.8% American Indian/Alaska Native, 0.0% Native Hawaiian/Other Pacific Islander, 13.5% Other, 18.7% Hispanic of any race (2010); Average household size: 2.37 (2010); Median age: 40.2 (2010); Males per 100 females: 97.1 (2010); Marriage status: 40.7% never married, 42.9% now married, 5.6% widowed, 10.7% divorced (2006-2010 5-year est.); Foreign born: 11.5% (2006-2010 5-year est.); Ancestry (includes multiple ancestries): 19.7% Irish, 18.5% German, 16.6% Italian, 11.2% English, 7.3% American (2006-2010 5-year est.).

**Economy:** Employment by occupation: 8.1% management, 5.6% professional, 7.3% services, 15.1% sales, 5.9% farming, 15.9% construction, 8.5% production (2006-2010 5-year est.).

**Income:** Per capita income: $29,006 (2006-2010 5-year est.); Median household income: $65,192 (2006-2010 5-year est.); Average household income: $71,339 (2006-2010 5-year est.); Percent of households with income of $100,000 or more: 26.2% (2006-2010 5-year est.); Poverty rate: 10.9% (2006-2010 5-year est.).

**Education:** Percent of population age 25 and over with: High school diploma (including GED) or higher: 88.6% (2006-2010 5-year est.); Bachelor's degree or higher: 31.7% (2006-2010 5-year est.); Master's degree or higher: 18.0% (2006-2010 5-year est.).

**School District(s)**

Highland Falls Central School District (PK-12)

    2009-10 Enrollment: 1,111 . . . . . . . . . . . . . . . . . . . . (845) 446-9575

**Housing:** Homeownership rate: 49.8% (2010); Median home value: $279,900 (2006-2010 5-year est.); Median contract rent: $852 per month (2006-2010 5-year est.); Median year structure built: before 1940 (2006-2010 5-year est.).

**Safety:** Violent crime rate: 0.0 per 10,000 population; Property crime rate: 127.9 per 10,000 population (2010).

**Newspapers:** News Of The Highlands (Community news; Circulation 2,800)

**Transportation:** Commute to work: 83.2% car, 2.9% public transportation, 12.3% walk, 0.6% work from home (2006-2010 5-year est.); Travel time to work: 55.7% less than 15 minutes, 20.0% 15 to 30 minutes, 6.3% 30 to 45 minutes, 6.3% 45 to 60 minutes, 11.8% 60 minutes or more (2006-2010 5-year est.)

**HIGHLANDS** (town). Covers a land area of 30.409 square miles and a water area of 3.060 square miles. Located at 41.36° N. Lat; 74.00° W. Long.

**Population:** 13,667 (1990); 12,484 (2000); 12,492 (2010); Density: 410.8 persons per square mile (2010); Race: 78.2% White, 8.2% Black, 3.4% Asian, 0.6% American Indian/Alaska Native, 0.1% Native Hawaiian/Other Pacific Islander, 9.5% Other, 12.7% Hispanic of any race (2010); Average household size: 2.69 (2010); Median age: 22.3 (2010); Males per 100 females: 163.2 (2010); Marriage status: 76.0% never married, 20.3% now

married, 1.4% widowed, 2.3% divorced (2006-2010 5-year est.); Foreign born: 4.9% (2006-2010 5-year est.); Ancestry (includes multiple ancestries): 27.0% German, 19.9% Irish, 16.9% Italian, 11.5% English, 7.0% Polish (2006-2010 5-year est.).

**Economy:** Single-family building permits issued: 1 (2011); Multi-family building permits issued: 0 (2011); Employment by occupation: 6.5% management, 4.4% professional, 7.4% services, 16.9% sales, 6.1% farming, 15.3% construction, 7.1% production (2006-2010 5-year est.).

**Income:** Per capita income: $19,328 (2006-2010 5-year est.); Median household income: $74,906 (2006-2010 5-year est.); Average household income: $89,853 (2006-2010 5-year est.); Percent of households with income of $100,000 or more: 32.5% (2006-2010 5-year est.); Poverty rate: 5.0% (2006-2010 5-year est.).

**Education:** Percent of population age 25 and over with: High school diploma (including GED) or higher: 93.9% (2006-2010 5-year est.); Bachelor's degree or higher: 44.5% (2006-2010 5-year est.); Master's degree or higher: 25.9% (2006-2010 5-year est.).

**Housing:** Homeownership rate: 45.2% (2010); Median home value: $267,200 (2006-2010 5-year est.); Median contract rent: $1,127 per month (2006-2010 5-year est.); Median year structure built: 1950 (2006-2010 5-year est.).

**Transportation:** Commute to work: 28.2% car, 1.3% public transportation, 34.7% walk, 34.1% work from home (2006-2010 5-year est.); Travel time to work: 79.4% less than 15 minutes, 8.4% 15 to 30 minutes, 4.9% 30 to 45 minutes, 2.3% 45 to 60 minutes, 5.0% 60 minutes or more (2006-2010 5-year est.)

**HOWELLS** (unincorporated postal area)

Zip Code: 10932

    Covers a land area of 0.149 square miles and a water area of <.001 square miles. Located at 41.48° N. Lat; 74.46° W. Long. Elevation is 679 feet. Population: 60 (2010); Density: 402.0 persons per square mile (2010); Race: 100.0% White, 0.0% Black, 0.0% Asian, 0.0% American Indian/Alaska Native, 0.0% Native Hawaiian/Other Pacific Islander, 0.0% Other, 8.3% Hispanic of any race (2010); Average household size: 2.61 (2010); Median age: 50.5 (2010); Males per 100 females: 71.4 (2010); Homeownership rate: 87.0% (2010)

**HUGUENOT** (unincorporated postal area)

Zip Code: 12746

    Covers a land area of 14.180 square miles and a water area of 0.323 square miles. Located at 41.44° N. Lat; 74.65° W. Long. Elevation is 469 feet. Population: 937 (2010); Density: 66.1 persons per square mile (2010); Race: 93.2% White, 1.8% Black, 1.9% Asian, 0.6% American Indian/Alaska Native, 0.0% Native Hawaiian/Other Pacific Islander, 2.5% Other, 5.0% Hispanic of any race (2010); Average household size: 2.79 (2010); Median age: 40.8 (2010); Males per 100 females: 97.7 (2010); Homeownership rate: 82.5% (2010)

**JOHNSON** (unincorporated postal area)

Zip Code: 10933

    Covers a land area of 1.092 square miles and a water area of 0.005 square miles. Located at 41.36° N. Lat; 74.51° W. Long. Elevation is 509 feet. Population: 473 (2010); Density: 433.1 persons per square mile (2010); Race: 93.0% White, 3.6% Black, 0.0% Asian, 0.0% American Indian/Alaska Native, 0.0% Native Hawaiian/Other Pacific Islander, 3.4% Other, 8.2% Hispanic of any race (2010); Average household size: 3.09 (2010); Median age: 37.9 (2010); Males per 100 females: 98.7 (2010); Homeownership rate: 86.3% (2010)

**KIRYAS JOEL** (village). Covers a land area of 1.108 square miles and a water area of 0.005 square miles. Located at 41.34° N. Lat; 74.16° W. Long. Elevation is 686 feet.

**History:** Founded in 1974 by the Satmar sect of Hasidic Jews to accommodate, in part, their burgeoning population in the Williamsburg section of Brooklyn.

**Population:** 7,437 (1990); 13,138 (2000); 20,175 (2010); Density: 18,198.7 persons per square mile (2010); Race: 99.2% White, 0.1% Black, 0.1% Asian, 0.0% American Indian/Alaska Native, 0.0% Native Hawaiian/Other Pacific Islander, 0.6% Other, 1.3% Hispanic of any race (2010); Average household size: 5.50 (2010); Median age: 13.2 (2010); Males per 100 females: 107.3 (2010); Marriage status: 18.2% never married, 78.8% now married, 2.3% widowed, 0.6% divorced (2006-2010 5-year est.); Foreign born: 7.7% (2006-2010 5-year est.); Ancestry (includes multiple

ancestries): 28.7% Hungarian, 12.0% Romanian, 7.0% European, 6.9% American, 5.0% Israeli (2006-2010 5-year est.).
**Economy:** Single-family building permits issued: 0 (2011); Multi-family building permits issued: 212 (2011); Employment by occupation: 10.4% management, 1.9% professional, 7.5% services, 16.1% sales, 8.2% farming, 6.5% construction, 2.9% production (2006-2010 5-year est.).
**Income:** Per capita income: $5,998 (2006-2010 5-year est.); Median household income: $19,775 (2006-2010 5-year est.); Average household income: $32,893 (2006-2010 5-year est.); Percent of households with income of $100,000 or more: 4.8% (2006-2010 5-year est.); Poverty rate: 63.8% (2006-2010 5-year est.).
**Education:** Percent of population age 25 and over with: High school diploma (including GED) or higher: 58.1% (2006-2010 5-year est.); Bachelor's degree or higher: 5.9% (2006-2010 5-year est.); Master's degree or higher: 1.6% (2006-2010 5-year est.).
**Housing:** Homeownership rate: 28.9% (2010); Median home value: $382,300 (2006-2010 5-year est.); Median contract rent: $794 per month (2006-2010 5-year est.); Median year structure built: 1993 (2006-2010 5-year est.).
**Transportation:** Commute to work: 43.3% car, 24.3% public transportation, 26.3% walk, 5.9% work from home (2006-2010 5-year est.); Travel time to work: 50.9% less than 15 minutes, 20.1% 15 to 30 minutes, 8.2% 30 to 45 minutes, 1.8% 45 to 60 minutes, 19.0% 60 minutes or more (2006-2010 5-year est.)

**MAYBROOK** (village). Covers a land area of 1.354 square miles and a water area of 0.005 square miles. Located at 41.48° N. Lat; 74.21° W. Long. Elevation is 420 feet.
**History:** Incorporated 1925.
**Population:** 2,802 (1990); 3,084 (2000); 2,958 (2010); Density: 2,184.3 persons per square mile (2010); Race: 76.6% White, 11.4% Black, 1.9% Asian, 0.5% American Indian/Alaska Native, 0.0% Native Hawaiian/Other Pacific Islander, 9.6% Other, 20.2% Hispanic of any race (2010); Average household size: 2.70 (2010); Median age: 37.0 (2010); Males per 100 females: 86.0 (2010); Marriage status: 31.8% never married, 50.6% now married, 5.1% widowed, 12.5% divorced (2006-2010 5-year est.); Foreign born: 12.4% (2006-2010 5-year est.); Ancestry (includes multiple ancestries): 27.1% Irish, 18.6% German, 13.7% Italian, 11.0% English, 4.0% Polish (2006-2010 5-year est.).
**Economy:** Single-family building permits issued: 3 (2011); Multi-family building permits issued: 0 (2011); Employment by occupation: 6.4% management, 3.0% professional, 10.6% services, 17.8% sales, 3.5% farming, 7.4% construction, 9.3% production (2006-2010 5-year est.).
**Income:** Per capita income: $25,651 (2006-2010 5-year est.); Median household income: $57,303 (2006-2010 5-year est.); Average household income: $64,642 (2006-2010 5-year est.); Percent of households with income of $100,000 or more: 20.8% (2006-2010 5-year est.); Poverty rate: 9.8% (2006-2010 5-year est.).
**Education:** Percent of population age 25 and over with: High school diploma (including GED) or higher: 84.9% (2006-2010 5-year est.); Bachelor's degree or higher: 19.1% (2006-2010 5-year est.); Master's degree or higher: 7.5% (2006-2010 5-year est.).
**School District(s)**
Valley Central School District (montgomery) (KG-12)
    2009-10 Enrollment: 4,853 . . . . . . . . . . . . . . . . . . . . . (845) 457-2400
**Housing:** Homeownership rate: 59.0% (2010); Median home value: $208,200 (2006-2010 5-year est.); Median contract rent: $798 per month (2006-2010 5-year est.); Median year structure built: 1977 (2006-2010 5-year est.).
**Transportation:** Commute to work: 87.7% car, 10.4% public transportation, 0.6% walk, 1.2% work from home (2006-2010 5-year est.); Travel time to work: 22.8% less than 15 minutes, 36.4% 15 to 30 minutes, 9.6% 30 to 45 minutes, 8.5% 45 to 60 minutes, 22.7% 60 minutes or more (2006-2010 5-year est.)
**Additional Information Contacts**
Village of Maybrook . . . . . . . . . . . . . . . . . . . . . . . . . . . (845) 427-2717
    http://www.villageofmaybrook.com

**MECHANICSTOWN** (CDP). Covers a land area of 3.344 square miles and a water area of 0.055 square miles. Located at 41.45° N. Lat; 74.38° W. Long. Elevation is 531 feet.
**Population:** 5,013 (1990); 6,061 (2000); 6,858 (2010); Density: 2,050.4 persons per square mile (2010); Race: 58.9% White, 20.9% Black, 3.1% Asian, 0.4% American Indian/Alaska Native, 0.1% Native Hawaiian/Other Pacific Islander, 16.6% Other, 28.6% Hispanic of any race (2010); Average

household size: 2.42 (2010); Median age: 40.7 (2010); Males per 100 females: 84.7 (2010); Marriage status: 40.4% never married, 38.7% now married, 9.9% widowed, 11.1% divorced (2006-2010 5-year est.); Foreign born: 19.9% (2006-2010 5-year est.); Ancestry (includes multiple ancestries): 15.3% Italian, 12.2% Irish, 8.4% German, 5.1% American, 4.3% Polish (2006-2010 5-year est.).
**Economy:** Employment by occupation: 10.5% management, 2.1% professional, 9.2% services, 22.5% sales, 2.8% farming, 13.9% construction, 7.8% production (2006-2010 5-year est.).
**Income:** Per capita income: $24,339 (2006-2010 5-year est.); Median household income: $50,238 (2006-2010 5-year est.); Average household income: $60,299 (2006-2010 5-year est.); Percent of households with income of $100,000 or more: 18.2% (2006-2010 5-year est.); Poverty rate: 16.9% (2006-2010 5-year est.).
**Education:** Percent of population age 25 and over with: High school diploma (including GED) or higher: 83.7% (2006-2010 5-year est.); Bachelor's degree or higher: 24.5% (2006-2010 5-year est.); Master's degree or higher: 8.6% (2006-2010 5-year est.).
**Housing:** Homeownership rate: 47.8% (2010); Median home value: $238,900 (2006-2010 5-year est.); Median contract rent: $896 per month (2006-2010 5-year est.); Median year structure built: 1982 (2006-2010 5-year est.).
**Transportation:** Commute to work: 90.2% car, 6.4% public transportation, 1.3% walk, 0.8% work from home (2006-2010 5-year est.); Travel time to work: 29.4% less than 15 minutes, 23.2% 15 to 30 minutes, 12.5% 30 to 45 minutes, 7.9% 45 to 60 minutes, 27.0% 60 minutes or more (2006-2010 5-year est.)

**MIDDLETOWN** (city). Covers a land area of 5.075 square miles and a water area of 0.025 square miles. Located at 41.44° N. Lat; 74.42° W. Long. Elevation is 558 feet.
**History:** Settled 1756, Incorporated as a city 1888.
**Population:** 24,224 (1990); 25,388 (2000); 28,086 (2010); Density: 5,533.2 persons per square mile (2010); Race: 52.4% White, 21.0% Black, 1.9% Asian, 0.8% American Indian/Alaska Native, 0.0% Native Hawaiian/Other Pacific Islander, 23.9% Other, 39.7% Hispanic of any race (2010); Average household size: 2.77 (2010); Median age: 33.7 (2010); Males per 100 females: 95.6 (2010); Marriage status: 37.5% never married, 45.6% now married, 5.8% widowed, 11.1% divorced (2006-2010 5-year est.); Foreign born: 19.9% (2006-2010 5-year est.); Ancestry (includes multiple ancestries): 11.4% Irish, 11.2% Italian, 8.8% German, 6.9% American, 5.3% English (2006-2010 5-year est.).
**Economy:** Unemployment rate: 9.3% (February 2012); Total civilian labor force: 12,739 (February 2012); Single-family building permits issued: 16 (2011); Multi-family building permits issued: 0 (2011); Employment by occupation: 7.6% management, 1.8% professional, 12.8% services, 17.0% sales, 5.4% farming, 10.5% construction, 7.1% production (2006-2010 5-year est.).
**Income:** Per capita income: $22,614 (2006-2010 5-year est.); Median household income: $54,354 (2006-2010 5-year est.); Average household income: $63,669 (2006-2010 5-year est.); Percent of households with income of $100,000 or more: 17.0% (2006-2010 5-year est.); Poverty rate: 17.8% (2006-2010 5-year est.).
**Taxes:** Total city taxes per capita: $574 (2009); City property taxes per capita: $512 (2009).
**Education:** Percent of population age 25 and over with: High school diploma (including GED) or higher: 75.3% (2006-2010 5-year est.); Bachelor's degree or higher: 17.1% (2006-2010 5-year est.); Master's degree or higher: 6.5% (2006-2010 5-year est.).
**School District(s)**
Middletown City School District (PK-12)
    2009-10 Enrollment: 6,767 . . . . . . . . . . . . . . . . . . . . . (845) 326-1158
Minisink Valley Central School District (KG-12)
    2009-10 Enrollment: 4,543 . . . . . . . . . . . . . . . . . . . . . (845) 355-5110
**Two-year College(s)**
Orange County Community College (Public)
    Fall 2010 Enrollment: 4,753 . . . . . . . . . . . . . . . . . . . . (845) 344-6222
    2011-12 Tuition: In-state $4,336; Out-of-state $8,236
**Vocational/Technical School(s)**
Beauty School of Middletown (Private, For-profit)
    Fall 2010 Enrollment: 119 . . . . . . . . . . . . . . . . . . . . . (8.4) 534-3E+1
    2011-12 Tuition: $13,100
**Housing:** Homeownership rate: 49.0% (2010); Median home value: $228,300 (2006-2010 5-year est.); Median contract rent: $868 per month

(2006-2010 5-year est.); Median year structure built: before 1940 (2006-2010 5-year est.).
**Hospitals:** Orange Regional Medical Center (286 beds)
**Safety:** Violent crime rate: 58.4 per 10,000 population; Property crime rate: 455.6 per 10,000 population (2010).
**Newspapers:** Times Herald-Record (Local news; Circulation 87,366)
**Transportation:** Commute to work: 81.2% car, 5.7% public transportation, 6.6% walk, 2.5% work from home (2006-2010 5-year est.); Travel time to work: 39.4% less than 15 minutes, 29.3% 15 to 30 minutes, 11.2% 30 to 45 minutes, 6.1% 45 to 60 minutes, 14.0% 60 minutes or more (2006-2010 5-year est.)
**Additional Information Contacts**
City of Middletown . . . . . . . . . . . . . . . . . . . . . . . . . . . . (845) 346-4166
  http://www.middletown-ny.com

**MINISINK** (town). Covers a land area of 23.029 square miles and a water area of 0.144 square miles. Located at 41.32° N. Lat; 74.54° W. Long.
**Population:** 2,981 (1990); 3,585 (2000); 4,490 (2010); Density: 195.0 persons per square mile (2010); Race: 91.6% White, 2.9% Black, 1.1% Asian, 0.1% American Indian/Alaska Native, 0.0% Native Hawaiian/Other Pacific Islander, 4.3% Other, 9.1% Hispanic of any race (2010); Average household size: 3.01 (2010); Median age: 39.3 (2010); Males per 100 females: 99.6 (2010); Marriage status: 23.2% never married, 67.5% now married, 3.9% widowed, 5.4% divorced (2006-2010 5-year est.); Foreign born: 2.3% (2006-2010 5-year est.); Ancestry (includes multiple ancestries): 35.9% German, 31.6% Irish, 19.1% English, 18.0% Italian, 8.7% American (2006-2010 5-year est.).
**Economy:** Single-family building permits issued: 11 (2011); Multi-family building permits issued: 0 (2011); Employment by occupation: 15.1% management, 6.3% professional, 8.0% services, 18.2% sales, 1.4% farming, 14.9% construction, 7.0% production (2006-2010 5-year est.).
**Income:** Per capita income: $32,554 (2006-2010 5-year est.); Median household income: $85,941 (2006-2010 5-year est.); Average household income: $95,411 (2006-2010 5-year est.); Percent of households with income of $100,000 or more: 39.6% (2006-2010 5-year est.); Poverty rate: 0.8% (2006-2010 5-year est.).
**Education:** Percent of population age 25 and over with: High school diploma (including GED) or higher: 94.8% (2006-2010 5-year est.); Bachelor's degree or higher: 30.0% (2006-2010 5-year est.); Master's degree or higher: 11.2% (2006-2010 5-year est.).
**Housing:** Homeownership rate: 82.8% (2010); Median home value: $379,300 (2006-2010 5-year est.); Median contract rent: $1,443 per month (2006-2010 5-year est.); Median year structure built: 1978 (2006-2010 5-year est.).
**Transportation:** Commute to work: 91.1% car, 1.4% public transportation, 1.3% walk, 5.8% work from home (2006-2010 5-year est.); Travel time to work: 11.4% less than 15 minutes, 37.4% 15 to 30 minutes, 17.7% 30 to 45 minutes, 8.8% 45 to 60 minutes, 24.8% 60 minutes or more (2006-2010 5-year est.)

**MONROE** (village). Covers a land area of 3.453 square miles and a water area of 0.064 square miles. Located at 41.32° N. Lat; 74.18° W. Long. Elevation is 643 feet.
**Population:** 6,798 (1990); 7,780 (2000); 8,364 (2010); Density: 2,422.0 persons per square mile (2010); Race: 82.5% White, 4.1% Black, 4.3% Asian, 0.2% American Indian/Alaska Native, 0.0% Native Hawaiian/Other Pacific Islander, 8.9% Other, 19.6% Hispanic of any race (2010); Average household size: 3.04 (2010); Median age: 38.4 (2010); Males per 100 females: 102.1 (2010); Marriage status: 23.5% never married, 69.0% now married, 2.3% widowed, 5.2% divorced (2006-2010 5-year est.); Foreign born: 12.1% (2006-2010 5-year est.); Ancestry (includes multiple ancestries): 29.8% Italian, 22.6% Irish, 13.7% German, 5.5% Polish, 5.0% American (2006-2010 5-year est.).
**Economy:** Single-family building permits issued: 37 (2011); Multi-family building permits issued: 0 (2011); Employment by occupation: 13.7% management, 7.2% professional, 6.6% services, 15.9% sales, 3.5% farming, 5.6% construction, 1.9% production (2006-2010 5-year est.).
**Income:** Per capita income: $34,140 (2006-2010 5-year est.); Median household income: $97,863 (2006-2010 5-year est.); Average household income: $105,781 (2006-2010 5-year est.); Percent of households with income of $100,000 or more: 47.3% (2006-2010 5-year est.); Poverty rate: 10.2% (2006-2010 5-year est.).
**Education:** Percent of population age 25 and over with: High school diploma (including GED) or higher: 89.0% (2006-2010 5-year est.);

Bachelor's degree or higher: 38.4% (2006-2010 5-year est.); Master's degree or higher: 14.2% (2006-2010 5-year est.).

**School District(s)**

Greenwood Lake Union Free School District (KG-08)
  2009-10 Enrollment: 596 . . . . . . . . . . . . . . . . . . . . (845) 782-8678
Kiryas Joel Village Union Free School District (PK-KG)
  2009-10 Enrollment: 159 . . . . . . . . . . . . . . . . . . . . (845) 782-2300
Monroe-Woodbury Central School District (KG-12)
  2009-10 Enrollment: 7,400 . . . . . . . . . . . . . . . . . . . (845) 460-6200

**Four-year College(s)**

Uta Mesivta of Kiryas Joel (Private, Not-for-profit, Jewish)
  Fall 2010 Enrollment: 1,315 . . . . . . . . . . . . . . . . . (8.4) 578-4E+1
  2011-12 Tuition: In-state $7,300; Out-of-state $7,300
**Housing:** Homeownership rate: 81.5% (2010); Median home value: $362,700 (2006-2010 5-year est.); Median contract rent: $1,103 per month (2006-2010 5-year est.); Median year structure built: 1973 (2006-2010 5-year est.).
**Safety:** Violent crime rate: 23.3 per 10,000 population; Property crime rate: 425.8 per 10,000 population (2010).
**Newspapers:** Monroe Photo News (Community news; Circulation 9,000); Warwick Advertiser (Local news; Circulation 8,900)
**Transportation:** Commute to work: 90.2% car, 4.2% public transportation, 0.9% walk, 2.2% work from home (2006-2010 5-year est.); Travel time to work: 21.3% less than 15 minutes, 17.2% 15 to 30 minutes, 24.9% 30 to 45 minutes, 13.0% 45 to 60 minutes, 23.6% 60 minutes or more (2006-2010 5-year est.)

**MONROE** (town). Covers a land area of 19.975 square miles and a water area of 1.280 square miles. Located at 41.30° N. Lat; 74.19° W. Long. Elevation is 643 feet.
**History:** Incorporated 1894.
**Population:** 23,035 (1990); 31,407 (2000); 39,912 (2010); Density: 1,998.0 persons per square mile (2010); Race: 91.3% White, 2.2% Black, 2.5% Asian, 0.1% American Indian/Alaska Native, 0.0% Native Hawaiian/Other Pacific Islander, 3.9% Other, 8.4% Hispanic of any race (2010); Average household size: 3.86 (2010); Median age: 21.8 (2010); Males per 100 females: 103.2 (2010); Marriage status: 23.0% never married, 69.3% now married, 2.8% widowed, 4.8% divorced (2006-2010 5-year est.); Foreign born: 11.5% (2006-2010 5-year est.); Ancestry (includes multiple ancestries): 14.5% Hungarian, 12.0% Italian, 11.5% Irish, 9.3% German, 6.3% Romanian (2006-2010 5-year est.).
**Economy:** Unemployment rate: 7.0% (February 2012); Total civilian labor force: 14,363 (February 2012); Single-family building permits issued: 32 (2011); Multi-family building permits issued: 0 (2011); Employment by occupation: 13.8% management, 4.8% professional, 5.9% services, 16.3% sales, 4.3% farming, 6.8% construction, 2.7% production (2006-2010 5-year est.).
**Income:** Per capita income: $21,167 (2006-2010 5-year est.); Median household income: $62,826 (2006-2010 5-year est.); Average household income: $81,822 (2006-2010 5-year est.); Percent of households with income of $100,000 or more: 33.6% (2006-2010 5-year est.); Poverty rate: 34.2% (2006-2010 5-year est.).
**Education:** Percent of population age 25 and over with: High school diploma (including GED) or higher: 81.9% (2006-2010 5-year est.); Bachelor's degree or higher: 30.3% (2006-2010 5-year est.); Master's degree or higher: 12.7% (2006-2010 5-year est.).

**School District(s)**

Greenwood Lake Union Free School District (KG-08)
  2009-10 Enrollment: 596 . . . . . . . . . . . . . . . . . . . . (845) 782-8678
Kiryas Joel Village Union Free School District (PK-KG)
  2009-10 Enrollment: 159 . . . . . . . . . . . . . . . . . . . . (845) 782-2300
Monroe-Woodbury Central School District (KG-12)
  2009-10 Enrollment: 7,400 . . . . . . . . . . . . . . . . . . . (845) 460-6200

**Four-year College(s)**

Uta Mesivta of Kiryas Joel (Private, Not-for-profit, Jewish)
  Fall 2010 Enrollment: 1,315 . . . . . . . . . . . . . . . . . (8.4) 578-4E+1
  2011-12 Tuition: In-state $7,300; Out-of-state $7,300
**Housing:** Homeownership rate: 62.5% (2010); Median home value: $365,500 (2006-2010 5-year est.); Median contract rent: $874 per month (2006-2010 5-year est.); Median year structure built: 1983 (2006-2010 5-year est.).
**Newspapers:** Monroe Photo News (Community news; Circulation 9,000); Warwick Advertiser (Local news; Circulation 8,900)
**Transportation:** Commute to work: 74.9% car, 11.3% public transportation, 8.1% walk, 3.6% work from home (2006-2010 5-year est.);

Travel time to work: 29.2% less than 15 minutes, 19.6% 15 to 30 minutes, 17.4% 30 to 45 minutes, 10.2% 45 to 60 minutes, 23.6% 60 minutes or more (2006-2010 5-year est.)

**Additional Information Contacts**

Town of Monroe . . . . . . . . . . . . . . . . . . . . . . . . . . . (845) 783-1900
http://www.monroeny.org

## MONTGOMERY (village).
Covers a land area of 1.405 square miles and a water area of 0.042 square miles. Located at 41.52° N. Lat; 74.23° W. Long. Elevation is 358 feet.

**Population:** 2,900 (1990); 3,636 (2000); 3,814 (2010); Density: 2,713.3 persons per square mile (2010); Race: 85.0% White, 7.0% Black, 1.1% Asian, 0.1% American Indian/Alaska Native, 0.0% Native Hawaiian/Other Pacific Islander, 6.8% Other, 13.0% Hispanic of any race (2010); Average household size: 2.60 (2010); Median age: 39.5 (2010); Males per 100 females: 91.9 (2010); Marriage status: 30.8% never married, 57.8% now married, 6.6% widowed, 4.8% divorced (2006-2010 5-year est.); Foreign born: 2.0% (2006-2010 5-year est.); Ancestry (includes multiple ancestries): 37.0% Irish, 30.1% Italian, 12.4% German, 9.3% English, 6.5% Dutch (2006-2010 5-year est.).

**Economy:** Single-family building permits issued: 5 (2011); Multi-family building permits issued: 70 (2011); Employment by occupation: 10.4% management, 3.6% professional, 7.9% services, 21.2% sales, 8.2% farming, 10.1% construction, 5.6% production (2006-2010 5-year est.).

**Income:** Per capita income: $29,832 (2006-2010 5-year est.); Median household income: $71,367 (2006-2010 5-year est.); Average household income: $82,543 (2006-2010 5-year est.); Percent of households with income of $100,000 or more: 31.2% (2006-2010 5-year est.); Poverty rate: 3.5% (2006-2010 5-year est.).

**Education:** Percent of population age 25 and over with: High school diploma (including GED) or higher: 95.7% (2006-2010 5-year est.); Bachelor's degree or higher: 25.3% (2006-2010 5-year est.); Master's degree or higher: 6.9% (2006-2010 5-year est.).

**School District(s)**

Valley Central School District (montgomery) (KG-12)
    2009-10 Enrollment: 4,853 . . . . . . . . . . . . . . . . . . . (845) 457-2400

**Housing:** Homeownership rate: 67.5% (2010); Median home value: $292,000 (2006-2010 5-year est.); Median contract rent: $796 per month (2006-2010 5-year est.); Median year structure built: 1980 (2006-2010 5-year est.).

**Safety:** Violent crime rate: 0.0 per 10,000 population; Property crime rate: 22.1 per 10,000 population (2010).

**Transportation:** Commute to work: 90.2% car, 5.6% public transportation, 1.9% walk, 2.3% work from home (2006-2010 5-year est.); Travel time to work: 22.7% less than 15 minutes, 35.5% 15 to 30 minutes, 23.0% 30 to 45 minutes, 2.9% 45 to 60 minutes, 15.9% 60 minutes or more (2006-2010 5-year est.).

**Airports:** Orange County (general aviation)

## MONTGOMERY (town).
Covers a land area of 50.256 square miles and a water area of 0.933 square miles. Located at 41.53° N. Lat; 74.20° W. Long. Elevation is 358 feet.

**Population:** 18,495 (1990); 20,891 (2000); 22,606 (2010); Density: 449.8 persons per square mile (2010); Race: 84.6% White, 7.2% Black, 1.4% Asian, 0.2% American Indian/Alaska Native, 0.0% Native Hawaiian/Other Pacific Islander, 6.6% Other, 14.0% Hispanic of any race (2010); Average household size: 2.78 (2010); Median age: 38.6 (2010); Males per 100 females: 94.9 (2010); Marriage status: 28.4% never married, 57.5% now married, 6.6% widowed, 7.5% divorced (2006-2010 5-year est.); Foreign born: 5.5% (2006-2010 5-year est.); Ancestry (includes multiple ancestries): 25.8% Irish, 22.7% Italian, 16.6% German, 10.0% English, 7.3% American (2006-2010 5-year est.).

**Economy:** Single-family building permits issued: 22 (2011); Multi-family building permits issued: 4 (2011); Employment by occupation: 12.1% management, 2.3% professional, 9.6% services, 19.6% sales, 5.3% farming, 9.4% construction, 7.7% production (2006-2010 5-year est.).

**Income:** Per capita income: $27,185 (2006-2010 5-year est.); Median household income: $67,449 (2006-2010 5-year est.); Average household income: $74,824 (2006-2010 5-year est.); Percent of households with income of $100,000 or more: 27.5% (2006-2010 5-year est.); Poverty rate: 5.6% (2006-2010 5-year est.).

**Education:** Percent of population age 25 and over with: High school diploma (including GED) or higher: 88.3% (2006-2010 5-year est.); Bachelor's degree or higher: 22.9% (2006-2010 5-year est.); Master's degree or higher: 9.5% (2006-2010 5-year est.).

**School District(s)**

Valley Central School District (montgomery) (KG-12)
    2009-10 Enrollment: 4,853 . . . . . . . . . . . . . . . . . . . (845) 457-2400

**Housing:** Homeownership rate: 71.5% (2010); Median home value: $283,800 (2006-2010 5-year est.); Median contract rent: $808 per month (2006-2010 5-year est.); Median year structure built: 1974 (2006-2010 5-year est.).

**Transportation:** Commute to work: 90.4% car, 4.9% public transportation, 1.4% walk, 2.4% work from home (2006-2010 5-year est.); Travel time to work: 26.0% less than 15 minutes, 34.2% 15 to 30 minutes, 15.1% 30 to 45 minutes, 5.4% 45 to 60 minutes, 19.3% 60 minutes or more (2006-2010 5-year est.).

**Airports:** Orange County (general aviation)

## MOUNT HOPE (town).
Covers a land area of 25.133 square miles and a water area of 0.361 square miles. Located at 41.45° N. Lat; 74.52° W. Long. Elevation is 823 feet.

**Population:** 5,971 (1990); 6,639 (2000); 7,018 (2010); Density: 279.2 persons per square mile (2010); Race: 74.6% White, 16.3% Black, 1.6% Asian, 0.7% American Indian/Alaska Native, 0.0% Native Hawaiian/Other Pacific Islander, 6.8% Other, 16.0% Hispanic of any race (2010); Average household size: 2.96 (2010); Median age: 39.3 (2010); Males per 100 females: 165.2 (2010); Marriage status: 29.5% never married, 55.5% now married, 2.3% widowed, 12.7% divorced (2006-2010 5-year est.); Foreign born: 10.6% (2006-2010 5-year est.); Ancestry (includes multiple ancestries): 23.7% Italian, 21.6% Irish, 12.9% German, 8.6% Polish, 6.0% English (2006-2010 5-year est.).

**Economy:** Single-family building permits issued: 9 (2011); Multi-family building permits issued: 0 (2011); Employment by occupation: 10.6% management, 2.1% professional, 12.2% services, 19.1% sales, 3.7% farming, 9.9% construction, 5.6% production (2006-2010 5-year est.).

**Income:** Per capita income: $26,596 (2006-2010 5-year est.); Median household income: $76,427 (2006-2010 5-year est.); Average household income: $86,709 (2006-2010 5-year est.); Percent of households with income of $100,000 or more: 32.9% (2006-2010 5-year est.); Poverty rate: 4.5% (2006-2010 5-year est.).

**Education:** Percent of population age 25 and over with: High school diploma (including GED) or higher: 87.1% (2006-2010 5-year est.); Bachelor's degree or higher: 21.0% (2006-2010 5-year est.); Master's degree or higher: 6.4% (2006-2010 5-year est.).

**Housing:** Homeownership rate: 83.7% (2010); Median home value: $288,100 (2006-2010 5-year est.); Median contract rent: $665 per month (2006-2010 5-year est.); Median year structure built: 1973 (2006-2010 5-year est.).

**Safety:** Violent crime rate: 2.7 per 10,000 population; Property crime rate: 38.5 per 10,000 population (2010).

**Transportation:** Commute to work: 93.6% car, 2.7% public transportation, 0.4% walk, 3.0% work from home (2006-2010 5-year est.); Travel time to work: 14.4% less than 15 minutes, 45.2% 15 to 30 minutes, 18.1% 30 to 45 minutes, 8.6% 45 to 60 minutes, 13.6% 60 minutes or more (2006-2010 5-year est.).

## MOUNTAIN LODGE PARK (CDP).
Covers a land area of 1.185 square miles and a water area of <.001 square miles. Located at 41.38° N. Lat; 74.13° W. Long. Elevation is 784 feet.

**Population:** n/a (1990); n/a (2000); 1,588 (2010); Density: 1,340.0 persons per square mile (2010); Race: 83.7% White, 5.0% Black, 0.9% Asian, 2.6% American Indian/Alaska Native, 0.0% Native Hawaiian/Other Pacific Islander, 7.8% Other, 18.1% Hispanic of any race (2010); Average household size: 2.63 (2010); Median age: 38.7 (2010); Males per 100 females: 100.3 (2010); Marriage status: 19.8% never married, 66.5% now married, 0.0% widowed, 13.7% divorced (2006-2010 5-year est.); Foreign born: 13.3% (2006-2010 5-year est.); Ancestry (includes multiple ancestries): 21.8% Irish, 18.7% German, 11.5% Italian, 9.4% Ukrainian, 7.4% Swedish (2006-2010 5-year est.).

**Economy:** Employment by occupation: 11.3% management, 6.6% professional, 4.3% services, 17.6% sales, 12.0% farming, 23.8% construction, 7.0% production (2006-2010 5-year est.).

**Income:** Per capita income: $25,865 (2006-2010 5-year est.); Median household income: $69,970 (2006-2010 5-year est.); Average household income: $71,446 (2006-2010 5-year est.); Percent of households with income of $100,000 or more: 18.6% (2006-2010 5-year est.); Poverty rate: 23.9% (2006-2010 5-year est.).

**Education:** Percent of population age 25 and over with: High school diploma (including GED) or higher: 82.4% (2006-2010 5-year est.);

Bachelor's degree or higher: 21.9% (2006-2010 5-year est.); Master's degree or higher: 7.7% (2006-2010 5-year est.).
**Housing:** Homeownership rate: 85.4% (2010); Median home value: $185,100 (2006-2010 5-year est.); Median contract rent: $788 per month (2006-2010 5-year est.); Median year structure built: 1947 (2006-2010 5-year est.).
**Transportation:** Commute to work: 98.7% car, 0.0% public transportation, 0.0% walk, 1.3% work from home (2006-2010 5-year est.); Travel time to work: 15.4% less than 15 minutes, 7.3% 15 to 30 minutes, 22.7% 30 to 45 minutes, 14.1% 45 to 60 minutes, 40.5% 60 minutes or more (2006-2010 5-year est.).

## MOUNTAINVILLE (unincorporated postal area)
Zip Code: 10953

Covers a land area of 1.102 square miles and a water area of 0.013 square miles. Located at 41.40° N. Lat; 74.07° W. Long. Elevation is 299 feet. Population: 252 (2010); Density: 228.7 persons per square mile (2010); Race: 93.3% White, 0.4% Black, 2.0% Asian, 0.0% American Indian/Alaska Native, 0.0% Native Hawaiian/Other Pacific Islander, 4.3% Other, 6.0% Hispanic of any race (2010); Average household size: 2.56 (2010); Median age: 44.0 (2010); Males per 100 females: 121.1 (2010); Homeownership rate: 85.6% (2010)

## NEW HAMPTON (unincorporated postal area)
Zip Code: 10958

Covers a land area of 22.865 square miles and a water area of 0.138 square miles. Located at 41.37° N. Lat; 74.43° W. Long. Elevation is 538 feet. Population: 3,291 (2010); Density: 143.9 persons per square mile (2010); Race: 85.6% White, 7.5% Black, 1.6% Asian, 0.1% American Indian/Alaska Native, 0.1% Native Hawaiian/Other Pacific Islander, 5.1% Other, 10.3% Hispanic of any race (2010); Average household size: 2.96 (2010); Median age: 40.5 (2010); Males per 100 females: 112.5 (2010); Homeownership rate: 83.8% (2010)

## NEW WINDSOR (town). Aka New Windsor Center. Covers a land area of 34.069 square miles and a water area of 2.994 square miles. Located at 41.47° N. Lat; 74.11° W. Long. Elevation is 161 feet.
**History:** Was home of George Clinton. De Witt Clinton was born here.
**Population:** 22,937 (1990); 22,866 (2000); 25,244 (2010); Density: 741.0 persons per square mile (2010); Race: 74.7% White, 11.5% Black, 3.5% Asian, 0.2% American Indian/Alaska Native, 0.0% Native Hawaiian/Other Pacific Islander, 10.1% Other, 19.5% Hispanic of any race (2010); Average household size: 2.69 (2010); Median age: 39.2 (2010); Males per 100 females: 95.4 (2010); Marriage status: 28.8% never married, 54.1% now married, 6.9% widowed, 10.2% divorced (2006-2010 5-year est.); Foreign born: 11.4% (2006-2010 5-year est.); Ancestry (includes multiple ancestries): 22.3% Irish, 20.5% Italian, 10.9% German, 7.6% American, 6.8% English (2006-2010 5-year est.).
**Economy:** Unemployment rate: 8.8% (February 2012); Total civilian labor force: 12,628 (February 2012); Single-family building permits issued: 50 (2011); Multi-family building permits issued: 174 (2011); Employment by occupation: 15.5% management, 4.7% professional, 11.1% services, 17.6% sales, 2.6% farming, 7.6% construction, 4.7% production (2006-2010 5-year est.).
**Income:** Per capita income: $31,652 (2006-2010 5-year est.); Median household income: $72,336 (2006-2010 5-year est.); Average household income: $82,443 (2006-2010 5-year est.); Percent of households with income of $100,000 or more: 31.9% (2006-2010 5-year est.); Poverty rate: 5.1% (2006-2010 5-year est.).
**Education:** Percent of population age 25 and over with: High school diploma (including GED) or higher: 87.7% (2006-2010 5-year est.); Bachelor's degree or higher: 27.4% (2006-2010 5-year est.); Master's degree or higher: 11.6% (2006-2010 5-year est.).
### School District(s)
Cornwall Central School District (KG-12)
   2009-10 Enrollment: 3,434 . . . . . . . . . . . . . . . . . . (845) 534-8009
Newburgh City School District (PK-12)
   2009-10 Enrollment: 12,094 . . . . . . . . . . . . . . . . . (845) 563-3500
Washingtonville Central School District (PK-12)
   2009-10 Enrollment: 4,630 . . . . . . . . . . . . . . . . . . (845) 497-4000
**Housing:** Homeownership rate: 74.4% (2010); Median home value: $298,900 (2006-2010 5-year est.); Median contract rent: $966 per month (2006-2010 5-year est.); Median year structure built: 1973 (2006-2010 5-year est.).

**Safety:** Violent crime rate: 9.5 per 10,000 population; Property crime rate: 187.2 per 10,000 population (2010).
**Newspapers:** Sentinel (Community news; Circulation 5,700)
**Transportation:** Commute to work: 90.7% car, 5.8% public transportation, 0.9% walk, 1.7% work from home (2006-2010 5-year est.); Travel time to work: 24.6% less than 15 minutes, 32.1% 15 to 30 minutes, 14.6% 30 to 45 minutes, 10.3% 45 to 60 minutes, 18.4% 60 minutes or more (2006-2010 5-year est.)
**Additional Information Contacts**
Town of New Windsor . . . . . . . . . . . . . . . . . . . . . . (845) 563-4611
  http://town.new-windsor.ny.us

## NEW WINDSOR (CDP). Covers a land area of 3.761 square miles and a water area of 0.041 square miles. Located at 41.46° N. Lat; 74.03° W. Long. Elevation is 161 feet.
**Population:** 8,898 (1990); 9,077 (2000); 8,922 (2010); Density: 2,371.9 persons per square mile (2010); Race: 75.9% White, 11.6% Black, 1.9% Asian, 0.3% American Indian/Alaska Native, 0.0% Native Hawaiian/Other Pacific Islander, 10.3% Other, 21.3% Hispanic of any race (2010); Average household size: 2.53 (2010); Median age: 40.5 (2010); Males per 100 females: 95.3 (2010); Marriage status: 29.2% never married, 53.0% now married, 7.6% widowed, 10.2% divorced (2006-2010 5-year est.); Foreign born: 11.2% (2006-2010 5-year est.); Ancestry (includes multiple ancestries): 21.2% Irish, 18.6% Italian, 10.0% German, 9.3% American, 8.2% English (2006-2010 5-year est.).
**Economy:** Employment by occupation: 14.2% management, 4.8% professional, 13.0% services, 16.6% sales, 2.8% farming, 7.6% construction, 4.1% production (2006-2010 5-year est.).
**Income:** Per capita income: $32,795 (2006-2010 5-year est.); Median household income: $71,546 (2006-2010 5-year est.); Average household income: $83,050 (2006-2010 5-year est.); Percent of households with income of $100,000 or more: 32.9% (2006-2010 5-year est.); Poverty rate: 5.4% (2006-2010 5-year est.).
**Education:** Percent of population age 25 and over with: High school diploma (including GED) or higher: 86.0% (2006-2010 5-year est.); Bachelor's degree or higher: 25.5% (2006-2010 5-year est.); Master's degree or higher: 9.5% (2006-2010 5-year est.).
### School District(s)
Cornwall Central School District (KG-12)
   2009-10 Enrollment: 3,434 . . . . . . . . . . . . . . . . . . (845) 534-8009
Newburgh City School District (PK-12)
   2009-10 Enrollment: 12,094 . . . . . . . . . . . . . . . . . (845) 563-3500
Washingtonville Central School District (PK-12)
   2009-10 Enrollment: 4,630 . . . . . . . . . . . . . . . . . . (845) 497-4000
**Housing:** Homeownership rate: 74.1% (2010); Median home value: $277,200 (2006-2010 5-year est.); Median contract rent: $910 per month (2006-2010 5-year est.); Median year structure built: 1964 (2006-2010 5-year est.).
**Transportation:** Commute to work: 89.6% car, 7.6% public transportation, 1.2% walk, 1.4% work from home (2006-2010 5-year est.); Travel time to work: 22.0% less than 15 minutes, 32.2% 15 to 30 minutes, 17.5% 30 to 45 minutes, 8.5% 45 to 60 minutes, 19.8% 60 minutes or more (2006-2010 5-year est.)

## NEWBURGH (city). Covers a land area of 3.804 square miles and a water area of 0.980 square miles. Located at 41.50° N. Lat; 74.01° W. Long. Elevation is 128 feet.
**History:** Has many old houses, and the streets run sharply to the river. At Hasbrouck House (1750; now a Museum), Washington made his headquarters from April 1782 to Aug. 1783. It was in Newburgh that the Continental Army was disbanded. Mt. St. Mary College is in the city. West Point is located a few miles to the south. Settled 1709 by Palatines; Incorporated 1800.
**Population:** 26,440 (1990); 28,259 (2000); 28,866 (2010); Density: 7,587.7 persons per square mile (2010); Race: 39.4% White, 30.2% Black, 1.0% Asian, 1.7% American Indian/Alaska Native, 0.1% Native Hawaiian/Other Pacific Islander, 27.6% Other, 47.9% Hispanic of any race (2010); Average household size: 3.09 (2010); Median age: 28.2 (2010); Males per 100 females: 94.6 (2010); Marriage status: 46.9% never married, 39.7% now married, 5.5% widowed, 7.9% divorced (2006-2010 5-year est.); Foreign born: 25.0% (2006-2010 5-year est.); Ancestry (includes multiple ancestries): 7.7% Italian, 6.0% Irish, 5.7% American, 3.9% German, 2.1% English (2006-2010 5-year est.).
**Economy:** Unemployment rate: 11.2% (February 2012); Total civilian labor force: 11,675 (February 2012); Single-family building permits issued: 2

(2011); Multi-family building permits issued: 0 (2011); Employment by occupation: 3.6% management, 0.7% professional, 15.7% services, 15.9% sales, 5.7% farming, 9.6% construction, 9.2% production (2006-2010 5-year est.).

**Income:** Per capita income: $15,897 (2006-2010 5-year est.); Median household income: $36,153 (2006-2010 5-year est.); Average household income: $48,046 (2006-2010 5-year est.); Percent of households with income of $100,000 or more: 10.5% (2006-2010 5-year est.); Poverty rate: 25.8% (2006-2010 5-year est.).

**Taxes:** Total city taxes per capita: $549 (2009); City property taxes per capita: $444 (2009).

**Education:** Percent of population age 25 and over with: High school diploma (including GED) or higher: 67.2% (2006-2010 5-year est.); Bachelor's degree or higher: 12.3% (2006-2010 5-year est.); Master's degree or higher: 4.6% (2006-2010 5-year est.).

### School District(s)
Marlboro Central School District (KG-12)
  2009-10 Enrollment: 2,051 . . . . . . . . . . . . . . . . . . (845) 236-5802
Newburgh City School District (PK-12)
  2009-10 Enrollment: 12,094 . . . . . . . . . . . . . . . . (845) 563-3500
Valley Central School District (montgomery) (KG-12)
  2009-10 Enrollment: 4,853 . . . . . . . . . . . . . . . . . (845) 457-2400

### Four-year College(s)
Mount Saint Mary College (Private, Not-for-profit, Roman Catholic)
  Fall 2010 Enrollment: 2,261 . . . . . . . . . . . . . . . . (845) 561-0800
  2011-12 Tuition: In-state $24,410; Out-of-state $24,410

**Housing:** Homeownership rate: 31.8% (2010); Median home value: $219,100 (2006-2010 5-year est.); Median contract rent: $799 per month (2006-2010 5-year est.); Median year structure built: before 1940 (2006-2010 5-year est.).

**Hospitals:** St. Luke's Hospital (367 beds)

**Safety:** Violent crime rate: 187.5 per 10,000 population; Property crime rate: 406.7 per 10,000 population (2010).

**Newspapers:** Hospital Newspaper (National news; Circulation 100,000); Hudson Valley Black Press (Regional news; Circulation 42,500); Mid-Hudson Times (Local news; Circulation 4,600)

**Transportation:** Commute to work: 74.4% car, 4.2% public transportation, 8.7% walk, 2.9% work from home (2006-2010 5-year est.); Travel time to work: 36.9% less than 15 minutes, 34.4% 15 to 30 minutes, 18.8% 30 to 45 minutes, 4.1% 45 to 60 minutes, 5.8% 60 minutes or more (2006-2010 5-year est.)

**Airports:** Stewart International (primary service/small hub)

**Additional Information Contacts**
City of Newburgh . . . . . . . . . . . . . . . . . . . . . . . . . (845) 569-7311
  http://www.cityofnewburgh-ny.gov

## NEWBURGH (town).
Covers a land area of 42.677 square miles and a water area of 4.265 square miles. Located at 41.55° N. Lat; 74.05° W. Long. Elevation is 128 feet.

**Population:** 24,066 (1990); 27,568 (2000); 29,801 (2010); Density: 698.3 persons per square mile (2010); Race: 76.5% White, 12.2% Black, 3.0% Asian, 0.3% American Indian/Alaska Native, 0.0% Native Hawaiian/Other Pacific Islander, 8.0% Other, 15.7% Hispanic of any race (2010); Average household size: 2.74 (2010); Median age: 41.8 (2010); Males per 100 females: 95.7 (2010); Marriage status: 25.9% never married, 57.4% now married, 6.6% widowed, 10.0% divorced (2006-2010 5-year est.); Foreign born: 10.4% (2006-2010 5-year est.); Ancestry (includes multiple ancestries): 21.9% Italian, 18.2% Irish, 14.0% German, 7.8% English, 5.4% American (2006-2010 5-year est.).

**Economy:** Unemployment rate: 8.6% (February 2012); Total civilian labor force: 15,629 (February 2012); Single-family building permits issued: 26 (2011); Multi-family building permits issued: 4 (2011); Employment by occupation: 14.4% management, 4.3% professional, 8.3% services, 18.9% sales, 4.5% farming, 8.3% construction, 6.2% production (2006-2010 5-year est.).

**Income:** Per capita income: $33,906 (2006-2010 5-year est.); Median household income: $77,027 (2006-2010 5-year est.); Average household income: $91,468 (2006-2010 5-year est.); Percent of households with income of $100,000 or more: 35.5% (2006-2010 5-year est.); Poverty rate: 6.0% (2006-2010 5-year est.).

**Taxes:** Total city taxes per capita: $596 (2009); City property taxes per capita: $520 (2009).

**Education:** Percent of population age 25 and over with: High school diploma (including GED) or higher: 90.2% (2006-2010 5-year est.);

Bachelor's degree or higher: 27.9% (2006-2010 5-year est.); Master's degree or higher: 12.1% (2006-2010 5-year est.).

### School District(s)
Marlboro Central School District (KG-12)
  2009-10 Enrollment: 2,051 . . . . . . . . . . . . . . . . . . (845) 236-5802
Newburgh City School District (PK-12)
  2009-10 Enrollment: 12,094 . . . . . . . . . . . . . . . . (845) 563-3500
Valley Central School District (montgomery) (KG-12)
  2009-10 Enrollment: 4,853 . . . . . . . . . . . . . . . . . (845) 457-2400

### Four-year College(s)
Mount Saint Mary College (Private, Not-for-profit, Roman Catholic)
  Fall 2010 Enrollment: 2,261 . . . . . . . . . . . . . . . . (845) 561-0800
  2011-12 Tuition: In-state $24,410; Out-of-state $24,410

**Housing:** Homeownership rate: 83.9% (2010); Median home value: $304,300 (2006-2010 5-year est.); Median contract rent: $955 per month (2006-2010 5-year est.); Median year structure built: 1968 (2006-2010 5-year est.).

**Hospitals:** St. Luke's Hospital (367 beds)

**Safety:** Violent crime rate: 9.9 per 10,000 population; Property crime rate: 402.3 per 10,000 population (2010).

**Newspapers:** Hospital Newspaper (National news; Circulation 100,000); Hudson Valley Black Press (Regional news; Circulation 42,500); Mid-Hudson Times (Local news; Circulation 4,600)

**Transportation:** Commute to work: 89.7% car, 5.5% public transportation, 0.7% walk, 2.9% work from home (2006-2010 5-year est.); Travel time to work: 27.4% less than 15 minutes, 31.3% 15 to 30 minutes, 14.7% 30 to 45 minutes, 7.3% 45 to 60 minutes, 19.2% 60 minutes or more (2006-2010 5-year est.)

**Airports:** Stewart International (primary service/small hub)

## ORANGE LAKE (CDP).
Covers a land area of 6.044 square miles and a water area of 0.656 square miles. Located at 41.53° N. Lat; 74.09° W. Long. Elevation is 492 feet.

**Population:** 5,196 (1990); 6,085 (2000); 6,982 (2010); Density: 1,155.1 persons per square mile (2010); Race: 67.9% White, 18.7% Black, 4.1% Asian, 0.4% American Indian/Alaska Native, 0.1% Native Hawaiian/Other Pacific Islander, 8.8% Other, 18.6% Hispanic of any race (2010); Average household size: 2.72 (2010); Median age: 42.1 (2010); Males per 100 females: 93.4 (2010); Marriage status: 22.0% never married, 61.9% now married, 6.7% widowed, 9.4% divorced (2006-2010 5-year est.); Foreign born: 10.5% (2006-2010 5-year est.); Ancestry (includes multiple ancestries): 17.6% Italian, 15.0% Irish, 12.5% German, 5.1% American, 4.6% English (2006-2010 5-year est.).

**Economy:** Employment by occupation: 15.0% management, 4.7% professional, 7.1% services, 22.9% sales, 3.0% farming, 4.1% construction, 4.2% production (2006-2010 5-year est.).

**Income:** Per capita income: $34,938 (2006-2010 5-year est.); Median household income: $75,788 (2006-2010 5-year est.); Average household income: $96,613 (2006-2010 5-year est.); Percent of households with income of $100,000 or more: 37.1% (2006-2010 5-year est.); Poverty rate: 9.0% (2006-2010 5-year est.).

**Education:** Percent of population age 25 and over with: High school diploma (including GED) or higher: 89.2% (2006-2010 5-year est.); Bachelor's degree or higher: 28.6% (2006-2010 5-year est.); Master's degree or higher: 10.6% (2006-2010 5-year est.).

**Housing:** Homeownership rate: 88.1% (2010); Median home value: $294,000 (2006-2010 5-year est.); Median contract rent: $927 per month (2006-2010 5-year est.); Median year structure built: 1976 (2006-2010 5-year est.).

**Transportation:** Commute to work: 87.4% car, 8.8% public transportation, 1.5% walk, 1.3% work from home (2006-2010 5-year est.); Travel time to work: 22.6% less than 15 minutes, 33.8% 15 to 30 minutes, 15.4% 30 to 45 minutes, 6.6% 45 to 60 minutes, 21.7% 60 minutes or more (2006-2010 5-year est.)

## OTISVILLE (village).
Covers a land area of 0.764 square miles and a water area of 0 square miles. Located at 41.47° N. Lat; 74.53° W. Long. Elevation is 853 feet.

**Population:** 1,060 (1990); 989 (2000); 1,068 (2010); Density: 1,397.6 persons per square mile (2010); Race: 88.7% White, 6.7% Black, 2.1% Asian, 0.2% American Indian/Alaska Native, 0.0% Native Hawaiian/Other Pacific Islander, 2.3% Other, 11.2% Hispanic of any race (2010); Average household size: 2.85 (2010); Median age: 36.7 (2010); Males per 100 females: 106.6 (2010); Marriage status: 31.3% never married, 50.9% now married, 7.1% widowed, 10.7% divorced (2006-2010 5-year est.); Foreign

born: 2.6% (2006-2010 5-year est.); Ancestry (includes multiple ancestries): 34.3% Italian, 25.9% Irish, 16.9% German, 7.8% Dutch, 7.4% English (2006-2010 5-year est.).
**Economy:** Single-family building permits issued: 0 (2011); Multi-family building permits issued: 0 (2011); Employment by occupation: 4.9% management, 2.6% professional, 15.7% services, 16.2% sales, 6.3% farming, 10.4% construction, 7.7% production (2006-2010 5-year est.).
**Income:** Per capita income: $29,728 (2006-2010 5-year est.); Median household income: $61,875 (2006-2010 5-year est.); Average household income: $74,562 (2006-2010 5-year est.); Percent of households with income of $100,000 or more: 30.6% (2006-2010 5-year est.); Poverty rate: 5.9% (2006-2010 5-year est.).
**Education:** Percent of population age 25 and over with: High school diploma (including GED) or higher: 85.5% (2006-2010 5-year est.); Bachelor's degree or higher: 18.2% (2006-2010 5-year est.); Master's degree or higher: 8.5% (2006-2010 5-year est.).

### School District(s)
Minisink Valley Central School District (KG-12)
  2009-10 Enrollment: 4,543 . . . . . . . . . . . . . . . . . . . . . . . (845) 355-5110
**Housing:** Homeownership rate: 73.9% (2010); Median home value: $215,200 (2006-2010 5-year est.); Median contract rent: $660 per month (2006-2010 5-year est.); Median year structure built: before 1940 (2006-2010 5-year est.).
**Transportation:** Commute to work: 97.8% car, 1.4% public transportation, 0.0% walk, 0.7% work from home (2006-2010 5-year est.); Travel time to work: 10.4% less than 15 minutes, 55.3% 15 to 30 minutes, 18.1% 30 to 45 minutes, 4.6% 45 to 60 minutes, 11.7% 60 minutes or more (2006-2010 5-year est.)
**Additional Information Contacts**
Village of Otisville. . . . . . . . . . . . . . . . . . . . . . . . . . . . . (845) 386-5172
  http://villageofotisville.com

## PINE BUSH (CDP). Covers a land area of 2.106 square miles and a water area of 0.003 square miles. Located at 41.60° N. Lat; 74.29° W. Long. Elevation is 387 feet.
**Population:** 1,387 (1990); 1,539 (2000); 1,780 (2010); Density: 845.1 persons per square mile (2010); Race: 90.8% White, 2.5% Black, 1.6% Asian, 0.1% American Indian/Alaska Native, 0.2% Native Hawaiian/Other Pacific Islander, 4.8% Other, 9.2% Hispanic of any race (2010); Average household size: 2.29 (2010); Median age: 43.7 (2010); Males per 100 females: 81.8 (2010); Marriage status: 26.3% never married, 57.1% now married, 8.1% widowed, 8.5% divorced (2006-2010 5-year est.); Foreign born: 8.0% (2006-2010 5-year est.); Ancestry (includes multiple ancestries): 27.1% Irish, 20.2% American, 11.3% Dutch, 11.1% German, 10.6% English (2006-2010 5-year est.).
**Economy:** Employment by occupation: 8.9% management, 2.8% professional, 3.0% services, 14.8% sales, 6.3% farming, 27.7% construction, 8.6% production (2006-2010 5-year est.).
**Income:** Per capita income: $27,856 (2006-2010 5-year est.); Median household income: $61,083 (2006-2010 5-year est.); Average household income: $67,895 (2006-2010 5-year est.); Percent of households with income of $100,000 or more: 16.7% (2006-2010 5-year est.); Poverty rate: 3.9% (2006-2010 5-year est.).
**Education:** Percent of population age 25 and over with: High school diploma (including GED) or higher: 77.8% (2006-2010 5-year est.); Bachelor's degree or higher: 15.4% (2006-2010 5-year est.); Master's degree or higher: 7.1% (2006-2010 5-year est.).

### School District(s)
Pine Bush Central School District (PK-12)
  2009-10 Enrollment: 5,991 . . . . . . . . . . . . . . . . . . . . . . . (845) 744-2031
**Housing:** Homeownership rate: 55.0% (2010); Median home value: $240,800 (2006-2010 5-year est.); Median contract rent: $677 per month (2006-2010 5-year est.); Median year structure built: 1962 (2006-2010 5-year est.).
**Transportation:** Commute to work: 92.7% car, 5.2% public transportation, 0.0% walk, 2.1% work from home (2006-2010 5-year est.); Travel time to work: 30.0% less than 15 minutes, 15.8% 15 to 30 minutes, 30.8% 30 to 45 minutes, 11.2% 45 to 60 minutes, 12.2% 60 minutes or more (2006-2010 5-year est.)

## PINE ISLAND (unincorporated postal area)
Zip Code: 10969
  Covers a land area of 11.220 square miles and a water area of 0.007 square miles. Located at 41.29° N. Lat; 74.48° W. Long. Elevation is 410 feet. Population: 1,267 (2010); Density: 112.9 persons per square mile

(2010); Race: 92.8% White, 2.5% Black, 0.9% Asian, 0.1% American Indian/Alaska Native, 0.0% Native Hawaiian/Other Pacific Islander, 3.7% Other, 10.2% Hispanic of any race (2010); Average household size: 2.74 (2010); Median age: 42.4 (2010); Males per 100 females: 106.4 (2010); Homeownership rate: 74.9% (2010)

## PORT JERVIS (city). Covers a land area of 2.528 square miles and a water area of 0.179 square miles. Located at 41.37° N. Lat; 74.69° W. Long. Elevation is 446 feet.
**History:** Grew after opening (1828) of Delaware and Hudson Canal. It is one of the largest equestrian centers in nation. Settled before 1700, Incorporated 1907.
**Population:** 9,060 (1990); 8,860 (2000); 8,828 (2010); Density: 3,490.8 persons per square mile (2010); Race: 82.2% White, 7.4% Black, 1.3% Asian, 0.7% American Indian/Alaska Native, 0.0% Native Hawaiian/Other Pacific Islander, 8.4% Other, 11.9% Hispanic of any race (2010); Average household size: 2.45 (2010); Median age: 37.3 (2010); Males per 100 females: 92.9 (2010); Marriage status: 30.7% never married, 48.9% now married, 9.6% widowed, 10.7% divorced (2006-2010 5-year est.); Foreign born: 4.8% (2006-2010 5-year est.); Ancestry (includes multiple ancestries): 23.6% German, 20.5% Irish, 13.8% Italian, 12.6% American, 12.6% English (2006-2010 5-year est.).
**Economy:** Single-family building permits issued: 0 (2011); Multi-family building permits issued: 0 (2011); Employment by occupation: 2.9% management, 2.9% professional, 11.4% services, 19.4% sales, 3.7% farming, 9.4% construction, 6.9% production (2006-2010 5-year est.).
**Income:** Per capita income: $22,226 (2006-2010 5-year est.); Median household income: $42,938 (2006-2010 5-year est.); Average household income: $56,146 (2006-2010 5-year est.); Percent of households with income of $100,000 or more: 13.8% (2006-2010 5-year est.); Poverty rate: 13.7% (2006-2010 5-year est.).
**Education:** Percent of population age 25 and over with: High school diploma (including GED) or higher: 81.1% (2006-2010 5-year est.); Bachelor's degree or higher: 14.6% (2006-2010 5-year est.); Master's degree or higher: 5.4% (2006-2010 5-year est.).

### School District(s)
Port Jervis City School District (KG-12)
  2009-10 Enrollment: 3,064 . . . . . . . . . . . . . . . . . . . . . . . (845) 858-3175
**Housing:** Homeownership rate: 45.9% (2010); Median home value: $198,600 (2006-2010 5-year est.); Median contract rent: $714 per month (2006-2010 5-year est.); Median year structure built: before 1940 (2006-2010 5-year est.).
**Hospitals:** Bon Secours Community Hospital (183 beds)
**Safety:** Violent crime rate: 32.0 per 10,000 population; Property crime rate: 341.0 per 10,000 population (2010).
**Newspapers:** Gazette (Community news; Circulation 8,900)
**Transportation:** Commute to work: 85.7% car, 3.9% public transportation, 6.2% walk, 3.5% work from home (2006-2010 5-year est.); Travel time to work: 41.8% less than 15 minutes, 20.0% 15 to 30 minutes, 12.4% 30 to 45 minutes, 5.7% 45 to 60 minutes, 20.1% 60 minutes or more (2006-2010 5-year est.)
**Additional Information Contacts**
City of Port Jervis. . . . . . . . . . . . . . . . . . . . . . . . . . . . . (845) 858-4014
  http://portjervisny.org
Tri-State Chamber of Commerce. . . . . . . . . . . . . . . . . . . (845) 856-6694
  http://www.tristatechamber.org

## ROCK TAVERN (unincorporated postal area)
Zip Code: 12575
  Covers a land area of 9.893 square miles and a water area of 0.254 square miles. Located at 41.46° N. Lat; 74.17° W. Long. Elevation is 413 feet. Population: 2,258 (2010); Density: 228.2 persons per square mile (2010); Race: 88.0% White, 3.8% Black, 1.2% Asian, 0.4% American Indian/Alaska Native, 0.0% Native Hawaiian/Other Pacific Islander, 6.6% Other, 11.3% Hispanic of any race (2010); Average household size: 3.05 (2010); Median age: 40.5 (2010); Males per 100 females: 94.7 (2010); Homeownership rate: 90.0% (2010)

## SALISBURY MILLS (CDP). Covers a land area of 0.498 square miles and a water area of 0.004 square miles. Located at 41.43° N. Lat; 74.10° W. Long. Elevation is 305 feet.
**Population:** n/a (1990); n/a (2000); 536 (2010); Density: 1,074.7 persons per square mile (2010); Race: 96.3% White, 0.2% Black, 1.3% Asian, 0.4% American Indian/Alaska Native, 0.0% Native Hawaiian/Other Pacific Islander, 1.8% Other, 7.3% Hispanic of any race (2010); Average

household size: 3.02 (2010); Median age: 37.8 (2010); Males per 100 females: 103.8 (2010); Marriage status: 22.5% never married, 72.7% now married, 0.0% widowed, 4.8% divorced (2006-2010 5-year est.); Foreign born: 12.3% (2006-2010 5-year est.); Ancestry (includes multiple ancestries): 45.2% Irish, 26.7% German, 16.8% Italian, 12.3% British, 10.3% English (2006-2010 5-year est.).

**Economy:** Employment by occupation: 3.6% management, 17.3% professional, 0.0% services, 0.0% sales, 0.0% farming, 7.9% construction, 7.9% production (2006-2010 5-year est.).

**Income:** Per capita income: $33,213 (2006-2010 5-year est.); Median household income: $68,000 (2006-2010 5-year est.); Average household income: $73,548 (2006-2010 5-year est.); Percent of households with income of $100,000 or more: 29.3% (2006-2010 5-year est.); Poverty rate: 0.0% (2006-2010 5-year est.).

**Education:** Percent of population age 25 and over with: High school diploma (including GED) or higher: 100.0% (2006-2010 5-year est.); Bachelor's degree or higher: 33.3% (2006-2010 5-year est.); Master's degree or higher: 31.2% (2006-2010 5-year est.).

**Housing:** Homeownership rate: 81.3% (2010); Median home value: $257,400 (2006-2010 5-year est.); Median contract rent: $933 per month (2006-2010 5-year est.); Median year structure built: 1985 (2006-2010 5-year est.).

**Transportation:** Commute to work: 87.8% car, 12.2% public transportation, 0.0% walk, 0.0% work from home (2006-2010 5-year est.); Travel time to work: 23.0% less than 15 minutes, 8.6% 15 to 30 minutes, 15.8% 30 to 45 minutes, 32.4% 45 to 60 minutes, 20.1% 60 minutes or more (2006-2010 5-year est.)

**SCOTCHTOWN** (CDP). Covers a land area of 4.225 square miles and a water area of 0.012 square miles. Located at 41.47° N. Lat; 74.36° W. Long. Elevation is 722 feet.

**Population:** 8,765 (1990); 8,954 (2000); 9,212 (2010); Density: 2,180.1 persons per square mile (2010); Race: 61.7% White, 20.9% Black, 4.1% Asian, 0.4% American Indian/Alaska Native, 0.0% Native Hawaiian/Other Pacific Islander, 12.9% Other, 25.1% Hispanic of any race (2010); Average household size: 2.80 (2010); Median age: 36.6 (2010); Males per 100 females: 94.5 (2010); Marriage status: 33.2% never married, 52.5% now married, 2.7% widowed, 11.6% divorced (2006-2010 5-year est.); Foreign born: 13.2% (2006-2010 5-year est.); Ancestry (includes multiple ancestries): 17.4% Irish, 16.8% Italian, 13.0% German, 5.9% American, 4.3% Polish (2006-2010 5-year est.).

**Economy:** Employment by occupation: 8.4% management, 4.8% professional, 11.8% services, 23.7% sales, 6.8% farming, 6.1% construction, 6.4% production (2006-2010 5-year est.).

**Income:** Per capita income: $27,942 (2006-2010 5-year est.); Median household income: $68,723 (2006-2010 5-year est.); Average household income: $76,573 (2006-2010 5-year est.); Percent of households with income of $100,000 or more: 26.7% (2006-2010 5-year est.); Poverty rate: 4.8% (2006-2010 5-year est.).

**Education:** Percent of population age 25 and over with: High school diploma (including GED) or higher: 90.1% (2006-2010 5-year est.); Bachelor's degree or higher: 21.8% (2006-2010 5-year est.); Master's degree or higher: 7.6% (2006-2010 5-year est.).

**Housing:** Homeownership rate: 58.4% (2010); Median home value: $299,100 (2006-2010 5-year est.); Median contract rent: $946 per month (2006-2010 5-year est.); Median year structure built: 1976 (2006-2010 5-year est.).

**Transportation:** Commute to work: 91.4% car, 2.8% public transportation, 1.2% walk, 1.9% work from home (2006-2010 5-year est.); Travel time to work: 32.5% less than 15 minutes, 26.3% 15 to 30 minutes, 13.9% 30 to 45 minutes, 9.7% 45 to 60 minutes, 17.6% 60 minutes or more (2006-2010 5-year est.)

**SLATE HILL** (unincorporated postal area)

Zip Code: 10973

Covers a land area of 8.394 square miles and a water area of 0.128 square miles. Located at 41.38° N. Lat; 74.48° W. Long. Elevation is 499 feet. Population: 2,126 (2010); Density: 253.3 persons per square mile (2010); Race: 90.9% White, 1.9% Black, 1.7% Asian, 0.3% American Indian/Alaska Native, 0.0% Native Hawaiian/Other Pacific Islander, 5.2% Other, 10.1% Hispanic of any race (2010); Average household size: 2.88 (2010); Median age: 40.9 (2010); Males per 100 females: 100.9 (2010); Homeownership rate: 83.4% (2010)

**SOUTH BLOOMING GROVE** (village). Covers a land area of 4.673 square miles and a water area of 0.033 square miles. Located at 41.37° N. Lat; 74.16° W. Long.

**Population:** n/a (1990); n/a (2000); 3,234 (2010); Density: 691.9 persons per square mile (2010); Race: 84.8% White, 6.7% Black, 2.2% Asian, 0.4% American Indian/Alaska Native, 0.0% Native Hawaiian/Other Pacific Islander, 5.9% Other, 15.2% Hispanic of any race (2010); Average household size: 2.84 (2010); Median age: 40.9 (2010); Males per 100 females: 97.8 (2010); Marriage status: 28.4% never married, 59.7% now married, 4.2% widowed, 7.7% divorced (2006-2010 5-year est.); Foreign born: 8.1% (2006-2010 5-year est.); Ancestry (includes multiple ancestries): 37.5% Irish, 19.9% Italian, 18.0% German, 5.6% Polish, 4.1% African (2006-2010 5-year est.).

**Economy:** Employment by occupation: 11.6% management, 2.5% professional, 3.0% services, 20.0% sales, 4.8% farming, 11.3% construction, 3.5% production (2006-2010 5-year est.).

**Income:** Per capita income: $34,596 (2006-2010 5-year est.); Median household income: $85,332 (2006-2010 5-year est.); Average household income: $93,195 (2006-2010 5-year est.); Percent of households with income of $100,000 or more: 35.6% (2006-2010 5-year est.); Poverty rate: 4.2% (2006-2010 5-year est.).

**Education:** Percent of population age 25 and over with: High school diploma (including GED) or higher: 94.6% (2006-2010 5-year est.); Bachelor's degree or higher: 25.3% (2006-2010 5-year est.); Master's degree or higher: 10.0% (2006-2010 5-year est.).

**Housing:** Homeownership rate: 82.2% (2010); Median home value: $324,900 (2006-2010 5-year est.); Median contract rent: $918 per month (2006-2010 5-year est.); Median year structure built: 1968 (2006-2010 5-year est.).

**Transportation:** Commute to work: 91.6% car, 5.3% public transportation, 0.0% walk, 1.2% work from home (2006-2010 5-year est.); Travel time to work: 17.1% less than 15 minutes, 17.8% 15 to 30 minutes, 23.1% 30 to 45 minutes, 14.4% 45 to 60 minutes, 27.5% 60 minutes or more (2006-2010 5-year est.)

**SOUTHFIELDS** (unincorporated postal area)

Zip Code: 10975

Covers a land area of 5.883 square miles and a water area of 0.121 square miles. Located at 41.26° N. Lat; 74.17° W. Long. Elevation is 505 feet. Population: 281 (2010); Density: 47.8 persons per square mile (2010); Race: 89.7% White, 5.3% Black, 1.4% Asian, 0.0% American Indian/Alaska Native, 0.0% Native Hawaiian/Other Pacific Islander, 3.6% Other, 8.5% Hispanic of any race (2010); Average household size: 1.82 (2010); Median age: 47.1 (2010); Males per 100 females: 124.8 (2010); Homeownership rate: 51.3% (2010)

**SPARROW BUSH** (unincorporated postal area)

Zip Code: 12780

Covers a land area of 23.825 square miles and a water area of 0.716 square miles. Located at 41.44° N. Lat; 74.72° W. Long. Elevation is 509 feet. Population: 2,312 (2010); Density: 97.0 persons per square mile (2010); Race: 92.2% White, 2.8% Black, 0.7% Asian, 0.2% American Indian/Alaska Native, 0.0% Native Hawaiian/Other Pacific Islander, 4.1% Other, 5.4% Hispanic of any race (2010); Average household size: 2.50 (2010); Median age: 44.4 (2010); Males per 100 females: 105.9 (2010); Homeownership rate: 85.1% (2010)

**STERLING FOREST** (unincorporated postal area)

Zip Code: 10979

Covers a land area of 0.145 square miles and a water area of 0 square miles. Located at 41.18° N. Lat; 74.31° W. Long. Elevation is 656 feet. Population: 234 (2010); Density: 1,605.8 persons per square mile (2010); Race: 93.6% White, 0.4% Black, 1.7% Asian, 0.4% American Indian/Alaska Native, 0.0% Native Hawaiian/Other Pacific Islander, 3.9% Other, 6.8% Hispanic of any race (2010); Average household size: 2.27 (2010); Median age: 45.0 (2010); Males per 100 females: 107.1 (2010); Homeownership rate: 89.3% (2010)

**THOMPSON RIDGE** (unincorporated postal area)

Zip Code: 10985

Covers a land area of 0.257 square miles and a water area of 0 square miles. Located at 41.58° N. Lat; 74.37° W. Long. Elevation is 456 feet. Population: 58 (2010); Density: 225.6 persons per square mile (2010); Race: 89.7% White, 10.3% Black, 0.0% Asian, 0.0% American Indian/Alaska Native, 0.0% Native Hawaiian/Other Pacific Islander, 0.0%

Other, 1.7% Hispanic of any race (2010); Average household size: 3.05 (2010); Median age: 46.8 (2010); Males per 100 females: 81.3 (2010); Homeownership rate: 89.4% (2010)

## TUXEDO (town).
Covers a land area of 47.046 square miles and a water area of 2.299 square miles. Located at 41.24° N. Lat; 74.17° W. Long.

**History:** Tuxedo Park colony here, a private residential development begun (1886) by Pierre Lorillard, became known for its sports and social functions. King's College relocated here from Briarcliff Manor.

**Population:** 3,023 (1990); 3,334 (2000); 3,624 (2010); Density: 77.0 persons per square mile (2010); Race: 89.0% White, 2.3% Black, 5.3% Asian, 0.1% American Indian/Alaska Native, 0.0% Native Hawaiian/Other Pacific Islander, 3.3% Other, 7.1% Hispanic of any race (2010); Average household size: 2.46 (2010); Median age: 45.7 (2010); Males per 100 females: 99.8 (2010); Marriage status: 18.0% never married, 67.5% now married, 5.8% widowed, 8.6% divorced (2006-2010 5-year est.); Foreign born: 10.8% (2006-2010 5-year est.); Ancestry (includes multiple ancestries): 26.6% Italian, 17.4% German, 17.1% Irish, 13.0% English, 7.6% American (2006-2010 5-year est.).

**Economy:** Single-family building permits issued: 2 (2011); Multi-family building permits issued: 0 (2011); Employment by occupation: 16.9% management, 1.8% professional, 7.9% services, 21.6% sales, 0.5% farming, 5.5% construction, 3.1% production (2006-2010 5-year est.).

**Income:** Per capita income: $52,673 (2006-2010 5-year est.); Median household income: $78,571 (2006-2010 5-year est.); Average household income: $125,222 (2006-2010 5-year est.); Percent of households with income of $100,000 or more: 39.7% (2006-2010 5-year est.); Poverty rate: 2.9% (2006-2010 5-year est.).

**Education:** Percent of population age 25 and over with: High school diploma (including GED) or higher: 97.3% (2006-2010 5-year est.); Bachelor's degree or higher: 53.6% (2006-2010 5-year est.); Master's degree or higher: 21.5% (2006-2010 5-year est.).

**Housing:** Homeownership rate: 74.9% (2010); Median home value: $520,800 (2006-2010 5-year est.); Median contract rent: $875 per month (2006-2010 5-year est.); Median year structure built: 1966 (2006-2010 5-year est.).

**Safety:** Violent crime rate: 3.4 per 10,000 population; Property crime rate: 6.8 per 10,000 population (2010).

**Transportation:** Commute to work: 75.2% car, 10.9% public transportation, 1.1% walk, 12.3% work from home (2006-2010 5-year est.); Travel time to work: 17.1% less than 15 minutes, 30.9% 15 to 30 minutes, 28.5% 30 to 45 minutes, 5.5% 45 to 60 minutes, 18.0% 60 minutes or more (2006-2010 5-year est.)

**Additional Information Contacts**

Town of Tuxedo . . . . . . . . . . . . . . . . . . . . . . . . . . . . . . . . (845) 351-4411
   http://www.tuxedogov.org

## TUXEDO PARK (village).
Aka Tuxedo. Covers a land area of 2.655 square miles and a water area of 0.565 square miles. Located at 41.19° N. Lat; 74.21° W. Long. Elevation is 407 feet.

**Population:** 706 (1990); 731 (2000); 623 (2010); Density: 234.6 persons per square mile (2010); Race: 87.5% White, 0.8% Black, 6.3% Asian, 0.2% American Indian/Alaska Native, 0.0% Native Hawaiian/Other Pacific Islander, 5.2% Other, 5.1% Hispanic of any race (2010); Average household size: 2.51 (2010); Median age: 47.2 (2010); Males per 100 females: 104.3 (2010); Marriage status: 16.9% never married, 78.2% now married, 1.5% widowed, 3.4% divorced (2006-2010 5-year est.); Foreign born: 9.4% (2006-2010 5-year est.); Ancestry (includes multiple ancestries): 26.2% English, 21.2% Irish, 19.0% Italian, 17.2% German, 6.8% French (2006-2010 5-year est.).

**Economy:** Single-family building permits issued: 0 (2011); Multi-family building permits issued: 0 (2011); Employment by occupation: 32.0% management, 0.6% professional, 6.0% services, 13.8% sales, 0.9% farming, 3.1% construction, 2.2% production (2006-2010 5-year est.).

**Income:** Per capita income: $102,589 (2006-2010 5-year est.); Median household income: $128,333 (2006-2010 5-year est.); Average household income: $266,375 (2006-2010 5-year est.); Percent of households with income of $100,000 or more: 66.7% (2006-2010 5-year est.); Poverty rate: 2.0% (2006-2010 5-year est.).

**Education:** Percent of population age 25 and over with: High school diploma (including GED) or higher: 98.7% (2006-2010 5-year est.); Bachelor's degree or higher: 75.4% (2006-2010 5-year est.); Master's degree or higher: 39.4% (2006-2010 5-year est.).

Tuxedo Union Free School District (KG-12)
   2009-10 Enrollment: 618 . . . . . . . . . . . . . . . . . . . . . . . (845) 351-4799

**Housing:** Homeownership rate: 81.8% (2010); Median home value: $1 (2006-2010 5-year est.); Median contract rent: $1,069 per month (2006-2010 5-year est.); Median year structure built: before 1940 (2006-2010 5-year est.).

**Safety:** Violent crime rate: 0.0 per 10,000 population; Property crime rate: 0.0 per 10,000 population (2010).

**Transportation:** Commute to work: 65.2% car, 13.6% public transportation, 4.9% walk, 15.7% work from home (2006-2010 5-year est.); Travel time to work: 31.0% less than 15 minutes, 16.1% 15 to 30 minutes, 17.8% 30 to 45 minutes, 6.6% 45 to 60 minutes, 28.5% 60 minutes or more (2006-2010 5-year est.)

## UNIONVILLE (village).
Covers a land area of 0.310 square miles and a water area of 0 square miles. Located at 41.30° N. Lat; 74.56° W. Long. Elevation is 535 feet.

**Population:** 548 (1990); 536 (2000); 612 (2010); Density: 1,971.6 persons per square mile (2010); Race: 93.6% White, 2.9% Black, 0.5% Asian, 0.2% American Indian/Alaska Native, 0.0% Native Hawaiian/Other Pacific Islander, 2.8% Other, 8.7% Hispanic of any race (2010); Average household size: 2.63 (2010); Median age: 38.7 (2010); Males per 100 females: 90.1 (2010); Marriage status: 26.1% never married, 55.2% now married, 4.8% widowed, 13.9% divorced (2006-2010 5-year est.); Foreign born: 1.6% (2006-2010 5-year est.); Ancestry (includes multiple ancestries): 26.1% Irish, 17.2% German, 14.9% Italian, 11.7% American, 11.2% English (2006-2010 5-year est.).

**Economy:** Single-family building permits issued: 0 (2011); Multi-family building permits issued: 0 (2011); Employment by occupation: 8.7% management, 7.1% professional, 11.6% services, 18.3% sales, 0.0% farming, 17.0% construction, 16.6% production (2006-2010 5-year est.).

**Income:** Per capita income: $27,040 (2006-2010 5-year est.); Median household income: $46,750 (2006-2010 5-year est.); Average household income: $68,126 (2006-2010 5-year est.); Percent of households with income of $100,000 or more: 22.4% (2006-2010 5-year est.); Poverty rate: 2.9% (2006-2010 5-year est.).

**Education:** Percent of population age 25 and over with: High school diploma (including GED) or higher: 98.9% (2006-2010 5-year est.); Bachelor's degree or higher: 17.5% (2006-2010 5-year est.); Master's degree or higher: 6.5% (2006-2010 5-year est.).

**Housing:** Homeownership rate: 71.9% (2010); Median home value: $225,000 (2006-2010 5-year est.); Median contract rent: $850 per month (2006-2010 5-year est.); Median year structure built: before 1940 (2006-2010 5-year est.).

**Transportation:** Commute to work: 92.9% car, 0.0% public transportation, 0.8% walk, 3.3% work from home (2006-2010 5-year est.); Travel time to work: 17.6% less than 15 minutes, 30.5% 15 to 30 minutes, 30.9% 30 to 45 minutes, 0.9% 45 to 60 minutes, 20.2% 60 minutes or more (2006-2010 5-year est.)

## VAILS GATE (CDP).
Covers a land area of 1.061 square miles and a water area of 0 square miles. Located at 41.45° N. Lat; 74.05° W. Long. Elevation is 282 feet.

**Population:** 3,014 (1990); 3,319 (2000); 3,369 (2010); Density: 3,174.9 persons per square mile (2010); Race: 61.7% White, 16.5% Black, 6.4% Asian, 0.2% American Indian/Alaska Native, 0.1% Native Hawaiian/Other Pacific Islander, 15.1% Other, 26.2% Hispanic of any race (2010); Average household size: 2.30 (2010); Median age: 38.3 (2010); Males per 100 females: 87.0 (2010); Marriage status: 35.2% never married, 37.4% now married, 10.2% widowed, 17.2% divorced (2006-2010 5-year est.); Foreign born: 20.7% (2006-2010 5-year est.); Ancestry (includes multiple ancestries): 23.3% Irish, 21.7% Italian, 8.8% German, 8.6% English, 5.0% Dutch (2006-2010 5-year est.).

**Economy:** Employment by occupation: 12.6% management, 1.3% professional, 12.0% services, 18.4% sales, 1.9% farming, 1.5% construction, 8.1% production (2006-2010 5-year est.).

**Income:** Per capita income: $25,354 (2006-2010 5-year est.); Median household income: $42,277 (2006-2010 5-year est.); Average household income: $52,053 (2006-2010 5-year est.); Percent of households with income of $100,000 or more: 12.2% (2006-2010 5-year est.); Poverty rate: 10.5% (2006-2010 5-year est.).

**Education:** Percent of population age 25 and over with: High school diploma (including GED) or higher: 79.5% (2006-2010 5-year est.); Bachelor's degree or higher: 18.8% (2006-2010 5-year est.); Master's degree or higher: 8.0% (2006-2010 5-year est.).

**Housing:** Homeownership rate: 42.9% (2010); Median home value: $229,300 (2006-2010 5-year est.); Median contract rent: $950 per month (2006-2010 5-year est.); Median year structure built: 1969 (2006-2010 5-year est.).

**Transportation:** Commute to work: 95.5% car, 2.4% public transportation, 0.0% walk, 1.2% work from home (2006-2010 5-year est.); Travel time to work: 43.6% less than 15 minutes, 27.1% 15 to 30 minutes, 15.1% 30 to 45 minutes, 3.8% 45 to 60 minutes, 10.4% 60 minutes or more (2006-2010 5-year est.).

**WALDEN** (village). Covers a land area of 1.968 square miles and a water area of 0.081 square miles. Located at 41.55° N. Lat; 74.18° W. Long. Elevation is 374 feet.

**History:** Former factory town. Incorporated 1855.

**Population:** 5,817 (1990); 6,164 (2000); 6,978 (2010); Density: 3,545.6 persons per square mile (2010); Race: 78.9% White, 11.0% Black, 1.4% Asian, 0.2% American Indian/Alaska Native, 0.0% Native Hawaiian/Other Pacific Islander, 8.5% Other, 18.5% Hispanic of any race (2010); Average household size: 2.81 (2010); Median age: 35.0 (2010); Males per 100 females: 93.2 (2010); Marriage status: 29.0% never married, 55.3% now married, 7.2% widowed, 8.5% divorced (2006-2010 5-year est.); Foreign born: 5.7% (2006-2010 5-year est.); Ancestry (includes multiple ancestries): 20.6% Italian, 20.6% Irish, 15.9% German, 7.1% English, 7.1% American (2006-2010 5-year est.).

**Economy:** Single-family building permits issued: 1 (2011); Multi-family building permits issued: 0 (2011); Employment by occupation: 6.4% management, 1.8% professional, 13.1% services, 18.4% sales, 7.0% farming, 6.9% construction, 5.0% production (2006-2010 5-year est.).

**Income:** Per capita income: $27,326 (2006-2010 5-year est.); Median household income: $55,760 (2006-2010 5-year est.); Average household income: $67,918 (2006-2010 5-year est.); Percent of households with income of $100,000 or more: 20.8% (2006-2010 5-year est.); Poverty rate: 6.2% (2006-2010 5-year est.).

**Taxes:** Total city taxes per capita: $638 (2009); City property taxes per capita: $598 (2009).

**Education:** Percent of population age 25 and over with: High school diploma (including GED) or higher: 82.2% (2006-2010 5-year est.); Bachelor's degree or higher: 18.5% (2006-2010 5-year est.); Master's degree or higher: 9.1% (2006-2010 5-year est.).

**School District(s)**

Valley Central School District (montgomery) (KG-12)
　2009-10 Enrollment: 4,853 . . . . . . . . . . . . . . . . . . . . (845) 457-2400

**Housing:** Homeownership rate: 65.4% (2010); Median home value: $249,000 (2006-2010 5-year est.); Median contract rent: $754 per month (2006-2010 5-year est.); Median year structure built: 1964 (2006-2010 5-year est.).

**Safety:** Violent crime rate: 41.5 per 10,000 population; Property crime rate: 73.0 per 10,000 population (2010).

**Newspapers:** Wallkill Valley Times (Community news; Circulation 5,000)

**Transportation:** Commute to work: 89.6% car, 5.5% public transportation, 1.4% walk, 2.9% work from home (2006-2010 5-year est.); Travel time to work: 25.8% less than 15 minutes, 36.4% 15 to 30 minutes, 12.7% 30 to 45 minutes, 6.3% 45 to 60 minutes, 18.8% 60 minutes or more (2006-2010 5-year est.).

**WALLKILL** (town). Covers a land area of 62.106 square miles and a water area of 0.735 square miles. Located at 41.48° N. Lat; 74.40° W. Long.

**Population:** 23,025 (1990); 24,659 (2000); 27,426 (2010); Density: 441.6 persons per square mile (2010); Race: 68.2% White, 16.0% Black, 3.2% Asian, 0.5% American Indian/Alaska Native, 0.0% Native Hawaiian/Other Pacific Islander, 12.1% Other, 22.5% Hispanic of any race (2010); Average household size: 2.67 (2010); Median age: 39.1 (2010); Males per 100 females: 92.5 (2010); Marriage status: 31.6% never married, 52.2% now married, 5.6% widowed, 10.6% divorced (2006-2010 5-year est.); Foreign born: 13.0% (2006-2010 5-year est.); Ancestry (includes multiple ancestries): 19.0% Irish, 17.6% Italian, 14.8% German, 6.9% American, 5.2% English (2006-2010 5-year est.).

**Economy:** Unemployment rate: 8.0% (February 2012); Total civilian labor force: 14,135 (February 2012); Single-family building permits issued: 40 (2011); Multi-family building permits issued: 30 (2011); Employment by occupation: 9.1% management, 3.2% professional, 10.2% services, 24.4% sales, 4.1% farming, 11.2% construction, 5.7% production (2006-2010 5-year est.).

**Income:** Per capita income: $28,625 (2006-2010 5-year est.); Median household income: $65,949 (2006-2010 5-year est.); Average household income: $75,338 (2006-2010 5-year est.); Percent of households with income of $100,000 or more: 27.5% (2006-2010 5-year est.); Poverty rate: 8.1% (2006-2010 5-year est.).

**Education:** Percent of population age 25 and over with: High school diploma (including GED) or higher: 88.8% (2006-2010 5-year est.); Bachelor's degree or higher: 24.9% (2006-2010 5-year est.); Master's degree or higher: 9.5% (2006-2010 5-year est.).

**School District(s)**

Wallkill Central School District (KG-12)
　2009-10 Enrollment: 3,491 . . . . . . . . . . . . . . . . . . . . (845) 895-7101

**Housing:** Homeownership rate: 63.6% (2010); Median home value: $287,100 (2006-2010 5-year est.); Median contract rent: $919 per month (2006-2010 5-year est.); Median year structure built: 1976 (2006-2010 5-year est.).

**Safety:** Violent crime rate: 9.7 per 10,000 population; Property crime rate: 307.1 per 10,000 population (2010).

**Transportation:** Commute to work: 91.6% car, 3.7% public transportation, 1.0% walk, 2.0% work from home (2006-2010 5-year est.); Travel time to work: 29.5% less than 15 minutes, 28.5% 15 to 30 minutes, 13.5% 30 to 45 minutes, 8.8% 45 to 60 minutes, 19.8% 60 minutes or more (2006-2010 5-year est.).

**Additional Information Contacts**

Town of Wallkill . . . . . . . . . . . . . . . . . . . . . . . . . . . . . (845) 692-7800
　http://www.townofwallkill.com

**WALTON PARK** (CDP). Covers a land area of 2.329 square miles and a water area of 0.348 square miles. Located at 41.31° N. Lat; 74.22° W. Long. Elevation is 843 feet.

**Population:** 2,231 (1990); 2,330 (2000); 2,669 (2010); Density: 1,145.9 persons per square mile (2010); Race: 86.8% White, 4.3% Black, 3.9% Asian, 0.1% American Indian/Alaska Native, 0.0% Native Hawaiian/Other Pacific Islander, 4.9% Other, 13.0% Hispanic of any race (2010); Average household size: 2.99 (2010); Median age: 39.7 (2010); Males per 100 females: 98.7 (2010); Marriage status: 31.4% never married, 45.2% now married, 7.8% widowed, 15.6% divorced (2006-2010 5-year est.); Foreign born: 5.5% (2006-2010 5-year est.); Ancestry (includes multiple ancestries): 23.7% Italian, 20.2% Irish, 8.3% German, 7.2% American, 6.9% Polish (2006-2010 5-year est.).

**Economy:** Employment by occupation: 5.0% management, 7.4% professional, 4.9% services, 21.4% sales, 3.0% farming, 4.3% construction, 3.9% production (2006-2010 5-year est.).

**Income:** Per capita income: $38,392 (2006-2010 5-year est.); Median household income: $123,458 (2006-2010 5-year est.); Average household income: $121,541 (2006-2010 5-year est.); Percent of households with income of $100,000 or more: 57.6% (2006-2010 5-year est.); Poverty rate: 3.0% (2006-2010 5-year est.).

**Education:** Percent of population age 25 and over with: High school diploma (including GED) or higher: 98.3% (2006-2010 5-year est.); Bachelor's degree or higher: 40.0% (2006-2010 5-year est.); Master's degree or higher: 15.2% (2006-2010 5-year est.).

**Housing:** Homeownership rate: 89.4% (2010); Median home value: $342,100 (2006-2010 5-year est.); Median contract rent: $586 per month (2006-2010 5-year est.); Median year structure built: 1966 (2006-2010 5-year est.).

**Transportation:** Commute to work: 87.1% car, 7.7% public transportation, 1.0% walk, 2.7% work from home (2006-2010 5-year est.); Travel time to work: 16.1% less than 15 minutes, 32.5% 15 to 30 minutes, 10.0% 30 to 45 minutes, 9.3% 45 to 60 minutes, 32.1% 60 minutes or more (2006-2010 5-year est.).

**WARWICK** (village). Covers a land area of 2.416 square miles and a water area of 0.003 square miles. Located at 41.25° N. Lat; 74.35° W. Long. Elevation is 518 feet.

**Population:** 6,107 (1990); 6,412 (2000); 6,731 (2010); Density: 2,785.2 persons per square mile (2010); Race: 91.5% White, 2.9% Black, 1.2% Asian, 0.2% American Indian/Alaska Native, 0.0% Native Hawaiian/Other Pacific Islander, 4.2% Other, 9.1% Hispanic of any race (2010); Average household size: 2.28 (2010); Median age: 46.2 (2010); Males per 100 females: 82.8 (2010); Marriage status: 23.5% never married, 49.9% now married, 12.8% widowed, 13.7% divorced (2006-2010 5-year est.); Foreign born: 4.5% (2006-2010 5-year est.); Ancestry (includes multiple ancestries): 31.9% Irish, 25.5% Italian, 20.8% German, 9.4% English, 6.1% Polish (2006-2010 5-year est.).

**Economy:** Single-family building permits issued: 13 (2011); Multi-family building permits issued: 0 (2011); Employment by occupation: 13.1% management, 3.6% professional, 9.8% services, 10.8% sales, 1.3% farming, 13.2% construction, 8.8% production (2006-2010 5-year est.).
**Income:** Per capita income: $37,369 (2006-2010 5-year est.); Median household income: $66,111 (2006-2010 5-year est.); Average household income: $86,570 (2006-2010 5-year est.); Percent of households with income of $100,000 or more: 30.2% (2006-2010 5-year est.); Poverty rate: 3.7% (2006-2010 5-year est.).
**Education:** Percent of population age 25 and over with: High school diploma (including GED) or higher: 92.1% (2006-2010 5-year est.); Bachelor's degree or higher: 39.5% (2006-2010 5-year est.); Master's degree or higher: 17.4% (2006-2010 5-year est.).

### School District(s)
Warwick Valley Central School District (KG-12)
   2009-10 Enrollment: 4,283 . . . . . . . . . . . . . . . . . . . . (845) 987-3010
**Housing:** Homeownership rate: 61.6% (2010); Median home value: $324,300 (2006-2010 5-year est.); Median contract rent: $882 per month (2006-2010 5-year est.); Median year structure built: 1979 (2006-2010 5-year est.).
**Hospitals:** St. Anthony Community Hospital (73 beds)
**Newspapers:** Warwick Valley Dispatch (Local news; Circulation 2,300)
**Transportation:** Commute to work: 87.2% car, 1.6% public transportation, 2.6% walk, 8.2% work from home (2006-2010 5-year est.); Travel time to work: 36.4% less than 15 minutes, 14.9% 15 to 30 minutes, 11.8% 30 to 45 minutes, 20.2% 45 to 60 minutes, 16.7% 60 minutes or more (2006-2010 5-year est.)
**Additional Information Contacts**
Warwick Valley Chamber of Commerce . . . . . . . . . . . . (845) 986-2720
   http://www.warwickcc.org

**WARWICK** (town). Covers a land area of 101.340 square miles and a water area of 3.546 square miles. Located at 41.25° N. Lat; 74.36° W. Long. Elevation is 518 feet.
**History:** Warwick was settled in 1746 by English immigrants from Warwickshire. Warwick Village Historic District. Incorporated in 1867.
**Population:** 27,174 (1990); 30,764 (2000); 32,065 (2010); Density: 316.4 persons per square mile (2010); Race: 88.4% White, 5.1% Black, 1.5% Asian, 0.3% American Indian/Alaska Native, 0.0% Native Hawaiian/Other Pacific Islander, 4.7% Other, 10.2% Hispanic of any race (2010); Average household size: 2.64 (2010); Median age: 43.2 (2010); Males per 100 females: 100.0 (2010); Marriage status: 25.6% never married, 59.0% now married, 6.4% widowed, 9.1% divorced (2006-2010 5-year est.); Foreign born: 8.4% (2006-2010 5-year est.); Ancestry (includes multiple ancestries): 31.2% Irish, 22.2% German, 21.3% Italian, 8.9% Polish, 6.8% English (2006-2010 5-year est.).
**Economy:** Unemployment rate: 7.5% (February 2012); Total civilian labor force: 15,717 (February 2012); Single-family building permits issued: 11 (2011); Multi-family building permits issued: 0 (2011); Employment by occupation: 14.2% management, 4.3% professional, 8.7% services, 15.0% sales, 2.5% farming, 11.9% construction, 5.6% production (2006-2010 5-year est.).
**Income:** Per capita income: $38,033 (2006-2010 5-year est.); Median household income: $84,104 (2006-2010 5-year est.); Average household income: $100,122 (2006-2010 5-year est.); Percent of households with income of $100,000 or more: 39.4% (2006-2010 5-year est.); Poverty rate: 3.8% (2006-2010 5-year est.).
**Taxes:** Total city taxes per capita: $314 (2009); City property taxes per capita: $266 (2009).
**Education:** Percent of population age 25 and over with: High school diploma (including GED) or higher: 93.3% (2006-2010 5-year est.); Bachelor's degree or higher: 35.4% (2006-2010 5-year est.); Master's degree or higher: 15.2% (2006-2010 5-year est.).

### School District(s)
Warwick Valley Central School District (KG-12)
   2009-10 Enrollment: 4,283 . . . . . . . . . . . . . . . . . . . . (845) 987-3010
**Housing:** Homeownership rate: 79.0% (2010); Median home value: $343,200 (2006-2010 5-year est.); Median contract rent: $912 per month (2006-2010 5-year est.); Median year structure built: 1967 (2006-2010 5-year est.).
**Hospitals:** St. Anthony Community Hospital (73 beds)
**Newspapers:** Warwick Valley Dispatch (Local news; Circulation 2,300)
**Transportation:** Commute to work: 87.2% car, 3.8% public transportation, 2.4% walk, 6.0% work from home (2006-2010 5-year est.); Travel time to work: 26.0% less than 15 minutes, 18.8% 15 to 30 minutes, 15.9% 30 to 45

minutes, 15.4% 45 to 60 minutes, 24.0% 60 minutes or more (2006-2010 5-year est.)

**WASHINGTON HEIGHTS** (CDP). Covers a land area of 1.486 square miles and a water area of 0.004 square miles. Located at 41.46° N. Lat; 74.41° W. Long. Elevation is 666 feet.
**Population:** 1,164 (1990); 1,318 (2000); 1,689 (2010); Density: 1,136.3 persons per square mile (2010); Race: 65.6% White, 16.3% Black, 3.2% Asian, 1.0% American Indian/Alaska Native, 0.0% Native Hawaiian/Other Pacific Islander, 13.9% Other, 29.7% Hispanic of any race (2010); Average household size: 2.69 (2010); Median age: 37.4 (2010); Males per 100 females: 93.0 (2010); Marriage status: 22.0% never married, 61.0% now married, 7.0% widowed, 9.9% divorced (2006-2010 5-year est.); Foreign born: 7.6% (2006-2010 5-year est.); Ancestry (includes multiple ancestries): 22.8% Irish, 13.1% American, 12.9% German, 8.6% Dutch, 8.5% English (2006-2010 5-year est.).
**Economy:** Employment by occupation: 12.0% management, 0.0% professional, 13.6% services, 30.5% sales, 6.2% farming, 16.5% construction, 5.4% production (2006-2010 5-year est.).
**Income:** Per capita income: $34,864 (2006-2010 5-year est.); Median household income: $78,214 (2006-2010 5-year est.); Average household income: $79,864 (2006-2010 5-year est.); Percent of households with income of $100,000 or more: 31.1% (2006-2010 5-year est.); Poverty rate: 0.0% (2006-2010 5-year est.).
**Education:** Percent of population age 25 and over with: High school diploma (including GED) or higher: 92.1% (2006-2010 5-year est.); Bachelor's degree or higher: 20.8% (2006-2010 5-year est.); Master's degree or higher: 9.7% (2006-2010 5-year est.).
**Housing:** Homeownership rate: 79.6% (2010); Median home value: $243,100 (2006-2010 5-year est.); Median contract rent: $440 per month (2006-2010 5-year est.); Median year structure built: 1957 (2006-2010 5-year est.).
**Transportation:** Commute to work: 100.0% car, 0.0% public transportation, 0.0% walk, 0.0% work from home (2006-2010 5-year est.); Travel time to work: 26.0% less than 15 minutes, 15.5% 15 to 30 minutes, 13.9% 30 to 45 minutes, 2.2% 45 to 60 minutes, 42.3% 60 minutes or more (2006-2010 5-year est.)

**WASHINGTONVILLE** (village). Covers a land area of 2.538 square miles and a water area of 0.013 square miles. Located at 41.42° N. Lat; 74.15° W. Long. Elevation is 305 feet.
**Population:** 4,911 (1990); 5,851 (2000); 5,899 (2010); Density: 2,324.1 persons per square mile (2010); Race: 80.3% White, 8.2% Black, 2.5% Asian, 0.5% American Indian/Alaska Native, 0.0% Native Hawaiian/Other Pacific Islander, 8.5% Other, 18.3% Hispanic of any race (2010); Average household size: 2.71 (2010); Median age: 41.1 (2010); Males per 100 females: 93.9 (2010); Marriage status: 25.6% never married, 56.5% now married, 6.6% widowed, 11.4% divorced (2006-2010 5-year est.); Foreign born: 6.3% (2006-2010 5-year est.); Ancestry (includes multiple ancestries): 28.6% Italian, 23.9% Irish, 14.0% German, 7.2% Polish, 4.6% American (2006-2010 5-year est.).
**Economy:** Single-family building permits issued: 0 (2011); Multi-family building permits issued: 0 (2011); Employment by occupation: 7.1% management, 4.1% professional, 5.9% services, 21.8% sales, 2.8% farming, 8.1% construction, 4.9% production (2006-2010 5-year est.).
**Income:** Per capita income: $30,455 (2006-2010 5-year est.); Median household income: $85,297 (2006-2010 5-year est.); Average household income: $82,969 (2006-2010 5-year est.); Percent of households with income of $100,000 or more: 36.8% (2006-2010 5-year est.); Poverty rate: 5.6% (2006-2010 5-year est.).
**Education:** Percent of population age 25 and over with: High school diploma (including GED) or higher: 88.8% (2006-2010 5-year est.); Bachelor's degree or higher: 19.9% (2006-2010 5-year est.); Master's degree or higher: 7.8% (2006-2010 5-year est.).

### School District(s)
Washingtonville Central School District (PK-12)
   2009-10 Enrollment: 4,630 . . . . . . . . . . . . . . . . . . . . (845) 497-4000
**Housing:** Homeownership rate: 78.0% (2010); Median home value: $304,000 (2006-2010 5-year est.); Median contract rent: $732 per month (2006-2010 5-year est.); Median year structure built: 1986 (2006-2010 5-year est.).
**Safety:** Violent crime rate: 13.1 per 10,000 population; Property crime rate: 120.9 per 10,000 population (2010).
**Newspapers:** Orange County Post (Community news; Circulation 2,800)

**Transportation:** Commute to work: 90.4% car, 5.7% public transportation, 0.4% walk, 2.5% work from home (2006-2010 5-year est.); Travel time to work: 13.8% less than 15 minutes, 28.2% 15 to 30 minutes, 13.2% 30 to 45 minutes, 15.1% 45 to 60 minutes, 29.8% 60 minutes or more (2006-2010 5-year est.)

**Additional Information Contacts**
Village of Washingtonville . . . . . . . . . . . . . . . . . . . . . . . . . . . (845) 496-3221

## WAWAYANDA (town). Covers a land area of 34.720 square miles and a water area of 0.308 square miles. Located at 41.38° N. Lat; 74.46° W. Long.

**Population:** 5,445 (1990); 6,273 (2000); 7,266 (2010); Density: 209.3 persons per square mile (2010); Race: 87.3% White, 5.0% Black, 1.9% Asian, 0.2% American Indian/Alaska Native, 0.0% Native Hawaiian/Other Pacific Islander, 5.6% Other, 12.2% Hispanic of any race (2010); Average household size: 2.95 (2010); Median age: 39.6 (2010); Males per 100 females: 98.2 (2010); Marriage status: 28.3% never married, 57.1% now married, 5.3% widowed, 9.2% divorced (2006-2010 5-year est.); Foreign born: 7.0% (2006-2010 5-year est.); Ancestry (includes multiple ancestries): 23.6% Italian, 21.1% Irish, 16.9% German, 14.6% Polish, 6.6% English (2006-2010 5-year est.).

**Economy:** Single-family building permits issued: 8 (2011); Multi-family building permits issued: 0 (2011); Employment by occupation: 11.8% management, 2.3% professional, 5.1% services, 20.0% sales, 1.8% farming, 12.8% construction, 7.2% production (2006-2010 5-year est.).

**Income:** Per capita income: $32,715 (2006-2010 5-year est.); Median household income: $93,354 (2006-2010 5-year est.); Average household income: $103,041 (2006-2010 5-year est.); Percent of households with income of $100,000 or more: 47.6% (2006-2010 5-year est.); Poverty rate: 5.1% (2006-2010 5-year est.).

**Education:** Percent of population age 25 and over with: High school diploma (including GED) or higher: 93.4% (2006-2010 5-year est.); Bachelor's degree or higher: 29.4% (2006-2010 5-year est.); Master's degree or higher: 11.6% (2006-2010 5-year est.).

**Housing:** Homeownership rate: 82.5% (2010); Median home value: $334,200 (2006-2010 5-year est.); Median contract rent: $951 per month (2006-2010 5-year est.); Median year structure built: 1977 (2006-2010 5-year est.).

**Transportation:** Commute to work: 92.8% car, 1.3% public transportation, 0.4% walk, 5.6% work from home (2006-2010 5-year est.); Travel time to work: 29.4% less than 15 minutes, 29.8% 15 to 30 minutes, 9.8% 30 to 45 minutes, 8.7% 45 to 60 minutes, 22.3% 60 minutes or more (2006-2010 5-year est.)

## WEST POINT (CDP). Covers a land area of 19.749 square miles and a water area of 0.901 square miles. Located at 41.36° N. Lat; 74.01° W. Long. Elevation is 154 feet.

**History:** The site of the United States Military Reservation has been known as West Point since Revolutionary times. In 1802, Congress authorized the establishment of the military academy here. It became a military school of the first order under Major Sylvanus Thayer, superintendent from 1817 to 1833. Many Civil War leaders on both sides were graduates of West Point.

**Population:** 8,024 (1990); 7,138 (2000); 6,763 (2010); Density: 342.4 persons per square mile (2010); Race: 80.4% White, 6.8% Black, 4.7% Asian, 0.4% American Indian/Alaska Native, 0.1% Native Hawaiian/Other Pacific Islander, 7.6% Other, 9.7% Hispanic of any race (2010); Average household size: 3.84 (2010); Median age: 20.9 (2010); Males per 100 females: 261.1 (2010); Marriage status: 88.2% never married, 11.4% now married, 0.0% widowed, 0.4% divorced (2006-2010 5-year est.); Foreign born: 3.1% (2006-2010 5-year est.); Ancestry (includes multiple ancestries): 29.0% German, 19.4% Irish, 16.0% Italian, 11.9% English, 6.6% Polish (2006-2010 5-year est.).

**Economy:** Employment by occupation: 5.1% management, 2.0% professional, 3.7% services, 15.5% sales, 7.1% farming, 19.4% construction, 6.2% production (2006-2010 5-year est.).

**Income:** Per capita income: $15,567 (2006-2010 5-year est.); Median household income: $92,841 (2006-2010 5-year est.); Average household income: $126,289 (2006-2010 5-year est.); Percent of households with income of $100,000 or more: 44.0% (2006-2010 5-year est.); Poverty rate: 0.0% (2006-2010 5-year est.).

**Education:** Percent of population age 25 and over with: High school diploma (including GED) or higher: 98.3% (2006-2010 5-year est.); Bachelor's degree or higher: 69.2% (2006-2010 5-year est.); Master's degree or higher: 47.5% (2006-2010 5-year est.).

United States Military Academy (Public)
Fall 2010 Enrollment: 4,728 . . . . . . . . . . . . . . . . . . . . . . . . (845) 938-4011

**Housing:** Homeownership rate: 0.5% (2010); Median home value: n/a (2006-2010 5-year est.); Median contract rent: n/a per month (2006-2010 5-year est.); Median year structure built: 1970 (2006-2010 5-year est.).

**Hospitals:** Keller Army Community Hospital (35 beds)

**Transportation:** Commute to work: 12.5% car, 0.4% public transportation, 41.9% walk, 43.3% work from home (2006-2010 5-year est.); Travel time to work: 95.9% less than 15 minutes, 2.4% 15 to 30 minutes, 0.3% 30 to 45 minutes, 0.2% 45 to 60 minutes, 1.2% 60 minutes or more (2006-2010 5-year est.)

## WESTTOWN (unincorporated postal area)
Zip Code: 10998

Covers a land area of 18.653 square miles and a water area of 0.141 square miles. Located at 41.32° N. Lat; 74.54° W. Long. Elevation is 502 feet. Population: 3,122 (2010); Density: 167.4 persons per square mile (2010); Race: 90.6% White, 2.9% Black, 1.4% Asian, 0.2% American Indian/Alaska Native, 0.0% Native Hawaiian/Other Pacific Islander, 4.9% Other, 9.2% Hispanic of any race (2010); Average household size: 3.07 (2010); Median age: 39.6 (2010); Males per 100 females: 100.0 (2010); Homeownership rate: 84.6% (2010)

## WOODBURY (town). Covers a land area of 36.124 square miles and a water area of 1.075 square miles. Located at 41.32° N. Lat; 74.10° W. Long. Elevation is 482 feet.

**Population:** 8,236 (1990); 9,460 (2000); 11,353 (2010); Density: 314.3 persons per square mile (2010); Race: 79.1% White, 6.5% Black, 6.1% Asian, 0.3% American Indian/Alaska Native, 0.1% Native Hawaiian/Other Pacific Islander, 7.9% Other, 14.7% Hispanic of any race (2010); Average household size: 3.13 (2010); Median age: 38.1 (2010); Males per 100 females: 98.7 (2010); Marriage status: 23.8% never married, 64.5% now married, 5.4% widowed, 6.3% divorced (2006-2010 5-year est.); Foreign born: 16.2% (2006-2010 5-year est.); Ancestry (includes multiple ancestries): 25.5% Irish, 18.1% Italian, 12.3% German, 8.4% American, 4.9% Polish (2006-2010 5-year est.).

**Economy:** Single-family building permits issued: 0 (2011); Multi-family building permits issued: 0 (2011); Employment by occupation: 14.8% management, 5.6% professional, 3.4% services, 14.3% sales, 3.9% farming, 9.2% construction, 6.5% production (2006-2010 5-year est.).

**Income:** Per capita income: $40,966 (2006-2010 5-year est.); Median household income: $106,084 (2006-2010 5-year est.); Average household income: $120,664 (2006-2010 5-year est.); Percent of households with income of $100,000 or more: 55.0% (2006-2010 5-year est.); Poverty rate: 3.2% (2006-2010 5-year est.).

**Education:** Percent of population age 25 and over with: High school diploma (including GED) or higher: 95.8% (2006-2010 5-year est.); Bachelor's degree or higher: 46.8% (2006-2010 5-year est.); Master's degree or higher: 21.8% (2006-2010 5-year est.).

**Housing:** Homeownership rate: 83.9% (2010); Median home value: $372,000 (2006-2010 5-year est.); Median contract rent: $1,142 per month (2006-2010 5-year est.); Median year structure built: 1981 (2006-2010 5-year est.).

**Safety:** Violent crime rate: 2.9 per 10,000 population; Property crime rate: 354.4 per 10,000 population (2010).

**Transportation:** Commute to work: 85.1% car, 7.8% public transportation, 1.1% walk, 4.3% work from home (2006-2010 5-year est.); Travel time to work: 19.0% less than 15 minutes, 18.6% 15 to 30 minutes, 20.2% 30 to 45 minutes, 15.5% 45 to 60 minutes, 26.7% 60 minutes or more (2006-2010 5-year est.)

## WOODBURY (village). Covers a land area of 35.602 square miles and a water area of 1.061 square miles. Located at 41.32° N. Lat; 74.10° W. Long. Elevation is 482 feet.

**Population:** n/a (1990); n/a (2000); 10,686 (2010); Density: 300.1 persons per square mile (2010); Race: 80.9% White, 5.7% Black, 5.2% Asian, 0.2% American Indian/Alaska Native, 0.0% Native Hawaiian/Other Pacific Islander, 8.0% Other, 14.5% Hispanic of any race (2010); Average household size: 3.14 (2010); Median age: 38.1 (2010); Males per 100 females: 98.2 (2010); Marriage status: 24.1% never married, 64.7% now married, 5.6% widowed, 5.6% divorced (2006-2010 5-year est.); Foreign born: 15.3% (2006-2010 5-year est.); Ancestry (includes multiple ancestries): 26.4% Irish, 18.8% Italian, 12.6% German, 8.7% American, 5.0% Polish (2006-2010 5-year est.).

**Economy:** Single-family building permits issued: 22 (2011); Multi-family building permits issued: 0 (2011); Employment by occupation: 14.8% management, 4.9% professional, 3.5% services, 14.5% sales, 3.9% farming, 9.4% construction, 6.8% production (2006-2010 5-year est.).
**Income:** Per capita income: $40,319 (2006-2010 5-year est.); Median household income: $106,454 (2006-2010 5-year est.); Average household income: $120,915 (2006-2010 5-year est.); Percent of households with income of $100,000 or more: 55.3% (2006-2010 5-year est.); Poverty rate: 3.4% (2006-2010 5-year est.).
**Education:** Percent of population age 25 and over with: High school diploma (including GED) or higher: 95.6% (2006-2010 5-year est.); Bachelor's degree or higher: 47.1% (2006-2010 5-year est.); Master's degree or higher: 21.5% (2006-2010 5-year est.).
**Housing:** Homeownership rate: 85.7% (2010); Median home value: $374,700 (2006-2010 5-year est.); Median contract rent: $1,035 per month (2006-2010 5-year est.); Median year structure built: 1980 (2006-2010 5-year est.).
**Transportation:** Commute to work: 84.5% car, 8.1% public transportation, 1.1% walk, 4.5% work from home (2006-2010 5-year est.); Travel time to work: 19.5% less than 15 minutes, 18.2% 15 to 30 minutes, 20.6% 30 to 45 minutes, 15.3% 45 to 60 minutes, 26.4% 60 minutes or more (2006-2010 5-year est.)

# Orleans County

Located in western New York; bounded on the north by Lake Ontario; drained by Oak Orchard Creek. Covers a land area of 391.40 square miles, a water area of 426.07 square miles, and is located in the Eastern Time Zone at 43.25° N. Lat., 78.23° W. Long. The county was founded in 1824. County seat is Albion.

Orleans County is part of the Rochester, NY Metropolitan Statistical Area. The entire metro area includes: Livingston County, NY; Monroe County, NY; Ontario County, NY; Orleans County, NY; Wayne County, NY

Weather Station: Albion 2 NE                                Elevation: 439 feet

|        | Jan  | Feb  | Mar  | Apr | May | Jun | Jul | Aug | Sep | Oct | Nov | Dec  |
|--------|------|------|------|-----|-----|-----|-----|-----|-----|-----|-----|------|
| High   | 32   | 35   | 44   | 57  | 69  | 78  | 82  | 80  | 73  | 61  | 49  | 37   |
| Low    | 18   | 19   | 26   | 37  | 47  | 57  | 62  | 61  | 54  | 43  | 34  | 24   |
| Precip | 2.7  | 2.0  | 2.8  | 3.0 | 3.0 | 3.1 | 3.0 | 3.0 | 3.6 | 3.1 | 3.2 | 3.0  |
| Snow   | 19.5 | 13.6 | 11.1 | 2.1 | 0.3 | 0.0 | 0.0 | 0.0 | 0.0 | 0.2 | 4.5 | 15.1 |

*High and Low temperatures in degrees Fahrenheit; Precipitation and Snow in inches*

**Population:** 41,846 (1990); 44,171 (2000); 42,883 (2010); Race: 89.8% White, 5.9% Black, 0.4% Asian, 0.6% American Indian/Alaska Native, 0.0% Native Hawaiian/Other Pacific Islander, 3.3% Other, 4.1% Hispanic of any race (2010); Density: 109.6 persons per square mile (2010); Average household size: 2.50 (2010); Median age: 41.0 (2010); Males per 100 females: 98.1 (2010).
**Religion:** Six largest groups: 15.9% Catholicism, 8.4% Baptist, 5.5% Methodist/Pietist, 2.3% Lutheran, 1.8% Non-Denominational, 1.8% Presbyterian-Reformed (2010)
**Economy:** Unemployment rate: 10.7% (February 2012); Total civilian labor force: 19,255 (February 2012); Leading industries: 25.8% manufacturing; 18.8% health care and social assistance; 15.5% retail trade (2009); Farms: 554 totaling 139,764 acres (2007); Companies that employ 500 or more persons: 1 (2009); Companies that employ 100 to 499 persons: 10 (2009); Companies that employ less than 100 persons: 671 (2009); Black-owned businesses: n/a (2007); Hispanic-owned businesses: n/a (2007); Asian-owned businesses: n/a (2007); Women-owned businesses: 757 (2007); Retail sales per capita: $6,573 (2010). Single-family building permits issued: 20 (2011); Multi-family building permits issued: 10 (2011).
**Income:** Per capita income: $20,812 (2006-2010 5-year est.); Median household income: $48,063 (2006-2010 5-year est.); Average household income: $56,420 (2006-2010 5-year est.); Percent of households with income of $100,000 or more: 12.7% (2006-2010 5-year est.); Poverty rate: 12.1% (2006-2010 5-year est.); Bankruptcy rate: 2.81% (2011).
**Taxes:** Total county taxes per capita: $687 (2009); County property taxes per capita: $341 (2009).
**Education:** Percent of population age 25 and over with: High school diploma (including GED) or higher: 84.2% (2006-2010 5-year est.); Bachelor's degree or higher: 15.1% (2006-2010 5-year est.); Master's degree or higher: 5.5% (2006-2010 5-year est.).
**Housing:** Homeownership rate: 75.3% (2010); Median home value: $86,400 (2006-2010 5-year est.); Median contract rent: $456 per month

(2006-2010 5-year est.); Median year structure built: 1949 (2006-2010 5-year est.)
**Health:** Birth rate: 100.7 per 10,000 population (2011); Death rate: 94.3 per 10,000 population (2011); Age-adjusted cancer mortality rate: 194.6 deaths per 100,000 population (2009); Number of physicians: 6.4 per 10,000 population (2008); Hospital beds: 23.8 per 10,000 population (2007); Hospital admissions: 672.4 per 10,000 population (2007).
**Elections:** 2008 Presidential election results: 39.9% Obama, 58.5% McCain, 0.8% Nader
**National and State Parks:** Golden Hill State Park; Lakeside Beach State Park
**Additional Information Contacts**
Orleans County Government . . . . . . . . . . . . . . . . . . (585) 589-5334
  http://www.orleansny.com
Orleans County Chamber of Commerce . . . . . . . . . (585) 589-7727
  http://www.orleanschamber.com
Village of Medina . . . . . . . . . . . . . . . . . . . . . . . . . (585) 798-1790
  http://villagemedina.org/content

## Orleans County Communities

**ALBION** (village). County seat. Covers a land area of 2.919 square miles and a water area of 0 square miles. Located at 43.24° N. Lat; 78.19° W. Long. Elevation is 538 feet.
**Population:** 5,904 (1990); 7,438 (2000); 6,056 (2010); Density: 2,074.3 persons per square mile (2010); Race: 83.7% White, 9.2% Black, 0.7% Asian, 0.5% American Indian/Alaska Native, 0.0% Native Hawaiian/Other Pacific Islander, 5.9% Other, 6.3% Hispanic of any race (2010); Average household size: 2.36 (2010); Median age: 36.7 (2010); Males per 100 females: 90.7 (2010); Marriage status: 29.8% never married, 41.6% now married, 11.8% widowed, 16.7% divorced (2006-2010 5-year est.); Foreign born: 4.4% (2006-2010 5-year est.); Ancestry (includes multiple ancestries): 21.0% Italian, 18.0% English, 16.1% Irish, 14.8% German, 7.8% Polish (2006-2010 5-year est.).
**Economy:** Single-family building permits issued: 0 (2011); Multi-family building permits issued: 0 (2011); Employment by occupation: 10.5% management, 1.9% professional, 7.4% services, 16.0% sales, 4.6% farming, 11.3% construction, 16.6% production (2006-2010 5-year est.).
**Income:** Per capita income: $19,423 (2006-2010 5-year est.); Median household income: $35,576 (2006-2010 5-year est.); Average household income: $46,636 (2006-2010 5-year est.); Percent of households with income of $100,000 or more: 6.6% (2006-2010 5-year est.); Poverty rate: 15.4% (2006-2010 5-year est.).
**Education:** Percent of population age 25 and over with: High school diploma (including GED) or higher: 87.4% (2006-2010 5-year est.); Bachelor's degree or higher: 12.9% (2006-2010 5-year est.); Master's degree or higher: 0.9% (2006-2010 5-year est.).
**School District(s)**
Albion Central School District (PK-12)
    2009-10 Enrollment: 2,268 . . . . . . . . . . . . . . . . . (585) 589-2056
**Housing:** Homeownership rate: 57.3% (2010); Median home value: $65,400 (2006-2010 5-year est.); Median contract rent: $452 per month (2006-2010 5-year est.); Median year structure built: before 1940 (2006-2010 5-year est.).
**Newspapers:** Albion Advertiser (Community news; Circulation 1,450); Lake Country Pennysaver (Community news; Circulation 20,300)
**Transportation:** Commute to work: 93.0% car, 2.0% public transportation, 2.0% walk, 1.3% work from home (2006-2010 5-year est.); Travel time to work: 38.5% less than 15 minutes, 27.0% 15 to 30 minutes, 18.6% 30 to 45 minutes, 8.2% 45 to 60 minutes, 7.7% 60 minutes or more (2006-2010 5-year est.)
**Additional Information Contacts**
Orleans County Chamber of Commerce . . . . . . . . . (585) 589-7727
  http://www.orleanschamber.com

**ALBION** (town). Covers a land area of 25.257 square miles and a water area of 0.093 square miles. Located at 43.22° N. Lat; 78.20° W. Long. Elevation is 538 feet.
**History:** Albion was the home of George M. Pullman (1831-1897), originator of the Pullman railroad cars. Pullman was a cabinetmaker here from 1848 to 1855. Disgusted with the dirt, discomfort, and inconvenience of early railroad passenger cars, he conceived the idea of a car with the luxuries of beds and upholstered seats. Incorporated in 1828.
**Population:** 8,178 (1990); 8,042 (2000); 8,468 (2010); Density: 335.3 persons per square mile (2010); Race: 76.3% White, 17.6% Black, 0.5%

Asian, 0.6% American Indian/Alaska Native, 0.0% Native Hawaiian/Other Pacific Islander, 5.0% Other, 7.4% Hispanic of any race (2010); Average household size: 2.48 (2010); Median age: 36.7 (2010); Males per 100 females: 99.0 (2010); Marriage status: 39.1% never married, 36.9% now married, 7.5% widowed, 16.5% divorced (2006-2010 5-year est.); Foreign born: 6.7% (2006-2010 5-year est.); Ancestry (includes multiple ancestries): 16.2% Italian, 14.8% English, 14.1% German, 13.9% Irish, 7.2% Polish (2006-2010 5-year est.).
**Economy:** Single-family building permits issued: 3 (2011); Multi-family building permits issued: 0 (2011); Employment by occupation: 11.2% management, 2.4% professional, 7.6% services, 17.3% sales, 3.6% farming, 11.4% construction, 12.3% production (2006-2010 5-year est.).
**Income:** Per capita income: $15,515 (2006-2010 5-year est.); Median household income: $36,563 (2006-2010 5-year est.); Average household income: $50,727 (2006-2010 5-year est.); Percent of households with income of $100,000 or more: 9.0% (2006-2010 5-year est.); Poverty rate: 16.4% (2006-2010 5-year est.).
**Education:** Percent of population age 25 and over with: High school diploma (including GED) or higher: 82.1% (2006-2010 5-year est.); Bachelor's degree or higher: 12.7% (2006-2010 5-year est.); Master's degree or higher: 1.9% (2006-2010 5-year est.).
**School District(s)**
Albion Central School District (PK-12)
    2009-10 Enrollment: 2,268 . . . . . . . . . . . . . . . . . (585) 589-2056
**Housing:** Homeownership rate: 59.7% (2010); Median home value: $78,700 (2006-2010 5-year est.); Median contract rent: $440 per month (2006-2010 5-year est.); Median year structure built: before 1940 (2006-2010 5-year est.).
**Newspapers:** Albion Advertiser (Community news; Circulation 1,450); Lake Country Pennysaver (Community news; Circulation 20,300)
**Transportation:** Commute to work: 92.4% car, 1.8% public transportation, 2.4% walk, 2.7% work from home (2006-2010 5-year est.); Travel time to work: 41.7% less than 15 minutes, 26.7% 15 to 30 minutes, 14.6% 30 to 45 minutes, 9.8% 45 to 60 minutes, 7.2% 60 minutes or more (2006-2010 5-year est.)

**BARRE** (town). Covers a land area of 55.040 square miles and a water area of 0.010 square miles. Located at 43.17° N. Lat; 78.21° W. Long.
**Population:** 2,093 (1990); 2,124 (2000); 2,025 (2010); Density: 36.8 persons per square mile (2010); Race: 94.8% White, 0.9% Black, 0.8% Asian, 0.6% American Indian/Alaska Native, 0.0% Native Hawaiian/Other Pacific Islander, 2.9% Other, 3.3% Hispanic of any race (2010); Average household size: 2.62 (2010); Median age: 43.1 (2010); Males per 100 females: 105.6 (2010); Marriage status: 27.4% never married, 61.5% now married, 5.0% widowed, 6.0% divorced (2006-2010 5-year est.); Foreign born: 0.9% (2006-2010 5-year est.); Ancestry (includes multiple ancestries): 33.0% German, 28.4% English, 17.4% Irish, 9.4% Italian, 8.8% Polish (2006-2010 5-year est.).
**Economy:** Single-family building permits issued: 0 (2011); Multi-family building permits issued: 0 (2011); Employment by occupation: 9.8% management, 0.3% professional, 13.3% services, 19.4% sales, 2.3% farming, 16.1% construction, 9.5% production (2006-2010 5-year est.).
**Income:** Per capita income: $21,241 (2006-2010 5-year est.); Median household income: $56,696 (2006-2010 5-year est.); Average household income: $59,934 (2006-2010 5-year est.); Percent of households with income of $100,000 or more: 12.3% (2006-2010 5-year est.); Poverty rate: 10.1% (2006-2010 5-year est.).
**Education:** Percent of population age 25 and over with: High school diploma (including GED) or higher: 87.9% (2006-2010 5-year est.); Bachelor's degree or higher: 13.0% (2006-2010 5-year est.); Master's degree or higher: 4.9% (2006-2010 5-year est.).
**Housing:** Homeownership rate: 88.0% (2010); Median home value: $90,100 (2006-2010 5-year est.); Median contract rent: $538 per month (2006-2010 5-year est.); Median year structure built: 1946 (2006-2010 5-year est.).
**Transportation:** Commute to work: 93.3% car, 0.4% public transportation, 1.2% walk, 3.9% work from home (2006-2010 5-year est.); Travel time to work: 32.8% less than 15 minutes, 33.3% 15 to 30 minutes, 13.9% 30 to 45 minutes, 12.3% 45 to 60 minutes, 7.6% 60 minutes or more (2006-2010 5-year est.)

**CARLTON** (town). Covers a land area of 43.607 square miles and a water area of 0.800 square miles. Located at 43.33° N. Lat; 78.20° W. Long. Elevation is 344 feet.
**Population:** 2,808 (1990); 2,960 (2000); 2,994 (2010); Density: 68.7 persons per square mile (2010); Race: 93.2% White, 2.2% Black, 0.3% Asian, 0.9% American Indian/Alaska Native, 0.0% Native Hawaiian/Other Pacific Islander, 3.4% Other, 3.6% Hispanic of any race (2010); Average household size: 2.51 (2010); Median age: 44.2 (2010); Males per 100 females: 102.3 (2010); Marriage status: 20.4% never married, 66.3% now married, 2.8% widowed, 10.5% divorced (2006-2010 5-year est.); Foreign born: 3.7% (2006-2010 5-year est.); Ancestry (includes multiple ancestries): 24.6% German, 20.7% English, 15.8% Irish, 11.1% Italian, 9.6% Polish (2006-2010 5-year est.).
**Economy:** Single-family building permits issued: 6 (2011); Multi-family building permits issued: 0 (2011); Employment by occupation: 9.0% management, 2.1% professional, 8.6% services, 18.1% sales, 1.6% farming, 19.3% construction, 14.7% production (2006-2010 5-year est.).
**Income:** Per capita income: $22,207 (2006-2010 5-year est.); Median household income: $55,750 (2006-2010 5-year est.); Average household income: $61,648 (2006-2010 5-year est.); Percent of households with income of $100,000 or more: 9.2% (2006-2010 5-year est.); Poverty rate: 11.2% (2006-2010 5-year est.).
**Education:** Percent of population age 25 and over with: High school diploma (including GED) or higher: 89.0% (2006-2010 5-year est.); Bachelor's degree or higher: 18.0% (2006-2010 5-year est.); Master's degree or higher: 6.9% (2006-2010 5-year est.).
**Housing:** Homeownership rate: 83.4% (2010); Median home value: $96,600 (2006-2010 5-year est.); Median contract rent: $510 per month (2006-2010 5-year est.); Median year structure built: 1954 (2006-2010 5-year est.).
**Transportation:** Commute to work: 91.2% car, 0.0% public transportation, 2.9% walk, 2.8% work from home (2006-2010 5-year est.); Travel time to work: 17.7% less than 15 minutes, 45.0% 15 to 30 minutes, 19.5% 30 to 45 minutes, 9.0% 45 to 60 minutes, 8.8% 60 minutes or more (2006-2010 5-year est.)

**CLARENDON** (town). Covers a land area of 35.218 square miles and a water area of 0 square miles. Located at 43.17° N. Lat; 78.05° W. Long. Elevation is 607 feet.
**Population:** 2,705 (1990); 3,392 (2000); 3,648 (2010); Density: 103.6 persons per square mile (2010); Race: 96.8% White, 1.0% Black, 0.4% Asian, 0.3% American Indian/Alaska Native, 0.0% Native Hawaiian/Other Pacific Islander, 1.5% Other, 2.3% Hispanic of any race (2010); Average household size: 2.58 (2010); Median age: 43.2 (2010); Males per 100 females: 95.4 (2010); Marriage status: 17.8% never married, 68.0% now married, 6.2% widowed, 8.0% divorced (2006-2010 5-year est.); Foreign born: 0.9% (2006-2010 5-year est.); Ancestry (includes multiple ancestries): 34.2% German, 22.0% Irish, 17.0% English, 12.9% American, 10.7% Italian (2006-2010 5-year est.).
**Economy:** Single-family building permits issued: 3 (2011); Multi-family building permits issued: 10 (2011); Employment by occupation: 4.3% management, 6.3% professional, 13.5% services, 15.5% sales, 2.4% farming, 15.2% construction, 11.5% production (2006-2010 5-year est.).
**Income:** Per capita income: $24,293 (2006-2010 5-year est.); Median household income: $66,155 (2006-2010 5-year est.); Average household income: $70,556 (2006-2010 5-year est.); Percent of households with income of $100,000 or more: 23.2% (2006-2010 5-year est.); Poverty rate: 1.5% (2006-2010 5-year est.).
**Education:** Percent of population age 25 and over with: High school diploma (including GED) or higher: 87.3% (2006-2010 5-year est.); Bachelor's degree or higher: 16.3% (2006-2010 5-year est.); Master's degree or higher: 6.7% (2006-2010 5-year est.).
**Housing:** Homeownership rate: 89.1% (2010); Median home value: $101,100 (2006-2010 5-year est.); Median contract rent: $429 per month (2006-2010 5-year est.); Median year structure built: 1987 (2006-2010 5-year est.).
**Transportation:** Commute to work: 96.0% car, 0.8% public transportation, 0.6% walk, 1.2% work from home (2006-2010 5-year est.); Travel time to work: 19.4% less than 15 minutes, 37.2% 15 to 30 minutes, 27.0% 30 to 45 minutes, 11.4% 45 to 60 minutes, 5.0% 60 minutes or more (2006-2010 5-year est.)

**GAINES** (town). Covers a land area of 34.419 square miles and a water area of 0.039 square miles. Located at 43.27° N. Lat; 78.19° W. Long. Elevation is 423 feet.
**Population:** 3,025 (1990); 3,740 (2000); 3,378 (2010); Density: 98.1 persons per square mile (2010); Race: 91.7% White, 4.2% Black, 0.4% Asian, 0.3% American Indian/Alaska Native, 0.1% Native Hawaiian/Other Pacific Islander, 3.3% Other, 4.1% Hispanic of any race (2010); Average household size: 2.35 (2010); Median age: 45.4 (2010); Males per 100 females: 94.9 (2010); Marriage status: 27.5% never married, 46.7% now married, 14.4% widowed, 11.4% divorced (2006-2010 5-year est.); Foreign born: 4.3% (2006-2010 5-year est.); Ancestry (includes multiple ancestries): 29.3% English, 19.1% Italian, 19.0% German, 16.7% Irish, 12.3% Polish (2006-2010 5-year est.).
**Economy:** Single-family building permits issued: 1 (2011); Multi-family building permits issued: 0 (2011); Employment by occupation: 11.0% management, 0.0% professional, 9.8% services, 9.9% sales, 10.0% farming, 14.6% construction, 15.6% production (2006-2010 5-year est.).
**Income:** Per capita income: $24,061 (2006-2010 5-year est.); Median household income: $46,146 (2006-2010 5-year est.); Average household income: $54,976 (2006-2010 5-year est.); Percent of households with income of $100,000 or more: 11.8% (2006-2010 5-year est.); Poverty rate: 10.2% (2006-2010 5-year est.).
**Education:** Percent of population age 25 and over with: High school diploma (including GED) or higher: 86.3% (2006-2010 5-year est.); Bachelor's degree or higher: 17.6% (2006-2010 5-year est.); Master's degree or higher: 7.7% (2006-2010 5-year est.).
**Housing:** Homeownership rate: 79.3% (2010); Median home value: $74,700 (2006-2010 5-year est.); Median contract rent: $287 per month (2006-2010 5-year est.); Median year structure built: 1974 (2006-2010 5-year est.).
**Transportation:** Commute to work: 93.5% car, 0.0% public transportation, 0.0% walk, 1.6% work from home (2006-2010 5-year est.); Travel time to work: 40.0% less than 15 minutes, 24.1% 15 to 30 minutes, 16.8% 30 to 45 minutes, 13.8% 45 to 60 minutes, 5.3% 60 minutes or more (2006-2010 5-year est.)

**HOLLEY** (village). Covers a land area of 1.268 square miles and a water area of 0 square miles. Located at 43.22° N. Lat; 78.02° W. Long. Elevation is 541 feet.
**History:** Incorporated 1867.
**Population:** 1,925 (1990); 1,802 (2000); 1,811 (2010); Density: 1,428.1 persons per square mile (2010); Race: 96.2% White, 1.1% Black, 0.1% Asian, 0.2% American Indian/Alaska Native, 0.0% Native Hawaiian/Other Pacific Islander, 2.4% Other, 3.0% Hispanic of any race (2010); Average household size: 2.36 (2010); Median age: 36.4 (2010); Males per 100 females: 94.7 (2010); Marriage status: 29.4% never married, 53.5% now married, 7.3% widowed, 9.9% divorced (2006-2010 5-year est.); Foreign born: 2.3% (2006-2010 5-year est.); Ancestry (includes multiple ancestries): 26.9% Italian, 26.1% Irish, 24.0% German, 19.9% English, 5.6% Polish (2006-2010 5-year est.).
**Economy:** Single-family building permits issued: 0 (2011); Multi-family building permits issued: 0 (2011); Employment by occupation: 8.6% management, 3.2% professional, 15.9% services, 13.0% sales, 4.6% farming, 11.8% construction, 13.4% production (2006-2010 5-year est.).
**Income:** Per capita income: $19,093 (2006-2010 5-year est.); Median household income: $42,539 (2006-2010 5-year est.); Average household income: $46,646 (2006-2010 5-year est.); Percent of households with income of $100,000 or more: 5.3% (2006-2010 5-year est.); Poverty rate: 9.0% (2006-2010 5-year est.).
**Education:** Percent of population age 25 and over with: High school diploma (including GED) or higher: 88.8% (2006-2010 5-year est.); Bachelor's degree or higher: 13.5% (2006-2010 5-year est.); Master's degree or higher: 2.7% (2006-2010 5-year est.).
**School District(s)**
Holley Central School District (PK-12)
   2009-10 Enrollment: 1,254 . . . . . . . . . . . . . . . . . . . . . . . (585) 638-6316
**Housing:** Homeownership rate: 53.3% (2010); Median home value: $84,800 (2006-2010 5-year est.); Median contract rent: $514 per month (2006-2010 5-year est.); Median year structure built: before 1940 (2006-2010 5-year est.).
**Safety:** Violent crime rate: 36.5 per 10,000 population; Property crime rate: 243.2 per 10,000 population (2010).
**Transportation:** Commute to work: 93.5% car, 0.6% public transportation, 3.6% walk, 1.4% work from home (2006-2010 5-year est.); Travel time to work: 35.1% less than 15 minutes, 18.1% 15 to 30 minutes, 29.5% 30 to 45

minutes, 14.9% 45 to 60 minutes, 2.4% 60 minutes or more (2006-2010 5-year est.)

**KENDALL** (town). Covers a land area of 32.856 square miles and a water area of 0.060 square miles. Located at 43.32° N. Lat; 78.05° W. Long. Elevation is 338 feet.
**Population:** 2,769 (1990); 2,838 (2000); 2,724 (2010); Density: 82.9 persons per square mile (2010); Race: 96.7% White, 0.6% Black, 0.3% Asian, 0.7% American Indian/Alaska Native, 0.0% Native Hawaiian/Other Pacific Islander, 1.7% Other, 2.1% Hispanic of any race (2010); Average household size: 2.65 (2010); Median age: 44.7 (2010); Males per 100 females: 101.9 (2010); Marriage status: 23.6% never married, 65.5% now married, 5.1% widowed, 5.8% divorced (2006-2010 5-year est.); Foreign born: 0.7% (2006-2010 5-year est.); Ancestry (includes multiple ancestries): 32.4% German, 24.6% English, 16.0% Italian, 15.2% Irish, 11.2% Polish (2006-2010 5-year est.).
**Economy:** Single-family building permits issued: 1 (2011); Multi-family building permits issued: 0 (2011); Employment by occupation: 7.8% management, 6.8% professional, 7.1% services, 16.9% sales, 4.5% farming, 15.7% construction, 9.1% production (2006-2010 5-year est.).
**Income:** Per capita income: $28,019 (2006-2010 5-year est.); Median household income: $70,673 (2006-2010 5-year est.); Average household income: $74,699 (2006-2010 5-year est.); Percent of households with income of $100,000 or more: 22.7% (2006-2010 5-year est.); Poverty rate: 8.7% (2006-2010 5-year est.).
**Education:** Percent of population age 25 and over with: High school diploma (including GED) or higher: 92.1% (2006-2010 5-year est.); Bachelor's degree or higher: 26.9% (2006-2010 5-year est.); Master's degree or higher: 11.4% (2006-2010 5-year est.).
**School District(s)**
Kendall Central School District (PK-12)
   2009-10 Enrollment: 834 . . . . . . . . . . . . . . . . . . . . . . . (585) 659-2741
**Housing:** Homeownership rate: 89.4% (2010); Median home value: $113,300 (2006-2010 5-year est.); Median contract rent: $593 per month (2006-2010 5-year est.); Median year structure built: 1958 (2006-2010 5-year est.).
**Transportation:** Commute to work: 94.9% car, 0.5% public transportation, 2.7% walk, 1.9% work from home (2006-2010 5-year est.); Travel time to work: 19.6% less than 15 minutes, 23.5% 15 to 30 minutes, 35.6% 30 to 45 minutes, 14.3% 45 to 60 minutes, 7.1% 60 minutes or more (2006-2010 5-year est.)

**KENT** (unincorporated postal area)
Zip Code: 14477
   Covers a land area of 26.177 square miles and a water area of 0.117 square miles. Located at 43.33° N. Lat; 78.14° W. Long. Elevation is 341 feet. Population: 1,732 (2010); Density: 66.2 persons per square mile (2010); Race: 93.6% White, 1.9% Black, 0.2% Asian, 0.9% American Indian/Alaska Native, 0.0% Native Hawaiian/Other Pacific Islander, 3.4% Other, 3.8% Hispanic of any race (2010); Average household size: 2.69 (2010); Median age: 42.7 (2010); Males per 100 females: 97.3 (2010); Homeownership rate: 84.6% (2010)

**KNOWLESVILLE** (unincorporated postal area)
Zip Code: 14479
   Covers a land area of 1.480 square miles and a water area of 0 square miles. Located at 43.23° N. Lat; 78.31° W. Long. Elevation is 512 feet. Population: 275 (2010); Density: 185.8 persons per square mile (2010); Race: 97.1% White, 0.7% Black, 0.0% Asian, 0.0% American Indian/Alaska Native, 0.0% Native Hawaiian/Other Pacific Islander, 2.2% Other, 0.0% Hispanic of any race (2010); Average household size: 2.78 (2010); Median age: 40.6 (2010); Males per 100 females: 97.8 (2010); Homeownership rate: 86.9% (2010)

**LYNDONVILLE** (village). Covers a land area of 1.024 square miles and a water area of 0 square miles. Located at 43.32° N. Lat; 78.38° W. Long. Elevation is 322 feet.
**History:** Incorporated 1903.
**Population:** 953 (1990); 862 (2000); 838 (2010); Density: 818.0 persons per square mile (2010); Race: 94.3% White, 1.6% Black, 0.5% Asian, 1.3% American Indian/Alaska Native, 0.0% Native Hawaiian/Other Pacific Islander, 2.3% Other, 2.3% Hispanic of any race (2010); Average household size: 2.54 (2010); Median age: 39.9 (2010); Males per 100 females: 98.6 (2010); Marriage status: 34.9% never married, 45.4% now married, 10.2% widowed, 9.6% divorced (2006-2010 5-year est.); Foreign

born: 1.5% (2006-2010 5-year est.); Ancestry (includes multiple ancestries): 30.9% German, 24.4% English, 16.6% Irish, 11.5% Polish, 10.5% Italian (2006-2010 5-year est.).

**Economy:** Single-family building permits issued: 0 (2011); Multi-family building permits issued: 0 (2011); Employment by occupation: 10.8% management, 1.7% professional, 6.8% services, 15.7% sales, 2.8% farming, 6.0% construction, 7.4% production (2006-2010 5-year est.).

**Income:** Per capita income: $16,840 (2006-2010 5-year est.); Median household income: $39,904 (2006-2010 5-year est.); Average household income: $44,835 (2006-2010 5-year est.); Percent of households with income of $100,000 or more: 6.4% (2006-2010 5-year est.); Poverty rate: 16.8% (2006-2010 5-year est.).

**Education:** Percent of population age 25 and over with: High school diploma (including GED) or higher: 83.7% (2006-2010 5-year est.); Bachelor's degree or higher: 12.8% (2006-2010 5-year est.); Master's degree or higher: 5.3% (2006-2010 5-year est.).

#### School District(s)
Lyndonville Central School District (PK-12)
  2009-10 Enrollment: 720 . . . . . . . . . . . . . . . . . . . . . . . . (585) 765-3101

**Housing:** Homeownership rate: 73.6% (2010); Median home value: $76,700 (2006-2010 5-year est.); Median contract rent: $389 per month (2006-2010 5-year est.); Median year structure built: before 1940 (2006-2010 5-year est.).

**Transportation:** Commute to work: 89.3% car, 0.0% public transportation, 9.2% walk, 0.0% work from home (2006-2010 5-year est.); Travel time to work: 34.3% less than 15 minutes, 37.2% 15 to 30 minutes, 8.4% 30 to 45 minutes, 6.3% 45 to 60 minutes, 13.8% 60 minutes or more (2006-2010 5-year est.)

## MEDINA (village).
Covers a land area of 3.298 square miles and a water area of 0.077 square miles. Located at 43.21° N. Lat; 78.38° W. Long. Elevation is 531 feet.

**History:** Incorporated 1832.

**Population:** 6,686 (1990); 6,415 (2000); 6,065 (2010); Density: 1,838.6 persons per square mile (2010); Race: 87.2% White, 6.8% Black, 0.7% Asian, 0.8% American Indian/Alaska Native, 0.0% Native Hawaiian/Other Pacific Islander, 4.5% Other, 5.0% Hispanic of any race (2010); Average household size: 2.34 (2010); Median age: 39.9 (2010); Males per 100 females: 87.8 (2010); Marriage status: 32.8% never married, 44.2% now married, 7.9% widowed, 15.0% divorced (2006-2010 5-year est.); Foreign born: 3.3% (2006-2010 5-year est.); Ancestry (includes multiple ancestries): 26.9% German, 20.8% English, 15.6% Irish, 11.0% Polish, 7.0% Italian (2006-2010 5-year est.).

**Economy:** Single-family building permits issued: 0 (2011); Multi-family building permits issued: 0 (2011); Employment by occupation: 6.3% management, 2.1% professional, 14.2% services, 15.7% sales, 2.1% farming, 10.1% construction, 12.1% production (2006-2010 5-year est.).

**Income:** Per capita income: $19,995 (2006-2010 5-year est.); Median household income: $39,621 (2006-2010 5-year est.); Average household income: $50,062 (2006-2010 5-year est.); Percent of households with income of $100,000 or more: 10.5% (2006-2010 5-year est.); Poverty rate: 18.2% (2006-2010 5-year est.).

**Education:** Percent of population age 25 and over with: High school diploma (including GED) or higher: 78.4% (2006-2010 5-year est.); Bachelor's degree or higher: 15.7% (2006-2010 5-year est.); Master's degree or higher: 6.9% (2006-2010 5-year est.).

#### School District(s)
Medina Central School District (PK-12)
  2009-10 Enrollment: 1,904 . . . . . . . . . . . . . . . . . . . . . . (585) 798-2700
Orleans-Niagara Boces
  2009-10 Enrollment: n/a . . . . . . . . . . . . . . . . . . . . . . (800) 836-7510

**Housing:** Homeownership rate: 59.1% (2010); Median home value: $68,500 (2006-2010 5-year est.); Median contract rent: $441 per month (2006-2010 5-year est.); Median year structure built: before 1940 (2006-2010 5-year est.).

**Hospitals:** Medina Memorial Hospital (101 beds)

**Safety:** Violent crime rate: 37.1 per 10,000 population; Property crime rate: 401.1 per 10,000 population (2010).

**Newspapers:** The Journal-Register (Local news; Circulation 4,401); Medina Journal-Register (Local news; Circulation 4,401)

**Transportation:** Commute to work: 95.0% car, 0.0% public transportation, 3.6% walk, 0.4% work from home (2006-2010 5-year est.); Travel time to work: 44.5% less than 15 minutes, 29.7% 15 to 30 minutes, 10.7% 30 to 45 minutes, 6.1% 45 to 60 minutes, 9.0% 60 minutes or more (2006-2010 5-year est.)

**Additional Information Contacts**
Orleans County Chamber of Commerce . . . . . . . . . . . . . . (585) 589-7727
  http://www.orleanschamber.com
Village of Medina . . . . . . . . . . . . . . . . . . . . . . . . . (585) 798-1790
  http://villagemedina.org/content

## MURRAY (town).
Covers a land area of 31.058 square miles and a water area of 0.039 square miles. Located at 43.25° N. Lat; 78.05° W. Long. Elevation is 410 feet.

**Population:** 4,921 (1990); 6,259 (2000); 4,988 (2010); Density: 160.6 persons per square mile (2010); Race: 95.8% White, 0.9% Black, 0.1% Asian, 0.3% American Indian/Alaska Native, 0.0% Native Hawaiian/Other Pacific Islander, 2.9% Other, 3.4% Hispanic of any race (2010); Average household size: 2.47 (2010); Median age: 40.1 (2010); Males per 100 females: 97.0 (2010); Marriage status: 28.7% never married, 53.8% now married, 5.8% widowed, 11.6% divorced (2006-2010 5-year est.); Foreign born: 2.0% (2006-2010 5-year est.); Ancestry (includes multiple ancestries): 29.4% German, 22.2% Irish, 20.5% English, 20.1% Italian, 9.3% Polish (2006-2010 5-year est.).

**Economy:** Single-family building permits issued: 2 (2011); Multi-family building permits issued: 0 (2011); Employment by occupation: 8.6% management, 5.6% professional, 12.7% services, 14.5% sales, 2.5% farming, 9.9% construction, 14.4% production (2006-2010 5-year est.).

**Income:** Per capita income: $22,158 (2006-2010 5-year est.); Median household income: $47,850 (2006-2010 5-year est.); Average household income: $55,027 (2006-2010 5-year est.); Percent of households with income of $100,000 or more: 13.8% (2006-2010 5-year est.); Poverty rate: 10.9% (2006-2010 5-year est.).

**Education:** Percent of population age 25 and over with: High school diploma (including GED) or higher: 85.7% (2006-2010 5-year est.); Bachelor's degree or higher: 15.0% (2006-2010 5-year est.); Master's degree or higher: 3.9% (2006-2010 5-year est.).

**Housing:** Homeownership rate: 74.5% (2010); Median home value: $94,200 (2006-2010 5-year est.); Median contract rent: $514 per month (2006-2010 5-year est.); Median year structure built: 1962 (2006-2010 5-year est.).

**Transportation:** Commute to work: 93.5% car, 1.1% public transportation, 1.7% walk, 2.6% work from home (2006-2010 5-year est.); Travel time to work: 26.4% less than 15 minutes, 19.6% 15 to 30 minutes, 27.3% 30 to 45 minutes, 21.0% 45 to 60 minutes, 5.6% 60 minutes or more (2006-2010 5-year est.)

## RIDGEWAY (town).
Covers a land area of 50.025 square miles and a water area of 0.216 square miles. Located at 43.26° N. Lat; 78.37° W. Long. Elevation is 417 feet.

**Population:** 7,341 (1990); 6,886 (2000); 6,780 (2010); Density: 135.5 persons per square mile (2010); Race: 92.0% White, 3.4% Black, 0.6% Asian, 0.6% American Indian/Alaska Native, 0.0% Native Hawaiian/Other Pacific Islander, 3.4% Other, 3.7% Hispanic of any race (2010); Average household size: 2.50 (2010); Median age: 40.8 (2010); Males per 100 females: 97.2 (2010); Marriage status: 25.4% never married, 57.0% now married, 5.8% widowed, 11.8% divorced (2006-2010 5-year est.); Foreign born: 2.7% (2006-2010 5-year est.); Ancestry (includes multiple ancestries): 32.3% German, 25.5% English, 19.9% Irish, 12.6% Polish, 6.9% Italian (2006-2010 5-year est.).

**Economy:** Single-family building permits issued: 0 (2011); Multi-family building permits issued: 0 (2011); Employment by occupation: 5.7% management, 2.1% professional, 15.7% services, 17.9% sales, 3.3% farming, 12.7% construction, 10.7% production (2006-2010 5-year est.).

**Income:** Per capita income: $22,235 (2006-2010 5-year est.); Median household income: $44,518 (2006-2010 5-year est.); Average household income: $54,766 (2006-2010 5-year est.); Percent of households with income of $100,000 or more: 12.9% (2006-2010 5-year est.); Poverty rate: 11.5% (2006-2010 5-year est.).

**Education:** Percent of population age 25 and over with: High school diploma (including GED) or higher: 79.5% (2006-2010 5-year est.); Bachelor's degree or higher: 15.0% (2006-2010 5-year est.); Master's degree or higher: 7.9% (2006-2010 5-year est.).

**Housing:** Homeownership rate: 71.5% (2010); Median home value: $77,300 (2006-2010 5-year est.); Median contract rent: $465 per month (2006-2010 5-year est.); Median year structure built: before 1940 (2006-2010 5-year est.).

**Transportation:** Commute to work: 94.2% car, 0.0% public transportation, 2.9% walk, 2.1% work from home (2006-2010 5-year est.); Travel time to work: 40.6% less than 15 minutes, 31.2% 15 to 30 minutes, 16.3% 30 to 45

minutes, 3.9% 45 to 60 minutes, 8.0% 60 minutes or more (2006-2010 5-year est.)

## SHELBY (town). Aka Shelby Center. Covers a land area of 46.389 square miles and a water area of 0.338 square miles. Located at 43.17° N. Lat; 78.38° W. Long. Elevation is 600 feet.

**Population:** 5,509 (1990); 5,420 (2000); 5,319 (2010); Density: 114.7 persons per square mile (2010); Race: 87.3% White, 8.4% Black, 0.3% Asian, 0.6% American Indian/Alaska Native, 0.0% Native Hawaiian/Other Pacific Islander, 3.4% Other, 3.6% Hispanic of any race (2010); Average household size: 2.40 (2010); Median age: 40.3 (2010); Males per 100 females: 93.1 (2010); Marriage status: 35.0% never married, 43.6% now married, 9.4% widowed, 12.0% divorced (2006-2010 5-year est.); Foreign born: 1.6% (2006-2010 5-year est.); Ancestry (includes multiple ancestries): 31.9% German, 21.3% English, 17.6% Irish, 8.3% Italian, 7.8% American (2006-2010 5-year est.).
**Economy:** Single-family building permits issued: 1 (2011); Multi-family building permits issued: 0 (2011); Employment by occupation: 6.9% management, 0.5% professional, 9.9% services, 12.0% sales, 2.2% farming, 9.8% construction, 12.3% production (2006-2010 5-year est.).
**Income:** Per capita income: $18,201 (2006-2010 5-year est.); Median household income: $34,898 (2006-2010 5-year est.); Average household income: $48,983 (2006-2010 5-year est.); Percent of households with income of $100,000 or more: 10.0% (2006-2010 5-year est.); Poverty rate: 22.0% (2006-2010 5-year est.).
**Education:** Percent of population age 25 and over with: High school diploma (including GED) or higher: 81.2% (2006-2010 5-year est.); Bachelor's degree or higher: 11.2% (2006-2010 5-year est.); Master's degree or higher: 4.1% (2006-2010 5-year est.).
**Housing:** Homeownership rate: 68.6% (2010); Median home value: $76,300 (2006-2010 5-year est.); Median contract rent: $461 per month (2006-2010 5-year est.); Median year structure built: before 1940 (2006-2010 5-year est.).
**Transportation:** Commute to work: 96.6% car, 0.0% public transportation, 0.5% walk, 2.3% work from home (2006-2010 5-year est.); Travel time to work: 49.8% less than 15 minutes, 28.0% 15 to 30 minutes, 9.3% 30 to 45 minutes, 7.9% 45 to 60 minutes, 5.1% 60 minutes or more (2006-2010 5-year est.)

## WATERPORT (unincorporated postal area)
Zip Code: 14571

Covers a land area of 18.355 square miles and a water area of 0.505 square miles. Located at 43.34° N. Lat; 78.25° W. Long. Elevation is 351 feet. Population: 1,176 (2010); Density: 64.1 persons per square mile (2010); Race: 93.5% White, 2.6% Black, 0.1% Asian, 0.7% American Indian/Alaska Native, 0.0% Native Hawaiian/Other Pacific Islander, 3.1% Other, 2.6% Hispanic of any race (2010); Average household size: 2.37 (2010); Median age: 47.7 (2010); Males per 100 females: 103.5 (2010); Homeownership rate: 87.1% (2010)

## YATES (town). Aka Yates Center. Covers a land area of 37.386 square miles and a water area of 0 square miles. Located at 43.33° N. Lat; 78.38° W. Long. Elevation is 325 feet.
**Population:** 2,497 (1990); 2,510 (2000); 2,559 (2010); Density: 68.4 persons per square mile (2010); Race: 95.2% White, 1.1% Black, 0.2% Asian, 1.0% American Indian/Alaska Native, 0.0% Native Hawaiian/Other Pacific Islander, 2.5% Other, 2.8% Hispanic of any race (2010); Average household size: 2.63 (2010); Median age: 41.0 (2010); Males per 100 females: 103.9 (2010); Marriage status: 26.4% never married, 53.5% now married, 9.1% widowed, 11.0% divorced (2006-2010 5-year est.); Foreign born: 1.5% (2006-2010 5-year est.); Ancestry (includes multiple ancestries): 35.0% German, 27.6% English, 13.6% Irish, 12.2% American, 10.1% Polish (2006-2010 5-year est.).
**Economy:** Single-family building permits issued: 3 (2011); Multi-family building permits issued: 0 (2011); Employment by occupation: 7.0% management, 0.6% professional, 9.0% services, 16.6% sales, 4.9% farming, 10.1% construction, 8.6% production (2006-2010 5-year est.).
**Income:** Per capita income: $18,593 (2006-2010 5-year est.); Median household income: $42,917 (2006-2010 5-year est.); Average household income: $48,731 (2006-2010 5-year est.); Percent of households with income of $100,000 or more: 5.7% (2006-2010 5-year est.); Poverty rate: 9.9% (2006-2010 5-year est.).
**Education:** Percent of population age 25 and over with: High school diploma (including GED) or higher: 82.1% (2006-2010 5-year est.);

Bachelor's degree or higher: 10.2% (2006-2010 5-year est.); Master's degree or higher: 5.2% (2006-2010 5-year est.).
**Housing:** Homeownership rate: 82.2% (2010); Median home value: $80,700 (2006-2010 5-year est.); Median contract rent: $419 per month (2006-2010 5-year est.); Median year structure built: 1952 (2006-2010 5-year est.).
**Transportation:** Commute to work: 88.0% car, 0.0% public transportation, 5.8% walk, 4.9% work from home (2006-2010 5-year est.); Travel time to work: 33.2% less than 15 minutes, 30.3% 15 to 30 minutes, 13.0% 30 to 45 minutes, 9.1% 45 to 60 minutes, 14.4% 60 minutes or more (2006-2010 5-year est.)

# Oswego County

Located in north central New York; bounded on the northwest by Lake Ontario, and on the south by Oneida Lake and the Oneida River; drained by the Oswego and Salmon Rivers. Covers a land area of 953.30 square miles, a water area of 358.88 square miles, and is located in the Eastern Time Zone at 43.41° N. Lat., 76.24° W. Long. The county was founded in 1816. County seat is Oswego.

Oswego County is part of the Syracuse, NY Metropolitan Statistical Area. The entire metro area includes: Madison County, NY; Onondaga County, NY; Oswego County, NY

Weather Station: Oswego East                        Elevation: 350 feet

|        | Jan  | Feb  | Mar  | Apr | May | Jun | Jul | Aug | Sep | Oct | Nov | Dec  |
|--------|------|------|------|-----|-----|-----|-----|-----|-----|-----|-----|------|
| High   | 31   | 33   | 41   | 54  | 65  | 75  | 80  | 79  | 71  | 59  | 47  | 36   |
| Low    | 18   | 19   | 26   | 37  | 47  | 56  | 62  | 61  | 54  | 44  | 35  | 24   |
| Precip | 3.6  | 2.8  | 3.2  | 3.5 | 3.3 | 3.0 | 3.1 | 3.4 | 3.9 | 4.1 | 4.5 | 3.8  |
| Snow   | 45.0 | 32.8 | 17.1 | 3.8 | tr  | 0.0 | 0.0 | 0.0 | tr  | 0.2 | 8.5 | 34.6 |

*High and Low temperatures in degrees Fahrenheit; Precipitation and Snow in inches*

**Population:** 121,771 (1990); 122,377 (2000); 122,109 (2010); Race: 96.3% White, 0.8% Black, 0.6% Asian, 0.4% American Indian/Alaska Native, 0.0% Native Hawaiian/Other Pacific Islander, 1.9% Other, 2.1% Hispanic of any race (2010); Density: 128.1 persons per square mile (2010); Average household size: 2.52 (2010); Median age: 38.5 (2010); Males per 100 females: 99.4 (2010).
**Religion:** Six largest groups: 20.8% Catholicism, 6.3% Methodist/Pietist, 1.8% Holiness, 1.7% Non-Denominational, 0.9% Baptist, 0.7% Presbyterian-Reformed (2010)
**Economy:** Unemployment rate: 12.2% (February 2012); Total civilian labor force: 57,760 (February 2012); Leading industries: 20.5% health care and social assistance; 19.0% retail trade; 14.1% accommodation & food services (2009); Farms: 639 totaling 100,195 acres (2007); Companies that employ 500 or more persons: 6 (2009); Companies that employ 100 to 499 persons: 23 (2009); Companies that employ less than 100 persons: 2,078 (2009); Black-owned businesses: n/a (2007); Hispanic-owned businesses: n/a (2007); Asian-owned businesses: n/a (2007); Women-owned businesses: 2,349 (2007); Retail sales per capita: $9,955 (2010). Single-family building permits issued: 159 (2011); Multi-family building permits issued: 56 (2011).
**Income:** Per capita income: $21,604 (2006-2010 5-year est.); Median household income: $45,333 (2006-2010 5-year est.); Average household income: $56,390 (2006-2010 5-year est.); Percent of households with income of $100,000 or more: 13.9% (2006-2010 5-year est.); Poverty rate: 15.3% (2006-2010 5-year est.); Bankruptcy rate: 3.86% (2011).
**Taxes:** Total county taxes per capita: $654 (2009); County property taxes per capita: $328 (2009).
**Education:** Percent of population age 25 and over with: High school diploma (including GED) or higher: 86.3% (2006-2010 5-year est.); Bachelor's degree or higher: 15.7% (2006-2010 5-year est.); Master's degree or higher: 6.1% (2006-2010 5-year est.).
**Housing:** Homeownership rate: 72.3% (2010); Median home value: $88,000 (2006-2010 5-year est.); Median contract rent: $492 per month (2006-2010 5-year est.); Median year structure built: 1966 (2006-2010 5-year est.).
**Health:** Birth rate: 113.3 per 10,000 population (2011); Death rate: 80.8 per 10,000 population (2011); Age-adjusted cancer mortality rate: 209.4 deaths per 100,000 population (2009); Number of physicians: 8.4 per 10,000 population (2008); Hospital beds: 11.9 per 10,000 population (2007); Hospital admissions: 629.1 per 10,000 population (2007).
**Environment:** Air Quality Index: 94.2% good, 5.8% moderate, 0.0% unhealthy for sensitive individuals, 0.0% unhealthy (percent of days in 2010)

**Elections:** 2008 Presidential election results: 50.2% Obama, 47.8% McCain, 0.9% Nader

**National and State Parks:** Battle Island State Park; Fort Brewerton State Park; Littlejohn State Game Management Area; Selkirk Shores State Park; Threemile Bay State Game Management Area

**Additional Information Contacts**

Oswego County Government............................(315) 349-8385
  http://www.co.oswego.ny.us
City of Fulton...........................................(315) 592-4340
  http://www.cityoffulton.com
City of Oswego.........................................(315) 342-8116
  http://www.oswegony.org
Fort Brewerton/Greater Oneida Lake Chamber of Commerce ......(315) 668-3408
  http://www.oneidalakechamber.com
Greater Mexico Chamber of Commerce ................(315) 963-1042
  http://commerce.mexicony.net
Greater Oswego-Fulton Chamber of Commerce .........(315) 343-7681
  http://oswegofultonchamber.com
Greater Oswego-Fulton Chamber of Commerce .........(315) 343-7681
  http://www.oswegofultonchamber.com
Pulaski Chamber of Commerce.......................(315) 298-2213
  http://www.pulaskinychamber.com
Town of Constantia....................................(315) 623-7771
  http://townconstantia.org
Town of Oswego.......................................(315) 343-2586
  http://www.townofoswego.com
Town of Scriba.........................................(315) 343-3375
  http://scribany.org

## Oswego County Communities

**ALBION** (town). Covers a land area of 47.286 square miles and a water area of 0.532 square miles. Located at 43.48° N. Lat; 76.03° W. Long.
**Population:** 2,043 (1990); 2,083 (2000); 2,073 (2010); Density: 43.8 persons per square mile (2010); Race: 96.8% White, 0.4% Black, 0.3% Asian, 0.5% American Indian/Alaska Native, 0.0% Native Hawaiian/Other Pacific Islander, 2.0% Other, 0.8% Hispanic of any race (2010); Average household size: 2.82 (2010); Median age: 36.1 (2010); Males per 100 females: 106.1 (2010); Marriage status: 24.9% never married, 60.8% now married, 3.5% widowed, 10.9% divorced (2006-2010 5-year est.); Foreign born: 1.8% (2006-2010 5-year est.); Ancestry (includes multiple ancestries): 23.6% Irish, 22.1% German, 18.4% English, 8.7% Italian, 8.0% French (2006-2010 5-year est.).
**Economy:** Single-family building permits issued: 15 (2011); Multi-family building permits issued: 0 (2011); Employment by occupation: 8.9% management, 0.9% professional, 10.9% services, 10.8% sales, 2.5% farming, 14.0% construction, 12.3% production (2006-2010 5-year est.).
**Income:** Per capita income: $20,356 (2006-2010 5-year est.); Median household income: $49,167 (2006-2010 5-year est.); Average household income: $56,189 (2006-2010 5-year est.); Percent of households with income of $100,000 or more: 12.6% (2006-2010 5-year est.); Poverty rate: 11.8% (2006-2010 5-year est.).
**Education:** Percent of population age 25 and over with: High school diploma (including GED) or higher: 86.6% (2006-2010 5-year est.); Bachelor's degree or higher: 9.4% (2006-2010 5-year est.); Master's degree or higher: 3.5% (2006-2010 5-year est.).
**Housing:** Homeownership rate: 80.8% (2010); Median home value: $76,000 (2006-2010 5-year est.); Median contract rent: $426 per month (2006-2010 5-year est.); Median year structure built: 1979 (2006-2010 5-year est.).
**Transportation:** Commute to work: 91.3% car, 0.0% public transportation, 3.2% walk, 5.5% work from home (2006-2010 5-year est.); Travel time to work: 23.2% less than 15 minutes, 30.6% 15 to 30 minutes, 24.5% 30 to 45 minutes, 17.3% 45 to 60 minutes, 4.4% 60 minutes or more (2006-2010 5-year est.)

**ALTMAR** (village). Covers a land area of 2.069 square miles and a water area of 0.010 square miles. Located at 43.51° N. Lat; 76.00° W. Long. Elevation is 574 feet.
**Population:** 336 (1990); 351 (2000); 407 (2010); Density: 196.7 persons per square mile (2010); Race: 96.3% White, 1.0% Black, 0.0% Asian, 0.5% American Indian/Alaska Native, 0.0% Native Hawaiian/Other Pacific Islander, 2.2% Other, 1.2% Hispanic of any race (2010); Average household size: 2.89 (2010); Median age: 30.5 (2010); Males per 100

females: 116.5 (2010); Marriage status: 27.9% never married, 57.3% now married, 0.0% widowed, 14.9% divorced (2006-2010 5-year est.); Foreign born: 4.6% (2006-2010 5-year est.); Ancestry (includes multiple ancestries): 25.2% Irish, 24.4% German, 13.8% English, 9.8% French, 8.1% French Canadian (2006-2010 5-year est.).
**Economy:** Single-family building permits issued: 0 (2011); Multi-family building permits issued: 0 (2011); Employment by occupation: 9.9% management, 1.3% professional, 6.6% services, 8.6% sales, 4.6% farming, 5.3% construction, 15.2% production (2006-2010 5-year est.).
**Income:** Per capita income: $15,831 (2006-2010 5-year est.); Median household income: $32,000 (2006-2010 5-year est.); Average household income: $39,794 (2006-2010 5-year est.); Percent of households with income of $100,000 or more: 11.6% (2006-2010 5-year est.); Poverty rate: 38.5% (2006-2010 5-year est.).
**Education:** Percent of population age 25 and over with: High school diploma (including GED) or higher: 79.1% (2006-2010 5-year est.); Bachelor's degree or higher: 9.0% (2006-2010 5-year est.); Master's degree or higher: 1.9% (2006-2010 5-year est.).

**School District(s)**
Altmar-Parish-Williamstown Central School District (PK-12)
  2009-10 Enrollment: 1,435 ......................(315) 625-5251
**Housing:** Homeownership rate: 61.7% (2010); Median home value: $77,300 (2006-2010 5-year est.); Median contract rent: $423 per month (2006-2010 5-year est.); Median year structure built: 1976 (2006-2010 5-year est.).
**Transportation:** Commute to work: 95.4% car, 0.0% public transportation, 2.0% walk, 2.6% work from home (2006-2010 5-year est.); Travel time to work: 19.0% less than 15 minutes, 38.1% 15 to 30 minutes, 12.2% 30 to 45 minutes, 26.5% 45 to 60 minutes, 4.1% 60 minutes or more (2006-2010 5-year est.)

**AMBOY** (town). Covers a land area of 37.048 square miles and a water area of 0.691 square miles. Located at 43.37° N. Lat; 75.91° W. Long.
**Population:** 1,010 (1990); 1,312 (2000); 1,263 (2010); Density: 34.1 persons per square mile (2010); Race: 97.1% White, 0.2% Black, 0.2% Asian, 0.6% American Indian/Alaska Native, 0.0% Native Hawaiian/Other Pacific Islander, 1.9% Other, 0.9% Hispanic of any race (2010); Average household size: 2.70 (2010); Median age: 40.1 (2010); Males per 100 females: 108.1 (2010); Marriage status: 18.9% never married, 59.5% now married, 7.1% widowed, 14.5% divorced (2006-2010 5-year est.); Foreign born: 0.5% (2006-2010 5-year est.); Ancestry (includes multiple ancestries): 27.6% German, 18.4% French, 18.2% Irish, 17.9% English, 8.3% American (2006-2010 5-year est.).
**Economy:** Single-family building permits issued: 8 (2011); Multi-family building permits issued: 0 (2011); Employment by occupation: 7.2% management, 1.4% professional, 5.8% services, 15.3% sales, 2.8% farming, 14.5% construction, 12.0% production (2006-2010 5-year est.).
**Income:** Per capita income: $20,025 (2006-2010 5-year est.); Median household income: $42,083 (2006-2010 5-year est.); Average household income: $48,375 (2006-2010 5-year est.); Percent of households with income of $100,000 or more: 6.7% (2006-2010 5-year est.); Poverty rate: 16.1% (2006-2010 5-year est.).
**Education:** Percent of population age 25 and over with: High school diploma (including GED) or higher: 80.5% (2006-2010 5-year est.); Bachelor's degree or higher: 6.9% (2006-2010 5-year est.); Master's degree or higher: 1.3% (2006-2010 5-year est.).
**Housing:** Homeownership rate: 84.0% (2010); Median home value: $83,100 (2006-2010 5-year est.); Median contract rent: $501 per month (2006-2010 5-year est.); Median year structure built: 1982 (2006-2010 5-year est.).
**Transportation:** Commute to work: 95.7% car, 1.4% public transportation, 1.6% walk, 1.3% work from home (2006-2010 5-year est.); Travel time to work: 10.1% less than 15 minutes, 16.5% 15 to 30 minutes, 32.1% 30 to 45 minutes, 25.9% 45 to 60 minutes, 15.4% 60 minutes or more (2006-2010 5-year est.)

**BERNHARDS BAY** (unincorporated postal area)
Zip Code: 13028
  Covers a land area of 18.687 square miles and a water area of 0.301 square miles. Located at 43.30° N. Lat; 75.92° W. Long. Elevation is 390 feet. Population: 1,350 (2010); Density: 72.2 persons per square mile (2010); Race: 97.7% White, 0.3% Black, 0.1% Asian, 0.4% American Indian/Alaska Native, 0.0% Native Hawaiian/Other Pacific Islander, 1.5% Other, 0.4% Hispanic of any race (2010); Average household size: 2.53

(2010); Median age: 44.2 (2010); Males per 100 females: 113.3 (2010); Homeownership rate: 88.2% (2010)

**BOYLSTON** (town). Covers a land area of 39.152 square miles and a water area of 0.021 square miles. Located at 43.65° N. Lat; 75.95° W. Long.
**Population:** 443 (1990); 505 (2000); 549 (2010); Density: 14.0 persons per square mile (2010); Race: 98.5% White, 0.0% Black, 0.4% Asian, 0.2% American Indian/Alaska Native, 0.0% Native Hawaiian/Other Pacific Islander, 0.9% Other, 0.7% Hispanic of any race (2010); Average household size: 2.65 (2010); Median age: 39.7 (2010); Males per 100 females: 115.3 (2010); Marriage status: 22.1% never married, 62.5% now married, 4.0% widowed, 11.4% divorced (2006-2010 5-year est.); Foreign born: 0.0% (2006-2010 5-year est.); Ancestry (includes multiple ancestries): 17.2% Irish, 15.7% German, 12.8% English, 8.2% French Canadian, 7.8% Italian (2006-2010 5-year est.).
**Economy:** Single-family building permits issued: 1 (2011); Multi-family building permits issued: 0 (2011); Employment by occupation: 1.6% management, 2.1% professional, 9.5% services, 19.6% sales, 2.1% farming, 22.2% construction, 14.3% production (2006-2010 5-year est.).
**Income:** Per capita income: $18,536 (2006-2010 5-year est.); Median household income: $39,844 (2006-2010 5-year est.); Average household income: $45,991 (2006-2010 5-year est.); Percent of households with income of $100,000 or more: 9.0% (2006-2010 5-year est.); Poverty rate: 17.5% (2006-2010 5-year est.).
**Education:** Percent of population age 25 and over with: High school diploma (including GED) or higher: 83.9% (2006-2010 5-year est.); Bachelor's degree or higher: 12.1% (2006-2010 5-year est.); Master's degree or higher: 3.0% (2006-2010 5-year est.).
**Housing:** Homeownership rate: 86.0% (2010); Median home value: $88,800 (2006-2010 5-year est.); Median contract rent: $325 per month (2006-2010 5-year est.); Median year structure built: 1979 (2006-2010 5-year est.).
**Transportation:** Commute to work: 84.8% car, 0.0% public transportation, 2.5% walk, 5.1% work from home (2006-2010 5-year est.); Travel time to work: 26.2% less than 15 minutes, 38.5% 15 to 30 minutes, 17.1% 30 to 45 minutes, 11.8% 45 to 60 minutes, 6.4% 60 minutes or more (2006-2010 5-year est.)

**CENTRAL SQUARE** (village). Covers a land area of 1.906 square miles and a water area of 0 square miles. Located at 43.28° N. Lat; 76.14° W. Long. Elevation is 449 feet.
**Population:** 1,632 (1990); 1,646 (2000); 1,848 (2010); Density: 969.4 persons per square mile (2010); Race: 97.7% White, 0.1% Black, 0.5% Asian, 0.5% American Indian/Alaska Native, 0.0% Native Hawaiian/Other Pacific Islander, 1.2% Other, 1.2% Hispanic of any race (2010); Average household size: 2.20 (2010); Median age: 42.3 (2010); Males per 100 females: 83.5 (2010); Marriage status: 27.6% never married, 49.6% now married, 10.0% widowed, 12.9% divorced (2006-2010 5-year est.); Foreign born: 1.1% (2006-2010 5-year est.); Ancestry (includes multiple ancestries): 25.1% German, 21.8% Italian, 20.9% Irish, 18.0% English, 7.2% French (2006-2010 5-year est.).
**Economy:** Single-family building permits issued: 1 (2011); Multi-family building permits issued: 0 (2011); Employment by occupation: 6.9% management, 2.4% professional, 5.7% services, 24.3% sales, 5.5% farming, 13.6% construction, 9.3% production (2006-2010 5-year est.).
**Income:** Per capita income: $26,192 (2006-2010 5-year est.); Median household income: $39,324 (2006-2010 5-year est.); Average household income: $58,977 (2006-2010 5-year est.); Percent of households with income of $100,000 or more: 23.5% (2006-2010 5-year est.); Poverty rate: 5.9% (2006-2010 5-year est.).
**Education:** Percent of population age 25 and over with: High school diploma (including GED) or higher: 88.5% (2006-2010 5-year est.); Bachelor's degree or higher: 20.2% (2006-2010 5-year est.); Master's degree or higher: 8.9% (2006-2010 5-year est.).
**School District(s)**
Central Square Central School District (PK-12)
2009-10 Enrollment: 4,634 . . . . . . . . . . . . . . . . . . . . . . (315) 668-4220
**Housing:** Homeownership rate: 57.9% (2010); Median home value: $125,400 (2006-2010 5-year est.); Median contract rent: $505 per month (2006-2010 5-year est.); Median year structure built: 1977 (2006-2010 5-year est.).
**Safety:** Violent crime rate: 0.0 per 10,000 population; Property crime rate: 200.1 per 10,000 population (2010).

**Transportation:** Commute to work: 97.0% car, 0.0% public transportation, 1.5% walk, 1.5% work from home (2006-2010 5-year est.); Travel time to work: 14.3% less than 15 minutes, 52.1% 15 to 30 minutes, 23.7% 30 to 45 minutes, 5.5% 45 to 60 minutes, 4.4% 60 minutes or more (2006-2010 5-year est.)
**Additional Information Contacts**
Fort Brewerton/Greater Oneida Lake Chamber of Commerce . . . . . . (315) 668-3408
http://www.oneidalakechamber.com

**CLEVELAND** (village). Covers a land area of 1.131 square miles and a water area of 0.093 square miles. Located at 43.24° N. Lat; 75.88° W. Long. Elevation is 436 feet.
**Population:** 784 (1990); 758 (2000); 750 (2010); Density: 662.9 persons per square mile (2010); Race: 97.2% White, 0.4% Black, 0.9% Asian, 0.7% American Indian/Alaska Native, 0.0% Native Hawaiian/Other Pacific Islander, 0.8% Other, 1.2% Hispanic of any race (2010); Average household size: 2.61 (2010); Median age: 39.4 (2010); Males per 100 females: 106.0 (2010); Marriage status: 35.4% never married, 49.2% now married, 4.6% widowed, 10.8% divorced (2006-2010 5-year est.); Foreign born: 0.7% (2006-2010 5-year est.); Ancestry (includes multiple ancestries): 29.8% Irish, 29.4% German, 15.3% English, 10.7% French, 8.8% Italian (2006-2010 5-year est.).
**Economy:** Employment by occupation: 7.3% management, 5.5% professional, 11.4% services, 19.0% sales, 6.2% farming, 15.8% construction, 4.7% production (2006-2010 5-year est.).
**Income:** Per capita income: $21,962 (2006-2010 5-year est.); Median household income: $50,714 (2006-2010 5-year est.); Average household income: $57,162 (2006-2010 5-year est.); Percent of households with income of $100,000 or more: 10.1% (2006-2010 5-year est.); Poverty rate: 6.3% (2006-2010 5-year est.).
**Education:** Percent of population age 25 and over with: High school diploma (including GED) or higher: 83.6% (2006-2010 5-year est.); Bachelor's degree or higher: 11.4% (2006-2010 5-year est.); Master's degree or higher: 3.9% (2006-2010 5-year est.).
**School District(s)**
Central Square Central School District (PK-12)
2009-10 Enrollment: 4,634 . . . . . . . . . . . . . . . . . . . . . . (315) 668-4220
**Housing:** Homeownership rate: 79.4% (2010); Median home value: $88,300 (2006-2010 5-year est.); Median contract rent: $558 per month (2006-2010 5-year est.); Median year structure built: 1943 (2006-2010 5-year est.).
**Transportation:** Commute to work: 91.3% car, 0.0% public transportation, 0.0% walk, 8.7% work from home (2006-2010 5-year est.); Travel time to work: 6.9% less than 15 minutes, 19.2% 15 to 30 minutes, 31.7% 30 to 45 minutes, 27.5% 45 to 60 minutes, 14.7% 60 minutes or more (2006-2010 5-year est.)

**CONSTANTIA** (town). Covers a land area of 56.765 square miles and a water area of 42.914 square miles. Located at 43.25° N. Lat; 75.96° W. Long. Elevation is 384 feet.
**Population:** 4,868 (1990); 5,141 (2000); 4,973 (2010); Density: 87.6 persons per square mile (2010); Race: 97.9% White, 0.2% Black, 0.3% Asian, 0.4% American Indian/Alaska Native, 0.0% Native Hawaiian/Other Pacific Islander, 1.2% Other, 0.5% Hispanic of any race (2010); Average household size: 2.55 (2010); Median age: 42.8 (2010); Males per 100 females: 109.3 (2010); Marriage status: 28.6% never married, 55.8% now married, 5.5% widowed, 10.2% divorced (2006-2010 5-year est.); Foreign born: 1.2% (2006-2010 5-year est.); Ancestry (includes multiple ancestries): 28.8% German, 19.6% Irish, 18.1% English, 13.4% French, 10.2% Italian (2006-2010 5-year est.).
**Economy:** Single-family building permits issued: 7 (2011); Multi-family building permits issued: 0 (2011); Employment by occupation: 4.2% management, 4.5% professional, 11.2% services, 16.7% sales, 6.0% farming, 12.4% construction, 6.0% production (2006-2010 5-year est.).
**Income:** Per capita income: $22,048 (2006-2010 5-year est.); Median household income: $48,780 (2006-2010 5-year est.); Average household income: $58,805 (2006-2010 5-year est.); Percent of households with income of $100,000 or more: 14.3% (2006-2010 5-year est.); Poverty rate: 8.5% (2006-2010 5-year est.).
**Education:** Percent of population age 25 and over with: High school diploma (including GED) or higher: 88.2% (2006-2010 5-year est.); Bachelor's degree or higher: 14.7% (2006-2010 5-year est.); Master's degree or higher: 5.5% (2006-2010 5-year est.).

**School District(s)**

Central Square Central School District (PK-12)

2009-10 Enrollment: 4,634 . . . . . . . . . . . . . . . . . . . . . . . . (315) 668-4220

**Housing:** Homeownership rate: 85.2% (2010); Median home value: $91,500 (2006-2010 5-year est.); Median contract rent: $609 per month (2006-2010 5-year est.); Median year structure built: 1971 (2006-2010 5-year est.).

**Transportation:** Commute to work: 90.2% car, 1.0% public transportation, 0.0% walk, 8.0% work from home (2006-2010 5-year est.); Travel time to work: 10.9% less than 15 minutes, 21.2% 15 to 30 minutes, 41.8% 30 to 45 minutes, 20.0% 45 to 60 minutes, 6.2% 60 minutes or more (2006-2010 5-year est.)

**Additional Information Contacts**

Town of Constantia . . . . . . . . . . . . . . . . . . . . . . . . . . . . . . . (315) 623-7771

http://townconstantia.org

**CONSTANTIA** (CDP). Covers a land area of 3.009 square miles and a water area of 0.006 square miles. Located at 43.25° N. Lat; 76.00° W. Long. Elevation is 384 feet.

**Population:** 1,140 (1990); 1,107 (2000); 1,182 (2010); Density: 392.8 persons per square mile (2010); Race: 97.8% White, 0.1% Black, 0.2% Asian, 0.7% American Indian/Alaska Native, 0.0% Native Hawaiian/Other Pacific Islander, 1.2% Other, 0.7% Hispanic of any race (2010); Average household size: 2.34 (2010); Median age: 45.2 (2010); Males per 100 females: 106.3 (2010); Marriage status: 33.9% never married, 49.3% now married, 6.4% widowed, 10.4% divorced (2006-2010 5-year est.); Foreign born: 1.3% (2006-2010 5-year est.); Ancestry (includes multiple ancestries): 33.2% German, 19.6% French, 13.3% Irish, 12.7% English, 8.9% Italian (2006-2010 5-year est.).

**Economy:** Employment by occupation: 3.7% management, 3.2% professional, 9.6% services, 17.6% sales, 8.5% farming, 7.7% construction, 5.1% production (2006-2010 5-year est.).

**Income:** Per capita income: $22,909 (2006-2010 5-year est.); Median household income: $64,000 (2006-2010 5-year est.); Average household income: $64,458 (2006-2010 5-year est.); Percent of households with income of $100,000 or more: 17.1% (2006-2010 5-year est.); Poverty rate: 12.9% (2006-2010 5-year est.).

**Education:** Percent of population age 25 and over with: High school diploma (including GED) or higher: 93.0% (2006-2010 5-year est.); Bachelor's degree or higher: 15.5% (2006-2010 5-year est.); Master's degree or higher: 4.8% (2006-2010 5-year est.).

**School District(s)**

Central Square Central School District (PK-12)

2009-10 Enrollment: 4,634 . . . . . . . . . . . . . . . . . . . . . . . . (315) 668-4220

**Housing:** Homeownership rate: 80.0% (2010); Median home value: $95,300 (2006-2010 5-year est.); Median contract rent: $1,281 per month (2006-2010 5-year est.); Median year structure built: 1971 (2006-2010 5-year est.).

**Transportation:** Commute to work: 81.8% car, 2.9% public transportation, 0.0% walk, 15.3% work from home (2006-2010 5-year est.); Travel time to work: 10.8% less than 15 minutes, 19.4% 15 to 30 minutes, 50.1% 30 to 45 minutes, 18.3% 45 to 60 minutes, 1.5% 60 minutes or more (2006-2010 5-year est.)

**FULTON** (city). Covers a land area of 3.754 square miles and a water area of 1.000 square miles. Located at 43.30° N. Lat; 76.39° W. Long. Elevation is 361 feet.

**History:** Incorporated as village in 1835, as city in 1902.

**Population:** 12,929 (1990); 11,855 (2000); 11,896 (2010); Density: 3,168.4 persons per square mile (2010); Race: 95.5% White, 1.0% Black, 0.5% Asian, 0.5% American Indian/Alaska Native, 0.0% Native Hawaiian/Other Pacific Islander, 2.5% Other, 3.1% Hispanic of any race (2010); Average household size: 2.44 (2010); Median age: 35.9 (2010); Males per 100 females: 91.9 (2010); Marriage status: 31.0% never married, 47.4% now married, 8.7% widowed, 12.9% divorced (2006-2010 5-year est.); Foreign born: 2.2% (2006-2010 5-year est.); Ancestry (includes multiple ancestries): 20.3% Irish, 18.3% German, 15.4% Italian, 14.1% English, 8.7% French (2006-2010 5-year est.).

**Economy:** Single-family building permits issued: 4 (2011); Multi-family building permits issued: 0 (2011); Employment by occupation: 5.9% management, 1.6% professional, 12.6% services, 15.3% sales, 6.2% farming, 9.7% construction, 7.7% production (2006-2010 5-year est.).

**Income:** Per capita income: $19,587 (2006-2010 5-year est.); Median household income: $35,896 (2006-2010 5-year est.); Average household income: $44,919 (2006-2010 5-year est.); Percent of households with income of $100,000 or more: 9.4% (2006-2010 5-year est.); Poverty rate: 24.4% (2006-2010 5-year est.).

**Education:** Percent of population age 25 and over with: High school diploma (including GED) or higher: 83.6% (2006-2010 5-year est.); Bachelor's degree or higher: 13.2% (2006-2010 5-year est.); Master's degree or higher: 4.6% (2006-2010 5-year est.).

**School District(s)**

Fulton City School District (KG-12)

2009-10 Enrollment: 3,683 . . . . . . . . . . . . . . . . . . . . . . . . (315) 593-5510

Mexico Central School District (KG-12)

2009-10 Enrollment: 2,281 . . . . . . . . . . . . . . . . . . . . . . . . (315) 963-8400

**Housing:** Homeownership rate: 51.5% (2010); Median home value: $75,200 (2006-2010 5-year est.); Median contract rent: $458 per month (2006-2010 5-year est.); Median year structure built: before 1940 (2006-2010 5-year est.).

**Hospitals:** Albert Lindley Lee Memorial Hospital (67 beds)

**Safety:** Violent crime rate: 31.0 per 10,000 population; Property crime rate: 477.4 per 10,000 population (2010).

**Newspapers:** Fulton Patriot (Community news; Circulation 6,235); Oswego Daily News (Local news); The Post-Standard - Oswego County Bureau (Regional news); Valley News (Local news; Circulation 8,000)

**Transportation:** Commute to work: 83.4% car, 2.4% public transportation, 9.7% walk, 2.9% work from home (2006-2010 5-year est.); Travel time to work: 46.3% less than 15 minutes, 25.5% 15 to 30 minutes, 20.6% 30 to 45 minutes, 5.2% 45 to 60 minutes, 2.5% 60 minutes or more (2006-2010 5-year est.)

**Additional Information Contacts**

City of Fulton . . . . . . . . . . . . . . . . . . . . . . . . . . . . . . . . . . (315) 592-4340

http://www.cityoffulton.com

Greater Oswego-Fulton Chamber of Commerce . . . . . . . . . (315) 343-7681

http://oswegofultonchamber.com

**GRANBY** (town). Covers a land area of 44.712 square miles and a water area of 1.729 square miles. Located at 43.28° N. Lat; 76.44° W. Long.

**Population:** 7,013 (1990); 7,009 (2000); 6,821 (2010); Density: 152.6 persons per square mile (2010); Race: 96.8% White, 0.5% Black, 0.3% Asian, 0.7% American Indian/Alaska Native, 0.0% Native Hawaiian/Other Pacific Islander, 1.7% Other, 1.5% Hispanic of any race (2010); Average household size: 2.64 (2010); Median age: 40.6 (2010); Males per 100 females: 104.7 (2010); Marriage status: 27.0% never married, 57.3% now married, 3.8% widowed, 11.8% divorced (2006-2010 5-year est.); Foreign born: 1.4% (2006-2010 5-year est.); Ancestry (includes multiple ancestries): 21.3% German, 19.7% Irish, 18.5% Italian, 14.6% English, 14.3% French (2006-2010 5-year est.).

**Economy:** Single-family building permits issued: 4 (2011); Multi-family building permits issued: 0 (2011); Employment by occupation: 6.4% management, 1.8% professional, 13.8% services, 17.8% sales, 3.0% farming, 11.6% construction, 13.5% production (2006-2010 5-year est.).

**Income:** Per capita income: $24,051 (2006-2010 5-year est.); Median household income: $37,406 (2006-2010 5-year est.); Average household income: $59,737 (2006-2010 5-year est.); Percent of households with income of $100,000 or more: 13.6% (2006-2010 5-year est.); Poverty rate: 18.5% (2006-2010 5-year est.).

**Education:** Percent of population age 25 and over with: High school diploma (including GED) or higher: 88.6% (2006-2010 5-year est.); Bachelor's degree or higher: 13.6% (2006-2010 5-year est.); Master's degree or higher: 7.9% (2006-2010 5-year est.).

**Housing:** Homeownership rate: 80.2% (2010); Median home value: $77,800 (2006-2010 5-year est.); Median contract rent: $444 per month (2006-2010 5-year est.); Median year structure built: 1972 (2006-2010 5-year est.).

**Transportation:** Commute to work: 93.5% car, 0.3% public transportation, 2.6% walk, 2.3% work from home (2006-2010 5-year est.); Travel time to work: 25.8% less than 15 minutes, 38.8% 15 to 30 minutes, 23.8% 30 to 45 minutes, 8.9% 45 to 60 minutes, 2.7% 60 minutes or more (2006-2010 5-year est.)

**HANNIBAL** (village). Covers a land area of 1.152 square miles and a water area of 0 square miles. Located at 43.31° N. Lat; 76.57° W. Long. Elevation is 328 feet.

**Population:** 613 (1990); 542 (2000); 555 (2010); Density: 481.6 persons per square mile (2010); Race: 97.8% White, 0.0% Black, 0.2% Asian, 0.5% American Indian/Alaska Native, 0.0% Native Hawaiian/Other Pacific Islander, 1.5% Other, 0.4% Hispanic of any race (2010); Average

household size: 2.57 (2010); Median age: 42.4 (2010); Males per 100 females: 89.4 (2010); Marriage status: 31.0% never married, 57.0% now married, 5.4% widowed, 6.6% divorced (2006-2010 5-year est.); Foreign born: 2.3% (2006-2010 5-year est.); Ancestry (includes multiple ancestries): 23.9% English, 15.4% Irish, 12.4% French, 10.8% German, 8.7% Dutch (2006-2010 5-year est.).

**Economy:** Single-family building permits issued: 0 (2011); Multi-family building permits issued: 0 (2011); Employment by occupation: 1.6% management, 5.4% professional, 7.8% services, 17.1% sales, 0.0% farming, 14.4% construction, 16.3% production (2006-2010 5-year est.).

**Income:** Per capita income: $20,878 (2006-2010 5-year est.); Median household income: $50,147 (2006-2010 5-year est.); Average household income: $48,796 (2006-2010 5-year est.); Percent of households with income of $100,000 or more: 0.8% (2006-2010 5-year est.); Poverty rate: 12.6% (2006-2010 5-year est.).

**Education:** Percent of population age 25 and over with: High school diploma (including GED) or higher: 94.9% (2006-2010 5-year est.); Bachelor's degree or higher: 15.3% (2006-2010 5-year est.); Master's degree or higher: 4.1% (2006-2010 5-year est.).

**School District(s)**

Hannibal Central School District (PK-12)

   2009-10 Enrollment: 1,617 . . . . . . . . . . . . . . . . . . . (315) 564-7900

**Housing:** Homeownership rate: 72.7% (2010); Median home value: $79,400 (2006-2010 5-year est.); Median contract rent: $467 per month (2006-2010 5-year est.); Median year structure built: before 1940 (2006-2010 5-year est.).

**Transportation:** Commute to work: 88.6% car, 0.0% public transportation, 5.3% walk, 4.9% work from home (2006-2010 5-year est.); Travel time to work: 18.0% less than 15 minutes, 49.4% 15 to 30 minutes, 20.2% 30 to 45 minutes, 8.6% 45 to 60 minutes, 3.9% 60 minutes or more (2006-2010 5-year est.)

**HANNIBAL** (town). Covers a land area of 44.655 square miles and a water area of 0.171 square miles. Located at 43.31° N. Lat; 76.54° W. Long. Elevation is 328 feet.

**Population:** 4,616 (1990); 4,957 (2000); 4,854 (2010); Density: 108.7 persons per square mile (2010); Race: 97.0% White, 0.5% Black, 0.2% Asian, 0.4% American Indian/Alaska Native, 0.0% Native Hawaiian/Other Pacific Islander, 1.9% Other, 1.4% Hispanic of any race (2010); Average household size: 2.73 (2010); Median age: 37.7 (2010); Males per 100 females: 102.5 (2010); Marriage status: 23.8% never married, 56.9% now married, 8.3% widowed, 10.9% divorced (2006-2010 5-year est.); Foreign born: 3.2% (2006-2010 5-year est.); Ancestry (includes multiple ancestries): 20.9% German, 19.5% Irish, 18.7% English, 13.2% French, 11.0% Italian (2006-2010 5-year est.).

**Economy:** Single-family building permits issued: 0 (2011); Multi-family building permits issued: 0 (2011); Employment by occupation: 4.5% management, 1.3% professional, 9.8% services, 18.2% sales, 2.5% farming, 13.7% construction, 15.3% production (2006-2010 5-year est.).

**Income:** Per capita income: $17,794 (2006-2010 5-year est.); Median household income: $39,506 (2006-2010 5-year est.); Average household income: $47,170 (2006-2010 5-year est.); Percent of households with income of $100,000 or more: 4.6% (2006-2010 5-year est.); Poverty rate: 19.3% (2006-2010 5-year est.).

**Education:** Percent of population age 25 and over with: High school diploma (including GED) or higher: 83.6% (2006-2010 5-year est.); Bachelor's degree or higher: 13.8% (2006-2010 5-year est.); Master's degree or higher: 3.7% (2006-2010 5-year est.).

**School District(s)**

Hannibal Central School District (PK-12)

   2009-10 Enrollment: 1,617 . . . . . . . . . . . . . . . . . . . (315) 564-7900

**Housing:** Homeownership rate: 78.9% (2010); Median home value: $84,700 (2006-2010 5-year est.); Median contract rent: $455 per month (2006-2010 5-year est.); Median year structure built: 1975 (2006-2010 5-year est.).

**Transportation:** Commute to work: 91.8% car, 0.7% public transportation, 4.0% walk, 2.2% work from home (2006-2010 5-year est.); Travel time to work: 24.6% less than 15 minutes, 40.1% 15 to 30 minutes, 20.0% 30 to 45 minutes, 10.6% 45 to 60 minutes, 4.7% 60 minutes or more (2006-2010 5-year est.)

**HASTINGS** (town). Covers a land area of 45.645 square miles and a water area of 0.352 square miles. Located at 43.32° N. Lat; 76.15° W. Long. Elevation is 476 feet.

**Population:** 8,113 (1990); 8,803 (2000); 9,450 (2010); Density: 207.0 persons per square mile (2010); Race: 97.4% White, 0.3% Black, 0.3% Asian, 0.5% American Indian/Alaska Native, 0.0% Native Hawaiian/Other Pacific Islander, 1.5% Other, 0.9% Hispanic of any race (2010); Average household size: 2.59 (2010); Median age: 40.6 (2010); Males per 100 females: 97.3 (2010); Marriage status: 25.3% never married, 54.3% now married, 6.9% widowed, 13.4% divorced (2006-2010 5-year est.); Foreign born: 1.8% (2006-2010 5-year est.); Ancestry (includes multiple ancestries): 22.2% German, 21.0% Irish, 15.9% English, 15.7% Italian, 9.8% Polish (2006-2010 5-year est.).

**Economy:** Single-family building permits issued: 8 (2011); Multi-family building permits issued: 0 (2011); Employment by occupation: 7.3% management, 2.4% professional, 7.4% services, 20.1% sales, 4.5% farming, 18.2% construction, 11.4% production (2006-2010 5-year est.).

**Income:** Per capita income: $24,236 (2006-2010 5-year est.); Median household income: $52,897 (2006-2010 5-year est.); Average household income: $62,163 (2006-2010 5-year est.); Percent of households with income of $100,000 or more: 19.5% (2006-2010 5-year est.); Poverty rate: 9.1% (2006-2010 5-year est.).

**Taxes:** Total city taxes per capita: $290 (2009); City property taxes per capita: $267 (2009).

**Education:** Percent of population age 25 and over with: High school diploma (including GED) or higher: 90.2% (2006-2010 5-year est.); Bachelor's degree or higher: 13.9% (2006-2010 5-year est.); Master's degree or higher: 3.8% (2006-2010 5-year est.).

**Housing:** Homeownership rate: 79.7% (2010); Median home value: $105,900 (2006-2010 5-year est.); Median contract rent: $534 per month (2006-2010 5-year est.); Median year structure built: 1979 (2006-2010 5-year est.).

**Transportation:** Commute to work: 97.1% car, 0.4% public transportation, 0.3% walk, 1.9% work from home (2006-2010 5-year est.); Travel time to work: 15.3% less than 15 minutes, 39.1% 15 to 30 minutes, 34.7% 30 to 45 minutes, 7.2% 45 to 60 minutes, 3.7% 60 minutes or more (2006-2010 5-year est.)

**LACONA** (village). Covers a land area of 1.109 square miles and a water area of 0.002 square miles. Located at 43.64° N. Lat; 76.06° W. Long. Elevation is 558 feet.

**Population:** 593 (1990); 590 (2000); 582 (2010); Density: 524.4 persons per square mile (2010); Race: 96.9% White, 0.7% Black, 0.7% Asian, 0.2% American Indian/Alaska Native, 0.0% Native Hawaiian/Other Pacific Islander, 1.5% Other, 1.5% Hispanic of any race (2010); Average household size: 2.44 (2010); Median age: 38.1 (2010); Males per 100 females: 110.1 (2010); Marriage status: 27.9% never married, 55.5% now married, 9.3% widowed, 7.3% divorced (2006-2010 5-year est.); Foreign born: 1.1% (2006-2010 5-year est.); Ancestry (includes multiple ancestries): 40.9% Irish, 29.7% English, 14.1% German, 12.6% French, 8.7% Italian (2006-2010 5-year est.).

**Economy:** Single-family building permits issued: 0 (2011); Multi-family building permits issued: 0 (2011); Employment by occupation: 6.6% management, 0.0% professional, 9.8% services, 11.7% sales, 2.7% farming, 13.7% construction, 0.0% production (2006-2010 5-year est.).

**Income:** Per capita income: $22,147 (2006-2010 5-year est.); Median household income: $40,000 (2006-2010 5-year est.); Average household income: $53,240 (2006-2010 5-year est.); Percent of households with income of $100,000 or more: 11.3% (2006-2010 5-year est.); Poverty rate: 12.8% (2006-2010 5-year est.).

**Education:** Percent of population age 25 and over with: High school diploma (including GED) or higher: 96.1% (2006-2010 5-year est.); Bachelor's degree or higher: 23.6% (2006-2010 5-year est.); Master's degree or higher: 8.3% (2006-2010 5-year est.).

**Housing:** Homeownership rate: 66.4% (2010); Median home value: $88,900 (2006-2010 5-year est.); Median contract rent: $483 per month (2006-2010 5-year est.); Median year structure built: before 1940 (2006-2010 5-year est.).

**Transportation:** Commute to work: 92.7% car, 0.0% public transportation, 0.0% walk, 7.3% work from home (2006-2010 5-year est.); Travel time to work: 33.9% less than 15 minutes, 21.7% 15 to 30 minutes, 21.3% 30 to 45 minutes, 16.5% 45 to 60 minutes, 6.5% 60 minutes or more (2006-2010 5-year est.)

## MALLORY (unincorporated postal area)

Zip Code: 13103

Covers a land area of 0.341 square miles and a water area of 0.014 square miles. Located at 43.32° N. Lat; 76.10° W. Long. Elevation is 413 feet. Population: 326 (2010); Density: 953.2 persons per square mile (2010); Race: 95.4% White, 0.6% Black, 0.0% Asian, 1.2% American Indian/Alaska Native, 0.0% Native Hawaiian/Other Pacific Islander, 2.8% Other, 1.5% Hispanic of any race (2010); Average household size: 2.83 (2010); Median age: 31.7 (2010); Males per 100 females: 109.0 (2010); Homeownership rate: 82.6% (2010)

## MEXICO (village).

Covers a land area of 2.144 square miles and a water area of 0 square miles. Located at 43.46° N. Lat; 76.23° W. Long. Elevation is 410 feet.

**Population:** 1,555 (1990); 1,572 (2000); 1,624 (2010); Density: 757.2 persons per square mile (2010); Race: 96.6% White, 0.3% Black, 0.4% Asian, 0.6% American Indian/Alaska Native, 0.0% Native Hawaiian/Other Pacific Islander, 2.1% Other, 1.7% Hispanic of any race (2010); Average household size: 2.44 (2010); Median age: 38.2 (2010); Males per 100 females: 84.1 (2010); Marriage status: 28.2% never married, 48.0% now married, 9.1% widowed, 14.7% divorced (2006-2010 5-year est.); Foreign born: 0.2% (2006-2010 5-year est.); Ancestry (includes multiple ancestries): 25.3% Irish, 22.7% German, 19.5% English, 10.6% French, 7.6% Italian (2006-2010 5-year est.).

**Economy:** Single-family building permits issued: 1 (2011); Multi-family building permits issued: 0 (2011); Employment by occupation: 9.2% management, 3.8% professional, 4.1% services, 13.5% sales, 4.0% farming, 8.0% construction, 9.1% production (2006-2010 5-year est.).

**Income:** Per capita income: $23,893 (2006-2010 5-year est.); Median household income: $43,462 (2006-2010 5-year est.); Average household income: $56,005 (2006-2010 5-year est.); Percent of households with income of $100,000 or more: 14.7% (2006-2010 5-year est.); Poverty rate: 11.4% (2006-2010 5-year est.).

**Education:** Percent of population age 25 and over with: High school diploma (including GED) or higher: 91.6% (2006-2010 5-year est.); Bachelor's degree or higher: 22.5% (2006-2010 5-year est.); Master's degree or higher: 7.0% (2006-2010 5-year est.).

### School District(s)

Mexico Central School District (KG-12)

    2009-10 Enrollment: 2,281 . . . . . . . . . . . . . . . . . . . . . . . (315) 963-8400

Oswego Boces

    2009-10 Enrollment: n/a . . . . . . . . . . . . . . . . . . . . . . . (315) 963-4222

### Vocational/Technical School(s)

Oswego County BOCES (Public)

    Fall 2010 Enrollment: 48 . . . . . . . . . . . . . . . . . . . . . . . (315) 963-4251

    2011-12 Tuition: $8,220

**Housing:** Homeownership rate: 57.7% (2010); Median home value: $88,400 (2006-2010 5-year est.); Median contract rent: $450 per month (2006-2010 5-year est.); Median year structure built: 1952 (2006-2010 5-year est.).

**Newspapers:** Citizen Outlet (Community news; Circulation 5,500); Mexico Independent Mirror (Community news; Circulation 3,400); Oswego Shopper (Community news; Circulation 14,202); Phoenix Register (Community news; Circulation 3,100); Pulaski/Salmon River News (Community news; Circulation 7,500)

**Transportation:** Commute to work: 87.5% car, 0.5% public transportation, 8.4% walk, 3.6% work from home (2006-2010 5-year est.); Travel time to work: 31.3% less than 15 minutes, 34.2% 15 to 30 minutes, 13.2% 30 to 45 minutes, 16.4% 45 to 60 minutes, 4.9% 60 minutes or more (2006-2010 5-year est.)

**Additional Information Contacts**

Greater Mexico Chamber of Commerce . . . . . . . . . . . . . . . (315) 963-1042

    http://commerce.mexicony.net

## MEXICO (town).

Covers a land area of 46.271 square miles and a water area of 0.716 square miles. Located at 43.45° N. Lat; 76.20° W. Long. Elevation is 410 feet.

**Population:** 5,050 (1990); 5,181 (2000); 5,197 (2010); Density: 112.3 persons per square mile (2010); Race: 96.9% White, 0.6% Black, 0.2% Asian, 0.6% American Indian/Alaska Native, 0.0% Native Hawaiian/Other Pacific Islander, 1.7% Other, 1.5% Hispanic of any race (2010); Average household size: 2.63 (2010); Median age: 39.4 (2010); Males per 100 females: 98.4 (2010); Marriage status: 24.4% never married, 58.0% now married, 5.5% widowed, 12.1% divorced (2006-2010 5-year est.); Foreign born: 1.4% (2006-2010 5-year est.); Ancestry (includes multiple

ancestries): 23.9% Irish, 19.6% German, 17.9% English, 11.2% French, 10.0% Polish (2006-2010 5-year est.).

**Economy:** Single-family building permits issued: 12 (2011); Multi-family building permits issued: 0 (2011); Employment by occupation: 6.4% management, 1.2% professional, 7.5% services, 18.0% sales, 4.0% farming, 13.6% construction, 11.3% production (2006-2010 5-year est.).

**Income:** Per capita income: $24,523 (2006-2010 5-year est.); Median household income: $49,334 (2006-2010 5-year est.); Average household income: $58,506 (2006-2010 5-year est.); Percent of households with income of $100,000 or more: 16.7% (2006-2010 5-year est.); Poverty rate: 10.8% (2006-2010 5-year est.).

**Education:** Percent of population age 25 and over with: High school diploma (including GED) or higher: 86.3% (2006-2010 5-year est.); Bachelor's degree or higher: 13.8% (2006-2010 5-year est.); Master's degree or higher: 3.9% (2006-2010 5-year est.).

### School District(s)

Mexico Central School District (KG-12)

    2009-10 Enrollment: 2,281 . . . . . . . . . . . . . . . . . . . . . (315) 963-8400

Oswego Boces

    2009-10 Enrollment: n/a . . . . . . . . . . . . . . . . . . . . . . . (315) 963-4222

### Vocational/Technical School(s)

Oswego County BOCES (Public)

    Fall 2010 Enrollment: 48 . . . . . . . . . . . . . . . . . . . . . . . (315) 963-4251

    2011-12 Tuition: $8,220

**Housing:** Homeownership rate: 77.2% (2010); Median home value: $88,500 (2006-2010 5-year est.); Median contract rent: $433 per month (2006-2010 5-year est.); Median year structure built: 1973 (2006-2010 5-year est.).

**Newspapers:** Citizen Outlet (Community news; Circulation 5,500); Mexico Independent Mirror (Community news; Circulation 3,400); Oswego Shopper (Community news; Circulation 14,202); Phoenix Register (Community news; Circulation 3,100); Pulaski/Salmon River News (Community news; Circulation 7,500)

**Transportation:** Commute to work: 92.3% car, 0.2% public transportation, 3.4% walk, 3.6% work from home (2006-2010 5-year est.); Travel time to work: 25.2% less than 15 minutes, 28.0% 15 to 30 minutes, 27.4% 30 to 45 minutes, 11.7% 45 to 60 minutes, 7.8% 60 minutes or more (2006-2010 5-year est.)

## MINETTO (town).

Covers a land area of 5.761 square miles and a water area of 0.279 square miles. Located at 43.39° N. Lat; 76.48° W. Long. Elevation is 325 feet.

**Population:** 1,822 (1990); 1,663 (2000); 1,659 (2010); Density: 287.9 persons per square mile (2010); Race: 97.5% White, 0.5% Black, 0.8% Asian, 0.2% American Indian/Alaska Native, 0.0% Native Hawaiian/Other Pacific Islander, 1.0% Other, 1.1% Hispanic of any race (2010); Average household size: 2.43 (2010); Median age: 46.1 (2010); Males per 100 females: 98.2 (2010); Marriage status: 25.7% never married, 61.6% now married, 4.4% widowed, 8.2% divorced (2006-2010 5-year est.); Foreign born: 3.2% (2006-2010 5-year est.); Ancestry (includes multiple ancestries): 25.4% Irish, 20.7% German, 19.0% English, 17.4% Italian, 8.0% French (2006-2010 5-year est.).

**Economy:** Single-family building permits issued: 0 (2011); Multi-family building permits issued: 0 (2011); Employment by occupation: 6.4% management, 2.7% professional, 4.1% services, 12.1% sales, 1.2% farming, 8.0% construction, 6.9% production (2006-2010 5-year est.).

**Income:** Per capita income: $34,893 (2006-2010 5-year est.); Median household income: $63,611 (2006-2010 5-year est.); Average household income: $88,825 (2006-2010 5-year est.); Percent of households with income of $100,000 or more: 25.1% (2006-2010 5-year est.); Poverty rate: 8.0% (2006-2010 5-year est.).

**Education:** Percent of population age 25 and over with: High school diploma (including GED) or higher: 93.4% (2006-2010 5-year est.); Bachelor's degree or higher: 37.3% (2006-2010 5-year est.); Master's degree or higher: 18.9% (2006-2010 5-year est.).

### School District(s)

Oswego City School District (PK-12)

    2009-10 Enrollment: 4,301 . . . . . . . . . . . . . . . . . . . . . (315) 341-2001

**Housing:** Homeownership rate: 83.1% (2010); Median home value: $110,100 (2006-2010 5-year est.); Median contract rent: $490 per month (2006-2010 5-year est.); Median year structure built: 1965 (2006-2010 5-year est.).

**Transportation:** Commute to work: 93.4% car, 0.5% public transportation, 1.8% walk, 3.5% work from home (2006-2010 5-year est.); Travel time to work: 41.2% less than 15 minutes, 38.2% 15 to 30 minutes, 9.9% 30 to 45

minutes, 6.6% 45 to 60 minutes, 4.0% 60 minutes or more (2006-2010 5-year est.)

**MINETTO** (CDP). Covers a land area of 3.322 square miles and a water area of 0.262 square miles. Located at 43.40° N. Lat; 76.48° W. Long. Elevation is 325 feet.
**Population:** 1,252 (1990); 1,086 (2000); 1,069 (2010); Density: 321.7 persons per square mile (2010); Race: 97.5% White, 0.1% Black, 0.8% Asian, 0.4% American Indian/Alaska Native, 0.0% Native Hawaiian/Other Pacific Islander, 1.2% Other, 1.0% Hispanic of any race (2010); Average household size: 2.37 (2010); Median age: 47.5 (2010); Males per 100 females: 100.9 (2010); Marriage status: 26.2% never married, 57.5% now married, 5.1% widowed, 11.2% divorced (2006-2010 5-year est.); Foreign born: 3.7% (2006-2010 5-year est.); Ancestry (includes multiple ancestries): 23.7% Irish, 20.6% German, 18.7% Italian, 15.9% English, 9.7% French (2006-2010 5-year est.).
**Economy:** Employment by occupation: 6.8% management, 1.2% professional, 3.1% services, 14.1% sales, 0.6% farming, 4.3% construction, 6.3% production (2006-2010 5-year est.).
**Income:** Per capita income: $30,877 (2006-2010 5-year est.); Median household income: $56,786 (2006-2010 5-year est.); Average household income: $81,975 (2006-2010 5-year est.); Percent of households with income of $100,000 or more: 21.5% (2006-2010 5-year est.); Poverty rate: 11.0% (2006-2010 5-year est.).
**Education:** Percent of population age 25 and over with: High school diploma (including GED) or higher: 96.0% (2006-2010 5-year est.); Bachelor's degree or higher: 36.5% (2006-2010 5-year est.); Master's degree or higher: 20.3% (2006-2010 5-year est.).

### School District(s)
Oswego City School District (PK-12)
   2009-10 Enrollment: 4,301 . . . . . . . . . . . . . . . . . . . . . . (315) 341-2001
**Housing:** Homeownership rate: 82.4% (2010); Median home value: $106,600 (2006-2010 5-year est.); Median contract rent: $437 per month (2006-2010 5-year est.); Median year structure built: 1960 (2006-2010 5-year est.).
**Transportation:** Commute to work: 91.5% car, 0.8% public transportation, 2.9% walk, 3.3% work from home (2006-2010 5-year est.); Travel time to work: 41.5% less than 15 minutes, 40.6% 15 to 30 minutes, 7.1% 30 to 45 minutes, 5.4% 45 to 60 minutes, 5.4% 60 minutes or more (2006-2010 5-year est.)

**NEW HAVEN** (town). Covers a land area of 31.098 square miles and a water area of 2.314 square miles. Located at 43.47° N. Lat; 76.31° W. Long. Elevation is 423 feet.
**Population:** 2,778 (1990); 2,930 (2000); 2,856 (2010); Density: 91.8 persons per square mile (2010); Race: 97.7% White, 0.3% Black, 0.4% Asian, 0.3% American Indian/Alaska Native, 0.0% Native Hawaiian/Other Pacific Islander, 1.3% Other, 1.3% Hispanic of any race (2010); Average household size: 2.63 (2010); Median age: 40.0 (2010); Males per 100 females: 102.1 (2010); Marriage status: 32.5% never married, 53.2% now married, 5.2% widowed, 9.1% divorced (2006-2010 5-year est.); Foreign born: 2.2% (2006-2010 5-year est.); Ancestry (includes multiple ancestries): 22.3% Irish, 20.8% English, 10.2% Italian, 10.0% French, 9.6% German (2006-2010 5-year est.).
**Economy:** Single-family building permits issued: 12 (2011); Multi-family building permits issued: 0 (2011); Employment by occupation: 6.8% management, 4.8% professional, 12.4% services, 11.1% sales, 2.2% farming, 10.8% construction, 14.9% production (2006-2010 5-year est.).
**Income:** Per capita income: $19,688 (2006-2010 5-year est.); Median household income: $49,189 (2006-2010 5-year est.); Average household income: $57,596 (2006-2010 5-year est.); Percent of households with income of $100,000 or more: 13.3% (2006-2010 5-year est.); Poverty rate: 15.7% (2006-2010 5-year est.).
**Education:** Percent of population age 25 and over with: High school diploma (including GED) or higher: 85.2% (2006-2010 5-year est.); Bachelor's degree or higher: 10.0% (2006-2010 5-year est.); Master's degree or higher: 3.6% (2006-2010 5-year est.).

### School District(s)
Mexico Central School District (KG-12)
   2009-10 Enrollment: 2,281 . . . . . . . . . . . . . . . . . . . . . . (315) 963-8400
**Housing:** Homeownership rate: 83.7% (2010); Median home value: $79,700 (2006-2010 5-year est.); Median contract rent: $479 per month (2006-2010 5-year est.); Median year structure built: 1977 (2006-2010 5-year est.).

**Transportation:** Commute to work: 95.5% car, 0.0% public transportation, 0.8% walk, 1.4% work from home (2006-2010 5-year est.); Travel time to work: 32.3% less than 15 minutes, 39.8% 15 to 30 minutes, 14.8% 30 to 45 minutes, 7.5% 45 to 60 minutes, 5.6% 60 minutes or more (2006-2010 5-year est.)

**ORWELL** (town). Covers a land area of 39.581 square miles and a water area of 1.684 square miles. Located at 43.56° N. Lat; 75.95° W. Long. Elevation is 801 feet.
**Population:** 1,171 (1990); 1,254 (2000); 1,167 (2010); Density: 29.5 persons per square mile (2010); Race: 95.5% White, 1.7% Black, 0.3% Asian, 1.1% American Indian/Alaska Native, 0.0% Native Hawaiian/Other Pacific Islander, 1.4% Other, 0.6% Hispanic of any race (2010); Average household size: 2.59 (2010); Median age: 43.1 (2010); Males per 100 females: 117.3 (2010); Marriage status: 28.2% never married, 56.4% now married, 7.9% widowed, 7.5% divorced (2006-2010 5-year est.); Foreign born: 5.3% (2006-2010 5-year est.); Ancestry (includes multiple ancestries): 18.8% English, 16.7% German, 10.4% Irish, 9.0% Italian, 8.1% French (2006-2010 5-year est.).
**Economy:** Single-family building permits issued: 16 (2011); Multi-family building permits issued: 0 (2011); Employment by occupation: 9.7% management, 4.7% professional, 6.5% services, 15.6% sales, 0.7% farming, 13.6% construction, 7.3% production (2006-2010 5-year est.).
**Income:** Per capita income: $18,809 (2006-2010 5-year est.); Median household income: $44,904 (2006-2010 5-year est.); Average household income: $53,378 (2006-2010 5-year est.); Percent of households with income of $100,000 or more: 7.9% (2006-2010 5-year est.); Poverty rate: 16.6% (2006-2010 5-year est.).
**Education:** Percent of population age 25 and over with: High school diploma (including GED) or higher: 89.7% (2006-2010 5-year est.); Bachelor's degree or higher: 21.1% (2006-2010 5-year est.); Master's degree or higher: 8.4% (2006-2010 5-year est.).
**Housing:** Homeownership rate: 83.7% (2010); Median home value: $80,900 (2006-2010 5-year est.); Median contract rent: $481 per month (2006-2010 5-year est.); Median year structure built: 1971 (2006-2010 5-year est.).
**Transportation:** Commute to work: 94.6% car, 0.0% public transportation, 2.2% walk, 1.5% work from home (2006-2010 5-year est.); Travel time to work: 8.9% less than 15 minutes, 29.6% 15 to 30 minutes, 22.6% 30 to 45 minutes, 24.5% 45 to 60 minutes, 14.3% 60 minutes or more (2006-2010 5-year est.)

**OSWEGO** (city). County seat. Covers a land area of 7.613 square miles and a water area of 3.613 square miles. Located at 43.45° N. Lat; 76.50° W. Long. Elevation is 285 feet.
**History:** The name of Oswego is of Indian origin, meaning "pouring out of waters." The strategic importance of the place led to the erection of a fort in 1722. Soon after military occupation ceased, settlement began. Its commanding position at the terminus of the inland water route made Oswego a busy port.
**Population:** 19,195 (1990); 17,954 (2000); 18,142 (2010); Density: 2,382.7 persons per square mile (2010); Race: 94.8% White, 1.3% Black, 1.2% Asian, 0.3% American Indian/Alaska Native, 0.0% Native Hawaiian/Other Pacific Islander, 2.4% Other, 4.4% Hispanic of any race (2010); Average household size: 2.30 (2010); Median age: 33.8 (2010); Males per 100 females: 93.4 (2010); Marriage status: 39.6% never married, 41.1% now married, 8.9% widowed, 10.4% divorced (2006-2010 5-year est.); Foreign born: 2.4% (2006-2010 5-year est.); Ancestry (includes multiple ancestries): 29.4% Irish, 18.5% German, 17.9% Italian, 12.5% English, 9.7% French (2006-2010 5-year est.).
**Economy:** Single-family building permits issued: 10 (2011); Multi-family building permits issued: 56 (2011); Employment by occupation: 8.2% management, 3.0% professional, 13.5% services, 16.5% sales, 4.0% farming, 6.9% construction, 5.5% production (2006-2010 5-year est.).
**Income:** Per capita income: $20,621 (2006-2010 5-year est.); Median household income: $37,070 (2006-2010 5-year est.); Average household income: $49,945 (2006-2010 5-year est.); Percent of households with income of $100,000 or more: 13.3% (2006-2010 5-year est.); Poverty rate: 21.9% (2006-2010 5-year est.).
**Taxes:** Total city taxes per capita: $1,123 (2009); City property taxes per capita: $399 (2009).
**Education:** Percent of population age 25 and over with: High school diploma (including GED) or higher: 85.2% (2006-2010 5-year est.); Bachelor's degree or higher: 22.3% (2006-2010 5-year est.); Master's degree or higher: 9.8% (2006-2010 5-year est.).

### School District(s)

Oswego City School District (PK-12)

  2009-10 Enrollment: 4,301 . . . . . . . . . . . . . . . . . . . . . . . (315) 341-2001

### Four-year College(s)

SUNY College at Oswego (Public)

  Fall 2010 Enrollment: 7,716 . . . . . . . . . . . . . . . . . . . . (315) 312-2500

  2011-12 Tuition: In-state $6,510; Out-of-state $15,560

**Housing:** Homeownership rate: 51.3% (2010); Median home value: $80,800 (2006-2010 5-year est.); Median contract rent: $514 per month (2006-2010 5-year est.); Median year structure built: before 1940 (2006-2010 5-year est.).

**Hospitals:** Oswego Hospital (74 beds)

**Safety:** Violent crime rate: 37.9 per 10,000 population; Property crime rate: 431.4 per 10,000 population (2010).

**Newspapers:** Palladium-Times (Local news; Circulation 8,500)

**Transportation:** Commute to work: 88.2% car, 0.9% public transportation, 7.3% walk, 2.6% work from home (2006-2010 5-year est.); Travel time to work: 58.3% less than 15 minutes, 23.2% 15 to 30 minutes, 7.8% 30 to 45 minutes, 5.9% 45 to 60 minutes, 4.9% 60 minutes or more (2006-2010 5-year est.)

### Additional Information Contacts

City of Oswego . . . . . . . . . . . . . . . . . . . . . . . . . . . . . . . (315) 342-8116

  http://www.oswegony.org

Greater Oswego-Fulton Chamber of Commerce . . . . . . . . (315) 343-7681

  http://oswegofultonchamber.com

---

**OSWEGO** (town). Covers a land area of 27.333 square miles and a water area of 2.016 square miles. Located at 43.40° N. Lat; 76.55° W. Long. Elevation is 285 feet.

**History:** Trading post established here after the English founded Oswego (1722) became vital to the Albany fur trade. Its strategic location prompted the building of Fort Oswego (1727), Fort George (1755) and Fort Ontario (1755), which were much contested in the colonial wars. Importance as a lake port came with the completion of the Barge Canal (1917) and the St. Lawrence Seaway (1959). Seat of State University College of Arts and Science at Oswego. Founded 1722, Incorporated as a city 1848.

**Population:** 8,027 (1990); 7,287 (2000); 7,984 (2010); Density: 292.1 persons per square mile (2010); Race: 91.4% White, 3.4% Black, 2.0% Asian, 0.2% American Indian/Alaska Native, 0.1% Native Hawaiian/Other Pacific Islander, 2.9% Other, 3.9% Hispanic of any race (2010); Average household size: 2.50 (2010); Median age: 21.3 (2010); Males per 100 females: 101.2 (2010); Marriage status: 69.3% never married, 26.7% now married, 1.0% widowed, 3.0% divorced (2006-2010 5-year est.); Foreign born: 4.3% (2006-2010 5-year est.); Ancestry (includes multiple ancestries): 25.3% Irish, 21.7% Italian, 21.5% German, 10.5% English, 8.3% Polish (2006-2010 5-year est.).

**Economy:** Single-family building permits issued: 5 (2011); Multi-family building permits issued: 0 (2011); Employment by occupation: 3.2% management, 5.0% professional, 15.9% services, 19.3% sales, 5.7% farming, 12.3% construction, 7.2% production (2006-2010 5-year est.).

**Income:** Per capita income: $14,609 (2006-2010 5-year est.); Median household income: $61,801 (2006-2010 5-year est.); Average household income: $68,782 (2006-2010 5-year est.); Percent of households with income of $100,000 or more: 17.2% (2006-2010 5-year est.); Poverty rate: 7.3% (2006-2010 5-year est.).

**Education:** Percent of population age 25 and over with: High school diploma (including GED) or higher: 90.0% (2006-2010 5-year est.); Bachelor's degree or higher: 27.4% (2006-2010 5-year est.); Master's degree or higher: 17.4% (2006-2010 5-year est.).

### School District(s)

Oswego City School District (PK-12)

  2009-10 Enrollment: 4,301 . . . . . . . . . . . . . . . . . . . . . . (315) 341-2001

### Four-year College(s)

SUNY College at Oswego (Public)

  Fall 2010 Enrollment: 7,716 . . . . . . . . . . . . . . . . . . . . (315) 312-2500

  2011-12 Tuition: In-state $6,510; Out-of-state $15,560

**Housing:** Homeownership rate: 85.8% (2010); Median home value: $113,900 (2006-2010 5-year est.); Median contract rent: $529 per month (2006-2010 5-year est.); Median year structure built: 1973 (2006-2010 5-year est.).

**Hospitals:** Oswego Hospital (74 beds)

**Newspapers:** Palladium-Times (Local news; Circulation 8,500)

**Transportation:** Commute to work: 66.6% car, 0.2% public transportation, 28.0% walk, 4.0% work from home (2006-2010 5-year est.); Travel time to work: 56.7% less than 15 minutes, 25.7% 15 to 30 minutes, 7.2% 30 to 45

minutes, 9.3% 45 to 60 minutes, 1.1% 60 minutes or more (2006-2010 5-year est.)

### Additional Information Contacts

Town of Oswego . . . . . . . . . . . . . . . . . . . . . . . . . . . . . . (315) 343-2586

  http://www.townofoswego.com

---

**PALERMO** (town). Covers a land area of 40.463 square miles and a water area of 0.278 square miles. Located at 43.36° N. Lat; 76.25° W. Long. Elevation is 469 feet.

**Population:** 3,582 (1990); 3,686 (2000); 3,664 (2010); Density: 90.6 persons per square mile (2010); Race: 97.2% White, 0.3% Black, 0.3% Asian, 0.3% American Indian/Alaska Native, 0.0% Native Hawaiian/Other Pacific Islander, 1.9% Other, 1.6% Hispanic of any race (2010); Average household size: 2.73 (2010); Median age: 39.4 (2010); Males per 100 females: 101.5 (2010); Marriage status: 27.4% never married, 61.8% now married, 2.8% widowed, 8.0% divorced (2006-2010 5-year est.); Foreign born: 0.3% (2006-2010 5-year est.); Ancestry (includes multiple ancestries): 20.0% German, 17.9% Irish, 16.1% French, 15.6% English, 14.2% Italian (2006-2010 5-year est.).

**Economy:** Single-family building permits issued: 8 (2011); Multi-family building permits issued: 0 (2011); Employment by occupation: 11.9% management, 3.7% professional, 15.4% services, 6.1% sales, 0.9% farming, 23.4% construction, 16.7% production (2006-2010 5-year est.).

**Income:** Per capita income: $23,599 (2006-2010 5-year est.); Median household income: $50,462 (2006-2010 5-year est.); Average household income: $60,937 (2006-2010 5-year est.); Percent of households with income of $100,000 or more: 14.4% (2006-2010 5-year est.); Poverty rate: 9.4% (2006-2010 5-year est.).

**Education:** Percent of population age 25 and over with: High school diploma (including GED) or higher: 81.6% (2006-2010 5-year est.); Bachelor's degree or higher: 9.2% (2006-2010 5-year est.); Master's degree or higher: 2.9% (2006-2010 5-year est.).

**Housing:** Homeownership rate: 84.7% (2010); Median home value: $96,700 (2006-2010 5-year est.); Median contract rent: $532 per month (2006-2010 5-year est.); Median year structure built: 1978 (2006-2010 5-year est.).

**Transportation:** Commute to work: 91.7% car, 0.4% public transportation, 1.2% walk, 5.1% work from home (2006-2010 5-year est.); Travel time to work: 16.6% less than 15 minutes, 29.6% 15 to 30 minutes, 38.3% 30 to 45 minutes, 9.2% 45 to 60 minutes, 6.2% 60 minutes or more (2006-2010 5-year est.)

---

**PARISH** (village). Covers a land area of 1.605 square miles and a water area of 0 square miles. Located at 43.40° N. Lat; 76.12° W. Long. Elevation is 495 feet.

**Population:** 477 (1990); 512 (2000); 450 (2010); Density: 280.3 persons per square mile (2010); Race: 97.3% White, 0.9% Black, 0.7% Asian, 0.0% American Indian/Alaska Native, 0.0% Native Hawaiian/Other Pacific Islander, 1.1% Other, 1.6% Hispanic of any race (2010); Average household size: 2.50 (2010); Median age: 42.0 (2010); Males per 100 females: 99.1 (2010); Marriage status: 27.2% never married, 59.9% now married, 5.2% widowed, 7.6% divorced (2006-2010 5-year est.); Foreign born: 0.6% (2006-2010 5-year est.); Ancestry (includes multiple ancestries): 28.3% German, 21.5% English, 18.9% Irish, 12.9% Scotch-Irish, 7.8% French Canadian (2006-2010 5-year est.).

**Economy:** Single-family building permits issued: 0 (2011); Multi-family building permits issued: 0 (2011); Employment by occupation: 6.7% management, 11.5% professional, 4.8% services, 25.0% sales, 3.8% farming, 14.4% construction, 4.3% production (2006-2010 5-year est.).

**Income:** Per capita income: $20,859 (2006-2010 5-year est.); Median household income: $55,089 (2006-2010 5-year est.); Average household income: $57,897 (2006-2010 5-year est.); Percent of households with income of $100,000 or more: 16.8% (2006-2010 5-year est.); Poverty rate: 3.1% (2006-2010 5-year est.).

**Education:** Percent of population age 25 and over with: High school diploma (including GED) or higher: 88.6% (2006-2010 5-year est.); Bachelor's degree or higher: 18.3% (2006-2010 5-year est.); Master's degree or higher: 3.9% (2006-2010 5-year est.).

### School District(s)

Altmar-Parish-Williamstown Central School District (PK-12)

  2009-10 Enrollment: 1,435 . . . . . . . . . . . . . . . . . . . . (315) 625-5251

**Housing:** Homeownership rate: 74.5% (2010); Median home value: $95,200 (2006-2010 5-year est.); Median contract rent: $454 per month (2006-2010 5-year est.); Median year structure built: before 1940 (2006-2010 5-year est.).

**Transportation:** Commute to work: 97.5% car, 0.0% public transportation, 0.0% walk, 2.5% work from home (2006-2010 5-year est.); Travel time to work: 20.4% less than 15 minutes, 32.1% 15 to 30 minutes, 25.5% 30 to 45 minutes, 15.8% 45 to 60 minutes, 6.1% 60 minutes or more (2006-2010 5-year est.)

## PARISH (town).
Covers a land area of 41.725 square miles and a water area of 0.224 square miles. Located at 43.40° N. Lat; 76.05° W. Long. Elevation is 495 feet.

**Population:** 2,425 (1990); 2,694 (2000); 2,558 (2010); Density: 61.3 persons per square mile (2010); Race: 97.4% White, 0.4% Black, 0.2% Asian, 0.6% American Indian/Alaska Native, 0.0% Native Hawaiian/Other Pacific Islander, 1.4% Other, 1.6% Hispanic of any race (2010); Average household size: 2.62 (2010); Median age: 41.0 (2010); Males per 100 females: 98.0 (2010); Marriage status: 25.2% never married, 58.9% now married, 8.6% widowed, 7.3% divorced (2006-2010 5-year est.); Foreign born: 0.4% (2006-2010 5-year est.); Ancestry (includes multiple ancestries): 23.5% German, 23.2% Irish, 12.7% English, 8.9% French, 8.3% Italian (2006-2010 5-year est.).

**Economy:** Single-family building permits issued: 0 (2011); Multi-family building permits issued: 0 (2011); Employment by occupation: 5.5% management, 4.6% professional, 6.3% services, 18.0% sales, 5.0% farming, 22.8% construction, 14.4% production (2006-2010 5-year est.).

**Income:** Per capita income: $21,472 (2006-2010 5-year est.); Median household income: $46,200 (2006-2010 5-year est.); Average household income: $58,512 (2006-2010 5-year est.); Percent of households with income of $100,000 or more: 13.7% (2006-2010 5-year est.); Poverty rate: 10.3% (2006-2010 5-year est.).

**Education:** Percent of population age 25 and over with: High school diploma (including GED) or higher: 84.9% (2006-2010 5-year est.); Bachelor's degree or higher: 13.2% (2006-2010 5-year est.); Master's degree or higher: 3.0% (2006-2010 5-year est.).

**School District(s)**
Altmar-Parish-Williamstown Central School District (PK-12)
   2009-10 Enrollment: 1,435 . . . . . . . . . . . . . . . . . . . (315) 625-5251

**Housing:** Homeownership rate: 84.6% (2010); Median home value: $88,500 (2006-2010 5-year est.); Median contract rent: $484 per month (2006-2010 5-year est.); Median year structure built: 1972 (2006-2010 5-year est.).

**Transportation:** Commute to work: 96.5% car, 0.0% public transportation, 0.6% walk, 2.9% work from home (2006-2010 5-year est.); Travel time to work: 13.2% less than 15 minutes, 27.5% 15 to 30 minutes, 35.2% 30 to 45 minutes, 14.7% 45 to 60 minutes, 9.3% 60 minutes or more (2006-2010 5-year est.)

## PENNELLVILLE (unincorporated postal area)
Zip Code: 13132
   Covers a land area of 23.725 square miles and a water area of 0.406 square miles. Located at 43.27° N. Lat; 76.25° W. Long. Elevation is 413 feet. Population: 4,244 (2010); Density: 178.9 persons per square mile (2010); Race: 97.0% White, 0.6% Black, 0.4% Asian, 0.8% American Indian/Alaska Native, 0.0% Native Hawaiian/Other Pacific Islander, 1.2% Other, 1.3% Hispanic of any race (2010); Average household size: 2.61 (2010); Median age: 41.9 (2010); Males per 100 females: 104.7 (2010); Homeownership rate: 88.4% (2010)

## PHOENIX (village).
Covers a land area of 1.170 square miles and a water area of 0.119 square miles. Located at 43.23° N. Lat; 76.29° W. Long. Elevation is 371 feet.

**History:** Incorporated 1849.

**Population:** 2,486 (1990); 2,251 (2000); 2,382 (2010); Density: 2,034.9 persons per square mile (2010); Race: 96.1% White, 0.8% Black, 0.5% Asian, 0.7% American Indian/Alaska Native, 0.0% Native Hawaiian/Other Pacific Islander, 1.9% Other, 1.3% Hispanic of any race (2010); Average household size: 2.35 (2010); Median age: 35.3 (2010); Males per 100 females: 90.7 (2010); Marriage status: 31.2% never married, 46.3% now married, 6.4% widowed, 16.1% divorced (2006-2010 5-year est.); Foreign born: 0.5% (2006-2010 5-year est.); Ancestry (includes multiple ancestries): 25.0% Irish, 24.9% German, 14.5% English, 12.3% Italian, 10.9% French (2006-2010 5-year est.).

**Economy:** Single-family building permits issued: 0 (2011); Multi-family building permits issued: 0 (2011); Employment by occupation: 4.7% management, 0.8% professional, 10.6% services, 16.8% sales, 8.6% farming, 18.1% construction, 14.2% production (2006-2010 5-year est.).

**Income:** Per capita income: $20,552 (2006-2010 5-year est.); Median household income: $42,378 (2006-2010 5-year est.); Average household income: $51,300 (2006-2010 5-year est.); Percent of households with income of $100,000 or more: 5.8% (2006-2010 5-year est.); Poverty rate: 12.8% (2006-2010 5-year est.).

**Education:** Percent of population age 25 and over with: High school diploma (including GED) or higher: 85.1% (2006-2010 5-year est.); Bachelor's degree or higher: 14.3% (2006-2010 5-year est.); Master's degree or higher: 3.9% (2006-2010 5-year est.).

**School District(s)**
Phoenix Central School District (PK-12)
   2009-10 Enrollment: 2,239 . . . . . . . . . . . . . . . . . . . (315) 695-1555

**Housing:** Homeownership rate: 46.6% (2010); Median home value: $88,200 (2006-2010 5-year est.); Median contract rent: $470 per month (2006-2010 5-year est.); Median year structure built: 1941 (2006-2010 5-year est.).

**Transportation:** Commute to work: 92.9% car, 1.7% public transportation, 1.8% walk, 1.6% work from home (2006-2010 5-year est.); Travel time to work: 22.9% less than 15 minutes, 40.5% 15 to 30 minutes, 28.2% 30 to 45 minutes, 3.0% 45 to 60 minutes, 5.4% 60 minutes or more (2006-2010 5-year est.)

**Additional Information Contacts**
Greater Oswego-Fulton Chamber of Commerce . . . . . . . . . (315) 343-7681
   http://www.oswegofultonchamber.com

## PULASKI (village).
Covers a land area of 3.483 square miles and a water area of 0.105 square miles. Located at 43.56° N. Lat; 76.12° W. Long. Elevation is 371 feet.

**History:** Incorporated 1832.

**Population:** 2,525 (1990); 2,398 (2000); 2,365 (2010); Density: 678.9 persons per square mile (2010); Race: 97.3% White, 0.8% Black, 0.4% Asian, 0.5% American Indian/Alaska Native, 0.0% Native Hawaiian/Other Pacific Islander, 1.0% Other, 1.6% Hispanic of any race (2010); Average household size: 2.25 (2010); Median age: 41.2 (2010); Males per 100 females: 93.9 (2010); Marriage status: 27.3% never married, 51.0% now married, 9.7% widowed, 12.1% divorced (2006-2010 5-year est.); Foreign born: 2.5% (2006-2010 5-year est.); Ancestry (includes multiple ancestries): 24.0% German, 19.1% Irish, 15.8% English, 10.9% Italian, 8.2% American (2006-2010 5-year est.).

**Economy:** Single-family building permits issued: 3 (2011); Multi-family building permits issued: 0 (2011); Employment by occupation: 7.2% management, 3.0% professional, 12.4% services, 15.8% sales, 2.6% farming, 9.7% construction, 6.9% production (2006-2010 5-year est.).

**Income:** Per capita income: $24,699 (2006-2010 5-year est.); Median household income: $37,793 (2006-2010 5-year est.); Average household income: $58,653 (2006-2010 5-year est.); Percent of households with income of $100,000 or more: 8.9% (2006-2010 5-year est.); Poverty rate: 23.9% (2006-2010 5-year est.).

**Education:** Percent of population age 25 and over with: High school diploma (including GED) or higher: 90.3% (2006-2010 5-year est.); Bachelor's degree or higher: 15.4% (2006-2010 5-year est.); Master's degree or higher: 6.6% (2006-2010 5-year est.).

**School District(s)**
Pulaski Central School District (PK-12)
   2009-10 Enrollment: 921 . . . . . . . . . . . . . . . . . . . . (315) 298-5188

**Housing:** Homeownership rate: 47.9% (2010); Median home value: $91,100 (2006-2010 5-year est.); Median contract rent: $457 per month (2006-2010 5-year est.); Median year structure built: 1961 (2006-2010 5-year est.).

**Safety:** Violent crime rate: 0.0 per 10,000 population; Property crime rate: 294.1 per 10,000 population (2010).

**Newspapers:** Salmon River News (Local news)

**Transportation:** Commute to work: 90.0% car, 2.4% public transportation, 4.6% walk, 2.8% work from home (2006-2010 5-year est.); Travel time to work: 49.4% less than 15 minutes, 9.4% 15 to 30 minutes, 21.3% 30 to 45 minutes, 7.8% 45 to 60 minutes, 12.0% 60 minutes or more (2006-2010 5-year est.)

**Additional Information Contacts**
Pulaski Chamber of Commerce . . . . . . . . . . . . . . . . . . . (315) 298-2213
   http://www.pulaskinychamber.com

**REDFIELD** (town). Covers a land area of 89.817 square miles and a water area of 3.606 square miles. Located at 43.58° N. Lat; 75.82° W. Long. Elevation is 951 feet.
**Population:** 564 (1990); 607 (2000); 550 (2010); Density: 6.1 persons per square mile (2010); Race: 98.2% White, 0.2% Black, 0.0% Asian, 0.4% American Indian/Alaska Native, 0.0% Native Hawaiian/Other Pacific Islander, 1.2% Other, 0.5% Hispanic of any race (2010); Average household size: 2.50 (2010); Median age: 43.5 (2010); Males per 100 females: 103.7 (2010); Marriage status: 14.9% never married, 60.9% now married, 13.1% widowed, 11.1% divorced (2006-2010 5-year est.); Foreign born: 1.9% (2006-2010 5-year est.); Ancestry (includes multiple ancestries): 27.7% German, 23.0% Irish, 12.3% English, 12.3% Italian, 6.4% Dutch (2006-2010 5-year est.).
**Economy:** Single-family building permits issued: 14 (2011); Multi-family building permits issued: 0 (2011); Employment by occupation: 1.5% management, 5.4% professional, 7.4% services, 9.8% sales, 0.0% farming, 18.1% construction, 17.2% production (2006-2010 5-year est.).
**Income:** Per capita income: $18,219 (2006-2010 5-year est.); Median household income: $26,813 (2006-2010 5-year est.); Average household income: $39,518 (2006-2010 5-year est.); Percent of households with income of $100,000 or more: 10.4% (2006-2010 5-year est.); Poverty rate: 21.3% (2006-2010 5-year est.).
**Education:** Percent of population age 25 and over with: High school diploma (including GED) or higher: 82.3% (2006-2010 5-year est.); Bachelor's degree or higher: 15.7% (2006-2010 5-year est.); Master's degree or higher: 5.5% (2006-2010 5-year est.).
**Housing:** Homeownership rate: 87.8% (2010); Median home value: $72,900 (2006-2010 5-year est.); Median contract rent: $288 per month (2006-2010 5-year est.); Median year structure built: 1976 (2006-2010 5-year est.).
**Transportation:** Commute to work: 95.9% car, 0.0% public transportation, 0.0% walk, 4.1% work from home (2006-2010 5-year est.); Travel time to work: 7.9% less than 15 minutes, 19.0% 15 to 30 minutes, 19.0% 30 to 45 minutes, 25.4% 45 to 60 minutes, 28.6% 60 minutes or more (2006-2010 5-year est.)

**RICHLAND** (town). Covers a land area of 57.247 square miles and a water area of 2.801 square miles. Located at 43.54° N. Lat; 76.15° W. Long. Elevation is 548 feet.
**Population:** 5,917 (1990); 5,824 (2000); 5,718 (2010); Density: 99.9 persons per square mile (2010); Race: 97.8% White, 0.4% Black, 0.3% Asian, 0.4% American Indian/Alaska Native, 0.0% Native Hawaiian/Other Pacific Islander, 1.1% Other, 1.5% Hispanic of any race (2010); Average household size: 2.51 (2010); Median age: 39.8 (2010); Males per 100 females: 99.2 (2010); Marriage status: 28.2% never married, 49.6% now married, 8.7% widowed, 13.4% divorced (2006-2010 5-year est.); Foreign born: 3.3% (2006-2010 5-year est.); Ancestry (includes multiple ancestries): 22.9% German, 18.1% Irish, 14.2% English, 9.8% American, 8.9% Italian (2006-2010 5-year est.).
**Economy:** Single-family building permits issued: 7 (2011); Multi-family building permits issued: 0 (2011); Employment by occupation: 9.5% management, 4.5% professional, 11.9% services, 14.7% sales, 5.2% farming, 12.1% construction, 6.1% production (2006-2010 5-year est.).
**Income:** Per capita income: $22,505 (2006-2010 5-year est.); Median household income: $44,731 (2006-2010 5-year est.); Average household income: $56,600 (2006-2010 5-year est.); Percent of households with income of $100,000 or more: 10.4% (2006-2010 5-year est.); Poverty rate: 17.3% (2006-2010 5-year est.).
**Education:** Percent of population age 25 and over with: High school diploma (including GED) or higher: 85.9% (2006-2010 5-year est.); Bachelor's degree or higher: 16.5% (2006-2010 5-year est.); Master's degree or higher: 5.5% (2006-2010 5-year est.).
**Housing:** Homeownership rate: 67.4% (2010); Median home value: $85,200 (2006-2010 5-year est.); Median contract rent: $465 per month (2006-2010 5-year est.); Median year structure built: 1969 (2006-2010 5-year est.).
**Transportation:** Commute to work: 93.4% car, 1.1% public transportation, 2.5% walk, 3.0% work from home (2006-2010 5-year est.); Travel time to work: 41.6% less than 15 minutes, 15.4% 15 to 30 minutes, 21.8% 30 to 45 minutes, 13.3% 45 to 60 minutes, 7.9% 60 minutes or more (2006-2010 5-year est.)

**SAND RIDGE** (CDP). Covers a land area of 2.398 square miles and a water area of 0.035 square miles. Located at 43.25° N. Lat; 76.24° W. Long. Elevation is 433 feet.
**Population:** 1,312 (1990); 906 (2000); 849 (2010); Density: 353.9 persons per square mile (2010); Race: 97.1% White, 1.1% Black, 0.0% Asian, 0.5% American Indian/Alaska Native, 0.0% Native Hawaiian/Other Pacific Islander, 1.3% Other, 1.5% Hispanic of any race (2010); Average household size: 2.39 (2010); Median age: 43.2 (2010); Males per 100 females: 105.6 (2010); Marriage status: 19.9% never married, 58.9% now married, 8.6% widowed, 12.6% divorced (2006-2010 5-year est.); Foreign born: 0.7% (2006-2010 5-year est.); Ancestry (includes multiple ancestries): 33.8% German, 27.0% Irish, 19.2% French, 11.0% English, 8.9% French Canadian (2006-2010 5-year est.).
**Economy:** Employment by occupation: 4.8% management, 0.0% professional, 2.9% services, 25.5% sales, 16.6% farming, 13.9% construction, 16.0% production (2006-2010 5-year est.).
**Income:** Per capita income: $19,547 (2006-2010 5-year est.); Median household income: $39,314 (2006-2010 5-year est.); Average household income: $51,946 (2006-2010 5-year est.); Percent of households with income of $100,000 or more: 18.1% (2006-2010 5-year est.); Poverty rate: 11.0% (2006-2010 5-year est.).
**Education:** Percent of population age 25 and over with: High school diploma (including GED) or higher: 90.0% (2006-2010 5-year est.); Bachelor's degree or higher: 0.6% (2006-2010 5-year est.); Master's degree or higher: 0.0% (2006-2010 5-year est.).
**Housing:** Homeownership rate: 87.9% (2010); Median home value: $58,300 (2006-2010 5-year est.); Median contract rent: n/a per month (2006-2010 5-year est.); Median year structure built: 1978 (2006-2010 5-year est.).
**Transportation:** Commute to work: 88.7% car, 0.0% public transportation, 8.3% walk, 3.0% work from home (2006-2010 5-year est.); Travel time to work: 22.9% less than 15 minutes, 54.7% 15 to 30 minutes, 19.1% 30 to 45 minutes, 2.5% 45 to 60 minutes, 0.9% 60 minutes or more (2006-2010 5-year est.)

**SANDY CREEK** (village). Covers a land area of 1.351 square miles and a water area of 0 square miles. Located at 43.64° N. Lat; 76.08° W. Long. Elevation is 499 feet.
**Population:** 793 (1990); 789 (2000); 771 (2010); Density: 570.5 persons per square mile (2010); Race: 96.9% White, 0.5% Black, 0.8% Asian, 1.0% American Indian/Alaska Native, 0.0% Native Hawaiian/Other Pacific Islander, 0.8% Other, 2.1% Hispanic of any race (2010); Average household size: 2.50 (2010); Median age: 36.7 (2010); Males per 100 females: 95.7 (2010); Marriage status: 28.2% never married, 48.0% now married, 6.5% widowed, 17.3% divorced (2006-2010 5-year est.); Foreign born: 4.3% (2006-2010 5-year est.); Ancestry (includes multiple ancestries): 28.9% German, 27.2% Irish, 17.6% English, 9.3% French, 3.5% Scottish (2006-2010 5-year est.).
**Economy:** Single-family building permits issued: 0 (2011); Multi-family building permits issued: 0 (2011); Employment by occupation: 2.7% management, 8.6% professional, 22.6% services, 21.6% sales, 0.0% farming, 4.3% construction, 5.3% production (2006-2010 5-year est.).
**Income:** Per capita income: $21,221 (2006-2010 5-year est.); Median household income: $47,917 (2006-2010 5-year est.); Average household income: $52,738 (2006-2010 5-year est.); Percent of households with income of $100,000 or more: 11.6% (2006-2010 5-year est.); Poverty rate: 14.1% (2006-2010 5-year est.).
**Education:** Percent of population age 25 and over with: High school diploma (including GED) or higher: 90.0% (2006-2010 5-year est.); Bachelor's degree or higher: 19.0% (2006-2010 5-year est.); Master's degree or higher: 4.2% (2006-2010 5-year est.).
**School District(s)**
Sandy Creek Central School District (PK-12)
    2009-10 Enrollment: 934 . . . . . . . . . . . . . . . . . . . . (315) 387-3445
**Housing:** Homeownership rate: 65.1% (2010); Median home value: $70,400 (2006-2010 5-year est.); Median contract rent: $487 per month (2006-2010 5-year est.); Median year structure built: before 1940 (2006-2010 5-year est.).
**Transportation:** Commute to work: 91.4% car, 0.0% public transportation, 6.0% walk, 2.6% work from home (2006-2010 5-year est.); Travel time to work: 18.5% less than 15 minutes, 20.4% 15 to 30 minutes, 32.3% 30 to 45 minutes, 17.3% 45 to 60 minutes, 11.5% 60 minutes or more (2006-2010 5-year est.)

**SANDY CREEK** (town). Covers a land area of 42.284 square miles and a water area of 4.157 square miles. Located at 43.63° N. Lat; 76.12° W. Long. Elevation is 499 feet.
**Population:** 3,454 (1990); 3,863 (2000); 3,939 (2010); Density: 93.2 persons per square mile (2010); Race: 97.5% White, 0.3% Black, 0.5% Asian, 0.5% American Indian/Alaska Native, 0.0% Native Hawaiian/Other Pacific Islander, 1.2% Other, 1.2% Hispanic of any race (2010); Average household size: 2.44 (2010); Median age: 42.6 (2010); Males per 100 females: 102.9 (2010); Marriage status: 23.7% never married, 57.8% now married, 7.2% widowed, 11.3% divorced (2006-2010 5-year est.); Foreign born: 1.7% (2006-2010 5-year est.); Ancestry (includes multiple ancestries): 23.9% Irish, 22.3% German, 19.2% English, 9.0% French, 7.1% Dutch (2006-2010 5-year est.).
**Economy:** Single-family building permits issued: 4 (2011); Multi-family building permits issued: 0 (2011); Employment by occupation: 9.5% management, 4.7% professional, 7.5% services, 19.3% sales, 0.5% farming, 15.2% construction, 6.9% production (2006-2010 5-year est.).
**Income:** Per capita income: $22,876 (2006-2010 5-year est.); Median household income: $44,201 (2006-2010 5-year est.); Average household income: $58,535 (2006-2010 5-year est.); Percent of households with income of $100,000 or more: 11.8% (2006-2010 5-year est.); Poverty rate: 16.6% (2006-2010 5-year est.).
**Education:** Percent of population age 25 and over with: High school diploma (including GED) or higher: 84.4% (2006-2010 5-year est.); Bachelor's degree or higher: 17.6% (2006-2010 5-year est.); Master's degree or higher: 7.9% (2006-2010 5-year est.).

**School District(s)**
Sandy Creek Central School District (PK-12)
    2009-10 Enrollment: 934 . . . . . . . . . . . . . . . . . . . . . . . . (315) 387-3445
**Housing:** Homeownership rate: 78.1% (2010); Median home value: $86,400 (2006-2010 5-year est.); Median contract rent: $488 per month (2006-2010 5-year est.); Median year structure built: 1963 (2006-2010 5-year est.).
**Transportation:** Commute to work: 87.5% car, 0.0% public transportation, 5.8% walk, 5.5% work from home (2006-2010 5-year est.); Travel time to work: 30.3% less than 15 minutes, 20.8% 15 to 30 minutes, 18.7% 30 to 45 minutes, 18.4% 45 to 60 minutes, 11.9% 60 minutes or more (2006-2010 5-year est.)

**SCHROEPPEL** (town). Covers a land area of 42.200 square miles and a water area of 0.996 square miles. Located at 43.25° N. Lat; 76.27° W. Long.
**Population:** 8,931 (1990); 8,566 (2000); 8,501 (2010); Density: 201.4 persons per square mile (2010); Race: 96.8% White, 0.6% Black, 0.4% Asian, 0.7% American Indian/Alaska Native, 0.0% Native Hawaiian/Other Pacific Islander, 1.5% Other, 1.3% Hispanic of any race (2010); Average household size: 2.54 (2010); Median age: 40.0 (2010); Males per 100 females: 99.8 (2010); Marriage status: 28.1% never married, 53.9% now married, 7.3% widowed, 10.7% divorced (2006-2010 5-year est.); Foreign born: 1.4% (2006-2010 5-year est.); Ancestry (includes multiple ancestries): 26.6% German, 22.6% Irish, 17.6% Italian, 13.7% English, 10.6% French (2006-2010 5-year est.).
**Economy:** Single-family building permits issued: 6 (2011); Multi-family building permits issued: 0 (2011); Employment by occupation: 5.2% management, 2.4% professional, 6.5% services, 23.3% sales, 6.6% farming, 14.5% construction, 10.5% production (2006-2010 5-year est.).
**Income:** Per capita income: $22,686 (2006-2010 5-year est.); Median household income: $47,675 (2006-2010 5-year est.); Average household income: $59,037 (2006-2010 5-year est.); Percent of households with income of $100,000 or more: 14.8% (2006-2010 5-year est.); Poverty rate: 7.3% (2006-2010 5-year est.).
**Education:** Percent of population age 25 and over with: High school diploma (including GED) or higher: 87.4% (2006-2010 5-year est.); Bachelor's degree or higher: 13.1% (2006-2010 5-year est.); Master's degree or higher: 5.9% (2006-2010 5-year est.).
**Housing:** Homeownership rate: 75.8% (2010); Median home value: $94,300 (2006-2010 5-year est.); Median contract rent: $556 per month (2006-2010 5-year est.); Median year structure built: 1970 (2006-2010 5-year est.).
**Transportation:** Commute to work: 91.7% car, 0.5% public transportation, 2.2% walk, 4.3% work from home (2006-2010 5-year est.); Travel time to work: 21.8% less than 15 minutes, 47.4% 15 to 30 minutes, 24.7% 30 to 45 minutes, 2.9% 45 to 60 minutes, 3.2% 60 minutes or more (2006-2010 5-year est.)

**SCRIBA** (town). Covers a land area of 40.570 square miles and a water area of 3.341 square miles. Located at 43.45° N. Lat; 76.41° W. Long. Elevation is 367 feet.
**Population:** 6,472 (1990); 7,331 (2000); 6,840 (2010); Density: 168.6 persons per square mile (2010); Race: 97.1% White, 0.5% Black, 0.6% Asian, 0.2% American Indian/Alaska Native, 0.0% Native Hawaiian/Other Pacific Islander, 1.6% Other, 1.9% Hispanic of any race (2010); Average household size: 2.49 (2010); Median age: 40.9 (2010); Males per 100 females: 98.0 (2010); Marriage status: 25.7% never married, 64.1% now married, 3.5% widowed, 6.7% divorced (2006-2010 5-year est.); Foreign born: 1.8% (2006-2010 5-year est.); Ancestry (includes multiple ancestries): 26.8% Irish, 19.2% English, 18.8% German, 17.9% Italian, 13.0% French (2006-2010 5-year est.).
**Economy:** Single-family building permits issued: 6 (2011); Multi-family building permits issued: 0 (2011); Employment by occupation: 6.7% management, 1.6% professional, 14.0% services, 12.6% sales, 3.2% farming, 15.3% construction, 8.8% production (2006-2010 5-year est.).
**Income:** Per capita income: $24,475 (2006-2010 5-year est.); Median household income: $53,906 (2006-2010 5-year est.); Average household income: $63,653 (2006-2010 5-year est.); Percent of households with income of $100,000 or more: 20.3% (2006-2010 5-year est.); Poverty rate: 15.2% (2006-2010 5-year est.).
**Education:** Percent of population age 25 and over with: High school diploma (including GED) or higher: 88.9% (2006-2010 5-year est.); Bachelor's degree or higher: 15.5% (2006-2010 5-year est.); Master's degree or higher: 4.8% (2006-2010 5-year est.).
**Housing:** Homeownership rate: 74.1% (2010); Median home value: $98,900 (2006-2010 5-year est.); Median contract rent: $511 per month (2006-2010 5-year est.); Median year structure built: 1981 (2006-2010 5-year est.).
**Transportation:** Commute to work: 98.4% car, 0.3% public transportation, 0.0% walk, 0.4% work from home (2006-2010 5-year est.); Travel time to work: 44.0% less than 15 minutes, 35.5% 15 to 30 minutes, 5.0% 30 to 45 minutes, 11.1% 45 to 60 minutes, 4.4% 60 minutes or more (2006-2010 5-year est.)
**Additional Information Contacts**
Town of Scriba . . . . . . . . . . . . . . . . . . . . . . . . . . . . . (315) 343-3375
    http://scribany.org

**SUNY OSWEGO** (CDP). Covers a land area of 0.324 square miles and a water area of 0.301 square miles. Located at 43.45° N. Lat; 76.54° W. Long.
**Population:** n/a (1990); n/a (2000); 3,676 (2010); Density: 11,330.1 persons per square mile (2010); Race: 85.1% White, 6.0% Black, 3.3% Asian, 0.2% American Indian/Alaska Native, 0.1% Native Hawaiian/Other Pacific Islander, 5.3% Other, 6.7% Hispanic of any race (2010); Average household size: 1.59 (2010); Median age: 19.9 (2010); Males per 100 females: 95.7 (2010); Marriage status: 99.8% never married, 0.0% now married, 0.0% widowed, 0.2% divorced (2006-2010 5-year est.); Foreign born: 4.8% (2006-2010 5-year est.); Ancestry (includes multiple ancestries): 29.3% Irish, 23.7% German, 23.2% Italian, 9.0% Polish, 6.1% English (2006-2010 5-year est.).
**Economy:** Employment by occupation: 2.0% management, 7.4% professional, 20.0% services, 23.6% sales, 10.4% farming, 0.9% construction, 0.0% production (2006-2010 5-year est.).
**Income:** Per capita income: $4,594 (2006-2010 5-year est.); Median household income: $0 (2006-2010 5-year est.); Average household income: $0 (2006-2010 5-year est.); Percent of households with income of $100,000 or more: 0.0% (2006-2010 5-year est.); Poverty rate: 0.0% (2006-2010 5-year est.).
**Education:** Percent of population age 25 and over with: High school diploma (including GED) or higher: 100.0% (2006-2010 5-year est.); Bachelor's degree or higher: 42.9% (2006-2010 5-year est.); Master's degree or higher: 14.3% (2006-2010 5-year est.).
**Housing:** Homeownership rate: 40.9% (2010); Median home value: n/a (2006-2010 5-year est.); Median contract rent: n/a per month (2006-2010 5-year est.); Median year structure built: n/a (2006-2010 5-year est.).
**Transportation:** Commute to work: 33.9% car, 0.0% public transportation, 61.4% walk, 3.8% work from home (2006-2010 5-year est.); Travel time to work: 75.9% less than 15 minutes, 13.5% 15 to 30 minutes, 3.4% 30 to 45 minutes, 7.2% 45 to 60 minutes, 0.0% 60 minutes or more (2006-2010 5-year est.)

**VOLNEY** (town). Covers a land area of 48.240 square miles and a water area of 0.916 square miles. Located at 43.36° N. Lat; 76.36° W. Long. Elevation is 446 feet.
**Population:** 5,676 (1990); 6,094 (2000); 5,926 (2010); Density: 122.8 persons per square mile (2010); Race: 97.8% White, 0.4% Black, 0.2% Asian, 0.3% American Indian/Alaska Native, 0.0% Native Hawaiian/Other Pacific Islander, 1.3% Other, 1.1% Hispanic of any race (2010); Average household size: 2.60 (2010); Median age: 42.1 (2010); Males per 100 females: 101.5 (2010); Marriage status: 25.7% never married, 56.7% now married, 3.9% widowed, 13.7% divorced (2006-2010 5-year est.); Foreign born: 0.6% (2006-2010 5-year est.); Ancestry (includes multiple ancestries): 26.6% Irish, 22.3% German, 18.5% English, 14.9% French, 13.5% Italian (2006-2010 5-year est.).
**Economy:** Single-family building permits issued: 3 (2011); Multi-family building permits issued: 0 (2011); Employment by occupation: 8.4% management, 1.4% professional, 10.6% services, 14.6% sales, 3.1% farming, 16.5% construction, 6.5% production (2006-2010 5-year est.).
**Income:** Per capita income: $23,549 (2006-2010 5-year est.); Median household income: $53,542 (2006-2010 5-year est.); Average household income: $64,075 (2006-2010 5-year est.); Percent of households with income of $100,000 or more: 19.0% (2006-2010 5-year est.); Poverty rate: 12.1% (2006-2010 5-year est.).
**Education:** Percent of population age 25 and over with: High school diploma (including GED) or higher: 82.8% (2006-2010 5-year est.); Bachelor's degree or higher: 15.6% (2006-2010 5-year est.); Master's degree or higher: 4.0% (2006-2010 5-year est.).
**Housing:** Homeownership rate: 82.7% (2010); Median home value: $83,100 (2006-2010 5-year est.); Median contract rent: $592 per month (2006-2010 5-year est.); Median year structure built: 1974 (2006-2010 5-year est.).
**Transportation:** Commute to work: 96.4% car, 0.5% public transportation, 0.3% walk, 2.3% work from home (2006-2010 5-year est.); Travel time to work: 26.6% less than 15 minutes, 40.1% 15 to 30 minutes, 22.1% 30 to 45 minutes, 4.3% 45 to 60 minutes, 6.9% 60 minutes or more (2006-2010 5-year est.)

**WEST MONROE** (town). Covers a land area of 33.746 square miles and a water area of 4.840 square miles. Located at 43.30° N. Lat; 76.08° W. Long. Elevation is 397 feet.
**Population:** 4,393 (1990); 4,428 (2000); 4,252 (2010); Density: 126.0 persons per square mile (2010); Race: 97.6% White, 0.3% Black, 0.4% Asian, 0.5% American Indian/Alaska Native, 0.0% Native Hawaiian/Other Pacific Islander, 1.2% Other, 0.9% Hispanic of any race (2010); Average household size: 2.57 (2010); Median age: 41.7 (2010); Males per 100 females: 106.4 (2010); Marriage status: 22.2% never married, 61.1% now married, 4.5% widowed, 12.1% divorced (2006-2010 5-year est.); Foreign born: 2.4% (2006-2010 5-year est.); Ancestry (includes multiple ancestries): 20.6% German, 17.1% English, 16.7% Irish, 14.3% American, 10.5% Italian (2006-2010 5-year est.).
**Economy:** Single-family building permits issued: 2 (2011); Multi-family building permits issued: 0 (2011); Employment by occupation: 12.1% management, 4.8% professional, 8.0% services, 25.2% sales, 2.6% farming, 12.7% construction, 8.2% production (2006-2010 5-year est.).
**Income:** Per capita income: $21,350 (2006-2010 5-year est.); Median household income: $50,060 (2006-2010 5-year est.); Average household income: $56,830 (2006-2010 5-year est.); Percent of households with income of $100,000 or more: 12.3% (2006-2010 5-year est.); Poverty rate: 13.4% (2006-2010 5-year est.).
**Education:** Percent of population age 25 and over with: High school diploma (including GED) or higher: 88.3% (2006-2010 5-year est.); Bachelor's degree or higher: 10.2% (2006-2010 5-year est.); Master's degree or higher: 2.8% (2006-2010 5-year est.).
**Housing:** Homeownership rate: 84.7% (2010); Median home value: $105,000 (2006-2010 5-year est.); Median contract rent: $623 per month (2006-2010 5-year est.); Median year structure built: 1984 (2006-2010 5-year est.).
**Transportation:** Commute to work: 91.4% car, 0.3% public transportation, 0.5% walk, 6.7% work from home (2006-2010 5-year est.); Travel time to work: 9.2% less than 15 minutes, 31.6% 15 to 30 minutes, 39.2% 30 to 45 minutes, 8.6% 45 to 60 minutes, 11.4% 60 minutes or more (2006-2010 5-year est.)

**WILLIAMSTOWN** (town). Covers a land area of 38.672 square miles and a water area of 0.491 square miles. Located at 43.45° N. Lat; 75.88° W. Long. Elevation is 600 feet.
**Population:** 1,279 (1990); 1,350 (2000); 1,277 (2010); Density: 33.0 persons per square mile (2010); Race: 95.5% White, 0.3% Black, 0.1% Asian, 0.3% American Indian/Alaska Native, 0.0% Native Hawaiian/Other Pacific Islander, 3.8% Other, 3.1% Hispanic of any race (2010); Average household size: 2.97 (2010); Median age: 35.0 (2010); Males per 100 females: 102.1 (2010); Marriage status: 24.6% never married, 60.7% now married, 5.5% widowed, 9.1% divorced (2006-2010 5-year est.); Foreign born: 1.0% (2006-2010 5-year est.); Ancestry (includes multiple ancestries): 23.5% Irish, 20.4% English, 17.7% German, 15.1% French, 6.1% American (2006-2010 5-year est.).
**Economy:** Single-family building permits issued: 2 (2011); Multi-family building permits issued: 0 (2011); Employment by occupation: 8.4% management, 0.9% professional, 9.0% services, 17.4% sales, 2.4% farming, 9.9% construction, 9.3% production (2006-2010 5-year est.).
**Income:** Per capita income: $18,079 (2006-2010 5-year est.); Median household income: $45,978 (2006-2010 5-year est.); Average household income: $51,005 (2006-2010 5-year est.); Percent of households with income of $100,000 or more: 7.6% (2006-2010 5-year est.); Poverty rate: 16.4% (2006-2010 5-year est.).
**Education:** Percent of population age 25 and over with: High school diploma (including GED) or higher: 84.9% (2006-2010 5-year est.); Bachelor's degree or higher: 7.4% (2006-2010 5-year est.); Master's degree or higher: 1.1% (2006-2010 5-year est.).
**Housing:** Homeownership rate: 86.5% (2010); Median home value: $65,700 (2006-2010 5-year est.); Median contract rent: $484 per month (2006-2010 5-year est.); Median year structure built: 1980 (2006-2010 5-year est.).
**Transportation:** Commute to work: 95.0% car, 0.0% public transportation, 2.3% walk, 1.3% work from home (2006-2010 5-year est.); Travel time to work: 23.0% less than 15 minutes, 31.9% 15 to 30 minutes, 22.9% 30 to 45 minutes, 15.0% 45 to 60 minutes, 7.2% 60 minutes or more (2006-2010 5-year est.)

# Otsego County

Located in central New York; bounded on the west by the Unadilla River; drained by the Susquehanna River; includes Canadarago Lake and other lakes. Covers a land area of 1,002.80 square miles, a water area of 12.31 square miles, and is located in the Eastern Time Zone at 42.61° N. Lat., 75.03° W. Long. The county was founded in 1791. County seat is Cooperstown.

Otsego County is part of the Oneonta, NY Micropolitan Statistical Area. The entire metro area includes: Otsego County, NY

Weather Station: Cherry Valley 2 NNE                    Elevation: 1,359 feet

|        | Jan  | Feb  | Mar  | Apr  | May  | Jun  | Jul  | Aug  | Sep  | Oct  | Nov  | Dec  |
|--------|------|------|------|------|------|------|------|------|------|------|------|------|
| High   | 28   | 32   | 40   | 54   | 66   | 74   | 78   | 76   | 69   | 57   | 46   | 33   |
| Low    | 12   | 14   | 22   | 34   | 44   | 53   | 58   | 57   | 49   | 38   | 30   | 18   |
| Precip | 3.3  | 2.8  | 3.9  | 4.1  | 4.4  | 4.5  | 4.5  | 4.2  | 4.0  | 3.9  | 3.8  | 3.3  |
| Snow   | 32.8 | 21.1 | 22.1 | 5.9  | 0.4  | 0.0  | 0.0  | 0.0  | tr   | 1.1  | 9.2  | 24.5 |

*High and Low temperatures in degrees Fahrenheit; Precipitation and Snow in inches*

Weather Station: Cooperstown                             Elevation: 1,200 feet

|        | Jan  | Feb  | Mar  | Apr  | May  | Jun  | Jul  | Aug  | Sep  | Oct  | Nov  | Dec  |
|--------|------|------|------|------|------|------|------|------|------|------|------|------|
| High   | 31   | 34   | 42   | 56   | 68   | 76   | 80   | 78   | 71   | 59   | 47   | 35   |
| Low    | 12   | 13   | 21   | 33   | 43   | 52   | 57   | 56   | 48   | 37   | 29   | 19   |
| Precip | 2.9  | 2.4  | 3.4  | 3.7  | 3.9  | 4.5  | 4.3  | 4.0  | 3.8  | 3.8  | 3.3  | 3.1  |
| Snow   | 21.7 | 16.4 | 15.3 | 4.0  | 0.1  | 0.0  | 0.0  | 0.0  | tr   | 0.5  | 6.1  | 18.0 |

*High and Low temperatures in degrees Fahrenheit; Precipitation and Snow in inches*

Weather Station: Maryland 6 SW                           Elevation: 3,911 feet

|        | Jan  | Feb  | Mar  | Apr  | May  | Jun  | Jul  | Aug  | Sep  | Oct  | Nov  | Dec  |
|--------|------|------|------|------|------|------|------|------|------|------|------|------|
| High   | 31   | 33   | 42   | 56   | 67   | 75   | 79   | 78   | 70   | 59   | 47   | 35   |
| Low    | 12   | 12   | 20   | 32   | 41   | 51   | 55   | 54   | 47   | 36   | 29   | 19   |
| Precip | 3.2  | 2.4  | 3.4  | 3.5  | 3.6  | 4.3  | 4.4  | 3.5  | 3.6  | 3.5  | 3.4  | 3.2  |
| Snow   | 21.2 | 16.0 | 13.3 | 3.3  | 0.2  | 0.0  | 0.0  | 0.0  | 0.0  | 0.8  | 6.0  | 16.0 |

*High and Low temperatures in degrees Fahrenheit; Precipitation and Snow in inches*

**Population:** 60,479 (1990); 61,676 (2000); 62,259 (2010); Race: 94.7% White, 1.7% Black, 1.1% Asian, 0.2% American Indian/Alaska Native, 0.0% Native Hawaiian/Other Pacific Islander, 2.3% Other, 3.1% Hispanic of any race (2010); Density: 62.1 persons per square mile (2010); Average household size: 2.31 (2010); Median age: 40.9 (2010); Males per 100 females: 93.7 (2010).

**Religion:** Six largest groups: 18.6% Catholicism, 8.5% Methodist/Pietist, 2.1% Episcopalianism/Anglicanism, 1.8% Presbyterian-Reformed, 1.7% Baptist, 1.6% Non-Denominational (2010)

**Economy:** Unemployment rate: 9.3% (February 2012); Total civilian labor force: 30,845 (February 2012); Leading industries: 27.3% health care and social assistance; 18.8% retail trade; 13.1% accommodation & food services (2009); Farms: 980 totaling 176,481 acres (2007); Companies that employ 500 or more persons: 3 (2009); Companies that employ 100 to 499 persons: 19 (2009); Companies that employ less than 100 persons: 1,412 (2009); Black-owned businesses: n/a (2007); Hispanic-owned businesses: n/a (2007); Asian-owned businesses: n/a (2007); Women-owned businesses: 1,557 (2007); Retail sales per capita: $14,836 (2010). Single-family building permits issued: 37 (2011); Multi-family building permits issued: 0 (2011).

**Income:** Per capita income: $22,902 (2006-2010 5-year est.); Median household income: $45,268 (2006-2010 5-year est.); Average household income: $56,813 (2006-2010 5-year est.); Percent of households with income of $100,000 or more: 12.6% (2006-2010 5-year est.); Poverty rate: 14.9% (2006-2010 5-year est.); Bankruptcy rate: 2.34% (2011).

**Taxes**: Total county taxes per capita: $747 (2009); County property taxes per capita: $182 (2009).

**Education:** Percent of population age 25 and over with: High school diploma (including GED) or higher: 88.3% (2006-2010 5-year est.); Bachelor's degree or higher: 25.5% (2006-2010 5-year est.); Master's degree or higher: 11.0% (2006-2010 5-year est.).

**Housing:** Homeownership rate: 72.7% (2010); Median home value: $129,000 (2006-2010 5-year est.); Median contract rent: $555 per month (2006-2010 5-year est.); Median year structure built: 1955 (2006-2010 5-year est.).

**Health:** Birth rate: 77.2 per 10,000 population (2011); Death rate: 97.7 per 10,000 population (2011); Age-adjusted cancer mortality rate: 180.4 deaths per 100,000 population (2009); Number of physicians: 52.4 per 10,000 population (2008); Hospital beds: 61.9 per 10,000 population (2007); Hospital admissions: 2,176.9 per 10,000 population (2007).

**Elections:** 2008 Presidential election results: 52.0% Obama, 46.0% McCain, 1.1% Nader

**National and State Parks:** Gilbert Lake State Park

**Additional Information Contacts**

Otsego County Government . . . . . . . . . . . . . . . . . . . . . . . . (607) 547-4276
    http://www.otsegocounty.com
City of Oneonta . . . . . . . . . . . . . . . . . . . . . . . . . . . . . . (607) 432-6450
    http://www.oneonta.ny.us
Cooperstown Chamber of Commerce . . . . . . . . . . . . . . . (607) 547-9983
    http://www.cooperstownchamber.org
Otsego County Chamber of Commerce . . . . . . . . . . . . . . (607) 432-4500
    http://www.otsegocountychamber.com
Town of Hartwick . . . . . . . . . . . . . . . . . . . . . . . . . . . . . (607) 293-8123
    http://townofhartwick.org

## Otsego County Communities

**BURLINGTON** (town). Covers a land area of 44.891 square miles and a water area of 0.122 square miles. Located at 42.71° N. Lat; 75.14° W. Long. Elevation is 1,535 feet.

**Population:** 1,036 (1990); 1,085 (2000); 1,140 (2010); Density: 25.4 persons per square mile (2010); Race: 97.3% White, 0.9% Black, 0.3% Asian, 0.0% American Indian/Alaska Native, 0.0% Native Hawaiian/Other Pacific Islander, 1.5% Other, 0.8% Hispanic of any race (2010); Average household size: 2.55 (2010); Median age: 44.4 (2010); Males per 100 females: 108.4 (2010); Marriage status: 25.1% never married, 60.4% now married, 3.9% widowed, 10.6% divorced (2006-2010 5-year est.); Foreign born: 0.9% (2006-2010 5-year est.); Ancestry (includes multiple ancestries): 17.6% American, 17.5% Irish, 14.6% German, 10.9% English, 7.9% Italian (2006-2010 5-year est.).

**Economy:** Employment by occupation: 11.7% management, 3.1% professional, 10.3% services, 15.7% sales, 5.9% farming, 18.3% construction, 7.1% production (2006-2010 5-year est.).

**Income:** Per capita income: $24,565 (2006-2010 5-year est.); Median household income: $54,643 (2006-2010 5-year est.); Average household income: $63,887 (2006-2010 5-year est.); Percent of households with income of $100,000 or more: 19.4% (2006-2010 5-year est.); Poverty rate: 8.4% (2006-2010 5-year est.).

**Education:** Percent of population age 25 and over with: High school diploma (including GED) or higher: 87.8% (2006-2010 5-year est.); Bachelor's degree or higher: 11.2% (2006-2010 5-year est.); Master's degree or higher: 4.6% (2006-2010 5-year est.).

**Housing:** Homeownership rate: 89.5% (2010); Median home value: $125,300 (2006-2010 5-year est.); Median contract rent: $344 per month (2006-2010 5-year est.); Median year structure built: 1968 (2006-2010 5-year est.).

**Transportation:** Commute to work: 80.7% car, 1.1% public transportation, 0.5% walk, 17.4% work from home (2006-2010 5-year est.); Travel time to work: 23.0% less than 15 minutes, 36.4% 15 to 30 minutes, 24.9% 30 to 45 minutes, 7.7% 45 to 60 minutes, 8.0% 60 minutes or more (2006-2010 5-year est.)

**BURLINGTON FLATS** (unincorporated postal area)

Zip Code: 13315

    Covers a land area of 49.097 square miles and a water area of 0.169 square miles. Located at 42.74° N. Lat; 75.14° W. Long. Elevation is 1,289 feet. Population: 1,419 (2010); Density: 28.9 persons per square mile (2010); Race: 97.3% White, 0.8% Black, 0.1% Asian, 0.1% American Indian/Alaska Native, 0.0% Native Hawaiian/Other Pacific Islander, 1.7% Other, 1.0% Hispanic of any race (2010); Average household size: 2.62 (2010); Median age: 43.4 (2010); Males per 100 females: 109.0 (2010); Homeownership rate: 89.3% (2010)

**BUTTERNUTS** (town). Covers a land area of 53.829 square miles and a water area of 0.039 square miles. Located at 42.46° N. Lat; 75.32° W. Long.

**Population:** 1,626 (1990); 1,792 (2000); 1,786 (2010); Density: 33.2 persons per square mile (2010); Race: 97.8% White, 0.4% Black, 0.2% Asian, 0.2% American Indian/Alaska Native, 0.0% Native Hawaiian/Other Pacific Islander, 1.4% Other, 1.5% Hispanic of any race (2010); Average household size: 2.32 (2010); Median age: 48.2 (2010); Males per 100 females: 97.6 (2010); Marriage status: 23.1% never married, 62.3% now married, 7.3% widowed, 7.3% divorced (2006-2010 5-year est.); Foreign born: 2.0% (2006-2010 5-year est.); Ancestry (includes multiple ancestries): 21.4% German, 16.0% English, 14.1% American, 13.4% Irish, 8.9% Italian (2006-2010 5-year est.).

**Economy:** Employment by occupation: 11.6% management, 0.0% professional, 6.4% services, 18.7% sales, 8.4% farming, 10.3% construction, 7.5% production (2006-2010 5-year est.).

**Income:** Per capita income: $23,767 (2006-2010 5-year est.); Median household income: $47,446 (2006-2010 5-year est.); Average household income: $61,120 (2006-2010 5-year est.); Percent of households with income of $100,000 or more: 16.2% (2006-2010 5-year est.); Poverty rate: 9.1% (2006-2010 5-year est.).

**Education:** Percent of population age 25 and over with: High school diploma (including GED) or higher: 90.4% (2006-2010 5-year est.); Bachelor's degree or higher: 19.9% (2006-2010 5-year est.); Master's degree or higher: 11.0% (2006-2010 5-year est.).

**Housing:** Homeownership rate: 84.8% (2010); Median home value: $128,300 (2006-2010 5-year est.); Median contract rent: $394 per month (2006-2010 5-year est.); Median year structure built: 1977 (2006-2010 5-year est.).

**Transportation:** Commute to work: 88.0% car, 3.1% public transportation, 1.2% walk, 7.4% work from home (2006-2010 5-year est.); Travel time to work: 17.6% less than 15 minutes, 40.8% 15 to 30 minutes, 19.5% 30 to 45 minutes, 15.4% 45 to 60 minutes, 6.6% 60 minutes or more (2006-2010 5-year est.)

**CHERRY VALLEY** (village). Covers a land area of 0.509 square miles and a water area of <.001 square miles. Located at 42.79° N. Lat; 74.75° W. Long. Elevation is 1,345 feet.

**Population:** 617 (1990); 592 (2000); 520 (2010); Density: 1,020.4 persons per square mile (2010); Race: 96.2% White, 1.2% Black, 0.0% Asian, 0.6% American Indian/Alaska Native, 0.0% Native Hawaiian/Other Pacific Islander, 2.0% Other, 1.0% Hispanic of any race (2010); Average household size: 2.23 (2010); Median age: 47.7 (2010); Males per 100 females: 81.2 (2010); Marriage status: 26.5% never married, 54.6% now married, 8.1% widowed, 10.9% divorced (2006-2010 5-year est.); Foreign born: 1.1% (2006-2010 5-year est.); Ancestry (includes multiple ancestries): 33.6% German, 22.3% Irish, 19.3% American, 16.1% English, 7.5% Italian (2006-2010 5-year est.).

**Economy:** Employment by occupation: 9.9% management, 3.4% professional, 4.3% services, 28.0% sales, 4.3% farming, 9.1% construction, 6.5% production (2006-2010 5-year est.).
**Income:** Per capita income: $21,508 (2006-2010 5-year est.); Median household income: $40,417 (2006-2010 5-year est.); Average household income: $48,420 (2006-2010 5-year est.); Percent of households with income of $100,000 or more: 5.2% (2006-2010 5-year est.); Poverty rate: 7.0% (2006-2010 5-year est.).
**Education:** Percent of population age 25 and over with: High school diploma (including GED) or higher: 91.7% (2006-2010 5-year est.); Bachelor's degree or higher: 24.8% (2006-2010 5-year est.); Master's degree or higher: 7.2% (2006-2010 5-year est.).

### School District(s)

Cherry Valley-Springfield Central School District (PK-12)
  2009-10 Enrollment: 583 . . . . . . . . . . . . . . . . . . . (607) 264-9332
**Housing:** Homeownership rate: 66.9% (2010); Median home value: $117,200 (2006-2010 5-year est.); Median contract rent: $403 per month (2006-2010 5-year est.); Median year structure built: before 1940 (2006-2010 5-year est.).
**Transportation:** Commute to work: 85.8% car, 0.9% public transportation, 4.0% walk, 9.3% work from home (2006-2010 5-year est.); Travel time to work: 26.5% less than 15 minutes, 44.1% 15 to 30 minutes, 12.3% 30 to 45 minutes, 7.4% 45 to 60 minutes, 9.8% 60 minutes or more (2006-2010 5-year est.)

## CHERRY VALLEY (town). Covers a land area of 40.375 square miles and a water area of 0.006 square miles. Located at 42.80° N. Lat; 74.72° W. Long. Elevation is 1,345 feet.

**History:** Burned (Nov. 11, 1778) during American Revolution by Native American and Tory forces; over 40 people killed. Settled c.1740.
**Population:** 1,210 (1990); 1,266 (2000); 1,223 (2010); Density: 30.3 persons per square mile (2010); Race: 97.6% White, 0.7% Black, 0.2% Asian, 0.4% American Indian/Alaska Native, 0.0% Native Hawaiian/Other Pacific Islander, 1.1% Other, 0.7% Hispanic of any race (2010); Average household size: 2.39 (2010); Median age: 46.1 (2010); Males per 100 females: 92.9 (2010); Marriage status: 19.8% never married, 64.7% now married, 7.1% widowed, 8.4% divorced (2006-2010 5-year est.); Foreign born: 1.1% (2006-2010 5-year est.); Ancestry (includes multiple ancestries): 31.0% German, 23.1% Irish, 21.5% English, 9.6% American, 9.4% Dutch (2006-2010 5-year est.).
**Economy:** Employment by occupation: 7.6% management, 4.7% professional, 4.5% services, 22.2% sales, 3.3% farming, 13.7% construction, 6.8% production (2006-2010 5-year est.).
**Income:** Per capita income: $24,899 (2006-2010 5-year est.); Median household income: $49,000 (2006-2010 5-year est.); Average household income: $56,915 (2006-2010 5-year est.); Percent of households with income of $100,000 or more: 11.8% (2006-2010 5-year est.); Poverty rate: 5.3% (2006-2010 5-year est.).
**Education:** Percent of population age 25 and over with: High school diploma (including GED) or higher: 90.4% (2006-2010 5-year est.); Bachelor's degree or higher: 24.3% (2006-2010 5-year est.); Master's degree or higher: 8.3% (2006-2010 5-year est.).

### School District(s)

Cherry Valley-Springfield Central School District (PK-12)
  2009-10 Enrollment: 583 . . . . . . . . . . . . . . . . . . . (607) 264-9332
**Housing:** Homeownership rate: 76.7% (2010); Median home value: $135,200 (2006-2010 5-year est.); Median contract rent: $409 per month (2006-2010 5-year est.); Median year structure built: before 1940 (2006-2010 5-year est.).
**Transportation:** Commute to work: 86.7% car, 0.4% public transportation, 1.6% walk, 10.6% work from home (2006-2010 5-year est.); Travel time to work: 24.5% less than 15 minutes, 42.9% 15 to 30 minutes, 15.8% 30 to 45 minutes, 7.5% 45 to 60 minutes, 9.3% 60 minutes or more (2006-2010 5-year est.)

## COOPERSTOWN (village). County seat. Covers a land area of 1.634 square miles and a water area of 0.210 square miles. Located at 42.69° N. Lat; 74.93° W. Long. Elevation is 1,227 feet.

**History:** Founded by William Cooper, who brought his family here in 1787. His son, James Fenimore Cooper, made his home here after returning from abroad in 1833, and the region is described in his Leatherstocking Tales. Fenimore House is the headquarters of N.Y. State Historical Association. Other attractions include Farmers' Museum and the famous National Baseball Hall of Fame and Museum, which commemorates the founding (1839) of baseball here by Abner Doubleday. Incorporated 1807.

**Population:** 2,180 (1990); 2,032 (2000); 1,852 (2010); Density: 1,133.0 persons per square mile (2010); Race: 94.0% White, 0.4% Black, 4.2% Asian, 0.1% American Indian/Alaska Native, 0.0% Native Hawaiian/Other Pacific Islander, 1.3% Other, 3.1% Hispanic of any race (2010); Average household size: 1.97 (2010); Median age: 47.1 (2010); Males per 100 females: 81.4 (2010); Marriage status: 37.0% never married, 50.0% now married, 7.5% widowed, 5.5% divorced (2006-2010 5-year est.); Foreign born: 7.6% (2006-2010 5-year est.); Ancestry (includes multiple ancestries): 26.6% Irish, 18.9% English, 18.2% German, 12.9% Italian, 12.6% American (2006-2010 5-year est.).
**Economy:** Employment by occupation: 20.5% management, 2.1% professional, 6.2% services, 16.6% sales, 0.6% farming, 1.2% construction, 0.9% production (2006-2010 5-year est.).
**Income:** Per capita income: $36,562 (2006-2010 5-year est.); Median household income: $49,419 (2006-2010 5-year est.); Average household income: $76,696 (2006-2010 5-year est.); Percent of households with income of $100,000 or more: 23.2% (2006-2010 5-year est.); Poverty rate: 17.1% (2006-2010 5-year est.).
**Education:** Percent of population age 25 and over with: High school diploma (including GED) or higher: 96.4% (2006-2010 5-year est.); Bachelor's degree or higher: 58.3% (2006-2010 5-year est.); Master's degree or higher: 33.6% (2006-2010 5-year est.).

### School District(s)

Cooperstown Central School District (KG-12)
  2009-10 Enrollment: 971 . . . . . . . . . . . . . . . . . . . (607) 547-5364
**Housing:** Homeownership rate: 50.8% (2010); Median home value: $341,700 (2006-2010 5-year est.); Median contract rent: $711 per month (2006-2010 5-year est.); Median year structure built: before 1940 (2006-2010 5-year est.).
**Hospitals:** Bassett Healthcare (180 beds)
**Safety:** Violent crime rate: 5.4 per 10,000 population; Property crime rate: 151.4 per 10,000 population (2010).
**Newspapers:** Cooperstown Crier (Community news; Circulation 6,000); The Freeman's Journal (Local news; Circulation 2,300)
**Transportation:** Commute to work: 61.0% car, 1.7% public transportation, 28.3% walk, 7.8% work from home (2006-2010 5-year est.); Travel time to work: 65.2% less than 15 minutes, 15.4% 15 to 30 minutes, 8.6% 30 to 45 minutes, 4.6% 45 to 60 minutes, 6.1% 60 minutes or more (2006-2010 5-year est.)

**Additional Information Contacts**

Cooperstown Chamber of Commerce . . . . . . . . . . . . . . . (607) 547-9983
  http://www.cooperstownchamber.org

## DECATUR (town). Covers a land area of 20.562 square miles and a water area of 0.196 square miles. Located at 42.65° N. Lat; 74.70° W. Long. Elevation is 1,617 feet.

**Population:** 356 (1990); 410 (2000); 353 (2010); Density: 17.2 persons per square mile (2010); Race: 97.7% White, 0.8% Black, 0.3% Asian, 0.0% American Indian/Alaska Native, 0.0% Native Hawaiian/Other Pacific Islander, 1.2% Other, 1.4% Hispanic of any race (2010); Average household size: 2.32 (2010); Median age: 51.2 (2010); Males per 100 females: 105.2 (2010); Marriage status: 15.1% never married, 70.5% now married, 6.8% widowed, 7.5% divorced (2006-2010 5-year est.); Foreign born: 6.4% (2006-2010 5-year est.); Ancestry (includes multiple ancestries): 32.8% German, 21.7% Irish, 11.8% English, 11.1% Italian, 8.9% Dutch (2006-2010 5-year est.).
**Economy:** Employment by occupation: 5.2% management, 0.9% professional, 8.6% services, 9.5% sales, 2.6% farming, 19.0% construction, 5.2% production (2006-2010 5-year est.).
**Income:** Per capita income: $22,154 (2006-2010 5-year est.); Median household income: $35,714 (2006-2010 5-year est.); Average household income: $46,361 (2006-2010 5-year est.); Percent of households with income of $100,000 or more: 8.1% (2006-2010 5-year est.); Poverty rate: 18.5% (2006-2010 5-year est.).
**Education:** Percent of population age 25 and over with: High school diploma (including GED) or higher: 80.6% (2006-2010 5-year est.); Bachelor's degree or higher: 14.2% (2006-2010 5-year est.); Master's degree or higher: 7.3% (2006-2010 5-year est.).
**Housing:** Homeownership rate: 88.2% (2010); Median home value: $165,900 (2006-2010 5-year est.); Median contract rent: $525 per month (2006-2010 5-year est.); Median year structure built: 1962 (2006-2010 5-year est.).
**Transportation:** Commute to work: 89.7% car, 1.7% public transportation, 4.3% walk, 4.3% work from home (2006-2010 5-year est.); Travel time to work: 18.9% less than 15 minutes, 29.7% 15 to 30 minutes, 38.7% 30 to 45

minutes, 1.8% 45 to 60 minutes, 10.8% 60 minutes or more (2006-2010 5-year est.)

## EAST SPRINGFIELD (unincorporated postal area)
Zip Code: 13333

Covers a land area of 1.700 square miles and a water area of 0.002 square miles. Located at 42.83° N. Lat; 74.81° W. Long. Elevation is 1,322 feet. Population: 62 (2010); Density: 36.5 persons per square mile (2010); Race: 90.3% White, 1.6% Black, 1.6% Asian, 0.0% American Indian/Alaska Native, 0.0% Native Hawaiian/Other Pacific Islander, 6.5% Other, 3.2% Hispanic of any race (2010); Average household size: 2.38 (2010); Median age: 55.0 (2010); Males per 100 females: 106.7 (2010); Homeownership rate: 84.6% (2010)

## EAST WORCESTER (unincorporated postal area)
Zip Code: 12064

Covers a land area of 11.428 square miles and a water area of 0.013 square miles. Located at 42.61° N. Lat; 74.65° W. Long. Elevation is 1,463 feet. Population: 563 (2010); Density: 49.3 persons per square mile (2010); Race: 94.5% White, 1.2% Black, 0.7% Asian, 0.0% American Indian/Alaska Native, 0.0% Native Hawaiian/Other Pacific Islander, 3.6% Other, 5.3% Hispanic of any race (2010); Average household size: 2.43 (2010); Median age: 40.1 (2010); Males per 100 females: 121.7 (2010); Homeownership rate: 74.1% (2010)

## EDMESTON (town). Covers a land area of 44.296 square miles and a water area of 0.083 square miles. Located at 42.72° N. Lat; 75.26° W. Long. Elevation is 1,204 feet.
**Population:** 1,717 (1990); 1,824 (2000); 1,826 (2010); Density: 41.2 persons per square mile (2010); Race: 97.6% White, 0.3% Black, 0.5% Asian, 0.0% American Indian/Alaska Native, 0.0% Native Hawaiian/Other Pacific Islander, 1.6% Other, 1.5% Hispanic of any race (2010); Average household size: 2.56 (2010); Median age: 42.0 (2010); Males per 100 females: 97.2 (2010); Marriage status: 26.0% never married, 60.5% now married, 5.0% widowed, 8.5% divorced (2006-2010 5-year est.); Foreign born: 0.9% (2006-2010 5-year est.); Ancestry (includes multiple ancestries): 21.6% English, 19.8% German, 14.8% American, 13.7% Irish, 9.0% Dutch (2006-2010 5-year est.).
**Economy:** Employment by occupation: 11.6% management, 3.6% professional, 13.3% services, 26.1% sales, 1.3% farming, 11.4% construction, 10.2% production (2006-2010 5-year est.).
**Income:** Per capita income: $21,165 (2006-2010 5-year est.); Median household income: $47,111 (2006-2010 5-year est.); Average household income: $53,959 (2006-2010 5-year est.); Percent of households with income of $100,000 or more: 13.9% (2006-2010 5-year est.); Poverty rate: 15.7% (2006-2010 5-year est.).
**Education:** Percent of population age 25 and over with: High school diploma (including GED) or higher: 82.4% (2006-2010 5-year est.); Bachelor's degree or higher: 11.2% (2006-2010 5-year est.); Master's degree or higher: 3.8% (2006-2010 5-year est.).
### School District(s)
Edmeston Central School District (PK-12)
   2009-10 Enrollment: 485 . . . . . . . . . . . . . . . . . . . . (607) 965-8931
**Housing:** Homeownership rate: 81.5% (2010); Median home value: $102,600 (2006-2010 5-year est.); Median contract rent: $413 per month (2006-2010 5-year est.); Median year structure built: 1950 (2006-2010 5-year est.).
**Transportation:** Commute to work: 83.5% car, 1.7% public transportation, 9.2% walk, 5.5% work from home (2006-2010 5-year est.); Travel time to work: 49.4% less than 15 minutes, 12.1% 15 to 30 minutes, 22.2% 30 to 45 minutes, 7.8% 45 to 60 minutes, 8.5% 60 minutes or more (2006-2010 5-year est.)

## EDMESTON (CDP). Covers a land area of 4.344 square miles and a water area of 0 square miles. Located at 42.69° N. Lat; 75.25° W. Long. Elevation is 1,204 feet.
**Population:** n/a (1990); n/a (2000); 657 (2010); Density: 151.2 persons per square mile (2010); Race: 96.7% White, 0.6% Black, 0.5% Asian, 0.0% American Indian/Alaska Native, 0.0% Native Hawaiian/Other Pacific Islander, 2.2% Other, 2.4% Hispanic of any race (2010); Average household size: 2.42 (2010); Median age: 43.8 (2010); Males per 100 females: 93.8 (2010); Marriage status: 29.3% never married, 59.7% now married, 4.1% widowed, 6.9% divorced (2006-2010 5-year est.); Foreign born: 1.8% (2006-2010 5-year est.); Ancestry (includes multiple

ancestries): 25.1% German, 16.9% English, 12.9% Irish, 9.8% Dutch, 5.9% Welsh (2006-2010 5-year est.).
**Economy:** Employment by occupation: 10.8% management, 6.1% professional, 11.6% services, 31.8% sales, 2.1% farming, 10.5% construction, 8.2% production (2006-2010 5-year est.).
**Income:** Per capita income: $24,170 (2006-2010 5-year est.); Median household income: $48,897 (2006-2010 5-year est.); Average household income: $57,610 (2006-2010 5-year est.); Percent of households with income of $100,000 or more: 16.9% (2006-2010 5-year est.); Poverty rate: 9.3% (2006-2010 5-year est.).
**Education:** Percent of population age 25 and over with: High school diploma (including GED) or higher: 82.6% (2006-2010 5-year est.); Bachelor's degree or higher: 15.9% (2006-2010 5-year est.); Master's degree or higher: 7.5% (2006-2010 5-year est.).
### School District(s)
Edmeston Central School District (PK-12)
   2009-10 Enrollment: 485 . . . . . . . . . . . . . . . . . . . . (607) 965-8931
**Housing:** Homeownership rate: 73.1% (2010); Median home value: $87,000 (2006-2010 5-year est.); Median contract rent: $406 per month (2006-2010 5-year est.); Median year structure built: before 1940 (2006-2010 5-year est.).
**Transportation:** Commute to work: 77.0% car, 4.0% public transportation, 15.9% walk, 3.2% work from home (2006-2010 5-year est.); Travel time to work: 62.6% less than 15 minutes, 11.5% 15 to 30 minutes, 15.8% 30 to 45 minutes, 5.5% 45 to 60 minutes, 4.6% 60 minutes or more (2006-2010 5-year est.)

## EXETER (town). Covers a land area of 32.077 square miles and a water area of 0.614 square miles. Located at 42.79° N. Lat; 75.07° W. Long.
**Population:** 967 (1990); 954 (2000); 987 (2010); Density: 30.8 persons per square mile (2010); Race: 96.5% White, 0.7% Black, 0.8% Asian, 0.4% American Indian/Alaska Native, 0.2% Native Hawaiian/Other Pacific Islander, 1.4% Other, 1.5% Hispanic of any race (2010); Average household size: 2.46 (2010); Median age: 43.9 (2010); Males per 100 females: 90.9 (2010); Marriage status: 20.3% never married, 64.5% now married, 7.5% widowed, 7.7% divorced (2006-2010 5-year est.); Foreign born: 2.3% (2006-2010 5-year est.); Ancestry (includes multiple ancestries): 15.9% Irish, 14.5% Dutch, 14.0% German, 13.6% English, 11.9% American (2006-2010 5-year est.).
**Economy:** Employment by occupation: 6.6% management, 0.0% professional, 14.4% services, 16.8% sales, 0.0% farming, 21.9% construction, 10.5% production (2006-2010 5-year est.).
**Income:** Per capita income: $20,933 (2006-2010 5-year est.); Median household income: $43,750 (2006-2010 5-year est.); Average household income: $51,052 (2006-2010 5-year est.); Percent of households with income of $100,000 or more: 8.9% (2006-2010 5-year est.); Poverty rate: 13.3% (2006-2010 5-year est.).
**Education:** Percent of population age 25 and over with: High school diploma (including GED) or higher: 81.6% (2006-2010 5-year est.); Bachelor's degree or higher: 13.9% (2006-2010 5-year est.); Master's degree or higher: 4.0% (2006-2010 5-year est.).
**Housing:** Homeownership rate: 85.5% (2010); Median home value: $118,900 (2006-2010 5-year est.); Median contract rent: $396 per month (2006-2010 5-year est.); Median year structure built: 1971 (2006-2010 5-year est.).
**Transportation:** Commute to work: 95.5% car, 0.0% public transportation, 0.0% walk, 4.5% work from home (2006-2010 5-year est.); Travel time to work: 22.3% less than 15 minutes, 50.0% 15 to 30 minutes, 13.2% 30 to 45 minutes, 7.8% 45 to 60 minutes, 6.7% 60 minutes or more (2006-2010 5-year est.)

## FLY CREEK (unincorporated postal area)
Zip Code: 13337

Covers a land area of 18.497 square miles and a water area of 0.115 square miles. Located at 42.75° N. Lat; 74.99° W. Long. Elevation is 1,302 feet. Population: 790 (2010); Density: 42.7 persons per square mile (2010); Race: 95.6% White, 0.9% Black, 0.9% Asian, 0.5% American Indian/Alaska Native, 0.0% Native Hawaiian/Other Pacific Islander, 2.1% Other, 1.1% Hispanic of any race (2010); Average household size: 2.36 (2010); Median age: 47.0 (2010); Males per 100 females: 101.5 (2010); Homeownership rate: 83.8% (2010)

## GARRATTSVILLE (unincorporated postal area)
Zip Code: 13342

Covers a land area of 7.940 square miles and a water area of 0.056 square miles. Located at 42.65° N. Lat; 75.19° W. Long. Elevation is 1,302 feet. Population: 165 (2010); Density: 20.8 persons per square mile (2010); Race: 97.0% White, 1.8% Black, 0.0% Asian, 0.0% American Indian/Alaska Native, 0.0% Native Hawaiian/Other Pacific Islander, 1.2% Other, 0.6% Hispanic of any race (2010); Average household size: 2.23 (2010); Median age: 49.9 (2010); Males per 100 females: 79.3 (2010); Homeownership rate: 94.6% (2010)

**GILBERTSVILLE** (village). Covers a land area of 1.002 square miles and a water area of 0 square miles. Located at 42.46° N. Lat; 75.32° W. Long. Elevation is 1,093 feet.
**Population:** 388 (1990); 375 (2000); 399 (2010); Density: 397.9 persons per square mile (2010); Race: 98.5% White, 0.5% Black, 0.3% Asian, 0.3% American Indian/Alaska Native, 0.0% Native Hawaiian/Other Pacific Islander, 0.4% Other, 1.0% Hispanic of any race (2010); Average household size: 2.27 (2010); Median age: 49.9 (2010); Males per 100 females: 70.5 (2010); Marriage status: 11.5% never married, 70.4% now married, 15.0% widowed, 3.2% divorced (2006-2010 5-year est.); Foreign born: 2.0% (2006-2010 5-year est.); Ancestry (includes multiple ancestries): 31.4% English, 21.4% American, 19.7% Irish, 14.0% Italian, 11.1% German (2006-2010 5-year est.).
**Economy:** Single-family building permits issued: 0 (2011); Multi-family building permits issued: 0 (2011); Employment by occupation: 14.4% management, 0.0% professional, 6.5% services, 15.8% sales, 0.0% farming, 11.5% construction, 12.9% production (2006-2010 5-year est.).
**Income:** Per capita income: $27,567 (2006-2010 5-year est.); Median household income: $49,375 (2006-2010 5-year est.); Average household income: $63,893 (2006-2010 5-year est.); Percent of households with income of $100,000 or more: 25.8% (2006-2010 5-year est.); Poverty rate: 9.4% (2006-2010 5-year est.).
**Education:** Percent of population age 25 and over with: High school diploma (including GED) or higher: 87.8% (2006-2010 5-year est.); Bachelor's degree or higher: 29.4% (2006-2010 5-year est.); Master's degree or higher: 17.6% (2006-2010 5-year est.).

**School District(s)**
Gilbertsville-Mount Upton Central School District (PK-12)
   2009-10 Enrollment: 460 . . . . . . . . . . . . . . . . . . . . . . . (607) 783-2207
**Housing:** Homeownership rate: 72.2% (2010); Median home value: $157,400 (2006-2010 5-year est.); Median contract rent: $372 per month (2006-2010 5-year est.); Median year structure built: before 1940 (2006-2010 5-year est.).
**Transportation:** Commute to work: 91.6% car, 1.7% public transportation, 0.0% walk, 6.7% work from home (2006-2010 5-year est.); Travel time to work: 17.1% less than 15 minutes, 59.5% 15 to 30 minutes, 19.8% 30 to 45 minutes, 0.0% 45 to 60 minutes, 3.6% 60 minutes or more (2006-2010 5-year est.)

**HARTWICK** (town). Covers a land area of 40.081 square miles and a water area of 0.342 square miles. Located at 42.64° N. Lat; 75.01° W. Long. Elevation is 1,329 feet.
**Population:** 2,045 (1990); 2,203 (2000); 2,110 (2010); Density: 52.6 persons per square mile (2010); Race: 96.5% White, 0.3% Black, 0.9% Asian, 0.2% American Indian/Alaska Native, 0.0% Native Hawaiian/Other Pacific Islander, 2.1% Other, 2.0% Hispanic of any race (2010); Average household size: 2.42 (2010); Median age: 43.3 (2010); Males per 100 females: 100.4 (2010); Marriage status: 32.5% never married, 50.4% now married, 6.9% widowed, 10.2% divorced (2006-2010 5-year est.); Foreign born: 1.3% (2006-2010 5-year est.); Ancestry (includes multiple ancestries): 22.4% German, 21.6% Irish, 18.8% English, 11.3% Polish, 9.5% American (2006-2010 5-year est.).
**Economy:** Employment by occupation: 13.1% management, 3.0% professional, 18.7% services, 13.3% sales, 1.0% farming, 10.2% construction, 5.4% production (2006-2010 5-year est.).
**Income:** Per capita income: $22,267 (2006-2010 5-year est.); Median household income: $42,500 (2006-2010 5-year est.); Average household income: $60,273 (2006-2010 5-year est.); Percent of households with income of $100,000 or more: 14.0% (2006-2010 5-year est.); Poverty rate: 18.9% (2006-2010 5-year est.).
**Education:** Percent of population age 25 and over with: High school diploma (including GED) or higher: 87.7% (2006-2010 5-year est.); Bachelor's degree or higher: 28.5% (2006-2010 5-year est.); Master's degree or higher: 10.1% (2006-2010 5-year est.).
**Housing:** Homeownership rate: 78.9% (2010); Median home value: $157,700 (2006-2010 5-year est.); Median contract rent: $495 per month

(2006-2010 5-year est.); Median year structure built: 1958 (2006-2010 5-year est.).
**Transportation:** Commute to work: 84.0% car, 4.1% public transportation, 8.9% walk, 2.1% work from home (2006-2010 5-year est.); Travel time to work: 39.1% less than 15 minutes, 41.3% 15 to 30 minutes, 10.8% 30 to 45 minutes, 7.1% 45 to 60 minutes, 1.8% 60 minutes or more (2006-2010 5-year est.)
**Additional Information Contacts**
Town of Hartwick . . . . . . . . . . . . . . . . . . . . . . . . . . . . (607) 293-8123
   http://townofhartwick.org

**HARTWICK** (CDP). Covers a land area of 3.457 square miles and a water area of 0 square miles. Located at 42.65° N. Lat; 75.06° W. Long. Elevation is 1,329 feet.
**Population:** n/a (1990); n/a (2000); 629 (2010); Density: 181.9 persons per square mile (2010); Race: 96.5% White, 0.0% Black, 0.2% Asian, 0.3% American Indian/Alaska Native, 0.0% Native Hawaiian/Other Pacific Islander, 3.0% Other, 1.3% Hispanic of any race (2010); Average household size: 2.54 (2010); Median age: 37.8 (2010); Males per 100 females: 96.6 (2010); Marriage status: 33.5% never married, 58.8% now married, 2.4% widowed, 5.3% divorced (2006-2010 5-year est.); Foreign born: 0.0% (2006-2010 5-year est.); Ancestry (includes multiple ancestries): 25.2% German, 24.2% English, 16.4% American, 15.6% Polish, 13.2% Irish (2006-2010 5-year est.).
**Economy:** Employment by occupation: 11.0% management, 3.9% professional, 32.6% services, 7.0% sales, 0.0% farming, 8.1% construction, 7.0% production (2006-2010 5-year est.).
**Income:** Per capita income: $24,517 (2006-2010 5-year est.); Median household income: $48,681 (2006-2010 5-year est.); Average household income: $61,191 (2006-2010 5-year est.); Percent of households with income of $100,000 or more: 5.2% (2006-2010 5-year est.); Poverty rate: 12.2% (2006-2010 5-year est.).
**Education:** Percent of population age 25 and over with: High school diploma (including GED) or higher: 86.8% (2006-2010 5-year est.); Bachelor's degree or higher: 29.1% (2006-2010 5-year est.); Master's degree or higher: 12.3% (2006-2010 5-year est.).
**Housing:** Homeownership rate: 71.4% (2010); Median home value: $156,300 (2006-2010 5-year est.); Median contract rent: $475 per month (2006-2010 5-year est.); Median year structure built: before 1940 (2006-2010 5-year est.).
**Transportation:** Commute to work: 85.2% car, 6.0% public transportation, 8.8% walk, 0.0% work from home (2006-2010 5-year est.); Travel time to work: 32.7% less than 15 minutes, 37.1% 15 to 30 minutes, 9.3% 30 to 45 minutes, 15.1% 45 to 60 minutes, 5.8% 60 minutes or more (2006-2010 5-year est.)

**LAURENS** (village). Covers a land area of 0.128 square miles and a water area of 0 square miles. Located at 42.53° N. Lat; 75.08° W. Long. Elevation is 1,112 feet.
**Population:** 293 (1990); 277 (2000); 263 (2010); Density: 2,048.2 persons per square mile (2010); Race: 97.3% White, 0.0% Black, 0.4% Asian, 0.0% American Indian/Alaska Native, 0.0% Native Hawaiian/Other Pacific Islander, 2.3% Other, 3.4% Hispanic of any race (2010); Average household size: 2.44 (2010); Median age: 34.8 (2010); Males per 100 females: 67.5 (2010); Marriage status: 28.9% never married, 38.6% now married, 4.8% widowed, 27.7% divorced (2006-2010 5-year est.); Foreign born: 0.0% (2006-2010 5-year est.); Ancestry (includes multiple ancestries): 22.3% English, 20.3% Italian, 19.3% Irish, 17.3% Scotch-Irish, 13.4% German (2006-2010 5-year est.).
**Economy:** Employment by occupation: 22.0% management, 0.0% professional, 20.7% services, 4.9% sales, 6.1% farming, 2.4% construction, 1.2% production (2006-2010 5-year est.).
**Income:** Per capita income: $21,815 (2006-2010 5-year est.); Median household income: $47,500 (2006-2010 5-year est.); Average household income: $50,693 (2006-2010 5-year est.); Percent of households with income of $100,000 or more: 16.3% (2006-2010 5-year est.); Poverty rate: 20.5% (2006-2010 5-year est.).
**Education:** Percent of population age 25 and over with: High school diploma (including GED) or higher: 93.2% (2006-2010 5-year est.); Bachelor's degree or higher: 12.0% (2006-2010 5-year est.); Master's degree or higher: 0.0% (2006-2010 5-year est.).
**School District(s)**
Laurens Central School District (KG-12)
   2009-10 Enrollment: 374 . . . . . . . . . . . . . . . . . . . . . . (607) 432-2050

**Housing:** Homeownership rate: 54.7% (2010); Median home value: $97,900 (2006-2010 5-year est.); Median contract rent: $522 per month (2006-2010 5-year est.); Median year structure built: before 1940 (2006-2010 5-year est.).
**Transportation:** Commute to work: 92.7% car, 2.4% public transportation, 2.4% walk, 2.4% work from home (2006-2010 5-year est.); Travel time to work: 28.7% less than 15 minutes, 61.3% 15 to 30 minutes, 1.3% 30 to 45 minutes, 0.0% 45 to 60 minutes, 8.8% 60 minutes or more (2006-2010 5-year est.)

**LAURENS** (town). Covers a land area of 42.049 square miles and a water area of 0.118 square miles. Located at 42.53° N. Lat; 75.11° W. Long. Elevation is 1,112 feet.
**Population:** 2,349 (1990); 2,402 (2000); 2,424 (2010); Density: 57.6 persons per square mile (2010); Race: 96.1% White, 0.4% Black, 0.6% Asian, 0.1% American Indian/Alaska Native, 0.0% Native Hawaiian/Other Pacific Islander, 2.8% Other, 2.7% Hispanic of any race (2010); Average household size: 2.31 (2010); Median age: 46.5 (2010); Males per 100 females: 91.2 (2010); Marriage status: 15.7% never married, 64.5% now married, 4.4% widowed, 15.4% divorced (2006-2010 5-year est.); Foreign born: 2.7% (2006-2010 5-year est.); Ancestry (includes multiple ancestries): 23.1% German, 18.6% English, 13.7% Irish, 9.8% American, 8.7% Italian (2006-2010 5-year est.).
**Economy:** Employment by occupation: 13.6% management, 1.3% professional, 11.7% services, 14.1% sales, 2.4% farming, 9.2% construction, 6.5% production (2006-2010 5-year est.).
**Income:** Per capita income: $22,873 (2006-2010 5-year est.); Median household income: $47,540 (2006-2010 5-year est.); Average household income: $53,067 (2006-2010 5-year est.); Percent of households with income of $100,000 or more: 9.9% (2006-2010 5-year est.); Poverty rate: 14.0% (2006-2010 5-year est.).
**Education:** Percent of population age 25 and over with: High school diploma (including GED) or higher: 89.7% (2006-2010 5-year est.); Bachelor's degree or higher: 22.9% (2006-2010 5-year est.); Master's degree or higher: 7.1% (2006-2010 5-year est.).

### School District(s)
Laurens Central School District (KG-12)
    2009-10 Enrollment: 374 . . . . . . . . . . . . . . . . . . . . . . . . . (607) 432-2050
**Housing:** Homeownership rate: 79.2% (2010); Median home value: $108,300 (2006-2010 5-year est.); Median contract rent: $462 per month (2006-2010 5-year est.); Median year structure built: 1961 (2006-2010 5-year est.).
**Transportation:** Commute to work: 90.9% car, 0.6% public transportation, 4.3% walk, 3.2% work from home (2006-2010 5-year est.); Travel time to work: 22.5% less than 15 minutes, 52.3% 15 to 30 minutes, 14.9% 30 to 45 minutes, 3.5% 45 to 60 minutes, 6.7% 60 minutes or more (2006-2010 5-year est.)

**MARYLAND** (town). Covers a land area of 52.405 square miles and a water area of 0.134 square miles. Located at 42.55° N. Lat; 74.86° W. Long. Elevation is 1,230 feet.
**Population:** 1,716 (1990); 1,920 (2000); 1,897 (2010); Density: 36.2 persons per square mile (2010); Race: 97.0% White, 1.1% Black, 0.2% Asian, 0.0% American Indian/Alaska Native, 0.0% Native Hawaiian/Other Pacific Islander, 1.7% Other, 2.6% Hispanic of any race (2010); Average household size: 2.39 (2010); Median age: 45.4 (2010); Males per 100 females: 97.6 (2010); Marriage status: 22.2% never married, 62.6% now married, 6.7% widowed, 8.5% divorced (2006-2010 5-year est.); Foreign born: 2.0% (2006-2010 5-year est.); Ancestry (includes multiple ancestries): 34.1% German, 22.9% Irish, 15.2% English, 9.0% American, 7.3% Dutch (2006-2010 5-year est.).
**Economy:** Employment by occupation: 11.0% management, 0.6% professional, 11.5% services, 17.9% sales, 2.3% farming, 8.6% construction, 8.3% production (2006-2010 5-year est.).
**Income:** Per capita income: $22,248 (2006-2010 5-year est.); Median household income: $43,833 (2006-2010 5-year est.); Average household income: $54,215 (2006-2010 5-year est.); Percent of households with income of $100,000 or more: 14.0% (2006-2010 5-year est.); Poverty rate: 9.1% (2006-2010 5-year est.).
**Education:** Percent of population age 25 and over with: High school diploma (including GED) or higher: 89.6% (2006-2010 5-year est.); Bachelor's degree or higher: 12.9% (2006-2010 5-year est.); Master's degree or higher: 6.4% (2006-2010 5-year est.).
**Housing:** Homeownership rate: 79.3% (2010); Median home value: $120,800 (2006-2010 5-year est.); Median contract rent: $513 per month

(2006-2010 5-year est.); Median year structure built: 1972 (2006-2010 5-year est.).
**Transportation:** Commute to work: 89.9% car, 1.0% public transportation, 0.2% walk, 8.9% work from home (2006-2010 5-year est.); Travel time to work: 11.1% less than 15 minutes, 44.2% 15 to 30 minutes, 21.1% 30 to 45 minutes, 16.2% 45 to 60 minutes, 7.3% 60 minutes or more (2006-2010 5-year est.)

**MIDDLEFIELD** (town). Covers a land area of 63.334 square miles and a water area of 0.371 square miles. Located at 42.69° N. Lat; 74.85° W. Long. Elevation is 1,250 feet.
**Population:** 2,231 (1990); 2,249 (2000); 2,114 (2010); Density: 33.4 persons per square mile (2010); Race: 95.3% White, 0.6% Black, 2.6% Asian, 0.1% American Indian/Alaska Native, 0.0% Native Hawaiian/Other Pacific Islander, 1.4% Other, 1.3% Hispanic of any race (2010); Average household size: 2.32 (2010); Median age: 46.2 (2010); Males per 100 females: 100.4 (2010); Marriage status: 29.8% never married, 58.8% now married, 4.3% widowed, 7.1% divorced (2006-2010 5-year est.); Foreign born: 2.5% (2006-2010 5-year est.); Ancestry (includes multiple ancestries): 22.2% Irish, 21.5% German, 16.7% Italian, 15.4% English, 7.0% Dutch (2006-2010 5-year est.).
**Economy:** Employment by occupation: 13.3% management, 2.8% professional, 15.1% services, 12.4% sales, 3.6% farming, 17.4% construction, 8.3% production (2006-2010 5-year est.).
**Income:** Per capita income: $32,151 (2006-2010 5-year est.); Median household income: $62,639 (2006-2010 5-year est.); Average household income: $76,575 (2006-2010 5-year est.); Percent of households with income of $100,000 or more: 23.9% (2006-2010 5-year est.); Poverty rate: 8.7% (2006-2010 5-year est.).
**Education:** Percent of population age 25 and over with: High school diploma (including GED) or higher: 94.0% (2006-2010 5-year est.); Bachelor's degree or higher: 39.1% (2006-2010 5-year est.); Master's degree or higher: 22.4% (2006-2010 5-year est.).
**Housing:** Homeownership rate: 80.2% (2010); Median home value: $228,400 (2006-2010 5-year est.); Median contract rent: $540 per month (2006-2010 5-year est.); Median year structure built: 1967 (2006-2010 5-year est.).
**Transportation:** Commute to work: 87.7% car, 0.0% public transportation, 6.3% walk, 3.2% work from home (2006-2010 5-year est.); Travel time to work: 56.6% less than 15 minutes, 25.1% 15 to 30 minutes, 6.7% 30 to 45 minutes, 2.5% 45 to 60 minutes, 9.1% 60 minutes or more (2006-2010 5-year est.)

**MILFORD** (village). Covers a land area of 0.424 square miles and a water area of 0 square miles. Located at 42.59° N. Lat; 74.94° W. Long. Elevation is 1,207 feet.
**Population:** 462 (1990); 511 (2000); 415 (2010); Density: 978.2 persons per square mile (2010); Race: 94.9% White, 1.2% Black, 1.2% Asian, 0.2% American Indian/Alaska Native, 0.0% Native Hawaiian/Other Pacific Islander, 2.5% Other, 1.7% Hispanic of any race (2010); Average household size: 2.31 (2010); Median age: 44.3 (2010); Males per 100 females: 91.2 (2010); Marriage status: 33.5% never married, 50.8% now married, 5.3% widowed, 10.4% divorced (2006-2010 5-year est.); Foreign born: 1.4% (2006-2010 5-year est.); Ancestry (includes multiple ancestries): 23.1% English, 19.6% German, 14.3% Italian, 13.3% Irish, 12.7% American (2006-2010 5-year est.).
**Economy:** Employment by occupation: 10.1% management, 0.0% professional, 10.5% services, 16.1% sales, 8.7% farming, 1.7% construction, 0.0% production (2006-2010 5-year est.).
**Income:** Per capita income: $23,039 (2006-2010 5-year est.); Median household income: $40,729 (2006-2010 5-year est.); Average household income: $49,399 (2006-2010 5-year est.); Percent of households with income of $100,000 or more: 7.8% (2006-2010 5-year est.); Poverty rate: 14.7% (2006-2010 5-year est.).
**Education:** Percent of population age 25 and over with: High school diploma (including GED) or higher: 94.7% (2006-2010 5-year est.); Bachelor's degree or higher: 27.4% (2006-2010 5-year est.); Master's degree or higher: 7.1% (2006-2010 5-year est.).

### School District(s)
Milford Central School District (PK-12)
    2009-10 Enrollment: 451 . . . . . . . . . . . . . . . . . . . . . . . . . (607) 286-3341
**Housing:** Homeownership rate: 65.5% (2010); Median home value: $106,800 (2006-2010 5-year est.); Median contract rent: $460 per month (2006-2010 5-year est.); Median year structure built: before 1940 (2006-2010 5-year est.).

**Transportation:** Commute to work: 73.6% car, 2.9% public transportation, 16.4% walk, 7.1% work from home (2006-2010 5-year est.); Travel time to work: 60.8% less than 15 minutes, 23.8% 15 to 30 minutes, 13.5% 30 to 45 minutes, 1.9% 45 to 60 minutes, 0.0% 60 minutes or more (2006-2010 5-year est.)

**MILFORD** (town). Covers a land area of 46.117 square miles and a water area of 1.029 square miles. Located at 42.54° N. Lat; 74.97° W. Long. Elevation is 1,207 feet.
**Population:** 2,845 (1990); 2,938 (2000); 3,044 (2010); Density: 66.0 persons per square mile (2010); Race: 96.1% White, 1.1% Black, 1.0% Asian, 0.1% American Indian/Alaska Native, 0.2% Native Hawaiian/Other Pacific Islander, 1.5% Other, 1.8% Hispanic of any race (2010); Average household size: 2.30 (2010); Median age: 46.3 (2010); Males per 100 females: 99.9 (2010); Marriage status: 28.6% never married, 59.4% now married, 5.5% widowed, 6.4% divorced (2006-2010 5-year est.); Foreign born: 0.7% (2006-2010 5-year est.); Ancestry (includes multiple ancestries): 23.1% German, 19.5% English, 19.2% Irish, 9.5% Italian, 9.0% American (2006-2010 5-year est.).
**Economy:** Employment by occupation: 11.6% management, 0.6% professional, 14.2% services, 13.0% sales, 2.6% farming, 10.7% construction, 7.7% production (2006-2010 5-year est.).
**Income:** Per capita income: $23,948 (2006-2010 5-year est.); Median household income: $44,806 (2006-2010 5-year est.); Average household income: $56,152 (2006-2010 5-year est.); Percent of households with income of $100,000 or more: 15.0% (2006-2010 5-year est.); Poverty rate: 17.6% (2006-2010 5-year est.).
**Education:** Percent of population age 25 and over with: High school diploma (including GED) or higher: 88.5% (2006-2010 5-year est.); Bachelor's degree or higher: 19.8% (2006-2010 5-year est.); Master's degree or higher: 4.3% (2006-2010 5-year est.).

**School District(s)**
Milford Central School District (PK-12)
   2009-10 Enrollment: 451 . . . . . . . . . . . . . . . . . . . (607) 286-3341
**Housing:** Homeownership rate: 79.9% (2010); Median home value: $136,300 (2006-2010 5-year est.); Median contract rent: $497 per month (2006-2010 5-year est.); Median year structure built: 1969 (2006-2010 5-year est.).
**Transportation:** Commute to work: 88.8% car, 5.1% public transportation, 4.4% walk, 1.7% work from home (2006-2010 5-year est.); Travel time to work: 32.9% less than 15 minutes, 51.0% 15 to 30 minutes, 10.1% 30 to 45 minutes, 3.2% 45 to 60 minutes, 2.8% 60 minutes or more (2006-2010 5-year est.)

**MORRIS** (village). Covers a land area of 0.745 square miles and a water area of 0.007 square miles. Located at 42.54° N. Lat; 75.24° W. Long. Elevation is 1,145 feet.
**Population:** 642 (1990); 591 (2000); 583 (2010); Density: 781.9 persons per square mile (2010); Race: 96.6% White, 1.0% Black, 0.0% Asian, 0.0% American Indian/Alaska Native, 0.0% Native Hawaiian/Other Pacific Islander, 2.4% Other, 3.3% Hispanic of any race (2010); Average household size: 2.26 (2010); Median age: 43.4 (2010); Males per 100 females: 95.6 (2010); Marriage status: 14.8% never married, 50.8% now married, 8.7% widowed, 25.8% divorced (2006-2010 5-year est.); Foreign born: 0.0% (2006-2010 5-year est.); Ancestry (includes multiple ancestries): 43.1% German, 33.9% Irish, 11.9% English, 9.8% Dutch, 6.7% Italian (2006-2010 5-year est.).
**Economy:** Employment by occupation: 6.9% management, 0.0% professional, 16.4% services, 9.1% sales, 0.0% farming, 11.6% construction, 10.3% production (2006-2010 5-year est.).
**Income:** Per capita income: $24,671 (2006-2010 5-year est.); Median household income: $38,846 (2006-2010 5-year est.); Average household income: $52,251 (2006-2010 5-year est.); Percent of households with income of $100,000 or more: 13.6% (2006-2010 5-year est.); Poverty rate: 14.9% (2006-2010 5-year est.).
**Education:** Percent of population age 25 and over with: High school diploma (including GED) or higher: 91.2% (2006-2010 5-year est.); Bachelor's degree or higher: 28.9% (2006-2010 5-year est.); Master's degree or higher: 8.6% (2006-2010 5-year est.).

**School District(s)**
Morris Central School District (PK-12)
   2009-10 Enrollment: 437 . . . . . . . . . . . . . . . . . . . (607) 263-6102
**Housing:** Homeownership rate: 67.8% (2010); Median home value: $106,300 (2006-2010 5-year est.); Median contract rent: $453 per month

(2006-2010 5-year est.); Median year structure built: before 1940 (2006-2010 5-year est.).
**Transportation:** Commute to work: 74.0% car, 0.0% public transportation, 19.3% walk, 5.4% work from home (2006-2010 5-year est.); Travel time to work: 36.5% less than 15 minutes, 52.1% 15 to 30 minutes, 11.4% 30 to 45 minutes, 0.0% 45 to 60 minutes, 0.0% 60 minutes or more (2006-2010 5-year est.)

**MORRIS** (town). Covers a land area of 39.067 square miles and a water area of 0.126 square miles. Located at 42.54° N. Lat; 75.26° W. Long. Elevation is 1,145 feet.
**Population:** 1,787 (1990); 1,867 (2000); 1,878 (2010); Density: 48.1 persons per square mile (2010); Race: 97.2% White, 0.4% Black, 0.1% Asian, 0.1% American Indian/Alaska Native, 0.0% Native Hawaiian/Other Pacific Islander, 2.2% Other, 2.8% Hispanic of any race (2010); Average household size: 2.38 (2010); Median age: 45.0 (2010); Males per 100 females: 97.9 (2010); Marriage status: 17.0% never married, 62.0% now married, 6.5% widowed, 14.5% divorced (2006-2010 5-year est.); Foreign born: 0.6% (2006-2010 5-year est.); Ancestry (includes multiple ancestries): 27.9% German, 22.0% Irish, 19.5% English, 11.9% American, 10.5% Italian (2006-2010 5-year est.).
**Economy:** Employment by occupation: 8.1% management, 0.6% professional, 11.4% services, 14.7% sales, 3.7% farming, 18.1% construction, 9.0% production (2006-2010 5-year est.).
**Income:** Per capita income: $22,003 (2006-2010 5-year est.); Median household income: $44,461 (2006-2010 5-year est.); Average household income: $50,172 (2006-2010 5-year est.); Percent of households with income of $100,000 or more: 10.2% (2006-2010 5-year est.); Poverty rate: 12.4% (2006-2010 5-year est.).
**Education:** Percent of population age 25 and over with: High school diploma (including GED) or higher: 88.0% (2006-2010 5-year est.); Bachelor's degree or higher: 19.8% (2006-2010 5-year est.); Master's degree or higher: 7.5% (2006-2010 5-year est.).

**School District(s)**
Morris Central School District (PK-12)
   2009-10 Enrollment: 437 . . . . . . . . . . . . . . . . . . . (607) 263-6102
**Housing:** Homeownership rate: 77.4% (2010); Median home value: $114,000 (2006-2010 5-year est.); Median contract rent: $428 per month (2006-2010 5-year est.); Median year structure built: 1950 (2006-2010 5-year est.).
**Transportation:** Commute to work: 85.4% car, 0.0% public transportation, 9.4% walk, 4.8% work from home (2006-2010 5-year est.); Travel time to work: 36.2% less than 15 minutes, 36.2% 15 to 30 minutes, 20.8% 30 to 45 minutes, 3.1% 45 to 60 minutes, 3.8% 60 minutes or more (2006-2010 5-year est.)

**MOUNT VISION** (unincorporated postal area)
Zip Code: 13810
   Covers a land area of 40.028 square miles and a water area of 0.183 square miles. Located at 42.60° N. Lat; 75.10° W. Long. Elevation is 1,171 feet. Population: 1,149 (2010); Density: 28.7 persons per square mile (2010); Race: 98.4% White, 0.3% Black, 0.0% Asian, 0.3% American Indian/Alaska Native, 0.0% Native Hawaiian/Other Pacific Islander, 1.0% Other, 2.3% Hispanic of any race (2010); Average household size: 2.26 (2010); Median age: 46.8 (2010); Males per 100 females: 93.4 (2010); Homeownership rate: 82.5% (2010)

**NEW LISBON** (town). Covers a land area of 44.354 square miles and a water area of 0.301 square miles. Located at 42.62° N. Lat; 75.13° W. Long. Elevation is 1,247 feet.
**Population:** 996 (1990); 1,116 (2000); 1,114 (2010); Density: 25.1 persons per square mile (2010); Race: 97.9% White, 0.3% Black, 0.0% Asian, 0.3% American Indian/Alaska Native, 0.0% Native Hawaiian/Other Pacific Islander, 1.5% Other, 2.2% Hispanic of any race (2010); Average household size: 2.35 (2010); Median age: 45.5 (2010); Males per 100 females: 90.8 (2010); Marriage status: 19.9% never married, 69.0% now married, 6.6% widowed, 4.6% divorced (2006-2010 5-year est.); Foreign born: 1.6% (2006-2010 5-year est.); Ancestry (includes multiple ancestries): 21.2% German, 17.9% English, 15.0% Irish, 13.4% Italian, 9.7% American (2006-2010 5-year est.).
**Economy:** Employment by occupation: 9.3% management, 1.7% professional, 9.8% services, 13.9% sales, 6.8% farming, 12.2% construction, 5.6% production (2006-2010 5-year est.).
**Income:** Per capita income: $21,744 (2006-2010 5-year est.); Median household income: $45,114 (2006-2010 5-year est.); Average household

income: $55,410 (2006-2010 5-year est.); Percent of households with income of $100,000 or more: 7.4% (2006-2010 5-year est.); Poverty rate: 6.2% (2006-2010 5-year est.).

**Education:** Percent of population age 25 and over with: High school diploma (including GED) or higher: 89.4% (2006-2010 5-year est.); Bachelor's degree or higher: 20.4% (2006-2010 5-year est.); Master's degree or higher: 8.6% (2006-2010 5-year est.).

**Housing:** Homeownership rate: 89.4% (2010); Median home value: $136,000 (2006-2010 5-year est.); Median contract rent: $435 per month (2006-2010 5-year est.); Median year structure built: 1974 (2006-2010 5-year est.).

**Transportation:** Commute to work: 89.8% car, 0.0% public transportation, 3.6% walk, 6.6% work from home (2006-2010 5-year est.); Travel time to work: 22.4% less than 15 minutes, 42.4% 15 to 30 minutes, 20.2% 30 to 45 minutes, 6.7% 45 to 60 minutes, 8.4% 60 minutes or more (2006-2010 5-year est.).

## ONEONTA (city). Covers a land area of 4.361 square miles and a water area of 0.004 square miles. Located at 42.45° N. Lat; 75.06° W. Long. Elevation is 1,112 feet.

**History:** Oneonta grew after the coming of the railroad in 1865; however, no vestiges of importance as a railroad center exist today. Brotherhood of Railroad Brakemen founded here in 1883), which was renamed Brotherhood of Railroad Trainmen in 1889. Seat of the State University of N.Y. College at Oneonta and Hartwick College. National Soccer Hall of Fame. Settled c.1780, Incorporated as a city 1909.

**Population:** 14,051 (1990); 13,292 (2000); 13,901 (2010); Density: 3,187.3 persons per square mile (2010); Race: 89.6% White, 3.5% Black, 2.4% Asian, 0.2% American Indian/Alaska Native, 0.0% Native Hawaiian/Other Pacific Islander, 4.3% Other, 5.9% Hispanic of any race (2010); Average household size: 2.17 (2010); Median age: 22.0 (2010); Males per 100 females: 83.9 (2010); Marriage status: 62.2% never married, 26.4% now married, 4.6% widowed, 6.7% divorced (2006-2010 5-year est.); Foreign born: 4.6% (2006-2010 5-year est.); Ancestry (includes multiple ancestries): 21.7% Irish, 20.3% Italian, 17.0% German, 11.0% English, 6.6% American (2006-2010 5-year est.).

**Economy:** Single-family building permits issued: 0 (2011); Multi-family building permits issued: 0 (2011); Employment by occupation: 9.3% management, 2.6% professional, 16.0% services, 15.7% sales, 3.9% farming, 3.7% construction, 2.8% production (2006-2010 5-year est.).

**Income:** Per capita income: $18,084 (2006-2010 5-year est.); Median household income: $33,545 (2006-2010 5-year est.); Average household income: $50,152 (2006-2010 5-year est.); Percent of households with income of $100,000 or more: 10.6% (2006-2010 5-year est.); Poverty rate: 25.4% (2006-2010 5-year est.).

**Education:** Percent of population age 25 and over with: High school diploma (including GED) or higher: 87.3% (2006-2010 5-year est.); Bachelor's degree or higher: 41.0% (2006-2010 5-year est.); Master's degree or higher: 17.8% (2006-2010 5-year est.).

### School District(s)
Oneonta City School District (PK-12)
    2009-10 Enrollment: 1,886 . . . . . . . . . . . . . . . . . . . . . . (607) 433-8232

### Four-year College(s)
Hartwick College (Private, Not-for-profit)
    Fall 2010 Enrollment: 1,539. . . . . . . . . . . . . . . . . . . . (607) 431-4000
    2011-12 Tuition: In-state $36,040; Out-of-state $36,040
SUNY College at Oneonta (Public)
    Fall 2010 Enrollment: 6,096. . . . . . . . . . . . . . . . . . . . (607) 436-3500
    2011-12 Tuition: In-state $6,559; Out-of-state $15,609

### Vocational/Technical School(s)
Otsego Area BOCES-School of Practical Nursing (Public)
    Fall 2010 Enrollment: 59 . . . . . . . . . . . . . . . . . . . . . . . (607) 431-2562
    2011-12 Tuition: $9,720

**Housing:** Homeownership rate: 43.3% (2010); Median home value: $126,700 (2006-2010 5-year est.); Median contract rent: $674 per month (2006-2010 5-year est.); Median year structure built: before 1940 (2006-2010 5-year est.).

**Hospitals:** AO Fox Memorial Hospital (128 beds)

**Safety:** Violent crime rate: 58.7 per 10,000 population; Property crime rate: 276.1 per 10,000 population (2010).

**Newspapers:** The Daily Star (Local news; Circulation 17,114)

**Transportation:** Commute to work: 63.3% car, 4.4% public transportation, 23.2% walk, 5.4% work from home (2006-2010 5-year est.); Travel time to work: 72.0% less than 15 minutes, 13.8% 15 to 30 minutes, 8.8% 30 to 45

minutes, 1.9% 45 to 60 minutes, 3.6% 60 minutes or more (2006-2010 5-year est.)

**Airports:** Oneonta Municipal (general aviation)

**Additional Information Contacts**
City of Oneonta . . . . . . . . . . . . . . . . . . . . . . . . . . . . . . (607) 432-6450
    http://www.oneonta.ny.us
Otsego County Chamber of Commerce. . . . . . . . . . . . (607) 432-4500
    http://www.otsegocountychamber.com

## ONEONTA (town). Covers a land area of 32.911 square miles and a water area of 0.251 square miles. Located at 42.42° N. Lat; 75.09° W. Long. Elevation is 1,112 feet.

**Population:** 4,828 (1990); 4,994 (2000); 5,229 (2010); Density: 158.9 persons per square mile (2010); Race: 90.5% White, 6.0% Black, 1.1% Asian, 0.3% American Indian/Alaska Native, 0.0% Native Hawaiian/Other Pacific Islander, 2.1% Other, 4.4% Hispanic of any race (2010); Average household size: 2.24 (2010); Median age: 44.4 (2010); Males per 100 females: 97.1 (2010); Marriage status: 31.9% never married, 52.2% now married, 6.6% widowed, 9.2% divorced (2006-2010 5-year est.); Foreign born: 11.6% (2006-2010 5-year est.); Ancestry (includes multiple ancestries): 26.9% German, 15.9% Italian, 15.2% English, 14.6% Irish, 8.5% American (2006-2010 5-year est.).

**Economy:** Single-family building permits issued: 4 (2011); Multi-family building permits issued: 0 (2011); Employment by occupation: 5.9% management, 4.5% professional, 14.9% services, 13.8% sales, 4.5% farming, 7.0% construction, 7.0% production (2006-2010 5-year est.).

**Income:** Per capita income: $26,659 (2006-2010 5-year est.); Median household income: $50,297 (2006-2010 5-year est.); Average household income: $63,424 (2006-2010 5-year est.); Percent of households with income of $100,000 or more: 17.5% (2006-2010 5-year est.); Poverty rate: 16.4% (2006-2010 5-year est.).

**Education:** Percent of population age 25 and over with: High school diploma (including GED) or higher: 91.6% (2006-2010 5-year est.); Bachelor's degree or higher: 31.3% (2006-2010 5-year est.); Master's degree or higher: 14.8% (2006-2010 5-year est.).

### School District(s)
Oneonta City School District (PK-12)
    2009-10 Enrollment: 1,886 . . . . . . . . . . . . . . . . . . . . . . (607) 433-8232

### Four-year College(s)
Hartwick College (Private, Not-for-profit)
    Fall 2010 Enrollment: 1,539. . . . . . . . . . . . . . . . . . . . (607) 431-4000
    2011-12 Tuition: In-state $36,040; Out-of-state $36,040
SUNY College at Oneonta (Public)
    Fall 2010 Enrollment: 6,096. . . . . . . . . . . . . . . . . . . . (607) 436-3500
    2011-12 Tuition: In-state $6,559; Out-of-state $15,609

### Vocational/Technical School(s)
Otsego Area BOCES-School of Practical Nursing (Public)
    Fall 2010 Enrollment: 59 . . . . . . . . . . . . . . . . . . . . . . . (607) 431-2562
    2011-12 Tuition: $9,720

**Housing:** Homeownership rate: 75.9% (2010); Median home value: $157,000 (2006-2010 5-year est.); Median contract rent: $583 per month (2006-2010 5-year est.); Median year structure built: 1969 (2006-2010 5-year est.).

**Hospitals:** AO Fox Memorial Hospital (128 beds)

**Newspapers:** The Daily Star (Local news; Circulation 17,114)

**Transportation:** Commute to work: 83.3% car, 2.7% public transportation, 9.1% walk, 4.9% work from home (2006-2010 5-year est.); Travel time to work: 54.4% less than 15 minutes, 30.2% 15 to 30 minutes, 7.4% 30 to 45 minutes, 4.7% 45 to 60 minutes, 3.4% 60 minutes or more (2006-2010 5-year est.)

**Airports:** Oneonta Municipal (general aviation)

## OTEGO (village). Covers a land area of 1.159 square miles and a water area of 0 square miles. Located at 42.39° N. Lat; 75.18° W. Long. Elevation is 1,070 feet.

**Population:** 1,068 (1990); 1,052 (2000); 1,010 (2010); Density: 871.1 persons per square mile (2010); Race: 93.5% White, 1.6% Black, 1.3% Asian, 0.1% American Indian/Alaska Native, 0.1% Native Hawaiian/Other Pacific Islander, 3.4% Other, 2.6% Hispanic of any race (2010); Average household size: 2.39 (2010); Median age: 41.9 (2010); Males per 100 females: 90.2 (2010); Marriage status: 26.3% never married, 59.0% now married, 5.4% widowed, 9.3% divorced (2006-2010 5-year est.); Foreign born: 6.1% (2006-2010 5-year est.); Ancestry (includes multiple ancestries): 27.6% German, 21.4% Irish, 15.2% English, 12.9% Italian, 12.3% French (2006-2010 5-year est.).

**Economy:** Single-family building permits issued: 0 (2011); Multi-family building permits issued: 0 (2011); Employment by occupation: 3.7% management, 1.1% professional, 4.9% services, 19.2% sales, 2.2% farming, 14.1% construction, 12.2% production (2006-2010 5-year est.).
**Income:** Per capita income: $24,004 (2006-2010 5-year est.); Median household income: $52,566 (2006-2010 5-year est.); Average household income: $56,839 (2006-2010 5-year est.); Percent of households with income of $100,000 or more: 14.1% (2006-2010 5-year est.); Poverty rate: 10.8% (2006-2010 5-year est.).
**Education:** Percent of population age 25 and over with: High school diploma (including GED) or higher: 85.2% (2006-2010 5-year est.); Bachelor's degree or higher: 28.2% (2006-2010 5-year est.); Master's degree or higher: 11.0% (2006-2010 5-year est.).

**School District(s)**
Otego-Unadilla Central School District (KG-12)
    2009-10 Enrollment: 1,067 . . . . . . . . . . . . . . . . . (607) 988-5038
**Housing:** Homeownership rate: 69.6% (2010); Median home value: $131,300 (2006-2010 5-year est.); Median contract rent: $635 per month (2006-2010 5-year est.); Median year structure built: before 1940 (2006-2010 5-year est.).
**Transportation:** Commute to work: 87.2% car, 0.0% public transportation, 8.9% walk, 3.9% work from home (2006-2010 5-year est.); Travel time to work: 49.1% less than 15 minutes, 27.9% 15 to 30 minutes, 16.1% 30 to 45 minutes, 5.3% 45 to 60 minutes, 1.7% 60 minutes or more (2006-2010 5-year est.)

**OTEGO** (town). Covers a land area of 45.632 square miles and a water area of 0.075 square miles. Located at 42.45° N. Lat; 75.19° W. Long. Elevation is 1,070 feet.
**Population:** 3,128 (1990); 3,183 (2000); 3,115 (2010); Density: 68.3 persons per square mile (2010); Race: 96.0% White, 0.7% Black, 0.6% Asian, 0.0% American Indian/Alaska Native, 0.0% Native Hawaiian/Other Pacific Islander, 2.7% Other, 2.6% Hispanic of any race (2010); Average household size: 2.41 (2010); Median age: 42.9 (2010); Males per 100 females: 94.1 (2010); Marriage status: 25.3% never married, 58.8% now married, 4.7% widowed, 11.3% divorced (2006-2010 5-year est.); Foreign born: 5.2% (2006-2010 5-year est.); Ancestry (includes multiple ancestries): 25.5% German, 19.8% English, 18.6% Irish, 13.0% Italian, 11.9% French (2006-2010 5-year est.).
**Economy:** Single-family building permits issued: 1 (2011); Multi-family building permits issued: 0 (2011); Employment by occupation: 8.0% management, 0.5% professional, 8.1% services, 23.2% sales, 2.1% farming, 16.3% construction, 9.6% production (2006-2010 5-year est.).
**Income:** Per capita income: $25,076 (2006-2010 5-year est.); Median household income: $47,827 (2006-2010 5-year est.); Average household income: $57,387 (2006-2010 5-year est.); Percent of households with income of $100,000 or more: 10.7% (2006-2010 5-year est.); Poverty rate: 12.5% (2006-2010 5-year est.).
**Education:** Percent of population age 25 and over with: High school diploma (including GED) or higher: 85.1% (2006-2010 5-year est.); Bachelor's degree or higher: 22.6% (2006-2010 5-year est.); Master's degree or higher: 11.3% (2006-2010 5-year est.).

**School District(s)**
Otego-Unadilla Central School District (KG-12)
    2009-10 Enrollment: 1,067 . . . . . . . . . . . . . . . . . (607) 988-5038
**Housing:** Homeownership rate: 76.7% (2010); Median home value: $127,900 (2006-2010 5-year est.); Median contract rent: $507 per month (2006-2010 5-year est.); Median year structure built: 1973 (2006-2010 5-year est.).
**Transportation:** Commute to work: 93.9% car, 0.0% public transportation, 3.6% walk, 2.6% work from home (2006-2010 5-year est.); Travel time to work: 30.6% less than 15 minutes, 44.7% 15 to 30 minutes, 13.5% 30 to 45 minutes, 6.4% 45 to 60 minutes, 4.7% 60 minutes or more (2006-2010 5-year est.).

**OTSEGO** (town). Covers a land area of 53.889 square miles and a water area of 5.161 square miles. Located at 42.75° N. Lat; 74.96° W. Long.
**Population:** 3,932 (1990); 3,904 (2000); 3,900 (2010); Density: 72.4 persons per square mile (2010); Race: 96.7% White, 0.4% Black, 1.2% Asian, 0.2% American Indian/Alaska Native, 0.0% Native Hawaiian/Other Pacific Islander, 1.5% Other, 2.0% Hispanic of any race (2010); Average household size: 2.13 (2010); Median age: 49.5 (2010); Males per 100 females: 85.6 (2010); Marriage status: 26.8% never married, 53.8% now married, 13.6% widowed, 5.8% divorced (2006-2010 5-year est.); Foreign

born: 4.4% (2006-2010 5-year est.); Ancestry (includes multiple ancestries): 23.0% Irish, 21.4% German, 20.7% American, 18.8% English, 9.3% Italian (2006-2010 5-year est.).
**Economy:** Employment by occupation: 17.2% management, 1.4% professional, 6.0% services, 16.0% sales, 0.9% farming, 4.2% construction, 1.3% production (2006-2010 5-year est.).
**Income:** Per capita income: $33,902 (2006-2010 5-year est.); Median household income: $54,158 (2006-2010 5-year est.); Average household income: $75,166 (2006-2010 5-year est.); Percent of households with income of $100,000 or more: 19.1% (2006-2010 5-year est.); Poverty rate: 12.8% (2006-2010 5-year est.).
**Education:** Percent of population age 25 and over with: High school diploma (including GED) or higher: 90.0% (2006-2010 5-year est.); Bachelor's degree or higher: 40.9% (2006-2010 5-year est.); Master's degree or higher: 20.2% (2006-2010 5-year est.).
**Housing:** Homeownership rate: 67.7% (2010); Median home value: $239,700 (2006-2010 5-year est.); Median contract rent: $723 per month (2006-2010 5-year est.); Median year structure built: 1943 (2006-2010 5-year est.).
**Transportation:** Commute to work: 81.8% car, 0.8% public transportation, 10.5% walk, 5.8% work from home (2006-2010 5-year est.); Travel time to work: 50.7% less than 15 minutes, 28.3% 15 to 30 minutes, 13.7% 30 to 45 minutes, 3.7% 45 to 60 minutes, 3.6% 60 minutes or more (2006-2010 5-year est.)

**PITTSFIELD** (town). Aka Pecktown. Covers a land area of 37.986 square miles and a water area of 0.115 square miles. Located at 42.61° N. Lat; 75.27° W. Long. Elevation is 1,155 feet.
**Population:** 1,116 (1990); 1,295 (2000); 1,366 (2010); Density: 36.0 persons per square mile (2010); Race: 96.3% White, 0.7% Black, 0.7% Asian, 0.1% American Indian/Alaska Native, 0.0% Native Hawaiian/Other Pacific Islander, 2.2% Other, 1.7% Hispanic of any race (2010); Average household size: 2.54 (2010); Median age: 44.4 (2010); Males per 100 females: 103.0 (2010); Marriage status: 26.1% never married, 63.9% now married, 2.6% widowed, 7.4% divorced (2006-2010 5-year est.); Foreign born: 3.6% (2006-2010 5-year est.); Ancestry (includes multiple ancestries): 17.3% Irish, 16.8% English, 16.5% American, 13.1% German, 7.8% Italian (2006-2010 5-year est.).
**Economy:** Employment by occupation: 12.6% management, 3.3% professional, 16.8% services, 15.9% sales, 0.9% farming, 10.6% construction, 5.0% production (2006-2010 5-year est.).
**Income:** Per capita income: $19,942 (2006-2010 5-year est.); Median household income: $44,219 (2006-2010 5-year est.); Average household income: $55,122 (2006-2010 5-year est.); Percent of households with income of $100,000 or more: 12.8% (2006-2010 5-year est.); Poverty rate: 16.8% (2006-2010 5-year est.).
**Education:** Percent of population age 25 and over with: High school diploma (including GED) or higher: 84.9% (2006-2010 5-year est.); Bachelor's degree or higher: 11.8% (2006-2010 5-year est.); Master's degree or higher: 4.0% (2006-2010 5-year est.).
**Housing:** Homeownership rate: 86.0% (2010); Median home value: $103,400 (2006-2010 5-year est.); Median contract rent: $334 per month (2006-2010 5-year est.); Median year structure built: 1978 (2006-2010 5-year est.).
**Transportation:** Commute to work: 89.3% car, 0.3% public transportation, 1.7% walk, 7.2% work from home (2006-2010 5-year est.); Travel time to work: 27.7% less than 15 minutes, 26.7% 15 to 30 minutes, 26.3% 30 to 45 minutes, 8.3% 45 to 60 minutes, 11.0% 60 minutes or more (2006-2010 5-year est.)

**PLAINFIELD** (town). Covers a land area of 29.499 square miles and a water area of 0 square miles. Located at 42.82° N. Lat; 75.19° W. Long.
**Population:** 850 (1990); 986 (2000); 915 (2010); Density: 31.0 persons per square mile (2010); Race: 98.5% White, 0.4% Black, 0.4% Asian, 0.2% American Indian/Alaska Native, 0.0% Native Hawaiian/Other Pacific Islander, 0.5% Other, 1.1% Hispanic of any race (2010); Average household size: 2.60 (2010); Median age: 41.8 (2010); Males per 100 females: 102.4 (2010); Marriage status: 25.1% never married, 61.1% now married, 6.9% widowed, 6.9% divorced (2006-2010 5-year est.); Foreign born: 1.3% (2006-2010 5-year est.); Ancestry (includes multiple ancestries): 24.7% German, 16.3% American, 15.1% Irish, 15.1% English, 7.2% Dutch (2006-2010 5-year est.).
**Economy:** Employment by occupation: 5.0% management, 2.0% professional, 11.4% services, 16.6% sales, 1.8% farming, 20.7% construction, 8.0% production (2006-2010 5-year est.).

**Income:** Per capita income: $21,583 (2006-2010 5-year est.); Median household income: $48,641 (2006-2010 5-year est.); Average household income: $52,397 (2006-2010 5-year est.); Percent of households with income of $100,000 or more: 6.2% (2006-2010 5-year est.); Poverty rate: 16.2% (2006-2010 5-year est.).

**Education:** Percent of population age 25 and over with: High school diploma (including GED) or higher: 88.0% (2006-2010 5-year est.); Bachelor's degree or higher: 13.3% (2006-2010 5-year est.); Master's degree or higher: 5.7% (2006-2010 5-year est.).

**Housing:** Homeownership rate: 87.0% (2010); Median home value: $86,900 (2006-2010 5-year est.); Median contract rent: $538 per month (2006-2010 5-year est.); Median year structure built: before 1940 (2006-2010 5-year est.).

**Transportation:** Commute to work: 90.5% car, 2.4% public transportation, 4.5% walk, 1.9% work from home (2006-2010 5-year est.); Travel time to work: 15.5% less than 15 minutes, 37.8% 15 to 30 minutes, 33.7% 30 to 45 minutes, 8.7% 45 to 60 minutes, 4.4% 60 minutes or more (2006-2010 5-year est.)

## PORTLANDVILLE (unincorporated postal area)
Zip Code: 13834

Covers a land area of 0.347 square miles and a water area of 0.041 square miles. Located at 42.53° N. Lat; 74.96° W. Long. Elevation is 1,152 feet. Population: 118 (2010); Density: 339.3 persons per square mile (2010); Race: 97.5% White, 0.8% Black, 0.0% Asian, 0.0% American Indian/Alaska Native, 0.0% Native Hawaiian/Other Pacific Islander, 1.7% Other, 5.1% Hispanic of any race (2010); Average household size: 1.97 (2010); Median age: 44.5 (2010); Males per 100 females: 114.5 (2010); Homeownership rate: 66.7% (2010)

## RICHFIELD (town). Aka Monticello. Covers a land area of 30.858 square miles and a water area of 1.598 square miles. Located at 42.85° N. Lat; 75.04° W. Long. Elevation is 1,476 feet.

**History:** Health resort until mid-20th century; sulphur springs. Incorporated 1934.

**Population:** 2,711 (1990); 2,423 (2000); 2,388 (2010); Density: 77.4 persons per square mile (2010); Race: 97.4% White, 0.3% Black, 0.7% Asian, 0.5% American Indian/Alaska Native, 0.0% Native Hawaiian/Other Pacific Islander, 1.1% Other, 0.9% Hispanic of any race (2010); Average household size: 2.28 (2010); Median age: 46.4 (2010); Males per 100 females: 95.6 (2010); Marriage status: 23.4% never married, 62.8% now married, 6.4% widowed, 7.4% divorced (2006-2010 5-year est.); Foreign born: 3.2% (2006-2010 5-year est.); Ancestry (includes multiple ancestries): 19.9% English, 18.5% German, 17.4% Irish, 11.6% American, 11.4% Italian (2006-2010 5-year est.).

**Economy:** Employment by occupation: 13.8% management, 3.7% professional, 16.1% services, 17.0% sales, 3.0% farming, 3.7% construction, 1.8% production (2006-2010 5-year est.).

**Income:** Per capita income: $21,195 (2006-2010 5-year est.); Median household income: $32,282 (2006-2010 5-year est.); Average household income: $49,793 (2006-2010 5-year est.); Percent of households with income of $100,000 or more: 9.6% (2006-2010 5-year est.); Poverty rate: 8.8% (2006-2010 5-year est.).

**Education:** Percent of population age 25 and over with: High school diploma (including GED) or higher: 82.1% (2006-2010 5-year est.); Bachelor's degree or higher: 22.0% (2006-2010 5-year est.); Master's degree or higher: 7.8% (2006-2010 5-year est.).

**Housing:** Homeownership rate: 71.1% (2010); Median home value: $95,900 (2006-2010 5-year est.); Median contract rent: $420 per month (2006-2010 5-year est.); Median year structure built: 1948 (2006-2010 5-year est.).

**Transportation:** Commute to work: 87.4% car, 2.2% public transportation, 3.1% walk, 5.7% work from home (2006-2010 5-year est.); Travel time to work: 29.6% less than 15 minutes, 26.2% 15 to 30 minutes, 28.1% 30 to 45 minutes, 11.7% 45 to 60 minutes, 4.4% 60 minutes or more (2006-2010 5-year est.)

## RICHFIELD SPRINGS (village). Covers a land area of 1.006 square miles and a water area of 0 square miles. Located at 42.85° N. Lat; 74.98° W. Long. Elevation is 1,312 feet.

**Population:** 1,543 (1990); 1,255 (2000); 1,264 (2010); Density: 1,255.8 persons per square mile (2010); Race: 96.5% White, 0.4% Black, 1.0% Asian, 0.9% American Indian/Alaska Native, 0.0% Native Hawaiian/Other Pacific Islander, 1.2% Other, 1.3% Hispanic of any race (2010); Average household size: 2.15 (2010); Median age: 47.1 (2010); Males per 100

females: 89.5 (2010); Marriage status: 25.7% never married, 55.6% now married, 10.2% widowed, 8.4% divorced (2006-2010 5-year est.); Foreign born: 6.2% (2006-2010 5-year est.); Ancestry (includes multiple ancestries): 23.1% Irish, 23.1% German, 21.5% English, 12.6% Italian, 12.5% French (2006-2010 5-year est.).

**Economy:** Employment by occupation: 11.5% management, 0.5% professional, 31.9% services, 16.2% sales, 7.3% farming, 1.3% construction, 1.0% production (2006-2010 5-year est.).

**Income:** Per capita income: $20,663 (2006-2010 5-year est.); Median household income: $29,792 (2006-2010 5-year est.); Average household income: $45,582 (2006-2010 5-year est.); Percent of households with income of $100,000 or more: 4.6% (2006-2010 5-year est.); Poverty rate: 9.6% (2006-2010 5-year est.).

**Education:** Percent of population age 25 and over with: High school diploma (including GED) or higher: 85.1% (2006-2010 5-year est.); Bachelor's degree or higher: 19.8% (2006-2010 5-year est.); Master's degree or higher: 8.6% (2006-2010 5-year est.).

### School District(s)
Richfield Springs Central School District (PK-12)
   2009-10 Enrollment: 583 . . . . . . . . . . . . . . . . . . . . . (315) 858-0610

**Housing:** Homeownership rate: 61.0% (2010); Median home value: $120,700 (2006-2010 5-year est.); Median contract rent: $407 per month (2006-2010 5-year est.); Median year structure built: before 1940 (2006-2010 5-year est.).

**Newspapers:** The Hall of Fame Pennysaver (Community news; Circulation 10,480); Richfield Springs Mercury (Community news); The Turnpike Pennysaver (Community news; Circulation 7,250)

**Transportation:** Commute to work: 90.9% car, 3.4% public transportation, 2.6% walk, 2.6% work from home (2006-2010 5-year est.); Travel time to work: 32.7% less than 15 minutes, 37.3% 15 to 30 minutes, 24.2% 30 to 45 minutes, 4.4% 45 to 60 minutes, 1.5% 60 minutes or more (2006-2010 5-year est.)

## ROSEBOOM (town). Covers a land area of 33.407 square miles and a water area of 0.104 square miles. Located at 42.72° N. Lat; 74.71° W. Long. Elevation is 1,289 feet.

**Population:** 668 (1990); 684 (2000); 711 (2010); Density: 21.3 persons per square mile (2010); Race: 97.7% White, 0.7% Black, 0.3% Asian, 0.3% American Indian/Alaska Native, 0.0% Native Hawaiian/Other Pacific Islander, 1.0% Other, 1.5% Hispanic of any race (2010); Average household size: 2.26 (2010); Median age: 46.5 (2010); Males per 100 females: 102.6 (2010); Marriage status: 19.5% never married, 70.8% now married, 3.9% widowed, 5.8% divorced (2006-2010 5-year est.); Foreign born: 1.9% (2006-2010 5-year est.); Ancestry (includes multiple ancestries): 29.8% German, 17.7% Dutch, 16.2% English, 15.1% Italian, 13.6% Irish (2006-2010 5-year est.).

**Economy:** Single-family building permits issued: 0 (2011); Multi-family building permits issued: 0 (2011); Employment by occupation: 3.3% management, 0.0% professional, 24.0% services, 9.3% sales, 1.3% farming, 17.9% construction, 7.1% production (2006-2010 5-year est.).

**Income:** Per capita income: $22,111 (2006-2010 5-year est.); Median household income: $48,594 (2006-2010 5-year est.); Average household income: $57,380 (2006-2010 5-year est.); Percent of households with income of $100,000 or more: 12.4% (2006-2010 5-year est.); Poverty rate: 6.7% (2006-2010 5-year est.).

**Education:** Percent of population age 25 and over with: High school diploma (including GED) or higher: 88.0% (2006-2010 5-year est.); Bachelor's degree or higher: 19.2% (2006-2010 5-year est.); Master's degree or higher: 11.1% (2006-2010 5-year est.).

**Housing:** Homeownership rate: 87.7% (2010); Median home value: $144,400 (2006-2010 5-year est.); Median contract rent: $419 per month (2006-2010 5-year est.); Median year structure built: 1971 (2006-2010 5-year est.).

**Transportation:** Commute to work: 95.2% car, 0.0% public transportation, 0.0% walk, 3.0% work from home (2006-2010 5-year est.); Travel time to work: 11.7% less than 15 minutes, 54.9% 15 to 30 minutes, 20.1% 30 to 45 minutes, 4.4% 45 to 60 minutes, 8.9% 60 minutes or more (2006-2010 5-year est.)

## SCHENEVUS (CDP). Covers a land area of 1.028 square miles and a water area of 0 square miles. Located at 42.54° N. Lat; 74.82° W. Long. Elevation is 1,302 feet.

**Population:** n/a (1990); n/a (2000); 551 (2010); Density: 535.7 persons per square mile (2010); Race: 97.1% White, 1.3% Black, 0.2% Asian, 0.0% American Indian/Alaska Native, 0.0% Native Hawaiian/Other Pacific

Islander, 1.4% Other, 1.8% Hispanic of any race (2010); Average household size: 2.30 (2010); Median age: 43.8 (2010); Males per 100 females: 88.7 (2010); Marriage status: 21.5% never married, 63.6% now married, 5.7% widowed, 9.3% divorced (2006-2010 5-year est.); Foreign born: 0.0% (2006-2010 5-year est.); Ancestry (includes multiple ancestries): 18.9% Irish, 18.2% German, 14.2% Dutch, 14.2% French Canadian, 12.4% English (2006-2010 5-year est.).

**Economy:** Employment by occupation: 11.2% management, 0.0% professional, 4.1% services, 15.3% sales, 0.0% farming, 8.8% construction, 9.4% production (2006-2010 5-year est.).

**Income:** Per capita income: $28,605 (2006-2010 5-year est.); Median household income: $52,500 (2006-2010 5-year est.); Average household income: $62,173 (2006-2010 5-year est.); Percent of households with income of $100,000 or more: 24.6% (2006-2010 5-year est.); Poverty rate: 8.7% (2006-2010 5-year est.).

**Education:** Percent of population age 25 and over with: High school diploma (including GED) or higher: 95.3% (2006-2010 5-year est.); Bachelor's degree or higher: 10.3% (2006-2010 5-year est.); Master's degree or higher: 9.4% (2006-2010 5-year est.).

**School District(s)**
Schenevus Central School District (PK-12)
    2009-10 Enrollment: 365 . . . . . . . . . . . . . . . . (607) 638-5530

**Housing:** Homeownership rate: 69.2% (2010); Median home value: $103,300 (2006-2010 5-year est.); Median contract rent: $581 per month (2006-2010 5-year est.); Median year structure built: before 1940 (2006-2010 5-year est.).

**Transportation:** Commute to work: 91.9% car, 0.0% public transportation, 0.0% walk, 8.1% work from home (2006-2010 5-year est.); Travel time to work: 0.0% less than 15 minutes, 43.9% 15 to 30 minutes, 19.6% 30 to 45 minutes, 14.2% 45 to 60 minutes, 22.3% 60 minutes or more (2006-2010 5-year est.)

**SPRINGFIELD** (town). Covers a land area of 42.894 square miles and a water area of 2.613 square miles. Located at 42.83° N. Lat; 74.86° W. Long. Elevation is 1,355 feet.

**Population:** 1,267 (1990); 1,350 (2000); 1,358 (2010); Density: 31.7 persons per square mile (2010); Race: 97.7% White, 0.8% Black, 0.4% Asian, 0.1% American Indian/Alaska Native, 0.0% Native Hawaiian/Other Pacific Islander, 1.0% Other, 1.0% Hispanic of any race (2010); Average household size: 2.39 (2010); Median age: 46.8 (2010); Males per 100 females: 105.8 (2010); Marriage status: 23.6% never married, 59.8% now married, 7.9% widowed, 8.7% divorced (2006-2010 5-year est.); Foreign born: 1.5% (2006-2010 5-year est.); Ancestry (includes multiple ancestries): 18.8% German, 17.1% American, 15.5% Irish, 12.5% English, 5.6% Dutch (2006-2010 5-year est.).

**Economy:** Employment by occupation: 18.1% management, 0.6% professional, 6.6% services, 10.4% sales, 4.1% farming, 12.7% construction, 6.6% production (2006-2010 5-year est.).

**Income:** Per capita income: $28,119 (2006-2010 5-year est.); Median household income: $48,261 (2006-2010 5-year est.); Average household income: $68,511 (2006-2010 5-year est.); Percent of households with income of $100,000 or more: 11.4% (2006-2010 5-year est.); Poverty rate: 11.7% (2006-2010 5-year est.).

**Education:** Percent of population age 25 and over with: High school diploma (including GED) or higher: 88.8% (2006-2010 5-year est.); Bachelor's degree or higher: 30.6% (2006-2010 5-year est.); Master's degree or higher: 14.2% (2006-2010 5-year est.).

**Housing:** Homeownership rate: 77.3% (2010); Median home value: $140,100 (2006-2010 5-year est.); Median contract rent: $496 per month (2006-2010 5-year est.); Median year structure built: before 1940 (2006-2010 5-year est.).

**Transportation:** Commute to work: 80.1% car, 0.0% public transportation, 5.7% walk, 11.3% work from home (2006-2010 5-year est.); Travel time to work: 29.0% less than 15 minutes, 36.3% 15 to 30 minutes, 23.4% 30 to 45 minutes, 5.3% 45 to 60 minutes, 5.9% 60 minutes or more (2006-2010 5-year est.)

**SPRINGFIELD CENTER** (unincorporated postal area)
Zip Code: 13468
    Covers a land area of 9.726 square miles and a water area of 0.108 square miles. Located at 42.84° N. Lat; 74.85° W. Long. Elevation is 1,260 feet. Population: 451 (2010); Density: 46.4 persons per square mile (2010); Race: 98.2% White, 0.0% Black, 0.0% Asian, 0.4% American Indian/Alaska Native, 0.0% Native Hawaiian/Other Pacific Islander, 1.4% Other, 1.1% Hispanic of any race (2010); Average

household size: 2.41 (2010); Median age: 47.7 (2010); Males per 100 females: 93.6 (2010); Homeownership rate: 72.2% (2010)

**UNADILLA** (village). Covers a land area of 1.036 square miles and a water area of 0.048 square miles. Located at 42.32° N. Lat; 75.31° W. Long. Elevation is 1,010 feet.

**Population:** 1,265 (1990); 1,127 (2000); 1,128 (2010); Density: 1,088.2 persons per square mile (2010); Race: 96.3% White, 1.1% Black, 0.7% Asian, 0.3% American Indian/Alaska Native, 0.0% Native Hawaiian/Other Pacific Islander, 1.6% Other, 2.2% Hispanic of any race (2010); Average household size: 2.37 (2010); Median age: 43.0 (2010); Males per 100 females: 90.9 (2010); Marriage status: 22.7% never married, 54.9% now married, 9.1% widowed, 13.4% divorced (2006-2010 5-year est.); Foreign born: 1.2% (2006-2010 5-year est.); Ancestry (includes multiple ancestries): 21.9% German, 18.5% English, 15.6% Irish, 10.8% Italian, 9.1% Scottish (2006-2010 5-year est.).

**Economy:** Employment by occupation: 7.1% management, 2.2% professional, 18.9% services, 18.9% sales, 0.9% farming, 7.8% construction, 6.9% production (2006-2010 5-year est.).

**Income:** Per capita income: $21,233 (2006-2010 5-year est.); Median household income: $41,813 (2006-2010 5-year est.); Average household income: $50,618 (2006-2010 5-year est.); Percent of households with income of $100,000 or more: 7.2% (2006-2010 5-year est.); Poverty rate: 14.0% (2006-2010 5-year est.).

**Education:** Percent of population age 25 and over with: High school diploma (including GED) or higher: 91.7% (2006-2010 5-year est.); Bachelor's degree or higher: 20.4% (2006-2010 5-year est.); Master's degree or higher: 10.3% (2006-2010 5-year est.).

**School District(s)**
Otego-Unadilla Central School District (KG-12)
    2009-10 Enrollment: 1,067 . . . . . . . . . . . . . . . . (607) 988-5038

**Housing:** Homeownership rate: 72.7% (2010); Median home value: $91,400 (2006-2010 5-year est.); Median contract rent: $363 per month (2006-2010 5-year est.); Median year structure built: before 1940 (2006-2010 5-year est.).

**Transportation:** Commute to work: 77.6% car, 0.0% public transportation, 14.6% walk, 3.9% work from home (2006-2010 5-year est.); Travel time to work: 39.6% less than 15 minutes, 37.9% 15 to 30 minutes, 15.7% 30 to 45 minutes, 0.0% 45 to 60 minutes, 6.8% 60 minutes or more (2006-2010 5-year est.)

**UNADILLA** (town). Covers a land area of 46.253 square miles and a water area of 0.418 square miles. Located at 42.36° N. Lat; 75.33° W. Long. Elevation is 1,010 feet.

**History:** During the early years of the Revolution, Native American villages in the vicinity of Unadilla were gathering places for Tories bent on destruction of frontier patriot settlements. In 1778, an American force destroyed the villages. The place began to grow with construction of the Catskill Turnpike soon after 1800. Settled in 1790, incorporated in 1827.

**Population:** 4,343 (1990); 4,548 (2000); 4,392 (2010); Density: 95.0 persons per square mile (2010); Race: 97.4% White, 0.8% Black, 0.3% Asian, 0.2% American Indian/Alaska Native, 0.0% Native Hawaiian/Other Pacific Islander, 1.3% Other, 2.1% Hispanic of any race (2010); Average household size: 2.37 (2010); Median age: 44.5 (2010); Males per 100 females: 98.0 (2010); Marriage status: 22.7% never married, 56.5% now married, 9.3% widowed, 11.5% divorced (2006-2010 5-year est.); Foreign born: 1.9% (2006-2010 5-year est.); Ancestry (includes multiple ancestries): 25.7% German, 20.9% Irish, 18.0% English, 11.2% American, 7.4% Scottish (2006-2010 5-year est.).

**Economy:** Employment by occupation: 7.2% management, 1.6% professional, 11.2% services, 21.8% sales, 1.9% farming, 9.9% construction, 12.1% production (2006-2010 5-year est.).

**Income:** Per capita income: $21,076 (2006-2010 5-year est.); Median household income: $45,900 (2006-2010 5-year est.); Average household income: $49,531 (2006-2010 5-year est.); Percent of households with income of $100,000 or more: 4.4% (2006-2010 5-year est.); Poverty rate: 9.5% (2006-2010 5-year est.).

**Education:** Percent of population age 25 and over with: High school diploma (including GED) or higher: 90.4% (2006-2010 5-year est.); Bachelor's degree or higher: 12.8% (2006-2010 5-year est.); Master's degree or higher: 5.4% (2006-2010 5-year est.).

**School District(s)**
Otego-Unadilla Central School District (KG-12)
    2009-10 Enrollment: 1,067 . . . . . . . . . . . . . . . . (607) 988-5038

**Housing:** Homeownership rate: 82.5% (2010); Median home value: $88,600 (2006-2010 5-year est.); Median contract rent: $399 per month (2006-2010 5-year est.); Median year structure built: 1965 (2006-2010 5-year est.).

**Transportation:** Commute to work: 92.3% car, 0.0% public transportation, 3.4% walk, 3.5% work from home (2006-2010 5-year est.); Travel time to work: 26.9% less than 15 minutes, 40.6% 15 to 30 minutes, 18.0% 30 to 45 minutes, 3.1% 45 to 60 minutes, 11.4% 60 minutes or more (2006-2010 5-year est.)

## WELLS BRIDGE (unincorporated postal area)
Zip Code: 13859

Covers a land area of 0.479 square miles and a water area of 0.030 square miles. Located at 42.37° N. Lat; 75.24° W. Long. Elevation is 1,043 feet. Population: 182 (2010); Density: 379.3 persons per square mile (2010); Race: 94.0% White, 2.2% Black, 0.0% Asian, 1.1% American Indian/Alaska Native, 0.0% Native Hawaiian/Other Pacific Islander, 2.7% Other, 6.0% Hispanic of any race (2010); Average household size: 2.28 (2010); Median age: 45.3 (2010); Males per 100 females: 104.5 (2010); Homeownership rate: 76.3% (2010)

## WEST EDMESTON (unincorporated postal area)
Zip Code: 13485

Covers a land area of 44.170 square miles and a water area of 0.160 square miles. Located at 42.78° N. Lat; 75.31° W. Long. Population: 1,132 (2010); Density: 25.6 persons per square mile (2010); Race: 97.3% White, 0.2% Black, 0.5% Asian, 1.1% American Indian/Alaska Native, 0.0% Native Hawaiian/Other Pacific Islander, 0.9% Other, 1.1% Hispanic of any race (2010); Average household size: 2.56 (2010); Median age: 44.1 (2010); Males per 100 females: 101.4 (2010); Homeownership rate: 86.2% (2010)

## WEST END (CDP). 
Covers a land area of 3.652 square miles and a water area of 0.075 square miles. Located at 42.47° N. Lat; 75.09° W. Long. Elevation is 1,476 feet.

**Population:** 1,728 (1990); 1,813 (2000); 1,940 (2010); Density: 531.1 persons per square mile (2010); Race: 94.7% White, 1.8% Black, 1.6% Asian, 0.2% American Indian/Alaska Native, 0.0% Native Hawaiian/Other Pacific Islander, 1.7% Other, 3.1% Hispanic of any race (2010); Average household size: 2.17 (2010); Median age: 46.6 (2010); Males per 100 females: 92.8 (2010); Marriage status: 32.0% never married, 41.5% now married, 8.1% widowed, 18.4% divorced (2006-2010 5-year est.); Foreign born: 20.3% (2006-2010 5-year est.); Ancestry (includes multiple ancestries): 20.6% German, 20.4% Italian, 12.8% Irish, 9.7% English, 5.8% American (2006-2010 5-year est.).

**Economy:** Employment by occupation: 4.2% management, 4.7% professional, 17.6% services, 17.1% sales, 4.4% farming, 8.6% construction, 7.7% production (2006-2010 5-year est.).

**Income:** Per capita income: $28,189 (2006-2010 5-year est.); Median household income: $42,396 (2006-2010 5-year est.); Average household income: $54,395 (2006-2010 5-year est.); Percent of households with income of $100,000 or more: 14.5% (2006-2010 5-year est.); Poverty rate: 6.1% (2006-2010 5-year est.).

**Education:** Percent of population age 25 and over with: High school diploma (including GED) or higher: 84.8% (2006-2010 5-year est.); Bachelor's degree or higher: 19.9% (2006-2010 5-year est.); Master's degree or higher: 12.9% (2006-2010 5-year est.).

**Housing:** Homeownership rate: 77.6% (2010); Median home value: $119,600 (2006-2010 5-year est.); Median contract rent: $446 per month (2006-2010 5-year est.); Median year structure built: 1963 (2006-2010 5-year est.).

**Transportation:** Commute to work: 83.9% car, 8.0% public transportation, 6.6% walk, 1.5% work from home (2006-2010 5-year est.); Travel time to work: 63.0% less than 15 minutes, 20.6% 15 to 30 minutes, 4.2% 30 to 45 minutes, 4.8% 45 to 60 minutes, 7.4% 60 minutes or more (2006-2010 5-year est.)

## WEST ONEONTA (unincorporated postal area)
Zip Code: 13861

Covers a land area of 4.409 square miles and a water area of 0.017 square miles. Located at 42.50° N. Lat; 75.15° W. Long. Elevation is 1,138 feet. Population: 432 (2010); Density: 98.0 persons per square mile (2010); Race: 94.0% White, 1.2% Black, 0.7% Asian, 0.2% American Indian/Alaska Native, 0.0% Native Hawaiian/Other Pacific Islander, 3.9% Other, 3.2% Hispanic of any race (2010); Average

household size: 2.56 (2010); Median age: 44.9 (2010); Males per 100 females: 100.0 (2010); Homeownership rate: 87.6% (2010)

## WESTFORD (town). 
Covers a land area of 33.853 square miles and a water area of 0.055 square miles. Located at 42.64° N. Lat; 74.81° W. Long. Elevation is 1,562 feet.

**Population:** 634 (1990); 784 (2000); 868 (2010); Density: 25.6 persons per square mile (2010); Race: 96.4% White, 0.3% Black, 0.8% Asian, 0.0% American Indian/Alaska Native, 0.0% Native Hawaiian/Other Pacific Islander, 2.5% Other, 2.4% Hispanic of any race (2010); Average household size: 2.48 (2010); Median age: 43.7 (2010); Males per 100 females: 99.5 (2010); Marriage status: 20.0% never married, 67.7% now married, 4.3% widowed, 8.0% divorced (2006-2010 5-year est.); Foreign born: 2.2% (2006-2010 5-year est.); Ancestry (includes multiple ancestries): 28.4% German, 16.0% American, 14.8% English, 14.7% Italian, 12.8% Irish (2006-2010 5-year est.).

**Economy:** Employment by occupation: 16.5% management, 2.1% professional, 11.9% services, 14.7% sales, 4.4% farming, 14.2% construction, 11.0% production (2006-2010 5-year est.).

**Income:** Per capita income: $25,496 (2006-2010 5-year est.); Median household income: $46,250 (2006-2010 5-year est.); Average household income: $58,607 (2006-2010 5-year est.); Percent of households with income of $100,000 or more: 13.8% (2006-2010 5-year est.); Poverty rate: 15.2% (2006-2010 5-year est.).

**Education:** Percent of population age 25 and over with: High school diploma (including GED) or higher: 87.8% (2006-2010 5-year est.); Bachelor's degree or higher: 21.4% (2006-2010 5-year est.); Master's degree or higher: 9.5% (2006-2010 5-year est.).

**Housing:** Homeownership rate: 90.3% (2010); Median home value: $115,900 (2006-2010 5-year est.); Median contract rent: $429 per month (2006-2010 5-year est.); Median year structure built: 1960 (2006-2010 5-year est.).

**Transportation:** Commute to work: 82.6% car, 0.0% public transportation, 1.4% walk, 15.0% work from home (2006-2010 5-year est.); Travel time to work: 18.8% less than 15 minutes, 43.1% 15 to 30 minutes, 20.7% 30 to 45 minutes, 10.2% 45 to 60 minutes, 7.2% 60 minutes or more (2006-2010 5-year est.)

## WORCESTER (town). 
Covers a land area of 46.710 square miles and a water area of 0.163 square miles. Located at 42.58° N. Lat; 74.72° W. Long. Elevation is 1,335 feet.

**Population:** 2,070 (1990); 2,207 (2000); 2,220 (2010); Density: 47.5 persons per square mile (2010); Race: 95.5% White, 0.6% Black, 0.3% Asian, 0.3% American Indian/Alaska Native, 0.1% Native Hawaiian/Other Pacific Islander, 3.2% Other, 4.6% Hispanic of any race (2010); Average household size: 2.33 (2010); Median age: 45.2 (2010); Males per 100 females: 97.9 (2010); Marriage status: 32.0% never married, 53.7% now married, 7.1% widowed, 7.1% divorced (2006-2010 5-year est.); Foreign born: 1.3% (2006-2010 5-year est.); Ancestry (includes multiple ancestries): 20.8% German, 15.8% English, 14.9% Irish, 10.3% American, 10.3% Dutch (2006-2010 5-year est.).

**Economy:** Employment by occupation: 8.2% management, 3.0% professional, 11.4% services, 14.8% sales, 5.5% farming, 10.5% construction, 5.7% production (2006-2010 5-year est.).

**Income:** Per capita income: $19,573 (2006-2010 5-year est.); Median household income: $43,429 (2006-2010 5-year est.); Average household income: $49,322 (2006-2010 5-year est.); Percent of households with income of $100,000 or more: 10.6% (2006-2010 5-year est.); Poverty rate: 12.4% (2006-2010 5-year est.).

**Education:** Percent of population age 25 and over with: High school diploma (including GED) or higher: 89.6% (2006-2010 5-year est.); Bachelor's degree or higher: 18.5% (2006-2010 5-year est.); Master's degree or higher: 6.8% (2006-2010 5-year est.).

**School District(s)**
Worcester Central School District (PK-12)
   2009-10 Enrollment: 406 . . . . . . . . . . . . . . . . . . . . . . . (607) 397-8785

**Housing:** Homeownership rate: 77.5% (2010); Median home value: $112,500 (2006-2010 5-year est.); Median contract rent: $459 per month (2006-2010 5-year est.); Median year structure built: before 1940 (2006-2010 5-year est.).

**Transportation:** Commute to work: 89.7% car, 0.4% public transportation, 6.4% walk, 3.6% work from home (2006-2010 5-year est.); Travel time to work: 22.1% less than 15 minutes, 26.5% 15 to 30 minutes, 33.3% 30 to 45 minutes, 8.3% 45 to 60 minutes, 9.8% 60 minutes or more (2006-2010 5-year est.)

## WORCESTER (CDP).

**WORCESTER** (CDP). Covers a land area of 8.562 square miles and a water area of 0.045 square miles. Located at 42.61° N. Lat; 74.73° W. Long. Elevation is 1,335 feet.

**Population:** n/a (1990); n/a (2000); 1,113 (2010); Density: 130.0 persons per square mile (2010); Race: 96.0% White, 0.6% Black, 0.2% Asian, 0.1% American Indian/Alaska Native, 0.3% Native Hawaiian/Other Pacific Islander, 2.8% Other, 4.4% Hispanic of any race (2010); Average household size: 2.35 (2010); Median age: 45.6 (2010); Males per 100 females: 90.9 (2010); Marriage status: 30.5% never married, 53.5% now married, 6.8% widowed, 9.2% divorced (2006-2010 5-year est.); Foreign born: 1.3% (2006-2010 5-year est.); Ancestry (includes multiple ancestries): 27.5% German, 17.7% English, 12.3% Irish, 12.1% Dutch, 11.0% American (2006-2010 5-year est.).

**Economy:** Employment by occupation: 8.4% management, 2.6% professional, 13.8% services, 16.9% sales, 5.8% farming, 6.7% construction, 4.7% production (2006-2010 5-year est.).

**Income:** Per capita income: $20,521 (2006-2010 5-year est.); Median household income: $44,271 (2006-2010 5-year est.); Average household income: $52,592 (2006-2010 5-year est.); Percent of households with income of $100,000 or more: 13.8% (2006-2010 5-year est.); Poverty rate: 13.9% (2006-2010 5-year est.).

**Education:** Percent of population age 25 and over with: High school diploma (including GED) or higher: 94.6% (2006-2010 5-year est.); Bachelor's degree or higher: 17.9% (2006-2010 5-year est.); Master's degree or higher: 5.4% (2006-2010 5-year est.).

### School District(s)
Worcester Central School District (PK-12)

    2009-10 Enrollment: 406 . . . . . . . . . . . . . . . . . . . . . . . . (607) 397-8785

**Housing:** Homeownership rate: 74.9% (2010); Median home value: $128,500 (2006-2010 5-year est.); Median contract rent: $454 per month (2006-2010 5-year est.); Median year structure built: before 1940 (2006-2010 5-year est.).

**Transportation:** Commute to work: 92.8% car, 0.0% public transportation, 4.8% walk, 2.5% work from home (2006-2010 5-year est.); Travel time to work: 20.6% less than 15 minutes, 25.7% 15 to 30 minutes, 35.6% 30 to 45 minutes, 6.0% 45 to 60 minutes, 12.2% 60 minutes or more (2006-2010 5-year est.)

# Putnam County

Located in southeastern New York; bounded on the west by the Hudson River, and on the east by Connecticut; includes part of the Taconic Mountains. Covers a land area of 231.28 square miles, a water area of 14.97 square miles, and is located in the Eastern Time Zone at 41.41° N. Lat., 73.73° W. Long. The county was founded in 1812. County seat is Carmel.

Putnam County is part of the New York-Northern New Jersey-Long Island, NY-NJ-PA Metropolitan Statistical Area. The entire metro area includes: Edison-New Brunswick, NJ Metropolitan Division (Middlesex County, NJ; Monmouth County, NJ; Ocean County, NJ; Somerset County, NJ); Nassau-Suffolk, NY Metropolitan Division (Nassau County, NY; Suffolk County, NY); New York-White Plains-Wayne, NY-NJ Metropolitan Division (Bergen County, NJ; Hudson County, NJ; Passaic County, NJ; Bronx County, NY; Kings County, NY; New York County, NY; Putnam County, NY; Queens County, NY; Richmond County, NY; Rockland County, NY; Westchester County, NY); Newark-Union, NJ-PA Metropolitan Division (Essex County, NJ; Hunterdon County, NJ; Morris County, NJ; Sussex County, NJ; Union County, NJ; Pike County, PA)

**Population:** 83,941 (1990); 95,745 (2000); 99,710 (2010); Race: 90.7% White, 2.4% Black, 1.9% Asian, 0.2% American Indian/Alaska Native, 0.0% Native Hawaiian/Other Pacific Islander, 4.8% Other, 11.7% Hispanic of any race (2010); Density: 431.1 persons per square mile (2010); Average household size: 2.77 (2010); Median age: 41.9 (2010); Males per 100 females: 99.7 (2010).

**Religion:** Six largest groups: 41.5% Catholicism, 1.2% Methodist/Pietist, 1.2% Lutheran, 1.2% Judaism, 1.0% Episcopalianism/Anglicanism, 0.8% Presbyterian-Reformed (2010)

**Economy:** Unemployment rate: 7.0% (February 2012); Total civilian labor force: 53,292 (February 2012); Leading industries: 20.6% health care and social assistance; 14.0% retail trade; 10.9% construction (2009); Farms: 72 totaling 5,635 acres (2007); Companies that employ 500 or more persons: 1 (2009); Companies that employ 100 to 499 persons: 24 (2009); Companies that employ less than 100 persons: 2,901 (2009); Black-owned businesses: 591 (2007); Hispanic-owned businesses: 710 (2007); Asian-owned businesses: 223 (2007); Women-owned businesses: 3,180 (2007); Retail sales per capita: $8,750 (2010). Single-family building permits issued: 38 (2011); Multi-family building permits issued: 113 (2011).

**Income:** Per capita income: $37,915 (2006-2010 5-year est.); Median household income: $89,218 (2006-2010 5-year est.); Average household income: $108,365 (2006-2010 5-year est.); Percent of households with income of $100,000 or more: 43.3% (2006-2010 5-year est.); Poverty rate: 7.0% (2006-2010 5-year est.); Bankruptcy rate: 2.84% (2011).

**Taxes:** Total county taxes per capita: $903 (2009); County property taxes per capita: $352 (2009).

**Education:** Percent of population age 25 and over with: High school diploma (including GED) or higher: 93.7% (2006-2010 5-year est.); Bachelor's degree or higher: 38.0% (2006-2010 5-year est.); Master's degree or higher: 16.0% (2006-2010 5-year est.).

**Housing:** Homeownership rate: 81.9% (2010); Median home value: $418,100 (2006-2010 5-year est.); Median contract rent: $1,092 per month (2006-2010 5-year est.); Median year structure built: 1967 (2006-2010 5-year est.)

**Health:** Birth rate: 86.7 per 10,000 population (2011); Death rate: 63.5 per 10,000 population (2011); Age-adjusted cancer mortality rate: 168.1 deaths per 100,000 population (2009); Number of physicians: 19.2 per 10,000 population (2008); Hospital beds: 27.6 per 10,000 population (2007); Hospital admissions: 1,112.6 per 10,000 population (2007).

**Environment:** Air Quality Index: 89.9% good, 9.0% moderate, 1.1% unhealthy for sensitive individuals, 0.0% unhealthy (percent of days in 2010)

**Elections:** 2008 Presidential election results: 45.7% Obama, 53.2% McCain, 0.5% Nader

**National and State Parks:** Appalachian National Scenic Trail; Clarence Fahnestock Memorial State Park

**Additional Information Contacts**

Putnam County Government . . . . . . . . . . . . . . . . . . . . . . (845) 225-3641
   http://www.putnamcountyny.com
Brewster Chamber of Commerce . . . . . . . . . . . . . . . . . (845) 279-2477
   http://www.brewsterchamber.com
Greater Mahopac-Carmel Chamber of Commerce . . . . . (845) 628-5553
   http://www.mahopaccarmelonline.com
Patterson Chamber of Commerce . . . . . . . . . . . . . . . . . (845) 363-6304
   http://www.pcofc.org
Town of Carmel . . . . . . . . . . . . . . . . . . . . . . . . . . . . . . (845) 628-1500
   http://www.ci.carmel.ny.us
Town of Kent . . . . . . . . . . . . . . . . . . . . . . . . . . . . . . . . (845) 225-3943
   http://www.townofkentny.com
Town of Patterson . . . . . . . . . . . . . . . . . . . . . . . . . . . . (845) 878-6500
   http://www.pattersonny.org
Town of Putnam Valley . . . . . . . . . . . . . . . . . . . . . . . . . (845) 526-2121
   http://www.putnamvalley.com
Town of Southeast . . . . . . . . . . . . . . . . . . . . . . . . . . . . (845) 279-4313
   http://www.townofsoutheast-ny.com/Home

# Putnam County Communities

**BREWSTER** (village). Covers a land area of 0.467 square miles and a water area of 0.004 square miles. Located at 41.39° N. Lat; 73.61° W. Long. Elevation is 466 feet.

**History:** Jurist James Kent born nearby, 1763. Settled 1850, incorporated 1894.

**Population:** 1,566 (1990); 2,162 (2000); 2,390 (2010); Density: 5,115.4 persons per square mile (2010); Race: 75.7% White, 2.9% Black, 3.4% Asian, 0.6% American Indian/Alaska Native, 0.5% Native Hawaiian/Other Pacific Islander, 16.9% Other, 56.0% Hispanic of any race (2010); Average household size: 2.73 (2010); Median age: 32.7 (2010); Males per 100 females: 161.2 (2010); Marriage status: 33.0% never married, 53.0% now married, 4.2% widowed, 9.8% divorced (2006-2010 5-year est.); Foreign born: 36.0% (2006-2010 5-year est.); Ancestry (includes multiple ancestries): 17.6% Irish, 12.8% Italian, 8.8% German, 6.5% Trinidadian and Tobagonian, 5.1% English (2006-2010 5-year est.).

**Economy:** Single-family building permits issued: 0 (2011); Multi-family building permits issued: 0 (2011); Employment by occupation: 6.5% management, 0.7% professional, 17.0% services, 14.2% sales, 4.5% farming, 14.7% construction, 3.4% production (2006-2010 5-year est.).

**Income:** Per capita income: $23,155 (2006-2010 5-year est.); Median household income: $53,542 (2006-2010 5-year est.); Average household income: $60,973 (2006-2010 5-year est.); Percent of households with

income of $100,000 or more: 17.0% (2006-2010 5-year est.); Poverty rate: 13.5% (2006-2010 5-year est.).
**Education:** Percent of population age 25 and over with: High school diploma (including GED) or higher: 68.1% (2006-2010 5-year est.); Bachelor's degree or higher: 18.7% (2006-2010 5-year est.); Master's degree or higher: 5.0% (2006-2010 5-year est.).

**School District(s)**
Brewster Central School District (KG-12)
   2009-10 Enrollment: 3,497 . . . . . . . . . . . . . . . . . . . . (845) 279-8000
**Housing:** Homeownership rate: 22.5% (2010); Median home value: $346,200 (2006-2010 5-year est.); Median contract rent: $1,004 per month (2006-2010 5-year est.); Median year structure built: 1948 (2006-2010 5-year est.).
**Safety:** Violent crime rate: 0.0 per 10,000 population; Property crime rate: 33.5 per 10,000 population (2010).
**Transportation:** Commute to work: 77.7% car, 11.8% public transportation, 10.5% walk, 0.0% work from home (2006-2010 5-year est.); Travel time to work: 21.4% less than 15 minutes, 41.0% 15 to 30 minutes, 15.2% 30 to 45 minutes, 5.3% 45 to 60 minutes, 17.2% 60 minutes or more (2006-2010 5-year est.)
**Additional Information Contacts**
Brewster Chamber of Commerce . . . . . . . . . . . . . . . . . . . (845) 279-2477
   http://www.brewsterchamber.com

**BREWSTER HILL** (CDP). Aka Tonetta Lake Heights. Covers a land area of 0.870 square miles and a water area of 0.110 square miles. Located at 41.42° N. Lat; 73.60° W. Long. Elevation is 617 feet.
**Population:** 2,226 (1990); 2,226 (2000); 2,089 (2010); Density: 2,400.5 persons per square mile (2010); Race: 92.0% White, 2.0% Black, 2.2% Asian, 0.0% American Indian/Alaska Native, 0.0% Native Hawaiian/Other Pacific Islander, 3.8% Other, 11.6% Hispanic of any race (2010); Average household size: 2.84 (2010); Median age: 43.1 (2010); Males per 100 females: 98.0 (2010); Marriage status: 30.5% never married, 49.7% now married, 8.3% widowed, 11.5% divorced (2006-2010 5-year est.); Foreign born: 15.8% (2006-2010 5-year est.); Ancestry (includes multiple ancestries): 30.4% Italian, 24.0% Irish, 11.4% German, 6.0% Scottish, 5.1% French Canadian (2006-2010 5-year est.).
**Economy:** Employment by occupation: 7.0% management, 1.7% professional, 6.6% services, 16.6% sales, 3.0% farming, 17.0% construction, 3.9% production (2006-2010 5-year est.).
**Income:** Per capita income: $37,638 (2006-2010 5-year est.); Median household income: $91,504 (2006-2010 5-year est.); Average household income: $100,515 (2006-2010 5-year est.); Percent of households with income of $100,000 or more: 44.0% (2006-2010 5-year est.); Poverty rate: 4.5% (2006-2010 5-year est.).
**Education:** Percent of population age 25 and over with: High school diploma (including GED) or higher: 92.0% (2006-2010 5-year est.); Bachelor's degree or higher: 21.3% (2006-2010 5-year est.); Master's degree or higher: 5.9% (2006-2010 5-year est.).
**Housing:** Homeownership rate: 91.0% (2010); Median home value: $360,800 (2006-2010 5-year est.); Median contract rent: $1,340 per month (2006-2010 5-year est.); Median year structure built: 1958 (2006-2010 5-year est.).
**Transportation:** Commute to work: 86.9% car, 5.6% public transportation, 0.0% walk, 3.8% work from home (2006-2010 5-year est.); Travel time to work: 36.4% less than 15 minutes, 22.3% 15 to 30 minutes, 13.6% 30 to 45 minutes, 11.2% 45 to 60 minutes, 16.5% 60 minutes or more (2006-2010 5-year est.)

**CARMEL** (town). County seat. Covers a land area of 35.906 square miles and a water area of 4.786 square miles. Located at 41.38° N. Lat; 73.72° W. Long. Elevation is 561 feet.
**Population:** 28,816 (1990); 33,006 (2000); 34,305 (2010); Density: 955.4 persons per square mile (2010); Race: 92.1% White, 2.0% Black, 1.8% Asian, 0.1% American Indian/Alaska Native, 0.0% Native Hawaiian/Other Pacific Islander, 4.0% Other, 10.1% Hispanic of any race (2010); Average household size: 2.90 (2010); Median age: 41.3 (2010); Males per 100 females: 98.4 (2010); Marriage status: 24.6% never married, 65.5% now married, 4.4% widowed, 5.5% divorced (2006-2010 5-year est.); Foreign born: 11.2% (2006-2010 5-year est.); Ancestry (includes multiple ancestries): 36.1% Italian, 26.4% Irish, 17.5% German, 6.7% Polish, 5.6% English (2006-2010 5-year est.).
**Economy:** Unemployment rate: 7.0% (February 2012); Total civilian labor force: 18,307 (February 2012); Single-family building permits issued: 7 (2011); Multi-family building permits issued: 101 (2011); Employment by

occupation: 14.4% management, 4.9% professional, 6.2% services, 17.0% sales, 3.1% farming, 9.1% construction, 3.9% production (2006-2010 5-year est.).
**Income:** Per capita income: $39,060 (2006-2010 5-year est.); Median household income: $98,226 (2006-2010 5-year est.); Average household income: $114,496 (2006-2010 5-year est.); Percent of households with income of $100,000 or more: 48.8% (2006-2010 5-year est.); Poverty rate: 3.4% (2006-2010 5-year est.).
**Taxes:** Total city taxes per capita: $613 (2009); City property taxes per capita: $544 (2009).
**Education:** Percent of population age 25 and over with: High school diploma (including GED) or higher: 93.4% (2006-2010 5-year est.); Bachelor's degree or higher: 39.7% (2006-2010 5-year est.); Master's degree or higher: 16.7% (2006-2010 5-year est.).

**School District(s)**
Carmel Central School District (KG-12)
   2009-10 Enrollment: 4,630 . . . . . . . . . . . . . . . . . . . . . (845) 878-2094
**Housing:** Homeownership rate: 82.8% (2010); Median home value: $459,200 (2006-2010 5-year est.); Median contract rent: $1,141 per month (2006-2010 5-year est.); Median year structure built: 1969 (2006-2010 5-year est.).
**Hospitals:** Arms Acres (129 beds); Putnam Hospital Center (164 beds)
**Safety:** Violent crime rate: 3.5 per 10,000 population; Property crime rate: 79.7 per 10,000 population (2010).
**Newspapers:** The Journal News - Putnam County Edition (Regional news); Putnam County Courier (Community news; Circulation 6,000)
**Transportation:** Commute to work: 89.7% car, 4.8% public transportation, 1.2% walk, 3.7% work from home (2006-2010 5-year est.); Travel time to work: 20.5% less than 15 minutes, 22.9% 15 to 30 minutes, 24.4% 30 to 45 minutes, 13.6% 45 to 60 minutes, 18.6% 60 minutes or more (2006-2010 5-year est.)
**Additional Information Contacts**
Town of Carmel . . . . . . . . . . . . . . . . . . . . . . . . . . . . . . . . (845) 628-1500
   http://www.ci.carmel.ny.us

**CARMEL HAMLET** (CDP). Covers a land area of 8.335 square miles and a water area of 2.055 square miles. Located at 41.42° N. Lat; 73.68° W. Long.
**Population:** 4,800 (1990); 5,650 (2000); 6,817 (2010); Density: 817.8 persons per square mile (2010); Race: 90.3% White, 3.0% Black, 1.9% Asian, 0.2% American Indian/Alaska Native, 0.0% Native Hawaiian/Other Pacific Islander, 4.6% Other, 13.1% Hispanic of any race (2010); Average household size: 2.78 (2010); Median age: 40.9 (2010); Males per 100 females: 98.6 (2010); Marriage status: 26.1% never married, 63.8% now married, 5.3% widowed, 4.7% divorced (2006-2010 5-year est.); Foreign born: 9.5% (2006-2010 5-year est.); Ancestry (includes multiple ancestries): 30.6% Irish, 29.9% Italian, 16.5% German, 6.5% Polish, 5.4% English (2006-2010 5-year est.).
**Economy:** Employment by occupation: 18.5% management, 7.7% professional, 5.5% services, 14.0% sales, 3.2% farming, 8.2% construction, 4.1% production (2006-2010 5-year est.).
**Income:** Per capita income: $36,456 (2006-2010 5-year est.); Median household income: $94,151 (2006-2010 5-year est.); Average household income: $112,122 (2006-2010 5-year est.); Percent of households with income of $100,000 or more: 46.5% (2006-2010 5-year est.); Poverty rate: 5.5% (2006-2010 5-year est.).
**Education:** Percent of population age 25 and over with: High school diploma (including GED) or higher: 93.8% (2006-2010 5-year est.); Bachelor's degree or higher: 40.0% (2006-2010 5-year est.); Master's degree or higher: 14.8% (2006-2010 5-year est.).
**Housing:** Homeownership rate: 75.6% (2010); Median home value: $470,500 (2006-2010 5-year est.); Median contract rent: $1,078 per month (2006-2010 5-year est.); Median year structure built: 1975 (2006-2010 5-year est.).
**Transportation:** Commute to work: 83.5% car, 8.1% public transportation, 0.6% walk, 7.9% work from home (2006-2010 5-year est.); Travel time to work: 17.5% less than 15 minutes, 22.3% 15 to 30 minutes, 15.3% 30 to 45 minutes, 19.2% 45 to 60 minutes, 25.7% 60 minutes or more (2006-2010 5-year est.)

**COLD SPRING** (village). Covers a land area of 0.593 square miles and a water area of 0.005 square miles. Located at 41.41° N. Lat; 73.95° W. Long. Elevation is 115 feet.
**History:** Settled before the American Revolution; incorporated 1846.

**Population:** 1,998 (1990); 1,983 (2000); 2,013 (2010); Density: 3,390.5 persons per square mile (2010); Race: 93.2% White, 0.7% Black, 2.0% Asian, 0.3% Native Hawaiian/Other Pacific Islander, 3.7% Other, 5.8% Hispanic of any race (2010); Average household size: 2.21 (2010); Median age: 46.4 (2010); Males per 100 females: 90.6 (2010); Marriage status: 15.5% never married, 59.4% now married, 13.2% widowed, 11.8% divorced (2006-2010 5-year est.); Foreign born: 4.5% (2006-2010 5-year est.); Ancestry (includes multiple ancestries): 44.5% Irish, 22.0% Italian, 18.2% German, 15.8% English, 5.5% Dutch (2006-2010 5-year est.).
**Economy:** Single-family building permits issued: 0 (2011); Multi-family building permits issued: 0 (2011); Employment by occupation: 15.9% management, 7.0% professional, 11.0% services, 13.7% sales, 2.3% farming, 5.8% construction, 2.1% production (2006-2010 5-year est.).
**Income:** Per capita income: $37,614 (2006-2010 5-year est.); Median household income: $63,000 (2006-2010 5-year est.); Average household income: $76,986 (2006-2010 5-year est.); Percent of households with income of $100,000 or more: 29.1% (2006-2010 5-year est.); Poverty rate: 3.7% (2006-2010 5-year est.).
**Education:** Percent of population age 25 and over with: High school diploma (including GED) or higher: 96.0% (2006-2010 5-year est.); Bachelor's degree or higher: 43.7% (2006-2010 5-year est.); Master's degree or higher: 20.3% (2006-2010 5-year est.).

**School District(s)**
Haldane Central School District (KG-12)
    2009-10 Enrollment: 902 . . . . . . . . . . . . . . . . . . . . . (845) 265-9254
**Housing:** Homeownership rate: 62.1% (2010); Median home value: $432,100 (2006-2010 5-year est.); Median contract rent: $685 per month (2006-2010 5-year est.); Median year structure built: 1940 (2006-2010 5-year est.).
**Newspapers:** Putnam County News And Recorder (Community news; Circulation 4,200)
**Transportation:** Commute to work: 48.4% car, 33.6% public transportation, 5.1% walk, 12.9% work from home (2006-2010 5-year est.); Travel time to work: 28.4% less than 15 minutes, 11.1% 15 to 30 minutes, 7.8% 30 to 45 minutes, 7.6% 45 to 60 minutes, 45.1% 60 minutes or more (2006-2010 5-year est.)

**GARRISON** (unincorporated postal area)
Zip Code: 10524
    Covers a land area of 20.801 square miles and a water area of 0.324 square miles. Located at 41.37° N. Lat; 73.92° W. Long. Elevation is 49 feet. Population: 4,421 (2010); Density: 212.5 persons per square mile (2010); Race: 92.7% White, 2.6% Black, 1.1% Asian, 0.1% American Indian/Alaska Native, 0.1% Native Hawaiian/Other Pacific Islander, 3.4% Other, 8.1% Hispanic of any race (2010); Average household size: 2.67 (2010); Median age: 45.6 (2010); Males per 100 females: 95.4 (2010); Homeownership rate: 85.4% (2010)

**KENT** (town). Covers a land area of 40.503 square miles and a water area of 2.822 square miles. Located at 41.45° N. Lat; 73.72° W. Long.
**Population:** 13,183 (1990); 14,009 (2000); 13,507 (2010); Density: 333.5 persons per square mile (2010); Race: 89.6% White, 2.6% Black, 1.9% Asian, 0.3% American Indian/Alaska Native, 0.0% Native Hawaiian/Other Pacific Islander, 5.6% Other, 13.0% Hispanic of any race (2010); Average household size: 2.72 (2010); Median age: 42.8 (2010); Males per 100 females: 98.9 (2010); Marriage status: 24.4% never married, 64.4% now married, 4.6% widowed, 6.6% divorced (2006-2010 5-year est.); Foreign born: 8.5% (2006-2010 5-year est.); Ancestry (includes multiple ancestries): 36.2% Italian, 30.7% Irish, 19.7% German, 6.8% English, 5.4% Polish (2006-2010 5-year est.).
**Economy:** Single-family building permits issued: 4 (2011); Multi-family building permits issued: 0 (2011); Employment by occupation: 12.8% management, 2.6% professional, 4.0% services, 21.1% sales, 3.4% farming, 10.9% construction, 4.8% production (2006-2010 5-year est.).
**Income:** Per capita income: $37,919 (2006-2010 5-year est.); Median household income: $86,458 (2006-2010 5-year est.); Average household income: $104,217 (2006-2010 5-year est.); Percent of households with income of $100,000 or more: 42.1% (2006-2010 5-year est.); Poverty rate: 3.4% (2006-2010 5-year est.).
**Taxes:** Total city taxes per capita: $1,020 (2009); City property taxes per capita: $967 (2009).
**Education:** Percent of population age 25 and over with: High school diploma (including GED) or higher: 94.8% (2006-2010 5-year est.);

Bachelor's degree or higher: 32.2% (2006-2010 5-year est.); Master's degree or higher: 14.3% (2006-2010 5-year est.).
**Housing:** Homeownership rate: 84.9% (2010); Median home value: $351,000 (2006-2010 5-year est.); Median contract rent: $1,022 per month (2006-2010 5-year est.); Median year structure built: 1961 (2006-2010 5-year est.).
**Safety:** Violent crime rate: 3.6 per 10,000 population; Property crime rate: 65.0 per 10,000 population (2010).
**Transportation:** Commute to work: 86.8% car, 8.1% public transportation, 1.1% walk, 3.9% work from home (2006-2010 5-year est.); Travel time to work: 16.0% less than 15 minutes, 26.4% 15 to 30 minutes, 19.1% 30 to 45 minutes, 10.3% 45 to 60 minutes, 28.2% 60 minutes or more (2006-2010 5-year est.)
**Additional Information Contacts**
Town of Kent . . . . . . . . . . . . . . . . . . . . . . . . . . . . . (845) 225-3943
    http://www.townofkentny.com

**LAKE CARMEL** (CDP). Covers a land area of 5.161 square miles and a water area of 0.332 square miles. Located at 41.46° N. Lat; 73.66° W. Long. Elevation is 801 feet.
**Population:** 8,482 (1990); 8,663 (2000); 8,282 (2010); Density: 1,604.7 persons per square mile (2010); Race: 89.1% White, 2.6% Black, 1.7% Asian, 0.4% American Indian/Alaska Native, 0.0% Native Hawaiian/Other Pacific Islander, 6.2% Other, 15.1% Hispanic of any race (2010); Average household size: 2.72 (2010); Median age: 41.5 (2010); Males per 100 females: 99.9 (2010); Marriage status: 23.4% never married, 66.8% now married, 3.7% widowed, 6.1% divorced (2006-2010 5-year est.); Foreign born: 8.6% (2006-2010 5-year est.); Ancestry (includes multiple ancestries): 36.3% Italian, 32.2% Irish, 19.5% German, 5.2% English, 4.3% Polish (2006-2010 5-year est.).
**Economy:** Employment by occupation: 9.0% management, 3.9% professional, 4.6% services, 24.6% sales, 4.2% farming, 12.4% construction, 5.6% production (2006-2010 5-year est.).
**Income:** Per capita income: $33,776 (2006-2010 5-year est.); Median household income: $78,340 (2006-2010 5-year est.); Average household income: $88,967 (2006-2010 5-year est.); Percent of households with income of $100,000 or more: 32.2% (2006-2010 5-year est.); Poverty rate: 4.2% (2006-2010 5-year est.).
**Education:** Percent of population age 25 and over with: High school diploma (including GED) or higher: 95.4% (2006-2010 5-year est.); Bachelor's degree or higher: 24.6% (2006-2010 5-year est.); Master's degree or higher: 9.4% (2006-2010 5-year est.).
**Housing:** Homeownership rate: 85.8% (2010); Median home value: $317,400 (2006-2010 5-year est.); Median contract rent: $1,122 per month (2006-2010 5-year est.); Median year structure built: 1956 (2006-2010 5-year est.).
**Transportation:** Commute to work: 89.9% car, 6.8% public transportation, 0.6% walk, 2.6% work from home (2006-2010 5-year est.); Travel time to work: 21.0% less than 15 minutes, 25.7% 15 to 30 minutes, 16.1% 30 to 45 minutes, 12.8% 45 to 60 minutes, 24.5% 60 minutes or more (2006-2010 5-year est.)

**LAKE PEEKSKILL** (unincorporated postal area)
Zip Code: 10537
    Covers a land area of 1.076 square miles and a water area of 0.095 square miles. Located at 41.33° N. Lat; 73.88° W. Long. Elevation is 315 feet. Population: 2,416 (2010); Density: 2,243.4 persons per square mile (2010); Race: 85.8% White, 5.3% Black, 1.6% Asian, 0.1% American Indian/Alaska Native, 0.0% Native Hawaiian/Other Pacific Islander, 7.2% Other, 15.2% Hispanic of any race (2010); Average household size: 2.63 (2010); Median age: 39.7 (2010); Males per 100 females: 101.0 (2010); Homeownership rate: 79.6% (2010)

**MAHOPAC** (CDP). Covers a land area of 5.279 square miles and a water area of 1.171 square miles. Located at 41.36° N. Lat; 73.74° W. Long. Elevation is 666 feet.
**Population:** 7,688 (1990); 8,478 (2000); 8,369 (2010); Density: 1,585.2 persons per square mile (2010); Race: 91.1% White, 2.1% Black, 2.0% Asian, 0.1% American Indian/Alaska Native, 0.0% Native Hawaiian/Other Pacific Islander, 4.7% Other, 10.9% Hispanic of any race (2010); Average household size: 2.74 (2010); Median age: 41.4 (2010); Males per 100 females: 101.2 (2010); Marriage status: 26.4% never married, 59.9% now married, 6.8% widowed, 6.9% divorced (2006-2010 5-year est.); Foreign born: 14.0% (2006-2010 5-year est.); Ancestry (includes multiple

ancestries): 38.3% Italian, 25.8% Irish, 14.7% German, 10.7% Polish, 7.8% English (2006-2010 5-year est.).
**Economy:** Employment by occupation: 14.0% management, 3.1% professional, 7.0% services, 15.4% sales, 2.9% farming, 11.5% construction, 5.7% production (2006-2010 5-year est.).
**Income:** Per capita income: $42,689 (2006-2010 5-year est.); Median household income: $88,708 (2006-2010 5-year est.); Average household income: $111,070 (2006-2010 5-year est.); Percent of households with income of $100,000 or more: 43.2% (2006-2010 5-year est.); Poverty rate: 4.6% (2006-2010 5-year est.).
**Education:** Percent of population age 25 and over with: High school diploma (including GED) or higher: 92.2% (2006-2010 5-year est.); Bachelor's degree or higher: 42.7% (2006-2010 5-year est.); Master's degree or higher: 19.1% (2006-2010 5-year est.).

**School District(s)**
Mahopac Central School District (KG-12)
   2009-10 Enrollment: 5,112 . . . . . . . . . . . . . . . . . . . . . . . . (845) 628-3415
**Housing:** Homeownership rate: 75.0% (2010); Median home value: $451,100 (2006-2010 5-year est.); Median contract rent: $1,209 per month (2006-2010 5-year est.); Median year structure built: 1966 (2006-2010 5-year est.).
**Newspapers:** Brewster Times (Community news; Circulation 8,200); Carmel Times (Community news; Circulation 11,800); East Fishkill Record (Community news); Fishkill Standard (Community news); Lagrange Independent (Local news); Mahopac Press (Community news)
**Transportation:** Commute to work: 86.9% car, 5.8% public transportation, 4.0% walk, 2.7% work from home (2006-2010 5-year est.); Travel time to work: 23.0% less than 15 minutes, 22.2% 15 to 30 minutes, 23.5% 30 to 45 minutes, 14.7% 45 to 60 minutes, 16.6% 60 minutes or more (2006-2010 5-year est.)

**NELSONVILLE** (village). Covers a land area of 1.033 square miles and a water area of 0.001 square miles. Located at 41.42° N. Lat; 73.95° W. Long. Elevation is 187 feet.
**Population:** 585 (1990); 565 (2000); 628 (2010); Density: 607.4 persons per square mile (2010); Race: 93.3% White, 0.5% Black, 1.1% Asian, 0.2% American Indian/Alaska Native, 0.2% Native Hawaiian/Other Pacific Islander, 4.7% Other, 7.8% Hispanic of any race (2010); Average household size: 2.57 (2010); Median age: 41.1 (2010); Males per 100 females: 97.5 (2010); Marriage status: 21.7% never married, 64.6% now married, 4.3% widowed, 9.4% divorced (2006-2010 5-year est.); Foreign born: 13.3% (2006-2010 5-year est.); Ancestry (includes multiple ancestries): 41.8% Irish, 26.4% Italian, 20.3% German, 5.5% English, 4.7% Polish (2006-2010 5-year est.).
**Economy:** Single-family building permits issued: 0 (2011); Multi-family building permits issued: 0 (2011); Employment by occupation: 13.0% management, 3.1% professional, 17.6% services, 15.8% sales, 0.9% farming, 8.4% construction, 4.3% production (2006-2010 5-year est.).
**Income:** Per capita income: $35,112 (2006-2010 5-year est.); Median household income: $81,250 (2006-2010 5-year est.); Average household income: $97,204 (2006-2010 5-year est.); Percent of households with income of $100,000 or more: 39.7% (2006-2010 5-year est.); Poverty rate: 1.4% (2006-2010 5-year est.).
**Education:** Percent of population age 25 and over with: High school diploma (including GED) or higher: 87.2% (2006-2010 5-year est.); Bachelor's degree or higher: 41.8% (2006-2010 5-year est.); Master's degree or higher: 14.0% (2006-2010 5-year est.).
**Housing:** Homeownership rate: 68.8% (2010); Median home value: $465,700 (2006-2010 5-year est.); Median contract rent: $1,478 per month (2006-2010 5-year est.); Median year structure built: before 1940 (2006-2010 5-year est.).
**Transportation:** Commute to work: 67.2% car, 11.7% public transportation, 9.1% walk, 12.0% work from home (2006-2010 5-year est.); Travel time to work: 27.6% less than 15 minutes, 29.7% 15 to 30 minutes, 12.2% 30 to 45 minutes, 5.7% 45 to 60 minutes, 24.7% 60 minutes or more (2006-2010 5-year est.)

**PATTERSON** (town). Covers a land area of 32.208 square miles and a water area of 0.695 square miles. Located at 41.48° N. Lat; 73.58° W. Long. Elevation is 443 feet.
**History:** Patterson is located in a valley which was formerly part of the Patterson Great Swamp. The village, originally named Franklin, was settled about 1770 by Scots discharged from the British army after service in the French and Indian War. The present name was adopted in 1808 when the

legislature passed a law abolishing the numerous "Franklins" in the state. The town was then named after Matthew Patterson, an early settler.
**Population:** 8,679 (1990); 11,306 (2000); 12,023 (2010); Density: 373.3 persons per square mile (2010); Race: 87.5% White, 4.4% Black, 1.8% Asian, 0.2% American Indian/Alaska Native, 0.0% Native Hawaiian/Other Pacific Islander, 6.1% Other, 12.9% Hispanic of any race (2010); Average household size: 2.74 (2010); Median age: 40.0 (2010); Males per 100 females: 102.4 (2010); Marriage status: 27.0% never married, 60.6% now married, 5.2% widowed, 7.2% divorced (2006-2010 5-year est.); Foreign born: 11.2% (2006-2010 5-year est.); Ancestry (includes multiple ancestries): 24.4% Italian, 21.4% Irish, 14.6% German, 9.4% English, 4.7% Polish (2006-2010 5-year est.).
**Economy:** Single-family building permits issued: 3 (2011); Multi-family building permits issued: 10 (2011); Employment by occupation: 9.7% management, 6.9% professional, 7.2% services, 18.1% sales, 3.5% farming, 11.7% construction, 4.9% production (2006-2010 5-year est.).
**Income:** Per capita income: $27,876 (2006-2010 5-year est.); Median household income: $81,836 (2006-2010 5-year est.); Average household income: $96,071 (2006-2010 5-year est.); Percent of households with income of $100,000 or more: 39.3% (2006-2010 5-year est.); Poverty rate: 25.5% (2006-2010 5-year est.).
**Education:** Percent of population age 25 and over with: High school diploma (including GED) or higher: 93.9% (2006-2010 5-year est.); Bachelor's degree or higher: 27.5% (2006-2010 5-year est.); Master's degree or higher: 10.3% (2006-2010 5-year est.).

**School District(s)**
Carmel Central School District (KG-12)
   2009-10 Enrollment: 4,630 . . . . . . . . . . . . . . . . . . . . . . . (845) 878-2094
**Housing:** Homeownership rate: 81.2% (2010); Median home value: $356,000 (2006-2010 5-year est.); Median contract rent: $1,083 per month (2006-2010 5-year est.); Median year structure built: 1971 (2006-2010 5-year est.).
**Transportation:** Commute to work: 86.0% car, 5.0% public transportation, 2.7% walk, 4.9% work from home (2006-2010 5-year est.); Travel time to work: 17.8% less than 15 minutes, 23.2% 15 to 30 minutes, 12.7% 30 to 45 minutes, 20.6% 45 to 60 minutes, 25.8% 60 minutes or more (2006-2010 5-year est.)
**Additional Information Contacts**
Patterson Chamber of Commerce . . . . . . . . . . . . . . . . . . . . (845) 363-6304
  http://www.pcofc.org
Town of Patterson . . . . . . . . . . . . . . . . . . . . . . . . . . . . . . . (845) 878-6500
  http://www.pattersonny.org

**PEACH LAKE** (CDP). Covers a land area of 2.663 square miles and a water area of 0.380 square miles. Located at 41.36° N. Lat; 73.57° W. Long. Elevation is 561 feet.
**Population:** 1,499 (1990); 1,671 (2000); 1,629 (2010); Density: 611.5 persons per square mile (2010); Race: 96.6% White, 0.3% Black, 1.0% Asian, 0.1% American Indian/Alaska Native, 0.0% Native Hawaiian/Other Pacific Islander, 2.0% Other, 4.5% Hispanic of any race (2010); Average household size: 2.63 (2010); Median age: 45.4 (2010); Males per 100 females: 95.8 (2010); Marriage status: 28.8% never married, 58.9% now married, 3.4% widowed, 8.8% divorced (2006-2010 5-year est.); Foreign born: 5.3% (2006-2010 5-year est.); Ancestry (includes multiple ancestries): 38.3% Italian, 27.7% German, 25.4% Irish, 17.0% English, 7.9% French (2006-2010 5-year est.).
**Economy:** Employment by occupation: 11.1% management, 1.3% professional, 10.5% services, 17.9% sales, 1.1% farming, 9.1% construction, 3.9% production (2006-2010 5-year est.).
**Income:** Per capita income: $46,598 (2006-2010 5-year est.); Median household income: $75,341 (2006-2010 5-year est.); Average household income: $120,593 (2006-2010 5-year est.); Percent of households with income of $100,000 or more: 37.8% (2006-2010 5-year est.); Poverty rate: 0.0% (2006-2010 5-year est.).
**Education:** Percent of population age 25 and over with: High school diploma (including GED) or higher: 98.1% (2006-2010 5-year est.); Bachelor's degree or higher: 36.3% (2006-2010 5-year est.); Master's degree or higher: 13.5% (2006-2010 5-year est.).
**Housing:** Homeownership rate: 91.8% (2010); Median home value: $465,000 (2006-2010 5-year est.); Median contract rent: $1,243 per month (2006-2010 5-year est.); Median year structure built: 1961 (2006-2010 5-year est.).
**Transportation:** Commute to work: 93.0% car, 5.0% public transportation, 0.0% walk, 2.1% work from home (2006-2010 5-year est.); Travel time to work: 25.1% less than 15 minutes, 23.0% 15 to 30 minutes, 25.0% 30 to 45

minutes, 16.1% 45 to 60 minutes, 10.8% 60 minutes or more (2006-2010 5-year est.)

**PHILIPSTOWN** (town). Covers a land area of 48.784 square miles and a water area of 2.784 square miles. Located at 41.41° N. Lat; 73.92° W. Long.

**Population:** 9,242 (1990); 9,422 (2000); 9,662 (2010); Density: 198.1 persons per square mile (2010); Race: 93.1% White, 1.6% Black, 1.4% Asian, 0.2% American Indian/Alaska Native, 0.1% Native Hawaiian/Other Pacific Islander, 3.6% Other, 6.9% Hispanic of any race (2010); Average household size: 2.53 (2010); Median age: 45.4 (2010); Males per 100 females: 95.8 (2010); Marriage status: 27.8% never married, 59.5% now married, 5.4% widowed, 7.3% divorced (2006-2010 5-year est.); Foreign born: 10.5% (2006-2010 5-year est.); Ancestry (includes multiple ancestries): 36.9% Irish, 22.5% Italian, 17.6% German, 12.1% English, 4.7% Polish (2006-2010 5-year est.).

**Economy:** Single-family building permits issued: 13 (2011); Multi-family building permits issued: 0 (2011); Employment by occupation: 18.4% management, 4.5% professional, 8.1% services, 13.6% sales, 2.1% farming, 6.0% construction, 3.8% production (2006-2010 5-year est.).

**Income:** Per capita income: $42,000 (2006-2010 5-year est.); Median household income: $77,784 (2006-2010 5-year est.); Average household income: $110,962 (2006-2010 5-year est.); Percent of households with income of $100,000 or more: 39.4% (2006-2010 5-year est.); Poverty rate: 9.6% (2006-2010 5-year est.).

**Education:** Percent of population age 25 and over with: High school diploma (including GED) or higher: 94.6% (2006-2010 5-year est.); Bachelor's degree or higher: 47.2% (2006-2010 5-year est.); Master's degree or higher: 23.2% (2006-2010 5-year est.).

**Housing:** Homeownership rate: 78.3% (2010); Median home value: $500,000 (2006-2010 5-year est.); Median contract rent: $1,072 per month (2006-2010 5-year est.); Median year structure built: 1962 (2006-2010 5-year est.).

**Transportation:** Commute to work: 67.4% car, 16.7% public transportation, 2.9% walk, 11.3% work from home (2006-2010 5-year est.); Travel time to work: 20.5% less than 15 minutes, 22.9% 15 to 30 minutes, 16.4% 30 to 45 minutes, 11.0% 45 to 60 minutes, 29.2% 60 minutes or more (2006-2010 5-year est.)

**PUTNAM LAKE** (CDP). Covers a land area of 3.841 square miles and a water area of 0.419 square miles. Located at 41.47° N. Lat; 73.54° W. Long. Elevation is 512 feet.

**Population:** 3,459 (1990); 3,855 (2000); 3,844 (2010); Density: 1,000.7 persons per square mile (2010); Race: 88.0% White, 3.8% Black, 1.7% Asian, 0.2% American Indian/Alaska Native, 0.0% Native Hawaiian/Other Pacific Islander, 6.3% Other, 13.8% Hispanic of any race (2010); Average household size: 2.66 (2010); Median age: 40.4 (2010); Males per 100 females: 102.4 (2010); Marriage status: 28.3% never married, 53.2% now married, 7.9% widowed, 10.7% divorced (2006-2010 5-year est.); Foreign born: 9.6% (2006-2010 5-year est.); Ancestry (includes multiple ancestries): 35.0% Italian, 27.3% Irish, 14.7% German, 9.4% English, 5.4% French (2006-2010 5-year est.).

**Economy:** Employment by occupation: 4.7% management, 9.4% professional, 7.9% services, 21.4% sales, 4.3% farming, 14.2% construction, 5.6% production (2006-2010 5-year est.).

**Income:** Per capita income: $28,043 (2006-2010 5-year est.); Median household income: $74,194 (2006-2010 5-year est.); Average household income: $77,788 (2006-2010 5-year est.); Percent of households with income of $100,000 or more: 32.9% (2006-2010 5-year est.); Poverty rate: 4.9% (2006-2010 5-year est.).

**Education:** Percent of population age 25 and over with: High school diploma (including GED) or higher: 90.3% (2006-2010 5-year est.); Bachelor's degree or higher: 24.3% (2006-2010 5-year est.); Master's degree or higher: 7.4% (2006-2010 5-year est.).

**Housing:** Homeownership rate: 85.5% (2010); Median home value: $318,500 (2006-2010 5-year est.); Median contract rent: $779 per month (2006-2010 5-year est.); Median year structure built: 1957 (2006-2010 5-year est.).

**Transportation:** Commute to work: 93.9% car, 2.9% public transportation, 1.8% walk, 1.5% work from home (2006-2010 5-year est.); Travel time to work: 15.9% less than 15 minutes, 19.1% 15 to 30 minutes, 8.6% 30 to 45 minutes, 27.7% 45 to 60 minutes, 28.7% 60 minutes or more (2006-2010 5-year est.)

**PUTNAM VALLEY** (town). Covers a land area of 41.174 square miles and a water area of 1.604 square miles. Located at 41.39° N. Lat; 73.83° W. Long. Elevation is 167 feet.

**Population:** 9,094 (1990); 10,686 (2000); 11,809 (2010); Density: 286.8 persons per square mile (2010); Race: 91.4% White, 2.2% Black, 1.8% Asian, 0.1% American Indian/Alaska Native, 0.0% Native Hawaiian/Other Pacific Islander, 4.5% Other, 9.8% Hispanic of any race (2010); Average household size: 2.80 (2010); Median age: 42.1 (2010); Males per 100 females: 101.1 (2010); Marriage status: 20.9% never married, 66.6% now married, 4.6% widowed, 8.0% divorced (2006-2010 5-year est.); Foreign born: 11.6% (2006-2010 5-year est.); Ancestry (includes multiple ancestries): 33.4% Italian, 28.5% Irish, 18.6% German, 6.4% Polish, 6.2% English (2006-2010 5-year est.).

**Economy:** Single-family building permits issued: 6 (2011); Multi-family building permits issued: 0 (2011); Employment by occupation: 17.0% management, 3.5% professional, 6.0% services, 16.4% sales, 4.1% farming, 10.5% construction, 3.5% production (2006-2010 5-year est.).

**Income:** Per capita income: $36,538 (2006-2010 5-year est.); Median household income: $90,743 (2006-2010 5-year est.); Average household income: $101,694 (2006-2010 5-year est.); Percent of households with income of $100,000 or more: 40.1% (2006-2010 5-year est.); Poverty rate: 5.1% (2006-2010 5-year est.).

**Education:** Percent of population age 25 and over with: High school diploma (including GED) or higher: 94.1% (2006-2010 5-year est.); Bachelor's degree or higher: 39.8% (2006-2010 5-year est.); Master's degree or higher: 16.9% (2006-2010 5-year est.).

### School District(s)
Putnam Valley Central School District (KG-12)
   2009-10 Enrollment: 1,835 . . . . . . . . . . . . . . . . . . . . . . . (845) 528-8143

**Housing:** Homeownership rate: 86.8% (2010); Median home value: $427,800 (2006-2010 5-year est.); Median contract rent: $968 per month (2006-2010 5-year est.); Median year structure built: 1959 (2006-2010 5-year est.).

**Transportation:** Commute to work: 88.5% car, 4.9% public transportation, 0.3% walk, 3.8% work from home (2006-2010 5-year est.); Travel time to work: 20.9% less than 15 minutes, 28.2% 15 to 30 minutes, 18.0% 30 to 45 minutes, 19.1% 45 to 60 minutes, 13.8% 60 minutes or more (2006-2010 5-year est.)

**Additional Information Contacts**
Town of Putnam Valley . . . . . . . . . . . . . . . . . . . . . . . . . . . (845) 526-2121
   http://www.putnamvalley.com

**SOUTHEAST** (town). Covers a land area of 31.733 square miles and a water area of 3.245 square miles. Located at 41.40° N. Lat; 73.60° W. Long.

**History:** The Tilly Foster Iron Mine (established 1790), located on a 128-acre farm owned by Tilly Foster, was the largest of a number of mines in the area. The town was named after this mine. For a time high-grade iron ore was shipped from here to Pennsylvania. Became open-pit mine in 1889, closed in 1897 after an avalanche.

**Population:** 14,927 (1990); 17,316 (2000); 18,404 (2010); Density: 579.9 persons per square mile (2010); Race: 89.4% White, 2.0% Black, 2.5% Asian, 0.2% American Indian/Alaska Native, 0.1% Native Hawaiian/Other Pacific Islander, 5.8% Other, 16.6% Hispanic of any race (2010); Average household size: 2.71 (2010); Median age: 41.7 (2010); Males per 100 females: 102.5 (2010); Marriage status: 28.2% never married, 56.9% now married, 5.3% widowed, 9.6% divorced (2006-2010 5-year est.); Foreign born: 12.1% (2006-2010 5-year est.); Ancestry (includes multiple ancestries): 28.0% Italian, 26.4% Irish, 17.7% German, 8.6% English, 4.4% Polish (2006-2010 5-year est.).

**Economy:** Single-family building permits issued: 5 (2011); Multi-family building permits issued: 2 (2011); Employment by occupation: 12.6% management, 4.5% professional, 6.9% services, 17.9% sales, 3.9% farming, 9.4% construction, 3.7% production (2006-2010 5-year est.).

**Income:** Per capita income: $41,051 (2006-2010 5-year est.); Median household income: $86,931 (2006-2010 5-year est.); Average household income: $109,785 (2006-2010 5-year est.); Percent of households with income of $100,000 or more: 41.0% (2006-2010 5-year est.); Poverty rate: 4.5% (2006-2010 5-year est.).

**Education:** Percent of population age 25 and over with: High school diploma (including GED) or higher: 92.3% (2006-2010 5-year est.); Bachelor's degree or higher: 40.2% (2006-2010 5-year est.); Master's degree or higher: 15.4% (2006-2010 5-year est.).

**Housing:** Homeownership rate: 77.4% (2010); Median home value: $386,700 (2006-2010 5-year est.); Median contract rent: $1,089 per month

(2006-2010 5-year est.); Median year structure built: 1974 (2006-2010 5-year est.).

**Transportation:** Commute to work: 85.4% car, 8.5% public transportation, 1.2% walk, 4.0% work from home (2006-2010 5-year est.); Travel time to work: 24.3% less than 15 minutes, 24.5% 15 to 30 minutes, 17.5% 30 to 45 minutes, 15.4% 45 to 60 minutes, 18.4% 60 minutes or more (2006-2010 5-year est.)

**Additional Information Contacts**
Town of Southeast . . . . . . . . . . . . . . . . . . . . . . . . . . . . (845) 279-4313
    http://www.townofsoutheast-ny.com/Home

# Queens County and Borough

*See New York City*

# Rensselaer County

Located in eastern New York; bounded on the west by the Hudson River, and on the east by Massachusetts and Vermont; includes part of the Taconic Mountains; drained by the Hoosic River. Covers a land area of 653.96 square miles, a water area of 11.43 square miles, and is located in the Eastern Time Zone at 42.69° N. Lat., 73.59° W. Long. The county was founded in 1791. County seat is Troy.

Rensselaer County is part of the Albany-Schenectady-Troy, NY Metropolitan Statistical Area. The entire metro area includes: Albany County, NY; Rensselaer County, NY; Saratoga County, NY; Schenectady County, NY; Schoharie County, NY

Weather Station: Grafton                                    Elevation: 1,560 feet

| | Jan | Feb | Mar | Apr | May | Jun | Jul | Aug | Sep | Oct | Nov | Dec |
|---|---|---|---|---|---|---|---|---|---|---|---|---|
| High | 28 | 32 | 41 | 54 | 66 | 74 | 78 | 76 | 68 | 57 | 45 | 33 |
| Low | 12 | 15 | 23 | 34 | 45 | 53 | 58 | 57 | 50 | 39 | 29 | 18 |
| Precip | 2.9 | 2.6 | 3.6 | 3.9 | 4.5 | 4.1 | 4.5 | 4.5 | 4.2 | 4.0 | 4.0 | 3.2 |
| Snow | 20.6 | 14.9 | 15.4 | 5.9 | 0.2 | 0.0 | 0.0 | 0.0 | tr | 1.3 | 7.2 | 17.8 |

*High and Low temperatures in degrees Fahrenheit; Precipitation and Snow in inches*

Weather Station: Troy Lock and Dam                      Elevation: 23 feet

| | Jan | Feb | Mar | Apr | May | Jun | Jul | Aug | Sep | Oct | Nov | Dec |
|---|---|---|---|---|---|---|---|---|---|---|---|---|
| High | 32 | 35 | 44 | 59 | 70 | 79 | 84 | 82 | 74 | 62 | 49 | 37 |
| Low | 15 | 17 | 25 | 37 | 48 | 58 | 63 | 61 | 53 | 41 | 32 | 22 |
| Precip | 2.2 | 1.9 | 3.0 | 3.3 | 3.7 | 4.2 | 4.4 | 4.1 | 3.3 | 3.7 | 3.1 | 2.6 |
| Snow | 12.7 | 8.0 | 7.5 | 1.3 | 0.0 | 0.0 | 0.0 | 0.0 | 0.0 | 0.1 | 1.8 | 7.2 |

*High and Low temperatures in degrees Fahrenheit; Precipitation and Snow in inches*

**Population:** 154,429 (1990); 152,538 (2000); 159,429 (2010); Race: 87.5% White, 6.5% Black, 2.2% Asian, 0.2% American Indian/Alaska Native, 0.0% Native Hawaiian/Other Pacific Islander, 3.6% Other, 3.8% Hispanic of any race (2010); Density: 243.8 persons per square mile (2010); Average household size: 2.38 (2010); Median age: 39.2 (2010); Males per 100 females: 97.5 (2010).

**Religion:** Six largest groups: 28.1% Catholicism, 3.4% Methodist/Pietist, 1.9% Presbyterian-Reformed, 1.5% Lutheran, 1.3% Baptist, 1.3% Non-Denominational (2010)

**Economy:** Unemployment rate: 8.7% (February 2012); Total civilian labor force: 81,997 (February 2012); Leading industries: 21.2% health care and social assistance; 14.3% retail trade; 12.2% educational services (2009); Farms: 506 totaling 85,034 acres (2007); Companies that employ 500 or more persons: 5 (2009); Companies that employ 100 to 499 persons: 52 (2009); Companies that employ less than 100 persons: 2,909 (2009); Black-owned businesses: 291 (2007); Hispanic-owned businesses: 172 (2007); Asian-owned businesses: 299 (2007); Women-owned businesses: 3,246 (2007); Retail sales per capita: $9,031 (2010). Single-family building permits issued: 105 (2011); Multi-family building permits issued: 50 (2011).

**Income:** Per capita income: $27,457 (2006-2010 5-year est.); Median household income: $54,152 (2006-2010 5-year est.); Average household income: $67,091 (2006-2010 5-year est.); Percent of households with income of $100,000 or more: 20.7% (2006-2010 5-year est.); Poverty rate: 11.7% (2006-2010 5-year est.); Bankruptcy rate: 3.23% (2011).

**Taxes:** Total county taxes per capita: $811 (2009); County property taxes per capita: $337 (2009).

**Education:** Percent of population age 25 and over with: High school diploma (including GED) or higher: 89.2% (2006-2010 5-year est.); Bachelor's degree or higher: 26.7% (2006-2010 5-year est.); Master's degree or higher: 11.8% (2006-2010 5-year est.).

**Housing:** Homeownership rate: 63.8% (2010); Median home value: $171,200 (2006-2010 5-year est.); Median contract rent: $625 per month (2006-2010 5-year est.); Median year structure built: 1955 (2006-2010 5-year est.)

**Health:** Birth rate: 110.0 per 10,000 population (2011); Death rate: 93.2 per 10,000 population (2011); Age-adjusted cancer mortality rate: 181.1 deaths per 100,000 population (2009); Number of physicians: 18.2 per 10,000 population (2008); Hospital beds: 26.7 per 10,000 population (2007); Hospital admissions: 1,091.0 per 10,000 population (2007).

**Environment:** Air Quality Index: 93.2% good, 6.6% moderate, 0.3% unhealthy for sensitive individuals, 0.0% unhealthy (percent of days in 2010)

**Elections:** 2008 Presidential election results: 53.7% Obama, 44.4% McCain, 1.1% Nader

**National and State Parks:** State Forest Rensselaer Number 3

**Additional Information Contacts**
Rensselaer County Government . . . . . . . . . . . . . . . . . . . . (518) 270-4080
    http://www.rensco.com
City of Troy. . . . . . . . . . . . . . . . . . . . . . . . . . . . . . . . . . (518) 279-7134
    http://www.troyny.gov
Rensselaer County Regional Chamber of Commerce . . . . . (518) 274-7020
    http://www.renscochamber.com
Town of Brunswick. . . . . . . . . . . . . . . . . . . . . . . . . . . . . (518) 279-3461
    http://www.townofbrunswick.org
Town of East Greenbush . . . . . . . . . . . . . . . . . . . . . . . . (518) 477-4775
    http://eastgreenbush.org
Town of Schodack . . . . . . . . . . . . . . . . . . . . . . . . . . . . . (518) 477-7918
    http://www.schodack.org

## *Rensselaer County Communities*

**AVERILL PARK** (CDP). Covers a land area of 2.932 square miles and a water area of 0.118 square miles. Located at 42.63° N. Lat; 73.55° W. Long. Elevation is 784 feet.

**Population:** 1,656 (1990); 1,517 (2000); 1,693 (2010); Density: 577.3 persons per square mile (2010); Race: 97.2% White, 0.6% Black, 0.6% Asian, 0.0% American Indian/Alaska Native, 0.0% Native Hawaiian/Other Pacific Islander, 1.6% Other, 2.1% Hispanic of any race (2010); Average household size: 2.56 (2010); Median age: 41.8 (2010); Males per 100 females: 99.9 (2010); Marriage status: 21.4% never married, 67.2% now married, 4.7% widowed, 6.7% divorced (2006-2010 5-year est.); Foreign born: 7.3% (2006-2010 5-year est.); Ancestry (includes multiple ancestries): 28.6% Irish, 26.3% German, 12.1% English, 9.4% Italian, 7.9% French (2006-2010 5-year est.).

**Economy:** Employment by occupation: 10.5% management, 8.8% professional, 10.0% services, 6.5% sales, 7.0% farming, 14.1% construction, 6.3% production (2006-2010 5-year est.).

**Income:** Per capita income: $35,262 (2006-2010 5-year est.); Median household income: $72,188 (2006-2010 5-year est.); Average household income: $82,474 (2006-2010 5-year est.); Percent of households with income of $100,000 or more: 28.8% (2006-2010 5-year est.); Poverty rate: 1.5% (2006-2010 5-year est.).

**Education:** Percent of population age 25 and over with: High school diploma (including GED) or higher: 96.0% (2006-2010 5-year est.); Bachelor's degree or higher: 39.2% (2006-2010 5-year est.); Master's degree or higher: 17.8% (2006-2010 5-year est.).

**School District(s)**
Averill Park Central School District (KG-12)
    2009-10 Enrollment: 3,367 . . . . . . . . . . . . . . . . . . . . (518) 674-7055

**Housing:** Homeownership rate: 75.2% (2010); Median home value: $186,100 (2006-2010 5-year est.); Median contract rent: $576 per month (2006-2010 5-year est.); Median year structure built: before 1940 (2006-2010 5-year est.).

**Transportation:** Commute to work: 94.1% car, 0.0% public transportation, 2.1% walk, 3.8% work from home (2006-2010 5-year est.); Travel time to work: 11.6% less than 15 minutes, 51.8% 15 to 30 minutes, 30.2% 30 to 45 minutes, 6.5% 45 to 60 minutes, 0.0% 60 minutes or more (2006-2010 5-year est.)

**BERLIN** (town). Covers a land area of 59.603 square miles and a water area of 0.319 square miles. Located at 42.66° N. Lat; 73.38° W. Long. Elevation is 840 feet.

**Population:** 1,921 (1990); 1,901 (2000); 1,880 (2010); Density: 31.5 persons per square mile (2010); Race: 97.3% White, 0.1% Black, 0.2% Asian, 0.2% American Indian/Alaska Native, 0.0% Native Hawaiian/Other

Pacific Islander, 2.2% Other, 1.0% Hispanic of any race (2010); Average household size: 2.38 (2010); Median age: 44.6 (2010); Males per 100 females: 96.9 (2010); Marriage status: 24.2% never married, 58.5% now married, 7.3% widowed, 10.1% divorced (2006-2010 5-year est.); Foreign born: 2.4% (2006-2010 5-year est.); Ancestry (includes multiple ancestries): 31.4% German, 22.9% Irish, 17.3% English, 11.1% French, 10.8% Italian (2006-2010 5-year est.).

**Economy:** Single-family building permits issued: 2 (2011); Multi-family building permits issued: 0 (2011); Employment by occupation: 8.9% management, 7.4% professional, 8.5% services, 16.2% sales, 3.7% farming, 14.9% construction, 6.4% production (2006-2010 5-year est.).

**Income:** Per capita income: $26,437 (2006-2010 5-year est.); Median household income: $57,321 (2006-2010 5-year est.); Average household income: $62,944 (2006-2010 5-year est.); Percent of households with income of $100,000 or more: 12.5% (2006-2010 5-year est.); Poverty rate: 5.8% (2006-2010 5-year est.).

**Education:** Percent of population age 25 and over with: High school diploma (including GED) or higher: 85.5% (2006-2010 5-year est.); Bachelor's degree or higher: 25.5% (2006-2010 5-year est.); Master's degree or higher: 7.9% (2006-2010 5-year est.).

### School District(s)
Berlin Central School District (PK-12)
   2009-10 Enrollment: 914 . . . . . . . . . . . . . . . . . . . . . . . . . (518) 658-2690

**Housing:** Homeownership rate: 77.0% (2010); Median home value: $157,100 (2006-2010 5-year est.); Median contract rent: $468 per month (2006-2010 5-year est.); Median year structure built: 1967 (2006-2010 5-year est.).

**Transportation:** Commute to work: 89.8% car, 0.0% public transportation, 4.7% walk, 4.9% work from home (2006-2010 5-year est.); Travel time to work: 22.4% less than 15 minutes, 21.6% 15 to 30 minutes, 25.4% 30 to 45 minutes, 24.0% 45 to 60 minutes, 6.6% 60 minutes or more (2006-2010 5-year est.)

## BRAINARD (unincorporated postal area)
Zip Code: 12024

Covers a land area of 1.041 square miles and a water area of 0 square miles. Located at 42.47° N. Lat; 73.53° W. Long. Elevation is 679 feet. Population: 31 (2010); Density: 29.8 persons per square mile (2010); Race: 96.8% White, 0.0% Black, 3.2% Asian, 0.0% American Indian/Alaska Native, 0.0% Native Hawaiian/Other Pacific Islander, 0.0% Other, 0.0% Hispanic of any race (2010); Average household size: 2.38 (2010); Median age: 44.5 (2010); Males per 100 females: 93.8 (2010); Homeownership rate: 92.3% (2010)

## BRUNSWICK (town). 
Covers a land area of 44.347 square miles and a water area of 0.280 square miles. Located at 42.74° N. Lat; 73.58° W. Long. Elevation is 518 feet.

Population: 11,093 (1990); 11,664 (2000); 11,941 (2010); Density: 269.3 persons per square mile (2010); Race: 94.5% White, 1.8% Black, 1.6% Asian, 0.2% American Indian/Alaska Native, 0.0% Native Hawaiian/Other Pacific Islander, 1.9% Other, 1.7% Hispanic of any race (2010); Average household size: 2.39 (2010); Median age: 44.7 (2010); Males per 100 females: 97.5 (2010); Marriage status: 27.0% never married, 59.2% now married, 6.0% widowed, 7.8% divorced (2006-2010 5-year est.); Foreign born: 3.5% (2006-2010 5-year est.); Ancestry (includes multiple ancestries): 32.9% Irish, 21.8% Italian, 20.8% German, 12.8% French, 11.8% English (2006-2010 5-year est.).

**Economy:** Single-family building permits issued: 6 (2011); Multi-family building permits issued: 0 (2011); Employment by occupation: 12.0% management, 5.6% professional, 6.0% services, 23.0% sales, 5.2% farming, 9.8% construction, 3.8% production (2006-2010 5-year est.).

**Income:** Per capita income: $33,414 (2006-2010 5-year est.); Median household income: $63,750 (2006-2010 5-year est.); Average household income: $80,672 (2006-2010 5-year est.); Percent of households with income of $100,000 or more: 29.9% (2006-2010 5-year est.); Poverty rate: 4.8% (2006-2010 5-year est.).

**Education:** Percent of population age 25 and over with: High school diploma (including GED) or higher: 93.8% (2006-2010 5-year est.); Bachelor's degree or higher: 30.4% (2006-2010 5-year est.); Master's degree or higher: 15.1% (2006-2010 5-year est.).

**Housing:** Homeownership rate: 78.7% (2010); Median home value: $194,700 (2006-2010 5-year est.); Median contract rent: $781 per month (2006-2010 5-year est.); Median year structure built: 1963 (2006-2010 5-year est.).

**Transportation:** Commute to work: 94.9% car, 0.2% public transportation, 0.9% walk, 3.2% work from home (2006-2010 5-year est.); Travel time to work: 26.5% less than 15 minutes, 47.6% 15 to 30 minutes, 17.7% 30 to 45 minutes, 6.0% 45 to 60 minutes, 2.2% 60 minutes or more (2006-2010 5-year est.)

**Additional Information Contacts**
Town of Brunswick. . . . . . . . . . . . . . . . . . . . . . . . . . . . . . . . (518) 279-3461
  http://www.townofbrunswick.org

## BUSKIRK (unincorporated postal area)
Zip Code: 12028

Covers a land area of 22.572 square miles and a water area of 0.274 square miles. Located at 42.93° N. Lat; 73.44° W. Long. Population: 1,172 (2010); Density: 51.9 persons per square mile (2010); Race: 97.2% White, 1.1% Black, 0.3% Asian, 0.2% American Indian/Alaska Native, 0.0% Native Hawaiian/Other Pacific Islander, 1.2% Other, 1.2% Hispanic of any race (2010); Average household size: 2.63 (2010); Median age: 42.4 (2010); Males per 100 females: 102.8 (2010); Homeownership rate: 86.5% (2010)

## CASTLETON-ON-HUDSON (village). Aka Castleton on Hudson.
Covers a land area of 0.714 square miles and a water area of <.001 square miles. Located at 42.53° N. Lat; 73.75° W. Long. Elevation is 151 feet.

**History:** Settled by the Dutch c.1630; incorporated 1827.

**Population:** 1,455 (1990); 1,619 (2000); 1,473 (2010); Density: 2,062.9 persons per square mile (2010); Race: 97.0% White, 1.3% Black, 0.3% Asian, 0.0% American Indian/Alaska Native, 0.0% Native Hawaiian/Other Pacific Islander, 1.4% Other, 2.6% Hispanic of any race (2010); Average household size: 2.43 (2010); Median age: 39.5 (2010); Males per 100 females: 88.4 (2010); Marriage status: 27.5% never married, 46.2% now married, 12.1% widowed, 14.2% divorced (2006-2010 5-year est.); Foreign born: 1.8% (2006-2010 5-year est.); Ancestry (includes multiple ancestries): 32.1% Irish, 22.1% German, 17.0% Italian, 12.2% English, 9.1% French (2006-2010 5-year est.).

**Economy:** Single-family building permits issued: 2 (2011); Multi-family building permits issued: 0 (2011); Employment by occupation: 13.4% management, 2.1% professional, 7.6% services, 23.1% sales, 7.2% farming, 8.5% construction, 2.9% production (2006-2010 5-year est.).

**Income:** Per capita income: $23,710 (2006-2010 5-year est.); Median household income: $58,906 (2006-2010 5-year est.); Average household income: $66,177 (2006-2010 5-year est.); Percent of households with income of $100,000 or more: 20.6% (2006-2010 5-year est.); Poverty rate: 5.0% (2006-2010 5-year est.).

**Education:** Percent of population age 25 and over with: High school diploma (including GED) or higher: 87.2% (2006-2010 5-year est.); Bachelor's degree or higher: 26.2% (2006-2010 5-year est.); Master's degree or higher: 10.1% (2006-2010 5-year est.).

### School District(s)
East Greenbush Central School District (KG-12)
   2009-10 Enrollment: 4,482 . . . . . . . . . . . . . . . . . . . . . (518) 207-2531
Questar Iii Boces (r-C-G)
   2009-10 Enrollment: n/a . . . . . . . . . . . . . . . . . . . . . . . (518) 477-8771
Schodack Central School District (KG-12)
   2009-10 Enrollment: 1,078 . . . . . . . . . . . . . . . . . . . . . (518) 732-2297

**Housing:** Homeownership rate: 68.0% (2010); Median home value: $164,100 (2006-2010 5-year est.); Median contract rent: $645 per month (2006-2010 5-year est.); Median year structure built: before 1940 (2006-2010 5-year est.).

**Transportation:** Commute to work: 95.8% car, 0.0% public transportation, 2.0% walk, 1.8% work from home (2006-2010 5-year est.); Travel time to work: 25.8% less than 15 minutes, 46.7% 15 to 30 minutes, 25.6% 30 to 45 minutes, 0.8% 45 to 60 minutes, 1.1% 60 minutes or more (2006-2010 5-year est.)

## CHERRY PLAIN (unincorporated postal area)
Zip Code: 12040

Covers a land area of 1.306 square miles and a water area of 0 square miles. Located at 42.63° N. Lat; 73.35° W. Long. Population: 113 (2010); Density: 86.5 persons per square mile (2010); Race: 95.6% White, 0.0% Black, 0.9% Asian, 0.0% American Indian/Alaska Native, 0.0% Native Hawaiian/Other Pacific Islander, 3.5% Other, 4.4% Hispanic of any race (2010); Average household size: 2.22 (2010); Median age: 51.9 (2010); Males per 100 females: 105.5 (2010); Homeownership rate: 94.1% (2010)

## CROPSEYVILLE (unincorporated postal area)
Zip Code: 12052

Covers a land area of 30.301 square miles and a water area of 1.046 square miles. Located at 42.75° N. Lat; 73.47° W. Long. Elevation is 561 feet. Population: 1,568 (2010); Density: 51.7 persons per square mile (2010); Race: 97.2% White, 0.1% Black, 1.3% Asian, 0.1% American Indian/Alaska Native, 0.0% Native Hawaiian/Other Pacific Islander, 1.3% Other, 0.4% Hispanic of any race (2010); Average household size: 2.60 (2010); Median age: 41.5 (2010); Males per 100 females: 105.8 (2010); Homeownership rate: 88.8% (2010)

## EAGLE BRIDGE (unincorporated postal area)
Zip Code: 12057

Covers a land area of 35.162 square miles and a water area of 0.012 square miles. Located at 42.96° N. Lat; 73.34° W. Long. Elevation is 414 feet. Population: 1,835 (2010); Density: 52.2 persons per square mile (2010); Race: 97.0% White, 0.3% Black, 1.0% Asian, 0.2% American Indian/Alaska Native, 0.1% Native Hawaiian/Other Pacific Islander, 1.4% Other, 1.8% Hispanic of any race (2010); Average household size: 2.59 (2010); Median age: 43.7 (2010); Males per 100 females: 99.5 (2010); Homeownership rate: 86.0% (2010)

## EAST GREENBUSH (town). Covers a land area of 24.020 square miles and a water area of 0.274 square miles. Located at 42.60° N. Lat; 73.70° W. Long. Elevation is 341 feet.
**Population:** 14,234 (1990); 15,560 (2000); 16,473 (2010); Density: 685.8 persons per square mile (2010); Race: 91.3% White, 3.1% Black, 3.2% Asian, 0.2% American Indian/Alaska Native, 0.0% Native Hawaiian/Other Pacific Islander, 2.2% Other, 2.4% Hispanic of any race (2010); Average household size: 2.41 (2010); Median age: 41.9 (2010); Males per 100 females: 91.2 (2010); Marriage status: 27.4% never married, 55.2% now married, 8.5% widowed, 8.9% divorced (2006-2010 5-year est.); Foreign born: 5.1% (2006-2010 5-year est.); Ancestry (includes multiple ancestries): 30.3% Irish, 22.1% German, 17.4% Italian, 13.6% English, 11.4% Polish (2006-2010 5-year est.).
**Economy:** Single-family building permits issued: 15 (2011); Multi-family building permits issued: 0 (2011); Employment by occupation: 14.7% management, 8.2% professional, 5.2% services, 17.8% sales, 5.0% farming, 5.7% construction, 2.7% production (2006-2010 5-year est.).
**Income:** Per capita income: $34,444 (2006-2010 5-year est.); Median household income: $70,111 (2006-2010 5-year est.); Average household income: $84,059 (2006-2010 5-year est.); Percent of households with income of $100,000 or more: 29.6% (2006-2010 5-year est.); Poverty rate: 3.2% (2006-2010 5-year est.).
**Education:** Percent of population age 25 and over with: High school diploma (including GED) or higher: 93.8% (2006-2010 5-year est.); Bachelor's degree or higher: 39.6% (2006-2010 5-year est.); Master's degree or higher: 17.7% (2006-2010 5-year est.).

**School District(s)**
East Greenbush Central School District (KG-12)
   2009-10 Enrollment: 4,482 . . . . . . . . . . . . . . . . . (518) 207-2531
**Housing:** Homeownership rate: 74.8% (2010); Median home value: $196,900 (2006-2010 5-year est.); Median contract rent: $808 per month (2006-2010 5-year est.); Median year structure built: 1972 (2006-2010 5-year est.).
**Safety:** Violent crime rate: 8.3 per 10,000 population; Property crime rate: 240.0 per 10,000 population (2010).
**Transportation:** Commute to work: 93.2% car, 2.0% public transportation, 1.2% walk, 3.7% work from home (2006-2010 5-year est.); Travel time to work: 35.6% less than 15 minutes, 52.0% 15 to 30 minutes, 8.4% 30 to 45 minutes, 2.1% 45 to 60 minutes, 1.9% 60 minutes or more (2006-2010 5-year est.)
**Additional Information Contacts**
Town of East Greenbush . . . . . . . . . . . . . . . . . . . . . . (518) 477-4775
   http://eastgreenbush.org

## EAST GREENBUSH (CDP). Covers a land area of 2.664 square miles and a water area of 0.006 square miles. Located at 42.59° N. Lat; 73.70° W. Long. Elevation is 341 feet.
**Population:** 3,784 (1990); 4,085 (2000); 4,487 (2010); Density: 1,684.3 persons per square mile (2010); Race: 90.8% White, 2.4% Black, 4.4% Asian, 0.1% American Indian/Alaska Native, 0.0% Native Hawaiian/Other Pacific Islander, 2.3% Other, 2.5% Hispanic of any race (2010); Average household size: 2.49 (2010); Median age: 39.7 (2010); Males per 100 females: 95.3 (2010); Marriage status: 30.3% never married, 59.9% now

married, 2.3% widowed, 7.5% divorced (2006-2010 5-year est.); Foreign born: 6.2% (2006-2010 5-year est.); Ancestry (includes multiple ancestries): 29.1% Irish, 21.7% German, 16.9% Italian, 16.1% English, 7.9% Polish (2006-2010 5-year est.).
**Economy:** Employment by occupation: 21.7% management, 11.1% professional, 3.3% services, 10.8% sales, 7.0% farming, 5.7% construction, 2.0% production (2006-2010 5-year est.).
**Income:** Per capita income: $37,633 (2006-2010 5-year est.); Median household income: $80,750 (2006-2010 5-year est.); Average household income: $90,915 (2006-2010 5-year est.); Percent of households with income of $100,000 or more: 36.1% (2006-2010 5-year est.); Poverty rate: 4.0% (2006-2010 5-year est.).
**Education:** Percent of population age 25 and over with: High school diploma (including GED) or higher: 97.1% (2006-2010 5-year est.); Bachelor's degree or higher: 55.5% (2006-2010 5-year est.); Master's degree or higher: 24.8% (2006-2010 5-year est.).

**School District(s)**
East Greenbush Central School District (KG-12)
   2009-10 Enrollment: 4,482 . . . . . . . . . . . . . . . . . (518) 207-2531
**Housing:** Homeownership rate: 66.4% (2010); Median home value: $224,200 (2006-2010 5-year est.); Median contract rent: $791 per month (2006-2010 5-year est.); Median year structure built: 1973 (2006-2010 5-year est.).
**Transportation:** Commute to work: 94.2% car, 1.2% public transportation, 1.9% walk, 2.7% work from home (2006-2010 5-year est.); Travel time to work: 26.5% less than 15 minutes, 58.0% 15 to 30 minutes, 10.3% 30 to 45 minutes, 2.0% 45 to 60 minutes, 3.2% 60 minutes or more (2006-2010 5-year est.)

## EAST NASSAU (village). Covers a land area of 4.862 square miles and a water area of 0.008 square miles. Located at 42.53° N. Lat; 73.50° W. Long. Elevation is 571 feet.
**Population:** 587 (1990); 571 (2000); 587 (2010); Density: 120.7 persons per square mile (2010); Race: 94.7% White, 1.7% Black, 1.4% Asian, 0.3% American Indian/Alaska Native, 0.0% Native Hawaiian/Other Pacific Islander, 1.9% Other, 2.4% Hispanic of any race (2010); Average household size: 2.59 (2010); Median age: 41.7 (2010); Males per 100 females: 105.2 (2010); Marriage status: 21.5% never married, 68.1% now married, 3.7% widowed, 6.7% divorced (2006-2010 5-year est.); Foreign born: 2.8% (2006-2010 5-year est.); Ancestry (includes multiple ancestries): 29.2% German, 20.8% Irish, 14.2% English, 11.2% French, 10.5% Italian (2006-2010 5-year est.).
**Economy:** Single-family building permits issued: 0 (2011); Multi-family building permits issued: 0 (2011); Employment by occupation: 11.2% management, 1.9% professional, 7.4% services, 12.9% sales, 3.1% farming, 13.2% construction, 9.3% production (2006-2010 5-year est.).
**Income:** Per capita income: $27,741 (2006-2010 5-year est.); Median household income: $58,125 (2006-2010 5-year est.); Average household income: $71,942 (2006-2010 5-year est.); Percent of households with income of $100,000 or more: 24.7% (2006-2010 5-year est.); Poverty rate: 2.3% (2006-2010 5-year est.).
**Education:** Percent of population age 25 and over with: High school diploma (including GED) or higher: 93.7% (2006-2010 5-year est.); Bachelor's degree or higher: 19.9% (2006-2010 5-year est.); Master's degree or higher: 8.6% (2006-2010 5-year est.).
**Housing:** Homeownership rate: 79.8% (2010); Median home value: $175,000 (2006-2010 5-year est.); Median contract rent: $599 per month (2006-2010 5-year est.); Median year structure built: 1952 (2006-2010 5-year est.).
**Transportation:** Commute to work: 95.5% car, 0.0% public transportation, 0.0% walk, 3.0% work from home (2006-2010 5-year est.); Travel time to work: 8.5% less than 15 minutes, 30.3% 15 to 30 minutes, 49.0% 30 to 45 minutes, 11.0% 45 to 60 minutes, 1.3% 60 minutes or more (2006-2010 5-year est.)

## EAST SCHODACK (unincorporated postal area)
Zip Code: 12063

Covers a land area of 1.424 square miles and a water area of 0.004 square miles. Located at 42.56° N. Lat; 73.63° W. Long. Elevation is 456 feet. Population: 444 (2010); Density: 311.6 persons per square mile (2010); Race: 93.7% White, 1.8% Black, 2.3% Asian, 0.0% American Indian/Alaska Native, 0.0% Native Hawaiian/Other Pacific Islander, 2.2% Other, 1.6% Hispanic of any race (2010); Average household size: 2.61 (2010); Median age: 44.4 (2010); Males per 100 females: 93.0 (2010); Homeownership rate: 87.6% (2010)

## GRAFTON (town).

Covers a land area of 44.720 square miles and a water area of 1.241 square miles. Located at 42.76° N. Lat; 73.45° W. Long. Elevation is 1,473 feet.

**Population:** 1,917 (1990); 1,987 (2000); 2,130 (2010); Density: 47.6 persons per square mile (2010); Race: 96.9% White, 0.2% Black, 1.0% Asian, 0.3% American Indian/Alaska Native, 0.0% Native Hawaiian/Other Pacific Islander, 1.6% Other, 0.9% Hispanic of any race (2010); Average household size: 2.57 (2010); Median age: 41.6 (2010); Males per 100 females: 102.5 (2010); Marriage status: 26.0% never married, 60.6% now married, 5.2% widowed, 8.2% divorced (2006-2010 5-year est.); Foreign born: 2.6% (2006-2010 5-year est.); Ancestry (includes multiple ancestries): 28.5% German, 20.0% Irish, 16.3% English, 15.8% French, 10.2% Italian (2006-2010 5-year est.).

**Economy:** Single-family building permits issued: 7 (2011); Multi-family building permits issued: 0 (2011); Employment by occupation: 13.0% management, 7.2% professional, 8.9% services, 18.1% sales, 3.9% farming, 8.6% construction, 6.4% production (2006-2010 5-year est.).

**Income:** Per capita income: $29,440 (2006-2010 5-year est.); Median household income: $65,417 (2006-2010 5-year est.); Average household income: $69,189 (2006-2010 5-year est.); Percent of households with income of $100,000 or more: 19.3% (2006-2010 5-year est.); Poverty rate: 5.5% (2006-2010 5-year est.).

**Education:** Percent of population age 25 and over with: High school diploma (including GED) or higher: 91.6% (2006-2010 5-year est.); Bachelor's degree or higher: 21.4% (2006-2010 5-year est.); Master's degree or higher: 9.9% (2006-2010 5-year est.).

**Housing:** Homeownership rate: 88.4% (2010); Median home value: $161,000 (2006-2010 5-year est.); Median contract rent: $752 per month (2006-2010 5-year est.); Median year structure built: 1973 (2006-2010 5-year est.).

**Transportation:** Commute to work: 93.9% car, 0.4% public transportation, 1.0% walk, 4.7% work from home (2006-2010 5-year est.); Travel time to work: 5.9% less than 15 minutes, 42.1% 15 to 30 minutes, 27.1% 30 to 45 minutes, 19.0% 45 to 60 minutes, 6.0% 60 minutes or more (2006-2010 5-year est.)

## HAMPTON MANOR (CDP).

Covers a land area of 0.624 square miles and a water area of 0.023 square miles. Located at 42.62° N. Lat; 73.72° W. Long. Elevation is 207 feet.

**Population:** 2,655 (1990); 2,525 (2000); 2,417 (2010); Density: 3,872.8 persons per square mile (2010); Race: 91.6% White, 3.4% Black, 2.1% Asian, 0.2% American Indian/Alaska Native, 0.0% Native Hawaiian/Other Pacific Islander, 2.7% Other, 1.9% Hispanic of any race (2010); Average household size: 2.31 (2010); Median age: 41.3 (2010); Males per 100 females: 90.9 (2010); Marriage status: 31.3% never married, 42.7% now married, 15.0% widowed, 10.9% divorced (2006-2010 5-year est.); Foreign born: 2.4% (2006-2010 5-year est.); Ancestry (includes multiple ancestries): 38.4% German, 18.7% Irish, 18.0% Italian, 13.0% English, 12.1% Polish (2006-2010 5-year est.).

**Economy:** Employment by occupation: 7.6% management, 1.3% professional, 11.2% services, 16.1% sales, 11.3% farming, 10.2% construction, 7.8% production (2006-2010 5-year est.).

**Income:** Per capita income: $27,035 (2006-2010 5-year est.); Median household income: $47,013 (2006-2010 5-year est.); Average household income: $54,257 (2006-2010 5-year est.); Percent of households with income of $100,000 or more: 8.4% (2006-2010 5-year est.); Poverty rate: 2.3% (2006-2010 5-year est.).

**Education:** Percent of population age 25 and over with: High school diploma (including GED) or higher: 87.1% (2006-2010 5-year est.); Bachelor's degree or higher: 17.1% (2006-2010 5-year est.); Master's degree or higher: 5.4% (2006-2010 5-year est.).

**Housing:** Homeownership rate: 76.3% (2010); Median home value: $153,100 (2006-2010 5-year est.); Median contract rent: $642 per month (2006-2010 5-year est.); Median year structure built: 1953 (2006-2010 5-year est.).

**Transportation:** Commute to work: 95.1% car, 3.6% public transportation, 1.3% walk, 0.0% work from home (2006-2010 5-year est.); Travel time to work: 39.2% less than 15 minutes, 54.1% 15 to 30 minutes, 3.6% 30 to 45 minutes, 1.9% 45 to 60 minutes, 1.1% 60 minutes or more (2006-2010 5-year est.)

## HOOSICK (town).

Covers a land area of 63.031 square miles and a water area of 0.112 square miles. Located at 42.87° N. Lat; 73.35° W. Long. Elevation is 482 feet.

**History:** Bennington Battlefield Park is Northeast. Hoosick Falls Historic District. Incorporated 1827.

**Population:** 6,696 (1990); 6,759 (2000); 6,924 (2010); Density: 109.8 persons per square mile (2010); Race: 96.9% White, 0.7% Black, 0.5% Asian, 0.2% American Indian/Alaska Native, 0.0% Native Hawaiian/Other Pacific Islander, 1.7% Other, 1.2% Hispanic of any race (2010); Average household size: 2.47 (2010); Median age: 42.6 (2010); Males per 100 females: 90.7 (2010); Marriage status: 30.0% never married, 50.4% now married, 8.6% widowed, 10.9% divorced (2006-2010 5-year est.); Foreign born: 1.8% (2006-2010 5-year est.); Ancestry (includes multiple ancestries): 22.5% Irish, 16.5% German, 11.9% American, 11.8% English, 10.7% French (2006-2010 5-year est.).

**Economy:** Single-family building permits issued: 6 (2011); Multi-family building permits issued: 0 (2011); Employment by occupation: 10.0% management, 4.2% professional, 10.1% services, 15.6% sales, 2.7% farming, 9.8% construction, 7.7% production (2006-2010 5-year est.).

**Income:** Per capita income: $23,972 (2006-2010 5-year est.); Median household income: $49,637 (2006-2010 5-year est.); Average household income: $59,992 (2006-2010 5-year est.); Percent of households with income of $100,000 or more: 15.8% (2006-2010 5-year est.); Poverty rate: 11.3% (2006-2010 5-year est.).

**Education:** Percent of population age 25 and over with: High school diploma (including GED) or higher: 88.1% (2006-2010 5-year est.); Bachelor's degree or higher: 21.7% (2006-2010 5-year est.); Master's degree or higher: 7.7% (2006-2010 5-year est.).

**Housing:** Homeownership rate: 70.8% (2010); Median home value: $133,700 (2006-2010 5-year est.); Median contract rent: $662 per month (2006-2010 5-year est.); Median year structure built: 1946 (2006-2010 5-year est.).

**Transportation:** Commute to work: 94.3% car, 0.2% public transportation, 3.1% walk, 2.0% work from home (2006-2010 5-year est.); Travel time to work: 26.4% less than 15 minutes, 29.1% 15 to 30 minutes, 16.5% 30 to 45 minutes, 16.4% 45 to 60 minutes, 11.7% 60 minutes or more (2006-2010 5-year est.)

## HOOSICK FALLS (village).

Covers a land area of 1.597 square miles and a water area of 0 square miles. Located at 42.90° N. Lat; 73.34° W. Long. Elevation is 443 feet.

**Population:** 3,490 (1990); 3,436 (2000); 3,501 (2010); Density: 2,190.9 persons per square mile (2010); Race: 96.7% White, 0.8% Black, 0.5% Asian, 0.2% American Indian/Alaska Native, 0.0% Native Hawaiian/Other Pacific Islander, 1.8% Other, 1.2% Hispanic of any race (2010); Average household size: 2.39 (2010); Median age: 40.5 (2010); Males per 100 females: 87.5 (2010); Marriage status: 31.9% never married, 45.5% now married, 11.3% widowed, 11.4% divorced (2006-2010 5-year est.); Foreign born: 2.1% (2006-2010 5-year est.); Ancestry (includes multiple ancestries): 24.6% Irish, 13.3% English, 13.3% German, 9.7% French, 8.5% American (2006-2010 5-year est.).

**Economy:** Single-family building permits issued: 0 (2011); Multi-family building permits issued: 0 (2011); Employment by occupation: 11.8% management, 3.1% professional, 9.5% services, 17.7% sales, 2.3% farming, 7.6% construction, 5.0% production (2006-2010 5-year est.).

**Income:** Per capita income: $23,000 (2006-2010 5-year est.); Median household income: $43,405 (2006-2010 5-year est.); Average household income: $57,991 (2006-2010 5-year est.); Percent of households with income of $100,000 or more: 17.3% (2006-2010 5-year est.); Poverty rate: 14.4% (2006-2010 5-year est.).

**Education:** Percent of population age 25 and over with: High school diploma (including GED) or higher: 86.0% (2006-2010 5-year est.); Bachelor's degree or higher: 26.3% (2006-2010 5-year est.); Master's degree or higher: 9.7% (2006-2010 5-year est.).

### School District(s)

Hoosick Falls Central School District (KG-12)
    2009-10 Enrollment: 1,238 . . . . . . . . . . . . . . . . . . . . . . (518) 686-7012

**Housing:** Homeownership rate: 60.2% (2010); Median home value: $120,400 (2006-2010 5-year est.); Median contract rent: $630 per month (2006-2010 5-year est.); Median year structure built: before 1940 (2006-2010 5-year est.).

**Transportation:** Commute to work: 93.8% car, 0.0% public transportation, 3.5% walk, 1.9% work from home (2006-2010 5-year est.); Travel time to work: 29.1% less than 15 minutes, 26.7% 15 to 30 minutes, 13.2% 30 to 45

minutes, 22.8% 45 to 60 minutes, 8.2% 60 minutes or more (2006-2010 5-year est.)

## JOHNSONVILLE (unincorporated postal area)
Zip Code: 12094

Covers a land area of 28.234 square miles and a water area of 0.581 square miles. Located at 42.89° N. Lat; 73.48° W. Long. Elevation is 377 feet. Population: 2,268 (2010); Density: 80.3 persons per square mile (2010); Race: 97.4% White, 0.1% Black, 0.3% Asian, 0.5% American Indian/Alaska Native, 0.0% Native Hawaiian/Other Pacific Islander, 1.7% Other, 0.6% Hispanic of any race (2010); Average household size: 2.74 (2010); Median age: 40.6 (2010); Males per 100 females: 100.4 (2010); Homeownership rate: 84.8% (2010)

## MELROSE (unincorporated postal area)
Zip Code: 12121

Covers a land area of 20.614 square miles and a water area of 2.959 square miles. Located at 42.83° N. Lat; 73.60° W. Long. Elevation is 390 feet. Population: 1,916 (2010); Density: 92.9 persons per square mile (2010); Race: 97.5% White, 1.0% Black, 1.0% Asian, 0.2% American Indian/Alaska Native, 0.0% Native Hawaiian/Other Pacific Islander, 0.3% Other, 0.7% Hispanic of any race (2010); Average household size: 2.66 (2010); Median age: 44.3 (2010); Males per 100 females: 97.3 (2010); Homeownership rate: 92.4% (2010)

## NASSAU (village). Covers a land area of 0.698 square miles and a water area of 0 square miles. Located at 42.51° N. Lat; 73.61° W. Long. Elevation is 404 feet.
**Population:** 1,254 (1990); 1,161 (2000); 1,133 (2010); Density: 1,621.5 persons per square mile (2010); Race: 96.4% White, 1.1% Black, 0.2% Asian, 0.1% American Indian/Alaska Native, 0.0% Native Hawaiian/Other Pacific Islander, 2.2% Other, 1.1% Hispanic of any race (2010); Average household size: 2.28 (2010); Median age: 39.3 (2010); Males per 100 females: 94.0 (2010); Marriage status: 32.1% never married, 41.8% now married, 13.9% widowed, 12.3% divorced (2006-2010 5-year est.); Foreign born: 1.3% (2006-2010 5-year est.); Ancestry (includes multiple ancestries): 25.5% German, 23.6% Irish, 17.5% English, 11.6% Italian, 9.1% French (2006-2010 5-year est.).
**Economy:** Single-family building permits issued: 0 (2011); Multi-family building permits issued: 0 (2011); Employment by occupation: 7.5% management, 4.7% professional, 6.6% services, 15.1% sales, 4.5% farming, 17.6% construction, 12.7% production (2006-2010 5-year est.).
**Income:** Per capita income: $26,761 (2006-2010 5-year est.); Median household income: $44,648 (2006-2010 5-year est.); Average household income: $58,341 (2006-2010 5-year est.); Percent of households with income of $100,000 or more: 17.1% (2006-2010 5-year est.); Poverty rate: 5.9% (2006-2010 5-year est.).
**Education:** Percent of population age 25 and over with: High school diploma (including GED) or higher: 87.8% (2006-2010 5-year est.); Bachelor's degree or higher: 13.3% (2006-2010 5-year est.); Master's degree or higher: 6.3% (2006-2010 5-year est.).
### School District(s)
East Greenbush Central School District (KG-12)
    2009-10 Enrollment: 4,482 . . . . . . . . . . . . . . . . . . . . . . (518) 207-2531
**Housing:** Homeownership rate: 57.4% (2010); Median home value: $125,900 (2006-2010 5-year est.); Median contract rent: $564 per month (2006-2010 5-year est.); Median year structure built: 1949 (2006-2010 5-year est.).
**Safety:** Violent crime rate: 36.4 per 10,000 population; Property crime rate: 264.1 per 10,000 population (2010).
**Transportation:** Commute to work: 93.4% car, 0.9% public transportation, 1.8% walk, 2.9% work from home (2006-2010 5-year est.); Travel time to work: 28.3% less than 15 minutes, 39.1% 15 to 30 minutes, 20.9% 30 to 45 minutes, 6.1% 45 to 60 minutes, 5.7% 60 minutes or more (2006-2010 5-year est.)

## NASSAU (town). Covers a land area of 44.444 square miles and a water area of 0.791 square miles. Located at 42.54° N. Lat; 73.54° W. Long. Elevation is 404 feet.
**Population:** 4,989 (1990); 4,818 (2000); 4,789 (2010); Density: 107.8 persons per square mile (2010); Race: 96.6% White, 0.8% Black, 0.6% Asian, 0.2% American Indian/Alaska Native, 0.0% Native Hawaiian/Other Pacific Islander, 1.8% Other, 1.6% Hispanic of any race (2010); Average household size: 2.46 (2010); Median age: 42.4 (2010); Males per 100 females: 102.0 (2010); Marriage status: 24.5% never married, 60.5% now

married, 7.6% widowed, 7.4% divorced (2006-2010 5-year est.); Foreign born: 1.7% (2006-2010 5-year est.); Ancestry (includes multiple ancestries): 34.5% German, 26.6% Irish, 12.9% English, 11.8% Italian, 7.5% French (2006-2010 5-year est.).
**Economy:** Single-family building permits issued: 7 (2011); Multi-family building permits issued: 2 (2011); Employment by occupation: 11.7% management, 4.3% professional, 5.2% services, 17.8% sales, 3.4% farming, 14.8% construction, 11.2% production (2006-2010 5-year est.).
**Income:** Per capita income: $29,149 (2006-2010 5-year est.); Median household income: $57,177 (2006-2010 5-year est.); Average household income: $70,762 (2006-2010 5-year est.); Percent of households with income of $100,000 or more: 22.0% (2006-2010 5-year est.); Poverty rate: 4.5% (2006-2010 5-year est.).
**Education:** Percent of population age 25 and over with: High school diploma (including GED) or higher: 92.6% (2006-2010 5-year est.); Bachelor's degree or higher: 22.3% (2006-2010 5-year est.); Master's degree or higher: 9.7% (2006-2010 5-year est.).
### School District(s)
East Greenbush Central School District (KG-12)
    2009-10 Enrollment: 4,482 . . . . . . . . . . . . . . . . . . . . . . (518) 207-2531
**Housing:** Homeownership rate: 75.8% (2010); Median home value: $168,400 (2006-2010 5-year est.); Median contract rent: $576 per month (2006-2010 5-year est.); Median year structure built: 1954 (2006-2010 5-year est.).
**Transportation:** Commute to work: 87.0% car, 1.0% public transportation, 2.8% walk, 8.7% work from home (2006-2010 5-year est.); Travel time to work: 18.8% less than 15 minutes, 29.0% 15 to 30 minutes, 36.2% 30 to 45 minutes, 9.8% 45 to 60 minutes, 6.2% 60 minutes or more (2006-2010 5-year est.)

## NORTH GREENBUSH (town). Covers a land area of 18.545 square miles and a water area of 0.363 square miles. Located at 42.67° N. Lat; 73.66° W. Long.
**Population:** 10,628 (1990); 10,805 (2000); 12,075 (2010); Density: 651.1 persons per square mile (2010); Race: 95.4% White, 1.7% Black, 1.3% Asian, 0.2% American Indian/Alaska Native, 0.0% Native Hawaiian/Other Pacific Islander, 1.4% Other, 1.6% Hispanic of any race (2010); Average household size: 2.41 (2010); Median age: 43.4 (2010); Males per 100 females: 88.8 (2010); Marriage status: 29.2% never married, 54.2% now married, 8.7% widowed, 7.9% divorced (2006-2010 5-year est.); Foreign born: 3.0% (2006-2010 5-year est.); Ancestry (includes multiple ancestries): 32.1% Irish, 22.1% German, 20.9% Italian, 10.8% French, 9.4% English (2006-2010 5-year est.).
**Economy:** Single-family building permits issued: 11 (2011); Multi-family building permits issued: 14 (2011); Employment by occupation: 14.6% management, 5.8% professional, 6.8% services, 18.1% sales, 5.5% farming, 6.5% construction, 5.1% production (2006-2010 5-year est.).
**Income:** Per capita income: $32,218 (2006-2010 5-year est.); Median household income: $68,551 (2006-2010 5-year est.); Average household income: $81,881 (2006-2010 5-year est.); Percent of households with income of $100,000 or more: 26.4% (2006-2010 5-year est.); Poverty rate: 3.4% (2006-2010 5-year est.).
**Education:** Percent of population age 25 and over with: High school diploma (including GED) or higher: 91.4% (2006-2010 5-year est.); Bachelor's degree or higher: 31.8% (2006-2010 5-year est.); Master's degree or higher: 15.1% (2006-2010 5-year est.).
**Housing:** Homeownership rate: 77.7% (2010); Median home value: $193,300 (2006-2010 5-year est.); Median contract rent: $817 per month (2006-2010 5-year est.); Median year structure built: 1965 (2006-2010 5-year est.).
**Safety:** Violent crime rate: 11.8 per 10,000 population; Property crime rate: 215.5 per 10,000 population (2010).
**Transportation:** Commute to work: 94.9% car, 1.6% public transportation, 0.9% walk, 2.5% work from home (2006-2010 5-year est.); Travel time to work: 28.7% less than 15 minutes, 54.4% 15 to 30 minutes, 12.7% 30 to 45 minutes, 2.1% 45 to 60 minutes, 2.0% 60 minutes or more (2006-2010 5-year est.)

## PETERSBURG (unincorporated postal area)
Zip Code: 12138

Covers a land area of 80.259 square miles and a water area of 0.410 square miles. Located at 42.74° N. Lat; 73.37° W. Long. Elevation is 712 feet. Population: 3,168 (2010); Density: 39.5 persons per square mile (2010); Race: 97.4% White, 0.3% Black, 0.3% Asian, 0.2% American Indian/Alaska Native, 0.0% Native Hawaiian/Other Pacific Islander, 1.8%

Other, 1.3% Hispanic of any race (2010); Average household size: 2.52 (2010); Median age: 43.7 (2010); Males per 100 females: 103.6 (2010); Homeownership rate: 86.7% (2010)

## PETERSBURGH (town).
Covers a land area of 41.604 square miles and a water area of 0.002 square miles. Located at 42.77° N. Lat; 73.32° W. Long.
**Population:** 1,469 (1990); 1,563 (2000); 1,525 (2010); Density: 36.7 persons per square mile (2010); Race: 97.3% White, 0.3% Black, 0.5% Asian, 0.1% American Indian/Alaska Native, 0.0% Native Hawaiian/Other Pacific Islander, 1.8% Other, 1.5% Hispanic of any race (2010); Average household size: 2.48 (2010); Median age: 45.4 (2010); Males per 100 females: 110.9 (2010); Marriage status: 22.1% never married, 61.0% now married, 6.2% widowed, 10.8% divorced (2006-2010 5-year est.); Foreign born: 2.3% (2006-2010 5-year est.); Ancestry (includes multiple ancestries): 27.5% Irish, 17.4% German, 13.2% American, 12.5% English, 11.7% French (2006-2010 5-year est.).
**Economy:** Single-family building permits issued: 1 (2011); Multi-family building permits issued: 0 (2011); Employment by occupation: 13.5% management, 2.5% professional, 6.2% services, 14.6% sales, 3.9% farming, 15.1% construction, 8.3% production (2006-2010 5-year est.).
**Income:** Per capita income: $22,670 (2006-2010 5-year est.); Median household income: $49,205 (2006-2010 5-year est.); Average household income: $59,387 (2006-2010 5-year est.); Percent of households with income of $100,000 or more: 10.6% (2006-2010 5-year est.); Poverty rate: 5.7% (2006-2010 5-year est.).
**Education:** Percent of population age 25 and over with: High school diploma (including GED) or higher: 85.3% (2006-2010 5-year est.); Bachelor's degree or higher: 16.0% (2006-2010 5-year est.); Master's degree or higher: 7.0% (2006-2010 5-year est.).
**Housing:** Homeownership rate: 86.2% (2010); Median home value: $129,000 (2006-2010 5-year est.); Median contract rent: $525 per month (2006-2010 5-year est.); Median year structure built: 1968 (2006-2010 5-year est.).
**Transportation:** Commute to work: 86.5% car, 2.7% public transportation, 5.2% walk, 4.9% work from home (2006-2010 5-year est.); Travel time to work: 24.2% less than 15 minutes, 25.4% 15 to 30 minutes, 24.1% 30 to 45 minutes, 16.5% 45 to 60 minutes, 9.8% 60 minutes or more (2006-2010 5-year est.)

## PITTSTOWN (town).
Covers a land area of 61.627 square miles and a water area of 3.215 square miles. Located at 42.86° N. Lat; 73.51° W. Long. Elevation is 568 feet.
**Population:** 5,468 (1990); 5,644 (2000); 5,735 (2010); Density: 93.1 persons per square mile (2010); Race: 97.4% White, 0.5% Black, 0.5% Asian, 0.5% American Indian/Alaska Native, 0.0% Native Hawaiian/Other Pacific Islander, 1.1% Other, 1.0% Hispanic of any race (2010); Average household size: 2.69 (2010); Median age: 41.7 (2010); Males per 100 females: 99.5 (2010); Marriage status: 24.9% never married, 60.0% now married, 5.6% widowed, 9.4% divorced (2006-2010 5-year est.); Foreign born: 0.7% (2006-2010 5-year est.); Ancestry (includes multiple ancestries): 29.7% Irish, 17.2% German, 17.0% Italian, 16.0% English, 15.2% French (2006-2010 5-year est.).
**Economy:** Single-family building permits issued: 8 (2011); Multi-family building permits issued: 0 (2011); Employment by occupation: 11.2% management, 3.1% professional, 9.8% services, 20.7% sales, 2.1% farming, 10.4% construction, 7.0% production (2006-2010 5-year est.).
**Income:** Per capita income: $26,059 (2006-2010 5-year est.); Median household income: $54,245 (2006-2010 5-year est.); Average household income: $70,356 (2006-2010 5-year est.); Percent of households with income of $100,000 or more: 22.6% (2006-2010 5-year est.); Poverty rate: 5.6% (2006-2010 5-year est.).
**Education:** Percent of population age 25 and over with: High school diploma (including GED) or higher: 92.2% (2006-2010 5-year est.); Bachelor's degree or higher: 20.3% (2006-2010 5-year est.); Master's degree or higher: 8.5% (2006-2010 5-year est.).
**Housing:** Homeownership rate: 85.3% (2010); Median home value: $169,900 (2006-2010 5-year est.); Median contract rent: $588 per month (2006-2010 5-year est.); Median year structure built: 1978 (2006-2010 5-year est.).
**Transportation:** Commute to work: 95.3% car, 0.4% public transportation, 0.0% walk, 4.4% work from home (2006-2010 5-year est.); Travel time to work: 10.8% less than 15 minutes, 35.0% 15 to 30 minutes, 36.1% 30 to 45 minutes, 12.2% 45 to 60 minutes, 5.9% 60 minutes or more (2006-2010 5-year est.)

## POESTENKILL (town).
Covers a land area of 32.355 square miles and a water area of 0.219 square miles. Located at 42.70° N. Lat; 73.52° W. Long. Elevation is 479 feet.
**Population:** 3,809 (1990); 4,054 (2000); 4,530 (2010); Density: 140.0 persons per square mile (2010); Race: 97.7% White, 0.3% Black, 0.4% Asian, 0.1% American Indian/Alaska Native, 0.0% Native Hawaiian/Other Pacific Islander, 1.5% Other, 1.1% Hispanic of any race (2010); Average household size: 2.69 (2010); Median age: 41.5 (2010); Males per 100 females: 98.4 (2010); Marriage status: 26.6% never married, 61.3% now married, 4.0% widowed, 8.1% divorced (2006-2010 5-year est.); Foreign born: 2.6% (2006-2010 5-year est.); Ancestry (includes multiple ancestries): 32.6% German, 29.4% Irish, 15.4% English, 12.9% French, 9.9% Italian (2006-2010 5-year est.).
**Economy:** Single-family building permits issued: 3 (2011); Multi-family building permits issued: 0 (2011); Employment by occupation: 12.9% management, 7.2% professional, 6.4% services, 19.2% sales, 5.2% farming, 12.0% construction, 5.3% production (2006-2010 5-year est.).
**Income:** Per capita income: $28,575 (2006-2010 5-year est.); Median household income: $78,045 (2006-2010 5-year est.); Average household income: $78,198 (2006-2010 5-year est.); Percent of households with income of $100,000 or more: 29.6% (2006-2010 5-year est.); Poverty rate: 1.1% (2006-2010 5-year est.).
**Education:** Percent of population age 25 and over with: High school diploma (including GED) or higher: 94.6% (2006-2010 5-year est.); Bachelor's degree or higher: 31.5% (2006-2010 5-year est.); Master's degree or higher: 14.7% (2006-2010 5-year est.).
**School District(s)**
Averill Park Central School District (KG-12)
    2009-10 Enrollment: 3,367 . . . . . . . . . . . . . . . . . . . . . . . . (518) 674-7055
**Housing:** Homeownership rate: 85.0% (2010); Median home value: $208,300 (2006-2010 5-year est.); Median contract rent: $722 per month (2006-2010 5-year est.); Median year structure built: 1968 (2006-2010 5-year est.).
**Transportation:** Commute to work: 92.9% car, 0.4% public transportation, 0.9% walk, 3.9% work from home (2006-2010 5-year est.); Travel time to work: 21.5% less than 15 minutes, 40.8% 15 to 30 minutes, 27.1% 30 to 45 minutes, 6.6% 45 to 60 minutes, 4.1% 60 minutes or more (2006-2010 5-year est.)

## POESTENKILL (CDP).
Covers a land area of 5.876 square miles and a water area of 0.066 square miles. Located at 42.69° N. Lat; 73.54° W. Long. Elevation is 479 feet.
**Population:** 1,028 (1990); 1,024 (2000); 1,061 (2010); Density: 180.6 persons per square mile (2010); Race: 98.2% White, 0.1% Black, 0.2% Asian, 0.3% American Indian/Alaska Native, 0.0% Native Hawaiian/Other Pacific Islander, 1.2% Other, 1.1% Hispanic of any race (2010); Average household size: 2.54 (2010); Median age: 44.1 (2010); Males per 100 females: 90.8 (2010); Marriage status: 30.4% never married, 59.1% now married, 5.8% widowed, 4.6% divorced (2006-2010 5-year est.); Foreign born: 0.0% (2006-2010 5-year est.); Ancestry (includes multiple ancestries): 46.1% Irish, 38.4% German, 17.7% French, 11.9% Italian, 8.2% English (2006-2010 5-year est.).
**Economy:** Employment by occupation: 13.8% management, 0.0% professional, 14.1% services, 16.1% sales, 2.5% farming, 15.4% construction, 3.1% production (2006-2010 5-year est.).
**Income:** Per capita income: $25,897 (2006-2010 5-year est.); Median household income: $47,500 (2006-2010 5-year est.); Average household income: $67,738 (2006-2010 5-year est.); Percent of households with income of $100,000 or more: 27.4% (2006-2010 5-year est.); Poverty rate: 1.9% (2006-2010 5-year est.).
**Education:** Percent of population age 25 and over with: High school diploma (including GED) or higher: 91.5% (2006-2010 5-year est.); Bachelor's degree or higher: 18.7% (2006-2010 5-year est.); Master's degree or higher: 9.1% (2006-2010 5-year est.).
**School District(s)**
Averill Park Central School District (KG-12)
    2009-10 Enrollment: 3,367 . . . . . . . . . . . . . . . . . . . . . . . . (518) 674-7055
**Housing:** Homeownership rate: 84.4% (2010); Median home value: $158,700 (2006-2010 5-year est.); Median contract rent: $317 per month (2006-2010 5-year est.); Median year structure built: 1959 (2006-2010 5-year est.).
**Transportation:** Commute to work: 92.5% car, 0.0% public transportation, 2.0% walk, 2.3% work from home (2006-2010 5-year est.); Travel time to work: 11.6% less than 15 minutes, 49.1% 15 to 30 minutes, 26.5% 30 to 45 minutes

minutes, 8.6% 45 to 60 minutes, 4.2% 60 minutes or more (2006-2010 5-year est.)

## RENSSELAER (city). Covers a land area of 3.170 square miles and a water area of 0.334 square miles. Located at 42.64° N. Lat; 73.73° W. Long. Elevation is 16 feet.

**History:** The city was formed by the union of several villages within the tract granted to Kiliaen Van Rensselaer by the chartered Dutch West Indies Company. At the 17th-century Fort Crailo, now a museum, the British surgeon Richard Shuckburg is said to have written "Yankee Doodle." Settled 1630 by Dutch, incorporated 1897.

**Population:** 8,360 (1990); 7,761 (2000); 9,392 (2010); Density: 2,962.3 persons per square mile (2010); Race: 80.2% White, 8.0% Black, 6.1% Asian, 0.3% American Indian/Alaska Native, 0.0% Native Hawaiian/Other Pacific Islander, 5.4% Other, 4.8% Hispanic of any race (2010); Average household size: 2.14 (2010); Median age: 37.1 (2010); Males per 100 females: 92.7 (2010); Marriage status: 41.6% never married, 35.5% now married, 7.7% widowed, 15.2% divorced (2006-2010 5-year est.); Foreign born: 9.0% (2006-2010 5-year est.); Ancestry (includes multiple ancestries): 24.5% Irish, 19.5% Italian, 18.0% German, 11.9% English, 8.5% Dutch (2006-2010 5-year est.).

**Economy:** Single-family building permits issued: 2 (2011); Multi-family building permits issued: 0 (2011); Employment by occupation: 8.1% management, 4.6% professional, 12.0% services, 20.7% sales, 6.9% farming, 4.3% construction, 3.6% production (2006-2010 5-year est.).

**Income:** Per capita income: $27,073 (2006-2010 5-year est.); Median household income: $45,420 (2006-2010 5-year est.); Average household income: $57,435 (2006-2010 5-year est.); Percent of households with income of $100,000 or more: 12.5% (2006-2010 5-year est.); Poverty rate: 17.9% (2006-2010 5-year est.).

**Education:** Percent of population age 25 and over with: High school diploma (including GED) or higher: 84.1% (2006-2010 5-year est.); Bachelor's degree or higher: 22.6% (2006-2010 5-year est.); Master's degree or higher: 9.4% (2006-2010 5-year est.).

### School District(s)

East Greenbush Central School District (KG-12)

   2009-10 Enrollment: 4,482 . . . . . . . . . . . . . . . . . . . . . . . (518) 207-2531

NYS Office of Children and Family Services (06-12)

   2009-10 Enrollment: n/a . . . . . . . . . . . . . . . . . . . . . . . . . (518) 473-7793

Rensselaer City School District (PK-12)

   2009-10 Enrollment: 1,079 . . . . . . . . . . . . . . . . . . . . . . . (518) 465-7509

**Housing:** Homeownership rate: 43.0% (2010); Median home value: $147,200 (2006-2010 5-year est.); Median contract rent: $593 per month (2006-2010 5-year est.); Median year structure built: 1948 (2006-2010 5-year est.).

**Safety:** Violent crime rate: 24.5 per 10,000 population; Property crime rate: 274.5 per 10,000 population (2010).

**Transportation:** Commute to work: 88.0% car, 6.6% public transportation, 3.1% walk, 0.3% work from home (2006-2010 5-year est.); Travel time to work: 39.1% less than 15 minutes, 45.8% 15 to 30 minutes, 11.9% 30 to 45 minutes, 1.0% 45 to 60 minutes, 2.1% 60 minutes or more (2006-2010 5-year est.); Amtrak: train service available.

## SAND LAKE (town). Covers a land area of 35.049 square miles and a water area of 1.119 square miles. Located at 42.63° N. Lat; 73.54° W. Long. Elevation is 781 feet.

**Population:** 7,642 (1990); 7,987 (2000); 8,530 (2010); Density: 243.4 persons per square mile (2010); Race: 97.6% White, 0.4% Black, 0.5% Asian, 0.1% American Indian/Alaska Native, 0.0% Native Hawaiian/Other Pacific Islander, 1.4% Other, 1.5% Hispanic of any race (2010); Average household size: 2.54 (2010); Median age: 43.4 (2010); Males per 100 females: 98.3 (2010); Marriage status: 23.5% never married, 58.8% now married, 5.9% widowed, 11.7% divorced (2006-2010 5-year est.); Foreign born: 3.7% (2006-2010 5-year est.); Ancestry (includes multiple ancestries): 28.8% German, 22.5% Irish, 18.9% English, 12.4% Italian, 7.8% French (2006-2010 5-year est.).

**Economy:** Single-family building permits issued: 0 (2011); Multi-family building permits issued: 0 (2011); Employment by occupation: 13.3% management, 7.5% professional, 7.6% services, 13.8% sales, 5.3% farming, 9.6% construction, 4.7% production (2006-2010 5-year est.).

**Income:** Per capita income: $33,300 (2006-2010 5-year est.); Median household income: $72,130 (2006-2010 5-year est.); Average household income: $82,519 (2006-2010 5-year est.); Percent of households with income of $100,000 or more: 31.1% (2006-2010 5-year est.); Poverty rate: 3.5% (2006-2010 5-year est.).

**Education:** Percent of population age 25 and over with: High school diploma (including GED) or higher: 94.3% (2006-2010 5-year est.); Bachelor's degree or higher: 37.0% (2006-2010 5-year est.); Master's degree or higher: 16.5% (2006-2010 5-year est.).

**Housing:** Homeownership rate: 82.2% (2010); Median home value: $194,700 (2006-2010 5-year est.); Median contract rent: $608 per month (2006-2010 5-year est.); Median year structure built: 1960 (2006-2010 5-year est.).

**Transportation:** Commute to work: 95.4% car, 0.4% public transportation, 1.0% walk, 3.3% work from home (2006-2010 5-year est.); Travel time to work: 15.8% less than 15 minutes, 47.4% 15 to 30 minutes, 28.8% 30 to 45 minutes, 6.8% 45 to 60 minutes, 1.2% 60 minutes or more (2006-2010 5-year est.)

## SCHAGHTICOKE (village). Covers a land area of 0.758 square miles and a water area of 0.235 square miles. Located at 42.90° N. Lat; 73.58° W. Long. Elevation is 358 feet.

**Population:** 794 (1990); 676 (2000); 592 (2010); Density: 780.9 persons per square mile (2010); Race: 96.3% White, 1.2% Black, 0.8% Asian, 1.0% American Indian/Alaska Native, 0.0% Native Hawaiian/Other Pacific Islander, 0.7% Other, 0.8% Hispanic of any race (2010); Average household size: 2.45 (2010); Median age: 37.2 (2010); Males per 100 females: 110.7 (2010); Marriage status: 36.1% never married, 51.4% now married, 6.7% widowed, 5.7% divorced (2006-2010 5-year est.); Foreign born: 0.0% (2006-2010 5-year est.); Ancestry (includes multiple ancestries): 25.7% French, 22.5% Irish, 20.3% German, 18.2% Italian, 13.0% English (2006-2010 5-year est.).

**Economy:** Single-family building permits issued: 4 (2011); Multi-family building permits issued: 0 (2011); Employment by occupation: 8.8% management, 2.4% professional, 6.1% services, 25.0% sales, 3.0% farming, 8.5% construction, 6.1% production (2006-2010 5-year est.).

**Income:** Per capita income: $25,351 (2006-2010 5-year est.); Median household income: $44,539 (2006-2010 5-year est.); Average household income: $67,290 (2006-2010 5-year est.); Percent of households with income of $100,000 or more: 19.7% (2006-2010 5-year est.); Poverty rate: 8.8% (2006-2010 5-year est.).

**Education:** Percent of population age 25 and over with: High school diploma (including GED) or higher: 94.0% (2006-2010 5-year est.); Bachelor's degree or higher: 9.6% (2006-2010 5-year est.); Master's degree or higher: 3.1% (2006-2010 5-year est.).

### School District(s)

Hoosic Valley Central School District (PK-12)

   2009-10 Enrollment: 1,196 . . . . . . . . . . . . . . . . . . . . . . . (518) 753-4450

**Housing:** Homeownership rate: 66.5% (2010); Median home value: $156,300 (2006-2010 5-year est.); Median contract rent: $726 per month (2006-2010 5-year est.); Median year structure built: before 1940 (2006-2010 5-year est.).

**Transportation:** Commute to work: 92.2% car, 0.0% public transportation, 5.3% walk, 1.2% work from home (2006-2010 5-year est.); Travel time to work: 33.4% less than 15 minutes, 22.4% 15 to 30 minutes, 38.2% 30 to 45 minutes, 4.7% 45 to 60 minutes, 1.3% 60 minutes or more (2006-2010 5-year est.)

## SCHAGHTICOKE (town). Covers a land area of 49.747 square miles and a water area of 2.114 square miles. Located at 42.88° N. Lat; 73.61° W. Long. Elevation is 358 feet.

**Population:** 7,574 (1990); 7,456 (2000); 7,679 (2010); Density: 154.4 persons per square mile (2010); Race: 96.4% White, 1.7% Black, 0.6% Asian, 0.2% American Indian/Alaska Native, 0.1% Native Hawaiian/Other Pacific Islander, 1.0% Other, 1.0% Hispanic of any race (2010); Average household size: 2.61 (2010); Median age: 43.4 (2010); Males per 100 females: 98.8 (2010); Marriage status: 23.4% never married, 65.0% now married, 4.5% widowed, 7.1% divorced (2006-2010 5-year est.); Foreign born: 2.5% (2006-2010 5-year est.); Ancestry (includes multiple ancestries): 30.5% Irish, 20.5% Italian, 15.5% German, 14.3% French, 13.3% English (2006-2010 5-year est.).

**Economy:** Employment by occupation: 8.0% management, 1.9% professional, 8.4% services, 24.1% sales, 3.2% farming, 10.6% construction, 6.8% production (2006-2010 5-year est.).

**Income:** Per capita income: $28,328 (2006-2010 5-year est.); Median household income: $69,417 (2006-2010 5-year est.); Average household income: $76,268 (2006-2010 5-year est.); Percent of households with income of $100,000 or more: 25.3% (2006-2010 5-year est.); Poverty rate: 2.7% (2006-2010 5-year est.).

**Education:** Percent of population age 25 and over with: High school diploma (including GED) or higher: 92.8% (2006-2010 5-year est.); Bachelor's degree or higher: 16.3% (2006-2010 5-year est.); Master's degree or higher: 6.2% (2006-2010 5-year est.).

**School District(s)**

Hoosic Valley Central School District (PK-12)

  2009-10 Enrollment: 1,196 . . . . . . . . . . . . . . . . . . . . . . (518) 753-4450

**Housing:** Homeownership rate: 86.6% (2010); Median home value: $182,500 (2006-2010 5-year est.); Median contract rent: $626 per month (2006-2010 5-year est.); Median year structure built: 1962 (2006-2010 5-year est.).

**Transportation:** Commute to work: 95.0% car, 0.3% public transportation, 1.1% walk, 2.9% work from home (2006-2010 5-year est.); Travel time to work: 19.8% less than 15 minutes, 38.1% 15 to 30 minutes, 32.6% 30 to 45 minutes, 6.4% 45 to 60 minutes, 3.1% 60 minutes or more (2006-2010 5-year est.)

## SCHODACK (town). Covers a land area of 61.926 square miles and a water area of 1.676 square miles. Located at 42.53° N. Lat; 73.68° W. Long.

**Population:** 11,839 (1990); 12,536 (2000); 12,794 (2010); Density: 206.6 persons per square mile (2010); Race: 96.6% White, 0.9% Black, 0.7% Asian, 0.1% American Indian/Alaska Native, 0.0% Native Hawaiian/Other Pacific Islander, 1.7% Other, 2.2% Hispanic of any race (2010); Average household size: 2.50 (2010); Median age: 43.4 (2010); Males per 100 females: 97.2 (2010); Marriage status: 21.5% never married, 63.4% now married, 6.4% widowed, 8.7% divorced (2006-2010 5-year est.); Foreign born: 2.2% (2006-2010 5-year est.); Ancestry (includes multiple ancestries): 31.2% Irish, 31.1% German, 14.8% Italian, 12.3% English, 9.0% Dutch (2006-2010 5-year est.).

**Economy:** Single-family building permits issued: 20 (2011); Multi-family building permits issued: 34 (2011); Employment by occupation: 12.9% management, 6.7% professional, 4.7% services, 18.3% sales, 4.8% farming, 9.7% construction, 6.5% production (2006-2010 5-year est.).

**Income:** Per capita income: $32,655 (2006-2010 5-year est.); Median household income: $72,032 (2006-2010 5-year est.); Average household income: $82,141 (2006-2010 5-year est.); Percent of households with income of $100,000 or more: 33.1% (2006-2010 5-year est.); Poverty rate: 6.4% (2006-2010 5-year est.).

**Education:** Percent of population age 25 and over with: High school diploma (including GED) or higher: 91.5% (2006-2010 5-year est.); Bachelor's degree or higher: 31.5% (2006-2010 5-year est.); Master's degree or higher: 13.0% (2006-2010 5-year est.).

**Housing:** Homeownership rate: 81.6% (2010); Median home value: $212,300 (2006-2010 5-year est.); Median contract rent: $628 per month (2006-2010 5-year est.); Median year structure built: 1965 (2006-2010 5-year est.).

**Safety:** Violent crime rate: 7.9 per 10,000 population; Property crime rate: 79.5 per 10,000 population (2010).

**Transportation:** Commute to work: 93.3% car, 0.5% public transportation, 1.4% walk, 3.3% work from home (2006-2010 5-year est.); Travel time to work: 25.1% less than 15 minutes, 42.6% 15 to 30 minutes, 24.1% 30 to 45 minutes, 5.7% 45 to 60 minutes, 2.5% 60 minutes or more (2006-2010 5-year est.).

**Additional Information Contacts**

Town of Schodack . . . . . . . . . . . . . . . . . . . . . . . . . . (518) 477-7918
  http://www.schodack.org

## SCHODACK LANDING (unincorporated postal area)

Zip Code: 12156

Covers a land area of 14.344 square miles and a water area of 0.682 square miles. Located at 42.48° N. Lat; 73.74° W. Long. Elevation is 59 feet. Population: 848 (2010); Density: 59.1 persons per square mile (2010); Race: 95.8% White, 0.2% Black, 0.4% Asian, 0.0% American Indian/Alaska Native, 0.0% Native Hawaiian/Other Pacific Islander, 3.6% Other, 1.5% Hispanic of any race (2010); Average household size: 2.47 (2010); Median age: 42.6 (2010); Males per 100 females: 103.4 (2010); Homeownership rate: 80.8% (2010)

## STEPHENTOWN (town). Covers a land area of 57.880 square miles and a water area of 0.196 square miles. Located at 42.55° N. Lat; 73.41° W. Long. Elevation is 876 feet.

**Population:** 2,521 (1990); 2,873 (2000); 2,903 (2010); Density: 50.2 persons per square mile (2010); Race: 95.2% White, 1.1% Black, 1.1% Asian, 0.3% American Indian/Alaska Native, 0.0% Native Hawaiian/Other

Pacific Islander, 2.3% Other, 1.8% Hispanic of any race (2010); Average household size: 2.44 (2010); Median age: 44.3 (2010); Males per 100 females: 100.5 (2010); Marriage status: 24.2% never married, 57.9% now married, 5.6% widowed, 12.3% divorced (2006-2010 5-year est.); Foreign born: 2.2% (2006-2010 5-year est.); Ancestry (includes multiple ancestries): 24.7% Irish, 21.8% German, 13.2% English, 12.1% Italian, 10.5% French (2006-2010 5-year est.).

**Economy:** Single-family building permits issued: 6 (2011); Multi-family building permits issued: 0 (2011); Employment by occupation: 13.4% management, 5.3% professional, 13.4% services, 21.2% sales, 2.2% farming, 15.7% construction, 7.2% production (2006-2010 5-year est.).

**Income:** Per capita income: $27,683 (2006-2010 5-year est.); Median household income: $63,750 (2006-2010 5-year est.); Average household income: $71,919 (2006-2010 5-year est.); Percent of households with income of $100,000 or more: 27.1% (2006-2010 5-year est.); Poverty rate: 7.2% (2006-2010 5-year est.).

**Education:** Percent of population age 25 and over with: High school diploma (including GED) or higher: 90.9% (2006-2010 5-year est.); Bachelor's degree or higher: 20.4% (2006-2010 5-year est.); Master's degree or higher: 10.1% (2006-2010 5-year est.).

**Housing:** Homeownership rate: 83.0% (2010); Median home value: $158,500 (2006-2010 5-year est.); Median contract rent: $602 per month (2006-2010 5-year est.); Median year structure built: 1977 (2006-2010 5-year est.).

**Transportation:** Commute to work: 91.7% car, 0.0% public transportation, 0.7% walk, 6.1% work from home (2006-2010 5-year est.); Travel time to work: 16.1% less than 15 minutes, 19.0% 15 to 30 minutes, 32.4% 30 to 45 minutes, 24.8% 45 to 60 minutes, 7.6% 60 minutes or more (2006-2010 5-year est.)

## TROY (city). County seat. Covers a land area of 10.357 square miles and a water area of 0.699 square miles. Located at 42.73° N. Lat; 73.67° W. Long. Elevation is 33 feet.

**History:** The early name of Troy was Pa-an-pa-ack, "field of standing corn." The site was part of the patroonship granted to Kiliaen Van Rensselaer by the Dutch West India Company. For 120 years, it was occupied by Dutch farmers. Some argument took place about the name, but "Troy" was selected in 1789 at a public meeting.

**Population:** 54,269 (1990); 49,170 (2000); 50,129 (2010); Density: 4,840.0 persons per square mile (2010); Race: 72.9% White, 16.4% Black, 3.4% Asian, 0.3% American Indian/Alaska Native, 0.0% Native Hawaiian/Other Pacific Islander, 7.0% Other, 7.9% Hispanic of any race (2010); Average household size: 2.22 (2010); Median age: 30.2 (2010); Males per 100 females: 102.1 (2010); Marriage status: 47.4% never married, 35.5% now married, 6.3% widowed, 10.9% divorced (2006-2010 5-year est.); Foreign born: 8.7% (2006-2010 5-year est.); Ancestry (includes multiple ancestries): 24.8% Irish, 13.3% Italian, 12.8% German, 9.7% French, 8.0% English (2006-2010 5-year est.).

**Economy:** Unemployment rate: 10.1% (February 2012); Total civilian labor force: 23,616 (February 2012); Single-family building permits issued: 4 (2011); Multi-family building permits issued: 0 (2011); Employment by occupation: 7.3% management, 5.6% professional, 12.1% services, 19.2% sales, 7.3% farming, 6.6% construction, 3.9% production (2006-2010 5-year est.).

**Income:** Per capita income: $20,736 (2006-2010 5-year est.); Median household income: $36,675 (2006-2010 5-year est.); Average household income: $48,936 (2006-2010 5-year est.); Percent of households with income of $100,000 or more: 10.8% (2006-2010 5-year est.); Poverty rate: 25.1% (2006-2010 5-year est.).

**Taxes:** Total city taxes per capita: $442 (2009); City property taxes per capita: $375 (2009).

**Education:** Percent of population age 25 and over with: High school diploma (including GED) or higher: 83.4% (2006-2010 5-year est.); Bachelor's degree or higher: 21.5% (2006-2010 5-year est.); Master's degree or higher: 9.4% (2006-2010 5-year est.).

**School District(s)**

Ark Community Charter School (KG-06)

  2009-10 Enrollment: 208 . . . . . . . . . . . . . . . . . . . . . (518) 274-6312

Averill Park Central School District (KG-12)

  2009-10 Enrollment: 3,367 . . . . . . . . . . . . . . . . . . . . (518) 674-7055

Brunswick Central School District (brittonkill) (PK-12)

  2009-10 Enrollment: 1,372 . . . . . . . . . . . . . . . . . . . . (518) 279-4600

East Greenbush Central School District (KG-12)

  2009-10 Enrollment: 4,482 . . . . . . . . . . . . . . . . . . . . (518) 207-2531

Lansingburgh Central School District (KG-12)
2009-10 Enrollment: 2,426 . . . . . . . . . . . . . . . . . . . . . (518) 233-6850
North Greenbush Common School District (williams) (KG-01)
2009-10 Enrollment: 19 . . . . . . . . . . . . . . . . . . . . . . . . (518) 283-6748
Troy City School District (PK-12)
2009-10 Enrollment: 4,040 . . . . . . . . . . . . . . . . . . . . . (518) 328-5052
True North Troy Preparatory Charter School (05-05)
2009-10 Enrollment: 60 . . . . . . . . . . . . . . . . . . . . . . . . (518) 445-3100

**Four-year College(s)**

Rensselaer Polytechnic Institute (Private, Not-for-profit)
Fall 2010 Enrollment: 6,888 . . . . . . . . . . . . . . . . . . . (518) 276-6000
2011-12 Tuition: In-state $42,704; Out-of-state $42,704
The Sage Colleges (Private, Not-for-profit)
Fall 2010 Enrollment: 2,419 . . . . . . . . . . . . . . . . . . . (518) 244-2000
2011-12 Tuition: In-state $28,000; Out-of-state $28,000

**Two-year College(s)**

Hudson Valley Community College (Public)
Fall 2010 Enrollment: 10,318 . . . . . . . . . . . . . . . . . . (518) 629-4822
2011-12 Tuition: In-state $4,476; Out-of-state $11,876
Samaritan Hospital School of Nursing (Private, Not-for-profit)
Fall 2010 Enrollment: 87 . . . . . . . . . . . . . . . . . . . . . . (518) 271-3285
2011-12 Tuition: In-state $9,264; Out-of-state $9,264

**Vocational/Technical School(s)**

Rensselaer BOCES-School of Practical Nursing (Public)
Fall 2010 Enrollment: 111 . . . . . . . . . . . . . . . . . . . . . (518) 273-2264
2011-12 Tuition: $10,600
**Housing:** Homeownership rate: 38.1% (2010); Median home value: $134,500 (2006-2010 5-year est.); Median contract rent: $586 per month (2006-2010 5-year est.); Median year structure built: before 1940 (2006-2010 5-year est.).
**Hospitals:** Samaritan Hospital (238 beds); Seton Health St.Mary's (201 beds)
**Safety:** Violent crime rate: 90.3 per 10,000 population; Property crime rate: 501.9 per 10,000 population (2010).
**Newspapers:** Progress - Troy Record (Local news); Times Union - Rensselaer County Bureau (Local news); The Troy Record (Local news; Circulation 15,000)
**Transportation:** Commute to work: 76.6% car, 8.7% public transportation, 9.8% walk, 3.5% work from home (2006-2010 5-year est.); Travel time to work: 35.8% less than 15 minutes, 40.6% 15 to 30 minutes, 13.6% 30 to 45 minutes, 4.8% 45 to 60 minutes, 5.2% 60 minutes or more (2006-2010 5-year est.)
**Additional Information Contacts**
City of Troy. . . . . . . . . . . . . . . . . . . . . . . . . . . . . . . . (518) 279-7134
http://www.troyny.gov
Rensselaer County Regional Chamber of Commerce. . . . . (518) 274-7020
http://www.renscochamber.com

---

**VALLEY FALLS** (village). Covers a land area of 0.463 square miles and a water area of 0.024 square miles. Located at 42.90° N. Lat; 73.56° W. Long. Elevation is 335 feet.
**Population:** 527 (1990); 491 (2000); 466 (2010); Density: 1,005.5 persons per square mile (2010); Race: 96.8% White, 0.2% Black, 1.1% Asian, 0.4% American Indian/Alaska Native, 0.0% Native Hawaiian/Other Pacific Islander, 1.5% Other, 1.5% Hispanic of any race (2010); Average household size: 2.60 (2010); Median age: 38.2 (2010); Males per 100 females: 86.4 (2010); Marriage status: 31.9% never married, 50.1% now married, 8.4% widowed, 9.6% divorced (2006-2010 5-year est.); Foreign born: 2.0% (2006-2010 5-year est.); Ancestry (includes multiple ancestries): 44.3% Irish, 20.8% German, 18.6% Italian, 14.7% English, 12.2% French (2006-2010 5-year est.).
**Economy:** Single-family building permits issued: 1 (2011); Multi-family building permits issued: 0 (2011); Employment by occupation: 9.9% management, 7.2% professional, 5.9% services, 17.1% sales, 4.1% farming, 4.5% construction, 2.7% production (2006-2010 5-year est.).
**Income:** Per capita income: $32,900 (2006-2010 5-year est.); Median household income: $61,875 (2006-2010 5-year est.); Average household income: $80,484 (2006-2010 5-year est.); Percent of households with income of $100,000 or more: 31.3% (2006-2010 5-year est.); Poverty rate: 10.0% (2006-2010 5-year est.).
**Education:** Percent of population age 25 and over with: High school diploma (including GED) or higher: 91.9% (2006-2010 5-year est.); Bachelor's degree or higher: 26.9% (2006-2010 5-year est.); Master's degree or higher: 15.2% (2006-2010 5-year est.).

**Housing:** Homeownership rate: 61.5% (2010); Median home value: $138,800 (2006-2010 5-year est.); Median contract rent: $546 per month (2006-2010 5-year est.); Median year structure built: before 1940 (2006-2010 5-year est.).
**Transportation:** Commute to work: 99.1% car, 0.0% public transportation, 0.0% walk, 0.9% work from home (2006-2010 5-year est.); Travel time to work: 14.9% less than 15 minutes, 26.5% 15 to 30 minutes, 32.1% 30 to 45 minutes, 24.2% 45 to 60 minutes, 2.3% 60 minutes or more (2006-2010 5-year est.)

---

**WEST SAND LAKE** (CDP). Covers a land area of 4.704 square miles and a water area of 0.088 square miles. Located at 42.63° N. Lat; 73.59° W. Long. Elevation is 525 feet.
**Population:** 2,145 (1990); 2,439 (2000); 2,660 (2010); Density: 565.5 persons per square mile (2010); Race: 97.3% White, 0.2% Black, 0.6% Asian, 0.1% American Indian/Alaska Native, 0.0% Native Hawaiian/Other Pacific Islander, 1.8% Other, 1.7% Hispanic of any race (2010); Average household size: 2.60 (2010); Median age: 42.0 (2010); Males per 100 females: 94.7 (2010); Marriage status: 25.4% never married, 51.5% now married, 6.6% widowed, 16.5% divorced (2006-2010 5-year est.); Foreign born: 5.1% (2006-2010 5-year est.); Ancestry (includes multiple ancestries): 25.4% German, 18.3% Irish, 18.2% English, 16.0% Italian, 9.6% Dutch (2006-2010 5-year est.).
**Economy:** Employment by occupation: 10.6% management, 8.8% professional, 8.9% services, 12.9% sales, 0.6% farming, 7.1% construction, 4.8% production (2006-2010 5-year est.).
**Income:** Per capita income: $31,073 (2006-2010 5-year est.); Median household income: $66,415 (2006-2010 5-year est.); Average household income: $77,941 (2006-2010 5-year est.); Percent of households with income of $100,000 or more: 32.6% (2006-2010 5-year est.); Poverty rate: 1.8% (2006-2010 5-year est.).
**Education:** Percent of population age 25 and over with: High school diploma (including GED) or higher: 89.6% (2006-2010 5-year est.); Bachelor's degree or higher: 31.1% (2006-2010 5-year est.); Master's degree or higher: 10.8% (2006-2010 5-year est.).

**School District(s)**

Averill Park Central School District (KG-12)
2009-10 Enrollment: 3,367 . . . . . . . . . . . . . . . . . . . (518) 674-7055
**Housing:** Homeownership rate: 81.4% (2010); Median home value: $184,600 (2006-2010 5-year est.); Median contract rent: $503 per month (2006-2010 5-year est.); Median year structure built: 1964 (2006-2010 5-year est.).
**Transportation:** Commute to work: 91.8% car, 1.0% public transportation, 1.6% walk, 5.6% work from home (2006-2010 5-year est.); Travel time to work: 21.4% less than 15 minutes, 57.7% 15 to 30 minutes, 14.6% 30 to 45 minutes, 4.4% 45 to 60 minutes, 2.0% 60 minutes or more (2006-2010 5-year est.)

---

**WYNANTSKILL** (CDP). Covers a land area of 2.359 square miles and a water area of 0.002 square miles. Located at 42.68° N. Lat; 73.64° W. Long. Elevation is 335 feet.
**Population:** 3,360 (1990); 3,018 (2000); 3,276 (2010); Density: 1,388.3 persons per square mile (2010); Race: 95.7% White, 1.6% Black, 0.9% Asian, 0.3% American Indian/Alaska Native, 0.1% Native Hawaiian/Other Pacific Islander, 1.4% Other, 1.5% Hispanic of any race (2010); Average household size: 2.36 (2010); Median age: 43.2 (2010); Males per 100 females: 90.2 (2010); Marriage status: 26.0% never married, 61.1% now married, 6.7% widowed, 6.1% divorced (2006-2010 5-year est.); Foreign born: 1.3% (2006-2010 5-year est.); Ancestry (includes multiple ancestries): 38.2% Irish, 24.2% German, 19.6% Italian, 10.6% French, 9.5% Polish (2006-2010 5-year est.).
**Economy:** Employment by occupation: 12.9% management, 4.7% professional, 5.1% services, 18.8% sales, 4.7% farming, 7.9% construction, 5.9% production (2006-2010 5-year est.).
**Income:** Per capita income: $29,032 (2006-2010 5-year est.); Median household income: $64,617 (2006-2010 5-year est.); Average household income: $72,740 (2006-2010 5-year est.); Percent of households with income of $100,000 or more: 23.0% (2006-2010 5-year est.); Poverty rate: 1.6% (2006-2010 5-year est.).
**Education:** Percent of population age 25 and over with: High school diploma (including GED) or higher: 93.5% (2006-2010 5-year est.); Bachelor's degree or higher: 26.6% (2006-2010 5-year est.); Master's degree or higher: 14.1% (2006-2010 5-year est.).

**School District(s)**

Wynantskill Union Free School District (KG-08)

2009-10 Enrollment: 331 .................... (518) 283-4679

**Housing:** Homeownership rate: 81.8% (2010); Median home value: $171,200 (2006-2010 5-year est.); Median contract rent: $702 per month (2006-2010 5-year est.); Median year structure built: 1956 (2006-2010 5-year est.).

**Transportation:** Commute to work: 97.1% car, 0.0% public transportation, 0.2% walk, 2.8% work from home (2006-2010 5-year est.); Travel time to work: 22.1% less than 15 minutes, 61.4% 15 to 30 minutes, 13.9% 30 to 45 minutes, 1.6% 45 to 60 minutes, 0.9% 60 minutes or more (2006-2010 5-year est.)

# Richmond County

*See New York City*

# Rockland County

Located in southeastern New York; bounded on the east by the Hudson River, and on the southwest and south by New Jersey; includes part of the Ramapo Mountains; drained by the Hackensack and Ramapo Rivers. Covers a land area of 174.22 square miles, a water area of 25.12 square miles, and is located in the Eastern Time Zone at 41.12° N. Lat., 74.01° W. Long. The county was founded in 1798. County seat is New City.

Rockland County is part of the New York-Northern New Jersey-Long Island, NY-NJ-PA Metropolitan Statistical Area. The entire metro area includes: Edison-New Brunswick, NJ Metropolitan Division (Middlesex County, NJ; Monmouth County, NJ; Ocean County, NJ; Somerset County, NJ); Nassau-Suffolk, NY Metropolitan Division (Nassau County, NY; Suffolk County, NY); New York-White Plains-Wayne, NY-NJ Metropolitan Division (Bergen County, NJ; Hudson County, NJ; Passaic County, NJ; Bronx County, NY; Kings County, NY; New York County, NY; Putnam County, NY; Queens County, NY; Richmond County, NY; Rockland County, NY; Westchester County, NY); Newark-Union, NJ-PA Metropolitan Division (Essex County, NJ; Hunterdon County, NJ; Morris County, NJ; Sussex County, NJ; Union County, NJ; Pike County, PA)

**Population:** 265,475 (1990); 286,753 (2000); 311,687 (2010); Race: 73.2% White, 11.9% Black, 6.2% Asian, 0.3% American Indian/Alaska Native, 0.0% Native Hawaiian/Other Pacific Islander, 8.4% Other, 15.7% Hispanic of any race (2010); Density: 1,789.1 persons per square mile (2010); Average household size: 3.07 (2010); Median age: 36.7 (2010); Males per 100 females: 96.3 (2010).

**Religion:** Six largest groups: 35.1% Catholicism, 22.0% Judaism, 2.8% Non-Denominational, 1.5% Muslim Estimate, 1.3% Baptist, 0.9% Eastern Liturgical (Orthodox) (2010)

**Economy:** Unemployment rate: 7.2% (February 2012); Total civilian labor force: 154,022 (February 2012); Leading industries: 21.4% health care and social assistance; 13.1% retail trade; 9.8% manufacturing (2009); Farms: 21 totaling n/a acres (2007); Companies that employ 500 or more persons: 16 (2009); Companies that employ 100 to 499 persons: 133 (2009); Companies that employ less than 100 persons: 8,999 (2009); Black-owned businesses: 2,386 (2007); Hispanic-owned businesses: 2,220 (2007); Asian-owned businesses: 2,137 (2007); Women-owned businesses: 8,689 (2007); Retail sales per capita: $13,926 (2010). Single-family building permits issued: 92 (2011); Multi-family building permits issued: 197 (2011).

**Income:** Per capita income: $34,304 (2006-2010 5-year est.); Median household income: $82,534 (2006-2010 5-year est.); Average household income: $105,450 (2006-2010 5-year est.); Percent of households with income of $100,000 or more: 41.2% (2006-2010 5-year est.); Poverty rate: 11.3% (2006-2010 5-year est.); Bankruptcy rate: 2.21% (2011).

**Taxes:** Total county taxes per capita: $1,004 (2009); County property taxes per capita: $389 (2009).

**Education:** Percent of population age 25 and over with: High school diploma (including GED) or higher: 87.9% (2006-2010 5-year est.); Bachelor's degree or higher: 40.7% (2006-2010 5-year est.); Master's degree or higher: 18.2% (2006-2010 5-year est.).

**Housing:** Homeownership rate: 69.3% (2010); Median home value: $476,900 (2006-2010 5-year est.); Median contract rent: $1,121 per month (2006-2010 5-year est.); Median year structure built: 1969 (2006-2010 5-year est.)

**Health:** Birth rate: 153.2 per 10,000 population (2011); Death rate: 65.0 per 10,000 population (2011); Age-adjusted cancer mortality rate: 144.4 deaths per 100,000 population (2009); Number of physicians: 39.1 per 10,000 population (2008); Hospital beds: 57.8 per 10,000 population (2007); Hospital admissions: 1,124.7 per 10,000 population (2007).

**Environment:** Air Quality Index: 85.8% good, 13.2% moderate, 1.1% unhealthy for sensitive individuals, 0.0% unhealthy (percent of days in 2010)

**Elections:** 2008 Presidential election results: 52.6% Obama, 46.7% McCain, 0.3% Nader

**National and State Parks:** Bear Mountain State Park; Bear Mountain State Park; Blauvelt State Park; High Tor State Park; Hook Mountain State Park; Palisades State Park; Rockland Lake State Park; Stony Point State Park; Tallman Mountain State Park

**Additional Information Contacts**

Rockland County Government ................... (845) 638-5070
   http://www.co.rockland.ny.us
Rockland County Office of Tourism .............. (845) 708-7300
   http://www.rocktourism.com
Suffern Chamber of Commerce ................. (845) 357-8424
   http://www.suffernchamberofcommerce.com
Town of Clarkstown ......................... (845) 639-2000
   http://www.town.clarkstown.ny.us
Town of Orangetown ........................ (845) 359-5100
   http://www.orangetown.com
Town of Ramapo ........................... (845) 357-5100
   http://www.ramapo.org
Village of Hillburn .......................... (845) 357-2036
   http://www.hillburn.org
Village of Nyack ........................... (845) 358-0548
   http://nyack-ny.gov
Village of Spring Valley ...................... (845) 352-1100
   http://www.villagespringvalley.org
Village of Suffern .......................... (845) 357-2600
   http://www.suffernvillage.com

# Rockland County Communities

**AIRMONT** (village). Covers a land area of 4.643 square miles and a water area of 0.001 square miles. Located at 41.09° N. Lat; 74.09° W. Long. Elevation is 584 feet.

**Population:** 7,739 (1990); 7,799 (2000); 8,628 (2010); Density: 1,858.3 persons per square mile (2010); Race: 86.3% White, 4.6% Black, 5.0% Asian, 0.3% American Indian/Alaska Native, 0.0% Native Hawaiian/Other Pacific Islander, 3.8% Other, 8.2% Hispanic of any race (2010); Average household size: 3.13 (2010); Median age: 40.9 (2010); Males per 100 females: 90.6 (2010); Marriage status: 23.9% never married, 63.4% now married, 8.3% widowed, 4.5% divorced (2006-2010 5-year est.); Foreign born: 16.0% (2006-2010 5-year est.); Ancestry (includes multiple ancestries): 19.6% Italian, 16.1% Irish, 13.6% German, 8.5% Russian, 6.2% Polish (2006-2010 5-year est.).

**Economy:** Single-family building permits issued: 2 (2011); Multi-family building permits issued: 0 (2011); Employment by occupation: 15.5% management, 8.0% professional, 6.5% services, 16.4% sales, 3.5% farming, 4.5% construction, 2.0% production (2006-2010 5-year est.).

**Income:** Per capita income: $39,716 (2006-2010 5-year est.); Median household income: $96,875 (2006-2010 5-year est.); Average household income: $120,811 (2006-2010 5-year est.); Percent of households with income of $100,000 or more: 49.8% (2006-2010 5-year est.); Poverty rate: 5.0% (2006-2010 5-year est.).

**Education:** Percent of population age 25 and over with: High school diploma (including GED) or higher: 91.5% (2006-2010 5-year est.); Bachelor's degree or higher: 49.2% (2006-2010 5-year est.); Master's degree or higher: 21.7% (2006-2010 5-year est.).

**Housing:** Homeownership rate: 84.7% (2010); Median home value: $520,100 (2006-2010 5-year est.); Median contract rent: $445 per month (2006-2010 5-year est.); Median year structure built: 1969 (2006-2010 5-year est.).

**Transportation:** Commute to work: 82.1% car, 6.7% public transportation, 3.2% walk, 7.8% work from home (2006-2010 5-year est.); Travel time to work: 36.4% less than 15 minutes, 22.8% 15 to 30 minutes, 11.7% 30 to 45 minutes, 7.1% 45 to 60 minutes, 21.9% 60 minutes or more (2006-2010 5-year est.)

**BARDONIA** (CDP). Covers a land area of 2.573 square miles and a water area of 0.354 square miles. Located at 41.11° N. Lat; 73.97° W. Long. Elevation is 295 feet.

**History:** Bardonia is named for the Bardon Brothers - John and the twins Phillip and Conrad - who came from Bavaria in the 1849 and opened several businesses.

**Population:** 4,473 (1990); 4,367 (2000); 4,108 (2010); Density: 1,596.0 persons per square mile (2010); Race: 84.3% White, 2.1% Black, 10.8% Asian, 0.1% American Indian/Alaska Native, 0.0% Native Hawaiian/Other Pacific Islander, 2.7% Other, 6.6% Hispanic of any race (2010); Average household size: 2.83 (2010); Median age: 46.4 (2010); Males per 100 females: 93.0 (2010); Marriage status: 26.7% never married, 58.3% now married, 6.6% widowed, 8.4% divorced (2006-2010 5-year est.); Foreign born: 14.4% (2006-2010 5-year est.); Ancestry (includes multiple ancestries): 25.7% Irish, 22.1% Italian, 11.9% German, 5.7% English, 5.5% Russian (2006-2010 5-year est.).

**Economy:** Employment by occupation: 23.9% management, 2.9% professional, 5.4% services, 14.0% sales, 2.2% farming, 1.6% construction, 1.9% production (2006-2010 5-year est.).

**Income:** Per capita income: $45,333 (2006-2010 5-year est.); Median household income: $97,083 (2006-2010 5-year est.); Average household income: $138,234 (2006-2010 5-year est.); Percent of households with income of $100,000 or more: 48.9% (2006-2010 5-year est.); Poverty rate: 2.7% (2006-2010 5-year est.).

**Education:** Percent of population age 25 and over with: High school diploma (including GED) or higher: 91.8% (2006-2010 5-year est.); Bachelor's degree or higher: 53.7% (2006-2010 5-year est.); Master's degree or higher: 28.8% (2006-2010 5-year est.).

**School District(s)**

Clarkstown Central School District (KG-12)

   2009-10 Enrollment: 9,196 . . . . . . . . . . . . . . . . . . . (845) 639-6419

**Housing:** Homeownership rate: 85.9% (2010); Median home value: $611,300 (2006-2010 5-year est.); Median contract rent: $559 per month (2006-2010 5-year est.); Median year structure built: 1973 (2006-2010 5-year est.).

**Transportation:** Commute to work: 89.9% car, 5.2% public transportation, 1.3% walk, 3.6% work from home (2006-2010 5-year est.); Travel time to work: 27.1% less than 15 minutes, 31.0% 15 to 30 minutes, 20.2% 30 to 45 minutes, 4.8% 45 to 60 minutes, 16.8% 60 minutes or more (2006-2010 5-year est.)

---

**BEAR MOUNTAIN** (unincorporated postal area)

Zip Code: 10911

   Covers a land area of 1.042 square miles and a water area of 0.021 square miles. Located at 41.31° N. Lat; 74.00° W. Long. Population: 2 (2010); Density: 1.9 persons per square mile (2010); Race: 100.0% White, 0.0% Black, 0.0% Asian, 0.0% American Indian/Alaska Native, 0.0% Native Hawaiian/Other Pacific Islander, 0.0% Other, 0.0% Hispanic of any race (2010); Average household size: 2.00 (2010); Median age: 43.5 (2010); Males per 100 females: 100.0 (2010); Homeownership rate: 0.0% (2010)

---

**BLAUVELT** (CDP). Covers a land area of 4.502 square miles and a water area of 0.105 square miles. Located at 41.06° N. Lat; 73.95° W. Long. Elevation is 200 feet.

**History:** Blauvelt section of Palisades Interstate Park is here.

**Population:** 4,844 (1990); 5,207 (2000); 5,689 (2010); Density: 1,263.6 persons per square mile (2010); Race: 84.8% White, 2.6% Black, 6.7% Asian, 0.2% American Indian/Alaska Native, 0.0% Native Hawaiian/Other Pacific Islander, 5.7% Other, 10.8% Hispanic of any race (2010); Average household size: 3.17 (2010); Median age: 39.7 (2010); Males per 100 females: 95.0 (2010); Marriage status: 34.0% never married, 57.5% now married, 5.4% widowed, 3.1% divorced (2006-2010 5-year est.); Foreign born: 16.4% (2006-2010 5-year est.); Ancestry (includes multiple ancestries): 41.0% Irish, 21.2% Italian, 6.3% Greek, 6.2% German, 5.5% English (2006-2010 5-year est.).

**Economy:** Employment by occupation: 18.0% management, 2.8% professional, 4.7% services, 16.2% sales, 6.6% farming, 6.8% construction, 3.0% production (2006-2010 5-year est.).

**Income:** Per capita income: $39,955 (2006-2010 5-year est.); Median household income: $120,702 (2006-2010 5-year est.); Average household income: $134,779 (2006-2010 5-year est.); Percent of households with income of $100,000 or more: 57.8% (2006-2010 5-year est.); Poverty rate: 1.3% (2006-2010 5-year est.).

**Education:** Percent of population age 25 and over with: High school diploma (including GED) or higher: 88.1% (2006-2010 5-year est.); Bachelor's degree or higher: 40.8% (2006-2010 5-year est.); Master's degree or higher: 20.5% (2006-2010 5-year est.).

**School District(s)**

South Orangetown Central School District (PK-12)

   2009-10 Enrollment: 3,519 . . . . . . . . . . . . . . . . . . . (845) 680-1050

**Housing:** Homeownership rate: 92.5% (2010); Median home value: $562,600 (2006-2010 5-year est.); Median contract rent: $1,281 per month (2006-2010 5-year est.); Median year structure built: 1961 (2006-2010 5-year est.).

**Transportation:** Commute to work: 86.0% car, 4.5% public transportation, 3.4% walk, 4.4% work from home (2006-2010 5-year est.); Travel time to work: 31.1% less than 15 minutes, 24.7% 15 to 30 minutes, 18.0% 30 to 45 minutes, 8.6% 45 to 60 minutes, 17.6% 60 minutes or more (2006-2010 5-year est.)

---

**CHESTNUT RIDGE** (village). Covers a land area of 4.967 square miles and a water area of 0.002 square miles. Located at 41.08° N. Lat; 74.04° W. Long. Elevation is 413 feet.

**Population:** 7,517 (1990); 7,829 (2000); 7,916 (2010); Density: 1,593.4 persons per square mile (2010); Race: 68.7% White, 17.5% Black, 8.1% Asian, 0.1% American Indian/Alaska Native, 0.1% Native Hawaiian/Other Pacific Islander, 5.5% Other, 11.1% Hispanic of any race (2010); Average household size: 2.89 (2010); Median age: 44.7 (2010); Males per 100 females: 94.6 (2010); Marriage status: 21.7% never married, 58.2% now married, 12.1% widowed, 8.1% divorced (2006-2010 5-year est.); Foreign born: 29.9% (2006-2010 5-year est.); Ancestry (includes multiple ancestries): 16.3% Italian, 9.9% Irish, 8.9% German, 7.3% Haitian, 5.5% Polish (2006-2010 5-year est.).

**Economy:** Single-family building permits issued: 0 (2011); Multi-family building permits issued: 0 (2011); Employment by occupation: 13.9% management, 5.5% professional, 6.3% services, 12.6% sales, 1.1% farming, 11.3% construction, 1.8% production (2006-2010 5-year est.).

**Income:** Per capita income: $38,768 (2006-2010 5-year est.); Median household income: $110,799 (2006-2010 5-year est.); Average household income: $122,257 (2006-2010 5-year est.); Percent of households with income of $100,000 or more: 57.9% (2006-2010 5-year est.); Poverty rate: 6.2% (2006-2010 5-year est.).

**Education:** Percent of population age 25 and over with: High school diploma (including GED) or higher: 85.8% (2006-2010 5-year est.); Bachelor's degree or higher: 47.7% (2006-2010 5-year est.); Master's degree or higher: 24.2% (2006-2010 5-year est.).

**School District(s)**

East Ramapo Central School District (spring Valley) (PK-12)

   2009-10 Enrollment: 8,116 . . . . . . . . . . . . . . . . . . . (845) 577-6011

**Housing:** Homeownership rate: 81.6% (2010); Median home value: $498,400 (2006-2010 5-year est.); Median contract rent: $795 per month (2006-2010 5-year est.); Median year structure built: 1967 (2006-2010 5-year est.).

**Transportation:** Commute to work: 87.1% car, 5.2% public transportation, 1.1% walk, 6.1% work from home (2006-2010 5-year est.); Travel time to work: 28.6% less than 15 minutes, 26.5% 15 to 30 minutes, 18.5% 30 to 45 minutes, 8.7% 45 to 60 minutes, 17.6% 60 minutes or more (2006-2010 5-year est.)

---

**CLARKSTOWN** (town). Covers a land area of 38.475 square miles and a water area of 8.593 square miles. Located at 41.13° N. Lat; 73.96° W. Long.

**Population:** 79,346 (1990); 82,082 (2000); 84,187 (2010); Density: 2,188.1 persons per square mile (2010); Race: 73.9% White, 9.6% Black, 10.5% Asian, 0.2% American Indian/Alaska Native, 0.0% Native Hawaiian/Other Pacific Islander, 5.8% Other, 11.7% Hispanic of any race (2010); Average household size: 2.84 (2010); Median age: 42.8 (2010); Males per 100 females: 94.1 (2010); Marriage status: 26.5% never married, 61.2% now married, 6.1% widowed, 6.1% divorced (2006-2010 5-year est.); Foreign born: 20.3% (2006-2010 5-year est.); Ancestry (includes multiple ancestries): 20.1% Italian, 19.0% Irish, 9.3% German, 6.4% Russian, 5.0% Polish (2006-2010 5-year est.).

**Economy:** Unemployment rate: 6.7% (February 2012); Total civilian labor force: 45,785 (February 2012); Single-family building permits issued: 25 (2011); Multi-family building permits issued: 0 (2011); Employment by occupation: 15.6% management, 4.1% professional, 6.7% services, 14.1% sales, 3.4% farming, 5.5% construction, 3.3% production (2006-2010 5-year est.).

**Income:** Per capita income: $42,042 (2006-2010 5-year est.); Median household income: $99,005 (2006-2010 5-year est.); Average household income: $119,415 (2006-2010 5-year est.); Percent of households with income of $100,000 or more: 49.5% (2006-2010 5-year est.); Poverty rate: 5.0% (2006-2010 5-year est.).

**Taxes:** Total city taxes per capita: $1,191 (2009); City property taxes per capita: $1,108 (2009).

**Education:** Percent of population age 25 and over with: High school diploma (including GED) or higher: 91.9% (2006-2010 5-year est.); Bachelor's degree or higher: 49.4% (2006-2010 5-year est.); Master's degree or higher: 23.2% (2006-2010 5-year est.).

**Housing:** Homeownership rate: 79.5% (2010); Median home value: $501,500 (2006-2010 5-year est.); Median contract rent: $1,309 per month (2006-2010 5-year est.); Median year structure built: 1970 (2006-2010 5-year est.).

**Safety:** Violent crime rate: 11.7 per 10,000 population; Property crime rate: 216.9 per 10,000 population (2010).

**Transportation:** Commute to work: 86.6% car, 7.3% public transportation, 1.4% walk, 3.8% work from home (2006-2010 5-year est.); Travel time to work: 25.6% less than 15 minutes, 28.8% 15 to 30 minutes, 17.4% 30 to 45 minutes, 11.1% 45 to 60 minutes, 17.1% 60 minutes or more (2006-2010 5-year est.)

**Additional Information Contacts**

Town of Clarkstown . . . . . . . . . . . . . . . . . . . . . . . . . . . . (845) 639-2000
   http://www.town.clarkstown.ny.us

---

**CONGERS** (CDP). Covers a land area of 3.067 square miles and a water area of 0.744 square miles. Located at 41.14° N. Lat; 73.94° W. Long. Elevation is 177 feet.

**Population:** 7,946 (1990); 8,303 (2000); 8,363 (2010); Density: 2,725.9 persons per square mile (2010); Race: 80.4% White, 3.3% Black, 11.7% Asian, 0.4% American Indian/Alaska Native, 0.0% Native Hawaiian/Other Pacific Islander, 4.2% Other, 11.4% Hispanic of any race (2010); Average household size: 2.96 (2010); Median age: 42.5 (2010); Males per 100 females: 93.6 (2010); Marriage status: 22.7% never married, 68.3% now married, 4.3% widowed, 4.8% divorced (2006-2010 5-year est.); Foreign born: 15.2% (2006-2010 5-year est.); Ancestry (includes multiple ancestries): 27.2% Italian, 25.5% Irish, 12.7% German, 5.2% Polish, 4.4% Russian (2006-2010 5-year est.).

**Economy:** Employment by occupation: 16.8% management, 3.3% professional, 7.7% services, 14.6% sales, 3.7% farming, 7.6% construction, 3.7% production (2006-2010 5-year est.).

**Income:** Per capita income: $39,132 (2006-2010 5-year est.); Median household income: $94,241 (2006-2010 5-year est.); Average household income: $113,387 (2006-2010 5-year est.); Percent of households with income of $100,000 or more: 48.5% (2006-2010 5-year est.); Poverty rate: 4.0% (2006-2010 5-year est.).

**Education:** Percent of population age 25 and over with: High school diploma (including GED) or higher: 94.0% (2006-2010 5-year est.); Bachelor's degree or higher: 43.5% (2006-2010 5-year est.); Master's degree or higher: 18.3% (2006-2010 5-year est.).

**School District(s)**

Clarkstown Central School District (KG-12)
   2009-10 Enrollment: 9,196 . . . . . . . . . . . . . . . . . . (845) 639-6419

**Housing:** Homeownership rate: 85.7% (2010); Median home value: $486,900 (2006-2010 5-year est.); Median contract rent: $1,555 per month (2006-2010 5-year est.); Median year structure built: 1969 (2006-2010 5-year est.).

**Transportation:** Commute to work: 90.2% car, 5.0% public transportation, 0.0% walk, 4.2% work from home (2006-2010 5-year est.); Travel time to work: 26.8% less than 15 minutes, 30.0% 15 to 30 minutes, 17.6% 30 to 45 minutes, 13.4% 45 to 60 minutes, 12.3% 60 minutes or more (2006-2010 5-year est.)

---

**GARNERVILLE** (unincorporated postal area)

Zip Code: 10923

   Covers a land area of 1.966 square miles and a water area of 0.035 square miles. Located at 41.20° N. Lat; 74.00° W. Long. Elevation is 210 feet. Population: 8,732 (2010); Density: 4,439.9 persons per square mile (2010); Race: 65.1% White, 14.9% Black, 3.8% Asian, 0.2% American Indian/Alaska Native, 0.0% Native Hawaiian/Other Pacific Islander, 16.0% Other, 31.3% Hispanic of any race (2010); Average household size: 2.94 (2010); Median age: 38.1 (2010); Males per 100 females: 94.2 (2010); Homeownership rate: 62.3% (2010)

---

**GRAND VIEW-ON-HUDSON** (village). Aka Grand View. Covers a land area of 0.175 square miles and a water area of <.001 square miles. Located at 41.06° N. Lat; 73.92° W. Long. Elevation is 43 feet.

**Population:** 267 (1990); 284 (2000); 285 (2010); Density: 1,622.8 persons per square mile (2010); Race: 91.2% White, 5.6% Black, 1.1% Asian, 0.0% American Indian/Alaska Native, 0.0% Native Hawaiian/Other Pacific Islander, 2.1% Other, 6.0% Hispanic of any race (2010); Average household size: 2.23 (2010); Median age: 50.9 (2010); Males per 100 females: 80.4 (2010); Marriage status: 29.8% never married, 45.6% now married, 9.7% widowed, 14.9% divorced (2006-2010 5-year est.); Foreign born: 11.3% (2006-2010 5-year est.); Ancestry (includes multiple ancestries): 21.8% Russian, 18.0% German, 13.4% Italian, 12.0% Irish, 11.6% Polish (2006-2010 5-year est.).

**Economy:** Single-family building permits issued: 0 (2011); Multi-family building permits issued: 0 (2011); Employment by occupation: 23.0% management, 3.7% professional, 6.8% services, 13.0% sales, 1.9% farming, 1.2% construction, 1.2% production (2006-2010 5-year est.).

**Income:** Per capita income: $96,539 (2006-2010 5-year est.); Median household income: $143,750 (2006-2010 5-year est.); Average household income: $213,685 (2006-2010 5-year est.); Percent of households with income of $100,000 or more: 64.8% (2006-2010 5-year est.); Poverty rate: 4.2% (2006-2010 5-year est.).

**Education:** Percent of population age 25 and over with: High school diploma (including GED) or higher: 99.1% (2006-2010 5-year est.); Bachelor's degree or higher: 58.4% (2006-2010 5-year est.); Master's degree or higher: 35.0% (2006-2010 5-year est.).

**Housing:** Homeownership rate: 82.0% (2010); Median home value: $1 (2006-2010 5-year est.); Median contract rent: n/a per month (2006-2010 5-year est.); Median year structure built: before 1940 (2006-2010 5-year est.).

**Transportation:** Commute to work: 59.1% car, 3.2% public transportation, 1.3% walk, 36.4% work from home (2006-2010 5-year est.); Travel time to work: 13.3% less than 15 minutes, 28.6% 15 to 30 minutes, 18.4% 30 to 45 minutes, 7.1% 45 to 60 minutes, 32.7% 60 minutes or more (2006-2010 5-year est.)

---

**HAVERSTRAW** (village). Covers a land area of 1.980 square miles and a water area of 3.056 square miles. Located at 41.17° N. Lat; 73.94° W. Long. Elevation is 30 feet.

**Population:** 9,438 (1990); 10,117 (2000); 11,910 (2010); Density: 6,014.9 persons per square mile (2010); Race: 47.9% White, 12.7% Black, 2.3% Asian, 0.8% American Indian/Alaska Native, 0.2% Native Hawaiian/Other Pacific Islander, 36.1% Other, 67.1% Hispanic of any race (2010); Average household size: 3.36 (2010); Median age: 32.5 (2010); Males per 100 females: 94.4 (2010); Marriage status: 37.6% never married, 46.8% now married, 8.1% widowed, 7.5% divorced (2006-2010 5-year est.); Foreign born: 39.0% (2006-2010 5-year est.); Ancestry (includes multiple ancestries): 5.3% Italian, 4.2% Irish, 3.6% Haitian, 2.4% American, 2.1% German (2006-2010 5-year est.).

**Economy:** Single-family building permits issued: 0 (2011); Multi-family building permits issued: 0 (2011); Employment by occupation: 3.6% management, 2.2% professional, 16.0% services, 17.4% sales, 1.8% farming, 8.9% construction, 7.9% production (2006-2010 5-year est.).

**Income:** Per capita income: $21,005 (2006-2010 5-year est.); Median household income: $47,668 (2006-2010 5-year est.); Average household income: $64,725 (2006-2010 5-year est.); Percent of households with income of $100,000 or more: 18.4% (2006-2010 5-year est.); Poverty rate: 18.6% (2006-2010 5-year est.).

**Taxes:** Total city taxes per capita: $553 (2009); City property taxes per capita: $519 (2009).

**Education:** Percent of population age 25 and over with: High school diploma (including GED) or higher: 65.6% (2006-2010 5-year est.); Bachelor's degree or higher: 17.2% (2006-2010 5-year est.); Master's degree or higher: 5.3% (2006-2010 5-year est.).

**School District(s)**

Haverstraw-Stony Point Csd (north Rockland) (KG-12)
   2009-10 Enrollment: 7,959 . . . . . . . . . . . . . . . . . . (845) 942-3002

**Housing:** Homeownership rate: 41.5% (2010); Median home value: $346,100 (2006-2010 5-year est.); Median contract rent: $1,047 per month (2006-2010 5-year est.); Median year structure built: 1954 (2006-2010 5-year est.).

**Transportation:** Commute to work: 72.0% car, 18.7% public transportation, 3.5% walk, 2.2% work from home (2006-2010 5-year est.); Travel time to work: 17.4% less than 15 minutes, 41.4% 15 to 30 minutes,

24.5% 30 to 45 minutes, 6.9% 45 to 60 minutes, 9.7% 60 minutes or more (2006-2010 5-year est.)

## HAVERSTRAW (town). Covers a land area of 22.155 square miles and a water area of 5.260 square miles. Located at 41.20° N. Lat; 74.03° W. Long. Elevation is 30 feet.

**History:** In Haverstraw, James Wood discovered the modern system of burning brick, and set up brickyards in the town. At its peak, the industry included 40 brickyards.

**Population:** 32,712 (1990); 33,811 (2000); 36,634 (2010); Density: 1,653.5 persons per square mile (2010); Race: 59.2% White, 14.7% Black, 4.4% Asian, 0.5% American Indian/Alaska Native, 0.1% Native Hawaiian/Other Pacific Islander, 21.1% Other, 41.0% Hispanic of any race (2010); Average household size: 2.96 (2010); Median age: 37.1 (2010); Males per 100 females: 94.0 (2010); Marriage status: 33.8% never married, 51.6% now married, 6.4% widowed, 8.2% divorced (2006-2010 5-year est.); Foreign born: 27.1% (2006-2010 5-year est.); Ancestry (includes multiple ancestries): 13.7% Italian, 12.7% Irish, 6.3% German, 4.0% American, 3.3% Haitian (2006-2010 5-year est.).

**Economy:** Unemployment rate: 10.2% (February 2012); Total civilian labor force: 18,641 (February 2012); Single-family building permits issued: 2 (2011); Multi-family building permits issued: 0 (2011); Employment by occupation: 7.9% management, 3.3% professional, 10.8% services, 19.1% sales, 3.1% farming, 7.7% construction, 6.7% production (2006-2010 5-year est.).

**Income:** Per capita income: $30,080 (2006-2010 5-year est.); Median household income: $66,633 (2006-2010 5-year est.); Average household income: $86,759 (2006-2010 5-year est.); Percent of households with income of $100,000 or more: 32.4% (2006-2010 5-year est.); Poverty rate: 10.9% (2006-2010 5-year est.).

**Taxes:** Total city taxes per capita: $594 (2009); City property taxes per capita: $564 (2009).

**Education:** Percent of population age 25 and over with: High school diploma (including GED) or higher: 79.7% (2006-2010 5-year est.); Bachelor's degree or higher: 28.4% (2006-2010 5-year est.); Master's degree or higher: 11.1% (2006-2010 5-year est.).

### School District(s)
Haverstraw-Stony Point Csd (north Rockland) (KG-12)
    2009-10 Enrollment: 7,959 . . . . . . . . . . . . . . . . . . . . . . (845) 942-3002

**Housing:** Homeownership rate: 62.5% (2010); Median home value: $372,600 (2006-2010 5-year est.); Median contract rent: $1,092 per month (2006-2010 5-year est.); Median year structure built: 1971 (2006-2010 5-year est.).

**Safety:** Violent crime rate: 17.3 per 10,000 population; Property crime rate: 116.8 per 10,000 population (2010).

**Transportation:** Commute to work: 85.1% car, 9.2% public transportation, 2.1% walk, 2.3% work from home (2006-2010 5-year est.); Travel time to work: 20.7% less than 15 minutes, 37.2% 15 to 30 minutes, 19.9% 30 to 45 minutes, 10.3% 45 to 60 minutes, 11.9% 60 minutes or more (2006-2010 5-year est.)

## HILLBURN (village). Covers a land area of 2.250 square miles and a water area of 0.017 square miles. Located at 41.12° N. Lat; 74.17° W. Long. Elevation is 305 feet.

**History:** Incorporated 1893.

**Population:** 892 (1990); 881 (2000); 951 (2010); Density: 422.5 persons per square mile (2010); Race: 52.6% White, 17.1% Black, 3.8% Asian, 9.0% American Indian/Alaska Native, 0.0% Native Hawaiian/Other Pacific Islander, 17.5% Other, 20.0% Hispanic of any race (2010); Average household size: 2.93 (2010); Median age: 40.1 (2010); Males per 100 females: 108.6 (2010); Marriage status: 33.2% never married, 56.8% now married, 4.5% widowed, 5.5% divorced (2006-2010 5-year est.); Foreign born: 21.3% (2006-2010 5-year est.); Ancestry (includes multiple ancestries): 13.5% Irish, 12.3% Italian, 9.3% Haitian, 7.9% Polish, 6.2% European (2006-2010 5-year est.).

**Economy:** Single-family building permits issued: 0 (2011); Multi-family building permits issued: 0 (2011); Employment by occupation: 12.6% management, 0.7% professional, 8.9% services, 22.8% sales, 5.7% farming, 10.1% construction, 7.5% production (2006-2010 5-year est.).

**Income:** Per capita income: $32,469 (2006-2010 5-year est.); Median household income: $84,545 (2006-2010 5-year est.); Average household income: $96,156 (2006-2010 5-year est.); Percent of households with income of $100,000 or more: 32.3% (2006-2010 5-year est.); Poverty rate: 1.8% (2006-2010 5-year est.).

**Education:** Percent of population age 25 and over with: High school diploma (including GED) or higher: 90.3% (2006-2010 5-year est.); Bachelor's degree or higher: 20.9% (2006-2010 5-year est.); Master's degree or higher: 8.5% (2006-2010 5-year est.).

**Housing:** Homeownership rate: 63.1% (2010); Median home value: $346,800 (2006-2010 5-year est.); Median contract rent: $1,103 per month (2006-2010 5-year est.); Median year structure built: before 1940 (2006-2010 5-year est.).

**Transportation:** Commute to work: 92.3% car, 5.9% public transportation, 1.8% walk, 0.0% work from home (2006-2010 5-year est.); Travel time to work: 28.7% less than 15 minutes, 29.8% 15 to 30 minutes, 27.6% 30 to 45 minutes, 6.8% 45 to 60 minutes, 7.1% 60 minutes or more (2006-2010 5-year est.)

**Additional Information Contacts**
Village of Hillburn . . . . . . . . . . . . . . . . . . . . . . . . . . . . . . . (845) 357-2036
    http://www.hillburn.org

## HILLCREST (CDP). Covers a land area of 1.297 square miles and a water area of 0 square miles. Located at 41.12° N. Lat; 74.03° W. Long. Elevation is 512 feet.

**Population:** 6,545 (1990); 7,106 (2000); 7,558 (2010); Density: 5,825.4 persons per square mile (2010); Race: 21.7% White, 55.8% Black, 10.9% Asian, 0.4% American Indian/Alaska Native, 0.1% Native Hawaiian/Other Pacific Islander, 11.1% Other, 20.0% Hispanic of any race (2010); Average household size: 3.85 (2010); Median age: 37.5 (2010); Males per 100 females: 96.1 (2010); Marriage status: 41.1% never married, 45.5% now married, 8.1% widowed, 5.3% divorced (2006-2010 5-year est.); Foreign born: 42.7% (2006-2010 5-year est.); Ancestry (includes multiple ancestries): 16.0% Haitian, 10.4% Jamaican, 4.5% Trinidadian and Tobagonian, 4.1% American, 3.4% Guyanese (2006-2010 5-year est.).

**Economy:** Employment by occupation: 11.8% management, 7.0% professional, 15.5% services, 8.8% sales, 3.6% farming, 10.1% construction, 6.8% production (2006-2010 5-year est.).

**Income:** Per capita income: $29,421 (2006-2010 5-year est.); Median household income: $98,317 (2006-2010 5-year est.); Average household income: $108,974 (2006-2010 5-year est.); Percent of households with income of $100,000 or more: 48.4% (2006-2010 5-year est.); Poverty rate: 7.9% (2006-2010 5-year est.).

**Education:** Percent of population age 25 and over with: High school diploma (including GED) or higher: 85.1% (2006-2010 5-year est.); Bachelor's degree or higher: 31.9% (2006-2010 5-year est.); Master's degree or higher: 10.4% (2006-2010 5-year est.).

**Housing:** Homeownership rate: 81.0% (2010); Median home value: $435,600 (2006-2010 5-year est.); Median contract rent: $940 per month (2006-2010 5-year est.); Median year structure built: 1962 (2006-2010 5-year est.).

**Transportation:** Commute to work: 83.0% car, 9.0% public transportation, 0.6% walk, 3.9% work from home (2006-2010 5-year est.); Travel time to work: 16.9% less than 15 minutes, 34.2% 15 to 30 minutes, 14.4% 30 to 45 minutes, 12.0% 45 to 60 minutes, 22.5% 60 minutes or more (2006-2010 5-year est.)

## KASER (village). Covers a land area of 0.172 square miles and a water area of 0 square miles. Located at 41.12° N. Lat; 74.06° W. Long. Elevation is 541 feet.

**Population:** 2,661 (1990); 3,316 (2000); 4,724 (2010); Density: 27,420.0 persons per square mile (2010); Race: 99.5% White, 0.0% Black, 0.1% Asian, 0.0% American Indian/Alaska Native, 0.0% Native Hawaiian/Other Pacific Islander, 0.4% Other, 0.9% Hispanic of any race (2010); Average household size: 5.39 (2010); Median age: 12.9 (2010); Males per 100 females: 105.5 (2010); Marriage status: 18.7% never married, 79.8% now married, 1.2% widowed, 0.4% divorced (2006-2010 5-year est.); Foreign born: 6.6% (2006-2010 5-year est.); Ancestry (includes multiple ancestries): 29.1% European, 23.3% Hungarian, 12.2% Israeli, 11.2% Romanian, 7.6% Polish (2006-2010 5-year est.).

**Economy:** Single-family building permits issued: 0 (2011); Multi-family building permits issued: 8 (2011); Employment by occupation: 7.7% management, 13.2% professional, 2.0% services, 6.7% sales, 5.6% farming, 5.2% construction, 1.7% production (2006-2010 5-year est.).

**Income:** Per capita income: $6,307 (2006-2010 5-year est.); Median household income: $18,470 (2006-2010 5-year est.); Average household income: $35,195 (2006-2010 5-year est.); Percent of households with income of $100,000 or more: 4.7% (2006-2010 5-year est.); Poverty rate: 63.8% (2006-2010 5-year est.).

**Education:** Percent of population age 25 and over with: High school diploma (including GED) or higher: 79.3% (2006-2010 5-year est.); Bachelor's degree or higher: 7.4% (2006-2010 5-year est.); Master's degree or higher: 1.2% (2006-2010 5-year est.).
**Housing:** Homeownership rate: 7.6% (2010); Median home value: $492,900 (2006-2010 5-year est.); Median contract rent: $1,127 per month (2006-2010 5-year est.); Median year structure built: 1995 (2006-2010 5-year est.).
**Transportation:** Commute to work: 38.9% car, 11.9% public transportation, 41.9% walk, 5.0% work from home (2006-2010 5-year est.); Travel time to work: 59.1% less than 15 minutes, 28.1% 15 to 30 minutes, 5.1% 30 to 45 minutes, 0.8% 45 to 60 minutes, 6.9% 60 minutes or more (2006-2010 5-year est.)

**MONSEY** (CDP). Covers a land area of 2.272 square miles and a water area of 0.013 square miles. Located at 41.10° N. Lat; 74.07° W. Long. Elevation is 548 feet.
**Population:** 11,325 (1990); 14,504 (2000); 18,412 (2010); Density: 8,101.2 persons per square mile (2010); Race: 95.1% White, 2.5% Black, 0.2% Asian, 0.1% American Indian/Alaska Native, 0.0% Native Hawaiian/Other Pacific Islander, 2.1% Other, 3.6% Hispanic of any race (2010); Average household size: 5.05 (2010); Median age: 17.4 (2010); Males per 100 females: 106.0 (2010); Marriage status: 31.1% never married, 64.1% now married, 3.2% widowed, 1.6% divorced (2006-2010 5-year est.); Foreign born: 15.9% (2006-2010 5-year est.); Ancestry (includes multiple ancestries): 22.3% European, 12.9% Polish, 9.9% Hungarian, 5.6% Russian, 4.6% German (2006-2010 5-year est.).
**Economy:** Employment by occupation: 13.5% management, 5.8% professional, 4.3% services, 13.4% sales, 7.5% farming, 4.5% construction, 1.0% production (2006-2010 5-year est.).
**Income:** Per capita income: $13,050 (2006-2010 5-year est.); Median household income: $34,150 (2006-2010 5-year est.); Average household income: $63,080 (2006-2010 5-year est.); Percent of households with income of $100,000 or more: 20.0% (2006-2010 5-year est.); Poverty rate: 42.1% (2006-2010 5-year est.).
**Education:** Percent of population age 25 and over with: High school diploma (including GED) or higher: 84.9% (2006-2010 5-year est.); Bachelor's degree or higher: 22.8% (2006-2010 5-year est.); Master's degree or higher: 9.1% (2006-2010 5-year est.).

**School District(s)**
East Ramapo Central School District (spring Valley (PK-12)
    2009-10 Enrollment: 8,116 . . . . . . . . . . . . . . . . . (845) 577-6011
**Four-year College(s)**
Bais Medrash Elyon (Private, Not-for-profit)
    Fall 2010 Enrollment: 17 . . . . . . . . . . . . . . . . . (845) 371-2481
    2011-12 Tuition: In-state $7,800; Out-of-state $7,800
Kol Yaakov Torah Center (Private, Not-for-profit)
    Fall 2010 Enrollment: 26 . . . . . . . . . . . . . . . . . (845) 425-3863
    2011-12 Tuition: In-state $6,500; Out-of-state $6,500
Rabbinical College Beth Shraga (Private, Not-for-profit)
    Fall 2010 Enrollment: 48 . . . . . . . . . . . . . . . . . (845) 356-1980
    2011-12 Tuition: In-state $10,050; Out-of-state $10,050
Yeshiva D'monsey Rabbinical College (Private, Not-for-profit)
    Fall 2010 Enrollment: 89 . . . . . . . . . . . . . . . . . (845) 352-5852
    2011-12 Tuition: In-state $4,750; Out-of-state $4,750
Yeshivath Viznitz (Private, Not-for-profit)
    Fall 2010 Enrollment: 542 . . . . . . . . . . . . . . . . (845) 731-3700
    2011-12 Tuition: In-state $6,400; Out-of-state $6,400
**Housing:** Homeownership rate: 41.8% (2010); Median home value: $590,600 (2006-2010 5-year est.); Median contract rent: $1,154 per month (2006-2010 5-year est.); Median year structure built: 1975 (2006-2010 5-year est.).
**Transportation:** Commute to work: 67.5% car, 8.9% public transportation, 15.2% walk, 7.3% work from home (2006-2010 5-year est.); Travel time to work: 52.6% less than 15 minutes, 17.1% 15 to 30 minutes, 9.7% 30 to 45 minutes, 6.2% 45 to 60 minutes, 14.4% 60 minutes or more (2006-2010 5-year est.)

**MONTEBELLO** (village). Covers a land area of 4.346 square miles and a water area of 0.009 square miles. Located at 41.13° N. Lat; 74.11° W. Long. Elevation is 318 feet.
**History:** Montebello was incorporated in 1986.
**Population:** 3,021 (1990); 3,688 (2000); 4,526 (2010); Density: 1,041.3 persons per square mile (2010); Race: 88.3% White, 3.2% Black, 5.7% Asian, 0.1% American Indian/Alaska Native, 0.0% Native Hawaiian/Other

Pacific Islander, 2.7% Other, 5.5% Hispanic of any race (2010); Average household size: 3.00 (2010); Median age: 43.7 (2010); Males per 100 females: 93.1 (2010); Marriage status: 25.1% never married, 60.0% now married, 6.6% widowed, 8.3% divorced (2006-2010 5-year est.); Foreign born: 7.5% (2006-2010 5-year est.); Ancestry (includes multiple ancestries): 15.0% Irish, 13.0% Italian, 10.1% Russian, 8.5% German, 8.1% Polish (2006-2010 5-year est.).
**Economy:** Single-family building permits issued: 0 (2011); Multi-family building permits issued: 0 (2011); Employment by occupation: 25.5% management, 5.9% professional, 1.9% services, 21.3% sales, 1.6% farming, 4.8% construction, 4.0% production (2006-2010 5-year est.).
**Income:** Per capita income: $60,005 (2006-2010 5-year est.); Median household income: $135,952 (2006-2010 5-year est.); Average household income: $182,296 (2006-2010 5-year est.); Percent of households with income of $100,000 or more: 62.6% (2006-2010 5-year est.); Poverty rate: 2.3% (2006-2010 5-year est.).
**Education:** Percent of population age 25 and over with: High school diploma (including GED) or higher: 94.3% (2006-2010 5-year est.); Bachelor's degree or higher: 59.3% (2006-2010 5-year est.); Master's degree or higher: 35.3% (2006-2010 5-year est.).
**Housing:** Homeownership rate: 85.9% (2010); Median home value: $668,300 (2006-2010 5-year est.); Median contract rent: $1,674 per month (2006-2010 5-year est.); Median year structure built: 1975 (2006-2010 5-year est.).
**Transportation:** Commute to work: 76.8% car, 10.0% public transportation, 1.8% walk, 10.1% work from home (2006-2010 5-year est.); Travel time to work: 26.8% less than 15 minutes, 29.4% 15 to 30 minutes, 16.6% 30 to 45 minutes, 6.8% 45 to 60 minutes, 20.4% 60 minutes or more (2006-2010 5-year est.)

**MOUNT IVY** (CDP). Covers a land area of 1.466 square miles and a water area of 0 square miles. Located at 41.19° N. Lat; 74.02° W. Long. Elevation is 459 feet.
**Population:** 6,013 (1990); 6,536 (2000); 6,878 (2010); Density: 4,688.8 persons per square mile (2010); Race: 65.6% White, 15.9% Black, 6.0% Asian, 0.4% American Indian/Alaska Native, 0.1% Native Hawaiian/Other Pacific Islander, 12.0% Other, 24.3% Hispanic of any race (2010); Average household size: 2.46 (2010); Median age: 39.0 (2010); Males per 100 females: 90.2 (2010); Marriage status: 34.1% never married, 49.2% now married, 6.9% widowed, 9.9% divorced (2006-2010 5-year est.); Foreign born: 26.2% (2006-2010 5-year est.); Ancestry (includes multiple ancestries): 16.9% Italian, 14.8% Irish, 10.0% German, 3.9% English, 3.2% Polish (2006-2010 5-year est.).
**Economy:** Employment by occupation: 8.3% management, 3.2% professional, 8.7% services, 25.3% sales, 3.0% farming, 6.2% construction, 4.2% production (2006-2010 5-year est.).
**Income:** Per capita income: $33,280 (2006-2010 5-year est.); Median household income: $62,071 (2006-2010 5-year est.); Average household income: $75,911 (2006-2010 5-year est.); Percent of households with income of $100,000 or more: 28.0% (2006-2010 5-year est.); Poverty rate: 13.0% (2006-2010 5-year est.).
**Education:** Percent of population age 25 and over with: High school diploma (including GED) or higher: 85.5% (2006-2010 5-year est.); Bachelor's degree or higher: 37.1% (2006-2010 5-year est.); Master's degree or higher: 13.7% (2006-2010 5-year est.).
**Housing:** Homeownership rate: 68.6% (2010); Median home value: $303,600 (2006-2010 5-year est.); Median contract rent: $1,158 per month (2006-2010 5-year est.); Median year structure built: 1976 (2006-2010 5-year est.).
**Transportation:** Commute to work: 91.7% car, 6.6% public transportation, 0.0% walk, 1.4% work from home (2006-2010 5-year est.); Travel time to work: 26.6% less than 15 minutes, 29.5% 15 to 30 minutes, 17.2% 30 to 45 minutes, 14.4% 45 to 60 minutes, 12.4% 60 minutes or more (2006-2010 5-year est.)

**NANUET** (CDP). Covers a land area of 5.432 square miles and a water area of 0.005 square miles. Located at 41.09° N. Lat; 74.01° W. Long. Elevation is 299 feet.
**History:** Named for a local Indian chief. International Shrine of St. Anthony is here.
**Population:** 14,065 (1990); 16,707 (2000); 17,882 (2010); Density: 3,291.5 persons per square mile (2010); Race: 66.0% White, 14.9% Black, 12.4% Asian, 0.2% American Indian/Alaska Native, 0.0% Native Hawaiian/Other Pacific Islander, 6.5% Other, 13.7% Hispanic of any race (2010); Average household size: 2.69 (2010); Median age: 41.6 (2010); Males per 100

females: 89.4 (2010); Marriage status: 28.5% never married, 54.7% now married, 9.0% widowed, 7.8% divorced (2006-2010 5-year est.); Foreign born: 25.3% (2006-2010 5-year est.); Ancestry (includes multiple ancestries): 20.7% Irish, 18.1% Italian, 8.5% German, 5.7% Haitian, 4.9% Russian (2006-2010 5-year est.).

**Economy:** Employment by occupation: 13.7% management, 4.4% professional, 8.3% services, 13.2% sales, 3.8% farming, 5.3% construction, 3.5% production (2006-2010 5-year est.).

**Income:** Per capita income: $37,854 (2006-2010 5-year est.); Median household income: $90,605 (2006-2010 5-year est.); Average household income: $99,409 (2006-2010 5-year est.); Percent of households with income of $100,000 or more: 44.2% (2006-2010 5-year est.); Poverty rate: 7.1% (2006-2010 5-year est.).

**Education:** Percent of population age 25 and over with: High school diploma (including GED) or higher: 89.1% (2006-2010 5-year est.); Bachelor's degree or higher: 44.0% (2006-2010 5-year est.); Master's degree or higher: 18.8% (2006-2010 5-year est.).

**School District(s)**

Nanuet Union Free School District (KG-12)
  2009-10 Enrollment: 2,299 . . . . . . . . . . . . . . . . . (845) 627-9888

**Vocational/Technical School(s)**

Capri School of Hair Design (Private, For-profit)
  Fall 2010 Enrollment: 254 . . . . . . . . . . . . . . . . . (845) 623-6339
  2011-12 Tuition: $12,100

**Housing:** Homeownership rate: 68.8% (2010); Median home value: $439,100 (2006-2010 5-year est.); Median contract rent: $1,560 per month (2006-2010 5-year est.); Median year structure built: 1976 (2006-2010 5-year est.).

**Newspapers:** Central Rockland Pennysaver (Community news; Circulation 10,000); Clarkstown East Pennysaver (Community news; Circulation 12,550); Clarkstown West Pennysaver (Community news; Circulation 12,600); East Ramapo Pennysaver (Community news; Circulation 13,564); North Rockland Pennysaver (Community news; Circulation 12,300); Orangetown Pennysaver (Community news; Circulation 13,900); Rockland County Times (Community news; Circulation 8,000); West Ramapo Pennysaver (Community news; Circulation 11,500)

**Transportation:** Commute to work: 87.9% car, 7.4% public transportation, 1.0% walk, 3.0% work from home (2006-2010 5-year est.); Travel time to work: 26.0% less than 15 minutes, 31.1% 15 to 30 minutes, 18.3% 30 to 45 minutes, 9.0% 45 to 60 minutes, 15.6% 60 minutes or more (2006-2010 5-year est.)

**NEW CITY** (CDP). County seat. Covers a land area of 15.582 square miles and a water area of 0.792 square miles. Located at 41.15° N. Lat; 73.99° W. Long. Elevation is 157 feet.

**Population:** 33,745 (1990); 34,038 (2000); 33,559 (2010); Density: 2,153.7 persons per square mile (2010); Race: 78.7% White, 6.4% Black, 10.3% Asian, 0.2% American Indian/Alaska Native, 0.0% Native Hawaiian/Other Pacific Islander, 4.4% Other, 9.0% Hispanic of any race (2010); Average household size: 2.96 (2010); Median age: 44.1 (2010); Males per 100 females: 96.4 (2010); Marriage status: 22.9% never married, 67.9% now married, 5.1% widowed, 4.1% divorced (2006-2010 5-year est.); Foreign born: 16.5% (2006-2010 5-year est.); Ancestry (includes multiple ancestries): 19.7% Italian, 17.3% Irish, 8.9% Russian, 8.8% German, 7.3% American (2006-2010 5-year est.).

**Economy:** Employment by occupation: 17.9% management, 3.9% professional, 4.7% services, 15.9% sales, 3.3% farming, 4.8% construction, 2.5% production (2006-2010 5-year est.).

**Income:** Per capita income: $47,247 (2006-2010 5-year est.); Median household income: $113,922 (2006-2010 5-year est.); Average household income: $139,514 (2006-2010 5-year est.); Percent of households with income of $100,000 or more: 58.7% (2006-2010 5-year est.); Poverty rate: 2.7% (2006-2010 5-year est.).

**Education:** Percent of population age 25 and over with: High school diploma (including GED) or higher: 94.6% (2006-2010 5-year est.); Bachelor's degree or higher: 54.6% (2006-2010 5-year est.); Master's degree or higher: 27.3% (2006-2010 5-year est.).

**School District(s)**

Clarkstown Central School District (KG-12)
  2009-10 Enrollment: 9,196 . . . . . . . . . . . . . . . . . (845) 639-6419
East Ramapo Central School District (spring Valley (PK-12)
  2009-10 Enrollment: 8,116 . . . . . . . . . . . . . . . . . (845) 577-6011

**Housing:** Homeownership rate: 89.5% (2010); Median home value: $558,100 (2006-2010 5-year est.); Median contract rent: $1,202 per month

(2006-2010 5-year est.); Median year structure built: 1968 (2006-2010 5-year est.).

**Newspapers:** Rockland Jewish Reporter (Local news; Circulation 22,000)

**Transportation:** Commute to work: 85.6% car, 7.8% public transportation, 1.2% walk, 4.7% work from home (2006-2010 5-year est.); Travel time to work: 24.3% less than 15 minutes, 24.7% 15 to 30 minutes, 17.2% 30 to 45 minutes, 13.1% 45 to 60 minutes, 20.7% 60 minutes or more (2006-2010 5-year est.)

**Additional Information Contacts**

Rockland County Office of Tourism . . . . . . . . . . . . . . (845) 708-7300
  http://www.rocktourism.com

**NEW HEMPSTEAD** (village). Aka Hempstead. Covers a land area of 2.853 square miles and a water area of 0.009 square miles. Located at 41.14° N. Lat; 74.05° W. Long.

**History:** New Hempstead, formally known as Kakiat, is a village in the Town of Ramapo. Joseph Berger of The New York Times said in a 1997 article that New Hempstead was one of several Town of Ramapo villages formed by non-Jewish people and more secular Jewish people "to preserve the sparse Better Homes and Gardens ambiance that attracted them to Rockland County.

**Population:** 4,096 (1990); 4,767 (2000); 5,132 (2010); Density: 1,798.7 persons per square mile (2010); Race: 71.6% White, 16.0% Black, 6.8% Asian, 0.1% American Indian/Alaska Native, 0.0% Native Hawaiian/Other Pacific Islander, 5.5% Other, 9.3% Hispanic of any race (2010); Average household size: 4.03 (2010); Median age: 29.4 (2010); Males per 100 females: 99.6 (2010); Marriage status: 25.7% never married, 67.1% now married, 3.7% widowed, 3.5% divorced (2006-2010 5-year est.); Foreign born: 20.7% (2006-2010 5-year est.); Ancestry (includes multiple ancestries): 9.3% Polish, 8.4% Russian, 7.4% American, 6.9% German, 6.3% Haitian (2006-2010 5-year est.).

**Economy:** Single-family building permits issued: 0 (2011); Multi-family building permits issued: 0 (2011); Employment by occupation: 15.0% management, 6.8% professional, 7.4% services, 14.6% sales, 1.0% farming, 7.5% construction, 5.5% production (2006-2010 5-year est.).

**Income:** Per capita income: $34,564 (2006-2010 5-year est.); Median household income: $111,196 (2006-2010 5-year est.); Average household income: $127,753 (2006-2010 5-year est.); Percent of households with income of $100,000 or more: 54.6% (2006-2010 5-year est.); Poverty rate: 1.8% (2006-2010 5-year est.).

**Education:** Percent of population age 25 and over with: High school diploma (including GED) or higher: 92.2% (2006-2010 5-year est.); Bachelor's degree or higher: 51.2% (2006-2010 5-year est.); Master's degree or higher: 26.0% (2006-2010 5-year est.).

**Housing:** Homeownership rate: 91.8% (2010); Median home value: $495,400 (2006-2010 5-year est.); Median contract rent: $942 per month (2006-2010 5-year est.); Median year structure built: 1967 (2006-2010 5-year est.).

**Transportation:** Commute to work: 81.7% car, 10.5% public transportation, 1.6% walk, 5.6% work from home (2006-2010 5-year est.); Travel time to work: 24.5% less than 15 minutes, 30.2% 15 to 30 minutes, 18.4% 30 to 45 minutes, 7.2% 45 to 60 minutes, 19.8% 60 minutes or more (2006-2010 5-year est.)

**NEW SQUARE** (village). Covers a land area of 0.356 square miles and a water area of 0 square miles. Located at 41.14° N. Lat; 74.02° W. Long. Elevation is 492 feet.

**History:** A community of Orthodox Hasidic Jews of the Skvirer sect lives here.

**Population:** 2,605 (1990); 4,624 (2000); 6,944 (2010); Density: 19,488.9 persons per square mile (2010); Race: 99.2% White, 0.1% Black, 0.1% Asian, 0.0% American Indian/Alaska Native, 0.0% Native Hawaiian/Other Pacific Islander, 0.6% Other, 0.4% Hispanic of any race (2010); Average household size: 5.54 (2010); Median age: 13.6 (2010); Males per 100 females: 107.5 (2010); Marriage status: 27.0% never married, 70.2% now married, 1.7% widowed, 1.1% divorced (2006-2010 5-year est.); Foreign born: 6.0% (2006-2010 5-year est.); Ancestry (includes multiple ancestries): 27.7% Hungarian, 17.8% European, 16.5% Polish, 4.6% American, 4.5% Russian (2006-2010 5-year est.).

**Economy:** Single-family building permits issued: 29 (2011); Multi-family building permits issued: 9 (2011); Employment by occupation: 8.0% management, 2.6% professional, 8.2% services, 12.0% sales, 8.4% farming, 5.9% construction, 2.4% production (2006-2010 5-year est.).

**Income:** Per capita income: $6,585 (2006-2010 5-year est.); Median household income: $21,172 (2006-2010 5-year est.); Average household

income: $35,603 (2006-2010 5-year est.); Percent of households with income of $100,000 or more: 3.7% (2006-2010 5-year est.); Poverty rate: 58.7% (2006-2010 5-year est.).

**Education:** Percent of population age 25 and over with: High school diploma (including GED) or higher: 71.4% (2006-2010 5-year est.); Bachelor's degree or higher: 6.1% (2006-2010 5-year est.); Master's degree or higher: 1.6% (2006-2010 5-year est.).

**Housing:** Homeownership rate: 12.5% (2010); Median home value: $500,000 (2006-2010 5-year est.); Median contract rent: $926 per month (2006-2010 5-year est.); Median year structure built: 1994 (2006-2010 5-year est.).

**Transportation:** Commute to work: 29.4% car, 1.3% public transportation, 61.3% walk, 4.5% work from home (2006-2010 5-year est.); Travel time to work: 69.2% less than 15 minutes, 24.7% 15 to 30 minutes, 0.0% 30 to 45 minutes, 1.3% 45 to 60 minutes, 4.8% 60 minutes or more (2006-2010 5-year est.)

**NYACK** (village). Covers a land area of 0.769 square miles and a water area of 0.837 square miles. Located at 41.08° N. Lat; 73.91° W. Long. Elevation is 72 feet.

**History:** Was a 19th-century health resort, port, and boat-building center. Birthplace of artist Edward Hopper. Settled 1684, incorporated 1833.

**Population:** 6,558 (1990); 6,737 (2000); 6,765 (2010); Density: 8,789.4 persons per square mile (2010); Race: 63.3% White, 24.0% Black, 4.0% Asian, 0.4% American Indian/Alaska Native, 0.0% Native Hawaiian/Other Pacific Islander, 8.3% Other, 13.9% Hispanic of any race (2010); Average household size: 2.03 (2010); Median age: 40.9 (2010); Males per 100 females: 86.3 (2010); Marriage status: 36.6% never married, 40.3% now married, 9.3% widowed, 13.9% divorced (2006-2010 5-year est.); Foreign born: 25.3% (2006-2010 5-year est.); Ancestry (includes multiple ancestries): 12.9% Italian, 12.0% Irish, 11.9% Russian, 8.3% Haitian, 5.6% English (2006-2010 5-year est.).

**Economy:** Single-family building permits issued: 2 (2011); Multi-family building permits issued: 0 (2011); Employment by occupation: 9.0% management, 3.6% professional, 10.2% services, 13.0% sales, 4.5% farming, 6.6% construction, 3.2% production (2006-2010 5-year est.).

**Income:** Per capita income: $33,127 (2006-2010 5-year est.); Median household income: $51,244 (2006-2010 5-year est.); Average household income: $68,263 (2006-2010 5-year est.); Percent of households with income of $100,000 or more: 23.0% (2006-2010 5-year est.); Poverty rate: 7.0% (2006-2010 5-year est.).

**Education:** Percent of population age 25 and over with: High school diploma (including GED) or higher: 82.4% (2006-2010 5-year est.); Bachelor's degree or higher: 40.3% (2006-2010 5-year est.); Master's degree or higher: 18.2% (2006-2010 5-year est.).

**School District(s)**
Nyack Union Free School District (KG-12)
   2009-10 Enrollment: 2,919 . . . . . . . . . . . . . . . . . . . . (845) 353-7015
**Four-year College(s)**
Nyack College (Private, Not-for-profit, Christ and Missionary Alliance Church)
   Fall 2010 Enrollment: 2,753 . . . . . . . . . . . . . . . . . . . (845) 675-4400
   2011-12 Tuition: In-state $21,500; Out-of-state $21,500

**Housing:** Homeownership rate: 33.9% (2010); Median home value: $477,700 (2006-2010 5-year est.); Median contract rent: $1,156 per month (2006-2010 5-year est.); Median year structure built: 1960 (2006-2010 5-year est.).

**Hospitals:** Nyack Hospital (375 beds)

**Transportation:** Commute to work: 73.7% car, 13.6% public transportation, 5.0% walk, 4.2% work from home (2006-2010 5-year est.); Travel time to work: 34.3% less than 15 minutes, 36.1% 15 to 30 minutes, 15.5% 30 to 45 minutes, 6.2% 45 to 60 minutes, 7.9% 60 minutes or more (2006-2010 5-year est.)

**Additional Information Contacts**
Village of Nyack . . . . . . . . . . . . . . . . . . . . . . . . . . . . . (845) 358-0548
   http://nyack-ny.gov

**ORANGEBURG** (CDP). Covers a land area of 3.072 square miles and a water area of 0 square miles. Located at 41.04° N. Lat; 73.94° W. Long. Elevation is 112 feet.

**Population:** 3,583 (1990); 3,388 (2000); 4,568 (2010); Density: 1,486.7 persons per square mile (2010); Race: 77.3% White, 4.0% Black, 13.2% Asian, 0.2% American Indian/Alaska Native, 0.0% Native Hawaiian/Other Pacific Islander, 5.3% Other, 10.9% Hispanic of any race (2010); Average household size: 2.35 (2010); Median age: 44.1 (2010); Males per 100

females: 73.8 (2010); Marriage status: 48.8% never married, 37.0% now married, 9.8% widowed, 4.4% divorced (2006-2010 5-year est.); Foreign born: 15.6% (2006-2010 5-year est.); Ancestry (includes multiple ancestries): 27.8% Irish, 25.4% Italian, 8.2% German, 5.5% American, 2.0% Scottish (2006-2010 5-year est.).

**Economy:** Employment by occupation: 15.4% management, 4.4% professional, 4.3% services, 20.9% sales, 4.8% farming, 2.7% construction, 1.3% production (2006-2010 5-year est.).

**Income:** Per capita income: $30,547 (2006-2010 5-year est.); Median household income: $70,859 (2006-2010 5-year est.); Average household income: $92,073 (2006-2010 5-year est.); Percent of households with income of $100,000 or more: 41.2% (2006-2010 5-year est.); Poverty rate: 27.0% (2006-2010 5-year est.).

**Education:** Percent of population age 25 and over with: High school diploma (including GED) or higher: 91.0% (2006-2010 5-year est.); Bachelor's degree or higher: 49.8% (2006-2010 5-year est.); Master's degree or higher: 23.0% (2006-2010 5-year est.).

**School District(s)**
South Orangetown Central School District (PK-12)
   2009-10 Enrollment: 3,519 . . . . . . . . . . . . . . . . . . . (845) 680-1050
**Four-year College(s)**
Dominican College of Blauvelt (Private, Not-for-profit)
   Fall 2010 Enrollment: 1,920 . . . . . . . . . . . . . . . . . . (845) 359-7800
   2011-12 Tuition: In-state $22,940; Out-of-state $22,940
Long Island University-Rockland Campus (Private, Not-for-profit)
   Fall 2010 Enrollment: 315 . . . . . . . . . . . . . . . . . . . . (845) 359-7200

**Housing:** Homeownership rate: 70.9% (2010); Median home value: $469,800 (2006-2010 5-year est.); Median contract rent: $756 per month (2006-2010 5-year est.); Median year structure built: 1967 (2006-2010 5-year est.).

**Hospitals:** Rockland Childrens Psychiatric Center (54 beds); Rockland Psychiatric Center (550 beds)

**Transportation:** Commute to work: 76.0% car, 8.9% public transportation, 8.0% walk, 7.0% work from home (2006-2010 5-year est.); Travel time to work: 37.9% less than 15 minutes, 27.4% 15 to 30 minutes, 9.4% 30 to 45 minutes, 6.4% 45 to 60 minutes, 18.9% 60 minutes or more (2006-2010 5-year est.)

**ORANGETOWN** (town). Covers a land area of 24.098 square miles and a water area of 7.267 square miles. Located at 41.05° N. Lat; 73.94° W. Long. Elevation is 112 feet.

**Population:** 46,742 (1990); 47,711 (2000); 49,212 (2010); Density: 2,042.2 persons per square mile (2010); Race: 81.9% White, 6.0% Black, 6.9% Asian, 0.2% American Indian/Alaska Native, 0.0% Native Hawaiian/Other Pacific Islander, 5.0% Other, 9.7% Hispanic of any race (2010); Average household size: 2.59 (2010); Median age: 42.4 (2010); Males per 100 females: 92.3 (2010); Marriage status: 36.5% never married, 50.8% now married, 6.3% widowed, 6.4% divorced (2006-2010 5-year est.); Foreign born: 16.2% (2006-2010 5-year est.); Ancestry (includes multiple ancestries): 31.4% Irish, 19.5% Italian, 10.2% German, 5.8% English, 4.0% Polish (2006-2010 5-year est.).

**Economy:** Unemployment rate: 6.6% (February 2012); Total civilian labor force: 26,150 (February 2012); Single-family building permits issued: 5 (2011); Multi-family building permits issued: 0 (2011); Employment by occupation: 15.9% management, 3.9% professional, 6.4% services, 16.5% sales, 4.3% farming, 6.5% construction, 2.7% production (2006-2010 5-year est.).

**Income:** Per capita income: $40,401 (2006-2010 5-year est.); Median household income: $91,264 (2006-2010 5-year est.); Average household income: $116,628 (2006-2010 5-year est.); Percent of households with income of $100,000 or more: 45.5% (2006-2010 5-year est.); Poverty rate: 5.6% (2006-2010 5-year est.).

**Education:** Percent of population age 25 and over with: High school diploma (including GED) or higher: 92.4% (2006-2010 5-year est.); Bachelor's degree or higher: 46.8% (2006-2010 5-year est.); Master's degree or higher: 21.4% (2006-2010 5-year est.).

**Housing:** Homeownership rate: 72.1% (2010); Median home value: $528,800 (2006-2010 5-year est.); Median contract rent: $1,199 per month (2006-2010 5-year est.); Median year structure built: 1959 (2006-2010 5-year est.).

**Safety:** Violent crime rate: 11.9 per 10,000 population; Property crime rate: 131.0 per 10,000 population (2010).

**Transportation:** Commute to work: 78.6% car, 8.1% public transportation, 5.1% walk, 7.0% work from home (2006-2010 5-year est.); Travel time to work: 31.4% less than 15 minutes, 28.3% 15 to 30 minutes, 16.2% 30 to 45

minutes, 8.6% 45 to 60 minutes, 15.4% 60 minutes or more (2006-2010 5-year est.)
**Additional Information Contacts**
Town of Orangetown . . . . . . . . . . . . . . . . . . . . . . . . . (845) 359-5100
http://www.orangetown.com

## PALISADES (unincorporated postal area)
Zip Code: 10964
Covers a land area of 2.466 square miles and a water area of 0 square miles. Located at 41.01° N. Lat; 73.91° W. Long. Elevation is 197 feet.
Population: 1,472 (2010); Density: 596.8 persons per square mile (2010); Race: 81.7% White, 1.6% Black, 13.4% Asian, 0.3% American Indian/Alaska Native, 0.0% Native Hawaiian/Other Pacific Islander, 3.0% Other, 5.9% Hispanic of any race (2010); Average household size: 2.59 (2010); Median age: 48.2 (2010); Males per 100 females: 95.2 (2010); Homeownership rate: 75.0% (2010)

## PEARL RIVER (CDP). Covers a land area of 6.798 square miles and a water area of 0.400 square miles. Located at 41.06° N. Lat; 74.00° W. Long. Elevation is 240 feet.
Population: 15,314 (1990); 15,553 (2000); 15,876 (2010); Density: 2,335.1 persons per square mile (2010); Race: 92.6% White, 0.8% Black, 3.8% Asian, 0.2% American Indian/Alaska Native, 0.1% Native Hawaiian/Other Pacific Islander, 2.5% Other, 7.0% Hispanic of any race (2010); Average household size: 2.79 (2010); Median age: 42.0 (2010); Males per 100 females: 95.8 (2010); Marriage status: 26.7% never married, 60.5% now married, 6.0% widowed, 6.7% divorced (2006-2010 5-year est.); Foreign born: 12.4% (2006-2010 5-year est.); Ancestry (includes multiple ancestries): 52.5% Irish, 19.8% Italian, 11.2% German, 5.9% English, 3.5% Polish (2006-2010 5-year est.).
Economy: Employment by occupation: 17.6% management, 3.7% professional, 5.7% services, 14.7% sales, 5.4% farming, 9.9% construction, 3.0% production (2006-2010 5-year est.).
Income: Per capita income: $42,011 (2006-2010 5-year est.); Median household income: $99,167 (2006-2010 5-year est.); Average household income: $123,933 (2006-2010 5-year est.); Percent of households with income of $100,000 or more: 49.6% (2006-2010 5-year est.); Poverty rate: 1.6% (2006-2010 5-year est.).
Education: Percent of population age 25 and over with: High school diploma (including GED) or higher: 95.5% (2006-2010 5-year est.); Bachelor's degree or higher: 45.4% (2006-2010 5-year est.); Master's degree or higher: 20.2% (2006-2010 5-year est.).
School District(s)
Pearl River Union Free School District (KG-12)
    2009-10 Enrollment: 2,664 . . . . . . . . . . . . . . . . . . . . (845) 620-3900
Housing: Homeownership rate: 80.2% (2010); Median home value: $493,500 (2006-2010 5-year est.); Median contract rent: $1,194 per month (2006-2010 5-year est.); Median year structure built: 1959 (2006-2010 5-year est.).
Newspapers: Clarkstown Courier (Local news; Circulation 13,000); Rockland Independent (Local news; Circulation 14,000)
Transportation: Commute to work: 81.9% car, 7.7% public transportation, 3.9% walk, 6.0% work from home (2006-2010 5-year est.); Travel time to work: 28.1% less than 15 minutes, 28.6% 15 to 30 minutes, 16.5% 30 to 45 minutes, 10.4% 45 to 60 minutes, 16.3% 60 minutes or more (2006-2010 5-year est.)

## PIERMONT (village). Covers a land area of 0.679 square miles and a water area of 0.473 square miles. Located at 41.04° N. Lat; 73.91° W. Long. Elevation is 95 feet.
History: Until the 1980s, manufacturing (paperboard, silk ribbons). Site of Camp Shanks, which was operational during World Wars I and II. Pier (1 mile long) from which village takes its name was used for embarkation of troops. Site where 1983 Woody Allen movie The Purple Rose of Cairo was filmed. Incorporated 1847.
Population: 2,163 (1990); 2,607 (2000); 2,510 (2010); Density: 3,694.0 persons per square mile (2010); Race: 86.1% White, 3.3% Black, 6.1% Asian, 0.0% American Indian/Alaska Native, 0.0% Native Hawaiian/Other Pacific Islander, 4.5% Other, 9.9% Hispanic of any race (2010); Average household size: 2.03 (2010); Median age: 47.7 (2010); Males per 100 females: 89.9 (2010); Marriage status: 18.0% never married, 60.7% now married, 4.0% widowed, 17.3% divorced (2006-2010 5-year est.); Foreign born: 16.3% (2006-2010 5-year est.); Ancestry (includes multiple ancestries): 21.1% Italian, 16.9% Irish, 15.8% German, 10.9% English, 8.7% Russian (2006-2010 5-year est.).

Economy: Single-family building permits issued: 0 (2011); Multi-family building permits issued: 0 (2011); Employment by occupation: 27.8% management, 1.0% professional, 5.9% services, 18.1% sales, 0.7% farming, 5.9% construction, 4.5% production (2006-2010 5-year est.).
Income: Per capita income: $67,966 (2006-2010 5-year est.); Median household income: $92,045 (2006-2010 5-year est.); Average household income: $129,292 (2006-2010 5-year est.); Percent of households with income of $100,000 or more: 46.9% (2006-2010 5-year est.); Poverty rate: 3.9% (2006-2010 5-year est.).
Education: Percent of population age 25 and over with: High school diploma (including GED) or higher: 98.3% (2006-2010 5-year est.); Bachelor's degree or higher: 49.0% (2006-2010 5-year est.); Master's degree or higher: 24.3% (2006-2010 5-year est.).
School District(s)
South Orangetown Central School District (PK-12)
    2009-10 Enrollment: 3,519 . . . . . . . . . . . . . . . . . . . . (845) 680-1050
Housing: Homeownership rate: 62.0% (2010); Median home value: $716,100 (2006-2010 5-year est.); Median contract rent: $1,363 per month (2006-2010 5-year est.); Median year structure built: 1963 (2006-2010 5-year est.).
Safety: Violent crime rate: 7.9 per 10,000 population; Property crime rate: 102.3 per 10,000 population (2010).
Transportation: Commute to work: 85.4% car, 4.8% public transportation, 0.0% walk, 9.8% work from home (2006-2010 5-year est.); Travel time to work: 34.5% less than 15 minutes, 25.5% 15 to 30 minutes, 8.3% 30 to 45 minutes, 6.2% 45 to 60 minutes, 25.4% 60 minutes or more (2006-2010 5-year est.)

## POMONA (village). Covers a land area of 2.397 square miles and a water area of 0 square miles. Located at 41.18° N. Lat; 74.05° W. Long. Elevation is 453 feet.
Population: 2,611 (1990); 2,726 (2000); 3,103 (2010); Density: 1,294.4 persons per square mile (2010); Race: 66.0% White, 19.1% Black, 9.3% Asian, 0.2% American Indian/Alaska Native, 0.0% Native Hawaiian/Other Pacific Islander, 5.4% Other, 7.1% Hispanic of any race (2010); Average household size: 3.01 (2010); Median age: 45.5 (2010); Males per 100 females: 99.2 (2010); Marriage status: 26.7% never married, 64.7% now married, 3.9% widowed, 4.8% divorced (2006-2010 5-year est.); Foreign born: 19.8% (2006-2010 5-year est.); Ancestry (includes multiple ancestries): 10.9% Italian, 9.9% American, 7.3% Polish, 6.6% Irish, 6.4% Haitian (2006-2010 5-year est.).
Economy: Single-family building permits issued: 0 (2011); Multi-family building permits issued: 0 (2011); Employment by occupation: 18.4% management, 3.9% professional, 3.2% services, 14.2% sales, 6.1% farming, 5.8% construction, 2.0% production (2006-2010 5-year est.).
Income: Per capita income: $56,164 (2006-2010 5-year est.); Median household income: $147,083 (2006-2010 5-year est.); Average household income: $171,383 (2006-2010 5-year est.); Percent of households with income of $100,000 or more: 68.2% (2006-2010 5-year est.); Poverty rate: 5.3% (2006-2010 5-year est.).
Education: Percent of population age 25 and over with: High school diploma (including GED) or higher: 86.1% (2006-2010 5-year est.); Bachelor's degree or higher: 54.7% (2006-2010 5-year est.); Master's degree or higher: 28.9% (2006-2010 5-year est.).
Housing: Homeownership rate: 93.9% (2010); Median home value: $646,200 (2006-2010 5-year est.); Median contract rent: $1,955 per month (2006-2010 5-year est.); Median year structure built: 1979 (2006-2010 5-year est.).
Hospitals: Summit Park Hospital (57 beds)
Transportation: Commute to work: 87.1% car, 4.9% public transportation, 0.3% walk, 5.3% work from home (2006-2010 5-year est.); Travel time to work: 17.3% less than 15 minutes, 36.6% 15 to 30 minutes, 15.1% 30 to 45 minutes, 9.4% 45 to 60 minutes, 21.5% 60 minutes or more (2006-2010 5-year est.)

## RAMAPO (town). Covers a land area of 61.197 square miles and a water area of 0.696 square miles. Located at 41.14° N. Lat; 74.10° W. Long. Elevation is 331 feet.
Population: 93,861 (1990); 108,905 (2000); 126,595 (2010); Density: 2,068.6 persons per square mile (2010); Race: 71.8% White, 15.8% Black, 4.0% Asian, 0.3% American Indian/Alaska Native, 0.0% Native Hawaiian/Other Pacific Islander, 8.1% Other, 13.6% Hispanic of any race (2010); Average household size: 3.58 (2010); Median age: 28.9 (2010); Males per 100 females: 100.0 (2010); Marriage status: 30.5% never married, 57.7% now married, 5.9% widowed, 5.8% divorced (2006-2010

5-year est.); Foreign born: 25.6% (2006-2010 5-year est.); Ancestry (includes multiple ancestries): 7.7% Polish, 7.3% Haitian, 7.2% European, 7.1% Italian, 6.6% Irish (2006-2010 5-year est.).

**Economy:** Unemployment rate: 6.5% (February 2012); Total civilian labor force: 55,462 (February 2012); Single-family building permits issued: 6 (2011); Multi-family building permits issued: 170 (2011); Employment by occupation: 11.6% management, 4.7% professional, 10.7% services, 14.0% sales, 4.2% farming, 8.1% construction, 4.0% production (2006-2010 5-year est.).

**Income:** Per capita income: $27,345 (2006-2010 5-year est.); Median household income: $68,819 (2006-2010 5-year est.); Average household income: $94,544 (2006-2010 5-year est.); Percent of households with income of $100,000 or more: 34.7% (2006-2010 5-year est.); Poverty rate: 18.6% (2006-2010 5-year est.).

**Taxes:** Total city taxes per capita: $513 (2009); City property taxes per capita: $482 (2009).

**Education:** Percent of population age 25 and over with: High school diploma (including GED) or higher: 85.3% (2006-2010 5-year est.); Bachelor's degree or higher: 36.1% (2006-2010 5-year est.); Master's degree or higher: 15.8% (2006-2010 5-year est.).

**Housing:** Homeownership rate: 59.8% (2010); Median home value: $468,500 (2006-2010 5-year est.); Median contract rent: $1,031 per month (2006-2010 5-year est.); Median year structure built: 1971 (2006-2010 5-year est.).

**Safety:** Violent crime rate: 10.3 per 10,000 population; Property crime rate: 97.8 per 10,000 population (2010).

**Transportation:** Commute to work: 76.4% car, 11.1% public transportation, 5.8% walk, 4.2% work from home (2006-2010 5-year est.); Travel time to work: 31.0% less than 15 minutes, 31.4% 15 to 30 minutes, 14.4% 30 to 45 minutes, 7.2% 45 to 60 minutes, 15.9% 60 minutes or more (2006-2010 5-year est.)

**Additional Information Contacts**

Town of Ramapo . . . . . . . . . . . . . . . . . . . . . . . . . . (845) 357-5100
  http://www.ramapo.org

## SLOATSBURG (village). Covers a land area of 2.467 square miles and a water area of 0.038 square miles. Located at 41.16° N. Lat; 74.19° W. Long. Elevation is 344 feet.

**History:** Settled before 1775, incorporated 1929.

**Population:** 3,035 (1990); 3,117 (2000); 3,039 (2010); Density: 1,231.9 persons per square mile (2010); Race: 87.4% White, 3.5% Black, 2.9% Asian, 0.5% American Indian/Alaska Native, 0.0% Native Hawaiian/Other Pacific Islander, 5.7% Other, 14.2% Hispanic of any race (2010); Average household size: 2.93 (2010); Median age: 39.3 (2010); Males per 100 females: 104.2 (2010); Marriage status: 28.2% never married, 57.6% now married, 4.7% widowed, 9.5% divorced (2006-2010 5-year est.); Foreign born: 13.2% (2006-2010 5-year est.); Ancestry (includes multiple ancestries): 34.0% Irish, 20.1% Italian, 18.4% German, 10.1% English, 8.5% American (2006-2010 5-year est.).

**Economy:** Single-family building permits issued: 1 (2011); Multi-family building permits issued: 0 (2011); Employment by occupation: 13.1% management, 6.3% professional, 5.7% services, 21.3% sales, 3.1% farming, 8.3% construction, 5.6% production (2006-2010 5-year est.).

**Income:** Per capita income: $35,780 (2006-2010 5-year est.); Median household income: $85,919 (2006-2010 5-year est.); Average household income: $97,870 (2006-2010 5-year est.); Percent of households with income of $100,000 or more: 42.3% (2006-2010 5-year est.); Poverty rate: 3.7% (2006-2010 5-year est.).

**Taxes:** Total city taxes per capita: $547 (2009); City property taxes per capita: $487 (2009).

**Education:** Percent of population age 25 and over with: High school diploma (including GED) or higher: 89.4% (2006-2010 5-year est.); Bachelor's degree or higher: 35.1% (2006-2010 5-year est.); Master's degree or higher: 9.6% (2006-2010 5-year est.).

**School District(s)**

Ramapo Central School District (suffern) (KG-12)
  2009-10 Enrollment: 4,641 . . . . . . . . . . . . . . . . . . (845) 357-7783

**Housing:** Homeownership rate: 78.9% (2010); Median home value: $412,400 (2006-2010 5-year est.); Median contract rent: $1,243 per month (2006-2010 5-year est.); Median year structure built: 1958 (2006-2010 5-year est.).

**Transportation:** Commute to work: 86.3% car, 5.3% public transportation, 3.2% walk, 4.8% work from home (2006-2010 5-year est.); Travel time to work: 20.8% less than 15 minutes, 38.1% 15 to 30 minutes, 21.3% 30 to 45 minutes, 4.1% 45 to 60 minutes, 15.6% 60 minutes or more (2006-2010 5-year est.)

## SOUTH NYACK (village). Covers a land area of 0.605 square miles and a water area of 1.078 square miles. Located at 41.07° N. Lat; 73.91° W. Long. Elevation is 72 feet.

**History:** Incorporated 1878.

**Population:** 3,346 (1990); 3,473 (2000); 3,510 (2010); Density: 5,801.6 persons per square mile (2010); Race: 67.1% White, 17.4% Black, 5.4% Asian, 0.2% American Indian/Alaska Native, 0.0% Native Hawaiian/Other Pacific Islander, 9.9% Other, 12.3% Hispanic of any race (2010); Average household size: 2.37 (2010); Median age: 31.4 (2010); Males per 100 females: 87.1 (2010); Marriage status: 72.6% never married, 22.4% now married, 2.8% widowed, 2.2% divorced (2006-2010 5-year est.); Foreign born: 13.5% (2006-2010 5-year est.); Ancestry (includes multiple ancestries): 16.9% Irish, 15.4% German, 14.1% Italian, 7.9% Dutch, 7.7% English (2006-2010 5-year est.).

**Economy:** Single-family building permits issued: 0 (2011); Multi-family building permits issued: 0 (2011); Employment by occupation: 9.1% management, 4.2% professional, 15.2% services, 20.0% sales, 2.2% farming, 3.3% construction, 3.1% production (2006-2010 5-year est.).

**Income:** Per capita income: $29,972 (2006-2010 5-year est.); Median household income: $99,250 (2006-2010 5-year est.); Average household income: $149,635 (2006-2010 5-year est.); Percent of households with income of $100,000 or more: 49.6% (2006-2010 5-year est.); Poverty rate: 4.6% (2006-2010 5-year est.).

**Education:** Percent of population age 25 and over with: High school diploma (including GED) or higher: 97.2% (2006-2010 5-year est.); Bachelor's degree or higher: 67.3% (2006-2010 5-year est.); Master's degree or higher: 34.2% (2006-2010 5-year est.).

**Housing:** Homeownership rate: 54.9% (2010); Median home value: $533,100 (2006-2010 5-year est.); Median contract rent: $1,475 per month (2006-2010 5-year est.); Median year structure built: before 1940 (2006-2010 5-year est.).

**Safety:** Violent crime rate: 6.1 per 10,000 population; Property crime rate: 142.2 per 10,000 population (2010).

**Transportation:** Commute to work: 55.1% car, 13.4% public transportation, 17.6% walk, 13.1% work from home (2006-2010 5-year est.); Travel time to work: 39.9% less than 15 minutes, 35.4% 15 to 30 minutes, 13.8% 30 to 45 minutes, 1.5% 45 to 60 minutes, 9.5% 60 minutes or more (2006-2010 5-year est.)

## SPARKILL (CDP). Covers a land area of 0.529 square miles and a water area of 0 square miles. Located at 41.02° N. Lat; 73.93° W. Long. Elevation is 52 feet.

**Population:** n/a (1990); n/a (2000); 1,565 (2010); Density: 2,956.0 persons per square mile (2010); Race: 83.2% White, 2.0% Black, 9.8% Asian, 0.1% American Indian/Alaska Native, 0.0% Native Hawaiian/Other Pacific Islander, 4.9% Other, 12.2% Hispanic of any race (2010); Average household size: 3.11 (2010); Median age: 39.9 (2010); Males per 100 females: 96.9 (2010); Marriage status: 28.3% never married, 60.4% now married, 9.8% widowed, 1.5% divorced (2006-2010 5-year est.); Foreign born: 10.4% (2006-2010 5-year est.); Ancestry (includes multiple ancestries): 38.7% Italian, 36.6% Irish, 11.2% German, 8.3% Greek, 3.7% English (2006-2010 5-year est.).

**Economy:** Employment by occupation: 13.7% management, 7.6% professional, 2.5% services, 19.5% sales, 2.4% farming, 8.0% construction, 0.0% production (2006-2010 5-year est.).

**Income:** Per capita income: $37,258 (2006-2010 5-year est.); Median household income: $72,375 (2006-2010 5-year est.); Average household income: $94,078 (2006-2010 5-year est.); Percent of households with income of $100,000 or more: 39.6% (2006-2010 5-year est.); Poverty rate: 3.7% (2006-2010 5-year est.).

**Education:** Percent of population age 25 and over with: High school diploma (including GED) or higher: 97.7% (2006-2010 5-year est.); Bachelor's degree or higher: 36.4% (2006-2010 5-year est.); Master's degree or higher: 19.8% (2006-2010 5-year est.).

**Four-year College(s)**

Saint Thomas Aquinas College (Private, Not-for-profit)
  Fall 2010 Enrollment: 1,332 . . . . . . . . . . . . . . . . . (845) 398-4000
  2011-12 Tuition: In-state $23,720; Out-of-state $23,720

**Housing:** Homeownership rate: 89.9% (2010); Median home value: $541,700 (2006-2010 5-year est.); Median contract rent: $2,000 per month (2006-2010 5-year est.); Median year structure built: 1977 (2006-2010 5-year est.).

**Transportation:** Commute to work: 85.8% car, 5.7% public transportation, 0.0% walk, 8.6% work from home (2006-2010 5-year est.); Travel time to work: 40.9% less than 15 minutes, 28.6% 15 to 30 minutes, 6.8% 30 to 45 minutes, 14.6% 45 to 60 minutes, 9.1% 60 minutes or more (2006-2010 5-year est.)

**SPRING VALLEY** (village). Covers a land area of 2.015 square miles and a water area of 0.002 square miles. Located at 41.11° N. Lat; 74.04° W. Long. Elevation is 443 feet.
**History:** Named for a spring in the area. Incorporated 1902.
**Population:** 21,802 (1990); 25,464 (2000); 31,347 (2010); Density: 15,551.2 persons per square mile (2010); Race: 39.4% White, 36.8% Black, 3.8% Asian, 0.6% American Indian/Alaska Native, 0.1% Native Hawaiian/Other Pacific Islander, 19.3% Other, 30.6% Hispanic of any race (2010); Average household size: 3.56 (2010); Median age: 28.8 (2010); Males per 100 females: 103.1 (2010); Marriage status: 37.5% never married, 51.6% now married, 4.0% widowed, 7.0% divorced (2006-2010 5-year est.); Foreign born: 47.7% (2006-2010 5-year est.); Ancestry (includes multiple ancestries): 22.0% Haitian, 3.2% Polish, 2.9% Jamaican, 2.5% Hungarian, 2.4% Russian (2006-2010 5-year est.).
**Economy:** Single-family building permits issued: 1 (2011); Multi-family building permits issued: 10 (2011); Employment by occupation: 4.2% management, 1.9% professional, 22.9% services, 12.2% sales, 5.2% farming, 9.2% construction, 5.3% production (2006-2010 5-year est.).
**Income:** Per capita income: $18,033 (2006-2010 5-year est.); Median household income: $48,125 (2006-2010 5-year est.); Average household income: $60,887 (2006-2010 5-year est.); Percent of households with income of $100,000 or more: 15.1% (2006-2010 5-year est.); Poverty rate: 21.0% (2006-2010 5-year est.).
**Education:** Percent of population age 25 and over with: High school diploma (including GED) or higher: 74.8% (2006-2010 5-year est.); Bachelor's degree or higher: 22.3% (2006-2010 5-year est.); Master's degree or higher: 7.1% (2006-2010 5-year est.).

###### School District(s)
East Ramapo Central School District (spring Valley (PK-12)
   2009-10 Enrollment: 8,116 . . . . . . . . . . . . . . . . . . . . (845) 577-6011
**Housing:** Homeownership rate: 28.7% (2010); Median home value: $301,500 (2006-2010 5-year est.); Median contract rent: $1,004 per month (2006-2010 5-year est.); Median year structure built: 1971 (2006-2010 5-year est.).
**Safety:** Violent crime rate: 55.7 per 10,000 population; Property crime rate: 249.5 per 10,000 population (2010).
**Transportation:** Commute to work: 70.6% car, 18.4% public transportation, 3.9% walk, 1.1% work from home (2006-2010 5-year est.); Travel time to work: 29.8% less than 15 minutes, 39.0% 15 to 30 minutes, 15.5% 30 to 45 minutes, 5.1% 45 to 60 minutes, 10.6% 60 minutes or more (2006-2010 5-year est.)
**Additional Information Contacts**
Village of Spring Valley . . . . . . . . . . . . . . . . . . . . . . . (845) 352-1100
  http://www.villagespringvalley.org

**STONY POINT** (town). Covers a land area of 27.624 square miles and a water area of 3.974 square miles. Located at 41.25° N. Lat; 74.00° W. Long. Elevation is 118 feet.
**History:** Named for a local rocky bluff that projects into the Hudson River. Nearby is Stony Point Museum (1936) in battlefield reservation (part of Palisades Interstate Park), commemorating storming of Stony Point by "Mad" Anthony Wayne's Continental forces in July 1779.
**Population:** 12,814 (1990); 14,244 (2000); 15,059 (2010); Density: 545.1 persons per square mile (2010); Race: 87.4% White, 3.8% Black, 2.6% Asian, 0.2% American Indian/Alaska Native, 0.1% Native Hawaiian/Other Pacific Islander, 5.9% Other, 12.8% Hispanic of any race (2010); Average household size: 2.84 (2010); Median age: 43.1 (2010); Males per 100 females: 97.1 (2010); Marriage status: 24.5% never married, 60.5% now married, 7.3% widowed, 7.7% divorced (2006-2010 5-year est.); Foreign born: 10.5% (2006-2010 5-year est.); Ancestry (includes multiple ancestries): 30.1% Italian, 25.2% Irish, 14.0% German, 10.2% American, 5.2% English (2006-2010 5-year est.).
**Economy:** Single-family building permits issued: 4 (2011); Multi-family building permits issued: 0 (2011); Employment by occupation: 14.8% management, 4.0% professional, 9.2% services, 12.2% sales, 3.3% farming, 13.6% construction, 4.0% production (2006-2010 5-year est.).
**Income:** Per capita income: $38,594 (2006-2010 5-year est.); Median household income: $95,748 (2006-2010 5-year est.); Average household income: $109,289 (2006-2010 5-year est.); Percent of households with

income of $100,000 or more: 45.2% (2006-2010 5-year est.); Poverty rate: 4.1% (2006-2010 5-year est.).
**Taxes:** Total city taxes per capita: $1,102 (2009); City property taxes per capita: $1,034 (2009).
**Education:** Percent of population age 25 and over with: High school diploma (including GED) or higher: 88.8% (2006-2010 5-year est.); Bachelor's degree or higher: 33.2% (2006-2010 5-year est.); Master's degree or higher: 13.5% (2006-2010 5-year est.).

###### School District(s)
Haverstraw-Stony Point Csd (north Rockland) (KG-12)
   2009-10 Enrollment: 7,959 . . . . . . . . . . . . . . . . . (845) 942-3002
**Housing:** Homeownership rate: 82.2% (2010); Median home value: $456,400 (2006-2010 5-year est.); Median contract rent: $1,059 per month (2006-2010 5-year est.); Median year structure built: 1968 (2006-2010 5-year est.).
**Safety:** Violent crime rate: 6.0 per 10,000 population; Property crime rate: 64.5 per 10,000 population (2010).
**Transportation:** Commute to work: 92.9% car, 1.8% public transportation, 0.8% walk, 3.8% work from home (2006-2010 5-year est.); Travel time to work: 20.7% less than 15 minutes, 30.9% 15 to 30 minutes, 20.1% 30 to 45 minutes, 15.0% 45 to 60 minutes, 13.2% 60 minutes or more (2006-2010 5-year est.)

**STONY POINT** (CDP). Covers a land area of 5.441 square miles and a water area of 1.293 square miles. Located at 41.22° N. Lat; 73.99° W. Long. Elevation is 118 feet.
**Population:** 10,587 (1990); 11,744 (2000); 12,147 (2010); Density: 2,232.3 persons per square mile (2010); Race: 86.2% White, 4.1% Black, 3.0% Asian, 0.2% American Indian/Alaska Native, 0.1% Native Hawaiian/Other Pacific Islander, 6.4% Other, 14.0% Hispanic of any race (2010); Average household size: 2.81 (2010); Median age: 43.3 (2010); Males per 100 females: 96.5 (2010); Marriage status: 25.8% never married, 58.2% now married, 8.0% widowed, 8.1% divorced (2006-2010 5-year est.); Foreign born: 11.7% (2006-2010 5-year est.); Ancestry (includes multiple ancestries): 29.3% Italian, 25.1% Irish, 14.2% German, 7.9% American, 4.6% English (2006-2010 5-year est.).
**Economy:** Employment by occupation: 13.8% management, 4.8% professional, 10.4% services, 11.6% sales, 3.2% farming, 12.9% construction, 4.0% production (2006-2010 5-year est.).
**Income:** Per capita income: $37,357 (2006-2010 5-year est.); Median household income: $95,696 (2006-2010 5-year est.); Average household income: $105,427 (2006-2010 5-year est.); Percent of households with income of $100,000 or more: 44.9% (2006-2010 5-year est.); Poverty rate: 4.3% (2006-2010 5-year est.).
**Education:** Percent of population age 25 and over with: High school diploma (including GED) or higher: 87.8% (2006-2010 5-year est.); Bachelor's degree or higher: 32.0% (2006-2010 5-year est.); Master's degree or higher: 12.4% (2006-2010 5-year est.).

###### School District(s)
Haverstraw-Stony Point Csd (north Rockland) (KG-12)
   2009-10 Enrollment: 7,959 . . . . . . . . . . . . . . . . . (845) 942-3002
**Housing:** Homeownership rate: 82.5% (2010); Median home value: $437,000 (2006-2010 5-year est.); Median contract rent: $1,018 per month (2006-2010 5-year est.); Median year structure built: 1969 (2006-2010 5-year est.).
**Transportation:** Commute to work: 92.0% car, 2.1% public transportation, 1.1% walk, 4.0% work from home (2006-2010 5-year est.); Travel time to work: 22.2% less than 15 minutes, 32.0% 15 to 30 minutes, 18.6% 30 to 45 minutes, 14.5% 45 to 60 minutes, 12.7% 60 minutes or more (2006-2010 5-year est.)

**SUFFERN** (village). Covers a land area of 2.088 square miles and a water area of 0.027 square miles. Located at 41.11° N. Lat; 74.14° W. Long. Elevation is 312 feet.
**History:** Named for John Suffern, original member of the first state legislature. Incorporated 1896.
**Population:** 11,055 (1990); 11,006 (2000); 10,723 (2010); Density: 5,133.9 persons per square mile (2010); Race: 79.3% White, 4.6% Black, 5.5% Asian, 0.3% American Indian/Alaska Native, 0.0% Native Hawaiian/Other Pacific Islander, 10.3% Other, 17.9% Hispanic of any race (2010); Average household size: 2.31 (2010); Median age: 41.6 (2010); Males per 100 females: 94.6 (2010); Marriage status: 31.3% never married, 53.3% now married, 5.6% widowed, 9.8% divorced (2006-2010 5-year est.); Foreign born: 16.5% (2006-2010 5-year est.); Ancestry (includes multiple

ancestries): 20.2% Irish, 18.2% Italian, 10.3% German, 6.8% Polish, 5.2% Russian (2006-2010 5-year est.).
**Economy:** Single-family building permits issued: 0 (2011); Multi-family building permits issued: 0 (2011); Employment by occupation: 14.0% management, 3.9% professional, 7.7% services, 16.4% sales, 4.7% farming, 8.2% construction, 4.1% production (2006-2010 5-year est.).
**Income:** Per capita income: $37,372 (2006-2010 5-year est.); Median household income: $70,285 (2006-2010 5-year est.); Average household income: $87,152 (2006-2010 5-year est.); Percent of households with income of $100,000 or more: 33.9% (2006-2010 5-year est.); Poverty rate: 3.7% (2006-2010 5-year est.).
**Education:** Percent of population age 25 and over with: High school diploma (including GED) or higher: 95.5% (2006-2010 5-year est.); Bachelor's degree or higher: 43.8% (2006-2010 5-year est.); Master's degree or higher: 18.6% (2006-2010 5-year est.).

### School District(s)
East Ramapo Central School District (spring Valley) (PK-12)
2009-10 Enrollment: 8,116 . . . . . . . . . . . . . . . . . . . (845) 577-6011
Ramapo Central School District (suffern) (KG-12)
2009-10 Enrollment: 4,641 . . . . . . . . . . . . . . . . . . . (845) 357-7783
### Four-year College(s)
Yeshiva Shaarei Torah of Rockland (Private, Not-for-profit, Jewish)
Fall 2010 Enrollment: 9 . . . . . . . . . . . . . . . . . . . . . (845) 352-3431
2011-12 Tuition: In-state $9,000; Out-of-state $9,000
### Two-year College(s)
Rockland Community College (Public)
Fall 2010 Enrollment: 6,228. . . . . . . . . . . . . . . . . . (845) 574-4000
2011-12 Tuition: In-state $3,985; Out-of-state $7,610
**Housing:** Homeownership rate: 70.7% (2010); Median home value: $338,100 (2006-2010 5-year est.); Median contract rent: $1,097 per month (2006-2010 5-year est.); Median year structure built: 1972 (2006-2010 5-year est.).
**Hospitals:** Good Samaritan Hospital (370 beds)
**Safety:** Violent crime rate: 3.7 per 10,000 population; Property crime rate: 51.3 per 10,000 population (2010).
**Transportation:** Commute to work: 84.8% car, 10.3% public transportation, 2.0% walk, 2.4% work from home (2006-2010 5-year est.); Travel time to work: 26.2% less than 15 minutes, 35.5% 15 to 30 minutes, 15.7% 30 to 45 minutes, 7.5% 45 to 60 minutes, 15.0% 60 minutes or more (2006-2010 5-year est.)
**Additional Information Contacts**
Suffern Chamber of Commerce. . . . . . . . . . . . . . . . . (845) 357-8424
http://www.suffernchamberofcommerce.com
Village of Suffern . . . . . . . . . . . . . . . . . . . . . . . . . . (845) 357-2600
http://www.suffernvillage.com

**TAPPAN** (CDP). Covers a land area of 2.770 square miles and a water area of 0.006 square miles. Located at 41.02° N. Lat; 73.95° W. Long. Elevation is 46 feet.
**History:** De Wint Mansion was Washington's headquarters in 1780 and 1783. John Andre, British spy in the American Revolution, was tried and hanged here.
**Population:** 6,867 (1990); 6,757 (2000); 6,613 (2010); Density: 2,386.7 persons per square mile (2010); Race: 79.0% White, 1.5% Black, 14.3% Asian, 0.1% American Indian/Alaska Native, 0.0% Native Hawaiian/Other Pacific Islander, 5.1% Other, 9.3% Hispanic of any race (2010); Average household size: 2.92 (2010); Median age: 44.1 (2010); Males per 100 females: 95.4 (2010); Marriage status: 24.1% never married, 66.6% now married, 5.9% widowed, 3.3% divorced (2006-2010 5-year est.); Foreign born: 23.2% (2006-2010 5-year est.); Ancestry (includes multiple ancestries): 22.6% Italian, 19.1% Irish, 8.4% German, 4.8% English, 4.8% American (2006-2010 5-year est.).
**Economy:** Employment by occupation: 14.0% management, 5.7% professional, 2.9% services, 20.0% sales, 3.0% farming, 4.6% construction, 3.5% production (2006-2010 5-year est.).
**Income:** Per capita income: $43,838 (2006-2010 5-year est.); Median household income: $99,886 (2006-2010 5-year est.); Average household income: $126,661 (2006-2010 5-year est.); Percent of households with income of $100,000 or more: 50.0% (2006-2010 5-year est.); Poverty rate: 1.3% (2006-2010 5-year est.).
**Education:** Percent of population age 25 and over with: High school diploma (including GED) or higher: 96.5% (2006-2010 5-year est.); Bachelor's degree or higher: 51.2% (2006-2010 5-year est.); Master's degree or higher: 18.9% (2006-2010 5-year est.).

### School District(s)
South Orangetown Central School District (PK-12)
2009-10 Enrollment: 3,519 . . . . . . . . . . . . . . . . . . . (845) 680-1050
**Housing:** Homeownership rate: 92.3% (2010); Median home value: $532,800 (2006-2010 5-year est.); Median contract rent: $1,240 per month (2006-2010 5-year est.); Median year structure built: 1961 (2006-2010 5-year est.).
**Transportation:** Commute to work: 89.5% car, 2.9% public transportation, 0.5% walk, 5.5% work from home (2006-2010 5-year est.); Travel time to work: 28.3% less than 15 minutes, 17.5% 15 to 30 minutes, 24.6% 30 to 45 minutes, 13.9% 45 to 60 minutes, 15.7% 60 minutes or more (2006-2010 5-year est.)

**THIELLS** (CDP). Covers a land area of 1.826 square miles and a water area of 0.031 square miles. Located at 41.20° N. Lat; 74.01° W. Long. Elevation is 276 feet.
**Population:** 5,204 (1990); 4,758 (2000); 5,032 (2010); Density: 2,754.5 persons per square mile (2010); Race: 79.6% White, 8.6% Black, 4.1% Asian, 0.2% American Indian/Alaska Native, 0.0% Native Hawaiian/Other Pacific Islander, 7.5% Other, 18.7% Hispanic of any race (2010); Average household size: 3.10 (2010); Median age: 42.1 (2010); Males per 100 females: 94.9 (2010); Marriage status: 30.5% never married, 60.3% now married, 4.9% widowed, 4.3% divorced (2006-2010 5-year est.); Foreign born: 11.4% (2006-2010 5-year est.); Ancestry (includes multiple ancestries): 28.3% Irish, 25.8% Italian, 10.7% German, 5.9% English, 3.5% Polish (2006-2010 5-year est.).
**Economy:** Employment by occupation: 11.9% management, 5.8% professional, 8.5% services, 14.3% sales, 4.2% farming, 8.0% construction, 4.6% production (2006-2010 5-year est.).
**Income:** Per capita income: $38,679 (2006-2010 5-year est.); Median household income: $106,420 (2006-2010 5-year est.); Average household income: $124,119 (2006-2010 5-year est.); Percent of households with income of $100,000 or more: 58.8% (2006-2010 5-year est.); Poverty rate: 3.0% (2006-2010 5-year est.).
**Education:** Percent of population age 25 and over with: High school diploma (including GED) or higher: 95.0% (2006-2010 5-year est.); Bachelor's degree or higher: 42.4% (2006-2010 5-year est.); Master's degree or higher: 18.9% (2006-2010 5-year est.).

### School District(s)
Haverstraw-Stony Point Csd (north Rockland) (KG-12)
2009-10 Enrollment: 7,959 . . . . . . . . . . . . . . . . . . . (845) 942-3002
**Housing:** Homeownership rate: 90.0% (2010); Median home value: $432,700 (2006-2010 5-year est.); Median contract rent: $954 per month (2006-2010 5-year est.); Median year structure built: 1972 (2006-2010 5-year est.).
**Transportation:** Commute to work: 91.3% car, 3.4% public transportation, 0.6% walk, 4.3% work from home (2006-2010 5-year est.); Travel time to work: 21.1% less than 15 minutes, 39.6% 15 to 30 minutes, 11.0% 30 to 45 minutes, 14.0% 45 to 60 minutes, 14.2% 60 minutes or more (2006-2010 5-year est.)

**TOMKINS COVE** (unincorporated postal area)
Zip Code: 10986
Covers a land area of 10.800 square miles and a water area of 0.172 square miles. Located at 41.28° N. Lat; 73.99° W. Long. Elevation is 144 feet. Population: 1,974 (2010); Density: 182.8 persons per square mile (2010); Race: 91.8% White, 2.8% Black, 0.8% Asian, 0.2% American Indian/Alaska Native, 0.1% Native Hawaiian/Other Pacific Islander, 4.3% Other, 8.9% Hispanic of any race (2010); Average household size: 2.95 (2010); Median age: 42.4 (2010); Males per 100 females: 100.6 (2010); Homeownership rate: 77.7% (2010)

**UPPER NYACK** (village). Covers a land area of 1.221 square miles and a water area of 3.143 square miles. Located at 41.12° N. Lat; 73.91° W. Long. Elevation is 190 feet.
**Population:** 2,084 (1990); 1,863 (2000); 2,063 (2010); Density: 1,688.6 persons per square mile (2010); Race: 89.3% White, 3.9% Black, 2.5% Asian, 0.1% American Indian/Alaska Native, 0.0% Native Hawaiian/Other Pacific Islander, 4.2% Other, 6.5% Hispanic of any race (2010); Average household size: 2.65 (2010); Median age: 44.9 (2010); Males per 100 females: 100.1 (2010); Marriage status: 24.4% never married, 64.6% now married, 4.3% widowed, 6.7% divorced (2006-2010 5-year est.); Foreign born: 11.2% (2006-2010 5-year est.); Ancestry (includes multiple ancestries): 21.5% Irish, 14.3% Italian, 13.1% German, 12.5% English, 6.1% Eastern European (2006-2010 5-year est.).

**Economy:** Single-family building permits issued: 1 (2011); Multi-family building permits issued: 0 (2011); Employment by occupation: 17.4% management, 6.5% professional, 3.7% services, 10.3% sales, 3.0% farming, 3.9% construction, 1.2% production (2006-2010 5-year est.).
**Income:** Per capita income: $53,161 (2006-2010 5-year est.); Median household income: $111,167 (2006-2010 5-year est.); Average household income: $143,670 (2006-2010 5-year est.); Percent of households with income of $100,000 or more: 55.3% (2006-2010 5-year est.); Poverty rate: 4.8% (2006-2010 5-year est.).
**Education:** Percent of population age 25 and over with: High school diploma (including GED) or higher: 97.3% (2006-2010 5-year est.); Bachelor's degree or higher: 70.4% (2006-2010 5-year est.); Master's degree or higher: 41.8% (2006-2010 5-year est.).

**School District(s)**
Nyack Union Free School District (KG-12)
   2009-10 Enrollment: 2,919 . . . . . . . . . . . . . . . . . . . . . . (845) 353-7015
**Housing:** Homeownership rate: 85.7% (2010); Median home value: $641,800 (2006-2010 5-year est.); Median contract rent: $1,517 per month (2006-2010 5-year est.); Median year structure built: 1954 (2006-2010 5-year est.).
**Transportation:** Commute to work: 86.5% car, 3.8% public transportation, 1.3% walk, 8.2% work from home (2006-2010 5-year est.); Travel time to work: 23.6% less than 15 minutes, 33.6% 15 to 30 minutes, 16.0% 30 to 45 minutes, 9.9% 45 to 60 minutes, 16.9% 60 minutes or more (2006-2010 5-year est.)

## VALLEY COTTAGE (CDP).
Covers a land area of 4.308 square miles and a water area of 0.022 square miles. Located at 41.11° N. Lat; 73.94° W. Long. Elevation is 177 feet.
**Population:** 9,006 (1990); 9,269 (2000); 9,107 (2010); Density: 2,113.7 persons per square mile (2010); Race: 78.1% White, 5.7% Black, 10.7% Asian, 0.3% American Indian/Alaska Native, 0.0% Native Hawaiian/Other Pacific Islander, 5.2% Other, 10.9% Hispanic of any race (2010); Average household size: 2.59 (2010); Median age: 44.8 (2010); Males per 100 females: 92.1 (2010); Marriage status: 29.1% never married, 54.9% now married, 7.2% widowed, 8.9% divorced (2006-2010 5-year est.); Foreign born: 24.4% (2006-2010 5-year est.); Ancestry (includes multiple ancestries): 26.1% Italian, 16.9% Irish, 9.4% German, 5.5% Russian, 5.3% English (2006-2010 5-year est.).
**Economy:** Employment by occupation: 11.6% management, 2.6% professional, 4.4% services, 14.0% sales, 3.4% farming, 6.1% construction, 4.7% production (2006-2010 5-year est.).
**Income:** Per capita income: $40,543 (2006-2010 5-year est.); Median household income: $87,917 (2006-2010 5-year est.); Average household income: $106,373 (2006-2010 5-year est.); Percent of households with income of $100,000 or more: 41.5% (2006-2010 5-year est.); Poverty rate: 5.9% (2006-2010 5-year est.).
**Education:** Percent of population age 25 and over with: High school diploma (including GED) or higher: 89.9% (2006-2010 5-year est.); Bachelor's degree or higher: 46.6% (2006-2010 5-year est.); Master's degree or higher: 18.8% (2006-2010 5-year est.).

**School District(s)**
Nyack Union Free School District (KG-12)
   2009-10 Enrollment: 2,919 . . . . . . . . . . . . . . . . . . . . . . (845) 353-7015
**Housing:** Homeownership rate: 82.9% (2010); Median home value: $442,600 (2006-2010 5-year est.); Median contract rent: $1,114 per month (2006-2010 5-year est.); Median year structure built: 1973 (2006-2010 5-year est.).
**Transportation:** Commute to work: 86.8% car, 7.1% public transportation, 2.7% walk, 3.2% work from home (2006-2010 5-year est.); Travel time to work: 24.8% less than 15 minutes, 31.5% 15 to 30 minutes, 18.3% 30 to 45 minutes, 12.3% 45 to 60 minutes, 13.1% 60 minutes or more (2006-2010 5-year est.)

## VIOLA (CDP).
Covers a land area of 2.678 square miles and a water area of <.001 square miles. Located at 41.13° N. Lat; 74.08° W. Long. Elevation is 568 feet.
**History:** Viola was originally known as Mechanicsville. The well known Alms House (or "County Poor House") was established in 1837, at Viola, in the Town of Ramapo, for the poor and destitute (debtors). The inmates contributed to their upkeep by tending the farm.
**Population:** 4,433 (1990); 5,931 (2000); 6,868 (2010); Density: 2,564.5 persons per square mile (2010); Race: 96.3% White, 1.5% Black, 0.6% Asian, 0.1% American Indian/Alaska Native, 0.0% Native Hawaiian/Other Pacific Islander, 1.5% Other, 3.8% Hispanic of any race (2010); Average

household size: 3.78 (2010); Median age: 24.1 (2010); Males per 100 females: 96.0 (2010); Marriage status: 30.8% never married, 56.2% now married, 10.3% widowed, 2.7% divorced (2006-2010 5-year est.); Foreign born: 12.9% (2006-2010 5-year est.); Ancestry (includes multiple ancestries): 19.4% Polish, 11.3% Russian, 11.2% Israeli, 9.2% German, 8.6% Hungarian (2006-2010 5-year est.).
**Economy:** Employment by occupation: 14.5% management, 6.4% professional, 1.8% services, 17.9% sales, 2.1% farming, 1.6% construction, 3.0% production (2006-2010 5-year est.).
**Income:** Per capita income: $29,019 (2006-2010 5-year est.); Median household income: $64,413 (2006-2010 5-year est.); Average household income: $104,464 (2006-2010 5-year est.); Percent of households with income of $100,000 or more: 38.6% (2006-2010 5-year est.); Poverty rate: 14.8% (2006-2010 5-year est.).
**Education:** Percent of population age 25 and over with: High school diploma (including GED) or higher: 92.9% (2006-2010 5-year est.); Bachelor's degree or higher: 43.6% (2006-2010 5-year est.); Master's degree or higher: 25.5% (2006-2010 5-year est.).
**Housing:** Homeownership rate: 65.0% (2010); Median home value: $610,900 (2006-2010 5-year est.); Median contract rent: $560 per month (2006-2010 5-year est.); Median year structure built: 1977 (2006-2010 5-year est.).
**Transportation:** Commute to work: 81.8% car, 7.5% public transportation, 0.7% walk, 6.5% work from home (2006-2010 5-year est.); Travel time to work: 40.4% less than 15 minutes, 20.3% 15 to 30 minutes, 10.6% 30 to 45 minutes, 11.2% 45 to 60 minutes, 17.4% 60 minutes or more (2006-2010 5-year est.)

## WESLEY HILLS (village).
Covers a land area of 3.352 square miles and a water area of 0.023 square miles. Located at 41.15° N. Lat; 74.07° W. Long. Elevation is 538 feet.
**History:** Wesley Hills, originally named Wesley Chapel,named after a chapel built in 1829 by a circuit-riding preacher named James Sherwood. The northeast corner of Grandview Avenue and Route 202 was the Kakiat Airstrip. Early air-mail delivery was flown from there.
**Population:** 4,305 (1990); 4,848 (2000); 5,628 (2010); Density: 1,678.7 persons per square mile (2010); Race: 90.7% White, 4.5% Black, 2.8% Asian, 0.1% American Indian/Alaska Native, 0.0% Native Hawaiian/Other Pacific Islander, 1.9% Other, 3.7% Hispanic of any race (2010); Average household size: 3.73 (2010); Median age: 31.4 (2010); Males per 100 females: 101.0 (2010); Marriage status: 23.3% never married, 67.6% now married, 1.4% widowed, 7.7% divorced (2006-2010 5-year est.); Foreign born: 16.7% (2006-2010 5-year est.); Ancestry (includes multiple ancestries): 10.1% European, 9.3% Polish, 9.1% German, 8.5% Russian, 7.6% American (2006-2010 5-year est.).
**Economy:** Single-family building permits issued: 14 (2011); Multi-family building permits issued: 0 (2011); Employment by occupation: 16.3% management, 4.8% professional, 1.6% services, 11.2% sales, 4.4% farming, 6.6% construction, 0.9% production (2006-2010 5-year est.).
**Income:** Per capita income: $50,927 (2006-2010 5-year est.); Median household income: $128,839 (2006-2010 5-year est.); Average household income: $178,700 (2006-2010 5-year est.); Percent of households with income of $100,000 or more: 63.0% (2006-2010 5-year est.); Poverty rate: 4.2% (2006-2010 5-year est.).
**Education:** Percent of population age 25 and over with: High school diploma (including GED) or higher: 97.3% (2006-2010 5-year est.); Bachelor's degree or higher: 69.1% (2006-2010 5-year est.); Master's degree or higher: 32.2% (2006-2010 5-year est.).
**Housing:** Homeownership rate: 92.1% (2010); Median home value: $609,900 (2006-2010 5-year est.); Median contract rent: n/a per month (2006-2010 5-year est.); Median year structure built: 1969 (2006-2010 5-year est.).
**Transportation:** Commute to work: 78.3% car, 15.4% public transportation, 0.5% walk, 5.9% work from home (2006-2010 5-year est.); Travel time to work: 19.3% less than 15 minutes, 24.6% 15 to 30 minutes, 15.9% 30 to 45 minutes, 12.0% 45 to 60 minutes, 28.3% 60 minutes or more (2006-2010 5-year est.)

## WEST HAVERSTRAW (village).
Covers a land area of 1.519 square miles and a water area of 0.023 square miles. Located at 41.20° N. Lat; 73.98° W. Long. Elevation is 108 feet.
**History:** Named, probably, for a variation of the Dutch translation of "oat-straw," or for a Dutch name. Incorporated 1883.
**Population:** 9,183 (1990); 10,295 (2000); 10,165 (2010); Density: 6,689.9 persons per square mile (2010); Race: 56.6% White, 18.1% Black, 4.6%

Asian, 0.3% American Indian/Alaska Native, 0.1% Native Hawaiian/Other Pacific Islander, 20.3% Other, 40.9% Hispanic of any race (2010); Average household size: 3.02 (2010); Median age: 35.8 (2010); Males per 100 females: 94.8 (2010); Marriage status: 33.6% never married, 51.8% now married, 4.4% widowed, 10.2% divorced (2006-2010 5-year est.); Foreign born: 24.6% (2006-2010 5-year est.); Ancestry (includes multiple ancestries): 14.8% Italian, 13.1% Irish, 7.2% American, 6.4% German, 4.3% Haitian (2006-2010 5-year est.).

**Economy:** Single-family building permits issued: 0 (2011); Multi-family building permits issued: 0 (2011); Employment by occupation: 7.5% management, 2.2% professional, 9.8% services, 20.0% sales, 3.8% farming, 8.5% construction, 9.9% production (2006-2010 5-year est.).

**Income:** Per capita income: $26,952 (2006-2010 5-year est.); Median household income: $73,825 (2006-2010 5-year est.); Average household income: $83,559 (2006-2010 5-year est.); Percent of households with income of $100,000 or more: 31.2% (2006-2010 5-year est.); Poverty rate: 5.9% (2006-2010 5-year est.).

**Education:** Percent of population age 25 and over with: High school diploma (including GED) or higher: 81.1% (2006-2010 5-year est.); Bachelor's degree or higher: 19.0% (2006-2010 5-year est.); Master's degree or higher: 5.8% (2006-2010 5-year est.).

**School District(s)**

Haverstraw-Stony Point Csd (north Rockland) (KG-12)

    2009-10 Enrollment: 7,959 . . . . . . . . . . . . . . . . . . . .(845) 942-3002

**Housing:** Homeownership rate: 61.5% (2010); Median home value: $355,300 (2006-2010 5-year est.); Median contract rent: $1,205 per month (2006-2010 5-year est.); Median year structure built: 1964 (2006-2010 5-year est.).

**Hospitals:** Helen Hayes Hospital (155 beds)

**Transportation:** Commute to work: 89.6% car, 5.8% public transportation, 3.4% walk, 1.2% work from home (2006-2010 5-year est.); Travel time to work: 21.9% less than 15 minutes, 38.0% 15 to 30 minutes, 22.2% 30 to 45 minutes, 7.7% 45 to 60 minutes, 10.2% 60 minutes or more (2006-2010 5-year est.)

**WEST NYACK** (CDP). Covers a land area of 2.939 square miles and a water area of 0.021 square miles. Located at 41.09° N. Lat; 73.96° W. Long. Elevation is 79 feet.

**Population:** 3,437 (1990); 3,282 (2000); 3,439 (2010); Density: 1,169.8 persons per square mile (2010); Race: 82.6% White, 2.7% Black, 10.2% Asian, 0.1% American Indian/Alaska Native, 0.1% Native Hawaiian/Other Pacific Islander, 4.3% Other, 9.9% Hispanic of any race (2010); Average household size: 2.95 (2010); Median age: 42.9 (2010); Males per 100 females: 96.0 (2010); Marriage status: 31.4% never married, 59.0% now married, 6.6% widowed, 3.0% divorced (2006-2010 5-year est.); Foreign born: 11.3% (2006-2010 5-year est.); Ancestry (includes multiple ancestries): 29.7% Irish, 23.9% Italian, 10.0% German, 4.9% English, 4.8% Polish (2006-2010 5-year est.).

**Economy:** Employment by occupation: 17.3% management, 6.1% professional, 5.0% services, 6.5% sales, 6.8% farming, 6.3% construction, 5.1% production (2006-2010 5-year est.).

**Income:** Per capita income: $43,081 (2006-2010 5-year est.); Median household income: $105,536 (2006-2010 5-year est.); Average household income: $127,350 (2006-2010 5-year est.); Percent of households with income of $100,000 or more: 52.7% (2006-2010 5-year est.); Poverty rate: 2.8% (2006-2010 5-year est.).

**Education:** Percent of population age 25 and over with: High school diploma (including GED) or higher: 94.1% (2006-2010 5-year est.); Bachelor's degree or higher: 48.9% (2006-2010 5-year est.); Master's degree or higher: 27.6% (2006-2010 5-year est.).

**School District(s)**

Clarkstown Central School District (KG-12)

    2009-10 Enrollment: 9,196 . . . . . . . . . . . . . . . . . . . . (845) 639-6419

Rockland Boces

    2009-10 Enrollment: n/a . . . . . . . . . . . . . . . . . . . (845) 627-4701

**Vocational/Technical School(s)**

Rockland County BOCES-Practical Nursing Program (Public)

    Fall 2010 Enrollment: 110 . . . . . . . . . . . . . . . . . . (845) 627-4770

    2011-12 Tuition: $10,199

**Housing:** Homeownership rate: 86.1% (2010); Median home value: $499,300 (2006-2010 5-year est.); Median contract rent: $1,157 per month (2006-2010 5-year est.); Median year structure built: 1960 (2006-2010 5-year est.).

**Newspapers:** The Journal News - Rockland Edition (Local news); Rockland Review (Community news; Circulation 26,000)

**Transportation:** Commute to work: 88.8% car, 4.9% public transportation, 2.9% walk, 2.3% work from home (2006-2010 5-year est.); Travel time to work: 33.3% less than 15 minutes, 23.4% 15 to 30 minutes, 11.4% 30 to 45 minutes, 9.0% 45 to 60 minutes, 22.8% 60 minutes or more (2006-2010 5-year est.)

# Saint Lawrence County

Located in northern New York; bounded on the northwest by the St. Lawrence River; drained by the St. Regis, Indian, Grass, Oswegatchie, and Raquette Rivers; plains area, rising to the Adirondacks in the southeast; includes Black and Cranberry Lakes. Covers a land area of 2,685.60 square miles, a water area of 135.88 square miles, and is located in the Eastern Time Zone at 44.59° N. Lat., 75.16° W. Long. The county was founded in 1802. County seat is Canton.

Saint Lawrence County is part of the Ogdensburg-Massena, NY Micropolitan Statistical Area. The entire metro area includes: St. Lawrence County, NY

| Weather Station: Canton 4 SE | | | | | | | | | | Elevation: 399 feet | | |
|---|---|---|---|---|---|---|---|---|---|---|---|---|
|  | Jan | Feb | Mar | Apr | May | Jun | Jul | Aug | Sep | Oct | Nov | Dec |
| High | 26 | 29 | 39 | 53 | 66 | 74 | 79 | 77 | 69 | 57 | 45 | 32 |
| Low | 5 | 8 | 18 | 33 | 44 | 54 | 58 | 56 | 48 | 37 | 28 | 14 |
| Precip | 2.1 | 1.8 | 2.1 | 2.9 | 3.1 | 3.3 | 3.9 | 3.7 | 4.0 | 3.9 | 3.4 | 2.6 |
| Snow | 20.1 | 16.9 | 12.4 | 3.7 | tr | 0.0 | 0.0 | 0.0 | tr | 0.6 | 5.8 | 18.5 |

*High and Low temperatures in degrees Fahrenheit; Precipitation and Snow in inches*

| Weather Station: Gouverneur 3 NW | | | | | | | | | | Elevation: 419 feet | | |
|---|---|---|---|---|---|---|---|---|---|---|---|---|
|  | Jan | Feb | Mar | Apr | May | Jun | Jul | Aug | Sep | Oct | Nov | Dec |
| High | 27 | 31 | 40 | 55 | 67 | 76 | 80 | 79 | 71 | 58 | 45 | 33 |
| Low | 6 | 8 | 18 | 32 | 42 | 52 | 56 | 55 | 46 | 36 | 28 | 14 |
| Precip | 2.3 | 2.0 | 2.2 | 3.0 | 3.1 | 3.3 | 3.6 | 3.4 | 3.9 | 4.0 | 3.7 | 2.7 |
| Snow | 21.9 | 18.2 | 13.6 | 3.9 | tr | tr | 0.0 | 0.0 | tr | 1.0 | 6.8 | 19.2 |

*High and Low temperatures in degrees Fahrenheit; Precipitation and Snow in inches*

| Weather Station: Lawrenceville 3 SW | | | | | | | | | | Elevation: 500 feet | | |
|---|---|---|---|---|---|---|---|---|---|---|---|---|
|  | Jan | Feb | Mar | Apr | May | Jun | Jul | Aug | Sep | Oct | Nov | Dec |
| High | 27 | 30 | 40 | 55 | 68 | 76 | 80 | 79 | 71 | 58 | 45 | 32 |
| Low | 8 | 10 | 20 | 33 | 45 | 54 | 59 | 57 | 49 | 39 | 29 | 15 |
| Precip | 2.2 | 1.9 | 2.3 | 3.0 | 3.0 | 3.9 | 4.1 | 3.9 | 4.1 | 3.7 | 3.5 | 2.7 |
| Snow | 15.7 | 14.0 | 13.3 | 4.1 | 0.2 | 0.0 | 0.0 | 0.0 | 0.0 | 0.5 | 6.3 | 14.3 |

*High and Low temperatures in degrees Fahrenheit; Precipitation and Snow in inches*

| Weather Station: Massena Arpt | | | | | | | | | | Elevation: 213 feet | | |
|---|---|---|---|---|---|---|---|---|---|---|---|---|
|  | Jan | Feb | Mar | Apr | May | Jun | Jul | Aug | Sep | Oct | Nov | Dec |
| High | 24 | 28 | 39 | 54 | 67 | 76 | 81 | 78 | 70 | 57 | 44 | 31 |
| Low | 5 | 8 | 19 | 33 | 45 | 53 | 58 | 56 | 48 | 37 | 28 | 14 |
| Precip | 2.2 | 1.9 | 2.3 | 2.8 | 3.1 | 3.4 | 3.5 | 3.6 | 3.1 | 3.1 | 2.6 |
| Snow | na | na | na | na | na | na | na | na | na | na | na | na |

*High and Low temperatures in degrees Fahrenheit; Precipitation and Snow in inches*

| Weather Station: Wanakena Ranger School | | | | | | | | | | Elevation: 1,509 feet | | |
|---|---|---|---|---|---|---|---|---|---|---|---|---|
|  | Jan | Feb | Mar | Apr | May | Jun | Jul | Aug | Sep | Oct | Nov | Dec |
| High | 27 | 30 | 38 | 52 | 66 | 74 | 78 | 76 | 68 | 55 | 43 | 31 |
| Low | 4 | 5 | 14 | 30 | 41 | 50 | 54 | 53 | 45 | 35 | 25 | 12 |
| Precip | 2.8 | 2.3 | 2.7 | 3.0 | 3.8 | 4.0 | 4.7 | 4.2 | 4.6 | 4.1 | 3.9 | 3.1 |
| Snow | 29.6 | 25.3 | 17.3 | 6.0 | 0.3 | 0.0 | 0.0 | 0.0 | tr | 1.6 | 11.2 | 25.8 |

*High and Low temperatures in degrees Fahrenheit; Precipitation and Snow in inches*

**Population:** 111,974 (1990); 111,931 (2000); 111,944 (2010); Race: 93.9% White, 2.2% Black, 1.0% Asian, 1.0% American Indian/Alaska Native, 0.0% Native Hawaiian/Other Pacific Islander, 1.9% Other, 1.9% Hispanic of any race (2010); Density: 41.7 persons per square mile (2010); Average household size: 2.43 (2010); Median age: 37.5 (2010); Males per 100 females: 103.2 (2010).

**Religion:** Six largest groups: 21.9% Catholicism, 3.8% Methodist/Pietist, 2.3% Presbyterian-Reformed, 1.7% European Free-Church, 1.2% Non-Denominational, 1.1% Episcopalianism/Anglicanism (2010)

**Economy:** Unemployment rate: 11.3% (February 2012); Total civilian labor force: 48,821 (February 2012); Leading industries: 23.1% health care and social assistance; 20.0% retail trade; 11.1% accommodation & food services (2009); Farms: 1,330 totaling 347,246 acres (2007); Companies that employ 500 or more persons: 5 (2009); Companies that employ 100 to 499 persons: 28 (2009); Companies that employ less than 100 persons: 2,047 (2009); Black-owned businesses: n/a (2007); Hispanic-owned businesses: n/a (2007); Asian-owned businesses: n/a (2007); Women-owned businesses: n/a (2007); Retail sales per capita: $10,561

(2010). Single-family building permits issued: 154 (2011); Multi-family building permits issued: 6 (2011).

**Income:** Per capita income: $20,143 (2006-2010 5-year est.); Median household income: $42,303 (2006-2010 5-year est.); Average household income: $52,241 (2006-2010 5-year est.); Percent of households with income of $100,000 or more: 11.0% (2006-2010 5-year est.); Poverty rate: 16.9% (2006-2010 5-year est.); Bankruptcy rate: 3.05% (2011).

**Taxes:** Total county taxes per capita: $729 (2009); County property taxes per capita: $339 (2009).

**Education:** Percent of population age 25 and over with: High school diploma (including GED) or higher: 85.8% (2006-2010 5-year est.); Bachelor's degree or higher: 18.7% (2006-2010 5-year est.); Master's degree or higher: 8.6% (2006-2010 5-year est.).

**Housing:** Homeownership rate: 70.8% (2010); Median home value: $79,600 (2006-2010 5-year est.); Median contract rent: $460 per month (2006-2010 5-year est.); Median year structure built: 1958 (2006-2010 5-year est.)

**Health:** Birth rate: 104.1 per 10,000 population (2011); Death rate: 88.6 per 10,000 population (2011); Age-adjusted cancer mortality rate: 201.7 deaths per 100,000 population (2009); Number of physicians: 15.1 per 10,000 population (2008); Hospital beds: 47.8 per 10,000 population (2007); Hospital admissions: 1,284.2 per 10,000 population (2007).

**Elections:** 2008 Presidential election results: 57.4% Obama, 41.0% McCain, 0.7% Nader

**National and State Parks:** Adirondack State Park; Cedar Island State Park; Cold Spring Brook State Forest; Degrasse State Forest; Donnerville State Forest; Greenwood Creek State Forest; Higley Flow State Park; Jacques Cartier State Park; Orebed Creek State Forest; Saint Lawrence State Forest; Saint Lawrence State Forest Number 10; Saint Lawrence State Forest Number 12; Saint Lawrence State Forest Number 15; Saint Lawrence State Forest Number 2; Saint Lawrence State Forest Number 23; Saint Lawrence State Forest Number 28; Saint Lawrence State Forest Number 31; Saint Lawrence State Forest Number 6; Saint Lawrence State Forest Number 8; Saint Lawrence State Park; Silver Hill State Forest; Stammer Creek State Forest; Taylor Creek State Forest; Trout Lake State Forest; Whippoorwill Corners State Forest; Wilson Hill State Fish And Game Managemen

**Additional Information Contacts**

Saint Lawrence County Government . . . . . . . . . . . . . . . . . . . (315) 379-2276
 http://www.co.st-lawrence.ny.us
Black Lake Chamber of Commerce . . . . . . . . . . . . . . . . . . . (315) 375-8640
 http://www.blacklakeny.com/chamber.html
Canton Chamber of Commerce . . . . . . . . . . . . . . . . . . . . . . (315) 386-8255
 http://cantonnychamber.org
City of Ogdensburg . . . . . . . . . . . . . . . . . . . . . . . . . . . . . . (315) 393-3540
 http://www.ogdensburg.org
Greater Gouverneur Area Chamber of Commerce . . . . . . . (315) 287-0331
 http://www.gouverneurchamber.net
Greater Massena Chamber of Commerce . . . . . . . . . . . . . . (315) 769-3525
 http://www.massenachamber.com
Ogdensburg Chamber of Commerce . . . . . . . . . . . . . . . . . . (315) 393-3620
 http://www.ogdensburgny.com
Potsdam Chamber of Commerce . . . . . . . . . . . . . . . . . . . . . (315) 274-9000
 http://www.potsdam.ny.us/chamber
Saint Lawrence County Chamber of Commerce . . . . . . . . . (315) 386-4000
 http://www.northcountryguide.com
Village of Canton . . . . . . . . . . . . . . . . . . . . . . . . . . . . . . . . (315) 386-2871
 http://www.cantonnewyork.us
Village of Massena . . . . . . . . . . . . . . . . . . . . . . . . . . . . . . . (315) 769-8625
 http://www.massenaworks.com
Waddington Chamber of Commerce . . . . . . . . . . . . . . . . . . (315) 388-4765
 http://www.waddingtonny.us./chamber

## Saint Lawrence County Communities

**BRASHER** (town). Covers a land area of 91.103 square miles and a water area of 0.966 square miles. Located at 44.88° N. Lat; 74.72° W. Long.

**Population:** 2,124 (1990); 2,337 (2000); 2,512 (2010); Density: 27.6 persons per square mile (2010); Race: 93.8% White, 0.2% Black, 0.2% Asian, 3.0% American Indian/Alaska Native, 0.0% Native Hawaiian/Other Pacific Islander, 2.8% Other, 1.8% Hispanic of any race (2010); Average household size: 2.54 (2010); Median age: 40.1 (2010); Males per 100 females: 96.4 (2010); Marriage status: 13.3% never married, 68.9% now married, 10.0% widowed, 7.8% divorced (2006-2010 5-year est.); Foreign

born: 4.1% (2006-2010 5-year est.); Ancestry (includes multiple ancestries): 18.3% Irish, 15.4% French, 14.2% American, 13.5% French Canadian, 8.0% English (2006-2010 5-year est.).

**Economy:** Single-family building permits issued: 6 (2011); Multi-family building permits issued: 0 (2011); Employment by occupation: 9.2% management, 4.4% professional, 12.6% services, 17.0% sales, 0.9% farming, 13.9% construction, 10.1% production (2006-2010 5-year est.).

**Income:** Per capita income: $19,243 (2006-2010 5-year est.); Median household income: $40,885 (2006-2010 5-year est.); Average household income: $48,699 (2006-2010 5-year est.); Percent of households with income of $100,000 or more: 7.7% (2006-2010 5-year est.); Poverty rate: 11.6% (2006-2010 5-year est.).

**Education:** Percent of population age 25 and over with: High school diploma (including GED) or higher: 86.8% (2006-2010 5-year est.); Bachelor's degree or higher: 12.8% (2006-2010 5-year est.); Master's degree or higher: 4.1% (2006-2010 5-year est.).

**Housing:** Homeownership rate: 75.7% (2010); Median home value: $86,600 (2006-2010 5-year est.); Median contract rent: $472 per month (2006-2010 5-year est.); Median year structure built: 1963 (2006-2010 5-year est.).

**Transportation:** Commute to work: 88.8% car, 0.0% public transportation, 4.4% walk, 6.8% work from home (2006-2010 5-year est.); Travel time to work: 29.5% less than 15 minutes, 40.8% 15 to 30 minutes, 23.6% 30 to 45 minutes, 3.8% 45 to 60 minutes, 2.3% 60 minutes or more (2006-2010 5-year est.)

**BRASHER FALLS** (CDP). Covers a land area of 1.638 square miles and a water area of 0.101 square miles. Located at 44.81° N. Lat; 74.78° W. Long. Elevation is 289 feet.

**Population:** n/a (1990); n/a (2000); 669 (2010); Density: 408.4 persons per square mile (2010); Race: 96.0% White, 0.1% Black, 0.3% Asian, 0.7% American Indian/Alaska Native, 0.0% Native Hawaiian/Other Pacific Islander, 2.9% Other, 1.8% Hispanic of any race (2010); Average household size: 2.31 (2010); Median age: 43.1 (2010); Males per 100 females: 89.5 (2010); Marriage status: 10.5% never married, 66.5% now married, 15.2% widowed, 7.8% divorced (2006-2010 5-year est.); Foreign born: 0.5% (2006-2010 5-year est.); Ancestry (includes multiple ancestries): 23.5% American, 20.3% Irish, 13.1% German, 13.1% French, 8.1% French Canadian (2006-2010 5-year est.).

**Economy:** Employment by occupation: 17.0% management, 9.4% professional, 4.2% services, 19.4% sales, 2.4% farming, 7.9% construction, 10.3% production (2006-2010 5-year est.).

**Income:** Per capita income: $17,483 (2006-2010 5-year est.); Median household income: $27,157 (2006-2010 5-year est.); Average household income: $45,201 (2006-2010 5-year est.); Percent of households with income of $100,000 or more: 8.6% (2006-2010 5-year est.); Poverty rate: 4.4% (2006-2010 5-year est.).

**Education:** Percent of population age 25 and over with: High school diploma (including GED) or higher: 89.9% (2006-2010 5-year est.); Bachelor's degree or higher: 20.1% (2006-2010 5-year est.); Master's degree or higher: 9.0% (2006-2010 5-year est.).

**School District(s)**

Brasher Falls Central School District (PK-12)
 2009-10 Enrollment: 1,077 . . . . . . . . . . . . . . . . . (315) 389-5131

**Housing:** Homeownership rate: 63.3% (2010); Median home value: $88,000 (2006-2010 5-year est.); Median contract rent: $491 per month (2006-2010 5-year est.); Median year structure built: before 1940 (2006-2010 5-year est.).

**Transportation:** Commute to work: 75.5% car, 0.0% public transportation, 12.0% walk, 12.6% work from home (2006-2010 5-year est.); Travel time to work: 38.9% less than 15 minutes, 27.4% 15 to 30 minutes, 28.4% 30 to 45 minutes, 2.8% 45 to 60 minutes, 2.5% 60 minutes or more (2006-2010 5-year est.)

**BRIER HILL** (unincorporated postal area)

Zip Code: 13614

Covers a land area of 8.965 square miles and a water area of 0 square miles. Located at 44.53° N. Lat; 75.69° W. Long. Elevation is 341 feet.

Population: 357 (2010); Density: 39.8 persons per square mile (2010); Race: 97.2% White, 0.0% Black, 0.6% Asian, 0.8% American Indian/Alaska Native, 0.0% Native Hawaiian/Other Pacific Islander, 1.4% Other, 0.3% Hispanic of any race (2010); Average household size: 2.95 (2010); Median age: 31.7 (2010); Males per 100 females: 85.9 (2010); Homeownership rate: 66.1% (2010)

**CANTON** (village). County seat. Covers a land area of 3.576 square miles and a water area of 0.099 square miles. Located at 44.59° N. Lat; 75.17° W. Long. Elevation is 377 feet.
**Population:** 6,495 (1990); 5,882 (2000); 6,314 (2010); Density: 1,765.5 persons per square mile (2010); Race: 88.0% White, 6.2% Black, 1.9% Asian, 0.5% American Indian/Alaska Native, 0.0% Native Hawaiian/Other Pacific Islander, 3.4% Other, 4.4% Hispanic of any race (2010); Average household size: 2.04 (2010); Median age: 21.8 (2010); Males per 100 females: 97.7 (2010); Marriage status: 73.9% never married, 19.6% now married, 4.0% widowed, 2.5% divorced (2006-2010 5-year est.); Foreign born: 7.5% (2006-2010 5-year est.); Ancestry (includes multiple ancestries): 19.4% English, 17.5% Irish, 8.2% German, 7.2% Italian, 4.7% French (2006-2010 5-year est.).
**Economy:** Single-family building permits issued: 2 (2011); Multi-family building permits issued: 0 (2011); Employment by occupation: 7.4% management, 0.4% professional, 12.0% services, 24.2% sales, 6.9% farming, 1.6% construction, 1.6% production (2006-2010 5-year est.).
**Income:** Per capita income: $16,854 (2006-2010 5-year est.); Median household income: $53,111 (2006-2010 5-year est.); Average household income: $62,344 (2006-2010 5-year est.); Percent of households with income of $100,000 or more: 19.7% (2006-2010 5-year est.); Poverty rate: 11.9% (2006-2010 5-year est.).
**Education:** Percent of population age 25 and over with: High school diploma (including GED) or higher: 93.2% (2006-2010 5-year est.); Bachelor's degree or higher: 45.7% (2006-2010 5-year est.); Master's degree or higher: 33.2% (2006-2010 5-year est.).
### School District(s)
Canton Central School District (PK-12)
    2009-10 Enrollment: 1,410 . . . . . . . . . . . . . . . . . . . . . . . (315) 386-8561
Saint Lawrence-Lewis Boces
    2009-10 Enrollment: n/a . . . . . . . . . . . . . . . . . . . . . . (315) 386-4504
### Four-year College(s)
SUNY College of Technology at Canton (Public)
    Fall 2010 Enrollment: 2,999 . . . . . . . . . . . . . . . . . . . (315) 386-7011
    2011-12 Tuition: In-state $6,629; Out-of-state $11,099
St Lawrence University (Private, Not-for-profit)
    Fall 2010 Enrollment: 2,345 . . . . . . . . . . . . . . . . . . . (315) 229-5011
    2011-12 Tuition: In-state $42,735; Out-of-state $42,735
**Housing:** Homeownership rate: 44.3% (2010); Median home value: $139,800 (2006-2010 5-year est.); Median contract rent: $503 per month (2006-2010 5-year est.); Median year structure built: 1946 (2006-2010 5-year est.).
**Safety:** Violent crime rate: 3.3 per 10,000 population; Property crime rate: 145.1 per 10,000 population (2010).
**Newspapers:** Saint Lawrence Plaindealer (Community news; Circulation 3,500)
**Transportation:** Commute to work: 46.7% car, 0.0% public transportation, 41.1% walk, 9.6% work from home (2006-2010 5-year est.); Travel time to work: 70.4% less than 15 minutes, 20.4% 15 to 30 minutes, 6.9% 30 to 45 minutes, 0.8% 45 to 60 minutes, 1.6% 60 minutes or more (2006-2010 5-year est.)
**Additional Information Contacts**
Canton Chamber of Commerce . . . . . . . . . . . . . . . . . . . . (315) 386-8255
    http://cantonnychamber.org
Saint Lawrence County Chamber of Commerce . . . . . . . . (315) 386-4000
    http://www.northcountryguide.com
Village of Canton . . . . . . . . . . . . . . . . . . . . . . . . . . . . . (315) 386-2871
    http://www.cantonnewyork.us

**CANTON** (town). Covers a land area of 104.764 square miles and a water area of 1.098 square miles. Located at 44.57° N. Lat; 75.21° W. Long. Elevation is 377 feet.
**History:** Seat of Saint Lawrence University and the State University of N.Y. College of Technology. Frederic Remington born here. Irving Bacheller born in nearby Pierrepont. Settled 1799, incorporated 1845.
**Population:** 11,120 (1990); 10,334 (2000); 10,995 (2010); Density: 104.9 persons per square mile (2010); Race: 91.9% White, 3.7% Black, 1.2% Asian, 0.4% American Indian/Alaska Native, 0.0% Native Hawaiian/Other Pacific Islander, 2.8% Other, 2.9% Hispanic of any race (2010); Average household size: 2.35 (2010); Median age: 25.3 (2010); Males per 100 females: 96.2 (2010); Marriage status: 54.2% never married, 35.8% now married, 4.2% widowed, 5.8% divorced (2006-2010 5-year est.); Foreign born: 5.0% (2006-2010 5-year est.); Ancestry (includes multiple ancestries): 17.9% English, 15.2% Irish, 12.1% French, 9.4% German, 7.7% Italian (2006-2010 5-year est.).

**Economy:** Single-family building permits issued: 7 (2011); Multi-family building permits issued: 0 (2011); Employment by occupation: 9.4% management, 0.8% professional, 10.7% services, 19.9% sales, 4.8% farming, 6.6% construction, 2.8% production (2006-2010 5-year est.).
**Income:** Per capita income: $19,589 (2006-2010 5-year est.); Median household income: $53,179 (2006-2010 5-year est.); Average household income: $59,357 (2006-2010 5-year est.); Percent of households with income of $100,000 or more: 16.8% (2006-2010 5-year est.); Poverty rate: 16.7% (2006-2010 5-year est.).
**Education:** Percent of population age 25 and over with: High school diploma (including GED) or higher: 88.5% (2006-2010 5-year est.); Bachelor's degree or higher: 32.4% (2006-2010 5-year est.); Master's degree or higher: 19.8% (2006-2010 5-year est.).
### School District(s)
Canton Central School District (PK-12)
    2009-10 Enrollment: 1,410 . . . . . . . . . . . . . . . . . . . . . . (315) 386-8561
Saint Lawrence-Lewis Boces
    2009-10 Enrollment: n/a . . . . . . . . . . . . . . . . . . . . . . (315) 386-4504
### Four-year College(s)
SUNY College of Technology at Canton (Public)
    Fall 2010 Enrollment: 2,999 . . . . . . . . . . . . . . . . . . . (315) 386-7011
    2011-12 Tuition: In-state $6,629; Out-of-state $11,099
St Lawrence University (Private, Not-for-profit)
    Fall 2010 Enrollment: 2,345 . . . . . . . . . . . . . . . . . . . (315) 229-5011
    2011-12 Tuition: In-state $42,735; Out-of-state $42,735
**Housing:** Homeownership rate: 63.3% (2010); Median home value: $102,300 (2006-2010 5-year est.); Median contract rent: $502 per month (2006-2010 5-year est.); Median year structure built: 1958 (2006-2010 5-year est.).
**Newspapers:** Saint Lawrence Plaindealer (Community news; Circulation 3,500)
**Transportation:** Commute to work: 64.4% car, 0.0% public transportation, 24.1% walk, 9.4% work from home (2006-2010 5-year est.); Travel time to work: 60.1% less than 15 minutes, 24.1% 15 to 30 minutes, 10.1% 30 to 45 minutes, 2.3% 45 to 60 minutes, 3.3% 60 minutes or more (2006-2010 5-year est.)

**CHASE MILLS** (unincorporated postal area)
Zip Code: 13621
    Covers a land area of 27.206 square miles and a water area of 0.824 square miles. Located at 44.83° N. Lat; 75.08° W. Long. Elevation is 269 feet. Population: 650 (2010); Density: 23.9 persons per square mile (2010); Race: 98.6% White, 0.0% Black, 0.2% Asian, 0.6% American Indian/Alaska Native, 0.0% Native Hawaiian/Other Pacific Islander, 0.6% Other, 0.6% Hispanic of any race (2010); Average household size: 2.52 (2010); Median age: 41.0 (2010); Males per 100 females: 101.2 (2010); Homeownership rate: 86.5% (2010)

**CHILDWOLD** (unincorporated postal area)
Zip Code: 12922
    Covers a land area of 43.967 square miles and a water area of 1.404 square miles. Located at 44.28° N. Lat; 74.70° W. Long. Elevation is 1,627 feet. Population: 65 (2010); Density: 1.5 persons per square mile (2010); Race: 98.5% White, 0.0% Black, 0.0% Asian, 1.5% American Indian/Alaska Native, 0.0% Native Hawaiian/Other Pacific Islander, 0.0% Other, 0.0% Hispanic of any race (2010); Average household size: 2.03 (2010); Median age: 50.2 (2010); Males per 100 females: 103.1 (2010); Homeownership rate: 90.6% (2010)

**CHIPPEWA BAY** (unincorporated postal area)
Zip Code: 13623
    Covers a land area of 0.396 square miles and a water area of 0 square miles. Located at 44.44° N. Lat; 75.75° W. Long. Elevation is 289 feet. Population: 49 (2010); Density: 123.6 persons per square mile (2010); Race: 100.0% White, 0.0% Black, 0.0% Asian, 0.0% American Indian/Alaska Native, 0.0% Native Hawaiian/Other Pacific Islander, 0.0% Other, 0.0% Hispanic of any race (2010); Average household size: 2.04 (2010); Median age: 50.1 (2010); Males per 100 females: 104.2 (2010); Homeownership rate: 91.6% (2010)

**CLARE** (town). Covers a land area of 96.556 square miles and a water area of 0.698 square miles. Located at 44.35° N. Lat; 75.01° W. Long. Elevation is 820 feet.
**Population:** 78 (1990); 112 (2000); 105 (2010); Density: 1.1 persons per square mile (2010); Race: 95.2% White, 1.9% Black, 0.0% Asian, 1.0%

American Indian/Alaska Native, 0.0% Native Hawaiian/Other Pacific Islander, 1.9% Other, 0.0% Hispanic of any race (2010); Average household size: 2.50 (2010); Median age: 41.9 (2010); Males per 100 females: 98.1 (2010); Marriage status: 26.1% never married, 64.3% now married, 4.3% widowed, 5.2% divorced (2006-2010 5-year est.); Foreign born: 3.6% (2006-2010 5-year est.); Ancestry (includes multiple ancestries): 34.1% German, 12.3% Irish, 10.1% French, 7.2% Italian, 6.5% English (2006-2010 5-year est.).
**Economy:** Single-family building permits issued: 0 (2011); Multi-family building permits issued: 0 (2011); Employment by occupation: 5.9% management, 0.0% professional, 13.2% services, 16.2% sales, 1.5% farming, 13.2% construction, 0.0% production (2006-2010 5-year est.).
**Income:** Per capita income: $18,185 (2006-2010 5-year est.); Median household income: $30,972 (2006-2010 5-year est.); Average household income: $51,638 (2006-2010 5-year est.); Percent of households with income of $100,000 or more: 21.2% (2006-2010 5-year est.); Poverty rate: 17.4% (2006-2010 5-year est.).
**Education:** Percent of population age 25 and over with: High school diploma (including GED) or higher: 79.5% (2006-2010 5-year est.); Bachelor's degree or higher: 8.4% (2006-2010 5-year est.); Master's degree or higher: 3.6% (2006-2010 5-year est.).
**Housing:** Homeownership rate: 76.2% (2010); Median home value: $110,200 (2006-2010 5-year est.); Median contract rent: $700 per month (2006-2010 5-year est.); Median year structure built: before 1940 (2006-2010 5-year est.).
**Transportation:** Commute to work: 88.2% car, 0.0% public transportation, 0.0% walk, 7.4% work from home (2006-2010 5-year est.); Travel time to work: 31.7% less than 15 minutes, 55.6% 15 to 30 minutes, 0.0% 30 to 45 minutes, 12.7% 45 to 60 minutes, 0.0% 60 minutes or more (2006-2010 5-year est.)

**CLIFTON** (town). Covers a land area of 134.360 square miles and a water area of 15.985 square miles. Located at 44.20° N. Lat; 74.88° W. Long.
**Population:** 917 (1990); 791 (2000); 751 (2010); Density: 5.6 persons per square mile (2010); Race: 96.4% White, 0.1% Black, 0.0% Asian, 0.4% American Indian/Alaska Native, 0.0% Native Hawaiian/Other Pacific Islander, 3.1% Other, 1.6% Hispanic of any race (2010); Average household size: 2.48 (2010); Median age: 44.5 (2010); Males per 100 females: 109.2 (2010); Marriage status: 26.6% never married, 55.5% now married, 6.3% widowed, 11.5% divorced (2006-2010 5-year est.); Foreign born: 0.6% (2006-2010 5-year est.); Ancestry (includes multiple ancestries): 22.8% American, 19.0% Irish, 10.3% French, 10.3% German, 6.9% English (2006-2010 5-year est.).
**Economy:** Single-family building permits issued: 3 (2011); Multi-family building permits issued: 0 (2011); Employment by occupation: 5.5% management, 2.0% professional, 16.4% services, 5.1% sales, 4.1% farming, 13.7% construction, 10.6% production (2006-2010 5-year est.).
**Income:** Per capita income: $18,817 (2006-2010 5-year est.); Median household income: $42,805 (2006-2010 5-year est.); Average household income: $45,068 (2006-2010 5-year est.); Percent of households with income of $100,000 or more: 5.2% (2006-2010 5-year est.); Poverty rate: 20.7% (2006-2010 5-year est.).
**Education:** Percent of population age 25 and over with: High school diploma (including GED) or higher: 87.4% (2006-2010 5-year est.); Bachelor's degree or higher: 13.9% (2006-2010 5-year est.); Master's degree or higher: 4.2% (2006-2010 5-year est.).
**Housing:** Homeownership rate: 82.1% (2010); Median home value: $59,000 (2006-2010 5-year est.); Median contract rent: $445 per month (2006-2010 5-year est.); Median year structure built: 1958 (2006-2010 5-year est.).
**Transportation:** Commute to work: 97.2% car, 0.0% public transportation, 0.0% walk, 2.8% work from home (2006-2010 5-year est.); Travel time to work: 43.8% less than 15 minutes, 15.7% 15 to 30 minutes, 11.7% 30 to 45 minutes, 16.8% 45 to 60 minutes, 12.0% 60 minutes or more (2006-2010 5-year est.)

**COLTON** (town). Covers a land area of 241.701 square miles and a water area of 13.251 square miles. Located at 44.36° N. Lat; 74.81° W. Long. Elevation is 873 feet.
**Population:** 1,274 (1990); 1,453 (2000); 1,451 (2010); Density: 6.0 persons per square mile (2010); Race: 98.1% White, 0.2% Black, 0.7% Asian, 0.3% American Indian/Alaska Native, 0.0% Native Hawaiian/Other Pacific Islander, 0.7% Other, 0.4% Hispanic of any race (2010); Average household size: 2.22 (2010); Median age: 47.7 (2010); Males per 100

females: 104.9 (2010); Marriage status: 22.5% never married, 62.9% now married, 6.6% widowed, 7.9% divorced (2006-2010 5-year est.); Foreign born: 3.3% (2006-2010 5-year est.); Ancestry (includes multiple ancestries): 23.3% Irish, 18.9% English, 16.7% French, 11.6% German, 7.1% American (2006-2010 5-year est.).
**Economy:** Single-family building permits issued: 8 (2011); Multi-family building permits issued: 0 (2011); Employment by occupation: 10.3% management, 4.2% professional, 11.5% services, 16.2% sales, 1.8% farming, 16.1% construction, 7.4% production (2006-2010 5-year est.).
**Income:** Per capita income: $26,986 (2006-2010 5-year est.); Median household income: $51,786 (2006-2010 5-year est.); Average household income: $61,480 (2006-2010 5-year est.); Percent of households with income of $100,000 or more: 18.1% (2006-2010 5-year est.); Poverty rate: 7.3% (2006-2010 5-year est.).
**Education:** Percent of population age 25 and over with: High school diploma (including GED) or higher: 94.4% (2006-2010 5-year est.); Bachelor's degree or higher: 29.2% (2006-2010 5-year est.); Master's degree or higher: 13.7% (2006-2010 5-year est.).
**School District(s)**
Colton-Pierrepont Central School District (PK-12)
    2009-10 Enrollment: 324 . . . . . . . . . . . . . . . . . . . . . . . . (315) 262-2100
**Housing:** Homeownership rate: 85.0% (2010); Median home value: $114,200 (2006-2010 5-year est.); Median contract rent: $504 per month (2006-2010 5-year est.); Median year structure built: 1967 (2006-2010 5-year est.).
**Transportation:** Commute to work: 92.8% car, 0.0% public transportation, 1.6% walk, 5.1% work from home (2006-2010 5-year est.); Travel time to work: 27.1% less than 15 minutes, 43.1% 15 to 30 minutes, 12.4% 30 to 45 minutes, 6.6% 45 to 60 minutes, 10.7% 60 minutes or more (2006-2010 5-year est.)

**COLTON** (CDP). Covers a land area of 1.688 square miles and a water area of 0.072 square miles. Located at 44.56° N. Lat; 74.94° W. Long. Elevation is 873 feet.
**Population:** n/a (1990); n/a (2000); 345 (2010); Density: 204.3 persons per square mile (2010); Race: 96.5% White, 0.3% Black, 2.0% Asian, 0.6% American Indian/Alaska Native, 0.0% Native Hawaiian/Other Pacific Islander, 0.6% Other, 0.9% Hispanic of any race (2010); Average household size: 2.25 (2010); Median age: 39.1 (2010); Males per 100 females: 93.8 (2010); Marriage status: 26.5% never married, 53.1% now married, 6.8% widowed, 13.6% divorced (2006-2010 5-year est.); Foreign born: 2.6% (2006-2010 5-year est.); Ancestry (includes multiple ancestries): 25.4% French, 20.2% German, 16.8% Scottish, 15.7% English, 11.5% Irish (2006-2010 5-year est.).
**Economy:** Employment by occupation: 14.0% management, 2.8% professional, 9.5% services, 18.4% sales, 2.8% farming, 21.2% construction, 8.4% production (2006-2010 5-year est.).
**Income:** Per capita income: $21,818 (2006-2010 5-year est.); Median household income: $43,158 (2006-2010 5-year est.); Average household income: $49,266 (2006-2010 5-year est.); Percent of households with income of $100,000 or more: 10.7% (2006-2010 5-year est.); Poverty rate: 11.5% (2006-2010 5-year est.).
**Education:** Percent of population age 25 and over with: High school diploma (including GED) or higher: 91.3% (2006-2010 5-year est.); Bachelor's degree or higher: 24.0% (2006-2010 5-year est.); Master's degree or higher: 15.7% (2006-2010 5-year est.).
**School District(s)**
Colton-Pierrepont Central School District (PK-12)
    2009-10 Enrollment: 324 . . . . . . . . . . . . . . . . . . . . . . . . (315) 262-2100
**Housing:** Homeownership rate: 71.2% (2010); Median home value: $71,400 (2006-2010 5-year est.); Median contract rent: $475 per month (2006-2010 5-year est.); Median year structure built: before 1940 (2006-2010 5-year est.).
**Transportation:** Commute to work: 85.5% car, 0.0% public transportation, 1.8% walk, 10.9% work from home (2006-2010 5-year est.); Travel time to work: 34.0% less than 15 minutes, 38.1% 15 to 30 minutes, 8.8% 30 to 45 minutes, 4.1% 45 to 60 minutes, 15.0% 60 minutes or more (2006-2010 5-year est.)

**CRANBERRY LAKE** (CDP). Covers a land area of 19.436 square miles and a water area of 0.275 square miles. Located at 44.18° N. Lat; 74.86° W. Long. Elevation is 1,489 feet.
**Population:** n/a (1990); n/a (2000); 200 (2010); Density: 10.3 persons per square mile (2010); Race: 99.5% White, 0.0% Black, 0.0% Asian, 0.5% American Indian/Alaska Native, 0.0% Native Hawaiian/Other Pacific

Islander, 0.0% Other, 0.0% Hispanic of any race (2010); Average household size: 2.28 (2010); Median age: 51.2 (2010); Males per 100 females: 115.1 (2010); Marriage status: 15.4% never married, 64.0% now married, 6.9% widowed, 13.7% divorced (2006-2010 5-year est.); Foreign born: 0.0% (2006-2010 5-year est.); Ancestry (includes multiple ancestries): 26.8% American, 22.6% Irish, 21.1% English, 10.0% German, 7.9% Italian (2006-2010 5-year est.).
**Economy:** Employment by occupation: 5.6% management, 7.0% professional, 0.0% services, 9.9% sales, 0.0% farming, 15.5% construction, 15.5% production (2006-2010 5-year est.).
**Income:** Per capita income: $30,520 (2006-2010 5-year est.); Median household income: $54,625 (2006-2010 5-year est.); Average household income: $61,380 (2006-2010 5-year est.); Percent of households with income of $100,000 or more: 18.6% (2006-2010 5-year est.); Poverty rate: 10.5% (2006-2010 5-year est.).
**Education:** Percent of population age 25 and over with: High school diploma (including GED) or higher: 94.0% (2006-2010 5-year est.); Bachelor's degree or higher: 34.7% (2006-2010 5-year est.); Master's degree or higher: 2.7% (2006-2010 5-year est.).
**Housing:** Homeownership rate: 90.7% (2010); Median home value: $136,100 (2006-2010 5-year est.); Median contract rent: n/a per month (2006-2010 5-year est.); Median year structure built: 1959 (2006-2010 5-year est.).
**Transportation:** Commute to work: 100.0% car, 0.0% public transportation, 0.0% walk, 0.0% work from home (2006-2010 5-year est.); Travel time to work: 26.2% less than 15 minutes, 15.4% 15 to 30 minutes, 38.5% 30 to 45 minutes, 16.9% 45 to 60 minutes, 3.1% 60 minutes or more (2006-2010 5-year est.)

**DE KALB** (town). Aka Old De Kalb. Covers a land area of 82.523 square miles and a water area of 0.683 square miles. Located at 44.47° N. Lat; 75.36° W. Long. Elevation is 331 feet.
**Population:** 2,153 (1990); 2,213 (2000); 2,434 (2010); Density: 29.5 persons per square mile (2010); Race: 97.6% White, 0.5% Black, 0.1% Asian, 0.5% American Indian/Alaska Native, 0.0% Native Hawaiian/Other Pacific Islander, 1.3% Other, 1.3% Hispanic of any race (2010); Average household size: 2.84 (2010); Median age: 36.5 (2010); Males per 100 females: 103.9 (2010); Marriage status: 26.4% never married, 60.0% now married, 7.0% widowed, 6.6% divorced (2006-2010 5-year est.); Foreign born: 1.5% (2006-2010 5-year est.); Ancestry (includes multiple ancestries): 15.7% American, 11.2% French, 10.2% English, 9.6% Irish, 6.4% German (2006-2010 5-year est.).
**Economy:** Single-family building permits issued: 10 (2011); Multi-family building permits issued: 0 (2011); Employment by occupation: 11.4% management, 0.9% professional, 17.0% services, 11.9% sales, 4.7% farming, 16.8% construction, 4.0% production (2006-2010 5-year est.).
**Income:** Per capita income: $18,787 (2006-2010 5-year est.); Median household income: $40,263 (2006-2010 5-year est.); Average household income: $50,928 (2006-2010 5-year est.); Percent of households with income of $100,000 or more: 9.7% (2006-2010 5-year est.); Poverty rate: 19.2% (2006-2010 5-year est.).
**Education:** Percent of population age 25 and over with: High school diploma (including GED) or higher: 82.6% (2006-2010 5-year est.); Bachelor's degree or higher: 14.3% (2006-2010 5-year est.); Master's degree or higher: 3.2% (2006-2010 5-year est.).
**Housing:** Homeownership rate: 81.2% (2010); Median home value: $76,600 (2006-2010 5-year est.); Median contract rent: $382 per month (2006-2010 5-year est.); Median year structure built: 1948 (2006-2010 5-year est.).
**Transportation:** Commute to work: 91.3% car, 0.0% public transportation, 0.4% walk, 3.7% work from home (2006-2010 5-year est.); Travel time to work: 21.4% less than 15 minutes, 38.8% 15 to 30 minutes, 22.3% 30 to 45 minutes, 4.9% 45 to 60 minutes, 12.6% 60 minutes or more (2006-2010 5-year est.)

**DE PEYSTER** (town). Covers a land area of 42.927 square miles and a water area of 2.169 square miles. Located at 44.53° N. Lat; 75.45° W. Long. Elevation is 374 feet.
**Population:** 913 (1990); 936 (2000); 998 (2010); Density: 23.2 persons per square mile (2010); Race: 98.2% White, 1.0% Black, 0.0% Asian, 0.0% American Indian/Alaska Native, 0.0% Native Hawaiian/Other Pacific Islander, 0.8% Other, 1.9% Hispanic of any race (2010); Average household size: 3.43 (2010); Median age: 28.1 (2010); Males per 100 females: 102.0 (2010); Marriage status: 30.7% never married, 58.5% now married, 5.6% widowed, 5.3% divorced (2006-2010 5-year est.); Foreign

born: 0.5% (2006-2010 5-year est.); Ancestry (includes multiple ancestries): 15.3% Pennsylvania German, 11.9% Irish, 10.0% American, 9.7% Dutch, 8.2% English (2006-2010 5-year est.).
**Economy:** Single-family building permits issued: 4 (2011); Multi-family building permits issued: 0 (2011); Employment by occupation: 17.1% management, 1.8% professional, 6.3% services, 14.4% sales, 3.3% farming, 19.4% construction, 18.4% production (2006-2010 5-year est.).
**Income:** Per capita income: $14,311 (2006-2010 5-year est.); Median household income: $45,074 (2006-2010 5-year est.); Average household income: $45,637 (2006-2010 5-year est.); Percent of households with income of $100,000 or more: 6.8% (2006-2010 5-year est.); Poverty rate: 24.5% (2006-2010 5-year est.).
**Education:** Percent of population age 25 and over with: High school diploma (including GED) or higher: 71.2% (2006-2010 5-year est.); Bachelor's degree or higher: 7.5% (2006-2010 5-year est.); Master's degree or higher: 2.5% (2006-2010 5-year est.).
**Housing:** Homeownership rate: 86.6% (2010); Median home value: $48,900 (2006-2010 5-year est.); Median contract rent: $1,167 per month (2006-2010 5-year est.); Median year structure built: 1975 (2006-2010 5-year est.).
**Transportation:** Commute to work: 74.9% car, 0.0% public transportation, 6.5% walk, 13.7% work from home (2006-2010 5-year est.); Travel time to work: 40.7% less than 15 minutes, 37.4% 15 to 30 minutes, 9.6% 30 to 45 minutes, 8.7% 45 to 60 minutes, 3.6% 60 minutes or more (2006-2010 5-year est.)

**DEKALB JUNCTION** (CDP). Covers a land area of 3.883 square miles and a water area of 0.062 square miles. Located at 44.51° N. Lat; 75.29° W. Long.
**Population:** n/a (1990); n/a (2000); 519 (2010); Density: 133.6 persons per square mile (2010); Race: 98.8% White, 0.0% Black, 0.0% Asian, 0.0% American Indian/Alaska Native, 0.0% Native Hawaiian/Other Pacific Islander, 1.2% Other, 1.3% Hispanic of any race (2010); Average household size: 2.72 (2010); Median age: 37.6 (2010); Males per 100 females: 107.6 (2010); Marriage status: 14.5% never married, 72.0% now married, 5.9% widowed, 7.6% divorced (2006-2010 5-year est.); Foreign born: 5.2% (2006-2010 5-year est.); Ancestry (includes multiple ancestries): 23.3% American, 12.6% Belgian, 12.3% Irish, 7.7% English, 7.4% French (2006-2010 5-year est.).
**Economy:** Employment by occupation: 23.2% management, 3.2% professional, 7.1% services, 18.7% sales, 8.4% farming, 9.0% construction, 0.0% production (2006-2010 5-year est.).
**Income:** Per capita income: $16,732 (2006-2010 5-year est.); Median household income: $31,779 (2006-2010 5-year est.); Average household income: $39,369 (2006-2010 5-year est.); Percent of households with income of $100,000 or more: 0.0% (2006-2010 5-year est.); Poverty rate: 12.9% (2006-2010 5-year est.).
**Education:** Percent of population age 25 and over with: High school diploma (including GED) or higher: 82.6% (2006-2010 5-year est.); Bachelor's degree or higher: 19.3% (2006-2010 5-year est.); Master's degree or higher: 4.4% (2006-2010 5-year est.).
**School District(s)**
Hermon-Dekalb Central School District (PK-12)
   2009-10 Enrollment: 405 . . . . . . . . . . . . . . . . . . . (315) 347-3442
**Housing:** Homeownership rate: 73.3% (2010); Median home value: $56,300 (2006-2010 5-year est.); Median contract rent: n/a per month (2006-2010 5-year est.); Median year structure built: before 1940 (2006-2010 5-year est.).
**Transportation:** Commute to work: 100.0% car, 0.0% public transportation, 0.0% walk, 0.0% work from home (2006-2010 5-year est.); Travel time to work: 6.8% less than 15 minutes, 43.8% 15 to 30 minutes, 24.0% 30 to 45 minutes, 3.4% 45 to 60 minutes, 21.9% 60 minutes or more (2006-2010 5-year est.)

**EDWARDS** (village). Covers a land area of 0.974 square miles and a water area of 0.011 square miles. Located at 44.32° N. Lat; 75.24° W. Long. Elevation is 669 feet.
**Population:** 487 (1990); 465 (2000); 439 (2010); Density: 450.7 persons per square mile (2010); Race: 99.1% White, 0.2% Black, 0.0% Asian, 0.0% American Indian/Alaska Native, 0.0% Native Hawaiian/Other Pacific Islander, 0.7% Other, 0.7% Hispanic of any race (2010); Average household size: 2.39 (2010); Median age: 41.6 (2010); Males per 100 females: 82.2 (2010); Marriage status: 21.0% never married, 62.1% now married, 10.7% widowed, 6.2% divorced (2006-2010 5-year est.); Foreign born: 0.0% (2006-2010 5-year est.); Ancestry (includes multiple

ancestries): 23.8% Irish, 15.5% Polish, 15.0% German, 14.7% English, 14.2% French (2006-2010 5-year est.).
**Economy:** Single-family building permits issued: 0 (2011); Multi-family building permits issued: 0 (2011); Employment by occupation: 4.8% management, 2.0% professional, 13.6% services, 27.2% sales, 1.4% farming, 19.0% construction, 13.6% production (2006-2010 5-year est.).
**Income:** Per capita income: $16,928 (2006-2010 5-year est.); Median household income: $38,393 (2006-2010 5-year est.); Average household income: $45,321 (2006-2010 5-year est.); Percent of households with income of $100,000 or more: 2.6% (2006-2010 5-year est.); Poverty rate: 18.9% (2006-2010 5-year est.).
**Education:** Percent of population age 25 and over with: High school diploma (including GED) or higher: 85.5% (2006-2010 5-year est.); Bachelor's degree or higher: 11.4% (2006-2010 5-year est.); Master's degree or higher: 3.5% (2006-2010 5-year est.).
**Housing:** Homeownership rate: 64.6% (2010); Median home value: $49,700 (2006-2010 5-year est.); Median contract rent: $331 per month (2006-2010 5-year est.); Median year structure built: 1943 (2006-2010 5-year est.).
**Transportation:** Commute to work: 88.3% car, 3.6% public transportation, 0.0% walk, 8.0% work from home (2006-2010 5-year est.); Travel time to work: 20.6% less than 15 minutes, 34.1% 15 to 30 minutes, 22.2% 30 to 45 minutes, 10.3% 45 to 60 minutes, 12.7% 60 minutes or more (2006-2010 5-year est.)

**EDWARDS** (town). Covers a land area of 50.470 square miles and a water area of 0.831 square miles. Located at 44.28° N. Lat; 75.28° W. Long. Elevation is 669 feet.
**Population:** 1,083 (1990); 1,148 (2000); 1,156 (2010); Density: 22.9 persons per square mile (2010); Race: 98.4% White, 0.3% Black, 0.2% Asian, 0.3% American Indian/Alaska Native, 0.1% Native Hawaiian/Other Pacific Islander, 0.7% Other, 0.9% Hispanic of any race (2010); Average household size: 2.49 (2010); Median age: 41.7 (2010); Males per 100 females: 94.9 (2010); Marriage status: 19.9% never married, 60.5% now married, 8.7% widowed, 10.9% divorced (2006-2010 5-year est.); Foreign born: 0.7% (2006-2010 5-year est.); Ancestry (includes multiple ancestries): 21.9% Irish, 21.4% French, 17.9% English, 10.1% American, 9.6% Polish (2006-2010 5-year est.).
**Economy:** Single-family building permits issued: 0 (2011); Multi-family building permits issued: 0 (2011); Employment by occupation: 9.9% management, 2.0% professional, 15.0% services, 18.8% sales, 1.7% farming, 16.4% construction, 6.8% production (2006-2010 5-year est.).
**Income:** Per capita income: $20,464 (2006-2010 5-year est.); Median household income: $47,115 (2006-2010 5-year est.); Average household income: $52,401 (2006-2010 5-year est.); Percent of households with income of $100,000 or more: 9.6% (2006-2010 5-year est.); Poverty rate: 22.2% (2006-2010 5-year est.).
**Education:** Percent of population age 25 and over with: High school diploma (including GED) or higher: 84.8% (2006-2010 5-year est.); Bachelor's degree or higher: 12.5% (2006-2010 5-year est.); Master's degree or higher: 5.3% (2006-2010 5-year est.).
**Housing:** Homeownership rate: 74.8% (2010); Median home value: $63,700 (2006-2010 5-year est.); Median contract rent: $383 per month (2006-2010 5-year est.); Median year structure built: 1957 (2006-2010 5-year est.).
**Transportation:** Commute to work: 92.1% car, 1.7% public transportation, 1.4% walk, 4.8% work from home (2006-2010 5-year est.); Travel time to work: 18.1% less than 15 minutes, 33.3% 15 to 30 minutes, 28.3% 30 to 45 minutes, 6.9% 45 to 60 minutes, 13.4% 60 minutes or more (2006-2010 5-year est.)

**FINE** (town). Covers a land area of 166.798 square miles and a water area of 2.618 square miles. Located at 44.15° N. Lat; 75.08° W. Long. Elevation is 965 feet.
**Population:** 1,813 (1990); 1,622 (2000); 1,512 (2010); Density: 9.1 persons per square mile (2010); Race: 96.6% White, 0.4% Black, 1.0% Asian, 0.9% American Indian/Alaska Native, 0.0% Native Hawaiian/Other Pacific Islander, 1.1% Other, 1.2% Hispanic of any race (2010); Average household size: 2.30 (2010); Median age: 46.0 (2010); Males per 100 females: 108.6 (2010); Marriage status: 18.5% never married, 66.0% now married, 6.9% widowed, 8.5% divorced (2006-2010 5-year est.); Foreign born: 1.2% (2006-2010 5-year est.); Ancestry (includes multiple ancestries): 19.1% Irish, 18.2% American, 17.7% French, 16.7% English, 12.7% German (2006-2010 5-year est.).

**Economy:** Single-family building permits issued: 7 (2011); Multi-family building permits issued: 0 (2011); Employment by occupation: 9.0% management, 4.1% professional, 8.7% services, 16.4% sales, 3.3% farming, 11.6% construction, 3.9% production (2006-2010 5-year est.).
**Income:** Per capita income: $19,736 (2006-2010 5-year est.); Median household income: $35,524 (2006-2010 5-year est.); Average household income: $43,705 (2006-2010 5-year est.); Percent of households with income of $100,000 or more: 7.8% (2006-2010 5-year est.); Poverty rate: 10.0% (2006-2010 5-year est.).
**Education:** Percent of population age 25 and over with: High school diploma (including GED) or higher: 88.5% (2006-2010 5-year est.); Bachelor's degree or higher: 16.4% (2006-2010 5-year est.); Master's degree or higher: 7.1% (2006-2010 5-year est.).
**Housing:** Homeownership rate: 82.8% (2010); Median home value: $59,200 (2006-2010 5-year est.); Median contract rent: $325 per month (2006-2010 5-year est.); Median year structure built: 1950 (2006-2010 5-year est.).
**Transportation:** Commute to work: 84.8% car, 0.0% public transportation, 3.3% walk, 11.9% work from home (2006-2010 5-year est.); Travel time to work: 44.6% less than 15 minutes, 17.5% 15 to 30 minutes, 6.8% 30 to 45 minutes, 13.3% 45 to 60 minutes, 17.8% 60 minutes or more (2006-2010 5-year est.)

**FOWLER** (town). Covers a land area of 59.325 square miles and a water area of 1.368 square miles. Located at 44.27° N. Lat; 75.40° W. Long. Elevation is 591 feet.
**Population:** 1,885 (1990); 2,180 (2000); 2,202 (2010); Density: 37.1 persons per square mile (2010); Race: 98.4% White, 0.2% Black, 0.2% Asian, 0.3% American Indian/Alaska Native, 0.0% Native Hawaiian/Other Pacific Islander, 0.9% Other, 1.1% Hispanic of any race (2010); Average household size: 2.57 (2010); Median age: 41.0 (2010); Males per 100 females: 102.0 (2010); Marriage status: 21.7% never married, 70.3% now married, 4.3% widowed, 3.7% divorced (2006-2010 5-year est.); Foreign born: 0.8% (2006-2010 5-year est.); Ancestry (includes multiple ancestries): 18.6% English, 16.1% French, 15.0% Irish, 13.7% American, 7.9% Italian (2006-2010 5-year est.).
**Economy:** Single-family building permits issued: 0 (2011); Multi-family building permits issued: 0 (2011); Employment by occupation: 6.9% management, 1.1% professional, 10.7% services, 20.2% sales, 6.7% farming, 23.0% construction, 7.0% production (2006-2010 5-year est.).
**Income:** Per capita income: $19,510 (2006-2010 5-year est.); Median household income: $48,984 (2006-2010 5-year est.); Average household income: $52,038 (2006-2010 5-year est.); Percent of households with income of $100,000 or more: 6.6% (2006-2010 5-year est.); Poverty rate: 10.0% (2006-2010 5-year est.).
**Education:** Percent of population age 25 and over with: High school diploma (including GED) or higher: 81.0% (2006-2010 5-year est.); Bachelor's degree or higher: 10.5% (2006-2010 5-year est.); Master's degree or higher: 1.6% (2006-2010 5-year est.).
**Housing:** Homeownership rate: 84.9% (2010); Median home value: $96,300 (2006-2010 5-year est.); Median contract rent: $535 per month (2006-2010 5-year est.); Median year structure built: 1982 (2006-2010 5-year est.).
**Transportation:** Commute to work: 97.3% car, 0.0% public transportation, 0.8% walk, 1.3% work from home (2006-2010 5-year est.); Travel time to work: 42.3% less than 15 minutes, 24.8% 15 to 30 minutes, 14.8% 30 to 45 minutes, 11.3% 45 to 60 minutes, 6.8% 60 minutes or more (2006-2010 5-year est.)

**GOUVERNEUR** (village). Covers a land area of 2.190 square miles and a water area of 0.087 square miles. Located at 44.33° N. Lat; 75.46° W. Long. Elevation is 440 feet.
**Population:** 4,604 (1990); 4,263 (2000); 3,949 (2010); Density: 1,802.6 persons per square mile (2010); Race: 95.3% White, 1.1% Black, 0.8% Asian, 0.5% American Indian/Alaska Native, 0.1% Native Hawaiian/Other Pacific Islander, 2.2% Other, 2.2% Hispanic of any race (2010); Average household size: 2.38 (2010); Median age: 35.9 (2010); Males per 100 females: 93.8 (2010); Marriage status: 28.1% never married, 50.0% now married, 11.5% widowed, 10.4% divorced (2006-2010 5-year est.); Foreign born: 1.5% (2006-2010 5-year est.); Ancestry (includes multiple ancestries): 28.2% Irish, 22.1% German, 17.1% French, 15.8% English, 10.3% American (2006-2010 5-year est.).
**Economy:** Single-family building permits issued: 0 (2011); Multi-family building permits issued: 0 (2011); Employment by occupation: 10.3%

management, 4.8% professional, 11.0% services, 20.3% sales, 0.2% farming, 12.1% construction, 7.4% production (2006-2010 5-year est.).
**Income:** Per capita income: $22,615 (2006-2010 5-year est.); Median household income: $42,641 (2006-2010 5-year est.); Average household income: $52,931 (2006-2010 5-year est.); Percent of households with income of $100,000 or more: 12.9% (2006-2010 5-year est.); Poverty rate: 10.9% (2006-2010 5-year est.).
**Education:** Percent of population age 25 and over with: High school diploma (including GED) or higher: 89.9% (2006-2010 5-year est.); Bachelor's degree or higher: 20.0% (2006-2010 5-year est.); Master's degree or higher: 8.5% (2006-2010 5-year est.).

### School District(s)
Gouverneur Central School District (PK-12)
    2009-10 Enrollment: 1,697 . . . . . . . . . . . . . . . . . . . . (315) 287-4870
**Housing:** Homeownership rate: 53.1% (2010); Median home value: $71,100 (2006-2010 5-year est.); Median contract rent: $483 per month (2006-2010 5-year est.); Median year structure built: before 1940 (2006-2010 5-year est.).
**Hospitals:** EJ Noble Hospital of Gouverneur (87 beds)
**Safety:** Violent crime rate: 15.3 per 10,000 population; Property crime rate: 514.7 per 10,000 population (2010).
**Newspapers:** Tribune-Press (Local news; Circulation 4,500)
**Transportation:** Commute to work: 83.3% car, 0.0% public transportation, 10.6% walk, 4.6% work from home (2006-2010 5-year est.); Travel time to work: 48.9% less than 15 minutes, 7.3% 15 to 30 minutes, 16.5% 30 to 45 minutes, 26.6% 45 to 60 minutes, 0.7% 60 minutes or more (2006-2010 5-year est.)
**Additional Information Contacts**
Greater Gouverneur Area Chamber of Commerce . . . . . . . (315) 287-0331
    http://www.gouverneurchamber.net

**GOUVERNEUR** (town). Covers a land area of 71.217 square miles and a water area of 1.074 square miles. Located at 44.35° N. Lat; 75.48° W. Long. Elevation is 440 feet.
**History:** Named for Gouverneur Morris, whose mansion still stands. Laid out 1787, Incorporated 1850.
**Population:** 6,986 (1990); 7,418 (2000); 7,085 (2010); Density: 99.5 persons per square mile (2010); Race: 86.1% White, 9.5% Black, 0.6% Asian, 0.5% American Indian/Alaska Native, 0.1% Native Hawaiian/Other Pacific Islander, 3.2% Other, 4.6% Hispanic of any race (2010); Average household size: 2.45 (2010); Median age: 36.2 (2010); Males per 100 females: 127.8 (2010); Marriage status: 35.2% never married, 47.3% now married, 8.8% widowed, 8.7% divorced (2006-2010 5-year est.); Foreign born: 4.9% (2006-2010 5-year est.); Ancestry (includes multiple ancestries): 20.5% Irish, 16.4% English, 14.9% German, 11.7% French, 7.3% American (2006-2010 5-year est.).
**Economy:** Single-family building permits issued: 4 (2011); Multi-family building permits issued: 0 (2011); Employment by occupation: 8.5% management, 3.5% professional, 12.2% services, 17.9% sales, 1.3% farming, 13.4% construction, 6.8% production (2006-2010 5-year est.).
**Income:** Per capita income: $17,299 (2006-2010 5-year est.); Median household income: $42,837 (2006-2010 5-year est.); Average household income: $52,178 (2006-2010 5-year est.); Percent of households with income of $100,000 or more: 13.2% (2006-2010 5-year est.); Poverty rate: 10.4% (2006-2010 5-year est.).
**Education:** Percent of population age 25 and over with: High school diploma (including GED) or higher: 80.8% (2006-2010 5-year est.); Bachelor's degree or higher: 14.3% (2006-2010 5-year est.); Master's degree or higher: 5.4% (2006-2010 5-year est.).

### School District(s)
Gouverneur Central School District (PK-12)
    2009-10 Enrollment: 1,697 . . . . . . . . . . . . . . . . . . . . (315) 287-4870
**Housing:** Homeownership rate: 61.8% (2010); Median home value: $69,400 (2006-2010 5-year est.); Median contract rent: $463 per month (2006-2010 5-year est.); Median year structure built: before 1940 (2006-2010 5-year est.).
**Hospitals:** EJ Noble Hospital of Gouverneur (87 beds)
**Newspapers:** Tribune-Press (Local news; Circulation 4,500)
**Transportation:** Commute to work: 84.1% car, 0.0% public transportation, 10.0% walk, 4.8% work from home (2006-2010 5-year est.); Travel time to work: 43.3% less than 15 minutes, 11.8% 15 to 30 minutes, 18.2% 30 to 45 minutes, 23.6% 45 to 60 minutes, 3.1% 60 minutes or more (2006-2010 5-year est.)

**HAILESBORO** (CDP). Covers a land area of 4.726 square miles and a water area of 0.079 square miles. Located at 44.31° N. Lat; 75.43° W. Long. Elevation is 492 feet.
**Population:** n/a (1990); n/a (2000); 624 (2010); Density: 132.0 persons per square mile (2010); Race: 97.3% White, 0.5% Black, 0.2% Asian, 0.3% American Indian/Alaska Native, 0.0% Native Hawaiian/Other Pacific Islander, 1.7% Other, 1.4% Hispanic of any race (2010); Average household size: 2.36 (2010); Median age: 44.1 (2010); Males per 100 females: 89.1 (2010); Marriage status: 19.1% never married, 65.9% now married, 11.5% widowed, 3.5% divorced (2006-2010 5-year est.); Foreign born: 0.0% (2006-2010 5-year est.); Ancestry (includes multiple ancestries): 22.8% American, 16.7% Italian, 13.7% Irish, 12.1% English, 10.2% French (2006-2010 5-year est.).
**Economy:** Employment by occupation: 5.3% management, 1.8% professional, 6.3% services, 19.7% sales, 8.8% farming, 13.4% construction, 6.3% production (2006-2010 5-year est.).
**Income:** Per capita income: $23,273 (2006-2010 5-year est.); Median household income: $50,833 (2006-2010 5-year est.); Average household income: $53,232 (2006-2010 5-year est.); Percent of households with income of $100,000 or more: 9.5% (2006-2010 5-year est.); Poverty rate: 5.0% (2006-2010 5-year est.).
**Education:** Percent of population age 25 and over with: High school diploma (including GED) or higher: 87.5% (2006-2010 5-year est.); Bachelor's degree or higher: 14.9% (2006-2010 5-year est.); Master's degree or higher: 2.9% (2006-2010 5-year est.).
**Housing:** Homeownership rate: 79.4% (2010); Median home value: $117,200 (2006-2010 5-year est.); Median contract rent: $617 per month (2006-2010 5-year est.); Median year structure built: 1984 (2006-2010 5-year est.).
**Transportation:** Commute to work: 95.2% car, 0.0% public transportation, 2.6% walk, 2.2% work from home (2006-2010 5-year est.); Travel time to work: 62.7% less than 15 minutes, 5.7% 15 to 30 minutes, 16.7% 30 to 45 minutes, 14.1% 45 to 60 minutes, 0.8% 60 minutes or more (2006-2010 5-year est.)

**HAMMOND** (village). Covers a land area of 0.585 square miles and a water area of 0 square miles. Located at 44.44° N. Lat; 75.69° W. Long. Elevation is 358 feet.
**Population:** 270 (1990); 302 (2000); 280 (2010); Density: 478.1 persons per square mile (2010); Race: 95.7% White, 0.7% Black, 1.1% Asian, 1.8% American Indian/Alaska Native, 0.0% Native Hawaiian/Other Pacific Islander, 0.7% Other, 0.7% Hispanic of any race (2010); Average household size: 2.46 (2010); Median age: 41.8 (2010); Males per 100 females: 78.3 (2010); Marriage status: 19.7% never married, 46.8% now married, 21.7% widowed, 11.8% divorced (2006-2010 5-year est.); Foreign born: 1.2% (2006-2010 5-year est.); Ancestry (includes multiple ancestries): 16.0% Italian, 14.4% German, 13.6% American, 10.7% English, 9.9% French (2006-2010 5-year est.).
**Economy:** Employment by occupation: 20.6% management, 0.0% professional, 24.3% services, 7.5% sales, 1.9% farming, 9.3% construction, 3.7% production (2006-2010 5-year est.).
**Income:** Per capita income: $20,921 (2006-2010 5-year est.); Median household income: $32,143 (2006-2010 5-year est.); Average household income: $48,364 (2006-2010 5-year est.); Percent of households with income of $100,000 or more: 12.5% (2006-2010 5-year est.); Poverty rate: 14.0% (2006-2010 5-year est.).
**Education:** Percent of population age 25 and over with: High school diploma (including GED) or higher: 79.4% (2006-2010 5-year est.); Bachelor's degree or higher: 18.0% (2006-2010 5-year est.); Master's degree or higher: 6.3% (2006-2010 5-year est.).

### School District(s)
Hammond Central School District (PK-12)
    2009-10 Enrollment: 329 . . . . . . . . . . . . . . . . . . . . (315) 324-5931
**Housing:** Homeownership rate: 73.6% (2010); Median home value: $69,600 (2006-2010 5-year est.); Median contract rent: $308 per month (2006-2010 5-year est.); Median year structure built: before 1940 (2006-2010 5-year est.).
**Transportation:** Commute to work: 76.5% car, 0.0% public transportation, 21.6% walk, 2.0% work from home (2006-2010 5-year est.); Travel time to work: 45.0% less than 15 minutes, 19.0% 15 to 30 minutes, 31.0% 30 to 45 minutes, 3.0% 45 to 60 minutes, 2.0% 60 minutes or more (2006-2010 5-year est.)
**Additional Information Contacts**
Black Lake Chamber of Commerce . . . . . . . . . . . . . . . . . . (315) 375-8640
    http://www.blacklakeny.com/chamber.html

**HAMMOND** (town). Covers a land area of 62.196 square miles and a water area of 15.708 square miles. Located at 44.43° N. Lat; 75.72° W. Long. Elevation is 358 feet.
**Population:** 1,168 (1990); 1,207 (2000); 1,191 (2010); Density: 19.1 persons per square mile (2010); Race: 96.6% White, 0.3% Black, 0.4% Asian, 0.8% American Indian/Alaska Native, 0.0% Native Hawaiian/Other Pacific Islander, 1.9% Other, 2.1% Hispanic of any race (2010); Average household size: 2.48 (2010); Median age: 42.9 (2010); Males per 100 females: 97.2 (2010); Marriage status: 22.5% never married, 62.8% now married, 8.6% widowed, 6.1% divorced (2006-2010 5-year est.); Foreign born: 1.1% (2006-2010 5-year est.); Ancestry (includes multiple ancestries): 16.9% German, 16.3% English, 14.4% Irish, 12.0% French, 10.5% Italian (2006-2010 5-year est.).
**Economy:** Single-family building permits issued: 4 (2011); Multi-family building permits issued: 0 (2011); Employment by occupation: 14.2% management, 0.4% professional, 9.7% services, 17.2% sales, 3.2% farming, 15.4% construction, 7.2% production (2006-2010 5-year est.).
**Income:** Per capita income: $24,271 (2006-2010 5-year est.); Median household income: $50,568 (2006-2010 5-year est.); Average household income: $61,270 (2006-2010 5-year est.); Percent of households with income of $100,000 or more: 10.7% (2006-2010 5-year est.); Poverty rate: 16.0% (2006-2010 5-year est.).
**Education:** Percent of population age 25 and over with: High school diploma (including GED) or higher: 90.0% (2006-2010 5-year est.); Bachelor's degree or higher: 25.0% (2006-2010 5-year est.); Master's degree or higher: 10.3% (2006-2010 5-year est.).

**School District(s)**
Hammond Central School District (PK-12)
   2009-10 Enrollment: 329 . . . . . . . . . . . . . . . . . . . . . . . (315) 324-5931
**Housing:** Homeownership rate: 82.8% (2010); Median home value: $102,900 (2006-2010 5-year est.); Median contract rent: $471 per month (2006-2010 5-year est.); Median year structure built: 1973 (2006-2010 5-year est.).
**Transportation:** Commute to work: 88.5% car, 0.0% public transportation, 4.3% walk, 3.3% work from home (2006-2010 5-year est.); Travel time to work: 29.7% less than 15 minutes, 27.8% 15 to 30 minutes, 23.6% 30 to 45 minutes, 15.1% 45 to 60 minutes, 3.8% 60 minutes or more (2006-2010 5-year est.)

**HANNAWA FALLS** (CDP). Covers a land area of 5.110 square miles and a water area of 0.301 square miles. Located at 44.60° N. Lat; 74.97° W. Long. Elevation is 558 feet.
**Population:** n/a (1990); n/a (2000); 1,042 (2010); Density: 203.9 persons per square mile (2010); Race: 98.3% White, 0.4% Black, 0.3% Asian, 0.3% American Indian/Alaska Native, 0.0% Native Hawaiian/Other Pacific Islander, 0.7% Other, 0.9% Hispanic of any race (2010); Average household size: 2.28 (2010); Median age: 47.2 (2010); Males per 100 females: 107.6 (2010); Marriage status: 18.5% never married, 62.5% now married, 4.7% widowed, 14.4% divorced (2006-2010 5-year est.); Foreign born: 3.7% (2006-2010 5-year est.); Ancestry (includes multiple ancestries): 24.1% Irish, 18.6% German, 12.1% French, 10.6% English, 7.2% Italian (2006-2010 5-year est.).
**Economy:** Employment by occupation: 16.1% management, 1.0% professional, 3.5% services, 24.8% sales, 5.0% farming, 6.1% construction, 1.3% production (2006-2010 5-year est.).
**Income:** Per capita income: $28,984 (2006-2010 5-year est.); Median household income: $58,600 (2006-2010 5-year est.); Average household income: $62,143 (2006-2010 5-year est.); Percent of households with income of $100,000 or more: 6.7% (2006-2010 5-year est.); Poverty rate: 6.7% (2006-2010 5-year est.).
**Education:** Percent of population age 25 and over with: High school diploma (including GED) or higher: 89.4% (2006-2010 5-year est.); Bachelor's degree or higher: 31.6% (2006-2010 5-year est.); Master's degree or higher: 16.2% (2006-2010 5-year est.).
**Housing:** Homeownership rate: 80.1% (2010); Median home value: $138,800 (2006-2010 5-year est.); Median contract rent: $590 per month (2006-2010 5-year est.); Median year structure built: 1968 (2006-2010 5-year est.).
**Transportation:** Commute to work: 92.1% car, 0.0% public transportation, 0.0% walk, 6.9% work from home (2006-2010 5-year est.); Travel time to work: 27.8% less than 15 minutes, 42.1% 15 to 30 minutes, 13.6% 30 to 45 minutes, 12.6% 45 to 60 minutes, 3.8% 60 minutes or more (2006-2010 5-year est.)

**HERMON** (village). Covers a land area of 0.379 square miles and a water area of 0 square miles. Located at 44.46° N. Lat; 75.23° W. Long. Elevation is 499 feet.
**Population:** 407 (1990); 402 (2000); 422 (2010); Density: 1,110.9 persons per square mile (2010); Race: 95.0% White, 0.2% Black, 0.9% Asian, 0.9% American Indian/Alaska Native, 0.0% Native Hawaiian/Other Pacific Islander, 3.0% Other, 4.0% Hispanic of any race (2010); Average household size: 2.40 (2010); Median age: 37.1 (2010); Males per 100 females: 84.3 (2010); Marriage status: 21.9% never married, 53.6% now married, 7.2% widowed, 17.2% divorced (2006-2010 5-year est.); Foreign born: 0.4% (2006-2010 5-year est.); Ancestry (includes multiple ancestries): 30.8% English, 16.4% Irish, 13.5% French, 12.4% Italian, 10.4% American (2006-2010 5-year est.).
**Economy:** Single-family building permits issued: 0 (2011); Multi-family building permits issued: 0 (2011); Employment by occupation: 11.3% management, 3.6% professional, 13.7% services, 20.2% sales, 2.4% farming, 17.9% construction, 3.0% production (2006-2010 5-year est.).
**Income:** Per capita income: $16,536 (2006-2010 5-year est.); Median household income: $40,417 (2006-2010 5-year est.); Average household income: $44,830 (2006-2010 5-year est.); Percent of households with income of $100,000 or more: 2.4% (2006-2010 5-year est.); Poverty rate: 9.7% (2006-2010 5-year est.).
**Education:** Percent of population age 25 and over with: High school diploma (including GED) or higher: 83.7% (2006-2010 5-year est.); Bachelor's degree or higher: 14.5% (2006-2010 5-year est.); Master's degree or higher: 2.1% (2006-2010 5-year est.).
**Housing:** Homeownership rate: 63.0% (2010); Median home value: $63,000 (2006-2010 5-year est.); Median contract rent: $410 per month (2006-2010 5-year est.); Median year structure built: before 1940 (2006-2010 5-year est.).
**Transportation:** Commute to work: 87.2% car, 0.0% public transportation, 6.1% walk, 1.2% work from home (2006-2010 5-year est.); Travel time to work: 25.9% less than 15 minutes, 42.6% 15 to 30 minutes, 24.1% 30 to 45 minutes, 5.6% 45 to 60 minutes, 1.9% 60 minutes or more (2006-2010 5-year est.)

**HERMON** (town). Covers a land area of 53.146 square miles and a water area of 1.079 square miles. Located at 44.39° N. Lat; 75.28° W. Long. Elevation is 499 feet.
**Population:** 1,041 (1990); 1,069 (2000); 1,108 (2010); Density: 20.8 persons per square mile (2010); Race: 97.7% White, 0.1% Black, 0.5% Asian, 0.5% American Indian/Alaska Native, 0.0% Native Hawaiian/Other Pacific Islander, 1.2% Other, 2.0% Hispanic of any race (2010); Average household size: 2.56 (2010); Median age: 38.2 (2010); Males per 100 females: 97.5 (2010); Marriage status: 24.2% never married, 56.1% now married, 7.5% widowed, 12.1% divorced (2006-2010 5-year est.); Foreign born: 1.1% (2006-2010 5-year est.); Ancestry (includes multiple ancestries): 26.4% English, 18.5% Irish, 14.8% French, 7.8% German, 7.7% American (2006-2010 5-year est.).
**Economy:** Single-family building permits issued: 2 (2011); Multi-family building permits issued: 0 (2011); Employment by occupation: 11.4% management, 3.6% professional, 14.6% services, 15.8% sales, 2.9% farming, 16.0% construction, 4.1% production (2006-2010 5-year est.).
**Income:** Per capita income: $19,916 (2006-2010 5-year est.); Median household income: $44,286 (2006-2010 5-year est.); Average household income: $55,295 (2006-2010 5-year est.); Percent of households with income of $100,000 or more: 11.6% (2006-2010 5-year est.); Poverty rate: 15.8% (2006-2010 5-year est.).
**Education:** Percent of population age 25 and over with: High school diploma (including GED) or higher: 83.9% (2006-2010 5-year est.); Bachelor's degree or higher: 18.1% (2006-2010 5-year est.); Master's degree or higher: 5.0% (2006-2010 5-year est.).
**Housing:** Homeownership rate: 77.2% (2010); Median home value: $67,600 (2006-2010 5-year est.); Median contract rent: $444 per month (2006-2010 5-year est.); Median year structure built: 1956 (2006-2010 5-year est.).
**Transportation:** Commute to work: 88.6% car, 1.5% public transportation, 2.5% walk, 1.5% work from home (2006-2010 5-year est.); Travel time to work: 21.4% less than 15 minutes, 45.7% 15 to 30 minutes, 18.3% 30 to 45 minutes, 7.0% 45 to 60 minutes, 7.5% 60 minutes or more (2006-2010 5-year est.)

**HEUVELTON** (village). Covers a land area of 0.760 square miles and a water area of 0.106 square miles. Located at 44.61° N. Lat; 75.40° W. Long. Elevation is 315 feet.
**Population:** 771 (1990); 804 (2000); 714 (2010); Density: 938.6 persons per square mile (2010); Race: 98.7% White, 0.1% Black, 0.1% Asian, 0.4% American Indian/Alaska Native, 0.1% Native Hawaiian/Other Pacific Islander, 0.6% Other, 0.3% Hispanic of any race (2010); Average household size: 2.33 (2010); Median age: 40.9 (2010); Males per 100 females: 84.0 (2010); Marriage status: 27.6% never married, 51.8% now married, 7.2% widowed, 13.5% divorced (2006-2010 5-year est.); Foreign born: 0.7% (2006-2010 5-year est.); Ancestry (includes multiple ancestries): 28.6% English, 14.7% French, 13.5% German, 12.8% Irish, 9.0% French Canadian (2006-2010 5-year est.).
**Economy:** Single-family building permits issued: 1 (2011); Multi-family building permits issued: 0 (2011); Employment by occupation: 6.5% management, 2.7% professional, 13.8% services, 15.1% sales, 4.3% farming, 8.1% construction, 5.1% production (2006-2010 5-year est.).
**Income:** Per capita income: $23,238 (2006-2010 5-year est.); Median household income: $43,810 (2006-2010 5-year est.); Average household income: $51,205 (2006-2010 5-year est.); Percent of households with income of $100,000 or more: 13.2% (2006-2010 5-year est.); Poverty rate: 17.4% (2006-2010 5-year est.).
**Education:** Percent of population age 25 and over with: High school diploma (including GED) or higher: 89.8% (2006-2010 5-year est.); Bachelor's degree or higher: 21.3% (2006-2010 5-year est.); Master's degree or higher: 14.4% (2006-2010 5-year est.).
### School District(s)
Heuvelton Central School District (PK-12)
    2009-10 Enrollment: 564 . . . . . . . . . . . . . . . . . . (315) 344-2414
**Housing:** Homeownership rate: 72.2% (2010); Median home value: $63,300 (2006-2010 5-year est.); Median contract rent: $440 per month (2006-2010 5-year est.); Median year structure built: before 1940 (2006-2010 5-year est.).
**Transportation:** Commute to work: 87.5% car, 0.0% public transportation, 6.3% walk, 6.3% work from home (2006-2010 5-year est.); Travel time to work: 48.5% less than 15 minutes, 38.4% 15 to 30 minutes, 1.7% 30 to 45 minutes, 5.8% 45 to 60 minutes, 5.5% 60 minutes or more (2006-2010 5-year est.)

**HOPKINTON** (town). Covers a land area of 185.340 square miles and a water area of 1.703 square miles. Located at 44.53° N. Lat; 74.66° W. Long. Elevation is 794 feet.
**Population:** 957 (1990); 1,020 (2000); 1,077 (2010); Density: 5.8 persons per square mile (2010); Race: 97.3% White, 0.3% Black, 0.0% Asian, 0.8% American Indian/Alaska Native, 0.0% Native Hawaiian/Other Pacific Islander, 1.6% Other, 1.8% Hispanic of any race (2010); Average household size: 2.57 (2010); Median age: 41.9 (2010); Males per 100 females: 104.8 (2010); Marriage status: 21.8% never married, 64.4% now married, 5.7% widowed, 8.1% divorced (2006-2010 5-year est.); Foreign born: 1.7% (2006-2010 5-year est.); Ancestry (includes multiple ancestries): 17.6% Irish, 16.3% English, 15.2% German, 10.8% French, 9.7% American (2006-2010 5-year est.).
**Economy:** Single-family building permits issued: 3 (2011); Multi-family building permits issued: 0 (2011); Employment by occupation: 7.2% management, 1.3% professional, 14.5% services, 11.4% sales, 4.0% farming, 12.3% construction, 6.7% production (2006-2010 5-year est.).
**Income:** Per capita income: $19,601 (2006-2010 5-year est.); Median household income: $35,938 (2006-2010 5-year est.); Average household income: $48,796 (2006-2010 5-year est.); Percent of households with income of $100,000 or more: 9.8% (2006-2010 5-year est.); Poverty rate: 15.2% (2006-2010 5-year est.).
**Education:** Percent of population age 25 and over with: High school diploma (including GED) or higher: 86.5% (2006-2010 5-year est.); Bachelor's degree or higher: 19.9% (2006-2010 5-year est.); Master's degree or higher: 8.8% (2006-2010 5-year est.).
**Housing:** Homeownership rate: 87.1% (2010); Median home value: $69,300 (2006-2010 5-year est.); Median contract rent: $385 per month (2006-2010 5-year est.); Median year structure built: 1960 (2006-2010 5-year est.).
**Transportation:** Commute to work: 93.6% car, 0.0% public transportation, 1.1% walk, 4.6% work from home (2006-2010 5-year est.); Travel time to work: 13.3% less than 15 minutes, 47.7% 15 to 30 minutes, 25.3% 30 to 45 minutes, 8.2% 45 to 60 minutes, 5.5% 60 minutes or more (2006-2010 5-year est.)

**LAWRENCE** (town). Covers a land area of 47.610 square miles and a water area of 0.057 square miles. Located at 44.74° N. Lat; 74.67° W. Long.
**Population:** 1,516 (1990); 1,545 (2000); 1,826 (2010); Density: 38.4 persons per square mile (2010); Race: 98.1% White, 0.3% Black, 0.1% Asian, 0.4% American Indian/Alaska Native, 0.0% Native Hawaiian/Other Pacific Islander, 1.1% Other, 0.9% Hispanic of any race (2010); Average household size: 2.81 (2010); Median age: 35.5 (2010); Males per 100 females: 102.9 (2010); Marriage status: 19.8% never married, 64.7% now married, 6.6% widowed, 8.9% divorced (2006-2010 5-year est.); Foreign born: 2.9% (2006-2010 5-year est.); Ancestry (includes multiple ancestries): 19.3% French, 16.1% Irish, 15.2% English, 13.8% German, 9.5% American (2006-2010 5-year est.).
**Economy:** Single-family building permits issued: 5 (2011); Multi-family building permits issued: 0 (2011); Employment by occupation: 7.5% management, 0.0% professional, 17.0% services, 12.8% sales, 0.7% farming, 21.4% construction, 14.9% production (2006-2010 5-year est.).
**Income:** Per capita income: $18,098 (2006-2010 5-year est.); Median household income: $43,155 (2006-2010 5-year est.); Average household income: $49,839 (2006-2010 5-year est.); Percent of households with income of $100,000 or more: 3.9% (2006-2010 5-year est.); Poverty rate: 16.6% (2006-2010 5-year est.).
**Education:** Percent of population age 25 and over with: High school diploma (including GED) or higher: 82.1% (2006-2010 5-year est.); Bachelor's degree or higher: 12.5% (2006-2010 5-year est.); Master's degree or higher: 5.1% (2006-2010 5-year est.).
**Housing:** Homeownership rate: 81.6% (2010); Median home value: $71,000 (2006-2010 5-year est.); Median contract rent: $409 per month (2006-2010 5-year est.); Median year structure built: 1972 (2006-2010 5-year est.).
**Transportation:** Commute to work: 91.0% car, 0.0% public transportation, 1.0% walk, 1.9% work from home (2006-2010 5-year est.); Travel time to work: 23.1% less than 15 minutes, 33.8% 15 to 30 minutes, 23.2% 30 to 45 minutes, 6.6% 45 to 60 minutes, 13.3% 60 minutes or more (2006-2010 5-year est.)

**LISBON** (town). Covers a land area of 108.280 square miles and a water area of 5.636 square miles. Located at 44.69° N. Lat; 75.30° W. Long. Elevation is 338 feet.
**Population:** 3,746 (1990); 4,047 (2000); 4,102 (2010); Density: 37.9 persons per square mile (2010); Race: 97.5% White, 0.3% Black, 0.2% Asian, 0.5% American Indian/Alaska Native, 0.0% Native Hawaiian/Other Pacific Islander, 1.5% Other, 0.8% Hispanic of any race (2010); Average household size: 2.64 (2010); Median age: 40.2 (2010); Males per 100 females: 101.3 (2010); Marriage status: 18.6% never married, 64.4% now married, 4.1% widowed, 12.9% divorced (2006-2010 5-year est.); Foreign born: 2.2% (2006-2010 5-year est.); Ancestry (includes multiple ancestries): 16.0% Irish, 13.7% American, 12.5% English, 11.7% French Canadian, 11.6% German (2006-2010 5-year est.).
**Economy:** Single-family building permits issued: 11 (2011); Multi-family building permits issued: 0 (2011); Employment by occupation: 12.7% management, 1.7% professional, 5.3% services, 13.4% sales, 1.6% farming, 15.4% construction, 2.9% production (2006-2010 5-year est.).
**Income:** Per capita income: $21,677 (2006-2010 5-year est.); Median household income: $44,866 (2006-2010 5-year est.); Average household income: $56,189 (2006-2010 5-year est.); Percent of households with income of $100,000 or more: 12.8% (2006-2010 5-year est.); Poverty rate: 14.6% (2006-2010 5-year est.).
**Education:** Percent of population age 25 and over with: High school diploma (including GED) or higher: 87.8% (2006-2010 5-year est.); Bachelor's degree or higher: 19.6% (2006-2010 5-year est.); Master's degree or higher: 7.6% (2006-2010 5-year est.).
### School District(s)
Lisbon Central School District (PK-12)
    2009-10 Enrollment: 610 . . . . . . . . . . . . . . . . . . (315) 393-4951
**Housing:** Homeownership rate: 83.7% (2010); Median home value: $82,800 (2006-2010 5-year est.); Median contract rent: $403 per month (2006-2010 5-year est.); Median year structure built: 1977 (2006-2010 5-year est.).
**Transportation:** Commute to work: 88.9% car, 0.0% public transportation, 5.6% walk, 4.9% work from home (2006-2010 5-year est.); Travel time to work: 37.3% less than 15 minutes, 42.8% 15 to 30 minutes, 11.6% 30 to 45 minutes, 6.9% 45 to 60 minutes, 1.4% 60 minutes or more (2006-2010 5-year est.)

**LOUISVILLE** (town). Covers a land area of 48.524 square miles and a water area of 15.341 square miles. Located at 44.90° N. Lat; 75.01° W. Long. Elevation is 217 feet.

**Population:** 3,040 (1990); 3,195 (2000); 3,145 (2010); Density: 64.8 persons per square mile (2010); Race: 96.7% White, 0.2% Black, 0.8% Asian, 1.4% American Indian/Alaska Native, 0.0% Native Hawaiian/Other Pacific Islander, 0.9% Other, 1.1% Hispanic of any race (2010); Average household size: 2.34 (2010); Median age: 44.3 (2010); Males per 100 females: 93.2 (2010); Marriage status: 25.7% never married, 57.4% now married, 6.7% widowed, 10.2% divorced (2006-2010 5-year est.); Foreign born: 7.1% (2006-2010 5-year est.); Ancestry (includes multiple ancestries): 26.0% French, 20.6% Irish, 15.4% German, 13.0% English, 8.5% American (2006-2010 5-year est.).

**Economy:** Single-family building permits issued: 1 (2011); Multi-family building permits issued: 0 (2011); Employment by occupation: 10.7% management, 3.4% professional, 7.3% services, 19.5% sales, 0.7% farming, 11.3% construction, 8.1% production (2006-2010 5-year est.).

**Income:** Per capita income: $29,275 (2006-2010 5-year est.); Median household income: $55,529 (2006-2010 5-year est.); Average household income: $66,469 (2006-2010 5-year est.); Percent of households with income of $100,000 or more: 23.4% (2006-2010 5-year est.); Poverty rate: 9.4% (2006-2010 5-year est.).

**Education:** Percent of population age 25 and over with: High school diploma (including GED) or higher: 90.9% (2006-2010 5-year est.); Bachelor's degree or higher: 29.8% (2006-2010 5-year est.); Master's degree or higher: 11.7% (2006-2010 5-year est.).

**Housing:** Homeownership rate: 77.8% (2010); Median home value: $102,200 (2006-2010 5-year est.); Median contract rent: $614 per month (2006-2010 5-year est.); Median year structure built: 1975 (2006-2010 5-year est.).

**Transportation:** Commute to work: 90.4% car, 1.2% public transportation, 2.9% walk, 4.8% work from home (2006-2010 5-year est.); Travel time to work: 43.8% less than 15 minutes, 31.7% 15 to 30 minutes, 21.1% 30 to 45 minutes, 1.5% 45 to 60 minutes, 1.8% 60 minutes or more (2006-2010 5-year est.)

**MACOMB** (town). Covers a land area of 60.717 square miles and a water area of 2.428 square miles. Located at 44.43° N. Lat; 75.57° W. Long.

**Population:** 789 (1990); 846 (2000); 906 (2010); Density: 14.9 persons per square mile (2010); Race: 98.6% White, 0.0% Black, 0.0% Asian, 0.3% American Indian/Alaska Native, 0.0% Native Hawaiian/Other Pacific Islander, 1.1% Other, 0.8% Hispanic of any race (2010); Average household size: 2.72 (2010); Median age: 40.9 (2010); Males per 100 females: 116.7 (2010); Marriage status: 23.0% never married, 67.9% now married, 3.0% widowed, 6.1% divorced (2006-2010 5-year est.); Foreign born: 3.4% (2006-2010 5-year est.); Ancestry (includes multiple ancestries): 19.0% Irish, 17.9% French, 17.4% English, 10.4% German, 6.9% Polish (2006-2010 5-year est.).

**Economy:** Single-family building permits issued: 6 (2011); Multi-family building permits issued: 0 (2011); Employment by occupation: 14.0% management, 0.0% professional, 14.3% services, 13.6% sales, 2.7% farming, 21.3% construction, 5.4% production (2006-2010 5-year est.).

**Income:** Per capita income: $21,689 (2006-2010 5-year est.); Median household income: $41,131 (2006-2010 5-year est.); Average household income: $56,225 (2006-2010 5-year est.); Percent of households with income of $100,000 or more: 14.8% (2006-2010 5-year est.); Poverty rate: 10.4% (2006-2010 5-year est.).

**Education:** Percent of population age 25 and over with: High school diploma (including GED) or higher: 86.1% (2006-2010 5-year est.); Bachelor's degree or higher: 18.6% (2006-2010 5-year est.); Master's degree or higher: 10.0% (2006-2010 5-year est.).

**Housing:** Homeownership rate: 81.0% (2010); Median home value: $89,200 (2006-2010 5-year est.); Median contract rent: $418 per month (2006-2010 5-year est.); Median year structure built: 1972 (2006-2010 5-year est.).

**Transportation:** Commute to work: 88.1% car, 1.4% public transportation, 3.4% walk, 6.2% work from home (2006-2010 5-year est.); Travel time to work: 12.9% less than 15 minutes, 34.4% 15 to 30 minutes, 25.6% 30 to 45 minutes, 21.5% 45 to 60 minutes, 5.6% 60 minutes or more (2006-2010 5-year est.)

**MADRID** (town). Covers a land area of 52.983 square miles and a water area of 0.598 square miles. Located at 44.77° N. Lat; 75.12° W. Long. Elevation is 325 feet.

**Population:** 1,568 (1990); 1,828 (2000); 1,735 (2010); Density: 32.7 persons per square mile (2010); Race: 97.1% White, 0.6% Black, 0.3% Asian, 0.3% American Indian/Alaska Native, 0.1% Native Hawaiian/Other Pacific Islander, 1.6% Other, 1.3% Hispanic of any race (2010); Average household size: 2.64 (2010); Median age: 41.1 (2010); Males per 100 females: 101.7 (2010); Marriage status: 23.0% never married, 62.6% now married, 5.4% widowed, 9.0% divorced (2006-2010 5-year est.); Foreign born: 2.1% (2006-2010 5-year est.); Ancestry (includes multiple ancestries): 23.6% English, 21.9% French, 18.0% Irish, 8.6% American, 8.6% German (2006-2010 5-year est.).

**Economy:** Single-family building permits issued: 2 (2011); Multi-family building permits issued: 0 (2011); Employment by occupation: 9.7% management, 1.4% professional, 14.2% services, 12.0% sales, 2.1% farming, 18.5% construction, 6.1% production (2006-2010 5-year est.).

**Income:** Per capita income: $23,487 (2006-2010 5-year est.); Median household income: $44,615 (2006-2010 5-year est.); Average household income: $58,067 (2006-2010 5-year est.); Percent of households with income of $100,000 or more: 11.9% (2006-2010 5-year est.); Poverty rate: 12.0% (2006-2010 5-year est.).

**Education:** Percent of population age 25 and over with: High school diploma (including GED) or higher: 81.6% (2006-2010 5-year est.); Bachelor's degree or higher: 14.7% (2006-2010 5-year est.); Master's degree or higher: 6.3% (2006-2010 5-year est.).

**School District(s)**
Madrid-Waddington Central School District (PK-12)
   2009-10 Enrollment: 767 . . . . . . . . . . . . . . . . (315) 322-5746

**Housing:** Homeownership rate: 79.9% (2010); Median home value: $76,900 (2006-2010 5-year est.); Median contract rent: $513 per month (2006-2010 5-year est.); Median year structure built: 1958 (2006-2010 5-year est.).

**Transportation:** Commute to work: 91.2% car, 0.0% public transportation, 2.2% walk, 6.2% work from home (2006-2010 5-year est.); Travel time to work: 27.1% less than 15 minutes, 44.5% 15 to 30 minutes, 21.1% 30 to 45 minutes, 4.3% 45 to 60 minutes, 3.0% 60 minutes or more (2006-2010 5-year est.)

**MADRID** (CDP). Covers a land area of 3.727 square miles and a water area of 0.133 square miles. Located at 44.74° N. Lat; 75.12° W. Long. Elevation is 325 feet.

**Population:** n/a (1990); n/a (2000); 757 (2010); Density: 203.1 persons per square mile (2010); Race: 97.1% White, 1.1% Black, 0.1% Asian, 0.4% American Indian/Alaska Native, 0.0% Native Hawaiian/Other Pacific Islander, 1.3% Other, 1.6% Hispanic of any race (2010); Average household size: 2.70 (2010); Median age: 39.6 (2010); Males per 100 females: 102.4 (2010); Marriage status: 18.5% never married, 65.9% now married, 6.4% widowed, 9.2% divorced (2006-2010 5-year est.); Foreign born: 1.4% (2006-2010 5-year est.); Ancestry (includes multiple ancestries): 27.3% English, 22.3% French, 20.8% Irish, 9.0% German, 7.8% French Canadian (2006-2010 5-year est.).

**Economy:** Employment by occupation: 8.4% management, 2.6% professional, 10.6% services, 12.9% sales, 1.0% farming, 17.1% construction, 2.9% production (2006-2010 5-year est.).

**Income:** Per capita income: $19,942 (2006-2010 5-year est.); Median household income: $46,250 (2006-2010 5-year est.); Average household income: $49,891 (2006-2010 5-year est.); Percent of households with income of $100,000 or more: 6.8% (2006-2010 5-year est.); Poverty rate: 8.1% (2006-2010 5-year est.).

**Education:** Percent of population age 25 and over with: High school diploma (including GED) or higher: 82.1% (2006-2010 5-year est.); Bachelor's degree or higher: 17.7% (2006-2010 5-year est.); Master's degree or higher: 10.1% (2006-2010 5-year est.).

**School District(s)**
Madrid-Waddington Central School District (PK-12)
   2009-10 Enrollment: 767 . . . . . . . . . . . . . . . . (315) 322-5746

**Housing:** Homeownership rate: 74.6% (2010); Median home value: $72,600 (2006-2010 5-year est.); Median contract rent: $509 per month (2006-2010 5-year est.); Median year structure built: before 1940 (2006-2010 5-year est.).

**Transportation:** Commute to work: 97.1% car, 0.0% public transportation, 1.3% walk, 1.6% work from home (2006-2010 5-year est.); Travel time to work: 29.2% less than 15 minutes, 39.2% 15 to 30 minutes, 20.3% 30 to 45

minutes, 7.0% 45 to 60 minutes, 4.3% 60 minutes or more (2006-2010 5-year est.)

**MASSENA** (village). Covers a land area of 4.524 square miles and a water area of 0.200 square miles. Located at 44.92° N. Lat; 74.89° W. Long. Elevation is 230 feet.
**Population:** 11,846 (1990); 11,209 (2000); 10,936 (2010); Density: 2,417.1 persons per square mile (2010); Race: 93.4% White, 0.6% Black, 1.0% Asian, 2.9% American Indian/Alaska Native, 0.0% Native Hawaiian/Other Pacific Islander, 2.1% Other, 1.9% Hispanic of any race (2010); Average household size: 2.27 (2010); Median age: 40.4 (2010); Males per 100 females: 90.6 (2010); Marriage status: 25.3% never married, 54.4% now married, 8.9% widowed, 11.4% divorced (2006-2010 5-year est.); Foreign born: 5.3% (2006-2010 5-year est.); Ancestry (includes multiple ancestries): 23.6% French, 20.0% Irish, 12.0% English, 10.6% German, 9.8% American (2006-2010 5-year est.).
**Economy:** Single-family building permits issued: 1 (2011); Multi-family building permits issued: 2 (2011); Employment by occupation: 6.9% management, 2.1% professional, 14.1% services, 15.4% sales, 3.3% farming, 10.8% construction, 5.5% production (2006-2010 5-year est.).
**Income:** Per capita income: $21,564 (2006-2010 5-year est.); Median household income: $38,371 (2006-2010 5-year est.); Average household income: $47,789 (2006-2010 5-year est.); Percent of households with income of $100,000 or more: 10.6% (2006-2010 5-year est.); Poverty rate: 19.9% (2006-2010 5-year est.).
**Education:** Percent of population age 25 and over with: High school diploma (including GED) or higher: 87.3% (2006-2010 5-year est.); Bachelor's degree or higher: 15.4% (2006-2010 5-year est.); Master's degree or higher: 5.3% (2006-2010 5-year est.).
**School District(s)**
Massena Central School District (PK-12)
    2009-10 Enrollment: 2,857 . . . . . . . . . . . . . . . . . . . (315) 764-3700
**Housing:** Homeownership rate: 60.7% (2010); Median home value: $76,200 (2006-2010 5-year est.); Median contract rent: $432 per month (2006-2010 5-year est.); Median year structure built: 1952 (2006-2010 5-year est.).
**Hospitals:** Massena Memorial Hospital
**Safety:** Violent crime rate: 18.5 per 10,000 population; Property crime rate: 386.0 per 10,000 population (2010).
**Newspapers:** Courier Observer (Local news; Circulation 8,500)
**Transportation:** Commute to work: 91.2% car, 0.0% public transportation, 4.4% walk, 1.9% work from home (2006-2010 5-year est.); Travel time to work: 59.4% less than 15 minutes, 20.9% 15 to 30 minutes, 10.9% 30 to 45 minutes, 5.9% 45 to 60 minutes, 2.9% 60 minutes or more (2006-2010 5-year est.)
**Airports:** Massena International-Richards Field (general aviation)
**Additional Information Contacts**
Greater Massena Chamber of Commerce . . . . . . . . . . . . . (315) 769-3525
   http://www.massenachamber.com
Village of Massena . . . . . . . . . . . . . . . . . . . . . . . . . . . (315) 769-8625
   http://www.massenaworks.com

**MASSENA** (town). Covers a land area of 44.369 square miles and a water area of 11.774 square miles. Located at 44.96° N. Lat; 74.83° W. Long. Elevation is 230 feet.
**History:** Settled 1792, incorporated 1886.
**Population:** 13,561 (1990); 13,121 (2000); 12,883 (2010); Density: 290.4 persons per square mile (2010); Race: 92.4% White, 0.6% Black, 0.8% Asian, 4.1% American Indian/Alaska Native, 0.0% Native Hawaiian/Other Pacific Islander, 2.1% Other, 1.8% Hispanic of any race (2010); Average household size: 2.28 (2010); Median age: 41.2 (2010); Males per 100 females: 91.9 (2010); Marriage status: 24.9% never married, 55.1% now married, 8.2% widowed, 11.8% divorced (2006-2010 5-year est.); Foreign born: 5.3% (2006-2010 5-year est.); Ancestry (includes multiple ancestries): 23.8% French, 19.5% Irish, 11.4% English, 10.7% German, 10.1% American (2006-2010 5-year est.).
**Economy:** Single-family building permits issued: 1 (2011); Multi-family building permits issued: 0 (2011); Employment by occupation: 5.5% management, 2.2% professional, 14.2% services, 16.6% sales, 3.2% farming, 11.0% construction, 5.5% production (2006-2010 5-year est.).
**Income:** Per capita income: $21,017 (2006-2010 5-year est.); Median household income: $39,266 (2006-2010 5-year est.); Average household income: $47,067 (2006-2010 5-year est.); Percent of households with income of $100,000 or more: 8.4% (2006-2010 5-year est.); Poverty rate: 19.0% (2006-2010 5-year est.).

**Taxes:** Total city taxes per capita: $182 (2009); City property taxes per capita: $169 (2009).
**Education:** Percent of population age 25 and over with: High school diploma (including GED) or higher: 86.3% (2006-2010 5-year est.); Bachelor's degree or higher: 13.7% (2006-2010 5-year est.); Master's degree or higher: 5.3% (2006-2010 5-year est.).
**School District(s)**
Massena Central School District (PK-12)
    2009-10 Enrollment: 2,857 . . . . . . . . . . . . . . . . . . . (315) 764-3700
**Housing:** Homeownership rate: 62.0% (2010); Median home value: $73,800 (2006-2010 5-year est.); Median contract rent: $436 per month (2006-2010 5-year est.); Median year structure built: 1952 (2006-2010 5-year est.).
**Hospitals:** Massena Memorial Hospital
**Newspapers:** Courier Observer (Local news; Circulation 8,500)
**Transportation:** Commute to work: 92.1% car, 0.1% public transportation, 3.7% walk, 2.0% work from home (2006-2010 5-year est.); Travel time to work: 60.5% less than 15 minutes, 20.3% 15 to 30 minutes, 11.2% 30 to 45 minutes, 5.3% 45 to 60 minutes, 2.8% 60 minutes or more (2006-2010 5-year est.)
**Airports:** Massena International-Richards Field (general aviation)

**MORRISTOWN** (village). Covers a land area of 0.980 square miles and a water area of 0.041 square miles. Located at 44.58° N. Lat; 75.64° W. Long. Elevation is 289 feet.
**Population:** 490 (1990); 456 (2000); 395 (2010); Density: 403.0 persons per square mile (2010); Race: 98.2% White, 0.8% Black, 0.3% Asian, 0.8% American Indian/Alaska Native, 0.0% Native Hawaiian/Other Pacific Islander, 0.0% Other, 0.5% Hispanic of any race (2010); Average household size: 2.32 (2010); Median age: 45.2 (2010); Males per 100 females: 85.4 (2010); Marriage status: 33.4% never married, 46.6% now married, 6.1% widowed, 13.9% divorced (2006-2010 5-year est.); Foreign born: 3.9% (2006-2010 5-year est.); Ancestry (includes multiple ancestries): 24.5% English, 20.9% Irish, 15.4% French, 8.8% Scottish, 8.1% American (2006-2010 5-year est.).
**Economy:** Employment by occupation: 6.4% management, 1.6% professional, 12.0% services, 18.8% sales, 2.8% farming, 5.2% construction, 6.4% production (2006-2010 5-year est.).
**Income:** Per capita income: $32,625 (2006-2010 5-year est.); Median household income: $48,750 (2006-2010 5-year est.); Average household income: $73,462 (2006-2010 5-year est.); Percent of households with income of $100,000 or more: 22.6% (2006-2010 5-year est.); Poverty rate: 20.8% (2006-2010 5-year est.).
**Education:** Percent of population age 25 and over with: High school diploma (including GED) or higher: 89.9% (2006-2010 5-year est.); Bachelor's degree or higher: 27.3% (2006-2010 5-year est.); Master's degree or higher: 20.4% (2006-2010 5-year est.).
**School District(s)**
Morristown Central School District (PK-12)
    2009-10 Enrollment: 410 . . . . . . . . . . . . . . . . . . . . (315) 375-8814
**Housing:** Homeownership rate: 73.9% (2010); Median home value: $86,700 (2006-2010 5-year est.); Median contract rent: $775 per month (2006-2010 5-year est.); Median year structure built: before 1940 (2006-2010 5-year est.).
**Transportation:** Commute to work: 81.0% car, 2.9% public transportation, 10.3% walk, 3.3% work from home (2006-2010 5-year est.); Travel time to work: 19.7% less than 15 minutes, 41.5% 15 to 30 minutes, 10.7% 30 to 45 minutes, 7.7% 45 to 60 minutes, 20.5% 60 minutes or more (2006-2010 5-year est.)

**MORRISTOWN** (town). Covers a land area of 45.720 square miles and a water area of 13.724 square miles. Located at 44.53° N. Lat; 75.63° W. Long. Elevation is 289 feet.
**Population:** 2,019 (1990); 2,050 (2000); 1,974 (2010); Density: 43.2 persons per square mile (2010); Race: 97.5% White, 0.3% Black, 0.4% Asian, 0.5% American Indian/Alaska Native, 0.1% Native Hawaiian/Other Pacific Islander, 1.2% Other, 0.4% Hispanic of any race (2010); Average household size: 2.56 (2010); Median age: 42.0 (2010); Males per 100 females: 96.4 (2010); Marriage status: 20.3% never married, 68.5% now married, 3.6% widowed, 7.6% divorced (2006-2010 5-year est.); Foreign born: 3.2% (2006-2010 5-year est.); Ancestry (includes multiple ancestries): 15.8% Pennsylvania German, 13.8% English, 13.3% Irish, 11.6% German, 9.4% French (2006-2010 5-year est.).
**Economy:** Single-family building permits issued: 7 (2011); Multi-family building permits issued: 0 (2011); Employment by occupation: 18.6%

management, 0.5% professional, 8.4% services, 18.6% sales, 1.5% farming, 6.7% construction, 6.2% production (2006-2010 5-year est.).
**Income:** Per capita income: $21,866 (2006-2010 5-year est.); Median household income: $48,482 (2006-2010 5-year est.); Average household income: $64,087 (2006-2010 5-year est.); Percent of households with income of $100,000 or more: 16.2% (2006-2010 5-year est.); Poverty rate: 24.5% (2006-2010 5-year est.).
**Education:** Percent of population age 25 and over with: High school diploma (including GED) or higher: 79.4% (2006-2010 5-year est.); Bachelor's degree or higher: 20.4% (2006-2010 5-year est.); Master's degree or higher: 14.9% (2006-2010 5-year est.).

**School District(s)**
Morristown Central School District (PK-12)
    2009-10 Enrollment: 410 . . . . . . . . . . . . . . . . . . . (315) 375-8814
**Housing:** Homeownership rate: 80.3% (2010); Median home value: $84,000 (2006-2010 5-year est.); Median contract rent: $625 per month (2006-2010 5-year est.); Median year structure built: 1966 (2006-2010 5-year est.).
**Transportation:** Commute to work: 78.3% car, 0.9% public transportation, 4.9% walk, 15.2% work from home (2006-2010 5-year est.); Travel time to work: 19.4% less than 15 minutes, 46.0% 15 to 30 minutes, 17.0% 30 to 45 minutes, 5.8% 45 to 60 minutes, 11.8% 60 minutes or more (2006-2010 5-year est.)

**NEWTON FALLS** (unincorporated postal area)
Zip Code: 13666
    Covers a land area of 39.110 square miles and a water area of 3.441 square miles. Located at 44.21° N. Lat; 74.92° W. Long. Elevation is 1,496 feet. Population: 266 (2010); Density: 6.8 persons per square mile (2010); Race: 96.2% White, 0.0% Black, 0.0% Asian, 0.4% American Indian/Alaska Native, 0.0% Native Hawaiian/Other Pacific Islander, 3.4% Other, 0.4% Hispanic of any race (2010); Average household size: 2.58 (2010); Median age: 41.2 (2010); Males per 100 females: 101.5 (2010); Homeownership rate: 75.7% (2010)

**NICHOLVILLE** (unincorporated postal area)
Zip Code: 12965
    Covers a land area of 9.535 square miles and a water area of 0.024 square miles. Located at 44.70° N. Lat; 74.68° W. Long. Elevation is 791 feet. Population: 516 (2010); Density: 54.1 persons per square mile (2010); Race: 97.5% White, 0.8% Black, 0.0% Asian, 0.0% American Indian/Alaska Native, 0.0% Native Hawaiian/Other Pacific Islander, 1.7% Other, 1.7% Hispanic of any race (2010); Average household size: 2.76 (2010); Median age: 37.9 (2010); Males per 100 females: 91.8 (2010); Homeownership rate: 82.9% (2010)

**NORFOLK** (town). Aka Norfolk Center. Covers a land area of 56.739 square miles and a water area of 1.003 square miles. Located at 44.83° N. Lat; 74.93° W. Long. Elevation is 259 feet.
**History:** Settled in 1809. Amish people moved into the area in the mid-1970s and opened a cheese mill, cheese factories, sawmills, and gristmills; they are no longer here. William P. Rogers, who grew up here, was appointed U.S. Attorney General in 1958.
**Population:** 4,523 (1990); 4,565 (2000); 4,668 (2010); Density: 82.3 persons per square mile (2010); Race: 96.5% White, 0.5% Black, 0.4% Asian, 1.0% American Indian/Alaska Native, 0.0% Native Hawaiian/Other Pacific Islander, 1.6% Other, 0.6% Hispanic of any race (2010); Average household size: 2.48 (2010); Median age: 41.4 (2010); Males per 100 females: 99.0 (2010); Marriage status: 24.5% never married, 57.4% now married, 7.3% widowed, 10.8% divorced (2006-2010 5-year est.); Foreign born: 5.5% (2006-2010 5-year est.); Ancestry (includes multiple ancestries): 26.9% French, 16.7% Irish, 16.7% English, 10.3% Italian, 9.4% German (2006-2010 5-year est.).
**Economy:** Single-family building permits issued: 5 (2011); Multi-family building permits issued: 0 (2011); Employment by occupation: 2.1% management, 0.0% professional, 21.5% services, 18.4% sales, 2.0% farming, 16.5% construction, 10.5% production (2006-2010 5-year est.).
**Income:** Per capita income: $23,425 (2006-2010 5-year est.); Median household income: $37,224 (2006-2010 5-year est.); Average household income: $53,910 (2006-2010 5-year est.); Percent of households with income of $100,000 or more: 6.4% (2006-2010 5-year est.); Poverty rate: 19.4% (2006-2010 5-year est.).
**Education:** Percent of population age 25 and over with: High school diploma (including GED) or higher: 86.1% (2006-2010 5-year est.);

Bachelor's degree or higher: 9.9% (2006-2010 5-year est.); Master's degree or higher: 4.5% (2006-2010 5-year est.).
**Housing:** Homeownership rate: 75.9% (2010); Median home value: $82,000 (2006-2010 5-year est.); Median contract rent: $519 per month (2006-2010 5-year est.); Median year structure built: 1960 (2006-2010 5-year est.).
**Safety:** Violent crime rate: 0.0 per 10,000 population; Property crime rate: 107.4 per 10,000 population (2010).
**Transportation:** Commute to work: 93.1% car, 0.0% public transportation, 2.5% walk, 4.0% work from home (2006-2010 5-year est.); Travel time to work: 26.8% less than 15 minutes, 45.0% 15 to 30 minutes, 24.3% 30 to 45 minutes, 2.3% 45 to 60 minutes, 1.7% 60 minutes or more (2006-2010 5-year est.)

**NORFOLK** (CDP). Covers a land area of 2.701 square miles and a water area of 0.111 square miles. Located at 44.78° N. Lat; 74.98° W. Long. Elevation is 259 feet.
**Population:** 1,483 (1990); 1,334 (2000); 1,327 (2010); Density: 491.1 persons per square mile (2010); Race: 96.8% White, 0.3% Black, 0.1% Asian, 0.5% American Indian/Alaska Native, 0.1% Native Hawaiian/Other Pacific Islander, 2.2% Other, 0.9% Hispanic of any race (2010); Average household size: 2.36 (2010); Median age: 39.0 (2010); Males per 100 females: 98.1 (2010); Marriage status: 31.5% never married, 52.8% now married, 4.2% widowed, 11.5% divorced (2006-2010 5-year est.); Foreign born: 6.8% (2006-2010 5-year est.); Ancestry (includes multiple ancestries): 37.1% French, 18.8% Irish, 18.2% German, 16.6% English, 9.5% American (2006-2010 5-year est.).
**Economy:** Employment by occupation: 0.0% management, 0.0% professional, 36.2% services, 21.0% sales, 0.0% farming, 15.7% construction, 7.4% production (2006-2010 5-year est.).
**Income:** Per capita income: $19,000 (2006-2010 5-year est.); Median household income: $29,213 (2006-2010 5-year est.); Average household income: $40,138 (2006-2010 5-year est.); Percent of households with income of $100,000 or more: 6.2% (2006-2010 5-year est.); Poverty rate: 16.0% (2006-2010 5-year est.).
**Education:** Percent of population age 25 and over with: High school diploma (including GED) or higher: 82.0% (2006-2010 5-year est.); Bachelor's degree or higher: 2.4% (2006-2010 5-year est.); Master's degree or higher: 0.0% (2006-2010 5-year est.).
**Housing:** Homeownership rate: 64.3% (2010); Median home value: $52,700 (2006-2010 5-year est.); Median contract rent: $517 per month (2006-2010 5-year est.); Median year structure built: before 1940 (2006-2010 5-year est.).
**Transportation:** Commute to work: 92.8% car, 0.0% public transportation, 7.2% walk, 0.0% work from home (2006-2010 5-year est.); Travel time to work: 25.7% less than 15 minutes, 51.9% 15 to 30 minutes, 19.5% 30 to 45 minutes, 2.9% 45 to 60 minutes, 0.0% 60 minutes or more (2006-2010 5-year est.)

**NORTH LAWRENCE** (unincorporated postal area)
Zip Code: 12967
    Covers a land area of 37.607 square miles and a water area of 0.032 square miles. Located at 44.77° N. Lat; 74.65° W. Long. Elevation is 338 feet. Population: 1,223 (2010); Density: 32.5 persons per square mile (2010); Race: 97.7% White, 0.3% Black, 0.1% Asian, 0.7% American Indian/Alaska Native, 0.0% Native Hawaiian/Other Pacific Islander, 1.2% Other, 1.2% Hispanic of any race (2010); Average household size: 2.77 (2010); Median age: 35.7 (2010); Males per 100 females: 106.6 (2010); Homeownership rate: 81.2% (2010)

**NORWOOD** (village). Covers a land area of 2.094 square miles and a water area of 0.169 square miles. Located at 44.74° N. Lat; 74.99° W. Long. Elevation is 331 feet.
**History:** Originally an Adirondack-Saint Lawrence Valley railroad center and industrial village, but now purely a residential community. Incorporated 1871.
**Population:** 1,841 (1990); 1,685 (2000); 1,657 (2010); Density: 791.0 persons per square mile (2010); Race: 96.1% White, 0.3% Black, 0.7% Asian, 0.5% American Indian/Alaska Native, 0.1% Native Hawaiian/Other Pacific Islander, 2.3% Other, 1.1% Hispanic of any race (2010); Average household size: 2.34 (2010); Median age: 41.9 (2010); Males per 100 females: 97.0 (2010); Marriage status: 32.5% never married, 48.2% now married, 7.6% widowed, 11.7% divorced (2006-2010 5-year est.); Foreign born: 4.7% (2006-2010 5-year est.); Ancestry (includes multiple

ancestries): 21.2% Irish, 19.8% English, 19.3% French, 9.1% German, 8.9% American (2006-2010 5-year est.).

**Economy:** Single-family building permits issued: 0 (2011); Multi-family building permits issued: 0 (2011); Employment by occupation: 8.7% management, 3.7% professional, 15.8% services, 12.7% sales, 1.3% farming, 12.9% construction, 5.5% production (2006-2010 5-year est.).

**Income:** Per capita income: $19,255 (2006-2010 5-year est.); Median household income: $38,083 (2006-2010 5-year est.); Average household income: $47,164 (2006-2010 5-year est.); Percent of households with income of $100,000 or more: 5.9% (2006-2010 5-year est.); Poverty rate: 19.7% (2006-2010 5-year est.).

**Education:** Percent of population age 25 and over with: High school diploma (including GED) or higher: 84.2% (2006-2010 5-year est.); Bachelor's degree or higher: 23.5% (2006-2010 5-year est.); Master's degree or higher: 8.1% (2006-2010 5-year est.).

### School District(s)
Norwood-Norfolk Central School District (PK-12)
   2009-10 Enrollment: 1,037 . . . . . . . . . . . . . . . . . . (315) 353-6631

**Housing:** Homeownership rate: 71.0% (2010); Median home value: $67,100 (2006-2010 5-year est.); Median contract rent: $488 per month (2006-2010 5-year est.); Median year structure built: before 1940 (2006-2010 5-year est.).

**Transportation:** Commute to work: 86.3% car, 0.5% public transportation, 7.1% walk, 5.1% work from home (2006-2010 5-year est.); Travel time to work: 37.1% less than 15 minutes, 37.6% 15 to 30 minutes, 14.6% 30 to 45 minutes, 4.6% 45 to 60 minutes, 6.1% 60 minutes or more (2006-2010 5-year est.)

## OGDENSBURG (city).
Covers a land area of 4.955 square miles and a water area of 3.180 square miles. Located at 44.70° N. Lat; 75.46° W. Long. Elevation is 295 feet.

**History:** Settled by French missionaries and trappers 1749; was strategically important in the War of 1812. Seat of Mater Dei, and Wadhams Hall Seminary and College and a Museum with works of Frederic Remington, who lived here. Rhoda Fox Graves was the first woman to serve the state's Assembly and Senate. Incorporated as a city 1868.

**Population:** 13,521 (1990); 12,364 (2000); 11,128 (2010); Density: 2,245.5 persons per square mile (2010); Race: 88.3% White, 7.3% Black, 0.8% Asian, 0.8% American Indian/Alaska Native, 0.0% Native Hawaiian/Other Pacific Islander, 2.8% Other, 3.5% Hispanic of any race (2010); Average household size: 2.36 (2010); Median age: 39.1 (2010); Males per 100 females: 120.6 (2010); Marriage status: 36.3% never married, 42.6% now married, 8.3% widowed, 12.7% divorced (2006-2010 5-year est.); Foreign born: 4.0% (2006-2010 5-year est.); Ancestry (includes multiple ancestries): 17.9% French, 14.6% Irish, 11.8% English, 8.9% French Canadian, 8.7% American (2006-2010 5-year est.).

**Economy:** Single-family building permits issued: 2 (2011); Multi-family building permits issued: 2 (2011); Employment by occupation: 7.8% management, 2.6% professional, 15.8% services, 19.3% sales, 4.8% farming, 9.8% construction, 3.4% production (2006-2010 5-year est.).

**Income:** Per capita income: $17,651 (2006-2010 5-year est.); Median household income: $34,148 (2006-2010 5-year est.); Average household income: $44,094 (2006-2010 5-year est.); Percent of households with income of $100,000 or more: 8.1% (2006-2010 5-year est.); Poverty rate: 21.8% (2006-2010 5-year est.).

**Education:** Percent of population age 25 and over with: High school diploma (including GED) or higher: 82.0% (2006-2010 5-year est.); Bachelor's degree or higher: 14.6% (2006-2010 5-year est.); Master's degree or higher: 5.3% (2006-2010 5-year est.).

### School District(s)
Ogdensburg City School District (PK-12)
   2009-10 Enrollment: 1,747 . . . . . . . . . . . . . . . . . . (315) 393-0900

**Housing:** Homeownership rate: 61.8% (2010); Median home value: $66,700 (2006-2010 5-year est.); Median contract rent: $441 per month (2006-2010 5-year est.); Median year structure built: before 1940 (2006-2010 5-year est.).

**Hospitals:** Claxton - Hepburn Medical Center (159 beds); St. Lawrence Psychiatric Center (85 beds)

**Safety:** Violent crime rate: 28.7 per 10,000 population; Property crime rate: 521.5 per 10,000 population (2010).

**Newspapers:** The Journal (Local news; Circulation 700); North Country Catholic (Regional news; Circulation 9,500); Ogdensburg Journal And Advance News (Community news; Circulation 5,152); Rural News (Local news; Circulation 10,500)

**Transportation:** Commute to work: 88.8% car, 0.3% public transportation, 4.6% walk, 2.2% work from home (2006-2010 5-year est.); Travel time to work: 72.4% less than 15 minutes, 14.2% 15 to 30 minutes, 6.5% 30 to 45 minutes, 3.4% 45 to 60 minutes, 3.5% 60 minutes or more (2006-2010 5-year est.)

**Airports:** Ogdensburg International (general aviation)

**Additional Information Contacts**
City of Ogdensburg . . . . . . . . . . . . . . . . . . . . . . . . . (315) 393-3540
   http://www.ogdensburg.org
Ogdensburg Chamber of Commerce . . . . . . . . . . . . . (315) 393-3620
   http://www.ogdensburgny.com

## OSWEGATCHIE (town).
Covers a land area of 65.498 square miles and a water area of 5.704 square miles. Located at 44.63° N. Lat; 75.49° W. Long. Elevation is 1,355 feet.

**Population:** 4,036 (1990); 4,370 (2000); 4,397 (2010); Density: 67.1 persons per square mile (2010); Race: 97.8% White, 0.3% Black, 0.5% Asian, 0.5% American Indian/Alaska Native, 0.0% Native Hawaiian/Other Pacific Islander, 0.9% Other, 0.6% Hispanic of any race (2010); Average household size: 2.52 (2010); Median age: 44.3 (2010); Males per 100 females: 91.7 (2010); Marriage status: 21.5% never married, 57.6% now married, 8.6% widowed, 12.3% divorced (2006-2010 5-year est.); Foreign born: 2.9% (2006-2010 5-year est.); Ancestry (includes multiple ancestries): 19.9% English, 15.6% French, 15.1% Irish, 9.9% German, 8.1% French Canadian (2006-2010 5-year est.).

**Economy:** Single-family building permits issued: 13 (2011); Multi-family building permits issued: 0 (2011); Employment by occupation: 9.8% management, 1.4% professional, 10.6% services, 20.5% sales, 4.4% farming, 6.9% construction, 5.9% production (2006-2010 5-year est.).

**Income:** Per capita income: $25,926 (2006-2010 5-year est.); Median household income: $51,189 (2006-2010 5-year est.); Average household income: $59,577 (2006-2010 5-year est.); Percent of households with income of $100,000 or more: 15.5% (2006-2010 5-year est.); Poverty rate: 8.7% (2006-2010 5-year est.).

**Education:** Percent of population age 25 and over with: High school diploma (including GED) or higher: 84.7% (2006-2010 5-year est.); Bachelor's degree or higher: 17.0% (2006-2010 5-year est.); Master's degree or higher: 8.2% (2006-2010 5-year est.).

**Housing:** Homeownership rate: 81.7% (2010); Median home value: $76,500 (2006-2010 5-year est.); Median contract rent: $444 per month (2006-2010 5-year est.); Median year structure built: 1972 (2006-2010 5-year est.).

**Transportation:** Commute to work: 95.6% car, 0.0% public transportation, 1.5% walk, 2.2% work from home (2006-2010 5-year est.); Travel time to work: 44.6% less than 15 minutes, 41.1% 15 to 30 minutes, 8.1% 30 to 45 minutes, 2.0% 45 to 60 minutes, 4.1% 60 minutes or more (2006-2010 5-year est.)

## PARISHVILLE (town).
Covers a land area of 98.159 square miles and a water area of 3.270 square miles. Located at 44.55° N. Lat; 74.78° W. Long. Elevation is 892 feet.

**Population:** 1,901 (1990); 2,049 (2000); 2,153 (2010); Density: 21.9 persons per square mile (2010); Race: 98.7% White, 0.0% Black, 0.0% Asian, 0.3% American Indian/Alaska Native, 0.0% Native Hawaiian/Other Pacific Islander, 1.0% Other, 0.9% Hispanic of any race (2010); Average household size: 2.42 (2010); Median age: 41.9 (2010); Males per 100 females: 103.3 (2010); Marriage status: 27.9% never married, 53.6% now married, 4.2% widowed, 14.3% divorced (2006-2010 5-year est.); Foreign born: 0.0% (2006-2010 5-year est.); Ancestry (includes multiple ancestries): 23.0% Irish, 15.9% American, 13.7% French, 13.7% English, 8.5% German (2006-2010 5-year est.).

**Economy:** Single-family building permits issued: 0 (2011); Multi-family building permits issued: 0 (2011); Employment by occupation: 4.0% management, 3.5% professional, 3.8% services, 25.8% sales, 3.3% farming, 17.2% construction, 14.2% production (2006-2010 5-year est.).

**Income:** Per capita income: $22,400 (2006-2010 5-year est.); Median household income: $37,589 (2006-2010 5-year est.); Average household income: $51,455 (2006-2010 5-year est.); Percent of households with income of $100,000 or more: 7.3% (2006-2010 5-year est.); Poverty rate: 19.9% (2006-2010 5-year est.).

**Education:** Percent of population age 25 and over with: High school diploma (including GED) or higher: 88.5% (2006-2010 5-year est.); Bachelor's degree or higher: 16.0% (2006-2010 5-year est.); Master's degree or higher: 7.8% (2006-2010 5-year est.).

**School District(s)**
Parishville-Hopkinton Central School District (PK-12)
  2009-10 Enrollment: 507 . . . . . . . . . . . . . . . . . . . . . . . . . (315) 265-4642
**Housing:** Homeownership rate: 78.0% (2010); Median home value:
$83,100 (2006-2010 5-year est.); Median contract rent: $391 per month
(2006-2010 5-year est.); Median year structure built: 1970 (2006-2010
5-year est.).
**Transportation:** Commute to work: 96.4% car, 0.0% public transportation,
0.6% walk, 3.0% work from home (2006-2010 5-year est.); Travel time to
work: 38.9% less than 15 minutes, 37.8% 15 to 30 minutes, 11.5% 30 to 45
minutes, 4.6% 45 to 60 minutes, 7.2% 60 minutes or more (2006-2010
5-year est.)

**PARISHVILLE** (CDP). Covers a land area of 3.292 square miles and
a water area of 0.066 square miles. Located at 44.62° N. Lat; 74.79° W.
Long. Elevation is 892 feet.
**Population:** n/a (1990); n/a (2000); 647 (2010); Density: 196.5 persons per
square mile (2010); Race: 98.3% White, 0.2% Black, 0.2% Asian, 0.3%
American Indian/Alaska Native, 0.2% Native Hawaiian/Other Pacific
Islander, 0.8% Other, 0.9% Hispanic of any race (2010); Average
household size: 2.32 (2010); Median age: 40.1 (2010); Males per 100
females: 93.7 (2010); Marriage status: 25.4% never married, 43.6% now
married, 7.9% widowed, 23.0% divorced (2006-2010 5-year est.); Foreign
born: 0.0% (2006-2010 5-year est.); Ancestry (includes multiple
ancestries): 23.5% Irish, 23.2% American, 14.0% English, 7.1% French,
6.7% Welsh (2006-2010 5-year est.).
**Economy:** Employment by occupation: 0.0% management, 0.0%
professional, 6.5% services, 16.7% sales, 0.0% farming, 25.9%
construction, 33.3% production (2006-2010 5-year est.).
**Income:** Per capita income: $19,543 (2006-2010 5-year est.); Median
household income: $39,063 (2006-2010 5-year est.); Average household
income: $42,519 (2006-2010 5-year est.); Percent of households with
income of $100,000 or more: 1.2% (2006-2010 5-year est.); Poverty rate:
17.8% (2006-2010 5-year est.).
**Education:** Percent of population age 25 and over with: High school
diploma (including GED) or higher: 94.1% (2006-2010 5-year est.);
Bachelor's degree or higher: 18.1% (2006-2010 5-year est.); Master's
degree or higher: 7.9% (2006-2010 5-year est.).
**School District(s)**
Parishville-Hopkinton Central School District (PK-12)
  2009-10 Enrollment: 507 . . . . . . . . . . . . . . . . . . . . . . . . . (315) 265-4642
**Housing:** Homeownership rate: 73.4% (2010); Median home value:
$85,200 (2006-2010 5-year est.); Median contract rent: $675 per month
(2006-2010 5-year est.); Median year structure built: 1965 (2006-2010
5-year est.).
**Transportation:** Commute to work: 91.8% car, 0.0% public transportation,
2.2% walk, 6.0% work from home (2006-2010 5-year est.); Travel time to
work: 14.5% less than 15 minutes, 67.4% 15 to 30 minutes, 9.9% 30 to 45
minutes, 0.6% 45 to 60 minutes, 7.6% 60 minutes or more (2006-2010
5-year est.)

**PIERCEFIELD** (town). Covers a land area of 104.155 square miles
and a water area of 6.910 square miles. Located at 44.22° N. Lat; 74.60°
W. Long. Elevation is 1,572 feet.
**Population:** 285 (1990); 305 (2000); 310 (2010); Density: 3.0 persons per
square mile (2010); Race: 99.7% White, 0.0% Black, 0.0% Asian, 0.3%
American Indian/Alaska Native, 0.0% Native Hawaiian/Other Pacific
Islander, 0.0% Other, 0.6% Hispanic of any race (2010); Average
household size: 2.23 (2010); Median age: 48.4 (2010); Males per 100
females: 93.8 (2010); Marriage status: 18.3% never married, 63.9% now
married, 7.5% widowed, 10.3% divorced (2006-2010 5-year est.); Foreign
born: 0.7% (2006-2010 5-year est.); Ancestry (includes multiple
ancestries): 21.6% English, 20.1% French, 15.8% German, 15.1% Irish,
13.3% Scottish (2006-2010 5-year est.).
**Economy:** Single-family building permits issued: 0 (2011); Multi-family
building permits issued: 0 (2011); Employment by occupation: 8.0%
management, 0.0% professional, 19.5% services, 8.8% sales, 2.7%
farming, 15.9% construction, 8.0% production (2006-2010 5-year est.).
**Income:** Per capita income: $23,557 (2006-2010 5-year est.); Median
household income: $50,500 (2006-2010 5-year est.); Average household
income: $52,808 (2006-2010 5-year est.); Percent of households with
income of $100,000 or more: 10.3% (2006-2010 5-year est.); Poverty rate:
6.8% (2006-2010 5-year est.).
**Education:** Percent of population age 25 and over with: High school
diploma (including GED) or higher: 84.1% (2006-2010 5-year est.);

Bachelor's degree or higher: 27.0% (2006-2010 5-year est.); Master's
degree or higher: 10.6% (2006-2010 5-year est.).
**Housing:** Homeownership rate: 90.0% (2010); Median home value:
$83,800 (2006-2010 5-year est.); Median contract rent: n/a per month
(2006-2010 5-year est.); Median year structure built: 1949 (2006-2010
5-year est.).
**Transportation:** Commute to work: 84.1% car, 0.0% public transportation,
0.0% walk, 15.9% work from home (2006-2010 5-year est.); Travel time to
work: 28.4% less than 15 minutes, 29.5% 15 to 30 minutes, 24.2% 30 to 45
minutes, 11.6% 45 to 60 minutes, 6.3% 60 minutes or more (2006-2010
5-year est.).

**PIERREPONT** (town). Covers a land area of 60.251 square miles and
a water area of 0.467 square miles. Located at 44.52° N. Lat; 75.01° W.
Long. Elevation is 741 feet.
**Population:** 2,375 (1990); 2,674 (2000); 2,589 (2010); Density: 43.0
persons per square mile (2010); Race: 98.1% White, 0.5% Black, 0.5%
Asian, 0.2% American Indian/Alaska Native, 0.0% Native Hawaiian/Other
Pacific Islander, 0.7% Other, 0.5% Hispanic of any race (2010); Average
household size: 2.46 (2010); Median age: 44.1 (2010); Males per 100
females: 103.2 (2010); Marriage status: 21.7% never married, 60.1% now
married, 6.5% widowed, 11.6% divorced (2006-2010 5-year est.); Foreign
born: 2.2% (2006-2010 5-year est.); Ancestry (includes multiple
ancestries): 17.0% Irish, 16.5% English, 14.5% American, 13.6% French,
12.0% German (2006-2010 5-year est.).
**Economy:** Single-family building permits issued: 6 (2011); Multi-family
building permits issued: 0 (2011); Employment by occupation: 12.2%
management, 4.0% professional, 8.3% services, 19.4% sales, 3.8%
farming, 13.7% construction, 5.9% production (2006-2010 5-year est.).
**Income:** Per capita income: $24,109 (2006-2010 5-year est.); Median
household income: $51,719 (2006-2010 5-year est.); Average household
income: $55,937 (2006-2010 5-year est.); Percent of households with
income of $100,000 or more: 9.2% (2006-2010 5-year est.); Poverty rate:
8.7% (2006-2010 5-year est.).
**Education:** Percent of population age 25 and over with: High school
diploma (including GED) or higher: 90.3% (2006-2010 5-year est.);
Bachelor's degree or higher: 24.0% (2006-2010 5-year est.); Master's
degree or higher: 11.1% (2006-2010 5-year est.).
**Housing:** Homeownership rate: 85.4% (2010); Median home value:
$102,600 (2006-2010 5-year est.); Median contract rent: $587 per month
(2006-2010 5-year est.); Median year structure built: 1974 (2006-2010
5-year est.).
**Transportation:** Commute to work: 93.0% car, 0.1% public transportation,
0.8% walk, 5.2% work from home (2006-2010 5-year est.); Travel time to
work: 24.5% less than 15 minutes, 48.6% 15 to 30 minutes, 14.7% 30 to 45
minutes, 8.0% 45 to 60 minutes, 4.2% 60 minutes or more (2006-2010
5-year est.)

**PITCAIRN** (town). Covers a land area of 58.517 square miles and a
water area of 0.937 square miles. Located at 44.22° N. Lat; 75.26° W.
Long. Elevation is 781 feet.
**Population:** 751 (1990); 783 (2000); 846 (2010); Density: 14.5 persons per
square mile (2010); Race: 97.8% White, 0.4% Black, 0.4% Asian, 0.1%
American Indian/Alaska Native, 0.0% Native Hawaiian/Other Pacific
Islander, 1.3% Other, 0.8% Hispanic of any race (2010); Average
household size: 2.54 (2010); Median age: 41.1 (2010); Males per 100
females: 105.8 (2010); Marriage status: 21.3% never married, 59.7% now
married, 6.2% widowed, 12.7% divorced (2006-2010 5-year est.); Foreign
born: 1.3% (2006-2010 5-year est.); Ancestry (includes multiple
ancestries): 24.5% Irish, 16.4% American, 11.7% French, 11.1% English,
7.0% German (2006-2010 5-year est.).
**Economy:** Single-family building permits issued: 0 (2011); Multi-family
building permits issued: 0 (2011); Employment by occupation: 3.3%
management, 0.0% professional, 9.3% services, 15.1% sales, 1.2%
farming, 21.1% construction, 17.5% production (2006-2010 5-year est.).
**Income:** Per capita income: $16,275 (2006-2010 5-year est.); Median
household income: $40,600 (2006-2010 5-year est.); Average household
income: $40,699 (2006-2010 5-year est.); Percent of households with
income of $100,000 or more: 3.7% (2006-2010 5-year est.); Poverty rate:
18.1% (2006-2010 5-year est.).
**Education:** Percent of population age 25 and over with: High school
diploma (including GED) or higher: 78.0% (2006-2010 5-year est.);
Bachelor's degree or higher: 6.9% (2006-2010 5-year est.); Master's
degree or higher: 2.9% (2006-2010 5-year est.).

**Housing:** Homeownership rate: 87.6% (2010); Median home value: $66,300 (2006-2010 5-year est.); Median contract rent: $414 per month (2006-2010 5-year est.); Median year structure built: 1973 (2006-2010 5-year est.).

**Transportation:** Commute to work: 97.9% car, 0.0% public transportation, 0.0% walk, 0.0% work from home (2006-2010 5-year est.); Travel time to work: 25.7% less than 15 minutes, 28.1% 15 to 30 minutes, 16.2% 30 to 45 minutes, 16.8% 45 to 60 minutes, 13.2% 60 minutes or more (2006-2010 5-year est.)

**POTSDAM** (village). Covers a land area of 4.447 square miles and a water area of 0.494 square miles. Located at 44.66° N. Lat; 74.98° W. Long. Elevation is 433 feet.

**Population:** 10,438 (1990); 9,425 (2000); 9,428 (2010); Density: 2,120.1 persons per square mile (2010); Race: 88.9% White, 2.8% Black, 4.9% Asian, 0.4% American Indian/Alaska Native, 0.0% Native Hawaiian/Other Pacific Islander, 3.0% Other, 2.9% Hispanic of any race (2010); Average household size: 2.08 (2010); Median age: 21.4 (2010); Males per 100 females: 113.9 (2010); Marriage status: 77.7% never married, 17.2% now married, 2.3% widowed, 2.9% divorced (2006-2010 5-year est.); Foreign born: 7.6% (2006-2010 5-year est.); Ancestry (includes multiple ancestries): 15.8% Irish, 15.7% English, 13.4% German, 12.1% Italian, 9.2% French (2006-2010 5-year est.).

**Economy:** Single-family building permits issued: 0 (2011); Multi-family building permits issued: 0 (2011); Employment by occupation: 7.7% management, 3.8% professional, 15.7% services, 20.4% sales, 8.8% farming, 1.7% construction, 0.6% production (2006-2010 5-year est.).

**Income:** Per capita income: $11,919 (2006-2010 5-year est.); Median household income: $23,144 (2006-2010 5-year est.); Average household income: $42,754 (2006-2010 5-year est.); Percent of households with income of $100,000 or more: 9.9% (2006-2010 5-year est.); Poverty rate: 37.2% (2006-2010 5-year est.).

**Education:** Percent of population age 25 and over with: High school diploma (including GED) or higher: 92.8% (2006-2010 5-year est.); Bachelor's degree or higher: 42.8% (2006-2010 5-year est.); Master's degree or higher: 22.6% (2006-2010 5-year est.).

**School District(s)**
Potsdam Central School District (PK-12)
    2009-10 Enrollment: 1,493 . . . . . . . . . . . . . . . . (315) 265-2000
**Four-year College(s)**
Clarkson University (Private, Not-for-profit)
    Fall 2010 Enrollment: 3,290 . . . . . . . . . . . . . . . (315) 268-6400
    2011-12 Tuition: In-state $36,780; Out-of-state $36,780
SUNY College at Potsdam (Public)
    Fall 2010 Enrollment: 4,504 . . . . . . . . . . . . . . . (315) 267-2000
    2011-12 Tuition: In-state $6,506; Out-of-state $15,556
**Housing:** Homeownership rate: 32.4% (2010); Median home value: $90,600 (2006-2010 5-year est.); Median contract rent: $526 per month (2006-2010 5-year est.); Median year structure built: 1955 (2006-2010 5-year est.).
**Hospitals:** Canton-Potsdam Hospital (94 beds)
**Newspapers:** Daily Courier - Observer (Local news; Circulation 8,000); North Country This Week (Community news; Circulation 10,600)
**Transportation:** Commute to work: 57.0% car, 0.0% public transportation, 30.6% walk, 10.9% work from home (2006-2010 5-year est.); Travel time to work: 67.6% less than 15 minutes, 24.8% 15 to 30 minutes, 3.5% 30 to 45 minutes, 2.7% 45 to 60 minutes, 1.3% 60 minutes or more (2006-2010 5-year est.)
**Airports:** Potsdam Municipal/Damon Field (general aviation)
**Additional Information Contacts**
Potsdam Chamber of Commerce . . . . . . . . . . . . . . . (315) 274-9000
    http://www.potsdam.ny.us/chamber

**POTSDAM** (town). Covers a land area of 101.403 square miles and a water area of 2.048 square miles. Located at 44.68° N. Lat; 75.03° W. Long. Elevation is 433 feet.

**History:** In 1804, William Bullard and others came to Potsdam from Massachusetts, pooled their resources, and purchased a tract of land on which they established the "Union." Property was held in common, an accurate account of labor and materials contributed by each member was kept, and all proceeds were divided pro rata annually. The group prospered for a few years but dissolved in 1810, when the land was evenly divided among the members. In the 19th century, sandstone quarries near Potsdam employed hundreds of workers. Seat of State University of New York College at Potsdam and Clarkson University. Incorporated in 1831.

**Population:** 16,822 (1990); 15,957 (2000); 16,041 (2010); Density: 158.2 persons per square mile (2010); Race: 91.9% White, 1.8% Black, 3.4% Asian, 0.4% American Indian/Alaska Native, 0.1% Native Hawaiian/Other Pacific Islander, 2.4% Other, 2.3% Hispanic of any race (2010); Average household size: 2.30 (2010); Median age: 23.1 (2010); Males per 100 females: 107.9 (2010); Marriage status: 59.5% never married, 31.7% now married, 3.4% widowed, 5.4% divorced (2006-2010 5-year est.); Foreign born: 5.6% (2006-2010 5-year est.); Ancestry (includes multiple ancestries): 19.5% Irish, 15.5% English, 12.2% French, 11.5% German, 10.3% Italian (2006-2010 5-year est.).

**Economy:** Single-family building permits issued: 15 (2011); Multi-family building permits issued: 0 (2011); Employment by occupation: 8.6% management, 4.4% professional, 13.0% services, 17.5% sales, 5.7% farming, 6.5% construction, 2.5% production (2006-2010 5-year est.).

**Income:** Per capita income: $16,384 (2006-2010 5-year est.); Median household income: $36,452 (2006-2010 5-year est.); Average household income: $51,384 (2006-2010 5-year est.); Percent of households with income of $100,000 or more: 12.3% (2006-2010 5-year est.); Poverty rate: 23.6% (2006-2010 5-year est.).

**Education:** Percent of population age 25 and over with: High school diploma (including GED) or higher: 91.0% (2006-2010 5-year est.); Bachelor's degree or higher: 34.3% (2006-2010 5-year est.); Master's degree or higher: 18.0% (2006-2010 5-year est.).

**School District(s)**
Potsdam Central School District (PK-12)
    2009-10 Enrollment: 1,493 . . . . . . . . . . . . . . . . (315) 265-2000
**Four-year College(s)**
Clarkson University (Private, Not-for-profit)
    Fall 2010 Enrollment: 3,290 . . . . . . . . . . . . . . . (315) 268-6400
    2011-12 Tuition: In-state $36,780; Out-of-state $36,780
SUNY College at Potsdam (Public)
    Fall 2010 Enrollment: 4,504 . . . . . . . . . . . . . . . (315) 267-2000
    2011-12 Tuition: In-state $6,506; Out-of-state $15,556
**Housing:** Homeownership rate: 55.5% (2010); Median home value: $86,900 (2006-2010 5-year est.); Median contract rent: $519 per month (2006-2010 5-year est.); Median year structure built: 1959 (2006-2010 5-year est.).
**Hospitals:** Canton-Potsdam Hospital (94 beds)
**Newspapers:** Daily Courier - Observer (Local news; Circulation 8,000); North Country This Week (Community news; Circulation 10,600)
**Transportation:** Commute to work: 72.8% car, 0.0% public transportation, 18.4% walk, 7.4% work from home (2006-2010 5-year est.); Travel time to work: 59.3% less than 15 minutes, 28.6% 15 to 30 minutes, 5.8% 30 to 45 minutes, 3.2% 45 to 60 minutes, 2.9% 60 minutes or more (2006-2010 5-year est.)
**Airports:** Potsdam Municipal/Damon Field (general aviation)

**PYRITES** (unincorporated postal area)
Zip Code: 13677
    Covers a land area of 0.196 square miles and a water area of 0.030 square miles. Located at 44.51° N. Lat; 75.17° W. Long. Elevation is 502 feet. Population: 93 (2010); Density: 473.3 persons per square mile (2010); Race: 84.9% White, 1.1% Black, 0.0% Asian, 0.0% American Indian/Alaska Native, 0.0% Native Hawaiian/Other Pacific Islander, 14.0% Other, 3.2% Hispanic of any race (2010); Average household size: 3.00 (2010); Median age: 32.5 (2010); Males per 100 females: 78.8 (2010); Homeownership rate: 71.0% (2010)

**RAYMONDVILLE** (unincorporated postal area)
Zip Code: 13678
    Covers a land area of 0.785 square miles and a water area of 0.038 square miles. Located at 44.81° N. Lat; 74.99° W. Long. Elevation is 253 feet. Population: 211 (2010); Density: 268.7 persons per square mile (2010); Race: 91.9% White, 2.8% Black, 1.4% Asian, 1.9% American Indian/Alaska Native, 0.0% Native Hawaiian/Other Pacific Islander, 2.0% Other, 0.9% Hispanic of any race (2010); Average household size: 2.29 (2010); Median age: 39.3 (2010); Males per 100 females: 93.6 (2010); Homeownership rate: 46.8% (2010)

**RENSSELAER FALLS** (village). Covers a land area of 0.290 square miles and a water area of 0.026 square miles. Located at 44.59° N. Lat; 75.31° W. Long. Elevation is 328 feet.
**Population:** 323 (1990); 337 (2000); 332 (2010); Density: 1,142.6 persons per square mile (2010); Race: 95.5% White, 0.9% Black, 0.3% Asian, 1.2% American Indian/Alaska Native, 0.0% Native Hawaiian/Other Pacific

Islander, 2.1% Other, 3.0% Hispanic of any race (2010); Average household size: 2.50 (2010); Median age: 34.3 (2010); Males per 100 females: 91.9 (2010); Marriage status: 24.4% never married, 54.6% now married, 11.4% widowed, 9.7% divorced (2006-2010 5-year est.); Foreign born: 3.1% (2006-2010 5-year est.); Ancestry (includes multiple ancestries): 23.2% English, 15.6% French Canadian, 13.3% Irish, 11.4% Italian, 11.2% French (2006-2010 5-year est.).
**Economy:** Single-family building permits issued: 0 (2011); Multi-family building permits issued: 0 (2011); Employment by occupation: 5.3% management, 1.5% professional, 16.3% services, 15.9% sales, 3.4% farming, 7.2% construction, 4.5% production (2006-2010 5-year est.).
**Income:** Per capita income: $23,747 (2006-2010 5-year est.); Median household income: $73,750 (2006-2010 5-year est.); Average household income: $68,043 (2006-2010 5-year est.); Percent of households with income of $100,000 or more: 6.6% (2006-2010 5-year est.); Poverty rate: 5.1% (2006-2010 5-year est.).
**Education:** Percent of population age 25 and over with: High school diploma (including GED) or higher: 98.2% (2006-2010 5-year est.); Bachelor's degree or higher: 28.2% (2006-2010 5-year est.); Master's degree or higher: 18.2% (2006-2010 5-year est.).
**Housing:** Homeownership rate: 78.0% (2010); Median home value: $78,100 (2006-2010 5-year est.); Median contract rent: $850 per month (2006-2010 5-year est.); Median year structure built: before 1940 (2006-2010 5-year est.).
**Transportation:** Commute to work: 93.8% car, 0.0% public transportation, 2.3% walk, 3.1% work from home (2006-2010 5-year est.); Travel time to work: 31.9% less than 15 minutes, 33.5% 15 to 30 minutes, 5.6% 30 to 45 minutes, 17.9% 45 to 60 minutes, 11.2% 60 minutes or more (2006-2010 5-year est.)

**RICHVILLE** (village). Aka Bigelow. Covers a land area of 0.738 square miles and a water area of 0 square miles. Located at 44.41° N. Lat; 75.39° W. Long. Elevation is 407 feet.
**Population:** 311 (1990); 274 (2000); 323 (2010); Density: 437.5 persons per square mile (2010); Race: 98.5% White, 0.3% Black, 0.0% Asian, 0.0% American Indian/Alaska Native, 0.0% Native Hawaiian/Other Pacific Islander, 1.2% Other, 0.9% Hispanic of any race (2010); Average household size: 2.91 (2010); Median age: 32.6 (2010); Males per 100 females: 105.7 (2010); Marriage status: 23.2% never married, 60.7% now married, 7.6% widowed, 8.5% divorced (2006-2010 5-year est.); Foreign born: 0.0% (2006-2010 5-year est.); Ancestry (includes multiple ancestries): 12.6% French, 11.6% English, 10.2% French Canadian, 9.2% American, 8.2% Italian (2006-2010 5-year est.).
**Economy:** Single-family building permits issued: 1 (2011); Multi-family building permits issued: 0 (2011); Employment by occupation: 8.6% management, 3.1% professional, 10.9% services, 8.6% sales, 6.3% farming, 26.6% construction, 12.5% production (2006-2010 5-year est.).
**Income:** Per capita income: $17,264 (2006-2010 5-year est.); Median household income: $42,500 (2006-2010 5-year est.); Average household income: $47,983 (2006-2010 5-year est.); Percent of households with income of $100,000 or more: 8.4% (2006-2010 5-year est.); Poverty rate: 26.5% (2006-2010 5-year est.).
**Education:** Percent of population age 25 and over with: High school diploma (including GED) or higher: 81.7% (2006-2010 5-year est.); Bachelor's degree or higher: 15.0% (2006-2010 5-year est.); Master's degree or higher: 3.9% (2006-2010 5-year est.).
**Housing:** Homeownership rate: 82.0% (2010); Median home value: $72,100 (2006-2010 5-year est.); Median contract rent: $558 per month (2006-2010 5-year est.); Median year structure built: before 1940 (2006-2010 5-year est.).
**Transportation:** Commute to work: 85.4% car, 0.0% public transportation, 2.4% walk, 1.6% work from home (2006-2010 5-year est.); Travel time to work: 44.6% less than 15 minutes, 30.6% 15 to 30 minutes, 9.9% 30 to 45 minutes, 10.7% 45 to 60 minutes, 4.1% 60 minutes or more (2006-2010 5-year est.)

**ROSSIE** (town). Covers a land area of 37.879 square miles and a water area of 1.362 square miles. Located at 44.32° N. Lat; 75.62° W. Long. Elevation is 276 feet.
**Population:** 770 (1990); 787 (2000); 877 (2010); Density: 23.2 persons per square mile (2010); Race: 98.6% White, 0.2% Black, 0.1% Asian, 0.2% American Indian/Alaska Native, 0.0% Native Hawaiian/Other Pacific Islander, 0.9% Other, 0.1% Hispanic of any race (2010); Average household size: 2.58 (2010); Median age: 39.2 (2010); Males per 100 females: 99.3 (2010); Marriage status: 31.0% never married, 54.6% now

married, 4.9% widowed, 9.5% divorced (2006-2010 5-year est.); Foreign born: 1.8% (2006-2010 5-year est.); Ancestry (includes multiple ancestries): 19.6% English, 14.8% German, 13.0% Irish, 12.1% American, 9.5% French (2006-2010 5-year est.).
**Economy:** Single-family building permits issued: 1 (2011); Multi-family building permits issued: 0 (2011); Employment by occupation: 2.1% management, 0.0% professional, 15.7% services, 16.4% sales, 2.1% farming, 31.4% construction, 7.7% production (2006-2010 5-year est.).
**Income:** Per capita income: $17,773 (2006-2010 5-year est.); Median household income: $41,513 (2006-2010 5-year est.); Average household income: $44,150 (2006-2010 5-year est.); Percent of households with income of $100,000 or more: 7.5% (2006-2010 5-year est.); Poverty rate: 15.0% (2006-2010 5-year est.).
**Education:** Percent of population age 25 and over with: High school diploma (including GED) or higher: 83.3% (2006-2010 5-year est.); Bachelor's degree or higher: 9.3% (2006-2010 5-year est.); Master's degree or higher: 6.1% (2006-2010 5-year est.).
**Housing:** Homeownership rate: 76.5% (2010); Median home value: $53,300 (2006-2010 5-year est.); Median contract rent: $437 per month (2006-2010 5-year est.); Median year structure built: 1976 (2006-2010 5-year est.).
**Transportation:** Commute to work: 96.4% car, 0.0% public transportation, 1.1% walk, 2.5% work from home (2006-2010 5-year est.); Travel time to work: 11.4% less than 15 minutes, 29.3% 15 to 30 minutes, 17.6% 30 to 45 minutes, 31.5% 45 to 60 minutes, 10.3% 60 minutes or more (2006-2010 5-year est.)

**RUSSELL** (town). Covers a land area of 96.675 square miles and a water area of 0.618 square miles. Located at 44.40° N. Lat; 75.14° W. Long. Elevation is 617 feet.
**Population:** 1,716 (1990); 1,801 (2000); 1,856 (2010); Density: 19.2 persons per square mile (2010); Race: 97.8% White, 0.2% Black, 0.4% Asian, 0.4% American Indian/Alaska Native, 0.1% Native Hawaiian/Other Pacific Islander, 1.1% Other, 0.5% Hispanic of any race (2010); Average household size: 2.57 (2010); Median age: 40.6 (2010); Males per 100 females: 103.7 (2010); Marriage status: 26.8% never married, 61.7% now married, 4.3% widowed, 7.2% divorced (2006-2010 5-year est.); Foreign born: 2.0% (2006-2010 5-year est.); Ancestry (includes multiple ancestries): 17.2% Irish, 14.3% French, 12.9% English, 12.5% German, 11.7% American (2006-2010 5-year est.).
**Economy:** Single-family building permits issued: 2 (2011); Multi-family building permits issued: 0 (2011); Employment by occupation: 6.8% management, 2.1% professional, 10.6% services, 12.9% sales, 2.7% farming, 18.2% construction, 8.7% production (2006-2010 5-year est.).
**Income:** Per capita income: $20,295 (2006-2010 5-year est.); Median household income: $41,618 (2006-2010 5-year est.); Average household income: $48,600 (2006-2010 5-year est.); Percent of households with income of $100,000 or more: 8.2% (2006-2010 5-year est.); Poverty rate: 18.5% (2006-2010 5-year est.).
**Education:** Percent of population age 25 and over with: High school diploma (including GED) or higher: 84.6% (2006-2010 5-year est.); Bachelor's degree or higher: 13.7% (2006-2010 5-year est.); Master's degree or higher: 5.5% (2006-2010 5-year est.).
**School District(s)**
Edwards-Knox Central School District (PK-12)
   2009-10 Enrollment: 636 . . . . . . . . . . . . . . . . . . . . . . . . . (315) 562-8326
**Housing:** Homeownership rate: 85.3% (2010); Median home value: $68,900 (2006-2010 5-year est.); Median contract rent: $409 per month (2006-2010 5-year est.); Median year structure built: 1976 (2006-2010 5-year est.).
**Transportation:** Commute to work: 94.3% car, 0.0% public transportation, 1.2% walk, 4.1% work from home (2006-2010 5-year est.); Travel time to work: 19.4% less than 15 minutes, 39.4% 15 to 30 minutes, 22.4% 30 to 45 minutes, 6.0% 45 to 60 minutes, 12.8% 60 minutes or more (2006-2010 5-year est.)

**SOUTH COLTON** (unincorporated postal area)
Zip Code: 13687
   Covers a land area of 134.416 square miles and a water area of 9.783 square miles. Located at 44.43° N. Lat; 74.83° W. Long. Elevation is 935 feet. Population: 479 (2010); Density: 3.6 persons per square mile (2010); Race: 99.2% White, 0.2% Black, 0.2% Asian, 0.0% American Indian/Alaska Native, 0.0% Native Hawaiian/Other Pacific Islander, 0.4% Other, 0.0% Hispanic of any race (2010); Average household size: 2.24

(2010); Median age: 51.1 (2010); Males per 100 females: 108.3 (2010); Homeownership rate: 90.7% (2010)

**STAR LAKE** (CDP). Covers a land area of 4.337 square miles and a water area of 0.425 square miles. Located at 44.16° N. Lat; 75.03° W. Long. Elevation is 1,486 feet.
**Population:** 1,092 (1990); 860 (2000); 809 (2010); Density: 186.5 persons per square mile (2010); Race: 96.4% White, 0.2% Black, 0.7% Asian, 0.4% American Indian/Alaska Native, 0.0% Native Hawaiian/Other Pacific Islander, 2.3% Other, 2.1% Hispanic of any race (2010); Average household size: 2.32 (2010); Median age: 46.2 (2010); Males per 100 females: 105.3 (2010); Marriage status: 20.0% never married, 66.2% now married, 7.1% widowed, 6.8% divorced (2006-2010 5-year est.); Foreign born: 1.7% (2006-2010 5-year est.); Ancestry (includes multiple ancestries): 23.1% French, 21.0% American, 18.3% Irish, 15.5% English, 13.1% German (2006-2010 5-year est.).
**Economy:** Employment by occupation: 9.8% management, 2.2% professional, 14.5% services, 17.2% sales, 0.9% farming, 8.0% construction, 1.8% production (2006-2010 5-year est.).
**Income:** Per capita income: $18,430 (2006-2010 5-year est.); Median household income: $40,417 (2006-2010 5-year est.); Average household income: $43,397 (2006-2010 5-year est.); Percent of households with income of $100,000 or more: 7.9% (2006-2010 5-year est.); Poverty rate: 10.7% (2006-2010 5-year est.).
**Education:** Percent of population age 25 and over with: High school diploma (including GED) or higher: 89.6% (2006-2010 5-year est.); Bachelor's degree or higher: 16.5% (2006-2010 5-year est.); Master's degree or higher: 7.8% (2006-2010 5-year est.).
**School District(s)**
Clifton-Fine Central School District (PK-12)
    2009-10 Enrollment: 340 . . . . . . . . . . . . . . . . . . . . . . . . . (315) 848-3333
**Housing:** Homeownership rate: 80.1% (2010); Median home value: $53,100 (2006-2010 5-year est.); Median contract rent: $386 per month (2006-2010 5-year est.); Median year structure built: 1951 (2006-2010 5-year est.).
**Hospitals:** Clifton-Fine Hospital (20 beds)
**Transportation:** Commute to work: 86.6% car, 0.0% public transportation, 3.4% walk, 10.0% work from home (2006-2010 5-year est.); Travel time to work: 46.5% less than 15 minutes, 13.2% 15 to 30 minutes, 5.2% 30 to 45 minutes, 17.7% 45 to 60 minutes, 17.4% 60 minutes or more (2006-2010 5-year est.)

**STOCKHOLM** (town). Covers a land area of 93.896 square miles and a water area of 0.392 square miles. Located at 44.74° N. Lat; 74.85° W. Long.
**Population:** 3,533 (1990); 3,592 (2000); 3,665 (2010); Density: 39.0 persons per square mile (2010); Race: 97.1% White, 0.1% Black, 0.3% Asian, 1.0% American Indian/Alaska Native, 0.0% Native Hawaiian/Other Pacific Islander, 1.5% Other, 1.0% Hispanic of any race (2010); Average household size: 2.51 (2010); Median age: 40.3 (2010); Males per 100 females: 104.9 (2010); Marriage status: 21.7% never married, 65.0% now married, 8.0% widowed, 5.3% divorced (2006-2010 5-year est.); Foreign born: 0.7% (2006-2010 5-year est.); Ancestry (includes multiple ancestries): 25.4% Irish, 25.1% French, 13.4% English, 11.3% American, 7.6% Italian (2006-2010 5-year est.).
**Economy:** Single-family building permits issued: 9 (2011); Multi-family building permits issued: 2 (2011); Employment by occupation: 6.4% management, 0.0% professional, 18.5% services, 9.9% sales, 0.9% farming, 20.8% construction, 8.6% production (2006-2010 5-year est.).
**Income:** Per capita income: $19,931 (2006-2010 5-year est.); Median household income: $38,800 (2006-2010 5-year est.); Average household income: $49,522 (2006-2010 5-year est.); Percent of households with income of $100,000 or more: 11.0% (2006-2010 5-year est.); Poverty rate: 21.7% (2006-2010 5-year est.).
**Education:** Percent of population age 25 and over with: High school diploma (including GED) or higher: 85.9% (2006-2010 5-year est.); Bachelor's degree or higher: 12.8% (2006-2010 5-year est.); Master's degree or higher: 6.9% (2006-2010 5-year est.).
**Housing:** Homeownership rate: 80.3% (2010); Median home value: $78,400 (2006-2010 5-year est.); Median contract rent: $396 per month (2006-2010 5-year est.); Median year structure built: 1959 (2006-2010 5-year est.).
**Transportation:** Commute to work: 85.7% car, 0.0% public transportation, 3.5% walk, 8.8% work from home (2006-2010 5-year est.); Travel time to work: 17.0% less than 15 minutes, 38.1% 15 to 30 minutes, 32.2% 30 to 45

minutes, 7.1% 45 to 60 minutes, 5.7% 60 minutes or more (2006-2010 5-year est.)

**WADDINGTON** (village). Covers a land area of 2.180 square miles and a water area of 0.187 square miles. Located at 44.86° N. Lat; 75.19° W. Long. Elevation is 272 feet.
**Population:** 944 (1990); 923 (2000); 972 (2010); Density: 445.9 persons per square mile (2010); Race: 97.7% White, 0.5% Black, 0.1% Asian, 1.2% American Indian/Alaska Native, 0.0% Native Hawaiian/Other Pacific Islander, 0.5% Other, 0.5% Hispanic of any race (2010); Average household size: 2.18 (2010); Median age: 48.8 (2010); Males per 100 females: 82.0 (2010); Marriage status: 15.1% never married, 59.3% now married, 15.9% widowed, 9.6% divorced (2006-2010 5-year est.); Foreign born: 5.1% (2006-2010 5-year est.); Ancestry (includes multiple ancestries): 17.9% English, 16.0% French, 15.1% Irish, 12.5% American, 9.6% German (2006-2010 5-year est.).
**Economy:** Single-family building permits issued: 2 (2011); Multi-family building permits issued: 0 (2011); Employment by occupation: 8.7% management, 3.8% professional, 9.1% services, 15.3% sales, 0.0% farming, 11.1% construction, 4.5% production (2006-2010 5-year est.).
**Income:** Per capita income: $24,789 (2006-2010 5-year est.); Median household income: $36,538 (2006-2010 5-year est.); Average household income: $49,648 (2006-2010 5-year est.); Percent of households with income of $100,000 or more: 10.7% (2006-2010 5-year est.); Poverty rate: 13.2% (2006-2010 5-year est.).
**Education:** Percent of population age 25 and over with: High school diploma (including GED) or higher: 90.7% (2006-2010 5-year est.); Bachelor's degree or higher: 18.5% (2006-2010 5-year est.); Master's degree or higher: 9.5% (2006-2010 5-year est.).
**Housing:** Homeownership rate: 70.4% (2010); Median home value: $107,600 (2006-2010 5-year est.); Median contract rent: $425 per month (2006-2010 5-year est.); Median year structure built: 1951 (2006-2010 5-year est.).
**Transportation:** Commute to work: 90.3% car, 2.9% public transportation, 1.4% walk, 4.3% work from home (2006-2010 5-year est.); Travel time to work: 30.8% less than 15 minutes, 18.8% 15 to 30 minutes, 45.5% 30 to 45 minutes, 1.1% 45 to 60 minutes, 3.8% 60 minutes or more (2006-2010 5-year est.)
**Additional Information Contacts**
Waddington Chamber of Commerce . . . . . . . . . . . . . . . . . (315) 388-4765
    http://www.waddingtonny.us./chamber

**WADDINGTON** (town). Covers a land area of 51.605 square miles and a water area of 6.366 square miles. Located at 44.83° N. Lat; 75.19° W. Long. Elevation is 272 feet.
**Population:** 1,990 (1990); 2,212 (2000); 2,266 (2010); Density: 43.9 persons per square mile (2010); Race: 98.0% White, 0.3% Black, 0.0% Asian, 0.8% American Indian/Alaska Native, 0.0% Native Hawaiian/Other Pacific Islander, 0.9% Other, 0.9% Hispanic of any race (2010); Average household size: 2.39 (2010); Median age: 44.8 (2010); Males per 100 females: 91.9 (2010); Marriage status: 17.8% never married, 60.5% now married, 11.2% widowed, 10.6% divorced (2006-2010 5-year est.); Foreign born: 3.7% (2006-2010 5-year est.); Ancestry (includes multiple ancestries): 23.6% French, 23.2% English, 14.8% Irish, 9.7% American, 6.9% German (2006-2010 5-year est.).
**Economy:** Single-family building permits issued: 3 (2011); Multi-family building permits issued: 0 (2011); Employment by occupation: 6.8% management, 1.8% professional, 9.6% services, 12.2% sales, 1.3% farming, 11.4% construction, 10.0% production (2006-2010 5-year est.).
**Income:** Per capita income: $23,758 (2006-2010 5-year est.); Median household income: $47,547 (2006-2010 5-year est.); Average household income: $55,251 (2006-2010 5-year est.); Percent of households with income of $100,000 or more: 11.6% (2006-2010 5-year est.); Poverty rate: 9.4% (2006-2010 5-year est.).
**Education:** Percent of population age 25 and over with: High school diploma (including GED) or higher: 91.9% (2006-2010 5-year est.); Bachelor's degree or higher: 18.2% (2006-2010 5-year est.); Master's degree or higher: 11.2% (2006-2010 5-year est.).
**Housing:** Homeownership rate: 77.5% (2010); Median home value: $94,200 (2006-2010 5-year est.); Median contract rent: $434 per month (2006-2010 5-year est.); Median year structure built: 1961 (2006-2010 5-year est.).
**Transportation:** Commute to work: 92.3% car, 0.9% public transportation, 1.2% walk, 4.7% work from home (2006-2010 5-year est.); Travel time to work: 16.5% less than 15 minutes, 39.6% 15 to 30 minutes, 35.3% 30 to 45

minutes, 0.8% 45 to 60 minutes, 7.8% 60 minutes or more (2006-2010 5-year est.)

## WANAKENA (unincorporated postal area)
Zip Code: 13695

Covers a land area of 17.000 square miles and a water area of 0.333 square miles. Located at 44.10° N. Lat; 74.92° W. Long. Elevation is 1,503 feet. Population: 134 (2010); Density: 7.9 persons per square mile (2010); Race: 99.3% White, 0.0% Black, 0.0% Asian, 0.7% American Indian/Alaska Native, 0.0% Native Hawaiian/Other Pacific Islander, 0.0% Other, 0.7% Hispanic of any race (2010); Average household size: 2.10 (2010); Median age: 33.0 (2010); Males per 100 females: 179.2 (2010); Homeownership rate: 84.6% (2010)

## WEST STOCKHOLM (unincorporated postal area)
Zip Code: 13696

Covers a land area of 1.862 square miles and a water area of 0 square miles. Located at 44.69° N. Lat; 74.88° W. Long. Elevation is 384 feet. Population: 87 (2010); Density: 46.7 persons per square mile (2010); Race: 95.4% White, 1.1% Black, 2.3% Asian, 0.0% American Indian/Alaska Native, 0.0% Native Hawaiian/Other Pacific Islander, 1.2% Other, 0.0% Hispanic of any race (2010); Average household size: 2.02 (2010); Median age: 45.8 (2010); Males per 100 females: 102.3 (2010); Homeownership rate: 72.1% (2010)

## WINTHROP (CDP). Covers a land area of 2.776 square miles and a
water area of 0.022 square miles. Located at 44.80° N. Lat; 74.80° W. Long. Elevation is 325 feet.
**Population:** n/a (1990); n/a (2000); 510 (2010); Density: 183.7 persons per square mile (2010); Race: 94.7% White, 0.0% Black, 0.4% Asian, 1.8% American Indian/Alaska Native, 0.0% Native Hawaiian/Other Pacific Islander, 3.1% Other, 1.8% Hispanic of any race (2010); Average household size: 2.52 (2010); Median age: 36.0 (2010); Males per 100 females: 96.9 (2010); Marriage status: 11.5% never married, 55.8% now married, 12.6% widowed, 20.1% divorced (2006-2010 5-year est.); Foreign born: 0.0% (2006-2010 5-year est.); Ancestry (includes multiple ancestries): 51.0% Irish, 29.4% French, 11.9% Italian, 11.0% Dutch, 6.3% English (2006-2010 5-year est.).
**Economy:** Employment by occupation: 11.0% management, 0.0% professional, 6.5% services, 5.1% sales, 0.0% farming, 18.8% construction, 17.8% production (2006-2010 5-year est.).
**Income:** Per capita income: $26,352 (2006-2010 5-year est.); Median household income: $37,755 (2006-2010 5-year est.); Average household income: $48,858 (2006-2010 5-year est.); Percent of households with income of $100,000 or more: 22.4% (2006-2010 5-year est.); Poverty rate: 25.7% (2006-2010 5-year est.).
**Education:** Percent of population age 25 and over with: High school diploma (including GED) or higher: 85.6% (2006-2010 5-year est.); Bachelor's degree or higher: 19.1% (2006-2010 5-year est.); Master's degree or higher: 5.1% (2006-2010 5-year est.).
**Housing:** Homeownership rate: 74.8% (2010); Median home value: $139,300 (2006-2010 5-year est.); Median contract rent: $395 per month (2006-2010 5-year est.); Median year structure built: 1941 (2006-2010 5-year est.).
**Transportation:** Commute to work: 82.2% car, 0.0% public transportation, 17.8% walk, 0.0% work from home (2006-2010 5-year est.); Travel time to work: 22.6% less than 15 minutes, 58.6% 15 to 30 minutes, 13.0% 30 to 45 minutes, 0.0% 45 to 60 minutes, 5.8% 60 minutes or more (2006-2010 5-year est.)

# Saratoga County

Located in eastern New York, partly in the Adirondacks; bounded on the east by the Hudson River, and on the south by the Mohawk River; includes Saratoga Lake. Covers a land area of 811.84 square miles, a water area of 31.87 square miles, and is located in the Eastern Time Zone at 43.03° N. Lat., 73.80° W. Long. The county was founded in 1791. County seat is Ballston Spa.

Saratoga County is part of the Albany-Schenectady-Troy, NY Metropolitan Statistical Area. The entire metro area includes: Albany County, NY; Rensselaer County, NY; Saratoga County, NY; Schenectady County, NY; Schoharie County, NY

**Weather Station: Conklingville Dam**  Elevation: 808 feet

|        | Jan | Feb | Mar | Apr | May | Jun | Jul | Aug | Sep | Oct | Nov | Dec |
|--------|-----|-----|-----|-----|-----|-----|-----|-----|-----|-----|-----|-----|
| High   | 29  | 33  | 41  | 54  | 66  | 74  | 78  | 77  | 69  | 58  | 46  | 33  |
| Low    | 9   | 12  | 21  | 33  | 45  | 54  | 58  | 57  | 49  | 38  | 30  | 17  |
| Precip | 3.4 | 2.8 | 4.0 | 3.7 | 4.1 | 4.1 | 4.2 | 4.0 | 3.8 | 3.7 | 3.8 | 3.8 |
| Snow   | 19.9| 13.8| 13.8| 2.6 | tr  | 0.0 | 0.0 | 0.0 | 0.0 | 0.1 | 3.7 | 16.5|

*High and Low temperatures in degrees Fahrenheit; Precipitation and Snow in inches*

**Weather Station: Saratoga Springs 4 SW**  Elevation: 310 feet

|        | Jan | Feb | Mar | Apr | May | Jun | Jul | Aug | Sep | Oct | Nov | Dec |
|--------|-----|-----|-----|-----|-----|-----|-----|-----|-----|-----|-----|-----|
| High   | 31  | 35  | 45  | 60  | 72  | 80  | 83  | 82  | 74  | 61  | 48  | 36  |
| Low    | 12  | 15  | 24  | 35  | 46  | 55  | 60  | 58  | 50  | 39  | 30  | 19  |
| Precip | 3.2 | 2.5 | 3.5 | 3.7 | 4.1 | 4.3 | 4.3 | 4.1 | 3.7 | 3.8 | 3.8 | 3.6 |
| Snow   | 19.1| 12.6| 11.6| 2.3 | tr  | 0.0 | 0.0 | 0.0 | tr  | 0.1 | 3.1 | 14.2|

*High and Low temperatures in degrees Fahrenheit; Precipitation and Snow in inches*

**Population:** 181,276 (1990); 200,635 (2000); 219,607 (2010); Race: 94.3% White, 1.5% Black, 1.8% Asian, 0.2% American Indian/Alaska Native, 0.0% Native Hawaiian/Other Pacific Islander, 2.2% Other, 2.4% Hispanic of any race (2010); Density: 270.5 persons per square mile (2010); Average household size: 2.44 (2010); Median age: 40.9 (2010); Males per 100 females: 96.9 (2010).
**Religion:** Six largest groups: 23.9% Catholicism, 4.1% Methodist/Pietist, 3.1% Non-Denominational, 1.9% Episcopalianism/Anglicanism, 1.2% Lutheran, 1.2% Presbyterian-Reformed (2010)
**Economy:** Unemployment rate: 7.6% (February 2012); Total civilian labor force: 116,150 (February 2012); Leading industries: 18.5% retail trade; 12.8% health care and social assistance; 11.4% accommodation & food services (2009); Farms: 641 totaling 75,660 acres (2007); Companies that employ 500 or more persons: 13 (2009); Companies that employ 100 to 499 persons: 62 (2009); Companies that employ less than 100 persons: 4,844 (2009); Black-owned businesses: 193 (2007); Hispanic-owned businesses: n/a (2007); Asian-owned businesses: n/a (2007); Women-owned businesses: 5,377 (2007); Retail sales per capita: $13,153 (2010). Single-family building permits issued: 456 (2011); Multi-family building permits issued: 642 (2011).
**Income:** Per capita income: $32,186 (2006-2010 5-year est.); Median household income: $65,100 (2006-2010 5-year est.); Average household income: $79,681 (2006-2010 5-year est.); Percent of households with income of $100,000 or more: 27.0% (2006-2010 5-year est.); Poverty rate: 6.4% (2006-2010 5-year est.); Bankruptcy rate: 3.57% (2011).
**Taxes:** Total county taxes per capita: $702 (2009); County property taxes per capita: $217 (2009).
**Education:** Percent of population age 25 and over with: High school diploma (including GED) or higher: 91.8% (2006-2010 5-year est.); Bachelor's degree or higher: 34.6% (2006-2010 5-year est.); Master's degree or higher: 14.8% (2006-2010 5-year est.).
**Housing:** Homeownership rate: 72.7% (2010); Median home value: $221,100 (2006-2010 5-year est.); Median contract rent: $726 per month (2006-2010 5-year est.); Median year structure built: 1977 (2006-2010 5-year est.)
**Health:** Birth rate: 97.1 per 10,000 population (2011); Death rate: 76.3 per 10,000 population (2011); Age-adjusted cancer mortality rate: 197.1 deaths per 100,000 population (2009); Number of physicians: 21.0 per 10,000 population (2008); Hospital beds: 13.7 per 10,000 population (2007); Hospital admissions: 483.8 per 10,000 population (2007).
**Environment:** Air Quality Index: 94.2% good, 5.8% moderate, 0.0% unhealthy for sensitive individuals, 0.0% unhealthy (percent of days in 2010)
**Elections:** 2008 Presidential election results: 50.9% Obama, 47.5% McCain, 0.9% Nader
**National and State Parks:** Moreau Lake State Park; New York State Game Management Area; Peebles Island State Park; Saratoga National Historical Park; Saratoga Spa State Park
**Additional Information Contacts**
Saratoga County Government . . . . . . . . . . . . . . . . . . . . (518) 885-2213
  http://www.co.saratoga.ny.us
Chamber of Southern Saratoga County. . . . . . . . . . . . . (518) 371-7748
  http://www.southernsaratoga.org
City of Mechanicville . . . . . . . . . . . . . . . . . . . . . . . . (518) 664-8331
  http://www.mechanicville.com
City of Saratoga Springs . . . . . . . . . . . . . . . . . . . . . (518) 587-3550
  http://www.saratoga-springs.org
Mechanicville-Stillwater Chamber of Commerce . . . . . . . (518) 664-8322
  http://mechanicvillestillwaterchamber.com

Saratoga County Chamber of Commerce . . . . . . . . . . . . (518) 584-3255
  http://www.saratoga.org
Town of Ballston . . . . . . . . . . . . . . . . . . . . . . . . . . . (518) 885-8502
  http://www.townofballstonny.org
Town of Charlton . . . . . . . . . . . . . . . . . . . . . . . . . . . (518) 384-0152
  http://www.townofcharlton.org
Town of Clifton Park. . . . . . . . . . . . . . . . . . . . . . . . . (518) 371-6651
  http://www.cliftonpark.org
Town of Corinth . . . . . . . . . . . . . . . . . . . . . . . . . . . . (518) 654-9232
  http://townofcorinthny.com
Town of Edinburg . . . . . . . . . . . . . . . . . . . . . . . . . . . (518) 863-2034
  http://www.edinburgny.com
Town of Greenfield. . . . . . . . . . . . . . . . . . . . . . . . . . (518) 893-7432
  http://www.townofgreenfield.com
Town of Hadley . . . . . . . . . . . . . . . . . . . . . . . . . . . . (518) 696-3112
  http://www.townofhadley.org
Town of Halfmoon . . . . . . . . . . . . . . . . . . . . . . . . . . (518) 371-2592
  http://www.townofhalfmoon.org
Town of Malta . . . . . . . . . . . . . . . . . . . . . . . . . . . . . (518) 899-2552
  http://www.malta-town.org
Town of Milton . . . . . . . . . . . . . . . . . . . . . . . . . . . . . (518) 885-9220
  http://www.townofmiltonny.org
Town of Wilton . . . . . . . . . . . . . . . . . . . . . . . . . . . . (518) 587-1939
  http://www.townofwilton.com
Village of Round Lake . . . . . . . . . . . . . . . . . . . . . . . (518) 899-2800
  http://www.roundlakevillage.org
Village of Waterford . . . . . . . . . . . . . . . . . . . . . . . . . (518) 235-9898
  http://www.waterfordny.org

## Saratoga County Communities

**BALLSTON** (town). Covers a land area of 29.575 square miles and a water area of 0.462 square miles. Located at 42.95° N. Lat; 73.88° W. Long.
**Population:** 8,078 (1990); 8,729 (2000); 9,776 (2010); Density: 330.5 persons per square mile (2010); Race: 96.1% White, 1.1% Black, 1.0% Asian, 0.2% American Indian/Alaska Native, 0.0% Native Hawaiian/Other Pacific Islander, 1.6% Other, 1.9% Hispanic of any race (2010); Average household size: 2.55 (2010); Median age: 42.7 (2010); Males per 100 females: 91.5 (2010); Marriage status: 25.0% never married, 54.5% now married, 12.4% widowed, 8.1% divorced (2006-2010 5-year est.); Foreign born: 2.8% (2006-2010 5-year est.); Ancestry (includes multiple ancestries): 24.6% Irish, 19.8% German, 14.4% Italian, 13.3% English, 10.7% French (2006-2010 5-year est.).
**Economy:** Single-family building permits issued: 46 (2011); Multi-family building permits issued: 0 (2011); Employment by occupation: 11.7% management, 9.3% professional, 9.0% services, 15.3% sales, 3.3% farming, 10.6% construction, 6.9% production (2006-2010 5-year est.).
**Income:** Per capita income: $28,420 (2006-2010 5-year est.); Median household income: $72,969 (2006-2010 5-year est.); Average household income: $79,285 (2006-2010 5-year est.); Percent of households with income of $100,000 or more: 32.4% (2006-2010 5-year est.); Poverty rate: 9.5% (2006-2010 5-year est.).
**Education:** Percent of population age 25 and over with: High school diploma (including GED) or higher: 89.7% (2006-2010 5-year est.); Bachelor's degree or higher: 31.9% (2006-2010 5-year est.); Master's degree or higher: 14.4% (2006-2010 5-year est.).
**Housing:** Homeownership rate: 78.5% (2010); Median home value: $238,300 (2006-2010 5-year est.); Median contract rent: $636 per month (2006-2010 5-year est.); Median year structure built: 1965 (2006-2010 5-year est.).
**Transportation:** Commute to work: 86.2% car, 2.7% public transportation, 3.9% walk, 5.4% work from home (2006-2010 5-year est.); Travel time to work: 24.7% less than 15 minutes, 38.4% 15 to 30 minutes, 23.2% 30 to 45 minutes, 6.9% 45 to 60 minutes, 6.8% 60 minutes or more (2006-2010 5-year est.)
**Additional Information Contacts**
Town of Ballston . . . . . . . . . . . . . . . . . . . . . . . . . . . (518) 885-8502
  http://www.townofballstonny.org

**BALLSTON LAKE** (unincorporated postal area)
Zip Code: 12019
  Covers a land area of 29.500 square miles and a water area of 0.493 square miles. Located at 42.93° N. Lat; 73.88° W. Long. Elevation is 266 feet. Population: 14,740 (2010); Density: 499.7 persons per square mile

(2010); Race: 96.1% White, 0.8% Black, 1.4% Asian, 0.1% American Indian/Alaska Native, 0.0% Native Hawaiian/Other Pacific Islander, 1.6% Other, 2.0% Hispanic of any race (2010); Average household size: 2.57 (2010); Median age: 43.1 (2010); Males per 100 females: 98.9 (2010); Homeownership rate: 78.9% (2010)

**BALLSTON SPA** (village). County seat. Covers a land area of 1.598 square miles and a water area of 0.009 square miles. Located at 43.00° N. Lat; 73.85° W. Long. Elevation is 315 feet.
**History:** Formerly a popular resort. Settled 1771, incorporated 1807.
**Population:** 4,893 (1990); 5,556 (2000); 5,409 (2010); Density: 3,383.8 persons per square mile (2010); Race: 93.9% White, 1.2% Black, 1.0% Asian, 0.2% American Indian/Alaska Native, 0.1% Native Hawaiian/Other Pacific Islander, 3.6% Other, 3.2% Hispanic of any race (2010); Average household size: 2.25 (2010); Median age: 39.3 (2010); Males per 100 females: 94.2 (2010); Marriage status: 40.7% never married, 35.4% now married, 15.8% widowed, 8.2% divorced (2006-2010 5-year est.); Foreign born: 1.5% (2006-2010 5-year est.); Ancestry (includes multiple ancestries): 31.6% Irish, 14.9% French, 14.8% Italian, 13.3% German, 11.4% English (2006-2010 5-year est.).
**Economy:** Single-family building permits issued: 2 (2011); Multi-family building permits issued: 16 (2011); Employment by occupation: 6.2% management, 2.7% professional, 15.0% services, 13.5% sales, 4.0% farming, 7.6% construction, 7.5% production (2006-2010 5-year est.).
**Income:** Per capita income: $23,365 (2006-2010 5-year est.); Median household income: $42,010 (2006-2010 5-year est.); Average household income: $55,228 (2006-2010 5-year est.); Percent of households with income of $100,000 or more: 12.9% (2006-2010 5-year est.); Poverty rate: 11.0% (2006-2010 5-year est.).
**Education:** Percent of population age 25 and over with: High school diploma (including GED) or higher: 81.1% (2006-2010 5-year est.); Bachelor's degree or higher: 20.3% (2006-2010 5-year est.); Master's degree or higher: 8.0% (2006-2010 5-year est.).
**School District(s)**
Ballston Spa Central School District (KG-12)
  2009-10 Enrollment: 4,300 . . . . . . . . . . . . . . . . . (518) 884-7195
**Vocational/Technical School(s)**
John Paolo's Xtreme Beauty Institute/Goldwell Product Artistry (Private, For-profit)
  Fall 2010 Enrollment: 51 . . . . . . . . . . . . . . . . . . (518) 583-3700
  2011-12 Tuition: $12,400
**Housing:** Homeownership rate: 53.5% (2010); Median home value: $189,700 (2006-2010 5-year est.); Median contract rent: $675 per month (2006-2010 5-year est.); Median year structure built: before 1940 (2006-2010 5-year est.).
**Safety:** Violent crime rate: 14.7 per 10,000 population; Property crime rate: 264.5 per 10,000 population (2010).
**Newspapers:** Daily Gazette - Ballston Spa Bureau (Local news; Circulation 50,000); Malta Messenger (Community news; Circulation 6,685)
**Transportation:** Commute to work: 87.3% car, 2.0% public transportation, 8.9% walk, 1.2% work from home (2006-2010 5-year est.); Travel time to work: 30.4% less than 15 minutes, 42.6% 15 to 30 minutes, 19.0% 30 to 45 minutes, 4.7% 45 to 60 minutes, 3.3% 60 minutes or more (2006-2010 5-year est.)

**BURNT HILLS** (unincorporated postal area)
Zip Code: 12027
  Covers a land area of 7.171 square miles and a water area of 0.022 square miles. Located at 42.93° N. Lat; 73.90° W. Long. Elevation is 407 feet. Population: 3,882 (2010); Density: 541.3 persons per square mile (2010); Race: 98.0% White, 0.3% Black, 0.7% Asian, 0.3% American Indian/Alaska Native, 0.0% Native Hawaiian/Other Pacific Islander, 0.7% Other, 1.3% Hispanic of any race (2010); Average household size: 2.60 (2010); Median age: 44.4 (2010); Males per 100 females: 91.4 (2010); Homeownership rate: 87.0% (2010)

**CHARLTON** (town). Covers a land area of 32.773 square miles and a water area of 0.188 square miles. Located at 42.95° N. Lat; 73.99° W. Long. Elevation is 495 feet.
**Population:** 3,984 (1990); 3,954 (2000); 4,133 (2010); Density: 126.1 persons per square mile (2010); Race: 97.8% White, 0.3% Black, 0.5% Asian, 0.1% American Indian/Alaska Native, 0.0% Native Hawaiian/Other Pacific Islander, 1.3% Other, 1.6% Hispanic of any race (2010); Average household size: 2.62 (2010); Median age: 47.1 (2010); Males per 100 females: 96.5 (2010); Marriage status: 22.3% never married, 65.4% now

married, 5.7% widowed, 6.6% divorced (2006-2010 5-year est.); Foreign born: 2.8% (2006-2010 5-year est.); Ancestry (includes multiple ancestries): 21.5% Irish, 17.6% German, 15.9% Italian, 11.4% Polish, 11.4% English (2006-2010 5-year est.).

**Economy:** Single-family building permits issued: 3 (2011); Multi-family building permits issued: 0 (2011); Employment by occupation: 14.3% management, 5.5% professional, 9.6% services, 22.2% sales, 3.1% farming, 7.5% construction, 3.5% production (2006-2010 5-year est.).

**Income:** Per capita income: $36,862 (2006-2010 5-year est.); Median household income: $77,197 (2006-2010 5-year est.); Average household income: $87,364 (2006-2010 5-year est.); Percent of households with income of $100,000 or more: 32.7% (2006-2010 5-year est.); Poverty rate: 2.1% (2006-2010 5-year est.).

**Education:** Percent of population age 25 and over with: High school diploma (including GED) or higher: 94.7% (2006-2010 5-year est.); Bachelor's degree or higher: 39.1% (2006-2010 5-year est.); Master's degree or higher: 15.4% (2006-2010 5-year est.).

**Housing:** Homeownership rate: 95.9% (2010); Median home value: $250,300 (2006-2010 5-year est.); Median contract rent: $623 per month (2006-2010 5-year est.); Median year structure built: 1964 (2006-2010 5-year est.).

**Transportation:** Commute to work: 95.3% car, 0.5% public transportation, 0.6% walk, 3.6% work from home (2006-2010 5-year est.); Travel time to work: 21.6% less than 15 minutes, 46.8% 15 to 30 minutes, 18.9% 30 to 45 minutes, 7.0% 45 to 60 minutes, 5.6% 60 minutes or more (2006-2010 5-year est.)

**Additional Information Contacts**

Town of Charlton . . . . . . . . . . . . . . . . . . . . . . . . . . (518) 384-0152
  http://www.townofcharlton.org

## CLIFTON PARK (town).
Covers a land area of 48.202 square miles and a water area of 2.004 square miles. Located at 42.85° N. Lat; 73.82° W. Long. Elevation is 344 feet.

**Population:** 30,117 (1990); 32,995 (2000); 36,705 (2010); Density: 761.5 persons per square mile (2010); Race: 91.0% White, 1.9% Black, 4.6% Asian, 0.1% American Indian/Alaska Native, 0.0% Native Hawaiian/Other Pacific Islander, 2.4% Other, 2.7% Hispanic of any race (2010); Average household size: 2.59 (2010); Median age: 42.1 (2010); Males per 100 females: 95.2 (2010); Marriage status: 22.8% never married, 64.2% now married, 4.5% widowed, 8.5% divorced (2006-2010 5-year est.); Foreign born: 8.5% (2006-2010 5-year est.); Ancestry (includes multiple ancestries): 25.4% Irish, 20.8% Italian, 19.7% German, 13.7% English, 8.7% Polish (2006-2010 5-year est.).

**Economy:** Unemployment rate: 6.1% (February 2012); Total civilian labor force: 20,192 (February 2012); Single-family building permits issued: 57 (2011); Multi-family building permits issued: 0 (2011); Employment by occupation: 17.2% management, 8.9% professional, 7.4% services, 14.1% sales, 3.4% farming, 4.1% construction, 2.1% production (2006-2010 5-year est.).

**Income:** Per capita income: $38,846 (2006-2010 5-year est.); Median household income: $87,747 (2006-2010 5-year est.); Average household income: $103,105 (2006-2010 5-year est.); Percent of households with income of $100,000 or more: 42.2% (2006-2010 5-year est.); Poverty rate: 2.7% (2006-2010 5-year est.).

**Taxes:** Total city taxes per capita: $130 (2009); City property taxes per capita: $79 (2009).

**Education:** Percent of population age 25 and over with: High school diploma (including GED) or higher: 96.2% (2006-2010 5-year est.); Bachelor's degree or higher: 51.8% (2006-2010 5-year est.); Master's degree or higher: 23.1% (2006-2010 5-year est.).

### School District(s)

Shenendehowa Central School District (KG-12)
  2009-10 Enrollment: 9,854 . . . . . . . . . . . . . . . . . . . . . . . (518) 881-0610

**Housing:** Homeownership rate: 82.2% (2010); Median home value: $274,400 (2006-2010 5-year est.); Median contract rent: $881 per month (2006-2010 5-year est.); Median year structure built: 1979 (2006-2010 5-year est.).

**Newspapers:** Community News (Community news; Circulation 28,500); Daily Gazette - Clifton Park Bureau (Local news)

**Transportation:** Commute to work: 93.2% car, 0.6% public transportation, 0.7% walk, 4.6% work from home (2006-2010 5-year est.); Travel time to work: 23.9% less than 15 minutes, 43.6% 15 to 30 minutes, 24.6% 30 to 45 minutes, 3.9% 45 to 60 minutes, 4.0% 60 minutes or more (2006-2010 5-year est.)

**Additional Information Contacts**

Chamber of Southern Saratoga County . . . . . . . . . . . . . (518) 371-7748
  http://www.southernsaratoga.org
Town of Clifton Park . . . . . . . . . . . . . . . . . . . . . . . . (518) 371-6651
  http://www.cliftonpark.org

## CORINTH (village).
Covers a land area of 1.066 square miles and a water area of 0.039 square miles. Located at 43.24° N. Lat; 73.83° W. Long. Elevation is 610 feet.

**Population:** 2,760 (1990); 2,474 (2000); 2,559 (2010); Density: 2,399.1 persons per square mile (2010); Race: 96.1% White, 0.5% Black, 0.7% Asian, 0.2% American Indian/Alaska Native, 0.1% Native Hawaiian/Other Pacific Islander, 2.4% Other, 1.3% Hispanic of any race (2010); Average household size: 2.49 (2010); Median age: 37.2 (2010); Males per 100 females: 93.3 (2010); Marriage status: 32.1% never married, 48.1% now married, 7.2% widowed, 12.7% divorced (2006-2010 5-year est.); Foreign born: 2.1% (2006-2010 5-year est.); Ancestry (includes multiple ancestries): 17.3% American, 16.8% English, 12.9% Irish, 11.4% German, 9.9% Italian (2006-2010 5-year est.).

**Economy:** Single-family building permits issued: 0 (2011); Multi-family building permits issued: 0 (2011); Employment by occupation: 8.2% management, 3.4% professional, 7.6% services, 18.8% sales, 3.8% farming, 12.8% construction, 5.7% production (2006-2010 5-year est.).

**Income:** Per capita income: $22,911 (2006-2010 5-year est.); Median household income: $47,835 (2006-2010 5-year est.); Average household income: $54,367 (2006-2010 5-year est.); Percent of households with income of $100,000 or more: 9.9% (2006-2010 5-year est.); Poverty rate: 13.5% (2006-2010 5-year est.).

**Taxes:** Total city taxes per capita: $640 (2009); City property taxes per capita: $597 (2009).

**Education:** Percent of population age 25 and over with: High school diploma (including GED) or higher: 90.7% (2006-2010 5-year est.); Bachelor's degree or higher: 18.2% (2006-2010 5-year est.); Master's degree or higher: 5.7% (2006-2010 5-year est.).

### School District(s)

Corinth Central School District (PK-12)
  2009-10 Enrollment: 1,280 . . . . . . . . . . . . . . . . . . . . . (518) 654-2601

**Housing:** Homeownership rate: 60.1% (2010); Median home value: $122,400 (2006-2010 5-year est.); Median contract rent: $607 per month (2006-2010 5-year est.); Median year structure built: before 1940 (2006-2010 5-year est.).

**Newspapers:** Pennysaver News (Community news; Circulation 13,000)

**Transportation:** Commute to work: 83.3% car, 0.0% public transportation, 6.3% walk, 6.8% work from home (2006-2010 5-year est.); Travel time to work: 24.5% less than 15 minutes, 35.8% 15 to 30 minutes, 31.4% 30 to 45 minutes, 4.8% 45 to 60 minutes, 3.5% 60 minutes or more (2006-2010 5-year est.)

## CORINTH (town).
Covers a land area of 56.763 square miles and a water area of 1.372 square miles. Located at 43.22° N. Lat; 73.92° W. Long. Elevation is 610 feet.

**History:** Incorporated 1886.

**Population:** 5,923 (1990); 5,985 (2000); 6,531 (2010); Density: 115.1 persons per square mile (2010); Race: 97.0% White, 0.4% Black, 0.4% Asian, 0.2% American Indian/Alaska Native, 0.1% Native Hawaiian/Other Pacific Islander, 1.9% Other, 1.2% Hispanic of any race (2010); Average household size: 2.56 (2010); Median age: 39.7 (2010); Males per 100 females: 96.5 (2010); Marriage status: 30.6% never married, 52.3% now married, 6.9% widowed, 10.2% divorced (2006-2010 5-year est.); Foreign born: 1.6% (2006-2010 5-year est.); Ancestry (includes multiple ancestries): 23.9% American, 16.4% English, 11.4% French, 10.3% Irish, 9.5% German (2006-2010 5-year est.).

**Economy:** Single-family building permits issued: 9 (2011); Multi-family building permits issued: 0 (2011); Employment by occupation: 6.3% management, 2.7% professional, 14.4% services, 17.6% sales, 2.8% farming, 14.4% construction, 8.7% production (2006-2010 5-year est.).

**Income:** Per capita income: $21,881 (2006-2010 5-year est.); Median household income: $49,390 (2006-2010 5-year est.); Average household income: $56,403 (2006-2010 5-year est.); Percent of households with income of $100,000 or more: 12.0% (2006-2010 5-year est.); Poverty rate: 14.6% (2006-2010 5-year est.).

**Taxes:** Total city taxes per capita: $209 (2009); City property taxes per capita: $182 (2009).

**Education:** Percent of population age 25 and over with: High school diploma (including GED) or higher: 84.9% (2006-2010 5-year est.);

Bachelor's degree or higher: 15.5% (2006-2010 5-year est.); Master's degree or higher: 3.4% (2006-2010 5-year est.).

Corinth Central School District (PK-12)

2009-10 Enrollment: 1,280 . . . . . . . . . . . . . . . . . . . .(518) 654-2601

**Housing:** Homeownership rate: 75.6% (2010); Median home value: $128,300 (2006-2010 5-year est.); Median contract rent: $652 per month (2006-2010 5-year est.); Median year structure built: 1957 (2006-2010 5-year est.).

**Newspapers:** Pennysaver News (Community news; Circulation 13,000)

**Transportation:** Commute to work: 89.0% car, 0.0% public transportation, 2.4% walk, 5.7% work from home (2006-2010 5-year est.); Travel time to work: 19.0% less than 15 minutes, 38.7% 15 to 30 minutes, 31.8% 30 to 45 minutes, 6.0% 45 to 60 minutes, 4.4% 60 minutes or more (2006-2010 5-year est.)

**Additional Information Contacts**

Town of Corinth . . . . . . . . . . . . . . . . . . . . . . . . . . . . . . . . . (518) 654-9232
  http://townofcorinthny.com

**COUNTRY KNOLLS** (CDP). Covers a land area of 1.581 square miles and a water area of <.001 square miles. Located at 42.91° N. Lat; 73.80° W. Long. Elevation is 282 feet.

**Population:** 2,287 (1990); 2,155 (2000); 2,224 (2010); Density: 1,405.8 persons per square mile (2010); Race: 95.2% White, 0.6% Black, 2.0% Asian, 0.0% American Indian/Alaska Native, 0.0% Native Hawaiian/Other Pacific Islander, 2.2% Other, 2.5% Hispanic of any race (2010); Average household size: 2.86 (2010); Median age: 44.0 (2010); Males per 100 females: 100.0 (2010); Marriage status: 13.7% never married, 78.4% now married, 2.9% widowed, 5.0% divorced (2006-2010 5-year est.); Foreign born: 7.1% (2006-2010 5-year est.); Ancestry (includes multiple ancestries): 22.4% Irish, 20.7% Italian, 20.0% German, 12.1% English, 7.1% Polish (2006-2010 5-year est.).

**Economy:** Employment by occupation: 18.9% management, 11.4% professional, 5.9% services, 13.8% sales, 1.0% farming, 1.2% construction, 0.0% production (2006-2010 5-year est.).

**Income:** Per capita income: $39,777 (2006-2010 5-year est.); Median household income: $106,691 (2006-2010 5-year est.); Average household income: $113,835 (2006-2010 5-year est.); Percent of households with income of $100,000 or more: 61.3% (2006-2010 5-year est.); Poverty rate: 0.6% (2006-2010 5-year est.).

**Education:** Percent of population age 25 and over with: High school diploma (including GED) or higher: 95.2% (2006-2010 5-year est.); Bachelor's degree or higher: 60.0% (2006-2010 5-year est.); Master's degree or higher: 29.5% (2006-2010 5-year est.).

**Housing:** Homeownership rate: 97.5% (2010); Median home value: $276,700 (2006-2010 5-year est.); Median contract rent: n/a per month (2006-2010 5-year est.); Median year structure built: 1970 (2006-2010 5-year est.).

**Transportation:** Commute to work: 95.4% car, 0.7% public transportation, 0.0% walk, 3.9% work from home (2006-2010 5-year est.); Travel time to work: 16.7% less than 15 minutes, 44.4% 15 to 30 minutes, 29.2% 30 to 45 minutes, 5.0% 45 to 60 minutes, 4.7% 60 minutes or more (2006-2010 5-year est.)

**DAY** (town). Covers a land area of 64.112 square miles and a water area of 5.420 square miles. Located at 43.32° N. Lat; 74.02° W. Long.

**Population:** 746 (1990); 920 (2000); 856 (2010); Density: 13.4 persons per square mile (2010); Race: 96.6% White, 1.6% Black, 0.0% Asian, 0.0% American Indian/Alaska Native, 0.0% Native Hawaiian/Other Pacific Islander, 1.8% Other, 1.6% Hispanic of any race (2010); Average household size: 2.40 (2010); Median age: 49.2 (2010); Males per 100 females: 110.8 (2010); Marriage status: 20.6% never married, 68.4% now married, 4.5% widowed, 6.5% divorced (2006-2010 5-year est.); Foreign born: 0.9% (2006-2010 5-year est.); Ancestry (includes multiple ancestries): 18.8% Irish, 17.8% American, 14.3% English, 11.4% Italian, 10.8% German (2006-2010 5-year est.).

**Economy:** Single-family building permits issued: 2 (2011); Multi-family building permits issued: 0 (2011); Employment by occupation: 4.9% management, 2.7% professional, 18.4% services, 11.6% sales, 0.0% farming, 23.1% construction, 4.5% production (2006-2010 5-year est.).

**Income:** Per capita income: $24,128 (2006-2010 5-year est.); Median household income: $49,833 (2006-2010 5-year est.); Average household income: $56,885 (2006-2010 5-year est.); Percent of households with income of $100,000 or more: 10.7% (2006-2010 5-year est.); Poverty rate: 16.6% (2006-2010 5-year est.).

**Education:** Percent of population age 25 and over with: High school diploma (including GED) or higher: 79.8% (2006-2010 5-year est.); Bachelor's degree or higher: 18.3% (2006-2010 5-year est.); Master's degree or higher: 8.8% (2006-2010 5-year est.).

**Housing:** Homeownership rate: 90.5% (2010); Median home value: $143,800 (2006-2010 5-year est.); Median contract rent: $446 per month (2006-2010 5-year est.); Median year structure built: 1967 (2006-2010 5-year est.).

**Transportation:** Commute to work: 91.0% car, 0.0% public transportation, 0.0% walk, 7.7% work from home (2006-2010 5-year est.); Travel time to work: 20.6% less than 15 minutes, 24.2% 15 to 30 minutes, 24.2% 30 to 45 minutes, 15.2% 45 to 60 minutes, 15.7% 60 minutes or more (2006-2010 5-year est.)

**EDINBURG** (town). Covers a land area of 60.169 square miles and a water area of 6.925 square miles. Located at 43.22° N. Lat; 74.06° W. Long. Elevation is 886 feet.

**Population:** 1,041 (1990); 1,384 (2000); 1,214 (2010); Density: 20.2 persons per square mile (2010); Race: 98.8% White, 0.1% Black, 0.1% Asian, 0.2% American Indian/Alaska Native, 0.0% Native Hawaiian/Other Pacific Islander, 0.8% Other, 0.4% Hispanic of any race (2010); Average household size: 2.22 (2010); Median age: 49.2 (2010); Males per 100 females: 106.5 (2010); Marriage status: 19.9% never married, 63.7% now married, 7.9% widowed, 8.6% divorced (2006-2010 5-year est.); Foreign born: 0.4% (2006-2010 5-year est.); Ancestry (includes multiple ancestries): 24.3% American, 18.9% German, 15.7% English, 12.6% Italian, 8.5% Irish (2006-2010 5-year est.).

**Economy:** Single-family building permits issued: 10 (2011); Multi-family building permits issued: 0 (2011); Employment by occupation: 6.4% management, 2.9% professional, 15.3% services, 10.7% sales, 5.4% farming, 14.9% construction, 8.1% production (2006-2010 5-year est.).

**Income:** Per capita income: $25,192 (2006-2010 5-year est.); Median household income: $47,045 (2006-2010 5-year est.); Average household income: $55,749 (2006-2010 5-year est.); Percent of households with income of $100,000 or more: 11.3% (2006-2010 5-year est.); Poverty rate: 9.5% (2006-2010 5-year est.).

**Education:** Percent of population age 25 and over with: High school diploma (including GED) or higher: 86.4% (2006-2010 5-year est.); Bachelor's degree or higher: 17.8% (2006-2010 5-year est.); Master's degree or higher: 5.0% (2006-2010 5-year est.).

Edinburg Common School District (PK-06)

2009-10 Enrollment: 79 . . . . . . . . . . . . . . . . . . . . . . . .(518) 863-8412

**Housing:** Homeownership rate: 86.1% (2010); Median home value: $182,300 (2006-2010 5-year est.); Median contract rent: n/a per month (2006-2010 5-year est.); Median year structure built: 1973 (2006-2010 5-year est.).

**Transportation:** Commute to work: 95.3% car, 1.9% public transportation, 2.8% walk, 0.0% work from home (2006-2010 5-year est.); Travel time to work: 18.5% less than 15 minutes, 13.8% 15 to 30 minutes, 29.8% 30 to 45 minutes, 10.6% 45 to 60 minutes, 27.2% 60 minutes or more (2006-2010 5-year est.)

**Additional Information Contacts**

Town of Edinburg. . . . . . . . . . . . . . . . . . . . . . . . . . . . . . . . (518) 863-2034
  http://www.edinburgny.com

**GALWAY** (village). Covers a land area of 0.255 square miles and a water area of 0 square miles. Located at 43.01° N. Lat; 74.03° W. Long. Elevation is 830 feet.

**Population:** 151 (1990); 214 (2000); 200 (2010); Density: 781.3 persons per square mile (2010); Race: 99.5% White, 0.0% Black, 0.0% Asian, 0.0% American Indian/Alaska Native, 0.0% Native Hawaiian/Other Pacific Islander, 0.5% Other, 1.0% Hispanic of any race (2010); Average household size: 2.70 (2010); Median age: 40.5 (2010); Males per 100 females: 92.3 (2010); Marriage status: 34.5% never married, 41.4% now married, 12.6% widowed, 11.5% divorced (2006-2010 5-year est.); Foreign born: 0.0% (2006-2010 5-year est.); Ancestry (includes multiple ancestries): 30.6% English, 24.1% American, 24.1% Dutch, 18.5% Irish, 10.2% Italian (2006-2010 5-year est.).

**Economy:** Single-family building permits issued: 0 (2011); Multi-family building permits issued: 0 (2011); Employment by occupation: 15.3% management, 0.0% professional, 6.8% services, 16.9% sales, 0.0% farming, 13.6% construction, 6.8% production (2006-2010 5-year est.).

**Income:** Per capita income: $21,572 (2006-2010 5-year est.); Median household income: $40,000 (2006-2010 5-year est.); Average household

income: $45,926 (2006-2010 5-year est.); Percent of households with income of $100,000 or more: 10.0% (2006-2010 5-year est.); Poverty rate: 17.6% (2006-2010 5-year est.).

**Education:** Percent of population age 25 and over with: High school diploma (including GED) or higher: 96.1% (2006-2010 5-year est.); Bachelor's degree or higher: 21.1% (2006-2010 5-year est.); Master's degree or higher: 3.9% (2006-2010 5-year est.).

**School District(s)**

Galway Central School District (KG-12)

  2009-10 Enrollment: 1,112 . . . . . . . . . . . . . . . . . . . (518) 882-1033

**Housing:** Homeownership rate: 70.3% (2010); Median home value: $159,700 (2006-2010 5-year est.); Median contract rent: $758 per month (2006-2010 5-year est.); Median year structure built: before 1940 (2006-2010 5-year est.).

**Transportation:** Commute to work: 94.9% car, 0.0% public transportation, 0.0% walk, 5.1% work from home (2006-2010 5-year est.); Travel time to work: 0.0% less than 15 minutes, 42.9% 15 to 30 minutes, 21.4% 30 to 45 minutes, 21.4% 45 to 60 minutes, 14.3% 60 minutes or more (2006-2010 5-year est.)

**GALWAY** (town). Covers a land area of 43.824 square miles and a water area of 1.180 square miles. Located at 43.03° N. Lat; 74.03° W. Long. Elevation is 830 feet.

**Population:** 3,266 (1990); 3,589 (2000); 3,545 (2010); Density: 80.9 persons per square mile (2010); Race: 98.4% White, 0.3% Black, 0.2% Asian, 0.2% American Indian/Alaska Native, 0.0% Native Hawaiian/Other Pacific Islander, 0.9% Other, 1.3% Hispanic of any race (2010); Average household size: 2.45 (2010); Median age: 45.9 (2010); Males per 100 females: 105.3 (2010); Marriage status: 23.7% never married, 61.5% now married, 5.2% widowed, 9.6% divorced (2006-2010 5-year est.); Foreign born: 2.2% (2006-2010 5-year est.); Ancestry (includes multiple ancestries): 23.0% Irish, 22.5% German, 15.3% English, 11.9% Italian, 11.9% American (2006-2010 5-year est.).

**Economy:** Single-family building permits issued: 5 (2011); Multi-family building permits issued: 0 (2011); Employment by occupation: 15.0% management, 6.3% professional, 8.2% services, 19.7% sales, 2.9% farming, 5.8% construction, 3.7% production (2006-2010 5-year est.).

**Income:** Per capita income: $34,819 (2006-2010 5-year est.); Median household income: $72,404 (2006-2010 5-year est.); Average household income: $88,709 (2006-2010 5-year est.); Percent of households with income of $100,000 or more: 32.0% (2006-2010 5-year est.); Poverty rate: 6.9% (2006-2010 5-year est.).

**Education:** Percent of population age 25 and over with: High school diploma (including GED) or higher: 93.8% (2006-2010 5-year est.); Bachelor's degree or higher: 33.1% (2006-2010 5-year est.); Master's degree or higher: 11.7% (2006-2010 5-year est.).

**School District(s)**

Galway Central School District (KG-12)

  2009-10 Enrollment: 1,112 . . . . . . . . . . . . . . . . . . . (518) 882-1033

**Housing:** Homeownership rate: 88.7% (2010); Median home value: $214,700 (2006-2010 5-year est.); Median contract rent: $763 per month (2006-2010 5-year est.); Median year structure built: 1968 (2006-2010 5-year est.).

**Transportation:** Commute to work: 94.7% car, 0.0% public transportation, 1.3% walk, 3.6% work from home (2006-2010 5-year est.); Travel time to work: 8.9% less than 15 minutes, 34.1% 15 to 30 minutes, 37.5% 30 to 45 minutes, 12.5% 45 to 60 minutes, 7.1% 60 minutes or more (2006-2010 5-year est.)

**GANSEVOORT** (unincorporated postal area)

Zip Code: 12831

  Covers a land area of 67.168 square miles and a water area of 0.991 square miles. Located at 43.19° N. Lat; 73.69° W. Long. Elevation is 240 feet. Population: 17,416 (2010); Density: 259.3 persons per square mile (2010); Race: 94.6% White, 2.4% Black, 0.9% Asian, 0.2% American Indian/Alaska Native, 0.0% Native Hawaiian/Other Pacific Islander, 1.9% Other, 2.4% Hispanic of any race (2010); Average household size: 2.67 (2010); Median age: 39.5 (2010); Males per 100 females: 102.5 (2010); Homeownership rate: 79.3% (2010)

**GREENFIELD** (town). Covers a land area of 67.388 square miles and a water area of 0.298 square miles. Located at 43.13° N. Lat; 73.87° W. Long. Elevation is 591 feet.

**Population:** 6,338 (1990); 7,362 (2000); 7,775 (2010); Density: 115.4 persons per square mile (2010); Race: 97.0% White, 0.7% Black, 0.3%

Asian, 0.1% American Indian/Alaska Native, 0.0% Native Hawaiian/Other Pacific Islander, 1.9% Other, 1.8% Hispanic of any race (2010); Average household size: 2.53 (2010); Median age: 41.5 (2010); Males per 100 females: 98.0 (2010); Marriage status: 24.0% never married, 60.8% now married, 5.7% widowed, 9.5% divorced (2006-2010 5-year est.); Foreign born: 3.9% (2006-2010 5-year est.); Ancestry (includes multiple ancestries): 20.7% American, 18.2% Irish, 15.9% German, 13.1% English, 9.0% Italian (2006-2010 5-year est.).

**Economy:** Single-family building permits issued: 16 (2011); Multi-family building permits issued: 0 (2011); Employment by occupation: 14.2% management, 3.8% professional, 11.6% services, 13.1% sales, 2.0% farming, 15.5% construction, 7.9% production (2006-2010 5-year est.).

**Income:** Per capita income: $35,885 (2006-2010 5-year est.); Median household income: $54,076 (2006-2010 5-year est.); Average household income: $86,344 (2006-2010 5-year est.); Percent of households with income of $100,000 or more: 23.3% (2006-2010 5-year est.); Poverty rate: 5.8% (2006-2010 5-year est.).

**Education:** Percent of population age 25 and over with: High school diploma (including GED) or higher: 87.5% (2006-2010 5-year est.); Bachelor's degree or higher: 30.6% (2006-2010 5-year est.); Master's degree or higher: 12.3% (2006-2010 5-year est.).

**Housing:** Homeownership rate: 81.2% (2010); Median home value: $217,300 (2006-2010 5-year est.); Median contract rent: $844 per month (2006-2010 5-year est.); Median year structure built: 1983 (2006-2010 5-year est.).

**Transportation:** Commute to work: 94.9% car, 1.4% public transportation, 0.0% walk, 1.7% work from home (2006-2010 5-year est.); Travel time to work: 22.7% less than 15 minutes, 41.0% 15 to 30 minutes, 18.4% 30 to 45 minutes, 9.0% 45 to 60 minutes, 8.9% 60 minutes or more (2006-2010 5-year est.)

**Additional Information Contacts**

Town of Greenfield. . . . . . . . . . . . . . . . . . . . . . . . . (518) 893-7432
  http://www.townofgreenfield.com

**GREENFIELD CENTER** (unincorporated postal area)

Zip Code: 12833

  Covers a land area of 35.245 square miles and a water area of 0.152 square miles. Located at 43.15° N. Lat; 73.84° W. Long. Elevation is 686 feet. Population: 4,401 (2010); Density: 124.9 persons per square mile (2010); Race: 96.9% White, 0.7% Black, 0.3% Asian, 0.1% American Indian/Alaska Native, 0.0% Native Hawaiian/Other Pacific Islander, 2.0% Other, 1.6% Hispanic of any race (2010); Average household size: 2.57 (2010); Median age: 41.6 (2010); Males per 100 females: 100.0 (2010); Homeownership rate: 86.0% (2010)

**HADLEY** (town). Covers a land area of 39.704 square miles and a water area of 1.379 square miles. Located at 43.33° N. Lat; 73.90° W. Long. Elevation is 633 feet.

**Population:** 1,628 (1990); 1,971 (2000); 2,048 (2010); Density: 51.6 persons per square mile (2010); Race: 96.0% White, 1.0% Black, 0.3% Asian, 0.7% American Indian/Alaska Native, 0.0% Native Hawaiian/Other Pacific Islander, 2.0% Other, 2.0% Hispanic of any race (2010); Average household size: 2.51 (2010); Median age: 43.6 (2010); Males per 100 females: 99.6 (2010); Marriage status: 21.9% never married, 60.7% now married, 5.8% widowed, 11.7% divorced (2006-2010 5-year est.); Foreign born: 1.5% (2006-2010 5-year est.); Ancestry (includes multiple ancestries): 26.8% American, 14.3% Irish, 13.3% English, 13.1% German, 11.7% French (2006-2010 5-year est.).

**Economy:** Single-family building permits issued: 5 (2011); Multi-family building permits issued: 0 (2011); Employment by occupation: 5.8% management, 1.6% professional, 14.6% services, 19.2% sales, 4.5% farming, 13.4% construction, 12.3% production (2006-2010 5-year est.).

**Income:** Per capita income: $25,896 (2006-2010 5-year est.); Median household income: $44,153 (2006-2010 5-year est.); Average household income: $58,604 (2006-2010 5-year est.); Percent of households with income of $100,000 or more: 9.9% (2006-2010 5-year est.); Poverty rate: 9.8% (2006-2010 5-year est.).

**Education:** Percent of population age 25 and over with: High school diploma (including GED) or higher: 91.7% (2006-2010 5-year est.); Bachelor's degree or higher: 16.4% (2006-2010 5-year est.); Master's degree or higher: 6.4% (2006-2010 5-year est.).

**Housing:** Homeownership rate: 78.1% (2010); Median home value: $157,100 (2006-2010 5-year est.); Median contract rent: $487 per month (2006-2010 5-year est.); Median year structure built: 1973 (2006-2010 5-year est.).

**Transportation:** Commute to work: 96.5% car, 0.7% public transportation, 0.8% walk, 2.1% work from home (2006-2010 5-year est.); Travel time to work: 22.1% less than 15 minutes, 18.5% 15 to 30 minutes, 37.5% 30 to 45 minutes, 15.4% 45 to 60 minutes, 6.4% 60 minutes or more (2006-2010 5-year est.)

**Additional Information Contacts**
Town of Hadley . . . . . . . . . . . . . . . . . . . . . . . . . . . . . . . . . . . . . . . (518) 696-3112
  http://www.townofhadley.org

**HADLEY** (CDP). Covers a land area of 1.117 square miles and a water area of 0.198 square miles. Located at 43.29° N. Lat; 73.82° W. Long. Elevation is 633 feet.
**Population:** n/a (1990); n/a (2000); 1,009 (2010); Density: 903.0 persons per square mile (2010); Race: 95.6% White, 1.5% Black, 0.2% Asian, 0.9% American Indian/Alaska Native, 0.0% Native Hawaiian/Other Pacific Islander, 1.8% Other, 2.7% Hispanic of any race (2010); Average household size: 2.47 (2010); Median age: 39.8 (2010); Males per 100 females: 94.4 (2010); Marriage status: 27.8% never married, 55.4% now married, 5.0% widowed, 11.9% divorced (2006-2010 5-year est.); Foreign born: 0.7% (2006-2010 5-year est.); Ancestry (includes multiple ancestries): 29.0% American, 13.9% Irish, 11.7% English, 11.0% German, 10.6% Italian (2006-2010 5-year est.).
**Economy:** Employment by occupation: 6.9% management, 1.5% professional, 15.6% services, 16.7% sales, 5.6% farming, 9.8% construction, 14.8% production (2006-2010 5-year est.).
**Income:** Per capita income: $25,443 (2006-2010 5-year est.); Median household income: $41,678 (2006-2010 5-year est.); Average household income: $57,407 (2006-2010 5-year est.); Percent of households with income of $100,000 or more: 12.4% (2006-2010 5-year est.); Poverty rate: 12.0% (2006-2010 5-year est.).
**Education:** Percent of population age 25 and over with: High school diploma (including GED) or higher: 92.1% (2006-2010 5-year est.); Bachelor's degree or higher: 19.8% (2006-2010 5-year est.); Master's degree or higher: 5.6% (2006-2010 5-year est.).
**Housing:** Homeownership rate: 68.9% (2010); Median home value: $153,000 (2006-2010 5-year est.); Median contract rent: $494 per month (2006-2010 5-year est.); Median year structure built: 1966 (2006-2010 5-year est.).
**Transportation:** Commute to work: 94.8% car, 1.2% public transportation, 1.3% walk, 2.7% work from home (2006-2010 5-year est.); Travel time to work: 19.0% less than 15 minutes, 20.6% 15 to 30 minutes, 40.9% 30 to 45 minutes, 11.5% 45 to 60 minutes, 8.1% 60 minutes or more (2006-2010 5-year est.)

**HALFMOON** (town). Covers a land area of 32.579 square miles and a water area of 1.050 square miles. Located at 42.86° N. Lat; 73.73° W. Long. Elevation is 276 feet.
**Population:** 13,879 (1990); 18,474 (2000); 21,535 (2010); Density: 661.0 persons per square mile (2010); Race: 91.6% White, 1.9% Black, 3.3% Asian, 0.2% American Indian/Alaska Native, 0.1% Native Hawaiian/Other Pacific Islander, 2.9% Other, 2.8% Hispanic of any race (2010); Average household size: 2.32 (2010); Median age: 40.5 (2010); Males per 100 females: 95.6 (2010); Marriage status: 26.6% never married, 56.7% now married, 4.9% widowed, 11.8% divorced (2006-2010 5-year est.); Foreign born: 6.0% (2006-2010 5-year est.); Ancestry (includes multiple ancestries): 24.3% Irish, 19.2% German, 16.7% Italian, 12.5% French, 12.2% English (2006-2010 5-year est.).
**Economy:** Single-family building permits issued: 113 (2011); Multi-family building permits issued: 99 (2011); Employment by occupation: 13.3% management, 7.4% professional, 9.4% services, 17.0% sales, 4.2% farming, 6.0% construction, 4.6% production (2006-2010 5-year est.).
**Income:** Per capita income: $34,034 (2006-2010 5-year est.); Median household income: $63,501 (2006-2010 5-year est.); Average household income: $78,409 (2006-2010 5-year est.); Percent of households with income of $100,000 or more: 26.1% (2006-2010 5-year est.); Poverty rate: 6.7% (2006-2010 5-year est.).
**Taxes:** Total city taxes per capita: $197 (2009); City property taxes per capita: $136 (2009).
**Education:** Percent of population age 25 and over with: High school diploma (including GED) or higher: 91.3% (2006-2010 5-year est.); Bachelor's degree or higher: 37.5% (2006-2010 5-year est.); Master's degree or higher: 15.8% (2006-2010 5-year est.).
**Housing:** Homeownership rate: 64.2% (2010); Median home value: $214,600 (2006-2010 5-year est.); Median contract rent: $793 per month

(2006-2010 5-year est.); Median year structure built: 1985 (2006-2010 5-year est.).
**Transportation:** Commute to work: 92.9% car, 0.6% public transportation, 1.3% walk, 4.6% work from home (2006-2010 5-year est.); Travel time to work: 22.9% less than 15 minutes, 40.8% 15 to 30 minutes, 29.0% 30 to 45 minutes, 4.2% 45 to 60 minutes, 3.2% 60 minutes or more (2006-2010 5-year est.).
**Additional Information Contacts**
Town of Halfmoon . . . . . . . . . . . . . . . . . . . . . . . . . . . . . . . . . . . (518) 371-2592
  http://www.townofhalfmoon.org

**MALTA** (town). Covers a land area of 27.922 square miles and a water area of 3.532 square miles. Located at 42.98° N. Lat; 73.78° W. Long. Elevation is 341 feet.
**Population:** 11,709 (1990); 13,005 (2000); 14,765 (2010); Density: 528.8 persons per square mile (2010); Race: 95.3% White, 1.2% Black, 1.3% Asian, 0.3% American Indian/Alaska Native, 0.0% Native Hawaiian/Other Pacific Islander, 1.9% Other, 2.5% Hispanic of any race (2010); Average household size: 2.33 (2010); Median age: 40.7 (2010); Males per 100 females: 98.6 (2010); Marriage status: 30.3% never married, 53.5% now married, 5.5% widowed, 10.7% divorced (2006-2010 5-year est.); Foreign born: 5.1% (2006-2010 5-year est.); Ancestry (includes multiple ancestries): 25.5% Irish, 18.0% Italian, 16.6% German, 13.6% English, 9.7% French (2006-2010 5-year est.).
**Economy:** Single-family building permits issued: 32 (2011); Multi-family building permits issued: 0 (2011); Employment by occupation: 15.1% management, 6.3% professional, 6.0% services, 17.8% sales, 3.5% farming, 6.6% construction, 2.2% production (2006-2010 5-year est.).
**Income:** Per capita income: $34,449 (2006-2010 5-year est.); Median household income: $67,790 (2006-2010 5-year est.); Average household income: $80,506 (2006-2010 5-year est.); Percent of households with income of $100,000 or more: 28.1% (2006-2010 5-year est.); Poverty rate: 3.5% (2006-2010 5-year est.).
**Education:** Percent of population age 25 and over with: High school diploma (including GED) or higher: 93.5% (2006-2010 5-year est.); Bachelor's degree or higher: 40.3% (2006-2010 5-year est.); Master's degree or higher: 14.7% (2006-2010 5-year est.).
**Housing:** Homeownership rate: 68.3% (2010); Median home value: $223,700 (2006-2010 5-year est.); Median contract rent: $782 per month (2006-2010 5-year est.); Median year structure built: 1985 (2006-2010 5-year est.).
**Transportation:** Commute to work: 92.8% car, 0.7% public transportation, 0.4% walk, 5.3% work from home (2006-2010 5-year est.); Travel time to work: 22.1% less than 15 minutes, 38.7% 15 to 30 minutes, 25.8% 30 to 45 minutes, 9.8% 45 to 60 minutes, 3.5% 60 minutes or more (2006-2010 5-year est.).
**Additional Information Contacts**
Town of Malta . . . . . . . . . . . . . . . . . . . . . . . . . . . . . . . . . . . . . . . (518) 899-2552
  http://www.malta-town.org

**MECHANICVILLE** (city). Covers a land area of 0.840 square miles and a water area of 0.078 square miles. Located at 42.90° N. Lat; 73.68° W. Long. Elevation is 89 feet.
**History:** Settled before 1700; incorporated as village in 1859, as city in 1915.
**Population:** 5,249 (1990); 5,019 (2000); 5,196 (2010); Density: 6,181.0 persons per square mile (2010); Race: 95.3% White, 0.8% Black, 1.0% Asian, 0.2% American Indian/Alaska Native, 0.0% Native Hawaiian/Other Pacific Islander, 2.7% Other, 2.5% Hispanic of any race (2010); Average household size: 2.22 (2010); Median age: 34.7 (2010); Males per 100 females: 87.0 (2010); Marriage status: 36.5% never married, 42.1% now married, 11.1% widowed, 10.4% divorced (2006-2010 5-year est.); Foreign born: 3.0% (2006-2010 5-year est.); Ancestry (includes multiple ancestries): 35.5% Italian, 23.0% Irish, 11.9% German, 9.6% French, 9.4% English (2006-2010 5-year est.).
**Economy:** Single-family building permits issued: 1 (2011); Multi-family building permits issued: 3 (2011); Employment by occupation: 5.6% management, 2.4% professional, 10.9% services, 24.1% sales, 5.1% farming, 14.9% construction, 5.4% production (2006-2010 5-year est.).
**Income:** Per capita income: $21,178 (2006-2010 5-year est.); Median household income: $37,739 (2006-2010 5-year est.); Average household income: $46,946 (2006-2010 5-year est.); Percent of households with income of $100,000 or more: 7.9% (2006-2010 5-year est.); Poverty rate: 15.1% (2006-2010 5-year est.).

**Education:** Percent of population age 25 and over with: High school diploma (including GED) or higher: 86.2% (2006-2010 5-year est.); Bachelor's degree or higher: 12.5% (2006-2010 5-year est.); Master's degree or higher: 4.8% (2006-2010 5-year est.).

**School District(s)**

Mechanicville City School District (KG-12)

    2009-10 Enrollment: 1,390 . . . . . . . . . . . . . . . . . . . . . . . (518) 664-5727

**Housing:** Homeownership rate: 37.2% (2010); Median home value: $149,100 (2006-2010 5-year est.); Median contract rent: $598 per month (2006-2010 5-year est.); Median year structure built: before 1940 (2006-2010 5-year est.).

**Safety:** Violent crime rate: 10.4 per 10,000 population; Property crime rate: 217.5 per 10,000 population (2010).

**Newspapers:** The Express (Community news; Circulation 2,650)

**Transportation:** Commute to work: 89.6% car, 0.0% public transportation, 4.9% walk, 2.8% work from home (2006-2010 5-year est.); Travel time to work: 35.4% less than 15 minutes, 33.2% 15 to 30 minutes, 23.5% 30 to 45 minutes, 6.3% 45 to 60 minutes, 1.6% 60 minutes or more (2006-2010 5-year est.)

**Additional Information Contacts**

City of Mechanicville . . . . . . . . . . . . . . . . . . . . . . . . . . . (518) 664-8331

    http://www.mechanicville.com

Mechanicville-Stillwater Chamber of Commerce . . . . . . . . (518) 664-8322

    http://mechanicvillestillwaterchamber.com


## MIDDLE GROVE (unincorporated postal area)

Zip Code: 12850

    Covers a land area of 46.763 square miles and a water area of 0.882 square miles. Located at 43.10° N. Lat; 73.98° W. Long. Elevation is 551 feet. Population: 2,835 (2010); Density: 60.6 persons per square mile (2010); Race: 96.9% White, 0.6% Black, 0.3% Asian, 0.1% American Indian/Alaska Native, 0.0% Native Hawaiian/Other Pacific Islander, 2.1% Other, 2.5% Hispanic of any race (2010); Average household size: 2.63 (2010); Median age: 40.7 (2010); Males per 100 females: 109.2 (2010); Homeownership rate: 85.8% (2010)


## MILTON (town). Covers a land area of 35.689 square miles and a water area of 0.064 square miles. Located at 43.04° N. Lat; 73.89° W. Long. Elevation is 420 feet.

**Population:** 14,658 (1990); 17,103 (2000); 18,575 (2010); Density: 520.5 persons per square mile (2010); Race: 95.6% White, 1.0% Black, 0.7% Asian, 0.1% American Indian/Alaska Native, 0.0% Native Hawaiian/Other Pacific Islander, 2.6% Other, 2.5% Hispanic of any race (2010); Average household size: 2.54 (2010); Median age: 38.3 (2010); Males per 100 females: 100.9 (2010); Marriage status: 31.0% never married, 56.3% now married, 3.6% widowed, 9.1% divorced (2006-2010 5-year est.); Foreign born: 1.2% (2006-2010 5-year est.); Ancestry (includes multiple ancestries): 28.4% Irish, 17.8% German, 14.2% French, 14.0% Italian, 13.6% English (2006-2010 5-year est.).

**Economy:** Single-family building permits issued: 18 (2011); Multi-family building permits issued: 50 (2011); Employment by occupation: 10.3% management, 4.6% professional, 9.3% services, 18.3% sales, 4.0% farming, 9.4% construction, 5.6% production (2006-2010 5-year est.).

**Income:** Per capita income: $28,532 (2006-2010 5-year est.); Median household income: $60,184 (2006-2010 5-year est.); Average household income: $70,945 (2006-2010 5-year est.); Percent of households with income of $100,000 or more: 21.8% (2006-2010 5-year est.); Poverty rate: 7.3% (2006-2010 5-year est.).

**Education:** Percent of population age 25 and over with: High school diploma (including GED) or higher: 91.2% (2006-2010 5-year est.); Bachelor's degree or higher: 26.3% (2006-2010 5-year est.); Master's degree or higher: 10.7% (2006-2010 5-year est.).

**Housing:** Homeownership rate: 75.7% (2010); Median home value: $190,100 (2006-2010 5-year est.); Median contract rent: $691 per month (2006-2010 5-year est.); Median year structure built: 1979 (2006-2010 5-year est.).

**Transportation:** Commute to work: 93.0% car, 1.5% public transportation, 2.4% walk, 2.6% work from home (2006-2010 5-year est.); Travel time to work: 26.6% less than 15 minutes, 34.9% 15 to 30 minutes, 23.6% 30 to 45 minutes, 8.5% 45 to 60 minutes, 6.4% 60 minutes or more (2006-2010 5-year est.)

**Additional Information Contacts**

Town of Milton . . . . . . . . . . . . . . . . . . . . . . . . . . . . . . . (518) 885-9220

    http://www.townofmiltonny.org


## MILTON (CDP). Covers a land area of 1.486 square miles and a water area of 0.004 square miles. Located at 43.03° N. Lat; 73.85° W. Long. Elevation is 420 feet.

**Population:** 1,892 (1990); 2,692 (2000); 3,087 (2010); Density: 2,076.6 persons per square mile (2010); Race: 96.1% White, 1.0% Black, 1.0% Asian, 0.0% American Indian/Alaska Native, 0.1% Native Hawaiian/Other Pacific Islander, 1.8% Other, 1.5% Hispanic of any race (2010); Average household size: 2.50 (2010); Median age: 41.2 (2010); Males per 100 females: 91.4 (2010); Marriage status: 23.1% never married, 64.1% now married, 6.5% widowed, 6.3% divorced (2006-2010 5-year est.); Foreign born: 3.4% (2006-2010 5-year est.); Ancestry (includes multiple ancestries): 23.7% Irish, 18.2% American, 16.7% German, 14.3% English, 13.6% Italian (2006-2010 5-year est.).

**Economy:** Employment by occupation: 15.9% management, 6.0% professional, 6.4% services, 19.3% sales, 2.1% farming, 5.8% construction, 4.4% production (2006-2010 5-year est.).

**Income:** Per capita income: $28,940 (2006-2010 5-year est.); Median household income: $64,018 (2006-2010 5-year est.); Average household income: $69,030 (2006-2010 5-year est.); Percent of households with income of $100,000 or more: 20.2% (2006-2010 5-year est.); Poverty rate: 5.6% (2006-2010 5-year est.).

**Education:** Percent of population age 25 and over with: High school diploma (including GED) or higher: 94.0% (2006-2010 5-year est.); Bachelor's degree or higher: 25.4% (2006-2010 5-year est.); Master's degree or higher: 9.9% (2006-2010 5-year est.).

**Housing:** Homeownership rate: 85.4% (2010); Median home value: $198,300 (2006-2010 5-year est.); Median contract rent: $503 per month (2006-2010 5-year est.); Median year structure built: 1989 (2006-2010 5-year est.).

**Transportation:** Commute to work: 92.2% car, 2.6% public transportation, 0.7% walk, 1.6% work from home (2006-2010 5-year est.); Travel time to work: 32.2% less than 15 minutes, 30.3% 15 to 30 minutes, 19.0% 30 to 45 minutes, 12.3% 45 to 60 minutes, 6.2% 60 minutes or more (2006-2010 5-year est.)


## MOREAU (town). Covers a land area of 41.923 square miles and a water area of 1.657 square miles. Located at 43.24° N. Lat; 73.66° W. Long.

**Population:** 13,022 (1990); 13,826 (2000); 14,728 (2010); Density: 351.3 persons per square mile (2010); Race: 95.6% White, 2.2% Black, 0.4% Asian, 0.1% American Indian/Alaska Native, 0.0% Native Hawaiian/Other Pacific Islander, 1.7% Other, 2.2% Hispanic of any race (2010); Average household size: 2.50 (2010); Median age: 41.4 (2010); Males per 100 females: 100.2 (2010); Marriage status: 25.5% never married, 59.8% now married, 5.5% widowed, 9.1% divorced (2006-2010 5-year est.); Foreign born: 1.6% (2006-2010 5-year est.); Ancestry (includes multiple ancestries): 25.8% American, 18.2% Irish, 15.3% French, 10.7% Italian, 10.0% English (2006-2010 5-year est.).

**Economy:** Single-family building permits issued: 30 (2011); Multi-family building permits issued: 152 (2011); Employment by occupation: 7.5% management, 3.8% professional, 11.8% services, 18.1% sales, 3.9% farming, 11.0% construction, 5.7% production (2006-2010 5-year est.).

**Income:** Per capita income: $24,621 (2006-2010 5-year est.); Median household income: $56,008 (2006-2010 5-year est.); Average household income: $61,820 (2006-2010 5-year est.); Percent of households with income of $100,000 or more: 15.7% (2006-2010 5-year est.); Poverty rate: 6.7% (2006-2010 5-year est.).

**Education:** Percent of population age 25 and over with: High school diploma (including GED) or higher: 89.7% (2006-2010 5-year est.); Bachelor's degree or higher: 15.1% (2006-2010 5-year est.); Master's degree or higher: 6.7% (2006-2010 5-year est.).

**Housing:** Homeownership rate: 76.7% (2010); Median home value: $160,000 (2006-2010 5-year est.); Median contract rent: $613 per month (2006-2010 5-year est.); Median year structure built: 1974 (2006-2010 5-year est.).

**Transportation:** Commute to work: 92.9% car, 0.2% public transportation, 1.3% walk, 5.0% work from home (2006-2010 5-year est.); Travel time to work: 30.9% less than 15 minutes, 43.0% 15 to 30 minutes, 12.5% 30 to 45 minutes, 6.5% 45 to 60 minutes, 7.0% 60 minutes or more (2006-2010 5-year est.)

## NORTH BALLSTON SPA (CDP).
Covers a land area of 0.823 square miles and a water area of 0.003 square miles. Located at 43.01° N. Lat; 73.85° W. Long.
**Population:** 1,357 (1990); 1,237 (2000); 1,338 (2010); Density: 1,623.9 persons per square mile (2010); Race: 97.5% White, 0.4% Black, 0.3% Asian, 0.0% American Indian/Alaska Native, 0.1% Native Hawaiian/Other Pacific Islander, 1.7% Other, 3.7% Hispanic of any race (2010); Average household size: 2.48 (2010); Median age: 42.5 (2010); Males per 100 females: 96.8 (2010); Marriage status: 19.2% never married, 60.4% now married, 6.0% widowed, 14.4% divorced (2006-2010 5-year est.); Foreign born: 0.0% (2006-2010 5-year est.); Ancestry (includes multiple ancestries): 24.6% Irish, 22.4% French, 17.8% Italian, 15.5% English, 9.1% American (2006-2010 5-year est.).
**Economy:** Employment by occupation: 7.1% management, 10.3% professional, 2.4% services, 25.6% sales, 11.0% farming, 13.6% construction, 2.7% production (2006-2010 5-year est.).
**Income:** Per capita income: $31,197 (2006-2010 5-year est.); Median household income: $76,250 (2006-2010 5-year est.); Average household income: $76,927 (2006-2010 5-year est.); Percent of households with income of $100,000 or more: 28.6% (2006-2010 5-year est.); Poverty rate: 4.1% (2006-2010 5-year est.).
**Education:** Percent of population age 25 and over with: High school diploma (including GED) or higher: 91.4% (2006-2010 5-year est.); Bachelor's degree or higher: 23.6% (2006-2010 5-year est.); Master's degree or higher: 8.2% (2006-2010 5-year est.).
**Housing:** Homeownership rate: 84.8% (2010); Median home value: $148,700 (2006-2010 5-year est.); Median contract rent: n/a per month (2006-2010 5-year est.); Median year structure built: 1965 (2006-2010 5-year est.).
**Transportation:** Commute to work: 92.4% car, 3.9% public transportation, 1.9% walk, 1.8% work from home (2006-2010 5-year est.); Travel time to work: 29.7% less than 15 minutes, 26.9% 15 to 30 minutes, 25.0% 30 to 45 minutes, 12.5% 45 to 60 minutes, 5.9% 60 minutes or more (2006-2010 5-year est.)

## NORTHUMBERLAND (town).
Covers a land area of 32.298 square miles and a water area of 0.619 square miles. Located at 43.16° N. Lat; 73.62° W. Long. Elevation is 112 feet.
**Population:** 3,645 (1990); 4,603 (2000); 5,087 (2010); Density: 157.5 persons per square mile (2010); Race: 96.0% White, 0.9% Black, 0.6% Asian, 0.4% American Indian/Alaska Native, 0.0% Native Hawaiian/Other Pacific Islander, 2.1% Other, 2.5% Hispanic of any race (2010); Average household size: 2.83 (2010); Median age: 38.7 (2010); Males per 100 females: 103.5 (2010); Marriage status: 25.7% never married, 62.9% now married, 3.8% widowed, 7.5% divorced (2006-2010 5-year est.); Foreign born: 1.5% (2006-2010 5-year est.); Ancestry (includes multiple ancestries): 30.3% American, 18.2% Irish, 14.1% German, 9.7% English, 9.6% French (2006-2010 5-year est.).
**Economy:** Single-family building permits issued: 10 (2011); Multi-family building permits issued: 0 (2011); Employment by occupation: 13.5% management, 5.2% professional, 10.9% services, 16.5% sales, 4.0% farming, 10.7% construction, 7.8% production (2006-2010 5-year est.).
**Income:** Per capita income: $27,433 (2006-2010 5-year est.); Median household income: $61,984 (2006-2010 5-year est.); Average household income: $76,333 (2006-2010 5-year est.); Percent of households with income of $100,000 or more: 20.6% (2006-2010 5-year est.); Poverty rate: 7.5% (2006-2010 5-year est.).
**Education:** Percent of population age 25 and over with: High school diploma (including GED) or higher: 85.0% (2006-2010 5-year est.); Bachelor's degree or higher: 15.6% (2006-2010 5-year est.); Master's degree or higher: 4.4% (2006-2010 5-year est.).
**Housing:** Homeownership rate: 87.9% (2010); Median home value: $187,000 (2006-2010 5-year est.); Median contract rent: $546 per month (2006-2010 5-year est.); Median year structure built: 1984 (2006-2010 5-year est.).
**Transportation:** Commute to work: 92.9% car, 1.2% public transportation, 1.5% walk, 3.9% work from home (2006-2010 5-year est.); Travel time to work: 22.3% less than 15 minutes, 41.0% 15 to 30 minutes, 21.8% 30 to 45 minutes, 7.8% 45 to 60 minutes, 7.1% 60 minutes or more (2006-2010 5-year est.)

## PORTER CORNERS (unincorporated postal area)
Zip Code: 12859
Covers a land area of 22.017 square miles and a water area of 0.058 square miles. Located at 43.17° N. Lat; 73.92° W. Long. Elevation is 663 feet. Population: 2,220 (2010); Density: 100.8 persons per square mile (2010); Race: 97.8% White, 0.6% Black, 0.2% Asian, 0.0% American Indian/Alaska Native, 0.0% Native Hawaiian/Other Pacific Islander, 1.4% Other, 1.6% Hispanic of any race (2010); Average household size: 2.72 (2010); Median age: 39.1 (2010); Males per 100 females: 101.1 (2010); Homeownership rate: 88.0% (2010)

## PROVIDENCE (town).
Covers a land area of 43.996 square miles and a water area of 1.097 square miles. Located at 43.11° N. Lat; 74.04° W. Long.
**Population:** 1,360 (1990); 1,841 (2000); 1,995 (2010); Density: 45.3 persons per square mile (2010); Race: 97.4% White, 0.7% Black, 0.3% Asian, 0.0% American Indian/Alaska Native, 0.0% Native Hawaiian/Other Pacific Islander, 1.6% Other, 1.9% Hispanic of any race (2010); Average household size: 2.60 (2010); Median age: 42.3 (2010); Males per 100 females: 111.1 (2010); Marriage status: 28.5% never married, 59.4% now married, 4.4% widowed, 7.6% divorced (2006-2010 5-year est.); Foreign born: 1.3% (2006-2010 5-year est.); Ancestry (includes multiple ancestries): 21.0% German, 20.6% American, 20.0% Irish, 15.6% English, 11.0% French (2006-2010 5-year est.).
**Economy:** Single-family building permits issued: 9 (2011); Multi-family building permits issued: 0 (2011); Employment by occupation: 5.7% management, 5.2% professional, 10.6% services, 14.0% sales, 0.6% farming, 16.3% construction, 11.0% production (2006-2010 5-year est.).
**Income:** Per capita income: $23,173 (2006-2010 5-year est.); Median household income: $54,950 (2006-2010 5-year est.); Average household income: $60,906 (2006-2010 5-year est.); Percent of households with income of $100,000 or more: 20.1% (2006-2010 5-year est.); Poverty rate: 11.7% (2006-2010 5-year est.).
**Education:** Percent of population age 25 and over with: High school diploma (including GED) or higher: 89.5% (2006-2010 5-year est.); Bachelor's degree or higher: 16.2% (2006-2010 5-year est.); Master's degree or higher: 7.5% (2006-2010 5-year est.).
**Housing:** Homeownership rate: 89.2% (2010); Median home value: $162,900 (2006-2010 5-year est.); Median contract rent: $685 per month (2006-2010 5-year est.); Median year structure built: 1980 (2006-2010 5-year est.).
**Transportation:** Commute to work: 93.7% car, 0.0% public transportation, 1.8% walk, 4.0% work from home (2006-2010 5-year est.); Travel time to work: 10.2% less than 15 minutes, 31.6% 15 to 30 minutes, 29.3% 30 to 45 minutes, 19.3% 45 to 60 minutes, 9.6% 60 minutes or more (2006-2010 5-year est.)

## REXFORD (unincorporated postal area)
Zip Code: 12148
Covers a land area of 15.649 square miles and a water area of 1.279 square miles. Located at 42.82° N. Lat; 73.84° W. Long. Elevation is 249 feet. Population: 4,569 (2010); Density: 292.0 persons per square mile (2010); Race: 90.6% White, 1.4% Black, 5.0% Asian, 0.0% American Indian/Alaska Native, 0.0% Native Hawaiian/Other Pacific Islander, 3.0% Other, 1.5% Hispanic of any race (2010); Average household size: 2.62 (2010); Median age: 42.2 (2010); Males per 100 females: 93.2 (2010); Homeownership rate: 83.5% (2010)

## ROCK CITY FALLS (unincorporated postal area)
Zip Code: 12863
Covers a land area of 3.593 square miles and a water area of 0 square miles. Located at 43.06° N. Lat; 73.93° W. Long. Elevation is 453 feet. Population: 533 (2010); Density: 148.3 persons per square mile (2010); Race: 98.5% White, 0.2% Black, 0.0% Asian, 0.0% American Indian/Alaska Native, 0.0% Native Hawaiian/Other Pacific Islander, 1.3% Other, 1.7% Hispanic of any race (2010); Average household size: 2.42 (2010); Median age: 41.2 (2010); Males per 100 females: 98.1 (2010); Homeownership rate: 84.5% (2010)

## ROUND LAKE (village).
Covers a land area of 1.123 square miles and a water area of 0.106 square miles. Located at 42.93° N. Lat; 73.79° W. Long. Elevation is 164 feet.
**Population:** 765 (1990); 604 (2000); 623 (2010); Density: 554.7 persons per square mile (2010); Race: 94.4% White, 0.8% Black, 1.4% Asian, 0.6% American Indian/Alaska Native, 0.0% Native Hawaiian/Other Pacific Islander, 2.8% Other, 1.8% Hispanic of any race (2010); Average household size: 2.29 (2010); Median age: 45.1 (2010); Males per 100 females: 89.4 (2010); Marriage status: 17.3% never married, 64.3% now married, 5.6% widowed, 12.8% divorced (2006-2010 5-year est.); Foreign

born: 6.0% (2006-2010 5-year est.); Ancestry (includes multiple ancestries): 28.0% Irish, 24.8% Italian, 16.6% French, 15.9% English, 12.0% German (2006-2010 5-year est.).
**Economy:** Single-family building permits issued: 0 (2011); Multi-family building permits issued: 0 (2011); Employment by occupation: 14.2% management, 8.7% professional, 9.1% services, 12.3% sales, 4.3% farming, 4.7% construction, 0.0% production (2006-2010 5-year est.).
**Income:** Per capita income: $35,463 (2006-2010 5-year est.); Median household income: $74,250 (2006-2010 5-year est.); Average household income: $75,391 (2006-2010 5-year est.); Percent of households with income of $100,000 or more: 28.7% (2006-2010 5-year est.); Poverty rate: 5.5% (2006-2010 5-year est.).
**Education:** Percent of population age 25 and over with: High school diploma (including GED) or higher: 97.5% (2006-2010 5-year est.); Bachelor's degree or higher: 50.5% (2006-2010 5-year est.); Master's degree or higher: 23.7% (2006-2010 5-year est.).
**Housing:** Homeownership rate: 81.6% (2010); Median home value: $192,900 (2006-2010 5-year est.); Median contract rent: $904 per month (2006-2010 5-year est.); Median year structure built: before 1940 (2006-2010 5-year est.).
**Transportation:** Commute to work: 89.6% car, 1.3% public transportation, 3.8% walk, 2.9% work from home (2006-2010 5-year est.); Travel time to work: 37.3% less than 15 minutes, 41.6% 15 to 30 minutes, 12.0% 30 to 45 minutes, 6.4% 45 to 60 minutes, 2.6% 60 minutes or more (2006-2010 5-year est.)
**Additional Information Contacts**
Village of Round Lake . . . . . . . . . . . . . . . . . . . . . . . . (518) 899-2800
  http://www.roundlakevillage.org

**SARATOGA** (town). Covers a land area of 40.561 square miles and a water area of 2.338 square miles. Located at 43.05° N. Lat; 73.65° W. Long.
**Population:** 5,069 (1990); 5,141 (2000); 5,674 (2010); Density: 139.9 persons per square mile (2010); Race: 96.9% White, 0.8% Black, 0.4% Asian, 0.2% American Indian/Alaska Native, 0.0% Native Hawaiian/Other Pacific Islander, 1.7% Other, 2.8% Hispanic of any race (2010); Average household size: 2.48 (2010); Median age: 41.4 (2010); Males per 100 females: 98.5 (2010); Marriage status: 24.9% never married, 57.7% now married, 5.5% widowed, 11.9% divorced (2006-2010 5-year est.); Foreign born: 2.6% (2006-2010 5-year est.); Ancestry (includes multiple ancestries): 21.8% American, 18.7% Irish, 12.8% French, 12.8% German, 12.2% Italian (2006-2010 5-year est.).
**Economy:** Single-family building permits issued: 8 (2011); Multi-family building permits issued: 0 (2011); Employment by occupation: 12.0% management, 3.7% professional, 11.5% services, 15.9% sales, 4.6% farming, 9.1% construction, 7.7% production (2006-2010 5-year est.).
**Income:** Per capita income: $29,138 (2006-2010 5-year est.); Median household income: $59,504 (2006-2010 5-year est.); Average household income: $73,883 (2006-2010 5-year est.); Percent of households with income of $100,000 or more: 22.9% (2006-2010 5-year est.); Poverty rate: 5.4% (2006-2010 5-year est.).
**Education:** Percent of population age 25 and over with: High school diploma (including GED) or higher: 87.4% (2006-2010 5-year est.); Bachelor's degree or higher: 27.8% (2006-2010 5-year est.); Master's degree or higher: 9.9% (2006-2010 5-year est.).
**Housing:** Homeownership rate: 76.8% (2010); Median home value: $183,300 (2006-2010 5-year est.); Median contract rent: $623 per month (2006-2010 5-year est.); Median year structure built: 1967 (2006-2010 5-year est.).
**Transportation:** Commute to work: 91.9% car, 0.1% public transportation, 2.0% walk, 4.7% work from home (2006-2010 5-year est.); Travel time to work: 21.9% less than 15 minutes, 31.8% 15 to 30 minutes, 23.5% 30 to 45 minutes, 15.0% 45 to 60 minutes, 7.8% 60 minutes or more (2006-2010 5-year est.)

**SARATOGA SPRINGS** (city). Covers a land area of 28.064 square miles and a water area of 0.807 square miles. Located at 43.06° N. Lat; 73.77° W. Long. Elevation is 299 feet.
**History:** The growth and development of Saratoga Springs has been closely associated with its mineral springs, the waters of which began to be used in 1774. Rumors of the healing powers of the water circulated. In 1789, Gideon Putnam arrived and in 1802 he erected the three-story Union Hall, a hotel for visitors. People were attracted to the spot, and Putnam was ready to sell them lots around his hotel.

**Population:** 25,001 (1990); 26,186 (2000); 26,586 (2010); Density: 947.3 persons per square mile (2010); Race: 92.3% White, 2.6% Black, 2.0% Asian, 0.2% American Indian/Alaska Native, 0.0% Native Hawaiian/Other Pacific Islander, 2.9% Other, 3.2% Hispanic of any race (2010); Average household size: 2.13 (2010); Median age: 39.8 (2010); Males per 100 females: 93.4 (2010); Marriage status: 33.3% never married, 50.5% now married, 7.0% widowed, 9.2% divorced (2006-2010 5-year est.); Foreign born: 4.3% (2006-2010 5-year est.); Ancestry (includes multiple ancestries): 27.2% Irish, 15.7% Italian, 14.9% American, 13.6% German, 12.6% English (2006-2010 5-year est.).
**Economy:** Unemployment rate: 7.1% (February 2012); Total civilian labor force: 14,136 (February 2012); Single-family building permits issued: 27 (2011); Multi-family building permits issued: 214 (2011); Employment by occupation: 15.2% management, 4.4% professional, 9.4% services, 14.4% sales, 4.0% farming, 4.1% construction, 1.3% production (2006-2010 5-year est.).
**Income:** Per capita income: $35,342 (2006-2010 5-year est.); Median household income: $61,184 (2006-2010 5-year est.); Average household income: $79,979 (2006-2010 5-year est.); Percent of households with income of $100,000 or more: 26.9% (2006-2010 5-year est.); Poverty rate: 8.1% (2006-2010 5-year est.).
**Education:** Percent of population age 25 and over with: High school diploma (including GED) or higher: 93.7% (2006-2010 5-year est.); Bachelor's degree or higher: 48.8% (2006-2010 5-year est.); Master's degree or higher: 22.9% (2006-2010 5-year est.).

**School District(s)**
Saratoga Springs City School District (KG-12)
  2009-10 Enrollment: 6,807 . . . . . . . . . . . . . . . . . (518) 583-4708
**Four-year College(s)**
SUNY Empire State College (Public)
  Fall 2010 Enrollment: 9,396 . . . . . . . . . . . . . . . . . (518) 587-2100
  2011-12 Tuition: In-state $5,545; Out-of-state $14,595
Skidmore College (Private, Not-for-profit)
  Fall 2010 Enrollment: 2,892 . . . . . . . . . . . . . . . . . (518) 580-5000
  2011-12 Tuition: In-state $42,380; Out-of-state $42,380
**Vocational/Technical School(s)**
Washington Saratoga Warren Hamilton Essex BOCES-Practical Nursing (Public)
  Fall 2010 Enrollment: 97 . . . . . . . . . . . . . . . . . . (518) 581-3550
  2011-12 Tuition: $8,950
**Housing:** Homeownership rate: 56.8% (2010); Median home value: $293,200 (2006-2010 5-year est.); Median contract rent: $727 per month (2006-2010 5-year est.); Median year structure built: 1963 (2006-2010 5-year est.).
**Hospitals:** Saratoga Care (243 beds)
**Safety:** Violent crime rate: 10.7 per 10,000 population; Property crime rate: 206.0 per 10,000 population (2010).
**Newspapers:** Daily Gazette - Saratoga Springs Bureau (Local news); The Saratogian (Local news; Circulation 12,000)
**Transportation:** Commute to work: 80.9% car, 0.9% public transportation, 7.8% walk, 7.5% work from home (2006-2010 5-year est.); Travel time to work: 43.6% less than 15 minutes, 23.6% 15 to 30 minutes, 19.1% 30 to 45 minutes, 9.8% 45 to 60 minutes, 3.8% 60 minutes or more (2006-2010 5-year est.); Amtrak: train and bus service available.
**Airports:** Saratoga County (general aviation)
**Additional Information Contacts**
City of Saratoga Springs . . . . . . . . . . . . . . . . . . . . . . (518) 587-3550
  http://www.saratoga-springs.org
Saratoga County Chamber of Commerce . . . . . . . . . . . . (518) 584-3255
  http://www.saratoga.org

**SCHUYLERVILLE** (village). Covers a land area of 0.533 square miles and a water area of 0.054 square miles. Located at 43.10° N. Lat; 73.58° W. Long. Elevation is 128 feet.
**Population:** 1,366 (1990); 1,197 (2000); 1,386 (2010); Density: 2,600.3 persons per square mile (2010); Race: 96.4% White, 1.2% Black, 0.6% Asian, 0.1% American Indian/Alaska Native, 0.0% Native Hawaiian/Other Pacific Islander, 1.7% Other, 3.3% Hispanic of any race (2010); Average household size: 2.31 (2010); Median age: 37.1 (2010); Males per 100 females: 89.3 (2010); Marriage status: 32.5% never married, 50.3% now married, 6.0% widowed, 11.2% divorced (2006-2010 5-year est.); Foreign born: 3.2% (2006-2010 5-year est.); Ancestry (includes multiple ancestries): 29.7% American, 22.7% Irish, 12.1% French, 12.1% Italian, 11.4% German (2006-2010 5-year est.).

**Economy:** Single-family building permits issued: 5 (2011); Multi-family building permits issued: 0 (2011); Employment by occupation: 9.4% management, 6.3% professional, 10.7% services, 17.2% sales, 6.7% farming, 6.9% construction, 5.9% production (2006-2010 5-year est.).
**Income:** Per capita income: $23,757 (2006-2010 5-year est.); Median household income: $55,694 (2006-2010 5-year est.); Average household income: $56,381 (2006-2010 5-year est.); Percent of households with income of $100,000 or more: 9.3% (2006-2010 5-year est.); Poverty rate: 9.3% (2006-2010 5-year est.).
**Education:** Percent of population age 25 and over with: High school diploma (including GED) or higher: 88.9% (2006-2010 5-year est.); Bachelor's degree or higher: 19.5% (2006-2010 5-year est.); Master's degree or higher: 5.7% (2006-2010 5-year est.).

**School District(s)**
Schuylerville Central School District (KG-12)
   2009-10 Enrollment: 1,794 . . . . . . . . . . . . . . . . . . . . . . (518) 695-3255
**Housing:** Homeownership rate: 57.0% (2010); Median home value: $159,000 (2006-2010 5-year est.); Median contract rent: $577 per month (2006-2010 5-year est.); Median year structure built: before 1940 (2006-2010 5-year est.).
**Transportation:** Commute to work: 94.0% car, 0.0% public transportation, 2.2% walk, 3.4% work from home (2006-2010 5-year est.); Travel time to work: 20.1% less than 15 minutes, 30.5% 15 to 30 minutes, 29.6% 30 to 45 minutes, 10.7% 45 to 60 minutes, 9.2% 60 minutes or more (2006-2010 5-year est.).

**SOUTH GLENS FALLS** (village). Covers a land area of 1.358 square miles and a water area of 0.131 square miles. Located at 43.29° N. Lat; 73.63° W. Long. Elevation is 344 feet.
**History:** Incorporated 1895.
**Population:** 3,506 (1990); 3,368 (2000); 3,518 (2010); Density: 2,589.8 persons per square mile (2010); Race: 97.1% White, 1.0% Black, 0.5% Asian, 0.1% American Indian/Alaska Native, 0.0% Native Hawaiian/Other Pacific Islander, 1.3% Other, 2.0% Hispanic of any race (2010); Average household size: 2.19 (2010); Median age: 40.4 (2010); Males per 100 females: 90.2 (2010); Marriage status: 30.8% never married, 45.0% now married, 9.9% widowed, 14.3% divorced (2006-2010 5-year est.); Foreign born: 1.8% (2006-2010 5-year est.); Ancestry (includes multiple ancestries): 24.6% American, 22.4% Irish, 15.5% German, 15.3% French, 9.6% English (2006-2010 5-year est.).
**Economy:** Employment by occupation: 7.9% management, 1.3% professional, 9.1% services, 19.9% sales, 2.4% farming, 14.8% construction, 7.9% production (2006-2010 5-year est.).
**Income:** Per capita income: $25,650 (2006-2010 5-year est.); Median household income: $48,327 (2006-2010 5-year est.); Average household income: $55,821 (2006-2010 5-year est.); Percent of households with income of $100,000 or more: 14.1% (2006-2010 5-year est.); Poverty rate: 7.1% (2006-2010 5-year est.).
**Education:** Percent of population age 25 and over with: High school diploma (including GED) or higher: 91.1% (2006-2010 5-year est.); Bachelor's degree or higher: 12.3% (2006-2010 5-year est.); Master's degree or higher: 5.1% (2006-2010 5-year est.).

**School District(s)**
South Glens Falls Central School District (KG-12)
   2009-10 Enrollment: 3,266 . . . . . . . . . . . . . . . . . . . . . (518) 793-9617
**Housing:** Homeownership rate: 54.2% (2010); Median home value: $141,300 (2006-2010 5-year est.); Median contract rent: $566 per month (2006-2010 5-year est.); Median year structure built: 1949 (2006-2010 5-year est.).
**Safety:** Violent crime rate: 23.7 per 10,000 population; Property crime rate: 252.2 per 10,000 population (2010).
**Transportation:** Commute to work: 92.6% car, 0.6% public transportation, 1.9% walk, 3.7% work from home (2006-2010 5-year est.); Travel time to work: 39.9% less than 15 minutes, 32.8% 15 to 30 minutes, 15.2% 30 to 45 minutes, 6.5% 45 to 60 minutes, 5.6% 60 minutes or more (2006-2010 5-year est.).

**STILLWATER** (village). Covers a land area of 1.258 square miles and a water area of 0.203 square miles. Located at 42.94° N. Lat; 73.64° W. Long. Elevation is 92 feet.
**Population:** 1,531 (1990); 1,644 (2000); 1,738 (2010); Density: 1,381.5 persons per square mile (2010); Race: 96.8% White, 0.4% Black, 0.3% Asian, 0.1% American Indian/Alaska Native, 0.0% Native Hawaiian/Other Pacific Islander, 2.4% Other, 2.8% Hispanic of any race (2010); Average household size: 2.56 (2010); Median age: 38.4 (2010); Males per 100

females: 93.8 (2010); Marriage status: 27.9% never married, 59.7% now married, 2.7% widowed, 9.7% divorced (2006-2010 5-year est.); Foreign born: 2.3% (2006-2010 5-year est.); Ancestry (includes multiple ancestries): 26.9% Irish, 19.5% Italian, 16.8% French, 15.9% Polish, 13.3% English (2006-2010 5-year est.).
**Economy:** Single-family building permits issued: 1 (2011); Multi-family building permits issued: 0 (2011); Employment by occupation: 11.0% management, 1.7% professional, 8.9% services, 17.6% sales, 4.8% farming, 11.4% construction, 6.9% production (2006-2010 5-year est.).
**Income:** Per capita income: $23,960 (2006-2010 5-year est.); Median household income: $61,298 (2006-2010 5-year est.); Average household income: $67,959 (2006-2010 5-year est.); Percent of households with income of $100,000 or more: 24.6% (2006-2010 5-year est.); Poverty rate: 12.2% (2006-2010 5-year est.).
**Education:** Percent of population age 25 and over with: High school diploma (including GED) or higher: 92.6% (2006-2010 5-year est.); Bachelor's degree or higher: 16.3% (2006-2010 5-year est.); Master's degree or higher: 6.7% (2006-2010 5-year est.).

**School District(s)**
Stillwater Central School District (PK-12)
   2009-10 Enrollment: 1,256 . . . . . . . . . . . . . . . . . . . . . (518) 373-6100
**Housing:** Homeownership rate: 65.8% (2010); Median home value: $178,700 (2006-2010 5-year est.); Median contract rent: $598 per month (2006-2010 5-year est.); Median year structure built: 1953 (2006-2010 5-year est.).
**Transportation:** Commute to work: 92.1% car, 0.0% public transportation, 2.1% walk, 4.9% work from home (2006-2010 5-year est.); Travel time to work: 20.9% less than 15 minutes, 30.8% 15 to 30 minutes, 27.3% 30 to 45 minutes, 14.9% 45 to 60 minutes, 6.2% 60 minutes or more (2006-2010 5-year est.).

**STILLWATER** (town). Covers a land area of 41.190 square miles and a water area of 2.383 square miles. Located at 42.96° N. Lat; 73.68° W. Long. Elevation is 92 feet.
**History:** The American Revolutionary battles (Sept. 19, 1777, and Oct. 7, 1777) fought near here are commemorated by Saratoga National Historical Park, 9 miles Southeast of Saratoga Springs.
**Population:** 7,233 (1990); 7,522 (2000); 8,287 (2010); Density: 201.2 persons per square mile (2010); Race: 97.3% White, 0.6% Black, 0.4% Asian, 0.2% American Indian/Alaska Native, 0.0% Native Hawaiian/Other Pacific Islander, 1.5% Other, 1.5% Hispanic of any race (2010); Average household size: 2.61 (2010); Median age: 41.0 (2010); Males per 100 females: 100.8 (2010); Marriage status: 24.7% never married, 63.1% now married, 4.0% widowed, 8.2% divorced (2006-2010 5-year est.); Foreign born: 2.8% (2006-2010 5-year est.); Ancestry (includes multiple ancestries): 29.1% Irish, 18.1% German, 18.1% Italian, 13.4% Polish, 10.9% English (2006-2010 5-year est.).
**Economy:** Single-family building permits issued: 15 (2011); Multi-family building permits issued: 0 (2011); Employment by occupation: 9.9% management, 7.6% professional, 7.1% services, 18.9% sales, 2.8% farming, 9.6% construction, 4.2% production (2006-2010 5-year est.).
**Income:** Per capita income: $29,417 (2006-2010 5-year est.); Median household income: $67,746 (2006-2010 5-year est.); Average household income: $77,614 (2006-2010 5-year est.); Percent of households with income of $100,000 or more: 22.3% (2006-2010 5-year est.); Poverty rate: 5.4% (2006-2010 5-year est.).
**Education:** Percent of population age 25 and over with: High school diploma (including GED) or higher: 91.9% (2006-2010 5-year est.); Bachelor's degree or higher: 21.1% (2006-2010 5-year est.); Master's degree or higher: 9.2% (2006-2010 5-year est.).

**School District(s)**
Stillwater Central School District (PK-12)
   2009-10 Enrollment: 1,256 . . . . . . . . . . . . . . . . . . . . . (518) 373-6100
**Housing:** Homeownership rate: 82.0% (2010); Median home value: $191,700 (2006-2010 5-year est.); Median contract rent: $665 per month (2006-2010 5-year est.); Median year structure built: 1975 (2006-2010 5-year est.).
**Safety:** Violent crime rate: 0.0 per 10,000 population; Property crime rate: 41.2 per 10,000 population (2010).
**Transportation:** Commute to work: 95.7% car, 0.0% public transportation, 0.6% walk, 3.4% work from home (2006-2010 5-year est.); Travel time to work: 22.9% less than 15 minutes, 28.3% 15 to 30 minutes, 27.1% 30 to 45 minutes, 16.8% 45 to 60 minutes, 4.9% 60 minutes or more (2006-2010 5-year est.).

**VICTORY** (village). Aka Victory Mills. Covers a land area of 0.525 square miles and a water area of 0 square miles. Located at 43.09° N. Lat; 73.59° W. Long. Elevation is 203 feet.
**Population:** 598 (1990); 544 (2000); 605 (2010); Density: 1,151.3 persons per square mile (2010); Race: 94.5% White, 0.5% Black, 0.0% Asian, 0.2% American Indian/Alaska Native, 0.0% Native Hawaiian/Other Pacific Islander, 4.8% Other, 2.5% Hispanic of any race (2010); Average household size: 2.71 (2010); Median age: 36.5 (2010); Males per 100 females: 101.0 (2010); Marriage status: 37.0% never married, 49.5% now married, 4.3% widowed, 9.1% divorced (2006-2010 5-year est.); Foreign born: 4.9% (2006-2010 5-year est.); Ancestry (includes multiple ancestries): 27.2% American, 21.7% Irish, 18.0% Italian, 15.7% French, 10.4% English (2006-2010 5-year est.).
**Economy:** Single-family building permits issued: 1 (2011); Multi-family building permits issued: 0 (2011); Employment by occupation: 6.6% management, 0.8% professional, 24.5% services, 10.9% sales, 6.6% farming, 12.5% construction, 4.7% production (2006-2010 5-year est.).
**Income:** Per capita income: $20,494 (2006-2010 5-year est.); Median household income: $50,417 (2006-2010 5-year est.); Average household income: $55,414 (2006-2010 5-year est.); Percent of households with income of $100,000 or more: 11.3% (2006-2010 5-year est.); Poverty rate: 9.5% (2006-2010 5-year est.).
**Education:** Percent of population age 25 and over with: High school diploma (including GED) or higher: 88.4% (2006-2010 5-year est.); Bachelor's degree or higher: 12.2% (2006-2010 5-year est.); Master's degree or higher: 5.2% (2006-2010 5-year est.).
**Housing:** Homeownership rate: 75.3% (2010); Median home value: $136,300 (2006-2010 5-year est.); Median contract rent: $638 per month (2006-2010 5-year est.); Median year structure built: before 1940 (2006-2010 5-year est.).
**Transportation:** Commute to work: 95.7% car, 0.8% public transportation, 2.7% walk, 0.8% work from home (2006-2010 5-year est.); Travel time to work: 20.4% less than 15 minutes, 34.1% 15 to 30 minutes, 26.7% 30 to 45 minutes, 14.5% 45 to 60 minutes, 4.3% 60 minutes or more (2006-2010 5-year est.)

**VICTORY MILLS** (unincorporated postal area)
Zip Code: 12884
Covers a land area of 0.498 square miles and a water area of 0 square miles. Located at 43.08° N. Lat; 73.59° W. Long. Elevation is 203 feet. Population: 486 (2010); Density: 975.7 persons per square mile (2010); Race: 94.7% White, 0.0% Black, 0.0% Asian, 0.4% American Indian/Alaska Native, 0.0% Native Hawaiian/Other Pacific Islander, 4.9% Other, 1.9% Hispanic of any race (2010); Average household size: 2.75 (2010); Median age: 38.7 (2010); Males per 100 females: 98.4 (2010); Homeownership rate: 78.0% (2010)

**WATERFORD** (village). Covers a land area of 0.282 square miles and a water area of 0.074 square miles. Located at 42.79° N. Lat; 73.67° W. Long. Elevation is 69 feet.
**Population:** 2,370 (1990); 2,204 (2000); 1,990 (2010); Density: 7,035.8 persons per square mile (2010); Race: 94.8% White, 1.7% Black, 1.5% Asian, 0.2% American Indian/Alaska Native, 0.0% Native Hawaiian/Other Pacific Islander, 1.8% Other, 2.8% Hispanic of any race (2010); Average household size: 2.07 (2010); Median age: 39.1 (2010); Males per 100 females: 97.2 (2010); Marriage status: 32.1% never married, 49.0% now married, 9.3% widowed, 9.6% divorced (2006-2010 5-year est.); Foreign born: 4.3% (2006-2010 5-year est.); Ancestry (includes multiple ancestries): 27.1% Irish, 22.0% Italian, 15.5% German, 13.3% French, 10.0% Polish (2006-2010 5-year est.).
**Economy:** Single-family building permits issued: 0 (2011); Multi-family building permits issued: 0 (2011); Employment by occupation: 9.4% management, 4.7% professional, 8.2% services, 18.6% sales, 3.6% farming, 16.7% construction, 8.5% production (2006-2010 5-year est.).
**Income:** Per capita income: $29,420 (2006-2010 5-year est.); Median household income: $52,899 (2006-2010 5-year est.); Average household income: $65,778 (2006-2010 5-year est.); Percent of households with income of $100,000 or more: 16.6% (2006-2010 5-year est.); Poverty rate: 7.7% (2006-2010 5-year est.).
**Education:** Percent of population age 25 and over with: High school diploma (including GED) or higher: 88.5% (2006-2010 5-year est.); Bachelor's degree or higher: 24.0% (2006-2010 5-year est.); Master's degree or higher: 7.3% (2006-2010 5-year est.).

**School District(s)**
Waterford-Halfmoon Union Free School District (KG-12)
2009-10 Enrollment: 851 . . . . . . . . . . . . . . . . . . . . (518) 237-0800
**Housing:** Homeownership rate: 44.4% (2010); Median home value: $149,500 (2006-2010 5-year est.); Median contract rent: $511 per month (2006-2010 5-year est.); Median year structure built: before 1940 (2006-2010 5-year est.).
**Transportation:** Commute to work: 92.4% car, 4.7% public transportation, 1.8% walk, 0.6% work from home (2006-2010 5-year est.); Travel time to work: 27.3% less than 15 minutes, 36.6% 15 to 30 minutes, 26.3% 30 to 45 minutes, 6.4% 45 to 60 minutes, 3.3% 60 minutes or more (2006-2010 5-year est.)
**Additional Information Contacts**
Village of Waterford . . . . . . . . . . . . . . . . . . . . . . . . . (518) 235-9898
  http://www.waterfordny.org

**WATERFORD** (town). Covers a land area of 6.566 square miles and a water area of 0.845 square miles. Located at 42.80° N. Lat; 73.68° W. Long. Elevation is 69 feet.
**History:** Incorporated 1794.
**Population:** 8,695 (1990); 8,515 (2000); 8,423 (2010); Density: 1,282.7 persons per square mile (2010); Race: 94.8% White, 1.3% Black, 1.5% Asian, 0.1% American Indian/Alaska Native, 0.0% Native Hawaiian/Other Pacific Islander, 2.3% Other, 1.8% Hispanic of any race (2010); Average household size: 2.32 (2010); Median age: 40.4 (2010); Males per 100 females: 96.0 (2010); Marriage status: 31.2% never married, 56.5% now married, 5.3% widowed, 7.0% divorced (2006-2010 5-year est.); Foreign born: 3.3% (2006-2010 5-year est.); Ancestry (includes multiple ancestries): 30.2% Irish, 18.6% French, 17.2% Italian, 12.5% German, 9.7% Polish (2006-2010 5-year est.).
**Economy:** Single-family building permits issued: 9 (2011); Multi-family building permits issued: 0 (2011); Employment by occupation: 8.4% management, 3.9% professional, 7.8% services, 21.4% sales, 4.7% farming, 11.0% construction, 5.0% production (2006-2010 5-year est.).
**Income:** Per capita income: $28,737 (2006-2010 5-year est.); Median household income: $61,879 (2006-2010 5-year est.); Average household income: $71,099 (2006-2010 5-year est.); Percent of households with income of $100,000 or more: 18.9% (2006-2010 5-year est.); Poverty rate: 8.8% (2006-2010 5-year est.).
**Education:** Percent of population age 25 and over with: High school diploma (including GED) or higher: 90.2% (2006-2010 5-year est.); Bachelor's degree or higher: 21.0% (2006-2010 5-year est.); Master's degree or higher: 7.0% (2006-2010 5-year est.).
**School District(s)**
Waterford-Halfmoon Union Free School District (KG-12)
2009-10 Enrollment: 851 . . . . . . . . . . . . . . . . . . . . (518) 237-0800
**Housing:** Homeownership rate: 60.6% (2010); Median home value: $198,100 (2006-2010 5-year est.); Median contract rent: $629 per month (2006-2010 5-year est.); Median year structure built: 1952 (2006-2010 5-year est.).
**Safety:** Violent crime rate: 4.7 per 10,000 population; Property crime rate: 106.8 per 10,000 population.
**Transportation:** Commute to work: 92.5% car, 2.2% public transportation, 2.6% walk, 1.9% work from home (2006-2010 5-year est.); Travel time to work: 23.4% less than 15 minutes, 43.4% 15 to 30 minutes, 25.1% 30 to 45 minutes, 4.1% 45 to 60 minutes, 3.9% 60 minutes or more (2006-2010 5-year est.)

**WILTON** (town). Covers a land area of 35.833 square miles and a water area of 0.118 square miles. Located at 43.15° N. Lat; 73.72° W. Long. Elevation is 348 feet.
**Population:** 10,635 (1990); 12,511 (2000); 16,173 (2010); Density: 451.3 persons per square mile (2010); Race: 95.6% White, 1.3% Black, 1.0% Asian, 0.2% American Indian/Alaska Native, 0.0% Native Hawaiian/Other Pacific Islander, 1.9% Other, 2.3% Hispanic of any race (2010); Average household size: 2.54 (2010); Median age: 40.9 (2010); Males per 100 females: 96.3 (2010); Marriage status: 24.1% never married, 63.0% now married, 4.0% widowed, 8.9% divorced (2006-2010 5-year est.); Foreign born: 2.6% (2006-2010 5-year est.); Ancestry (includes multiple ancestries): 24.5% Irish, 15.2% German, 15.0% Italian, 14.8% American, 11.3% English (2006-2010 5-year est.).
**Economy:** Single-family building permits issued: 22 (2011); Multi-family building permits issued: 108 (2011); Employment by occupation: 14.6% management, 5.0% professional, 4.4% services, 16.5% sales, 3.4% farming, 7.5% construction, 6.3% production (2006-2010 5-year est.).

**Income:** Per capita income: $33,711 (2006-2010 5-year est.); Median household income: $70,183 (2006-2010 5-year est.); Average household income: $87,544 (2006-2010 5-year est.); Percent of households with income of $100,000 or more: 36.4% (2006-2010 5-year est.); Poverty rate: 3.4% (2006-2010 5-year est.).

**Education:** Percent of population age 25 and over with: High school diploma (including GED) or higher: 93.4% (2006-2010 5-year est.); Bachelor's degree or higher: 37.8% (2006-2010 5-year est.); Master's degree or higher: 18.3% (2006-2010 5-year est.).

### School District(s)
South Glens Falls Central School District (KG-12)
    2009-10 Enrollment: 3,266 . . . . . . . . . . . . . . . . . . (518) 793-9617

**Housing:** Homeownership rate: 77.0% (2010); Median home value: $232,000 (2006-2010 5-year est.); Median contract rent: $730 per month (2006-2010 5-year est.); Median year structure built: 1990 (2006-2010 5-year est.).

**Transportation:** Commute to work: 94.4% car, 1.0% public transportation, 0.6% walk, 4.0% work from home (2006-2010 5-year est.); Travel time to work: 30.1% less than 15 minutes, 38.5% 15 to 30 minutes, 14.5% 30 to 45 minutes, 11.2% 45 to 60 minutes, 5.7% 60 minutes or more (2006-2010 5-year est.)

**Additional Information Contacts**
Town of Wilton . . . . . . . . . . . . . . . . . . . . . . . . . . . . (518) 587-1939
    http://www.townofwilton.com

## Schenectady County

Located in eastern New York; bounded on the north by Schoharie Creek; crossed by the Mohawk River. Covers a land area of 206.10 square miles, a water area of 3.52 square miles, and is located in the Eastern Time Zone at 42.80° N. Lat., 73.97° W. Long. The county was founded in 1809. County seat is Schenectady.

Schenectady County is part of the Albany-Schenectady-Troy, NY Metropolitan Statistical Area. The entire metro area includes: Albany County, NY; Rensselaer County, NY; Saratoga County, NY; Schenectady County, NY; Schoharie County, NY

**Population:** 149,285 (1990); 146,555 (2000); 154,727 (2010); Race: 79.6% White, 9.5% Black, 3.2% Asian, 0.4% American Indian/Alaska Native, 0.1% Native Hawaiian/Other Pacific Islander, 7.2% Other, 5.7% Hispanic of any race (2010); Density: 750.7 persons per square mile (2010); Average household size: 2.39 (2010); Median age: 39.8 (2010); Males per 100 females: 93.7 (2010).

**Religion:** Six largest groups: 28.6% Catholicism, 3.9% Muslim Estimate, 3.7% Presbyterian-Reformed, 2.1% Lutheran, 2.1% Methodist/Pietist, 1.5% Judaism (2010)

**Economy:** Unemployment rate: 8.3% (February 2012); Total civilian labor force: 74,218 (February 2012); Leading industries: 21.6% health care and social assistance; 14.3% retail trade; 8.2% manufacturing (2009); Farms: 194 totaling 19,129 acres (2007); Companies that employ 500 or more persons: 10 (2009); Companies that employ 100 to 499 persons: 54 (2009); Companies that employ less than 100 persons: 3,026 (2009); Black-owned businesses: 598 (2007); Hispanic-owned businesses: 387 (2007); Asian-owned businesses: n/a (2007); Women-owned businesses: 3,841 (2007); Retail sales per capita: $11,902 (2010). Single-family building permits issued: 118 (2011); Multi-family building permits issued: 5 (2011).

**Income:** Per capita income: $27,500 (2006-2010 5-year est.); Median household income: $55,188 (2006-2010 5-year est.); Average household income: $68,161 (2006-2010 5-year est.); Percent of households with income of $100,000 or more: 20.9% (2006-2010 5-year est.); Poverty rate: 11.1% (2006-2010 5-year est.); Bankruptcy rate: 3.91% (2011).

**Taxes:** Total county taxes per capita: $1,033 (2009); County property taxes per capita: $420 (2009).

**Education:** Percent of population age 25 and over with: High school diploma (including GED) or higher: 90.0% (2006-2010 5-year est.); Bachelor's degree or higher: 28.7% (2006-2010 5-year est.); Master's degree or higher: 13.0% (2006-2010 5-year est.).

**Housing:** Homeownership rate: 64.7% (2010); Median home value: $160,200 (2006-2010 5-year est.); Median contract rent: $626 per month (2006-2010 5-year est.); Median year structure built: 1950 (2006-2010 5-year est.).

**Health:** Birth rate: 118.3 per 10,000 population (2011); Death rate: 95.5 per 10,000 population (2011); Age-adjusted cancer mortality rate: 186.4 deaths per 100,000 population (2009); Number of physicians: 30.6 per 10,000

population (2008); Hospital beds: 55.6 per 10,000 population (2007); Hospital admissions: 1,864.6 per 10,000 population (2007).

**Environment:** Air Quality Index: 97.0% good, 2.7% moderate, 0.3% unhealthy for sensitive individuals, 0.0% unhealthy (percent of days in 2010)

**Elections:** 2008 Presidential election results: 55.3% Obama, 42.6% McCain, 1.3% Nader

**Additional Information Contacts**
Schenectady County Government . . . . . . . . . . . . . . . . . . (518) 388-4282
    http://www.schenectadycounty.com
Chamber of Schenectady County . . . . . . . . . . . . . . . . . (518) 372-5656
    http://www.schenectadychamber.net
Town of Duanesburg . . . . . . . . . . . . . . . . . . . . . . . . . (518) 895-8920
    http://www.duanesburg.net
Town of Glenville . . . . . . . . . . . . . . . . . . . . . . . . . . . (518) 688-1200
    http://www.townofglenville.org
Town of Niskayuna . . . . . . . . . . . . . . . . . . . . . . . . . . (518) 386-4500
    http://www.niskayuna.org

## Schenectady County Communities

### ALPLAUS (unincorporated postal area)
Zip Code: 12008

Covers a land area of 0.831 square miles and a water area of 0.174 square miles. Located at 42.85° N. Lat; 73.90° W. Long. Elevation is 259 feet. Population: 497 (2010); Density: 597.8 persons per square mile (2010); Race: 98.6% White, 0.0% Black, 0.6% Asian, 0.0% American Indian/Alaska Native, 0.0% Native Hawaiian/Other Pacific Islander, 0.8% Other, 2.0% Hispanic of any race (2010); Average household size: 2.63 (2010); Median age: 40.5 (2010); Males per 100 females: 103.7 (2010); Homeownership rate: 87.6% (2010)

### DELANSON (village). Covers a land area of 0.643 square miles and a water area of 0.002 square miles. Located at 42.74° N. Lat; 74.18° W. Long. Elevation is 817 feet.

**Population:** 361 (1990); 385 (2000); 377 (2010); Density: 585.6 persons per square mile (2010); Race: 97.3% White, 0.3% Black, 0.3% Asian, 0.0% American Indian/Alaska Native, 0.0% Native Hawaiian/Other Pacific Islander, 2.1% Other, 1.3% Hispanic of any race (2010); Average household size: 2.79 (2010); Median age: 36.3 (2010); Males per 100 females: 96.4 (2010); Marriage status: 13.2% never married, 65.8% now married, 2.6% widowed, 18.4% divorced (2006-2010 5-year est.); Foreign born: 2.0% (2006-2010 5-year est.); Ancestry (includes multiple ancestries): 24.7% German, 23.1% Irish, 21.4% Italian, 11.9% American, 10.2% English (2006-2010 5-year est.).

**Economy:** Single-family building permits issued: 0 (2011); Multi-family building permits issued: 0 (2011); Employment by occupation: 11.6% management, 11.6% professional, 7.8% services, 18.6% sales, 2.3% farming, 13.2% construction, 7.8% production (2006-2010 5-year est.).

**Income:** Per capita income: $27,754 (2006-2010 5-year est.); Median household income: $70,000 (2006-2010 5-year est.); Average household income: $73,354 (2006-2010 5-year est.); Percent of households with income of $100,000 or more: 28.6% (2006-2010 5-year est.); Poverty rate: 9.8% (2006-2010 5-year est.).

**Education:** Percent of population age 25 and over with: High school diploma (including GED) or higher: 94.6% (2006-2010 5-year est.); Bachelor's degree or higher: 26.3% (2006-2010 5-year est.); Master's degree or higher: 11.2% (2006-2010 5-year est.).

### School District(s)
Duanesburg Central School District (KG-12)
    2009-10 Enrollment: 911 . . . . . . . . . . . . . . . . . . (518) 895-2279

**Housing:** Homeownership rate: 75.6% (2010); Median home value: $183,800 (2006-2010 5-year est.); Median contract rent: $875 per month (2006-2010 5-year est.); Median year structure built: before 1940 (2006-2010 5-year est.).

**Transportation:** Commute to work: 90.2% car, 0.0% public transportation, 4.9% walk, 4.9% work from home (2006-2010 5-year est.); Travel time to work: 22.2% less than 15 minutes, 24.8% 15 to 30 minutes, 41.9% 30 to 45 minutes, 7.7% 45 to 60 minutes, 3.4% 60 minutes or more (2006-2010 5-year est.)

**DUANE LAKE** (CDP). Covers a land area of 2.401 square miles and a water area of 0.194 square miles. Located at 42.75° N. Lat; 74.10° W. Long. Elevation is 922 feet.

**Population:** 358 (1990); 357 (2000); 323 (2010); Density: 134.5 persons per square mile (2010); Race: 98.5% White, 0.0% Black, 1.2% Asian, 0.0% American Indian/Alaska Native, 0.0% Native Hawaiian/Other Pacific Islander, 0.3% Other, 1.5% Hispanic of any race (2010); Average household size: 2.34 (2010); Median age: 49.3 (2010); Males per 100 females: 97.0 (2010); Marriage status: 11.2% never married, 81.0% now married, 0.0% widowed, 7.8% divorced (2006-2010 5-year est.); Foreign born: 0.0% (2006-2010 5-year est.); Ancestry (includes multiple ancestries): 43.8% Italian, 30.2% Polish, 24.4% English, 21.1% German, 17.4% Irish (2006-2010 5-year est.).

**Economy:** Employment by occupation: 15.5% management, 0.0% professional, 0.0% services, 27.2% sales, 0.0% farming, 10.7% construction, 0.0% production (2006-2010 5-year est.).

**Income:** Per capita income: $37,077 (2006-2010 5-year est.); Median household income: $85,417 (2006-2010 5-year est.); Average household income: $87,561 (2006-2010 5-year est.); Percent of households with income of $100,000 or more: 29.1% (2006-2010 5-year est.); Poverty rate: 0.0% (2006-2010 5-year est.).

**Education:** Percent of population age 25 and over with: High school diploma (including GED) or higher: 100.0% (2006-2010 5-year est.); Bachelor's degree or higher: 47.3% (2006-2010 5-year est.); Master's degree or higher: 0.0% (2006-2010 5-year est.).

**Housing:** Homeownership rate: 92.7% (2010); Median home value: $257,700 (2006-2010 5-year est.); Median contract rent: n/a per month (2006-2010 5-year est.); Median year structure built: 1948 (2006-2010 5-year est.).

**Transportation:** Commute to work: 87.4% car, 0.0% public transportation, 12.6% walk, 0.0% work from home (2006-2010 5-year est.); Travel time to work: 28.2% less than 15 minutes, 49.5% 15 to 30 minutes, 22.3% 30 to 45 minutes, 0.0% 45 to 60 minutes, 0.0% 60 minutes or more (2006-2010 5-year est.).

**DUANESBURG** (town). Covers a land area of 70.781 square miles and a water area of 1.249 square miles. Located at 42.77° N. Lat; 74.17° W. Long. Elevation is 719 feet.

**Population:** 5,474 (1990); 5,808 (2000); 6,122 (2010); Density: 86.5 persons per square mile (2010); Race: 97.7% White, 0.4% Black, 0.4% Asian, 0.1% American Indian/Alaska Native, 0.0% Native Hawaiian/Other Pacific Islander, 1.4% Other, 1.7% Hispanic of any race (2010); Average household size: 2.62 (2010); Median age: 44.1 (2010); Males per 100 females: 100.5 (2010); Marriage status: 22.1% never married, 67.8% now married, 4.6% widowed, 5.5% divorced (2006-2010 5-year est.); Foreign born: 1.6% (2006-2010 5-year est.); Ancestry (includes multiple ancestries): 22.2% Irish, 21.1% German, 18.6% English, 11.9% Italian, 11.3% French (2006-2010 5-year est.).

**Economy:** Single-family building permits issued: 9 (2011); Multi-family building permits issued: 0 (2011); Employment by occupation: 15.3% management, 6.7% professional, 7.2% services, 17.8% sales, 3.3% farming, 11.4% construction, 5.1% production (2006-2010 5-year est.).

**Income:** Per capita income: $31,586 (2006-2010 5-year est.); Median household income: $75,561 (2006-2010 5-year est.); Average household income: $80,973 (2006-2010 5-year est.); Percent of households with income of $100,000 or more: 30.4% (2006-2010 5-year est.); Poverty rate: 3.8% (2006-2010 5-year est.).

**Education:** Percent of population age 25 and over with: High school diploma (including GED) or higher: 92.5% (2006-2010 5-year est.); Bachelor's degree or higher: 27.9% (2006-2010 5-year est.); Master's degree or higher: 12.2% (2006-2010 5-year est.).

**Housing:** Homeownership rate: 88.6% (2010); Median home value: $198,000 (2006-2010 5-year est.); Median contract rent: $470 per month (2006-2010 5-year est.); Median year structure built: 1971 (2006-2010 5-year est.).

**Transportation:** Commute to work: 91.9% car, 0.6% public transportation, 1.4% walk, 5.1% work from home (2006-2010 5-year est.); Travel time to work: 13.1% less than 15 minutes, 38.7% 15 to 30 minutes, 34.6% 30 to 45 minutes, 12.1% 45 to 60 minutes, 1.5% 60 minutes or more (2006-2010 5-year est.)

**Additional Information Contacts**

Town of Duanesburg . . . . . . . . . . . . . . . . . . . . . . . . . . . . (518) 895-8920
  http://www.duanesburg.net

**DUANESBURG** (CDP). Covers a land area of 2.449 square miles and a water area of 0.096 square miles. Located at 42.76° N. Lat; 74.13° W. Long. Elevation is 719 feet.

**Population:** 344 (1990); 339 (2000); 391 (2010); Density: 159.6 persons per square mile (2010); Race: 97.2% White, 1.0% Black, 0.8% Asian, 0.0% American Indian/Alaska Native, 0.0% Native Hawaiian/Other Pacific Islander, 1.0% Other, 5.9% Hispanic of any race (2010); Average household size: 2.43 (2010); Median age: 40.8 (2010); Males per 100 females: 89.8 (2010); Marriage status: 27.3% never married, 55.8% now married, 9.1% widowed, 7.9% divorced (2006-2010 5-year est.); Foreign born: 0.0% (2006-2010 5-year est.); Ancestry (includes multiple ancestries): 17.1% English, 16.6% Italian, 16.0% Welsh, 16.0% Dutch, 12.0% Northern European (2006-2010 5-year est.).

**Economy:** Employment by occupation: 35.9% management, 6.4% professional, 0.0% services, 0.0% sales, 0.0% farming, 0.0% construction, 0.0% production (2006-2010 5-year est.).

**Income:** Per capita income: $29,101 (2006-2010 5-year est.); Median household income: $75,288 (2006-2010 5-year est.); Average household income: $56,789 (2006-2010 5-year est.); Percent of households with income of $100,000 or more: 6.6% (2006-2010 5-year est.); Poverty rate: 9.1% (2006-2010 5-year est.).

**Education:** Percent of population age 25 and over with: High school diploma (including GED) or higher: 100.0% (2006-2010 5-year est.); Bachelor's degree or higher: 24.8% (2006-2010 5-year est.); Master's degree or higher: 24.8% (2006-2010 5-year est.).

**Housing:** Homeownership rate: 69.6% (2010); Median home value: $164,300 (2006-2010 5-year est.); Median contract rent: n/a per month (2006-2010 5-year est.); Median year structure built: 1971 (2006-2010 5-year est.).

**Transportation:** Commute to work: 92.3% car, 0.0% public transportation, 0.0% walk, 7.7% work from home (2006-2010 5-year est.); Travel time to work: 0.0% less than 15 minutes, 54.2% 15 to 30 minutes, 25.0% 30 to 45 minutes, 20.8% 45 to 60 minutes, 0.0% 60 minutes or more (2006-2010 5-year est.)

**EAST GLENVILLE** (CDP). Covers a land area of 7.165 square miles and a water area of 0.287 square miles. Located at 42.86° N. Lat; 73.91° W. Long. Elevation is 361 feet.

**Population:** 6,518 (1990); 6,064 (2000); 6,616 (2010); Density: 923.3 persons per square mile (2010); Race: 94.0% White, 0.8% Black, 3.0% Asian, 0.0% American Indian/Alaska Native, 0.0% Native Hawaiian/Other Pacific Islander, 2.2% Other, 1.9% Hispanic of any race (2010); Average household size: 2.42 (2010); Median age: 43.9 (2010); Males per 100 females: 92.5 (2010); Marriage status: 23.7% never married, 60.2% now married, 6.5% widowed, 9.5% divorced (2006-2010 5-year est.); Foreign born: 4.3% (2006-2010 5-year est.); Ancestry (includes multiple ancestries): 23.6% Italian, 21.0% Irish, 16.7% German, 16.5% English, 9.0% Polish (2006-2010 5-year est.).

**Economy:** Employment by occupation: 13.5% management, 6.0% professional, 9.1% services, 9.5% sales, 5.8% farming, 4.9% construction, 2.4% production (2006-2010 5-year est.).

**Income:** Per capita income: $32,976 (2006-2010 5-year est.); Median household income: $76,494 (2006-2010 5-year est.); Average household income: $86,171 (2006-2010 5-year est.); Percent of households with income of $100,000 or more: 36.0% (2006-2010 5-year est.); Poverty rate: 5.8% (2006-2010 5-year est.).

**Education:** Percent of population age 25 and over with: High school diploma (including GED) or higher: 93.3% (2006-2010 5-year est.); Bachelor's degree or higher: 38.1% (2006-2010 5-year est.); Master's degree or higher: 21.9% (2006-2010 5-year est.).

**Housing:** Homeownership rate: 76.6% (2010); Median home value: $202,700 (2006-2010 5-year est.); Median contract rent: $794 per month (2006-2010 5-year est.); Median year structure built: 1964 (2006-2010 5-year est.).

**Transportation:** Commute to work: 95.7% car, 0.0% public transportation, 2.3% walk, 1.6% work from home (2006-2010 5-year est.); Travel time to work: 27.8% less than 15 minutes, 36.5% 15 to 30 minutes, 28.4% 30 to 45 minutes, 6.1% 45 to 60 minutes, 1.2% 60 minutes or more (2006-2010 5-year est.)

**GLENVILLE** (town). Covers a land area of 49.186 square miles and a water area of 1.489 square miles. Located at 42.88° N. Lat; 73.98° W. Long. Elevation is 705 feet.

**Population:** 28,771 (1990); 28,183 (2000); 29,480 (2010); Density: 599.4 persons per square mile (2010); Race: 95.9% White, 1.0% Black, 1.4%

Asian, 0.1% American Indian/Alaska Native, 0.0% Native Hawaiian/Other Pacific Islander, 1.6% Other, 2.0% Hispanic of any race (2010); Average household size: 2.39 (2010); Median age: 44.2 (2010); Males per 100 females: 94.0 (2010); Marriage status: 25.7% never married, 57.1% now married, 7.1% widowed, 10.1% divorced (2006-2010 5-year est.); Foreign born: 2.9% (2006-2010 5-year est.); Ancestry (includes multiple ancestries): 21.9% Irish, 20.8% Italian, 19.1% German, 13.8% English, 10.9% Polish (2006-2010 5-year est.).

**Economy:** Unemployment rate: 7.1% (February 2012); Total civilian labor force: 14,354 (February 2012); Single-family building permits issued: 18 (2011); Multi-family building permits issued: 5 (2011); Employment by occupation: 13.5% management, 6.8% professional, 7.3% services, 16.3% sales, 5.0% farming, 5.8% construction, 3.5% production (2006-2010 5-year est.).

**Income:** Per capita income: $31,363 (2006-2010 5-year est.); Median household income: $68,066 (2006-2010 5-year est.); Average household income: $77,759 (2006-2010 5-year est.); Percent of households with income of $100,000 or more: 29.0% (2006-2010 5-year est.); Poverty rate: 5.0% (2006-2010 5-year est.).

**Education:** Percent of population age 25 and over with: High school diploma (including GED) or higher: 95.8% (2006-2010 5-year est.); Bachelor's degree or higher: 34.9% (2006-2010 5-year est.); Master's degree or higher: 16.0% (2006-2010 5-year est.).

**Housing:** Homeownership rate: 78.4% (2010); Median home value: $179,800 (2006-2010 5-year est.); Median contract rent: $696 per month (2006-2010 5-year est.); Median year structure built: 1957 (2006-2010 5-year est.).

**Hospitals:** Conifer Park (225 beds)

**Safety:** Violent crime rate: 6.9 per 10,000 population; Property crime rate: 170.3 per 10,000 population (2010).

**Transportation:** Commute to work: 95.9% car, 0.2% public transportation, 1.2% walk, 1.9% work from home (2006-2010 5-year est.); Travel time to work: 29.9% less than 15 minutes, 36.9% 15 to 30 minutes, 26.3% 30 to 45 minutes, 4.6% 45 to 60 minutes, 2.2% 60 minutes or more (2006-2010 5-year est.)

**Additional Information Contacts**

Town of Glenville . . . . . . . . . . . . . . . . . . . . . . . . . . . . (518) 688-1200
  http://www.townofglenville.org

**MARIAVILLE LAKE** (CDP). Covers a land area of 5.623 square miles and a water area of 0.379 square miles. Located at 42.82° N. Lat; 74.13° W. Long. Elevation is 1,289 feet.

**Population:** 636 (1990); 710 (2000); 722 (2010); Density: 128.4 persons per square mile (2010); Race: 97.0% White, 0.7% Black, 1.1% Asian, 0.0% American Indian/Alaska Native, 0.0% Native Hawaiian/Other Pacific Islander, 1.2% Other, 1.4% Hispanic of any race (2010); Average household size: 2.56 (2010); Median age: 45.5 (2010); Males per 100 females: 109.9 (2010); Marriage status: 29.4% never married, 54.2% now married, 6.1% widowed, 10.3% divorced (2006-2010 5-year est.); Foreign born: 5.6% (2006-2010 5-year est.); Ancestry (includes multiple ancestries): 29.4% English, 25.0% Irish, 20.0% German, 13.4% Italian, 11.6% Polish (2006-2010 5-year est.).

**Economy:** Employment by occupation: 8.7% management, 0.0% professional, 9.9% services, 21.7% sales, 8.7% farming, 9.6% construction, 3.8% production (2006-2010 5-year est.).

**Income:** Per capita income: $32,525 (2006-2010 5-year est.); Median household income: $85,375 (2006-2010 5-year est.); Average household income: $76,462 (2006-2010 5-year est.); Percent of households with income of $100,000 or more: 34.4% (2006-2010 5-year est.); Poverty rate: 8.1% (2006-2010 5-year est.).

**Education:** Percent of population age 25 and over with: High school diploma (including GED) or higher: 90.5% (2006-2010 5-year est.); Bachelor's degree or higher: 19.7% (2006-2010 5-year est.); Master's degree or higher: 13.1% (2006-2010 5-year est.).

**Housing:** Homeownership rate: 91.5% (2010); Median home value: $175,500 (2006-2010 5-year est.); Median contract rent: n/a per month (2006-2010 5-year est.); Median year structure built: 1967 (2006-2010 5-year est.).

**Transportation:** Commute to work: 91.7% car, 0.0% public transportation, 6.6% walk, 1.7% work from home (2006-2010 5-year est.); Travel time to work: 8.4% less than 15 minutes, 48.3% 15 to 30 minutes, 28.8% 30 to 45 minutes, 14.5% 45 to 60 minutes, 0.0% 60 minutes or more (2006-2010 5-year est.)

**NISKAYUNA** (town). Covers a land area of 14.151 square miles and a water area of 0.890 square miles. Located at 42.80° N. Lat; 73.87° W. Long. Elevation is 292 feet.

**Population:** 19,048 (1990); 20,295 (2000); 21,781 (2010); Density: 1,539.1 persons per square mile (2010); Race: 86.1% White, 2.7% Black, 8.1% Asian, 0.1% American Indian/Alaska Native, 0.0% Native Hawaiian/Other Pacific Islander, 3.0% Other, 2.5% Hispanic of any race (2010); Average household size: 2.48 (2010); Median age: 44.2 (2010); Males per 100 females: 93.0 (2010); Marriage status: 20.8% never married, 64.4% now married, 7.9% widowed, 7.0% divorced (2006-2010 5-year est.); Foreign born: 13.3% (2006-2010 5-year est.); Ancestry (includes multiple ancestries): 19.5% Irish, 18.8% Italian, 14.5% German, 12.6% English, 7.9% Polish (2006-2010 5-year est.).

**Economy:** Single-family building permits issued: 62 (2011); Multi-family building permits issued: 0 (2011); Employment by occupation: 17.9% management, 12.1% professional, 3.7% services, 14.0% sales, 2.9% farming, 2.5% construction, 1.8% production (2006-2010 5-year est.).

**Income:** Per capita income: $42,570 (2006-2010 5-year est.); Median household income: $87,348 (2006-2010 5-year est.); Average household income: $110,546 (2006-2010 5-year est.); Percent of households with income of $100,000 or more: 42.4% (2006-2010 5-year est.); Poverty rate: 3.1% (2006-2010 5-year est.).

**Education:** Percent of population age 25 and over with: High school diploma (including GED) or higher: 95.9% (2006-2010 5-year est.); Bachelor's degree or higher: 59.6% (2006-2010 5-year est.); Master's degree or higher: 32.0% (2006-2010 5-year est.).

**Housing:** Homeownership rate: 80.6% (2010); Median home value: $244,200 (2006-2010 5-year est.); Median contract rent: $747 per month (2006-2010 5-year est.); Median year structure built: 1963 (2006-2010 5-year est.).

**Hospitals:** Bellevue Woman's Hospital (40 beds)

**Safety:** Violent crime rate: 6.0 per 10,000 population; Property crime rate: 181.3 per 10,000 population (2010).

**Transportation:** Commute to work: 91.7% car, 1.0% public transportation, 2.5% walk, 4.5% work from home (2006-2010 5-year est.); Travel time to work: 32.3% less than 15 minutes, 38.5% 15 to 30 minutes, 23.6% 30 to 45 minutes, 3.7% 45 to 60 minutes, 1.9% 60 minutes or more (2006-2010 5-year est.)

**Additional Information Contacts**

Town of Niskayuna . . . . . . . . . . . . . . . . . . . . . . . . . . . (518) 386-4500
  http://www.niskayuna.org

**NISKAYUNA** (CDP). Covers a land area of 1.007 square miles and a water area of 0 square miles. Located at 42.81° N. Lat; 73.89° W. Long. Elevation is 292 feet.

**Population:** 4,942 (1990); 4,892 (2000); 4,859 (2010); Density: 4,822.3 persons per square mile (2010); Race: 91.0% White, 3.1% Black, 3.0% Asian, 0.1% American Indian/Alaska Native, 0.0% Native Hawaiian/Other Pacific Islander, 2.8% Other, 2.9% Hispanic of any race (2010); Average household size: 2.51 (2010); Median age: 40.5 (2010); Males per 100 females: 95.1 (2010); Marriage status: 21.2% never married, 63.0% now married, 4.1% widowed, 11.7% divorced (2006-2010 5-year est.); Foreign born: 5.8% (2006-2010 5-year est.); Ancestry (includes multiple ancestries): 21.4% Italian, 19.7% German, 19.2% Irish, 19.0% English, 7.7% American (2006-2010 5-year est.).

**Economy:** Employment by occupation: 13.1% management, 16.1% professional, 1.0% services, 15.4% sales, 4.0% farming, 3.6% construction, 0.7% production (2006-2010 5-year est.).

**Income:** Per capita income: $35,577 (2006-2010 5-year est.); Median household income: $82,336 (2006-2010 5-year est.); Average household income: $91,144 (2006-2010 5-year est.); Percent of households with income of $100,000 or more: 34.8% (2006-2010 5-year est.); Poverty rate: 3.2% (2006-2010 5-year est.).

**Education:** Percent of population age 25 and over with: High school diploma (including GED) or higher: 94.9% (2006-2010 5-year est.); Bachelor's degree or higher: 62.4% (2006-2010 5-year est.); Master's degree or higher: 30.9% (2006-2010 5-year est.).

**Housing:** Homeownership rate: 87.9% (2010); Median home value: $199,500 (2006-2010 5-year est.); Median contract rent: $805 per month (2006-2010 5-year est.); Median year structure built: 1942 (2006-2010 5-year est.).

**Hospitals:** Bellevue Woman's Hospital (40 beds)

**Transportation:** Commute to work: 90.8% car, 1.9% public transportation, 0.4% walk, 6.0% work from home (2006-2010 5-year est.); Travel time to work: 31.9% less than 15 minutes, 32.2% 15 to 30 minutes, 29.4% 30 to 45

minutes, 4.7% 45 to 60 minutes, 1.8% 60 minutes or more (2006-2010 5-year est.)

## PATTERSONVILLE (unincorporated postal area)
Zip Code: 12137

Covers a land area of 23.977 square miles and a water area of 0.395 square miles. Located at 42.86° N. Lat; 74.13° W. Long. Elevation is 269 feet. Population: 1,679 (2010); Density: 70.0 persons per square mile (2010); Race: 96.7% White, 0.2% Black, 1.0% Asian, 0.2% American Indian/Alaska Native, 0.0% Native Hawaiian/Other Pacific Islander, 1.9% Other, 1.7% Hispanic of any race (2010); Average household size: 2.53 (2010); Median age: 44.6 (2010); Males per 100 females: 98.7 (2010); Homeownership rate: 87.8% (2010)

## PRINCETOWN (town). Covers a land area of 23.924 square miles and a water area of 0.286 square miles. Located at 42.81° N. Lat; 74.07° W. Long. Elevation is 420 feet.
Population: 2,031 (1990); 2,132 (2000); 2,115 (2010); Density: 88.4 persons per square mile (2010); Race: 96.8% White, 0.4% Black, 1.2% Asian, 0.4% American Indian/Alaska Native, 0.0% Native Hawaiian/Other Pacific Islander, 1.2% Other, 1.1% Hispanic of any race (2010); Average household size: 2.54 (2010); Median age: 46.5 (2010); Males per 100 females: 100.5 (2010); Marriage status: 23.4% never married, 59.4% now married, 4.6% widowed, 12.7% divorced (2006-2010 5-year est.); Foreign born: 6.4% (2006-2010 5-year est.); Ancestry (includes multiple ancestries): 22.7% German, 17.6% Irish, 16.8% Italian, 14.7% English, 10.9% American (2006-2010 5-year est.).
Economy: Single-family building permits issued: 1 (2011); Multi-family building permits issued: 0 (2011); Employment by occupation: 6.9% management, 5.8% professional, 8.6% services, 15.3% sales, 3.0% farming, 9.8% construction, 6.0% production (2006-2010 5-year est.).
Income: Per capita income: $32,217 (2006-2010 5-year est.); Median household income: $78,077 (2006-2010 5-year est.); Average household income: $84,981 (2006-2010 5-year est.); Percent of households with income of $100,000 or more: 32.2% (2006-2010 5-year est.); Poverty rate: 6.9% (2006-2010 5-year est.).
Education: Percent of population age 25 and over with: High school diploma (including GED) or higher: 93.9% (2006-2010 5-year est.); Bachelor's degree or higher: 29.1% (2006-2010 5-year est.); Master's degree or higher: 11.4% (2006-2010 5-year est.).
Housing: Homeownership rate: 89.0% (2010); Median home value: $209,900 (2006-2010 5-year est.); Median contract rent: $634 per month (2006-2010 5-year est.); Median year structure built: 1972 (2006-2010 5-year est.).
Transportation: Commute to work: 89.6% car, 0.0% public transportation, 4.0% walk, 5.9% work from home (2006-2010 5-year est.); Travel time to work: 20.8% less than 15 minutes, 37.2% 15 to 30 minutes, 29.9% 30 to 45 minutes, 7.2% 45 to 60 minutes, 4.9% 60 minutes or more (2006-2010 5-year est.)

## ROTTERDAM (town). Aka South Schenectady. Covers a land area of 35.692 square miles and a water area of 0.767 square miles. Located at 42.81° N. Lat; 74.01° W. Long. Elevation is 338 feet.
History: Settled c.1670, incorporated 1821.
Population: 28,395 (1990); 28,316 (2000); 29,094 (2010); Density: 815.1 persons per square mile (2010); Race: 94.7% White, 1.5% Black, 1.2% Asian, 0.2% American Indian/Alaska Native, 0.0% Native Hawaiian/Other Pacific Islander, 2.4% Other, 2.3% Hispanic of any race (2010); Average household size: 2.35 (2010); Median age: 43.5 (2010); Males per 100 females: 92.2 (2010); Marriage status: 26.0% never married, 55.5% now married, 8.6% widowed, 9.8% divorced (2006-2010 5-year est.); Foreign born: 4.8% (2006-2010 5-year est.); Ancestry (includes multiple ancestries): 32.2% Italian, 20.0% Irish, 17.8% German, 11.0% Polish, 8.9% English (2006-2010 5-year est.).
Economy: Unemployment rate: 8.0% (February 2012); Total civilian labor force: 14,367 (February 2012); Single-family building permits issued: 21 (2011); Multi-family building permits issued: 0 (2011); Employment by occupation: 10.7% management, 4.6% professional, 8.4% services, 20.6% sales, 5.4% farming, 7.9% construction, 5.6% production (2006-2010 5-year est.).
Income: Per capita income: $28,557 (2006-2010 5-year est.); Median household income: $59,664 (2006-2010 5-year est.); Average household income: $67,415 (2006-2010 5-year est.); Percent of households with income of $100,000 or more: 20.3% (2006-2010 5-year est.); Poverty rate: 4.7% (2006-2010 5-year est.).

Taxes: Total city taxes per capita: $438 (2009); City property taxes per capita: $395 (2009).
Education: Percent of population age 25 and over with: High school diploma (including GED) or higher: 92.0% (2006-2010 5-year est.); Bachelor's degree or higher: 21.2% (2006-2010 5-year est.); Master's degree or higher: 8.1% (2006-2010 5-year est.).
Housing: Homeownership rate: 79.3% (2010); Median home value: $161,500 (2006-2010 5-year est.); Median contract rent: $602 per month (2006-2010 5-year est.); Median year structure built: 1956 (2006-2010 5-year est.).
Safety: Violent crime rate: 8.7 per 10,000 population; Property crime rate: 260.1 per 10,000 population (2010).
Transportation: Commute to work: 96.7% car, 0.2% public transportation, 0.7% walk, 2.3% work from home (2006-2010 5-year est.); Travel time to work: 32.0% less than 15 minutes, 41.6% 15 to 30 minutes, 20.0% 30 to 45 minutes, 4.4% 45 to 60 minutes, 2.0% 60 minutes or more (2006-2010 5-year est.)

## ROTTERDAM (CDP). Covers a land area of 6.933 square miles and a water area of 0.005 square miles. Located at 42.77° N. Lat; 73.95° W. Long. Elevation is 338 feet.
Population: 21,228 (1990); 20,536 (2000); 20,652 (2010); Density: 2,978.6 persons per square mile (2010); Race: 94.4% White, 1.5% Black, 1.2% Asian, 0.2% American Indian/Alaska Native, 0.0% Native Hawaiian/Other Pacific Islander, 2.7% Other, 2.5% Hispanic of any race (2010); Average household size: 2.33 (2010); Median age: 43.2 (2010); Males per 100 females: 90.9 (2010); Marriage status: 25.7% never married, 54.3% now married, 9.6% widowed, 10.4% divorced (2006-2010 5-year est.); Foreign born: 5.3% (2006-2010 5-year est.); Ancestry (includes multiple ancestries): 32.0% Italian, 19.8% Irish, 17.0% German, 10.8% Polish, 8.5% English (2006-2010 5-year est.).
Economy: Employment by occupation: 10.2% management, 4.7% professional, 9.2% services, 21.0% sales, 5.1% farming, 8.5% construction, 5.6% production (2006-2010 5-year est.).
Income: Per capita income: $27,226 (2006-2010 5-year est.); Median household income: $57,658 (2006-2010 5-year est.); Average household income: $63,180 (2006-2010 5-year est.); Percent of households with income of $100,000 or more: 16.6% (2006-2010 5-year est.); Poverty rate: 5.0% (2006-2010 5-year est.).
Education: Percent of population age 25 and over with: High school diploma (including GED) or higher: 90.9% (2006-2010 5-year est.); Bachelor's degree or higher: 18.5% (2006-2010 5-year est.); Master's degree or higher: 7.4% (2006-2010 5-year est.).
Housing: Homeownership rate: 80.8% (2010); Median home value: $152,500 (2006-2010 5-year est.); Median contract rent: $638 per month (2006-2010 5-year est.); Median year structure built: 1954 (2006-2010 5-year est.).
Transportation: Commute to work: 96.2% car, 0.1% public transportation, 0.8% walk, 2.8% work from home (2006-2010 5-year est.); Travel time to work: 32.5% less than 15 minutes, 43.2% 15 to 30 minutes, 18.6% 30 to 45 minutes, 3.6% 45 to 60 minutes, 2.0% 60 minutes or more (2006-2010 5-year est.)

## ROTTERDAM JUNCTION (unincorporated postal area)
Zip Code: 12150

Covers a land area of 1.096 square miles and a water area of 0.094 square miles. Located at 42.88° N. Lat; 74.05° W. Long. Elevation is 249 feet. Population: 914 (2010); Density: 833.7 persons per square mile (2010); Race: 96.6% White, 1.1% Black, 0.3% Asian, 0.2% American Indian/Alaska Native, 0.0% Native Hawaiian/Other Pacific Islander, 1.8% Other, 1.1% Hispanic of any race (2010); Average household size: 2.33 (2010); Median age: 44.9 (2010); Males per 100 females: 91.2 (2010); Homeownership rate: 79.7% (2010)

## SCHENECTADY (city). County seat. Covers a land area of 10.779 square miles and a water area of 0.185 square miles. Located at 42.80° N. Lat; 73.92° W. Long. Elevation is 243 feet.
History: The site of Schenectady was called "Schonowe" meaning "big flats" by the Mohawk people. In 1662, Arent Van Curler, with a small group of Dutchmen, emigrated from Albany to the "Groote Vlachte" ("big flats") and purchased land. The first major migration of English into Schenectady began about 1700. In 1848, a locomotive factory was organized that was Schenectady's largest industry for a half century. In 1886, Thomas A. Edison bought two abandoned factory buildings for the Edison Company. In 1892 it was consolidated with the Thompson-Huston Company of Lynn,

Massachusetts, to form the General Electric Company. Schenectady became the city that "lights and hauls the world."

**Population:** 65,566 (1990); 61,821 (2000); 66,135 (2010); Density: 6,135.3 persons per square mile (2010); Race: 61.4% White, 20.2% Black, 3.6% Asian, 0.7% American Indian/Alaska Native, 0.1% Native Hawaiian/Other Pacific Islander, 14.0% Other, 10.5% Hispanic of any race (2010); Average household size: 2.35 (2010); Median age: 33.4 (2010); Males per 100 females: 93.7 (2010); Marriage status: 43.1% never married, 37.9% now married, 8.2% widowed, 10.8% divorced (2006-2010 5-year est.); Foreign born: 12.3% (2006-2010 5-year est.); Ancestry (includes multiple ancestries): 15.1% Italian, 13.2% Irish, 10.5% German, 6.1% English, 6.1% Polish (2006-2010 5-year est.).

**Economy:** Unemployment rate: 9.7% (February 2012); Total civilian labor force: 30,548 (February 2012); Single-family building permits issued: 7 (2011); Multi-family building permits issued: 0 (2011); Employment by occupation: 8.5% management, 4.1% professional, 14.4% services, 19.2% sales, 6.1% farming, 6.0% construction, 4.1% production (2006-2010 5-year est.).

**Income:** Per capita income: $19,810 (2006-2010 5-year est.); Median household income: $37,607 (2006-2010 5-year est.); Average household income: $48,630 (2006-2010 5-year est.); Percent of households with income of $100,000 or more: 9.2% (2006-2010 5-year est.); Poverty rate: 20.6% (2006-2010 5-year est.).

**Taxes:** Total city taxes per capita: $526 (2009); City property taxes per capita: $467 (2009).

**Education:** Percent of population age 25 and over with: High school diploma (including GED) or higher: 83.6% (2006-2010 5-year est.); Bachelor's degree or higher: 18.3% (2006-2010 5-year est.); Master's degree or higher: 7.3% (2006-2010 5-year est.).

### School District(s)

Guilderland Central School District (KG-12)

    2009-10 Enrollment: 5,274 . . . . . . . . . . . . . . . . (518) 456-6200

Niskayuna Central School District (KG-12)

    2009-10 Enrollment: 4,224 . . . . . . . . . . . . . . . . (518) 377-4666

Rotterdam-Mohonasen Central School District (KG-12)

    2009-10 Enrollment: 3,079 . . . . . . . . . . . . . . . . (518) 356-8200

Schalmont Central School District (KG-12)

    2009-10 Enrollment: 1,973 . . . . . . . . . . . . . . . . (518) 355-9200

Schenectady City School District (PK-12)

    2009-10 Enrollment: 9,903 . . . . . . . . . . . . . . . . (518) 370-8100

### Four-year College(s)

Union College (Private, Not-for-profit)

    Fall 2010 Enrollment: 2,162 . . . . . . . . . . . . . . . . (518) 388-6000

    2011-12 Tuition: In-state $43,602; Out-of-state $43,602

Union Graduate College (Private, Not-for-profit)

    Fall 2010 Enrollment: 431 . . . . . . . . . . . . . . . . (518) 631-9900

### Two-year College(s)

Ellis School of Nursing (Private, Not-for-profit)

    Fall 2010 Enrollment: 92 . . . . . . . . . . . . . . . . (518) 243-4471

    2011-12 Tuition: In-state $7,855; Out-of-state $7,855

Schenectady County Community College (Public)

    Fall 2010 Enrollment: 3,686 . . . . . . . . . . . . . . . . (518) 381-1200

    2011-12 Tuition: In-state $3,681; Out-of-state $7,065

### Vocational/Technical School(s)

Modern Welding School (Private, For-profit)

    Fall 2010 Enrollment: 120 . . . . . . . . . . . . . . . . (518) 374-1216

    2011-12 Tuition: $12,600

**Housing:** Homeownership rate: 43.8% (2010); Median home value: $109,500 (2006-2010 5-year est.); Median contract rent: $612 per month (2006-2010 5-year est.); Median year structure built: before 1940 (2006-2010 5-year est.).

**Hospitals:** Ellis Hospital (368 beds); St. Clare's Hospital of Schenectady (200 beds); Sunnyview Hospital & Rehabilitation Center (104 beds)

**Safety:** Violent crime rate: 111.8 per 10,000 population; Property crime rate: 557.5 per 10,000 population (2010).

**Newspapers:** Daily Gazette (Local news; Circulation 49,453)

**Transportation:** Commute to work: 82.3% car, 5.8% public transportation, 6.9% walk, 3.0% work from home (2006-2010 5-year est.); Travel time to work: 34.5% less than 15 minutes, 32.1% 15 to 30 minutes, 25.4% 30 to 45 minutes, 3.7% 45 to 60 minutes, 4.3% 60 minutes or more (2006-2010 5-year est.); Amtrak: train service available.

**Airports:** Schenectady County (general aviation)

**Additional Information Contacts**

Chamber of Schenectady County . . . . . . . . . . . . . . . . (518) 372-5656

    http://www.schenectadychamber.net

**SCOTIA** (village). Covers a land area of 1.685 square miles and a water area of 0.104 square miles. Located at 42.83° N. Lat; 73.96° W. Long. Elevation is 243 feet.

**History:** Scotia Naval Supply Depot closed. Settled before 1660, incorporated 1904.

**Population:** 7,417 (1990); 7,957 (2000); 7,729 (2010); Density: 4,585.8 persons per square mile (2010); Race: 95.4% White, 1.2% Black, 1.1% Asian, 0.2% American Indian/Alaska Native, 0.1% Native Hawaiian/Other Pacific Islander, 2.0% Other, 2.8% Hispanic of any race (2010); Average household size: 2.30 (2010); Median age: 39.5 (2010); Males per 100 females: 93.9 (2010); Marriage status: 29.2% never married, 50.6% now married, 6.2% widowed, 14.0% divorced (2006-2010 5-year est.); Foreign born: 2.9% (2006-2010 5-year est.); Ancestry (includes multiple ancestries): 22.0% Irish, 17.5% German, 15.7% Italian, 13.5% English, 9.4% American (2006-2010 5-year est.).

**Economy:** Single-family building permits issued: 0 (2011); Multi-family building permits issued: 0 (2011); Employment by occupation: 11.8% management, 6.1% professional, 6.2% services, 19.6% sales, 5.5% farming, 7.3% construction, 4.4% production (2006-2010 5-year est.).

**Income:** Per capita income: $27,092 (2006-2010 5-year est.); Median household income: $58,927 (2006-2010 5-year est.); Average household income: $64,968 (2006-2010 5-year est.); Percent of households with income of $100,000 or more: 15.5% (2006-2010 5-year est.); Poverty rate: 4.9% (2006-2010 5-year est.).

**Taxes:** Total city taxes per capita: $494 (2009); City property taxes per capita: $459 (2009).

**Education:** Percent of population age 25 and over with: High school diploma (including GED) or higher: 95.6% (2006-2010 5-year est.); Bachelor's degree or higher: 29.0% (2006-2010 5-year est.); Master's degree or higher: 11.9% (2006-2010 5-year est.).

### School District(s)

Burnt Hills-Ballston Lake Central School District (KG-12)

    2009-10 Enrollment: 3,379 . . . . . . . . . . . . . . . . (518) 399-9141

Scotia-Glenville Central School District (KG-12)

    2009-10 Enrollment: 2,745 . . . . . . . . . . . . . . . . (518) 382-1215

**Housing:** Homeownership rate: 69.2% (2010); Median home value: $143,000 (2006-2010 5-year est.); Median contract rent: $628 per month (2006-2010 5-year est.); Median year structure built: before 1940 (2006-2010 5-year est.).

**Safety:** Violent crime rate: 10.0 per 10,000 population; Property crime rate: 274.5 per 10,000 population (2010).

**Transportation:** Commute to work: 95.2% car, 0.4% public transportation, 1.2% walk, 0.8% work from home (2006-2010 5-year est.); Travel time to work: 33.9% less than 15 minutes, 31.5% 15 to 30 minutes, 31.2% 30 to 45 minutes, 2.5% 45 to 60 minutes, 0.9% 60 minutes or more (2006-2010 5-year est.)

# Schoharie County

Located in east central New York, partly in the Catskills; crossed by The Helderbergs; drained by Schoharie and Catskill Creeks. Covers a land area of 622.02 square miles, a water area of 4.34 square miles, and is located in the Eastern Time Zone at 42.61° N. Lat., 74.43° W. Long. The county was founded in 1795. County seat is Schoharie.

Schoharie County is part of the Albany-Schenectady-Troy, NY Metropolitan Statistical Area. The entire metro area includes: Albany County, NY; Rensselaer County, NY; Saratoga County, NY; Schenectady County, NY; Schoharie County, NY

Weather Station: Lansing Manor                      Elevation: 1,100 feet

| | Jan | Feb | Mar | Apr | May | Jun | Jul | Aug | Sep | Oct | Nov | Dec |
|---|---|---|---|---|---|---|---|---|---|---|---|---|
| High | 34 | 35 | 44 | 57 | 68 | 77 | 81 | 80 | 72 | 60 | 49 | 38 |
| Low | 13 | 13 | 22 | 33 | 43 | 53 | 57 | 56 | 49 | 37 | 30 | 19 |
| Precip | 2.5 | 2.0 | 3.0 | 3.4 | 3.7 | 4.1 | 4.7 | 3.5 | 3.6 | 4.3 | 2.9 | 2.4 |
| Snow | 17.0 | 9.8 | 10.9 | 2.1 | tr | 0.0 | 0.0 | 0.0 | 0.0 | 0.6 | 3.6 | 11.2 |

*High and Low temperatures in degrees Fahrenheit; Precipitation and Snow in inches*

**Population:** 31,876 (1990); 31,582 (2000); 32,749 (2010); Race: 95.9% White, 1.3% Black, 0.7% Asian, 0.2% American Indian/Alaska Native, 0.0% Native Hawaiian/Other Pacific Islander, 1.9% Other, 2.8% Hispanic of any race (2010); Density: 52.6 persons per square mile (2010); Average household size: 2.37 (2010); Median age: 42.5 (2010); Males per 100 females: 100.0 (2010).

**Religion:** Six largest groups: 20.7% Catholicism, 6.3% Methodist/Pietist, 4.6% Lutheran, 2.4% Presbyterian-Reformed, 1.6% Non-Denominational, 1.2% Latter-day Saints (2010)

**Economy:** Unemployment rate: 11.8% (February 2012); Total civilian labor force: 15,725 (February 2012); Leading industries: 20.5% retail trade; 18.8% health care and social assistance; 9.9% accommodation & food services (2009); Farms: 525 totaling 95,490 acres (2007); Companies that employ 500 or more persons: 1 (2009); Companies that employ 100 to 499 persons: 5 (2009); Companies that employ less than 100 persons: 561 (2009); Black-owned businesses: n/a (2007); Hispanic-owned businesses: n/a (2007); Asian-owned businesses: n/a (2007); Women-owned businesses: n/a (2007); Retail sales per capita: $8,715 (2010). Single-family building permits issued: 25 (2011); Multi-family building permits issued: 3 (2011).

**Income:** Per capita income: $25,105 (2006-2010 5-year est.); Median household income: $50,864 (2006-2010 5-year est.); Average household income: $62,093 (2006-2010 5-year est.); Percent of households with income of $100,000 or more: 17.7% (2006-2010 5-year est.); Poverty rate: 11.4% (2006-2010 5-year est.); Bankruptcy rate: 3.81% (2011).

**Taxes:** Total county taxes per capita: $954 (2009); County property taxes per capita: $516 (2009).

**Education:** Percent of population age 25 and over with: High school diploma (including GED) or higher: 86.5% (2006-2010 5-year est.); Bachelor's degree or higher: 21.0% (2006-2010 5-year est.); Master's degree or higher: 8.7% (2006-2010 5-year est.).

**Housing:** Homeownership rate: 75.2% (2010); Median home value: $139,000 (2006-2010 5-year est.); Median contract rent: $533 per month (2006-2010 5-year est.); Median year structure built: 1968 (2006-2010 5-year est.)

**Health:** Birth rate: 84.1 per 10,000 population (2011); Death rate: 86.3 per 10,000 population (2011); Age-adjusted cancer mortality rate: 204.3 deaths per 100,000 population (2009); Number of physicians: 6.0 per 10,000 population (2008); Hospital beds: 12.5 per 10,000 population (2007); Hospital admissions: 259.3 per 10,000 population (2007).

**Elections:** 2008 Presidential election results: 41.7% Obama, 56.0% McCain, 1.4% Nader

**National and State Parks:** Max V Shaul State Park

**Additional Information Contacts**

Schoharie County Government . . . . . . . . . . . . . . . . . . . . . (518) 295-8114
   http://www.schohariecounty-ny.gov
Schoharie County Chamber of Commerce . . . . . . . . . . . (518) 296-8820
   http://www.schohariechamber.com
Town of Esperance . . . . . . . . . . . . . . . . . . . . . . . . . . . (518) 875-6109
   http://townofesperance.org
Village of Cobleskill . . . . . . . . . . . . . . . . . . . . . . . . . . (518) 234-3891
   http://www.schohariecounty-ny.gov/CountyWebSite/villcob

## Schoharie County Communities

**BLENHEIM** (town). Covers a land area of 33.933 square miles and a water area of 0.460 square miles. Located at 42.48° N. Lat; 74.52° W. Long.

**Population:** 332 (1990); 330 (2000); 377 (2010); Density: 11.1 persons per square mile (2010); Race: 97.3% White, 0.8% Black, 0.0% Asian, 0.0% American Indian/Alaska Native, 0.0% Native Hawaiian/Other Pacific Islander, 1.9% Other, 1.6% Hispanic of any race (2010); Average household size: 2.39 (2010); Median age: 46.6 (2010); Males per 100 females: 96.4 (2010); Marriage status: 10.0% never married, 63.5% now married, 11.8% widowed, 14.8% divorced (2006-2010 5-year est.); Foreign born: 4.8% (2006-2010 5-year est.); Ancestry (includes multiple ancestries): 34.5% German, 23.0% Irish, 19.4% Dutch, 12.1% English, 8.8% Italian (2006-2010 5-year est.).

**Economy:** Single-family building permits issued: 2 (2011); Multi-family building permits issued: 0 (2011); Employment by occupation: 4.2% management, 10.8% professional, 12.5% services, 10.8% sales, 0.0% farming, 20.0% construction, 8.3% production (2006-2010 5-year est.).

**Income:** Per capita income: $20,865 (2006-2010 5-year est.); Median household income: $50,833 (2006-2010 5-year est.); Average household income: $48,023 (2006-2010 5-year est.); Percent of households with income of $100,000 or more: 4.3% (2006-2010 5-year est.); Poverty rate: 18.3% (2006-2010 5-year est.).

**Education:** Percent of population age 25 and over with: High school diploma (including GED) or higher: 78.3% (2006-2010 5-year est.); Bachelor's degree or higher: 12.6% (2006-2010 5-year est.); Master's degree or higher: 2.0% (2006-2010 5-year est.).

**Housing:** Homeownership rate: 88.6% (2010); Median home value: $100,800 (2006-2010 5-year est.); Median contract rent: $621 per month (2006-2010 5-year est.); Median year structure built: 1974 (2006-2010 5-year est.)

**Transportation:** Commute to work: 94.0% car, 0.0% public transportation, 0.0% walk, 6.0% work from home (2006-2010 5-year est.); Travel time to work: 26.4% less than 15 minutes, 21.8% 15 to 30 minutes, 19.1% 30 to 45 minutes, 2.7% 45 to 60 minutes, 30.0% 60 minutes or more (2006-2010 5-year est.)

**BROOME** (town). Covers a land area of 47.741 square miles and a water area of 0.250 square miles. Located at 42.50° N. Lat; 74.29° W. Long.

**Population:** 949 (1990); 947 (2000); 973 (2010); Density: 20.4 persons per square mile (2010); Race: 96.8% White, 0.7% Black, 0.4% Asian, 1.0% American Indian/Alaska Native, 0.0% Native Hawaiian/Other Pacific Islander, 1.1% Other, 3.5% Hispanic of any race (2010); Average household size: 2.21 (2010); Median age: 49.0 (2010); Males per 100 females: 107.9 (2010); Marriage status: 18.9% never married, 59.4% now married, 10.7% widowed, 11.0% divorced (2006-2010 5-year est.); Foreign born: 2.5% (2006-2010 5-year est.); Ancestry (includes multiple ancestries): 43.8% German, 35.6% Irish, 14.2% Italian, 12.8% English, 11.6% Dutch (2006-2010 5-year est.).

**Economy:** Employment by occupation: 13.5% management, 0.0% professional, 12.9% services, 18.8% sales, 1.1% farming, 25.9% construction, 7.0% production (2006-2010 5-year est.).

**Income:** Per capita income: $29,244 (2006-2010 5-year est.); Median household income: $42,273 (2006-2010 5-year est.); Average household income: $61,555 (2006-2010 5-year est.); Percent of households with income of $100,000 or more: 14.5% (2006-2010 5-year est.); Poverty rate: 5.5% (2006-2010 5-year est.).

**Education:** Percent of population age 25 and over with: High school diploma (including GED) or higher: 90.1% (2006-2010 5-year est.); Bachelor's degree or higher: 9.7% (2006-2010 5-year est.); Master's degree or higher: 2.7% (2006-2010 5-year est.).

**Housing:** Homeownership rate: 87.5% (2010); Median home value: $132,000 (2006-2010 5-year est.); Median contract rent: $372 per month (2006-2010 5-year est.); Median year structure built: 1970 (2006-2010 5-year est.)

**Transportation:** Commute to work: 95.5% car, 0.0% public transportation, 0.0% walk, 4.5% work from home (2006-2010 5-year est.); Travel time to work: 15.8% less than 15 minutes, 20.6% 15 to 30 minutes, 32.6% 30 to 45 minutes, 11.3% 45 to 60 minutes, 19.7% 60 minutes or more (2006-2010 5-year est.)

**CARLISLE** (town). Covers a land area of 34.123 square miles and a water area of 0.128 square miles. Located at 42.74° N. Lat; 74.43° W. Long. Elevation is 1,283 feet.

**Population:** 1,672 (1990); 1,758 (2000); 1,948 (2010); Density: 57.1 persons per square mile (2010); Race: 96.3% White, 1.2% Black, 0.3% Asian, 0.3% American Indian/Alaska Native, 0.0% Native Hawaiian/Other Pacific Islander, 1.9% Other, 3.6% Hispanic of any race (2010); Average household size: 2.68 (2010); Median age: 40.4 (2010); Males per 100 females: 100.0 (2010); Marriage status: 26.3% never married, 60.2% now married, 5.0% widowed, 8.5% divorced (2006-2010 5-year est.); Foreign born: 1.5% (2006-2010 5-year est.); Ancestry (includes multiple ancestries): 34.6% German, 20.8% Irish, 19.6% American, 16.0% English, 5.1% Italian (2006-2010 5-year est.).

**Economy:** Single-family building permits issued: 2 (2011); Multi-family building permits issued: 0 (2011); Employment by occupation: 16.2% management, 6.3% professional, 6.1% services, 20.5% sales, 1.1% farming, 18.5% construction, 9.6% production (2006-2010 5-year est.).

**Income:** Per capita income: $24,500 (2006-2010 5-year est.); Median household income: $63,750 (2006-2010 5-year est.); Average household income: $67,406 (2006-2010 5-year est.); Percent of households with income of $100,000 or more: 20.9% (2006-2010 5-year est.); Poverty rate: 8.4% (2006-2010 5-year est.).

**Education:** Percent of population age 25 and over with: High school diploma (including GED) or higher: 87.6% (2006-2010 5-year est.); Bachelor's degree or higher: 20.4% (2006-2010 5-year est.); Master's degree or higher: 6.6% (2006-2010 5-year est.).

**Housing:** Homeownership rate: 79.6% (2010); Median home value: $143,600 (2006-2010 5-year est.); Median contract rent: $569 per month (2006-2010 5-year est.); Median year structure built: 1970 (2006-2010 5-year est.)

**Transportation:** Commute to work: 86.2% car, 1.7% public transportation, 1.9% walk, 7.6% work from home (2006-2010 5-year est.); Travel time to work: 21.4% less than 15 minutes, 31.2% 15 to 30 minutes, 12.8% 30 to 45 minutes, 28.3% 45 to 60 minutes, 6.3% 60 minutes or more (2006-2010 5-year est.)

**CENTRAL BRIDGE** (CDP). Covers a land area of 1.843 square miles and a water area of 0.013 square miles. Located at 42.70° N. Lat; 74.34° W. Long. Elevation is 620 feet.

**Population:** n/a (1990); n/a (2000); 593 (2010); Density: 321.7 persons per square mile (2010); Race: 97.5% White, 0.5% Black, 0.5% Asian, 0.0% American Indian/Alaska Native, 0.0% Native Hawaiian/Other Pacific Islander, 1.5% Other, 1.3% Hispanic of any race (2010); Average household size: 2.22 (2010); Median age: 38.1 (2010); Males per 100 females: 97.7 (2010); Marriage status: 19.2% never married, 49.7% now married, 23.7% widowed, 7.4% divorced (2006-2010 5-year est.); Foreign born: 0.0% (2006-2010 5-year est.); Ancestry (includes multiple ancestries): 51.2% German, 34.6% English, 14.5% French, 9.0% Irish, 7.0% European (2006-2010 5-year est.).

**Economy:** Employment by occupation: 0.0% management, 0.0% professional, 19.0% services, 43.5% sales, 0.0% farming, 5.8% construction, 4.8% production (2006-2010 5-year est.).

**Income:** Per capita income: $18,416 (2006-2010 5-year est.); Median household income: $31,321 (2006-2010 5-year est.); Average household income: $39,187 (2006-2010 5-year est.); Percent of households with income of $100,000 or more: 14.4% (2006-2010 5-year est.); Poverty rate: 23.6% (2006-2010 5-year est.).

**Education:** Percent of population age 25 and over with: High school diploma (including GED) or higher: 91.0% (2006-2010 5-year est.); Bachelor's degree or higher: 31.1% (2006-2010 5-year est.); Master's degree or higher: 21.6% (2006-2010 5-year est.).

**Housing:** Homeownership rate: 55.5% (2010); Median home value: $149,300 (2006-2010 5-year est.); Median contract rent: $373 per month (2006-2010 5-year est.); Median year structure built: 1946 (2006-2010 5-year est.).

**Transportation:** Commute to work: 92.9% car, 0.0% public transportation, 0.0% walk, 0.0% work from home (2006-2010 5-year est.); Travel time to work: 16.7% less than 15 minutes, 46.9% 15 to 30 minutes, 20.1% 30 to 45 minutes, 16.3% 45 to 60 minutes, 0.0% 60 minutes or more (2006-2010 5-year est.)

**CHARLOTTEVILLE** (unincorporated postal area)

Zip Code: 12036

Covers a land area of 7.406 square miles and a water area of 0.008 square miles. Located at 42.54° N. Lat; 74.67° W. Long. Elevation is 1,604 feet. Population: 228 (2010); Density: 30.8 persons per square mile (2010); Race: 97.4% White, 0.4% Black, 0.4% Asian, 0.0% American Indian/Alaska Native, 0.0% Native Hawaiian/Other Pacific Islander, 1.8% Other, 3.5% Hispanic of any race (2010); Average household size: 2.43 (2010); Median age: 47.0 (2010); Males per 100 females: 103.6 (2010); Homeownership rate: 86.2% (2010)

**COBLESKILL** (village). Covers a land area of 3.571 square miles and a water area of 0.003 square miles. Located at 42.67° N. Lat; 74.48° W. Long. Elevation is 922 feet.

**Population:** 5,256 (1990); 4,533 (2000); 4,678 (2010); Density: 1,309.6 persons per square mile (2010); Race: 90.2% White, 4.2% Black, 1.9% Asian, 0.3% American Indian/Alaska Native, 0.0% Native Hawaiian/Other Pacific Islander, 3.4% Other, 4.7% Hispanic of any race (2010); Average household size: 2.07 (2010); Median age: 24.5 (2010); Males per 100 females: 93.0 (2010); Marriage status: 57.2% never married, 25.5% now married, 9.1% widowed, 8.3% divorced (2006-2010 5-year est.); Foreign born: 2.9% (2006-2010 5-year est.); Ancestry (includes multiple ancestries): 25.8% Irish, 24.8% German, 17.7% Italian, 9.8% Polish, 8.7% American (2006-2010 5-year est.).

**Economy:** Single-family building permits issued: 0 (2011); Multi-family building permits issued: 3 (2011); Employment by occupation: 14.7% management, 1.1% professional, 8.2% services, 15.8% sales, 6.6% farming, 9.8% construction, 6.2% production (2006-2010 5-year est.).

**Income:** Per capita income: $18,624 (2006-2010 5-year est.); Median household income: $30,455 (2006-2010 5-year est.); Average household income: $49,998 (2006-2010 5-year est.); Percent of households with income of $100,000 or more: 11.0% (2006-2010 5-year est.); Poverty rate: 29.1% (2006-2010 5-year est.).

**Education:** Percent of population age 25 and over with: High school diploma (including GED) or higher: 84.7% (2006-2010 5-year est.); Bachelor's degree or higher: 31.9% (2006-2010 5-year est.); Master's degree or higher: 20.2% (2006-2010 5-year est.).

### School District(s)
Cobleskill-Richmondville Central School District (PK-12)
   2009-10 Enrollment: 2,064 . . . . . . . . . . . . . . . . . . (518) 234-4032

### Four-year College(s)
SUNY College of Agriculture and Technology at Cobleskill (Public)
   Fall 2010 Enrollment: 2,556. . . . . . . . . . . . . . . . . . (518) 255-5525
   2011-12 Tuition: In-state $6,519; Out-of-state $15,569

**Housing:** Homeownership rate: 39.9% (2010); Median home value: $142,900 (2006-2010 5-year est.); Median contract rent: $581 per month (2006-2010 5-year est.); Median year structure built: 1952 (2006-2010 5-year est.).

**Hospitals:** Bassett Hospital of Schoharie County (40 beds)

**Safety:** Violent crime rate: 8.9 per 10,000 population; Property crime rate: 361.1 per 10,000 population (2010).

**Newspapers:** My Shopper/Schoharie Valley Edition (Community news; Circulation 15,442); Times-Journal (Community news; Circulation 6,400)

**Transportation:** Commute to work: 65.7% car, 5.3% public transportation, 16.7% walk, 3.7% work from home (2006-2010 5-year est.); Travel time to work: 59.8% less than 15 minutes, 20.9% 15 to 30 minutes, 7.7% 30 to 45 minutes, 3.8% 45 to 60 minutes, 7.8% 60 minutes or more (2006-2010 5-year est.)

**Additional Information Contacts**

Village of Cobleskill . . . . . . . . . . . . . . . . . . . . . . . (518) 234-3891
   http://www.schohariecounty-ny.gov/CountyWebSite/villcob

**COBLESKILL** (town). Covers a land area of 30.599 square miles and a water area of 0.178 square miles. Located at 42.68° N. Lat; 74.44° W. Long. Elevation is 922 feet.

**History:** The Borst & Burnhans Plant began in Cobleskill in 1800 as a feed, flour, and grist mill, and became famous for its pancake flour in 1890. The Harder Refrigerator Plant, established in 1859, made threshing machines, silos, manure spreaders, and refrigerators. Seat of State University of N.Y. College. of Agriculture and Technology at Cobleskill. Cobleskill Historic District. Settled in 1752, incorporated in 1868.

**Population:** 7,276 (1990); 6,407 (2000); 6,625 (2010); Density: 216.5 persons per square mile (2010); Race: 92.3% White, 3.1% Black, 1.6% Asian, 0.2% American Indian/Alaska Native, 0.0% Native Hawaiian/Other Pacific Islander, 2.8% Other, 4.1% Hispanic of any race (2010); Average household size: 2.19 (2010); Median age: 31.1 (2010); Males per 100 females: 94.9 (2010); Marriage status: 49.3% never married, 32.5% now married, 9.5% widowed, 8.7% divorced (2006-2010 5-year est.); Foreign born: 2.3% (2006-2010 5-year est.); Ancestry (includes multiple ancestries): 25.4% German, 23.8% Irish, 16.9% Italian, 10.5% English, 9.8% American (2006-2010 5-year est.).

**Economy:** Single-family building permits issued: 4 (2011); Multi-family building permits issued: 0 (2011); Employment by occupation: 16.1% management, 1.7% professional, 6.5% services, 18.2% sales, 5.0% farming, 12.4% construction, 8.3% production (2006-2010 5-year est.).

**Income:** Per capita income: $22,269 (2006-2010 5-year est.); Median household income: $41,144 (2006-2010 5-year est.); Average household income: $57,943 (2006-2010 5-year est.); Percent of households with income of $100,000 or more: 16.5% (2006-2010 5-year est.); Poverty rate: 20.8% (2006-2010 5-year est.).

**Education:** Percent of population age 25 and over with: High school diploma (including GED) or higher: 85.0% (2006-2010 5-year est.); Bachelor's degree or higher: 29.8% (2006-2010 5-year est.); Master's degree or higher: 18.6% (2006-2010 5-year est.).

### School District(s)
Cobleskill-Richmondville Central School District (PK-12)
   2009-10 Enrollment: 2,064 . . . . . . . . . . . . . . . . . . (518) 234-4032

### Four-year College(s)
SUNY College of Agriculture and Technology at Cobleskill (Public)
   Fall 2010 Enrollment: 2,556. . . . . . . . . . . . . . . . . . (518) 255-5525
   2011-12 Tuition: In-state $6,519; Out-of-state $15,569

**Housing:** Homeownership rate: 53.7% (2010); Median home value: $141,100 (2006-2010 5-year est.); Median contract rent: $583 per month (2006-2010 5-year est.); Median year structure built: 1954 (2006-2010 5-year est.).

**Hospitals:** Bassett Hospital of Schoharie County (40 beds)

**Newspapers:** My Shopper/Schoharie Valley Edition (Community news; Circulation 15,442); Times-Journal (Community news; Circulation 6,400)

**Transportation:** Commute to work: 73.9% car, 3.9% public transportation, 13.1% walk, 2.7% work from home (2006-2010 5-year est.); Travel time to work: 58.9% less than 15 minutes, 17.4% 15 to 30 minutes, 9.7% 30 to 45 minutes, 5.9% 45 to 60 minutes, 8.2% 60 minutes or more (2006-2010 5-year est.)

## CONESVILLE (town). Covers a land area of 39.465 square miles and a water area of 0.403 square miles. Located at 42.39° N. Lat; 74.33° W. Long. Elevation is 1,381 feet.

**Population:** 684 (1990); 726 (2000); 734 (2010); Density: 18.6 persons per square mile (2010); Race: 96.9% White, 1.0% Black, 0.3% Asian, 0.3% American Indian/Alaska Native, 0.0% Native Hawaiian/Other Pacific Islander, 1.5% Other, 2.7% Hispanic of any race (2010); Average household size: 2.17 (2010); Median age: 49.3 (2010); Males per 100 females: 96.3 (2010); Marriage status: 23.3% never married, 64.4% now married, 8.8% widowed, 3.5% divorced (2006-2010 5-year est.); Foreign born: 8.2% (2006-2010 5-year est.); Ancestry (includes multiple ancestries): 31.7% Irish, 27.7% German, 19.6% English, 11.7% Italian, 10.9% Dutch (2006-2010 5-year est.).
**Economy:** Single-family building permits issued: 2 (2011); Multi-family building permits issued: 0 (2011); Employment by occupation: 7.2% management, 0.0% professional, 6.2% services, 13.6% sales, 0.0% farming, 18.9% construction, 14.8% production (2006-2010 5-year est.).
**Income:** Per capita income: $27,031 (2006-2010 5-year est.); Median household income: $57,386 (2006-2010 5-year est.); Average household income: $57,733 (2006-2010 5-year est.); Percent of households with income of $100,000 or more: 10.8% (2006-2010 5-year est.); Poverty rate: 9.8% (2006-2010 5-year est.).
**Education:** Percent of population age 25 and over with: High school diploma (including GED) or higher: 92.8% (2006-2010 5-year est.); Bachelor's degree or higher: 17.8% (2006-2010 5-year est.); Master's degree or higher: 8.9% (2006-2010 5-year est.).
**Housing:** Homeownership rate: 90.0% (2010); Median home value: $124,400 (2006-2010 5-year est.); Median contract rent: $427 per month (2006-2010 5-year est.); Median year structure built: 1978 (2006-2010 5-year est.).
**Transportation:** Commute to work: 94.5% car, 0.0% public transportation, 0.0% walk, 5.5% work from home (2006-2010 5-year est.); Travel time to work: 19.3% less than 15 minutes, 39.4% 15 to 30 minutes, 20.6% 30 to 45 minutes, 3.2% 45 to 60 minutes, 17.5% 60 minutes or more (2006-2010 5-year est.)

## ESPERANCE (village). Covers a land area of 0.491 square miles and a water area of 0.030 square miles. Located at 42.76° N. Lat; 74.25° W. Long. Elevation is 581 feet.

**Population:** 324 (1990); 380 (2000); 345 (2010); Density: 702.5 persons per square mile (2010); Race: 93.0% White, 3.5% Black, 0.3% Asian, 0.0% American Indian/Alaska Native, 0.0% Native Hawaiian/Other Pacific Islander, 3.2% Other, 4.9% Hispanic of any race (2010); Average household size: 2.33 (2010); Median age: 40.4 (2010); Males per 100 females: 106.6 (2010); Marriage status: 20.9% never married, 58.7% now married, 3.2% widowed, 17.2% divorced (2006-2010 5-year est.); Foreign born: 8.9% (2006-2010 5-year est.); Ancestry (includes multiple ancestries): 28.1% German, 23.0% English, 16.1% Italian, 11.8% Dutch, 8.5% Irish (2006-2010 5-year est.).
**Economy:** Single-family building permits issued: 1 (2011); Multi-family building permits issued: 0 (2011); Employment by occupation: 7.5% management, 0.0% professional, 16.5% services, 13.2% sales, 7.5% farming, 18.0% construction, 9.0% production (2006-2010 5-year est.).
**Income:** Per capita income: $27,727 (2006-2010 5-year est.); Median household income: $67,750 (2006-2010 5-year est.); Average household income: $69,942 (2006-2010 5-year est.); Percent of households with income of $100,000 or more: 19.3% (2006-2010 5-year est.); Poverty rate: 4.0% (2006-2010 5-year est.).
**Education:** Percent of population age 25 and over with: High school diploma (including GED) or higher: 88.9% (2006-2010 5-year est.); Bachelor's degree or higher: 16.2% (2006-2010 5-year est.); Master's degree or higher: 8.5% (2006-2010 5-year est.).
**Housing:** Homeownership rate: 81.1% (2010); Median home value: $135,200 (2006-2010 5-year est.); Median contract rent: $504 per month (2006-2010 5-year est.); Median year structure built: 1952 (2006-2010 5-year est.).
**Transportation:** Commute to work: 91.5% car, 0.0% public transportation, 0.0% walk, 6.1% work from home (2006-2010 5-year est.); Travel time to work: 29.0% less than 15 minutes, 22.9% 15 to 30 minutes, 28.6% 30 to 45

minutes, 17.3% 45 to 60 minutes, 2.2% 60 minutes or more (2006-2010 5-year est.)

## ESPERANCE (town). Covers a land area of 19.666 square miles and a water area of 0.370 square miles. Located at 42.75° N. Lat; 74.31° W. Long. Elevation is 581 feet.

**Population:** 2,101 (1990); 2,043 (2000); 2,076 (2010); Density: 105.6 persons per square mile (2010); Race: 96.9% White, 0.8% Black, 0.2% Asian, 0.2% American Indian/Alaska Native, 0.0% Native Hawaiian/Other Pacific Islander, 1.9% Other, 2.3% Hispanic of any race (2010); Average household size: 2.49 (2010); Median age: 42.0 (2010); Males per 100 females: 101.6 (2010); Marriage status: 21.6% never married, 59.8% now married, 4.1% widowed, 14.4% divorced (2006-2010 5-year est.); Foreign born: 3.3% (2006-2010 5-year est.); Ancestry (includes multiple ancestries): 25.3% German, 18.3% English, 17.6% American, 12.3% Irish, 9.8% Italian (2006-2010 5-year est.).
**Economy:** Single-family building permits issued: 3 (2011); Multi-family building permits issued: 0 (2011); Employment by occupation: 9.4% management, 3.5% professional, 13.0% services, 13.0% sales, 5.2% farming, 18.2% construction, 8.6% production (2006-2010 5-year est.).
**Income:** Per capita income: $29,504 (2006-2010 5-year est.); Median household income: $59,451 (2006-2010 5-year est.); Average household income: $73,790 (2006-2010 5-year est.); Percent of households with income of $100,000 or more: 22.2% (2006-2010 5-year est.); Poverty rate: 6.0% (2006-2010 5-year est.).
**Education:** Percent of population age 25 and over with: High school diploma (including GED) or higher: 90.0% (2006-2010 5-year est.); Bachelor's degree or higher: 18.3% (2006-2010 5-year est.); Master's degree or higher: 5.6% (2006-2010 5-year est.).
**Housing:** Homeownership rate: 81.9% (2010); Median home value: $121,200 (2006-2010 5-year est.); Median contract rent: $444 per month (2006-2010 5-year est.); Median year structure built: 1971 (2006-2010 5-year est.).
**Transportation:** Commute to work: 96.7% car, 0.0% public transportation, 0.0% walk, 1.4% work from home (2006-2010 5-year est.); Travel time to work: 14.9% less than 15 minutes, 29.8% 15 to 30 minutes, 32.6% 30 to 45 minutes, 16.1% 45 to 60 minutes, 6.7% 60 minutes or more (2006-2010 5-year est.)
**Additional Information Contacts**
Town of Esperance . . . . . . . . . . . . . . . . . . . . . . . . . . . . . (518) 875-6109
  http://townofesperance.org

## FULTON (town). Covers a land area of 64.978 square miles and a water area of 0.027 square miles. Located at 42.58° N. Lat; 74.45° W. Long.

**Population:** 1,514 (1990); 1,495 (2000); 1,442 (2010); Density: 22.2 persons per square mile (2010); Race: 93.1% White, 4.3% Black, 0.7% Asian, 0.6% American Indian/Alaska Native, 0.0% Native Hawaiian/Other Pacific Islander, 1.3% Other, 2.6% Hispanic of any race (2010); Average household size: 2.39 (2010); Median age: 42.5 (2010); Males per 100 females: 127.8 (2010); Marriage status: 35.1% never married, 52.5% now married, 4.2% widowed, 8.2% divorced (2006-2010 5-year est.); Foreign born: 1.4% (2006-2010 5-year est.); Ancestry (includes multiple ancestries): 30.7% German, 23.4% Irish, 14.0% Italian, 13.7% Dutch, 10.9% English (2006-2010 5-year est.).
**Economy:** Employment by occupation: 8.0% management, 0.0% professional, 14.7% services, 18.2% sales, 4.9% farming, 17.1% construction, 8.5% production (2006-2010 5-year est.).
**Income:** Per capita income: $20,881 (2006-2010 5-year est.); Median household income: $45,870 (2006-2010 5-year est.); Average household income: $50,849 (2006-2010 5-year est.); Percent of households with income of $100,000 or more: 7.1% (2006-2010 5-year est.); Poverty rate: 12.4% (2006-2010 5-year est.).
**Education:** Percent of population age 25 and over with: High school diploma (including GED) or higher: 73.3% (2006-2010 5-year est.); Bachelor's degree or higher: 15.9% (2006-2010 5-year est.); Master's degree or higher: 5.3% (2006-2010 5-year est.).
**Housing:** Homeownership rate: 86.4% (2010); Median home value: $113,100 (2006-2010 5-year est.); Median contract rent: $502 per month (2006-2010 5-year est.); Median year structure built: 1974 (2006-2010 5-year est.).
**Transportation:** Commute to work: 94.5% car, 0.0% public transportation, 0.4% walk, 5.2% work from home (2006-2010 5-year est.); Travel time to work: 13.9% less than 15 minutes, 39.0% 15 to 30 minutes, 16.1% 30 to 45

minutes, 8.3% 45 to 60 minutes, 22.7% 60 minutes or more (2006-2010 5-year est.)

## FULTONHAM (unincorporated postal area)
Zip Code: 12071

Covers a land area of 9.231 square miles and a water area of 0 square miles. Located at 42.55° N. Lat; 74.42° W. Long. Elevation is 702 feet. Population: 270 (2010); Density: 29.2 persons per square mile (2010); Race: 97.0% White, 0.4% Black, 0.7% Asian, 0.0% American Indian/Alaska Native, 0.0% Native Hawaiian/Other Pacific Islander, 1.9% Other, 1.1% Hispanic of any race (2010); Average household size: 2.41 (2010); Median age: 43.0 (2010); Males per 100 females: 104.5 (2010); Homeownership rate: 80.3% (2010)

## GILBOA (town). Covers a land area of 57.800 square miles and a water area of 1.575 square miles. Located at 42.43° N. Lat; 74.45° W. Long. Elevation is 1,027 feet.
Population: 1,207 (1990); 1,215 (2000); 1,307 (2010); Density: 22.6 persons per square mile (2010); Race: 97.2% White, 0.6% Black, 0.3% Asian, 0.1% American Indian/Alaska Native, 0.0% Native Hawaiian/Other Pacific Islander, 1.8% Other, 3.3% Hispanic of any race (2010); Average household size: 2.40 (2010); Median age: 48.7 (2010); Males per 100 females: 104.9 (2010); Marriage status: 18.5% never married, 62.5% now married, 9.3% widowed, 9.7% divorced (2006-2010 5-year est.); Foreign born: 4.4% (2006-2010 5-year est.); Ancestry (includes multiple ancestries): 24.9% Irish, 23.0% German, 15.4% English, 15.0% Italian, 10.4% Dutch (2006-2010 5-year est.).
Economy: Single-family building permits issued: 2 (2011); Multi-family building permits issued: 0 (2011); Employment by occupation: 7.0% management, 0.0% professional, 6.3% services, 18.6% sales, 1.6% farming, 23.9% construction, 9.4% production (2006-2010 5-year est.).
Income: Per capita income: $27,275 (2006-2010 5-year est.); Median household income: $55,703 (2006-2010 5-year est.); Average household income: $61,813 (2006-2010 5-year est.); Percent of households with income of $100,000 or more: 14.1% (2006-2010 5-year est.); Poverty rate: 10.0% (2006-2010 5-year est.).
Education: Percent of population age 25 and over with: High school diploma (including GED) or higher: 89.7% (2006-2010 5-year est.); Bachelor's degree or higher: 12.1% (2006-2010 5-year est.); Master's degree or higher: 3.6% (2006-2010 5-year est.).
### School District(s)
Gilboa-Conesville Central School District (PK-12)
   2009-10 Enrollment: 414 . . . . . . . . . . . . . . . . . . (607) 588-7541
Housing: Homeownership rate: 90.7% (2010); Median home value: $162,900 (2006-2010 5-year est.); Median contract rent: $663 per month (2006-2010 5-year est.); Median year structure built: 1969 (2006-2010 5-year est.).
Transportation: Commute to work: 94.6% car, 0.8% public transportation, 1.0% walk, 3.5% work from home (2006-2010 5-year est.); Travel time to work: 17.7% less than 15 minutes, 34.4% 15 to 30 minutes, 25.8% 30 to 45 minutes, 11.5% 45 to 60 minutes, 10.6% 60 minutes or more (2006-2010 5-year est.)

## HOWES CAVE (unincorporated postal area)
Zip Code: 12092

Covers a land area of 14.957 square miles and a water area of 0.171 square miles. Located at 42.69° N. Lat; 74.37° W. Long. Elevation is 781 feet. Population: 1,304 (2010); Density: 87.2 persons per square mile (2010); Race: 96.5% White, 0.8% Black, 1.2% Asian, 0.1% American Indian/Alaska Native, 0.0% Native Hawaiian/Other Pacific Islander, 1.4% Other, 1.3% Hispanic of any race (2010); Average household size: 2.39 (2010); Median age: 42.5 (2010); Males per 100 females: 97.0 (2010); Homeownership rate: 70.3% (2010)

## JEFFERSON (town). Covers a land area of 43.250 square miles and a water area of 0.163 square miles. Located at 42.48° N. Lat; 74.60° W. Long. Elevation is 1,867 feet.
Population: 1,190 (1990); 1,285 (2000); 1,410 (2010); Density: 32.6 persons per square mile (2010); Race: 97.2% White, 0.7% Black, 0.1% Asian, 0.4% American Indian/Alaska Native, 0.0% Native Hawaiian/Other Pacific Islander, 1.6% Other, 2.8% Hispanic of any race (2010); Average household size: 2.41 (2010); Median age: 46.4 (2010); Males per 100 females: 105.8 (2010); Marriage status: 25.4% never married, 57.0% now married, 8.2% widowed, 9.4% divorced (2006-2010 5-year est.); Foreign born: 1.7% (2006-2010 5-year est.); Ancestry (includes multiple

ancestries): 28.1% Irish, 26.5% Italian, 24.3% German, 9.2% English, 7.6% French (2006-2010 5-year est.).
Economy: Employment by occupation: 21.5% management, 1.7% professional, 13.6% services, 14.3% sales, 2.9% farming, 13.6% construction, 7.1% production (2006-2010 5-year est.).
Income: Per capita income: $24,956 (2006-2010 5-year est.); Median household income: $48,618 (2006-2010 5-year est.); Average household income: $62,418 (2006-2010 5-year est.); Percent of households with income of $100,000 or more: 15.8% (2006-2010 5-year est.); Poverty rate: 13.1% (2006-2010 5-year est.).
Education: Percent of population age 25 and over with: High school diploma (including GED) or higher: 85.4% (2006-2010 5-year est.); Bachelor's degree or higher: 19.4% (2006-2010 5-year est.); Master's degree or higher: 6.9% (2006-2010 5-year est.).
### School District(s)
Jefferson Central School District (PK-12)
   2009-10 Enrollment: 294 . . . . . . . . . . . . . . . . . . (607) 652-7821
Housing: Homeownership rate: 86.8% (2010); Median home value: $161,400 (2006-2010 5-year est.); Median contract rent: $645 per month (2006-2010 5-year est.); Median year structure built: 1975 (2006-2010 5-year est.).
Transportation: Commute to work: 86.2% car, 1.2% public transportation, 2.6% walk, 10.0% work from home (2006-2010 5-year est.); Travel time to work: 28.3% less than 15 minutes, 23.9% 15 to 30 minutes, 29.5% 30 to 45 minutes, 3.6% 45 to 60 minutes, 14.8% 60 minutes or more (2006-2010 5-year est.)

## MIDDLEBURGH (village). Covers a land area of 1.247 square miles and a water area of 0 square miles. Located at 42.59° N. Lat; 74.32° W. Long. Elevation is 640 feet.
Population: 1,455 (1990); 1,398 (2000); 1,500 (2010); Density: 1,202.6 persons per square mile (2010); Race: 95.7% White, 0.5% Black, 0.6% Asian, 0.4% American Indian/Alaska Native, 0.0% Native Hawaiian/Other Pacific Islander, 2.8% Other, 2.7% Hispanic of any race (2010); Average household size: 2.17 (2010); Median age: 43.0 (2010); Males per 100 females: 85.9 (2010); Marriage status: 28.3% never married, 51.7% now married, 12.6% widowed, 7.5% divorced (2006-2010 5-year est.); Foreign born: 3.2% (2006-2010 5-year est.); Ancestry (includes multiple ancestries): 31.9% German, 26.0% Irish, 17.6% Italian, 12.6% English, 12.1% Dutch (2006-2010 5-year est.).
Economy: Single-family building permits issued: 1 (2011); Multi-family building permits issued: 0 (2011); Employment by occupation: 9.2% management, 4.4% professional, 12.7% services, 15.0% sales, 3.7% farming, 14.2% construction, 7.7% production (2006-2010 5-year est.).
Income: Per capita income: $24,226 (2006-2010 5-year est.); Median household income: $45,175 (2006-2010 5-year est.); Average household income: $53,505 (2006-2010 5-year est.); Percent of households with income of $100,000 or more: 13.0% (2006-2010 5-year est.); Poverty rate: 12.6% (2006-2010 5-year est.).
Education: Percent of population age 25 and over with: High school diploma (including GED) or higher: 90.2% (2006-2010 5-year est.); Bachelor's degree or higher: 15.3% (2006-2010 5-year est.); Master's degree or higher: 6.0% (2006-2010 5-year est.).
### School District(s)
Middleburgh Central School District (PK-12)
   2009-10 Enrollment: 922 . . . . . . . . . . . . . . . . . . (518) 827-3625
Housing: Homeownership rate: 58.0% (2010); Median home value: $142,600 (2006-2010 5-year est.); Median contract rent: $543 per month (2006-2010 5-year est.); Median year structure built: 1960 (2006-2010 5-year est.).
Transportation: Commute to work: 88.3% car, 1.9% public transportation, 7.5% walk, 1.6% work from home (2006-2010 5-year est.); Travel time to work: 36.5% less than 15 minutes, 29.3% 15 to 30 minutes, 14.2% 30 to 45 minutes, 13.6% 45 to 60 minutes, 6.4% 60 minutes or more (2006-2010 5-year est.)

## MIDDLEBURGH (town). Covers a land area of 49.110 square miles and a water area of 0.098 square miles. Located at 42.62° N. Lat; 74.31° W. Long. Elevation is 640 feet.
Population: 3,290 (1990); 3,515 (2000); 3,746 (2010); Density: 76.3 persons per square mile (2010); Race: 97.3% White, 0.3% Black, 0.2% Asian, 0.2% American Indian/Alaska Native, 0.0% Native Hawaiian/Other Pacific Islander, 2.0% Other, 2.1% Hispanic of any race (2010); Average household size: 2.39 (2010); Median age: 43.5 (2010); Males per 100 females: 94.6 (2010); Marriage status: 29.4% never married, 55.2% now

married, 6.4% widowed, 9.0% divorced (2006-2010 5-year est.); Foreign born: 2.3% (2006-2010 5-year est.); Ancestry (includes multiple ancestries): 36.6% German, 21.5% Irish, 15.3% Dutch, 14.1% Italian, 11.2% English (2006-2010 5-year est.).

**Economy:** Single-family building permits issued: 2 (2011); Multi-family building permits issued: 0 (2011); Employment by occupation: 5.5% management, 1.9% professional, 12.6% services, 15.4% sales, 3.4% farming, 15.7% construction, 8.4% production (2006-2010 5-year est.).

**Income:** Per capita income: $25,353 (2006-2010 5-year est.); Median household income: $51,444 (2006-2010 5-year est.); Average household income: $64,001 (2006-2010 5-year est.); Percent of households with income of $100,000 or more: 16.9% (2006-2010 5-year est.); Poverty rate: 12.1% (2006-2010 5-year est.).

**Education:** Percent of population age 25 and over with: High school diploma (including GED) or higher: 85.9% (2006-2010 5-year est.); Bachelor's degree or higher: 18.4% (2006-2010 5-year est.); Master's degree or higher: 7.0% (2006-2010 5-year est.).

**School District(s)**
Middleburgh Central School District (PK-12)
    2009-10 Enrollment: 922 . . . . . . . . . . . . . . . . . . . . (518) 827-3625

**Housing:** Homeownership rate: 71.6% (2010); Median home value: $124,900 (2006-2010 5-year est.); Median contract rent: $529 per month (2006-2010 5-year est.); Median year structure built: 1967 (2006-2010 5-year est.).

**Transportation:** Commute to work: 89.7% car, 0.8% public transportation, 3.1% walk, 5.0% work from home (2006-2010 5-year est.); Travel time to work: 32.9% less than 15 minutes, 31.4% 15 to 30 minutes, 14.6% 30 to 45 minutes, 15.2% 45 to 60 minutes, 5.9% 60 minutes or more (2006-2010 5-year est.).

## NORTH BLENHEIM (unincorporated postal area)
Zip Code: 12131
    Covers a land area of 7.065 square miles and a water area of 0.404 square miles. Located at 42.45° N. Lat; 74.46° W. Long. Elevation is 791 feet. Population: 115 (2010); Density: 16.3 persons per square mile (2010); Race: 96.5% White, 0.0% Black, 0.0% Asian, 0.0% American Indian/Alaska Native, 0.0% Native Hawaiian/Other Pacific Islander, 3.5% Other, 0.9% Hispanic of any race (2010); Average household size: 2.45 (2010); Median age: 48.2 (2010); Males per 100 females: 117.0 (2010); Homeownership rate: 91.5% (2010)

## RICHMONDVILLE (village). Covers a land area of 1.846 square miles and a water area of 0 square miles. Located at 42.63° N. Lat; 74.56° W. Long. Elevation is 1,096 feet.
**Population:** 843 (1990); 786 (2000); 918 (2010); Density: 497.2 persons per square mile (2010); Race: 95.9% White, 1.3% Black, 0.3% Asian, 0.5% American Indian/Alaska Native, 0.0% Native Hawaiian/Other Pacific Islander, 2.0% Other, 3.3% Hispanic of any race (2010); Average household size: 2.47 (2010); Median age: 35.7 (2010); Males per 100 females: 82.5 (2010); Marriage status: 24.8% never married, 48.1% now married, 12.6% widowed, 14.5% divorced (2006-2010 5-year est.); Foreign born: 4.6% (2006-2010 5-year est.); Ancestry (includes multiple ancestries): 24.1% German, 21.7% American, 21.7% Irish, 10.1% English, 9.7% Italian (2006-2010 5-year est.).

**Economy:** Single-family building permits issued: 0 (2011); Multi-family building permits issued: 0 (2011); Employment by occupation: 6.2% management, 0.0% professional, 10.3% services, 23.2% sales, 0.0% farming, 10.7% construction, 8.1% production (2006-2010 5-year est.).

**Income:** Per capita income: $23,693 (2006-2010 5-year est.); Median household income: $43,587 (2006-2010 5-year est.); Average household income: $54,176 (2006-2010 5-year est.); Percent of households with income of $100,000 or more: 11.8% (2006-2010 5-year est.); Poverty rate: 8.7% (2006-2010 5-year est.).

**Education:** Percent of population age 25 and over with: High school diploma (including GED) or higher: 91.0% (2006-2010 5-year est.); Bachelor's degree or higher: 21.6% (2006-2010 5-year est.); Master's degree or higher: 7.0% (2006-2010 5-year est.).

**School District(s)**
Cobleskill-Richmondville Central School District (PK-12)
    2009-10 Enrollment: 2,064 . . . . . . . . . . . . . . . . . . (518) 234-4032

**Housing:** Homeownership rate: 58.8% (2010); Median home value: $134,900 (2006-2010 5-year est.); Median contract rent: $550 per month (2006-2010 5-year est.); Median year structure built: before 1940 (2006-2010 5-year est.).

**Transportation:** Commute to work: 92.4% car, 0.0% public transportation, 0.0% walk, 7.6% work from home (2006-2010 5-year est.); Travel time to work: 41.3% less than 15 minutes, 21.4% 15 to 30 minutes, 26.1% 30 to 45 minutes, 5.7% 45 to 60 minutes, 5.4% 60 minutes or more (2006-2010 5-year est.)

## RICHMONDVILLE (town). Covers a land area of 30.159 square miles and a water area of 0.064 square miles. Located at 42.63° N. Lat; 74.54° W. Long. Elevation is 1,096 feet.
**Population:** 2,391 (1990); 2,412 (2000); 2,610 (2010); Density: 86.5 persons per square mile (2010); Race: 96.9% White, 0.8% Black, 0.6% Asian, 0.3% American Indian/Alaska Native, 0.0% Native Hawaiian/Other Pacific Islander, 1.4% Other, 2.2% Hispanic of any race (2010); Average household size: 2.39 (2010); Median age: 42.1 (2010); Males per 100 females: 94.5 (2010); Marriage status: 26.5% never married, 55.3% now married, 6.7% widowed, 11.5% divorced (2006-2010 5-year est.); Foreign born: 1.6% (2006-2010 5-year est.); Ancestry (includes multiple ancestries): 29.9% German, 27.6% Irish, 14.3% American, 13.2% English, 12.0% Italian (2006-2010 5-year est.).

**Economy:** Single-family building permits issued: 1 (2011); Multi-family building permits issued: 0 (2011); Employment by occupation: 5.4% management, 0.7% professional, 12.3% services, 21.6% sales, 0.0% farming, 10.7% construction, 7.6% production (2006-2010 5-year est.).

**Income:** Per capita income: $20,146 (2006-2010 5-year est.); Median household income: $44,269 (2006-2010 5-year est.); Average household income: $48,609 (2006-2010 5-year est.); Percent of households with income of $100,000 or more: 6.8% (2006-2010 5-year est.); Poverty rate: 17.3% (2006-2010 5-year est.).

**Education:** Percent of population age 25 and over with: High school diploma (including GED) or higher: 90.0% (2006-2010 5-year est.); Bachelor's degree or higher: 15.4% (2006-2010 5-year est.); Master's degree or higher: 6.5% (2006-2010 5-year est.).

**School District(s)**
Cobleskill-Richmondville Central School District (PK-12)
    2009-10 Enrollment: 2,064 . . . . . . . . . . . . . . . . . . (518) 234-4032

**Housing:** Homeownership rate: 71.3% (2010); Median home value: $131,100 (2006-2010 5-year est.); Median contract rent: $581 per month (2006-2010 5-year est.); Median year structure built: 1970 (2006-2010 5-year est.).

**Transportation:** Commute to work: 88.5% car, 0.0% public transportation, 0.0% walk, 10.7% work from home (2006-2010 5-year est.); Travel time to work: 44.7% less than 15 minutes, 17.0% 15 to 30 minutes, 15.0% 30 to 45 minutes, 16.4% 45 to 60 minutes, 6.9% 60 minutes or more (2006-2010 5-year est.)

## SCHOHARIE (village). County seat. Covers a land area of 1.658 square miles and a water area of <.001 square miles. Located at 42.66° N. Lat; 74.31° W. Long. Elevation is 600 feet.
**Population:** 1,045 (1990); 1,030 (2000); 922 (2010); Density: 556.0 persons per square mile (2010); Race: 97.0% White, 1.2% Black, 0.1% Asian, 0.1% American Indian/Alaska Native, 0.0% Native Hawaiian/Other Pacific Islander, 1.6% Other, 2.5% Hispanic of any race (2010); Average household size: 1.99 (2010); Median age: 46.7 (2010); Males per 100 females: 91.7 (2010); Marriage status: 24.6% never married, 50.6% now married, 15.0% widowed, 9.7% divorced (2006-2010 5-year est.); Foreign born: 2.4% (2006-2010 5-year est.); Ancestry (includes multiple ancestries): 30.1% German, 22.6% Irish, 13.4% Italian, 13.4% English, 9.1% Polish (2006-2010 5-year est.).

**Economy:** Single-family building permits issued: 0 (2011); Multi-family building permits issued: 0 (2011); Employment by occupation: 12.6% management, 6.1% professional, 6.9% services, 12.6% sales, 4.0% farming, 10.1% construction, 8.4% production (2006-2010 5-year est.).

**Income:** Per capita income: $30,148 (2006-2010 5-year est.); Median household income: $60,909 (2006-2010 5-year est.); Average household income: $66,472 (2006-2010 5-year est.); Percent of households with income of $100,000 or more: 25.5% (2006-2010 5-year est.); Poverty rate: 6.2% (2006-2010 5-year est.).

**Education:** Percent of population age 25 and over with: High school diploma (including GED) or higher: 87.4% (2006-2010 5-year est.); Bachelor's degree or higher: 29.8% (2006-2010 5-year est.); Master's degree or higher: 13.8% (2006-2010 5-year est.).

**School District(s)**
Schoharie Central School District (KG-12)
    2009-10 Enrollment: 938 . . . . . . . . . . . . . . . . . . . (518) 295-6679

**Housing:** Homeownership rate: 56.1% (2010); Median home value: $160,300 (2006-2010 5-year est.); Median contract rent: $405 per month (2006-2010 5-year est.); Median year structure built: 1946 (2006-2010 5-year est.).
**Safety:** Violent crime rate: 20.9 per 10,000 population; Property crime rate: 83.6 per 10,000 population (2010).
**Transportation:** Commute to work: 82.4% car, 3.9% public transportation, 7.3% walk, 6.4% work from home (2006-2010 5-year est.); Travel time to work: 35.5% less than 15 minutes, 27.0% 15 to 30 minutes, 20.8% 30 to 45 minutes, 6.4% 45 to 60 minutes, 10.3% 60 minutes or more (2006-2010 5-year est.)
**Additional Information Contacts**
Schoharie County Chamber of Commerce . . . . . . . . . . . . . (518) 296-8820
  http://www.schohariechamber.com

**SCHOHARIE** (town). Covers a land area of 29.830 square miles and a water area of 0.129 square miles. Located at 42.67° N. Lat; 74.31° W. Long. Elevation is 600 feet.
**History:** Has 18th-century buildings including Old Stone Fort; 1772, now a museum. Incorporated 1867.
**Population:** 3,369 (1990); 3,299 (2000); 3,205 (2010); Density: 107.4 persons per square mile (2010); Race: 97.7% White, 0.6% Black, 0.4% Asian, 0.0% American Indian/Alaska Native, 0.0% Native Hawaiian/Other Pacific Islander, 1.3% Other, 1.5% Hispanic of any race (2010); Average household size: 2.27 (2010); Median age: 45.4 (2010); Males per 100 females: 93.5 (2010); Marriage status: 27.4% never married, 51.3% now married, 10.0% widowed, 11.4% divorced (2006-2010 5-year est.); Foreign born: 2.2% (2006-2010 5-year est.); Ancestry (includes multiple ancestries): 46.0% German, 25.8% English, 18.0% Irish, 11.4% American, 8.9% Italian (2006-2010 5-year est.).
**Economy:** Single-family building permits issued: 1 (2011); Multi-family building permits issued: 0 (2011); Employment by occupation: 6.7% management, 1.6% professional, 15.0% services, 18.0% sales, 5.6% farming, 8.6% construction, 10.3% production (2006-2010 5-year est.).
**Income:** Per capita income: $30,258 (2006-2010 5-year est.); Median household income: $53,065 (2006-2010 5-year est.); Average household income: $69,524 (2006-2010 5-year est.); Percent of households with income of $100,000 or more: 29.3% (2006-2010 5-year est.); Poverty rate: 8.1% (2006-2010 5-year est.).
**Education:** Percent of population age 25 and over with: High school diploma (including GED) or higher: 87.7% (2006-2010 5-year est.); Bachelor's degree or higher: 26.6% (2006-2010 5-year est.); Master's degree or higher: 10.0% (2006-2010 5-year est.).

**School District(s)**
Schoharie Central School District (KG-12)
  2009-10 Enrollment: 938 . . . . . . . . . . . . . . . . . . . . (518) 295-6679
**Housing:** Homeownership rate: 71.1% (2010); Median home value: $163,700 (2006-2010 5-year est.); Median contract rent: $387 per month (2006-2010 5-year est.); Median year structure built: 1959 (2006-2010 5-year est.).
**Transportation:** Commute to work: 87.5% car, 1.0% public transportation, 7.9% walk, 2.3% work from home (2006-2010 5-year est.); Travel time to work: 32.2% less than 15 minutes, 25.4% 15 to 30 minutes, 12.4% 30 to 45 minutes, 25.6% 45 to 60 minutes, 4.4% 60 minutes or more (2006-2010 5-year est.)

**SEWARD** (town). Covers a land area of 36.376 square miles and a water area of 0.079 square miles. Located at 42.70° N. Lat; 74.58° W. Long. Elevation is 1,184 feet.
**Population:** 1,653 (1990); 1,637 (2000); 1,763 (2010); Density: 48.5 persons per square mile (2010); Race: 96.1% White, 0.6% Black, 0.7% Asian, 0.0% American Indian/Alaska Native, 0.1% Native Hawaiian/Other Pacific Islander, 2.5% Other, 3.8% Hispanic of any race (2010); Average household size: 2.61 (2010); Median age: 43.6 (2010); Males per 100 females: 100.8 (2010); Marriage status: 19.9% never married, 64.3% now married, 4.9% widowed, 10.9% divorced (2006-2010 5-year est.); Foreign born: 2.9% (2006-2010 5-year est.); Ancestry (includes multiple ancestries): 30.0% German, 19.2% American, 16.8% Irish, 11.0% English, 7.2% Italian (2006-2010 5-year est.).
**Economy:** Single-family building permits issued: 2 (2011); Multi-family building permits issued: 0 (2011); Employment by occupation: 7.0% management, 5.4% professional, 4.4% services, 21.5% sales, 4.4% farming, 7.0% construction, 4.1% production (2006-2010 5-year est.).
**Income:** Per capita income: $26,497 (2006-2010 5-year est.); Median household income: $66,450 (2006-2010 5-year est.); Average household

income: $70,895 (2006-2010 5-year est.); Percent of households with income of $100,000 or more: 24.2% (2006-2010 5-year est.); Poverty rate: 2.6% (2006-2010 5-year est.).
**Education:** Percent of population age 25 and over with: High school diploma (including GED) or higher: 83.3% (2006-2010 5-year est.); Bachelor's degree or higher: 22.6% (2006-2010 5-year est.); Master's degree or higher: 7.7% (2006-2010 5-year est.).
**Housing:** Homeownership rate: 89.7% (2010); Median home value: $120,800 (2006-2010 5-year est.); Median contract rent: $450 per month (2006-2010 5-year est.); Median year structure built: 1961 (2006-2010 5-year est.).
**Transportation:** Commute to work: 86.8% car, 2.6% public transportation, 1.5% walk, 8.5% work from home (2006-2010 5-year est.); Travel time to work: 26.5% less than 15 minutes, 33.1% 15 to 30 minutes, 17.9% 30 to 45 minutes, 13.0% 45 to 60 minutes, 9.5% 60 minutes or more (2006-2010 5-year est.)

**SHARON** (town). Covers a land area of 39.062 square miles and a water area of 0.098 square miles. Located at 42.77° N. Lat; 74.61° W. Long. Elevation is 1,184 feet.
**History:** Former health resort, with sulphur springs.
**Population:** 1,890 (1990); 1,843 (2000); 1,846 (2010); Density: 47.3 persons per square mile (2010); Race: 96.2% White, 0.9% Black, 0.5% Asian, 0.1% American Indian/Alaska Native, 0.2% Native Hawaiian/Other Pacific Islander, 2.1% Other, 3.0% Hispanic of any race (2010); Average household size: 2.44 (2010); Median age: 42.4 (2010); Males per 100 females: 105.6 (2010); Marriage status: 28.6% never married, 52.7% now married, 8.3% widowed, 10.3% divorced (2006-2010 5-year est.); Foreign born: 5.1% (2006-2010 5-year est.); Ancestry (includes multiple ancestries): 24.7% German, 18.4% American, 16.7% English, 15.0% Irish, 13.4% Dutch (2006-2010 5-year est.).
**Economy:** Single-family building permits issued: 1 (2011); Multi-family building permits issued: 0 (2011); Employment by occupation: 15.2% management, 0.0% professional, 9.7% services, 14.2% sales, 2.1% farming, 13.1% construction, 6.3% production (2006-2010 5-year est.).
**Income:** Per capita income: $24,343 (2006-2010 5-year est.); Median household income: $49,426 (2006-2010 5-year est.); Average household income: $54,007 (2006-2010 5-year est.); Percent of households with income of $100,000 or more: 12.4% (2006-2010 5-year est.); Poverty rate: 8.6% (2006-2010 5-year est.).
**Education:** Percent of population age 25 and over with: High school diploma (including GED) or higher: 91.6% (2006-2010 5-year est.); Bachelor's degree or higher: 18.9% (2006-2010 5-year est.); Master's degree or higher: 7.1% (2006-2010 5-year est.).
**Housing:** Homeownership rate: 73.2% (2010); Median home value: $112,100 (2006-2010 5-year est.); Median contract rent: $463 per month (2006-2010 5-year est.); Median year structure built: 1944 (2006-2010 5-year est.).
**Transportation:** Commute to work: 82.1% car, 0.0% public transportation, 6.9% walk, 10.5% work from home (2006-2010 5-year est.); Travel time to work: 33.9% less than 15 minutes, 25.0% 15 to 30 minutes, 16.5% 30 to 45 minutes, 12.3% 45 to 60 minutes, 12.3% 60 minutes or more (2006-2010 5-year est.)

**SHARON SPRINGS** (village). Covers a land area of 1.826 square miles and a water area of 0 square miles. Located at 42.79° N. Lat; 74.61° W. Long. Elevation is 1,102 feet.
**Population:** 591 (1990); 547 (2000); 558 (2010); Density: 305.5 persons per square mile (2010); Race: 94.6% White, 0.7% Black, 1.4% Asian, 0.2% American Indian/Alaska Native, 0.0% Native Hawaiian/Other Pacific Islander, 3.1% Other, 4.3% Hispanic of any race (2010); Average household size: 2.33 (2010); Median age: 42.6 (2010); Males per 100 females: 100.7 (2010); Marriage status: 29.3% never married, 42.4% now married, 9.8% widowed, 18.5% divorced (2006-2010 5-year est.); Foreign born: 17.2% (2006-2010 5-year est.); Ancestry (includes multiple ancestries): 16.6% German, 14.4% Italian, 13.6% English, 11.6% American, 10.5% Irish (2006-2010 5-year est.).
**Economy:** Single-family building permits issued: 0 (2011); Multi-family building permits issued: 0 (2011); Employment by occupation: 18.8% management, 0.0% professional, 8.3% services, 3.9% sales, 1.7% farming, 11.0% construction, 1.7% production (2006-2010 5-year est.).
**Income:** Per capita income: $28,360 (2006-2010 5-year est.); Median household income: $53,182 (2006-2010 5-year est.); Average household income: $56,275 (2006-2010 5-year est.); Percent of households with

income of $100,000 or more: 18.6% (2006-2010 5-year est.); Poverty rate: 12.5% (2006-2010 5-year est.).
**Education:** Percent of population age 25 and over with: High school diploma (including GED) or higher: 94.6% (2006-2010 5-year est.); Bachelor's degree or higher: 43.6% (2006-2010 5-year est.); Master's degree or higher: 14.0% (2006-2010 5-year est.).

### School District(s)

Sharon Springs Central School District (PK-12)
2009-10 Enrollment: 349 . . . . . . . . . . . . . . . . . . . . . . . (518) 284-2266
**Housing:** Homeownership rate: 58.6% (2010); Median home value: $89,000 (2006-2010 5-year est.); Median contract rent: $377 per month (2006-2010 5-year est.); Median year structure built: before 1940 (2006-2010 5-year est.).
**Transportation:** Commute to work: 81.2% car, 0.0% public transportation, 12.2% walk, 4.4% work from home (2006-2010 5-year est.); Travel time to work: 48.6% less than 15 minutes, 19.7% 15 to 30 minutes, 15.6% 30 to 45 minutes, 1.7% 45 to 60 minutes, 14.5% 60 minutes or more (2006-2010 5-year est.)

**SLOANSVILLE** (unincorporated postal area)
Zip Code: 12160
Covers a land area of 17.719 square miles and a water area of 0.139 square miles. Located at 42.76° N. Lat; 74.38° W. Long. Elevation is 679 feet. Population: 944 (2010); Density: 53.3 persons per square mile (2010); Race: 97.2% White, 0.5% Black, 0.2% Asian, 0.3% American Indian/Alaska Native, 0.0% Native Hawaiian/Other Pacific Islander, 1.8% Other, 3.1% Hispanic of any race (2010); Average household size: 2.57 (2010); Median age: 43.1 (2010); Males per 100 females: 104.8 (2010); Homeownership rate: 83.1% (2010)

**SUMMIT** (town). Covers a land area of 37.084 square miles and a water area of 0.398 square miles. Located at 42.57° N. Lat; 74.59° W. Long. Elevation is 2,116 feet.
**Population:** 973 (1990); 1,123 (2000); 1,148 (2010); Density: 31.0 persons per square mile (2010); Race: 96.9% White, 0.6% Black, 1.0% Asian, 0.1% American Indian/Alaska Native, 0.0% Native Hawaiian/Other Pacific Islander, 1.4% Other, 2.5% Hispanic of any race (2010); Average household size: 2.33 (2010); Median age: 46.4 (2010); Males per 100 females: 115.4 (2010); Marriage status: 22.4% never married, 60.5% now married, 7.7% widowed, 9.4% divorced (2006-2010 5-year est.); Foreign born: 0.0% (2006-2010 5-year est.); Ancestry (includes multiple ancestries): 26.0% American, 25.3% German, 20.6% Irish, 14.9% Italian, 7.4% English (2006-2010 5-year est.).
**Economy:** Single-family building permits issued: 1 (2011); Multi-family building permits issued: 0 (2011); Employment by occupation: 9.2% management, 5.7% professional, 12.9% services, 14.0% sales, 0.0% farming, 10.1% construction, 1.8% production (2006-2010 5-year est.).
**Income:** Per capita income: $24,643 (2006-2010 5-year est.); Median household income: $47,167 (2006-2010 5-year est.); Average household income: $63,239 (2006-2010 5-year est.); Percent of households with income of $100,000 or more: 16.0% (2006-2010 5-year est.); Poverty rate: 5.2% (2006-2010 5-year est.).
**Education:** Percent of population age 25 and over with: High school diploma (including GED) or higher: 74.3% (2006-2010 5-year est.); Bachelor's degree or higher: 19.6% (2006-2010 5-year est.); Master's degree or higher: 9.4% (2006-2010 5-year est.).
**Housing:** Homeownership rate: 90.9% (2010); Median home value: $134,800 (2006-2010 5-year est.); Median contract rent: $706 per month (2006-2010 5-year est.); Median year structure built: 1974 (2006-2010 5-year est.).
**Transportation:** Commute to work: 85.7% car, 0.0% public transportation, 3.2% walk, 4.6% work from home (2006-2010 5-year est.); Travel time to work: 29.3% less than 15 minutes, 37.9% 15 to 30 minutes, 14.8% 30 to 45 minutes, 2.4% 45 to 60 minutes, 15.6% 60 minutes or more (2006-2010 5-year est.)

**WARNERVILLE** (unincorporated postal area)
Zip Code: 12187
Covers a land area of 23.019 square miles and a water area of 0.022 square miles. Located at 42.61° N. Lat; 74.46° W. Long. Elevation is 925 feet. Population: 697 (2010); Density: 30.3 persons per square mile (2010); Race: 97.6% White, 0.4% Black, 0.6% Asian, 0.4% American Indian/Alaska Native, 0.0% Native Hawaiian/Other Pacific Islander, 1.0% Other, 3.0% Hispanic of any race (2010); Average household size: 2.47

(2010); Median age: 45.3 (2010); Males per 100 females: 108.1 (2010); Homeownership rate: 81.5% (2010)

**WEST FULTON** (unincorporated postal area)
Zip Code: 12194
Covers a land area of 15.429 square miles and a water area of 0.008 square miles. Located at 42.52° N. Lat; 74.44° W. Long. Elevation is 1,158 feet. Population: 207 (2010); Density: 13.4 persons per square mile (2010); Race: 98.6% White, 0.0% Black, 1.0% Asian, 0.0% American Indian/Alaska Native, 0.0% Native Hawaiian/Other Pacific Islander, 0.4% Other, 0.0% Hispanic of any race (2010); Average household size: 2.52 (2010); Median age: 36.8 (2010); Males per 100 females: 99.0 (2010); Homeownership rate: 89.0% (2010)

**WRIGHT** (town). Covers a land area of 28.636 square miles and a water area of 0.081 square miles. Located at 42.67° N. Lat; 74.20° W. Long.
**Population:** 1,385 (1990); 1,547 (2000); 1,539 (2010); Density: 53.7 persons per square mile (2010); Race: 98.1% White, 0.5% Black, 0.4% Asian, 0.0% American Indian/Alaska Native, 0.0% Native Hawaiian/Other Pacific Islander, 1.0% Other, 1.3% Hispanic of any race (2010); Average household size: 2.50 (2010); Median age: 44.3 (2010); Males per 100 females: 105.5 (2010); Marriage status: 15.7% never married, 75.6% now married, 4.0% widowed, 4.8% divorced (2006-2010 5-year est.); Foreign born: 2.5% (2006-2010 5-year est.); Ancestry (includes multiple ancestries): 29.2% German, 28.2% Irish, 13.9% English, 9.7% Dutch, 9.7% Italian (2006-2010 5-year est.).
**Economy:** Single-family building permits issued: 0 (2011); Multi-family building permits issued: 0 (2011); Employment by occupation: 11.2% management, 6.5% professional, 7.1% services, 18.8% sales, 2.5% farming, 14.9% construction, 6.2% production (2006-2010 5-year est.).
**Income:** Per capita income: $28,375 (2006-2010 5-year est.); Median household income: $63,333 (2006-2010 5-year est.); Average household income: $73,925 (2006-2010 5-year est.); Percent of households with income of $100,000 or more: 30.3% (2006-2010 5-year est.); Poverty rate: 6.8% (2006-2010 5-year est.).
**Education:** Percent of population age 25 and over with: High school diploma (including GED) or higher: 93.7% (2006-2010 5-year est.); Bachelor's degree or higher: 25.7% (2006-2010 5-year est.); Master's degree or higher: 6.2% (2006-2010 5-year est.).
**Housing:** Homeownership rate: 88.4% (2010); Median home value: $166,000 (2006-2010 5-year est.); Median contract rent: $542 per month (2006-2010 5-year est.); Median year structure built: 1978 (2006-2010 5-year est.).
**Transportation:** Commute to work: 88.0% car, 0.6% public transportation, 1.9% walk, 5.6% work from home (2006-2010 5-year est.); Travel time to work: 20.4% less than 15 minutes, 25.7% 15 to 30 minutes, 29.2% 30 to 45 minutes, 13.2% 45 to 60 minutes, 11.5% 60 minutes or more (2006-2010 5-year est.)

# Schuyler County

Located in west central New York, in the Finger Lakes region; drained by Cayuta and Catherine Creeks; includes Lamoka and Cayuta Lakes and part of Seneca Lake. Covers a land area of 328.71 square miles, a water area of 13.51 square miles, and is located in the Eastern Time Zone at 42.38° N. Lat., 76.87° W. Long. The county was founded in 1854. County seat is Watkins Glen.
**Population:** 18,662 (1990); 19,224 (2000); 18,343 (2010); Race: 97.1% White, 0.9% Black, 0.3% Asian, 0.3% American Indian/Alaska Native, 0.0% Native Hawaiian/Other Pacific Islander, 1.4% Other, 1.3% Hispanic of any race (2010); Density: 55.8 persons per square mile (2010); Average household size: 2.39 (2010); Median age: 44.2 (2010); Males per 100 females: 98.9 (2010).
**Religion:** Six largest groups: 12.9% Catholicism, 6.1% Methodist/Pietist, 3.2% Baptist, 2.7% Presbyterian-Reformed, 0.8% Episcopalianism/Anglicanism, 0.8% Non-Denominational (2010)
**Economy:** Unemployment rate: 9.7% (February 2012); Total civilian labor force: 9,695 (February 2012); Leading industries: 21.5% retail trade; 14.8% manufacturing; 12.8% accommodation & food services (2009); Farms: 394 totaling 66,368 acres (2007); Companies that employ 500 or more persons: 0 (2009); Companies that employ 100 to 499 persons: 9 (2009); Companies that employ less than 100 persons: 345 (2009); Black-owned businesses: n/a (2007); Hispanic-owned businesses: n/a (2007); Asian-owned businesses: n/a (2007); Women-owned businesses: 454

(2007); Retail sales per capita: $11,705 (2010). Single-family building permits issued: 35 (2011); Multi-family building permits issued: 0 (2011).
**Income:** Per capita income: $22,123 (2006-2010 5-year est.); Median household income: $47,404 (2006-2010 5-year est.); Average household income: $54,844 (2006-2010 5-year est.); Percent of households with income of $100,000 or more: 12.0% (2006-2010 5-year est.); Poverty rate: 8.3% (2006-2010 5-year est.); Bankruptcy rate: 1.20% (2011).
**Education:** Percent of population age 25 and over with: High school diploma (including GED) or higher: 87.4% (2006-2010 5-year est.); Bachelor's degree or higher: 17.4% (2006-2010 5-year est.); Master's degree or higher: 7.8% (2006-2010 5-year est.).
**Housing:** Homeownership rate: 76.2% (2010); Median home value: $86,700 (2006-2010 5-year est.); Median contract rent: $454 per month (2006-2010 5-year est.); Median year structure built: 1959 (2006-2010 5-year est.)
**Health:** Birth rate: 81.2 per 10,000 population (2011); Death rate: 98.0 per 10,000 population (2011); Age-adjusted cancer mortality rate: 152.2 deaths per 100,000 population (2009); Number of physicians: 10.6 per 10,000 population (2008); Hospital beds: 76.6 per 10,000 population (2007); Hospital admissions: 884.6 per 10,000 population (2007).
**Elections:** 2008 Presidential election results: 45.7% Obama, 52.8% McCain, 0.8% Nader
**National and State Parks:** Cliffside State Forest; Connecticut Hill State Game Management Area; Finger Lakes National Forest; Green Mountain National Forest-Hector Ranger District; Watkins Glen State Park
**Additional Information Contacts**
Schuyler County Government . . . . . . . . . . . . . . . . . . (607) 535-8133
  http://www.schuylercounty.us
Watkins Glen Area Chamber of Commerce. . . . . . . . . . . . . (607) 535-4300
  http://www.watkinsglenchamber.com

## Schuyler County Communities

**ALPINE** (unincorporated postal area)
Zip Code: 14805
Covers a land area of 27.655 square miles and a water area of 0.598 square miles. Located at 42.35° N. Lat; 76.72° W. Long. Elevation is 1,165 feet. Population: 1,100 (2010); Density: 39.8 persons per square mile (2010); Race: 97.7% White, 0.5% Black, 0.2% Asian, 0.5% American Indian/Alaska Native, 0.0% Native Hawaiian/Other Pacific Islander, 1.1% Other, 1.5% Hispanic of any race (2010); Average household size: 2.53 (2010); Median age: 43.2 (2010); Males per 100 females: 100.0 (2010); Homeownership rate: 85.7% (2010)

**BEAVER DAMS** (unincorporated postal area)
Zip Code: 14812
Covers a land area of 77.542 square miles and a water area of 0.084 square miles. Located at 42.30° N. Lat; 77.00° W. Long. Elevation is 1,263 feet. Population: 3,478 (2010); Density: 44.9 persons per square mile (2010); Race: 96.1% White, 1.6% Black, 0.5% Asian, 0.7% American Indian/Alaska Native, 0.0% Native Hawaiian/Other Pacific Islander, 1.1% Other, 1.6% Hispanic of any race (2010); Average household size: 2.55 (2010); Median age: 39.9 (2010); Males per 100 females: 111.6 (2010); Homeownership rate: 83.9% (2010)

**BURDETT** (village). Covers a land area of 0.962 square miles and a water area of 0 square miles. Located at 42.41° N. Lat; 76.84° W. Long. Elevation is 978 feet.
**Population:** 372 (1990); 357 (2000); 340 (2010); Density: 353.3 persons per square mile (2010); Race: 96.2% White, 0.9% Black, 0.3% Asian, 0.3% American Indian/Alaska Native, 0.0% Native Hawaiian/Other Pacific Islander, 2.3% Other, 0.9% Hispanic of any race (2010); Average household size: 2.43 (2010); Median age: 41.0 (2010); Males per 100 females: 87.8 (2010); Marriage status: 22.9% never married, 55.3% now married, 14.7% widowed, 7.1% divorced (2006-2010 5-year est.); Foreign born: 0.0% (2006-2010 5-year est.); Ancestry (includes multiple ancestries): 33.9% German, 24.3% Italian, 21.9% English, 10.3% Irish, 9.9% French (2006-2010 5-year est.).
**Economy:** Single-family building permits issued: 0 (2011); Multi-family building permits issued: 0 (2011); Employment by occupation: 22.1% management, 3.8% professional, 9.9% services, 14.5% sales, 1.5% farming, 4.6% construction, 3.1% production (2006-2010 5-year est.).
**Income:** Per capita income: $23,848 (2006-2010 5-year est.); Median household income: $43,125 (2006-2010 5-year est.); Average household income: $48,826 (2006-2010 5-year est.); Percent of households with

income of $100,000 or more: 11.3% (2006-2010 5-year est.); Poverty rate: 7.9% (2006-2010 5-year est.).
**Education:** Percent of population age 25 and over with: High school diploma (including GED) or higher: 83.6% (2006-2010 5-year est.); Bachelor's degree or higher: 12.9% (2006-2010 5-year est.); Master's degree or higher: 3.0% (2006-2010 5-year est.).
**Housing:** Homeownership rate: 80.0% (2010); Median home value: $95,800 (2006-2010 5-year est.); Median contract rent: $425 per month (2006-2010 5-year est.); Median year structure built: before 1940 (2006-2010 5-year est.).
**Transportation:** Commute to work: 89.0% car, 3.9% public transportation, 0.0% walk, 5.5% work from home (2006-2010 5-year est.); Travel time to work: 36.7% less than 15 minutes, 25.8% 15 to 30 minutes, 19.2% 30 to 45 minutes, 14.2% 45 to 60 minutes, 4.2% 60 minutes or more (2006-2010 5-year est.)

**CATHARINE** (town). Aka Catherine. Covers a land area of 32.295 square miles and a water area of 0.604 square miles. Located at 42.33° N. Lat; 76.73° W. Long. Elevation is 1,178 feet.
**Population:** 1,978 (1990); 1,930 (2000); 1,762 (2010); Density: 54.6 persons per square mile (2010); Race: 97.6% White, 0.6% Black, 0.0% Asian, 0.4% American Indian/Alaska Native, 0.0% Native Hawaiian/Other Pacific Islander, 1.4% Other, 0.7% Hispanic of any race (2010); Average household size: 2.44 (2010); Median age: 42.7 (2010); Males per 100 females: 96.2 (2010); Marriage status: 25.3% never married, 57.2% now married, 7.4% widowed, 10.2% divorced (2006-2010 5-year est.); Foreign born: 0.4% (2006-2010 5-year est.); Ancestry (includes multiple ancestries): 21.5% German, 19.9% English, 17.6% American, 14.3% Irish, 7.7% Italian (2006-2010 5-year est.).
**Economy:** Single-family building permits issued: 1 (2011); Multi-family building permits issued: 0 (2011); Employment by occupation: 9.8% management, 1.5% professional, 14.8% services, 13.8% sales, 3.1% farming, 15.6% construction, 10.6% production (2006-2010 5-year est.).
**Income:** Per capita income: $20,631 (2006-2010 5-year est.); Median household income: $45,347 (2006-2010 5-year est.); Average household income: $51,358 (2006-2010 5-year est.); Percent of households with income of $100,000 or more: 10.7% (2006-2010 5-year est.); Poverty rate: 12.0% (2006-2010 5-year est.).
**Education:** Percent of population age 25 and over with: High school diploma (including GED) or higher: 90.5% (2006-2010 5-year est.); Bachelor's degree or higher: 19.2% (2006-2010 5-year est.); Master's degree or higher: 6.9% (2006-2010 5-year est.).
**Housing:** Homeownership rate: 78.1% (2010); Median home value: $78,800 (2006-2010 5-year est.); Median contract rent: $429 per month (2006-2010 5-year est.); Median year structure built: 1952 (2006-2010 5-year est.).
**Transportation:** Commute to work: 91.5% car, 2.2% public transportation, 0.7% walk, 5.5% work from home (2006-2010 5-year est.); Travel time to work: 21.6% less than 15 minutes, 25.1% 15 to 30 minutes, 38.7% 30 to 45 minutes, 9.5% 45 to 60 minutes, 5.1% 60 minutes or more (2006-2010 5-year est.)

**CAYUTA** (town). Covers a land area of 20.319 square miles and a water area of <.001 square miles. Located at 42.27° N. Lat; 76.68° W. Long. Elevation is 1,102 feet.
**Population:** 612 (1990); 545 (2000); 556 (2010); Density: 27.4 persons per square mile (2010); Race: 95.7% White, 0.7% Black, 1.1% Asian, 0.4% American Indian/Alaska Native, 0.0% Native Hawaiian/Other Pacific Islander, 2.1% Other, 0.7% Hispanic of any race (2010); Average household size: 2.59 (2010); Median age: 39.1 (2010); Males per 100 females: 100.7 (2010); Marriage status: 28.3% never married, 56.1% now married, 6.9% widowed, 8.7% divorced (2006-2010 5-year est.); Foreign born: 0.0% (2006-2010 5-year est.); Ancestry (includes multiple ancestries): 20.5% Irish, 17.1% American, 16.5% German, 9.5% English, 7.0% Italian (2006-2010 5-year est.).
**Economy:** Single-family building permits issued: 0 (2011); Multi-family building permits issued: 0 (2011); Employment by occupation: 5.8% management, 2.7% professional, 19.6% services, 21.3% sales, 2.7% farming, 7.6% construction, 8.4% production (2006-2010 5-year est.).
**Income:** Per capita income: $18,861 (2006-2010 5-year est.); Median household income: $44,625 (2006-2010 5-year est.); Average household income: $47,374 (2006-2010 5-year est.); Percent of households with income of $100,000 or more: 4.3% (2006-2010 5-year est.); Poverty rate: 15.4% (2006-2010 5-year est.).

**Education:** Percent of population age 25 and over with: High school diploma (including GED) or higher: 73.2% (2006-2010 5-year est.); Bachelor's degree or higher: 8.6% (2006-2010 5-year est.); Master's degree or higher: 3.6% (2006-2010 5-year est.).
**Housing:** Homeownership rate: 70.6% (2010); Median home value: $64,200 (2006-2010 5-year est.); Median contract rent: $469 per month (2006-2010 5-year est.); Median year structure built: 1975 (2006-2010 5-year est.).
**Transportation:** Commute to work: 90.8% car, 1.8% public transportation, 1.4% walk, 4.6% work from home (2006-2010 5-year est.); Travel time to work: 19.7% less than 15 minutes, 35.6% 15 to 30 minutes, 32.2% 30 to 45 minutes, 4.8% 45 to 60 minutes, 7.7% 60 minutes or more (2006-2010 5-year est.)

**DIX** (town). Covers a land area of 36.257 square miles and a water area of 0.454 square miles. Located at 42.33° N. Lat; 76.89° W. Long.
**Population:** 4,130 (1990); 4,197 (2000); 3,864 (2010); Density: 106.6 persons per square mile (2010); Race: 96.9% White, 0.3% Black, 0.6% Asian, 0.4% American Indian/Alaska Native, 0.0% Native Hawaiian/Other Pacific Islander, 1.8% Other, 1.1% Hispanic of any race (2010); Average household size: 2.30 (2010); Median age: 44.1 (2010); Males per 100 females: 93.0 (2010); Marriage status: 22.2% never married, 57.3% now married, 7.4% widowed, 13.1% divorced (2006-2010 5-year est.); Foreign born: 3.9% (2006-2010 5-year est.); Ancestry (includes multiple ancestries): 19.2% German, 15.6% Irish, 15.5% English, 14.4% American, 13.2% Italian (2006-2010 5-year est.).
**Economy:** Single-family building permits issued: 13 (2011); Multi-family building permits issued: 0 (2011); Employment by occupation: 8.1% management, 4.9% professional, 13.4% services, 15.3% sales, 1.7% farming, 10.2% construction, 5.3% production (2006-2010 5-year est.).
**Income:** Per capita income: $22,630 (2006-2010 5-year est.); Median household income: $41,875 (2006-2010 5-year est.); Average household income: $50,188 (2006-2010 5-year est.); Percent of households with income of $100,000 or more: 11.0% (2006-2010 5-year est.); Poverty rate: 6.7% (2006-2010 5-year est.).
**Education:** Percent of population age 25 and over with: High school diploma (including GED) or higher: 88.0% (2006-2010 5-year est.); Bachelor's degree or higher: 18.7% (2006-2010 5-year est.); Master's degree or higher: 9.7% (2006-2010 5-year est.).
**Housing:** Homeownership rate: 66.4% (2010); Median home value: $76,800 (2006-2010 5-year est.); Median contract rent: $449 per month (2006-2010 5-year est.); Median year structure built: 1954 (2006-2010 5-year est.).
**Transportation:** Commute to work: 85.8% car, 2.2% public transportation, 3.8% walk, 4.9% work from home (2006-2010 5-year est.); Travel time to work: 42.2% less than 15 minutes, 23.1% 15 to 30 minutes, 21.7% 30 to 45 minutes, 4.8% 45 to 60 minutes, 8.2% 60 minutes or more (2006-2010 5-year est.)

**HECTOR** (town). Covers a land area of 102.368 square miles and a water area of 10.214 square miles. Located at 42.46° N. Lat; 76.78° W. Long. Elevation is 853 feet.
**Population:** 4,423 (1990); 4,854 (2000); 4,940 (2010); Density: 48.3 persons per square mile (2010); Race: 97.7% White, 0.6% Black, 0.3% Asian, 0.1% American Indian/Alaska Native, 0.1% Native Hawaiian/Other Pacific Islander, 1.2% Other, 1.5% Hispanic of any race (2010); Average household size: 2.46 (2010); Median age: 44.4 (2010); Males per 100 females: 102.2 (2010); Marriage status: 21.1% never married, 68.4% now married, 4.5% widowed, 6.0% divorced (2006-2010 5-year est.); Foreign born: 2.8% (2006-2010 5-year est.); Ancestry (includes multiple ancestries): 23.4% Irish, 20.0% English, 13.7% German, 11.5% American, 6.2% Dutch (2006-2010 5-year est.).
**Economy:** Single-family building permits issued: 6 (2011); Multi-family building permits issued: 0 (2011); Employment by occupation: 10.7% management, 6.8% professional, 13.9% services, 18.2% sales, 3.1% farming, 12.2% construction, 3.6% production (2006-2010 5-year est.).
**Income:** Per capita income: $24,090 (2006-2010 5-year est.); Median household income: $54,382 (2006-2010 5-year est.); Average household income: $61,912 (2006-2010 5-year est.); Percent of households with income of $100,000 or more: 15.6% (2006-2010 5-year est.); Poverty rate: 2.9% (2006-2010 5-year est.).
**Education:** Percent of population age 25 and over with: High school diploma (including GED) or higher: 89.4% (2006-2010 5-year est.); Bachelor's degree or higher: 19.3% (2006-2010 5-year est.); Master's degree or higher: 9.2% (2006-2010 5-year est.).

**Housing:** Homeownership rate: 84.6% (2010); Median home value: $92,500 (2006-2010 5-year est.); Median contract rent: $488 per month (2006-2010 5-year est.); Median year structure built: 1956 (2006-2010 5-year est.).
**Transportation:** Commute to work: 88.9% car, 2.8% public transportation, 3.9% walk, 4.4% work from home (2006-2010 5-year est.); Travel time to work: 24.1% less than 15 minutes, 28.2% 15 to 30 minutes, 27.1% 30 to 45 minutes, 15.4% 45 to 60 minutes, 5.2% 60 minutes or more (2006-2010 5-year est.)

**MONTOUR** (town). Covers a land area of 18.578 square miles and a water area of 0.004 square miles. Located at 42.33° N. Lat; 76.82° W. Long. Elevation is 482 feet.
**History:** Chequaga (or Shequaga) Falls here attract tourists, especially when snowmelt in the spring enhances the awesome spectacle.
**Population:** 2,528 (1990); 2,446 (2000); 2,308 (2010); Density: 124.2 persons per square mile (2010); Race: 97.1% White, 0.7% Black, 0.3% Asian, 0.1% American Indian/Alaska Native, 0.0% Native Hawaiian/Other Pacific Islander, 1.8% Other, 1.3% Hispanic of any race (2010); Average household size: 2.18 (2010); Median age: 46.8 (2010); Males per 100 females: 92.5 (2010); Marriage status: 21.5% never married, 57.5% now married, 10.4% widowed, 10.6% divorced (2006-2010 5-year est.); Foreign born: 0.5% (2006-2010 5-year est.); Ancestry (includes multiple ancestries): 25.5% German, 16.5% American, 16.4% English, 11.7% Irish, 10.8% Italian (2006-2010 5-year est.).
**Economy:** Single-family building permits issued: 4 (2011); Multi-family building permits issued: 0 (2011); Employment by occupation: 13.0% management, 0.0% professional, 13.8% services, 20.1% sales, 3.1% farming, 11.6% construction, 4.5% production (2006-2010 5-year est.).
**Income:** Per capita income: $21,297 (2006-2010 5-year est.); Median household income: $39,491 (2006-2010 5-year est.); Average household income: $48,334 (2006-2010 5-year est.); Percent of households with income of $100,000 or more: 6.6% (2006-2010 5-year est.); Poverty rate: 16.0% (2006-2010 5-year est.).
**Education:** Percent of population age 25 and over with: High school diploma (including GED) or higher: 85.6% (2006-2010 5-year est.); Bachelor's degree or higher: 15.9% (2006-2010 5-year est.); Master's degree or higher: 5.6% (2006-2010 5-year est.).
**Housing:** Homeownership rate: 62.9% (2010); Median home value: $85,000 (2006-2010 5-year est.); Median contract rent: $473 per month (2006-2010 5-year est.); Median year structure built: 1955 (2006-2010 5-year est.).
**Transportation:** Commute to work: 91.6% car, 1.7% public transportation, 3.3% walk, 2.7% work from home (2006-2010 5-year est.); Travel time to work: 46.0% less than 15 minutes, 19.1% 15 to 30 minutes, 24.4% 30 to 45 minutes, 6.8% 45 to 60 minutes, 3.7% 60 minutes or more (2006-2010 5-year est.)

**MONTOUR FALLS** (village). Covers a land area of 3.008 square miles and a water area of 0.024 square miles. Located at 42.34° N. Lat; 76.84° W. Long. Elevation is 449 feet.
**Population:** 1,845 (1990); 1,797 (2000); 1,711 (2010); Density: 568.8 persons per square mile (2010); Race: 97.0% White, 0.9% Black, 0.1% Asian, 0.1% American Indian/Alaska Native, 0.0% Native Hawaiian/Other Pacific Islander, 1.9% Other, 1.4% Hispanic of any race (2010); Average household size: 2.10 (2010); Median age: 48.8 (2010); Males per 100 females: 81.6 (2010); Marriage status: 23.3% never married, 52.9% now married, 10.9% widowed, 12.9% divorced (2006-2010 5-year est.); Foreign born: 0.2% (2006-2010 5-year est.); Ancestry (includes multiple ancestries): 24.3% German, 19.5% American, 16.8% English, 12.7% Irish, 10.3% Italian (2006-2010 5-year est.).
**Economy:** Single-family building permits issued: 1 (2011); Multi-family building permits issued: 0 (2011); Employment by occupation: 10.8% management, 0.0% professional, 14.5% services, 19.2% sales, 4.6% farming, 10.1% construction, 4.6% production (2006-2010 5-year est.).
**Income:** Per capita income: $21,199 (2006-2010 5-year est.); Median household income: $38,988 (2006-2010 5-year est.); Average household income: $46,740 (2006-2010 5-year est.); Percent of households with income of $100,000 or more: 6.2% (2006-2010 5-year est.); Poverty rate: 14.9% (2006-2010 5-year est.).
**Education:** Percent of population age 25 and over with: High school diploma (including GED) or higher: 85.8% (2006-2010 5-year est.); Bachelor's degree or higher: 16.6% (2006-2010 5-year est.); Master's degree or higher: 8.9% (2006-2010 5-year est.).

**School District(s)**
Odessa-Montour Central School District (PK-12)
    2009-10 Enrollment: 802 . . . . . . . . . . . . . . . . . . . . . . . (607) 594-3341
**Housing:** Homeownership rate: 51.4% (2010); Median home value: $83,200 (2006-2010 5-year est.); Median contract rent: $466 per month (2006-2010 5-year est.); Median year structure built: 1945 (2006-2010 5-year est.).
**Hospitals:** Schuyler Hospital (169 beds)
**Transportation:** Commute to work: 92.7% car, 1.6% public transportation, 4.7% walk, 0.9% work from home (2006-2010 5-year est.); Travel time to work: 51.1% less than 15 minutes, 18.4% 15 to 30 minutes, 21.9% 30 to 45 minutes, 5.9% 45 to 60 minutes, 2.7% 60 minutes or more (2006-2010 5-year est.)

**ODESSA** (village). Covers a land area of 1.136 square miles and a water area of 0 square miles. Located at 42.33° N. Lat; 76.78° W. Long. Elevation is 1,043 feet.
**Population:** 683 (1990); 617 (2000); 591 (2010); Density: 520.0 persons per square mile (2010); Race: 98.5% White, 0.0% Black, 0.0% Asian, 0.0% American Indian/Alaska Native, 0.0% Native Hawaiian/Other Pacific Islander, 1.5% Other, 0.5% Hispanic of any race (2010); Average household size: 2.35 (2010); Median age: 42.9 (2010); Males per 100 females: 94.4 (2010); Marriage status: 25.3% never married, 51.9% now married, 11.6% widowed, 11.2% divorced (2006-2010 5-year est.); Foreign born: 0.0% (2006-2010 5-year est.); Ancestry (includes multiple ancestries): 30.9% English, 19.6% German, 14.3% Irish, 12.0% Italian, 10.1% American (2006-2010 5-year est.).
**Economy:** Single-family building permits issued: 0 (2011); Multi-family building permits issued: 0 (2011); Employment by occupation: 11.0% management, 0.0% professional, 10.6% services, 15.9% sales, 0.0% farming, 7.0% construction, 12.8% production (2006-2010 5-year est.).
**Income:** Per capita income: $20,217 (2006-2010 5-year est.); Median household income: $40,455 (2006-2010 5-year est.); Average household income: $44,100 (2006-2010 5-year est.); Percent of households with income of $100,000 or more: 8.1% (2006-2010 5-year est.); Poverty rate: 10.5% (2006-2010 5-year est.).
**Education:** Percent of population age 25 and over with: High school diploma (including GED) or higher: 87.6% (2006-2010 5-year est.); Bachelor's degree or higher: 17.9% (2006-2010 5-year est.); Master's degree or higher: 4.5% (2006-2010 5-year est.).
**School District(s)**
Odessa-Montour Central School District (PK-12)
    2009-10 Enrollment: 802 . . . . . . . . . . . . . . . . . . . . . . . (607) 594-3341
**Housing:** Homeownership rate: 70.0% (2010); Median home value: $79,300 (2006-2010 5-year est.); Median contract rent: $453 per month (2006-2010 5-year est.); Median year structure built: 1941 (2006-2010 5-year est.).
**Transportation:** Commute to work: 92.1% car, 4.0% public transportation, 2.6% walk, 1.3% work from home (2006-2010 5-year est.); Travel time to work: 27.7% less than 15 minutes, 22.8% 15 to 30 minutes, 29.9% 30 to 45 minutes, 13.8% 45 to 60 minutes, 5.8% 60 minutes or more (2006-2010 5-year est.)

**ORANGE** (town). Covers a land area of 54.068 square miles and a water area of 0.384 square miles. Located at 42.34° N. Lat; 77.03° W. Long.
**Population:** 1,561 (1990); 1,752 (2000); 1,609 (2010); Density: 29.8 persons per square mile (2010); Race: 95.2% White, 3.2% Black, 0.1% Asian, 0.2% American Indian/Alaska Native, 0.1% Native Hawaiian/Other Pacific Islander, 1.2% Other, 2.3% Hispanic of any race (2010); Average household size: 2.52 (2010); Median age: 40.3 (2010); Males per 100 females: 126.0 (2010); Marriage status: 46.8% never married, 43.3% now married, 2.8% widowed, 7.1% divorced (2006-2010 5-year est.); Foreign born: 2.2% (2006-2010 5-year est.); Ancestry (includes multiple ancestries): 17.6% German, 16.9% Irish, 10.3% English, 10.1% Italian, 8.6% American (2006-2010 5-year est.).
**Economy:** Single-family building permits issued: 0 (2011); Multi-family building permits issued: 0 (2011); Employment by occupation: 5.7% management, 1.8% professional, 8.5% services, 19.5% sales, 4.0% farming, 11.1% construction, 5.1% production (2006-2010 5-year est.).
**Income:** Per capita income: $18,366 (2006-2010 5-year est.); Median household income: $55,714 (2006-2010 5-year est.); Average household income: $58,770 (2006-2010 5-year est.); Percent of households with income of $100,000 or more: 13.5% (2006-2010 5-year est.); Poverty rate: 11.5% (2006-2010 5-year est.).

**Education:** Percent of population age 25 and over with: High school diploma (including GED) or higher: 84.2% (2006-2010 5-year est.); Bachelor's degree or higher: 10.2% (2006-2010 5-year est.); Master's degree or higher: 3.8% (2006-2010 5-year est.).
**Housing:** Homeownership rate: 83.7% (2010); Median home value: $77,100 (2006-2010 5-year est.); Median contract rent: $468 per month (2006-2010 5-year est.); Median year structure built: 1975 (2006-2010 5-year est.).
**Transportation:** Commute to work: 95.5% car, 0.4% public transportation, 1.7% walk, 1.9% work from home (2006-2010 5-year est.); Travel time to work: 13.9% less than 15 minutes, 42.8% 15 to 30 minutes, 29.7% 30 to 45 minutes, 8.0% 45 to 60 minutes, 5.6% 60 minutes or more (2006-2010 5-year est.)

**READING** (town). Covers a land area of 27.149 square miles and a water area of 0 square miles. Located at 42.41° N. Lat; 76.93° W. Long.
**Population:** 1,810 (1990); 1,786 (2000); 1,707 (2010); Density: 62.9 persons per square mile (2010); Race: 96.5% White, 1.5% Black, 0.3% Asian, 0.4% American Indian/Alaska Native, 0.0% Native Hawaiian/Other Pacific Islander, 1.3% Other, 1.8% Hispanic of any race (2010); Average household size: 2.43 (2010); Median age: 46.0 (2010); Males per 100 females: 95.3 (2010); Marriage status: 17.4% never married, 69.6% now married, 6.6% widowed, 6.3% divorced (2006-2010 5-year est.); Foreign born: 3.3% (2006-2010 5-year est.); Ancestry (includes multiple ancestries): 27.0% Italian, 16.9% German, 16.3% Irish, 15.7% English, 7.7% American (2006-2010 5-year est.).
**Economy:** Single-family building permits issued: 2 (2011); Multi-family building permits issued: 0 (2011); Employment by occupation: 17.5% management, 2.5% professional, 9.8% services, 8.7% sales, 3.8% farming, 5.8% construction, 5.8% production (2006-2010 5-year est.).
**Income:** Per capita income: $26,415 (2006-2010 5-year est.); Median household income: $57,130 (2006-2010 5-year est.); Average household income: $67,353 (2006-2010 5-year est.); Percent of households with income of $100,000 or more: 19.0% (2006-2010 5-year est.); Poverty rate: 2.5% (2006-2010 5-year est.).
**Education:** Percent of population age 25 and over with: High school diploma (including GED) or higher: 91.6% (2006-2010 5-year est.); Bachelor's degree or higher: 19.8% (2006-2010 5-year est.); Master's degree or higher: 9.9% (2006-2010 5-year est.).
**Housing:** Homeownership rate: 83.6% (2010); Median home value: $131,000 (2006-2010 5-year est.); Median contract rent: $472 per month (2006-2010 5-year est.); Median year structure built: 1963 (2006-2010 5-year est.).
**Transportation:** Commute to work: 88.4% car, 0.4% public transportation, 1.1% walk, 9.0% work from home (2006-2010 5-year est.); Travel time to work: 38.7% less than 15 minutes, 31.1% 15 to 30 minutes, 17.9% 30 to 45 minutes, 6.6% 45 to 60 minutes, 5.7% 60 minutes or more (2006-2010 5-year est.)

**TYRONE** (town). Covers a land area of 37.296 square miles and a water area of 2.331 square miles. Located at 42.44° N. Lat; 77.04° W. Long. Elevation is 1,171 feet.
**Population:** 1,620 (1990); 1,714 (2000); 1,597 (2010); Density: 42.8 persons per square mile (2010); Race: 97.6% White, 0.4% Black, 0.0% Asian, 0.3% American Indian/Alaska Native, 0.0% Native Hawaiian/Other Pacific Islander, 1.7% Other, 0.4% Hispanic of any race (2010); Average household size: 2.44 (2010); Median age: 45.6 (2010); Males per 100 females: 95.7 (2010); Marriage status: 28.4% never married, 56.6% now married, 6.9% widowed, 8.0% divorced (2006-2010 5-year est.); Foreign born: 0.4% (2006-2010 5-year est.); Ancestry (includes multiple ancestries): 22.8% German, 22.0% Irish, 15.3% English, 11.0% American, 7.1% Polish (2006-2010 5-year est.).
**Economy:** Single-family building permits issued: 7 (2011); Multi-family building permits issued: 0 (2011); Employment by occupation: 12.1% management, 3.2% professional, 11.6% services, 13.0% sales, 4.3% farming, 14.7% construction, 11.5% production (2006-2010 5-year est.).
**Income:** Per capita income: $18,111 (2006-2010 5-year est.); Median household income: $40,303 (2006-2010 5-year est.); Average household income: $45,554 (2006-2010 5-year est.); Percent of households with income of $100,000 or more: 5.9% (2006-2010 5-year est.); Poverty rate: 16.2% (2006-2010 5-year est.).
**Education:** Percent of population age 25 and over with: High school diploma (including GED) or higher: 81.0% (2006-2010 5-year est.); Bachelor's degree or higher: 14.4% (2006-2010 5-year est.); Master's degree or higher: 5.5% (2006-2010 5-year est.).

**Housing:** Homeownership rate: 79.6% (2010); Median home value: $87,600 (2006-2010 5-year est.); Median contract rent: $406 per month (2006-2010 5-year est.); Median year structure built: 1962 (2006-2010 5-year est.).

**Transportation:** Commute to work: 89.4% car, 0.5% public transportation, 1.3% walk, 8.0% work from home (2006-2010 5-year est.); Travel time to work: 10.4% less than 15 minutes, 44.7% 15 to 30 minutes, 23.1% 30 to 45 minutes, 16.8% 45 to 60 minutes, 5.1% 60 minutes or more (2006-2010 5-year est.)

**WATKINS GLEN** (village). County seat. Covers a land area of 1.559 square miles and a water area of 0.383 square miles. Located at 42.38° N. Lat; 76.86° W. Long. Elevation is 463 feet.

**History:** The resort hotel here is famed for its mineral spring water. An international Grand Prix sports-car race was held here annually until 1981. Incorporated 1842.

**Population:** 2,230 (1990); 2,149 (2000); 1,859 (2010); Density: 1,192.4 persons per square mile (2010); Race: 96.2% White, 0.5% Black, 0.5% Asian, 0.4% American Indian/Alaska Native, 0.0% Native Hawaiian/Other Pacific Islander, 2.4% Other, 1.4% Hispanic of any race (2010); Average household size: 2.09 (2010); Median age: 43.2 (2010); Males per 100 females: 87.2 (2010); Marriage status: 30.5% never married, 48.2% now married, 12.0% widowed, 9.3% divorced (2006-2010 5-year est.); Foreign born: 2.8% (2006-2010 5-year est.); Ancestry (includes multiple ancestries): 28.5% Italian, 19.2% Irish, 16.7% English, 12.1% German, 10.3% American (2006-2010 5-year est.).

**Economy:** Single-family building permits issued: 1 (2011); Multi-family building permits issued: 0 (2011); Employment by occupation: 2.8% management, 5.9% professional, 12.7% services, 13.5% sales, 1.3% farming, 8.2% construction, 5.5% production (2006-2010 5-year est.).

**Income:** Per capita income: $22,332 (2006-2010 5-year est.); Median household income: $33,886 (2006-2010 5-year est.); Average household income: $45,093 (2006-2010 5-year est.); Percent of households with income of $100,000 or more: 6.5% (2006-2010 5-year est.); Poverty rate: 5.0% (2006-2010 5-year est.).

**Education:** Percent of population age 25 and over with: High school diploma (including GED) or higher: 83.4% (2006-2010 5-year est.); Bachelor's degree or higher: 25.1% (2006-2010 5-year est.); Master's degree or higher: 11.1% (2006-2010 5-year est.).

**School District(s)**

Watkins Glen Central School District (PK-12)

    2009-10 Enrollment: 1,245 . . . . . . . . . . . . . . . . . (607) 535-3219

**Housing:** Homeownership rate: 55.5% (2010); Median home value: $88,400 (2006-2010 5-year est.); Median contract rent: $463 per month (2006-2010 5-year est.); Median year structure built: before 1940 (2006-2010 5-year est.).

**Safety:** Violent crime rate: 0.0 per 10,000 population; Property crime rate: 486.9 per 10,000 population (2010).

**Newspapers:** The Daily News (Local news; Circulation 1,500); Watkins Review & Express (Community news; Circulation 3,200)

**Transportation:** Commute to work: 78.7% car, 4.6% public transportation, 8.0% walk, 7.4% work from home (2006-2010 5-year est.); Travel time to work: 44.2% less than 15 minutes, 10.0% 15 to 30 minutes, 26.9% 30 to 45 minutes, 4.8% 45 to 60 minutes, 14.1% 60 minutes or more (2006-2010 5-year est.)

**Additional Information Contacts**

Watkins Glen Area Chamber of Commerce. . . . . . . . . . . . . (607) 535-4300
   http://www.watkinsglenchamber.com

# Seneca County

Located in west central New York, in the Finger Lakes region; bounded on the east by Cayuga Lake and the Seneca River, and partly on the west by Seneca Lake. Covers a land area of 324.91 square miles, a water area of 65.60 square miles, and is located in the Eastern Time Zone at 42.80° N. Lat., 76.82° W. Long. The county was founded in 1804. County seat is Waterloo.

Seneca County is part of the Seneca Falls, NY Micropolitan Statistical Area. The entire metro area includes: Seneca County, NY

**Population:** 33,683 (1990); 33,342 (2000); 35,251 (2010); Race: 92.5% White, 4.6% Black, 0.7% Asian, 0.3% American Indian/Alaska Native, 0.0% Native Hawaiian/Other Pacific Islander, 1.9% Other, 2.7% Hispanic of any race (2010); Density: 108.5 persons per square mile (2010); Average

household size: 2.42 (2010); Median age: 41.0 (2010); Males per 100 females: 109.9 (2010).

**Religion:** Six largest groups: 3.1% Methodist/Pietist, 2.7% Catholicism, 2.1% European Free-Church, 1.9% Presbyterian-Reformed, 1.7% Non-Denominational, 1.4% Latter-day Saints (2010)

**Economy:** Unemployment rate: 9.0% (February 2012); Total civilian labor force: 16,705 (February 2012); Leading industries: 25.7% retail trade; 16.0% health care and social assistance; 15.8% manufacturing (2009); Farms: 513 totaling 127,972 acres (2007); Companies that employ 500 or more persons: 1 (2009); Companies that employ 100 to 499 persons: 10 (2009); Companies that employ less than 100 persons: 691 (2009); Black-owned businesses: 33 (2007); Hispanic-owned businesses: n/a (2007); Asian-owned businesses: 32 (2007); Women-owned businesses: 673 (2007); Retail sales per capita: $14,616 (2010). Single-family building permits issued: 26 (2011); Multi-family building permits issued: 43 (2011).

**Income:** Per capita income: $21,818 (2006-2010 5-year est.); Median household income: $46,707 (2006-2010 5-year est.); Average household income: $56,681 (2006-2010 5-year est.); Percent of households with income of $100,000 or more: 13.0% (2006-2010 5-year est.); Poverty rate: 13.9% (2006-2010 5-year est.); Bankruptcy rate: 1.47% (2011).

**Taxes:** Total county taxes per capita: $892 (2009); County property taxes per capita: $282 (2009).

**Education:** Percent of population age 25 and over with: High school diploma (including GED) or higher: 83.7% (2006-2010 5-year est.); Bachelor's degree or higher: 18.1% (2006-2010 5-year est.); Master's degree or higher: 6.5% (2006-2010 5-year est.).

**Housing:** Homeownership rate: 73.4% (2010); Median home value: $88,900 (2006-2010 5-year est.); Median contract rent: $529 per month (2006-2010 5-year est.); Median year structure built: 1956 (2006-2010 5-year est.).

**Health:** Birth rate: 101.4 per 10,000 population (2011); Death rate: 92.9 per 10,000 population (2011); Age-adjusted cancer mortality rate: 179.8 deaths per 100,000 population (2009); Number of physicians: 4.7 per 10,000 population (2008); Hospital beds: 0.0 per 10,000 population (2007); Hospital admissions: 0.0 per 10,000 population (2007).

**Elections:** 2008 Presidential election results: 50.3% Obama, 47.7% McCain, 0.9% Nader

**National and State Parks:** Cayuga Lake State Park; Montezuma National Wildlife Refuge; Sampson State Park; Seneca Lake State Park; Womens Rights National Historical Park

**Additional Information Contacts**

Seneca County Government . . . . . . . . . . . . . . . . . (315) 539-1771
   http://www.co.seneca.ny.us
Seneca County Chamber of Commerce . . . . . . . . . . . . . (315) 568-2906
   http://www.senecachamber.org

## *Seneca County Communities*

**COVERT** (town). Covers a land area of 31.385 square miles and a water area of 6.195 square miles. Located at 42.58° N. Lat; 76.69° W. Long. Elevation is 906 feet.

**Population:** 2,246 (1990); 2,227 (2000); 2,154 (2010); Density: 68.6 persons per square mile (2010); Race: 96.6% White, 0.8% Black, 0.8% Asian, 0.3% American Indian/Alaska Native, 0.0% Native Hawaiian/Other Pacific Islander, 1.5% Other, 1.0% Hispanic of any race (2010); Average household size: 2.41 (2010); Median age: 45.4 (2010); Males per 100 females: 105.9 (2010); Marriage status: 20.9% never married, 53.5% now married, 8.7% widowed, 16.9% divorced (2006-2010 5-year est.); Foreign born: 4.6% (2006-2010 5-year est.); Ancestry (includes multiple ancestries): 29.4% English, 16.9% German, 13.7% Irish, 8.9% American, 5.1% Dutch (2006-2010 5-year est.).

**Economy:** Employment by occupation: 9.5% management, 4.4% professional, 10.2% services, 10.8% sales, 4.4% farming, 10.7% construction, 11.2% production (2006-2010 5-year est.).

**Income:** Per capita income: $27,344 (2006-2010 5-year est.); Median household income: $44,831 (2006-2010 5-year est.); Average household income: $63,361 (2006-2010 5-year est.); Percent of households with income of $100,000 or more: 19.0% (2006-2010 5-year est.); Poverty rate: 15.7% (2006-2010 5-year est.).

**Education:** Percent of population age 25 and over with: High school diploma (including GED) or higher: 87.9% (2006-2010 5-year est.); Bachelor's degree or higher: 30.4% (2006-2010 5-year est.); Master's degree or higher: 14.9% (2006-2010 5-year est.).

**Housing:** Homeownership rate: 81.4% (2010); Median home value: $99,500 (2006-2010 5-year est.); Median contract rent: $568 per month

(2006-2010 5-year est.); Median year structure built: 1950 (2006-2010 5-year est.).
**Transportation:** Commute to work: 82.0% car, 1.4% public transportation, 7.4% walk, 9.0% work from home (2006-2010 5-year est.); Travel time to work: 33.8% less than 15 minutes, 32.7% 15 to 30 minutes, 22.6% 30 to 45 minutes, 7.3% 45 to 60 minutes, 3.5% 60 minutes or more (2006-2010 5-year est.)

## FAYETTE (town). Covers a land area of 54.818 square miles and a water area of 11.583 square miles. Located at 42.84° N. Lat; 76.85° W. Long. Elevation is 607 feet.
**Population:** 3,636 (1990); 3,643 (2000); 3,929 (2010); Density: 71.7 persons per square mile (2010); Race: 97.7% White, 0.6% Black, 0.4% Asian, 0.1% American Indian/Alaska Native, 0.0% Native Hawaiian/Other Pacific Islander, 1.2% Other, 1.6% Hispanic of any race (2010); Average household size: 2.54 (2010); Median age: 43.8 (2010); Males per 100 females: 97.2 (2010); Marriage status: 19.6% never married, 64.7% now married, 7.4% widowed, 8.3% divorced (2006-2010 5-year est.); Foreign born: 0.7% (2006-2010 5-year est.); Ancestry (includes multiple ancestries): 29.6% German, 23.6% Italian, 21.8% Irish, 16.7% English, 8.0% American (2006-2010 5-year est.).
**Economy:** Employment by occupation: 11.2% management, 1.9% professional, 7.6% services, 14.6% sales, 5.9% farming, 10.6% construction, 5.4% production (2006-2010 5-year est.).
**Income:** Per capita income: $23,699 (2006-2010 5-year est.); Median household income: $52,245 (2006-2010 5-year est.); Average household income: $62,085 (2006-2010 5-year est.); Percent of households with income of $100,000 or more: 14.3% (2006-2010 5-year est.); Poverty rate: 16.2% (2006-2010 5-year est.).
**Education:** Percent of population age 25 and over with: High school diploma (including GED) or higher: 85.1% (2006-2010 5-year est.); Bachelor's degree or higher: 17.7% (2006-2010 5-year est.); Master's degree or higher: 6.2% (2006-2010 5-year est.).
**Housing:** Homeownership rate: 84.7% (2010); Median home value: $113,500 (2006-2010 5-year est.); Median contract rent: $520 per month (2006-2010 5-year est.); Median year structure built: 1968 (2006-2010 5-year est.).
**Transportation:** Commute to work: 89.7% car, 0.0% public transportation, 2.5% walk, 3.6% work from home (2006-2010 5-year est.); Travel time to work: 34.2% less than 15 minutes, 35.0% 15 to 30 minutes, 17.2% 30 to 45 minutes, 2.8% 45 to 60 minutes, 10.9% 60 minutes or more (2006-2010 5-year est.)

## INTERLAKEN (village). Covers a land area of 0.267 square miles and a water area of 0 square miles. Located at 42.61° N. Lat; 76.72° W. Long. Elevation is 906 feet.
**Population:** 680 (1990); 674 (2000); 602 (2010); Density: 2,251.3 persons per square mile (2010); Race: 95.2% White, 1.7% Black, 1.5% Asian, 0.3% American Indian/Alaska Native, 0.0% Native Hawaiian/Other Pacific Islander, 1.3% Other, 0.7% Hispanic of any race (2010); Average household size: 2.36 (2010); Median age: 38.1 (2010); Males per 100 females: 99.3 (2010); Marriage status: 27.3% never married, 53.1% now married, 13.3% widowed, 6.3% divorced (2006-2010 5-year est.); Foreign born: 7.1% (2006-2010 5-year est.); Ancestry (includes multiple ancestries): 27.8% English, 15.6% German, 10.2% Irish, 10.2% French, 6.4% American (2006-2010 5-year est.).
**Economy:** Employment by occupation: 3.1% management, 3.7% professional, 9.3% services, 10.9% sales, 5.3% farming, 8.1% construction, 12.5% production (2006-2010 5-year est.).
**Income:** Per capita income: $22,483 (2006-2010 5-year est.); Median household income: $42,500 (2006-2010 5-year est.); Average household income: $55,934 (2006-2010 5-year est.); Percent of households with income of $100,000 or more: 12.5% (2006-2010 5-year est.); Poverty rate: 16.4% (2006-2010 5-year est.).
**Education:** Percent of population age 25 and over with: High school diploma (including GED) or higher: 85.2% (2006-2010 5-year est.); Bachelor's degree or higher: 26.4% (2006-2010 5-year est.); Master's degree or higher: 7.6% (2006-2010 5-year est.).
### School District(s)
South Seneca Central School District (PK-12)
    2009-10 Enrollment: 845 . . . . . . . . . . . . . . . . . . . . . . (607) 869-9636
**Housing:** Homeownership rate: 67.9% (2010); Median home value: $90,000 (2006-2010 5-year est.); Median contract rent: $489 per month (2006-2010 5-year est.); Median year structure built: before 1940 (2006-2010 5-year est.).

**Newspapers:** Ithaca Pennysaver (Community news; Circulation 27,278); Tri-Village Pennysaver (Community news; Circulation 32,500)
**Transportation:** Commute to work: 95.6% car, 0.9% public transportation, 1.6% walk, 0.9% work from home (2006-2010 5-year est.); Travel time to work: 32.1% less than 15 minutes, 33.7% 15 to 30 minutes, 27.9% 30 to 45 minutes, 4.1% 45 to 60 minutes, 2.2% 60 minutes or more (2006-2010 5-year est.)

## JUNIUS (town). Covers a land area of 26.708 square miles and a water area of 0.145 square miles. Located at 42.97° N. Lat; 76.90° W. Long. Elevation is 443 feet.
**Population:** 1,354 (1990); 1,362 (2000); 1,471 (2010); Density: 55.1 persons per square mile (2010); Race: 97.6% White, 0.3% Black, 0.2% Asian, 0.3% American Indian/Alaska Native, 0.0% Native Hawaiian/Other Pacific Islander, 1.6% Other, 2.5% Hispanic of any race (2010); Average household size: 2.71 (2010); Median age: 39.4 (2010); Males per 100 females: 103.5 (2010); Marriage status: 21.1% never married, 57.3% now married, 9.2% widowed, 12.4% divorced (2006-2010 5-year est.); Foreign born: 0.8% (2006-2010 5-year est.); Ancestry (includes multiple ancestries): 24.5% German, 12.1% English, 11.4% Irish, 10.1% Pennsylvania German, 8.6% Dutch (2006-2010 5-year est.).
**Economy:** Employment by occupation: 13.9% management, 1.9% professional, 8.7% services, 17.3% sales, 2.2% farming, 17.5% construction, 15.5% production (2006-2010 5-year est.).
**Income:** Per capita income: $18,278 (2006-2010 5-year est.); Median household income: $44,338 (2006-2010 5-year est.); Average household income: $51,803 (2006-2010 5-year est.); Percent of households with income of $100,000 or more: 7.3% (2006-2010 5-year est.); Poverty rate: 32.4% (2006-2010 5-year est.).
**Education:** Percent of population age 25 and over with: High school diploma (including GED) or higher: 74.5% (2006-2010 5-year est.); Bachelor's degree or higher: 8.8% (2006-2010 5-year est.); Master's degree or higher: 1.1% (2006-2010 5-year est.).
**Housing:** Homeownership rate: 82.0% (2010); Median home value: $87,500 (2006-2010 5-year est.); Median contract rent: $460 per month (2006-2010 5-year est.); Median year structure built: 1973 (2006-2010 5-year est.).
**Transportation:** Commute to work: 85.4% car, 0.0% public transportation, 2.6% walk, 7.3% work from home (2006-2010 5-year est.); Travel time to work: 28.3% less than 15 minutes, 51.1% 15 to 30 minutes, 13.2% 30 to 45 minutes, 4.4% 45 to 60 minutes, 3.0% 60 minutes or more (2006-2010 5-year est.)

## LODI (village). Covers a land area of 0.551 square miles and a water area of 0.002 square miles. Located at 42.61° N. Lat; 76.82° W. Long. Elevation is 1,106 feet.
**Population:** 364 (1990); 338 (2000); 291 (2010); Density: 528.0 persons per square mile (2010); Race: 97.6% White, 0.0% Black, 1.0% Asian, 0.7% American Indian/Alaska Native, 0.0% Native Hawaiian/Other Pacific Islander, 0.7% Other, 1.4% Hispanic of any race (2010); Average household size: 2.47 (2010); Median age: 40.3 (2010); Males per 100 females: 122.1 (2010); Marriage status: 28.8% never married, 59.9% now married, 1.7% widowed, 9.6% divorced (2006-2010 5-year est.); Foreign born: 0.0% (2006-2010 5-year est.); Ancestry (includes multiple ancestries): 28.8% American, 18.3% German, 12.4% English, 6.5% Irish, 5.5% Scottish (2006-2010 5-year est.).
**Economy:** Employment by occupation: 10.9% management, 0.0% professional, 23.8% services, 9.2% sales, 2.1% farming, 25.1% construction, 10.5% production (2006-2010 5-year est.).
**Income:** Per capita income: $14,835 (2006-2010 5-year est.); Median household income: $38,346 (2006-2010 5-year est.); Average household income: $41,564 (2006-2010 5-year est.); Percent of households with income of $100,000 or more: 2.5% (2006-2010 5-year est.); Poverty rate: 6.5% (2006-2010 5-year est.).
**Education:** Percent of population age 25 and over with: High school diploma (including GED) or higher: 95.7% (2006-2010 5-year est.); Bachelor's degree or higher: 8.5% (2006-2010 5-year est.); Master's degree or higher: 4.6% (2006-2010 5-year est.).
**Housing:** Homeownership rate: 82.2% (2010); Median home value: $48,600 (2006-2010 5-year est.); Median contract rent: $509 per month (2006-2010 5-year est.); Median year structure built: before 1940 (2006-2010 5-year est.).
**Transportation:** Commute to work: 91.8% car, 0.0% public transportation, 6.4% walk, 1.7% work from home (2006-2010 5-year est.); Travel time to work: 34.9% less than 15 minutes, 29.7% 15 to 30 minutes, 25.3% 30 to 45

minutes, 4.4% 45 to 60 minutes, 5.7% 60 minutes or more (2006-2010 5-year est.)

**LODI** (town). Covers a land area of 34.190 square miles and a water area of 5.574 square miles. Located at 42.59° N. Lat; 76.83° W. Long. Elevation is 1,106 feet.
**Population:** 1,429 (1990); 1,476 (2000); 1,550 (2010); Density: 45.3 persons per square mile (2010); Race: 96.4% White, 0.5% Black, 0.5% Asian, 0.7% American Indian/Alaska Native, 0.0% Native Hawaiian/Other Pacific Islander, 1.9% Other, 1.3% Hispanic of any race (2010); Average household size: 2.45 (2010); Median age: 42.7 (2010); Males per 100 females: 104.2 (2010); Marriage status: 24.8% never married, 58.8% now married, 6.3% widowed, 10.1% divorced (2006-2010 5-year est.); Foreign born: 1.3% (2006-2010 5-year est.); Ancestry (includes multiple ancestries): 20.4% English, 20.1% German, 19.6% American, 7.0% Irish, 6.8% Dutch (2006-2010 5-year est.).
**Economy:** Employment by occupation: 12.3% management, 4.0% professional, 19.2% services, 9.5% sales, 3.1% farming, 17.9% construction, 9.8% production (2006-2010 5-year est.).
**Income:** Per capita income: $18,136 (2006-2010 5-year est.); Median household income: $38,542 (2006-2010 5-year est.); Average household income: $45,409 (2006-2010 5-year est.); Percent of households with income of $100,000 or more: 5.9% (2006-2010 5-year est.); Poverty rate: 16.0% (2006-2010 5-year est.).
**Education:** Percent of population age 25 and over with: High school diploma (including GED) or higher: 85.5% (2006-2010 5-year est.); Bachelor's degree or higher: 13.9% (2006-2010 5-year est.); Master's degree or higher: 7.6% (2006-2010 5-year est.).
**Housing:** Homeownership rate: 86.1% (2010); Median home value: $83,800 (2006-2010 5-year est.); Median contract rent: $333 per month (2006-2010 5-year est.); Median year structure built: 1962 (2006-2010 5-year est.).
**Transportation:** Commute to work: 91.3% car, 0.8% public transportation, 4.8% walk, 2.5% work from home (2006-2010 5-year est.); Travel time to work: 26.1% less than 15 minutes, 29.6% 15 to 30 minutes, 30.1% 30 to 45 minutes, 10.1% 45 to 60 minutes, 4.1% 60 minutes or more (2006-2010 5-year est.).

**OVID** (village). Covers a land area of 0.397 square miles and a water area of 0 square miles. Located at 42.67° N. Lat; 76.82° W. Long. Elevation is 968 feet.
**Population:** 660 (1990); 612 (2000); 602 (2010); Density: 1,514.3 persons per square mile (2010); Race: 93.7% White, 1.7% Black, 0.8% Asian, 0.2% American Indian/Alaska Native, 0.0% Native Hawaiian/Other Pacific Islander, 3.6% Other, 2.3% Hispanic of any race (2010); Average household size: 2.37 (2010); Median age: 39.3 (2010); Males per 100 females: 93.6 (2010); Marriage status: 30.4% never married, 35.5% now married, 7.9% widowed, 26.3% divorced (2006-2010 5-year est.); Foreign born: 0.6% (2006-2010 5-year est.); Ancestry (includes multiple ancestries): 33.1% German, 27.9% Irish, 22.2% English, 6.3% Dutch, 4.6% Italian (2006-2010 5-year est.).
**Economy:** Employment by occupation: 8.8% management, 2.6% professional, 11.4% services, 18.7% sales, 4.7% farming, 8.8% construction, 9.3% production (2006-2010 5-year est.).
**Income:** Per capita income: $19,289 (2006-2010 5-year est.); Median household income: $40,074 (2006-2010 5-year est.); Average household income: $43,627 (2006-2010 5-year est.); Percent of households with income of $100,000 or more: 4.3% (2006-2010 5-year est.); Poverty rate: 10.9% (2006-2010 5-year est.).
**Education:** Percent of population age 25 and over with: High school diploma (including GED) or higher: 79.2% (2006-2010 5-year est.); Bachelor's degree or higher: 17.3% (2006-2010 5-year est.); Master's degree or higher: 3.9% (2006-2010 5-year est.).
**School District(s)**
South Seneca Central School District (PK-12)
    2009-10 Enrollment: 845 . . . . . . . . . . . . . . . . . . . . . . (607) 869-9636
**Housing:** Homeownership rate: 61.0% (2010); Median home value: $80,600 (2006-2010 5-year est.); Median contract rent: $469 per month (2006-2010 5-year est.); Median year structure built: before 1940 (2006-2010 5-year est.).
**Newspapers:** Reveille Between the Lakes (Community news; Circulation 2,200)
**Transportation:** Commute to work: 94.3% car, 0.0% public transportation, 4.7% walk, 1.0% work from home (2006-2010 5-year est.); Travel time to work: 43.5% less than 15 minutes, 24.6% 15 to 30 minutes, 17.8% 30 to 45

minutes, 14.1% 45 to 60 minutes, 0.0% 60 minutes or more (2006-2010 5-year est.)

**OVID** (town). Covers a land area of 30.861 square miles and a water area of 7.892 square miles. Located at 42.65° N. Lat; 76.79° W. Long. Elevation is 968 feet.
**Population:** 2,306 (1990); 2,757 (2000); 2,311 (2010); Density: 74.9 persons per square mile (2010); Race: 97.1% White, 0.6% Black, 0.3% Asian, 0.1% American Indian/Alaska Native, 0.0% Native Hawaiian/Other Pacific Islander, 1.9% Other, 1.6% Hispanic of any race (2010); Average household size: 2.39 (2010); Median age: 43.9 (2010); Males per 100 females: 101.1 (2010); Marriage status: 35.8% never married, 41.6% now married, 7.5% widowed, 15.0% divorced (2006-2010 5-year est.); Foreign born: 1.1% (2006-2010 5-year est.); Ancestry (includes multiple ancestries): 19.3% English, 17.9% German, 14.5% Irish, 6.3% American, 5.7% Italian (2006-2010 5-year est.).
**Economy:** Employment by occupation: 12.5% management, 1.2% professional, 11.5% services, 12.1% sales, 3.1% farming, 17.7% construction, 13.9% production (2006-2010 5-year est.).
**Income:** Per capita income: $20,509 (2006-2010 5-year est.); Median household income: $40,107 (2006-2010 5-year est.); Average household income: $51,816 (2006-2010 5-year est.); Percent of households with income of $100,000 or more: 13.7% (2006-2010 5-year est.); Poverty rate: 13.7% (2006-2010 5-year est.).
**Education:** Percent of population age 25 and over with: High school diploma (including GED) or higher: 81.1% (2006-2010 5-year est.); Bachelor's degree or higher: 13.2% (2006-2010 5-year est.); Master's degree or higher: 5.2% (2006-2010 5-year est.).
**School District(s)**
South Seneca Central School District (PK-12)
    2009-10 Enrollment: 845 . . . . . . . . . . . . . . . . . . . . . . (607) 869-9636
**Housing:** Homeownership rate: 74.3% (2010); Median home value: $91,800 (2006-2010 5-year est.); Median contract rent: $453 per month (2006-2010 5-year est.); Median year structure built: 1952 (2006-2010 5-year est.).
**Newspapers:** Reveille Between the Lakes (Community news; Circulation 2,200)
**Transportation:** Commute to work: 91.1% car, 2.5% public transportation, 3.6% walk, 2.8% work from home (2006-2010 5-year est.); Travel time to work: 29.3% less than 15 minutes, 19.9% 15 to 30 minutes, 34.6% 30 to 45 minutes, 12.7% 45 to 60 minutes, 3.5% 60 minutes or more (2006-2010 5-year est.)

**ROMULUS** (town). Covers a land area of 37.791 square miles and a water area of 13.590 square miles. Located at 42.71° N. Lat; 76.83° W. Long. Elevation is 719 feet.
**Population:** 2,532 (1990); 2,036 (2000); 4,316 (2010); Density: 114.2 persons per square mile (2010); Race: 66.5% White, 29.2% Black, 0.3% Asian, 0.5% American Indian/Alaska Native, 0.0% Native Hawaiian/Other Pacific Islander, 3.5% Other, 9.2% Hispanic of any race (2010); Average household size: 2.71 (2010); Median age: 33.4 (2010); Males per 100 females: 264.2 (2010); Marriage status: 47.6% never married, 41.1% now married, 2.5% widowed, 8.8% divorced (2006-2010 5-year est.); Foreign born: 3.4% (2006-2010 5-year est.); Ancestry (includes multiple ancestries): 15.0% German, 14.9% Irish, 10.1% Italian, 8.6% English, 4.3% Polish (2006-2010 5-year est.).
**Economy:** Employment by occupation: 11.0% management, 1.4% professional, 11.0% services, 11.1% sales, 3.2% farming, 7.7% construction, 7.2% production (2006-2010 5-year est.).
**Income:** Per capita income: $13,854 (2006-2010 5-year est.); Median household income: $56,053 (2006-2010 5-year est.); Average household income: $64,320 (2006-2010 5-year est.); Percent of households with income of $100,000 or more: 14.1% (2006-2010 5-year est.); Poverty rate: 11.5% (2006-2010 5-year est.).
**Education:** Percent of population age 25 and over with: High school diploma (including GED) or higher: 69.7% (2006-2010 5-year est.); Bachelor's degree or higher: 11.0% (2006-2010 5-year est.); Master's degree or higher: 2.8% (2006-2010 5-year est.).
**School District(s)**
Romulus Central School District (PK-12)
    2009-10 Enrollment: 476 . . . . . . . . . . . . . . . . . . . . . . (866) 810-0345
**Housing:** Homeownership rate: 69.6% (2010); Median home value: $111,400 (2006-2010 5-year est.); Median contract rent: $583 per month (2006-2010 5-year est.); Median year structure built: 1957 (2006-2010 5-year est.).

**Transportation:** Commute to work: 89.7% car, 1.3% public transportation, 5.2% walk, 3.9% work from home (2006-2010 5-year est.); Travel time to work: 32.0% less than 15 minutes, 35.4% 15 to 30 minutes, 18.0% 30 to 45 minutes, 9.8% 45 to 60 minutes, 4.8% 60 minutes or more (2006-2010 5-year est.)

## ROMULUS (CDP).

Covers a land area of 0.608 square miles and a water area of 0 square miles. Located at 42.75° N. Lat; 76.83° W. Long. Elevation is 719 feet.

**Population:** n/a (1990); n/a (2000); 409 (2010); Density: 672.0 persons per square mile (2010); Race: 94.9% White, 2.0% Black, 0.0% Asian, 0.5% American Indian/Alaska Native, 0.0% Native Hawaiian/Other Pacific Islander, 2.6% Other, 2.4% Hispanic of any race (2010); Average household size: 2.64 (2010); Median age: 37.8 (2010); Males per 100 females: 96.6 (2010); Marriage status: 33.5% never married, 56.8% now married, 3.1% widowed, 6.7% divorced (2006-2010 5-year est.); Foreign born: 1.4% (2006-2010 5-year est.); Ancestry (includes multiple ancestries): 40.0% German, 21.7% Irish, 13.1% English, 6.4% Swiss, 4.4% Italian (2006-2010 5-year est.).

**Economy:** Employment by occupation: 13.7% management, 0.0% professional, 4.9% services, 12.5% sales, 8.0% farming, 7.6% construction, 8.0% production (2006-2010 5-year est.).

**Income:** Per capita income: $17,924 (2006-2010 5-year est.); Median household income: $50,938 (2006-2010 5-year est.); Average household income: $53,643 (2006-2010 5-year est.); Percent of households with income of $100,000 or more: 11.5% (2006-2010 5-year est.); Poverty rate: 24.4% (2006-2010 5-year est.).

**Education:** Percent of population age 25 and over with: High school diploma (including GED) or higher: 75.5% (2006-2010 5-year est.); Bachelor's degree or higher: 10.0% (2006-2010 5-year est.); Master's degree or higher: 2.1% (2006-2010 5-year est.).

### School District(s)
Romulus Central School District (PK-12)
    2009-10 Enrollment: 476 . . . . . . . . . . . . . . . . . . . . . . . . (866) 810-0345

**Housing:** Homeownership rate: 73.0% (2010); Median home value: $81,400 (2006-2010 5-year est.); Median contract rent: $493 per month (2006-2010 5-year est.); Median year structure built: 1951 (2006-2010 5-year est.).

**Transportation:** Commute to work: 91.6% car, 5.7% public transportation, 1.1% walk, 1.5% work from home (2006-2010 5-year est.); Travel time to work: 20.8% less than 15 minutes, 29.0% 15 to 30 minutes, 36.3% 30 to 45 minutes, 7.3% 45 to 60 minutes, 6.6% 60 minutes or more (2006-2010 5-year est.)

## SENECA FALLS (village).

Covers a land area of 4.413 square miles and a water area of 0.157 square miles. Located at 42.90° N. Lat; 76.79° W. Long. Elevation is 449 feet.

**History:** Elizabeth Cady Stanton lived here and helped organize first women's rights convention in U.S., held here in 1848. Women's Rights National Historic Park and Museum, located in the restored Elizabeth Cady Stanton House, and the National Women's Hall of Fame are here. Settled 1787, Incorporated 1831.

**Population:** 7,448 (1990); 6,861 (2000); 6,681 (2010); Density: 1,513.7 persons per square mile (2010); Race: 95.1% White, 1.2% Black, 1.6% Asian, 0.4% American Indian/Alaska Native, 0.0% Native Hawaiian/Other Pacific Islander, 1.7% Other, 1.7% Hispanic of any race (2010); Average household size: 2.27 (2010); Median age: 41.0 (2010); Males per 100 females: 95.5 (2010); Marriage status: 31.3% never married, 50.4% now married, 6.8% widowed, 11.5% divorced (2006-2010 5-year est.); Foreign born: 2.5% (2006-2010 5-year est.); Ancestry (includes multiple ancestries): 33.2% Italian, 26.1% German, 24.4% Irish, 16.0% English, 5.4% Polish (2006-2010 5-year est.).

**Economy:** Employment by occupation: 12.1% management, 4.4% professional, 9.5% services, 18.4% sales, 3.6% farming, 9.1% construction, 4.2% production (2006-2010 5-year est.).

**Income:** Per capita income: $24,114 (2006-2010 5-year est.); Median household income: $47,283 (2006-2010 5-year est.); Average household income: $56,498 (2006-2010 5-year est.); Percent of households with income of $100,000 or more: 14.6% (2006-2010 5-year est.); Poverty rate: 13.2% (2006-2010 5-year est.).

**Taxes:** Total city taxes per capita: $526 (2009); City property taxes per capita: $498 (2009).

**Education:** Percent of population age 25 and over with: High school diploma (including GED) or higher: 88.1% (2006-2010 5-year est.);

Bachelor's degree or higher: 22.7% (2006-2010 5-year est.); Master's degree or higher: 6.9% (2006-2010 5-year est.).

### School District(s)
Seneca Falls Central School District (KG-12)
    2009-10 Enrollment: 1,304 . . . . . . . . . . . . . . . . . . . (315) 568-5818

### Four-year College(s)
New York Chiropractic College (Private, Not-for-profit)
    Fall 2010 Enrollment: 898 . . . . . . . . . . . . . . . . . . . . . (315) 568-3000

**Housing:** Homeownership rate: 63.1% (2010); Median home value: $82,900 (2006-2010 5-year est.); Median contract rent: $555 per month (2006-2010 5-year est.); Median year structure built: 1943 (2006-2010 5-year est.).

**Safety:** Violent crime rate: 16.8 per 10,000 population; Property crime rate: 93.3 per 10,000 population (2010).

**Newspapers:** Reveille/Between The Lake (Community news; Circulation 2,500)

**Transportation:** Commute to work: 94.3% car, 0.1% public transportation, 2.8% walk, 1.5% work from home (2006-2010 5-year est.); Travel time to work: 43.0% less than 15 minutes, 35.1% 15 to 30 minutes, 11.9% 30 to 45 minutes, 3.8% 45 to 60 minutes, 6.1% 60 minutes or more (2006-2010 5-year est.)

**Additional Information Contacts**
Seneca County Chamber of Commerce . . . . . . . . . . . . . (315) 568-2906
    http://www.senecachamber.org

## SENECA FALLS (town).

Covers a land area of 24.217 square miles and a water area of 3.241 square miles. Located at 42.91° N. Lat; 76.79° W. Long. Elevation is 449 feet.

**History:** Seneca Falls owes its early industrial development to the 50-foot waterfall which provided power, and its fame to great women who mothered the causes of woman's suffrage, anti-slavery, and temperance. Amelia Jenks Bloomer (1818-1894), wife of the local postmaster, did not invent the bloomers but she introduced them and advocated them as a uniform for women fighting for suffrage. Elizabeth Cady Stanton (1815-1902) moved to Seneca Falls in 1847, and the two called together the first convention of women fighting for suffrage. Susan B. Anthony (1820-1906) also joined the group and was president of the American Women's Suffrage Association until 1900.

**Population:** 9,384 (1990); 9,347 (2000); 9,040 (2010); Density: 373.3 persons per square mile (2010); Race: 94.9% White, 1.3% Black, 1.6% Asian, 0.4% American Indian/Alaska Native, 0.0% Native Hawaiian/Other Pacific Islander, 1.8% Other, 1.7% Hispanic of any race (2010); Average household size: 2.28 (2010); Median age: 41.5 (2010); Males per 100 females: 97.5 (2010); Marriage status: 32.1% never married, 51.3% now married, 6.5% widowed, 10.0% divorced (2006-2010 5-year est.); Foreign born: 3.2% (2006-2010 5-year est.); Ancestry (includes multiple ancestries): 30.0% Italian, 24.5% German, 22.0% Irish, 18.5% English, 4.7% Polish (2006-2010 5-year est.).

**Economy:** Employment by occupation: 11.3% management, 4.6% professional, 10.3% services, 18.0% sales, 3.5% farming, 9.2% construction, 5.1% production (2006-2010 5-year est.).

**Income:** Per capita income: $23,841 (2006-2010 5-year est.); Median household income: $46,127 (2006-2010 5-year est.); Average household income: $56,964 (2006-2010 5-year est.); Percent of households with income of $100,000 or more: 15.2% (2006-2010 5-year est.); Poverty rate: 12.0% (2006-2010 5-year est.).

**Education:** Percent of population age 25 and over with: High school diploma (including GED) or higher: 88.1% (2006-2010 5-year est.); Bachelor's degree or higher: 24.4% (2006-2010 5-year est.); Master's degree or higher: 7.6% (2006-2010 5-year est.).

### School District(s)
Seneca Falls Central School District (KG-12)
    2009-10 Enrollment: 1,304 . . . . . . . . . . . . . . . . . . . (315) 568-5818

### Four-year College(s)
New York Chiropractic College (Private, Not-for-profit)
    Fall 2010 Enrollment: 898 . . . . . . . . . . . . . . . . . . . . . (315) 568-3000

**Housing:** Homeownership rate: 64.1% (2010); Median home value: $90,800 (2006-2010 5-year est.); Median contract rent: $533 per month (2006-2010 5-year est.); Median year structure built: 1953 (2006-2010 5-year est.).

**Newspapers:** Reveille/Between The Lake (Community news; Circulation 2,500)

**Transportation:** Commute to work: 93.1% car, 0.6% public transportation, 3.0% walk, 2.1% work from home (2006-2010 5-year est.); Travel time to work: 42.4% less than 15 minutes, 34.9% 15 to 30 minutes, 12.4% 30 to 45

minutes, 3.9% 45 to 60 minutes, 6.3% 60 minutes or more (2006-2010 5-year est.)

**TYRE** (town). Covers a land area of 30.054 square miles and a water area of 3.059 square miles. Located at 42.98° N. Lat; 76.78° W. Long. Elevation is 410 feet.

**Population:** 870 (1990); 899 (2000); 981 (2010); Density: 32.6 persons per square mile (2010); Race: 97.6% White, 0.0% Black, 0.3% Asian, 0.2% American Indian/Alaska Native, 0.0% Native Hawaiian/Other Pacific Islander, 1.9% Other, 1.4% Hispanic of any race (2010); Average household size: 2.76 (2010); Median age: 40.0 (2010); Males per 100 females: 101.9 (2010); Marriage status: 26.2% never married, 58.6% now married, 3.8% widowed, 11.4% divorced (2006-2010 5-year est.); Foreign born: 2.3% (2006-2010 5-year est.); Ancestry (includes multiple ancestries): 28.2% German, 18.3% Italian, 15.9% Irish, 12.5% American, 11.9% English (2006-2010 5-year est.).

**Economy:** Employment by occupation: 14.8% management, 4.0% professional, 6.0% services, 15.4% sales, 2.9% farming, 18.3% construction, 8.7% production (2006-2010 5-year est.).

**Income:** Per capita income: $22,139 (2006-2010 5-year est.); Median household income: $50,000 (2006-2010 5-year est.); Average household income: $57,299 (2006-2010 5-year est.); Percent of households with income of $100,000 or more: 16.9% (2006-2010 5-year est.); Poverty rate: 15.3% (2006-2010 5-year est.).

**Education:** Percent of population age 25 and over with: High school diploma (including GED) or higher: 76.9% (2006-2010 5-year est.); Bachelor's degree or higher: 13.7% (2006-2010 5-year est.); Master's degree or higher: 5.6% (2006-2010 5-year est.).

**Housing:** Homeownership rate: 85.1% (2010); Median home value: $89,400 (2006-2010 5-year est.); Median contract rent: $555 per month (2006-2010 5-year est.); Median year structure built: 1955 (2006-2010 5-year est.).

**Transportation:** Commute to work: 83.7% car, 0.0% public transportation, 9.3% walk, 5.4% work from home (2006-2010 5-year est.); Travel time to work: 37.6% less than 15 minutes, 35.6% 15 to 30 minutes, 16.5% 30 to 45 minutes, 7.2% 45 to 60 minutes, 3.1% 60 minutes or more (2006-2010 5-year est.)

**VARICK** (town). Covers a land area of 31.994 square miles and a water area of 13.675 square miles. Located at 42.78° N. Lat; 76.84° W. Long.

**Population:** 2,161 (1990); 1,729 (2000); 1,857 (2010); Density: 58.0 persons per square mile (2010); Race: 95.2% White, 2.5% Black, 0.2% Asian, 0.2% American Indian/Alaska Native, 0.0% Native Hawaiian/Other Pacific Islander, 1.9% Other, 1.1% Hispanic of any race (2010); Average household size: 2.58 (2010); Median age: 40.7 (2010); Males per 100 females: 105.4 (2010); Marriage status: 21.4% never married, 60.4% now married, 5.3% widowed, 12.9% divorced (2006-2010 5-year est.); Foreign born: 0.8% (2006-2010 5-year est.); Ancestry (includes multiple ancestries): 31.4% German, 18.7% English, 13.3% Irish, 12.5% Italian, 6.0% American (2006-2010 5-year est.).

**Economy:** Employment by occupation: 12.2% management, 3.4% professional, 7.3% services, 10.5% sales, 4.1% farming, 12.2% construction, 7.7% production (2006-2010 5-year est.).

**Income:** Per capita income: $26,127 (2006-2010 5-year est.); Median household income: $53,542 (2006-2010 5-year est.); Average household income: $63,444 (2006-2010 5-year est.); Percent of households with income of $100,000 or more: 16.4% (2006-2010 5-year est.); Poverty rate: 14.5% (2006-2010 5-year est.).

**Education:** Percent of population age 25 and over with: High school diploma (including GED) or higher: 87.2% (2006-2010 5-year est.); Bachelor's degree or higher: 18.2% (2006-2010 5-year est.); Master's degree or higher: 7.4% (2006-2010 5-year est.).

**Housing:** Homeownership rate: 84.3% (2010); Median home value: $122,900 (2006-2010 5-year est.); Median contract rent: $539 per month (2006-2010 5-year est.); Median year structure built: 1957 (2006-2010 5-year est.).

**Transportation:** Commute to work: 90.1% car, 0.8% public transportation, 2.9% walk, 6.0% work from home (2006-2010 5-year est.); Travel time to work: 23.4% less than 15 minutes, 41.6% 15 to 30 minutes, 21.4% 30 to 45 minutes, 6.7% 45 to 60 minutes, 6.8% 60 minutes or more (2006-2010 5-year est.)

**WATERLOO** (village). County seat. Covers a land area of 2.156 square miles and a water area of 0.046 square miles. Located at 42.90° N. Lat; 76.85° W. Long. Elevation is 453 feet.

**Population:** 5,181 (1990); 5,111 (2000); 5,171 (2010); Density: 2,397.3 persons per square mile (2010); Race: 96.6% White, 1.1% Black, 0.4% Asian, 0.0% American Indian/Alaska Native, 0.0% Native Hawaiian/Other Pacific Islander, 1.9% Other, 2.2% Hispanic of any race (2010); Average household size: 2.39 (2010); Median age: 42.3 (2010); Males per 100 females: 86.5 (2010); Marriage status: 22.2% never married, 55.5% now married, 11.8% widowed, 10.5% divorced (2006-2010 5-year est.); Foreign born: 1.1% (2006-2010 5-year est.); Ancestry (includes multiple ancestries): 25.0% Irish, 22.2% English, 19.1% German, 18.2% Italian, 7.0% French (2006-2010 5-year est.).

**Economy:** Employment by occupation: 8.2% management, 2.6% professional, 10.0% services, 20.6% sales, 2.2% farming, 9.3% construction, 6.2% production (2006-2010 5-year est.).

**Income:** Per capita income: $21,649 (2006-2010 5-year est.); Median household income: $48,087 (2006-2010 5-year est.); Average household income: $54,125 (2006-2010 5-year est.); Percent of households with income of $100,000 or more: 8.2% (2006-2010 5-year est.); Poverty rate: 12.4% (2006-2010 5-year est.).

**Education:** Percent of population age 25 and over with: High school diploma (including GED) or higher: 89.0% (2006-2010 5-year est.); Bachelor's degree or higher: 16.8% (2006-2010 5-year est.); Master's degree or higher: 6.9% (2006-2010 5-year est.).

**School District(s)**
Waterloo Central School District (KG-12)
   2009-10 Enrollment: 1,807 . . . . . . . . . . . . . . . . . . . . (315) 539-1500

**Housing:** Homeownership rate: 69.8% (2010); Median home value: $76,100 (2006-2010 5-year est.); Median contract rent: $520 per month (2006-2010 5-year est.); Median year structure built: before 1940 (2006-2010 5-year est.).

**Safety:** Violent crime rate: 26.5 per 10,000 population; Property crime rate: 326.2 per 10,000 population (2010).

**Transportation:** Commute to work: 93.7% car, 0.4% public transportation, 2.5% walk, 2.5% work from home (2006-2010 5-year est.); Travel time to work: 50.0% less than 15 minutes, 24.1% 15 to 30 minutes, 12.7% 30 to 45 minutes, 5.4% 45 to 60 minutes, 7.8% 60 minutes or more (2006-2010 5-year est.)

**WATERLOO** (town). Covers a land area of 21.668 square miles and a water area of 0.147 square miles. Located at 42.91° N. Lat; 76.91° W. Long. Elevation is 453 feet.

**History:** Official birthplace of the Memorial Day celebaration, May 5, 1866 (celebrated on May 30). Incorporated 1824.

**Population:** 7,765 (1990); 7,866 (2000); 7,642 (2010); Density: 352.7 persons per square mile (2010); Race: 95.9% White, 1.5% Black, 0.3% Asian, 0.1% American Indian/Alaska Native, 0.0% Native Hawaiian/Other Pacific Islander, 2.2% Other, 2.5% Hispanic of any race (2010); Average household size: 2.35 (2010); Median age: 43.3 (2010); Males per 100 females: 92.3 (2010); Marriage status: 25.9% never married, 51.3% now married, 10.9% widowed, 11.8% divorced (2006-2010 5-year est.); Foreign born: 1.1% (2006-2010 5-year est.); Ancestry (includes multiple ancestries): 22.1% Irish, 21.8% German, 21.3% English, 16.1% Italian, 6.0% Dutch (2006-2010 5-year est.).

**Economy:** Employment by occupation: 7.4% management, 1.7% professional, 10.7% services, 20.3% sales, 3.4% farming, 12.0% construction, 7.2% production (2006-2010 5-year est.).

**Income:** Per capita income: $21,941 (2006-2010 5-year est.); Median household income: $44,872 (2006-2010 5-year est.); Average household income: $52,527 (2006-2010 5-year est.); Percent of households with income of $100,000 or more: 8.5% (2006-2010 5-year est.); Poverty rate: 10.3% (2006-2010 5-year est.).

**Taxes:** Total city taxes per capita: $141 (2009); City property taxes per capita: $133 (2009).

**Education:** Percent of population age 25 and over with: High school diploma (including GED) or higher: 85.9% (2006-2010 5-year est.); Bachelor's degree or higher: 15.4% (2006-2010 5-year est.); Master's degree or higher: 6.0% (2006-2010 5-year est.).

**School District(s)**
Waterloo Central School District (KG-12)
   2009-10 Enrollment: 1,807 . . . . . . . . . . . . . . . . . . . . (315) 539-1500

**Housing:** Homeownership rate: 69.9% (2010); Median home value: $74,500 (2006-2010 5-year est.); Median contract rent: $538 per month

(2006-2010 5-year est.); Median year structure built: 1954 (2006-2010 5-year est.).

**Transportation:** Commute to work: 95.6% car, 0.2% public transportation, 2.0% walk, 2.1% work from home (2006-2010 5-year est.); Travel time to work: 45.5% less than 15 minutes, 29.4% 15 to 30 minutes, 13.5% 30 to 45 minutes, 7.2% 45 to 60 minutes, 4.5% 60 minutes or more (2006-2010 5-year est.)

## WILLARD (unincorporated postal area)
Zip Code: 14588

Covers a land area of 0.240 square miles and a water area of 0 square miles. Located at 42.68° N. Lat; 76.87° W. Long. Elevation is 600 feet. Population: 749 (2010); Density: 3,110.5 persons per square mile (2010); Race: 44.7% White, 49.0% Black, 0.8% Asian, 0.9% American Indian/Alaska Native, 0.0% Native Hawaiian/Other Pacific Islander, 4.6% Other, 10.4% Hispanic of any race (2010); Average household size: 2.94 (2010); Median age: 29.6 (2010); Males per 100 females: 813.4 (2010); Homeownership rate: 78.2% (2010)

# Staten Island Borough

*See New York City*

# Steuben County

Located in southern New York, partly in the Finger Lakes region; bounded on the south by Pennsylvania; drained by the Canisteo, Cohocton, Tioga, and Chemung Rivers; includes part of Keuka Lake. Covers a land area of 1,392.64 square miles, a water area of 11.45 square miles, and is located in the Eastern Time Zone at 42.28° N. Lat., 77.36° W. Long. The county was founded in 1796. County seat is Bath.

Steuben County is part of the Corning, NY Micropolitan Statistical Area. The entire metro area includes: Steuben County, NY

Weather Station: Bath                                    Elevation: 1,120 feet

| | Jan | Feb | Mar | Apr | May | Jun | Jul | Aug | Sep | Oct | Nov | Dec |
|---|---|---|---|---|---|---|---|---|---|---|---|---|
| High | 32 | 35 | 43 | 56 | 68 | 77 | 81 | 79 | 72 | 60 | 47 | 36 |
| Low | 13 | 14 | 21 | 32 | 41 | 50 | 55 | 54 | 46 | 35 | 29 | 19 |
| Precip | 1.7 | 1.5 | 2.1 | 2.8 | 2.9 | 3.8 | 3.2 | 2.8 | 3.4 | 2.5 | 2.7 | 2.1 |
| Snow | 11.1 | 9.1 | 10.3 | 1.5 | tr | tr | 0.0 | 0.0 | 0.0 | tr | 3.6 | 9.2 |

*High and Low temperatures in degrees Fahrenheit; Precipitation and Snow in inches*

**Population:** 99,088 (1990); 98,726 (2000); 98,990 (2010); Race: 95.3% White, 1.6% Black, 1.2% Asian, 0.2% American Indian/Alaska Native, 0.0% Native Hawaiian/Other Pacific Islander, 1.7% Other, 1.4% Hispanic of any race (2010); Density: 71.1 persons per square mile (2010); Average household size: 2.41 (2010); Median age: 41.4 (2010); Males per 100 females: 98.5 (2010).
**Religion:** Six largest groups: 14.1% Catholicism, 6.4% Methodist/Pietist, 3.9% Holiness, 2.5% Non-Denominational, 1.9% Presbyterian-Reformed, 1.8% Baptist (2010)
**Economy:** Unemployment rate: 10.7% (February 2012); Total civilian labor force: 44,186 (February 2012); Leading industries: 22.5% manufacturing; 20.6% health care and social assistance; 15.2% retail trade (2009); Farms: 1,578 totaling 371,932 acres (2007); Companies that employ 500 or more persons: 9 (2009); Companies that employ 100 to 499 persons: 32 (2009); Companies that employ less than 100 persons: 1,797 (2009); Black-owned businesses: n/a (2007); Hispanic-owned businesses: 97 (2007); Asian-owned businesses: 53 (2007); Women-owned businesses: 2,228 (2007); Retail sales per capita: $10,030 (2010). Single-family building permits issued: 96 (2011); Multi-family building permits issued: 214 (2011).
**Income:** Per capita income: $23,279 (2006-2010 5-year est.); Median household income: $43,867 (2006-2010 5-year est.); Average household income: $56,222 (2006-2010 5-year est.); Percent of households with income of $100,000 or more: 13.7% (2006-2010 5-year est.); Poverty rate: 13.5% (2006-2010 5-year est.); Bankruptcy rate: 1.47% (2011).
**Taxes**: Total county taxes per capita: $784 (2009); County property taxes per capita: $377 (2009).
**Education:** Percent of population age 25 and over with: High school diploma (including GED) or higher: 87.5% (2006-2010 5-year est.); Bachelor's degree or higher: 19.9% (2006-2010 5-year est.); Master's degree or higher: 9.5% (2006-2010 5-year est.).
**Housing:** Homeownership rate: 72.1% (2010); Median home value: $83,000 (2006-2010 5-year est.); Median contract rent: $444 per month

(2006-2010 5-year est.); Median year structure built: 1956 (2006-2010 5-year est.).
**Health:** Birth rate: 109.8 per 10,000 population (2011); Death rate: 96.8 per 10,000 population (2011); Age-adjusted cancer mortality rate: 186.4 deaths per 100,000 population (2009); Number of physicians: 14.8 per 10,000 population (2008); Hospital beds: 82.3 per 10,000 population (2007); Hospital admissions: 1,244.9 per 10,000 population (2007).
**Environment:** Air Quality Index: 91.0% good, 9.0% moderate, 0.0% unhealthy for sensitive individuals, 0.0% unhealthy (percent of days in 2010)
**Elections:** 2008 Presidential election results: 40.9% Obama, 57.7% McCain, 0.6% Nader
**National and State Parks:** Stony Brook State Park
**Additional Information Contacts**
Steuben County Government .................... (607) 776-9631
  http://www.steubencony.org
City of Hornell ............................ (607) 324-7421
  http://www.cityofhornell.com
Corning Area Chamber of Commerce .................. (607) 936-4686
  http://www.corningny.com
Dansville Area Chamber of Commerce ............... (585) 335-6920
  http://www.dansvilleny.net
Hammondsport Chamber of Commerce ............. (607) 569-2989
  http://www.hammondsport.org
Hornell Area Chamber of Commerce ............... (607) 324-0310
  http://www.hornellny.com
Town of Erwin ............................ (607) 936-3652
  http://www.erwinny.org

# *Steuben County Communities*

**ADDISON** (village). Covers a land area of 1.892 square miles and a water area of 0 square miles. Located at 42.10° N. Lat; 77.23° W. Long. Elevation is 997 feet.
**Population:** 1,913 (1990); 1,797 (2000); 1,763 (2010); Density: 931.4 persons per square mile (2010); Race: 96.9% White, 0.5% Black, 0.7% Asian, 0.2% American Indian/Alaska Native, 0.0% Native Hawaiian/Other Pacific Islander, 1.7% Other, 1.8% Hispanic of any race (2010); Average household size: 2.53 (2010); Median age: 36.7 (2010); Males per 100 females: 91.4 (2010); Marriage status: 24.7% never married, 55.7% now married, 9.1% widowed, 10.4% divorced (2006-2010 5-year est.); Foreign born: 0.4% (2006-2010 5-year est.); Ancestry (includes multiple ancestries): 20.5% English, 18.3% Irish, 16.8% German, 7.2% American, 5.3% Italian (2006-2010 5-year est.).
**Economy:** Single-family building permits issued: 0 (2011); Multi-family building permits issued: 0 (2011); Employment by occupation: 9.7% management, 4.9% professional, 12.1% services, 14.5% sales, 4.2% farming, 7.2% construction, 6.0% production (2006-2010 5-year est.).
**Income:** Per capita income: $21,500 (2006-2010 5-year est.); Median household income: $44,583 (2006-2010 5-year est.); Average household income: $49,638 (2006-2010 5-year est.); Percent of households with income of $100,000 or more: 9.9% (2006-2010 5-year est.); Poverty rate: 14.1% (2006-2010 5-year est.).
**Education:** Percent of population age 25 and over with: High school diploma (including GED) or higher: 83.7% (2006-2010 5-year est.); Bachelor's degree or higher: 12.4% (2006-2010 5-year est.); Master's degree or higher: 5.3% (2006-2010 5-year est.).
**School District(s)**
Addison Central School District (PK-12)
  2009-10 Enrollment: 1,177 ................ (607) 359-2244
**Housing:** Homeownership rate: 65.8% (2010); Median home value: $74,100 (2006-2010 5-year est.); Median contract rent: $368 per month (2006-2010 5-year est.); Median year structure built: before 1940 (2006-2010 5-year est.).
**Transportation:** Commute to work: 90.7% car, 0.0% public transportation, 5.0% walk, 2.7% work from home (2006-2010 5-year est.); Travel time to work: 24.3% less than 15 minutes, 40.6% 15 to 30 minutes, 16.3% 30 to 45 minutes, 11.6% 45 to 60 minutes, 7.3% 60 minutes or more (2006-2010 5-year est.)

**ADDISON** (town). Covers a land area of 25.545 square miles and a water area of 0.142 square miles. Located at 42.13° N. Lat; 77.23° W. Long. Elevation is 997 feet.
**History:** Incorporated 1873.

**Population:** 2,645 (1990); 2,640 (2000); 2,595 (2010); Density: 101.6 persons per square mile (2010); Race: 96.5% White, 0.4% Black, 0.7% Asian, 0.2% American Indian/Alaska Native, 0.0% Native Hawaiian/Other Pacific Islander, 2.2% Other, 1.5% Hispanic of any race (2010); Average household size: 2.60 (2010); Median age: 37.2 (2010); Males per 100 females: 93.7 (2010); Marriage status: 21.9% never married, 60.6% now married, 7.0% widowed, 10.5% divorced (2006-2010 5-year est.); Foreign born: 1.9% (2006-2010 5-year est.); Ancestry (includes multiple ancestries): 22.5% English, 17.9% Irish, 15.9% German, 8.4% Dutch, 5.8% American (2006-2010 5-year est.).
**Economy:** Employment by occupation: 9.1% management, 3.5% professional, 11.1% services, 12.7% sales, 3.7% farming, 12.3% construction, 7.8% production (2006-2010 5-year est.).
**Income:** Per capita income: $20,731 (2006-2010 5-year est.); Median household income: $44,779 (2006-2010 5-year est.); Average household income: $49,364 (2006-2010 5-year est.); Percent of households with income of $100,000 or more: 8.1% (2006-2010 5-year est.); Poverty rate: 13.2% (2006-2010 5-year est.).
**Education:** Percent of population age 25 and over with: High school diploma (including GED) or higher: 84.7% (2006-2010 5-year est.); Bachelor's degree or higher: 10.8% (2006-2010 5-year est.); Master's degree or higher: 4.7% (2006-2010 5-year est.).

#### School District(s)
Addison Central School District (PK-12)
   2009-10 Enrollment: 1,177 . . . . . . . . . . . . . . . . . (607) 359-2244
**Housing:** Homeownership rate: 71.0% (2010); Median home value: $75,800 (2006-2010 5-year est.); Median contract rent: $413 per month (2006-2010 5-year est.); Median year structure built: 1953 (2006-2010 5-year est.).
**Safety:** Violent crime rate: 16.2 per 10,000 population; Property crime rate: 231.1 per 10,000 population (2010).
**Transportation:** Commute to work: 93.6% car, 0.0% public transportation, 3.6% walk, 1.7% work from home (2006-2010 5-year est.); Travel time to work: 22.0% less than 15 minutes, 45.0% 15 to 30 minutes, 21.3% 30 to 45 minutes, 7.2% 45 to 60 minutes, 4.5% 60 minutes or more (2006-2010 5-year est.)

**ARKPORT** (village). Covers a land area of 0.694 square miles and a water area of 0 square miles. Located at 42.39° N. Lat; 77.69° W. Long. Elevation is 1,184 feet.
**Population:** 770 (1990); 832 (2000); 844 (2010); Density: 1,215.7 persons per square mile (2010); Race: 98.6% White, 0.1% Black, 0.5% Asian, 0.1% American Indian/Alaska Native, 0.0% Native Hawaiian/Other Pacific Islander, 0.7% Other, 0.4% Hispanic of any race (2010); Average household size: 2.33 (2010); Median age: 43.2 (2010); Males per 100 females: 83.1 (2010); Marriage status: 18.7% never married, 62.5% now married, 7.5% widowed, 11.4% divorced (2006-2010 5-year est.); Foreign born: 0.8% (2006-2010 5-year est.); Ancestry (includes multiple ancestries): 35.0% German, 27.4% Irish, 13.8% English, 12.7% Italian, 10.6% American (2006-2010 5-year est.).
**Economy:** Single-family building permits issued: 0 (2011); Multi-family building permits issued: 0 (2011); Employment by occupation: 4.2% management, 2.5% professional, 15.0% services, 11.3% sales, 0.0% farming, 16.7% construction, 5.9% production (2006-2010 5-year est.).
**Income:** Per capita income: $18,000 (2006-2010 5-year est.); Median household income: $46,375 (2006-2010 5-year est.); Average household income: $50,095 (2006-2010 5-year est.); Percent of households with income of $100,000 or more: 4.1% (2006-2010 5-year est.); Poverty rate: 2.2% (2006-2010 5-year est.).
**Education:** Percent of population age 25 and over with: High school diploma (including GED) or higher: 96.9% (2006-2010 5-year est.); Bachelor's degree or higher: 20.1% (2006-2010 5-year est.); Master's degree or higher: 8.2% (2006-2010 5-year est.).

#### School District(s)
Arkport Central School District (PK-12)
   2009-10 Enrollment: 589 . . . . . . . . . . . . . . . . . . (607) 295-7471
**Housing:** Homeownership rate: 73.0% (2010); Median home value: $81,400 (2006-2010 5-year est.); Median contract rent: $417 per month (2006-2010 5-year est.); Median year structure built: 1949 (2006-2010 5-year est.).
**Transportation:** Commute to work: 94.6% car, 2.0% public transportation, 2.6% walk, 0.9% work from home (2006-2010 5-year est.); Travel time to work: 41.1% less than 15 minutes, 25.6% 15 to 30 minutes, 10.6% 30 to 45 minutes, 1.7% 45 to 60 minutes, 21.0% 60 minutes or more (2006-2010 5-year est.)

**ATLANTA** (unincorporated postal area)
Zip Code: 14808
   Covers a land area of 3.369 square miles and a water area of 0 square miles. Located at 42.55° N. Lat; 77.46° W. Long. Elevation is 1,309 feet. Population: 591 (2010); Density: 175.4 persons per square mile (2010); Race: 96.6% White, 0.2% Black, 0.3% Asian, 0.5% American Indian/Alaska Native, 0.0% Native Hawaiian/Other Pacific Islander, 2.4% Other, 1.9% Hispanic of any race (2010); Average household size: 2.62 (2010); Median age: 39.6 (2010); Males per 100 females: 119.7 (2010); Homeownership rate: 77.1% (2010)

**AVOCA** (village). Covers a land area of 1.326 square miles and a water area of 0.002 square miles. Located at 42.41° N. Lat; 77.42° W. Long. Elevation is 1,194 feet.
**Population:** 1,017 (1990); 1,008 (2000); 946 (2010); Density: 713.4 persons per square mile (2010); Race: 96.5% White, 0.6% Black, 0.1% Asian, 0.2% American Indian/Alaska Native, 0.0% Native Hawaiian/Other Pacific Islander, 2.6% Other, 3.5% Hispanic of any race (2010); Average household size: 2.62 (2010); Median age: 37.1 (2010); Males per 100 females: 100.4 (2010); Marriage status: 25.7% never married, 56.9% now married, 3.6% widowed, 13.8% divorced (2006-2010 5-year est.); Foreign born: 0.0% (2006-2010 5-year est.); Ancestry (includes multiple ancestries): 29.8% German, 19.0% Irish, 13.5% English, 11.7% Italian, 9.0% Polish (2006-2010 5-year est.).
**Economy:** Single-family building permits issued: 0 (2011); Multi-family building permits issued: 0 (2011); Employment by occupation: 10.1% management, 0.5% professional, 13.2% services, 16.7% sales, 1.6% farming, 8.2% construction, 6.3% production (2006-2010 5-year est.).
**Income:** Per capita income: $18,841 (2006-2010 5-year est.); Median household income: $43,684 (2006-2010 5-year est.); Average household income: $51,875 (2006-2010 5-year est.); Percent of households with income of $100,000 or more: 9.1% (2006-2010 5-year est.); Poverty rate: 10.6% (2006-2010 5-year est.).
**Education:** Percent of population age 25 and over with: High school diploma (including GED) or higher: 92.4% (2006-2010 5-year est.); Bachelor's degree or higher: 17.2% (2006-2010 5-year est.); Master's degree or higher: 5.6% (2006-2010 5-year est.).

#### School District(s)
Avoca Central School District (KG-12)
   2009-10 Enrollment: 561 . . . . . . . . . . . . . . . . . . (607) 566-2221
**Housing:** Homeownership rate: 70.9% (2010); Median home value: $60,600 (2006-2010 5-year est.); Median contract rent: $417 per month (2006-2010 5-year est.); Median year structure built: before 1940 (2006-2010 5-year est.).
**Transportation:** Commute to work: 90.4% car, 0.0% public transportation, 5.9% walk, 2.8% work from home (2006-2010 5-year est.); Travel time to work: 35.0% less than 15 minutes, 37.6% 15 to 30 minutes, 17.2% 30 to 45 minutes, 4.1% 45 to 60 minutes, 6.1% 60 minutes or more (2006-2010 5-year est.)

**AVOCA** (town). Covers a land area of 36.248 square miles and a water area of 0.040 square miles. Located at 42.42° N. Lat; 77.44° W. Long. Elevation is 1,194 feet.
**History:** Settled 1843, incorporated 1883.
**Population:** 2,269 (1990); 2,314 (2000); 2,264 (2010); Density: 62.5 persons per square mile (2010); Race: 97.2% White, 0.5% Black, 0.1% Asian, 0.4% American Indian/Alaska Native, 0.0% Native Hawaiian/Other Pacific Islander, 1.8% Other, 1.9% Hispanic of any race (2010); Average household size: 2.53 (2010); Median age: 40.8 (2010); Males per 100 females: 104.7 (2010); Marriage status: 23.8% never married, 59.2% now married, 3.7% widowed, 13.4% divorced (2006-2010 5-year est.); Foreign born: 0.3% (2006-2010 5-year est.); Ancestry (includes multiple ancestries): 24.7% German, 17.3% English, 11.5% Irish, 9.8% American, 8.9% French (2006-2010 5-year est.).
**Economy:** Single-family building permits issued: 0 (2011); Multi-family building permits issued: 0 (2011); Employment by occupation: 10.7% management, 0.9% professional, 9.0% services, 20.3% sales, 5.9% farming, 9.8% construction, 7.8% production (2006-2010 5-year est.).
**Income:** Per capita income: $19,279 (2006-2010 5-year est.); Median household income: $44,605 (2006-2010 5-year est.); Average household income: $50,603 (2006-2010 5-year est.); Percent of households with income of $100,000 or more: 10.0% (2006-2010 5-year est.); Poverty rate: 12.0% (2006-2010 5-year est.).
**Education:** Percent of population age 25 and over with: High school diploma (including GED) or higher: 88.5% (2006-2010 5-year est.);

Bachelor's degree or higher: 14.9% (2006-2010 5-year est.); Master's degree or higher: 6.1% (2006-2010 5-year est.).

### School District(s)

Avoca Central School District (KG-12)

   2009-10 Enrollment: 561 . . . . . . . . . . . . . . . . . . . . . . . (607) 566-2221

**Housing:** Homeownership rate: 76.9% (2010); Median home value: $74,400 (2006-2010 5-year est.); Median contract rent: $413 per month (2006-2010 5-year est.); Median year structure built: 1953 (2006-2010 5-year est.).

**Transportation:** Commute to work: 87.4% car, 0.0% public transportation, 2.5% walk, 9.7% work from home (2006-2010 5-year est.); Travel time to work: 31.7% less than 15 minutes, 42.0% 15 to 30 minutes, 13.8% 30 to 45 minutes, 7.2% 45 to 60 minutes, 5.2% 60 minutes or more (2006-2010 5-year est.)

## BATH (village). County seat. Covers a land area of 3.174 square miles and a water area of <.001 square miles. Located at 42.33° N. Lat; 77.31° W. Long. Elevation is 1,109 feet.

**Population:** 5,801 (1990); 5,641 (2000); 5,786 (2010); Density: 1,822.6 persons per square mile (2010); Race: 93.7% White, 3.0% Black, 0.6% Asian, 0.3% American Indian/Alaska Native, 0.0% Native Hawaiian/Other Pacific Islander, 2.4% Other, 1.3% Hispanic of any race (2010); Average household size: 2.10 (2010); Median age: 43.8 (2010); Males per 100 females: 93.1 (2010); Marriage status: 28.1% never married, 43.8% now married, 10.0% widowed, 18.1% divorced (2006-2010 5-year est.); Foreign born: 0.7% (2006-2010 5-year est.); Ancestry (includes multiple ancestries): 20.7% German, 19.4% English, 14.2% Irish, 10.1% American, 9.1% Polish (2006-2010 5-year est.).

**Economy:** Single-family building permits issued: 2 (2011); Multi-family building permits issued: 0 (2011); Employment by occupation: 8.8% management, 1.1% professional, 13.8% services, 16.3% sales, 1.0% farming, 9.7% construction, 7.1% production (2006-2010 5-year est.).

**Income:** Per capita income: $22,217 (2006-2010 5-year est.); Median household income: $30,432 (2006-2010 5-year est.); Average household income: $44,822 (2006-2010 5-year est.); Percent of households with income of $100,000 or more: 11.4% (2006-2010 5-year est.); Poverty rate: 16.3% (2006-2010 5-year est.).

**Education:** Percent of population age 25 and over with: High school diploma (including GED) or higher: 82.8% (2006-2010 5-year est.); Bachelor's degree or higher: 15.8% (2006-2010 5-year est.); Master's degree or higher: 7.3% (2006-2010 5-year est.).

### School District(s)

Bath Central School District (PK-12)

   2009-10 Enrollment: 1,759 . . . . . . . . . . . . . . . . . . . . (607) 776-3301

**Housing:** Homeownership rate: 52.6% (2010); Median home value: $84,500 (2006-2010 5-year est.); Median contract rent: $433 per month (2006-2010 5-year est.); Median year structure built: 1948 (2006-2010 5-year est.).

**Hospitals:** Bath VA Medical Center (440 beds)

**Safety:** Violent crime rate: 31.9 per 10,000 population; Property crime rate: 384.6 per 10,000 population (2010).

**Newspapers:** Steuben Courier-Advocate (Community news; Circulation 11,022)

**Transportation:** Commute to work: 83.8% car, 3.9% public transportation, 6.5% walk, 1.9% work from home (2006-2010 5-year est.); Travel time to work: 59.5% less than 15 minutes, 21.0% 15 to 30 minutes, 13.2% 30 to 45 minutes, 3.8% 45 to 60 minutes, 2.5% 60 minutes or more (2006-2010 5-year est.)

## BATH (town). Covers a land area of 95.318 square miles and a water area of 0.558 square miles. Located at 42.32° N. Lat; 77.31° W. Long. Elevation is 1,109 feet.

**History:** Bath is the site of the first clearing in Steuben County, made in 1793 by Colonel Charles Williamson (1757-1808), agent for the Pulteney Estate. Williamson chose the site of Bath on the Cohocton River as the location of a future metropolis that was to be the trading, industrial, and distribution center for the entire region. He was too energetic to wait for the normal processes of settlement. His plan was to build the city first, which would then attract settlers. Williamson's overhasty promotions cost his principals more than a million dollars, and he was dismissed from his position in 1801. Incorporated in 1816.

**Population:** 12,724 (1990); 12,097 (2000); 12,379 (2010); Density: 129.9 persons per square mile (2010); Race: 94.9% White, 2.9% Black, 0.5% Asian, 0.3% American Indian/Alaska Native, 0.0% Native Hawaiian/Other Pacific Islander, 1.4% Other, 1.2% Hispanic of any race (2010); Average

household size: 2.26 (2010); Median age: 43.8 (2010); Males per 100 females: 103.4 (2010); Marriage status: 25.2% never married, 51.4% now married, 8.4% widowed, 15.0% divorced (2006-2010 5-year est.); Foreign born: 1.1% (2006-2010 5-year est.); Ancestry (includes multiple ancestries): 20.7% German, 18.9% English, 17.4% Irish, 9.2% American, 8.0% Polish (2006-2010 5-year est.).

**Economy:** Single-family building permits issued: 9 (2011); Multi-family building permits issued: 0 (2011); Employment by occupation: 10.4% management, 2.1% professional, 13.6% services, 17.1% sales, 2.9% farming, 11.0% construction, 7.8% production (2006-2010 5-year est.).

**Income:** Per capita income: $22,551 (2006-2010 5-year est.); Median household income: $38,497 (2006-2010 5-year est.); Average household income: $50,822 (2006-2010 5-year est.); Percent of households with income of $100,000 or more: 13.0% (2006-2010 5-year est.); Poverty rate: 12.6% (2006-2010 5-year est.).

**Education:** Percent of population age 25 and over with: High school diploma (including GED) or higher: 81.1% (2006-2010 5-year est.); Bachelor's degree or higher: 14.0% (2006-2010 5-year est.); Master's degree or higher: 6.6% (2006-2010 5-year est.).

### School District(s)

Bath Central School District (PK-12)

   2009-10 Enrollment: 1,759 . . . . . . . . . . . . . . . . . . . . (607) 776-3301

**Housing:** Homeownership rate: 64.8% (2010); Median home value: $82,500 (2006-2010 5-year est.); Median contract rent: $433 per month (2006-2010 5-year est.); Median year structure built: 1959 (2006-2010 5-year est.).

**Hospitals:** Bath VA Medical Center (440 beds); Ira Davenport Memorial Hospital (66 beds); Ira Davenport Memorial Hospital (66 beds)

**Newspapers:** Steuben Courier-Advocate (Community news; Circulation 11,022)

**Transportation:** Commute to work: 89.0% car, 1.9% public transportation, 3.4% walk, 2.9% work from home (2006-2010 5-year est.); Travel time to work: 50.0% less than 15 minutes, 25.8% 15 to 30 minutes, 14.8% 30 to 45 minutes, 5.4% 45 to 60 minutes, 3.9% 60 minutes or more (2006-2010 5-year est.)

## BRADFORD (town). Covers a land area of 25.121 square miles and a water area of 0.114 square miles. Located at 42.33° N. Lat; 77.13° W. Long. Elevation is 1,119 feet.

**Population:** 699 (1990); 763 (2000); 855 (2010); Density: 34.0 persons per square mile (2010); Race: 98.4% White, 0.1% Black, 0.1% Asian, 0.2% American Indian/Alaska Native, 0.0% Native Hawaiian/Other Pacific Islander, 1.2% Other, 0.6% Hispanic of any race (2010); Average household size: 2.51 (2010); Median age: 39.3 (2010); Males per 100 females: 104.1 (2010); Marriage status: 25.4% never married, 58.3% now married, 5.7% widowed, 10.6% divorced (2006-2010 5-year est.); Foreign born: 4.1% (2006-2010 5-year est.); Ancestry (includes multiple ancestries): 23.1% Irish, 17.7% Polish, 17.5% German, 10.2% English, 5.7% American (2006-2010 5-year est.).

**Economy:** Single-family building permits issued: 0 (2011); Multi-family building permits issued: 0 (2011); Employment by occupation: 11.2% management, 2.4% professional, 10.5% services, 16.9% sales, 3.5% farming, 15.4% construction, 13.4% production (2006-2010 5-year est.).

**Income:** Per capita income: $18,521 (2006-2010 5-year est.); Median household income: $47,721 (2006-2010 5-year est.); Average household income: $56,342 (2006-2010 5-year est.); Percent of households with income of $100,000 or more: 15.6% (2006-2010 5-year est.); Poverty rate: 26.3% (2006-2010 5-year est.).

**Education:** Percent of population age 25 and over with: High school diploma (including GED) or higher: 89.1% (2006-2010 5-year est.); Bachelor's degree or higher: 11.7% (2006-2010 5-year est.); Master's degree or higher: 2.7% (2006-2010 5-year est.).

### School District(s)

Bradford Central School District (PK-12)

   2009-10 Enrollment: 279 . . . . . . . . . . . . . . . . . . . . . . (607) 583-4616

**Housing:** Homeownership rate: 82.9% (2010); Median home value: $73,100 (2006-2010 5-year est.); Median contract rent: $385 per month (2006-2010 5-year est.); Median year structure built: 1977 (2006-2010 5-year est.).

**Transportation:** Commute to work: 92.6% car, 0.0% public transportation, 1.6% walk, 1.6% work from home (2006-2010 5-year est.); Travel time to work: 9.3% less than 15 minutes, 50.8% 15 to 30 minutes, 24.6% 30 to 45 minutes, 9.8% 45 to 60 minutes, 5.5% 60 minutes or more (2006-2010 5-year est.)

**CAMERON** (town). Covers a land area of 46.703 square miles and a water area of 0.057 square miles. Located at 42.22° N. Lat; 77.42° W. Long. Elevation is 1,070 feet.
**Population:** 916 (1990); 1,034 (2000); 945 (2010); Density: 20.2 persons per square mile (2010); Race: 97.6% White, 0.8% Black, 0.0% Asian, 0.3% American Indian/Alaska Native, 0.0% Native Hawaiian/Other Pacific Islander, 1.3% Other, 1.2% Hispanic of any race (2010); Average household size: 2.68 (2010); Median age: 40.1 (2010); Males per 100 females: 106.8 (2010); Marriage status: 24.1% never married, 56.4% now married, 2.9% widowed, 16.6% divorced (2006-2010 5-year est.); Foreign born: 1.9% (2006-2010 5-year est.); Ancestry (includes multiple ancestries): 22.5% German, 13.5% Irish, 12.6% English, 9.1% French, 7.7% American (2006-2010 5-year est.).
**Economy:** Single-family building permits issued: 2 (2011); Multi-family building permits issued: 0 (2011); Employment by occupation: 6.5% management, 1.5% professional, 9.0% services, 14.0% sales, 1.7% farming, 15.5% construction, 15.5% production (2006-2010 5-year est.).
**Income:** Per capita income: $16,043 (2006-2010 5-year est.); Median household income: $33,269 (2006-2010 5-year est.); Average household income: $41,005 (2006-2010 5-year est.); Percent of households with income of $100,000 or more: 3.8% (2006-2010 5-year est.); Poverty rate: 20.5% (2006-2010 5-year est.).
**Education:** Percent of population age 25 and over with: High school diploma (including GED) or higher: 77.5% (2006-2010 5-year est.); Bachelor's degree or higher: 3.3% (2006-2010 5-year est.); Master's degree or higher: 1.8% (2006-2010 5-year est.).
**Housing:** Homeownership rate: 81.5% (2010); Median home value: $72,700 (2006-2010 5-year est.); Median contract rent: $406 per month (2006-2010 5-year est.); Median year structure built: 1975 (2006-2010 5-year est.).
**Transportation:** Commute to work: 95.7% car, 0.0% public transportation, 1.3% walk, 2.5% work from home (2006-2010 5-year est.); Travel time to work: 17.0% less than 15 minutes, 36.3% 15 to 30 minutes, 32.6% 30 to 45 minutes, 6.5% 45 to 60 minutes, 7.6% 60 minutes or more (2006-2010 5-year est.)

**CAMERON MILLS** (unincorporated postal area)
Zip Code: 14820
   Covers a land area of 30.739 square miles and a water area of 0.025 square miles. Located at 42.19° N. Lat; 77.35° W. Long. Elevation is 1,033 feet. Population: 784 (2010); Density: 25.5 persons per square mile (2010); Race: 98.0% White, 0.1% Black, 0.0% Asian, 0.4% American Indian/Alaska Native, 0.0% Native Hawaiian/Other Pacific Islander, 1.5% Other, 0.3% Hispanic of any race (2010); Average household size: 2.80 (2010); Median age: 37.8 (2010); Males per 100 females: 100.0 (2010); Homeownership rate: 82.1% (2010)

**CAMPBELL** (town). Covers a land area of 40.684 square miles and a water area of 0.094 square miles. Located at 42.23° N. Lat; 77.16° W. Long. Elevation is 1,014 feet.
**Population:** 3,658 (1990); 3,691 (2000); 3,406 (2010); Density: 83.7 persons per square mile (2010); Race: 97.4% White, 0.4% Black, 0.3% Asian, 0.1% American Indian/Alaska Native, 0.0% Native Hawaiian/Other Pacific Islander, 1.8% Other, 1.1% Hispanic of any race (2010); Average household size: 2.47 (2010); Median age: 43.0 (2010); Males per 100 females: 96.5 (2010); Marriage status: 28.8% never married, 62.7% now married, 3.4% widowed, 5.2% divorced (2006-2010 5-year est.); Foreign born: 0.9% (2006-2010 5-year est.); Ancestry (includes multiple ancestries): 19.3% Irish, 18.8% German, 14.8% English, 14.4% American, 9.1% Italian (2006-2010 5-year est.).
**Economy:** Single-family building permits issued: 3 (2011); Multi-family building permits issued: 0 (2011); Employment by occupation: 5.1% management, 2.6% professional, 8.9% services, 17.3% sales, 2.4% farming, 14.4% construction, 10.2% production (2006-2010 5-year est.).
**Income:** Per capita income: $20,619 (2006-2010 5-year est.); Median household income: $45,042 (2006-2010 5-year est.); Average household income: $57,479 (2006-2010 5-year est.); Percent of households with income of $100,000 or more: 13.0% (2006-2010 5-year est.); Poverty rate: 12.7% (2006-2010 5-year est.).
**Education:** Percent of population age 25 and over with: High school diploma (including GED) or higher: 84.6% (2006-2010 5-year est.); Bachelor's degree or higher: 18.1% (2006-2010 5-year est.); Master's degree or higher: 6.4% (2006-2010 5-year est.).

**School District(s)**
Campbell-Savona Central School District (PK-12)
   2009-10 Enrollment: 1,007 . . . . . . . . . . . . . . . . (607) 527-9800
**Housing:** Homeownership rate: 83.3% (2010); Median home value: $77,400 (2006-2010 5-year est.); Median contract rent: $487 per month (2006-2010 5-year est.); Median year structure built: 1974 (2006-2010 5-year est.).
**Transportation:** Commute to work: 88.7% car, 1.8% public transportation, 2.9% walk, 5.9% work from home (2006-2010 5-year est.); Travel time to work: 20.4% less than 15 minutes, 57.7% 15 to 30 minutes, 15.1% 30 to 45 minutes, 2.4% 45 to 60 minutes, 4.5% 60 minutes or more (2006-2010 5-year est.)

**CAMPBELL** (CDP). Covers a land area of 1.761 square miles and a water area of 0 square miles. Located at 42.23° N. Lat; 77.19° W. Long. Elevation is 1,014 feet.
**Population:** n/a (1990); n/a (2000); 713 (2010); Density: 404.8 persons per square mile (2010); Race: 97.2% White, 0.1% Black, 0.1% Asian, 0.0% American Indian/Alaska Native, 0.0% Native Hawaiian/Other Pacific Islander, 2.6% Other, 0.7% Hispanic of any race (2010); Average household size: 2.45 (2010); Median age: 44.0 (2010); Males per 100 females: 90.6 (2010); Marriage status: 26.5% never married, 62.1% now married, 1.6% widowed, 9.9% divorced (2006-2010 5-year est.); Foreign born: 0.0% (2006-2010 5-year est.); Ancestry (includes multiple ancestries): 24.4% German, 19.7% American, 16.2% Irish, 14.9% English, 9.6% Italian (2006-2010 5-year est.).
**Economy:** Employment by occupation: 0.0% management, 0.0% professional, 6.6% services, 15.7% sales, 3.8% farming, 28.6% construction, 24.2% production (2006-2010 5-year est.).
**Income:** Per capita income: $16,243 (2006-2010 5-year est.); Median household income: $32,348 (2006-2010 5-year est.); Average household income: $50,064 (2006-2010 5-year est.); Percent of households with income of $100,000 or more: 13.2% (2006-2010 5-year est.); Poverty rate: 22.2% (2006-2010 5-year est.).
**Education:** Percent of population age 25 and over with: High school diploma (including GED) or higher: 94.1% (2006-2010 5-year est.); Bachelor's degree or higher: 18.7% (2006-2010 5-year est.); Master's degree or higher: 2.4% (2006-2010 5-year est.).

**School District(s)**
Campbell-Savona Central School District (PK-12)
   2009-10 Enrollment: 1,007 . . . . . . . . . . . . . . . . . . . . . (607) 527-9800
**Housing:** Homeownership rate: 78.7% (2010); Median home value: $76,600 (2006-2010 5-year est.); Median contract rent: $481 per month (2006-2010 5-year est.); Median year structure built: 1982 (2006-2010 5-year est.).
**Transportation:** Commute to work: 81.5% car, 0.0% public transportation, 4.0% walk, 10.7% work from home (2006-2010 5-year est.); Travel time to work: 8.3% less than 15 minutes, 59.0% 15 to 30 minutes, 12.0% 30 to 45 minutes, 8.6% 45 to 60 minutes, 12.0% 60 minutes or more (2006-2010 5-year est.)

**CANISTEO** (village). Covers a land area of 0.933 square miles and a water area of 0 square miles. Located at 42.27° N. Lat; 77.60° W. Long. Elevation is 1,135 feet.
**Population:** 2,423 (1990); 2,336 (2000); 2,270 (2010); Density: 2,431.3 persons per square mile (2010); Race: 98.5% White, 0.5% Black, 0.4% Asian, 0.1% American Indian/Alaska Native, 0.0% Native Hawaiian/Other Pacific Islander, 0.5% Other, 1.1% Hispanic of any race (2010); Average household size: 2.49 (2010); Median age: 40.5 (2010); Males per 100 females: 90.8 (2010); Marriage status: 24.0% never married, 59.2% now married, 7.2% widowed, 9.6% divorced (2006-2010 5-year est.); Foreign born: 1.6% (2006-2010 5-year est.); Ancestry (includes multiple ancestries): 27.5% English, 22.4% Irish, 20.5% German, 10.0% American, 8.5% Italian (2006-2010 5-year est.).
**Economy:** Single-family building permits issued: 0 (2011); Multi-family building permits issued: 0 (2011); Employment by occupation: 6.8% management, 0.9% professional, 10.5% services, 13.7% sales, 1.9% farming, 15.1% construction, 6.3% production (2006-2010 5-year est.).
**Income:** Per capita income: $22,041 (2006-2010 5-year est.); Median household income: $49,917 (2006-2010 5-year est.); Average household income: $56,052 (2006-2010 5-year est.); Percent of households with income of $100,000 or more: 15.5% (2006-2010 5-year est.); Poverty rate: 9.5% (2006-2010 5-year est.).
**Education:** Percent of population age 25 and over with: High school diploma (including GED) or higher: 94.0% (2006-2010 5-year est.);

Bachelor's degree or higher: 22.0% (2006-2010 5-year est.); Master's degree or higher: 15.1% (2006-2010 5-year est.).

### School District(s)

Canisteo-Greenwood Csd (PK-12)

    2009-10 Enrollment: 968 . . . . . . . . . . . . . . . . . . . . . (607) 698-4225

**Housing:** Homeownership rate: 73.0% (2010); Median home value: $68,200 (2006-2010 5-year est.); Median contract rent: $379 per month (2006-2010 5-year est.); Median year structure built: before 1940 (2006-2010 5-year est.).

**Safety:** Violent crime rate: 13.8 per 10,000 population; Property crime rate: 197.7 per 10,000 population (2010).

**Transportation:** Commute to work: 97.5% car, 0.7% public transportation, 1.5% walk, 0.3% work from home (2006-2010 5-year est.); Travel time to work: 44.9% less than 15 minutes, 26.0% 15 to 30 minutes, 16.2% 30 to 45 minutes, 4.8% 45 to 60 minutes, 8.1% 60 minutes or more (2006-2010 5-year est.)

**CANISTEO** (town). Covers a land area of 54.350 square miles and a water area of 0.009 square miles. Located at 42.23° N. Lat; 77.53° W. Long. Elevation is 1,135 feet.

**History:** Settled before 1790, incorporated 1873.

**Population:** 3,636 (1990); 3,583 (2000); 3,391 (2010); Density: 62.4 persons per square mile (2010); Race: 98.6% White, 0.4% Black, 0.3% Asian, 0.1% American Indian/Alaska Native, 0.0% Native Hawaiian/Other Pacific Islander, 0.6% Other, 0.9% Hispanic of any race (2010); Average household size: 2.48 (2010); Median age: 42.2 (2010); Males per 100 females: 95.8 (2010); Marriage status: 28.0% never married, 55.3% now married, 5.6% widowed, 11.2% divorced (2006-2010 5-year est.); Foreign born: 1.7% (2006-2010 5-year est.); Ancestry (includes multiple ancestries): 22.1% German, 21.1% Irish, 20.8% English, 10.6% American, 8.4% French (2006-2010 5-year est.).

**Economy:** Single-family building permits issued: 2 (2011); Multi-family building permits issued: 0 (2011); Employment by occupation: 7.5% management, 0.6% professional, 9.7% services, 18.8% sales, 1.9% farming, 14.6% construction, 5.8% production (2006-2010 5-year est.).

**Income:** Per capita income: $21,368 (2006-2010 5-year est.); Median household income: $50,191 (2006-2010 5-year est.); Average household income: $55,753 (2006-2010 5-year est.); Percent of households with income of $100,000 or more: 15.0% (2006-2010 5-year est.); Poverty rate: 9.6% (2006-2010 5-year est.).

**Education:** Percent of population age 25 and over with: High school diploma (including GED) or higher: 91.6% (2006-2010 5-year est.); Bachelor's degree or higher: 19.0% (2006-2010 5-year est.); Master's degree or higher: 11.5% (2006-2010 5-year est.).

### School District(s)

Canisteo-Greenwood Csd (PK-12)

    2009-10 Enrollment: 968 . . . . . . . . . . . . . . . . . . . . . (607) 698-4225

**Housing:** Homeownership rate: 76.5% (2010); Median home value: $71,300 (2006-2010 5-year est.); Median contract rent: $394 per month (2006-2010 5-year est.); Median year structure built: before 1940 (2006-2010 5-year est.).

**Transportation:** Commute to work: 95.7% car, 0.5% public transportation, 1.3% walk, 2.5% work from home (2006-2010 5-year est.); Travel time to work: 45.2% less than 15 minutes, 28.7% 15 to 30 minutes, 13.7% 30 to 45 minutes, 4.5% 45 to 60 minutes, 7.9% 60 minutes or more (2006-2010 5-year est.)

**CATON** (town). Covers a land area of 37.565 square miles and a water area of 0.434 square miles. Located at 42.03° N. Lat; 77.02° W. Long. Elevation is 1,424 feet.

**Population:** 1,888 (1990); 2,097 (2000); 2,179 (2010); Density: 58.0 persons per square mile (2010); Race: 97.8% White, 0.4% Black, 0.2% Asian, 0.0% American Indian/Alaska Native, 0.0% Native Hawaiian/Other Pacific Islander, 1.6% Other, 0.6% Hispanic of any race (2010); Average household size: 2.63 (2010); Median age: 42.8 (2010); Males per 100 females: 101.0 (2010); Marriage status: 16.9% never married, 70.0% now married, 6.2% widowed, 6.9% divorced (2006-2010 5-year est.); Foreign born: 2.8% (2006-2010 5-year est.); Ancestry (includes multiple ancestries): 22.5% German, 21.8% English, 17.7% Irish, 8.6% American, 6.3% Italian (2006-2010 5-year est.).

**Economy:** Single-family building permits issued: 3 (2011); Multi-family building permits issued: 0 (2011); Employment by occupation: 13.4% management, 6.9% professional, 7.4% services, 14.3% sales, 1.3% farming, 8.2% construction, 6.8% production (2006-2010 5-year est.).

**Income:** Per capita income: $25,694 (2006-2010 5-year est.); Median household income: $58,214 (2006-2010 5-year est.); Average household income: $67,074 (2006-2010 5-year est.); Percent of households with income of $100,000 or more: 19.6% (2006-2010 5-year est.); Poverty rate: 4.5% (2006-2010 5-year est.).

**Education:** Percent of population age 25 and over with: High school diploma (including GED) or higher: 92.5% (2006-2010 5-year est.); Bachelor's degree or higher: 27.0% (2006-2010 5-year est.); Master's degree or higher: 11.0% (2006-2010 5-year est.).

**Housing:** Homeownership rate: 91.4% (2010); Median home value: $98,200 (2006-2010 5-year est.); Median contract rent: $543 per month (2006-2010 5-year est.); Median year structure built: 1969 (2006-2010 5-year est.).

**Transportation:** Commute to work: 93.2% car, 0.3% public transportation, 4.4% walk, 1.4% work from home (2006-2010 5-year est.); Travel time to work: 14.4% less than 15 minutes, 58.0% 15 to 30 minutes, 18.9% 30 to 45 minutes, 5.2% 45 to 60 minutes, 3.6% 60 minutes or more (2006-2010 5-year est.)

**COHOCTON** (village). Covers a land area of 1.501 square miles and a water area of 0 square miles. Located at 42.49° N. Lat; 77.50° W. Long. Elevation is 1,319 feet.

**Population:** 859 (1990); 854 (2000); 838 (2010); Density: 558.1 persons per square mile (2010); Race: 96.8% White, 0.4% Black, 0.1% Asian, 0.1% American Indian/Alaska Native, 0.0% Native Hawaiian/Other Pacific Islander, 2.6% Other, 1.3% Hispanic of any race (2010); Average household size: 2.67 (2010); Median age: 38.8 (2010); Males per 100 females: 93.5 (2010); Marriage status: 23.1% never married, 67.4% now married, 5.0% widowed, 4.5% divorced (2006-2010 5-year est.); Foreign born: 0.3% (2006-2010 5-year est.); Ancestry (includes multiple ancestries): 34.0% German, 25.1% Irish, 11.0% English, 9.8% American, 9.6% Dutch (2006-2010 5-year est.).

**Economy:** Single-family building permits issued: 0 (2011); Multi-family building permits issued: 0 (2011); Employment by occupation: 5.2% management, 0.9% professional, 15.6% services, 10.8% sales, 0.7% farming, 22.1% construction, 6.5% production (2006-2010 5-year est.).

**Income:** Per capita income: $19,205 (2006-2010 5-year est.); Median household income: $48,750 (2006-2010 5-year est.); Average household income: $56,822 (2006-2010 5-year est.); Percent of households with income of $100,000 or more: 18.3% (2006-2010 5-year est.); Poverty rate: 6.2% (2006-2010 5-year est.).

**Education:** Percent of population age 25 and over with: High school diploma (including GED) or higher: 83.3% (2006-2010 5-year est.); Bachelor's degree or higher: 14.0% (2006-2010 5-year est.); Master's degree or higher: 7.8% (2006-2010 5-year est.).

### School District(s)

Wayland-Cohocton Central School District (PK-12)

    2009-10 Enrollment: 1,581 . . . . . . . . . . . . . . . . . . . . (585) 728-2211

**Housing:** Homeownership rate: 78.4% (2010); Median home value: $68,200 (2006-2010 5-year est.); Median contract rent: $483 per month (2006-2010 5-year est.); Median year structure built: before 1940 (2006-2010 5-year est.).

**Transportation:** Commute to work: 89.8% car, 1.0% public transportation, 4.8% walk, 3.6% work from home (2006-2010 5-year est.); Travel time to work: 27.8% less than 15 minutes, 40.4% 15 to 30 minutes, 10.3% 30 to 45 minutes, 5.2% 45 to 60 minutes, 16.3% 60 minutes or more (2006-2010 5-year est.)

**COHOCTON** (town). Covers a land area of 56.082 square miles and a water area of 0.007 square miles. Located at 42.51° N. Lat; 77.48° W. Long. Elevation is 1,319 feet.

**History:** The glass industry, for which the city . . .

**Population:** 2,520 (1990); 2,626 (2000); 2,561 (2010); Density: 45.7 persons per square mile (2010); Race: 97.5% White, 0.2% Black, 0.3% Asian, 0.2% American Indian/Alaska Native, 0.0% Native Hawaiian/Other Pacific Islander, 1.8% Other, 1.2% Hispanic of any race (2010); Average household size: 2.61 (2010); Median age: 41.4 (2010); Males per 100 females: 105.0 (2010); Marriage status: 21.2% never married, 66.6% now married, 6.3% widowed, 5.9% divorced (2006-2010 5-year est.); Foreign born: 1.1% (2006-2010 5-year est.); Ancestry (includes multiple ancestries): 38.4% German, 22.6% Irish, 15.6% English, 9.7% Italian, 6.8% American (2006-2010 5-year est.).

**Economy:** Single-family building permits issued: 3 (2011); Multi-family building permits issued: 0 (2011); Employment by occupation: 6.9% management, 0.3% professional, 13.1% services, 13.5% sales, 1.3% farming, 18.5% construction, 15.6% production (2006-2010 5-year est.).

**Income:** Per capita income: $22,041 (2006-2010 5-year est.); Median household income: $49,028 (2006-2010 5-year est.); Average household income: $57,449 (2006-2010 5-year est.); Percent of households with income of $100,000 or more: 15.0% (2006-2010 5-year est.); Poverty rate: 6.6% (2006-2010 5-year est.).

**Education:** Percent of population age 25 and over with: High school diploma (including GED) or higher: 87.4% (2006-2010 5-year est.); Bachelor's degree or higher: 13.8% (2006-2010 5-year est.); Master's degree or higher: 6.0% (2006-2010 5-year est.).

**School District(s)**

Wayland-Cohocton Central School District (PK-12)

    2009-10 Enrollment: 1,581 . . . . . . . . . . . . . . . . . . . . . . (585) 728-2211

**Housing:** Homeownership rate: 82.4% (2010); Median home value: $74,300 (2006-2010 5-year est.); Median contract rent: $391 per month (2006-2010 5-year est.); Median year structure built: before 1940 (2006-2010 5-year est.).

**Transportation:** Commute to work: 91.2% car, 0.3% public transportation, 4.9% walk, 3.3% work from home (2006-2010 5-year est.); Travel time to work: 34.5% less than 15 minutes, 35.1% 15 to 30 minutes, 11.1% 30 to 45 minutes, 6.7% 45 to 60 minutes, 12.5% 60 minutes or more (2006-2010 5-year est.)

**COOPERS PLAINS** (CDP). Covers a land area of 0.824 square miles and a water area of 0 square miles. Located at 42.17° N. Lat; 77.13° W. Long. Elevation is 981 feet.

**Population:** n/a (1990); n/a (2000); 598 (2010); Density: 725.3 persons per square mile (2010); Race: 97.0% White, 1.2% Black, 0.0% Asian, 0.2% American Indian/Alaska Native, 0.0% Native Hawaiian/Other Pacific Islander, 1.6% Other, 1.2% Hispanic of any race (2010); Average household size: 2.21 (2010); Median age: 48.6 (2010); Males per 100 females: 101.3 (2010); Marriage status: 5.0% never married, 40.1% now married, 40.1% widowed, 14.9% divorced (2006-2010 5-year est.); Foreign born: 0.0% (2006-2010 5-year est.); Ancestry (includes multiple ancestries): 19.8% English, 16.8% Dutch, 16.8% Irish, 14.1% French, 10.7% Italian (2006-2010 5-year est.).

**Economy:** Employment by occupation: 6.6% management, 13.2% professional, 27.4% services, 9.4% sales, 13.2% farming, 0.0% construction, 0.0% production (2006-2010 5-year est.).

**Income:** Per capita income: $30,389 (2006-2010 5-year est.); Median household income: $24,774 (2006-2010 5-year est.); Average household income: $37,774 (2006-2010 5-year est.); Percent of households with income of $100,000 or more: 6.7% (2006-2010 5-year est.); Poverty rate: 0.0% (2006-2010 5-year est.).

**Education:** Percent of population age 25 and over with: High school diploma (including GED) or higher: 90.8% (2006-2010 5-year est.); Bachelor's degree or higher: 40.5% (2006-2010 5-year est.); Master's degree or higher: 36.6% (2006-2010 5-year est.).

**Housing:** Homeownership rate: 77.5% (2010); Median home value: $62,500 (2006-2010 5-year est.); Median contract rent: n/a per month (2006-2010 5-year est.); Median year structure built: 1943 (2006-2010 5-year est.).

**Transportation:** Commute to work: 100.0% car, 0.0% public transportation, 0.0% walk, 0.0% work from home (2006-2010 5-year est.); Travel time to work: 58.5% less than 15 minutes, 22.6% 15 to 30 minutes, 0.0% 30 to 45 minutes, 0.0% 45 to 60 minutes, 18.9% 60 minutes or more (2006-2010 5-year est.)

**CORNING** (city). Covers a land area of 3.083 square miles and a water area of 0.177 square miles. Located at 42.14° N. Lat; 77.05° W. Long. Elevation is 932 feet.

**History:** The glass industry, for which the city is famous, began in 1868. Corning glass Museum and the Rockwell Museum, with the largest collection of Western art in the Eastern U.S. and the world's largest collection of Steuben glass, are located in the city. In 1972 the city was heavily damaged by flooding in the wake of Hurricane Agnes. Settled 1788; Incorporated as a city 1890.

**Population:** 11,938 (1990); 10,842 (2000); 11,183 (2010); Density: 3,626.4 persons per square mile (2010); Race: 91.8% White, 3.2% Black, 1.8% Asian, 0.3% American Indian/Alaska Native, 0.0% Native Hawaiian/Other Pacific Islander, 2.9% Other, 2.4% Hispanic of any race (2010); Average household size: 2.17 (2010); Median age: 36.5 (2010); Males per 100 females: 93.1 (2010); Marriage status: 31.5% never married, 49.3% now married, 6.7% widowed, 12.5% divorced (2006-2010 5-year est.); Foreign born: 3.8% (2006-2010 5-year est.); Ancestry (includes multiple

ancestries): 22.7% Irish, 22.4% German, 16.6% English, 14.5% Italian, 5.9% American (2006-2010 5-year est.).

**Economy:** Single-family building permits issued: 6 (2011); Multi-family building permits issued: 0 (2011); Employment by occupation: 9.0% management, 5.3% professional, 13.0% services, 15.8% sales, 2.8% farming, 6.8% construction, 4.3% production (2006-2010 5-year est.).

**Income:** Per capita income: $23,180 (2006-2010 5-year est.); Median household income: $37,224 (2006-2010 5-year est.); Average household income: $50,130 (2006-2010 5-year est.); Percent of households with income of $100,000 or more: 12.1% (2006-2010 5-year est.); Poverty rate: 20.4% (2006-2010 5-year est.).

**Taxes:** Total city taxes per capita: $852 (2009); City property taxes per capita: $500 (2009).

**Education:** Percent of population age 25 and over with: High school diploma (including GED) or higher: 92.7% (2006-2010 5-year est.); Bachelor's degree or higher: 26.8% (2006-2010 5-year est.); Master's degree or higher: 12.3% (2006-2010 5-year est.).

**School District(s)**

Corning City School District (PK-12)

    2009-10 Enrollment: 5,418 . . . . . . . . . . . . . . . . . . . . . . (607) 936-3704

**Two-year College(s)**

Corning Community College (Public)

    Fall 2010 Enrollment: 3,451 . . . . . . . . . . . . . . . . . . . . (607) 962-9011

    2011-12 Tuition: In-state $4,360; Out-of-state $8,230

**Housing:** Homeownership rate: 51.3% (2010); Median home value: $83,700 (2006-2010 5-year est.); Median contract rent: $505 per month (2006-2010 5-year est.); Median year structure built: before 1940 (2006-2010 5-year est.).

**Hospitals:** Corning Hospital (99 beds)

**Safety:** Violent crime rate: 50.8 per 10,000 population; Property crime rate: 396.2 per 10,000 population (2010).

**Newspapers:** The Corning Leader (Local news; Circulation 15,500)

**Transportation:** Commute to work: 87.6% car, 0.4% public transportation, 4.5% walk, 4.6% work from home (2006-2010 5-year est.); Travel time to work: 59.1% less than 15 minutes, 26.3% 15 to 30 minutes, 10.4% 30 to 45 minutes, 1.5% 45 to 60 minutes, 2.7% 60 minutes or more (2006-2010 5-year est.)

**Airports:** Elmira/Corning Regional (primary service)

**Additional Information Contacts**

Corning Area Chamber of Commerce . . . . . . . . . . . . . . . . (607) 936-4686

    http://www.corningny.com

**CORNING** (town). Covers a land area of 36.849 square miles and a water area of 0.502 square miles. Located at 42.14° N. Lat; 77.01° W. Long. Elevation is 932 feet.

**Population:** 6,367 (1990); 6,426 (2000); 6,270 (2010); Density: 170.1 persons per square mile (2010); Race: 94.1% White, 2.8% Black, 1.5% Asian, 0.3% American Indian/Alaska Native, 0.0% Native Hawaiian/Other Pacific Islander, 1.3% Other, 1.1% Hispanic of any race (2010); Average household size: 2.45 (2010); Median age: 42.7 (2010); Males per 100 females: 99.4 (2010); Marriage status: 23.4% never married, 59.0% now married, 5.6% widowed, 12.0% divorced (2006-2010 5-year est.); Foreign born: 1.5% (2006-2010 5-year est.); Ancestry (includes multiple ancestries): 21.3% German, 20.7% Irish, 15.9% English, 10.7% Italian, 10.2% American (2006-2010 5-year est.).

**Economy:** Single-family building permits issued: 7 (2011); Multi-family building permits issued: 0 (2011); Employment by occupation: 12.5% management, 5.8% professional, 10.6% services, 12.4% sales, 4.0% farming, 8.0% construction, 8.9% production (2006-2010 5-year est.).

**Income:** Per capita income: $30,024 (2006-2010 5-year est.); Median household income: $52,750 (2006-2010 5-year est.); Average household income: $74,485 (2006-2010 5-year est.); Percent of households with income of $100,000 or more: 22.8% (2006-2010 5-year est.); Poverty rate: 12.2% (2006-2010 5-year est.).

**Education:** Percent of population age 25 and over with: High school diploma (including GED) or higher: 86.1% (2006-2010 5-year est.); Bachelor's degree or higher: 27.5% (2006-2010 5-year est.); Master's degree or higher: 11.5% (2006-2010 5-year est.).

**School District(s)**

Corning City School District (PK-12)

    2009-10 Enrollment: 5,418 . . . . . . . . . . . . . . . . . . . . . . (607) 936-3704

**Two-year College(s)**

Corning Community College (Public)

    Fall 2010 Enrollment: 3,451 . . . . . . . . . . . . . . . . . . . . (607) 962-9011

    2011-12 Tuition: In-state $4,360; Out-of-state $8,230

**Housing:** Homeownership rate: 82.6% (2010); Median home value: $95,200 (2006-2010 5-year est.); Median contract rent: $492 per month (2006-2010 5-year est.); Median year structure built: 1956 (2006-2010 5-year est.).

**Hospitals:** Corning Hospital (99 beds)

**Newspapers:** The Corning Leader (Local news; Circulation 15,500)

**Transportation:** Commute to work: 93.8% car, 0.6% public transportation, 1.6% walk, 3.5% work from home (2006-2010 5-year est.); Travel time to work: 37.6% less than 15 minutes, 38.7% 15 to 30 minutes, 13.9% 30 to 45 minutes, 2.4% 45 to 60 minutes, 7.4% 60 minutes or more (2006-2010 5-year est.)

**Airports:** Elmira/Corning Regional (primary service)

**DANSVILLE** (town). Covers a land area of 48.367 square miles and a water area of 0.067 square miles. Located at 42.46° N. Lat; 77.66° W. Long.

**Population:** 1,811 (1990); 1,977 (2000); 1,842 (2010); Density: 38.1 persons per square mile (2010); Race: 96.6% White, 0.8% Black, 0.1% Asian, 0.2% American Indian/Alaska Native, 0.0% Native Hawaiian/Other Pacific Islander, 2.3% Other, 2.0% Hispanic of any race (2010); Average household size: 2.53 (2010); Median age: 44.2 (2010); Males per 100 females: 104.0 (2010); Marriage status: 23.2% never married, 61.6% now married, 4.0% widowed, 11.2% divorced (2006-2010 5-year est.); Foreign born: 0.6% (2006-2010 5-year est.); Ancestry (includes multiple ancestries): 29.4% German, 22.9% English, 17.6% Irish, 9.2% American, 8.9% Italian (2006-2010 5-year est.).

**Economy:** Single-family building permits issued: 2 (2011); Multi-family building permits issued: 0 (2011); Employment by occupation: 8.0% management, 0.4% professional, 8.4% services, 16.1% sales, 3.9% farming, 15.9% construction, 9.7% production (2006-2010 5-year est.).

**Income:** Per capita income: $21,332 (2006-2010 5-year est.); Median household income: $48,281 (2006-2010 5-year est.); Average household income: $54,663 (2006-2010 5-year est.); Percent of households with income of $100,000 or more: 9.5% (2006-2010 5-year est.); Poverty rate: 11.7% (2006-2010 5-year est.).

**Education:** Percent of population age 25 and over with: High school diploma (including GED) or higher: 86.5% (2006-2010 5-year est.); Bachelor's degree or higher: 10.6% (2006-2010 5-year est.); Master's degree or higher: 4.1% (2006-2010 5-year est.).

**Housing:** Homeownership rate: 82.8% (2010); Median home value: $86,200 (2006-2010 5-year est.); Median contract rent: $380 per month (2006-2010 5-year est.); Median year structure built: 1979 (2006-2010 5-year est.).

**Newspapers:** Genesee Country Express (Local news; Circulation 3,000); Genesee Way Shopper (Community news; Circulation 3,000)

**Transportation:** Commute to work: 90.8% car, 0.0% public transportation, 2.4% walk, 4.9% work from home (2006-2010 5-year est.); Travel time to work: 27.0% less than 15 minutes, 35.0% 15 to 30 minutes, 16.8% 30 to 45 minutes, 11.4% 45 to 60 minutes, 9.8% 60 minutes or more (2006-2010 5-year est.)

**Additional Information Contacts**

Dansville Area Chamber of Commerce . . . . . . . . . . . . . . . (585) 335-6920
http://www.dansvilleny.net

**ERWIN** (town). Covers a land area of 38.656 square miles and a water area of 0.500 square miles. Located at 42.13° N. Lat; 77.15° W. Long.

**Population:** 6,763 (1990); 7,227 (2000); 8,037 (2010); Density: 207.9 persons per square mile (2010); Race: 87.7% White, 2.6% Black, 7.3% Asian, 0.2% American Indian/Alaska Native, 0.0% Native Hawaiian/Other Pacific Islander, 2.2% Other, 1.4% Hispanic of any race (2010); Average household size: 2.36 (2010); Median age: 42.5 (2010); Males per 100 females: 95.0 (2010); Marriage status: 18.9% never married, 60.4% now married, 8.6% widowed, 12.0% divorced (2006-2010 5-year est.); Foreign born: 9.7% (2006-2010 5-year est.); Ancestry (includes multiple ancestries): 18.4% German, 16.1% English, 14.5% Irish, 9.1% Italian, 8.8% American (2006-2010 5-year est.).

**Economy:** Single-family building permits issued: 7 (2011); Multi-family building permits issued: 107 (2011); Employment by occupation: 19.5% management, 12.7% professional, 7.8% services, 11.6% sales, 2.4% farming, 5.3% construction, 3.7% production (2006-2010 5-year est.).

**Income:** Per capita income: $34,848 (2006-2010 5-year est.); Median household income: $52,176 (2006-2010 5-year est.); Average household income: $81,437 (2006-2010 5-year est.); Percent of households with income of $100,000 or more: 26.8% (2006-2010 5-year est.); Poverty rate: 11.9% (2006-2010 5-year est.).

**Taxes:** Total city taxes per capita: $343 (2009); City property taxes per capita: $315 (2009).

**Education:** Percent of population age 25 and over with: High school diploma (including GED) or higher: 90.1% (2006-2010 5-year est.); Bachelor's degree or higher: 41.6% (2006-2010 5-year est.); Master's degree or higher: 25.2% (2006-2010 5-year est.).

**Housing:** Homeownership rate: 67.5% (2010); Median home value: $119,100 (2006-2010 5-year est.); Median contract rent: $615 per month (2006-2010 5-year est.); Median year structure built: 1972 (2006-2010 5-year est.).

**Transportation:** Commute to work: 90.7% car, 0.3% public transportation, 2.5% walk, 5.1% work from home (2006-2010 5-year est.); Travel time to work: 58.8% less than 15 minutes, 26.9% 15 to 30 minutes, 6.8% 30 to 45 minutes, 1.9% 45 to 60 minutes, 5.7% 60 minutes or more (2006-2010 5-year est.).

**Additional Information Contacts**

Town of Erwin . . . . . . . . . . . . . . . . . . . . . . . . . . . . . . (607) 936-3652
http://www.erwinny.org

**FREMONT** (town). Covers a land area of 32.036 square miles and a water area of 0.153 square miles. Located at 42.39° N. Lat; 77.61° W. Long. Elevation is 1,529 feet.

**Population:** 912 (1990); 964 (2000); 1,008 (2010); Density: 31.5 persons per square mile (2010); Race: 97.3% White, 0.3% Black, 0.1% Asian, 0.0% American Indian/Alaska Native, 0.0% Native Hawaiian/Other Pacific Islander, 2.3% Other, 2.5% Hispanic of any race (2010); Average household size: 2.45 (2010); Median age: 44.2 (2010); Males per 100 females: 104.0 (2010); Marriage status: 26.9% never married, 57.0% now married, 6.0% widowed, 10.1% divorced (2006-2010 5-year est.); Foreign born: 1.8% (2006-2010 5-year est.); Ancestry (includes multiple ancestries): 34.4% German, 19.9% Irish, 18.2% English, 13.3% American, 8.6% Italian (2006-2010 5-year est.).

**Economy:** Single-family building permits issued: 0 (2011); Multi-family building permits issued: 0 (2011); Employment by occupation: 11.0% management, 5.8% professional, 7.1% services, 11.6% sales, 2.3% farming, 15.8% construction, 9.1% production (2006-2010 5-year est.).

**Income:** Per capita income: $24,685 (2006-2010 5-year est.); Median household income: $47,212 (2006-2010 5-year est.); Average household income: $58,060 (2006-2010 5-year est.); Percent of households with income of $100,000 or more: 17.0% (2006-2010 5-year est.); Poverty rate: 7.5% (2006-2010 5-year est.).

**Education:** Percent of population age 25 and over with: High school diploma (including GED) or higher: 90.9% (2006-2010 5-year est.); Bachelor's degree or higher: 11.8% (2006-2010 5-year est.); Master's degree or higher: 4.4% (2006-2010 5-year est.).

**Housing:** Homeownership rate: 86.1% (2010); Median home value: $93,100 (2006-2010 5-year est.); Median contract rent: $529 per month (2006-2010 5-year est.); Median year structure built: 1970 (2006-2010 5-year est.).

**Transportation:** Commute to work: 87.8% car, 0.6% public transportation, 7.8% walk, 3.1% work from home (2006-2010 5-year est.); Travel time to work: 42.5% less than 15 minutes, 29.1% 15 to 30 minutes, 15.0% 30 to 45 minutes, 4.3% 45 to 60 minutes, 9.1% 60 minutes or more (2006-2010 5-year est.).

**GANG MILLS** (CDP). Covers a land area of 4.377 square miles and a water area of 0.023 square miles. Located at 42.16° N. Lat; 77.12° W. Long. Elevation is 935 feet.

**Population:** 2,699 (1990); 3,304 (2000); 4,185 (2010); Density: 955.9 persons per square mile (2010); Race: 80.5% White, 3.7% Black, 13.3% Asian, 0.3% American Indian/Alaska Native, 0.0% Native Hawaiian/Other Pacific Islander, 2.2% Other, 1.8% Hispanic of any race (2010); Average household size: 2.50 (2010); Median age: 39.8 (2010); Males per 100 females: 95.1 (2010); Marriage status: 14.3% never married, 66.8% now married, 8.5% widowed, 10.4% divorced (2006-2010 5-year est.); Foreign born: 16.6% (2006-2010 5-year est.); Ancestry (includes multiple ancestries): 18.7% German, 14.2% English, 12.1% Irish, 10.3% Italian, 5.5% American (2006-2010 5-year est.).

**Economy:** Employment by occupation: 23.1% management, 13.6% professional, 6.1% services, 10.2% sales, 1.9% farming, 4.5% construction, 3.2% production (2006-2010 5-year est.).

**Income:** Per capita income: $38,131 (2006-2010 5-year est.); Median household income: $61,821 (2006-2010 5-year est.); Average household income: $93,514 (2006-2010 5-year est.); Percent of households with

income of $100,000 or more: 35.3% (2006-2010 5-year est.); Poverty rate: 11.8% (2006-2010 5-year est.).

**Education:** Percent of population age 25 and over with: High school diploma (including GED) or higher: 93.9% (2006-2010 5-year est.); Bachelor's degree or higher: 53.7% (2006-2010 5-year est.); Master's degree or higher: 32.9% (2006-2010 5-year est.).

**Housing:** Homeownership rate: 61.0% (2010); Median home value: $185,100 (2006-2010 5-year est.); Median contract rent: $790 per month (2006-2010 5-year est.); Median year structure built: 1979 (2006-2010 5-year est.).

**Transportation:** Commute to work: 92.3% car, 0.6% public transportation, 0.8% walk, 5.1% work from home (2006-2010 5-year est.); Travel time to work: 58.4% less than 15 minutes, 30.5% 15 to 30 minutes, 3.4% 30 to 45 minutes, 1.3% 45 to 60 minutes, 6.4% 60 minutes or more (2006-2010 5-year est.)

## GREENWOOD (town). Covers a land area of 41.338 square miles and a water area of 0.007 square miles. Located at 42.14° N. Lat; 77.66° W. Long. Elevation is 1,562 feet.

**Population:** 898 (1990); 849 (2000); 801 (2010); Density: 19.4 persons per square mile (2010); Race: 98.5% White, 0.0% Black, 0.9% Asian, 0.2% American Indian/Alaska Native, 0.0% Native Hawaiian/Other Pacific Islander, 0.4% Other, 0.4% Hispanic of any race (2010); Average household size: 2.45 (2010); Median age: 41.8 (2010); Males per 100 females: 103.8 (2010); Marriage status: 27.1% never married, 55.9% now married, 7.5% widowed, 9.4% divorced (2006-2010 5-year est.); Foreign born: 3.9% (2006-2010 5-year est.); Ancestry (includes multiple ancestries): 28.4% Irish, 23.9% German, 15.0% English, 9.0% American, 5.6% French (2006-2010 5-year est.).

**Economy:** Single-family building permits issued: 2 (2011); Multi-family building permits issued: 0 (2011); Employment by occupation: 9.8% management, 0.0% professional, 21.5% services, 7.0% sales, 6.0% farming, 27.2% construction, 8.9% production (2006-2010 5-year est.).

**Income:** Per capita income: $18,005 (2006-2010 5-year est.); Median household income: $36,250 (2006-2010 5-year est.); Average household income: $42,065 (2006-2010 5-year est.); Percent of households with income of $100,000 or more: 6.2% (2006-2010 5-year est.); Poverty rate: 8.0% (2006-2010 5-year est.).

**Education:** Percent of population age 25 and over with: High school diploma (including GED) or higher: 88.3% (2006-2010 5-year est.); Bachelor's degree or higher: 11.7% (2006-2010 5-year est.); Master's degree or higher: 5.0% (2006-2010 5-year est.).

**School District(s)**

Canisteo-Greenwood Csd (PK-12)

    2009-10 Enrollment: 968 . . . . . . . . . . . . . . . . . . . . . . . . . (607) 698-4225

**Housing:** Homeownership rate: 80.2% (2010); Median home value: $63,800 (2006-2010 5-year est.); Median contract rent: $470 per month (2006-2010 5-year est.); Median year structure built: before 1940 (2006-2010 5-year est.).

**Transportation:** Commute to work: 94.2% car, 0.0% public transportation, 3.2% walk, 2.6% work from home (2006-2010 5-year est.); Travel time to work: 20.5% less than 15 minutes, 32.8% 15 to 30 minutes, 31.5% 30 to 45 minutes, 5.3% 45 to 60 minutes, 9.9% 60 minutes or more (2006-2010 5-year est.)

## HAMMONDSPORT (village). Covers a land area of 0.345 square miles and a water area of 0.020 square miles. Located at 42.40° N. Lat; 77.22° W. Long. Elevation is 755 feet.

**History:** Birthplace of Glenn Curtiss, who made aviation experiments in the village. Museum. Incorporated 1871.

**Population:** 929 (1990); 731 (2000); 661 (2010); Density: 1,915.3 persons per square mile (2010); Race: 97.3% White, 0.9% Black, 0.6% Asian, 0.2% American Indian/Alaska Native, 0.0% Native Hawaiian/Other Pacific Islander, 1.0% Other, 0.3% Hispanic of any race (2010); Average household size: 2.05 (2010); Median age: 49.6 (2010); Males per 100 females: 95.0 (2010); Marriage status: 22.7% never married, 60.3% now married, 10.0% widowed, 7.0% divorced (2006-2010 5-year est.); Foreign born: 1.8% (2006-2010 5-year est.); Ancestry (includes multiple ancestries): 25.9% German, 20.1% Irish, 20.0% English, 7.0% Italian, 6.6% Dutch (2006-2010 5-year est.).

**Economy:** Single-family building permits issued: 0 (2011); Multi-family building permits issued: 0 (2011); Employment by occupation: 13.0% management, 2.5% professional, 0.7% services, 18.6% sales, 1.8% farming, 3.9% construction, 4.2% production (2006-2010 5-year est.).

**Income:** Per capita income: $23,205 (2006-2010 5-year est.); Median household income: $49,821 (2006-2010 5-year est.); Average household income: $52,110 (2006-2010 5-year est.); Percent of households with income of $100,000 or more: 10.3% (2006-2010 5-year est.); Poverty rate: 6.5% (2006-2010 5-year est.).

**Education:** Percent of population age 25 and over with: High school diploma (including GED) or higher: 92.5% (2006-2010 5-year est.); Bachelor's degree or higher: 27.6% (2006-2010 5-year est.); Master's degree or higher: 11.2% (2006-2010 5-year est.).

**School District(s)**

Hammondsport Central School District (PK-12)

    2009-10 Enrollment: 525 . . . . . . . . . . . . . . . . . . . . . . . . . (607) 569-5200

**Housing:** Homeownership rate: 63.0% (2010); Median home value: $122,600 (2006-2010 5-year est.); Median contract rent: $478 per month (2006-2010 5-year est.); Median year structure built: before 1940 (2006-2010 5-year est.).

**Safety:** Violent crime rate: 0.0 per 10,000 population; Property crime rate: 237.1 per 10,000 population (2010).

**Transportation:** Commute to work: 78.4% car, 0.0% public transportation, 14.5% walk, 5.9% work from home (2006-2010 5-year est.); Travel time to work: 67.2% less than 15 minutes, 14.6% 15 to 30 minutes, 11.1% 30 to 45 minutes, 1.6% 45 to 60 minutes, 5.5% 60 minutes or more (2006-2010 5-year est.)

**Additional Information Contacts**

Hammondsport Chamber of Commerce . . . . . . . . . . . . . . . (607) 569-2989

    http://www.hammondsport.org

## HARTSVILLE (town). Covers a land area of 36.142 square miles and a water area of 0.056 square miles. Located at 42.22° N. Lat; 77.66° W. Long. Elevation is 1,480 feet.

**Population:** 546 (1990); 585 (2000); 609 (2010); Density: 16.8 persons per square mile (2010); Race: 99.2% White, 0.2% Black, 0.0% Asian, 0.2% American Indian/Alaska Native, 0.0% Native Hawaiian/Other Pacific Islander, 0.4% Other, 0.5% Hispanic of any race (2010); Average household size: 2.49 (2010); Median age: 45.5 (2010); Males per 100 females: 116.7 (2010); Marriage status: 20.2% never married, 67.0% now married, 4.0% widowed, 8.8% divorced (2006-2010 5-year est.); Foreign born: 2.0% (2006-2010 5-year est.); Ancestry (includes multiple ancestries): 26.3% Irish, 22.6% English, 18.6% German, 12.9% American, 7.1% Italian (2006-2010 5-year est.).

**Economy:** Single-family building permits issued: 0 (2011); Multi-family building permits issued: 0 (2011); Employment by occupation: 5.4% management, 14.0% professional, 8.9% services, 15.5% sales, 3.3% farming, 16.7% construction, 9.8% production (2006-2010 5-year est.).

**Income:** Per capita income: $23,348 (2006-2010 5-year est.); Median household income: $47,000 (2006-2010 5-year est.); Average household income: $55,144 (2006-2010 5-year est.); Percent of households with income of $100,000 or more: 9.0% (2006-2010 5-year est.); Poverty rate: 11.0% (2006-2010 5-year est.).

**Education:** Percent of population age 25 and over with: High school diploma (including GED) or higher: 91.6% (2006-2010 5-year est.); Bachelor's degree or higher: 17.4% (2006-2010 5-year est.); Master's degree or higher: 3.2% (2006-2010 5-year est.).

**Housing:** Homeownership rate: 90.2% (2010); Median home value: $72,100 (2006-2010 5-year est.); Median contract rent: $500 per month (2006-2010 5-year est.); Median year structure built: 1965 (2006-2010 5-year est.).

**Transportation:** Commute to work: 98.2% car, 0.0% public transportation, 0.9% walk, 0.9% work from home (2006-2010 5-year est.); Travel time to work: 24.1% less than 15 minutes, 47.0% 15 to 30 minutes, 22.6% 30 to 45 minutes, 2.1% 45 to 60 minutes, 4.3% 60 minutes or more (2006-2010 5-year est.)

## HORNBY (town). Covers a land area of 40.849 square miles and a water area of 0.038 square miles. Located at 42.23° N. Lat; 77.02° W. Long. Elevation is 1,522 feet.

**Population:** 1,655 (1990); 1,742 (2000); 1,706 (2010); Density: 41.8 persons per square mile (2010); Race: 96.5% White, 0.4% Black, 0.4% Asian, 0.9% American Indian/Alaska Native, 0.0% Native Hawaiian/Other Pacific Islander, 1.8% Other, 1.6% Hispanic of any race (2010); Average household size: 2.62 (2010); Median age: 42.8 (2010); Males per 100 females: 99.5 (2010); Marriage status: 19.4% never married, 67.5% now married, 4.3% widowed, 8.9% divorced (2006-2010 5-year est.); Foreign born: 1.5% (2006-2010 5-year est.); Ancestry (includes multiple

ancestries): 21.0% German, 18.8% Irish, 14.6% English, 12.8% American, 6.5% Polish (2006-2010 5-year est.).
**Economy:** Single-family building permits issued: 4 (2011); Multi-family building permits issued: 0 (2011); Employment by occupation: 10.6% management, 4.7% professional, 14.5% services, 17.0% sales, 2.3% farming, 13.4% construction, 6.8% production (2006-2010 5-year est.).
**Income:** Per capita income: $23,357 (2006-2010 5-year est.); Median household income: $47,656 (2006-2010 5-year est.); Average household income: $59,432 (2006-2010 5-year est.); Percent of households with income of $100,000 or more: 14.6% (2006-2010 5-year est.); Poverty rate: 10.9% (2006-2010 5-year est.).
**Taxes:** Total city taxes per capita: $379 (2009); City property taxes per capita: $373 (2009).
**Education:** Percent of population age 25 and over with: High school diploma (including GED) or higher: 85.0% (2006-2010 5-year est.); Bachelor's degree or higher: 16.6% (2006-2010 5-year est.); Master's degree or higher: 8.1% (2006-2010 5-year est.).
**Housing:** Homeownership rate: 86.7% (2010); Median home value: $87,700 (2006-2010 5-year est.); Median contract rent: $417 per month (2006-2010 5-year est.); Median year structure built: 1972 (2006-2010 5-year est.).
**Transportation:** Commute to work: 90.4% car, 0.5% public transportation, 1.3% walk, 5.7% work from home (2006-2010 5-year est.); Travel time to work: 19.4% less than 15 minutes, 55.8% 15 to 30 minutes, 19.4% 30 to 45 minutes, 4.9% 45 to 60 minutes, 0.5% 60 minutes or more (2006-2010 5-year est.)

## HORNELL (city). Covers a land area of 2.837 square miles and a water area of 0 square miles. Located at 42.32° N. Lat; 77.66° W. Long. Elevation is 1,161 feet.
**History:** Settled 1790, incorporated 1906.
**Population:** 9,877 (1990); 9,019 (2000); 8,563 (2010); Density: 3,018.1 persons per square mile (2010); Race: 93.8% White, 2.3% Black, 0.7% Asian, 0.2% American Indian/Alaska Native, 0.1% Native Hawaiian/Other Pacific Islander, 2.9% Other, 2.0% Hispanic of any race (2010); Average household size: 2.36 (2010); Median age: 36.6 (2010); Males per 100 females: 93.6 (2010); Marriage status: 27.1% never married, 53.0% now married, 7.0% widowed, 12.8% divorced (2006-2010 5-year est.); Foreign born: 1.6% (2006-2010 5-year est.); Ancestry (includes multiple ancestries): 32.8% Irish, 24.1% German, 14.8% English, 13.9% Italian, 8.6% American (2006-2010 5-year est.).
**Economy:** Single-family building permits issued: 2 (2011); Multi-family building permits issued: 0 (2011); Employment by occupation: 8.9% management, 1.9% professional, 14.4% services, 19.2% sales, 5.5% farming, 6.6% construction, 5.4% production (2006-2010 5-year est.).
**Income:** Per capita income: $19,938 (2006-2010 5-year est.); Median household income: $34,713 (2006-2010 5-year est.); Average household income: $45,918 (2006-2010 5-year est.); Percent of households with income of $100,000 or more: 7.6% (2006-2010 5-year est.); Poverty rate: 17.9% (2006-2010 5-year est.).
**Education:** Percent of population age 25 and over with: High school diploma (including GED) or higher: 90.6% (2006-2010 5-year est.); Bachelor's degree or higher: 17.8% (2006-2010 5-year est.); Master's degree or higher: 8.9% (2006-2010 5-year est.).

### School District(s)
Hornell City School District (PK-12)
    2009-10 Enrollment: 1,805 . . . . . . . . . . . . . . . . . (607) 324-1302
### Two-year College(s)
St James Mercy Hospital School of Radiologic Science (Private, Not-for-profit, Roman Catholic)
    Fall 2010 Enrollment: 26 . . . . . . . . . . . . . . . . . . . (607) 324-8265
    2011-12 Tuition: In-state $5,000; Out-of-state $5,000
**Housing:** Homeownership rate: 54.4% (2010); Median home value: $60,200 (2006-2010 5-year est.); Median contract rent: $416 per month (2006-2010 5-year est.); Median year structure built: before 1940 (2006-2010 5-year est.).
**Hospitals:** Saint James Mercy Hospital (297 beds)
**Safety:** Violent crime rate: 22.5 per 10,000 population; Property crime rate: 186.0 per 10,000 population (2010).
**Newspapers:** The Evening Tribune (Local news; Circulation 8,500); Tribune (Local news; Circulation 1,300)
**Transportation:** Commute to work: 81.4% car, 1.9% public transportation, 10.4% walk, 5.4% work from home (2006-2010 5-year est.); Travel time to work: 64.5% less than 15 minutes, 15.1% 15 to 30 minutes, 8.4% 30 to 45

minutes, 5.6% 45 to 60 minutes, 6.4% 60 minutes or more (2006-2010 5-year est.)
**Airports:** Hornell Municipal (general aviation)
**Additional Information Contacts**
City of Hornell . . . . . . . . . . . . . . . . . . . . . . . . . . . . . . (607) 324-7421
  http://www.cityofhornell.com
Hornell Area Chamber of Commerce. . . . . . . . . . . . . (607) 324-0310
  http://www.hornellny.com

## HORNELLSVILLE (town). Covers a land area of 43.325 square miles and a water area of 0.216 square miles. Located at 42.33° N. Lat; 77.67° W. Long.
**Population:** 4,149 (1990); 4,042 (2000); 4,151 (2010); Density: 95.8 persons per square mile (2010); Race: 97.9% White, 0.2% Black, 0.7% Asian, 0.1% American Indian/Alaska Native, 0.0% Native Hawaiian/Other Pacific Islander, 1.1% Other, 0.7% Hispanic of any race (2010); Average household size: 2.26 (2010); Median age: 48.1 (2010); Males per 100 females: 89.7 (2010); Marriage status: 20.9% never married, 57.8% now married, 10.2% widowed, 11.1% divorced (2006-2010 5-year est.); Foreign born: 2.3% (2006-2010 5-year est.); Ancestry (includes multiple ancestries): 28.3% German, 24.6% Irish, 19.6% English, 10.3% Italian, 7.1% American (2006-2010 5-year est.).
**Economy:** Single-family building permits issued: 4 (2011); Multi-family building permits issued: 0 (2011); Employment by occupation: 9.1% management, 2.9% professional, 7.6% services, 17.4% sales, 3.4% farming, 14.2% construction, 7.9% production (2006-2010 5-year est.).
**Income:** Per capita income: $24,168 (2006-2010 5-year est.); Median household income: $42,105 (2006-2010 5-year est.); Average household income: $57,552 (2006-2010 5-year est.); Percent of households with income of $100,000 or more: 16.5% (2006-2010 5-year est.); Poverty rate: 8.6% (2006-2010 5-year est.).
**Education:** Percent of population age 25 and over with: High school diploma (including GED) or higher: 90.3% (2006-2010 5-year est.); Bachelor's degree or higher: 22.0% (2006-2010 5-year est.); Master's degree or higher: 8.9% (2006-2010 5-year est.).
**Housing:** Homeownership rate: 81.6% (2010); Median home value: $92,400 (2006-2010 5-year est.); Median contract rent: $365 per month (2006-2010 5-year est.); Median year structure built: 1959 (2006-2010 5-year est.).
**Transportation:** Commute to work: 92.1% car, 0.7% public transportation, 2.9% walk, 3.4% work from home (2006-2010 5-year est.); Travel time to work: 59.3% less than 15 minutes, 24.9% 15 to 30 minutes, 6.4% 30 to 45 minutes, 1.1% 45 to 60 minutes, 8.3% 60 minutes or more (2006-2010 5-year est.)

## HOWARD (town). Covers a land area of 60.545 square miles and a water area of 0.219 square miles. Located at 42.33° N. Lat; 77.51° W. Long. Elevation is 1,650 feet.
**Population:** 1,331 (1990); 1,430 (2000); 1,467 (2010); Density: 24.2 persons per square mile (2010); Race: 97.7% White, 0.4% Black, 0.2% Asian, 0.2% American Indian/Alaska Native, 0.0% Native Hawaiian/Other Pacific Islander, 1.5% Other, 1.8% Hispanic of any race (2010); Average household size: 2.64 (2010); Median age: 42.2 (2010); Males per 100 females: 106.6 (2010); Marriage status: 25.6% never married, 65.4% now married, 2.8% widowed, 6.3% divorced (2006-2010 5-year est.); Foreign born: 2.6% (2006-2010 5-year est.); Ancestry (includes multiple ancestries): 24.3% English, 24.1% German, 20.0% Irish, 6.9% American, 5.4% Dutch (2006-2010 5-year est.).
**Economy:** Single-family building permits issued: 1 (2011); Multi-family building permits issued: 0 (2011); Employment by occupation: 10.1% management, 2.2% professional, 7.1% services, 16.0% sales, 1.1% farming, 14.5% construction, 9.2% production (2006-2010 5-year est.).
**Income:** Per capita income: $19,824 (2006-2010 5-year est.); Median household income: $50,139 (2006-2010 5-year est.); Average household income: $54,399 (2006-2010 5-year est.); Percent of households with income of $100,000 or more: 10.2% (2006-2010 5-year est.); Poverty rate: 11.9% (2006-2010 5-year est.).
**Education:** Percent of population age 25 and over with: High school diploma (including GED) or higher: 93.3% (2006-2010 5-year est.); Bachelor's degree or higher: 16.7% (2006-2010 5-year est.); Master's degree or higher: 10.1% (2006-2010 5-year est.).
**Housing:** Homeownership rate: 86.3% (2010); Median home value: $87,000 (2006-2010 5-year est.); Median contract rent: $540 per month (2006-2010 5-year est.); Median year structure built: 1974 (2006-2010 5-year est.).

**Transportation:** Commute to work: 87.1% car, 1.0% public transportation, 5.7% walk, 4.8% work from home (2006-2010 5-year est.); Travel time to work: 25.0% less than 15 minutes, 49.1% 15 to 30 minutes, 17.8% 30 to 45 minutes, 4.5% 45 to 60 minutes, 3.5% 60 minutes or more (2006-2010 5-year est.)

**JASPER** (town). Covers a land area of 52.643 square miles and a water area of 0.022 square miles. Located at 42.14° N. Lat; 77.53° W. Long. Elevation is 1,572 feet.
**Population:** 1,232 (1990); 1,270 (2000); 1,424 (2010); Density: 27.0 persons per square mile (2010); Race: 99.2% White, 0.0% Black, 0.2% Asian, 0.1% American Indian/Alaska Native, 0.0% Native Hawaiian/Other Pacific Islander, 0.5% Other, 0.9% Hispanic of any race (2010); Average household size: 3.17 (2010); Median age: 32.2 (2010); Males per 100 females: 100.3 (2010); Marriage status: 27.2% never married, 60.1% now married, 5.4% widowed, 7.3% divorced (2006-2010 5-year est.); Foreign born: 3.3% (2006-2010 5-year est.); Ancestry (includes multiple ancestries): 21.6% English, 19.8% German, 17.5% Irish, 7.5% American, 5.0% Italian (2006-2010 5-year est.).
**Economy:** Single-family building permits issued: 3 (2011); Multi-family building permits issued: 0 (2011); Employment by occupation: 20.9% management, 1.9% professional, 7.6% services, 13.3% sales, 2.9% farming, 10.8% construction, 9.1% production (2006-2010 5-year est.).
**Income:** Per capita income: $17,209 (2006-2010 5-year est.); Median household income: $44,023 (2006-2010 5-year est.); Average household income: $49,231 (2006-2010 5-year est.); Percent of households with income of $100,000 or more: 6.9% (2006-2010 5-year est.); Poverty rate: 18.6% (2006-2010 5-year est.).
**Education:** Percent of population age 25 and over with: High school diploma (including GED) or higher: 90.6% (2006-2010 5-year est.); Bachelor's degree or higher: 13.4% (2006-2010 5-year est.); Master's degree or higher: 6.7% (2006-2010 5-year est.).
**School District(s)**
Jasper-Troupsburg Central School District (KG-12)
   2009-10 Enrollment: 583 . . . . . . . . . . . . . . . . . . . . . (607) 792-3675
**Housing:** Homeownership rate: 83.0% (2010); Median home value: $85,600 (2006-2010 5-year est.); Median contract rent: $352 per month (2006-2010 5-year est.); Median year structure built: 1955 (2006-2010 5-year est.).
**Transportation:** Commute to work: 75.6% car, 0.0% public transportation, 14.4% walk, 8.8% work from home (2006-2010 5-year est.); Travel time to work: 30.2% less than 15 minutes, 24.7% 15 to 30 minutes, 28.3% 30 to 45 minutes, 8.4% 45 to 60 minutes, 8.4% 60 minutes or more (2006-2010 5-year est.)

**KANONA** (unincorporated postal area)
Zip Code: 14856
   Covers a land area of 0.377 square miles and a water area of 0 square miles. Located at 42.37° N. Lat; 77.36° W. Long. Elevation is 1,145 feet.
Population: 215 (2010); Density: 570.2 persons per square mile (2010); Race: 98.1% White, 0.0% Black, 0.0% Asian, 0.0% American Indian/Alaska Native, 0.0% Native Hawaiian/Other Pacific Islander, 1.9% Other, 0.5% Hispanic of any race (2010); Average household size: 2.69 (2010); Median age: 38.6 (2010); Males per 100 females: 117.2 (2010); Homeownership rate: 66.3% (2010)

**LINDLEY** (town). Covers a land area of 37.596 square miles and a water area of 0.270 square miles. Located at 42.03° N. Lat; 77.14° W. Long. Elevation is 1,014 feet.
**Population:** 1,862 (1990); 1,913 (2000); 1,967 (2010); Density: 52.3 persons per square mile (2010); Race: 98.5% White, 0.2% Black, 0.2% Asian, 0.3% American Indian/Alaska Native, 0.0% Native Hawaiian/Other Pacific Islander, 0.8% Other, 0.4% Hispanic of any race (2010); Average household size: 2.69 (2010); Median age: 39.8 (2010); Males per 100 females: 102.6 (2010); Marriage status: 16.6% never married, 71.9% now married, 4.5% widowed, 7.1% divorced (2006-2010 5-year est.); Foreign born: 4.0% (2006-2010 5-year est.); Ancestry (includes multiple ancestries): 27.5% German, 24.5% English, 17.9% Irish, 8.1% American, 6.7% Dutch (2006-2010 5-year est.).
**Economy:** Single-family building permits issued: 2 (2011); Multi-family building permits issued: 0 (2011); Employment by occupation: 10.0% management, 4.0% professional, 10.4% services, 14.7% sales, 4.7% farming, 11.7% construction, 9.5% production (2006-2010 5-year est.).
**Income:** Per capita income: $21,054 (2006-2010 5-year est.); Median household income: $42,614 (2006-2010 5-year est.); Average household

income: $52,172 (2006-2010 5-year est.); Percent of households with income of $100,000 or more: 11.0% (2006-2010 5-year est.); Poverty rate: 11.7% (2006-2010 5-year est.).
**Education:** Percent of population age 25 and over with: High school diploma (including GED) or higher: 86.1% (2006-2010 5-year est.); Bachelor's degree or higher: 12.2% (2006-2010 5-year est.); Master's degree or higher: 4.1% (2006-2010 5-year est.).
**Housing:** Homeownership rate: 84.1% (2010); Median home value: $93,500 (2006-2010 5-year est.); Median contract rent: $316 per month (2006-2010 5-year est.); Median year structure built: 1975 (2006-2010 5-year est.).
**Transportation:** Commute to work: 95.9% car, 0.0% public transportation, 0.0% walk, 3.4% work from home (2006-2010 5-year est.); Travel time to work: 26.8% less than 15 minutes, 46.0% 15 to 30 minutes, 19.6% 30 to 45 minutes, 3.8% 45 to 60 minutes, 3.8% 60 minutes or more (2006-2010 5-year est.)

**NORTH HORNELL** (village). Covers a land area of 0.497 square miles and a water area of 0 square miles. Located at 42.34° N. Lat; 77.66° W. Long. Elevation is 1,165 feet.
**Population:** 822 (1990); 851 (2000); 778 (2010); Density: 1,563.1 persons per square mile (2010); Race: 97.4% White, 0.0% Black, 0.6% Asian, 0.1% American Indian/Alaska Native, 0.0% Native Hawaiian/Other Pacific Islander, 1.9% Other, 2.2% Hispanic of any race (2010); Average household size: 2.22 (2010); Median age: 54.7 (2010); Males per 100 females: 76.4 (2010); Marriage status: 20.5% never married, 58.2% now married, 11.5% widowed, 9.9% divorced (2006-2010 5-year est.); Foreign born: 1.0% (2006-2010 5-year est.); Ancestry (includes multiple ancestries): 33.3% Irish, 25.9% German, 20.3% English, 11.6% Italian, 6.7% Polish (2006-2010 5-year est.).
**Economy:** Single-family building permits issued: 0 (2011); Multi-family building permits issued: 0 (2011); Employment by occupation: 12.7% management, 4.3% professional, 6.8% services, 25.7% sales, 4.3% farming, 8.7% construction, 1.4% production (2006-2010 5-year est.).
**Income:** Per capita income: $34,253 (2006-2010 5-year est.); Median household income: $72,000 (2006-2010 5-year est.); Average household income: $73,524 (2006-2010 5-year est.); Percent of households with income of $100,000 or more: 27.3% (2006-2010 5-year est.); Poverty rate: 3.2% (2006-2010 5-year est.).
**Education:** Percent of population age 25 and over with: High school diploma (including GED) or higher: 96.0% (2006-2010 5-year est.); Bachelor's degree or higher: 41.0% (2006-2010 5-year est.); Master's degree or higher: 16.1% (2006-2010 5-year est.).
**Housing:** Homeownership rate: 87.5% (2010); Median home value: $109,600 (2006-2010 5-year est.); Median contract rent: $378 per month (2006-2010 5-year est.); Median year structure built: 1947 (2006-2010 5-year est.).
**Transportation:** Commute to work: 89.8% car, 1.6% public transportation, 1.6% walk, 4.9% work from home (2006-2010 5-year est.); Travel time to work: 60.7% less than 15 minutes, 24.3% 15 to 30 minutes, 3.8% 30 to 45 minutes, 3.2% 45 to 60 minutes, 8.1% 60 minutes or more (2006-2010 5-year est.)

**PAINTED POST** (village). Covers a land area of 1.272 square miles and a water area of 0.059 square miles. Located at 42.16° N. Lat; 77.09° W. Long. Elevation is 942 feet.
**History:** Settled before 1790; incorporated 1893.
**Population:** 1,950 (1990); 1,842 (2000); 1,809 (2010); Density: 1,421.9 persons per square mile (2010); Race: 95.1% White, 1.9% Black, 0.9% Asian, 0.3% American Indian/Alaska Native, 0.0% Native Hawaiian/Other Pacific Islander, 1.8% Other, 0.8% Hispanic of any race (2010); Average household size: 2.14 (2010); Median age: 42.7 (2010); Males per 100 females: 93.3 (2010); Marriage status: 31.2% never married, 47.5% now married, 8.7% widowed, 12.6% divorced (2006-2010 5-year est.); Foreign born: 1.6% (2006-2010 5-year est.); Ancestry (includes multiple ancestries): 20.7% English, 18.3% Irish, 18.2% German, 9.8% American, 6.9% Italian (2006-2010 5-year est.).
**Economy:** Single-family building permits issued: 7 (2011); Multi-family building permits issued: 107 (2011); Employment by occupation: 14.7% management, 9.9% professional, 7.8% services, 14.6% sales, 3.7% farming, 5.6% construction, 3.6% production (2006-2010 5-year est.).
**Income:** Per capita income: $26,832 (2006-2010 5-year est.); Median household income: $42,778 (2006-2010 5-year est.); Average household income: $60,402 (2006-2010 5-year est.); Percent of households with

income of $100,000 or more: 19.8% (2006-2010 5-year est.); Poverty rate: 12.7% (2006-2010 5-year est.).

**Education:** Percent of population age 25 and over with: High school diploma (including GED) or higher: 86.4% (2006-2010 5-year est.); Bachelor's degree or higher: 27.0% (2006-2010 5-year est.); Master's degree or higher: 16.1% (2006-2010 5-year est.).

### School District(s)
Corning City School District (PK-12)

   2009-10 Enrollment: 5,418 . . . . . . . . . . . . . . . . . . . . . . . (607) 936-3704

Schuyler-Steuben-Chemung-Tioga-Allegany Boces

   2009-10 Enrollment: n/a . . . . . . . . . . . . . . . . . . . . . . . . . (607) 654-2283

**Housing:** Homeownership rate: 58.6% (2010); Median home value: $107,900 (2006-2010 5-year est.); Median contract rent: $508 per month (2006-2010 5-year est.); Median year structure built: 1948 (2006-2010 5-year est.).

**Safety:** Violent crime rate: 11.5 per 10,000 population; Property crime rate: 425.8 per 10,000 population (2010).

**Transportation:** Commute to work: 89.4% car, 0.0% public transportation, 4.0% walk, 5.4% work from home (2006-2010 5-year est.); Travel time to work: 62.2% less than 15 minutes, 17.9% 15 to 30 minutes, 12.3% 30 to 45 minutes, 4.6% 45 to 60 minutes, 3.0% 60 minutes or more (2006-2010 5-year est.)

## PERKINSVILLE (unincorporated postal area)
Zip Code: 14529

   Covers a land area of 0.390 square miles and a water area of 0 square miles. Located at 42.53° N. Lat; 77.63° W. Long. Elevation is 1,365 feet.

   Population: 67 (2010); Density: 171.8 persons per square mile (2010); Race: 100.0% White, 0.0% Black, 0.0% Asian, 0.0% American Indian/Alaska Native, 0.0% Native Hawaiian/Other Pacific Islander, 0.0% Other, 1.5% Hispanic of any race (2010); Average household size: 2.16 (2010); Median age: 49.3 (2010); Males per 100 females: 97.1 (2010); Homeownership rate: 87.1% (2010)

## PRATTSBURGH (town). Covers a land area of 51.666 square miles and a water area of 0.049 square miles. Located at 42.53° N. Lat; 77.33° W. Long. Elevation is 1,481 feet.

**Population:** 1,894 (1990); 2,064 (2000); 2,085 (2010); Density: 40.4 persons per square mile (2010); Race: 96.8% White, 0.8% Black, 0.2% Asian, 0.5% American Indian/Alaska Native, 0.0% Native Hawaiian/Other Pacific Islander, 1.7% Other, 1.2% Hispanic of any race (2010); Average household size: 2.43 (2010); Median age: 42.4 (2010); Males per 100 females: 100.3 (2010); Marriage status: 26.4% never married, 56.0% now married, 6.5% widowed, 11.0% divorced (2006-2010 5-year est.); Foreign born: 1.7% (2006-2010 5-year est.); Ancestry (includes multiple ancestries): 30.4% German, 16.0% Irish, 15.1% English, 11.2% American, 8.3% French (2006-2010 5-year est.).

**Economy:** Single-family building permits issued: 1 (2011); Multi-family building permits issued: 0 (2011); Employment by occupation: 10.7% management, 3.3% professional, 18.9% services, 12.9% sales, 6.9% farming, 15.2% construction, 8.2% production (2006-2010 5-year est.).

**Income:** Per capita income: $20,049 (2006-2010 5-year est.); Median household income: $37,039 (2006-2010 5-year est.); Average household income: $47,302 (2006-2010 5-year est.); Percent of households with income of $100,000 or more: 10.7% (2006-2010 5-year est.); Poverty rate: 14.8% (2006-2010 5-year est.).

**Education:** Percent of population age 25 and over with: High school diploma (including GED) or higher: 86.6% (2006-2010 5-year est.); Bachelor's degree or higher: 14.8% (2006-2010 5-year est.); Master's degree or higher: 5.6% (2006-2010 5-year est.).

### School District(s)
Prattsburgh Central School District (PK-12)

   2009-10 Enrollment: 474 . . . . . . . . . . . . . . . . . . . . . . . (607) 522-3795

**Housing:** Homeownership rate: 81.4% (2010); Median home value: $77,100 (2006-2010 5-year est.); Median contract rent: $382 per month (2006-2010 5-year est.); Median year structure built: 1975 (2006-2010 5-year est.).

**Transportation:** Commute to work: 85.7% car, 0.0% public transportation, 7.4% walk, 4.4% work from home (2006-2010 5-year est.); Travel time to work: 39.5% less than 15 minutes, 26.7% 15 to 30 minutes, 16.5% 30 to 45 minutes, 9.7% 45 to 60 minutes, 7.8% 60 minutes or more (2006-2010 5-year est.)

## PRATTSBURGH (CDP). Covers a land area of 1.640 square miles and a water area of 0 square miles. Located at 42.52° N. Lat; 77.28° W. Long. Elevation is 1,463 feet.

**Population:** n/a (1990); n/a (2000); 656 (2010); Density: 399.9 persons per square mile (2010); Race: 96.6% White, 1.8% Black, 0.2% Asian, 0.2% American Indian/Alaska Native, 0.0% Native Hawaiian/Other Pacific Islander, 1.2% Other, 1.4% Hispanic of any race (2010); Average household size: 2.44 (2010); Median age: 37.7 (2010); Males per 100 females: 85.3 (2010); Marriage status: 26.0% never married, 59.2% now married, 9.5% widowed, 5.3% divorced (2006-2010 5-year est.); Foreign born: 2.7% (2006-2010 5-year est.); Ancestry (includes multiple ancestries): 32.3% German, 16.3% Irish, 12.5% American, 11.9% French, 10.7% English (2006-2010 5-year est.).

**Economy:** Employment by occupation: 10.8% management, 2.2% professional, 24.8% services, 7.6% sales, 8.6% farming, 8.0% construction, 5.7% production (2006-2010 5-year est.).

**Income:** Per capita income: $18,063 (2006-2010 5-year est.); Median household income: $37,813 (2006-2010 5-year est.); Average household income: $46,135 (2006-2010 5-year est.); Percent of households with income of $100,000 or more: 9.9% (2006-2010 5-year est.); Poverty rate: 13.1% (2006-2010 5-year est.).

**Education:** Percent of population age 25 and over with: High school diploma (including GED) or higher: 85.2% (2006-2010 5-year est.); Bachelor's degree or higher: 11.1% (2006-2010 5-year est.); Master's degree or higher: 5.6% (2006-2010 5-year est.).

### School District(s)
Prattsburgh Central School District (PK-12)

   2009-10 Enrollment: 474 . . . . . . . . . . . . . . . . . . . . . . . (607) 522-3795

**Housing:** Homeownership rate: 73.6% (2010); Median home value: $65,900 (2006-2010 5-year est.); Median contract rent: $388 per month (2006-2010 5-year est.); Median year structure built: before 1940 (2006-2010 5-year est.).

**Transportation:** Commute to work: 75.3% car, 0.0% public transportation, 17.7% walk, 6.9% work from home (2006-2010 5-year est.); Travel time to work: 42.9% less than 15 minutes, 30.6% 15 to 30 minutes, 12.7% 30 to 45 minutes, 2.2% 45 to 60 minutes, 11.6% 60 minutes or more (2006-2010 5-year est.)

## PULTENEY (town). Covers a land area of 33.137 square miles and a water area of 3.316 square miles. Located at 42.52° N. Lat; 77.20° W. Long. Elevation is 1,053 feet.

**Population:** 1,417 (1990); 1,405 (2000); 1,285 (2010); Density: 38.8 persons per square mile (2010); Race: 98.7% White, 0.1% Black, 0.1% Asian, 0.1% American Indian/Alaska Native, 0.0% Native Hawaiian/Other Pacific Islander, 1.0% Other, 1.2% Hispanic of any race (2010); Average household size: 2.24 (2010); Median age: 49.9 (2010); Males per 100 females: 96.8 (2010); Marriage status: 18.5% never married, 61.1% now married, 8.6% widowed, 11.7% divorced (2006-2010 5-year est.); Foreign born: 1.7% (2006-2010 5-year est.); Ancestry (includes multiple ancestries): 32.7% German, 19.8% English, 14.3% Irish, 11.3% American, 6.1% Italian (2006-2010 5-year est.).

**Economy:** Single-family building permits issued: 3 (2011); Multi-family building permits issued: 0 (2011); Employment by occupation: 5.9% management, 2.7% professional, 11.9% services, 19.8% sales, 4.3% farming, 11.9% construction, 6.7% production (2006-2010 5-year est.).

**Income:** Per capita income: $24,095 (2006-2010 5-year est.); Median household income: $46,799 (2006-2010 5-year est.); Average household income: $54,272 (2006-2010 5-year est.); Percent of households with income of $100,000 or more: 9.4% (2006-2010 5-year est.); Poverty rate: 15.5% (2006-2010 5-year est.).

**Education:** Percent of population age 25 and over with: High school diploma (including GED) or higher: 87.8% (2006-2010 5-year est.); Bachelor's degree or higher: 25.5% (2006-2010 5-year est.); Master's degree or higher: 7.9% (2006-2010 5-year est.).

**Housing:** Homeownership rate: 86.2% (2010); Median home value: $116,100 (2006-2010 5-year est.); Median contract rent: $525 per month (2006-2010 5-year est.); Median year structure built: 1957 (2006-2010 5-year est.).

**Transportation:** Commute to work: 92.1% car, 0.0% public transportation, 0.9% walk, 6.5% work from home (2006-2010 5-year est.); Travel time to work: 20.5% less than 15 minutes, 41.7% 15 to 30 minutes, 16.6% 30 to 45 minutes, 13.3% 45 to 60 minutes, 8.0% 60 minutes or more (2006-2010 5-year est.)

**RATHBONE** (town). Covers a land area of 36.016 square miles and a water area of 0.101 square miles. Located at 42.12° N. Lat; 77.34° W. Long. Elevation is 1,001 feet.
**Population:** 892 (1990); 1,080 (2000); 1,126 (2010); Density: 31.3 persons per square mile (2010); Race: 97.7% White, 0.3% Black, 0.1% Asian, 0.6% American Indian/Alaska Native, 0.0% Native Hawaiian/Other Pacific Islander, 1.3% Other, 0.6% Hispanic of any race (2010); Average household size: 2.90 (2010); Median age: 35.8 (2010); Males per 100 females: 110.5 (2010); Marriage status: 20.1% never married, 66.4% now married, 6.8% widowed, 6.7% divorced (2006-2010 5-year est.); Foreign born: 0.9% (2006-2010 5-year est.); Ancestry (includes multiple ancestries): 16.0% German, 14.8% English, 13.2% Irish, 8.4% Dutch, 6.6% American (2006-2010 5-year est.).
**Economy:** Single-family building permits issued: 1 (2011); Multi-family building permits issued: 0 (2011); Employment by occupation: 6.5% management, 5.0% professional, 12.0% services, 14.1% sales, 2.4% farming, 18.2% construction, 13.2% production (2006-2010 5-year est.).
**Income:** Per capita income: $16,156 (2006-2010 5-year est.); Median household income: $41,136 (2006-2010 5-year est.); Average household income: $47,090 (2006-2010 5-year est.); Percent of households with income of $100,000 or more: 3.9% (2006-2010 5-year est.); Poverty rate: 23.0% (2006-2010 5-year est.).
**Education:** Percent of population age 25 and over with: High school diploma (including GED) or higher: 86.8% (2006-2010 5-year est.); Bachelor's degree or higher: 9.0% (2006-2010 5-year est.); Master's degree or higher: 3.6% (2006-2010 5-year est.).
**Housing:** Homeownership rate: 85.6% (2010); Median home value: $59,800 (2006-2010 5-year est.); Median contract rent: $354 per month (2006-2010 5-year est.); Median year structure built: 1973 (2006-2010 5-year est.).
**Transportation:** Commute to work: 84.0% car, 0.0% public transportation, 10.3% walk, 4.2% work from home (2006-2010 5-year est.); Travel time to work: 23.3% less than 15 minutes, 27.9% 15 to 30 minutes, 35.4% 30 to 45 minutes, 4.1% 45 to 60 minutes, 9.2% 60 minutes or more (2006-2010 5-year est.).

**REXVILLE** (unincorporated postal area)
Zip Code: 14877
Covers a land area of 42.288 square miles and a water area of 0.145 square miles. Located at 42.05° N. Lat; 77.68° W. Long. Elevation is 1,841 feet. Population: 401 (2010); Density: 9.5 persons per square mile (2010); Race: 100.0% White, 0.0% Black, 0.0% Asian, 0.0% American Indian/Alaska Native, 0.0% Native Hawaiian/Other Pacific Islander, 0.0% Other, 0.5% Hispanic of any race (2010); Average household size: 2.36 (2010); Median age: 47.2 (2010); Males per 100 females: 114.4 (2010); Homeownership rate: 77.0% (2010)

**RIVERSIDE** (village). Covers a land area of 0.301 square miles and a water area of 0.005 square miles. Located at 42.15° N. Lat; 77.07° W. Long. Elevation is 938 feet.
**Population:** 585 (1990); 594 (2000); 497 (2010); Density: 1,648.5 persons per square mile (2010); Race: 95.8% White, 3.0% Black, 0.0% Asian, 0.4% American Indian/Alaska Native, 0.0% Native Hawaiian/Other Pacific Islander, 0.8% Other, 2.2% Hispanic of any race (2010); Average household size: 2.27 (2010); Median age: 41.3 (2010); Males per 100 females: 96.4 (2010); Marriage status: 33.4% never married, 45.9% now married, 8.3% widowed, 12.4% divorced (2006-2010 5-year est.); Foreign born: 1.2% (2006-2010 5-year est.); Ancestry (includes multiple ancestries): 31.8% German, 24.1% English, 15.9% Irish, 10.4% American, 7.2% Italian (2006-2010 5-year est.).
**Economy:** Single-family building permits issued: 0 (2011); Multi-family building permits issued: 0 (2011); Employment by occupation: 3.2% management, 6.5% professional, 13.4% services, 24.7% sales, 3.2% farming, 1.1% construction, 7.5% production (2006-2010 5-year est.).
**Income:** Per capita income: $19,148 (2006-2010 5-year est.); Median household income: $31,607 (2006-2010 5-year est.); Average household income: $37,772 (2006-2010 5-year est.); Percent of households with income of $100,000 or more: 3.0% (2006-2010 5-year est.); Poverty rate: 10.4% (2006-2010 5-year est.).
**Education:** Percent of population age 25 and over with: High school diploma (including GED) or higher: 90.2% (2006-2010 5-year est.); Bachelor's degree or higher: 8.1% (2006-2010 5-year est.); Master's degree or higher: 3.4% (2006-2010 5-year est.).
**Housing:** Homeownership rate: 76.7% (2010); Median home value: $66,300 (2006-2010 5-year est.); Median contract rent: $497 per month

(2006-2010 5-year est.); Median year structure built: 1951 (2006-2010 5-year est.).
**Transportation:** Commute to work: 89.9% car, 0.0% public transportation, 4.8% walk, 3.7% work from home (2006-2010 5-year est.); Travel time to work: 59.9% less than 15 minutes, 22.0% 15 to 30 minutes, 13.7% 30 to 45 minutes, 1.6% 45 to 60 minutes, 2.7% 60 minutes or more (2006-2010 5-year est.)

**SAVONA** (village). Covers a land area of 1.039 square miles and a water area of 0 square miles. Located at 42.28° N. Lat; 77.22° W. Long. Elevation is 1,053 feet.
**Population:** 974 (1990); 822 (2000); 827 (2010); Density: 795.5 persons per square mile (2010); Race: 97.5% White, 0.8% Black, 0.2% Asian, 0.1% American Indian/Alaska Native, 0.0% Native Hawaiian/Other Pacific Islander, 1.4% Other, 0.7% Hispanic of any race (2010); Average household size: 2.72 (2010); Median age: 32.9 (2010); Males per 100 females: 93.2 (2010); Marriage status: 31.9% never married, 47.6% now married, 8.8% widowed, 11.8% divorced (2006-2010 5-year est.); Foreign born: 0.5% (2006-2010 5-year est.); Ancestry (includes multiple ancestries): 30.8% Irish, 17.5% German, 12.3% English, 11.6% Dutch, 7.4% Polish (2006-2010 5-year est.).
**Economy:** Single-family building permits issued: 1 (2011); Multi-family building permits issued: 0 (2011); Employment by occupation: 11.6% management, 1.8% professional, 9.5% services, 31.8% sales, 4.6% farming, 6.7% construction, 10.4% production (2006-2010 5-year est.).
**Income:** Per capita income: $17,146 (2006-2010 5-year est.); Median household income: $38,654 (2006-2010 5-year est.); Average household income: $44,885 (2006-2010 5-year est.); Percent of households with income of $100,000 or more: 2.1% (2006-2010 5-year est.); Poverty rate: 15.8% (2006-2010 5-year est.).
**Education:** Percent of population age 25 and over with: High school diploma (including GED) or higher: 86.6% (2006-2010 5-year est.); Bachelor's degree or higher: 7.8% (2006-2010 5-year est.); Master's degree or higher: 3.1% (2006-2010 5-year est.).
**School District(s)**
Campbell-Savona Central School District (PK-12)
    2009-10 Enrollment: 1,007 . . . . . . . . . . . . . . . . . . . (607) 527-9800
**Housing:** Homeownership rate: 72.4% (2010); Median home value: $73,800 (2006-2010 5-year est.); Median contract rent: $458 per month (2006-2010 5-year est.); Median year structure built: before 1940 (2006-2010 5-year est.).
**Transportation:** Commute to work: 98.7% car, 0.0% public transportation, 0.0% walk, 0.0% work from home (2006-2010 5-year est.); Travel time to work: 27.2% less than 15 minutes, 43.7% 15 to 30 minutes, 20.5% 30 to 45 minutes, 6.6% 45 to 60 minutes, 2.0% 60 minutes or more (2006-2010 5-year est.)

**SOUTH CORNING** (village). Covers a land area of 0.616 square miles and a water area of 0 square miles. Located at 42.12° N. Lat; 77.03° W. Long. Elevation is 951 feet.
**Population:** 1,025 (1990); 1,147 (2000); 1,145 (2010); Density: 1,856.7 persons per square mile (2010); Race: 89.5% White, 6.2% Black, 2.6% Asian, 0.5% American Indian/Alaska Native, 0.0% Native Hawaiian/Other Pacific Islander, 1.2% Other, 1.0% Hispanic of any race (2010); Average household size: 2.24 (2010); Median age: 40.8 (2010); Males per 100 females: 95.7 (2010); Marriage status: 24.6% never married, 54.6% now married, 8.5% widowed, 12.3% divorced (2006-2010 5-year est.); Foreign born: 2.2% (2006-2010 5-year est.); Ancestry (includes multiple ancestries): 23.6% Irish, 16.7% English, 15.5% German, 13.1% Italian, 7.1% American (2006-2010 5-year est.).
**Economy:** Single-family building permits issued: 0 (2011); Multi-family building permits issued: 0 (2011); Employment by occupation: 12.9% management, 4.4% professional, 11.7% services, 17.3% sales, 3.8% farming, 6.1% construction, 3.7% production (2006-2010 5-year est.).
**Income:** Per capita income: $27,437 (2006-2010 5-year est.); Median household income: $54,038 (2006-2010 5-year est.); Average household income: $63,831 (2006-2010 5-year est.); Percent of households with income of $100,000 or more: 18.1% (2006-2010 5-year est.); Poverty rate: 10.1% (2006-2010 5-year est.).
**Education:** Percent of population age 25 and over with: High school diploma (including GED) or higher: 89.2% (2006-2010 5-year est.); Bachelor's degree or higher: 22.3% (2006-2010 5-year est.); Master's degree or higher: 6.4% (2006-2010 5-year est.).
**Housing:** Homeownership rate: 68.1% (2010); Median home value: $79,100 (2006-2010 5-year est.); Median contract rent: $575 per month

(2006-2010 5-year est.); Median year structure built: 1954 (2006-2010 5-year est.).

**Transportation:** Commute to work: 95.9% car, 0.0% public transportation, 2.5% walk, 1.6% work from home (2006-2010 5-year est.); Travel time to work: 37.2% less than 15 minutes, 43.0% 15 to 30 minutes, 10.2% 30 to 45 minutes, 3.1% 45 to 60 minutes, 6.5% 60 minutes or more (2006-2010 5-year est.)

**THURSTON** (town). Covers a land area of 36.352 square miles and a water area of 0.165 square miles. Located at 42.22° N. Lat; 77.27° W. Long. Elevation is 1,263 feet.

**Population:** 1,054 (1990); 1,309 (2000); 1,350 (2010); Density: 37.1 persons per square mile (2010); Race: 97.5% White, 0.6% Black, 0.1% Asian, 0.1% American Indian/Alaska Native, 0.1% Native Hawaiian/Other Pacific Islander, 1.6% Other, 1.3% Hispanic of any race (2010); Average household size: 2.72 (2010); Median age: 41.8 (2010); Males per 100 females: 102.4 (2010); Marriage status: 24.6% never married, 63.4% now married, 2.1% widowed, 9.9% divorced (2006-2010 5-year est.); Foreign born: 0.2% (2006-2010 5-year est.); Ancestry (includes multiple ancestries): 20.5% German, 20.2% Irish, 14.1% English, 11.5% American, 7.7% Polish (2006-2010 5-year est.).

**Economy:** Single-family building permits issued: 0 (2011); Multi-family building permits issued: 0 (2011); Employment by occupation: 4.3% management, 4.0% professional, 7.3% services, 16.8% sales, 16.8% farming, 16.7% construction, 14.8% production (2006-2010 5-year est.).

**Income:** Per capita income: $21,723 (2006-2010 5-year est.); Median household income: $51,016 (2006-2010 5-year est.); Average household income: $56,696 (2006-2010 5-year est.); Percent of households with income of $100,000 or more: 11.1% (2006-2010 5-year est.); Poverty rate: 7.9% (2006-2010 5-year est.).

**Education:** Percent of population age 25 and over with: High school diploma (including GED) or higher: 87.5% (2006-2010 5-year est.); Bachelor's degree or higher: 10.1% (2006-2010 5-year est.); Master's degree or higher: 3.8% (2006-2010 5-year est.).

**Housing:** Homeownership rate: 85.5% (2010); Median home value: $80,100 (2006-2010 5-year est.); Median contract rent: $369 per month (2006-2010 5-year est.); Median year structure built: 1981 (2006-2010 5-year est.).

**Transportation:** Commute to work: 93.9% car, 0.0% public transportation, 1.6% walk, 2.4% work from home (2006-2010 5-year est.); Travel time to work: 12.2% less than 15 minutes, 57.2% 15 to 30 minutes, 21.2% 30 to 45 minutes, 3.9% 45 to 60 minutes, 5.4% 60 minutes or more (2006-2010 5-year est.).

**TROUPSBURG** (town). Covers a land area of 61.238 square miles and a water area of 0.028 square miles. Located at 42.07° N. Lat; 77.53° W. Long. Elevation is 1,663 feet.

**Population:** 1,006 (1990); 1,126 (2000); 1,291 (2010); Density: 21.1 persons per square mile (2010); Race: 98.4% White, 1.1% Black, 0.2% Asian, 0.1% American Indian/Alaska Native, 0.0% Native Hawaiian/Other Pacific Islander, 0.2% Other, 0.9% Hispanic of any race (2010); Average household size: 3.10 (2010); Median age: 31.2 (2010); Males per 100 females: 103.6 (2010); Marriage status: 21.4% never married, 65.6% now married, 4.9% widowed, 8.0% divorced (2006-2010 5-year est.); Foreign born: 0.2% (2006-2010 5-year est.); Ancestry (includes multiple ancestries): 23.3% Pennsylvania German, 14.5% English, 14.2% German, 13.1% Irish, 7.2% American (2006-2010 5-year est.).

**Economy:** Single-family building permits issued: 5 (2011); Multi-family building permits issued: 0 (2011); Employment by occupation: 11.5% management, 0.6% professional, 10.5% services, 14.1% sales, 4.6% farming, 25.4% construction, 11.9% production (2006-2010 5-year est.).

**Income:** Per capita income: $14,199 (2006-2010 5-year est.); Median household income: $34,934 (2006-2010 5-year est.); Average household income: $45,597 (2006-2010 5-year est.); Percent of households with income of $100,000 or more: 8.3% (2006-2010 5-year est.); Poverty rate: 22.4% (2006-2010 5-year est.).

**Education:** Percent of population age 25 and over with: High school diploma (including GED) or higher: 85.9% (2006-2010 5-year est.); Bachelor's degree or higher: 9.6% (2006-2010 5-year est.); Master's degree or higher: 5.4% (2006-2010 5-year est.).

**School District(s)**

Jasper-Troupsburg Central School District (KG-12)
   2009-10 Enrollment: 583 . . . . . . . . . . . . . . . . . . . . (607) 792-3675

**Housing:** Homeownership rate: 86.8% (2010); Median home value: $70,600 (2006-2010 5-year est.); Median contract rent: $375 per month

(2006-2010 5-year est.); Median year structure built: 1973 (2006-2010 5-year est.).

**Transportation:** Commute to work: 78.7% car, 0.0% public transportation, 6.2% walk, 6.8% work from home (2006-2010 5-year est.); Travel time to work: 29.8% less than 15 minutes, 22.5% 15 to 30 minutes, 22.7% 30 to 45 minutes, 20.3% 45 to 60 minutes, 4.8% 60 minutes or more (2006-2010 5-year est.)

**TUSCARORA** (town). Covers a land area of 37.627 square miles and a water area of 0.085 square miles. Located at 42.04° N. Lat; 77.25° W. Long.

**Population:** 1,368 (1990); 1,400 (2000); 1,473 (2010); Density: 39.1 persons per square mile (2010); Race: 97.8% White, 0.1% Black, 0.3% Asian, 0.3% American Indian/Alaska Native, 0.1% Native Hawaiian/Other Pacific Islander, 1.4% Other, 0.7% Hispanic of any race (2010); Average household size: 2.64 (2010); Median age: 36.4 (2010); Males per 100 females: 101.8 (2010); Marriage status: 26.1% never married, 56.0% now married, 6.6% widowed, 11.3% divorced (2006-2010 5-year est.); Foreign born: 0.0% (2006-2010 5-year est.); Ancestry (includes multiple ancestries): 19.7% German, 12.8% English, 10.3% Irish, 8.4% American, 5.8% Italian (2006-2010 5-year est.).

**Economy:** Single-family building permits issued: 2 (2011); Multi-family building permits issued: 0 (2011); Employment by occupation: 11.2% management, 2.0% professional, 8.8% services, 9.2% sales, 3.1% farming, 9.0% construction, 7.9% production (2006-2010 5-year est.).

**Income:** Per capita income: $19,108 (2006-2010 5-year est.); Median household income: $41,150 (2006-2010 5-year est.); Average household income: $47,287 (2006-2010 5-year est.); Percent of households with income of $100,000 or more: 6.9% (2006-2010 5-year est.); Poverty rate: 17.3% (2006-2010 5-year est.).

**Education:** Percent of population age 25 and over with: High school diploma (including GED) or higher: 77.8% (2006-2010 5-year est.); Bachelor's degree or higher: 11.2% (2006-2010 5-year est.); Master's degree or higher: 4.5% (2006-2010 5-year est.).

**Housing:** Homeownership rate: 81.3% (2010); Median home value: $68,200 (2006-2010 5-year est.); Median contract rent: $429 per month (2006-2010 5-year est.); Median year structure built: 1971 (2006-2010 5-year est.).

**Transportation:** Commute to work: 94.7% car, 0.6% public transportation, 2.1% walk, 2.6% work from home (2006-2010 5-year est.); Travel time to work: 17.1% less than 15 minutes, 32.4% 15 to 30 minutes, 27.0% 30 to 45 minutes, 15.9% 45 to 60 minutes, 7.6% 60 minutes or more (2006-2010 5-year est.)

**URBANA** (town). Covers a land area of 40.945 square miles and a water area of 3.231 square miles. Located at 42.41° N. Lat; 77.22° W. Long. Elevation is 728 feet.

**Population:** 2,807 (1990); 2,546 (2000); 2,343 (2010); Density: 57.2 persons per square mile (2010); Race: 97.1% White, 1.0% Black, 0.3% Asian, 0.2% American Indian/Alaska Native, 0.0% Native Hawaiian/Other Pacific Islander, 1.4% Other, 1.6% Hispanic of any race (2010); Average household size: 2.27 (2010); Median age: 50.3 (2010); Males per 100 females: 100.1 (2010); Marriage status: 21.2% never married, 60.8% now married, 9.0% widowed, 9.0% divorced (2006-2010 5-year est.); Foreign born: 1.7% (2006-2010 5-year est.); Ancestry (includes multiple ancestries): 22.3% German, 20.6% Irish, 18.3% English, 8.8% American, 6.6% French (2006-2010 5-year est.).

**Economy:** Single-family building permits issued: 3 (2011); Multi-family building permits issued: 0 (2011); Employment by occupation: 8.5% management, 0.7% professional, 6.3% services, 13.1% sales, 2.3% farming, 8.7% construction, 10.9% production (2006-2010 5-year est.).

**Income:** Per capita income: $26,728 (2006-2010 5-year est.); Median household income: $49,946 (2006-2010 5-year est.); Average household income: $58,805 (2006-2010 5-year est.); Percent of households with income of $100,000 or more: 11.0% (2006-2010 5-year est.); Poverty rate: 6.5% (2006-2010 5-year est.).

**Education:** Percent of population age 25 and over with: High school diploma (including GED) or higher: 90.4% (2006-2010 5-year est.); Bachelor's degree or higher: 23.8% (2006-2010 5-year est.); Master's degree or higher: 12.3% (2006-2010 5-year est.).

**Housing:** Homeownership rate: 76.9% (2010); Median home value: $107,600 (2006-2010 5-year est.); Median contract rent: $459 per month (2006-2010 5-year est.); Median year structure built: 1942 (2006-2010 5-year est.).

**Transportation:** Commute to work: 87.1% car, 0.0% public transportation, 3.9% walk, 4.9% work from home (2006-2010 5-year est.); Travel time to work: 55.8% less than 15 minutes, 22.7% 15 to 30 minutes, 13.6% 30 to 45 minutes, 2.5% 45 to 60 minutes, 5.3% 60 minutes or more (2006-2010 5-year est.)

---

**WAYLAND** (village). Covers a land area of 1.129 square miles and a water area of 0.057 square miles. Located at 42.56° N. Lat; 77.59° W. Long. Elevation is 1,375 feet.

**Population:** 1,976 (1990); 1,893 (2000); 1,865 (2010); Density: 1,651.0 persons per square mile (2010); Race: 96.2% White, 1.3% Black, 0.8% Asian, 0.2% American Indian/Alaska Native, 0.0% Native Hawaiian/Other Pacific Islander, 1.5% Other, 1.1% Hispanic of any race (2010); Average household size: 2.45 (2010); Median age: 39.2 (2010); Males per 100 females: 94.3 (2010); Marriage status: 25.6% never married, 53.0% now married, 8.7% widowed, 12.6% divorced (2006-2010 5-year est.); Foreign born: 1.2% (2006-2010 5-year est.); Ancestry (includes multiple ancestries): 37.2% German, 23.3% Irish, 20.0% English, 6.8% American, 6.4% Italian (2006-2010 5-year est.).

**Economy:** Single-family building permits issued: 0 (2011); Multi-family building permits issued: 0 (2011); Employment by occupation: 7.8% management, 1.8% professional, 9.4% services, 11.6% sales, 2.4% farming, 15.6% construction, 8.9% production (2006-2010 5-year est.).

**Income:** Per capita income: $20,504 (2006-2010 5-year est.); Median household income: $38,565 (2006-2010 5-year est.); Average household income: $47,667 (2006-2010 5-year est.); Percent of households with income of $100,000 or more: 10.3% (2006-2010 5-year est.); Poverty rate: 10.7% (2006-2010 5-year est.).

**Education:** Percent of population age 25 and over with: High school diploma (including GED) or higher: 86.8% (2006-2010 5-year est.); Bachelor's degree or higher: 19.1% (2006-2010 5-year est.); Master's degree or higher: 8.4% (2006-2010 5-year est.).

**School District(s)**
Wayland-Cohocton Central School District (PK-12)
    2009-10 Enrollment: 1,581 . . . . . . . . . . . . . . . . . . . . . . (585) 728-2211
**Housing:** Homeownership rate: 63.8% (2010); Median home value: $86,500 (2006-2010 5-year est.); Median contract rent: $443 per month (2006-2010 5-year est.); Median year structure built: before 1940 (2006-2010 5-year est.).
**Safety:** Violent crime rate: 0.0 per 10,000 population; Property crime rate: 154.6 per 10,000 population (2010).
**Transportation:** Commute to work: 86.0% car, 0.4% public transportation, 9.4% walk, 4.0% work from home (2006-2010 5-year est.); Travel time to work: 40.4% less than 15 minutes, 16.2% 15 to 30 minutes, 21.9% 30 to 45 minutes, 13.5% 45 to 60 minutes, 7.9% 60 minutes or more (2006-2010 5-year est.)

---

**WAYLAND** (town). Covers a land area of 38.737 square miles and a water area of 0.599 square miles. Located at 42.52° N. Lat; 77.59° W. Long. Elevation is 1,375 feet.
**History:** Incorporated 1877.
**Population:** 4,311 (1990); 4,314 (2000); 4,102 (2010); Density: 105.9 persons per square mile (2010); Race: 97.0% White, 1.0% Black, 0.5% Asian, 0.3% American Indian/Alaska Native, 0.0% Native Hawaiian/Other Pacific Islander, 1.2% Other, 0.9% Hispanic of any race (2010); Average household size: 2.41 (2010); Median age: 42.6 (2010); Males per 100 females: 95.0 (2010); Marriage status: 22.4% never married, 59.1% now married, 8.4% widowed, 10.2% divorced (2006-2010 5-year est.); Foreign born: 0.9% (2006-2010 5-year est.); Ancestry (includes multiple ancestries): 35.2% German, 23.9% Irish, 16.4% English, 9.8% American, 8.5% Italian (2006-2010 5-year est.).

**Economy:** Single-family building permits issued: 0 (2011); Multi-family building permits issued: 0 (2011); Employment by occupation: 8.1% management, 1.4% professional, 9.9% services, 12.8% sales, 4.2% farming, 14.2% construction, 10.5% production (2006-2010 5-year est.).

**Income:** Per capita income: $22,437 (2006-2010 5-year est.); Median household income: $42,057 (2006-2010 5-year est.); Average household income: $54,757 (2006-2010 5-year est.); Percent of households with income of $100,000 or more: 10.6% (2006-2010 5-year est.); Poverty rate: 10.5% (2006-2010 5-year est.).

**Education:** Percent of population age 25 and over with: High school diploma (including GED) or higher: 83.7% (2006-2010 5-year est.); Bachelor's degree or higher: 15.7% (2006-2010 5-year est.); Master's degree or higher: 8.2% (2006-2010 5-year est.).

**School District(s)**
Wayland-Cohocton Central School District (PK-12)
    2009-10 Enrollment: 1,581 . . . . . . . . . . . . . . . . . . . . . . (585) 728-2211
**Housing:** Homeownership rate: 73.3% (2010); Median home value: $79,300 (2006-2010 5-year est.); Median contract rent: $429 per month (2006-2010 5-year est.); Median year structure built: before 1940 (2006-2010 5-year est.).
**Transportation:** Commute to work: 91.6% car, 0.2% public transportation, 4.9% walk, 3.1% work from home (2006-2010 5-year est.); Travel time to work: 42.0% less than 15 minutes, 19.3% 15 to 30 minutes, 14.3% 30 to 45 minutes, 14.3% 45 to 60 minutes, 10.2% 60 minutes or more (2006-2010 5-year est.)

---

**WAYNE** (town). Covers a land area of 20.581 square miles and a water area of 2.013 square miles. Located at 42.43° N. Lat; 77.13° W. Long. Elevation is 1,168 feet.
**Population:** 1,029 (1990); 1,165 (2000); 1,041 (2010); Density: 50.6 persons per square mile (2010); Race: 99.1% White, 0.2% Black, 0.2% Asian, 0.0% American Indian/Alaska Native, 0.0% Native Hawaiian/Other Pacific Islander, 0.5% Other, 0.6% Hispanic of any race (2010); Average household size: 2.16 (2010); Median age: 52.3 (2010); Males per 100 females: 97.2 (2010); Marriage status: 20.1% never married, 62.7% now married, 6.0% widowed, 11.2% divorced (2006-2010 5-year est.); Foreign born: 1.0% (2006-2010 5-year est.); Ancestry (includes multiple ancestries): 30.6% German, 22.1% English, 14.3% Irish, 11.3% Polish, 9.3% Italian (2006-2010 5-year est.).

**Economy:** Single-family building permits issued: 2 (2011); Multi-family building permits issued: 0 (2011); Employment by occupation: 20.0% management, 1.2% professional, 10.7% services, 10.9% sales, 10.9% farming, 10.5% construction, 3.4% production (2006-2010 5-year est.).

**Income:** Per capita income: $32,676 (2006-2010 5-year est.); Median household income: $52,250 (2006-2010 5-year est.); Average household income: $74,176 (2006-2010 5-year est.); Percent of households with income of $100,000 or more: 27.1% (2006-2010 5-year est.); Poverty rate: 8.1% (2006-2010 5-year est.).

**Education:** Percent of population age 25 and over with: High school diploma (including GED) or higher: 89.0% (2006-2010 5-year est.); Bachelor's degree or higher: 28.6% (2006-2010 5-year est.); Master's degree or higher: 15.9% (2006-2010 5-year est.).

**Housing:** Homeownership rate: 89.4% (2010); Median home value: $171,900 (2006-2010 5-year est.); Median contract rent: $527 per month (2006-2010 5-year est.); Median year structure built: 1964 (2006-2010 5-year est.).
**Transportation:** Commute to work: 94.6% car, 0.0% public transportation, 3.7% walk, 1.7% work from home (2006-2010 5-year est.); Travel time to work: 14.3% less than 15 minutes, 37.8% 15 to 30 minutes, 25.2% 30 to 45 minutes, 8.6% 45 to 60 minutes, 14.1% 60 minutes or more (2006-2010 5-year est.)

---

**WEST UNION** (town). Covers a land area of 40.903 square miles and a water area of 0.145 square miles. Located at 42.04° N. Lat; 77.68° W. Long. Elevation is 2,257 feet.
**Population:** 412 (1990); 399 (2000); 312 (2010); Density: 7.6 persons per square mile (2010); Race: 100.0% White, 0.0% Black, 0.0% Asian, 0.0% American Indian/Alaska Native, 0.0% Native Hawaiian/Other Pacific Islander, 0.0% Other, 0.6% Hispanic of any race (2010); Average household size: 2.42 (2010); Median age: 47.8 (2010); Males per 100 females: 113.7 (2010); Marriage status: 18.8% never married, 58.2% now married, 12.5% widowed, 10.5% divorced (2006-2010 5-year est.); Foreign born: 0.6% (2006-2010 5-year est.); Ancestry (includes multiple ancestries): 27.9% German, 16.6% English, 15.6% Irish, 14.0% American, 12.7% Italian (2006-2010 5-year est.).

**Economy:** Single-family building permits issued: 0 (2011); Multi-family building permits issued: 0 (2011); Employment by occupation: 13.8% management, 1.3% professional, 22.4% services, 15.1% sales, 7.2% farming, 15.8% construction, 5.3% production (2006-2010 5-year est.).

**Income:** Per capita income: $23,364 (2006-2010 5-year est.); Median household income: $35,000 (2006-2010 5-year est.); Average household income: $48,918 (2006-2010 5-year est.); Percent of households with income of $100,000 or more: 10.6% (2006-2010 5-year est.); Poverty rate: 11.0% (2006-2010 5-year est.).

**Education:** Percent of population age 25 and over with: High school diploma (including GED) or higher: 88.0% (2006-2010 5-year est.); Bachelor's degree or higher: 12.4% (2006-2010 5-year est.); Master's degree or higher: 0.9% (2006-2010 5-year est.).

**Housing:** Homeownership rate: 76.0% (2010); Median home value: $107,800 (2006-2010 5-year est.); Median contract rent: $342 per month (2006-2010 5-year est.); Median year structure built: 1971 (2006-2010 5-year est.).

**Transportation:** Commute to work: 79.6% car, 0.0% public transportation, 7.2% walk, 8.6% work from home (2006-2010 5-year est.); Travel time to work: 30.9% less than 15 minutes, 43.2% 15 to 30 minutes, 15.1% 30 to 45 minutes, 7.2% 45 to 60 minutes, 3.6% 60 minutes or more (2006-2010 5-year est.)

**WHEELER** (town). Covers a land area of 46.065 square miles and a water area of 0.060 square miles. Located at 42.43° N. Lat; 77.33° W. Long. Elevation is 1,257 feet.

**Population:** 1,084 (1990); 1,263 (2000); 1,260 (2010); Density: 27.4 persons per square mile (2010); Race: 96.1% White, 1.7% Black, 0.3% Asian, 0.0% American Indian/Alaska Native, 0.0% Native Hawaiian/Other Pacific Islander, 1.9% Other, 0.8% Hispanic of any race (2010); Average household size: 2.70 (2010); Median age: 40.5 (2010); Males per 100 females: 106.9 (2010); Marriage status: 25.5% never married, 58.3% now married, 5.6% widowed, 10.6% divorced (2006-2010 5-year est.); Foreign born: 0.3% (2006-2010 5-year est.); Ancestry (includes multiple ancestries): 26.4% German, 14.4% English, 13.1% Irish, 11.3% American, 5.8% Dutch (2006-2010 5-year est.).

**Economy:** Single-family building permits issued: 3 (2011); Multi-family building permits issued: 0 (2011); Employment by occupation: 12.1% management, 1.8% professional, 9.4% services, 19.1% sales, 6.2% farming, 14.4% construction, 5.1% production (2006-2010 5-year est.).

**Income:** Per capita income: $20,064 (2006-2010 5-year est.); Median household income: $44,018 (2006-2010 5-year est.); Average household income: $52,845 (2006-2010 5-year est.); Percent of households with income of $100,000 or more: 11.1% (2006-2010 5-year est.); Poverty rate: 13.1% (2006-2010 5-year est.).

**Education:** Percent of population age 25 and over with: High school diploma (including GED) or higher: 78.8% (2006-2010 5-year est.); Bachelor's degree or higher: 12.6% (2006-2010 5-year est.); Master's degree or higher: 5.4% (2006-2010 5-year est.).

**Housing:** Homeownership rate: 86.7% (2010); Median home value: $82,000 (2006-2010 5-year est.); Median contract rent: $425 per month (2006-2010 5-year est.); Median year structure built: 1977 (2006-2010 5-year est.).

**Transportation:** Commute to work: 85.3% car, 0.6% public transportation, 6.2% walk, 5.6% work from home (2006-2010 5-year est.); Travel time to work: 29.4% less than 15 minutes, 40.3% 15 to 30 minutes, 18.1% 30 to 45 minutes, 5.3% 45 to 60 minutes, 6.8% 60 minutes or more (2006-2010 5-year est.)

**WOODHULL** (town). Covers a land area of 55.390 square miles and a water area of 0.032 square miles. Located at 42.05° N. Lat; 77.39° W. Long. Elevation is 1,322 feet.

**Population:** 1,518 (1990); 1,524 (2000); 1,719 (2010); Density: 31.0 persons per square mile (2010); Race: 98.6% White, 0.3% Black, 0.3% Asian, 0.2% American Indian/Alaska Native, 0.0% Native Hawaiian/Other Pacific Islander, 0.6% Other, 1.3% Hispanic of any race (2010); Average household size: 2.80 (2010); Median age: 37.4 (2010); Males per 100 females: 101.3 (2010); Marriage status: 26.9% never married, 63.1% now married, 3.4% widowed, 6.7% divorced (2006-2010 5-year est.); Foreign born: 0.2% (2006-2010 5-year est.); Ancestry (includes multiple ancestries): 18.6% German, 17.7% English, 16.7% Irish, 13.7% American, 5.5% Italian (2006-2010 5-year est.).

**Economy:** Single-family building permits issued: 1 (2011); Multi-family building permits issued: 0 (2011); Employment by occupation: 5.3% management, 1.6% professional, 11.7% services, 15.7% sales, 2.1% farming, 17.9% construction, 10.3% production (2006-2010 5-year est.).

**Income:** Per capita income: $16,684 (2006-2010 5-year est.); Median household income: $41,818 (2006-2010 5-year est.); Average household income: $48,083 (2006-2010 5-year est.); Percent of households with income of $100,000 or more: 7.9% (2006-2010 5-year est.); Poverty rate: 17.2% (2006-2010 5-year est.).

**Education:** Percent of population age 25 and over with: High school diploma (including GED) or higher: 84.1% (2006-2010 5-year est.); Bachelor's degree or higher: 6.2% (2006-2010 5-year est.); Master's degree or higher: 3.2% (2006-2010 5-year est.).

**Housing:** Homeownership rate: 83.4% (2010); Median home value: $64,100 (2006-2010 5-year est.); Median contract rent: $424 per month

(2006-2010 5-year est.); Median year structure built: 1971 (2006-2010 5-year est.).

**Transportation:** Commute to work: 89.2% car, 0.0% public transportation, 4.7% walk, 4.6% work from home (2006-2010 5-year est.); Travel time to work: 19.5% less than 15 minutes, 23.2% 15 to 30 minutes, 29.3% 30 to 45 minutes, 14.8% 45 to 60 minutes, 13.2% 60 minutes or more (2006-2010 5-year est.)

# Suffolk County

Located in southeastern New York; on Long Island, bounded on the south by the Atlantic Ocean, on the east by Block Island Sound, and on the north by Long Island Sound; includes many bays and inlets. Covers a land area of 912.20 square miles, a water area of 1,460.87 square miles, and is located in the Eastern Time Zone at 40.83° N. Lat., 73.02° W. Long. The county was founded in 1683. County seat is Riverhead.

Suffolk County is part of the New York-Northern New Jersey-Long Island, NY-NJ-PA Metropolitan Statistical Area. The entire metro area includes: Edison-New Brunswick, NJ Metropolitan Division (Middlesex County, NJ; Monmouth County, NJ; Ocean County, NJ; Somerset County, NJ); Nassau-Suffolk, NY Metropolitan Division (Nassau County, NY; Suffolk County, NY); New York-White Plains-Wayne, NY-NJ Metropolitan Division (Bergen County, NJ; Hudson County, NJ; Passaic County, NJ; Bronx County, NY; Kings County, NY; New York County, NY; Putnam County, NY; Queens County, NY; Richmond County, NY; Rockland County, NY; Westchester County, NY); Newark-Union, NJ-PA Metropolitan Division (Essex County, NJ; Hunterdon County, NJ; Morris County, NJ; Sussex County, NJ; Union County, NJ; Pike County, PA)

| Weather Station: Bridgehampton | | | | | | | | | | | Elevation: 60 feet | |
|---|---|---|---|---|---|---|---|---|---|---|---|---|
| | Jan | Feb | Mar | Apr | May | Jun | Jul | Aug | Sep | Oct | Nov | Dec |
| High | 39 | 40 | 47 | 56 | 66 | 75 | 81 | 80 | 74 | 63 | 54 | 44 |
| Low | 23 | 25 | 30 | 39 | 48 | 57 | 63 | 63 | 55 | 44 | 37 | 28 |
| Precip | 4.0 | 3.5 | 4.9 | 4.7 | 3.7 | 4.2 | 3.4 | 4.0 | 4.4 | 4.2 | 4.4 | 4.3 |
| Snow | 7.7 | 7.9 | 5.3 | 0.9 | 0.0 | 0.0 | 0.0 | 0.0 | 0.0 | tr | 0.7 | 4.0 |

*High and Low temperatures in degrees Fahrenheit; Precipitation and Snow in inches*

| Weather Station: Islip-Macarthur Arpt | | | | | | | | | | | Elevation: 83 feet | |
|---|---|---|---|---|---|---|---|---|---|---|---|---|
| | Jan | Feb | Mar | Apr | May | Jun | Jul | Aug | Sep | Oct | Nov | Dec |
| High | 39 | 41 | 48 | 58 | 68 | 77 | 82 | 81 | 74 | 64 | 54 | 44 |
| Low | 24 | 25 | 31 | 41 | 50 | 60 | 66 | 65 | 58 | 46 | 37 | 28 |
| Precip | 3.8 | 3.0 | 4.4 | 4.3 | 3.8 | 4.1 | 3.3 | 4.3 | 3.8 | 4.0 | 3.6 | 4.2 |
| Snow | na | na | na | na | na | na | na | na | na | na | na | na |

*High and Low temperatures in degrees Fahrenheit; Precipitation and Snow in inches*

| Weather Station: Riverhead Research Farm | | | | | | | | | | | Elevation: 100 feet | |
|---|---|---|---|---|---|---|---|---|---|---|---|---|
| | Jan | Feb | Mar | Apr | May | Jun | Jul | Aug | Sep | Oct | Nov | Dec |
| High | 40 | 42 | 49 | 60 | 71 | 79 | 84 | 83 | 76 | 65 | 55 | 45 |
| Low | 25 | 26 | 32 | 41 | 50 | 60 | 65 | 65 | 58 | 48 | 40 | 30 |
| Precip | 3.7 | 3.1 | 4.5 | 4.5 | 3.9 | 4.1 | 3.2 | 3.9 | 3.8 | 4.2 | 4.3 | 4.0 |
| Snow | 8.5 | 7.6 | 5.1 | 0.7 | 0.0 | 0.0 | 0.0 | 0.0 | 0.0 | 0.0 | 0.5 | 4.7 |

*High and Low temperatures in degrees Fahrenheit; Precipitation and Snow in inches*

| Weather Station: Setauket Strong | | | | | | | | | | | Elevation: 40 feet | |
|---|---|---|---|---|---|---|---|---|---|---|---|---|
| | Jan | Feb | Mar | Apr | May | Jun | Jul | Aug | Sep | Oct | Nov | Dec |
| High | 40 | 42 | 50 | 61 | 71 | 79 | 83 | 82 | 76 | 65 | 55 | 45 |
| Low | 25 | 26 | 31 | 41 | 49 | 59 | 65 | 64 | 58 | 47 | 38 | 30 |
| Precip | 3.4 | 2.7 | 4.0 | 4.4 | 3.7 | 3.9 | na | 3.6 | 3.8 | 3.6 | 3.6 | 3.5 |
| Snow | 2.5 | 3.3 | 1.3 | 0.2 | 0.0 | 0.0 | 0.0 | 0.0 | 0.0 | 0.0 | tr | na |

*High and Low temperatures in degrees Fahrenheit; Precipitation and Snow in inches*

**Population:** 1,321,330 (1990); 1,419,369 (2000); 1,493,350 (2010); Race: 80.8% White, 7.4% Black, 3.4% Asian, 0.4% American Indian/Alaska Native, 0.0% Native Hawaiian/Other Pacific Islander, 8.0% Other, 16.5% Hispanic of any race (2010); Density: 1,637.1 persons per square mile (2010); Average household size: 2.93 (2010); Median age: 39.8 (2010); Males per 100 females: 96.8 (2010).

**Religion:** Six largest groups: 58.9% Catholicism, 2.2% Lutheran, 1.7% Methodist/Pietist, 1.6% Non-Denominational, 1.4% Judaism, 1.3% Muslim Estimate (2010)

**Economy:** Unemployment rate: 8.3% (February 2012); Total civilian labor force: 773,535 (February 2012); Leading industries: 16.5% health care and social assistance; 14.2% retail trade; 10.2% manufacturing (2009); Farms: 585 totaling 34,404 acres (2007); Companies that employ 500 or more persons: 65 (2009); Companies that employ 100 to 499 persons: 755 (2009); Companies that employ less than 100 persons: 46,753 (2009);

Black-owned businesses: 7,176 (2007); Hispanic-owned businesses: 11,380 (2007); Asian-owned businesses: 6,813 (2007); Women-owned businesses: 43,092 (2007); Retail sales per capita: $17,325 (2010). Single-family building permits issued: 759 (2011); Multi-family building permits issued: 97 (2011).

**Income:** Per capita income: $35,755 (2006-2010 5-year est.); Median household income: $84,506 (2006-2010 5-year est.); Average household income: $104,548 (2006-2010 5-year est.); Percent of households with income of $100,000 or more: 41.0% (2006-2010 5-year est.); Poverty rate: 5.7% (2006-2010 5-year est.); Bankruptcy rate: 4.01% (2011).

**Taxes:** Total county taxes per capita: $1,212 (2009); County property taxes per capita: $389 (2009).

**Education:** Percent of population age 25 and over with: High school diploma (including GED) or higher: 89.4% (2006-2010 5-year est.); Bachelor's degree or higher: 31.9% (2006-2010 5-year est.); Master's degree or higher: 14.2% (2006-2010 5-year est.).

**Housing:** Homeownership rate: 78.8% (2010); Median home value: $424,200 (2006-2010 5-year est.); Median contract rent: $1,293 per month (2006-2010 5-year est.); Median year structure built: 1967 (2006-2010 5-year est.)

**Health:** Birth rate: 112.4 per 10,000 population (2011); Death rate: 75.2 per 10,000 population (2011); Age-adjusted cancer mortality rate: 175.8 deaths per 100,000 population (2009); Number of physicians: 30.1 per 10,000 population (2008); Hospital beds: 32.6 per 10,000 population (2007); Hospital admissions: 1,079.8 per 10,000 population (2007).

**Environment:** Air Quality Index: 80.8% good, 15.6% moderate, 3.6% unhealthy for sensitive individuals, 0.0% unhealthy (percent of days in 2010)

**Elections:** 2008 Presidential election results: 52.5% Obama, 46.5% McCain, 0.5% Nader

**National and State Parks:** Belmont Lake State Park; Captree State Park; Caumsett State Park; Fire Island National Seashore; Gilgo State Park; Heckscher State Park; Hither Hills State Park; Middle Island State Game Farm; Morton National Wildlife Refuge; Orient Beach State Park; Robert Moses State Park; Sunken Meadow State Park; Wertheim National Wildlife Refuge; Wildwood State Park

**Additional Information Contacts**

Suffolk County Government . . . . . . . . . . . . . . . . . . . . . . . . (631) 852-2000
  http://www.co.suffolk.ny.us
Babylon Chamber of Commerce . . . . . . . . . . . . . . . . . . . (631) 482-1482
  http://www.babylonvillagechamber.org
Chamber of Commerce of Greater Bay Shore . . . . . . . . . . (631) 665-7003
  http://www.bayshorecommerce.com
Chamber of Commerce of the Greater Ronkonkomas . . . . (631) 963-2796
  http://www.ronkonkomachamber.com
Copiague Chamber of Commerce . . . . . . . . . . . . . . . . . . (631) 226-2956
  http://copiaguechamber.org
East Hampton Chamber of Commerce . . . . . . . . . . . . . . . (631) 324-0362
  http://www.easthamptonchamber.com
East Northport Chamber of Commerce . . . . . . . . . . . . . . (631) 261-3573
  http://www.eastnorthport.com
East Quogue Chamber of Commerce . . . . . . . . . . . . . . . (631) 728-5555
  http://www.eqny.com
Greater Patchogue Chamber of Commerce . . . . . . . . . . . (631) 207-1000
  http://www.patchoguechamber.com
Greater Sayville Chamber of Commerce . . . . . . . . . . . . . (631) 567-5257
  http://www.greatersayvillechamber.com
Greater Smithtown Chamber of Commerce . . . . . . . . . . . (631) 979-8069
  http://www.smithtownchamber.org
Greater Westhampton Beach Chamber of Commerce . . . . (631) 288-3337
  http://www.whbcc.com
Hampton Bays Chamber of Commerce . . . . . . . . . . . . . . (631) 728-2211
  http://www.hamptonbayschamber.com
Holbrook Chamber of Commerce . . . . . . . . . . . . . . . . . . (631) 471-2725
  http://www.holbrookchamber.com
Huntington Township Chamber of Commerce . . . . . . . . . . (631) 423-6100
  http://www.huntingtonchamber.com
Islip Chamber of Commerce . . . . . . . . . . . . . . . . . . . . . (631) 581-2720
  http://www.islipchamberofcommerce.com
Islip Chamber of Commerce . . . . . . . . . . . . . . . . . . . . . (631) 581-2720
  http://www.longislandweb.com/islipchamber
Kings Park Chamber of Commerce . . . . . . . . . . . . . . . . . (631) 269-7678
  http://www.kingsparkli.com
Lindenhurst Chamber of Commerce . . . . . . . . . . . . . . . . (631) 226-4641
  http://www.lindenhurstchamber.org

Mastics and Shirley Chamber of Commerce . . . . . . . . . . . (631) 399-2228
  http://www.masticsshirleychamber.com
Mattituck Chamber of Commerce . . . . . . . . . . . . . . . . . . (631) 953-9389
  http://www.mattituckchamber.org
Montauk Chamber of Commerce . . . . . . . . . . . . . . . . . . (631) 668-2428
  http://www.montaukchamber.com
North Brookhaven Chamber of Commerce . . . . . . . . . . . . (631) 821-1313
  http://northbrookhavenchamber.org
North Fork Chamber of Commerce . . . . . . . . . . . . . . . . . (631) 765-3161
  http://northforkchamberofcommerce.org
North Fork Chamber of Commerce . . . . . . . . . . . . . . . . . (631) 765-3161
  http://www.greenportsoutholdchamber.org
North Fork Promotional Council . . . . . . . . . . . . . . . . . . . (631) 477-1383
  http://northfork.org
Northport Chamber of Commerce . . . . . . . . . . . . . . . . . . (631) 754-3905
  http://www.northportny.com
Port Jefferson Chamber of Commerce . . . . . . . . . . . . . . (631) 473-1414
  http://www.portjeffchamber.com
Riverhead Chamber of Commerce . . . . . . . . . . . . . . . . . (631) 727-7600
  http://www.riverheadchamber.com
Sag Harbor Chamber of Commerce . . . . . . . . . . . . . . . . (631) 725-0011
  http://www.sagharborchamber.com
Saint James Chamber of Commerce . . . . . . . . . . . . . . . . (631) 584-8510
  http://www.stjameschamber.org
Shelter Island Chamber of Commerce . . . . . . . . . . . . . . . (631) 749-0399
  http://www.shelterislandchamber.org
Southampton Chamber of Commerce . . . . . . . . . . . . . . . (631) 283-0402
  http://www.southamptonchamber.com
Town of Babylon . . . . . . . . . . . . . . . . . . . . . . . . . . . . . (631) 957-3005
  http://www.townofbabylon.com
Town of Brookhaven . . . . . . . . . . . . . . . . . . . . . . . . . . (631) 451-9101
  http://www.brookhaven.org
Town of East Hampton . . . . . . . . . . . . . . . . . . . . . . . . . (631) 324-4142
  http://www.town.east-hampton.ny.us
Town of Huntington . . . . . . . . . . . . . . . . . . . . . . . . . . . (631) 351-3206
  http://www.huntingtonny.gov
Town of Islip . . . . . . . . . . . . . . . . . . . . . . . . . . . . . . . . (631) 224-5490
  http://www.townofislip-ny.gov
Town of Riverhead . . . . . . . . . . . . . . . . . . . . . . . . . . . . (631) 727-3200
  http://www.townofriverheadny.gov
Town of Smithtown . . . . . . . . . . . . . . . . . . . . . . . . . . . . (631) 360-7620
  http://www.smithtowninfo.com
Town of Southampton . . . . . . . . . . . . . . . . . . . . . . . . . (631) 287-5740
  http://www.southamptontownny.gov
Town of Southold . . . . . . . . . . . . . . . . . . . . . . . . . . . . (631) 765-1800
  http://southoldtown.northfork.net
Village of Amityville . . . . . . . . . . . . . . . . . . . . . . . . . . . (631) 264-6000
  http://www.amityville.com
Village of Bellport . . . . . . . . . . . . . . . . . . . . . . . . . . . . (631) 286-0327
  http://www.bellportvillage.com
Village of Lindenhurst . . . . . . . . . . . . . . . . . . . . . . . . . . (631) 957-7500
  http://www.villageoflindenhurst.com
Village of Ocean Beach . . . . . . . . . . . . . . . . . . . . . . . . (631) 583-5940
  http://www.villageofoceanbeach.org
Village of Old Field . . . . . . . . . . . . . . . . . . . . . . . . . . . (631) 941-9412
  http://www.oldfieldny.org
Village of Patchogue . . . . . . . . . . . . . . . . . . . . . . . . . . (631) 475-4300
  http://www.patchoguevillage.org
Village of Port Jefferson . . . . . . . . . . . . . . . . . . . . . . . . (631) 473-4724
  http://www.portjeff.com
Village of Saltaire . . . . . . . . . . . . . . . . . . . . . . . . . . . . (631) 583-5566
  http://www.saltaire.org
Village of Westhampton Beach . . . . . . . . . . . . . . . . . . . (631) 288-1654
  http://www.whbvillage.com
West Islip Chamber of Commerce . . . . . . . . . . . . . . . . . (631) 661-3838
  http://westislipchamber.org

## Suffolk County Communities

**AMAGANSETT** (CDP). Covers a land area of 6.527 square miles and a water area of 0.024 square miles. Located at 40.98° N. Lat; 72.12° W. Long. Elevation is 30 feet.

**Population:** 894 (1990); 1,067 (2000); 1,165 (2010); Density: 178.5 persons per square mile (2010); Race: 92.3% White, 1.1% Black, 1.9% Asian, 0.2% American Indian/Alaska Native, 0.0% Native Hawaiian/Other

Pacific Islander, 4.5% Other, 10.2% Hispanic of any race (2010); Average household size: 2.27 (2010); Median age: 52.2 (2010); Males per 100 females: 107.3 (2010); Marriage status: 14.4% never married, 51.5% now married, 9.7% widowed, 24.5% divorced (2006-2010 5-year est.); Foreign born: 16.2% (2006-2010 5-year est.); Ancestry (includes multiple ancestries): 16.8% Irish, 16.7% Italian, 14.1% German, 13.4% English, 7.8% French (2006-2010 5-year est.).

**Economy:** Employment by occupation: 28.6% management, 4.8% professional, 0.8% services, 18.0% sales, 1.5% farming, 2.0% construction, 0.0% production (2006-2010 5-year est.).

**Income:** Per capita income: $59,719 (2006-2010 5-year est.); Median household income: $71,650 (2006-2010 5-year est.); Average household income: $112,554 (2006-2010 5-year est.); Percent of households with income of $100,000 or more: 35.9% (2006-2010 5-year est.); Poverty rate: 10.5% (2006-2010 5-year est.).

**Education:** Percent of population age 25 and over with: High school diploma (including GED) or higher: 96.8% (2006-2010 5-year est.); Bachelor's degree or higher: 63.1% (2006-2010 5-year est.); Master's degree or higher: 29.9% (2006-2010 5-year est.).

### School District(s)
Amagansett Union Free School District (PK-06)
  2009-10 Enrollment: 121 . . . . . . . . . . . . . . (631) 267-3572

**Housing:** Homeownership rate: 79.8% (2010); Median home value: $1 (2006-2010 5-year est.); Median contract rent: $1,371 per month (2006-2010 5-year est.); Median year structure built: 1974 (2006-2010 5-year est.).

**Transportation:** Commute to work: 65.0% car, 1.5% public transportation, 13.9% walk, 18.0% work from home (2006-2010 5-year est.); Travel time to work: 76.5% less than 15 minutes, 17.6% 15 to 30 minutes, 0.0% 30 to 45 minutes, 0.0% 45 to 60 minutes, 6.0% 60 minutes or more (2006-2010 5-year est.)

## AMITYVILLE (village).
Covers a land area of 2.112 square miles and a water area of 0.362 square miles. Located at 40.66° N. Lat; 73.41° W. Long. Elevation is 20 feet.

**History:** Settled 1780, incorporated 1894.

**Population:** 9,197 (1990); 9,441 (2000); 9,523 (2010); Density: 4,506.9 persons per square mile (2010); Race: 81.7% White, 9.7% Black, 1.8% Asian, 0.3% American Indian/Alaska Native, 0.0% Native Hawaiian/Other Pacific Islander, 6.5% Other, 13.1% Hispanic of any race (2010); Average household size: 2.43 (2010); Median age: 46.4 (2010); Males per 100 females: 91.5 (2010); Marriage status: 36.3% never married, 47.2% now married, 9.2% widowed, 7.4% divorced (2006-2010 5-year est.); Foreign born: 14.9% (2006-2010 5-year est.); Ancestry (includes multiple ancestries): 26.8% Irish, 22.1% German, 19.2% Italian, 8.4% English, 5.8% Polish (2006-2010 5-year est.).

**Economy:** Single-family building permits issued: 0 (2011); Multi-family building permits issued: 0 (2011); Employment by occupation: 11.9% management, 4.7% professional, 7.0% services, 15.7% sales, 5.1% farming, 7.3% construction, 4.4% production (2006-2010 5-year est.).

**Income:** Per capita income: $35,411 (2006-2010 5-year est.); Median household income: $74,366 (2006-2010 5-year est.); Average household income: $99,438 (2006-2010 5-year est.); Percent of households with income of $100,000 or more: 37.8% (2006-2010 5-year est.); Poverty rate: 6.5% (2006-2010 5-year est.).

**Education:** Percent of population age 25 and over with: High school diploma (including GED) or higher: 90.1% (2006-2010 5-year est.); Bachelor's degree or higher: 30.7% (2006-2010 5-year est.); Master's degree or higher: 13.4% (2006-2010 5-year est.).

### School District(s)
Amityville Union Free School District (PK-12)
  2009-10 Enrollment: 2,826 . . . . . . . . . . . . . (631) 598-6520

### Two-year College(s)
Island Drafting and Technical Institute (Private, For-profit)
  Fall 2010 Enrollment: 148 . . . . . . . . . . . . . . . . (631) 691-8733
  2011-12 Tuition: In-state $15,200; Out-of-state $15,200

**Housing:** Homeownership rate: 70.9% (2010); Median home value: $443,500 (2006-2010 5-year est.); Median contract rent: $1,155 per month (2006-2010 5-year est.); Median year structure built: 1954 (2006-2010 5-year est.).

**Hospitals:** Brunswick Hospital Center (474 beds); South Oaks Hospital (217 beds)

**Safety:** Violent crime rate: 10.0 per 10,000 population; Property crime rate: 153.6 per 10,000 population (2010).

**Newspapers:** Record (Community news; Circulation 3,500)

**Transportation:** Commute to work: 83.4% car, 10.0% public transportation, 2.4% walk, 2.3% work from home (2006-2010 5-year est.); Travel time to work: 39.9% less than 15 minutes, 20.8% 15 to 30 minutes, 18.0% 30 to 45 minutes, 7.3% 45 to 60 minutes, 14.0% 60 minutes or more (2006-2010 5-year est.)

**Additional Information Contacts**
Village of Amityville . . . . . . . . . . . . . . . . . . . (631) 264-6000
  http://www.amityville.com

## AQUEBOGUE (CDP).
Covers a land area of 3.811 square miles and a water area of 0.098 square miles. Located at 40.94° N. Lat; 72.61° W. Long. Elevation is 39 feet.

**Population:** 2,072 (1990); 2,254 (2000); 2,438 (2010); Density: 639.6 persons per square mile (2010); Race: 90.7% White, 4.2% Black, 0.2% Asian, 0.0% American Indian/Alaska Native, 0.5% Native Hawaiian/Other Pacific Islander, 4.4% Other, 11.9% Hispanic of any race (2010); Average household size: 2.59 (2010); Median age: 45.1 (2010); Males per 100 females: 92.4 (2010); Marriage status: 21.0% never married, 69.9% now married, 5.5% widowed, 3.6% divorced (2006-2010 5-year est.); Foreign born: 8.8% (2006-2010 5-year est.); Ancestry (includes multiple ancestries): 32.4% Irish, 28.0% Italian, 16.7% German, 15.0% Polish, 6.6% English (2006-2010 5-year est.).

**Economy:** Employment by occupation: 17.1% management, 0.0% professional, 4.2% services, 18.4% sales, 2.9% farming, 19.9% construction, 8.3% production (2006-2010 5-year est.).

**Income:** Per capita income: $35,358 (2006-2010 5-year est.); Median household income: $86,154 (2006-2010 5-year est.); Average household income: $88,502 (2006-2010 5-year est.); Percent of households with income of $100,000 or more: 37.9% (2006-2010 5-year est.); Poverty rate: 13.4% (2006-2010 5-year est.).

**Education:** Percent of population age 25 and over with: High school diploma (including GED) or higher: 94.4% (2006-2010 5-year est.); Bachelor's degree or higher: 33.3% (2006-2010 5-year est.); Master's degree or higher: 24.0% (2006-2010 5-year est.).

### School District(s)
Riverhead Central School District (KG-12)
  2009-10 Enrollment: 4,816 . . . . . . . . . . . . . (631) 369-6717

**Housing:** Homeownership rate: 82.8% (2010); Median home value: $450,000 (2006-2010 5-year est.); Median contract rent: $1,259 per month (2006-2010 5-year est.); Median year structure built: 1983 (2006-2010 5-year est.).

**Transportation:** Commute to work: 93.2% car, 3.9% public transportation, 0.0% walk, 2.9% work from home (2006-2010 5-year est.); Travel time to work: 42.8% less than 15 minutes, 26.0% 15 to 30 minutes, 7.9% 30 to 45 minutes, 10.7% 45 to 60 minutes, 12.6% 60 minutes or more (2006-2010 5-year est.)

## ASHAROKEN (village).
Covers a land area of 1.470 square miles and a water area of 5.015 square miles. Located at 40.93° N. Lat; 73.38° W. Long. Elevation is 13 feet.

**Population:** 807 (1990); 625 (2000); 654 (2010); Density: 444.7 persons per square mile (2010); Race: 95.9% White, 0.2% Black, 2.0% Asian, 0.2% American Indian/Alaska Native, 0.0% Native Hawaiian/Other Pacific Islander, 1.7% Other, 3.1% Hispanic of any race (2010); Average household size: 2.56 (2010); Median age: 51.5 (2010); Males per 100 females: 107.6 (2010); Marriage status: 19.5% never married, 66.4% now married, 9.7% widowed, 4.5% divorced (2006-2010 5-year est.); Foreign born: 8.4% (2006-2010 5-year est.); Ancestry (includes multiple ancestries): 26.6% German, 25.7% Irish, 23.8% Italian, 6.8% Russian, 6.4% English (2006-2010 5-year est.).

**Economy:** Single-family building permits issued: 0 (2011); Multi-family building permits issued: 0 (2011); Employment by occupation: 16.4% management, 3.6% professional, 5.3% services, 18.9% sales, 1.1% farming, 6.8% construction, 3.6% production (2006-2010 5-year est.).

**Income:** Per capita income: $81,618 (2006-2010 5-year est.); Median household income: $131,563 (2006-2010 5-year est.); Average household income: $228,772 (2006-2010 5-year est.); Percent of households with income of $100,000 or more: 57.7% (2006-2010 5-year est.); Poverty rate: 6.8% (2006-2010 5-year est.).

**Education:** Percent of population age 25 and over with: High school diploma (including GED) or higher: 98.5% (2006-2010 5-year est.); Bachelor's degree or higher: 57.6% (2006-2010 5-year est.); Master's degree or higher: 27.1% (2006-2010 5-year est.).

**Housing:** Homeownership rate: 89.0% (2010); Median home value: $1 (2006-2010 5-year est.); Median contract rent: n/a per month (2006-2010 5-year est.); Median year structure built: 1961 (2006-2010 5-year est.).
**Safety:** Violent crime rate: 0.0 per 10,000 population; Property crime rate: 15.2 per 10,000 population (2010).
**Transportation:** Commute to work: 75.6% car; 14.9% public transportation, 0.0% walk, 5.8% work from home (2006-2010 5-year est.); Travel time to work: 12.0% less than 15 minutes, 23.6% 15 to 30 minutes, 27.4% 30 to 45 minutes, 10.4% 45 to 60 minutes, 26.6% 60 minutes or more (2006-2010 5-year est.)

**BABYLON** (village). Covers a land area of 2.444 square miles and a water area of 0.342 square miles. Located at 40.69° N. Lat; 73.32° W. Long. Elevation is 7 feet.
**Population:** 12,346 (1990); 12,615 (2000); 12,166 (2010); Density: 4,976.0 persons per square mile (2010); Race: 91.9% White, 2.0% Black, 2.2% Asian, 0.1% American Indian/Alaska Native, 0.0% Native Hawaiian/Other Pacific Islander, 3.8% Other, 6.7% Hispanic of any race (2010); Average household size: 2.64 (2010); Median age: 41.6 (2010); Males per 100 females: 94.5 (2010); Marriage status: 27.5% never married, 59.3% now married, 6.1% widowed, 7.1% divorced (2006-2010 5-year est.); Foreign born: 8.8% (2006-2010 5-year est.); Ancestry (includes multiple ancestries): 34.8% Irish, 31.3% Italian, 23.9% German, 9.0% English, 6.1% Polish (2006-2010 5-year est.).
**Economy:** Single-family building permits issued: 1 (2011); Multi-family building permits issued: 0 (2011); Employment by occupation: 12.7% management, 4.1% professional, 6.1% services, 17.0% sales, 2.6% farming, 8.3% construction, 5.5% production (2006-2010 5-year est.).
**Income:** Per capita income: $44,293 (2006-2010 5-year est.); Median household income: $97,407 (2006-2010 5-year est.); Average household income: $120,340 (2006-2010 5-year est.); Percent of households with income of $100,000 or more: 47.8% (2006-2010 5-year est.); Poverty rate: 4.5% (2006-2010 5-year est.).
**Taxes:** Total city taxes per capita: $444 (2009); City property taxes per capita: $375 (2009).
**Education:** Percent of population age 25 and over with: High school diploma (including GED) or higher: 95.1% (2006-2010 5-year est.); Bachelor's degree or higher: 39.6% (2006-2010 5-year est.); Master's degree or higher: 19.2% (2006-2010 5-year est.).
**School District(s)**
Babylon Union Free School District (KG-12)
    2009-10 Enrollment: 1,807 . . . . . . . . . . . . . . . . . . (631) 893-7925
**Housing:** Homeownership rate: 76.4% (2010); Median home value: $481,000 (2006-2010 5-year est.); Median contract rent: $1,265 per month (2006-2010 5-year est.); Median year structure built: 1953 (2006-2010 5-year est.).
**Newspapers:** The Beacon (Community news; Circulation 20,000)
**Transportation:** Commute to work: 81.0% car, 12.3% public transportation, 2.7% walk, 3.3% work from home (2006-2010 5-year est.); Travel time to work: 28.4% less than 15 minutes, 30.2% 15 to 30 minutes, 15.6% 30 to 45 minutes, 8.0% 45 to 60 minutes, 17.7% 60 minutes or more (2006-2010 5-year est.)
**Additional Information Contacts**
Babylon Chamber of Commerce . . . . . . . . . . . . . . . (631) 482-1482
    http://www.babylonvillagechamber.org

**BABYLON** (town). Covers a land area of 52.318 square miles and a water area of 61.861 square miles. Located at 40.68° N. Lat; 73.31° W. Long. Elevation is 7 feet.
**History:** The 1st U.S. wireless station was built here by Marconi. Settled 1689, incorporated as a village 1893.
**Population:** 202,355 (1990); 211,792 (2000); 213,603 (2010); Density: 4,082.7 persons per square mile (2010); Race: 71.7% White, 16.3% Black, 3.1% Asian, 0.3% American Indian/Alaska Native, 0.0% Native Hawaiian/Other Pacific Islander, 8.6% Other, 16.8% Hispanic of any race (2010); Average household size: 2.98 (2010); Median age: 39.2 (2010); Males per 100 females: 93.7 (2010); Marriage status: 32.7% never married, 52.8% now married, 6.8% widowed, 7.7% divorced (2006-2010 5-year est.); Foreign born: 17.0% (2006-2010 5-year est.); Ancestry (includes multiple ancestries): 28.9% Italian, 19.8% Irish, 14.8% German, 5.8% Polish, 4.0% English (2006-2010 5-year est.).
**Economy:** Unemployment rate: 8.7% (February 2012); Total civilian labor force: 108,816 (February 2012); Single-family building permits issued: 15 (2011); Multi-family building permits issued: 0 (2011); Employment by occupation: 9.6% management, 3.1% professional, 9.4% services, 19.1%

sales, 4.8% farming, 10.0% construction, 6.8% production (2006-2010 5-year est.).
**Income:** Per capita income: $30,107 (2006-2010 5-year est.); Median household income: $77,407 (2006-2010 5-year est.); Average household income: $89,527 (2006-2010 5-year est.); Percent of households with income of $100,000 or more: 35.8% (2006-2010 5-year est.); Poverty rate: 6.1% (2006-2010 5-year est.).
**Taxes:** Total city taxes per capita: $481 (2009); City property taxes per capita: $419 (2009).
**Education:** Percent of population age 25 and over with: High school diploma (including GED) or higher: 86.8% (2006-2010 5-year est.); Bachelor's degree or higher: 22.4% (2006-2010 5-year est.); Master's degree or higher: 8.3% (2006-2010 5-year est.).
**School District(s)**
Babylon Union Free School District (KG-12)
    2009-10 Enrollment: 1,807 . . . . . . . . . . . . . . . . . . (631) 893-7925
**Housing:** Homeownership rate: 74.2% (2010); Median home value: $387,800 (2006-2010 5-year est.); Median contract rent: $1,269 per month (2006-2010 5-year est.); Median year structure built: 1959 (2006-2010 5-year est.).
**Newspapers:** The Beacon (Community news; Circulation 20,000)
**Transportation:** Commute to work: 85.2% car, 9.0% public transportation, 1.3% walk, 3.2% work from home (2006-2010 5-year est.); Travel time to work: 26.7% less than 15 minutes, 32.4% 15 to 30 minutes, 18.6% 30 to 45 minutes, 6.9% 45 to 60 minutes, 15.4% 60 minutes or more (2006-2010 5-year est.)
**Additional Information Contacts**
Town of Babylon . . . . . . . . . . . . . . . . . . . . . . . . . (631) 957-3005
    http://www.townofbabylon.com

**BAITING HOLLOW** (CDP). Covers a land area of 3.212 square miles and a water area of 0 square miles. Located at 40.96° N. Lat; 72.74° W. Long. Elevation is 105 feet.
**Population:** 997 (1990); 1,449 (2000); 1,642 (2010); Density: 511.1 persons per square mile (2010); Race: 96.8% White, 0.9% Black, 0.7% Asian, 0.1% American Indian/Alaska Native, 0.1% Native Hawaiian/Other Pacific Islander, 1.4% Other, 6.0% Hispanic of any race (2010); Average household size: 2.26 (2010); Median age: 51.8 (2010); Males per 100 females: 97.1 (2010); Marriage status: 13.9% never married, 66.0% now married, 9.9% widowed, 10.2% divorced (2006-2010 5-year est.); Foreign born: 18.0% (2006-2010 5-year est.); Ancestry (includes multiple ancestries): 23.0% English, 21.4% German, 21.2% Italian, 19.6% Irish, 11.1% Dutch (2006-2010 5-year est.).
**Economy:** Employment by occupation: 11.4% management, 4.3% professional, 1.2% services, 12.4% sales, 1.8% farming, 12.2% construction, 2.0% production (2006-2010 5-year est.).
**Income:** Per capita income: $53,625 (2006-2010 5-year est.); Median household income: $97,868 (2006-2010 5-year est.); Average household income: $119,718 (2006-2010 5-year est.); Percent of households with income of $100,000 or more: 48.2% (2006-2010 5-year est.); Poverty rate: 1.1% (2006-2010 5-year est.).
**Education:** Percent of population age 25 and over with: High school diploma (including GED) or higher: 93.1% (2006-2010 5-year est.); Bachelor's degree or higher: 32.8% (2006-2010 5-year est.); Master's degree or higher: 17.3% (2006-2010 5-year est.).
**Housing:** Homeownership rate: 87.1% (2010); Median home value: $423,600 (2006-2010 5-year est.); Median contract rent: $1,672 per month (2006-2010 5-year est.); Median year structure built: 1983 (2006-2010 5-year est.).
**Transportation:** Commute to work: 79.0% car, 1.8% public transportation, 3.6% walk, 10.2% work from home (2006-2010 5-year est.); Travel time to work: 38.1% less than 15 minutes, 33.6% 15 to 30 minutes, 16.4% 30 to 45 minutes, 0.1% 45 to 60 minutes, 11.8% 60 minutes or more (2006-2010 5-year est.)

**BAY SHORE** (CDP). Covers a land area of 5.367 square miles and a water area of 0.159 square miles. Located at 40.73° N. Lat; 73.24° W. Long. Elevation is 16 feet.
**History:** Named for its location on Great South Bay. Founded 1708.
**Population:** 21,279 (1990); 23,852 (2000); 26,337 (2010); Density: 4,906.7 persons per square mile (2010); Race: 61.0% White, 19.6% Black, 3.2% Asian, 0.7% American Indian/Alaska Native, 0.0% Native Hawaiian/Other Pacific Islander, 15.5% Other, 30.8% Hispanic of any race (2010); Average household size: 2.88 (2010); Median age: 37.4 (2010); Males per 100 females: 94.1 (2010); Marriage status: 35.6% never married, 46.2% now

married, 6.5% widowed, 11.7% divorced (2006-2010 5-year est.); Foreign born: 18.9% (2006-2010 5-year est.); Ancestry (includes multiple ancestries): 18.1% Italian, 15.7% Irish, 9.5% German, 4.5% Polish, 3.4% English (2006-2010 5-year est.).

**Economy:** Employment by occupation: 9.8% management, 3.1% professional, 10.1% services, 17.1% sales, 4.3% farming, 10.4% construction, 9.2% production (2006-2010 5-year est.).

**Income:** Per capita income: $27,648 (2006-2010 5-year est.); Median household income: $66,382 (2006-2010 5-year est.); Average household income: $81,306 (2006-2010 5-year est.); Percent of households with income of $100,000 or more: 28.2% (2006-2010 5-year est.); Poverty rate: 9.1% (2006-2010 5-year est.).

**Education:** Percent of population age 25 and over with: High school diploma (including GED) or higher: 84.3% (2006-2010 5-year est.); Bachelor's degree or higher: 23.2% (2006-2010 5-year est.); Master's degree or higher: 8.8% (2006-2010 5-year est.).

### School District(s)
Bay Shore Union Free School District (KG-12)
   2009-10 Enrollment: 5,756 . . . . . . . . . . . . . . . . . . . . (631) 968-1117
Brentwood Union Free School District (PK-12)
   2009-10 Enrollment: 16,517 . . . . . . . . . . . . . . . . . . . (631) 434-2325
Fire Island Union Free School District (PK-06)
   2009-10 Enrollment: 27 . . . . . . . . . . . . . . . . . . . . . . . (631) 583-5626

**Housing:** Homeownership rate: 59.0% (2010); Median home value: $359,900 (2006-2010 5-year est.); Median contract rent: $1,203 per month (2006-2010 5-year est.); Median year structure built: 1960 (2006-2010 5-year est.).

**Hospitals:** Southside Hospital (377 beds)

**Transportation:** Commute to work: 84.1% car, 7.6% public transportation, 2.5% walk, 3.2% work from home (2006-2010 5-year est.); Travel time to work: 31.7% less than 15 minutes, 32.9% 15 to 30 minutes, 18.1% 30 to 45 minutes, 4.6% 45 to 60 minutes, 12.8% 60 minutes or more (2006-2010 5-year est.)

**Additional Information Contacts**
Chamber of Commerce of Greater Bay Shore. . . . . . . . . . . (631) 665-7003
   http://www.bayshorecommerce.com

**BAYPORT** (CDP). Covers a land area of 3.719 square miles and a water area of 0.075 square miles. Located at 40.74° N. Lat; 73.05° W. Long. Elevation is 16 feet.

**Population:** 7,702 (1990); 8,662 (2000); 8,896 (2010); Density: 2,391.6 persons per square mile (2010); Race: 94.6% White, 1.4% Black, 1.7% Asian, 0.1% American Indian/Alaska Native, 0.0% Native Hawaiian/Other Pacific Islander, 2.2% Other, 5.3% Hispanic of any race (2010); Average household size: 2.65 (2010); Median age: 42.9 (2010); Males per 100 females: 92.2 (2010); Marriage status: 28.1% never married, 55.8% now married, 8.2% widowed, 7.9% divorced (2006-2010 5-year est.); Foreign born: 3.6% (2006-2010 5-year est.); Ancestry (includes multiple ancestries): 37.8% Italian, 33.3% Irish, 23.1% German, 11.5% English, 2.6% American (2006-2010 5-year est.).

**Economy:** Employment by occupation: 12.9% management, 3.5% professional, 6.0% services, 17.3% sales, 2.7% farming, 6.6% construction, 2.6% production (2006-2010 5-year est.).

**Income:** Per capita income: $37,577 (2006-2010 5-year est.); Median household income: $81,283 (2006-2010 5-year est.); Average household income: $97,851 (2006-2010 5-year est.); Percent of households with income of $100,000 or more: 37.1% (2006-2010 5-year est.); Poverty rate: 3.7% (2006-2010 5-year est.).

**Education:** Percent of population age 25 and over with: High school diploma (including GED) or higher: 94.1% (2006-2010 5-year est.); Bachelor's degree or higher: 36.9% (2006-2010 5-year est.); Master's degree or higher: 18.5% (2006-2010 5-year est.).

### School District(s)
Bayport-Blue Point Union Free School District (KG-12)
   2009-10 Enrollment: 2,502 . . . . . . . . . . . . . . . . . . . (631) 472-7860

**Housing:** Homeownership rate: 69.4% (2010); Median home value: $483,500 (2006-2010 5-year est.); Median contract rent: $1,187 per month (2006-2010 5-year est.); Median year structure built: 1964 (2006-2010 5-year est.).

**Transportation:** Commute to work: 89.7% car, 5.8% public transportation, 0.8% walk, 3.7% work from home (2006-2010 5-year est.); Travel time to work: 23.1% less than 15 minutes, 39.3% 15 to 30 minutes, 19.6% 30 to 45 minutes, 7.0% 45 to 60 minutes, 10.9% 60 minutes or more (2006-2010 5-year est.)

**BAYWOOD** (CDP). Covers a land area of 2.260 square miles and a water area of 0 square miles. Located at 40.75° N. Lat; 73.29° W. Long. Elevation is 59 feet.

**Population:** 7,351 (1990); 7,571 (2000); 7,350 (2010); Density: 3,251.7 persons per square mile (2010); Race: 63.8% White, 14.8% Black, 4.0% Asian, 0.8% American Indian/Alaska Native, 0.0% Native Hawaiian/Other Pacific Islander, 16.6% Other, 34.7% Hispanic of any race (2010); Average household size: 3.38 (2010); Median age: 37.4 (2010); Males per 100 females: 100.5 (2010); Marriage status: 35.0% never married, 53.9% now married, 5.1% widowed, 6.0% divorced (2006-2010 5-year est.); Foreign born: 29.0% (2006-2010 5-year est.); Ancestry (includes multiple ancestries): 18.8% Irish, 15.7% Italian, 15.0% German, 4.0% Polish, 2.1% Jamaican (2006-2010 5-year est.).

**Economy:** Employment by occupation: 7.7% management, 1.3% professional, 10.4% services, 17.0% sales, 5.3% farming, 10.6% construction, 11.4% production (2006-2010 5-year est.).

**Income:** Per capita income: $25,672 (2006-2010 5-year est.); Median household income: $76,650 (2006-2010 5-year est.); Average household income: $85,499 (2006-2010 5-year est.); Percent of households with income of $100,000 or more: 36.4% (2006-2010 5-year est.); Poverty rate: 5.0% (2006-2010 5-year est.).

**Education:** Percent of population age 25 and over with: High school diploma (including GED) or higher: 84.6% (2006-2010 5-year est.); Bachelor's degree or higher: 17.7% (2006-2010 5-year est.); Master's degree or higher: 4.8% (2006-2010 5-year est.).

**Housing:** Homeownership rate: 82.3% (2010); Median home value: $351,500 (2006-2010 5-year est.); Median contract rent: $1,333 per month (2006-2010 5-year est.); Median year structure built: 1959 (2006-2010 5-year est.).

**Transportation:** Commute to work: 87.3% car, 5.8% public transportation, 2.5% walk, 3.3% work from home (2006-2010 5-year est.); Travel time to work: 27.5% less than 15 minutes, 37.2% 15 to 30 minutes, 16.9% 30 to 45 minutes, 6.9% 45 to 60 minutes, 11.5% 60 minutes or more (2006-2010 5-year est.)

**BELLE TERRE** (village). Covers a land area of 0.884 square miles and a water area of 0 square miles. Located at 40.96° N. Lat; 73.06° W. Long. Elevation is 161 feet.

**Population:** 839 (1990); 832 (2000); 792 (2010); Density: 895.1 persons per square mile (2010); Race: 92.6% White, 1.3% Black, 3.3% Asian, 0.1% American Indian/Alaska Native, 0.0% Native Hawaiian/Other Pacific Islander, 2.7% Other, 3.9% Hispanic of any race (2010); Average household size: 2.77 (2010); Median age: 48.2 (2010); Males per 100 females: 101.0 (2010); Marriage status: 19.6% never married, 72.4% now married, 5.6% widowed, 2.5% divorced (2006-2010 5-year est.); Foreign born: 17.5% (2006-2010 5-year est.); Ancestry (includes multiple ancestries): 26.8% Irish, 23.7% German, 19.3% Italian, 8.4% Russian, 6.4% Polish (2006-2010 5-year est.).

**Economy:** Single-family building permits issued: 1 (2011); Multi-family building permits issued: 0 (2011); Employment by occupation: 22.4% management, 5.7% professional, 3.0% services, 12.1% sales, 0.5% farming, 9.1% construction, 3.0% production (2006-2010 5-year est.).

**Income:** Per capita income: $77,997 (2006-2010 5-year est.); Median household income: $158,295 (2006-2010 5-year est.); Average household income: $210,097 (2006-2010 5-year est.); Percent of households with income of $100,000 or more: 64.4% (2006-2010 5-year est.); Poverty rate: 9.4% (2006-2010 5-year est.).

**Education:** Percent of population age 25 and over with: High school diploma (including GED) or higher: 99.6% (2006-2010 5-year est.); Bachelor's degree or higher: 72.2% (2006-2010 5-year est.); Master's degree or higher: 43.9% (2006-2010 5-year est.).

**Housing:** Homeownership rate: 98.2% (2010); Median home value: $849,700 (2006-2010 5-year est.); Median contract rent: n/a per month (2006-2010 5-year est.); Median year structure built: 1964 (2006-2010 5-year est.).

**Transportation:** Commute to work: 88.7% car, 6.2% public transportation, 0.0% walk, 5.2% work from home (2006-2010 5-year est.); Travel time to work: 42.6% less than 15 minutes, 20.0% 15 to 30 minutes, 11.2% 30 to 45 minutes, 6.5% 45 to 60 minutes, 19.7% 60 minutes or more (2006-2010 5-year est.)

**BELLPORT** (village). Covers a land area of 1.445 square miles and a water area of 0.091 square miles. Located at 40.75° N. Lat; 72.94° W. Long. Elevation is 26 feet.
**Population:** 2,572 (1990); 2,363 (2000); 2,084 (2010); Density: 1,442.2 persons per square mile (2010); Race: 94.2% White, 1.7% Black, 1.3% Asian, 0.4% American Indian/Alaska Native, 0.0% Native Hawaiian/Other Pacific Islander, 2.4% Other, 4.2% Hispanic of any race (2010); Average household size: 2.26 (2010); Median age: 51.3 (2010); Males per 100 females: 93.5 (2010); Marriage status: 25.6% never married, 61.3% now married, 5.7% widowed, 7.4% divorced (2006-2010 5-year est.); Foreign born: 8.5% (2006-2010 5-year est.); Ancestry (includes multiple ancestries): 29.1% Irish, 20.4% Italian, 15.6% German, 12.9% English, 4.4% American (2006-2010 5-year est.).
**Economy:** Single-family building permits issued: 0 (2011); Multi-family building permits issued: 0 (2011); Employment by occupation: 16.9% management, 5.8% professional, 5.1% services, 12.0% sales, 1.9% farming, 9.3% construction, 1.3% production (2006-2010 5-year est.).
**Income:** Per capita income: $54,743 (2006-2010 5-year est.); Median household income: $80,724 (2006-2010 5-year est.); Average household income: $119,206 (2006-2010 5-year est.); Percent of households with income of $100,000 or more: 35.9% (2006-2010 5-year est.); Poverty rate: 4.1% (2006-2010 5-year est.).
**Education:** Percent of population age 25 and over with: High school diploma (including GED) or higher: 95.8% (2006-2010 5-year est.); Bachelor's degree or higher: 54.1% (2006-2010 5-year est.); Master's degree or higher: 34.5% (2006-2010 5-year est.).

**School District(s)**
South Country Central School District (PK-12)
    2009-10 Enrollment: 4,600 . . . . . . . . . . . . . . . . . . . . . . . (631) 730-1510
**Housing:** Homeownership rate: 84.1% (2010); Median home value: $465,000 (2006-2010 5-year est.); Median contract rent: $1,186 per month (2006-2010 5-year est.); Median year structure built: 1956 (2006-2010 5-year est.).
**Transportation:** Commute to work: 81.1% car, 9.2% public transportation, 2.7% walk, 5.7% work from home (2006-2010 5-year est.); Travel time to work: 18.2% less than 15 minutes, 40.8% 15 to 30 minutes, 17.8% 30 to 45 minutes, 11.5% 45 to 60 minutes, 11.6% 60 minutes or more (2006-2010 5-year est.)
**Additional Information Contacts**
Village of Bellport . . . . . . . . . . . . . . . . . . . . . . . . . . . . . . . (631) 286-0327
  http://www.bellportvillage.com

**BLUE POINT** (CDP). Covers a land area of 1.793 square miles and a water area of 0.005 square miles. Located at 40.75° N. Lat; 73.03° W. Long. Elevation is 10 feet.
**History:** Bluepoint oysters take their name from here.
**Population:** 4,230 (1990); 4,407 (2000); 4,773 (2010); Density: 2,661.1 persons per square mile (2010); Race: 95.3% White, 0.8% Black, 1.7% Asian, 0.2% American Indian/Alaska Native, 0.0% Native Hawaiian/Other Pacific Islander, 2.0% Other, 4.2% Hispanic of any race (2010); Average household size: 2.81 (2010); Median age: 41.3 (2010); Males per 100 females: 96.7 (2010); Marriage status: 27.9% never married, 58.3% now married, 5.8% widowed, 8.1% divorced (2006-2010 5-year est.); Foreign born: 6.5% (2006-2010 5-year est.); Ancestry (includes multiple ancestries): 35.7% Italian, 32.4% Irish, 27.5% German, 12.8% English, 4.8% Dutch (2006-2010 5-year est.).
**Economy:** Employment by occupation: 9.4% management, 2.7% professional, 11.5% services, 14.6% sales, 2.3% farming, 12.2% construction, 5.4% production (2006-2010 5-year est.).
**Income:** Per capita income: $35,372 (2006-2010 5-year est.); Median household income: $90,393 (2006-2010 5-year est.); Average household income: $99,009 (2006-2010 5-year est.); Percent of households with income of $100,000 or more: 44.2% (2006-2010 5-year est.); Poverty rate: 2.2% (2006-2010 5-year est.).
**Education:** Percent of population age 25 and over with: High school diploma (including GED) or higher: 96.1% (2006-2010 5-year est.); Bachelor's degree or higher: 40.1% (2006-2010 5-year est.); Master's degree or higher: 22.2% (2006-2010 5-year est.).

**School District(s)**
Bayport-Blue Point Union Free School District (KG-12)
    2009-10 Enrollment: 2,502 . . . . . . . . . . . . . . . . . . . . . . . (631) 472-7860
**Housing:** Homeownership rate: 88.7% (2010); Median home value: $413,400 (2006-2010 5-year est.); Median contract rent: $1,371 per month (2006-2010 5-year est.); Median year structure built: 1956 (2006-2010 5-year est.).

**Newspapers:** Times Beacon Record (Local news)
**Transportation:** Commute to work: 93.1% car, 3.6% public transportation, 0.3% walk, 3.0% work from home (2006-2010 5-year est.); Travel time to work: 32.7% less than 15 minutes, 34.8% 15 to 30 minutes, 14.7% 30 to 45 minutes, 4.5% 45 to 60 minutes, 13.2% 60 minutes or more (2006-2010 5-year est.)

**BOHEMIA** (CDP). Covers a land area of 8.619 square miles and a water area of 0.036 square miles. Located at 40.77° N. Lat; 73.13° W. Long. Elevation is 66 feet.
**Population:** 9,556 (1990); 9,871 (2000); 10,180 (2010); Density: 1,181.0 persons per square mile (2010); Race: 93.9% White, 1.0% Black, 2.3% Asian, 0.1% American Indian/Alaska Native, 0.0% Native Hawaiian/Other Pacific Islander, 2.7% Other, 7.1% Hispanic of any race (2010); Average household size: 2.77 (2010); Median age: 42.5 (2010); Males per 100 females: 97.0 (2010); Marriage status: 26.1% never married, 57.1% now married, 7.0% widowed, 9.8% divorced (2006-2010 5-year est.); Foreign born: 5.5% (2006-2010 5-year est.); Ancestry (includes multiple ancestries): 37.1% Italian, 29.4% Irish, 26.9% German, 8.7% Polish, 4.0% English (2006-2010 5-year est.).
**Economy:** Employment by occupation: 8.2% management, 6.2% professional, 6.6% services, 17.3% sales, 6.5% farming, 8.2% construction, 5.2% production (2006-2010 5-year est.).
**Income:** Per capita income: $37,686 (2006-2010 5-year est.); Median household income: $91,047 (2006-2010 5-year est.); Average household income: $104,947 (2006-2010 5-year est.); Percent of households with income of $100,000 or more: 47.0% (2006-2010 5-year est.); Poverty rate: 1.8% (2006-2010 5-year est.).
**Education:** Percent of population age 25 and over with: High school diploma (including GED) or higher: 92.5% (2006-2010 5-year est.); Bachelor's degree or higher: 28.7% (2006-2010 5-year est.); Master's degree or higher: 14.0% (2006-2010 5-year est.).

**School District(s)**
Connetquot Central School District (PK-12)
    2009-10 Enrollment: 6,757 . . . . . . . . . . . . . . . . . . . . . . . (631) 244-2215
**Vocational/Technical School(s)**
Branford Hall Career Institute-Bohemia Campus (Private, For-profit)
    Fall 2010 Enrollment: 922 . . . . . . . . . . . . . . . . . . . . . . . (631) 589-1222
    2011-12 Tuition: $10,600
**Housing:** Homeownership rate: 78.7% (2010); Median home value: $441,700 (2006-2010 5-year est.); Median contract rent: $1,242 per month (2006-2010 5-year est.); Median year structure built: 1970 (2006-2010 5-year est.).
**Newspapers:** Carrier Pigeon - Huntington/Cold Spring Harbor Edition (Local news; Circulation 15,000); Our Place (Ronkonkoma Lake Edition) (Local news; Circulation 32,000); Pennysaver News (Community news; Circulation 1,000,000); Pennysaver News Bayport/Blue Point Edition (Local news; Circulation 1,000,000); Pennysaver News Bellport/East Patchogue Edition (Local news; Circulation 1,000,000); Pennysaver News Center & East Moriches/Manorville/Eastport (Local news; Circulation 1,000,000); Pennysaver News Centereach/Lake Grove Edition (Local news; Circulation 1,000,000); Pennysaver News Coram Edition (Local news; Circulation 1,000,000); Pennysaver News East Setauket/Setauket/South Setauket (Local news; Circulation 1,000,000); Pennysaver News Farmingville/Holtsville Edition (Local news; Circulation 1,000,000); Pennysaver News Holbrook Edition (Local news; Circulation 1,000,000); Pennysaver News Medford/Yaphank Edition (Local news; Circulation 1,000,000); Pennysaver News Middle Island/Ridge Edition (Local news; Circulation 1,000,000); Pennysaver News Miller Place/Mount Sinai/Sound Beach Edition (Local news; Circulation 1,000,000); Pennysaver News North Shirley/Mastic Edition (Local news; Circulation 1,000,000); Pennysaver News Oakdale/Bohemia Edition (Community news; Circulation 1,000,000); Pennysaver News Patchogue Edition (Local news; Circulation 1,000,000); Pennysaver News Riverhead/Flanders/Calverton Edition (Local news; Circulation 1,000,000); Pennysaver News Rocky Point/Leisure Knoll/Glenn/Village (Local news; Circulation 1,000,000); Pennysaver News Ronkonkoma Edition (Local news; Circulation 1,000,000); Pennysaver News Selden Edition (Local news; Circulation 1,000,000); Pennysaver News Shoreham/Wading River Edition (Local news; Circulation 1,000,000); Pennysaver News South Shirley/Mastic Beach Edition (Local news; Circulation 8,900); Pennysaver News Stony Brook Edition (Local news); Pennysaver News Westhampton/Quoque/Speonk Edition (Local news; Circulation 1,000,000); Pennysaver South Shore-Bay Shore Edition (Local news; Circulation 16,000); Pennysaver South Shore-Brentwood Edition (Local news; Circulation 1,000,000); Pennysaver South Shore-Deer Park

Edition (Local news; Circulation 1,000,000); Pennysaver South Shore-Islip Edition (Local news; Circulation 1,000,000); Pennysaver South Shore-North Babylon Edition (Local news; Circulation 9,700); Springville Pennysaver (Community news; Circulation 12,150)
**Transportation:** Commute to work: 91.4% car, 3.5% public transportation, 0.4% walk, 2.5% work from home (2006-2010 5-year est.); Travel time to work: 31.1% less than 15 minutes, 34.0% 15 to 30 minutes, 17.7% 30 to 45 minutes, 5.9% 45 to 60 minutes, 11.3% 60 minutes or more (2006-2010 5-year est.)

## BRENTWOOD (CDP).
Covers a land area of 10.980 square miles and a water area of 0 square miles. Located at 40.78° N. Lat; 73.25° W. Long. Elevation is 79 feet.
**History:** Josiah Warren led (1851) an experiment in communal living in Brentwood.
**Population:** 45,218 (1990); 53,917 (2000); 60,664 (2010); Density: 5,524.6 persons per square mile (2010); Race: 48.4% White, 16.4% Black, 2.0% Asian, 1.2% American Indian/Alaska Native, 0.0% Native Hawaiian/Other Pacific Islander, 32.0% Other, 68.5% Hispanic of any race (2010); Average household size: 4.35 (2010); Median age: 32.0 (2010); Males per 100 females: 103.6 (2010); Marriage status: 41.3% never married, 47.0% now married, 5.5% widowed, 6.3% divorced (2006-2010 5-year est.); Foreign born: 42.3% (2006-2010 5-year est.); Ancestry (includes multiple ancestries): 5.9% Italian, 4.7% Irish, 3.9% Haitian, 3.6% German, 1.6% English (2006-2010 5-year est.).
**Economy:** Employment by occupation: 4.8% management, 0.9% professional, 12.0% services, 12.4% sales, 5.8% farming, 9.4% construction, 11.4% production (2006-2010 5-year est.).
**Income:** Per capita income: $20,705 (2006-2010 5-year est.); Median household income: $68,750 (2006-2010 5-year est.); Average household income: $79,089 (2006-2010 5-year est.); Percent of households with income of $100,000 or more: 29.8% (2006-2010 5-year est.); Poverty rate: 8.2% (2006-2010 5-year est.).
**Education:** Percent of population age 25 and over with: High school diploma (including GED) or higher: 69.0% (2006-2010 5-year est.); Bachelor's degree or higher: 14.4% (2006-2010 5-year est.); Master's degree or higher: 5.2% (2006-2010 5-year est.).
**School District(s)**
Brentwood Union Free School District (PK-12)
    2009-10 Enrollment: 16,517 . . . . . . . . . . . . . . (631) 434-2325
**Four-year College(s)**
Long Island University-Brentwood Campus (Private, Not-for-profit)
    Fall 2010 Enrollment: 388 . . . . . . . . . . . . . . . (631) 273-5112
**Housing:** Homeownership rate: 69.6% (2010); Median home value: $343,300 (2006-2010 5-year est.); Median contract rent: $1,137 per month (2006-2010 5-year est.); Median year structure built: 1964 (2006-2010 5-year est.).
**Hospitals:** Pilgrim Psychiatric Center (800 beds)
**Transportation:** Commute to work: 86.7% car, 6.5% public transportation, 1.2% walk, 2.0% work from home (2006-2010 5-year est.); Travel time to work: 22.6% less than 15 minutes, 43.8% 15 to 30 minutes, 17.5% 30 to 45 minutes, 6.3% 45 to 60 minutes, 9.7% 60 minutes or more (2006-2010 5-year est.)

## BRIDGEHAMPTON (CDP).
Covers a land area of 13.010 square miles and a water area of 0.623 square miles. Located at 40.95° N. Lat; 72.31° W. Long. Elevation is 43 feet.
**Population:** 1,518 (1990); 1,381 (2000); 1,756 (2010); Density: 135.0 persons per square mile (2010); Race: 76.3% White, 13.4% Black, 1.2% Asian, 0.3% American Indian/Alaska Native, 0.0% Native Hawaiian/Other Pacific Islander, 8.8% Other, 14.6% Hispanic of any race (2010); Average household size: 2.35 (2010); Median age: 48.3 (2010); Males per 100 females: 101.1 (2010); Marriage status: 22.0% never married, 56.4% now married, 9.4% widowed, 12.2% divorced (2006-2010 5-year est.); Foreign born: 9.8% (2006-2010 5-year est.); Ancestry (includes multiple ancestries): 19.1% English, 14.8% Irish, 10.6% Italian, 7.8% Hungarian, 7.3% German (2006-2010 5-year est.).
**Economy:** Employment by occupation: 20.2% management, 0.8% professional, 10.3% services, 13.9% sales, 5.1% farming, 11.6% construction, 4.6% production (2006-2010 5-year est.).
**Income:** Per capita income: $70,508 (2006-2010 5-year est.); Median household income: $95,000 (2006-2010 5-year est.); Average household income: $144,752 (2006-2010 5-year est.); Percent of households with income of $100,000 or more: 46.6% (2006-2010 5-year est.); Poverty rate: 5.3% (2006-2010 5-year est.).

**Education:** Percent of population age 25 and over with: High school diploma (including GED) or higher: 89.8% (2006-2010 5-year est.); Bachelor's degree or higher: 52.7% (2006-2010 5-year est.); Master's degree or higher: 24.0% (2006-2010 5-year est.).
**School District(s)**
Bridgehampton Union Free School District (PK-12)
    2009-10 Enrollment: 159 . . . . . . . . . . . . . . . (631) 537-0271
**Housing:** Homeownership rate: 77.4% (2010); Median home value: $1 (2006-2010 5-year est.); Median contract rent: $1,375 per month (2006-2010 5-year est.); Median year structure built: 1980 (2006-2010 5-year est.).
**Newspapers:** Dan's Papers (Community news; Circulation 71,000); Montauk Pioneer (Community news; Circulation 10,000)
**Transportation:** Commute to work: 73.2% car, 10.3% public transportation, 4.2% walk, 10.7% work from home (2006-2010 5-year est.); Travel time to work: 44.8% less than 15 minutes, 31.3% 15 to 30 minutes, 15.2% 30 to 45 minutes, 0.0% 45 to 60 minutes, 8.6% 60 minutes or more (2006-2010 5-year est.)

## BRIGHTWATERS (village).
Covers a land area of 0.976 square miles and a water area of 0.022 square miles. Located at 40.71° N. Lat; 73.26° W. Long. Elevation is 23 feet.
**History:** Laid out 1907, incorporated 1916.
**Population:** 3,265 (1990); 3,248 (2000); 3,103 (2010); Density: 3,178.3 persons per square mile (2010); Race: 94.3% White, 1.5% Black, 1.6% Asian, 0.0% American Indian/Alaska Native, 0.0% Native Hawaiian/Other Pacific Islander, 2.6% Other, 5.1% Hispanic of any race (2010); Average household size: 2.75 (2010); Median age: 43.7 (2010); Males per 100 females: 97.6 (2010); Marriage status: 22.6% never married, 69.8% now married, 2.9% widowed, 4.6% divorced (2006-2010 5-year est.); Foreign born: 5.3% (2006-2010 5-year est.); Ancestry (includes multiple ancestries): 37.1% Italian, 36.1% Irish, 22.1% German, 8.4% English, 7.6% Polish (2006-2010 5-year est.).
**Economy:** Single-family building permits issued: 0 (2011); Multi-family building permits issued: 0 (2011); Employment by occupation: 16.2% management, 6.2% professional, 5.9% services, 14.0% sales, 3.9% farming, 4.7% construction, 3.4% production (2006-2010 5-year est.).
**Income:** Per capita income: $48,393 (2006-2010 5-year est.); Median household income: $124,722 (2006-2010 5-year est.); Average household income: $140,355 (2006-2010 5-year est.); Percent of households with income of $100,000 or more: 58.8% (2006-2010 5-year est.); Poverty rate: 4.1% (2006-2010 5-year est.).
**Education:** Percent of population age 25 and over with: High school diploma (including GED) or higher: 96.8% (2006-2010 5-year est.); Bachelor's degree or higher: 53.8% (2006-2010 5-year est.); Master's degree or higher: 26.5% (2006-2010 5-year est.).
**Housing:** Homeownership rate: 90.7% (2010); Median home value: $586,800 (2006-2010 5-year est.); Median contract rent: $1,149 per month (2006-2010 5-year est.); Median year structure built: 1943 (2006-2010 5-year est.).
**Transportation:** Commute to work: 79.8% car, 12.1% public transportation, 1.2% walk, 3.0% work from home (2006-2010 5-year est.); Travel time to work: 34.7% less than 15 minutes, 29.0% 15 to 30 minutes, 13.9% 30 to 45 minutes, 5.4% 45 to 60 minutes, 17.0% 60 minutes or more (2006-2010 5-year est.)

## BROOKHAVEN (town).
Covers a land area of 259.438 square miles and a water area of 272.096 square miles. Located at 40.85° N. Lat; 72.95° W. Long. Elevation is 10 feet.
**History:** Brookhaven was the home of William Floyd (1743-1821), Revolutionary War soldier, statesman, and signer of the Declaration of Independence.
**Population:** 407,832 (1990); 448,248 (2000); 486,040 (2010); Density: 1,873.4 persons per square mile (2010); Race: 84.5% White, 5.5% Black, 3.9% Asian, 0.3% American Indian/Alaska Native, 0.0% Native Hawaiian/Other Pacific Islander, 5.8% Other, 12.4% Hispanic of any race (2010); Average household size: 2.89 (2010); Median age: 38.5 (2010); Males per 100 females: 97.2 (2010); Marriage status: 30.2% never married, 56.1% now married, 6.0% widowed, 7.8% divorced (2006-2010 5-year est.); Foreign born: 10.6% (2006-2010 5-year est.); Ancestry (includes multiple ancestries): 32.4% Italian, 25.5% Irish, 18.7% German, 6.3% English, 5.7% Polish (2006-2010 5-year est.).
**Economy:** Unemployment rate: 8.0% (February 2012); Total civilian labor force: 254,842 (February 2012); Single-family building permits issued: 208 (2011); Multi-family building permits issued: 0 (2011); Employment by

occupation: 10.9% management, 4.4% professional, 8.3% services, 18.7% sales, 4.1% farming, 9.7% construction, 5.7% production (2006-2010 5-year est.).

**Income:** Per capita income: $33,324 (2006-2010 5-year est.); Median household income: $81,937 (2006-2010 5-year est.); Average household income: $96,849 (2006-2010 5-year est.); Percent of households with income of $100,000 or more: 39.0% (2006-2010 5-year est.); Poverty rate: 6.5% (2006-2010 5-year est.).

**Taxes:** Total city taxes per capita: $366 (2009); City property taxes per capita: $315 (2009).

**Education:** Percent of population age 25 and over with: High school diploma (including GED) or higher: 90.4% (2006-2010 5-year est.); Bachelor's degree or higher: 29.4% (2006-2010 5-year est.); Master's degree or higher: 13.6% (2006-2010 5-year est.).

**School District(s)**

South Country Central School District (PK-12)

   2009-10 Enrollment: 4,600 . . . . . . . . . . . . . . . . . . (631) 730-1510

**Housing:** Homeownership rate: 78.8% (2010); Median home value: $371,300 (2006-2010 5-year est.); Median contract rent: $1,313 per month (2006-2010 5-year est.); Median year structure built: 1973 (2006-2010 5-year est.).

**Transportation:** Commute to work: 91.3% car, 3.9% public transportation, 1.4% walk, 2.7% work from home (2006-2010 5-year est.); Travel time to work: 23.0% less than 15 minutes, 33.2% 15 to 30 minutes, 19.9% 30 to 45 minutes, 9.0% 45 to 60 minutes, 14.9% 60 minutes or more (2006-2010 5-year est.)

**Additional Information Contacts**

Town of Brookhaven . . . . . . . . . . . . . . . . . . . . . . . (631) 451-9101
  http://www.brookhaven.org

**BROOKHAVEN** (CDP). Covers a land area of 5.760 square miles and a water area of 0.145 square miles. Located at 40.77° N. Lat; 72.90° W. Long. Elevation is 10 feet.

**Population:** 3,311 (1990); 3,570 (2000); 3,451 (2010); Density: 599.0 persons per square mile (2010); Race: 89.3% White, 6.6% Black, 0.7% Asian, 0.1% American Indian/Alaska Native, 0.0% Native Hawaiian/Other Pacific Islander, 3.3% Other, 6.1% Hispanic of any race (2010); Average household size: 2.55 (2010); Median age: 47.3 (2010); Males per 100 females: 93.2 (2010); Marriage status: 24.0% never married, 57.4% now married, 8.4% widowed, 10.1% divorced (2006-2010 5-year est.); Foreign born: 3.2% (2006-2010 5-year est.); Ancestry (includes multiple ancestries): 26.1% Italian, 22.1% German, 17.3% Irish, 9.9% English, 4.0% Scottish (2006-2010 5-year est.).

**Economy:** Employment by occupation: 9.3% management, 0.0% professional, 9.3% services, 21.3% sales, 3.7% farming, 7.3% construction, 2.0% production (2006-2010 5-year est.).

**Income:** Per capita income: $36,334 (2006-2010 5-year est.); Median household income: $78,452 (2006-2010 5-year est.); Average household income: $98,882 (2006-2010 5-year est.); Percent of households with income of $100,000 or more: 38.3% (2006-2010 5-year est.); Poverty rate: 10.8% (2006-2010 5-year est.).

**Education:** Percent of population age 25 and over with: High school diploma (including GED) or higher: 88.4% (2006-2010 5-year est.); Bachelor's degree or higher: 29.2% (2006-2010 5-year est.); Master's degree or higher: 12.9% (2006-2010 5-year est.).

**School District(s)**

South Country Central School District (PK-12)

   2009-10 Enrollment: 4,600 . . . . . . . . . . . . . . . . . . (631) 730-1510

**Housing:** Homeownership rate: 79.3% (2010); Median home value: $454,700 (2006-2010 5-year est.); Median contract rent: n/a per month (2006-2010 5-year est.); Median year structure built: 1971 (2006-2010 5-year est.).

**Transportation:** Commute to work: 87.5% car, 7.9% public transportation, 1.1% walk, 3.4% work from home (2006-2010 5-year est.); Travel time to work: 15.8% less than 15 minutes, 35.8% 15 to 30 minutes, 16.6% 30 to 45 minutes, 22.8% 45 to 60 minutes, 8.9% 60 minutes or more (2006-2010 5-year est.).

**CALVERTON** (CDP). Covers a land area of 28.026 square miles and a water area of 0.501 square miles. Located at 40.92° N. Lat; 72.76° W. Long. Elevation is 30 feet.

**Population:** 4,759 (1990); 5,704 (2000); 6,510 (2010); Density: 232.3 persons per square mile (2010); Race: 87.2% White, 8.0% Black, 0.9% Asian, 0.2% American Indian/Alaska Native, 0.0% Native Hawaiian/Other Pacific Islander, 3.7% Other, 7.0% Hispanic of any race (2010); Average

household size: 2.19 (2010); Median age: 48.5 (2010); Males per 100 females: 91.5 (2010); Marriage status: 17.9% never married, 58.4% now married, 11.7% widowed, 12.0% divorced (2006-2010 5-year est.); Foreign born: 7.9% (2006-2010 5-year est.); Ancestry (includes multiple ancestries): 26.2% Irish, 23.1% German, 21.8% Italian, 16.3% Polish, 8.3% English (2006-2010 5-year est.).

**Economy:** Employment by occupation: 5.2% management, 3.7% professional, 4.7% services, 14.9% sales, 3.4% farming, 14.2% construction, 6.8% production (2006-2010 5-year est.).

**Income:** Per capita income: $33,079 (2006-2010 5-year est.); Median household income: $56,104 (2006-2010 5-year est.); Average household income: $73,404 (2006-2010 5-year est.); Percent of households with income of $100,000 or more: 28.5% (2006-2010 5-year est.); Poverty rate: 9.1% (2006-2010 5-year est.).

**Education:** Percent of population age 25 and over with: High school diploma (including GED) or higher: 86.7% (2006-2010 5-year est.); Bachelor's degree or higher: 23.1% (2006-2010 5-year est.); Master's degree or higher: 12.3% (2006-2010 5-year est.).

**School District(s)**

Riverhead Central School District (KG-12)

   2009-10 Enrollment: 4,816 . . . . . . . . . . . . . . . . . . (631) 369-6717

Riverhead Charter School (KG-06)

   2009-10 Enrollment: 233 . . . . . . . . . . . . . . . . . . . (631) 369-5800

**Housing:** Homeownership rate: 85.8% (2010); Median home value: $291,100 (2006-2010 5-year est.); Median contract rent: $890 per month (2006-2010 5-year est.); Median year structure built: 1983 (2006-2010 5-year est.).

**Transportation:** Commute to work: 93.4% car, 0.6% public transportation, 0.7% walk, 3.2% work from home (2006-2010 5-year est.); Travel time to work: 22.0% less than 15 minutes, 34.1% 15 to 30 minutes, 17.9% 30 to 45 minutes, 12.8% 45 to 60 minutes, 13.2% 60 minutes or more (2006-2010 5-year est.)

**CENTER MORICHES** (CDP). Covers a land area of 5.216 square miles and a water area of 0.414 square miles. Located at 40.80° N. Lat; 72.79° W. Long. Elevation is 26 feet.

**Population:** 5,987 (1990); 6,655 (2000); 7,580 (2010); Density: 1,453.0 persons per square mile (2010); Race: 89.5% White, 3.5% Black, 1.4% Asian, 0.2% American Indian/Alaska Native, 0.0% Native Hawaiian/Other Pacific Islander, 5.4% Other, 10.2% Hispanic of any race (2010); Average household size: 2.88 (2010); Median age: 39.5 (2010); Males per 100 females: 102.0 (2010); Marriage status: 28.4% never married, 61.4% now married, 5.8% widowed, 4.5% divorced (2006-2010 5-year est.); Foreign born: 9.6% (2006-2010 5-year est.); Ancestry (includes multiple ancestries): 29.2% Italian, 29.1% Irish, 21.9% German, 11.0% English, 9.7% Polish (2006-2010 5-year est.).

**Economy:** Employment by occupation: 15.4% management, 1.6% professional, 4.4% services, 15.3% sales, 5.0% farming, 11.6% construction, 4.1% production (2006-2010 5-year est.).

**Income:** Per capita income: $36,374 (2006-2010 5-year est.); Median household income: $91,250 (2006-2010 5-year est.); Average household income: $104,446 (2006-2010 5-year est.); Percent of households with income of $100,000 or more: 44.4% (2006-2010 5-year est.); Poverty rate: 4.2% (2006-2010 5-year est.).

**Education:** Percent of population age 25 and over with: High school diploma (including GED) or higher: 86.9% (2006-2010 5-year est.); Bachelor's degree or higher: 27.9% (2006-2010 5-year est.); Master's degree or higher: 12.4% (2006-2010 5-year est.).

**School District(s)**

Center Moriches Union Free School District (PK-12)

   2009-10 Enrollment: 1,593 . . . . . . . . . . . . . . . . . . (631) 878-0052

**Housing:** Homeownership rate: 80.6% (2010); Median home value: $413,400 (2006-2010 5-year est.); Median contract rent: $1,292 per month (2006-2010 5-year est.); Median year structure built: 1969 (2006-2010 5-year est.).

**Transportation:** Commute to work: 94.0% car, 1.6% public transportation, 1.2% walk, 2.9% work from home (2006-2010 5-year est.); Travel time to work: 26.0% less than 15 minutes, 30.4% 15 to 30 minutes, 21.4% 30 to 45 minutes, 11.0% 45 to 60 minutes, 11.1% 60 minutes or more (2006-2010 5-year est.)

**CENTEREACH** (CDP). Covers a land area of 8.714 square miles and a water area of 0 square miles. Located at 40.86° N. Lat; 73.08° W. Long. Elevation is 98 feet.
**Population:** 26,720 (1990); 27,285 (2000); 31,578 (2010); Density: 3,623.6 persons per square mile (2010); Race: 85.4% White, 3.1% Black, 6.2% Asian, 0.1% American Indian/Alaska Native, 0.0% Native Hawaiian/Other Pacific Islander, 5.2% Other, 11.3% Hispanic of any race (2010); Average household size: 3.13 (2010); Median age: 38.9 (2010); Males per 100 females: 99.7 (2010); Marriage status: 28.6% never married, 58.2% now married, 6.0% widowed, 7.2% divorced (2006-2010 5-year est.); Foreign born: 12.9% (2006-2010 5-year est.); Ancestry (includes multiple ancestries): 36.0% Italian, 23.5% Irish, 17.0% German, 6.6% Polish, 5.3% English (2006-2010 5-year est.).
**Economy:** Employment by occupation: 11.1% management, 3.6% professional, 7.5% services, 20.4% sales, 3.7% farming, 8.8% construction, 6.8% production (2006-2010 5-year est.).
**Income:** Per capita income: $33,008 (2006-2010 5-year est.); Median household income: $90,930 (2006-2010 5-year est.); Average household income: $101,826 (2006-2010 5-year est.); Percent of households with income of $100,000 or more: 44.2% (2006-2010 5-year est.); Poverty rate: 4.5% (2006-2010 5-year est.).
**Education:** Percent of population age 25 and over with: High school diploma (including GED) or higher: 89.7% (2006-2010 5-year est.); Bachelor's degree or higher: 27.4% (2006-2010 5-year est.); Master's degree or higher: 10.7% (2006-2010 5-year est.).

#### School District(s)
Middle Country Central School District (PK-12)
    2009-10 Enrollment: 10,929 . . . . . . . . . . . . . . . . . . . . . (631) 285-8005
**Housing:** Homeownership rate: 84.3% (2010); Median home value: $376,600 (2006-2010 5-year est.); Median contract rent: $1,549 per month (2006-2010 5-year est.); Median year structure built: 1967 (2006-2010 5-year est.).
**Transportation:** Commute to work: 93.3% car, 3.1% public transportation, 0.9% walk, 1.9% work from home (2006-2010 5-year est.); Travel time to work: 23.5% less than 15 minutes, 31.5% 15 to 30 minutes, 21.3% 30 to 45 minutes, 9.4% 45 to 60 minutes, 14.3% 60 minutes or more (2006-2010 5-year est.)

**CENTERPORT** (CDP). Covers a land area of 2.104 square miles and a water area of 0.190 square miles. Located at 40.90° N. Lat; 73.37° W. Long. Elevation is 49 feet.
**History:** Formerly known as Little Cow Harbor about 1700, Centreport in 1836, and then the present Centerport after 1895. The name refers to its geographic position midway between the east and west boundaries of the township of Huntington.
**Population:** 5,333 (1990); 5,446 (2000); 5,508 (2010); Density: 2,617.5 persons per square mile (2010); Race: 96.3% White, 0.5% Black, 1.9% Asian, 0.1% American Indian/Alaska Native, 0.0% Native Hawaiian/Other Pacific Islander, 1.2% Other, 3.5% Hispanic of any race (2010); Average household size: 2.71 (2010); Median age: 44.7 (2010); Males per 100 females: 91.1 (2010); Marriage status: 22.5% never married, 63.4% now married, 5.3% widowed, 8.8% divorced (2006-2010 5-year est.); Foreign born: 8.1% (2006-2010 5-year est.); Ancestry (includes multiple ancestries): 31.1% Italian, 24.3% Irish, 21.6% German, 8.6% English, 4.3% Polish (2006-2010 5-year est.).
**Economy:** Employment by occupation: 21.8% management, 3.7% professional, 4.8% services, 13.1% sales, 2.1% farming, 6.0% construction, 3.4% production (2006-2010 5-year est.).
**Income:** Per capita income: $47,831 (2006-2010 5-year est.); Median household income: $98,843 (2006-2010 5-year est.); Average household income: $129,447 (2006-2010 5-year est.); Percent of households with income of $100,000 or more: 48.2% (2006-2010 5-year est.); Poverty rate: 3.7% (2006-2010 5-year est.).
**Education:** Percent of population age 25 and over with: High school diploma (including GED) or higher: 96.4% (2006-2010 5-year est.); Bachelor's degree or higher: 57.7% (2006-2010 5-year est.); Master's degree or higher: 28.0% (2006-2010 5-year est.).

#### School District(s)
Harborfields Central School District (KG-12)
    2009-10 Enrollment: 3,664 . . . . . . . . . . . . . . . . . . . . . . (631) 754-5320
**Housing:** Homeownership rate: 90.7% (2010); Median home value: $608,400 (2006-2010 5-year est.); Median contract rent: $1,607 per month (2006-2010 5-year est.); Median year structure built: 1954 (2006-2010 5-year est.).

**Transportation:** Commute to work: 79.5% car, 7.5% public transportation, 1.0% walk, 11.4% work from home (2006-2010 5-year est.); Travel time to work: 17.4% less than 15 minutes, 24.0% 15 to 30 minutes, 31.2% 30 to 45 minutes, 10.0% 45 to 60 minutes, 17.3% 60 minutes or more (2006-2010 5-year est.)

**CENTRAL ISLIP** (CDP). Covers a land area of 7.111 square miles and a water area of 0 square miles. Located at 40.78° N. Lat; 73.19° W. Long. Elevation is 85 feet.
**Population:** 27,789 (1990); 31,950 (2000); 34,450 (2010); Density: 4,844.5 persons per square mile (2010); Race: 43.6% White, 25.0% Black, 3.4% Asian, 0.9% American Indian/Alaska Native, 0.0% Native Hawaiian/Other Pacific Islander, 27.1% Other, 52.1% Hispanic of any race (2010); Average household size: 3.66 (2010); Median age: 32.6 (2010); Males per 100 females: 98.5 (2010); Marriage status: 40.3% never married, 46.4% now married, 4.9% widowed, 8.4% divorced (2006-2010 5-year est.); Foreign born: 36.7% (2006-2010 5-year est.); Ancestry (includes multiple ancestries): 6.6% Italian, 6.5% Irish, 4.9% German, 4.3% Haitian, 1.9% Polish (2006-2010 5-year est.).
**Economy:** Employment by occupation: 6.4% management, 3.7% professional, 12.7% services, 16.7% sales, 5.3% farming, 10.3% construction, 10.2% production (2006-2010 5-year est.).
**Income:** Per capita income: $21,925 (2006-2010 5-year est.); Median household income: $68,876 (2006-2010 5-year est.); Average household income: $77,350 (2006-2010 5-year est.); Percent of households with income of $100,000 or more: 24.8% (2006-2010 5-year est.); Poverty rate: 9.4% (2006-2010 5-year est.).
**Education:** Percent of population age 25 and over with: High school diploma (including GED) or higher: 72.9% (2006-2010 5-year est.); Bachelor's degree or higher: 16.5% (2006-2010 5-year est.); Master's degree or higher: 6.7% (2006-2010 5-year est.).

#### School District(s)
Central Islip Union Free School District (PK-12)
    2009-10 Enrollment: 6,500 . . . . . . . . . . . . . . . . . . . . . . (631) 348-5001
**Housing:** Homeownership rate: 68.9% (2010); Median home value: $327,000 (2006-2010 5-year est.); Median contract rent: $1,277 per month (2006-2010 5-year est.); Median year structure built: 1969 (2006-2010 5-year est.).
**Transportation:** Commute to work: 89.9% car, 4.4% public transportation, 1.0% walk, 1.2% work from home (2006-2010 5-year est.); Travel time to work: 24.3% less than 15 minutes, 37.3% 15 to 30 minutes, 20.8% 30 to 45 minutes, 6.5% 45 to 60 minutes, 11.1% 60 minutes or more (2006-2010 5-year est.)
**Additional Information Contacts**
Islip Chamber of Commerce . . . . . . . . . . . . . . . . . . . . . . . (631) 581-2720
    http://www.islipchamberofcommerce.com

**COLD SPRING HARBOR** (CDP). Covers a land area of 3.665 square miles and a water area of 0.169 square miles. Located at 40.85° N. Lat; 73.45° W. Long. Elevation is 33 feet.
**History:** Was 19th-century whaling port.
**Population:** 4,789 (1990); 4,975 (2000); 5,070 (2010); Density: 1,383.3 persons per square mile (2010); Race: 95.4% White, 0.7% Black, 2.3% Asian, 0.0% American Indian/Alaska Native, 0.0% Native Hawaiian/Other Pacific Islander, 1.6% Other, 3.8% Hispanic of any race (2010); Average household size: 2.87 (2010); Median age: 43.8 (2010); Males per 100 females: 96.3 (2010); Marriage status: 18.9% never married, 71.3% now married, 5.1% widowed, 4.7% divorced (2006-2010 5-year est.); Foreign born: 7.6% (2006-2010 5-year est.); Ancestry (includes multiple ancestries): 31.9% Irish, 31.3% Italian, 13.2% German, 8.8% English, 6.5% Polish (2006-2010 5-year est.).
**Economy:** Employment by occupation: 24.0% management, 7.1% professional, 3.9% services, 11.6% sales, 1.4% farming, 4.3% construction, 1.6% production (2006-2010 5-year est.).
**Income:** Per capita income: $63,436 (2006-2010 5-year est.); Median household income: $134,821 (2006-2010 5-year est.); Average household income: $187,828 (2006-2010 5-year est.); Percent of households with income of $100,000 or more: 68.6% (2006-2010 5-year est.); Poverty rate: 2.5% (2006-2010 5-year est.).
**Education:** Percent of population age 25 and over with: High school diploma (including GED) or higher: 95.4% (2006-2010 5-year est.); Bachelor's degree or higher: 64.3% (2006-2010 5-year est.); Master's degree or higher: 33.0% (2006-2010 5-year est.).

**School District(s)**
Cold Spring Harbor Central School District (KG-12)
2009-10 Enrollment: 2,018 . . . . . . . . . . . . . . . . . . . . . . . . . (631) 367-5931
**Housing:** Homeownership rate: 88.1% (2010); Median home value: $827,100 (2006-2010 5-year est.); Median contract rent: $638 per month (2006-2010 5-year est.); Median year structure built: 1957 (2006-2010 5-year est.).
**Transportation:** Commute to work: 77.9% car, 13.0% public transportation, 1.2% walk, 7.5% work from home (2006-2010 5-year est.); Travel time to work: 23.7% less than 15 minutes, 24.3% 15 to 30 minutes, 25.6% 30 to 45 minutes, 5.7% 45 to 60 minutes, 20.7% 60 minutes or more (2006-2010 5-year est.)

**COMMACK** (CDP). Covers a land area of 11.968 square miles and a water area of 0 square miles. Located at 40.84° N. Lat; 73.28° W. Long. Elevation is 131 feet.
**Population:** 36,124 (1990); 36,367 (2000); 36,124 (2010); Density: 3,018.2 persons per square mile (2010); Race: 91.6% White, 0.9% Black, 5.4% Asian, 0.1% American Indian/Alaska Native, 0.0% Native Hawaiian/Other Pacific Islander, 2.0% Other, 4.8% Hispanic of any race (2010); Average household size: 2.99 (2010); Median age: 43.0 (2010); Males per 100 females: 94.1 (2010); Marriage status: 23.1% never married, 66.3% now married, 6.8% widowed, 3.8% divorced (2006-2010 5-year est.); Foreign born: 9.9% (2006-2010 5-year est.); Ancestry (includes multiple ancestries): 36.7% Italian, 21.2% Irish, 17.1% German, 9.0% Polish, 7.1% Russian (2006-2010 5-year est.).
**Economy:** Employment by occupation: 19.0% management, 4.6% professional, 5.3% services, 16.2% sales, 3.2% farming, 6.0% construction, 2.8% production (2006-2010 5-year est.).
**Income:** Per capita income: $40,773 (2006-2010 5-year est.); Median household income: $107,512 (2006-2010 5-year est.); Average household income: $126,686 (2006-2010 5-year est.); Percent of households with income of $100,000 or more: 55.1% (2006-2010 5-year est.); Poverty rate: 1.9% (2006-2010 5-year est.).
**Education:** Percent of population age 25 and over with: High school diploma (including GED) or higher: 95.9% (2006-2010 5-year est.); Bachelor's degree or higher: 45.3% (2006-2010 5-year est.); Master's degree or higher: 20.0% (2006-2010 5-year est.).

**School District(s)**
Commack Union Free School District (KG-12)
2009-10 Enrollment: 7,671 . . . . . . . . . . . . . . . . . . . . . . . (631) 912-2010
**Housing:** Homeownership rate: 91.2% (2010); Median home value: $524,200 (2006-2010 5-year est.); Median contract rent: $1,641 per month (2006-2010 5-year est.); Median year structure built: 1963 (2006-2010 5-year est.).
**Transportation:** Commute to work: 88.6% car, 6.4% public transportation, 0.9% walk, 4.1% work from home (2006-2010 5-year est.); Travel time to work: 23.8% less than 15 minutes, 32.7% 15 to 30 minutes, 19.5% 30 to 45 minutes, 7.3% 45 to 60 minutes, 16.8% 60 minutes or more (2006-2010 5-year est.)

**COPIAGUE** (CDP). Covers a land area of 3.218 square miles and a water area of 0.028 square miles. Located at 40.67° N. Lat; 73.39° W. Long. Elevation is 23 feet.
**Population:** 20,769 (1990); 21,922 (2000); 22,993 (2010); Density: 7,144.3 persons per square mile (2010); Race: 73.5% White, 7.6% Black, 2.2% Asian, 0.3% American Indian/Alaska Native, 0.0% Native Hawaiian/Other Pacific Islander, 16.4% Other, 32.7% Hispanic of any race (2010); Average household size: 3.04 (2010); Median age: 38.4 (2010); Males per 100 females: 99.2 (2010); Marriage status: 31.4% never married, 53.8% now married, 5.9% widowed, 8.9% divorced (2006-2010 5-year est.); Foreign born: 26.9% (2006-2010 5-year est.); Ancestry (includes multiple ancestries): 28.6% Italian, 16.2% German, 16.1% Irish, 11.1% Polish, 3.2% English (2006-2010 5-year est.).
**Economy:** Employment by occupation: 8.0% management, 3.5% professional, 8.7% services, 18.7% sales, 4.9% farming, 12.9% construction, 11.1% production (2006-2010 5-year est.).
**Income:** Per capita income: $30,276 (2006-2010 5-year est.); Median household income: $71,828 (2006-2010 5-year est.); Average household income: $86,089 (2006-2010 5-year est.); Percent of households with income of $100,000 or more: 29.6% (2006-2010 5-year est.); Poverty rate: 6.5% (2006-2010 5-year est.).
**Education:** Percent of population age 25 and over with: High school diploma (including GED) or higher: 82.9% (2006-2010 5-year est.);

Bachelor's degree or higher: 19.5% (2006-2010 5-year est.); Master's degree or higher: 6.8% (2006-2010 5-year est.).
**School District(s)**
Copiague Union Free School District (KG-12)
2009-10 Enrollment: 4,663 . . . . . . . . . . . . . . . . . . . . . . . (631) 842-4015
**Housing:** Homeownership rate: 72.0% (2010); Median home value: $369,400 (2006-2010 5-year est.); Median contract rent: $1,200 per month (2006-2010 5-year est.); Median year structure built: 1959 (2006-2010 5-year est.).
**Transportation:** Commute to work: 84.9% car, 7.4% public transportation, 1.2% walk, 4.3% work from home (2006-2010 5-year est.); Travel time to work: 26.3% less than 15 minutes, 30.9% 15 to 30 minutes, 25.6% 30 to 45 minutes, 7.4% 45 to 60 minutes, 9.8% 60 minutes or more (2006-2010 5-year est.)
**Additional Information Contacts**
Copiague Chamber of Commerce . . . . . . . . . . . . . . . . . . . . (631) 226-2956
http://copiaguechamber.org

**CORAM** (CDP). Covers a land area of 13.824 square miles and a water area of 0 square miles. Located at 40.88° N. Lat; 73.00° W. Long. Elevation is 95 feet.
**Population:** 30,173 (1990); 34,923 (2000); 39,113 (2010); Density: 2,829.3 persons per square mile (2010); Race: 77.4% White, 10.6% Black, 5.0% Asian, 0.2% American Indian/Alaska Native, 0.0% Native Hawaiian/Other Pacific Islander, 6.8% Other, 13.6% Hispanic of any race (2010); Average household size: 2.66 (2010); Median age: 38.7 (2010); Males per 100 females: 93.2 (2010); Marriage status: 28.4% never married, 53.5% now married, 6.4% widowed, 11.6% divorced (2006-2010 5-year est.); Foreign born: 14.9% (2006-2010 5-year est.); Ancestry (includes multiple ancestries): 30.2% Italian, 19.8% Irish, 16.6% German, 6.2% Polish, 4.5% English (2006-2010 5-year est.).
**Economy:** Employment by occupation: 9.8% management, 5.1% professional, 7.5% services, 20.2% sales, 4.1% farming, 6.7% construction, 5.6% production (2006-2010 5-year est.).
**Income:** Per capita income: $34,546 (2006-2010 5-year est.); Median household income: $77,692 (2006-2010 5-year est.); Average household income: $90,334 (2006-2010 5-year est.); Percent of households with income of $100,000 or more: 36.2% (2006-2010 5-year est.); Poverty rate: 7.3% (2006-2010 5-year est.).
**Education:** Percent of population age 25 and over with: High school diploma (including GED) or higher: 92.0% (2006-2010 5-year est.); Bachelor's degree or higher: 31.2% (2006-2010 5-year est.); Master's degree or higher: 12.9% (2006-2010 5-year est.).
**School District(s)**
Longwood Central School District (KG-12)
2009-10 Enrollment: 9,154 . . . . . . . . . . . . . . . . . . . . . . . (631) 345-2172
**Housing:** Homeownership rate: 67.9% (2010); Median home value: $346,500 (2006-2010 5-year est.); Median contract rent: $1,348 per month (2006-2010 5-year est.); Median year structure built: 1978 (2006-2010 5-year est.).
**Transportation:** Commute to work: 92.6% car, 4.2% public transportation, 0.5% walk, 1.8% work from home (2006-2010 5-year est.); Travel time to work: 15.9% less than 15 minutes, 38.0% 15 to 30 minutes, 19.2% 30 to 45 minutes, 9.6% 45 to 60 minutes, 17.3% 60 minutes or more (2006-2010 5-year est.)

**CUTCHOGUE** (CDP). Covers a land area of 9.723 square miles and a water area of 0.427 square miles. Located at 41.02° N. Lat; 72.48° W. Long. Elevation is 30 feet.
**Population:** 2,627 (1990); 2,849 (2000); 3,349 (2010); Density: 344.4 persons per square mile (2010); Race: 94.7% White, 1.8% Black, 0.8% Asian, 0.0% American Indian/Alaska Native, 0.0% Native Hawaiian/Other Pacific Islander, 2.7% Other, 7.2% Hispanic of any race (2010); Average household size: 2.46 (2010); Median age: 49.4 (2010); Males per 100 females: 102.0 (2010); Marriage status: 22.0% never married, 60.3% now married, 11.0% widowed, 6.7% divorced (2006-2010 5-year est.); Foreign born: 3.9% (2006-2010 5-year est.); Ancestry (includes multiple ancestries): 29.5% German, 27.3% Irish, 17.0% Italian, 13.5% Polish, 10.3% English (2006-2010 5-year est.).
**Economy:** Employment by occupation: 16.7% management, 2.4% professional, 6.2% services, 17.7% sales, 4.3% farming, 8.7% construction, 2.9% production (2006-2010 5-year est.).
**Income:** Per capita income: $40,594 (2006-2010 5-year est.); Median household income: $82,574 (2006-2010 5-year est.); Average household income: $100,040 (2006-2010 5-year est.); Percent of households with

income of $100,000 or more: 39.9% (2006-2010 5-year est.); Poverty rate: 4.1% (2006-2010 5-year est.).

**Education:** Percent of population age 25 and over with: High school diploma (including GED) or higher: 88.6% (2006-2010 5-year est.); Bachelor's degree or higher: 38.1% (2006-2010 5-year est.); Master's degree or higher: 20.5% (2006-2010 5-year est.).

**School District(s)**

Mattituck-Cutchogue Union Free School District (KG-12)

   2009-10 Enrollment: 1,514 . . . . . . . . . . . . . . . . . . . . . . (631) 298-4242

**Housing:** Homeownership rate: 84.2% (2010); Median home value: $640,100 (2006-2010 5-year est.); Median contract rent: $727 per month (2006-2010 5-year est.); Median year structure built: 1968 (2006-2010 5-year est.).

**Transportation:** Commute to work: 95.1% car, 2.3% public transportation, 0.0% walk, 0.8% work from home (2006-2010 5-year est.); Travel time to work: 42.3% less than 15 minutes, 23.0% 15 to 30 minutes, 13.3% 30 to 45 minutes, 3.6% 45 to 60 minutes, 17.8% 60 minutes or more (2006-2010 5-year est.)

**Additional Information Contacts**

North Fork Chamber of Commerce . . . . . . . . . . . . . . . . . (631) 765-3161

   http://northforkchamberofcommerce.org

**DEER PARK** (CDP). Covers a land area of 6.167 square miles and a water area of 0.003 square miles. Located at 40.76° N. Lat; 73.32° W. Long. Elevation is 85 feet.

**Population:** 29,019 (1990); 28,316 (2000); 27,745 (2010); Density: 4,498.5 persons per square mile (2010); Race: 74.9% White, 12.0% Black, 6.8% Asian, 0.2% American Indian/Alaska Native, 0.0% Native Hawaiian/Other Pacific Islander, 6.1% Other, 12.1% Hispanic of any race (2010); Average household size: 2.95 (2010); Median age: 40.7 (2010); Males per 100 females: 93.8 (2010); Marriage status: 28.5% never married, 56.8% now married, 7.7% widowed, 7.0% divorced (2006-2010 5-year est.); Foreign born: 15.8% (2006-2010 5-year est.); Ancestry (includes multiple ancestries): 36.0% Italian, 19.0% Irish, 13.4% German, 3.7% English, 3.4% Polish (2006-2010 5-year est.).

**Economy:** Employment by occupation: 11.1% management, 4.9% professional, 7.0% services, 19.6% sales, 4.0% farming, 10.4% construction, 6.5% production (2006-2010 5-year est.).

**Income:** Per capita income: $30,020 (2006-2010 5-year est.); Median household income: $78,325 (2006-2010 5-year est.); Average household income: $86,821 (2006-2010 5-year est.); Percent of households with income of $100,000 or more: 37.1% (2006-2010 5-year est.); Poverty rate: 6.0% (2006-2010 5-year est.).

**Education:** Percent of population age 25 and over with: High school diploma (including GED) or higher: 88.8% (2006-2010 5-year est.); Bachelor's degree or higher: 23.5% (2006-2010 5-year est.); Master's degree or higher: 7.9% (2006-2010 5-year est.).

**School District(s)**

Deer Park Union Free School District (PK-12)

   2009-10 Enrollment: 4,386 . . . . . . . . . . . . . . . . . . . . . . (631) 274-4010

**Housing:** Homeownership rate: 80.8% (2010); Median home value: $393,600 (2006-2010 5-year est.); Median contract rent: $1,206 per month (2006-2010 5-year est.); Median year structure built: 1962 (2006-2010 5-year est.).

**Transportation:** Commute to work: 86.8% car, 8.3% public transportation, 0.9% walk, 3.5% work from home (2006-2010 5-year est.); Travel time to work: 18.9% less than 15 minutes, 36.0% 15 to 30 minutes, 20.3% 30 to 45 minutes, 7.3% 45 to 60 minutes, 17.5% 60 minutes or more (2006-2010 5-year est.)

**DERING HARBOR** (village). Covers a land area of 0.245 square miles and a water area of 0.013 square miles. Located at 41.09° N. Lat; 72.34° W. Long. Elevation is 7 feet.

**Population:** 28 (1990); 13 (2000); 11 (2010); Density: 44.8 persons per square mile (2010); Race: 100.0% White, 0.0% Black, 0.0% Asian, 0.0% American Indian/Alaska Native, 0.0% Native Hawaiian/Other Pacific Islander, 0.0% Other, 0.0% Hispanic of any race (2010); Average household size: 2.20 (2010); Median age: 61.5 (2010); Males per 100 females: 120.0 (2010); Marriage status: 0.0% never married, 100.0% now married, 0.0% widowed, 0.0% divorced (2006-2010 5-year est.); Foreign born: 31.3% (2006-2010 5-year est.); Ancestry (includes multiple ancestries): 50.0% English, 31.3% Turkish, 31.3% Scottish (2006-2010 5-year est.).

**Economy:** Single-family building permits issued: 0 (2011); Multi-family building permits issued: 0 (2011); Employment by occupation: 0.0%

management, 0.0% professional, 50.0% services, 0.0% sales, 0.0% farming, 0.0% construction, 0.0% production (2006-2010 5-year est.).

**Income:** Per capita income: $30,338 (2006-2010 5-year est.); Median household income: $75,500 (2006-2010 5-year est.); Average household income: $0 (2006-2010 5-year est.); Percent of households with income of $100,000 or more: 0.0% (2006-2010 5-year est.); Poverty rate: 0.0% (2006-2010 5-year est.).

**Education:** Percent of population age 25 and over with: High school diploma (including GED) or higher: 100.0% (2006-2010 5-year est.); Bachelor's degree or higher: 100.0% (2006-2010 5-year est.); Master's degree or higher: 62.5% (2006-2010 5-year est.).

**Housing:** Homeownership rate: 100.0% (2010); Median home value: $950,000 (2006-2010 5-year est.); Median contract rent: n/a per month (2006-2010 5-year est.); Median year structure built: before 1940 (2006-2010 5-year est.).

**Transportation:** Commute to work: 0.0% car, 50.0% public transportation, 0.0% walk, 50.0% work from home (2006-2010 5-year est.); Travel time to work: 0.0% less than 15 minutes, 0.0% 15 to 30 minutes, 0.0% 30 to 45 minutes, 0.0% 45 to 60 minutes, 100.0% 60 minutes or more (2006-2010 5-year est.)

**DIX HILLS** (CDP). Covers a land area of 15.946 square miles and a water area of 0 square miles. Located at 40.80° N. Lat; 73.33° W. Long. Elevation is 203 feet.

**Population:** 25,849 (1990); 26,024 (2000); 26,892 (2010); Density: 1,686.4 persons per square mile (2010); Race: 79.9% White, 5.5% Black, 11.2% Asian, 0.1% American Indian/Alaska Native, 0.0% Native Hawaiian/Other Pacific Islander, 3.3% Other, 5.7% Hispanic of any race (2010); Average household size: 3.19 (2010); Median age: 42.4 (2010); Males per 100 females: 98.9 (2010); Marriage status: 23.8% never married, 67.1% now married, 4.4% widowed, 4.7% divorced (2006-2010 5-year est.); Foreign born: 16.7% (2006-2010 5-year est.); Ancestry (includes multiple ancestries): 27.7% Italian, 12.9% Irish, 11.4% German, 7.4% Polish, 7.3% Russian (2006-2010 5-year est.).

**Economy:** Employment by occupation: 21.0% management, 3.3% professional, 3.3% services, 16.1% sales, 2.4% farming, 4.9% construction, 2.9% production (2006-2010 5-year est.).

**Income:** Per capita income: $55,881 (2006-2010 5-year est.); Median household income: $146,316 (2006-2010 5-year est.); Average household income: $180,838 (2006-2010 5-year est.); Percent of households with income of $100,000 or more: 70.1% (2006-2010 5-year est.); Poverty rate: 1.4% (2006-2010 5-year est.).

**Education:** Percent of population age 25 and over with: High school diploma (including GED) or higher: 95.5% (2006-2010 5-year est.); Bachelor's degree or higher: 56.9% (2006-2010 5-year est.); Master's degree or higher: 29.4% (2006-2010 5-year est.).

**School District(s)**

Commack Union Free School District (KG-12)

   2009-10 Enrollment: 7,671 . . . . . . . . . . . . . . . . . . . . . (631) 912-2010

Half Hollow Hills Central School District (KG-12)

   2009-10 Enrollment: 10,037 . . . . . . . . . . . . . . . . . . . . (631) 592-3008

Western Suffolk Boces

   2009-10 Enrollment: n/a . . . . . . . . . . . . . . . . . . . . . . . (631) 549-4900

**Four-year College(s)**

Five Towns College (Private, For-profit)

   Fall 2010 Enrollment: 1,071 . . . . . . . . . . . . . . . . . . . . (631) 424-7000

   2011-12 Tuition: In-state $19,570; Out-of-state $19,570

**Housing:** Homeownership rate: 92.9% (2010); Median home value: $750,800 (2006-2010 5-year est.); Median contract rent: $1,375 per month (2006-2010 5-year est.); Median year structure built: 1968 (2006-2010 5-year est.).

**Hospitals:** Sagamore Childrens Psychiatric Center (69 beds)

**Transportation:** Commute to work: 84.4% car, 9.2% public transportation, 0.9% walk, 5.4% work from home (2006-2010 5-year est.); Travel time to work: 19.7% less than 15 minutes, 34.3% 15 to 30 minutes, 14.9% 30 to 45 minutes, 8.0% 45 to 60 minutes, 23.1% 60 minutes or more (2006-2010 5-year est.)

**EAST FARMINGDALE** (CDP). Covers a land area of 5.715 square miles and a water area of 0.019 square miles. Located at 40.73° N. Lat; 73.41° W. Long. Elevation is 69 feet.

**Population:** 4,255 (1990); 5,400 (2000); 6,484 (2010); Density: 1,134.6 persons per square mile (2010); Race: 71.6% White, 12.5% Black, 5.1% Asian, 0.2% American Indian/Alaska Native, 0.1% Native Hawaiian/Other Pacific Islander, 10.5% Other, 20.9% Hispanic of any race (2010); Average

household size: 3.00 (2010); Median age: 35.6 (2010); Males per 100 females: 100.9 (2010); Marriage status: 36.8% never married, 52.9% now married, 5.2% widowed, 5.1% divorced (2006-2010 5-year est.); Foreign born: 20.3% (2006-2010 5-year est.); Ancestry (includes multiple ancestries): 24.6% Italian, 20.2% Irish, 12.9% German, 4.9% Polish, 4.5% Haitian (2006-2010 5-year est.).

**Economy:** Employment by occupation: 11.2% management, 3.0% professional, 13.4% services, 18.6% sales, 4.1% farming, 8.6% construction, 8.4% production (2006-2010 5-year est.).

**Income:** Per capita income: $32,187 (2006-2010 5-year est.); Median household income: $90,577 (2006-2010 5-year est.); Average household income: $94,703 (2006-2010 5-year est.); Percent of households with income of $100,000 or more: 43.3% (2006-2010 5-year est.); Poverty rate: 2.9% (2006-2010 5-year est.).

**Education:** Percent of population age 25 and over with: High school diploma (including GED) or higher: 84.9% (2006-2010 5-year est.); Bachelor's degree or higher: 20.7% (2006-2010 5-year est.); Master's degree or higher: 7.1% (2006-2010 5-year est.).

**Housing:** Homeownership rate: 68.7% (2010); Median home value: $443,700 (2006-2010 5-year est.); Median contract rent: $1,208 per month (2006-2010 5-year est.); Median year structure built: 1959 (2006-2010 5-year est.).

**Transportation:** Commute to work: 82.1% car, 8.5% public transportation, 3.1% walk, 3.1% work from home (2006-2010 5-year est.); Travel time to work: 32.9% less than 15 minutes, 35.2% 15 to 30 minutes, 15.8% 30 to 45 minutes, 8.3% 45 to 60 minutes, 7.8% 60 minutes or more (2006-2010 5-year est.)

**EAST HAMPTON** (village). Covers a land area of 4.763 square miles and a water area of 0.138 square miles. Located at 40.95° N. Lat; 72.19° W. Long. Elevation is 33 feet.

**Population:** 1,403 (1990); 1,334 (2000); 1,083 (2010); Density: 227.3 persons per square mile (2010); Race: 92.7% White, 0.7% Black, 1.1% Asian, 0.0% American Indian/Alaska Native, 0.0% Native Hawaiian/Other Pacific Islander, 5.5% Other, 11.8% Hispanic of any race (2010); Average household size: 2.03 (2010); Median age: 55.5 (2010); Males per 100 females: 90.7 (2010); Marriage status: 21.3% never married, 62.8% now married, 8.2% widowed, 7.8% divorced (2006-2010 5-year est.); Foreign born: 11.0% (2006-2010 5-year est.); Ancestry (includes multiple ancestries): 17.3% German, 15.2% Irish, 13.3% English, 8.0% Scottish, 7.8% Italian (2006-2010 5-year est.).

**Economy:** Single-family building permits issued: 9 (2011); Multi-family building permits issued: 0 (2011); Employment by occupation: 18.5% management, 6.2% professional, 2.1% services, 27.6% sales, 4.9% farming, 4.5% construction, 0.9% production (2006-2010 5-year est.).

**Income:** Per capita income: $89,830 (2006-2010 5-year est.); Median household income: $84,234 (2006-2010 5-year est.); Average household income: $169,031 (2006-2010 5-year est.); Percent of households with income of $100,000 or more: 44.2% (2006-2010 5-year est.); Poverty rate: 5.7% (2006-2010 5-year est.).

**Education:** Percent of population age 25 and over with: High school diploma (including GED) or higher: 96.2% (2006-2010 5-year est.); Bachelor's degree or higher: 58.2% (2006-2010 5-year est.); Master's degree or higher: 30.4% (2006-2010 5-year est.).

### School District(s)
East Hampton Union Free School District (KG-12)
    2009-10 Enrollment: 1,818 . . . . . . . . . . . . . . . . . . . . (631) 329-4104
Springs Union Free School District (PK-08)
    2009-10 Enrollment: 641 . . . . . . . . . . . . . . . . . . . . (631) 324-0144

**Housing:** Homeownership rate: 72.2% (2010); Median home value: $1 (2006-2010 5-year est.); Median contract rent: n/a per month (2006-2010 5-year est.); Median year structure built: 1957 (2006-2010 5-year est.).

**Safety:** Violent crime rate: 21.5 per 10,000 population; Property crime rate: 982.1 per 10,000 population (2010).

**Newspapers:** East Hampton Independent (Community news; Circulation 12,000); East Hampton Star (Community news; Circulation 11,628)

**Transportation:** Commute to work: 64.8% car, 7.7% public transportation, 10.6% walk, 7.5% work from home (2006-2010 5-year est.); Travel time to work: 53.1% less than 15 minutes, 28.2% 15 to 30 minutes, 12.3% 30 to 45 minutes, 0.6% 45 to 60 minutes, 5.6% 60 minutes or more (2006-2010 5-year est.)

**Airports:** East Hampton (general aviation)

**Additional Information Contacts**
East Hampton Chamber of Commerce . . . . . . . . . . . . . . . (631) 324-0362
  http://www.easthamptonchamber.com

**EAST HAMPTON** (town). Covers a land area of 74.327 square miles and a water area of 312.224 square miles. Located at 41.09° N. Lat; 72.10° W. Long. Elevation is 33 feet.

**History:** Birthplace of John Howard Payne, whose home is now a museum. The village has 3 historic districts containing other significant buildings. Settled 1648, incorporated 1920.

**Population:** 16,132 (1990); 19,719 (2000); 21,457 (2010); Density: 288.7 persons per square mile (2010); Race: 84.8% White, 3.4% Black, 1.3% Asian, 0.6% American Indian/Alaska Native, 0.1% Native Hawaiian/Other Pacific Islander, 9.8% Other, 26.4% Hispanic of any race (2010); Average household size: 2.54 (2010); Median age: 43.8 (2010); Males per 100 females: 101.5 (2010); Marriage status: 27.1% never married, 58.1% now married, 5.9% widowed, 9.0% divorced (2006-2010 5-year est.); Foreign born: 24.5% (2006-2010 5-year est.); Ancestry (includes multiple ancestries): 16.1% Irish, 14.0% Italian, 12.9% German, 12.5% English, 4.6% Polish (2006-2010 5-year est.).

**Economy:** Single-family building permits issued: 68 (2011); Multi-family building permits issued: 0 (2011); Employment by occupation: 13.1% management, 2.5% professional, 9.2% services, 13.8% sales, 1.1% farming, 15.1% construction, 2.5% production (2006-2010 5-year est.).

**Income:** Per capita income: $51,639 (2006-2010 5-year est.); Median household income: $76,769 (2006-2010 5-year est.); Average household income: $124,502 (2006-2010 5-year est.); Percent of households with income of $100,000 or more: 36.6% (2006-2010 5-year est.); Poverty rate: 7.7% (2006-2010 5-year est.).

**Taxes:** Total city taxes per capita: $2,302 (2009); City property taxes per capita: $2,028 (2009).

**Education:** Percent of population age 25 and over with: High school diploma (including GED) or higher: 92.8% (2006-2010 5-year est.); Bachelor's degree or higher: 45.4% (2006-2010 5-year est.); Master's degree or higher: 22.2% (2006-2010 5-year est.).

### School District(s)
East Hampton Union Free School District (KG-12)
    2009-10 Enrollment: 1,818 . . . . . . . . . . . . . . . . . . . . (631) 329-4104
Springs Union Free School District (PK-08)
    2009-10 Enrollment: 641 . . . . . . . . . . . . . . . . . . . . (631) 324-0144

**Housing:** Homeownership rate: 75.2% (2010); Median home value: $847,100 (2006-2010 5-year est.); Median contract rent: $1,525 per month (2006-2010 5-year est.); Median year structure built: 1979 (2006-2010 5-year est.).

**Safety:** Violent crime rate: 4.5 per 10,000 population; Property crime rate: 248.7 per 10,000 population (2010).

**Newspapers:** East Hampton Independent (Community news; Circulation 12,000); East Hampton Star (Community news; Circulation 11,628)

**Transportation:** Commute to work: 81.4% car, 5.8% public transportation, 3.1% walk, 7.5% work from home (2006-2010 5-year est.); Travel time to work: 43.9% less than 15 minutes, 30.1% 15 to 30 minutes, 13.4% 30 to 45 minutes, 3.6% 45 to 60 minutes, 9.0% 60 minutes or more (2006-2010 5-year est.)

**Airports:** East Hampton (general aviation)

**Additional Information Contacts**
Town of East Hampton . . . . . . . . . . . . . . . . . . . . . . . . . (631) 324-4142
  http://www.town.east-hampton.ny.us

**EAST HAMPTON NORTH** (CDP). Covers a land area of 5.638 square miles and a water area of 0 square miles. Located at 40.97° N. Lat; 72.18° W. Long.

**Population:** 2,779 (1990); 3,587 (2000); 4,142 (2010); Density: 734.5 persons per square mile (2010); Race: 76.1% White, 6.0% Black, 1.1% Asian, 0.7% American Indian/Alaska Native, 0.0% Native Hawaiian/Other Pacific Islander, 16.1% Other, 38.5% Hispanic of any race (2010); Average household size: 2.69 (2010); Median age: 40.0 (2010); Males per 100 females: 99.3 (2010); Marriage status: 31.8% never married, 56.1% now married, 4.4% widowed, 7.7% divorced (2006-2010 5-year est.); Foreign born: 26.9% (2006-2010 5-year est.); Ancestry (includes multiple ancestries): 18.3% Irish, 11.4% English, 10.6% Italian, 8.1% German, 3.9% Polish (2006-2010 5-year est.).

**Economy:** Employment by occupation: 5.5% management, 1.6% professional, 5.6% services, 14.4% sales, 0.0% farming, 6.0% construction, 0.4% production (2006-2010 5-year est.).

**Income:** Per capita income: $35,763 (2006-2010 5-year est.); Median household income: $53,391 (2006-2010 5-year est.); Average household income: $95,260 (2006-2010 5-year est.); Percent of households with income of $100,000 or more: 28.0% (2006-2010 5-year est.); Poverty rate: 16.5% (2006-2010 5-year est.).

**Education:** Percent of population age 25 and over with: High school diploma (including GED) or higher: 89.7% (2006-2010 5-year est.); Bachelor's degree or higher: 34.5% (2006-2010 5-year est.); Master's degree or higher: 15.1% (2006-2010 5-year est.).
**Housing:** Homeownership rate: 67.1% (2010); Median home value: $734,500 (2006-2010 5-year est.); Median contract rent: $1,265 per month (2006-2010 5-year est.); Median year structure built: 1982 (2006-2010 5-year est.).
**Transportation:** Commute to work: 88.1% car, 1.7% public transportation, 3.8% walk, 5.5% work from home (2006-2010 5-year est.); Travel time to work: 55.0% less than 15 minutes, 36.4% 15 to 30 minutes, 7.2% 30 to 45 minutes, 0.7% 45 to 60 minutes, 0.7% 60 minutes or more (2006-2010 5-year est.)

**EAST ISLIP** (CDP). Covers a land area of 3.949 square miles and a water area of 0.108 square miles. Located at 40.72° N. Lat; 73.18° W. Long. Elevation is 16 feet.
**Population:** 13,867 (1990); 14,078 (2000); 14,475 (2010); Density: 3,664.7 persons per square mile (2010); Race: 94.5% White, 1.0% Black, 1.6% Asian, 0.1% American Indian/Alaska Native, 0.0% Native Hawaiian/Other Pacific Islander, 2.8% Other, 6.2% Hispanic of any race (2010); Average household size: 2.98 (2010); Median age: 41.3 (2010); Males per 100 females: 96.2 (2010); Marriage status: 25.6% never married, 59.1% now married, 8.6% widowed, 6.7% divorced (2006-2010 5-year est.); Foreign born: 6.1% (2006-2010 5-year est.); Ancestry (includes multiple ancestries): 37.1% Italian, 34.6% Irish, 20.0% German, 9.4% English, 4.7% Polish (2006-2010 5-year est.).
**Economy:** Employment by occupation: 15.8% management, 2.9% professional, 6.4% services, 19.7% sales, 2.7% farming, 7.9% construction, 2.7% production (2006-2010 5-year est.).
**Income:** Per capita income: $42,019 (2006-2010 5-year est.); Median household income: $94,250 (2006-2010 5-year est.); Average household income: $125,759 (2006-2010 5-year est.); Percent of households with income of $100,000 or more: 45.8% (2006-2010 5-year est.); Poverty rate: 3.9% (2006-2010 5-year est.).
**Education:** Percent of population age 25 and over with: High school diploma (including GED) or higher: 92.8% (2006-2010 5-year est.); Bachelor's degree or higher: 29.8% (2006-2010 5-year est.); Master's degree or higher: 12.2% (2006-2010 5-year est.).
**School District(s)**
East Islip Union Free School District (PK-12)
    2009-10 Enrollment: 4,876 . . . . . . . . . . . . . . . . . (631) 224-2000
**Housing:** Homeownership rate: 85.7% (2010); Median home value: $441,800 (2006-2010 5-year est.); Median contract rent: $1,441 per month (2006-2010 5-year est.); Median year structure built: 1960 (2006-2010 5-year est.).
**Transportation:** Commute to work: 88.9% car, 4.4% public transportation, 0.8% walk, 5.9% work from home (2006-2010 5-year est.); Travel time to work: 27.3% less than 15 minutes, 33.8% 15 to 30 minutes, 19.3% 30 to 45 minutes, 6.5% 45 to 60 minutes, 13.1% 60 minutes or more (2006-2010 5-year est.)
**Additional Information Contacts**
Islip Chamber of Commerce . . . . . . . . . . . . . . . . (631) 581-2720
    http://www.longislandweb.com/islipchamber

**EAST MARION** (CDP). Covers a land area of 2.238 square miles and a water area of 0.128 square miles. Located at 41.13° N. Lat; 72.34° W. Long. Elevation is 33 feet.
**Population:** 717 (1990); 756 (2000); 926 (2010); Density: 413.7 persons per square mile (2010); Race: 95.2% White, 0.8% Black, 0.9% Asian, 0.0% American Indian/Alaska Native, 0.0% Native Hawaiian/Other Pacific Islander, 3.1% Other, 6.7% Hispanic of any race (2010); Average household size: 2.26 (2010); Median age: 53.7 (2010); Males per 100 females: 102.2 (2010); Marriage status: 21.7% never married, 65.7% now married, 7.4% widowed, 5.2% divorced (2006-2010 5-year est.); Foreign born: 14.6% (2006-2010 5-year est.); Ancestry (includes multiple ancestries): 24.0% German, 20.5% Italian, 13.8% Irish, 11.6% Polish, 10.0% English (2006-2010 5-year est.).
**Economy:** Employment by occupation: 19.9% management, 5.5% professional, 8.2% services, 12.4% sales, 0.0% farming, 8.0% construction, 3.3% production (2006-2010 5-year est.).
**Income:** Per capita income: $39,321 (2006-2010 5-year est.); Median household income: $73,050 (2006-2010 5-year est.); Average household income: $98,420 (2006-2010 5-year est.); Percent of households with

income of $100,000 or more: 35.6% (2006-2010 5-year est.); Poverty rate: 6.7% (2006-2010 5-year est.).
**Education:** Percent of population age 25 and over with: High school diploma (including GED) or higher: 90.4% (2006-2010 5-year est.); Bachelor's degree or higher: 37.4% (2006-2010 5-year est.); Master's degree or higher: 16.1% (2006-2010 5-year est.).
**Housing:** Homeownership rate: 82.6% (2010); Median home value: $590,700 (2006-2010 5-year est.); Median contract rent: $1,280 per month (2006-2010 5-year est.); Median year structure built: 1975 (2006-2010 5-year est.).
**Transportation:** Commute to work: 94.2% car, 0.8% public transportation, 2.4% walk, 1.3% work from home (2006-2010 5-year est.); Travel time to work: 41.8% less than 15 minutes, 20.2% 15 to 30 minutes, 18.9% 30 to 45 minutes, 1.7% 45 to 60 minutes, 17.4% 60 minutes or more (2006-2010 5-year est.)

**EAST MORICHES** (CDP). Covers a land area of 5.476 square miles and a water area of 0.149 square miles. Located at 40.80° N. Lat; 72.75° W. Long. Elevation is 30 feet.
**Population:** 4,021 (1990); 4,550 (2000); 5,249 (2010); Density: 958.4 persons per square mile (2010); Race: 94.5% White, 1.4% Black, 0.9% Asian, 0.3% American Indian/Alaska Native, 0.0% Native Hawaiian/Other Pacific Islander, 2.9% Other, 5.9% Hispanic of any race (2010); Average household size: 2.69 (2010); Median age: 44.8 (2010); Males per 100 females: 96.4 (2010); Marriage status: 24.8% never married, 63.9% now married, 7.2% widowed, 4.1% divorced (2006-2010 5-year est.); Foreign born: 3.9% (2006-2010 5-year est.); Ancestry (includes multiple ancestries): 37.4% Italian, 25.2% Irish, 23.1% German, 13.0% English, 8.4% Polish (2006-2010 5-year est.).
**Economy:** Employment by occupation: 15.1% management, 3.5% professional, 8.3% services, 18.2% sales, 0.9% farming, 12.0% construction, 3.8% production (2006-2010 5-year est.).
**Income:** Per capita income: $45,950 (2006-2010 5-year est.); Median household income: $85,341 (2006-2010 5-year est.); Average household income: $120,958 (2006-2010 5-year est.); Percent of households with income of $100,000 or more: 41.8% (2006-2010 5-year est.); Poverty rate: 2.3% (2006-2010 5-year est.).
**Education:** Percent of population age 25 and over with: High school diploma (including GED) or higher: 90.9% (2006-2010 5-year est.); Bachelor's degree or higher: 35.9% (2006-2010 5-year est.); Master's degree or higher: 19.6% (2006-2010 5-year est.).
**School District(s)**
East Moriches Union Free School District (KG-08)
    2009-10 Enrollment: 735 . . . . . . . . . . . . . . . . . (631) 878-0162
**Housing:** Homeownership rate: 74.7% (2010); Median home value: $455,400 (2006-2010 5-year est.); Median contract rent: $1,414 per month (2006-2010 5-year est.); Median year structure built: 1978 (2006-2010 5-year est.).
**Transportation:** Commute to work: 90.8% car, 3.5% public transportation, 0.4% walk, 4.9% work from home (2006-2010 5-year est.); Travel time to work: 21.0% less than 15 minutes, 38.7% 15 to 30 minutes, 21.6% 30 to 45 minutes, 6.4% 45 to 60 minutes, 12.4% 60 minutes or more (2006-2010 5-year est.)

**EAST NORTHPORT** (CDP). Covers a land area of 5.160 square miles and a water area of 0 square miles. Located at 40.87° N. Lat; 73.32° W. Long. Elevation is 223 feet.
**Population:** 20,703 (1990); 20,845 (2000); 20,217 (2010); Density: 3,917.3 persons per square mile (2010); Race: 93.1% White, 0.8% Black, 2.8% Asian, 0.0% American Indian/Alaska Native, 0.0% Native Hawaiian/Other Pacific Islander, 3.3% Other, 6.7% Hispanic of any race (2010); Average household size: 2.84 (2010); Median age: 41.8 (2010); Males per 100 females: 97.8 (2010); Marriage status: 26.3% never married, 60.1% now married, 6.2% widowed, 7.4% divorced (2006-2010 5-year est.); Foreign born: 5.8% (2006-2010 5-year est.); Ancestry (includes multiple ancestries): 35.5% Italian, 34.5% Irish, 24.9% German, 8.0% English, 6.3% Polish (2006-2010 5-year est.).
**Economy:** Employment by occupation: 14.6% management, 4.0% professional, 6.3% services, 15.0% sales, 4.2% farming, 8.5% construction, 4.1% production (2006-2010 5-year est.).
**Income:** Per capita income: $37,079 (2006-2010 5-year est.); Median household income: $98,918 (2006-2010 5-year est.); Average household income: $110,200 (2006-2010 5-year est.); Percent of households with income of $100,000 or more: 49.5% (2006-2010 5-year est.); Poverty rate: 4.0% (2006-2010 5-year est.).

**Education:** Percent of population age 25 and over with: High school diploma (including GED) or higher: 94.5% (2006-2010 5-year est.); Bachelor's degree or higher: 39.8% (2006-2010 5-year est.); Master's degree or higher: 16.2% (2006-2010 5-year est.).

**School District(s)**

Northport-East Northport Union Free School Distric (KG-12)

   2009-10 Enrollment: 6,333 . . . . . . . . . . . . . . . . . (631) 262-6604

**Housing:** Homeownership rate: 83.6% (2010); Median home value: $474,600 (2006-2010 5-year est.); Median contract rent: $1,325 per month (2006-2010 5-year est.); Median year structure built: 1957 (2006-2010 5-year est.).

**Transportation:** Commute to work: 83.8% car, 10.2% public transportation, 1.3% walk, 3.5% work from home (2006-2010 5-year est.); Travel time to work: 26.8% less than 15 minutes, 27.2% 15 to 30 minutes, 20.5% 30 to 45 minutes, 9.1% 45 to 60 minutes, 16.5% 60 minutes or more (2006-2010 5-year est.)

**Additional Information Contacts**

East Northport Chamber of Commerce . . . . . . . . . . . . (631) 261-3573
  http://www.eastnorthport.com

## EAST PATCHOGUE (CDP). Covers a land area of 8.345 square miles and a water area of 0.131 square miles. Located at 40.77° N. Lat; 72.98° W. Long. Elevation is 23 feet.

**Population:** 20,195 (1990); 20,824 (2000); 22,469 (2010); Density: 2,692.2 persons per square mile (2010); Race: 84.3% White, 4.4% Black, 2.3% Asian, 0.3% American Indian/Alaska Native, 0.0% Native Hawaiian/Other Pacific Islander, 8.7% Other, 17.6% Hispanic of any race (2010); Average household size: 2.66 (2010); Median age: 40.5 (2010); Males per 100 females: 95.3 (2010); Marriage status: 27.5% never married, 53.9% now married, 8.8% widowed, 9.8% divorced (2006-2010 5-year est.); Foreign born: 10.3% (2006-2010 5-year est.); Ancestry (includes multiple ancestries): 28.7% Irish, 28.2% Italian, 16.5% German, 6.1% English, 5.3% Polish (2006-2010 5-year est.).

**Economy:** Employment by occupation: 10.1% management, 3.6% professional, 10.2% services, 16.5% sales, 5.7% farming, 12.0% construction, 6.5% production (2006-2010 5-year est.).

**Income:** Per capita income: $30,530 (2006-2010 5-year est.); Median household income: $68,888 (2006-2010 5-year est.); Average household income: $79,640 (2006-2010 5-year est.); Percent of households with income of $100,000 or more: 32.1% (2006-2010 5-year est.); Poverty rate: 12.2% (2006-2010 5-year est.).

**Education:** Percent of population age 25 and over with: High school diploma (including GED) or higher: 88.1% (2006-2010 5-year est.); Bachelor's degree or higher: 23.0% (2006-2010 5-year est.); Master's degree or higher: 9.5% (2006-2010 5-year est.).

**School District(s)**

South Country Central School District (PK-12)

   2009-10 Enrollment: 4,600 . . . . . . . . . . . . . . . . . . . . (631) 730-1510

**Housing:** Homeownership rate: 62.7% (2010); Median home value: $366,600 (2006-2010 5-year est.); Median contract rent: $1,157 per month (2006-2010 5-year est.); Median year structure built: 1969 (2006-2010 5-year est.).

**Hospitals:** Brookhaven Memorial Hospital Medical Center (321 beds)

**Transportation:** Commute to work: 91.1% car, 4.8% public transportation, 1.8% walk, 1.6% work from home (2006-2010 5-year est.); Travel time to work: 31.2% less than 15 minutes, 28.7% 15 to 30 minutes, 21.3% 30 to 45 minutes, 7.6% 45 to 60 minutes, 11.2% 60 minutes or more (2006-2010 5-year est.)

## EAST QUOGUE (CDP). Covers a land area of 8.873 square miles and a water area of 2.685 square miles. Located at 40.84° N. Lat; 72.57° W. Long. Elevation is 13 feet.

**Population:** 3,519 (1990); 4,265 (2000); 4,757 (2010); Density: 536.1 persons per square mile (2010); Race: 93.0% White, 1.7% Black, 1.3% Asian, 0.2% American Indian/Alaska Native, 0.0% Native Hawaiian/Other Pacific Islander, 3.8% Other, 8.9% Hispanic of any race (2010); Average household size: 2.59 (2010); Median age: 42.7 (2010); Males per 100 females: 96.4 (2010); Marriage status: 29.1% never married, 57.0% now married, 6.3% widowed, 7.6% divorced (2006-2010 5-year est.); Foreign born: 5.5% (2006-2010 5-year est.); Ancestry (includes multiple ancestries): 32.6% Irish, 20.4% Italian, 18.3% German, 9.8% English, 8.7% Polish (2006-2010 5-year est.).

**Economy:** Employment by occupation: 11.7% management, 2.4% professional, 7.3% services, 17.8% sales, 4.7% farming, 14.3% construction, 7.8% production (2006-2010 5-year est.).

**Income:** Per capita income: $40,882 (2006-2010 5-year est.); Median household income: $81,808 (2006-2010 5-year est.); Average household income: $105,025 (2006-2010 5-year est.); Percent of households with income of $100,000 or more: 35.5% (2006-2010 5-year est.); Poverty rate: 8.0% (2006-2010 5-year est.).

**Education:** Percent of population age 25 and over with: High school diploma (including GED) or higher: 93.5% (2006-2010 5-year est.); Bachelor's degree or higher: 39.9% (2006-2010 5-year est.); Master's degree or higher: 17.9% (2006-2010 5-year est.).

**School District(s)**

East Quogue Union Free School District (KG-06)

   2009-10 Enrollment: 445 . . . . . . . . . . . . . . . . . . . . (631) 653-5210

**Housing:** Homeownership rate: 82.5% (2010); Median home value: $558,300 (2006-2010 5-year est.); Median contract rent: $1,056 per month (2006-2010 5-year est.); Median year structure built: 1975 (2006-2010 5-year est.).

**Transportation:** Commute to work: 90.6% car, 2.3% public transportation, 2.3% walk, 1.6% work from home (2006-2010 5-year est.); Travel time to work: 24.0% less than 15 minutes, 30.5% 15 to 30 minutes, 23.4% 30 to 45 minutes, 9.9% 45 to 60 minutes, 12.2% 60 minutes or more (2006-2010 5-year est.)

**Additional Information Contacts**

East Quogue Chamber of Commerce . . . . . . . . . . . . . . (631) 728-5555
  http://www.eqny.com

## EAST SETAUKET (unincorporated postal area)

Zip Code: 11733

   Covers a land area of 11.842 square miles and a water area of 4.743 square miles. Located at 40.94° N. Lat; 73.11° W. Long. Elevation is 66 feet. Population: 18,949 (2010); Density: 1,600.0 persons per square mile (2010); Race: 88.7% White, 2.0% Black, 6.8% Asian, 0.2% American Indian/Alaska Native, 0.0% Native Hawaiian/Other Pacific Islander, 2.3% Other, 5.0% Hispanic of any race (2010); Average household size: 2.92 (2010); Median age: 42.4 (2010); Males per 100 females: 100.1 (2010); Homeownership rate: 92.4% (2010)

## EAST SHOREHAM (CDP). Covers a land area of 5.367 square miles and a water area of 0 square miles. Located at 40.94° N. Lat; 72.88° W. Long. Elevation is 121 feet.

**Population:** 5,276 (1990); 5,809 (2000); 6,666 (2010); Density: 1,242.0 persons per square mile (2010); Race: 94.6% White, 1.4% Black, 2.4% Asian, 0.1% American Indian/Alaska Native, 0.0% Native Hawaiian/Other Pacific Islander, 1.5% Other, 5.5% Hispanic of any race (2010); Average household size: 3.20 (2010); Median age: 40.1 (2010); Males per 100 females: 101.8 (2010); Marriage status: 24.1% never married, 67.2% now married, 4.8% widowed, 3.9% divorced (2006-2010 5-year est.); Foreign born: 6.6% (2006-2010 5-year est.); Ancestry (includes multiple ancestries): 37.9% Italian, 28.8% Irish, 23.4% German, 9.4% English, 6.5% Polish (2006-2010 5-year est.).

**Economy:** Employment by occupation: 12.7% management, 8.4% professional, 4.0% services, 13.6% sales, 1.2% farming, 10.1% construction, 3.6% production (2006-2010 5-year est.).

**Income:** Per capita income: $41,317 (2006-2010 5-year est.); Median household income: $119,788 (2006-2010 5-year est.); Average household income: $130,739 (2006-2010 5-year est.); Percent of households with income of $100,000 or more: 66.1% (2006-2010 5-year est.); Poverty rate: 2.1% (2006-2010 5-year est.).

**Education:** Percent of population age 25 and over with: High school diploma (including GED) or higher: 97.3% (2006-2010 5-year est.); Bachelor's degree or higher: 46.6% (2006-2010 5-year est.); Master's degree or higher: 27.0% (2006-2010 5-year est.).

**Housing:** Homeownership rate: 95.2% (2010); Median home value: $465,700 (2006-2010 5-year est.); Median contract rent: $1,579 per month (2006-2010 5-year est.); Median year structure built: 1975 (2006-2010 5-year est.).

**Transportation:** Commute to work: 92.0% car, 2.1% public transportation, 1.0% walk, 4.5% work from home (2006-2010 5-year est.); Travel time to work: 24.9% less than 15 minutes, 35.5% 15 to 30 minutes, 19.9% 30 to 45 minutes, 9.8% 45 to 60 minutes, 9.8% 60 minutes or more (2006-2010 5-year est.)

**EASTPORT** (CDP). Covers a land area of 5.258 square miles and a water area of 0.129 square miles. Located at 40.84° N. Lat; 72.72° W. Long. Elevation is 30 feet.
**Population:** 1,333 (1990); 1,454 (2000); 1,831 (2010); Density: 348.2 persons per square mile (2010); Race: 94.3% White, 1.4% Black, 0.6% Asian, 0.0% American Indian/Alaska Native, 0.0% Native Hawaiian/Other Pacific Islander, 3.7% Other, 8.7% Hispanic of any race (2010); Average household size: 2.59 (2010); Median age: 44.4 (2010); Males per 100 females: 99.2 (2010); Marriage status: 29.0% never married, 53.8% now married, 10.8% widowed, 6.3% divorced (2006-2010 5-year est.); Foreign born: 10.1% (2006-2010 5-year est.); Ancestry (includes multiple ancestries): 27.0% Irish, 23.4% German, 18.5% Italian, 14.7% Polish, 12.3% English (2006-2010 5-year est.).
**Economy:** Employment by occupation: 17.0% management, 3.8% professional, 16.9% services, 7.4% sales, 0.0% farming, 14.5% construction, 2.2% production (2006-2010 5-year est.).
**Income:** Per capita income: $43,287 (2006-2010 5-year est.); Median household income: $52,069 (2006-2010 5-year est.); Average household income: $93,471 (2006-2010 5-year est.); Percent of households with income of $100,000 or more: 25.8% (2006-2010 5-year est.); Poverty rate: 15.2% (2006-2010 5-year est.).
**Education:** Percent of population age 25 and over with: High school diploma (including GED) or higher: 87.1% (2006-2010 5-year est.); Bachelor's degree or higher: 28.3% (2006-2010 5-year est.); Master's degree or higher: 14.5% (2006-2010 5-year est.).
**School District(s)**
Eastport-South Manor Csd (KG-12)
   2009-10 Enrollment: 3,897 . . . . . . . . . . . . . . . . . . . (631) 874-6720
**Housing:** Homeownership rate: 84.6% (2010); Median home value: $468,600 (2006-2010 5-year est.); Median contract rent: $910 per month (2006-2010 5-year est.); Median year structure built: 1973 (2006-2010 5-year est.).
**Transportation:** Commute to work: 74.0% car, 3.8% public transportation, 3.2% walk, 19.0% work from home (2006-2010 5-year est.); Travel time to work: 26.7% less than 15 minutes, 33.9% 15 to 30 minutes, 22.0% 30 to 45 minutes, 8.7% 45 to 60 minutes, 8.7% 60 minutes or more (2006-2010 5-year est.)

**EATONS NECK** (CDP). Covers a land area of 1.004 square miles and a water area of 0 square miles. Located at 40.93° N. Lat; 73.39° W. Long. Elevation is 16 feet.
**Population:** 1,499 (1990); 1,388 (2000); 1,406 (2010); Density: 1,399.6 persons per square mile (2010); Race: 97.4% White, 0.2% Black, 0.9% Asian, 0.0% American Indian/Alaska Native, 0.0% Native Hawaiian/Other Pacific Islander, 1.5% Other, 2.6% Hispanic of any race (2010); Average household size: 2.71 (2010); Median age: 47.4 (2010); Males per 100 females: 96.1 (2010); Marriage status: 12.8% never married, 81.4% now married, 3.7% widowed, 2.1% divorced (2006-2010 5-year est.); Foreign born: 3.6% (2006-2010 5-year est.); Ancestry (includes multiple ancestries): 35.4% Irish, 28.2% Italian, 21.5% German, 9.8% English, 5.3% Scotch-Irish (2006-2010 5-year est.).
**Economy:** Employment by occupation: 23.9% management, 5.7% professional, 0.5% services, 24.0% sales, 0.0% farming, 2.1% construction, 0.5% production (2006-2010 5-year est.).
**Income:** Per capita income: $74,639 (2006-2010 5-year est.); Median household income: $124,167 (2006-2010 5-year est.); Average household income: $200,523 (2006-2010 5-year est.); Percent of households with income of $100,000 or more: 70.4% (2006-2010 5-year est.); Poverty rate: 2.6% (2006-2010 5-year est.).
**Education:** Percent of population age 25 and over with: High school diploma (including GED) or higher: 100.0% (2006-2010 5-year est.); Bachelor's degree or higher: 64.7% (2006-2010 5-year est.); Master's degree or higher: 31.3% (2006-2010 5-year est.).
**Housing:** Homeownership rate: 94.0% (2010); Median home value: $698,200 (2006-2010 5-year est.); Median contract rent: $1,975 per month (2006-2010 5-year est.); Median year structure built: 1964 (2006-2010 5-year est.).
**Transportation:** Commute to work: 80.4% car, 8.0% public transportation, 3.6% walk, 6.1% work from home (2006-2010 5-year est.); Travel time to work: 9.9% less than 15 minutes, 26.2% 15 to 30 minutes, 31.1% 30 to 45 minutes, 7.6% 45 to 60 minutes, 25.2% 60 minutes or more (2006-2010 5-year est.)

**ELWOOD** (CDP). Covers a land area of 4.781 square miles and a water area of 0 square miles. Located at 40.84° N. Lat; 73.33° W. Long. Elevation is 184 feet.
**Population:** 10,916 (1990); 10,916 (2000); 11,177 (2010); Density: 2,337.5 persons per square mile (2010); Race: 82.1% White, 6.2% Black, 8.0% Asian, 0.1% American Indian/Alaska Native, 0.0% Native Hawaiian/Other Pacific Islander, 3.6% Other, 8.2% Hispanic of any race (2010); Average household size: 3.15 (2010); Median age: 42.0 (2010); Males per 100 females: 94.0 (2010); Marriage status: 23.1% never married, 66.0% now married, 6.5% widowed, 4.4% divorced (2006-2010 5-year est.); Foreign born: 12.3% (2006-2010 5-year est.); Ancestry (includes multiple ancestries): 30.8% Italian, 25.5% Irish, 17.1% German, 6.7% Polish, 4.3% English (2006-2010 5-year est.).
**Economy:** Employment by occupation: 16.0% management, 5.1% professional, 7.3% services, 15.0% sales, 4.4% farming, 9.7% construction, 5.8% production (2006-2010 5-year est.).
**Income:** Per capita income: $35,705 (2006-2010 5-year est.); Median household income: $91,163 (2006-2010 5-year est.); Average household income: $110,192 (2006-2010 5-year est.); Percent of households with income of $100,000 or more: 42.2% (2006-2010 5-year est.); Poverty rate: 1.1% (2006-2010 5-year est.).
**Education:** Percent of population age 25 and over with: High school diploma (including GED) or higher: 95.2% (2006-2010 5-year est.); Bachelor's degree or higher: 45.4% (2006-2010 5-year est.); Master's degree or higher: 18.0% (2006-2010 5-year est.).
**School District(s)**
Elwood Union Free School District (KG-12)
   2009-10 Enrollment: 2,616 . . . . . . . . . . . . . . . . . . . (631) 266-5402
**Housing:** Homeownership rate: 92.0% (2010); Median home value: $509,500 (2006-2010 5-year est.); Median contract rent: n/a per month (2006-2010 5-year est.); Median year structure built: 1963 (2006-2010 5-year est.).
**Transportation:** Commute to work: 90.8% car, 3.7% public transportation, 0.3% walk, 4.4% work from home (2006-2010 5-year est.); Travel time to work: 26.1% less than 15 minutes, 36.6% 15 to 30 minutes, 16.2% 30 to 45 minutes, 9.6% 45 to 60 minutes, 11.5% 60 minutes or more (2006-2010 5-year est.)

**FARMINGVILLE** (CDP). Covers a land area of 4.123 square miles and a water area of 0 square miles. Located at 40.83° N. Lat; 73.04° W. Long. Elevation is 105 feet.
**Population:** 14,842 (1990); 16,458 (2000); 15,481 (2010); Density: 3,753.9 persons per square mile (2010); Race: 88.2% White, 2.4% Black, 3.7% Asian, 0.3% American Indian/Alaska Native, 0.0% Native Hawaiian/Other Pacific Islander, 5.4% Other, 12.5% Hispanic of any race (2010); Average household size: 3.26 (2010); Median age: 37.0 (2010); Males per 100 females: 99.7 (2010); Marriage status: 29.8% never married, 59.9% now married, 3.0% widowed, 7.3% divorced (2006-2010 5-year est.); Foreign born: 13.6% (2006-2010 5-year est.); Ancestry (includes multiple ancestries): 42.6% Italian, 23.4% Irish, 18.5% German, 7.3% Polish, 6.9% Portuguese (2006-2010 5-year est.).
**Economy:** Employment by occupation: 10.9% management, 3.1% professional, 10.5% services, 20.1% sales, 3.1% farming, 14.2% construction, 4.0% production (2006-2010 5-year est.).
**Income:** Per capita income: $28,173 (2006-2010 5-year est.); Median household income: $82,603 (2006-2010 5-year est.); Average household income: $91,740 (2006-2010 5-year est.); Percent of households with income of $100,000 or more: 36.6% (2006-2010 5-year est.); Poverty rate: 8.3% (2006-2010 5-year est.).
**Education:** Percent of population age 25 and over with: High school diploma (including GED) or higher: 86.0% (2006-2010 5-year est.); Bachelor's degree or higher: 21.7% (2006-2010 5-year est.); Master's degree or higher: 8.2% (2006-2010 5-year est.).
**School District(s)**
Sachem Central School District (KG-12)
   2009-10 Enrollment: 14,760 . . . . . . . . . . . . . . . . . . (631) 471-1336
**Housing:** Homeownership rate: 82.9% (2010); Median home value: $371,200 (2006-2010 5-year est.); Median contract rent: $1,736 per month (2006-2010 5-year est.); Median year structure built: 1970 (2006-2010 5-year est.).
**Newspapers:** Pennysaver News Hampton Bays/East Quogue Edition (Local news; Circulation 6,000)
**Transportation:** Commute to work: 90.0% car, 3.5% public transportation, 1.4% walk, 3.7% work from home (2006-2010 5-year est.); Travel time to work: 22.5% less than 15 minutes, 36.7% 15 to 30 minutes, 20.4% 30 to 45

minutes, 6.4% 45 to 60 minutes, 14.1% 60 minutes or more (2006-2010 5-year est.)

**FIRE ISLAND** (CDP). Covers a land area of 9.225 square miles and a water area of 29.043 square miles. Located at 40.63° N. Lat; 73.20° W. Long. Elevation is 3 feet.
**Population:** 250 (1990); 310 (2000); 292 (2010); Density: 31.7 persons per square mile (2010); Race: 91.1% White, 4.1% Black, 0.3% Asian, 0.0% American Indian/Alaska Native, 0.0% Native Hawaiian/Other Pacific Islander, 4.5% Other, 7.9% Hispanic of any race (2010); Average household size: 2.18 (2010); Median age: 45.8 (2010); Males per 100 females: 121.2 (2010); Marriage status: 29.5% never married, 58.5% now married, 6.3% widowed, 5.8% divorced (2006-2010 5-year est.); Foreign born: 15.9% (2006-2010 5-year est.); Ancestry (includes multiple ancestries): 29.2% Irish, 16.7% Italian, 13.6% English, 10.2% French, 8.0% German (2006-2010 5-year est.).
**Economy:** Employment by occupation: 18.9% management, 2.7% professional, 0.0% services, 16.2% sales, 0.0% farming, 4.5% construction, 0.0% production (2006-2010 5-year est.).
**Income:** Per capita income: $41,109 (2006-2010 5-year est.); Median household income: $64,250 (2006-2010 5-year est.); Average household income: $96,416 (2006-2010 5-year est.); Percent of households with income of $100,000 or more: 41.4% (2006-2010 5-year est.); Poverty rate: 3.8% (2006-2010 5-year est.).
**Education:** Percent of population age 25 and over with: High school diploma (including GED) or higher: 89.3% (2006-2010 5-year est.); Bachelor's degree or higher: 47.8% (2006-2010 5-year est.); Master's degree or higher: 28.8% (2006-2010 5-year est.).
**Housing:** Homeownership rate: 69.4% (2010); Median home value: $378,600 (2006-2010 5-year est.); Median contract rent: $343 per month (2006-2010 5-year est.); Median year structure built: 1960 (2006-2010 5-year est.).
**Transportation:** Commute to work: 46.2% car, 17.0% public transportation, 17.9% walk, 6.6% work from home (2006-2010 5-year est.); Travel time to work: 38.4% less than 15 minutes, 30.3% 15 to 30 minutes, 3.0% 30 to 45 minutes, 3.0% 45 to 60 minutes, 25.3% 60 minutes or more (2006-2010 5-year est.)

**FISHERS ISLAND** (CDP). Covers a land area of 4.075 square miles and a water area of 0.147 square miles. Located at 41.27° N. Lat; 71.96° W. Long. Elevation is 16 feet.
**Population:** 329 (1990); 289 (2000); 236 (2010); Density: 57.9 persons per square mile (2010); Race: 96.2% White, 0.8% Black, 0.8% Asian, 0.0% American Indian/Alaska Native, 0.0% Native Hawaiian/Other Pacific Islander, 2.2% Other, 0.8% Hispanic of any race (2010); Average household size: 1.97 (2010); Median age: 49.4 (2010); Males per 100 females: 100.0 (2010); Marriage status: 32.3% never married, 59.2% now married, 4.5% widowed, 4.0% divorced (2006-2010 5-year est.); Foreign born: 8.0% (2006-2010 5-year est.); Ancestry (includes multiple ancestries): 22.8% English, 21.6% Irish, 17.2% French, 14.4% Italian, 14.4% German (2006-2010 5-year est.).
**Economy:** Employment by occupation: 16.6% management, 0.0% professional, 3.1% services, 31.3% sales, 0.0% farming, 23.9% construction, 9.8% production (2006-2010 5-year est.).
**Income:** Per capita income: $44,722 (2006-2010 5-year est.); Median household income: $67,045 (2006-2010 5-year est.); Average household income: $91,458 (2006-2010 5-year est.); Percent of households with income of $100,000 or more: 33.6% (2006-2010 5-year est.); Poverty rate: 6.4% (2006-2010 5-year est.).
**Education:** Percent of population age 25 and over with: High school diploma (including GED) or higher: 97.9% (2006-2010 5-year est.); Bachelor's degree or higher: 32.6% (2006-2010 5-year est.); Master's degree or higher: 9.6% (2006-2010 5-year est.).
**Housing:** Homeownership rate: 48.4% (2010); Median home value: $800,000 (2006-2010 5-year est.); Median contract rent: $490 per month (2006-2010 5-year est.); Median year structure built: 1956 (2006-2010 5-year est.).
**Transportation:** Commute to work: 76.7% car, 1.8% public transportation, 12.3% walk, 6.7% work from home (2006-2010 5-year est.); Travel time to work: 90.1% less than 15 minutes, 7.9% 15 to 30 minutes, 2.0% 30 to 45 minutes, 0.0% 45 to 60 minutes, 0.0% 60 minutes or more (2006-2010 5-year est.)
**Airports:** Elizabeth Field (general aviation)

**FLANDERS** (CDP). Covers a land area of 11.460 square miles and a water area of 0.173 square miles. Located at 40.88° N. Lat; 72.60° W. Long. Elevation is 7 feet.
**Population:** 3,246 (1990); 3,646 (2000); 4,472 (2010); Density: 390.2 persons per square mile (2010); Race: 65.3% White, 13.8% Black, 1.1% Asian, 1.5% American Indian/Alaska Native, 0.0% Native Hawaiian/Other Pacific Islander, 18.3% Other, 37.5% Hispanic of any race (2010); Average household size: 3.30 (2010); Median age: 32.7 (2010); Males per 100 females: 114.6 (2010); Marriage status: 39.0% never married, 46.4% now married, 5.6% widowed, 9.0% divorced (2006-2010 5-year est.); Foreign born: 33.9% (2006-2010 5-year est.); Ancestry (includes multiple ancestries): 16.5% Irish, 11.9% Italian, 7.1% German, 5.0% Polish, 4.4% English (2006-2010 5-year est.).
**Economy:** Employment by occupation: 5.7% management, 2.9% professional, 14.8% services, 8.0% sales, 3.0% farming, 23.1% construction, 5.6% production (2006-2010 5-year est.).
**Income:** Per capita income: $25,125 (2006-2010 5-year est.); Median household income: $68,276 (2006-2010 5-year est.); Average household income: $75,583 (2006-2010 5-year est.); Percent of households with income of $100,000 or more: 32.4% (2006-2010 5-year est.); Poverty rate: 7.4% (2006-2010 5-year est.).
**Education:** Percent of population age 25 and over with: High school diploma (including GED) or higher: 69.5% (2006-2010 5-year est.); Bachelor's degree or higher: 21.0% (2006-2010 5-year est.); Master's degree or higher: 12.9% (2006-2010 5-year est.).
**Housing:** Homeownership rate: 68.1% (2010); Median home value: $360,300 (2006-2010 5-year est.); Median contract rent: $1,330 per month (2006-2010 5-year est.); Median year structure built: 1967 (2006-2010 5-year est.).
**Transportation:** Commute to work: 91.5% car, 7.8% public transportation, 0.0% walk, 0.0% work from home (2006-2010 5-year est.); Travel time to work: 29.8% less than 15 minutes, 26.1% 15 to 30 minutes, 17.4% 30 to 45 minutes, 13.9% 45 to 60 minutes, 12.9% 60 minutes or more (2006-2010 5-year est.)

**FORT SALONGA** (CDP). Covers a land area of 9.829 square miles and a water area of 0.111 square miles. Located at 40.90° N. Lat; 73.30° W. Long. Elevation is 33 feet.
**History:** The name evolved from the Revolutionary War British Fort Salonga, or Fort Slongo, (named after one of the fort's architects) once located near the border of Huntington Township and The Town of Smithtown, overlooking the Long Island Sound.
**Population:** 9,032 (1990); 9,634 (2000); 10,008 (2010); Density: 1,018.2 persons per square mile (2010); Race: 95.2% White, 0.9% Black, 2.2% Asian, 0.1% American Indian/Alaska Native, 0.1% Native Hawaiian/Other Pacific Islander, 1.5% Other, 3.9% Hispanic of any race (2010); Average household size: 2.92 (2010); Median age: 45.1 (2010); Males per 100 females: 100.5 (2010); Marriage status: 24.2% never married, 66.8% now married, 5.2% widowed, 3.8% divorced (2006-2010 5-year est.); Foreign born: 7.9% (2006-2010 5-year est.); Ancestry (includes multiple ancestries): 29.6% Irish, 24.9% Italian, 18.0% German, 8.7% English, 5.4% Polish (2006-2010 5-year est.).
**Economy:** Employment by occupation: 23.1% management, 5.7% professional, 2.1% services, 14.4% sales, 4.2% farming, 6.2% construction, 1.2% production (2006-2010 5-year est.).
**Income:** Per capita income: $56,041 (2006-2010 5-year est.); Median household income: $125,199 (2006-2010 5-year est.); Average household income: $171,200 (2006-2010 5-year est.); Percent of households with income of $100,000 or more: 62.6% (2006-2010 5-year est.); Poverty rate: 2.1% (2006-2010 5-year est.).
**Education:** Percent of population age 25 and over with: High school diploma (including GED) or higher: 94.1% (2006-2010 5-year est.); Bachelor's degree or higher: 53.6% (2006-2010 5-year est.); Master's degree or higher: 22.9% (2006-2010 5-year est.).
**Housing:** Homeownership rate: 91.5% (2010); Median home value: $704,600 (2006-2010 5-year est.); Median contract rent: $1,799 per month (2006-2010 5-year est.); Median year structure built: 1965 (2006-2010 5-year est.).
**Transportation:** Commute to work: 84.5% car, 9.1% public transportation, 0.2% walk, 5.0% work from home (2006-2010 5-year est.); Travel time to work: 21.8% less than 15 minutes, 28.2% 15 to 30 minutes, 16.9% 30 to 45 minutes, 10.6% 45 to 60 minutes, 22.5% 60 minutes or more (2006-2010 5-year est.)

**GILGO** (CDP). Covers a land area of 4.995 square miles and a water area of 6.706 square miles. Located at 40.63° N. Lat; 73.38° W. Long.
**Population:** n/a (1990); n/a (2000); 131 (2010); Density: 26.2 persons per square mile (2010); Race: 100.0% White, 0.0% Black, 0.0% Asian, 0.0% American Indian/Alaska Native, 0.0% Native Hawaiian/Other Pacific Islander, 0.0% Other, 2.3% Hispanic of any race (2010); Average household size: 2.47 (2010); Median age: 50.6 (2010); Males per 100 females: 118.3 (2010); Marriage status: 20.4% never married, 66.4% now married, 13.3% widowed, 0.0% divorced (2006-2010 5-year est.); Foreign born: 21.2% (2006-2010 5-year est.); Ancestry (includes multiple ancestries): 46.9% Irish, 24.8% Italian, 12.4% English, 9.7% German, 1.8% Scottish (2006-2010 5-year est.).
**Economy:** Employment by occupation: 0.0% management, 0.0% professional, 0.0% services, 13.2% sales, 0.0% farming, 0.0% construction, 0.0% production (2006-2010 5-year est.).
**Income:** Per capita income: $64,759 (2006-2010 5-year est.); Median household income: $90,625 (2006-2010 5-year est.); Average household income: $143,486 (2006-2010 5-year est.); Percent of households with income of $100,000 or more: 47.1% (2006-2010 5-year est.); Poverty rate: 1.8% (2006-2010 5-year est.).
**Education:** Percent of population age 25 and over with: High school diploma (including GED) or higher: 100.0% (2006-2010 5-year est.); Bachelor's degree or higher: 85.6% (2006-2010 5-year est.); Master's degree or higher: 58.9% (2006-2010 5-year est.).
**Housing:** Homeownership rate: 100.0% (2010); Median home value: $812,500 (2006-2010 5-year est.); Median contract rent: n/a per month (2006-2010 5-year est.); Median year structure built: 1952 (2006-2010 5-year est.).
**Transportation:** Commute to work: 58.5% car, 0.0% public transportation, 0.0% walk, 41.5% work from home (2006-2010 5-year est.); Travel time to work: 71.0% less than 15 minutes, 22.6% 15 to 30 minutes, 0.0% 30 to 45 minutes, 0.0% 45 to 60 minutes, 6.5% 60 minutes or more (2006-2010 5-year est.)

**GORDON HEIGHTS** (CDP). Covers a land area of 1.704 square miles and a water area of 0.013 square miles. Located at 40.86° N. Lat; 72.96° W. Long. Elevation is 154 feet.
**Population:** 2,200 (1990); 3,094 (2000); 4,042 (2010); Density: 2,371.0 persons per square mile (2010); Race: 28.7% White, 52.9% Black, 1.9% Asian, 1.9% American Indian/Alaska Native, 0.3% Native Hawaiian/Other Pacific Islander, 14.3% Other, 25.0% Hispanic of any race (2010); Average household size: 3.69 (2010); Median age: 32.3 (2010); Males per 100 females: 100.2 (2010); Marriage status: 39.6% never married, 41.0% now married, 9.8% widowed, 9.6% divorced (2006-2010 5-year est.); Foreign born: 16.3% (2006-2010 5-year est.); Ancestry (includes multiple ancestries): 6.9% Italian, 6.1% African, 4.6% Irish, 3.4% Romanian, 2.4% Jamaican (2006-2010 5-year est.).
**Economy:** Employment by occupation: 11.6% management, 0.0% professional, 10.0% services, 18.1% sales, 3.3% farming, 19.5% construction, 5.9% production (2006-2010 5-year est.).
**Income:** Per capita income: $23,713 (2006-2010 5-year est.); Median household income: $58,401 (2006-2010 5-year est.); Average household income: $66,258 (2006-2010 5-year est.); Percent of households with income of $100,000 or more: 17.8% (2006-2010 5-year est.); Poverty rate: 14.0% (2006-2010 5-year est.).
**Education:** Percent of population age 25 and over with: High school diploma (including GED) or higher: 90.6% (2006-2010 5-year est.); Bachelor's degree or higher: 28.3% (2006-2010 5-year est.); Master's degree or higher: 13.4% (2006-2010 5-year est.).
**Housing:** Homeownership rate: 75.4% (2010); Median home value: $304,600 (2006-2010 5-year est.); Median contract rent: $964 per month (2006-2010 5-year est.); Median year structure built: 1982 (2006-2010 5-year est.).
**Transportation:** Commute to work: 93.0% car, 6.6% public transportation, 0.0% walk, 0.5% work from home (2006-2010 5-year est.); Travel time to work: 12.3% less than 15 minutes, 30.7% 15 to 30 minutes, 20.7% 30 to 45 minutes, 2.7% 45 to 60 minutes, 33.5% 60 minutes or more (2006-2010 5-year est.)

**GREAT RIVER** (CDP). Covers a land area of 4.597 square miles and a water area of 0.594 square miles. Located at 40.71° N. Lat; 73.16° W. Long. Elevation is 13 feet.
**Population:** 1,442 (1990); 1,546 (2000); 1,489 (2010); Density: 323.9 persons per square mile (2010); Race: 96.8% White, 0.5% Black, 1.8% Asian, 0.0% American Indian/Alaska Native, 0.0% Native Hawaiian/Other

Pacific Islander, 0.9% Other, 4.2% Hispanic of any race (2010); Average household size: 2.96 (2010); Median age: 45.5 (2010); Males per 100 females: 105.4 (2010); Marriage status: 37.8% never married, 46.4% now married, 9.3% widowed, 6.4% divorced (2006-2010 5-year est.); Foreign born: 3.3% (2006-2010 5-year est.); Ancestry (includes multiple ancestries): 48.8% Italian, 29.1% Irish, 25.3% German, 8.6% Polish, 8.3% French (2006-2010 5-year est.).
**Economy:** Employment by occupation: 31.7% management, 2.8% professional, 2.3% services, 15.6% sales, 3.3% farming, 2.4% construction, 0.0% production (2006-2010 5-year est.).
**Income:** Per capita income: $56,410 (2006-2010 5-year est.); Median household income: $173,438 (2006-2010 5-year est.); Average household income: $183,585 (2006-2010 5-year est.); Percent of households with income of $100,000 or more: 80.5% (2006-2010 5-year est.); Poverty rate: 0.0% (2006-2010 5-year est.).
**Education:** Percent of population age 25 and over with: High school diploma (including GED) or higher: 100.0% (2006-2010 5-year est.); Bachelor's degree or higher: 60.9% (2006-2010 5-year est.); Master's degree or higher: 30.6% (2006-2010 5-year est.).
**Housing:** Homeownership rate: 88.5% (2010); Median home value: $683,900 (2006-2010 5-year est.); Median contract rent: $1,670 per month (2006-2010 5-year est.); Median year structure built: 1963 (2006-2010 5-year est.).
**Transportation:** Commute to work: 82.9% car, 7.4% public transportation, 8.3% walk, 1.5% work from home (2006-2010 5-year est.); Travel time to work: 25.7% less than 15 minutes, 39.2% 15 to 30 minutes, 19.0% 30 to 45 minutes, 5.3% 45 to 60 minutes, 10.8% 60 minutes or more (2006-2010 5-year est.)

**GREENLAWN** (CDP). Covers a land area of 3.721 square miles and a water area of 0.002 square miles. Located at 40.86° N. Lat; 73.36° W. Long. Elevation is 226 feet.
**Population:** 13,208 (1990); 13,286 (2000); 13,742 (2010); Density: 3,692.4 persons per square mile (2010); Race: 74.0% White, 13.9% Black, 4.1% Asian, 0.4% American Indian/Alaska Native, 0.0% Native Hawaiian/Other Pacific Islander, 7.6% Other, 12.5% Hispanic of any race (2010); Average household size: 2.94 (2010); Median age: 41.9 (2010); Males per 100 females: 92.4 (2010); Marriage status: 26.2% never married, 59.7% now married, 7.7% widowed, 6.4% divorced (2006-2010 5-year est.); Foreign born: 13.5% (2006-2010 5-year est.); Ancestry (includes multiple ancestries): 22.7% Italian, 21.9% Irish, 15.6% German, 8.5% English, 6.1% Polish (2006-2010 5-year est.).
**Economy:** Employment by occupation: 19.8% management, 7.3% professional, 5.8% services, 14.4% sales, 2.7% farming, 6.2% construction, 4.0% production (2006-2010 5-year est.).
**Income:** Per capita income: $41,559 (2006-2010 5-year est.); Median household income: $92,571 (2006-2010 5-year est.); Average household income: $115,576 (2006-2010 5-year est.); Percent of households with income of $100,000 or more: 47.8% (2006-2010 5-year est.); Poverty rate: 3.6% (2006-2010 5-year est.).
**Education:** Percent of population age 25 and over with: High school diploma (including GED) or higher: 94.0% (2006-2010 5-year est.); Bachelor's degree or higher: 40.5% (2006-2010 5-year est.); Master's degree or higher: 16.3% (2006-2010 5-year est.).
**School District(s)**
Harborfields Central School District (KG-12)
    2009-10 Enrollment: 3,664 . . . . . . . . . . . . . . . . . . . . . . . . (631) 754-5320
**Housing:** Homeownership rate: 77.8% (2010); Median home value: $492,000 (2006-2010 5-year est.); Median contract rent: $736 per month (2006-2010 5-year est.); Median year structure built: 1961 (2006-2010 5-year est.).
**Transportation:** Commute to work: 80.1% car, 12.8% public transportation, 0.7% walk, 5.1% work from home (2006-2010 5-year est.); Travel time to work: 21.3% less than 15 minutes, 32.2% 15 to 30 minutes, 16.4% 30 to 45 minutes, 10.6% 45 to 60 minutes, 19.6% 60 minutes or more (2006-2010 5-year est.)

**GREENPORT** (village). Covers a land area of 0.955 square miles and a water area of 0.248 square miles. Located at 41.10° N. Lat; 72.36° W. Long. Elevation is 10 feet.
**History:** By 1840 pursuit of offshore whaling, practiced by both Native Americans and European residents, had turned into a way of industry with ships leaving Cold Springs Harbor, Sag Harbor, and Greenport on 3-year whaling voyages. Greenport Village Historic District. Incorporated 1838.

**Population:** 1,998 (1990); 2,048 (2000); 2,197 (2010); Density: 2,298.4 persons per square mile (2010); Race: 66.5% White, 10.4% Black, 0.6% Asian, 0.2% American Indian/Alaska Native, 0.0% Native Hawaiian/Other Pacific Islander, 22.3% Other, 34.0% Hispanic of any race (2010); Average household size: 2.52 (2010); Median age: 40.7 (2010); Males per 100 females: 100.8 (2010); Marriage status: 31.1% never married, 51.0% now married, 9.7% widowed, 8.2% divorced (2006-2010 5-year est.); Foreign born: 27.4% (2006-2010 5-year est.); Ancestry (includes multiple ancestries): 15.3% English, 14.2% Irish, 13.0% German, 11.5% Italian, 2.5% Polish (2006-2010 5-year est.).

**Economy:** Single-family building permits issued: 2 (2011); Multi-family building permits issued: 0 (2011); Employment by occupation: 3.3% management, 4.5% professional, 9.6% services, 11.9% sales, 0.6% farming, 27.0% construction, 5.8% production (2006-2010 5-year est.).

**Income:** Per capita income: $30,746 (2006-2010 5-year est.); Median household income: $48,398 (2006-2010 5-year est.); Average household income: $73,494 (2006-2010 5-year est.); Percent of households with income of $100,000 or more: 21.1% (2006-2010 5-year est.); Poverty rate: 22.6% (2006-2010 5-year est.).

**Education:** Percent of population age 25 and over with: High school diploma (including GED) or higher: 74.9% (2006-2010 5-year est.); Bachelor's degree or higher: 26.0% (2006-2010 5-year est.); Master's degree or higher: 13.4% (2006-2010 5-year est.).

**School District(s)**
Greenport Union Free School District (KG-12)
   2009-10 Enrollment: 605 . . . . . . . . . . . . . . . . . . . . . . (631) 477-1950
**Housing:** Homeownership rate: 47.6% (2010); Median home value: $470,900 (2006-2010 5-year est.); Median contract rent: $1,109 per month (2006-2010 5-year est.); Median year structure built: before 1940 (2006-2010 5-year est.).
**Hospitals:** Eastern Long Island Hospital (90 beds)
**Transportation:** Commute to work: 59.8% car, 12.0% public transportation, 17.5% walk, 3.3% work from home (2006-2010 5-year est.); Travel time to work: 31.0% less than 15 minutes, 38.1% 15 to 30 minutes, 19.6% 30 to 45 minutes, 3.4% 45 to 60 minutes, 7.8% 60 minutes or more (2006-2010 5-year est.)
**Additional Information Contacts**
North Fork Promotional Council . . . . . . . . . . . . . . . . . . . (631) 477-1383
   http://northfork.org

**GREENPORT WEST** (CDP). Covers a land area of 3.209 square miles and a water area of 0.125 square miles. Located at 41.09° N. Lat; 72.38° W. Long. Elevation is 7 feet.
**Population:** 1,678 (1990); 1,679 (2000); 2,124 (2010); Density: 661.8 persons per square mile (2010); Race: 81.5% White, 5.4% Black, 0.8% Asian, 0.4% American Indian/Alaska Native, 0.1% Native Hawaiian/Other Pacific Islander, 11.8% Other, 15.4% Hispanic of any race (2010); Average household size: 2.09 (2010); Median age: 55.1 (2010); Males per 100 females: 82.8 (2010); Marriage status: 15.3% never married, 53.0% now married, 20.8% widowed, 10.9% divorced (2006-2010 5-year est.); Foreign born: 6.5% (2006-2010 5-year est.); Ancestry (includes multiple ancestries): 28.0% Irish, 19.7% Italian, 15.9% English, 15.5% Polish, 13.5% German (2006-2010 5-year est.).
**Economy:** Employment by occupation: 14.5% management, 2.7% professional, 7.7% services, 15.6% sales, 5.9% farming, 8.9% construction, 8.6% production (2006-2010 5-year est.).
**Income:** Per capita income: $43,572 (2006-2010 5-year est.); Median household income: $63,153 (2006-2010 5-year est.); Average household income: $89,042 (2006-2010 5-year est.); Percent of households with income of $100,000 or more: 31.3% (2006-2010 5-year est.); Poverty rate: 2.4% (2006-2010 5-year est.).
**Education:** Percent of population age 25 and over with: High school diploma (including GED) or higher: 95.1% (2006-2010 5-year est.); Bachelor's degree or higher: 35.5% (2006-2010 5-year est.); Master's degree or higher: 17.6% (2006-2010 5-year est.).
**Housing:** Homeownership rate: 79.6% (2010); Median home value: $456,800 (2006-2010 5-year est.); Median contract rent: $946 per month (2006-2010 5-year est.); Median year structure built: 1978 (2006-2010 5-year est.).
**Transportation:** Commute to work: 78.1% car, 6.7% public transportation, 4.4% walk, 3.0% work from home (2006-2010 5-year est.); Travel time to work: 65.9% less than 15 minutes, 8.1% 15 to 30 minutes, 12.7% 30 to 45 minutes, 1.0% 45 to 60 minutes, 12.2% 60 minutes or more (2006-2010 5-year est.)

**HALESITE** (CDP). Covers a land area of 0.888 square miles and a water area of 0.092 square miles. Located at 40.88° N. Lat; 73.41° W. Long. Elevation is 26 feet.
**Population:** 2,687 (1990); 2,582 (2000); 2,498 (2010); Density: 2,810.3 persons per square mile (2010); Race: 96.1% White, 0.8% Black, 1.5% Asian, 0.0% American Indian/Alaska Native, 0.1% Native Hawaiian/Other Pacific Islander, 1.5% Other, 4.2% Hispanic of any race (2010); Average household size: 2.48 (2010); Median age: 46.1 (2010); Males per 100 females: 101.0 (2010); Marriage status: 32.4% never married, 57.3% now married, 6.0% widowed, 4.2% divorced (2006-2010 5-year est.); Foreign born: 2.2% (2006-2010 5-year est.); Ancestry (includes multiple ancestries): 35.3% Irish, 32.7% Italian, 15.8% German, 13.4% English, 7.0% Polish (2006-2010 5-year est.).
**Economy:** Employment by occupation: 29.2% management, 4.3% professional, 7.6% services, 15.9% sales, 6.0% farming, 1.2% construction, 1.2% production (2006-2010 5-year est.).
**Income:** Per capita income: $57,394 (2006-2010 5-year est.); Median household income: $104,671 (2006-2010 5-year est.); Average household income: $136,594 (2006-2010 5-year est.); Percent of households with income of $100,000 or more: 57.2% (2006-2010 5-year est.); Poverty rate: 4.1% (2006-2010 5-year est.).
**Education:** Percent of population age 25 and over with: High school diploma (including GED) or higher: 98.3% (2006-2010 5-year est.); Bachelor's degree or higher: 58.6% (2006-2010 5-year est.); Master's degree or higher: 22.4% (2006-2010 5-year est.).
**Housing:** Homeownership rate: 85.8% (2010); Median home value: $618,200 (2006-2010 5-year est.); Median contract rent: $1,342 per month (2006-2010 5-year est.); Median year structure built: 1955 (2006-2010 5-year est.).
**Transportation:** Commute to work: 88.7% car, 9.9% public transportation, 0.0% walk, 1.4% work from home (2006-2010 5-year est.); Travel time to work: 27.2% less than 15 minutes, 20.6% 15 to 30 minutes, 20.1% 30 to 45 minutes, 9.1% 45 to 60 minutes, 23.0% 60 minutes or more (2006-2010 5-year est.)

**HAMPTON BAYS** (CDP). Covers a land area of 12.953 square miles and a water area of 5.174 square miles. Located at 40.87° N. Lat; 72.52° W. Long. Elevation is 33 feet.
**History:** Until 1922 called Good Ground.
**Population:** 9,348 (1990); 12,236 (2000); 13,603 (2010); Density: 1,050.1 persons per square mile (2010); Race: 84.3% White, 1.5% Black, 0.8% Asian, 0.3% American Indian/Alaska Native, 0.2% Native Hawaiian/Other Pacific Islander, 12.9% Other, 28.6% Hispanic of any race (2010); Average household size: 2.64 (2010); Median age: 39.3 (2010); Males per 100 females: 106.0 (2010); Marriage status: 23.2% never married, 59.8% now married, 6.6% widowed, 10.4% divorced (2006-2010 5-year est.); Foreign born: 18.2% (2006-2010 5-year est.); Ancestry (includes multiple ancestries): 25.9% Irish, 16.7% Italian, 15.6% German, 10.0% English, 7.4% Polish (2006-2010 5-year est.).
**Economy:** Employment by occupation: 8.8% management, 1.3% professional, 11.8% services, 14.2% sales, 2.1% farming, 17.5% construction, 4.1% production (2006-2010 5-year est.).
**Income:** Per capita income: $32,796 (2006-2010 5-year est.); Median household income: $64,935 (2006-2010 5-year est.); Average household income: $81,614 (2006-2010 5-year est.); Percent of households with income of $100,000 or more: 24.6% (2006-2010 5-year est.); Poverty rate: 7.6% (2006-2010 5-year est.).
**Education:** Percent of population age 25 and over with: High school diploma (including GED) or higher: 88.0% (2006-2010 5-year est.); Bachelor's degree or higher: 33.8% (2006-2010 5-year est.); Master's degree or higher: 13.3% (2006-2010 5-year est.).
**School District(s)**
Hampton Bays Union Free School District (KG-12)
   2009-10 Enrollment: 1,916 . . . . . . . . . . . . . . . . . . . . . (631) 723-2100
**Housing:** Homeownership rate: 66.6% (2010); Median home value: $497,600 (2006-2010 5-year est.); Median contract rent: $1,318 per month (2006-2010 5-year est.); Median year structure built: 1969 (2006-2010 5-year est.).
**Transportation:** Commute to work: 86.8% car, 3.1% public transportation, 3.7% walk, 3.6% work from home (2006-2010 5-year est.); Travel time to work: 20.6% less than 15 minutes, 31.5% 15 to 30 minutes, 24.3% 30 to 45 minutes, 6.9% 45 to 60 minutes, 16.7% 60 minutes or more (2006-2010 5-year est.)
**Additional Information Contacts**

Hampton Bays Chamber of Commerce . . . . . . . . . . . . . . . . (631) 728-2211
  http://www.hamptonbayschamber.com

## HAUPPAUGE (CDP). Covers a land area of 10.712 square miles and a water area of 0.148 square miles. Located at 40.82° N. Lat; 73.21° W. Long. Elevation is 62 feet.

**Population:** 19,750 (1990); 20,100 (2000); 20,882 (2010); Density: 1,949.3 persons per square mile (2010); Race: 89.2% White, 2.2% Black, 5.9% Asian, 0.1% American Indian/Alaska Native, 0.0% Native Hawaiian/Other Pacific Islander, 2.6% Other, 7.1% Hispanic of any race (2010); Average household size: 2.81 (2010); Median age: 42.5 (2010); Males per 100 females: 96.4 (2010); Marriage status: 26.1% never married, 62.2% now married, 5.0% widowed, 6.7% divorced (2006-2010 5-year est.); Foreign born: 9.5% (2006-2010 5-year est.); Ancestry (includes multiple ancestries): 35.4% Italian, 23.0% Irish, 20.9% German, 8.0% Polish, 4.6% Russian (2006-2010 5-year est.).
**Economy:** Employment by occupation: 12.6% management, 5.4% professional, 6.2% services, 20.3% sales, 3.9% farming, 6.6% construction, 3.4% production (2006-2010 5-year est.).
**Income:** Per capita income: $39,144 (2006-2010 5-year est.); Median household income: $100,054 (2006-2010 5-year est.); Average household income: $113,988 (2006-2010 5-year est.); Percent of households with income of $100,000 or more: 50.0% (2006-2010 5-year est.); Poverty rate: 3.7% (2006-2010 5-year est.).
**Education:** Percent of population age 25 and over with: High school diploma (including GED) or higher: 95.7% (2006-2010 5-year est.); Bachelor's degree or higher: 39.9% (2006-2010 5-year est.); Master's degree or higher: 18.0% (2006-2010 5-year est.).

### School District(s)
Hauppauge Union Free School District (KG-12)
  2009-10 Enrollment: 4,076 . . . . . . . . . . . . . . . . . . . . . (631) 761-8208

### Vocational/Technical School(s)
Long Island Beauty School-Hauppauge (Private, For-profit)
  Fall 2010 Enrollment: 243 . . . . . . . . . . . . . . . . . . . . . (631) 724-0440
  2011-12 Tuition: $12,200
**Housing:** Homeownership rate: 82.1% (2010); Median home value: $533,700 (2006-2010 5-year est.); Median contract rent: $1,474 per month (2006-2010 5-year est.); Median year structure built: 1967 (2006-2010 5-year est.).
**Transportation:** Commute to work: 90.4% car, 4.3% public transportation, 0.6% walk, 4.1% work from home (2006-2010 5-year est.); Travel time to work: 28.5% less than 15 minutes, 36.4% 15 to 30 minutes, 15.7% 30 to 45 minutes, 7.3% 45 to 60 minutes, 12.0% 60 minutes or more (2006-2010 5-year est.).

## HEAD OF THE HARBOR (village). Covers a land area of 2.807 square miles and a water area of 0.228 square miles. Located at 40.89° N. Lat; 73.16° W. Long. Elevation is 121 feet.

**Population:** 1,354 (1990); 1,447 (2000); 1,472 (2010); Density: 524.4 persons per square mile (2010); Race: 95.4% White, 0.7% Black, 2.6% Asian, 0.0% American Indian/Alaska Native, 0.0% Native Hawaiian/Other Pacific Islander, 1.3% Other, 3.1% Hispanic of any race (2010); Average household size: 2.88 (2010); Median age: 45.6 (2010); Males per 100 females: 102.2 (2010); Marriage status: 23.2% never married, 66.5% now married, 6.7% widowed, 3.5% divorced (2006-2010 5-year est.); Foreign born: 4.7% (2006-2010 5-year est.); Ancestry (includes multiple ancestries): 42.0% Italian, 25.4% Irish, 18.4% German, 8.9% English, 6.6% Polish (2006-2010 5-year est.).
**Economy:** Single-family building permits issued: 1 (2011); Multi-family building permits issued: 0 (2011); Employment by occupation: 27.8% management, 1.5% professional, 1.1% services, 11.2% sales, 4.0% farming, 4.0% construction, 2.5% production (2006-2010 5-year est.).
**Income:** Per capita income: $66,497 (2006-2010 5-year est.); Median household income: $152,813 (2006-2010 5-year est.); Average household income: $198,585 (2006-2010 5-year est.); Percent of households with income of $100,000 or more: 65.0% (2006-2010 5-year est.); Poverty rate: 2.9% (2006-2010 5-year est.).
**Education:** Percent of population age 25 and over with: High school diploma (including GED) or higher: 96.6% (2006-2010 5-year est.); Bachelor's degree or higher: 62.6% (2006-2010 5-year est.); Master's degree or higher: 33.3% (2006-2010 5-year est.).
**Housing:** Homeownership rate: 87.5% (2010); Median home value: $1 (2006-2010 5-year est.); Median contract rent: $1,125 per month (2006-2010 5-year est.); Median year structure built: 1972 (2006-2010 5-year est.).

**Transportation:** Commute to work: 89.9% car, 1.8% public transportation, 0.0% walk, 6.9% work from home (2006-2010 5-year est.); Travel time to work: 22.1% less than 15 minutes, 36.7% 15 to 30 minutes, 22.7% 30 to 45 minutes, 8.1% 45 to 60 minutes, 10.4% 60 minutes or more (2006-2010 5-year est.)

## HOLBROOK (CDP). Covers a land area of 7.182 square miles and a water area of 0 square miles. Located at 40.79° N. Lat; 73.07° W. Long. Elevation is 118 feet.

**Population:** 25,273 (1990); 27,512 (2000); 27,195 (2010); Density: 3,786.2 persons per square mile (2010); Race: 91.7% White, 1.6% Black, 3.7% Asian, 0.1% American Indian/Alaska Native, 0.0% Native Hawaiian/Other Pacific Islander, 2.9% Other, 8.5% Hispanic of any race (2010); Average household size: 2.83 (2010); Median age: 40.1 (2010); Males per 100 females: 93.2 (2010); Marriage status: 29.1% never married, 57.1% now married, 5.3% widowed, 8.6% divorced (2006-2010 5-year est.); Foreign born: 8.6% (2006-2010 5-year est.); Ancestry (includes multiple ancestries): 41.7% Italian, 24.9% Irish, 18.3% German, 6.8% Polish, 5.6% English (2006-2010 5-year est.).
**Economy:** Employment by occupation: 13.0% management, 5.1% professional, 7.4% services, 18.6% sales, 4.2% farming, 9.4% construction, 4.9% production (2006-2010 5-year est.).
**Income:** Per capita income: $35,481 (2006-2010 5-year est.); Median household income: $91,826 (2006-2010 5-year est.); Average household income: $101,464 (2006-2010 5-year est.); Percent of households with income of $100,000 or more: 45.7% (2006-2010 5-year est.); Poverty rate: 3.5% (2006-2010 5-year est.).
**Education:** Percent of population age 25 and over with: High school diploma (including GED) or higher: 91.4% (2006-2010 5-year est.); Bachelor's degree or higher: 28.9% (2006-2010 5-year est.); Master's degree or higher: 11.4% (2006-2010 5-year est.).

### School District(s)
Sachem Central School District (KG-12)
  2009-10 Enrollment: 14,760 . . . . . . . . . . . . . . . . . . . . . (631) 471-1336
**Housing:** Homeownership rate: 77.1% (2010); Median home value: $403,100 (2006-2010 5-year est.); Median contract rent: $1,394 per month (2006-2010 5-year est.); Median year structure built: 1974 (2006-2010 5-year est.).
**Transportation:** Commute to work: 90.5% car, 5.2% public transportation, 1.3% walk, 2.6% work from home (2006-2010 5-year est.); Travel time to work: 27.7% less than 15 minutes, 31.4% 15 to 30 minutes, 21.5% 30 to 45 minutes, 6.9% 45 to 60 minutes, 12.5% 60 minutes or more (2006-2010 5-year est.)

## HOLTSVILLE (CDP). Covers a land area of 7.113 square miles and a water area of 0 square miles. Located at 40.81° N. Lat; 73.04° W. Long. Elevation is 105 feet.

**Population:** 14,972 (1990); 17,006 (2000); 19,714 (2010); Density: 2,771.5 persons per square mile (2010); Race: 90.2% White, 1.8% Black, 4.4% Asian, 0.2% American Indian/Alaska Native, 0.0% Native Hawaiian/Other Pacific Islander, 3.4% Other, 10.1% Hispanic of any race (2010); Average household size: 2.92 (2010); Median age: 39.3 (2010); Males per 100 females: 93.5 (2010); Marriage status: 26.9% never married, 61.1% now married, 4.2% widowed, 7.9% divorced (2006-2010 5-year est.); Foreign born: 9.0% (2006-2010 5-year est.); Ancestry (includes multiple ancestries): 42.4% Italian, 27.0% Irish, 20.2% German, 6.5% English, 4.9% Polish (2006-2010 5-year est.).
**Economy:** Employment by occupation: 10.6% management, 3.9% professional, 7.7% services, 22.9% sales, 4.9% farming, 8.9% construction, 4.6% production (2006-2010 5-year est.).
**Income:** Per capita income: $34,341 (2006-2010 5-year est.); Median household income: $91,091 (2006-2010 5-year est.); Average household income: $102,628 (2006-2010 5-year est.); Percent of households with income of $100,000 or more: 43.7% (2006-2010 5-year est.); Poverty rate: 3.6% (2006-2010 5-year est.).
**Education:** Percent of population age 25 and over with: High school diploma (including GED) or higher: 92.8% (2006-2010 5-year est.); Bachelor's degree or higher: 26.2% (2006-2010 5-year est.); Master's degree or higher: 11.3% (2006-2010 5-year est.).

### School District(s)
Sachem Central School District (KG-12)
  2009-10 Enrollment: 14,760 . . . . . . . . . . . . . . . . . . . . . (631) 471-1336
**Housing:** Homeownership rate: 81.4% (2010); Median home value: $382,000 (2006-2010 5-year est.); Median contract rent: $1,505 per month

(2006-2010 5-year est.); Median year structure built: 1975 (2006-2010 5-year est.).
**Transportation:** Commute to work: 92.4% car, 4.3% public transportation, 0.3% walk, 2.5% work from home (2006-2010 5-year est.); Travel time to work: 21.7% less than 15 minutes, 33.5% 15 to 30 minutes, 20.1% 30 to 45 minutes, 8.8% 45 to 60 minutes, 16.0% 60 minutes or more (2006-2010 5-year est.)

**HUNTINGTON** (town). Covers a land area of 94.123 square miles and a water area of 42.988 square miles. Located at 40.88° N. Lat; 73.37° W. Long. Elevation is 75 feet.
**History:** Named for Huntingdon, England, or to mean "hunting town" for its abundance of game. Seat of Immaculate Conception College, World Friends College. Settled 1653.
**Population:** 191,474 (1990); 195,289 (2000); 203,264 (2010); Density: 2,159.5 persons per square mile (2010); Race: 84.2% White, 4.7% Black, 5.0% Asian, 0.2% American Indian/Alaska Native, 0.0% Native Hawaiian/Other Pacific Islander, 5.9% Other, 11.0% Hispanic of any race (2010); Average household size: 2.89 (2010); Median age: 42.5 (2010); Males per 100 females: 96.9 (2010); Marriage status: 26.4% never married, 60.9% now married, 6.2% widowed, 6.4% divorced (2006-2010 5-year est.); Foreign born: 13.5% (2006-2010 5-year est.); Ancestry (includes multiple ancestries): 27.7% Italian, 22.6% Irish, 16.7% German, 6.5% Polish, 6.4% English (2006-2010 5-year est.).
**Economy:** Unemployment rate: 7.2% (February 2012); Total civilian labor force: 105,069 (February 2012); Single-family building permits issued: 40 (2011); Multi-family building permits issued: 0 (2011); Employment by occupation: 18.6% management, 4.4% professional, 5.9% services, 15.3% sales, 3.0% farming, 6.7% construction, 3.5% production (2006-2010 5-year est.).
**Income:** Per capita income: $46,862 (2006-2010 5-year est.); Median household income: $102,782 (2006-2010 5-year est.); Average household income: $136,356 (2006-2010 5-year est.); Percent of households with income of $100,000 or more: 52.3% (2006-2010 5-year est.); Poverty rate: 4.4% (2006-2010 5-year est.).
**Taxes:** Total city taxes per capita: $657 (2009); City property taxes per capita: $569 (2009).
**Education:** Percent of population age 25 and over with: High school diploma (including GED) or higher: 93.0% (2006-2010 5-year est.); Bachelor's degree or higher: 47.5% (2006-2010 5-year est.); Master's degree or higher: 21.7% (2006-2010 5-year est.).
**School District(s)**
Cold Spring Harbor Central School District (KG-12)
    2009-10 Enrollment: 2,018 . . . . . . . . . . . . . . . . . . . . . . (631) 367-5931
Elwood Union Free School District (KG-12)
    2009-10 Enrollment: 2,616 . . . . . . . . . . . . . . . . . . . . . . (631) 266-5402
Huntington Union Free School District (KG-12)
    2009-10 Enrollment: 4,445 . . . . . . . . . . . . . . . . . . . . . . (631) 673-2038
South Huntington Union Free School District (KG-12)
    2009-10 Enrollment: 6,019 . . . . . . . . . . . . . . . . . . . . . . (631) 812-3070
**Four-year College(s)**
Seminary of the Immaculate Conception (Private, Not-for-profit, Roman Catholic)
    Fall 2010 Enrollment: 71 . . . . . . . . . . . . . . . . . . . . . . (6.3) 142-3E+1
**Housing:** Homeownership rate: 83.9% (2010); Median home value: $573,300 (2006-2010 5-year est.); Median contract rent: $1,269 per month (2006-2010 5-year est.); Median year structure built: 1961 (2006-2010 5-year est.).
**Hospitals:** Huntington Hospital (396 beds)
**Newspapers:** Half Hollow Hills (Community news; Circulation 15,000); Huntington Record (Community news; Circulation 6,600); Long Islander Half Hollow Hills (Local news; Circulation 15,000); The Long Islander (Community news; Circulation 7,993); Northport Journal (Community news; Circulation 1,213); The Pennysaver - Huntington (Community news); canvas (Regional news)
**Transportation:** Commute to work: 82.2% car, 9.8% public transportation, 1.4% walk, 5.8% work from home (2006-2010 5-year est.); Travel time to work: 25.0% less than 15 minutes, 30.6% 15 to 30 minutes, 18.9% 30 to 45 minutes, 8.1% 45 to 60 minutes, 17.4% 60 minutes or more (2006-2010 5-year est.)
**Additional Information Contacts**
Huntington Township Chamber of Commerce. . . . . . . . . . . (631) 423-6100
    http://www.huntingtonchamber.com
Town of Huntington . . . . . . . . . . . . . . . . . . . . . . . . . (631) 351-3206
    http://www.huntingtonny.gov

**HUNTINGTON** (CDP). Covers a land area of 7.593 square miles and a water area of 0.139 square miles. Located at 40.87° N. Lat; 73.40° W. Long. Elevation is 75 feet.
**History:** The central business district, called Huntington Village locally, is old and well developed, but it is not incorporated and does not have a village form of government. Huntington is the birthplace of singer Mariah Carey and actor Ralph Macchio. It is also where world-renowned jazz musicians John Coltrane and his wife Alice Coltrane (harpist and pianist) lived in the later years of their life together; he died in Huntington in 1967.
**Population:** 18,217 (1990); 18,403 (2000); 18,046 (2010); Density: 2,376.4 persons per square mile (2010); Race: 93.2% White, 2.2% Black, 2.2% Asian, 0.1% American Indian/Alaska Native, 0.0% Native Hawaiian/Other Pacific Islander, 2.3% Other, 5.0% Hispanic of any race (2010); Average household size: 2.50 (2010); Median age: 44.9 (2010); Males per 100 females: 96.5 (2010); Marriage status: 26.7% never married, 59.7% now married, 6.7% widowed, 6.9% divorced (2006-2010 5-year est.); Foreign born: 10.2% (2006-2010 5-year est.); Ancestry (includes multiple ancestries): 29.0% Italian, 27.6% Irish, 19.5% German, 9.0% English, 6.3% Polish (2006-2010 5-year est.).
**Economy:** Employment by occupation: 22.7% management, 5.2% professional, 4.1% services, 14.4% sales, 2.1% farming, 4.8% construction, 1.6% production (2006-2010 5-year est.).
**Income:** Per capita income: $55,975 (2006-2010 5-year est.); Median household income: $110,988 (2006-2010 5-year est.); Average household income: $146,901 (2006-2010 5-year est.); Percent of households with income of $100,000 or more: 56.2% (2006-2010 5-year est.); Poverty rate: 3.2% (2006-2010 5-year est.).
**Education:** Percent of population age 25 and over with: High school diploma (including GED) or higher: 95.7% (2006-2010 5-year est.); Bachelor's degree or higher: 57.6% (2006-2010 5-year est.); Master's degree or higher: 28.5% (2006-2010 5-year est.).
**School District(s)**
Cold Spring Harbor Central School District (KG-12)
    2009-10 Enrollment: 2,018 . . . . . . . . . . . . . . . . . . . . . . (631) 367-5931
Elwood Union Free School District (KG-12)
    2009-10 Enrollment: 2,616 . . . . . . . . . . . . . . . . . . . . . . (631) 266-5402
Huntington Union Free School District (KG-12)
    2009-10 Enrollment: 4,445 . . . . . . . . . . . . . . . . . . . . . . (631) 673-2038
South Huntington Union Free School District (KG-12)
    2009-10 Enrollment: 6,019 . . . . . . . . . . . . . . . . . . . . . . (631) 812-3070
**Four-year College(s)**
Seminary of the Immaculate Conception (Private, Not-for-profit, Roman Catholic)
    Fall 2010 Enrollment: 71 . . . . . . . . . . . . . . . . . . . . . . (6.3) 142-3E+1
**Housing:** Homeownership rate: 80.3% (2010); Median home value: $631,700 (2006-2010 5-year est.); Median contract rent: $1,456 per month (2006-2010 5-year est.); Median year structure built: 1954 (2006-2010 5-year est.).
**Hospitals:** Huntington Hospital (396 beds)
**Transportation:** Commute to work: 77.2% car, 11.4% public transportation, 2.6% walk, 7.6% work from home (2006-2010 5-year est.); Travel time to work: 26.2% less than 15 minutes, 26.3% 15 to 30 minutes, 20.1% 30 to 45 minutes, 9.2% 45 to 60 minutes, 18.2% 60 minutes or more (2006-2010 5-year est.)

**HUNTINGTON BAY** (village). Covers a land area of 0.998 square miles and a water area of 0.896 square miles. Located at 40.90° N. Lat; 73.41° W. Long. Elevation is 16 feet.
**History:** Site of capture of Nathan Hale by British forces during American Revolution.
**Population:** 1,521 (1990); 1,496 (2000); 1,425 (2010); Density: 1,427.5 persons per square mile (2010); Race: 96.4% White, 0.5% Black, 1.8% Asian, 0.0% American Indian/Alaska Native, 0.0% Native Hawaiian/Other Pacific Islander, 1.3% Other, 3.4% Hispanic of any race (2010); Average household size: 2.67 (2010); Median age: 50.7 (2010); Males per 100 females: 97.9 (2010); Marriage status: 19.1% never married, 69.7% now married, 6.1% widowed, 5.2% divorced (2006-2010 5-year est.); Foreign born: 9.7% (2006-2010 5-year est.); Ancestry (includes multiple ancestries): 35.2% Irish, 27.4% Italian, 18.8% German, 12.6% English, 5.8% Polish (2006-2010 5-year est.).
**Economy:** Single-family building permits issued: 1 (2011); Multi-family building permits issued: 0 (2011); Employment by occupation: 27.0% management, 3.8% professional, 0.5% services, 11.8% sales, 0.9% farming, 3.1% construction, 1.3% production (2006-2010 5-year est.).

**Income:** Per capita income: $99,326 (2006-2010 5-year est.); Median household income: $133,333 (2006-2010 5-year est.); Average household income: $253,094 (2006-2010 5-year est.); Percent of households with income of $100,000 or more: 63.6% (2006-2010 5-year est.); Poverty rate: 2.4% (2006-2010 5-year est.).

**Education:** Percent of population age 25 and over with: High school diploma (including GED) or higher: 98.7% (2006-2010 5-year est.); Bachelor's degree or higher: 69.1% (2006-2010 5-year est.); Master's degree or higher: 37.9% (2006-2010 5-year est.).

**Housing:** Homeownership rate: 95.7% (2010); Median home value: $1 (2006-2010 5-year est.); Median contract rent: n/a per month (2006-2010 5-year est.); Median year structure built: 1951 (2006-2010 5-year est.).

**Safety:** Violent crime rate: 0.0 per 10,000 population; Property crime rate: 93.1 per 10,000 population (2010).

**Transportation:** Commute to work: 72.0% car, 13.1% public transportation, 0.0% walk, 13.1% work from home (2006-2010 5-year est.); Travel time to work: 19.7% less than 15 minutes, 18.0% 15 to 30 minutes, 24.5% 30 to 45 minutes, 15.5% 45 to 60 minutes, 22.3% 60 minutes or more (2006-2010 5-year est.)

---

**HUNTINGTON STATION** (CDP). Covers a land area of 5.474 square miles and a water area of 0.003 square miles. Located at 40.84° N. Lat; 73.40° W. Long. Elevation is 217 feet.

**History:** Named for Huntingdon, England, or to mean "hunting town". Walt Whitman born here.

**Population:** 28,247 (1990); 29,910 (2000); 33,029 (2010); Density: 6,033.7 persons per square mile (2010); Race: 64.0% White, 10.9% Black, 3.5% Asian, 0.6% American Indian/Alaska Native, 0.0% Native Hawaiian/Other Pacific Islander, 21.0% Other, 36.7% Hispanic of any race (2010); Average household size: 3.26 (2010); Median age: 35.4 (2010); Males per 100 females: 104.4 (2010); Marriage status: 36.3% never married, 51.1% now married, 5.0% widowed, 7.5% divorced (2006-2010 5-year est.); Foreign born: 27.3% (2006-2010 5-year est.); Ancestry (includes multiple ancestries): 20.8% Italian, 17.0% Irish, 13.1% German, 5.1% English, 3.8% Polish (2006-2010 5-year est.).

**Economy:** Employment by occupation: 9.9% management, 3.3% professional, 10.3% services, 18.1% sales, 3.0% farming, 10.4% construction, 5.6% production (2006-2010 5-year est.).

**Income:** Per capita income: $30,052 (2006-2010 5-year est.); Median household income: $74,667 (2006-2010 5-year est.); Average household income: $90,035 (2006-2010 5-year est.); Percent of households with income of $100,000 or more: 34.5% (2006-2010 5-year est.); Poverty rate: 11.3% (2006-2010 5-year est.).

**Education:** Percent of population age 25 and over with: High school diploma (including GED) or higher: 81.0% (2006-2010 5-year est.); Bachelor's degree or higher: 29.5% (2006-2010 5-year est.); Master's degree or higher: 11.6% (2006-2010 5-year est.).

**School District(s)**
Huntington Union Free School District (KG-12)
    2009-10 Enrollment: 4,445 . . . . . . . . . . . . . . . . . . . . . (631) 673-2038
South Huntington Union Free School District (KG-12)
    2009-10 Enrollment: 6,019 . . . . . . . . . . . . . . . . . . . . . (631) 812-3070

**Housing:** Homeownership rate: 69.5% (2010); Median home value: $419,100 (2006-2010 5-year est.); Median contract rent: $1,219 per month (2006-2010 5-year est.); Median year structure built: 1957 (2006-2010 5-year est.).

**Transportation:** Commute to work: 82.9% car, 9.0% public transportation, 2.5% walk, 4.4% work from home (2006-2010 5-year est.); Travel time to work: 31.5% less than 15 minutes, 31.9% 15 to 30 minutes, 20.2% 30 to 45 minutes, 6.3% 45 to 60 minutes, 10.1% 60 minutes or more (2006-2010 5-year est.)

---

**ISLANDIA** (village). Covers a land area of 2.219 square miles and a water area of 0 square miles. Located at 40.80° N. Lat; 73.17° W. Long. Elevation is 66 feet.

**Population:** 2,769 (1990); 3,057 (2000); 3,335 (2010); Density: 1,502.4 persons per square mile (2010); Race: 62.8% White, 14.0% Black, 6.1% Asian, 0.4% American Indian/Alaska Native, 0.0% Native Hawaiian/Other Pacific Islander, 16.7% Other, 28.3% Hispanic of any race (2010); Average household size: 3.05 (2010); Median age: 40.7 (2010); Males per 100 females: 88.1 (2010); Marriage status: 29.5% never married, 54.7% now married, 4.7% widowed, 11.1% divorced (2006-2010 5-year est.); Foreign born: 25.0% (2006-2010 5-year est.); Ancestry (includes multiple ancestries): 19.8% Italian, 15.3% Irish, 8.4% German, 6.2% American, 5.1% Jamaican (2006-2010 5-year est.).

**Economy:** Single-family building permits issued: 1 (2011); Multi-family building permits issued: 0 (2011); Employment by occupation: 10.1% management, 3.9% professional, 11.8% services, 16.3% sales, 4.2% farming, 10.3% construction, 8.3% production (2006-2010 5-year est.).

**Income:** Per capita income: $31,698 (2006-2010 5-year est.); Median household income: $91,721 (2006-2010 5-year est.); Average household income: $91,564 (2006-2010 5-year est.); Percent of households with income of $100,000 or more: 38.2% (2006-2010 5-year est.); Poverty rate: 3.9% (2006-2010 5-year est.).

**Education:** Percent of population age 25 and over with: High school diploma (including GED) or higher: 93.0% (2006-2010 5-year est.); Bachelor's degree or higher: 27.8% (2006-2010 5-year est.); Master's degree or higher: 11.0% (2006-2010 5-year est.).

**School District(s)**
Central Islip Union Free School District (PK-12)
    2009-10 Enrollment: 6,500 . . . . . . . . . . . . . . . . . . . . . (631) 348-5001

**Housing:** Homeownership rate: 89.7% (2010); Median home value: $359,300 (2006-2010 5-year est.); Median contract rent: $1,643 per month (2006-2010 5-year est.); Median year structure built: 1969 (2006-2010 5-year est.).

**Transportation:** Commute to work: 88.7% car, 6.9% public transportation, 0.0% walk, 3.0% work from home (2006-2010 5-year est.); Travel time to work: 22.2% less than 15 minutes, 38.7% 15 to 30 minutes, 13.9% 30 to 45 minutes, 8.6% 45 to 60 minutes, 16.6% 60 minutes or more (2006-2010 5-year est.)

---

**ISLIP** (town). Covers a land area of 104.113 square miles and a water area of 58.890 square miles. Located at 40.71° N. Lat; 73.19° W. Long. Elevation is 13 feet.

**Population:** 299,587 (1990); 322,612 (2000); 335,543 (2010); Density: 3,222.8 persons per square mile (2010); Race: 73.3% White, 9.5% Black, 2.9% Asian, 0.5% American Indian/Alaska Native, 0.0% Native Hawaiian/Other Pacific Islander, 13.8% Other, 29.0% Hispanic of any race (2010); Average household size: 3.20 (2010); Median age: 37.6 (2010); Males per 100 females: 97.2 (2010); Marriage status: 32.2% never married, 54.0% now married, 5.9% widowed, 7.8% divorced (2006-2010 5-year est.); Foreign born: 19.3% (2006-2010 5-year est.); Ancestry (includes multiple ancestries): 25.3% Italian, 20.6% Irish, 14.5% German, 4.5% Polish, 4.2% English (2006-2010 5-year est.).

**Economy:** Unemployment rate: 8.5% (February 2012); Total civilian labor force: 174,736 (February 2012); Single-family building permits issued: 47 (2011); Multi-family building permits issued: 32 (2011); Employment by occupation: 10.0% management, 3.3% professional, 8.9% services, 17.1% sales, 4.3% farming, 9.4% construction, 7.8% production (2006-2010 5-year est.).

**Income:** Per capita income: $30,893 (2006-2010 5-year est.); Median household income: $82,160 (2006-2010 5-year est.); Average household income: $97,067 (2006-2010 5-year est.); Percent of households with income of $100,000 or more: 38.7% (2006-2010 5-year est.); Poverty rate: 5.5% (2006-2010 5-year est.).

**Taxes:** Total city taxes per capita: $348 (2009); City property taxes per capita: $293 (2009).

**Education:** Percent of population age 25 and over with: High school diploma (including GED) or higher: 85.2% (2006-2010 5-year est.); Bachelor's degree or higher: 25.5% (2006-2010 5-year est.); Master's degree or higher: 10.8% (2006-2010 5-year est.).

**School District(s)**
Islip Union Free School District (KG-12)
    2009-10 Enrollment: 3,433 . . . . . . . . . . . . . . . . . . . . . (631) 859-2209

**Housing:** Homeownership rate: 76.4% (2010); Median home value: $395,500 (2006-2010 5-year est.); Median contract rent: $1,313 per month (2006-2010 5-year est.); Median year structure built: 1965 (2006-2010 5-year est.).

**Transportation:** Commute to work: 88.7% car, 5.8% public transportation, 1.1% walk, 2.7% work from home (2006-2010 5-year est.); Travel time to work: 26.3% less than 15 minutes, 35.9% 15 to 30 minutes, 19.1% 30 to 45 minutes, 6.2% 45 to 60 minutes, 12.4% 60 minutes or more (2006-2010 5-year est.)

**Airports:** Long Island MacArthur (primary service/small hub)

**Additional Information Contacts**
Islip Chamber of Commerce . . . . . . . . . . . . . . . . . . . . . . . (631) 581-2720
    http://www.islipchamberofcommerce.com
Town of Islip. . . . . . . . . . . . . . . . . . . . . . . . . . . . . . . . (631) 224-5490
    http://www.townofislip-ny.gov

**ISLIP** (CDP). Covers a land area of 4.800 square miles and a water area of 0.119 square miles. Located at 40.73° N. Lat; 73.21° W. Long. Elevation is 13 feet.

**Population:** 18,924 (1990); 20,575 (2000); 18,689 (2010); Density: 3,893.5 persons per square mile (2010); Race: 86.4% White, 4.7% Black, 2.5% Asian, 0.2% American Indian/Alaska Native, 0.1% Native Hawaiian/Other Pacific Islander, 6.1% Other, 13.8% Hispanic of any race (2010); Average household size: 2.89 (2010); Median age: 40.1 (2010); Males per 100 females: 95.6 (2010); Marriage status: 30.5% never married, 55.9% now married, 5.3% widowed, 8.3% divorced (2006-2010 5-year est.); Foreign born: 7.6% (2006-2010 5-year est.); Ancestry (includes multiple ancestries): 32.5% Italian, 30.0% Irish, 18.4% German, 6.0% Polish, 5.6% English (2006-2010 5-year est.).

**Economy:** Employment by occupation: 12.1% management, 3.0% professional, 9.7% services, 16.3% sales, 2.9% farming, 10.9% construction, 6.5% production (2006-2010 5-year est.).

**Income:** Per capita income: $33,657 (2006-2010 5-year est.); Median household income: $88,631 (2006-2010 5-year est.); Average household income: $98,429 (2006-2010 5-year est.); Percent of households with income of $100,000 or more: 42.0% (2006-2010 5-year est.); Poverty rate: 4.3% (2006-2010 5-year est.).

**Education:** Percent of population age 25 and over with: High school diploma (including GED) or higher: 90.9% (2006-2010 5-year est.); Bachelor's degree or higher: 29.3% (2006-2010 5-year est.); Master's degree or higher: 11.4% (2006-2010 5-year est.).

### School District(s)

Islip Union Free School District (KG-12)

    2009-10 Enrollment: 3,433 . . . . . . . . . . . . . . . . . . . . . . . (631) 859-2209

**Housing:** Homeownership rate: 80.6% (2010); Median home value: $401,800 (2006-2010 5-year est.); Median contract rent: $1,307 per month (2006-2010 5-year est.); Median year structure built: 1963 (2006-2010 5-year est.).

**Transportation:** Commute to work: 89.1% car, 7.7% public transportation, 0.5% walk, 1.7% work from home (2006-2010 5-year est.); Travel time to work: 26.6% less than 15 minutes, 31.2% 15 to 30 minutes, 17.8% 30 to 45 minutes, 8.4% 45 to 60 minutes, 16.0% 60 minutes or more (2006-2010 5-year est.)

**Airports:** Long Island MacArthur (primary service/small hub)

**ISLIP TERRACE** (CDP). Covers a land area of 1.347 square miles and a water area of 0 square miles. Located at 40.75° N. Lat; 73.18° W. Long. Elevation is 23 feet.

**Population:** 5,530 (1990); 5,641 (2000); 5,389 (2010); Density: 4,000.1 persons per square mile (2010); Race: 92.5% White, 1.9% Black, 2.3% Asian, 0.2% American Indian/Alaska Native, 0.0% Native Hawaiian/Other Pacific Islander, 3.1% Other, 8.9% Hispanic of any race (2010); Average household size: 3.16 (2010); Median age: 38.4 (2010); Males per 100 females: 99.7 (2010); Marriage status: 26.0% never married, 62.7% now married, 5.3% widowed, 6.0% divorced (2006-2010 5-year est.); Foreign born: 5.0% (2006-2010 5-year est.); Ancestry (includes multiple ancestries): 38.4% Italian, 32.1% German, 24.7% Irish, 6.6% English, 6.1% Austrian (2006-2010 5-year est.).

**Economy:** Employment by occupation: 9.8% management, 5.3% professional, 7.5% services, 27.3% sales, 2.8% farming, 12.4% construction, 7.8% production (2006-2010 5-year est.).

**Income:** Per capita income: $30,781 (2006-2010 5-year est.); Median household income: $88,992 (2006-2010 5-year est.); Average household income: $98,941 (2006-2010 5-year est.); Percent of households with income of $100,000 or more: 41.3% (2006-2010 5-year est.); Poverty rate: 1.9% (2006-2010 5-year est.).

**Education:** Percent of population age 25 and over with: High school diploma (including GED) or higher: 92.1% (2006-2010 5-year est.); Bachelor's degree or higher: 20.1% (2006-2010 5-year est.); Master's degree or higher: 7.4% (2006-2010 5-year est.).

### School District(s)

East Islip Union Free School District (PK-12)

    2009-10 Enrollment: 4,876 . . . . . . . . . . . . . . . . . . . . . . . (631) 224-2000

**Housing:** Homeownership rate: 88.8% (2010); Median home value: $399,800 (2006-2010 5-year est.); Median contract rent: $1,618 per month (2006-2010 5-year est.); Median year structure built: 1961 (2006-2010 5-year est.).

**Transportation:** Commute to work: 86.1% car, 5.4% public transportation, 4.0% walk, 3.1% work from home (2006-2010 5-year est.); Travel time to work: 20.7% less than 15 minutes, 39.2% 15 to 30 minutes, 21.8% 30 to 45

minutes, 6.9% 45 to 60 minutes, 11.4% 60 minutes or more (2006-2010 5-year est.)

**JAMESPORT** (CDP). Covers a land area of 4.496 square miles and a water area of 0.027 square miles. Located at 40.96° N. Lat; 72.58° W. Long. Elevation is 16 feet.

**Population:** 1,520 (1990); 1,526 (2000); 1,710 (2010); Density: 380.3 persons per square mile (2010); Race: 95.7% White, 1.1% Black, 0.4% Asian, 0.1% American Indian/Alaska Native, 0.0% Native Hawaiian/Other Pacific Islander, 2.7% Other, 8.3% Hispanic of any race (2010); Average household size: 2.37 (2010); Median age: 48.7 (2010); Males per 100 females: 97.2 (2010); Marriage status: 21.4% never married, 62.8% now married, 5.1% widowed, 10.7% divorced (2006-2010 5-year est.); Foreign born: 8.1% (2006-2010 5-year est.); Ancestry (includes multiple ancestries): 23.0% German, 22.5% Italian, 20.0% English, 19.7% Irish, 15.2% French (2006-2010 5-year est.).

**Economy:** Employment by occupation: 16.0% management, 2.2% professional, 3.3% services, 15.5% sales, 8.8% farming, 18.8% construction, 0.0% production (2006-2010 5-year est.).

**Income:** Per capita income: $39,042 (2006-2010 5-year est.); Median household income: $76,792 (2006-2010 5-year est.); Average household income: $83,431 (2006-2010 5-year est.); Percent of households with income of $100,000 or more: 39.3% (2006-2010 5-year est.); Poverty rate: 6.0% (2006-2010 5-year est.).

**Education:** Percent of population age 25 and over with: High school diploma (including GED) or higher: 98.6% (2006-2010 5-year est.); Bachelor's degree or higher: 40.3% (2006-2010 5-year est.); Master's degree or higher: 22.3% (2006-2010 5-year est.).

**Housing:** Homeownership rate: 81.1% (2010); Median home value: $406,700 (2006-2010 5-year est.); Median contract rent: $1,061 per month (2006-2010 5-year est.); Median year structure built: 1971 (2006-2010 5-year est.).

**Transportation:** Commute to work: 92.4% car, 2.2% public transportation, 2.2% walk, 3.1% work from home (2006-2010 5-year est.); Travel time to work: 21.3% less than 15 minutes, 44.3% 15 to 30 minutes, 9.1% 30 to 45 minutes, 16.2% 45 to 60 minutes, 9.1% 60 minutes or more (2006-2010 5-year est.)

**KINGS PARK** (CDP). Covers a land area of 6.199 square miles and a water area of 0.391 square miles. Located at 40.88° N. Lat; 73.24° W. Long. Elevation is 174 feet.

**History:** Developed as utopian community in 1872; became farm for insane in 1885. State psychiatric center opened 1892.

**Population:** 17,655 (1990); 16,146 (2000); 17,282 (2010); Density: 2,787.8 persons per square mile (2010); Race: 94.1% White, 1.1% Black, 2.4% Asian, 0.1% American Indian/Alaska Native, 0.0% Native Hawaiian/Other Pacific Islander, 2.3% Other, 5.3% Hispanic of any race (2010); Average household size: 2.71 (2010); Median age: 43.3 (2010); Males per 100 females: 93.7 (2010); Marriage status: 25.9% never married, 59.8% now married, 8.0% widowed, 6.2% divorced (2006-2010 5-year est.); Foreign born: 5.1% (2006-2010 5-year est.); Ancestry (includes multiple ancestries): 39.8% Italian, 33.5% Irish, 22.8% German, 8.0% Polish, 6.3% English (2006-2010 5-year est.).

**Economy:** Employment by occupation: 14.3% management, 5.4% professional, 7.0% services, 15.4% sales, 4.8% farming, 10.3% construction, 6.2% production (2006-2010 5-year est.).

**Income:** Per capita income: $36,294 (2006-2010 5-year est.); Median household income: $90,357 (2006-2010 5-year est.); Average household income: $103,072 (2006-2010 5-year est.); Percent of households with income of $100,000 or more: 45.5% (2006-2010 5-year est.); Poverty rate: 2.7% (2006-2010 5-year est.).

**Education:** Percent of population age 25 and over with: High school diploma (including GED) or higher: 94.6% (2006-2010 5-year est.); Bachelor's degree or higher: 36.3% (2006-2010 5-year est.); Master's degree or higher: 15.6% (2006-2010 5-year est.).

### School District(s)

Kings Park Central School District (KG-12)

    2009-10 Enrollment: 3,955 . . . . . . . . . . . . . . . . . . . . . . . (631) 269-3310

**Housing:** Homeownership rate: 81.2% (2010); Median home value: $458,500 (2006-2010 5-year est.); Median contract rent: $1,130 per month (2006-2010 5-year est.); Median year structure built: 1964 (2006-2010 5-year est.).

**Transportation:** Commute to work: 89.6% car, 6.3% public transportation, 1.5% walk, 2.1% work from home (2006-2010 5-year est.); Travel time to work: 25.4% less than 15 minutes, 31.6% 15 to 30 minutes, 20.6% 30 to 45

minutes, 7.2% 45 to 60 minutes, 15.2% 60 minutes or more (2006-2010 5-year est.)

**Additional Information Contacts**

Kings Park Chamber of Commerce ............ (631) 269-7678
  http://www.kingsparkli.com

## LAKE GROVE (village). Covers a land area of 2.946 square miles and a water area of 0.001 square miles. Located at 40.85° N. Lat; 73.11° W. Long. Elevation is 118 feet.

**Population:** 9,612 (1990); 10,250 (2000); 11,163 (2010); Density: 3,788.2 persons per square mile (2010); Race: 87.9% White, 2.2% Black, 6.7% Asian, 0.2% American Indian/Alaska Native, 0.0% Native Hawaiian/Other Pacific Islander, 3.0% Other, 7.8% Hispanic of any race (2010); Average household size: 2.92 (2010); Median age: 39.4 (2010); Males per 100 females: 98.6 (2010); Marriage status: 26.2% never married, 62.7% now married, 4.3% widowed, 6.8% divorced (2006-2010 5-year est.); Foreign born: 8.9% (2006-2010 5-year est.); Ancestry (includes multiple ancestries): 42.7% Italian, 28.3% Irish, 18.4% German, 5.4% English, 5.4% Polish (2006-2010 5-year est.).

**Economy:** Single-family building permits issued: 3 (2011); Multi-family building permits issued: 0 (2011); Employment by occupation: 14.8% management, 6.3% professional, 4.8% services, 19.8% sales, 2.3% farming, 6.9% construction, 5.2% production (2006-2010 5-year est.).

**Income:** Per capita income: $37,010 (2006-2010 5-year est.); Median household income: $94,983 (2006-2010 5-year est.); Average household income: $107,608 (2006-2010 5-year est.); Percent of households with income of $100,000 or more: 47.6% (2006-2010 5-year est.); Poverty rate: 4.9% (2006-2010 5-year est.).

**Education:** Percent of population age 25 and over with: High school diploma (including GED) or higher: 93.5% (2006-2010 5-year est.); Bachelor's degree or higher: 34.4% (2006-2010 5-year est.); Master's degree or higher: 14.2% (2006-2010 5-year est.).

### School District(s)

Middle Country Central School District (PK-12)

  2009-10 Enrollment: 10,929 .................... (631) 285-8005

Sachem Central School District (KG-12)

  2009-10 Enrollment: 14,760 .................... (631) 471-1336

**Housing:** Homeownership rate: 82.0% (2010); Median home value: $429,800 (2006-2010 5-year est.); Median contract rent: $1,413 per month (2006-2010 5-year est.); Median year structure built: 1969 (2006-2010 5-year est.).

**Transportation:** Commute to work: 87.1% car, 6.5% public transportation, 1.1% walk, 5.0% work from home (2006-2010 5-year est.); Travel time to work: 23.0% less than 15 minutes, 31.1% 15 to 30 minutes, 18.2% 30 to 45 minutes, 6.8% 45 to 60 minutes, 20.9% 60 minutes or more (2006-2010 5-year est.)

## LAKE RONKONKOMA (CDP). Covers a land area of 4.940 square miles and a water area of 0.002 square miles. Located at 40.83° N. Lat; 73.11° W. Long. Elevation is 72 feet.

**Population:** 18,997 (1990); 19,701 (2000); 20,155 (2010); Density: 4,079.7 persons per square mile (2010); Race: 89.2% White, 2.4% Black, 4.5% Asian, 0.2% American Indian/Alaska Native, 0.0% Native Hawaiian/Other Pacific Islander, 3.7% Other, 10.0% Hispanic of any race (2010); Average household size: 2.85 (2010); Median age: 39.9 (2010); Males per 100 females: 94.6 (2010); Marriage status: 25.7% never married, 57.7% now married, 8.5% widowed, 8.1% divorced (2006-2010 5-year est.); Foreign born: 7.3% (2006-2010 5-year est.); Ancestry (includes multiple ancestries): 35.5% Italian, 31.0% Irish, 20.5% German, 6.6% Polish, 4.8% English (2006-2010 5-year est.).

**Economy:** Employment by occupation: 10.6% management, 3.8% professional, 7.1% services, 21.4% sales, 4.0% farming, 10.1% construction, 7.1% production (2006-2010 5-year est.).

**Income:** Per capita income: $31,331 (2006-2010 5-year est.); Median household income: $81,764 (2006-2010 5-year est.); Average household income: $92,558 (2006-2010 5-year est.); Percent of households with income of $100,000 or more: 39.3% (2006-2010 5-year est.); Poverty rate: 4.9% (2006-2010 5-year est.).

**Education:** Percent of population age 25 and over with: High school diploma (including GED) or higher: 89.2% (2006-2010 5-year est.); Bachelor's degree or higher: 25.6% (2006-2010 5-year est.); Master's degree or higher: 10.7% (2006-2010 5-year est.).

### School District(s)

Sachem Central School District (KG-12)

  2009-10 Enrollment: 14,760 .................... (631) 471-1336

**Housing:** Homeownership rate: 72.2% (2010); Median home value: $390,700 (2006-2010 5-year est.); Median contract rent: $1,243 per month (2006-2010 5-year est.); Median year structure built: 1968 (2006-2010 5-year est.).

**Transportation:** Commute to work: 91.2% car, 6.9% public transportation, 0.6% walk, 1.1% work from home (2006-2010 5-year est.); Travel time to work: 24.0% less than 15 minutes, 34.2% 15 to 30 minutes, 19.7% 30 to 45 minutes, 6.7% 45 to 60 minutes, 15.4% 60 minutes or more (2006-2010 5-year est.)

## LAUREL (CDP). Covers a land area of 2.999 square miles and a water area of 0.073 square miles. Located at 40.97° N. Lat; 72.55° W. Long. Elevation is 20 feet.

**Population:** 1,091 (1990); 1,188 (2000); 1,394 (2010); Density: 464.7 persons per square mile (2010); Race: 92.0% White, 1.7% Black, 0.4% Asian, 0.0% American Indian/Alaska Native, 0.0% Native Hawaiian/Other Pacific Islander, 5.9% Other, 8.9% Hispanic of any race (2010); Average household size: 2.65 (2010); Median age: 43.8 (2010); Males per 100 females: 102.9 (2010); Marriage status: 26.3% never married, 58.1% now married, 9.3% widowed, 6.3% divorced (2006-2010 5-year est.); Foreign born: 1.4% (2006-2010 5-year est.); Ancestry (includes multiple ancestries): 38.1% Italian, 21.7% Irish, 21.7% German, 15.0% Polish, 14.1% Scottish (2006-2010 5-year est.).

**Economy:** Employment by occupation: 18.6% management, 2.5% professional, 9.7% services, 24.1% sales, 2.7% farming, 4.3% construction, 0.0% production (2006-2010 5-year est.).

**Income:** Per capita income: $44,569 (2006-2010 5-year est.); Median household income: $105,119 (2006-2010 5-year est.); Average household income: $107,512 (2006-2010 5-year est.); Percent of households with income of $100,000 or more: 50.6% (2006-2010 5-year est.); Poverty rate: 3.3% (2006-2010 5-year est.).

**Education:** Percent of population age 25 and over with: High school diploma (including GED) or higher: 94.9% (2006-2010 5-year est.); Bachelor's degree or higher: 38.0% (2006-2010 5-year est.); Master's degree or higher: 12.9% (2006-2010 5-year est.).

**Housing:** Homeownership rate: 82.8% (2010); Median home value: $531,000 (2006-2010 5-year est.); Median contract rent: n/a per month (2006-2010 5-year est.); Median year structure built: 1959 (2006-2010 5-year est.).

**Transportation:** Commute to work: 91.8% car, 5.7% public transportation, 0.0% walk, 2.5% work from home (2006-2010 5-year est.); Travel time to work: 26.5% less than 15 minutes, 36.8% 15 to 30 minutes, 20.3% 30 to 45 minutes, 2.8% 45 to 60 minutes, 13.6% 60 minutes or more (2006-2010 5-year est.)

## LINDENHURST (village). Covers a land area of 3.760 square miles and a water area of 0.056 square miles. Located at 40.68° N. Lat; 73.37° W. Long. Elevation is 30 feet.

**History:** Named for Linden, Germany. Incorporated 1923.

**Population:** 26,879 (1990); 27,819 (2000); 27,253 (2010); Density: 7,247.8 persons per square mile (2010); Race: 92.1% White, 1.5% Black, 1.9% Asian, 0.1% American Indian/Alaska Native, 0.0% Native Hawaiian/Other Pacific Islander, 4.4% Other, 9.7% Hispanic of any race (2010); Average household size: 2.92 (2010); Median age: 40.3 (2010); Males per 100 females: 94.6 (2010); Marriage status: 29.5% never married, 55.8% now married, 7.1% widowed, 7.6% divorced (2006-2010 5-year est.); Foreign born: 13.0% (2006-2010 5-year est.); Ancestry (includes multiple ancestries): 38.9% Italian, 26.8% Irish, 20.3% German, 8.8% Polish, 4.7% English (2006-2010 5-year est.).

**Economy:** Unemployment rate: 8.8% (February 2012); Total civilian labor force: 14,254 (February 2012); Single-family building permits issued: 3 (2011); Multi-family building permits issued: 0 (2011); Employment by occupation: 9.5% management, 2.9% professional, 8.6% services, 19.9% sales, 5.9% farming, 11.9% construction, 5.6% production (2006-2010 5-year est.).

**Income:** Per capita income: $31,275 (2006-2010 5-year est.); Median household income: $85,345 (2006-2010 5-year est.); Average household income: $96,334 (2006-2010 5-year est.); Percent of households with income of $100,000 or more: 41.3% (2006-2010 5-year est.); Poverty rate: 2.7% (2006-2010 5-year est.).

**Education:** Percent of population age 25 and over with: High school diploma (including GED) or higher: 88.3% (2006-2010 5-year est.); Bachelor's degree or higher: 21.2% (2006-2010 5-year est.); Master's degree or higher: 7.3% (2006-2010 5-year est.).

Lindenhurst Union Free School District (KG-12)
    2009-10 Enrollment: 6,810 . . . . . . . . . . . . . . . . . . (631) 226-6511
**Housing:** Homeownership rate: 79.3% (2010); Median home value: $392,100 (2006-2010 5-year est.); Median contract rent: $1,256 per month (2006-2010 5-year est.); Median year structure built: 1956 (2006-2010 5-year est.).
**Newspapers:** Babylon South Bay (Local news; Circulation 96,200); Lindenhurst South Bay's (Local news; Circulation 23,100); Seaford South Bay (Local news; Circulation 18,300)
**Transportation:** Commute to work: 85.9% car, 9.3% public transportation, 1.2% walk, 3.0% work from home (2006-2010 5-year est.); Travel time to work: 24.7% less than 15 minutes, 29.5% 15 to 30 minutes, 21.2% 30 to 45 minutes, 7.6% 45 to 60 minutes, 16.9% 60 minutes or more (2006-2010 5-year est.)
**Additional Information Contacts**
Lindenhurst Chamber of Commerce . . . . . . . . . . . . . . . (631) 226-4641
    http://www.lindenhurstchamber.org
Village of Lindenhurst . . . . . . . . . . . . . . . . . . . . . . . . (631) 957-7500
    http://www.villageoflindenhurst.com

**LLOYD HARBOR** (village). Covers a land area of 9.363 square miles and a water area of 1.295 square miles. Located at 40.92° N. Lat; 73.44° W. Long. Elevation is 138 feet.
**History:** In 1654, the Matinecock Native Americans sold 3,000 acres (12 km²) of what is now called Lloyd Neck to English settlers from Oyster Bay. The Matinecock referred to the region as Caumsett (place by sharp rock). In 1676, James Lloyd acquired the neck, which was then taken over by his son Henry.
**Population:** 3,369 (1990); 3,675 (2000); 3,660 (2010); Density: 390.9 persons per square mile (2010); Race: 95.3% White, 1.0% Black, 2.2% Asian, 0.1% American Indian/Alaska Native, 0.0% Native Hawaiian/Other Pacific Islander, 1.4% Other, 3.3% Hispanic of any race (2010); Average household size: 3.11 (2010); Median age: 45.4 (2010); Males per 100 females: 99.7 (2010); Marriage status: 21.1% never married, 70.4% now married, 5.2% widowed, 3.2% divorced (2006-2010 5-year est.); Foreign born: 5.9% (2006-2010 5-year est.); Ancestry (includes multiple ancestries): 28.2% Italian, 24.6% Irish, 20.3% German, 10.9% English, 5.2% Russian (2006-2010 5-year est.).
**Economy:** Single-family building permits issued: 2 (2011); Multi-family building permits issued: 0 (2011); Employment by occupation: 25.7% management, 1.6% professional, 4.3% services, 9.5% sales, 1.4% farming, 2.6% construction, 2.1% production (2006-2010 5-year est.).
**Income:** Per capita income: $104,813 (2006-2010 5-year est.); Median household income: $186,500 (2006-2010 5-year est.); Average household income: $326,295 (2006-2010 5-year est.); Percent of households with income of $100,000 or more: 70.8% (2006-2010 5-year est.); Poverty rate: 3.9% (2006-2010 5-year est.).
**Education:** Percent of population age 25 and over with: High school diploma (including GED) or higher: 97.7% (2006-2010 5-year est.); Bachelor's degree or higher: 71.4% (2006-2010 5-year est.); Master's degree or higher: 34.7% (2006-2010 5-year est.).
**Housing:** Homeownership rate: 95.2% (2010); Median home value: $1 (2006-2010 5-year est.); Median contract rent: n/a per month (2006-2010 5-year est.); Median year structure built: 1964 (2006-2010 5-year est.).
**Safety:** Violent crime rate: 2.7 per 10,000 population; Property crime rate: 43.0 per 10,000 population (2010).
**Transportation:** Commute to work: 75.0% car, 15.5% public transportation, 1.1% walk, 7.9% work from home (2006-2010 5-year est.); Travel time to work: 17.3% less than 15 minutes, 20.7% 15 to 30 minutes, 27.0% 30 to 45 minutes, 8.1% 45 to 60 minutes, 26.9% 60 minutes or more (2006-2010 5-year est.)

**MANORVILLE** (CDP). Covers a land area of 25.469 square miles and a water area of 0.041 square miles. Located at 40.86° N. Lat; 72.78° W. Long. Elevation is 52 feet.
**Population:** 5,876 (1990); 11,131 (2000); 14,314 (2010); Density: 562.0 persons per square mile (2010); Race: 93.9% White, 1.6% Black, 1.7% Asian, 0.2% American Indian/Alaska Native, 0.0% Native Hawaiian/Other Pacific Islander, 2.6% Other, 6.6% Hispanic of any race (2010); Average household size: 2.84 (2010); Median age: 39.9 (2010); Males per 100 females: 98.0 (2010); Marriage status: 28.2% never married, 58.8% now married, 5.0% widowed, 8.0% divorced (2006-2010 5-year est.); Foreign born: 4.1% (2006-2010 5-year est.); Ancestry (includes multiple ancestries): 36.2% Irish, 35.0% Italian, 21.6% German, 6.4% English, 6.1% Polish (2006-2010 5-year est.).

**Economy:** Employment by occupation: 11.0% management, 6.3% professional, 4.6% services, 14.8% sales, 3.8% farming, 10.4% construction, 5.5% production (2006-2010 5-year est.).
**Income:** Per capita income: $40,652 (2006-2010 5-year est.); Median household income: $93,070 (2006-2010 5-year est.); Average household income: $110,418 (2006-2010 5-year est.); Percent of households with income of $100,000 or more: 46.7% (2006-2010 5-year est.); Poverty rate: 1.5% (2006-2010 5-year est.).
**Education:** Percent of population age 25 and over with: High school diploma (including GED) or higher: 96.1% (2006-2010 5-year est.); Bachelor's degree or higher: 38.3% (2006-2010 5-year est.); Master's degree or higher: 17.9% (2006-2010 5-year est.).
Eastport-South Manor Csd (KG-12)
    2009-10 Enrollment: 3,897 . . . . . . . . . . . . . . . . . . (631) 874-6720
**Housing:** Homeownership rate: 81.5% (2010); Median home value: $437,600 (2006-2010 5-year est.); Median contract rent: $1,201 per month (2006-2010 5-year est.); Median year structure built: 1992 (2006-2010 5-year est.).
**Transportation:** Commute to work: 95.8% car, 1.6% public transportation, 0.2% walk, 2.0% work from home (2006-2010 5-year est.); Travel time to work: 16.0% less than 15 minutes, 38.0% 15 to 30 minutes, 20.6% 30 to 45 minutes, 10.7% 45 to 60 minutes, 14.8% 60 minutes or more (2006-2010 5-year est.)

**MASTIC** (CDP). Covers a land area of 3.896 square miles and a water area of 0.084 square miles. Located at 40.81° N. Lat; 72.84° W. Long. Elevation is 30 feet.
**Population:** 13,887 (1990); 15,436 (2000); 15,481 (2010); Density: 3,972.6 persons per square mile (2010); Race: 76.5% White, 9.0% Black, 2.1% Asian, 0.7% American Indian/Alaska Native, 0.1% Native Hawaiian/Other Pacific Islander, 11.6% Other, 21.8% Hispanic of any race (2010); Average household size: 3.41 (2010); Median age: 33.1 (2010); Males per 100 females: 100.1 (2010); Marriage status: 38.9% never married, 49.8% now married, 4.4% widowed, 6.9% divorced (2006-2010 5-year est.); Foreign born: 8.5% (2006-2010 5-year est.); Ancestry (includes multiple ancestries): 36.1% Italian, 23.9% Irish, 21.7% German, 3.1% English, 2.8% Polish (2006-2010 5-year est.).
**Economy:** Employment by occupation: 7.2% management, 4.3% professional, 13.7% services, 19.1% sales, 1.9% farming, 11.2% construction, 8.3% production (2006-2010 5-year est.).
**Income:** Per capita income: $25,595 (2006-2010 5-year est.); Median household income: $75,306 (2006-2010 5-year est.); Average household income: $78,812 (2006-2010 5-year est.); Percent of households with income of $100,000 or more: 28.0% (2006-2010 5-year est.); Poverty rate: 12.6% (2006-2010 5-year est.).
**Education:** Percent of population age 25 and over with: High school diploma (including GED) or higher: 85.4% (2006-2010 5-year est.); Bachelor's degree or higher: 13.3% (2006-2010 5-year est.); Master's degree or higher: 5.7% (2006-2010 5-year est.).
**Housing:** Homeownership rate: 80.1% (2010); Median home value: $311,200 (2006-2010 5-year est.); Median contract rent: $1,264 per month (2006-2010 5-year est.); Median year structure built: 1975 (2006-2010 5-year est.).
**Transportation:** Commute to work: 93.8% car, 2.5% public transportation, 0.5% walk, 1.4% work from home (2006-2010 5-year est.); Travel time to work: 19.4% less than 15 minutes, 30.6% 15 to 30 minutes, 20.7% 30 to 45 minutes, 11.4% 45 to 60 minutes, 17.9% 60 minutes or more (2006-2010 5-year est.)

**MASTIC BEACH** (CDP). Covers a land area of 4.714 square miles and a water area of 0.264 square miles. Located at 40.76° N. Lat; 72.83° W. Long. Elevation is 7 feet.
**Population:** 10,293 (1990); 11,543 (2000); 12,930 (2010); Density: 2,742.4 persons per square mile (2010); Race: 80.5% White, 9.5% Black, 1.5% Asian, 0.4% American Indian/Alaska Native, 0.1% Native Hawaiian/Other Pacific Islander, 8.0% Other, 15.6% Hispanic of any race (2010); Average household size: 3.05 (2010); Median age: 35.4 (2010); Males per 100 females: 98.6 (2010); Marriage status: 31.9% never married, 52.7% now married, 7.6% widowed, 7.8% divorced (2006-2010 5-year est.); Foreign born: 6.0% (2006-2010 5-year est.); Ancestry (includes multiple ancestries): 30.5% Irish, 27.6% Italian, 23.5% German, 7.5% English, 5.4% Polish (2006-2010 5-year est.).

**Economy:** Employment by occupation: 7.0% management, 4.2% professional, 12.7% services, 20.0% sales, 5.2% farming, 12.6% construction, 9.2% production (2006-2010 5-year est.).
**Income:** Per capita income: $23,252 (2006-2010 5-year est.); Median household income: $67,462 (2006-2010 5-year est.); Average household income: $70,515 (2006-2010 5-year est.); Percent of households with income of $100,000 or more: 22.6% (2006-2010 5-year est.); Poverty rate: 12.8% (2006-2010 5-year est.).
**Education:** Percent of population age 25 and over with: High school diploma (including GED) or higher: 81.4% (2006-2010 5-year est.); Bachelor's degree or higher: 11.3% (2006-2010 5-year est.); Master's degree or higher: 5.9% (2006-2010 5-year est.).

### School District(s)
William Floyd Union Free School District (KG-12)
    2009-10 Enrollment: 9,398 . . . . . . . . . . . . . . . . . . . . . . (631) 874-1201
**Housing:** Homeownership rate: 75.9% (2010); Median home value: $273,100 (2006-2010 5-year est.); Median contract rent: $1,453 per month (2006-2010 5-year est.); Median year structure built: 1968 (2006-2010 5-year est.).
**Transportation:** Commute to work: 91.2% car, 4.2% public transportation, 0.5% walk, 1.8% work from home (2006-2010 5-year est.); Travel time to work: 11.9% less than 15 minutes, 23.6% 15 to 30 minutes, 29.4% 30 to 45 minutes, 14.7% 45 to 60 minutes, 20.4% 60 minutes or more (2006-2010 5-year est.)

## MATTITUCK (CDP).
Covers a land area of 8.995 square miles and a water area of 0.363 square miles. Located at 41.00° N. Lat; 72.54° W. Long. Elevation is 13 feet.
**Population:** 3,905 (1990); 4,198 (2000); 4,219 (2010); Density: 469.0 persons per square mile (2010); Race: 93.6% White, 1.6% Black, 0.9% Asian, 0.0% American Indian/Alaska Native, 0.0% Native Hawaiian/Other Pacific Islander, 3.9% Other, 6.8% Hispanic of any race (2010); Average household size: 2.48 (2010); Median age: 47.4 (2010); Males per 100 females: 98.2 (2010); Marriage status: 21.8% never married, 64.6% now married, 7.9% widowed, 5.7% divorced (2006-2010 5-year est.); Foreign born: 3.6% (2006-2010 5-year est.); Ancestry (includes multiple ancestries): 27.6% Irish, 24.6% German, 21.5% Italian, 16.9% Polish, 15.4% English (2006-2010 5-year est.).
**Economy:** Employment by occupation: 19.1% management, 0.0% professional, 7.0% services, 17.4% sales, 2.1% farming, 13.7% construction, 3.2% production (2006-2010 5-year est.).
**Income:** Per capita income: $43,131 (2006-2010 5-year est.); Median household income: $90,015 (2006-2010 5-year est.); Average household income: $100,770 (2006-2010 5-year est.); Percent of households with income of $100,000 or more: 40.4% (2006-2010 5-year est.); Poverty rate: 1.9% (2006-2010 5-year est.).
**Education:** Percent of population age 25 and over with: High school diploma (including GED) or higher: 92.1% (2006-2010 5-year est.); Bachelor's degree or higher: 38.8% (2006-2010 5-year est.); Master's degree or higher: 14.2% (2006-2010 5-year est.).

### School District(s)
Mattituck-Cutchogue Union Free School District (KG-12)
    2009-10 Enrollment: 1,514 . . . . . . . . . . . . . . . . . . . . . . (631) 298-4242
**Housing:** Homeownership rate: 83.9% (2010); Median home value: $555,100 (2006-2010 5-year est.); Median contract rent: $1,399 per month (2006-2010 5-year est.); Median year structure built: 1966 (2006-2010 5-year est.).
**Newspapers:** News-Review (Community news; Circulation 15,000); Suffolk Times (Community news; Circulation 15,000)
**Transportation:** Commute to work: 86.0% car, 3.2% public transportation, 0.6% walk, 6.1% work from home (2006-2010 5-year est.); Travel time to work: 51.4% less than 15 minutes, 23.6% 15 to 30 minutes, 6.2% 30 to 45 minutes, 7.8% 45 to 60 minutes, 11.0% 60 minutes or more (2006-2010 5-year est.)
**Additional Information Contacts**
Mattituck Chamber of Commerce . . . . . . . . . . . . . . . . . . . (631) 953-9389
    http://www.mattituckchamber.org

## MEDFORD (CDP).
Covers a land area of 10.796 square miles and a water area of 0 square miles. Located at 40.82° N. Lat; 72.98° W. Long. Elevation is 89 feet.
**Population:** 21,070 (1990); 21,985 (2000); 24,142 (2010); Density: 2,236.0 persons per square mile (2010); Race: 83.3% White, 6.0% Black, 2.6% Asian, 0.4% American Indian/Alaska Native, 0.0% Native Hawaiian/Other Pacific Islander, 7.7% Other, 17.8% Hispanic of any race (2010); Average

household size: 3.04 (2010); Median age: 38.7 (2010); Males per 100 females: 96.5 (2010); Marriage status: 28.8% never married, 56.8% now married, 5.6% widowed, 8.7% divorced (2006-2010 5-year est.); Foreign born: 11.6% (2006-2010 5-year est.); Ancestry (includes multiple ancestries): 34.2% Italian, 24.4% Irish, 13.9% German, 5.9% Polish, 5.4% English (2006-2010 5-year est.).
**Economy:** Employment by occupation: 10.5% management, 2.7% professional, 8.9% services, 16.9% sales, 6.4% farming, 8.2% construction, 7.4% production (2006-2010 5-year est.).
**Income:** Per capita income: $29,670 (2006-2010 5-year est.); Median household income: $83,480 (2006-2010 5-year est.); Average household income: $91,313 (2006-2010 5-year est.); Percent of households with income of $100,000 or more: 41.3% (2006-2010 5-year est.); Poverty rate: 6.0% (2006-2010 5-year est.).
**Education:** Percent of population age 25 and over with: High school diploma (including GED) or higher: 87.5% (2006-2010 5-year est.); Bachelor's degree or higher: 21.4% (2006-2010 5-year est.); Master's degree or higher: 9.0% (2006-2010 5-year est.).

### School District(s)
Patchogue-Medford Union Free School District (PK-12)
    2009-10 Enrollment: 8,571 . . . . . . . . . . . . . . . . . . . . . . (631) 687-6380
**Housing:** Homeownership rate: 83.2% (2010); Median home value: $349,800 (2006-2010 5-year est.); Median contract rent: $1,196 per month (2006-2010 5-year est.); Median year structure built: 1975 (2006-2010 5-year est.).
**Transportation:** Commute to work: 91.0% car, 5.4% public transportation, 0.7% walk, 2.2% work from home (2006-2010 5-year est.); Travel time to work: 26.3% less than 15 minutes, 34.3% 15 to 30 minutes, 17.3% 30 to 45 minutes, 7.7% 45 to 60 minutes, 14.5% 60 minutes or more (2006-2010 5-year est.)

## MELVILLE (CDP).
Covers a land area of 12.085 square miles and a water area of <.001 square miles. Located at 40.78° N. Lat; 73.40° W. Long. Elevation is 135 feet.
**History:** Poet Walt Whitman was born in a shingle-sided farmhouse that still sits, though rather improbably, on a heavily commercial stretch of Route 110 in Melville, squeezed between a film developer and a furniture store.
**Population:** 12,586 (1990); 14,533 (2000); 18,985 (2010); Density: 1,570.9 persons per square mile (2010); Race: 86.6% White, 3.4% Black, 7.2% Asian, 0.1% American Indian/Alaska Native, 0.0% Native Hawaiian/Other Pacific Islander, 2.7% Other, 5.0% Hispanic of any race (2010); Average household size: 2.68 (2010); Median age: 45.5 (2010); Males per 100 females: 89.9 (2010); Marriage status: 23.7% never married, 63.6% now married, 7.4% widowed, 5.3% divorced (2006-2010 5-year est.); Foreign born: 11.9% (2006-2010 5-year est.); Ancestry (includes multiple ancestries): 28.3% Italian, 12.4% Irish, 11.5% German, 9.2% Polish, 8.4% Russian (2006-2010 5-year est.).
**Economy:** Employment by occupation: 23.7% management, 4.9% professional, 4.9% services, 13.6% sales, 3.1% farming, 3.0% construction, 1.1% production (2006-2010 5-year est.).
**Income:** Per capita income: $52,952 (2006-2010 5-year est.); Median household income: $104,603 (2006-2010 5-year est.); Average household income: $147,166 (2006-2010 5-year est.); Percent of households with income of $100,000 or more: 53.0% (2006-2010 5-year est.); Poverty rate: 4.8% (2006-2010 5-year est.).
**Education:** Percent of population age 25 and over with: High school diploma (including GED) or higher: 93.7% (2006-2010 5-year est.); Bachelor's degree or higher: 53.0% (2006-2010 5-year est.); Master's degree or higher: 25.3% (2006-2010 5-year est.).

### School District(s)
Half Hollow Hills Central School District (KG-12)
    2009-10 Enrollment: 10,037 . . . . . . . . . . . . . . . . . . . . . . (631) 592-3008
South Huntington Union Free School District (KG-12)
    2009-10 Enrollment: 6,019 . . . . . . . . . . . . . . . . . . . . . . (631) 812-3070
### Two-year College(s)
SBI Campus-An Affiliate of Sanford-Brown (Private, For-profit)
    Fall 2010 Enrollment: 871 . . . . . . . . . . . . . . . . . . . . . . (631) 370-3300
    2011-12 Tuition: In-state $11,208; Out-of-state $11,208
**Housing:** Homeownership rate: 85.2% (2010); Median home value: $665,500 (2006-2010 5-year est.); Median contract rent: $1,668 per month (2006-2010 5-year est.); Median year structure built: 1980 (2006-2010 5-year est.).
**Newspapers:** Coping - Newsday (Local news); FanFare - Newsday (Community news); Fitness File - Newsday (Community news); Kidsday -

Newsday (Local news); LI LIfe - Newsday (Community news); Money & Careers - Newsday (Local news); Newsday (Local news; Circulation 427,771); Real Estate - Newsday (Local news); Student Briefing Page - Newsday (Local news); TV Plus Home Entertainment Guide (Local news); Travel - Newsday (Community news); Weekend Amusement - Newsday (Local news)

**Transportation:** Commute to work: 81.8% car, 10.4% public transportation, 1.4% walk, 5.9% work from home (2006-2010 5-year est.); Travel time to work: 28.3% less than 15 minutes, 32.5% 15 to 30 minutes, 14.2% 30 to 45 minutes, 5.8% 45 to 60 minutes, 19.2% 60 minutes or more (2006-2010 5-year est.)

## MIDDLE ISLAND (CDP). Covers a land area of 8.239 square miles and a water area of 0.058 square miles. Located at 40.88° N. Lat; 72.94° W. Long. Elevation is 82 feet.

**Population:** 7,848 (1990); 9,702 (2000); 10,483 (2010); Density: 1,272.3 persons per square mile (2010); Race: 83.6% White, 8.2% Black, 3.5% Asian, 0.4% American Indian/Alaska Native, 0.0% Native Hawaiian/Other Pacific Islander, 4.3% Other, 9.3% Hispanic of any race (2010); Average household size: 2.41 (2010); Median age: 42.0 (2010); Males per 100 females: 92.7 (2010); Marriage status: 28.6% never married, 54.8% now married, 7.2% widowed, 9.4% divorced (2006-2010 5-year est.); Foreign born: 11.5% (2006-2010 5-year est.); Ancestry (includes multiple ancestries): 28.9% Italian, 21.1% Irish, 17.6% German, 6.8% Polish, 4.6% English (2006-2010 5-year est.).

**Economy:** Employment by occupation: 11.7% management, 3.1% professional, 9.5% services, 22.5% sales, 5.0% farming, 7.3% construction, 6.3% production (2006-2010 5-year est.).

**Income:** Per capita income: $30,802 (2006-2010 5-year est.); Median household income: $66,838 (2006-2010 5-year est.); Average household income: $76,639 (2006-2010 5-year est.); Percent of households with income of $100,000 or more: 23.8% (2006-2010 5-year est.); Poverty rate: 6.1% (2006-2010 5-year est.).

**Education:** Percent of population age 25 and over with: High school diploma (including GED) or higher: 90.0% (2006-2010 5-year est.); Bachelor's degree or higher: 25.5% (2006-2010 5-year est.); Master's degree or higher: 10.6% (2006-2010 5-year est.).

### School District(s)
Longwood Central School District (KG-12)
   2009-10 Enrollment: 9,154 . . . . . . . . . . . . . . . . . . (631) 345-2172

**Housing:** Homeownership rate: 77.0% (2010); Median home value: $302,700 (2006-2010 5-year est.); Median contract rent: $1,251 per month (2006-2010 5-year est.); Median year structure built: 1981 (2006-2010 5-year est.).

**Transportation:** Commute to work: 95.8% car, 1.5% public transportation, 0.7% walk, 2.0% work from home (2006-2010 5-year est.); Travel time to work: 15.7% less than 15 minutes, 41.7% 15 to 30 minutes, 20.0% 30 to 45 minutes, 8.6% 45 to 60 minutes, 13.9% 60 minutes or more (2006-2010 5-year est.)

## MILLER PLACE (CDP). Covers a land area of 6.551 square miles and a water area of 0 square miles. Located at 40.93° N. Lat; 72.98° W. Long. Elevation is 131 feet.

**Population:** 9,514 (1990); 10,580 (2000); 12,339 (2010); Density: 1,883.4 persons per square mile (2010); Race: 93.5% White, 1.7% Black, 2.9% Asian, 0.1% American Indian/Alaska Native, 0.0% Native Hawaiian/Other Pacific Islander, 1.8% Other, 5.0% Hispanic of any race (2010); Average household size: 3.07 (2010); Median age: 39.7 (2010); Males per 100 females: 98.4 (2010); Marriage status: 22.5% never married, 66.3% now married, 4.1% widowed, 7.1% divorced (2006-2010 5-year est.); Foreign born: 6.1% (2006-2010 5-year est.); Ancestry (includes multiple ancestries): 33.8% Italian, 29.2% Irish, 24.9% German, 9.7% English, 6.5% Polish (2006-2010 5-year est.).

**Economy:** Employment by occupation: 12.9% management, 3.7% professional, 7.7% services, 14.7% sales, 3.6% farming, 7.5% construction, 2.7% production (2006-2010 5-year est.).

**Income:** Per capita income: $40,604 (2006-2010 5-year est.); Median household income: $107,774 (2006-2010 5-year est.); Average household income: $122,112 (2006-2010 5-year est.); Percent of households with income of $100,000 or more: 56.4% (2006-2010 5-year est.); Poverty rate: 1.1% (2006-2010 5-year est.).

**Education:** Percent of population age 25 and over with: High school diploma (including GED) or higher: 96.9% (2006-2010 5-year est.); Bachelor's degree or higher: 42.1% (2006-2010 5-year est.); Master's degree or higher: 22.1% (2006-2010 5-year est.).

### School District(s)
Miller Place Union Free School District (KG-12)
   2009-10 Enrollment: 3,098 . . . . . . . . . . . . . . . . . (631) 474-2733

**Housing:** Homeownership rate: 91.6% (2010); Median home value: $467,500 (2006-2010 5-year est.); Median contract rent: $1,214 per month (2006-2010 5-year est.); Median year structure built: 1974 (2006-2010 5-year est.).

**Transportation:** Commute to work: 89.5% car, 5.4% public transportation, 0.6% walk, 4.0% work from home (2006-2010 5-year est.); Travel time to work: 16.3% less than 15 minutes, 29.6% 15 to 30 minutes, 20.2% 30 to 45 minutes, 9.6% 45 to 60 minutes, 24.2% 60 minutes or more (2006-2010 5-year est.)

**Additional Information Contacts**
North Brookhaven Chamber of Commerce . . . . . . . . . . . . . (631) 821-1313
  http://northbrookhavenchamber.org

## MONTAUK (CDP). Covers a land area of 17.479 square miles and a water area of 2.252 square miles. Located at 41.04° N. Lat; 71.94° W. Long. Elevation is 33 feet.

**History:** Name derived from Montauk word for hilly land. Founded on land bought from Montauks in 1686 by settlers from nearby East Hampton to raise cattle. Site of oldest cattle ranch in U.S.

**Population:** 3,003 (1990); 3,851 (2000); 3,326 (2010); Density: 190.3 persons per square mile (2010); Race: 90.3% White, 2.8% Black, 0.9% Asian, 0.2% American Indian/Alaska Native, 0.1% Native Hawaiian/Other Pacific Islander, 5.7% Other, 16.1% Hispanic of any race (2010); Average household size: 2.30 (2010); Median age: 47.9 (2010); Males per 100 females: 99.8 (2010); Marriage status: 24.7% never married, 55.8% now married, 9.2% widowed, 10.3% divorced (2006-2010 5-year est.); Foreign born: 23.3% (2006-2010 5-year est.); Ancestry (includes multiple ancestries): 20.5% Irish, 19.3% Italian, 16.9% German, 8.7% English, 4.0% Russian (2006-2010 5-year est.).

**Economy:** Employment by occupation: 14.2% management, 4.9% professional, 13.7% services, 14.4% sales, 0.5% farming, 15.0% construction, 2.4% production (2006-2010 5-year est.).

**Income:** Per capita income: $43,660 (2006-2010 5-year est.); Median household income: $69,917 (2006-2010 5-year est.); Average household income: $92,273 (2006-2010 5-year est.); Percent of households with income of $100,000 or more: 31.8% (2006-2010 5-year est.); Poverty rate: 4.7% (2006-2010 5-year est.).

**Education:** Percent of population age 25 and over with: High school diploma (including GED) or higher: 94.0% (2006-2010 5-year est.); Bachelor's degree or higher: 37.2% (2006-2010 5-year est.); Master's degree or higher: 16.8% (2006-2010 5-year est.).

### School District(s)
Montauk Union Free School District (PK-08)
   2009-10 Enrollment: 313 . . . . . . . . . . . . . . . . . . . . . (631) 668-2474

**Housing:** Homeownership rate: 73.3% (2010); Median home value: $819,600 (2006-2010 5-year est.); Median contract rent: $1,165 per month (2006-2010 5-year est.); Median year structure built: 1978 (2006-2010 5-year est.).

**Transportation:** Commute to work: 75.3% car, 11.5% public transportation, 5.7% walk, 3.9% work from home (2006-2010 5-year est.); Travel time to work: 46.4% less than 15 minutes, 15.5% 15 to 30 minutes, 17.3% 30 to 45 minutes, 11.3% 45 to 60 minutes, 9.6% 60 minutes or more (2006-2010 5-year est.)

**Airports:** Montauk (general aviation)

**Additional Information Contacts**
Montauk Chamber of Commerce. . . . . . . . . . . . . . . . . . . . . (631) 668-2428
  http://www.montaukchamber.com

## MORICHES (CDP). Covers a land area of 2.049 square miles and a water area of 0.227 square miles. Located at 40.80° N. Lat; 72.82° W. Long. Elevation is 23 feet.

**Population:** 2,067 (1990); 2,319 (2000); 2,838 (2010); Density: 1,384.6 persons per square mile (2010); Race: 89.8% White, 2.8% Black, 2.8% Asian, 0.2% American Indian/Alaska Native, 0.0% Native Hawaiian/Other Pacific Islander, 4.4% Other, 8.7% Hispanic of any race (2010); Average household size: 2.14 (2010); Median age: 44.5 (2010); Males per 100 females: 93.6 (2010); Marriage status: 19.5% never married, 61.2% now married, 8.3% widowed, 11.0% divorced (2006-2010 5-year est.); Foreign born: 3.8% (2006-2010 5-year est.); Ancestry (includes multiple ancestries): 46.9% Italian, 28.8% Irish, 22.4% German, 7.3% English, 6.5% Polish (2006-2010 5-year est.).

**Economy:** Employment by occupation: 7.2% management, 4.1% professional, 2.0% services, 30.3% sales, 4.6% farming, 11.1% construction, 5.4% production (2006-2010 5-year est.).
**Income:** Per capita income: $40,310 (2006-2010 5-year est.); Median household income: $73,047 (2006-2010 5-year est.); Average household income: $89,702 (2006-2010 5-year est.); Percent of households with income of $100,000 or more: 34.0% (2006-2010 5-year est.); Poverty rate: 0.0% (2006-2010 5-year est.).
**Education:** Percent of population age 25 and over with: High school diploma (including GED) or higher: 96.1% (2006-2010 5-year est.); Bachelor's degree or higher: 25.2% (2006-2010 5-year est.); Master's degree or higher: 12.0% (2006-2010 5-year est.).

### School District(s)

William Floyd Union Free School District (KG-12)
    2009-10 Enrollment: 9,398 . . . . . . . . . . . . . . . . . . . (631) 874-1201
**Housing:** Homeownership rate: 49.7% (2010); Median home value: $462,900 (2006-2010 5-year est.); Median contract rent: $1,297 per month (2006-2010 5-year est.); Median year structure built: 1986 (2006-2010 5-year est.).
**Newspapers:** South Shore Press (Community news; Circulation 27,000)
**Transportation:** Commute to work: 85.6% car, 0.0% public transportation, 5.3% walk, 9.1% work from home (2006-2010 5-year est.); Travel time to work: 18.1% less than 15 minutes, 39.5% 15 to 30 minutes, 22.3% 30 to 45 minutes, 11.7% 45 to 60 minutes, 8.3% 60 minutes or more (2006-2010 5-year est.)

## MOUNT SINAI (CDP). Covers a land area of 5.999 square miles and a water area of 0.419 square miles. Located at 40.94° N. Lat; 73.02° W. Long. Elevation is 33 feet.

**Population:** 7,762 (1990); 8,734 (2000); 12,118 (2010); Density: 2,020.0 persons per square mile (2010); Race: 92.1% White, 1.5% Black, 4.0% Asian, 0.1% American Indian/Alaska Native, 0.1% Native Hawaiian/Other Pacific Islander, 2.2% Other, 5.8% Hispanic of any race (2010); Average household size: 2.96 (2010); Median age: 41.9 (2010); Males per 100 females: 95.3 (2010); Marriage status: 18.8% never married, 68.6% now married, 6.5% widowed, 6.1% divorced (2006-2010 5-year est.); Foreign born: 7.3% (2006-2010 5-year est.); Ancestry (includes multiple ancestries): 34.5% Italian, 28.9% Irish, 21.9% German, 5.1% Polish, 4.9% English (2006-2010 5-year est.).
**Economy:** Employment by occupation: 13.2% management, 7.0% professional, 2.9% services, 19.0% sales, 3.3% farming, 6.5% construction, 2.4% production (2006-2010 5-year est.).
**Income:** Per capita income: $45,247 (2006-2010 5-year est.); Median household income: $111,069 (2006-2010 5-year est.); Average household income: $135,855 (2006-2010 5-year est.); Percent of households with income of $100,000 or more: 57.2% (2006-2010 5-year est.); Poverty rate: 1.9% (2006-2010 5-year est.).
**Education:** Percent of population age 25 and over with: High school diploma (including GED) or higher: 93.3% (2006-2010 5-year est.); Bachelor's degree or higher: 40.6% (2006-2010 5-year est.); Master's degree or higher: 19.6% (2006-2010 5-year est.).

### School District(s)

Mount Sinai Union Free School District (KG-12)
    2009-10 Enrollment: 2,609 . . . . . . . . . . . . . . . . . . . (631) 870-2550
**Housing:** Homeownership rate: 93.8% (2010); Median home value: $484,200 (2006-2010 5-year est.); Median contract rent: $1,213 per month (2006-2010 5-year est.); Median year structure built: 1984 (2006-2010 5-year est.).
**Transportation:** Commute to work: 88.4% car, 6.3% public transportation, 0.1% walk, 5.1% work from home (2006-2010 5-year est.); Travel time to work: 19.9% less than 15 minutes, 24.9% 15 to 30 minutes, 21.1% 30 to 45 minutes, 10.8% 45 to 60 minutes, 23.3% 60 minutes or more (2006-2010 5-year est.)
**Additional Information Contacts**
North Brookhaven Chamber of Commerce . . . . . . . . . . . . (631) 821-1313
    http://northbrookhavenchamber.org

## NAPEAGUE (CDP). Covers a land area of 3.678 square miles and a water area of 0.079 square miles. Located at 40.99° N. Lat; 72.07° W. Long. Elevation is 7 feet.

**Population:** 175 (1990); 223 (2000); 200 (2010); Density: 54.4 persons per square mile (2010); Race: 95.5% White, 1.0% Black, 1.5% Asian, 0.5% American Indian/Alaska Native, 0.0% Native Hawaiian/Other Pacific Islander, 1.5% Other, 3.0% Hispanic of any race (2010); Average household size: 1.87 (2010); Median age: 55.4 (2010); Males per 100

females: 92.3 (2010); Marriage status: 29.7% never married, 63.6% now married, 3.3% widowed, 3.3% divorced (2006-2010 5-year est.); Foreign born: 0.0% (2006-2010 5-year est.); Ancestry (includes multiple ancestries): 29.2% Polish, 24.4% Yugoslavian, 23.9% Irish, 19.6% German, 18.7% American (2006-2010 5-year est.).
**Economy:** Employment by occupation: 10.4% management, 0.0% professional, 16.5% services, 14.0% sales, 0.0% farming, 19.5% construction, 0.0% production (2006-2010 5-year est.).
**Income:** Per capita income: $44,863 (2006-2010 5-year est.); Median household income: $83,375 (2006-2010 5-year est.); Average household income: $102,992 (2006-2010 5-year est.); Percent of households with income of $100,000 or more: 32.6% (2006-2010 5-year est.); Poverty rate: 0.0% (2006-2010 5-year est.).
**Education:** Percent of population age 25 and over with: High school diploma (including GED) or higher: 100.0% (2006-2010 5-year est.); Bachelor's degree or higher: 21.2% (2006-2010 5-year est.); Master's degree or higher: 5.5% (2006-2010 5-year est.).
**Housing:** Homeownership rate: 84.1% (2010); Median home value: $886,400 (2006-2010 5-year est.); Median contract rent: n/a per month (2006-2010 5-year est.); Median year structure built: 1981 (2006-2010 5-year est.).
**Transportation:** Commute to work: 82.3% car, 6.1% public transportation, 0.0% walk, 11.6% work from home (2006-2010 5-year est.); Travel time to work: 51.0% less than 15 minutes, 35.9% 15 to 30 minutes, 0.0% 30 to 45 minutes, 6.9% 45 to 60 minutes, 6.2% 60 minutes or more (2006-2010 5-year est.)

## NESCONSET (CDP). Covers a land area of 3.821 square miles and a water area of 0.002 square miles. Located at 40.84° N. Lat; 73.15° W. Long. Elevation is 118 feet.

**Population:** 10,712 (1990); 11,992 (2000); 13,387 (2010); Density: 3,503.5 persons per square mile (2010); Race: 91.8% White, 1.3% Black, 4.9% Asian, 0.1% American Indian/Alaska Native, 0.0% Native Hawaiian/Other Pacific Islander, 1.9% Other, 6.2% Hispanic of any race (2010); Average household size: 2.88 (2010); Median age: 40.9 (2010); Males per 100 females: 94.6 (2010); Marriage status: 25.1% never married, 60.4% now married, 6.9% widowed, 7.5% divorced (2006-2010 5-year est.); Foreign born: 8.3% (2006-2010 5-year est.); Ancestry (includes multiple ancestries): 42.7% Italian, 27.5% Irish, 19.7% German, 6.9% Polish, 3.4% English (2006-2010 5-year est.).
**Economy:** Employment by occupation: 17.4% management, 3.9% professional, 6.1% services, 16.6% sales, 3.7% farming, 6.5% construction, 4.4% production (2006-2010 5-year est.).
**Income:** Per capita income: $41,010 (2006-2010 5-year est.); Median household income: $108,141 (2006-2010 5-year est.); Average household income: $122,116 (2006-2010 5-year est.); Percent of households with income of $100,000 or more: 55.7% (2006-2010 5-year est.); Poverty rate: 3.5% (2006-2010 5-year est.).
**Education:** Percent of population age 25 and over with: High school diploma (including GED) or higher: 95.6% (2006-2010 5-year est.); Bachelor's degree or higher: 40.8% (2006-2010 5-year est.); Master's degree or higher: 19.0% (2006-2010 5-year est.).

### School District(s)

Smithtown Central School District (KG-12)
    2009-10 Enrollment: 10,862 . . . . . . . . . . . . . . . . . . (631) 382-2005
**Housing:** Homeownership rate: 82.6% (2010); Median home value: $495,200 (2006-2010 5-year est.); Median contract rent: $1,409 per month (2006-2010 5-year est.); Median year structure built: 1976 (2006-2010 5-year est.).
**Newspapers:** Brookhaven Review (Community news); Ronkonkoma Review (Community news); Smithtown Messenger (Community news)
**Transportation:** Commute to work: 93.0% car, 4.5% public transportation, 0.2% walk, 2.3% work from home (2006-2010 5-year est.); Travel time to work: 16.8% less than 15 minutes, 34.9% 15 to 30 minutes, 22.5% 30 to 45 minutes, 10.7% 45 to 60 minutes, 15.2% 60 minutes or more (2006-2010 5-year est.)

## NEW SUFFOLK (CDP). Covers a land area of 0.556 square miles and a water area of 0.053 square miles. Located at 40.99° N. Lat; 72.47° W. Long. Elevation is 26 feet.

**Population:** 374 (1990); 337 (2000); 349 (2010); Density: 627.2 persons per square mile (2010); Race: 98.0% White, 0.6% Black, 0.0% Asian, 0.3% American Indian/Alaska Native, 0.0% Native Hawaiian/Other Pacific Islander, 1.1% Other, 6.3% Hispanic of any race (2010); Average household size: 1.97 (2010); Median age: 56.3 (2010); Males per 100 females: 84.7 (2010); Marriage status: 18.7% never married, 57.7% now married, 12.6% widowed, 11.0% divorced (2006-2010 5-year est.); Foreign born: 12.2% (2006-2010 5-year est.); Ancestry (includes multiple ancestries): 26.6% English, 22.9% Irish, 12.2% Italian, 10.1% German, 6.4% French (2006-2010 5-year est.).

**Economy:** Employment by occupation: 0.0% management, 0.0% professional, 0.0% services, 21.9% sales, 3.1% farming, 15.6% construction, 9.4% production (2006-2010 5-year est.).

**Income:** Per capita income: $35,351 (2006-2010 5-year est.); Median household income: $44,643 (2006-2010 5-year est.); Average household income: $61,265 (2006-2010 5-year est.); Percent of households with income of $100,000 or more: 17.6% (2006-2010 5-year est.); Poverty rate: 5.3% (2006-2010 5-year est.).

**Education:** Percent of population age 25 and over with: High school diploma (including GED) or higher: 96.7% (2006-2010 5-year est.); Bachelor's degree or higher: 53.3% (2006-2010 5-year est.); Master's degree or higher: 23.9% (2006-2010 5-year est.).

**School District(s)**
New Suffolk Common School District (PK-06)
   2009-10 Enrollment: 18 . . . . . . . . . . . . . . . . . . . . . . . (631) 734-6940

**Housing:** Homeownership rate: 81.4% (2010); Median home value: $694,700 (2006-2010 5-year est.); Median contract rent: n/a per month (2006-2010 5-year est.); Median year structure built: 1958 (2006-2010 5-year est.).

**Transportation:** Commute to work: 71.9% car, 0.0% public transportation, 10.9% walk, 17.2% work from home (2006-2010 5-year est.); Travel time to work: 26.4% less than 15 minutes, 39.6% 15 to 30 minutes, 11.3% 30 to 45 minutes, 3.8% 45 to 60 minutes, 18.9% 60 minutes or more (2006-2010 5-year est.)

## NISSEQUOGUE (village). Covers a land area of 3.782 square miles and a water area of 0.194 square miles. Located at 40.90° N. Lat; 73.18° W. Long. Elevation is 85 feet.

**Population:** 1,620 (1990); 1,543 (2000); 1,749 (2010); Density: 462.4 persons per square mile (2010); Race: 92.5% White, 0.9% Black, 5.0% Asian, 0.0% American Indian/Alaska Native, 0.0% Native Hawaiian/Other Pacific Islander, 1.6% Other, 3.4% Hispanic of any race (2010); Average household size: 2.84 (2010); Median age: 45.8 (2010); Males per 100 females: 107.5 (2010); Marriage status: 26.7% never married, 62.8% now married, 5.4% widowed, 5.2% divorced (2006-2010 5-year est.); Foreign born: 7.0% (2006-2010 5-year est.); Ancestry (includes multiple ancestries): 31.6% Italian, 27.0% Irish, 19.4% German, 12.1% English, 8.7% Polish (2006-2010 5-year est.).

**Economy:** Single-family building permits issued: 0 (2011); Multi-family building permits issued: 0 (2011); Employment by occupation: 28.4% management, 3.6% professional, 2.4% services, 14.4% sales, 3.1% farming, 5.7% construction, 1.2% production (2006-2010 5-year est.).

**Income:** Per capita income: $86,965 (2006-2010 5-year est.); Median household income: $175,833 (2006-2010 5-year est.); Average household income: $243,612 (2006-2010 5-year est.); Percent of households with income of $100,000 or more: 77.5% (2006-2010 5-year est.); Poverty rate: 1.1% (2006-2010 5-year est.).

**Education:** Percent of population age 25 and over with: High school diploma (including GED) or higher: 98.5% (2006-2010 5-year est.); Bachelor's degree or higher: 58.1% (2006-2010 5-year est.); Master's degree or higher: 30.3% (2006-2010 5-year est.).

**Housing:** Homeownership rate: 92.3% (2010); Median home value: $1 (2006-2010 5-year est.); Median contract rent: $1,313 per month (2006-2010 5-year est.); Median year structure built: 1975 (2006-2010 5-year est.).

**Safety:** Violent crime rate: 0.0 per 10,000 population; Property crime rate: 56.0 per 10,000 population (2010).

**Transportation:** Commute to work: 90.7% car, 2.4% public transportation, 2.4% walk, 3.6% work from home (2006-2010 5-year est.); Travel time to work: 19.3% less than 15 minutes, 35.9% 15 to 30 minutes, 22.8% 30 to 45 minutes, 10.5% 45 to 60 minutes, 11.6% 60 minutes or more (2006-2010 5-year est.)

## NORTH AMITYVILLE (CDP). Covers a land area of 2.354 square miles and a water area of 0 square miles. Located at 40.70° N. Lat; 73.41° W. Long. Elevation is 33 feet.

**Population:** 13,775 (1990); 16,572 (2000); 17,862 (2010); Density: 7,587.5 persons per square mile (2010); Race: 21.9% White, 58.9% Black, 1.0% Asian, 1.1% American Indian/Alaska Native, 0.1% Native Hawaiian/Other Pacific Islander, 17.0% Other, 28.5% Hispanic of any race (2010); Average

household size: 3.32 (2010); Median age: 34.4 (2010); Males per 100 females: 85.7 (2010); Marriage status: 46.2% never married, 40.4% now married, 6.1% widowed, 7.3% divorced (2006-2010 5-year est.); Foreign born: 27.4% (2006-2010 5-year est.); Ancestry (includes multiple ancestries): 12.6% Jamaican, 3.7% Haitian, 3.3% Irish, 2.4% Italian, 2.1% West Indian (2006-2010 5-year est.).

**Economy:** Employment by occupation: 5.7% management, 0.3% professional, 19.3% services, 17.5% sales, 4.0% farming, 9.6% construction, 6.5% production (2006-2010 5-year est.).

**Income:** Per capita income: $21,571 (2006-2010 5-year est.); Median household income: $57,231 (2006-2010 5-year est.); Average household income: $67,281 (2006-2010 5-year est.); Percent of households with income of $100,000 or more: 18.6% (2006-2010 5-year est.); Poverty rate: 11.8% (2006-2010 5-year est.).

**Education:** Percent of population age 25 and over with: High school diploma (including GED) or higher: 75.5% (2006-2010 5-year est.); Bachelor's degree or higher: 12.7% (2006-2010 5-year est.); Master's degree or higher: 2.6% (2006-2010 5-year est.).

**Housing:** Homeownership rate: 60.6% (2010); Median home value: $339,100 (2006-2010 5-year est.); Median contract rent: $1,314 per month (2006-2010 5-year est.); Median year structure built: 1971 (2006-2010 5-year est.).

**Transportation:** Commute to work: 85.0% car, 8.0% public transportation, 2.8% walk, 0.9% work from home (2006-2010 5-year est.); Travel time to work: 30.9% less than 15 minutes, 35.5% 15 to 30 minutes, 14.7% 30 to 45 minutes, 8.2% 45 to 60 minutes, 10.6% 60 minutes or more (2006-2010 5-year est.)

## NORTH BABYLON (CDP). Covers a land area of 3.369 square miles and a water area of 0.052 square miles. Located at 40.72° N. Lat; 73.32° W. Long. Elevation is 23 feet.

**Population:** 17,984 (1990); 17,877 (2000); 17,509 (2010); Density: 5,195.9 persons per square mile (2010); Race: 84.9% White, 6.2% Black, 4.1% Asian, 0.1% American Indian/Alaska Native, 0.0% Native Hawaiian/Other Pacific Islander, 4.7% Other, 12.7% Hispanic of any race (2010); Average household size: 2.85 (2010); Median age: 40.9 (2010); Males per 100 females: 93.8 (2010); Marriage status: 30.4% never married, 55.2% now married, 6.7% widowed, 7.6% divorced (2006-2010 5-year est.); Foreign born: 11.1% (2006-2010 5-year est.); Ancestry (includes multiple ancestries): 33.8% Italian, 23.4% Irish, 17.9% German, 5.5% Polish, 4.9% English (2006-2010 5-year est.).

**Economy:** Employment by occupation: 11.5% management, 3.3% professional, 7.1% services, 19.9% sales, 5.0% farming, 9.2% construction, 5.5% production (2006-2010 5-year est.).

**Income:** Per capita income: $32,785 (2006-2010 5-year est.); Median household income: $82,745 (2006-2010 5-year est.); Average household income: $91,736 (2006-2010 5-year est.); Percent of households with income of $100,000 or more: 39.9% (2006-2010 5-year est.); Poverty rate: 6.0% (2006-2010 5-year est.).

**Education:** Percent of population age 25 and over with: High school diploma (including GED) or higher: 92.4% (2006-2010 5-year est.); Bachelor's degree or higher: 21.6% (2006-2010 5-year est.); Master's degree or higher: 8.3% (2006-2010 5-year est.).

**School District(s)**
North Babylon Union Free School District (KG-12)
   2009-10 Enrollment: 4,840 . . . . . . . . . . . . . . . . . (631) 321-3226

**Housing:** Homeownership rate: 82.9% (2010); Median home value: $379,800 (2006-2010 5-year est.); Median contract rent: $1,489 per month (2006-2010 5-year est.); Median year structure built: 1957 (2006-2010 5-year est.).

**Transportation:** Commute to work: 84.3% car, 8.8% public transportation, 0.7% walk, 5.5% work from home (2006-2010 5-year est.); Travel time to work: 26.3% less than 15 minutes, 32.0% 15 to 30 minutes, 17.5% 30 to 45 minutes, 5.6% 45 to 60 minutes, 18.6% 60 minutes or more (2006-2010 5-year est.)

**Airports:** Republic (general aviation)

## NORTH BAY SHORE (CDP). Covers a land area of 3.251 square miles and a water area of 0 square miles. Located at 40.76° N. Lat; 73.26° W. Long. Elevation is 36 feet.

**Population:** 12,799 (1990); 14,992 (2000); 18,944 (2010); Density: 5,825.4 persons per square mile (2010); Race: 43.6% White, 18.3% Black, 3.8% Asian, 0.7% American Indian/Alaska Native, 0.0% Native Hawaiian/Other Pacific Islander, 33.6% Other, 65.0% Hispanic of any race (2010); Average household size: 4.30 (2010); Median age: 31.7 (2010); Males per 100

females: 103.7 (2010); Marriage status: 38.8% never married, 51.0% now married, 4.1% widowed, 6.1% divorced (2006-2010 5-year est.); Foreign born: 38.0% (2006-2010 5-year est.); Ancestry (includes multiple ancestries): 5.7% Italian, 5.7% Irish, 5.4% German, 4.3% Haitian, 1.7% Jamaican (2006-2010 5-year est.).
**Economy:** Employment by occupation: 7.5% management, 1.8% professional, 9.8% services, 18.2% sales, 5.2% farming, 7.3% construction, 14.3% production (2006-2010 5-year est.).
**Income:** Per capita income: $21,257 (2006-2010 5-year est.); Median household income: $72,540 (2006-2010 5-year est.); Average household income: $83,237 (2006-2010 5-year est.); Percent of households with income of $100,000 or more: 30.6% (2006-2010 5-year est.); Poverty rate: 6.0% (2006-2010 5-year est.).
**Education:** Percent of population age 25 and over with: High school diploma (including GED) or higher: 70.4% (2006-2010 5-year est.); Bachelor's degree or higher: 13.9% (2006-2010 5-year est.); Master's degree or higher: 4.6% (2006-2010 5-year est.).
**Housing:** Homeownership rate: 70.7% (2010); Median home value: $350,500 (2006-2010 5-year est.); Median contract rent: $1,263 per month (2006-2010 5-year est.); Median year structure built: 1965 (2006-2010 5-year est.).
**Transportation:** Commute to work: 89.4% car, 4.9% public transportation, 0.3% walk, 2.3% work from home (2006-2010 5-year est.); Travel time to work: 28.2% less than 15 minutes, 42.4% 15 to 30 minutes, 17.2% 30 to 45 minutes, 4.7% 45 to 60 minutes, 7.6% 60 minutes or more (2006-2010 5-year est.).

**NORTH BELLPORT** (CDP). Covers a land area of 4.936 square miles and a water area of 0 square miles. Located at 40.78° N. Lat; 72.94° W. Long. Elevation is 46 feet.
**Population:** 7,989 (1990); 9,007 (2000); 11,545 (2010); Density: 2,338.7 persons per square mile (2010); Race: 53.9% White, 26.5% Black, 2.6% Asian, 1.4% American Indian/Alaska Native, 0.1% Native Hawaiian/Other Pacific Islander, 15.5% Other, 29.3% Hispanic of any race (2010); Average household size: 3.42 (2010); Median age: 31.6 (2010); Males per 100 females: 98.5 (2010); Marriage status: 41.7% never married, 47.8% now married, 3.0% widowed, 7.5% divorced (2006-2010 5-year est.); Foreign born: 15.0% (2006-2010 5-year est.); Ancestry (includes multiple ancestries): 15.2% Italian, 13.3% Irish, 11.2% German, 6.5% African, 4.4% English (2006-2010 5-year est.).
**Economy:** Employment by occupation: 5.2% management, 4.2% professional, 8.0% services, 17.8% sales, 6.1% farming, 11.1% construction, 11.8% production (2006-2010 5-year est.).
**Income:** Per capita income: $24,794 (2006-2010 5-year est.); Median household income: $76,607 (2006-2010 5-year est.); Average household income: $81,299 (2006-2010 5-year est.); Percent of households with income of $100,000 or more: 27.2% (2006-2010 5-year est.); Poverty rate: 11.9% (2006-2010 5-year est.).
**Education:** Percent of population age 25 and over with: High school diploma (including GED) or higher: 86.5% (2006-2010 5-year est.); Bachelor's degree or higher: 16.8% (2006-2010 5-year est.); Master's degree or higher: 7.5% (2006-2010 5-year est.).
**Housing:** Homeownership rate: 59.7% (2010); Median home value: $322,600 (2006-2010 5-year est.); Median contract rent: $1,724 per month (2006-2010 5-year est.); Median year structure built: 1978 (2006-2010 5-year est.).
**Transportation:** Commute to work: 93.4% car, 3.4% public transportation, 1.7% walk, 1.1% work from home (2006-2010 5-year est.); Travel time to work: 23.7% less than 15 minutes, 35.8% 15 to 30 minutes, 21.3% 30 to 45 minutes, 8.4% 45 to 60 minutes, 10.8% 60 minutes or more (2006-2010 5-year est.).

**NORTH GREAT RIVER** (CDP). Covers a land area of 2.325 square miles and a water area of 0.023 square miles. Located at 40.75° N. Lat; 73.16° W. Long. Elevation is 30 feet.
**Population:** 3,964 (1990); 3,929 (2000); 4,001 (2010); Density: 1,720.8 persons per square mile (2010); Race: 90.0% White, 3.0% Black, 2.0% Asian, 0.3% American Indian/Alaska Native, 0.0% Native Hawaiian/Other Pacific Islander, 4.7% Other, 11.7% Hispanic of any race (2010); Average household size: 3.16 (2010); Median age: 41.3 (2010); Males per 100 females: 97.9 (2010); Marriage status: 24.7% never married, 65.5% now married, 3.5% widowed, 6.3% divorced (2006-2010 5-year est.); Foreign born: 11.0% (2006-2010 5-year est.); Ancestry (includes multiple ancestries): 34.7% Italian, 31.1% Irish, 25.4% German, 3.6% Polish, 3.3% French (2006-2010 5-year est.).

**Economy:** Employment by occupation: 5.8% management, 3.8% professional, 10.8% services, 23.5% sales, 3.4% farming, 13.2% construction, 7.2% production (2006-2010 5-year est.).
**Income:** Per capita income: $32,174 (2006-2010 5-year est.); Median household income: $85,000 (2006-2010 5-year est.); Average household income: $96,438 (2006-2010 5-year est.); Percent of households with income of $100,000 or more: 40.8% (2006-2010 5-year est.); Poverty rate: 1.4% (2006-2010 5-year est.).
**Education:** Percent of population age 25 and over with: High school diploma (including GED) or higher: 92.7% (2006-2010 5-year est.); Bachelor's degree or higher: 19.6% (2006-2010 5-year est.); Master's degree or higher: 3.6% (2006-2010 5-year est.).
**Housing:** Homeownership rate: 90.8% (2010); Median home value: $407,300 (2006-2010 5-year est.); Median contract rent: n/a per month (2006-2010 5-year est.); Median year structure built: 1965 (2006-2010 5-year est.).
**Transportation:** Commute to work: 91.0% car, 4.1% public transportation, 0.4% walk, 3.1% work from home (2006-2010 5-year est.); Travel time to work: 20.4% less than 15 minutes, 33.9% 15 to 30 minutes, 23.3% 30 to 45 minutes, 3.9% 45 to 60 minutes, 18.5% 60 minutes or more (2006-2010 5-year est.)

**NORTH HAVEN** (village). Covers a land area of 2.712 square miles and a water area of 0 square miles. Located at 41.02° N. Lat; 72.31° W. Long. Elevation is 20 feet.
**Population:** 713 (1990); 743 (2000); 833 (2010); Density: 307.1 persons per square mile (2010); Race: 97.6% White, 0.1% Black, 1.4% Asian, 0.0% American Indian/Alaska Native, 0.0% Native Hawaiian/Other Pacific Islander, 0.9% Other, 2.9% Hispanic of any race (2010); Average household size: 2.51 (2010); Median age: 47.3 (2010); Males per 100 females: 91.5 (2010); Marriage status: 18.5% never married, 66.3% now married, 7.1% widowed, 8.1% divorced (2006-2010 5-year est.); Foreign born: 10.8% (2006-2010 5-year est.); Ancestry (includes multiple ancestries): 28.9% Irish, 23.2% English, 19.7% Italian, 16.2% German, 5.7% Polish (2006-2010 5-year est.).
**Economy:** Single-family building permits issued: 4 (2011); Multi-family building permits issued: 0 (2011); Employment by occupation: 14.8% management, 3.4% professional, 9.4% services, 19.4% sales, 1.4% farming, 8.4% construction, 4.8% production (2006-2010 5-year est.).
**Income:** Per capita income: $83,677 (2006-2010 5-year est.); Median household income: $112,679 (2006-2010 5-year est.); Average household income: $204,852 (2006-2010 5-year est.); Percent of households with income of $100,000 or more: 53.4% (2006-2010 5-year est.); Poverty rate: 0.6% (2006-2010 5-year est.).
**Education:** Percent of population age 25 and over with: High school diploma (including GED) or higher: 97.9% (2006-2010 5-year est.); Bachelor's degree or higher: 51.8% (2006-2010 5-year est.); Master's degree or higher: 26.1% (2006-2010 5-year est.).
**Housing:** Homeownership rate: 86.1% (2010); Median home value: $960,200 (2006-2010 5-year est.); Median contract rent: $1,700 per month (2006-2010 5-year est.); Median year structure built: 1977 (2006-2010 5-year est.).
**Transportation:** Commute to work: 72.2% car, 7.6% public transportation, 2.1% walk, 16.3% work from home (2006-2010 5-year est.); Travel time to work: 43.2% less than 15 minutes, 33.7% 15 to 30 minutes, 6.6% 30 to 45 minutes, 6.4% 45 to 60 minutes, 10.1% 60 minutes or more (2006-2010 5-year est.)

**NORTH LINDENHURST** (CDP). Covers a land area of 1.919 square miles and a water area of 0 square miles. Located at 40.70° N. Lat; 73.38° W. Long. Elevation is 43 feet.
**Population:** 10,563 (1990); 11,767 (2000); 11,652 (2010); Density: 6,070.0 persons per square mile (2010); Race: 81.5% White, 5.1% Black, 3.1% Asian, 0.3% American Indian/Alaska Native, 0.0% Native Hawaiian/Other Pacific Islander, 10.0% Other, 19.3% Hispanic of any race (2010); Average household size: 3.07 (2010); Median age: 38.0 (2010); Males per 100 females: 96.3 (2010); Marriage status: 29.9% never married, 56.7% now married, 6.1% widowed, 7.2% divorced (2006-2010 5-year est.); Foreign born: 19.8% (2006-2010 5-year est.); Ancestry (includes multiple ancestries): 34.1% Italian, 18.7% Irish, 15.6% German, 9.4% Polish, 4.0% English (2006-2010 5-year est.).
**Economy:** Employment by occupation: 7.7% management, 1.2% professional, 6.9% services, 22.7% sales, 4.7% farming, 12.6% construction, 8.3% production (2006-2010 5-year est.).

**Income:** Per capita income: $28,604 (2006-2010 5-year est.); Median household income: $74,510 (2006-2010 5-year est.); Average household income: $84,924 (2006-2010 5-year est.); Percent of households with income of $100,000 or more: 35.0% (2006-2010 5-year est.); Poverty rate: 3.9% (2006-2010 5-year est.).
**Education:** Percent of population age 25 and over with: High school diploma (including GED) or higher: 85.7% (2006-2010 5-year est.); Bachelor's degree or higher: 16.2% (2006-2010 5-year est.); Master's degree or higher: 5.0% (2006-2010 5-year est.).
**Housing:** Homeownership rate: 69.4% (2010); Median home value: $370,100 (2006-2010 5-year est.); Median contract rent: $1,203 per month (2006-2010 5-year est.); Median year structure built: 1959 (2006-2010 5-year est.).
**Transportation:** Commute to work: 87.7% car, 7.1% public transportation, 1.4% walk, 2.9% work from home (2006-2010 5-year est.); Travel time to work: 30.6% less than 15 minutes, 33.6% 15 to 30 minutes, 19.2% 30 to 45 minutes, 5.9% 45 to 60 minutes, 10.8% 60 minutes or more (2006-2010 5-year est.).

**NORTH PATCHOGUE** (CDP). Covers a land area of 1.977 square miles and a water area of 0.052 square miles. Located at 40.78° N. Lat; 73.02° W. Long. Elevation is 49 feet.
**Population:** 7,374 (1990); 7,825 (2000); 7,246 (2010); Density: 3,664.1 persons per square mile (2010); Race: 86.9% White, 2.3% Black, 1.8% Asian, 0.2% American Indian/Alaska Native, 0.0% Native Hawaiian/Other Pacific Islander, 8.8% Other, 20.6% Hispanic of any race (2010); Average household size: 3.10 (2010); Median age: 37.1 (2010); Males per 100 females: 98.2 (2010); Marriage status: 34.4% never married, 49.6% now married, 8.8% widowed, 7.2% divorced (2006-2010 5-year est.); Foreign born: 12.5% (2006-2010 5-year est.); Ancestry (includes multiple ancestries): 33.1% Italian, 32.8% Irish, 24.6% German, 6.5% Polish, 6.0% English (2006-2010 5-year est.).
**Economy:** Employment by occupation: 11.0% management, 2.8% professional, 13.4% services, 16.7% sales, 3.4% farming, 10.4% construction, 9.1% production (2006-2010 5-year est.).
**Income:** Per capita income: $26,190 (2006-2010 5-year est.); Median household income: $76,411 (2006-2010 5-year est.); Average household income: $80,711 (2006-2010 5-year est.); Percent of households with income of $100,000 or more: 37.0% (2006-2010 5-year est.); Poverty rate: 10.8% (2006-2010 5-year est.).
**Education:** Percent of population age 25 and over with: High school diploma (including GED) or higher: 82.9% (2006-2010 5-year est.); Bachelor's degree or higher: 19.5% (2006-2010 5-year est.); Master's degree or higher: 6.1% (2006-2010 5-year est.).
**Housing:** Homeownership rate: 84.4% (2010); Median home value: $345,000 (2006-2010 5-year est.); Median contract rent: $1,364 per month (2006-2010 5-year est.); Median year structure built: 1960 (2006-2010 5-year est.).
**Transportation:** Commute to work: 93.9% car, 3.1% public transportation, 0.9% walk, 2.2% work from home (2006-2010 5-year est.); Travel time to work: 32.1% less than 15 minutes, 45.8% 15 to 30 minutes, 14.5% 30 to 45 minutes, 1.6% 45 to 60 minutes, 6.0% 60 minutes or more (2006-2010 5-year est.).

**NORTH SEA** (CDP). Covers a land area of 11.051 square miles and a water area of 1.041 square miles. Located at 40.93° N. Lat; 72.40° W. Long. Elevation is 16 feet.
**Population:** 3,592 (1990); 4,493 (2000); 4,458 (2010); Density: 403.4 persons per square mile (2010); Race: 92.8% White, 1.1% Black, 1.5% Asian, 0.1% American Indian/Alaska Native, 0.1% Native Hawaiian/Other Pacific Islander, 4.4% Other, 16.8% Hispanic of any race (2010); Average household size: 2.52 (2010); Median age: 43.1 (2010); Males per 100 females: 103.7 (2010); Marriage status: 27.5% never married, 56.6% now married, 5.2% widowed, 10.7% divorced (2006-2010 5-year est.); Foreign born: 17.8% (2006-2010 5-year est.); Ancestry (includes multiple ancestries): 30.4% Irish, 17.7% Italian, 16.0% German, 12.3% English, 5.5% Polish (2006-2010 5-year est.).
**Economy:** Employment by occupation: 8.9% management, 2.4% professional, 11.8% services, 16.4% sales, 0.4% farming, 9.9% construction, 4.1% production (2006-2010 5-year est.).
**Income:** Per capita income: $49,502 (2006-2010 5-year est.); Median household income: $90,331 (2006-2010 5-year est.); Average household income: $123,055 (2006-2010 5-year est.); Percent of households with income of $100,000 or more: 42.4% (2006-2010 5-year est.); Poverty rate: 3.0% (2006-2010 5-year est.).

**Education:** Percent of population age 25 and over with: High school diploma (including GED) or higher: 90.5% (2006-2010 5-year est.); Bachelor's degree or higher: 43.1% (2006-2010 5-year est.); Master's degree or higher: 18.5% (2006-2010 5-year est.).
**Housing:** Homeownership rate: 73.2% (2010); Median home value: $772,800 (2006-2010 5-year est.); Median contract rent: $1,213 per month (2006-2010 5-year est.); Median year structure built: 1976 (2006-2010 5-year est.).
**Transportation:** Commute to work: 87.2% car, 5.2% public transportation, 0.9% walk, 5.8% work from home (2006-2010 5-year est.); Travel time to work: 40.9% less than 15 minutes, 31.1% 15 to 30 minutes, 16.3% 30 to 45 minutes, 5.1% 45 to 60 minutes, 6.6% 60 minutes or more (2006-2010 5-year est.).

**NORTHAMPTON** (CDP). Covers a land area of 11.550 square miles and a water area of 0.100 square miles. Located at 40.87° N. Lat; 72.68° W. Long. Elevation is 151 feet.
**Population:** 397 (1990); 468 (2000); 570 (2010); Density: 49.3 persons per square mile (2010); Race: 53.7% White, 27.5% Black, 0.4% Asian, 0.0% American Indian/Alaska Native, 0.4% Native Hawaiian/Other Pacific Islander, 18.0% Other, 19.6% Hispanic of any race (2010); Average household size: 2.95 (2010); Median age: 37.9 (2010); Males per 100 females: 108.8 (2010); Marriage status: 38.1% never married, 57.0% now married, 3.1% widowed, 1.8% divorced (2006-2010 5-year est.); Foreign born: 2.6% (2006-2010 5-year est.); Ancestry (includes multiple ancestries): 24.6% Polish, 23.0% German, 21.2% English, 13.9% Irish, 10.7% Italian (2006-2010 5-year est.).
**Economy:** Employment by occupation: 7.6% management, 0.0% professional, 0.0% services, 5.0% sales, 9.3% farming, 15.2% construction, 6.1% production (2006-2010 5-year est.).
**Income:** Per capita income: $25,375 (2006-2010 5-year est.); Median household income: $66,875 (2006-2010 5-year est.); Average household income: $72,595 (2006-2010 5-year est.); Percent of households with income of $100,000 or more: 24.8% (2006-2010 5-year est.); Poverty rate: 0.0% (2006-2010 5-year est.).
**Education:** Percent of population age 25 and over with: High school diploma (including GED) or higher: 92.1% (2006-2010 5-year est.); Bachelor's degree or higher: 17.7% (2006-2010 5-year est.); Master's degree or higher: 8.2% (2006-2010 5-year est.).
**Housing:** Homeownership rate: 75.4% (2010); Median home value: $320,000 (2006-2010 5-year est.); Median contract rent: n/a per month (2006-2010 5-year est.); Median year structure built: 1969 (2006-2010 5-year est.).
**Transportation:** Commute to work: 90.4% car, 5.2% public transportation, 4.4% walk, 0.0% work from home (2006-2010 5-year est.); Travel time to work: 45.2% less than 15 minutes, 38.5% 15 to 30 minutes, 0.0% 30 to 45 minutes, 0.0% 45 to 60 minutes, 16.3% 60 minutes or more (2006-2010 5-year est.).

**NORTHPORT** (village). Aka Old Northport. Covers a land area of 2.308 square miles and a water area of 0.221 square miles. Located at 40.90° N. Lat; 73.34° W. Long. Elevation is 59 feet.
**History:** Although it was known by the name of Northport since at least 1837, the village of Northport was formally incorporated in 1894, the first village to do so in Huntington Township. Over the years Northport has expanded from its original borders, annexing other established communities.
**Population:** 7,572 (1990); 7,606 (2000); 7,401 (2010); Density: 3,206.2 persons per square mile (2010); Race: 96.1% White, 0.6% Black, 1.7% Asian, 0.0% American Indian/Alaska Native, 0.0% Native Hawaiian/Other Pacific Islander, 1.6% Other, 3.6% Hispanic of any race (2010); Average household size: 2.52 (2010); Median age: 45.7 (2010); Males per 100 females: 95.5 (2010); Marriage status: 24.0% never married, 57.7% now married, 5.8% widowed, 12.6% divorced (2006-2010 5-year est.); Foreign born: 9.2% (2006-2010 5-year est.); Ancestry (includes multiple ancestries): 28.0% Irish, 22.6% German, 16.8% Italian, 15.2% English, 6.6% Polish (2006-2010 5-year est.).
**Economy:** Single-family building permits issued: 4 (2011); Multi-family building permits issued: 0 (2011); Employment by occupation: 15.6% management, 5.9% professional, 5.9% services, 10.5% sales, 2.7% farming, 7.9% construction, 4.3% production (2006-2010 5-year est.).
**Income:** Per capita income: $51,798 (2006-2010 5-year est.); Median household income: $107,962 (2006-2010 5-year est.); Average household income: $136,769 (2006-2010 5-year est.); Percent of households with

income of $100,000 or more: 54.6% (2006-2010 5-year est.); Poverty rate: 2.8% (2006-2010 5-year est.).

**Education:** Percent of population age 25 and over with: High school diploma (including GED) or higher: 99.2% (2006-2010 5-year est.); Bachelor's degree or higher: 54.4% (2006-2010 5-year est.); Master's degree or higher: 26.1% (2006-2010 5-year est.).

**School District(s)**

Kings Park Central School District (KG-12)

   2009-10 Enrollment: 3,955 . . . . . . . . . . . . . . . (631) 269-3310

Northport-East Northport Union Free School Distric (KG-12)

   2009-10 Enrollment: 6,333 . . . . . . . . . . . . . . . (631) 262-6604

**Two-year College(s)**

Western Suffolk BOCES (Public)

   Fall 2010 Enrollment: 724 . . . . . . . . . . . . . . . . . (6.3) 166-8E+1

**Housing:** Homeownership rate: 75.9% (2010); Median home value: $631,100 (2006-2010 5-year est.); Median contract rent: $1,054 per month (2006-2010 5-year est.); Median year structure built: 1953 (2006-2010 5-year est.).

**Hospitals:** Northport VA Medical Center (524 beds)

**Safety:** Violent crime rate: 1.3 per 10,000 population; Property crime rate: 98.3 per 10,000 population (2010).

**Transportation:** Commute to work: 74.1% car, 11.8% public transportation, 1.5% walk, 12.7% work from home (2006-2010 5-year est.); Travel time to work: 20.6% less than 15 minutes, 23.5% 15 to 30 minutes, 19.8% 30 to 45 minutes, 12.3% 45 to 60 minutes, 23.7% 60 minutes or more (2006-2010 5-year est.)

**Additional Information Contacts**

Northport Chamber of Commerce . . . . . . . . . . . . . (631) 754-3905

   http://www.northportny.com

## NORTHVILLE (CDP). Covers a land area of 7.403 square miles and a water area of 0.020 square miles. Located at 40.97° N. Lat; 72.63° W. Long. Elevation is 59 feet.

**Population:** 641 (1990); 801 (2000); 1,340 (2010); Density: 181.0 persons per square mile (2010); Race: 92.6% White, 1.1% Black, 0.7% Asian, 0.2% American Indian/Alaska Native, 0.0% Native Hawaiian/Other Pacific Islander, 5.4% Other, 5.8% Hispanic of any race (2010); Average household size: 2.49 (2010); Median age: 49.6 (2010); Males per 100 females: 99.4 (2010); Marriage status: 14.9% never married, 75.6% now married, 6.7% widowed, 2.8% divorced (2006-2010 5-year est.); Foreign born: 3.9% (2006-2010 5-year est.); Ancestry (includes multiple ancestries): 38.9% Irish, 21.6% Italian, 16.8% German, 10.8% Polish, 7.4% Norwegian (2006-2010 5-year est.).

**Economy:** Employment by occupation: 22.4% management, 0.0% professional, 15.8% services, 22.2% sales, 7.0% farming, 2.8% construction, 0.0% production (2006-2010 5-year est.).

**Income:** Per capita income: $40,092 (2006-2010 5-year est.); Median household income: $69,639 (2006-2010 5-year est.); Average household income: $98,038 (2006-2010 5-year est.); Percent of households with income of $100,000 or more: 29.8% (2006-2010 5-year est.); Poverty rate: 17.4% (2006-2010 5-year est.).

**Education:** Percent of population age 25 and over with: High school diploma (including GED) or higher: 98.4% (2006-2010 5-year est.); Bachelor's degree or higher: 32.6% (2006-2010 5-year est.); Master's degree or higher: 9.3% (2006-2010 5-year est.).

**Housing:** Homeownership rate: 90.8% (2010); Median home value: $615,500 (2006-2010 5-year est.); Median contract rent: n/a per month (2006-2010 5-year est.); Median year structure built: 2001 (2006-2010 5-year est.).

**Transportation:** Commute to work: 81.3% car, 5.5% public transportation, 0.0% walk, 13.2% work from home (2006-2010 5-year est.); Travel time to work: 21.1% less than 15 minutes, 26.3% 15 to 30 minutes, 17.6% 30 to 45 minutes, 14.7% 45 to 60 minutes, 20.3% 60 minutes or more (2006-2010 5-year est.)

## NORTHWEST HARBOR (CDP). Covers a land area of 14.473 square miles and a water area of 1.579 square miles. Located at 41.00° N. Lat; 72.22° W. Long. Elevation is 79 feet.

**History:** Northwest Harbor is named for the bay on the South Fork of Long Island connecting Sag Harbor, Shelter Island and East Hampton town to Gardiners Bay and the open waters of the Atlantic Ocean. The bay derives its name from being northwest of East Hampton village.

**Population:** 2,107 (1990); 3,059 (2000); 3,317 (2010); Density: 229.2 persons per square mile (2010); Race: 88.1% White, 2.6% Black, 1.7% Asian, 0.4% American Indian/Alaska Native, 0.4% Native Hawaiian/Other

Pacific Islander, 6.8% Other, 18.2% Hispanic of any race (2010); Average household size: 2.52 (2010); Median age: 47.0 (2010); Males per 100 females: 96.6 (2010); Marriage status: 30.3% never married, 60.9% now married, 1.8% widowed, 7.0% divorced (2006-2010 5-year est.); Foreign born: 17.8% (2006-2010 5-year est.); Ancestry (includes multiple ancestries): 20.1% Italian, 17.9% German, 15.9% Irish, 15.8% English, 9.0% Russian (2006-2010 5-year est.).

**Economy:** Employment by occupation: 14.4% management, 0.5% professional, 6.4% services, 13.8% sales, 0.0% farming, 7.4% construction, 3.9% production (2006-2010 5-year est.).

**Income:** Per capita income: $82,049 (2006-2010 5-year est.); Median household income: $125,757 (2006-2010 5-year est.); Average household income: $205,981 (2006-2010 5-year est.); Percent of households with income of $100,000 or more: 58.4% (2006-2010 5-year est.); Poverty rate: 1.4% (2006-2010 5-year est.).

**Education:** Percent of population age 25 and over with: High school diploma (including GED) or higher: 96.1% (2006-2010 5-year est.); Bachelor's degree or higher: 56.1% (2006-2010 5-year est.); Master's degree or higher: 27.8% (2006-2010 5-year est.).

**Housing:** Homeownership rate: 83.3% (2010); Median home value: $941,900 (2006-2010 5-year est.); Median contract rent: $1,545 per month (2006-2010 5-year est.); Median year structure built: 1986 (2006-2010 5-year est.).

**Transportation:** Commute to work: 74.9% car, 6.8% public transportation, 1.6% walk, 12.5% work from home (2006-2010 5-year est.); Travel time to work: 54.1% less than 15 minutes, 28.3% 15 to 30 minutes, 4.0% 30 to 45 minutes, 2.3% 45 to 60 minutes, 11.3% 60 minutes or more (2006-2010 5-year est.)

## NOYACK (CDP). Covers a land area of 8.403 square miles and a water area of 0.322 square miles. Located at 40.97° N. Lat; 72.34° W. Long. Elevation is 26 feet.

**Population:** 2,001 (1990); 2,696 (2000); 3,568 (2010); Density: 424.6 persons per square mile (2010); Race: 93.0% White, 1.2% Black, 1.5% Asian, 0.3% American Indian/Alaska Native, 0.1% Native Hawaiian/Other Pacific Islander, 3.9% Other, 9.4% Hispanic of any race (2010); Average household size: 2.36 (2010); Median age: 45.9 (2010); Males per 100 females: 93.1 (2010); Marriage status: 21.8% never married, 65.4% now married, 7.3% widowed, 5.5% divorced (2006-2010 5-year est.); Foreign born: 11.5% (2006-2010 5-year est.); Ancestry (includes multiple ancestries): 27.0% Italian, 26.4% Irish, 17.9% German, 13.0% English, 3.7% Scottish (2006-2010 5-year est.).

**Economy:** Employment by occupation: 16.3% management, 1.5% professional, 3.2% services, 16.0% sales, 4.9% farming, 12.7% construction, 2.8% production (2006-2010 5-year est.).

**Income:** Per capita income: $52,207 (2006-2010 5-year est.); Median household income: $87,842 (2006-2010 5-year est.); Average household income: $121,738 (2006-2010 5-year est.); Percent of households with income of $100,000 or more: 40.6% (2006-2010 5-year est.); Poverty rate: 1.7% (2006-2010 5-year est.).

**Education:** Percent of population age 25 and over with: High school diploma (including GED) or higher: 98.4% (2006-2010 5-year est.); Bachelor's degree or higher: 55.2% (2006-2010 5-year est.); Master's degree or higher: 25.4% (2006-2010 5-year est.).

**Housing:** Homeownership rate: 76.3% (2010); Median home value: $757,900 (2006-2010 5-year est.); Median contract rent: $1,904 per month (2006-2010 5-year est.); Median year structure built: 1979 (2006-2010 5-year est.).

**Transportation:** Commute to work: 88.7% car, 2.4% public transportation, 1.3% walk, 4.9% work from home (2006-2010 5-year est.); Travel time to work: 53.0% less than 15 minutes, 28.0% 15 to 30 minutes, 2.9% 30 to 45 minutes, 4.0% 45 to 60 minutes, 12.0% 60 minutes or more (2006-2010 5-year est.)

## OAK BEACH-CAPTREE (CDP). Covers a land area of 2.755 square miles and a water area of 0.920 square miles. Located at 40.65° N. Lat; 73.27° W. Long.

**Population:** n/a (1990); n/a (2000); 286 (2010); Density: 103.8 persons per square mile (2010); Race: 97.6% White, 0.3% Black, 1.0% Asian, 0.0% American Indian/Alaska Native, 0.0% Native Hawaiian/Other Pacific Islander, 1.1% Other, 8.0% Hispanic of any race (2010); Average household size: 2.22 (2010); Median age: 51.4 (2010); Males per 100 females: 100.0 (2010); Marriage status: 1.7% never married, 72.8% now married, 4.0% widowed, 21.5% divorced (2006-2010 5-year est.); Foreign born: 1.1% (2006-2010 5-year est.); Ancestry (includes multiple

ancestries): 73.3% Irish, 19.8% Polish, 17.5% German, 15.8% Italian, 14.5% English (2006-2010 5-year est.).
**Economy:** Employment by occupation: 20.1% management, 0.0% professional, 9.9% services, 20.7% sales, 0.0% farming, 0.6% construction, 0.0% production (2006-2010 5-year est.).
**Income:** Per capita income: $91,513 (2006-2010 5-year est.); Median household income: $142,583 (2006-2010 5-year est.); Average household income: $239,354 (2006-2010 5-year est.); Percent of households with income of $100,000 or more: 54.9% (2006-2010 5-year est.); Poverty rate: 1.7% (2006-2010 5-year est.).
**Education:** Percent of population age 25 and over with: High school diploma (including GED) or higher: 100.0% (2006-2010 5-year est.); Bachelor's degree or higher: 61.3% (2006-2010 5-year est.); Master's degree or higher: 41.3% (2006-2010 5-year est.).
**Housing:** Homeownership rate: 93.0% (2010); Median home value: $701,500 (2006-2010 5-year est.); Median contract rent: n/a per month (2006-2010 5-year est.); Median year structure built: 1946 (2006-2010 5-year est.).
**Transportation:** Commute to work: 78.9% car, 16.1% public transportation, 0.0% walk, 5.0% work from home (2006-2010 5-year est.); Travel time to work: 21.2% less than 15 minutes, 24.2% 15 to 30 minutes, 32.7% 30 to 45 minutes, 3.3% 45 to 60 minutes, 18.6% 60 minutes or more (2006-2010 5-year est.)

## OAKDALE (CDP).
Covers a land area of 3.417 square miles and a water area of 0.394 square miles. Located at 40.73° N. Lat; 73.13° W. Long. Elevation is 10 feet.
**History:** Seat of Dowling College.
**Population:** 7,875 (1990); 8,075 (2000); 7,974 (2010); Density: 2,333.4 persons per square mile (2010); Race: 96.5% White, 1.2% Black, 1.3% Asian, 0.0% American Indian/Alaska Native, 0.0% Native Hawaiian/Other Pacific Islander, 1.0% Other, 3.9% Hispanic of any race (2010); Average household size: 2.49 (2010); Median age: 45.0 (2010); Males per 100 females: 91.1 (2010); Marriage status: 25.5% never married, 60.3% now married, 8.5% widowed, 5.8% divorced (2006-2010 5-year est.); Foreign born: 6.5% (2006-2010 5-year est.); Ancestry (includes multiple ancestries): 36.5% Italian, 32.8% Irish, 22.6% German, 7.4% English, 4.6% Polish (2006-2010 5-year est.).
**Economy:** Employment by occupation: 20.2% management, 4.6% professional, 5.1% services, 15.7% sales, 2.2% farming, 7.8% construction, 4.1% production (2006-2010 5-year est.).
**Income:** Per capita income: $41,104 (2006-2010 5-year est.); Median household income: $78,310 (2006-2010 5-year est.); Average household income: $100,938 (2006-2010 5-year est.); Percent of households with income of $100,000 or more: 43.1% (2006-2010 5-year est.); Poverty rate: 2.2% (2006-2010 5-year est.).
**Education:** Percent of population age 25 and over with: High school diploma (including GED) or higher: 94.8% (2006-2010 5-year est.); Bachelor's degree or higher: 38.3% (2006-2010 5-year est.); Master's degree or higher: 17.3% (2006-2010 5-year est.).

#### School District(s)
Connetquot Central School District (PK-12)
    2009-10 Enrollment: 6,757 . . . . . . . . . . . . . . . . . . . (631) 244-2215

#### Four-year College(s)
Dowling College (Private, Not-for-profit)
    Fall 2010 Enrollment: 3,611 . . . . . . . . . . . . . . . . . . . (631) 244-3000
    2011-12 Tuition: In-state $25,908; Out-of-state $25,908
**Housing:** Homeownership rate: 79.7% (2010); Median home value: $477,400 (2006-2010 5-year est.); Median contract rent: $1,359 per month (2006-2010 5-year est.); Median year structure built: 1965 (2006-2010 5-year est.).
**Transportation:** Commute to work: 89.3% car, 7.2% public transportation, 1.2% walk, 2.0% work from home (2006-2010 5-year est.); Travel time to work: 22.9% less than 15 minutes, 35.3% 15 to 30 minutes, 19.7% 30 to 45 minutes, 6.4% 45 to 60 minutes, 15.7% 60 minutes or more (2006-2010 5-year est.)

## OCEAN BEACH (village).
Covers a land area of 0.141 square miles and a water area of 0 square miles. Located at 40.64° N. Lat; 73.15° W. Long. Elevation is 3 feet.
**Population:** 129 (1990); 138 (2000); 79 (2010); Density: 559.0 persons per square mile (2010); Race: 100.0% White, 0.0% Black, 0.0% Asian, 0.0% American Indian/Alaska Native, 0.0% Native Hawaiian/Other Pacific Islander, 0.0% Other, 1.3% Hispanic of any race (2010); Average household size: 2.03 (2010); Median age: 54.8 (2010); Males per 100

females: 146.9 (2010); Marriage status: 37.3% never married, 27.3% now married, 17.3% widowed, 18.2% divorced (2006-2010 5-year est.); Foreign born: 0.9% (2006-2010 5-year est.); Ancestry (includes multiple ancestries): 39.1% Irish, 25.2% German, 20.0% Italian, 9.6% English, 8.7% Russian (2006-2010 5-year est.).
**Economy:** Single-family building permits issued: 2 (2011); Multi-family building permits issued: 0 (2011); Employment by occupation: 9.4% management, 1.6% professional, 34.4% services, 17.2% sales, 0.0% farming, 0.0% construction, 0.0% production (2006-2010 5-year est.).
**Income:** Per capita income: $53,207 (2006-2010 5-year est.); Median household income: $60,833 (2006-2010 5-year est.); Average household income: $98,067 (2006-2010 5-year est.); Percent of households with income of $100,000 or more: 31.3% (2006-2010 5-year est.); Poverty rate: 17.4% (2006-2010 5-year est.).
**Education:** Percent of population age 25 and over with: High school diploma (including GED) or higher: 100.0% (2006-2010 5-year est.); Bachelor's degree or higher: 56.7% (2006-2010 5-year est.); Master's degree or higher: 13.3% (2006-2010 5-year est.).
**Housing:** Homeownership rate: 92.3% (2010); Median home value: $820,800 (2006-2010 5-year est.); Median contract rent: $842 per month (2006-2010 5-year est.); Median year structure built: 1953 (2006-2010 5-year est.).
**Safety:** Violent crime rate: 0.0 per 10,000 population; Property crime rate: 3,741.5 per 10,000 population (2010).
**Newspapers:** Fire Island News (Community news; Circulation 20,000)
**Transportation:** Commute to work: 15.0% car, 6.7% public transportation, 51.7% walk, 5.0% work from home (2006-2010 5-year est.); Travel time to work: 63.2% less than 15 minutes, 8.8% 15 to 30 minutes, 19.3% 30 to 45 minutes, 1.8% 45 to 60 minutes, 7.0% 60 minutes or more (2006-2010 5-year est.)
**Additional Information Contacts**
Village of Ocean Beach . . . . . . . . . . . . . . . . . . . . . . . . (631) 583-5940
    http://www.villageofoceanbeach.org

## OLD FIELD (village).
Covers a land area of 2.069 square miles and a water area of 0.120 square miles. Located at 40.96° N. Lat; 73.14° W. Long. Elevation is 7 feet.
**Population:** 765 (1990); 947 (2000); 918 (2010); Density: 443.6 persons per square mile (2010); Race: 89.8% White, 0.9% Black, 6.3% Asian, 0.7% American Indian/Alaska Native, 0.0% Native Hawaiian/Other Pacific Islander, 2.3% Other, 2.8% Hispanic of any race (2010); Average household size: 2.79 (2010); Median age: 49.7 (2010); Males per 100 females: 104.5 (2010); Marriage status: 24.5% never married, 67.4% now married, 4.9% widowed, 3.2% divorced (2006-2010 5-year est.); Foreign born: 12.6% (2006-2010 5-year est.); Ancestry (includes multiple ancestries): 38.8% Irish, 20.7% German, 19.4% Italian, 12.4% English, 6.1% Polish (2006-2010 5-year est.).
**Economy:** Single-family building permits issued: 0 (2011); Multi-family building permits issued: 0 (2011); Employment by occupation: 18.4% management, 7.6% professional, 4.3% services, 8.3% sales, 0.9% farming, 4.9% construction, 0.9% production (2006-2010 5-year est.).
**Income:** Per capita income: $124,944 (2006-2010 5-year est.); Median household income: $219,107 (2006-2010 5-year est.); Average household income: $378,848 (2006-2010 5-year est.); Percent of households with income of $100,000 or more: 85.3% (2006-2010 5-year est.); Poverty rate: 0.0% (2006-2010 5-year est.).
**Education:** Percent of population age 25 and over with: High school diploma (including GED) or higher: 99.2% (2006-2010 5-year est.); Bachelor's degree or higher: 82.3% (2006-2010 5-year est.); Master's degree or higher: 52.7% (2006-2010 5-year est.).
**Housing:** Homeownership rate: 94.8% (2010); Median home value: $1 (2006-2010 5-year est.); Median contract rent: n/a per month (2006-2010 5-year est.); Median year structure built: 1964 (2006-2010 5-year est.).
**Transportation:** Commute to work: 81.8% car, 6.1% public transportation, 0.0% walk, 12.0% work from home (2006-2010 5-year est.); Travel time to work: 35.7% less than 15 minutes, 24.8% 15 to 30 minutes, 15.0% 30 to 45 minutes, 6.7% 45 to 60 minutes, 17.8% 60 minutes or more (2006-2010 5-year est.)
**Additional Information Contacts**
Village of Old Field . . . . . . . . . . . . . . . . . . . . . . . . . . . (631) 941-9412
    http://www.oldfieldny.org

**ORIENT** (CDP). Covers a land area of 5.121 square miles and a water area of 1.031 square miles. Located at 41.14° N. Lat; 72.25° W. Long. Elevation is 13 feet.
**Population:** 817 (1990); 709 (2000); 743 (2010); Density: 145.1 persons per square mile (2010); Race: 96.1% White, 1.1% Black, 0.8% Asian, 0.1% American Indian/Alaska Native, 0.0% Native Hawaiian/Other Pacific Islander, 1.9% Other, 2.2% Hispanic of any race (2010); Average household size: 2.10 (2010); Median age: 57.3 (2010); Males per 100 females: 89.5 (2010); Marriage status: 30.8% never married, 51.4% now married, 8.0% widowed, 9.8% divorced (2006-2010 5-year est.); Foreign born: 6.5% (2006-2010 5-year est.); Ancestry (includes multiple ancestries): 24.3% German, 20.7% Irish, 13.3% English, 13.2% Italian, 8.3% Polish (2006-2010 5-year est.).
**Economy:** Employment by occupation: 16.2% management, 0.0% professional, 17.2% services, 11.3% sales, 1.3% farming, 10.7% construction, 2.9% production (2006-2010 5-year est.).
**Income:** Per capita income: $49,000 (2006-2010 5-year est.); Median household income: $77,000 (2006-2010 5-year est.); Average household income: $100,738 (2006-2010 5-year est.); Percent of households with income of $100,000 or more: 28.1% (2006-2010 5-year est.); Poverty rate: 7.3% (2006-2010 5-year est.).
**Education:** Percent of population age 25 and over with: High school diploma (including GED) or higher: 95.9% (2006-2010 5-year est.); Bachelor's degree or higher: 48.0% (2006-2010 5-year est.); Master's degree or higher: 21.9% (2006-2010 5-year est.).
### School District(s)
Oysterponds Union Free School District (KG-06)
    2009-10 Enrollment: 100 . . . . . . . . . . . . . . . . . . . . . . . . (631) 323-2410
**Housing:** Homeownership rate: 84.2% (2010); Median home value: $740,500 (2006-2010 5-year est.); Median contract rent: $1,256 per month (2006-2010 5-year est.); Median year structure built: 1964 (2006-2010 5-year est.).
**Transportation:** Commute to work: 77.8% car, 7.1% public transportation, 0.0% walk, 13.8% work from home (2006-2010 5-year est.); Travel time to work: 28.1% less than 15 minutes, 29.3% 15 to 30 minutes, 15.6% 30 to 45 minutes, 3.5% 45 to 60 minutes, 23.4% 60 minutes or more (2006-2010 5-year est.)

**PATCHOGUE** (village). Covers a land area of 2.255 square miles and a water area of 0.261 square miles. Located at 40.76° N. Lat; 73.01° W. Long. Elevation is 20 feet.
**Population:** 10,967 (1990); 11,919 (2000); 11,798 (2010); Density: 5,230.9 persons per square mile (2010); Race: 76.2% White, 5.8% Black, 1.6% Asian, 0.5% American Indian/Alaska Native, 0.0% Native Hawaiian/Other Pacific Islander, 15.9% Other, 29.6% Hispanic of any race (2010); Average household size: 2.50 (2010); Median age: 37.3 (2010); Males per 100 females: 100.2 (2010); Marriage status: 38.3% never married, 45.4% now married, 7.6% widowed, 8.7% divorced (2006-2010 5-year est.); Foreign born: 15.8% (2006-2010 5-year est.); Ancestry (includes multiple ancestries): 29.6% Italian, 20.5% Irish, 17.9% German, 6.9% English, 3.3% American (2006-2010 5-year est.).
**Economy:** Single-family building permits issued: 24 (2011); Multi-family building permits issued: 0 (2011); Employment by occupation: 4.5% management, 7.3% professional, 9.2% services, 17.2% sales, 4.0% farming, 10.0% construction, 4.9% production (2006-2010 5-year est.).
**Income:** Per capita income: $29,857 (2006-2010 5-year est.); Median household income: $55,929 (2006-2010 5-year est.); Average household income: $67,738 (2006-2010 5-year est.); Percent of households with income of $100,000 or more: 23.5% (2006-2010 5-year est.); Poverty rate: 18.4% (2006-2010 5-year est.).
**Education:** Percent of population age 25 and over with: High school diploma (including GED) or higher: 87.2% (2006-2010 5-year est.); Bachelor's degree or higher: 25.9% (2006-2010 5-year est.); Master's degree or higher: 10.4% (2006-2010 5-year est.).
### School District(s)
Eastern Suffolk Boces
    2009-10 Enrollment: n/a . . . . . . . . . . . . . . . . . . . . . . . (631) 687-3006
Patchogue-Medford Union Free School District (PK-12)
    2009-10 Enrollment: 8,571 . . . . . . . . . . . . . . . . . . . . . (631) 687-6380
### Vocational/Technical School(s)
Eastern Suffolk BOCES-School of Practical Nursing (Public)
    Fall 2010 Enrollment: 434 . . . . . . . . . . . . . . . . . . . . . (631) 582-2387
    2011-12 Tuition: $12,500
**Housing:** Homeownership rate: 54.6% (2010); Median home value: $318,100 (2006-2010 5-year est.); Median contract rent: $1,163 per month

(2006-2010 5-year est.); Median year structure built: 1958 (2006-2010 5-year est.).
**Newspapers:** Long Island Advance (Community news; Circulation 11,522)
**Transportation:** Commute to work: 93.7% car, 3.9% public transportation, 1.2% walk, 0.5% work from home (2006-2010 5-year est.); Travel time to work: 33.0% less than 15 minutes, 28.8% 15 to 30 minutes, 19.4% 30 to 45 minutes, 6.7% 45 to 60 minutes, 12.1% 60 minutes or more (2006-2010 5-year est.)
**Additional Information Contacts**
Greater Patchogue Chamber of Commerce . . . . . . . . . . . . (631) 207-1000
    http://www.patchoguechamber.com
Village of Patchogue . . . . . . . . . . . . . . . . . . . . . . . . . (631) 475-4300
    http://www.patchoguevillage.org

**PECONIC** (CDP). Covers a land area of 3.379 square miles and a water area of 0.125 square miles. Located at 41.03° N. Lat; 72.46° W. Long. Elevation is 30 feet.
**Population:** 1,100 (1990); 1,081 (2000); 683 (2010); Density: 202.1 persons per square mile (2010); Race: 90.0% White, 4.2% Black, 0.1% Asian, 0.0% American Indian/Alaska Native, 0.0% Native Hawaiian/Other Pacific Islander, 5.7% Other, 10.2% Hispanic of any race (2010); Average household size: 2.50 (2010); Median age: 49.7 (2010); Males per 100 females: 109.5 (2010); Marriage status: 10.8% never married, 81.2% now married, 5.6% widowed, 2.4% divorced (2006-2010 5-year est.); Foreign born: 2.8% (2006-2010 5-year est.); Ancestry (includes multiple ancestries): 27.9% Italian, 21.9% Polish, 19.3% Irish, 13.1% English, 9.2% German (2006-2010 5-year est.).
**Economy:** Employment by occupation: 12.3% management, 4.3% professional, 4.3% services, 17.8% sales, 0.0% farming, 9.1% construction, 0.0% production (2006-2010 5-year est.).
**Income:** Per capita income: $59,320 (2006-2010 5-year est.); Median household income: $78,295 (2006-2010 5-year est.); Average household income: $135,350 (2006-2010 5-year est.); Percent of households with income of $100,000 or more: 36.5% (2006-2010 5-year est.); Poverty rate: 1.8% (2006-2010 5-year est.).
**Education:** Percent of population age 25 and over with: High school diploma (including GED) or higher: 93.7% (2006-2010 5-year est.); Bachelor's degree or higher: 50.7% (2006-2010 5-year est.); Master's degree or higher: 15.4% (2006-2010 5-year est.).
**Housing:** Homeownership rate: 83.9% (2010); Median home value: $658,600 (2006-2010 5-year est.); Median contract rent: n/a per month (2006-2010 5-year est.); Median year structure built: 1961 (2006-2010 5-year est.).
**Transportation:** Commute to work: 85.8% car, 0.0% public transportation, 0.0% walk, 14.2% work from home (2006-2010 5-year est.); Travel time to work: 50.2% less than 15 minutes, 20.7% 15 to 30 minutes, 16.1% 30 to 45 minutes, 4.6% 45 to 60 minutes, 8.3% 60 minutes or more (2006-2010 5-year est.)

**POOSPATUCK RESERVATION** (Reservation). Covers a land area of 0.112 square miles and a water area of 0.057 square miles. Located at 40.78° N. Lat; 72.83° W. Long.
**Population:** 136 (1990); 271 (2000); 324 (2010); Density: 2,875.6 persons per square mile (2010); Race: 12.3% White, 16.4% Black, 0.9% Asian, 44.1% American Indian/Alaska Native, 0.0% Native Hawaiian/Other Pacific Islander, 26.3% Other, 8.3% Hispanic of any race (2010); Average household size: 2.95 (2010); Median age: 31.0 (2010); Males per 100 females: 88.4 (2010); Marriage status: 64.5% never married, 21.6% now married, 2.7% widowed, 11.1% divorced (2006-2010 5-year est.); Foreign born: 7.4% (2006-2010 5-year est.); Ancestry (includes multiple ancestries): 1.5% Haitian, 0.9% Irish (2006-2010 5-year est.).
**Economy:** Employment by occupation: 3.4% management, 0.0% professional, 31.3% services, 13.6% sales, 4.8% farming, 6.8% construction, 6.8% production (2006-2010 5-year est.).
**Income:** Per capita income: $23,962 (2006-2010 5-year est.); Median household income: $49,792 (2006-2010 5-year est.); Average household income: $73,447 (2006-2010 5-year est.); Percent of households with income of $100,000 or more: 20.9% (2006-2010 5-year est.); Poverty rate: 9.8% (2006-2010 5-year est.).
**Education:** Percent of population age 25 and over with: High school diploma (including GED) or higher: 66.3% (2006-2010 5-year est.); Bachelor's degree or higher: 10.0% (2006-2010 5-year est.); Master's degree or higher: 4.4% (2006-2010 5-year est.).
**Housing:** Homeownership rate: 78.2% (2010); Median home value: $315,000 (2006-2010 5-year est.); Median contract rent: $1,063 per month

(2006-2010 5-year est.); Median year structure built: 1966 (2006-2010 5-year est.).

**Transportation:** Commute to work: 57.1% car, 0.0% public transportation, 34.0% walk, 4.1% work from home (2006-2010 5-year est.); Travel time to work: 40.4% less than 15 minutes, 38.3% 15 to 30 minutes, 7.8% 30 to 45 minutes, 5.0% 45 to 60 minutes, 8.5% 60 minutes or more (2006-2010 5-year est.)

**POQUOTT** (village). Covers a land area of 0.439 square miles and a water area of 0.147 square miles. Located at 40.95° N. Lat; 73.09° W. Long. Elevation is 66 feet.

**Population:** 770 (1990); 975 (2000); 953 (2010); Density: 2,169.6 persons per square mile (2010); Race: 88.2% White, 2.0% Black, 6.6% Asian, 0.4% American Indian/Alaska Native, 0.0% Native Hawaiian/Other Pacific Islander, 2.8% Other, 4.2% Hispanic of any race (2010); Average household size: 2.70 (2010); Median age: 46.5 (2010); Males per 100 females: 97.3 (2010); Marriage status: 26.0% never married, 63.6% now married, 5.8% widowed, 4.6% divorced (2006-2010 5-year est.); Foreign born: 18.0% (2006-2010 5-year est.); Ancestry (includes multiple ancestries): 30.5% Italian, 17.1% German, 15.7% Irish, 8.5% Polish, 7.8% Russian (2006-2010 5-year est.).

**Economy:** Single-family building permits issued: 0 (2011); Multi-family building permits issued: 0 (2011); Employment by occupation: 12.6% management, 9.2% professional, 3.4% services, 9.0% sales, 2.8% farming, 10.2% construction, 7.8% production (2006-2010 5-year est.).

**Income:** Per capita income: $65,813 (2006-2010 5-year est.); Median household income: $145,625 (2006-2010 5-year est.); Average household income: $194,967 (2006-2010 5-year est.); Percent of households with income of $100,000 or more: 65.9% (2006-2010 5-year est.); Poverty rate: 0.9% (2006-2010 5-year est.).

**Education:** Percent of population age 25 and over with: High school diploma (including GED) or higher: 98.6% (2006-2010 5-year est.); Bachelor's degree or higher: 62.1% (2006-2010 5-year est.); Master's degree or higher: 42.4% (2006-2010 5-year est.).

**Housing:** Homeownership rate: 89.3% (2010); Median home value: $663,400 (2006-2010 5-year est.); Median contract rent: $1,286 per month (2006-2010 5-year est.); Median year structure built: 1957 (2006-2010 5-year est.).

**Transportation:** Commute to work: 85.7% car, 4.0% public transportation, 4.9% walk, 3.8% work from home (2006-2010 5-year est.); Travel time to work: 42.0% less than 15 minutes, 25.4% 15 to 30 minutes, 14.8% 30 to 45 minutes, 11.7% 45 to 60 minutes, 6.0% 60 minutes or more (2006-2010 5-year est.)

**PORT JEFFERSON** (village). Covers a land area of 3.056 square miles and a water area of 0.026 square miles. Located at 40.94° N. Lat; 73.05° W. Long. Elevation is 3 feet.

**History:** Port Jefferson at one time was a small ship building community, with the name Drowned Meadow. The community leaders, realizing this was a poor name for the ship building business, eventually changed its name to Port Jefferson in 1836 after President Thomas Jefferson. The town was once a major whaling port, especially in the 1880s. The Village of Port Jefferson was incorporated in 1964.

**Population:** 7,455 (1990); 7,837 (2000); 7,750 (2010); Density: 2,535.3 persons per square mile (2010); Race: 88.5% White, 1.6% Black, 6.1% Asian, 0.2% American Indian/Alaska Native, 0.0% Native Hawaiian/Other Pacific Islander, 3.6% Other, 6.5% Hispanic of any race (2010); Average household size: 2.40 (2010); Median age: 43.6 (2010); Males per 100 females: 97.5 (2010); Marriage status: 36.8% never married, 46.8% now married, 5.8% widowed, 10.7% divorced (2006-2010 5-year est.); Foreign born: 12.1% (2006-2010 5-year est.); Ancestry (includes multiple ancestries): 23.9% Irish, 21.1% Italian, 17.1% German, 12.3% English, 6.8% Russian (2006-2010 5-year est.).

**Economy:** Single-family building permits issued: 6 (2011); Multi-family building permits issued: 0 (2011); Employment by occupation: 16.9% management, 6.3% professional, 7.5% services, 11.5% sales, 2.9% farming, 4.8% construction, 1.7% production (2006-2010 5-year est.).

**Income:** Per capita income: $45,558 (2006-2010 5-year est.); Median household income: $98,355 (2006-2010 5-year est.); Average household income: $121,980 (2006-2010 5-year est.); Percent of households with income of $100,000 or more: 49.6% (2006-2010 5-year est.); Poverty rate: 11.6% (2006-2010 5-year est.).

**Education:** Percent of population age 25 and over with: High school diploma (including GED) or higher: 97.3% (2006-2010 5-year est.);

Bachelor's degree or higher: 59.9% (2006-2010 5-year est.); Master's degree or higher: 38.1% (2006-2010 5-year est.).

**School District(s)**
Port Jefferson Union Free School District (PK-12)
    2009-10 Enrollment: 1,252 ..................... (631) 476-4404
**Housing:** Homeownership rate: 69.8% (2010); Median home value: $567,800 (2006-2010 5-year est.); Median contract rent: $1,480 per month (2006-2010 5-year est.); Median year structure built: 1969 (2006-2010 5-year est.).
**Hospitals:** John Mather Memorial Hospital (248 beds)
**Transportation:** Commute to work: 85.9% car, 2.2% public transportation, 3.5% walk, 5.4% work from home (2006-2010 5-year est.); Travel time to work: 23.4% less than 15 minutes, 35.8% 15 to 30 minutes, 19.0% 30 to 45 minutes, 8.8% 45 to 60 minutes, 12.9% 60 minutes or more (2006-2010 5-year est.)
**Additional Information Contacts**
Port Jefferson Chamber of Commerce ............... (631) 473-1414
    http://www.portjeffchamber.com
Village of Port Jefferson....................... (631) 473-4724
    http://www.portjeff.com

**PORT JEFFERSON STATION** (CDP). Covers a land area of 2.665 square miles and a water area of 0 square miles. Located at 40.92° N. Lat; 73.06° W. Long. Elevation is 177 feet.

**Population:** 7,232 (1990); 7,527 (2000); 7,838 (2010); Density: 2,940.1 persons per square mile (2010); Race: 85.2% White, 2.5% Black, 5.4% Asian, 0.1% American Indian/Alaska Native, 0.0% Native Hawaiian/Other Pacific Islander, 6.8% Other, 14.8% Hispanic of any race (2010); Average household size: 2.75 (2010); Median age: 39.2 (2010); Males per 100 females: 95.8 (2010); Marriage status: 27.3% never married, 58.1% now married, 5.9% widowed, 8.7% divorced (2006-2010 5-year est.); Foreign born: 15.9% (2006-2010 5-year est.); Ancestry (includes multiple ancestries): 28.6% Italian, 25.5% Irish, 13.8% German, 7.8% English, 3.7% Greek (2006-2010 5-year est.).

**Economy:** Employment by occupation: 9.2% management, 2.8% professional, 13.1% services, 20.2% sales, 1.7% farming, 8.6% construction, 3.4% production (2006-2010 5-year est.).

**Income:** Per capita income: $32,926 (2006-2010 5-year est.); Median household income: $69,962 (2006-2010 5-year est.); Average household income: $88,269 (2006-2010 5-year est.); Percent of households with income of $100,000 or more: 29.5% (2006-2010 5-year est.); Poverty rate: 2.3% (2006-2010 5-year est.).

**Education:** Percent of population age 25 and over with: High school diploma (including GED) or higher: 85.3% (2006-2010 5-year est.); Bachelor's degree or higher: 29.4% (2006-2010 5-year est.); Master's degree or higher: 14.5% (2006-2010 5-year est.).

**School District(s)**
Brookhaven-Comsewogue Union Free School District (KG-12)
    2009-10 Enrollment: 3,963 ..................... (631) 474-8105
**Housing:** Homeownership rate: 71.3% (2010); Median home value: $373,400 (2006-2010 5-year est.); Median contract rent: $1,338 per month (2006-2010 5-year est.); Median year structure built: 1968 (2006-2010 5-year est.).
**Hospitals:** St. Charles Hospital and Rehabilitation Center (289 beds)
**Transportation:** Commute to work: 95.8% car, 1.9% public transportation, 0.8% walk, 1.5% work from home (2006-2010 5-year est.); Travel time to work: 33.8% less than 15 minutes, 38.3% 15 to 30 minutes, 8.4% 30 to 45 minutes, 9.7% 45 to 60 minutes, 9.9% 60 minutes or more (2006-2010 5-year est.)
**Additional Information Contacts**
North Brookhaven Chamber of Commerce ............. (631) 821-1313
    http://northbrookhavenchamber.org

**QUIOQUE** (CDP). Covers a land area of 1.257 square miles and a water area of 0.430 square miles. Located at 40.81° N. Lat; 72.62° W. Long. Elevation is 23 feet.

**Population:** 584 (1990); 800 (2000); 816 (2010); Density: 648.7 persons per square mile (2010); Race: 80.0% White, 8.2% Black, 2.1% Asian, 1.0% American Indian/Alaska Native, 1.6% Native Hawaiian/Other Pacific Islander, 7.1% Other, 19.0% Hispanic of any race (2010); Average household size: 2.65 (2010); Median age: 40.8 (2010); Males per 100 females: 112.5 (2010); Marriage status: 26.4% never married, 60.6% now married, 0.0% widowed, 13.0% divorced (2006-2010 5-year est.); Foreign born: 20.7% (2006-2010 5-year est.); Ancestry (includes multiple

ancestries): 19.8% Irish, 18.2% Italian, 12.9% German, 11.6% Polish, 8.4% Russian (2006-2010 5-year est.).

**Economy:** Employment by occupation: 9.0% management, 4.2% professional, 12.1% services, 25.3% sales, 3.5% farming, 6.2% construction, 4.8% production (2006-2010 5-year est.).

**Income:** Per capita income: $46,689 (2006-2010 5-year est.); Median household income: $67,361 (2006-2010 5-year est.); Average household income: $107,464 (2006-2010 5-year est.); Percent of households with income of $100,000 or more: 46.1% (2006-2010 5-year est.); Poverty rate: 11.7% (2006-2010 5-year est.).

**Education:** Percent of population age 25 and over with: High school diploma (including GED) or higher: 80.4% (2006-2010 5-year est.); Bachelor's degree or higher: 38.0% (2006-2010 5-year est.); Master's degree or higher: 19.1% (2006-2010 5-year est.).

**Housing:** Homeownership rate: 75.9% (2010); Median home value: $604,500 (2006-2010 5-year est.); Median contract rent: $1,425 per month (2006-2010 5-year est.); Median year structure built: 1962 (2006-2010 5-year est.).

**Transportation:** Commute to work: 80.1% car, 0.0% public transportation, 0.0% walk, 19.9% work from home (2006-2010 5-year est.); Travel time to work: 62.7% less than 15 minutes, 10.4% 15 to 30 minutes, 8.5% 30 to 45 minutes, 0.0% 45 to 60 minutes, 18.4% 60 minutes or more (2006-2010 5-year est.)

**QUOGUE** (village). Covers a land area of 4.191 square miles and a water area of 0.772 square miles. Located at 40.82° N. Lat; 72.59° W. Long. Elevation is 16 feet.

**History:** Region originally occupied by Native American tribe of Shinnecocks because of rich hunting and fishing. Nearby Hampton Bays was called Good Ground until 1922. Settled in 1686, when known as Fourth Neck, then Atlanticville, until adoption of present name in 1891.

**Population:** 898 (1990); 1,018 (2000); 967 (2010); Density: 230.7 persons per square mile (2010); Race: 91.8% White, 1.8% Black, 1.0% Asian, 0.2% American Indian/Alaska Native, 0.0% Native Hawaiian/Other Pacific Islander, 5.2% Other, 6.0% Hispanic of any race (2010); Average household size: 2.26 (2010); Median age: 51.5 (2010); Males per 100 females: 91.9 (2010); Marriage status: 16.8% never married, 60.8% now married, 11.8% widowed, 10.7% divorced (2006-2010 5-year est.); Foreign born: 4.8% (2006-2010 5-year est.); Ancestry (includes multiple ancestries): 18.1% German, 15.1% Italian, 11.2% English, 8.4% Irish, 4.2% Scottish (2006-2010 5-year est.).

**Economy:** Single-family building permits issued: 5 (2011); Multi-family building permits issued: 0 (2011); Employment by occupation: 19.4% management, 0.0% professional, 6.2% services, 19.2% sales, 5.2% farming, 10.1% construction, 3.9% production (2006-2010 5-year est.).

**Income:** Per capita income: $52,661 (2006-2010 5-year est.); Median household income: $65,365 (2006-2010 5-year est.); Average household income: $111,757 (2006-2010 5-year est.); Percent of households with income of $100,000 or more: 36.9% (2006-2010 5-year est.); Poverty rate: 3.8% (2006-2010 5-year est.).

**Education:** Percent of population age 25 and over with: High school diploma (including GED) or higher: 92.1% (2006-2010 5-year est.); Bachelor's degree or higher: 42.4% (2006-2010 5-year est.); Master's degree or higher: 23.1% (2006-2010 5-year est.).

**School District(s)**
Quogue Union Free School District (PK-06)
    2009-10 Enrollment: 120 . . . . . . . . . . . . . . . . . . . . . . . (631) 653-4285
**Housing:** Homeownership rate: 82.6% (2010); Median home value: $1 (2006-2010 5-year est.); Median contract rent: $1,395 per month (2006-2010 5-year est.); Median year structure built: 1975 (2006-2010 5-year est.).

**Safety:** Violent crime rate: 0.0 per 10,000 population; Property crime rate: 340.7 per 10,000 population (2010).

**Transportation:** Commute to work: 82.9% car, 5.4% public transportation, 1.9% walk, 9.8% work from home (2006-2010 5-year est.); Travel time to work: 32.5% less than 15 minutes, 37.0% 15 to 30 minutes, 10.5% 30 to 45 minutes, 5.7% 45 to 60 minutes, 14.2% 60 minutes or more (2006-2010 5-year est.)

**REMSENBURG** (unincorporated postal area)
Zip Code: 11960
    Covers a land area of 1.887 square miles and a water area of 0.073 square miles. Located at 40.81° N. Lat; 72.70° W. Long. Elevation is 10 feet. Population: 1,084 (2010); Density: 574.3 persons per square mile (2010); Race: 96.0% White, 0.3% Black, 0.8% Asian, 0.1% American

Indian/Alaska Native, 0.0% Native Hawaiian/Other Pacific Islander, 2.8% Other, 3.7% Hispanic of any race (2010); Average household size: 2.47 (2010); Median age: 50.5 (2010); Males per 100 females: 95.3 (2010); Homeownership rate: 89.1% (2010)

**REMSENBURG-SPEONK** (CDP). Covers a land area of 3.602 square miles and a water area of 0.081 square miles. Located at 40.81° N. Lat; 72.70° W. Long. Elevation is 30 feet.

**Population:** 1,992 (1990); 2,675 (2000); 2,642 (2010); Density: 733.5 persons per square mile (2010); Race: 93.1% White, 1.2% Black, 0.8% Asian, 0.1% American Indian/Alaska Native, 0.0% Native Hawaiian/Other Pacific Islander, 4.8% Other, 7.9% Hispanic of any race (2010); Average household size: 2.67 (2010); Median age: 44.5 (2010); Males per 100 females: 94.4 (2010); Marriage status: 20.9% never married, 66.0% now married, 5.8% widowed, 7.3% divorced (2006-2010 5-year est.); Foreign born: 7.8% (2006-2010 5-year est.); Ancestry (includes multiple ancestries): 31.5% Italian, 28.4% Irish, 19.2% German, 5.7% Polish, 4.8% American (2006-2010 5-year est.).

**Economy:** Employment by occupation: 9.7% management, 0.7% professional, 12.0% services, 20.5% sales, 5.7% farming, 11.4% construction, 0.3% production (2006-2010 5-year est.).

**Income:** Per capita income: $43,715 (2006-2010 5-year est.); Median household income: $76,667 (2006-2010 5-year est.); Average household income: $112,671 (2006-2010 5-year est.); Percent of households with income of $100,000 or more: 37.7% (2006-2010 5-year est.); Poverty rate: 3.7% (2006-2010 5-year est.).

**Education:** Percent of population age 25 and over with: High school diploma (including GED) or higher: 94.4% (2006-2010 5-year est.); Bachelor's degree or higher: 52.3% (2006-2010 5-year est.); Master's degree or higher: 16.4% (2006-2010 5-year est.).

**Housing:** Homeownership rate: 84.5% (2010); Median home value: $625,500 (2006-2010 5-year est.); Median contract rent: $1,435 per month (2006-2010 5-year est.); Median year structure built: 1975 (2006-2010 5-year est.).

**Transportation:** Commute to work: 93.7% car, 2.0% public transportation, 0.0% walk, 4.3% work from home (2006-2010 5-year est.); Travel time to work: 29.6% less than 15 minutes, 17.9% 15 to 30 minutes, 22.7% 30 to 45 minutes, 18.1% 45 to 60 minutes, 11.7% 60 minutes or more (2006-2010 5-year est.)

**RIDGE** (CDP). Covers a land area of 13.210 square miles and a water area of 0.092 square miles. Located at 40.90° N. Lat; 72.88° W. Long. Elevation is 92 feet.

**Population:** 11,972 (1990); 13,380 (2000); 13,336 (2010); Density: 1,009.5 persons per square mile (2010); Race: 90.8% White, 4.9% Black, 1.8% Asian, 0.2% American Indian/Alaska Native, 0.0% Native Hawaiian/Other Pacific Islander, 2.3% Other, 5.6% Hispanic of any race (2010); Average household size: 2.30 (2010); Median age: 48.2 (2010); Males per 100 females: 85.0 (2010); Marriage status: 17.2% never married, 59.5% now married, 14.8% widowed, 8.5% divorced (2006-2010 5-year est.); Foreign born: 5.3% (2006-2010 5-year est.); Ancestry (includes multiple ancestries): 36.3% Italian, 28.0% Irish, 19.6% German, 7.8% Polish, 5.3% English (2006-2010 5-year est.).

**Economy:** Employment by occupation: 14.8% management, 6.1% professional, 7.3% services, 19.3% sales, 4.1% farming, 7.7% construction, 4.1% production (2006-2010 5-year est.).

**Income:** Per capita income: $32,623 (2006-2010 5-year est.); Median household income: $53,273 (2006-2010 5-year est.); Average household income: $73,181 (2006-2010 5-year est.); Percent of households with income of $100,000 or more: 24.8% (2006-2010 5-year est.); Poverty rate: 7.2% (2006-2010 5-year est.).

**Education:** Percent of population age 25 and over with: High school diploma (including GED) or higher: 88.2% (2006-2010 5-year est.); Bachelor's degree or higher: 23.1% (2006-2010 5-year est.); Master's degree or higher: 11.1% (2006-2010 5-year est.).

**School District(s)**
Longwood Central School District (KG-12)
    2009-10 Enrollment: 9,154 . . . . . . . . . . . . . . . . . . . . . (631) 345-2172
**Housing:** Homeownership rate: 87.3% (2010); Median home value: $301,900 (2006-2010 5-year est.); Median contract rent: $1,070 per month (2006-2010 5-year est.); Median year structure built: 1977 (2006-2010 5-year est.).

**Transportation:** Commute to work: 91.7% car, 3.6% public transportation, 0.4% walk, 3.5% work from home (2006-2010 5-year est.); Travel time to work: 18.4% less than 15 minutes, 36.1% 15 to 30 minutes, 22.1% 30 to 45

minutes, 7.8% 45 to 60 minutes, 15.6% 60 minutes or more (2006-2010 5-year est.)

## RIVERHEAD (town). County seat. Covers a land area of 67.426 square miles and a water area of 133.840 square miles. Located at 40.97° N. Lat; 72.70° W. Long. Elevation is 13 feet.

**History:** Named for its location at the head of the Peconic River. Museum of Suffolk County Historical Society is here.

**Population:** 22,958 (1990); 27,680 (2000); 33,506 (2010); Density: 496.9 persons per square mile (2010); Race: 82.7% White, 7.7% Black, 1.1% Asian, 0.3% American Indian/Alaska Native, 0.1% Native Hawaiian/Other Pacific Islander, 8.1% Other, 13.9% Hispanic of any race (2010); Average household size: 2.52 (2010); Median age: 44.1 (2010); Males per 100 females: 99.0 (2010); Marriage status: 23.9% never married, 59.6% now married, 8.2% widowed, 8.3% divorced (2006-2010 5-year est.); Foreign born: 12.7% (2006-2010 5-year est.); Ancestry (includes multiple ancestries): 21.6% Irish, 21.2% Italian, 15.9% German, 14.7% Polish, 9.1% English (2006-2010 5-year est.).

**Economy:** Unemployment rate: 9.7% (February 2012); Total civilian labor force: 16,516 (February 2012); Single-family building permits issued: 32 (2011); Multi-family building permits issued: 0 (2011); Employment by occupation: 9.5% management, 3.2% professional, 6.9% services, 16.9% sales, 2.9% farming, 11.5% construction, 5.2% production (2006-2010 5-year est.).

**Income:** Per capita income: $33,461 (2006-2010 5-year est.); Median household income: $68,254 (2006-2010 5-year est.); Average household income: $83,211 (2006-2010 5-year est.); Percent of households with income of $100,000 or more: 32.8% (2006-2010 5-year est.); Poverty rate: 9.4% (2006-2010 5-year est.).

**Taxes:** Total city taxes per capita: $1,334 (2009); City property taxes per capita: $1,178 (2009).

**Education:** Percent of population age 25 and over with: High school diploma (including GED) or higher: 88.8% (2006-2010 5-year est.); Bachelor's degree or higher: 29.5% (2006-2010 5-year est.); Master's degree or higher: 16.2% (2006-2010 5-year est.).

### School District(s)
Riverhead Central School District (KG-12)

    2009-10 Enrollment: 4,816 . . . . . . . . . . . . . . . . . . . . (631) 369-6717

### Four-year College(s)
Long Island University-Riverhead Campus (Private, Not-for-profit)

    Fall 2010 Enrollment: 163 . . . . . . . . . . . . . . . . . . . . (631) 287-8010

**Housing:** Homeownership rate: 77.5% (2010); Median home value: $382,000 (2006-2010 5-year est.); Median contract rent: $1,033 per month (2006-2010 5-year est.); Median year structure built: 1979 (2006-2010 5-year est.).

**Hospitals:** Peconic Bay Medical Center (214 beds)

**Safety:** Violent crime rate: 22.7 per 10,000 population; Property crime rate: 294.0 per 10,000 population (2010).

**Newspapers:** Amityville Suffolk Life (Community news; Circulation 17,500); Bay Shore Suffolk Life (Community news; Circulation 16,976); Bellport/East Patchogue Suffolk Life (Community news; Circulation 11,123); Brentwood Suffolk Life (Local news; Circulation 14,305); Centereach/Lake Grove Suffolk Life (Community news; Circulation 12,342); Central Islip/Hauppauge Suffolk Life (Community news; Circulation 35,000); Commack/Kings Park Suffolk Life (Local news; Circulation 17,629); Coram/Middle Island Suffolk Life (Local news; Circulation 19,172); Deer Park Suffolk Life (Community news; Circulation 19,844); Dix Hills Suffolk Life (Local news; Circulation 13,773); East Islip Suffolk Life (Community news; Circulation 13,927); Hampton/East Suffolk Life (Local news; Circulation 17,165); Hampton/West Suffolk Life (Local news; Circulation 16,562); Holbrook/Bohemia Suffolk Life (Community news; Circulation 14,389); Huntington Station Suffolk Life (Community news; Circulation 18,761); Huntington Suffolk Life (Community news; Circulation 18,761); Lindenhurst Suffolk Life (Community news; Circulation 14,606); Mastic/Shirley Suffolk Life (Local news; Circulation 16,394); Medford/Holtsville Suffolk Life (Community news; Circulation 13,329); Mid-Hampton Suffolk Life (Local news; Circulation 17,244); Moriches Suffolk Life (Community news; Circulation 11,529); North Fork Suffolk Life (Community news; Circulation 13,976); Patchogue Suffolk Life (Community news; Circulation 12,261); Port Jefferson Suffolk Life (Community news; Circulation 14,625); Riverhead Suffolk Life (Community news; Circulation 18,186); Rocky Point Suffolk Life (Community news; Circulation 15,854); Ronkonkoma Suffolk Life (Community news; Circulation 13,416); Sayville/Oakdale Suffolk Life (Community news; Circulation 13,294); Selden/Farmingville Suffolk Life (Community news; Circulation 12,294);

Smithtown Suffolk Life (Community news; Circulation 14,622); St. James Nesonset Suffolk Life (Local news; Circulation 350,000); Stony Brook/Setauket Suffolk Life (Local news; Circulation 13,090); West Babylon Suffolk Life (Local news; Circulation 19,264); West Islip Suffolk Life (Local news; Circulation 8,531)

**Transportation:** Commute to work: 91.8% car, 2.1% public transportation, 1.4% walk, 3.5% work from home (2006-2010 5-year est.); Travel time to work: 29.2% less than 15 minutes, 30.8% 15 to 30 minutes, 20.6% 30 to 45 minutes, 9.0% 45 to 60 minutes, 10.4% 60 minutes or more (2006-2010 5-year est.)

**Additional Information Contacts**

Riverhead Chamber of Commerce . . . . . . . . . . . . . (631) 727-7600
    http://www.riverheadchamber.com
Town of Riverhead . . . . . . . . . . . . . . . . . . . . . . . (631) 727-3200
    http://www.townofriverheadny.gov

## RIVERHEAD (CDP). Covers a land area of 15.082 square miles and a water area of 0.305 square miles. Located at 40.94° N. Lat; 72.67° W. Long. Elevation is 13 feet.

**Population:** 8,814 (1990); 10,513 (2000); 13,299 (2010); Density: 881.8 persons per square mile (2010); Race: 66.1% White, 15.8% Black, 1.7% Asian, 0.6% American Indian/Alaska Native, 0.1% Native Hawaiian/Other Pacific Islander, 15.7% Other, 25.3% Hispanic of any race (2010); Average household size: 2.64 (2010); Median age: 40.2 (2010); Males per 100 females: 103.5 (2010); Marriage status: 31.9% never married, 50.7% now married, 8.7% widowed, 8.7% divorced (2006-2010 5-year est.); Foreign born: 19.3% (2006-2010 5-year est.); Ancestry (includes multiple ancestries): 20.1% Polish, 12.0% Irish, 11.6% Italian, 11.4% German, 7.4% English (2006-2010 5-year est.).

**Economy:** Employment by occupation: 7.6% management, 1.9% professional, 11.5% services, 18.1% sales, 2.6% farming, 10.3% construction, 4.0% production (2006-2010 5-year est.).

**Income:** Per capita income: $26,987 (2006-2010 5-year est.); Median household income: $52,211 (2006-2010 5-year est.); Average household income: $66,534 (2006-2010 5-year est.); Percent of households with income of $100,000 or more: 20.9% (2006-2010 5-year est.); Poverty rate: 12.0% (2006-2010 5-year est.).

**Education:** Percent of population age 25 and over with: High school diploma (including GED) or higher: 82.4% (2006-2010 5-year est.); Bachelor's degree or higher: 21.4% (2006-2010 5-year est.); Master's degree or higher: 11.3% (2006-2010 5-year est.).

### School District(s)
Riverhead Central School District (KG-12)

    2009-10 Enrollment: 4,816 . . . . . . . . . . . . . . . . . . . . (631) 369-6717

### Four-year College(s)
Long Island University-Riverhead Campus (Private, Not-for-profit)

    Fall 2010 Enrollment: 163 . . . . . . . . . . . . . . . . . . . . (631) 287-8010

**Housing:** Homeownership rate: 59.6% (2010); Median home value: $348,100 (2006-2010 5-year est.); Median contract rent: $1,024 per month (2006-2010 5-year est.); Median year structure built: 1972 (2006-2010 5-year est.).

**Hospitals:** Peconic Bay Medical Center (214 beds)

**Transportation:** Commute to work: 92.3% car, 1.8% public transportation, 2.2% walk, 2.6% work from home (2006-2010 5-year est.); Travel time to work: 38.1% less than 15 minutes, 26.9% 15 to 30 minutes, 21.9% 30 to 45 minutes, 6.6% 45 to 60 minutes, 6.5% 60 minutes or more (2006-2010 5-year est.)

## RIVERSIDE (CDP). Covers a land area of 2.717 square miles and a water area of 0.113 square miles. Located at 40.90° N. Lat; 72.67° W. Long. Elevation is 180 feet.

**Population:** 2,389 (1990); 2,875 (2000); 2,911 (2010); Density: 1,071.3 persons per square mile (2010); Race: 56.4% White, 25.7% Black, 0.3% Asian, 1.2% American Indian/Alaska Native, 0.0% Native Hawaiian/Other Pacific Islander, 16.4% Other, 30.0% Hispanic of any race (2010); Average household size: 2.60 (2010); Median age: 34.9 (2010); Males per 100 females: 178.0 (2010); Marriage status: 52.4% never married, 29.1% now married, 8.2% widowed, 10.4% divorced (2006-2010 5-year est.); Foreign born: 20.9% (2006-2010 5-year est.); Ancestry (includes multiple ancestries): 14.6% Italian, 11.4% Irish, 8.1% Polish, 6.9% German, 3.5% English (2006-2010 5-year est.).

**Economy:** Employment by occupation: 4.4% management, 4.7% professional, 20.8% services, 11.9% sales, 8.9% farming, 18.5% construction, 11.6% production (2006-2010 5-year est.).

**Income:** Per capita income: $20,179 (2006-2010 5-year est.); Median household income: $35,175 (2006-2010 5-year est.); Average household income: $54,879 (2006-2010 5-year est.); Percent of households with income of $100,000 or more: 10.2% (2006-2010 5-year est.); Poverty rate: 17.4% (2006-2010 5-year est.).
**Education:** Percent of population age 25 and over with: High school diploma (including GED) or higher: 65.3% (2006-2010 5-year est.); Bachelor's degree or higher: 10.4% (2006-2010 5-year est.); Master's degree or higher: 3.3% (2006-2010 5-year est.).
**Housing:** Homeownership rate: 73.3% (2010); Median home value: $78,500 (2006-2010 5-year est.); Median contract rent: $897 per month (2006-2010 5-year est.); Median year structure built: 1973 (2006-2010 5-year est.).
**Transportation:** Commute to work: 89.8% car, 0.0% public transportation, 2.4% walk, 0.0% work from home (2006-2010 5-year est.); Travel time to work: 16.1% less than 15 minutes, 36.3% 15 to 30 minutes, 25.3% 30 to 45 minutes, 11.5% 45 to 60 minutes, 10.8% 60 minutes or more (2006-2010 5-year est.)

## ROCKY POINT (CDP).

Covers a land area of 11.298 square miles and a water area of 0 square miles. Located at 40.93° N. Lat; 72.93° W. Long. Elevation is 194 feet.
**Population:** 8,596 (1990); 10,185 (2000); 14,014 (2010); Density: 1,240.3 persons per square mile (2010); Race: 93.7% White, 1.5% Black, 1.6% Asian, 0.1% American Indian/Alaska Native, 0.0% Native Hawaiian/Other Pacific Islander, 3.1% Other, 7.0% Hispanic of any race (2010); Average household size: 2.89 (2010); Median age: 36.8 (2010); Males per 100 females: 98.7 (2010); Marriage status: 29.6% never married, 56.1% now married, 4.2% widowed, 10.1% divorced (2006-2010 5-year est.); Foreign born: 4.6% (2006-2010 5-year est.); Ancestry (includes multiple ancestries): 34.9% Italian, 29.8% Irish, 27.5% German, 9.4% English, 5.9% Polish (2006-2010 5-year est.).
**Economy:** Employment by occupation: 11.9% management, 3.1% professional, 9.7% services, 15.2% sales, 3.0% farming, 15.5% construction, 7.4% production (2006-2010 5-year est.).
**Income:** Per capita income: $32,501 (2006-2010 5-year est.); Median household income: $80,189 (2006-2010 5-year est.); Average household income: $91,737 (2006-2010 5-year est.); Percent of households with income of $100,000 or more: 35.2% (2006-2010 5-year est.); Poverty rate: 6.5% (2006-2010 5-year est.).
**Education:** Percent of population age 25 and over with: High school diploma (including GED) or higher: 93.0% (2006-2010 5-year est.); Bachelor's degree or higher: 27.2% (2006-2010 5-year est.); Master's degree or higher: 13.9% (2006-2010 5-year est.).
**School District(s)**
Rocky Point Union Free School District (KG-12)
   2009-10 Enrollment: 3,433 . . . . . . . . . . . . . . (631) 849-7561
**Housing:** Homeownership rate: 83.2% (2010); Median home value: $344,800 (2006-2010 5-year est.); Median contract rent: $1,134 per month (2006-2010 5-year est.); Median year structure built: 1964 (2006-2010 5-year est.).
**Transportation:** Commute to work: 95.7% car, 1.2% public transportation, 0.6% walk, 1.7% work from home (2006-2010 5-year est.); Travel time to work: 18.6% less than 15 minutes, 29.2% 15 to 30 minutes, 22.5% 30 to 45 minutes, 12.6% 45 to 60 minutes, 17.0% 60 minutes or more (2006-2010 5-year est.)
**Additional Information Contacts**
North Brookhaven Chamber of Commerce . . . . . . . . . . . . . (631) 821-1313
   http://northbrookhavenchamber.org

## RONKONKOMA (CDP).

Covers a land area of 7.832 square miles and a water area of 0.331 square miles. Located at 40.80° N. Lat; 73.12° W. Long. Elevation is 112 feet.
**Population:** 20,391 (1990); 20,029 (2000); 19,082 (2010); Density: 2,436.1 persons per square mile (2010); Race: 89.0% White, 2.1% Black, 4.6% Asian, 0.1% American Indian/Alaska Native, 0.0% Native Hawaiian/Other Pacific Islander, 4.2% Other, 10.2% Hispanic of any race (2010); Average household size: 2.93 (2010); Median age: 39.0 (2010); Males per 100 females: 98.3 (2010); Marriage status: 30.6% never married, 54.4% now married, 4.9% widowed, 10.1% divorced (2006-2010 5-year est.); Foreign born: 9.6% (2006-2010 5-year est.); Ancestry (includes multiple ancestries): 39.3% Italian, 28.9% Irish, 18.3% German, 6.1% English, 5.9% Polish (2006-2010 5-year est.).

**Economy:** Employment by occupation: 9.8% management, 4.8% professional, 8.8% services, 19.3% sales, 2.8% farming, 12.3% construction, 8.4% production (2006-2010 5-year est.).
**Income:** Per capita income: $32,749 (2006-2010 5-year est.); Median household income: $86,793 (2006-2010 5-year est.); Average household income: $97,388 (2006-2010 5-year est.); Percent of households with income of $100,000 or more: 40.6% (2006-2010 5-year est.); Poverty rate: 5.0% (2006-2010 5-year est.).
**Education:** Percent of population age 25 and over with: High school diploma (including GED) or higher: 93.3% (2006-2010 5-year est.); Bachelor's degree or higher: 24.5% (2006-2010 5-year est.); Master's degree or higher: 10.2% (2006-2010 5-year est.).
**School District(s)**
Connetquot Central School District (PK-12)
   2009-10 Enrollment: 6,757 . . . . . . . . . . . . . . (631) 244-2215
**Housing:** Homeownership rate: 81.1% (2010); Median home value: $386,800 (2006-2010 5-year est.); Median contract rent: $1,405 per month (2006-2010 5-year est.); Median year structure built: 1971 (2006-2010 5-year est.).
**Newspapers:** Our Place In Holbrook (Community news; Circulation 18,900)
**Transportation:** Commute to work: 92.6% car, 4.5% public transportation, 0.0% walk, 2.3% work from home (2006-2010 5-year est.); Travel time to work: 22.9% less than 15 minutes, 36.3% 15 to 30 minutes, 20.5% 30 to 45 minutes, 5.4% 45 to 60 minutes, 14.8% 60 minutes or more (2006-2010 5-year est.)
**Additional Information Contacts**
Chamber of Commerce of the Greater Ronkonkomas . . . . (631) 963-2796
   http://www.ronkonkomachamber.com

## SAG HARBOR (village).

Covers a land area of 1.804 square miles and a water area of 0.521 square miles. Located at 40.99° N. Lat; 72.28° W. Long. Elevation is 26 feet.
**History:** An important 19th-century whaling port. National Historic District. The *Long Island Herald* (1791) was L.I.'s first local paper. The Whalers' Church and Whalers' Museum, noted for their architecture, are among its historic buildings. Had first customhouse in N.Y., and first post office on L.I., established 1794. Settled 1720—1730, Incorporated 1846.
**Population:** 2,134 (1990); 2,313 (2000); 2,169 (2010); Density: 1,202.3 persons per square mile (2010); Race: 87.0% White, 7.2% Black, 1.4% Asian, 1.0% American Indian/Alaska Native, 0.0% Native Hawaiian/Other Pacific Islander, 3.4% Other, 13.1% Hispanic of any race (2010); Average household size: 2.15 (2010); Median age: 47.3 (2010); Males per 100 females: 88.4 (2010); Marriage status: 26.1% never married, 47.0% now married, 13.1% widowed, 13.8% divorced (2006-2010 5-year est.); Foreign born: 15.0% (2006-2010 5-year est.); Ancestry (includes multiple ancestries): 19.9% German, 14.8% English, 12.8% Irish, 10.1% Italian, 7.5% Polish (2006-2010 5-year est.).
**Economy:** Single-family building permits issued: 4 (2011); Multi-family building permits issued: 65 (2011); Employment by occupation: 25.8% management, 1.3% professional, 9.7% services, 17.8% sales, 0.0% farming, 10.6% construction, 1.4% production (2006-2010 5-year est.).
**Income:** Per capita income: $63,726 (2006-2010 5-year est.); Median household income: $85,401 (2006-2010 5-year est.); Average household income: $126,777 (2006-2010 5-year est.); Percent of households with income of $100,000 or more: 39.7% (2006-2010 5-year est.); Poverty rate: 7.6% (2006-2010 5-year est.).
**Education:** Percent of population age 25 and over with: High school diploma (including GED) or higher: 98.3% (2006-2010 5-year est.); Bachelor's degree or higher: 57.9% (2006-2010 5-year est.); Master's degree or higher: 29.8% (2006-2010 5-year est.).
**School District(s)**
Sag Harbor Union Free School District (KG-12)
   2009-10 Enrollment: 935 . . . . . . . . . . . . . . . . (631) 725-5300
**Housing:** Homeownership rate: 68.2% (2010); Median home value: $852,400 (2006-2010 5-year est.); Median contract rent: $1,684 per month (2006-2010 5-year est.); Median year structure built: 1956 (2006-2010 5-year est.).
**Safety:** Violent crime rate: 4.1 per 10,000 population; Property crime rate: 132.1 per 10,000 population (2010).
**Newspapers:** Express (Local news; Circulation 3,000)
**Transportation:** Commute to work: 69.3% car, 12.4% public transportation, 7.4% walk, 9.7% work from home (2006-2010 5-year est.); Travel time to work: 39.2% less than 15 minutes, 35.9% 15 to 30 minutes,

7.3% 30 to 45 minutes, 2.7% 45 to 60 minutes, 14.9% 60 minutes or more (2006-2010 5-year est.)
**Additional Information Contacts**
Sag Harbor Chamber of Commerce . . . . . . . . . . . . . . . . . . (631) 725-0011
  http://www.sagharborchamber.com

**SAGAPONACK** (village). Covers a land area of 4.413 square miles and a water area of 0.239 square miles. Located at 40.93° N. Lat; 72.26° W. Long. Elevation is 23 feet.
**Population:** 490 (1990); 582 (2000); 313 (2010); Density: 70.9 persons per square mile (2010); Race: 96.2% White, 1.3% Black, 0.6% Asian, 0.0% American Indian/Alaska Native, 0.3% Native Hawaiian/Other Pacific Islander, 1.6% Other, 2.2% Hispanic of any race (2010); Average household size: 2.14 (2010); Median age: 55.5 (2010); Males per 100 females: 93.2 (2010); Marriage status: 20.8% never married, 63.2% now married, 5.6% widowed, 10.4% divorced (2006-2010 5-year est.); Foreign born: 8.2% (2006-2010 5-year est.); Ancestry (includes multiple ancestries): 33.2% Irish, 26.2% English, 17.6% American, 10.9% German, 5.1% Scottish (2006-2010 5-year est.).
**Economy:** Single-family building permits issued: 4 (2011); Multi-family building permits issued: 0 (2011); Employment by occupation: 13.1% management, 0.0% professional, 27.9% services, 19.7% sales, 0.0% farming, 0.0% construction, 0.0% production (2006-2010 5-year est.).
**Income:** Per capita income: $49,193 (2006-2010 5-year est.); Median household income: $98,500 (2006-2010 5-year est.); Average household income: $106,747 (2006-2010 5-year est.); Percent of households with income of $100,000 or more: 39.6% (2006-2010 5-year est.); Poverty rate: 1.6% (2006-2010 5-year est.).
**Education:** Percent of population age 25 and over with: High school diploma (including GED) or higher: 100.0% (2006-2010 5-year est.); Bachelor's degree or higher: 54.7% (2006-2010 5-year est.); Master's degree or higher: 10.7% (2006-2010 5-year est.).
### School District(s)
Sagaponack Common School District (01-04)
  2009-10 Enrollment: 21 . . . . . . . . . . . . . . . . . . . . . (631) 537-0651
**Housing:** Homeownership rate: 85.7% (2010); Median home value: $1 (2006-2010 5-year est.); Median contract rent: n/a per month (2006-2010 5-year est.); Median year structure built: 1979 (2006-2010 5-year est.).
**Transportation:** Commute to work: 59.3% car, 2.5% public transportation, 12.7% walk, 20.3% work from home (2006-2010 5-year est.); Travel time to work: 57.4% less than 15 minutes, 39.4% 15 to 30 minutes, 3.2% 30 to 45 minutes, 0.0% 45 to 60 minutes, 0.0% 60 minutes or more (2006-2010 5-year est.)

**SAINT JAMES** (CDP). Covers a land area of 4.559 square miles and a water area of <.001 square miles. Located at 40.87° N. Lat; 73.15° W. Long. Elevation is 151 feet.
**Population:** 12,703 (1990); 13,268 (2000); 13,338 (2010); Density: 2,925.3 persons per square mile (2010); Race: 95.1% White, 0.6% Black, 2.0% Asian, 0.1% American Indian/Alaska Native, 0.0% Native Hawaiian/Other Pacific Islander, 2.2% Other, 5.6% Hispanic of any race (2010); Average household size: 2.84 (2010); Median age: 43.0 (2010); Males per 100 females: 90.8 (2010); Marriage status: 22.1% never married, 61.4% now married, 10.3% widowed, 6.1% divorced (2006-2010 5-year est.); Foreign born: 5.3% (2006-2010 5-year est.); Ancestry (includes multiple ancestries): 41.7% Italian, 28.9% Irish, 21.5% German, 7.0% Polish, 5.4% English (2006-2010 5-year est.).
**Economy:** Employment by occupation: 16.5% management, 4.3% professional, 5.7% services, 17.5% sales, 2.9% farming, 8.1% construction, 3.7% production (2006-2010 5-year est.).
**Income:** Per capita income: $38,759 (2006-2010 5-year est.); Median household income: $96,473 (2006-2010 5-year est.); Average household income: $107,148 (2006-2010 5-year est.); Percent of households with income of $100,000 or more: 48.2% (2006-2010 5-year est.); Poverty rate: 3.5% (2006-2010 5-year est.).
**Education:** Percent of population age 25 and over with: High school diploma (including GED) or higher: 95.1% (2006-2010 5-year est.); Bachelor's degree or higher: 41.0% (2006-2010 5-year est.); Master's degree or higher: 18.0% (2006-2010 5-year est.).
### School District(s)
Smithtown Central School District (KG-12)
  2009-10 Enrollment: 10,862 . . . . . . . . . . . . . . . . . . (631) 382-2005
**Housing:** Homeownership rate: 89.6% (2010); Median home value: $485,100 (2006-2010 5-year est.); Median contract rent: $1,127 per month

(2006-2010 5-year est.); Median year structure built: 1966 (2006-2010 5-year est.).
**Newspapers:** Our Town-Saint James (Local news; Circulation 6,022)
**Transportation:** Commute to work: 86.6% car, 4.0% public transportation, 2.5% walk, 6.0% work from home (2006-2010 5-year est.); Travel time to work: 25.9% less than 15 minutes, 31.1% 15 to 30 minutes, 22.7% 30 to 45 minutes, 7.3% 45 to 60 minutes, 12.9% 60 minutes or more (2006-2010 5-year est.)
**Additional Information Contacts**
Holbrook Chamber of Commerce . . . . . . . . . . . . . . . . . (631) 471-2725
  http://www.holbrookchamber.com
Saint James Chamber of Commerce . . . . . . . . . . . . . . (631) 584-8510
  http://www.stjameschamber.org

**SALTAIRE** (village). Covers a land area of 0.232 square miles and a water area of 0.051 square miles. Located at 40.63° N. Lat; 73.19° W. Long. Elevation is 3 feet.
**Population:** 38 (1990); 43 (2000); 37 (2010); Density: 158.9 persons per square mile (2010); Race: 100.0% White, 0.0% Black, 0.0% Asian, 0.0% American Indian/Alaska Native, 0.0% Native Hawaiian/Other Pacific Islander, 0.0% Other, 0.0% Hispanic of any race (2010); Average household size: 2.47 (2010); Median age: 54.8 (2010); Males per 100 females: 105.6 (2010); Marriage status: 17.0% never married, 70.2% now married, 4.3% widowed, 8.5% divorced (2006-2010 5-year est.); Foreign born: 10.3% (2006-2010 5-year est.); Ancestry (includes multiple ancestries): 34.5% English, 32.8% Italian, 32.8% German, 17.2% Irish, 13.8% Norwegian (2006-2010 5-year est.).
**Economy:** Single-family building permits issued: 0 (2011); Multi-family building permits issued: 0 (2011); Employment by occupation: 26.9% management, 0.0% professional, 7.7% services, 23.1% sales, 0.0% farming, 0.0% construction, 0.0% production (2006-2010 5-year est.).
**Income:** Per capita income: $72,057 (2006-2010 5-year est.); Median household income: $81,786 (2006-2010 5-year est.); Average household income: $191,414 (2006-2010 5-year est.); Percent of households with income of $100,000 or more: 40.9% (2006-2010 5-year est.); Poverty rate: 0.0% (2006-2010 5-year est.).
**Education:** Percent of population age 25 and over with: High school diploma (including GED) or higher: 100.0% (2006-2010 5-year est.); Bachelor's degree or higher: 61.0% (2006-2010 5-year est.); Master's degree or higher: 24.4% (2006-2010 5-year est.).
**Housing:** Homeownership rate: 93.3% (2010); Median home value: $1 (2006-2010 5-year est.); Median contract rent: n/a per month (2006-2010 5-year est.); Median year structure built: 1964 (2006-2010 5-year est.).
**Transportation:** Commute to work: 0.0% car, 8.7% public transportation, 34.8% walk, 56.5% work from home (2006-2010 5-year est.); Travel time to work: 100.0% less than 15 minutes, 0.0% 15 to 30 minutes, 0.0% 30 to 45 minutes, 0.0% 45 to 60 minutes, 0.0% 60 minutes or more (2006-2010 5-year est.)
**Additional Information Contacts**
Village of Saltaire . . . . . . . . . . . . . . . . . . . . . . . . . . . . (631) 583-5566
  http://www.saltaire.org

**SAYVILLE** (CDP). Covers a land area of 5.289 square miles and a water area of 0.064 square miles. Located at 40.74° N. Lat; 73.08° W. Long. Elevation is 20 feet.
**Population:** 16,550 (1990); 16,735 (2000); 16,853 (2010); Density: 3,186.3 persons per square mile (2010); Race: 95.4% White, 1.1% Black, 1.8% Asian, 0.1% American Indian/Alaska Native, 0.0% Native Hawaiian/Other Pacific Islander, 1.6% Other, 4.8% Hispanic of any race (2010); Average household size: 2.72 (2010); Median age: 43.0 (2010); Males per 100 females: 89.5 (2010); Marriage status: 22.5% never married, 58.7% now married, 9.3% widowed, 9.4% divorced (2006-2010 5-year est.); Foreign born: 4.6% (2006-2010 5-year est.); Ancestry (includes multiple ancestries): 36.0% Irish, 32.9% Italian, 24.7% German, 5.4% English, 5.0% Polish (2006-2010 5-year est.).
**Economy:** Employment by occupation: 13.7% management, 4.1% professional, 4.8% services, 16.1% sales, 3.6% farming, 9.7% construction, 4.8% production (2006-2010 5-year est.).
**Income:** Per capita income: $38,914 (2006-2010 5-year est.); Median household income: $94,031 (2006-2010 5-year est.); Average household income: $106,363 (2006-2010 5-year est.); Percent of households with income of $100,000 or more: 46.7% (2006-2010 5-year est.); Poverty rate: 3.8% (2006-2010 5-year est.).
**Education:** Percent of population age 25 and over with: High school diploma (including GED) or higher: 95.1% (2006-2010 5-year est.);

Bachelor's degree or higher: 36.9% (2006-2010 5-year est.); Master's degree or higher: 19.4% (2006-2010 5-year est.).

**School District(s)**

Sayville Union Free School District (KG-12)

   2009-10 Enrollment: 3,335 . . . . . . . . . . . . . . . . . . . . (631) 244-6510

**Housing:** Homeownership rate: 78.8% (2010); Median home value: $462,500 (2006-2010 5-year est.); Median contract rent: $1,372 per month (2006-2010 5-year est.); Median year structure built: 1964 (2006-2010 5-year est.).

**Newspapers:** Fire Island Tide (Local news; Circulation 35,000); Islip Bulletin (Community news; Circulation 6,000); Suffolk County News (Community news; Circulation 15,000)

**Transportation:** Commute to work: 91.4% car, 3.5% public transportation, 0.8% walk, 3.9% work from home (2006-2010 5-year est.); Travel time to work: 27.7% less than 15 minutes, 28.4% 15 to 30 minutes, 23.8% 30 to 45 minutes, 6.7% 45 to 60 minutes, 13.3% 60 minutes or more (2006-2010 5-year est.)

**Additional Information Contacts**

Greater Sayville Chamber of Commerce . . . . . . . . . . . . . (631) 567-5257

   http://www.greatersayvillechamber.com

## SELDEN (CDP). Covers a land area of 4.321 square miles and a water area of 0 square miles. Located at 40.87° N. Lat; 73.04° W. Long. Elevation is 89 feet.

**Population:** 20,608 (1990); 21,861 (2000); 19,851 (2010); Density: 4,593.8 persons per square mile (2010); Race: 86.0% White, 3.3% Black, 4.4% Asian, 0.2% American Indian/Alaska Native, 0.0% Native Hawaiian/Other Pacific Islander, 6.1% Other, 13.9% Hispanic of any race (2010); Average household size: 3.08 (2010); Median age: 37.0 (2010); Males per 100 females: 98.4 (2010); Marriage status: 30.5% never married, 57.4% now married, 5.1% widowed, 7.1% divorced (2006-2010 5-year est.); Foreign born: 12.4% (2006-2010 5-year est.); Ancestry (includes multiple ancestries): 39.8% Italian, 24.5% Irish, 20.3% German, 5.5% English, 4.3% Polish (2006-2010 5-year est.).

**Economy:** Employment by occupation: 11.0% management, 4.3% professional, 9.1% services, 19.2% sales, 5.7% farming, 10.6% construction, 4.7% production (2006-2010 5-year est.).

**Income:** Per capita income: $27,710 (2006-2010 5-year est.); Median household income: $74,819 (2006-2010 5-year est.); Average household income: $81,900 (2006-2010 5-year est.); Percent of households with income of $100,000 or more: 30.9% (2006-2010 5-year est.); Poverty rate: 3.8% (2006-2010 5-year est.).

**Education:** Percent of population age 25 and over with: High school diploma (including GED) or higher: 89.2% (2006-2010 5-year est.); Bachelor's degree or higher: 21.4% (2006-2010 5-year est.); Master's degree or higher: 7.3% (2006-2010 5-year est.).

**School District(s)**

Middle Country Central School District (PK-12)

   2009-10 Enrollment: 10,929 . . . . . . . . . . . . . . . . . . (631) 285-8005

**Two-year College(s)**

Suffolk County Community College (Public)

   Fall 2010 Enrollment: 19,319 . . . . . . . . . . . . . . . . . . (631) 451-4110

   2011-12 Tuition: In-state $4,830; Out-of-state $8,820

**Housing:** Homeownership rate: 78.1% (2010); Median home value: $344,500 (2006-2010 5-year est.); Median contract rent: $1,260 per month (2006-2010 5-year est.); Median year structure built: 1967 (2006-2010 5-year est.).

**Transportation:** Commute to work: 92.6% car, 3.1% public transportation, 0.7% walk, 2.8% work from home (2006-2010 5-year est.); Travel time to work: 20.0% less than 15 minutes, 40.2% 15 to 30 minutes, 19.3% 30 to 45 minutes, 6.2% 45 to 60 minutes, 14.4% 60 minutes or more (2006-2010 5-year est.).

## SETAUKET-EAST SETAUKET (CDP). Covers a land area of 8.519 square miles and a water area of 0.805 square miles. Located at 40.92° N. Lat; 73.10° W. Long.

**History:** The region was first settled in the 1650s. During the American Revolutionary War, the Culper Spy Ring headed by Benjamin Tallmadge passed information about British troop movements gathered in New York City to George Washington. The 1777 Battle of Setauket was fought here.

**Population:** 13,634 (1990); 15,931 (2000); 15,477 (2010); Density: 1,816.6 persons per square mile (2010); Race: 89.1% White, 1.2% Black, 7.4% Asian, 0.1% American Indian/Alaska Native, 0.0% Native Hawaiian/Other Pacific Islander, 2.2% Other, 5.2% Hispanic of any race (2010); Average household size: 2.86 (2010); Median age: 42.6 (2010); Males per 100

females: 94.7 (2010); Marriage status: 25.5% never married, 65.4% now married, 3.3% widowed, 5.8% divorced (2006-2010 5-year est.); Foreign born: 9.3% (2006-2010 5-year est.); Ancestry (includes multiple ancestries): 27.9% Italian, 27.1% Irish, 16.1% German, 10.9% English, 10.0% Polish (2006-2010 5-year est.).

**Economy:** Employment by occupation: 16.5% management, 5.7% professional, 6.6% services, 14.7% sales, 3.7% farming, 5.6% construction, 3.1% production (2006-2010 5-year est.).

**Income:** Per capita income: $48,218 (2006-2010 5-year est.); Median household income: $116,148 (2006-2010 5-year est.); Average household income: $138,042 (2006-2010 5-year est.); Percent of households with income of $100,000 or more: 57.5% (2006-2010 5-year est.); Poverty rate: 2.5% (2006-2010 5-year est.).

**Education:** Percent of population age 25 and over with: High school diploma (including GED) or higher: 96.4% (2006-2010 5-year est.); Bachelor's degree or higher: 59.1% (2006-2010 5-year est.); Master's degree or higher: 34.2% (2006-2010 5-year est.).

**School District(s)**

Three Village Central School District (KG-12)

   2009-10 Enrollment: 7,572 . . . . . . . . . . . . . . . . . . . . (631) 730-4010

**Housing:** Homeownership rate: 90.8% (2010); Median home value: $552,000 (2006-2010 5-year est.); Median contract rent: $1,431 per month (2006-2010 5-year est.); Median year structure built: 1969 (2006-2010 5-year est.).

**Transportation:** Commute to work: 89.6% car, 4.2% public transportation, 2.3% walk, 3.3% work from home (2006-2010 5-year est.); Travel time to work: 37.1% less than 15 minutes, 23.9% 15 to 30 minutes, 18.4% 30 to 45 minutes, 9.3% 45 to 60 minutes, 11.3% 60 minutes or more (2006-2010 5-year est.).

## SHELTER ISLAND (town). Covers a land area of 12.164 square miles and a water area of 16.944 square miles. Located at 41.06° N. Lat; 72.31° W. Long. Elevation is 52 feet.

**Population:** 2,263 (1990); 2,228 (2000); 2,392 (2010); Density: 196.6 persons per square mile (2010); Race: 94.4% White, 1.2% Black, 0.4% Asian, 0.9% American Indian/Alaska Native, 0.0% Native Hawaiian/Other Pacific Islander, 3.1% Other, 4.8% Hispanic of any race (2010); Average household size: 2.12 (2010); Median age: 52.5 (2010); Males per 100 females: 97.2 (2010); Marriage status: 15.8% never married, 65.4% now married, 9.3% widowed, 9.4% divorced (2006-2010 5-year est.); Foreign born: 5.0% (2006-2010 5-year est.); Ancestry (includes multiple ancestries): 29.5% Irish, 27.0% German, 17.9% Italian, 15.4% English, 5.4% Swedish (2006-2010 5-year est.).

**Economy:** Single-family building permits issued: 4 (2011); Multi-family building permits issued: 0 (2011); Employment by occupation: 20.3% management, 4.5% professional, 12.9% services, 21.9% sales, 0.0% farming, 8.1% construction, 0.8% production (2006-2010 5-year est.).

**Income:** Per capita income: $44,111 (2006-2010 5-year est.); Median household income: $71,384 (2006-2010 5-year est.); Average household income: $93,974 (2006-2010 5-year est.); Percent of households with income of $100,000 or more: 30.9% (2006-2010 5-year est.); Poverty rate: 1.7% (2006-2010 5-year est.).

**Education:** Percent of population age 25 and over with: High school diploma (including GED) or higher: 92.6% (2006-2010 5-year est.); Bachelor's degree or higher: 43.7% (2006-2010 5-year est.); Master's degree or higher: 21.4% (2006-2010 5-year est.).

**School District(s)**

Shelter Island Union Free School District (KG-12)

   2009-10 Enrollment: 262 . . . . . . . . . . . . . . . . . . . . . . (631) 749-0302

**Housing:** Homeownership rate: 78.4% (2010); Median home value: $845,400 (2006-2010 5-year est.); Median contract rent: $1,128 per month (2006-2010 5-year est.); Median year structure built: 1969 (2006-2010 5-year est.).

**Safety:** Violent crime rate: 0.0 per 10,000 population; Property crime rate: 199.6 per 10,000 population (2010).

**Newspapers:** Shelter Island Reporter (Community news; Circulation 3,000)

**Transportation:** Commute to work: 71.3% car, 8.7% public transportation, 6.7% walk, 7.8% work from home (2006-2010 5-year est.); Travel time to work: 49.6% less than 15 minutes, 15.9% 15 to 30 minutes, 19.0% 30 to 45 minutes, 2.2% 45 to 60 minutes, 13.3% 60 minutes or more (2006-2010 5-year est.)

**Additional Information Contacts**

Shelter Island Chamber of Commerce . . . . . . . . . . . . . . (631) 749-0399

   http://www.shelterislandchamber.org

**SHELTER ISLAND** (CDP). Covers a land area of 6.549 square miles and a water area of 0.142 square miles. Located at 41.05° N. Lat; 72.31° W. Long. Elevation is 52 feet.
**Population:** 1,193 (1990); 1,234 (2000); 1,333 (2010); Density: 203.5 persons per square mile (2010); Race: 94.4% White, 0.9% Black, 0.5% Asian, 1.4% American Indian/Alaska Native, 0.0% Native Hawaiian/Other Pacific Islander, 2.8% Other, 5.6% Hispanic of any race (2010); Average household size: 2.23 (2010); Median age: 48.2 (2010); Males per 100 females: 103.5 (2010); Marriage status: 18.8% never married, 61.4% now married, 9.6% widowed, 10.2% divorced (2006-2010 5-year est.); Foreign born: 8.9% (2006-2010 5-year est.); Ancestry (includes multiple ancestries): 26.5% Irish, 24.3% German, 17.5% Italian, 11.3% English, 5.2% Scottish (2006-2010 5-year est.).
**Economy:** Employment by occupation: 21.6% management, 2.5% professional, 13.2% services, 23.7% sales, 0.0% farming, 12.5% construction, 1.4% production (2006-2010 5-year est.).
**Income:** Per capita income: $48,036 (2006-2010 5-year est.); Median household income: $61,438 (2006-2010 5-year est.); Average household income: $102,386 (2006-2010 5-year est.); Percent of households with income of $100,000 or more: 36.1% (2006-2010 5-year est.); Poverty rate: 2.9% (2006-2010 5-year est.).
**Education:** Percent of population age 25 and over with: High school diploma (including GED) or higher: 85.1% (2006-2010 5-year est.); Bachelor's degree or higher: 31.7% (2006-2010 5-year est.); Master's degree or higher: 21.5% (2006-2010 5-year est.).
**School District(s)**
Shelter Island Union Free School District (KG-12)
   2009-10 Enrollment: 262 . . . . . . . . . . . . . . . . . . (631) 749-0302
**Housing:** Homeownership rate: 76.2% (2010); Median home value: $845,400 (2006-2010 5-year est.); Median contract rent: $1,026 per month (2006-2010 5-year est.); Median year structure built: 1974 (2006-2010 5-year est.).
**Transportation:** Commute to work: 67.0% car, 7.1% public transportation, 11.2% walk, 5.3% work from home (2006-2010 5-year est.); Travel time to work: 56.6% less than 15 minutes, 14.1% 15 to 30 minutes, 26.4% 30 to 45 minutes, 0.0% 45 to 60 minutes, 2.9% 60 minutes or more (2006-2010 5-year est.)
**Additional Information Contacts**
Shelter Island Chamber of Commerce . . . . . . . . . . . (631) 749-0399
   http://www.shelterislandchamber.org

**SHELTER ISLAND HEIGHTS** (CDP). Covers a land area of 5.369 square miles and a water area of 0.278 square miles. Located at 41.06° N. Lat; 72.36° W. Long. Elevation is 56 feet.
**Population:** 1,042 (1990); 981 (2000); 1,048 (2010); Density: 195.2 persons per square mile (2010); Race: 94.3% White, 1.5% Black, 0.4% Asian, 0.3% American Indian/Alaska Native, 0.0% Native Hawaiian/Other Pacific Islander, 3.5% Other, 3.9% Hispanic of any race (2010); Average household size: 2.00 (2010); Median age: 58.0 (2010); Males per 100 females: 89.5 (2010); Marriage status: 13.3% never married, 68.7% now married, 9.1% widowed, 8.9% divorced (2006-2010 5-year est.); Foreign born: 0.8% (2006-2010 5-year est.); Ancestry (includes multiple ancestries): 33.0% Irish, 30.1% German, 19.1% English, 18.4% Italian, 10.7% Swedish (2006-2010 5-year est.).
**Economy:** Employment by occupation: 19.0% management, 7.4% professional, 11.8% services, 19.8% sales, 0.0% farming, 1.8% construction, 0.0% production (2006-2010 5-year est.).
**Income:** Per capita income: $40,302 (2006-2010 5-year est.); Median household income: $75,724 (2006-2010 5-year est.); Average household income: $85,853 (2006-2010 5-year est.); Percent of households with income of $100,000 or more: 25.8% (2006-2010 5-year est.); Poverty rate: 0.5% (2006-2010 5-year est.).
**Education:** Percent of population age 25 and over with: High school diploma (including GED) or higher: 100.0% (2006-2010 5-year est.); Bachelor's degree or higher: 54.8% (2006-2010 5-year est.); Master's degree or higher: 20.8% (2006-2010 5-year est.).
**Housing:** Homeownership rate: 80.6% (2010); Median home value: $841,800 (2006-2010 5-year est.); Median contract rent: n/a per month (2006-2010 5-year est.); Median year structure built: 1968 (2006-2010 5-year est.).
**Transportation:** Commute to work: 79.1% car, 10.2% public transportation, 0.0% walk, 10.6% work from home (2006-2010 5-year est.); Travel time to work: 39.0% less than 15 minutes, 19.0% 15 to 30 minutes, 7.4% 30 to 45 minutes, 5.7% 45 to 60 minutes, 28.8% 60 minutes or more (2006-2010 5-year est.)

**SHINNECOCK HILLS** (CDP). Covers a land area of 2.838 square miles and a water area of 0.200 square miles. Located at 40.88° N. Lat; 72.45° W. Long. Elevation is 79 feet.
**Population:** 1,607 (1990); 1,749 (2000); 2,188 (2010); Density: 770.7 persons per square mile (2010); Race: 86.1% White, 2.1% Black, 1.1% Asian, 2.3% American Indian/Alaska Native, 0.2% Native Hawaiian/Other Pacific Islander, 8.2% Other, 29.9% Hispanic of any race (2010); Average household size: 2.69 (2010); Median age: 35.2 (2010); Males per 100 females: 104.9 (2010); Marriage status: 29.1% never married, 60.8% now married, 5.7% widowed, 4.5% divorced (2006-2010 5-year est.); Foreign born: 27.1% (2006-2010 5-year est.); Ancestry (includes multiple ancestries): 20.6% Italian, 17.3% German, 12.5% Irish, 9.1% English, 7.2% Greek (2006-2010 5-year est.).
**Economy:** Employment by occupation: 9.6% management, 1.1% professional, 8.3% services, 20.1% sales, 2.4% farming, 12.8% construction, 1.1% production (2006-2010 5-year est.).
**Income:** Per capita income: $41,308 (2006-2010 5-year est.); Median household income: $65,774 (2006-2010 5-year est.); Average household income: $106,111 (2006-2010 5-year est.); Percent of households with income of $100,000 or more: 38.8% (2006-2010 5-year est.); Poverty rate: 18.5% (2006-2010 5-year est.).
**Education:** Percent of population age 25 and over with: High school diploma (including GED) or higher: 92.6% (2006-2010 5-year est.); Bachelor's degree or higher: 42.7% (2006-2010 5-year est.); Master's degree or higher: 21.2% (2006-2010 5-year est.).
**Housing:** Homeownership rate: 67.4% (2010); Median home value: $721,600 (2006-2010 5-year est.); Median contract rent: $1,592 per month (2006-2010 5-year est.); Median year structure built: 1980 (2006-2010 5-year est.).
**Transportation:** Commute to work: 91.4% car, 5.3% public transportation, 0.0% walk, 3.2% work from home (2006-2010 5-year est.); Travel time to work: 12.8% less than 15 minutes, 44.8% 15 to 30 minutes, 34.4% 30 to 45 minutes, 2.3% 45 to 60 minutes, 5.7% 60 minutes or more (2006-2010 5-year est.)

**SHINNECOCK RESERVATION** (Reservation). Covers a land area of 1.349 square miles and a water area of 0 square miles. Located at 40.87° N. Lat; 72.43° W. Long.
**Population:** 375 (1990); 504 (2000); 662 (2010); Density: 490.7 persons per square mile (2010); Race: 6.0% White, 4.5% Black, 0.5% Asian, 76.6% American Indian/Alaska Native, 0.0% Native Hawaiian/Other Pacific Islander, 12.4% Other, 6.3% Hispanic of any race (2010); Average household size: 2.93 (2010); Median age: 36.7 (2010); Males per 100 females: 88.1 (2010); Marriage status: 31.4% never married, 40.7% now married, 18.6% widowed, 9.3% divorced (2006-2010 5-year est.); Foreign born: 0.0% (2006-2010 5-year est.); Ancestry (includes multiple ancestries): 1.3% Italian, 1.3% German, 1.1% English (2006-2010 5-year est.).
**Economy:** Employment by occupation: 0.0% management, 0.0% professional, 21.8% services, 14.9% sales, 5.9% farming, 6.9% construction, 0.0% production (2006-2010 5-year est.).
**Income:** Per capita income: $15,423 (2006-2010 5-year est.); Median household income: $25,536 (2006-2010 5-year est.); Average household income: $33,850 (2006-2010 5-year est.); Percent of households with income of $100,000 or more: 3.6% (2006-2010 5-year est.); Poverty rate: 22.6% (2006-2010 5-year est.).
**Education:** Percent of population age 25 and over with: High school diploma (including GED) or higher: 81.3% (2006-2010 5-year est.); Bachelor's degree or higher: 9.6% (2006-2010 5-year est.); Master's degree or higher: 4.8% (2006-2010 5-year est.).
**Housing:** Homeownership rate: 90.3% (2010); Median home value: $363,900 (2006-2010 5-year est.); Median contract rent: n/a per month (2006-2010 5-year est.); Median year structure built: 1971 (2006-2010 5-year est.).
**Transportation:** Commute to work: 67.3% car, 0.0% public transportation, 18.8% walk, 0.0% work from home (2006-2010 5-year est.); Travel time to work: 56.4% less than 15 minutes, 33.7% 15 to 30 minutes, 5.0% 30 to 45 minutes, 0.0% 45 to 60 minutes, 5.0% 60 minutes or more (2006-2010 5-year est.)

**SHIRLEY** (CDP). Covers a land area of 11.455 square miles and a water area of 0.432 square miles. Located at 40.79° N. Lat; 72.87° W. Long. Elevation is 52 feet.
**Population:** 23,149 (1990); 25,395 (2000); 27,854 (2010); Density: 2,431.6 persons per square mile (2010); Race: 81.5% White, 7.2% Black, 2.6%

Asian, 0.4% American Indian/Alaska Native, 0.0% Native Hawaiian/Other Pacific Islander, 8.3% Other, 17.2% Hispanic of any race (2010); Average household size: 3.30 (2010); Median age: 34.7 (2010); Males per 100 females: 99.4 (2010); Marriage status: 31.1% never married, 58.3% now married, 4.5% widowed, 6.0% divorced (2006-2010 5-year est.); Foreign born: 9.4% (2006-2010 5-year est.); Ancestry (includes multiple ancestries): 36.9% Italian, 21.8% Irish, 15.7% German, 5.4% Polish, 5.3% English (2006-2010 5-year est.).

**Economy:** Employment by occupation: 8.6% management, 3.0% professional, 10.3% services, 21.9% sales, 4.5% farming, 13.2% construction, 9.2% production (2006-2010 5-year est.).

**Income:** Per capita income: $26,562 (2006-2010 5-year est.); Median household income: $82,762 (2006-2010 5-year est.); Average household income: $86,260 (2006-2010 5-year est.); Percent of households with income of $100,000 or more: 34.3% (2006-2010 5-year est.); Poverty rate: 8.1% (2006-2010 5-year est.).

**Education:** Percent of population age 25 and over with: High school diploma (including GED) or higher: 88.3% (2006-2010 5-year est.); Bachelor's degree or higher: 16.9% (2006-2010 5-year est.); Master's degree or higher: 5.1% (2006-2010 5-year est.).

### School District(s)

William Floyd Union Free School District (KG-12)
   2009-10 Enrollment: 9,398 . . . . . . . . . . . . . . . . . . . . . . . (631) 874-1201

**Housing:** Homeownership rate: 84.4% (2010); Median home value: $311,000 (2006-2010 5-year est.); Median contract rent: $1,495 per month (2006-2010 5-year est.); Median year structure built: 1976 (2006-2010 5-year est.).

**Transportation:** Commute to work: 92.7% car, 2.5% public transportation, 0.5% walk, 3.9% work from home (2006-2010 5-year est.); Travel time to work: 15.5% less than 15 minutes, 35.8% 15 to 30 minutes, 24.0% 30 to 45 minutes, 11.5% 45 to 60 minutes, 13.2% 60 minutes or more (2006-2010 5-year est.)

**Additional Information Contacts**
Mastics and Shirley Chamber of Commerce . . . . . . . . . . . (631) 399-2228
   http://www.masticshirleychamber.com

**SHOREHAM** (village). Covers a land area of 0.448 square miles and a water area of 0 square miles. Located at 40.95° N. Lat; 72.90° W. Long. Elevation is 66 feet.

**Population:** 540 (1990); 417 (2000); 531 (2010); Density: 1,184.2 persons per square mile (2010); Race: 95.1% White, 1.3% Black, 3.0% Asian, 0.0% American Indian/Alaska Native, 0.0% Native Hawaiian/Other Pacific Islander, 0.6% Other, 2.8% Hispanic of any race (2010); Average household size: 2.77 (2010); Median age: 46.3 (2010); Males per 100 females: 101.1 (2010); Marriage status: 23.7% never married, 68.3% now married, 2.5% widowed, 5.6% divorced (2006-2010 5-year est.); Foreign born: 7.9% (2006-2010 5-year est.); Ancestry (includes multiple ancestries): 36.2% Irish, 26.2% German, 17.5% Italian, 16.1% English, 7.8% French (2006-2010 5-year est.).

**Economy:** Single-family building permits issued: 0 (2011); Multi-family building permits issued: 0 (2011); Employment by occupation: 15.1% management, 12.0% professional, 4.0% services, 8.4% sales, 6.0% farming, 2.8% construction, 0.8% production (2006-2010 5-year est.).

**Income:** Per capita income: $44,030 (2006-2010 5-year est.); Median household income: $125,833 (2006-2010 5-year est.); Average household income: $144,854 (2006-2010 5-year est.); Percent of households with income of $100,000 or more: 71.6% (2006-2010 5-year est.); Poverty rate: 5.9% (2006-2010 5-year est.).

**Education:** Percent of population age 25 and over with: High school diploma (including GED) or higher: 95.5% (2006-2010 5-year est.); Bachelor's degree or higher: 62.8% (2006-2010 5-year est.); Master's degree or higher: 38.7% (2006-2010 5-year est.).

### School District(s)

Shoreham-Wading River Central School District (KG-12)
   2009-10 Enrollment: 2,692 . . . . . . . . . . . . . . . . . . . (631) 821-8105

**Housing:** Homeownership rate: 92.2% (2010); Median home value: $620,100 (2006-2010 5-year est.); Median contract rent: $1,625 per month (2006-2010 5-year est.); Median year structure built: 1962 (2006-2010 5-year est.).

**Transportation:** Commute to work: 90.3% car, 1.2% public transportation, 0.4% walk, 8.1% work from home (2006-2010 5-year est.); Travel time to work: 27.6% less than 15 minutes, 30.7% 15 to 30 minutes, 16.7% 30 to 45 minutes, 2.2% 45 to 60 minutes, 22.8% 60 minutes or more (2006-2010 5-year est.)

**SMITHTOWN** (town). Covers a land area of 53.697 square miles and a water area of 57.752 square miles. Located at 40.91° N. Lat; 73.17° W. Long. Elevation is 59 feet.

**Population:** 113,406 (1990); 115,715 (2000); 117,801 (2010); Density: 2,193.8 persons per square mile (2010); Race: 93.2% White, 1.1% Black, 3.6% Asian, 0.1% American Indian/Alaska Native, 0.0% Native Hawaiian/Other Pacific Islander, 2.0% Other, 5.3% Hispanic of any race (2010); Average household size: 2.89 (2010); Median age: 42.7 (2010); Males per 100 females: 94.8 (2010); Marriage status: 24.9% never married, 62.9% now married, 6.4% widowed, 5.8% divorced (2006-2010 5-year est.); Foreign born: 6.8% (2006-2010 5-year est.); Ancestry (includes multiple ancestries): 38.6% Italian, 27.2% Irish, 20.1% German, 7.4% Polish, 5.6% English (2006-2010 5-year est.).

**Economy:** Unemployment rate: 6.7% (February 2012); Total civilian labor force: 59,642 (February 2012); Single-family building permits issued: 36 (2011); Multi-family building permits issued: 0 (2011); Employment by occupation: 16.4% management, 4.7% professional, 5.7% services, 16.3% sales, 3.5% farming, 7.2% construction, 3.7% production (2006-2010 5-year est.).

**Income:** Per capita income: $41,847 (2006-2010 5-year est.); Median household income: $104,665 (2006-2010 5-year est.); Average household income: $125,305 (2006-2010 5-year est.); Percent of households with income of $100,000 or more: 53.4% (2006-2010 5-year est.); Poverty rate: 2.9% (2006-2010 5-year est.).

**Taxes:** Total city taxes per capita: $533 (2009); City property taxes per capita: $447 (2009).

**Education:** Percent of population age 25 and over with: High school diploma (including GED) or higher: 95.4% (2006-2010 5-year est.); Bachelor's degree or higher: 42.5% (2006-2010 5-year est.); Master's degree or higher: 19.0% (2006-2010 5-year est.).

### School District(s)

Hauppauge Union Free School District (KG-12)
   2009-10 Enrollment: 4,076 . . . . . . . . . . . . . . . . . . . (631) 761-8208
Smithtown Central School District (KG-12)
   2009-10 Enrollment: 10,862 . . . . . . . . . . . . . . . . . . . (631) 382-2005

**Housing:** Homeownership rate: 87.3% (2010); Median home value: $511,400 (2006-2010 5-year est.); Median contract rent: $1,273 per month (2006-2010 5-year est.); Median year structure built: 1966 (2006-2010 5-year est.).

**Hospitals:** St Catherine of Siena Medical Center (311 beds)

**Newspapers:** Commack News (Community news; Circulation 3,862); Huntington News (Community news; Circulation 4,952); Islip News (Community news; Circulation 2,043); Mid Island News (Local news; Circulation 2,263); Observer (Local news; Circulation 9,360); Smithtown News (Local news; Circulation 10,426)

**Transportation:** Commute to work: 89.8% car, 5.1% public transportation, 1.0% walk, 3.8% work from home (2006-2010 5-year est.); Travel time to work: 23.9% less than 15 minutes, 32.9% 15 to 30 minutes, 21.3% 30 to 45 minutes, 7.3% 45 to 60 minutes, 14.5% 60 minutes or more (2006-2010 5-year est.)

**Additional Information Contacts**
Greater Smithtown Chamber of Commerce . . . . . . . . . . . . (631) 979-8069
   http://www.smithtownchamber.org
Town of Smithtown . . . . . . . . . . . . . . . . . . . . . . . . . . . (631) 360-7620
   http://www.smithtowninfo.com

**SMITHTOWN** (CDP). Covers a land area of 11.628 square miles and a water area of 0.484 square miles. Located at 40.86° N. Lat; 73.22° W. Long. Elevation is 59 feet.

**Population:** 25,786 (1990); 26,901 (2000); 26,470 (2010); Density: 2,276.2 persons per square mile (2010); Race: 94.0% White, 1.1% Black, 2.9% Asian, 0.1% American Indian/Alaska Native, 0.0% Native Hawaiian/Other Pacific Islander, 1.9% Other, 5.1% Hispanic of any race (2010); Average household size: 2.93 (2010); Median age: 42.9 (2010); Males per 100 females: 94.5 (2010); Marriage status: 26.0% never married, 62.3% now married, 5.2% widowed, 6.5% divorced (2006-2010 5-year est.); Foreign born: 5.4% (2006-2010 5-year est.); Ancestry (includes multiple ancestries): 37.8% Italian, 29.1% Irish, 21.0% German, 7.0% English, 6.9% Polish (2006-2010 5-year est.).

**Economy:** Employment by occupation: 15.5% management, 4.4% professional, 6.7% services, 14.4% sales, 3.0% farming, 7.6% construction, 3.3% production (2006-2010 5-year est.).

**Income:** Per capita income: $42,513 (2006-2010 5-year est.); Median household income: $107,814 (2006-2010 5-year est.); Average household income: $131,975 (2006-2010 5-year est.); Percent of households with

income of $100,000 or more: 54.1% (2006-2010 5-year est.); Poverty rate: 4.1% (2006-2010 5-year est.).
**Education:** Percent of population age 25 and over with: High school diploma (including GED) or higher: 95.0% (2006-2010 5-year est.); Bachelor's degree or higher: 41.9% (2006-2010 5-year est.); Master's degree or higher: 19.6% (2006-2010 5-year est.).

### School District(s)
Hauppauge Union Free School District (KG-12)
   2009-10 Enrollment: 4,076 . . . . . . . . . . . . . . . . . . (631) 761-8208
Smithtown Central School District (KG-12)
   2009-10 Enrollment: 10,862 . . . . . . . . . . . . . . . . . (631) 382-2005
**Housing:** Homeownership rate: 86.7% (2010); Median home value: $542,100 (2006-2010 5-year est.); Median contract rent: $1,159 per month (2006-2010 5-year est.); Median year structure built: 1964 (2006-2010 5-year est.).
**Hospitals:** St Catherine of Siena Medical Center (311 beds)
**Transportation:** Commute to work: 89.4% car, 4.9% public transportation, 1.0% walk, 4.4% work from home (2006-2010 5-year est.); Travel time to work: 23.6% less than 15 minutes, 31.2% 15 to 30 minutes, 25.8% 30 to 45 minutes, 5.9% 45 to 60 minutes, 13.5% 60 minutes or more (2006-2010 5-year est.)

**SOUND BEACH** (CDP). Covers a land area of 1.636 square miles and a water area of 0 square miles. Located at 40.95° N. Lat; 72.97° W. Long. Elevation is 177 feet.
**Population:** 9,102 (1990); 9,807 (2000); 7,612 (2010); Density: 4,651.0 persons per square mile (2010); Race: 94.2% White, 1.2% Black, 1.8% Asian, 0.2% American Indian/Alaska Native, 0.1% Native Hawaiian/Other Pacific Islander, 2.5% Other, 6.2% Hispanic of any race (2010); Average household size: 2.78 (2010); Median age: 37.0 (2010); Males per 100 females: 97.0 (2010); Marriage status: 29.2% never married, 58.7% now married, 3.1% widowed, 9.1% divorced (2006-2010 5-year est.); Foreign born: 7.1% (2006-2010 5-year est.); Ancestry (includes multiple ancestries): 38.1% Irish, 29.8% Italian, 21.0% German, 6.4% English, 5.1% Polish (2006-2010 5-year est.).
**Economy:** Employment by occupation: 4.4% management, 3.3% professional, 8.8% services, 14.4% sales, 2.7% farming, 11.5% construction, 6.6% production (2006-2010 5-year est.).
**Income:** Per capita income: $31,225 (2006-2010 5-year est.); Median household income: $77,115 (2006-2010 5-year est.); Average household income: $89,523 (2006-2010 5-year est.); Percent of households with income of $100,000 or more: 31.6% (2006-2010 5-year est.); Poverty rate: 4.9% (2006-2010 5-year est.).
**Education:** Percent of population age 25 and over with: High school diploma (including GED) or higher: 95.9% (2006-2010 5-year est.); Bachelor's degree or higher: 36.5% (2006-2010 5-year est.); Master's degree or higher: 16.8% (2006-2010 5-year est.).
**Housing:** Homeownership rate: 80.9% (2010); Median home value: $342,200 (2006-2010 5-year est.); Median contract rent: $1,334 per month (2006-2010 5-year est.); Median year structure built: 1958 (2006-2010 5-year est.).
**Transportation:** Commute to work: 94.6% car, 2.9% public transportation, 0.4% walk, 1.9% work from home (2006-2010 5-year est.); Travel time to work: 18.4% less than 15 minutes, 28.2% 15 to 30 minutes, 26.9% 30 to 45 minutes, 11.4% 45 to 60 minutes, 15.1% 60 minutes or more (2006-2010 5-year est.)
**Additional Information Contacts**
North Brookhaven Chamber of Commerce . . . . . . . . . . . . (631) 821-1313
   http://northbrookhavenchamber.org

**SOUTH HUNTINGTON** (CDP). Covers a land area of 3.408 square miles and a water area of 0 square miles. Located at 40.82° N. Lat; 73.39° W. Long. Elevation is 207 feet.
**Population:** 9,624 (1990); 9,465 (2000); 9,422 (2010); Density: 2,764.2 persons per square mile (2010); Race: 87.1% White, 2.3% Black, 5.8% Asian, 0.1% American Indian/Alaska Native, 0.0% Native Hawaiian/Other Pacific Islander, 4.7% Other, 8.0% Hispanic of any race (2010); Average household size: 2.73 (2010); Median age: 43.7 (2010); Males per 100 females: 96.7 (2010); Marriage status: 31.0% never married, 51.4% now married, 8.4% widowed, 9.2% divorced (2006-2010 5-year est.); Foreign born: 11.9% (2006-2010 5-year est.); Ancestry (includes multiple ancestries): 33.2% Italian, 23.4% Irish, 19.5% German, 6.3% Polish, 4.3% Russian (2006-2010 5-year est.).

**Economy:** Employment by occupation: 19.9% management, 4.1% professional, 5.2% services, 18.8% sales, 4.1% farming, 7.5% construction, 3.7% production (2006-2010 5-year est.).
**Income:** Per capita income: $39,302 (2006-2010 5-year est.); Median household income: $89,417 (2006-2010 5-year est.); Average household income: $111,188 (2006-2010 5-year est.); Percent of households with income of $100,000 or more: 46.4% (2006-2010 5-year est.); Poverty rate: 4.6% (2006-2010 5-year est.).
**Education:** Percent of population age 25 and over with: High school diploma (including GED) or higher: 95.9% (2006-2010 5-year est.); Bachelor's degree or higher: 40.1% (2006-2010 5-year est.); Master's degree or higher: 16.8% (2006-2010 5-year est.).
**Housing:** Homeownership rate: 85.3% (2010); Median home value: $479,400 (2006-2010 5-year est.); Median contract rent: $1,382 per month (2006-2010 5-year est.); Median year structure built: 1957 (2006-2010 5-year est.).
**Transportation:** Commute to work: 84.1% car, 8.2% public transportation, 0.9% walk, 6.2% work from home (2006-2010 5-year est.); Travel time to work: 28.3% less than 15 minutes, 36.4% 15 to 30 minutes, 17.2% 30 to 45 minutes, 5.1% 45 to 60 minutes, 13.0% 60 minutes or more (2006-2010 5-year est.)

**SOUTH JAMESPORT** (unincorporated postal area)
Zip Code: 11970
   Covers a land area of 0.561 square miles and a water area of 0.027 square miles. Located at 40.93° N. Lat; 72.57° W. Long. Elevation is 3 feet. Population: 522 (2010); Density: 929.5 persons per square mile (2010); Race: 97.9% White, 1.3% Black, 0.2% Asian, 0.0% American Indian/Alaska Native, 0.0% Native Hawaiian/Other Pacific Islander, 0.6% Other, 2.3% Hispanic of any race (2010); Average household size: 2.10 (2010); Median age: 57.6 (2010); Males per 100 females: 83.2 (2010); Homeownership rate: 79.2% (2010)

**SOUTHAMPTON** (village). Covers a land area of 6.422 square miles and a water area of 0.796 square miles. Located at 40.87° N. Lat; 72.39° W. Long. Elevation is 26 feet.
**Population:** 3,980 (1990); 3,965 (2000); 3,109 (2010); Density: 484.1 persons per square mile (2010); Race: 81.8% White, 9.9% Black, 1.8% Asian, 0.6% American Indian/Alaska Native, 0.2% Native Hawaiian/Other Pacific Islander, 5.7% Other, 16.2% Hispanic of any race (2010); Average household size: 2.26 (2010); Median age: 50.2 (2010); Males per 100 females: 96.2 (2010); Marriage status: 21.0% never married, 59.5% now married, 10.7% widowed, 8.8% divorced (2006-2010 5-year est.); Foreign born: 22.3% (2006-2010 5-year est.); Ancestry (includes multiple ancestries): 15.7% Irish, 12.0% English, 10.6% German, 9.7% American, 9.6% Polish (2006-2010 5-year est.).
**Economy:** Single-family building permits issued: 20 (2011); Multi-family building permits issued: 0 (2011); Employment by occupation: 13.9% management, 2.0% professional, 11.5% services, 12.3% sales, 1.0% farming, 5.7% construction, 0.8% production (2006-2010 5-year est.).
**Income:** Per capita income: $100,953 (2006-2010 5-year est.); Median household income: $81,250 (2006-2010 5-year est.); Average household income: $228,411 (2006-2010 5-year est.); Percent of households with income of $100,000 or more: 43.1% (2006-2010 5-year est.); Poverty rate: 3.2% (2006-2010 5-year est.).
**Education:** Percent of population age 25 and over with: High school diploma (including GED) or higher: 96.6% (2006-2010 5-year est.); Bachelor's degree or higher: 52.5% (2006-2010 5-year est.); Master's degree or higher: 24.7% (2006-2010 5-year est.).

### School District(s)
Southampton Union Free School District (PK-12)
   2009-10 Enrollment: 1,590 . . . . . . . . . . . . . . . . . . (631) 591-4510
Tuckahoe Common School District (PK-08)
   2009-10 Enrollment: 355 . . . . . . . . . . . . . . . . . . . (631) 283-3550
**Housing:** Homeownership rate: 68.5% (2010); Median home value: $1 (2006-2010 5-year est.); Median contract rent: $1,227 per month (2006-2010 5-year est.); Median year structure built: 1958 (2006-2010 5-year est.).
**Hospitals:** Southampton Hospital (168 beds)
**Safety:** Violent crime rate: 4.4 per 10,000 population; Property crime rate: 342.1 per 10,000 population (2010).
**Newspapers:** Southampton Independent (Community news; Circulation 10,000); Southampton Press (Community news; Circulation 40,000)
**Transportation:** Commute to work: 60.6% car, 5.2% public transportation, 12.1% walk, 15.8% work from home (2006-2010 5-year est.); Travel time to

work: 58.0% less than 15 minutes, 21.8% 15 to 30 minutes, 13.5% 30 to 45 minutes, 2.2% 45 to 60 minutes, 4.4% 60 minutes or more (2006-2010 5-year est.)
**Airports:** Southampton (general aviation)
**Additional Information Contacts**
Southampton Chamber of Commerce . . . . . . . . . . . . . . . . . (631) 283-0402
   http://www.southamptonchamber.com

## SOUTHAMPTON (town). Covers a land area of 139.194 square miles and a water area of 154.509 square miles. Located at 40.88° N. Lat; 72.45° W. Long. Elevation is 26 feet.

**History:** Known for its many fine estates and celebrity residents. Parrish Memorial Art Museum is here, as is Southampton College of Long Island University. Settled 1640 as first English settlement in state, incorporated 1894.
**Population:** 44,976 (1990); 54,712 (2000); 56,790 (2010); Density: 408.0 persons per square mile (2010); Race: 84.2% White, 5.2% Black, 1.1% Asian, 0.5% American Indian/Alaska Native, 0.1% Native Hawaiian/Other Pacific Islander, 8.9% Other, 19.9% Hispanic of any race (2010); Average household size: 2.59 (2010); Median age: 41.9 (2010); Males per 100 females: 104.6 (2010); Marriage status: 26.7% never married, 57.1% now married, 7.2% widowed, 9.0% divorced (2006-2010 5-year est.); Foreign born: 16.6% (2006-2010 5-year est.); Ancestry (includes multiple ancestries): 23.0% Irish, 17.3% Italian, 14.7% German, 10.2% English, 7.4% Polish (2006-2010 5-year est.).
**Economy:** Unemployment rate: 10.5% (February 2012); Total civilian labor force: 29,579 (February 2012); Single-family building permits issued: 165 (2011); Multi-family building permits issued: 0 (2011); Employment by occupation: 11.7% management, 2.0% professional, 10.3% services, 15.2% sales, 3.0% farming, 13.6% construction, 4.1% production (2006-2010 5-year est.).
**Income:** Per capita income: $47,111 (2006-2010 5-year est.); Median household income: $74,316 (2006-2010 5-year est.); Average household income: $118,171 (2006-2010 5-year est.); Percent of households with income of $100,000 or more: 36.0% (2006-2010 5-year est.); Poverty rate: 7.2% (2006-2010 5-year est.).
**Taxes:** Total city taxes per capita: $1,665 (2009); City property taxes per capita: $918 (2009).
**Education:** Percent of population age 25 and over with: High school diploma (including GED) or higher: 88.5% (2006-2010 5-year est.); Bachelor's degree or higher: 39.8% (2006-2010 5-year est.); Master's degree or higher: 17.5% (2006-2010 5-year est.).
### School District(s)
Southampton Union Free School District (PK-12)
   2009-10 Enrollment: 1,590 . . . . . . . . . . . . . . . . . . . . (631) 591-4510
Tuckahoe Common School District (PK-08)
   2009-10 Enrollment: 355 . . . . . . . . . . . . . . . . . . . . . . (631) 283-3550
**Housing:** Homeownership rate: 73.1% (2010); Median home value: $646,800 (2006-2010 5-year est.); Median contract rent: $1,359 per month (2006-2010 5-year est.); Median year structure built: 1972 (2006-2010 5-year est.).
**Hospitals:** Southampton Hospital (168 beds)
**Safety:** Violent crime rate: 10.5 per 10,000 population; Property crime rate: 217.5 per 10,000 population (2010).
**Newspapers:** Southampton Independent (Community news; Circulation 10,000); Southampton Press (Community news; Circulation 40,000)
**Transportation:** Commute to work: 84.1% car, 4.6% public transportation, 3.5% walk, 5.7% work from home (2006-2010 5-year est.); Travel time to work: 34.3% less than 15 minutes, 28.5% 15 to 30 minutes, 17.4% 30 to 45 minutes, 6.8% 45 to 60 minutes, 12.9% 60 minutes or more (2006-2010 5-year est.).
**Airports:** Southampton (general aviation)
**Additional Information Contacts**
Town of Southampton . . . . . . . . . . . . . . . . . . . . . . . . . . . (631) 287-5740
   http://www.southamptontownny.gov

## SOUTHOLD (town). Covers a land area of 53.782 square miles and a water area of 349.916 square miles. Located at 41.13° N. Lat; 72.31° W. Long. Elevation is 23 feet.

**Population:** 19,836 (1990); 20,599 (2000); 21,968 (2010); Density: 408.5 persons per square mile (2010); Race: 90.0% White, 2.7% Black, 0.8% Asian, 0.1% American Indian/Alaska Native, 0.1% Native Hawaiian/Other Pacific Islander, 6.3% Other, 10.8% Hispanic of any race (2010); Average household size: 2.38 (2010); Median age: 49.0 (2010); Males per 100 females: 96.9 (2010); Marriage status: 21.1% never married, 62.6% now

married, 9.6% widowed, 6.8% divorced (2006-2010 5-year est.); Foreign born: 8.1% (2006-2010 5-year est.); Ancestry (includes multiple ancestries): 24.7% Irish, 21.7% German, 19.4% Italian, 13.4% Polish, 13.3% English (2006-2010 5-year est.).
**Economy:** Single-family building permits issued: 40 (2011); Multi-family building permits issued: 0 (2011); Employment by occupation: 14.4% management, 3.5% professional, 8.3% services, 15.9% sales, 2.5% farming, 13.3% construction, 4.7% production (2006-2010 5-year est.).
**Income:** Per capita income: $41,284 (2006-2010 5-year est.); Median household income: $73,171 (2006-2010 5-year est.); Average household income: $95,603 (2006-2010 5-year est.); Percent of households with income of $100,000 or more: 34.2% (2006-2010 5-year est.); Poverty rate: 5.2% (2006-2010 5-year est.).
**Education:** Percent of population age 25 and over with: High school diploma (including GED) or higher: 90.2% (2006-2010 5-year est.); Bachelor's degree or higher: 38.0% (2006-2010 5-year est.); Master's degree or higher: 16.5% (2006-2010 5-year est.).
### School District(s)
Southold Union Free School District (KG-12)
   2009-10 Enrollment: 926 . . . . . . . . . . . . . . . . . . . . . . (631) 765-5400
**Housing:** Homeownership rate: 79.6% (2010); Median home value: $558,800 (2006-2010 5-year est.); Median contract rent: $1,033 per month (2006-2010 5-year est.); Median year structure built: 1966 (2006-2010 5-year est.).
**Safety:** Violent crime rate: 0.0 per 10,000 population; Property crime rate: 133.0 per 10,000 population (2010).
**Newspapers:** Traveler-Watchman (Local news; Circulation 21,500)
**Transportation:** Commute to work: 86.2% car, 3.6% public transportation, 2.8% walk, 4.7% work from home (2006-2010 5-year est.); Travel time to work: 44.5% less than 15 minutes, 23.0% 15 to 30 minutes, 12.0% 30 to 45 minutes, 4.9% 45 to 60 minutes, 15.6% 60 minutes or more (2006-2010 5-year est.).
**Additional Information Contacts**
North Fork Chamber of Commerce . . . . . . . . . . . . . . . . . . (631) 765-3161
   http://www.greenportsoutholdchamber.org
Town of Southold . . . . . . . . . . . . . . . . . . . . . . . . . . . . . . (631) 765-1800
   http://southoldtown.northfork.net

## SOUTHOLD (CDP). Covers a land area of 10.464 square miles and a water area of 0.854 square miles. Located at 41.05° N. Lat; 72.42° W. Long. Elevation is 23 feet.

**Population:** 5,200 (1990); 5,465 (2000); 5,748 (2010); Density: 549.3 persons per square mile (2010); Race: 93.9% White, 0.8% Black, 0.8% Asian, 0.0% American Indian/Alaska Native, 0.4% Native Hawaiian/Other Pacific Islander, 4.1% Other, 8.4% Hispanic of any race (2010); Average household size: 2.37 (2010); Median age: 49.7 (2010); Males per 100 females: 95.1 (2010); Marriage status: 16.2% never married, 71.0% now married, 6.8% widowed, 6.0% divorced (2006-2010 5-year est.); Foreign born: 6.7% (2006-2010 5-year est.); Ancestry (includes multiple ancestries): 28.3% Irish, 22.3% German, 19.0% Italian, 14.8% Polish, 13.1% English (2006-2010 5-year est.).
**Economy:** Employment by occupation: 11.9% management, 6.9% professional, 9.7% services, 13.5% sales, 2.7% farming, 14.3% construction, 7.1% production (2006-2010 5-year est.).
**Income:** Per capita income: $41,201 (2006-2010 5-year est.); Median household income: $70,903 (2006-2010 5-year est.); Average household income: $94,883 (2006-2010 5-year est.); Percent of households with income of $100,000 or more: 30.7% (2006-2010 5-year est.); Poverty rate: 2.2% (2006-2010 5-year est.).
**Education:** Percent of population age 25 and over with: High school diploma (including GED) or higher: 91.9% (2006-2010 5-year est.); Bachelor's degree or higher: 40.8% (2006-2010 5-year est.); Master's degree or higher: 16.9% (2006-2010 5-year est.).
### School District(s)
Southold Union Free School District (KG-12)
   2009-10 Enrollment: 926 . . . . . . . . . . . . . . . . . . . . . . (631) 765-5400
**Housing:** Homeownership rate: 84.0% (2010); Median home value: $509,800 (2006-2010 5-year est.); Median contract rent: $971 per month (2006-2010 5-year est.); Median year structure built: 1969 (2006-2010 5-year est.).
**Transportation:** Commute to work: 92.4% car, 0.9% public transportation, 0.4% walk, 5.6% work from home (2006-2010 5-year est.); Travel time to work: 44.1% less than 15 minutes, 17.7% 15 to 30 minutes, 8.9% 30 to 45 minutes, 6.6% 45 to 60 minutes, 22.7% 60 minutes or more (2006-2010 5-year est.).

**SPEONK** (unincorporated postal area)
Zip Code: 11972
Covers a land area of 2.413 square miles and a water area of 0.006 square miles. Located at 40.84° N. Lat; 72.70° W. Long. Elevation is 30 feet. Population: 1,321 (2010); Density: 547.2 persons per square mile (2010); Race: 89.8% White, 2.3% Black, 0.5% Asian, 0.1% American Indian/Alaska Native, 0.1% Native Hawaiian/Other Pacific Islander, 7.2% Other, 12.1% Hispanic of any race (2010); Average household size: 2.79 (2010); Median age: 40.4 (2010); Males per 100 females: 95.7 (2010); Homeownership rate: 79.3% (2010)

**SPRINGS** (CDP). Aka The Springs. Covers a land area of 8.479 square miles and a water area of 0.756 square miles. Located at 41.02° N. Lat; 72.16° W. Long. Elevation is 10 feet.
Population: 4,355 (1990); 4,950 (2000); 6,592 (2010); Density: 777.4 persons per square mile (2010); Race: 83.3% White, 1.7% Black, 1.5% Asian, 0.7% American Indian/Alaska Native, 0.0% Native Hawaiian/Other Pacific Islander, 12.8% Other, 36.6% Hispanic of any race (2010); Average household size: 2.84 (2010); Median age: 38.5 (2010); Males per 100 females: 108.5 (2010); Marriage status: 26.6% never married, 59.1% now married, 6.3% widowed, 8.0% divorced (2006-2010 5-year est.); Foreign born: 34.4% (2006-2010 5-year est.); Ancestry (includes multiple ancestries): 13.0% English, 12.3% Irish, 10.3% Italian, 9.7% German, 3.5% Polish (2006-2010 5-year est.).
Economy: Employment by occupation: 11.0% management, 2.1% professional, 11.0% services, 10.6% sales, 2.2% farming, 27.7% construction, 3.3% production (2006-2010 5-year est.).
Income: Per capita income: $36,341 (2006-2010 5-year est.); Median household income: $68,828 (2006-2010 5-year est.); Average household income: $97,588 (2006-2010 5-year est.); Percent of households with income of $100,000 or more: 26.9% (2006-2010 5-year est.); Poverty rate: 9.1% (2006-2010 5-year est.).
Education: Percent of population age 25 and over with: High school diploma (including GED) or higher: 88.9% (2006-2010 5-year est.); Bachelor's degree or higher: 40.1% (2006-2010 5-year est.); Master's degree or higher: 20.8% (2006-2010 5-year est.).
Housing: Homeownership rate: 76.8% (2010); Median home value: $701,200 (2006-2010 5-year est.); Median contract rent: $1,654 per month (2006-2010 5-year est.); Median year structure built: 1980 (2006-2010 5-year est.).
Transportation: Commute to work: 89.6% car, 3.9% public transportation, 0.9% walk, 5.2% work from home (2006-2010 5-year est.); Travel time to work: 26.6% less than 15 minutes, 37.2% 15 to 30 minutes, 22.0% 30 to 45 minutes, 1.6% 45 to 60 minutes, 12.5% 60 minutes or more (2006-2010 5-year est.)

**STONY BROOK** (CDP). Covers a land area of 5.814 square miles and a water area of 0.138 square miles. Located at 40.90° N. Lat; 73.12° W. Long. Elevation is 89 feet.
History: Named for its location, and to promote the town. Restored 1941 to resemble 18th-century village. State University of New York at Stony Brook, one of the university's four graduate centers, and the State University of New York Health Science Center are here.
Population: 13,726 (1990); 13,727 (2000); 13,740 (2010); Density: 2,363.0 persons per square mile (2010); Race: 88.6% White, 1.7% Black, 7.5% Asian, 0.1% American Indian/Alaska Native, 0.0% Native Hawaiian/Other Pacific Islander, 2.1% Other, 4.4% Hispanic of any race (2010); Average household size: 2.82 (2010); Median age: 43.0 (2010); Males per 100 females: 95.9 (2010); Marriage status: 27.1% never married, 61.6% now married, 6.5% widowed, 4.8% divorced (2006-2010 5-year est.); Foreign born: 10.0% (2006-2010 5-year est.); Ancestry (includes multiple ancestries): 29.8% Italian, 28.1% Irish, 19.2% German, 9.2% English, 4.6% Polish (2006-2010 5-year est.).
Economy: Employment by occupation: 14.9% management, 7.9% professional, 3.4% services, 16.2% sales, 3.9% farming, 6.0% construction, 2.4% production (2006-2010 5-year est.).
Income: Per capita income: $48,061 (2006-2010 5-year est.); Median household income: $118,397 (2006-2010 5-year est.); Average household income: $138,975 (2006-2010 5-year est.); Percent of households with income of $100,000 or more: 58.8% (2006-2010 5-year est.); Poverty rate: 1.7% (2006-2010 5-year est.).
Education: Percent of population age 25 and over with: High school diploma (including GED) or higher: 97.0% (2006-2010 5-year est.); Bachelor's degree or higher: 56.2% (2006-2010 5-year est.); Master's degree or higher: 31.0% (2006-2010 5-year est.).

School District(s)
Three Village Central School District (KG-12)
2009-10 Enrollment: 7,572 . . . . . . . . . . . . . . . . . . . . . . (631) 730-4010
Four-year College(s)
Stony Brook University (Public)
Fall 2010 Enrollment: 23,095. . . . . . . . . . . . . . . . . . . . (631) 632-6000
2011-12 Tuition: In-state $6,994; Out-of-state $16,444
Housing: Homeownership rate: 90.0% (2010); Median home value: $487,800 (2006-2010 5-year est.); Median contract rent: $1,279 per month (2006-2010 5-year est.); Median year structure built: 1966 (2006-2010 5-year est.).
Hospitals: Stony Brook University Hospital (504 beds)
Transportation: Commute to work: 89.2% car, 4.1% public transportation, 1.9% walk, 3.5% work from home (2006-2010 5-year est.); Travel time to work: 24.6% less than 15 minutes, 28.7% 15 to 30 minutes, 21.5% 30 to 45 minutes, 7.8% 45 to 60 minutes, 17.4% 60 minutes or more (2006-2010 5-year est.)
Airports: Health Sciences Center Unv Hospital (general aviation)

**STONY BROOK UNIVERSITY** (CDP). Covers a land area of 1.697 square miles and a water area of 0 square miles. Located at 40.90° N. Lat; 73.12° W. Long.
Population: n/a (1990); n/a (2000); 9,216 (2010); Density: 5,429.4 persons per square mile (2010); Race: 60.8% White, 14.0% Black, 20.5% Asian, 0.4% American Indian/Alaska Native, 0.0% Native Hawaiian/Other Pacific Islander, 4.3% Other, 6.6% Hispanic of any race (2010); Average household size: 3.65 (2010); Median age: 20.7 (2010); Males per 100 females: 110.0 (2010); Marriage status: 91.6% never married, 6.2% now married, 1.8% widowed, 0.5% divorced (2006-2010 5-year est.); Foreign born: 33.2% (2006-2010 5-year est.); Ancestry (includes multiple ancestries): 8.9% Italian, 6.1% Irish, 5.4% German, 3.1% Russian, 2.8% Polish (2006-2010 5-year est.).
Economy: Employment by occupation: 4.1% management, 9.5% professional, 7.9% services, 35.5% sales, 5.9% farming, 1.1% construction, 1.1% production (2006-2010 5-year est.).
Income: Per capita income: $4,634 (2006-2010 5-year est.); Median household income: $60,167 (2006-2010 5-year est.); Average household income: $51,569 (2006-2010 5-year est.); Percent of households with income of $100,000 or more: 8.5% (2006-2010 5-year est.); Poverty rate: 41.2% (2006-2010 5-year est.).
Education: Percent of population age 25 and over with: High school diploma (including GED) or higher: 94.3% (2006-2010 5-year est.); Bachelor's degree or higher: 71.1% (2006-2010 5-year est.); Master's degree or higher: 49.4% (2006-2010 5-year est.).
Housing: Homeownership rate: 88.5% (2010); Median home value: $587,500 (2006-2010 5-year est.); Median contract rent: $763 per month (2006-2010 5-year est.); Median year structure built: 1967 (2006-2010 5-year est.).
Transportation: Commute to work: 37.7% car, 9.6% public transportation, 45.0% walk, 5.8% work from home (2006-2010 5-year est.); Travel time to work: 57.7% less than 15 minutes, 25.9% 15 to 30 minutes, 6.9% 30 to 45 minutes, 1.5% 45 to 60 minutes, 7.9% 60 minutes or more (2006-2010 5-year est.)

**TERRYVILLE** (CDP). Covers a land area of 3.212 square miles and a water area of 0 square miles. Located at 40.90° N. Lat; 73.04° W. Long. Elevation is 151 feet.
Population: 10,275 (1990); 10,589 (2000); 11,849 (2010); Density: 3,687.9 persons per square mile (2010); Race: 87.0% White, 2.6% Black, 3.2% Asian, 0.4% American Indian/Alaska Native, 0.0% Native Hawaiian/Other Pacific Islander, 6.8% Other, 15.5% Hispanic of any race (2010); Average household size: 3.07 (2010); Median age: 38.5 (2010); Males per 100 females: 93.5 (2010); Marriage status: 25.1% never married, 59.6% now married, 6.0% widowed, 9.3% divorced (2006-2010 5-year est.); Foreign born: 11.1% (2006-2010 5-year est.); Ancestry (includes multiple ancestries): 27.9% Italian, 26.9% Irish, 17.1% German, 6.8% Polish, 6.0% English (2006-2010 5-year est.).
Economy: Employment by occupation: 14.1% management, 4.8% professional, 8.6% services, 17.3% sales, 6.8% farming, 10.0% construction, 2.9% production (2006-2010 5-year est.).
Income: Per capita income: $34,343 (2006-2010 5-year est.); Median household income: $88,785 (2006-2010 5-year est.); Average household income: $106,613 (2006-2010 5-year est.); Percent of households with income of $100,000 or more: 45.1% (2006-2010 5-year est.); Poverty rate: 4.3% (2006-2010 5-year est.).

**Education:** Percent of population age 25 and over with: High school diploma (including GED) or higher: 90.6% (2006-2010 5-year est.); Bachelor's degree or higher: 28.9% (2006-2010 5-year est.); Master's degree or higher: 11.2% (2006-2010 5-year est.).

**Housing:** Homeownership rate: 76.5% (2010); Median home value: $392,400 (2006-2010 5-year est.); Median contract rent: $1,904 per month (2006-2010 5-year est.); Median year structure built: 1972 (2006-2010 5-year est.).

**Transportation:** Commute to work: 92.5% car, 3.9% public transportation, 0.9% walk, 1.8% work from home (2006-2010 5-year est.); Travel time to work: 32.6% less than 15 minutes, 25.1% 15 to 30 minutes, 17.7% 30 to 45 minutes, 10.4% 45 to 60 minutes, 14.2% 60 minutes or more (2006-2010 5-year est.)

**Additional Information Contacts**

North Brookhaven Chamber of Commerce . . . . . . . . . . . . (631) 821-1313
    http://northbrookhavenchamber.org

## TUCKAHOE (CDP). Covers a land area of 4.140 square miles and a water area of 0.458 square miles. Located at 40.90° N. Lat; 72.43° W. Long. Elevation is 49 feet.

**Population:** 1,397 (1990); 1,741 (2000); 1,373 (2010); Density: 331.6 persons per square mile (2010); Race: 78.8% White, 9.6% Black, 1.3% Asian, 0.5% American Indian/Alaska Native, 0.1% Native Hawaiian/Other Pacific Islander, 9.7% Other, 26.7% Hispanic of any race (2010); Average household size: 2.83 (2010); Median age: 39.8 (2010); Males per 100 females: 101.0 (2010); Marriage status: 33.8% never married, 53.2% now married, 6.9% widowed, 6.0% divorced (2006-2010 5-year est.); Foreign born: 31.6% (2006-2010 5-year est.); Ancestry (includes multiple ancestries): 18.5% Irish, 12.9% Italian, 9.7% German, 8.8% English, 7.0% Polish (2006-2010 5-year est.).

**Economy:** Employment by occupation: 15.6% management, 1.4% professional, 9.4% services, 8.8% sales, 2.7% farming, 15.6% construction, 4.8% production (2006-2010 5-year est.).

**Income:** Per capita income: $65,746 (2006-2010 5-year est.); Median household income: $73,750 (2006-2010 5-year est.); Average household income: $166,486 (2006-2010 5-year est.); Percent of households with income of $100,000 or more: 40.7% (2006-2010 5-year est.); Poverty rate: 25.4% (2006-2010 5-year est.).

**Education:** Percent of population age 25 and over with: High school diploma (including GED) or higher: 84.8% (2006-2010 5-year est.); Bachelor's degree or higher: 41.4% (2006-2010 5-year est.); Master's degree or higher: 16.4% (2006-2010 5-year est.).

**Housing:** Homeownership rate: 68.4% (2010); Median home value: $688,000 (2006-2010 5-year est.); Median contract rent: $1,213 per month (2006-2010 5-year est.); Median year structure built: 1970 (2006-2010 5-year est.).

**Transportation:** Commute to work: 87.7% car, 5.3% public transportation, 2.0% walk, 2.2% work from home (2006-2010 5-year est.); Travel time to work: 45.8% less than 15 minutes, 14.1% 15 to 30 minutes, 10.1% 30 to 45 minutes, 2.7% 45 to 60 minutes, 27.3% 60 minutes or more (2006-2010 5-year est.)

## UPTON (unincorporated postal area)
Zip Code: 11973

Covers a land area of 4.408 square miles and a water area of 0.004 square miles. Located at 40.86° N. Lat; 72.88° W. Long. Elevation is 89 feet. Population: 9 (2010); Density: 2.0 persons per square mile (2010); Race: 0.0% White, 0.0% Black, 100.0% Asian, 0.0% American Indian/Alaska Native, 0.0% Native Hawaiian/Other Pacific Islander, 0.0% Other, 11.1% Hispanic of any race (2010); Average household size: 0.00 (2010); Median age: 19.5 (2010); Males per 100 females: ***.* (2010); Homeownership rate: 0.0% (2010)

## VILLAGE OF THE BRANCH (village). Aka The Branch. Covers a land area of 0.947 square miles and a water area of 0.029 square miles. Located at 40.85° N. Lat; 73.18° W. Long. Elevation is 62 feet.

**Population:** 1,642 (1990); 1,895 (2000); 1,807 (2010); Density: 1,906.3 persons per square mile (2010); Race: 94.2% White, 1.3% Black, 2.3% Asian, 0.0% American Indian/Alaska Native, 0.1% Native Hawaiian/Other Pacific Islander, 2.1% Other, 2.8% Hispanic of any race (2010); Average household size: 2.86 (2010); Median age: 43.2 (2010); Males per 100 females: 89.4 (2010); Marriage status: 30.2% never married, 60.7% now married, 4.7% widowed, 4.4% divorced (2006-2010 5-year est.); Foreign born: 6.3% (2006-2010 5-year est.); Ancestry (includes multiple

ancestries): 32.3% Italian, 30.1% Irish, 20.5% German, 5.4% English, 4.8% Russian (2006-2010 5-year est.).

**Economy:** Single-family building permits issued: 0 (2011); Multi-family building permits issued: 0 (2011); Employment by occupation: 14.8% management, 6.4% professional, 2.3% services, 14.2% sales, 1.7% farming, 5.2% construction, 3.9% production (2006-2010 5-year est.).

**Income:** Per capita income: $43,165 (2006-2010 5-year est.); Median household income: $114,135 (2006-2010 5-year est.); Average household income: $142,926 (2006-2010 5-year est.); Percent of households with income of $100,000 or more: 61.5% (2006-2010 5-year est.); Poverty rate: 5.8% (2006-2010 5-year est.).

**Education:** Percent of population age 25 and over with: High school diploma (including GED) or higher: 91.6% (2006-2010 5-year est.); Bachelor's degree or higher: 54.3% (2006-2010 5-year est.); Master's degree or higher: 23.3% (2006-2010 5-year est.).

**Housing:** Homeownership rate: 84.8% (2010); Median home value: $591,400 (2006-2010 5-year est.); Median contract rent: $1,313 per month (2006-2010 5-year est.); Median year structure built: 1968 (2006-2010 5-year est.).

**Transportation:** Commute to work: 83.8% car, 8.2% public transportation, 1.4% walk, 5.7% work from home (2006-2010 5-year est.); Travel time to work: 26.3% less than 15 minutes, 30.1% 15 to 30 minutes, 21.1% 30 to 45 minutes, 5.4% 45 to 60 minutes, 17.1% 60 minutes or more (2006-2010 5-year est.)

## WADING RIVER (CDP). Covers a land area of 9.803 square miles and a water area of 0.039 square miles. Located at 40.94° N. Lat; 72.82° W. Long. Elevation is 92 feet.

**Population:** 5,248 (1990); 6,668 (2000); 7,719 (2010); Density: 787.4 persons per square mile (2010); Race: 94.5% White, 2.0% Black, 1.0% Asian, 0.1% American Indian/Alaska Native, 0.0% Native Hawaiian/Other Pacific Islander, 2.4% Other, 4.5% Hispanic of any race (2010); Average household size: 2.79 (2010); Median age: 41.4 (2010); Males per 100 females: 100.1 (2010); Marriage status: 24.8% never married, 64.7% now married, 4.7% widowed, 5.9% divorced (2006-2010 5-year est.); Foreign born: 8.2% (2006-2010 5-year est.); Ancestry (includes multiple ancestries): 31.8% Italian, 29.4% Irish, 15.3% German, 8.7% English, 8.5% Polish (2006-2010 5-year est.).

**Economy:** Employment by occupation: 9.9% management, 6.2% professional, 2.2% services, 16.1% sales, 3.0% farming, 9.3% construction, 7.2% production (2006-2010 5-year est.).

**Income:** Per capita income: $36,371 (2006-2010 5-year est.); Median household income: $101,162 (2006-2010 5-year est.); Average household income: $108,377 (2006-2010 5-year est.); Percent of households with income of $100,000 or more: 51.7% (2006-2010 5-year est.); Poverty rate: 5.6% (2006-2010 5-year est.).

**Education:** Percent of population age 25 and over with: High school diploma (including GED) or higher: 95.9% (2006-2010 5-year est.); Bachelor's degree or higher: 42.8% (2006-2010 5-year est.); Master's degree or higher: 24.2% (2006-2010 5-year est.).

### School District(s)

Little Flower Union Free School District (04-12)
    2009-10 Enrollment: 91 . . . . . . . . . . . . . . . . . . . (631) 929-4300
Shoreham-Wading River Central School District (KG-12)
    2009-10 Enrollment: 2,692 . . . . . . . . . . . . . . . . . (631) 821-8105

**Housing:** Homeownership rate: 91.4% (2010); Median home value: $426,400 (2006-2010 5-year est.); Median contract rent: $1,523 per month (2006-2010 5-year est.); Median year structure built: 1976 (2006-2010 5-year est.).

**Newspapers:** Community Journal (Community news; Circulation 7,000)

**Transportation:** Commute to work: 95.2% car, 2.4% public transportation, 0.5% walk, 1.6% work from home (2006-2010 5-year est.); Travel time to work: 19.6% less than 15 minutes, 34.4% 15 to 30 minutes, 24.7% 30 to 45 minutes, 10.4% 45 to 60 minutes, 10.9% 60 minutes or more (2006-2010 5-year est.)

## WAINSCOTT (CDP). Covers a land area of 6.728 square miles and a water area of 0.496 square miles. Located at 40.95° N. Lat; 72.25° W. Long. Elevation is 23 feet.

**Population:** 506 (1990); 628 (2000); 650 (2010); Density: 96.6 persons per square mile (2010); Race: 93.1% White, 2.3% Black, 0.5% Asian, 1.7% American Indian/Alaska Native, 0.0% Native Hawaiian/Other Pacific Islander, 2.4% Other, 14.3% Hispanic of any race (2010); Average household size: 2.30 (2010); Median age: 44.1 (2010); Males per 100 females: 115.9 (2010); Marriage status: 22.4% never married, 57.3% now

married, 4.5% widowed, 15.8% divorced (2006-2010 5-year est.); Foreign born: 8.5% (2006-2010 5-year est.); Ancestry (includes multiple ancestries): 16.7% Italian, 16.7% German, 14.4% Irish, 8.5% Scotch-Irish, 7.6% English (2006-2010 5-year est.).
**Economy:** Employment by occupation: 26.8% management, 0.0% professional, 14.5% services, 17.1% sales, 2.2% farming, 9.2% construction, 0.0% production (2006-2010 5-year est.).
**Income:** Per capita income: $61,233 (2006-2010 5-year est.); Median household income: $98,125 (2006-2010 5-year est.); Average household income: $135,918 (2006-2010 5-year est.); Percent of households with income of $100,000 or more: 46.9% (2006-2010 5-year est.); Poverty rate: 3.7% (2006-2010 5-year est.).
**Education:** Percent of population age 25 and over with: High school diploma (including GED) or higher: 95.3% (2006-2010 5-year est.); Bachelor's degree or higher: 58.0% (2006-2010 5-year est.); Master's degree or higher: 20.2% (2006-2010 5-year est.).

**School District(s)**
Child Development Center of the Hamptons Charter S (KG-05)
    2009-10 Enrollment: 61 . . . . . . . . . . . . . . . . . . . . . . (631) 324-0207
Wainscott Common School District (KG-03)
    2009-10 Enrollment: 21 . . . . . . . . . . . . . . . . . . . . . . (631) 537-1080
**Housing:** Homeownership rate: 76.2% (2010); Median home value: $1 (2006-2010 5-year est.); Median contract rent: $1,488 per month (2006-2010 5-year est.); Median year structure built: 1985 (2006-2010 5-year est.).
**Transportation:** Commute to work: 82.0% car, 7.8% public transportation, 0.0% walk, 10.1% work from home (2006-2010 5-year est.); Travel time to work: 50.8% less than 15 minutes, 11.3% 15 to 30 minutes, 15.9% 30 to 45 minutes, 11.8% 45 to 60 minutes, 10.3% 60 minutes or more (2006-2010 5-year est.)

**WATER MILL** (unincorporated postal area)
Zip Code: 11976
    Covers a land area of 12.271 square miles and a water area of 2.253 square miles. Located at 40.92° N. Lat; 72.35° W. Long. Elevation is 33 feet. Population: 1,565 (2010); Density: 127.5 persons per square mile (2010); Race: 93.7% White, 1.0% Black, 1.5% Asian, 0.0% American Indian/Alaska Native, 0.0% Native Hawaiian/Other Pacific Islander, 3.8% Other, 7.9% Hispanic of any race (2010); Average household size: 2.37 (2010); Median age: 50.6 (2010); Males per 100 females: 100.6 (2010); Homeownership rate: 85.9% (2010)

**WATERMILL** (CDP). Covers a land area of 10.540 square miles and a water area of 1.483 square miles. Located at 40.92° N. Lat; 72.35° W. Long. Elevation is 39 feet.
**Population:** 1,303 (1990); 1,724 (2000); 1,559 (2010); Density: 147.9 persons per square mile (2010); Race: 93.8% White, 1.0% Black, 1.4% Asian, 0.0% American Indian/Alaska Native, 0.0% Native Hawaiian/Other Pacific Islander, 3.8% Other, 7.0% Hispanic of any race (2010); Average household size: 2.38 (2010); Median age: 51.0 (2010); Males per 100 females: 102.2 (2010); Marriage status: 26.7% never married, 66.3% now married, 1.8% widowed, 5.2% divorced (2006-2010 5-year est.); Foreign born: 7.4% (2006-2010 5-year est.); Ancestry (includes multiple ancestries): 25.2% Irish, 19.8% German, 17.6% Italian, 15.9% English, 10.0% Polish (2006-2010 5-year est.).
**Economy:** Employment by occupation: 28.5% management, 4.2% professional, 5.8% services, 12.1% sales, 1.9% farming, 5.0% construction, 1.6% production (2006-2010 5-year est.).
**Income:** Per capita income: $96,867 (2006-2010 5-year est.); Median household income: $118,011 (2006-2010 5-year est.); Average household income: $227,549 (2006-2010 5-year est.); Percent of households with income of $100,000 or more: 62.1% (2006-2010 5-year est.); Poverty rate: 7.2% (2006-2010 5-year est.).
**Education:** Percent of population age 25 and over with: High school diploma (including GED) or higher: 98.0% (2006-2010 5-year est.); Bachelor's degree or higher: 55.5% (2006-2010 5-year est.); Master's degree or higher: 26.6% (2006-2010 5-year est.).
**Housing:** Homeownership rate: 88.1% (2010); Median home value: $1 (2006-2010 5-year est.); Median contract rent: $1,771 per month (2006-2010 5-year est.); Median year structure built: 1976 (2006-2010 5-year est.).
**Transportation:** Commute to work: 65.9% car, 13.3% public transportation, 11.9% walk, 8.9% work from home (2006-2010 5-year est.); Travel time to work: 45.5% less than 15 minutes, 19.8% 15 to 30 minutes,

12.0% 30 to 45 minutes, 5.3% 45 to 60 minutes, 17.4% 60 minutes or more (2006-2010 5-year est.)

**WEST BABYLON** (CDP). Covers a land area of 7.766 square miles and a water area of 0.309 square miles. Located at 40.71° N. Lat; 73.35° W. Long. Elevation is 39 feet.
**Population:** 42,410 (1990); 43,452 (2000); 43,213 (2010); Density: 5,563.7 persons per square mile (2010); Race: 79.9% White, 11.2% Black, 2.7% Asian, 0.2% American Indian/Alaska Native, 0.0% Native Hawaiian/Other Pacific Islander, 6.0% Other, 12.2% Hispanic of any race (2010); Average household size: 2.93 (2010); Median age: 40.0 (2010); Males per 100 females: 91.8 (2010); Marriage status: 30.5% never married, 53.2% now married, 7.8% widowed, 8.5% divorced (2006-2010 5-year est.); Foreign born: 12.1% (2006-2010 5-year est.); Ancestry (includes multiple ancestries): 38.0% Italian, 23.2% Irish, 16.5% German, 6.2% Polish, 4.3% English (2006-2010 5-year est.).
**Economy:** Employment by occupation: 10.0% management, 3.2% professional, 10.0% services, 20.6% sales, 5.1% farming, 10.1% construction, 6.5% production (2006-2010 5-year est.).
**Income:** Per capita income: $29,425 (2006-2010 5-year est.); Median household income: $79,591 (2006-2010 5-year est.); Average household income: $87,513 (2006-2010 5-year est.); Percent of households with income of $100,000 or more: 37.1% (2006-2010 5-year est.); Poverty rate: 5.2% (2006-2010 5-year est.).
**Education:** Percent of population age 25 and over with: High school diploma (including GED) or higher: 88.1% (2006-2010 5-year est.); Bachelor's degree or higher: 22.6% (2006-2010 5-year est.); Master's degree or higher: 8.6% (2006-2010 5-year est.).
**School District(s)**
West Babylon Union Free School District (KG-12)
    2009-10 Enrollment: 4,484 . . . . . . . . . . . . . . . . . . . . . . (631) 376-7001
**Housing:** Homeownership rate: 73.2% (2010); Median home value: $378,800 (2006-2010 5-year est.); Median contract rent: $1,357 per month (2006-2010 5-year est.); Median year structure built: 1961 (2006-2010 5-year est.).
**Transportation:** Commute to work: 86.9% car, 8.3% public transportation, 0.6% walk, 2.8% work from home (2006-2010 5-year est.); Travel time to work: 27.3% less than 15 minutes, 34.1% 15 to 30 minutes, 15.3% 30 to 45 minutes, 5.5% 45 to 60 minutes, 17.8% 60 minutes or more (2006-2010 5-year est.)

**WEST BAY SHORE** (CDP). Covers a land area of 2.192 square miles and a water area of 0.094 square miles. Located at 40.70° N. Lat; 73.27° W. Long. Elevation is 13 feet.
**Population:** 4,907 (1990); 4,775 (2000); 4,648 (2010); Density: 2,119.9 persons per square mile (2010); Race: 92.1% White, 2.2% Black, 2.3% Asian, 0.0% American Indian/Alaska Native, 0.0% Native Hawaiian/Other Pacific Islander, 3.4% Other, 7.4% Hispanic of any race (2010); Average household size: 2.69 (2010); Median age: 45.6 (2010); Males per 100 females: 96.7 (2010); Marriage status: 21.9% never married, 63.4% now married, 5.5% widowed, 9.2% divorced (2006-2010 5-year est.); Foreign born: 7.7% (2006-2010 5-year est.); Ancestry (includes multiple ancestries): 36.6% Italian, 28.5% Irish, 21.3% German, 6.0% Polish, 3.7% English (2006-2010 5-year est.).
**Economy:** Employment by occupation: 16.0% management, 2.8% professional, 5.2% services, 21.2% sales, 5.2% farming, 10.3% construction, 4.2% production (2006-2010 5-year est.).
**Income:** Per capita income: $51,337 (2006-2010 5-year est.); Median household income: $109,375 (2006-2010 5-year est.); Average household income: $132,464 (2006-2010 5-year est.); Percent of households with income of $100,000 or more: 55.7% (2006-2010 5-year est.); Poverty rate: 0.9% (2006-2010 5-year est.).
**Education:** Percent of population age 25 and over with: High school diploma (including GED) or higher: 95.9% (2006-2010 5-year est.); Bachelor's degree or higher: 45.8% (2006-2010 5-year est.); Master's degree or higher: 22.6% (2006-2010 5-year est.).
**Housing:** Homeownership rate: 93.7% (2010); Median home value: $470,400 (2006-2010 5-year est.); Median contract rent: n/a per month (2006-2010 5-year est.); Median year structure built: 1959 (2006-2010 5-year est.).
**Transportation:** Commute to work: 86.1% car, 10.1% public transportation, 0.0% walk, 3.9% work from home (2006-2010 5-year est.); Travel time to work: 25.8% less than 15 minutes, 26.6% 15 to 30 minutes, 24.2% 30 to 45 minutes, 1.2% 45 to 60 minutes, 22.3% 60 minutes or more (2006-2010 5-year est.)

## WEST HAMPTON DUNES (village). Covers a land area of 0.329 square miles and a water area of 0.084 square miles. Located at 40.77° N. Lat; 72.70° W. Long. Elevation is 7 feet.

**Population:** 6 (1990); 11 (2000); 55 (2010); Density: 167.0 persons per square mile (2010); Race: 98.2% White, 0.0% Black, 1.8% Asian, 0.0% American Indian/Alaska Native, 0.0% Native Hawaiian/Other Pacific Islander, 0.0% Other, 3.6% Hispanic of any race (2010); Average household size: 2.29 (2010); Median age: 56.5 (2010); Males per 100 females: 139.1 (2010); Marriage status: 0.0% never married, 81.4% now married, 18.6% widowed, 0.0% divorced (2006-2010 5-year est.); Foreign born: 0.0% (2006-2010 5-year est.); Ancestry (includes multiple ancestries): 37.2% Irish, 23.3% Italian, 18.6% Austrian, 14.0% Czech, 14.0% European (2006-2010 5-year est.).
**Economy:** Single-family building permits issued: 3 (2011); Multi-family building permits issued: 0 (2011); Employment by occupation: n/a management, n/a professional, n/a services, n/a sales, n/a farming, n/a construction, n/a production (2006-2010 5-year est.).
**Income:** Per capita income: $39,114 (2006-2010 5-year est.); Median household income: $67,500 (2006-2010 5-year est.); Average household income: $70,238 (2006-2010 5-year est.); Percent of households with income of $100,000 or more: 50.0% (2006-2010 5-year est.); Poverty rate: 4.7% (2006-2010 5-year est.).
**Education:** Percent of population age 25 and over with: High school diploma (including GED) or higher: 100.0% (2006-2010 5-year est.); Bachelor's degree or higher: 55.8% (2006-2010 5-year est.); Master's degree or higher: 41.9% (2006-2010 5-year est.).
**Housing:** Homeownership rate: 95.9% (2010); Median home value: $833,300 (2006-2010 5-year est.); Median contract rent: n/a per month (2006-2010 5-year est.); Median year structure built: 1977 (2006-2010 5-year est.).
**Transportation:** Commute to work: n/a car, n/a public transportation, n/a walk, n/a work from home (2006-2010 5-year est.); Travel time to work: n/a less than 15 minutes, n/a 15 to 30 minutes, n/a 30 to 45 minutes, n/a 45 to 60 minutes, n/a 60 minutes or more (2006-2010 5-year est.)

## WEST HILLS (CDP). Covers a land area of 4.925 square miles and a water area of 0 square miles. Located at 40.81° N. Lat; 73.43° W. Long. Elevation is 348 feet.

**History:** The community of West Hills is home to West Hills County Park, the location of Jayne's Hill which is the natural highest point on Long Island (400 feet). This area includes picturesque, well-groomed nature trails, including the historic Walt Whitman Trail.
**Population:** 5,849 (1990); 5,607 (2000); 5,592 (2010); Density: 1,135.3 persons per square mile (2010); Race: 90.6% White, 1.3% Black, 5.4% Asian, 0.0% American Indian/Alaska Native, 0.1% Native Hawaiian/Other Pacific Islander, 2.6% Other, 5.4% Hispanic of any race (2010); Average household size: 2.82 (2010); Median age: 45.2 (2010); Males per 100 females: 97.4 (2010); Marriage status: 21.4% never married, 64.1% now married, 5.8% widowed, 8.7% divorced (2006-2010 5-year est.); Foreign born: 10.9% (2006-2010 5-year est.); Ancestry (includes multiple ancestries): 33.9% Italian, 28.8% Irish, 15.2% German, 11.5% Polish, 7.9% Russian (2006-2010 5-year est.).
**Economy:** Employment by occupation: 22.7% management, 3.8% professional, 4.0% services, 14.2% sales, 2.8% farming, 3.9% construction, 4.1% production (2006-2010 5-year est.).
**Income:** Per capita income: $57,678 (2006-2010 5-year est.); Median household income: $122,560 (2006-2010 5-year est.); Average household income: $154,961 (2006-2010 5-year est.); Percent of households with income of $100,000 or more: 63.6% (2006-2010 5-year est.); Poverty rate: 2.4% (2006-2010 5-year est.).
**Education:** Percent of population age 25 and over with: High school diploma (including GED) or higher: 94.2% (2006-2010 5-year est.); Bachelor's degree or higher: 52.8% (2006-2010 5-year est.); Master's degree or higher: 24.5% (2006-2010 5-year est.).
**Housing:** Homeownership rate: 93.5% (2010); Median home value: $619,300 (2006-2010 5-year est.); Median contract rent: $875 per month (2006-2010 5-year est.); Median year structure built: 1960 (2006-2010 5-year est.).
**Transportation:** Commute to work: 82.0% car, 12.3% public transportation, 0.0% walk, 5.0% work from home (2006-2010 5-year est.); Travel time to work: 25.3% less than 15 minutes, 35.3% 15 to 30 minutes, 17.7% 30 to 45 minutes, 4.8% 45 to 60 minutes, 17.0% 60 minutes or more (2006-2010 5-year est.)

## WEST ISLIP (CDP). Covers a land area of 6.328 square miles and a water area of 0.437 square miles. Located at 40.71° N. Lat; 73.29° W. Long. Elevation is 20 feet.

**Population:** 28,419 (1990); 28,907 (2000); 28,335 (2010); Density: 4,477.2 persons per square mile (2010); Race: 95.9% White, 0.6% Black, 1.7% Asian, 0.0% American Indian/Alaska Native, 0.0% Native Hawaiian/Other Pacific Islander, 1.8% Other, 5.5% Hispanic of any race (2010); Average household size: 3.09 (2010); Median age: 41.3 (2010); Males per 100 females: 96.2 (2010); Marriage status: 24.5% never married, 62.4% now married, 6.8% widowed, 6.3% divorced (2006-2010 5-year est.); Foreign born: 5.0% (2006-2010 5-year est.); Ancestry (includes multiple ancestries): 41.9% Italian, 35.2% Irish, 20.8% German, 8.2% Polish, 6.5% English (2006-2010 5-year est.).
**Economy:** Employment by occupation: 13.9% management, 3.3% professional, 6.1% services, 18.4% sales, 3.4% farming, 8.6% construction, 5.5% production (2006-2010 5-year est.).
**Income:** Per capita income: $37,735 (2006-2010 5-year est.); Median household income: $97,242 (2006-2010 5-year est.); Average household income: $117,238 (2006-2010 5-year est.); Percent of households with income of $100,000 or more: 49.2% (2006-2010 5-year est.); Poverty rate: 3.0% (2006-2010 5-year est.).
**Education:** Percent of population age 25 and over with: High school diploma (including GED) or higher: 93.3% (2006-2010 5-year est.); Bachelor's degree or higher: 33.3% (2006-2010 5-year est.); Master's degree or higher: 14.1% (2006-2010 5-year est.).
### School District(s)
West Islip Union Free School District (KG-12)
   2009-10 Enrollment: 5,451 . . . . . . . . . . . . . . . . . . . . . (631) 893-3200
**Housing:** Homeownership rate: 92.1% (2010); Median home value: $455,600 (2006-2010 5-year est.); Median contract rent: $1,256 per month (2006-2010 5-year est.); Median year structure built: 1959 (2006-2010 5-year est.).
**Hospitals:** Good Samaritan Hospital Medical Center (437 beds)
**Transportation:** Commute to work: 87.5% car, 7.0% public transportation, 0.5% walk, 4.4% work from home (2006-2010 5-year est.); Travel time to work: 31.3% less than 15 minutes, 30.5% 15 to 30 minutes, 16.2% 30 to 45 minutes, 7.1% 45 to 60 minutes, 14.9% 60 minutes or more (2006-2010 5-year est.)
**Additional Information Contacts**
West Islip Chamber of Commerce . . . . . . . . . . . . . . . . . . . . (631) 661-3838
   http://westislipchamber.org

## WEST SAYVILLE (CDP). Covers a land area of 2.099 square miles and a water area of 0.006 square miles. Located at 40.72° N. Lat; 73.10° W. Long. Elevation is 13 feet.

**Population:** 4,680 (1990); 5,003 (2000); 5,011 (2010); Density: 2,386.7 persons per square mile (2010); Race: 96.8% White, 0.7% Black, 1.1% Asian, 0.1% American Indian/Alaska Native, 0.0% Native Hawaiian/Other Pacific Islander, 1.3% Other, 3.7% Hispanic of any race (2010); Average household size: 2.78 (2010); Median age: 42.8 (2010); Males per 100 females: 92.4 (2010); Marriage status: 25.5% never married, 61.0% now married, 6.9% widowed, 6.6% divorced (2006-2010 5-year est.); Foreign born: 2.8% (2006-2010 5-year est.); Ancestry (includes multiple ancestries): 40.6% Italian, 34.2% Irish, 30.6% German, 6.0% Polish, 4.4% French (2006-2010 5-year est.).
**Economy:** Employment by occupation: 12.6% management, 2.8% professional, 5.6% services, 19.7% sales, 2.5% farming, 10.3% construction, 4.6% production (2006-2010 5-year est.).
**Income:** Per capita income: $34,314 (2006-2010 5-year est.); Median household income: $87,929 (2006-2010 5-year est.); Average household income: $97,182 (2006-2010 5-year est.); Percent of households with income of $100,000 or more: 35.5% (2006-2010 5-year est.); Poverty rate: 2.8% (2006-2010 5-year est.).
**Education:** Percent of population age 25 and over with: High school diploma (including GED) or higher: 96.4% (2006-2010 5-year est.); Bachelor's degree or higher: 24.7% (2006-2010 5-year est.); Master's degree or higher: 13.6% (2006-2010 5-year est.).
### School District(s)
Sayville Union Free School District (KG-12)
   2009-10 Enrollment: 3,335 . . . . . . . . . . . . . . . . . . . . . (631) 244-6510
**Housing:** Homeownership rate: 83.8% (2010); Median home value: $430,900 (2006-2010 5-year est.); Median contract rent: $1,363 per month (2006-2010 5-year est.); Median year structure built: 1957 (2006-2010 5-year est.).

**Transportation:** Commute to work: 89.3% car, 8.2% public transportation, 0.4% walk, 1.5% work from home (2006-2010 5-year est.); Travel time to work: 23.3% less than 15 minutes, 34.4% 15 to 30 minutes, 22.2% 30 to 45 minutes, 5.5% 45 to 60 minutes, 14.7% 60 minutes or more (2006-2010 5-year est.)

## WESTHAMPTON (CDP).
Covers a land area of 12.674 square miles and a water area of 2.191 square miles. Located at 40.84° N. Lat; 72.65° W. Long. Elevation is 36 feet.

**History:** Like most of Southern Long Island shore zone, suffering from significant beach erosion due to a succession of mid-1990s Atlantic hurricanes. Part of the original Quogue Purchase of 1666. Westhampton's first summerhouse built by Gen. John A. Dix in 1879; then a three-day journey by stage from Brooklyn until L.I. Railroad extended to Sag Harbor in 1870. By 1920s Westhampton and The Hamptons were the summering place for the rich and famous. Incorporated 1928.

**Population:** 1,849 (1990); 2,869 (2000); 3,079 (2010); Density: 242.9 persons per square mile (2010); Race: 86.0% White, 3.6% Black, 1.2% Asian, 0.5% American Indian/Alaska Native, 0.2% Native Hawaiian/Other Pacific Islander, 8.5% Other, 12.3% Hispanic of any race (2010); Average household size: 2.74 (2010); Median age: 44.7 (2010); Males per 100 females: 97.2 (2010); Marriage status: 19.6% never married, 58.7% now married, 12.8% widowed, 8.8% divorced (2006-2010 5-year est.); Foreign born: 8.2% (2006-2010 5-year est.); Ancestry (includes multiple ancestries): 20.5% Italian, 17.4% Irish, 14.4% German, 10.8% Polish, 6.7% European (2006-2010 5-year est.).

**Economy:** Employment by occupation: 9.6% management, 2.5% professional, 9.9% services, 18.2% sales, 5.0% farming, 9.6% construction, 5.9% production (2006-2010 5-year est.).

**Income:** Per capita income: $50,649 (2006-2010 5-year est.); Median household income: $88,478 (2006-2010 5-year est.); Average household income: $144,726 (2006-2010 5-year est.); Percent of households with income of $100,000 or more: 47.5% (2006-2010 5-year est.); Poverty rate: 3.9% (2006-2010 5-year est.).

**Education:** Percent of population age 25 and over with: High school diploma (including GED) or higher: 87.7% (2006-2010 5-year est.); Bachelor's degree or higher: 44.9% (2006-2010 5-year est.); Master's degree or higher: 20.5% (2006-2010 5-year est.).

**Housing:** Homeownership rate: 74.6% (2010); Median home value: $655,200 (2006-2010 5-year est.); Median contract rent: $1,229 per month (2006-2010 5-year est.); Median year structure built: 1975 (2006-2010 5-year est.).

**Transportation:** Commute to work: 80.3% car, 1.3% public transportation, 6.9% walk, 10.8% work from home (2006-2010 5-year est.); Travel time to work: 51.4% less than 15 minutes, 27.1% 15 to 30 minutes, 8.6% 30 to 45 minutes, 4.8% 45 to 60 minutes, 8.0% 60 minutes or more (2006-2010 5-year est.)

## WESTHAMPTON BEACH (village).
Covers a land area of 2.931 square miles and a water area of 0.072 square miles. Located at 40.80° N. Lat; 72.64° W. Long. Elevation is 7 feet.

**Population:** 1,571 (1990); 1,902 (2000); 1,721 (2010); Density: 587.2 persons per square mile (2010); Race: 87.2% White, 2.7% Black, 1.0% Asian, 1.0% American Indian/Alaska Native, 0.0% Native Hawaiian/Other Pacific Islander, 8.1% Other, 19.8% Hispanic of any race (2010); Average household size: 2.44 (2010); Median age: 42.5 (2010); Males per 100 females: 109.6 (2010); Marriage status: 19.3% never married, 65.9% now married, 8.3% widowed, 6.5% divorced (2006-2010 5-year est.); Foreign born: 12.9% (2006-2010 5-year est.); Ancestry (includes multiple ancestries): 28.4% Irish, 15.8% Italian, 12.3% English, 12.1% German, 7.0% Polish (2006-2010 5-year est.).

**Economy:** Single-family building permits issued: 4 (2011); Multi-family building permits issued: 0 (2011); Employment by occupation: 16.9% management, 4.5% professional, 0.6% services, 24.1% sales, 4.3% farming, 8.6% construction, 0.0% production (2006-2010 5-year est.).

**Income:** Per capita income: $60,291 (2006-2010 5-year est.); Median household income: $85,000 (2006-2010 5-year est.); Average household income: $133,797 (2006-2010 5-year est.); Percent of households with income of $100,000 or more: 45.8% (2006-2010 5-year est.); Poverty rate: 5.3% (2006-2010 5-year est.).

**Education:** Percent of population age 25 and over with: High school diploma (including GED) or higher: 90.7% (2006-2010 5-year est.); Bachelor's degree or higher: 50.5% (2006-2010 5-year est.); Master's degree or higher: 21.3% (2006-2010 5-year est.).

**School District(s)**
Westhampton Beach Union Free School District (KG-12)
    2009-10 Enrollment: 1,786 . . . . . . . . . . . . . . . . . . . . (631) 288-3800
**Housing:** Homeownership rate: 63.3% (2010); Median home value: $754,100 (2006-2010 5-year est.); Median contract rent: $1,432 per month (2006-2010 5-year est.); Median year structure built: 1965 (2006-2010 5-year est.).

**Safety:** Violent crime rate: 34.8 per 10,000 population; Property crime rate: 263.8 per 10,000 population (2010).

**Transportation:** Commute to work: 87.1% car, 6.6% public transportation, 1.5% walk, 3.5% work from home (2006-2010 5-year est.); Travel time to work: 37.6% less than 15 minutes, 16.5% 15 to 30 minutes, 16.1% 30 to 45 minutes, 4.4% 45 to 60 minutes, 25.3% 60 minutes or more (2006-2010 5-year est.)

**Airports:** Francis S Gabreski (general aviation)

**Additional Information Contacts**
Greater Westhampton Beach Chamber of Commerce . . . . (631) 288-3337
    http://www.whbcc.com
Village of Westhampton Beach . . . . . . . . . . . . . . . . . . . (631) 288-1654
    http://www.whbvillage.com

## WHEATLEY HEIGHTS (CDP).
Covers a land area of 1.301 square miles and a water area of 0 square miles. Located at 40.76° N. Lat; 73.37° W. Long. Elevation is 102 feet.

**Population:** 5,027 (1990); 5,013 (2000); 5,130 (2010); Density: 3,940.9 persons per square mile (2010); Race: 30.3% White, 54.6% Black, 5.6% Asian, 0.5% American Indian/Alaska Native, 0.0% Native Hawaiian/Other Pacific Islander, 9.0% Other, 13.5% Hispanic of any race (2010); Average household size: 3.43 (2010); Median age: 37.2 (2010); Males per 100 females: 91.6 (2010); Marriage status: 33.6% never married, 56.0% now married, 4.9% widowed, 5.6% divorced (2006-2010 5-year est.); Foreign born: 26.1% (2006-2010 5-year est.); Ancestry (includes multiple ancestries): 9.3% Irish, 8.8% Haitian, 5.9% African, 5.9% Italian, 5.2% German (2006-2010 5-year est.).

**Economy:** Employment by occupation: 11.9% management, 5.1% professional, 7.7% services, 17.3% sales, 6.2% farming, 4.7% construction, 4.2% production (2006-2010 5-year est.).

**Income:** Per capita income: $26,367 (2006-2010 5-year est.); Median household income: $88,191 (2006-2010 5-year est.); Average household income: $99,513 (2006-2010 5-year est.); Percent of households with income of $100,000 or more: 46.1% (2006-2010 5-year est.); Poverty rate: 4.3% (2006-2010 5-year est.).

**Education:** Percent of population age 25 and over with: High school diploma (including GED) or higher: 92.3% (2006-2010 5-year est.); Bachelor's degree or higher: 32.3% (2006-2010 5-year est.); Master's degree or higher: 14.5% (2006-2010 5-year est.).

**Housing:** Homeownership rate: 85.5% (2010); Median home value: $502,900 (2006-2010 5-year est.); Median contract rent: $985 per month (2006-2010 5-year est.); Median year structure built: 1965 (2006-2010 5-year est.).

**Transportation:** Commute to work: 85.8% car, 8.3% public transportation, 0.4% walk, 5.5% work from home (2006-2010 5-year est.); Travel time to work: 22.3% less than 15 minutes, 34.9% 15 to 30 minutes, 12.6% 30 to 45 minutes, 9.4% 45 to 60 minutes, 20.8% 60 minutes or more (2006-2010 5-year est.)

## WYANDANCH (CDP).
Covers a land area of 4.473 square miles and a water area of 0.003 square miles. Located at 40.74° N. Lat; 73.37° W. Long. Elevation is 56 feet.

**Population:** 8,771 (1990); 10,546 (2000); 11,647 (2010); Density: 2,603.6 persons per square mile (2010); Race: 16.4% White, 65.0% Black, 1.2% Asian, 1.0% American Indian/Alaska Native, 0.0% Native Hawaiian/Other Pacific Islander, 16.4% Other, 28.2% Hispanic of any race (2010); Average household size: 3.95 (2010); Median age: 30.4 (2010); Males per 100 females: 96.4 (2010); Marriage status: 50.3% never married, 38.1% now married, 4.1% widowed, 7.4% divorced (2006-2010 5-year est.); Foreign born: 25.6% (2006-2010 5-year est.); Ancestry (includes multiple ancestries): 4.8% Haitian, 2.2% Jamaican, 1.9% African, 1.6% Italian, 1.6% Nigerian (2006-2010 5-year est.).

**Economy:** Employment by occupation: 4.7% management, 0.9% professional, 13.5% services, 14.0% sales, 5.8% farming, 4.6% construction, 9.0% production (2006-2010 5-year est.).

**Income:** Per capita income: $18,426 (2006-2010 5-year est.); Median household income: $54,052 (2006-2010 5-year est.); Average household income: $63,149 (2006-2010 5-year est.); Percent of households with

income of $100,000 or more: 17.2% (2006-2010 5-year est.); Poverty rate: 16.2% (2006-2010 5-year est.).

**Education:** Percent of population age 25 and over with: High school diploma (including GED) or higher: 72.2% (2006-2010 5-year est.); Bachelor's degree or higher: 14.3% (2006-2010 5-year est.); Master's degree or higher: 3.7% (2006-2010 5-year est.).

### School District(s)

Wyandanch Union Free School District (PK-12)

    2009-10 Enrollment: 2,141 . . . . . . . . . . . . . . . . . . . . . . (631) 870-0401

**Housing:** Homeownership rate: 58.7% (2010); Median home value: $296,700 (2006-2010 5-year est.); Median contract rent: $1,253 per month (2006-2010 5-year est.); Median year structure built: 1964 (2006-2010 5-year est.).

**Transportation:** Commute to work: 80.9% car, 15.9% public transportation, 0.6% walk, 1.2% work from home (2006-2010 5-year est.); Travel time to work: 26.0% less than 15 minutes, 30.2% 15 to 30 minutes, 21.7% 30 to 45 minutes, 6.2% 45 to 60 minutes, 15.8% 60 minutes or more (2006-2010 5-year est.)

**YAPHANK** (CDP). Covers a land area of 13.648 square miles and a water area of 0.122 square miles. Located at 40.83° N. Lat; 72.92° W. Long. Elevation is 43 feet.

**History:** US Camp Upton here was a US Army induction center in World Wars I and II.

**Population:** 4,841 (1990); 5,025 (2000); 5,945 (2010); Density: 435.6 persons per square mile (2010); Race: 87.9% White, 7.2% Black, 1.8% Asian, 0.2% American Indian/Alaska Native, 0.0% Native Hawaiian/Other Pacific Islander, 2.9% Other, 11.4% Hispanic of any race (2010); Average household size: 2.68 (2010); Median age: 40.1 (2010); Males per 100 females: 119.4 (2010); Marriage status: 35.4% never married, 50.0% now married, 4.0% widowed, 10.6% divorced (2006-2010 5-year est.); Foreign born: 5.4% (2006-2010 5-year est.); Ancestry (includes multiple ancestries): 31.5% Italian, 27.7% German, 26.5% Irish, 4.6% Polish, 4.3% French (2006-2010 5-year est.).

**Economy:** Employment by occupation: 8.0% management, 2.4% professional, 8.0% services, 24.7% sales, 2.7% farming, 12.0% construction, 8.4% production (2006-2010 5-year est.).

**Income:** Per capita income: $27,558 (2006-2010 5-year est.); Median household income: $83,015 (2006-2010 5-year est.); Average household income: $88,168 (2006-2010 5-year est.); Percent of households with income of $100,000 or more: 40.5% (2006-2010 5-year est.); Poverty rate: 12.3% (2006-2010 5-year est.).

**Education:** Percent of population age 25 and over with: High school diploma (including GED) or higher: 87.9% (2006-2010 5-year est.); Bachelor's degree or higher: 22.6% (2006-2010 5-year est.); Master's degree or higher: 10.2% (2006-2010 5-year est.).

### School District(s)

Longwood Central School District (KG-12)

    2009-10 Enrollment: 9,154 . . . . . . . . . . . . . . . . . . . . . . (631) 345-2172

**Housing:** Homeownership rate: 87.9% (2010); Median home value: $349,000 (2006-2010 5-year est.); Median contract rent: $1,353 per month (2006-2010 5-year est.); Median year structure built: 1981 (2006-2010 5-year est.).

**Transportation:** Commute to work: 95.0% car, 3.3% public transportation, 0.0% walk, 1.0% work from home (2006-2010 5-year est.); Travel time to work: 23.2% less than 15 minutes, 40.0% 15 to 30 minutes, 18.3% 30 to 45 minutes, 7.5% 45 to 60 minutes, 11.0% 60 minutes or more (2006-2010 5-year est.)

# Sullivan County

Located in southeastern New York; bounded on the west and southwest by the Delaware River and the Pennsylvania border; drained by the Neversink River; includes parts of the Catskills and the Shawangunk Range, and many lakes. Covers a land area of 969.71 square miles, a water area of 27.14 square miles, and is located in the Eastern Time Zone at 41.70° N. Lat., 74.74° W. Long. The county was founded in 1809. County seat is Monticello.

| Weather Station: Liberty 1 NE | | | | | | | | | Elevation: 1,548 feet | | |
|---|---|---|---|---|---|---|---|---|---|---|---|
| | Jan | Feb | Mar | Apr | May | Jun | Jul | Aug | Sep | Oct | Nov | Dec |
| High | 30 | 34 | 42 | 55 | 66 | 74 | 79 | 78 | 70 | 59 | 47 | 34 |
| Low | 12 | 14 | 22 | 33 | 43 | 51 | 56 | 55 | 47 | 36 | 28 | 18 |
| Precip | 3.7 | 2.8 | 3.8 | 4.6 | 4.8 | 5.0 | 4.9 | 4.5 | 4.9 | 4.5 | 3.9 | 4.2 |
| Snow | 18.6 | 12.7 | 12.7 | 3.3 | tr | 0.0 | 0.0 | 0.0 | 0.0 | 0.3 | 4.0 | 15.1 |

*High and Low temperatures in degrees Fahrenheit; Precipitation and Snow in inches*

**Population:** 69,277 (1990); 73,966 (2000); 77,547 (2010); Race: 82.0% White, 9.1% Black, 1.4% Asian, 0.5% American Indian/Alaska Native, 0.0% Native Hawaiian/Other Pacific Islander, 7.0% Other, 13.6% Hispanic of any race (2010); Density: 80.0 persons per square mile (2010); Average household size: 2.45 (2010); Median age: 41.7 (2010); Males per 100 females: 104.4 (2010).

**Religion:** Six largest groups: 19.8% Catholicism, 5.6% Judaism, 4.0% Methodist/Pietist, 3.9% Muslim Estimate, 1.7% Hindu, 1.5% Presbyterian-Reformed (2010)

**Economy:** Unemployment rate: 10.7% (February 2012); Total civilian labor force: 33,468 (February 2012); Leading industries: 27.5% health care and social assistance; 16.6% retail trade; 9.3% accommodation & food services (2009); Farms: 323 totaling 50,443 acres (2007); Companies that employ 500 or more persons: 2 (2009); Companies that employ 100 to 499 persons: 22 (2009); Companies that employ less than 100 persons: 1,971 (2009); Black-owned businesses: 349 (2007); Hispanic-owned businesses: 462 (2007); Asian-owned businesses: 281 (2007); Women-owned businesses: n/a (2007); Retail sales per capita: $11,492 (2010). Single-family building permits issued: 233 (2011); Multi-family building permits issued: 6 (2011).

**Income:** Per capita income: $23,422 (2006-2010 5-year est.); Median household income: $48,103 (2006-2010 5-year est.); Average household income: $60,596 (2006-2010 5-year est.); Percent of households with income of $100,000 or more: 15.7% (2006-2010 5-year est.); Poverty rate: 16.6% (2006-2010 5-year est.); Bankruptcy rate: 3.37% (2011).

**Taxes:** Total county taxes per capita: $1,104 (2009); County property taxes per capita: $571 (2009).

**Education:** Percent of population age 25 and over with: High school diploma (including GED) or higher: 83.9% (2006-2010 5-year est.); Bachelor's degree or higher: 20.3% (2006-2010 5-year est.); Master's degree or higher: 8.8% (2006-2010 5-year est.).

**Housing:** Homeownership rate: 67.0% (2010); Median home value: $186,900 (2006-2010 5-year est.); Median contract rent: $657 per month (2006-2010 5-year est.); Median year structure built: 1969 (2006-2010 5-year est.)

**Health:** Birth rate: 111.1 per 10,000 population (2011); Death rate: 94.1 per 10,000 population (2011); Age-adjusted cancer mortality rate: 179.0 deaths per 100,000 population (2009); Number of physicians: 14.0 per 10,000 population (2008); Hospital beds: 30.9 per 10,000 population (2007); Hospital admissions: 964.1 per 10,000 population (2007).

**Elections:** 2008 Presidential election results: 54.0% Obama, 44.6% McCain, 0.7% Nader

**Additional Information Contacts**

Sullivan County Government . . . . . . . . . . . . . . . . . . . . . . . (845) 794-3000
    http://co.sullivan.ny.us
Jeffersonville Area Chamber of Commerce . . . . . . . . . . . . (845) 482-5688
    http://jeffersonvilleny.com
Narrowsburg Chamber of Commerce . . . . . . . . . . . . . . . . (845) 252-7234
    http://www.narrowsburg.org
Sullivan County Chamber of Commerce . . . . . . . . . . . . . . (845) 791-4200
    http://www.catskills.com
Town of Bethel . . . . . . . . . . . . . . . . . . . . . . . . . . . . . . . . (845) 583-4350
    http://www.town.bethel.ny.us
Town of Liberty . . . . . . . . . . . . . . . . . . . . . . . . . . . . . . . . (845) 292-5110
    http://www.townofliberty.org
Town of Thompson . . . . . . . . . . . . . . . . . . . . . . . . . . . . . (845) 794-2500
    http://www.townofthompson.com
Village of Monticello . . . . . . . . . . . . . . . . . . . . . . . . . . . . (845) 794-6130
    http://www.villageofmonticello.com

# Sullivan County Communities

**BARRYVILLE** (unincorporated postal area)

Zip Code: 12719

    Covers a land area of 17.232 square miles and a water area of 0.443 square miles. Located at 41.49° N. Lat; 74.90° W. Long. Elevation is 594 feet. Population: 1,207 (2010); Density: 70.0 persons per square mile (2010); Race: 88.6% White, 6.2% Black, 0.8% Asian, 0.0% American Indian/Alaska Native, 0.0% Native Hawaiian/Other Pacific Islander, 4.4% Other, 7.3% Hispanic of any race (2010); Average household size: 2.38 (2010); Median age: 44.4 (2010); Males per 100 females: 109.5 (2010); Homeownership rate: 80.6% (2010)

**BETHEL** (town). Covers a land area of 85.264 square miles and a water area of 4.692 square miles. Located at 41.68° N. Lat; 74.85° W. Long. Elevation is 1,325 feet.
**History:** Site of the 3-day Woodstock rock festival, July 1969.
**Population:** 3,693 (1990); 4,362 (2000); 4,255 (2010); Density: 49.9 persons per square mile (2010); Race: 88.9% White, 3.6% Black, 0.9% Asian, 0.4% American Indian/Alaska Native, 0.0% Native Hawaiian/Other Pacific Islander, 6.2% Other, 11.4% Hispanic of any race (2010); Average household size: 2.35 (2010); Median age: 46.3 (2010); Males per 100 females: 110.6 (2010); Marriage status: 28.6% never married, 53.5% now married, 6.6% widowed, 11.2% divorced (2006-2010 5-year est.); Foreign born: 6.6% (2006-2010 5-year est.); Ancestry (includes multiple ancestries): 21.9% Irish, 18.5% Italian, 18.4% German, 8.2% American, 7.5% Russian (2006-2010 5-year est.).
**Economy:** Single-family building permits issued: 10 (2011); Multi-family building permits issued: 6 (2011); Employment by occupation: 18.1% management, 2.6% professional, 11.6% services, 10.5% sales, 7.5% farming, 14.1% construction, 1.2% production (2006-2010 5-year est.).
**Income:** Per capita income: $24,777 (2006-2010 5-year est.); Median household income: $49,508 (2006-2010 5-year est.); Average household income: $60,020 (2006-2010 5-year est.); Percent of households with income of $100,000 or more: 14.4% (2006-2010 5-year est.); Poverty rate: 12.8% (2006-2010 5-year est.).
**Education:** Percent of population age 25 and over with: High school diploma (including GED) or higher: 85.5% (2006-2010 5-year est.); Bachelor's degree or higher: 19.7% (2006-2010 5-year est.); Master's degree or higher: 6.4% (2006-2010 5-year est.).
**Housing:** Homeownership rate: 77.7% (2010); Median home value: $218,400 (2006-2010 5-year est.); Median contract rent: $739 per month (2006-2010 5-year est.); Median year structure built: 1963 (2006-2010 5-year est.).
**Transportation:** Commute to work: 91.4% car, 0.9% public transportation, 0.0% walk, 6.1% work from home (2006-2010 5-year est.); Travel time to work: 27.8% less than 15 minutes, 43.7% 15 to 30 minutes, 15.9% 30 to 45 minutes, 6.9% 45 to 60 minutes, 5.7% 60 minutes or more (2006-2010 5-year est.)
**Additional Information Contacts**
Town of Bethel . . . . . . . . . . . . . . . . . . . . . . . . . . . . . . . (845) 583-4350
  http://www.town.bethel.ny.us

**BLOOMINGBURG** (village). Aka Bloomingburgh. Covers a land area of 0.308 square miles and a water area of 0 square miles. Located at 41.55° N. Lat; 74.44° W. Long. Elevation is 515 feet.
**History:** Also spelled Bloomingburgh.
**Population:** 332 (1990); 353 (2000); 420 (2010); Density: 1,360.3 persons per square mile (2010); Race: 84.3% White, 4.5% Black, 1.0% Asian, 0.5% American Indian/Alaska Native, 0.0% Native Hawaiian/Other Pacific Islander, 9.7% Other, 13.3% Hispanic of any race (2010); Average household size: 2.21 (2010); Median age: 37.0 (2010); Males per 100 females: 92.7 (2010); Marriage status: 33.7% never married, 31.3% now married, 13.2% widowed, 21.9% divorced (2006-2010 5-year est.); Foreign born: 0.0% (2006-2010 5-year est.); Ancestry (includes multiple ancestries): 25.6% Irish, 24.7% Italian, 21.2% German, 16.7% American, 3.8% English (2006-2010 5-year est.).
**Economy:** Single-family building permits issued: 1 (2011); Multi-family building permits issued: 0 (2011); Employment by occupation: 2.8% management, 0.0% professional, 13.5% services, 17.0% sales, 6.4% farming, 5.7% construction, 0.0% production (2006-2010 5-year est.).
**Income:** Per capita income: $18,066 (2006-2010 5-year est.); Median household income: $29,063 (2006-2010 5-year est.); Average household income: $43,060 (2006-2010 5-year est.); Percent of households with income of $100,000 or more: 15.6% (2006-2010 5-year est.); Poverty rate: 29.8% (2006-2010 5-year est.).
**Education:** Percent of population age 25 and over with: High school diploma (including GED) or higher: 82.6% (2006-2010 5-year est.); Bachelor's degree or higher: 5.2% (2006-2010 5-year est.); Master's degree or higher: 3.3% (2006-2010 5-year est.).
**Housing:** Homeownership rate: 33.2% (2010); Median home value: $170,800 (2006-2010 5-year est.); Median contract rent: $748 per month (2006-2010 5-year est.); Median year structure built: before 1940 (2006-2010 5-year est.).
**Transportation:** Commute to work: 97.9% car, 0.0% public transportation, 2.1% walk, 0.0% work from home (2006-2010 5-year est.); Travel time to work: 18.4% less than 15 minutes, 68.1% 15 to 30 minutes, 10.6% 30 to 45

minutes, 0.0% 45 to 60 minutes, 2.8% 60 minutes or more (2006-2010 5-year est.)

**BURLINGHAM** (unincorporated postal area)
Zip Code: 12722
  Covers a land area of 0.278 square miles and a water area of 0 square miles. Located at 41.59° N. Lat; 74.37° W. Long. Elevation is 400 feet.
Population: 158 (2010); Density: 567.6 persons per square mile (2010); Race: 94.3% White, 0.0% Black, 0.0% Asian, 1.9% American Indian/Alaska Native, 0.0% Native Hawaiian/Other Pacific Islander, 3.8% Other, 9.5% Hispanic of any race (2010); Average household size: 2.23 (2010); Median age: 40.5 (2010); Males per 100 females: 100.0 (2010); Homeownership rate: 81.6% (2010)

**CALLICOON** (town). Covers a land area of 48.591 square miles and a water area of 0.354 square miles. Located at 41.83° N. Lat; 74.92° W. Long. Elevation is 846 feet.
**History:** Seat of St. Joseph Seraphic Seminary.
**Population:** 3,024 (1990); 3,052 (2000); 3,057 (2010); Density: 62.9 persons per square mile (2010); Race: 94.5% White, 1.1% Black, 1.8% Asian, 0.1% American Indian/Alaska Native, 0.0% Native Hawaiian/Other Pacific Islander, 2.5% Other, 4.1% Hispanic of any race (2010); Average household size: 2.30 (2010); Median age: 46.6 (2010); Males per 100 females: 99.3 (2010); Marriage status: 13.7% never married, 72.3% now married, 6.9% widowed, 7.0% divorced (2006-2010 5-year est.); Foreign born: 3.5% (2006-2010 5-year est.); Ancestry (includes multiple ancestries): 36.9% German, 19.4% Irish, 8.8% English, 8.8% Italian, 8.5% American (2006-2010 5-year est.).
**Economy:** Single-family building permits issued: 4 (2011); Multi-family building permits issued: 0 (2011); Employment by occupation: 5.1% management, 2.1% professional, 13.2% services, 11.8% sales, 2.8% farming, 16.6% construction, 6.0% production (2006-2010 5-year est.).
**Income:** Per capita income: $26,138 (2006-2010 5-year est.); Median household income: $52,182 (2006-2010 5-year est.); Average household income: $55,568 (2006-2010 5-year est.); Percent of households with income of $100,000 or more: 13.1% (2006-2010 5-year est.); Poverty rate: 11.1% (2006-2010 5-year est.).
**Education:** Percent of population age 25 and over with: High school diploma (including GED) or higher: 86.3% (2006-2010 5-year est.); Bachelor's degree or higher: 23.9% (2006-2010 5-year est.); Master's degree or higher: 10.8% (2006-2010 5-year est.).
**Housing:** Homeownership rate: 79.6% (2010); Median home value: $178,200 (2006-2010 5-year est.); Median contract rent: $582 per month (2006-2010 5-year est.); Median year structure built: 1967 (2006-2010 5-year est.).
**Newspapers:** Sullivan County Democrat (Local news; Circulation 8,275)
**Transportation:** Commute to work: 93.8% car, 0.0% public transportation, 2.8% walk, 3.4% work from home (2006-2010 5-year est.); Travel time to work: 19.6% less than 15 minutes, 41.2% 15 to 30 minutes, 20.0% 30 to 45 minutes, 3.4% 45 to 60 minutes, 15.7% 60 minutes or more (2006-2010 5-year est.)

**CALLICOON** (CDP). Covers a land area of 0.358 square miles and a water area of 0.086 square miles. Located at 41.76° N. Lat; 75.06° W. Long. Elevation is 846 feet.
**Population:** 222 (1990); 216 (2000); 167 (2010); Density: 465.6 persons per square mile (2010); Race: 97.6% White, 0.6% Black, 0.6% Asian, 0.0% American Indian/Alaska Native, 0.0% Native Hawaiian/Other Pacific Islander, 1.2% Other, 8.4% Hispanic of any race (2010); Average household size: 1.88 (2010); Median age: 50.8 (2010); Males per 100 females: 85.6 (2010); Marriage status: 20.5% never married, 37.5% now married, 9.8% widowed, 32.1% divorced (2006-2010 5-year est.); Foreign born: 0.0% (2006-2010 5-year est.); Ancestry (includes multiple ancestries): 18.8% English, 18.8% Swedish, 18.8% Scottish, 17.0% Polish, 17.0% Dutch (2006-2010 5-year est.).
**Economy:** Employment by occupation: 25.0% management, 11.9% professional, 3.6% services, 0.0% sales, 25.0% farming, 0.0% construction, 0.0% production (2006-2010 5-year est.).
**Income:** Per capita income: $53,628 (2006-2010 5-year est.); Median household income: $77,500 (2006-2010 5-year est.); Average household income: $80,280 (2006-2010 5-year est.); Percent of households with income of $100,000 or more: 50.0% (2006-2010 5-year est.); Poverty rate: 6.3% (2006-2010 5-year est.).
**Education:** Percent of population age 25 and over with: High school diploma (including GED) or higher: 100.0% (2006-2010 5-year est.);

Bachelor's degree or higher: 20.2% (2006-2010 5-year est.); Master's degree or higher: 0.0% (2006-2010 5-year est.).
**Housing:** Homeownership rate: 66.3% (2010); Median home value: $186,400 (2006-2010 5-year est.); Median contract rent: $850 per month (2006-2010 5-year est.); Median year structure built: before 1940 (2006-2010 5-year est.).
**Transportation:** Commute to work: 81.0% car, 8.3% public transportation, 3.6% walk, 7.1% work from home (2006-2010 5-year est.); Travel time to work: 12.8% less than 15 minutes, 53.8% 15 to 30 minutes, 33.3% 30 to 45 minutes, 0.0% 45 to 60 minutes, 0.0% 60 minutes or more (2006-2010 5-year est.)

**CALLICOON CENTER** (unincorporated postal area)
Zip Code: 12724
Covers a land area of 7.556 square miles and a water area of <.001 square miles. Located at 41.83° N. Lat; 74.95° W. Long. Elevation is 1,253 feet. Population: 245 (2010); Density: 32.4 persons per square mile (2010); Race: 91.0% White, 0.4% Black, 2.0% Asian, 0.0% American Indian/Alaska Native, 0.0% Native Hawaiian/Other Pacific Islander, 6.6% Other, 3.3% Hispanic of any race (2010); Average household size: 2.09 (2010); Median age: 49.9 (2010); Males per 100 females: 100.8 (2010); Homeownership rate: 89.7% (2010)

**CLARYVILLE** (unincorporated postal area)
Zip Code: 12725
Covers a land area of 67.785 square miles and a water area of 0.103 square miles. Located at 41.98° N. Lat; 74.56° W. Long. Population: 277 (2010); Density: 4.1 persons per square mile (2010); Race: 94.9% White, 1.1% Black, 0.4% Asian, 1.4% American Indian/Alaska Native, 0.0% Native Hawaiian/Other Pacific Islander, 2.2% Other, 1.8% Hispanic of any race (2010); Average household size: 2.17 (2010); Median age: 45.6 (2010); Males per 100 females: 102.2 (2010); Homeownership rate: 70.0% (2010)

**COCHECTON** (town). Covers a land area of 36.240 square miles and a water area of 0.789 square miles. Located at 41.68° N. Lat; 74.99° W. Long. Elevation is 738 feet.
**Population:** 1,318 (1990); 1,328 (2000); 1,372 (2010); Density: 37.9 persons per square mile (2010); Race: 95.1% White, 2.4% Black, 0.7% Asian, 0.1% American Indian/Alaska Native, 0.0% Native Hawaiian/Other Pacific Islander, 1.7% Other, 4.2% Hispanic of any race (2010); Average household size: 2.26 (2010); Median age: 47.9 (2010); Males per 100 females: 100.6 (2010); Marriage status: 20.6% never married, 65.5% now married, 6.3% widowed, 7.5% divorced (2006-2010 5-year est.); Foreign born: 5.9% (2006-2010 5-year est.); Ancestry (includes multiple ancestries): 33.3% German, 21.1% Irish, 15.7% Italian, 7.6% English, 7.5% Polish (2006-2010 5-year est.).
**Economy:** Single-family building permits issued: 4 (2011); Multi-family building permits issued: 0 (2011); Employment by occupation: 6.5% management, 1.0% professional, 7.8% services, 22.3% sales, 2.1% farming, 15.6% construction, 4.5% production (2006-2010 5-year est.).
**Income:** Per capita income: $26,784 (2006-2010 5-year est.); Median household income: $57,917 (2006-2010 5-year est.); Average household income: $67,389 (2006-2010 5-year est.); Percent of households with income of $100,000 or more: 18.6% (2006-2010 5-year est.); Poverty rate: 13.3% (2006-2010 5-year est.).
**Education:** Percent of population age 25 and over with: High school diploma (including GED) or higher: 94.9% (2006-2010 5-year est.); Bachelor's degree or higher: 20.4% (2006-2010 5-year est.); Master's degree or higher: 10.1% (2006-2010 5-year est.).
**Housing:** Homeownership rate: 82.1% (2010); Median home value: $196,900 (2006-2010 5-year est.); Median contract rent: $598 per month (2006-2010 5-year est.); Median year structure built: 1972 (2006-2010 5-year est.).
**Transportation:** Commute to work: 92.2% car, 2.5% public transportation, 0.8% walk, 3.7% work from home (2006-2010 5-year est.); Travel time to work: 22.7% less than 15 minutes, 27.3% 15 to 30 minutes, 29.2% 30 to 45 minutes, 10.4% 45 to 60 minutes, 10.4% 60 minutes or more (2006-2010 5-year est.).

**DELAWARE** (town). Covers a land area of 34.941 square miles and a water area of 0.703 square miles. Located at 41.75° N. Lat; 75.00° W. Long.
**Population:** 2,633 (1990); 2,719 (2000); 2,670 (2010); Density: 76.4 persons per square mile (2010); Race: 84.3% White, 12.1% Black, 0.4%

Asian, 0.3% American Indian/Alaska Native, 0.1% Native Hawaiian/Other Pacific Islander, 2.8% Other, 6.9% Hispanic of any race (2010); Average household size: 2.28 (2010); Median age: 41.7 (2010); Males per 100 females: 96.3 (2010); Marriage status: 32.1% never married, 52.4% now married, 6.4% widowed, 9.1% divorced (2006-2010 5-year est.); Foreign born: 6.6% (2006-2010 5-year est.); Ancestry (includes multiple ancestries): 37.9% German, 21.8% Irish, 9.7% English, 9.1% Italian, 6.6% American (2006-2010 5-year est.).
**Economy:** Single-family building permits issued: 2 (2011); Multi-family building permits issued: 0 (2011); Employment by occupation: 8.7% management, 2.6% professional, 9.3% services, 13.8% sales, 2.0% farming, 11.4% construction, 4.5% production (2006-2010 5-year est.).
**Income:** Per capita income: $28,349 (2006-2010 5-year est.); Median household income: $53,598 (2006-2010 5-year est.); Average household income: $66,185 (2006-2010 5-year est.); Percent of households with income of $100,000 or more: 15.4% (2006-2010 5-year est.); Poverty rate: 15.3% (2006-2010 5-year est.).
**Education:** Percent of population age 25 and over with: High school diploma (including GED) or higher: 90.1% (2006-2010 5-year est.); Bachelor's degree or higher: 26.6% (2006-2010 5-year est.); Master's degree or higher: 9.4% (2006-2010 5-year est.).
**Housing:** Homeownership rate: 75.3% (2010); Median home value: $170,500 (2006-2010 5-year est.); Median contract rent: $613 per month (2006-2010 5-year est.); Median year structure built: 1957 (2006-2010 5-year est.).
**Transportation:** Commute to work: 88.5% car, 1.6% public transportation, 4.8% walk, 5.1% work from home (2006-2010 5-year est.); Travel time to work: 33.3% less than 15 minutes, 26.3% 15 to 30 minutes, 18.5% 30 to 45 minutes, 9.1% 45 to 60 minutes, 12.8% 60 minutes or more (2006-2010 5-year est.)

**ELDRED** (unincorporated postal area)
Zip Code: 12732
Covers a land area of 25.066 square miles and a water area of 0.759 square miles. Located at 41.55° N. Lat; 74.87° W. Long. Elevation is 971 feet. Population: 786 (2010); Density: 31.4 persons per square mile (2010); Race: 94.8% White, 1.8% Black, 0.5% Asian, 0.3% American Indian/Alaska Native, 0.0% Native Hawaiian/Other Pacific Islander, 2.6% Other, 4.5% Hispanic of any race (2010); Average household size: 2.16 (2010); Median age: 48.6 (2010); Males per 100 females: 91.2 (2010); Homeownership rate: 82.1% (2010)

**FALLSBURG** (town). Aka Fallsburgh. Covers a land area of 77.621 square miles and a water area of 1.488 square miles. Located at 41.73° N. Lat; 74.60° W. Long. Elevation is 1,204 feet.
**Population:** 11,445 (1990); 12,234 (2000); 12,870 (2010); Density: 165.8 persons per square mile (2010); Race: 72.9% White, 14.4% Black, 1.5% Asian, 0.6% American Indian/Alaska Native, 0.1% Native Hawaiian/Other Pacific Islander, 10.5% Other, 21.9% Hispanic of any race (2010); Average household size: 2.65 (2010); Median age: 37.1 (2010); Males per 100 females: 124.0 (2010); Marriage status: 40.1% never married, 44.1% now married, 4.4% widowed, 11.4% divorced (2006-2010 5-year est.); Foreign born: 15.6% (2006-2010 5-year est.); Ancestry (includes multiple ancestries): 14.7% Irish, 10.8% German, 7.9% Italian, 7.2% English, 5.7% Polish (2006-2010 5-year est.).
**Economy:** Single-family building permits issued: 71 (2011); Multi-family building permits issued: 0 (2011); Employment by occupation: 13.3% management, 3.9% professional, 12.1% services, 18.0% sales, 3.6% farming, 10.5% construction, 6.2% production (2006-2010 5-year est.).
**Income:** Per capita income: $16,614 (2006-2010 5-year est.); Median household income: $43,009 (2006-2010 5-year est.); Average household income: $53,182 (2006-2010 5-year est.); Percent of households with income of $100,000 or more: 12.9% (2006-2010 5-year est.); Poverty rate: 22.7% (2006-2010 5-year est.).
**Education:** Percent of population age 25 and over with: High school diploma (including GED) or higher: 77.6% (2006-2010 5-year est.); Bachelor's degree or higher: 19.6% (2006-2010 5-year est.); Master's degree or higher: 7.5% (2006-2010 5-year est.).
**School District(s)**
Fallsburg Central School District (PK-12)
2009-10 Enrollment: 1,389 . . . . . . . . . . . . . . . . (845) 434-5884
**Housing:** Homeownership rate: 56.5% (2010); Median home value: $155,000 (2006-2010 5-year est.); Median contract rent: $677 per month (2006-2010 5-year est.); Median year structure built: 1976 (2006-2010 5-year est.).

**Safety:** Violent crime rate: 24.4 per 10,000 population; Property crime rate: 168.5 per 10,000 population (2010).
**Transportation:** Commute to work: 72.2% car, 1.9% public transportation, 10.1% walk, 13.0% work from home (2006-2010 5-year est.); Travel time to work: 44.5% less than 15 minutes, 34.0% 15 to 30 minutes, 10.7% 30 to 45 minutes, 2.4% 45 to 60 minutes, 8.3% 60 minutes or more (2006-2010 5-year est.)

## FERNDALE (unincorporated postal area)
Zip Code: 12734

Covers a land area of 13.771 square miles and a water area of 0.036 square miles. Located at 41.73° N. Lat; 74.75° W. Long. Elevation is 1,345 feet. Population: 867 (2010); Density: 63.0 persons per square mile (2010); Race: 84.0% White, 3.0% Black, 1.4% Asian, 0.5% American Indian/Alaska Native, 0.0% Native Hawaiian/Other Pacific Islander, 11.1% Other, 23.6% Hispanic of any race (2010); Average household size: 2.48 (2010); Median age: 42.4 (2010); Males per 100 females: 114.1 (2010); Homeownership rate: 65.2% (2010)

## FORESTBURGH (town). Covers a land area of 54.780 square miles and a water area of 1.531 square miles. Located at 41.56° N. Lat; 74.70° W. Long.
**Population:** 624 (1990); 833 (2000); 819 (2010); Density: 15.0 persons per square mile (2010); Race: 90.5% White, 4.4% Black, 0.9% Asian, 0.4% American Indian/Alaska Native, 0.2% Native Hawaiian/Other Pacific Islander, 3.6% Other, 4.4% Hispanic of any race (2010); Average household size: 2.27 (2010); Median age: 49.4 (2010); Males per 100 females: 99.3 (2010); Marriage status: 24.1% never married, 59.8% now married, 7.6% widowed, 8.5% divorced (2006-2010 5-year est.); Foreign born: 4.5% (2006-2010 5-year est.); Ancestry (includes multiple ancestries): 30.4% Irish, 22.4% German, 13.2% Italian, 7.8% English, 6.8% Polish (2006-2010 5-year est.).
**Economy:** Single-family building permits issued: 0 (2011); Multi-family building permits issued: 0 (2011); Employment by occupation: 15.8% management, 2.4% professional, 4.9% services, 15.8% sales, 7.1% farming, 9.9% construction, 3.0% production (2006-2010 5-year est.).
**Income:** Per capita income: $44,186 (2006-2010 5-year est.); Median household income: $66,042 (2006-2010 5-year est.); Average household income: $98,040 (2006-2010 5-year est.); Percent of households with income of $100,000 or more: 28.9% (2006-2010 5-year est.); Poverty rate: 8.6% (2006-2010 5-year est.).
**Education:** Percent of population age 25 and over with: High school diploma (including GED) or higher: 95.0% (2006-2010 5-year est.); Bachelor's degree or higher: 36.2% (2006-2010 5-year est.); Master's degree or higher: 21.1% (2006-2010 5-year est.).
**Housing:** Homeownership rate: 82.5% (2010); Median home value: $190,400 (2006-2010 5-year est.); Median contract rent: $736 per month (2006-2010 5-year est.); Median year structure built: 1968 (2006-2010 5-year est.).
**Transportation:** Commute to work: 93.0% car, 1.4% public transportation, 0.0% walk, 4.8% work from home (2006-2010 5-year est.); Travel time to work: 28.2% less than 15 minutes, 36.0% 15 to 30 minutes, 22.2% 30 to 45 minutes, 9.1% 45 to 60 minutes, 4.5% 60 minutes or more (2006-2010 5-year est.)

## FREMONT (town). Covers a land area of 50.185 square miles and a water area of 1.045 square miles. Located at 41.87° N. Lat; 75.03° W. Long.
**Population:** 1,332 (1990); 1,391 (2000); 1,381 (2010); Density: 27.5 persons per square mile (2010); Race: 93.7% White, 2.3% Black, 0.9% Asian, 0.1% American Indian/Alaska Native, 0.2% Native Hawaiian/Other Pacific Islander, 2.8% Other, 3.5% Hispanic of any race (2010); Average household size: 2.24 (2010); Median age: 46.7 (2010); Males per 100 females: 106.4 (2010); Marriage status: 22.3% never married, 53.2% now married, 12.2% widowed, 12.3% divorced (2006-2010 5-year est.); Foreign born: 3.6% (2006-2010 5-year est.); Ancestry (includes multiple ancestries): 30.5% German, 23.4% Irish, 18.7% English, 17.1% Italian, 5.5% Polish (2006-2010 5-year est.).
**Economy:** Single-family building permits issued: 6 (2011); Multi-family building permits issued: 0 (2011); Employment by occupation: 16.1% management, 1.7% professional, 10.1% services, 9.9% sales, 2.4% farming, 11.4% construction, 3.1% production (2006-2010 5-year est.).
**Income:** Per capita income: $32,205 (2006-2010 5-year est.); Median household income: $59,650 (2006-2010 5-year est.); Average household income: $68,641 (2006-2010 5-year est.); Percent of households with

income of $100,000 or more: 18.0% (2006-2010 5-year est.); Poverty rate: 7.8% (2006-2010 5-year est.).
**Education:** Percent of population age 25 and over with: High school diploma (including GED) or higher: 88.3% (2006-2010 5-year est.); Bachelor's degree or higher: 21.2% (2006-2010 5-year est.); Master's degree or higher: 10.3% (2006-2010 5-year est.).
**Housing:** Homeownership rate: 79.4% (2010); Median home value: $180,200 (2006-2010 5-year est.); Median contract rent: $550 per month (2006-2010 5-year est.); Median year structure built: 1963 (2006-2010 5-year est.).
**Transportation:** Commute to work: 89.2% car, 1.5% public transportation, 1.9% walk, 6.9% work from home (2006-2010 5-year est.); Travel time to work: 19.9% less than 15 minutes, 32.7% 15 to 30 minutes, 25.3% 30 to 45 minutes, 14.7% 45 to 60 minutes, 7.4% 60 minutes or more (2006-2010 5-year est.)

## FREMONT CENTER (unincorporated postal area)
Zip Code: 12736

Covers a land area of 6.086 square miles and a water area of <.001 square miles. Located at 41.85° N. Lat; 75.02° W. Long. Elevation is 1,240 feet. Population: 118 (2010); Density: 19.4 persons per square mile (2010); Race: 95.8% White, 0.0% Black, 1.7% Asian, 0.8% American Indian/Alaska Native, 0.0% Native Hawaiian/Other Pacific Islander, 1.7% Other, 6.8% Hispanic of any race (2010); Average household size: 2.23 (2010); Median age: 57.0 (2010); Males per 100 females: 114.5 (2010); Homeownership rate: 88.7% (2010)

## GLEN SPEY (unincorporated postal area)
Zip Code: 12737

Covers a land area of 35.800 square miles and a water area of 2.321 square miles. Located at 41.50° N. Lat; 74.79° W. Long. Elevation is 1,283 feet. Population: 1,910 (2010); Density: 53.4 persons per square mile (2010); Race: 94.1% White, 1.4% Black, 1.0% Asian, 0.1% American Indian/Alaska Native, 0.0% Native Hawaiian/Other Pacific Islander, 3.4% Other, 5.1% Hispanic of any race (2010); Average household size: 2.55 (2010); Median age: 41.9 (2010); Males per 100 females: 101.7 (2010); Homeownership rate: 83.4% (2010)

## GLEN WILD (unincorporated postal area)
Zip Code: 12738

Covers a land area of 6.559 square miles and a water area of 0.047 square miles. Located at 41.67° N. Lat; 74.58° W. Long. Elevation is 1,322 feet. Population: 320 (2010); Density: 48.8 persons per square mile (2010); Race: 85.9% White, 4.4% Black, 0.9% Asian, 2.2% American Indian/Alaska Native, 0.0% Native Hawaiian/Other Pacific Islander, 6.6% Other, 9.7% Hispanic of any race (2010); Average household size: 2.37 (2010); Median age: 43.4 (2010); Males per 100 females: 93.9 (2010); Homeownership rate: 74.0% (2010)

## GRAHAMSVILLE (unincorporated postal area)
Zip Code: 12740

Covers a land area of 74.354 square miles and a water area of 1.050 square miles. Located at 41.93° N. Lat; 74.43° W. Long. Elevation is 968 feet. Population: 1,886 (2010); Density: 25.4 persons per square mile (2010); Race: 94.8% White, 1.5% Black, 0.4% Asian, 0.2% American Indian/Alaska Native, 0.0% Native Hawaiian/Other Pacific Islander, 3.1% Other, 3.8% Hispanic of any race (2010); Average household size: 2.35 (2010); Median age: 46.6 (2010); Males per 100 females: 98.5 (2010); Homeownership rate: 77.9% (2010)

## HANKINS (unincorporated postal area)
Zip Code: 12741

Covers a land area of 8.248 square miles and a water area of 0.122 square miles. Located at 41.83° N. Lat; 75.07° W. Long. Elevation is 807 feet. Population: 351 (2010); Density: 42.6 persons per square mile (2010); Race: 94.3% White, 2.3% Black, 0.0% Asian, 0.3% American Indian/Alaska Native, 0.0% Native Hawaiian/Other Pacific Islander, 3.1% Other, 3.1% Hispanic of any race (2010); Average household size: 2.24 (2010); Median age: 40.9 (2010); Males per 100 females: 104.1 (2010); Homeownership rate: 66.9% (2010)

## HARRIS (unincorporated postal area)
Zip Code: 12742

Covers a land area of 2.150 square miles and a water area of 0.008 square miles. Located at 41.72° N. Lat; 74.72° W. Long. Elevation is

1,181 feet. Population: 181 (2010); Density: 84.2 persons per square mile (2010); Race: 81.8% White, 11.0% Black, 0.6% Asian, 0.0% American Indian/Alaska Native, 0.0% Native Hawaiian/Other Pacific Islander, 6.6% Other, 17.7% Hispanic of any race (2010); Average household size: 2.29 (2010); Median age: 42.9 (2010); Males per 100 females: 101.1 (2010); Homeownership rate: 59.5% (2010)

## HIGHLAND (town).
Covers a land area of 50.056 square miles and a water area of 1.866 square miles. Located at 41.56° N. Lat; 74.88° W. Long.

**Population:** 2,147 (1990); 2,404 (2000); 2,530 (2010); Density: 50.5 persons per square mile (2010); Race: 91.2% White, 3.6% Black, 0.9% Asian, 0.0% American Indian/Alaska Native, 0.0% Native Hawaiian/Other Pacific Islander, 4.3% Other, 5.8% Hispanic of any race (2010); Average household size: 2.29 (2010); Median age: 45.4 (2010); Males per 100 females: 102.4 (2010); Marriage status: 31.2% never married, 47.9% now married, 5.5% widowed, 15.3% divorced (2006-2010 5-year est.); Foreign born: 4.6% (2006-2010 5-year est.); Ancestry (includes multiple ancestries): 31.1% German, 29.6% Irish, 11.7% Italian, 9.8% English, 6.5% Dutch (2006-2010 5-year est.).
**Economy:** Single-family building permits issued: 5 (2011); Multi-family building permits issued: 0 (2011); Employment by occupation: 3.6% management, 2.2% professional, 13.8% services, 14.5% sales, 3.0% farming, 23.6% construction, 8.5% production (2006-2010 5-year est.).
**Income:** Per capita income: $27,241 (2006-2010 5-year est.); Median household income: $51,523 (2006-2010 5-year est.); Average household income: $69,302 (2006-2010 5-year est.); Percent of households with income of $100,000 or more: 18.7% (2006-2010 5-year est.); Poverty rate: 17.2% (2006-2010 5-year est.).
**Education:** Percent of population age 25 and over with: High school diploma (including GED) or higher: 74.5% (2006-2010 5-year est.); Bachelor's degree or higher: 21.1% (2006-2010 5-year est.); Master's degree or higher: 7.0% (2006-2010 5-year est.).
**Housing:** Homeownership rate: 77.9% (2010); Median home value: $187,700 (2006-2010 5-year est.); Median contract rent: $704 per month (2006-2010 5-year est.); Median year structure built: 1966 (2006-2010 5-year est.).
**Transportation:** Commute to work: 86.6% car, 3.8% public transportation, 5.0% walk, 3.4% work from home (2006-2010 5-year est.); Travel time to work: 26.2% less than 15 minutes, 18.3% 15 to 30 minutes, 29.1% 30 to 45 minutes, 6.6% 45 to 60 minutes, 19.7% 60 minutes or more (2006-2010 5-year est.).

## HIGHLAND LAKE (unincorporated postal area)
Zip Code: 12743

Covers a land area of 8.192 square miles and a water area of 0.623 square miles. Located at 41.54° N. Lat; 74.83° W. Long. Elevation is 1,332 feet. Population: 389 (2010); Density: 47.5 persons per square mile (2010); Race: 94.3% White, 1.0% Black, 1.0% Asian, 0.0% American Indian/Alaska Native, 0.0% Native Hawaiian/Other Pacific Islander, 3.7% Other, 2.8% Hispanic of any race (2010); Average household size: 2.34 (2010); Median age: 45.1 (2010); Males per 100 females: 103.7 (2010); Homeownership rate: 72.9% (2010)

## HORTONVILLE (CDP).
Covers a land area of 0.755 square miles and a water area of 0 square miles. Located at 41.76° N. Lat; 75.02° W. Long. Elevation is 804 feet.

**Population:** n/a (1990); n/a (2000); 218 (2010); Density: 288.4 persons per square mile (2010); Race: 98.2% White, 1.8% Black, 0.0% Asian, 0.0% American Indian/Alaska Native, 0.0% Native Hawaiian/Other Pacific Islander, 0.0% Other, 3.2% Hispanic of any race (2010); Average household size: 2.37 (2010); Median age: 42.2 (2010); Males per 100 females: 96.4 (2010); Marriage status: 0.0% never married, 87.9% now married, 12.1% widowed, 0.0% divorced (2006-2010 5-year est.); Foreign born: 8.6% (2006-2010 5-year est.); Ancestry (includes multiple ancestries): 47.9% German, 24.3% American, 17.8% Irish, 15.7% French, 15.1% English (2006-2010 5-year est.).
**Economy:** Employment by occupation: 15.9% management, 9.7% professional, 10.3% services, 11.7% sales, 0.0% farming, 0.0% construction, 0.0% production (2006-2010 5-year est.).
**Income:** Per capita income: $27,076 (2006-2010 5-year est.); Median household income: $62,917 (2006-2010 5-year est.); Average household income: $63,286 (2006-2010 5-year est.); Percent of households with income of $100,000 or more: 13.7% (2006-2010 5-year est.); Poverty rate: 0.0% (2006-2010 5-year est.).

**Education:** Percent of population age 25 and over with: High school diploma (including GED) or higher: 100.0% (2006-2010 5-year est.); Bachelor's degree or higher: 36.4% (2006-2010 5-year est.); Master's degree or higher: 25.8% (2006-2010 5-year est.).
**Housing:** Homeownership rate: 62.0% (2010); Median home value: $168,800 (2006-2010 5-year est.); Median contract rent: $661 per month (2006-2010 5-year est.); Median year structure built: 1951 (2006-2010 5-year est.).
**Transportation:** Commute to work: 86.2% car, 0.0% public transportation, 0.0% walk, 13.8% work from home (2006-2010 5-year est.); Travel time to work: 45.6% less than 15 minutes, 14.4% 15 to 30 minutes, 28.0% 30 to 45 minutes, 0.0% 45 to 60 minutes, 12.0% 60 minutes or more (2006-2010 5-year est.)

## HURLEYVILLE (unincorporated postal area)
Zip Code: 12747

Covers a land area of 13.953 square miles and a water area of 0.451 square miles. Located at 41.75° N. Lat; 74.69° W. Long. Elevation is 1,319 feet. Population: 1,714 (2010); Density: 122.8 persons per square mile (2010); Race: 84.4% White, 6.8% Black, 1.6% Asian, 1.0% American Indian/Alaska Native, 0.1% Native Hawaiian/Other Pacific Islander, 6.1% Other, 14.4% Hispanic of any race (2010); Average household size: 2.62 (2010); Median age: 40.7 (2010); Males per 100 females: 95.7 (2010); Homeownership rate: 65.5% (2010)

## JEFFERSONVILLE (village).
Covers a land area of 0.405 square miles and a water area of 0.032 square miles. Located at 41.77° N. Lat; 74.92° W. Long. Elevation is 1,050 feet.

**Population:** 484 (1990); 420 (2000); 359 (2010); Density: 885.4 persons per square mile (2010); Race: 85.0% White, 3.3% Black, 4.7% Asian, 0.0% American Indian/Alaska Native, 0.0% Native Hawaiian/Other Pacific Islander, 7.0% Other, 11.1% Hispanic of any race (2010); Average household size: 2.11 (2010); Median age: 48.3 (2010); Males per 100 females: 106.3 (2010); Marriage status: 20.4% never married, 58.1% now married, 19.6% widowed, 1.9% divorced (2006-2010 5-year est.); Foreign born: 5.0% (2006-2010 5-year est.); Ancestry (includes multiple ancestries): 52.2% German, 26.4% Irish, 11.8% Italian, 9.6% Swiss, 9.0% English (2006-2010 5-year est.).
**Economy:** Single-family building permits issued: 0 (2011); Multi-family building permits issued: 0 (2011); Employment by occupation: 17.0% management, 4.1% professional, 8.2% services, 7.5% sales, 8.2% farming, 10.9% construction, 2.0% production (2006-2010 5-year est.).
**Income:** Per capita income: $24,453 (2006-2010 5-year est.); Median household income: $57,188 (2006-2010 5-year est.); Average household income: $55,441 (2006-2010 5-year est.); Percent of households with income of $100,000 or more: 10.9% (2006-2010 5-year est.); Poverty rate: 10.6% (2006-2010 5-year est.).
**Education:** Percent of population age 25 and over with: High school diploma (including GED) or higher: 90.9% (2006-2010 5-year est.); Bachelor's degree or higher: 26.7% (2006-2010 5-year est.); Master's degree or higher: 14.2% (2006-2010 5-year est.).
**School District(s)**
Sullivan West Central School District (PK-12)
    2009-10 Enrollment: 1,354 ..................... (845) 482-4610
**Housing:** Homeownership rate: 61.2% (2010); Median home value: $161,800 (2006-2010 5-year est.); Median contract rent: $621 per month (2006-2010 5-year est.); Median year structure built: before 1940 (2006-2010 5-year est.).
**Transportation:** Commute to work: 89.6% car, 0.0% public transportation, 6.9% walk, 3.5% work from home (2006-2010 5-year est.); Travel time to work: 31.7% less than 15 minutes, 41.7% 15 to 30 minutes, 23.7% 30 to 45 minutes, 0.0% 45 to 60 minutes, 2.9% 60 minutes or more (2006-2010 5-year est.)
**Additional Information Contacts**
Jeffersonville Area Chamber of Commerce ............. (845) 482-5688
    http://jeffersonvilleny.com

## KAUNEONGA LAKE (unincorporated postal area)
Zip Code: 12749

Covers a land area of 2.941 square miles and a water area of 0.025 square miles. Located at 41.69° N. Lat; 74.84° W. Long. Elevation is 1,348 feet. Population: 300 (2010); Density: 102.0 persons per square mile (2010); Race: 90.7% White, 3.0% Black, 1.7% Asian, 0.0% American Indian/Alaska Native, 0.0% Native Hawaiian/Other Pacific Islander, 4.6% Other, 8.3% Hispanic of any race (2010); Average household size: 2.07 (2010); Median age: 51.0 (2010); Males per 100 females: 106.9 (2010); Homeownership rate: 60.7% (2010)

## KENOZA LAKE (unincorporated postal area)
Zip Code: 12750

Covers a land area of 4.254 square miles and a water area of 0.220 square miles. Located at 41.72° N. Lat; 74.96° W. Long. Elevation is 1,060 feet. Population: 187 (2010); Density: 44.0 persons per square mile (2010); Race: 97.3% White, 0.0% Black, 0.5% Asian, 0.0% American Indian/Alaska Native, 0.0% Native Hawaiian/Other Pacific Islander, 2.2% Other, 1.6% Hispanic of any race (2010); Average household size: 2.49 (2010); Median age: 44.4 (2010); Males per 100 females: 88.9 (2010); Homeownership rate: 80.0% (2010)

## KIAMESHA LAKE (unincorporated postal area)
Zip Code: 12751

Covers a land area of 3.417 square miles and a water area of 0.464 square miles. Located at 41.69° N. Lat; 74.66° W. Long. Elevation is 1,417 feet. Population: 1,054 (2010); Density: 308.4 persons per square mile (2010); Race: 82.0% White, 8.9% Black, 0.4% Asian, 0.8% American Indian/Alaska Native, 0.1% Native Hawaiian/Other Pacific Islander, 7.8% Other, 12.3% Hispanic of any race (2010); Average household size: 3.30 (2010); Median age: 23.3 (2010); Males per 100 females: 98.5 (2010); Homeownership rate: 46.6% (2010)

## LAKE HUNTINGTON (unincorporated postal area)
Zip Code: 12752

Covers a land area of 1.732 square miles and a water area of 0.141 square miles. Located at 41.68° N. Lat; 74.99° W. Long. Elevation is 1,217 feet. Population: 242 (2010); Density: 139.7 persons per square mile (2010); Race: 98.3% White, 0.8% Black, 0.4% Asian, 0.0% American Indian/Alaska Native, 0.0% Native Hawaiian/Other Pacific Islander, 0.5% Other, 3.7% Hispanic of any race (2010); Average household size: 2.02 (2010); Median age: 49.8 (2010); Males per 100 females: 112.3 (2010); Homeownership rate: 67.5% (2010)

## LIBERTY (village). Covers a land area of 2.602 square miles and a water area of 0.003 square miles. Located at 41.79° N. Lat; 74.74° W. Long. Elevation is 1,506 feet.
Population: 4,211 (1990); 3,975 (2000); 4,392 (2010); Density: 1,687.7 persons per square mile (2010); Race: 66.5% White, 14.9% Black, 1.8% Asian, 0.8% American Indian/Alaska Native, 0.0% Native Hawaiian/Other Pacific Islander, 16.0% Other, 25.1% Hispanic of any race (2010); Average household size: 2.40 (2010); Median age: 37.7 (2010); Males per 100 females: 93.4 (2010); Marriage status: 40.9% never married, 35.1% now married, 11.7% widowed, 12.4% divorced (2006-2010 5-year est.); Foreign born: 10.1% (2006-2010 5-year est.); Ancestry (includes multiple ancestries): 21.9% Irish, 18.0% German, 9.0% Italian, 7.7% Polish, 5.6% English (2006-2010 5-year est.).
Economy: Single-family building permits issued: 0 (2011); Multi-family building permits issued: 0 (2011); Employment by occupation: 4.7% management, 1.9% professional, 12.8% services, 19.5% sales, 0.6% farming, 15.8% construction, 7.9% production (2006-2010 5-year est.).
Income: Per capita income: $17,231 (2006-2010 5-year est.); Median household income: $23,423 (2006-2010 5-year est.); Average household income: $43,714 (2006-2010 5-year est.); Percent of households with income of $100,000 or more: 8.2% (2006-2010 5-year est.); Poverty rate: 21.5% (2006-2010 5-year est.).
Education: Percent of population age 25 and over with: High school diploma (including GED) or higher: 76.3% (2006-2010 5-year est.); Bachelor's degree or higher: 15.2% (2006-2010 5-year est.); Master's degree or higher: 5.9% (2006-2010 5-year est.).
### School District(s)
Liberty Central School District (PK-12)
   2009-10 Enrollment: 1,541 . . . . . . . . . . . . . . . . . . . . . . . (845) 292-6990
Sullivan Boces
   2009-10 Enrollment: n/a . . . . . . . . . . . . . . . . . . . . . . . (845) 295-4016
### Vocational/Technical School(s)
Sullivan County BOCES-Practical Nursing Program (Public)
   Fall 2010 Enrollment: 78 . . . . . . . . . . . . . . . . . . . . (845) 295-4136
   2011-12 Tuition: $7,980
Housing: Homeownership rate: 37.6% (2010); Median home value: $139,700 (2006-2010 5-year est.); Median contract rent: $623 per month (2006-2010 5-year est.); Median year structure built: 1954 (2006-2010 5-year est.).

**Safety:** Violent crime rate: 52.6 per 10,000 population; Property crime rate: 457.4 per 10,000 population (2010).
**Newspapers:** Catskill Shopper (Community news; Circulation 40,000)
**Transportation:** Commute to work: 76.7% car, 1.2% public transportation, 11.2% walk, 10.9% work from home (2006-2010 5-year est.); Travel time to work: 40.1% less than 15 minutes, 36.9% 15 to 30 minutes, 13.4% 30 to 45 minutes, 4.5% 45 to 60 minutes, 5.0% 60 minutes or more (2006-2010 5-year est.)
**Additional Information Contacts**
Sullivan County Chamber of Commerce . . . . . . . . . . . . . (845) 791-4200
  http://www.catskills.com

## LIBERTY (town). Covers a land area of 79.579 square miles and a water area of 1.157 square miles. Located at 41.81° N. Lat; 74.77° W. Long. Elevation is 1,506 feet.
History: Settled 1793, incorporated 1870.
Population: 9,825 (1990); 9,632 (2000); 9,885 (2010); Density: 124.2 persons per square mile (2010); Race: 77.8% White, 9.3% Black, 1.5% Asian, 0.6% American Indian/Alaska Native, 0.0% Native Hawaiian/Other Pacific Islander, 10.8% Other, 18.8% Hispanic of any race (2010); Average household size: 2.43 (2010); Median age: 41.7 (2010); Males per 100 females: 99.0 (2010); Marriage status: 31.8% never married, 45.8% now married, 10.4% widowed, 12.0% divorced (2006-2010 5-year est.); Foreign born: 8.9% (2006-2010 5-year est.); Ancestry (includes multiple ancestries): 19.5% German, 19.4% Irish, 13.9% Italian, 9.3% English, 5.2% Polish (2006-2010 5-year est.).
Economy: Single-family building permits issued: 4 (2011); Multi-family building permits issued: 0 (2011); Employment by occupation: 11.2% management, 1.2% professional, 10.8% services, 16.7% sales, 3.0% farming, 13.7% construction, 6.2% production (2006-2010 5-year est.).
Income: Per capita income: $22,037 (2006-2010 5-year est.); Median household income: $37,743 (2006-2010 5-year est.); Average household income: $56,014 (2006-2010 5-year est.); Percent of households with income of $100,000 or more: 14.2% (2006-2010 5-year est.); Poverty rate: 19.8% (2006-2010 5-year est.).
Education: Percent of population age 25 and over with: High school diploma (including GED) or higher: 80.1% (2006-2010 5-year est.); Bachelor's degree or higher: 16.7% (2006-2010 5-year est.); Master's degree or higher: 8.6% (2006-2010 5-year est.).
### School District(s)
Liberty Central School District (PK-12)
   2009-10 Enrollment: 1,541 . . . . . . . . . . . . . . . . . . . . . . . (845) 292-6990
Sullivan Boces
   2009-10 Enrollment: n/a . . . . . . . . . . . . . . . . . . . . . . . (845) 295-4016
### Vocational/Technical School(s)
Sullivan County BOCES-Practical Nursing Program (Public)
   Fall 2010 Enrollment: 78 . . . . . . . . . . . . . . . . . . . . (845) 295-4136
   2011-12 Tuition: $7,980
Housing: Homeownership rate: 56.1% (2010); Median home value: $165,300 (2006-2010 5-year est.); Median contract rent: $620 per month (2006-2010 5-year est.); Median year structure built: 1961 (2006-2010 5-year est.).
Newspapers: Catskill Shopper (Community news; Circulation 40,000)
Transportation: Commute to work: 86.2% car, 0.6% public transportation, 5.2% walk, 6.9% work from home (2006-2010 5-year est.); Travel time to work: 36.2% less than 15 minutes, 42.7% 15 to 30 minutes, 12.1% 30 to 45 minutes, 3.5% 45 to 60 minutes, 5.4% 60 minutes or more (2006-2010 5-year est.)
**Additional Information Contacts**
Town of Liberty . . . . . . . . . . . . . . . . . . . . . . . . . . . . (845) 292-5110
  http://www.townofliberty.org

## LIVINGSTON MANOR (CDP). Covers a land area of 3.080 square miles and a water area of 0.011 square miles. Located at 41.88° N. Lat; 74.82° W. Long. Elevation is 1,401 feet.
Population: 1,482 (1990); 1,355 (2000); 1,221 (2010); Density: 396.3 persons per square mile (2010); Race: 88.4% White, 5.0% Black, 1.5% Asian, 0.7% American Indian/Alaska Native, 0.0% Native Hawaiian/Other Pacific Islander, 4.4% Other, 10.3% Hispanic of any race (2010); Average household size: 2.38 (2010); Median age: 41.2 (2010); Males per 100 females: 96.6 (2010); Marriage status: 33.0% never married, 45.7% now married, 8.9% widowed, 12.4% divorced (2006-2010 5-year est.); Foreign born: 9.0% (2006-2010 5-year est.); Ancestry (includes multiple ancestries): 24.1% Italian, 19.0% German, 17.2% American, 16.5% Irish, 9.7% English (2006-2010 5-year est.).

**Economy:** Employment by occupation: 16.8% management, 0.0% professional, 23.5% services, 9.4% sales, 3.5% farming, 7.2% construction, 0.0% production (2006-2010 5-year est.).
**Income:** Per capita income: $23,214 (2006-2010 5-year est.); Median household income: $33,306 (2006-2010 5-year est.); Average household income: $50,282 (2006-2010 5-year est.); Percent of households with income of $100,000 or more: 8.1% (2006-2010 5-year est.); Poverty rate: 22.2% (2006-2010 5-year est.).
**Education:** Percent of population age 25 and over with: High school diploma (including GED) or higher: 77.4% (2006-2010 5-year est.); Bachelor's degree or higher: 21.9% (2006-2010 5-year est.); Master's degree or higher: 5.7% (2006-2010 5-year est.).

**School District(s)**
Livingston Manor Central School District (PK-12)
    2009-10 Enrollment: 559 . . . . . . . . . . . . . . . . . (845) 439-4400
**Housing:** Homeownership rate: 54.5% (2010); Median home value: $162,500 (2006-2010 5-year est.); Median contract rent: $528 per month (2006-2010 5-year est.); Median year structure built: before 1940 (2006-2010 5-year est.).
**Transportation:** Commute to work: 71.2% car, 16.2% public transportation, 9.6% walk, 2.9% work from home (2006-2010 5-year est.); Travel time to work: 25.6% less than 15 minutes, 37.3% 15 to 30 minutes, 26.6% 30 to 45 minutes, 0.0% 45 to 60 minutes, 10.5% 60 minutes or more (2006-2010 5-year est.)

**LOCH SHELDRAKE** (unincorporated postal area)
Zip Code: 12759
    Covers a land area of 6.185 square miles and a water area of 0.221 square miles. Located at 41.78° N. Lat; 74.65° W. Long. Elevation is 1,457 feet. Population: 1,649 (2010); Density: 266.6 persons per square mile (2010); Race: 77.1% White, 11.6% Black, 2.5% Asian, 0.4% American Indian/Alaska Native, 0.0% Native Hawaiian/Other Pacific Islander, 8.4% Other, 16.3% Hispanic of any race (2010); Average household size: 2.74 (2010); Median age: 32.8 (2010); Males per 100 females: 96.8 (2010); Homeownership rate: 63.8% (2010).

**LONG EDDY** (unincorporated postal area)
Zip Code: 12760
    Covers a land area of 42.315 square miles and a water area of 0.403 square miles. Located at 41.90° N. Lat; 75.10° W. Long. Elevation is 846 feet. Population: 482 (2010); Density: 11.4 persons per square mile (2010); Race: 95.2% White, 2.1% Black, 0.8% Asian, 0.0% American Indian/Alaska Native, 0.0% Native Hawaiian/Other Pacific Islander, 1.9% Other, 3.5% Hispanic of any race (2010); Average household size: 2.15 (2010); Median age: 48.8 (2010); Males per 100 females: 115.2 (2010); Homeownership rate: 83.0% (2010).

**LUMBERLAND** (town). Covers a land area of 46.538 square miles and a water area of 2.806 square miles. Located at 41.49° N. Lat; 74.81° W. Long.
**Population:** 1,425 (1990); 1,939 (2000); 2,468 (2010); Density: 53.0 persons per square mile (2010); Race: 94.4% White, 1.5% Black, 0.9% Asian, 0.2% American Indian/Alaska Native, 0.0% Native Hawaiian/Other Pacific Islander, 3.0% Other, 5.1% Hispanic of any race (2010); Average household size: 2.52 (2010); Median age: 42.9 (2010); Males per 100 females: 100.5 (2010); Marriage status: 19.0% never married, 71.5% now married, 5.4% widowed, 4.0% divorced (2006-2010 5-year est.); Foreign born: 8.7% (2006-2010 5-year est.); Ancestry (includes multiple ancestries): 27.6% Irish, 26.4% German, 12.9% Italian, 8.8% Polish, 7.2% American (2006-2010 5-year est.).
**Economy:** Single-family building permits issued: 5 (2011); Multi-family building permits issued: 0 (2011); Employment by occupation: 7.3% management, 2.6% professional, 7.2% services, 13.6% sales, 1.3% farming, 19.8% construction, 15.7% production (2006-2010 5-year est.).
**Income:** Per capita income: $24,095 (2006-2010 5-year est.); Median household income: $48,011 (2006-2010 5-year est.); Average household income: $62,473 (2006-2010 5-year est.); Percent of households with income of $100,000 or more: 20.6% (2006-2010 5-year est.); Poverty rate: 13.7% (2006-2010 5-year est.).
**Education:** Percent of population age 25 and over with: High school diploma (including GED) or higher: 86.5% (2006-2010 5-year est.); Bachelor's degree or higher: 19.4% (2006-2010 5-year est.); Master's degree or higher: 10.6% (2006-2010 5-year est.).
**Housing:** Homeownership rate: 84.0% (2010); Median home value: $214,900 (2006-2010 5-year est.); Median contract rent: $738 per month

(2006-2010 5-year est.); Median year structure built: 1968 (2006-2010 5-year est.).
**Transportation:** Commute to work: 89.9% car, 2.8% public transportation, 0.6% walk, 3.4% work from home (2006-2010 5-year est.); Travel time to work: 14.0% less than 15 minutes, 19.1% 15 to 30 minutes, 23.1% 30 to 45 minutes, 23.3% 45 to 60 minutes, 20.4% 60 minutes or more (2006-2010 5-year est.)

**MAMAKATING** (town). Covers a land area of 96.108 square miles and a water area of 2.560 square miles. Located at 41.58° N. Lat; 74.49° W. Long. Elevation is 577 feet.
**Population:** 9,782 (1990); 11,002 (2000); 12,085 (2010); Density: 125.7 persons per square mile (2010); Race: 90.8% White, 3.5% Black, 1.1% Asian, 0.5% American Indian/Alaska Native, 0.0% Native Hawaiian/Other Pacific Islander, 4.1% Other, 8.5% Hispanic of any race (2010); Average household size: 2.54 (2010); Median age: 40.9 (2010); Males per 100 females: 102.2 (2010); Marriage status: 27.0% never married, 53.9% now married, 5.6% widowed, 13.6% divorced (2006-2010 5-year est.); Foreign born: 5.3% (2006-2010 5-year est.); Ancestry (includes multiple ancestries): 29.1% Irish, 22.3% Italian, 19.5% German, 9.2% American, 7.3% English (2006-2010 5-year est.).
**Economy:** Single-family building permits issued: 15 (2011); Multi-family building permits issued: 0 (2011); Employment by occupation: 9.0% management, 2.0% professional, 10.6% services, 16.6% sales, 4.1% farming, 15.0% construction, 7.4% production (2006-2010 5-year est.).
**Income:** Per capita income: $28,333 (2006-2010 5-year est.); Median household income: $59,302 (2006-2010 5-year est.); Average household income: $71,042 (2006-2010 5-year est.); Percent of households with income of $100,000 or more: 20.2% (2006-2010 5-year est.); Poverty rate: 6.3% (2006-2010 5-year est.).
**Education:** Percent of population age 25 and over with: High school diploma (including GED) or higher: 87.5% (2006-2010 5-year est.); Bachelor's degree or higher: 19.4% (2006-2010 5-year est.); Master's degree or higher: 8.3% (2006-2010 5-year est.).
**Housing:** Homeownership rate: 77.2% (2010); Median home value: $226,400 (2006-2010 5-year est.); Median contract rent: $739 per month (2006-2010 5-year est.); Median year structure built: 1964 (2006-2010 5-year est.).
**Transportation:** Commute to work: 95.8% car, 0.9% public transportation, 1.5% walk, 1.8% work from home (2006-2010 5-year est.); Travel time to work: 12.9% less than 15 minutes, 40.3% 15 to 30 minutes, 22.3% 30 to 45 minutes, 7.1% 45 to 60 minutes, 17.4% 60 minutes or more (2006-2010 5-year est.)

**MONGAUP VALLEY** (unincorporated postal area)
Zip Code: 12762
    Covers a land area of 6.341 square miles and a water area of 0.490 square miles. Located at 41.66° N. Lat; 74.79° W. Long. Elevation is 1,112 feet. Population: 512 (2010); Density: 80.7 persons per square mile (2010); Race: 86.1% White, 2.0% Black, 0.8% Asian, 0.4% American Indian/Alaska Native, 0.0% Native Hawaiian/Other Pacific Islander, 10.7% Other, 16.8% Hispanic of any race (2010); Average household size: 2.71 (2010); Median age: 41.9 (2010); Males per 100 females: 101.6 (2010); Homeownership rate: 66.7% (2010)

**MONTICELLO** (village). County seat. Covers a land area of 3.984 square miles and a water area of 0.023 square miles. Located at 41.65° N. Lat; 74.68° W. Long. Elevation is 1,512 feet.
**History:** Incorporated 1830.
**Population:** 6,623 (1990); 6,512 (2000); 6,726 (2010); Density: 1,687.9 persons per square mile (2010); Race: 49.4% White, 32.1% Black, 2.4% Asian, 0.6% American Indian/Alaska Native, 0.0% Native Hawaiian/Other Pacific Islander, 15.5% Other, 29.9% Hispanic of any race (2010); Average household size: 2.38 (2010); Median age: 34.1 (2010); Males per 100 females: 97.1 (2010); Marriage status: 34.9% never married, 45.9% now married, 7.7% widowed, 11.5% divorced (2006-2010 5-year est.); Foreign born: 18.0% (2006-2010 5-year est.); Ancestry (includes multiple ancestries): 5.1% Irish, 4.8% German, 3.9% Italian, 3.8% American, 2.8% Polish (2006-2010 5-year est.).
**Economy:** Single-family building permits issued: 1 (2011); Multi-family building permits issued: 0 (2011); Employment by occupation: 6.1% management, 0.0% professional, 17.8% services, 23.5% sales, 1.7% farming, 5.1% construction, 2.7% production (2006-2010 5-year est.).
**Income:** Per capita income: $14,034 (2006-2010 5-year est.); Median household income: $26,879 (2006-2010 5-year est.); Average household

income: $35,848 (2006-2010 5-year est.); Percent of households with income of $100,000 or more: 4.0% (2006-2010 5-year est.); Poverty rate: 30.2% (2006-2010 5-year est.).

**Education:** Percent of population age 25 and over with: High school diploma (including GED) or higher: 79.6% (2006-2010 5-year est.); Bachelor's degree or higher: 11.2% (2006-2010 5-year est.); Master's degree or higher: 3.8% (2006-2010 5-year est.).

**School District(s)**

Monticello Central School District (KG-12)
    2009-10 Enrollment: 3,226 . . . . . . . . . . . . . . . (845) 794-7700

**Housing:** Homeownership rate: 27.3% (2010); Median home value: $125,800 (2006-2010 5-year est.); Median contract rent: $700 per month (2006-2010 5-year est.); Median year structure built: 1970 (2006-2010 5-year est.).

**Safety:** Violent crime rate: 94.6 per 10,000 population; Property crime rate: 269.2 per 10,000 population (2010).

**Transportation:** Commute to work: 83.3% car, 3.2% public transportation, 6.2% walk, 4.2% work from home (2006-2010 5-year est.); Travel time to work: 52.2% less than 15 minutes, 35.2% 15 to 30 minutes, 5.7% 30 to 45 minutes, 1.7% 45 to 60 minutes, 5.3% 60 minutes or more (2006-2010 5-year est.)

**Airports:** MMC (general aviation); Sullivan County International (general aviation)

**Additional Information Contacts**

Village of Monticello . . . . . . . . . . . . . . . . . . . . . (845) 794-6130
    http://www.villageofmonticello.com

**MOUNTAIN DALE** (unincorporated postal area)

Zip Code: 12763

Covers a land area of 14.268 square miles and a water area of 0.177 square miles. Located at 41.67° N. Lat; 74.52° W. Long. Elevation is 1,010 feet. Population: 942 (2010); Density: 66.0 persons per square mile (2010); Race: 89.9% White, 3.3% Black, 1.4% Asian, 0.6% American Indian/Alaska Native, 0.0% Native Hawaiian/Other Pacific Islander, 4.8% Other, 14.0% Hispanic of any race (2010); Average household size: 2.46 (2010); Median age: 44.4 (2010); Males per 100 females: 112.2 (2010); Homeownership rate: 78.7% (2010)

**NARROWSBURG** (CDP). Covers a land area of 1.366 square miles and a water area of 0.134 square miles. Located at 41.59° N. Lat; 75.05° W. Long. Elevation is 663 feet.

**Population:** 402 (1990); 414 (2000); 431 (2010); Density: 315.5 persons per square mile (2010); Race: 91.9% White, 1.6% Black, 2.6% Asian, 0.0% American Indian/Alaska Native, 0.0% Native Hawaiian/Other Pacific Islander, 3.9% Other, 4.2% Hispanic of any race (2010); Average household size: 2.27 (2010); Median age: 46.4 (2010); Males per 100 females: 109.2 (2010); Marriage status: 13.3% never married, 69.0% now married, 9.0% widowed, 8.7% divorced (2006-2010 5-year est.); Foreign born: 6.2% (2006-2010 5-year est.); Ancestry (includes multiple ancestries): 26.3% Irish, 24.3% German, 11.4% Italian, 8.3% English, 5.2% European (2006-2010 5-year est.).

**Economy:** Employment by occupation: 8.9% management, 0.0% professional, 6.5% services, 15.4% sales, 1.9% farming, 17.3% construction, 1.4% production (2006-2010 5-year est.).

**Income:** Per capita income: $24,696 (2006-2010 5-year est.); Median household income: $58,750 (2006-2010 5-year est.); Average household income: $62,004 (2006-2010 5-year est.); Percent of households with income of $100,000 or more: 11.9% (2006-2010 5-year est.); Poverty rate: 4.7% (2006-2010 5-year est.).

**Education:** Percent of population age 25 and over with: High school diploma (including GED) or higher: 88.8% (2006-2010 5-year est.); Bachelor's degree or higher: 37.1% (2006-2010 5-year est.); Master's degree or higher: 15.0% (2006-2010 5-year est.).

**Housing:** Homeownership rate: 78.5% (2010); Median home value: $174,300 (2006-2010 5-year est.); Median contract rent: $837 per month (2006-2010 5-year est.); Median year structure built: 1952 (2006-2010 5-year est.).

**Newspapers:** River Reporter (Local news; Circulation 3,700)

**Transportation:** Commute to work: 81.4% car, 4.9% public transportation, 0.0% walk, 12.3% work from home (2006-2010 5-year est.); Travel time to work: 11.2% less than 15 minutes, 46.9% 15 to 30 minutes, 31.8% 30 to 45 minutes, 3.9% 45 to 60 minutes, 6.1% 60 minutes or more (2006-2010 5-year est.)

**Additional Information Contacts**

Narrowsburg Chamber of Commerce . . . . . . . . . . . . . . (845) 252-7234
    http://www.narrowsburg.org

**NEVERSINK** (town). Covers a land area of 82.773 square miles and a water area of 3.490 square miles. Located at 41.86° N. Lat; 74.59° W. Long. Elevation is 1,634 feet.

**Population:** 2,951 (1990); 3,553 (2000); 3,557 (2010); Density: 43.0 persons per square mile (2010); Race: 95.6% White, 1.5% Black, 0.6% Asian, 0.3% American Indian/Alaska Native, 0.0% Native Hawaiian/Other Pacific Islander, 2.0% Other, 3.6% Hispanic of any race (2010); Average household size: 2.43 (2010); Median age: 44.8 (2010); Males per 100 females: 96.5 (2010); Marriage status: 23.4% never married, 63.0% now married, 2.6% widowed, 11.0% divorced (2006-2010 5-year est.); Foreign born: 3.0% (2006-2010 5-year est.); Ancestry (includes multiple ancestries): 30.5% German, 29.9% Irish, 12.9% English, 12.1% Italian, 7.7% Dutch (2006-2010 5-year est.).

**Economy:** Single-family building permits issued: 7 (2011); Multi-family building permits issued: 0 (2011); Employment by occupation: 14.2% management, 2.7% professional, 4.4% services, 16.7% sales, 0.6% farming, 17.8% construction, 8.6% production (2006-2010 5-year est.).

**Income:** Per capita income: $25,076 (2006-2010 5-year est.); Median household income: $50,795 (2006-2010 5-year est.); Average household income: $63,495 (2006-2010 5-year est.); Percent of households with income of $100,000 or more: 16.6% (2006-2010 5-year est.); Poverty rate: 13.0% (2006-2010 5-year est.).

**Education:** Percent of population age 25 and over with: High school diploma (including GED) or higher: 92.3% (2006-2010 5-year est.); Bachelor's degree or higher: 27.4% (2006-2010 5-year est.); Master's degree or higher: 9.3% (2006-2010 5-year est.).

**Housing:** Homeownership rate: 79.8% (2010); Median home value: $191,600 (2006-2010 5-year est.); Median contract rent: $667 per month (2006-2010 5-year est.); Median year structure built: 1975 (2006-2010 5-year est.).

**Transportation:** Commute to work: 88.7% car, 1.4% public transportation, 3.8% walk, 6.1% work from home (2006-2010 5-year est.); Travel time to work: 38.9% less than 15 minutes, 26.7% 15 to 30 minutes, 16.6% 30 to 45 minutes, 4.9% 45 to 60 minutes, 12.8% 60 minutes or more (2006-2010 5-year est.)

**NORTH BRANCH** (unincorporated postal area)

Zip Code: 12766

Covers a land area of 8.037 square miles and a water area of 0.005 square miles. Located at 41.81° N. Lat; 74.97° W. Long. Elevation is 1,037 feet. Population: 437 (2010); Density: 54.4 persons per square mile (2010); Race: 94.1% White, 1.6% Black, 2.7% Asian, 0.2% American Indian/Alaska Native, 0.0% Native Hawaiian/Other Pacific Islander, 1.4% Other, 1.6% Hispanic of any race (2010); Average household size: 2.44 (2010); Median age: 43.1 (2010); Males per 100 females: 98.6 (2010); Homeownership rate: 82.1% (2010)

**OBERNBURG** (unincorporated postal area)

Zip Code: 12767

Covers a land area of 2.956 square miles and a water area of 0.015 square miles. Located at 41.83° N. Lat; 74.99° W. Long. Elevation is 1,657 feet. Population: 126 (2010); Density: 42.6 persons per square mile (2010); Race: 99.2% White, 0.0% Black, 0.8% Asian, 0.0% American Indian/Alaska Native, 0.0% Native Hawaiian/Other Pacific Islander, 0.0% Other, 4.0% Hispanic of any race (2010); Average household size: 2.42 (2010); Median age: 40.7 (2010); Males per 100 females: 103.2 (2010); Homeownership rate: 77.0% (2010)

**PARKSVILLE** (unincorporated postal area)

Zip Code: 12768

Covers a land area of 34.839 square miles and a water area of 0.521 square miles. Located at 41.86° N. Lat; 74.73° W. Long. Elevation is 1,670 feet. Population: 1,131 (2010); Density: 32.5 persons per square mile (2010); Race: 85.3% White, 6.5% Black, 1.1% Asian, 0.2% American Indian/Alaska Native, 0.0% Native Hawaiian/Other Pacific Islander, 6.9% Other, 9.8% Hispanic of any race (2010); Average household size: 2.42 (2010); Median age: 43.6 (2010); Males per 100 females: 134.6 (2010); Homeownership rate: 78.5% (2010)

**PHILLIPSPORT** (unincorporated postal area)

Zip Code: 12769

Covers a land area of 4.935 square miles and a water area of 0 square miles. Located at 41.65° N. Lat; 74.46° W. Long. Elevation is 499 feet. Population: 253 (2010); Density: 51.3 persons per square mile (2010); Race: 90.5% White, 7.1% Black, 0.4% Asian, 0.0% American Indian/Alaska Native, 0.0% Native Hawaiian/Other Pacific Islander, 2.0% Other, 7.1% Hispanic of any race (2010); Average household size: 2.24 (2010); Median age: 47.3 (2010); Males per 100 females: 107.4 (2010); Homeownership rate: 78.7% (2010)

## POND EDDY (unincorporated postal area)
Zip Code: 12770

Covers a land area of 4.498 square miles and a water area of 0.274 square miles. Located at 41.44° N. Lat; 74.84° W. Long. Elevation is 558 feet. Population: 296 (2010); Density: 65.8 persons per square mile (2010); Race: 93.2% White, 3.0% Black, 0.3% Asian, 0.7% American Indian/Alaska Native, 0.3% Native Hawaiian/Other Pacific Islander, 2.5% Other, 6.8% Hispanic of any race (2010); Average household size: 2.45 (2010); Median age: 43.7 (2010); Males per 100 females: 88.5 (2010); Homeownership rate: 82.6% (2010)

## ROCK HILL (CDP). Covers a land area of 3.657 square miles and a water area of 0.946 square miles. Located at 41.60° N. Lat; 74.58° W. Long. Elevation is 1,378 feet.
Population: 696 (1990); 1,056 (2000); 1,742 (2010); Density: 476.3 persons per square mile (2010); Race: 81.1% White, 9.4% Black, 4.9% Asian, 0.5% American Indian/Alaska Native, 0.0% Native Hawaiian/Other Pacific Islander, 4.1% Other, 12.4% Hispanic of any race (2010); Average household size: 2.53 (2010); Median age: 43.0 (2010); Males per 100 females: 97.7 (2010); Marriage status: 27.7% never married, 59.6% now married, 7.0% widowed, 5.7% divorced (2006-2010 5-year est.); Foreign born: 7.9% (2006-2010 5-year est.); Ancestry (includes multiple ancestries): 14.8% Italian, 13.7% Irish, 8.5% English, 8.4% Scottish, 7.2% Hungarian (2006-2010 5-year est.).
Economy: Employment by occupation: 5.2% management, 3.3% professional, 4.6% services, 19.0% sales, 1.4% farming, 12.5% construction, 2.4% production (2006-2010 5-year est.).
Income: Per capita income: $30,547 (2006-2010 5-year est.); Median household income: $61,292 (2006-2010 5-year est.); Average household income: $85,124 (2006-2010 5-year est.); Percent of households with income of $100,000 or more: 28.9% (2006-2010 5-year est.); Poverty rate: 10.5% (2006-2010 5-year est.).
Education: Percent of population age 25 and over with: High school diploma (including GED) or higher: 88.6% (2006-2010 5-year est.); Bachelor's degree or higher: 32.8% (2006-2010 5-year est.); Master's degree or higher: 16.5% (2006-2010 5-year est.).
Housing: Homeownership rate: 85.4% (2010); Median home value: $258,400 (2006-2010 5-year est.); Median contract rent: $1,221 per month (2006-2010 5-year est.); Median year structure built: 1976 (2006-2010 5-year est.).
Transportation: Commute to work: 88.3% car, 1.1% public transportation, 5.7% walk, 4.0% work from home (2006-2010 5-year est.); Travel time to work: 19.9% less than 15 minutes, 36.7% 15 to 30 minutes, 29.8% 30 to 45 minutes, 5.2% 45 to 60 minutes, 8.4% 60 minutes or more (2006-2010 5-year est.)

## ROCKLAND (town). Covers a land area of 94.155 square miles and a water area of 1.113 square miles. Located at 41.96° N. Lat; 74.78° W. Long. Elevation is 1,293 feet.
Population: 4,096 (1990); 3,913 (2000); 3,775 (2010); Density: 40.1 persons per square mile (2010); Race: 90.7% White, 2.8% Black, 1.4% Asian, 0.7% American Indian/Alaska Native, 0.0% Native Hawaiian/Other Pacific Islander, 4.4% Other, 8.5% Hispanic of any race (2010); Average household size: 2.36 (2010); Median age: 44.6 (2010); Males per 100 females: 101.7 (2010); Marriage status: 26.7% never married, 56.1% now married, 5.9% widowed, 11.3% divorced (2006-2010 5-year est.); Foreign born: 8.0% (2006-2010 5-year est.); Ancestry (includes multiple ancestries): 24.9% German, 20.7% Italian, 18.7% Irish, 9.6% English, 8.4% American (2006-2010 5-year est.).
Economy: Single-family building permits issued: 9 (2011); Multi-family building permits issued: 0 (2011); Employment by occupation: 17.0% management, 0.4% professional, 18.3% services, 15.1% sales, 1.8% farming, 7.0% construction, 1.3% production (2006-2010 5-year est.).
Income: Per capita income: $28,778 (2006-2010 5-year est.); Median household income: $53,171 (2006-2010 5-year est.); Average household income: $67,247 (2006-2010 5-year est.); Percent of households with

income of $100,000 or more: 16.1% (2006-2010 5-year est.); Poverty rate: 13.4% (2006-2010 5-year est.).
Taxes: Total city taxes per capita: $553 (2009); City property taxes per capita: $523 (2009).
Education: Percent of population age 25 and over with: High school diploma (including GED) or higher: 87.8% (2006-2010 5-year est.); Bachelor's degree or higher: 22.7% (2006-2010 5-year est.); Master's degree or higher: 11.2% (2006-2010 5-year est.).
Housing: Homeownership rate: 70.4% (2010); Median home value: $175,500 (2006-2010 5-year est.); Median contract rent: $528 per month (2006-2010 5-year est.); Median year structure built: 1966 (2006-2010 5-year est.).
Transportation: Commute to work: 82.8% car, 5.4% public transportation, 6.4% walk, 5.1% work from home (2006-2010 5-year est.); Travel time to work: 29.7% less than 15 minutes, 32.1% 15 to 30 minutes, 27.1% 30 to 45 minutes, 3.3% 45 to 60 minutes, 7.8% 60 minutes or more (2006-2010 5-year est.)

## ROSCOE (CDP). Covers a land area of 0.718 square miles and a water area of 0.001 square miles. Located at 41.93° N. Lat; 74.91° W. Long. Elevation is 1,296 feet.
Population: 665 (1990); 597 (2000); 541 (2010); Density: 753.4 persons per square mile (2010); Race: 95.0% White, 1.5% Black, 1.3% Asian, 0.0% American Indian/Alaska Native, 0.0% Native Hawaiian/Other Pacific Islander, 2.2% Other, 5.2% Hispanic of any race (2010); Average household size: 2.17 (2010); Median age: 47.9 (2010); Males per 100 females: 88.5 (2010); Marriage status: 23.9% never married, 60.8% now married, 8.7% widowed, 6.6% divorced (2006-2010 5-year est.); Foreign born: 9.0% (2006-2010 5-year est.); Ancestry (includes multiple ancestries): 35.9% German, 31.5% Irish, 23.0% Italian, 14.2% English, 8.8% Welsh (2006-2010 5-year est.).
Economy: Employment by occupation: 15.5% management, 0.0% professional, 15.2% services, 9.5% sales, 6.4% farming, 15.5% construction, 9.2% production (2006-2010 5-year est.).
Income: Per capita income: $26,287 (2006-2010 5-year est.); Median household income: $39,097 (2006-2010 5-year est.); Average household income: $55,837 (2006-2010 5-year est.); Percent of households with income of $100,000 or more: 19.1% (2006-2010 5-year est.); Poverty rate: 20.1% (2006-2010 5-year est.).
Education: Percent of population age 25 and over with: High school diploma (including GED) or higher: 93.6% (2006-2010 5-year est.); Bachelor's degree or higher: 21.7% (2006-2010 5-year est.); Master's degree or higher: 10.2% (2006-2010 5-year est.).

### School District(s)
Roscoe Central School District (PK-12)
   2009-10 Enrollment: 248 . . . . . . . . . . . . . . . . . . . . (607) 498-4126
Housing: Homeownership rate: 69.8% (2010); Median home value: $157,400 (2006-2010 5-year est.); Median contract rent: $525 per month (2006-2010 5-year est.); Median year structure built: before 1940 (2006-2010 5-year est.).
Transportation: Commute to work: 75.0% car, 0.0% public transportation, 19.4% walk, 3.0% work from home (2006-2010 5-year est.); Travel time to work: 62.7% less than 15 minutes, 14.6% 15 to 30 minutes, 10.8% 30 to 45 minutes, 4.2% 45 to 60 minutes, 7.7% 60 minutes or more (2006-2010 5-year est.)

## SMALLWOOD (CDP). Covers a land area of 1.504 square miles and a water area of 0.118 square miles. Located at 41.66° N. Lat; 74.82° W. Long. Elevation is 1,201 feet.
Population: 431 (1990); 566 (2000); 580 (2010); Density: 385.5 persons per square mile (2010); Race: 92.9% White, 2.2% Black, 0.3% Asian, 0.2% American Indian/Alaska Native, 0.0% Native Hawaiian/Other Pacific Islander, 4.4% Other, 6.7% Hispanic of any race (2010); Average household size: 2.19 (2010); Median age: 49.0 (2010); Males per 100 females: 99.3 (2010); Marriage status: 35.5% never married, 46.9% now married, 2.5% widowed, 15.2% divorced (2006-2010 5-year est.); Foreign born: 10.0% (2006-2010 5-year est.); Ancestry (includes multiple ancestries): 23.0% Irish, 21.1% Czechoslovakian, 16.1% English, 13.2% Italian, 12.9% German (2006-2010 5-year est.).
Economy: Employment by occupation: 41.6% management, 4.4% professional, 6.7% services, 5.0% sales, 0.0% farming, 2.6% construction, 7.3% production (2006-2010 5-year est.).
Income: Per capita income: $27,890 (2006-2010 5-year est.); Median household income: $50,667 (2006-2010 5-year est.); Average household income: $69,786 (2006-2010 5-year est.); Percent of households with

income of $100,000 or more: 30.7% (2006-2010 5-year est.); Poverty rate: 6.3% (2006-2010 5-year est.).

**Education:** Percent of population age 25 and over with: High school diploma (including GED) or higher: 76.7% (2006-2010 5-year est.); Bachelor's degree or higher: 30.4% (2006-2010 5-year est.); Master's degree or higher: 11.8% (2006-2010 5-year est.).

**Housing:** Homeownership rate: 87.2% (2010); Median home value: $188,700 (2006-2010 5-year est.); Median contract rent: n/a per month (2006-2010 5-year est.); Median year structure built: 1945 (2006-2010 5-year est.).

**Transportation:** Commute to work: 80.6% car, 5.8% public transportation, 0.0% walk, 3.1% work from home (2006-2010 5-year est.); Travel time to work: 22.2% less than 15 minutes, 34.6% 15 to 30 minutes, 12.7% 30 to 45 minutes, 19.7% 45 to 60 minutes, 10.8% 60 minutes or more (2006-2010 5-year est.)

**SOUTH FALLSBURG** (CDP). Aka South Fallsburgh. Covers a land area of 5.946 square miles and a water area of 0.154 square miles. Located at 41.72° N. Lat; 74.63° W. Long. Elevation is 1,266 feet.

**Population:** 2,115 (1990); 2,061 (2000); 2,870 (2010); Density: 482.6 persons per square mile (2010); Race: 63.7% White, 14.2% Black, 0.9% Asian, 1.0% American Indian/Alaska Native, 0.2% Native Hawaiian/Other Pacific Islander, 20.0% Other, 38.5% Hispanic of any race (2010); Average household size: 3.15 (2010); Median age: 27.4 (2010); Males per 100 females: 99.0 (2010); Marriage status: 38.3% never married, 49.3% now married, 4.8% widowed, 7.6% divorced (2006-2010 5-year est.); Foreign born: 21.2% (2006-2010 5-year est.); Ancestry (includes multiple ancestries): 16.1% German, 13.3% English, 6.4% Polish, 4.3% Russian, 4.0% Hungarian (2006-2010 5-year est.).

**Economy:** Employment by occupation: 0.0% management, 0.0% professional, 8.9% services, 13.9% sales, 1.0% farming, 15.5% construction, 12.2% production (2006-2010 5-year est.).

**Income:** Per capita income: $17,225 (2006-2010 5-year est.); Median household income: $43,385 (2006-2010 5-year est.); Average household income: $56,837 (2006-2010 5-year est.); Percent of households with income of $100,000 or more: 16.8% (2006-2010 5-year est.); Poverty rate: 32.4% (2006-2010 5-year est.).

**Education:** Percent of population age 25 and over with: High school diploma (including GED) or higher: 67.4% (2006-2010 5-year est.); Bachelor's degree or higher: 24.6% (2006-2010 5-year est.); Master's degree or higher: 13.9% (2006-2010 5-year est.).

**Four-year College(s)**
Yeshivath Zichron Moshe (Private, Not-for-profit)
    Fall 2010 Enrollment: 201 . . . . . . . . . . . . . . . . . . . . . (914) 434-5240
    2011-12 Tuition: In-state $10,800; Out-of-state $10,800

**Housing:** Homeownership rate: 29.5% (2010); Median home value: $176,400 (2006-2010 5-year est.); Median contract rent: $625 per month (2006-2010 5-year est.); Median year structure built: 1975 (2006-2010 5-year est.).

**Transportation:** Commute to work: 80.2% car, 4.2% public transportation, 7.3% walk, 6.7% work from home (2006-2010 5-year est.); Travel time to work: 45.5% less than 15 minutes, 48.9% 15 to 30 minutes, 3.4% 30 to 45 minutes, 0.0% 45 to 60 minutes, 2.2% 60 minutes or more (2006-2010 5-year est.)

**SUMMITVILLE** (unincorporated postal area)
Zip Code: 12781
    Covers a land area of 4.266 square miles and a water area of 0 square miles. Located at 41.61° N. Lat; 74.46° W. Long. Elevation is 548 feet. Population: 307 (2010); Density: 71.9 persons per square mile (2010); Race: 91.9% White, 1.0% Black, 2.6% Asian, 0.0% American Indian/Alaska Native, 0.0% Native Hawaiian/Other Pacific Islander, 4.5% Other, 4.9% Hispanic of any race (2010); Average household size: 2.42 (2010); Median age: 44.3 (2010); Males per 100 females: 106.0 (2010); Homeownership rate: 74.8% (2010)

**SWAN LAKE** (unincorporated postal area)
Zip Code: 12783
    Covers a land area of 33.250 square miles and a water area of 1.096 square miles. Located at 41.73° N. Lat; 74.83° W. Long. Elevation is 1,345 feet. Population: 1,668 (2010); Density: 50.2 persons per square mile (2010); Race: 84.5% White, 7.7% Black, 0.8% Asian, 0.7% American Indian/Alaska Native, 0.0% Native Hawaiian/Other Pacific Islander, 6.3% Other, 15.4% Hispanic of any race (2010); Average

household size: 2.36 (2010); Median age: 45.4 (2010); Males per 100 females: 137.3 (2010); Homeownership rate: 74.9% (2010)

**THOMPSON** (town). Covers a land area of 84.089 square miles and a water area of 3.407 square miles. Located at 41.64° N. Lat; 74.67° W. Long.

**Population:** 13,711 (1990); 14,189 (2000); 15,308 (2010); Density: 182.0 persons per square mile (2010); Race: 68.0% White, 18.7% Black, 2.2% Asian, 0.6% American Indian/Alaska Native, 0.0% Native Hawaiian/Other Pacific Islander, 10.5% Other, 20.3% Hispanic of any race (2010); Average household size: 2.45 (2010); Median age: 38.5 (2010); Males per 100 females: 99.3 (2010); Marriage status: 34.7% never married, 49.6% now married, 6.9% widowed, 8.8% divorced (2006-2010 5-year est.); Foreign born: 12.9% (2006-2010 5-year est.); Ancestry (includes multiple ancestries): 9.2% Irish, 9.0% Italian, 7.9% German, 5.5% American, 5.1% English (2006-2010 5-year est.).

**Economy:** Single-family building permits issued: 77 (2011); Multi-family building permits issued: 0 (2011); Employment by occupation: 9.1% management, 1.2% professional, 10.2% services, 20.5% sales, 3.5% farming, 10.6% construction, 4.5% production (2006-2010 5-year est.).

**Income:** Per capita income: $19,439 (2006-2010 5-year est.); Median household income: $37,417 (2006-2010 5-year est.); Average household income: $51,047 (2006-2010 5-year est.); Percent of households with income of $100,000 or more: 12.0% (2006-2010 5-year est.); Poverty rate: 25.4% (2006-2010 5-year est.).

**Education:** Percent of population age 25 and over with: High school diploma (including GED) or higher: 82.6% (2006-2010 5-year est.); Bachelor's degree or higher: 18.0% (2006-2010 5-year est.); Master's degree or higher: 9.2% (2006-2010 5-year est.).

**Housing:** Homeownership rate: 52.4% (2010); Median home value: $171,300 (2006-2010 5-year est.); Median contract rent: $676 per month (2006-2010 5-year est.); Median year structure built: 1973 (2006-2010 5-year est.).

**Transportation:** Commute to work: 86.7% car, 2.0% public transportation, 4.5% walk, 5.4% work from home (2006-2010 5-year est.); Travel time to work: 47.0% less than 15 minutes, 32.5% 15 to 30 minutes, 12.3% 30 to 45 minutes, 2.0% 45 to 60 minutes, 6.3% 60 minutes or more (2006-2010 5-year est.)

**Additional Information Contacts**
Town of Thompson . . . . . . . . . . . . . . . . . . . . . . . . . . (845) 794-2500
    http://www.townofthompson.com

**THOMPSONVILLE** (unincorporated postal area)
Zip Code: 12784
    Covers a land area of 2.260 square miles and a water area of 0.006 square miles. Located at 41.66° N. Lat; 74.63° W. Long. Elevation is 1,168 feet. Population: 94 (2010); Density: 41.6 persons per square mile (2010); Race: 77.7% White, 4.3% Black, 6.4% Asian, 0.0% American Indian/Alaska Native, 0.0% Native Hawaiian/Other Pacific Islander, 11.6% Other, 12.8% Hispanic of any race (2010); Average household size: 2.69 (2010); Median age: 35.7 (2010); Males per 100 females: 100.0 (2010); Homeownership rate: 54.2% (2010)

**TUSTEN** (town). Covers a land area of 47.205 square miles and a water area of 1.579 square miles. Located at 41.57° N. Lat; 74.99° W. Long. Elevation is 689 feet.

**Population:** 1,271 (1990); 1,415 (2000); 1,515 (2010); Density: 32.1 persons per square mile (2010); Race: 90.3% White, 4.5% Black, 0.9% Asian, 0.4% American Indian/Alaska Native, 0.0% Native Hawaiian/Other Pacific Islander, 3.9% Other, 5.1% Hispanic of any race (2010); Average household size: 2.22 (2010); Median age: 48.2 (2010); Males per 100 females: 109.5 (2010); Marriage status: 24.6% never married, 57.8% now married, 9.0% widowed, 8.7% divorced (2006-2010 5-year est.); Foreign born: 5.2% (2006-2010 5-year est.); Ancestry (includes multiple ancestries): 27.0% German, 16.9% Irish, 11.3% Italian, 6.9% English, 6.0% Polish (2006-2010 5-year est.).

**Economy:** Single-family building permits issued: 12 (2011); Multi-family building permits issued: 0 (2011); Employment by occupation: 8.8% management, 1.3% professional, 17.2% services, 14.5% sales, 1.0% farming, 18.0% construction, 6.7% production (2006-2010 5-year est.).

**Income:** Per capita income: $26,592 (2006-2010 5-year est.); Median household income: $55,952 (2006-2010 5-year est.); Average household income: $66,545 (2006-2010 5-year est.); Percent of households with income of $100,000 or more: 21.1% (2006-2010 5-year est.); Poverty rate: 6.4% (2006-2010 5-year est.).

**Education:** Percent of population age 25 and over with: High school diploma (including GED) or higher: 84.8% (2006-2010 5-year est.); Bachelor's degree or higher: 23.3% (2006-2010 5-year est.); Master's degree or higher: 7.5% (2006-2010 5-year est.).
**Housing:** Homeownership rate: 81.3% (2010); Median home value: $189,400 (2006-2010 5-year est.); Median contract rent: $806 per month (2006-2010 5-year est.); Median year structure built: 1959 (2006-2010 5-year est.).
**Transportation:** Commute to work: 85.4% car, 4.4% public transportation, 1.8% walk, 7.0% work from home (2006-2010 5-year est.); Travel time to work: 14.1% less than 15 minutes, 41.3% 15 to 30 minutes, 25.0% 30 to 45 minutes, 6.3% 45 to 60 minutes, 13.3% 60 minutes or more (2006-2010 5-year est.)

## WESTBROOKVILLE (unincorporated postal area)
Zip Code: 12785

Covers a land area of 16.665 square miles and a water area of 0.893 square miles. Located at 41.53° N. Lat; 74.56° W. Long. Population: 1,024 (2010); Density: 61.4 persons per square mile (2010); Race: 90.5% White, 3.1% Black, 1.0% Asian, 0.2% American Indian/Alaska Native, 0.1% Native Hawaiian/Other Pacific Islander, 5.1% Other, 9.8% Hispanic of any race (2010); Average household size: 2.65 (2010); Median age: 42.4 (2010); Males per 100 females: 101.6 (2010); Homeownership rate: 84.4% (2010)

## WHITE LAKE (unincorporated postal area)
Zip Code: 12786

Covers a land area of 14.962 square miles and a water area of 2.790 square miles. Located at 41.63° N. Lat; 74.85° W. Long. Elevation is 1,335 feet. Population: 665 (2010); Density: 44.4 persons per square mile (2010); Race: 89.3% White, 2.0% Black, 0.9% Asian, 0.0% American Indian/Alaska Native, 0.0% Native Hawaiian/Other Pacific Islander, 7.8% Other, 11.6% Hispanic of any race (2010); Average household size: 2.28 (2010); Median age: 49.8 (2010); Males per 100 females: 97.9 (2010); Homeownership rate: 80.9% (2010)

## WHITE SULPHUR SPRINGS (unincorporated postal area)
Zip Code: 12787

Covers a land area of 3.509 square miles and a water area of 0.001 square miles. Located at 41.79° N. Lat; 74.84° W. Long. Elevation is 1,362 feet. Population: 452 (2010); Density: 128.8 persons per square mile (2010); Race: 86.7% White, 5.3% Black, 1.1% Asian, 0.2% American Indian/Alaska Native, 0.0% Native Hawaiian/Other Pacific Islander, 6.7% Other, 14.8% Hispanic of any race (2010); Average household size: 2.35 (2010); Median age: 45.0 (2010); Males per 100 females: 97.4 (2010); Homeownership rate: 63.0% (2010)

## WOODBOURNE (unincorporated postal area)
Zip Code: 12788

Covers a land area of 23.498 square miles and a water area of 0.211 square miles. Located at 41.78° N. Lat; 74.58° W. Long. Elevation is 1,188 feet. Population: 2,908 (2010); Density: 123.8 persons per square mile (2010); Race: 72.7% White, 18.7% Black, 1.8% Asian, 0.3% American Indian/Alaska Native, 0.0% Native Hawaiian/Other Pacific Islander, 6.5% Other, 14.0% Hispanic of any race (2010); Average household size: 2.50 (2010); Median age: 42.4 (2010); Males per 100 females: 178.3 (2010); Homeownership rate: 73.1% (2010)

## WOODRIDGE (village).
Covers a land area of 1.603 square miles and a water area of 0.104 square miles. Located at 41.72° N. Lat; 74.58° W. Long. Elevation is 1,161 feet.
**Population:** 798 (1990); 902 (2000); 847 (2010); Density: 528.3 persons per square mile (2010); Race: 70.7% White, 11.9% Black, 2.2% Asian, 0.4% American Indian/Alaska Native, 0.1% Native Hawaiian/Other Pacific Islander, 14.7% Other, 34.6% Hispanic of any race (2010); Average household size: 2.46 (2010); Median age: 34.8 (2010); Males per 100 females: 105.1 (2010); Marriage status: 49.3% never married, 37.2% now married, 5.2% widowed, 8.3% divorced (2006-2010 5-year est.); Foreign born: 16.5% (2006-2010 5-year est.); Ancestry (includes multiple ancestries): 8.2% Russian, 7.9% Irish, 5.5% Polish, 5.0% Italian, 5.0% German (2006-2010 5-year est.).
**Economy:** Single-family building permits issued: 0 (2011); Multi-family building permits issued: 0 (2011); Employment by occupation: 15.3% management, 1.5% professional, 18.8% services, 6.1% sales, 7.7% farming, 11.5% construction, 6.5% production (2006-2010 5-year est.).

**Income:** Per capita income: $16,850 (2006-2010 5-year est.); Median household income: $30,324 (2006-2010 5-year est.); Average household income: $40,224 (2006-2010 5-year est.); Percent of households with income of $100,000 or more: 9.3% (2006-2010 5-year est.); Poverty rate: 21.6% (2006-2010 5-year est.).
**Education:** Percent of population age 25 and over with: High school diploma (including GED) or higher: 71.6% (2006-2010 5-year est.); Bachelor's degree or higher: 18.3% (2006-2010 5-year est.); Master's degree or higher: 7.4% (2006-2010 5-year est.).
**Housing:** Homeownership rate: 36.8% (2010); Median home value: $166,700 (2006-2010 5-year est.); Median contract rent: $569 per month (2006-2010 5-year est.); Median year structure built: 1970 (2006-2010 5-year est.).
**Transportation:** Commute to work: 84.2% car, 3.6% public transportation, 4.0% walk, 8.1% work from home (2006-2010 5-year est.); Travel time to work: 30.0% less than 15 minutes, 39.6% 15 to 30 minutes, 26.4% 30 to 45 minutes, 1.3% 45 to 60 minutes, 2.6% 60 minutes or more (2006-2010 5-year est.)

## WURTSBORO (village).
Covers a land area of 1.266 square miles and a water area of 0 square miles. Located at 41.57° N. Lat; 74.48° W. Long. Elevation is 577 feet.
**Population:** 1,048 (1990); 1,234 (2000); 1,246 (2010); Density: 984.0 persons per square mile (2010); Race: 88.7% White, 4.0% Black, 1.4% Asian, 0.7% American Indian/Alaska Native, 0.0% Native Hawaiian/Other Pacific Islander, 5.2% Other, 8.9% Hispanic of any race (2010); Average household size: 2.28 (2010); Median age: 44.4 (2010); Males per 100 females: 89.1 (2010); Marriage status: 32.9% never married, 41.7% now married, 7.8% widowed, 17.6% divorced (2006-2010 5-year est.); Foreign born: 2.7% (2006-2010 5-year est.); Ancestry (includes multiple ancestries): 28.4% Irish, 23.2% Italian, 23.2% German, 11.8% English, 8.0% American (2006-2010 5-year est.).
**Economy:** Single-family building permits issued: 0 (2011); Multi-family building permits issued: 0 (2011); Employment by occupation: 10.0% management, 0.0% professional, 12.3% services, 15.1% sales, 0.4% farming, 11.0% construction, 5.7% production (2006-2010 5-year est.).
**Income:** Per capita income: $23,810 (2006-2010 5-year est.); Median household income: $57,098 (2006-2010 5-year est.); Average household income: $61,391 (2006-2010 5-year est.); Percent of households with income of $100,000 or more: 12.7% (2006-2010 5-year est.); Poverty rate: 8.2% (2006-2010 5-year est.).
**Education:** Percent of population age 25 and over with: High school diploma (including GED) or higher: 84.3% (2006-2010 5-year est.); Bachelor's degree or higher: 15.4% (2006-2010 5-year est.); Master's degree or higher: 7.9% (2006-2010 5-year est.).
### School District(s)
Monticello Central School District (KG-12)
    2009-10 Enrollment: 3,226 . . . . . . . . . . . . . . . . . . . . . . . (845) 794-7700
**Housing:** Homeownership rate: 59.8% (2010); Median home value: $190,800 (2006-2010 5-year est.); Median contract rent: $877 per month (2006-2010 5-year est.); Median year structure built: 1968 (2006-2010 5-year est.).
**Transportation:** Commute to work: 96.7% car, 1.2% public transportation, 1.0% walk, 1.0% work from home (2006-2010 5-year est.); Travel time to work: 23.3% less than 15 minutes, 29.4% 15 to 30 minutes, 28.1% 30 to 45 minutes, 3.1% 45 to 60 minutes, 16.0% 60 minutes or more (2006-2010 5-year est.)

## YOUNGSVILLE (unincorporated postal area)
Zip Code: 12791

Covers a land area of 6.557 square miles and a water area of 0.009 square miles. Located at 41.81° N. Lat; 74.89° W. Long. Elevation is 1,198 feet. Population: 737 (2010); Density: 112.4 persons per square mile (2010); Race: 96.3% White, 1.2% Black, 1.1% Asian, 0.0% American Indian/Alaska Native, 0.0% Native Hawaiian/Other Pacific Islander, 1.4% Other, 6.1% Hispanic of any race (2010); Average household size: 2.25 (2010); Median age: 47.2 (2010); Males per 100 females: 90.4 (2010); Homeownership rate: 68.9% (2010)

## YULAN (unincorporated postal area)
Zip Code: 12792

Covers a land area of 3.391 square miles and a water area of 0.002 square miles. Located at 41.51° N. Lat; 74.95° W. Long. Elevation is 1,070 feet. Population: 335 (2010); Density: 98.8 persons per square mile (2010); Race: 91.9% White, 0.0% Black, 1.8% Asian, 0.0%

American Indian/Alaska Native, 0.0% Native Hawaiian/Other Pacific Islander, 6.3% Other, 6.0% Hispanic of any race (2010); Average household size: 2.41 (2010); Median age: 46.1 (2010); Males per 100 females: 108.1 (2010); Homeownership rate: 72.0% (2010)

## Tioga County

Located in southern New York; bounded on the south by Pennsylvania; crossed by the Susquehanna River. Covers a land area of 518.69 square miles, a water area of 4.21 square miles, and is located in the Eastern Time Zone at 42.14° N. Lat., 76.32° W. Long. The county was founded in 1791. County seat is Owego.

Tioga County is part of the Binghamton, NY Metropolitan Statistical Area. The entire metro area includes: Broome County, NY; Tioga County, NY

**Population:** 52,337 (1990); 51,784 (2000); 51,125 (2010); Race: 96.9% White, 0.7% Black, 0.7% Asian, 0.2% American Indian/Alaska Native, 0.0% Native Hawaiian/Other Pacific Islander, 1.5% Other, 1.4% Hispanic of any race (2010); Density: 98.6 persons per square mile (2010); Average household size: 2.49 (2010); Median age: 42.5 (2010); Males per 100 females: 98.3 (2010).
**Religion:** Six largest groups: 11.4% Catholicism, 10.3% Methodist/Pietist, 2.2% Baptist, 2.1% Non-Denominational, 1.8% Holiness, 1.5% Presbyterian-Reformed (2010)
**Economy:** Unemployment rate: 9.2% (February 2012); Total civilian labor force: 25,035 (February 2012); Leading industries: 12.1% manufacturing; 11.2% health care and social assistance; 10.3% retail trade (2009); Farms: 565 totaling 106,834 acres (2007); Companies that employ 500 or more persons: 3 (2009); Companies that employ 100 to 499 persons: 11 (2009); Companies that employ less than 100 persons: 782 (2009); Black-owned businesses: n/a (2007); Hispanic-owned businesses: n/a (2007); Asian-owned businesses: n/a (2007); Women-owned businesses: 1,108 (2007); Retail sales per capita: $6,970 (2010). Single-family building permits issued: 72 (2011); Multi-family building permits issued: 0 (2011).
**Income:** Per capita income: $24,596 (2006-2010 5-year est.); Median household income: $51,948 (2006-2010 5-year est.); Average household income: $61,956 (2006-2010 5-year est.); Percent of households with income of $100,000 or more: 15.2% (2006-2010 5-year est.); Poverty rate: 9.6% (2006-2010 5-year est.); Bankruptcy rate: 1.89% (2011).
**Education:** Percent of population age 25 and over with: High school diploma (including GED) or higher: 89.1% (2006-2010 5-year est.); Bachelor's degree or higher: 22.7% (2006-2010 5-year est.); Master's degree or higher: 9.1% (2006-2010 5-year est.).
**Housing:** Homeownership rate: 77.7% (2010); Median home value: $98,200 (2006-2010 5-year est.); Median contract rent: $443 per month (2006-2010 5-year est.); Median year structure built: 1963 (2006-2010 5-year est.)
**Health:** Birth rate: 102.1 per 10,000 population (2011); Death rate: 81.7 per 10,000 population (2011); Age-adjusted cancer mortality rate: 168.1 deaths per 100,000 population (2009); Number of physicians: 7.4 per 10,000 population (2008); Hospital beds: 0.0 per 10,000 population (2007); Hospital admissions: 0.0 per 10,000 population (2007).
**Elections:** 2008 Presidential election results: 44.0% Obama, 54.2% McCain, 0.9% Nader
**National and State Parks:** Fairfield State Forest; Ketchumville State Forest; Oakley Corners State Forest; Robinson Hollow State Forest
**Additional Information Contacts**
Tioga County Government . . . . . . . . . . . . . . . . . . . (607) 687-8660
  http://www.tiogacountyny.com
Tioga County Chamber of Commerce . . . . . . . . . . . . . . . . (607) 687-2020
  http://www.tiogachamber.com
Town of Berkshire . . . . . . . . . . . . . . . . . . . . . . . (607) 657-8678
  http://berkshireny.com

## Tioga County Communities

**APALACHIN** (CDP). Covers a land area of 1.459 square miles and a water area of 0 square miles. Located at 42.07° N. Lat; 76.16° W. Long. Elevation is 843 feet.
**Population:** 1,208 (1990); 1,126 (2000); 1,131 (2010); Density: 775.0 persons per square mile (2010); Race: 97.2% White, 0.3% Black, 0.6% Asian, 0.1% American Indian/Alaska Native, 0.0% Native Hawaiian/Other Pacific Islander, 1.8% Other, 1.1% Hispanic of any race (2010); Average household size: 2.26 (2010); Median age: 40.7 (2010); Males per 100

females: 105.3 (2010); Marriage status: 34.9% never married, 33.0% now married, 5.0% widowed, 27.1% divorced (2006-2010 5-year est.); Foreign born: 0.0% (2006-2010 5-year est.); Ancestry (includes multiple ancestries): 17.4% German, 15.0% Irish, 9.7% Italian, 9.0% English, 6.7% Russian (2006-2010 5-year est.).
**Economy:** Employment by occupation: 11.2% management, 3.0% professional, 12.6% services, 27.3% sales, 1.7% farming, 6.2% construction, 2.0% production (2006-2010 5-year est.).
**Income:** Per capita income: $21,324 (2006-2010 5-year est.); Median household income: $60,096 (2006-2010 5-year est.); Average household income: $53,639 (2006-2010 5-year est.); Percent of households with income of $100,000 or more: 8.9% (2006-2010 5-year est.); Poverty rate: 14.0% (2006-2010 5-year est.).
**Education:** Percent of population age 25 and over with: High school diploma (including GED) or higher: 95.8% (2006-2010 5-year est.); Bachelor's degree or higher: 19.2% (2006-2010 5-year est.); Master's degree or higher: 5.5% (2006-2010 5-year est.).
**School District(s)**
Owego-Apalachin Central School District (KG-12)
  2009-10 Enrollment: 2,148 . . . . . . . . . . . . . . . . . (607) 687-6224
Vestal Central School District (KG-12)
  2009-10 Enrollment: 3,767 . . . . . . . . . . . . . . . . . (607) 757-2241
**Housing:** Homeownership rate: 57.9% (2010); Median home value: $86,400 (2006-2010 5-year est.); Median contract rent: $544 per month (2006-2010 5-year est.); Median year structure built: before 1940 (2006-2010 5-year est.).
**Transportation:** Commute to work: 97.6% car, 0.0% public transportation, 0.0% walk, 0.0% work from home (2006-2010 5-year est.); Travel time to work: 41.2% less than 15 minutes, 41.4% 15 to 30 minutes, 7.6% 30 to 45 minutes, 0.0% 45 to 60 minutes, 9.8% 60 minutes or more (2006-2010 5-year est.)

**BARTON** (town). Covers a land area of 59.275 square miles and a water area of 0.413 square miles. Located at 42.07° N. Lat; 76.49° W. Long. Elevation is 804 feet.
**Population:** 8,925 (1990); 9,066 (2000); 8,858 (2010); Density: 149.4 persons per square mile (2010); Race: 97.6% White, 0.5% Black, 0.3% Asian, 0.3% American Indian/Alaska Native, 0.0% Native Hawaiian/Other Pacific Islander, 1.3% Other, 1.4% Hispanic of any race (2010); Average household size: 2.40 (2010); Median age: 40.9 (2010); Males per 100 females: 92.1 (2010); Marriage status: 24.4% never married, 55.0% now married, 9.0% widowed, 11.6% divorced (2006-2010 5-year est.); Foreign born: 1.8% (2006-2010 5-year est.); Ancestry (includes multiple ancestries): 22.9% German, 20.4% Irish, 16.8% English, 11.3% Italian, 9.1% American (2006-2010 5-year est.).
**Economy:** Single-family building permits issued: 8 (2011); Multi-family building permits issued: 0 (2011); Employment by occupation: 7.4% management, 3.9% professional, 9.8% services, 15.4% sales, 2.6% farming, 10.9% construction, 11.2% production (2006-2010 5-year est.).
**Income:** Per capita income: $22,096 (2006-2010 5-year est.); Median household income: $43,771 (2006-2010 5-year est.); Average household income: $52,362 (2006-2010 5-year est.); Percent of households with income of $100,000 or more: 10.1% (2006-2010 5-year est.); Poverty rate: 15.4% (2006-2010 5-year est.).
**Taxes:** Total city taxes per capita: $85 (2009); City property taxes per capita: $70 (2009).
**Education:** Percent of population age 25 and over with: High school diploma (including GED) or higher: 86.2% (2006-2010 5-year est.); Bachelor's degree or higher: 16.0% (2006-2010 5-year est.); Master's degree or higher: 6.0% (2006-2010 5-year est.).
**Housing:** Homeownership rate: 67.2% (2010); Median home value: $85,200 (2006-2010 5-year est.); Median contract rent: $422 per month (2006-2010 5-year est.); Median year structure built: 1949 (2006-2010 5-year est.).
**Transportation:** Commute to work: 90.5% car, 0.9% public transportation, 3.6% walk, 2.6% work from home (2006-2010 5-year est.); Travel time to work: 40.7% less than 15 minutes, 30.9% 15 to 30 minutes, 14.9% 30 to 45 minutes, 6.1% 45 to 60 minutes, 7.5% 60 minutes or more (2006-2010 5-year est.)

**BERKSHIRE** (town). Covers a land area of 30.216 square miles and a water area of 0.009 square miles. Located at 42.29° N. Lat; 76.16° W. Long. Elevation is 1,047 feet.
**Population:** 1,303 (1990); 1,366 (2000); 1,412 (2010); Density: 46.7 persons per square mile (2010); Race: 98.0% White, 0.5% Black, 0.6%

Asian, 0.1% American Indian/Alaska Native, 0.0% Native Hawaiian/Other Pacific Islander, 0.8% Other, 0.6% Hispanic of any race (2010); Average household size: 2.61 (2010); Median age: 42.0 (2010); Males per 100 females: 100.9 (2010); Marriage status: 24.2% never married, 60.4% now married, 4.2% widowed, 11.1% divorced (2006-2010 5-year est.); Foreign born: 1.8% (2006-2010 5-year est.); Ancestry (includes multiple ancestries): 25.5% English, 23.7% German, 14.8% Irish, 9.5% American, 5.3% Italian (2006-2010 5-year est.).

**Economy:** Single-family building permits issued: 2 (2011); Multi-family building permits issued: 0 (2011); Employment by occupation: 8.5% management, 3.8% professional, 8.2% services, 13.6% sales, 3.8% farming, 16.2% construction, 13.0% production (2006-2010 5-year est.).

**Income:** Per capita income: $20,100 (2006-2010 5-year est.); Median household income: $50,750 (2006-2010 5-year est.); Average household income: $57,737 (2006-2010 5-year est.); Percent of households with income of $100,000 or more: 12.4% (2006-2010 5-year est.); Poverty rate: 11.5% (2006-2010 5-year est.).

**Education:** Percent of population age 25 and over with: High school diploma (including GED) or higher: 85.1% (2006-2010 5-year est.); Bachelor's degree or higher: 12.0% (2006-2010 5-year est.); Master's degree or higher: 5.4% (2006-2010 5-year est.).

**Housing:** Homeownership rate: 87.8% (2010); Median home value: $95,000 (2006-2010 5-year est.); Median contract rent: $432 per month (2006-2010 5-year est.); Median year structure built: 1972 (2006-2010 5-year est.).

**Transportation:** Commute to work: 91.1% car, 1.2% public transportation, 1.3% walk, 6.1% work from home (2006-2010 5-year est.); Travel time to work: 11.8% less than 15 minutes, 26.9% 15 to 30 minutes, 48.2% 30 to 45 minutes, 8.6% 45 to 60 minutes, 4.6% 60 minutes or more (2006-2010 5-year est.)

**Additional Information Contacts**
Town of Berkshire . . . . . . . . . . . . . . . . . . . . . . . . . . . (607) 657-8678
    http://berkshireny.com

**CANDOR** (village). Covers a land area of 0.440 square miles and a water area of 0 square miles. Located at 42.22° N. Lat; 76.33° W. Long. Elevation is 902 feet.

**Population:** 869 (1990); 855 (2000); 851 (2010); Density: 1,931.9 persons per square mile (2010); Race: 97.3% White, 0.8% Black, 0.0% Asian, 0.1% American Indian/Alaska Native, 0.0% Native Hawaiian/Other Pacific Islander, 1.8% Other, 1.6% Hispanic of any race (2010); Average household size: 2.45 (2010); Median age: 37.5 (2010); Males per 100 females: 88.3 (2010); Marriage status: 25.0% never married, 55.4% now married, 4.4% widowed, 15.1% divorced (2006-2010 5-year est.); Foreign born: 0.0% (2006-2010 5-year est.); Ancestry (includes multiple ancestries): 25.3% Irish, 20.1% English, 16.7% German, 10.4% American, 9.1% Italian (2006-2010 5-year est.).

**Economy:** Single-family building permits issued: 0 (2011); Multi-family building permits issued: 0 (2011); Employment by occupation: 12.5% management, 5.2% professional, 8.0% services, 22.1% sales, 6.6% farming, 10.5% construction, 3.0% production (2006-2010 5-year est.).

**Income:** Per capita income: $25,099 (2006-2010 5-year est.); Median household income: $50,481 (2006-2010 5-year est.); Average household income: $61,164 (2006-2010 5-year est.); Percent of households with income of $100,000 or more: 18.5% (2006-2010 5-year est.); Poverty rate: 11.7% (2006-2010 5-year est.).

**Education:** Percent of population age 25 and over with: High school diploma (including GED) or higher: 89.7% (2006-2010 5-year est.); Bachelor's degree or higher: 17.4% (2006-2010 5-year est.); Master's degree or higher: 5.9% (2006-2010 5-year est.).

**School District(s)**
Candor Central School District (KG-12)
    2009-10 Enrollment: 832 . . . . . . . . . . . . . . . . . . . . . (607) 659-5010
**Housing:** Homeownership rate: 65.6% (2010); Median home value: $81,500 (2006-2010 5-year est.); Median contract rent: $425 per month (2006-2010 5-year est.); Median year structure built: before 1940 (2006-2010 5-year est.).

**Transportation:** Commute to work: 85.9% car, 1.6% public transportation, 7.8% walk, 1.8% work from home (2006-2010 5-year est.); Travel time to work: 20.7% less than 15 minutes, 27.5% 15 to 30 minutes, 37.3% 30 to 45 minutes, 9.9% 45 to 60 minutes, 4.7% 60 minutes or more (2006-2010 5-year est.)

**CANDOR** (town). Covers a land area of 94.510 square miles and a water area of 0.109 square miles. Located at 42.23° N. Lat; 76.33° W. Long. Elevation is 902 feet.

**Population:** 5,310 (1990); 5,317 (2000); 5,305 (2010); Density: 56.1 persons per square mile (2010); Race: 96.7% White, 1.1% Black, 0.1% Asian, 0.2% American Indian/Alaska Native, 0.0% Native Hawaiian/Other Pacific Islander, 1.9% Other, 1.9% Hispanic of any race (2010); Average household size: 2.50 (2010); Median age: 41.7 (2010); Males per 100 females: 95.3 (2010); Marriage status: 18.4% never married, 66.5% now married, 5.6% widowed, 9.5% divorced (2006-2010 5-year est.); Foreign born: 2.2% (2006-2010 5-year est.); Ancestry (includes multiple ancestries): 24.3% German, 17.8% English, 15.2% Irish, 9.8% Italian, 9.5% American (2006-2010 5-year est.).

**Economy:** Single-family building permits issued: 3 (2011); Multi-family building permits issued: 0 (2011); Employment by occupation: 11.9% management, 4.2% professional, 12.9% services, 13.7% sales, 5.2% farming, 11.6% construction, 6.6% production (2006-2010 5-year est.).

**Income:** Per capita income: $22,957 (2006-2010 5-year est.); Median household income: $49,152 (2006-2010 5-year est.); Average household income: $58,120 (2006-2010 5-year est.); Percent of households with income of $100,000 or more: 14.0% (2006-2010 5-year est.); Poverty rate: 9.1% (2006-2010 5-year est.).

**Education:** Percent of population age 25 and over with: High school diploma (including GED) or higher: 88.5% (2006-2010 5-year est.); Bachelor's degree or higher: 15.9% (2006-2010 5-year est.); Master's degree or higher: 5.0% (2006-2010 5-year est.).

**School District(s)**
Candor Central School District (KG-12)
    2009-10 Enrollment: 832 . . . . . . . . . . . . . . . . . . . . . (607) 659-5010
**Housing:** Homeownership rate: 78.4% (2010); Median home value: $89,500 (2006-2010 5-year est.); Median contract rent: $412 per month (2006-2010 5-year est.); Median year structure built: 1974 (2006-2010 5-year est.).

**Transportation:** Commute to work: 92.7% car, 0.3% public transportation, 3.5% walk, 3.0% work from home (2006-2010 5-year est.); Travel time to work: 21.7% less than 15 minutes, 27.9% 15 to 30 minutes, 37.2% 30 to 45 minutes, 9.4% 45 to 60 minutes, 3.8% 60 minutes or more (2006-2010 5-year est.)

**LOCKWOOD** (unincorporated postal area)
Zip Code: 14859
    Covers a land area of 31.161 square miles and a water area of 0.060 square miles. Located at 42.11° N. Lat; 76.53° W. Long. Elevation is 902 feet. Population: 1,029 (2010); Density: 33.0 persons per square mile (2010); Race: 97.6% White, 0.7% Black, 0.1% Asian, 0.4% American Indian/Alaska Native, 0.0% Native Hawaiian/Other Pacific Islander, 1.2% Other, 1.9% Hispanic of any race (2010); Average household size: 2.57 (2010); Median age: 43.7 (2010); Males per 100 females: 97.1 (2010); Homeownership rate: 86.3% (2010)

**NEWARK VALLEY** (village). Covers a land area of 0.987 square miles and a water area of 0 square miles. Located at 42.22° N. Lat; 76.18° W. Long. Elevation is 968 feet.

**Population:** 1,082 (1990); 1,071 (2000); 997 (2010); Density: 1,009.3 persons per square mile (2010); Race: 96.8% White, 0.0% Black, 0.6% Asian, 0.2% American Indian/Alaska Native, 0.0% Native Hawaiian/Other Pacific Islander, 2.4% Other, 1.7% Hispanic of any race (2010); Average household size: 2.57 (2010); Median age: 37.0 (2010); Males per 100 females: 89.2 (2010); Marriage status: 23.2% never married, 53.7% now married, 10.5% widowed, 12.6% divorced (2006-2010 5-year est.); Foreign born: 1.5% (2006-2010 5-year est.); Ancestry (includes multiple ancestries): 20.1% Irish, 15.1% English, 14.0% German, 10.0% Italian, 7.8% Polish (2006-2010 5-year est.).

**Economy:** Single-family building permits issued: 0 (2011); Multi-family building permits issued: 0 (2011); Employment by occupation: 5.5% management, 6.7% professional, 9.9% services, 21.0% sales, 5.5% farming, 9.9% construction, 5.0% production (2006-2010 5-year est.).

**Income:** Per capita income: $23,678 (2006-2010 5-year est.); Median household income: $51,875 (2006-2010 5-year est.); Average household income: $62,232 (2006-2010 5-year est.); Percent of households with income of $100,000 or more: 13.3% (2006-2010 5-year est.); Poverty rate: 10.6% (2006-2010 5-year est.).

**Education:** Percent of population age 25 and over with: High school diploma (including GED) or higher: 92.8% (2006-2010 5-year est.);

Bachelor's degree or higher: 26.6% (2006-2010 5-year est.); Master's degree or higher: 9.6% (2006-2010 5-year est.).

Newark Valley Central School District (KG-12)

    2009-10 Enrollment: 1,236 . . . . . . . . . . . . . . . . . . . . . . . (607) 642-3221

**Housing:** Homeownership rate: 71.4% (2010); Median home value: $90,100 (2006-2010 5-year est.); Median contract rent: $443 per month (2006-2010 5-year est.); Median year structure built: before 1940 (2006-2010 5-year est.).

**Transportation:** Commute to work: 88.1% car, 2.1% public transportation, 4.6% walk, 4.4% work from home (2006-2010 5-year est.); Travel time to work: 28.7% less than 15 minutes, 36.1% 15 to 30 minutes, 25.7% 30 to 45 minutes, 6.4% 45 to 60 minutes, 3.2% 60 minutes or more (2006-2010 5-year est.)

**NEWARK VALLEY** (town). Covers a land area of 50.294 square miles and a water area of 0.100 square miles. Located at 42.23° N. Lat; 76.16° W. Long. Elevation is 968 feet.

**Population:** 4,189 (1990); 4,097 (2000); 3,946 (2010); Density: 78.5 persons per square mile (2010); Race: 97.9% White, 0.2% Black, 0.6% Asian, 0.2% American Indian/Alaska Native, 0.0% Native Hawaiian/Other Pacific Islander, 1.1% Other, 1.0% Hispanic of any race (2010); Average household size: 2.57 (2010); Median age: 42.3 (2010); Males per 100 females: 101.2 (2010); Marriage status: 22.5% never married, 59.0% now married, 5.6% widowed, 13.0% divorced (2006-2010 5-year est.); Foreign born: 2.3% (2006-2010 5-year est.); Ancestry (includes multiple ancestries): 21.6% English, 17.7% German, 12.7% Irish, 7.5% Polish, 7.0% French (2006-2010 5-year est.).

**Economy:** Single-family building permits issued: 4 (2011); Multi-family building permits issued: 0 (2011); Employment by occupation: 5.5% management, 2.4% professional, 8.6% services, 19.6% sales, 7.2% farming, 12.6% construction, 8.9% production (2006-2010 5-year est.).

**Income:** Per capita income: $21,623 (2006-2010 5-year est.); Median household income: $49,710 (2006-2010 5-year est.); Average household income: $57,064 (2006-2010 5-year est.); Percent of households with income of $100,000 or more: 12.5% (2006-2010 5-year est.); Poverty rate: 12.6% (2006-2010 5-year est.).

**Education:** Percent of population age 25 and over with: High school diploma (including GED) or higher: 87.3% (2006-2010 5-year est.); Bachelor's degree or higher: 18.6% (2006-2010 5-year est.); Master's degree or higher: 5.5% (2006-2010 5-year est.).

Newark Valley Central School District (KG-12)

    2009-10 Enrollment: 1,236 . . . . . . . . . . . . . . . . . . . . . . . (607) 642-3221

**Housing:** Homeownership rate: 81.9% (2010); Median home value: $90,300 (2006-2010 5-year est.); Median contract rent: $445 per month (2006-2010 5-year est.); Median year structure built: 1968 (2006-2010 5-year est.).

**Transportation:** Commute to work: 91.5% car, 0.6% public transportation, 1.3% walk, 5.5% work from home (2006-2010 5-year est.); Travel time to work: 17.8% less than 15 minutes, 35.9% 15 to 30 minutes, 28.4% 30 to 45 minutes, 11.3% 45 to 60 minutes, 6.5% 60 minutes or more (2006-2010 5-year est.)

**NICHOLS** (village). Covers a land area of 0.518 square miles and a water area of 0 square miles. Located at 42.02° N. Lat; 76.37° W. Long. Elevation is 791 feet.

**Population:** 573 (1990); 574 (2000); 512 (2010); Density: 987.6 persons per square mile (2010); Race: 99.6% White, 0.2% Black, 0.2% Asian, 0.0% American Indian/Alaska Native, 0.0% Native Hawaiian/Other Pacific Islander, 0.0% Other, 0.8% Hispanic of any race (2010); Average household size: 2.47 (2010); Median age: 41.5 (2010); Males per 100 females: 96.9 (2010); Marriage status: 15.7% never married, 63.9% now married, 9.0% widowed, 11.4% divorced (2006-2010 5-year est.); Foreign born: 3.6% (2006-2010 5-year est.); Ancestry (includes multiple ancestries): 35.7% Irish, 21.7% German, 16.4% English, 13.5% American, 6.5% Dutch (2006-2010 5-year est.).

**Economy:** Single-family building permits issued: 0 (2011); Multi-family building permits issued: 0 (2011); Employment by occupation: 12.8% management, 1.1% professional, 7.8% services, 16.2% sales, 2.2% farming, 5.0% construction, 7.8% production (2006-2010 5-year est.).

**Income:** Per capita income: $19,360 (2006-2010 5-year est.); Median household income: $36,705 (2006-2010 5-year est.); Average household income: $49,423 (2006-2010 5-year est.); Percent of households with

income of $100,000 or more: 9.7% (2006-2010 5-year est.); Poverty rate: 5.6% (2006-2010 5-year est.).

**Education:** Percent of population age 25 and over with: High school diploma (including GED) or higher: 80.6% (2006-2010 5-year est.); Bachelor's degree or higher: 13.8% (2006-2010 5-year est.); Master's degree or higher: 7.4% (2006-2010 5-year est.).

Tioga Central School District (PK-12)

    2009-10 Enrollment: 1,115 . . . . . . . . . . . . . . . . . . . . . . . (607) 687-8000

**Housing:** Homeownership rate: 64.2% (2010); Median home value: $86,900 (2006-2010 5-year est.); Median contract rent: $406 per month (2006-2010 5-year est.); Median year structure built: before 1940 (2006-2010 5-year est.).

**Transportation:** Commute to work: 100.0% car, 0.0% public transportation, 0.0% walk, 0.0% work from home (2006-2010 5-year est.); Travel time to work: 21.2% less than 15 minutes, 39.7% 15 to 30 minutes, 15.6% 30 to 45 minutes, 11.7% 45 to 60 minutes, 11.7% 60 minutes or more (2006-2010 5-year est.)

**NICHOLS** (town). Covers a land area of 33.727 square miles and a water area of 0.938 square miles. Located at 42.03° N. Lat; 76.34° W. Long. Elevation is 791 feet.

**Population:** 2,525 (1990); 2,584 (2000); 2,525 (2010); Density: 74.9 persons per square mile (2010); Race: 98.8% White, 0.4% Black, 0.0% Asian, 0.0% American Indian/Alaska Native, 0.0% Native Hawaiian/Other Pacific Islander, 0.8% Other, 1.0% Hispanic of any race (2010); Average household size: 2.55 (2010); Median age: 43.0 (2010); Males per 100 females: 101.5 (2010); Marriage status: 29.4% never married, 55.9% now married, 5.7% widowed, 9.0% divorced (2006-2010 5-year est.); Foreign born: 0.9% (2006-2010 5-year est.); Ancestry (includes multiple ancestries): 24.7% English, 24.1% German, 15.8% Irish, 11.8% American, 5.9% Italian (2006-2010 5-year est.).

**Economy:** Single-family building permits issued: 18 (2011); Multi-family building permits issued: 0 (2011); Employment by occupation: 8.2% management, 0.4% professional, 11.2% services, 13.2% sales, 1.1% farming, 12.6% construction, 7.8% production (2006-2010 5-year est.).

**Income:** Per capita income: $20,216 (2006-2010 5-year est.); Median household income: $46,154 (2006-2010 5-year est.); Average household income: $54,001 (2006-2010 5-year est.); Percent of households with income of $100,000 or more: 8.2% (2006-2010 5-year est.); Poverty rate: 13.8% (2006-2010 5-year est.).

**Education:** Percent of population age 25 and over with: High school diploma (including GED) or higher: 85.1% (2006-2010 5-year est.); Bachelor's degree or higher: 13.2% (2006-2010 5-year est.); Master's degree or higher: 6.6% (2006-2010 5-year est.).

Tioga Central School District (PK-12)

    2009-10 Enrollment: 1,115 . . . . . . . . . . . . . . . . . . . . . . . (607) 687-8000

**Housing:** Homeownership rate: 80.0% (2010); Median home value: $87,400 (2006-2010 5-year est.); Median contract rent: $432 per month (2006-2010 5-year est.); Median year structure built: 1959 (2006-2010 5-year est.).

**Transportation:** Commute to work: 87.6% car, 3.0% public transportation, 3.2% walk, 2.7% work from home (2006-2010 5-year est.); Travel time to work: 32.7% less than 15 minutes, 36.6% 15 to 30 minutes, 19.3% 30 to 45 minutes, 3.7% 45 to 60 minutes, 7.7% 60 minutes or more (2006-2010 5-year est.)

**OWEGO** (village). County seat. Covers a land area of 2.453 square miles and a water area of 0.214 square miles. Located at 42.10° N. Lat; 76.26° W. Long. Elevation is 814 feet.

**Population:** 4,442 (1990); 3,911 (2000); 3,896 (2010); Density: 1,587.7 persons per square mile (2010); Race: 93.8% White, 1.7% Black, 1.5% Asian, 0.3% American Indian/Alaska Native, 0.0% Native Hawaiian/Other Pacific Islander, 2.7% Other, 2.4% Hispanic of any race (2010); Average household size: 2.25 (2010); Median age: 39.6 (2010); Males per 100 females: 95.3 (2010); Marriage status: 32.2% never married, 52.8% now married, 5.5% widowed, 9.6% divorced (2006-2010 5-year est.); Foreign born: 0.8% (2006-2010 5-year est.); Ancestry (includes multiple ancestries): 23.4% German, 19.9% Irish, 16.5% English, 16.5% Italian, 5.7% American (2006-2010 5-year est.).

**Economy:** Single-family building permits issued: 0 (2011); Multi-family building permits issued: 0 (2011); Employment by occupation: 7.7% management, 7.4% professional, 8.2% services, 17.1% sales, 4.1% farming, 8.0% construction, 5.4% production (2006-2010 5-year est.).

**Income:** Per capita income: $22,886 (2006-2010 5-year est.); Median household income: $51,288 (2006-2010 5-year est.); Average household income: $58,382 (2006-2010 5-year est.); Percent of households with income of $100,000 or more: 12.7% (2006-2010 5-year est.); Poverty rate: 11.3% (2006-2010 5-year est.).

**Education:** Percent of population age 25 and over with: High school diploma (including GED) or higher: 89.5% (2006-2010 5-year est.); Bachelor's degree or higher: 23.5% (2006-2010 5-year est.); Master's degree or higher: 11.4% (2006-2010 5-year est.).

### School District(s)

Owego-Apalachin Central School District (KG-12)

   2009-10 Enrollment: 2,148 . . . . . . . . . . . . . . . . . . . . . (607) 687-6224

**Housing:** Homeownership rate: 49.6% (2010); Median home value: $91,900 (2006-2010 5-year est.); Median contract rent: $433 per month (2006-2010 5-year est.); Median year structure built: before 1940 (2006-2010 5-year est.).

**Newspapers:** Owego Pennysaver Press (Community news; Circulation 20,833); Tioga County Courier (Community news; Circulation 1,340)

**Transportation:** Commute to work: 86.6% car, 1.0% public transportation, 6.5% walk, 4.7% work from home (2006-2010 5-year est.); Travel time to work: 44.9% less than 15 minutes, 30.7% 15 to 30 minutes, 13.8% 30 to 45 minutes, 3.5% 45 to 60 minutes, 7.1% 60 minutes or more (2006-2010 5-year est.)

**Additional Information Contacts**

Tioga County Chamber of Commerce . . . . . . . . . . . . . . . . (607) 687-2020
   http://www.tiogachamber.com

**OWEGO** (town). Covers a land area of 104.221 square miles and a water area of 1.521 square miles. Located at 42.08° N. Lat; 76.19° W. Long. Elevation is 814 feet.

**History:** Owego came into existence as Ah-wah-ga, "where the valley widens." Thomas C. Platt born here. Settled in 1787 and incorporated in 1827 on site of Native American village destroyed (1779) in Sullivan campaign.

**Population:** 21,279 (1990); 20,365 (2000); 19,883 (2010); Density: 190.8 persons per square mile (2010); Race: 95.9% White, 1.0% Black, 1.3% Asian, 0.1% American Indian/Alaska Native, 0.0% Native Hawaiian/Other Pacific Islander, 1.7% Other, 1.4% Hispanic of any race (2010); Average household size: 2.48 (2010); Median age: 43.9 (2010); Males per 100 females: 100.4 (2010); Marriage status: 23.8% never married, 62.5% now married, 4.8% widowed, 8.9% divorced (2006-2010 5-year est.); Foreign born: 1.5% (2006-2010 5-year est.); Ancestry (includes multiple ancestries): 25.4% German, 20.3% Irish, 18.8% English, 10.4% Italian, 6.6% Polish (2006-2010 5-year est.).

**Economy:** Single-family building permits issued: 14 (2011); Multi-family building permits issued: 0 (2011); Employment by occupation: 10.2% management, 11.4% professional, 7.5% services, 16.3% sales, 3.7% farming, 7.8% construction, 4.8% production (2006-2010 5-year est.).

**Income:** Per capita income: $29,083 (2006-2010 5-year est.); Median household income: $62,262 (2006-2010 5-year est.); Average household income: $74,427 (2006-2010 5-year est.); Percent of households with income of $100,000 or more: 22.4% (2006-2010 5-year est.); Poverty rate: 5.9% (2006-2010 5-year est.).

**Education:** Percent of population age 25 and over with: High school diploma (including GED) or higher: 93.2% (2006-2010 5-year est.); Bachelor's degree or higher: 33.2% (2006-2010 5-year est.); Master's degree or higher: 13.6% (2006-2010 5-year est.).

### School District(s)

Owego-Apalachin Central School District (KG-12)

   2009-10 Enrollment: 2,148 . . . . . . . . . . . . . . . . . . . . . (607) 687-6224

**Housing:** Homeownership rate: 79.6% (2010); Median home value: $118,100 (2006-2010 5-year est.); Median contract rent: $469 per month (2006-2010 5-year est.); Median year structure built: 1962 (2006-2010 5-year est.).

**Newspapers:** Owego Pennysaver Press (Community news; Circulation 20,833); Tioga County Courier (Community news; Circulation 1,340)

**Transportation:** Commute to work: 93.7% car, 0.5% public transportation, 1.8% walk, 3.2% work from home (2006-2010 5-year est.); Travel time to work: 33.2% less than 15 minutes, 45.0% 15 to 30 minutes, 14.2% 30 to 45 minutes, 3.1% 45 to 60 minutes, 4.4% 60 minutes or more (2006-2010 5-year est.)

**RICHFORD** (town). Covers a land area of 38.186 square miles and a water area of 0.019 square miles. Located at 42.37° N. Lat; 76.19° W. Long. Elevation is 1,115 feet.

**Population:** 1,153 (1990); 1,170 (2000); 1,172 (2010); Density: 30.7 persons per square mile (2010); Race: 98.0% White, 0.4% Black, 0.2% Asian, 0.1% American Indian/Alaska Native, 0.0% Native Hawaiian/Other Pacific Islander, 1.3% Other, 0.3% Hispanic of any race (2010); Average household size: 2.48 (2010); Median age: 42.7 (2010); Males per 100 females: 104.5 (2010); Marriage status: 23.3% never married, 61.9% now married, 5.4% widowed, 9.4% divorced (2006-2010 5-year est.); Foreign born: 1.1% (2006-2010 5-year est.); Ancestry (includes multiple ancestries): 21.1% German, 17.9% English, 12.7% Irish, 5.7% American, 5.7% Dutch (2006-2010 5-year est.).

**Economy:** Single-family building permits issued: 2 (2011); Multi-family building permits issued: 0 (2011); Employment by occupation: 6.2% management, 1.8% professional, 9.6% services, 13.6% sales, 1.9% farming, 16.5% construction, 8.6% production (2006-2010 5-year est.).

**Income:** Per capita income: $20,318 (2006-2010 5-year est.); Median household income: $40,781 (2006-2010 5-year est.); Average household income: $50,381 (2006-2010 5-year est.); Percent of households with income of $100,000 or more: 8.5% (2006-2010 5-year est.); Poverty rate: 18.9% (2006-2010 5-year est.).

**Education:** Percent of population age 25 and over with: High school diploma (including GED) or higher: 84.2% (2006-2010 5-year est.); Bachelor's degree or higher: 15.4% (2006-2010 5-year est.); Master's degree or higher: 6.7% (2006-2010 5-year est.).

**Housing:** Homeownership rate: 85.2% (2010); Median home value: $69,900 (2006-2010 5-year est.); Median contract rent: $342 per month (2006-2010 5-year est.); Median year structure built: 1973 (2006-2010 5-year est.).

**Transportation:** Commute to work: 92.9% car, 1.2% public transportation, 1.3% walk, 3.6% work from home (2006-2010 5-year est.); Travel time to work: 5.7% less than 15 minutes, 28.5% 15 to 30 minutes, 44.3% 30 to 45 minutes, 15.6% 45 to 60 minutes, 6.0% 60 minutes or more (2006-2010 5-year est.)

**SPENCER** (village). Covers a land area of 1.014 square miles and a water area of 0.013 square miles. Located at 42.21° N. Lat; 76.49° W. Long. Elevation is 994 feet.

**Population:** 815 (1990); 731 (2000); 759 (2010); Density: 748.2 persons per square mile (2010); Race: 95.4% White, 2.1% Black, 0.4% Asian, 0.1% American Indian/Alaska Native, 0.0% Native Hawaiian/Other Pacific Islander, 2.0% Other, 0.9% Hispanic of any race (2010); Average household size: 2.40 (2010); Median age: 41.0 (2010); Males per 100 females: 88.8 (2010); Marriage status: 22.9% never married, 59.1% now married, 9.6% widowed, 8.4% divorced (2006-2010 5-year est.); Foreign born: 2.2% (2006-2010 5-year est.); Ancestry (includes multiple ancestries): 21.6% German, 18.0% Italian, 16.0% Irish, 14.8% English, 7.3% American (2006-2010 5-year est.).

**Economy:** Single-family building permits issued: 1 (2011); Multi-family building permits issued: 0 (2011); Employment by occupation: 13.4% management, 4.3% professional, 9.1% services, 21.7% sales, 0.0% farming, 12.9% construction, 4.0% production (2006-2010 5-year est.).

**Income:** Per capita income: $19,178 (2006-2010 5-year est.); Median household income: $34,200 (2006-2010 5-year est.); Average household income: $44,218 (2006-2010 5-year est.); Percent of households with income of $100,000 or more: 7.2% (2006-2010 5-year est.); Poverty rate: 17.7% (2006-2010 5-year est.).

**Education:** Percent of population age 25 and over with: High school diploma (including GED) or higher: 87.1% (2006-2010 5-year est.); Bachelor's degree or higher: 25.7% (2006-2010 5-year est.); Master's degree or higher: 12.9% (2006-2010 5-year est.).

### School District(s)

Spencer-Van Etten Central School District (PK-12)

   2009-10 Enrollment: 1,019 . . . . . . . . . . . . . . . . . . . . . (607) 589-7100

**Housing:** Homeownership rate: 64.3% (2010); Median home value: $96,200 (2006-2010 5-year est.); Median contract rent: $401 per month (2006-2010 5-year est.); Median year structure built: 1943 (2006-2010 5-year est.).

**Transportation:** Commute to work: 84.8% car, 2.8% public transportation, 5.6% walk, 6.8% work from home (2006-2010 5-year est.); Travel time to work: 21.6% less than 15 minutes, 31.9% 15 to 30 minutes, 32.9% 30 to 45 minutes, 6.6% 45 to 60 minutes, 7.0% 60 minutes or more (2006-2010 5-year est.)

**SPENCER** (town). Covers a land area of 49.550 square miles and a water area of 0.325 square miles. Located at 42.22° N. Lat; 76.46° W. Long. Elevation is 994 feet.
**Population:** 2,881 (1990); 2,979 (2000); 3,153 (2010); Density: 63.6 persons per square mile (2010); Race: 96.3% White, 1.1% Black, 0.5% Asian, 0.1% American Indian/Alaska Native, 0.1% Native Hawaiian/Other Pacific Islander, 1.9% Other, 1.7% Hispanic of any race (2010); Average household size: 2.48 (2010); Median age: 41.3 (2010); Males per 100 females: 101.6 (2010); Marriage status: 21.7% never married, 55.8% now married, 7.4% widowed, 15.1% divorced (2006-2010 5-year est.); Foreign born: 1.5% (2006-2010 5-year est.); Ancestry (includes multiple ancestries): 19.9% German, 16.9% English, 14.9% Irish, 13.6% Italian, 6.7% American (2006-2010 5-year est.).
**Economy:** Single-family building permits issued: 3 (2011); Multi-family building permits issued: 0 (2011); Employment by occupation: 10.9% management, 2.3% professional, 7.2% services, 14.1% sales, 1.0% farming, 13.8% construction, 7.1% production (2006-2010 5-year est.).
**Income:** Per capita income: $23,117 (2006-2010 5-year est.); Median household income: $50,865 (2006-2010 5-year est.); Average household income: $53,801 (2006-2010 5-year est.); Percent of households with income of $100,000 or more: 8.3% (2006-2010 5-year est.); Poverty rate: 8.9% (2006-2010 5-year est.).
**Education:** Percent of population age 25 and over with: High school diploma (including GED) or higher: 94.2% (2006-2010 5-year est.); Bachelor's degree or higher: 24.7% (2006-2010 5-year est.); Master's degree or higher: 13.3% (2006-2010 5-year est.).
School District(s)
Spencer-Van Etten Central School District (PK-12)
   2009-10 Enrollment: 1,019 . . . . . . . . . . . . . . . . . . . . . (607) 589-7100
**Housing:** Homeownership rate: 77.0% (2010); Median home value: $98,000 (2006-2010 5-year est.); Median contract rent: $453 per month (2006-2010 5-year est.); Median year structure built: 1969 (2006-2010 5-year est.).
**Transportation:** Commute to work: 92.5% car, 1.6% public transportation, 1.2% walk, 4.8% work from home (2006-2010 5-year est.); Travel time to work: 19.9% less than 15 minutes, 27.4% 15 to 30 minutes, 36.8% 30 to 45 minutes, 8.1% 45 to 60 minutes, 7.7% 60 minutes or more (2006-2010 5-year est.)

**TIOGA** (town). Covers a land area of 58.620 square miles and a water area of 0.839 square miles. Located at 42.10° N. Lat; 76.36° W. Long.
**Population:** 4,772 (1990); 4,840 (2000); 4,871 (2010); Density: 83.1 persons per square mile (2010); Race: 98.2% White, 0.3% Black, 0.4% Asian, 0.2% American Indian/Alaska Native, 0.0% Native Hawaiian/Other Pacific Islander, 0.9% Other, 1.2% Hispanic of any race (2010); Average household size: 2.54 (2010); Median age: 42.3 (2010); Males per 100 females: 96.7 (2010); Marriage status: 23.6% never married, 56.6% now married, 6.1% widowed, 13.7% divorced (2006-2010 5-year est.); Foreign born: 1.4% (2006-2010 5-year est.); Ancestry (includes multiple ancestries): 21.7% German, 17.0% English, 14.7% Irish, 12.9% American, 8.5% Italian (2006-2010 5-year est.).
**Economy:** Single-family building permits issued: 16 (2011); Multi-family building permits issued: 0 (2011); Employment by occupation: 3.9% management, 5.7% professional, 7.8% services, 19.9% sales, 2.7% farming, 14.4% construction, 11.4% production (2006-2010 5-year est.).
**Income:** Per capita income: $20,524 (2006-2010 5-year est.); Median household income: $43,914 (2006-2010 5-year est.); Average household income: $51,702 (2006-2010 5-year est.); Percent of households with income of $100,000 or more: 9.9% (2006-2010 5-year est.); Poverty rate: 8.3% (2006-2010 5-year est.).
**Education:** Percent of population age 25 and over with: High school diploma (including GED) or higher: 80.8% (2006-2010 5-year est.); Bachelor's degree or higher: 11.4% (2006-2010 5-year est.); Master's degree or higher: 4.4% (2006-2010 5-year est.).
**Housing:** Homeownership rate: 79.8% (2010); Median home value: $84,000 (2006-2010 5-year est.); Median contract rent: $446 per month (2006-2010 5-year est.); Median year structure built: 1972 (2006-2010 5-year est.).
**Transportation:** Commute to work: 94.4% car, 0.0% public transportation, 1.0% walk, 4.7% work from home (2006-2010 5-year est.); Travel time to work: 23.2% less than 15 minutes, 42.6% 15 to 30 minutes, 22.3% 30 to 45 minutes, 6.7% 45 to 60 minutes, 5.3% 60 minutes or more (2006-2010 5-year est.)

**TIOGA CENTER** (unincorporated postal area)
Zip Code: 13845
   Covers a land area of 0.388 square miles and a water area of 0.003 square miles. Located at 42.05° N. Lat; 76.35° W. Long. Elevation is 797 feet. Population: 83 (2010); Density: 213.9 persons per square mile (2010); Race: 96.4% White, 1.2% Black, 0.0% Asian, 0.0% American Indian/Alaska Native, 0.0% Native Hawaiian/Other Pacific Islander, 2.4% Other, 0.0% Hispanic of any race (2010); Average household size: 2.59 (2010); Median age: 35.5 (2010); Males per 100 females: 97.6 (2010); Homeownership rate: 65.7% (2010)

**WAVERLY** (village). Covers a land area of 2.293 square miles and a water area of 0.026 square miles. Located at 42.01° N. Lat; 76.54° W. Long. Elevation is 814 feet.
**History:** Incorporated 1853.
**Population:** 4,847 (1990); 4,607 (2000); 4,444 (2010); Density: 1,937.8 persons per square mile (2010); Race: 97.0% White, 0.8% Black, 0.4% Asian, 0.3% American Indian/Alaska Native, 0.0% Native Hawaiian/Other Pacific Islander, 1.5% Other, 1.2% Hispanic of any race (2010); Average household size: 2.27 (2010); Median age: 39.7 (2010); Males per 100 females: 86.0 (2010); Marriage status: 28.4% never married, 48.5% now married, 12.1% widowed, 10.9% divorced (2006-2010 5-year est.); Foreign born: 1.9% (2006-2010 5-year est.); Ancestry (includes multiple ancestries): 25.0% German, 17.6% Irish, 14.6% English, 11.2% Italian, 9.5% American (2006-2010 5-year est.).
**Economy:** Single-family building permits issued: 1 (2011); Multi-family building permits issued: 0 (2011); Employment by occupation: 10.0% management, 4.5% professional, 7.3% services, 16.1% sales, 2.4% farming, 9.6% construction, 9.8% production (2006-2010 5-year est.).
**Income:** Per capita income: $22,913 (2006-2010 5-year est.); Median household income: $39,821 (2006-2010 5-year est.); Average household income: $50,138 (2006-2010 5-year est.); Percent of households with income of $100,000 or more: 10.0% (2006-2010 5-year est.); Poverty rate: 18.8% (2006-2010 5-year est.).
**Education:** Percent of population age 25 and over with: High school diploma (including GED) or higher: 88.8% (2006-2010 5-year est.); Bachelor's degree or higher: 18.7% (2006-2010 5-year est.); Master's degree or higher: 6.0% (2006-2010 5-year est.).
School District(s)
Waverly Central School District (PK-12)
   2009-10 Enrollment: 1,724 . . . . . . . . . . . . . . . . . . . . . (607) 565-2841
**Housing:** Homeownership rate: 54.2% (2010); Median home value: $80,600 (2006-2010 5-year est.); Median contract rent: $423 per month (2006-2010 5-year est.); Median year structure built: before 1940 (2006-2010 5-year est.).
**Safety:** Violent crime rate: 7.1 per 10,000 population; Property crime rate: 301.2 per 10,000 population (2010).
**Transportation:** Commute to work: 86.7% car, 0.9% public transportation, 6.0% walk, 4.0% work from home (2006-2010 5-year est.); Travel time to work: 49.5% less than 15 minutes, 25.2% 15 to 30 minutes, 15.1% 30 to 45 minutes, 5.8% 45 to 60 minutes, 4.4% 60 minutes or more (2006-2010 5-year est.)

**WILLSEYVILLE** (unincorporated postal area)
Zip Code: 13864
   Covers a land area of 26.650 square miles and a water area of 0.005 square miles. Located at 42.27° N. Lat; 76.38° W. Long. Elevation is 948 feet. Population: 1,149 (2010); Density: 43.1 persons per square mile (2010); Race: 95.9% White, 1.4% Black, 0.3% Asian, 1.0% American Indian/Alaska Native, 0.0% Native Hawaiian/Other Pacific Islander, 1.4% Other, 1.0% Hispanic of any race (2010); Average household size: 2.34 (2010); Median age: 42.2 (2010); Males per 100 females: 100.5 (2010); Homeownership rate: 78.2% (2010)

## Tompkins County

Located in west central New York; includes part of Cayuga Lake. Covers a land area of 476.05 square miles, a water area of 15.57 square miles, and is located in the Eastern Time Zone at 42.46° N. Lat., 76.48° W. Long. The county was founded in 1817. County seat is Ithaca.

Tompkins County is part of the Ithaca, NY Metropolitan Statistical Area. The entire metro area includes: Tompkins County, NY

Weather Station: Ithaca Cornell Univ         Elevation: 959 feet

| | Jan | Feb | Mar | Apr | May | Jun | Jul | Aug | Sep | Oct | Nov | Dec |
|---|---|---|---|---|---|---|---|---|---|---|---|---|
| High | 31 | 34 | 41 | 55 | 67 | 76 | 80 | 79 | 71 | 59 | 47 | 36 |
| Low | 15 | 16 | 23 | 34 | 44 | 53 | 58 | 57 | 49 | 39 | 31 | 21 |
| Precip | 2.0 | 1.8 | 2.8 | 3.3 | 3.2 | 3.9 | 3.9 | 3.5 | 3.7 | 3.3 | 3.2 | 2.3 |
| Snow | 17.4 | 12.7 | 12.2 | 3.6 | 0.0 | 0.0 | 0.0 | 0.0 | 0.0 | 0.4 | 4.8 | 12.9 |

*High and Low temperatures in degrees Fahrenheit; Precipitation and Snow in inches*

**Population:** 94,097 (1990); 96,501 (2000); 101,564 (2010); Race: 82.6% White, 4.0% Black, 8.6% Asian, 0.4% American Indian/Alaska Native, 0.0% Native Hawaiian/Other Pacific Islander, 4.4% Other, 4.2% Hispanic of any race (2010); Density: 213.3 persons per square mile (2010); Average household size: 2.27 (2010); Median age: 29.8 (2010); Males per 100 females: 97.1 (2010).

**Religion:** Six largest groups: 7.2% Catholicism, 4.0% Methodist/Pietist, 2.1% Non-Denominational, 2.0% Presbyterian-Reformed, 1.3% Pentecostal, 1.2% Lutheran (2010)

**Economy:** Unemployment rate: 6.5% (February 2012); Total civilian labor force: 54,232 (February 2012); Leading industries: 11.4% health care and social assistance; 11.2% retail trade; 8.7% accommodation & food services (2009); Farms: 588 totaling 108,739 acres (2007); Companies that employ 500 or more persons: 4 (2009); Companies that employ 100 to 499 persons: 39 (2009); Companies that employ less than 100 persons: 2,254 (2009); Black-owned businesses: 88 (2007); Hispanic-owned businesses: n/a (2007); Asian-owned businesses: 510 (2007); Women-owned businesses: 3,101 (2007); Retail sales per capita: $10,525 (2010). Single-family building permits issued: 102 (2011); Multi-family building permits issued: 51 (2011).

**Income:** Per capita income: $25,737 (2006-2010 5-year est.); Median household income: $48,655 (2006-2010 5-year est.); Average household income: $66,115 (2006-2010 5-year est.); Percent of households with income of $100,000 or more: 20.6% (2006-2010 5-year est.); Poverty rate: 18.8% (2006-2010 5-year est.); Bankruptcy rate: 1.22% (2011).

**Taxes:** Total county taxes per capita: $792 (2009); County property taxes per capita: $337 (2009).

**Education:** Percent of population age 25 and over with: High school diploma (including GED) or higher: 92.4% (2006-2010 5-year est.); Bachelor's degree or higher: 49.7% (2006-2010 5-year est.); Master's degree or higher: 28.5% (2006-2010 5-year est.).

**Housing:** Homeownership rate: 54.2% (2010); Median home value: $162,100 (2006-2010 5-year est.); Median contract rent: $744 per month (2006-2010 5-year est.); Median year structure built: 1969 (2006-2010 5-year est.)

**Health:** Birth rate: 89.5 per 10,000 population (2011); Death rate: 57.7 per 10,000 population (2011); Age-adjusted cancer mortality rate: 146.8 deaths per 100,000 population (2009); Number of physicians: 25.6 per 10,000 population (2008); Hospital beds: 20.8 per 10,000 population (2007); Hospital admissions: 707.9 per 10,000 population (2007).

**Elections:** 2008 Presidential election results: 70.1% Obama, 28.0% McCain, 0.7% Nader

**National and State Parks:** Buttermilk Falls State Park; Buttermilk Falls State Park; Danby State Forest; Hammond Hill State Forest; Newfield State Forest; Potato Hill State Forest; Robert H Treman State Park; Shindagin Hollow State Forest; Taughannock Falls State Park; Yellow Barn State Forest

**Additional Information Contacts**

Tompkins County Government . . . . . . . . . . . . . . . . . . . . . (607) 274-5431
  http://www.co.tompkins.ny.us
City of Ithaca . . . . . . . . . . . . . . . . . . . . . . . . . . . . . . . . . (607) 274-6570
  http://www.ci.ithaca.ny.us
Tompkins County Chamber of Commerce. . . . . . . . . . . . (607) 273-7080
  http://www.tompkinschamber.org
Town of Dryden . . . . . . . . . . . . . . . . . . . . . . . . . . . . . . . (607) 844-8888
  http://www.dryden.ny.us
Town of Ithaca . . . . . . . . . . . . . . . . . . . . . . . . . . . . . . . . (607) 273-1721
  http://www.town.ithaca.ny.us
Town of Lansing. . . . . . . . . . . . . . . . . . . . . . . . . . . . . . . (607) 533-4142
  http://www.lansingtown.com
Town of Ulysses. . . . . . . . . . . . . . . . . . . . . . . . . . . . . . . (607) 387-5767
  http://www.ulysses.ny.us
Trumansburg Area Chamber of Commerce. . . . . . . . . . . (607) 387-9254
  http://www.trumansburgchamber.com
Village of Dryden . . . . . . . . . . . . . . . . . . . . . . . . . . . . . . (607) 844-8122
  http://www.dryden-ny.org
Village of Lansing. . . . . . . . . . . . . . . . . . . . . . . . . . . . . . (607) 257-0424
  http://www.vlansing.org
Village of Trumansburg . . . . . . . . . . . . . . . . . . . . . . . . . (607) 387-6501
  http://www.trumansburg-ny.gov

## Tompkins County Communities

### BROOKTONDALE (unincorporated postal area)
Zip Code: 14817

Covers a land area of 40.293 square miles and a water area of 0.097 square miles. Located at 42.35° N. Lat; 76.33° W. Long. Elevation is 915 feet. Population: 2,380 (2010); Density: 59.1 persons per square mile (2010); Race: 93.1% White, 2.1% Black, 0.7% Asian, 0.3% American Indian/Alaska Native, 0.0% Native Hawaiian/Other Pacific Islander, 3.8% Other, 1.7% Hispanic of any race (2010); Average household size: 2.34 (2010); Median age: 39.3 (2010); Males per 100 females: 101.9 (2010); Homeownership rate: 71.8% (2010)

### CAROLINE (town). Covers a land area of 54.763 square miles and a water area of 0.130 square miles. Located at 42.35° N. Lat; 76.33° W. Long. Elevation is 968 feet.

**Population:** 3,044 (1990); 2,910 (2000); 3,282 (2010); Density: 59.9 persons per square mile (2010); Race: 93.6% White, 2.1% Black, 0.9% Asian, 0.3% American Indian/Alaska Native, 0.1% Native Hawaiian/Other Pacific Islander, 3.0% Other, 1.7% Hispanic of any race (2010); Average household size: 2.32 (2010); Median age: 40.3 (2010); Males per 100 females: 99.9 (2010); Marriage status: 26.3% never married, 63.0% now married, 6.1% widowed, 4.6% divorced (2006-2010 5-year est.); Foreign born: 1.3% (2006-2010 5-year est.); Ancestry (includes multiple ancestries): 27.4% German, 18.4% Irish, 14.6% English, 11.9% American, 8.5% Italian (2006-2010 5-year est.).

**Economy:** Single-family building permits issued: 0 (2011); Multi-family building permits issued: 0 (2011); Employment by occupation: 10.4% management, 5.7% professional, 7.7% services, 8.2% sales, 4.3% farming, 12.3% construction, 2.9% production (2006-2010 5-year est.).

**Income:** Per capita income: $25,347 (2006-2010 5-year est.); Median household income: $53,186 (2006-2010 5-year est.); Average household income: $61,751 (2006-2010 5-year est.); Percent of households with income of $100,000 or more: 17.9% (2006-2010 5-year est.); Poverty rate: 3.3% (2006-2010 5-year est.).

**Education:** Percent of population age 25 and over with: High school diploma (including GED) or higher: 96.3% (2006-2010 5-year est.); Bachelor's degree or higher: 39.0% (2006-2010 5-year est.); Master's degree or higher: 20.2% (2006-2010 5-year est.).

**Housing:** Homeownership rate: 70.4% (2010); Median home value: $131,000 (2006-2010 5-year est.); Median contract rent: $545 per month (2006-2010 5-year est.); Median year structure built: 1972 (2006-2010 5-year est.)

**Transportation:** Commute to work: 92.3% car, 0.0% public transportation, 0.0% walk, 6.9% work from home (2006-2010 5-year est.); Travel time to work: 14.5% less than 15 minutes, 51.8% 15 to 30 minutes, 18.2% 30 to 45 minutes, 11.7% 45 to 60 minutes, 3.8% 60 minutes or more (2006-2010 5-year est.)

### CAYUGA HEIGHTS (village). Covers a land area of 1.766 square miles and a water area of 0.001 square miles. Located at 42.46° N. Lat; 76.48° W. Long. Elevation is 787 feet.

**Population:** 3,457 (1990); 3,273 (2000); 3,729 (2010); Density: 2,110.7 persons per square mile (2010); Race: 79.5% White, 2.1% Black, 14.7% Asian, 0.1% American Indian/Alaska Native, 0.0% Native Hawaiian/Other Pacific Islander, 3.6% Other, 4.7% Hispanic of any race (2010); Average household size: 2.04 (2010); Median age: 34.7 (2010); Males per 100 females: 94.1 (2010); Marriage status: 39.1% never married, 45.1% now married, 8.9% widowed, 6.9% divorced (2006-2010 5-year est.); Foreign born: 26.9% (2006-2010 5-year est.); Ancestry (includes multiple ancestries): 14.0% German, 11.1% Irish, 11.0% English, 10.4% Italian, 5.1% American (2006-2010 5-year est.).

**Economy:** Single-family building permits issued: 0 (2011); Multi-family building permits issued: 0 (2011); Employment by occupation: 11.7% management, 13.5% professional, 3.1% services, 7.7% sales, 4.7% farming, 1.6% construction, 0.0% production (2006-2010 5-year est.).

**Income:** Per capita income: $46,743 (2006-2010 5-year est.); Median household income: $79,375 (2006-2010 5-year est.); Average household income: $108,211 (2006-2010 5-year est.); Percent of households with income of $100,000 or more: 40.4% (2006-2010 5-year est.); Poverty rate: 12.9% (2006-2010 5-year est.).

**Education:** Percent of population age 25 and over with: High school diploma (including GED) or higher: 100.0% (2006-2010 5-year est.); Bachelor's degree or higher: 86.6% (2006-2010 5-year est.); Master's degree or higher: 65.9% (2006-2010 5-year est.).
**Housing:** Homeownership rate: 50.4% (2010); Median home value: $326,300 (2006-2010 5-year est.); Median contract rent: $1,046 per month (2006-2010 5-year est.); Median year structure built: 1962 (2006-2010 5-year est.).
**Safety:** Violent crime rate: 2.8 per 10,000 population; Property crime rate: 135.1 per 10,000 population (2010).
**Transportation:** Commute to work: 55.5% car, 9.7% public transportation, 18.1% walk, 11.7% work from home (2006-2010 5-year est.); Travel time to work: 62.6% less than 15 minutes, 27.9% 15 to 30 minutes, 7.5% 30 to 45 minutes, 1.2% 45 to 60 minutes, 0.7% 60 minutes or more (2006-2010 5-year est.).

**DANBY** (town). Covers a land area of 53.553 square miles and a water area of 0.222 square miles. Located at 42.33° N. Lat; 76.47° W. Long. Elevation is 1,237 feet.
**Population:** 2,858 (1990); 3,007 (2000); 3,329 (2010); Density: 62.2 persons per square mile (2010); Race: 91.8% White, 2.5% Black, 1.3% Asian, 0.8% American Indian/Alaska Native, 0.0% Native Hawaiian/Other Pacific Islander, 3.6% Other, 2.6% Hispanic of any race (2010); Average household size: 2.42 (2010); Median age: 43.5 (2010); Males per 100 females: 97.6 (2010); Marriage status: 18.7% never married, 68.4% now married, 6.8% widowed, 6.1% divorced (2006-2010 5-year est.); Foreign born: 4.8% (2006-2010 5-year est.); Ancestry (includes multiple ancestries): 21.0% German, 20.2% English, 15.0% Irish, 7.3% Italian, 6.5% Scottish (2006-2010 5-year est.).
**Economy:** Single-family building permits issued: 13 (2011); Multi-family building permits issued: 2 (2011); Employment by occupation: 14.2% management, 5.8% professional, 5.0% services, 14.1% sales, 4.9% farming, 6.7% construction, 3.2% production (2006-2010 5-year est.).
**Income:** Per capita income: $31,323 (2006-2010 5-year est.); Median household income: $55,703 (2006-2010 5-year est.); Average household income: $72,440 (2006-2010 5-year est.); Percent of households with income of $100,000 or more: 26.5% (2006-2010 5-year est.); Poverty rate: 12.5% (2006-2010 5-year est.).
**Education:** Percent of population age 25 and over with: High school diploma (including GED) or higher: 90.6% (2006-2010 5-year est.); Bachelor's degree or higher: 39.3% (2006-2010 5-year est.); Master's degree or higher: 21.1% (2006-2010 5-year est.).
**Housing:** Homeownership rate: 81.9% (2010); Median home value: $160,000 (2006-2010 5-year est.); Median contract rent: $598 per month (2006-2010 5-year est.); Median year structure built: 1970 (2006-2010 5-year est.).
**Transportation:** Commute to work: 88.1% car, 0.0% public transportation, 3.6% walk, 4.7% work from home (2006-2010 5-year est.); Travel time to work: 33.1% less than 15 minutes, 40.1% 15 to 30 minutes, 17.2% 30 to 45 minutes, 6.0% 45 to 60 minutes, 3.6% 60 minutes or more (2006-2010 5-year est.).

**DRYDEN** (village). Covers a land area of 1.756 square miles and a water area of 0.013 square miles. Located at 42.49° N. Lat; 76.30° W. Long. Elevation is 1,089 feet.
**Population:** 1,908 (1990); 1,832 (2000); 1,890 (2010); Density: 1,076.2 persons per square mile (2010); Race: 94.7% White, 1.3% Black, 0.7% Asian, 0.4% American Indian/Alaska Native, 0.0% Native Hawaiian/Other Pacific Islander, 2.9% Other, 2.5% Hispanic of any race (2010); Average household size: 2.31 (2010); Median age: 41.4 (2010); Males per 100 females: 96.9 (2010); Marriage status: 27.5% never married, 56.1% now married, 7.7% widowed, 8.7% divorced (2006-2010 5-year est.); Foreign born: 5.8% (2006-2010 5-year est.); Ancestry (includes multiple ancestries): 25.5% German, 20.4% Irish, 15.2% English, 13.8% Italian, 6.1% Dutch (2006-2010 5-year est.).
**Economy:** Single-family building permits issued: 2 (2011); Multi-family building permits issued: 0 (2011); Employment by occupation: 9.0% management, 9.4% professional, 15.1% services, 10.6% sales, 3.7% farming, 4.2% construction, 3.4% production (2006-2010 5-year est.).
**Income:** Per capita income: $27,025 (2006-2010 5-year est.); Median household income: $59,231 (2006-2010 5-year est.); Average household income: $61,300 (2006-2010 5-year est.); Percent of households with income of $100,000 or more: 14.3% (2006-2010 5-year est.); Poverty rate: 10.0% (2006-2010 5-year est.).

**Education:** Percent of population age 25 and over with: High school diploma (including GED) or higher: 95.9% (2006-2010 5-year est.); Bachelor's degree or higher: 38.1% (2006-2010 5-year est.); Master's degree or higher: 18.9% (2006-2010 5-year est.).
**School District(s)**
Dryden Central School District (KG-12)
   2009-10 Enrollment: 1,778 . . . . . . . . . . . . . . . . . . . . . . . . . . (607) 844-5361
**Two-year College(s)**
Tompkins Cortland Community College (Public)
   Fall 2010 Enrollment: 3,935 . . . . . . . . . . . . . . . . . . . . . . . (607) 844-8211
   2011-12 Tuition: In-state $4,615; Out-of-state $8,865
**Housing:** Homeownership rate: 61.5% (2010); Median home value: $144,200 (2006-2010 5-year est.); Median contract rent: $498 per month (2006-2010 5-year est.); Median year structure built: 1956 (2006-2010 5-year est.).
**Safety:** Violent crime rate: 16.6 per 10,000 population; Property crime rate: 630.9 per 10,000 population (2010).
**Transportation:** Commute to work: 92.2% car, 2.7% public transportation, 2.1% walk, 2.3% work from home (2006-2010 5-year est.); Travel time to work: 36.2% less than 15 minutes, 51.8% 15 to 30 minutes, 7.2% 30 to 45 minutes, 1.7% 45 to 60 minutes, 3.1% 60 minutes or more (2006-2010 5-year est.).
**Additional Information Contacts**
Village of Dryden . . . . . . . . . . . . . . . . . . . . . . . . . . . . . . (607) 844-8122
   http://www.dryden-ny.org

**DRYDEN** (town). Covers a land area of 93.639 square miles and a water area of 0.690 square miles. Located at 42.47° N. Lat; 76.36° W. Long. Elevation is 1,089 feet.
**Population:** 13,251 (1990); 13,532 (2000); 14,435 (2010); Density: 154.2 persons per square mile (2010); Race: 91.0% White, 2.9% Black, 1.9% Asian, 0.3% American Indian/Alaska Native, 0.0% Native Hawaiian/Other Pacific Islander, 3.9% Other, 3.1% Hispanic of any race (2010); Average household size: 2.36 (2010); Median age: 37.6 (2010); Males per 100 females: 100.1 (2010); Marriage status: 30.9% never married, 56.0% now married, 4.0% widowed, 9.0% divorced (2006-2010 5-year est.); Foreign born: 5.2% (2006-2010 5-year est.); Ancestry (includes multiple ancestries): 17.9% German, 16.9% English, 16.8% Irish, 9.6% Italian, 8.5% American (2006-2010 5-year est.).
**Economy:** Single-family building permits issued: 11 (2011); Multi-family building permits issued: 12 (2011); Employment by occupation: 11.0% management, 6.0% professional, 9.1% services, 15.1% sales, 2.3% farming, 8.2% construction, 5.5% production (2006-2010 5-year est.).
**Income:** Per capita income: $30,866 (2006-2010 5-year est.); Median household income: $60,514 (2006-2010 5-year est.); Average household income: $73,754 (2006-2010 5-year est.); Percent of households with income of $100,000 or more: 22.9% (2006-2010 5-year est.); Poverty rate: 9.5% (2006-2010 5-year est.).
**Education:** Percent of population age 25 and over with: High school diploma (including GED) or higher: 92.9% (2006-2010 5-year est.); Bachelor's degree or higher: 43.7% (2006-2010 5-year est.); Master's degree or higher: 23.5% (2006-2010 5-year est.).
**School District(s)**
Dryden Central School District (KG-12)
   2009-10 Enrollment: 1,778 . . . . . . . . . . . . . . . . . . . . . . . . . . (607) 844-5361
**Two-year College(s)**
Tompkins Cortland Community College (Public)
   Fall 2010 Enrollment: 3,935 . . . . . . . . . . . . . . . . . . . . . . . (607) 844-8211
   2011-12 Tuition: In-state $4,615; Out-of-state $8,865
**Housing:** Homeownership rate: 65.4% (2010); Median home value: $155,800 (2006-2010 5-year est.); Median contract rent: $616 per month (2006-2010 5-year est.); Median year structure built: 1975 (2006-2010 5-year est.).
**Transportation:** Commute to work: 90.3% car, 2.6% public transportation, 1.4% walk, 4.3% work from home (2006-2010 5-year est.); Travel time to work: 32.7% less than 15 minutes, 52.1% 15 to 30 minutes, 8.0% 30 to 45 minutes, 2.7% 45 to 60 minutes, 4.5% 60 minutes or more (2006-2010 5-year est.).
**Additional Information Contacts**
Town of Dryden . . . . . . . . . . . . . . . . . . . . . . . . . . . . . . . (607) 844-8888
   http://www.dryden.ny.us

## EAST ITHACA (CDP).
Covers a land area of 1.733 square miles and a water area of 0.049 square miles. Located at 42.42° N. Lat; 76.46° W. Long. Elevation is 804 feet.

**Population:** 2,164 (1990); 2,192 (2000); 2,231 (2010); Density: 1,287.3 persons per square mile (2010); Race: 69.7% White, 4.8% Black, 20.3% Asian, 0.4% American Indian/Alaska Native, 0.0% Native Hawaiian/Other Pacific Islander, 4.8% Other, 5.0% Hispanic of any race (2010); Average household size: 1.97 (2010); Median age: 31.6 (2010); Males per 100 females: 98.3 (2010); Marriage status: 29.3% never married, 58.2% now married, 4.7% widowed, 7.8% divorced (2006-2010 5-year est.); Foreign born: 39.3% (2006-2010 5-year est.); Ancestry (includes multiple ancestries): 23.9% English, 19.9% German, 12.3% Irish, 8.0% Italian, 7.6% Russian (2006-2010 5-year est.).

**Economy:** Employment by occupation: 7.6% management, 12.7% professional, 3.3% services, 8.1% sales, 2.0% farming, 3.6% construction, 0.0% production (2006-2010 5-year est.).

**Income:** Per capita income: $33,948 (2006-2010 5-year est.); Median household income: $58,442 (2006-2010 5-year est.); Average household income: $72,214 (2006-2010 5-year est.); Percent of households with income of $100,000 or more: 29.3% (2006-2010 5-year est.); Poverty rate: 15.3% (2006-2010 5-year est.).

**Education:** Percent of population age 25 and over with: High school diploma (including GED) or higher: 95.0% (2006-2010 5-year est.); Bachelor's degree or higher: 74.6% (2006-2010 5-year est.); Master's degree or higher: 55.1% (2006-2010 5-year est.).

**Housing:** Homeownership rate: 49.7% (2010); Median home value: $175,500 (2006-2010 5-year est.); Median contract rent: $807 per month (2006-2010 5-year est.); Median year structure built: 1980 (2006-2010 5-year est.).

**Transportation:** Commute to work: 61.5% car, 7.5% public transportation, 21.6% walk, 6.7% work from home (2006-2010 5-year est.); Travel time to work: 45.9% less than 15 minutes, 39.4% 15 to 30 minutes, 7.1% 30 to 45 minutes, 2.3% 45 to 60 minutes, 5.3% 60 minutes or more (2006-2010 5-year est.)

## ENFIELD (town).
Aka Enfield Center. Covers a land area of 36.732 square miles and a water area of 0.104 square miles. Located at 42.44° N. Lat; 76.62° W. Long. Elevation is 1,106 feet.

**Population:** 3,054 (1990); 3,369 (2000); 3,512 (2010); Density: 95.6 persons per square mile (2010); Race: 93.4% White, 2.0% Black, 0.4% Asian, 0.4% American Indian/Alaska Native, 0.0% Native Hawaiian/Other Pacific Islander, 3.8% Other, 2.3% Hispanic of any race (2010); Average household size: 2.43 (2010); Median age: 41.2 (2010); Males per 100 females: 95.2 (2010); Marriage status: 28.5% never married, 49.5% now married, 5.9% widowed, 16.2% divorced (2006-2010 5-year est.); Foreign born: 3.8% (2006-2010 5-year est.); Ancestry (includes multiple ancestries): 21.0% English, 16.1% German, 14.4% Irish, 8.3% American, 6.8% Italian (2006-2010 5-year est.).

**Economy:** Single-family building permits issued: 11 (2011); Multi-family building permits issued: 0 (2011); Employment by occupation: 11.4% management, 2.5% professional, 9.2% services, 15.4% sales, 4.7% farming, 20.2% construction, 11.9% production (2006-2010 5-year est.).

**Income:** Per capita income: $22,667 (2006-2010 5-year est.); Median household income: $42,997 (2006-2010 5-year est.); Average household income: $53,889 (2006-2010 5-year est.); Percent of households with income of $100,000 or more: 11.5% (2006-2010 5-year est.); Poverty rate: 13.6% (2006-2010 5-year est.).

**Education:** Percent of population age 25 and over with: High school diploma (including GED) or higher: 83.9% (2006-2010 5-year est.); Bachelor's degree or higher: 20.0% (2006-2010 5-year est.); Master's degree or higher: 9.1% (2006-2010 5-year est.).

**Housing:** Homeownership rate: 72.5% (2010); Median home value: $108,700 (2006-2010 5-year est.); Median contract rent: $652 per month (2006-2010 5-year est.); Median year structure built: 1976 (2006-2010 5-year est.).

**Transportation:** Commute to work: 86.4% car, 3.3% public transportation, 1.2% walk, 5.4% work from home (2006-2010 5-year est.); Travel time to work: 10.5% less than 15 minutes, 62.4% 15 to 30 minutes, 21.2% 30 to 45 minutes, 3.2% 45 to 60 minutes, 2.7% 60 minutes or more (2006-2010 5-year est.)

## ETNA (unincorporated postal area)
Zip Code: 13062

Covers a land area of 0.180 square miles and a water area of 0.006 square miles. Located at 42.48° N. Lat; 76.38° W. Long. Elevation is 1,020 feet. Population: 173 (2010); Density: 959.0 persons per square mile (2010); Race: 92.5% White, 1.7% Black, 2.3% Asian, 0.0% American Indian/Alaska Native, 0.0% Native Hawaiian/Other Pacific Islander, 3.5% Other, 0.0% Hispanic of any race (2010); Average household size: 2.28 (2010); Median age: 34.2 (2010); Males per 100 females: 94.4 (2010); Homeownership rate: 48.7% (2010)

## FOREST HOME (CDP).
Covers a land area of 0.251 square miles and a water area of 0.022 square miles. Located at 42.45° N. Lat; 76.47° W. Long. Elevation is 922 feet.

**Population:** 1,125 (1990); 941 (2000); 572 (2010); Density: 2,277.2 persons per square mile (2010); Race: 59.1% White, 2.1% Black, 35.5% Asian, 0.0% American Indian/Alaska Native, 0.0% Native Hawaiian/Other Pacific Islander, 3.3% Other, 5.6% Hispanic of any race (2010); Average household size: 2.13 (2010); Median age: 30.1 (2010); Males per 100 females: 102.8 (2010); Marriage status: 29.0% never married, 63.2% now married, 1.1% widowed, 6.6% divorced (2006-2010 5-year est.); Foreign born: 45.1% (2006-2010 5-year est.); Ancestry (includes multiple ancestries): 11.7% Italian, 9.8% German, 4.9% English, 4.8% Irish, 3.2% Norwegian (2006-2010 5-year est.).

**Economy:** Employment by occupation: 0.0% management, 21.8% professional, 8.7% services, 4.4% sales, 0.0% farming, 0.0% construction, 10.0% production (2006-2010 5-year est.).

**Income:** Per capita income: $29,578 (2006-2010 5-year est.); Median household income: $29,514 (2006-2010 5-year est.); Average household income: $73,931 (2006-2010 5-year est.); Percent of households with income of $100,000 or more: 14.4% (2006-2010 5-year est.); Poverty rate: 13.7% (2006-2010 5-year est.).

**Education:** Percent of population age 25 and over with: High school diploma (including GED) or higher: 87.1% (2006-2010 5-year est.); Bachelor's degree or higher: 65.6% (2006-2010 5-year est.); Master's degree or higher: 51.5% (2006-2010 5-year est.).

**Housing:** Homeownership rate: 27.2% (2010); Median home value: $263,300 (2006-2010 5-year est.); Median contract rent: $843 per month (2006-2010 5-year est.); Median year structure built: 1959 (2006-2010 5-year est.).

**Transportation:** Commute to work: 42.6% car, 31.2% public transportation, 23.7% walk, 2.5% work from home (2006-2010 5-year est.); Travel time to work: 51.4% less than 15 minutes, 37.1% 15 to 30 minutes, 4.0% 30 to 45 minutes, 2.6% 45 to 60 minutes, 4.9% 60 minutes or more (2006-2010 5-year est.)

## FREEVILLE (village).
Covers a land area of 1.058 square miles and a water area of 0.037 square miles. Located at 42.51° N. Lat; 76.34° W. Long. Elevation is 1,043 feet.

**Population:** 437 (1990); 505 (2000); 520 (2010); Density: 491.3 persons per square mile (2010); Race: 94.2% White, 3.5% Black, 0.2% Asian, 0.4% American Indian/Alaska Native, 0.0% Native Hawaiian/Other Pacific Islander, 1.7% Other, 1.0% Hispanic of any race (2010); Average household size: 2.29 (2010); Median age: 38.0 (2010); Males per 100 females: 98.5 (2010); Marriage status: 28.1% never married, 54.9% now married, 4.1% widowed, 13.0% divorced (2006-2010 5-year est.); Foreign born: 2.6% (2006-2010 5-year est.); Ancestry (includes multiple ancestries): 21.6% Irish, 18.6% English, 15.6% German, 8.6% Polish, 8.2% Italian (2006-2010 5-year est.).

**Economy:** Single-family building permits issued: 0 (2011); Multi-family building permits issued: 0 (2011); Employment by occupation: 18.7% management, 4.0% professional, 4.4% services, 17.9% sales, 4.0% farming, 7.5% construction, 1.2% production (2006-2010 5-year est.).

**Income:** Per capita income: $28,147 (2006-2010 5-year est.); Median household income: $54,750 (2006-2010 5-year est.); Average household income: $61,996 (2006-2010 5-year est.); Percent of households with income of $100,000 or more: 14.1% (2006-2010 5-year est.); Poverty rate: 5.6% (2006-2010 5-year est.).

**Education:** Percent of population age 25 and over with: High school diploma (including GED) or higher: 88.1% (2006-2010 5-year est.); Bachelor's degree or higher: 34.6% (2006-2010 5-year est.); Master's degree or higher: 10.3% (2006-2010 5-year est.).

**School District(s)**
Dryden Central School District (KG-12)
    2009-10 Enrollment: 1,778 . . . . . . . . . . . . . . . . . . . . . (607) 844-5361
George Junior Republic Union Free School District (07-12)
    2009-10 Enrollment: 192 . . . . . . . . . . . . . . . . . . . . . . (607) 844-6343
**Housing:** Homeownership rate: 60.9% (2010); Median home value: $120,100 (2006-2010 5-year est.); Median contract rent: $504 per month

(2006-2010 5-year est.); Median year structure built: 1952 (2006-2010 5-year est.).

**Transportation:** Commute to work: 91.7% car, 0.0% public transportation, 2.9% walk, 5.4% work from home (2006-2010 5-year est.); Travel time to work: 21.6% less than 15 minutes, 75.3% 15 to 30 minutes, 1.8% 30 to 45 minutes, 0.0% 45 to 60 minutes, 1.3% 60 minutes or more (2006-2010 5-year est.)

**GROTON** (village). Covers a land area of 1.738 square miles and a water area of <.001 square miles. Located at 42.58° N. Lat; 76.35° W. Long. Elevation is 997 feet.

**Population:** 2,452 (1990); 2,470 (2000); 2,363 (2010); Density: 1,359.5 persons per square mile (2010); Race: 95.4% White, 1.6% Black, 0.8% Asian, 0.0% American Indian/Alaska Native, 0.0% Native Hawaiian/Other Pacific Islander, 2.2% Other, 1.8% Hispanic of any race (2010); Average household size: 2.34 (2010); Median age: 40.0 (2010); Males per 100 females: 88.4 (2010); Marriage status: 27.1% never married, 45.5% now married, 13.2% widowed, 14.3% divorced (2006-2010 5-year est.); Foreign born: 2.1% (2006-2010 5-year est.); Ancestry (includes multiple ancestries): 17.6% German, 17.3% English, 15.5% Irish, 12.0% Italian, 7.1% French (2006-2010 5-year est.).

**Economy:** Single-family building permits issued: 2 (2011); Multi-family building permits issued: 0 (2011); Employment by occupation: 15.3% management, 5.1% professional, 8.8% services, 16.5% sales, 2.8% farming, 5.1% construction, 2.2% production (2006-2010 5-year est.).

**Income:** Per capita income: $22,199 (2006-2010 5-year est.); Median household income: $45,441 (2006-2010 5-year est.); Average household income: $53,506 (2006-2010 5-year est.); Percent of households with income of $100,000 or more: 9.7% (2006-2010 5-year est.); Poverty rate: 13.1% (2006-2010 5-year est.).

**Education:** Percent of population age 25 and over with: High school diploma (including GED) or higher: 84.1% (2006-2010 5-year est.); Bachelor's degree or higher: 19.5% (2006-2010 5-year est.); Master's degree or higher: 7.9% (2006-2010 5-year est.).

**School District(s)**

Groton Central School District (PK-12)

   2009-10 Enrollment: 1,015 . . . . . . . . . . . . . . . . . . . . . . . (607) 898-5301

**Housing:** Homeownership rate: 60.7% (2010); Median home value: $99,000 (2006-2010 5-year est.); Median contract rent: $481 per month (2006-2010 5-year est.); Median year structure built: before 1940 (2006-2010 5-year est.).

**Safety:** Violent crime rate: 12.6 per 10,000 population; Property crime rate: 277.3 per 10,000 population (2010).

**Transportation:** Commute to work: 91.5% car, 0.3% public transportation, 4.0% walk, 3.3% work from home (2006-2010 5-year est.); Travel time to work: 29.9% less than 15 minutes, 41.6% 15 to 30 minutes, 20.7% 30 to 45 minutes, 2.5% 45 to 60 minutes, 5.3% 60 minutes or more (2006-2010 5-year est.)

**GROTON** (town). Covers a land area of 49.406 square miles and a water area of 0.133 square miles. Located at 42.58° N. Lat; 76.35° W. Long. Elevation is 997 feet.

**History:** Incorporated 1860.

**Population:** 5,483 (1990); 5,794 (2000); 5,950 (2010); Density: 120.4 persons per square mile (2010); Race: 96.3% White, 1.0% Black, 0.7% Asian, 0.3% American Indian/Alaska Native, 0.0% Native Hawaiian/Other Pacific Islander, 1.7% Other, 1.9% Hispanic of any race (2010); Average household size: 2.52 (2010); Median age: 41.3 (2010); Males per 100 females: 96.3 (2010); Marriage status: 29.8% never married, 53.2% now married, 6.8% widowed, 10.2% divorced (2006-2010 5-year est.); Foreign born: 1.8% (2006-2010 5-year est.); Ancestry (includes multiple ancestries): 22.3% German, 20.0% Irish, 13.8% English, 8.8% Italian, 7.5% American (2006-2010 5-year est.).

**Economy:** Single-family building permits issued: 2 (2011); Multi-family building permits issued: 0 (2011); Employment by occupation: 10.1% management, 4.8% professional, 13.0% services, 14.8% sales, 3.3% farming, 10.7% construction, 6.0% production (2006-2010 5-year est.).

**Income:** Per capita income: $23,208 (2006-2010 5-year est.); Median household income: $53,772 (2006-2010 5-year est.); Average household income: $62,832 (2006-2010 5-year est.); Percent of households with income of $100,000 or more: 17.1% (2006-2010 5-year est.); Poverty rate: 11.9% (2006-2010 5-year est.).

**Education:** Percent of population age 25 and over with: High school diploma (including GED) or higher: 86.3% (2006-2010 5-year est.);

Bachelor's degree or higher: 19.3% (2006-2010 5-year est.); Master's degree or higher: 9.2% (2006-2010 5-year est.).

**School District(s)**

Groton Central School District (PK-12)

   2009-10 Enrollment: 1,015 . . . . . . . . . . . . . . . . . . . . . . . (607) 898-5301

**Housing:** Homeownership rate: 75.9% (2010); Median home value: $107,700 (2006-2010 5-year est.); Median contract rent: $480 per month (2006-2010 5-year est.); Median year structure built: 1953 (2006-2010 5-year est.).

**Transportation:** Commute to work: 91.3% car, 0.1% public transportation, 1.7% walk, 5.4% work from home (2006-2010 5-year est.); Travel time to work: 26.5% less than 15 minutes, 40.3% 15 to 30 minutes, 22.5% 30 to 45 minutes, 5.2% 45 to 60 minutes, 5.4% 60 minutes or more (2006-2010 5-year est.)

**ITHACA** (city). County seat. Covers a land area of 5.388 square miles and a water area of 0.684 square miles. Located at 42.44° N. Lat; 76.50° W. Long. Elevation is 410 feet.

**History:** Detachments of General John Sullivan's expedition crossed the site of Ithaca in 1779. The first settlers came in 1788 and 1789, but when the site was included within the Military Tract and title given to Revolutionary War veterans, these pioneers were obliged to move on. The land was later acquired by Simeon De Witt, surveyor-general of New York State, who gave the place its name. Solid growth began after the opening of Cornell University in 1868. In 1888, Ithaca became a city. For several years beginning in 1914, Ithaca was a center of the motion picture industry.

**Population:** 29,541 (1990); 29,287 (2000); 30,014 (2010); Density: 5,570.3 persons per square mile (2010); Race: 70.5% White, 6.6% Black, 16.2% Asian, 0.4% American Indian/Alaska Native, 0.0% Native Hawaiian/Other Pacific Islander, 6.3% Other, 6.9% Hispanic of any race (2010); Average household size: 2.14 (2010); Median age: 22.4 (2010); Males per 100 females: 101.5 (2010); Marriage status: 73.6% never married, 18.1% now married, 2.7% widowed, 5.6% divorced (2006-2010 5-year est.); Foreign born: 17.0% (2006-2010 5-year est.); Ancestry (includes multiple ancestries): 11.7% Irish, 11.6% German, 8.0% English, 7.1% Italian, 4.5% Polish (2006-2010 5-year est.).

**Economy:** Unemployment rate: 6.7% (February 2012); Total civilian labor force: 14,900 (February 2012); Single-family building permits issued: 4 (2011); Multi-family building permits issued: 35 (2011); Employment by occupation: 8.4% management, 8.2% professional, 7.1% services, 14.8% sales, 5.7% farming, 4.9% construction, 1.0% production (2006-2010 5-year est.).

**Income:** Per capita income: $17,346 (2006-2010 5-year est.); Median household income: $30,919 (2006-2010 5-year est.); Average household income: $46,315 (2006-2010 5-year est.); Percent of households with income of $100,000 or more: 11.4% (2006-2010 5-year est.); Poverty rate: 41.2% (2006-2010 5-year est.).

**Taxes:** Total city taxes per capita: $1,030 (2009); City property taxes per capita: $568 (2009).

**Education:** Percent of population age 25 and over with: High school diploma (including GED) or higher: 89.8% (2006-2010 5-year est.); Bachelor's degree or higher: 62.1% (2006-2010 5-year est.); Master's degree or higher: 34.9% (2006-2010 5-year est.).

**School District(s)**

Ithaca City School District (PK-12)

   2009-10 Enrollment: 5,374 . . . . . . . . . . . . . . . . . . . . . . (607) 274-2101

New Roots Charter School (09-10)

   2009-10 Enrollment: 102 . . . . . . . . . . . . . . . . . . . . . . . (607) 339-6994

Tompkins-Seneca-Tioga Boces

   2009-10 Enrollment: n/a . . . . . . . . . . . . . . . . . . . . . . . (607) 257-1551

**Four-year College(s)**

Cornell University (Private, Not-for-profit)

   Fall 2010 Enrollment: 21,515 . . . . . . . . . . . . . . . . . . . . (607) 255-2000

   2011-12 Tuition: In-state $41,541; Out-of-state $41,541

Ithaca College (Private, Not-for-profit)

   Fall 2010 Enrollment: 7,112 . . . . . . . . . . . . . . . . . . . . . (607) 274-3011

   2011-12 Tuition: In-state $35,278; Out-of-state $35,278

**Vocational/Technical School(s)**

Finger Lakes School of Massage (Private, For-profit)

   Fall 2010 Enrollment: 133 . . . . . . . . . . . . . . . . . . . . . . . (6.0) 727-3E+1

   2011-12 Tuition: $14,400

**Housing:** Homeownership rate: 26.4% (2010); Median home value: $171,400 (2006-2010 5-year est.); Median contract rent: $743 per month (2006-2010 5-year est.); Median year structure built: before 1940 (2006-2010 5-year est.).

**Hospitals:** Cayuga Medical Center of Ithaca (204 beds)
**Safety:** Violent crime rate: 20.1 per 10,000 population; Property crime rate: 383.7 per 10,000 population (2010).
**Newspapers:** The Ithaca Journal (Local news; Circulation 20,000); Ithaca Times (Local news; Circulation 24,500)
**Transportation:** Commute to work: 38.4% car, 11.8% public transportation, 40.1% walk, 7.1% work from home (2006-2010 5-year est.); Travel time to work: 50.2% less than 15 minutes, 37.8% 15 to 30 minutes, 8.7% 30 to 45 minutes, 2.0% 45 to 60 minutes, 1.4% 60 minutes or more (2006-2010 5-year est.)
**Airports:** Ithaca Tompkins Regional (primary service)
**Additional Information Contacts**
City of Ithaca . . . . . . . . . . . . . . . . . . . . . . . . . . . . . . . . . (607) 274-6570
   http://www.ci.ithaca.ny.us
Tompkins County Chamber of Commerce. . . . . . . . . . . . . (607) 273-7080
   http://www.tompkinschamber.org

**ITHACA** (town). Covers a land area of 28.945 square miles and a water area of 1.340 square miles. Located at 42.41° N. Lat; 76.54° W. Long. Elevation is 410 feet.
**History:** Settled 1789, Incorporated as a city 1888.
**Population:** 17,797 (1990); 18,198 (2000); 19,930 (2010); Density: 688.5 persons per square mile (2010); Race: 79.7% White, 4.1% Black, 11.4% Asian, 0.2% American Indian/Alaska Native, 0.1% Native Hawaiian/Other Pacific Islander, 4.5% Other, 4.4% Hispanic of any race (2010); Average household size: 2.15 (2010); Median age: 27.5 (2010); Males per 100 females: 89.1 (2010); Marriage status: 54.1% never married, 35.7% now married, 5.1% widowed, 5.1% divorced (2006-2010 5-year est.); Foreign born: 20.7% (2006-2010 5-year est.); Ancestry (includes multiple ancestries): 13.4% English, 13.3% German, 11.6% Irish, 9.2% Italian, 3.9% Polish (2006-2010 5-year est.).
**Economy:** Single-family building permits issued: 8 (2011); Multi-family building permits issued: 2 (2011); Employment by occupation: 10.5% management, 8.7% professional, 8.7% services, 15.8% sales, 4.0% farming, 2.3% construction, 1.8% production (2006-2010 5-year est.).
**Income:** Per capita income: $28,086 (2006-2010 5-year est.); Median household income: $59,525 (2006-2010 5-year est.); Average household income: $80,644 (2006-2010 5-year est.); Percent of households with income of $100,000 or more: 28.6% (2006-2010 5-year est.); Poverty rate: 15.9% (2006-2010 5-year est.).
**Education:** Percent of population age 25 and over with: High school diploma (including GED) or higher: 95.8% (2006-2010 5-year est.); Bachelor's degree or higher: 71.8% (2006-2010 5-year est.); Master's degree or higher: 49.7% (2006-2010 5-year est.).
**School District(s)**
Ithaca City School District (PK-12)
   2009-10 Enrollment: 5,374 . . . . . . . . . . . . . . . . . . . . . (607) 274-2101
New Roots Charter School (09-10)
   2009-10 Enrollment: 102 . . . . . . . . . . . . . . . . . . . . . . (607) 339-6994
Tompkins-Seneca-Tioga Boces
   2009-10 Enrollment: n/a . . . . . . . . . . . . . . . . . . . . . . . (607) 257-1551
**Four-year College(s)**
Cornell University (Private, Not-for-profit)
   Fall 2010 Enrollment: 21,515. . . . . . . . . . . . . . . . . . . (607) 255-2000
   2011-12 Tuition: In-state $41,541; Out-of-state $41,541
Ithaca College (Private, Not-for-profit)
   Fall 2010 Enrollment: 7,112. . . . . . . . . . . . . . . . . . . . (607) 274-3011
   2011-12 Tuition: In-state $35,278; Out-of-state $35,278
**Vocational/Technical School(s)**
Finger Lakes School of Massage (Private, For-profit)
   Fall 2010 Enrollment: 133 . . . . . . . . . . . . . . . . . . . . (6.0) 727-3E+1
   2011-12 Tuition: $14,400
**Housing:** Homeownership rate: 50.8% (2010); Median home value: $224,700 (2006-2010 5-year est.); Median contract rent: $886 per month (2006-2010 5-year est.); Median year structure built: 1974 (2006-2010 5-year est.).
**Hospitals:** Cayuga Medical Center of Ithaca (204 beds)
**Newspapers:** The Ithaca Journal (Local news; Circulation 20,000); Ithaca Times (Local news; Circulation 24,500)
**Transportation:** Commute to work: 58.9% car, 10.5% public transportation, 18.8% walk, 8.8% work from home (2006-2010 5-year est.); Travel time to work: 54.6% less than 15 minutes, 34.4% 15 to 30 minutes, 6.1% 30 to 45 minutes, 2.2% 45 to 60 minutes, 2.7% 60 minutes or more (2006-2010 5-year est.)
**Airports:** Ithaca Tompkins Regional (primary service)

**Additional Information Contacts**
Town of Ithaca . . . . . . . . . . . . . . . . . . . . . . . . . . . . . . (607) 273-1721
   http://www.town.ithaca.ny.us

**JACKSONVILLE** (unincorporated postal area)
Zip Code: 14854
   Covers a land area of 0.022 square miles and a water area of 0 square miles. Located at 42.50° N. Lat; 76.61° W. Long. Elevation is 1,024 feet. Population: 37 (2010); Density: 1,625.6 persons per square mile (2010); Race: 100.0% White, 0.0% Black, 0.0% Asian, 0.0% American Indian/Alaska Native, 0.0% Native Hawaiian/Other Pacific Islander, 0.0% Other, 0.0% Hispanic of any race (2010); Average household size: 2.58 (2010); Median age: 60.5 (2010); Males per 100 females: 48.0 (2010); Homeownership rate: 91.7% (2010)

**LANSING** (village). Aka South Lansing. Covers a land area of 4.610 square miles and a water area of 0.018 square miles. Located at 42.48° N. Lat; 76.48° W. Long. Elevation is 928 feet.
**Population:** 3,242 (1990); 3,417 (2000); 3,529 (2010); Density: 765.5 persons per square mile (2010); Race: 63.2% White, 6.5% Black, 25.0% Asian, 0.4% American Indian/Alaska Native, 0.1% Native Hawaiian/Other Pacific Islander, 4.8% Other, 4.8% Hispanic of any race (2010); Average household size: 2.04 (2010); Median age: 33.2 (2010); Males per 100 females: 102.0 (2010); Marriage status: 33.0% never married, 57.3% now married, 3.5% widowed, 6.3% divorced (2006-2010 5-year est.); Foreign born: 42.3% (2006-2010 5-year est.); Ancestry (includes multiple ancestries): 14.2% German, 12.5% Irish, 12.2% English, 7.8% Italian, 3.6% African (2006-2010 5-year est.).
**Economy:** Single-family building permits issued: 6 (2011); Multi-family building permits issued: 0 (2011); Employment by occupation: 11.2% management, 12.5% professional, 2.0% services, 5.0% sales, 1.8% farming, 7.2% construction, 3.9% production (2006-2010 5-year est.).
**Income:** Per capita income: $32,510 (2006-2010 5-year est.); Median household income: $54,721 (2006-2010 5-year est.); Average household income: $70,072 (2006-2010 5-year est.); Percent of households with income of $100,000 or more: 18.9% (2006-2010 5-year est.); Poverty rate: 6.3% (2006-2010 5-year est.).
**Education:** Percent of population age 25 and over with: High school diploma (including GED) or higher: 96.6% (2006-2010 5-year est.); Bachelor's degree or higher: 72.8% (2006-2010 5-year est.); Master's degree or higher: 45.4% (2006-2010 5-year est.).
**School District(s)**
Lansing Central School District (KG-12)
   2009-10 Enrollment: 1,222 . . . . . . . . . . . . . . . . . . . . (607) 533-4294
**Housing:** Homeownership rate: 30.9% (2010); Median home value: $263,800 (2006-2010 5-year est.); Median contract rent: $905 per month (2006-2010 5-year est.); Median year structure built: 1974 (2006-2010 5-year est.).
**Transportation:** Commute to work: 72.8% car, 14.1% public transportation, 5.5% walk, 5.4% work from home (2006-2010 5-year est.); Travel time to work: 40.6% less than 15 minutes, 42.4% 15 to 30 minutes, 10.2% 30 to 45 minutes, 0.5% 45 to 60 minutes, 6.3% 60 minutes or more (2006-2010 5-year est.)
**Additional Information Contacts**
Village of Lansing . . . . . . . . . . . . . . . . . . . . . . . . . . . (607) 257-0424
   http://www.vlansing.org

**LANSING** (town). Aka South Lansing. Covers a land area of 60.490 square miles and a water area of 9.451 square miles. Located at 42.56° N. Lat; 76.53° W. Long. Elevation is 928 feet.
**Population:** 9,296 (1990); 10,521 (2000); 11,033 (2010); Density: 182.4 persons per square mile (2010); Race: 82.3% White, 3.6% Black, 10.2% Asian, 0.4% American Indian/Alaska Native, 0.1% Native Hawaiian/Other Pacific Islander, 3.4% Other, 3.5% Hispanic of any race (2010); Average household size: 2.28 (2010); Median age: 39.6 (2010); Males per 100 females: 101.0 (2010); Marriage status: 29.1% never married, 59.8% now married, 4.8% widowed, 6.2% divorced (2006-2010 5-year est.); Foreign born: 18.3% (2006-2010 5-year est.); Ancestry (includes multiple ancestries): 18.3% German, 16.5% English, 13.9% Irish, 11.2% Italian, 6.4% American (2006-2010 5-year est.).
**Economy:** Single-family building permits issued: 22 (2011); Multi-family building permits issued: 0 (2011); Employment by occupation: 16.6% management, 9.8% professional, 4.4% services, 16.3% sales, 2.7% farming, 7.3% construction, 3.7% production (2006-2010 5-year est.).

**Income:** Per capita income: $37,460 (2006-2010 5-year est.); Median household income: $62,034 (2006-2010 5-year est.); Average household income: $84,234 (2006-2010 5-year est.); Percent of households with income of $100,000 or more: 28.5% (2006-2010 5-year est.); Poverty rate: 6.0% (2006-2010 5-year est.).

**Education:** Percent of population age 25 and over with: High school diploma (including GED) or higher: 96.6% (2006-2010 5-year est.); Bachelor's degree or higher: 56.2% (2006-2010 5-year est.); Master's degree or higher: 31.4% (2006-2010 5-year est.).

**School District(s)**

Lansing Central School District (KG-12)

    2009-10 Enrollment: 1,222 ............................ (607) 533-4294

**Housing:** Homeownership rate: 58.7% (2010); Median home value: $186,500 (2006-2010 5-year est.); Median contract rent: $843 per month (2006-2010 5-year est.); Median year structure built: 1977 (2006-2010 5-year est.).

**Transportation:** Commute to work: 86.8% car, 4.6% public transportation, 2.4% walk, 5.3% work from home (2006-2010 5-year est.); Travel time to work: 37.3% less than 15 minutes, 46.2% 15 to 30 minutes, 10.5% 30 to 45 minutes, 0.7% 45 to 60 minutes, 5.3% 60 minutes or more (2006-2010 5-year est.).

**Additional Information Contacts**

Town of Lansing ............................................ (607) 533-4142
    http://www.lansingtown.com

## MCLEAN (unincorporated postal area)

Zip Code: 13102

    Covers a land area of 0.058 square miles and a water area of 0.001 square miles. Located at 42.55° N. Lat; 76.29° W. Long. Elevation is 1,122 feet. Population: 85 (2010); Density: 1,460.5 persons per square mile (2010); Race: 96.5% White, 1.2% Black, 1.2% Asian, 0.0% American Indian/Alaska Native, 0.0% Native Hawaiian/Other Pacific Islander, 1.1% Other, 0.0% Hispanic of any race (2010); Average household size: 2.30 (2010); Median age: 45.5 (2010); Males per 100 females: 117.9 (2010); Homeownership rate: 64.8% (2010)

## NEWFIELD (town). Covers a land area of 58.840 square miles and a water area of 0.126 square miles. Located at 42.33° N. Lat; 76.61° W. Long. Elevation is 1,050 feet.

**Population:** 4,867 (1990); 5,108 (2000); 5,179 (2010); Density: 88.0 persons per square mile (2010); Race: 94.0% White, 1.6% Black, 0.6% Asian, 0.6% American Indian/Alaska Native, 0.0% Native Hawaiian/Other Pacific Islander, 3.2% Other, 1.4% Hispanic of any race (2010); Average household size: 2.44 (2010); Median age: 40.4 (2010); Males per 100 females: 94.7 (2010); Marriage status: 28.5% never married, 57.6% now married, 4.7% widowed, 9.2% divorced (2006-2010 5-year est.); Foreign born: 0.9% (2006-2010 5-year est.); Ancestry (includes multiple ancestries): 18.6% Irish, 18.2% German, 16.4% English, 9.0% Italian, 4.5% American (2006-2010 5-year est.).

**Economy:** Single-family building permits issued: 8 (2011); Multi-family building permits issued: 0 (2011); Employment by occupation: 5.8% management, 1.0% professional, 9.2% services, 15.1% sales, 3.4% farming, 11.9% construction, 9.1% production (2006-2010 5-year est.).

**Income:** Per capita income: $22,598 (2006-2010 5-year est.); Median household income: $46,493 (2006-2010 5-year est.); Average household income: $57,701 (2006-2010 5-year est.); Percent of households with income of $100,000 or more: 14.6% (2006-2010 5-year est.); Poverty rate: 9.9% (2006-2010 5-year est.).

**Education:** Percent of population age 25 and over with: High school diploma (including GED) or higher: 90.4% (2006-2010 5-year est.); Bachelor's degree or higher: 19.2% (2006-2010 5-year est.); Master's degree or higher: 6.5% (2006-2010 5-year est.).

**School District(s)**

Newfield Central School District (PK-12)

    2009-10 Enrollment: 965 ............................ (607) 564-9955

**Housing:** Homeownership rate: 74.4% (2010); Median home value: $105,700 (2006-2010 5-year est.); Median contract rent: $628 per month (2006-2010 5-year est.); Median year structure built: 1978 (2006-2010 5-year est.).

**Transportation:** Commute to work: 90.2% car, 1.2% public transportation, 0.5% walk, 7.0% work from home (2006-2010 5-year est.); Travel time to work: 14.3% less than 15 minutes, 54.3% 15 to 30 minutes, 29.3% 30 to 45 minutes, 1.6% 45 to 60 minutes, 0.5% 60 minutes or more (2006-2010 5-year est.)

## NEWFIELD HAMLET (CDP). Covers a land area of 1.257 square miles and a water area of <.001 square miles. Located at 42.35° N. Lat; 76.59° W. Long. Elevation is 1,050 feet.

**Population:** 692 (1990); 647 (2000); 759 (2010); Density: 603.8 persons per square mile (2010); Race: 93.4% White, 1.1% Black, 0.0% Asian, 1.1% American Indian/Alaska Native, 0.0% Native Hawaiian/Other Pacific Islander, 4.4% Other, 1.6% Hispanic of any race (2010); Average household size: 2.19 (2010); Median age: 42.7 (2010); Males per 100 females: 89.8 (2010); Marriage status: 30.3% never married, 49.6% now married, 11.8% widowed, 8.2% divorced (2006-2010 5-year est.); Foreign born: 4.3% (2006-2010 5-year est.); Ancestry (includes multiple ancestries): 28.7% English, 28.5% Irish, 17.5% German, 15.1% French, 10.7% Swedish (2006-2010 5-year est.).

**Economy:** Employment by occupation: 0.0% management, 0.0% professional, 8.7% services, 2.2% sales, 4.5% farming, 7.5% construction, 10.7% production (2006-2010 5-year est.).

**Income:** Per capita income: $30,304 (2006-2010 5-year est.); Median household income: $59,545 (2006-2010 5-year est.); Average household income: $72,288 (2006-2010 5-year est.); Percent of households with income of $100,000 or more: 41.0% (2006-2010 5-year est.); Poverty rate: 0.0% (2006-2010 5-year est.).

**Education:** Percent of population age 25 and over with: High school diploma (including GED) or higher: 94.9% (2006-2010 5-year est.); Bachelor's degree or higher: 30.3% (2006-2010 5-year est.); Master's degree or higher: 15.3% (2006-2010 5-year est.).

**Housing:** Homeownership rate: 62.0% (2010); Median home value: $113,700 (2006-2010 5-year est.); Median contract rent: $605 per month (2006-2010 5-year est.); Median year structure built: 1969 (2006-2010 5-year est.).

**Transportation:** Commute to work: 94.8% car, 0.0% public transportation, 2.7% walk, 2.5% work from home (2006-2010 5-year est.); Travel time to work: 2.8% less than 15 minutes, 70.8% 15 to 30 minutes, 23.5% 30 to 45 minutes, 0.0% 45 to 60 minutes, 2.8% 60 minutes or more (2006-2010 5-year est.)

## NORTHEAST ITHACA (CDP). Covers a land area of 1.469 square miles and a water area of 0.004 square miles. Located at 42.46° N. Lat; 76.46° W. Long.

**Population:** 2,533 (1990); 2,655 (2000); 2,641 (2010); Density: 1,797.2 persons per square mile (2010); Race: 71.5% White, 4.1% Black, 20.4% Asian, 0.2% American Indian/Alaska Native, 0.0% Native Hawaiian/Other Pacific Islander, 3.8% Other, 3.7% Hispanic of any race (2010); Average household size: 2.49 (2010); Median age: 34.7 (2010); Males per 100 females: 98.6 (2010); Marriage status: 36.1% never married, 55.4% now married, 3.9% widowed, 4.7% divorced (2006-2010 5-year est.); Foreign born: 28.1% (2006-2010 5-year est.); Ancestry (includes multiple ancestries): 17.6% English, 15.3% German, 12.3% Irish, 6.4% Italian, 4.2% Scottish (2006-2010 5-year est.).

**Economy:** Employment by occupation: 12.8% management, 15.2% professional, 1.7% services, 8.4% sales, 1.6% farming, 1.2% construction, 1.7% production (2006-2010 5-year est.).

**Income:** Per capita income: $33,208 (2006-2010 5-year est.); Median household income: $85,978 (2006-2010 5-year est.); Average household income: $90,984 (2006-2010 5-year est.); Percent of households with income of $100,000 or more: 37.9% (2006-2010 5-year est.); Poverty rate: 14.1% (2006-2010 5-year est.).

**Education:** Percent of population age 25 and over with: High school diploma (including GED) or higher: 96.5% (2006-2010 5-year est.); Bachelor's degree or higher: 80.0% (2006-2010 5-year est.); Master's degree or higher: 48.8% (2006-2010 5-year est.).

**Housing:** Homeownership rate: 52.1% (2010); Median home value: $215,700 (2006-2010 5-year est.); Median contract rent: $953 per month (2006-2010 5-year est.); Median year structure built: 1966 (2006-2010 5-year est.).

**Transportation:** Commute to work: 73.1% car, 18.8% public transportation, 2.3% walk, 3.4% work from home (2006-2010 5-year est.); Travel time to work: 51.4% less than 15 minutes, 39.2% 15 to 30 minutes, 4.5% 30 to 45 minutes, 0.6% 45 to 60 minutes, 4.3% 60 minutes or more (2006-2010 5-year est.)

## NORTHWEST ITHACA (CDP). Covers a land area of 2.907 square miles and a water area of 0.662 square miles. Located at 42.47° N. Lat; 76.54° W. Long. Elevation is 915 feet.

**Population:** 1,144 (1990); 1,115 (2000); 1,413 (2010); Density: 486.0 persons per square mile (2010); Race: 83.5% White, 8.4% Black, 3.0%

Asian, 0.1% American Indian/Alaska Native, 0.1% Native Hawaiian/Other Pacific Islander, 4.9% Other, 3.4% Hispanic of any race (2010); Average household size: 2.01 (2010); Median age: 45.8 (2010); Males per 100 females: 82.3 (2010); Marriage status: 34.6% never married, 38.5% now married, 11.7% widowed, 15.2% divorced (2006-2010 5-year est.); Foreign born: 9.3% (2006-2010 5-year est.); Ancestry (includes multiple ancestries): 16.5% English, 14.1% Irish, 8.2% German, 7.5% French, 7.2% Italian (2006-2010 5-year est.).

**Economy:** Employment by occupation: 5.3% management, 4.6% professional, 1.3% services, 25.3% sales, 0.5% farming, 1.4% construction, 1.9% production (2006-2010 5-year est.).

**Income:** Per capita income: $35,056 (2006-2010 5-year est.); Median household income: $49,955 (2006-2010 5-year est.); Average household income: $70,317 (2006-2010 5-year est.); Percent of households with income of $100,000 or more: 22.6% (2006-2010 5-year est.); Poverty rate: 14.7% (2006-2010 5-year est.).

**Education:** Percent of population age 25 and over with: High school diploma (including GED) or higher: 98.3% (2006-2010 5-year est.); Bachelor's degree or higher: 59.4% (2006-2010 5-year est.); Master's degree or higher: 40.7% (2006-2010 5-year est.).

**Housing:** Homeownership rate: 46.0% (2010); Median home value: $241,400 (2006-2010 5-year est.); Median contract rent: $793 per month (2006-2010 5-year est.); Median year structure built: 1974 (2006-2010 5-year est.).

**Transportation:** Commute to work: 73.7% car, 14.0% public transportation, 5.1% walk, 5.9% work from home (2006-2010 5-year est.); Travel time to work: 37.3% less than 15 minutes, 52.2% 15 to 30 minutes, 6.2% 30 to 45 minutes, 1.6% 45 to 60 minutes, 2.8% 60 minutes or more (2006-2010 5-year est.)

**SLATERVILLE SPRINGS** (unincorporated postal area)
Zip Code: 14881
Covers a land area of 1.228 square miles and a water area of 0.001 square miles. Located at 42.39° N. Lat; 76.35° W. Long. Elevation is 1,112 feet. Population: 192 (2010); Density: 156.3 persons per square mile (2010); Race: 92.2% White, 4.7% Black, 2.1% Asian, 0.0% American Indian/Alaska Native, 0.5% Native Hawaiian/Other Pacific Islander, 0.5% Other, 0.5% Hispanic of any race (2010); Average household size: 1.88 (2010); Median age: 46.4 (2010); Males per 100 females: 90.1 (2010); Homeownership rate: 50.9% (2010)

**SOUTH HILL** (CDP). Covers a land area of 5.895 square miles and a water area of 0.094 square miles. Located at 42.41° N. Lat; 76.49° W. Long. Elevation is 778 feet.
**Population:** 5,423 (1990); 6,003 (2000); 6,673 (2010); Density: 1,131.8 persons per square mile (2010); Race: 87.2% White, 3.4% Black, 4.3% Asian, 0.2% American Indian/Alaska Native, 0.1% Native Hawaiian/Other Pacific Islander, 4.8% Other, 4.9% Hispanic of any race (2010); Average household size: 2.32 (2010); Median age: 20.3 (2010); Males per 100 females: 80.0 (2010); Marriage status: 83.7% never married, 13.3% now married, 1.7% widowed, 1.3% divorced (2006-2010 5-year est.); Foreign born: 4.4% (2006-2010 5-year est.); Ancestry (includes multiple ancestries): 13.6% Irish, 12.0% German, 10.5% English, 10.5% Italian, 6.3% Polish (2006-2010 5-year est.).

**Economy:** Employment by occupation: 8.7% management, 3.6% professional, 19.5% services, 25.8% sales, 7.7% farming, 3.2% construction, 2.6% production (2006-2010 5-year est.).

**Income:** Per capita income: $11,357 (2006-2010 5-year est.); Median household income: $57,639 (2006-2010 5-year est.); Average household income: $69,317 (2006-2010 5-year est.); Percent of households with income of $100,000 or more: 22.7% (2006-2010 5-year est.); Poverty rate: 20.9% (2006-2010 5-year est.).

**Education:** Percent of population age 25 and over with: High school diploma (including GED) or higher: 95.2% (2006-2010 5-year est.); Bachelor's degree or higher: 59.5% (2006-2010 5-year est.); Master's degree or higher: 43.4% (2006-2010 5-year est.).

**Housing:** Homeownership rate: 57.7% (2010); Median home value: $188,500 (2006-2010 5-year est.); Median contract rent: $889 per month (2006-2010 5-year est.); Median year structure built: 1986 (2006-2010 5-year est.).

**Transportation:** Commute to work: 48.8% car, 3.3% public transportation, 33.6% walk, 11.1% work from home (2006-2010 5-year est.); Travel time to work: 66.0% less than 15 minutes, 26.0% 15 to 30 minutes, 3.8% 30 to 45 minutes, 2.3% 45 to 60 minutes, 1.9% 60 minutes or more (2006-2010 5-year est.)

**TRUMANSBURG** (village). Covers a land area of 1.387 square miles and a water area of 0.004 square miles. Located at 42.54° N. Lat; 76.66° W. Long. Elevation is 965 feet.
**History:** Settled 1792; incorporated 1865.
**Population:** 1,611 (1990); 1,581 (2000); 1,797 (2010); Density: 1,295.6 persons per square mile (2010); Race: 95.5% White, 1.1% Black, 0.8% Asian, 0.0% American Indian/Alaska Native, 0.0% Native Hawaiian/Other Pacific Islander, 2.6% Other, 2.1% Hispanic of any race (2010); Average household size: 2.20 (2010); Median age: 46.4 (2010); Males per 100 females: 84.3 (2010); Marriage status: 27.2% never married, 54.0% now married, 7.8% widowed, 11.1% divorced (2006-2010 5-year est.); Foreign born: 4.2% (2006-2010 5-year est.); Ancestry (includes multiple ancestries): 22.7% English, 22.1% Irish, 19.2% German, 5.8% Scotch-Irish, 5.6% American (2006-2010 5-year est.).

**Economy:** Single-family building permits issued: 0 (2011); Multi-family building permits issued: 0 (2011); Employment by occupation: 13.5% management, 7.7% professional, 7.0% services, 15.1% sales, 3.4% farming, 5.1% construction, 2.1% production (2006-2010 5-year est.).

**Income:** Per capita income: $29,821 (2006-2010 5-year est.); Median household income: $43,333 (2006-2010 5-year est.); Average household income: $68,440 (2006-2010 5-year est.); Percent of households with income of $100,000 or more: 21.6% (2006-2010 5-year est.); Poverty rate: 17.9% (2006-2010 5-year est.).

**Education:** Percent of population age 25 and over with: High school diploma (including GED) or higher: 94.6% (2006-2010 5-year est.); Bachelor's degree or higher: 43.3% (2006-2010 5-year est.); Master's degree or higher: 20.7% (2006-2010 5-year est.).

### School District(s)
Trumansburg Central School District (PK-12)
    2009-10 Enrollment: 1,196 . . . . . . . . . . . . . . . . . . . . . . (607) 387-7551
**Housing:** Homeownership rate: 63.8% (2010); Median home value: $180,300 (2006-2010 5-year est.); Median contract rent: $600 per month (2006-2010 5-year est.); Median year structure built: 1953 (2006-2010 5-year est.).

**Newspapers:** Candor Chronicle (Community news; Circulation 600); Free Press (Local news; Circulation 1,500); Interlaken Review (Community news; Circulation 650); Ovid Gazette (Community news; Circulation 750); Random Harvest (Community news; Circulation 1,200)

**Transportation:** Commute to work: 71.7% car, 10.1% public transportation, 10.1% walk, 5.4% work from home (2006-2010 5-year est.); Travel time to work: 24.9% less than 15 minutes, 44.6% 15 to 30 minutes, 21.3% 30 to 45 minutes, 7.2% 45 to 60 minutes, 2.1% 60 minutes or more (2006-2010 5-year est.)

**Additional Information Contacts**
Trumansburg Area Chamber of Commerce. . . . . . . . . . . . . (607) 387-9254
    http://www.trumansburgchamber.com
Village of Trumansburg . . . . . . . . . . . . . . . . . . . . . . . . . (607) 387-6501
    http://www.trumansburg-ny.gov

**ULYSSES** (town). Covers a land area of 32.888 square miles and a water area of 4.026 square miles. Located at 42.51° N. Lat; 76.61° W. Long.
**Population:** 4,906 (1990); 4,775 (2000); 4,900 (2010); Density: 149.0 persons per square mile (2010); Race: 95.0% White, 1.0% Black, 1.0% Asian, 0.3% American Indian/Alaska Native, 0.1% Native Hawaiian/Other Pacific Islander, 2.6% Other, 2.0% Hispanic of any race (2010); Average household size: 2.26 (2010); Median age: 45.9 (2010); Males per 100 females: 89.8 (2010); Marriage status: 25.8% never married, 59.4% now married, 5.2% widowed, 9.6% divorced (2006-2010 5-year est.); Foreign born: 5.2% (2006-2010 5-year est.); Ancestry (includes multiple ancestries): 21.6% German, 20.2% English, 19.0% Irish, 7.9% Italian, 7.5% American (2006-2010 5-year est.).

**Economy:** Single-family building permits issued: 13 (2011); Multi-family building permits issued: 0 (2011); Employment by occupation: 13.4% management, 6.1% professional, 9.2% services, 12.6% sales, 3.7% farming, 7.2% construction, 3.2% production (2006-2010 5-year est.).

**Income:** Per capita income: $31,290 (2006-2010 5-year est.); Median household income: $63,472 (2006-2010 5-year est.); Average household income: $76,841 (2006-2010 5-year est.); Percent of households with income of $100,000 or more: 30.1% (2006-2010 5-year est.); Poverty rate: 11.0% (2006-2010 5-year est.).

**Education:** Percent of population age 25 and over with: High school diploma (including GED) or higher: 93.4% (2006-2010 5-year est.); Bachelor's degree or higher: 44.1% (2006-2010 5-year est.); Master's degree or higher: 19.4% (2006-2010 5-year est.).

**Housing:** Homeownership rate: 73.5% (2010); Median home value: $189,300 (2006-2010 5-year est.); Median contract rent: $565 per month (2006-2010 5-year est.); Median year structure built: 1960 (2006-2010 5-year est.).

**Transportation:** Commute to work: 80.9% car, 5.2% public transportation, 5.4% walk, 6.8% work from home (2006-2010 5-year est.); Travel time to work: 29.7% less than 15 minutes, 48.9% 15 to 30 minutes, 13.5% 30 to 45 minutes, 4.9% 45 to 60 minutes, 2.9% 60 minutes or more (2006-2010 5-year est.).

**Additional Information Contacts**

Town of Ulysses . . . . . . . . . . . . . . . . . . . . . . . . . . . . . . . (607) 387-5767
  http://www.ulysses.ny.us

# Ulster County

Located in southeastern New York, mainly in the Catskills; bounded on the east by the Hudson River; drained by the Wallkill River; includes part of the Shawangunk Range and several small lakes. Covers a land area of 1,126.48 square miles, a water area of 34.28 square miles, and is located in the Eastern Time Zone at 41.85° N. Lat., 74.14° W. Long. The county was founded in 1683. County seat is Kingston.

Ulster County is part of the Kingston, NY Metropolitan Statistical Area. The entire metro area includes: Ulster County, NY

| Weather Station: Mohonk Lake | | | | | | | | | Elevation: 1,245 feet | | |
|---|---|---|---|---|---|---|---|---|---|---|---|
| | Jan | Feb | Mar | Apr | May | Jun | Jul | Aug | Sep | Oct | Nov | Dec |
| High | 32 | 36 | 45 | 59 | 69 | 77 | 81 | 79 | 71 | 60 | 48 | 37 |
| Low | 18 | 20 | 27 | 38 | 49 | 58 | 63 | 62 | 55 | 44 | 34 | 24 |
| Precip | 3.6 | 3.1 | 4.4 | 4.4 | 4.8 | 4.6 | 4.8 | 4.3 | 4.7 | 4.7 | 4.0 | 4.2 |
| Snow | 16.5 | 12.7 | 12.4 | 2.9 | tr | 0.0 | 0.0 | 0.0 | 0.0 | 0.1 | 3.2 | 13.4 |

*High and Low temperatures in degrees Fahrenheit; Precipitation and Snow in inches*

| Weather Station: Slide Mountain | | | | | | | | | Elevation: 2,649 feet | | |
|---|---|---|---|---|---|---|---|---|---|---|---|
| | Jan | Feb | Mar | Apr | May | Jun | Jul | Aug | Sep | Oct | Nov | Dec |
| High | 27 | 30 | 37 | 49 | 61 | 68 | 72 | 71 | 64 | 54 | 42 | 31 |
| Low | 11 | 12 | 19 | 31 | 41 | 50 | 54 | 53 | 46 | 36 | 27 | 16 |
| Precip | 4.4 | 3.9 | 5.3 | 5.5 | 5.5 | 5.5 | 5.5 | 4.9 | 5.8 | 6.0 | 5.7 | 4.9 |
| Snow | 24.3 | 18.9 | 20.0 | 6.3 | 0.3 | 0.0 | 0.0 | 0.0 | 0.0 | 2.0 | 7.5 | 20.1 |

*High and Low temperatures in degrees Fahrenheit; Precipitation and Snow in inches*

**Population:** 165,310 (1990); 177,749 (2000); 182,493 (2010); Race: 86.7% White, 6.0% Black, 1.7% Asian, 0.3% American Indian/Alaska Native, 0.0% Native Hawaiian/Other Pacific Islander, 5.3% Other, 8.7% Hispanic of any race (2010); Density: 162.0 persons per square mile (2010); Average household size: 2.40 (2010); Median age: 42.0 (2010); Males per 100 females: 99.0 (2010).

**Religion:** Six largest groups: 27.5% Catholicism, 3.6% Methodist/Pietist, 3.0% Presbyterian-Reformed, 1.4% Lutheran, 0.9% Non-Denominational, 0.8% Muslim Estimate (2010)

**Economy:** Unemployment rate: 9.1% (February 2012); Total civilian labor force: 88,335 (February 2012); Leading industries: 19.4% retail trade; 19.0% health care and social assistance; 13.5% accommodation & food services (2009); Farms: 501 totaling 75,205 acres (2007); Companies that employ 500 or more persons: 5 (2009); Companies that employ 100 to 499 persons: 64 (2009); Companies that employ less than 100 persons: 4,613 (2009); Black-owned businesses: n/a (2007); Hispanic-owned businesses: 763 (2007); Asian-owned businesses: 482 (2007); Women-owned businesses: 6,659 (2007); Retail sales per capita: $13,838 (2010). Single-family building permits issued: 128 (2011); Multi-family building permits issued: 102 (2011).

**Income:** Per capita income: $28,954 (2006-2010 5-year est.); Median household income: $57,584 (2006-2010 5-year est.); Average household income: $73,407 (2006-2010 5-year est.); Percent of households with income of $100,000 or more: 23.1% (2006-2010 5-year est.); Poverty rate: 11.3% (2006-2010 5-year est.); Bankruptcy rate: 3.46% (2011).

**Taxes:** Total county taxes per capita: $972 (2009); County property taxes per capita: $406 (2009).

**Education:** Percent of population age 25 and over with: High school diploma (including GED) or higher: 87.5% (2006-2010 5-year est.); Bachelor's degree or higher: 29.5% (2006-2010 5-year est.); Master's degree or higher: 13.6% (2006-2010 5-year est.).

**Housing:** Homeownership rate: 68.6% (2010); Median home value: $242,100 (2006-2010 5-year est.); Median contract rent: $790 per month (2006-2010 5-year est.); Median year structure built: 1961 (2006-2010 5-year est.)

**Health:** Birth rate: 89.4 per 10,000 population (2011); Death rate: 83.5 per 10,000 population (2011); Age-adjusted cancer mortality rate: 182.9 deaths per 100,000 population (2009); Number of physicians: 19.5 per 10,000 population (2008); Hospital beds: 19.5 per 10,000 population (2007); Hospital admissions: 774.7 per 10,000 population (2007).

**Environment:** Air Quality Index: 94.0% good, 6.0% moderate, 0.0% unhealthy for sensitive individuals, 0.0% unhealthy (percent of days in 2010)

**Elections:** 2008 Presidential election results: 60.7% Obama, 37.6% McCain, 0.9% Nader

**National and State Parks:** Catskill State Park; Home of Franklin D Roosevelt National Historic Site

**Additional Information Contacts**

Ulster County Government . . . . . . . . . . . . . . . . . . (845) 340-3288
  http://www.co.ulster.ny.us
City of Kingston . . . . . . . . . . . . . . . . . . . . . . . . . (845) 331-0080
  http://www.ci.kingston.ny.us
Ellenville-Wawarsing Chamber of Commerce . . . . (845) 647-4620
New Paltz Regional Chamber of Commerce . . . . . (845) 255-0243
  http://www.newpaltzchamber.org
Rondout Valley Business Association . . . . . . . . . . (845) 687-4567
  http://www.marbletown.org
Southern Ulster County Chamber of Commerce . . . (845) 691-6070
  http://www.southernulsterchamber.org
Town of Esopus . . . . . . . . . . . . . . . . . . . . . . . . . (845) 331-3709
  http://www.esopus.com
Town of Kingston . . . . . . . . . . . . . . . . . . . . . . . . (845) 336-8853
  http://www.townkingstonny.us
Town of Rosendale . . . . . . . . . . . . . . . . . . . . . . . (845) 658-3159
  http://www.townofrosendale.com
Town of Saugerties . . . . . . . . . . . . . . . . . . . . . . (845) 246-2800
  http://www.saugerties.ny.us
Town of Woodstock . . . . . . . . . . . . . . . . . . . . . . (845) 679-2113
  http://www.woodstockny.org
Ulster County Regional Chamber of Commerce . . . . . . (845) 338-5100
  http://www.ulsterchamber.org
Village of New Paltz . . . . . . . . . . . . . . . . . . . . . . (845) 255-0130
  http://villageofnewpaltz.org
Woodstock Chamber of Commerce & Arts . . . . . . . (845) 679-6234
  http://www.woodstockchamber.com

# Ulster County Communities

**ACCORD** (CDP). Part of the City of Rochester. Covers a land area of 3.400 square miles and a water area of 0.043 square miles. Located at 41.80° N. Lat; 74.23° W. Long. Elevation is 253 feet.

**Population:** 491 (1990); 622 (2000); 562 (2010); Density: 165.3 persons per square mile (2010); Race: 91.3% White, 2.7% Black, 0.9% Asian, 1.1% American Indian/Alaska Native, 0.2% Native Hawaiian/Other Pacific Islander, 3.8% Other, 7.1% Hispanic of any race (2010); Average household size: 2.57 (2010); Median age: 40.3 (2010); Males per 100 females: 100.0 (2010); Marriage status: 56.0% never married, 23.3% now married, 4.7% widowed, 16.0% divorced (2006-2010 5-year est.); Foreign born: 0.0% (2006-2010 5-year est.); Ancestry (includes multiple ancestries): 35.0% Italian, 30.1% Irish, 23.4% American, 11.9% German, 8.4% European (2006-2010 5-year est.).

**Economy:** Employment by occupation: 0.0% management, 4.6% professional, 0.0% services, 0.0% sales, 0.0% farming, 57.5% construction, 6.9% production (2006-2010 5-year est.).

**Income:** Per capita income: $17,049 (2006-2010 5-year est.); Median household income: $27,500 (2006-2010 5-year est.); Average household income: $47,629 (2006-2010 5-year est.); Percent of households with income of $100,000 or more: 19.6% (2006-2010 5-year est.); Poverty rate: 44.4% (2006-2010 5-year est.).

**Education:** Percent of population age 25 and over with: High school diploma (including GED) or higher: 74.3% (2006-2010 5-year est.); Bachelor's degree or higher: 21.4% (2006-2010 5-year est.); Master's degree or higher: 14.3% (2006-2010 5-year est.).

**School District(s)**
Rondout Valley Central School District (KG-12)
  2009-10 Enrollment: 2,316 . . . . . . . . . . . . . . . . . (845) 687-2400

**Housing:** Homeownership rate: 71.8% (2010); Median home value: $123,800 (2006-2010 5-year est.); Median contract rent: $739 per month (2006-2010 5-year est.); Median year structure built: 1991 (2006-2010 5-year est.).

**Transportation:** Commute to work: 100.0% car, 0.0% public transportation, 0.0% walk, 0.0% work from home (2006-2010 5-year est.); Travel time to work: 31.0% less than 15 minutes, 8.4% 15 to 30 minutes, 11.5% 30 to 45 minutes, 32.2% 45 to 60 minutes, 16.9% 60 minutes or more (2006-2010 5-year est.)

**Additional Information Contacts**

Ulster County Regional Chamber of Commerce . . . . . . . . . (845) 338-5100
  http://www.ulsterchamber.org

## BEARSVILLE (unincorporated postal area)
Zip Code: 12409

Covers a land area of 14.267 square miles and a water area of 0.222 square miles. Located at 42.03° N. Lat; 74.18° W. Long. Elevation is 699 feet. Population: 804 (2010); Density: 56.4 persons per square mile (2010); Race: 92.9% White, 0.7% Black, 1.9% Asian, 0.2% American Indian/Alaska Native, 0.0% Native Hawaiian/Other Pacific Islander, 4.3% Other, 3.1% Hispanic of any race (2010); Average household size: 1.97 (2010); Median age: 53.7 (2010); Males per 100 females: 84.4 (2010); Homeownership rate: 83.5% (2010)

## BIG INDIAN (unincorporated postal area)
Zip Code: 12410

Covers a land area of 41.180 square miles and a water area of 0.035 square miles. Located at 42.06° N. Lat; 74.42° W. Long. Elevation is 1,217 feet. Population: 397 (2010); Density: 9.6 persons per square mile (2010); Race: 93.2% White, 1.3% Black, 2.8% Asian, 0.3% American Indian/Alaska Native, 0.0% Native Hawaiian/Other Pacific Islander, 2.4% Other, 5.5% Hispanic of any race (2010); Average household size: 2.14 (2010); Median age: 50.2 (2010); Males per 100 females: 107.9 (2010); Homeownership rate: 81.4% (2010)

## BLOOMINGTON (unincorporated postal area)
Zip Code: 12411

Covers a land area of 0.937 square miles and a water area of 0.018 square miles. Located at 41.87° N. Lat; 74.04° W. Long. Elevation is 184 feet. Population: 497 (2010); Density: 530.3 persons per square mile (2010); Race: 95.0% White, 1.6% Black, 1.0% Asian, 0.0% American Indian/Alaska Native, 0.4% Native Hawaiian/Other Pacific Islander, 2.0% Other, 2.4% Hispanic of any race (2010); Average household size: 2.34 (2010); Median age: 43.1 (2010); Males per 100 females: 97.2 (2010); Homeownership rate: 83.5% (2010)

## BOICEVILLE (unincorporated postal area)
Zip Code: 12412

Covers a land area of 6.069 square miles and a water area of 0 square miles. Located at 42.01° N. Lat; 74.27° W. Long. Elevation is 630 feet. Population: 673 (2010); Density: 110.9 persons per square mile (2010); Race: 90.5% White, 0.3% Black, 2.2% Asian, 0.4% American Indian/Alaska Native, 0.0% Native Hawaiian/Other Pacific Islander, 6.6% Other, 5.6% Hispanic of any race (2010); Average household size: 2.38 (2010); Median age: 46.5 (2010); Males per 100 females: 103.3 (2010); Homeownership rate: 74.5% (2010)

## CHICHESTER (unincorporated postal area)
Zip Code: 12416

Covers a land area of 5.085 square miles and a water area of <.001 square miles. Located at 42.10° N. Lat; 74.28° W. Long. Elevation is 965 feet. Population: 277 (2010); Density: 54.5 persons per square mile (2010); Race: 89.2% White, 0.0% Black, 3.2% Asian, 0.7% American Indian/Alaska Native, 0.0% Native Hawaiian/Other Pacific Islander, 6.9% Other, 5.8% Hispanic of any race (2010); Average household size: 2.23 (2010); Median age: 42.5 (2010); Males per 100 females: 102.2 (2010); Homeownership rate: 75.8% (2010)

## CLINTONDALE (CDP). Covers a land area of 5.572 square miles and a water area of 0.039 square miles. Located at 41.69° N. Lat; 74.04° W. Long. Elevation is 545 feet.

**Population:** 1,394 (1990); 1,424 (2000); 1,452 (2010); Density: 260.6 persons per square mile (2010); Race: 89.5% White, 3.6% Black, 2.3% Asian, 0.1% American Indian/Alaska Native, 0.0% Native Hawaiian/Other Pacific Islander, 4.5% Other, 8.3% Hispanic of any race (2010); Average household size: 2.61 (2010); Median age: 40.1 (2010); Males per 100 females: 101.9 (2010); Marriage status: 27.1% never married, 62.2% now married, 1.0% widowed, 9.6% divorced (2006-2010 5-year est.); Foreign born: 11.2% (2006-2010 5-year est.); Ancestry (includes multiple

ancestries): 29.3% Irish, 25.7% Italian, 19.8% German, 17.2% English, 7.8% American (2006-2010 5-year est.).

**Economy:** Employment by occupation: 4.3% management, 5.6% professional, 7.6% services, 21.8% sales, 5.8% farming, 26.5% construction, 0.0% production (2006-2010 5-year est.).

**Income:** Per capita income: $28,528 (2006-2010 5-year est.); Median household income: $52,727 (2006-2010 5-year est.); Average household income: $70,564 (2006-2010 5-year est.); Percent of households with income of $100,000 or more: 17.7% (2006-2010 5-year est.); Poverty rate: 5.3% (2006-2010 5-year est.).

**Education:** Percent of population age 25 and over with: High school diploma (including GED) or higher: 77.1% (2006-2010 5-year est.); Bachelor's degree or higher: 26.8% (2006-2010 5-year est.); Master's degree or higher: 17.8% (2006-2010 5-year est.).

**Housing:** Homeownership rate: 65.4% (2010); Median home value: $234,800 (2006-2010 5-year est.); Median contract rent: $897 per month (2006-2010 5-year est.); Median year structure built: 1957 (2006-2010 5-year est.).

**Transportation:** Commute to work: 71.7% car, 5.0% public transportation, 18.1% walk, 5.2% work from home (2006-2010 5-year est.); Travel time to work: 32.4% less than 15 minutes, 30.8% 15 to 30 minutes, 27.4% 30 to 45 minutes, 1.1% 45 to 60 minutes, 8.3% 60 minutes or more (2006-2010 5-year est.)

## CONNELLY (unincorporated postal area)
Zip Code: 12417

Covers a land area of 0.315 square miles and a water area of 0.028 square miles. Located at 41.90° N. Lat; 73.99° W. Long. Elevation is 23 feet. Population: 581 (2010); Density: 1,841.5 persons per square mile (2010); Race: 86.2% White, 6.0% Black, 0.3% Asian, 0.0% American Indian/Alaska Native, 0.0% Native Hawaiian/Other Pacific Islander, 7.5% Other, 2.2% Hispanic of any race (2010); Average household size: 2.48 (2010); Median age: 41.6 (2010); Males per 100 females: 90.5 (2010); Homeownership rate: 82.5% (2010)

## COTTEKILL (unincorporated postal area)
Zip Code: 12419

Covers a land area of 2.394 square miles and a water area of 0.020 square miles. Located at 41.86° N. Lat; 74.10° W. Long. Elevation is 253 feet. Population: 722 (2010); Density: 301.5 persons per square mile (2010); Race: 95.6% White, 0.6% Black, 0.3% Asian, 0.1% American Indian/Alaska Native, 0.0% Native Hawaiian/Other Pacific Islander, 3.4% Other, 2.8% Hispanic of any race (2010); Average household size: 2.52 (2010); Median age: 43.9 (2010); Males per 100 females: 96.2 (2010); Homeownership rate: 77.7% (2010)

## CRAGSMOOR (CDP). Covers a land area of 4.351 square miles and a water area of 0 square miles. Located at 41.66° N. Lat; 74.39° W. Long. Elevation is 1,864 feet.

**Population:** 362 (1990); 474 (2000); 449 (2010); Density: 103.2 persons per square mile (2010); Race: 96.9% White, 0.7% Black, 0.9% Asian, 0.0% American Indian/Alaska Native, 0.0% Native Hawaiian/Other Pacific Islander, 1.5% Other, 4.5% Hispanic of any race (2010); Average household size: 2.35 (2010); Median age: 49.7 (2010); Males per 100 females: 102.3 (2010); Marriage status: 21.4% never married, 64.1% now married, 0.0% widowed, 14.5% divorced (2006-2010 5-year est.); Foreign born: 8.3% (2006-2010 5-year est.); Ancestry (includes multiple ancestries): 33.3% German, 18.1% English, 16.1% Italian, 11.9% Ukrainian, 11.7% American (2006-2010 5-year est.).

**Economy:** Employment by occupation: 4.2% management, 0.0% professional, 0.0% services, 27.8% sales, 10.8% farming, 0.0% construction, 0.0% production (2006-2010 5-year est.).

**Income:** Per capita income: $50,770 (2006-2010 5-year est.); Median household income: $94,493 (2006-2010 5-year est.); Average household income: $99,983 (2006-2010 5-year est.); Percent of households with income of $100,000 or more: 45.9% (2006-2010 5-year est.); Poverty rate: 0.0% (2006-2010 5-year est.).

**Education:** Percent of population age 25 and over with: High school diploma (including GED) or higher: 94.8% (2006-2010 5-year est.); Bachelor's degree or higher: 69.9% (2006-2010 5-year est.); Master's degree or higher: 40.0% (2006-2010 5-year est.).

**Housing:** Homeownership rate: 86.4% (2010); Median home value: $406,800 (2006-2010 5-year est.); Median contract rent: n/a per month (2006-2010 5-year est.); Median year structure built: before 1940 (2006-2010 5-year est.).

**Transportation:** Commute to work: 91.5% car, 4.7% public transportation, 0.0% walk, 3.8% work from home (2006-2010 5-year est.); Travel time to work: 3.9% less than 15 minutes, 36.8% 15 to 30 minutes, 26.0% 30 to 45 minutes, 13.2% 45 to 60 minutes, 20.1% 60 minutes or more (2006-2010 5-year est.)

**DENNING** (town). Covers a land area of 105.666 square miles and a water area of 0.099 square miles. Located at 41.95° N. Lat; 74.48° W. Long. Elevation is 1,959 feet.
**Population:** 524 (1990); 516 (2000); 551 (2010); Density: 5.2 persons per square mile (2010); Race: 94.9% White, 1.1% Black, 0.2% Asian, 0.7% American Indian/Alaska Native, 0.0% Native Hawaiian/Other Pacific Islander, 3.1% Other, 1.3% Hispanic of any race (2010); Average household size: 2.26 (2010); Median age: 46.2 (2010); Males per 100 females: 106.4 (2010); Marriage status: 18.1% never married, 73.2% now married, 1.7% widowed, 7.0% divorced (2006-2010 5-year est.); Foreign born: 1.7% (2006-2010 5-year est.); Ancestry (includes multiple ancestries): 38.7% English, 17.8% German, 16.9% Italian, 8.8% American, 6.7% Dutch (2006-2010 5-year est.).
**Economy:** Single-family building permits issued: 1 (2011); Multi-family building permits issued: 0 (2011); Employment by occupation: 18.2% management, 0.0% professional, 4.7% services, 17.2% sales, 5.7% farming, 13.0% construction, 4.2% production (2006-2010 5-year est.).
**Income:** Per capita income: $25,747 (2006-2010 5-year est.); Median household income: $53,125 (2006-2010 5-year est.); Average household income: $58,305 (2006-2010 5-year est.); Percent of households with income of $100,000 or more: 3.5% (2006-2010 5-year est.); Poverty rate: 4.8% (2006-2010 5-year est.).
**Education:** Percent of population age 25 and over with: High school diploma (including GED) or higher: 83.8% (2006-2010 5-year est.); Bachelor's degree or higher: 23.0% (2006-2010 5-year est.); Master's degree or higher: 8.1% (2006-2010 5-year est.).
**Housing:** Homeownership rate: 75.2% (2010); Median home value: $209,800 (2006-2010 5-year est.); Median contract rent: $578 per month (2006-2010 5-year est.); Median year structure built: 1963 (2006-2010 5-year est.).
**Transportation:** Commute to work: 96.7% car, 0.0% public transportation, 1.6% walk, 1.6% work from home (2006-2010 5-year est.); Travel time to work: 21.2% less than 15 minutes, 30.2% 15 to 30 minutes, 19.0% 30 to 45 minutes, 6.7% 45 to 60 minutes, 22.9% 60 minutes or more (2006-2010 5-year est.)

**EAST KINGSTON** (CDP). Covers a land area of 0.673 square miles and a water area of 0.022 square miles. Located at 41.95° N. Lat; 73.97° W. Long. Elevation is 151 feet.
**Population:** 300 (1990); 285 (2000); 276 (2010); Density: 409.6 persons per square mile (2010); Race: 85.5% White, 10.9% Black, 0.0% Asian, 0.0% American Indian/Alaska Native, 0.0% Native Hawaiian/Other Pacific Islander, 3.6% Other, 8.0% Hispanic of any race (2010); Average household size: 2.42 (2010); Median age: 39.0 (2010); Males per 100 females: 110.7 (2010); Marriage status: 52.5% never married, 31.6% now married, 12.4% widowed, 3.5% divorced (2006-2010 5-year est.); Foreign born: 0.0% (2006-2010 5-year est.); Ancestry (includes multiple ancestries): 49.6% Italian, 32.9% German, 20.7% Irish, 16.0% Dutch, 8.2% Hungarian (2006-2010 5-year est.).
**Economy:** Employment by occupation: 4.7% management, 0.0% professional, 9.4% services, 33.3% sales, 10.9% farming, 12.0% construction, 12.5% production (2006-2010 5-year est.).
**Income:** Per capita income: $18,878 (2006-2010 5-year est.); Median household income: $46,250 (2006-2010 5-year est.); Average household income: $52,661 (2006-2010 5-year est.); Percent of households with income of $100,000 or more: 14.0% (2006-2010 5-year est.); Poverty rate: 7.0% (2006-2010 5-year est.).
**Education:** Percent of population age 25 and over with: High school diploma (including GED) or higher: 66.0% (2006-2010 5-year est.); Bachelor's degree or higher: 0.0% (2006-2010 5-year est.); Master's degree or higher: 0.0% (2006-2010 5-year est.).
**Housing:** Homeownership rate: 64.0% (2010); Median home value: $134,700 (2006-2010 5-year est.); Median contract rent: n/a per month (2006-2010 5-year est.); Median year structure built: before 1940 (2006-2010 5-year est.).
**Transportation:** Commute to work: 100.0% car, 0.0% public transportation, 0.0% walk, 0.0% work from home (2006-2010 5-year est.); Travel time to work: 59.4% less than 15 minutes, 24.5% 15 to 30 minutes,

16.1% 30 to 45 minutes, 0.0% 45 to 60 minutes, 0.0% 60 minutes or more (2006-2010 5-year est.)

**ELLENVILLE** (village). Covers a land area of 8.724 square miles and a water area of 0.086 square miles. Located at 41.70° N. Lat; 74.36° W. Long. Elevation is 338 feet.
**History:** Incorporated 1856.
**Population:** 4,259 (1990); 4,130 (2000); 4,135 (2010); Density: 474.0 persons per square mile (2010); Race: 68.1% White, 13.7% Black, 2.4% Asian, 1.3% American Indian/Alaska Native, 0.1% Native Hawaiian/Other Pacific Islander, 14.4% Other, 27.9% Hispanic of any race (2010); Average household size: 2.58 (2010); Median age: 35.9 (2010); Males per 100 females: 94.1 (2010); Marriage status: 31.2% never married, 50.7% now married, 7.6% widowed, 10.5% divorced (2006-2010 5-year est.); Foreign born: 11.3% (2006-2010 5-year est.); Ancestry (includes multiple ancestries): 12.3% Irish, 8.4% English, 7.5% German, 5.8% Italian, 5.7% Polish (2006-2010 5-year est.).
**Economy:** Single-family building permits issued: 0 (2011); Multi-family building permits issued: 0 (2011); Employment by occupation: 5.6% management, 2.3% professional, 18.7% services, 11.3% sales, 7.0% farming, 5.9% construction, 4.4% production (2006-2010 5-year est.).
**Income:** Per capita income: $17,735 (2006-2010 5-year est.); Median household income: $40,223 (2006-2010 5-year est.); Average household income: $47,036 (2006-2010 5-year est.); Percent of households with income of $100,000 or more: 8.4% (2006-2010 5-year est.); Poverty rate: 27.0% (2006-2010 5-year est.).
**Education:** Percent of population age 25 and over with: High school diploma (including GED) or higher: 71.7% (2006-2010 5-year est.); Bachelor's degree or higher: 21.4% (2006-2010 5-year est.); Master's degree or higher: 13.0% (2006-2010 5-year est.).
**School District(s)**
Ellenville Central School District (PK-12)
    2009-10 Enrollment: 1,822 . . . . . . . . . . . . . . . . . . . . . . (845) 647-0100
**Housing:** Homeownership rate: 47.4% (2010); Median home value: $168,700 (2006-2010 5-year est.); Median contract rent: $766 per month (2006-2010 5-year est.); Median year structure built: 1948 (2006-2010 5-year est.).
**Hospitals:** Ellenville Regional Hospital (25 beds)
**Safety:** Violent crime rate: 85.7 per 10,000 population; Property crime rate: 246.7 per 10,000 population (2010).
**Newspapers:** The Ellenville Press (Community news; Circulation 2,400)
**Transportation:** Commute to work: 83.4% car, 2.5% public transportation, 6.3% walk, 7.2% work from home (2006-2010 5-year est.); Travel time to work: 40.9% less than 15 minutes, 24.7% 15 to 30 minutes, 19.6% 30 to 45 minutes, 6.9% 45 to 60 minutes, 7.9% 60 minutes or more (2006-2010 5-year est.)
**Additional Information Contacts**
Ellenville-Wawarsing Chamber of Commerce . . . . . . . . . . . (845) 647-4620

**ESOPUS** (town). Covers a land area of 37.312 square miles and a water area of 4.628 square miles. Located at 41.83° N. Lat; 73.98° W. Long. Elevation is 125 feet.
**History:** Seat of Mt. St. Alphonsus Theological Seminary. John Burroughs lived near here. Town was formed in 1811, and was partly annexed by Kingston in 1818.
**Population:** 8,860 (1990); 9,331 (2000); 9,041 (2010); Density: 242.3 persons per square mile (2010); Race: 89.1% White, 5.0% Black, 1.4% Asian, 0.4% American Indian/Alaska Native, 0.0% Native Hawaiian/Other Pacific Islander, 4.1% Other, 5.4% Hispanic of any race (2010); Average household size: 2.37 (2010); Median age: 43.6 (2010); Males per 100 females: 93.4 (2010); Marriage status: 26.7% never married, 56.0% now married, 6.8% widowed, 10.5% divorced (2006-2010 5-year est.); Foreign born: 3.6% (2006-2010 5-year est.); Ancestry (includes multiple ancestries): 28.5% German, 27.6% Irish, 17.4% Italian, 10.9% American, 10.2% English (2006-2010 5-year est.).
**Economy:** Single-family building permits issued: 7 (2011); Multi-family building permits issued: 2 (2011); Employment by occupation: 7.7% management, 2.4% professional, 9.3% services, 17.0% sales, 2.9% farming, 10.6% construction, 4.6% production (2006-2010 5-year est.).
**Income:** Per capita income: $31,173 (2006-2010 5-year est.); Median household income: $65,617 (2006-2010 5-year est.); Average household income: $79,911 (2006-2010 5-year est.); Percent of households with income of $100,000 or more: 25.9% (2006-2010 5-year est.); Poverty rate: 7.3% (2006-2010 5-year est.).

**Education:** Percent of population age 25 and over with: High school diploma (including GED) or higher: 90.8% (2006-2010 5-year est.); Bachelor's degree or higher: 29.4% (2006-2010 5-year est.); Master's degree or higher: 14.4% (2006-2010 5-year est.).

**Housing:** Homeownership rate: 73.9% (2010); Median home value: $234,900 (2006-2010 5-year est.); Median contract rent: $726 per month (2006-2010 5-year est.); Median year structure built: 1965 (2006-2010 5-year est.).

**Transportation:** Commute to work: 93.3% car, 1.0% public transportation, 1.6% walk, 3.3% work from home (2006-2010 5-year est.); Travel time to work: 33.9% less than 15 minutes, 31.8% 15 to 30 minutes, 21.0% 30 to 45 minutes, 4.9% 45 to 60 minutes, 8.4% 60 minutes or more (2006-2010 5-year est.)

**Additional Information Contacts**

Town of Esopus . . . . . . . . . . . . . . . . . . . . . . . . . . . . . . . (845) 331-3709
http://www.esopus.com

**GARDINER** (town). Covers a land area of 43.434 square miles and a water area of 0.510 square miles. Located at 41.69° N. Lat; 74.18° W. Long. Elevation is 315 feet.

**History:** A 17th-century gristmill is here.

**Population:** 4,380 (1990); 5,238 (2000); 5,713 (2010); Density: 131.5 persons per square mile (2010); Race: 93.2% White, 1.5% Black, 1.1% Asian, 0.1% American Indian/Alaska Native, 0.0% Native Hawaiian/Other Pacific Islander, 4.1% Other, 6.7% Hispanic of any race (2010); Average household size: 2.53 (2010); Median age: 43.2 (2010); Males per 100 females: 100.7 (2010); Marriage status: 25.6% never married, 60.0% now married, 2.5% widowed, 11.8% divorced (2006-2010 5-year est.); Foreign born: 5.6% (2006-2010 5-year est.); Ancestry (includes multiple ancestries): 24.6% Italian, 20.1% German, 17.0% Irish, 12.8% English, 7.0% French (2006-2010 5-year est.).

**Economy:** Single-family building permits issued: 8 (2011); Multi-family building permits issued: 2 (2011); Employment by occupation: 11.1% management, 5.8% professional, 5.0% services, 15.3% sales, 3.3% farming, 8.0% construction, 3.6% production (2006-2010 5-year est.).

**Income:** Per capita income: $40,901 (2006-2010 5-year est.); Median household income: $84,161 (2006-2010 5-year est.); Average household income: $100,451 (2006-2010 5-year est.); Percent of households with income of $100,000 or more: 36.9% (2006-2010 5-year est.); Poverty rate: 5.8% (2006-2010 5-year est.).

**Education:** Percent of population age 25 and over with: High school diploma (including GED) or higher: 95.7% (2006-2010 5-year est.); Bachelor's degree or higher: 45.1% (2006-2010 5-year est.); Master's degree or higher: 22.2% (2006-2010 5-year est.).

**Housing:** Homeownership rate: 78.1% (2010); Median home value: $336,900 (2006-2010 5-year est.); Median contract rent: $950 per month (2006-2010 5-year est.); Median year structure built: 1977 (2006-2010 5-year est.).

**Transportation:** Commute to work: 87.8% car, 0.7% public transportation, 2.5% walk, 8.3% work from home (2006-2010 5-year est.); Travel time to work: 28.6% less than 15 minutes, 21.5% 15 to 30 minutes, 30.7% 30 to 45 minutes, 8.9% 45 to 60 minutes, 10.4% 60 minutes or more (2006-2010 5-year est.)

**GARDINER** (CDP). Covers a land area of 3.862 square miles and a water area of 0 square miles. Located at 41.67° N. Lat; 74.14° W. Long. Elevation is 315 feet.

**Population:** 726 (1990); 856 (2000); 950 (2010); Density: 246.0 persons per square mile (2010); Race: 91.4% White, 1.5% Black, 0.4% Asian, 0.2% American Indian/Alaska Native, 0.0% Native Hawaiian/Other Pacific Islander, 6.5% Other, 8.9% Hispanic of any race (2010); Average household size: 2.47 (2010); Median age: 40.2 (2010); Males per 100 females: 95.5 (2010); Marriage status: 27.1% never married, 65.1% now married, 4.6% widowed, 3.2% divorced (2006-2010 5-year est.); Foreign born: 0.0% (2006-2010 5-year est.); Ancestry (includes multiple ancestries): 30.9% German, 27.9% Italian, 21.6% Irish, 17.3% English, 11.9% French (2006-2010 5-year est.).

**Economy:** Employment by occupation: 6.0% management, 15.3% professional, 0.0% services, 8.0% sales, 2.6% farming, 15.1% construction, 3.0% production (2006-2010 5-year est.).

**Income:** Per capita income: $25,263 (2006-2010 5-year est.); Median household income: $68,750 (2006-2010 5-year est.); Average household income: $59,169 (2006-2010 5-year est.); Percent of households with income of $100,000 or more: 10.2% (2006-2010 5-year est.); Poverty rate: 1.1% (2006-2010 5-year est.).

**Education:** Percent of population age 25 and over with: High school diploma (including GED) or higher: 89.1% (2006-2010 5-year est.); Bachelor's degree or higher: 33.9% (2006-2010 5-year est.); Master's degree or higher: 19.6% (2006-2010 5-year est.).

**Housing:** Homeownership rate: 65.9% (2010); Median home value: $258,800 (2006-2010 5-year est.); Median contract rent: $958 per month (2006-2010 5-year est.); Median year structure built: 1959 (2006-2010 5-year est.).

**Transportation:** Commute to work: 94.8% car, 0.0% public transportation, 0.0% walk, 5.2% work from home (2006-2010 5-year est.); Travel time to work: 29.4% less than 15 minutes, 8.9% 15 to 30 minutes, 41.7% 30 to 45 minutes, 9.6% 45 to 60 minutes, 10.5% 60 minutes or more (2006-2010 5-year est.)

**GLASCO** (CDP). Covers a land area of 1.762 square miles and a water area of 0.683 square miles. Located at 42.04° N. Lat; 73.95° W. Long. Elevation is 151 feet.

**Population:** 1,538 (1990); 1,692 (2000); 2,099 (2010); Density: 1,191.0 persons per square mile (2010); Race: 92.8% White, 1.7% Black, 2.3% Asian, 0.1% American Indian/Alaska Native, 0.0% Native Hawaiian/Other Pacific Islander, 3.1% Other, 5.2% Hispanic of any race (2010); Average household size: 2.32 (2010); Median age: 43.1 (2010); Males per 100 females: 82.0 (2010); Marriage status: 42.5% never married, 39.8% now married, 8.5% widowed, 9.3% divorced (2006-2010 5-year est.); Foreign born: 9.5% (2006-2010 5-year est.); Ancestry (includes multiple ancestries): 25.1% Italian, 15.6% Irish, 11.6% German, 7.9% English, 6.4% American (2006-2010 5-year est.).

**Economy:** Employment by occupation: 12.4% management, 1.7% professional, 4.6% services, 24.4% sales, 6.6% farming, 6.5% construction, 4.1% production (2006-2010 5-year est.).

**Income:** Per capita income: $30,783 (2006-2010 5-year est.); Median household income: $52,132 (2006-2010 5-year est.); Average household income: $76,338 (2006-2010 5-year est.); Percent of households with income of $100,000 or more: 16.8% (2006-2010 5-year est.); Poverty rate: 2.7% (2006-2010 5-year est.).

**Education:** Percent of population age 25 and over with: High school diploma (including GED) or higher: 91.4% (2006-2010 5-year est.); Bachelor's degree or higher: 28.2% (2006-2010 5-year est.); Master's degree or higher: 11.5% (2006-2010 5-year est.).

**School District(s)**

Saugerties Central School District (KG-12)
    2009-10 Enrollment: 3,083 . . . . . . . . . . . . . . . . . . . . . . . (845) 247-6500

**Housing:** Homeownership rate: 67.5% (2010); Median home value: $204,300 (2006-2010 5-year est.); Median contract rent: $826 per month (2006-2010 5-year est.); Median year structure built: 1986 (2006-2010 5-year est.).

**Transportation:** Commute to work: 87.7% car, 3.2% public transportation, 1.6% walk, 1.2% work from home (2006-2010 5-year est.); Travel time to work: 35.3% less than 15 minutes, 39.9% 15 to 30 minutes, 12.4% 30 to 45 minutes, 2.4% 45 to 60 minutes, 10.0% 60 minutes or more (2006-2010 5-year est.)

**GLENFORD** (unincorporated postal area)

Zip Code: 12433
    Covers a land area of 3.819 square miles and a water area of 0.086 square miles. Located at 42.00° N. Lat; 74.15° W. Long. Elevation is 659 feet. Population: 483 (2010); Density: 126.4 persons per square mile (2010); Race: 95.2% White, 0.6% Black, 0.8% Asian, 0.0% American Indian/Alaska Native, 0.0% Native Hawaiian/Other Pacific Islander, 3.4% Other, 2.7% Hispanic of any race (2010); Average household size: 2.16 (2010); Median age: 51.2 (2010); Males per 100 females: 98.8 (2010); Homeownership rate: 84.0% (2010)

**GREENFIELD PARK** (unincorporated postal area)

Zip Code: 12435
    Covers a land area of 9.957 square miles and a water area of 0.076 square miles. Located at 41.73° N. Lat; 74.51° W. Long. Elevation is 873 feet. Population: 326 (2010); Density: 32.7 persons per square mile (2010); Race: 93.9% White, 4.0% Black, 0.0% Asian, 2.1% American Indian/Alaska Native, 0.0% Native Hawaiian/Other Pacific Islander, 0.0% Other, 7.1% Hispanic of any race (2010); Average household size: 2.35 (2010); Median age: 48.0 (2010); Males per 100 females: 109.0 (2010); Homeownership rate: 74.8% (2010)

**HARDENBURGH** (town). Covers a land area of 80.786 square miles and a water area of 0.235 square miles. Located at 42.04° N. Lat; 74.62° W. Long.

**Population:** 204 (1990); 208 (2000); 238 (2010); Density: 2.9 persons per square mile (2010); Race: 92.4% White, 0.0% Black, 2.1% Asian, 4.2% American Indian/Alaska Native, 0.0% Native Hawaiian/Other Pacific Islander, 1.3% Other, 2.9% Hispanic of any race (2010); Average household size: 2.13 (2010); Median age: 50.3 (2010); Males per 100 females: 116.4 (2010); Marriage status: 26.8% never married, 52.8% now married, 2.1% widowed, 18.3% divorced (2006-2010 5-year est.); Foreign born: 1.3% (2006-2010 5-year est.); Ancestry (includes multiple ancestries): 36.2% German, 22.4% Italian, 15.8% English, 12.5% Irish, 10.5% Scottish (2006-2010 5-year est.).

**Economy:** Single-family building permits issued: 0 (2011); Multi-family building permits issued: 0 (2011); Employment by occupation: 31.8% management, 0.0% professional, 16.5% services, 10.6% sales, 0.0% farming, 15.3% construction, 2.4% production (2006-2010 5-year est.).

**Income:** Per capita income: $22,299 (2006-2010 5-year est.); Median household income: $35,357 (2006-2010 5-year est.); Average household income: $46,247 (2006-2010 5-year est.); Percent of households with income of $100,000 or more: 12.5% (2006-2010 5-year est.); Poverty rate: 9.2% (2006-2010 5-year est.).

**Education:** Percent of population age 25 and over with: High school diploma (including GED) or higher: 94.3% (2006-2010 5-year est.); Bachelor's degree or higher: 23.0% (2006-2010 5-year est.); Master's degree or higher: 9.8% (2006-2010 5-year est.).

**Housing:** Homeownership rate: 76.8% (2010); Median home value: $275,000 (2006-2010 5-year est.); Median contract rent: $444 per month (2006-2010 5-year est.); Median year structure built: 1966 (2006-2010 5-year est.).

**Transportation:** Commute to work: 68.2% car, 0.0% public transportation, 11.8% walk, 20.0% work from home (2006-2010 5-year est.); Travel time to work: 35.3% less than 15 minutes, 29.4% 15 to 30 minutes, 1.5% 30 to 45 minutes, 33.8% 45 to 60 minutes, 0.0% 60 minutes or more (2006-2010 5-year est.)

**HIGH FALLS** (CDP). Covers a land area of 1.196 square miles and a water area of 0 square miles. Located at 41.82° N. Lat; 74.11° W. Long. Elevation is 161 feet.

**Population:** 661 (1990); 627 (2000); 627 (2010); Density: 524.2 persons per square mile (2010); Race: 93.1% White, 2.9% Black, 1.8% Asian, 0.0% American Indian/Alaska Native, 0.0% Native Hawaiian/Other Pacific Islander, 2.2% Other, 3.7% Hispanic of any race (2010); Average household size: 2.40 (2010); Median age: 42.8 (2010); Males per 100 females: 93.5 (2010); Marriage status: 42.8% never married, 40.8% now married, 13.9% widowed, 2.5% divorced (2006-2010 5-year est.); Foreign born: 0.0% (2006-2010 5-year est.); Ancestry (includes multiple ancestries): 36.7% Irish, 25.1% English, 12.5% German, 9.3% Italian, 7.9% French (2006-2010 5-year est.).

**Economy:** Employment by occupation: 5.1% management, 0.0% professional, 0.0% services, 14.7% sales, 5.9% farming, 17.6% construction, 0.0% production (2006-2010 5-year est.).

**Income:** Per capita income: $37,357 (2006-2010 5-year est.); Median household income: $55,625 (2006-2010 5-year est.); Average household income: $79,244 (2006-2010 5-year est.); Percent of households with income of $100,000 or more: 19.0% (2006-2010 5-year est.); Poverty rate: 1.6% (2006-2010 5-year est.).

**Education:** Percent of population age 25 and over with: High school diploma (including GED) or higher: 87.9% (2006-2010 5-year est.); Bachelor's degree or higher: 41.3% (2006-2010 5-year est.); Master's degree or higher: 26.6% (2006-2010 5-year est.).

**Housing:** Homeownership rate: 75.1% (2010); Median home value: $237,700 (2006-2010 5-year est.); Median contract rent: $883 per month (2006-2010 5-year est.); Median year structure built: before 1940 (2006-2010 5-year est.).

**Transportation:** Commute to work: 85.8% car, 0.0% public transportation, 0.0% walk, 14.2% work from home (2006-2010 5-year est.); Travel time to work: 11.7% less than 15 minutes, 42.1% 15 to 30 minutes, 13.7% 30 to 45 minutes, 8.8% 45 to 60 minutes, 23.8% 60 minutes or more (2006-2010 5-year est.)

**HIGHLAND** (CDP). Covers a land area of 4.685 square miles and a water area of 0.390 square miles. Located at 41.71° N. Lat; 73.96° W. Long. Elevation is 174 feet.

**Population:** 4,494 (1990); 5,060 (2000); 5,647 (2010); Density: 1,205.2 persons per square mile (2010); Race: 84.4% White, 6.9% Black, 4.0% Asian, 0.3% American Indian/Alaska Native, 0.0% Native Hawaiian/Other Pacific Islander, 4.4% Other, 7.8% Hispanic of any race (2010); Average household size: 2.40 (2010); Median age: 40.6 (2010); Males per 100 females: 88.7 (2010); Marriage status: 26.7% never married, 48.5% now married, 12.4% widowed, 12.5% divorced (2006-2010 5-year est.); Foreign born: 9.0% (2006-2010 5-year est.); Ancestry (includes multiple ancestries): 29.9% Italian, 17.9% Irish, 10.2% American, 7.8% German, 5.5% English (2006-2010 5-year est.).

**Economy:** Employment by occupation: 11.4% management, 8.6% professional, 13.9% services, 13.8% sales, 2.4% farming, 9.7% construction, 4.7% production (2006-2010 5-year est.).

**Income:** Per capita income: $27,348 (2006-2010 5-year est.); Median household income: $53,049 (2006-2010 5-year est.); Average household income: $66,104 (2006-2010 5-year est.); Percent of households with income of $100,000 or more: 17.3% (2006-2010 5-year est.); Poverty rate: 11.9% (2006-2010 5-year est.).

**Education:** Percent of population age 25 and over with: High school diploma (including GED) or higher: 84.1% (2006-2010 5-year est.); Bachelor's degree or higher: 35.5% (2006-2010 5-year est.); Master's degree or higher: 16.0% (2006-2010 5-year est.).

**School District(s)**

Highland Central School District (KG-12)
    2009-10 Enrollment: 1,929 . . . . . . . . . . . . . . . . . . . . . . . . (845) 691-1012

**Housing:** Homeownership rate: 62.3% (2010); Median home value: $245,000 (2006-2010 5-year est.); Median contract rent: $863 per month (2006-2010 5-year est.); Median year structure built: 1969 (2006-2010 5-year est.).

**Newspapers:** Pioneer (Local news)

**Transportation:** Commute to work: 89.9% car, 2.6% public transportation, 3.8% walk, 3.2% work from home (2006-2010 5-year est.); Travel time to work: 22.0% less than 15 minutes, 33.4% 15 to 30 minutes, 24.6% 30 to 45 minutes, 5.6% 45 to 60 minutes, 14.5% 60 minutes or more (2006-2010 5-year est.)

**Additional Information Contacts**

Southern Ulster County Chamber of Commerce . . . . . . . . (845) 691-6070
http://www.southernulsterchamber.org

**HIGHMOUNT** (unincorporated postal area)

Zip Code: 12441

Covers a land area of 6.326 square miles and a water area of 0.001 square miles. Located at 42.13° N. Lat; 74.50° W. Long. Elevation is 1,854 feet. Population: 114 (2010); Density: 18.0 persons per square mile (2010); Race: 93.0% White, 1.8% Black, 0.0% Asian, 0.0% American Indian/Alaska Native, 0.0% Native Hawaiian/Other Pacific Islander, 5.2% Other, 6.1% Hispanic of any race (2010); Average household size: 1.93 (2010); Median age: 54.7 (2010); Males per 100 females: 119.2 (2010); Homeownership rate: 81.4% (2010)

**HILLSIDE** (CDP). Covers a land area of 0.825 square miles and a water area of 0.003 square miles. Located at 41.91° N. Lat; 74.03° W. Long. Elevation is 318 feet.

**Population:** 1,008 (1990); 882 (2000); 877 (2010); Density: 1,062.8 persons per square mile (2010); Race: 93.5% White, 1.7% Black, 3.1% Asian, 0.0% American Indian/Alaska Native, 0.0% Native Hawaiian/Other Pacific Islander, 1.7% Other, 3.4% Hispanic of any race (2010); Average household size: 2.65 (2010); Median age: 48.6 (2010); Males per 100 females: 98.4 (2010); Marriage status: 9.4% never married, 76.1% now married, 8.5% widowed, 6.0% divorced (2006-2010 5-year est.); Foreign born: 14.3% (2006-2010 5-year est.); Ancestry (includes multiple ancestries): 26.0% Italian, 24.4% Irish, 19.5% German, 13.0% American, 6.6% French (2006-2010 5-year est.).

**Economy:** Employment by occupation: 20.7% management, 2.4% professional, 0.0% services, 8.8% sales, 0.0% farming, 3.0% construction, 0.0% production (2006-2010 5-year est.).

**Income:** Per capita income: $56,627 (2006-2010 5-year est.); Median household income: $101,905 (2006-2010 5-year est.); Average household income: $134,103 (2006-2010 5-year est.); Percent of households with income of $100,000 or more: 55.1% (2006-2010 5-year est.); Poverty rate: 4.0% (2006-2010 5-year est.).

**Education:** Percent of population age 25 and over with: High school diploma (including GED) or higher: 98.7% (2006-2010 5-year est.); Bachelor's degree or higher: 66.1% (2006-2010 5-year est.); Master's degree or higher: 34.7% (2006-2010 5-year est.).
**Housing:** Homeownership rate: 97.2% (2010); Median home value: $283,300 (2006-2010 5-year est.); Median contract rent: n/a per month (2006-2010 5-year est.); Median year structure built: 1970 (2006-2010 5-year est.).
**Transportation:** Commute to work: 94.3% car, 0.0% public transportation, 0.0% walk, 5.7% work from home (2006-2010 5-year est.); Travel time to work: 42.7% less than 15 minutes, 36.0% 15 to 30 minutes, 0.0% 30 to 45 minutes, 17.0% 45 to 60 minutes, 4.3% 60 minutes or more (2006-2010 5-year est.)

**HURLEY** (town). Covers a land area of 29.910 square miles and a water area of 6.055 square miles. Located at 41.95° N. Lat; 74.12° W. Long. Elevation is 197 feet.
**Population:** 6,741 (1990); 6,564 (2000); 6,314 (2010); Density: 211.1 persons per square mile (2010); Race: 94.5% White, 1.6% Black, 1.4% Asian, 0.1% American Indian/Alaska Native, 0.1% Native Hawaiian/Other Pacific Islander, 2.3% Other, 2.9% Hispanic of any race (2010); Average household size: 2.32 (2010); Median age: 48.6 (2010); Males per 100 females: 92.9 (2010); Marriage status: 23.6% never married, 63.2% now married, 5.6% widowed, 7.6% divorced (2006-2010 5-year est.); Foreign born: 5.3% (2006-2010 5-year est.); Ancestry (includes multiple ancestries): 33.8% German, 22.5% Irish, 18.9% Italian, 12.7% English, 6.2% Polish (2006-2010 5-year est.).
**Economy:** Single-family building permits issued: 6 (2011); Multi-family building permits issued: 0 (2011); Employment by occupation: 16.8% management, 3.2% professional, 6.0% services, 16.2% sales, 3.0% farming, 7.8% construction, 2.7% production (2006-2010 5-year est.).
**Income:** Per capita income: $36,343 (2006-2010 5-year est.); Median household income: $67,798 (2006-2010 5-year est.); Average household income: $86,311 (2006-2010 5-year est.); Percent of households with income of $100,000 or more: 27.8% (2006-2010 5-year est.); Poverty rate: 3.1% (2006-2010 5-year est.).
**Education:** Percent of population age 25 and over with: High school diploma (including GED) or higher: 94.0% (2006-2010 5-year est.); Bachelor's degree or higher: 43.9% (2006-2010 5-year est.); Master's degree or higher: 20.7% (2006-2010 5-year est.).
**School District(s)**
Kingston City School District (PK-12)
    2009-10 Enrollment: 7,120 . . . . . . . . . . . . . . . . . . . . . (845) 339-3000
**Housing:** Homeownership rate: 86.3% (2010); Median home value: $251,200 (2006-2010 5-year est.); Median contract rent: $825 per month (2006-2010 5-year est.); Median year structure built: 1961 (2006-2010 5-year est.).
**Transportation:** Commute to work: 90.8% car, 0.0% public transportation, 1.1% walk, 7.6% work from home (2006-2010 5-year est.); Travel time to work: 23.1% less than 15 minutes, 46.4% 15 to 30 minutes, 10.9% 30 to 45 minutes, 10.4% 45 to 60 minutes, 9.2% 60 minutes or more (2006-2010 5-year est.)

**HURLEY** (CDP). Covers a land area of 5.485 square miles and a water area of 0.032 square miles. Located at 41.91° N. Lat; 74.06° W. Long. Elevation is 197 feet.
**Population:** 3,771 (1990); 3,561 (2000); 3,458 (2010); Density: 630.4 persons per square mile (2010); Race: 93.9% White, 1.4% Black, 2.0% Asian, 0.0% American Indian/Alaska Native, 0.0% Native Hawaiian/Other Pacific Islander, 2.7% Other, 3.4% Hispanic of any race (2010); Average household size: 2.47 (2010); Median age: 46.5 (2010); Males per 100 females: 95.7 (2010); Marriage status: 25.1% never married, 62.6% now married, 5.7% widowed, 6.6% divorced (2006-2010 5-year est.); Foreign born: 4.0% (2006-2010 5-year est.); Ancestry (includes multiple ancestries): 30.1% German, 29.2% Irish, 20.6% Italian, 12.9% English, 7.2% Dutch (2006-2010 5-year est.).
**Economy:** Employment by occupation: 16.0% management, 5.6% professional, 7.8% services, 12.9% sales, 2.7% farming, 4.8% construction, 2.2% production (2006-2010 5-year est.).
**Income:** Per capita income: $34,053 (2006-2010 5-year est.); Median household income: $71,952 (2006-2010 5-year est.); Average household income: $83,643 (2006-2010 5-year est.); Percent of households with income of $100,000 or more: 29.8% (2006-2010 5-year est.); Poverty rate: 5.1% (2006-2010 5-year est.).

**Education:** Percent of population age 25 and over with: High school diploma (including GED) or higher: 91.8% (2006-2010 5-year est.); Bachelor's degree or higher: 42.7% (2006-2010 5-year est.); Master's degree or higher: 22.2% (2006-2010 5-year est.).
**School District(s)**
Kingston City School District (PK-12)
    2009-10 Enrollment: 7,120 . . . . . . . . . . . . . . . . . . . . . (845) 339-3000
**Housing:** Homeownership rate: 91.1% (2010); Median home value: $233,700 (2006-2010 5-year est.); Median contract rent: $794 per month (2006-2010 5-year est.); Median year structure built: 1959 (2006-2010 5-year est.).
**Transportation:** Commute to work: 94.0% car, 0.0% public transportation, 0.0% walk, 5.5% work from home (2006-2010 5-year est.); Travel time to work: 27.2% less than 15 minutes, 36.6% 15 to 30 minutes, 14.5% 30 to 45 minutes, 14.2% 45 to 60 minutes, 7.4% 60 minutes or more (2006-2010 5-year est.)

**KERHONKSON** (CDP). Covers a land area of 5.277 square miles and a water area of 0.017 square miles. Located at 41.77° N. Lat; 74.29° W. Long. Elevation is 262 feet.
**Population:** 1,640 (1990); 1,732 (2000); 1,684 (2010); Density: 319.1 persons per square mile (2010); Race: 92.6% White, 1.8% Black, 1.3% Asian, 0.7% American Indian/Alaska Native, 0.1% Native Hawaiian/Other Pacific Islander, 3.5% Other, 7.8% Hispanic of any race (2010); Average household size: 2.46 (2010); Median age: 39.4 (2010); Males per 100 females: 97.7 (2010); Marriage status: 19.3% never married, 64.3% now married, 12.0% widowed, 4.5% divorced (2006-2010 5-year est.); Foreign born: 32.1% (2006-2010 5-year est.); Ancestry (includes multiple ancestries): 18.8% Irish, 16.0% Ukrainian, 7.2% Italian, 6.6% American, 6.6% German (2006-2010 5-year est.).
**Economy:** Employment by occupation: 2.0% management, 9.5% professional, 7.7% services, 19.4% sales, 6.7% farming, 6.9% construction, 4.8% production (2006-2010 5-year est.).
**Income:** Per capita income: $21,890 (2006-2010 5-year est.); Median household income: $37,841 (2006-2010 5-year est.); Average household income: $45,835 (2006-2010 5-year est.); Percent of households with income of $100,000 or more: 9.7% (2006-2010 5-year est.); Poverty rate: 14.0% (2006-2010 5-year est.).
**Education:** Percent of population age 25 and over with: High school diploma (including GED) or higher: 71.3% (2006-2010 5-year est.); Bachelor's degree or higher: 11.3% (2006-2010 5-year est.); Master's degree or higher: 8.9% (2006-2010 5-year est.).
**School District(s)**
Rondout Valley Central School District (KG-12)
    2009-10 Enrollment: 2,316 . . . . . . . . . . . . . . . . . . . . . (845) 687-2400
**Housing:** Homeownership rate: 67.7% (2010); Median home value: $177,700 (2006-2010 5-year est.); Median contract rent: $634 per month (2006-2010 5-year est.); Median year structure built: 1948 (2006-2010 5-year est.).
**Transportation:** Commute to work: 91.3% car, 1.9% public transportation, 6.7% walk, 0.0% work from home (2006-2010 5-year est.); Travel time to work: 34.6% less than 15 minutes, 14.7% 15 to 30 minutes, 31.0% 30 to 45 minutes, 14.5% 45 to 60 minutes, 5.2% 60 minutes or more (2006-2010 5-year est.)

**KINGSTON** (city). County seat. Covers a land area of 7.486 square miles and a water area of 1.287 square miles. Located at 41.93° N. Lat; 73.99° W. Long. Elevation is 197 feet.
**History:** In 1615, Dutch traders established a trading post at the present site of Kingston and named it Esopus. A group of Dutch colonists from Albany made the first permanent settlement in 1653. In 1658, Director General Peter Stuyvesant erected a stockade and blockhouse and in 1661 granted a charter to the village, which he called Wiltwyck. In 1669, the English Governor Francis Lovelace gave it its present name in honor of Kingston L'Isle, his family seat in England. Kingston was the site of the New York government during 1777. Boat building and the cement industry both began about 1830.
**Population:** 23,059 (1990); 23,456 (2000); 23,893 (2010); Density: 3,191.5 persons per square mile (2010); Race: 73.2% White, 14.6% Black, 1.8% Asian, 0.5% American Indian/Alaska Native, 0.0% Native Hawaiian/Other Pacific Islander, 9.9% Other, 13.4% Hispanic of any race (2010); Average household size: 2.27 (2010); Median age: 39.2 (2010); Males per 100 females: 92.7 (2010); Marriage status: 35.7% never married, 45.4% now married, 6.9% widowed, 11.9% divorced (2006-2010 5-year est.); Foreign born: 10.9% (2006-2010 5-year est.); Ancestry (includes multiple

ancestries): 21.8% Irish, 18.7% German, 14.0% Italian, 9.2% English, 5.5% Dutch (2006-2010 5-year est.).
**Economy:** Single-family building permits issued: 6 (2011); Multi-family building permits issued: 46 (2011); Employment by occupation: 9.7% management, 2.8% professional, 13.3% services, 18.1% sales, 4.5% farming, 7.0% construction, 4.8% production (2006-2010 5-year est.).
**Income:** Per capita income: $24,368 (2006-2010 5-year est.); Median household income: $46,098 (2006-2010 5-year est.); Average household income: $57,260 (2006-2010 5-year est.); Percent of households with income of $100,000 or more: 13.1% (2006-2010 5-year est.); Poverty rate: 14.6% (2006-2010 5-year est.).
**Education:** Percent of population age 25 and over with: High school diploma (including GED) or higher: 83.5% (2006-2010 5-year est.); Bachelor's degree or higher: 22.8% (2006-2010 5-year est.); Master's degree or higher: 9.8% (2006-2010 5-year est.).

**School District(s)**
Kingston City School District (PK-12)
    2009-10 Enrollment: 7,120 . . . . . . . . . . . . . . . . . . (845) 339-3000
**Housing:** Homeownership rate: 46.5% (2010); Median home value: $195,700 (2006-2010 5-year est.); Median contract rent: $766 per month (2006-2010 5-year est.); Median year structure built: before 1940 (2006-2010 5-year est.).
**Hospitals:** Benedictine Hospital (222 beds)
**Safety:** Violent crime rate: 36.8 per 10,000 population; Property crime rate: 277.6 per 10,000 population (2010).
**Newspapers:** Daily Freeman (Local news; Circulation 22,911); Daily Freeman - Rhinebeck Bureau (Local news); Las Noticias (Local news); Southern Ulster Pioneer (Community news; Circulation 2,422); Woodstock Times (Community news; Circulation 5,000)
**Transportation:** Commute to work: 84.2% car, 2.1% public transportation, 5.6% walk, 5.2% work from home (2006-2010 5-year est.); Travel time to work: 48.2% less than 15 minutes, 30.6% 15 to 30 minutes, 10.9% 30 to 45 minutes, 4.7% 45 to 60 minutes, 5.5% 60 minutes or more (2006-2010 5-year est.)
**Additional Information Contacts**
City of Kingston . . . . . . . . . . . . . . . . . . . . . . . . . (845) 331-0080
    http://www.ci.kingston.ny.us
Ulster County Regional Chamber of Commerce . . . . . . . . . (845) 338-5100
    http://www.ulsterchamber.org

**KINGSTON** (town). Covers a land area of 7.702 square miles and a water area of 0.048 square miles. Located at 41.97° N. Lat; 74.03° W. Long. Elevation is 197 feet.
**History:** First permanent settlement (Wiltwyck) was established in 1652. Served as the first capital of New York State until it was burned by the British in Oct. 1777. Many old Dutch stone houses; the Senate house (1676 meeting place of the first state legislature); the old Dutch church (1659) and cemetery (1661); and the burial place of James Clinton. Incorporated as a village 1805, and as a city through the union (1872) of Kingston and Rondout.
**Population:** 864 (1990); 908 (2000); 889 (2010); Density: 115.4 persons per square mile (2010); Race: 93.0% White, 3.9% Black, 1.2% Asian, 0.3% American Indian/Alaska Native, 0.0% Native Hawaiian/Other Pacific Islander, 1.6% Other, 3.1% Hispanic of any race (2010); Average household size: 2.34 (2010); Median age: 46.4 (2010); Males per 100 females: 101.6 (2010); Marriage status: 21.4% never married, 59.0% now married, 6.7% widowed, 12.9% divorced (2006-2010 5-year est.); Foreign born: 2.4% (2006-2010 5-year est.); Ancestry (includes multiple ancestries): 35.0% Irish, 32.3% Italian, 24.5% German, 11.7% English, 5.0% Dutch (2006-2010 5-year est.).
**Economy:** Single-family building permits issued: 0 (2011); Multi-family building permits issued: 0 (2011); Employment by occupation: 27.9% management, 3.8% professional, 4.6% services, 20.6% sales, 6.1% farming, 8.0% construction, 6.7% production (2006-2010 5-year est.).
**Income:** Per capita income: $27,447 (2006-2010 5-year est.); Median household income: $54,063 (2006-2010 5-year est.); Average household income: $59,617 (2006-2010 5-year est.); Percent of households with income of $100,000 or more: 19.2% (2006-2010 5-year est.); Poverty rate: 5.7% (2006-2010 5-year est.).
**Education:** Percent of population age 25 and over with: High school diploma (including GED) or higher: 88.9% (2006-2010 5-year est.); Bachelor's degree or higher: 20.2% (2006-2010 5-year est.); Master's degree or higher: 6.1% (2006-2010 5-year est.).

**School District(s)**
Kingston City School District (PK-12)
    2009-10 Enrollment: 7,120 . . . . . . . . . . . . . . . . . . (845) 339-3000
**Housing:** Homeownership rate: 85.3% (2010); Median home value: $202,200 (2006-2010 5-year est.); Median contract rent: $850 per month (2006-2010 5-year est.); Median year structure built: 1972 (2006-2010 5-year est.).
**Hospitals:** Benedictine Hospital (222 beds); Kingston Hospital (160 beds); Kingston Hospital (160 beds)
**Newspapers:** Daily Freeman (Local news; Circulation 22,911); Daily Freeman - Rhinebeck Bureau (Local news); Las Noticias (Local news); Southern Ulster Pioneer (Community news; Circulation 2,422); Woodstock Times (Community news; Circulation 5,000)
**Transportation:** Commute to work: 78.0% car, 0.0% public transportation, 0.0% walk, 22.0% work from home (2006-2010 5-year est.); Travel time to work: 29.3% less than 15 minutes, 50.0% 15 to 30 minutes, 6.9% 30 to 45 minutes, 2.9% 45 to 60 minutes, 10.9% 60 minutes or more (2006-2010 5-year est.)
**Additional Information Contacts**
Town of Kingston . . . . . . . . . . . . . . . . . . . . . . . . (845) 336-8853
    http://www.townkingstonny.us

**LAKE HILL** (unincorporated postal area)
Zip Code: 12448
    Covers a land area of 11.661 square miles and a water area of 0.243 square miles. Located at 42.09° N. Lat; 74.15° W. Long. Elevation is 1,109 feet. Population: 388 (2010); Density: 33.3 persons per square mile (2010); Race: 95.9% White, 0.5% Black, 0.8% Asian, 0.0% American Indian/Alaska Native, 0.0% Native Hawaiian/Other Pacific Islander, 2.8% Other, 2.1% Hispanic of any race (2010); Average household size: 1.88 (2010); Median age: 54.8 (2010); Males per 100 females: 103.1 (2010); Homeownership rate: 79.1% (2010)

**LAKE KATRINE** (CDP). Covers a land area of 2.254 square miles and a water area of 0.040 square miles. Located at 41.98° N. Lat; 73.98° W. Long. Elevation is 184 feet.
**Population:** 1,998 (1990); 2,396 (2000); 2,397 (2010); Density: 1,063.3 persons per square mile (2010); Race: 90.6% White, 3.0% Black, 1.9% Asian, 0.2% American Indian/Alaska Native, 0.0% Native Hawaiian/Other Pacific Islander, 4.3% Other, 4.3% Hispanic of any race (2010); Average household size: 2.22 (2010); Median age: 49.0 (2010); Males per 100 females: 89.6 (2010); Marriage status: 32.6% never married, 44.1% now married, 10.1% widowed, 13.2% divorced (2006-2010 5-year est.); Foreign born: 6.3% (2006-2010 5-year est.); Ancestry (includes multiple ancestries): 23.1% German, 18.9% Italian, 13.6% Irish, 11.7% English, 9.5% American (2006-2010 5-year est.).
**Economy:** Employment by occupation: 6.6% management, 2.1% professional, 5.3% services, 22.0% sales, 4.6% farming, 14.1% construction, 9.9% production (2006-2010 5-year est.).
**Income:** Per capita income: $25,138 (2006-2010 5-year est.); Median household income: $50,000 (2006-2010 5-year est.); Average household income: $63,940 (2006-2010 5-year est.); Percent of households with income of $100,000 or more: 14.4% (2006-2010 5-year est.); Poverty rate: 7.5% (2006-2010 5-year est.).
**Education:** Percent of population age 25 and over with: High school diploma (including GED) or higher: 84.3% (2006-2010 5-year est.); Bachelor's degree or higher: 17.4% (2006-2010 5-year est.); Master's degree or higher: 9.3% (2006-2010 5-year est.).

**School District(s)**
Kingston City School District (PK-12)
    2009-10 Enrollment: 7,120 . . . . . . . . . . . . . . . . . . (845) 339-3000
**Housing:** Homeownership rate: 58.9% (2010); Median home value: $174,100 (2006-2010 5-year est.); Median contract rent: $845 per month (2006-2010 5-year est.); Median year structure built: 1969 (2006-2010 5-year est.).
**Transportation:** Commute to work: 95.1% car, 1.0% public transportation, 0.0% walk, 3.9% work from home (2006-2010 5-year est.); Travel time to work: 50.7% less than 15 minutes, 26.4% 15 to 30 minutes, 8.9% 30 to 45 minutes, 4.1% 45 to 60 minutes, 9.8% 60 minutes or more (2006-2010 5-year est.)

**LINCOLN PARK** (CDP). Covers a land area of 1.433 square miles and a water area of 0.030 square miles. Located at 41.95° N. Lat; 74.00° W. Long. Elevation is 187 feet.
**Population:** 2,481 (1990); 2,337 (2000); 2,366 (2010); Density: 1,650.1 persons per square mile (2010); Race: 87.1% White, 4.5% Black, 2.2% Asian, 0.5% American Indian/Alaska Native, 0.0% Native Hawaiian/Other Pacific Islander, 5.7% Other, 6.7% Hispanic of any race (2010); Average household size: 2.14 (2010); Median age: 44.3 (2010); Males per 100 females: 84.1 (2010); Marriage status: 30.4% never married, 40.6% now married, 12.3% widowed, 16.6% divorced (2006-2010 5-year est.); Foreign born: 10.1% (2006-2010 5-year est.); Ancestry (includes multiple ancestries): 30.8% Italian, 22.8% German, 18.1% Irish, 15.5% English, 10.0% Polish (2006-2010 5-year est.).
**Economy:** Employment by occupation: 6.8% management, 2.9% professional, 14.2% services, 18.4% sales, 1.0% farming, 5.4% construction, 7.2% production (2006-2010 5-year est.).
**Income:** Per capita income: $25,354 (2006-2010 5-year est.); Median household income: $45,805 (2006-2010 5-year est.); Average household income: $53,573 (2006-2010 5-year est.); Percent of households with income of $100,000 or more: 18.9% (2006-2010 5-year est.); Poverty rate: 6.3% (2006-2010 5-year est.).
**Education:** Percent of population age 25 and over with: High school diploma (including GED) or higher: 82.0% (2006-2010 5-year est.); Bachelor's degree or higher: 19.3% (2006-2010 5-year est.); Master's degree or higher: 4.8% (2006-2010 5-year est.).
**Housing:** Homeownership rate: 51.8% (2010); Median home value: $195,100 (2006-2010 5-year est.); Median contract rent: $788 per month (2006-2010 5-year est.); Median year structure built: 1961 (2006-2010 5-year est.).
**Transportation:** Commute to work: 88.0% car, 5.2% public transportation, 1.8% walk, 5.0% work from home (2006-2010 5-year est.); Travel time to work: 60.2% less than 15 minutes, 20.7% 15 to 30 minutes, 5.9% 30 to 45 minutes, 4.9% 45 to 60 minutes, 8.3% 60 minutes or more (2006-2010 5-year est.)

**LLOYD** (town). Covers a land area of 31.266 square miles and a water area of 2.019 square miles. Located at 41.71° N. Lat; 73.99° W. Long. Elevation is 381 feet.
**Population:** 9,275 (1990); 9,941 (2000); 10,863 (2010); Density: 347.4 persons per square mile (2010); Race: 86.1% White, 6.4% Black, 2.9% Asian, 0.2% American Indian/Alaska Native, 0.0% Native Hawaiian/Other Pacific Islander, 4.4% Other, 7.3% Hispanic of any race (2010); Average household size: 2.52 (2010); Median age: 40.7 (2010); Males per 100 females: 95.3 (2010); Marriage status: 28.4% never married, 51.2% now married, 8.2% widowed, 12.2% divorced (2006-2010 5-year est.); Foreign born: 7.0% (2006-2010 5-year est.); Ancestry (includes multiple ancestries): 31.3% Italian, 18.5% Irish, 11.5% German, 7.5% American, 6.7% English (2006-2010 5-year est.).
**Economy:** Single-family building permits issued: 8 (2011); Multi-family building permits issued: 0 (2011); Employment by occupation: 11.8% management, 8.0% professional, 10.9% services, 12.9% sales, 4.1% farming, 10.7% construction, 4.4% production (2006-2010 5-year est.).
**Income:** Per capita income: $30,979 (2006-2010 5-year est.); Median household income: $64,030 (2006-2010 5-year est.); Average household income: $78,536 (2006-2010 5-year est.); Percent of households with income of $100,000 or more: 25.7% (2006-2010 5-year est.); Poverty rate: 9.3% (2006-2010 5-year est.).
**Education:** Percent of population age 25 and over with: High school diploma (including GED) or higher: 86.2% (2006-2010 5-year est.); Bachelor's degree or higher: 35.1% (2006-2010 5-year est.); Master's degree or higher: 15.6% (2006-2010 5-year est.).
**Housing:** Homeownership rate: 69.0% (2010); Median home value: $268,600 (2006-2010 5-year est.); Median contract rent: $885 per month (2006-2010 5-year est.); Median year structure built: 1970 (2006-2010 5-year est.).
**Safety:** Violent crime rate: 8.5 per 10,000 population; Property crime rate: 110.1 per 10,000 population (2010).
**Transportation:** Commute to work: 87.4% car, 4.4% public transportation, 4.5% walk, 2.7% work from home (2006-2010 5-year est.); Travel time to work: 25.2% less than 15 minutes, 31.7% 15 to 30 minutes, 22.4% 30 to 45 minutes, 5.9% 45 to 60 minutes, 14.8% 60 minutes or more (2006-2010 5-year est.)

**MALDEN-ON-HUDSON** (CDP). Covers a land area of 0.501 square miles and a water area of 0 square miles. Located at 42.09° N. Lat; 73.93° W. Long. Elevation is 85 feet.
**Population:** n/a (1990); n/a (2000); 405 (2010); Density: 808.3 persons per square mile (2010); Race: 96.5% White, 1.5% Black, 0.0% Asian, 0.0% American Indian/Alaska Native, 0.0% Native Hawaiian/Other Pacific Islander, 2.0% Other, 10.4% Hispanic of any race (2010); Average household size: 2.50 (2010); Median age: 44.1 (2010); Males per 100 females: 88.4 (2010); Marriage status: 11.4% never married, 50.4% now married, 14.3% widowed, 23.9% divorced (2006-2010 5-year est.); Foreign born: 0.0% (2006-2010 5-year est.); Ancestry (includes multiple ancestries): 32.2% Dutch, 29.1% German, 15.2% American, 14.2% Irish, 13.3% Polish (2006-2010 5-year est.).
**Economy:** Employment by occupation: 7.8% management, 0.0% professional, 21.6% services, 0.0% sales, 0.0% farming, 22.5% construction, 0.0% production (2006-2010 5-year est.).
**Income:** Per capita income: $26,055 (2006-2010 5-year est.); Median household income: $62,917 (2006-2010 5-year est.); Average household income: $70,125 (2006-2010 5-year est.); Percent of households with income of $100,000 or more: 19.1% (2006-2010 5-year est.); Poverty rate: 0.0% (2006-2010 5-year est.).
**Education:** Percent of population age 25 and over with: High school diploma (including GED) or higher: 100.0% (2006-2010 5-year est.); Bachelor's degree or higher: 15.4% (2006-2010 5-year est.); Master's degree or higher: 12.5% (2006-2010 5-year est.).
**Housing:** Homeownership rate: 72.2% (2010); Median home value: $262,500 (2006-2010 5-year est.); Median contract rent: n/a per month (2006-2010 5-year est.); Median year structure built: before 1940 (2006-2010 5-year est.).
**Transportation:** Commute to work: 100.0% car, 0.0% public transportation, 0.0% walk, 0.0% work from home (2006-2010 5-year est.); Travel time to work: 21.6% less than 15 minutes, 70.6% 15 to 30 minutes, 7.8% 30 to 45 minutes, 0.0% 45 to 60 minutes, 0.0% 60 minutes or more (2006-2010 5-year est.)

**MARBLETOWN** (town). Covers a land area of 54.471 square miles and a water area of 0.709 square miles. Located at 41.87° N. Lat; 74.16° W. Long. Elevation is 220 feet.
**Population:** 5,285 (1990); 5,854 (2000); 5,607 (2010); Density: 102.9 persons per square mile (2010); Race: 94.6% White, 1.6% Black, 1.2% Asian, 0.2% American Indian/Alaska Native, 0.0% Native Hawaiian/Other Pacific Islander, 2.4% Other, 2.8% Hispanic of any race (2010); Average household size: 2.30 (2010); Median age: 47.7 (2010); Males per 100 females: 97.4 (2010); Marriage status: 31.4% never married, 55.2% now married, 5.9% widowed, 7.4% divorced (2006-2010 5-year est.); Foreign born: 4.0% (2006-2010 5-year est.); Ancestry (includes multiple ancestries): 25.2% German, 22.6% Irish, 16.2% English, 11.9% Italian, 9.0% Dutch (2006-2010 5-year est.).
**Economy:** Single-family building permits issued: 12 (2011); Multi-family building permits issued: 0 (2011); Employment by occupation: 11.2% management, 4.2% professional, 5.7% services, 14.3% sales, 1.6% farming, 10.1% construction, 4.3% production (2006-2010 5-year est.).
**Income:** Per capita income: $42,459 (2006-2010 5-year est.); Median household income: $81,865 (2006-2010 5-year est.); Average household income: $98,390 (2006-2010 5-year est.); Percent of households with income of $100,000 or more: 44.7% (2006-2010 5-year est.); Poverty rate: 4.0% (2006-2010 5-year est.).
**Education:** Percent of population age 25 and over with: High school diploma (including GED) or higher: 93.9% (2006-2010 5-year est.); Bachelor's degree or higher: 49.2% (2006-2010 5-year est.); Master's degree or higher: 24.9% (2006-2010 5-year est.).
**Housing:** Homeownership rate: 81.5% (2010); Median home value: $305,100 (2006-2010 5-year est.); Median contract rent: $912 per month (2006-2010 5-year est.); Median year structure built: 1969 (2006-2010 5-year est.).
**Transportation:** Commute to work: 83.2% car, 3.7% public transportation, 0.4% walk, 12.3% work from home (2006-2010 5-year est.); Travel time to work: 22.1% less than 15 minutes, 37.9% 15 to 30 minutes, 21.6% 30 to 45 minutes, 4.5% 45 to 60 minutes, 13.9% 60 minutes or more (2006-2010 5-year est.)

**MARLBORO** (CDP). Aka Marlborough. Covers a land area of 4.455 square miles and a water area of 0.635 square miles. Located at 41.60° N. Lat; 73.97° W. Long. Elevation is 180 feet.
**History:** Also spelled Marlborough.

**Population:** 2,208 (1990); 2,339 (2000); 3,669 (2010); Density: 823.4 persons per square mile (2010); Race: 91.0% White, 3.7% Black, 1.0% Asian, 0.2% American Indian/Alaska Native, 0.0% Native Hawaiian/Other Pacific Islander, 4.1% Other, 8.0% Hispanic of any race (2010); Average household size: 2.57 (2010); Median age: 41.8 (2010); Males per 100 females: 94.0 (2010); Marriage status: 20.4% never married, 57.5% now married, 9.5% widowed, 12.6% divorced (2006-2010 5-year est.); Foreign born: 7.7% (2006-2010 5-year est.); Ancestry (includes multiple ancestries): 32.5% Italian, 19.4% Irish, 11.0% American, 8.0% English, 7.8% German (2006-2010 5-year est.).
**Economy:** Employment by occupation: 16.3% management, 2.2% professional, 11.4% services, 15.5% sales, 5.5% farming, 11.5% construction, 4.6% production (2006-2010 5-year est.).
**Income:** Per capita income: $28,665 (2006-2010 5-year est.); Median household income: $58,672 (2006-2010 5-year est.); Average household income: $70,969 (2006-2010 5-year est.); Percent of households with income of $100,000 or more: 20.8% (2006-2010 5-year est.); Poverty rate: 6.4% (2006-2010 5-year est.).
**Education:** Percent of population age 25 and over with: High school diploma (including GED) or higher: 89.3% (2006-2010 5-year est.); Bachelor's degree or higher: 21.9% (2006-2010 5-year est.); Master's degree or higher: 8.5% (2006-2010 5-year est.).

**School District(s)**
Marlboro Central School District (KG-12)
   2009-10 Enrollment: 2,051 . . . . . . . . . . . . . . . . . . . . . . . . (845) 236-5802
**Housing:** Homeownership rate: 64.4% (2010); Median home value: $275,900 (2006-2010 5-year est.); Median contract rent: $815 per month (2006-2010 5-year est.); Median year structure built: 1962 (2006-2010 5-year est.).
**Transportation:** Commute to work: 91.1% car, 3.7% public transportation, 1.1% walk, 3.6% work from home (2006-2010 5-year est.); Travel time to work: 21.0% less than 15 minutes, 42.7% 15 to 30 minutes, 20.4% 30 to 45 minutes, 3.9% 45 to 60 minutes, 12.0% 60 minutes or more (2006-2010 5-year est.)

**MARLBOROUGH** (town). Covers a land area of 24.470 square miles and a water area of 2.029 square miles. Located at 41.63° N. Lat; 73.98° W. Long.
**Population:** 7,430 (1990); 8,263 (2000); 8,808 (2010); Density: 359.9 persons per square mile (2010); Race: 89.7% White, 4.1% Black, 0.9% Asian, 0.2% American Indian/Alaska Native, 0.0% Native Hawaiian/Other Pacific Islander, 5.1% Other, 8.7% Hispanic of any race (2010); Average household size: 2.63 (2010); Median age: 41.3 (2010); Males per 100 females: 97.1 (2010); Marriage status: 25.6% never married, 58.2% now married, 6.2% widowed, 10.0% divorced (2006-2010 5-year est.); Foreign born: 6.7% (2006-2010 5-year est.); Ancestry (includes multiple ancestries): 31.1% Italian, 20.8% Irish, 14.2% German, 11.1% American, 10.7% English (2006-2010 5-year est.).
**Economy:** Single-family building permits issued: 0 (2011); Multi-family building permits issued: 0 (2011); Employment by occupation: 14.8% management, 3.1% professional, 10.1% services, 14.6% sales, 4.2% farming, 12.1% construction, 6.2% production (2006-2010 5-year est.).
**Income:** Per capita income: $30,135 (2006-2010 5-year est.); Median household income: $64,405 (2006-2010 5-year est.); Average household income: $77,603 (2006-2010 5-year est.); Percent of households with income of $100,000 or more: 27.9% (2006-2010 5-year est.); Poverty rate: 8.3% (2006-2010 5-year est.).
**Education:** Percent of population age 25 and over with: High school diploma (including GED) or higher: 90.1% (2006-2010 5-year est.); Bachelor's degree or higher: 25.1% (2006-2010 5-year est.); Master's degree or higher: 9.7% (2006-2010 5-year est.).
**Housing:** Homeownership rate: 69.8% (2010); Median home value: $291,900 (2006-2010 5-year est.); Median contract rent: $830 per month (2006-2010 5-year est.); Median year structure built: 1967 (2006-2010 5-year est.).
**Safety:** Violent crime rate: 20.8 per 10,000 population; Property crime rate: 173.6 per 10,000 population (2010).
**Transportation:** Commute to work: 90.2% car, 2.8% public transportation, 1.6% walk, 5.0% work from home (2006-2010 5-year est.); Travel time to work: 26.3% less than 15 minutes, 41.3% 15 to 30 minutes, 19.8% 30 to 45 minutes, 4.3% 45 to 60 minutes, 8.2% 60 minutes or more (2006-2010 5-year est.)

**MILTON** (CDP). Covers a land area of 2.962 square miles and a water area of 0.049 square miles. Located at 41.65° N. Lat; 73.96° W. Long. Elevation is 154 feet.
**Population:** 1,308 (1990); 1,251 (2000); 1,403 (2010); Density: 473.6 persons per square mile (2010); Race: 90.2% White, 4.6% Black, 0.8% Asian, 0.6% American Indian/Alaska Native, 0.0% Native Hawaiian/Other Pacific Islander, 3.8% Other, 10.0% Hispanic of any race (2010); Average household size: 2.59 (2010); Median age: 40.6 (2010); Males per 100 females: 103.9 (2010); Marriage status: 27.8% never married, 62.4% now married, 0.9% widowed, 8.9% divorced (2006-2010 5-year est.); Foreign born: 8.3% (2006-2010 5-year est.); Ancestry (includes multiple ancestries): 23.4% German, 19.2% Italian, 19.0% Irish, 18.3% English, 8.7% Albanian (2006-2010 5-year est.).
**Economy:** Employment by occupation: 15.3% management, 0.0% professional, 15.0% services, 11.4% sales, 3.9% farming, 8.4% construction, 6.8% production (2006-2010 5-year est.).
**Income:** Per capita income: $32,848 (2006-2010 5-year est.); Median household income: $58,929 (2006-2010 5-year est.); Average household income: $84,662 (2006-2010 5-year est.); Percent of households with income of $100,000 or more: 37.2% (2006-2010 5-year est.); Poverty rate: 5.2% (2006-2010 5-year est.).
**Education:** Percent of population age 25 and over with: High school diploma (including GED) or higher: 89.4% (2006-2010 5-year est.); Bachelor's degree or higher: 34.2% (2006-2010 5-year est.); Master's degree or higher: 13.2% (2006-2010 5-year est.).

**School District(s)**
Marlboro Central School District (KG-12)
   2009-10 Enrollment: 2,051 . . . . . . . . . . . . . . . . . . . . . . . . (845) 236-5802
**Housing:** Homeownership rate: 71.1% (2010); Median home value: $261,400 (2006-2010 5-year est.); Median contract rent: $678 per month (2006-2010 5-year est.); Median year structure built: 1976 (2006-2010 5-year est.).
**Transportation:** Commute to work: 90.5% car, 1.6% public transportation, 1.0% walk, 6.9% work from home (2006-2010 5-year est.); Travel time to work: 33.5% less than 15 minutes, 39.0% 15 to 30 minutes, 17.1% 30 to 45 minutes, 3.6% 45 to 60 minutes, 6.7% 60 minutes or more (2006-2010 5-year est.)

**MODENA** (unincorporated postal area)
Zip Code: 12548
   Covers a land area of 5.870 square miles and a water area of 0.207 square miles. Located at 41.65° N. Lat; 74.10° W. Long. Elevation is 456 feet. Population: 1,494 (2010); Density: 254.5 persons per square mile (2010); Race: 85.7% White, 5.8% Black, 1.3% Asian, 0.1% American Indian/Alaska Native, 0.0% Native Hawaiian/Other Pacific Islander, 7.1% Other, 12.3% Hispanic of any race (2010); Average household size: 2.67 (2010); Median age: 39.8 (2010); Males per 100 females: 102.2 (2010); Homeownership rate: 67.6% (2010)

**MOUNT MARION** (unincorporated postal area)
Zip Code: 12456
   Covers a land area of 0.540 square miles and a water area of 0.020 square miles. Located at 42.03° N. Lat; 73.99° W. Long. Elevation is 174 feet. Population: 639 (2010); Density: 1,182.8 persons per square mile (2010); Race: 95.5% White, 2.5% Black, 0.6% Asian, 0.0% American Indian/Alaska Native, 0.0% Native Hawaiian/Other Pacific Islander, 1.4% Other, 2.7% Hispanic of any race (2010); Average household size: 2.74 (2010); Median age: 40.3 (2010); Males per 100 females: 99.7 (2010); Homeownership rate: 88.0% (2010)

**MOUNT TREMPER** (unincorporated postal area)
Zip Code: 12457
   Covers a land area of 13.972 square miles and a water area of 0 square miles. Located at 42.04° N. Lat; 74.25° W. Long. Elevation is 725 feet. Population: 763 (2010); Density: 54.6 persons per square mile (2010); Race: 92.4% White, 0.5% Black, 1.6% Asian, 0.3% American Indian/Alaska Native, 0.0% Native Hawaiian/Other Pacific Islander, 5.2% Other, 4.2% Hispanic of any race (2010); Average household size: 2.02 (2010); Median age: 50.8 (2010); Males per 100 females: 108.5 (2010); Homeownership rate: 75.1% (2010)

**NAPANOCH** (CDP). Covers a land area of 1.220 square miles and a water area of 0.025 square miles. Located at 41.75° N. Lat; 74.37° W. Long. Elevation is 312 feet.
**Population:** 1,068 (1990); 1,168 (2000); 1,174 (2010); Density: 961.9 persons per square mile (2010); Race: 89.4% White, 3.4% Black, 0.5% Asian, 0.6% American Indian/Alaska Native, 0.0% Native Hawaiian/Other Pacific Islander, 6.1% Other, 11.8% Hispanic of any race (2010); Average household size: 2.50 (2010); Median age: 39.6 (2010); Males per 100 females: 92.5 (2010); Marriage status: 26.3% never married, 49.7% now married, 7.8% widowed, 16.2% divorced (2006-2010 5-year est.); Foreign born: 6.6% (2006-2010 5-year est.); Ancestry (includes multiple ancestries): 38.9% German, 19.7% Irish, 14.5% English, 8.1% Italian, 7.7% Dutch (2006-2010 5-year est.).
**Economy:** Employment by occupation: 5.0% management, 0.0% professional, 16.4% services, 13.6% sales, 2.0% farming, 7.3% construction, 9.1% production (2006-2010 5-year est.).
**Income:** Per capita income: $27,308 (2006-2010 5-year est.); Median household income: $42,361 (2006-2010 5-year est.); Average household income: $58,318 (2006-2010 5-year est.); Percent of households with income of $100,000 or more: 18.8% (2006-2010 5-year est.); Poverty rate: 9.2% (2006-2010 5-year est.).
**Education:** Percent of population age 25 and over with: High school diploma (including GED) or higher: 81.4% (2006-2010 5-year est.); Bachelor's degree or higher: 15.2% (2006-2010 5-year est.); Master's degree or higher: 2.2% (2006-2010 5-year est.).
**Housing:** Homeownership rate: 79.6% (2010); Median home value: $135,800 (2006-2010 5-year est.); Median contract rent: $632 per month (2006-2010 5-year est.); Median year structure built: 1953 (2006-2010 5-year est.).
**Transportation:** Commute to work: 88.2% car, 0.0% public transportation, 0.0% walk, 11.8% work from home (2006-2010 5-year est.); Travel time to work: 45.3% less than 15 minutes, 15.3% 15 to 30 minutes, 19.3% 30 to 45 minutes, 8.9% 45 to 60 minutes, 11.1% 60 minutes or more (2006-2010 5-year est.)

**NEW PALTZ** (village). Covers a land area of 1.715 square miles and a water area of 0.037 square miles. Located at 41.74° N. Lat; 74.07° W. Long. Elevation is 240 feet.
**Population:** 5,504 (1990); 6,034 (2000); 6,818 (2010); Density: 3,975.0 persons per square mile (2010); Race: 80.5% White, 6.4% Black, 6.0% Asian, 0.3% American Indian/Alaska Native, 0.0% Native Hawaiian/Other Pacific Islander, 6.8% Other, 11.1% Hispanic of any race (2010); Average household size: 2.20 (2010); Median age: 21.5 (2010); Males per 100 females: 71.5 (2010); Marriage status: 83.9% never married, 10.1% now married, 1.9% widowed, 4.1% divorced (2006-2010 5-year est.); Foreign born: 9.6% (2006-2010 5-year est.); Ancestry (includes multiple ancestries): 24.0% Irish, 19.1% Italian, 13.2% German, 5.5% Polish, 5.1% English (2006-2010 5-year est.).
**Economy:** Single-family building permits issued: 0 (2011); Multi-family building permits issued: 0 (2011); Employment by occupation: 5.6% management, 4.4% professional, 17.6% services, 24.3% sales, 3.5% farming, 4.0% construction, 0.3% production (2006-2010 5-year est.).
**Income:** Per capita income: $15,857 (2006-2010 5-year est.); Median household income: $41,722 (2006-2010 5-year est.); Average household income: $59,002 (2006-2010 5-year est.); Percent of households with income of $100,000 or more: 18.9% (2006-2010 5-year est.); Poverty rate: 38.9% (2006-2010 5-year est.).
**Education:** Percent of population age 25 and over with: High school diploma (including GED) or higher: 98.4% (2006-2010 5-year est.); Bachelor's degree or higher: 60.6% (2006-2010 5-year est.); Master's degree or higher: 34.1% (2006-2010 5-year est.).
**School District(s)**
New Paltz Central School District (PK-12)
    2009-10 Enrollment: 2,290 . . . . . . . . . . . . . . . . . . . (845) 256-4020
Ulster Boces
    2009-10 Enrollment: n/a . . . . . . . . . . . . . . . . . . . . (845) 255-3040
**Four-year College(s)**
State University of New York at New Paltz (Public)
    Fall 2010 Enrollment: 7,286 . . . . . . . . . . . . . . . . . (877) 696-7411
    2011-12 Tuition: In-state $6,458; Out-of-state $15,508
**Housing:** Homeownership rate: 29.0% (2010); Median home value: $264,600 (2006-2010 5-year est.); Median contract rent: $993 per month (2006-2010 5-year est.); Median year structure built: 1968 (2006-2010 5-year est.).

**Newspapers:** Mid-Hudson Post (Local news; Circulation 1,580); New Paltz News (Community news; Circulation 6,083)
**Transportation:** Commute to work: 53.6% car, 1.3% public transportation, 31.0% walk, 9.3% work from home (2006-2010 5-year est.); Travel time to work: 58.2% less than 15 minutes, 21.4% 15 to 30 minutes, 12.4% 30 to 45 minutes, 3.4% 45 to 60 minutes, 4.6% 60 minutes or more (2006-2010 5-year est.)
**Additional Information Contacts**
New Paltz Regional Chamber of Commerce . . . . . . . . . . (845) 255-0243
    http://www.newpaltzchamber.org
Village of New Paltz . . . . . . . . . . . . . . . . . . . . . . . . . (845) 255-0130
    http://villageofnewpaltz.org

**NEW PALTZ** (town). Covers a land area of 33.874 square miles and a water area of 0.431 square miles. Located at 41.76° N. Lat; 74.08° W. Long. Elevation is 240 feet.
**History:** State University of N.Y. College at New Paltz is here. Settled by Huguenots in 1677; incorporated 1887.
**Population:** 11,286 (1990); 12,830 (2000); 14,003 (2010); Density: 413.4 persons per square mile (2010); Race: 84.7% White, 5.3% Black, 4.4% Asian, 0.3% American Indian/Alaska Native, 0.0% Native Hawaiian/Other Pacific Islander, 5.3% Other, 8.8% Hispanic of any race (2010); Average household size: 2.45 (2010); Median age: 25.3 (2010); Males per 100 females: 83.9 (2010); Marriage status: 58.5% never married, 32.2% now married, 3.7% widowed, 5.6% divorced (2006-2010 5-year est.); Foreign born: 9.1% (2006-2010 5-year est.); Ancestry (includes multiple ancestries): 22.1% Irish, 18.4% Italian, 15.0% German, 8.3% English, 6.5% American (2006-2010 5-year est.).
**Economy:** Single-family building permits issued: 10 (2011); Multi-family building permits issued: 0 (2011); Employment by occupation: 10.1% management, 5.4% professional, 12.9% services, 17.9% sales, 2.5% farming, 7.3% construction, 3.9% production (2006-2010 5-year est.).
**Income:** Per capita income: $26,846 (2006-2010 5-year est.); Median household income: $63,217 (2006-2010 5-year est.); Average household income: $83,755 (2006-2010 5-year est.); Percent of households with income of $100,000 or more: 30.0% (2006-2010 5-year est.); Poverty rate: 19.1% (2006-2010 5-year est.).
**Education:** Percent of population age 25 and over with: High school diploma (including GED) or higher: 92.6% (2006-2010 5-year est.); Bachelor's degree or higher: 51.8% (2006-2010 5-year est.); Master's degree or higher: 27.9% (2006-2010 5-year est.).
**School District(s)**
New Paltz Central School District (PK-12)
    2009-10 Enrollment: 2,290 . . . . . . . . . . . . . . . . . . . (845) 256-4020
Ulster Boces
    2009-10 Enrollment: n/a . . . . . . . . . . . . . . . . . . . . (845) 255-3040
**Four-year College(s)**
State University of New York at New Paltz (Public)
    Fall 2010 Enrollment: 7,286 . . . . . . . . . . . . . . . . . (877) 696-7411
    2011-12 Tuition: In-state $6,458; Out-of-state $15,508
**Housing:** Homeownership rate: 57.2% (2010); Median home value: $317,000 (2006-2010 5-year est.); Median contract rent: $929 per month (2006-2010 5-year est.); Median year structure built: 1971 (2006-2010 5-year est.).
**Safety:** Violent crime rate: 38.5 per 10,000 population; Property crime rate: 170.9 per 10,000 population (2010).
**Newspapers:** Mid-Hudson Post (Local news; Circulation 1,580); New Paltz News (Community news; Circulation 6,083)
**Transportation:** Commute to work: 69.6% car, 2.4% public transportation, 16.2% walk, 9.2% work from home (2006-2010 5-year est.); Travel time to work: 41.4% less than 15 minutes, 25.5% 15 to 30 minutes, 22.2% 30 to 45 minutes, 2.7% 45 to 60 minutes, 8.3% 60 minutes or more (2006-2010 5-year est.)

**OLIVE** (town). Covers a land area of 58.449 square miles and a water area of 6.743 square miles. Located at 41.94° N. Lat; 74.26° W. Long.
**Population:** 4,086 (1990); 4,579 (2000); 4,419 (2010); Density: 75.6 persons per square mile (2010); Race: 94.0% White, 1.2% Black, 1.3% Asian, 0.1% American Indian/Alaska Native, 0.0% Native Hawaiian/Other Pacific Islander, 3.4% Other, 3.1% Hispanic of any race (2010); Average household size: 2.25 (2010); Median age: 48.9 (2010); Males per 100 females: 99.6 (2010); Marriage status: 25.7% never married, 58.4% now married, 8.8% widowed, 7.0% divorced (2006-2010 5-year est.); Foreign born: 3.1% (2006-2010 5-year est.); Ancestry (includes multiple

ancestries): 25.6% Irish, 24.1% German, 17.2% Italian, 12.1% English, 9.4% Dutch (2006-2010 5-year est.).
**Economy:** Single-family building permits issued: 0 (2011); Multi-family building permits issued: 0 (2011); Employment by occupation: 16.4% management, 3.3% professional, 3.8% services, 15.0% sales, 1.8% farming, 11.8% construction, 5.1% production (2006-2010 5-year est.).
**Income:** Per capita income: $39,019 (2006-2010 5-year est.); Median household income: $53,553 (2006-2010 5-year est.); Average household income: $82,596 (2006-2010 5-year est.); Percent of households with income of $100,000 or more: 23.9% (2006-2010 5-year est.); Poverty rate: 10.3% (2006-2010 5-year est.).
**Education:** Percent of population age 25 and over with: High school diploma (including GED) or higher: 92.0% (2006-2010 5-year est.); Bachelor's degree or higher: 37.4% (2006-2010 5-year est.); Master's degree or higher: 21.1% (2006-2010 5-year est.).
**Housing:** Homeownership rate: 80.1% (2010); Median home value: $275,600 (2006-2010 5-year est.); Median contract rent: $544 per month (2006-2010 5-year est.); Median year structure built: 1966 (2006-2010 5-year est.).
**Transportation:** Commute to work: 73.5% car, 5.1% public transportation, 6.5% walk, 13.2% work from home (2006-2010 5-year est.); Travel time to work: 20.9% less than 15 minutes, 23.3% 15 to 30 minutes, 27.3% 30 to 45 minutes, 10.3% 45 to 60 minutes, 18.2% 60 minutes or more (2006-2010 5-year est.)

## OLIVEBRIDGE (unincorporated postal area)

Zip Code: 12461

Covers a land area of 23.888 square miles and a water area of 0.022 square miles. Located at 41.90° N. Lat; 74.26° W. Long. Elevation is 571 feet. Population: 1,634 (2010); Density: 68.4 persons per square mile (2010); Race: 95.5% White, 0.9% Black, 1.5% Asian, 0.1% American Indian/Alaska Native, 0.0% Native Hawaiian/Other Pacific Islander, 2.0% Other, 2.9% Hispanic of any race (2010); Average household size: 2.23 (2010); Median age: 48.7 (2010); Males per 100 females: 99.8 (2010); Homeownership rate: 80.1% (2010)

## PHOENICIA (CDP). Covers a land area of 0.455 square miles and a water area of 0 square miles. Located at 42.08° N. Lat; 74.31° W. Long. Elevation is 827 feet.

**Population:** 371 (1990); 381 (2000); 309 (2010); Density: 678.3 persons per square mile (2010); Race: 96.1% White, 0.0% Black, 1.0% Asian, 0.0% American Indian/Alaska Native, 0.0% Native Hawaiian/Other Pacific Islander, 2.9% Other, 1.9% Hispanic of any race (2010); Average household size: 1.80 (2010); Median age: 52.4 (2010); Males per 100 females: 87.3 (2010); Marriage status: 34.9% never married, 43.8% now married, 0.0% widowed, 21.3% divorced (2006-2010 5-year est.); Foreign born: 3.3% (2006-2010 5-year est.); Ancestry (includes multiple ancestries): 34.2% Italian, 25.8% German, 16.2% Irish, 13.7% French, 7.9% English (2006-2010 5-year est.).
**Economy:** Employment by occupation: 4.1% management, 0.0% professional, 12.4% services, 19.5% sales, 9.5% farming, 10.0% construction, 4.1% production (2006-2010 5-year est.).
**Income:** Per capita income: $31,696 (2006-2010 5-year est.); Median household income: $57,031 (2006-2010 5-year est.); Average household income: $58,929 (2006-2010 5-year est.); Percent of households with income of $100,000 or more: 14.2% (2006-2010 5-year est.); Poverty rate: 0.0% (2006-2010 5-year est.).
**Education:** Percent of population age 25 and over with: High school diploma (including GED) or higher: 88.9% (2006-2010 5-year est.); Bachelor's degree or higher: 28.7% (2006-2010 5-year est.); Master's degree or higher: 9.6% (2006-2010 5-year est.).
### School District(s)
Onteora Central School District (KG-12)
   2009-10 Enrollment: 1,651 . . . . . . . . . . . . . . . . . . . . . . (845) 657-6383
**Housing:** Homeownership rate: 50.6% (2010); Median home value: $264,400 (2006-2010 5-year est.); Median contract rent: $573 per month (2006-2010 5-year est.); Median year structure built: 1956 (2006-2010 5-year est.).
**Transportation:** Commute to work: 76.2% car, 0.0% public transportation, 3.0% walk, 20.8% work from home (2006-2010 5-year est.); Travel time to work: 39.9% less than 15 minutes, 0.0% 15 to 30 minutes, 49.7% 30 to 45 minutes, 10.4% 45 to 60 minutes, 0.0% 60 minutes or more (2006-2010 5-year est.)

## PINE HILL (CDP). Covers a land area of 2.077 square miles and a water area of 0.009 square miles. Located at 42.13° N. Lat; 74.47° W. Long. Elevation is 1,499 feet.

**Population:** 278 (1990); 308 (2000); 275 (2010); Density: 132.3 persons per square mile (2010); Race: 91.6% White, 1.5% Black, 0.4% Asian, 0.4% American Indian/Alaska Native, 0.0% Native Hawaiian/Other Pacific Islander, 6.1% Other, 9.5% Hispanic of any race (2010); Average household size: 1.85 (2010); Median age: 52.6 (2010); Males per 100 females: 99.3 (2010); Marriage status: 52.7% never married, 34.6% now married, 12.8% widowed, 0.0% divorced (2006-2010 5-year est.); Foreign born: 0.0% (2006-2010 5-year est.); Ancestry (includes multiple ancestries): 36.6% Irish, 21.4% German, 16.7% English, 13.6% Italian, 8.9% Danish (2006-2010 5-year est.).
**Economy:** Employment by occupation: 18.8% management, 0.0% professional, 5.8% services, 5.8% sales, 9.1% farming, 17.5% construction, 0.0% production (2006-2010 5-year est.).
**Income:** Per capita income: $64,780 (2006-2010 5-year est.); Median household income: $49,107 (2006-2010 5-year est.); Average household income: $88,832 (2006-2010 5-year est.); Percent of households with income of $100,000 or more: 24.5% (2006-2010 5-year est.); Poverty rate: 19.5% (2006-2010 5-year est.).
**Education:** Percent of population age 25 and over with: High school diploma (including GED) or higher: 100.0% (2006-2010 5-year est.); Bachelor's degree or higher: 32.1% (2006-2010 5-year est.); Master's degree or higher: 6.2% (2006-2010 5-year est.).
**Housing:** Homeownership rate: 59.1% (2010); Median home value: $318,000 (2006-2010 5-year est.); Median contract rent: $517 per month (2006-2010 5-year est.); Median year structure built: 1960 (2006-2010 5-year est.).
**Transportation:** Commute to work: 87.0% car, 0.0% public transportation, 13.0% walk, 0.0% work from home (2006-2010 5-year est.); Travel time to work: 42.2% less than 15 minutes, 14.3% 15 to 30 minutes, 26.0% 30 to 45 minutes, 9.1% 45 to 60 minutes, 8.4% 60 minutes or more (2006-2010 5-year est.)

## PLATTEKILL (town). Covers a land area of 35.110 square miles and a water area of 0.627 square miles. Located at 41.65° N. Lat; 74.07° W. Long. Elevation is 568 feet.

**Population:** 8,853 (1990); 9,892 (2000); 10,499 (2010); Density: 299.0 persons per square mile (2010); Race: 84.8% White, 5.9% Black, 0.8% Asian, 0.3% American Indian/Alaska Native, 0.0% Native Hawaiian/Other Pacific Islander, 8.2% Other, 18.4% Hispanic of any race (2010); Average household size: 2.71 (2010); Median age: 39.7 (2010); Males per 100 females: 97.6 (2010); Marriage status: 37.1% never married, 50.5% now married, 4.1% widowed, 8.3% divorced (2006-2010 5-year est.); Foreign born: 10.8% (2006-2010 5-year est.); Ancestry (includes multiple ancestries): 23.9% Italian, 18.6% Irish, 16.1% German, 7.2% American, 6.6% English (2006-2010 5-year est.).
**Economy:** Single-family building permits issued: 7 (2011); Multi-family building permits issued: 0 (2011); Employment by occupation: 7.4% management, 3.2% professional, 9.7% services, 21.2% sales, 5.4% farming, 10.5% construction, 3.9% production (2006-2010 5-year est.).
**Income:** Per capita income: $23,972 (2006-2010 5-year est.); Median household income: $54,529 (2006-2010 5-year est.); Average household income: $66,741 (2006-2010 5-year est.); Percent of households with income of $100,000 or more: 19.7% (2006-2010 5-year est.); Poverty rate: 11.2% (2006-2010 5-year est.).
**Education:** Percent of population age 25 and over with: High school diploma (including GED) or higher: 81.0% (2006-2010 5-year est.); Bachelor's degree or higher: 18.7% (2006-2010 5-year est.); Master's degree or higher: 8.0% (2006-2010 5-year est.).
### School District(s)
Wallkill Central School District (KG-12)
   2009-10 Enrollment: 3,491 . . . . . . . . . . . . . . . . . . . . . . (845) 895-7101
**Housing:** Homeownership rate: 72.7% (2010); Median home value: $247,000 (2006-2010 5-year est.); Median contract rent: $807 per month (2006-2010 5-year est.); Median year structure built: 1978 (2006-2010 5-year est.).
**Safety:** Violent crime rate: 15.8 per 10,000 population; Property crime rate: 111.6 per 10,000 population (2010).
**Transportation:** Commute to work: 91.1% car, 1.0% public transportation, 4.8% walk, 3.2% work from home (2006-2010 5-year est.); Travel time to work: 21.1% less than 15 minutes, 38.5% 15 to 30 minutes, 20.8% 30 to 45 minutes, 7.0% 45 to 60 minutes, 12.7% 60 minutes or more (2006-2010 5-year est.)

## PLATTEKILL

**PLATTEKILL** (CDP). Covers a land area of 2.550 square miles and a water area of 0.072 square miles. Located at 41.61° N. Lat; 74.05° W. Long. Elevation is 568 feet.

**Population:** 906 (1990); 1,050 (2000); 1,260 (2010); Density: 494.1 persons per square mile (2010); Race: 64.5% White, 11.0% Black, 0.2% Asian, 0.2% American Indian/Alaska Native, 0.0% Native Hawaiian/Other Pacific Islander, 24.1% Other, 44.4% Hispanic of any race (2010); Average household size: 3.11 (2010); Median age: 34.0 (2010); Males per 100 females: 97.8 (2010); Marriage status: 43.3% never married, 42.8% now married, 4.0% widowed, 9.9% divorced (2006-2010 5-year est.); Foreign born: 10.7% (2006-2010 5-year est.); Ancestry (includes multiple ancestries): 14.3% American, 13.6% Italian, 7.2% Irish, 4.9% Dutch, 4.6% English (2006-2010 5-year est.).

**Economy:** Employment by occupation: 8.1% management, 3.6% professional, 14.2% services, 18.8% sales, 2.6% farming, 6.7% construction, 9.4% production (2006-2010 5-year est.).

**Income:** Per capita income: $23,770 (2006-2010 5-year est.); Median household income: $63,315 (2006-2010 5-year est.); Average household income: $67,012 (2006-2010 5-year est.); Percent of households with income of $100,000 or more: 22.0% (2006-2010 5-year est.); Poverty rate: 11.8% (2006-2010 5-year est.).

**Education:** Percent of population age 25 and over with: High school diploma (including GED) or higher: 82.4% (2006-2010 5-year est.); Bachelor's degree or higher: 14.2% (2006-2010 5-year est.); Master's degree or higher: 5.1% (2006-2010 5-year est.).

**School District(s)**

Wallkill Central School District (KG-12)

    2009-10 Enrollment: 3,491 . . . . . . . . . . . . . . . . . . . . . . (845) 895-7101

**Housing:** Homeownership rate: 60.5% (2010); Median home value: $245,800 (2006-2010 5-year est.); Median contract rent: $865 per month (2006-2010 5-year est.); Median year structure built: 1963 (2006-2010 5-year est.).

**Transportation:** Commute to work: 100.0% car, 0.0% public transportation, 0.0% walk, 0.0% work from home (2006-2010 5-year est.); Travel time to work: 1.2% less than 15 minutes, 59.0% 15 to 30 minutes, 30.6% 30 to 45 minutes, 2.7% 45 to 60 minutes, 6.5% 60 minutes or more (2006-2010 5-year est.)

## PORT EWEN

**PORT EWEN** (CDP). Covers a land area of 1.973 square miles and a water area of 0.653 square miles. Located at 41.90° N. Lat; 73.97° W. Long. Elevation is 184 feet.

**Population:** 3,444 (1990); 3,650 (2000); 3,546 (2010); Density: 1,797.3 persons per square mile (2010); Race: 89.9% White, 4.0% Black, 1.6% Asian, 0.2% American Indian/Alaska Native, 0.0% Native Hawaiian/Other Pacific Islander, 4.3% Other, 3.8% Hispanic of any race (2010); Average household size: 2.28 (2010); Median age: 46.8 (2010); Males per 100 females: 86.8 (2010); Marriage status: 26.7% never married, 54.8% now married, 5.3% widowed, 13.3% divorced (2006-2010 5-year est.); Foreign born: 4.5% (2006-2010 5-year est.); Ancestry (includes multiple ancestries): 32.5% Irish, 29.5% German, 17.9% Italian, 10.1% American, 8.4% English (2006-2010 5-year est.).

**Economy:** Employment by occupation: 7.6% management, 2.4% professional, 11.8% services, 19.7% sales, 4.0% farming, 9.9% construction, 1.6% production (2006-2010 5-year est.).

**Income:** Per capita income: $30,061 (2006-2010 5-year est.); Median household income: $62,309 (2006-2010 5-year est.); Average household income: $72,161 (2006-2010 5-year est.); Percent of households with income of $100,000 or more: 18.2% (2006-2010 5-year est.); Poverty rate: 7.3% (2006-2010 5-year est.).

**Education:** Percent of population age 25 and over with: High school diploma (including GED) or higher: 89.1% (2006-2010 5-year est.); Bachelor's degree or higher: 25.5% (2006-2010 5-year est.); Master's degree or higher: 12.3% (2006-2010 5-year est.).

**School District(s)**

Kingston City School District (PK-12)

    2009-10 Enrollment: 7,120 . . . . . . . . . . . . . . . . . . . . . . (845) 339-3000

**Vocational/Technical School(s)**

Ulster County BOCES-School of Practical Nursing (Public)

    Fall 2010 Enrollment: 166 . . . . . . . . . . . . . . . . . . . . . . (8.4) 533-2E+1

    2011-12 Tuition: $10,390

**Housing:** Homeownership rate: 74.6% (2010); Median home value: $216,900 (2006-2010 5-year est.); Median contract rent: $726 per month (2006-2010 5-year est.); Median year structure built: 1972 (2006-2010 5-year est.).

## RIFTON

**RIFTON** (CDP). Covers a land area of 1.175 square miles and a water area of 0 square miles. Located at 41.82° N. Lat; 74.03° W. Long. Elevation is 180 feet.

**Population:** 519 (1990); 501 (2000); 456 (2010); Density: 387.9 persons per square mile (2010); Race: 92.8% White, 2.0% Black, 1.1% Asian, 0.2% American Indian/Alaska Native, 0.0% Native Hawaiian/Other Pacific Islander, 3.9% Other, 6.4% Hispanic of any race (2010); Average household size: 2.41 (2010); Median age: 47.6 (2010); Males per 100 females: 95.7 (2010); Marriage status: 7.3% never married, 79.5% now married, 13.3% widowed, 0.0% divorced (2006-2010 5-year est.); Foreign born: 0.0% (2006-2010 5-year est.); Ancestry (includes multiple ancestries): 27.3% Italian, 24.3% Irish, 15.4% German, 10.1% Dutch, 6.6% English (2006-2010 5-year est.).

**Economy:** Employment by occupation: 0.0% management, 6.2% professional, 13.8% services, 0.0% sales, 0.0% farming, 0.0% construction, 0.0% production (2006-2010 5-year est.).

**Income:** Per capita income: $29,294 (2006-2010 5-year est.); Median household income: $65,139 (2006-2010 5-year est.); Average household income: $64,643 (2006-2010 5-year est.); Percent of households with income of $100,000 or more: 7.0% (2006-2010 5-year est.); Poverty rate: 0.0% (2006-2010 5-year est.).

**Education:** Percent of population age 25 and over with: High school diploma (including GED) or higher: 87.2% (2006-2010 5-year est.); Bachelor's degree or higher: 40.0% (2006-2010 5-year est.); Master's degree or higher: 30.0% (2006-2010 5-year est.).

**Housing:** Homeownership rate: 82.1% (2010); Median home value: $313,800 (2006-2010 5-year est.); Median contract rent: n/a per month (2006-2010 5-year est.); Median year structure built: 1954 (2006-2010 5-year est.).

**Transportation:** Commute to work: 100.0% car, 0.0% public transportation, 0.0% walk, 0.0% work from home (2006-2010 5-year est.); Travel time to work: 18.1% less than 15 minutes, 8.1% 15 to 30 minutes, 62.9% 30 to 45 minutes, 0.0% 45 to 60 minutes, 10.9% 60 minutes or more (2006-2010 5-year est.)

## ROCHESTER

**ROCHESTER** (town). Covers a land area of 89.303 square miles and a water area of 0.415 square miles. Located at 41.81° N. Lat; 74.27° W. Long.

**Population:** 5,679 (1990); 7,018 (2000); 7,313 (2010); Density: 81.9 persons per square mile (2010); Race: 92.6% White, 2.2% Black, 0.9% Asian, 0.4% American Indian/Alaska Native, 0.0% Native Hawaiian/Other Pacific Islander, 3.9% Other, 5.6% Hispanic of any race (2010); Average household size: 2.48 (2010); Median age: 42.9 (2010); Males per 100 females: 101.5 (2010); Marriage status: 29.5% never married, 55.9% now married, 7.3% widowed, 7.3% divorced (2006-2010 5-year est.); Foreign born: 5.9% (2006-2010 5-year est.); Ancestry (includes multiple ancestries): 19.3% Irish, 18.4% German, 15.3% Italian, 8.1% English, 6.9% Polish (2006-2010 5-year est.).

**Economy:** Single-family building permits issued: 9 (2011); Multi-family building permits issued: 0 (2011); Employment by occupation: 6.6% management, 5.8% professional, 6.4% services, 18.2% sales, 1.1% farming, 17.3% construction, 6.4% production (2006-2010 5-year est.).

**Income:** Per capita income: $26,873 (2006-2010 5-year est.); Median household income: $55,326 (2006-2010 5-year est.); Average household income: $62,045 (2006-2010 5-year est.); Percent of households with income of $100,000 or more: 16.4% (2006-2010 5-year est.); Poverty rate: 12.2% (2006-2010 5-year est.).

**Education:** Percent of population age 25 and over with: High school diploma (including GED) or higher: 86.3% (2006-2010 5-year est.); Bachelor's degree or higher: 26.1% (2006-2010 5-year est.); Master's degree or higher: 13.1% (2006-2010 5-year est.).

**Housing:** Homeownership rate: 78.4% (2010); Median home value: $227,200 (2006-2010 5-year est.); Median contract rent: $610 per month (2006-2010 5-year est.); Median year structure built: 1976 (2006-2010 5-year est.).

**Transportation:** Commute to work: 86.7% car, 1.8% public transportation, 3.0% walk, 8.5% work from home (2006-2010 5-year est.); Travel time to work: 26.2% less than 15 minutes, 25.9% 15 to 30 minutes, 25.6% 30 to 45

minutes, 12.5% 45 to 60 minutes, 9.8% 60 minutes or more (2006-2010 5-year est.)

## ROSENDALE (town). Covers a land area of 19.978 square miles and a water area of 0.766 square miles. Located at 41.84° N. Lat; 74.07° W. Long. Elevation is 66 feet.

**History:** Incorporated 1890.
**Population:** 6,220 (1990); 6,352 (2000); 6,075 (2010); Density: 304.1 persons per square mile (2010); Race: 93.8% White, 1.8% Black, 0.8% Asian, 0.1% American Indian/Alaska Native, 0.0% Native Hawaiian/Other Pacific Islander, 3.5% Other, 5.0% Hispanic of any race (2010); Average household size: 2.35 (2010); Median age: 42.8 (2010); Males per 100 females: 95.1 (2010); Marriage status: 29.7% never married, 52.6% now married, 8.1% widowed, 9.6% divorced (2006-2010 5-year est.); Foreign born: 2.6% (2006-2010 5-year est.); Ancestry (includes multiple ancestries): 27.2% Irish, 25.4% German, 18.9% Italian, 10.3% English, 8.7% American (2006-2010 5-year est.).
**Economy:** Single-family building permits issued: 7 (2011); Multi-family building permits issued: 0 (2011); Employment by occupation: 5.4% management, 3.1% professional, 8.6% services, 17.9% sales, 3.7% farming, 8.5% construction, 4.4% production (2006-2010 5-year est.).
**Income:** Per capita income: $30,009 (2006-2010 5-year est.); Median household income: $56,639 (2006-2010 5-year est.); Average household income: $69,247 (2006-2010 5-year est.); Percent of households with income of $100,000 or more: 19.8% (2006-2010 5-year est.); Poverty rate: 5.6% (2006-2010 5-year est.).
**Education:** Percent of population age 25 and over with: High school diploma (including GED) or higher: 90.2% (2006-2010 5-year est.); Bachelor's degree or higher: 35.1% (2006-2010 5-year est.); Master's degree or higher: 15.0% (2006-2010 5-year est.).
**Housing:** Homeownership rate: 73.3% (2010); Median home value: $214,000 (2006-2010 5-year est.); Median contract rent: $852 per month (2006-2010 5-year est.); Median year structure built: 1951 (2006-2010 5-year est.).
**Safety:** Violent crime rate: 1.6 per 10,000 population; Property crime rate: 89.6 per 10,000 population (2010).
**Transportation:** Commute to work: 90.8% car, 0.3% public transportation, 1.7% walk, 6.4% work from home (2006-2010 5-year est.); Travel time to work: 27.9% less than 15 minutes, 33.6% 15 to 30 minutes, 19.2% 30 to 45 minutes, 7.3% 45 to 60 minutes, 12.1% 60 minutes or more (2006-2010 5-year est.)
**Additional Information Contacts**
Town of Rosendale . . . . . . . . . . . . . . . . . . . . . . . . . . . . . . (845) 658-3159
  http://www.townofrosendale.com

## ROSENDALE VILLAGE (CDP). Covers a land area of 1.904 square miles and a water area of 0.055 square miles. Located at 41.85° N. Lat; 74.07° W. Long.

**Population:** 1,353 (1990); 1,374 (2000); 1,349 (2010); Density: 708.5 persons per square mile (2010); Race: 90.9% White, 2.9% Black, 1.0% Asian, 0.0% American Indian/Alaska Native, 0.0% Native Hawaiian/Other Pacific Islander, 5.2% Other, 7.9% Hispanic of any race (2010); Average household size: 2.19 (2010); Median age: 43.6 (2010); Males per 100 females: 91.6 (2010); Marriage status: 36.4% never married, 39.4% now married, 16.8% widowed, 7.5% divorced (2006-2010 5-year est.); Foreign born: 0.9% (2006-2010 5-year est.); Ancestry (includes multiple ancestries): 25.7% German, 24.2% Irish, 21.5% Italian, 8.9% Dutch, 7.2% American (2006-2010 5-year est.).
**Economy:** Employment by occupation: 4.3% management, 8.6% professional, 7.7% services, 18.0% sales, 0.0% farming, 8.5% construction, 1.0% production (2006-2010 5-year est.).
**Income:** Per capita income: $25,738 (2006-2010 5-year est.); Median household income: $43,415 (2006-2010 5-year est.); Average household income: $55,166 (2006-2010 5-year est.); Percent of households with income of $100,000 or more: 12.0% (2006-2010 5-year est.); Poverty rate: 10.9% (2006-2010 5-year est.).
**Education:** Percent of population age 25 and over with: High school diploma (including GED) or higher: 84.0% (2006-2010 5-year est.); Bachelor's degree or higher: 39.6% (2006-2010 5-year est.); Master's degree or higher: 16.9% (2006-2010 5-year est.).
**Housing:** Homeownership rate: 61.2% (2010); Median home value: $171,400 (2006-2010 5-year est.); Median contract rent: $771 per month (2006-2010 5-year est.); Median year structure built: before 1940 (2006-2010 5-year est.).

**Transportation:** Commute to work: 89.3% car, 0.0% public transportation, 4.1% walk, 4.7% work from home (2006-2010 5-year est.); Travel time to work: 28.8% less than 15 minutes, 33.3% 15 to 30 minutes, 19.3% 30 to 45 minutes, 5.5% 45 to 60 minutes, 13.1% 60 minutes or more (2006-2010 5-year est.)

## RUBY (unincorporated postal area)
Zip Code: 12475
  Covers a land area of 1.228 square miles and a water area of 0 square miles. Located at 42.01° N. Lat; 74.01° W. Long. Elevation is 312 feet. Population: 354 (2010); Density: 288.0 persons per square mile (2010); Race: 97.5% White, 0.0% Black, 0.0% Asian, 0.0% American Indian/Alaska Native, 0.0% Native Hawaiian/Other Pacific Islander, 2.5% Other, 2.0% Hispanic of any race (2010); Average household size: 2.38 (2010); Median age: 42.8 (2010); Males per 100 females: 108.2 (2010); Homeownership rate: 75.1% (2010)

## SAUGERTIES (village). Covers a land area of 1.783 square miles and a water area of 0.476 square miles. Located at 42.07° N. Lat; 73.94° W. Long. Elevation is 154 feet.

**Population:** 3,915 (1990); 4,955 (2000); 3,971 (2010); Density: 2,226.5 persons per square mile (2010); Race: 91.8% White, 2.3% Black, 1.1% Asian, 0.5% American Indian/Alaska Native, 0.0% Native Hawaiian/Other Pacific Islander, 4.3% Other, 7.6% Hispanic of any race (2010); Average household size: 2.11 (2010); Median age: 42.8 (2010); Males per 100 females: 93.9 (2010); Marriage status: 32.8% never married, 47.3% now married, 4.7% widowed, 15.2% divorced (2006-2010 5-year est.); Foreign born: 5.7% (2006-2010 5-year est.); Ancestry (includes multiple ancestries): 28.6% German, 25.0% Irish, 20.9% Italian, 10.4% Dutch, 6.6% French (2006-2010 5-year est.).
**Economy:** Single-family building permits issued: 2 (2011); Multi-family building permits issued: 0 (2011); Employment by occupation: 12.8% management, 3.8% professional, 9.2% services, 14.1% sales, 4.7% farming, 5.0% construction, 5.0% production (2006-2010 5-year est.).
**Income:** Per capita income: $28,057 (2006-2010 5-year est.); Median household income: $50,592 (2006-2010 5-year est.); Average household income: $58,411 (2006-2010 5-year est.); Percent of households with income of $100,000 or more: 13.3% (2006-2010 5-year est.); Poverty rate: 10.4% (2006-2010 5-year est.).
**Taxes:** Total city taxes per capita: $567 (2009); City property taxes per capita: $515 (2009).
**Education:** Percent of population age 25 and over with: High school diploma (including GED) or higher: 83.7% (2006-2010 5-year est.); Bachelor's degree or higher: 22.3% (2006-2010 5-year est.); Master's degree or higher: 8.1% (2006-2010 5-year est.).
**School District(s)**
Saugerties Central School District (KG-12)
  2009-10 Enrollment: 3,083 . . . . . . . . . . . . . . . . . . . . . (845) 247-6500
**Housing:** Homeownership rate: 43.5% (2010); Median home value: $229,800 (2006-2010 5-year est.); Median contract rent: $680 per month (2006-2010 5-year est.); Median year structure built: before 1940 (2006-2010 5-year est.).
**Newspapers:** Saugerties Post Star (Community news; Circulation 2,330); Star Newspaper (Community news; Circulation 2,330)
**Transportation:** Commute to work: 83.3% car, 3.5% public transportation, 2.8% walk, 7.4% work from home (2006-2010 5-year est.); Travel time to work: 31.3% less than 15 minutes, 40.1% 15 to 30 minutes, 13.3% 30 to 45 minutes, 4.9% 45 to 60 minutes, 10.4% 60 minutes or more (2006-2010 5-year est.)

## SAUGERTIES (town). Covers a land area of 64.574 square miles and a water area of 3.386 square miles. Located at 42.09° N. Lat; 73.99° W. Long. Elevation is 154 feet.

**History:** Former summer resort. Incorporated 1831.
**Population:** 18,467 (1990); 19,868 (2000); 19,482 (2010); Density: 301.7 persons per square mile (2010); Race: 94.2% White, 1.7% Black, 1.1% Asian, 0.3% American Indian/Alaska Native, 0.0% Native Hawaiian/Other Pacific Islander, 2.7% Other, 5.0% Hispanic of any race (2010); Average household size: 2.37 (2010); Median age: 43.7 (2010); Males per 100 females: 95.2 (2010); Marriage status: 31.1% never married, 53.4% now married, 5.8% widowed, 9.8% divorced (2006-2010 5-year est.); Foreign born: 5.2% (2006-2010 5-year est.); Ancestry (includes multiple ancestries): 24.3% German, 22.6% Irish, 20.4% Italian, 9.6% English, 8.2% Dutch (2006-2010 5-year est.).

**Economy:** Single-family building permits issued: 18 (2011); Multi-family building permits issued: 0 (2011); Employment by occupation: 11.3% management, 3.4% professional, 9.6% services, 18.8% sales, 4.4% farming, 8.5% construction, 4.8% production (2006-2010 5-year est.).
**Income:** Per capita income: $29,598 (2006-2010 5-year est.); Median household income: $54,190 (2006-2010 5-year est.); Average household income: $71,443 (2006-2010 5-year est.); Percent of households with income of $100,000 or more: 20.5% (2006-2010 5-year est.); Poverty rate: 8.3% (2006-2010 5-year est.).
**Education:** Percent of population age 25 and over with: High school diploma (including GED) or higher: 88.4% (2006-2010 5-year est.); Bachelor's degree or higher: 24.9% (2006-2010 5-year est.); Master's degree or higher: 12.1% (2006-2010 5-year est.).

### School District(s)
Saugerties Central School District (KG-12)
    2009-10 Enrollment: 3,083 . . . . . . . . . . . . . . . . (845) 247-6500
**Housing:** Homeownership rate: 69.8% (2010); Median home value: $219,400 (2006-2010 5-year est.); Median contract rent: $748 per month (2006-2010 5-year est.); Median year structure built: 1959 (2006-2010 5-year est.).
**Safety:** Violent crime rate: 2.1 per 10,000 population; Property crime rate: 143.5 per 10,000 population (2010).
**Newspapers:** Saugerties Post Star (Community news; Circulation 2,330); Star Newspaper (Community news; Circulation 2,330)
**Transportation:** Commute to work: 89.9% car, 1.9% public transportation, 1.9% walk, 4.8% work from home (2006-2010 5-year est.); Travel time to work: 30.1% less than 15 minutes, 43.4% 15 to 30 minutes, 14.1% 30 to 45 minutes, 5.1% 45 to 60 minutes, 7.4% 60 minutes or more (2006-2010 5-year est.)
**Additional Information Contacts**
Town of Saugerties . . . . . . . . . . . . . . . . . . . . . (845) 246-2800
    http://www.saugerties.ny.us

## SAUGERTIES SOUTH (CDP). Covers a land area of 0.952 square miles and a water area of 0.209 square miles. Located at 42.05° N. Lat; 73.94° W. Long.
**Population:** 2,346 (1990); 2,285 (2000); 2,218 (2010); Density: 2,328.3 persons per square mile (2010); Race: 94.0% White, 1.6% Black, 0.9% Asian, 0.4% American Indian/Alaska Native, 0.0% Native Hawaiian/Other Pacific Islander, 3.1% Other, 6.2% Hispanic of any race (2010); Average household size: 2.44 (2010); Median age: 44.0 (2010); Males per 100 females: 92.0 (2010); Marriage status: 35.7% never married, 46.9% now married, 6.2% widowed, 11.2% divorced (2006-2010 5-year est.); Foreign born: 7.1% (2006-2010 5-year est.); Ancestry (includes multiple ancestries): 26.2% Irish, 25.6% German, 19.5% Italian, 10.2% American, 8.7% English (2006-2010 5-year est.).
**Economy:** Employment by occupation: 10.2% management, 3.2% professional, 10.4% services, 19.1% sales, 7.3% farming, 6.8% construction, 5.3% production (2006-2010 5-year est.).
**Income:** Per capita income: $28,753 (2006-2010 5-year est.); Median household income: $65,263 (2006-2010 5-year est.); Average household income: $76,422 (2006-2010 5-year est.); Percent of households with income of $100,000 or more: 21.4% (2006-2010 5-year est.); Poverty rate: 9.1% (2006-2010 5-year est.).
**Education:** Percent of population age 25 and over with: High school diploma (including GED) or higher: 84.0% (2006-2010 5-year est.); Bachelor's degree or higher: 29.6% (2006-2010 5-year est.); Master's degree or higher: 14.5% (2006-2010 5-year est.).
**Housing:** Homeownership rate: 77.1% (2010); Median home value: $215,000 (2006-2010 5-year est.); Median contract rent: $598 per month (2006-2010 5-year est.); Median year structure built: 1963 (2006-2010 5-year est.).
**Transportation:** Commute to work: 93.0% car, 0.8% public transportation, 1.8% walk, 4.5% work from home (2006-2010 5-year est.); Travel time to work: 39.2% less than 15 minutes, 38.8% 15 to 30 minutes, 11.7% 30 to 45 minutes, 3.7% 45 to 60 minutes, 6.6% 60 minutes or more (2006-2010 5-year est.)

## SHANDAKEN (town). Covers a land area of 119.783 square miles and a water area of 0.057 square miles. Located at 42.02° N. Lat; 74.35° W. Long. Elevation is 1,056 feet.
**Population:** 3,013 (1990); 3,235 (2000); 3,085 (2010); Density: 25.8 persons per square mile (2010); Race: 92.9% White, 0.9% Black, 1.6% Asian, 0.5% American Indian/Alaska Native, 0.0% Native Hawaiian/Other Pacific Islander, 4.1% Other, 5.0% Hispanic of any race (2010); Average

household size: 2.02 (2010); Median age: 50.2 (2010); Males per 100 females: 101.2 (2010); Marriage status: 29.4% never married, 51.9% now married, 7.1% widowed, 11.6% divorced (2006-2010 5-year est.); Foreign born: 7.8% (2006-2010 5-year est.); Ancestry (includes multiple ancestries): 21.6% German, 19.6% Italian, 13.7% Irish, 12.7% English, 7.8% Dutch (2006-2010 5-year est.).
**Economy:** Single-family building permits issued: 0 (2011); Multi-family building permits issued: 0 (2011); Employment by occupation: 10.4% management, 3.6% professional, 9.5% services, 10.9% sales, 4.4% farming, 14.6% construction, 4.0% production (2006-2010 5-year est.).
**Income:** Per capita income: $29,768 (2006-2010 5-year est.); Median household income: $43,349 (2006-2010 5-year est.); Average household income: $60,331 (2006-2010 5-year est.); Percent of households with income of $100,000 or more: 15.4% (2006-2010 5-year est.); Poverty rate: 16.4% (2006-2010 5-year est.).
**Education:** Percent of population age 25 and over with: High school diploma (including GED) or higher: 88.6% (2006-2010 5-year est.); Bachelor's degree or higher: 28.1% (2006-2010 5-year est.); Master's degree or higher: 8.9% (2006-2010 5-year est.).
**Housing:** Homeownership rate: 72.0% (2010); Median home value: $218,800 (2006-2010 5-year est.); Median contract rent: $601 per month (2006-2010 5-year est.); Median year structure built: 1953 (2006-2010 5-year est.).
**Safety:** Violent crime rate: 16.7 per 10,000 population; Property crime rate: 337.8 per 10,000 population (2010).
**Transportation:** Commute to work: 81.8% car, 1.7% public transportation, 3.2% walk, 12.6% work from home (2006-2010 5-year est.); Travel time to work: 32.6% less than 15 minutes, 17.3% 15 to 30 minutes, 26.3% 30 to 45 minutes, 9.7% 45 to 60 minutes, 14.2% 60 minutes or more (2006-2010 5-year est.)

## SHAWANGUNK (town). Covers a land area of 56.056 square miles and a water area of 0.494 square miles. Located at 41.63° N. Lat; 74.26° W. Long. Elevation is 299 feet.
**Population:** 10,081 (1990); 12,022 (2000); 14,332 (2010); Density: 255.7 persons per square mile (2010); Race: 86.7% White, 8.1% Black, 1.6% Asian, 0.2% American Indian/Alaska Native, 0.0% Native Hawaiian/Other Pacific Islander, 3.4% Other, 9.1% Hispanic of any race (2010); Average household size: 2.78 (2010); Median age: 38.7 (2010); Males per 100 females: 131.2 (2010); Marriage status: 28.8% never married, 58.2% now married, 4.5% widowed, 8.5% divorced (2006-2010 5-year est.); Foreign born: 3.4% (2006-2010 5-year est.); Ancestry (includes multiple ancestries): 23.7% Irish, 21.1% Italian, 17.8% German, 11.3% American, 10.1% English (2006-2010 5-year est.).
**Economy:** Single-family building permits issued: 5 (2011); Multi-family building permits issued: 0 (2011); Employment by occupation: 11.8% management, 3.4% professional, 7.8% services, 19.7% sales, 4.3% farming, 13.4% construction, 6.9% production (2006-2010 5-year est.).
**Income:** Per capita income: $26,038 (2006-2010 5-year est.); Median household income: $78,740 (2006-2010 5-year est.); Average household income: $89,418 (2006-2010 5-year est.); Percent of households with income of $100,000 or more: 37.2% (2006-2010 5-year est.); Poverty rate: 12.2% (2006-2010 5-year est.).
**Education:** Percent of population age 25 and over with: High school diploma (including GED) or higher: 89.4% (2006-2010 5-year est.); Bachelor's degree or higher: 20.4% (2006-2010 5-year est.); Master's degree or higher: 8.3% (2006-2010 5-year est.).
**Housing:** Homeownership rate: 79.6% (2010); Median home value: $295,000 (2006-2010 5-year est.); Median contract rent: $848 per month (2006-2010 5-year est.); Median year structure built: 1971 (2006-2010 5-year est.).
**Safety:** Violent crime rate: 9.5 per 10,000 population; Property crime rate: 96.3 per 10,000 population (2010).
**Transportation:** Commute to work: 89.0% car, 0.9% public transportation, 2.5% walk, 7.5% work from home (2006-2010 5-year est.); Travel time to work: 20.9% less than 15 minutes, 28.4% 15 to 30 minutes, 31.2% 30 to 45 minutes, 6.0% 45 to 60 minutes, 13.5% 60 minutes or more (2006-2010 5-year est.)

## SHOKAN (CDP). Covers a land area of 3.891 square miles and a water area of 0 square miles. Located at 41.98° N. Lat; 74.21° W. Long. Elevation is 709 feet.
**Population:** 1,157 (1990); 1,252 (2000); 1,183 (2010); Density: 304.0 persons per square mile (2010); Race: 92.5% White, 2.4% Black, 1.1% Asian, 0.0% American Indian/Alaska Native, 0.0% Native Hawaiian/Other

Pacific Islander, 4.0% Other, 3.0% Hispanic of any race (2010); Average household size: 2.32 (2010); Median age: 48.8 (2010); Males per 100 females: 98.5 (2010); Marriage status: 22.3% never married, 64.0% now married, 7.9% widowed, 5.7% divorced (2006-2010 5-year est.); Foreign born: 5.6% (2006-2010 5-year est.); Ancestry (includes multiple ancestries): 31.1% Italian, 14.5% German, 12.9% Irish, 9.2% English, 9.2% Polish (2006-2010 5-year est.).

**Economy:** Employment by occupation: 18.9% management, 1.7% professional, 0.0% services, 7.9% sales, 2.2% farming, 14.6% construction, 2.2% production (2006-2010 5-year est.).

**Income:** Per capita income: $34,203 (2006-2010 5-year est.); Median household income: $52,083 (2006-2010 5-year est.); Average household income: $62,805 (2006-2010 5-year est.); Percent of households with income of $100,000 or more: 11.8% (2006-2010 5-year est.); Poverty rate: 1.4% (2006-2010 5-year est.).

**Education:** Percent of population age 25 and over with: High school diploma (including GED) or higher: 95.0% (2006-2010 5-year est.); Bachelor's degree or higher: 41.2% (2006-2010 5-year est.); Master's degree or higher: 19.6% (2006-2010 5-year est.).

**Housing:** Homeownership rate: 83.0% (2010); Median home value: $304,800 (2006-2010 5-year est.); Median contract rent: $814 per month (2006-2010 5-year est.); Median year structure built: 1964 (2006-2010 5-year est.).

**Transportation:** Commute to work: 79.5% car, 2.2% public transportation, 0.0% walk, 18.3% work from home (2006-2010 5-year est.); Travel time to work: 10.9% less than 15 minutes, 31.4% 15 to 30 minutes, 20.8% 30 to 45 minutes, 18.4% 45 to 60 minutes, 18.4% 60 minutes or more (2006-2010 5-year est.).

**SPRING GLEN** (unincorporated postal area)

Zip Code: 12483

Covers a land area of 3.323 square miles and a water area of 0.029 square miles. Located at 41.67° N. Lat; 74.42° W. Long. Elevation is 400 feet. Population: 259 (2010); Density: 77.9 persons per square mile (2010); Race: 86.9% White, 5.4% Black, 0.0% Asian, 0.8% American Indian/Alaska Native, 0.0% Native Hawaiian/Other Pacific Islander, 6.9% Other, 14.7% Hispanic of any race (2010); Average household size: 2.38 (2010); Median age: 41.7 (2010); Males per 100 females: 90.4 (2010); Homeownership rate: 62.4% (2010).

**STONE RIDGE** (CDP). Covers a land area of 5.190 square miles and a water area of 0.040 square miles. Located at 41.84° N. Lat; 74.15° W. Long. Elevation is 364 feet.

**Population:** 1,000 (1990); 1,173 (2000); 1,173 (2010); Density: 226.0 persons per square mile (2010); Race: 92.0% White, 1.4% Black, 2.4% Asian, 0.3% American Indian/Alaska Native, 0.1% Native Hawaiian/Other Pacific Islander, 3.8% Other, 2.9% Hispanic of any race (2010); Average household size: 2.44 (2010); Median age: 46.5 (2010); Males per 100 females: 92.9 (2010); Marriage status: 21.3% never married, 68.6% now married, 7.8% widowed, 2.3% divorced (2006-2010 5-year est.); Foreign born: 6.6% (2006-2010 5-year est.); Ancestry (includes multiple ancestries): 27.2% English, 24.9% Italian, 24.4% German, 14.7% Irish, 10.9% Polish (2006-2010 5-year est.).

**Economy:** Employment by occupation: 15.8% management, 8.0% professional, 7.4% services, 14.5% sales, 0.0% farming, 5.3% construction, 1.8% production (2006-2010 5-year est.).

**Income:** Per capita income: $45,539 (2006-2010 5-year est.); Median household income: $133,182 (2006-2010 5-year est.); Average household income: $115,661 (2006-2010 5-year est.); Percent of households with income of $100,000 or more: 62.8% (2006-2010 5-year est.); Poverty rate: 0.0% (2006-2010 5-year est.).

**Education:** Percent of population age 25 and over with: High school diploma (including GED) or higher: 97.4% (2006-2010 5-year est.); Bachelor's degree or higher: 47.1% (2006-2010 5-year est.); Master's degree or higher: 21.0% (2006-2010 5-year est.).

**School District(s)**

Rondout Valley Central School District (KG-12)

2009-10 Enrollment: 2,316 . . . . . . . . . . . . . . . . . . . . . . (845) 687-2400

**Two-year College(s)**

Ulster County Community College (Public)

Fall 2010 Enrollment: 2,278 . . . . . . . . . . . . . . . . . . . (845) 687-5000

2011-12 Tuition: In-state $4,628; Out-of-state $8,618

**Housing:** Homeownership rate: 83.3% (2010); Median home value: $311,100 (2006-2010 5-year est.); Median contract rent: n/a per month

(2006-2010 5-year est.); Median year structure built: 1966 (2006-2010 5-year est.).

**Transportation:** Commute to work: 93.4% car, 1.5% public transportation, 0.0% walk, 5.1% work from home (2006-2010 5-year est.); Travel time to work: 24.4% less than 15 minutes, 55.9% 15 to 30 minutes, 4.7% 30 to 45 minutes, 7.6% 45 to 60 minutes, 7.4% 60 minutes or more (2006-2010 5-year est.)

**Additional Information Contacts**

Rondout Valley Business Association . . . . . . . . . . . . . . (845) 687-4567

http://www.marbletown.org

**TILLSON** (CDP). Covers a land area of 2.344 square miles and a water area of 0.024 square miles. Located at 41.83° N. Lat; 74.07° W. Long. Elevation is 233 feet.

**Population:** 1,619 (1990); 1,709 (2000); 1,586 (2010); Density: 676.3 persons per square mile (2010); Race: 94.6% White, 1.5% Black, 1.1% Asian, 0.1% American Indian/Alaska Native, 0.0% Native Hawaiian/Other Pacific Islander, 2.7% Other, 3.8% Hispanic of any race (2010); Average household size: 2.48 (2010); Median age: 43.2 (2010); Males per 100 females: 91.5 (2010); Marriage status: 16.4% never married, 64.6% now married, 7.6% widowed, 11.4% divorced (2006-2010 5-year est.); Foreign born: 1.6% (2006-2010 5-year est.); Ancestry (includes multiple ancestries): 37.9% Irish, 30.5% German, 19.0% Italian, 10.5% English, 6.7% American (2006-2010 5-year est.).

**Economy:** Employment by occupation: 8.1% management, 3.0% professional, 9.0% services, 14.7% sales, 6.7% farming, 4.6% construction, 2.6% production (2006-2010 5-year est.).

**Income:** Per capita income: $33,300 (2006-2010 5-year est.); Median household income: $74,545 (2006-2010 5-year est.); Average household income: $82,926 (2006-2010 5-year est.); Percent of households with income of $100,000 or more: 28.9% (2006-2010 5-year est.); Poverty rate: 0.7% (2006-2010 5-year est.).

**Education:** Percent of population age 25 and over with: High school diploma (including GED) or higher: 92.3% (2006-2010 5-year est.); Bachelor's degree or higher: 34.4% (2006-2010 5-year est.); Master's degree or higher: 11.7% (2006-2010 5-year est.).

**Housing:** Homeownership rate: 85.0% (2010); Median home value: $229,800 (2006-2010 5-year est.); Median contract rent: n/a per month (2006-2010 5-year est.); Median year structure built: 1959 (2006-2010 5-year est.).

**Transportation:** Commute to work: 87.8% car, 1.3% public transportation, 3.5% walk, 7.4% work from home (2006-2010 5-year est.); Travel time to work: 17.0% less than 15 minutes, 38.3% 15 to 30 minutes, 30.8% 30 to 45 minutes, 6.6% 45 to 60 minutes, 7.3% 60 minutes or more (2006-2010 5-year est.)

**ULSTER** (town). Covers a land area of 26.803 square miles and a water area of 2.077 square miles. Located at 41.97° N. Lat; 74.00° W. Long.

**Population:** 12,365 (1990); 12,544 (2000); 12,327 (2010); Density: 459.9 persons per square mile (2010); Race: 90.2% White, 3.1% Black, 2.2% Asian, 0.3% American Indian/Alaska Native, 0.0% Native Hawaiian/Other Pacific Islander, 4.2% Other, 5.4% Hispanic of any race (2010); Average household size: 2.36 (2010); Median age: 45.7 (2010); Males per 100 females: 93.8 (2010); Marriage status: 29.3% never married, 48.9% now married, 8.9% widowed, 12.9% divorced (2006-2010 5-year est.); Foreign born: 7.0% (2006-2010 5-year est.); Ancestry (includes multiple ancestries): 26.1% Italian, 24.0% German, 19.4% Irish, 11.4% English, 6.6% Polish (2006-2010 5-year est.).

**Economy:** Single-family building permits issued: 5 (2011); Multi-family building permits issued: 0 (2011); Employment by occupation: 9.8% management, 3.1% professional, 10.1% services, 18.6% sales, 3.9% farming, 8.5% construction, 5.9% production (2006-2010 5-year est.).

**Income:** Per capita income: $29,689 (2006-2010 5-year est.); Median household income: $53,183 (2006-2010 5-year est.); Average household income: $69,496 (2006-2010 5-year est.); Percent of households with income of $100,000 or more: 20.5% (2006-2010 5-year est.); Poverty rate: 9.1% (2006-2010 5-year est.).

**Taxes:** Total city taxes per capita: $719 (2009); City property taxes per capita: $650 (2009).

**Education:** Percent of population age 25 and over with: High school diploma (including GED) or higher: 84.9% (2006-2010 5-year est.); Bachelor's degree or higher: 21.5% (2006-2010 5-year est.); Master's degree or higher: 9.6% (2006-2010 5-year est.).

**Housing:** Homeownership rate: 70.6% (2010); Median home value: $207,400 (2006-2010 5-year est.); Median contract rent: $801 per month

(2006-2010 5-year est.); Median year structure built: 1965 (2006-2010 5-year est.).
**Safety:** Violent crime rate: 6.4 per 10,000 population; Property crime rate: 386.6 per 10,000 population (2010).
**Transportation:** Commute to work: 91.8% car, 1.6% public transportation, 0.4% walk, 5.3% work from home (2006-2010 5-year est.); Travel time to work: 43.0% less than 15 minutes, 30.8% 15 to 30 minutes, 12.9% 30 to 45 minutes, 6.3% 45 to 60 minutes, 7.0% 60 minutes or more (2006-2010 5-year est.)

**ULSTER PARK** (unincorporated postal area)
Zip Code: 12487
Covers a land area of 15.704 square miles and a water area of 0.283 square miles. Located at 41.86° N. Lat; 73.99° W. Long. Elevation is 157 feet. Population: 3,268 (2010); Density: 208.1 persons per square mile (2010); Race: 89.7% White, 5.4% Black, 1.3% Asian, 0.3% American Indian/Alaska Native, 0.0% Native Hawaiian/Other Pacific Islander, 3.3% Other, 5.9% Hispanic of any race (2010); Average household size: 2.34 (2010); Median age: 43.3 (2010); Males per 100 females: 93.7 (2010); Homeownership rate: 66.9% (2010)

**WALKER VALLEY** (CDP). Covers a land area of 2.120 square miles and a water area of 0.009 square miles. Located at 41.64° N. Lat; 74.38° W. Long. Elevation is 663 feet.
Population: 546 (1990); 758 (2000); 853 (2010); Density: 402.3 persons per square mile (2010); Race: 93.8% White, 1.9% Black, 0.1% Asian, 0.4% American Indian/Alaska Native, 0.0% Native Hawaiian/Other Pacific Islander, 3.8% Other, 7.4% Hispanic of any race (2010); Average household size: 2.87 (2010); Median age: 39.7 (2010); Males per 100 females: 106.0 (2010); Marriage status: 22.2% never married, 61.6% now married, 2.6% widowed, 13.6% divorced (2006-2010 5-year est.); Foreign born: 7.6% (2006-2010 5-year est.); Ancestry (includes multiple ancestries): 59.5% Irish, 28.7% Italian, 11.8% English, 9.5% German, 9.5% Dutch (2006-2010 5-year est.).
**Economy:** Employment by occupation: 10.7% management, 0.0% professional, 6.3% services, 31.7% sales, 0.0% farming, 26.0% construction, 14.7% production (2006-2010 5-year est.).
**Income:** Per capita income: $32,841 (2006-2010 5-year est.); Median household income: $66,940 (2006-2010 5-year est.); Average household income: $77,238 (2006-2010 5-year est.); Percent of households with income of $100,000 or more: 19.4% (2006-2010 5-year est.); Poverty rate: 0.0% (2006-2010 5-year est.).
**Education:** Percent of population age 25 and over with: High school diploma (including GED) or higher: 100.0% (2006-2010 5-year est.); Bachelor's degree or higher: 28.8% (2006-2010 5-year est.); Master's degree or higher: 13.1% (2006-2010 5-year est.).
**Housing:** Homeownership rate: 83.1% (2010); Median home value: $226,500 (2006-2010 5-year est.); Median contract rent: $784 per month (2006-2010 5-year est.); Median year structure built: 1957 (2006-2010 5-year est.).
**Transportation:** Commute to work: 100.0% car, 0.0% public transportation, 0.0% walk, 0.0% work from home (2006-2010 5-year est.); Travel time to work: 10.0% less than 15 minutes, 19.0% 15 to 30 minutes, 39.1% 30 to 45 minutes, 5.0% 45 to 60 minutes, 26.9% 60 minutes or more (2006-2010 5-year est.)

**WALLKILL** (CDP). Covers a land area of 3.067 square miles and a water area of 0 square miles. Located at 41.60° N. Lat; 74.16° W. Long. Elevation is 262 feet.
Population: 2,125 (1990); 2,143 (2000); 2,288 (2010); Density: 746.0 persons per square mile (2010); Race: 93.0% White, 2.5% Black, 0.9% Asian, 0.3% American Indian/Alaska Native, 0.0% Native Hawaiian/Other Pacific Islander, 3.3% Other, 8.4% Hispanic of any race (2010); Average household size: 2.69 (2010); Median age: 38.8 (2010); Males per 100 females: 97.8 (2010); Marriage status: 21.4% never married, 60.1% now married, 4.6% widowed, 13.9% divorced (2006-2010 5-year est.); Foreign born: 1.3% (2006-2010 5-year est.); Ancestry (includes multiple ancestries): 39.1% Irish, 22.5% Italian, 16.9% German, 14.5% American, 9.7% Dutch (2006-2010 5-year est.).
**Economy:** Employment by occupation: 18.8% management, 0.0% professional, 11.8% services, 17.0% sales, 5.8% farming, 8.9% construction, 7.0% production (2006-2010 5-year est.).
**Income:** Per capita income: $30,162 (2006-2010 5-year est.); Median household income: $72,170 (2006-2010 5-year est.); Average household income: $81,014 (2006-2010 5-year est.); Percent of households with

income of $100,000 or more: 30.6% (2006-2010 5-year est.); Poverty rate: 4.8% (2006-2010 5-year est.).
**Education:** Percent of population age 25 and over with: High school diploma (including GED) or higher: 93.1% (2006-2010 5-year est.); Bachelor's degree or higher: 20.4% (2006-2010 5-year est.); Master's degree or higher: 7.1% (2006-2010 5-year est.).
**School District(s)**
Wallkill Central School District (KG-12)
   2009-10 Enrollment: 3,491 . . . . . . . . . . . . . . . . . (845) 895-7101
**Housing:** Homeownership rate: 68.3% (2010); Median home value: $257,100 (2006-2010 5-year est.); Median contract rent: $862 per month (2006-2010 5-year est.); Median year structure built: 1964 (2006-2010 5-year est.).
**Transportation:** Commute to work: 87.3% car, 0.9% public transportation, 4.6% walk, 7.1% work from home (2006-2010 5-year est.); Travel time to work: 26.9% less than 15 minutes, 38.5% 15 to 30 minutes, 11.3% 30 to 45 minutes, 11.6% 45 to 60 minutes, 11.8% 60 minutes or more (2006-2010 5-year est.)

**WATCHTOWER** (CDP). Covers a land area of 0.777 square miles and a water area of 0 square miles. Located at 41.63° N. Lat; 74.26° W. Long.
Population: n/a (1990); n/a (2000); 2,381 (2010); Density: 3,063.5 persons per square mile (2010); Race: 80.8% White, 10.4% Black, 5.5% Asian, 0.0% American Indian/Alaska Native, 0.0% Native Hawaiian/Other Pacific Islander, 3.3% Other, 11.4% Hispanic of any race (2010); Average household size: 0.00 (2010); Median age: 32.4 (2010); Males per 100 females: 183.5 (2010); Marriage status: 36.6% never married, 61.1% now married, 1.9% widowed, 0.5% divorced (2006-2010 5-year est.); Foreign born: 5.8% (2006-2010 5-year est.); Ancestry (includes multiple ancestries): 21.5% German, 16.2% American, 14.4% English, 4.8% Irish, 4.1% Polish (2006-2010 5-year est.).
**Economy:** Employment by occupation: 0.0% management, 5.3% professional, 5.8% services, 5.8% sales, 17.5% farming, 15.2% construction, 11.6% production (2006-2010 5-year est.).
**Income:** Per capita income: $12,379 (2006-2010 5-year est.); Median household income: $0 (2006-2010 5-year est.); Average household income: $0 (2006-2010 5-year est.); Percent of households with income of $100,000 or more: 0.0% (2006-2010 5-year est.); Poverty rate: 63.7% (2006-2010 5-year est.).
**Education:** Percent of population age 25 and over with: High school diploma (including GED) or higher: 94.5% (2006-2010 5-year est.); Bachelor's degree or higher: 8.0% (2006-2010 5-year est.); Master's degree or higher: 3.6% (2006-2010 5-year est.).
**Housing:** Homeownership rate: 0.0% (2010); Median home value: n/a (2006-2010 5-year est.); Median contract rent: n/a per month (2006-2010 5-year est.); Median year structure built: n/a (2006-2010 5-year est.).
**Transportation:** Commute to work: 14.3% car, 0.0% public transportation, 18.3% walk, 67.4% work from home (2006-2010 5-year est.); Travel time to work: 57.0% less than 15 minutes, 8.8% 15 to 30 minutes, 27.2% 30 to 45 minutes, 7.0% 45 to 60 minutes, 0.0% 60 minutes or more (2006-2010 5-year est.)

**WAWARSING** (town). Covers a land area of 130.504 square miles and a water area of 3.357 square miles. Located at 41.74° N. Lat; 74.41° W. Long. Elevation is 292 feet.
Population: 12,348 (1990); 12,889 (2000); 13,157 (2010); Density: 100.8 persons per square mile (2010); Race: 73.2% White, 15.3% Black, 1.4% Asian, 0.8% American Indian/Alaska Native, 0.0% Native Hawaiian/Other Pacific Islander, 9.3% Other, 19.3% Hispanic of any race (2010); Average household size: 2.46 (2010); Median age: 40.1 (2010); Males per 100 females: 128.3 (2010); Marriage status: 34.1% never married, 48.7% now married, 6.6% widowed, 10.5% divorced (2006-2010 5-year est.); Foreign born: 11.5% (2006-2010 5-year est.); Ancestry (includes multiple ancestries): 13.2% Irish, 12.5% German, 11.2% Italian, 6.4% American, 6.3% Polish (2006-2010 5-year est.).
**Economy:** Single-family building permits issued: 3 (2011); Multi-family building permits issued: 0 (2011); Employment by occupation: 3.6% management, 0.8% professional, 14.0% services, 12.2% sales, 4.8% farming, 10.1% construction, 6.5% production (2006-2010 5-year est.).
**Income:** Per capita income: $18,380 (2006-2010 5-year est.); Median household income: $43,690 (2006-2010 5-year est.); Average household income: $54,401 (2006-2010 5-year est.); Percent of households with income of $100,000 or more: 15.5% (2006-2010 5-year est.); Poverty rate: 23.0% (2006-2010 5-year est.).

**Education:** Percent of population age 25 and over with: High school diploma (including GED) or higher: 76.0% (2006-2010 5-year est.); Bachelor's degree or higher: 17.1% (2006-2010 5-year est.); Master's degree or higher: 8.1% (2006-2010 5-year est.).
**Housing:** Homeownership rate: 63.9% (2010); Median home value: $182,200 (2006-2010 5-year est.); Median contract rent: $764 per month (2006-2010 5-year est.); Median year structure built: 1954 (2006-2010 5-year est.).
**Transportation:** Commute to work: 86.6% car, 1.9% public transportation, 3.9% walk, 7.4% work from home (2006-2010 5-year est.); Travel time to work: 34.8% less than 15 minutes, 28.0% 15 to 30 minutes, 18.9% 30 to 45 minutes, 5.9% 45 to 60 minutes, 12.4% 60 minutes or more (2006-2010 5-year est.)

**WEST CAMP** (unincorporated postal area)
Zip Code: 12490
Covers a land area of 0.522 square miles and a water area of 0.003 square miles. Located at 42.12° N. Lat; 73.92° W. Long. Elevation is 184 feet. Population: 110 (2010); Density: 210.6 persons per square mile (2010); Race: 99.1% White, 0.0% Black, 0.0% Asian, 0.0% American Indian/Alaska Native, 0.0% Native Hawaiian/Other Pacific Islander, 0.9% Other, 10.0% Hispanic of any race (2010); Average household size: 2.44 (2010); Median age: 42.5 (2010); Males per 100 females: 103.7 (2010); Homeownership rate: 75.5% (2010).

**WEST HURLEY** (CDP). Covers a land area of 3.787 square miles and a water area of <.001 square miles. Located at 42.00° N. Lat; 74.10° W. Long. Elevation is 597 feet.
**Population:** 2,190 (1990); 2,105 (2000); 1,939 (2010); Density: 512.0 persons per square mile (2010); Race: 94.4% White, 2.0% Black, 1.8% Asian, 0.0% American Indian/Alaska Native, 0.0% Native Hawaiian/Other Pacific Islander, 1.8% Other, 2.3% Hispanic of any race (2010); Average household size: 2.17 (2010); Median age: 52.4 (2010); Males per 100 females: 84.7 (2010); Marriage status: 19.9% never married, 60.7% now married, 9.5% widowed, 9.9% divorced (2006-2010 5-year est.); Foreign born: 7.5% (2006-2010 5-year est.); Ancestry (includes multiple ancestries): 24.2% Italian, 20.7% German, 16.0% English, 15.8% Irish, 5.9% Polish (2006-2010 5-year est.).
**Economy:** Employment by occupation: 16.1% management, 1.7% professional, 6.1% services, 16.3% sales, 1.2% farming, 3.1% construction, 3.2% production (2006-2010 5-year est.).
**Income:** Per capita income: $36,248 (2006-2010 5-year est.); Median household income: $58,493 (2006-2010 5-year est.); Average household income: $71,616 (2006-2010 5-year est.); Percent of households with income of $100,000 or more: 23.7% (2006-2010 5-year est.); Poverty rate: 1.2% (2006-2010 5-year est.).
**Education:** Percent of population age 25 and over with: High school diploma (including GED) or higher: 97.4% (2006-2010 5-year est.); Bachelor's degree or higher: 54.7% (2006-2010 5-year est.); Master's degree or higher: 26.4% (2006-2010 5-year est.).
**Housing:** Homeownership rate: 83.2% (2010); Median home value: $260,400 (2006-2010 5-year est.); Median contract rent: $964 per month (2006-2010 5-year est.); Median year structure built: 1961 (2006-2010 5-year est.).
**Transportation:** Commute to work: 90.0% car, 0.0% public transportation, 0.0% walk, 10.0% work from home (2006-2010 5-year est.); Travel time to work: 26.2% less than 15 minutes, 56.9% 15 to 30 minutes, 7.8% 30 to 45 minutes, 5.8% 45 to 60 minutes, 3.3% 60 minutes or more (2006-2010 5-year est.)

**WEST PARK** (unincorporated postal area)
Zip Code: 12493
Covers a land area of 6.893 square miles and a water area of 0.020 square miles. Located at 41.78° N. Lat; 73.97° W. Long. Elevation is 102 feet. Population: 495 (2010); Density: 71.8 persons per square mile (2010); Race: 84.8% White, 7.3% Black, 1.0% Asian, 0.6% American Indian/Alaska Native, 0.0% Native Hawaiian/Other Pacific Islander, 6.3% Other, 7.3% Hispanic of any race (2010); Average household size: 2.23 (2010); Median age: 37.2 (2010); Males per 100 females: 113.4 (2010); Homeownership rate: 52.7% (2010).

**WEST SHOKAN** (unincorporated postal area)
Zip Code: 12494
Covers a land area of 18.743 square miles and a water area of 0 square miles. Located at 41.95° N. Lat; 74.29° W. Long. Elevation is 666 feet.

Population: 764 (2010); Density: 40.8 persons per square mile (2010); Race: 96.7% White, 0.9% Black, 0.5% Asian, 0.1% American Indian/Alaska Native, 0.0% Native Hawaiian/Other Pacific Islander, 1.8% Other, 2.5% Hispanic of any race (2010); Average household size: 2.16 (2010); Median age: 50.5 (2010); Males per 100 females: 97.4 (2010); Homeownership rate: 82.7% (2010)

**WILLOW** (unincorporated postal area)
Zip Code: 12495
Covers a land area of 9.140 square miles and a water area of 0 square miles. Located at 42.08° N. Lat; 74.24° W. Long. Elevation is 1,093 feet. Population: 265 (2010); Density: 29.0 persons per square mile (2010); Race: 95.1% White, 0.8% Black, 2.6% Asian, 0.0% American Indian/Alaska Native, 0.0% Native Hawaiian/Other Pacific Islander, 1.5% Other, 2.3% Hispanic of any race (2010); Average household size: 1.78 (2010); Median age: 56.3 (2010); Males per 100 females: 100.8 (2010); Homeownership rate: 84.5% (2010)

**WOODSTOCK** (town). Covers a land area of 67.288 square miles and a water area of 0.544 square miles. Located at 42.05° N. Lat; 74.16° W. Long. Elevation is 561 feet.
**History:** Best known for its association with the famous 3-day music festival in 1969, Woodstock had a reputation as an artists' colony and progressive retreat long before the 1960s. A tannery center in the 19th century, it became an art colony in 1902. In 1906 the Manhattan-based Arts Student League opened a summer school here, and the adjacent Maverick colony drew social reformers, artists, and performers. To this day the village remains a magnet for tourists, artists, and drifters.
**Population:** 6,290 (1990); 6,241 (2000); 5,884 (2010); Density: 87.4 persons per square mile (2010); Race: 92.3% White, 1.5% Black, 2.0% Asian, 0.2% American Indian/Alaska Native, 0.0% Native Hawaiian/Other Pacific Islander, 4.0% Other, 4.0% Hispanic of any race (2010); Average household size: 1.95 (2010); Median age: 53.8 (2010); Males per 100 females: 91.3 (2010); Marriage status: 26.0% never married, 56.1% now married, 5.6% widowed, 12.2% divorced (2006-2010 5-year est.); Foreign born: 9.4% (2006-2010 5-year est.); Ancestry (includes multiple ancestries): 22.5% Irish, 16.7% English, 14.8% German, 12.4% Italian, 8.7% American (2006-2010 5-year est.).
**Economy:** Single-family building permits issued: 11 (2011); Multi-family building permits issued: 52 (2011); Employment by occupation: 13.8% management, 5.7% professional, 6.7% services, 15.6% sales, 1.6% farming, 7.8% construction, 3.4% production (2006-2010 5-year est.).
**Income:** Per capita income: $41,221 (2006-2010 5-year est.); Median household income: $60,826 (2006-2010 5-year est.); Average household income: $89,293 (2006-2010 5-year est.); Percent of households with income of $100,000 or more: 28.0% (2006-2010 5-year est.); Poverty rate: 12.6% (2006-2010 5-year est.).
**Taxes:** Total city taxes per capita: $761 (2009); City property taxes per capita: $675 (2009).
**Education:** Percent of population age 25 and over with: High school diploma (including GED) or higher: 94.8% (2006-2010 5-year est.); Bachelor's degree or higher: 54.9% (2006-2010 5-year est.); Master's degree or higher: 20.8% (2006-2010 5-year est.).

**School District(s)**
Onteora Central School District (KG-12)
    2009-10 Enrollment: 1,651 . . . . . . . . . . . . . . . . . . . . . . (845) 657-6383
**Housing:** Homeownership rate: 76.3% (2010); Median home value: $367,900 (2006-2010 5-year est.); Median contract rent: $789 per month (2006-2010 5-year est.); Median year structure built: 1958 (2006-2010 5-year est.).
**Safety:** Violent crime rate: 8.3 per 10,000 population; Property crime rate: 108.2 per 10,000 population (2010).
**Newspapers:** Ulster County Townsman (Community news; Circulation 5,100)
**Transportation:** Commute to work: 60.9% car, 5.2% public transportation, 11.2% walk, 20.3% work from home (2006-2010 5-year est.); Travel time to work: 32.1% less than 15 minutes, 32.7% 15 to 30 minutes, 15.0% 30 to 45 minutes, 6.4% 45 to 60 minutes, 13.8% 60 minutes or more (2006-2010 5-year est.)
**Additional Information Contacts**
Town of Woodstock . . . . . . . . . . . . . . . . . . . . . . . . . . . (845) 679-2113
    http://www.woodstockny.org
Woodstock Chamber of Commerce & Arts . . . . . . . . . . . (845) 679-6234
    http://www.woodstockchamber.com

**WOODSTOCK** (CDP). Covers a land area of 5.916 square miles and a water area of 0.008 square miles. Located at 42.04° N. Lat; 74.10° W. Long. Elevation is 561 feet.

**Population:** 2,285 (1990); 2,187 (2000); 2,088 (2010); Density: 352.9 persons per square mile (2010); Race: 90.0% White, 2.6% Black, 1.2% Asian, 0.5% American Indian/Alaska Native, 0.0% Native Hawaiian/Other Pacific Islander, 5.7% Other, 6.8% Hispanic of any race (2010); Average household size: 1.85 (2010); Median age: 53.0 (2010); Males per 100 females: 86.1 (2010); Marriage status: 28.7% never married, 58.7% now married, 4.9% widowed, 7.7% divorced (2006-2010 5-year est.); Foreign born: 10.4% (2006-2010 5-year est.); Ancestry (includes multiple ancestries): 25.9% Irish, 15.8% German, 14.3% Italian, 11.3% American, 10.8% English (2006-2010 5-year est.).

**Economy:** Employment by occupation: 14.8% management, 3.1% professional, 4.4% services, 19.6% sales, 2.5% farming, 5.4% construction, 4.9% production (2006-2010 5-year est.).

**Income:** Per capita income: $37,159 (2006-2010 5-year est.); Median household income: $48,583 (2006-2010 5-year est.); Average household income: $76,538 (2006-2010 5-year est.); Percent of households with income of $100,000 or more: 21.2% (2006-2010 5-year est.); Poverty rate: 14.2% (2006-2010 5-year est.).

**Education:** Percent of population age 25 and over with: High school diploma (including GED) or higher: 92.8% (2006-2010 5-year est.); Bachelor's degree or higher: 52.6% (2006-2010 5-year est.); Master's degree or higher: 19.0% (2006-2010 5-year est.).

**School District(s)**
Onteora Central School District (KG-12)
   2009-10 Enrollment: 1,651 . . . . . . . . . . . . . . . . . . . . . . . . . (845) 657-6383

**Housing:** Homeownership rate: 62.5% (2010); Median home value: $350,600 (2006-2010 5-year est.); Median contract rent: $839 per month (2006-2010 5-year est.); Median year structure built: 1952 (2006-2010 5-year est.).

**Transportation:** Commute to work: 64.2% car, 5.4% public transportation, 12.9% walk, 14.9% work from home (2006-2010 5-year est.); Travel time to work: 30.4% less than 15 minutes, 37.1% 15 to 30 minutes, 12.9% 30 to 45 minutes, 8.6% 45 to 60 minutes, 11.0% 60 minutes or more (2006-2010 5-year est.)

**ZENA** (CDP). Covers a land area of 2.934 square miles and a water area of 0 square miles. Located at 42.02° N. Lat; 74.08° W. Long. Elevation is 377 feet.

**Population:** 1,208 (1990); 1,119 (2000); 1,031 (2010); Density: 351.3 persons per square mile (2010); Race: 94.6% White, 1.2% Black, 2.3% Asian, 0.0% American Indian/Alaska Native, 0.0% Native Hawaiian/Other Pacific Islander, 1.9% Other, 2.5% Hispanic of any race (2010); Average household size: 2.30 (2010); Median age: 51.1 (2010); Males per 100 females: 92.4 (2010); Marriage status: 29.3% never married, 55.3% now married, 7.4% widowed, 8.0% divorced (2006-2010 5-year est.); Foreign born: 9.4% (2006-2010 5-year est.); Ancestry (includes multiple ancestries): 28.6% Irish, 24.5% Italian, 15.4% German, 12.3% English, 7.8% Scotch-Irish (2006-2010 5-year est.).

**Economy:** Employment by occupation: 16.3% management, 8.4% professional, 0.0% services, 7.7% sales, 3.5% farming, 8.2% construction, 2.7% production (2006-2010 5-year est.).

**Income:** Per capita income: $36,145 (2006-2010 5-year est.); Median household income: $68,702 (2006-2010 5-year est.); Average household income: $102,251 (2006-2010 5-year est.); Percent of households with income of $100,000 or more: 31.2% (2006-2010 5-year est.); Poverty rate: 13.0% (2006-2010 5-year est.).

**Education:** Percent of population age 25 and over with: High school diploma (including GED) or higher: 87.9% (2006-2010 5-year est.); Bachelor's degree or higher: 47.9% (2006-2010 5-year est.); Master's degree or higher: 20.2% (2006-2010 5-year est.).

**Housing:** Homeownership rate: 89.9% (2010); Median home value: $324,200 (2006-2010 5-year est.); Median contract rent: $1,375 per month (2006-2010 5-year est.); Median year structure built: 1966 (2006-2010 5-year est.).

**Transportation:** Commute to work: 60.6% car, 7.1% public transportation, 23.2% walk, 9.1% work from home (2006-2010 5-year est.); Travel time to work: 40.6% less than 15 minutes, 28.6% 15 to 30 minutes, 19.4% 30 to 45 minutes, 1.9% 45 to 60 minutes, 9.4% 60 minutes or more (2006-2010 5-year est.)

# Warren County

Located in eastern New York, in the Adirondacks; bounded on the east by Lake George; drained by the Hudson and Schroon Rivers. Covers a land area of 869.29 square miles, a water area of 62.37 square miles, and is located in the Eastern Time Zone at 43.47° N. Lat., 73.75° W. Long. The county was founded in 1813. County seat is Lake George.

Warren County is part of the Glens Falls, NY Metropolitan Statistical Area. The entire metro area includes: Warren County, NY; Washington County, NY

Weather Station: Glens Falls Arpt                 Elevation: 320 feet

| | Jan | Feb | Mar | Apr | May | Jun | Jul | Aug | Sep | Oct | Nov | Dec |
|---|---|---|---|---|---|---|---|---|---|---|---|---|
| High | 29 | 33 | 42 | 57 | 68 | 77 | 81 | 79 | 71 | 58 | 46 | 34 |
| Low | 9 | 11 | 21 | 34 | 44 | 53 | 58 | 56 | 48 | 36 | 28 | 17 |
| Precip | 2.9 | 2.0 | 3.0 | 3.0 | 3.6 | 3.5 | 4.1 | 3.6 | 3.3 | 3.4 | 3.3 | 3.0 |
| Snow | na | 13.2 | 12.8 | 2.4 | tr | 0.0 | tr | na | na | na | na | na |

*High and Low temperatures in degrees Fahrenheit; Precipitation and Snow in inches*

Weather Station: Glens Falls Farm               Elevation: 503 feet

| | Jan | Feb | Mar | Apr | May | Jun | Jul | Aug | Sep | Oct | Nov | Dec |
|---|---|---|---|---|---|---|---|---|---|---|---|---|
| High | 31 | 35 | 44 | 59 | 70 | 79 | 82 | 80 | 73 | 60 | 48 | 35 |
| Low | 11 | 12 | 22 | 34 | 45 | 54 | 59 | 57 | 50 | 38 | 29 | 18 |
| Precip | 3.3 | 2.7 | 3.6 | 3.7 | 4.0 | 4.2 | 4.6 | 4.2 | 3.9 | 4.0 | 4.1 | 3.7 |
| Snow | 19.0 | 12.4 | 11.3 | 2.0 | 0.0 | 0.0 | 0.0 | 0.0 | 0.0 | tr | 2.5 | 12.4 |

*High and Low temperatures in degrees Fahrenheit; Precipitation and Snow in inches*

**Population:** 59,209 (1990); 63,303 (2000); 65,707 (2010); Race: 96.5% White, 0.9% Black, 0.7% Asian, 0.2% American Indian/Alaska Native, 0.0% Native Hawaiian/Other Pacific Islander, 1.7% Other, 1.8% Hispanic of any race (2010); Density: 75.6 persons per square mile (2010); Average household size: 2.32 (2010); Median age: 44.1 (2010); Males per 100 females: 95.4 (2010).

**Religion:** Six largest groups: 22.1% Catholicism, 3.2% Methodist/Pietist, 2.1% Presbyterian-Reformed, 1.7% Episcopalianism/Anglicanism, 1.4% Holiness, 1.3% Baptist (2010)

**Economy:** Unemployment rate: 10.1% (February 2012); Total civilian labor force: 36,246 (February 2012); Leading industries: 21.6% health care and social assistance; 17.8% retail trade; 13.1% manufacturing (2009); Farms: 86 totaling 8,555 acres (2007); Companies that employ 500 or more persons: 5 (2009); Companies that employ 100 to 499 persons: 37 (2009); Companies that employ less than 100 persons: 2,329 (2009); Black-owned businesses: n/a (2007); Hispanic-owned businesses: n/a (2007); Asian-owned businesses: n/a (2007); Women-owned businesses: 1,980 (2007); Retail sales per capita: $20,470 (2010). Single-family building permits issued: 125 (2011); Multi-family building permits issued: 8 (2011).

**Income:** Per capita income: $27,744 (2006-2010 5-year est.); Median household income: $51,619 (2006-2010 5-year est.); Average household income: $64,279 (2006-2010 5-year est.); Percent of households with income of $100,000 or more: 17.7% (2006-2010 5-year est.); Poverty rate: 10.0% (2006-2010 5-year est.); Bankruptcy rate: 4.93% (2011).

**Education:** Percent of population age 25 and over with: High school diploma (including GED) or higher: 89.6% (2006-2010 5-year est.); Bachelor's degree or higher: 27.3% (2006-2010 5-year est.); Master's degree or higher: 11.9% (2006-2010 5-year est.).

**Housing:** Homeownership rate: 69.3% (2010); Median home value: $183,000 (2006-2010 5-year est.); Median contract rent: $627 per month (2006-2010 5-year est.); Median year structure built: 1968 (2006-2010 5-year est.).

**Health:** Birth rate: 95.5 per 10,000 population (2011); Death rate: 93.4 per 10,000 population (2011); Age-adjusted cancer mortality rate: 181.4 deaths per 100,000 population (2009); Number of physicians: 33.8 per 10,000 population (2008); Hospital beds: 50.9 per 10,000 population (2007); Hospital admissions: 2,212.2 per 10,000 population (2007).

**Elections:** 2008 Presidential election results: 50.5% Obama, 47.8% McCain, 1.0% Nader

**National and State Parks:** Lake George Beach State Park

**Additional Information Contacts**
Warren County Government . . . . . . . . . . . . . . . . . . . . . . . . . (518) 761-6539
   http://www.co.warren.ny.us
Adirondack Regional Chamber of Commerce . . . . . . . . . . (518) 798-1761
   http://www.adirondackchamber.org
Bolton Landing Chamber of Commerce . . . . . . . . . . . . . . . (518) 644-3831
   http://www.boltonchamber.com
City of Glens Falls . . . . . . . . . . . . . . . . . . . . . . . . . . . . . . . . (518) 761-3800
   http://www.cityofglensfalls.com

Gore Mountain Region Chamber of Commerce ............ (518) 251-2612
http://www.gorechamber.com
Hague on Lake George Chamber of Commerce ......... (518) 543-6441
http://www.visithague.com
Lake George Regional Chamber of Commerce .......... (518) 668-5755
http://www.lakegeorgechamber.com
Lake Luzerne Regional Chamber of Commerce ......... (518) 696-3500
http://www.lakeluzernechamber.org
North Warren Chamber of Commerce ................. (518) 494-2722
http://www.northwarren.com/index/chamber
Town of Queensbury ............................. (518) 761-8234
http://www.queensbury.net
Warrensburg Chamber of Commerce ................. (518) 623-2161
http://www.warrensburgchamber.com

## Warren County Communities

**ADIRONDACK** (unincorporated postal area)
Zip Code: 12808
Covers a land area of 22.184 square miles and a water area of 2.849
square miles. Located at 43.76° N. Lat; 73.71° W. Long. Elevation is 814
feet. Population: 306 (2010); Density: 13.8 persons per square mile
(2010); Race: 98.7% White, 0.0% Black, 0.3% Asian, 0.0% American
Indian/Alaska Native, 0.0% Native Hawaiian/Other Pacific Islander, 1.0%
Other, 0.7% Hispanic of any race (2010); Average household size: 2.07
(2010); Median age: 57.8 (2010); Males per 100 females: 104.0 (2010);
Homeownership rate: 94.6% (2010)

**ATHOL** (unincorporated postal area)
Zip Code: 12810
Covers a land area of 66.404 square miles and a water area of 1.140
square miles. Located at 43.49° N. Lat; 73.98° W. Long. Elevation is 787
feet. Population: 627 (2010); Density: 9.4 persons per square mile
(2010); Race: 96.2% White, 0.2% Black, 0.5% Asian, 0.8% American
Indian/Alaska Native, 0.0% Native Hawaiian/Other Pacific Islander, 2.3%
Other, 0.3% Hispanic of any race (2010); Average household size: 2.43
(2010); Median age: 46.0 (2010); Males per 100 females: 112.5 (2010);
Homeownership rate: 88.8% (2010)

**BAKERS MILLS** (unincorporated postal area)
Zip Code: 12811
Covers a land area of 1.721 square miles and a water area of 0 square
miles. Located at 43.60° N. Lat; 74.02° W. Long. Elevation is 1,594 feet.
Population: 127 (2010); Density: 73.8 persons per square mile (2010);
Race: 97.6% White, 0.0% Black, 0.8% Asian, 0.0% American
Indian/Alaska Native, 0.0% Native Hawaiian/Other Pacific Islander, 1.6%
Other, 0.0% Hispanic of any race (2010); Average household size: 2.70
(2010); Median age: 42.5 (2010); Males per 100 females: 95.4 (2010);
Homeownership rate: 78.7% (2010)

**BOLTON** (town). Covers a land area of 63.270 square miles and a
water area of 26.771 square miles. Located at 43.57° N. Lat; 73.65° W.
Long. Elevation is 374 feet.
**Population:** 1,855 (1990); 2,117 (2000); 2,326 (2010); Density: 36.8
persons per square mile (2010); Race: 97.9% White, 0.2% Black, 0.4%
Asian, 0.0% American Indian/Alaska Native, 0.0% Native Hawaiian/Other
Pacific Islander, 1.5% Other, 1.8% Hispanic of any race (2010); Average
household size: 2.19 (2010); Median age: 52.2 (2010); Males per 100
females: 104.8 (2010); Marriage status: 22.0% never married, 58.1% now
married, 7.9% widowed, 11.9% divorced (2006-2010 5-year est.); Foreign
born: 3.8% (2006-2010 5-year est.); Ancestry (includes multiple
ancestries): 18.7% German, 14.5% English, 14.0% Irish, 9.4% Italian, 8.1%
French (2006-2010 5-year est.).
**Economy:** Employment by occupation: 15.2% management, 5.5%
professional, 13.4% services, 13.5% sales, 1.8% farming, 9.1%
construction, 5.2% production (2006-2010 5-year est.).
**Income:** Per capita income: $29,269 (2006-2010 5-year est.); Median
household income: $57,500 (2006-2010 5-year est.); Average household
income: $66,466 (2006-2010 5-year est.); Percent of households with
income of $100,000 or more: 15.8% (2006-2010 5-year est.); Poverty rate:
6.7% (2006-2010 5-year est.).
**Education:** Percent of population age 25 and over with: High school
diploma (including GED) or higher: 92.6% (2006-2010 5-year est.);
Bachelor's degree or higher: 32.8% (2006-2010 5-year est.); Master's
degree or higher: 10.8% (2006-2010 5-year est.).

**Housing:** Homeownership rate: 79.7% (2010); Median home value:
$356,800 (2006-2010 5-year est.); Median contract rent: $634 per month
(2006-2010 5-year est.); Median year structure built: 1967 (2006-2010
5-year est.).
**Safety:** Violent crime rate: 14.1 per 10,000 population; Property crime rate:
108.0 per 10,000 population (2010).
**Transportation:** Commute to work: 80.4% car, 0.6% public transportation,
2.1% walk, 14.4% work from home (2006-2010 5-year est.); Travel time to
work: 33.2% less than 15 minutes, 28.2% 15 to 30 minutes, 25.5% 30 to 45
minutes, 7.8% 45 to 60 minutes, 5.3% 60 minutes or more (2006-2010
5-year est.).

**BOLTON LANDING** (CDP). Covers a land area of 1.062 square
miles and a water area of 0.176 square miles. Located at 43.56° N. Lat;
73.65° W. Long. Elevation is 361 feet.
**Population:** n/a (1990); n/a (2000); 513 (2010); Density: 482.8 persons per
square mile (2010); Race: 95.5% White, 0.2% Black, 0.4% Asian, 0.2%
American Indian/Alaska Native, 0.0% Native Hawaiian/Other Pacific
Islander, 3.7% Other, 4.1% Hispanic of any race (2010); Average
household size: 1.91 (2010); Median age: 54.1 (2010); Males per 100
females: 101.2 (2010); Marriage status: 23.9% never married, 55.7% now
married, 6.1% widowed, 14.3% divorced (2006-2010 5-year est.); Foreign
born: 11.0% (2006-2010 5-year est.); Ancestry (includes multiple
ancestries): 24.0% German, 14.5% Italian, 13.5% English, 11.8% Irish,
5.9% Scottish (2006-2010 5-year est.).
**Economy:** Employment by occupation: 8.5% management, 2.4%
professional, 7.0% services, 13.5% sales, 4.1% farming, 7.7%
construction, 10.9% production (2006-2010 5-year est.).
**Income:** Per capita income: $27,909 (2006-2010 5-year est.); Median
household income: $54,875 (2006-2010 5-year est.); Average household
income: $60,839 (2006-2010 5-year est.); Percent of households with
income of $100,000 or more: 9.1% (2006-2010 5-year est.); Poverty rate:
1.6% (2006-2010 5-year est.).
**Education:** Percent of population age 25 and over with: High school
diploma (including GED) or higher: 96.7% (2006-2010 5-year est.);
Bachelor's degree or higher: 22.5% (2006-2010 5-year est.); Master's
degree or higher: 8.5% (2006-2010 5-year est.).
**School District(s)**
Bolton Central School District (PK-12)
2009-10 Enrollment: 249 .......................... (518) 644-2400
**Housing:** Homeownership rate: 68.0% (2010); Median home value:
$301,000 (2006-2010 5-year est.); Median contract rent: $706 per month
(2006-2010 5-year est.); Median year structure built: 1956 (2006-2010
5-year est.).
**Transportation:** Commute to work: 73.8% car, 0.0% public transportation,
6.7% walk, 11.1% work from home (2006-2010 5-year est.); Travel time to
work: 54.0% less than 15 minutes, 13.9% 15 to 30 minutes, 20.3% 30 to 45
minutes, 9.2% 45 to 60 minutes, 2.5% 60 minutes or more (2006-2010
5-year est.)

**BRANT LAKE** (unincorporated postal area)
Zip Code: 12815
Covers a land area of 36.591 square miles and a water area of 2.975
square miles. Located at 43.69° N. Lat; 73.66° W. Long. Elevation is 794
feet. Population: 871 (2010); Density: 23.8 persons per square mile
(2010); Race: 96.8% White, 0.6% Black, 0.1% Asian, 0.0% American
Indian/Alaska Native, 0.0% Native Hawaiian/Other Pacific Islander, 2.5%
Other, 0.8% Hispanic of any race (2010); Average household size: 2.26
(2010); Median age: 49.3 (2010); Males per 100 females: 98.9 (2010);
Homeownership rate: 80.8% (2010)

**CHESTER** (town). Covers a land area of 84.190 square miles and a
water area of 2.859 square miles. Located at 43.68° N. Lat; 73.87° W.
Long.
**Population:** 3,465 (1990); 3,614 (2000); 3,355 (2010); Density: 39.9
persons per square mile (2010); Race: 97.9% White, 0.4% Black, 0.4%
Asian, 0.1% American Indian/Alaska Native, 0.0% Native Hawaiian/Other
Pacific Islander, 1.2% Other, 1.5% Hispanic of any race (2010); Average
household size: 2.28 (2010); Median age: 48.1 (2010); Males per 100
females: 99.5 (2010); Marriage status: 37.3% never married, 51.2% now
married, 3.3% widowed, 8.2% divorced (2006-2010 5-year est.); Foreign
born: 3.6% (2006-2010 5-year est.); Ancestry (includes multiple
ancestries): 28.4% Irish, 19.7% German, 16.9% English, 14.6% French,
5.8% American (2006-2010 5-year est.).

**Economy:** Employment by occupation: 7.1% management, 0.9% professional, 11.1% services, 18.7% sales, 3.6% farming, 15.8% construction, 8.9% production (2006-2010 5-year est.).
**Income:** Per capita income: $19,806 (2006-2010 5-year est.); Median household income: $44,063 (2006-2010 5-year est.); Average household income: $55,250 (2006-2010 5-year est.); Percent of households with income of $100,000 or more: 12.4% (2006-2010 5-year est.); Poverty rate: 9.6% (2006-2010 5-year est.).
**Education:** Percent of population age 25 and over with: High school diploma (including GED) or higher: 81.6% (2006-2010 5-year est.); Bachelor's degree or higher: 22.3% (2006-2010 5-year est.); Master's degree or higher: 8.7% (2006-2010 5-year est.).
**Housing:** Homeownership rate: 83.0% (2010); Median home value: $169,300 (2006-2010 5-year est.); Median contract rent: $473 per month (2006-2010 5-year est.); Median year structure built: 1970 (2006-2010 5-year est.).
**Transportation:** Commute to work: 83.4% car, 0.0% public transportation, 5.0% walk, 10.2% work from home (2006-2010 5-year est.); Travel time to work: 45.1% less than 15 minutes, 19.9% 15 to 30 minutes, 20.1% 30 to 45 minutes, 2.2% 45 to 60 minutes, 12.7% 60 minutes or more (2006-2010 5-year est.)

## CHESTERTOWN (CDP).
Covers a land area of 3.842 square miles and a water area of 0.013 square miles. Located at 43.64° N. Lat; 73.78° W. Long. Elevation is 843 feet.
**Population:** n/a (1990); n/a (2000); 677 (2010); Density: 176.2 persons per square mile (2010); Race: 97.0% White, 0.6% Black, 0.1% Asian, 0.1% American Indian/Alaska Native, 0.0% Native Hawaiian/Other Pacific Islander, 2.2% Other, 4.4% Hispanic of any race (2010); Average household size: 2.21 (2010); Median age: 42.7 (2010); Males per 100 females: 94.5 (2010); Marriage status: 18.9% never married, 56.1% now married, 9.2% widowed, 15.8% divorced (2006-2010 5-year est.); Foreign born: 0.0% (2006-2010 5-year est.); Ancestry (includes multiple ancestries): 43.5% Irish, 23.5% English, 15.1% German, 10.6% French Canadian, 2.9% Italian (2006-2010 5-year est.).
**Economy:** Employment by occupation: 6.0% management, 3.7% professional, 21.0% services, 26.3% sales, 0.0% farming, 14.7% construction, 0.0% production (2006-2010 5-year est.).
**Income:** Per capita income: $21,813 (2006-2010 5-year est.); Median household income: $26,699 (2006-2010 5-year est.); Average household income: $44,507 (2006-2010 5-year est.); Percent of households with income of $100,000 or more: 8.7% (2006-2010 5-year est.); Poverty rate: 11.3% (2006-2010 5-year est.).
**Education:** Percent of population age 25 and over with: High school diploma (including GED) or higher: 77.5% (2006-2010 5-year est.); Bachelor's degree or higher: 10.1% (2006-2010 5-year est.); Master's degree or higher: 4.0% (2006-2010 5-year est.).
**School District(s)**
North Warren Central School District (PK-12)
    2009-10 Enrollment: 559 . . . . . . . . . . . . . . . . . . . . (518) 494-3015
**Housing:** Homeownership rate: 67.7% (2010); Median home value: $158,600 (2006-2010 5-year est.); Median contract rent: $438 per month (2006-2010 5-year est.); Median year structure built: before 1940 (2006-2010 5-year est.).
**Transportation:** Commute to work: 82.8% car, 0.0% public transportation, 13.4% walk, 3.8% work from home (2006-2010 5-year est.); Travel time to work: 63.2% less than 15 minutes, 25.0% 15 to 30 minutes, 11.8% 30 to 45 minutes, 0.0% 45 to 60 minutes, 0.0% 60 minutes or more (2006-2010 5-year est.)

## DIAMOND POINT (unincorporated postal area)
Zip Code: 12824
    Covers a land area of 15.163 square miles and a water area of 0.486 square miles. Located at 43.52° N. Lat; 73.72° W. Long. Elevation is 331 feet. Population: 894 (2010); Density: 59.0 persons per square mile (2010); Race: 97.9% White, 0.0% Black, 0.4% Asian, 0.0% American Indian/Alaska Native, 0.0% Native Hawaiian/Other Pacific Islander, 1.7% Other, 1.0% Hispanic of any race (2010); Average household size: 2.32 (2010); Median age: 50.7 (2010); Males per 100 females: 101.4 (2010); Homeownership rate: 85.7% (2010)

## GLENS FALLS (city).
Covers a land area of 3.851 square miles and a water area of 0.138 square miles. Located at 43.31° N. Lat; 73.64° W. Long. Elevation is 344 feet.
**History:** The site of Glens Falls was part of the Queensbury Patent, 23,000 acres of land granted in 1759 to 23 men. The water power provided by the 60-foot falls in the Hudson River determined the location of the settlement. During the Revolution the village was destroyed by the British. In 1788, Colonel John Glen of Schenectady acquired land and built mills here. There followed a succession of industrial activities, beginning with lumbering and followed by the manufacture of lime, cement, paper and cellulose.
**Population:** 15,099 (1990); 14,354 (2000); 14,700 (2010); Density: 3,817.2 persons per square mile (2010); Race: 94.7% White, 1.8% Black, 0.6% Asian, 0.3% American Indian/Alaska Native, 0.0% Native Hawaiian/Other Pacific Islander, 2.6% Other, 2.3% Hispanic of any race (2010); Average household size: 2.22 (2010); Median age: 37.6 (2010); Males per 100 females: 94.3 (2010); Marriage status: 33.5% never married, 44.8% now married, 6.2% widowed, 15.4% divorced (2006-2010 5-year est.); Foreign born: 2.8% (2006-2010 5-year est.); Ancestry (includes multiple ancestries): 22.3% Irish, 16.3% French, 15.0% English, 11.4% Italian, 10.9% German (2006-2010 5-year est.).
**Economy:** Single-family building permits issued: 16 (2011); Multi-family building permits issued: 0 (2011); Employment by occupation: 8.8% management, 2.0% professional, 10.5% services, 19.1% sales, 3.9% farming, 9.3% construction, 6.2% production (2006-2010 5-year est.).
**Income:** Per capita income: $24,302 (2006-2010 5-year est.); Median household income: $41,950 (2006-2010 5-year est.); Average household income: $52,955 (2006-2010 5-year est.); Percent of households with income of $100,000 or more: 10.4% (2006-2010 5-year est.); Poverty rate: 14.0% (2006-2010 5-year est.).
**Education:** Percent of population age 25 and over with: High school diploma (including GED) or higher: 90.4% (2006-2010 5-year est.); Bachelor's degree or higher: 23.3% (2006-2010 5-year est.); Master's degree or higher: 8.5% (2006-2010 5-year est.).
**School District(s)**
Glens Falls City School District (PK-12)
    2009-10 Enrollment: 2,280 . . . . . . . . . . . . . . . . . . . . (518) 792-1212
Glens Falls Common School District (KG-06)
    2009-10 Enrollment: 193 . . . . . . . . . . . . . . . . . . . . (518) 792-3231
**Vocational/Technical School(s)**
Adirondack Beauty School (Private, For-profit)
    Fall 2010 Enrollment: 30 . . . . . . . . . . . . . . . . . . . . (518) 745-1646
    2011-12 Tuition: $9,600
**Housing:** Homeownership rate: 49.5% (2010); Median home value: $148,800 (2006-2010 5-year est.); Median contract rent: $578 per month (2006-2010 5-year est.); Median year structure built: before 1940 (2006-2010 5-year est.).
**Hospitals:** Glens Falls Hospital (410 beds)
**Safety:** Violent crime rate: 30.8 per 10,000 population; Property crime rate: 153.1 per 10,000 population (2010).
**Newspapers:** The Chronicle (Local news; Circulation 25,000); The Post-Star (Local news; Circulation 33,870)
**Transportation:** Commute to work: 86.5% car, 2.0% public transportation, 6.2% walk, 1.9% work from home (2006-2010 5-year est.); Travel time to work: 57.9% less than 15 minutes, 25.7% 15 to 30 minutes, 8.6% 30 to 45 minutes, 3.2% 45 to 60 minutes, 4.7% 60 minutes or more (2006-2010 5-year est.); Amtrak: train service available.
**Airports:** Floyd Bennett Memorial (general aviation)
**Additional Information Contacts**
Adirondack Regional Chamber of Commerce . . . . . . . . . . (518) 798-1761
    http://www.adirondackchamber.org
City of Glens Falls . . . . . . . . . . . . . . . . . . . . . . . . . . (518) 761-3800
    http://www.cityofglensfalls.com

## GLENS FALLS NORTH (CDP).
Covers a land area of 8.232 square miles and a water area of 0.088 square miles. Located at 43.33° N. Lat; 73.67° W. Long.
**Population:** 8,139 (1990); 8,061 (2000); 8,443 (2010); Density: 1,025.6 persons per square mile (2010); Race: 95.8% White, 1.1% Black, 1.4% Asian, 0.2% American Indian/Alaska Native, 0.1% Native Hawaiian/Other Pacific Islander, 1.4% Other, 1.9% Hispanic of any race (2010); Average household size: 2.21 (2010); Median age: 45.7 (2010); Males per 100 females: 87.8 (2010); Marriage status: 22.5% never married, 56.0% now married, 11.4% widowed, 10.1% divorced (2006-2010 5-year est.); Foreign born: 3.6% (2006-2010 5-year est.); Ancestry (includes multiple

ancestries): 29.2% Irish, 16.3% Italian, 16.1% German, 15.0% French, 12.1% English (2006-2010 5-year est.).
**Economy:** Employment by occupation: 12.8% management, 4.5% professional, 8.4% services, 15.2% sales, 2.0% farming, 6.7% construction, 5.4% production (2006-2010 5-year est.).
**Income:** Per capita income: $31,645 (2006-2010 5-year est.); Median household income: $57,473 (2006-2010 5-year est.); Average household income: $68,357 (2006-2010 5-year est.); Percent of households with income of $100,000 or more: 23.4% (2006-2010 5-year est.); Poverty rate: 9.7% (2006-2010 5-year est.).
**Education:** Percent of population age 25 and over with: High school diploma (including GED) or higher: 92.9% (2006-2010 5-year est.); Bachelor's degree or higher: 37.7% (2006-2010 5-year est.); Master's degree or higher: 18.8% (2006-2010 5-year est.).
**Housing:** Homeownership rate: 61.1% (2010); Median home value: $220,500 (2006-2010 5-year est.); Median contract rent: $686 per month (2006-2010 5-year est.); Median year structure built: 1975 (2006-2010 5-year est.).
**Transportation:** Commute to work: 93.4% car, 0.0% public transportation, 0.6% walk, 5.1% work from home (2006-2010 5-year est.); Travel time to work: 44.6% less than 15 minutes, 31.9% 15 to 30 minutes, 13.3% 30 to 45 minutes, 5.4% 45 to 60 minutes, 4.9% 60 minutes or more (2006-2010 5-year est.)

**HAGUE** (town). Covers a land area of 63.760 square miles and a water area of 15.859 square miles. Located at 43.69° N. Lat; 73.54° W. Long. Elevation is 331 feet.
**Population:** 699 (1990); 854 (2000); 699 (2010); Density: 11.0 persons per square mile (2010); Race: 99.1% White, 0.0% Black, 0.0% Asian, 0.1% American Indian/Alaska Native, 0.0% Native Hawaiian/Other Pacific Islander, 0.8% Other, 0.7% Hispanic of any race (2010); Average household size: 2.11 (2010); Median age: 57.1 (2010); Males per 100 females: 97.5 (2010); Marriage status: 15.4% never married, 64.1% now married, 14.4% widowed, 6.1% divorced (2006-2010 5-year est.); Foreign born: 3.7% (2006-2010 5-year est.); Ancestry (includes multiple ancestries): 28.3% Irish, 27.6% English, 19.7% German, 8.2% French, 8.0% Polish (2006-2010 5-year est.).
**Economy:** Employment by occupation: 27.1% management, 0.0% professional, 2.7% services, 13.0% sales, 3.8% farming, 16.2% construction, 3.2% production (2006-2010 5-year est.).
**Income:** Per capita income: $36,903 (2006-2010 5-year est.); Median household income: $60,781 (2006-2010 5-year est.); Average household income: $74,273 (2006-2010 5-year est.); Percent of households with income of $100,000 or more: 24.2% (2006-2010 5-year est.); Poverty rate: 5.6% (2006-2010 5-year est.).
**Education:** Percent of population age 25 and over with: High school diploma (including GED) or higher: 88.4% (2006-2010 5-year est.); Bachelor's degree or higher: 38.3% (2006-2010 5-year est.); Master's degree or higher: 16.8% (2006-2010 5-year est.).
**Housing:** Homeownership rate: 90.1% (2010); Median home value: $186,600 (2006-2010 5-year est.); Median contract rent: $375 per month (2006-2010 5-year est.); Median year structure built: 1966 (2006-2010 5-year est.).
**Transportation:** Commute to work: 85.0% car, 0.0% public transportation, 3.3% walk, 11.8% work from home (2006-2010 5-year est.); Travel time to work: 33.7% less than 15 minutes, 31.5% 15 to 30 minutes, 21.1% 30 to 45 minutes, 7.4% 45 to 60 minutes, 6.3% 60 minutes or more (2006-2010 5-year est.)
**Additional Information Contacts**
Hague on Lake George Chamber of Commerce . . . . . . . . . (518) 543-6441
  http://www.visithague.com

**HORICON** (town). Covers a land area of 65.766 square miles and a water area of 6.099 square miles. Located at 43.71° N. Lat; 73.70° W. Long.
**Population:** 1,269 (1990); 1,479 (2000); 1,389 (2010); Density: 21.1 persons per square mile (2010); Race: 97.1% White, 0.4% Black, 0.1% Asian, 0.0% American Indian/Alaska Native, 0.0% Native Hawaiian/Other Pacific Islander, 2.4% Other, 0.8% Hispanic of any race (2010); Average household size: 2.21 (2010); Median age: 50.3 (2010); Males per 100 females: 100.4 (2010); Marriage status: 20.2% never married, 64.0% now married, 9.1% widowed, 6.7% divorced (2006-2010 5-year est.); Foreign born: 3.9% (2006-2010 5-year est.); Ancestry (includes multiple ancestries): 25.2% Irish, 18.7% German, 14.9% English, 13.3% Italian, 11.1% American (2006-2010 5-year est.).

**Economy:** Employment by occupation: 6.7% management, 0.3% professional, 12.7% services, 18.2% sales, 1.6% farming, 20.8% construction, 11.9% production (2006-2010 5-year est.).
**Income:** Per capita income: $30,892 (2006-2010 5-year est.); Median household income: $50,524 (2006-2010 5-year est.); Average household income: $63,426 (2006-2010 5-year est.); Percent of households with income of $100,000 or more: 17.2% (2006-2010 5-year est.); Poverty rate: 8.7% (2006-2010 5-year est.).
**Education:** Percent of population age 25 and over with: High school diploma (including GED) or higher: 88.8% (2006-2010 5-year est.); Bachelor's degree or higher: 28.0% (2006-2010 5-year est.); Master's degree or higher: 14.9% (2006-2010 5-year est.).
**Housing:** Homeownership rate: 85.4% (2010); Median home value: $210,700 (2006-2010 5-year est.); Median contract rent: $523 per month (2006-2010 5-year est.); Median year structure built: 1969 (2006-2010 5-year est.).
**Transportation:** Commute to work: 92.2% car, 0.0% public transportation, 2.9% walk, 4.4% work from home (2006-2010 5-year est.); Travel time to work: 33.6% less than 15 minutes, 28.6% 15 to 30 minutes, 18.4% 30 to 45 minutes, 9.1% 45 to 60 minutes, 10.3% 60 minutes or more (2006-2010 5-year est.)

**JOHNSBURG** (town). Covers a land area of 203.976 square miles and a water area of 2.767 square miles. Located at 43.65° N. Lat; 74.06° W. Long. Elevation is 1,283 feet.
**Population:** 2,352 (1990); 2,450 (2000); 2,395 (2010); Density: 11.7 persons per square mile (2010); Race: 98.0% White, 0.3% Black, 0.3% Asian, 0.3% American Indian/Alaska Native, 0.0% Native Hawaiian/Other Pacific Islander, 1.1% Other, 1.4% Hispanic of any race (2010); Average household size: 2.32 (2010); Median age: 46.8 (2010); Males per 100 females: 96.2 (2010); Marriage status: 21.3% never married, 51.8% now married, 13.6% widowed, 13.4% divorced (2006-2010 5-year est.); Foreign born: 1.3% (2006-2010 5-year est.); Ancestry (includes multiple ancestries): 19.2% Irish, 15.7% French, 15.4% German, 15.0% English, 9.1% Italian (2006-2010 5-year est.).
**Economy:** Employment by occupation: 0.8% management, 1.7% professional, 7.4% services, 16.7% sales, 7.2% farming, 29.8% construction, 9.2% production (2006-2010 5-year est.).
**Income:** Per capita income: $22,557 (2006-2010 5-year est.); Median household income: $40,391 (2006-2010 5-year est.); Average household income: $47,583 (2006-2010 5-year est.); Percent of households with income of $100,000 or more: 6.5% (2006-2010 5-year est.); Poverty rate: 10.5% (2006-2010 5-year est.).
**Education:** Percent of population age 25 and over with: High school diploma (including GED) or higher: 78.0% (2006-2010 5-year est.); Bachelor's degree or higher: 23.5% (2006-2010 5-year est.); Master's degree or higher: 10.9% (2006-2010 5-year est.).
**Housing:** Homeownership rate: 76.6% (2010); Median home value: $160,300 (2006-2010 5-year est.); Median contract rent: $579 per month (2006-2010 5-year est.); Median year structure built: 1964 (2006-2010 5-year est.).
**Transportation:** Commute to work: 93.1% car, 0.0% public transportation, 3.5% walk, 2.4% work from home (2006-2010 5-year est.); Travel time to work: 43.0% less than 15 minutes, 21.3% 15 to 30 minutes, 16.4% 30 to 45 minutes, 2.7% 45 to 60 minutes, 16.4% 60 minutes or more (2006-2010 5-year est.)

**KATTSKILL BAY** (unincorporated postal area)
Zip Code: 12844
  Covers a land area of 2.737 square miles and a water area of 0 square miles. Located at 43.48° N. Lat; 73.62° W. Long. Population: 199 (2010); Density: 72.7 persons per square mile (2010); Race: 97.0% White, 0.0% Black, 1.0% Asian, 0.0% American Indian/Alaska Native, 0.0% Native Hawaiian/Other Pacific Islander, 2.0% Other, 0.5% Hispanic of any race (2010); Average household size: 2.11 (2010); Median age: 53.9 (2010); Males per 100 females: 103.1 (2010); Homeownership rate: 80.4% (2010)

**LAKE GEORGE** (village). County seat. Covers a land area of 0.586 square miles and a water area of 0 square miles. Located at 43.42° N. Lat; 73.71° W. Long. Elevation is 344 feet.
**Population:** 969 (1990); 985 (2000); 906 (2010); Density: 1,546.0 persons per square mile (2010); Race: 96.6% White, 0.4% Black, 1.1% Asian, 0.1% American Indian/Alaska Native, 0.0% Native Hawaiian/Other Pacific Islander, 1.8% Other, 2.0% Hispanic of any race (2010); Average

household size: 2.01 (2010); Median age: 46.6 (2010); Males per 100 females: 95.7 (2010); Marriage status: 31.0% never married, 48.1% now married, 5.8% widowed, 15.1% divorced (2006-2010 5-year est.); Foreign born: 11.2% (2006-2010 5-year est.); Ancestry (includes multiple ancestries): 22.1% Irish, 16.2% Italian, 15.2% English, 10.2% Polish, 9.6% American (2006-2010 5-year est.).

**Economy:** Employment by occupation: 20.6% management, 1.2% professional, 11.4% services, 15.3% sales, 5.5% farming, 6.1% construction, 4.3% production (2006-2010 5-year est.).

**Income:** Per capita income: $31,583 (2006-2010 5-year est.); Median household income: $47,643 (2006-2010 5-year est.); Average household income: $58,917 (2006-2010 5-year est.); Percent of households with income of $100,000 or more: 15.4% (2006-2010 5-year est.); Poverty rate: 16.3% (2006-2010 5-year est.).

**Education:** Percent of population age 25 and over with: High school diploma (including GED) or higher: 87.3% (2006-2010 5-year est.); Bachelor's degree or higher: 32.5% (2006-2010 5-year est.); Master's degree or higher: 15.3% (2006-2010 5-year est.).

**School District(s)**

Lake George Central School District (KG-12)

    2009-10 Enrollment: 1,000 . . . . . . . . . . . . . . . . . . . (518) 668-5456

**Housing:** Homeownership rate: 46.7% (2010); Median home value: $222,900 (2006-2010 5-year est.); Median contract rent: $646 per month (2006-2010 5-year est.); Median year structure built: 1952 (2006-2010 5-year est.).

**Transportation:** Commute to work: 76.1% car, 0.5% public transportation, 14.2% walk, 8.7% work from home (2006-2010 5-year est.); Travel time to work: 37.1% less than 15 minutes, 38.3% 15 to 30 minutes, 14.0% 30 to 45 minutes, 9.1% 45 to 60 minutes, 1.6% 60 minutes or more (2006-2010 5-year est.)

**Additional Information Contacts**

Lake George Regional Chamber of Commerce . . . . . . . . . (518) 668-5755

    http://www.lakegeorgechamber.com

**LAKE GEORGE** (town). Covers a land area of 30.068 square miles and a water area of 2.549 square miles. Located at 43.43° N. Lat; 73.72° W. Long. Elevation is 344 feet.

**History:** Vestiges of Fort William Henry, built by Sir William Johnson, and Fort George are in the village. Incorporated 1903.

**Population:** 3,211 (1990); 3,578 (2000); 3,515 (2010); Density: 116.9 persons per square mile (2010); Race: 96.5% White, 0.6% Black, 0.7% Asian, 0.5% American Indian/Alaska Native, 0.0% Native Hawaiian/Other Pacific Islander, 1.7% Other, 1.5% Hispanic of any race (2010); Average household size: 2.25 (2010); Median age: 46.7 (2010); Males per 100 females: 101.9 (2010); Marriage status: 22.8% never married, 58.6% now married, 7.4% widowed, 11.2% divorced (2006-2010 5-year est.); Foreign born: 5.4% (2006-2010 5-year est.); Ancestry (includes multiple ancestries): 20.2% Irish, 17.5% English, 14.1% Italian, 13.0% German, 8.1% American (2006-2010 5-year est.).

**Economy:** Employment by occupation: 13.4% management, 3.1% professional, 8.8% services, 17.6% sales, 3.9% farming, 10.7% construction, 6.9% production (2006-2010 5-year est.).

**Income:** Per capita income: $34,350 (2006-2010 5-year est.); Median household income: $53,452 (2006-2010 5-year est.); Average household income: $70,950 (2006-2010 5-year est.); Percent of households with income of $100,000 or more: 21.9% (2006-2010 5-year est.); Poverty rate: 6.3% (2006-2010 5-year est.).

**Education:** Percent of population age 25 and over with: High school diploma (including GED) or higher: 89.5% (2006-2010 5-year est.); Bachelor's degree or higher: 38.2% (2006-2010 5-year est.); Master's degree or higher: 16.9% (2006-2010 5-year est.).

**School District(s)**

Lake George Central School District (KG-12)

    2009-10 Enrollment: 1,000 . . . . . . . . . . . . . . . . . . . (518) 668-5456

**Housing:** Homeownership rate: 67.5% (2010); Median home value: $236,300 (2006-2010 5-year est.); Median contract rent: $617 per month (2006-2010 5-year est.); Median year structure built: 1971 (2006-2010 5-year est.).

**Transportation:** Commute to work: 87.8% car, 0.7% public transportation, 6.6% walk, 4.1% work from home (2006-2010 5-year est.); Travel time to work: 37.6% less than 15 minutes, 44.2% 15 to 30 minutes, 7.8% 30 to 45 minutes, 5.2% 45 to 60 minutes, 5.2% 60 minutes or more (2006-2010 5-year est.)

**LAKE LUZERNE** (town). Covers a land area of 52.518 square miles and a water area of 1.539 square miles. Located at 43.34° N. Lat; 73.78° W. Long. Elevation is 564 feet.

**History:** Also called Luzerne.

**Population:** 2,816 (1990); 3,219 (2000); 3,347 (2010); Density: 63.7 persons per square mile (2010); Race: 97.4% White, 0.1% Black, 0.7% Asian, 0.2% American Indian/Alaska Native, 0.0% Native Hawaiian/Other Pacific Islander, 1.6% Other, 1.9% Hispanic of any race (2010); Average household size: 2.47 (2010); Median age: 44.1 (2010); Males per 100 females: 99.1 (2010); Marriage status: 30.6% never married, 55.7% now married, 3.8% widowed, 9.9% divorced (2006-2010 5-year est.); Foreign born: 1.6% (2006-2010 5-year est.); Ancestry (includes multiple ancestries): 22.0% Irish, 19.5% Italian, 15.4% German, 12.2% English, 12.2% French (2006-2010 5-year est.).

**Economy:** Employment by occupation: 6.7% management, 2.2% professional, 15.5% services, 19.4% sales, 5.7% farming, 9.9% construction, 10.9% production (2006-2010 5-year est.).

**Income:** Per capita income: $25,720 (2006-2010 5-year est.); Median household income: $56,696 (2006-2010 5-year est.); Average household income: $64,903 (2006-2010 5-year est.); Percent of households with income of $100,000 or more: 14.5% (2006-2010 5-year est.); Poverty rate: 7.1% (2006-2010 5-year est.).

**Education:** Percent of population age 25 and over with: High school diploma (including GED) or higher: 87.3% (2006-2010 5-year est.); Bachelor's degree or higher: 15.4% (2006-2010 5-year est.); Master's degree or higher: 6.0% (2006-2010 5-year est.).

**School District(s)**

Hadley-Luzerne Central School District (PK-12)

    2009-10 Enrollment: 921 . . . . . . . . . . . . . . . . . . . . (518) 696-2112

**Housing:** Homeownership rate: 80.3% (2010); Median home value: $163,400 (2006-2010 5-year est.); Median contract rent: $542 per month (2006-2010 5-year est.); Median year structure built: 1974 (2006-2010 5-year est.).

**Transportation:** Commute to work: 92.9% car, 0.0% public transportation, 1.2% walk, 4.1% work from home (2006-2010 5-year est.); Travel time to work: 21.5% less than 15 minutes, 39.2% 15 to 30 minutes, 21.9% 30 to 45 minutes, 8.3% 45 to 60 minutes, 9.0% 60 minutes or more (2006-2010 5-year est.)

**Additional Information Contacts**

Lake Luzerne Regional Chamber of Commerce . . . . . . . . . (518) 696-3500

    http://www.lakeluzernechamber.org

**LAKE LUZERNE** (CDP). Covers a land area of 2.508 square miles and a water area of 0.368 square miles. Located at 43.32° N. Lat; 73.83° W. Long. Elevation is 564 feet.

**Population:** n/a (1990); n/a (2000); 1,227 (2010); Density: 489.2 persons per square mile (2010); Race: 97.7% White, 0.2% Black, 0.7% Asian, 0.2% American Indian/Alaska Native, 0.0% Native Hawaiian/Other Pacific Islander, 1.2% Other, 1.5% Hispanic of any race (2010); Average household size: 2.42 (2010); Median age: 41.5 (2010); Males per 100 females: 90.8 (2010); Marriage status: 28.2% never married, 62.6% now married, 3.1% widowed, 6.1% divorced (2006-2010 5-year est.); Foreign born: 0.0% (2006-2010 5-year est.); Ancestry (includes multiple ancestries): 27.1% Italian, 23.9% Irish, 23.5% English, 23.0% German, 11.6% French (2006-2010 5-year est.).

**Economy:** Employment by occupation: 6.9% management, 4.9% professional, 19.1% services, 8.7% sales, 9.4% farming, 8.5% construction, 1.8% production (2006-2010 5-year est.).

**Income:** Per capita income: $25,396 (2006-2010 5-year est.); Median household income: $54,625 (2006-2010 5-year est.); Average household income: $68,384 (2006-2010 5-year est.); Percent of households with income of $100,000 or more: 11.4% (2006-2010 5-year est.); Poverty rate: 1.9% (2006-2010 5-year est.).

**Education:** Percent of population age 25 and over with: High school diploma (including GED) or higher: 90.6% (2006-2010 5-year est.); Bachelor's degree or higher: 19.2% (2006-2010 5-year est.); Master's degree or higher: 2.5% (2006-2010 5-year est.).

**School District(s)**

Hadley-Luzerne Central School District (PK-12)

    2009-10 Enrollment: 921 . . . . . . . . . . . . . . . . . . . . (518) 696-2112

**Housing:** Homeownership rate: 71.9% (2010); Median home value: $146,600 (2006-2010 5-year est.); Median contract rent: $588 per month (2006-2010 5-year est.); Median year structure built: 1956 (2006-2010 5-year est.).

**Transportation:** Commute to work: 85.0% car, 0.0% public transportation, 4.0% walk, 7.3% work from home (2006-2010 5-year est.); Travel time to work: 20.4% less than 15 minutes, 24.7% 15 to 30 minutes, 33.5% 30 to 45 minutes, 13.7% 45 to 60 minutes, 7.6% 60 minutes or more (2006-2010 5-year est.)

## NORTH CREEK (CDP).
Covers a land area of 1.594 square miles and a water area of 0.050 square miles. Located at 43.69° N. Lat; 73.98° W. Long. Elevation is 1,030 feet.
**Population:** n/a (1990); n/a (2000); 616 (2010); Density: 386.3 persons per square mile (2010); Race: 97.4% White, 0.3% Black, 0.6% Asian, 0.2% American Indian/Alaska Native, 0.0% Native Hawaiian/Other Pacific Islander, 1.5% Other, 2.3% Hispanic of any race (2010); Average household size: 2.18 (2010); Median age: 46.3 (2010); Males per 100 females: 96.8 (2010); Marriage status: 30.0% never married, 43.4% now married, 17.7% widowed, 8.9% divorced (2006-2010 5-year est.); Foreign born: 1.6% (2006-2010 5-year est.); Ancestry (includes multiple ancestries): 22.9% French, 22.1% English, 20.8% German, 7.3% Dutch, 7.0% Scottish (2006-2010 5-year est.).
**Economy:** Employment by occupation: 6.4% management, 0.0% professional, 0.0% services, 35.2% sales, 6.4% farming, 6.4% construction, 0.0% production (2006-2010 5-year est.).
**Income:** Per capita income: $15,679 (2006-2010 5-year est.); Median household income: $26,593 (2006-2010 5-year est.); Average household income: $28,488 (2006-2010 5-year est.); Percent of households with income of $100,000 or more: 0.0% (2006-2010 5-year est.); Poverty rate: 19.8% (2006-2010 5-year est.).
**Education:** Percent of population age 25 and over with: High school diploma (including GED) or higher: 68.0% (2006-2010 5-year est.); Bachelor's degree or higher: 12.7% (2006-2010 5-year est.); Master's degree or higher: 7.7% (2006-2010 5-year est.).
### School District(s)
Johnsburg Central School District (KG-12)
   2009-10 Enrollment: 342 . . . . . . . . . . . . . . . . . . . . . . . . (518) 251-2814
**Housing:** Homeownership rate: 56.9% (2010); Median home value: $151,400 (2006-2010 5-year est.); Median contract rent: $296 per month (2006-2010 5-year est.); Median year structure built: 1980 (2006-2010 5-year est.).
**Transportation:** Commute to work: 93.6% car, 0.0% public transportation, 6.4% walk, 0.0% work from home (2006-2010 5-year est.); Travel time to work: 65.6% less than 15 minutes, 6.4% 15 to 30 minutes, 21.6% 30 to 45 minutes, 0.0% 45 to 60 minutes, 6.4% 60 minutes or more (2006-2010 5-year est.).

## NORTH RIVER (unincorporated postal area)
Zip Code: 12856
   Covers a land area of 63.591 square miles and a water area of 1.072 square miles. Located at 43.66° N. Lat; 74.14° W. Long. Elevation is 1,073 feet. Population: 187 (2010); Density: 2.9 persons per square mile (2010); Race: 100.0% White, 0.0% Black, 0.0% Asian, 0.0% American Indian/Alaska Native, 0.0% Native Hawaiian/Other Pacific Islander, 0.0% Other, 1.1% Hispanic of any race (2010); Average household size: 2.10 (2010); Median age: 52.3 (2010); Males per 100 females: 94.8 (2010); Homeownership rate: 86.5% (2010)

## POTTERSVILLE (CDP).
Covers a land area of 2.278 square miles and a water area of 0.047 square miles. Located at 43.73° N. Lat; 73.82° W. Long. Elevation is 846 feet.
**Population:** n/a (1990); n/a (2000); 424 (2010); Density: 186.1 persons per square mile (2010); Race: 97.9% White, 0.2% Black, 0.9% Asian, 0.0% American Indian/Alaska Native, 0.0% Native Hawaiian/Other Pacific Islander, 1.0% Other, 0.7% Hispanic of any race (2010); Average household size: 2.49 (2010); Median age: 39.2 (2010); Males per 100 females: 91.9 (2010); Marriage status: 85.8% never married, 14.2% now married, 0.0% widowed, 0.0% divorced (2006-2010 5-year est.); Foreign born: 12.3% (2006-2010 5-year est.); Ancestry (includes multiple ancestries): 25.5% Irish, 22.3% German, 14.2% English, 10.2% American, 6.5% Italian (2006-2010 5-year est.).
**Economy:** Employment by occupation: 0.0% management, 0.0% professional, 0.0% services, 0.0% sales, 32.6% farming, 34.8% construction, 34.8% production (2006-2010 5-year est.).
**Income:** Per capita income: $6,372 (2006-2010 5-year est.); Median household income: $29,679 (2006-2010 5-year est.); Average household income: $40,704 (2006-2010 5-year est.); Percent of households with

income of $100,000 or more: 0.0% (2006-2010 5-year est.); Poverty rate: 25.9% (2006-2010 5-year est.).
**Education:** Percent of population age 25 and over with: High school diploma (including GED) or higher: 93.8% (2006-2010 5-year est.); Bachelor's degree or higher: 19.9% (2006-2010 5-year est.); Master's degree or higher: 0.0% (2006-2010 5-year est.).
### Two-year College(s)
Word of Life Bible Institute (Private, Not-for-profit, Interdenominational)
   Fall 2010 Enrollment: 597 . . . . . . . . . . . . . . . . . . . . . . . (518) 494-4723
   2011-12 Tuition: In-state $7,940; Out-of-state $7,940
**Housing:** Homeownership rate: 75.9% (2010); Median home value: $98,600 (2006-2010 5-year est.); Median contract rent: n/a per month (2006-2010 5-year est.); Median year structure built: 1942 (2006-2010 5-year est.).
**Transportation:** Commute to work: 89.5% car, 0.0% public transportation, 10.5% walk, 0.0% work from home (2006-2010 5-year est.); Travel time to work: 79.8% less than 15 minutes, 12.9% 15 to 30 minutes, 0.0% 30 to 45 minutes, 0.0% 45 to 60 minutes, 7.3% 60 minutes or more (2006-2010 5-year est.).

## QUEENSBURY (town).
Covers a land area of 62.829 square miles and a water area of 2.008 square miles. Located at 43.36° N. Lat; 73.67° W. Long. Elevation is 315 feet.
**Population:** 22,554 (1990); 25,441 (2000); 27,901 (2010); Density: 444.1 persons per square mile (2010); Race: 96.6% White, 0.9% Black, 0.9% Asian, 0.2% American Indian/Alaska Native, 0.0% Native Hawaiian/Other Pacific Islander, 1.4% Other, 1.7% Hispanic of any race (2010); Average household size: 2.39 (2010); Median age: 44.7 (2010); Males per 100 females: 92.6 (2010); Marriage status: 22.6% never married, 59.1% now married, 8.4% widowed, 10.0% divorced (2006-2010 5-year est.); Foreign born: 2.9% (2006-2010 5-year est.); Ancestry (includes multiple ancestries): 26.8% Irish, 15.9% Italian, 14.5% German, 14.4% English, 13.0% French (2006-2010 5-year est.).
**Economy:** Unemployment rate: 8.2% (February 2012); Total civilian labor force: 15,286 (February 2012); Single-family building permits issued: 34 (2011); Multi-family building permits issued: 8 (2011); Employment by occupation: 11.2% management, 3.1% professional, 8.3% services, 16.6% sales, 3.6% farming, 7.5% construction, 5.0% production (2006-2010 5-year est.).
**Income:** Per capita income: $30,450 (2006-2010 5-year est.); Median household income: $61,009 (2006-2010 5-year est.); Average household income: $73,641 (2006-2010 5-year est.); Percent of households with income of $100,000 or more: 25.1% (2006-2010 5-year est.); Poverty rate: 8.3% (2006-2010 5-year est.).
**Education:** Percent of population age 25 and over with: High school diploma (including GED) or higher: 92.3% (2006-2010 5-year est.); Bachelor's degree or higher: 32.0% (2006-2010 5-year est.); Master's degree or higher: 15.1% (2006-2010 5-year est.).
### School District(s)
Queensbury Union Free School District (KG-12)
   2009-10 Enrollment: 3,692 . . . . . . . . . . . . . . . . . . . . . (518) 824-5602
### Two-year College(s)
Adirondack Community College (Public)
   Fall 2010 Enrollment: 2,849. . . . . . . . . . . . . . . . . . . . . (518) 743-2200
   2011-12 Tuition: In-state $3,828; Out-of-state $7,384
**Housing:** Homeownership rate: 73.4% (2010); Median home value: $214,300 (2006-2010 5-year est.); Median contract rent: $698 per month (2006-2010 5-year est.); Median year structure built: 1978 (2006-2010 5-year est.).
**Transportation:** Commute to work: 94.6% car, 0.1% public transportation, 0.5% walk, 3.5% work from home (2006-2010 5-year est.); Travel time to work: 45.1% less than 15 minutes, 34.7% 15 to 30 minutes, 10.7% 30 to 45 minutes, 4.8% 45 to 60 minutes, 4.7% 60 minutes or more (2006-2010 5-year est.)
**Additional Information Contacts**
Town of Queensbury . . . . . . . . . . . . . . . . . . . . . . . . . . . (518) 761-8234
   http://www.queensbury.net

## RIPARIUS (unincorporated postal area)
Zip Code: 12862
   Covers a land area of 2.328 square miles and a water area of 0.200 square miles. Located at 43.68° N. Lat; 73.91° W. Long. Elevation is 883 feet. Population: 17 (2010); Density: 7.3 persons per square mile (2010); Race: 100.0% White, 0.0% Black, 0.0% Asian, 0.0% American Indian/Alaska Native, 0.0% Native Hawaiian/Other Pacific Islander, 0.0%

Other, 0.0% Hispanic of any race (2010); Average household size: 2.13 (2010); Median age: 51.5 (2010); Males per 100 females: 142.9 (2010); Homeownership rate: 87.5% (2010)

## SILVER BAY (unincorporated postal area)
Zip Code: 12874

Covers a land area of 21.418 square miles and a water area of 0.307 square miles. Located at 43.69° N. Lat; 73.54° W. Long. Elevation is 348 feet. Population: 142 (2010); Density: 6.6 persons per square mile (2010); Race: 97.9% White, 0.0% Black, 0.0% Asian, 0.0% American Indian/Alaska Native, 0.0% Native Hawaiian/Other Pacific Islander, 2.1% Other, 0.0% Hispanic of any race (2010); Average household size: 1.84 (2010); Median age: 62.8 (2010); Males per 100 females: 105.8 (2010); Homeownership rate: 91.0% (2010)

## STONY CREEK (town). Covers a land area of 82.162 square miles and a water area of 1.042 square miles. Located at 43.41° N. Lat; 74.02° W. Long. Elevation is 827 feet.
Population: 670 (1990); 743 (2000); 767 (2010); Density: 9.3 persons per square mile (2010); Race: 95.4% White, 0.7% Black, 0.5% Asian, 0.3% American Indian/Alaska Native, 0.0% Native Hawaiian/Other Pacific Islander, 3.1% Other, 3.0% Hispanic of any race (2010); Average household size: 2.30 (2010); Median age: 48.4 (2010); Males per 100 females: 102.9 (2010); Marriage status: 22.8% never married, 57.8% now married, 7.0% widowed, 12.3% divorced (2006-2010 5-year est.); Foreign born: 1.6% (2006-2010 5-year est.); Ancestry (includes multiple ancestries): 15.8% Irish, 15.5% German, 13.6% American, 9.9% English, 9.3% French (2006-2010 5-year est.).
Economy: Employment by occupation: 5.7% management, 2.8% professional, 13.9% services, 16.3% sales, 3.3% farming, 12.2% construction, 7.6% production (2006-2010 5-year est.).
Income: Per capita income: $23,663 (2006-2010 5-year est.); Median household income: $40,114 (2006-2010 5-year est.); Average household income: $53,271 (2006-2010 5-year est.); Percent of households with income of $100,000 or more: 10.9% (2006-2010 5-year est.); Poverty rate: 9.2% (2006-2010 5-year est.).
Education: Percent of population age 25 and over with: High school diploma (including GED) or higher: 86.9% (2006-2010 5-year est.); Bachelor's degree or higher: 23.4% (2006-2010 5-year est.); Master's degree or higher: 8.5% (2006-2010 5-year est.).
Housing: Homeownership rate: 81.0% (2010); Median home value: $118,500 (2006-2010 5-year est.); Median contract rent: $389 per month (2006-2010 5-year est.); Median year structure built: 1961 (2006-2010 5-year est.).
Transportation: Commute to work: 96.9% car, 0.0% public transportation, 0.0% walk, 2.4% work from home (2006-2010 5-year est.); Travel time to work: 14.2% less than 15 minutes, 23.6% 15 to 30 minutes, 29.4% 30 to 45 minutes, 18.4% 45 to 60 minutes, 14.4% 60 minutes or more (2006-2010 5-year est.)

## THURMAN (town). Covers a land area of 91.098 square miles and a water area of 1.678 square miles. Located at 43.49° N. Lat; 73.98° W. Long. Elevation is 1,316 feet.
Population: 1,045 (1990); 1,199 (2000); 1,219 (2010); Density: 13.4 persons per square mile (2010); Race: 97.0% White, 0.2% Black, 0.2% Asian, 0.5% American Indian/Alaska Native, 0.0% Native Hawaiian/Other Pacific Islander, 2.1% Other, 0.5% Hispanic of any race (2010); Average household size: 2.45 (2010); Median age: 46.2 (2010); Males per 100 females: 104.9 (2010); Marriage status: 14.7% never married, 70.7% now married, 6.3% widowed, 8.3% divorced (2006-2010 5-year est.); Foreign born: 2.8% (2006-2010 5-year est.); Ancestry (includes multiple ancestries): 18.8% English, 13.5% Irish, 10.9% French, 9.9% German, 8.2% Italian (2006-2010 5-year est.).
Economy: Employment by occupation: 6.4% management, 4.7% professional, 12.5% services, 12.5% sales, 2.1% farming, 22.8% construction, 9.2% production (2006-2010 5-year est.).
Income: Per capita income: $30,388 (2006-2010 5-year est.); Median household income: $48,472 (2006-2010 5-year est.); Average household income: $69,188 (2006-2010 5-year est.); Percent of households with income of $100,000 or more: 17.0% (2006-2010 5-year est.); Poverty rate: 9.1% (2006-2010 5-year est.).
Education: Percent of population age 25 and over with: High school diploma (including GED) or higher: 80.3% (2006-2010 5-year est.); Bachelor's degree or higher: 20.7% (2006-2010 5-year est.); Master's degree or higher: 11.4% (2006-2010 5-year est.).

Housing: Homeownership rate: 88.3% (2010); Median home value: $136,500 (2006-2010 5-year est.); Median contract rent: $535 per month (2006-2010 5-year est.); Median year structure built: 1976 (2006-2010 5-year est.).
Transportation: Commute to work: 95.4% car, 0.0% public transportation, 0.8% walk, 2.9% work from home (2006-2010 5-year est.); Travel time to work: 16.8% less than 15 minutes, 35.6% 15 to 30 minutes, 28.2% 30 to 45 minutes, 11.0% 45 to 60 minutes, 8.4% 60 minutes or more (2006-2010 5-year est.)

## WARRENSBURG (town). Aka Warrenburg Center. Covers a land area of 63.460 square miles and a water area of 1.338 square miles. Located at 43.52° N. Lat; 73.80° W. Long. Elevation is 745 feet.
Population: 4,174 (1990); 4,255 (2000); 4,094 (2010); Density: 64.5 persons per square mile (2010); Race: 97.6% White, 0.3% Black, 0.6% Asian, 0.2% American Indian/Alaska Native, 0.0% Native Hawaiian/Other Pacific Islander, 1.3% Other, 1.9% Hispanic of any race (2010); Average household size: 2.34 (2010); Median age: 43.9 (2010); Males per 100 females: 95.9 (2010); Marriage status: 21.0% never married, 56.4% now married, 6.7% widowed, 15.8% divorced (2006-2010 5-year est.); Foreign born: 1.6% (2006-2010 5-year est.); Ancestry (includes multiple ancestries): 17.4% Irish, 14.5% English, 13.1% German, 10.6% French, 9.3% Italian (2006-2010 5-year est.).
Economy: Employment by occupation: 5.0% management, 2.6% professional, 22.7% services, 15.8% sales, 5.9% farming, 15.8% construction, 9.7% production (2006-2010 5-year est.).
Income: Per capita income: $23,376 (2006-2010 5-year est.); Median household income: $38,146 (2006-2010 5-year est.); Average household income: $53,242 (2006-2010 5-year est.); Percent of households with income of $100,000 or more: 6.8% (2006-2010 5-year est.); Poverty rate: 16.4% (2006-2010 5-year est.).
Education: Percent of population age 25 and over with: High school diploma (including GED) or higher: 85.3% (2006-2010 5-year est.); Bachelor's degree or higher: 11.6% (2006-2010 5-year est.); Master's degree or higher: 5.0% (2006-2010 5-year est.).

### School District(s)
Warrensburg Central School District (PK-12)
    2009-10 Enrollment: 857 . . . . . . . . . . . . . . . . . . . . . (518) 623-2861
Housing: Homeownership rate: 69.6% (2010); Median home value: $125,700 (2006-2010 5-year est.); Median contract rent: $593 per month (2006-2010 5-year est.); Median year structure built: 1966 (2006-2010 5-year est.).
Transportation: Commute to work: 88.8% car, 0.8% public transportation, 6.5% walk, 2.9% work from home (2006-2010 5-year est.); Travel time to work: 34.3% less than 15 minutes, 37.4% 15 to 30 minutes, 16.8% 30 to 45 minutes, 5.0% 45 to 60 minutes, 6.4% 60 minutes or more (2006-2010 5-year est.)
**Additional Information Contacts**
Warrensburg Chamber of Commerce . . . . . . . . . . . . . . . . (518) 623-2161
    http://www.warrensburgchamber.com

## WARRENSBURG (CDP). Covers a land area of 11.028 square miles and a water area of 0.318 square miles. Located at 43.52° N. Lat; 73.77° W. Long. Elevation is 745 feet.
Population: 3,280 (1990); 3,208 (2000); 3,103 (2010); Density: 281.4 persons per square mile (2010); Race: 97.6% White, 0.3% Black, 0.6% Asian, 0.1% American Indian/Alaska Native, 0.0% Native Hawaiian/Other Pacific Islander, 1.4% Other, 2.3% Hispanic of any race (2010); Average household size: 2.36 (2010); Median age: 42.5 (2010); Males per 100 females: 92.1 (2010); Marriage status: 23.9% never married, 53.2% now married, 7.6% widowed, 15.4% divorced (2006-2010 5-year est.); Foreign born: 2.1% (2006-2010 5-year est.); Ancestry (includes multiple ancestries): 18.5% Irish, 15.6% English, 11.9% French, 11.8% German, 6.5% Italian (2006-2010 5-year est.).
Economy: Employment by occupation: 5.8% management, 1.9% professional, 20.8% services, 19.5% sales, 6.0% farming, 13.2% construction, 9.2% production (2006-2010 5-year est.).
Income: Per capita income: $20,129 (2006-2010 5-year est.); Median household income: $37,901 (2006-2010 5-year est.); Average household income: $46,026 (2006-2010 5-year est.); Percent of households with income of $100,000 or more: 6.3% (2006-2010 5-year est.); Poverty rate: 20.6% (2006-2010 5-year est.).
Education: Percent of population age 25 and over with: High school diploma (including GED) or higher: 85.4% (2006-2010 5-year est.);

Bachelor's degree or higher: 10.1% (2006-2010 5-year est.); Master's degree or higher: 4.8% (2006-2010 5-year est.).

**School District(s)**

Warrensburg Central School District (PK-12)

   2009-10 Enrollment: 857 . . . . . . . . . . . . . . . . . . . . . . . . . . . (518) 623-2861

**Housing:** Homeownership rate: 65.1% (2010); Median home value: $134,600 (2006-2010 5-year est.); Median contract rent: $592 per month (2006-2010 5-year est.); Median year structure built: 1955 (2006-2010 5-year est.).

**Transportation:** Commute to work: 86.2% car, 1.1% public transportation, 8.1% walk, 4.0% work from home (2006-2010 5-year est.); Travel time to work: 39.4% less than 15 minutes, 31.6% 15 to 30 minutes, 18.2% 30 to 45 minutes, 7.1% 45 to 60 minutes, 3.8% 60 minutes or more (2006-2010 5-year est.)

## WEST GLENS FALLS (CDP).

Covers a land area of 4.681 square miles and a water area of 0.130 square miles. Located at 43.30° N. Lat; 73.68° W. Long. Elevation is 381 feet.

**Population:** 5,939 (1990); 6,721 (2000); 7,071 (2010); Density: 1,510.3 persons per square mile (2010); Race: 96.7% White, 0.7% Black, 0.7% Asian, 0.2% American Indian/Alaska Native, 0.0% Native Hawaiian/Other Pacific Islander, 1.7% Other, 1.3% Hispanic of any race (2010); Average household size: 2.56 (2010); Median age: 40.9 (2010); Males per 100 females: 93.5 (2010); Marriage status: 26.7% never married, 51.8% now married, 8.8% widowed, 12.8% divorced (2006-2010 5-year est.); Foreign born: 2.9% (2006-2010 5-year est.); Ancestry (includes multiple ancestries): 22.3% Irish, 14.8% English, 13.3% American, 12.5% French, 10.3% Italian (2006-2010 5-year est.).

**Economy:** Employment by occupation: 9.5% management, 1.4% professional, 10.3% services, 18.7% sales, 4.6% farming, 10.2% construction, 3.9% production (2006-2010 5-year est.).

**Income:** Per capita income: $25,006 (2006-2010 5-year est.); Median household income: $49,257 (2006-2010 5-year est.); Average household income: $63,212 (2006-2010 5-year est.); Percent of households with income of $100,000 or more: 16.0% (2006-2010 5-year est.); Poverty rate: 15.3% (2006-2010 5-year est.).

**Education:** Percent of population age 25 and over with: High school diploma (including GED) or higher: 82.7% (2006-2010 5-year est.); Bachelor's degree or higher: 18.9% (2006-2010 5-year est.); Master's degree or higher: 7.3% (2006-2010 5-year est.).

**Housing:** Homeownership rate: 82.8% (2010); Median home value: $145,900 (2006-2010 5-year est.); Median contract rent: $668 per month (2006-2010 5-year est.); Median year structure built: 1978 (2006-2010 5-year est.).

**Transportation:** Commute to work: 95.6% car, 0.0% public transportation, 0.8% walk, 1.3% work from home (2006-2010 5-year est.); Travel time to work: 49.1% less than 15 minutes, 37.2% 15 to 30 minutes, 7.8% 30 to 45 minutes, 2.9% 45 to 60 minutes, 3.1% 60 minutes or more (2006-2010 5-year est.)

## WEVERTOWN (unincorporated postal area)

Zip Code: 12886

Covers a land area of 14.477 square miles and a water area of 0.053 square miles. Located at 43.68° N. Lat; 73.93° W. Long. Elevation is 1,066 feet. Population: 269 (2010); Density: 18.6 persons per square mile (2010); Race: 98.5% White, 0.7% Black, 0.0% Asian, 0.0% American Indian/Alaska Native, 0.0% Native Hawaiian/Other Pacific Islander, 0.8% Other, 2.2% Hispanic of any race (2010); Average household size: 2.16 (2010); Median age: 48.2 (2010); Males per 100 females: 99.3 (2010); Homeownership rate: 80.4% (2010)

## Washington County

Located in eastern New York; bounded on the northwest by Lake George, on the east by Vermont, and on the west by the Hudson River; drained by the Poultney, Mettawee, and Hoosic Rivers; includes part of Lake Champlain. Covers a land area of 835.44 square miles, a water area of 10.40 square miles, and is located in the Eastern Time Zone at 43.27° N. Lat., 73.44° W. Long. The county was founded in 1772. County seat is Hudson Falls.

Washington County is part of the Glens Falls, NY Metropolitan Statistical Area. The entire metro area includes: Warren County, NY; Washington County, NY

Weather Station: Whitehall                                 Elevation: 119 feet

| | Jan | Feb | Mar | Apr | May | Jun | Jul | Aug | Sep | Oct | Nov | Dec |
|---|---|---|---|---|---|---|---|---|---|---|---|---|
| High | 30 | 34 | 44 | 59 | 71 | 80 | 84 | 82 | 73 | 61 | 47 | 35 |
| Low | 12 | 14 | 24 | 36 | 47 | 57 | 61 | 60 | 52 | 41 | 32 | 20 |
| Precip | 3.0 | 2.5 | 3.0 | 3.2 | 3.7 | 3.9 | 4.5 | 4.2 | 3.7 | 3.7 | 3.6 | 3.2 |
| Snow | 16.6 | 12.0 | 12.5 | 2.2 | 0.0 | 0.0 | 0.0 | 0.0 | 0.0 | tr | 2.7 | 13.6 |

*High and Low temperatures in degrees Fahrenheit; Precipitation and Snow in inches*

**Population:** 59,330 (1990); 61,042 (2000); 63,216 (2010); Race: 94.6% White, 3.0% Black, 0.4% Asian, 0.2% American Indian/Alaska Native, 0.0% Native Hawaiian/Other Pacific Islander, 1.8% Other, 2.3% Hispanic of any race (2010); Density: 75.7 persons per square mile (2010); Average household size: 2.49 (2010); Median age: 41.7 (2010); Males per 100 females: 107.6 (2010).

**Religion:** Six largest groups: 21.5% Catholicism, 5.2% Methodist/Pietist, 2.5% Baptist, 2.0% Presbyterian-Reformed, 1.2% Non-Denominational, 0.8% Episcopalianism/Anglicanism (2010)

**Economy:** Unemployment rate: 8.7% (February 2012); Total civilian labor force: 32,406 (February 2012); Leading industries: 29.5% manufacturing; 19.4% retail trade; 14.9% health care and social assistance (2009); Farms: 843 totaling 202,877 acres (2007); Companies that employ 500 or more persons: 0 (2009); Companies that employ 100 to 499 persons: 15 (2009); Companies that employ less than 100 persons: 1,067 (2009); Black-owned businesses: n/a (2007); Hispanic-owned businesses: n/a (2007); Asian-owned businesses: n/a (2007); Women-owned businesses: 1,674 (2007); Retail sales per capita: $6,698 (2010). Single-family building permits issued: 97 (2011); Multi-family building permits issued: 12 (2011).

**Income:** Per capita income: $22,347 (2006-2010 5-year est.); Median household income: $48,327 (2006-2010 5-year est.); Average household income: $57,471 (2006-2010 5-year est.); Percent of households with income of $100,000 or more: 12.7% (2006-2010 5-year est.); Poverty rate: 11.5% (2006-2010 5-year est.); Bankruptcy rate: 4.55% (2011).

**Taxes:** Total county taxes per capita: $861 (2009); County property taxes per capita: $504 (2009).

**Education:** Percent of population age 25 and over with: High school diploma (including GED) or higher: 85.9% (2006-2010 5-year est.); Bachelor's degree or higher: 16.8% (2006-2010 5-year est.); Master's degree or higher: 7.3% (2006-2010 5-year est.).

**Housing:** Homeownership rate: 73.4% (2010); Median home value: $137,000 (2006-2010 5-year est.); Median contract rent: $560 per month (2006-2010 5-year est.); Median year structure built: 1958 (2006-2010 5-year est.)

**Health:** Birth rate: 98.6 per 10,000 population (2011); Death rate: 98.3 per 10,000 population (2011); Age-adjusted cancer mortality rate: 214.9 deaths per 100,000 population (2009); Number of physicians: 4.3 per 10,000 population (2008); Hospital beds: 0.0 per 10,000 population (2007); Hospital admissions: 0.0 per 10,000 population (2007).

**Elections:** 2008 Presidential election results: 49.5% Obama, 48.7% McCain, 1.0% Nader

**Additional Information Contacts**

Washington County Government . . . . . . . . . . . . . . . . . . . . . (518) 746-2210
   http://www.co.washington.ny.us
Fort Edward Chamber of Commerce . . . . . . . . . . . . . . . . . (518) 747-3000
   http://www.fortedwardchamber.com
Granville Chamber of Commerce . . . . . . . . . . . . . . . . . . . (518) 642-2815
   http://granvillechamber.com
Greater Greenwich Chamber of Commerce . . . . . . . . . . . . (518) 692-7979
   http://www.greenwichchamber.org
Whitehall Chamber of Commerce . . . . . . . . . . . . . . . . . . . (518) 499-4435
   http://www.whitehall-chamber.org

## Washington County Communities

## ARGYLE (village).

Covers a land area of 0.349 square miles and a water area of 0 square miles. Located at 43.23° N. Lat; 73.49° W. Long. Elevation is 285 feet.

**Population:** 295 (1990); 289 (2000); 306 (2010); Density: 874.4 persons per square mile (2010); Race: 98.4% White, 0.0% Black, 0.0% Asian, 0.7% American Indian/Alaska Native, 0.0% Native Hawaiian/Other Pacific Islander, 0.9% Other, 0.3% Hispanic of any race (2010); Average household size: 2.37 (2010); Median age: 42.7 (2010); Males per 100 females: 98.7 (2010); Marriage status: 23.5% never married, 49.2% now married, 16.5% widowed, 10.8% divorced (2006-2010 5-year est.); Foreign born: 1.9% (2006-2010 5-year est.); Ancestry (includes multiple ancestries): 25.3% Irish, 19.4% American, 14.2% English, 13.6% Scotch-Irish, 12.5% French (2006-2010 5-year est.).

**Economy:** Employment by occupation: 3.4% management, 1.4% professional, 13.5% services, 12.2% sales, 15.5% farming, 8.8% construction, 6.1% production (2006-2010 5-year est.).
**Income:** Per capita income: $21,298 (2006-2010 5-year est.); Median household income: $42,708 (2006-2010 5-year est.); Average household income: $51,019 (2006-2010 5-year est.); Percent of households with income of $100,000 or more: 13.8% (2006-2010 5-year est.); Poverty rate: 16.3% (2006-2010 5-year est.).
**Education:** Percent of population age 25 and over with: High school diploma (including GED) or higher: 90.3% (2006-2010 5-year est.); Bachelor's degree or higher: 29.1% (2006-2010 5-year est.); Master's degree or higher: 13.5% (2006-2010 5-year est.).

School District(s)

Argyle Central School District (KG-12)
    2009-10 Enrollment: 646 . . . . . . . . . . . . . . . . . . . . . . . . . (518) 638-8243
**Housing:** Homeownership rate: 60.5% (2010); Median home value: $116,800 (2006-2010 5-year est.); Median contract rent: $547 per month (2006-2010 5-year est.); Median year structure built: before 1940 (2006-2010 5-year est.).
**Transportation:** Commute to work: 91.5% car, 0.0% public transportation, 2.8% walk, 4.2% work from home (2006-2010 5-year est.); Travel time to work: 14.0% less than 15 minutes, 23.5% 15 to 30 minutes, 34.6% 30 to 45 minutes, 2.2% 45 to 60 minutes, 25.7% 60 minutes or more (2006-2010 5-year est.)

**ARGYLE** (town). Covers a land area of 56.535 square miles and a water area of 1.260 square miles. Located at 43.23° N. Lat; 73.47° W. Long. Elevation is 285 feet.
**Population:** 3,031 (1990); 3,688 (2000); 3,782 (2010); Density: 66.9 persons per square mile (2010); Race: 97.8% White, 0.3% Black, 0.5% Asian, 0.1% American Indian/Alaska Native, 0.0% Native Hawaiian/Other Pacific Islander, 1.3% Other, 1.1% Hispanic of any race (2010); Average household size: 2.55 (2010); Median age: 44.4 (2010); Males per 100 females: 100.6 (2010); Marriage status: 23.9% never married, 61.2% now married, 5.4% widowed, 9.4% divorced (2006-2010 5-year est.); Foreign born: 2.5% (2006-2010 5-year est.); Ancestry (includes multiple ancestries): 17.3% Irish, 15.5% French, 15.1% Italian, 10.9% German, 9.9% English (2006-2010 5-year est.).
**Economy:** Employment by occupation: 9.4% management, 0.6% professional, 10.7% services, 13.7% sales, 5.5% farming, 14.8% construction, 8.0% production (2006-2010 5-year est.).
**Income:** Per capita income: $26,736 (2006-2010 5-year est.); Median household income: $61,813 (2006-2010 5-year est.); Average household income: $65,625 (2006-2010 5-year est.); Percent of households with income of $100,000 or more: 13.9% (2006-2010 5-year est.); Poverty rate: 8.4% (2006-2010 5-year est.).
**Education:** Percent of population age 25 and over with: High school diploma (including GED) or higher: 88.1% (2006-2010 5-year est.); Bachelor's degree or higher: 21.6% (2006-2010 5-year est.); Master's degree or higher: 10.0% (2006-2010 5-year est.).

School District(s)

Argyle Central School District (KG-12)
    2009-10 Enrollment: 646 . . . . . . . . . . . . . . . . . . . . . . . . . (518) 638-8243
**Housing:** Homeownership rate: 85.8% (2010); Median home value: $152,500 (2006-2010 5-year est.); Median contract rent: $540 per month (2006-2010 5-year est.); Median year structure built: 1970 (2006-2010 5-year est.).
**Transportation:** Commute to work: 90.2% car, 0.4% public transportation, 1.7% walk, 6.1% work from home (2006-2010 5-year est.); Travel time to work: 20.3% less than 15 minutes, 44.1% 15 to 30 minutes, 19.7% 30 to 45 minutes, 9.6% 45 to 60 minutes, 6.3% 60 minutes or more (2006-2010 5-year est.)

**CAMBRIDGE** (village). Covers a land area of 1.677 square miles and a water area of 0 square miles. Located at 43.02° N. Lat; 73.38° W. Long. Elevation is 489 feet.
**Population:** 1,967 (1990); 1,925 (2000); 1,870 (2010); Density: 1,114.7 persons per square mile (2010); Race: 96.1% White, 1.1% Black, 0.9% Asian, 0.1% American Indian/Alaska Native, 0.0% Native Hawaiian/Other Pacific Islander, 1.8% Other, 1.3% Hispanic of any race (2010); Average household size: 2.33 (2010); Median age: 44.1 (2010); Males per 100 females: 89.5 (2010); Marriage status: 21.0% never married, 56.1% now married, 8.0% widowed, 14.9% divorced (2006-2010 5-year est.); Foreign born: 3.6% (2006-2010 5-year est.); Ancestry (includes multiple

ancestries): 29.9% Irish, 22.3% English, 22.1% German, 9.4% French, 8.6% Italian (2006-2010 5-year est.).
**Economy:** Employment by occupation: 4.0% management, 3.8% professional, 17.8% services, 11.6% sales, 7.4% farming, 14.2% construction, 7.3% production (2006-2010 5-year est.).
**Income:** Per capita income: $21,060 (2006-2010 5-year est.); Median household income: $36,667 (2006-2010 5-year est.); Average household income: $44,815 (2006-2010 5-year est.); Percent of households with income of $100,000 or more: 6.0% (2006-2010 5-year est.); Poverty rate: 12.5% (2006-2010 5-year est.).
**Taxes:** Total city taxes per capita: $351 (2009); City property taxes per capita: $334 (2009).
**Education:** Percent of population age 25 and over with: High school diploma (including GED) or higher: 89.7% (2006-2010 5-year est.); Bachelor's degree or higher: 20.9% (2006-2010 5-year est.); Master's degree or higher: 10.7% (2006-2010 5-year est.).

School District(s)

Cambridge Central School District (PK-12)
    2009-10 Enrollment: 980 . . . . . . . . . . . . . . . . . . . . . . . . . (518) 677-2653
**Housing:** Homeownership rate: 63.4% (2010); Median home value: $139,300 (2006-2010 5-year est.); Median contract rent: $518 per month (2006-2010 5-year est.); Median year structure built: before 1940 (2006-2010 5-year est.).
**Safety:** Violent crime rate: 11.2 per 10,000 population; Property crime rate: 196.0 per 10,000 population (2010).
**Newspapers:** Eagle (Community news; Circulation 4,860)
**Transportation:** Commute to work: 86.6% car, 0.0% public transportation, 4.7% walk, 6.1% work from home (2006-2010 5-year est.); Travel time to work: 43.7% less than 15 minutes, 15.5% 15 to 30 minutes, 18.4% 30 to 45 minutes, 14.6% 45 to 60 minutes, 7.8% 60 minutes or more (2006-2010 5-year est.)

**CAMBRIDGE** (town). Covers a land area of 36.356 square miles and a water area of 0.127 square miles. Located at 43.00° N. Lat; 73.44° W. Long. Elevation is 489 feet.
**History:** Cambridge Historical District within the village. Its weekly, *WASHINGTON COUNTY POST.ITAL WAS FOUNDED IN 1787. SETTLED C.1761, INCORPORATED 1866.*
**Population:** 1,938 (1990); 2,152 (2000); 2,021 (2010); Density: 55.6 persons per square mile (2010); Race: 97.5% White, 0.5% Black, 0.8% Asian, 0.1% American Indian/Alaska Native, 0.0% Native Hawaiian/Other Pacific Islander, 1.1% Other, 0.9% Hispanic of any race (2010); Average household size: 2.51 (2010); Median age: 45.2 (2010); Males per 100 females: 108.4 (2010); Marriage status: 22.3% never married, 64.7% now married, 5.8% widowed, 7.2% divorced (2006-2010 5-year est.); Foreign born: 1.9% (2006-2010 5-year est.); Ancestry (includes multiple ancestries): 22.6% German, 20.6% English, 19.8% Irish, 12.7% French, 8.9% American (2006-2010 5-year est.).
**Economy:** Single-family building permits issued: 3 (2011); Multi-family building permits issued: 0 (2011); Employment by occupation: 10.0% management, 4.6% professional, 8.3% services, 14.8% sales, 6.5% farming, 18.9% construction, 9.6% production (2006-2010 5-year est.).
**Income:** Per capita income: $26,246 (2006-2010 5-year est.); Median household income: $59,000 (2006-2010 5-year est.); Average household income: $68,170 (2006-2010 5-year est.); Percent of households with income of $100,000 or more: 20.2% (2006-2010 5-year est.); Poverty rate: 10.7% (2006-2010 5-year est.).
**Education:** Percent of population age 25 and over with: High school diploma (including GED) or higher: 87.0% (2006-2010 5-year est.); Bachelor's degree or higher: 29.5% (2006-2010 5-year est.); Master's degree or higher: 14.8% (2006-2010 5-year est.).

School District(s)

Cambridge Central School District (PK-12)
    2009-10 Enrollment: 980 . . . . . . . . . . . . . . . . . . . . . . . . . (518) 677-2653
**Housing:** Homeownership rate: 81.6% (2010); Median home value: $189,400 (2006-2010 5-year est.); Median contract rent: $656 per month (2006-2010 5-year est.); Median year structure built: before 1940 (2006-2010 5-year est.).
**Newspapers:** Eagle (Community news; Circulation 4,860)
**Transportation:** Commute to work: 92.6% car, 0.0% public transportation, 2.0% walk, 4.1% work from home (2006-2010 5-year est.); Travel time to work: 28.2% less than 15 minutes, 23.2% 15 to 30 minutes, 23.6% 30 to 45 minutes, 17.7% 45 to 60 minutes, 7.2% 60 minutes or more (2006-2010 5-year est.)

## CLEMONS (unincorporated postal area)
Zip Code: 12819

Covers a land area of 28.976 square miles and a water area of 0.464 square miles. Located at 43.59° N. Lat; 73.46° W. Long. Elevation is 377 feet. Population: 403 (2010); Density: 13.9 persons per square mile (2010); Race: 96.0% White, 1.0% Black, 0.0% Asian, 0.0% American Indian/Alaska Native, 0.0% Native Hawaiian/Other Pacific Islander, 3.0% Other, 2.2% Hispanic of any race (2010); Average household size: 2.46 (2010); Median age: 45.1 (2010); Males per 100 females: 97.5 (2010); Homeownership rate: 76.7% (2010)

## COMSTOCK (unincorporated postal area)
Zip Code: 12821

Covers a land area of 5.548 square miles and a water area of 0.061 square miles. Located at 43.45° N. Lat; 73.41° W. Long. Elevation is 128 feet. Population: 2,750 (2010); Density: 495.7 persons per square mile (2010); Race: 38.1% White, 54.5% Black, 0.5% Asian, 0.8% American Indian/Alaska Native, 0.0% Native Hawaiian/Other Pacific Islander, 6.1% Other, 16.1% Hispanic of any race (2010); Average household size: 2.66 (2010); Median age: 33.2 (2010); Males per 100 females: ***.* (2010); Homeownership rate: 84.8% (2010)

## COSSAYUNA (unincorporated postal area)
Zip Code: 12823

Covers a land area of 4.260 square miles and a water area of 0.080 square miles. Located at 43.17° N. Lat; 73.40° W. Long. Elevation is 479 feet. Population: 238 (2010); Density: 55.9 persons per square mile (2010); Race: 98.3% White, 0.0% Black, 0.0% Asian, 0.0% American Indian/Alaska Native, 1.3% Native Hawaiian/Other Pacific Islander, 0.4% Other, 0.8% Hispanic of any race (2010); Average household size: 2.40 (2010); Median age: 49.3 (2010); Males per 100 females: 100.0 (2010); Homeownership rate: 93.9% (2010)

## DRESDEN (town).
Covers a land area of 52.253 square miles and a water area of 2.745 square miles. Located at 43.59° N. Lat; 73.46° W. Long. Elevation is 138 feet.
**Population:** 561 (1990); 677 (2000); 652 (2010); Density: 12.5 persons per square mile (2010); Race: 97.2% White, 0.6% Black, 0.0% Asian, 0.0% American Indian/Alaska Native, 0.0% Native Hawaiian/Other Pacific Islander, 2.2% Other, 1.7% Hispanic of any race (2010); Average household size: 2.40 (2010); Median age: 48.9 (2010); Males per 100 females: 95.2 (2010); Marriage status: 8.3% never married, 64.8% now married, 9.4% widowed, 17.5% divorced (2006-2010 5-year est.); Foreign born: 1.0% (2006-2010 5-year est.); Ancestry (includes multiple ancestries): 33.7% French, 32.4% Irish, 18.8% German, 9.3% English, 7.3% Welsh (2006-2010 5-year est.).
**Economy:** Employment by occupation: 6.4% management, 0.0% professional, 16.5% services, 18.8% sales, 4.5% farming, 1.9% construction, 5.6% production (2006-2010 5-year est.).
**Income:** Per capita income: $21,249 (2006-2010 5-year est.); Median household income: $35,500 (2006-2010 5-year est.); Average household income: $48,676 (2006-2010 5-year est.); Percent of households with income of $100,000 or more: 12.8% (2006-2010 5-year est.); Poverty rate: 32.0% (2006-2010 5-year est.).
**Education:** Percent of population age 25 and over with: High school diploma (including GED) or higher: 84.8% (2006-2010 5-year est.); Bachelor's degree or higher: 25.3% (2006-2010 5-year est.); Master's degree or higher: 14.5% (2006-2010 5-year est.).
**Housing:** Homeownership rate: 77.9% (2010); Median home value: $99,700 (2006-2010 5-year est.); Median contract rent: $396 per month (2006-2010 5-year est.); Median year structure built: 1972 (2006-2010 5-year est.).
**Transportation:** Commute to work: 91.2% car, 2.2% public transportation, 2.2% walk, 3.9% work from home (2006-2010 5-year est.); Travel time to work: 10.5% less than 15 minutes, 26.5% 15 to 30 minutes, 33.8% 30 to 45 minutes, 22.4% 45 to 60 minutes, 6.8% 60 minutes or more (2006-2010 5-year est.)

## EASTON (town).
Covers a land area of 62.303 square miles and a water area of 0.934 square miles. Located at 43.02° N. Lat; 73.53° W. Long. Elevation is 436 feet.
**Population:** 2,203 (1990); 2,259 (2000); 2,336 (2010); Density: 37.5 persons per square mile (2010); Race: 96.4% White, 0.9% Black, 0.1% Asian, 0.3% American Indian/Alaska Native, 0.0% Native Hawaiian/Other Pacific Islander, 2.3% Other, 2.0% Hispanic of any race (2010); Average

household size: 2.55 (2010); Median age: 43.4 (2010); Males per 100 females: 103.1 (2010); Marriage status: 21.5% never married, 68.9% now married, 4.2% widowed, 5.4% divorced (2006-2010 5-year est.); Foreign born: 1.4% (2006-2010 5-year est.); Ancestry (includes multiple ancestries): 24.9% Irish, 14.2% English, 12.1% American, 12.0% German, 11.8% Italian (2006-2010 5-year est.).
**Economy:** Single-family building permits issued: 2 (2011); Multi-family building permits issued: 0 (2011); Employment by occupation: 17.0% management, 3.9% professional, 8.3% services, 12.1% sales, 3.5% farming, 17.8% construction, 7.6% production (2006-2010 5-year est.).
**Income:** Per capita income: $24,520 (2006-2010 5-year est.); Median household income: $58,875 (2006-2010 5-year est.); Average household income: $72,803 (2006-2010 5-year est.); Percent of households with income of $100,000 or more: 20.4% (2006-2010 5-year est.); Poverty rate: 16.3% (2006-2010 5-year est.).
**Education:** Percent of population age 25 and over with: High school diploma (including GED) or higher: 91.3% (2006-2010 5-year est.); Bachelor's degree or higher: 28.3% (2006-2010 5-year est.); Master's degree or higher: 10.1% (2006-2010 5-year est.).
**Housing:** Homeownership rate: 79.5% (2010); Median home value: $164,300 (2006-2010 5-year est.); Median contract rent: $547 per month (2006-2010 5-year est.); Median year structure built: 1957 (2006-2010 5-year est.).
**Transportation:** Commute to work: 85.8% car, 0.3% public transportation, 6.1% walk, 7.4% work from home (2006-2010 5-year est.); Travel time to work: 25.6% less than 15 minutes, 24.0% 15 to 30 minutes, 29.4% 30 to 45 minutes, 14.3% 45 to 60 minutes, 6.7% 60 minutes or more (2006-2010 5-year est.)

## FORT ANN (village).
Covers a land area of 0.292 square miles and a water area of 0.014 square miles. Located at 43.41° N. Lat; 73.48° W. Long. Elevation is 157 feet.
**Population:** 419 (1990); 471 (2000); 484 (2010); Density: 1,654.2 persons per square mile (2010); Race: 98.1% White, 0.0% Black, 0.6% Asian, 0.0% American Indian/Alaska Native, 0.0% Native Hawaiian/Other Pacific Islander, 1.3% Other, 4.5% Hispanic of any race (2010); Average household size: 2.59 (2010); Median age: 38.0 (2010); Males per 100 females: 96.0 (2010); Marriage status: 36.0% never married, 41.0% now married, 11.2% widowed, 11.8% divorced (2006-2010 5-year est.); Foreign born: 2.4% (2006-2010 5-year est.); Ancestry (includes multiple ancestries): 27.0% Irish, 21.8% French, 21.6% American, 17.5% Italian, 10.4% German (2006-2010 5-year est.).
**Economy:** Employment by occupation: 7.8% management, 0.0% professional, 11.9% services, 22.8% sales, 1.6% farming, 15.0% construction, 14.5% production (2006-2010 5-year est.).
**Income:** Per capita income: $22,163 (2006-2010 5-year est.); Median household income: $55,417 (2006-2010 5-year est.); Average household income: $56,466 (2006-2010 5-year est.); Percent of households with income of $100,000 or more: 9.5% (2006-2010 5-year est.); Poverty rate: 20.1% (2006-2010 5-year est.).
**Education:** Percent of population age 25 and over with: High school diploma (including GED) or higher: 76.8% (2006-2010 5-year est.); Bachelor's degree or higher: 8.4% (2006-2010 5-year est.); Master's degree or higher: 1.4% (2006-2010 5-year est.).
#### School District(s)
Fort Ann Central School District (PK-12)
   2009-10 Enrollment: 558 . . . . . . . . . . . . . . . . . . . . . . . . (518) 639-5594
**Housing:** Homeownership rate: 66.3% (2010); Median home value: $124,400 (2006-2010 5-year est.); Median contract rent: $448 per month (2006-2010 5-year est.); Median year structure built: before 1940 (2006-2010 5-year est.).
**Transportation:** Commute to work: 82.5% car, 0.0% public transportation, 14.7% walk, 2.8% work from home (2006-2010 5-year est.); Travel time to work: 38.4% less than 15 minutes, 39.0% 15 to 30 minutes, 14.5% 30 to 45 minutes, 2.9% 45 to 60 minutes, 5.2% 60 minutes or more (2006-2010 5-year est.)

## FORT ANN (town).
Covers a land area of 108.998 square miles and a water area of 1.779 square miles. Located at 43.46° N. Lat; 73.52° W. Long. Elevation is 157 feet.
**Population:** 6,368 (1990); 6,417 (2000); 6,190 (2010); Density: 56.8 persons per square mile (2010); Race: 71.2% White, 24.3% Black, 0.4% Asian, 0.4% American Indian/Alaska Native, 0.0% Native Hawaiian/Other Pacific Islander, 3.7% Other, 8.4% Hispanic of any race (2010); Average household size: 2.58 (2010); Median age: 37.9 (2010); Males per 100

females: 237.1 (2010); Marriage status: 47.4% never married, 40.6% now married, 4.1% widowed, 7.9% divorced (2006-2010 5-year est.); Foreign born: 3.8% (2006-2010 5-year est.); Ancestry (includes multiple ancestries): 15.6% Irish, 13.0% American, 10.8% English, 9.5% French, 6.9% Italian (2006-2010 5-year est.).

**Economy:** Employment by occupation: 9.0% management, 1.2% professional, 9.8% services, 18.9% sales, 1.0% farming, 13.5% construction, 10.9% production (2006-2010 5-year est.).

**Income:** Per capita income: $12,915 (2006-2010 5-year est.); Median household income: $51,361 (2006-2010 5-year est.); Average household income: $60,346 (2006-2010 5-year est.); Percent of households with income of $100,000 or more: 10.8% (2006-2010 5-year est.); Poverty rate: 6.4% (2006-2010 5-year est.).

**Education:** Percent of population age 25 and over with: High school diploma (including GED) or higher: 73.3% (2006-2010 5-year est.); Bachelor's degree or higher: 9.5% (2006-2010 5-year est.); Master's degree or higher: 3.7% (2006-2010 5-year est.).

#### School District(s)
Fort Ann Central School District (PK-12)
　　2009-10 Enrollment: 558 . . . . . . . . . . . . . . . . . . . . . . . . (518) 639-5594

**Housing:** Homeownership rate: 84.3% (2010); Median home value: $140,800 (2006-2010 5-year est.); Median contract rent: $531 per month (2006-2010 5-year est.); Median year structure built: 1974 (2006-2010 5-year est.).

**Transportation:** Commute to work: 95.4% car, 0.0% public transportation, 2.4% walk, 2.2% work from home (2006-2010 5-year est.); Travel time to work: 20.0% less than 15 minutes, 45.8% 15 to 30 minutes, 17.9% 30 to 45 minutes, 5.5% 45 to 60 minutes, 10.8% 60 minutes or more (2006-2010 5-year est.)

## FORT EDWARD (village). Covers a land area of 1.756 square miles and a water area of 0.180 square miles. Located at 43.26° N. Lat; 73.58° W. Long. Elevation is 138 feet.

**Population:** 3,564 (1990); 3,141 (2000); 3,375 (2010); Density: 1,921.7 persons per square mile (2010); Race: 96.9% White, 1.0% Black, 0.2% Asian, 0.2% American Indian/Alaska Native, 0.0% Native Hawaiian/Other Pacific Islander, 1.7% Other, 1.5% Hispanic of any race (2010); Average household size: 2.59 (2010); Median age: 36.0 (2010); Males per 100 females: 95.3 (2010); Marriage status: 21.9% never married, 59.2% now married, 6.4% widowed, 12.4% divorced (2006-2010 5-year est.); Foreign born: 3.3% (2006-2010 5-year est.); Ancestry (includes multiple ancestries): 28.9% Irish, 18.2% French, 12.4% English, 10.1% German, 8.9% Italian (2006-2010 5-year est.).

**Economy:** Employment by occupation: 5.4% management, 4.1% professional, 12.0% services, 8.5% sales, 3.1% farming, 16.5% construction, 17.1% production (2006-2010 5-year est.).

**Income:** Per capita income: $20,181 (2006-2010 5-year est.); Median household income: $42,062 (2006-2010 5-year est.); Average household income: $47,311 (2006-2010 5-year est.); Percent of households with income of $100,000 or more: 7.8% (2006-2010 5-year est.); Poverty rate: 18.6% (2006-2010 5-year est.).

**Education:** Percent of population age 25 and over with: High school diploma (including GED) or higher: 80.6% (2006-2010 5-year est.); Bachelor's degree or higher: 6.2% (2006-2010 5-year est.); Master's degree or higher: 3.9% (2006-2010 5-year est.).

#### School District(s)
Fort Edward Union Free School District (PK-12)
　　2009-10 Enrollment: 549 . . . . . . . . . . . . . . . . . . . . . . . . (518) 747-4594
Washington-Saratoga-Warren-Hamilton-Essex Boces
　　2009-10 Enrollment: n/a . . . . . . . . . . . . . . . . . . . . . . . . (518) 746-3310

**Housing:** Homeownership rate: 63.8% (2010); Median home value: $103,300 (2006-2010 5-year est.); Median contract rent: $573 per month (2006-2010 5-year est.); Median year structure built: before 1940 (2006-2010 5-year est.).

**Transportation:** Commute to work: 91.8% car, 1.2% public transportation, 1.5% walk, 3.7% work from home (2006-2010 5-year est.); Travel time to work: 20.7% less than 15 minutes, 35.0% 15 to 30 minutes, 21.4% 30 to 45 minutes, 9.4% 45 to 60 minutes, 13.6% 60 minutes or more (2006-2010 5-year est.); Amtrak: train service available.

**Additional Information Contacts**
Fort Edward Chamber of Commerce . . . . . . . . . . . . . . . (518) 747-3000
　　http://www.fortedwardchamber.com

## FORT EDWARD (town). Covers a land area of 26.630 square miles and a water area of 0.795 square miles. Located at 43.23° N. Lat; 73.55° W. Long. Elevation is 138 feet.

**History:** Fort built here in 1755 to protect portage between the Hudson River and Lake Champlain; it was occupied by Burgoyne in 1777. Incorporated 1849.

**Population:** 6,330 (1990); 5,892 (2000); 6,371 (2010); Density: 239.2 persons per square mile (2010); Race: 97.1% White, 0.9% Black, 0.3% Asian, 0.3% American Indian/Alaska Native, 0.0% Native Hawaiian/Other Pacific Islander, 1.4% Other, 1.9% Hispanic of any race (2010); Average household size: 2.53 (2010); Median age: 40.1 (2010); Males per 100 females: 98.9 (2010); Marriage status: 27.5% never married, 49.8% now married, 11.6% widowed, 11.0% divorced (2006-2010 5-year est.); Foreign born: 2.8% (2006-2010 5-year est.); Ancestry (includes multiple ancestries): 24.1% Irish, 16.4% French, 11.7% German, 11.0% English, 8.7% American (2006-2010 5-year est.).

**Economy:** Single-family building permits issued: 3 (2011); Multi-family building permits issued: 0 (2011); Employment by occupation: 4.1% management, 3.0% professional, 11.0% services, 13.7% sales, 2.1% farming, 12.8% construction, 12.3% production (2006-2010 5-year est.).

**Income:** Per capita income: $20,485 (2006-2010 5-year est.); Median household income: $42,852 (2006-2010 5-year est.); Average household income: $48,138 (2006-2010 5-year est.); Percent of households with income of $100,000 or more: 7.8% (2006-2010 5-year est.); Poverty rate: 16.1% (2006-2010 5-year est.).

**Education:** Percent of population age 25 and over with: High school diploma (including GED) or higher: 81.8% (2006-2010 5-year est.); Bachelor's degree or higher: 6.8% (2006-2010 5-year est.); Master's degree or higher: 3.0% (2006-2010 5-year est.).

#### School District(s)
Fort Edward Union Free School District (PK-12)
　　2009-10 Enrollment: 549 . . . . . . . . . . . . . . . . . . . . . . . . (518) 747-4594
Washington-Saratoga-Warren-Hamilton-Essex Boces
　　2009-10 Enrollment: n/a . . . . . . . . . . . . . . . . . . . . . . . . (518) 746-3310

**Housing:** Homeownership rate: 68.3% (2010); Median home value: $98,100 (2006-2010 5-year est.); Median contract rent: $573 per month (2006-2010 5-year est.); Median year structure built: before 1940 (2006-2010 5-year est.).

**Transportation:** Commute to work: 94.6% car, 0.7% public transportation, 1.1% walk, 2.6% work from home (2006-2010 5-year est.); Travel time to work: 27.0% less than 15 minutes, 37.6% 15 to 30 minutes, 15.2% 30 to 45 minutes, 10.4% 45 to 60 minutes, 9.8% 60 minutes or more (2006-2010 5-year est.); Amtrak: train service available.

## GRANVILLE (village). Covers a land area of 1.570 square miles and a water area of <.001 square miles. Located at 43.41° N. Lat; 73.27° W. Long. Elevation is 410 feet.

**Population:** 2,646 (1990); 2,644 (2000); 2,543 (2010); Density: 1,619.3 persons per square mile (2010); Race: 97.2% White, 0.6% Black, 0.4% Asian, 0.5% American Indian/Alaska Native, 0.0% Native Hawaiian/Other Pacific Islander, 1.3% Other, 1.3% Hispanic of any race (2010); Average household size: 2.47 (2010); Median age: 40.9 (2010); Males per 100 females: 85.9 (2010); Marriage status: 22.4% never married, 50.3% now married, 16.7% widowed, 10.5% divorced (2006-2010 5-year est.); Foreign born: 2.9% (2006-2010 5-year est.); Ancestry (includes multiple ancestries): 22.3% American, 19.5% Irish, 15.2% French, 11.4% German, 10.4% Welsh (2006-2010 5-year est.).

**Economy:** Single-family building permits issued: 0 (2011); Multi-family building permits issued: 0 (2011); Employment by occupation: 6.6% management, 0.5% professional, 17.4% services, 20.6% sales, 3.7% farming, 6.7% construction, 5.8% production (2006-2010 5-year est.).

**Income:** Per capita income: $19,121 (2006-2010 5-year est.); Median household income: $39,632 (2006-2010 5-year est.); Average household income: $45,932 (2006-2010 5-year est.); Percent of households with income of $100,000 or more: 8.1% (2006-2010 5-year est.); Poverty rate: 21.6% (2006-2010 5-year est.).

**Education:** Percent of population age 25 and over with: High school diploma (including GED) or higher: 82.9% (2006-2010 5-year est.); Bachelor's degree or higher: 11.4% (2006-2010 5-year est.); Master's degree or higher: 4.3% (2006-2010 5-year est.).

#### School District(s)
Granville Central School District (PK-12)
　　2009-10 Enrollment: 1,337 . . . . . . . . . . . . . . . . . . . . . . . . (518) 642-1051

**Housing:** Homeownership rate: 55.2% (2010); Median home value: $110,300 (2006-2010 5-year est.); Median contract rent: $471 per month

(2006-2010 5-year est.); Median year structure built: before 1940 (2006-2010 5-year est.).
**Safety:** Violent crime rate: 12.0 per 10,000 population; Property crime rate: 172.7 per 10,000 population (2010).
**Newspapers:** Lake Region Free Press (Local news); North Country Free Press (Community news); Northshire Free Press (Community news); Sentinel (Community news; Circulation 3,300); Whitehall Times (Community news; Circulation 2,200)
**Transportation:** Commute to work: 86.6% car, 0.0% public transportation, 10.8% walk, 2.6% work from home (2006-2010 5-year est.); Travel time to work: 41.6% less than 15 minutes, 18.8% 15 to 30 minutes, 20.4% 30 to 45 minutes, 17.4% 45 to 60 minutes, 1.7% 60 minutes or more (2006-2010 5-year est.)
**Additional Information Contacts**
Granville Chamber of Commerce . . . . . . . . . . . . . . . . . . . . (518) 642-2815
  http://granvillechamber.com

**GRANVILLE** (town). Covers a land area of 55.618 square miles and a water area of 0.500 square miles. Located at 43.42° N. Lat; 73.30° W. Long. Elevation is 410 feet.
**Population:** 5,935 (1990); 6,456 (2000); 6,669 (2010); Density: 119.9 persons per square mile (2010); Race: 97.8% White, 0.3% Black, 0.5% Asian, 0.3% American Indian/Alaska Native, 0.0% Native Hawaiian/Other Pacific Islander, 1.1% Other, 1.1% Hispanic of any race (2010); Average household size: 2.57 (2010); Median age: 42.2 (2010); Males per 100 females: 97.6 (2010); Marriage status: 27.4% never married, 52.2% now married, 9.5% widowed, 11.0% divorced (2006-2010 5-year est.); Foreign born: 1.1% (2006-2010 5-year est.); Ancestry (includes multiple ancestries): 18.9% Irish, 18.1% American, 12.6% French, 11.2% English, 10.7% German (2006-2010 5-year est.).
**Economy:** Employment by occupation: 5.0% management, 1.6% professional, 14.2% services, 19.4% sales, 1.9% farming, 11.7% construction, 14.5% production (2006-2010 5-year est.).
**Income:** Per capita income: $19,956 (2006-2010 5-year est.); Median household income: $44,874 (2006-2010 5-year est.); Average household income: $52,388 (2006-2010 5-year est.); Percent of households with income of $100,000 or more: 9.7% (2006-2010 5-year est.); Poverty rate: 15.3% (2006-2010 5-year est.).
**Education:** Percent of population age 25 and over with: High school diploma (including GED) or higher: 86.1% (2006-2010 5-year est.); Bachelor's degree or higher: 12.8% (2006-2010 5-year est.); Master's degree or higher: 5.3% (2006-2010 5-year est.).
**School District(s)**
Granville Central School District (PK-12)
  2009-10 Enrollment: 1,337 . . . . . . . . . . . . . . . . . . . (518) 642-1051
**Housing:** Homeownership rate: 72.7% (2010); Median home value: $109,900 (2006-2010 5-year est.); Median contract rent: $508 per month (2006-2010 5-year est.); Median year structure built: 1952 (2006-2010 5-year est.).
**Newspapers:** Lake Region Free Press (Local news); North Country Free Press (Community news); Northshire Free Press (Community news); Sentinel (Community news; Circulation 3,300); Whitehall Times (Community news; Circulation 2,200)
**Transportation:** Commute to work: 92.0% car, 0.0% public transportation, 4.9% walk, 2.6% work from home (2006-2010 5-year est.); Travel time to work: 36.8% less than 15 minutes, 17.3% 15 to 30 minutes, 26.3% 30 to 45 minutes, 9.5% 45 to 60 minutes, 10.0% 60 minutes or more (2006-2010 5-year est.)

**GREENWICH** (village). Covers a land area of 1.476 square miles and a water area of 0 square miles. Located at 43.08° N. Lat; 73.49° W. Long. Elevation is 374 feet.
**Population:** 1,961 (1990); 1,902 (2000); 1,777 (2010); Density: 1,203.2 persons per square mile (2010); Race: 97.4% White, 0.5% Black, 0.5% Asian, 0.3% American Indian/Alaska Native, 0.0% Native Hawaiian/Other Pacific Islander, 1.3% Other, 1.1% Hispanic of any race (2010); Average household size: 2.34 (2010); Median age: 41.8 (2010); Males per 100 females: 93.6 (2010); Marriage status: 23.3% never married, 59.7% now married, 7.0% widowed, 10.0% divorced (2006-2010 5-year est.); Foreign born: 0.9% (2006-2010 5-year est.); Ancestry (includes multiple ancestries): 33.7% Irish, 18.8% German, 12.2% Italian, 11.0% English, 6.7% French (2006-2010 5-year est.).
**Economy:** Employment by occupation: 11.2% management, 1.2% professional, 12.4% services, 20.3% sales, 1.8% farming, 6.4% construction, 4.5% production (2006-2010 5-year est.).

**Income:** Per capita income: $27,440 (2006-2010 5-year est.); Median household income: $49,000 (2006-2010 5-year est.); Average household income: $66,274 (2006-2010 5-year est.); Percent of households with income of $100,000 or more: 21.0% (2006-2010 5-year est.); Poverty rate: 8.6% (2006-2010 5-year est.).
**Education:** Percent of population age 25 and over with: High school diploma (including GED) or higher: 86.3% (2006-2010 5-year est.); Bachelor's degree or higher: 25.0% (2006-2010 5-year est.); Master's degree or higher: 8.8% (2006-2010 5-year est.).
**School District(s)**
Greenwich Central School District (KG-12)
  2009-10 Enrollment: 1,074 . . . . . . . . . . . . . . . . . . . (518) 692-9542
**Housing:** Homeownership rate: 57.0% (2010); Median home value: $162,100 (2006-2010 5-year est.); Median contract rent: $534 per month (2006-2010 5-year est.); Median year structure built: before 1940 (2006-2010 5-year est.).
**Safety:** Violent crime rate: 22.3 per 10,000 population; Property crime rate: 173.1 per 10,000 population (2010).
**Newspapers:** Greenwich Journal & Salem Press (Local news; Circulation 2,900)
**Transportation:** Commute to work: 94.1% car, 0.0% public transportation, 2.8% walk, 0.7% work from home (2006-2010 5-year est.); Travel time to work: 33.6% less than 15 minutes, 18.7% 15 to 30 minutes, 26.6% 30 to 45 minutes, 12.0% 45 to 60 minutes, 9.2% 60 minutes or more (2006-2010 5-year est.)
**Additional Information Contacts**
Greater Greenwich Chamber of Commerce . . . . . . . . . . . . (518) 692-7979
  http://www.greenwichchamber.org

**GREENWICH** (town). Covers a land area of 43.663 square miles and a water area of 0.597 square miles. Located at 43.14° N. Lat; 73.47° W. Long. Elevation is 374 feet.
**History:** Incorporated 1809.
**Population:** 4,557 (1990); 4,896 (2000); 4,942 (2010); Density: 113.2 persons per square mile (2010); Race: 97.6% White, 0.5% Black, 0.6% Asian, 0.1% American Indian/Alaska Native, 0.1% Native Hawaiian/Other Pacific Islander, 1.1% Other, 0.8% Hispanic of any race (2010); Average household size: 2.47 (2010); Median age: 43.8 (2010); Males per 100 females: 97.3 (2010); Marriage status: 19.7% never married, 65.1% now married, 6.8% widowed, 8.5% divorced (2006-2010 5-year est.); Foreign born: 2.2% (2006-2010 5-year est.); Ancestry (includes multiple ancestries): 31.1% Irish, 16.4% English, 15.1% German, 12.0% Italian, 7.6% French (2006-2010 5-year est.).
**Economy:** Employment by occupation: 9.9% management, 3.1% professional, 5.0% services, 17.0% sales, 2.8% farming, 16.8% construction, 8.5% production (2006-2010 5-year est.).
**Income:** Per capita income: $27,839 (2006-2010 5-year est.); Median household income: $56,088 (2006-2010 5-year est.); Average household income: $69,333 (2006-2010 5-year est.); Percent of households with income of $100,000 or more: 21.2% (2006-2010 5-year est.); Poverty rate: 6.7% (2006-2010 5-year est.).
**Education:** Percent of population age 25 and over with: High school diploma (including GED) or higher: 89.9% (2006-2010 5-year est.); Bachelor's degree or higher: 28.3% (2006-2010 5-year est.); Master's degree or higher: 12.9% (2006-2010 5-year est.).
**School District(s)**
Greenwich Central School District (KG-12)
  2009-10 Enrollment: 1,074 . . . . . . . . . . . . . . . . . . . (518) 692-9542
**Housing:** Homeownership rate: 76.0% (2010); Median home value: $181,300 (2006-2010 5-year est.); Median contract rent: $590 per month (2006-2010 5-year est.); Median year structure built: 1952 (2006-2010 5-year est.).
**Newspapers:** Greenwich Journal & Salem Press (Local news; Circulation 2,900)
**Transportation:** Commute to work: 92.4% car, 0.0% public transportation, 1.9% walk, 4.2% work from home (2006-2010 5-year est.); Travel time to work: 27.7% less than 15 minutes, 23.3% 15 to 30 minutes, 26.7% 30 to 45 minutes, 12.6% 45 to 60 minutes, 9.7% 60 minutes or more (2006-2010 5-year est.)

**HAMPTON** (town). Covers a land area of 22.241 square miles and a water area of 0.348 square miles. Located at 43.55° N. Lat; 73.29° W. Long. Elevation is 427 feet.
**Population:** 756 (1990); 871 (2000); 938 (2010); Density: 42.2 persons per square mile (2010); Race: 98.2% White, 0.3% Black, 0.1% Asian, 0.1%

American Indian/Alaska Native, 0.0% Native Hawaiian/Other Pacific Islander, 1.3% Other, 1.4% Hispanic of any race (2010); Average household size: 2.55 (2010); Median age: 40.8 (2010); Males per 100 females: 103.0 (2010); Marriage status: 24.6% never married, 58.6% now married, 4.3% widowed, 12.5% divorced (2006-2010 5-year est.); Foreign born: 0.3% (2006-2010 5-year est.); Ancestry (includes multiple ancestries): 16.8% Irish, 16.6% American, 14.8% French, 11.7% German, 10.2% English (2006-2010 5-year est.).
**Economy:** Employment by occupation: 9.8% management, 2.6% professional, 9.3% services, 22.1% sales, 2.6% farming, 12.4% construction, 11.4% production (2006-2010 5-year est.).
**Income:** Per capita income: $21,934 (2006-2010 5-year est.); Median household income: $46,000 (2006-2010 5-year est.); Average household income: $57,146 (2006-2010 5-year est.); Percent of households with income of $100,000 or more: 14.1% (2006-2010 5-year est.); Poverty rate: 8.7% (2006-2010 5-year est.).
**Education:** Percent of population age 25 and over with: High school diploma (including GED) or higher: 87.2% (2006-2010 5-year est.); Bachelor's degree or higher: 16.9% (2006-2010 5-year est.); Master's degree or higher: 6.9% (2006-2010 5-year est.).
**Housing:** Homeownership rate: 85.2% (2010); Median home value: $120,600 (2006-2010 5-year est.); Median contract rent: $635 per month (2006-2010 5-year est.); Median year structure built: 1981 (2006-2010 5-year est.).
**Transportation:** Commute to work: 93.0% car, 0.0% public transportation, 3.9% walk, 3.1% work from home (2006-2010 5-year est.); Travel time to work: 37.2% less than 15 minutes, 36.4% 15 to 30 minutes, 20.0% 30 to 45 minutes, 2.2% 45 to 60 minutes, 4.2% 60 minutes or more (2006-2010 5-year est.)

**HARTFORD** (town). Covers a land area of 43.384 square miles and a water area of 0.105 square miles. Located at 43.35° N. Lat; 73.41° W. Long. Elevation is 390 feet.
**Population:** 1,989 (1990); 2,279 (2000); 2,269 (2010); Density: 52.3 persons per square mile (2010); Race: 98.3% White, 0.2% Black, 0.3% Asian, 0.3% American Indian/Alaska Native, 0.0% Native Hawaiian/Other Pacific Islander, 0.9% Other, 1.5% Hispanic of any race (2010); Average household size: 2.66 (2010); Median age: 41.8 (2010); Males per 100 females: 101.9 (2010); Marriage status: 19.5% never married, 68.0% now married, 3.5% widowed, 9.1% divorced (2006-2010 5-year est.); Foreign born: 2.0% (2006-2010 5-year est.); Ancestry (includes multiple ancestries): 22.3% Irish, 20.5% English, 17.7% French, 12.4% German, 12.3% American (2006-2010 5-year est.).
**Economy:** Employment by occupation: 9.1% management, 2.1% professional, 12.3% services, 11.7% sales, 1.4% farming, 17.3% construction, 19.1% production (2006-2010 5-year est.).
**Income:** Per capita income: $24,930 (2006-2010 5-year est.); Median household income: $62,500 (2006-2010 5-year est.); Average household income: $67,959 (2006-2010 5-year est.); Percent of households with income of $100,000 or more: 16.5% (2006-2010 5-year est.); Poverty rate: 6.9% (2006-2010 5-year est.).
**Education:** Percent of population age 25 and over with: High school diploma (including GED) or higher: 92.1% (2006-2010 5-year est.); Bachelor's degree or higher: 15.3% (2006-2010 5-year est.); Master's degree or higher: 6.1% (2006-2010 5-year est.).

**School District(s)**
Hartford Central School District (PK-12)
    2009-10 Enrollment: 516 . . . . . . . . . . . . . . . . . . . . . (518) 632-5931
**Housing:** Homeownership rate: 83.7% (2010); Median home value: $158,600 (2006-2010 5-year est.); Median contract rent: $631 per month (2006-2010 5-year est.); Median year structure built: 1977 (2006-2010 5-year est.).
**Transportation:** Commute to work: 90.7% car, 0.4% public transportation, 3.6% walk, 5.0% work from home (2006-2010 5-year est.); Travel time to work: 13.9% less than 15 minutes, 49.5% 15 to 30 minutes, 25.3% 30 to 45 minutes, 4.1% 45 to 60 minutes, 7.2% 60 minutes or more (2006-2010 5-year est.)

**HEBRON** (town). Covers a land area of 56.108 square miles and a water area of 0.309 square miles. Located at 43.25° N. Lat; 73.34° W. Long.
**Population:** 1,540 (1990); 1,773 (2000); 1,853 (2010); Density: 33.0 persons per square mile (2010); Race: 96.5% White, 1.2% Black, 0.3% Asian, 0.1% American Indian/Alaska Native, 0.0% Native Hawaiian/Other Pacific Islander, 1.9% Other, 1.8% Hispanic of any race (2010); Average

household size: 2.47 (2010); Median age: 45.0 (2010); Males per 100 females: 104.1 (2010); Marriage status: 21.9% never married, 65.0% now married, 4.6% widowed, 8.5% divorced (2006-2010 5-year est.); Foreign born: 1.0% (2006-2010 5-year est.); Ancestry (includes multiple ancestries): 23.6% Irish, 15.1% German, 14.6% English, 12.8% French, 11.2% Italian (2006-2010 5-year est.).
**Economy:** Employment by occupation: 9.2% management, 4.7% professional, 6.4% services, 16.0% sales, 1.6% farming, 18.1% construction, 10.9% production (2006-2010 5-year est.).
**Income:** Per capita income: $25,592 (2006-2010 5-year est.); Median household income: $51,435 (2006-2010 5-year est.); Average household income: $62,392 (2006-2010 5-year est.); Percent of households with income of $100,000 or more: 18.5% (2006-2010 5-year est.); Poverty rate: 12.0% (2006-2010 5-year est.).
**Education:** Percent of population age 25 and over with: High school diploma (including GED) or higher: 85.4% (2006-2010 5-year est.); Bachelor's degree or higher: 22.7% (2006-2010 5-year est.); Master's degree or higher: 11.6% (2006-2010 5-year est.).
**Housing:** Homeownership rate: 85.8% (2010); Median home value: $125,900 (2006-2010 5-year est.); Median contract rent: $506 per month (2006-2010 5-year est.); Median year structure built: 1976 (2006-2010 5-year est.).
**Transportation:** Commute to work: 88.2% car, 1.7% public transportation, 2.6% walk, 7.2% work from home (2006-2010 5-year est.); Travel time to work: 18.1% less than 15 minutes, 31.8% 15 to 30 minutes, 23.1% 30 to 45 minutes, 9.8% 45 to 60 minutes, 17.3% 60 minutes or more (2006-2010 5-year est.)

**HUDSON FALLS** (village). County seat. Covers a land area of 1.831 square miles and a water area of 0.058 square miles. Located at 43.30° N. Lat; 73.58° W. Long. Elevation is 295 feet.
**History:** Settlers arrived in Hudson Falls in the 1760's and built gristmills and sawmills on the river near the 70-foot falls. The Burgoyne campaign delayed development and then the settlement was burned in 1780 by Sir Guy Carleton. In the 19th century, pulpwood, floated down the Hudson River from the Adirondack forests, helped to establish paper manufacturing as the dominant industry.
**Population:** 7,494 (1990); 6,927 (2000); 7,281 (2010); Density: 3,974.5 persons per square mile (2010); Race: 96.4% White, 1.1% Black, 0.4% Asian, 0.1% American Indian/Alaska Native, 0.0% Native Hawaiian/Other Pacific Islander, 2.0% Other, 1.5% Hispanic of any race (2010); Average household size: 2.41 (2010); Median age: 36.6 (2010); Males per 100 females: 92.3 (2010); Marriage status: 29.1% never married, 51.8% now married, 7.6% widowed, 11.6% divorced (2006-2010 5-year est.); Foreign born: 1.7% (2006-2010 5-year est.); Ancestry (includes multiple ancestries): 21.4% Irish, 18.7% English, 17.1% French, 10.0% German, 8.7% American (2006-2010 5-year est.).
**Economy:** Single-family building permits issued: 3 (2011); Multi-family building permits issued: 0 (2011); Employment by occupation: 6.0% management, 0.3% professional, 15.8% services, 19.5% sales, 4.4% farming, 7.2% construction, 7.5% production (2006-2010 5-year est.).
**Income:** Per capita income: $20,765 (2006-2010 5-year est.); Median household income: $39,361 (2006-2010 5-year est.); Average household income: $47,354 (2006-2010 5-year est.); Percent of households with income of $100,000 or more: 7.8% (2006-2010 5-year est.); Poverty rate: 14.5% (2006-2010 5-year est.).
**Education:** Percent of population age 25 and over with: High school diploma (including GED) or higher: 86.4% (2006-2010 5-year est.); Bachelor's degree or higher: 14.3% (2006-2010 5-year est.); Master's degree or higher: 6.1% (2006-2010 5-year est.).

**School District(s)**
Hudson Falls Central School District (PK-12)
    2009-10 Enrollment: 2,264 . . . . . . . . . . . . . . . . . . . . . . (518) 747-2121
**Housing:** Homeownership rate: 55.2% (2010); Median home value: $120,700 (2006-2010 5-year est.); Median contract rent: $557 per month (2006-2010 5-year est.); Median year structure built: 1946 (2006-2010 5-year est.).
**Safety:** Violent crime rate: 27.7 per 10,000 population; Property crime rate: 214.1 per 10,000 population (2010).
**Newspapers:** Washington County Wise Shoppers (Local news; Circulation 50,000)
**Transportation:** Commute to work: 93.2% car, 0.8% public transportation, 1.1% walk, 4.6% work from home (2006-2010 5-year est.); Travel time to work: 44.8% less than 15 minutes, 33.0% 15 to 30 minutes, 13.9% 30 to 45

minutes, 3.8% 45 to 60 minutes, 4.5% 60 minutes or more (2006-2010 5-year est.)

## HULETTS LANDING (unincorporated postal area)
Zip Code: 12841

Covers a land area of 16.967 square miles and a water area of 0.040 square miles. Located at 43.60° N. Lat; 73.53° W. Long. Elevation is 371 feet. Population: 77 (2010); Density: 4.5 persons per square mile (2010); Race: 98.7% White, 0.0% Black, 0.0% Asian, 0.0% American Indian/Alaska Native, 0.0% Native Hawaiian/Other Pacific Islander, 1.3% Other, 2.6% Hispanic of any race (2010); Average household size: 1.93 (2010); Median age: 61.8 (2010); Males per 100 females: 87.8 (2010); Homeownership rate: 87.5% (2010)

## JACKSON (town). Covers a land area of 37.159 square miles and a water area of 0.406 square miles. Located at 43.08° N. Lat; 73.38° W. Long.
**Population:** 1,581 (1990); 1,718 (2000); 1,800 (2010); Density: 48.4 persons per square mile (2010); Race: 96.6% White, 1.4% Black, 0.3% Asian, 0.1% American Indian/Alaska Native, 0.0% Native Hawaiian/Other Pacific Islander, 1.6% Other, 1.5% Hispanic of any race (2010); Average household size: 2.36 (2010); Median age: 46.9 (2010); Males per 100 females: 104.8 (2010); Marriage status: 21.3% never married, 63.3% now married, 2.7% widowed, 12.7% divorced (2006-2010 5-year est.); Foreign born: 0.5% (2006-2010 5-year est.); Ancestry (includes multiple ancestries): 27.2% Irish, 19.3% English, 19.0% German, 9.5% Italian, 9.5% French (2006-2010 5-year est.).
**Economy:** Employment by occupation: 11.1% management, 3.4% professional, 8.3% services, 19.7% sales, 4.7% farming, 9.5% construction, 7.7% production (2006-2010 5-year est.).
**Income:** Per capita income: $28,661 (2006-2010 5-year est.); Median household income: $58,795 (2006-2010 5-year est.); Average household income: $67,643 (2006-2010 5-year est.); Percent of households with income of $100,000 or more: 18.6% (2006-2010 5-year est.); Poverty rate: 10.1% (2006-2010 5-year est.).
**Education:** Percent of population age 25 and over with: High school diploma (including GED) or higher: 89.9% (2006-2010 5-year est.); Bachelor's degree or higher: 25.9% (2006-2010 5-year est.); Master's degree or higher: 11.2% (2006-2010 5-year est.).
**Housing:** Homeownership rate: 78.7% (2010); Median home value: $196,900 (2006-2010 5-year est.); Median contract rent: $566 per month (2006-2010 5-year est.); Median year structure built: 1971 (2006-2010 5-year est.).
**Transportation:** Commute to work: 91.3% car, 0.0% public transportation, 3.2% walk, 5.2% work from home (2006-2010 5-year est.); Travel time to work: 27.4% less than 15 minutes, 20.3% 15 to 30 minutes, 18.5% 30 to 45 minutes, 16.3% 45 to 60 minutes, 17.5% 60 minutes or more (2006-2010 5-year est.)

## KINGSBURY (town). Covers a land area of 39.678 square miles and a water area of 0.326 square miles. Located at 43.33° N. Lat; 73.55° W. Long. Elevation is 305 feet.
**Population:** 11,851 (1990); 11,171 (2000); 12,671 (2010); Density: 319.3 persons per square mile (2010); Race: 96.8% White, 0.9% Black, 0.4% Asian, 0.2% American Indian/Alaska Native, 0.0% Native Hawaiian/Other Pacific Islander, 1.7% Other, 1.9% Hispanic of any race (2010); Average household size: 2.41 (2010); Median age: 38.5 (2010); Males per 100 females: 96.4 (2010); Marriage status: 29.2% never married, 52.9% now married, 7.2% widowed, 10.6% divorced (2006-2010 5-year est.); Foreign born: 1.4% (2006-2010 5-year est.); Ancestry (includes multiple ancestries): 20.4% Irish, 19.6% French, 15.0% English, 10.8% German, 7.6% Italian (2006-2010 5-year est.).
**Economy:** Single-family building permits issued: 9 (2011); Multi-family building permits issued: 12 (2011); Employment by occupation: 7.0% management, 1.0% professional, 12.9% services, 20.7% sales, 4.1% farming, 7.2% construction, 7.5% production (2006-2010 5-year est.).
**Income:** Per capita income: $22,727 (2006-2010 5-year est.); Median household income: $44,574 (2006-2010 5-year est.); Average household income: $53,320 (2006-2010 5-year est.); Percent of households with income of $100,000 or more: 11.2% (2006-2010 5-year est.); Poverty rate: 10.8% (2006-2010 5-year est.).
**Education:** Percent of population age 25 and over with: High school diploma (including GED) or higher: 88.5% (2006-2010 5-year est.); Bachelor's degree or higher: 14.1% (2006-2010 5-year est.); Master's degree or higher: 5.4% (2006-2010 5-year est.).

**Housing:** Homeownership rate: 59.8% (2010); Median home value: $133,300 (2006-2010 5-year est.); Median contract rent: $575 per month (2006-2010 5-year est.); Median year structure built: 1956 (2006-2010 5-year est.).
**Transportation:** Commute to work: 94.8% car, 0.6% public transportation, 0.9% walk, 3.2% work from home (2006-2010 5-year est.); Travel time to work: 39.6% less than 15 minutes, 37.5% 15 to 30 minutes, 13.0% 30 to 45 minutes, 4.3% 45 to 60 minutes, 5.6% 60 minutes or more (2006-2010 5-year est.)

## MIDDLE GRANVILLE (unincorporated postal area)
Zip Code: 12849

Covers a land area of 2.719 square miles and a water area of 0.011 square miles. Located at 43.44° N. Lat; 73.29° W. Long. Elevation is 367 feet. Population: 385 (2010); Density: 141.6 persons per square mile (2010); Race: 98.2% White, 0.0% Black, 1.6% Asian, 0.0% American Indian/Alaska Native, 0.0% Native Hawaiian/Other Pacific Islander, 0.2% Other, 0.5% Hispanic of any race (2010); Average household size: 2.66 (2010); Median age: 45.2 (2010); Males per 100 females: 94.4 (2010); Homeownership rate: 93.6% (2010)

## PUTNAM (town). Covers a land area of 32.790 square miles and a water area of 2.627 square miles. Located at 43.74° N. Lat; 73.41° W. Long. Elevation is 335 feet.
**Population:** 477 (1990); 645 (2000); 609 (2010); Density: 18.6 persons per square mile (2010); Race: 99.2% White, 0.0% Black, 0.0% Asian, 0.0% American Indian/Alaska Native, 0.0% Native Hawaiian/Other Pacific Islander, 0.8% Other, 0.2% Hispanic of any race (2010); Average household size: 2.34 (2010); Median age: 49.4 (2010); Males per 100 females: 100.3 (2010); Marriage status: 8.4% never married, 80.0% now married, 6.6% widowed, 5.0% divorced (2006-2010 5-year est.); Foreign born: 0.6% (2006-2010 5-year est.); Ancestry (includes multiple ancestries): 26.4% Irish, 21.5% French, 19.3% English, 15.9% German, 10.3% Italian (2006-2010 5-year est.).
**Economy:** Single-family building permits issued: 0 (2011); Multi-family building permits issued: 0 (2011); Employment by occupation: 5.1% management, 0.0% professional, 13.4% services, 18.9% sales, 3.7% farming, 14.7% construction, 2.3% production (2006-2010 5-year est.).
**Income:** Per capita income: $25,635 (2006-2010 5-year est.); Median household income: $47,000 (2006-2010 5-year est.); Average household income: $59,345 (2006-2010 5-year est.); Percent of households with income of $100,000 or more: 19.8% (2006-2010 5-year est.); Poverty rate: 7.3% (2006-2010 5-year est.).
**Education:** Percent of population age 25 and over with: High school diploma (including GED) or higher: 90.5% (2006-2010 5-year est.); Bachelor's degree or higher: 23.6% (2006-2010 5-year est.); Master's degree or higher: 13.4% (2006-2010 5-year est.).
**Housing:** Homeownership rate: 88.0% (2010); Median home value: $200,800 (2006-2010 5-year est.); Median contract rent: $472 per month (2006-2010 5-year est.); Median year structure built: 1961 (2006-2010 5-year est.).
**Transportation:** Commute to work: 93.7% car, 0.0% public transportation, 0.0% walk, 3.9% work from home (2006-2010 5-year est.); Travel time to work: 52.0% less than 15 minutes, 20.2% 15 to 30 minutes, 16.7% 30 to 45 minutes, 2.5% 45 to 60 minutes, 8.6% 60 minutes or more (2006-2010 5-year est.)

## PUTNAM STATION (unincorporated postal area)
Zip Code: 12861

Covers a land area of 32.790 square miles and a water area of 0.565 square miles. Located at 43.74° N. Lat; 73.41° W. Long. Elevation is 118 feet. Population: 609 (2010); Density: 18.6 persons per square mile (2010); Race: 99.2% White, 0.0% Black, 0.0% Asian, 0.0% American Indian/Alaska Native, 0.0% Native Hawaiian/Other Pacific Islander, 0.8% Other, 0.2% Hispanic of any race (2010); Average household size: 2.34 (2010); Median age: 49.4 (2010); Males per 100 females: 100.3 (2010); Homeownership rate: 88.0% (2010)

## SALEM (village). Covers a land area of 2.928 square miles and a water area of 0 square miles. Located at 43.17° N. Lat; 73.32° W. Long. Elevation is 482 feet.
**Population:** 958 (1990); 964 (2000); 946 (2010); Density: 323.0 persons per square mile (2010); Race: 96.6% White, 1.5% Black, 0.2% Asian, 0.0% American Indian/Alaska Native, 0.0% Native Hawaiian/Other Pacific Islander, 1.7% Other, 1.5% Hispanic of any race (2010); Average

household size: 2.48 (2010); Median age: 42.1 (2010); Males per 100 females: 93.1 (2010); Marriage status: 31.0% never married, 46.5% now married, 7.2% widowed, 15.3% divorced (2006-2010 5-year est.); Foreign born: 1.4% (2006-2010 5-year est.); Ancestry (includes multiple ancestries): 27.6% Irish, 19.5% German, 19.5% French, 14.4% Italian, 13.3% English (2006-2010 5-year est.).
**Economy:** Employment by occupation: 5.1% management, 0.0% professional, 16.5% services, 21.6% sales, 3.3% farming, 8.4% construction, 4.1% production (2006-2010 5-year est.).
**Income:** Per capita income: $23,117 (2006-2010 5-year est.); Median household income: $38,500 (2006-2010 5-year est.); Average household income: $54,914 (2006-2010 5-year est.); Percent of households with income of $100,000 or more: 14.5% (2006-2010 5-year est.); Poverty rate: 11.6% (2006-2010 5-year est.).
**Education:** Percent of population age 25 and over with: High school diploma (including GED) or higher: 84.2% (2006-2010 5-year est.); Bachelor's degree or higher: 18.8% (2006-2010 5-year est.); Master's degree or higher: 6.6% (2006-2010 5-year est.).

**School District(s)**
Salem Central School District (KG-12)
    2009-10 Enrollment: 619 . . . . . . . . . . . . . . . . . (518) 854-7855
**Housing:** Homeownership rate: 73.3% (2010); Median home value: $117,100 (2006-2010 5-year est.); Median contract rent: $575 per month (2006-2010 5-year est.); Median year structure built: before 1940 (2006-2010 5-year est.).
**Transportation:** Commute to work: 80.5% car, 0.0% public transportation, 15.2% walk, 2.3% work from home (2006-2010 5-year est.); Travel time to work: 26.7% less than 15 minutes, 26.5% 15 to 30 minutes, 20.2% 30 to 45 minutes, 20.8% 45 to 60 minutes, 5.7% 60 minutes or more (2006-2010 5-year est.)

**SALEM** (town). Covers a land area of 52.361 square miles and a water area of 0.057 square miles. Located at 43.16° N. Lat; 73.32° W. Long. Elevation is 482 feet.
**History:** Settled 1764, incorporated 1803.
**Population:** 2,608 (1990); 2,702 (2000); 2,715 (2010); Density: 51.9 persons per square mile (2010); Race: 96.7% White, 1.3% Black, 0.1% Asian, 0.1% American Indian/Alaska Native, 0.1% Native Hawaiian/Other Pacific Islander, 1.7% Other, 2.0% Hispanic of any race (2010); Average household size: 2.37 (2010); Median age: 46.2 (2010); Males per 100 females: 100.4 (2010); Marriage status: 23.9% never married, 58.0% now married, 6.8% widowed, 11.3% divorced (2006-2010 5-year est.); Foreign born: 1.0% (2006-2010 5-year est.); Ancestry (includes multiple ancestries): 20.0% Irish, 18.8% English, 18.3% German, 11.8% French, 11.0% Italian (2006-2010 5-year est.).
**Economy:** Employment by occupation: 8.3% management, 1.7% professional, 9.1% services, 15.8% sales, 3.9% farming, 14.9% construction, 4.6% production (2006-2010 5-year est.).
**Income:** Per capita income: $28,019 (2006-2010 5-year est.); Median household income: $48,947 (2006-2010 5-year est.); Average household income: $60,189 (2006-2010 5-year est.); Percent of households with income of $100,000 or more: 13.2% (2006-2010 5-year est.); Poverty rate: 9.8% (2006-2010 5-year est.).
**Education:** Percent of population age 25 and over with: High school diploma (including GED) or higher: 90.0% (2006-2010 5-year est.); Bachelor's degree or higher: 23.1% (2006-2010 5-year est.); Master's degree or higher: 11.8% (2006-2010 5-year est.).

**School District(s)**
Salem Central School District (KG-12)
    2009-10 Enrollment: 619 . . . . . . . . . . . . . . . . . (518) 854-7855
**Housing:** Homeownership rate: 81.9% (2010); Median home value: $151,600 (2006-2010 5-year est.); Median contract rent: $563 per month (2006-2010 5-year est.); Median year structure built: 1944 (2006-2010 5-year est.).
**Transportation:** Commute to work: 82.5% car, 0.8% public transportation, 8.2% walk, 6.1% work from home (2006-2010 5-year est.); Travel time to work: 25.4% less than 15 minutes, 21.9% 15 to 30 minutes, 26.8% 30 to 45 minutes, 17.4% 45 to 60 minutes, 8.5% 60 minutes or more (2006-2010 5-year est.)

**SHUSHAN** (unincorporated postal area)
Zip Code: 12873
    Covers a land area of 21.118 square miles and a water area of <.001 square miles. Located at 43.11° N. Lat; 73.31° W. Long. Elevation is 469 feet. Population: 736 (2010); Density: 34.9 persons per square mile

(2010); Race: 96.2% White, 0.8% Black, 0.1% Asian, 0.4% American Indian/Alaska Native, 0.0% Native Hawaiian/Other Pacific Islander, 2.5% Other, 2.4% Hispanic of any race (2010); Average household size: 2.21 (2010); Median age: 50.8 (2010); Males per 100 females: 100.5 (2010); Homeownership rate: 89.1% (2010)

**WHITE CREEK** (town). Covers a land area of 47.923 square miles and a water area of 0.053 square miles. Located at 42.99° N. Lat; 73.32° W. Long. Elevation is 656 feet.
**Population:** 3,196 (1990); 3,411 (2000); 3,356 (2010); Density: 70.0 persons per square mile (2010); Race: 97.2% White, 0.5% Black, 0.6% Asian, 0.1% American Indian/Alaska Native, 0.0% Native Hawaiian/Other Pacific Islander, 1.6% Other, 1.7% Hispanic of any race (2010); Average household size: 2.48 (2010); Median age: 44.5 (2010); Males per 100 females: 93.5 (2010); Marriage status: 20.0% never married, 65.1% now married, 4.1% widowed, 10.8% divorced (2006-2010 5-year est.); Foreign born: 2.2% (2006-2010 5-year est.); Ancestry (includes multiple ancestries): 26.1% Irish, 17.6% English, 16.6% German, 13.9% American, 9.2% French (2006-2010 5-year est.).
**Economy:** Employment by occupation: 11.6% management, 3.7% professional, 13.9% services, 12.9% sales, 2.8% farming, 12.8% construction, 8.1% production (2006-2010 5-year est.).
**Income:** Per capita income: $21,216 (2006-2010 5-year est.); Median household income: $40,547 (2006-2010 5-year est.); Average household income: $50,891 (2006-2010 5-year est.); Percent of households with income of $100,000 or more: 6.5% (2006-2010 5-year est.); Poverty rate: 9.8% (2006-2010 5-year est.).
**Education:** Percent of population age 25 and over with: High school diploma (including GED) or higher: 87.4% (2006-2010 5-year est.); Bachelor's degree or higher: 19.6% (2006-2010 5-year est.); Master's degree or higher: 7.8% (2006-2010 5-year est.).
**Housing:** Homeownership rate: 75.9% (2010); Median home value: $148,600 (2006-2010 5-year est.); Median contract rent: $607 per month (2006-2010 5-year est.); Median year structure built: 1960 (2006-2010 5-year est.).
**Transportation:** Commute to work: 85.5% car, 0.0% public transportation, 4.1% walk, 9.1% work from home (2006-2010 5-year est.); Travel time to work: 28.9% less than 15 minutes, 30.9% 15 to 30 minutes, 18.9% 30 to 45 minutes, 13.1% 45 to 60 minutes, 8.2% 60 minutes or more (2006-2010 5-year est.)

**WHITEHALL** (village). Covers a land area of 4.702 square miles and a water area of 0.211 square miles. Located at 43.56° N. Lat; 73.41° W. Long. Elevation is 157 feet.
**Population:** 3,099 (1990); 2,667 (2000); 2,614 (2010); Density: 555.8 persons per square mile (2010); Race: 95.8% White, 0.5% Black, 0.3% Asian, 0.2% American Indian/Alaska Native, 0.1% Native Hawaiian/Other Pacific Islander, 3.1% Other, 2.5% Hispanic of any race (2010); Average household size: 2.40 (2010); Median age: 38.3 (2010); Males per 100 females: 104.1 (2010); Marriage status: 29.6% never married, 54.0% now married, 7.8% widowed, 8.6% divorced (2006-2010 5-year est.); Foreign born: 0.7% (2006-2010 5-year est.); Ancestry (includes multiple ancestries): 25.8% Irish, 21.4% French, 18.3% English, 11.3% American, 8.6% French Canadian (2006-2010 5-year est.).
**Economy:** Employment by occupation: 4.8% management, 3.6% professional, 11.9% services, 15.6% sales, 2.7% farming, 13.3% construction, 11.9% production (2006-2010 5-year est.).
**Income:** Per capita income: $17,304 (2006-2010 5-year est.); Median household income: $30,647 (2006-2010 5-year est.); Average household income: $39,965 (2006-2010 5-year est.); Percent of households with income of $100,000 or more: 5.5% (2006-2010 5-year est.); Poverty rate: 20.8% (2006-2010 5-year est.).
**Education:** Percent of population age 25 and over with: High school diploma (including GED) or higher: 81.4% (2006-2010 5-year est.); Bachelor's degree or higher: 7.9% (2006-2010 5-year est.); Master's degree or higher: 2.0% (2006-2010 5-year est.).

**School District(s)**
Whitehall Central School District (KG-12)
    2009-10 Enrollment: 779 . . . . . . . . . . . . . . . . . (518) 499-1772
**Housing:** Homeownership rate: 57.2% (2010); Median home value: $83,400 (2006-2010 5-year est.); Median contract rent: $508 per month (2006-2010 5-year est.); Median year structure built: before 1940 (2006-2010 5-year est.).
**Safety:** Violent crime rate: 19.9 per 10,000 population; Property crime rate: 135.0 per 10,000 population (2010).

**Transportation:** Commute to work: 89.8% car, 0.0% public transportation, 8.0% walk, 1.6% work from home (2006-2010 5-year est.); Travel time to work: 41.6% less than 15 minutes, 23.8% 15 to 30 minutes, 19.2% 30 to 45 minutes, 9.8% 45 to 60 minutes, 5.6% 60 minutes or more (2006-2010 5-year est.); Amtrak: train service available.

**Additional Information Contacts**
Whitehall Chamber of Commerce . . . . . . . . . . . . . . . . . (518) 499-4435
   http://www.whitehall-chamber.org

**WHITEHALL** (town). Covers a land area of 57.176 square miles and a water area of 1.728 square miles. Located at 43.53° N. Lat; 73.38° W. Long. Elevation is 157 feet.
**History:** Settled 1759, incorporated 1806.
**Population:** 4,409 (1990); 4,035 (2000); 4,042 (2010); Density: 70.7 persons per square mile (2010); Race: 96.2% White, 0.4% Black, 0.5% Asian, 0.1% American Indian/Alaska Native, 0.0% Native Hawaiian/Other Pacific Islander, 2.8% Other, 2.9% Hispanic of any race (2010); Average household size: 2.46 (2010); Median age: 40.7 (2010); Males per 100 females: 103.9 (2010); Marriage status: 26.6% never married, 60.0% now married, 6.4% widowed, 7.0% divorced (2006-2010 5-year est.); Foreign born: 0.5% (2006-2010 5-year est.); Ancestry (includes multiple ancestries): 24.0% Irish, 23.5% French, 18.2% English, 10.9% American, 8.9% Italian (2006-2010 5-year est.).
**Economy:** Employment by occupation: 8.8% management, 3.6% professional, 10.3% services, 18.1% sales, 2.3% farming, 11.0% construction, 11.6% production (2006-2010 5-year est.).
**Income:** Per capita income: $20,121 (2006-2010 5-year est.); Median household income: $42,779 (2006-2010 5-year est.); Average household income: $48,813 (2006-2010 5-year est.); Percent of households with income of $100,000 or more: 8.4% (2006-2010 5-year est.); Poverty rate: 14.0% (2006-2010 5-year est.).
**Education:** Percent of population age 25 and over with: High school diploma (including GED) or higher: 83.9% (2006-2010 5-year est.); Bachelor's degree or higher: 12.2% (2006-2010 5-year est.); Master's degree or higher: 5.3% (2006-2010 5-year est.).

**School District(s)**
Whitehall Central School District (KG-12)
   2009-10 Enrollment: 779 . . . . . . . . . . . . . . . . . . . (518) 499-1772
**Housing:** Homeownership rate: 67.1% (2010); Median home value: $91,200 (2006-2010 5-year est.); Median contract rent: $518 per month (2006-2010 5-year est.); Median year structure built: before 1940 (2006-2010 5-year est.).
**Transportation:** Commute to work: 91.1% car, 0.0% public transportation, 6.8% walk, 1.7% work from home (2006-2010 5-year est.); Travel time to work: 44.2% less than 15 minutes, 25.9% 15 to 30 minutes, 16.1% 30 to 45 minutes, 8.2% 45 to 60 minutes, 5.6% 60 minutes or more (2006-2010 5-year est.); Amtrak: train service available.

# Wayne County

Located in western New York; bounded on the north by Lake Ontario; drained by the Clyde River. Covers a land area of 604.21 square miles, a water area of 779.93 square miles, and is located in the Eastern Time Zone at 43.14° N. Lat., 77.05° W. Long. The county was founded in 1823. County seat is Lyons.

Wayne County is part of the Rochester, NY Metropolitan Statistical Area. The entire metro area includes: Livingston County, NY; Monroe County, NY; Ontario County, NY; Orleans County, NY; Wayne County, NY

| Weather Station: Sodus Center | | | | | | | | | | Elevation: 419 feet | |
| --- | --- | --- | --- | --- | --- | --- | --- | --- | --- | --- | --- |
| | Jan | Feb | Mar | Apr | May | Jun | Jul | Aug | Sep | Oct | Nov | Dec |
| High | 33 | 35 | 44 | 57 | 69 | 78 | 81 | 80 | 73 | 60 | 49 | 37 |
| Low | 18 | 19 | 26 | 37 | 46 | 55 | 61 | 60 | 53 | 42 | 34 | 24 |
| Precip | 2.7 | 2.1 | 2.7 | 3.1 | 3.2 | 3.5 | 3.3 | 3.3 | 3.7 | 4.0 | 4.0 | 3.2 |
| Snow | 29.7 | 16.3 | 12.9 | 2.8 | 0.1 | 0.0 | 0.0 | 0.0 | 0.0 | 0.1 | 7.1 | 23.7 |

*High and Low temperatures in degrees Fahrenheit; Precipitation and Snow in inches*

**Population:** 89,123 (1990); 93,765 (2000); 93,772 (2010); Race: 92.9% White, 3.1% Black, 0.5% Asian, 0.3% American Indian/Alaska Native, 0.0% Native Hawaiian/Other Pacific Islander, 3.2% Other, 3.7% Hispanic of any race (2010); Density: 155.2 persons per square mile (2010); Average household size: 2.53 (2010); Median age: 41.6 (2010); Males per 100 females: 98.5 (2010).

**Religion:** Six largest groups: 16.4% Catholicism, 5.2% Methodist/Pietist, 3.1% Presbyterian-Reformed, 2.4% Baptist, 2.1% Non-Denominational, 1.3% Holiness (2010)
**Economy:** Unemployment rate: 9.7% (February 2012); Total civilian labor force: 47,766 (February 2012); Leading industries: 29.1% manufacturing; 18.6% retail trade; 14.1% health care and social assistance (2009); Farms: 938 totaling 168,471 acres (2007); Companies that employ 500 or more persons: 4 (2009); Companies that employ 100 to 499 persons: 24 (2009); Companies that employ less than 100 persons: 1,700 (2009); Black-owned businesses: 70 (2007); Hispanic-owned businesses: 182 (2007); Asian-owned businesses: n/a (2007); Women-owned businesses: 1,956 (2007); Retail sales per capita: $10,041 (2010). Single-family building permits issued: 85 (2011); Multi-family building permits issued: 0 (2011).
**Income:** Per capita income: $24,092 (2006-2010 5-year est.); Median household income: $52,562 (2006-2010 5-year est.); Average household income: $61,072 (2006-2010 5-year est.); Percent of households with income of $100,000 or more: 15.7% (2006-2010 5-year est.); Poverty rate: 11.1% (2006-2010 5-year est.); Bankruptcy rate: 2.07% (2011).
**Education:** Percent of population age 25 and over with: High school diploma (including GED) or higher: 86.7% (2006-2010 5-year est.); Bachelor's degree or higher: 21.5% (2006-2010 5-year est.); Master's degree or higher: 8.5% (2006-2010 5-year est.).
**Housing:** Homeownership rate: 76.8% (2010); Median home value: $107,400 (2006-2010 5-year est.); Median contract rent: $507 per month (2006-2010 5-year est.); Median year structure built: 1964 (2006-2010 5-year est.).
**Health:** Birth rate: 112.1 per 10,000 population (2011); Death rate: 83.9 per 10,000 population (2011); Age-adjusted cancer mortality rate: 186.5 deaths per 100,000 population (2009); Number of physicians: 6.3 per 10,000 population (2008); Hospital beds: 28.7 per 10,000 population (2007); Hospital admissions: 353.4 per 10,000 population (2007).
**Environment:** Air Quality Index: 92.7% good, 7.3% moderate, 0.0% unhealthy for sensitive individuals, 0.0% unhealthy (percent of days in 2010)
**Elections:** 2008 Presidential election results: 44.3% Obama, 54.2% McCain, 0.7% Nader
**Additional Information Contacts**
Wayne County Government. . . . . . . . . . . . . . . . . . . . . . (315) 946-5400
   http://www.co.wayne.ny.us
Greater Newark Chamber of Commerce . . . . . . . . . . . . (315) 331-2705
   http://www.newarknychamber.org
Town of Palmyra . . . . . . . . . . . . . . . . . . . . . . . . . . . . (315) 597-5521
   http://www.palmyrany.com
Village of Palmyra . . . . . . . . . . . . . . . . . . . . . . . . . . . (315) 597-4849
   http://www.palmyrany.com
Village of Sodus Point . . . . . . . . . . . . . . . . . . . . . . . . (315) 483-9881
   http://www.soduspoint.info
Williamson Chamber of Commerce . . . . . . . . . . . . . . . (315) 589-8100
   http://williamsonchamberofcommerceny.org

# Wayne County Communities

**ARCADIA** (town). Covers a land area of 52.032 square miles and a water area of 0.110 square miles. Located at 43.09° N. Lat; 77.08° W. Long.
**Population:** 14,827 (1990); 14,889 (2000); 14,244 (2010); Density: 273.8 persons per square mile (2010); Race: 89.3% White, 4.6% Black, 0.5% Asian, 0.3% American Indian/Alaska Native, 0.1% Native Hawaiian/Other Pacific Islander, 5.2% Other, 6.8% Hispanic of any race (2010); Average household size: 2.38 (2010); Median age: 42.4 (2010); Males per 100 females: 93.6 (2010); Marriage status: 27.0% never married, 55.1% now married, 7.2% widowed, 10.7% divorced (2006-2010 5-year est.); Foreign born: 2.9% (2006-2010 5-year est.); Ancestry (includes multiple ancestries): 24.9% German, 17.3% Dutch, 15.9% Irish, 14.7% Italian, 14.2% English (2006-2010 5-year est.).
**Economy:** Single-family building permits issued: 4 (2011); Multi-family building permits issued: 0 (2011); Employment by occupation: 7.6% management, 5.4% professional, 12.5% services, 16.2% sales, 3.8% farming, 9.2% construction, 7.5% production (2006-2010 5-year est.).
**Income:** Per capita income: $23,068 (2006-2010 5-year est.); Median household income: $45,736 (2006-2010 5-year est.); Average household income: $53,065 (2006-2010 5-year est.); Percent of households with income of $100,000 or more: 10.8% (2006-2010 5-year est.); Poverty rate: 11.3% (2006-2010 5-year est.).

**Education:** Percent of population age 25 and over with: High school diploma (including GED) or higher: 83.6% (2006-2010 5-year est.); Bachelor's degree or higher: 16.6% (2006-2010 5-year est.); Master's degree or higher: 6.9% (2006-2010 5-year est.).
**Housing:** Homeownership rate: 65.6% (2010); Median home value: $89,600 (2006-2010 5-year est.); Median contract rent: $522 per month (2006-2010 5-year est.); Median year structure built: 1956 (2006-2010 5-year est.).
**Transportation:** Commute to work: 94.6% car, 0.2% public transportation, 3.1% walk, 1.5% work from home (2006-2010 5-year est.); Travel time to work: 43.9% less than 15 minutes, 26.8% 15 to 30 minutes, 15.0% 30 to 45 minutes, 7.2% 45 to 60 minutes, 7.1% 60 minutes or more (2006-2010 5-year est.)

**BUTLER** (town). Covers a land area of 37.089 square miles and a water area of 0.078 square miles. Located at 43.17° N. Lat; 76.76° W. Long.
**Population:** 2,152 (1990); 2,277 (2000); 2,064 (2010); Density: 55.6 persons per square mile (2010); Race: 92.5% White, 3.2% Black, 0.1% Asian, 0.2% American Indian/Alaska Native, 0.0% Native Hawaiian/Other Pacific Islander, 4.0% Other, 4.4% Hispanic of any race (2010); Average household size: 2.76 (2010); Median age: 38.1 (2010); Males per 100 females: 108.9 (2010); Marriage status: 28.0% never married, 55.9% now married, 5.5% widowed, 10.6% divorced (2006-2010 5-year est.); Foreign born: 2.0% (2006-2010 5-year est.); Ancestry (includes multiple ancestries): 21.0% German, 13.7% Irish, 11.3% English, 11.0% American, 8.5% Dutch (2006-2010 5-year est.).
**Economy:** Single-family building permits issued: 0 (2011); Multi-family building permits issued: 0 (2011); Employment by occupation: 8.2% management, 1.3% professional, 11.6% services, 14.9% sales, 4.2% farming, 17.7% construction, 10.9% production (2006-2010 5-year est.).
**Income:** Per capita income: $16,471 (2006-2010 5-year est.); Median household income: $44,573 (2006-2010 5-year est.); Average household income: $52,505 (2006-2010 5-year est.); Percent of households with income of $100,000 or more: 6.2% (2006-2010 5-year est.); Poverty rate: 21.5% (2006-2010 5-year est.).
**Education:** Percent of population age 25 and over with: High school diploma (including GED) or higher: 74.5% (2006-2010 5-year est.); Bachelor's degree or higher: 5.4% (2006-2010 5-year est.); Master's degree or higher: 1.4% (2006-2010 5-year est.).
**Housing:** Homeownership rate: 80.1% (2010); Median home value: $73,100 (2006-2010 5-year est.); Median contract rent: $404 per month (2006-2010 5-year est.); Median year structure built: 1963 (2006-2010 5-year est.).
**Transportation:** Commute to work: 89.7% car, 0.4% public transportation, 0.9% walk, 7.3% work from home (2006-2010 5-year est.); Travel time to work: 29.3% less than 15 minutes, 24.7% 15 to 30 minutes, 28.8% 30 to 45 minutes, 11.7% 45 to 60 minutes, 5.4% 60 minutes or more (2006-2010 5-year est.)

**CLYDE** (village). Covers a land area of 2.198 square miles and a water area of 0.059 square miles. Located at 43.08° N. Lat; 76.87° W. Long. Elevation is 400 feet.
**History:** Incorporated 1835.
**Population:** 2,409 (1990); 2,269 (2000); 2,093 (2010); Density: 952.2 persons per square mile (2010); Race: 90.2% White, 4.5% Black, 0.5% Asian, 0.2% American Indian/Alaska Native, 0.0% Native Hawaiian/Other Pacific Islander, 4.6% Other, 4.0% Hispanic of any race (2010); Average household size: 2.61 (2010); Median age: 37.1 (2010); Males per 100 females: 94.7 (2010); Marriage status: 27.6% never married, 56.5% now married, 7.4% widowed, 8.5% divorced (2006-2010 5-year est.); Foreign born: 1.2% (2006-2010 5-year est.); Ancestry (includes multiple ancestries): 32.6% Italian, 19.8% German, 16.7% Irish, 10.0% English, 8.2% Dutch (2006-2010 5-year est.).
**Economy:** Single-family building permits issued: 0 (2011); Multi-family building permits issued: 0 (2011); Employment by occupation: 9.2% management, 1.5% professional, 12.9% services, 17.8% sales, 4.3% farming, 17.2% construction, 8.4% production (2006-2010 5-year est.).
**Income:** Per capita income: $19,290 (2006-2010 5-year est.); Median household income: $39,896 (2006-2010 5-year est.); Average household income: $49,684 (2006-2010 5-year est.); Percent of households with income of $100,000 or more: 5.9% (2006-2010 5-year est.); Poverty rate: 14.2% (2006-2010 5-year est.).
**Education:** Percent of population age 25 and over with: High school diploma (including GED) or higher: 84.0% (2006-2010 5-year est.);

Bachelor's degree or higher: 8.0% (2006-2010 5-year est.); Master's degree or higher: 1.6% (2006-2010 5-year est.).
**School District(s)**
Clyde-Savannah Central School District (PK-12)
    2009-10 Enrollment: 885 . . . . . . . . . . . . . . . . . . . (315) 902-3000
**Housing:** Homeownership rate: 69.6% (2010); Median home value: $65,100 (2006-2010 5-year est.); Median contract rent: $444 per month (2006-2010 5-year est.); Median year structure built: before 1940 (2006-2010 5-year est.).
**Safety:** Violent crime rate: 19.6 per 10,000 population; Property crime rate: 156.6 per 10,000 population (2010).
**Transportation:** Commute to work: 91.1% car, 0.0% public transportation, 5.0% walk, 3.9% work from home (2006-2010 5-year est.); Travel time to work: 39.7% less than 15 minutes, 35.6% 15 to 30 minutes, 13.0% 30 to 45 minutes, 6.0% 45 to 60 minutes, 5.6% 60 minutes or more (2006-2010 5-year est.)

**GALEN** (town). Covers a land area of 59.477 square miles and a water area of 0.580 square miles. Located at 43.06° N. Lat; 76.88° W. Long.
**Population:** 4,413 (1990); 4,439 (2000); 4,290 (2010); Density: 72.1 persons per square mile (2010); Race: 92.8% White, 3.2% Black, 0.3% Asian, 0.2% American Indian/Alaska Native, 0.0% Native Hawaiian/Other Pacific Islander, 3.5% Other, 3.2% Hispanic of any race (2010); Average household size: 2.66 (2010); Median age: 39.0 (2010); Males per 100 females: 99.8 (2010); Marriage status: 23.6% never married, 61.5% now married, 6.2% widowed, 8.8% divorced (2006-2010 5-year est.); Foreign born: 4.4% (2006-2010 5-year est.); Ancestry (includes multiple ancestries): 24.4% German, 21.5% Italian, 12.8% Irish, 11.9% English, 9.3% Dutch (2006-2010 5-year est.).
**Economy:** Single-family building permits issued: 5 (2011); Multi-family building permits issued: 0 (2011); Employment by occupation: 6.4% management, 2.5% professional, 10.2% services, 17.5% sales, 3.9% farming, 18.9% construction, 11.5% production (2006-2010 5-year est.).
**Income:** Per capita income: $18,285 (2006-2010 5-year est.); Median household income: $44,153 (2006-2010 5-year est.); Average household income: $52,087 (2006-2010 5-year est.); Percent of households with income of $100,000 or more: 8.3% (2006-2010 5-year est.); Poverty rate: 15.5% (2006-2010 5-year est.).
**Education:** Percent of population age 25 and over with: High school diploma (including GED) or higher: 80.0% (2006-2010 5-year est.); Bachelor's degree or higher: 8.4% (2006-2010 5-year est.); Master's degree or higher: 1.7% (2006-2010 5-year est.).
**Housing:** Homeownership rate: 77.9% (2010); Median home value: $69,000 (2006-2010 5-year est.); Median contract rent: $441 per month (2006-2010 5-year est.); Median year structure built: 1944 (2006-2010 5-year est.).
**Transportation:** Commute to work: 89.9% car, 0.0% public transportation, 4.2% walk, 4.6% work from home (2006-2010 5-year est.); Travel time to work: 40.0% less than 15 minutes, 35.3% 15 to 30 minutes, 14.1% 30 to 45 minutes, 5.1% 45 to 60 minutes, 5.5% 60 minutes or more (2006-2010 5-year est.)

**HURON** (town). Covers a land area of 39.391 square miles and a water area of 3.710 square miles. Located at 43.24° N. Lat; 76.89° W. Long. Elevation is 390 feet.
**Population:** 2,025 (1990); 2,117 (2000); 2,118 (2010); Density: 53.8 persons per square mile (2010); Race: 93.5% White, 2.1% Black, 0.3% Asian, 0.2% American Indian/Alaska Native, 0.0% Native Hawaiian/Other Pacific Islander, 3.9% Other, 4.5% Hispanic of any race (2010); Average household size: 2.42 (2010); Median age: 46.4 (2010); Males per 100 females: 107.6 (2010); Marriage status: 26.7% never married, 58.5% now married, 5.1% widowed, 9.7% divorced (2006-2010 5-year est.); Foreign born: 8.7% (2006-2010 5-year est.); Ancestry (includes multiple ancestries): 16.6% German, 16.0% English, 12.5% Irish, 9.8% Dutch, 7.7% Italian (2006-2010 5-year est.).
**Economy:** Single-family building permits issued: 3 (2011); Multi-family building permits issued: 0 (2011); Employment by occupation: 9.5% management, 3.3% professional, 6.2% services, 15.3% sales, 3.6% farming, 20.2% construction, 7.6% production (2006-2010 5-year est.).
**Income:** Per capita income: $22,885 (2006-2010 5-year est.); Median household income: $51,528 (2006-2010 5-year est.); Average household income: $58,906 (2006-2010 5-year est.); Percent of households with income of $100,000 or more: 16.1% (2006-2010 5-year est.); Poverty rate: 19.0% (2006-2010 5-year est.).

**Education:** Percent of population age 25 and over with: High school diploma (including GED) or higher: 75.8% (2006-2010 5-year est.); Bachelor's degree or higher: 20.4% (2006-2010 5-year est.); Master's degree or higher: 9.5% (2006-2010 5-year est.).
**Housing:** Homeownership rate: 82.1% (2010); Median home value: $113,300 (2006-2010 5-year est.); Median contract rent: $520 per month (2006-2010 5-year est.); Median year structure built: 1962 (2006-2010 5-year est.).
**Transportation:** Commute to work: 86.5% car, 0.0% public transportation, 3.8% walk, 9.3% work from home (2006-2010 5-year est.); Travel time to work: 40.9% less than 15 minutes, 18.9% 15 to 30 minutes, 15.1% 30 to 45 minutes, 16.1% 45 to 60 minutes, 9.0% 60 minutes or more (2006-2010 5-year est.)

**LYONS** (village). County seat. Covers a land area of 4.073 square miles and a water area of 0.076 square miles. Located at 43.06° N. Lat; 76.99° W. Long. Elevation is 410 feet.
**Population:** 4,280 (1990); 3,695 (2000); 3,619 (2010); Density: 888.3 persons per square mile (2010); Race: 83.8% White, 10.6% Black, 0.3% Asian, 0.3% American Indian/Alaska Native, 0.0% Native Hawaiian/Other Pacific Islander, 5.0% Other, 5.0% Hispanic of any race (2010); Average household size: 2.36 (2010); Median age: 39.3 (2010); Males per 100 females: 92.4 (2010); Marriage status: 33.1% never married, 43.6% now married, 7.7% widowed, 15.6% divorced (2006-2010 5-year est.); Foreign born: 2.3% (2006-2010 5-year est.); Ancestry (includes multiple ancestries): 19.4% Italian, 16.2% German, 14.9% Irish, 11.9% Dutch, 9.0% English (2006-2010 5-year est.).
**Economy:** Single-family building permits issued: 0 (2011); Multi-family building permits issued: 0 (2011); Employment by occupation: 14.2% management, 0.5% professional, 14.7% services, 13.1% sales, 1.2% farming, 6.7% construction, 9.7% production (2006-2010 5-year est.).
**Income:** Per capita income: $17,564 (2006-2010 5-year est.); Median household income: $30,856 (2006-2010 5-year est.); Average household income: $41,575 (2006-2010 5-year est.); Percent of households with income of $100,000 or more: 8.1% (2006-2010 5-year est.); Poverty rate: 17.2% (2006-2010 5-year est.).
**Education:** Percent of population age 25 and over with: High school diploma (including GED) or higher: 83.5% (2006-2010 5-year est.); Bachelor's degree or higher: 15.2% (2006-2010 5-year est.); Master's degree or higher: 5.2% (2006-2010 5-year est.).
**School District(s)**
Lyons Central School District (PK-12)
   2009-10 Enrollment: 913 . . . . . . . . . . . . . . . . . . . . . . (315) 946-2200
**Housing:** Homeownership rate: 57.5% (2010); Median home value: $66,600 (2006-2010 5-year est.); Median contract rent: $466 per month (2006-2010 5-year est.); Median year structure built: before 1940 (2006-2010 5-year est.).
**Safety:** Violent crime rate: 72.0 per 10,000 population; Property crime rate: 452.9 per 10,000 population (2010).
**Transportation:** Commute to work: 87.2% car, 0.0% public transportation, 8.9% walk, 0.3% work from home (2006-2010 5-year est.); Travel time to work: 44.3% less than 15 minutes, 28.1% 15 to 30 minutes, 18.0% 30 to 45 minutes, 4.7% 45 to 60 minutes, 4.9% 60 minutes or more (2006-2010 5-year est.)

**LYONS** (town). Covers a land area of 37.484 square miles and a water area of 0.111 square miles. Located at 43.09° N. Lat; 77.00° W. Long. Elevation is 410 feet.
**History:** Settled 1800; incorporated 1831.
**Population:** 6,343 (1990); 5,831 (2000); 5,682 (2010); Density: 151.6 persons per square mile (2010); Race: 87.1% White, 8.1% Black, 0.2% Asian, 0.4% American Indian/Alaska Native, 0.0% Native Hawaiian/Other Pacific Islander, 4.2% Other, 4.7% Hispanic of any race (2010); Average household size: 2.41 (2010); Median age: 41.9 (2010); Males per 100 females: 96.0 (2010); Marriage status: 30.3% never married, 43.8% now married, 11.4% widowed, 14.6% divorced (2006-2010 5-year est.); Foreign born: 2.1% (2006-2010 5-year est.); Ancestry (includes multiple ancestries): 19.6% German, 17.5% Italian, 14.3% Irish, 11.1% English, 10.3% Dutch (2006-2010 5-year est.).
**Economy:** Single-family building permits issued: 3 (2011); Multi-family building permits issued: 0 (2011); Employment by occupation: 15.6% management, 0.3% professional, 10.3% services, 17.7% sales, 2.9% farming, 12.3% construction, 10.8% production (2006-2010 5-year est.).
**Income:** Per capita income: $19,220 (2006-2010 5-year est.); Median household income: $34,503 (2006-2010 5-year est.); Average household

income: $44,769 (2006-2010 5-year est.); Percent of households with income of $100,000 or more: 6.4% (2006-2010 5-year est.); Poverty rate: 15.1% (2006-2010 5-year est.).
**Education:** Percent of population age 25 and over with: High school diploma (including GED) or higher: 83.8% (2006-2010 5-year est.); Bachelor's degree or higher: 17.7% (2006-2010 5-year est.); Master's degree or higher: 4.5% (2006-2010 5-year est.).
**School District(s)**
Lyons Central School District (PK-12)
   2009-10 Enrollment: 913 . . . . . . . . . . . . . . . . . . . . . . (315) 946-2200
**Housing:** Homeownership rate: 65.4% (2010); Median home value: $78,000 (2006-2010 5-year est.); Median contract rent: $466 per month (2006-2010 5-year est.); Median year structure built: before 1940 (2006-2010 5-year est.).
**Transportation:** Commute to work: 91.0% car, 0.0% public transportation, 5.6% walk, 1.2% work from home (2006-2010 5-year est.); Travel time to work: 41.2% less than 15 minutes, 29.3% 15 to 30 minutes, 20.1% 30 to 45 minutes, 5.6% 45 to 60 minutes, 3.9% 60 minutes or more (2006-2010 5-year est.)

**MACEDON** (village). Covers a land area of 1.225 square miles and a water area of 0.006 square miles. Located at 43.06° N. Lat; 77.30° W. Long. Elevation is 472 feet.
**Population:** 1,400 (1990); 1,496 (2000); 1,523 (2010); Density: 1,243.1 persons per square mile (2010); Race: 96.2% White, 1.2% Black, 0.7% Asian, 0.1% American Indian/Alaska Native, 0.0% Native Hawaiian/Other Pacific Islander, 1.8% Other, 1.8% Hispanic of any race (2010); Average household size: 2.53 (2010); Median age: 41.0 (2010); Males per 100 females: 101.2 (2010); Marriage status: 26.9% never married, 56.8% now married, 5.9% widowed, 10.4% divorced (2006-2010 5-year est.); Foreign born: 1.6% (2006-2010 5-year est.); Ancestry (includes multiple ancestries): 26.7% German, 21.2% Irish, 19.3% English, 14.7% Italian, 13.2% Dutch (2006-2010 5-year est.).
**Economy:** Single-family building permits issued: 2 (2011); Multi-family building permits issued: 0 (2011); Employment by occupation: 4.9% management, 7.3% professional, 7.3% services, 20.4% sales, 2.2% farming, 11.2% construction, 4.6% production (2006-2010 5-year est.).
**Income:** Per capita income: $23,742 (2006-2010 5-year est.); Median household income: $52,037 (2006-2010 5-year est.); Average household income: $60,317 (2006-2010 5-year est.); Percent of households with income of $100,000 or more: 16.2% (2006-2010 5-year est.); Poverty rate: 7.2% (2006-2010 5-year est.).
**Education:** Percent of population age 25 and over with: High school diploma (including GED) or higher: 92.8% (2006-2010 5-year est.); Bachelor's degree or higher: 28.2% (2006-2010 5-year est.); Master's degree or higher: 6.0% (2006-2010 5-year est.).
**School District(s)**
Palmyra-Macedon Central School District (KG-12)
   2009-10 Enrollment: 2,037 . . . . . . . . . . . . . . . . . . . . . . (315) 597-3401
**Housing:** Homeownership rate: 75.0% (2010); Median home value: $117,000 (2006-2010 5-year est.); Median contract rent: $541 per month (2006-2010 5-year est.); Median year structure built: 1971 (2006-2010 5-year est.).
**Transportation:** Commute to work: 95.0% car, 0.8% public transportation, 1.6% walk, 2.4% work from home (2006-2010 5-year est.); Travel time to work: 24.1% less than 15 minutes, 43.4% 15 to 30 minutes, 24.5% 30 to 45 minutes, 5.9% 45 to 60 minutes, 2.1% 60 minutes or more (2006-2010 5-year est.)

**MACEDON** (town). Covers a land area of 38.681 square miles and a water area of 0.177 square miles. Located at 43.07° N. Lat; 77.31° W. Long. Elevation is 472 feet.
**Population:** 7,375 (1990); 8,688 (2000); 9,148 (2010); Density: 236.5 persons per square mile (2010); Race: 95.9% White, 0.8% Black, 1.1% Asian, 0.2% American Indian/Alaska Native, 0.0% Native Hawaiian/Other Pacific Islander, 2.0% Other, 2.5% Hispanic of any race (2010); Average household size: 2.50 (2010); Median age: 41.1 (2010); Males per 100 females: 99.5 (2010); Marriage status: 22.6% never married, 60.5% now married, 5.2% widowed, 11.7% divorced (2006-2010 5-year est.); Foreign born: 2.2% (2006-2010 5-year est.); Ancestry (includes multiple ancestries): 29.1% German, 21.4% Irish, 19.8% English, 14.2% Italian, 12.6% Dutch (2006-2010 5-year est.).
**Economy:** Single-family building permits issued: 16 (2011); Multi-family building permits issued: 0 (2011); Employment by occupation: 11.3%

management, 6.6% professional, 11.0% services, 17.9% sales, 3.2% farming, 8.9% construction, 5.2% production (2006-2010 5-year est.).
**Income:** Per capita income: $27,788 (2006-2010 5-year est.); Median household income: $55,918 (2006-2010 5-year est.); Average household income: $68,081 (2006-2010 5-year est.); Percent of households with income of $100,000 or more: 22.7% (2006-2010 5-year est.); Poverty rate: 8.7% (2006-2010 5-year est.).
**Education:** Percent of population age 25 and over with: High school diploma (including GED) or higher: 92.3% (2006-2010 5-year est.); Bachelor's degree or higher: 34.6% (2006-2010 5-year est.); Master's degree or higher: 15.3% (2006-2010 5-year est.).

**School District(s)**
Palmyra-Macedon Central School District (KG-12)
   2009-10 Enrollment: 2,037 . . . . . . . . . . . . . . . . . . . . . . (315) 597-3401
**Housing:** Homeownership rate: 77.6% (2010); Median home value: $142,600 (2006-2010 5-year est.); Median contract rent: $592 per month (2006-2010 5-year est.); Median year structure built: 1978 (2006-2010 5-year est.).
**Safety:** Violent crime rate: 5.7 per 10,000 population; Property crime rate: 68.4 per 10,000 population (2010).
**Transportation:** Commute to work: 94.7% car, 0.4% public transportation, 1.2% walk, 3.1% work from home (2006-2010 5-year est.); Travel time to work: 22.7% less than 15 minutes, 35.2% 15 to 30 minutes, 33.4% 30 to 45 minutes, 6.4% 45 to 60 minutes, 2.3% 60 minutes or more (2006-2010 5-year est.)

**MARION** (town). Covers a land area of 29.146 square miles and a water area of 0.102 square miles. Located at 43.16° N. Lat; 77.19° W. Long. Elevation is 459 feet.
**Population:** 4,901 (1990); 4,974 (2000); 4,746 (2010); Density: 162.8 persons per square mile (2010); Race: 96.7% White, 0.8% Black, 0.2% Asian, 0.2% American Indian/Alaska Native, 0.0% Native Hawaiian/Other Pacific Islander, 2.1% Other, 2.6% Hispanic of any race (2010); Average household size: 2.61 (2010); Median age: 41.1 (2010); Males per 100 females: 95.1 (2010); Marriage status: 26.3% never married, 59.6% now married, 6.5% widowed, 7.6% divorced (2006-2010 5-year est.); Foreign born: 4.5% (2006-2010 5-year est.); Ancestry (includes multiple ancestries): 25.3% German, 18.2% Dutch, 14.4% English, 12.8% Irish, 7.8% Italian (2006-2010 5-year est.).
**Economy:** Single-family building permits issued: 2 (2011); Multi-family building permits issued: 0 (2011); Employment by occupation: 8.9% management, 3.7% professional, 10.8% services, 14.9% sales, 6.0% farming, 13.7% construction, 9.2% production (2006-2010 5-year est.).
**Income:** Per capita income: $24,357 (2006-2010 5-year est.); Median household income: $56,109 (2006-2010 5-year est.); Average household income: $64,280 (2006-2010 5-year est.); Percent of households with income of $100,000 or more: 16.6% (2006-2010 5-year est.); Poverty rate: 10.8% (2006-2010 5-year est.).
**Education:** Percent of population age 25 and over with: High school diploma (including GED) or higher: 85.0% (2006-2010 5-year est.); Bachelor's degree or higher: 23.9% (2006-2010 5-year est.); Master's degree or higher: 9.5% (2006-2010 5-year est.).

**School District(s)**
Marion Central School District (KG-12)
   2009-10 Enrollment: 934 . . . . . . . . . . . . . . . . . . . . . . (315) 926-2300
**Housing:** Homeownership rate: 83.8% (2010); Median home value: $114,800 (2006-2010 5-year est.); Median contract rent: $410 per month (2006-2010 5-year est.); Median year structure built: 1967 (2006-2010 5-year est.).
**Transportation:** Commute to work: 90.2% car, 0.0% public transportation, 4.1% walk, 3.5% work from home (2006-2010 5-year est.); Travel time to work: 15.4% less than 15 minutes, 39.9% 15 to 30 minutes, 31.4% 30 to 45 minutes, 11.2% 45 to 60 minutes, 2.1% 60 minutes or more (2006-2010 5-year est.)

**MARION** (CDP). Covers a land area of 3.052 square miles and a water area of 0.005 square miles. Located at 43.14° N. Lat; 77.19° W. Long. Elevation is 459 feet.
**Population:** n/a (1990); n/a (2000); 1,511 (2010); Density: 494.9 persons per square mile (2010); Race: 95.4% White, 0.9% Black, 0.5% Asian, 0.6% American Indian/Alaska Native, 0.0% Native Hawaiian/Other Pacific Islander, 2.6% Other, 3.4% Hispanic of any race (2010); Average household size: 2.49 (2010); Median age: 37.8 (2010); Males per 100 females: 92.2 (2010); Marriage status: 30.0% never married, 47.8% now married, 10.8% widowed, 11.4% divorced (2006-2010 5-year est.); Foreign

born: 5.5% (2006-2010 5-year est.); Ancestry (includes multiple ancestries): 18.1% German, 16.5% Dutch, 13.8% Irish, 8.1% English, 6.4% American (2006-2010 5-year est.).
**Economy:** Employment by occupation: 2.7% management, 3.3% professional, 10.5% services, 16.1% sales, 9.2% farming, 16.1% construction, 5.3% production (2006-2010 5-year est.).
**Income:** Per capita income: $19,717 (2006-2010 5-year est.); Median household income: $38,359 (2006-2010 5-year est.); Average household income: $51,283 (2006-2010 5-year est.); Percent of households with income of $100,000 or more: 11.5% (2006-2010 5-year est.); Poverty rate: 19.6% (2006-2010 5-year est.).
**Education:** Percent of population age 25 and over with: High school diploma (including GED) or higher: 77.8% (2006-2010 5-year est.); Bachelor's degree or higher: 20.0% (2006-2010 5-year est.); Master's degree or higher: 11.1% (2006-2010 5-year est.).

**School District(s)**
Marion Central School District (KG-12)
   2009-10 Enrollment: 934 . . . . . . . . . . . . . . . . . . . . . . (315) 926-2300
**Housing:** Homeownership rate: 64.1% (2010); Median home value: $106,700 (2006-2010 5-year est.); Median contract rent: $400 per month (2006-2010 5-year est.); Median year structure built: 1941 (2006-2010 5-year est.).
**Transportation:** Commute to work: 86.4% car, 0.0% public transportation, 7.3% walk, 0.0% work from home (2006-2010 5-year est.); Travel time to work: 18.2% less than 15 minutes, 45.6% 15 to 30 minutes, 23.0% 30 to 45 minutes, 10.8% 45 to 60 minutes, 2.3% 60 minutes or more (2006-2010 5-year est.)

**NEWARK** (village). Covers a land area of 5.406 square miles and a water area of 0.004 square miles. Located at 43.04° N. Lat; 77.09° W. Long. Elevation is 443 feet.
**History:** Incorporated 1839.
**Population:** 9,979 (1990); 9,682 (2000); 9,145 (2010); Density: 1,691.6 persons per square mile (2010); Race: 86.3% White, 6.1% Black, 0.7% Asian, 0.4% American Indian/Alaska Native, 0.0% Native Hawaiian/Other Pacific Islander, 6.5% Other, 8.7% Hispanic of any race (2010); Average household size: 2.32 (2010); Median age: 39.3 (2010); Males per 100 females: 90.5 (2010); Marriage status: 28.1% never married, 53.3% now married, 8.6% widowed, 10.0% divorced (2006-2010 5-year est.); Foreign born: 4.1% (2006-2010 5-year est.); Ancestry (includes multiple ancestries): 21.1% German, 16.1% Dutch, 15.9% Italian, 14.8% Irish, 13.6% English (2006-2010 5-year est.).
**Economy:** Single-family building permits issued: 1 (2011); Multi-family building permits issued: 0 (2011); Employment by occupation: 8.6% management, 4.4% professional, 10.5% services, 16.4% sales, 3.8% farming, 6.6% construction, 5.6% production (2006-2010 5-year est.).
**Income:** Per capita income: $22,491 (2006-2010 5-year est.); Median household income: $42,574 (2006-2010 5-year est.); Average household income: $49,716 (2006-2010 5-year est.); Percent of households with income of $100,000 or more: 9.6% (2006-2010 5-year est.); Poverty rate: 14.7% (2006-2010 5-year est.).
**Education:** Percent of population age 25 and over with: High school diploma (including GED) or higher: 86.3% (2006-2010 5-year est.); Bachelor's degree or higher: 19.6% (2006-2010 5-year est.); Master's degree or higher: 9.8% (2006-2010 5-year est.).

**School District(s)**
Newark Central School District (PK-12)
   2009-10 Enrollment: 2,295 . . . . . . . . . . . . . . . . . . . (315) 332-3217
Wayne-Finger Lakes Boces
   2009-10 Enrollment: n/a . . . . . . . . . . . . . . . . . . . . . (315) 332-7284
**Vocational/Technical School(s)**
Wayne Finger Lakes BOCES-School of Practical Nursing (Public)
   Fall 2010 Enrollment: 187 . . . . . . . . . . . . . . . . . . . (315) 332-7400
   2011-12 Tuition: $14,385
**Housing:** Homeownership rate: 54.2% (2010); Median home value: $89,200 (2006-2010 5-year est.); Median contract rent: $534 per month (2006-2010 5-year est.); Median year structure built: 1951 (2006-2010 5-year est.).
**Hospitals:** Newark-Wayne Community Hospital
**Safety:** Violent crime rate: 46.2 per 10,000 population; Property crime rate: 330.3 per 10,000 population (2010).
**Newspapers:** Courier Gazette (Local news; Circulation 3,500); Lyons/Clyde/Savannah Shopping Guide (Community news; Circulation 6,500); Newark Pennysaver (Community news; Circulation 7,000)

**Transportation:** Commute to work: 93.7% car, 0.3% public transportation, 3.5% walk, 1.6% work from home (2006-2010 5-year est.); Travel time to work: 47.9% less than 15 minutes, 24.8% 15 to 30 minutes, 16.1% 30 to 45 minutes, 3.3% 45 to 60 minutes, 7.8% 60 minutes or more (2006-2010 5-year est.)

**Additional Information Contacts**

Greater Newark Chamber of Commerce . . . . . . . . . . . . . . . . (315) 331-2705
  http://www.newarknychamber.org

**NORTH ROSE** (CDP). Covers a land area of 1.690 square miles and a water area of 0 square miles. Located at 43.18° N. Lat; 76.88° W. Long. Elevation is 387 feet.

**Population:** n/a (1990); n/a (2000); 636 (2010); Density: 376.3 persons per square mile (2010); Race: 93.2% White, 0.8% Black, 0.2% Asian, 0.5% American Indian/Alaska Native, 0.0% Native Hawaiian/Other Pacific Islander, 5.3% Other, 4.2% Hispanic of any race (2010); Average household size: 2.46 (2010); Median age: 42.3 (2010); Males per 100 females: 88.7 (2010); Marriage status: 18.3% never married, 71.4% now married, 3.7% widowed, 6.7% divorced (2006-2010 5-year est.); Foreign born: 0.0% (2006-2010 5-year est.); Ancestry (includes multiple ancestries): 24.0% English, 17.9% Irish, 17.9% Italian, 17.5% German, 12.5% Polish (2006-2010 5-year est.).

**Economy:** Employment by occupation: 9.0% management, 2.3% professional, 7.5% services, 9.4% sales, 7.1% farming, 9.4% construction, 19.9% production (2006-2010 5-year est.).

**Income:** Per capita income: $23,206 (2006-2010 5-year est.); Median household income: $52,900 (2006-2010 5-year est.); Average household income: $52,861 (2006-2010 5-year est.); Percent of households with income of $100,000 or more: 5.4% (2006-2010 5-year est.); Poverty rate: 2.2% (2006-2010 5-year est.).

**Education:** Percent of population age 25 and over with: High school diploma (including GED) or higher: 87.9% (2006-2010 5-year est.); Bachelor's degree or higher: 22.8% (2006-2010 5-year est.); Master's degree or higher: 8.6% (2006-2010 5-year est.).

**School District(s)**

North Rose-Wolcott Central School District (KG-12)
  2009-10 Enrollment: 1,381 . . . . . . . . . . . . . . . . . . (315) 594-3141

**Housing:** Homeownership rate: 77.6% (2010); Median home value: $59,300 (2006-2010 5-year est.); Median contract rent: $431 per month (2006-2010 5-year est.); Median year structure built: before 1940 (2006-2010 5-year est.).

**Transportation:** Commute to work: 88.8% car, 0.0% public transportation, 8.8% walk, 2.4% work from home (2006-2010 5-year est.); Travel time to work: 34.3% less than 15 minutes, 21.6% 15 to 30 minutes, 20.8% 30 to 45 minutes, 12.7% 45 to 60 minutes, 10.6% 60 minutes or more (2006-2010 5-year est.)

**ONTARIO** (town). Covers a land area of 32.411 square miles and a water area of 0.085 square miles. Located at 43.24° N. Lat; 77.31° W. Long. Elevation is 440 feet.

**Population:** 8,560 (1990); 9,778 (2000); 10,136 (2010); Density: 312.7 persons per square mile (2010); Race: 96.7% White, 1.2% Black, 0.5% Asian, 0.2% American Indian/Alaska Native, 0.0% Native Hawaiian/Other Pacific Islander, 1.4% Other, 1.6% Hispanic of any race (2010); Average household size: 2.56 (2010); Median age: 42.1 (2010); Males per 100 females: 98.1 (2010); Marriage status: 22.8% never married, 63.6% now married, 2.9% widowed, 10.7% divorced (2006-2010 5-year est.); Foreign born: 2.3% (2006-2010 5-year est.); Ancestry (includes multiple ancestries): 27.3% German, 22.1% Italian, 16.5% Irish, 14.5% English, 10.9% Dutch (2006-2010 5-year est.).

**Economy:** Single-family building permits issued: 18 (2011); Multi-family building permits issued: 0 (2011); Employment by occupation: 11.9% management, 5.5% professional, 5.9% services, 15.7% sales, 3.2% farming, 8.8% construction, 7.4% production (2006-2010 5-year est.).

**Income:** Per capita income: $27,869 (2006-2010 5-year est.); Median household income: $63,871 (2006-2010 5-year est.); Average household income: $74,205 (2006-2010 5-year est.); Percent of households with income of $100,000 or more: 25.1% (2006-2010 5-year est.); Poverty rate: 6.2% (2006-2010 5-year est.).

**Education:** Percent of population age 25 and over with: High school diploma (including GED) or higher: 92.4% (2006-2010 5-year est.); Bachelor's degree or higher: 24.2% (2006-2010 5-year est.); Master's degree or higher: 8.4% (2006-2010 5-year est.).

**Housing:** Homeownership rate: 84.1% (2010); Median home value: $145,500 (2006-2010 5-year est.); Median contract rent: $641 per month

(2006-2010 5-year est.); Median year structure built: 1977 (2006-2010 5-year est.).

**Transportation:** Commute to work: 94.1% car, 0.8% public transportation, 1.3% walk, 2.7% work from home (2006-2010 5-year est.); Travel time to work: 27.6% less than 15 minutes, 39.4% 15 to 30 minutes, 26.4% 30 to 45 minutes, 4.1% 45 to 60 minutes, 2.5% 60 minutes or more (2006-2010 5-year est.)

**ONTARIO** (CDP). Covers a land area of 3.796 square miles and a water area of 0 square miles. Located at 43.21° N. Lat; 77.27° W. Long. Elevation is 440 feet.

**Population:** n/a (1990); n/a (2000); 2,160 (2010); Density: 569.0 persons per square mile (2010); Race: 96.3% White, 1.5% Black, 0.3% Asian, 0.2% American Indian/Alaska Native, 0.0% Native Hawaiian/Other Pacific Islander, 1.7% Other, 1.3% Hispanic of any race (2010); Average household size: 2.36 (2010); Median age: 40.1 (2010); Males per 100 females: 92.9 (2010); Marriage status: 19.2% never married, 62.9% now married, 5.5% widowed, 12.4% divorced (2006-2010 5-year est.); Foreign born: 2.4% (2006-2010 5-year est.); Ancestry (includes multiple ancestries): 30.1% German, 29.9% Italian, 18.3% English, 17.6% Irish, 13.0% Dutch (2006-2010 5-year est.).

**Economy:** Employment by occupation: 10.2% management, 1.3% professional, 8.5% services, 15.3% sales, 0.0% farming, 8.1% construction, 6.4% production (2006-2010 5-year est.).

**Income:** Per capita income: $26,836 (2006-2010 5-year est.); Median household income: $60,481 (2006-2010 5-year est.); Average household income: $61,824 (2006-2010 5-year est.); Percent of households with income of $100,000 or more: 25.2% (2006-2010 5-year est.); Poverty rate: 16.7% (2006-2010 5-year est.).

**Education:** Percent of population age 25 and over with: High school diploma (including GED) or higher: 91.0% (2006-2010 5-year est.); Bachelor's degree or higher: 12.2% (2006-2010 5-year est.); Master's degree or higher: 3.1% (2006-2010 5-year est.).

**Housing:** Homeownership rate: 69.8% (2010); Median home value: $120,400 (2006-2010 5-year est.); Median contract rent: $323 per month (2006-2010 5-year est.); Median year structure built: 1973 (2006-2010 5-year est.).

**Transportation:** Commute to work: 96.9% car, 0.0% public transportation, 0.0% walk, 0.0% work from home (2006-2010 5-year est.); Travel time to work: 31.3% less than 15 minutes, 42.3% 15 to 30 minutes, 24.9% 30 to 45 minutes, 1.4% 45 to 60 minutes, 0.0% 60 minutes or more (2006-2010 5-year est.)

**PALMYRA** (village). Covers a land area of 1.346 square miles and a water area of 0 square miles. Located at 43.06° N. Lat; 77.22° W. Long. Elevation is 486 feet.

**Population:** 3,621 (1990); 3,490 (2000); 3,536 (2010); Density: 2,625.3 persons per square mile (2010); Race: 96.6% White, 0.9% Black, 0.4% Asian, 0.4% American Indian/Alaska Native, 0.1% Native Hawaiian/Other Pacific Islander, 1.6% Other, 1.1% Hispanic of any race (2010); Average household size: 2.32 (2010); Median age: 39.4 (2010); Males per 100 females: 95.9 (2010); Marriage status: 35.9% never married, 42.7% now married, 8.9% widowed, 12.4% divorced (2006-2010 5-year est.); Foreign born: 0.7% (2006-2010 5-year est.); Ancestry (includes multiple ancestries): 27.2% German, 20.2% English, 20.2% Irish, 14.1% Dutch, 12.9% Italian (2006-2010 5-year est.).

**Economy:** Single-family building permits issued: 0 (2011); Multi-family building permits issued: 0 (2011); Employment by occupation: 5.5% management, 2.7% professional, 9.0% services, 19.1% sales, 0.0% farming, 7.7% construction, 13.4% production (2006-2010 5-year est.).

**Income:** Per capita income: $22,209 (2006-2010 5-year est.); Median household income: $45,989 (2006-2010 5-year est.); Average household income: $50,125 (2006-2010 5-year est.); Percent of households with income of $100,000 or more: 6.8% (2006-2010 5-year est.); Poverty rate: 15.7% (2006-2010 5-year est.).

**Education:** Percent of population age 25 and over with: High school diploma (including GED) or higher: 93.0% (2006-2010 5-year est.); Bachelor's degree or higher: 19.4% (2006-2010 5-year est.); Master's degree or higher: 9.0% (2006-2010 5-year est.).

**School District(s)**

Palmyra-Macedon Central School District (KG-12)
  2009-10 Enrollment: 2,037 . . . . . . . . . . . . . . . . . . . . (315) 597-3401

**Housing:** Homeownership rate: 52.3% (2010); Median home value: $88,300 (2006-2010 5-year est.); Median contract rent: $578 per month

(2006-2010 5-year est.); Median year structure built: before 1940 (2006-2010 5-year est.).
**Newspapers:** Courier Journal (Community news; Circulation 2,600); Second Section (Community news; Circulation 2,600); Timesaver Shopping Guide (Community news; Circulation 11,000)
**Transportation:** Commute to work: 92.9% car, 0.5% public transportation, 5.4% walk, 0.6% work from home (2006-2010 5-year est.); Travel time to work: 33.8% less than 15 minutes, 38.3% 15 to 30 minutes, 16.5% 30 to 45 minutes, 8.9% 45 to 60 minutes, 2.5% 60 minutes or more (2006-2010 5-year est.)
**Additional Information Contacts**
Village of Palmyra . . . . . . . . . . . . . . . . . . . . . . . . . . . (315) 597-4849
   http://www.palmyrany.com

**PALMYRA** (town). Covers a land area of 33.435 square miles and a water area of 0.234 square miles. Located at 43.08° N. Lat; 77.18° W. Long. Elevation is 486 feet.
**History:** Joseph Smith, founder and first president of the Mormon Church, lived and published *The Book of Mormon* here. Hill Cumorah Center pageant held each August atop the glacial drumlin where Smith buried his tablets four miles south of village.
**Population:** 7,690 (1990); 7,672 (2000); 7,975 (2010); Density: 238.5 persons per square mile (2010); Race: 96.7% White, 0.8% Black, 0.5% Asian, 0.4% American Indian/Alaska Native, 0.1% Native Hawaiian/Other Pacific Islander, 1.5% Other, 1.4% Hispanic of any race (2010); Average household size: 2.44 (2010); Median age: 41.7 (2010); Males per 100 females: 98.2 (2010); Marriage status: 31.6% never married, 53.6% now married, 6.0% widowed, 8.7% divorced (2006-2010 5-year est.); Foreign born: 0.8% (2006-2010 5-year est.); Ancestry (includes multiple ancestries): 29.2% German, 20.1% English, 18.1% Irish, 14.3% Dutch, 13.0% Italian (2006-2010 5-year est.).
**Economy:** Single-family building permits issued: 0 (2011); Multi-family building permits issued: 0 (2011); Employment by occupation: 7.0% management, 5.3% professional, 9.4% services, 18.5% sales, 1.8% farming, 10.7% construction, 10.8% production (2006-2010 5-year est.).
**Income:** Per capita income: $23,471 (2006-2010 5-year est.); Median household income: $53,617 (2006-2010 5-year est.); Average household income: $57,225 (2006-2010 5-year est.); Percent of households with income of $100,000 or more: 11.6% (2006-2010 5-year est.); Poverty rate: 13.4% (2006-2010 5-year est.).
**Education:** Percent of population age 25 and over with: High school diploma (including GED) or higher: 90.6% (2006-2010 5-year est.); Bachelor's degree or higher: 20.2% (2006-2010 5-year est.); Master's degree or higher: 6.7% (2006-2010 5-year est.).
**School District(s)**
Palmyra-Macedon Central School District (KG-12)
   2009-10 Enrollment: 2,037 . . . . . . . . . . . . . . . . . . . (315) 597-3401
**Housing:** Homeownership rate: 68.0% (2010); Median home value: $97,400 (2006-2010 5-year est.); Median contract rent: $564 per month (2006-2010 5-year est.); Median year structure built: 1955 (2006-2010 5-year est.).
**Newspapers:** Courier Journal (Community news; Circulation 2,600); Second Section (Community news; Circulation 2,600); Timesaver Shopping Guide (Community news; Circulation 11,000)
**Transportation:** Commute to work: 94.0% car, 0.3% public transportation, 3.3% walk, 1.8% work from home (2006-2010 5-year est.); Travel time to work: 30.9% less than 15 minutes, 35.0% 15 to 30 minutes, 20.3% 30 to 45 minutes, 10.0% 45 to 60 minutes, 3.8% 60 minutes or more (2006-2010 5-year est.)
**Additional Information Contacts**
Town of Palmyra . . . . . . . . . . . . . . . . . . . . . . . . . . . . (315) 597-5521
   http://www.palmyrany.com

**PULTNEYVILLE** (CDP). Covers a land area of 2.241 square miles and a water area of <.001 square miles. Located at 43.27° N. Lat; 77.17° W. Long. Elevation is 272 feet.
**Population:** n/a (1990); n/a (2000); 698 (2010); Density: 311.4 persons per square mile (2010); Race: 96.6% White, 1.0% Black, 0.1% Asian, 0.6% American Indian/Alaska Native, 0.0% Native Hawaiian/Other Pacific Islander, 1.7% Other, 0.9% Hispanic of any race (2010); Average household size: 2.38 (2010); Median age: 48.3 (2010); Males per 100 females: 94.4 (2010); Marriage status: 9.4% never married, 76.5% now married, 3.1% widowed, 10.9% divorced (2006-2010 5-year est.); Foreign born: 0.9% (2006-2010 5-year est.); Ancestry (includes multiple

ancestries): 28.9% English, 23.9% Dutch, 21.6% German, 20.7% Italian, 15.4% Irish (2006-2010 5-year est.).
**Economy:** Employment by occupation: 8.3% management, 6.3% professional, 6.9% services, 9.7% sales, 0.0% farming, 9.5% construction, 22.1% production (2006-2010 5-year est.).
**Income:** Per capita income: $36,504 (2006-2010 5-year est.); Median household income: $54,615 (2006-2010 5-year est.); Average household income: $78,013 (2006-2010 5-year est.); Percent of households with income of $100,000 or more: 25.7% (2006-2010 5-year est.); Poverty rate: 7.2% (2006-2010 5-year est.).
**Education:** Percent of population age 25 and over with: High school diploma (including GED) or higher: 94.2% (2006-2010 5-year est.); Bachelor's degree or higher: 53.9% (2006-2010 5-year est.); Master's degree or higher: 36.3% (2006-2010 5-year est.).
**Housing:** Homeownership rate: 92.5% (2010); Median home value: $139,300 (2006-2010 5-year est.); Median contract rent: n/a per month (2006-2010 5-year est.); Median year structure built: 1965 (2006-2010 5-year est.).
**Transportation:** Commute to work: 84.6% car, 0.0% public transportation, 0.0% walk, 15.4% work from home (2006-2010 5-year est.); Travel time to work: 8.8% less than 15 minutes, 41.8% 15 to 30 minutes, 41.8% 30 to 45 minutes, 5.7% 45 to 60 minutes, 2.0% 60 minutes or more (2006-2010 5-year est.)

**RED CREEK** (village). Covers a land area of 0.908 square miles and a water area of 0.026 square miles. Located at 43.24° N. Lat; 76.72° W. Long. Elevation is 341 feet.
**Population:** 566 (1990); 521 (2000); 532 (2010); Density: 585.5 persons per square mile (2010); Race: 97.0% White, 1.3% Black, 0.4% Asian, 0.9% American Indian/Alaska Native, 0.0% Native Hawaiian/Other Pacific Islander, 0.4% Other, 3.0% Hispanic of any race (2010); Average household size: 2.65 (2010); Median age: 33.9 (2010); Males per 100 females: 102.3 (2010); Marriage status: 22.8% never married, 64.3% now married, 6.2% widowed, 6.7% divorced (2006-2010 5-year est.); Foreign born: 0.0% (2006-2010 5-year est.); Ancestry (includes multiple ancestries): 14.0% English, 12.7% Italian, 11.2% Irish, 11.2% German, 9.5% French (2006-2010 5-year est.).
**Economy:** Single-family building permits issued: 0 (2011); Multi-family building permits issued: 0 (2011); Employment by occupation: 5.4% management, 2.9% professional, 12.6% services, 18.1% sales, 0.0% farming, 5.4% construction, 5.8% production (2006-2010 5-year est.).
**Income:** Per capita income: $19,110 (2006-2010 5-year est.); Median household income: $55,682 (2006-2010 5-year est.); Average household income: $57,464 (2006-2010 5-year est.); Percent of households with income of $100,000 or more: 17.5% (2006-2010 5-year est.); Poverty rate: 4.4% (2006-2010 5-year est.).
**Education:** Percent of population age 25 and over with: High school diploma (including GED) or higher: 92.7% (2006-2010 5-year est.); Bachelor's degree or higher: 25.7% (2006-2010 5-year est.); Master's degree or higher: 14.8% (2006-2010 5-year est.).
**School District(s)**
Red Creek Central School District (PK-12)
   2009-10 Enrollment: 985 . . . . . . . . . . . . . . . . . . . . . (315) 754-2010
**Housing:** Homeownership rate: 73.7% (2010); Median home value: $87,700 (2006-2010 5-year est.); Median contract rent: $431 per month (2006-2010 5-year est.); Median year structure built: 1948 (2006-2010 5-year est.).
**Newspapers:** Post-Herald (Community news; Circulation 2,400); The Shopper (Community news; Circulation 18,200)
**Transportation:** Commute to work: 84.6% car, 0.0% public transportation, 15.4% walk, 0.0% work from home (2006-2010 5-year est.); Travel time to work: 28.0% less than 15 minutes, 22.9% 15 to 30 minutes, 33.7% 30 to 45 minutes, 11.5% 45 to 60 minutes, 3.9% 60 minutes or more (2006-2010 5-year est.)

**ROSE** (town). Covers a land area of 33.896 square miles and a water area of 0.006 square miles. Located at 43.15° N. Lat; 76.90° W. Long. Elevation is 420 feet.
**Population:** 2,424 (1990); 2,442 (2000); 2,369 (2010); Density: 69.9 persons per square mile (2010); Race: 95.4% White, 0.5% Black, 0.2% Asian, 0.5% American Indian/Alaska Native, 0.0% Native Hawaiian/Other Pacific Islander, 3.4% Other, 3.3% Hispanic of any race (2010); Average household size: 2.61 (2010); Median age: 43.4 (2010); Males per 100 females: 93.2 (2010); Marriage status: 22.2% never married, 64.0% now married, 4.3% widowed, 9.5% divorced (2006-2010 5-year est.); Foreign

born: 0.9% (2006-2010 5-year est.); Ancestry (includes multiple ancestries): 20.9% German, 18.9% English, 13.6% Irish, 13.0% Italian, 9.0% Dutch (2006-2010 5-year est.).
**Economy:** Single-family building permits issued: 2 (2011); Multi-family building permits issued: 0 (2011); Employment by occupation: 8.8% management, 3.7% professional, 9.2% services, 12.7% sales, 3.7% farming, 8.5% construction, 15.4% production (2006-2010 5-year est.).
**Income:** Per capita income: $24,134 (2006-2010 5-year est.); Median household income: $53,006 (2006-2010 5-year est.); Average household income: $64,329 (2006-2010 5-year est.); Percent of households with income of $100,000 or more: 14.6% (2006-2010 5-year est.); Poverty rate: 6.4% (2006-2010 5-year est.).
**Education:** Percent of population age 25 and over with: High school diploma (including GED) or higher: 85.6% (2006-2010 5-year est.); Bachelor's degree or higher: 22.8% (2006-2010 5-year est.); Master's degree or higher: 8.0% (2006-2010 5-year est.).
**Housing:** Homeownership rate: 83.3% (2010); Median home value: $76,200 (2006-2010 5-year est.); Median contract rent: $490 per month (2006-2010 5-year est.); Median year structure built: before 1940 (2006-2010 5-year est.).
**Transportation:** Commute to work: 86.5% car, 0.0% public transportation, 7.8% walk, 2.8% work from home (2006-2010 5-year est.); Travel time to work: 24.9% less than 15 minutes, 31.3% 15 to 30 minutes, 18.4% 30 to 45 minutes, 9.1% 45 to 60 minutes, 16.3% 60 minutes or more (2006-2010 5-year est.)

**SAVANNAH** (town). Covers a land area of 35.967 square miles and a water area of 0.211 square miles. Located at 43.07° N. Lat; 76.75° W. Long. Elevation is 420 feet.
**Population:** 1,768 (1990); 1,838 (2000); 1,730 (2010); Density: 48.1 persons per square mile (2010); Race: 95.4% White, 1.6% Black, 0.3% Asian, 0.2% American Indian/Alaska Native, 0.0% Native Hawaiian/Other Pacific Islander, 2.5% Other, 4.4% Hispanic of any race (2010); Average household size: 2.73 (2010); Median age: 39.7 (2010); Males per 100 females: 99.1 (2010); Marriage status: 25.9% never married, 58.2% now married, 5.3% widowed, 10.6% divorced (2006-2010 5-year est.); Foreign born: 1.8% (2006-2010 5-year est.); Ancestry (includes multiple ancestries): 25.9% German, 14.5% Irish, 12.5% English, 12.5% Dutch, 8.6% American (2006-2010 5-year est.).
**Economy:** Single-family building permits issued: 2 (2011); Multi-family building permits issued: 0 (2011); Employment by occupation: 4.6% management, 2.7% professional, 7.6% services, 16.5% sales, 1.6% farming, 14.1% construction, 19.7% production (2006-2010 5-year est.).
**Income:** Per capita income: $19,018 (2006-2010 5-year est.); Median household income: $43,684 (2006-2010 5-year est.); Average household income: $49,556 (2006-2010 5-year est.); Percent of households with income of $100,000 or more: 7.0% (2006-2010 5-year est.); Poverty rate: 16.1% (2006-2010 5-year est.).
**Education:** Percent of population age 25 and over with: High school diploma (including GED) or higher: 74.2% (2006-2010 5-year est.); Bachelor's degree or higher: 10.9% (2006-2010 5-year est.); Master's degree or higher: 2.3% (2006-2010 5-year est.).
**School District(s)**
Clyde-Savannah Central School District (PK-12)
    2009-10 Enrollment: 885 . . . . . . . . . . . . . . . . . . . . . (315) 902-3000
**Housing:** Homeownership rate: 81.3% (2010); Median home value: $62,200 (2006-2010 5-year est.); Median contract rent: $363 per month (2006-2010 5-year est.); Median year structure built: 1962 (2006-2010 5-year est.).
**Transportation:** Commute to work: 88.7% car, 0.0% public transportation, 5.2% walk, 3.8% work from home (2006-2010 5-year est.); Travel time to work: 25.5% less than 15 minutes, 31.4% 15 to 30 minutes, 23.4% 30 to 45 minutes, 10.6% 45 to 60 minutes, 9.1% 60 minutes or more (2006-2010 5-year est.)

**SAVANNAH** (CDP). Covers a land area of 1.179 square miles and a water area of 0 square miles. Located at 43.06° N. Lat; 76.75° W. Long. Elevation is 420 feet.
**Population:** n/a (1990); n/a (2000); 558 (2010); Density: 473.0 persons per square mile (2010); Race: 98.2% White, 1.1% Black, 0.0% Asian, 0.4% American Indian/Alaska Native, 0.0% Native Hawaiian/Other Pacific Islander, 0.3% Other, 1.4% Hispanic of any race (2010); Average household size: 2.56 (2010); Median age: 41.8 (2010); Males per 100 females: 88.5 (2010); Marriage status: 26.2% never married, 57.5% now married, 6.5% widowed, 9.8% divorced (2006-2010 5-year est.); Foreign

born: 0.5% (2006-2010 5-year est.); Ancestry (includes multiple ancestries): 34.1% German, 17.3% Dutch, 13.9% English, 12.8% Irish, 9.4% American (2006-2010 5-year est.).
**Economy:** Employment by occupation: 0.0% management, 1.3% professional, 11.0% services, 23.3% sales, 2.5% farming, 11.9% construction, 10.6% production (2006-2010 5-year est.).
**Income:** Per capita income: $16,283 (2006-2010 5-year est.); Median household income: $33,958 (2006-2010 5-year est.); Average household income: $40,296 (2006-2010 5-year est.); Percent of households with income of $100,000 or more: 2.5% (2006-2010 5-year est.); Poverty rate: 24.1% (2006-2010 5-year est.).
**Education:** Percent of population age 25 and over with: High school diploma (including GED) or higher: 83.5% (2006-2010 5-year est.); Bachelor's degree or higher: 10.5% (2006-2010 5-year est.); Master's degree or higher: 2.9% (2006-2010 5-year est.).
**School District(s)**
Clyde-Savannah Central School District (PK-12)
    2009-10 Enrollment: 885 . . . . . . . . . . . . . . . . . . . . . (315) 902-3000
**Housing:** Homeownership rate: 77.5% (2010); Median home value: $56,600 (2006-2010 5-year est.); Median contract rent: $315 per month (2006-2010 5-year est.); Median year structure built: before 1940 (2006-2010 5-year est.).
**Transportation:** Commute to work: 82.8% car, 0.0% public transportation, 10.9% walk, 3.6% work from home (2006-2010 5-year est.); Travel time to work: 36.6% less than 15 minutes, 32.4% 15 to 30 minutes, 23.9% 30 to 45 minutes, 6.1% 45 to 60 minutes, 0.9% 60 minutes or more (2006-2010 5-year est.)

**SODUS** (village). Covers a land area of 0.940 square miles and a water area of 0 square miles. Located at 43.23° N. Lat; 77.06° W. Long. Elevation is 436 feet.
**Population:** 1,904 (1990); 1,735 (2000); 1,819 (2010); Density: 1,933.2 persons per square mile (2010); Race: 75.3% White, 15.7% Black, 0.6% Asian, 0.7% American Indian/Alaska Native, 0.0% Native Hawaiian/Other Pacific Islander, 7.7% Other, 8.4% Hispanic of any race (2010); Average household size: 2.55 (2010); Median age: 36.6 (2010); Males per 100 females: 89.5 (2010); Marriage status: 35.9% never married, 43.7% now married, 6.9% widowed, 13.5% divorced (2006-2010 5-year est.); Foreign born: 2.2% (2006-2010 5-year est.); Ancestry (includes multiple ancestries): 19.8% English, 16.3% German, 12.0% Dutch, 11.5% Irish, 7.5% Italian (2006-2010 5-year est.).
**Economy:** Single-family building permits issued: 0 (2011); Multi-family building permits issued: 0 (2011); Employment by occupation: 2.9% management, 2.0% professional, 15.7% services, 11.0% sales, 1.1% farming, 16.9% construction, 10.8% production (2006-2010 5-year est.).
**Income:** Per capita income: $17,119 (2006-2010 5-year est.); Median household income: $36,250 (2006-2010 5-year est.); Average household income: $44,129 (2006-2010 5-year est.); Percent of households with income of $100,000 or more: 6.9% (2006-2010 5-year est.); Poverty rate: 24.2% (2006-2010 5-year est.).
**Education:** Percent of population age 25 and over with: High school diploma (including GED) or higher: 73.0% (2006-2010 5-year est.); Bachelor's degree or higher: 15.3% (2006-2010 5-year est.); Master's degree or higher: 5.5% (2006-2010 5-year est.).
**School District(s)**
Sodus Central School District (PK-12)
    2009-10 Enrollment: 1,241 . . . . . . . . . . . . . . . . . . (315) 483-5201
**Housing:** Homeownership rate: 58.6% (2010); Median home value: $72,700 (2006-2010 5-year est.); Median contract rent: $479 per month (2006-2010 5-year est.); Median year structure built: before 1940 (2006-2010 5-year est.).
**Safety:** Violent crime rate: 6.4 per 10,000 population; Property crime rate: 299.0 per 10,000 population (2010).
**Newspapers:** Sodus/Williamson Pennysaver (Community news; Circulation 8,000)
**Transportation:** Commute to work: 91.1% car, 2.4% public transportation, 3.5% walk, 0.9% work from home (2006-2010 5-year est.); Travel time to work: 38.3% less than 15 minutes, 20.5% 15 to 30 minutes, 24.3% 30 to 45 minutes, 9.9% 45 to 60 minutes, 7.0% 60 minutes or more (2006-2010 5-year est.)
**Additional Information Contacts**
Sodus Chamber of Commerce . . . . . . . . . . . . . . . . (315) 576-3818
    http://sodusny.org

**SODUS** (town). Covers a land area of 67.268 square miles and a water area of 1.979 square miles. Located at 43.21° N. Lat; 77.04° W. Long. Elevation is 436 feet.

**History:** The raising of silkworms was attempted in Sodus in the 1830s. The attempt failed because mulberry trees could not withstand the severe winters. The lotuses of nearby Sodus Bay are famous. Incorporated in 1918.

**Population:** 8,877 (1990); 8,949 (2000); 8,384 (2010); Density: 124.6 persons per square mile (2010); Race: 84.8% White, 8.5% Black, 0.4% Asian, 0.3% American Indian/Alaska Native, 0.1% Native Hawaiian/Other Pacific Islander, 5.9% Other, 6.2% Hispanic of any race (2010); Average household size: 2.48 (2010); Median age: 43.8 (2010); Males per 100 females: 98.3 (2010); Marriage status: 26.3% never married, 51.5% now married, 7.3% widowed, 14.8% divorced (2006-2010 5-year est.); Foreign born: 2.0% (2006-2010 5-year est.); Ancestry (includes multiple ancestries): 21.5% German, 17.3% English, 16.2% Dutch, 14.1% Irish, 9.8% Italian (2006-2010 5-year est.).

**Economy:** Single-family building permits issued: 8 (2011); Multi-family building permits issued: 0 (2011); Employment by occupation: 9.8% management, 2.9% professional, 11.5% services, 13.8% sales, 1.5% farming, 13.6% construction, 12.3% production (2006-2010 5-year est.).

**Income:** Per capita income: $23,623 (2006-2010 5-year est.); Median household income: $50,204 (2006-2010 5-year est.); Average household income: $56,130 (2006-2010 5-year est.); Percent of households with income of $100,000 or more: 12.1% (2006-2010 5-year est.); Poverty rate: 16.0% (2006-2010 5-year est.).

**Education:** Percent of population age 25 and over with: High school diploma (including GED) or higher: 83.3% (2006-2010 5-year est.); Bachelor's degree or higher: 16.1% (2006-2010 5-year est.); Master's degree or higher: 7.1% (2006-2010 5-year est.).

### School District(s)
Sodus Central School District (PK-12)
    2009-10 Enrollment: 1,241 . . . . . . . . . . . . . . . . . . . . . . . (315) 483-5201

**Housing:** Homeownership rate: 77.7% (2010); Median home value: $89,300 (2006-2010 5-year est.); Median contract rent: $498 per month (2006-2010 5-year est.); Median year structure built: 1949 (2006-2010 5-year est.).

**Newspapers:** Sodus/Williamson Pennysaver (Community news; Circulation 8,000)

**Transportation:** Commute to work: 92.9% car, 2.1% public transportation, 2.4% walk, 1.6% work from home (2006-2010 5-year est.); Travel time to work: 30.2% less than 15 minutes, 28.3% 15 to 30 minutes, 24.5% 30 to 45 minutes, 11.8% 45 to 60 minutes, 5.2% 60 minutes or more (2006-2010 5-year est.)

**Additional Information Contacts**
Sodus Chamber of Commerce . . . . . . . . . . . . . . . . . . (315) 576-3818
    http://sodusny.org

**SODUS POINT** (village). Covers a land area of 1.467 square miles and a water area of 0.005 square miles. Located at 43.26° N. Lat; 76.99° W. Long. Elevation is 276 feet.

**History:** Fired upon by British in War of 1812.

**Population:** 1,190 (1990); 1,160 (2000); 900 (2010); Density: 613.1 persons per square mile (2010); Race: 93.0% White, 3.0% Black, 0.3% Asian, 0.0% American Indian/Alaska Native, 0.1% Native Hawaiian/Other Pacific Islander, 3.6% Other, 3.3% Hispanic of any race (2010); Average household size: 2.12 (2010); Median age: 51.8 (2010); Males per 100 females: 105.0 (2010); Marriage status: 18.9% never married, 64.0% now married, 5.8% widowed, 11.3% divorced (2006-2010 5-year est.); Foreign born: 4.1% (2006-2010 5-year est.); Ancestry (includes multiple ancestries): 28.2% German, 22.7% English, 19.6% Irish, 11.9% Dutch, 10.7% Italian (2006-2010 5-year est.).

**Economy:** Single-family building permits issued: 3 (2011); Multi-family building permits issued: 0 (2011); Employment by occupation: 19.4% management, 1.5% professional, 8.3% services, 14.9% sales, 1.7% farming, 14.3% construction, 9.4% production (2006-2010 5-year est.).

**Income:** Per capita income: $30,199 (2006-2010 5-year est.); Median household income: $59,583 (2006-2010 5-year est.); Average household income: $67,360 (2006-2010 5-year est.); Percent of households with income of $100,000 or more: 17.3% (2006-2010 5-year est.); Poverty rate: 8.2% (2006-2010 5-year est.).

**Education:** Percent of population age 25 and over with: High school diploma (including GED) or higher: 92.7% (2006-2010 5-year est.); Bachelor's degree or higher: 29.6% (2006-2010 5-year est.); Master's degree or higher: 11.2% (2006-2010 5-year est.).

**Housing:** Homeownership rate: 76.4% (2010); Median home value: $120,200 (2006-2010 5-year est.); Median contract rent: $544 per month (2006-2010 5-year est.); Median year structure built: before 1940 (2006-2010 5-year est.).

**Safety:** Violent crime rate: 18.3 per 10,000 population; Property crime rate: 73.3 per 10,000 population (2010).

**Transportation:** Commute to work: 87.2% car, 3.7% public transportation, 2.7% walk, 5.4% work from home (2006-2010 5-year est.); Travel time to work: 20.3% less than 15 minutes, 34.8% 15 to 30 minutes, 23.0% 30 to 45 minutes, 15.0% 45 to 60 minutes, 7.0% 60 minutes or more (2006-2010 5-year est.)

**Additional Information Contacts**
Village of Sodus Point . . . . . . . . . . . . . . . . . . . . . . . . . (315) 483-9881
    http://www.soduspoint.info

**WALWORTH** (town). Covers a land area of 33.853 square miles and a water area of 0.042 square miles. Located at 43.15° N. Lat; 77.31° W. Long. Elevation is 541 feet.

**Population:** 6,945 (1990); 8,402 (2000); 9,449 (2010); Density: 279.1 persons per square mile (2010); Race: 96.5% White, 0.9% Black, 0.8% Asian, 0.1% American Indian/Alaska Native, 0.0% Native Hawaiian/Other Pacific Islander, 1.7% Other, 1.9% Hispanic of any race (2010); Average household size: 2.81 (2010); Median age: 39.5 (2010); Males per 100 females: 99.3 (2010); Marriage status: 19.3% never married, 68.2% now married, 3.1% widowed, 9.4% divorced (2006-2010 5-year est.); Foreign born: 3.4% (2006-2010 5-year est.); Ancestry (includes multiple ancestries): 35.2% German, 21.9% Irish, 20.6% Italian, 19.0% English, 7.3% Polish (2006-2010 5-year est.).

**Economy:** Single-family building permits issued: 9 (2011); Multi-family building permits issued: 0 (2011); Employment by occupation: 12.5% management, 8.0% professional, 6.8% services, 13.1% sales, 2.7% farming, 9.6% construction, 6.2% production (2006-2010 5-year est.).

**Income:** Per capita income: $28,457 (2006-2010 5-year est.); Median household income: $76,660 (2006-2010 5-year est.); Average household income: $80,956 (2006-2010 5-year est.); Percent of households with income of $100,000 or more: 28.1% (2006-2010 5-year est.); Poverty rate: 3.7% (2006-2010 5-year est.).

**Education:** Percent of population age 25 and over with: High school diploma (including GED) or higher: 96.1% (2006-2010 5-year est.); Bachelor's degree or higher: 34.2% (2006-2010 5-year est.); Master's degree or higher: 14.9% (2006-2010 5-year est.).

### School District(s)
Gananda Central School District (KG-12)
    2009-10 Enrollment: 1,162 . . . . . . . . . . . . . . . . . . . . . . (315) 986-3521

**Housing:** Homeownership rate: 92.1% (2010); Median home value: $145,300 (2006-2010 5-year est.); Median contract rent: $574 per month (2006-2010 5-year est.); Median year structure built: 1981 (2006-2010 5-year est.).

**Transportation:** Commute to work: 94.5% car, 0.4% public transportation, 0.4% walk, 4.7% work from home (2006-2010 5-year est.); Travel time to work: 18.8% less than 15 minutes, 40.0% 15 to 30 minutes, 34.9% 30 to 45 minutes, 2.0% 45 to 60 minutes, 4.3% 60 minutes or more (2006-2010 5-year est.)

**WILLIAMSON** (town). Aka Williamson Center. Covers a land area of 34.639 square miles and a water area of 0.015 square miles. Located at 43.24° N. Lat; 77.19° W. Long. Elevation is 443 feet.

**Population:** 6,540 (1990); 6,777 (2000); 6,984 (2010); Density: 201.6 persons per square mile (2010); Race: 92.4% White, 3.3% Black, 0.4% Asian, 0.4% American Indian/Alaska Native, 0.0% Native Hawaiian/Other Pacific Islander, 3.5% Other, 3.9% Hispanic of any race (2010); Average household size: 2.51 (2010); Median age: 43.1 (2010); Males per 100 females: 100.0 (2010); Marriage status: 20.0% never married, 64.5% now married, 4.5% widowed, 11.1% divorced (2006-2010 5-year est.); Foreign born: 3.2% (2006-2010 5-year est.); Ancestry (includes multiple ancestries): 23.8% German, 17.8% English, 17.4% Dutch, 14.9% Irish, 9.0% Italian (2006-2010 5-year est.).

**Economy:** Single-family building permits issued: 4 (2011); Multi-family building permits issued: 0 (2011); Employment by occupation: 8.1% management, 7.9% professional, 7.5% services, 16.3% sales, 2.8% farming, 9.3% construction, 8.5% production (2006-2010 5-year est.).

**Income:** Per capita income: $25,760 (2006-2010 5-year est.); Median household income: $53,522 (2006-2010 5-year est.); Average household income: $66,842 (2006-2010 5-year est.); Percent of households with

income of $100,000 or more: 18.5% (2006-2010 5-year est.); Poverty rate: 7.3% (2006-2010 5-year est.).
**Education:** Percent of population age 25 and over with: High school diploma (including GED) or higher: 87.3% (2006-2010 5-year est.); Bachelor's degree or higher: 26.5% (2006-2010 5-year est.); Master's degree or higher: 11.5% (2006-2010 5-year est.).

**School District(s)**
Williamson Central School District (PK-12)
  2009-10 Enrollment: 1,213 . . . . . . . . . . . . . . . . . . . . . . (315) 589-9661
**Housing:** Homeownership rate: 80.4% (2010); Median home value: $116,100 (2006-2010 5-year est.); Median contract rent: $382 per month (2006-2010 5-year est.); Median year structure built: 1959 (2006-2010 5-year est.).
**Transportation:** Commute to work: 89.7% car, 0.8% public transportation, 4.2% walk, 4.2% work from home (2006-2010 5-year est.); Travel time to work: 34.6% less than 15 minutes, 31.3% 15 to 30 minutes, 22.2% 30 to 45 minutes, 8.0% 45 to 60 minutes, 4.0% 60 minutes or more (2006-2010 5-year est.)
**Additional Information Contacts**
Williamson Chamber of Commerce . . . . . . . . . . . . . . . . . . (315) 589-8100
  http://williamsonchamberofcommerceny.org

**WILLIAMSON** (CDP). Covers a land area of 3.840 square miles and a water area of 0.003 square miles. Located at 43.22° N. Lat; 77.18° W. Long. Elevation is 443 feet.
**Population:** n/a (1990); n/a (2000); 2,495 (2010); Density: 649.7 persons per square mile (2010); Race: 89.1% White, 5.0% Black, 0.5% Asian, 0.1% American Indian/Alaska Native, 0.0% Native Hawaiian/Other Pacific Islander, 5.3% Other, 4.8% Hispanic of any race (2010); Average household size: 2.29 (2010); Median age: 42.9 (2010); Males per 100 females: 93.3 (2010); Marriage status: 20.4% never married, 57.2% now married, 9.0% widowed, 13.5% divorced (2006-2010 5-year est.); Foreign born: 1.1% (2006-2010 5-year est.); Ancestry (includes multiple ancestries): 22.0% English, 18.5% German, 17.9% Irish, 14.8% Dutch, 10.6% Italian (2006-2010 5-year est.).
**Economy:** Employment by occupation: 6.2% management, 7.2% professional, 9.9% services, 10.5% sales, 3.7% farming, 6.2% construction, 9.1% production (2006-2010 5-year est.).
**Income:** Per capita income: $19,262 (2006-2010 5-year est.); Median household income: $37,930 (2006-2010 5-year est.); Average household income: $45,315 (2006-2010 5-year est.); Percent of households with income of $100,000 or more: 7.0% (2006-2010 5-year est.); Poverty rate: 12.8% (2006-2010 5-year est.).
**Education:** Percent of population age 25 and over with: High school diploma (including GED) or higher: 85.7% (2006-2010 5-year est.); Bachelor's degree or higher: 21.6% (2006-2010 5-year est.); Master's degree or higher: 6.7% (2006-2010 5-year est.).

**School District(s)**
Williamson Central School District (PK-12)
  2009-10 Enrollment: 1,213 . . . . . . . . . . . . . . . . . . . . . . (315) 589-9661
**Housing:** Homeownership rate: 65.6% (2010); Median home value: $96,600 (2006-2010 5-year est.); Median contract rent: $388 per month (2006-2010 5-year est.); Median year structure built: 1959 (2006-2010 5-year est.).
**Transportation:** Commute to work: 95.1% car, 0.0% public transportation, 2.0% walk, 1.2% work from home (2006-2010 5-year est.); Travel time to work: 38.9% less than 15 minutes, 31.4% 15 to 30 minutes, 19.2% 30 to 45 minutes, 3.7% 45 to 60 minutes, 6.7% 60 minutes or more (2006-2010 5-year est.)

**WOLCOTT** (village). Covers a land area of 1.947 square miles and a water area of 0.019 square miles. Located at 43.22° N. Lat; 76.81° W. Long. Elevation is 371 feet.
**Population:** 1,544 (1990); 1,712 (2000); 1,701 (2010); Density: 873.4 persons per square mile (2010); Race: 93.6% White, 3.0% Black, 0.2% Asian, 0.1% American Indian/Alaska Native, 0.0% Native Hawaiian/Other Pacific Islander, 3.1% Other, 5.4% Hispanic of any race (2010); Average household size: 2.41 (2010); Median age: 38.5 (2010); Males per 100 females: 97.8 (2010); Marriage status: 26.8% never married, 47.9% now married, 12.0% widowed, 13.3% divorced (2006-2010 5-year est.); Foreign born: 2.8% (2006-2010 5-year est.); Ancestry (includes multiple ancestries): 20.2% English, 19.1% German, 18.4% Irish, 13.7% Dutch, 7.5% Italian (2006-2010 5-year est.).
**Economy:** Single-family building permits issued: 0 (2011); Multi-family building permits issued: 0 (2011); Employment by occupation: 3.8%

management, 2.7% professional, 7.9% services, 11.5% sales, 3.8% farming, 14.4% construction, 13.2% production (2006-2010 5-year est.).
**Income:** Per capita income: $17,175 (2006-2010 5-year est.); Median household income: $27,736 (2006-2010 5-year est.); Average household income: $39,207 (2006-2010 5-year est.); Percent of households with income of $100,000 or more: 5.0% (2006-2010 5-year est.); Poverty rate: 30.7% (2006-2010 5-year est.).
**Education:** Percent of population age 25 and over with: High school diploma (including GED) or higher: 78.3% (2006-2010 5-year est.); Bachelor's degree or higher: 8.3% (2006-2010 5-year est.); Master's degree or higher: 2.6% (2006-2010 5-year est.).

**School District(s)**
North Rose-Wolcott Central School District (KG-12)
  2009-10 Enrollment: 1,381 . . . . . . . . . . . . . . . . . . . . . . (315) 594-3141
**Housing:** Homeownership rate: 59.1% (2010); Median home value: $60,600 (2006-2010 5-year est.); Median contract rent: $392 per month (2006-2010 5-year est.); Median year structure built: 1944 (2006-2010 5-year est.).
**Newspapers:** Wayne County Star (Local news; Circulation 7,200)
**Transportation:** Commute to work: 86.3% car, 1.1% public transportation, 7.4% walk, 2.5% work from home (2006-2010 5-year est.); Travel time to work: 40.1% less than 15 minutes, 24.7% 15 to 30 minutes, 16.7% 30 to 45 minutes, 8.2% 45 to 60 minutes, 10.2% 60 minutes or more (2006-2010 5-year est.)
**Additional Information Contacts**
Wolcott Chamber of Commerce . . . . . . . . . . . . . . . . . . . . . (315) 594-2506
  http://www.wolcottny.org/chamberindex.php

**WOLCOTT** (town). Covers a land area of 39.050 square miles and a water area of 0.900 square miles. Located at 43.27° N. Lat; 76.76° W. Long. Elevation is 371 feet.
**History:** Incorporated 1873.
**Population:** 4,283 (1990); 4,692 (2000); 4,453 (2010); Density: 114.0 persons per square mile (2010); Race: 93.1% White, 3.7% Black, 0.2% Asian, 0.3% American Indian/Alaska Native, 0.0% Native Hawaiian/Other Pacific Islander, 2.7% Other, 3.9% Hispanic of any race (2010); Average household size: 2.47 (2010); Median age: 39.9 (2010); Males per 100 females: 109.4 (2010); Marriage status: 26.0% never married, 54.5% now married, 7.1% widowed, 12.4% divorced (2006-2010 5-year est.); Foreign born: 1.8% (2006-2010 5-year est.); Ancestry (includes multiple ancestries): 23.8% German, 20.0% English, 13.4% Irish, 11.0% French, 9.2% Italian (2006-2010 5-year est.).
**Economy:** Single-family building permits issued: 3 (2011); Multi-family building permits issued: 0 (2011); Employment by occupation: 5.0% management, 1.5% professional, 7.5% services, 12.3% sales, 4.5% farming, 15.2% construction, 13.6% production (2006-2010 5-year est.).
**Income:** Per capita income: $19,750 (2006-2010 5-year est.); Median household income: $38,281 (2006-2010 5-year est.); Average household income: $50,893 (2006-2010 5-year est.); Percent of households with income of $100,000 or more: 11.0% (2006-2010 5-year est.); Poverty rate: 16.2% (2006-2010 5-year est.).
**Education:** Percent of population age 25 and over with: High school diploma (including GED) or higher: 81.3% (2006-2010 5-year est.); Bachelor's degree or higher: 10.7% (2006-2010 5-year est.); Master's degree or higher: 4.9% (2006-2010 5-year est.).

**School District(s)**
North Rose-Wolcott Central School District (KG-12)
  2009-10 Enrollment: 1,381 . . . . . . . . . . . . . . . . . . . . . . (315) 594-3141
**Housing:** Homeownership rate: 73.1% (2010); Median home value: $73,500 (2006-2010 5-year est.); Median contract rent: $405 per month (2006-2010 5-year est.); Median year structure built: 1958 (2006-2010 5-year est.).
**Newspapers:** Wayne County Star (Local news; Circulation 7,200)
**Transportation:** Commute to work: 91.4% car, 0.3% public transportation, 5.6% walk, 2.0% work from home (2006-2010 5-year est.); Travel time to work: 29.9% less than 15 minutes, 21.6% 15 to 30 minutes, 24.4% 30 to 45 minutes, 12.8% 45 to 60 minutes, 11.4% 60 minutes or more (2006-2010 5-year est.)
**Additional Information Contacts**
Wolcott Chamber of Commerce . . . . . . . . . . . . . . . . . . . . . (315) 594-2506
  http://www.wolcottny.org/chamberindex.php

# Westchester County

Located in southeastern New York; bounded on the west by the Hudson River, on the southeast by Long Island Sound, and on the east by Connecticut; drained by the Byram, Mianus, and Rippowam Rivers. Covers a land area of 432.82 square miles, a water area of 67.26 square miles, and is located in the Eastern Time Zone at 41.05° N. Lat., 73.79° W. Long. The county was founded in 1683. County seat is White Plains.

Westchester County is part of the New York-Northern New Jersey-Long Island, NY-NJ-PA Metropolitan Statistical Area. The entire metro area includes: Edison-New Brunswick, NJ Metropolitan Division (Middlesex County, NJ; Monmouth County, NJ; Ocean County, NJ; Somerset County, NJ); Nassau-Suffolk, NY Metropolitan Division (Nassau County, NY; Suffolk County, NY); New York-White Plains-Wayne, NY-NJ Metropolitan Division (Bergen County, NJ; Hudson County, NJ; Passaic County, NJ; Bronx County, NY; Kings County, NY; New York County, NY; Putnam County, NY; Queens County, NY; Richmond County, NY; Rockland County, NY; Westchester County, NY); Newark-Union, NJ-PA Metropolitan Division (Essex County, NJ; Hunterdon County, NJ; Morris County, NJ; Sussex County, NJ; Union County, NJ; Pike County, PA)

| Weather Station: Dobbs Ferry Ardsley | | | | | | | | | | | Elevation: 200 feet | |
|---|---|---|---|---|---|---|---|---|---|---|---|---|
| | Jan | Feb | Mar | Apr | May | Jun | Jul | Aug | Sep | Oct | Nov | Dec |
| High | 39 | 42 | 50 | 62 | 72 | 81 | 85 | 84 | 76 | 65 | 54 | 43 |
| Low | 23 | 25 | 31 | 40 | 50 | 59 | 64 | 64 | 56 | 45 | 36 | 28 |
| Precip | 3.8 | 3.0 | 4.5 | 4.7 | 4.5 | 4.4 | 4.6 | 4.2 | 4.6 | 4.5 | 4.4 | 4.3 |
| Snow | 9.0 | 8.4 | 5.7 | 0.9 | tr | 0.0 | 0.0 | 0.0 | 0.0 | 0.1 | 0.7 | 5.8 |

*High and Low temperatures in degrees Fahrenheit; Precipitation and Snow in inches*

| Weather Station: Yorktown Heights 1 W | | | | | | | | | | | Elevation: 669 feet | |
|---|---|---|---|---|---|---|---|---|---|---|---|---|
| | Jan | Feb | Mar | Apr | May | Jun | Jul | Aug | Sep | Oct | Nov | Dec |
| High | 34 | 38 | 47 | 59 | 69 | 78 | 82 | 81 | 73 | 62 | 51 | 40 |
| Low | 19 | 21 | 28 | 39 | 49 | 58 | 63 | 62 | 54 | 43 | 35 | 25 |
| Precip | 3.6 | 3.0 | 4.0 | 4.6 | 4.4 | 4.8 | 4.8 | 4.4 | 4.5 | 4.5 | 4.4 | 3.9 |
| Snow | 11.0 | 10.3 | 7.7 | 2.1 | 0.0 | 0.0 | 0.0 | 0.0 | 0.0 | tr | 1.3 | 7.6 |

*High and Low temperatures in degrees Fahrenheit; Precipitation and Snow in inches*

**Population:** 874,910 (1990); 923,459 (2000); 949,113 (2010); Race: 68.1% White, 14.6% Black, 5.4% Asian, 0.4% American Indian/Alaska Native, 0.0% Native Hawaiian/Other Pacific Islander, 11.5% Other, 21.8% Hispanic of any race (2010); Density: 2,192.8 persons per square mile (2010); Average household size: 2.65 (2010); Median age: 40.0 (2010); Males per 100 females: 92.7 (2010).
**Religion:** Six largest groups: 45.9% Catholicism, 5.2% Judaism, 1.7% Methodist/Pietist, 1.6% Baptist, 1.5% Episcopalianism/Anglicanism, 1.4% Presbyterian-Reformed (2010)
**Economy:** Unemployment rate: 7.4% (February 2012); Total civilian labor force: 467,047 (February 2012); Leading industries: 19.7% health care and social assistance; 12.7% retail trade; 7.4% professional, scientific & technical services (2009); Farms: 106 totaling 8,521 acres (2007); Companies that employ 500 or more persons: 63 (2009); Companies that employ 100 to 499 persons: 519 (2009); Companies that employ less than 100 persons: 31,008 (2009); Black-owned businesses: 10,756 (2007); Hispanic-owned businesses: 12,126 (2007); Asian-owned businesses: 6,618 (2007); Women-owned businesses: 35,757 (2007); Retail sales per capita: $17,096 (2010). Single-family building permits issued: 192 (2011); Multi-family building permits issued: 758 (2011).
**Income:** Per capita income: $47,814 (2006-2010 5-year est.); Median household income: $79,619 (2006-2010 5-year est.); Average household income: $128,127 (2006-2010 5-year est.); Percent of households with income of $100,000 or more: 40.5% (2006-2010 5-year est.); Poverty rate: 8.2% (2006-2010 5-year est.); Bankruptcy rate: 1.97% (2011).
**Taxes:** Total county taxes per capita: $1,211 (2009); County property taxes per capita: $700 (2009).
**Education:** Percent of population age 25 and over with: High school diploma (including GED) or higher: 87.4% (2006-2010 5-year est.); Bachelor's degree or higher: 44.5% (2006-2010 5-year est.); Master's degree or higher: 22.1% (2006-2010 5-year est.).
**Housing:** Homeownership rate: 61.6% (2010); Median home value: $556,900 (2006-2010 5-year est.); Median contract rent: $1,097 per month (2006-2010 5-year est.); Median year structure built: 1955 (2006-2010 5-year est.).
**Health:** Birth rate: 114.3 per 10,000 population (2011); Death rate: 70.3 per 10,000 population (2011); Age-adjusted cancer mortality rate: 159.1 deaths per 100,000 population (2009); Number of physicians: 67.7 per 10,000

population (2008); Hospital beds: 43.0 per 10,000 population (2007); Hospital admissions: 1,335.4 per 10,000 population (2007).
**Environment:** Air Quality Index: 85.8% good, 13.2% moderate, 1.1% unhealthy for sensitive individuals, 0.0% unhealthy (percent of days in 2010)
**Elections:** 2008 Presidential election results: 63.4% Obama, 35.8% McCain, 0.3% Nader
**National and State Parks:** Mohansic State Park; Saint Pauls Church National Historic Site
**Additional Information Contacts**

Westchester County Government . . . . . . . . . . . . . . . . . (914) 995-2900
  http://www.co.westchester.ny.us
Bronxville Chamber of Commerce . . . . . . . . . . . . . . . . (914) 337-6040
  http://www.bronxvillechamber.com
Business Council of Westchester . . . . . . . . . . . . . . . . . (914) 948-2110
  http://www.westchesterny.org
City of Mount Vernon . . . . . . . . . . . . . . . . . . . . . . . . . . (914) 665-2300
  http://www.cmvny.com
City of New Rochelle . . . . . . . . . . . . . . . . . . . . . . . . . . (914) 654-2000
  http://www.newrochelleny.com
City of Peekskill . . . . . . . . . . . . . . . . . . . . . . . . . . . . . . (914) 737-3400
  http://www.cityofpeekskill.com
City of Rye . . . . . . . . . . . . . . . . . . . . . . . . . . . . . . . . . . (914) 967-5400
  http://www.ryeny.gov
City of White Plains . . . . . . . . . . . . . . . . . . . . . . . . . . . (914) 422-1200
  http://www.ci.white-plains.ny.us
City of Yonkers . . . . . . . . . . . . . . . . . . . . . . . . . . . . . . (914) 377-6020
  http://www.cityofyonkers.com
Greater Ossining Chamber of Commerce . . . . . . . . . . (914) 941-0009
  http://www.ossiningchamber.org
Hudson Valley Gateway Chamber of Commerce . . . . . (914) 737-3600
  http://www.hvgatewaychamber.com
Irvington on Hudson Chamber of Commerce . . . . . . . . (914) 473-4819
  http://www.irvingtonnychamber.com
Katonah Chamber of Commerce . . . . . . . . . . . . . . . . . (914) 232-2668
  http://www.katonahchamber.org
Mamaroneck Chamber of Commerce . . . . . . . . . . . . . (914) 698-4400
  http://www.mamaroneckchamberofcommerce.org
Mount Kisco Chamber of Commerce . . . . . . . . . . . . . . (914) 666-7525
  http://www.mtkisco.com
Mt Vernon Chamber of Commerce . . . . . . . . . . . . . . . (888) 716-2460
  http://www.mtvernonchamber.org
New Rochelle Chamber of Commerce . . . . . . . . . . . . . (914) 632-5700
  http://www.newrochellechamber.org
Scarsdale Chamber of Commerce. . . . . . . . . . . . . . . . (914) 620-2426
  http://www.scarsdalechamber.org
Sleepy Hollow Tarrytown Chamber of Commerce. . . . . (914) 631-1705
  http://www.sleepyhollowchamber.com
Town of Bedford. . . . . . . . . . . . . . . . . . . . . . . . . . . . . . (914) 666-6530
  http://www.bedfordny.info
Town of Cortlandt. . . . . . . . . . . . . . . . . . . . . . . . . . . . . (914) 734-1020
  http://www.townofcortlandt.com
Town of Eastchester . . . . . . . . . . . . . . . . . . . . . . . . . . (914) 771-3351
  http://www.eastchester.org
Town of Greenburgh . . . . . . . . . . . . . . . . . . . . . . . . . . (914) 993-1500
  http://www.greenburghny.com
Town of Harrison . . . . . . . . . . . . . . . . . . . . . . . . . . . . . (914) 670-3030
  http://www.town.harrison.ny.us
Town of Lewisboro . . . . . . . . . . . . . . . . . . . . . . . . . . . . (914) 763-3511
  http://www.lewisborogov.com
Town of Mamaroneck . . . . . . . . . . . . . . . . . . . . . . . . . (914) 381-7870
  http://www.townofmamaroneck.org
Town of Mount Pleasant . . . . . . . . . . . . . . . . . . . . . . . (914) 742-2300
  http://www.mtpleasantny.com
Town of New Castle. . . . . . . . . . . . . . . . . . . . . . . . . . . (914) 238-7269
  http://www.mynewcastle.org
Town of North Castle . . . . . . . . . . . . . . . . . . . . . . . . . . (914) 273-3321
  http://www.northcastleny.com
Town of Ossining . . . . . . . . . . . . . . . . . . . . . . . . . . . . . (914) 762-6000
  http://www.townofossining.com
Town of Pelham. . . . . . . . . . . . . . . . . . . . . . . . . . . . . . (914) 738-0777
  http://townofpelham.com
Town of Pound Ridge . . . . . . . . . . . . . . . . . . . . . . . . . (914) 764-5511
  http://www.townofpoundridge.com
Town of Rye. . . . . . . . . . . . . . . . . . . . . . . . . . . . . . . . . (914) 939-3570
  http://www.townofryeny.com

Town of Somers. . . . . . . . . . . . . . . . . . . . . . . . . . . . . . (914) 277-3323
   http://www.somersny.com
Town of Yorktown. . . . . . . . . . . . . . . . . . . . . . . . . . . . (914) 962-5722
   http://www.yorktownny.org
Village of Ardsley. . . . . . . . . . . . . . . . . . . . . . . . . . . . (914) 693-1550
   http://www.ardsleyvillage.com
Village of Bronxville. . . . . . . . . . . . . . . . . . . . . . . . . . (914) 337-6500
   http://villageofbronxville.com
Village of Buchanan. . . . . . . . . . . . . . . . . . . . . . . . . . (914) 737-1033
   http://villageofbuchanan.com
Village of Croton-on-Hudson. . . . . . . . . . . . . . . . . . (914) 271-4781
   http://village.croton-on-hudson.ny.us/Home
Village of Dobbs Ferry. . . . . . . . . . . . . . . . . . . . . . . (914) 231-8504
   http://www.dobbsferry.com
Village of Elmsford. . . . . . . . . . . . . . . . . . . . . . . . . . (914) 592-6555
   http://www.elmsfordny.org
Village of Hastings-on-Hudson. . . . . . . . . . . . . . . . (914) 478-3400
   http://www.hastingsgov.org
Village of Irvington. . . . . . . . . . . . . . . . . . . . . . . . . . (914) 591-7070
   http://www.irvingtonny.gov
Village of Larchmont. . . . . . . . . . . . . . . . . . . . . . . . (914) 834-6230
   http://www.villageoflarchmont.org
Village of Mamaroneck. . . . . . . . . . . . . . . . . . . . . . (914) 777-7722
   http://www.village.mamaroneck.ny.us
Village of Ossining. . . . . . . . . . . . . . . . . . . . . . . . . (914) 762-8428
   http://www.villageofossining.org
Village of Pelham Manor. . . . . . . . . . . . . . . . . . . . . (914) 738-8820
   http://www.pelhammanor.org
Village of Pleasantville. . . . . . . . . . . . . . . . . . . . . . (914) 769-1900
   http://www.pleasantville-ny.gov
Village of Port Chester. . . . . . . . . . . . . . . . . . . . . . (914) 939-5202
   http://www.portchesterny.com
Village of Rye Brook. . . . . . . . . . . . . . . . . . . . . . . . (914) 939-1121
   http://www.ryebrook.org
Village of Scarsdale. . . . . . . . . . . . . . . . . . . . . . . . (914) 722-1175
   http://www.scarsdale.com
Village of Tuckahoe. . . . . . . . . . . . . . . . . . . . . . . . (914) 961-3100
   http://www.tuckahoe.com
Yonkers Chamber of Commerce. . . . . . . . . . . . . . . (914) 963-0332
   http://www.yonkerschamber.com
Yorktown Heights Chamber of Commerce. . . . . . . . (914) 245-4599
   http://www.yorktownchamber.org

## Westchester County Communities

### AMAWALK (unincorporated postal area)
Zip Code: 10501
   Covers a land area of 1.399 square miles and a water area of 0.001 square miles. Located at 41.29° N. Lat; 73.75° W. Long. Elevation is 413 feet. Population: 1,219 (2010); Density: 871.1 persons per square mile (2010); Race: 94.5% White, 0.6% Black, 3.0% Asian, 0.2% American Indian/Alaska Native, 0.0% Native Hawaiian/Other Pacific Islander, 1.7% Other, 6.2% Hispanic of any race (2010); Average household size: 3.20 (2010); Median age: 43.2 (2010); Males per 100 females: 103.8 (2010); Homeownership rate: 95.8% (2010)

### ARDSLEY (village). 
Covers a land area of 1.322 square miles and a water area of 0 square miles. Located at 41.01° N. Lat; 73.83° W. Long. Elevation is 210 feet.
**History:** The town took the name "Ardsley" after the name of a local baron's estate, and the first village postmaster was appointed in 1883. Incorporated in 1896, Ardsley would continue to grow at a steady pace, until a fire destroyed the village center in 1914.
**Population:** 4,272 (1990); 4,269 (2000); 4,452 (2010); Density: 3,366.2 persons per square mile (2010); Race: 77.9% White, 2.4% Black, 16.8% Asian, 0.0% American Indian/Alaska Native, 0.0% Native Hawaiian/Other Pacific Islander, 2.9% Other, 6.5% Hispanic of any race (2010); Average household size: 2.80 (2010); Median age: 45.2 (2010); Males per 100 females: 88.4 (2010); Marriage status: 26.5% never married, 58.3% now married, 9.2% widowed, 5.9% divorced (2006-2010 5-year est.); Foreign born: 18.9% (2006-2010 5-year est.); Ancestry (includes multiple ancestries): 12.8% Italian, 11.0% Irish, 10.4% Russian, 8.8% German, 8.1% Polish (2006-2010 5-year est.).
**Economy:** Single-family building permits issued: 1 (2011); Multi-family building permits issued: 0 (2011); Employment by occupation: 21.7%

management, 3.4% professional, 6.1% services, 11.9% sales, 2.9% farming, 4.4% construction, 1.8% production (2006-2010 5-year est.).
**Income:** Per capita income: $54,923 (2006-2010 5-year est.); Median household income: $114,394 (2006-2010 5-year est.); Average household income: $156,104 (2006-2010 5-year est.); Percent of households with income of $100,000 or more: 55.5% (2006-2010 5-year est.); Poverty rate: 2.3% (2006-2010 5-year est.).
**Education:** Percent of population age 25 and over with: High school diploma (including GED) or higher: 97.1% (2006-2010 5-year est.); Bachelor's degree or higher: 69.5% (2006-2010 5-year est.); Master's degree or higher: 43.3% (2006-2010 5-year est.).
#### School District(s)
Ardsley Union Free School District (KG-12)
   2009-10 Enrollment: 2,130 . . . . . . . . . . . . . . . . . (914) 693-6300
**Housing:** Homeownership rate: 81.9% (2010); Median home value: $690,200 (2006-2010 5-year est.); Median contract rent: $1,730 per month (2006-2010 5-year est.); Median year structure built: 1956 (2006-2010 5-year est.).
**Safety:** Violent crime rate: 2.1 per 10,000 population; Property crime rate: 49.4 per 10,000 population (2010).
**Transportation:** Commute to work: 75.3% car, 10.9% public transportation, 3.2% walk, 10.6% work from home (2006-2010 5-year est.); Travel time to work: 21.4% less than 15 minutes, 27.9% 15 to 30 minutes, 20.5% 30 to 45 minutes, 8.5% 45 to 60 minutes, 21.7% 60 minutes or more (2006-2010 5-year est.)
**Additional Information Contacts**
Village of Ardsley. . . . . . . . . . . . . . . . . . . . . . . . . . (914) 693-1550
   http://www.ardsleyvillage.com

### ARMONK (CDP). 
Covers a land area of 5.966 square miles and a water area of 0.093 square miles. Located at 41.13° N. Lat; 73.71° W. Long. Elevation is 387 feet.
**History:** The Indians of North Castle were the Siwanoys, who belonged to the Wappinger Confederacy, and were part of the Algonkian-speaking group. They gave the name of Armonck (the name the Indians called Byram River) undoubtedly gave us thw hamlet name of Armonk.
**Population:** 2,745 (1990); 3,461 (2000); 4,330 (2010); Density: 725.7 persons per square mile (2010); Race: 92.7% White, 0.7% Black, 4.7% Asian, 0.0% American Indian/Alaska Native, 0.0% Native Hawaiian/Other Pacific Islander, 1.9% Other, 5.1% Hispanic of any race (2010); Average household size: 3.06 (2010); Median age: 40.8 (2010); Males per 100 females: 97.0 (2010); Marriage status: 24.3% never married, 66.3% now married, 3.6% widowed, 5.7% divorced (2006-2010 5-year est.); Foreign born: 11.3% (2006-2010 5-year est.); Ancestry (includes multiple ancestries): 25.8% Italian, 16.4% Irish, 11.5% German, 7.0% Russian, 6.5% American (2006-2010 5-year est.).
**Economy:** Employment by occupation: 33.0% management, 2.7% professional, 3.6% services, 11.1% sales, 1.1% farming, 1.0% construction, 2.6% production (2006-2010 5-year est.).
**Income:** Per capita income: $79,508 (2006-2010 5-year est.); Median household income: $130,469 (2006-2010 5-year est.); Average household income: $252,243 (2006-2010 5-year est.); Percent of households with income of $100,000 or more: 65.5% (2006-2010 5-year est.); Poverty rate: 2.1% (2006-2010 5-year est.).
**Education:** Percent of population age 25 and over with: High school diploma (including GED) or higher: 96.5% (2006-2010 5-year est.); Bachelor's degree or higher: 65.6% (2006-2010 5-year est.); Master's degree or higher: 34.9% (2006-2010 5-year est.).
#### School District(s)
Byram Hills Central School District (KG-12)
   2009-10 Enrollment: 2,795 . . . . . . . . . . . . . . . . . (914) 273-4082
**Housing:** Homeownership rate: 90.1% (2010); Median home value: $921,100 (2006-2010 5-year est.); Median contract rent: $1,611 per month (2006-2010 5-year est.); Median year structure built: 1966 (2006-2010 5-year est.).
**Transportation:** Commute to work: 76.1% car, 16.6% public transportation, 0.6% walk, 6.8% work from home (2006-2010 5-year est.); Travel time to work: 17.4% less than 15 minutes, 33.6% 15 to 30 minutes, 13.3% 30 to 45 minutes, 6.5% 45 to 60 minutes, 29.2% 60 minutes or more (2006-2010 5-year est.)

### BALDWIN PLACE (unincorporated postal area)
Zip Code: 10505
   Covers a land area of 0.652 square miles and a water area of 0 square miles. Located at 41.34° N. Lat; 73.74° W. Long. Population: 851 (2010);

Density: 1,304.5 persons per square mile (2010); Race: 84.6% White, 2.0% Black, 11.5% Asian, 0.0% American Indian/Alaska Native, 0.0% Native Hawaiian/Other Pacific Islander, 1.9% Other, 3.9% Hispanic of any race (2010); Average household size: 3.73 (2010); Median age: 36.7 (2010); Males per 100 females: 98.4 (2010); Homeownership rate: 98.6% (2010)

## BEDFORD (town).
Covers a land area of 37.173 square miles and a water area of 2.246 square miles. Located at 41.22° N. Lat; 73.66° W. Long. Elevation is 377 feet.

**History:** Caramoor Art and Music Center. Maximum-security Tacoma Correctional Facility for Women is at nearby Bedford Hills village. Also known as Bedford Village.

**Population:** 16,906 (1990); 18,133 (2000); 17,335 (2010); Density: 466.3 persons per square mile (2010); Race: 85.7% White, 5.4% Black, 2.9% Asian, 0.2% American Indian/Alaska Native, 0.0% Native Hawaiian/Other Pacific Islander, 5.8% Other, 12.1% Hispanic of any race (2010); Average household size: 2.79 (2010); Median age: 41.5 (2010); Males per 100 females: 84.3 (2010); Marriage status: 25.6% never married, 60.5% now married, 4.4% widowed, 9.4% divorced (2006-2010 5-year est.); Foreign born: 13.8% (2006-2010 5-year est.); Ancestry (includes multiple ancestries): 19.5% Irish, 18.8% Italian, 12.1% German, 8.9% English, 5.8% Russian (2006-2010 5-year est.).

**Economy:** Single-family building permits issued: 8 (2011); Multi-family building permits issued: 0 (2011); Employment by occupation: 20.6% management, 3.7% professional, 7.2% services, 15.9% sales, 2.0% farming, 5.4% construction, 2.4% production (2006-2010 5-year est.).

**Income:** Per capita income: $65,577 (2006-2010 5-year est.); Median household income: $109,742 (2006-2010 5-year est.); Average household income: $200,190 (2006-2010 5-year est.); Percent of households with income of $100,000 or more: 54.9% (2006-2010 5-year est.); Poverty rate: 4.4% (2006-2010 5-year est.).

**Taxes:** Total city taxes per capita: $1,181 (2009); City property taxes per capita: $1,070 (2009).

**Education:** Percent of population age 25 and over with: High school diploma (including GED) or higher: 90.6% (2006-2010 5-year est.); Bachelor's degree or higher: 54.1% (2006-2010 5-year est.); Master's degree or higher: 26.3% (2006-2010 5-year est.).

**School District(s)**
Bedford Central School District (PK-12)
    2009-10 Enrollment: 4,362 . . . . . . . . . . . . . . . . . . . (914) 241-6010

**Housing:** Homeownership rate: 75.7% (2010); Median home value: $772,200 (2006-2010 5-year est.); Median contract rent: $1,344 per month (2006-2010 5-year est.); Median year structure built: 1962 (2006-2010 5-year est.).

**Safety:** Violent crime rate: 1.1 per 10,000 population; Property crime rate: 19.6 per 10,000 population (2010).

**Transportation:** Commute to work: 65.5% car, 18.4% public transportation, 5.9% walk, 8.6% work from home (2006-2010 5-year est.); Travel time to work: 24.8% less than 15 minutes, 21.1% 15 to 30 minutes, 23.2% 30 to 45 minutes, 5.9% 45 to 60 minutes, 25.0% 60 minutes or more (2006-2010 5-year est.)

**Additional Information Contacts**
Town of Bedford. . . . . . . . . . . . . . . . . . . . . . . . . . . (914) 666-6530
    http://www.bedfordny.info

## BEDFORD (CDP).
Covers a land area of 3.507 square miles and a water area of 0.048 square miles. Located at 41.19° N. Lat; 73.64° W. Long. Elevation is 377 feet.

**Population:** 1,828 (1990); 1,724 (2000); 1,834 (2010); Density: 522.9 persons per square mile (2010); Race: 93.9% White, 0.9% Black, 2.8% Asian, 0.1% American Indian/Alaska Native, 0.0% Native Hawaiian/Other Pacific Islander, 2.3% Other, 7.3% Hispanic of any race (2010); Average household size: 2.85 (2010); Median age: 43.7 (2010); Males per 100 females: 99.1 (2010); Marriage status: 20.4% never married, 72.4% now married, 2.0% widowed, 5.2% divorced (2006-2010 5-year est.); Foreign born: 9.0% (2006-2010 5-year est.); Ancestry (includes multiple ancestries): 31.5% Irish, 17.7% French, 16.8% Italian, 9.6% English, 9.5% German (2006-2010 5-year est.).

**Economy:** Employment by occupation: 22.6% management, 2.2% professional, 12.9% services, 17.9% sales, 0.9% farming, 3.7% construction, 0.0% production (2006-2010 5-year est.).

**Income:** Per capita income: $88,015 (2006-2010 5-year est.); Median household income: $170,888 (2006-2010 5-year est.); Average household income: $272,301 (2006-2010 5-year est.); Percent of households with

income of $100,000 or more: 70.6% (2006-2010 5-year est.); Poverty rate: 1.0% (2006-2010 5-year est.).

**Education:** Percent of population age 25 and over with: High school diploma (including GED) or higher: 98.7% (2006-2010 5-year est.); Bachelor's degree or higher: 62.2% (2006-2010 5-year est.); Master's degree or higher: 23.0% (2006-2010 5-year est.).

**School District(s)**
Bedford Central School District (PK-12)
    2009-10 Enrollment: 4,362 . . . . . . . . . . . . . . . . . . . (914) 241-6010

**Housing:** Homeownership rate: 86.8% (2010); Median home value: $923,400 (2006-2010 5-year est.); Median contract rent: $1,316 per month (2006-2010 5-year est.); Median year structure built: 1959 (2006-2010 5-year est.).

**Transportation:** Commute to work: 67.8% car, 11.7% public transportation, 2.2% walk, 16.4% work from home (2006-2010 5-year est.); Travel time to work: 24.7% less than 15 minutes, 17.4% 15 to 30 minutes, 36.0% 30 to 45 minutes, 1.8% 45 to 60 minutes, 20.1% 60 minutes or more (2006-2010 5-year est.)

## BEDFORD HILLS (CDP).
Covers a land area of 1.006 square miles and a water area of 0 square miles. Located at 41.24° N. Lat; 73.68° W. Long. Elevation is 341 feet.

**Population:** n/a (1990); n/a (2000); 3,001 (2010); Density: 2,982.9 persons per square mile (2010); Race: 73.6% White, 4.9% Black, 4.7% Asian, 0.4% American Indian/Alaska Native, 0.0% Native Hawaiian/Other Pacific Islander, 16.4% Other, 33.9% Hispanic of any race (2010); Average household size: 2.64 (2010); Median age: 37.4 (2010); Males per 100 females: 97.8 (2010); Marriage status: 24.6% never married, 56.6% now married, 2.4% widowed, 16.4% divorced (2006-2010 5-year est.); Foreign born: 28.9% (2006-2010 5-year est.); Ancestry (includes multiple ancestries): 20.6% Italian, 19.6% Irish, 11.2% German, 9.1% English, 6.7% Polish (2006-2010 5-year est.).

**Economy:** Employment by occupation: 7.3% management, 1.7% professional, 7.7% services, 26.8% sales, 6.9% farming, 13.7% construction, 8.2% production (2006-2010 5-year est.).

**Income:** Per capita income: $29,748 (2006-2010 5-year est.); Median household income: $55,663 (2006-2010 5-year est.); Average household income: $75,349 (2006-2010 5-year est.); Percent of households with income of $100,000 or more: 28.2% (2006-2010 5-year est.); Poverty rate: 3.7% (2006-2010 5-year est.).

**Education:** Percent of population age 25 and over with: High school diploma (including GED) or higher: 86.7% (2006-2010 5-year est.); Bachelor's degree or higher: 27.3% (2006-2010 5-year est.); Master's degree or higher: 8.4% (2006-2010 5-year est.).

**School District(s)**
Bedford Central School District (PK-12)
    2009-10 Enrollment: 4,362 . . . . . . . . . . . . . . . . . . . (914) 241-6010

**Housing:** Homeownership rate: 50.2% (2010); Median home value: $442,400 (2006-2010 5-year est.); Median contract rent: $1,264 per month (2006-2010 5-year est.); Median year structure built: 1965 (2006-2010 5-year est.).

**Transportation:** Commute to work: 77.5% car, 14.8% public transportation, 3.2% walk, 2.1% work from home (2006-2010 5-year est.); Travel time to work: 27.6% less than 15 minutes, 17.1% 15 to 30 minutes, 33.2% 30 to 45 minutes, 5.3% 45 to 60 minutes, 16.9% 60 minutes or more (2006-2010 5-year est.)

## BRIARCLIFF MANOR (village).
Covers a land area of 5.961 square miles and a water area of 0.849 square miles. Located at 41.14° N. Lat; 73.84° W. Long. Elevation is 249 feet.

**History:** Settled 1896, incorporated 1902.

**Population:** 7,070 (1990); 7,696 (2000); 7,867 (2010); Density: 1,319.6 persons per square mile (2010); Race: 86.4% White, 3.4% Black, 6.9% Asian, 0.1% American Indian/Alaska Native, 0.0% Native Hawaiian/Other Pacific Islander, 3.2% Other, 5.3% Hispanic of any race (2010); Average household size: 2.71 (2010); Median age: 43.4 (2010); Males per 100 females: 92.3 (2010); Marriage status: 24.7% never married, 63.1% now married, 8.5% widowed, 3.7% divorced (2006-2010 5-year est.); Foreign born: 11.1% (2006-2010 5-year est.); Ancestry (includes multiple ancestries): 22.9% Italian, 21.3% Irish, 10.0% German, 9.1% Russian, 8.6% Polish (2006-2010 5-year est.).

**Economy:** Single-family building permits issued: 1 (2011); Multi-family building permits issued: 0 (2011); Employment by occupation: 26.1% management, 5.1% professional, 5.0% services, 14.2% sales, 1.6% farming, 2.0% construction, 0.5% production (2006-2010 5-year est.).

**Income:** Per capita income: $79,359 (2006-2010 5-year est.); Median household income: $173,674 (2006-2010 5-year est.); Average household income: $244,875 (2006-2010 5-year est.); Percent of households with income of $100,000 or more: 70.9% (2006-2010 5-year est.); Poverty rate: 4.9% (2006-2010 5-year est.).
**Education:** Percent of population age 25 and over with: High school diploma (including GED) or higher: 96.0% (2006-2010 5-year est.); Bachelor's degree or higher: 75.9% (2006-2010 5-year est.); Master's degree or higher: 45.9% (2006-2010 5-year est.).

### School District(s)
Briarcliff Manor Union Free School District (KG-12)
    2009-10 Enrollment: 1,664 . . . . . . . . . . . . . . . . (914) 941-8880
**Housing:** Homeownership rate: 84.5% (2010); Median home value: $779,000 (2006-2010 5-year est.); Median contract rent: $1,240 per month (2006-2010 5-year est.); Median year structure built: 1964 (2006-2010 5-year est.).
**Hospitals:** Stony Lodge Hospital (61 beds)
**Safety:** Violent crime rate: 1.3 per 10,000 population; Property crime rate: 22.9 per 10,000 population (2010).
**Transportation:** Commute to work: 60.0% car, 29.2% public transportation, 2.0% walk, 8.4% work from home (2006-2010 5-year est.); Travel time to work: 18.1% less than 15 minutes, 24.3% 15 to 30 minutes, 15.0% 30 to 45 minutes, 12.9% 45 to 60 minutes, 29.7% 60 minutes or more (2006-2010 5-year est.)

## BRONXVILLE (village).
Covers a land area of 0.961 square miles and a water area of 0 square miles. Located at 40.93° N. Lat; 73.82° W. Long. Elevation is 92 feet.
**History:** Seat of Sarah Lawrence College. Settled 1664, incorporated 1898.
**Population:** 6,028 (1990); 6,543 (2000); 6,323 (2010); Density: 6,572.9 persons per square mile (2010); Race: 90.3% White, 1.4% Black, 5.2% Asian, 0.0% American Indian/Alaska Native, 0.0% Native Hawaiian/Other Pacific Islander, 3.1% Other, 4.4% Hispanic of any race (2010); Average household size: 2.69 (2010); Median age: 41.3 (2010); Males per 100 females: 88.7 (2010); Marriage status: 22.9% never married, 66.0% now married, 5.6% widowed, 5.5% divorced (2006-2010 5-year est.); Foreign born: 8.0% (2006-2010 5-year est.); Ancestry (includes multiple ancestries): 32.4% Irish, 19.7% German, 16.7% Italian, 14.5% English, 4.4% Russian (2006-2010 5-year est.).
**Economy:** Single-family building permits issued: 0 (2011); Multi-family building permits issued: 0 (2011); Employment by occupation: 26.4% management, 2.5% professional, 2.4% services, 12.1% sales, 3.0% farming, 0.6% construction, 0.4% production (2006-2010 5-year est.).
**Income:** Per capita income: $113,726 (2006-2010 5-year est.); Median household income: $178,465 (2006-2010 5-year est.); Average household income: $317,645 (2006-2010 5-year est.); Percent of households with income of $100,000 or more: 69.6% (2006-2010 5-year est.); Poverty rate: 2.2% (2006-2010 5-year est.).
**Education:** Percent of population age 25 and over with: High school diploma (including GED) or higher: 99.0% (2006-2010 5-year est.); Bachelor's degree or higher: 83.7% (2006-2010 5-year est.); Master's degree or higher: 45.2% (2006-2010 5-year est.).

### School District(s)
Bronxville Union Free School District (KG-12)
    2009-10 Enrollment: 1,526 . . . . . . . . . . . . . . . . (914) 395-0500

### Four-year College(s)
Concordia College-New York (Private, Not-for-profit, Lutheran Church - Missouri Synod)
    Fall 2010 Enrollment: 729 . . . . . . . . . . . . . . . . (914) 337-9300
    2011-12 Tuition: In-state $26,620; Out-of-state $26,620
Sarah Lawrence College (Private, Not-for-profit)
    Fall 2010 Enrollment: 1,583. . . . . . . . . . . . . . . (914) 337-0700
    2011-12 Tuition: In-state $45,212; Out-of-state $45,212
**Housing:** Homeownership rate: 78.4% (2010); Median home value: $1 (2006-2010 5-year est.); Median contract rent: $1,663 per month (2006-2010 5-year est.); Median year structure built: before 1940 (2006-2010 5-year est.).
**Hospitals:** Lawrence Hospital Center (281 beds)
**Safety:** Violent crime rate: 6.2 per 10,000 population; Property crime rate: 80.6 per 10,000 population (2010).
**Transportation:** Commute to work: 44.3% car, 40.3% public transportation, 7.5% walk, 7.0% work from home (2006-2010 5-year est.); Travel time to work: 15.3% less than 15 minutes, 18.1% 15 to 30 minutes,

20.8% 30 to 45 minutes, 21.3% 45 to 60 minutes, 24.5% 60 minutes or more (2006-2010 5-year est.)
**Additional Information Contacts**
Bronxville Chamber of Commerce . . . . . . . . . . . . . . (914) 337-6040
    http://www.bronxvillechamber.com
Village of Bronxville . . . . . . . . . . . . . . . . . . . . . . . . (914) 337-6500
    http://villageofbronxville.com

## BUCHANAN (village).
Covers a land area of 1.381 square miles and a water area of 0.338 square miles. Located at 41.26° N. Lat; 73.94° W. Long. Elevation is 39 feet.
**History:** Incorporated 1928.
**Population:** 1,970 (1990); 2,189 (2000); 2,230 (2010); Density: 1,614.0 persons per square mile (2010); Race: 90.2% White, 3.1% Black, 1.5% Asian, 0.0% American Indian/Alaska Native, 0.0% Native Hawaiian/Other Pacific Islander, 5.2% Other, 16.0% Hispanic of any race (2010); Average household size: 2.68 (2010); Median age: 40.1 (2010); Males per 100 females: 101.1 (2010); Marriage status: 25.5% never married, 58.0% now married, 6.9% widowed, 9.6% divorced (2006-2010 5-year est.); Foreign born: 14.5% (2006-2010 5-year est.); Ancestry (includes multiple ancestries): 32.1% Irish, 16.5% Italian, 15.0% German, 6.6% English, 5.4% American (2006-2010 5-year est.).
**Economy:** Single-family building permits issued: 0 (2011); Multi-family building permits issued: 0 (2011); Employment by occupation: 9.8% management, 1.8% professional, 14.0% services, 9.7% sales, 2.8% farming, 13.1% construction, 7.3% production (2006-2010 5-year est.).
**Income:** Per capita income: $46,316 (2006-2010 5-year est.); Median household income: $87,647 (2006-2010 5-year est.); Average household income: $126,919 (2006-2010 5-year est.); Percent of households with income of $100,000 or more: 39.0% (2006-2010 5-year est.); Poverty rate: 0.3% (2006-2010 5-year est.).
**Education:** Percent of population age 25 and over with: High school diploma (including GED) or higher: 92.0% (2006-2010 5-year est.); Bachelor's degree or higher: 30.5% (2006-2010 5-year est.); Master's degree or higher: 9.9% (2006-2010 5-year est.).

### School District(s)
Hendrick Hudson Central School District (KG-12)
    2009-10 Enrollment: 2,701 . . . . . . . . . . . . . . . . (914) 257-5100
**Housing:** Homeownership rate: 70.4% (2010); Median home value: $388,500 (2006-2010 5-year est.); Median contract rent: $1,164 per month (2006-2010 5-year est.); Median year structure built: 1954 (2006-2010 5-year est.).
**Safety:** Violent crime rate: 4.5 per 10,000 population; Property crime rate: 49.5 per 10,000 population (2010).
**Transportation:** Commute to work: 92.6% car, 2.5% public transportation, 0.0% walk, 4.5% work from home (2006-2010 5-year est.); Travel time to work: 31.4% less than 15 minutes, 19.2% 15 to 30 minutes, 23.1% 30 to 45 minutes, 16.0% 45 to 60 minutes, 10.2% 60 minutes or more (2006-2010 5-year est.)
**Additional Information Contacts**
Village of Buchanan . . . . . . . . . . . . . . . . . . . . . . . . (914) 737-1033
    http://villageofbuchanan.com

## CHAPPAQUA (CDP).
Covers a land area of 0.450 square miles and a water area of 0 square miles. Located at 41.16° N. Lat; 73.76° W. Long. Elevation is 492 feet.
**History:** Originally a Quaker community; later estate area. Horace Greeley lived here.
**Population:** 8,975 (1990); 9,468 (2000); 1,436 (2010); Density: 3,191.0 persons per square mile (2010); Race: 81.7% White, 1.9% Black, 12.5% Asian, 0.0% American Indian/Alaska Native, 0.0% Native Hawaiian/Other Pacific Islander, 3.9% Other, 7.8% Hispanic of any race (2010); Average household size: 2.54 (2010); Median age: 44.0 (2010); Males per 100 females: 88.2 (2010); Marriage status: 20.3% never married, 70.2% now married, 4.7% widowed, 4.7% divorced (2006-2010 5-year est.); Foreign born: 28.7% (2006-2010 5-year est.); Ancestry (includes multiple ancestries): 12.5% Irish, 11.3% Italian, 11.1% German, 10.3% English, 8.8% Russian (2006-2010 5-year est.).
**Economy:** Employment by occupation: 29.6% management, 5.4% professional, 2.2% services, 13.0% sales, 0.0% farming, 0.0% construction, 0.0% production (2006-2010 5-year est.).
**Income:** Per capita income: $75,100 (2006-2010 5-year est.); Median household income: $106,985 (2006-2010 5-year est.); Average household income: $175,307 (2006-2010 5-year est.); Percent of households with

income of $100,000 or more: 61.1% (2006-2010 5-year est.); Poverty rate: 0.0% (2006-2010 5-year est.).
**Education:** Percent of population age 25 and over with: High school diploma (including GED) or higher: 98.3% (2006-2010 5-year est.); Bachelor's degree or higher: 71.0% (2006-2010 5-year est.); Master's degree or higher: 46.5% (2006-2010 5-year est.).

**School District(s)**
Chappaqua Central School District (KG-12)
   2009-10 Enrollment: 4,166 . . . . . . . . . . . . . . . . . . . . (914) 238-7200
**Housing:** Homeownership rate: 78.6% (2010); Median home value: $560,700 (2006-2010 5-year est.); Median contract rent: $1,183 per month (2006-2010 5-year est.); Median year structure built: 1961 (2006-2010 5-year est.).
**Transportation:** Commute to work: 63.1% car, 26.3% public transportation, 0.0% walk, 9.3% work from home (2006-2010 5-year est.); Travel time to work: 18.9% less than 15 minutes, 20.6% 15 to 30 minutes, 24.2% 30 to 45 minutes, 3.4% 45 to 60 minutes, 32.8% 60 minutes or more (2006-2010 5-year est.)

**CORTLANDT** (town). Covers a land area of 39.254 square miles and a water area of 10.760 square miles. Located at 41.26° N. Lat; 73.90° W. Long.
**Population:** 37,357 (1990); 38,467 (2000); 41,592 (2010); Density: 1,059.5 persons per square mile (2010); Race: 84.5% White, 5.4% Black, 3.6% Asian, 0.2% American Indian/Alaska Native, 0.0% Native Hawaiian/Other Pacific Islander, 6.3% Other, 12.8% Hispanic of any race (2010); Average household size: 2.68 (2010); Median age: 43.3 (2010); Males per 100 females: 96.4 (2010); Marriage status: 24.1% never married, 60.9% now married, 7.2% widowed, 7.8% divorced (2006-2010 5-year est.); Foreign born: 14.2% (2006-2010 5-year est.); Ancestry (includes multiple ancestries): 26.9% Italian, 21.5% Irish, 12.1% German, 5.8% Polish, 5.2% English (2006-2010 5-year est.).
**Economy:** Unemployment rate: 6.5% (February 2012); Total civilian labor force: 21,422 (February 2012); Single-family building permits issued: 6 (2011); Multi-family building permits issued: 92 (2011); Employment by occupation: 18.3% management, 5.5% professional, 7.0% services, 15.1% sales, 4.0% farming, 8.5% construction, 3.6% production (2006-2010 5-year est.).
**Income:** Per capita income: $42,815 (2006-2010 5-year est.); Median household income: $92,342 (2006-2010 5-year est.); Average household income: $120,267 (2006-2010 5-year est.); Percent of households with income of $100,000 or more: 45.3% (2006-2010 5-year est.); Poverty rate: 4.8% (2006-2010 5-year est.).
**Education:** Percent of population age 25 and over with: High school diploma (including GED) or higher: 91.3% (2006-2010 5-year est.); Bachelor's degree or higher: 43.4% (2006-2010 5-year est.); Master's degree or higher: 20.3% (2006-2010 5-year est.).
**Housing:** Homeownership rate: 76.9% (2010); Median home value: $456,600 (2006-2010 5-year est.); Median contract rent: $1,108 per month (2006-2010 5-year est.); Median year structure built: 1960 (2006-2010 5-year est.).
**Transportation:** Commute to work: 77.4% car, 16.6% public transportation, 1.1% walk, 3.9% work from home (2006-2010 5-year est.); Travel time to work: 18.5% less than 15 minutes, 18.5% 15 to 30 minutes, 24.9% 30 to 45 minutes, 12.0% 45 to 60 minutes, 26.1% 60 minutes or more (2006-2010 5-year est.)
**Additional Information Contacts**
Town of Cortlandt. . . . . . . . . . . . . . . . . . . . . . . . . . . . . . (914) 734-1020
   http://www.townofcortlandt.com

**CORTLANDT MANOR** (unincorporated postal area)
Zip Code: 10567
   Covers a land area of 22.137 square miles and a water area of 0.452 square miles. Located at 41.28° N. Lat; 73.89° W. Long. Population: 19,929 (2010); Density: 900.2 persons per square mile (2010); Race: 82.4% White, 6.4% Black, 4.4% Asian, 0.2% American Indian/Alaska Native, 0.0% Native Hawaiian/Other Pacific Islander, 6.6% Other, 13.5% Hispanic of any race (2010); Average household size: 2.94 (2010); Median age: 42.2 (2010); Males per 100 females: 97.6 (2010); Homeownership rate: 90.6% (2010)

**CROMPOND** (CDP). Covers a land area of 2.419 square miles and a water area of 0.019 square miles. Located at 41.29° N. Lat; 73.83° W. Long. Elevation is 420 feet.
**Population:** 1,895 (1990); 2,050 (2000); 2,292 (2010); Density: 947.2 persons per square mile (2010); Race: 88.0% White, 4.4% Black, 5.6% Asian, 0.0% American Indian/Alaska Native, 0.0% Native Hawaiian/Other Pacific Islander, 2.0% Other, 7.0% Hispanic of any race (2010); Average household size: 2.96 (2010); Median age: 45.0 (2010); Males per 100 females: 85.1 (2010); Marriage status: 20.8% never married, 72.4% now married, 5.0% widowed, 1.8% divorced (2006-2010 5-year est.); Foreign born: 11.2% (2006-2010 5-year est.); Ancestry (includes multiple ancestries): 34.1% Italian, 28.9% Irish, 12.4% German, 9.7% American, 6.4% Russian (2006-2010 5-year est.).
**Economy:** Employment by occupation: 22.0% management, 13.9% professional, 5.0% services, 12.6% sales, 1.6% farming, 4.3% construction, 0.0% production (2006-2010 5-year est.).
**Income:** Per capita income: $50,940 (2006-2010 5-year est.); Median household income: $116,450 (2006-2010 5-year est.); Average household income: $151,197 (2006-2010 5-year est.); Percent of households with income of $100,000 or more: 62.6% (2006-2010 5-year est.); Poverty rate: 3.6% (2006-2010 5-year est.).
**Education:** Percent of population age 25 and over with: High school diploma (including GED) or higher: 92.0% (2006-2010 5-year est.); Bachelor's degree or higher: 57.8% (2006-2010 5-year est.); Master's degree or higher: 27.3% (2006-2010 5-year est.).

**School District(s)**
Lakeland Central School District (PK-12)
   2009-10 Enrollment: 6,439 . . . . . . . . . . . . . . . . . . . . (914) 245-1700
**Housing:** Homeownership rate: 91.1% (2010); Median home value: $536,600 (2006-2010 5-year est.); Median contract rent: $1,299 per month (2006-2010 5-year est.); Median year structure built: 1965 (2006-2010 5-year est.).
**Transportation:** Commute to work: 79.5% car, 7.8% public transportation, 0.0% walk, 12.7% work from home (2006-2010 5-year est.); Travel time to work: 20.3% less than 15 minutes, 27.7% 15 to 30 minutes, 23.8% 30 to 45 minutes, 9.3% 45 to 60 minutes, 18.9% 60 minutes or more (2006-2010 5-year est.)

**CROSS RIVER** (unincorporated postal area)
Zip Code: 10518
   Covers a land area of 3.447 square miles and a water area of 0.054 square miles. Located at 41.26° N. Lat; 73.58° W. Long. Elevation is 338 feet. Population: 1,268 (2010); Density: 367.8 persons per square mile (2010); Race: 90.8% White, 0.6% Black, 5.4% Asian, 0.2% American Indian/Alaska Native, 0.0% Native Hawaiian/Other Pacific Islander, 3.0% Other, 3.6% Hispanic of any race (2010); Average household size: 2.83 (2010); Median age: 43.1 (2010); Males per 100 females: 90.4 (2010); Homeownership rate: 89.9% (2010)

**CROTON FALLS** (unincorporated postal area)
Zip Code: 10519
   Covers a land area of 0.744 square miles and a water area of 0.025 square miles. Located at 41.35° N. Lat; 73.65° W. Long. Elevation is 266 feet. Population: 316 (2010); Density: 424.7 persons per square mile (2010); Race: 80.7% White, 6.0% Black, 2.5% Asian, 0.0% American Indian/Alaska Native, 0.0% Native Hawaiian/Other Pacific Islander, 10.8% Other, 12.0% Hispanic of any race (2010); Average household size: 2.68 (2010); Median age: 40.8 (2010); Males per 100 females: 91.5 (2010); Homeownership rate: 62.4% (2010)

**CROTON-ON-HUDSON** (village). Aka Croton-Harmon. Covers a land area of 4.642 square miles and a water area of 6.037 square miles. Located at 41.20° N. Lat; 73.90° W. Long. Elevation is 164 feet.
**History:** During 1920s, fashionable haven for intellectuals such as Edna St. Vincent Millay, Doris Stevens, Stuart Chase and John Reed. Van Cortlandt Manor, a restored 18th-century Dutch-English manorhouse on 20 acres of what was once 86,000-acre estate is located here. Settled 1609, Incorporated 1898.
**Population:** 7,018 (1990); 7,606 (2000); 8,070 (2010); Density: 1,738.3 persons per square mile (2010); Race: 86.6% White, 2.9% Black, 3.7% Asian, 0.2% American Indian/Alaska Native, 0.0% Native Hawaiian/Other Pacific Islander, 6.6% Other, 11.4% Hispanic of any race (2010); Average household size: 2.66 (2010); Median age: 43.2 (2010); Males per 100 females: 92.3 (2010); Marriage status: 19.4% never married, 68.9% now married, 5.2% widowed, 6.5% divorced (2006-2010 5-year est.); Foreign

born: 14.2% (2006-2010 5-year est.); Ancestry (includes multiple ancestries): 23.3% Italian, 22.7% Irish, 12.5% German, 8.1% English, 6.0% Russian (2006-2010 5-year est.).
**Economy:** Single-family building permits issued: 2 (2011); Multi-family building permits issued: 0 (2011); Employment by occupation: 20.4% management, 6.8% professional, 5.8% services, 15.3% sales, 2.2% farming, 5.8% construction, 3.2% production (2006-2010 5-year est.).
**Income:** Per capita income: $47,962 (2006-2010 5-year est.); Median household income: $97,500 (2006-2010 5-year est.); Average household income: $126,715 (2006-2010 5-year est.); Percent of households with income of $100,000 or more: 49.7% (2006-2010 5-year est.); Poverty rate: 4.7% (2006-2010 5-year est.).
**Taxes:** Total city taxes per capita: $1,339 (2009); City property taxes per capita: $1,289 (2009).
**Education:** Percent of population age 25 and over with: High school diploma (including GED) or higher: 92.6% (2006-2010 5-year est.); Bachelor's degree or higher: 57.1% (2006-2010 5-year est.); Master's degree or higher: 28.0% (2006-2010 5-year est.).

**School District(s)**
Croton-Harmon Union Free School District (KG-12)
   2009-10 Enrollment: 1,749 . . . . . . . . . . . . . . . . . . . . . . (914) 271-4793
**Housing:** Homeownership rate: 77.9% (2010); Median home value: $515,700 (2006-2010 5-year est.); Median contract rent: $1,186 per month (2006-2010 5-year est.); Median year structure built: 1955 (2006-2010 5-year est.).
**Newspapers:** Gazette (Community news; Circulation 3,000)
**Transportation:** Commute to work: 65.5% car, 26.2% public transportation, 3.5% walk, 4.0% work from home (2006-2010 5-year est.); Travel time to work: 22.9% less than 15 minutes, 13.5% 15 to 30 minutes, 21.3% 30 to 45 minutes, 12.1% 45 to 60 minutes, 30.1% 60 minutes or more (2006-2010 5-year est.); Amtrak: train service available.
**Additional Information Contacts**
Village of Croton-on-Hudson . . . . . . . . . . . . . . . . . . . . . . . (914) 271-4781
   http://village.croton-on-hudson.ny.us/Home

## CRUGERS (CDP).
Covers a land area of 0.660 square miles and a water area of 0.573 square miles. Located at 41.23° N. Lat; 73.92° W. Long. Elevation is 95 feet.
**Population:** 1,547 (1990); 1,752 (2000); 1,534 (2010); Density: 2,322.0 persons per square mile (2010); Race: 87.6% White, 6.9% Black, 1.2% Asian, 0.0% American Indian/Alaska Native, 0.0% Native Hawaiian/Other Pacific Islander, 4.3% Other, 9.3% Hispanic of any race (2010); Average household size: 1.68 (2010); Median age: 62.9 (2010); Males per 100 females: 81.3 (2010); Marriage status: 22.0% never married, 39.3% now married, 18.2% widowed, 20.6% divorced (2006-2010 5-year est.); Foreign born: 16.9% (2006-2010 5-year est.); Ancestry (includes multiple ancestries): 17.7% Irish, 16.1% Italian, 10.8% German, 7.7% French, 5.0% English (2006-2010 5-year est.).
**Economy:** Employment by occupation: 9.7% management, 7.6% professional, 13.6% services, 18.1% sales, 1.7% farming, 4.1% construction, 5.3% production (2006-2010 5-year est.).
**Income:** Per capita income: $39,400 (2006-2010 5-year est.); Median household income: $42,724 (2006-2010 5-year est.); Average household income: $68,047 (2006-2010 5-year est.); Percent of households with income of $100,000 or more: 21.2% (2006-2010 5-year est.); Poverty rate: 8.8% (2006-2010 5-year est.).
**Education:** Percent of population age 25 and over with: High school diploma (including GED) or higher: 88.9% (2006-2010 5-year est.); Bachelor's degree or higher: 32.0% (2006-2010 5-year est.); Master's degree or higher: 19.6% (2006-2010 5-year est.).
**Housing:** Homeownership rate: 25.1% (2010); Median home value: $469,600 (2006-2010 5-year est.); Median contract rent: $927 per month (2006-2010 5-year est.); Median year structure built: 1959 (2006-2010 5-year est.).
**Transportation:** Commute to work: 87.2% car, 9.1% public transportation, 2.3% walk, 1.4% work from home (2006-2010 5-year est.); Travel time to work: 15.7% less than 15 minutes, 18.3% 15 to 30 minutes, 39.1% 30 to 45 minutes, 6.9% 45 to 60 minutes, 19.9% 60 minutes or more (2006-2010 5-year est.)

## DOBBS FERRY (village).
Covers a land area of 2.429 square miles and a water area of 0.752 square miles. Located at 41.00° N. Lat; 73.86° W. Long. Elevation is 210 feet.
**History:** Named for Jeremiah Dobbs, who operated a ferry across the Hudson River. Site of Livingston Manor, where George Washington and

Marshal Rochambeau of France are said to have planned the Yorktown Campaign. Seat of Mercy College. Incorporated 1873.
**Population:** 9,940 (1990); 10,622 (2000); 10,875 (2010); Density: 4,476.7 persons per square mile (2010); Race: 78.6% White, 7.2% Black, 8.6% Asian, 0.1% American Indian/Alaska Native, 0.1% Native Hawaiian/Other Pacific Islander, 5.4% Other, 10.5% Hispanic of any race (2010); Average household size: 2.54 (2010); Median age: 41.4 (2010); Males per 100 females: 91.4 (2010); Marriage status: 31.0% never married, 54.1% now married, 6.8% widowed, 8.2% divorced (2006-2010 5-year est.); Foreign born: 15.5% (2006-2010 5-year est.); Ancestry (includes multiple ancestries): 26.9% Italian, 15.8% Irish, 8.5% German, 6.5% Polish, 5.1% Russian (2006-2010 5-year est.).
**Economy:** Single-family building permits issued: 4 (2011); Multi-family building permits issued: 0 (2011); Employment by occupation: 16.8% management, 4.6% professional, 7.7% services, 16.9% sales, 3.2% farming, 3.8% construction, 0.8% production (2006-2010 5-year est.).
**Income:** Per capita income: $47,732 (2006-2010 5-year est.); Median household income: $100,659 (2006-2010 5-year est.); Average household income: $133,103 (2006-2010 5-year est.); Percent of households with income of $100,000 or more: 51.0% (2006-2010 5-year est.); Poverty rate: 4.0% (2006-2010 5-year est.).
**Education:** Percent of population age 25 and over with: High school diploma (including GED) or higher: 94.2% (2006-2010 5-year est.); Bachelor's degree or higher: 55.1% (2006-2010 5-year est.); Master's degree or higher: 29.2% (2006-2010 5-year est.).

**School District(s)**
Dobbs Ferry Union Free School District (KG-12)
   2009-10 Enrollment: 1,461 . . . . . . . . . . . . . . . . . . . . . . (914) 693-1506
Greenburgh Eleven Union Free School District (01-12)
   2009-10 Enrollment: 364 . . . . . . . . . . . . . . . . . . . . . . . (914) 693-8500
Greenburgh-North Castle Union Free School District (07-12)
   2009-10 Enrollment: 354 . . . . . . . . . . . . . . . . . . . . . . . (914) 693-4309

**Four-year College(s)**
Mercy College (Private, Not-for-profit)
   Fall 2010 Enrollment: 8,401 . . . . . . . . . . . . . . . . . . . . . . (800) 637-2969
   2011-12 Tuition: In-state $17,360; Out-of-state $17,360
**Housing:** Homeownership rate: 60.7% (2010); Median home value: $633,100 (2006-2010 5-year est.); Median contract rent: $1,305 per month (2006-2010 5-year est.); Median year structure built: 1954 (2006-2010 5-year est.).
**Hospitals:** Community Hospital at Dobbs Ferry (50 beds)
**Safety:** Violent crime rate: 6.3 per 10,000 population; Property crime rate: 121.1 per 10,000 population (2010).
**Newspapers:** The Rivertowns Enterprise (Community news; Circulation 1,600)
**Transportation:** Commute to work: 59.2% car, 22.0% public transportation, 8.4% walk, 8.8% work from home (2006-2010 5-year est.); Travel time to work: 23.8% less than 15 minutes, 21.9% 15 to 30 minutes, 24.2% 30 to 45 minutes, 9.1% 45 to 60 minutes, 21.0% 60 minutes or more (2006-2010 5-year est.)
**Additional Information Contacts**
Village of Dobbs Ferry . . . . . . . . . . . . . . . . . . . . . . . . . . . . (914) 231-8504
   http://www.dobbsferry.com

## EASTCHESTER (town).
Covers a land area of 4.853 square miles and a water area of 0.088 square miles. Located at 40.95° N. Lat; 73.81° W. Long. Elevation is 52 feet.
**History:** Named for the town of Chester in England. Once a township (formed 1788) extending from the present Bronx North to Scarsdale; Mt. Vernon city was separated from it in 1892; the section South of Mt. Vernon was annexed by N.Y. city in 1895.
**Population:** 30,867 (1990); 31,318 (2000); 32,363 (2010); Density: 6,668.6 persons per square mile (2010); Race: 85.9% White, 3.3% Black, 7.3% Asian, 0.1% American Indian/Alaska Native, 0.0% Native Hawaiian/Other Pacific Islander, 3.4% Other, 7.2% Hispanic of any race (2010); Average household size: 2.48 (2010); Median age: 42.0 (2010); Males per 100 females: 88.7 (2010); Marriage status: 26.3% never married, 59.8% now married, 7.7% widowed, 6.3% divorced (2006-2010 5-year est.); Foreign born: 16.5% (2006-2010 5-year est.); Ancestry (includes multiple ancestries): 34.3% Italian, 21.1% Irish, 12.5% German, 7.2% English, 3.2% Polish (2006-2010 5-year est.).
**Economy:** Unemployment rate: 6.2% (February 2012); Total civilian labor force: 15,828 (February 2012); Single-family building permits issued: 0 (2011); Multi-family building permits issued: 0 (2011); Employment by occupation: 22.6% management, 3.8% professional, 3.8% services, 16.8%

sales, 3.4% farming, 5.2% construction, 2.8% production (2006-2010 5-year est.).

**Income:** Per capita income: $66,589 (2006-2010 5-year est.); Median household income: $100,518 (2006-2010 5-year est.); Average household income: $164,549 (2006-2010 5-year est.); Percent of households with income of $100,000 or more: 50.4% (2006-2010 5-year est.); Poverty rate: 3.8% (2006-2010 5-year est.).

**Education:** Percent of population age 25 and over with: High school diploma (including GED) or higher: 94.7% (2006-2010 5-year est.); Bachelor's degree or higher: 58.6% (2006-2010 5-year est.); Master's degree or higher: 27.5% (2006-2010 5-year est.).

### School District(s)

Eastchester Union Free School District (KG-12)

    2009-10 Enrollment: 3,114 . . . . . . . . . . . . . . . . . . . (914) 793-6130

Tuckahoe Union Free School District (KG-12)

    2009-10 Enrollment: 1,021 . . . . . . . . . . . . . . . . . . . (914) 337-6600

**Housing:** Homeownership rate: 73.1% (2010); Median home value: $598,900 (2006-2010 5-year est.); Median contract rent: $1,310 per month (2006-2010 5-year est.); Median year structure built: 1951 (2006-2010 5-year est.).

**Transportation:** Commute to work: 63.7% car, 25.6% public transportation, 4.2% walk, 6.1% work from home (2006-2010 5-year est.); Travel time to work: 21.7% less than 15 minutes, 26.8% 15 to 30 minutes, 18.8% 30 to 45 minutes, 12.3% 45 to 60 minutes, 20.3% 60 minutes or more (2006-2010 5-year est.).

**Additional Information Contacts**

Town of Eastchester . . . . . . . . . . . . . . . . . . . . . . . . (914) 771-3351

    http://www.eastchester.org

## EASTCHESTER (CDP).

Covers a land area of 3.293 square miles and a water area of 0.088 square miles. Located at 40.95° N. Lat; 73.80° W. Long. Elevation is 52 feet.

**History:** Laws for the region (of which Eastchester CDP is a part) were established in 1665, under an agreement called the "Eastchester Covenant." The covenant was a rare document for this period. It contained 26 provisions, such items as: education of children, disposition and upkeep of property, and support of a minister.

**Population:** 18,537 (1990); 18,564 (2000); 19,554 (2010); Density: 5,937.1 persons per square mile (2010); Race: 88.3% White, 1.3% Black, 7.7% Asian, 0.1% American Indian/Alaska Native, 0.0% Native Hawaiian/Other Pacific Islander, 2.6% Other, 6.5% Hispanic of any race (2010); Average household size: 2.49 (2010); Median age: 42.9 (2010); Males per 100 females: 89.4 (2010); Marriage status: 24.1% never married, 61.3% now married, 8.3% widowed, 6.3% divorced (2006-2010 5-year est.); Foreign born: 18.4% (2006-2010 5-year est.); Ancestry (includes multiple ancestries): 42.5% Italian, 18.2% Irish, 10.7% German, 5.3% English, 3.5% American (2006-2010 5-year est.).

**Economy:** Employment by occupation: 22.5% management, 4.4% professional, 3.4% services, 17.7% sales, 3.8% farming, 4.7% construction, 2.1% production (2006-2010 5-year est.).

**Income:** Per capita income: $59,003 (2006-2010 5-year est.); Median household income: $99,250 (2006-2010 5-year est.); Average household income: $141,864 (2006-2010 5-year est.); Percent of households with income of $100,000 or more: 49.4% (2006-2010 5-year est.); Poverty rate: 3.5% (2006-2010 5-year est.).

**Education:** Percent of population age 25 and over with: High school diploma (including GED) or higher: 93.3% (2006-2010 5-year est.); Bachelor's degree or higher: 56.5% (2006-2010 5-year est.); Master's degree or higher: 24.7% (2006-2010 5-year est.).

### School District(s)

Eastchester Union Free School District (KG-12)

    2009-10 Enrollment: 3,114 . . . . . . . . . . . . . . . . . . . (914) 793-6130

Tuckahoe Union Free School District (KG-12)

    2009-10 Enrollment: 1,021 . . . . . . . . . . . . . . . . . . . (914) 337-6600

**Housing:** Homeownership rate: 80.5% (2010); Median home value: $565,000 (2006-2010 5-year est.); Median contract rent: $1,339 per month (2006-2010 5-year est.); Median year structure built: 1953 (2006-2010 5-year est.).

**Transportation:** Commute to work: 70.0% car, 21.8% public transportation, 1.1% walk, 6.7% work from home (2006-2010 5-year est.); Travel time to work: 23.0% less than 15 minutes, 29.1% 15 to 30 minutes, 20.5% 30 to 45 minutes, 10.3% 45 to 60 minutes, 17.0% 60 minutes or more (2006-2010 5-year est.).

## ELMSFORD (village).

Covers a land area of 1.026 square miles and a water area of 0 square miles. Located at 41.05° N. Lat; 73.81° W. Long. Elevation is 177 feet.

**History:** Incorporated 1910.

**Population:** 4,114 (1990); 4,676 (2000); 4,664 (2010); Density: 4,542.7 persons per square mile (2010); Race: 46.4% White, 20.5% Black, 10.5% Asian, 0.6% American Indian/Alaska Native, 0.0% Native Hawaiian/Other Pacific Islander, 22.0% Other, 38.0% Hispanic of any race (2010); Average household size: 2.88 (2010); Median age: 35.1 (2010); Males per 100 females: 103.8 (2010); Marriage status: 35.9% never married, 53.3% now married, 5.8% widowed, 5.0% divorced (2006-2010 5-year est.); Foreign born: 30.3% (2006-2010 5-year est.); Ancestry (includes multiple ancestries): 17.9% Italian, 16.4% Irish, 4.3% Jamaican, 4.1% American, 3.7% German (2006-2010 5-year est.).

**Economy:** Single-family building permits issued: 1 (2011); Multi-family building permits issued: 0 (2011); Employment by occupation: 11.1% management, 6.3% professional, 5.2% services, 16.5% sales, 3.9% farming, 9.3% construction, 2.9% production (2006-2010 5-year est.).

**Income:** Per capita income: $31,484 (2006-2010 5-year est.); Median household income: $76,218 (2006-2010 5-year est.); Average household income: $81,656 (2006-2010 5-year est.); Percent of households with income of $100,000 or more: 32.5% (2006-2010 5-year est.); Poverty rate: 4.5% (2006-2010 5-year est.).

**Education:** Percent of population age 25 and over with: High school diploma (including GED) or higher: 90.2% (2006-2010 5-year est.); Bachelor's degree or higher: 37.7% (2006-2010 5-year est.); Master's degree or higher: 14.0% (2006-2010 5-year est.).

### School District(s)

Elmsford Union Free School District (PK-12)

    2009-10 Enrollment: 1,020 . . . . . . . . . . . . . . . . . . . (914) 592-6632

### Vocational/Technical School(s)

Southern Westchester BOCES-Practical Nursing Program (Public)

    Fall 2010 Enrollment: 152 . . . . . . . . . . . . . . . . . . . (914) 592-0849

    2011-12 Tuition: $10,200

**Housing:** Homeownership rate: 48.2% (2010); Median home value: $481,800 (2006-2010 5-year est.); Median contract rent: $1,627 per month (2006-2010 5-year est.); Median year structure built: 1960 (2006-2010 5-year est.).

**Safety:** Violent crime rate: 12.7 per 10,000 population; Property crime rate: 91.1 per 10,000 population (2010).

**Newspapers:** Ardsley/Hartsdale Pennysaver (Community news; Circulation 11,094); Bronxville/Eastchester and Tuckahoe Pennysaver (Community news; Circulation 9,700); City Island Pennysaver (Community news; Circulation 1,700); Co-Op City Pennysaver (Community news; Circulation 15,800); Greenwich/Byram Pennysaver (Community news; Circulation 10,700); Kingsbridge Pennysaver (Community news; Circulation 7,800); Larchmont/Mamaroneck Pennysaver (Community news; Circulation 11,800); Mount Vernon/Fleetwood Pennysaver (Community news; Circulation 10,900); New Rochelle/Pelhams Pennysaver (Community news; Circulation 10,900); New Rochelle/Wykagyl Pennysaver (Community news; Circulation 10,800); Parkchester Pennysaver (Community news; Circulation 12,300); Pelham Parkway North Pennysaver (Community news; Circulation 13,900); Purchase/Rye Brook/Port Chester Pennysaver (Community news; Circulation 10,000); Riverdale Pennysaver (Community news; Circulation 8,200); Rye/Harrison Pennysaver (Community news; Circulation 9,600); Scarsdale Pennysaver (Community news; Circulation 12,700); Throgs Neck Pennysaver (Community news; Circulation 18,200); Wakefield Pennysaver (Community news; Circulation 9,100); Westchester Square Pennysaver (Community news; Circulation 8,600); White Plains South Pennysaver (Community news; Circulation 9,300); Yonkers North Pennysaver (Community news; Circulation 13,700); Yonkers South Pennysaver (Community news; Circulation 11,400); Yonkers West Pennysaver (Community news; Circulation 13,500); Yonkers/Lincoln Park Pennysaver (Community news; Circulation 12,200)

**Transportation:** Commute to work: 77.4% car, 11.8% public transportation, 5.1% walk, 2.6% work from home (2006-2010 5-year est.); Travel time to work: 30.3% less than 15 minutes, 30.2% 15 to 30 minutes, 21.4% 30 to 45 minutes, 9.1% 45 to 60 minutes, 8.9% 60 minutes or more (2006-2010 5-year est.)

**Additional Information Contacts**

Village of Elmsford . . . . . . . . . . . . . . . . . . . . . . . . (914) 592-6555

    http://www.elmsfordny.org

**FAIRVIEW** (CDP). Covers a land area of 0.428 square miles and a water area of 0.002 square miles. Located at 41.04° N. Lat; 73.79° W. Long. Elevation is 217 feet.

**Population:** 2,688 (1990); 2,887 (2000); 3,099 (2010); Density: 7,238.3 persons per square mile (2010); Race: 16.0% White, 58.2% Black, 3.3% Asian, 0.4% American Indian/Alaska Native, 0.3% Native Hawaiian/Other Pacific Islander, 21.8% Other, 33.4% Hispanic of any race (2010); Average household size: 3.17 (2010); Median age: 34.5 (2010); Males per 100 females: 88.0 (2010); Marriage status: 39.2% never married, 44.7% now married, 6.2% widowed, 9.9% divorced (2006-2010 5-year est.); Foreign born: 24.7% (2006-2010 5-year est.); Ancestry (includes multiple ancestries): 9.1% Italian, 4.9% Haitian, 4.3% West Indian, 4.0% German, 1.8% Jamaican (2006-2010 5-year est.).

**Economy:** Employment by occupation: 6.5% management, 2.7% professional, 18.2% services, 15.4% sales, 9.5% farming, 7.9% construction, 4.3% production (2006-2010 5-year est.).

**Income:** Per capita income: $30,984 (2006-2010 5-year est.); Median household income: $78,194 (2006-2010 5-year est.); Average household income: $90,507 (2006-2010 5-year est.); Percent of households with income of $100,000 or more: 39.2% (2006-2010 5-year est.); Poverty rate: 6.2% (2006-2010 5-year est.).

**Education:** Percent of population age 25 and over with: High school diploma (including GED) or higher: 84.9% (2006-2010 5-year est.); Bachelor's degree or higher: 30.2% (2006-2010 5-year est.); Master's degree or higher: 19.1% (2006-2010 5-year est.).

**Housing:** Homeownership rate: 42.5% (2010); Median home value: $420,200 (2006-2010 5-year est.); Median contract rent: $1,174 per month (2006-2010 5-year est.); Median year structure built: 1969 (2006-2010 5-year est.).

**Transportation:** Commute to work: 76.2% car, 16.8% public transportation, 6.3% walk, 0.0% work from home (2006-2010 5-year est.); Travel time to work: 33.5% less than 15 minutes, 41.7% 15 to 30 minutes, 14.8% 30 to 45 minutes, 1.4% 45 to 60 minutes, 8.6% 60 minutes or more (2006-2010 5-year est.)

**GOLDEN'S BRIDGE** (CDP). Covers a land area of 2.429 square miles and a water area of 0.133 square miles. Located at 41.28° N. Lat; 73.67° W. Long. Elevation is 217 feet.

**Population:** 1,423 (1990); 1,578 (2000); 1,630 (2010); Density: 670.9 persons per square mile (2010); Race: 92.7% White, 2.5% Black, 2.6% Asian, 0.0% American Indian/Alaska Native, 0.0% Native Hawaiian/Other Pacific Islander, 2.2% Other, 5.6% Hispanic of any race (2010); Average household size: 2.56 (2010); Median age: 44.3 (2010); Males per 100 females: 92.4 (2010); Marriage status: 31.5% never married, 60.6% now married, 3.1% widowed, 4.9% divorced (2006-2010 5-year est.); Foreign born: 14.8% (2006-2010 5-year est.); Ancestry (includes multiple ancestries): 19.0% Italian, 18.2% Irish, 12.6% Russian, 9.9% Polish, 8.8% American (2006-2010 5-year est.).

**Economy:** Employment by occupation: 21.2% management, 7.5% professional, 6.1% services, 18.0% sales, 0.9% farming, 1.2% construction, 1.2% production (2006-2010 5-year est.).

**Income:** Per capita income: $73,948 (2006-2010 5-year est.); Median household income: $145,641 (2006-2010 5-year est.); Average household income: $205,713 (2006-2010 5-year est.); Percent of households with income of $100,000 or more: 61.2% (2006-2010 5-year est.); Poverty rate: 3.0% (2006-2010 5-year est.).

**Education:** Percent of population age 25 and over with: High school diploma (including GED) or higher: 97.3% (2006-2010 5-year est.); Bachelor's degree or higher: 72.8% (2006-2010 5-year est.); Master's degree or higher: 38.4% (2006-2010 5-year est.).

**Housing:** Homeownership rate: 82.7% (2010); Median home value: $578,500 (2006-2010 5-year est.); Median contract rent: n/a per month (2006-2010 5-year est.); Median year structure built: 1972 (2006-2010 5-year est.).

**Transportation:** Commute to work: 61.1% car, 22.5% public transportation, 1.4% walk, 13.5% work from home (2006-2010 5-year est.); Travel time to work: 14.5% less than 15 minutes, 29.3% 15 to 30 minutes, 14.0% 30 to 45 minutes, 7.7% 45 to 60 minutes, 34.5% 60 minutes or more (2006-2010 5-year est.)

**GOLDENS BRIDGE** (unincorporated postal area)
Zip Code: 10526

Covers a land area of 3.293 square miles and a water area of 0.531 square miles. Located at 41.29° N. Lat; 73.67° W. Long. Elevation is 217 feet. Population: 1,809 (2010); Density: 549.3 persons per square mile

(2010); Race: 92.4% White, 2.7% Black, 2.3% Asian, 0.1% American Indian/Alaska Native, 0.0% Native Hawaiian/Other Pacific Islander, 2.5% Other, 6.1% Hispanic of any race (2010); Average household size: 2.66 (2010); Median age: 43.6 (2010); Males per 100 females: 92.4 (2010); Homeownership rate: 81.5% (2010)

**GRANITE SPRINGS** (unincorporated postal area)
Zip Code: 10527

Covers a land area of 2.444 square miles and a water area of 0.007 square miles. Located at 41.32° N. Lat; 73.76° W. Long. Elevation is 515 feet. Population: 908 (2010); Density: 371.5 persons per square mile (2010); Race: 95.3% White, 1.2% Black, 1.8% Asian, 0.0% American Indian/Alaska Native, 0.0% Native Hawaiian/Other Pacific Islander, 1.7% Other, 4.1% Hispanic of any race (2010); Average household size: 3.16 (2010); Median age: 42.6 (2010); Males per 100 females: 102.2 (2010); Homeownership rate: 93.7% (2010)

**GREENBURGH** (town). Covers a land area of 30.309 square miles and a water area of 5.805 square miles. Located at 41.02° N. Lat; 73.84° W. Long. Elevation is 348 feet.

**Population:** 83,816 (1990); 86,764 (2000); 88,400 (2010); Density: 2,916.6 persons per square mile (2010); Race: 69.2% White, 12.6% Black, 10.4% Asian, 0.2% American Indian/Alaska Native, 0.0% Native Hawaiian/Other Pacific Islander, 7.6% Other, 14.0% Hispanic of any race (2010); Average household size: 2.55 (2010); Median age: 42.8 (2010); Males per 100 females: 89.5 (2010); Marriage status: 28.6% never married, 56.5% now married, 7.2% widowed, 7.7% divorced (2006-2010 5-year est.); Foreign born: 21.4% (2006-2010 5-year est.); Ancestry (includes multiple ancestries): 18.6% Italian, 13.0% Irish, 8.6% German, 5.8% Russian, 5.3% Polish (2006-2010 5-year est.).

**Economy:** Unemployment rate: 6.4% (February 2012); Total civilian labor force: 47,358 (February 2012); Single-family building permits issued: 12 (2011); Multi-family building permits issued: 350 (2011); Employment by occupation: 18.3% management, 4.8% professional, 7.0% services, 13.7% sales, 2.7% farming, 3.8% construction, 2.1% production (2006-2010 5-year est.).

**Income:** Per capita income: $54,963 (2006-2010 5-year est.); Median household income: $101,893 (2006-2010 5-year est.); Average household income: $143,607 (2006-2010 5-year est.); Percent of households with income of $100,000 or more: 51.4% (2006-2010 5-year est.); Poverty rate: 3.3% (2006-2010 5-year est.).

**Taxes:** Total city taxes per capita: $657 (2009); City property taxes per capita: $581 (2009).

**Education:** Percent of population age 25 and over with: High school diploma (including GED) or higher: 95.0% (2006-2010 5-year est.); Bachelor's degree or higher: 59.1% (2006-2010 5-year est.); Master's degree or higher: 31.8% (2006-2010 5-year est.).

**Housing:** Homeownership rate: 72.7% (2010); Median home value: $584,600 (2006-2010 5-year est.); Median contract rent: $1,331 per month (2006-2010 5-year est.); Median year structure built: 1957 (2006-2010 5-year est.).

**Safety:** Violent crime rate: 16.2 per 10,000 population; Property crime rate: 146.4 per 10,000 population (2010).

**Transportation:** Commute to work: 68.1% car, 20.5% public transportation, 3.3% walk, 6.6% work from home (2006-2010 5-year est.); Travel time to work: 22.8% less than 15 minutes, 29.7% 15 to 30 minutes, 19.6% 30 to 45 minutes, 9.8% 45 to 60 minutes, 18.1% 60 minutes or more (2006-2010 5-year est.)

**Additional Information Contacts**
Town of Greenburgh . . . . . . . . . . . . . . . . . . . . . . . . . . . . . . (914) 993-1500
   http://www.greenburghny.com

**GREENVILLE** (CDP). Covers a land area of 2.562 square miles and a water area of 0.034 square miles. Located at 40.99° N. Lat; 73.81° W. Long. Elevation is 249 feet.

**History:** Residents popularly refer to the Greenville area as "Edgemont". Edgemont was originally a development designed by different architects for summer homes for Manhattanites.

**Population:** 8,983 (1990); 8,648 (2000); 7,116 (2010); Density: 2,777.2 persons per square mile (2010); Race: 73.3% White, 1.5% Black, 22.2% Asian, 0.1% American Indian/Alaska Native, 0.0% Native Hawaiian/Other Pacific Islander, 2.9% Other, 4.8% Hispanic of any race (2010); Average household size: 2.89 (2010); Median age: 43.6 (2010); Males per 100 females: 94.4 (2010); Marriage status: 15.3% never married, 76.2% now married, 3.4% widowed, 5.1% divorced (2006-2010 5-year est.); Foreign

born: 20.1% (2006-2010 5-year est.); Ancestry (includes multiple ancestries): 16.9% Italian, 11.8% Irish, 10.2% Russian, 6.2% German, 5.9% American (2006-2010 5-year est.).
**Economy:** Employment by occupation: 22.3% management, 6.6% professional, 1.4% services, 7.8% sales, 1.3% farming, 2.4% construction, 1.4% production (2006-2010 5-year est.).
**Income:** Per capita income: $79,478 (2006-2010 5-year est.); Median household income: $192,885 (2006-2010 5-year est.); Average household income: $249,681 (2006-2010 5-year est.); Percent of households with income of $100,000 or more: 78.8% (2006-2010 5-year est.); Poverty rate: 3.3% (2006-2010 5-year est.).
**Education:** Percent of population age 25 and over with: High school diploma (including GED) or higher: 98.2% (2006-2010 5-year est.); Bachelor's degree or higher: 80.0% (2006-2010 5-year est.); Master's degree or higher: 52.8% (2006-2010 5-year est.).
**Housing:** Homeownership rate: 91.0% (2010); Median home value: $898,300 (2006-2010 5-year est.); Median contract rent: n/a per month (2006-2010 5-year est.); Median year structure built: 1957 (2006-2010 5-year est.).
**Transportation:** Commute to work: 68.2% car, 24.9% public transportation, 0.5% walk, 6.4% work from home (2006-2010 5-year est.); Travel time to work: 14.6% less than 15 minutes, 29.4% 15 to 30 minutes, 23.9% 30 to 45 minutes, 16.5% 45 to 60 minutes, 15.7% 60 minutes or more (2006-2010 5-year est.)

**HARRISON** (town and village). Covers a land area of 16.765 square miles and a water area of 0.603 square miles. Located at 41.02° N. Lat; 73.72° W. Long. Elevation is 69 feet.
**Population:** 23,308 (1990); 24,154 (2000); 27,472 (2010); Density: 1,638.6 persons per square mile (2010); Race: 84.1% White, 2.4% Black, 7.5% Asian, 0.2% American Indian/Alaska Native, 0.0% Native Hawaiian/Other Pacific Islander, 5.8% Other, 11.7% Hispanic of any race (2010); Average household size: 2.77 (2010); Median age: 34.6 (2010); Males per 100 females: 88.5 (2010); Marriage status: 34.9% never married, 55.2% now married, 5.1% widowed, 4.7% divorced (2006-2010 5-year est.); Foreign born: 20.9% (2006-2010 5-year est.); Ancestry (includes multiple ancestries): 28.7% Italian, 12.1% American, 11.8% Irish, 6.8% German, 3.9% Polish (2006-2010 5-year est.).
**Economy:** Single-family building permits issued: 18 (2011); Multi-family building permits issued: 0 (2011); Employment by occupation: 21.5% management, 2.2% professional, 8.0% services, 16.1% sales, 2.6% farming, 7.3% construction, 2.4% production (2006-2010 5-year est.).
**Income:** Per capita income: $66,547 (2006-2010 5-year est.); Median household income: $106,299 (2006-2010 5-year est.); Average household income: $205,046 (2006-2010 5-year est.); Percent of households with income of $100,000 or more: 52.4% (2006-2010 5-year est.); Poverty rate: 3.9% (2006-2010 5-year est.).
**Taxes:** Total city taxes per capita: $309 (2009); City property taxes per capita: $244 (2009).
**Education:** Percent of population age 25 and over with: High school diploma (including GED) or higher: 91.3% (2006-2010 5-year est.); Bachelor's degree or higher: 51.4% (2006-2010 5-year est.); Master's degree or higher: 22.8% (2006-2010 5-year est.).
### School District(s)
Harrison Central School District (KG-12)
   2009-10 Enrollment: 3,520 . . . . . . . . . . . . . . . . . . . (914) 630-3021
**Housing:** Homeownership rate: 65.6% (2010); Median home value: $871,500 (2006-2010 5-year est.); Median contract rent: $1,462 per month (2006-2010 5-year est.); Median year structure built: 1958 (2006-2010 5-year est.).
**Hospitals:** St. Vincent's Hospital-Westchester (133 beds)
**Transportation:** Commute to work: 68.3% car, 19.1% public transportation, 5.3% walk, 4.3% work from home (2006-2010 5-year est.); Travel time to work: 26.8% less than 15 minutes, 35.3% 15 to 30 minutes, 13.5% 30 to 45 minutes, 7.8% 45 to 60 minutes, 16.6% 60 minutes or more (2006-2010 5-year est.)

**HARRISON** (town). Covers a land area of 16.765 square miles and a water area of 0.603 square miles. Located at 41.02° N. Lat; 73.72° W. Long. Elevation is 69 feet.
**Population:** 23,308 (1990); 24,154 (2000); 27,472 (2010); Density: 1,638.6 persons per square mile (2010); Race: 84.1% White, 2.4% Black, 7.5% Asian, 0.2% American Indian/Alaska Native, 0.0% Native Hawaiian/Other Pacific Islander, 5.8% Other, 11.7% Hispanic of any race (2010); Average household size: 2.77 (2010); Median age: 34.6 (2010); Males per 100

females: 88.5 (2010); Marriage status: 34.9% never married, 55.2% now married, 5.1% widowed, 4.7% divorced (2006-2010 5-year est.); Foreign born: 20.9% (2006-2010 5-year est.); Ancestry (includes multiple ancestries): 28.7% Italian, 12.1% American, 11.8% Irish, 6.8% German, 3.9% Polish (2006-2010 5-year est.).
**Economy:** Employment by occupation: 21.5% management, 2.2% professional, 8.0% services, 16.1% sales, 2.6% farming, 7.3% construction, 2.4% production (2006-2010 5-year est.).
**Income:** Per capita income: $66,547 (2006-2010 5-year est.); Median household income: $106,299 (2006-2010 5-year est.); Average household income: $205,046 (2006-2010 5-year est.); Percent of households with income of $100,000 or more: 52.4% (2006-2010 5-year est.); Poverty rate: 3.9% (2006-2010 5-year est.).
**Taxes:** Total city taxes per capita: $1,327 (2009); City property taxes per capita: $1,203 (2009).
**Education:** Percent of population age 25 and over with: High school diploma (including GED) or higher: 91.3% (2006-2010 5-year est.); Bachelor's degree or higher: 51.4% (2006-2010 5-year est.); Master's degree or higher: 22.8% (2006-2010 5-year est.).
### School District(s)
Harrison Central School District (KG-12)
   2009-10 Enrollment: 3,520 . . . . . . . . . . . . . . . . . . . (914) 630-3021
**Housing:** Homeownership rate: 65.6% (2010); Median home value: $871,500 (2006-2010 5-year est.); Median contract rent: $1,462 per month (2006-2010 5-year est.); Median year structure built: 1958 (2006-2010 5-year est.).
**Hospitals:** St. Vincent's Hospital-Westchester (133 beds)
**Safety:** Violent crime rate: 7.5 per 10,000 population; Property crime rate: 95.1 per 10,000 population (2010).
**Transportation:** Commute to work: 68.3% car, 19.1% public transportation, 5.3% walk, 4.3% work from home (2006-2010 5-year est.); Travel time to work: 26.8% less than 15 minutes, 35.3% 15 to 30 minutes, 13.5% 30 to 45 minutes, 7.8% 45 to 60 minutes, 16.6% 60 minutes or more (2006-2010 5-year est.)
**Additional Information Contacts**
Town of Harrison . . . . . . . . . . . . . . . . . . . . . . . . . . . . . (914) 670-3030
   http://www.town.harrison.ny.us

**HARTSDALE** (CDP). Covers a land area of 0.895 square miles and a water area of 0 square miles. Located at 41.01° N. Lat; 73.80° W. Long. Elevation is 184 feet.
**History:** The intersection of Central Park Avenue and Hartsdale Avenue was named "Hart's Corners" after Robert Hart, one of these farmers who successfully bid for the land, and in the mid 1800s the entire area became known as "Hartsdale".
**Population:** 10,052 (1990); 9,830 (2000); 5,293 (2010); Density: 5,913.6 persons per square mile (2010); Race: 72.5% White, 5.5% Black, 16.7% Asian, 0.3% American Indian/Alaska Native, 0.1% Native Hawaiian/Other Pacific Islander, 4.9% Other, 12.1% Hispanic of any race (2010); Average household size: 1.97 (2010); Median age: 44.7 (2010); Males per 100 females: 80.9 (2010); Marriage status: 27.1% never married, 48.1% now married, 8.8% widowed, 16.0% divorced (2006-2010 5-year est.); Foreign born: 21.7% (2006-2010 5-year est.); Ancestry (includes multiple ancestries): 20.6% Italian, 15.3% Irish, 9.8% German, 8.8% Russian, 5.5% Polish (2006-2010 5-year est.).
**Economy:** Employment by occupation: 22.7% management, 5.1% professional, 4.7% services, 15.4% sales, 0.7% farming, 3.4% construction, 4.0% production (2006-2010 5-year est.).
**Income:** Per capita income: $58,204 (2006-2010 5-year est.); Median household income: $87,822 (2006-2010 5-year est.); Average household income: $111,265 (2006-2010 5-year est.); Percent of households with income of $100,000 or more: 43.7% (2006-2010 5-year est.); Poverty rate: 3.6% (2006-2010 5-year est.).
**Education:** Percent of population age 25 and over with: High school diploma (including GED) or higher: 97.2% (2006-2010 5-year est.); Bachelor's degree or higher: 67.3% (2006-2010 5-year est.); Master's degree or higher: 36.4% (2006-2010 5-year est.).
### School District(s)
Greenburgh Central School District (PK-12)
   2009-10 Enrollment: 1,786 . . . . . . . . . . . . . . . . . . . (914) 761-6000
**Housing:** Homeownership rate: 69.8% (2010); Median home value: $357,100 (2006-2010 5-year est.); Median contract rent: $1,365 per month (2006-2010 5-year est.); Median year structure built: 1958 (2006-2010 5-year est.).
**Newspapers:** DIE WELT (Local news)

**Transportation:** Commute to work: 55.8% car, 31.7% public transportation, 1.3% walk, 8.8% work from home (2006-2010 5-year est.); Travel time to work: 17.4% less than 15 minutes, 24.2% 15 to 30 minutes, 20.8% 30 to 45 minutes, 10.7% 45 to 60 minutes, 26.9% 60 minutes or more (2006-2010 5-year est.)

## HASTINGS-ON-HUDSON (village). Covers a land area of 1.952 square miles and a water area of 0.961 square miles. Located at 40.98° N. Lat; 73.88° W. Long. Elevation is 125 feet.

**History:** Incorporated 1879.
**Population:** 8,000 (1990); 7,648 (2000); 7,849 (2010); Density: 4,020.2 persons per square mile (2010); Race: 85.2% White, 4.6% Black, 4.7% Asian, 0.2% American Indian/Alaska Native, 0.0% Native Hawaiian/Other Pacific Islander, 5.3% Other, 9.0% Hispanic of any race (2010); Average household size: 2.46 (2010); Median age: 45.8 (2010); Males per 100 females: 89.4 (2010); Marriage status: 25.8% never married, 60.6% now married, 7.4% widowed, 6.2% divorced (2006-2010 5-year est.); Foreign born: 14.0% (2006-2010 5-year est.); Ancestry (includes multiple ancestries): 18.3% Irish, 16.4% Italian, 13.3% German, 10.4% Russian, 7.7% English (2006-2010 5-year est.).
**Economy:** Single-family building permits issued: 2 (2011); Multi-family building permits issued: 0 (2011); Employment by occupation: 16.7% management, 3.5% professional, 5.1% services, 10.2% sales, 1.1% farming, 2.7% construction, 0.6% production (2006-2010 5-year est.).
**Income:** Per capita income: $62,457 (2006-2010 5-year est.); Median household income: $122,941 (2006-2010 5-year est.); Average household income: $167,692 (2006-2010 5-year est.); Percent of households with income of $100,000 or more: 58.9% (2006-2010 5-year est.); Poverty rate: 2.5% (2006-2010 5-year est.).
**Taxes:** Total city taxes per capita: $1,198 (2009); City property taxes per capita: $1,133 (2009).
**Education:** Percent of population age 25 and over with: High school diploma (including GED) or higher: 95.8% (2006-2010 5-year est.); Bachelor's degree or higher: 65.2% (2006-2010 5-year est.); Master's degree or higher: 39.7% (2006-2010 5-year est.).

### School District(s)
Greenburgh-Graham Union Free School District (KG-12)
   2009-10 Enrollment: 330 . . . . . . . . . . . . . . . . . . . . . . . (914) 478-1106
Hastings-On-Hudson Union Free School District (KG-12)
   2009-10 Enrollment: 1,567 . . . . . . . . . . . . . . . . . . . . (914) 478-6200
**Housing:** Homeownership rate: 68.3% (2010); Median home value: $681,500 (2006-2010 5-year est.); Median contract rent: $1,092 per month (2006-2010 5-year est.); Median year structure built: before 1940 (2006-2010 5-year est.).
**Safety:** Violent crime rate: 8.9 per 10,000 population; Property crime rate: 176.2 per 10,000 population (2010).
**Transportation:** Commute to work: 61.1% car, 28.1% public transportation, 1.9% walk, 8.6% work from home (2006-2010 5-year est.); Travel time to work: 15.8% less than 15 minutes, 26.9% 15 to 30 minutes, 25.4% 30 to 45 minutes, 14.7% 45 to 60 minutes, 17.2% 60 minutes or more (2006-2010 5-year est.)
**Additional Information Contacts**
Village of Hastings-on-Hudson . . . . . . . . . . . . . . . . . . (914) 478-3400
   http://www.hastingsgov.org

## HAWTHORNE (CDP). Covers a land area of 1.092 square miles and a water area of 0 square miles. Located at 41.10° N. Lat; 73.79° W. Long. Elevation is 282 feet.

**Population:** 4,734 (1990); 5,083 (2000); 4,586 (2010); Density: 4,195.9 persons per square mile (2010); Race: 93.4% White, 0.9% Black, 2.7% Asian, 0.0% American Indian/Alaska Native, 0.0% Native Hawaiian/Other Pacific Islander, 3.0% Other, 7.3% Hispanic of any race (2010); Average household size: 2.83 (2010); Median age: 43.3 (2010); Males per 100 females: 95.8 (2010); Marriage status: 30.4% never married, 56.6% now married, 7.3% widowed, 5.7% divorced (2006-2010 5-year est.); Foreign born: 16.2% (2006-2010 5-year est.); Ancestry (includes multiple ancestries): 40.2% Italian, 24.3% Irish, 12.3% German, 5.5% English, 4.7% Yugoslavian (2006-2010 5-year est.).
**Economy:** Employment by occupation: 16.9% management, 3.8% professional, 8.5% services, 25.6% sales, 3.2% farming, 6.9% construction, 3.2% production (2006-2010 5-year est.).
**Income:** Per capita income: $45,765 (2006-2010 5-year est.); Median household income: $104,816 (2006-2010 5-year est.); Average household income: $126,941 (2006-2010 5-year est.); Percent of households with

income of $100,000 or more: 55.9% (2006-2010 5-year est.); Poverty rate: 1.5% (2006-2010 5-year est.).
**Education:** Percent of population age 25 and over with: High school diploma (including GED) or higher: 93.2% (2006-2010 5-year est.); Bachelor's degree or higher: 39.6% (2006-2010 5-year est.); Master's degree or higher: 17.9% (2006-2010 5-year est.).

### School District(s)
Hawthorne-Cedar Knolls Union Free School District (04-12)
   2009-10 Enrollment: 414 . . . . . . . . . . . . . . . . . . . . . . (914) 749-2903
Mount Pleasant Central School District (KG-12)
   2009-10 Enrollment: 1,977 . . . . . . . . . . . . . . . . . . . (914) 769-5500
**Housing:** Homeownership rate: 84.7% (2010); Median home value: $573,100 (2006-2010 5-year est.); Median contract rent: $1,599 per month (2006-2010 5-year est.); Median year structure built: 1954 (2006-2010 5-year est.).
**Transportation:** Commute to work: 83.8% car, 13.9% public transportation, 0.0% walk, 2.2% work from home (2006-2010 5-year est.); Travel time to work: 26.9% less than 15 minutes, 39.1% 15 to 30 minutes, 15.0% 30 to 45 minutes, 4.6% 45 to 60 minutes, 14.5% 60 minutes or more (2006-2010 5-year est.)

## HERITAGE HILLS (CDP). Covers a land area of 1.863 square miles and a water area of 0.038 square miles. Located at 41.33° N. Lat; 73.69° W. Long. Elevation is 587 feet.

**History:** This community in Northern Westchester is located in the town of Somers, N.Y. and was designed to enhance the quality of living for its residents. It is a self contained complex of over 2,500 units on 1,100 acres of beautiful countryside, 40% of which will remain as open space.
**Population:** 2,519 (1990); 3,683 (2000); 3,975 (2010); Density: 2,133.0 persons per square mile (2010); Race: 95.7% White, 1.3% Black, 2.1% Asian, 0.1% American Indian/Alaska Native, 0.1% Native Hawaiian/Other Pacific Islander, 0.7% Other, 2.2% Hispanic of any race (2010); Average household size: 1.62 (2010); Median age: 70.9 (2010); Males per 100 females: 65.0 (2010); Marriage status: 6.6% never married, 66.5% now married, 17.5% widowed, 9.4% divorced (2006-2010 5-year est.); Foreign born: 6.7% (2006-2010 5-year est.); Ancestry (includes multiple ancestries): 26.8% Italian, 18.0% Irish, 7.1% German, 6.5% Polish, 6.4% English (2006-2010 5-year est.).
**Economy:** Employment by occupation: 19.7% management, 3.5% professional, 0.4% services, 27.0% sales, 8.1% farming, 2.3% construction, 0.0% production (2006-2010 5-year est.).
**Income:** Per capita income: $58,242 (2006-2010 5-year est.); Median household income: $75,808 (2006-2010 5-year est.); Average household income: $89,988 (2006-2010 5-year est.); Percent of households with income of $100,000 or more: 36.9% (2006-2010 5-year est.); Poverty rate: 2.1% (2006-2010 5-year est.).
**Education:** Percent of population age 25 and over with: High school diploma (including GED) or higher: 96.2% (2006-2010 5-year est.); Bachelor's degree or higher: 46.0% (2006-2010 5-year est.); Master's degree or higher: 22.7% (2006-2010 5-year est.).
**Housing:** Homeownership rate: 90.6% (2010); Median home value: $449,900 (2006-2010 5-year est.); Median contract rent: n/a per month (2006-2010 5-year est.); Median year structure built: 1986 (2006-2010 5-year est.).
**Transportation:** Commute to work: 86.2% car, 11.5% public transportation, 0.0% walk, 2.2% work from home (2006-2010 5-year est.); Travel time to work: 10.1% less than 15 minutes, 25.3% 15 to 30 minutes, 30.4% 30 to 45 minutes, 9.8% 45 to 60 minutes, 24.5% 60 minutes or more (2006-2010 5-year est.)

## IRVINGTON (village). Covers a land area of 2.773 square miles and a water area of 1.290 square miles. Located at 41.03° N. Lat; 73.86° W. Long. Elevation is 151 feet.

**History:** Here at Nevis, once the estate of Alexander Hamilton's son, are a Columbia University arboretum and a children's Museum. Originally called Dearman; renamed (1857) for Washington Irving, who bought the estate Sunnyside (extant) here in 1835. Settled c.1655, Incorporated 1872.
**Population:** 6,348 (1990); 6,631 (2000); 6,420 (2010); Density: 2,314.9 persons per square mile (2010); Race: 87.1% White, 1.9% Black, 7.9% Asian, 0.1% American Indian/Alaska Native, 0.0% Native Hawaiian/Other Pacific Islander, 3.0% Other, 6.2% Hispanic of any race (2010); Average household size: 2.51 (2010); Median age: 44.6 (2010); Males per 100 females: 90.6 (2010); Marriage status: 18.6% never married, 64.4% now married, 8.9% widowed, 8.1% divorced (2006-2010 5-year est.); Foreign born: 13.8% (2006-2010 5-year est.); Ancestry (includes multiple

ancestries): 23.9% Italian, 15.7% Irish, 15.0% German, 11.4% English, 8.9% Russian (2006-2010 5-year est.).

**Economy:** Single-family building permits issued: 4 (2011); Multi-family building permits issued: 3 (2011); Employment by occupation: 26.5% management, 5.3% professional, 4.2% services, 16.0% sales, 2.4% farming, 0.5% construction, 2.7% production (2006-2010 5-year est.).

**Income:** Per capita income: $78,013 (2006-2010 5-year est.); Median household income: $115,875 (2006-2010 5-year est.); Average household income: $199,102 (2006-2010 5-year est.); Percent of households with income of $100,000 or more: 56.1% (2006-2010 5-year est.); Poverty rate: 2.8% (2006-2010 5-year est.).

**Education:** Percent of population age 25 and over with: High school diploma (including GED) or higher: 98.4% (2006-2010 5-year est.); Bachelor's degree or higher: 61.0% (2006-2010 5-year est.); Master's degree or higher: 31.8% (2006-2010 5-year est.).

### School District(s)

Abbott Union Free School District (01-08)

    2009-10 Enrollment: 80 . . . . . . . . . . . . . . . . . . . . . . . (914) 591-7428

Irvington Union Free School District (KG-12)

    2009-10 Enrollment: 1,799 . . . . . . . . . . . . . . . . . . . . (914) 591-8501

**Housing:** Homeownership rate: 77.8% (2010); Median home value: $644,300 (2006-2010 5-year est.); Median contract rent: $1,270 per month (2006-2010 5-year est.); Median year structure built: 1955 (2006-2010 5-year est.).

**Safety:** Violent crime rate: 0.0 per 10,000 population; Property crime rate: 43.8 per 10,000 population (2010).

**Transportation:** Commute to work: 57.9% car, 29.1% public transportation, 1.4% walk, 11.1% work from home (2006-2010 5-year est.); Travel time to work: 17.6% less than 15 minutes, 24.6% 15 to 30 minutes, 21.8% 30 to 45 minutes, 8.6% 45 to 60 minutes, 27.3% 60 minutes or more (2006-2010 5-year est.)

**Additional Information Contacts**

Irvington on Hudson Chamber of Commerce . . . . . . . . . (914) 473-4819
    http://www.irvingtonnychamber.com

Village of Irvington . . . . . . . . . . . . . . . . . . . . . . . . . . . (914) 591-7070
    http://www.irvingtonny.gov

## JEFFERSON VALLEY (unincorporated postal area)

**Zip Code:** 10535

Covers a land area of 0.451 square miles and a water area of 0.059 square miles. Located at 41.33° N. Lat; 73.79° W. Long. Elevation is 459 feet. Population: 555 (2010); Density: 1,228.8 persons per square mile (2010); Race: 78.4% White, 5.4% Black, 3.6% Asian, 0.2% American Indian/Alaska Native, 0.0% Native Hawaiian/Other Pacific Islander, 12.4% Other, 20.5% Hispanic of any race (2010); Average household size: 2.64 (2010); Median age: 40.0 (2010); Males per 100 females: 92.0 (2010); Homeownership rate: 47.1% (2010)

## JEFFERSON VALLEY-YORKTOWN (CDP). Covers a land

area of 6.925 square miles and a water area of 0.095 square miles. Located at 41.31° N. Lat; 73.80° W. Long.

**Population:** 14,118 (1990); 14,891 (2000); 14,142 (2010); Density: 2,042.0 persons per square mile (2010); Race: 89.2% White, 2.6% Black, 4.3% Asian, 0.2% American Indian/Alaska Native, 0.0% Native Hawaiian/Other Pacific Islander, 3.7% Other, 8.2% Hispanic of any race (2010); Average household size: 2.70 (2010); Median age: 44.7 (2010); Males per 100 females: 91.3 (2010); Marriage status: 21.3% never married, 64.7% now married, 8.4% widowed, 5.6% divorced (2006-2010 5-year est.); Foreign born: 10.3% (2006-2010 5-year est.); Ancestry (includes multiple ancestries): 34.4% Italian, 26.5% Irish, 13.6% German, 5.4% American, 5.2% Polish (2006-2010 5-year est.).

**Economy:** Employment by occupation: 15.7% management, 5.3% professional, 7.1% services, 16.8% sales, 2.2% farming, 7.6% construction, 4.7% production (2006-2010 5-year est.).

**Income:** Per capita income: $42,206 (2006-2010 5-year est.); Median household income: $88,137 (2006-2010 5-year est.); Average household income: $113,079 (2006-2010 5-year est.); Percent of households with income of $100,000 or more: 46.7% (2006-2010 5-year est.); Poverty rate: 1.7% (2006-2010 5-year est.).

**Education:** Percent of population age 25 and over with: High school diploma (including GED) or higher: 94.0% (2006-2010 5-year est.); Bachelor's degree or higher: 42.8% (2006-2010 5-year est.); Master's degree or higher: 20.2% (2006-2010 5-year est.).

**Housing:** Homeownership rate: 91.2% (2010); Median home value: $456,600 (2006-2010 5-year est.); Median contract rent: $1,354 per month

(2006-2010 5-year est.); Median year structure built: 1969 (2006-2010 5-year est.).

**Transportation:** Commute to work: 87.9% car, 6.9% public transportation, 1.1% walk, 3.9% work from home (2006-2010 5-year est.); Travel time to work: 22.3% less than 15 minutes, 22.7% 15 to 30 minutes, 26.9% 30 to 45 minutes, 13.2% 45 to 60 minutes, 14.8% 60 minutes or more (2006-2010 5-year est.)

## KATONAH (CDP). Covers a land area of 0.725 square miles and a

water area of 0.078 square miles. Located at 41.25° N. Lat; 73.68° W. Long. Elevation is 236 feet.

**Population:** n/a (1990); n/a (2000); 1,679 (2010); Density: 2,314.4 persons per square mile (2010); Race: 87.1% White, 2.5% Black, 2.6% Asian, 0.2% American Indian/Alaska Native, 0.0% Native Hawaiian/Other Pacific Islander, 7.6% Other, 11.9% Hispanic of any race (2010); Average household size: 2.83 (2010); Median age: 40.6 (2010); Males per 100 females: 88.0 (2010); Marriage status: 18.6% never married, 71.0% now married, 5.6% widowed, 4.9% divorced (2006-2010 5-year est.); Foreign born: 11.7% (2006-2010 5-year est.); Ancestry (includes multiple ancestries): 17.5% Irish, 14.9% Italian, 12.2% German, 9.1% English, 8.6% Russian (2006-2010 5-year est.).

**Economy:** Employment by occupation: 13.2% management, 7.8% professional, 3.0% services, 10.4% sales, 0.0% farming, 2.3% construction, 4.0% production (2006-2010 5-year est.).

**Income:** Per capita income: $44,056 (2006-2010 5-year est.); Median household income: $97,891 (2006-2010 5-year est.); Average household income: $128,246 (2006-2010 5-year est.); Percent of households with income of $100,000 or more: 47.3% (2006-2010 5-year est.); Poverty rate: 4.0% (2006-2010 5-year est.).

**Education:** Percent of population age 25 and over with: High school diploma (including GED) or higher: 91.3% (2006-2010 5-year est.); Bachelor's degree or higher: 62.8% (2006-2010 5-year est.); Master's degree or higher: 38.3% (2006-2010 5-year est.).

### School District(s)

Katonah-Lewisboro Union Free School District (KG-12)

    2009-10 Enrollment: 3,868 . . . . . . . . . . . . . . . . . . . (914) 763-7003

**Housing:** Homeownership rate: 72.5% (2010); Median home value: $712,500 (2006-2010 5-year est.); Median contract rent: $1,058 per month (2006-2010 5-year est.); Median year structure built: before 1940 (2006-2010 5-year est.).

**Transportation:** Commute to work: 61.6% car, 13.6% public transportation, 18.1% walk, 6.6% work from home (2006-2010 5-year est.); Travel time to work: 30.5% less than 15 minutes, 25.2% 15 to 30 minutes, 14.9% 30 to 45 minutes, 4.5% 45 to 60 minutes, 24.9% 60 minutes or more (2006-2010 5-year est.)

## LAKE MOHEGAN (CDP). Covers a land area of 2.875 square miles

and a water area of 0.198 square miles. Located at 41.31° N. Lat; 73.84° W. Long. Elevation is 522 feet.

**Population:** 4,831 (1990); 5,979 (2000); 6,010 (2010); Density: 2,089.9 persons per square mile (2010); Race: 82.2% White, 6.6% Black, 4.4% Asian, 0.3% American Indian/Alaska Native, 0.0% Native Hawaiian/Other Pacific Islander, 6.5% Other, 16.2% Hispanic of any race (2010); Average household size: 2.82 (2010); Median age: 39.9 (2010); Males per 100 females: 95.2 (2010); Marriage status: 21.4% never married, 64.9% now married, 5.3% widowed, 8.5% divorced (2006-2010 5-year est.); Foreign born: 14.0% (2006-2010 5-year est.); Ancestry (includes multiple ancestries): 28.5% Italian, 15.4% Irish, 10.3% German, 7.8% Polish, 6.7% Russian (2006-2010 5-year est.).

**Economy:** Employment by occupation: 11.9% management, 4.6% professional, 8.7% services, 20.3% sales, 4.4% farming, 10.6% construction, 4.3% production (2006-2010 5-year est.).

**Income:** Per capita income: $39,736 (2006-2010 5-year est.); Median household income: $82,833 (2006-2010 5-year est.); Average household income: $108,630 (2006-2010 5-year est.); Percent of households with income of $100,000 or more: 45.8% (2006-2010 5-year est.); Poverty rate: 2.5% (2006-2010 5-year est.).

**Education:** Percent of population age 25 and over with: High school diploma (including GED) or higher: 90.8% (2006-2010 5-year est.); Bachelor's degree or higher: 33.5% (2006-2010 5-year est.); Master's degree or higher: 16.5% (2006-2010 5-year est.).

**Housing:** Homeownership rate: 79.0% (2010); Median home value: $425,200 (2006-2010 5-year est.); Median contract rent: $1,114 per month (2006-2010 5-year est.); Median year structure built: 1960 (2006-2010 5-year est.).

**Transportation:** Commute to work: 93.4% car, 2.7% public transportation, 0.9% walk, 3.0% work from home (2006-2010 5-year est.); Travel time to work: 23.0% less than 15 minutes, 16.3% 15 to 30 minutes, 31.7% 30 to 45 minutes, 9.0% 45 to 60 minutes, 20.1% 60 minutes or more (2006-2010 5-year est.)

---

## LARCHMONT (village).

Covers a land area of 1.077 square miles and a water area of 0.001 square miles. Located at 40.92° N. Lat; 73.75° W. Long. Elevation is 52 feet.

**History:** Joyce Kilmer lived here. Developed c.1845, incorporated 1891.

**Population:** 6,181 (1990); 6,485 (2000); 5,864 (2010); Density: 5,442.9 persons per square mile (2010); Race: 92.7% White, 1.5% Black, 2.5% Asian, 0.2% American Indian/Alaska Native, 0.0% Native Hawaiian/Other Pacific Islander, 3.1% Other, 6.3% Hispanic of any race (2010); Average household size: 2.78 (2010); Median age: 39.8 (2010); Males per 100 females: 95.5 (2010); Marriage status: 23.3% never married, 71.4% now married, 2.2% widowed, 3.1% divorced (2006-2010 5-year est.); Foreign born: 14.8% (2006-2010 5-year est.); Ancestry (includes multiple ancestries): 22.3% Irish, 13.4% German, 13.2% Italian, 12.3% English, 8.3% Russian (2006-2010 5-year est.).

**Economy:** Single-family building permits issued: 2 (2011); Multi-family building permits issued: 0 (2011); Employment by occupation: 26.5% management, 2.9% professional, 6.1% services, 8.5% sales, 2.3% farming, 2.5% construction, 0.6% production (2006-2010 5-year est.).

**Income:** Per capita income: $96,499 (2006-2010 5-year est.); Median household income: $169,038 (2006-2010 5-year est.); Average household income: $276,620 (2006-2010 5-year est.); Percent of households with income of $100,000 or more: 67.3% (2006-2010 5-year est.); Poverty rate: 1.3% (2006-2010 5-year est.).

**Education:** Percent of population age 25 and over with: High school diploma (including GED) or higher: 99.2% (2006-2010 5-year est.); Bachelor's degree or higher: 86.0% (2006-2010 5-year est.); Master's degree or higher: 47.5% (2006-2010 5-year est.).

### School District(s)

Mamaroneck Union Free School District (PK-12)
   2009-10 Enrollment: 5,050 . . . . . . . . . . . . . . . . . (914) 220-3005

**Housing:** Homeownership rate: 72.5% (2010); Median home value: $1 (2006-2010 5-year est.); Median contract rent: $1,558 per month (2006-2010 5-year est.); Median year structure built: before 1940 (2006-2010 5-year est.).

**Safety:** Violent crime rate: 3.1 per 10,000 population; Property crime rate: 124.3 per 10,000 population (2010).

**Transportation:** Commute to work: 41.5% car, 40.7% public transportation, 5.0% walk, 9.3% work from home (2006-2010 5-year est.); Travel time to work: 18.1% less than 15 minutes, 10.0% 15 to 30 minutes, 18.8% 30 to 45 minutes, 22.4% 45 to 60 minutes, 30.7% 60 minutes or more (2006-2010 5-year est.)

**Additional Information Contacts**

Village of Larchmont . . . . . . . . . . . . . . . . . . . . . . . . . . . (914) 834-6230
   http://www.villageoflarchmont.org

---

## LEWISBORO (town).

Covers a land area of 27.745 square miles and a water area of 1.415 square miles. Located at 41.26° N. Lat; 73.58° W. Long. Elevation is 728 feet.

**History:** The town was formed in 1747 as the "Town of Salem." John Lewis, a financier, requested that the town be given his name and established a fund for the town, though he did not follow through on his promise of a railroad link.

**Population:** 11,313 (1990); 12,324 (2000); 12,411 (2010); Density: 447.3 persons per square mile (2010); Race: 93.9% White, 1.3% Black, 2.4% Asian, 0.1% American Indian/Alaska Native, 0.0% Native Hawaiian/Other Pacific Islander, 2.3% Other, 4.4% Hispanic of any race (2010); Average household size: 2.78 (2010); Median age: 44.8 (2010); Males per 100 females: 96.7 (2010); Marriage status: 24.0% never married, 66.6% now married, 3.0% widowed, 6.5% divorced (2006-2010 5-year est.); Foreign born: 8.9% (2006-2010 5-year est.); Ancestry (includes multiple ancestries): 24.3% Irish, 21.9% Italian, 14.1% German, 10.9% English, 7.0% Polish (2006-2010 5-year est.).

**Economy:** Single-family building permits issued: 4 (2011); Multi-family building permits issued: 0 (2011); Employment by occupation: 23.4% management, 6.3% professional, 4.1% services, 14.9% sales, 2.5% farming, 3.1% construction, 1.1% production (2006-2010 5-year est.).

**Income:** Per capita income: $71,725 (2006-2010 5-year est.); Median household income: $155,766 (2006-2010 5-year est.); Average household income: $204,540 (2006-2010 5-year est.); Percent of households with

income of $100,000 or more: 66.5% (2006-2010 5-year est.); Poverty rate: 2.0% (2006-2010 5-year est.).

**Education:** Percent of population age 25 and over with: High school diploma (including GED) or higher: 97.3% (2006-2010 5-year est.); Bachelor's degree or higher: 71.8% (2006-2010 5-year est.); Master's degree or higher: 35.9% (2006-2010 5-year est.).

**Housing:** Homeownership rate: 90.0% (2010); Median home value: $706,200 (2006-2010 5-year est.); Median contract rent: $1,625 per month (2006-2010 5-year est.); Median year structure built: 1974 (2006-2010 5-year est.).

**Safety:** Violent crime rate: 0.0 per 10,000 population; Property crime rate: 32.2 per 10,000 population (2010).

**Transportation:** Commute to work: 74.5% car, 15.2% public transportation, 0.6% walk, 8.6% work from home (2006-2010 5-year est.); Travel time to work: 14.6% less than 15 minutes, 25.8% 15 to 30 minutes, 23.8% 30 to 45 minutes, 9.6% 45 to 60 minutes, 26.2% 60 minutes or more (2006-2010 5-year est.)

**Additional Information Contacts**

Town of Lewisboro . . . . . . . . . . . . . . . . . . . . . . . . . . . (914) 763-3511
   http://www.lewisborogov.com

---

## LINCOLNDALE (CDP).

Covers a land area of 0.957 square miles and a water area of 0.041 square miles. Located at 41.33° N. Lat; 73.72° W. Long. Elevation is 338 feet.

**Population:** 2,287 (1990); 2,018 (2000); 1,521 (2010); Density: 1,588.5 persons per square mile (2010); Race: 95.2% White, 0.9% Black, 1.3% Asian, 0.1% American Indian/Alaska Native, 0.0% Native Hawaiian/Other Pacific Islander, 2.5% Other, 5.8% Hispanic of any race (2010); Average household size: 2.81 (2010); Median age: 42.5 (2010); Males per 100 females: 95.5 (2010); Marriage status: 16.0% never married, 69.7% now married, 2.8% widowed, 11.5% divorced (2006-2010 5-year est.); Foreign born: 3.4% (2006-2010 5-year est.); Ancestry (includes multiple ancestries): 39.9% Italian, 32.2% Irish, 17.3% German, 10.5% English, 7.4% Polish (2006-2010 5-year est.).

**Economy:** Employment by occupation: 31.2% management, 2.2% professional, 6.0% services, 19.8% sales, 0.0% farming, 10.0% construction, 4.5% production (2006-2010 5-year est.).

**Income:** Per capita income: $50,658 (2006-2010 5-year est.); Median household income: $128,646 (2006-2010 5-year est.); Average household income: $143,124 (2006-2010 5-year est.); Percent of households with income of $100,000 or more: 68.4% (2006-2010 5-year est.); Poverty rate: 1.2% (2006-2010 5-year est.).

**Education:** Percent of population age 25 and over with: High school diploma (including GED) or higher: 98.1% (2006-2010 5-year est.); Bachelor's degree or higher: 51.9% (2006-2010 5-year est.); Master's degree or higher: 16.2% (2006-2010 5-year est.).

### School District(s)

Somers Central School District (KG-12)
   2009-10 Enrollment: 3,422 . . . . . . . . . . . . . . . . (914) 277-2400

**Housing:** Homeownership rate: 91.5% (2010); Median home value: $450,600 (2006-2010 5-year est.); Median contract rent: n/a per month (2006-2010 5-year est.); Median year structure built: 1959 (2006-2010 5-year est.).

**Transportation:** Commute to work: 74.5% car, 18.1% public transportation, 2.1% walk, 5.3% work from home (2006-2010 5-year est.); Travel time to work: 22.2% less than 15 minutes, 17.8% 15 to 30 minutes, 22.3% 30 to 45 minutes, 16.0% 45 to 60 minutes, 21.7% 60 minutes or more (2006-2010 5-year est.)

---

## MAMARONECK (village).

Covers a land area of 3.169 square miles and a water area of 3.406 square miles. Located at 40.93° N. Lat; 73.72° W. Long. Elevation is 47 feet.

**Population:** 17,325 (1990); 18,752 (2000); 18,929 (2010); Density: 5,971.8 persons per square mile (2010); Race: 76.8% White, 4.1% Black, 4.9% Asian, 0.3% American Indian/Alaska Native, 0.1% Native Hawaiian/Other Pacific Islander, 13.8% Other, 24.3% Hispanic of any race (2010); Average household size: 2.65 (2010); Median age: 40.0 (2010); Males per 100 females: 95.1 (2010); Marriage status: 29.1% never married, 54.9% now married, 8.0% widowed, 7.9% divorced (2006-2010 5-year est.); Foreign born: 27.8% (2006-2010 5-year est.); Ancestry (includes multiple ancestries): 22.1% Italian, 10.0% American, 9.6% Irish, 6.8% German, 3.6% Polish (2006-2010 5-year est.).

**Economy:** Single-family building permits issued: 3 (2011); Multi-family building permits issued: 0 (2011); Employment by occupation: 17.0%

management, 5.1% professional, 9.6% services, 10.7% sales, 2.2% farming, 7.4% construction, 2.0% production (2006-2010 5-year est.).
**Income:** Per capita income: $52,750 (2006-2010 5-year est.); Median household income: $86,307 (2006-2010 5-year est.); Average household income: $140,626 (2006-2010 5-year est.); Percent of households with income of $100,000 or more: 43.3% (2006-2010 5-year est.); Poverty rate: 4.1% (2006-2010 5-year est.).
**Education:** Percent of population age 25 and over with: High school diploma (including GED) or higher: 88.9% (2006-2010 5-year est.); Bachelor's degree or higher: 48.3% (2006-2010 5-year est.); Master's degree or higher: 27.5% (2006-2010 5-year est.).

### School District(s)
Mamaroneck Union Free School District (PK-12)
    2009-10 Enrollment: 5,050 . . . . . . . . . . . . . . . . . (914) 220-3005
Rye Neck Union Free School District (KG-12)
    2009-10 Enrollment: 1,484 . . . . . . . . . . . . . . . . . (914) 777-5200
**Housing:** Homeownership rate: 58.7% (2010); Median home value: $596,100 (2006-2010 5-year est.); Median contract rent: $1,403 per month (2006-2010 5-year est.); Median year structure built: 1953 (2006-2010 5-year est.).
**Safety:** Violent crime rate: 8.2 per 10,000 population; Property crime rate: 73.7 per 10,000 population (2010).
**Transportation:** Commute to work: 65.9% car, 22.9% public transportation, 5.2% walk, 4.0% work from home (2006-2010 5-year est.); Travel time to work: 26.4% less than 15 minutes, 31.1% 15 to 30 minutes, 16.7% 30 to 45 minutes, 11.2% 45 to 60 minutes, 14.7% 60 minutes or more (2006-2010 5-year est.)
**Additional Information Contacts**
Mamaroneck Chamber of Commerce . . . . . . . . . . . . . . . . (914) 698-4400
    http://www.mamaroneckchamberofcommerce.org
Village of Mamaroneck . . . . . . . . . . . . . . . . . . . . . . . . (914) 777-7722
    http://www.village.mamaroneck.ny.us

**MAMARONECK** (town). Covers a land area of 6.654 square miles and a water area of 7.410 square miles. Located at 40.92° N. Lat; 73.74° W. Long. Elevation is 47 feet.
**History:** Initially a farming community. Settled 1661, incorporated 1895.
**Population:** 27,706 (1990); 28,967 (2000); 29,156 (2010); Density: 4,381.7 persons per square mile (2010); Race: 84.1% White, 2.9% Black, 3.9% Asian, 0.2% American Indian/Alaska Native, 0.0% Native Hawaiian/Other Pacific Islander, 8.9% Other, 15.5% Hispanic of any race (2010); Average household size: 2.65 (2010); Median age: 40.7 (2010); Males per 100 females: 93.9 (2010); Marriage status: 24.9% never married, 62.7% now married, 5.8% widowed, 6.6% divorced (2006-2010 5-year est.); Foreign born: 20.1% (2006-2010 5-year est.); Ancestry (includes multiple ancestries): 16.4% Italian, 15.7% Irish, 10.5% German, 7.5% English, 6.9% Russian (2006-2010 5-year est.).
**Economy:** Unemployment rate: 5.9% (February 2012); Total civilian labor force: 14,511 (February 2012); Single-family building permits issued: 6 (2011); Multi-family building permits issued: 0 (2011); Employment by occupation: 21.2% management, 4.9% professional, 7.4% services, 10.9% sales, 1.6% farming, 4.8% construction, 2.2% production (2006-2010 5-year est.).
**Income:** Per capita income: $78,335 (2006-2010 5-year est.); Median household income: $111,812 (2006-2010 5-year est.); Average household income: $207,825 (2006-2010 5-year est.); Percent of households with income of $100,000 or more: 55.6% (2006-2010 5-year est.); Poverty rate: 3.8% (2006-2010 5-year est.).
**Education:** Percent of population age 25 and over with: High school diploma (including GED) or higher: 93.9% (2006-2010 5-year est.); Bachelor's degree or higher: 65.6% (2006-2010 5-year est.); Master's degree or higher: 38.3% (2006-2010 5-year est.).

### School District(s)
Mamaroneck Union Free School District (PK-12)
    2009-10 Enrollment: 5,050 . . . . . . . . . . . . . . . . . (914) 220-3005
Rye Neck Union Free School District (KG-12)
    2009-10 Enrollment: 1,484 . . . . . . . . . . . . . . . . . (914) 777-5200
**Housing:** Homeownership rate: 68.8% (2010); Median home value: $798,600 (2006-2010 5-year est.); Median contract rent: $1,375 per month (2006-2010 5-year est.); Median year structure built: 1945 (2006-2010 5-year est.).
**Safety:** Violent crime rate: 7.0 per 10,000 population; Property crime rate: 125.6 per 10,000 population (2010).
**Transportation:** Commute to work: 55.2% car, 31.0% public transportation, 4.3% walk, 7.1% work from home (2006-2010 5-year est.);

Travel time to work: 20.1% less than 15 minutes, 23.9% 15 to 30 minutes, 19.1% 30 to 45 minutes, 16.9% 45 to 60 minutes, 19.9% 60 minutes or more (2006-2010 5-year est.).
**Additional Information Contacts**
Town of Mamaroneck . . . . . . . . . . . . . . . . . . . . . . . . . (914) 381-7870
    http://www.townofmamaroneck.org

**MARYKNOLL** (unincorporated postal area)
Zip Code: 10545
    Covers a land area of 0.125 square miles and a water area of 0 square miles. Located at 41.17° N. Lat; 73.83° W. Long. Population: 141 (2010); Density: 1,119.6 persons per square mile (2010); Race: 98.6% White, 0.7% Black, 0.7% Asian, 0.0% American Indian/Alaska Native, 0.0% Native Hawaiian/Other Pacific Islander, 0.0% Other, 1.4% Hispanic of any race (2010); Average household size: 2.00 (2010); Median age: 79.3 (2010); Males per 100 females: ***.* (2010); Homeownership rate: 100.0% (2010)

**MILLWOOD** (unincorporated postal area)
Zip Code: 10546
    Covers a land area of 1.123 square miles and a water area of 0.004 square miles. Located at 41.19° N. Lat; 73.80° W. Long. Elevation is 361 feet. Population: 1,277 (2010); Density: 1,137.1 persons per square mile (2010); Race: 84.3% White, 2.3% Black, 11.6% Asian, 0.0% American Indian/Alaska Native, 0.0% Native Hawaiian/Other Pacific Islander, 1.8% Other, 4.4% Hispanic of any race (2010); Average household size: 2.81 (2010); Median age: 42.0 (2010); Males per 100 females: 97.1 (2010); Homeownership rate: 89.2% (2010)

**MOHEGAN LAKE** (unincorporated postal area)
Zip Code: 10547
    Covers a land area of 5.065 square miles and a water area of 0.198 square miles. Located at 41.31° N. Lat; 73.84° W. Long. Elevation is 472 feet. Population: 7,647 (2010); Density: 1,509.5 persons per square mile (2010); Race: 80.2% White, 8.5% Black, 4.3% Asian, 0.3% American Indian/Alaska Native, 0.0% Native Hawaiian/Other Pacific Islander, 6.7% Other, 17.3% Hispanic of any race (2010); Average household size: 2.76 (2010); Median age: 40.0 (2010); Males per 100 females: 96.6 (2010); Homeownership rate: 71.9% (2010)

**MONTROSE** (CDP). Covers a land area of 1.614 square miles and a water area of 0.051 square miles. Located at 41.24° N. Lat; 73.93° W. Long. Elevation is 115 feet.
**Population:** n/a (1990); n/a (2000); 2,731 (2010); Density: 1,691.9 persons per square mile (2010); Race: 88.9% White, 2.2% Black, 3.0% Asian, 0.0% American Indian/Alaska Native, 0.0% Native Hawaiian/Other Pacific Islander, 5.9% Other, 11.9% Hispanic of any race (2010); Average household size: 2.56 (2010); Median age: 42.9 (2010); Males per 100 females: 97.0 (2010); Marriage status: 25.9% never married, 65.6% now married, 4.3% widowed, 4.2% divorced (2006-2010 5-year est.); Foreign born: 13.4% (2006-2010 5-year est.); Ancestry (includes multiple ancestries): 34.4% Italian, 27.9% Irish, 20.9% German, 7.6% Polish, 4.9% American (2006-2010 5-year est.).
**Economy:** Employment by occupation: 15.3% management, 9.3% professional, 6.2% services, 13.9% sales, 3.8% farming, 6.7% construction, 2.3% production (2006-2010 5-year est.).
**Income:** Per capita income: $43,026 (2006-2010 5-year est.); Median household income: $91,375 (2006-2010 5-year est.); Average household income: $113,042 (2006-2010 5-year est.); Percent of households with income of $100,000 or more: 48.3% (2006-2010 5-year est.); Poverty rate: 12.3% (2006-2010 5-year est.).
**Education:** Percent of population age 25 and over with: High school diploma (including GED) or higher: 92.5% (2006-2010 5-year est.); Bachelor's degree or higher: 42.9% (2006-2010 5-year est.); Master's degree or higher: 22.2% (2006-2010 5-year est.).

### School District(s)
Hendrick Hudson Central School District (KG-12)
    2009-10 Enrollment: 2,701 . . . . . . . . . . . . . . . . . (914) 257-5100
**Housing:** Homeownership rate: 80.8% (2010); Median home value: $375,800 (2006-2010 5-year est.); Median contract rent: $1,305 per month (2006-2010 5-year est.); Median year structure built: 1959 (2006-2010 5-year est.).
**Transportation:** Commute to work: 84.5% car, 14.9% public transportation, 0.6% walk, 0.0% work from home (2006-2010 5-year est.); Travel time to work: 12.2% less than 15 minutes, 18.9% 15 to 30 minutes,

33.3% 30 to 45 minutes, 9.9% 45 to 60 minutes, 25.7% 60 minutes or more (2006-2010 5-year est.)

## MOUNT KISCO (town and village). Covers a land area of 3.035 square miles and a water area of 0.030 square miles. Located at 41.20° N. Lat; 73.72° W. Long. Elevation is 302 feet.

**History:** Incorporated 1874.

**Population:** 9,108 (1990); 9,983 (2000); 10,877 (2010); Density: 3,583.6 persons per square mile (2010); Race: 69.5% White, 5.2% Black, 4.8% Asian, 0.8% American Indian/Alaska Native, 0.0% Native Hawaiian/Other Pacific Islander, 19.7% Other, 35.1% Hispanic of any race (2010); Average household size: 2.64 (2010); Median age: 38.0 (2010); Males per 100 females: 107.4 (2010); Marriage status: 28.5% never married, 57.6% now married, 5.0% widowed, 9.0% divorced (2006-2010 5-year est.); Foreign born: 32.6% (2006-2010 5-year est.); Ancestry (includes multiple ancestries): 21.4% Italian, 14.1% Irish, 9.0% German, 3.7% English, 3.1% Polish (2006-2010 5-year est.).

**Economy:** Single-family building permits issued: 0 (2011); Multi-family building permits issued: 0 (2011); Employment by occupation: 13.6% management, 3.2% professional, 13.6% services, 13.7% sales, 2.6% farming, 6.7% construction, 1.4% production (2006-2010 5-year est.).

**Income:** Per capita income: $38,859 (2006-2010 5-year est.); Median household income: $63,929 (2006-2010 5-year est.); Average household income: $95,814 (2006-2010 5-year est.); Percent of households with income of $100,000 or more: 31.6% (2006-2010 5-year est.); Poverty rate: 7.2% (2006-2010 5-year est.).

**Taxes:** Total city taxes per capita: $1,367 (2009); City property taxes per capita: $1,203 (2009).

**Education:** Percent of population age 25 and over with: High school diploma (including GED) or higher: 82.4% (2006-2010 5-year est.); Bachelor's degree or higher: 40.7% (2006-2010 5-year est.); Master's degree or higher: 17.6% (2006-2010 5-year est.).

#### School District(s)

Bedford Central School District (PK-12)

   2009-10 Enrollment: 4,362 . . . . . . . . . . . . . . . . . . . . . . (914) 241-6010

#### Four-year College(s)

Yeshiva of Nitra Rabbinical College (Private, Not-for-profit)

   Fall 2010 Enrollment: 250 . . . . . . . . . . . . . . . . . . . . . (7.1) 838-5E+1

   2011-12 Tuition: In-state $7,300; Out-of-state $7,300

#### Vocational/Technical School(s)

Finger Lakes School of Massage (Private, For-profit)

   Fall 2010 Enrollment: 79 . . . . . . . . . . . . . . . . . . . . . . (914) 241-7363

   2011-12 Tuition: $15,950

**Housing:** Homeownership rate: 57.3% (2010); Median home value: $440,800 (2006-2010 5-year est.); Median contract rent: $1,050 per month (2006-2010 5-year est.); Median year structure built: 1968 (2006-2010 5-year est.).

**Hospitals:** Northern Westchester Hospital (233 beds)

**Safety:** Violent crime rate: 26.2 per 10,000 population; Property crime rate: 159.0 per 10,000 population (2010).

**Transportation:** Commute to work: 69.8% car, 11.2% public transportation, 8.6% walk, 5.6% work from home (2006-2010 5-year est.); Travel time to work: 33.7% less than 15 minutes, 34.9% 15 to 30 minutes, 15.7% 30 to 45 minutes, 3.5% 45 to 60 minutes, 12.3% 60 minutes or more (2006-2010 5-year est.)

**Additional Information Contacts**

Mount Kisco Chamber of Commerce. . . . . . . . . . . . . . . . (914) 666-7525

   http://www.mtkisco.com

## MOUNT PLEASANT (town). Covers a land area of 27.422 square miles and a water area of 5.334 square miles. Located at 41.09° N. Lat; 73.82° W. Long. Elevation is 259 feet.

**Population:** 40,590 (1990); 43,221 (2000); 43,724 (2010); Density: 1,594.4 persons per square mile (2010); Race: 79.7% White, 5.5% Black, 4.8% Asian, 0.3% American Indian/Alaska Native, 0.0% Native Hawaiian/Other Pacific Islander, 9.7% Other, 18.0% Hispanic of any race (2010); Average household size: 2.84 (2010); Median age: 39.5 (2010); Males per 100 females: 101.8 (2010); Marriage status: 31.6% never married, 56.8% now married, 4.7% widowed, 6.9% divorced (2006-2010 5-year est.); Foreign born: 22.1% (2006-2010 5-year est.); Ancestry (includes multiple ancestries): 27.3% Italian, 16.7% Irish, 9.6% German, 4.9% English, 4.8% Polish (2006-2010 5-year est.).

**Economy:** Unemployment rate: 7.1% (February 2012); Total civilian labor force: 20,908 (February 2012); Single-family building permits issued: 8 (2011); Multi-family building permits issued: 0 (2011); Employment by

occupation: 16.2% management, 4.8% professional, 9.4% services, 15.7% sales, 4.2% farming, 6.7% construction, 3.0% production (2006-2010 5-year est.).

**Income:** Per capita income: $48,825 (2006-2010 5-year est.); Median household income: $102,938 (2006-2010 5-year est.); Average household income: $148,184 (2006-2010 5-year est.); Percent of households with income of $100,000 or more: 51.8% (2006-2010 5-year est.); Poverty rate: 5.5% (2006-2010 5-year est.).

**Taxes:** Total city taxes per capita: $760 (2009); City property taxes per capita: $666 (2009).

**Education:** Percent of population age 25 and over with: High school diploma (including GED) or higher: 89.1% (2006-2010 5-year est.); Bachelor's degree or higher: 48.0% (2006-2010 5-year est.); Master's degree or higher: 23.2% (2006-2010 5-year est.).

**Housing:** Homeownership rate: 70.5% (2010); Median home value: $657,200 (2006-2010 5-year est.); Median contract rent: $1,236 per month (2006-2010 5-year est.); Median year structure built: 1953 (2006-2010 5-year est.).

**Safety:** Violent crime rate: 3.4 per 10,000 population; Property crime rate: 70.8 per 10,000 population (2010).

**Transportation:** Commute to work: 72.4% car, 17.7% public transportation, 5.2% walk, 3.8% work from home (2006-2010 5-year est.); Travel time to work: 27.0% less than 15 minutes, 30.1% 15 to 30 minutes, 18.0% 30 to 45 minutes, 8.2% 45 to 60 minutes, 16.6% 60 minutes or more (2006-2010 5-year est.)

**Additional Information Contacts**

Town of Mount Pleasant . . . . . . . . . . . . . . . . . . . . . . . (914) 742-2300

   http://www.mtpleasantny.com

## MOUNT VERNON (city). Covers a land area of 4.385 square miles and a water area of 0.017 square miles. Located at 40.91° N. Lat; 73.82° W. Long. Elevation is 108 feet.

**History:** Named for George Washington's estate on the Potomac River, which was named for Edward Vernon, British admiral. John Peter Zenger was arrested here for libel in 1733. The city itself was not founded until 1851, when a cooperative group, the Industrial Home Association, bought the land and built a planned community. St. Paul's Church (c.1761), a national historic site, is here. The city, which has a large French-American population, has been the scene of a great deal of controversy over school and housing integration in the 1970s, 1980s, and 1990s.

**Population:** 67,076 (1990); 68,381 (2000); 67,292 (2010); Density: 15,343.6 persons per square mile (2010); Race: 24.3% White, 63.4% Black, 1.8% Asian, 0.5% American Indian/Alaska Native, 0.1% Native Hawaiian/Other Pacific Islander, 9.9% Other, 14.3% Hispanic of any race (2010); Average household size: 2.53 (2010); Median age: 38.4 (2010); Males per 100 females: 83.3 (2010); Marriage status: 41.7% never married, 41.8% now married, 7.3% widowed, 9.2% divorced (2006-2010 5-year est.); Foreign born: 31.1% (2006-2010 5-year est.); Ancestry (includes multiple ancestries): 15.6% Jamaican, 7.9% Italian, 4.3% Irish, 3.1% American, 3.0% Brazilian (2006-2010 5-year est.).

**Economy:** Unemployment rate: 9.3% (February 2012); Total civilian labor force: 32,668 (February 2012); Single-family building permits issued: 4 (2011); Multi-family building permits issued: 2 (2011); Employment by occupation: 10.2% management, 2.9% professional, 14.9% services, 16.2% sales, 4.5% farming, 9.0% construction, 3.6% production (2006-2010 5-year est.).

**Income:** Per capita income: $27,611 (2006-2010 5-year est.); Median household income: $49,862 (2006-2010 5-year est.); Average household income: $68,091 (2006-2010 5-year est.); Percent of households with income of $100,000 or more: 20.0% (2006-2010 5-year est.); Poverty rate: 12.8% (2006-2010 5-year est.).

**Taxes:** Total city taxes per capita: $992 (2009); City property taxes per capita: $614 (2009).

**Education:** Percent of population age 25 and over with: High school diploma (including GED) or higher: 81.7% (2006-2010 5-year est.); Bachelor's degree or higher: 24.8% (2006-2010 5-year est.); Master's degree or higher: 11.2% (2006-2010 5-year est.).

#### School District(s)

Mount Vernon City School District (PK-12)

   2009-10 Enrollment: 8,904 . . . . . . . . . . . . . . . . . . . . (914) 665-5201

#### Two-year College(s)

Dorothea Hopfer School of Nursing-Mt Vernon Hospital (Private, Not-for-profit)

   Fall 2010 Enrollment: 74 . . . . . . . . . . . . . . . . . . . . . . (914) 361-6537

## Vocational/Technical School(s)
Westchester School of Beauty Culture (Private, For-profit)
Fall 2010 Enrollment: 78 . . . . . . . . . . . . . . . . . . . . . . . . . . . (914) 699-2344
2011-12 Tuition: $8,923
**Housing:** Homeownership rate: 38.1% (2010); Median home value: $428,400 (2006-2010 5-year est.); Median contract rent: $982 per month (2006-2010 5-year est.); Median year structure built: 1945 (2006-2010 5-year est.).
**Hospitals:** Mount Vernon Hospital (228 beds)
**Safety:** Violent crime rate: 99.6 per 10,000 population; Property crime rate: 232.7 per 10,000 population (2010).
**Newspapers:** Westchester County Press (Local news; Circulation 15,000)
**Transportation:** Commute to work: 65.0% car, 21.1% public transportation, 8.0% walk, 2.6% work from home (2006-2010 5-year est.); Travel time to work: 20.2% less than 15 minutes, 38.0% 15 to 30 minutes, 21.8% 30 to 45 minutes, 9.1% 45 to 60 minutes, 11.0% 60 minutes or more (2006-2010 5-year est.)
**Additional Information Contacts**
City of Mount Vernon . . . . . . . . . . . . . . . . . . . . . . . . . . . . . (914) 665-2300
http://www.cmvny.com
Mt Vernon Chamber of Commerce . . . . . . . . . . . . . . . . . . . (888) 716-2460
http://www.mtvernonchamber.org

## NEW CASTLE (town). Covers a land area of 23.236 square miles and a water area of 0.382 square miles. Located at 41.18° N. Lat; 73.77° W. Long.
**History:** In 1696 Caleb Heathcote purchases a large tract of land including what is now New Castle from Wampus and other Native American sachems. In 1730 Quakers begin settling in the northern and western parts of North Castle, which will become New Castle.
**Population:** 16,801 (1990); 17,491 (2000); 17,569 (2010); Density: 756.1 persons per square mile (2010); Race: 88.3% White, 1.6% Black, 7.3% Asian, 0.0% American Indian/Alaska Native, 0.0% Native Hawaiian/Other Pacific Islander, 2.8% Other, 4.0% Hispanic of any race (2010); Average household size: 3.00 (2010); Median age: 42.3 (2010); Males per 100 females: 99.2 (2010); Marriage status: 21.7% never married, 70.8% now married, 3.2% widowed, 4.3% divorced (2006-2010 5-year est.); Foreign born: 12.2% (2006-2010 5-year est.); Ancestry (includes multiple ancestries): 13.6% Italian, 13.3% Irish, 11.7% German, 10.8% Russian, 8.5% English (2006-2010 5-year est.).
**Economy:** Single-family building permits issued: 4 (2011); Multi-family building permits issued: 0 (2011); Employment by occupation: 26.6% management, 5.8% professional, 5.1% services, 10.2% sales, 1.3% farming, 2.7% construction, 0.6% production (2006-2010 5-year est.).
**Income:** Per capita income: $93,183 (2006-2010 5-year est.); Median household income: $186,464 (2006-2010 5-year est.); Average household income: $274,966 (2006-2010 5-year est.); Percent of households with income of $100,000 or more: 74.6% (2006-2010 5-year est.); Poverty rate: 1.5% (2006-2010 5-year est.).
**Education:** Percent of population age 25 and over with: High school diploma (including GED) or higher: 97.7% (2006-2010 5-year est.); Bachelor's degree or higher: 76.3% (2006-2010 5-year est.); Master's degree or higher: 44.6% (2006-2010 5-year est.).
**Housing:** Homeownership rate: 91.0% (2010); Median home value: $897,200 (2006-2010 5-year est.); Median contract rent: $1,352 per month (2006-2010 5-year est.); Median year structure built: 1965 (2006-2010 5-year est.).
**Safety:** Violent crime rate: 1.7 per 10,000 population; Property crime rate: 60.8 per 10,000 population (2010).
**Transportation:** Commute to work: 63.5% car, 26.1% public transportation, 0.9% walk, 9.1% work from home (2006-2010 5-year est.); Travel time to work: 15.9% less than 15 minutes, 24.8% 15 to 30 minutes, 18.4% 30 to 45 minutes, 6.7% 45 to 60 minutes, 34.1% 60 minutes or more (2006-2010 5-year est.)
**Additional Information Contacts**
Town of New Castle. . . . . . . . . . . . . . . . . . . . . . . . . . . . . . . (914) 238-7269
http://www.mynewcastle.org

## NEW ROCHELLE (city). Covers a land area of 10.350 square miles and a water area of 2.885 square miles. Located at 40.92° N. Lat; 73.77° W. Long. Elevation is 85 feet.
**History:** New Rochelle occupies the site of the villages of the Siwanoy, principal nation of the Wappinger confederacy. In 1689, a group of Huguenot refugees purchased a tract of 6,000 acres and named the settlement for their old home in France, La Rochelle. New Rochelle was incorporated as a village in 1857 and as a city in 1899.

**Population:** 67,429 (1990); 72,182 (2000); 77,062 (2010); Density: 7,445.4 persons per square mile (2010); Race: 65.2% White, 19.3% Black, 4.2% Asian, 0.5% American Indian/Alaska Native, 0.1% Native Hawaiian/Other Pacific Islander, 10.7% Other, 27.8% Hispanic of any race (2010); Average household size: 2.64 (2010); Median age: 38.4 (2010); Males per 100 females: 92.3 (2010); Marriage status: 37.7% never married, 47.5% now married, 7.1% widowed, 7.8% divorced (2006-2010 5-year est.); Foreign born: 27.2% (2006-2010 5-year est.); Ancestry (includes multiple ancestries): 18.9% Italian, 9.8% Irish, 5.2% German, 4.1% Russian, 3.6% Polish (2006-2010 5-year est.).
**Economy:** Unemployment rate: 9.5% (February 2012); Total civilian labor force: 38,710 (February 2012); Single-family building permits issued: 20 (2011); Multi-family building permits issued: 201 (2011); Employment by occupation: 13.8% management, 3.3% professional, 10.9% services, 14.8% sales, 3.0% farming, 9.4% construction, 1.9% production (2006-2010 5-year est.).
**Income:** Per capita income: $40,787 (2006-2010 5-year est.); Median household income: $65,317 (2006-2010 5-year est.); Average household income: $108,529 (2006-2010 5-year est.); Percent of households with income of $100,000 or more: 33.5% (2006-2010 5-year est.); Poverty rate: 10.7% (2006-2010 5-year est.).
**Taxes:** Total city taxes per capita: $1,063 (2009); City property taxes per capita: $620 (2009).
**Education:** Percent of population age 25 and over with: High school diploma (including GED) or higher: 83.4% (2006-2010 5-year est.); Bachelor's degree or higher: 39.7% (2006-2010 5-year est.); Master's degree or higher: 20.4% (2006-2010 5-year est.).
### School District(s)
New Rochelle City School District (PK-12)
2009-10 Enrollment: 10,850 . . . . . . . . . . . . . . . . . . (914) 576-4200
### Four-year College(s)
Iona College (Private, Not-for-profit, Roman Catholic)
Fall 2010 Enrollment: 4,220. . . . . . . . . . . . . . . . . . . . . (914) 633-2000
2011-12 Tuition: In-state $30,192; Out-of-state $30,192
Monroe College-New Rochelle (Private, For-profit)
Fall 2010 Enrollment: 3,148. . . . . . . . . . . . . . . . . . . . . (914) 632-5400
2011-12 Tuition: In-state $12,440; Out-of-state $12,440
The College of New Rochelle (Private, Not-for-profit)
Fall 2010 Enrollment: 4,166. . . . . . . . . . . . . . . . . . . . . (914) 632-5300
2011-12 Tuition: In-state $29,100; Out-of-state $29,100
**Housing:** Homeownership rate: 51.2% (2010); Median home value: $605,500 (2006-2010 5-year est.); Median contract rent: $1,097 per month (2006-2010 5-year est.); Median year structure built: 1947 (2006-2010 5-year est.).
**Hospitals:** Sound Shore Medical Center of Westchester (476 beds)
**Safety:** Violent crime rate: 29.5 per 10,000 population; Property crime rate: 165.1 per 10,000 population (2010).
**Newspapers:** Bronx News (Community news; Circulation 10,000); City News (Community news); Parkchester News (Community news; Circulation 12,500); Town & Village (Local news; Circulation 8,300)
**Transportation:** Commute to work: 62.7% car, 19.3% public transportation, 9.1% walk, 6.3% work from home (2006-2010 5-year est.); Travel time to work: 27.5% less than 15 minutes, 31.1% 15 to 30 minutes, 18.9% 30 to 45 minutes, 8.8% 45 to 60 minutes, 13.7% 60 minutes or more (2006-2010 5-year est.); Amtrak: train service available.
**Additional Information Contacts**
City of New Rochelle . . . . . . . . . . . . . . . . . . . . . . . . . . . . . (914) 654-2000
http://www.newrochelleny.com
New Rochelle Chamber of Commerce . . . . . . . . . . . . . . . . (914) 632-5700
http://www.newrochellechamber.org

## NORTH CASTLE (town). Covers a land area of 23.757 square miles and a water area of 2.603 square miles. Located at 41.13° N. Lat; 73.69° W. Long.
**History:** Town got its name from a barrier built by the Mohicans to protect themselves from attack.
**Population:** 10,164 (1990); 10,849 (2000); 11,841 (2010); Density: 498.4 persons per square mile (2010); Race: 89.8% White, 1.6% Black, 5.0% Asian, 0.1% American Indian/Alaska Native, 0.0% Native Hawaiian/Other Pacific Islander, 3.5% Other, 7.7% Hispanic of any race (2010); Average household size: 3.02 (2010); Median age: 42.0 (2010); Males per 100 females: 98.2 (2010); Marriage status: 24.2% never married, 67.0% now married, 4.2% widowed, 4.6% divorced (2006-2010 5-year est.); Foreign born: 11.7% (2006-2010 5-year est.); Ancestry (includes multiple

ancestries): 24.4% Italian, 14.1% Irish, 9.1% German, 6.2% Russian, 5.5% English (2006-2010 5-year est.).
**Economy:** Single-family building permits issued: 12 (2011); Multi-family building permits issued: 0 (2011); Employment by occupation: 27.4% management, 2.4% professional, 5.0% services, 14.3% sales, 1.6% farming, 2.9% construction, 2.8% production (2006-2010 5-year est.).
**Income:** Per capita income: $76,063 (2006-2010 5-year est.); Median household income: $136,507 (2006-2010 5-year est.); Average household income: $250,272 (2006-2010 5-year est.); Percent of households with income of $100,000 or more: 68.2% (2006-2010 5-year est.); Poverty rate: 5.5% (2006-2010 5-year est.).
**Education:** Percent of population age 25 and over with: High school diploma (including GED) or higher: 95.7% (2006-2010 5-year est.); Bachelor's degree or higher: 62.9% (2006-2010 5-year est.); Master's degree or higher: 31.9% (2006-2010 5-year est.).
**Housing:** Homeownership rate: 86.6% (2010); Median home value: $967,500 (2006-2010 5-year est.); Median contract rent: $1,810 per month (2006-2010 5-year est.); Median year structure built: 1967 (2006-2010 5-year est.).
**Safety:** Violent crime rate: 0.8 per 10,000 population; Property crime rate: 58.3 per 10,000 population (2010).
**Transportation:** Commute to work: 69.3% car, 16.3% public transportation, 1.6% walk, 12.0% work from home (2006-2010 5-year est.); Travel time to work: 23.7% less than 15 minutes, 31.5% 15 to 30 minutes, 13.3% 30 to 45 minutes, 7.6% 45 to 60 minutes, 23.9% 60 minutes or more (2006-2010 5-year est.).
**Additional Information Contacts**
Town of North Castle . . . . . . . . . . . . . . . . . . . . . . . . . (914) 273-3321
  http://www.northcastleny.com

## NORTH SALEM (town). Covers a land area of 21.326 square miles and a water area of 1.518 square miles. Located at 41.34° N. Lat; 73.59° W. Long. Elevation is 505 feet.

**History:** DeLancey Town Hall, a restored 18th-century Georgian manor, is on the National Register of Historic Places; Museum, Japanese Stroll Garden also here.
**Population:** 4,725 (1990); 5,173 (2000); 5,104 (2010); Density: 239.3 persons per square mile (2010); Race: 93.6% White, 1.2% Black, 1.7% Asian, 0.2% American Indian/Alaska Native, 0.0% Native Hawaiian/Other Pacific Islander, 3.3% Other, 7.5% Hispanic of any race (2010); Average household size: 2.68 (2010); Median age: 45.8 (2010); Males per 100 females: 94.1 (2010); Marriage status: 20.8% never married, 63.6% now married, 10.4% widowed, 5.2% divorced (2006-2010 5-year est.); Foreign born: 10.0% (2006-2010 5-year est.); Ancestry (includes multiple ancestries): 27.8% Italian, 23.8% Irish, 18.9% German, 9.4% English, 8.0% Polish (2006-2010 5-year est.).
**Economy:** Single-family building permits issued: 0 (2011); Multi-family building permits issued: 0 (2011); Employment by occupation: 19.9% management, 1.5% professional, 6.6% services, 13.0% sales, 0.9% farming, 9.8% construction, 5.7% production (2006-2010 5-year est.).
**Income:** Per capita income: $69,054 (2006-2010 5-year est.); Median household income: $138,803 (2006-2010 5-year est.); Average household income: $215,121 (2006-2010 5-year est.); Percent of households with income of $100,000 or more: 64.5% (2006-2010 5-year est.); Poverty rate: 1.5% (2006-2010 5-year est.).
**Education:** Percent of population age 25 and over with: High school diploma (including GED) or higher: 91.1% (2006-2010 5-year est.); Bachelor's degree or higher: 51.4% (2006-2010 5-year est.); Master's degree or higher: 24.4% (2006-2010 5-year est.).
### School District(s)
North Salem Central School District (KG-12)
  2009-10 Enrollment: 1,331 . . . . . . . . . . . . . . . . . . . . (914) 669-5414
**Housing:** Homeownership rate: 84.3% (2010); Median home value: $655,300 (2006-2010 5-year est.); Median contract rent: $1,701 per month (2006-2010 5-year est.); Median year structure built: 1959 (2006-2010 5-year est.).
**Transportation:** Commute to work: 78.4% car, 9.7% public transportation, 3.8% walk, 8.2% work from home (2006-2010 5-year est.); Travel time to work: 18.4% less than 15 minutes, 21.1% 15 to 30 minutes, 35.1% 30 to 45 minutes, 8.8% 45 to 60 minutes, 16.6% 60 minutes or more (2006-2010 5-year est.)

## OSSINING (village). Covers a land area of 3.149 square miles and a water area of 3.282 square miles. Located at 41.15° N. Lat; 73.87° W. Long. Elevation is 161 feet.

**Population:** 22,582 (1990); 24,010 (2000); 25,060 (2010); Density: 7,957.4 persons per square mile (2010); Race: 54.6% White, 17.2% Black, 4.2% Asian, 0.6% American Indian/Alaska Native, 0.0% Native Hawaiian/Other Pacific Islander, 23.4% Other, 41.4% Hispanic of any race (2010); Average household size: 2.78 (2010); Median age: 36.6 (2010); Males per 100 females: 113.0 (2010); Marriage status: 35.4% never married, 50.0% now married, 5.5% widowed, 9.0% divorced (2006-2010 5-year est.); Foreign born: 34.7% (2006-2010 5-year est.); Ancestry (includes multiple ancestries): 14.7% Italian, 10.3% Irish, 6.2% German, 2.8% English, 2.7% American (2006-2010 5-year est.).
**Economy:** Single-family building permits issued: 0 (2011); Multi-family building permits issued: 0 (2011); Employment by occupation: 10.7% management, 4.7% professional, 11.8% services, 16.3% sales, 3.0% farming, 12.0% construction, 3.8% production (2006-2010 5-year est.).
**Income:** Per capita income: $31,192 (2006-2010 5-year est.); Median household income: $70,864 (2006-2010 5-year est.); Average household income: $88,483 (2006-2010 5-year est.); Percent of households with income of $100,000 or more: 34.0% (2006-2010 5-year est.); Poverty rate: 16.0% (2006-2010 5-year est.).
**Education:** Percent of population age 25 and over with: High school diploma (including GED) or higher: 76.5% (2006-2010 5-year est.); Bachelor's degree or higher: 35.7% (2006-2010 5-year est.); Master's degree or higher: 16.3% (2006-2010 5-year est.).
### School District(s)
Ossining Union Free School District (PK-12)
  2009-10 Enrollment: 4,450 . . . . . . . . . . . . . . . . . . . . (914) 941-7700
### Four-year College(s)
Kehilath Yakov Rabbinical Seminary (Private, Not-for-profit, Jewish)
  Fall 2010 Enrollment: 117 . . . . . . . . . . . . . . . . . . (7.1) 896-3E+1
  2011-12 Tuition: In-state $6,200; Out-of-state $6,200
**Housing:** Homeownership rate: 53.2% (2010); Median home value: $426,700 (2006-2010 5-year est.); Median contract rent: $1,194 per month (2006-2010 5-year est.); Median year structure built: 1952 (2006-2010 5-year est.).
**Safety:** Violent crime rate: 16.5 per 10,000 population; Property crime rate: 104.7 per 10,000 population (2010).
**Transportation:** Commute to work: 75.9% car, 14.3% public transportation, 4.0% walk, 3.3% work from home (2006-2010 5-year est.); Travel time to work: 26.3% less than 15 minutes, 32.3% 15 to 30 minutes, 19.6% 30 to 45 minutes, 8.3% 45 to 60 minutes, 13.5% 60 minutes or more (2006-2010 5-year est.)
**Additional Information Contacts**
Greater Ossining Chamber of Commerce . . . . . . . . . . . . . (914) 941-0009
  http://www.ossiningchamber.org
Village of Ossining . . . . . . . . . . . . . . . . . . . . . . . . . . . . (914) 762-8428
  http://www.villageofossining.org

## OSSINING (town). Covers a land area of 11.556 square miles and a water area of 4.167 square miles. Located at 41.15° N. Lat; 73.85° W. Long. Elevation is 161 feet.

**History:** Ossining is the site of Sing Sing state prison (built 1825—1828). This prison was long known for its extreme discipline, but under Thomas Mott Osborne and Lewis Edward Lawes, notable reforms were introduced. By end of 19th century, second-largest industrial center in Westchester. Brickyards produced bricks for Old Croton Aqueduct. Maryknoll, the headquarters of the Catholic Foreign Mission Society, is nearby. Settled c.1750, Incorporated 1813 as Sing Sing, renamed 1901.
**Population:** 34,124 (1990); 36,534 (2000); 37,674 (2010); Density: 3,260.1 persons per square mile (2010); Race: 65.0% White, 12.7% Black, 4.9% Asian, 0.5% American Indian/Alaska Native, 0.0% Native Hawaiian/Other Pacific Islander, 16.9% Other, 30.3% Hispanic of any race (2010); Average household size: 2.72 (2010); Median age: 39.3 (2010); Males per 100 females: 104.3 (2010); Marriage status: 31.5% never married, 53.7% now married, 6.9% widowed, 7.9% divorced (2006-2010 5-year est.); Foreign born: 28.3% (2006-2010 5-year est.); Ancestry (includes multiple ancestries): 17.8% Italian, 13.5% Irish, 7.5% German, 4.4% English, 4.0% Polish (2006-2010 5-year est.).
**Economy:** Unemployment rate: 7.1% (February 2012); Total civilian labor force: 18,432 (February 2012); Single-family building permits issued: 4 (2011); Multi-family building permits issued: 0 (2011); Employment by occupation: 14.3% management, 4.8% professional, 9.8% services, 15.5%

sales, 2.7% farming, 9.2% construction, 3.2% production (2006-2010 5-year est.).

**Income:** Per capita income: $43,721 (2006-2010 5-year est.); Median household income: $85,749 (2006-2010 5-year est.); Average household income: $125,865 (2006-2010 5-year est.); Percent of households with income of $100,000 or more: 44.2% (2006-2010 5-year est.); Poverty rate: 12.3% (2006-2010 5-year est.).

**Education:** Percent of population age 25 and over with: High school diploma (including GED) or higher: 82.3% (2006-2010 5-year est.); Bachelor's degree or higher: 46.0% (2006-2010 5-year est.); Master's degree or higher: 23.4% (2006-2010 5-year est.).

**School District(s)**
Ossining Union Free School District (PK-12)
    2009-10 Enrollment: 4,450 . . . . . . . . . . . . . . . . . . . . (914) 941-7700

**Four-year College(s)**
Kehilath Yakov Rabbinical Seminary (Private, Not-for-profit, Jewish)
    Fall 2010 Enrollment: 117 . . . . . . . . . . . . . . . . . . . . . (7.1) 896-3E+1
    2011-12 Tuition: In-state $6,200; Out-of-state $6,200

**Housing:** Homeownership rate: 64.2% (2010); Median home value: $483,500 (2006-2010 5-year est.); Median contract rent: $1,185 per month (2006-2010 5-year est.); Median year structure built: 1958 (2006-2010 5-year est.).

**Transportation:** Commute to work: 73.2% car, 17.0% public transportation, 3.3% walk, 4.7% work from home (2006-2010 5-year est.); Travel time to work: 23.7% less than 15 minutes, 30.6% 15 to 30 minutes, 19.5% 30 to 45 minutes, 9.6% 45 to 60 minutes, 16.6% 60 minutes or more (2006-2010 5-year est.)

**Additional Information Contacts**
Town of Ossining . . . . . . . . . . . . . . . . . . . . . . . . . . . . (914) 762-6000
    http://www.townofossining.com

**PEEKSKILL** (city). Covers a land area of 4.367 square miles and a water area of 1.230 square miles. Located at 41.28° N. Lat; 73.92° W. Long. Elevation is 128 feet.

**History:** Named for Jan Peeck, a Dutch trader from New Amsterdam. In the American Revolution, Peekskill was attacked and burned (1777) by the British; after the war the city became a prominent trade center. In 19th century had foundries based on Putnam County iron deposits. Peter Cooper and Henry Ward Beecher born here. St. Peter's Church, dedicated in 1767, has been restored. Settled 1665. Incorporated as a village 1816, as a city 1940.

**Population:** 19,536 (1990); 22,441 (2000); 23,583 (2010); Density: 5,399.6 persons per square mile (2010); Race: 51.3% White, 23.6% Black, 3.0% Asian, 0.6% American Indian/Alaska Native, 0.1% Native Hawaiian/Other Pacific Islander, 21.4% Other, 36.9% Hispanic of any race (2010); Average household size: 2.58 (2010); Median age: 37.5 (2010); Males per 100 females: 95.6 (2010); Marriage status: 37.5% never married, 49.1% now married, 4.7% widowed, 8.7% divorced (2006-2010 5-year est.); Foreign born: 34.1% (2006-2010 5-year est.); Ancestry (includes multiple ancestries): 14.2% Italian, 10.7% Irish, 5.1% German, 3.7% English, 3.5% Jamaican (2006-2010 5-year est.).

**Economy:** Single-family building permits issued: 4 (2011); Multi-family building permits issued: 0 (2011); Employment by occupation: 6.6% management, 1.6% professional, 14.6% services, 14.9% sales, 3.3% farming, 17.4% construction, 6.9% production (2006-2010 5-year est.).

**Income:** Per capita income: $27,965 (2006-2010 5-year est.); Median household income: $57,784 (2006-2010 5-year est.); Average household income: $73,041 (2006-2010 5-year est.); Percent of households with income of $100,000 or more: 25.4% (2006-2010 5-year est.); Poverty rate: 15.5% (2006-2010 5-year est.).

**Taxes:** Total city taxes per capita: $617 (2009); City property taxes per capita: $553 (2009).

**Education:** Percent of population age 25 and over with: High school diploma (including GED) or higher: 77.7% (2006-2010 5-year est.); Bachelor's degree or higher: 24.3% (2006-2010 5-year est.); Master's degree or higher: 11.1% (2006-2010 5-year est.).

**School District(s)**
Peekskill City School District (PK-12)
    2009-10 Enrollment: 2,905 . . . . . . . . . . . . . . . . . . . . (914) 737-3300

**Four-year College(s)**
Ohr Hameir Theological Seminary (Private, Not-for-profit)
    Fall 2010 Enrollment: 115 . . . . . . . . . . . . . . . . . . . . . (914) 736-1500
    2011-12 Tuition: In-state $8,100; Out-of-state $8,100

**Vocational/Technical School(s)**
North Westchester School of Hair-Cosmetology (Private, For-profit)
    Fall 2010 Enrollment: 74 . . . . . . . . . . . . . . . . . . . (800) 920-4593
    2011-12 Tuition: $11,750

**Housing:** Homeownership rate: 54.1% (2010); Median home value: $346,500 (2006-2010 5-year est.); Median contract rent: $1,107 per month (2006-2010 5-year est.); Median year structure built: 1958 (2006-2010 5-year est.).

**Safety:** Violent crime rate: 12.1 per 10,000 population; Property crime rate: 93.9 per 10,000 population (2010).

**Transportation:** Commute to work: 75.5% car, 13.8% public transportation, 5.7% walk, 2.5% work from home (2006-2010 5-year est.); Travel time to work: 28.7% less than 15 minutes, 21.8% 15 to 30 minutes, 21.5% 30 to 45 minutes, 11.0% 45 to 60 minutes, 17.0% 60 minutes or more (2006-2010 5-year est.)

**Additional Information Contacts**
City of Peekskill . . . . . . . . . . . . . . . . . . . . . . . . . . . . (914) 737-3400
    http://www.cityofpeekskill.com
Hudson Valley Gateway Chamber of Commerce . . . . . . . . (914) 737-3600
    http://www.hvgatewaychamber.com

**PELHAM** (village). Covers a land area of 0.829 square miles and a water area of 0.004 square miles. Located at 40.91° N. Lat; 73.80° W. Long. Elevation is 72 feet.

**History:** On June 27, 1654, Thomas Pell purchased 9,166 acres (37.09 sq. km.) from the Native American tribe of the Siwanoys. Among the land that he purchased, of course, was all the land that constitutes today's Village of Pelham. Upon his death in 1669, Thomas Pell left the land to his nephew and sole heir, John Pell.

**Population:** 6,373 (1990); 6,400 (2000); 6,910 (2010); Density: 8,332.8 persons per square mile (2010); Race: 76.9% White, 9.5% Black, 6.0% Asian, 0.1% American Indian/Alaska Native, 0.1% Native Hawaiian/Other Pacific Islander, 7.4% Other, 12.3% Hispanic of any race (2010); Average household size: 2.89 (2010); Median age: 39.1 (2010); Males per 100 females: 95.8 (2010); Marriage status: 26.9% never married, 58.5% now married, 5.4% widowed, 9.1% divorced (2006-2010 5-year est.); Foreign born: 14.3% (2006-2010 5-year est.); Ancestry (includes multiple ancestries): 18.2% Italian, 16.1% German, 16.1% Irish, 7.4% American, 7.3% English (2006-2010 5-year est.).

**Economy:** Single-family building permits issued: 0 (2011); Multi-family building permits issued: 0 (2011); Employment by occupation: 19.3% management, 3.5% professional, 5.3% services, 14.9% sales, 5.1% farming, 4.7% construction, 1.1% production (2006-2010 5-year est.).

**Income:** Per capita income: $63,951 (2006-2010 5-year est.); Median household income: $111,989 (2006-2010 5-year est.); Average household income: $179,404 (2006-2010 5-year est.); Percent of households with income of $100,000 or more: 55.4% (2006-2010 5-year est.); Poverty rate: 0.9% (2006-2010 5-year est.).

**Education:** Percent of population age 25 and over with: High school diploma (including GED) or higher: 94.5% (2006-2010 5-year est.); Bachelor's degree or higher: 61.2% (2006-2010 5-year est.); Master's degree or higher: 30.6% (2006-2010 5-year est.).

**School District(s)**
Pelham Union Free School District (KG-12)
    2009-10 Enrollment: 2,780 . . . . . . . . . . . . . . . . . . . . (914) 738-3434

**Housing:** Homeownership rate: 67.2% (2010); Median home value: $677,100 (2006-2010 5-year est.); Median contract rent: $1,274 per month (2006-2010 5-year est.); Median year structure built: before 1940 (2006-2010 5-year est.).

**Safety:** Violent crime rate: 31.2 per 10,000 population; Property crime rate: 155.8 per 10,000 population (2010).

**Newspapers:** Baychester Pennysaver (Community news; Circulation 9,600); Fordham Pennysaver (Community news; Circulation 9,100); Pelham Weekly (Community news; Circulation 1,600)

**Transportation:** Commute to work: 58.5% car, 29.1% public transportation, 3.0% walk, 8.7% work from home (2006-2010 5-year est.); Travel time to work: 16.1% less than 15 minutes, 28.2% 15 to 30 minutes, 22.4% 30 to 45 minutes, 19.2% 45 to 60 minutes, 14.0% 60 minutes or more (2006-2010 5-year est.)

**PELHAM** (town). Covers a land area of 2.171 square miles and a water area of 0.045 square miles. Located at 40.90° N. Lat; 73.80° W. Long. Elevation is 72 feet.

**History:** Settled in 17th century; incorporated 1896.

**Population:** 11,816 (1990); 11,866 (2000); 12,396 (2010); Density: 5,707.3 persons per square mile (2010); Race: 82.5% White, 6.2% Black, 5.3% Asian, 0.0% American Indian/Alaska Native, 0.1% Native Hawaiian/Other Pacific Islander, 5.9% Other, 10.0% Hispanic of any race (2010); Average household size: 2.91 (2010); Median age: 40.4 (2010); Males per 100 females: 96.4 (2010); Marriage status: 27.2% never married, 60.3% now married, 5.2% widowed, 7.3% divorced (2006-2010 5-year est.); Foreign born: 12.7% (2006-2010 5-year est.); Ancestry (includes multiple ancestries): 27.5% Italian, 19.1% Irish, 12.7% German, 8.7% English, 5.4% American (2006-2010 5-year est.).

**Economy:** Employment by occupation: 20.7% management, 3.5% professional, 5.0% services, 13.7% sales, 3.5% farming, 3.5% construction, 0.9% production (2006-2010 5-year est.).

**Income:** Per capita income: $71,707 (2006-2010 5-year est.); Median household income: $131,272 (2006-2010 5-year est.); Average household income: $210,362 (2006-2010 5-year est.); Percent of households with income of $100,000 or more: 62.8% (2006-2010 5-year est.); Poverty rate: 2.0% (2006-2010 5-year est.).

**Education:** Percent of population age 25 and over with: High school diploma (including GED) or higher: 95.6% (2006-2010 5-year est.); Bachelor's degree or higher: 66.1% (2006-2010 5-year est.); Master's degree or higher: 34.4% (2006-2010 5-year est.).

**School District(s)**

Pelham Union Free School District (KG-12)

  2009-10 Enrollment: 2,780 . . . . . . . . . . . . . . . (914) 738-3434

**Housing:** Homeownership rate: 78.3% (2010); Median home value: $702,400 (2006-2010 5-year est.); Median contract rent: $1,256 per month (2006-2010 5-year est.); Median year structure built: before 1940 (2006-2010 5-year est.).

**Newspapers:** Baychester Pennysaver (Community news; Circulation 9,600); Fordham Pennysaver (Community news; Circulation 9,100); Pelham Weekly (Community news; Circulation 1,600)

**Transportation:** Commute to work: 65.1% car, 25.6% public transportation, 2.5% walk, 6.4% work from home (2006-2010 5-year est.); Travel time to work: 19.5% less than 15 minutes, 28.4% 15 to 30 minutes, 21.4% 30 to 45 minutes, 16.0% 45 to 60 minutes, 14.7% 60 minutes or more (2006-2010 5-year est.)

**Additional Information Contacts**

Town of Pelham . . . . . . . . . . . . . . . . . . . . . . . . . . (914) 738-0777

  http://townofpelham.com

## PELHAM MANOR (village).

Covers a land area of 1.342 square miles and a water area of 0.041 square miles. Located at 40.89° N. Lat; 73.80° W. Long. Elevation is 62 feet.

**History:** Settled in mid-17th century; incorporated 1891.

**Population:** 5,443 (1990); 5,466 (2000); 5,486 (2010); Density: 4,085.8 persons per square mile (2010); Race: 89.6% White, 2.1% Black, 4.3% Asian, 0.0% American Indian/Alaska Native, 0.0% Native Hawaiian/Other Pacific Islander, 4.0% Other, 7.2% Hispanic of any race (2010); Average household size: 2.94 (2010); Median age: 42.2 (2010); Males per 100 females: 97.1 (2010); Marriage status: 27.5% never married, 62.5% now married, 5.0% widowed, 5.0% divorced (2006-2010 5-year est.); Foreign born: 10.6% (2006-2010 5-year est.); Ancestry (includes multiple ancestries): 38.9% Italian, 22.7% Irish, 10.6% English, 8.4% German, 4.8% Polish (2006-2010 5-year est.).

**Economy:** Single-family building permits issued: 0 (2011); Multi-family building permits issued: 0 (2011); Employment by occupation: 22.4% management, 3.4% professional, 4.7% services, 12.3% sales, 1.6% farming, 2.1% construction, 0.6% production (2006-2010 5-year est.).

**Income:** Per capita income: $81,353 (2006-2010 5-year est.); Median household income: $154,865 (2006-2010 5-year est.); Average household income: $253,261 (2006-2010 5-year est.); Percent of households with income of $100,000 or more: 73.3% (2006-2010 5-year est.); Poverty rate: 3.4% (2006-2010 5-year est.).

**Education:** Percent of population age 25 and over with: High school diploma (including GED) or higher: 97.0% (2006-2010 5-year est.); Bachelor's degree or higher: 72.3% (2006-2010 5-year est.); Master's degree or higher: 39.2% (2006-2010 5-year est.).

**Housing:** Homeownership rate: 92.6% (2010); Median home value: $748,200 (2006-2010 5-year est.); Median contract rent: $1,030 per month (2006-2010 5-year est.); Median year structure built: 1943 (2006-2010 5-year est.).

**Transportation:** Commute to work: 73.0% car, 21.4% public transportation, 2.0% walk, 3.6% work from home (2006-2010 5-year est.); Travel time to work: 23.3% less than 15 minutes, 28.7% 15 to 30 minutes,

20.3% 30 to 45 minutes, 12.2% 45 to 60 minutes, 15.5% 60 minutes or more (2006-2010 5-year est.)

**Additional Information Contacts**

Village of Pelham Manor . . . . . . . . . . . . . . . . . . . . (914) 738-8820

  http://www.pelhammanor.org

## PLEASANTVILLE (village).

Covers a land area of 1.824 square miles and a water area of 0.002 square miles. Located at 41.13° N. Lat; 73.78° W. Long. Elevation is 292 feet.

**History:** French Huguenot Isaac See (sometimes spelled Sie) settled here as an agent for Dutch landowner Frederick Philipse in 1695, thus beginning the modern history of Pleasantville.

**Population:** 6,592 (1990); 7,172 (2000); 7,019 (2010); Density: 3,847.1 persons per square mile (2010); Race: 85.7% White, 4.2% Black, 4.5% Asian, 0.1% American Indian/Alaska Native, 0.0% Native Hawaiian/Other Pacific Islander, 5.5% Other, 11.7% Hispanic of any race (2010); Average household size: 2.60 (2010); Median age: 41.0 (2010); Males per 100 females: 95.4 (2010); Marriage status: 30.4% never married, 56.7% now married, 5.4% widowed, 7.5% divorced (2006-2010 5-year est.); Foreign born: 13.0% (2006-2010 5-year est.); Ancestry (includes multiple ancestries): 28.1% Italian, 25.3% Irish, 14.8% German, 9.4% English, 7.7% Polish (2006-2010 5-year est.).

**Economy:** Single-family building permits issued: 0 (2011); Multi-family building permits issued: 0 (2011); Employment by occupation: 11.9% management, 4.9% professional, 7.0% services, 16.3% sales, 3.8% farming, 3.0% construction, 0.0% production (2006-2010 5-year est.).

**Income:** Per capita income: $59,374 (2006-2010 5-year est.); Median household income: $100,417 (2006-2010 5-year est.); Average household income: $151,468 (2006-2010 5-year est.); Percent of households with income of $100,000 or more: 50.1% (2006-2010 5-year est.); Poverty rate: 1.9% (2006-2010 5-year est.).

**Taxes:** Total city taxes per capita: $1,393 (2009); City property taxes per capita: $1,319 (2009).

**Education:** Percent of population age 25 and over with: High school diploma (including GED) or higher: 95.2% (2006-2010 5-year est.); Bachelor's degree or higher: 63.0% (2006-2010 5-year est.); Master's degree or higher: 29.4% (2006-2010 5-year est.).

**School District(s)**

Mount Pleasant-Cottage Union Free School District (02-12)

  2009-10 Enrollment: 331 . . . . . . . . . . . . . . . . . (914) 769-0456

Pleasantville Union Free School District (KG-12)

  2009-10 Enrollment: 1,834 . . . . . . . . . . . . . . . (914) 741-1400

**Housing:** Homeownership rate: 72.8% (2010); Median home value: $611,500 (2006-2010 5-year est.); Median contract rent: $1,456 per month (2006-2010 5-year est.); Median year structure built: 1948 (2006-2010 5-year est.).

**Safety:** Violent crime rate: 2.8 per 10,000 population; Property crime rate: 4.2 per 10,000 population (2010).

**Transportation:** Commute to work: 67.7% car, 23.8% public transportation, 3.4% walk, 4.6% work from home (2006-2010 5-year est.); Travel time to work: 31.3% less than 15 minutes, 21.8% 15 to 30 minutes, 15.4% 30 to 45 minutes, 9.5% 45 to 60 minutes, 22.0% 60 minutes or more (2006-2010 5-year est.)

**Additional Information Contacts**

Village of Pleasantville . . . . . . . . . . . . . . . . . . . . (914) 769-1900

  http://www.pleasantville-ny.gov

## PORT CHESTER (village).

Covers a land area of 2.330 square miles and a water area of 0.071 square miles. Located at 41.00° N. Lat; 73.66° W. Long. Elevation is 43 feet.

**History:** Named for Chester, England, and for its location as a port on Long Island Sound. Gen. Israel Putnam had his headquarters here 1777—1778. Several Colonial homes remain. Previously called Saw Pits, village was renamed in 1837. Settled after 1660. Incorporated 1868.

**Population:** 24,728 (1990); 27,867 (2000); 28,967 (2010); Density: 12,428.8 persons per square mile (2010); Race: 61.1% White, 6.5% Black, 2.1% Asian, 0.9% American Indian/Alaska Native, 0.0% Native Hawaiian/Other Pacific Islander, 29.4% Other, 59.4% Hispanic of any race (2010); Average household size: 3.08 (2010); Median age: 34.4 (2010); Males per 100 females: 110.3 (2010); Marriage status: 37.7% never married, 48.4% now married, 6.2% widowed, 7.7% divorced (2006-2010 5-year est.); Foreign born: 45.1% (2006-2010 5-year est.); Ancestry (includes multiple ancestries): 14.7% Italian, 8.6% American, 4.7% Irish, 3.5% Polish, 2.8% Brazilian (2006-2010 5-year est.).

**Economy:** Unemployment rate: 7.3% (February 2012); Total civilian labor force: 14,662 (February 2012); Single-family building permits issued: 1 (2011); Multi-family building permits issued: 2 (2011); Employment by occupation: 8.5% management, 1.9% professional, 16.1% services, 11.2% sales, 5.5% farming, 12.2% construction, 5.5% production (2006-2010 5-year est.).
**Income:** Per capita income: $26,744 (2006-2010 5-year est.); Median household income: $52,758 (2006-2010 5-year est.); Average household income: $73,895 (2006-2010 5-year est.); Percent of households with income of $100,000 or more: 20.1% (2006-2010 5-year est.); Poverty rate: 16.0% (2006-2010 5-year est.).
**Taxes:** Total city taxes per capita: $856 (2009); City property taxes per capita: $801 (2009).
**Education:** Percent of population age 25 and over with: High school diploma (including GED) or higher: 72.1% (2006-2010 5-year est.); Bachelor's degree or higher: 23.2% (2006-2010 5-year est.); Master's degree or higher: 10.1% (2006-2010 5-year est.).

**School District(s)**
Port Chester-Rye Union Free School District (KG-12)
   2009-10 Enrollment: 4,057 . . . . . . . . . . . . . . . . . . . . . . . (914) 934-7901
**Housing:** Homeownership rate: 43.2% (2010); Median home value: $472,900 (2006-2010 5-year est.); Median contract rent: $1,181 per month (2006-2010 5-year est.); Median year structure built: 1952 (2006-2010 5-year est.).
**Safety:** Violent crime rate: 18.3 per 10,000 population; Property crime rate: 242.7 per 10,000 population (2010).
**Newspapers:** America Latina (Local news; Circulation 4,000); Westmore News (Community news; Circulation 3,500)
**Transportation:** Commute to work: 62.3% car, 17.0% public transportation, 9.0% walk, 1.0% work from home (2006-2010 5-year est.); Travel time to work: 34.7% less than 15 minutes, 35.6% 15 to 30 minutes, 15.4% 30 to 45 minutes, 5.8% 45 to 60 minutes, 8.5% 60 minutes or more (2006-2010 5-year est.)
**Additional Information Contacts**
Village of Port Chester. . . . . . . . . . . . . . . . . . . . . . . . . . . . (914) 939-5202
   http://www.portchesterny.com

## POUND RIDGE (town). Covers a land area of 22.637 square miles and a water area of 0.803 square miles. Located at 41.21° N. Lat; 73.58° W. Long. Elevation is 620 feet.

**History:** Originally home to the Siwanoy and Kitchawong Indians (Mohican tribes, a subgroup of the Algonquians), the town takes its name from a tribal "pound" or enclosure for game that was on one of the area's many "ridges". The Indians led a relatively peaceful life of planting, hunting, and fishing.
**Population:** 4,550 (1990); 4,726 (2000); 5,104 (2010); Density: 225.5 persons per square mile (2010); Race: 93.7% White, 1.3% Black, 1.9% Asian, 0.1% American Indian/Alaska Native, 0.0% Native Hawaiian/Other Pacific Islander, 3.0% Other, 4.6% Hispanic of any race (2010); Average household size: 2.76 (2010); Median age: 45.9 (2010); Males per 100 females: 96.7 (2010); Marriage status: 15.6% never married, 76.8% now married, 2.6% widowed, 4.9% divorced (2006-2010 5-year est.); Foreign born: 9.5% (2006-2010 5-year est.); Ancestry (includes multiple ancestries): 17.2% Italian, 14.2% Irish, 12.2% English, 12.1% German, 9.1% Russian (2006-2010 5-year est.).
**Economy:** Single-family building permits issued: 3 (2011); Multi-family building permits issued: 0 (2011); Employment by occupation: 33.0% management, 5.6% professional, 2.9% services, 8.4% sales, 1.8% farming, 1.4% construction, 2.0% production (2006-2010 5-year est.).
**Income:** Per capita income: $127,078 (2006-2010 5-year est.); Median household income: $223,088 (2006-2010 5-year est.); Average household income: $345,550 (2006-2010 5-year est.); Percent of households with income of $100,000 or more: 78.9% (2006-2010 5-year est.); Poverty rate: 4.1% (2006-2010 5-year est.).
**Education:** Percent of population age 25 and over with: High school diploma (including GED) or higher: 98.0% (2006-2010 5-year est.); Bachelor's degree or higher: 76.1% (2006-2010 5-year est.); Master's degree or higher: 43.8% (2006-2010 5-year est.).

**School District(s)**
Bedford Central School District (PK-12)
   2009-10 Enrollment: 4,362 . . . . . . . . . . . . . . . . . . . . . . (914) 241-6010
**Housing:** Homeownership rate: 89.9% (2010); Median home value: $1 (2006-2010 5-year est.); Median contract rent: $1,825 per month (2006-2010 5-year est.); Median year structure built: 1968 (2006-2010 5-year est.).

**Safety:** Violent crime rate: 0.0 per 10,000 population; Property crime rate: 197.4 per 10,000 population (2010).
**Newspapers:** Country Shopper (Community news; Circulation 22,000)
**Transportation:** Commute to work: 64.8% car, 15.0% public transportation, 3.5% walk, 10.9% work from home (2006-2010 5-year est.); Travel time to work: 11.3% less than 15 minutes, 26.0% 15 to 30 minutes, 23.1% 30 to 45 minutes, 5.4% 45 to 60 minutes, 34.2% 60 minutes or more (2006-2010 5-year est.)
**Additional Information Contacts**
Town of Pound Ridge . . . . . . . . . . . . . . . . . . . . . . . . . . . . (914) 764-5511
   http://www.townofpoundridge.com

## PURCHASE (unincorporated postal area)
**Zip Code:** 10577
   Covers a land area of 6.717 square miles and a water area of 0.032 square miles. Located at 41.03° N. Lat; 73.71° W. Long. Elevation is 351 feet. Population: 6,552 (2010); Density: 975.4 persons per square mile (2010); Race: 77.5% White, 7.0% Black, 8.5% Asian, 0.2% American Indian/Alaska Native, 0.1% Native Hawaiian/Other Pacific Islander, 6.7% Other, 11.3% Hispanic of any race (2010); Average household size: 3.01 (2010); Median age: 20.9 (2010); Males per 100 females: 78.3 (2010); Homeownership rate: 93.2% (2010)

## PURDYS (unincorporated postal area)
**Zip Code:** 10578
   Covers a land area of 1.583 square miles and a water area of 0.168 square miles. Located at 41.32° N. Lat; 73.67° W. Long. Elevation is 253 feet. Population: 681 (2010); Density: 430.0 persons per square mile (2010); Race: 92.4% White, 1.6% Black, 2.3% Asian, 0.0% American Indian/Alaska Native, 1.0% Native Hawaiian/Other Pacific Islander, 2.7% Other, 8.4% Hispanic of any race (2010); Average household size: 2.86 (2010); Median age: 41.0 (2010); Males per 100 females: 92.9 (2010); Homeownership rate: 87.4% (2010)

## RYE (city). Covers a land area of 5.848 square miles and a water area of 14.173 square miles. Located at 40.94° N. Lat; 73.68° W. Long. Elevation is 26 feet.

**History:** Named for Rye in Sussex, England. In colonial times, Rye was the first stop on the Boston Post Road after N.Y. city. The old Square House, an inn where many Revolutionary notables stayed, is now a museum. Playland, a large county-owned amusement park, is on the beach here. Chief Justice John Jay is buried in Rye. Settled 1660. Incorporated as a city 1942.
**Population:** 14,936 (1990); 14,955 (2000); 15,720 (2010); Density: 2,688.0 persons per square mile (2010); Race: 89.5% White, 1.5% Black, 6.0% Asian, 0.1% American Indian/Alaska Native, 0.0% Native Hawaiian/Other Pacific Islander, 2.9% Other, 6.5% Hispanic of any race (2010); Average household size: 2.82 (2010); Median age: 40.8 (2010); Males per 100 females: 92.7 (2010); Marriage status: 21.3% never married, 64.2% now married, 7.5% widowed, 7.0% divorced (2006-2010 5-year est.); Foreign born: 18.1% (2006-2010 5-year est.); Ancestry (includes multiple ancestries): 19.9% Irish, 19.4% American, 15.7% Italian, 11.4% German, 9.0% English (2006-2010 5-year est.).
**Economy:** Single-family building permits issued: 0 (2011); Multi-family building permits issued: 0 (2011); Employment by occupation: 29.2% management, 4.2% professional, 3.8% services, 12.1% sales, 1.6% farming, 2.5% construction, 0.7% production (2006-2010 5-year est.).
**Income:** Per capita income: $93,072 (2006-2010 5-year est.); Median household income: $146,069 (2006-2010 5-year est.); Average household income: $258,134 (2006-2010 5-year est.); Percent of households with income of $100,000 or more: 64.5% (2006-2010 5-year est.); Poverty rate: 1.3% (2006-2010 5-year est.).
**Taxes:** Total city taxes per capita: $1,450 (2009); City property taxes per capita: $1,193 (2009).
**Education:** Percent of population age 25 and over with: High school diploma (including GED) or higher: 96.3% (2006-2010 5-year est.); Bachelor's degree or higher: 70.4% (2006-2010 5-year est.); Master's degree or higher: 33.0% (2006-2010 5-year est.).

**School District(s)**
Rye City School District (KG-12)
   2009-10 Enrollment: 3,095 . . . . . . . . . . . . . . . . . . . . . . (914) 967-6108
**Housing:** Homeownership rate: 72.7% (2010); Median home value: $1 (2006-2010 5-year est.); Median contract rent: $1,530 per month (2006-2010 5-year est.); Median year structure built: 1949 (2006-2010 5-year est.).

**Hospitals:** Rye Hospital Center (34 beds)
**Transportation:** Commute to work: 57.1% car, 31.3% public transportation, 1.3% walk, 7.8% work from home (2006-2010 5-year est.); Travel time to work: 25.7% less than 15 minutes, 23.4% 15 to 30 minutes, 13.1% 30 to 45 minutes, 10.3% 45 to 60 minutes, 27.5% 60 minutes or more (2006-2010 5-year est.)
**Additional Information Contacts**
City of Rye . . . . . . . . . . . . . . . . . . . . . . . . . . . . . . . . . . (914) 967-5400
  http://www.ryeny.gov

**RYE** (town). Covers a land area of 6.918 square miles and a water area of 0.434 square miles. Located at 41.00° N. Lat; 73.68° W. Long. Elevation is 26 feet.
**Population:** 39,524 (1990); 43,880 (2000); 45,928 (2010); Density: 6,638.2 persons per square mile (2010); Race: 70.2% White, 4.9% Black, 3.3% Asian, 0.7% American Indian/Alaska Native, 0.0% Native Hawaiian/Other Pacific Islander, 20.9% Other, 42.4% Hispanic of any race (2010); Average household size: 2.93 (2010); Median age: 37.2 (2010); Males per 100 females: 102.9 (2010); Marriage status: 32.8% never married, 53.1% now married, 7.0% widowed, 7.1% divorced (2006-2010 5-year est.); Foreign born: 36.1% (2006-2010 5-year est.); Ancestry (includes multiple ancestries): 18.7% Italian, 8.8% American, 6.9% Irish, 4.7% German, 4.1% Polish (2006-2010 5-year est.).
**Economy:** Unemployment rate: 6.9% (February 2012); Total civilian labor force: 23,154 (February 2012); Employment by occupation: 11.7% management, 2.8% professional, 13.0% services, 11.7% sales, 4.4% farming, 10.6% construction, 4.0% production (2006-2010 5-year est.).
**Income:** Per capita income: $39,563 (2006-2010 5-year est.); Median household income: $67,083 (2006-2010 5-year est.); Average household income: $109,772 (2006-2010 5-year est.); Percent of households with income of $100,000 or more: 31.9% (2006-2010 5-year est.); Poverty rate: 11.6% (2006-2010 5-year est.).
**Taxes:** Total city taxes per capita: $56 (2009); City property taxes per capita: $35 (2009).
**Education:** Percent of population age 25 and over with: High school diploma (including GED) or higher: 79.9% (2006-2010 5-year est.); Bachelor's degree or higher: 34.1% (2006-2010 5-year est.); Master's degree or higher: 16.4% (2006-2010 5-year est.).
**School District(s)**
Rye City School District (KG-12)
  2009-10 Enrollment: 3,095 . . . . . . . . . . . . . . . . . . (914) 967-6108
**Housing:** Homeownership rate: 55.5% (2010); Median home value: $572,300 (2006-2010 5-year est.); Median contract rent: $1,237 per month (2006-2010 5-year est.); Median year structure built: 1955 (2006-2010 5-year est.).
**Hospitals:** Rye Hospital Center (34 beds)
**Transportation:** Commute to work: 64.8% car, 18.0% public transportation, 6.8% walk, 2.6% work from home (2006-2010 5-year est.); Travel time to work: 32.2% less than 15 minutes, 33.5% 15 to 30 minutes, 15.5% 30 to 45 minutes, 7.1% 45 to 60 minutes, 11.7% 60 minutes or more (2006-2010 5-year est.)
**Additional Information Contacts**
Town of Rye . . . . . . . . . . . . . . . . . . . . . . . . . . . . . . . . . . (914) 939-3570
  http://www.townofryeny.com

**RYE BROOK** (village). Covers a land area of 3.432 square miles and a water area of 0.031 square miles. Located at 41.03° N. Lat; 73.68° W. Long. Elevation is 249 feet.
**History:** Prior to the village's establishment on July 7, 1982, the area was an unincorporated section of the Town of Rye. The population was 8,602 according to the 2000 census. Rye Brook has been designated as a Tree City USA for 14 years.
**Population:** 7,765 (1990); 8,602 (2000); 9,347 (2010); Density: 2,722.9 persons per square mile (2010); Race: 89.0% White, 1.5% Black, 4.5% Asian, 0.2% American Indian/Alaska Native, 0.0% Native Hawaiian/Other Pacific Islander, 4.8% Other, 11.1% Hispanic of any race (2010); Average household size: 2.67 (2010); Median age: 44.1 (2010); Males per 100 females: 88.4 (2010); Marriage status: 20.6% never married, 64.4% now married, 9.1% widowed, 5.9% divorced (2006-2010 5-year est.); Foreign born: 17.4% (2006-2010 5-year est.); Ancestry (includes multiple ancestries): 24.7% Italian, 10.2% Russian, 9.6% Irish, 8.7% American, 7.8% German (2006-2010 5-year est.).
**Economy:** Single-family building permits issued: 1 (2011); Multi-family building permits issued: 0 (2011); Employment by occupation: 19.1%

management, 4.6% professional, 7.9% services, 13.1% sales, 0.6% farming, 7.3% construction, 1.4% production (2006-2010 5-year est.).
**Income:** Per capita income: $75,753 (2006-2010 5-year est.); Median household income: $122,974 (2006-2010 5-year est.); Average household income: $210,011 (2006-2010 5-year est.); Percent of households with income of $100,000 or more: 58.6% (2006-2010 5-year est.); Poverty rate: 5.9% (2006-2010 5-year est.).
**Education:** Percent of population age 25 and over with: High school diploma (including GED) or higher: 96.2% (2006-2010 5-year est.); Bachelor's degree or higher: 52.1% (2006-2010 5-year est.); Master's degree or higher: 27.4% (2006-2010 5-year est.).
**School District(s)**
Blind Brook-Rye Union Free School District (KG-12)
  2009-10 Enrollment: 1,524 . . . . . . . . . . . . . . . . . . (914) 937-3600
Westchester Boces
  2009-10 Enrollment: n/a . . . . . . . . . . . . . . . . . . . . (914) 937-3820
**Housing:** Homeownership rate: 80.2% (2010); Median home value: $739,700 (2006-2010 5-year est.); Median contract rent: $1,356 per month (2006-2010 5-year est.); Median year structure built: 1964 (2006-2010 5-year est.).
**Safety:** Violent crime rate: 2.1 per 10,000 population; Property crime rate: 96.1 per 10,000 population (2010).
**Transportation:** Commute to work: 72.4% car, 18.8% public transportation, 0.7% walk, 5.6% work from home (2006-2010 5-year est.); Travel time to work: 23.9% less than 15 minutes, 30.4% 15 to 30 minutes, 15.9% 30 to 45 minutes, 10.8% 45 to 60 minutes, 19.1% 60 minutes or more (2006-2010 5-year est.)
**Additional Information Contacts**
Village of Rye Brook . . . . . . . . . . . . . . . . . . . . . . . . . . . (914) 939-1121
  http://www.ryebrook.org

**SCARSDALE** (town and village). Aka Quaker Ridge. Covers a land area of 6.660 square miles and a water area of 0.008 square miles. Located at 40.99° N. Lat; 73.78° W. Long. Elevation is 217 feet.
**History:** Named for the Manor of Scarsdale in England, home of early town resident Caleb Heathcote. Settled c.1701, inc. 1915.
**Population:** 16,987 (1990); 17,823 (2000); 17,166 (2010); Density: 2,577.3 persons per square mile (2010); Race: 82.7% White, 1.5% Black, 13.0% Asian, 0.0% American Indian/Alaska Native, 0.0% Native Hawaiian/Other Pacific Islander, 2.8% Other, 3.9% Hispanic of any race (2010); Average household size: 3.16 (2010); Median age: 42.0 (2010); Males per 100 females: 95.1 (2010); Marriage status: 18.7% never married, 73.9% now married, 4.0% widowed, 3.4% divorced (2006-2010 5-year est.); Foreign born: 19.7% (2006-2010 5-year est.); Ancestry (includes multiple ancestries): 17.1% Russian, 10.4% German, 10.0% Irish, 9.7% Italian, 9.6% Polish (2006-2010 5-year est.).
**Economy:** Single-family building permits issued: 30 (2011); Multi-family building permits issued: 0 (2011); Employment by occupation: 27.3% management, 2.8% professional, 2.6% services, 8.6% sales, 0.8% farming, 1.1% construction, 0.7% production (2006-2010 5-year est.).
**Income:** Per capita income: $112,323 (2006-2010 5-year est.); Median household income: $237,135 (2006-2010 5-year est.); Average household income: $360,584 (2006-2010 5-year est.); Percent of households with income of $100,000 or more: 84.6% (2006-2010 5-year est.); Poverty rate: 2.1% (2006-2010 5-year est.).
**Education:** Percent of population age 25 and over with: High school diploma (including GED) or higher: 98.3% (2006-2010 5-year est.); Bachelor's degree or higher: 85.1% (2006-2010 5-year est.); Master's degree or higher: 56.5% (2006-2010 5-year est.).
**School District(s)**
Eastchester Union Free School District (KG-12)
  2009-10 Enrollment: 3,114 . . . . . . . . . . . . . . . . . . (914) 793-6130
Edgemont Union Free School District (KG-12)
  2009-10 Enrollment: 1,940 . . . . . . . . . . . . . . . . . . (914) 472-7768
Scarsdale Union Free School District (KG-12)
  2009-10 Enrollment: 4,718 . . . . . . . . . . . . . . . . . . (914) 721-2410
**Housing:** Homeownership rate: 91.3% (2010); Median home value: $1 (2006-2010 5-year est.); Median contract rent: n/a per month (2006-2010 5-year est.); Median year structure built: 1941 (2006-2010 5-year est.).
**Safety:** Violent crime rate: 2.9 per 10,000 population; Property crime rate: 122.6 per 10,000 population (2010).
**Newspapers:** Scarsdale Inquirer (Community news; Circulation 7,000)
**Transportation:** Commute to work: 52.9% car, 33.6% public transportation, 0.5% walk, 11.7% work from home (2006-2010 5-year est.); Travel time to work: 16.7% less than 15 minutes, 19.4% 15 to 30 minutes,

18.2% 30 to 45 minutes, 18.4% 45 to 60 minutes, 27.4% 60 minutes or more (2006-2010 5-year est.).
**Additional Information Contacts**
Scarsdale Chamber of Commerce.....................(914) 620-2426
  http://www.scarsdalechamber.org
Village of Scarsdale...............................(914) 722-1175
  http://www.scarsdale.com

## SCOTTS CORNERS (CDP). Covers a land area of 1.773 square miles and a water area of 0 square miles. Located at 41.18° N. Lat; 73.55° W. Long. Elevation is 397 feet.
**Population:** 659 (1990); 624 (2000); 711 (2010); Density: 401.0 persons per square mile (2010); Race: 95.8% White, 1.1% Black, 1.0% Asian, 0.0% American Indian/Alaska Native, 0.0% Native Hawaiian/Other Pacific Islander, 2.1% Other, 6.2% Hispanic of any race (2010); Average household size: 2.65 (2010); Median age: 46.6 (2010); Males per 100 females: 95.9 (2010); Marriage status: 20.0% never married, 73.3% now married, 1.9% widowed, 4.7% divorced (2006-2010 5-year est.); Foreign born: 4.6% (2006-2010 5-year est.); Ancestry (includes multiple ancestries): 40.8% Italian, 20.3% Russian, 14.5% English, 14.3% Polish, 10.1% Irish (2006-2010 5-year est.).
**Economy:** Employment by occupation: 24.5% management, 3.8% professional, 0.0% services, 15.9% sales, 8.3% farming, 0.0% construction, 0.0% production (2006-2010 5-year est.).
**Income:** Per capita income: $113,049 (2006-2010 5-year est.); Median household income: $166,875 (2006-2010 5-year est.); Average household income: $257,867 (2006-2010 5-year est.); Percent of households with income of $100,000 or more: 71.0% (2006-2010 5-year est.); Poverty rate: 0.0% (2006-2010 5-year est.).
**Education:** Percent of population age 25 and over with: High school diploma (including GED) or higher: 100.0% (2006-2010 5-year est.); Bachelor's degree or higher: 60.2% (2006-2010 5-year est.); Master's degree or higher: 34.4% (2006-2010 5-year est.).
**Housing:** Homeownership rate: 80.4% (2010); Median home value: $815,500 (2006-2010 5-year est.); Median contract rent: $1,205 per month (2006-2010 5-year est.); Median year structure built: 1966 (2006-2010 5-year est.).
**Transportation:** Commute to work: 77.4% car, 7.2% public transportation, 7.5% walk, 7.9% work from home (2006-2010 5-year est.); Travel time to work: 4.5% less than 15 minutes, 19.3% 15 to 30 minutes, 32.8% 30 to 45 minutes, 3.7% 45 to 60 minutes, 39.8% 60 minutes or more (2006-2010 5-year est.).

## SHENOROCK (CDP). Aka Lake Shenorock. Covers a land area of 0.699 square miles and a water area of 0.029 square miles. Located at 41.33° N. Lat; 73.74° W. Long. Elevation is 509 feet.
**Population:** 1,848 (1990); 1,887 (2000); 1,898 (2010); Density: 2,711.9 persons per square mile (2010); Race: 93.2% White, 0.7% Black, 2.4% Asian, 0.4% American Indian/Alaska Native, 0.0% Native Hawaiian/Other Pacific Islander, 3.3% Other, 7.4% Hispanic of any race (2010); Average household size: 2.82 (2010); Median age: 41.0 (2010); Males per 100 females: 94.9 (2010); Marriage status: 14.5% never married, 65.6% now married, 11.1% widowed, 8.8% divorced (2006-2010 5-year est.); Foreign born: 8.9% (2006-2010 5-year est.); Ancestry (includes multiple ancestries): 37.5% Italian, 23.6% Irish, 20.3% German, 8.3% Russian, 3.8% English (2006-2010 5-year est.).
**Economy:** Employment by occupation: 17.1% management, 10.6% professional, 0.8% services, 23.3% sales, 3.4% farming, 4.5% construction, 2.7% production (2006-2010 5-year est.).
**Income:** Per capita income: $41,090 (2006-2010 5-year est.); Median household income: $76,563 (2006-2010 5-year est.); Average household income: $112,083 (2006-2010 5-year est.); Percent of households with income of $100,000 or more: 39.2% (2006-2010 5-year est.); Poverty rate: 0.5% (2006-2010 5-year est.).
**Education:** Percent of population age 25 and over with: High school diploma (including GED) or higher: 98.2% (2006-2010 5-year est.); Bachelor's degree or higher: 40.7% (2006-2010 5-year est.); Master's degree or higher: 13.2% (2006-2010 5-year est.).
**Housing:** Homeownership rate: 92.8% (2010); Median home value: $405,100 (2006-2010 5-year est.); Median contract rent: n/a per month (2006-2010 5-year est.); Median year structure built: 1954 (2006-2010 5-year est.).
**Transportation:** Commute to work: 84.3% car, 8.5% public transportation, 1.3% walk, 5.9% work from home (2006-2010 5-year est.); Travel time to work: 11.8% less than 15 minutes, 34.8% 15 to 30 minutes, 25.6% 30 to 45

minutes, 10.0% 45 to 60 minutes, 17.8% 60 minutes or more (2006-2010 5-year est.).

## SHRUB OAK (CDP). Covers a land area of 1.580 square miles and a water area of 0.026 square miles. Located at 41.32° N. Lat; 73.82° W. Long. Elevation is 440 feet.
**Population:** 1,727 (1990); 1,812 (2000); 2,011 (2010); Density: 1,272.5 persons per square mile (2010); Race: 89.0% White, 3.4% Black, 3.1% Asian, 0.0% American Indian/Alaska Native, 0.0% Native Hawaiian/Other Pacific Islander, 4.5% Other, 10.9% Hispanic of any race (2010); Average household size: 2.64 (2010); Median age: 43.8 (2010); Males per 100 females: 89.2 (2010); Marriage status: 25.8% never married, 51.8% now married, 11.3% widowed, 11.1% divorced (2006-2010 5-year est.); Foreign born: 21.8% (2006-2010 5-year est.); Ancestry (includes multiple ancestries): 28.2% Italian, 16.4% Irish, 14.0% German, 7.4% Albanian, 6.1% Danish (2006-2010 5-year est.).
**Economy:** Employment by occupation: 19.5% management, 0.0% professional, 0.0% services, 15.1% sales, 1.4% farming, 6.7% construction, 4.5% production (2006-2010 5-year est.).
**Income:** Per capita income: $37,350 (2006-2010 5-year est.); Median household income: $93,021 (2006-2010 5-year est.); Average household income: $96,401 (2006-2010 5-year est.); Percent of households with income of $100,000 or more: 48.5% (2006-2010 5-year est.); Poverty rate: 3.3% (2006-2010 5-year est.).
**Education:** Percent of population age 25 and over with: High school diploma (including GED) or higher: 90.8% (2006-2010 5-year est.); Bachelor's degree or higher: 40.3% (2006-2010 5-year est.); Master's degree or higher: 15.3% (2006-2010 5-year est.).
**School District(s)**
Lakeland Central School District (PK-12)
  2009-10 Enrollment: 6,439 ..................(914) 245-1700
**Housing:** Homeownership rate: 74.3% (2010); Median home value: $395,800 (2006-2010 5-year est.); Median contract rent: $789 per month (2006-2010 5-year est.); Median year structure built: 1969 (2006-2010 5-year est.).
**Transportation:** Commute to work: 94.6% car, 1.4% public transportation, 1.6% walk, 2.3% work from home (2006-2010 5-year est.); Travel time to work: 17.6% less than 15 minutes, 25.7% 15 to 30 minutes, 34.0% 30 to 45 minutes, 14.2% 45 to 60 minutes, 8.5% 60 minutes or more (2006-2010 5-year est.).

## SLEEPY HOLLOW (village). Aka North Tarrytown. Covers a land area of 2.160 square miles and a water area of 2.918 square miles. Located at 41.09° N. Lat; 73.86° W. Long. Elevation is 89 feet.
**Population:** 8,152 (1990); 9,212 (2000); 9,870 (2010); Density: 4,568.0 persons per square mile (2010); Race: 61.0% White, 6.2% Black, 3.3% Asian, 0.8% American Indian/Alaska Native, 0.0% Native Hawaiian/Other Pacific Islander, 28.7% Other, 51.0% Hispanic of any race (2010); Average household size: 2.83 (2010); Median age: 36.7 (2010); Males per 100 females: 94.2 (2010); Marriage status: 35.3% never married, 53.8% now married, 3.2% widowed, 7.7% divorced (2006-2010 5-year est.); Foreign born: 45.4% (2006-2010 5-year est.); Ancestry (includes multiple ancestries): 11.2% Italian, 9.5% Irish, 5.7% German, 3.3% Portuguese, 3.0% English (2006-2010 5-year est.).
**Economy:** Single-family building permits issued: 1 (2011); Multi-family building permits issued: 0 (2011); Employment by occupation: 10.1% management, 4.6% professional, 14.5% services, 11.4% sales, 5.0% farming, 13.0% construction, 5.9% production (2006-2010 5-year est.).
**Income:** Per capita income: $35,455 (2006-2010 5-year est.); Median household income: $69,015 (2006-2010 5-year est.); Average household income: $104,671 (2006-2010 5-year est.); Percent of households with income of $100,000 or more: 30.2% (2006-2010 5-year est.); Poverty rate: 12.4% (2006-2010 5-year est.).
**Education:** Percent of population age 25 and over with: High school diploma (including GED) or higher: 75.6% (2006-2010 5-year est.); Bachelor's degree or higher: 36.0% (2006-2010 5-year est.); Master's degree or higher: 17.9% (2006-2010 5-year est.).
**School District(s)**
Pocantico Hills Central School District (PK-08)
  2009-10 Enrollment: 290 .....................(914) 631-2440
Union Free School District of the Tarrytowns (PK-12)
  2009-10 Enrollment: 2,653 ...................(914) 631-9404
**Housing:** Homeownership rate: 34.2% (2010); Median home value: $692,400 (2006-2010 5-year est.); Median contract rent: $1,155 per month

(2006-2010 5-year est.); Median year structure built: before 1940 (2006-2010 5-year est.).
**Hospitals:** Phelps Memorial Hospital Center (235 beds)
**Safety:** Violent crime rate: 10.8 per 10,000 population; Property crime rate: 99.9 per 10,000 population (2010).
**Transportation:** Commute to work: 64.7% car, 19.1% public transportation, 10.6% walk, 3.0% work from home (2006-2010 5-year est.); Travel time to work: 24.1% less than 15 minutes, 30.0% 15 to 30 minutes, 23.3% 30 to 45 minutes, 11.3% 45 to 60 minutes, 11.2% 60 minutes or more (2006-2010 5-year est.)
**Additional Information Contacts**
Sleepy Hollow Tarrytown Chamber of Commerce. . . . . . . . . (914) 631-1705
http://www.sleepyhollowchamber.com

## SOMERS (town).

Covers a land area of 29.641 square miles and a water area of 2.518 square miles. Located at 41.30° N. Lat; 73.72° W. Long. Elevation is 279 feet.
**History:** Formerly a rural, summer lake community. Early Dutch settlement, it was incorporated 1778 as Stephentown. Renamed Somerstown for US naval hero Captain Richard Somers.
**Population:** 16,216 (1990); 18,346 (2000); 20,434 (2010); Density: 689.4 persons per square mile (2010); Race: 92.9% White, 1.6% Black, 3.2% Asian, 0.1% American Indian/Alaska Native, 0.1% Native Hawaiian/Other Pacific Islander, 2.1% Other, 4.9% Hispanic of any race (2010); Average household size: 2.61 (2010); Median age: 46.6 (2010); Males per 100 females: 91.0 (2010); Marriage status: 17.1% never married, 68.1% now married, 8.4% widowed, 6.4% divorced (2006-2010 5-year est.); Foreign born: 9.8% (2006-2010 5-year est.); Ancestry (includes multiple ancestries): 34.5% Italian, 22.8% Irish, 12.3% German, 5.8% Polish, 5.4% English (2006-2010 5-year est.).
**Economy:** Single-family building permits issued: 0 (2011); Multi-family building permits issued: 0 (2011); Employment by occupation: 23.9% management, 5.1% professional, 1.8% services, 17.1% sales, 2.7% farming, 7.1% construction, 2.9% production (2006-2010 5-year est.).
**Income:** Per capita income: $55,441 (2006-2010 5-year est.); Median household income: $113,025 (2006-2010 5-year est.); Average household income: $146,180 (2006-2010 5-year est.); Percent of households with income of $100,000 or more: 56.9% (2006-2010 5-year est.); Poverty rate: 1.4% (2006-2010 5-year est.).
**Taxes:** Total city taxes per capita: $390 (2009); City property taxes per capita: $307 (2009).
**Education:** Percent of population age 25 and over with: High school diploma (including GED) or higher: 96.2% (2006-2010 5-year est.); Bachelor's degree or higher: 51.0% (2006-2010 5-year est.); Master's degree or higher: 23.4% (2006-2010 5-year est.).
### School District(s)
Somers Central School District (KG-12)
    2009-10 Enrollment: 3,422 . . . . . . . . . . . . . . . . . . . . . (914) 277-2400
**Housing:** Homeownership rate: 93.1% (2010); Median home value: $556,700 (2006-2010 5-year est.); Median contract rent: $1,862 per month (2006-2010 5-year est.); Median year structure built: 1980 (2006-2010 5-year est.).
**Transportation:** Commute to work: 84.4% car, 8.9% public transportation, 0.9% walk, 5.0% work from home (2006-2010 5-year est.); Travel time to work: 17.6% less than 15 minutes, 26.5% 15 to 30 minutes, 25.9% 30 to 45 minutes, 10.1% 45 to 60 minutes, 19.8% 60 minutes or more (2006-2010 5-year est.)
**Additional Information Contacts**
Town of Somers. . . . . . . . . . . . . . . . . . . . . . . . . . . . . . . . (914) 277-3323
http://www.somersny.com

## SOUTH SALEM (unincorporated postal area)

Zip Code: 10590
    Covers a land area of 13.496 square miles and a water area of 0.520 square miles. Located at 41.25° N. Lat; 73.53° W. Long. Elevation is 541 feet. Population: 6,767 (2010); Density: 501.4 persons per square mile (2010); Race: 93.9% White, 1.1% Black, 2.3% Asian, 0.1% American Indian/Alaska Native, 0.0% Native Hawaiian/Other Pacific Islander, 2.6% Other, 4.8% Hispanic of any race (2010); Average household size: 2.76 (2010); Median age: 44.7 (2010); Males per 100 females: 98.2 (2010); Homeownership rate: 91.1% (2010)

## TARRYTOWN (village).

Covers a land area of 2.926 square miles and a water area of 2.752 square miles. Located at 41.06° N. Lat; 73.86° W. Long. Elevation is 121 feet.
**History:** Named for a variation of the Dutch translation of "wheat". Of interest are Sunnyside, the home of Washington Irving; Sleepy Hollow cemetery, where Irving is buried; Philipsburg Manor, an estate; and Lyndhurst (1838), a Gothic Revival mansion. Philipsburg Manor, an early trading center complex northwest of village center, includes a Dutch farmhouse (c.1683) and a restored operating gristmill. Settled in the 17th century by Dutch. Incorporated 1870.
**Population:** 10,739 (1990); 11,090 (2000); 11,277 (2010); Density: 3,853.6 persons per square mile (2010); Race: 74.7% White, 7.8% Black, 8.0% Asian, 0.3% American Indian/Alaska Native, 0.0% Native Hawaiian/Other Pacific Islander, 9.2% Other, 20.0% Hispanic of any race (2010); Average household size: 2.36 (2010); Median age: 39.3 (2010); Males per 100 females: 87.7 (2010); Marriage status: 39.3% never married, 46.4% now married, 5.2% widowed, 9.1% divorced (2006-2010 5-year est.); Foreign born: 28.8% (2006-2010 5-year est.); Ancestry (includes multiple ancestries): 19.2% Italian, 17.2% Irish, 9.8% German, 6.0% English, 4.7% Polish (2006-2010 5-year est.).
**Economy:** Single-family building permits issued: 5 (2011); Multi-family building permits issued: 0 (2011); Employment by occupation: 17.4% management, 7.4% professional, 8.0% services, 14.9% sales, 1.0% farming, 2.6% construction, 0.9% production (2006-2010 5-year est.).
**Income:** Per capita income: $46,908 (2006-2010 5-year est.); Median household income: $80,683 (2006-2010 5-year est.); Average household income: $117,721 (2006-2010 5-year est.); Percent of households with income of $100,000 or more: 41.6% (2006-2010 5-year est.); Poverty rate: 5.8% (2006-2010 5-year est.).
**Taxes:** Total city taxes per capita: $1,311 (2009); City property taxes per capita: $1,238 (2009).
**Education:** Percent of population age 25 and over with: High school diploma (including GED) or higher: 93.4% (2006-2010 5-year est.); Bachelor's degree or higher: 58.3% (2006-2010 5-year est.); Master's degree or higher: 29.4% (2006-2010 5-year est.).
### School District(s)
Union Free School District of the Tarrytowns (PK-12)
    2009-10 Enrollment: 2,653 . . . . . . . . . . . . . . . . . . . . . (914) 631-9404
**Housing:** Homeownership rate: 56.6% (2010); Median home value: $556,800 (2006-2010 5-year est.); Median contract rent: $1,232 per month (2006-2010 5-year est.); Median year structure built: 1953 (2006-2010 5-year est.).
**Safety:** Violent crime rate: 6.3 per 10,000 population; Property crime rate: 72.4 per 10,000 population (2010).
**Transportation:** Commute to work: 63.5% car, 18.9% public transportation, 7.8% walk, 8.0% work from home (2006-2010 5-year est.); Travel time to work: 31.5% less than 15 minutes, 30.7% 15 to 30 minutes, 12.4% 30 to 45 minutes, 8.0% 45 to 60 minutes, 17.4% 60 minutes or more (2006-2010 5-year est.)
**Additional Information Contacts**
Sleepy Hollow Tarrytown Chamber of Commerce. . . . . . . . . (914) 631-1705
http://www.sleepyhollowchamber.com

## THORNWOOD (CDP).

Covers a land area of 1.107 square miles and a water area of 0 square miles. Located at 41.11° N. Lat; 73.77° W. Long. Elevation is 269 feet.
**History:** Thornwood once had a large and thriving marble quarry near its heart, the intersection of Route 141 and Kensico Road (known as Four Corners). The quarry pit was filled in the mid 1980s and the Town Center shopping center constructed over it.
**Population:** 5,635 (1990); 5,980 (2000); 3,759 (2010); Density: 3,395.2 persons per square mile (2010); Race: 89.5% White, 1.2% Black, 3.4% Asian, 0.1% American Indian/Alaska Native, 0.0% Native Hawaiian/Other Pacific Islander, 5.8% Other, 10.2% Hispanic of any race (2010); Average household size: 2.85 (2010); Median age: 42.7 (2010); Males per 100 females: 98.7 (2010); Marriage status: 27.2% never married, 56.6% now married, 7.2% widowed, 8.9% divorced (2006-2010 5-year est.); Foreign born: 21.0% (2006-2010 5-year est.); Ancestry (includes multiple ancestries): 40.4% Italian, 14.6% Irish, 6.8% German, 5.5% American, 1.9% English (2006-2010 5-year est.).
**Economy:** Employment by occupation: 14.9% management, 0.9% professional, 15.3% services, 23.4% sales, 2.9% farming, 1.1% construction, 4.6% production (2006-2010 5-year est.).
**Income:** Per capita income: $36,777 (2006-2010 5-year est.); Median household income: $88,558 (2006-2010 5-year est.); Average household

income: $112,254 (2006-2010 5-year est.); Percent of households with income of $100,000 or more: 39.5% (2006-2010 5-year est.); Poverty rate: 3.4% (2006-2010 5-year est.).

**Education:** Percent of population age 25 and over with: High school diploma (including GED) or higher: 93.8% (2006-2010 5-year est.); Bachelor's degree or higher: 34.6% (2006-2010 5-year est.); Master's degree or higher: 9.8% (2006-2010 5-year est.).

**School District(s)**

Mount Pleasant Central School District (KG-12)

2009-10 Enrollment: 1,977 . . . . . . . . . . . . . . . . . . . . . . . (914) 769-5500

**Housing:** Homeownership rate: 77.5% (2010); Median home value: $593,100 (2006-2010 5-year est.); Median contract rent: $1,344 per month (2006-2010 5-year est.); Median year structure built: 1956 (2006-2010 5-year est.).

**Transportation:** Commute to work: 79.4% car, 4.0% public transportation, 15.3% walk, 1.3% work from home (2006-2010 5-year est.); Travel time to work: 36.6% less than 15 minutes, 33.7% 15 to 30 minutes, 18.8% 30 to 45 minutes, 4.1% 45 to 60 minutes, 6.7% 60 minutes or more (2006-2010 5-year est.)

## TUCKAHOE (village).
Covers a land area of 0.597 square miles and a water area of 0 square miles. Located at 40.95° N. Lat; 73.82° W. Long. Elevation is 112 feet.

**History:** Settled 1684; incorporated 1903.

**Population:** 6,302 (1990); 6,211 (2000); 6,486 (2010); Density: 10,854.3 persons per square mile (2010); Race: 74.5% White, 11.0% Black, 8.3% Asian, 0.1% American Indian/Alaska Native, 0.0% Native Hawaiian/Other Pacific Islander, 6.1% Other, 12.1% Hispanic of any race (2010); Average household size: 2.27 (2010); Median age: 40.0 (2010); Males per 100 females: 86.6 (2010); Marriage status: 35.8% never married, 49.7% now married, 7.7% widowed, 6.8% divorced (2006-2010 5-year est.); Foreign born: 19.3% (2006-2010 5-year est.); Ancestry (includes multiple ancestries): 26.9% Italian, 18.8% Irish, 10.8% German, 5.8% English, 2.0% Polish (2006-2010 5-year est.).

**Economy:** Single-family building permits issued: 1 (2011); Multi-family building permits issued: 2 (2011); Employment by occupation: 19.7% management, 3.2% professional, 6.3% services, 18.4% sales, 2.3% farming, 10.5% construction, 7.0% production (2006-2010 5-year est.).

**Income:** Per capita income: $42,884 (2006-2010 5-year est.); Median household income: $81,341 (2006-2010 5-year est.); Average household income: $102,506 (2006-2010 5-year est.); Percent of households with income of $100,000 or more: 37.0% (2006-2010 5-year est.); Poverty rate: 6.1% (2006-2010 5-year est.).

**Taxes:** Total city taxes per capita: $1,095 (2009); City property taxes per capita: $987 (2009).

**Education:** Percent of population age 25 and over with: High school diploma (including GED) or higher: 95.0% (2006-2010 5-year est.); Bachelor's degree or higher: 43.4% (2006-2010 5-year est.); Master's degree or higher: 20.6% (2006-2010 5-year est.).

**Housing:** Homeownership rate: 48.2% (2010); Median home value: $564,800 (2006-2010 5-year est.); Median contract rent: $1,222 per month (2006-2010 5-year est.); Median year structure built: 1953 (2006-2010 5-year est.).

**Safety:** Violent crime rate: 6.5 per 10,000 population; Property crime rate: 12.9 per 10,000 population (2010).

**Transportation:** Commute to work: 62.7% car, 23.4% public transportation, 10.0% walk, 3.9% work from home (2006-2010 5-year est.); Travel time to work: 23.7% less than 15 minutes, 27.7% 15 to 30 minutes, 12.7% 30 to 45 minutes, 10.3% 45 to 60 minutes, 25.6% 60 minutes or more (2006-2010 5-year est.)

**Additional Information Contacts**

Village of Tuckahoe . . . . . . . . . . . . . . . . . . . . . . . . . . (914) 961-3100
http://www.tuckahoe.com

## VALHALLA (CDP).
Covers a land area of 0.829 square miles and a water area of 0 square miles. Located at 41.07° N. Lat; 73.77° W. Long. Elevation is 256 feet.

**Population:** 5,167 (1990); 5,379 (2000); 3,162 (2010); Density: 3,809.7 persons per square mile (2010); Race: 86.0% White, 1.3% Black, 6.3% Asian, 0.1% American Indian/Alaska Native, 0.0% Native Hawaiian/Other Pacific Islander, 6.3% Other, 10.1% Hispanic of any race (2010); Average household size: 2.73 (2010); Median age: 41.5 (2010); Males per 100 females: 94.1 (2010); Marriage status: 26.4% never married, 57.9% now married, 3.6% widowed, 12.1% divorced (2006-2010 5-year est.); Foreign born: 21.0% (2006-2010 5-year est.); Ancestry (includes multiple

ancestries): 29.0% Italian, 18.0% Irish, 7.3% German, 4.8% American, 4.7% English (2006-2010 5-year est.).

**Economy:** Employment by occupation: 21.6% management, 9.2% professional, 4.5% services, 10.5% sales, 7.3% farming, 7.6% construction, 1.9% production (2006-2010 5-year est.).

**Income:** Per capita income: $41,676 (2006-2010 5-year est.); Median household income: $97,220 (2006-2010 5-year est.); Average household income: $108,660 (2006-2010 5-year est.); Percent of households with income of $100,000 or more: 46.0% (2006-2010 5-year est.); Poverty rate: 1.3% (2006-2010 5-year est.).

**Education:** Percent of population age 25 and over with: High school diploma (including GED) or higher: 98.2% (2006-2010 5-year est.); Bachelor's degree or higher: 43.5% (2006-2010 5-year est.); Master's degree or higher: 21.3% (2006-2010 5-year est.).

**School District(s)**

Greenburgh-North Castle Union Free School District (07-12)

2009-10 Enrollment: 354 . . . . . . . . . . . . . . . . . . . . . . (914) 693-4309

Mount Pleasant-Blythedale Union Free School Distri (KG-12)

2009-10 Enrollment: 115 . . . . . . . . . . . . . . . . . . . . . . (914) 347-1800

Valhalla Union Free School District (KG-12)

2009-10 Enrollment: 1,519 . . . . . . . . . . . . . . . . . . . . (914) 683-5040

**Four-year College(s)**

New York Medical College (Private, Not-for-profit, Jewish)

Fall 2010 Enrollment: 1,356 . . . . . . . . . . . . . . . . . . . (914) 594-4000

**Two-year College(s)**

SUNY Westchester Community College (Public)

Fall 2010 Enrollment: 10,323 . . . . . . . . . . . . . . . . . . (914) 606-6600

2011-12 Tuition: In-state $4,513; Out-of-state $12,813

**Housing:** Homeownership rate: 77.1% (2010); Median home value: $590,500 (2006-2010 5-year est.); Median contract rent: $1,529 per month (2006-2010 5-year est.); Median year structure built: 1953 (2006-2010 5-year est.).

**Hospitals:** Blythedale Childrens Hospital (92 beds); Westchester Medical Center (635 beds)

**Transportation:** Commute to work: 78.6% car, 14.4% public transportation, 1.2% walk, 5.8% work from home (2006-2010 5-year est.); Travel time to work: 28.5% less than 15 minutes, 27.9% 15 to 30 minutes, 27.3% 30 to 45 minutes, 7.1% 45 to 60 minutes, 9.1% 60 minutes or more (2006-2010 5-year est.)

## VERPLANCK (CDP).
Covers a land area of 0.622 square miles and a water area of 0.104 square miles. Located at 41.25° N. Lat; 73.95° W. Long. Elevation is 59 feet.

**Population:** 1,088 (1990); 777 (2000); 1,729 (2010); Density: 2,778.4 persons per square mile (2010); Race: 89.4% White, 1.4% Black, 1.9% Asian, 0.2% American Indian/Alaska Native, 0.0% Native Hawaiian/Other Pacific Islander, 7.1% Other, 14.1% Hispanic of any race (2010); Average household size: 2.53 (2010); Median age: 41.0 (2010); Males per 100 females: 92.1 (2010); Marriage status: 22.0% never married, 42.3% now married, 17.8% widowed, 18.0% divorced (2006-2010 5-year est.); Foreign born: 15.1% (2006-2010 5-year est.); Ancestry (includes multiple ancestries): 35.5% Irish, 16.4% Italian, 10.0% French, 9.8% German, 6.4% Polish (2006-2010 5-year est.).

**Economy:** Employment by occupation: 17.0% management, 14.3% professional, 9.7% services, 7.7% sales, 9.7% farming, 17.8% construction, 3.5% production (2006-2010 5-year est.).

**Income:** Per capita income: $32,207 (2006-2010 5-year est.); Median household income: $60,000 (2006-2010 5-year est.); Average household income: $60,131 (2006-2010 5-year est.); Percent of households with income of $100,000 or more: 14.8% (2006-2010 5-year est.); Poverty rate: 3.6% (2006-2010 5-year est.).

**Education:** Percent of population age 25 and over with: High school diploma (including GED) or higher: 86.3% (2006-2010 5-year est.); Bachelor's degree or higher: 27.2% (2006-2010 5-year est.); Master's degree or higher: 14.7% (2006-2010 5-year est.).

**Housing:** Homeownership rate: 60.0% (2010); Median home value: $362,400 (2006-2010 5-year est.); Median contract rent: $950 per month (2006-2010 5-year est.); Median year structure built: before 1940 (2006-2010 5-year est.).

**Transportation:** Commute to work: 92.3% car, 0.0% public transportation, 0.0% walk, 0.0% work from home (2006-2010 5-year est.); Travel time to work: 23.9% less than 15 minutes, 31.7% 15 to 30 minutes, 44.4% 30 to 45 minutes, 0.0% 45 to 60 minutes, 0.0% 60 minutes or more (2006-2010 5-year est.)

## WACCABUC (unincorporated postal area)

Zip Code: 10597

Covers a land area of 3.338 square miles and a water area of 0.249 square miles. Located at 41.29° N. Lat; 73.59° W. Long. Elevation is 554 feet. Population: 968 (2010); Density: 289.9 persons per square mile (2010); Race: 97.4% White, 0.4% Black, 1.3% Asian, 0.1% American Indian/Alaska Native, 0.0% Native Hawaiian/Other Pacific Islander, 0.8% Other, 3.2% Hispanic of any race (2010); Average household size: 2.97 (2010); Median age: 46.9 (2010); Males per 100 females: 100.4 (2010); Homeownership rate: 93.0% (2010)

## WEST HARRISON (unincorporated postal area)

Zip Code: 10604

Covers a land area of 6.813 square miles and a water area of 1.252 square miles. Located at 41.06° N. Lat; 73.74° W. Long. Population: 11,250 (2010); Density: 1,651.2 persons per square mile (2010); Race: 77.1% White, 6.8% Black, 4.8% Asian, 0.3% American Indian/Alaska Native, 0.1% Native Hawaiian/Other Pacific Islander, 10.9% Other, 23.2% Hispanic of any race (2010); Average household size: 2.79 (2010); Median age: 39.5 (2010); Males per 100 females: 92.0 (2010); Homeownership rate: 57.4% (2010)

## WHITE PLAINS (city). County seat. Covers a land area of 9.767 square miles and a water area of 0.117 square miles. Located at 41.02° N. Lat; 73.75° W. Long. Elevation is 213 feet.

History: Named for the Weckquaeskeck word "quaropas," meaning "white marshes or plains". Settled by Puritans in 1683. The state convention that ratified the Declaration of Independence met (1776) here. The battle of White Plains (1776), a principal engagement of the American Revolution occurred here. Gen. George Washington briefly made his headquarters here at Elijah Miller House, which still stands. Other buildings from the revolutionary period are also preserved. Incorporated as a village 1866 (originally named Quarrapas by Siwanoy people), as a city 1916.

Population: 48,615 (1990); 53,077 (2000); 56,853 (2010); Density: 5,820.5 persons per square mile (2010); Race: 63.6% White, 14.2% Black, 6.4% Asian, 0.7% American Indian/Alaska Native, 0.0% Native Hawaiian/Other Pacific Islander, 15.1% Other, 29.6% Hispanic of any race (2010); Average household size: 2.40 (2010); Median age: 39.2 (2010); Males per 100 females: 92.7 (2010); Marriage status: 34.5% never married, 49.1% now married, 7.0% widowed, 9.3% divorced (2006-2010 5-year est.); Foreign born: 29.9% (2006-2010 5-year est.); Ancestry (includes multiple ancestries): 16.3% Italian, 10.1% Irish, 5.9% German, 4.9% American, 4.1% Russian (2006-2010 5-year est.).

Economy: Unemployment rate: 6.5% (February 2012); Total civilian labor force: 29,397 (February 2012); Single-family building permits issued: 9 (2011); Multi-family building permits issued: 4 (2011); Employment by occupation: 16.8% management, 5.2% professional, 11.9% services, 13.1% sales, 2.7% farming, 5.6% construction, 2.4% production (2006-2010 5-year est.).

Income: Per capita income: $43,938 (2006-2010 5-year est.); Median household income: $73,522 (2006-2010 5-year est.); Average household income: $105,025 (2006-2010 5-year est.); Percent of households with income of $100,000 or more: 36.4% (2006-2010 5-year est.); Poverty rate: 8.9% (2006-2010 5-year est.).

Taxes: Total city taxes per capita: $1,663 (2009); City property taxes per capita: $741 (2009).

Education: Percent of population age 25 and over with: High school diploma (including GED) or higher: 87.2% (2006-2010 5-year est.); Bachelor's degree or higher: 46.7% (2006-2010 5-year est.); Master's degree or higher: 23.7% (2006-2010 5-year est.).

### School District(s)

Academic Leadership Charter School (KG-01)
    2009-10 Enrollment: 117 . . . . . . . . . . . . . . . . . . . . . . . . . . . . (917) 687-0949
Greenburgh Central School District (PK-12)
    2009-10 Enrollment: 1,786 . . . . . . . . . . . . . . . . . . . . . . . . (914) 761-6000
Valhalla Union Free School District (KG-12)
    2009-10 Enrollment: 1,519 . . . . . . . . . . . . . . . . . . . . . . . . (914) 683-5040
White Plains City School District (PK-12)
    2009-10 Enrollment: 7,104 . . . . . . . . . . . . . . . . . . . . . . . . (914) 422-2019

### Four-year College(s)

The College of Westchester (Private, For-profit)
    Fall 2010 Enrollment: 1,972 . . . . . . . . . . . . . . . . . . . . . . (914) 948-4442
    2011-12 Tuition: In-state $20,070; Out-of-state $20,070

### Two-year College(s)

Sanford-Brown Institute-White Plains (Private, For-profit)
    Fall 2010 Enrollment: 830 . . . . . . . . . . . . . . . . . . . . . . . . (914) 874-2500

Housing: Homeownership rate: 53.8% (2010); Median home value: $510,400 (2006-2010 5-year est.); Median contract rent: $1,156 per month (2006-2010 5-year est.); Median year structure built: 1956 (2006-2010 5-year est.).

Hospitals: Burke Rehabilitation Hospital (150 beds); White Plains Hospital Center (292 beds)

Safety: Violent crime rate: 19.2 per 10,000 population; Property crime rate: 191.1 per 10,000 population (2010).

Newspapers: 60 Plus (Local news); El Aguila del Hudson Valley (Local news; Circulation 30,000); The Journal News - Northern Westchester Edition (Regional news); The Journal News (Local news; Circulation 146,187); Sound Shore Review (Local news; Circulation 10,000); The Star (Community news; Circulation 2,100); Suburban Street News (Local news; Circulation 27,000); White Plains Times (Local news; Circulation 27,000)

Transportation: Commute to work: 60.9% car, 20.5% public transportation, 9.7% walk, 6.5% work from home (2006-2010 5-year est.); Travel time to work: 28.9% less than 15 minutes, 34.5% 15 to 30 minutes, 17.0% 30 to 45 minutes, 6.7% 45 to 60 minutes, 12.9% 60 minutes or more (2006-2010 5-year est.)

Airports: Westchester County (primary service/small hub)

Additional Information Contacts

Business Council of Westchester . . . . . . . . . . . . . . . . . . (914) 948-2110
    http://www.westchesterny.org
City of White Plains . . . . . . . . . . . . . . . . . . . . . . . . . . . . (914) 422-1200
    http://www.ci.white-plains.ny.us

## WYKAGYL (unincorporated postal area)

Zip Code: 10804

Covers a land area of 4.333 square miles and a water area of 0.122 square miles. Located at 40.94° N. Lat; 73.78° W. Long. Elevation is 128 feet. Population: 14,146 (2010); Density: 3,264.0 persons per square mile (2010); Race: 85.2% White, 7.9% Black, 4.1% Asian, 0.0% American Indian/Alaska Native, 0.0% Native Hawaiian/Other Pacific Islander, 2.8% Other, 5.0% Hispanic of any race (2010); Average household size: 2.84 (2010); Median age: 44.8 (2010); Males per 100 females: 93.9 (2010); Homeownership rate: 94.9% (2010)

## YONKERS (city). Covers a land area of 18.011 square miles and a water area of 2.284 square miles. Located at 40.94° N. Lat; 73.86° W. Long. Elevation is 82 feet.

History: Named for Adriaen Van der Donck, whose title was "jonkheer," purchaser of the land. The village of Nappeckamack stood on the site of Yonkers before the Kekeskick Purchase (1639) made by the Dutch West India Company. The city site was included in a grant of land made in 1646 by the company to Adriaen Cornelissen Van der Donck, the first lawyer and first historian of New Netherland. By reason of his wealth and social position, Van der Donck enjoyed the courtesy title of "jonker," the Dutch equivalent of "his young lordship," from which was derived the name of the city.

Population: 188,126 (1990); 196,086 (2000); 195,976 (2010); Density: 10,880.3 persons per square mile (2010); Race: 55.8% White, 18.7% Black, 5.9% Asian, 0.7% American Indian/Alaska Native, 0.1% Native Hawaiian/Other Pacific Islander, 18.8% Other, 34.7% Hispanic of any race (2010); Average household size: 2.58 (2010); Median age: 37.6 (2010); Males per 100 females: 90.0 (2010); Marriage status: 35.8% never married, 48.6% now married, 7.5% widowed, 8.1% divorced (2006-2010 5-year est.); Foreign born: 30.2% (2006-2010 5-year est.); Ancestry (includes multiple ancestries): 16.5% Italian, 11.4% Irish, 4.4% German, 2.8% Polish, 2.6% American (2006-2010 5-year est.).

Economy: Unemployment rate: 8.9% (February 2012); Total civilian labor force: 89,804 (February 2012); Single-family building permits issued: 7 (2011); Multi-family building permits issued: 102 (2011); Employment by occupation: 10.9% management, 3.2% professional, 10.6% services, 17.3% sales, 4.3% farming, 8.8% construction, 4.5% production (2006-2010 5-year est.).

Income: Per capita income: $29,191 (2006-2010 5-year est.); Median household income: $55,715 (2006-2010 5-year est.); Average household income: $74,571 (2006-2010 5-year est.); Percent of households with income of $100,000 or more: 24.5% (2006-2010 5-year est.); Poverty rate: 13.8% (2006-2010 5-year est.).

Taxes: Total city taxes per capita: $1,842 (2009); City property taxes per capita: $1,259 (2009).

**Education:** Percent of population age 25 and over with: High school diploma (including GED) or higher: 80.9% (2006-2010 5-year est.); Bachelor's degree or higher: 29.1% (2006-2010 5-year est.); Master's degree or higher: 12.4% (2006-2010 5-year est.).

### School District(s)
Charter School of Educational Excellence (KG-05)
  2009-10 Enrollment: 378 . . . . . . . . . . . . . . . . . . . . . . . . . (914) 476-5070
Greenburgh-North Castle Union Free School District (07-12)
  2009-10 Enrollment: 354 . . . . . . . . . . . . . . . . . . . . . . . . . (914) 693-4309
Yonkers City School District (PK-12)
  2009-10 Enrollment: 24,956 . . . . . . . . . . . . . . . . . . . . . . (914) 376-8100

### Four-year College(s)
Saint Josephs Seminary and College (Private, Not-for-profit, Roman Catholic)
  Fall 2010 Enrollment: 82 . . . . . . . . . . . . . . . . . . . . . . . . (914) 968-6200

### Two-year College(s)
Cochran School of Nursing (Private, Not-for-profit)
  Fall 2010 Enrollment: 82 . . . . . . . . . . . . . . . . . . . . . . . . (914) 964-4296
St Joseph's Medical Center School of Radiography (Private, Not-for-profit)
  Fall 2010 Enrollment: 36 . . . . . . . . . . . . . . . . . . . . . . . . (914) 751-0391

**Housing:** Homeownership rate: 46.2% (2010); Median home value: $428,900 (2006-2010 5-year est.); Median contract rent: $966 per month (2006-2010 5-year est.); Median year structure built: 1953 (2006-2010 5-year est.).

**Hospitals:** St. John's Riverside Hospital (406 beds); St. Joseph's Medical Center (194 beds)

**Safety:** Violent crime rate: 44.9 per 10,000 population; Property crime rate: 143.1 per 10,000 population (2010).

**Newspapers:** Avance/Latino (Local news; Circulation 50,000); Eastchester Record (Community news; Circulation 4,058); Harrison Independent (Local news; Circulation 4,300); Home News & Times (Community news; Circulation 20,100); Mount Vernon Independent (Community news; Circulation 6,000); North Castle News (Community news; Circulation 3,300); Pelham Sun (Local news; Circulation 3,606); Rye Chronicle (Local news; Circulation 3,966); Sound View News (Local news; Circulation 6,000)

**Transportation:** Commute to work: 65.6% car, 25.8% public transportation, 5.1% walk, 2.3% work from home (2006-2010 5-year est.); Travel time to work: 16.5% less than 15 minutes, 32.8% 15 to 30 minutes, 22.1% 30 to 45 minutes, 10.3% 45 to 60 minutes, 18.3% 60 minutes or more (2006-2010 5-year est.); Amtrak: train service available.

**Additional Information Contacts**
City of Yonkers . . . . . . . . . . . . . . . . . . . . . . . . . . . . . . . (914) 377-6020
  http://www.cityofyonkers.com
Yonkers Chamber of Commerce . . . . . . . . . . . . . . . . . . . (914) 963-0332
  http://www.yonkerschamber.com

---

## YORKTOWN (town).
Covers a land area of 36.644 square miles and a water area of 2.612 square miles. Located at 41.26° N. Lat; 73.81° W. Long. Elevation is 505 feet.

**History:** Nearby, at Crompound (2.5 miles east of Peekskill), is the former anarchist Mohegan colony designed by Lewis Mumford in 1923 and led by American Harry Kelly and Englishmen Joseph Cohen and Leonard Abbott. Also known as the twelve Mohegan Colony and the Modern School Movement, the colony flourished both here and in the Stetton colony in N.J.

**Population:** 33,314 (1990); 36,318 (2000); 36,081 (2010); Density: 984.6 persons per square mile (2010); Race: 87.9% White, 3.3% Black, 4.7% Asian, 0.1% American Indian/Alaska Native, 0.0% Native Hawaiian/Other Pacific Islander, 4.0% Other, 9.4% Hispanic of any race (2010); Average household size: 2.75 (2010); Median age: 43.6 (2010); Males per 100 females: 93.0 (2010); Marriage status: 22.5% never married, 64.7% now married, 6.7% widowed, 6.0% divorced (2006-2010 5-year est.); Foreign born: 12.7% (2006-2010 5-year est.); Ancestry (includes multiple ancestries): 33.1% Italian, 22.5% Irish, 12.0% German, 5.4% Polish, 5.2% Russian (2006-2010 5-year est.).

**Economy:** Unemployment rate: 6.8% (February 2012); Total civilian labor force: 18,792 (February 2012); Single-family building permits issued: 4 (2011); Multi-family building permits issued: 0 (2011); Employment by occupation: 16.3% management, 6.0% professional, 7.0% services, 16.9% sales, 3.6% farming, 7.8% construction, 4.0% production (2006-2010 5-year est.).

**Income:** Per capita income: $44,667 (2006-2010 5-year est.); Median household income: $101,612 (2006-2010 5-year est.); Average household income: $122,674 (2006-2010 5-year est.); Percent of households with

income of $100,000 or more: 51.2% (2006-2010 5-year est.); Poverty rate: 1.7% (2006-2010 5-year est.).

**Education:** Percent of population age 25 and over with: High school diploma (including GED) or higher: 93.3% (2006-2010 5-year est.); Bachelor's degree or higher: 44.5% (2006-2010 5-year est.); Master's degree or higher: 21.3% (2006-2010 5-year est.).

**Housing:** Homeownership rate: 84.5% (2010); Median home value: $480,300 (2006-2010 5-year est.); Median contract rent: $1,135 per month (2006-2010 5-year est.); Median year structure built: 1967 (2006-2010 5-year est.).

**Safety:** Violent crime rate: 6.9 per 10,000 population; Property crime rate: 122.6 per 10,000 population (2010).

**Transportation:** Commute to work: 88.2% car, 6.0% public transportation, 1.0% walk, 4.7% work from home (2006-2010 5-year est.); Travel time to work: 23.4% less than 15 minutes, 22.3% 15 to 30 minutes, 28.0% 30 to 45 minutes, 10.9% 45 to 60 minutes, 15.3% 60 minutes or more (2006-2010 5-year est.)

**Additional Information Contacts**
Town of Yorktown . . . . . . . . . . . . . . . . . . . . . . . . . . . . . (914) 962-5722
  http://www.yorktownny.org

---

## YORKTOWN HEIGHTS (CDP).
Covers a land area of 0.914 square miles and a water area of 0.003 square miles. Located at 41.27° N. Lat; 73.77° W. Long. Elevation is 492 feet.

**Population:** 7,690 (1990); 7,972 (2000); 1,781 (2010); Density: 1,948.1 persons per square mile (2010); Race: 88.3% White, 2.8% Black, 5.4% Asian, 0.0% American Indian/Alaska Native, 0.0% Native Hawaiian/Other Pacific Islander, 3.5% Other, 8.2% Hispanic of any race (2010); Average household size: 2.85 (2010); Median age: 42.0 (2010); Males per 100 females: 94.9 (2010); Marriage status: 29.4% never married, 61.3% now married, 5.3% widowed, 4.0% divorced (2006-2010 5-year est.); Foreign born: 12.3% (2006-2010 5-year est.); Ancestry (includes multiple ancestries): 44.8% Italian, 21.6% Irish, 15.4% German, 10.2% Albanian, 7.9% Russian (2006-2010 5-year est.).

**Economy:** Employment by occupation: 9.1% management, 4.8% professional, 10.2% services, 30.0% sales, 5.4% farming, 14.5% construction, 11.5% production (2006-2010 5-year est.).

**Income:** Per capita income: $39,095 (2006-2010 5-year est.); Median household income: $105,417 (2006-2010 5-year est.); Average household income: $112,958 (2006-2010 5-year est.); Percent of households with income of $100,000 or more: 53.0% (2006-2010 5-year est.); Poverty rate: 1.2% (2006-2010 5-year est.).

**Education:** Percent of population age 25 and over with: High school diploma (including GED) or higher: 83.5% (2006-2010 5-year est.); Bachelor's degree or higher: 26.7% (2006-2010 5-year est.); Master's degree or higher: 9.7% (2006-2010 5-year est.).

### School District(s)
Lakeland Central School District (PK-12)
  2009-10 Enrollment: 6,439 . . . . . . . . . . . . . . . . . . . . . . (914) 245-1700
Putnam-Northern Westchester Boces
  2009-10 Enrollment: n/a . . . . . . . . . . . . . . . . . . . . . . . . (845) 248-2300
Yorktown Central School District (KG-12)
  2009-10 Enrollment: 3,940 . . . . . . . . . . . . . . . . . . . . . . (914) 243-8001

### Vocational/Technical School(s)
Putnam-Westchester BOCES Practical Nursing Program (Public)
  Fall 2010 Enrollment: 54 . . . . . . . . . . . . . . . . . . . . . . . . (914) 245-2700
  2011-12 Tuition: $12,600

**Housing:** Homeownership rate: 77.0% (2010); Median home value: $492,800 (2006-2010 5-year est.); Median contract rent: $677 per month (2006-2010 5-year est.); Median year structure built: 1959 (2006-2010 5-year est.).

**Newspapers:** Brewster/New Fairfield Pennysaver (Community news; Circulation 16,775); Carmel Pennysaver (Community news; Circulation 14,325); City of Poughkeepsie Pennysaver (Community news; Circulation 18,950); Croton/Ossining Pennysaver (Community news; Circulation 24,125); Fishkill/Beacon Pennysaver (Community news; Circulation 17,875); Hopewell Pennysaver (Community news; Circulation 12,300); Hyde Park Pennysaver (Community news; Circulation 11,275); Mahopac Pennysaver (Community news; Circulation 10,050); Mount Kisco/Katonah Pennysaver (Community news; Circulation 26,625); North County News (Community news; Circulation 9,200); North White Plains/Elmsford Pennysaver (Community news; Circulation 15,650); Pawling Pennysaver (Community news; Circulation 14,175); Peekskill Pennysaver (Community news; Circulation 25,075); Pleasantville Pennysaver (Community news; Circulation 17,525); Putnam Valley Pennysaver (Community news;

Circulation 4,925); Rhinebeck Pennysaver (Community news; Circulation 13,850); Tarrytown Pennysaver (Community news; Circulation 18,175); Town of Poughkeepsie Pennysaver (Community news; Circulation 24,850); Wappingers Falls Pennysaver (Community news; Circulation 15,025); Yorktown/Somers Pennysaver (Community news; Circulation 26,150)
**Transportation:** Commute to work: 90.1% car, 0.0% public transportation, 1.0% walk, 8.9% work from home (2006-2010 5-year est.); Travel time to work: 44.3% less than 15 minutes, 22.0% 15 to 30 minutes, 22.6% 30 to 45 minutes, 9.9% 45 to 60 minutes, 1.2% 60 minutes or more (2006-2010 5-year est.)
**Additional Information Contacts**
Yorktown Heights Chamber of Commerce . . . . . . . . . . . . . (914) 245-4599
  http://www.yorktownchamber.org

# Wyoming County

Located in western New York; drained by the Genesee River. Covers a land area of 592.91 square miles, a water area of 3.53 square miles, and is located in the Eastern Time Zone at 42.70° N. Lat., 78.19° W. Long. The county was founded in 1841. County seat is Warsaw.

Weather Station: Warsaw 6 SW — Elevation: 1,819 feet

|  | Jan | Feb | Mar | Apr | May | Jun | Jul | Aug | Sep | Oct | Nov | Dec |
|---|---|---|---|---|---|---|---|---|---|---|---|---|
| High | 28 | 30 | 38 | 52 | 64 | 72 | 76 | 75 | 68 | 56 | 44 | 32 |
| Low | 13 | 14 | 20 | 33 | 43 | 53 | 57 | 56 | 49 | 38 | 29 | 19 |
| Precip | 3.2 | 2.5 | 3.2 | 3.4 | 4.0 | 4.6 | 4.5 | 3.7 | 4.6 | 4.0 | 3.9 | 3.7 |
| Snow | 35.3 | 25.5 | 20.7 | 6.1 | 0.2 | 0.0 | 0.0 | 0.0 | 0.0 | 0.6 | 12.4 | 29.7 |

*High and Low temperatures in degrees Fahrenheit; Precipitation and Snow in inches*

**Population:** 42,507 (1990); 43,424 (2000); 42,155 (2010); Race: 91.6% White, 5.6% Black, 0.4% Asian, 0.3% American Indian/Alaska Native, 0.0% Native Hawaiian/Other Pacific Islander, 2.1% Other, 3.0% Hispanic of any race (2010); Density: 71.1 persons per square mile (2010); Average household size: 2.46 (2010); Median age: 40.9 (2010); Males per 100 females: 119.5 (2010).
**Religion:** Six largest groups: 18.9% Catholicism, 4.7% Methodist/Pietist, 4.3% Presbyterian-Reformed, 1.6% Baptist, 1.2% Non-Denominational, 1.0% Episcopalianism/Anglicanism (2010)
**Economy:** Unemployment rate: 10.5% (February 2012); Total civilian labor force: 20,209 (February 2012); Leading industries: 21.9% manufacturing; 16.1% retail trade; 14.5% health care and social assistance (2009); Farms: 761 totaling 218,028 acres (2007); Companies that employ 500 or more persons: 1 (2009); Companies that employ 100 to 499 persons: 11 (2009); Companies that employ less than 100 persons: 773 (2009); Black-owned businesses: n/a (2007); Hispanic-owned businesses: n/a (2007); Asian-owned businesses: n/a (2007); Women-owned businesses: 893 (2007); Retail sales per capita: $8,116 (2010). Single-family building permits issued: 21 (2011); Multi-family building permits issued: 8 (2011).
**Income:** Per capita income: $20,605 (2006-2010 5-year est.); Median household income: $50,075 (2006-2010 5-year est.); Average household income: $56,972 (2006-2010 5-year est.); Percent of households with income of $100,000 or more: 12.3% (2006-2010 5-year est.); Poverty rate: 10.9% (2006-2010 5-year est.); Bankruptcy rate: 2.53% (2011).
**Education:** Percent of population age 25 and over with: High school diploma (including GED) or higher: 85.5% (2006-2010 5-year est.); Bachelor's degree or higher: 14.8% (2006-2010 5-year est.); Master's degree or higher: 5.5% (2006-2010 5-year est.).
**Housing:** Homeownership rate: 75.9% (2010); Median home value: $97,300 (2006-2010 5-year est.); Median contract rent: $472 per month (2006-2010 5-year est.); Median year structure built: 1947 (2006-2010 5-year est.)
**Health:** Birth rate: 94.9 per 10,000 population (2011); Death rate: 77.7 per 10,000 population (2011); Age-adjusted cancer mortality rate: 205.3 deaths per 100,000 population (2009); Number of physicians: 10.1 per 10,000 population (2008); Hospital beds: 56.2 per 10,000 population (2007); Hospital admissions: 679.0 per 10,000 population (2007).
**Elections:** 2008 Presidential election results: 36.1% Obama, 62.3% McCain, 0.9% Nader
**National and State Parks:** Letchworth State Park; Silver Lake State Park
**Additional Information Contacts**
Wyoming County Government. . . . . . . . . . . . . . . . . . . . . . . (716) 786-8810
  http://www.wyomingco.net
Arcade Area Chamber of Commerce. . . . . . . . . . . . . . . . . (585) 492-2114
  http://www.arcadechamber.org
Perry Chamber of Commerce . . . . . . . . . . . . . . . . . . . . . . (585) 237-5040
  http://www.perrychamber.com

Village of Arcade . . . . . . . . . . . . . . . . . . . . . . . . . . . . . . (585) 492-1111
  http://www.villageofarcade.org
Village of Attica . . . . . . . . . . . . . . . . . . . . . . . . . . . . . . . (585) 591-0898
  http://attica.org
Village of Perry. . . . . . . . . . . . . . . . . . . . . . . . . . . . . . . . (585) 237-2216
  http://www.villageofperry.com
Wyoming County Chamber of Commerce . . . . . . . . . . . . . . (585) 237-0230
  http://www.wycochamber.org

## Wyoming County Communities

**ARCADE** (village). Covers a land area of 2.649 square miles and a water area of 0.003 square miles. Located at 42.53° N. Lat; 78.44° W. Long. Elevation is 1,476 feet.
**Population:** 2,148 (1990); 2,026 (2000); 2,071 (2010); Density: 781.7 persons per square mile (2010); Race: 97.4% White, 0.3% Black, 0.3% Asian, 0.3% American Indian/Alaska Native, 0.0% Native Hawaiian/Other Pacific Islander, 1.7% Other, 1.2% Hispanic of any race (2010); Average household size: 2.33 (2010); Median age: 35.2 (2010); Males per 100 females: 90.5 (2010); Marriage status: 31.9% never married, 52.5% now married, 4.9% widowed, 10.7% divorced (2006-2010 5-year est.); Foreign born: 1.2% (2006-2010 5-year est.); Ancestry (includes multiple ancestries): 37.2% German, 20.0% English, 16.0% Polish, 14.7% Italian, 13.9% Irish (2006-2010 5-year est.).
**Economy:** Employment by occupation: 3.9% management, 3.8% professional, 13.6% services, 15.7% sales, 1.5% farming, 11.7% construction, 9.5% production (2006-2010 5-year est.).
**Income:** Per capita income: $21,748 (2006-2010 5-year est.); Median household income: $41,705 (2006-2010 5-year est.); Average household income: $52,646 (2006-2010 5-year est.); Percent of households with income of $100,000 or more: 6.6% (2006-2010 5-year est.); Poverty rate: 20.2% (2006-2010 5-year est.).
**Taxes:** Total city taxes per capita: $582 (2009); City property taxes per capita: $566 (2009).
**Education:** Percent of population age 25 and over with: High school diploma (including GED) or higher: 91.7% (2006-2010 5-year est.); Bachelor's degree or higher: 22.0% (2006-2010 5-year est.); Master's degree or higher: 13.4% (2006-2010 5-year est.).
**School District(s)**
Yorkshire-Pioneer Central School District (PK-12)
  2009-10 Enrollment: 2,515 . . . . . . . . . . . . . . . . . (716) 492-9304
**Housing:** Homeownership rate: 54.8% (2010); Median home value: $99,900 (2006-2010 5-year est.); Median contract rent: $467 per month (2006-2010 5-year est.); Median year structure built: 1948 (2006-2010 5-year est.).
**Safety:** Violent crime rate: 5.4 per 10,000 population; Property crime rate: 245.1 per 10,000 population (2010).
**Newspapers:** Arcade Herald (Community news; Circulation 4,900); Arcade Pennysaver (Community news; Circulation 12,000)
**Transportation:** Commute to work: 88.0% car, 1.6% public transportation, 7.1% walk, 1.9% work from home (2006-2010 5-year est.); Travel time to work: 46.2% less than 15 minutes, 23.4% 15 to 30 minutes, 11.4% 30 to 45 minutes, 11.6% 45 to 60 minutes, 7.3% 60 minutes or more (2006-2010 5-year est.)
**Additional Information Contacts**
Arcade Area Chamber of Commerce. . . . . . . . . . . . . . . . . (585) 492-2114
  http://www.arcadechamber.org
Village of Arcade . . . . . . . . . . . . . . . . . . . . . . . . . . . . . . (585) 492-1111
  http://www.villageofarcade.org

**ARCADE** (town). Covers a land area of 47.004 square miles and a water area of 0.105 square miles. Located at 42.57° N. Lat; 78.36° W. Long. Elevation is 1,476 feet.
**Population:** 3,938 (1990); 4,184 (2000); 4,205 (2010); Density: 89.5 persons per square mile (2010); Race: 97.4% White, 0.4% Black, 0.5% Asian, 0.4% American Indian/Alaska Native, 0.0% Native Hawaiian/Other Pacific Islander, 1.3% Other, 1.2% Hispanic of any race (2010); Average household size: 2.34 (2010); Median age: 40.6 (2010); Males per 100 females: 95.3 (2010); Marriage status: 27.3% never married, 56.5% now married, 5.9% widowed, 10.4% divorced (2006-2010 5-year est.); Foreign born: 0.9% (2006-2010 5-year est.); Ancestry (includes multiple ancestries): 40.5% German, 17.5% Polish, 16.9% English, 10.2% Irish, 9.3% Italian (2006-2010 5-year est.).

**Economy:** Employment by occupation: 8.2% management, 2.5% professional, 8.9% services, 12.0% sales, 2.5% farming, 14.7% construction, 7.4% production (2006-2010 5-year est.).
**Income:** Per capita income: $23,499 (2006-2010 5-year est.); Median household income: $44,632 (2006-2010 5-year est.); Average household income: $54,705 (2006-2010 5-year est.); Percent of households with income of $100,000 or more: 11.4% (2006-2010 5-year est.); Poverty rate: 13.1% (2006-2010 5-year est.).
**Education:** Percent of population age 25 and over with: High school diploma (including GED) or higher: 91.2% (2006-2010 5-year est.); Bachelor's degree or higher: 20.2% (2006-2010 5-year est.); Master's degree or higher: 10.3% (2006-2010 5-year est.).

**School District(s)**
Yorkshire-Pioneer Central School District (PK-12)
   2009-10 Enrollment: 2,515 . . . . . . . . . . . . . . . . . . (716) 492-9304
**Housing:** Homeownership rate: 71.3% (2010); Median home value: $106,200 (2006-2010 5-year est.); Median contract rent: $477 per month (2006-2010 5-year est.); Median year structure built: 1968 (2006-2010 5-year est.).
**Newspapers:** Arcade Herald (Community news; Circulation 4,900); Arcade Pennysaver (Community news; Circulation 12,000)
**Transportation:** Commute to work: 87.8% car, 0.9% public transportation, 7.2% walk, 2.3% work from home (2006-2010 5-year est.); Travel time to work: 47.4% less than 15 minutes, 19.8% 15 to 30 minutes, 11.6% 30 to 45 minutes, 13.5% 45 to 60 minutes, 7.7% 60 minutes or more (2006-2010 5-year est.)

## ATTICA (village). Covers a land area of 1.691 square miles and a water area of 0 square miles. Located at 42.86° N. Lat; 78.27° W. Long. Elevation is 981 feet.

**Population:** 2,630 (1990); 2,597 (2000); 2,547 (2010); Density: 1,505.8 persons per square mile (2010); Race: 96.5% White, 0.5% Black, 0.5% Asian, 0.2% American Indian/Alaska Native, 0.0% Native Hawaiian/Other Pacific Islander, 2.3% Other, 1.7% Hispanic of any race (2010); Average household size: 2.39 (2010); Median age: 38.1 (2010); Males per 100 females: 93.7 (2010); Marriage status: 26.4% never married, 58.1% now married, 6.1% widowed, 9.4% divorced (2006-2010 5-year est.); Foreign born: 1.6% (2006-2010 5-year est.); Ancestry (includes multiple ancestries): 39.6% German, 17.9% Irish, 15.5% English, 11.2% Polish, 5.9% Dutch (2006-2010 5-year est.).
**Economy:** Employment by occupation: 8.5% management, 1.8% professional, 13.0% services, 19.3% sales, 3.9% farming, 7.8% construction, 9.1% production (2006-2010 5-year est.).
**Income:** Per capita income: $22,140 (2006-2010 5-year est.); Median household income: $47,196 (2006-2010 5-year est.); Average household income: $55,886 (2006-2010 5-year est.); Percent of households with income of $100,000 or more: 10.6% (2006-2010 5-year est.); Poverty rate: 20.2% (2006-2010 5-year est.).
**Education:** Percent of population age 25 and over with: High school diploma (including GED) or higher: 87.5% (2006-2010 5-year est.); Bachelor's degree or higher: 13.7% (2006-2010 5-year est.); Master's degree or higher: 4.8% (2006-2010 5-year est.).

**School District(s)**
Attica Central School District (KG-12)
   2009-10 Enrollment: 1,604 . . . . . . . . . . . . . . . . . . (585) 591-2173
**Housing:** Homeownership rate: 59.8% (2010); Median home value: $95,100 (2006-2010 5-year est.); Median contract rent: $478 per month (2006-2010 5-year est.); Median year structure built: before 1940 (2006-2010 5-year est.).
**Safety:** Violent crime rate: 17.0 per 10,000 population; Property crime rate: 46.8 per 10,000 population (2010).
**Transportation:** Commute to work: 95.4% car, 0.0% public transportation, 2.9% walk, 1.7% work from home (2006-2010 5-year est.); Travel time to work: 40.8% less than 15 minutes, 30.1% 15 to 30 minutes, 18.3% 30 to 45 minutes, 5.2% 45 to 60 minutes, 5.5% 60 minutes or more (2006-2010 5-year est.)
**Additional Information Contacts**
Attica Area Chamber of Commerce . . . . . . . . . . . . . . . (585) 591-1703
   http://www.atticachamberofcommerce.com
Village of Attica . . . . . . . . . . . . . . . . . . . . . . . . . . . . (585) 591-0898
   http://attica.org

## ATTICA (town). Covers a land area of 35.712 square miles and a water area of 0.315 square miles. Located at 42.82° N. Lat; 78.24° W. Long. Elevation is 981 feet.

**Population:** 7,383 (1990); 6,028 (2000); 7,702 (2010); Density: 215.7 persons per square mile (2010); Race: 64.4% White, 29.7% Black, 0.5% Asian, 0.6% American Indian/Alaska Native, 0.0% Native Hawaiian/Other Pacific Islander, 4.8% Other, 8.5% Hispanic of any race (2010); Average household size: 2.50 (2010); Median age: 38.0 (2010); Males per 100 females: 283.4 (2010); Marriage status: 47.9% never married, 39.0% now married, 3.5% widowed, 9.6% divorced (2006-2010 5-year est.); Foreign born: 5.7% (2006-2010 5-year est.); Ancestry (includes multiple ancestries): 20.3% German, 9.4% English, 7.9% Irish, 5.3% Polish, 4.2% Italian (2006-2010 5-year est.).
**Economy:** Employment by occupation: 12.0% management, 1.8% professional, 11.6% services, 17.3% sales, 3.9% farming, 9.1% construction, 6.8% production (2006-2010 5-year est.).
**Income:** Per capita income: $11,103 (2006-2010 5-year est.); Median household income: $52,147 (2006-2010 5-year est.); Average household income: $58,161 (2006-2010 5-year est.); Percent of households with income of $100,000 or more: 14.5% (2006-2010 5-year est.); Poverty rate: 13.6% (2006-2010 5-year est.).
**Education:** Percent of population age 25 and over with: High school diploma (including GED) or higher: 73.8% (2006-2010 5-year est.); Bachelor's degree or higher: 8.0% (2006-2010 5-year est.); Master's degree or higher: 2.8% (2006-2010 5-year est.).

**School District(s)**
Attica Central School District (KG-12)
   2009-10 Enrollment: 1,604 . . . . . . . . . . . . . . . . . . (585) 591-2173
**Housing:** Homeownership rate: 71.4% (2010); Median home value: $101,200 (2006-2010 5-year est.); Median contract rent: $483 per month (2006-2010 5-year est.); Median year structure built: before 1940 (2006-2010 5-year est.).
**Transportation:** Commute to work: 92.2% car, 0.0% public transportation, 4.2% walk, 3.0% work from home (2006-2010 5-year est.); Travel time to work: 42.2% less than 15 minutes, 30.6% 15 to 30 minutes, 16.0% 30 to 45 minutes, 6.1% 45 to 60 minutes, 5.1% 60 minutes or more (2006-2010 5-year est.)
**Additional Information Contacts**
Attica Area Chamber of Commerce . . . . . . . . . . . . . . . (585) 591-1703
   http://www.atticachamberofcommerce.com

## BENNINGTON (town). Covers a land area of 55.049 square miles and a water area of 0.215 square miles. Located at 42.81° N. Lat; 78.38° W. Long. Elevation is 1,207 feet.

**Population:** 3,046 (1990); 3,349 (2000); 3,359 (2010); Density: 61.0 persons per square mile (2010); Race: 99.1% White, 0.0% Black, 0.2% Asian, 0.1% American Indian/Alaska Native, 0.0% Native Hawaiian/Other Pacific Islander, 0.6% Other, 0.8% Hispanic of any race (2010); Average household size: 2.58 (2010); Median age: 45.6 (2010); Males per 100 females: 107.0 (2010); Marriage status: 17.5% never married, 75.0% now married, 3.6% widowed, 3.9% divorced (2006-2010 5-year est.); Foreign born: 2.7% (2006-2010 5-year est.); Ancestry (includes multiple ancestries): 47.4% German, 21.4% Polish, 14.9% Irish, 14.1% Italian, 13.7% English (2006-2010 5-year est.).
**Economy:** Employment by occupation: 7.3% management, 3.3% professional, 12.8% services, 9.8% sales, 3.2% farming, 11.7% construction, 8.6% production (2006-2010 5-year est.).
**Income:** Per capita income: $25,160 (2006-2010 5-year est.); Median household income: $60,170 (2006-2010 5-year est.); Average household income: $65,747 (2006-2010 5-year est.); Percent of households with income of $100,000 or more: 14.5% (2006-2010 5-year est.); Poverty rate: 6.6% (2006-2010 5-year est.).
**Education:** Percent of population age 25 and over with: High school diploma (including GED) or higher: 87.6% (2006-2010 5-year est.); Bachelor's degree or higher: 17.2% (2006-2010 5-year est.); Master's degree or higher: 5.2% (2006-2010 5-year est.).
**Housing:** Homeownership rate: 90.9% (2010); Median home value: $145,100 (2006-2010 5-year est.); Median contract rent: $430 per month (2006-2010 5-year est.); Median year structure built: 1965 (2006-2010 5-year est.).
**Transportation:** Commute to work: 90.2% car, 0.0% public transportation, 1.8% walk, 5.8% work from home (2006-2010 5-year est.); Travel time to work: 20.3% less than 15 minutes, 30.2% 15 to 30 minutes, 27.6% 30 to 45 minutes, 15.5% 45 to 60 minutes, 6.3% 60 minutes or more (2006-2010 5-year est.)

**BLISS** (CDP). Covers a land area of 9.791 square miles and a water area of 0 square miles. Located at 42.58° N. Lat; 78.25° W. Long. Elevation is 1,745 feet.
**Population:** n/a (1990); n/a (2000); 527 (2010); Density: 53.8 persons per square mile (2010); Race: 97.9% White, 1.5% Black, 0.2% Asian, 0.0% American Indian/Alaska Native, 0.0% Native Hawaiian/Other Pacific Islander, 0.4% Other, 1.1% Hispanic of any race (2010); Average household size: 2.58 (2010); Median age: 40.6 (2010); Males per 100 females: 92.3 (2010); Marriage status: 23.8% never married, 56.8% now married, 6.4% widowed, 12.9% divorced (2006-2010 5-year est.); Foreign born: 0.6% (2006-2010 5-year est.); Ancestry (includes multiple ancestries): 41.6% German, 27.8% Irish, 14.5% English, 12.5% Polish, 9.1% Italian (2006-2010 5-year est.).
**Economy:** Employment by occupation: 10.9% management, 0.9% professional, 8.9% services, 17.2% sales, 3.0% farming, 23.1% construction, 11.8% production (2006-2010 5-year est.).
**Income:** Per capita income: $17,755 (2006-2010 5-year est.); Median household income: $38,333 (2006-2010 5-year est.); Average household income: $46,278 (2006-2010 5-year est.); Percent of households with income of $100,000 or more: 4.0% (2006-2010 5-year est.); Poverty rate: 13.2% (2006-2010 5-year est.).
**Education:** Percent of population age 25 and over with: High school diploma (including GED) or higher: 87.7% (2006-2010 5-year est.); Bachelor's degree or higher: 9.6% (2006-2010 5-year est.); Master's degree or higher: 2.1% (2006-2010 5-year est.).
**Housing:** Homeownership rate: 86.8% (2010); Median home value: $65,400 (2006-2010 5-year est.); Median contract rent: $423 per month (2006-2010 5-year est.); Median year structure built: 1954 (2006-2010 5-year est.).
**Transportation:** Commute to work: 87.5% car, 2.7% public transportation, 0.9% walk, 7.9% work from home (2006-2010 5-year est.); Travel time to work: 12.2% less than 15 minutes, 37.6% 15 to 30 minutes, 13.2% 30 to 45 minutes, 16.5% 45 to 60 minutes, 20.5% 60 minutes or more (2006-2010 5-year est.).

**CASTILE** (village). Covers a land area of 1.351 square miles and a water area of 0 square miles. Located at 42.63° N. Lat; 78.05° W. Long. Elevation is 1,355 feet.
**Population:** 1,078 (1990); 1,051 (2000); 1,015 (2010); Density: 750.8 persons per square mile (2010); Race: 98.6% White, 0.3% Black, 0.2% Asian, 0.2% American Indian/Alaska Native, 0.0% Native Hawaiian/Other Pacific Islander, 0.7% Other, 1.3% Hispanic of any race (2010); Average household size: 2.42 (2010); Median age: 38.9 (2010); Males per 100 females: 93.0 (2010); Marriage status: 25.5% never married, 57.8% now married, 6.8% widowed, 9.9% divorced (2006-2010 5-year est.); Foreign born: 0.8% (2006-2010 5-year est.); Ancestry (includes multiple ancestries): 28.6% German, 23.9% Irish, 18.6% English, 18.3% Italian, 6.1% Welsh (2006-2010 5-year est.).
**Economy:** Employment by occupation: 7.9% management, 1.5% professional, 6.8% services, 20.3% sales, 2.1% farming, 13.2% construction, 4.1% production (2006-2010 5-year est.).
**Income:** Per capita income: $18,648 (2006-2010 5-year est.); Median household income: $44,464 (2006-2010 5-year est.); Average household income: $48,168 (2006-2010 5-year est.); Percent of households with income of $100,000 or more: 7.8% (2006-2010 5-year est.); Poverty rate: 13.3% (2006-2010 5-year est.).
**Education:** Percent of population age 25 and over with: High school diploma (including GED) or higher: 90.9% (2006-2010 5-year est.); Bachelor's degree or higher: 17.6% (2006-2010 5-year est.); Master's degree or higher: 6.5% (2006-2010 5-year est.).
**Housing:** Homeownership rate: 68.8% (2010); Median home value: $82,200 (2006-2010 5-year est.); Median contract rent: $450 per month (2006-2010 5-year est.); Median year structure built: before 1940 (2006-2010 5-year est.).
**Transportation:** Commute to work: 94.4% car, 2.0% public transportation, 3.2% walk, 0.4% work from home (2006-2010 5-year est.); Travel time to work: 43.0% less than 15 minutes, 27.1% 15 to 30 minutes, 12.7% 30 to 45 minutes, 3.4% 45 to 60 minutes, 13.7% 60 minutes or more (2006-2010 5-year est.).

**CASTILE** (town). Covers a land area of 36.980 square miles and a water area of 1.415 square miles. Located at 42.66° N. Lat; 78.02° W. Long. Elevation is 1,355 feet.
**Population:** 3,042 (1990); 2,873 (2000); 2,906 (2010); Density: 78.6 persons per square mile (2010); Race: 97.6% White, 0.5% Black, 0.1%

Asian, 0.2% American Indian/Alaska Native, 0.0% Native Hawaiian/Other Pacific Islander, 1.6% Other, 2.2% Hispanic of any race (2010); Average household size: 2.46 (2010); Median age: 42.5 (2010); Males per 100 females: 99.0 (2010); Marriage status: 24.4% never married, 59.2% now married, 7.3% widowed, 9.1% divorced (2006-2010 5-year est.); Foreign born: 0.9% (2006-2010 5-year est.); Ancestry (includes multiple ancestries): 28.1% German, 21.6% English, 18.9% Irish, 14.8% Italian, 6.0% Polish (2006-2010 5-year est.).
**Economy:** Employment by occupation: 14.9% management, 0.6% professional, 6.5% services, 12.3% sales, 3.5% farming, 16.6% construction, 7.3% production (2006-2010 5-year est.).
**Income:** Per capita income: $23,239 (2006-2010 5-year est.); Median household income: $50,167 (2006-2010 5-year est.); Average household income: $57,022 (2006-2010 5-year est.); Percent of households with income of $100,000 or more: 16.1% (2006-2010 5-year est.); Poverty rate: 10.6% (2006-2010 5-year est.).
**Education:** Percent of population age 25 and over with: High school diploma (including GED) or higher: 87.3% (2006-2010 5-year est.); Bachelor's degree or higher: 20.2% (2006-2010 5-year est.); Master's degree or higher: 8.6% (2006-2010 5-year est.).
**Housing:** Homeownership rate: 76.8% (2010); Median home value: $101,500 (2006-2010 5-year est.); Median contract rent: $451 per month (2006-2010 5-year est.); Median year structure built: before 1940 (2006-2010 5-year est.).
**Transportation:** Commute to work: 94.9% car, 0.8% public transportation, 2.0% walk, 2.3% work from home (2006-2010 5-year est.); Travel time to work: 47.5% less than 15 minutes, 21.0% 15 to 30 minutes, 15.0% 30 to 45 minutes, 3.3% 45 to 60 minutes, 13.1% 60 minutes or more (2006-2010 5-year est.).

**COVINGTON** (town). Covers a land area of 26.137 square miles and a water area of 0 square miles. Located at 42.83° N. Lat; 78.01° W. Long. Elevation is 1,102 feet.
**Population:** 1,266 (1990); 1,357 (2000); 1,232 (2010); Density: 47.1 persons per square mile (2010); Race: 98.5% White, 0.3% Black, 0.2% Asian, 0.2% American Indian/Alaska Native, 0.0% Native Hawaiian/Other Pacific Islander, 0.8% Other, 2.4% Hispanic of any race (2010); Average household size: 2.60 (2010); Median age: 40.9 (2010); Males per 100 females: 105.0 (2010); Marriage status: 25.0% never married, 61.8% now married, 4.6% widowed, 8.6% divorced (2006-2010 5-year est.); Foreign born: 0.5% (2006-2010 5-year est.); Ancestry (includes multiple ancestries): 30.3% German, 27.1% Irish, 21.8% English, 8.8% European, 8.6% Italian (2006-2010 5-year est.).
**Economy:** Employment by occupation: 9.9% management, 1.4% professional, 12.0% services, 14.5% sales, 4.6% farming, 18.9% construction, 12.8% production (2006-2010 5-year est.).
**Income:** Per capita income: $23,434 (2006-2010 5-year est.); Median household income: $60,227 (2006-2010 5-year est.); Average household income: $66,507 (2006-2010 5-year est.); Percent of households with income of $100,000 or more: 20.9% (2006-2010 5-year est.); Poverty rate: 8.6% (2006-2010 5-year est.).
**Education:** Percent of population age 25 and over with: High school diploma (including GED) or higher: 91.8% (2006-2010 5-year est.); Bachelor's degree or higher: 14.1% (2006-2010 5-year est.); Master's degree or higher: 6.1% (2006-2010 5-year est.).
**Housing:** Homeownership rate: 84.8% (2010); Median home value: $88,400 (2006-2010 5-year est.); Median contract rent: $607 per month (2006-2010 5-year est.); Median year structure built: 1965 (2006-2010 5-year est.).
**Transportation:** Commute to work: 93.4% car, 0.0% public transportation, 2.8% walk, 2.8% work from home (2006-2010 5-year est.); Travel time to work: 35.2% less than 15 minutes, 30.6% 15 to 30 minutes, 15.1% 30 to 45 minutes, 11.8% 45 to 60 minutes, 7.3% 60 minutes or more (2006-2010 5-year est.).

**COWLESVILLE** (unincorporated postal area)
Zip Code: 14037
Covers a land area of 17.307 square miles and a water area of 0.007 square miles. Located at 42.80° N. Lat; 78.45° W. Long. Elevation is 945 feet. Population: 1,166 (2010); Density: 67.4 persons per square mile (2010); Race: 98.5% White, 0.5% Black, 0.2% Asian, 0.3% American Indian/Alaska Native, 0.0% Native Hawaiian/Other Pacific Islander, 0.5% Other, 0.8% Hispanic of any race (2010); Average household size: 2.63 (2010); Median age: 45.4 (2010); Males per 100 females: 105.3 (2010); Homeownership rate: 87.6% (2010)

**DALE** (unincorporated postal area)
Zip Code: 14039
Covers a land area of 1.868 square miles and a water area of 0 square miles. Located at 42.85° N. Lat; 78.17° W. Long. Elevation is 1,201 feet.
Population: 101 (2010); Density: 54.1 persons per square mile (2010); Race: 100.0% White, 0.0% Black, 0.0% Asian, 0.0% American Indian/Alaska Native, 0.0% Native Hawaiian/Other Pacific Islander, 0.0% Other, 0.0% Hispanic of any race (2010); Average household size: 2.24 (2010); Median age: 44.8 (2010); Males per 100 females: 102.0 (2010); Homeownership rate: 73.3% (2010)

**EAGLE** (town). Covers a land area of 36.282 square miles and a water area of 0.187 square miles. Located at 42.56° N. Lat; 78.25° W. Long. Elevation is 1,768 feet.
Population: 1,155 (1990); 1,194 (2000); 1,192 (2010); Density: 32.9 persons per square mile (2010); Race: 97.7% White, 1.2% Black, 0.3% Asian, 0.2% American Indian/Alaska Native, 0.0% Native Hawaiian/Other Pacific Islander, 0.6% Other, 0.8% Hispanic of any race (2010); Average household size: 2.67 (2010); Median age: 40.7 (2010); Males per 100 females: 101.4 (2010); Marriage status: 21.6% never married, 56.8% now married, 8.4% widowed, 13.2% divorced (2006-2010 5-year est.); Foreign born: 1.5% (2006-2010 5-year est.); Ancestry (includes multiple ancestries): 38.6% German, 21.1% Irish, 19.7% English, 14.8% Polish, 10.6% Italian (2006-2010 5-year est.).
Economy: Employment by occupation: 10.4% management, 1.0% professional, 6.3% services, 20.7% sales, 2.0% farming, 20.4% construction, 13.8% production (2006-2010 5-year est.).
Income: Per capita income: $18,906 (2006-2010 5-year est.); Median household income: $38,906 (2006-2010 5-year est.); Average household income: $46,197 (2006-2010 5-year est.); Percent of households with income of $100,000 or more: 5.2% (2006-2010 5-year est.); Poverty rate: 13.9% (2006-2010 5-year est.).
Education: Percent of population age 25 and over with: High school diploma (including GED) or higher: 86.2% (2006-2010 5-year est.); Bachelor's degree or higher: 7.7% (2006-2010 5-year est.); Master's degree or higher: 1.2% (2006-2010 5-year est.).
Housing: Homeownership rate: 87.3% (2010); Median home value: $74,000 (2006-2010 5-year est.); Median contract rent: $425 per month (2006-2010 5-year est.); Median year structure built: 1956 (2006-2010 5-year est.).
Transportation: Commute to work: 88.7% car, 2.3% public transportation, 1.1% walk, 7.1% work from home (2006-2010 5-year est.); Travel time to work: 18.0% less than 15 minutes, 38.7% 15 to 30 minutes, 13.9% 30 to 45 minutes, 12.0% 45 to 60 minutes, 17.5% 60 minutes or more (2006-2010 5-year est.)

**GAINESVILLE** (village). Covers a land area of 0.855 square miles and a water area of 0 square miles. Located at 42.64° N. Lat; 78.13° W. Long. Elevation is 1,617 feet.
Population: 340 (1990); 304 (2000); 229 (2010); Density: 267.6 persons per square mile (2010); Race: 99.6% White, 0.0% Black, 0.0% Asian, 0.0% American Indian/Alaska Native, 0.0% Native Hawaiian/Other Pacific Islander, 0.4% Other, 0.9% Hispanic of any race (2010); Average household size: 2.36 (2010); Median age: 44.8 (2010); Males per 100 females: 110.1 (2010); Marriage status: 34.2% never married, 50.2% now married, 3.1% widowed, 12.4% divorced (2006-2010 5-year est.); Foreign born: 1.1% (2006-2010 5-year est.); Ancestry (includes multiple ancestries): 44.9% German, 25.7% English, 14.7% Irish, 9.8% Polish, 9.1% Italian (2006-2010 5-year est.).
Economy: Employment by occupation: 1.4% management, 0.7% professional, 11.4% services, 20.7% sales, 5.0% farming, 22.9% construction, 12.1% production (2006-2010 5-year est.).
Income: Per capita income: $19,050 (2006-2010 5-year est.); Median household income: $41,250 (2006-2010 5-year est.); Average household income: $47,708 (2006-2010 5-year est.); Percent of households with income of $100,000 or more: 4.7% (2006-2010 5-year est.); Poverty rate: 2.3% (2006-2010 5-year est.).
Education: Percent of population age 25 and over with: High school diploma (including GED) or higher: 88.4% (2006-2010 5-year est.); Bachelor's degree or higher: 13.3% (2006-2010 5-year est.); Master's degree or higher: 4.6% (2006-2010 5-year est.).
**School District(s)**
Letchworth Central School District (KG-12)
2009-10 Enrollment: 1,048 . . . . . . . . . . . . . . . . . . . . . . (585) 493-5450

**GAINESVILLE** (town). Covers a land area of 35.570 square miles and a water area of 0.137 square miles. Located at 42.65° N. Lat; 78.12° W. Long. Elevation is 1,617 feet.
Population: 2,288 (1990); 2,333 (2000); 2,182 (2010); Density: 61.3 persons per square mile (2010); Race: 98.0% White, 0.2% Black, 0.1% Asian, 0.2% American Indian/Alaska Native, 0.0% Native Hawaiian/Other Pacific Islander, 1.5% Other, 1.5% Hispanic of any race (2010); Average household size: 2.47 (2010); Median age: 42.3 (2010); Males per 100 females: 102.8 (2010); Marriage status: 33.1% never married, 48.6% now married, 4.7% widowed, 13.6% divorced (2006-2010 5-year est.); Foreign born: 2.2% (2006-2010 5-year est.); Ancestry (includes multiple ancestries): 35.8% German, 18.4% English, 17.8% Irish, 10.2% Italian, 8.7% Polish (2006-2010 5-year est.).
Economy: Employment by occupation: 4.4% management, 0.9% professional, 10.6% services, 14.3% sales, 3.1% farming, 24.6% construction, 10.1% production (2006-2010 5-year est.).
Income: Per capita income: $19,992 (2006-2010 5-year est.); Median household income: $46,484 (2006-2010 5-year est.); Average household income: $50,827 (2006-2010 5-year est.); Percent of households with income of $100,000 or more: 5.9% (2006-2010 5-year est.); Poverty rate: 7.7% (2006-2010 5-year est.).
Education: Percent of population age 25 and over with: High school diploma (including GED) or higher: 88.2% (2006-2010 5-year est.); Bachelor's degree or higher: 9.4% (2006-2010 5-year est.); Master's degree or higher: 3.5% (2006-2010 5-year est.).
**School District(s)**
Letchworth Central School District (KG-12)
2009-10 Enrollment: 1,048 . . . . . . . . . . . . . . . . . . . . . . (585) 493-5450
Housing: Homeownership rate: 77.6% (2010); Median home value: $79,400 (2006-2010 5-year est.); Median contract rent: $463 per month (2006-2010 5-year est.); Median year structure built: before 1940 (2006-2010 5-year est.).
Transportation: Commute to work: 94.3% car, 1.0% public transportation, 1.7% walk, 1.6% work from home (2006-2010 5-year est.); Travel time to work: 33.8% less than 15 minutes, 42.1% 15 to 30 minutes, 12.8% 30 to 45 minutes, 3.8% 45 to 60 minutes, 7.5% 60 minutes or more (2006-2010 5-year est.)

**GENESEE FALLS** (town). Covers a land area of 15.614 square miles and a water area of 0.085 square miles. Located at 42.57° N. Lat; 78.06° W. Long.
Population: 488 (1990); 460 (2000); 438 (2010); Density: 28.1 persons per square mile (2010); Race: 97.9% White, 0.0% Black, 1.4% Asian, 0.0% American Indian/Alaska Native, 0.0% Native Hawaiian/Other Pacific Islander, 0.7% Other, 0.5% Hispanic of any race (2010); Average household size: 2.27 (2010); Median age: 44.9 (2010); Males per 100 females: 96.4 (2010); Marriage status: 19.0% never married, 67.7% now married, 6.5% widowed, 6.8% divorced (2006-2010 5-year est.); Foreign born: 2.0% (2006-2010 5-year est.); Ancestry (includes multiple ancestries): 26.8% German, 20.7% Irish, 12.9% English, 8.0% American, 6.6% Scotch-Irish (2006-2010 5-year est.).
Economy: Employment by occupation: 9.4% management, 0.0% professional, 14.9% services, 12.8% sales, 0.0% farming, 17.0% construction, 13.2% production (2006-2010 5-year est.).
Income: Per capita income: $21,682 (2006-2010 5-year est.); Median household income: $37,500 (2006-2010 5-year est.); Average household income: $53,169 (2006-2010 5-year est.); Percent of households with income of $100,000 or more: 9.0% (2006-2010 5-year est.); Poverty rate: 8.2% (2006-2010 5-year est.).
Education: Percent of population age 25 and over with: High school diploma (including GED) or higher: 89.0% (2006-2010 5-year est.); Bachelor's degree or higher: 12.6% (2006-2010 5-year est.); Master's degree or higher: 4.6% (2006-2010 5-year est.).
Housing: Homeownership rate: 80.4% (2010); Median home value: $75,200 (2006-2010 5-year est.); Median contract rent: $447 per month

(2006-2010 5-year est.); Median year structure built: before 1940 (2006-2010 5-year est.).
**Transportation:** Commute to work: 92.0% car, 0.0% public transportation, 7.1% walk, 0.9% work from home (2006-2010 5-year est.); Travel time to work: 34.4% less than 15 minutes, 31.7% 15 to 30 minutes, 8.0% 30 to 45 minutes, 12.1% 45 to 60 minutes, 13.8% 60 minutes or more (2006-2010 5-year est.).

**JAVA** (town). Covers a land area of 47.128 square miles and a water area of 0.202 square miles. Located at 42.65° N. Lat; 78.38° W. Long. Elevation is 1,522 feet.
**Population:** 2,197 (1990); 2,222 (2000); 2,057 (2010); Density: 43.6 persons per square mile (2010); Race: 98.8% White, 0.0% Black, 0.3% Asian, 0.2% American Indian/Alaska Native, 0.1% Native Hawaiian/Other Pacific Islander, 0.6% Other, 1.4% Hispanic of any race (2010); Average household size: 2.57 (2010); Median age: 41.1 (2010); Males per 100 females: 106.5 (2010); Marriage status: 28.3% never married, 60.9% now married, 4.6% widowed, 6.2% divorced (2006-2010 5-year est.); Foreign born: 2.2% (2006-2010 5-year est.); Ancestry (includes multiple ancestries): 54.7% German, 18.2% Irish, 16.7% Polish, 10.6% English, 6.6% Italian (2006-2010 5-year est.).
**Economy:** Employment by occupation: 9.9% management, 2.5% professional, 7.8% services, 12.8% sales, 1.9% farming, 17.8% construction, 10.2% production (2006-2010 5-year est.).
**Income:** Per capita income: $25,103 (2006-2010 5-year est.); Median household income: $57,557 (2006-2010 5-year est.); Average household income: $67,469 (2006-2010 5-year est.); Percent of households with income of $100,000 or more: 15.8% (2006-2010 5-year est.); Poverty rate: 3.5% (2006-2010 5-year est.).
**Education:** Percent of population age 25 and over with: High school diploma (including GED) or higher: 90.2% (2006-2010 5-year est.); Bachelor's degree or higher: 18.8% (2006-2010 5-year est.); Master's degree or higher: 10.9% (2006-2010 5-year est.).
**Housing:** Homeownership rate: 86.0% (2010); Median home value: $119,200 (2006-2010 5-year est.); Median contract rent: $554 per month (2006-2010 5-year est.); Median year structure built: 1959 (2006-2010 5-year est.).
**Transportation:** Commute to work: 91.5% car, 0.0% public transportation, 2.6% walk, 5.3% work from home (2006-2010 5-year est.); Travel time to work: 24.6% less than 15 minutes, 34.6% 15 to 30 minutes, 21.5% 30 to 45 minutes, 15.3% 45 to 60 minutes, 4.1% 60 minutes or more (2006-2010 5-year est.).

**JAVA CENTER** (unincorporated postal area)
Zip Code: 14082
Covers a land area of 9.929 square miles and a water area of 0.111 square miles. Located at 42.65° N. Lat; 78.38° W. Long. Elevation is 1,522 feet. Population: 426 (2010); Density: 42.9 persons per square mile (2010); Race: 98.1% White, 0.0% Black, 0.9% Asian, 0.2% American Indian/Alaska Native, 0.0% Native Hawaiian/Other Pacific Islander, 0.8% Other, 1.6% Hispanic of any race (2010); Average household size: 2.43 (2010); Median age: 39.7 (2010); Males per 100 females: 105.8 (2010); Homeownership rate: 79.4% (2010)

**MIDDLEBURY** (town). Covers a land area of 35.642 square miles and a water area of 0.024 square miles. Located at 42.82° N. Lat; 78.13° W. Long.
**Population:** 1,532 (1990); 1,508 (2000); 1,441 (2010); Density: 40.4 persons per square mile (2010); Race: 97.4% White, 0.2% Black, 0.1% Asian, 0.1% American Indian/Alaska Native, 0.0% Native Hawaiian/Other Pacific Islander, 2.2% Other, 1.1% Hispanic of any race (2010); Average household size: 2.51 (2010); Median age: 43.0 (2010); Males per 100 females: 105.6 (2010); Marriage status: 25.9% never married, 60.8% now married, 4.0% widowed, 9.2% divorced (2006-2010 5-year est.); Foreign born: 0.7% (2006-2010 5-year est.); Ancestry (includes multiple ancestries): 34.9% German, 25.2% English, 19.1% Irish, 8.6% Italian, 8.5% Polish (2006-2010 5-year est.).
**Economy:** Employment by occupation: 15.3% management, 1.2% professional, 11.0% services, 17.3% sales, 3.0% farming, 11.6% construction, 6.1% production (2006-2010 5-year est.).
**Income:** Per capita income: $25,403 (2006-2010 5-year est.); Median household income: $56,625 (2006-2010 5-year est.); Average household income: $69,125 (2006-2010 5-year est.); Percent of households with income of $100,000 or more: 14.0% (2006-2010 5-year est.); Poverty rate: 7.0% (2006-2010 5-year est.).

**Education:** Percent of population age 25 and over with: High school diploma (including GED) or higher: 90.6% (2006-2010 5-year est.); Bachelor's degree or higher: 15.2% (2006-2010 5-year est.); Master's degree or higher: 6.0% (2006-2010 5-year est.).
**Housing:** Homeownership rate: 85.9% (2010); Median home value: $94,900 (2006-2010 5-year est.); Median contract rent: $485 per month (2006-2010 5-year est.); Median year structure built: before 1940 (2006-2010 5-year est.).
**Transportation:** Commute to work: 86.6% car, 0.2% public transportation, 8.1% walk, 3.7% work from home (2006-2010 5-year est.); Travel time to work: 36.8% less than 15 minutes, 33.8% 15 to 30 minutes, 13.4% 30 to 45 minutes, 9.0% 45 to 60 minutes, 7.0% 60 minutes or more (2006-2010 5-year est.)

**NORTH JAVA** (unincorporated postal area)
Zip Code: 14113
Covers a land area of 17.020 square miles and a water area of <.001 square miles. Located at 42.67° N. Lat; 78.33° W. Long. Elevation is 1,562 feet. Population: 703 (2010); Density: 41.3 persons per square mile (2010); Race: 98.2% White, 0.0% Black, 0.3% Asian, 0.4% American Indian/Alaska Native, 0.0% Native Hawaiian/Other Pacific Islander, 1.1% Other, 1.4% Hispanic of any race (2010); Average household size: 2.66 (2010); Median age: 41.0 (2010); Males per 100 females: 109.2 (2010); Homeownership rate: 88.2% (2010)

**ORANGEVILLE** (town). Covers a land area of 35.560 square miles and a water area of 0.081 square miles. Located at 42.74° N. Lat; 78.25° W. Long.
**Population:** 1,115 (1990); 1,301 (2000); 1,355 (2010); Density: 38.1 persons per square mile (2010); Race: 97.3% White, 0.1% Black, 0.1% Asian, 0.3% American Indian/Alaska Native, 0.1% Native Hawaiian/Other Pacific Islander, 2.1% Other, 3.4% Hispanic of any race (2010); Average household size: 2.55 (2010); Median age: 44.2 (2010); Males per 100 females: 108.5 (2010); Marriage status: 18.3% never married, 71.7% now married, 3.4% widowed, 6.6% divorced (2006-2010 5-year est.); Foreign born: 0.7% (2006-2010 5-year est.); Ancestry (includes multiple ancestries): 47.0% German, 21.4% English, 13.1% Irish, 12.8% Polish, 6.5% Italian (2006-2010 5-year est.).
**Economy:** Employment by occupation: 6.4% management, 2.0% professional, 10.9% services, 17.9% sales, 0.5% farming, 13.9% construction, 10.9% production (2006-2010 5-year est.).
**Income:** Per capita income: $26,079 (2006-2010 5-year est.); Median household income: $63,500 (2006-2010 5-year est.); Average household income: $66,052 (2006-2010 5-year est.); Percent of households with income of $100,000 or more: 15.5% (2006-2010 5-year est.); Poverty rate: 3.5% (2006-2010 5-year est.).
**Education:** Percent of population age 25 and over with: High school diploma (including GED) or higher: 93.9% (2006-2010 5-year est.); Bachelor's degree or higher: 19.5% (2006-2010 5-year est.); Master's degree or higher: 5.6% (2006-2010 5-year est.).
**Housing:** Homeownership rate: 89.3% (2010); Median home value: $118,200 (2006-2010 5-year est.); Median contract rent: $556 per month (2006-2010 5-year est.); Median year structure built: 1974 (2006-2010 5-year est.).
**Transportation:** Commute to work: 90.0% car, 1.1% public transportation, 3.8% walk, 3.5% work from home (2006-2010 5-year est.); Travel time to work: 25.2% less than 15 minutes, 34.5% 15 to 30 minutes, 26.0% 30 to 45 minutes, 11.0% 45 to 60 minutes, 3.3% 60 minutes or more (2006-2010 5-year est.)

**PERRY** (village). Covers a land area of 2.337 square miles and a water area of 0.111 square miles. Located at 42.71° N. Lat; 78.00° W. Long. Elevation is 1,371 feet.
**Population:** 4,219 (1990); 3,945 (2000); 3,673 (2010); Density: 1,571.4 persons per square mile (2010); Race: 97.0% White, 0.7% Black, 0.2% Asian, 0.3% American Indian/Alaska Native, 0.0% Native Hawaiian/Other Pacific Islander, 1.8% Other, 2.4% Hispanic of any race (2010); Average household size: 2.39 (2010); Median age: 38.7 (2010); Males per 100 females: 91.0 (2010); Marriage status: 31.5% never married, 52.9% now married, 6.9% widowed, 8.7% divorced (2006-2010 5-year est.); Foreign born: 1.1% (2006-2010 5-year est.); Ancestry (includes multiple ancestries): 29.4% German, 22.9% Irish, 18.0% English, 17.1% Italian, 6.6% Polish (2006-2010 5-year est.).

**Economy:** Employment by occupation: 10.2% management, 0.7% professional, 9.6% services, 13.3% sales, 6.7% farming, 15.0% construction, 12.2% production (2006-2010 5-year est.).
**Income:** Per capita income: $19,850 (2006-2010 5-year est.); Median household income: $42,589 (2006-2010 5-year est.); Average household income: $48,707 (2006-2010 5-year est.); Percent of households with income of $100,000 or more: 8.3% (2006-2010 5-year est.); Poverty rate: 18.9% (2006-2010 5-year est.).
**Education:** Percent of population age 25 and over with: High school diploma (including GED) or higher: 87.2% (2006-2010 5-year est.); Bachelor's degree or higher: 16.2% (2006-2010 5-year est.); Master's degree or higher: 5.7% (2006-2010 5-year est.).

**School District(s)**

Perry Central School District (PK-12)
    2009-10 Enrollment: 963 . . . . . . . . . . . . . . . . . (585) 237-0270
**Housing:** Homeownership rate: 62.5% (2010); Median home value: $76,000 (2006-2010 5-year est.); Median contract rent: $488 per month (2006-2010 5-year est.); Median year structure built: before 1940 (2006-2010 5-year est.).
**Safety:** Violent crime rate: 14.0 per 10,000 population; Property crime rate: 238.0 per 10,000 population (2010).
**Newspapers:** Perry Herald (Local news; Circulation 5,000); The Perry Shopper (Community news; Circulation 7,350)
**Transportation:** Commute to work: 92.0% car, 0.0% public transportation, 3.7% walk, 4.3% work from home (2006-2010 5-year est.); Travel time to work: 32.0% less than 15 minutes, 33.5% 15 to 30 minutes, 16.5% 30 to 45 minutes, 5.3% 45 to 60 minutes, 12.6% 60 minutes or more (2006-2010 5-year est.)
**Additional Information Contacts**

Perry Chamber of Commerce . . . . . . . . . . . . . . (585) 237-5040
    http://www.perrychamber.com
Village of Perry. . . . . . . . . . . . . . . . . . . . . . . (585) 237-2216
    http://www.villageofperry.com
Wyoming County Chamber of Commerce . . . . . . (585) 237-0230
    http://www.wycochamber.org

**PERRY** (town). Covers a land area of 36.405 square miles and a water area of 0.242 square miles. Located at 42.75° N. Lat; 78.01° W. Long. Elevation is 1,371 feet.
**History:** In 1833, the Reverend William Arthur became pastor of the First Baptist Church in Perry. His son, Chester Alan Arthur, then four yeas old, was destined to become the 21st President of the United States.
**Population:** 5,353 (1990); 6,654 (2000); 4,616 (2010); Density: 126.8 persons per square mile (2010); Race: 96.2% White, 0.5% Black, 0.3% Asian, 0.3% American Indian/Alaska Native, 0.0% Native Hawaiian/Other Pacific Islander, 2.7% Other, 3.3% Hispanic of any race (2010); Average household size: 2.45 (2010); Median age: 39.4 (2010); Males per 100 females: 94.8 (2010); Marriage status: 28.6% never married, 54.9% now married, 6.7% widowed, 9.8% divorced (2006-2010 5-year est.); Foreign born: 1.0% (2006-2010 5-year est.); Ancestry (includes multiple ancestries): 30.4% German, 20.8% English, 20.6% Irish, 15.6% Italian, 6.9% Polish (2006-2010 5-year est.).
**Economy:** Employment by occupation: 12.3% management, 3.0% professional, 8.8% services, 12.8% sales, 5.5% farming, 16.2% construction, 12.2% production (2006-2010 5-year est.).
**Income:** Per capita income: $19,858 (2006-2010 5-year est.); Median household income: $46,011 (2006-2010 5-year est.); Average household income: $49,178 (2006-2010 5-year est.); Percent of households with income of $100,000 or more: 8.6% (2006-2010 5-year est.); Poverty rate: 16.5% (2006-2010 5-year est.).
**Education:** Percent of population age 25 and over with: High school diploma (including GED) or higher: 86.9% (2006-2010 5-year est.); Bachelor's degree or higher: 16.0% (2006-2010 5-year est.); Master's degree or higher: 5.7% (2006-2010 5-year est.).

**School District(s)**

Perry Central School District (PK-12)
    2009-10 Enrollment: 963 . . . . . . . . . . . . . . . . . (585) 237-0270
**Housing:** Homeownership rate: 66.4% (2010); Median home value: $77,900 (2006-2010 5-year est.); Median contract rent: $487 per month (2006-2010 5-year est.); Median year structure built: before 1940 (2006-2010 5-year est.).
**Newspapers:** Perry Herald (Local news; Circulation 5,000); The Perry Shopper (Community news; Circulation 7,350)
**Transportation:** Commute to work: 92.5% car, 0.0% public transportation, 4.2% walk, 2.9% work from home (2006-2010 5-year est.); Travel time to

work: 31.4% less than 15 minutes, 33.4% 15 to 30 minutes, 13.4% 30 to 45 minutes, 6.9% 45 to 60 minutes, 15.0% 60 minutes or more (2006-2010 5-year est.)

**PIKE** (village). Covers a land area of 1.493 square miles and a water area of <.001 square miles. Located at 42.55° N. Lat; 78.14° W. Long. Elevation is 1,545 feet.
**Population:** 384 (1990); 382 (2000); 371 (2010); Density: 248.4 persons per square mile (2010); Race: 99.2% White, 0.0% Black, 0.3% Asian, 0.0% American Indian/Alaska Native, 0.0% Native Hawaiian/Other Pacific Islander, 0.5% Other, 1.9% Hispanic of any race (2010); Average household size: 2.90 (2010); Median age: 35.5 (2010); Males per 100 females: 101.6 (2010); Marriage status: 31.3% never married, 57.9% now married, 2.8% widowed, 7.9% divorced (2006-2010 5-year est.); Foreign born: 1.8% (2006-2010 5-year est.); Ancestry (includes multiple ancestries): 28.6% German, 24.5% English, 14.5% Irish, 10.5% French, 5.6% Dutch (2006-2010 5-year est.).
**Economy:** Employment by occupation: 10.8% management, 0.0% professional, 8.4% services, 12.7% sales, 5.4% farming, 12.7% construction, 21.1% production (2006-2010 5-year est.).
**Income:** Per capita income: $17,975 (2006-2010 5-year est.); Median household income: $53,000 (2006-2010 5-year est.); Average household income: $56,148 (2006-2010 5-year est.); Percent of households with income of $100,000 or more: 11.1% (2006-2010 5-year est.); Poverty rate: 11.7% (2006-2010 5-year est.).
**Education:** Percent of population age 25 and over with: High school diploma (including GED) or higher: 82.0% (2006-2010 5-year est.); Bachelor's degree or higher: 7.4% (2006-2010 5-year est.); Master's degree or higher: 0.8% (2006-2010 5-year est.).
**Housing:** Homeownership rate: 71.9% (2010); Median home value: $68,300 (2006-2010 5-year est.); Median contract rent: $475 per month (2006-2010 5-year est.); Median year structure built: before 1940 (2006-2010 5-year est.).
**Transportation:** Commute to work: 90.5% car, 4.4% public transportation, 2.5% walk, 2.5% work from home (2006-2010 5-year est.); Travel time to work: 20.1% less than 15 minutes, 41.6% 15 to 30 minutes, 18.2% 30 to 45 minutes, 9.7% 45 to 60 minutes, 10.4% 60 minutes or more (2006-2010 5-year est.)

**PIKE** (town). Covers a land area of 31.083 square miles and a water area of 0.145 square miles. Located at 42.56° N. Lat; 78.13° W. Long. Elevation is 1,545 feet.
**Population:** 1,081 (1990); 1,086 (2000); 1,114 (2010); Density: 35.8 persons per square mile (2010); Race: 97.7% White, 0.2% Black, 0.5% Asian, 0.6% American Indian/Alaska Native, 0.0% Native Hawaiian/Other Pacific Islander, 1.0% Other, 0.8% Hispanic of any race (2010); Average household size: 2.77 (2010); Median age: 38.8 (2010); Males per 100 females: 104.4 (2010); Marriage status: 26.5% never married, 63.2% now married, 2.8% widowed, 7.5% divorced (2006-2010 5-year est.); Foreign born: 1.4% (2006-2010 5-year est.); Ancestry (includes multiple ancestries): 33.6% German, 21.1% English, 10.0% Irish, 6.7% Polish, 6.5% French (2006-2010 5-year est.).
**Economy:** Employment by occupation: 13.4% management, 0.0% professional, 9.6% services, 20.6% sales, 3.5% farming, 17.7% construction, 11.0% production (2006-2010 5-year est.).
**Income:** Per capita income: $20,994 (2006-2010 5-year est.); Median household income: $61,033 (2006-2010 5-year est.); Average household income: $61,379 (2006-2010 5-year est.); Percent of households with income of $100,000 or more: 11.5% (2006-2010 5-year est.); Poverty rate: 11.9% (2006-2010 5-year est.).
**Education:** Percent of population age 25 and over with: High school diploma (including GED) or higher: 90.0% (2006-2010 5-year est.); Bachelor's degree or higher: 12.6% (2006-2010 5-year est.); Master's degree or higher: 4.3% (2006-2010 5-year est.).
**Housing:** Homeownership rate: 83.0% (2010); Median home value: $71,100 (2006-2010 5-year est.); Median contract rent: $484 per month (2006-2010 5-year est.); Median year structure built: 1952 (2006-2010 5-year est.).
**Transportation:** Commute to work: 91.7% car, 1.4% public transportation, 4.4% walk, 1.4% work from home (2006-2010 5-year est.); Travel time to work: 30.4% less than 15 minutes, 37.8% 15 to 30 minutes, 16.1% 30 to 45 minutes, 6.2% 45 to 60 minutes, 9.5% 60 minutes or more (2006-2010 5-year est.)

**PORTAGEVILLE** (unincorporated postal area)
Zip Code: 14536
Covers a land area of 18.221 square miles and a water area of 0.164 square miles. Located at 42.54° N. Lat; 78.08° W. Long. Elevation is 1,115 feet. Population: 687 (2010); Density: 37.7 persons per square mile (2010); Race: 97.2% White, 0.3% Black, 0.9% Asian, 0.1% American Indian/Alaska Native, 0.0% Native Hawaiian/Other Pacific Islander, 1.5% Other, 0.9% Hispanic of any race (2010); Average household size: 2.54 (2010); Median age: 40.7 (2010); Males per 100 females: 103.3 (2010); Homeownership rate: 78.6% (2010)

**SHELDON** (town). Covers a land area of 47.348 square miles and a water area of 0.025 square miles. Located at 42.74° N. Lat; 78.37° W. Long. Elevation is 1,512 feet.
**Population:** 2,487 (1990); 2,561 (2000); 2,409 (2010); Density: 50.9 persons per square mile (2010); Race: 98.5% White, 0.0% Black, 0.1% Asian, 0.2% American Indian/Alaska Native, 0.0% Native Hawaiian/Other Pacific Islander, 1.2% Other, 1.5% Hispanic of any race (2010); Average household size: 2.46 (2010); Median age: 43.1 (2010); Males per 100 females: 110.9 (2010); Marriage status: 23.1% never married, 65.0% now married, 5.4% widowed, 6.5% divorced (2006-2010 5-year est.); Foreign born: 1.5% (2006-2010 5-year est.); Ancestry (includes multiple ancestries): 49.6% German, 17.1% Irish, 16.8% Polish, 12.4% English, 9.9% Italian (2006-2010 5-year est.).
**Economy:** Employment by occupation: 14.5% management, 0.9% professional, 7.8% services, 10.0% sales, 2.5% farming, 22.2% construction, 11.6% production (2006-2010 5-year est.).
**Income:** Per capita income: $25,306 (2006-2010 5-year est.); Median household income: $51,433 (2006-2010 5-year est.); Average household income: $59,478 (2006-2010 5-year est.); Percent of households with income of $100,000 or more: 13.8% (2006-2010 5-year est.); Poverty rate: 7.1% (2006-2010 5-year est.).
**Education:** Percent of population age 25 and over with: High school diploma (including GED) or higher: 87.2% (2006-2010 5-year est.); Bachelor's degree or higher: 13.0% (2006-2010 5-year est.); Master's degree or higher: 3.9% (2006-2010 5-year est.).
**Housing:** Homeownership rate: 81.8% (2010); Median home value: $122,600 (2006-2010 5-year est.); Median contract rent: $444 per month (2006-2010 5-year est.); Median year structure built: 1958 (2006-2010 5-year est.).
**Transportation:** Commute to work: 85.5% car, 0.0% public transportation, 9.2% walk, 3.2% work from home (2006-2010 5-year est.); Travel time to work: 26.3% less than 15 minutes, 26.0% 15 to 30 minutes, 24.2% 30 to 45 minutes, 14.2% 45 to 60 minutes, 9.4% 60 minutes or more (2006-2010 5-year est.)

**SILVER LAKE** (unincorporated postal area)
Zip Code: 14549
Covers a land area of 0.112 square miles and a water area of 0 square miles. Located at 42.70° N. Lat; 78.01° W. Long. Elevation is 1,375 feet. Population: 91 (2010); Density: 809.7 persons per square mile (2010); Race: 98.9% White, 0.0% Black, 0.0% Asian, 0.0% American Indian/Alaska Native, 0.0% Native Hawaiian/Other Pacific Islander, 1.1% Other, 0.0% Hispanic of any race (2010); Average household size: 2.53 (2010); Median age: 41.5 (2010); Males per 100 females: 71.7 (2010); Homeownership rate: 69.4% (2010)

**SILVER SPRINGS** (village). Covers a land area of 0.952 square miles and a water area of 0.027 square miles. Located at 42.66° N. Lat; 78.08° W. Long. Elevation is 1,414 feet.
**Population:** 852 (1990); 844 (2000); 782 (2010); Density: 821.2 persons per square mile (2010); Race: 97.3% White, 0.3% Black, 0.0% Asian, 0.3% American Indian/Alaska Native, 0.0% Native Hawaiian/Other Pacific Islander, 2.1% Other, 1.7% Hispanic of any race (2010); Average household size: 2.30 (2010); Median age: 42.4 (2010); Males per 100 females: 89.3 (2010); Marriage status: 29.6% never married, 45.8% now married, 11.6% widowed, 13.0% divorced (2006-2010 5-year est.); Foreign born: 0.0% (2006-2010 5-year est.); Ancestry (includes multiple ancestries): 46.1% German, 23.8% English, 23.5% Irish, 7.4% Italian, 6.6% Polish (2006-2010 5-year est.).
**Economy:** Employment by occupation: 2.0% management, 2.5% professional, 9.3% services, 11.3% sales, 4.5% farming, 30.1% construction, 11.3% production (2006-2010 5-year est.).
**Income:** Per capita income: $19,056 (2006-2010 5-year est.); Median household income: $41,293 (2006-2010 5-year est.); Average household

income: $43,395 (2006-2010 5-year est.); Percent of households with income of $100,000 or more: 2.4% (2006-2010 5-year est.); Poverty rate: 12.9% (2006-2010 5-year est.).
**Education:** Percent of population age 25 and over with: High school diploma (including GED) or higher: 87.6% (2006-2010 5-year est.); Bachelor's degree or higher: 7.2% (2006-2010 5-year est.); Master's degree or higher: 4.4% (2006-2010 5-year est.).
**Housing:** Homeownership rate: 66.4% (2010); Median home value: $74,200 (2006-2010 5-year est.); Median contract rent: $376 per month (2006-2010 5-year est.); Median year structure built: before 1940 (2006-2010 5-year est.).
**Transportation:** Commute to work: 87.0% car, 2.3% public transportation, 4.6% walk, 4.3% work from home (2006-2010 5-year est.); Travel time to work: 42.4% less than 15 minutes, 31.2% 15 to 30 minutes, 16.1% 30 to 45 minutes, 3.0% 45 to 60 minutes, 7.3% 60 minutes or more (2006-2010 5-year est.)

**STRYKERSVILLE** (CDP). Covers a land area of 3.420 square miles and a water area of 0 square miles. Located at 42.70° N. Lat; 78.44° W. Long. Elevation is 1,083 feet.
**Population:** n/a (1990); n/a (2000); 647 (2010); Density: 189.2 persons per square mile (2010); Race: 97.8% White, 0.2% Black, 0.2% Asian, 0.2% American Indian/Alaska Native, 0.2% Native Hawaiian/Other Pacific Islander, 1.4% Other, 2.2% Hispanic of any race (2010); Average household size: 2.43 (2010); Median age: 42.5 (2010); Males per 100 females: 93.1 (2010); Marriage status: 25.8% never married, 61.9% now married, 6.5% widowed, 5.8% divorced (2006-2010 5-year est.); Foreign born: 1.2% (2006-2010 5-year est.); Ancestry (includes multiple ancestries): 38.5% German, 27.0% Irish, 18.1% English, 14.7% Polish, 13.9% French (2006-2010 5-year est.).
**Economy:** Employment by occupation: 14.4% management, 3.2% professional, 10.5% services, 13.4% sales, 3.5% farming, 11.8% construction, 8.3% production (2006-2010 5-year est.).
**Income:** Per capita income: $27,286 (2006-2010 5-year est.); Median household income: $61,250 (2006-2010 5-year est.); Average household income: $66,038 (2006-2010 5-year est.); Percent of households with income of $100,000 or more: 10.1% (2006-2010 5-year est.); Poverty rate: 0.0% (2006-2010 5-year est.).
**Education:** Percent of population age 25 and over with: High school diploma (including GED) or higher: 92.8% (2006-2010 5-year est.); Bachelor's degree or higher: 22.4% (2006-2010 5-year est.); Master's degree or higher: 7.5% (2006-2010 5-year est.).
**Housing:** Homeownership rate: 75.9% (2010); Median home value: $123,000 (2006-2010 5-year est.); Median contract rent: $517 per month (2006-2010 5-year est.); Median year structure built: 1961 (2006-2010 5-year est.).
**Transportation:** Commute to work: 90.0% car, 0.0% public transportation, 8.0% walk, 0.0% work from home (2006-2010 5-year est.); Travel time to work: 21.7% less than 15 minutes, 34.8% 15 to 30 minutes, 33.4% 30 to 45 minutes, 6.0% 45 to 60 minutes, 4.0% 60 minutes or more (2006-2010 5-year est.)

**VARYSBURG** (unincorporated postal area)
Zip Code: 14167
Covers a land area of 37.668 square miles and a water area of 0.003 square miles. Located at 42.75° N. Lat; 78.32° W. Long. Elevation is 1,158 feet. Population: 1,663 (2010); Density: 44.1 persons per square mile (2010); Race: 98.0% White, 0.1% Black, 0.2% Asian, 0.1% American Indian/Alaska Native, 0.1% Native Hawaiian/Other Pacific Islander, 1.5% Other, 2.5% Hispanic of any race (2010); Average household size: 2.42 (2010); Median age: 44.5 (2010); Males per 100 females: 117.1 (2010); Homeownership rate: 84.1% (2010)

**WARSAW** (village). County seat. Covers a land area of 4.105 square miles and a water area of 0 square miles. Located at 42.74° N. Lat; 78.14° W. Long. Elevation is 1,014 feet.
**Population:** 3,830 (1990); 3,814 (2000); 3,473 (2010); Density: 845.9 persons per square mile (2010); Race: 96.9% White, 0.2% Black, 0.9% Asian, 0.3% American Indian/Alaska Native, 0.0% Native Hawaiian/Other Pacific Islander, 1.7% Other, 1.6% Hispanic of any race (2010); Average household size: 2.20 (2010); Median age: 39.9 (2010); Males per 100 females: 90.5 (2010); Marriage status: 31.3% never married, 45.7% now married, 9.3% widowed, 13.6% divorced (2006-2010 5-year est.); Foreign born: 3.0% (2006-2010 5-year est.); Ancestry (includes multiple

ancestries): 34.3% English, 27.2% German, 20.9% Irish, 9.2% Italian, 4.2% Polish (2006-2010 5-year est.).
**Economy:** Single-family building permits issued: 0 (2011); Multi-family building permits issued: 8 (2011); Employment by occupation: 8.4% management, 1.6% professional, 11.3% services, 23.6% sales, 2.8% farming, 11.1% construction, 8.7% production (2006-2010 5-year est.).
**Income:** Per capita income: $20,920 (2006-2010 5-year est.); Median household income: $37,971 (2006-2010 5-year est.); Average household income: $50,118 (2006-2010 5-year est.); Percent of households with income of $100,000 or more: 10.5% (2006-2010 5-year est.); Poverty rate: 12.4% (2006-2010 5-year est.).
**Education:** Percent of population age 25 and over with: High school diploma (including GED) or higher: 85.0% (2006-2010 5-year est.); Bachelor's degree or higher: 18.2% (2006-2010 5-year est.); Master's degree or higher: 5.1% (2006-2010 5-year est.).

#### School District(s)
Warsaw Central School District (PK-12)
  2009-10 Enrollment: 1,035 . . . . . . . . . . . . . . . . . . . . . (585) 786-8000
**Housing:** Homeownership rate: 53.3% (2010); Median home value: $88,900 (2006-2010 5-year est.); Median contract rent: $468 per month (2006-2010 5-year est.); Median year structure built: before 1940 (2006-2010 5-year est.).
**Hospitals:** Wyoming County Community Health System (262 beds)
**Safety:** Violent crime rate: 5.7 per 10,000 population; Property crime rate: 215.5 per 10,000 population (2010).
**Transportation:** Commute to work: 93.1% car, 0.0% public transportation, 4.4% walk, 1.9% work from home (2006-2010 5-year est.); Travel time to work: 54.7% less than 15 minutes, 21.1% 15 to 30 minutes, 12.2% 30 to 45 minutes, 6.7% 45 to 60 minutes, 5.4% 60 minutes or more (2006-2010 5-year est.)

**WARSAW** (town). Covers a land area of 35.415 square miles and a water area of 0.050 square miles. Located at 42.73° N. Lat; 78.13° W. Long. Elevation is 1,014 feet.
**Population:** 5,342 (1990); 5,423 (2000); 5,064 (2010); Density: 143.0 persons per square mile (2010); Race: 96.8% White, 0.1% Black, 1.0% Asian, 0.3% American Indian/Alaska Native, 0.0% Native Hawaiian/Other Pacific Islander, 1.8% Other, 1.5% Hispanic of any race (2010); Average household size: 2.27 (2010); Median age: 42.1 (2010); Males per 100 females: 91.4 (2010); Marriage status: 28.4% never married, 50.0% now married, 8.9% widowed, 12.8% divorced (2006-2010 5-year est.); Foreign born: 3.3% (2006-2010 5-year est.); Ancestry (includes multiple ancestries): 31.6% German, 30.9% English, 21.6% Irish, 9.2% Italian, 4.1% Polish (2006-2010 5-year est.).
**Economy:** Employment by occupation: 8.3% management, 1.8% professional, 12.2% services, 22.5% sales, 3.8% farming, 11.8% construction, 9.3% production (2006-2010 5-year est.).
**Income:** Per capita income: $21,762 (2006-2010 5-year est.); Median household income: $42,746 (2006-2010 5-year est.); Average household income: $51,696 (2006-2010 5-year est.); Percent of households with income of $100,000 or more: 11.2% (2006-2010 5-year est.); Poverty rate: 12.9% (2006-2010 5-year est.).
**Education:** Percent of population age 25 and over with: High school diploma (including GED) or higher: 86.4% (2006-2010 5-year est.); Bachelor's degree or higher: 18.7% (2006-2010 5-year est.); Master's degree or higher: 5.1% (2006-2010 5-year est.).

#### School District(s)
Warsaw Central School District (PK-12)
  2009-10 Enrollment: 1,035 . . . . . . . . . . . . . . . . . . . . . (585) 786-8000
**Housing:** Homeownership rate: 62.4% (2010); Median home value: $92,300 (2006-2010 5-year est.); Median contract rent: $470 per month (2006-2010 5-year est.); Median year structure built: before 1940 (2006-2010 5-year est.).
**Hospitals:** Wyoming County Community Health System (262 beds)
**Transportation:** Commute to work: 91.4% car, 0.0% public transportation, 5.7% walk, 2.4% work from home (2006-2010 5-year est.); Travel time to work: 53.0% less than 15 minutes, 22.9% 15 to 30 minutes, 12.3% 30 to 45 minutes, 6.3% 45 to 60 minutes, 5.5% 60 minutes or more (2006-2010 5-year est.)

**WETHERSFIELD** (town). Covers a land area of 35.810 square miles and a water area of 0.307 square miles. Located at 42.64° N. Lat; 78.24° W. Long.
**Population:** 794 (1990); 891 (2000); 883 (2010); Density: 24.7 persons per square mile (2010); Race: 99.0% White, 0.1% Black, 0.0% Asian, 0.2%

American Indian/Alaska Native, 0.0% Native Hawaiian/Other Pacific Islander, 0.7% Other, 1.5% Hispanic of any race (2010); Average household size: 2.64 (2010); Median age: 39.7 (2010); Males per 100 females: 112.8 (2010); Marriage status: 21.6% never married, 65.7% now married, 7.8% widowed, 4.9% divorced (2006-2010 5-year est.); Foreign born: 1.8% (2006-2010 5-year est.); Ancestry (includes multiple ancestries): 51.3% German, 19.3% Irish, 12.3% Polish, 10.5% English, 7.9% French (2006-2010 5-year est.).
**Economy:** Employment by occupation: 18.1% management, 0.0% professional, 11.5% services, 13.0% sales, 1.7% farming, 21.1% construction, 12.3% production (2006-2010 5-year est.).
**Income:** Per capita income: $20,356 (2006-2010 5-year est.); Median household income: $43,958 (2006-2010 5-year est.); Average household income: $54,999 (2006-2010 5-year est.); Percent of households with income of $100,000 or more: 8.9% (2006-2010 5-year est.); Poverty rate: 19.2% (2006-2010 5-year est.).
**Education:** Percent of population age 25 and over with: High school diploma (including GED) or higher: 86.6% (2006-2010 5-year est.); Bachelor's degree or higher: 17.0% (2006-2010 5-year est.); Master's degree or higher: 4.6% (2006-2010 5-year est.).
**Housing:** Homeownership rate: 75.7% (2010); Median home value: $98,900 (2006-2010 5-year est.); Median contract rent: $550 per month (2006-2010 5-year est.); Median year structure built: 1967 (2006-2010 5-year est.).
**Transportation:** Commute to work: 93.5% car, 0.0% public transportation, 4.0% walk, 2.5% work from home (2006-2010 5-year est.); Travel time to work: 33.7% less than 15 minutes, 41.3% 15 to 30 minutes, 11.0% 30 to 45 minutes, 10.5% 45 to 60 minutes, 3.6% 60 minutes or more (2006-2010 5-year est.)

**WYOMING** (village). Covers a land area of 0.668 square miles and a water area of 0 square miles. Located at 42.82° N. Lat; 78.08° W. Long. Elevation is 988 feet.
**Population:** 478 (1990); 513 (2000); 434 (2010); Density: 648.9 persons per square mile (2010); Race: 97.7% White, 0.5% Black, 0.0% Asian, 0.0% American Indian/Alaska Native, 0.0% Native Hawaiian/Other Pacific Islander, 1.8% Other, 0.9% Hispanic of any race (2010); Average household size: 2.73 (2010); Median age: 35.8 (2010); Males per 100 females: 100.9 (2010); Marriage status: 27.0% never married, 54.0% now married, 3.7% widowed, 15.3% divorced (2006-2010 5-year est.); Foreign born: 0.3% (2006-2010 5-year est.); Ancestry (includes multiple ancestries): 31.0% German, 23.5% English, 21.4% Irish, 8.0% Polish, 6.4% American (2006-2010 5-year est.).
**Economy:** Employment by occupation: 4.2% management, 1.6% professional, 13.6% services, 14.7% sales, 3.7% farming, 9.4% construction, 12.6% production (2006-2010 5-year est.).
**Income:** Per capita income: $18,847 (2006-2010 5-year est.); Median household income: $39,792 (2006-2010 5-year est.); Average household income: $47,715 (2006-2010 5-year est.); Percent of households with income of $100,000 or more: 4.8% (2006-2010 5-year est.); Poverty rate: 6.0% (2006-2010 5-year est.).
**Education:** Percent of population age 25 and over with: High school diploma (including GED) or higher: 85.4% (2006-2010 5-year est.); Bachelor's degree or higher: 14.6% (2006-2010 5-year est.); Master's degree or higher: 5.3% (2006-2010 5-year est.).

#### School District(s)
Wyoming Central School District (KG-08)
  2009-10 Enrollment: 167 . . . . . . . . . . . . . . . . . . . . . . . (585) 495-6222
**Housing:** Homeownership rate: 78.6% (2010); Median home value: $86,700 (2006-2010 5-year est.); Median contract rent: $492 per month (2006-2010 5-year est.); Median year structure built: before 1940 (2006-2010 5-year est.).
**Transportation:** Commute to work: 92.9% car, 0.0% public transportation, 4.9% walk, 2.2% work from home (2006-2010 5-year est.); Travel time to work: 39.9% less than 15 minutes, 32.6% 15 to 30 minutes, 12.9% 30 to 45 minutes, 10.1% 45 to 60 minutes, 4.5% 60 minutes or more (2006-2010 5-year est.)

# Yates County

Located in west central New York; bounded on the east by Seneca Lake; includes parts of Keuka and Canandaigua Lakes. Covers a land area of 338.24 square miles, a water area of 37.52 square miles, and is located in the Eastern Time Zone at 42.63° N. Lat., 77.07° W. Long. The county was founded in 1823. County seat is Penn Yan.

**Population:** 22,810 (1990); 24,621 (2000); 25,348 (2010); Race: 97.2% White, 0.8% Black, 0.4% Asian, 0.1% American Indian/Alaska Native, 0.0% Native Hawaiian/Other Pacific Islander, 1.5% Other, 1.7% Hispanic of any race (2010); Density: 74.9 persons per square mile (2010); Average household size: 2.53 (2010); Median age: 40.7 (2010); Males per 100 females: 93.9 (2010).
**Religion:** Six largest groups: 11.3% Catholicism, 8.3% Methodist/Pietist, 4.0% Baptist, 2.0% Presbyterian-Reformed, 1.9% Lutheran, 0.8% Non-Denominational (2010)
**Economy:** Unemployment rate: 8.2% (February 2012); Total civilian labor force: 13,014 (February 2012); Leading industries: 23.1% health care and social assistance; 14.9% manufacturing; 14.2% retail trade (2009); Farms: 864 totaling 126,118 acres (2007); Companies that employ 500 or more persons: 1 (2009); Companies that employ 100 to 499 persons: 4 (2009); Companies that employ less than 100 persons: 529 (2009); Black-owned businesses: n/a (2007); Hispanic-owned businesses: n/a (2007); Asian-owned businesses: n/a (2007); Women-owned businesses: n/a (2007); Retail sales per capita: $6,722 (2010). Single-family building permits issued: 31 (2011); Multi-family building permits issued: 2 (2011).
**Income:** Per capita income: $23,255 (2006-2010 5-year est.); Median household income: $46,822 (2006-2010 5-year est.); Average household income: $61,417 (2006-2010 5-year est.); Percent of households with income of $100,000 or more: 14.0% (2006-2010 5-year est.); Poverty rate: 14.7% (2006-2010 5-year est.); Bankruptcy rate: 1.14% (2011).
**Taxes:** Total county taxes per capita: $925 (2009); County property taxes per capita: $502 (2009).
**Education:** Percent of population age 25 and over with: High school diploma (including GED) or higher: 83.9% (2006-2010 5-year est.); Bachelor's degree or higher: 22.1% (2006-2010 5-year est.); Master's degree or higher: 10.3% (2006-2010 5-year est.).
**Housing:** Homeownership rate: 75.6% (2010); Median home value: $114,200 (2006-2010 5-year est.); Median contract rent: $438 per month (2006-2010 5-year est.); Median year structure built: 1961 (2006-2010 5-year est.)
**Health:** Birth rate: 137.1 per 10,000 population (2011); Death rate: 101.0 per 10,000 population (2011); Age-adjusted cancer mortality rate: 208.4 deaths per 100,000 population (2009); Number of physicians: 9.4 per 10,000 population (2008); Hospital beds: 75.8 per 10,000 population (2007); Hospital admissions: 606.1 per 10,000 population (2007).
**Elections:** 2008 Presidential election results: 47.6% Obama, 51.3% McCain, 0.5% Nader

**Additional Information Contacts**

Yates County Government. . . . . . . . . . . . . . . . . . . . . . . . . . (315) 536-5120
   http://www.yatescounty.org
Yates County Chamber of Commerce. . . . . . . . . . . . . . . (800) 868-9283
   http://www.yatesny.com

## Yates County Communities

**BARRINGTON** (town). Covers a land area of 35.752 square miles and a water area of 1.378 square miles. Located at 42.52° N. Lat; 77.05° W. Long. Elevation is 1,565 feet.
**Population:** 1,195 (1990); 1,396 (2000); 1,681 (2010); Density: 47.0 persons per square mile (2010); Race: 98.8% White, 0.4% Black, 0.1% Asian, 0.2% American Indian/Alaska Native, 0.0% Native Hawaiian/Other Pacific Islander, 0.5% Other, 0.8% Hispanic of any race (2010); Average household size: 2.92 (2010); Median age: 39.5 (2010); Males per 100 females: 93.4 (2010); Marriage status: 22.5% never married, 68.7% now married, 4.1% widowed, 4.8% divorced (2006-2010 5-year est.); Foreign born: 0.3% (2006-2010 5-year est.); Ancestry (includes multiple ancestries): 26.8% German, 18.9% English, 10.8% Irish, 10.7% Swiss, 8.3% American (2006-2010 5-year est.).
**Economy:** Single-family building permits issued: 4 (2011); Multi-family building permits issued: 0 (2011); Employment by occupation: 16.0% management, 4.0% professional, 11.4% services, 11.8% sales, 3.0% farming, 13.6% construction, 7.7% production (2006-2010 5-year est.).
**Income:** Per capita income: $19,912 (2006-2010 5-year est.); Median household income: $56,518 (2006-2010 5-year est.); Average household income: $65,051 (2006-2010 5-year est.); Percent of households with income of $100,000 or more: 17.0% (2006-2010 5-year est.); Poverty rate: 9.0% (2006-2010 5-year est.).
**Education:** Percent of population age 25 and over with: High school diploma (including GED) or higher: 77.5% (2006-2010 5-year est.); Bachelor's degree or higher: 20.6% (2006-2010 5-year est.); Master's degree or higher: 8.7% (2006-2010 5-year est.).

**Housing:** Homeownership rate: 86.1% (2010); Median home value: $119,300 (2006-2010 5-year est.); Median contract rent: $445 per month (2006-2010 5-year est.); Median year structure built: 1975 (2006-2010 5-year est.).
**Transportation:** Commute to work: 76.6% car, 0.0% public transportation, 4.4% walk, 14.8% work from home (2006-2010 5-year est.); Travel time to work: 23.6% less than 15 minutes, 37.1% 15 to 30 minutes, 20.4% 30 to 45 minutes, 8.0% 45 to 60 minutes, 10.9% 60 minutes or more (2006-2010 5-year est.)

**BELLONA** (unincorporated postal area)
Zip Code: 14415
   Covers a land area of 1.452 square miles and a water area of 0 square miles. Located at 42.75° N. Lat; 77.01° W. Long. Elevation is 725 feet. Population: 132 (2010); Density: 90.9 persons per square mile (2010); Race: 100.0% White, 0.0% Black, 0.0% Asian, 0.0% American Indian/Alaska Native, 0.0% Native Hawaiian/Other Pacific Islander, 0.0% Other, 0.0% Hispanic of any race (2010); Average household size: 2.54 (2010); Median age: 34.5 (2010); Males per 100 females: 83.3 (2010); Homeownership rate: 69.2% (2010)

**BENTON** (town). Covers a land area of 41.472 square miles and a water area of 2.964 square miles. Located at 42.72° N. Lat; 77.04° W. Long. Elevation is 837 feet.
**Population:** 2,380 (1990); 2,640 (2000); 2,836 (2010); Density: 68.4 persons per square mile (2010); Race: 98.1% White, 0.4% Black, 0.3% Asian, 0.0% American Indian/Alaska Native, 0.0% Native Hawaiian/Other Pacific Islander, 1.2% Other, 1.2% Hispanic of any race (2010); Average household size: 2.76 (2010); Median age: 42.2 (2010); Males per 100 females: 94.6 (2010); Marriage status: 14.6% never married, 59.7% now married, 16.7% widowed, 9.0% divorced (2006-2010 5-year est.); Foreign born: 1.0% (2006-2010 5-year est.); Ancestry (includes multiple ancestries): 19.7% German, 17.9% Irish, 14.0% English, 12.3% American, 8.0% Danish (2006-2010 5-year est.).
**Economy:** Single-family building permits issued: 4 (2011); Multi-family building permits issued: 0 (2011); Employment by occupation: 12.5% management, 2.3% professional, 6.5% services, 16.6% sales, 3.1% farming, 25.5% construction, 13.1% production (2006-2010 5-year est.).
**Income:** Per capita income: $20,725 (2006-2010 5-year est.); Median household income: $48,942 (2006-2010 5-year est.); Average household income: $59,152 (2006-2010 5-year est.); Percent of households with income of $100,000 or more: 14.9% (2006-2010 5-year est.); Poverty rate: 6.1% (2006-2010 5-year est.).
**Education:** Percent of population age 25 and over with: High school diploma (including GED) or higher: 73.7% (2006-2010 5-year est.); Bachelor's degree or higher: 15.6% (2006-2010 5-year est.); Master's degree or higher: 5.2% (2006-2010 5-year est.).
**Housing:** Homeownership rate: 83.2% (2010); Median home value: $117,900 (2006-2010 5-year est.); Median contract rent: $528 per month (2006-2010 5-year est.); Median year structure built: 1954 (2006-2010 5-year est.).
**Transportation:** Commute to work: 82.2% car, 0.7% public transportation, 2.3% walk, 12.2% work from home (2006-2010 5-year est.); Travel time to work: 46.4% less than 15 minutes, 25.3% 15 to 30 minutes, 15.3% 30 to 45 minutes, 6.9% 45 to 60 minutes, 6.1% 60 minutes or more (2006-2010 5-year est.)

**BRANCHPORT** (unincorporated postal area)
Zip Code: 14418
   Covers a land area of 37.363 square miles and a water area of 0.040 square miles. Located at 42.60° N. Lat; 77.21° W. Long. Elevation is 741 feet. Population: 1,325 (2010); Density: 35.5 persons per square mile (2010); Race: 98.1% White, 0.7% Black, 0.2% Asian, 0.1% American Indian/Alaska Native, 0.0% Native Hawaiian/Other Pacific Islander, 0.9% Other, 0.5% Hispanic of any race (2010); Average household size: 2.39 (2010); Median age: 48.2 (2010); Males per 100 females: 99.5 (2010); Homeownership rate: 84.7% (2010)

**DRESDEN** (village). Covers a land area of 0.301 square miles and a water area of 0.005 square miles. Located at 42.68° N. Lat; 76.95° W. Long. Elevation is 509 feet.
**Population:** 339 (1990); 307 (2000); 308 (2010); Density: 1,020.7 persons per square mile (2010); Race: 96.4% White, 0.0% Black, 0.6% Asian, 0.6% American Indian/Alaska Native, 0.0% Native Hawaiian/Other Pacific Islander, 2.4% Other, 12.7% Hispanic of any race (2010); Average

household size: 2.57 (2010); Median age: 39.8 (2010); Males per 100 females: 115.4 (2010); Marriage status: 27.5% never married, 46.6% now married, 5.1% widowed, 20.8% divorced (2006-2010 5-year est.); Foreign born: 20.1% (2006-2010 5-year est.); Ancestry (includes multiple ancestries): 16.7% English, 16.3% American, 15.1% German, 10.0% Irish, 7.5% Danish (2006-2010 5-year est.).

**Economy:** Single-family building permits issued: 0 (2011); Multi-family building permits issued: 0 (2011); Employment by occupation: 11.6% management, 0.0% professional, 8.0% services, 8.0% sales, 4.5% farming, 36.6% construction, 0.0% production (2006-2010 5-year est.).

**Income:** Per capita income: $18,046 (2006-2010 5-year est.); Median household income: $46,458 (2006-2010 5-year est.); Average household income: $51,919 (2006-2010 5-year est.); Percent of households with income of $100,000 or more: 6.6% (2006-2010 5-year est.); Poverty rate: 20.2% (2006-2010 5-year est.).

**Education:** Percent of population age 25 and over with: High school diploma (including GED) or higher: 67.3% (2006-2010 5-year est.); Bachelor's degree or higher: 13.6% (2006-2010 5-year est.); Master's degree or higher: 5.4% (2006-2010 5-year est.).

**Housing:** Homeownership rate: 70.4% (2010); Median home value: $90,000 (2006-2010 5-year est.); Median contract rent: $529 per month (2006-2010 5-year est.); Median year structure built: before 1940 (2006-2010 5-year est.).

**Transportation:** Commute to work: 99.1% car, 0.0% public transportation, 0.0% walk, 0.9% work from home (2006-2010 5-year est.); Travel time to work: 19.3% less than 15 minutes, 23.9% 15 to 30 minutes, 5.5% 30 to 45 minutes, 5.5% 45 to 60 minutes, 45.9% 60 minutes or more (2006-2010 5-year est.)

**DUNDEE** (village). Covers a land area of 1.123 square miles and a water area of 0 square miles. Located at 42.52° N. Lat; 76.97° W. Long. Elevation is 984 feet.

**History:** Incorporated 1847.

**Population:** 1,598 (1990); 1,690 (2000); 1,725 (2010); Density: 1,534.7 persons per square mile (2010); Race: 97.7% White, 0.9% Black, 0.3% Asian, 0.1% American Indian/Alaska Native, 0.1% Native Hawaiian/Other Pacific Islander, 0.9% Other, 1.2% Hispanic of any race (2010); Average household size: 2.43 (2010); Median age: 39.1 (2010); Males per 100 females: 93.2 (2010); Marriage status: 27.5% never married, 51.5% now married, 9.3% widowed, 11.7% divorced (2006-2010 5-year est.); Foreign born: 1.5% (2006-2010 5-year est.); Ancestry (includes multiple ancestries): 21.4% Irish, 18.6% German, 15.4% English, 8.2% Polish, 6.9% Dutch (2006-2010 5-year est.).

**Economy:** Single-family building permits issued: 0 (2011); Multi-family building permits issued: 0 (2011); Employment by occupation: 4.1% management, 1.0% professional, 17.0% services, 15.1% sales, 3.1% farming, 12.5% construction, 12.0% production (2006-2010 5-year est.).

**Income:** Per capita income: $16,873 (2006-2010 5-year est.); Median household income: $37,056 (2006-2010 5-year est.); Average household income: $39,460 (2006-2010 5-year est.); Percent of households with income of $100,000 or more: 3.7% (2006-2010 5-year est.); Poverty rate: 19.4% (2006-2010 5-year est.).

**Education:** Percent of population age 25 and over with: High school diploma (including GED) or higher: 82.4% (2006-2010 5-year est.); Bachelor's degree or higher: 11.6% (2006-2010 5-year est.); Master's degree or higher: 6.9% (2006-2010 5-year est.).

**School District(s)**

Dundee Central School District (PK-12)

    2009-10 Enrollment: 895 . . . . . . . . . . . . . . . . . . . . . . (607) 243-5533

**Housing:** Homeownership rate: 55.1% (2010); Median home value: $71,000 (2006-2010 5-year est.); Median contract rent: $403 per month (2006-2010 5-year est.); Median year structure built: 1946 (2006-2010 5-year est.).

**Newspapers:** Observer (Local news; Circulation 3,100)

**Transportation:** Commute to work: 86.5% car, 1.6% public transportation, 8.7% walk, 2.2% work from home (2006-2010 5-year est.); Travel time to work: 36.2% less than 15 minutes, 37.1% 15 to 30 minutes, 14.5% 30 to 45 minutes, 9.0% 45 to 60 minutes, 3.2% 60 minutes or more (2006-2010 5-year est.)

**HIMROD** (unincorporated postal area)

Zip Code: 14842

    Covers a land area of 16.731 square miles and a water area of 0.006 square miles. Located at 42.60° N. Lat; 76.98° W. Long. Elevation is 797 feet. Population: 938 (2010); Density: 56.1 persons per square mile

(2010); Race: 99.4% White, 0.1% Black, 0.1% Asian, 0.0% American Indian/Alaska Native, 0.0% Native Hawaiian/Other Pacific Islander, 0.4% Other, 0.2% Hispanic of any race (2010); Average household size: 2.93 (2010); Median age: 35.4 (2010); Males per 100 females: 100.9 (2010); Homeownership rate: 86.9% (2010)

**ITALY** (town). Covers a land area of 40.139 square miles and a water area of 0.121 square miles. Located at 42.61° N. Lat; 77.31° W. Long. Elevation is 1,109 feet.

**Population:** 1,120 (1990); 1,087 (2000); 1,141 (2010); Density: 28.4 persons per square mile (2010); Race: 98.4% White, 0.3% Black, 0.2% Asian, 0.0% American Indian/Alaska Native, 0.0% Native Hawaiian/Other Pacific Islander, 1.1% Other, 0.9% Hispanic of any race (2010); Average household size: 2.42 (2010); Median age: 44.9 (2010); Males per 100 females: 103.0 (2010); Marriage status: 18.9% never married, 58.8% now married, 4.7% widowed, 17.6% divorced (2006-2010 5-year est.); Foreign born: 1.4% (2006-2010 5-year est.); Ancestry (includes multiple ancestries): 30.5% German, 18.9% English, 17.9% Irish, 9.8% American, 8.6% Italian (2006-2010 5-year est.).

**Economy:** Employment by occupation: 6.0% management, 2.1% professional, 12.6% services, 19.5% sales, 1.8% farming, 16.5% construction, 12.6% production (2006-2010 5-year est.).

**Income:** Per capita income: $21,271 (2006-2010 5-year est.); Median household income: $43,636 (2006-2010 5-year est.); Average household income: $48,603 (2006-2010 5-year est.); Percent of households with income of $100,000 or more: 6.6% (2006-2010 5-year est.); Poverty rate: 16.4% (2006-2010 5-year est.).

**Education:** Percent of population age 25 and over with: High school diploma (including GED) or higher: 87.5% (2006-2010 5-year est.); Bachelor's degree or higher: 17.4% (2006-2010 5-year est.); Master's degree or higher: 9.7% (2006-2010 5-year est.).

**Housing:** Homeownership rate: 86.2% (2010); Median home value: $79,200 (2006-2010 5-year est.); Median contract rent: $386 per month (2006-2010 5-year est.); Median year structure built: 1973 (2006-2010 5-year est.).

**Transportation:** Commute to work: 92.4% car, 0.0% public transportation, 0.0% walk, 6.7% work from home (2006-2010 5-year est.); Travel time to work: 18.5% less than 15 minutes, 25.2% 15 to 30 minutes, 27.9% 30 to 45 minutes, 14.3% 45 to 60 minutes, 14.1% 60 minutes or more (2006-2010 5-year est.)

**JERUSALEM** (town). Covers a land area of 58.639 square miles and a water area of 6.761 square miles. Located at 42.61° N. Lat; 77.15° W. Long.

**Population:** 3,784 (1990); 4,525 (2000); 4,469 (2010); Density: 76.2 persons per square mile (2010); Race: 96.7% White, 1.1% Black, 0.6% Asian, 0.2% American Indian/Alaska Native, 0.1% Native Hawaiian/Other Pacific Islander, 1.3% Other, 1.6% Hispanic of any race (2010); Average household size: 2.31 (2010); Median age: 42.3 (2010); Males per 100 females: 82.1 (2010); Marriage status: 42.8% never married, 48.9% now married, 2.5% widowed, 5.7% divorced (2006-2010 5-year est.); Foreign born: 1.9% (2006-2010 5-year est.); Ancestry (includes multiple ancestries): 26.9% German, 25.3% Irish, 19.2% English, 11.9% Italian, 7.8% American (2006-2010 5-year est.).

**Economy:** Single-family building permits issued: 0 (2011); Multi-family building permits issued: 2 (2011); Employment by occupation: 12.0% management, 2.8% professional, 13.4% services, 25.1% sales, 3.3% farming, 7.7% construction, 4.5% production (2006-2010 5-year est.).

**Income:** Per capita income: $25,772 (2006-2010 5-year est.); Median household income: $57,143 (2006-2010 5-year est.); Average household income: $75,369 (2006-2010 5-year est.); Percent of households with income of $100,000 or more: 19.5% (2006-2010 5-year est.); Poverty rate: 13.1% (2006-2010 5-year est.).

**Education:** Percent of population age 25 and over with: High school diploma (including GED) or higher: 91.1% (2006-2010 5-year est.); Bachelor's degree or higher: 30.3% (2006-2010 5-year est.); Master's degree or higher: 13.7% (2006-2010 5-year est.).

**Housing:** Homeownership rate: 85.7% (2010); Median home value: $169,000 (2006-2010 5-year est.); Median contract rent: $555 per month (2006-2010 5-year est.); Median year structure built: 1964 (2006-2010 5-year est.).

**Transportation:** Commute to work: 73.7% car, 0.0% public transportation, 15.6% walk, 10.0% work from home (2006-2010 5-year est.); Travel time to work: 49.7% less than 15 minutes, 27.4% 15 to 30 minutes, 15.6% 30 to 45

minutes, 3.3% 45 to 60 minutes, 4.1% 60 minutes or more (2006-2010 5-year est.)

**KEUKA PARK** (CDP). Covers a land area of 0.677 square miles and a water area of 0.559 square miles. Located at 42.61° N. Lat; 77.09° W. Long. Elevation is 774 feet.
**Population:** n/a (1990); n/a (2000); 1,137 (2010); Density: 1,677.5 persons per square mile (2010); Race: 93.5% White, 3.6% Black, 0.4% Asian, 0.6% American Indian/Alaska Native, 0.0% Native Hawaiian/Other Pacific Islander, 1.9% Other, 2.6% Hispanic of any race (2010); Average household size: 1.84 (2010); Median age: 21.3 (2010); Males per 100 females: 50.6 (2010); Marriage status: 88.5% never married, 6.7% now married, 3.5% widowed, 1.3% divorced (2006-2010 5-year est.); Foreign born: 1.9% (2006-2010 5-year est.); Ancestry (includes multiple ancestries): 36.3% Irish, 26.7% Italian, 23.4% German, 19.7% English, 9.5% Polish (2006-2010 5-year est.).
**Economy:** Employment by occupation: 0.0% management, 0.0% professional, 12.7% services, 43.3% sales, 7.6% farming, 0.0% construction, 0.0% production (2006-2010 5-year est.).
**Income:** Per capita income: $7,422 (2006-2010 5-year est.); Median household income: $34,194 (2006-2010 5-year est.); Average household income: $40,487 (2006-2010 5-year est.); Percent of households with income of $100,000 or more: 0.0% (2006-2010 5-year est.); Poverty rate: 0.0% (2006-2010 5-year est.).
**Education:** Percent of population age 25 and over with: High school diploma (including GED) or higher: 94.1% (2006-2010 5-year est.); Bachelor's degree or higher: 32.2% (2006-2010 5-year est.); Master's degree or higher: 17.8% (2006-2010 5-year est.).
### Four-year College(s)
Keuka College (Private, Not-for-profit, Baptist)
    Fall 2010 Enrollment: 1,908 . . . . . . . . . . . . . . . . . . . . . (315) 279-5000
    2011-12 Tuition: In-state $25,235; Out-of-state $25,235
**Housing:** Homeownership rate: 58.1% (2010); Median home value: $99,100 (2006-2010 5-year est.); Median contract rent: $667 per month (2006-2010 5-year est.); Median year structure built: before 1940 (2006-2010 5-year est.).
**Transportation:** Commute to work: 28.3% car, 0.0% public transportation, 52.0% walk, 19.6% work from home (2006-2010 5-year est.); Travel time to work: 77.1% less than 15 minutes, 22.9% 15 to 30 minutes, 0.0% 30 to 45 minutes, 0.0% 45 to 60 minutes, 0.0% 60 minutes or more (2006-2010 5-year est.)

**MIDDLESEX** (town). Covers a land area of 30.875 square miles and a water area of 3.229 square miles. Located at 42.71° N. Lat; 77.28° W. Long. Elevation is 771 feet.
**Population:** 1,249 (1990); 1,345 (2000); 1,495 (2010); Density: 48.4 persons per square mile (2010); Race: 98.3% White, 0.3% Black, 0.6% Asian, 0.1% American Indian/Alaska Native, 0.0% Native Hawaiian/Other Pacific Islander, 0.7% Other, 0.4% Hispanic of any race (2010); Average household size: 2.53 (2010); Median age: 45.3 (2010); Males per 100 females: 99.6 (2010); Marriage status: 16.7% never married, 69.6% now married, 4.2% widowed, 9.5% divorced (2006-2010 5-year est.); Foreign born: 2.1% (2006-2010 5-year est.); Ancestry (includes multiple ancestries): 29.9% German, 28.2% English, 17.0% Irish, 12.5% American, 7.8% Dutch (2006-2010 5-year est.).
**Economy:** Single-family building permits issued: 5 (2011); Multi-family building permits issued: 0 (2011); Employment by occupation: 10.0% management, 2.2% professional, 14.6% services, 11.8% sales, 2.8% farming, 14.6% construction, 7.4% production (2006-2010 5-year est.).
**Income:** Per capita income: $25,315 (2006-2010 5-year est.); Median household income: $51,976 (2006-2010 5-year est.); Average household income: $61,339 (2006-2010 5-year est.); Percent of households with income of $100,000 or more: 13.2% (2006-2010 5-year est.); Poverty rate: 9.3% (2006-2010 5-year est.).
**Education:** Percent of population age 25 and over with: High school diploma (including GED) or higher: 91.1% (2006-2010 5-year est.); Bachelor's degree or higher: 23.8% (2006-2010 5-year est.); Master's degree or higher: 6.8% (2006-2010 5-year est.).
**Housing:** Homeownership rate: 86.7% (2010); Median home value: $122,000 (2006-2010 5-year est.); Median contract rent: $502 per month (2006-2010 5-year est.); Median year structure built: 1972 (2006-2010 5-year est.).
**Transportation:** Commute to work: 91.1% car, 0.0% public transportation, 3.1% walk, 5.5% work from home (2006-2010 5-year est.); Travel time to work: 26.7% less than 15 minutes, 32.2% 15 to 30 minutes, 29.8% 30 to 45

minutes, 5.6% 45 to 60 minutes, 5.6% 60 minutes or more (2006-2010 5-year est.)

**MILO** (town). Covers a land area of 38.434 square miles and a water area of 5.901 square miles. Located at 42.61° N. Lat; 77.00° W. Long.
**Population:** 7,023 (1990); 7,026 (2000); 7,006 (2010); Density: 182.3 persons per square mile (2010); Race: 96.5% White, 0.9% Black, 0.4% Asian, 0.1% American Indian/Alaska Native, 0.0% Native Hawaiian/Other Pacific Islander, 2.1% Other, 2.2% Hispanic of any race (2010); Average household size: 2.36 (2010); Median age: 40.4 (2010); Males per 100 females: 92.3 (2010); Marriage status: 27.9% never married, 55.9% now married, 7.2% widowed, 9.1% divorced (2006-2010 5-year est.); Foreign born: 2.0% (2006-2010 5-year est.); Ancestry (includes multiple ancestries): 25.4% Irish, 20.3% German, 16.9% English, 12.4% American, 11.5% Italian (2006-2010 5-year est.).
**Economy:** Single-family building permits issued: 7 (2011); Multi-family building permits issued: 0 (2011); Employment by occupation: 12.3% management, 1.8% professional, 10.7% services, 15.8% sales, 5.4% farming, 11.6% construction, 6.2% production (2006-2010 5-year est.).
**Income:** Per capita income: $24,344 (2006-2010 5-year est.); Median household income: $36,645 (2006-2010 5-year est.); Average household income: $56,817 (2006-2010 5-year est.); Percent of households with income of $100,000 or more: 10.9% (2006-2010 5-year est.); Poverty rate: 19.5% (2006-2010 5-year est.).
**Education:** Percent of population age 25 and over with: High school diploma (including GED) or higher: 83.9% (2006-2010 5-year est.); Bachelor's degree or higher: 23.1% (2006-2010 5-year est.); Master's degree or higher: 12.6% (2006-2010 5-year est.).
**Housing:** Homeownership rate: 61.9% (2010); Median home value: $100,900 (2006-2010 5-year est.); Median contract rent: $423 per month (2006-2010 5-year est.); Median year structure built: before 1940 (2006-2010 5-year est.).
**Transportation:** Commute to work: 83.3% car, 1.0% public transportation, 7.6% walk, 5.5% work from home (2006-2010 5-year est.); Travel time to work: 55.1% less than 15 minutes, 18.3% 15 to 30 minutes, 16.6% 30 to 45 minutes, 5.1% 45 to 60 minutes, 4.8% 60 minutes or more (2006-2010 5-year est.)

**PENN YAN** (village). County seat. Covers a land area of 2.381 square miles and a water area of 0.056 square miles. Located at 42.66° N. Lat; 77.05° W. Long. Elevation is 728 feet.
**History:** Controversy between the settlers from Pennsylvania and New England over a name for this place was compromised by combining the first syllables of Pennsylvania and Yankee.
**Population:** 5,294 (1990); 5,219 (2000); 5,159 (2010); Density: 2,166.4 persons per square mile (2010); Race: 95.7% White, 1.1% Black, 0.6% Asian, 0.2% American Indian/Alaska Native, 0.0% Native Hawaiian/Other Pacific Islander, 2.4% Other, 2.7% Hispanic of any race (2010); Average household size: 2.21 (2010); Median age: 42.9 (2010); Males per 100 females: 86.7 (2010); Marriage status: 29.9% never married, 45.8% now married, 12.4% widowed, 11.9% divorced (2006-2010 5-year est.); Foreign born: 2.2% (2006-2010 5-year est.); Ancestry (includes multiple ancestries): 28.1% Irish, 16.5% German, 15.5% English, 12.1% American, 10.1% Italian (2006-2010 5-year est.).
**Economy:** Single-family building permits issued: 2 (2011); Multi-family building permits issued: 0 (2011); Employment by occupation: 7.3% management, 1.6% professional, 15.8% services, 17.1% sales, 4.5% farming, 9.7% construction, 6.8% production (2006-2010 5-year est.).
**Income:** Per capita income: $18,975 (2006-2010 5-year est.); Median household income: $31,585 (2006-2010 5-year est.); Average household income: $43,796 (2006-2010 5-year est.); Percent of households with income of $100,000 or more: 6.7% (2006-2010 5-year est.); Poverty rate: 20.8% (2006-2010 5-year est.).
**Education:** Percent of population age 25 and over with: High school diploma (including GED) or higher: 82.9% (2006-2010 5-year est.); Bachelor's degree or higher: 21.1% (2006-2010 5-year est.); Master's degree or higher: 8.8% (2006-2010 5-year est.).
### School District(s)
Penn Yan Central School District (PK-12)
    2009-10 Enrollment: 1,716 . . . . . . . . . . . . . . . . . . . . . (315) 536-3371
**Housing:** Homeownership rate: 53.3% (2010); Median home value: $94,400 (2006-2010 5-year est.); Median contract rent: $428 per month (2006-2010 5-year est.); Median year structure built: before 1940 (2006-2010 5-year est.).
**Hospitals:** Soldiers and Sailors Memorial Hospital (186 beds)

**Safety:** Violent crime rate: 8.0 per 10,000 population; Property crime rate: 352.2 per 10,000 population (2010).
**Newspapers:** Chronicle Ad-Viser (Community news; Circulation 13,500); Chronicle-Express (Community news; Circulation 4,200)
**Transportation:** Commute to work: 83.3% car, 1.4% public transportation, 9.5% walk, 4.1% work from home (2006-2010 5-year est.); Travel time to work: 60.6% less than 15 minutes, 17.1% 15 to 30 minutes, 14.9% 30 to 45 minutes, 3.7% 45 to 60 minutes, 3.6% 60 minutes or more (2006-2010 5-year est.)
**Airports:** Penn Yan (general aviation)
**Additional Information Contacts**
Yates County Chamber of Commerce . . . . . . . . . . . . . . . . (800) 868-9283
http://www.yatesny.com

**POTTER** (town). Covers a land area of 37.237 square miles and a water area of 0 square miles. Located at 42.71° N. Lat; 77.18° W. Long. Elevation is 896 feet.
**Population:** 1,617 (1990); 1,830 (2000); 1,865 (2010); Density: 50.1 persons per square mile (2010); Race: 97.7% White, 0.7% Black, 0.1% Asian, 0.1% American Indian/Alaska Native, 0.0% Native Hawaiian/Other Pacific Islander, 1.4% Other, 1.5% Hispanic of any race (2010); Average household size: 2.96 (2010); Median age: 34.4 (2010); Males per 100 females: 99.5 (2010); Marriage status: 22.0% never married, 61.9% now married, 6.7% widowed, 9.3% divorced (2006-2010 5-year est.); Foreign born: 2.4% (2006-2010 5-year est.); Ancestry (includes multiple ancestries): 29.6% German, 18.3% Irish, 14.9% English, 13.3% Italian, 7.4% American (2006-2010 5-year est.).
**Economy:** Single-family building permits issued: 1 (2011); Multi-family building permits issued: 0 (2011); Employment by occupation: 14.8% management, 0.4% professional, 8.9% services, 13.8% sales, 1.7% farming, 18.8% construction, 7.9% production (2006-2010 5-year est.).
**Income:** Per capita income: $18,817 (2006-2010 5-year est.); Median household income: $50,417 (2006-2010 5-year est.); Average household income: $57,136 (2006-2010 5-year est.); Percent of households with income of $100,000 or more: 10.8% (2006-2010 5-year est.); Poverty rate: 16.3% (2006-2010 5-year est.).
**Education:** Percent of population age 25 and over with: High school diploma (including GED) or higher: 80.5% (2006-2010 5-year est.); Bachelor's degree or higher: 12.3% (2006-2010 5-year est.); Master's degree or higher: 4.7% (2006-2010 5-year est.).
**Housing:** Homeownership rate: 83.2% (2010); Median home value: $97,000 (2006-2010 5-year est.); Median contract rent: $483 per month (2006-2010 5-year est.); Median year structure built: 1970 (2006-2010 5-year est.).
**Transportation:** Commute to work: 87.5% car, 0.0% public transportation, 3.1% walk, 7.3% work from home (2006-2010 5-year est.); Travel time to work: 29.0% less than 15 minutes, 37.2% 15 to 30 minutes, 16.0% 30 to 45 minutes, 7.3% 45 to 60 minutes, 10.5% 60 minutes or more (2006-2010 5-year est.)

**ROCK STREAM** (unincorporated postal area)
Zip Code: 14878
Covers a land area of 16.039 square miles and a water area of 0 square miles. Located at 42.45° N. Lat; 76.94° W. Long. Population: 781 (2010); Density: 48.7 persons per square mile (2010); Race: 99.0% White, 0.3% Black, 0.3% Asian, 0.1% American Indian/Alaska Native, 0.0% Native Hawaiian/Other Pacific Islander, 0.3% Other, 0.5% Hispanic of any race (2010); Average household size: 2.64 (2010); Median age: 44.1 (2010); Males per 100 females: 100.8 (2010); Homeownership rate: 85.9% (2010)

**RUSHVILLE** (village). Covers a land area of 0.639 square miles and a water area of 0 square miles. Located at 42.76° N. Lat; 77.22° W. Long. Elevation is 876 feet.
**Population:** 609 (1990); 621 (2000); 677 (2010); Density: 1,058.9 persons per square mile (2010); Race: 95.7% White, 0.9% Black, 0.3% Asian, 0.3% American Indian/Alaska Native, 0.0% Native Hawaiian/Other Pacific Islander, 2.8% Other, 1.0% Hispanic of any race (2010); Average household size: 2.53 (2010); Median age: 37.6 (2010); Males per 100 females: 91.8 (2010); Marriage status: 24.3% never married, 63.0% now married, 4.6% widowed, 8.1% divorced (2006-2010 5-year est.); Foreign born: 3.8% (2006-2010 5-year est.); Ancestry (includes multiple ancestries): 25.2% German, 19.7% Irish, 14.4% Italian, 14.3% English, 7.5% Scottish (2006-2010 5-year est.).

**Economy:** Single-family building permits issued: 0 (2011); Multi-family building permits issued: 0 (2011); Employment by occupation: 4.8% management, 0.0% professional, 6.3% services, 10.8% sales, 0.0% farming, 16.5% construction, 5.4% production (2006-2010 5-year est.).
**Income:** Per capita income: $20,913 (2006-2010 5-year est.); Median household income: $58,405 (2006-2010 5-year est.); Average household income: $55,667 (2006-2010 5-year est.); Percent of households with income of $100,000 or more: 10.5% (2006-2010 5-year est.); Poverty rate: 17.4% (2006-2010 5-year est.).
**Education:** Percent of population age 25 and over with: High school diploma (including GED) or higher: 92.6% (2006-2010 5-year est.); Bachelor's degree or higher: 16.6% (2006-2010 5-year est.); Master's degree or higher: 10.6% (2006-2010 5-year est.).
**School District(s)**
Gorham-Middlesex Central School District (marcus W (PK-12)
    2009-10 Enrollment: 1,395 . . . . . . . . . . . . . . . . . . . . . (585) 554-4848
**Housing:** Homeownership rate: 65.9% (2010); Median home value: $94,200 (2006-2010 5-year est.); Median contract rent: $481 per month (2006-2010 5-year est.); Median year structure built: before 1940 (2006-2010 5-year est.).
**Transportation:** Commute to work: 96.5% car, 0.0% public transportation, 0.0% walk, 3.5% work from home (2006-2010 5-year est.); Travel time to work: 25.3% less than 15 minutes, 41.4% 15 to 30 minutes, 13.5% 30 to 45 minutes, 11.8% 45 to 60 minutes, 7.9% 60 minutes or more (2006-2010 5-year est.)

**STARKEY** (town). Covers a land area of 32.830 square miles and a water area of 6.375 square miles. Located at 42.52° N. Lat; 76.94° W. Long. Elevation is 804 feet.
**Population:** 3,173 (1990); 3,465 (2000); 3,573 (2010); Density: 108.8 persons per square mile (2010); Race: 96.7% White, 1.2% Black, 0.4% Asian, 0.2% American Indian/Alaska Native, 0.0% Native Hawaiian/Other Pacific Islander, 1.5% Other, 1.7% Hispanic of any race (2010); Average household size: 2.61 (2010); Median age: 38.6 (2010); Males per 100 females: 101.1 (2010); Marriage status: 28.5% never married, 56.0% now married, 5.3% widowed, 10.1% divorced (2006-2010 5-year est.); Foreign born: 1.3% (2006-2010 5-year est.); Ancestry (includes multiple ancestries): 29.2% German, 20.7% Irish, 19.8% English, 5.9% American, 5.6% Italian (2006-2010 5-year est.).
**Economy:** Single-family building permits issued: 4 (2011); Multi-family building permits issued: 0 (2011); Employment by occupation: 10.9% management, 1.5% professional, 9.3% services, 14.3% sales, 1.5% farming, 15.1% construction, 12.6% production (2006-2010 5-year est.).
**Income:** Per capita income: $23,102 (2006-2010 5-year est.); Median household income: $44,306 (2006-2010 5-year est.); Average household income: $59,931 (2006-2010 5-year est.); Percent of households with income of $100,000 or more: 14.6% (2006-2010 5-year est.); Poverty rate: 18.2% (2006-2010 5-year est.).
**Education:** Percent of population age 25 and over with: High school diploma (including GED) or higher: 85.5% (2006-2010 5-year est.); Bachelor's degree or higher: 22.0% (2006-2010 5-year est.); Master's degree or higher: 10.7% (2006-2010 5-year est.).
**Housing:** Homeownership rate: 69.0% (2010); Median home value: $89,700 (2006-2010 5-year est.); Median contract rent: $407 per month (2006-2010 5-year est.); Median year structure built: 1965 (2006-2010 5-year est.).
**Transportation:** Commute to work: 82.6% car, 0.8% public transportation, 5.9% walk, 10.2% work from home (2006-2010 5-year est.); Travel time to work: 30.3% less than 15 minutes, 42.5% 15 to 30 minutes, 12.8% 30 to 45 minutes, 7.1% 45 to 60 minutes, 7.3% 60 minutes or more (2006-2010 5-year est.)

**TORREY** (town). Covers a land area of 22.759 square miles and a water area of 10.914 square miles. Located at 42.66° N. Lat; 76.95° W. Long. Elevation is 509 feet.
**Population:** 1,269 (1990); 1,307 (2000); 1,282 (2010); Density: 56.3 persons per square mile (2010); Race: 97.5% White, 0.7% Black, 0.3% Asian, 0.2% American Indian/Alaska Native, 0.0% Native Hawaiian/Other Pacific Islander, 1.3% Other, 3.5% Hispanic of any race (2010); Average household size: 2.67 (2010); Median age: 43.5 (2010); Males per 100 females: 105.4 (2010); Marriage status: 19.7% never married, 65.0% now married, 7.7% widowed, 7.6% divorced (2006-2010 5-year est.); Foreign born: 5.0% (2006-2010 5-year est.); Ancestry (includes multiple ancestries): 31.8% German, 18.0% English, 12.8% Irish, 9.7% American, 7.7% Swiss (2006-2010 5-year est.).

**Economy:** Single-family building permits issued: 0 (2011); Multi-family building permits issued: 0 (2011); Employment by occupation: 19.1% management, 4.6% professional, 7.4% services, 12.0% sales, 1.9% farming, 20.8% construction, 6.4% production (2006-2010 5-year est.).
**Income:** Per capita income: $25,534 (2006-2010 5-year est.); Median household income: $53,056 (2006-2010 5-year est.); Average household income: $69,477 (2006-2010 5-year est.); Percent of households with income of $100,000 or more: 20.7% (2006-2010 5-year est.); Poverty rate: 10.4% (2006-2010 5-year est.).
**Education:** Percent of population age 25 and over with: High school diploma (including GED) or higher: 80.6% (2006-2010 5-year est.); Bachelor's degree or higher: 24.1% (2006-2010 5-year est.); Master's degree or higher: 11.7% (2006-2010 5-year est.).
**Housing:** Homeownership rate: 83.1% (2010); Median home value: $171,000 (2006-2010 5-year est.); Median contract rent: $475 per month (2006-2010 5-year est.); Median year structure built: 1966 (2006-2010 5-year est.).
**Transportation:** Commute to work: 79.8% car, 1.1% public transportation, 1.8% walk, 12.8% work from home (2006-2010 5-year est.); Travel time to work: 32.0% less than 15 minutes, 32.6% 15 to 30 minutes, 7.9% 30 to 45 minutes, 5.6% 45 to 60 minutes, 21.9% 60 minutes or more (2006-2010 5-year est.)

## A

Accord CDP *Ulster County*, 584

Acra postal area *Greene County*, 189

Adams Center CDP *Jefferson County*, 212

Adams town *Jefferson County*, 211

Adams village *Jefferson County*, 211

Addison town *Steuben County*, 499

Addison village *Steuben County*, 499

Adirondack postal area *Warren County*, 602

Afton town *Chenango County*, 79

Afton village *Chenango County*, 79

Airmont village *Rockland County*, 439

Akron village *Erie County*, 139

Alabama town *Genesee County*, 182

Albany County, 1 - 8

Albany city *Albany County*, 1

Albertson CDP *Nassau County*, 276

Albion town *Orleans County*, 398

Albion town *Oswego County*, 403

Albion village *Orleans County*, 398

Alcove postal area *Albany County*, 2

Alden town *Erie County*, 140

Alden village *Erie County*, 140

Alder Creek postal area *Oneida County*, 339

Alexander town *Genesee County*, 183

Alexander village *Genesee County*, 182

Alexandria Bay village *Jefferson County*, 212

Alexandria town *Jefferson County*, 212

Alfred Station postal area *Allegany County*, 10

Alfred town *Allegany County*, 9

Alfred village *Allegany County*, 9

Allegany County, 9 - 21

Allegany Reservation Reservation *Cattaraugus County*, 31

Allegany town *Cattaraugus County*, 31

Allegany village *Cattaraugus County*, 31

Allen town *Allegany County*, 10

Alma town *Allegany County*, 10

Almond town *Allegany County*, 11

Almond village *Allegany County*, 10

Alpine postal area *Schuyler County*, 491

Alplaus postal area *Schenectady County*, 479

Altamont village *Albany County*, 2

Altmar village *Oswego County*, 403

Altona CDP *Clinton County*, 88

Altona town *Clinton County*, 88

Amagansett CDP *Suffolk County*, 514

Amawalk postal area *Westchester County*, 626

Amboy town *Oswego County*, 403

Amenia CDP *Dutchess County*, 123

Amenia town *Dutchess County*, 123

Ames village *Montgomery County*, 268

Amherst town *Erie County*, 140

Amity town *Allegany County*, 11

Amityville village *Suffolk County*, 515

Amsterdam city *Montgomery County*, 269

Amsterdam town *Montgomery County*, 269

Ancram town *Columbia County*, 97

Ancramdale postal area *Columbia County*, 97

Andes town *Delaware County*, 113

Andes village *Delaware County*, 112

Andover town *Allegany County*, 11

Andover village *Allegany County*, 11

Angelica town *Allegany County*, 12

Angelica village *Allegany County*, 12

Angola on the Lake CDP *Erie County*, 141

Angola village *Erie County*, 141

Annandale-On-Hudson postal area *Dutchess County*, 124

Annsville town *Oneida County*, 339

Antwerp town *Jefferson County*, 213

Antwerp village *Jefferson County*, 212

Apalachin CDP *Tioga County*, 572

Appleton postal area *Niagara County*, 330

Apulia Station postal area *Onondaga County*, 356

Aquebogue CDP *Suffolk County*, 515

Arcade town *Wyoming County*, 650

Arcade village *Wyoming County*, 650

Arcadia town *Wayne County*, 616

Arden postal area *Orange County*, 380

Ardsley village *Westchester County*, 626

Argyle town *Washington County*, 609

Argyle village *Washington County*, 608

Arietta town *Hamilton County*, 198

Arkport village *Steuben County*, 500

Arkville postal area *Delaware County*, 113

Arkwright town *Chautauqua County*, 57

Arlington CDP *Dutchess County*, 124

Armonk CDP *Westchester County*, 626

Arverne postal area *Queens County*, 325

Asharoken village *Suffolk County*, 515

Ashford town *Cattaraugus County*, 32

Ashland town *Chemung County*, 72

Ashland town *Greene County*, 189

Ashville postal area *Chautauqua County*, 57

Astoria postal area *Queens County*, 325

Athens town *Greene County*, 190

Athens village *Greene County*, 189

Athol postal area *Warren County*, 602

Atlanta postal area *Steuben County*, 500

Atlantic Beach village *Nassau County*, 276

Attica town *Wyoming County*, 651

Attica village *Wyoming County*, 651

Au Sable Forks CDP *Clinton County*, 89

Au Sable town *Clinton County*, 88

Auburn city *Cayuga County*, 47

Augusta town *Oneida County*, 339

Aurelius town *Cayuga County*, 47

Aurora town *Erie County*, 141

Aurora village *Cayuga County*, 47

Austerlitz town *Columbia County*, 97

Ava town *Oneida County*, 340

Averill Park CDP *Rensselaer County*, 430

Avoca town *Steuben County*, 500

Avoca village *Steuben County*, 500

Avon town *Livingston County*, 236

Avon village *Livingston County*, 235

## B

Babylon town *Suffolk County*, 516

Babylon village *Suffolk County*, 516

Bainbridge town *Chenango County*, 80

Bainbridge village *Chenango County*, 79

Baiting Hollow CDP *Suffolk County*, 516

Bakers Mills postal area *Warren County*, 602

Baldwin Harbor CDP *Nassau County*, 277

Baldwin Place postal area *Westchester County*, 626

Baldwin CDP *Nassau County*, 276

Baldwin town *Chemung County*, 72

Baldwinsville village *Onondaga County*, 356

Ballston Lake postal area *Saratoga County*, 469

Ballston Spa village *Saratoga County*, 469

Ballston town *Saratoga County*, 469

Balmville CDP *Orange County*, 380

Bangor town *Franklin County*, 169

Bardonia CDP *Rockland County*, 440

Barker town *Broome County*, 22

Barker village *Niagara County*, 330

Barneveld village *Oneida County*, 340

Barnum Island CDP *Nassau County*, 277

Barre town *Orleans County*, 399

Barrington town *Yates County*, 658

Barrytown postal area *Dutchess County*, 124

Barryville postal area *Sullivan County*, 561

Barton town *Tioga County*, 572

Basom postal area *Genesee County*, 183

Batavia city *Genesee County*, 183

Batavia town *Genesee County*, 183

Bath town *Steuben County*, 501

Bath village *Steuben County*, 501

Baxter Estates village *Nassau County*, 277

Bay Park CDP *Nassau County*, 277

Bay Shore CDP *Suffolk County*, 516

Bayport CDP *Suffolk County*, 517

Bayside postal area *Queens County*, 325

Bayville village *Nassau County*, 277

Baywood CDP *Suffolk County*, 517

Beacon city *Dutchess County*, 124

Bear Mountain postal area *Rockland County*, 440

Bearsville postal area *Ulster County*, 585

Beaver Dams postal area *Schuyler County*, 491

Beaver Falls postal area *Lewis County*, 228

Beaverdam Lake-Salisbury Mills CDP *Orange County*, 380

Bedford Hills CDP *Westchester County*, 627

Bedford CDP *Westchester County*, 627

Bedford town *Westchester County*, 627

Beekman town *Dutchess County*, 124

Beekmantown town *Clinton County*, 89

Belfast CDP *Allegany County*, 12

Belfast town *Allegany County*, 12

Belle Terre village *Suffolk County*, 517

Bellerose Terrace CDP *Nassau County*, 278

Bellerose village *Nassau County*, 278

Belleville CDP *Jefferson County*, 213

Bellmont town *Franklin County*, 169

Bellmore CDP *Nassau County*, 278

Bellona postal area *Yates County*, 658

Bellport village *Suffolk County*, 518

Belmont village *Allegany County*, 13

Bemus Point village *Chautauqua County*, 57

Bennington town *Wyoming County*, 651

Benson town *Hamilton County*, 198

Benton town *Yates County*, 658

Bergen town *Genesee County*, 184

Bergen village *Genesee County*, 184

Berkshire town *Tioga County*, 572

Berlin town *Rensselaer County*, 430

Berne town *Albany County*, 3

Bernhards Bay postal area *Oswego County*, 403

Bethany town *Genesee County*, 184

Bethel town *Sullivan County*, 562

*CDP = Census Designated Place*

**Bethlehem** town *Albany County*, 3
**Bethpage** CDP *Nassau County*, 279
**Big Flats** CDP *Chemung County*, 72
**Big Flats** town *Chemung County*, 72
**Big Indian** postal area *Ulster County*, 585
**Billington Heights** CDP *Erie County*, 141
**Binghamton University** CDP *Broome County*, 23
**Binghamton** city *Broome County*, 22
**Binghamton** town *Broome County*, 23
**Birdsall** town *Allegany County*, 13
**Black Brook** town *Clinton County*, 89
**Black Creek** postal area *Allegany County*, 13
**Black River** village *Jefferson County*, 213
**Blasdell** village *Erie County*, 142
**Blauvelt** CDP *Rockland County*, 440
**Bleecker** town *Fulton County*, 177
**Blenheim** town *Schoharie County*, 484
**Bliss** CDP *Wyoming County*, 652
**Blodgett Mills** CDP *Cortland County*, 106
**Bloomfield** village *Ontario County*, 371
**Blooming Grove** town *Orange County*, 381
**Bloomingburg** village *Sullivan County*, 562
**Bloomingdale** postal area *Essex County*, 160
**Bloomington** postal area *Ulster County*, 585
**Bloomville** CDP *Delaware County*, 113
**Blossvale** postal area *Oneida County*, 340
**Blue Mountain Lake** postal area *Hamilton County*, 198
**Blue Point** CDP *Suffolk County*, 518
**Bohemia** CDP *Suffolk County*, 518
**Boiceville** postal area *Ulster County*, 585
**Bolivar** town *Allegany County*, 13
**Bolivar** village *Allegany County*, 13
**Bolton Landing** CDP *Warren County*, 602
**Bolton** town *Warren County*, 602
**Bombay** town *Franklin County*, 169
**Boonville** town *Oneida County*, 340
**Boonville** village *Oneida County*, 340
**Boston** town *Erie County*, 142
**Bouckville** postal area *Madison County*, 249
**Bovina Center** postal area *Delaware County*, 113
**Bovina** town *Delaware County*, 113
**Bowmansville** postal area *Erie County*, 142
**Boylston** town *Oswego County*, 404
**Bradford** town *Steuben County*, 501
**Brainard** postal area *Rensselaer County*, 431
**Branchport** postal area *Yates County*, 658
**Brandon** town *Franklin County*, 169
**Brant Lake** postal area *Warren County*, 602
**Brant** town *Erie County*, 142
**Brantingham** postal area *Lewis County*, 228
**Brasher Falls** CDP *St. Lawrence County*, 452
**Brasher** town *Saint Lawrence County*, 452
**Breesport** CDP *Chemung County*, 73
**Breezy Point** postal area *Queens County*, 325
**Brentwood** CDP *Suffolk County*, 519
**Brewerton** CDP *Onondaga County*, 356
**Brewster Hill** CDP *Putnam County*, 426
**Brewster** village *Putnam County*, 425
**Briarcliff Manor** village *Westchester County*, 627
**Bridgehampton** CDP *Suffolk County*, 519
**Bridgeport** CDP *Onondaga County*, 356
**Bridgewater** town *Oneida County*, 341
**Bridgewater** village *Oneida County*, 341

**Brier Hill** postal area *Saint Lawrence County*, 452
**Brighton** town *Franklin County*, 170
**Brighton** town/CDP *Monroe County*, 257
**Brightwaters** village *Suffolk County*, 519
**Brinckerhoff** CDP *Dutchess County*, 125
**Bristol** town *Ontario County*, 371
**Broadalbin** town *Fulton County*, 178
**Broadalbin** village *Fulton County*, 178
**Brockport** village *Monroe County*, 258
**Brocton** village *Chautauqua County*, 58
**Bronx County**, 315
**Bronx** borough *Bronx County*, 315
**Bronxville** village *Westchester County*, 628
**Brookfield** town *Madison County*, 249
**Brookhaven** CDP *Suffolk County*, 520
**Brookhaven** town *Suffolk County*, 519
**Brooklyn** borough *Kings County*, 317
**Brooktondale** postal area *Tompkins County*, 577
**Brookville** village *Nassau County*, 279
**Broome County**, 22 - 29
**Broome** town *Schoharie County*, 484
**Brownville** town *Jefferson County*, 214
**Brownville** village *Jefferson County*, 213
**Brunswick** town *Rensselaer County*, 431
**Brushton** village *Franklin County*, 170
**Brutus** town *Cayuga County*, 48
**Buchanan** village *Westchester County*, 628
**Buffalo** city *Erie County*, 143
**Bullville** postal area *Orange County*, 381
**Burdett** village *Schuyler County*, 491
**Burke** town *Franklin County*, 170
**Burke** village *Franklin County*, 170
**Burlingham** postal area *Sullivan County*, 562
**Burlington Flats** postal area *Otsego County*, 414
**Burlington** town *Otsego County*, 414
**Burns** town *Allegany County*, 14
**Burnt Hills** postal area *Saratoga County*, 469
**Burt** postal area *Niagara County*, 331
**Buskirk** postal area *Rensselaer County*, 431
**Busti** CDP *Chautauqua County*, 58
**Busti** town *Chautauqua County*, 58
**Butler** town *Wayne County*, 617
**Butternuts** town *Otsego County*, 414
**Byersville** CDP *Livingston County*, 236
**Byron** town *Genesee County*, 185

**C**

**Cadyville** postal area *Clinton County*, 89
**Cairo** CDP *Greene County*, 190
**Cairo** town *Greene County*, 190
**Calcium** CDP *Jefferson County*, 214
**Caledonia** town *Livingston County*, 236
**Caledonia** village *Livingston County*, 236
**Callicoon Center** postal area *Sullivan County*, 563
**Callicoon** CDP *Sullivan County*, 562
**Callicoon** town *Sullivan County*, 562
**Calverton** CDP *Suffolk County*, 520
**Cambria Heights** postal area *Queens County*, 325
**Cambria** town *Niagara County*, 331
**Cambridge** town *Washington County*, 609
**Cambridge** village *Washington County*, 609
**Camden** town *Oneida County*, 342

**Camden** village *Oneida County*, 341
**Cameron Mills** postal area *Steuben County*, 502
**Cameron** town *Steuben County*, 502
**Camillus** town *Onondaga County*, 357
**Camillus** village *Onondaga County*, 357
**Campbell Hall** postal area *Orange County*, 381
**Campbell** CDP *Steuben County*, 502
**Campbell** town *Steuben County*, 502
**Canaan** town *Columbia County*, 98
**Canadice** town *Ontario County*, 371
**Canajoharie** town *Montgomery County*, 270
**Canajoharie** village *Montgomery County*, 269
**Canandaigua** city *Ontario County*, 372
**Canandaigua** town *Ontario County*, 372
**Canaseraga** village *Allegany County*, 14
**Canastota** village *Madison County*, 249
**Candor** town *Tioga County*, 573
**Candor** village *Tioga County*, 573
**Caneadea** town *Allegany County*, 14
**Canisteo** town *Steuben County*, 503
**Canisteo** village *Steuben County*, 502
**Canton** town *Saint Lawrence County*, 453
**Canton** village *Saint Lawrence County*, 453
**Cape Vincent** town *Jefferson County*, 214
**Cape Vincent** village *Jefferson County*, 214
**Carle Place** CDP *Nassau County*, 279
**Carlisle** town *Schoharie County*, 484
**Carlton** town *Orleans County*, 399
**Carmel Hamlet** CDP *Putnam County*, 426
**Carmel** town *Putnam County*, 426
**Caroga Lake** CDP *Fulton County*, 178
**Caroga** town *Fulton County*, 178
**Caroline** town *Tompkins County*, 577
**Carroll** town *Chautauqua County*, 58
**Carrollton** town *Cattaraugus County*, 32
**Carthage** village *Jefferson County*, 215
**Cassadaga** village *Chautauqua County*, 59
**Cassville** postal area *Oneida County*, 342
**Castile** town *Wyoming County*, 652
**Castile** village *Wyoming County*, 652
**Castle Creek** postal area *Broome County*, 24
**Castleton-on-Hudson** village *Rensselaer County*, 431
**Castorland** village *Lewis County*, 228
**Catharine** town *Schuyler County*, 491
**Catlin** town *Chemung County*, 73
**Cato** town *Cayuga County*, 48
**Cato** village *Cayuga County*, 48
**Caton** town *Steuben County*, 503
**Catskill** town *Greene County*, 191
**Catskill** village *Greene County*, 190
**Cattaraugus County**, 30 - 45
**Cattaraugus Reservation** Reservation *Cattaraugus County*, 32
**Cattaraugus Reservation** Reservation *Chautauqua County*, 59
**Cattaraugus Reservation** Reservation *Erie County*, 144
**Cattaraugus** village *Cattaraugus County*, 32
**Cayuga County**, 46 - 55
**Cayuga Heights** village *Tompkins County*, 577
**Cayuga** village *Cayuga County*, 48
**Cayuta** town *Schuyler County*, 491
**Cazenovia** town *Madison County*, 250
**Cazenovia** village *Madison County*, 249

*CDP = Census Designated Place*

**Cedarhurst** village *Nassau County*, 279

**Celoron** village *Chautauqua County*, 59

**Center Moriches** CDP *Suffolk County*, 520

**Centereach** CDP *Suffolk County*, 521

**Centerport** CDP *Suffolk County*, 521

**Centerville** town *Allegany County*, 14

**Central Bridge** CDP *Schoharie County*, 485

**Central Islip** CDP *Suffolk County*, 521

**Central Square** village *Oswego County*, 404

**Centre Island** village *Nassau County*, 280

**Ceres** postal area *Allegany County*, 15

**Chadwicks** CDP *Oneida County*, 342

**Chaffee** postal area *Erie County*, 144

**Champion** town *Jefferson County*, 215

**Champlain** town *Clinton County*, 90

**Champlain** village *Clinton County*, 89

**Chappaqua** CDP *Westchester County*, 628

**Charleston** town *Montgomery County*, 270

**Charlotte** town *Chautauqua County*, 59

**Charlotteville** postal area *Schoharie County*, 485

**Charlton** town *Saratoga County*, 469

**Chase Mills** postal area *Saint Lawrence County*, 453

**Chateaugay** town *Franklin County*, 171

**Chateaugay** village *Franklin County*, 171

**Chatham** town *Columbia County*, 98

**Chatham** village *Columbia County*, 98

**Chaumont** village *Jefferson County*, 215

**Chautauqua County**, 56 - 70

**Chautauqua** CDP *Chautauqua County*, 60

**Chautauqua** town *Chautauqua County*, 60

**Chazy** CDP *Clinton County*, 90

**Chazy** town *Clinton County*, 90

**Cheektowaga** CDP *Erie County*, 144

**Cheektowaga** town *Erie County*, 144

**Chelsea** postal area *Dutchess County*, 125

**Chemung County**, 71 - 77

**Chemung** town *Chemung County*, 73

**Chenango Bridge** CDP *Broome County*, 24

**Chenango County**, 78 - 86

**Chenango Forks** postal area *Broome County*, 24

**Chenango** town *Broome County*, 24

**Cherry Creek** town *Chautauqua County*, 60

**Cherry Creek** village *Chautauqua County*, 60

**Cherry Plain** postal area *Rensselaer County*, 431

**Cherry Valley** town *Otsego County*, 415

**Cherry Valley** village *Otsego County*, 414

**Chester** town *Orange County*, 381

**Chester** town *Warren County*, 602

**Chester** village *Orange County*, 381

**Chesterfield** town *Essex County*, 160

**Chestertown** CDP *Warren County*, 603

**Chestnut Ridge** village *Rockland County*, 440

**Chichester** postal area *Ulster County*, 585

**Childwold** postal area *Saint Lawrence County*, 453

**Chili** town *Monroe County*, 258

**Chippewa Bay** postal area *Saint Lawrence County*, 453

**Chittenango** village *Madison County*, 250

**Churchville** village *Monroe County*, 258

**Churubusco** postal area *Clinton County*, 91

**Cicero** town *Onondaga County*, 357

**Cincinnatus** town *Cortland County*, 106

**Circleville** postal area *Orange County*, 382

**Clare** town *Saint Lawrence County*, 453

**Clarence Center** CDP *Erie County*, 145

**Clarence** CDP *Erie County*, 145

**Clarence** town *Erie County*, 145

**Clarendon** town *Orleans County*, 399

**Clark Mills** CDP *Oneida County*, 342

**Clarkson** CDP *Monroe County*, 259

**Clarkson** town *Monroe County*, 258

**Clarkstown** town *Rockland County*, 440

**Clarksville** postal area *Albany County*, 3

**Clarksville** town *Allegany County*, 15

**Claryville** postal area *Sullivan County*, 563

**Claverack** town *Columbia County*, 98

**Claverack-Red Mills** CDP *Columbia County*, 99

**Clay** town *Onondaga County*, 358

**Clayton** town *Jefferson County*, 216

**Clayton** village *Jefferson County*, 216

**Clayville** village *Oneida County*, 342

**Clemons** postal area *Washington County*, 610

**Clermont** town *Columbia County*, 99

**Cleveland** village *Oswego County*, 404

**Clifton Park** town *Saratoga County*, 470

**Clifton Springs** village *Ontario County*, 372

**Clifton** town *Saint Lawrence County*, 454

**Climax** postal area *Greene County*, 191

**Clinton Corners** postal area *Dutchess County*, 125

**Clinton County**, 87 - 96

**Clinton** town *Clinton County*, 91

**Clinton** town *Dutchess County*, 125

**Clinton** village *Oneida County*, 343

**Clintondale** CDP *Ulster County*, 585

**Clyde** village *Wayne County*, 617

**Clymer** town *Chautauqua County*, 61

**Cobleskill** town *Schoharie County*, 485

**Cobleskill** village *Schoharie County*, 485

**Cochecton** town *Sullivan County*, 563

**Coeymans Hollow** postal area *Albany County*, 4

**Coeymans** town *Albany County*, 3

**Cohocton** town *Steuben County*, 503

**Cohocton** village *Steuben County*, 503

**Cohoes** city *Albany County*, 4

**Colchester** town *Delaware County*, 114

**Cold Brook** village *Herkimer County*, 202

**Cold Spring Harbor** CDP *Suffolk County*, 521

**Cold Spring** village *Putnam County*, 426

**Colden** town *Erie County*, 146

**Coldspring** town *Cattaraugus County*, 33

**Colesville** town *Broome County*, 24

**College Point** postal area *Queens County*, 325

**Collins Center** postal area *Erie County*, 146

**Collins** town *Erie County*, 146

**Colonie** town *Albany County*, 4

**Colonie** village *Albany County*, 4

**Colton** CDP *St. Lawrence County*, 454

**Colton** town *Saint Lawrence County*, 454

**Columbia County**, 97 - 105

**Columbia** town *Herkimer County*, 202

**Columbus** town *Chenango County*, 80

**Commack** CDP *Suffolk County*, 522

**Comstock** postal area *Washington County*, 610

**Concord** town *Erie County*, 146

**Conesus Hamlet** CDP *Livingston County*, 237

**Conesus Lake** CDP *Livingston County*, 237

**Conesus** town *Livingston County*, 237

**Conesville** town *Schoharie County*, 486

**Conewango Valley** postal area *Cattaraugus County*, 33

**Conewango** town *Cattaraugus County*, 33

**Congers** CDP *Rockland County*, 441

**Conklin** town *Broome County*, 24

**Connelly** postal area *Ulster County*, 585

**Conquest** town *Cayuga County*, 49

**Constable** town *Franklin County*, 171

**Constableville** village *Lewis County*, 228

**Constantia** CDP *Oswego County*, 405

**Constantia** town *Oswego County*, 404

**Coopers Plains** CDP *Steuben County*, 504

**Cooperstown** village *Otsego County*, 415

**Copake Falls** postal area *Columbia County*, 99

**Copake Lake** CDP *Columbia County*, 99

**Copake** town *Columbia County*, 99

**Copenhagen** village *Lewis County*, 229

**Copiague** CDP *Suffolk County*, 522

**Coram** CDP *Suffolk County*, 522

**Corfu** village *Genesee County*, 185

**Corinth** town *Saratoga County*, 470

**Corinth** village *Saratoga County*, 470

**Corning** city *Steuben County*, 504

**Corning** town *Steuben County*, 504

**Cornwall on Hudson** village *Orange County*, 382

**Cornwall** town *Orange County*, 382

**Cornwallville** postal area *Greene County*, 191

**Corona** postal area *Queens County*, 325

**Cortland County**, 106 - 111

**Cortland West** CDP *Cortland County*, 107

**Cortland** city *Cortland County*, 107

**Cortlandt Manor** postal area *Westchester County*, 629

**Cortlandt** town *Westchester County*, 629

**Cortlandville** town *Cortland County*, 107

**Cossayuna** postal area *Washington County*, 610

**Cottekill** postal area *Ulster County*, 585

**Country Knolls** CDP *Saratoga County*, 471

**Cove Neck** village *Nassau County*, 280

**Coventry** town *Chenango County*, 80

**Covert** town *Seneca County*, 494

**Covington** town *Wyoming County*, 652

**Cowlesville** postal area *Wyoming County*, 652

**Coxsackie** town *Greene County*, 191

**Coxsackie** village *Greene County*, 191

**Cragsmoor** CDP *Ulster County*, 585

**Cranberry Lake** CDP *St. Lawrence County*, 454

**Craryville** postal area *Columbia County*, 100

**Crawford** town *Orange County*, 382

**Croghan** town *Lewis County*, 229

**Croghan** village *Lewis County*, 229

**Crompond** CDP *Westchester County*, 629

**Cropseyville** postal area *Rensselaer County*, 432

**Cross River** postal area *Westchester County*, 629

**Croton Falls** postal area *Westchester County*, 629

*CDP = Census Designated Place*

**Croton-on-Hudson** village *Westchester County*, 629
**Crown Heights** CDP *Dutchess County*, 125
**Crown Point** town *Essex County*, 160
**Crugers** CDP *Westchester County*, 630
**Crystal Beach** CDP *Ontario County*, 373
**Cuba** town *Allegany County*, 15
**Cuba** village *Allegany County*, 15
**Cuddebackville** postal area *Orange County*, 383
**Cumberland Head** CDP *Clinton County*, 91
**Cumminsville** CDP *Livingston County*, 237
**Cutchogue** CDP *Suffolk County*, 522
**Cuyler** town *Cortland County*, 107
**Cuylerville** CDP *Livingston County*, 237

**D**

**Dale** postal area *Wyoming County*, 653
**Dalton** CDP *Livingston County*, 238
**Danby** town *Tompkins County*, 578
**Dannemora** town *Clinton County*, 91
**Dannemora** village *Clinton County*, 91
**Dansville** town *Steuben County*, 505
**Dansville** village *Livingston County*, 238
**Danube** town *Herkimer County*, 202
**Darien Center** postal area *Genesee County*, 185
**Darien** town *Genesee County*, 185
**Davenport Center** CDP *Delaware County*, 114
**Davenport** town *Delaware County*, 114
**Day** town *Saratoga County*, 471
**Dayton** town *Cattaraugus County*, 33
**De Kalb** town *Saint Lawrence County*, 455
**De Lancey** postal area *Delaware County*, 114
**De Peyster** town *Saint Lawrence County*, 455
**De Ruyter** town *Madison County*, 251
**De Ruyter** village *Madison County*, 250
**De Witt** town *Onondaga County*, 358
**Deansboro** postal area *Oneida County*, 343
**Decatur** town *Otsego County*, 415
**Deer Park** CDP *Suffolk County*, 523
**Deerfield** town *Oneida County*, 343
**Deerpark** town *Orange County*, 383
**Deferiet** village *Jefferson County*, 216
**DeKalb Junction** CDP *St. Lawrence County*, 455
**Delanson** village *Schenectady County*, 479
**Delaware County**, 112 - 121
**Delaware** town *Sullivan County*, 563
**Delevan** village *Cattaraugus County*, 33
**Delhi** town *Delaware County*, 115
**Delhi** village *Delaware County*, 114
**Delphi Falls** postal area *Onondaga County*, 358
**Denmark** town *Lewis County*, 229
**Denning** town *Ulster County*, 586
**Denver** postal area *Delaware County*, 115
**Depauville** CDP *Jefferson County*, 216
**Depew** village *Erie County*, 146
**Deposit** town *Delaware County*, 115
**Deposit** village *Delaware County*, 115
**Derby** postal area *Erie County*, 147
**Dering Harbor** village *Suffolk County*, 523
**Dewittville** postal area *Chautauqua County*, 61
**Dexter** village *Jefferson County*, 217

**Diamond Point** postal area *Warren County*, 603
**Diana** town *Lewis County*, 229
**Dickinson Center** postal area *Franklin County*, 172
**Dickinson** town *Broome County*, 25
**Dickinson** town *Franklin County*, 171
**Dix Hills** CDP *Suffolk County*, 523
**Dix** town *Schuyler County*, 492
**Dobbs Ferry** village *Westchester County*, 630
**Dolgeville** village *Herkimer County*, 202
**Dover Plains** CDP *Dutchess County*, 126
**Dover** town *Dutchess County*, 126
**Downsville** CDP *Delaware County*, 116
**Dresden** town *Washington County*, 610
**Dresden** village *Yates County*, 658
**Dryden** town *Tompkins County*, 578
**Dryden** village *Tompkins County*, 578
**Duane Lake** CDP *Schenectady County*, 480
**Duane** town *Franklin County*, 172
**Duanesburg** CDP *Schenectady County*, 480
**Duanesburg** town *Schenectady County*, 480
**Dundee** village *Yates County*, 659
**Dunkirk** city *Chautauqua County*, 61
**Dunkirk** town *Chautauqua County*, 61
**Durham** town *Greene County*, 192
**Durhamville** CDP *Oneida County*, 343
**Dutchess County**, 122 - 137

**E**

**Eagle Bay** postal area *Herkimer County*, 203
**Eagle Bridge** postal area *Rensselaer County*, 432
**Eagle** town *Wyoming County*, 653
**Earlton** postal area *Greene County*, 192
**Earlville** village *Madison County*, 251
**East Amherst** postal area *Erie County*, 147
**East Atlantic Beach** CDP *Nassau County*, 280
**East Aurora** village *Erie County*, 147
**East Avon** CDP *Livingston County*, 238
**East Berne** postal area *Albany County*, 5
**East Bethany** postal area *Genesee County*, 185
**East Bloomfield** town *Ontario County*, 373
**East Branch** postal area *Delaware County*, 116
**East Chatham** postal area *Columbia County*, 100
**East Concord** postal area *Erie County*, 147
**East Durham** postal area *Greene County*, 192
**East Elmhurst** postal area *Queens County*, 325
**East Farmingdale** CDP *Suffolk County*, 523
**East Fishkill** town *Dutchess County*, 126
**East Garden City** CDP *Nassau County*, 280
**East Glenville** CDP *Schenectady County*, 480
**East Greenbush** CDP *Rensselaer County*, 432
**East Greenbush** town *Rensselaer County*, 432
**East Hampton North** CDP *Suffolk County*, 524
**East Hampton** town *Suffolk County*, 524
**East Hampton** village *Suffolk County*, 524
**East Hills** village *Nassau County*, 281
**East Islip** CDP *Suffolk County*, 525
**East Ithaca** CDP *Tompkins County*, 579

**East Jewett** postal area *Greene County*, 192
**East Kingston** CDP *Ulster County*, 586
**East Marion** CDP *Suffolk County*, 525
**East Massapequa** CDP *Nassau County*, 281
**East Meadow** CDP *Nassau County*, 281
**East Meredith** postal area *Delaware County*, 116
**East Moriches** CDP *Suffolk County*, 525
**East Nassau** village *Rensselaer County*, 432
**East Northport** CDP *Suffolk County*, 525
**East Norwich** CDP *Nassau County*, 281
**East Otto** town *Cattaraugus County*, 34
**East Patchogue** CDP *Suffolk County*, 526
**East Quogue** CDP *Suffolk County*, 526
**East Randolph** village *Cattaraugus County*, 34
**East Rochester** town/village *Monroe County*, 259
**East Rockaway** village *Nassau County*, 282
**East Schodack** postal area *Rensselaer County*, 432
**East Setauket** postal area *Suffolk County*, 526
**East Shoreham** CDP *Suffolk County*, 526
**East Springfield** postal area *Otsego County*, 416
**East Syracuse** village *Onondaga County*, 358
**East Williston** village *Nassau County*, 282
**East Worcester** postal area *Otsego County*, 416
**Eastchester** CDP *Westchester County*, 631
**Eastchester** town *Westchester County*, 630
**Easton** town *Washington County*, 610
**Eastport** CDP *Suffolk County*, 527
**Eaton** town *Madison County*, 251
**Eatons Neck** CDP *Suffolk County*, 527
**Eden** CDP *Erie County*, 148
**Eden** town *Erie County*, 147
**Edinburg** town *Saratoga County*, 471
**Edmeston** CDP *Otsego County*, 416
**Edmeston** town *Otsego County*, 416
**Edwards** town *Saint Lawrence County*, 456
**Edwards** village *Saint Lawrence County*, 455
**Eggertsville** CDP *Erie County*, 148
**Elba** town *Genesee County*, 186
**Elba** village *Genesee County*, 186
**Elbridge** town *Onondaga County*, 359
**Elbridge** village *Onondaga County*, 359
**Eldred** postal area *Sullivan County*, 563
**Elizabethtown** CDP *Essex County*, 161
**Elizabethtown** town *Essex County*, 161
**Elizaville** postal area *Columbia County*, 100
**Elka Park** postal area *Greene County*, 192
**Ellenburg Center** postal area *Clinton County*, 92
**Ellenburg Depot** postal area *Clinton County*, 92
**Ellenburg** town *Clinton County*, 92
**Ellenville** village *Ulster County*, 586
**Ellery** town *Chautauqua County*, 61
**Ellicott** town *Chautauqua County*, 62
**Ellicottville** town *Cattaraugus County*, 34
**Ellicottville** village *Cattaraugus County*, 34
**Ellington** town *Chautauqua County*, 62
**Ellisburg** town *Jefferson County*, 217
**Ellisburg** village *Jefferson County*, 217
**Elma Center** CDP *Erie County*, 148
**Elma** town *Erie County*, 148

*CDP = Census Designated Place*

Elmhurst postal area *Queens County*, 326
Elmira Heights village *Chemung County*, 74
Elmira city *Chemung County*, 73
Elmira town *Chemung County*, 74
Elmont CDP *Nassau County*, 282
Elmsford village *Westchester County*, 631
Elwood CDP *Suffolk County*, 527
Endicott village *Broome County*, 25
Endwell CDP *Broome County*, 25
Enfield town *Tompkins County*, 579
Ephratah town *Fulton County*, 179
Erie County, 138 - 158
Erieville postal area *Madison County*, 251
Erin CDP *Chemung County*, 75
Erin town *Chemung County*, 75
Erwin town *Steuben County*, 505
Esopus town *Ulster County*, 586
Esperance town *Schoharie County*, 486
Esperance village *Schoharie County*, 486
Essex County, 159 - 167
Essex town *Essex County*, 161
Etna postal area *Tompkins County*, 579
Evans Mills village *Jefferson County*, 217
Evans town *Erie County*, 149
Exeter town *Otsego County*, 416

**F**

Fabius town *Onondaga County*, 359
Fabius village *Onondaga County*, 359
Fair Haven village *Cayuga County*, 49
Fairfield town *Herkimer County*, 203
Fairmount CDP *Onondaga County*, 360
Fairport village *Monroe County*, 259
Fairview CDP *Dutchess County*, 126
Fairview CDP *Westchester County*, 632
Falconer village *Chautauqua County*, 62
Fallsburg town *Sullivan County*, 563
Far Rockaway postal area *Queens County*, 326
Farmersville Station postal area *Cattaraugus County*, 35
Farmersville town *Cattaraugus County*, 35
Farmingdale village *Nassau County*, 283
Farmington town *Ontario County*, 373
Farmingville CDP *Suffolk County*, 527
Farnham village *Erie County*, 149
Fayette town *Seneca County*, 495
Fayetteville village *Onondaga County*, 360
Felts Mills CDP *Jefferson County*, 218
Fenner town *Madison County*, 251
Fenton town *Broome County*, 26
Ferndale postal area *Sullivan County*, 564
Feura Bush postal area *Albany County*, 5
Fillmore CDP *Allegany County*, 16
Findley Lake postal area *Chautauqua County*, 62
Fine town *Saint Lawrence County*, 456
Fire Island CDP *Suffolk County*, 528
Firthcliffe CDP *Orange County*, 383
Fishers Island CDP *Suffolk County*, 528
Fishers Landing CDP *Jefferson County*, 218
Fishkill town *Dutchess County*, 127
Fishkill village *Dutchess County*, 127
Fishs Eddy postal area *Delaware County*, 116
Flanders CDP *Suffolk County*, 528
Fleischmanns village *Delaware County*, 116
Fleming town *Cayuga County*, 49

Floral Park village *Nassau County*, 283
Florence town *Oneida County*, 343
Florida town *Montgomery County*, 270
Florida village *Orange County*, 383
Flower Hill village *Nassau County*, 283
Floyd town *Oneida County*, 344
Flushing postal area *Queens County*, 326
Fly Creek postal area *Otsego County*, 416
Fonda village *Montgomery County*, 270
Forest Hills postal area *Queens County*, 326
Forest Home CDP *Tompkins County*, 579
Forestburgh town *Sullivan County*, 564
Forestport town *Oneida County*, 344
Forestville village *Chautauqua County*, 63
Fort Ann town *Washington County*, 610
Fort Ann village *Washington County*, 610
Fort Covington Hamlet CDP *Franklin County*, 172
Fort Covington town *Franklin County*, 172
Fort Drum CDP *Jefferson County*, 218
Fort Edward town *Washington County*, 611
Fort Edward village *Washington County*, 611
Fort Hunter postal area *Montgomery County*, 271
Fort Johnson village *Montgomery County*, 271
Fort Montgomery CDP *Orange County*, 383
Fort Plain village *Montgomery County*, 271
Fort Salonga CDP *Suffolk County*, 528
Fowler town *Saint Lawrence County*, 456
Fowlerville CDP *Livingston County*, 239
Frankfort town *Herkimer County*, 203
Frankfort village *Herkimer County*, 203
Franklin County, 168 - 176
Franklin Springs postal area *Oneida County*, 344
Franklin Square CDP *Nassau County*, 284
Franklin town *Delaware County*, 117
Franklin town *Franklin County*, 173
Franklin village *Delaware County*, 116
Franklinville town *Cattaraugus County*, 35
Franklinville village *Cattaraugus County*, 35
Fredonia village *Chautauqua County*, 63
Freedom Plains CDP *Dutchess County*, 127
Freedom town *Cattaraugus County*, 36
Freehold postal area *Greene County*, 192
Freeport village *Nassau County*, 284
Freetown town *Cortland County*, 108
Freeville village *Tompkins County*, 579
Fremont Center postal area *Sullivan County*, 564
Fremont town *Steuben County*, 505
Fremont town *Sullivan County*, 564
French Creek town *Chautauqua County*, 63
Fresh Meadows postal area *Queens County*, 326
Frewsburg CDP *Chautauqua County*, 63
Friendship CDP *Allegany County*, 16
Friendship town *Allegany County*, 16
Fulton County, 177 - 181
Fulton city *Oswego County*, 405
Fulton town *Schoharie County*, 486
Fultonham postal area *Schoharie County*, 487
Fultonville village *Montgomery County*, 271

**G**

Gabriels postal area *Franklin County*, 173

Gaines town *Orleans County*, 400
Gainesville town *Wyoming County*, 653
Gainesville village *Wyoming County*, 653
Galen town *Wayne County*, 617
Galeville CDP *Onondaga County*, 360
Gallatin town *Columbia County*, 100
Galway town *Saratoga County*, 472
Galway village *Saratoga County*, 471
Gang Mills CDP *Steuben County*, 505
Gansevoort postal area *Saratoga County*, 472
Garden City Park CDP *Nassau County*, 285
Garden City South CDP *Nassau County*, 285
Garden City village *Nassau County*, 284
Gardiner CDP *Ulster County*, 587
Gardiner town *Ulster County*, 587
Gardnertown CDP *Orange County*, 384
Garnerville postal area *Rockland County*, 441
Garrattsville postal area *Otsego County*, 416
Garrison postal area *Putnam County*, 427
Gasport CDP *Niagara County*, 331
Gates CDP *Monroe County*, 260
Gates town *Monroe County*, 260
Geddes town *Onondaga County*, 360
Genesee County, 182 - 187
Genesee Falls town *Wyoming County*, 653
Genesee town *Allegany County*, 16
Geneseo town *Livingston County*, 239
Geneseo village *Livingston County*, 239
Geneva city *Ontario County*, 373
Geneva town *Ontario County*, 374
Genoa town *Cayuga County*, 50
Georgetown town *Madison County*, 252
German Flatts town *Herkimer County*, 203
German town *Chenango County*, 80
Germantown CDP *Columbia County*, 100
Germantown town *Columbia County*, 100
Gerry town *Chautauqua County*, 64
Getzville postal area *Erie County*, 149
Ghent CDP *Columbia County*, 101
Ghent town *Columbia County*, 101
Gilbertsville village *Otsego County*, 417
Gilboa town *Schoharie County*, 487
Gilgo CDP *Suffolk County*, 529
Glasco CDP *Ulster County*, 587
Glen Aubrey CDP *Broome County*, 26
Glen Cove city *Nassau County*, 285
Glen Head CDP *Nassau County*, 286
Glen Oaks postal area *Queens County*, 326
Glen Park village *Jefferson County*, 218
Glen Spey postal area *Sullivan County*, 564
Glen Wild postal area *Sullivan County*, 564
Glen town *Montgomery County*, 272
Glenfield postal area *Lewis County*, 230
Glenford postal area *Ulster County*, 587
Glenham postal area *Dutchess County*, 127
Glenmont postal area *Albany County*, 5
Glens Falls North CDP *Warren County*, 603
Glens Falls city *Warren County*, 603
Glenville town *Schenectady County*, 480
Glenwood Landing CDP *Nassau County*, 286
Glenwood postal area *Erie County*, 149
Gloversville city *Fulton County*, 179
Golden's Bridge CDP *Westchester County*, 632
Goldens Bridge postal area *Westchester County*, 632

*CDP = Census Designated Place*

**Gordon Heights** CDP *Suffolk County*, 529
**Gorham** CDP *Ontario County*, 374
**Gorham** town *Ontario County*, 374
**Goshen** town *Orange County*, 384
**Goshen** village *Orange County*, 384
**Gouverneur** town *Saint Lawrence County*, 457
**Gouverneur** village *Saint Lawrence County*, 456
**Gowanda** village *Cattaraugus County*, 36
**Grafton** town *Rensselaer County*, 433
**Grahamsville** postal area *Sullivan County*, 564
**Granby** town *Oswego County*, 405
**Grand Gorge** postal area *Delaware County*, 117
**Grand Island** town *Erie County*, 149
**Grand View-on-Hudson** village *Rockland County*, 441
**Grandyle Village** CDP *Erie County*, 150
**Granger** town *Allegany County*, 17
**Granite Springs** postal area *Westchester County*, 632
**Granville** town *Washington County*, 612
**Granville** village *Washington County*, 611
**Great Bend** CDP *Jefferson County*, 219
**Great Neck Estates** village *Nassau County*, 286
**Great Neck Gardens** CDP *Nassau County*, 287
**Great Neck Plaza** village *Nassau County*, 287
**Great Neck** village *Nassau County*, 286
**Great River** CDP *Suffolk County*, 529
**Great Valley** town *Cattaraugus County*, 36
**Greece** CDP *Monroe County*, 260
**Greece** town *Monroe County*, 260
**Green Island** town/village *Albany County*, 5
**Greenburgh** town *Westchester County*, 632
**Greene County**, 188 - 196
**Greene** town *Chenango County*, 81
**Greene** village *Chenango County*, 81
**Greenfield Center** postal area *Saratoga County*, 472
**Greenfield Park** postal area *Ulster County*, 587
**Greenfield** town *Saratoga County*, 472
**Greenhurst** postal area *Chautauqua County*, 64
**Greenlawn** CDP *Suffolk County*, 529
**Greenport West** CDP *Suffolk County*, 530
**Greenport** town *Columbia County*, 101
**Greenport** village *Suffolk County*, 529
**Greenvale** CDP *Nassau County*, 287
**Greenville** CDP *Greene County*, 193
**Greenville** CDP *Westchester County*, 632
**Greenville** town *Greene County*, 192
**Greenville** town *Orange County*, 385
**Greenwich** town *Washington County*, 612
**Greenwich** village *Washington County*, 612
**Greenwood Lake** village *Orange County*, 385
**Greenwood** town *Steuben County*, 506
**Greig** town *Lewis County*, 230
**Greigsville** CDP *Livingston County*, 239
**Groton** town *Tompkins County*, 580
**Groton** village *Tompkins County*, 580
**Grove** town *Allegany County*, 17
**Groveland Station** CDP *Livingston County*, 240

**Groveland** town *Livingston County*, 240
**Guilderland Center** postal area *Albany County*, 5
**Guilderland** town *Albany County*, 5
**Guilford** CDP *Chenango County*, 81
**Guilford** town *Chenango County*, 81

**H**

**Hadley** CDP *Saratoga County*, 473
**Hadley** town *Saratoga County*, 472
**Hagaman** village *Montgomery County*, 272
**Hague** town *Warren County*, 604
**Hailesboro** CDP *St. Lawrence County*, 457
**Haines Falls** postal area *Greene County*, 193
**Halcott** town *Greene County*, 193
**Halcottsville** postal area *Delaware County*, 117
**Halesite** CDP *Suffolk County*, 530
**Halfmoon** town *Saratoga County*, 473
**Hall** CDP *Ontario County*, 375
**Hamburg** town *Erie County*, 150
**Hamburg** village *Erie County*, 150
**Hamden** town *Delaware County*, 117
**Hamilton County**, 197 - 200
**Hamilton** town *Madison County*, 252
**Hamilton** village *Madison County*, 252
**Hamlin** CDP *Monroe County*, 261
**Hamlin** town *Monroe County*, 261
**Hammond** town *Saint Lawrence County*, 458
**Hammond** village *Saint Lawrence County*, 457
**Hammondsport** village *Steuben County*, 506
**Hampton Bays** CDP *Suffolk County*, 530
**Hampton Manor** CDP *Rensselaer County*, 433
**Hampton** town *Washington County*, 612
**Hamptonburgh** town *Orange County*, 385
**Hancock** town *Delaware County*, 118
**Hancock** village *Delaware County*, 117
**Hankins** postal area *Sullivan County*, 564
**Hannacroix** postal area *Greene County*, 193
**Hannawa Falls** CDP *St. Lawrence County*, 458
**Hannibal** town *Oswego County*, 406
**Hannibal** village *Oswego County*, 405
**Hanover** town *Chautauqua County*, 64
**Harbor Hills** CDP *Nassau County*, 287
**Harbor Isle** CDP *Nassau County*, 288
**Hardenburgh** town *Ulster County*, 588
**Harford** town *Cortland County*, 108
**Harmony** town *Chautauqua County*, 64
**Harpersfield** town *Delaware County*, 118
**Harpursville** postal area *Broome County*, 26
**Harrietstown** town *Franklin County*, 173
**Harriman** village *Orange County*, 385
**Harris Hill** CDP *Erie County*, 151
**Harris** postal area *Sullivan County*, 564
**Harrisburg** town *Lewis County*, 230
**Harrison** town *Westchester County*, 633
**Harrison** town/village *Westchester County*, 633
**Harrisville** village *Lewis County*, 230
**Hartford** town *Washington County*, 613
**Hartland** town *Niagara County*, 331
**Hartsdale** CDP *Westchester County*, 633
**Hartsville** town *Steuben County*, 506
**Hartwick** CDP *Otsego County*, 417
**Hartwick** town *Otsego County*, 417

**Hastings** town *Oswego County*, 406
**Hastings-on-Hudson** village *Westchester County*, 634
**Hauppauge** CDP *Suffolk County*, 531
**Haverstraw** town *Rockland County*, 442
**Haverstraw** village *Rockland County*, 441
**Haviland** CDP *Dutchess County*, 128
**Hawthorne** CDP *Westchester County*, 634
**Head of the Harbor** village *Suffolk County*, 531
**Hebron** town *Washington County*, 613
**Hector** town *Schuyler County*, 492
**Hemlock** CDP *Livingston County*, 240
**Hempstead** town *Nassau County*, 288
**Hempstead** village *Nassau County*, 288
**Henderson Harbor** postal area *Jefferson County*, 219
**Henderson** CDP *Jefferson County*, 219
**Henderson** town *Jefferson County*, 219
**Henrietta** town *Monroe County*, 261
**Hensonville** postal area *Greene County*, 193
**Heritage Hills** CDP *Westchester County*, 634
**Herkimer County**, 201 - 209
**Herkimer** town *Herkimer County*, 204
**Herkimer** village *Herkimer County*, 204
**Hermon** town *Saint Lawrence County*, 458
**Hermon** village *Saint Lawrence County*, 458
**Herricks** CDP *Nassau County*, 289
**Herrings** village *Jefferson County*, 219
**Heuvelton** village *Saint Lawrence County*, 459
**Hewlett Bay Park** village *Nassau County*, 289
**Hewlett Harbor** village *Nassau County*, 290
**Hewlett Neck** village *Nassau County*, 290
**Hewlett** CDP *Nassau County*, 289
**Hicksville** CDP *Nassau County*, 290
**High Falls** CDP *Ulster County*, 588
**Highland Falls** village *Orange County*, 386
**Highland Lake** postal area *Sullivan County*, 565
**Highland** CDP *Ulster County*, 588
**Highland** town *Sullivan County*, 565
**Highlands** town *Orange County*, 386
**Highmount** postal area *Ulster County*, 588
**Hillburn** village *Rockland County*, 442
**Hillcrest** CDP *Rockland County*, 442
**Hillsdale** town *Columbia County*, 101
**Hillside Lake** CDP *Dutchess County*, 128
**Hillside** CDP *Ulster County*, 588
**Hilton** village *Monroe County*, 261
**Himrod** postal area *Yates County*, 659
**Hinckley** postal area *Oneida County*, 344
**Hinsdale** town *Cattaraugus County*, 36
**Hobart** village *Delaware County*, 118
**Hoffmeister** postal area *Hamilton County*, 198
**Hogansburg** postal area *Franklin County*, 173
**Holbrook** CDP *Suffolk County*, 531
**Holland Patent** village *Oneida County*, 344
**Holland** CDP *Erie County*, 151
**Holland** town *Erie County*, 151
**Holley** village *Orleans County*, 400
**Hollis** postal area *Queens County*, 326
**Hollowville** postal area *Columbia County*, 102
**Holmes** postal area *Dutchess County*, 128
**Holtsville** CDP *Suffolk County*, 531
**Homer** town *Cortland County*, 108
**Homer** village *Cortland County*, 108

*CDP = Census Designated Place*

**Honeoye Falls** village *Monroe County*, 262
**Honeoye** CDP *Ontario County*, 375
**Hoosick Falls** village *Rensselaer County*, 433
**Hoosick** town *Rensselaer County*, 433
**Hope** town *Hamilton County*, 198
**Hopewell Junction** CDP *Dutchess County*, 128
**Hopewell** town *Ontario County*, 375
**Hopkinton** town *Saint Lawrence County*, 459
**Horicon** town *Warren County*, 604
**Hornby** town *Steuben County*, 506
**Hornell** city *Steuben County*, 507
**Hornellsville** town *Steuben County*, 507
**Horseheads North** CDP *Chemung County*, 76
**Horseheads** town *Chemung County*, 75
**Horseheads** village *Chemung County*, 75
**Hortonville** CDP *Sullivan County*, 565
**Houghton** CDP *Allegany County*, 17
**Hounsfield** town *Jefferson County*, 220
**Howard Beach** postal area *Queens County*, 326
**Howard** town *Steuben County*, 507
**Howells** postal area *Orange County*, 386
**Howes Cave** postal area *Schoharie County*, 487
**Hubbardsville** postal area *Madison County*, 253
**Hudson Falls** village *Washington County*, 613
**Hudson** city *Columbia County*, 102
**Huguenot** postal area *Orange County*, 386
**Huletts Landing** postal area *Washington County*, 614
**Hume** town *Allegany County*, 17
**Humphrey** town *Cattaraugus County*, 37
**Hunt** CDP *Livingston County*, 240
**Hunter** town *Greene County*, 194
**Hunter** village *Greene County*, 193
**Huntington Bay** village *Suffolk County*, 532
**Huntington Station** CDP *Suffolk County*, 533
**Huntington** CDP *Suffolk County*, 532
**Huntington** town *Suffolk County*, 532
**Hurley** CDP *Ulster County*, 589
**Hurley** town *Ulster County*, 589
**Hurleyville** postal area *Sullivan County*, 565
**Huron** town *Wayne County*, 617
**Hyde Park** CDP *Dutchess County*, 129
**Hyde Park** town *Dutchess County*, 128

**I**

**Ilion** village *Herkimer County*, 205
**Independence** town *Allegany County*, 18
**Indian Lake** town *Hamilton County*, 199
**Inlet** town *Hamilton County*, 199
**Interlaken** village *Seneca County*, 495
**Inwood** CDP *Nassau County*, 291
**Ionia** postal area *Ontario County*, 375
**Ira** town *Cayuga County*, 50
**Irondequoit** town/CDP *Monroe County*, 262
**Irving** postal area *Chautauqua County*, 64
**Irvington** village *Westchester County*, 634
**Ischua** town *Cattaraugus County*, 37
**Island Park** village *Nassau County*, 291
**Islandia** village *Suffolk County*, 533
**Islip Terrace** CDP *Suffolk County*, 534
**Islip** CDP *Suffolk County*, 534
**Islip** town *Suffolk County*, 533
**Italy** town *Yates County*, 659

**Ithaca** city *Tompkins County*, 580
**Ithaca** town *Tompkins County*, 581

**J**

**Jackson Heights** postal area *Queens County*, 327
**Jackson** town *Washington County*, 614
**Jacksonville** postal area *Tompkins County*, 581
**Jamaica** postal area *Queens County*, 327
**Jamesport** CDP *Suffolk County*, 534
**Jamestown West** CDP *Chautauqua County*, 65
**Jamestown** city *Chautauqua County*, 65
**Jamesville** postal area *Onondaga County*, 361
**Jasper** town *Steuben County*, 508
**Java Center** postal area *Wyoming County*, 654
**Java** town *Wyoming County*, 654
**Jay** town *Essex County*, 162
**Jefferson County**, 210 - 226
**Jefferson Heights** CDP *Greene County*, 194
**Jefferson Valley** postal area *Westchester County*, 635
**Jefferson Valley-Yorktown** CDP *Westchester County*, 635
**Jefferson** town *Schoharie County*, 487
**Jeffersonville** village *Sullivan County*, 565
**Jericho** CDP *Nassau County*, 291
**Jerusalem** town *Yates County*, 659
**Jewett** town *Greene County*, 194
**Johnsburg** town *Warren County*, 604
**Johnson City** village *Broome County*, 26
**Johnson** postal area *Orange County*, 386
**Johnsonville** postal area *Rensselaer County*, 434
**Johnstown** city *Fulton County*, 179
**Johnstown** town *Fulton County*, 180
**Jordan** village *Onondaga County*, 361
**Jordanville** postal area *Herkimer County*, 205
**Junius** town *Seneca County*, 495

**K**

**Kanona** postal area *Steuben County*, 508
**Kaser** village *Rockland County*, 442
**Katonah** CDP *Westchester County*, 635
**Kattskill Bay** postal area *Warren County*, 604
**Kauneonga Lake** postal area *Sullivan County*, 565
**Keene Valley** postal area *Essex County*, 162
**Keene** town *Essex County*, 162
**Keeseville** village *Clinton County*, 92
**Kendall** town *Orleans County*, 400
**Kenmore** village *Erie County*, 151
**Kennedy** CDP *Chautauqua County*, 65
**Kenoza Lake** postal area *Sullivan County*, 566
**Kensington** village *Nassau County*, 292
**Kent** postal area *Orleans County*, 400
**Kent** town *Putnam County*, 427
**Kerhonkson** CDP *Ulster County*, 589
**Keuka Park** CDP *Yates County*, 660
**Kew Gardens** postal area *Queens County*, 327
**Kiamesha Lake** postal area *Sullivan County*, 566
**Kiantone** town *Chautauqua County*, 66

**Kill Buck** postal area *Cattaraugus County*, 37
**Killawog** postal area *Broome County*, 26
**Kinderhook** town *Columbia County*, 102
**Kinderhook** village *Columbia County*, 102
**King Ferry** postal area *Cayuga County*, 50
**Kings County**, 317
**Kings Park** CDP *Suffolk County*, 534
**Kings Point** village *Nassau County*, 292
**Kingsbury** town *Washington County*, 614
**Kingston** city *Ulster County*, 589
**Kingston** town *Ulster County*, 590
**Kirkland** town *Oneida County*, 345
**Kirkville** postal area *Onondaga County*, 361
**Kirkwood** town *Broome County*, 27
**Kiryas Joel** village *Orange County*, 386
**Knowlesville** postal area *Orleans County*, 400
**Knox** town *Albany County*, 6
**Knoxboro** postal area *Oneida County*, 345
**Kortright** town *Delaware County*, 118
**Kysorville** CDP *Livingston County*, 241

**L**

**La Fargeville** CDP *Jefferson County*, 220
**La Fayette** postal area *Onondaga County*, 361
**La Fayette** town *Onondaga County*, 361
**La Grange** town *Dutchess County*, 129
**Lackawanna** city *Erie County*, 152
**Lacona** village *Oswego County*, 406
**Lagrangeville** postal area *Dutchess County*, 129
**Lake Carmel** CDP *Putnam County*, 427
**Lake Clear** postal area *Franklin County*, 173
**Lake Erie Beach** CDP *Erie County*, 152
**Lake George** town *Warren County*, 605
**Lake George** village *Warren County*, 604
**Lake Grove** village *Suffolk County*, 535
**Lake Hill** postal area *Ulster County*, 590
**Lake Huntington** postal area *Sullivan County*, 566
**Lake Katrine** CDP *Ulster County*, 590
**Lake Luzerne** CDP *Warren County*, 605
**Lake Luzerne** town *Warren County*, 605
**Lake Mohegan** CDP *Westchester County*, 635
**Lake Peekskill** postal area *Putnam County*, 427
**Lake Placid** village *Essex County*, 162
**Lake Pleasant** town *Hamilton County*, 199
**Lake Ronkonkoma** CDP *Suffolk County*, 535
**Lake Success** village *Nassau County*, 292
**Lake View** postal area *Erie County*, 152
**Lakeland** CDP *Onondaga County*, 361
**Lakeview** CDP *Nassau County*, 292
**Lakeville** CDP *Livingston County*, 241
**Lakewood** village *Chautauqua County*, 66
**Lancaster** town *Erie County*, 153
**Lancaster** village *Erie County*, 152
**Lanesville** postal area *Greene County*, 194
**Lansing** town *Tompkins County*, 581
**Lansing** village *Tompkins County*, 581
**Lapeer** town *Cortland County*, 109
**Larchmont** village *Westchester County*, 636
**Latham** postal area *Albany County*, 6
**Lattingtown** village *Nassau County*, 293
**Laurel Hollow** village *Nassau County*, 293
**Laurel** CDP *Suffolk County*, 535

**Laurens** town *Otsego County*, 418
**Laurens** village *Otsego County*, 417
**Lawrence** town *Saint Lawrence County*, 459
**Lawrence** village *Nassau County*, 293
**Lawtons** postal area *Erie County*, 153
**Le Ray** town *Jefferson County*, 220
**Le Roy** town *Genesee County*, 186
**Le Roy** village *Genesee County*, 186
**Lebanon** town *Madison County*, 253
**Ledyard** town *Cayuga County*, 50
**Lee Center** postal area *Oneida County*, 345
**Lee** town *Oneida County*, 345
**Leeds** CDP *Greene County*, 195
**Leicester** town *Livingston County*, 241
**Leicester** village *Livingston County*, 241
**Lenox** town *Madison County*, 253
**Leon** town *Cattaraugus County*, 37
**Leonardsville** postal area *Madison County*, 253
**Levittown** CDP *Nassau County*, 294
**Lewis County**, 227 - 234
**Lewis** town *Essex County*, 162
**Lewis** town *Lewis County*, 231
**Lewisboro** town *Westchester County*, 636
**Lewiston** town *Niagara County*, 332
**Lewiston** village *Niagara County*, 331
**Lexington** town *Greene County*, 195
**Leyden** town *Lewis County*, 231
**Liberty** town *Sullivan County*, 566
**Liberty** village *Sullivan County*, 566
**Lido Beach** CDP *Nassau County*, 294
**Lily Dale** postal area *Chautauqua County*, 66
**Lima** town *Livingston County*, 242
**Lima** village *Livingston County*, 242
**Lime Lake** CDP *Cattaraugus County*, 38
**Limestone** village *Cattaraugus County*, 38
**Lincklaen** town *Chenango County*, 82
**Lincoln Park** CDP *Ulster County*, 591
**Lincoln** town *Madison County*, 253
**Lincolndale** CDP *Westchester County*, 636
**Lindenhurst** village *Suffolk County*, 535
**Lindley** town *Steuben County*, 508
**Linwood** CDP *Livingston County*, 242
**Lisbon** town *Saint Lawrence County*, 459
**Lisle** town *Broome County*, 27
**Lisle** village *Broome County*, 27
**Litchfield** town *Herkimer County*, 205
**Little Falls** city *Herkimer County*, 205
**Little Falls** town *Herkimer County*, 205
**Little Genesee** postal area *Allegany County*, 18
**Little Neck** postal area *Queens County*, 327
**Little Valley** town *Cattaraugus County*, 38
**Little Valley** village *Cattaraugus County*, 38
**Little York** postal area *Cortland County*, 109
**Liverpool** village *Onondaga County*, 362
**Livingston County**, 235 - 247
**Livingston Manor** CDP *Sullivan County*, 566
**Livingston** town *Columbia County*, 103
**Livonia Center** CDP *Livingston County*, 243
**Livonia** town *Livingston County*, 243
**Livonia** village *Livingston County*, 242
**Lloyd Harbor** village *Suffolk County*, 536
**Lloyd** town *Ulster County*, 591
**Loch Sheldrake** postal area *Sullivan County*, 567
**Locke** town *Cayuga County*, 50

**Lockport** city *Niagara County*, 332
**Lockport** town *Niagara County*, 332
**Lockwood** postal area *Tioga County*, 573
**Locust Valley** CDP *Nassau County*, 294
**Lodi** town *Seneca County*, 496
**Lodi** village *Seneca County*, 495
**Long Beach** city *Nassau County*, 294
**Long Eddy** postal area *Sullivan County*, 567
**Long Island City** postal area *Queens County*, 327
**Long Lake** CDP *Hamilton County*, 200
**Long Lake** town *Hamilton County*, 200
**Lorenz Park** CDP *Columbia County*, 103
**Lorraine** CDP *Jefferson County*, 221
**Lorraine** town *Jefferson County*, 220
**Louisville** town *Saint Lawrence County*, 460
**Lowman** postal area *Chemung County*, 76
**Lowville** town *Lewis County*, 231
**Lowville** village *Lewis County*, 231
**Lumberland** town *Sullivan County*, 567
**Lyme** town *Jefferson County*, 221
**Lynbrook** village *Nassau County*, 295
**Lyncourt** CDP *Onondaga County*, 362
**Lyndon** town *Cattaraugus County*, 39
**Lyndonville** village *Orleans County*, 400
**Lyon Mountain** CDP *Clinton County*, 92
**Lyons Falls** village *Lewis County*, 232
**Lyons** town *Wayne County*, 618
**Lyons** village *Wayne County*, 618
**Lyonsdale** town *Lewis County*, 232
**Lysander** town *Onondaga County*, 362

## M

**Macedon** town *Wayne County*, 618
**Macedon** village *Wayne County*, 618
**Machias** CDP *Cattaraugus County*, 39
**Machias** town *Cattaraugus County*, 39
**Macomb** town *Saint Lawrence County*, 460
**Madison County**, 248 - 255
**Madison** town *Madison County*, 254
**Madison** village *Madison County*, 253
**Madrid** CDP *St. Lawrence County*, 460
**Madrid** town *Saint Lawrence County*, 460
**Mahopac** CDP *Putnam County*, 427
**Maine** town *Broome County*, 27
**Malden Bridge** postal area *Columbia County*, 103
**Malden-on-Hudson** CDP *Ulster County*, 591
**Mallory** postal area *Oswego County*, 407
**Malone** town *Franklin County*, 174
**Malone** village *Franklin County*, 173
**Malta** town *Saratoga County*, 473
**Malverne Park Oaks** CDP *Nassau County*, 295
**Malverne** village *Nassau County*, 295
**Mamakating** town *Sullivan County*, 567
**Mamaroneck** town *Westchester County*, 637
**Mamaroneck** village *Westchester County*, 636
**Manchester** town *Ontario County*, 376
**Manchester** village *Ontario County*, 376
**Manhasset Hills** CDP *Nassau County*, 296
**Manhasset** CDP *Nassau County*, 296
**Manhattan** borough *New York County*, 319
**Manheim** town *Herkimer County*, 206
**Manlius** town *Onondaga County*, 363
**Manlius** village *Onondaga County*, 363
**Mannsville** village *Jefferson County*, 221

**Manorhaven** village *Nassau County*, 296
**Manorville** CDP *Suffolk County*, 536
**Mansfield** town *Cattaraugus County*, 39
**Maple Springs** postal area *Chautauqua County*, 66
**Maplecrest** postal area *Greene County*, 195
**Marathon** town *Cortland County*, 109
**Marathon** village *Cortland County*, 109
**Marbletown** town *Ulster County*, 591
**Marcellus** town *Onondaga County*, 363
**Marcellus** village *Onondaga County*, 363
**Marcy** town *Oneida County*, 345
**Margaretville** village *Delaware County*, 119
**Mariaville Lake** CDP *Schenectady County*, 481
**Marietta** postal area *Onondaga County*, 364
**Marilla** town *Erie County*, 153
**Marion** CDP *Wayne County*, 619
**Marion** town *Wayne County*, 619
**Marlboro** CDP *Ulster County*, 591
**Marlborough** town *Ulster County*, 592
**Marshall** town *Oneida County*, 346
**Martinsburg** town *Lewis County*, 232
**Martville** postal area *Cayuga County*, 51
**Maryknoll** postal area *Westchester County*, 637
**Maryland** town *Otsego County*, 418
**Masonville** town *Delaware County*, 119
**Maspeth** postal area *Queens County*, 327
**Massapequa Park** village *Nassau County*, 297
**Massapequa** CDP *Nassau County*, 297
**Massena** town *Saint Lawrence County*, 461
**Massena** village *Saint Lawrence County*, 461
**Mastic Beach** CDP *Suffolk County*, 536
**Mastic** CDP *Suffolk County*, 536
**Matinecock** village *Nassau County*, 297
**Mattituck** CDP *Suffolk County*, 537
**Mattydale** CDP *Onondaga County*, 364
**Maybrook** village *Orange County*, 387
**Mayfield** town *Fulton County*, 180
**Mayfield** village *Fulton County*, 180
**Mayville** village *Chautauqua County*, 66
**McDonough** town *Chenango County*, 82
**McGraw** village *Cortland County*, 110
**Mclean** postal area *Tompkins County*, 582
**Mechanicstown** CDP *Orange County*, 387
**Mechanicville** city *Saratoga County*, 473
**Medford** CDP *Suffolk County*, 537
**Medina** village *Orleans County*, 401
**Melrose Park** CDP *Cayuga County*, 51
**Melrose** postal area *Rensselaer County*, 434
**Melville** CDP *Suffolk County*, 537
**Memphis** postal area *Onondaga County*, 364
**Menands** village *Albany County*, 6
**Mendon** town *Monroe County*, 262
**Mentz** town *Cayuga County*, 51
**Meredith** town *Delaware County*, 119
**Meridale** postal area *Delaware County*, 119
**Meridian** village *Cayuga County*, 51
**Merrick** CDP *Nassau County*, 297
**Merritt Park** CDP *Dutchess County*, 129
**Mexico** town *Oswego County*, 407
**Mexico** village *Oswego County*, 407
**Middle Granville** postal area *Washington County*, 614

*CDP = Census Designated Place*

**Middle Grove** postal area *Saratoga County,* 474

**Middle Island** CDP *Suffolk County,* 538

**Middle Village** postal area *Queens County,* 327

**Middleburgh** town *Schoharie County,* 487

**Middleburgh** village *Schoharie County,* 487

**Middlebury** town *Wyoming County,* 654

**Middlefield** town *Otsego County,* 418

**Middleport** village *Niagara County,* 333

**Middlesex** town *Yates County,* 660

**Middletown** city *Orange County,* 387

**Middletown** town *Delaware County,* 119

**Middleville** village *Herkimer County,* 206

**Milan** town *Dutchess County,* 130

**Milford** town *Otsego County,* 419

**Milford** village *Otsego County,* 418

**Mill Neck** village *Nassau County,* 298

**Millbrook** village *Dutchess County,* 130

**Miller Place** CDP *Suffolk County,* 538

**Millerton** village *Dutchess County,* 130

**Millport** village *Chemung County,* 76

**Millwood** postal area *Westchester County,* 637

**Milo** town *Yates County,* 660

**Milton** CDP *Saratoga County,* 474

**Milton** CDP *Ulster County,* 592

**Milton** town *Saratoga County,* 474

**Mina** town *Chautauqua County,* 66

**Minden** town *Montgomery County,* 272

**Mineola** village *Nassau County,* 298

**Minerva** town *Essex County,* 163

**Minetto** CDP *Oswego County,* 408

**Minetto** town *Oswego County,* 407

**Mineville** CDP *Essex County,* 163

**Minisink** town *Orange County,* 388

**Minoa** village *Onondaga County,* 364

**Modena** postal area *Ulster County,* 592

**Mohawk** town *Montgomery County,* 272

**Mohawk** village *Herkimer County,* 206

**Mohegan Lake** postal area *Westchester County,* 637

**Moira** town *Franklin County,* 174

**Mongaup Valley** postal area *Sullivan County,* 567

**Monroe County,** 256 - 267

**Monroe** town *Orange County,* 388

**Monroe** village *Orange County,* 388

**Monsey** CDP *Rockland County,* 443

**Montague** town *Lewis County,* 232

**Montauk** CDP *Suffolk County,* 538

**Montebello** village *Rockland County,* 443

**Montezuma** town *Cayuga County,* 52

**Montgomery County,** 268 - 273

**Montgomery** town *Orange County,* 389

**Montgomery** village *Orange County,* 389

**Monticello** village *Sullivan County,* 567

**Montour Falls** village *Schuyler County,* 492

**Montour** town *Schuyler County,* 492

**Montrose** CDP *Westchester County,* 637

**Mooers Forks** postal area *Clinton County,* 93

**Mooers** CDP *Clinton County,* 93

**Mooers** town *Clinton County,* 93

**Moravia** town *Cayuga County,* 52

**Moravia** village *Cayuga County,* 52

**Moreau** town *Saratoga County,* 474

**Morehouse** town *Hamilton County,* 200

**Moriah Center** postal area *Essex County,* 163

**Moriah** town *Essex County,* 163

**Moriches** CDP *Suffolk County,* 538

**Morris** town *Otsego County,* 419

**Morris** village *Otsego County,* 419

**Morrisonville** CDP *Clinton County,* 93

**Morristown** town *Saint Lawrence County,* 461

**Morristown** village *Saint Lawrence County,* 461

**Morrisville** village *Madison County,* 254

**Mount Hope** town *Orange County,* 389

**Mount Ivy** CDP *Rockland County,* 443

**Mount Kisco** town/village *Westchester County,* 638

**Mount Marion** postal area *Ulster County,* 592

**Mount Morris** town *Livingston County,* 243

**Mount Morris** village *Livingston County,* 243

**Mount Pleasant** town *Westchester County,* 638

**Mount Sinai** CDP *Suffolk County,* 539

**Mount Tremper** postal area *Ulster County,* 592

**Mount Upton** postal area *Chenango County,* 82

**Mount Vernon** city *Westchester County,* 638

**Mount Vision** postal area *Otsego County,* 419

**Mountain Dale** postal area *Sullivan County,* 568

**Mountain Lodge Park** CDP *Orange County,* 389

**Mountainville** postal area *Orange County,* 390

**Mumford** postal area *Monroe County,* 262

**Munnsville** village *Madison County,* 254

**Munsey Park** village *Nassau County,* 298

**Munsons Corners** CDP *Cortland County,* 110

**Murray** town *Orleans County,* 401

**Muttontown** village *Nassau County,* 299

**Myers Corner** CDP *Dutchess County,* 130

## N

**Nanticoke** town *Broome County,* 28

**Nanuet** CDP *Rockland County,* 443

**Napanoch** CDP *Ulster County,* 593

**Napeague** CDP *Suffolk County,* 539

**Naples** town *Ontario County,* 376

**Naples** village *Ontario County,* 376

**Napoli** town *Cattaraugus County,* 40

**Narrowsburg** CDP *Sullivan County,* 568

**Nassau County,** 274 - 314

**Nassau** town *Rensselaer County,* 434

**Nassau** village *Rensselaer County,* 434

**Natural Bridge** CDP *Jefferson County,* 221

**Nedrow** CDP *Onondaga County,* 364

**Nelliston** village *Montgomery County,* 273

**Nelson** town *Madison County,* 255

**Nelsonville** village *Putnam County,* 428

**Nesconset** CDP *Suffolk County,* 539

**Neversink** town *Sullivan County,* 568

**New Albion** town *Cattaraugus County,* 40

**New Baltimore** town *Greene County,* 195

**New Berlin** town *Chenango County,* 83

**New Berlin** village *Chenango County,* 82

**New Bremen** town *Lewis County,* 233

**New Cassel** CDP *Nassau County,* 299

**New Castle** town *Westchester County,* 639

**New City** CDP *Rockland County,* 444

**New Hampton** postal area *Orange County,* 390

**New Hartford** town *Oneida County,* 346

**New Hartford** village *Oneida County,* 346

**New Haven** town *Oswego County,* 408

**New Hempstead** village *Rockland County,* 444

**New Hudson** town *Allegany County,* 18

**New Hyde Park** village *Nassau County,* 299

**New Kingston** postal area *Delaware County,* 120

**New Lebanon** town *Columbia County,* 103

**New Lisbon** town *Otsego County,* 419

**New Paltz** town *Ulster County,* 593

**New Paltz** village *Ulster County,* 593

**New Rochelle** city *Westchester County,* 639

**New Russia** postal area *Essex County,* 163

**New Scotland** town *Albany County,* 6

**New Square** village *Rockland County,* 444

**New Suffolk** CDP *Suffolk County,* 539

**New Windsor** CDP *Orange County,* 390

**New Windsor** town *Orange County,* 390

**New Woodstock** postal area *Madison County,* 255

**New York City,** 315 - 329

**New York County,** 319

**New York Mills** village *Oneida County,* 346

**Newark Valley** town *Tioga County,* 574

**Newark Valley** village *Tioga County,* 573

**Newark** village *Wayne County,* 619

**Newburgh** city *Orange County,* 390

**Newburgh** town *Orange County,* 391

**Newcomb** town *Essex County,* 164

**Newfane** CDP *Niagara County,* 333

**Newfane** town *Niagara County,* 333

**Newfield Hamlet** CDP *Tompkins County,* 582

**Newfield** town *Tompkins County,* 582

**Newport** town *Herkimer County,* 207

**Newport** village *Herkimer County,* 207

**Newstead** town *Erie County,* 153

**Newton Falls** postal area *Saint Lawrence County,* 462

**Niagara County,** 330 - 337

**Niagara Falls** city *Niagara County,* 334

**Niagara University** postal area *Niagara County,* 334

**Niagara** town *Niagara County,* 333

**Nichols** town *Tioga County,* 574

**Nichols** village *Tioga County,* 574

**Nicholville** postal area *Saint Lawrence County,* 462

**Niles** town *Cayuga County,* 52

**Nineveh** postal area *Broome County,* 28

**Niskayuna** CDP *Schenectady County,* 481

**Niskayuna** town *Schenectady County,* 481

**Nissequogue** village *Suffolk County,* 540

**Niverville** CDP *Columbia County,* 104

**Norfolk** CDP *Saint Lawrence County,* 462

**Norfolk** town *Saint Lawrence County,* 462

**North Amityville** CDP *Suffolk County,* 540

**North Babylon** CDP *Suffolk County,* 540

**North Ballston Spa** CDP *Saratoga County,* 475

**North Bangor** postal area *Franklin County,* 174

**North Bay Shore** CDP *Suffolk County,* 540

**North Bay** postal area *Oneida County,* 347

**North Bellmore** CDP *Nassau County,* 300

**North Bellport** CDP *Suffolk County*, 541
**North Blenheim** postal area *Schoharie County*, 488
**North Boston** CDP *Erie County*, 154
**North Branch** postal area *Sullivan County*, 568
**North Brookfield** postal area *Madison County*, 255
**North Castle** town *Westchester County*, 639
**North Chatham** postal area *Columbia County*, 104
**North Chili** postal area *Monroe County*, 263
**North Collins** town *Erie County*, 154
**North Collins** village *Erie County*, 154
**North Creek** CDP *Warren County*, 606
**North Dansville** town *Livingston County*, 244
**North East** town *Dutchess County*, 131
**North Elba** town *Essex County*, 164
**North Evans** postal area *Erie County*, 154
**North Gates** CDP *Monroe County*, 263
**North Great River** CDP *Suffolk County*, 541
**North Greenbush** town *Rensselaer County*, 434
**North Harmony** town *Chautauqua County*, 67
**North Haven** village *Suffolk County*, 541
**North Hempstead** town *Nassau County*, 300
**North Hills** village *Nassau County*, 300
**North Hornell** village *Steuben County*, 508
**North Hudson** town *Essex County*, 164
**North Java** postal area *Wyoming County*, 654
**North Lawrence** postal area *Saint Lawrence County*, 462
**North Lindenhurst** CDP *Suffolk County*, 541
**North Lynbrook** CDP *Nassau County*, 300
**North Massapequa** CDP *Nassau County*, 301
**North Merrick** CDP *Nassau County*, 301
**North New Hyde Park** CDP *Nassau County*, 301
**North Norwich** town *Chenango County*, 83
**North Patchogue** CDP *Suffolk County*, 542
**North Pitcher** postal area *Chenango County*, 83
**North River** postal area *Warren County*, 606
**North Rose** CDP *Wayne County*, 620
**North Salem** town *Westchester County*, 640
**North Sea** CDP *Suffolk County*, 542
**North Syracuse** village *Onondaga County*, 365
**North Tonawanda** city *Niagara County*, 334
**North Valley Stream** CDP *Nassau County*, 301
**North Wantagh** CDP *Nassau County*, 302
**Northampton** CDP *Suffolk County*, 542
**Northampton** town *Fulton County*, 180
**Northeast Ithaca** CDP *Tompkins County*, 582
**Northport** village *Suffolk County*, 542
**Northumberland** town *Saratoga County*, 475
**Northville** CDP *Suffolk County*, 543
**Northville** village *Fulton County*, 181
**Northwest Harbor** CDP *Suffolk County*, 543
**Northwest Ithaca** CDP *Tompkins County*, 582
**Norway** town *Herkimer County*, 207
**Norwich** city *Chenango County*, 83
**Norwich** town *Chenango County*, 84
**Norwood** village *Saint Lawrence County*, 462
**Noyack** CDP *Suffolk County*, 543
**Nunda** town *Livingston County*, 244
**Nunda** village *Livingston County*, 244

**Nyack** village *Rockland County*, 445

## O

**Oak Beach-Captree** CDP *Suffolk County*, 543
**Oak Hill** postal area *Greene County*, 195
**Oakdale** CDP *Suffolk County*, 544
**Oakfield** town *Genesee County*, 187
**Oakfield** village *Genesee County*, 187
**Oakland Gardens** postal area *Queens County*, 327
**Obernburg** postal area *Sullivan County*, 568
**Ocean Beach** village *Suffolk County*, 544
**Oceanside** CDP *Nassau County*, 302
**Odessa** village *Schuyler County*, 493
**Ogden** town *Monroe County*, 263
**Ogdensburg** city *Saint Lawrence County*, 463
**Ohio** town *Herkimer County*, 207
**Olcott** CDP *Niagara County*, 335
**Old Bethpage** CDP *Nassau County*, 302
**Old Brookville** village *Nassau County*, 302
**Old Chatham** postal area *Columbia County*, 104
**Old Field** village *Suffolk County*, 544
**Old Forge** CDP *Herkimer County*, 208
**Old Westbury** village *Nassau County*, 303
**Olean** city *Cattaraugus County*, 40
**Olean** town *Cattaraugus County*, 40
**Olive** town *Ulster County*, 593
**Olivebridge** postal area *Ulster County*, 594
**Olmstedville** postal area *Essex County*, 164
**Oneida Castle** village *Oneida County*, 347
**Oneida County**, 338 - 354
**Oneida** city *Madison County*, 255
**Oneonta** city *Otsego County*, 420
**Oneonta** town *Otsego County*, 420
**Onondaga County**, 355 - 369
**Onondaga Reservation** Reservation *Onondaga County*, 365
**Onondaga** town *Onondaga County*, 365
**Ontario County**, 370 - 378
**Ontario** CDP *Wayne County*, 620
**Ontario** town *Wayne County*, 620
**Oppenheim** town *Fulton County*, 181
**Orange County**, 379 - 397
**Orange Lake** CDP *Orange County*, 391
**Orange** town *Schuyler County*, 493
**Orangeburg** CDP *Rockland County*, 445
**Orangetown** town *Rockland County*, 445
**Orangeville** town *Wyoming County*, 654
**Orchard Park** town *Erie County*, 155
**Orchard Park** village *Erie County*, 154
**Orient** CDP *Suffolk County*, 545
**Oriskany Falls** village *Oneida County*, 347
**Oriskany** village *Oneida County*, 347
**Orleans County**, 398 - 401
**Orleans** town *Jefferson County*, 222
**Orwell** town *Oswego County*, 408
**Osceola** town *Lewis County*, 233
**Ossian** town *Livingston County*, 244
**Ossining** town *Westchester County*, 640
**Ossining** village *Westchester County*, 640
**Oswegatchie** town *Saint Lawrence County*, 463
**Oswego County**, 402 - 412
**Oswego** city *Oswego County*, 408
**Oswego** town *Oswego County*, 409
**Otego** town *Otsego County*, 421

**Otego** village *Otsego County*, 420
**Otisco** town *Onondaga County*, 365
**Otisville** village *Orange County*, 391
**Otsego County**, 413 - 424
**Otsego** town *Otsego County*, 421
**Otselic** town *Chenango County*, 84
**Otto** town *Cattaraugus County*, 41
**Ouaquaga** postal area *Broome County*, 28
**Ovid** town *Seneca County*, 496
**Ovid** village *Seneca County*, 496
**Owasco** town *Cayuga County*, 53
**Owego** town *Tioga County*, 575
**Owego** village *Tioga County*, 574
**Owls Head** postal area *Franklin County*, 174
**Oxbow** CDP *Jefferson County*, 222
**Oxford** town *Chenango County*, 84
**Oxford** village *Chenango County*, 84
**Oyster Bay Cove** village *Nassau County*, 304
**Oyster Bay** CDP *Nassau County*, 303
**Oyster Bay** town *Nassau County*, 303
**Ozone Park** postal area *Queens County*, 328

## P

**Painted Post** village *Steuben County*, 508
**Palatine Bridge** village *Montgomery County*, 273
**Palatine** town *Montgomery County*, 273
**Palenville** CDP *Greene County*, 195
**Palermo** town *Oswego County*, 409
**Palisades** postal area *Rockland County*, 446
**Palmyra** town *Wayne County*, 621
**Palmyra** village *Wayne County*, 620
**Pamelia Center** CDP *Jefferson County*, 222
**Pamelia** town *Jefferson County*, 222
**Panama** village *Chautauqua County*, 67
**Paradox** postal area *Essex County*, 164
**Parc** CDP *Clinton County*, 93
**Paris** town *Oneida County*, 348
**Parish** town *Oswego County*, 410
**Parish** village *Oswego County*, 409
**Parishville** CDP *St. Lawrence County*, 464
**Parishville** town *Saint Lawrence County*, 463
**Parksville** postal area *Sullivan County*, 568
**Parma** town *Monroe County*, 263
**Patchogue** village *Suffolk County*, 545
**Patterson** town *Putnam County*, 428
**Pattersonville** postal area *Schenectady County*, 482
**Paul Smiths** CDP *Franklin County*, 174
**Pavilion** CDP *Genesee County*, 187
**Pavilion** town *Genesee County*, 187
**Pawling** town *Dutchess County*, 131
**Pawling** village *Dutchess County*, 131
**Peach Lake** CDP *Putnam County*, 428
**Pearl River** CDP *Rockland County*, 446
**Peconic** CDP *Suffolk County*, 545
**Peekskill** city *Westchester County*, 641
**Pelham Manor** village *Westchester County*, 642
**Pelham** town *Westchester County*, 641
**Pelham** village *Westchester County*, 641
**Pembroke** town *Genesee County*, 188
**Pendleton** town *Niagara County*, 335
**Penfield** town *Monroe County*, 263
**Penn Yan** village *Yates County*, 660
**Pennellville** postal area *Oswego County*, 410
**Perinton** town *Monroe County*, 264

*CDP = Census Designated Place*

Perkinsville postal area *Steuben County*, 509
Perry town *Wyoming County*, 655
Perry village *Wyoming County*, 654
Perrysburg town *Cattaraugus County*, 41
Perrysburg village *Cattaraugus County*, 41
Persia town *Cattaraugus County*, 42
Perth town *Fulton County*, 181
Peru CDP *Clinton County*, 94
Peru town *Clinton County*, 94
Peterboro postal area *Madison County*, 255
Petersburg postal area *Rensselaer County*, 434
Petersburgh town *Rensselaer County*, 435
Pharsalia town *Chenango County*, 85
Phelps town *Ontario County*, 377
Phelps village *Ontario County*, 377
Philadelphia town *Jefferson County*, 223
Philadelphia village *Jefferson County*, 223
Philipstown town *Putnam County*, 429
Phillipsport postal area *Sullivan County*, 568
Philmont village *Columbia County*, 104
Phoenicia CDP *Ulster County*, 594
Phoenix village *Oswego County*, 410
Piercefield town *Saint Lawrence County*, 464
Piermont village *Rockland County*, 446
Pierrepont Manor CDP *Jefferson County*, 223
Pierrepont town *Saint Lawrence County*, 464
Piffard CDP *Livingston County*, 245
Pike town *Wyoming County*, 655
Pike village *Wyoming County*, 655
Pinckney town *Lewis County*, 233
Pine Bush CDP *Orange County*, 392
Pine City postal area *Chemung County*, 76
Pine Hill CDP *Ulster County*, 594
Pine Island postal area *Orange County*, 392
Pine Plains CDP *Dutchess County*, 132
Pine Plains town *Dutchess County*, 132
Pine Valley CDP *Chemung County*, 76
Piseco postal area *Hamilton County*, 200
Pitcairn town *Saint Lawrence County*, 464
Pitcher town *Chenango County*, 85
Pittsfield town *Otsego County*, 421
Pittsford town *Monroe County*, 264
Pittsford village *Monroe County*, 264
Pittstown town *Rensselaer County*, 435
Plainedge CDP *Nassau County*, 304
Plainfield town *Otsego County*, 421
Plainview CDP *Nassau County*, 304
Plandome Heights village *Nassau County*, 305
Plandome Manor village *Nassau County*, 305
Plandome village *Nassau County*, 305
Plattekill CDP *Ulster County*, 595
Plattekill town *Ulster County*, 594
Plattsburgh West CDP *Clinton County*, 95
Plattsburgh city *Clinton County*, 94
Plattsburgh town *Clinton County*, 95
Pleasant Valley CDP *Dutchess County*, 132
Pleasant Valley town *Dutchess County*, 132
Pleasantville village *Westchester County*, 642
Plessis CDP *Jefferson County*, 223
Plymouth town *Chenango County*, 85
Poestenkill CDP *Rensselaer County*, 435
Poestenkill town *Rensselaer County*, 435
Point Lookout CDP *Nassau County*, 305
Poland town *Chautauqua County*, 67
Poland village *Herkimer County*, 208

Pomfret town *Chautauqua County*, 67
Pomona village *Rockland County*, 446
Pompey town *Onondaga County*, 366
Pond Eddy postal area *Sullivan County*, 569
Poospatuck Reservation Reservation *Suffolk County*, 545
Poquott village *Suffolk County*, 546
Port Byron village *Cayuga County*, 53
Port Chester village *Westchester County*, 642
Port Crane postal area *Broome County*, 28
Port Dickinson village *Broome County*, 28
Port Ewen CDP *Ulster County*, 595
Port Gibson CDP *Ontario County*, 377
Port Henry village *Essex County*, 165
Port Jefferson Station CDP *Suffolk County*, 546
Port Jefferson village *Suffolk County*, 546
Port Jervis city *Orange County*, 392
Port Kent postal area *Essex County*, 165
Port Leyden village *Lewis County*, 233
Port Washington North village *Nassau County*, 306
Port Washington CDP *Nassau County*, 306
Portage town *Livingston County*, 245
Portageville postal area *Wyoming County*, 656
Porter Corners postal area *Saratoga County*, 475
Porter town *Niagara County*, 335
Portland town *Chautauqua County*, 68
Portlandville postal area *Otsego County*, 422
Portville town *Cattaraugus County*, 42
Portville village *Cattaraugus County*, 42
Potsdam town *Saint Lawrence County*, 465
Potsdam village *Saint Lawrence County*, 465
Potter town *Yates County*, 661
Pottersville CDP *Warren County*, 606
Poughkeepsie city *Dutchess County*, 133
Poughkeepsie town *Dutchess County*, 133
Poughquag postal area *Dutchess County*, 134
Pound Ridge town *Westchester County*, 643
Prattsburgh CDP *Steuben County*, 509
Prattsburgh town *Steuben County*, 509
Prattsville CDP *Greene County*, 196
Prattsville town *Greene County*, 196
Preble town *Cortland County*, 110
Preston Hollow postal area *Albany County*, 6
Preston town *Chenango County*, 85
Preston-Potter Hollow CDP *Albany County*, 7
Princetown town *Schenectady County*, 482
Prospect village *Oneida County*, 348
Providence town *Saratoga County*, 475
Pulaski village *Oswego County*, 410
Pulteney town *Steuben County*, 509
Pultneyville CDP *Wayne County*, 621
Purchase postal area *Westchester County*, 643
Purdys postal area *Westchester County*, 643
Purling postal area *Greene County*, 196
Putnam County, 425 - 429
Putnam Lake CDP *Putnam County*, 429
Putnam Station postal area *Washington County*, 614
Putnam Valley town *Putnam County*, 429
Putnam town *Washington County*, 614

Pyrites postal area *Saint Lawrence County*, 465

**Q**

Queens Village postal area *Queens County*, 328
Queens borough *Queens County*, 323
Queens County, 323
Queensbury town *Warren County*, 606
Quioque CDP *Suffolk County*, 546
Quogue village *Suffolk County*, 547

**R**

Rainbow Lake postal area *Franklin County*, 175
Ramapo town *Rockland County*, 446
Randolph town *Cattaraugus County*, 43
Randolph village *Cattaraugus County*, 42
Ransomville CDP *Niagara County*, 335
Rapids CDP *Niagara County*, 336
Raquette Lake postal area *Hamilton County*, 200
Rathbone town *Steuben County*, 510
Ravena village *Albany County*, 7
Ray Brook postal area *Essex County*, 165
Raymondville postal area *Saint Lawrence County*, 465
Reading town *Schuyler County*, 493
Red Creek village *Wayne County*, 621
Red Hook town *Dutchess County*, 134
Red Hook village *Dutchess County*, 134
Red House town *Cattaraugus County*, 43
Red Oaks Mill CDP *Dutchess County*, 134
Redfield town *Oswego County*, 411
Redford CDP *Clinton County*, 95
Redwood CDP *Jefferson County*, 223
Rego Park postal area *Queens County*, 328
Remsen town *Oneida County*, 348
Remsen village *Oneida County*, 348
Remsenburg postal area *Suffolk County*, 547
Remsenburg-Speonk CDP *Suffolk County*, 547
Rensselaer County, 430 - 438
Rensselaer Falls village *Saint Lawrence County*, 465
Rensselaer city *Rensselaer County*, 436
Rensselaerville town *Albany County*, 7
Retsof CDP *Livingston County*, 245
Rexford postal area *Saratoga County*, 475
Rexville postal area *Steuben County*, 510
Rhinebeck town *Dutchess County*, 135
Rhinebeck village *Dutchess County*, 135
Rhinecliff CDP *Dutchess County*, 135
Richburg village *Allegany County*, 18
Richfield Springs village *Otsego County*, 422
Richfield town *Otsego County*, 422
Richford town *Tioga County*, 575
Richland town *Oswego County*, 411
Richmond County, 329
Richmond Hill postal area *Queens County*, 328
Richmond town *Ontario County*, 377
Richmondville town *Schoharie County*, 488
Richmondville village *Schoharie County*, 488
Richville village *Saint Lawrence County*, 466
Ridge CDP *Suffolk County*, 547
Ridgeway town *Orleans County*, 401
Ridgewood postal area *Queens County*, 328

*CDP = Census Designated Place*

Rifton CDP *Ulster County*, 595
Riga town *Monroe County*, 265
Riparius postal area *Warren County*, 606
Ripley CDP *Chautauqua County*, 68
Ripley town *Chautauqua County*, 68
Riverhead CDP *Suffolk County*, 548
Riverhead town *Suffolk County*, 548
Riverside CDP *Suffolk County*, 548
Riverside village *Steuben County*, 510
Rochester city *Monroe County*, 265
Rochester town *Ulster County*, 595
Rock City Falls postal area *Saratoga County*, 475
Rock Hill CDP *Sullivan County*, 569
Rock Stream postal area *Yates County*, 661
Rock Tavern postal area *Orange County*, 392
Rockaway Park postal area *Queens County*, 328
Rockland County, 439 - 450
Rockland town *Sullivan County*, 569
Rockville Centre village *Nassau County*, 306
Rocky Point CDP *Suffolk County*, 549
Rodman CDP *Jefferson County*, 224
Rodman town *Jefferson County*, 224
Rome city *Oneida County*, 349
Romulus CDP *Seneca County*, 497
Romulus town *Seneca County*, 496
Ronkonkoma CDP *Suffolk County*, 549
Roosevelt CDP *Nassau County*, 306
Root town *Montgomery County*, 273
Roscoe CDP *Sullivan County*, 569
Rose town *Wayne County*, 621
Roseboom town *Otsego County*, 422
Rosedale postal area *Queens County*, 328
Rosendale Village CDP *Ulster County*, 596
Rosendale town *Ulster County*, 596
Roslyn Estates village *Nassau County*, 307
Roslyn Harbor village *Nassau County*, 307
Roslyn Heights CDP *Nassau County*, 308
Roslyn village *Nassau County*, 307
Rossie town *Saint Lawrence County*, 466
Rotterdam Junction postal area *Schenectady County*, 482
Rotterdam CDP *Schenectady County*, 482
Rotterdam town *Schenectady County*, 482
Round Lake village *Saratoga County*, 475
Round Top postal area *Greene County*, 196
Rouses Point village *Clinton County*, 95
Roxbury town *Delaware County*, 120
Royalton town *Niagara County*, 336
Ruby postal area *Ulster County*, 596
Rush town *Monroe County*, 266
Rushford CDP *Allegany County*, 19
Rushford town *Allegany County*, 19
Rushville village *Yates County*, 661
Russell Gardens village *Nassau County*, 308
Russell town *Saint Lawrence County*, 466
Russia town *Herkimer County*, 208
Rutland town *Jefferson County*, 224
Rye Brook village *Westchester County*, 644
Rye city *Westchester County*, 643
Rye town *Westchester County*, 644

**S**

Sabael postal area *Hamilton County*, 200
Sackets Harbor village *Jefferson County*, 224

Saddle Rock Estates CDP *Nassau County*, 308
Saddle Rock village *Nassau County*, 308
Sag Harbor village *Suffolk County*, 549
Sagaponack village *Suffolk County*, 550
Saint Albans postal area *Queens County*, 328
Saint Armand town *Essex County*, 165
Saint Bonaventure CDP *Cattaraugus County*, 43
Saint James CDP *Suffolk County*, 550
Saint Johnsville town *Montgomery County*, 274
Saint Johnsville village *Montgomery County*, 274
Saint Lawrence County, 451 - 467
Saint Regis Mohawk Reservation Reservation *Franklin County*, 175
Salamanca city *Cattaraugus County*, 43
Salamanca town *Cattaraugus County*, 44
Salem town *Washington County*, 615
Salem village *Washington County*, 614
Salina town *Onondaga County*, 366
Salisbury Center postal area *Herkimer County*, 209
Salisbury Mills CDP *Orange County*, 392
Salisbury CDP *Nassau County*, 309
Salisbury town *Herkimer County*, 208
Salt Point CDP *Dutchess County*, 136
Saltaire village *Suffolk County*, 550
Sanborn CDP *Niagara County*, 336
Sand Lake town *Rensselaer County*, 436
Sand Ridge CDP *Oswego County*, 411
Sands Point village *Nassau County*, 309
Sandy Creek town *Oswego County*, 412
Sandy Creek village *Oswego County*, 411
Sanford town *Broome County*, 28
Sangerfield town *Oneida County*, 349
Santa Clara town *Franklin County*, 175
Saranac Lake village *Franklin County*, 175
Saranac town *Clinton County*, 96
Saratoga County, 468 - 478
Saratoga Springs city *Saratoga County*, 476
Saratoga town *Saratoga County*, 476
Sardinia town *Erie County*, 155
Saugerties South CDP *Ulster County*, 597
Saugerties town *Ulster County*, 596
Saugerties village *Ulster County*, 596
Sauquoit postal area *Oneida County*, 349
Savannah CDP *Wayne County*, 622
Savannah town *Wayne County*, 622
Savona village *Steuben County*, 510
Sayville CDP *Suffolk County*, 550
Scarsdale town/village *Westchester County*, 644
Schaghticoke town *Rensselaer County*, 436
Schaghticoke village *Rensselaer County*, 436
Schenectady County, 479 - 482
Schenectady city *Schenectady County*, 482
Schenevus CDP *Otsego County*, 422
Schodack Landing postal area *Rensselaer County*, 437
Schodack town *Rensselaer County*, 437
Schoharie County, 483 - 489
Schoharie town *Schoharie County*, 489
Schoharie village *Schoharie County*, 488
Schroeppel town *Oswego County*, 412
Schroon Lake CDP *Essex County*, 165
Schroon town *Essex County*, 165

Schuyler County, 490 - 493
Schuyler Falls town *Clinton County*, 96
Schuyler town *Herkimer County*, 209
Schuylerville village *Saratoga County*, 476
Scio CDP *Allegany County*, 19
Scio town *Allegany County*, 19
Scipio Center postal area *Cayuga County*, 53
Scipio town *Cayuga County*, 53
Scotchtown CDP *Orange County*, 393
Scotia village *Schenectady County*, 483
Scott town *Cortland County*, 110
Scotts Corners CDP *Westchester County*, 645
Scottsburg CDP *Livingston County*, 245
Scottsville village *Monroe County*, 266
Scriba town *Oswego County*, 412
Sea Cliff village *Nassau County*, 309
Seaford CDP *Nassau County*, 309
Searingtown CDP *Nassau County*, 310
Selden CDP *Suffolk County*, 551
Selkirk postal area *Albany County*, 7
Sempronius town *Cayuga County*, 54
Seneca County, 494 - 498
Seneca Falls town *Seneca County*, 497
Seneca Falls village *Seneca County*, 497
Seneca Knolls CDP *Onondaga County*, 366
Seneca town *Ontario County*, 378
Sennett town *Cayuga County*, 54
Setauket-East Setauket CDP *Suffolk County*, 551
Severance postal area *Essex County*, 166
Seward town *Schoharie County*, 489
Shandaken town *Ulster County*, 597
Sharon Springs village *Schoharie County*, 489
Sharon town *Schoharie County*, 489
Shawangunk town *Ulster County*, 597
Shelby town *Orleans County*, 402
Sheldon town *Wyoming County*, 656
Shelter Island Heights CDP *Suffolk County*, 552
Shelter Island CDP *Suffolk County*, 552
Shelter Island town *Suffolk County*, 551
Shenorock CDP *Westchester County*, 645
Sherburne town *Chenango County*, 86
Sherburne village *Chenango County*, 86
Sheridan town *Chautauqua County*, 68
Sherman town *Chautauqua County*, 69
Sherman village *Chautauqua County*, 69
Sherrill city *Oneida County*, 349
Shinnecock Hills CDP *Suffolk County*, 552
Shinnecock Reservation Reservation *Suffolk County*, 552
Shirley CDP *Suffolk County*, 552
Shokan CDP *Ulster County*, 597
Shoreham village *Suffolk County*, 553
Shortsville village *Ontario County*, 378
Shrub Oak CDP *Westchester County*, 645
Shushan postal area *Washington County*, 615
Sidney Center postal area *Delaware County*, 121
Sidney town *Delaware County*, 120
Sidney village *Delaware County*, 120
Silver Bay postal area *Warren County*, 607
Silver Creek village *Chautauqua County*, 69
Silver Lake postal area *Wyoming County*, 656
Silver Springs village *Wyoming County*, 656

*CDP = Census Designated Place*

**Sinclairville** village *Chautauqua County*, 70
**Skaneateles Falls** postal area *Onondaga County*, 367
**Skaneateles** town *Onondaga County*, 367
**Skaneateles** village *Onondaga County*, 366
**Slate Hill** postal area *Orange County*, 393
**Slaterville Springs** postal area *Tompkins County*, 583
**Sleepy Hollow** village *Westchester County*, 645
**Slingerlands** postal area *Albany County*, 7
**Sloan** village *Erie County*, 155
**Sloansville** postal area *Schoharie County*, 490
**Sloatsburg** village *Rockland County*, 447
**Smallwood** CDP *Sullivan County*, 569
**Smithfield** town *Madison County*, 255
**Smithtown** CDP *Suffolk County*, 553
**Smithtown** town *Suffolk County*, 553
**Smithville Flats** CDP *Chenango County*, 86
**Smithville** town *Chenango County*, 86
**Smyrna** town *Chenango County*, 87
**Smyrna** village *Chenango County*, 87
**Sodus Point** village *Wayne County*, 623
**Sodus** town *Wayne County*, 623
**Sodus** village *Wayne County*, 622
**Solon** town *Cortland County*, 111
**Solvay** village *Onondaga County*, 367
**Somers** town *Westchester County*, 646
**Somerset** town *Niagara County*, 336
**Sound Beach** CDP *Suffolk County*, 554
**South Bethlehem** postal area *Albany County*, 7
**South Blooming Grove** village *Orange County*, 393
**South Bristol** town *Ontario County*, 378
**South Cairo** postal area *Greene County*, 196
**South Colton** postal area *Saint Lawrence County*, 466
**South Corning** village *Steuben County*, 510
**South Dayton** village *Cattaraugus County*, 44
**South Fallsburg** CDP *Sullivan County*, 570
**South Farmingdale** CDP *Nassau County*, 310
**South Floral Park** village *Nassau County*, 310
**South Glens Falls** village *Saratoga County*, 477
**South Hempstead** CDP *Nassau County*, 310
**South Hill** CDP *Tompkins County*, 583
**South Huntington** CDP *Suffolk County*, 554
**South Jamesport** postal area *Suffolk County*, 554
**South Kortright** postal area *Delaware County*, 121
**South Lima** CDP *Livingston County*, 246
**South Lockport** CDP *Niagara County*, 337
**South New Berlin** postal area *Chenango County*, 87
**South Nyack** village *Rockland County*, 447
**South Otselic** postal area *Chenango County*, 87
**South Ozone Park** postal area *Queens County*, 328
**South Plymouth** postal area *Chenango County*, 87
**South Richmond Hill** postal area *Queens County*, 328
**South Salem** postal area *Westchester County*, 646

**South Valley Stream** CDP *Nassau County*, 311
**South Valley** town *Cattaraugus County*, 44
**South Wales** postal area *Erie County*, 156
**Southampton** town *Suffolk County*, 555
**Southampton** village *Suffolk County*, 554
**Southeast** town *Putnam County*, 429
**Southfields** postal area *Orange County*, 393
**Southold** CDP *Suffolk County*, 555
**Southold** town *Suffolk County*, 555
**Southport** CDP *Chemung County*, 77
**Southport** town *Chemung County*, 77
**Spackenkill** CDP *Dutchess County*, 136
**Spafford** town *Onondaga County*, 367
**Sparkill** CDP *Rockland County*, 447
**Sparrow Bush** postal area *Orange County*, 393
**Sparta** town *Livingston County*, 246
**Speculator** village *Hamilton County*, 201
**Spencer** town *Tioga County*, 576
**Spencer** village *Tioga County*, 575
**Spencerport** village *Monroe County*, 267
**Spencertown** postal area *Columbia County*, 104
**Speonk** postal area *Suffolk County*, 556
**Sprakers** postal area *Montgomery County*, 274
**Spring Glen** postal area *Ulster County*, 598
**Spring Valley** village *Rockland County*, 448
**Springfield Center** postal area *Otsego County*, 423
**Springfield Gardens** postal area *Queens County*, 328
**Springfield** town *Otsego County*, 423
**Springport** town *Cayuga County*, 54
**Springs** CDP *Suffolk County*, 556
**Springville** village *Erie County*, 156
**Springwater Hamlet** CDP *Livingston County*, 246
**Springwater** town *Livingston County*, 246
**St. Regis Falls** CDP *Franklin County*, 175
**Staatsburg** CDP *Dutchess County*, 136
**Stafford** town *Genesee County*, 188
**Stamford** town *Delaware County*, 121
**Stamford** village *Delaware County*, 121
**Stanford** town *Dutchess County*, 136
**Stanfordville** postal area *Dutchess County*, 136
**Stanley** postal area *Ontario County*, 378
**Stannards** CDP *Allegany County*, 20
**Star Lake** CDP *Saint Lawrence County*, 467
**Stark** town *Herkimer County*, 209
**Starkey** town *Yates County*, 661
**Staten Island** borough *Richmond County*, 329
**Steamburg** postal area *Cattaraugus County*, 45
**Stephentown** town *Rensselaer County*, 437
**Sterling Forest** postal area *Orange County*, 393
**Sterling** town *Cayuga County*, 54
**Steuben County**, 499 - 512
**Steuben** town *Oneida County*, 350
**Stewart Manor** village *Nassau County*, 311
**Stillwater** town *Saratoga County*, 477
**Stillwater** village *Saratoga County*, 477
**Stittville** postal area *Oneida County*, 350
**Stockbridge** town *Madison County*, 256
**Stockholm** town *Saint Lawrence County*, 467

**Stockport** town *Columbia County*, 104
**Stockton** town *Chautauqua County*, 70
**Stone Ridge** CDP *Ulster County*, 598
**Stony Brook University** CDP *Suffolk County*, 556
**Stony Brook** CDP *Suffolk County*, 556
**Stony Creek** town *Warren County*, 607
**Stony Point** CDP *Rockland County*, 448
**Stony Point** town *Rockland County*, 448
**Stormville** postal area *Dutchess County*, 137
**Stottville** CDP *Columbia County*, 105
**Stratford** town *Fulton County*, 181
**Strykersville** CDP *Wyoming County*, 656
**Stuyvesant Falls** postal area *Columbia County*, 105
**Stuyvesant** town *Columbia County*, 105
**Suffern** village *Rockland County*, 448
**Suffolk County**, 513 - 560
**Sullivan County**, 561 - 571
**Sullivan** town *Madison County*, 256
**Summerhill** town *Cayuga County*, 55
**Summit** town *Schoharie County*, 490
**Summitville** postal area *Sullivan County*, 570
**Sunnyside** postal area *Queens County*, 328
**Sunset Bay** CDP *Chautauqua County*, 70
**SUNY Oswego** CDP *Oswego County*, 412
**Surprise** postal area *Greene County*, 196
**Swain** postal area *Allegany County*, 20
**Swan Lake** postal area *Sullivan County*, 570
**Sweden** town *Monroe County*, 267
**Sylvan Beach** village *Oneida County*, 350
**Syosset** CDP *Nassau County*, 311
**Syracuse** city *Onondaga County*, 368

**T**

**Taberg** postal area *Oneida County*, 350
**Taghkanic** town *Columbia County*, 105
**Tannersville** village *Greene County*, 196
**Tappan** CDP *Rockland County*, 449
**Tarrytown** village *Westchester County*, 646
**Taylor** town *Cortland County*, 111
**Terryville** CDP *Suffolk County*, 556
**Thendara** postal area *Herkimer County*, 209
**Theresa** town *Jefferson County*, 225
**Theresa** village *Jefferson County*, 225
**Thiells** CDP *Rockland County*, 449
**Thomaston** village *Nassau County*, 312
**Thompson Ridge** postal area *Orange County*, 393
**Thompson** town *Sullivan County*, 570
**Thompsonville** postal area *Sullivan County*, 570
**Thornwood** CDP *Westchester County*, 646
**Thousand Island Park** CDP *Jefferson County*, 225
**Three Mile Bay** CDP *Jefferson County*, 225
**Throop** town *Cayuga County*, 55
**Thurman** town *Warren County*, 607
**Thurston** town *Steuben County*, 511
**Ticonderoga** CDP *Essex County*, 166
**Ticonderoga** town *Essex County*, 166
**Tillson** CDP *Ulster County*, 598
**Tioga Center** postal area *Tioga County*, 576
**Tioga County**, 572 - 575
**Tioga** town *Tioga County*, 576
**Titusville** CDP *Dutchess County*, 137
**Tivoli** village *Dutchess County*, 137

*CDP = Census Designated Place*

**Tomkins Cove** postal area *Rockland County*, 449

**Tompkins County**, 576 - 583

**Tompkins** town *Delaware County*, 121

**Tonawanda Reservation** Reservation *Erie County*, 157

**Tonawanda Reservation** Reservation *Genesee County*, 188

**Tonawanda** CDP *Erie County*, 157

**Tonawanda** city *Erie County*, 156

**Tonawanda** town *Erie County*, 156

**Torrey** town *Yates County*, 661

**Town Line** CDP *Erie County*, 157

**Treadwell** postal area *Delaware County*, 122

**Trenton** town *Oneida County*, 350

**Triangle** town *Broome County*, 29

**Tribes Hill** CDP *Montgomery County*, 274

**Troupsburg** town *Steuben County*, 511

**Trout Creek** postal area *Delaware County*, 122

**Troy** city *Rensselaer County*, 437

**Trumansburg** village *Tompkins County*, 583

**Truxton** town *Cortland County*, 111

**Tuckahoe** CDP *Suffolk County*, 557

**Tuckahoe** village *Westchester County*, 647

**Tully** town *Onondaga County*, 369

**Tully** village *Onondaga County*, 369

**Tupper Lake** town *Franklin County*, 176

**Tupper Lake** village *Franklin County*, 176

**Turin** town *Lewis County*, 234

**Turin** village *Lewis County*, 234

**Tuscarora Reservation** Reservation *Niagara County*, 337

**Tuscarora** CDP *Livingston County*, 247

**Tuscarora** town *Steuben County*, 511

**Tusten** town *Sullivan County*, 570

**Tuxedo Park** village *Orange County*, 394

**Tuxedo** town *Orange County*, 394

**Tyre** town *Seneca County*, 498

**Tyrone** town *Schuyler County*, 493

**U**

**Ulster County**, 584 - 600

**Ulster Park** postal area *Ulster County*, 599

**Ulster** town *Ulster County*, 598

**Ulysses** town *Tompkins County*, 583

**Unadilla** town *Otsego County*, 423

**Unadilla** village *Otsego County*, 423

**Union Springs** village *Cayuga County*, 55

**Union Vale** town *Dutchess County*, 137

**Union** town *Broome County*, 29

**Uniondale** CDP *Nassau County*, 312

**Unionville** village *Orange County*, 394

**University at Buffalo** CDP *Erie County*, 157

**University Gardens** CDP *Nassau County*, 312

**Upper Brookville** village *Nassau County*, 312

**Upper Jay** postal area *Essex County*, 166

**Upper Nyack** village *Rockland County*, 449

**Upton** postal area *Suffolk County*, 557

**Urbana** town *Steuben County*, 511

**Utica** city *Oneida County*, 351

**V**

**Vails Gate** CDP *Orange County*, 394

**Valatie** village *Columbia County*, 105

**Valhalla** CDP *Westchester County*, 647

**Valley Cottage** CDP *Rockland County*, 450

**Valley Falls** village *Rensselaer County*, 438

**Valley Stream** village *Nassau County*, 313

**Van Buren** town *Onondaga County*, 369

**Van Etten** town *Chemung County*, 77

**Van Etten** village *Chemung County*, 77

**Van Hornesville** postal area *Herkimer County*, 209

**Varick** town *Seneca County*, 498

**Varysburg** postal area *Wyoming County*, 656

**Venice** town *Cayuga County*, 55

**Verbank** postal area *Dutchess County*, 137

**Vermontville** postal area *Franklin County*, 176

**Vernon Center** postal area *Oneida County*, 352

**Vernon** town *Oneida County*, 351

**Vernon** village *Oneida County*, 351

**Verona Beach** postal area *Oneida County*, 352

**Verona** CDP *Oneida County*, 352

**Verona** town *Oneida County*, 352

**Verplanck** CDP *Westchester County*, 647

**Versailles** postal area *Cattaraugus County*, 45

**Vestal** town *Broome County*, 29

**Veteran** town *Chemung County*, 78

**Victor** town *Ontario County*, 379

**Victor** village *Ontario County*, 378

**Victory Mills** postal area *Saratoga County*, 478

**Victory** town *Cayuga County*, 56

**Victory** village *Saratoga County*, 478

**Vienna** town *Oneida County*, 352

**Village Green** CDP *Onondaga County*, 370

**Village of the Branch** village *Suffolk County*, 557

**Villenova** town *Chautauqua County*, 70

**Viola** CDP *Rockland County*, 450

**Virgil** town *Cortland County*, 111

**Volney** town *Oswego County*, 413

**Voorheesville** village *Albany County*, 8

**W**

**Waccabuc** postal area *Westchester County*, 648

**Waddington** town *Saint Lawrence County*, 467

**Waddington** village *Saint Lawrence County*, 467

**Wading River** CDP *Suffolk County*, 557

**Wadsworth** CDP *Livingston County*, 247

**Wainscott** CDP *Suffolk County*, 557

**Walden** village *Orange County*, 395

**Wales Center** postal area *Erie County*, 158

**Wales** town *Erie County*, 158

**Walker Valley** CDP *Ulster County*, 599

**Wallkill** CDP *Ulster County*, 599

**Wallkill** town *Orange County*, 395

**Walton Park** CDP *Orange County*, 395

**Walton** town *Delaware County*, 122

**Walton** village *Delaware County*, 122

**Walworth** town *Wayne County*, 623

**Wampsville** village *Madison County*, 256

**Wanakah** CDP *Erie County*, 158

**Wanakena** postal area *Saint Lawrence County*, 468

**Wantagh** CDP *Nassau County*, 313

**Wappinger** town *Dutchess County*, 137

**Wappingers Falls** village *Dutchess County*, 138

**Ward** town *Allegany County*, 20

**Warners** postal area *Onondaga County*, 370

**Warnerville** postal area *Schoharie County*, 490

**Warren County**, 601 - 607

**Warren** town *Herkimer County*, 209

**Warrensburg** CDP *Warren County*, 607

**Warrensburg** town *Warren County*, 607

**Warsaw** town *Wyoming County*, 657

**Warsaw** village *Wyoming County*, 656

**Warwick** town *Orange County*, 396

**Warwick** village *Orange County*, 395

**Washington County**, 608 - 615

**Washington Heights** CDP *Orange County*, 396

**Washington Mills** CDP *Oneida County*, 353

**Washington** town *Dutchess County*, 138

**Washingtonville** village *Orange County*, 396

**Wassaic** postal area *Dutchess County*, 138

**Watchtower** CDP *Ulster County*, 599

**Water Mill** postal area *Suffolk County*, 558

**Waterford** town *Saratoga County*, 478

**Waterford** village *Saratoga County*, 478

**Waterloo** town *Seneca County*, 498

**Waterloo** village *Seneca County*, 498

**Watermill** CDP *Suffolk County*, 558

**Waterport** postal area *Orleans County*, 402

**Watertown** city *Jefferson County*, 226

**Watertown** town *Jefferson County*, 226

**Waterville** village *Oneida County*, 353

**Watervliet** city *Albany County*, 8

**Watkins Glen** village *Schuyler County*, 494

**Watson** town *Lewis County*, 234

**Waverly** town *Franklin County*, 176

**Waverly** village *Tioga County*, 576

**Wawarsing** town *Ulster County*, 599

**Wawayanda** town *Orange County*, 397

**Wayland** town *Steuben County*, 512

**Wayland** village *Steuben County*, 512

**Wayne County**, 616 - 624

**Wayne** town *Steuben County*, 512

**Webb** town *Herkimer County*, 209

**Webster** town *Monroe County*, 267

**Webster** village *Monroe County*, 267

**Websters Crossing** CDP *Livingston County*, 247

**Weedsport** village *Cayuga County*, 56

**Wellesley Island** postal area *Jefferson County*, 227

**Wells Bridge** postal area *Otsego County*, 424

**Wells** town *Hamilton County*, 201

**Wellsburg** village *Chemung County*, 78

**Wellsville** town *Allegany County*, 20

**Wellsville** village *Allegany County*, 20

**Wesley Hills** village *Rockland County*, 450

**West Almond** town *Allegany County*, 21

**West Babylon** CDP *Suffolk County*, 558

**West Bay Shore** CDP *Suffolk County*, 558

**West Bloomfield** town *Ontario County*, 379

**West Camp** postal area *Ulster County*, 600

**West Carthage** village *Jefferson County*, 227

**West Chazy** CDP *Clinton County*, 96

**West Coxsackie** postal area *Greene County*, 197

**West Davenport** postal area *Delaware County*, 122

**West Eaton** postal area *Madison County*, 256
**West Edmeston** postal area *Otsego County*, 424
**West Elmira** CDP *Chemung County*, 78
**West End** CDP *Otsego County*, 424
**West Falls** postal area *Erie County*, 158
**West Fulton** postal area *Schoharie County*, 490
**West Glens Falls** CDP *Warren County*, 608
**West Hampton Dunes** village *Suffolk County*, 559
**West Harrison** postal area *Westchester County*, 648
**West Haverstraw** village *Rockland County*, 450
**West Hempstead** CDP *Nassau County*, 313
**West Henrietta** postal area *Monroe County*, 268
**West Hills** CDP *Suffolk County*, 559
**West Hurley** CDP *Ulster County*, 600
**West Islip** CDP *Suffolk County*, 559
**West Kill** postal area *Greene County*, 197
**West Lebanon** postal area *Columbia County*, 106
**West Leyden** postal area *Lewis County*, 234
**West Monroe** town *Oswego County*, 413
**West Nyack** CDP *Rockland County*, 451
**West Oneonta** postal area *Otsego County*, 424
**West Park** postal area *Ulster County*, 600
**West Point** CDP *Orange County*, 397
**West Sand Lake** CDP *Rensselaer County*, 438
**West Sayville** CDP *Suffolk County*, 559
**West Seneca** CDP *Erie County*, 159
**West Seneca** town/CDP *Erie County*, 158
**West Shokan** postal area *Ulster County*, 600
**West Sparta** town *Livingston County*, 247
**West Stockholm** postal area *Saint Lawrence County*, 468
**West Turin** town *Lewis County*, 234
**West Union** town *Steuben County*, 512
**West Valley** CDP *Cattaraugus County*, 45
**West Winfield** village *Herkimer County*, 210
**Westbrookville** postal area *Sullivan County*, 571
**Westbury** village *Nassau County*, 314
**Westchester County**, 625 - 649
**Westdale** postal area *Oneida County*, 353
**Westerlo** town *Albany County*, 8
**Western** town *Oneida County*, 353
**Westernville** postal area *Oneida County*, 354
**Westfield** town *Chautauqua County*, 71
**Westfield** village *Chautauqua County*, 71
**Westford** town *Otsego County*, 424

**Westhampton Beach** village *Suffolk County*, 560
**Westhampton** CDP *Suffolk County*, 560
**Westmere** CDP *Albany County*, 8
**Westmoreland** CDP *Oneida County*, 354
**Westmoreland** town *Oneida County*, 354
**Weston Mills** CDP *Cattaraugus County*, 45
**Westons Mills** postal area *Cattaraugus County*, 45
**Westport** CDP *Essex County*, 167
**Westport** town *Essex County*, 166
**Westtown** postal area *Orange County*, 397
**Westvale** CDP *Onondaga County*, 370
**Westville** town *Franklin County*, 177
**Wethersfield** town *Wyoming County*, 657
**Wevertown** postal area *Warren County*, 608
**Wheatfield** town *Niagara County*, 337
**Wheatland** town *Monroe County*, 268
**Wheatley Heights** CDP *Suffolk County*, 560
**Wheeler** town *Steuben County*, 513
**White Creek** town *Washington County*, 615
**White Lake** postal area *Sullivan County*, 571
**White Plains** city *Westchester County*, 648
**White Sulphur Springs** postal area *Sullivan County*, 571
**Whitehall** town *Washington County*, 616
**Whitehall** village *Washington County*, 615
**Whitesboro** village *Oneida County*, 354
**Whitestone** postal area *Queens County*, 329
**Whitestown** town *Oneida County*, 354
**Whitesville** postal area *Allegany County*, 21
**Whitney Point** village *Broome County*, 29
**Willard** postal area *Seneca County*, 499
**Willet** town *Cortland County*, 112
**Williamson** CDP *Wayne County*, 624
**Williamson** town *Wayne County*, 623
**Williamstown** town *Oswego County*, 413
**Williamsville** village *Erie County*, 159
**Willing** town *Allegany County*, 21
**Williston Park** village *Nassau County*, 314
**Willow** postal area *Ulster County*, 600
**Willsboro** CDP *Essex County*, 167
**Willsboro** town *Essex County*, 167
**Willseyville** postal area *Tioga County*, 576
**Wilmington** CDP *Essex County*, 168
**Wilmington** town *Essex County*, 167
**Wilna** town *Jefferson County*, 227
**Wilson** town *Niagara County*, 338
**Wilson** village *Niagara County*, 337
**Wilton** town *Saratoga County*, 478
**Windham** CDP *Greene County*, 197
**Windham** town *Greene County*, 197
**Windsor** town *Broome County*, 30
**Windsor** village *Broome County*, 30

**Winfield** town *Herkimer County*, 210
**Wingdale** postal area *Dutchess County*, 138
**Winthrop** CDP *St. Lawrence County*, 468
**Wirt** town *Allegany County*, 21
**Witherbee** CDP *Essex County*, 168
**Wolcott** town *Wayne County*, 624
**Wolcott** village *Wayne County*, 624
**Woodbourne** postal area *Sullivan County*, 571
**Woodbury** CDP *Nassau County*, 314
**Woodbury** town *Orange County*, 397
**Woodbury** village *Orange County*, 397
**Woodgate** postal area *Oneida County*, 355
**Woodhaven** postal area *Queens County*, 329
**Woodhull** town *Steuben County*, 513
**Woodmere** CDP *Nassau County*, 314
**Woodridge** village *Sullivan County*, 571
**Woodsburgh** village *Nassau County*, 315
**Woodside** postal area *Queens County*, 329
**Woodstock** CDP *Ulster County*, 601
**Woodstock** town *Ulster County*, 600
**Woodsville** CDP *Livingston County*, 248
**Worcester** CDP *Otsego County*, 425
**Worcester** town *Otsego County*, 424
**Worth** town *Jefferson County*, 227
**Wright** town *Schoharie County*, 490
**Wurtsboro** village *Sullivan County*, 571
**Wyandanch** CDP *Suffolk County*, 560
**Wykagyl** postal area *Westchester County*, 648
**Wynantskill** CDP *Rensselaer County*, 438
**Wyoming County**, 650 - 656
**Wyoming** village *Wyoming County*, 657

**Y**

**Yaphank** CDP *Suffolk County*, 561
**Yates County**, 657 - 662
**Yates** town *Orleans County*, 402
**Yonkers** city *Westchester County*, 648
**York Hamlet** CDP *Livingston County*, 248
**York** town *Livingston County*, 248
**Yorkshire** CDP *Cattaraugus County*, 46
**Yorkshire** town *Cattaraugus County*, 45
**Yorktown Heights** CDP *Westchester County*, 649
**Yorktown** town *Westchester County*, 649
**Yorkville** village *Oneida County*, 355
**Youngstown** village *Niagara County*, 338
**Youngsville** postal area *Sullivan County*, 571
**Yulan** postal area *Sullivan County*, 571

**Z**

**Zena** CDP *Ulster County*, 601

*CDP = Census Designated Place*

Westview postal area Orange County, 397

# Comparative
# Statistics

## Population

| Place | 1990 Census | 2000 Census | 2010 Census |
|---|---|---|---|
| **Albany** city *Albany Co.* | 100,756 | 95,658 | 97,856 |
| **Amherst** town *Erie Co.* | 111,711 | 116,510 | 122,366 |
| **Babylon** town *Suffolk Co.* | 202,355 | 211,792 | 213,603 |
| **Bethlehem** town *Albany Co.* | 27,552 | 31,304 | 33,656 |
| **Binghamton** city *Broome Co.* | 53,017 | 47,380 | 47,376 |
| **Brentwood** CDP *Suffolk Co.* | 45,218 | 53,917 | 60,664 |
| **Brighton** town and CDP *Monroe Co.* | 34,458 | 35,588 | 36,609 |
| **Brookhaven** town *Suffolk Co.* | 407,832 | 448,248 | 486,040 |
| **Buffalo** city *Erie Co.* | 328,123 | 292,648 | 261,310 |
| **Carmel** town *Putnam Co.* | 28,816 | 33,006 | 34,305 |
| **Centereach** CDP *Suffolk Co.* | 26,720 | 27,285 | 31,578 |
| **Central Islip** CDP *Suffolk Co.* | 27,789 | 31,950 | 34,450 |
| **Cheektowaga** town *Erie Co.* | 99,314 | 94,019 | 88,226 |
| **Cheektowaga** CDP *Erie Co.* | 84,387 | 79,988 | 75,178 |
| **Chili** town *Monroe Co.* | 25,178 | 27,638 | 28,625 |
| **Cicero** town *Onondaga Co.* | 25,560 | 27,982 | 31,632 |
| **Clarence** town *Erie Co.* | 20,041 | 26,123 | 30,673 |
| **Clarkstown** town *Rockland Co.* | 79,346 | 82,082 | 84,187 |
| **Clay** town *Onondaga Co.* | 59,749 | 58,805 | 58,206 |
| **Clifton Park** town *Saratoga Co.* | 30,117 | 32,995 | 36,705 |
| **Colonie** town *Albany Co.* | 76,536 | 79,258 | 81,591 |
| **Commack** CDP *Suffolk Co.* | 36,124 | 36,367 | 36,124 |
| **Coram** CDP *Suffolk Co.* | 30,173 | 34,923 | 39,113 |
| **Cortlandt** town *Westchester Co.* | 37,357 | 38,467 | 41,592 |
| **East Fishkill** town *Dutchess Co.* | 22,101 | 25,589 | 29,029 |
| **East Meadow** CDP *Nassau Co.* | 36,909 | 37,461 | 38,132 |
| **Eastchester** town *Westchester Co.* | 30,867 | 31,318 | 32,363 |
| **Elmira** city *Chemung Co.* | 33,719 | 30,940 | 29,200 |
| **Elmont** CDP *Nassau Co.* | 28,612 | 32,657 | 33,198 |
| **Franklin Square** CDP *Nassau Co.* | 28,205 | 29,342 | 29,320 |
| **Freeport** village *Nassau Co.* | 39,894 | 43,783 | 42,860 |
| **Glenville** town *Schenectady Co.* | 28,771 | 28,183 | 29,480 |
| **Greece** town *Monroe Co.* | 90,106 | 94,141 | 96,095 |
| **Greenburgh** town *Westchester Co.* | 83,816 | 86,764 | 88,400 |
| **Guilderland** town *Albany Co.* | 28,877 | 32,688 | 35,303 |
| **Hamburg** town *Erie Co.* | 53,735 | 56,259 | 56,936 |
| **Haverstraw** town *Rockland Co.* | 32,712 | 33,811 | 36,634 |
| **Hempstead** town *Nassau Co.* | 725,630 | 755,924 | 759,757 |
| **Hempstead** village *Nassau Co.* | 49,435 | 56,554 | 53,891 |
| **Henrietta** town *Monroe Co.* | 36,376 | 39,028 | 42,581 |
| **Hicksville** CDP *Nassau Co.* | 40,174 | 41,260 | 41,547 |
| **Huntington** town *Suffolk Co.* | 191,474 | 195,289 | 203,264 |
| **Huntington Station** CDP *Suffolk Co.* | 28,247 | 29,910 | 33,029 |
| **Irondequoit** town and CDP *Monroe Co.* | 52,371 | 52,354 | 51,692 |
| **Islip** town *Suffolk Co.* | 299,587 | 322,612 | 335,543 |
| **Ithaca** city *Tompkins Co.* | 29,541 | 29,287 | 30,014 |
| **Jamestown** city *Chautauqua Co.* | 34,689 | 31,730 | 31,146 |
| **Lancaster** town *Erie Co.* | 32,181 | 39,019 | 41,604 |
| **Levittown** CDP *Nassau Co.* | 53,296 | 53,067 | 51,881 |
| **Long Beach** city *Nassau Co.* | 33,510 | 35,462 | 33,275 |

| Place | 1990 Census | 2000 Census | 2010 Census |
|---|---|---|---|
| Mamaroneck town *Westchester Co.* | 27,706 | 28,967 | 29,156 |
| Manlius town *Onondaga Co.* | 30,656 | 31,872 | 32,370 |
| Monroe town *Orange Co.* | 23,035 | 31,407 | 39,912 |
| Mount Pleasant town *Westchester Co.* | 40,590 | 43,221 | 43,724 |
| Mount Vernon city *Westchester Co.* | 67,076 | 68,381 | 67,292 |
| New City CDP *Rockland Co.* | 33,745 | 34,038 | 33,559 |
| New Rochelle city *Westchester Co.* | 67,429 | 72,182 | 77,062 |
| New York city | 7,322,552 | 8,008,278 | 8,175,133 |
| Newburgh city *Orange Co.* | 26,440 | 28,259 | 28,866 |
| Newburgh town *Orange Co.* | 24,066 | 27,568 | 29,801 |
| Niagara Falls city *Niagara Co.* | 61,840 | 55,593 | 50,193 |
| North Hempstead town *Nassau Co.* | 211,355 | 222,611 | 226,322 |
| North Tonawanda city *Niagara Co.* | 34,989 | 33,262 | 31,568 |
| Oceanside CDP *Nassau Co.* | 32,423 | 32,733 | 32,109 |
| Orangetown town *Rockland Co.* | 46,742 | 47,711 | 49,212 |
| Orchard Park town *Erie Co.* | 24,632 | 27,637 | 29,054 |
| Ossining town *Westchester Co.* | 34,124 | 36,534 | 37,674 |
| Oyster Bay town *Nassau Co.* | 293,200 | 293,925 | 293,214 |
| Penfield town *Monroe Co.* | 30,216 | 34,645 | 36,242 |
| Perinton town *Monroe Co.* | 43,015 | 46,090 | 46,462 |
| Pittsford town *Monroe Co.* | 24,497 | 27,219 | 29,405 |
| Port Chester village *Westchester Co.* | 24,728 | 27,867 | 28,967 |
| Poughkeepsie town *Dutchess Co.* | 40,143 | 42,777 | 43,341 |
| Poughkeepsie city *Dutchess Co.* | 28,844 | 29,871 | 32,736 |
| Ramapo town *Rockland Co.* | 93,861 | 108,905 | 126,595 |
| Riverhead town *Suffolk Co.* | 22,958 | 27,680 | 33,506 |
| Rochester city *Monroe Co.* | 231,642 | 219,773 | 210,565 |
| Rome city *Oneida Co.* | 44,350 | 34,950 | 33,725 |
| Rotterdam town *Schenectady Co.* | 28,395 | 28,316 | 29,094 |
| Rye town *Westchester Co.* | 39,524 | 43,880 | 45,928 |
| Salina town *Onondaga Co.* | 35,145 | 33,290 | 33,710 |
| Schenectady city *Schenectady Co.* | 65,566 | 61,821 | 66,135 |
| Smithtown town *Suffolk Co.* | 113,406 | 115,715 | 117,801 |
| Southampton town *Suffolk Co.* | 44,976 | 54,712 | 56,790 |
| Spring Valley village *Rockland Co.* | 21,802 | 25,464 | 31,347 |
| Syracuse city *Onondaga Co.* | 163,860 | 147,306 | 145,170 |
| Tonawanda CDP *Erie Co.* | 65,284 | 61,729 | 58,144 |
| Tonawanda town *Erie Co.* | 82,464 | 78,155 | 73,567 |
| Troy city *Rensselaer Co.* | 54,269 | 49,170 | 50,129 |
| Union town *Broome Co.* | 59,786 | 56,298 | 56,346 |
| Utica city *Oneida Co.* | 68,637 | 60,651 | 62,235 |
| Valley Stream village *Nassau Co.* | 33,962 | 36,368 | 37,511 |
| Warwick town *Orange Co.* | 27,174 | 30,764 | 32,065 |
| Webster town *Monroe Co.* | 31,639 | 37,926 | 42,641 |
| West Babylon CDP *Suffolk Co.* | 42,410 | 43,452 | 43,213 |
| West Seneca CDP *Erie Co.* | 47,866 | 45,943 | 44,711 |
| West Seneca town and CDP *Erie Co.* | 47,830 | 45,920 | 44,711 |
| White Plains city *Westchester Co.* | 48,615 | 53,077 | 56,853 |
| Yonkers city *Westchester Co.* | 188,126 | 196,086 | 195,976 |
| Yorktown town *Westchester Co.* | 33,314 | 36,318 | 36,081 |

## Physical Characteristics

| Place | Density (persons per square mile) | Land Area (square miles) | Water Area (square miles) | Elevation (feet) |
|---|---|---|---|---|
| Albany city *Albany Co.* | 4,575.2 | 21.38 | 0.54 | 148 |
| Amherst town *Erie Co.* | 2,300.0 | 53.20 | 0.39 | 597 |
| Babylon town *Suffolk Co.* | 4,082.7 | 52.31 | 61.86 | 7 |
| Bethlehem town *Albany Co.* | 686.4 | 49.02 | 0.83 | 210 |
| Binghamton city *Broome Co.* | 4,516.8 | 10.48 | 0.64 | 866 |
| Brentwood CDP *Suffolk Co.* | 5,524.6 | 10.98 | 0.00 | 79 |
| Brighton town and CDP *Monroe Co.* | 2,374.8 | 15.41 | 0.16 | 446 |
| Brookhaven town *Suffolk Co.* | 1,873.4 | 259.43 | 272.09 | 10 |
| Buffalo city *Erie Co.* | 6,470.6 | 40.38 | 12.10 | 600 |
| Carmel town *Putnam Co.* | 955.4 | 35.90 | 4.78 | 561 |
| Centereach CDP *Suffolk Co.* | 3,623.6 | 8.71 | 0.00 | 98 |
| Central Islip CDP *Suffolk Co.* | 4,844.5 | 7.11 | 0.00 | 85 |
| Cheektowaga town *Erie Co.* | 2,998.6 | 29.42 | 0.06 | 650 |
| Cheektowaga CDP *Erie Co.* | 2,966.4 | 25.34 | 0.05 | 650 |
| Chili town *Monroe Co.* | 724.7 | 39.49 | 0.36 | n/a |
| Cicero town *Onondaga Co.* | 655.3 | 48.27 | 0.19 | 394 |
| Clarence town *Erie Co.* | 573.3 | 53.50 | 0.13 | 738 |
| Clarkstown town *Rockland Co.* | 2,188.1 | 38.47 | 8.59 | n/a |
| Clay town *Onondaga Co.* | 1,213.7 | 47.95 | 0.90 | 394 |
| Clifton Park town *Saratoga Co.* | 761.5 | 48.20 | 2.00 | 344 |
| Colonie town *Albany Co.* | 1,458.5 | 55.94 | 1.89 | 312 |
| Commack CDP *Suffolk Co.* | 3,018.2 | 11.96 | 0.00 | 131 |
| Coram CDP *Suffolk Co.* | 2,829.3 | 13.82 | 0.00 | 95 |
| Cortlandt town *Westchester Co.* | 1,059.5 | 39.25 | 10.76 | n/a |
| East Fishkill town *Dutchess Co.* | 513.8 | 56.50 | 0.88 | 276 |
| East Meadow CDP *Nassau Co.* | 6,048.9 | 6.30 | 0.02 | 72 |
| Eastchester town *Westchester Co.* | 6,668.6 | 4.85 | 0.08 | 52 |
| Elmira city *Chemung Co.* | 4,028.2 | 7.24 | 0.32 | 853 |
| Elmont CDP *Nassau Co.* | 9,854.8 | 3.36 | 0.01 | 39 |
| Franklin Square CDP *Nassau Co.* | 10,188.8 | 2.87 | 0.00 | 66 |
| Freeport village *Nassau Co.* | 9,260.5 | 4.62 | 0.24 | 20 |
| Glenville town *Schenectady Co.* | 599.4 | 49.18 | 1.48 | 705 |
| Greece town *Monroe Co.* | 2,022.3 | 47.51 | 3.87 | 430 |
| Greenburgh town *Westchester Co.* | 2,916.6 | 30.30 | 5.80 | 348 |
| Guilderland town *Albany Co.* | 609.7 | 57.90 | 0.88 | 207 |
| Hamburg town *Erie Co.* | 1,377.9 | 41.32 | 0.02 | 820 |
| Haverstraw town *Rockland Co.* | 1,653.5 | 22.15 | 5.26 | 30 |
| Hempstead town *Nassau Co.* | 6,406.7 | 118.58 | 72.99 | 56 |
| Hempstead village *Nassau Co.* | 14,636.2 | 3.68 | 0.00 | 56 |
| Henrietta town *Monroe Co.* | 1,204.5 | 35.35 | 0.29 | 600 |
| Hicksville CDP *Nassau Co.* | 6,118.0 | 6.79 | 0.01 | 148 |
| Huntington town *Suffolk Co.* | 2,159.5 | 94.12 | 42.98 | 75 |
| Huntington Station CDP *Suffolk Co.* | 6,033.7 | 5.47 | 0.00 | 217 |
| Irondequoit town and CDP *Monroe Co.* | 3,445.9 | 15.00 | 1.83 | 381 |
| Islip town *Suffolk Co.* | 3,222.8 | 104.11 | 58.89 | 13 |
| Ithaca city *Tompkins Co.* | 5,570.3 | 5.38 | 0.68 | 410 |
| Jamestown city *Chautauqua Co.* | 3,486.0 | 8.93 | 0.12 | 1,378 |
| Lancaster town *Erie Co.* | 1,103.5 | 37.70 | 0.23 | 669 |
| Levittown CDP *Nassau Co.* | 7,617.2 | 6.81 | 0.02 | 82 |
| Long Beach city *Nassau Co.* | 15,024.8 | 2.21 | 1.67 | 9 |

| Place | Density (persons per square mile) | Land Area (square miles) | Water Area (square miles) | Elevation (feet) |
|---|---|---|---|---|
| Mamaroneck town *Westchester Co.* | 4,381.7 | 6.65 | 7.41 | 47 |
| Manlius town *Onondaga Co.* | 657.7 | 49.21 | 0.73 | 591 |
| Monroe town *Orange Co.* | 1,998.0 | 19.97 | 1.28 | 643 |
| Mount Pleasant town *Westchester Co.* | 1,594.4 | 27.42 | 5.33 | 259 |
| Mount Vernon city *Westchester Co.* | 15,343.6 | 4.38 | 0.01 | 108 |
| New City CDP *Rockland Co.* | 2,153.7 | 15.58 | 0.79 | 157 |
| New Rochelle city *Westchester Co.* | 7,445.4 | 10.35 | 2.88 | 85 |
| New York city | 27,012.4 | 302.64 | 165.84 | 33 |
| Newburgh city *Orange Co.* | 7,587.7 | 3.80 | 0.98 | 128 |
| Newburgh town *Orange Co.* | 698.3 | 42.67 | 4.26 | 128 |
| Niagara Falls city *Niagara Co.* | 3,563.3 | 14.08 | 2.74 | 614 |
| North Hempstead town *Nassau Co.* | 4,229.3 | 53.51 | 15.59 | 157 |
| North Tonawanda city *Niagara Co.* | 3,125.4 | 10.10 | 0.80 | 574 |
| Oceanside CDP *Nassau Co.* | 6,495.0 | 4.94 | 0.47 | 10 |
| Orangetown town *Rockland Co.* | 2,042.2 | 24.09 | 7.26 | 112 |
| Orchard Park town *Erie Co.* | 755.8 | 38.44 | 0.07 | 863 |
| Ossining town *Westchester Co.* | 3,260.1 | 11.55 | 4.16 | 161 |
| Oyster Bay town *Nassau Co.* | 2,826.2 | 103.74 | 65.65 | 46 |
| Penfield town *Monroe Co.* | 974.0 | 37.21 | 0.63 | 423 |
| Perinton town *Monroe Co.* | 1,359.1 | 34.18 | 0.35 | n/a |
| Pittsford town *Monroe Co.* | 1,268.5 | 23.18 | 0.20 | 492 |
| Port Chester village *Westchester Co.* | 12,428.8 | 2.33 | 0.07 | 43 |
| Poughkeepsie town *Dutchess Co.* | 1,520.0 | 28.51 | 2.62 | 203 |
| Poughkeepsie city *Dutchess Co.* | 6,364.1 | 5.14 | 0.57 | 203 |
| Ramapo town *Rockland Co.* | 2,068.6 | 61.19 | 0.69 | 331 |
| Riverhead town *Suffolk Co.* | 496.9 | 67.42 | 133.84 | 13 |
| Rochester city *Monroe Co.* | 5,884.9 | 35.78 | 1.37 | 505 |
| Rome city *Oneida Co.* | 450.9 | 74.79 | 0.81 | 456 |
| Rotterdam town *Schenectady Co.* | 815.1 | 35.69 | 0.76 | 338 |
| Rye town *Westchester Co.* | 6,638.2 | 6.91 | 0.43 | 26 |
| Salina town *Onondaga Co.* | 2,451.6 | 13.74 | 1.31 | n/a |
| Schenectady city *Schenectady Co.* | 6,135.3 | 10.77 | 0.18 | 243 |
| Smithtown town *Suffolk Co.* | 2,193.8 | 53.69 | 57.75 | 59 |
| Southampton town *Suffolk Co.* | 408.0 | 139.19 | 154.50 | 26 |
| Spring Valley village *Rockland Co.* | 15,551.2 | 2.01 | 0.00 | 443 |
| Syracuse city *Onondaga Co.* | 5,796.7 | 25.04 | 0.56 | 397 |
| Tonawanda CDP *Erie Co.* | 3,361.0 | 17.29 | 1.33 | 574 |
| Tonawanda town *Erie Co.* | 3,926.7 | 18.73 | 1.54 | 574 |
| Troy city *Rensselaer Co.* | 4,840.0 | 10.35 | 0.69 | 33 |
| Union town *Broome Co.* | 1,589.4 | 35.45 | 0.53 | 846 |
| Utica city *Oneida Co.* | 3,713.6 | 16.75 | 0.25 | 456 |
| Valley Stream village *Nassau Co.* | 10,772.4 | 3.48 | 0.01 | 16 |
| Warwick town *Orange Co.* | 316.4 | 101.34 | 3.54 | 518 |
| Webster town *Monroe Co.* | 1,271.7 | 33.53 | 1.70 | 446 |
| West Babylon CDP *Suffolk Co.* | 5,563.7 | 7.76 | 0.30 | 39 |
| West Seneca CDP *Erie Co.* | 2,093.5 | 21.35 | 0.05 | 597 |
| West Seneca town and CDP *Erie Co.* | 2,093.5 | 21.35 | 0.05 | 597 |
| White Plains city *Westchester Co.* | 5,820.5 | 9.76 | 0.11 | 213 |
| Yonkers city *Westchester Co.* | 10,880.3 | 18.01 | 2.28 | 82 |
| Yorktown town *Westchester Co.* | 984.6 | 36.64 | 2.61 | 505 |

NOTE: Data as of 2010

## Population by Race/Hispanic Origin

| Place | White[1] (%) | Black[1] (%) | Asian[1] (%) | AIAN[1,2] (%) | NHOPI[1,3] (%) | Other (%) | Hispanic[4] (%) |
|---|---|---|---|---|---|---|---|
| **Albany** city *Albany Co.* | 57.0 | 30.8 | 5.0 | 0.3 | 0.1 | 6.8 | 8.6 |
| **Amherst** town *Erie Co.* | 83.8 | 5.7 | 7.9 | 0.2 | 0.0 | 2.4 | 2.3 |
| **Babylon** town *Suffolk Co.* | 71.7 | 16.3 | 3.1 | 0.3 | 0.0 | 8.6 | 16.8 |
| **Bethlehem** town *Albany Co.* | 91.9 | 2.6 | 3.2 | 0.1 | 0.0 | 2.2 | 2.7 |
| **Binghamton** city *Broome Co.* | 77.6 | 11.4 | 4.2 | 0.3 | 0.0 | 6.5 | 6.4 |
| **Brentwood** CDP *Suffolk Co.* | 48.4 | 16.4 | 2.0 | 1.2 | 0.0 | 32.0 | 68.5 |
| **Brighton** town and CDP *Monroe Co.* | 79.8 | 5.1 | 11.8 | 0.1 | 0.0 | 3.2 | 3.3 |
| **Brookhaven** town *Suffolk Co.* | 84.5 | 5.5 | 3.9 | 0.3 | 0.0 | 5.8 | 12.4 |
| **Buffalo** city *Erie Co.* | 50.4 | 38.6 | 3.2 | 0.8 | 0.0 | 7.0 | 10.5 |
| **Carmel** town *Putnam Co.* | 92.1 | 2.0 | 1.8 | 0.1 | 0.0 | 4.0 | 10.1 |
| **Centereach** CDP *Suffolk Co.* | 85.4 | 3.1 | 6.2 | 0.1 | 0.0 | 5.2 | 11.3 |
| **Central Islip** CDP *Suffolk Co.* | 43.6 | 25.0 | 3.4 | 0.9 | 0.0 | 27.1 | 52.1 |
| **Cheektowaga** town *Erie Co.* | 88.1 | 8.0 | 1.5 | 0.3 | 0.0 | 2.1 | 2.2 |
| **Cheektowaga** CDP *Erie Co.* | 86.8 | 9.2 | 1.7 | 0.3 | 0.0 | 2.0 | 2.2 |
| **Chili** town *Monroe Co.* | 87.6 | 7.6 | 2.1 | 0.2 | 0.0 | 2.5 | 2.8 |
| **Cicero** town *Onondaga Co.* | 95.2 | 1.7 | 1.0 | 0.3 | 0.0 | 1.8 | 1.6 |
| **Clarence** town *Erie Co.* | 93.8 | 1.1 | 3.6 | 0.1 | 0.0 | 1.4 | 1.4 |
| **Clarkstown** town *Rockland Co.* | 73.9 | 9.6 | 10.5 | 0.2 | 0.0 | 5.8 | 11.7 |
| **Clay** town *Onondaga Co.* | 89.9 | 4.3 | 2.5 | 0.5 | 0.0 | 2.8 | 2.5 |
| **Clifton Park** town *Saratoga Co.* | 91.0 | 1.9 | 4.6 | 0.1 | 0.0 | 2.4 | 2.7 |
| **Colonie** town *Albany Co.* | 85.2 | 5.3 | 6.6 | 0.1 | 0.0 | 2.8 | 3.1 |
| **Commack** CDP *Suffolk Co.* | 91.6 | 0.9 | 5.4 | 0.1 | 0.0 | 2.0 | 4.8 |
| **Coram** CDP *Suffolk Co.* | 77.4 | 10.6 | 5.0 | 0.2 | 0.0 | 6.8 | 13.6 |
| **Cortlandt** town *Westchester Co.* | 84.5 | 5.4 | 3.6 | 0.2 | 0.0 | 6.3 | 12.8 |
| **East Fishkill** town *Dutchess Co.* | 88.6 | 3.4 | 4.1 | 0.1 | 0.0 | 3.8 | 7.7 |
| **East Meadow** CDP *Nassau Co.* | 77.3 | 5.2 | 11.6 | 0.1 | 0.0 | 5.8 | 12.2 |
| **Eastchester** town *Westchester Co.* | 85.9 | 3.3 | 7.3 | 0.1 | 0.0 | 3.4 | 7.2 |
| **Elmira** city *Chemung Co.* | 78.3 | 14.6 | 0.6 | 0.4 | 0.0 | 6.1 | 4.3 |
| **Elmont** CDP *Nassau Co.* | 28.5 | 45.5 | 10.9 | 0.5 | 0.0 | 14.6 | 21.8 |
| **Franklin Square** CDP *Nassau Co.* | 83.3 | 3.2 | 7.2 | 0.3 | 0.0 | 6.0 | 13.3 |
| **Freeport** village *Nassau Co.* | 40.5 | 33.3 | 1.6 | 0.8 | 0.1 | 23.7 | 41.7 |
| **Glenville** town *Schenectady Co.* | 95.9 | 1.0 | 1.4 | 0.1 | 0.0 | 1.6 | 2.0 |
| **Greece** town *Monroe Co.* | 88.7 | 6.0 | 1.7 | 0.3 | 0.0 | 3.3 | 4.8 |
| **Greenburgh** town *Westchester Co.* | 69.2 | 12.6 | 10.4 | 0.2 | 0.0 | 7.6 | 14.0 |
| **Guilderland** town *Albany Co.* | 86.2 | 3.4 | 7.5 | 0.2 | 0.0 | 2.7 | 3.2 |
| **Hamburg** town *Erie Co.* | 97.0 | 0.8 | 0.6 | 0.3 | 0.0 | 1.3 | 2.1 |
| **Haverstraw** town *Rockland Co.* | 59.2 | 14.7 | 4.4 | 0.5 | 0.1 | 21.1 | 41.0 |
| **Hempstead** town *Nassau Co.* | 68.3 | 16.5 | 5.2 | 0.3 | 0.0 | 9.7 | 17.4 |
| **Hempstead** village *Nassau Co.* | 21.9 | 48.3 | 1.4 | 0.6 | 0.0 | 27.8 | 44.2 |
| **Henrietta** town *Monroe Co.* | 80.2 | 8.5 | 7.2 | 0.2 | 0.0 | 3.9 | 4.3 |
| **Hicksville** CDP *Nassau Co.* | 70.3 | 2.3 | 19.7 | 0.3 | 0.0 | 7.4 | 14.5 |
| **Huntington** town *Suffolk Co.* | 84.2 | 4.7 | 5.0 | 0.2 | 0.0 | 5.9 | 11.0 |
| **Huntington Station** CDP *Suffolk Co.* | 64.0 | 10.9 | 3.5 | 0.6 | 0.0 | 21.0 | 36.7 |
| **Irondequoit** town and CDP *Monroe Co.* | 86.8 | 7.7 | 1.3 | 0.2 | 0.0 | 4.0 | 6.2 |
| **Islip** town *Suffolk Co.* | 73.3 | 9.5 | 2.9 | 0.5 | 0.0 | 13.8 | 29.0 |
| **Ithaca** city *Tompkins Co.* | 70.5 | 6.6 | 16.2 | 0.4 | 0.0 | 6.3 | 6.9 |
| **Jamestown** city *Chautauqua Co.* | 88.4 | 4.1 | 0.4 | 0.6 | 0.0 | 6.5 | 8.8 |
| **Lancaster** town *Erie Co.* | 97.0 | 1.0 | 0.6 | 0.2 | 0.0 | 1.2 | 1.4 |
| **Levittown** CDP *Nassau Co.* | 88.9 | 0.9 | 5.7 | 0.1 | 0.0 | 4.4 | 11.5 |

| Place | White[1] (%) | Black[1] (%) | Asian[1] (%) | AIAN[1,2] (%) | NHOPI[1,3] (%) | Other (%) | Hispanic[4] (%) |
|---|---|---|---|---|---|---|---|
| Long Beach city Nassau Co. | 83.2 | 6.4 | 2.7 | 0.3 | 0.0 | 7.4 | 14.1 |
| Mamaroneck town Westchester Co. | 84.1 | 2.9 | 3.9 | 0.2 | 0.0 | 8.9 | 15.5 |
| Manlius town Onondaga Co. | 92.9 | 1.4 | 3.7 | 0.3 | 0.0 | 1.7 | 1.5 |
| Monroe town Orange Co. | 91.3 | 2.2 | 2.5 | 0.1 | 0.0 | 3.9 | 8.4 |
| Mount Pleasant town Westchester Co. | 79.7 | 5.5 | 4.8 | 0.3 | 0.0 | 9.7 | 18.0 |
| Mount Vernon city Westchester Co. | 24.3 | 63.4 | 1.8 | 0.5 | 0.1 | 9.9 | 14.3 |
| New City CDP Rockland Co. | 78.7 | 6.4 | 10.3 | 0.2 | 0.0 | 4.4 | 9.0 |
| New Rochelle city Westchester Co. | 65.2 | 19.3 | 4.2 | 0.5 | 0.1 | 10.7 | 27.8 |
| New York city | 44.0 | 25.5 | 12.7 | 0.7 | 0.1 | 17.0 | 28.6 |
| Newburgh city Orange Co. | 39.4 | 30.2 | 1.0 | 1.7 | 0.1 | 27.6 | 47.9 |
| Newburgh town Orange Co. | 76.5 | 12.2 | 3.0 | 0.3 | 0.0 | 8.0 | 15.7 |
| Niagara Falls city Niagara Co. | 70.5 | 21.6 | 1.2 | 1.9 | 0.0 | 4.8 | 3.0 |
| North Hempstead town Nassau Co. | 71.6 | 5.6 | 15.0 | 0.2 | 0.0 | 7.6 | 12.8 |
| North Tonawanda city Niagara Co. | 96.5 | 0.8 | 0.7 | 0.4 | 0.0 | 1.6 | 1.7 |
| Oceanside CDP Nassau Co. | 92.2 | 1.3 | 2.7 | 0.1 | 0.0 | 3.7 | 9.2 |
| Orangetown town Rockland Co. | 81.9 | 6.0 | 6.9 | 0.2 | 0.0 | 5.0 | 9.7 |
| Orchard Park town Erie Co. | 96.7 | 0.7 | 1.3 | 0.2 | 0.0 | 1.1 | 1.6 |
| Ossining town Westchester Co. | 65.0 | 12.7 | 4.9 | 0.5 | 0.0 | 16.9 | 30.3 |
| Oyster Bay town Nassau Co. | 85.0 | 2.3 | 9.1 | 0.2 | 0.0 | 3.4 | 7.5 |
| Penfield town Monroe Co. | 92.6 | 2.1 | 3.1 | 0.1 | 0.0 | 2.1 | 2.5 |
| Perinton town Monroe Co. | 93.0 | 2.0 | 2.9 | 0.1 | 0.0 | 2.0 | 2.1 |
| Pittsford town Monroe Co. | 89.3 | 1.7 | 6.8 | 0.1 | 0.0 | 2.1 | 2.3 |
| Port Chester village Westchester Co. | 61.1 | 6.5 | 2.1 | 0.9 | 0.0 | 29.4 | 59.4 |
| Poughkeepsie town Dutchess Co. | 77.4 | 9.8 | 6.1 | 0.2 | 0.0 | 6.5 | 9.8 |
| Poughkeepsie city Dutchess Co. | 50.9 | 33.5 | 1.6 | 0.9 | 0.1 | 13.0 | 19.5 |
| Ramapo town Rockland Co. | 71.8 | 15.8 | 4.0 | 0.3 | 0.0 | 8.1 | 13.6 |
| Riverhead town Suffolk Co. | 82.7 | 7.7 | 1.1 | 0.3 | 0.1 | 8.1 | 13.9 |
| Rochester city Monroe Co. | 43.7 | 41.7 | 3.1 | 0.5 | 0.0 | 11.0 | 16.4 |
| Rome city Oneida Co. | 87.4 | 7.1 | 1.1 | 0.3 | 0.0 | 4.1 | 5.3 |
| Rotterdam town Schenectady Co. | 94.7 | 1.5 | 1.2 | 0.2 | 0.0 | 2.4 | 2.3 |
| Rye town Westchester Co. | 70.2 | 4.9 | 3.3 | 0.7 | 0.0 | 20.9 | 42.4 |
| Salina town Onondaga Co. | 90.2 | 4.0 | 2.2 | 0.6 | 0.0 | 3.0 | 2.8 |
| Schenectady city Schenectady Co. | 61.4 | 20.2 | 3.6 | 0.7 | 0.1 | 14.0 | 10.5 |
| Smithtown town Suffolk Co. | 93.2 | 1.1 | 3.6 | 0.1 | 0.0 | 2.0 | 5.3 |
| Southampton town Suffolk Co. | 84.2 | 5.2 | 1.1 | 0.5 | 0.1 | 8.9 | 19.9 |
| Spring Valley village Rockland Co. | 39.4 | 36.8 | 3.8 | 0.6 | 0.1 | 19.3 | 30.6 |
| Syracuse city Onondaga Co. | 56.0 | 29.5 | 5.5 | 1.1 | 0.0 | 7.9 | 8.3 |
| Tonawanda CDP Erie Co. | 93.1 | 3.0 | 1.4 | 0.4 | 0.0 | 2.1 | 2.6 |
| Tonawanda town Erie Co. | 93.1 | 3.0 | 1.3 | 0.4 | 0.0 | 2.2 | 2.7 |
| Troy city Rensselaer Co. | 72.9 | 16.4 | 3.4 | 0.3 | 0.0 | 7.0 | 7.9 |
| Union town Broome Co. | 89.1 | 4.4 | 2.9 | 0.2 | 0.1 | 3.3 | 3.2 |
| Utica city Oneida Co. | 69.0 | 15.3 | 7.4 | 0.3 | 0.1 | 7.9 | 10.5 |
| Valley Stream village Nassau Co. | 57.2 | 18.6 | 11.4 | 0.3 | 0.1 | 12.4 | 22.2 |
| Warwick town Orange Co. | 88.4 | 5.1 | 1.5 | 0.3 | 0.0 | 4.7 | 10.2 |
| Webster town Monroe Co. | 92.8 | 2.0 | 2.8 | 0.2 | 0.0 | 2.2 | 2.9 |
| West Babylon CDP Suffolk Co. | 79.9 | 11.2 | 2.7 | 0.2 | 0.0 | 6.0 | 12.2 |
| West Seneca CDP Erie Co. | 97.2 | 0.9 | 0.6 | 0.2 | 0.0 | 1.1 | 1.7 |
| West Seneca town and CDP Erie Co. | 97.2 | 0.9 | 0.6 | 0.2 | 0.0 | 1.1 | 1.7 |
| White Plains city Westchester Co. | 63.6 | 14.2 | 6.4 | 0.7 | 0.0 | 15.1 | 29.6 |
| Yonkers city Westchester Co. | 55.8 | 18.7 | 5.9 | 0.7 | 0.1 | 18.8 | 34.7 |
| Yorktown town Westchester Co. | 87.9 | 3.3 | 4.7 | 0.1 | 0.0 | 4.0 | 9.4 |

NOTE: Data as of 2010; (1) Exclude multiple race combinations; (2) American Indian/Alaska Native; (3) Native Hawaiian/Other Pacific Islander; (4) May be of any race

## Avg. Household Size, Median Age, Male/Female Ratio & Foreign Born

| Place | Average Household Size (persons) | Median Age (years) | Males per 100 Females | Foreign Born (%) |
|---|---|---|---|---|
| Albany city Albany Co. | 2.13 | 30.3 | 93.6 | 11.6 |
| Amherst town Erie Co. | 2.33 | 40.2 | 89.9 | 12.1 |
| Babylon town Suffolk Co. | 2.98 | 39.2 | 93.7 | 17.0 |
| Bethlehem town Albany Co. | 2.46 | 43.6 | 92.2 | 6.2 |
| Binghamton city Broome Co. | 2.18 | 35.8 | 96.1 | 9.7 |
| Brentwood CDP Suffolk Co. | 4.35 | 32.0 | 103.6 | 42.3 |
| Brighton town and CDP Monroe Co. | 2.16 | 39.5 | 89.3 | 17.9 |
| Brookhaven town Suffolk Co. | 2.89 | 38.5 | 97.2 | 10.6 |
| Buffalo city Erie Co. | 2.24 | 33.2 | 92.0 | 7.0 |
| Carmel town Putnam Co. | 2.90 | 41.3 | 98.4 | 11.2 |
| Centereach CDP Suffolk Co. | 3.13 | 38.9 | 99.7 | 12.9 |
| Central Islip CDP Suffolk Co. | 3.66 | 32.6 | 98.5 | 36.7 |
| Cheektowaga town Erie Co. | 2.22 | 43.2 | 88.9 | 4.9 |
| Cheektowaga CDP Erie Co. | 2.21 | 43.0 | 88.5 | 4.9 |
| Chili town Monroe Co. | 2.50 | 40.8 | 93.5 | 5.7 |
| Cicero town Onondaga Co. | 2.55 | 39.9 | 96.1 | 3.8 |
| Clarence town Erie Co. | 2.68 | 43.7 | 94.2 | 7.2 |
| Clarkstown town Rockland Co. | 2.84 | 42.8 | 94.1 | 20.3 |
| Clay town Onondaga Co. | 2.50 | 38.9 | 93.9 | 5.1 |
| Clifton Park town Saratoga Co. | 2.59 | 42.1 | 95.2 | 8.5 |
| Colonie town Albany Co. | 2.35 | 42.6 | 92.8 | 9.1 |
| Commack CDP Suffolk Co. | 2.99 | 43.0 | 94.1 | 9.9 |
| Coram CDP Suffolk Co. | 2.66 | 38.7 | 93.2 | 14.9 |
| Cortlandt town Westchester Co. | 2.68 | 43.3 | 96.4 | 14.2 |
| East Fishkill town Dutchess Co. | 3.05 | 41.3 | 99.9 | 11.1 |
| East Meadow CDP Nassau Co. | 2.91 | 41.9 | 98.2 | 17.9 |
| Eastchester town Westchester Co. | 2.48 | 42.0 | 88.7 | 16.5 |
| Elmira city Chemung Co. | 2.34 | 33.9 | 102.4 | 2.9 |
| Elmont CDP Nassau Co. | 3.37 | 37.1 | 92.9 | 42.1 |
| Franklin Square CDP Nassau Co. | 2.92 | 42.4 | 91.1 | 21.9 |
| Freeport village Nassau Co. | 3.18 | 37.2 | 94.9 | 34.3 |
| Glenville town Schenectady Co. | 2.39 | 44.2 | 94.0 | 2.9 |
| Greece town Monroe Co. | 2.41 | 42.2 | 90.4 | 7.5 |
| Greenburgh town Westchester Co. | 2.55 | 42.8 | 89.5 | 21.4 |
| Guilderland town Albany Co. | 2.34 | 41.5 | 94.0 | 10.8 |
| Hamburg town Erie Co. | 2.40 | 42.2 | 92.1 | 3.4 |
| Haverstraw town Rockland Co. | 2.96 | 37.1 | 94.0 | 27.1 |
| Hempstead town Nassau Co. | 3.03 | 40.0 | 93.3 | 21.2 |
| Hempstead village Nassau Co. | 3.45 | 32.5 | 97.1 | 39.2 |
| Henrietta town Monroe Co. | 2.51 | 30.7 | 110.7 | 9.7 |
| Hicksville CDP Nassau Co. | 3.09 | 41.4 | 96.2 | 26.9 |
| Huntington town Suffolk Co. | 2.89 | 42.5 | 96.9 | 13.5 |
| Huntington Station CDP Suffolk Co. | 3.26 | 35.4 | 104.4 | 27.3 |
| Irondequoit town and CDP Monroe Co. | 2.26 | 44.1 | 86.6 | 8.6 |
| Islip town Suffolk Co. | 3.20 | 37.6 | 97.2 | 19.3 |
| Ithaca city Tompkins Co. | 2.14 | 22.4 | 101.5 | 17.0 |
| Jamestown city Chautauqua Co. | 2.29 | 36.9 | 94.6 | 1.9 |
| Lancaster town Erie Co. | 2.47 | 41.7 | 93.8 | 2.5 |
| Levittown CDP Nassau Co. | 3.05 | 41.0 | 94.7 | 12.5 |
| Long Beach city Nassau Co. | 2.17 | 42.5 | 93.3 | 14.9 |

| Place | Average Household Size (persons) | Median Age (years) | Males per 100 Females | Foreign Born (%) |
|---|---|---|---|---|
| Mamaroneck town *Westchester Co.* | 2.65 | 40.7 | 93.9 | 20.1 |
| Manlius town *Onondaga Co.* | 2.40 | 44.9 | 91.2 | 6.5 |
| Monroe town *Orange Co.* | 3.86 | 21.8 | 103.2 | 11.5 |
| Mount Pleasant town *Westchester Co.* | 2.84 | 39.5 | 101.8 | 22.1 |
| Mount Vernon city *Westchester Co.* | 2.53 | 38.4 | 83.3 | 31.1 |
| New City CDP *Rockland Co.* | 2.96 | 44.1 | 96.4 | 16.5 |
| New Rochelle city *Westchester Co.* | 2.64 | 38.4 | 92.3 | 27.2 |
| New York city | 2.57 | 35.5 | 90.4 | 36.8 |
| Newburgh city *Orange Co.* | 3.09 | 28.2 | 94.6 | 25.0 |
| Newburgh town *Orange Co.* | 2.74 | 41.8 | 95.7 | 10.4 |
| Niagara Falls city *Niagara Co.* | 2.20 | 39.8 | 91.2 | 4.4 |
| North Hempstead town *Nassau Co.* | 2.87 | 42.4 | 94.5 | 27.3 |
| North Tonawanda city *Niagara Co.* | 2.24 | 42.4 | 95.3 | 3.8 |
| Oceanside CDP *Nassau Co.* | 2.84 | 43.5 | 92.8 | 11.9 |
| Orangetown town *Rockland Co.* | 2.59 | 42.4 | 92.3 | 16.2 |
| Orchard Park town *Erie Co.* | 2.51 | 44.4 | 92.1 | 4.2 |
| Ossining town *Westchester Co.* | 2.72 | 39.3 | 104.3 | 28.3 |
| Oyster Bay town *Nassau Co.* | 2.89 | 43.1 | 94.0 | 14.3 |
| Penfield town *Monroe Co.* | 2.44 | 44.7 | 93.0 | 8.4 |
| Perinton town *Monroe Co.* | 2.44 | 44.2 | 92.6 | 6.2 |
| Pittsford town *Monroe Co.* | 2.57 | 42.9 | 86.7 | 11.2 |
| Port Chester village *Westchester Co.* | 3.08 | 34.4 | 110.3 | 45.1 |
| Poughkeepsie town *Dutchess Co.* | 2.55 | 37.0 | 91.4 | 11.2 |
| Poughkeepsie city *Dutchess Co.* | 2.41 | 32.4 | 92.4 | 22.1 |
| Ramapo town *Rockland Co.* | 3.58 | 28.9 | 100.0 | 25.6 |
| Riverhead town *Suffolk Co.* | 2.52 | 44.1 | 99.0 | 12.7 |
| Rochester city *Monroe Co.* | 2.30 | 30.8 | 93.4 | 8.2 |
| Rome city *Oneida Co.* | 2.28 | 40.2 | 105.6 | 4.4 |
| Rotterdam town *Schenectady Co.* | 2.35 | 43.5 | 92.2 | 4.8 |
| Rye town *Westchester Co.* | 2.93 | 37.2 | 102.9 | 36.1 |
| Salina town *Onondaga Co.* | 2.23 | 41.9 | 90.4 | 5.3 |
| Schenectady city *Schenectady Co.* | 2.35 | 33.4 | 93.7 | 12.3 |
| Smithtown town *Suffolk Co.* | 2.89 | 42.7 | 94.8 | 6.8 |
| Southampton town *Suffolk Co.* | 2.59 | 41.9 | 104.6 | 16.6 |
| Spring Valley village *Rockland Co.* | 3.56 | 28.8 | 103.1 | 47.7 |
| Syracuse city *Onondaga Co.* | 2.31 | 29.6 | 91.0 | 10.3 |
| Tonawanda CDP *Erie Co.* | 2.22 | 44.4 | 89.1 | 5.6 |
| Tonawanda town *Erie Co.* | 2.21 | 43.3 | 88.8 | 4.9 |
| Troy city *Rensselaer Co.* | 2.22 | 30.2 | 102.1 | 8.7 |
| Union town *Broome Co.* | 2.21 | 41.8 | 92.3 | 5.3 |
| Utica city *Oneida Co.* | 2.38 | 34.8 | 92.6 | 14.8 |
| Valley Stream village *Nassau Co.* | 3.07 | 39.7 | 92.6 | 33.0 |
| Warwick town *Orange Co.* | 2.64 | 43.2 | 100.0 | 8.4 |
| Webster town *Monroe Co.* | 2.47 | 42.9 | 93.7 | 9.0 |
| West Babylon CDP *Suffolk Co.* | 2.93 | 40.0 | 91.8 | 12.1 |
| West Seneca CDP *Erie Co.* | 2.31 | 44.7 | 91.7 | 3.7 |
| West Seneca town and CDP *Erie Co.* | 2.31 | 44.7 | 91.7 | 3.7 |
| White Plains city *Westchester Co.* | 2.40 | 39.2 | 92.7 | 29.9 |
| Yonkers city *Westchester Co.* | 2.58 | 37.6 | 90.0 | 30.2 |
| Yorktown town *Westchester Co.* | 2.75 | 43.6 | 93.0 | 12.7 |

NOTE: Average Household Size, Median Age, and Males per 100 Females as of 2010. Foreign Born figures are 2006-2010 5-year estimates.

# Five Largest Ancestry Groups

| Place | Group 1 | Group 2 | Group 3 | Group 4 | Group 5 |
|---|---|---|---|---|---|
| **Albany** city *Albany Co.* | Irish (18.2%) | Italian (13.1%) | German (10.4%) | English (5.4%) | Polish (4.6%) |
| **Amherst** town *Erie Co.* | German (25.3%) | Italian (19.5%) | Irish (18.3%) | Polish (14.1%) | English (9.8%) |
| **Babylon** town *Suffolk Co.* | Italian (28.9%) | Irish (19.8%) | German (14.8%) | Polish (5.8%) | English (4.0%) |
| **Bethlehem** town *Albany Co.* | Irish (26.0%) | German (20.1%) | Italian (19.1%) | English (13.3%) | Polish (6.4%) |
| **Binghamton** city *Broome Co.* | Irish (22.5%) | German (16.3%) | Italian (13.3%) | English (9.7%) | Polish (4.9%) |
| **Brentwood** CDP *Suffolk Co.* | Italian (5.9%) | Irish (4.7%) | Haitian (3.9%) | German (3.6%) | English (1.6%) |
| **Brighton** town and CDP *Monroe Co.* | German (17.9%) | Irish (17.7%) | English (14.7%) | Italian (13.1%) | Polish (6.3%) |
| **Brookhaven** town *Suffolk Co.* | Italian (32.4%) | Irish (25.5%) | German (18.7%) | English (6.3%) | Polish (5.7%) |
| **Buffalo** city *Erie Co.* | German (13.4%) | Irish (12.8%) | Italian (11.5%) | Polish (10.6%) | English (4.2%) |
| **Carmel** town *Putnam Co.* | Italian (36.1%) | Irish (26.4%) | German (17.5%) | Polish (6.7%) | English (5.6%) |
| **Centereach** CDP *Suffolk Co.* | Italian (36.0%) | Irish (23.5%) | German (17.0%) | Polish (6.6%) | English (5.3%) |
| **Central Islip** CDP *Suffolk Co.* | Italian (6.6%) | Irish (6.5%) | German (4.9%) | Haitian (4.3%) | Polish (1.9%) |
| **Cheektowaga** town *Erie Co.* | Polish (35.4%) | German (29.4%) | Italian (16.5%) | Irish (15.0%) | English (5.4%) |
| **Cheektowaga** CDP *Erie Co.* | Polish (34.6%) | German (28.8%) | Italian (16.3%) | Irish (14.9%) | English (5.6%) |
| **Chili** town *Monroe Co.* | German (28.7%) | Italian (22.4%) | Irish (20.7%) | English (14.4%) | Polish (5.0%) |
| **Cicero** town *Onondaga Co.* | Irish (26.6%) | German (24.4%) | Italian (20.7%) | English (16.2%) | Polish (11.3%) |
| **Clarence** town *Erie Co.* | German (34.9%) | Italian (21.8%) | Irish (19.0%) | Polish (14.8%) | English (10.1%) |
| **Clarkstown** town *Rockland Co.* | Italian (20.1%) | Irish (19.0%) | German (9.3%) | Russian (6.4%) | Polish (5.0%) |
| **Clay** town *Onondaga Co.* | German (24.5%) | Irish (24.4%) | Italian (22.8%) | English (14.2%) | Polish (8.1%) |
| **Clifton Park** town *Saratoga Co.* | Irish (25.4%) | Italian (20.8%) | German (19.7%) | English (13.7%) | Polish (8.7%) |
| **Colonie** town *Albany Co.* | Irish (28.3%) | Italian (20.1%) | German (17.8%) | English (10.2%) | Polish (8.5%) |
| **Commack** CDP *Suffolk Co.* | Italian (36.7%) | Irish (21.2%) | German (17.1%) | Polish (9.0%) | Russian (7.1%) |
| **Coram** CDP *Suffolk Co.* | Italian (30.2%) | Irish (19.8%) | German (16.6%) | Polish (6.2%) | English (4.5%) |
| **Cortlandt** town *Westchester Co.* | Italian (26.9%) | Irish (21.5%) | German (12.1%) | Polish (5.8%) | English (5.2%) |
| **East Fishkill** town *Dutchess Co.* | Italian (34.8%) | Irish (30.3%) | German (17.1%) | English (8.5%) | Polish (5.6%) |
| **East Meadow** CDP *Nassau Co.* | Italian (24.3%) | Irish (16.9%) | German (10.2%) | Polish (6.7%) | Russian (4.2%) |
| **Eastchester** town *Westchester Co.* | Italian (34.3%) | Irish (21.1%) | German (12.5%) | English (7.2%) | Polish (3.2%) |
| **Elmira** city *Chemung Co.* | Irish (19.6%) | German (16.6%) | Italian (11.5%) | English (9.5%) | American (6.8%) |
| **Elmont** CDP *Nassau Co.* | Haitian (16.2%) | Italian (11.3%) | Jamaican (8.6%) | Irish (5.1%) | German (3.8%) |
| **Franklin Square** CDP *Nassau Co.* | Italian (45.5%) | Irish (15.9%) | German (10.7%) | Polish (4.3%) | Greek (2.7%) |
| **Freeport** village *Nassau Co.* | Italian (8.4%) | Irish (7.3%) | German (6.6%) | Jamaican (4.3%) | English (2.4%) |
| **Glenville** town *Schenectady Co.* | Irish (21.9%) | Italian (20.8%) | German (19.1%) | English (13.8%) | Polish (10.9%) |
| **Greece** town *Monroe Co.* | Italian (27.4%) | German (26.9%) | Irish (19.9%) | English (13.2%) | Polish (6.2%) |
| **Greenburgh** town *Westchester Co.* | Italian (18.6%) | Irish (13.0%) | German (8.6%) | Russian (5.8%) | Polish (5.3%) |
| **Guilderland** town *Albany Co.* | Irish (24.2%) | Italian (21.1%) | German (19.9%) | English (12.0%) | Polish (7.8%) |
| **Hamburg** town *Erie Co.* | German (34.6%) | Irish (27.7%) | Polish (23.3%) | Italian (18.0%) | English (9.3%) |
| **Haverstraw** town *Rockland Co.* | Italian (13.7%) | Irish (12.7%) | German (6.3%) | American (4.0%) | Haitian (3.3%) |
| **Hempstead** town *Nassau Co.* | Italian (21.8%) | Irish (16.7%) | German (10.4%) | Polish (4.7%) | Russian (3.5%) |
| **Hempstead** village *Nassau Co.* | Jamaican (5.3%) | Haitian (3.9%) | African (1.6%) | West Indian (1.5%) | Irish (1.2%) |
| **Henrietta** town *Monroe Co.* | German (22.3%) | Irish (19.7%) | Italian (15.6%) | English (14.2%) | Polish (6.5%) |
| **Hicksville** CDP *Nassau Co.* | Italian (23.3%) | Irish (18.3%) | German (11.3%) | Polish (5.7%) | English (3.1%) |
| **Huntington** town *Suffolk Co.* | Italian (27.7%) | Irish (22.6%) | German (16.7%) | Polish (6.5%) | English (6.4%) |
| **Huntington Station** CDP *Suffolk Co.* | Italian (20.8%) | Irish (17.0%) | German (13.1%) | English (5.1%) | Polish (3.8%) |
| **Irondequoit** town and CDP *Monroe Co.* | Italian (28.2%) | German (22.9%) | Irish (17.6%) | English (14.0%) | Polish (7.4%) |
| **Islip** town *Suffolk Co.* | Italian (25.3%) | Irish (20.6%) | German (14.5%) | Polish (4.5%) | English (4.2%) |
| **Ithaca** city *Tompkins Co.* | Irish (11.7%) | German (11.6%) | English (8.0%) | Italian (7.1%) | Polish (4.5%) |
| **Jamestown** city *Chautauqua Co.* | Italian (21.7%) | German (18.8%) | Swedish (18.6%) | Irish (14.9%) | English (14.1%) |
| **Lancaster** town *Erie Co.* | Polish (36.7%) | German (34.9%) | Italian (20.3%) | Irish (17.6%) | English (7.3%) |
| **Levittown** CDP *Nassau Co.* | Italian (32.6%) | Irish (27.8%) | German (17.2%) | Polish (5.0%) | English (3.9%) |
| **Long Beach** city *Nassau Co.* | Irish (22.8%) | Italian (17.8%) | German (9.1%) | Russian (7.0%) | Polish (5.7%) |

| Place | Group 1 | Group 2 | Group 3 | Group 4 | Group 5 |
|-------|---------|---------|---------|---------|---------|
| **Mamaroneck** town *Westchester Co.* | Italian (16.4%) | Irish (15.7%) | German (10.5%) | English (7.5%) | Russian (6.9%) |
| **Manlius** town *Onondaga Co.* | Irish (28.0%) | German (24.3%) | Italian (15.8%) | English (15.3%) | Polish (8.3%) |
| **Monroe** town *Orange Co.* | Hungarian (14.5%) | Italian (12.0%) | Irish (11.5%) | German (9.3%) | Romanian (6.3%) |
| **Mount Pleasant** town *Westchester Co.* | Italian (27.3%) | Irish (16.7%) | German (9.6%) | English (4.9%) | Polish (4.8%) |
| **Mount Vernon** city *Westchester Co.* | Jamaican (15.6%) | Italian (7.9%) | Irish (4.3%) | American (3.1%) | Brazilian (3.0%) |
| **New City** CDP *Rockland Co.* | Italian (19.7%) | Irish (17.3%) | Russian (8.9%) | German (8.8%) | American (7.3%) |
| **New Rochelle** city *Westchester Co.* | Italian (18.9%) | Irish (9.8%) | German (5.2%) | Russian (4.1%) | Polish (3.6%) |
| **New York** city | Italian (7.7%) | Irish (5.1%) | German (3.4%) | Russian (3.0%) | Polish (2.7%) |
| **Newburgh** city *Orange Co.* | Italian (7.7%) | Irish (6.0%) | American (5.7%) | German (3.9%) | English (2.1%) |
| **Newburgh** town *Orange Co.* | Italian (21.9%) | Irish (18.2%) | German (14.0%) | English (7.8%) | American (5.4%) |
| **Niagara Falls** city *Niagara Co.* | Italian (22.6%) | German (17.0%) | Irish (13.8%) | English (11.9%) | Polish (9.8%) |
| **North Hempstead** town *Nassau Co.* | Italian (18.0%) | Irish (12.2%) | German (8.2%) | Russian (6.6%) | Polish (6.0%) |
| **North Tonawanda** city *Niagara Co.* | German (35.0%) | Polish (20.5%) | Irish (17.9%) | Italian (17.4%) | English (10.3%) |
| **Oceanside** CDP *Nassau Co.* | Italian (29.3%) | Irish (19.5%) | German (11.0%) | Russian (8.1%) | Polish (6.8%) |
| **Orangetown** town *Rockland Co.* | Irish (31.4%) | Italian (19.5%) | German (10.2%) | English (5.8%) | Polish (4.0%) |
| **Orchard Park** town *Erie Co.* | German (32.3%) | Irish (24.8%) | Polish (20.9%) | Italian (18.2%) | English (10.2%) |
| **Ossining** town *Westchester Co.* | Italian (17.8%) | Irish (13.5%) | German (7.5%) | English (4.4%) | Polish (4.0%) |
| **Oyster Bay** town *Nassau Co.* | Italian (30.4%) | Irish (20.5%) | German (14.2%) | Polish (6.7%) | Russian (5.0%) |
| **Penfield** town *Monroe Co.* | German (25.8%) | Italian (24.3%) | Irish (18.9%) | English (16.3%) | Polish (7.9%) |
| **Perinton** town *Monroe Co.* | German (25.5%) | Italian (22.4%) | Irish (21.3%) | English (17.9%) | Polish (6.5%) |
| **Pittsford** town *Monroe Co.* | Irish (22.6%) | German (20.1%) | English (17.1%) | Italian (15.3%) | Polish (7.0%) |
| **Port Chester** village *Westchester Co.* | Italian (14.7%) | American (8.6%) | Irish (4.7%) | Polish (3.5%) | Brazilian (2.8%) |
| **Poughkeepsie** town *Dutchess Co.* | Italian (23.4%) | Irish (22.3%) | German (18.3%) | English (9.6%) | Polish (5.0%) |
| **Poughkeepsie** city *Dutchess Co.* | Italian (12.6%) | Irish (11.3%) | Jamaican (9.5%) | German (9.0%) | English (5.0%) |
| **Ramapo** town *Rockland Co.* | Polish (7.7%) | Haitian (7.3%) | European (7.2%) | Italian (7.1%) | Irish (6.6%) |
| **Riverhead** town *Suffolk Co.* | Irish (21.6%) | Italian (21.2%) | German (15.9%) | Polish (14.7%) | English (9.1%) |
| **Rochester** city *Monroe Co.* | German (10.8%) | Italian (9.3%) | Irish (9.2%) | English (6.4%) | African (2.7%) |
| **Rome** city *Oneida Co.* | Italian (24.6%) | Irish (18.4%) | German (17.5%) | English (11.1%) | Polish (7.9%) |
| **Rotterdam** town *Schenectady Co.* | Italian (32.2%) | Irish (20.0%) | German (17.8%) | Polish (11.0%) | English (8.9%) |
| **Rye** town *Westchester Co.* | Italian (18.7%) | American (8.8%) | Irish (6.9%) | German (4.7%) | Polish (4.1%) |
| **Salina** town *Onondaga Co.* | Italian (25.8%) | Irish (24.6%) | German (23.9%) | English (13.0%) | Polish (7.4%) |
| **Schenectady** city *Schenectady Co.* | Italian (15.1%) | Irish (13.2%) | German (10.5%) | English (6.1%) | Polish (6.1%) |
| **Smithtown** town *Suffolk Co.* | Italian (38.6%) | Irish (27.2%) | German (20.1%) | Polish (7.4%) | English (5.6%) |
| **Southampton** town *Suffolk Co.* | Irish (23.0%) | Italian (17.3%) | German (14.7%) | English (10.2%) | Polish (7.4%) |
| **Spring Valley** village *Rockland Co.* | Haitian (22.0%) | Polish (3.2%) | Jamaican (2.9%) | Hungarian (2.5%) | Russian (2.4%) |
| **Syracuse** city *Onondaga Co.* | Irish (15.5%) | Italian (12.8%) | German (11.8%) | English (7.0%) | Polish (5.0%) |
| **Tonawanda** CDP *Erie Co.* | German (33.0%) | Italian (24.4%) | Irish (20.5%) | Polish (15.4%) | English (10.4%) |
| **Tonawanda** town *Erie Co.* | German (32.5%) | Italian (25.9%) | Irish (21.2%) | Polish (15.5%) | English (9.8%) |
| **Troy** city *Rensselaer Co.* | Irish (24.8%) | Italian (13.3%) | German (12.8%) | French (9.7%) | English (8.0%) |
| **Union** town *Broome Co.* | Irish (21.9%) | German (18.8%) | Italian (17.2%) | English (12.6%) | Polish (8.2%) |
| **Utica** city *Oneida Co.* | Italian (22.9%) | Irish (15.2%) | German (11.9%) | Polish (8.7%) | Yugoslavian (5.2%) |
| **Valley Stream** village *Nassau Co.* | Italian (21.6%) | Irish (11.4%) | German (8.6%) | Haitian (4.7%) | Jamaican (3.4%) |
| **Warwick** town *Orange Co.* | Irish (31.2%) | German (22.2%) | Italian (21.3%) | Polish (8.9%) | English (6.8%) |
| **Webster** town *Monroe Co.* | German (26.6%) | Italian (25.7%) | Irish (16.1%) | English (15.6%) | Polish (8.0%) |
| **West Babylon** CDP *Suffolk Co.* | Italian (38.0%) | Irish (23.2%) | German (16.5%) | Polish (6.2%) | English (4.3%) |
| **West Seneca** CDP *Erie Co.* | German (31.0%) | Polish (29.6%) | Irish (25.1%) | Italian (18.5%) | English (7.1%) |
| **West Seneca** town and CDP *Erie Co.* | German (31.0%) | Polish (29.6%) | Irish (25.1%) | Italian (18.5%) | English (7.1%) |
| **White Plains** city *Westchester Co.* | Italian (16.3%) | Irish (10.1%) | German (5.9%) | American (4.9%) | Russian (4.1%) |
| **Yonkers** city *Westchester Co.* | Italian (16.5%) | Irish (11.4%) | German (4.4%) | Polish (2.8%) | American (2.6%) |
| **Yorktown** town *Westchester Co.* | Italian (33.1%) | Irish (22.5%) | German (12.0%) | Polish (5.4%) | Russian (5.2%) |

NOTE: Figures are 2006-2010 5-year estimates; "French" excludes Basque; Please refer to the Explanation of Data for more information.

## Marriage Status

| Place | Never Married (%) | Now Married (%) | Widowed (%) | Divorced (%) |
|---|---|---|---|---|
| **Albany** city *Albany Co.* | 56.0 | 29.5 | 6.0 | 8.4 |
| **Amherst** town *Erie Co.* | 32.0 | 51.9 | 7.8 | 8.3 |
| **Babylon** town *Suffolk Co.* | 32.7 | 52.8 | 6.8 | 7.7 |
| **Bethlehem** town *Albany Co.* | 26.5 | 61.5 | 5.9 | 6.0 |
| **Binghamton** city *Broome Co.* | 40.0 | 38.4 | 9.2 | 12.3 |
| **Brentwood** CDP *Suffolk Co.* | 41.3 | 47.0 | 5.5 | 6.3 |
| **Brighton** town and CDP *Monroe Co.* | 32.4 | 52.3 | 8.5 | 6.8 |
| **Brookhaven** town *Suffolk Co.* | 30.2 | 56.1 | 6.0 | 7.8 |
| **Buffalo** city *Erie Co.* | 48.9 | 32.4 | 7.3 | 11.4 |
| **Carmel** town *Putnam Co.* | 24.6 | 65.5 | 4.4 | 5.5 |
| **Centereach** CDP *Suffolk Co.* | 28.6 | 58.2 | 6.0 | 7.2 |
| **Central Islip** CDP *Suffolk Co.* | 40.3 | 46.4 | 4.9 | 8.4 |
| **Cheektowaga** town *Erie Co.* | 30.7 | 50.1 | 9.5 | 9.8 |
| **Cheektowaga** CDP *Erie Co.* | 31.2 | 49.6 | 9.4 | 9.7 |
| **Chili** town *Monroe Co.* | 28.0 | 58.1 | 6.1 | 7.8 |
| **Cicero** town *Onondaga Co.* | 24.7 | 59.5 | 5.1 | 10.7 |
| **Clarence** town *Erie Co.* | 23.3 | 63.9 | 6.6 | 6.3 |
| **Clarkstown** town *Rockland Co.* | 26.5 | 61.2 | 6.1 | 6.1 |
| **Clay** town *Onondaga Co.* | 29.6 | 55.3 | 5.3 | 9.8 |
| **Clifton Park** town *Saratoga Co.* | 22.8 | 64.2 | 4.5 | 8.5 |
| **Colonie** town *Albany Co.* | 33.0 | 51.6 | 6.5 | 8.9 |
| **Commack** CDP *Suffolk Co.* | 23.1 | 66.3 | 6.8 | 3.8 |
| **Coram** CDP *Suffolk Co.* | 28.4 | 53.5 | 6.4 | 11.6 |
| **Cortlandt** town *Westchester Co.* | 24.1 | 60.9 | 7.2 | 7.8 |
| **East Fishkill** town *Dutchess Co.* | 24.3 | 65.2 | 4.4 | 6.2 |
| **East Meadow** CDP *Nassau Co.* | 29.1 | 57.6 | 7.9 | 5.5 |
| **Eastchester** town *Westchester Co.* | 26.3 | 59.8 | 7.7 | 6.3 |
| **Elmira** city *Chemung Co.* | 40.9 | 39.4 | 8.0 | 11.7 |
| **Elmont** CDP *Nassau Co.* | 36.2 | 50.1 | 6.3 | 7.4 |
| **Franklin Square** CDP *Nassau Co.* | 27.0 | 57.6 | 9.0 | 6.3 |
| **Freeport** village *Nassau Co.* | 35.5 | 46.9 | 6.7 | 10.8 |
| **Glenville** town *Schenectady Co.* | 25.7 | 57.1 | 7.1 | 10.1 |
| **Greece** town *Monroe Co.* | 27.6 | 54.5 | 8.1 | 9.8 |
| **Greenburgh** town *Westchester Co.* | 28.6 | 56.5 | 7.2 | 7.7 |
| **Guilderland** town *Albany Co.* | 30.3 | 55.4 | 6.3 | 8.0 |
| **Hamburg** town *Erie Co.* | 26.6 | 56.5 | 6.8 | 10.1 |
| **Haverstraw** town *Rockland Co.* | 33.8 | 51.6 | 6.4 | 8.2 |
| **Hempstead** town *Nassau Co.* | 31.8 | 54.8 | 6.8 | 6.6 |
| **Hempstead** village *Nassau Co.* | 47.4 | 38.3 | 6.2 | 8.1 |
| **Henrietta** town *Monroe Co.* | 47.2 | 43.3 | 4.4 | 5.1 |
| **Hicksville** CDP *Nassau Co.* | 28.3 | 59.4 | 6.8 | 5.5 |
| **Huntington** town *Suffolk Co.* | 26.4 | 60.9 | 6.2 | 6.4 |
| **Huntington Station** CDP *Suffolk Co.* | 36.3 | 51.1 | 5.0 | 7.5 |
| **Irondequoit** town and CDP *Monroe Co.* | 29.2 | 52.9 | 7.9 | 10.0 |
| **Islip** town *Suffolk Co.* | 32.2 | 54.0 | 5.9 | 7.8 |
| **Ithaca** city *Tompkins Co.* | 73.6 | 18.1 | 2.7 | 5.6 |
| **Jamestown** city *Chautauqua Co.* | 34.9 | 46.2 | 6.7 | 12.2 |
| **Lancaster** town *Erie Co.* | 28.4 | 55.2 | 7.5 | 8.9 |
| **Levittown** CDP *Nassau Co.* | 29.4 | 57.4 | 7.1 | 6.1 |
| **Long Beach** city *Nassau Co.* | 36.5 | 45.7 | 8.1 | 9.7 |
| **Mamaroneck** town *Westchester Co.* | 24.9 | 62.7 | 5.8 | 6.6 |

| Place | Never Married (%) | Now Married (%) | Widowed (%) | Divorced (%) |
|---|---|---|---|---|
| **Manlius** town *Onondaga Co.* | 24.5 | 60.0 | 7.5 | 8.0 |
| **Monroe** town *Orange Co.* | 23.0 | 69.3 | 2.8 | 4.8 |
| **Mount Pleasant** town *Westchester Co.* | 31.6 | 56.8 | 4.7 | 6.9 |
| **Mount Vernon** city *Westchester Co.* | 41.7 | 41.8 | 7.3 | 9.2 |
| **New City** CDP *Rockland Co.* | 22.9 | 67.9 | 5.1 | 4.1 |
| **New Rochelle** city *Westchester Co.* | 37.7 | 47.5 | 7.1 | 7.8 |
| **New York** city | 42.6 | 43.6 | 6.0 | 7.8 |
| **Newburgh** city *Orange Co.* | 46.9 | 39.7 | 5.5 | 7.9 |
| **Newburgh** town *Orange Co.* | 25.9 | 57.4 | 6.6 | 10.0 |
| **Niagara Falls** city *Niagara Co.* | 37.7 | 40.4 | 8.4 | 13.4 |
| **North Hempstead** town *Nassau Co.* | 26.9 | 60.3 | 7.1 | 5.8 |
| **North Tonawanda** city *Niagara Co.* | 27.4 | 53.6 | 7.1 | 11.8 |
| **Oceanside** CDP *Nassau Co.* | 27.2 | 58.8 | 7.6 | 6.3 |
| **Orangetown** town *Rockland Co.* | 36.5 | 50.8 | 6.3 | 6.4 |
| **Orchard Park** town *Erie Co.* | 25.7 | 59.1 | 8.6 | 6.6 |
| **Ossining** town *Westchester Co.* | 31.5 | 53.7 | 6.9 | 7.9 |
| **Oyster Bay** town *Nassau Co.* | 25.8 | 61.3 | 7.5 | 5.4 |
| **Penfield** town *Monroe Co.* | 24.1 | 59.0 | 8.1 | 8.8 |
| **Perinton** town *Monroe Co.* | 21.5 | 62.2 | 6.3 | 9.9 |
| **Pittsford** town *Monroe Co.* | 27.0 | 62.0 | 4.5 | 6.5 |
| **Port Chester** village *Westchester Co.* | 37.7 | 48.4 | 6.2 | 7.7 |
| **Poughkeepsie** town *Dutchess Co.* | 39.4 | 47.7 | 6.0 | 6.9 |
| **Poughkeepsie** city *Dutchess Co.* | 44.0 | 39.8 | 6.6 | 9.6 |
| **Ramapo** town *Rockland Co.* | 30.5 | 57.7 | 5.9 | 5.8 |
| **Riverhead** town *Suffolk Co.* | 23.9 | 59.6 | 8.2 | 8.3 |
| **Rochester** city *Monroe Co.* | 51.4 | 31.1 | 5.9 | 11.6 |
| **Rome** city *Oneida Co.* | 33.3 | 45.4 | 8.8 | 12.5 |
| **Rotterdam** town *Schenectady Co.* | 26.0 | 55.5 | 8.6 | 9.8 |
| **Rye** town *Westchester Co.* | 32.8 | 53.1 | 7.0 | 7.1 |
| **Salina** town *Onondaga Co.* | 31.3 | 48.2 | 9.3 | 11.2 |
| **Schenectady** city *Schenectady Co.* | 43.1 | 37.9 | 8.2 | 10.8 |
| **Smithtown** town *Suffolk Co.* | 24.9 | 62.9 | 6.4 | 5.8 |
| **Southampton** town *Suffolk Co.* | 26.7 | 57.1 | 7.2 | 9.0 |
| **Spring Valley** village *Rockland Co.* | 37.5 | 51.6 | 4.0 | 7.0 |
| **Syracuse** city *Onondaga Co.* | 51.4 | 31.8 | 6.0 | 10.8 |
| **Tonawanda** CDP *Erie Co.* | 31.0 | 50.4 | 9.2 | 9.5 |
| **Tonawanda** town *Erie Co.* | 31.8 | 50.0 | 8.7 | 9.6 |
| **Troy** city *Rensselaer Co.* | 47.4 | 35.5 | 6.3 | 10.9 |
| **Union** town *Broome Co.* | 31.7 | 46.7 | 9.2 | 12.4 |
| **Utica** city *Oneida Co.* | 40.1 | 41.7 | 8.2 | 10.0 |
| **Valley Stream** village *Nassau Co.* | 32.4 | 54.9 | 5.7 | 7.0 |
| **Warwick** town *Orange Co.* | 25.6 | 59.0 | 6.4 | 9.1 |
| **Webster** town *Monroe Co.* | 24.3 | 61.1 | 6.9 | 7.8 |
| **West Babylon** CDP *Suffolk Co.* | 30.5 | 53.2 | 7.8 | 8.5 |
| **West Seneca** CDP *Erie Co.* | 27.1 | 54.8 | 9.3 | 8.8 |
| **West Seneca** town and CDP *Erie Co.* | 27.1 | 54.8 | 9.3 | 8.8 |
| **White Plains** city *Westchester Co.* | 34.5 | 49.1 | 7.0 | 9.3 |
| **Yonkers** city *Westchester Co.* | 35.8 | 48.6 | 7.5 | 8.1 |
| **Yorktown** town *Westchester Co.* | 22.5 | 64.7 | 6.7 | 6.0 |

NOTE: Figures are 2006-2010 5-year estimates.

## Employment and Building Permits Issued

| Place | Unemployment Rate (%) | Total Civilian Labor Force | Single-Family Building Permits | Multi-Family Building Permits |
|---|---|---|---|---|
| Albany city Albany Co. | 8.2 | 46,317 | 17 | 6 |
| Amherst town Erie Co. | 6.6 | 62,142 | 65 | 233 |
| Babylon town Suffolk Co. | 8.7 | 108,816 | 15 | 0 |
| Bethlehem town Albany Co. | 5.8 | 17,005 | 22 | 107 |
| Binghamton city Broome Co. | 9.4 | 20,590 | 0 | 0 |
| Brentwood CDP Suffolk Co. | n/a | n/a | n/a | n/a |
| Brighton town and CDP Monroe Co. | 5.6 | 18,290 | 56 | 0 |
| Brookhaven town Suffolk Co. | 8.0 | 254,842 | 208 | 0 |
| Buffalo city Erie Co. | 10.9 | 113,951 | 6 | 26 |
| Carmel town Putnam Co. | 7.0 | 18,307 | 7 | 101 |
| Centereach CDP Suffolk Co. | n/a | n/a | n/a | n/a |
| Central Islip CDP Suffolk Co. | n/a | n/a | n/a | n/a |
| Cheektowaga town Erie Co. | 9.3 | 46,920 | 2 | 0 |
| Cheektowaga CDP Erie Co. | n/a | n/a | n/a | n/a |
| Chili town Monroe Co. | 7.3 | 14,997 | 32 | 0 |
| Cicero town Onondaga Co. | 8.2 | 16,571 | 38 | 0 |
| Clarence town Erie Co. | n/a | n/a | 73 | 0 |
| Clarkstown town Rockland Co. | 6.7 | 45,785 | 25 | 0 |
| Clay town Onondaga Co. | 7.5 | 31,298 | 83 | 58 |
| Clifton Park town Saratoga Co. | 6.1 | 20,192 | 57 | 0 |
| Colonie town Albany Co. | 6.8 | 42,248 | 72 | 28 |
| Commack CDP Suffolk Co. | n/a | n/a | n/a | n/a |
| Coram CDP Suffolk Co. | n/a | n/a | n/a | n/a |
| Cortlandt town Westchester Co. | 6.5 | 21,422 | 6 | 92 |
| East Fishkill town Dutchess Co. | 7.4 | 15,052 | 53 | 0 |
| East Meadow CDP Nassau Co. | n/a | n/a | n/a | n/a |
| Eastchester town Westchester Co. | 6.2 | 15,828 | 0 | 0 |
| Elmira city Chemung Co. | 11.1 | 11,235 | 0 | 0 |
| Elmont CDP Nassau Co. | n/a | n/a | n/a | n/a |
| Franklin Square CDP Nassau Co. | n/a | n/a | n/a | n/a |
| Freeport village Nassau Co. | 9.4 | 21,937 | 1 | 2 |
| Glenville town Schenectady Co. | 7.1 | 14,354 | 18 | 5 |
| Greece town Monroe Co. | 8.0 | 49,208 | 75 | 70 |
| Greenburgh town Westchester Co. | 6.4 | 47,358 | 12 | 350 |
| Guilderland town Albany Co. | 6.0 | 19,046 | 36 | 0 |
| Hamburg town Erie Co. | 8.3 | 31,054 | 108 | 124 |
| Haverstraw town Rockland Co. | 10.2 | 18,641 | 2 | 0 |
| Hempstead town Nassau Co. | 7.6 | 382,210 | 72 | 215 |
| Hempstead village Nassau Co. | 10.9 | 25,983 | 1 | 232 |
| Henrietta town Monroe Co. | 7.5 | 22,438 | 100 | 0 |
| Hicksville CDP Nassau Co. | n/a | n/a | n/a | n/a |
| Huntington town Suffolk Co. | 7.2 | 105,069 | 40 | 0 |
| Huntington Station CDP Suffolk Co. | n/a | n/a | n/a | n/a |
| Irondequoit town and CDP Monroe Co. | 8.1 | 24,648 | 2 | 0 |
| Islip town Suffolk Co. | 8.5 | 174,736 | 47 | 32 |
| Ithaca city Tompkins Co. | 6.7 | 14,900 | 4 | 35 |
| Jamestown city Chautauqua Co. | 9.8 | 14,143 | 1 | 35 |
| Lancaster town Erie Co. | 7.8 | 23,407 | 102 | 0 |
| Levittown CDP Nassau Co. | n/a | n/a | n/a | n/a |
| Long Beach city Nassau Co. | 7.2 | 17,944 | 9 | 0 |

| Place | Unemployment Rate (%) | Total Civilian Labor Force | Single-Family Building Permits | Multi-Family Building Permits |
|---|---|---|---|---|
| **Mamaroneck** town *Westchester Co.* | 5.9 | 14,511 | 6 | 0 |
| **Manlius** town *Onondaga Co.* | 6.8 | 15,902 | 30 | 0 |
| **Monroe** town *Orange Co.* | 7.0 | 14,363 | 32 | 0 |
| **Mount Pleasant** town *Westchester Co.* | 7.1 | 20,908 | 8 | 0 |
| **Mount Vernon** city *Westchester Co.* | 9.3 | 32,668 | 4 | 2 |
| **New City** CDP *Rockland Co.* | n/a | n/a | n/a | n/a |
| **New Rochelle** city *Westchester Co.* | 9.5 | 38,710 | 20 | 201 |
| **New York** city | 10.1 | 3,968,110 | 264 | 8,672 |
| **Newburgh** city *Orange Co.* | 11.2 | 11,675 | 2 | 0 |
| **Newburgh** town *Orange Co.* | 8.6 | 15,629 | 26 | 4 |
| **Niagara Falls** city *Niagara Co.* | 12.6 | 22,946 | 8 | 52 |
| **North Hempstead** town *Nassau Co.* | 6.4 | 112,195 | 28 | 0 |
| **North Tonawanda** city *Niagara Co.* | 8.4 | 17,155 | 13 | 0 |
| **Oceanside** CDP *Nassau Co.* | n/a | n/a | n/a | n/a |
| **Orangetown** town *Rockland Co.* | 6.6 | 26,150 | 5 | 0 |
| **Orchard Park** town *Erie Co.* | 7.3 | 15,190 | 25 | 0 |
| **Ossining** town *Westchester Co.* | 7.1 | 18,432 | 4 | 0 |
| **Oyster Bay** town *Nassau Co.* | 6.6 | 148,644 | 72 | 0 |
| **Penfield** town *Monroe Co.* | 6.6 | 18,617 | 121 | 0 |
| **Perinton** town *Monroe Co.* | 6.1 | 24,861 | 22 | 0 |
| **Pittsford** town *Monroe Co.* | 5.7 | 14,141 | 33 | 0 |
| **Port Chester** village *Westchester Co.* | 7.3 | 14,662 | 1 | 2 |
| **Poughkeepsie** town *Dutchess Co.* | 8.1 | 21,283 | 10 | 0 |
| **Poughkeepsie** city *Dutchess Co.* | 8.7 | 14,394 | 4 | 12 |
| **Ramapo** town *Rockland Co.* | 6.5 | 55,462 | 6 | 170 |
| **Riverhead** town *Suffolk Co.* | 9.7 | 16,516 | 32 | 0 |
| **Rochester** city *Monroe Co.* | 10.8 | 93,136 | 46 | 160 |
| **Rome** city *Oneida Co.* | 9.2 | 14,240 | 2 | 18 |
| **Rotterdam** town *Schenectady Co.* | 8.0 | 14,367 | 21 | 0 |
| **Rye** town *Westchester Co.* | 6.9 | 23,154 | n/a | n/a |
| **Salina** town *Onondaga Co.* | 8.1 | 17,429 | 0 | 0 |
| **Schenectady** city *Schenectady Co.* | 9.7 | 30,548 | 7 | 0 |
| **Smithtown** town *Suffolk Co.* | 6.7 | 59,642 | 36 | 0 |
| **Southampton** town *Suffolk Co.* | 10.5 | 29,579 | 165 | 0 |
| **Spring Valley** village *Rockland Co.* | n/a | n/a | 1 | 10 |
| **Syracuse** city *Onondaga Co.* | 10.1 | 62,393 | 61 | 275 |
| **Tonawanda** CDP *Erie Co.* | n/a | n/a | n/a | n/a |
| **Tonawanda** town *Erie Co.* | 8.0 | 38,324 | 7 | 0 |
| **Troy** city *Rensselaer Co.* | 10.1 | 23,616 | 4 | 0 |
| **Union** town *Broome Co.* | 9.0 | 27,634 | 4 | 0 |
| **Utica** city *Oneida Co.* | 9.7 | 26,496 | 10 | 0 |
| **Valley Stream** village *Nassau Co.* | 7.3 | 19,287 | 1 | 0 |
| **Warwick** town *Orange Co.* | 7.5 | 15,717 | 11 | 0 |
| **Webster** town *Monroe Co.* | 6.4 | 22,171 | 38 | 78 |
| **West Babylon** CDP *Suffolk Co.* | n/a | n/a | n/a | n/a |
| **West Seneca** CDP *Erie Co.* | n/a | n/a | n/a | n/a |
| **West Seneca** town and CDP *Erie Co.* | 8.1 | 23,916 | 44 | 2 |
| **White Plains** city *Westchester Co.* | 6.5 | 29,397 | 9 | 4 |
| **Yonkers** city *Westchester Co.* | 8.9 | 89,804 | 7 | 102 |
| **Yorktown** town *Westchester Co.* | 6.8 | 18,792 | 4 | 0 |

*NOTE: Unemployment Rate and Civilian Labor Force as of February 2012; Building permit data covers 2011; n/a not available.*

## Employment by Occupation

| Place | Sales (%) | Professional (%) | Management (%) | Services (%) | Production (%) | Construction (%) |
|---|---|---|---|---|---|---|
| **Albany** city *Albany Co.* | 19.2 | 4.7 | 11.2 | 12.7 | 2.3 | 3.5 |
| **Amherst** town *Erie Co.* | 15.9 | 6.4 | 14.8 | 7.8 | 2.8 | 3.2 |
| **Babylon** town *Suffolk Co.* | 19.1 | 3.1 | 9.6 | 9.4 | 6.8 | 10.0 |
| **Bethlehem** town *Albany Co.* | 13.8 | 7.4 | 16.1 | 7.1 | 2.1 | 4.4 |
| **Binghamton** city *Broome Co.* | 15.9 | 4.1 | 6.8 | 13.6 | 5.2 | 5.9 |
| **Brentwood** CDP *Suffolk Co.* | 12.4 | 0.9 | 4.8 | 12.0 | 11.4 | 9.4 |
| **Brighton** town and CDP *Monroe Co.* | 11.0 | 10.8 | 15.4 | 6.2 | 2.6 | 2.5 |
| **Brookhaven** town *Suffolk Co.* | 18.7 | 4.4 | 10.9 | 8.3 | 5.7 | 9.7 |
| **Buffalo** city *Erie Co.* | 17.1 | 2.5 | 7.1 | 13.4 | 6.4 | 5.4 |
| **Carmel** town *Putnam Co.* | 17.0 | 4.9 | 14.4 | 6.2 | 3.9 | 9.1 |
| **Centereach** CDP *Suffolk Co.* | 20.4 | 3.6 | 11.1 | 7.5 | 6.8 | 8.8 |
| **Central Islip** CDP *Suffolk Co.* | 16.7 | 3.7 | 6.4 | 12.7 | 10.2 | 10.3 |
| **Cheektowaga** town *Erie Co.* | 21.0 | 3.4 | 8.0 | 10.5 | 5.7 | 6.9 |
| **Cheektowaga** CDP *Erie Co.* | 20.7 | 3.3 | 8.3 | 10.6 | 5.4 | 6.8 |
| **Chili** town *Monroe Co.* | 17.8 | 6.7 | 12.7 | 8.1 | 6.4 | 7.7 |
| **Cicero** town *Onondaga Co.* | 20.0 | 4.8 | 11.8 | 7.5 | 5.7 | 7.9 |
| **Clarence** town *Erie Co.* | 16.9 | 5.7 | 16.2 | 6.1 | 3.1 | 4.6 |
| **Clarkstown** town *Rockland Co.* | 14.1 | 4.1 | 15.6 | 6.7 | 3.3 | 5.5 |
| **Clay** town *Onondaga Co.* | 19.1 | 6.1 | 11.2 | 8.3 | 5.6 | 7.1 |
| **Clifton Park** town *Saratoga Co.* | 14.1 | 8.9 | 17.2 | 7.4 | 2.1 | 4.1 |
| **Colonie** town *Albany Co.* | 19.6 | 7.1 | 13.4 | 7.8 | 3.1 | 5.4 |
| **Commack** CDP *Suffolk Co.* | 16.2 | 4.6 | 19.0 | 5.3 | 2.8 | 6.0 |
| **Coram** CDP *Suffolk Co.* | 20.2 | 5.1 | 9.8 | 7.5 | 5.6 | 6.7 |
| **Cortlandt** town *Westchester Co.* | 15.1 | 5.5 | 18.3 | 7.0 | 3.6 | 8.5 |
| **East Fishkill** town *Dutchess Co.* | 14.6 | 6.5 | 14.9 | 6.9 | 6.3 | 11.4 |
| **East Meadow** CDP *Nassau Co.* | 20.5 | 4.2 | 13.2 | 5.8 | 3.8 | 7.8 |
| **Eastchester** town *Westchester Co.* | 16.8 | 3.8 | 22.6 | 3.8 | 2.8 | 5.2 |
| **Elmira** city *Chemung Co.* | 21.8 | 2.1 | 5.6 | 16.0 | 6.1 | 7.0 |
| **Elmont** CDP *Nassau Co.* | 17.8 | 2.4 | 7.1 | 13.0 | 5.8 | 7.2 |
| **Franklin Square** CDP *Nassau Co.* | 19.0 | 2.6 | 13.4 | 9.0 | 5.6 | 11.3 |
| **Freeport** village *Nassau Co.* | 17.2 | 2.2 | 9.8 | 12.6 | 6.8 | 9.1 |
| **Glenville** town *Schenectady Co.* | 16.3 | 6.8 | 13.5 | 7.3 | 3.5 | 5.8 |
| **Greece** town *Monroe Co.* | 18.4 | 5.7 | 10.9 | 9.0 | 6.1 | 7.1 |
| **Greenburgh** town *Westchester Co.* | 13.7 | 4.8 | 18.3 | 7.0 | 2.1 | 3.8 |
| **Guilderland** town *Albany Co.* | 15.8 | 9.1 | 16.4 | 6.2 | 2.8 | 5.5 |
| **Hamburg** town *Erie Co.* | 19.7 | 4.0 | 10.8 | 9.6 | 5.0 | 6.3 |
| **Haverstraw** town *Rockland Co.* | 19.1 | 3.3 | 7.9 | 10.8 | 6.7 | 7.7 |
| **Hempstead** town *Nassau Co.* | 17.1 | 3.1 | 12.9 | 8.8 | 4.6 | 7.5 |
| **Hempstead** village *Nassau Co.* | 14.7 | 2.0 | 5.5 | 18.2 | 7.6 | 11.0 |
| **Henrietta** town *Monroe Co.* | 17.0 | 10.4 | 10.3 | 7.7 | 5.3 | 5.5 |
| **Hicksville** CDP *Nassau Co.* | 18.1 | 5.3 | 14.0 | 7.8 | 5.5 | 7.4 |
| **Huntington** town *Suffolk Co.* | 15.3 | 4.4 | 18.6 | 5.9 | 3.5 | 6.7 |
| **Huntington Station** CDP *Suffolk Co.* | 18.1 | 3.3 | 9.9 | 10.3 | 5.6 | 10.4 |
| **Irondequoit** town and CDP *Monroe Co.* | 18.3 | 5.3 | 10.1 | 9.5 | 4.7 | 6.0 |
| **Islip** town *Suffolk Co.* | 17.1 | 3.3 | 10.0 | 8.9 | 7.8 | 9.4 |
| **Ithaca** city *Tompkins Co.* | 14.8 | 8.2 | 8.4 | 7.1 | 1.0 | 4.9 |
| **Jamestown** city *Chautauqua Co.* | 15.8 | 2.9 | 8.2 | 15.2 | 6.6 | 5.0 |
| **Lancaster** town *Erie Co.* | 17.6 | 5.5 | 12.3 | 9.0 | 5.3 | 7.2 |
| **Levittown** CDP *Nassau Co.* | 18.9 | 4.5 | 12.4 | 8.9 | 4.7 | 8.5 |

| Place | Sales (%) | Professional (%) | Management (%) | Services (%) | Production (%) | Construction (%) |
|---|---|---|---|---|---|---|
| Long Beach city Nassau Co. | 15.5 | 1.7 | 14.7 | 5.6 | 3.2 | 5.7 |
| Mamaroneck town Westchester Co. | 10.9 | 4.9 | 21.2 | 7.4 | 2.2 | 4.8 |
| Manlius town Onondaga Co. | 15.0 | 5.9 | 14.3 | 6.3 | 4.0 | 4.7 |
| Monroe town Orange Co. | 16.3 | 4.8 | 13.8 | 5.9 | 2.7 | 6.8 |
| Mount Pleasant town Westchester Co. | 15.7 | 4.8 | 16.2 | 9.4 | 3.0 | 6.7 |
| Mount Vernon city Westchester Co. | 16.2 | 2.9 | 10.2 | 14.9 | 3.6 | 9.0 |
| New City CDP Rockland Co. | 15.9 | 3.9 | 17.9 | 4.7 | 2.5 | 4.8 |
| New Rochelle city Westchester Co. | 14.8 | 3.3 | 13.8 | 10.9 | 1.9 | 9.4 |
| New York city | 15.7 | 3.2 | 11.4 | 12.4 | 3.8 | 6.4 |
| Newburgh city Orange Co. | 15.9 | 0.7 | 3.6 | 15.7 | 9.2 | 9.6 |
| Newburgh town Orange Co. | 18.9 | 4.3 | 14.4 | 8.3 | 6.2 | 8.3 |
| Niagara Falls city Niagara Co. | 20.3 | 2.4 | 7.7 | 16.7 | 7.2 | 7.1 |
| North Hempstead town Nassau Co. | 14.9 | 3.8 | 17.3 | 5.6 | 3.5 | 5.2 |
| North Tonawanda city Niagara Co. | 20.2 | 3.8 | 7.4 | 8.4 | 6.8 | 7.2 |
| Oceanside CDP Nassau Co. | 17.2 | 2.9 | 14.5 | 6.9 | 3.3 | 7.6 |
| Orangetown town Rockland Co. | 16.5 | 3.9 | 15.9 | 6.4 | 2.7 | 6.5 |
| Orchard Park town Erie Co. | 16.0 | 5.2 | 15.2 | 5.7 | 4.3 | 5.4 |
| Ossining town Westchester Co. | 15.5 | 4.8 | 14.3 | 9.8 | 3.2 | 9.2 |
| Oyster Bay town Nassau Co. | 18.0 | 4.6 | 17.4 | 5.7 | 3.7 | 5.9 |
| Penfield town Monroe Co. | 14.9 | 9.3 | 17.2 | 5.9 | 4.4 | 4.2 |
| Perinton town Monroe Co. | 15.3 | 8.0 | 17.6 | 6.5 | 3.3 | 3.9 |
| Pittsford town Monroe Co. | 11.5 | 7.6 | 22.1 | 5.4 | 2.1 | 3.0 |
| Port Chester village Westchester Co. | 11.2 | 1.9 | 8.5 | 16.1 | 5.5 | 12.2 |
| Poughkeepsie town Dutchess Co. | 18.2 | 7.4 | 10.7 | 9.6 | 4.5 | 6.7 |
| Poughkeepsie city Dutchess Co. | 14.3 | 3.4 | 8.4 | 18.0 | 4.4 | 9.2 |
| Ramapo town Rockland Co. | 14.0 | 4.7 | 11.6 | 10.7 | 4.0 | 8.1 |
| Riverhead town Suffolk Co. | 16.9 | 3.2 | 9.5 | 6.9 | 5.2 | 11.5 |
| Rochester city Monroe Co. | 16.9 | 4.1 | 6.7 | 13.2 | 6.6 | 5.8 |
| Rome city Oneida Co. | 17.1 | 2.3 | 8.0 | 11.7 | 5.0 | 6.5 |
| Rotterdam town Schenectady Co. | 20.6 | 4.6 | 10.7 | 8.4 | 5.6 | 7.9 |
| Rye town Westchester Co. | 11.7 | 2.8 | 11.7 | 13.0 | 4.0 | 10.6 |
| Salina town Onondaga Co. | 22.1 | 4.1 | 8.4 | 10.7 | 6.5 | 6.9 |
| Schenectady city Schenectady Co. | 19.2 | 4.1 | 8.5 | 14.4 | 4.1 | 6.0 |
| Smithtown town Suffolk Co. | 16.3 | 4.7 | 16.4 | 5.7 | 3.7 | 7.2 |
| Southampton town Suffolk Co. | 15.2 | 2.0 | 11.7 | 10.3 | 4.1 | 13.6 |
| Spring Valley village Rockland Co. | 12.2 | 1.9 | 4.2 | 22.9 | 5.3 | 9.2 |
| Syracuse city Onondaga Co. | 16.4 | 3.3 | 7.5 | 14.5 | 5.3 | 6.3 |
| Tonawanda CDP Erie Co. | 19.8 | 3.8 | 9.6 | 9.6 | 4.2 | 5.5 |
| Tonawanda town Erie Co. | 19.5 | 3.7 | 9.4 | 9.8 | 4.3 | 5.7 |
| Troy city Rensselaer Co. | 19.2 | 5.6 | 7.3 | 12.1 | 3.9 | 6.6 |
| Union town Broome Co. | 17.8 | 6.0 | 9.8 | 10.3 | 4.4 | 5.5 |
| Utica city Oneida Co. | 18.5 | 2.0 | 7.7 | 13.2 | 6.9 | 6.2 |
| Valley Stream village Nassau Co. | 15.9 | 3.0 | 12.1 | 9.5 | 5.0 | 8.3 |
| Warwick town Orange Co. | 15.0 | 4.3 | 14.2 | 8.7 | 5.6 | 11.9 |
| Webster town Monroe Co. | 17.0 | 7.5 | 12.9 | 7.4 | 5.0 | 5.9 |
| West Babylon CDP Suffolk Co. | 20.6 | 3.2 | 10.0 | 10.0 | 6.5 | 10.1 |
| West Seneca CDP Erie Co. | 19.6 | 4.1 | 8.1 | 9.5 | 5.0 | 7.7 |
| West Seneca town and CDP Erie Co. | 19.6 | 4.1 | 8.1 | 9.5 | 5.0 | 7.7 |
| White Plains city Westchester Co. | 13.1 | 5.2 | 16.8 | 11.9 | 2.4 | 5.6 |
| Yonkers city Westchester Co. | 17.3 | 3.2 | 10.9 | 10.6 | 4.5 | 8.8 |
| Yorktown town Westchester Co. | 16.9 | 6.0 | 16.3 | 7.0 | 4.0 | 7.8 |

NOTE: Figures are 2006-2010 5-year estimates.

## Educational Attainment

| Place | Percent of Population 25 Years and Over with: | | |
|---|---|---|---|
| | High School Diploma including Equivalency | Bachelor's Degree or Higher | Master's Degree or Higher |
| **Albany** city *Albany Co.* | 86.0 | 37.2 | 18.2 |
| **Amherst** town *Erie Co.* | 94.4 | 51.6 | 26.6 |
| **Babylon** town *Suffolk Co.* | 86.8 | 22.4 | 8.3 |
| **Bethlehem** town *Albany Co.* | 95.9 | 54.3 | 29.5 |
| **Binghamton** city *Broome Co.* | 83.5 | 23.0 | 11.4 |
| **Brentwood** CDP *Suffolk Co.* | 69.0 | 14.4 | 5.2 |
| **Brighton** town and CDP *Monroe Co.* | 94.0 | 62.2 | 33.0 |
| **Brookhaven** town *Suffolk Co.* | 90.4 | 29.4 | 13.6 |
| **Buffalo** city *Erie Co.* | 80.6 | 21.7 | 9.3 |
| **Carmel** town *Putnam Co.* | 93.4 | 39.7 | 16.7 |
| **Centereach** CDP *Suffolk Co.* | 89.7 | 27.4 | 10.7 |
| **Central Islip** CDP *Suffolk Co.* | 72.9 | 16.5 | 6.7 |
| **Cheektowaga** town *Erie Co.* | 86.8 | 18.1 | 6.1 |
| **Cheektowaga** CDP *Erie Co.* | 87.0 | 18.7 | 6.5 |
| **Chili** town *Monroe Co.* | 91.8 | 35.2 | 13.4 |
| **Cicero** town *Onondaga Co.* | 91.2 | 28.0 | 11.1 |
| **Clarence** town *Erie Co.* | 95.7 | 50.1 | 24.5 |
| **Clarkstown** town *Rockland Co.* | 91.9 | 49.4 | 23.2 |
| **Clay** town *Onondaga Co.* | 93.0 | 30.5 | 11.2 |
| **Clifton Park** town *Saratoga Co.* | 96.2 | 51.8 | 23.1 |
| **Colonie** town *Albany Co.* | 93.0 | 37.5 | 16.3 |
| **Commack** CDP *Suffolk Co.* | 95.9 | 45.3 | 20.0 |
| **Coram** CDP *Suffolk Co.* | 92.0 | 31.2 | 12.9 |
| **Cortlandt** town *Westchester Co.* | 91.3 | 43.4 | 20.3 |
| **East Fishkill** town *Dutchess Co.* | 93.4 | 39.8 | 17.4 |
| **East Meadow** CDP *Nassau Co.* | 89.6 | 33.3 | 14.8 |
| **Eastchester** town *Westchester Co.* | 94.7 | 58.6 | 27.5 |
| **Elmira** city *Chemung Co.* | 82.3 | 13.3 | 5.6 |
| **Elmont** CDP *Nassau Co.* | 85.1 | 29.0 | 9.3 |
| **Franklin Square** CDP *Nassau Co.* | 85.3 | 28.5 | 10.2 |
| **Freeport** village *Nassau Co.* | 78.2 | 25.1 | 10.7 |
| **Glenville** town *Schenectady Co.* | 95.8 | 34.9 | 16.0 |
| **Greece** town *Monroe Co.* | 90.0 | 25.2 | 10.1 |
| **Greenburgh** town *Westchester Co.* | 95.0 | 59.1 | 31.8 |
| **Guilderland** town *Albany Co.* | 94.3 | 46.7 | 23.1 |
| **Hamburg** town *Erie Co.* | 93.0 | 30.0 | 11.9 |
| **Haverstraw** town *Rockland Co.* | 79.7 | 28.4 | 11.1 |
| **Hempstead** town *Nassau Co.* | 88.3 | 36.3 | 15.7 |
| **Hempstead** village *Nassau Co.* | 68.4 | 16.7 | 6.2 |
| **Henrietta** town *Monroe Co.* | 92.4 | 34.6 | 12.5 |
| **Hicksville** CDP *Nassau Co.* | 89.5 | 33.5 | 12.9 |
| **Huntington** town *Suffolk Co.* | 93.0 | 47.5 | 21.7 |
| **Huntington Station** CDP *Suffolk Co.* | 81.0 | 29.5 | 11.6 |
| **Irondequoit** town and CDP *Monroe Co.* | 87.7 | 31.9 | 13.4 |
| **Islip** town *Suffolk Co.* | 85.2 | 25.5 | 10.8 |
| **Ithaca** city *Tompkins Co.* | 89.8 | 62.1 | 34.9 |
| **Jamestown** city *Chautauqua Co.* | 84.3 | 16.7 | 7.0 |
| **Lancaster** town *Erie Co.* | 91.3 | 29.7 | 11.3 |
| **Levittown** CDP *Nassau Co.* | 91.6 | 28.7 | 11.4 |
| **Long Beach** city *Nassau Co.* | 92.3 | 45.7 | 20.6 |

| Place | Percent of Population 25 Years and Over with: | | |
| --- | --- | --- | --- |
| | High School Diploma including Equivalency | Bachelor's Degree or Higher | Master's Degree or Higher |
| Mamaroneck town *Westchester Co.* | 93.9 | 65.6 | 38.3 |
| Manlius town *Onondaga Co.* | 96.0 | 52.6 | 26.0 |
| Monroe town *Orange Co.* | 81.9 | 30.3 | 12.7 |
| Mount Pleasant town *Westchester Co.* | 89.1 | 48.0 | 23.2 |
| Mount Vernon city *Westchester Co.* | 81.7 | 24.8 | 11.2 |
| New City CDP *Rockland Co.* | 94.6 | 54.6 | 27.3 |
| New Rochelle city *Westchester Co.* | 83.4 | 39.7 | 20.4 |
| New York city | 79.0 | 33.3 | 13.5 |
| Newburgh city *Orange Co.* | 67.2 | 12.3 | 4.6 |
| Newburgh town *Orange Co.* | 90.2 | 27.9 | 12.1 |
| Niagara Falls city *Niagara Co.* | 84.5 | 12.9 | 5.7 |
| North Hempstead town *Nassau Co.* | 90.2 | 51.5 | 25.1 |
| North Tonawanda city *Niagara Co.* | 89.6 | 20.0 | 8.5 |
| Oceanside CDP *Nassau Co.* | 92.5 | 42.0 | 19.6 |
| Orangetown town *Rockland Co.* | 92.4 | 46.8 | 21.4 |
| Orchard Park town *Erie Co.* | 94.1 | 44.1 | 20.2 |
| Ossining town *Westchester Co.* | 82.3 | 46.0 | 23.4 |
| Oyster Bay town *Nassau Co.* | 93.2 | 44.1 | 19.2 |
| Penfield town *Monroe Co.* | 93.6 | 47.9 | 21.4 |
| Perinton town *Monroe Co.* | 96.1 | 54.1 | 24.1 |
| Pittsford town *Monroe Co.* | 98.1 | 70.4 | 37.7 |
| Port Chester village *Westchester Co.* | 72.1 | 23.2 | 10.1 |
| Poughkeepsie town *Dutchess Co.* | 90.8 | 34.6 | 16.0 |
| Poughkeepsie city *Dutchess Co.* | 77.5 | 21.9 | 8.9 |
| Ramapo town *Rockland Co.* | 85.3 | 36.1 | 15.8 |
| Riverhead town *Suffolk Co.* | 88.8 | 29.5 | 16.2 |
| Rochester city *Monroe Co.* | 78.2 | 24.1 | 10.2 |
| Rome city *Oneida Co.* | 83.0 | 16.9 | 6.6 |
| Rotterdam town *Schenectady Co.* | 92.0 | 21.2 | 8.1 |
| Rye town *Westchester Co.* | 79.9 | 34.1 | 16.4 |
| Salina town *Onondaga Co.* | 89.9 | 24.5 | 9.7 |
| Schenectady city *Schenectady Co.* | 83.6 | 18.3 | 7.3 |
| Smithtown town *Suffolk Co.* | 95.4 | 42.5 | 19.0 |
| Southampton town *Suffolk Co.* | 88.5 | 39.8 | 17.5 |
| Spring Valley village *Rockland Co.* | 74.8 | 22.3 | 7.1 |
| Syracuse city *Onondaga Co.* | 80.6 | 25.6 | 11.1 |
| Tonawanda CDP *Erie Co.* | 91.6 | 29.8 | 11.6 |
| Tonawanda town *Erie Co.* | 91.9 | 30.5 | 11.7 |
| Troy city *Rensselaer Co.* | 83.4 | 21.5 | 9.4 |
| Union town *Broome Co.* | 88.4 | 26.7 | 11.7 |
| Utica city *Oneida Co.* | 80.4 | 16.4 | 6.0 |
| Valley Stream village *Nassau Co.* | 89.2 | 33.0 | 12.9 |
| Warwick town *Orange Co.* | 93.3 | 35.4 | 15.2 |
| Webster town *Monroe Co.* | 94.2 | 39.2 | 16.8 |
| West Babylon CDP *Suffolk Co.* | 88.1 | 22.6 | 8.6 |
| West Seneca CDP *Erie Co.* | 92.0 | 23.6 | 9.7 |
| West Seneca town and CDP *Erie Co.* | 92.0 | 23.6 | 9.7 |
| White Plains city *Westchester Co.* | 87.2 | 46.7 | 23.7 |
| Yonkers city *Westchester Co.* | 80.9 | 29.1 | 12.4 |
| Yorktown town *Westchester Co.* | 93.3 | 44.5 | 21.3 |

NOTE: Figures are 2006-2010 5-year estimates.

## Income and Poverty

| Place | Average Household Income ($) | Median Household Income ($) | Per Capita Income ($) | Households w/$100,000+ Income (%) | Poverty Rate[1] (%) |
|---|---|---|---|---|---|
| Albany city Albany Co. | 53,425 | 39,158 | 23,341 | 13.8 | 25.3 |
| Amherst town Erie Co. | 84,333 | 65,439 | 34,312 | 29.3 | 8.2 |
| Babylon town Suffolk Co. | 89,527 | 77,407 | 30,107 | 35.8 | 6.1 |
| Bethlehem town Albany Co. | 101,025 | 87,711 | 39,867 | 41.2 | 5.1 |
| Binghamton city Broome Co. | 46,513 | 30,702 | 21,455 | 9.3 | 27.8 |
| Brentwood CDP Suffolk Co. | 79,089 | 68,750 | 20,705 | 29.8 | 8.2 |
| Brighton town and CDP Monroe Co. | 83,702 | 61,381 | 37,610 | 25.7 | 9.5 |
| Brookhaven town Suffolk Co. | 96,849 | 81,937 | 33,324 | 39.0 | 6.5 |
| Buffalo city Erie Co. | 44,120 | 30,043 | 19,409 | 8.5 | 29.6 |
| Carmel town Putnam Co. | 114,496 | 98,226 | 39,060 | 48.8 | 3.4 |
| Centereach CDP Suffolk Co. | 101,826 | 90,930 | 33,008 | 44.2 | 4.5 |
| Central Islip CDP Suffolk Co. | 77,350 | 68,876 | 21,925 | 24.8 | 9.4 |
| Cheektowaga town Erie Co. | 53,966 | 45,893 | 23,918 | 10.0 | 8.9 |
| Cheektowaga CDP Erie Co. | 54,475 | 45,998 | 24,085 | 10.3 | 9.1 |
| Chili town Monroe Co. | 72,710 | 63,937 | 28,219 | 24.3 | 4.1 |
| Cicero town Onondaga Co. | 73,241 | 65,226 | 29,393 | 25.1 | 6.3 |
| Clarence town Erie Co. | 103,633 | 81,623 | 37,745 | 38.8 | 4.1 |
| Clarkstown town Rockland Co. | 119,415 | 99,005 | 42,042 | 49.5 | 5.0 |
| Clay town Onondaga Co. | 72,093 | 62,193 | 28,637 | 22.7 | 4.7 |
| Clifton Park town Saratoga Co. | 103,105 | 87,747 | 38,846 | 42.2 | 2.7 |
| Colonie town Albany Co. | 86,844 | 68,134 | 35,075 | 30.3 | 5.7 |
| Commack CDP Suffolk Co. | 126,686 | 107,512 | 40,773 | 55.1 | 1.9 |
| Coram CDP Suffolk Co. | 90,334 | 77,692 | 34,546 | 36.2 | 7.3 |
| Cortlandt town Westchester Co. | 120,267 | 92,342 | 42,815 | 45.3 | 4.8 |
| East Fishkill town Dutchess Co. | 116,119 | 97,297 | 37,928 | 48.2 | 3.9 |
| East Meadow CDP Nassau Co. | 101,556 | 89,176 | 33,772 | 43.7 | 2.4 |
| Eastchester town Westchester Co. | 164,549 | 100,518 | 66,589 | 50.4 | 3.8 |
| Elmira city Chemung Co. | 44,261 | 31,724 | 17,399 | 7.4 | 25.9 |
| Elmont CDP Nassau Co. | 90,111 | 80,356 | 25,961 | 38.3 | 5.4 |
| Franklin Square CDP Nassau Co. | 93,680 | 80,200 | 32,569 | 38.0 | 3.3 |
| Freeport village Nassau Co. | 86,662 | 69,081 | 29,930 | 32.6 | 11.3 |
| Glenville town Schenectady Co. | 77,759 | 68,066 | 31,363 | 29.0 | 5.0 |
| Greece town Monroe Co. | 64,661 | 53,894 | 26,439 | 18.1 | 7.5 |
| Greenburgh town Westchester Co. | 143,607 | 101,893 | 54,963 | 51.4 | 3.3 |
| Guilderland town Albany Co. | 92,769 | 76,741 | 38,039 | 35.9 | 5.5 |
| Hamburg town Erie Co. | 71,343 | 59,477 | 29,730 | 21.4 | 6.3 |
| Haverstraw town Rockland Co. | 86,759 | 66,633 | 30,080 | 32.4 | 10.9 |
| Hempstead town Nassau Co. | 109,854 | 89,722 | 36,416 | 44.7 | 5.3 |
| Hempstead village Nassau Co. | 64,221 | 53,333 | 20,713 | 20.3 | 14.8 |
| Henrietta town Monroe Co. | 67,241 | 58,750 | 22,778 | 20.2 | 11.2 |
| Hicksville CDP Nassau Co. | 103,560 | 85,397 | 34,431 | 44.3 | 4.7 |
| Huntington town Suffolk Co. | 136,356 | 102,782 | 46,862 | 52.3 | 4.4 |
| Huntington Station CDP Suffolk Co. | 90,035 | 74,667 | 30,052 | 34.5 | 11.3 |
| Irondequoit town and CDP Monroe Co. | 63,192 | 51,683 | 27,341 | 15.5 | 10.0 |
| Islip town Suffolk Co. | 97,067 | 82,160 | 30,893 | 38.7 | 5.5 |
| Ithaca city Tompkins Co. | 46,315 | 30,919 | 17,346 | 11.4 | 41.2 |
| Jamestown city Chautauqua Co. | 42,215 | 33,092 | 18,374 | 6.6 | 23.4 |
| Lancaster town Erie Co. | 72,141 | 63,314 | 28,005 | 25.5 | 7.2 |
| Levittown CDP Nassau Co. | 104,910 | 91,814 | 34,485 | 44.5 | 2.5 |
| Long Beach city Nassau Co. | 96,946 | 77,673 | 43,377 | 38.3 | 8.9 |

| Place | Average Household Income ($) | Median Household Income ($) | Per Capita Income ($) | Households w/$100,000+ Income (%) | Poverty Rate[1] (%) |
|---|---|---|---|---|---|
| Mamaroneck town *Westchester Co.* | 207,825 | 111,812 | 78,335 | 55.6 | 3.8 |
| Manlius town *Onondaga Co.* | 93,916 | 72,428 | 38,170 | 33.5 | 4.2 |
| Monroe town *Orange Co.* | 81,822 | 62,826 | 21,167 | 33.6 | 34.2 |
| Mount Pleasant town *Westchester Co.* | 148,184 | 102,938 | 48,825 | 51.8 | 5.5 |
| Mount Vernon city *Westchester Co.* | 68,091 | 49,862 | 27,611 | 20.0 | 12.8 |
| New City CDP *Rockland Co.* | 139,514 | 113,922 | 47,247 | 58.7 | 2.7 |
| New Rochelle city *Westchester Co.* | 108,529 | 65,317 | 40,787 | 33.5 | 10.7 |
| New York city | 77,897 | 50,285 | 30,498 | 22.8 | 19.1 |
| Newburgh city *Orange Co.* | 48,046 | 36,153 | 15,897 | 10.5 | 25.8 |
| Newburgh town *Orange Co.* | 91,468 | 77,027 | 33,906 | 35.5 | 6.0 |
| Niagara Falls city *Niagara Co.* | 43,578 | 31,452 | 19,720 | 7.7 | 21.8 |
| North Hempstead town *Nassau Co.* | 147,254 | 100,760 | 51,663 | 50.5 | 4.7 |
| North Tonawanda city *Niagara Co.* | 55,819 | 45,278 | 24,957 | 12.8 | 9.2 |
| Oceanside CDP *Nassau Co.* | 112,053 | 101,521 | 40,109 | 51.2 | 3.1 |
| Orangetown town *Rockland Co.* | 116,628 | 91,264 | 40,401 | 45.5 | 5.6 |
| Orchard Park town *Erie Co.* | 95,968 | 75,158 | 37,932 | 34.7 | 3.9 |
| Ossining town *Westchester Co.* | 125,865 | 85,749 | 43,721 | 44.2 | 12.3 |
| Oyster Bay town *Nassau Co.* | 136,353 | 104,453 | 46,598 | 52.0 | 3.2 |
| Penfield town *Monroe Co.* | 87,882 | 71,550 | 34,767 | 34.4 | 3.7 |
| Perinton town *Monroe Co.* | 93,429 | 74,497 | 38,306 | 36.5 | 4.9 |
| Pittsford town *Monroe Co.* | 143,505 | 102,355 | 50,484 | 51.0 | 3.9 |
| Port Chester village *Westchester Co.* | 73,895 | 52,758 | 26,744 | 20.1 | 16.0 |
| Poughkeepsie town *Dutchess Co.* | 80,922 | 66,793 | 29,442 | 29.2 | 8.9 |
| Poughkeepsie city *Dutchess Co.* | 54,723 | 38,406 | 23,192 | 13.6 | 23.9 |
| Ramapo town *Rockland Co.* | 94,544 | 68,819 | 27,345 | 34.7 | 18.6 |
| Riverhead town *Suffolk Co.* | 83,211 | 68,254 | 33,461 | 32.8 | 9.4 |
| Rochester city *Monroe Co.* | 42,129 | 30,138 | 17,865 | 7.4 | 30.4 |
| Rome city *Oneida Co.* | 52,507 | 42,779 | 21,989 | 10.0 | 15.3 |
| Rotterdam town *Schenectady Co.* | 67,415 | 59,664 | 28,557 | 20.3 | 4.7 |
| Rye town *Westchester Co.* | 109,772 | 67,083 | 39,563 | 31.9 | 11.6 |
| Salina town *Onondaga Co.* | 57,544 | 49,124 | 25,864 | 12.4 | 7.4 |
| Schenectady city *Schenectady Co.* | 48,630 | 37,607 | 19,810 | 9.2 | 20.6 |
| Smithtown town *Suffolk Co.* | 125,305 | 104,665 | 41,847 | 53.4 | 2.9 |
| Southampton town *Suffolk Co.* | 118,171 | 74,316 | 47,111 | 36.0 | 7.2 |
| Spring Valley village *Rockland Co.* | 60,887 | 48,125 | 18,033 | 15.1 | 21.0 |
| Syracuse city *Onondaga Co.* | 43,385 | 30,891 | 17,866 | 8.4 | 31.1 |
| Tonawanda CDP *Erie Co.* | 58,831 | 48,330 | 26,253 | 13.4 | 9.8 |
| Tonawanda town *Erie Co.* | 58,741 | 47,871 | 25,999 | 13.4 | 9.6 |
| Troy city *Rensselaer Co.* | 48,936 | 36,675 | 20,736 | 10.8 | 25.1 |
| Union town *Broome Co.* | 56,634 | 43,543 | 25,732 | 13.9 | 13.7 |
| Utica city *Oneida Co.* | 43,669 | 31,381 | 17,754 | 7.9 | 29.0 |
| Valley Stream village *Nassau Co.* | 94,369 | 82,279 | 30,608 | 39.5 | 4.5 |
| Warwick town *Orange Co.* | 100,122 | 84,104 | 38,033 | 39.4 | 3.8 |
| Webster town *Monroe Co.* | 80,707 | 66,727 | 32,270 | 26.8 | 4.8 |
| West Babylon CDP *Suffolk Co.* | 87,513 | 79,591 | 29,425 | 37.1 | 5.2 |
| West Seneca CDP *Erie Co.* | 63,052 | 52,301 | 26,728 | 17.2 | 6.3 |
| West Seneca town and CDP *Erie Co.* | 63,052 | 52,301 | 26,728 | 17.2 | 6.3 |
| White Plains city *Westchester Co.* | 105,025 | 73,522 | 43,938 | 36.4 | 8.9 |
| Yonkers city *Westchester Co.* | 74,571 | 55,715 | 29,191 | 24.5 | 13.8 |
| Yorktown town *Westchester Co.* | 122,674 | 101,612 | 44,667 | 51.2 | 1.7 |

NOTE: Figures are 2006-2010 5-year estimates.

## Taxes

| Place | Total City Taxes Per Capita ($) | City Property Taxes Per Capita ($) |
|---|---|---|
| **Albany** city *Albany Co.* | 612 | 530 |
| **Amherst** town *Erie Co.* | 684 | 634 |
| **Babylon** town *Suffolk Co.* | 481 | 419 |
| **Bethlehem** town *Albany Co.* | 362 | 304 |
| **Binghamton** city *Broome Co.* | 623 | 585 |
| **Brentwood** CDP *Suffolk Co.* | n/a | n/a |
| **Brighton** town and CDP *Monroe Co.* | n/a | n/a |
| **Brookhaven** town *Suffolk Co.* | 366 | 315 |
| **Buffalo** city *Erie Co.* | 588 | 519 |
| **Carmel** town *Putnam Co.* | 613 | 544 |
| **Centereach** CDP *Suffolk Co.* | n/a | n/a |
| **Central Islip** CDP *Suffolk Co.* | n/a | n/a |
| **Cheektowaga** town *Erie Co.* | 644 | 611 |
| **Cheektowaga** CDP *Erie Co.* | n/a | n/a |
| **Chili** town *Monroe Co.* | 305 | 257 |
| **Cicero** town *Onondaga Co.* | n/a | n/a |
| **Clarence** town *Erie Co.* | 401 | 344 |
| **Clarkstown** town *Rockland Co.* | 1,191 | 1,108 |
| **Clay** town *Onondaga Co.* | 310 | 276 |
| **Clifton Park** town *Saratoga Co.* | 130 | 79 |
| **Colonie** town *Albany Co.* | 335 | 295 |
| **Commack** CDP *Suffolk Co.* | n/a | n/a |
| **Coram** CDP *Suffolk Co.* | n/a | n/a |
| **Cortlandt** town *Westchester Co.* | n/a | n/a |
| **East Fishkill** town *Dutchess Co.* | n/a | n/a |
| **East Meadow** CDP *Nassau Co.* | n/a | n/a |
| **Eastchester** town *Westchester Co.* | n/a | n/a |
| **Elmira** city *Chemung Co.* | 398 | 358 |
| **Elmont** CDP *Nassau Co.* | n/a | n/a |
| **Franklin Square** CDP *Nassau Co.* | n/a | n/a |
| **Freeport** village *Nassau Co.* | 904 | 854 |
| **Glenville** town *Schenectady Co.* | n/a | n/a |
| **Greece** town *Monroe Co.* | 413 | 370 |
| **Greenburgh** town *Westchester Co.* | 657 | 581 |
| **Guilderland** town *Albany Co.* | 281 | 231 |
| **Hamburg** town *Erie Co.* | 448 | 406 |
| **Haverstraw** town *Rockland Co.* | 594 | 564 |
| **Hempstead** town *Nassau Co.* | 366 | 313 |
| **Hempstead** village *Nassau Co.* | 1,074 | 1,030 |
| **Henrietta** town *Monroe Co.* | n/a | n/a |
| **Hicksville** CDP *Nassau Co.* | n/a | n/a |
| **Huntington** town *Suffolk Co.* | 657 | 569 |
| **Huntington Station** CDP *Suffolk Co.* | n/a | n/a |
| **Irondequoit** town and CDP *Monroe Co.* | 419 | 385 |
| **Islip** town *Suffolk Co.* | 348 | 293 |
| **Ithaca** city *Tompkins Co.* | 1,030 | 568 |
| **Jamestown** city *Chautauqua Co.* | 456 | 431 |
| **Lancaster** town *Erie Co.* | 469 | 423 |
| **Levittown** CDP *Nassau Co.* | n/a | n/a |
| **Long Beach** city *Nassau Co.* | 995 | 819 |

| Place | Total City Taxes Per Capita ($) | City Property Taxes Per Capita ($) |
|---|---|---|
| Mamaroneck town *Westchester Co.* | n/a | n/a |
| Manlius town *Onondaga Co.* | n/a | n/a |
| Monroe town *Orange Co.* | n/a | n/a |
| Mount Pleasant town *Westchester Co.* | 760 | 666 |
| Mount Vernon city *Westchester Co.* | 992 | 614 |
| New City CDP *Rockland Co.* | n/a | n/a |
| New Rochelle city *Westchester Co.* | 1,063 | 620 |
| New York city | 4,372 | 1,758 |
| Newburgh city *Orange Co.* | 549 | 444 |
| Newburgh town *Orange Co.* | 596 | 520 |
| Niagara Falls city *Niagara Co.* | 711 | 522 |
| North Hempstead town *Nassau Co.* | 567 | 507 |
| North Tonawanda city *Niagara Co.* | n/a | n/a |
| Oceanside CDP *Nassau Co.* | n/a | n/a |
| Orangetown town *Rockland Co.* | n/a | n/a |
| Orchard Park town *Erie Co.* | n/a | n/a |
| Ossining town *Westchester Co.* | n/a | n/a |
| Oyster Bay town *Nassau Co.* | 677 | 605 |
| Penfield town *Monroe Co.* | n/a | n/a |
| Perinton town *Monroe Co.* | n/a | n/a |
| Pittsford town *Monroe Co.* | n/a | n/a |
| Port Chester village *Westchester Co.* | 856 | 801 |
| Poughkeepsie town *Dutchess Co.* | 539 | 482 |
| Poughkeepsie city *Dutchess Co.* | 655 | 592 |
| Ramapo town *Rockland Co.* | 513 | 482 |
| Riverhead town *Suffolk Co.* | 1,334 | 1,178 |
| Rochester city *Monroe Co.* | 805 | 735 |
| Rome city *Oneida Co.* | 698 | 413 |
| Rotterdam town *Schenectady Co.* | 438 | 395 |
| Rye town *Westchester Co.* | 56 | 35 |
| Salina town *Onondaga Co.* | 356 | 322 |
| Schenectady city *Schenectady Co.* | 526 | 467 |
| Smithtown town *Suffolk Co.* | 533 | 447 |
| Southampton town *Suffolk Co.* | 1,665 | 918 |
| Spring Valley village *Rockland Co.* | n/a | n/a |
| Syracuse city *Onondaga Co.* | 631 | 582 |
| Tonawanda CDP *Erie Co.* | n/a | n/a |
| Tonawanda town *Erie Co.* | 510 | 475 |
| Troy city *Rensselaer Co.* | 442 | 375 |
| Union town *Broome Co.* | 171 | 155 |
| Utica city *Oneida Co.* | 576 | 338 |
| Valley Stream village *Nassau Co.* | n/a | n/a |
| Warwick town *Orange Co.* | 314 | 266 |
| Webster town *Monroe Co.* | n/a | n/a |
| West Babylon CDP *Suffolk Co.* | n/a | n/a |
| West Seneca CDP *Erie Co.* | n/a | n/a |
| West Seneca town and CDP *Erie Co.* | 637 | 609 |
| White Plains city *Westchester Co.* | 1,663 | 741 |
| Yonkers city *Westchester Co.* | 1,842 | 1,259 |
| Yorktown town *Westchester Co.* | n/a | n/a |

NOTE: Data as of 2009.

## Housing

| Place | Homeownership Rate (%) | Median Home Value ($) | Median Year Structure Built | Median Rent ($/month) |
|---|---|---|---|---|
| **Albany** city *Albany Co.* | 36.6 | 177,200 | before 1940 | 681 |
| **Amherst** town *Erie Co.* | 71.4 | 162,600 | 1969 | 731 |
| **Babylon** town *Suffolk Co.* | 74.2 | 387,800 | 1959 | 1,269 |
| **Bethlehem** town *Albany Co.* | 75.0 | 262,200 | 1972 | 885 |
| **Binghamton** city *Broome Co.* | 42.5 | 82,600 | before 1940 | 467 |
| **Brentwood** CDP *Suffolk Co.* | 69.6 | 343,300 | 1964 | 1,137 |
| **Brighton** town and CDP *Monroe Co.* | 56.7 | 165,300 | 1961 | 797 |
| **Brookhaven** town *Suffolk Co.* | 78.8 | 371,300 | 1973 | 1,313 |
| **Buffalo** city *Erie Co.* | 40.7 | 65,700 | before 1940 | 464 |
| **Carmel** town *Putnam Co.* | 82.8 | 459,200 | 1969 | 1,141 |
| **Centereach** CDP *Suffolk Co.* | 84.3 | 376,600 | 1967 | 1,549 |
| **Central Islip** CDP *Suffolk Co.* | 68.9 | 327,000 | 1969 | 1,277 |
| **Cheektowaga** town *Erie Co.* | 71.5 | 93,200 | 1959 | 591 |
| **Cheektowaga** CDP *Erie Co.* | 70.8 | 94,000 | 1959 | 589 |
| **Chili** town *Monroe Co.* | 78.1 | 135,100 | 1976 | 701 |
| **Cicero** town *Onondaga Co.* | 81.0 | 141,200 | 1975 | 584 |
| **Clarence** town *Erie Co.* | 84.9 | 222,800 | 1979 | 748 |
| **Clarkstown** town *Rockland Co.* | 79.5 | 501,500 | 1970 | 1,309 |
| **Clay** town *Onondaga Co.* | 74.3 | 131,200 | 1975 | 689 |
| **Clifton Park** town *Saratoga Co.* | 82.2 | 274,400 | 1979 | 881 |
| **Colonie** town *Albany Co.* | 71.1 | 210,700 | 1965 | 782 |
| **Commack** CDP *Suffolk Co.* | 91.2 | 524,200 | 1963 | 1,641 |
| **Coram** CDP *Suffolk Co.* | 67.9 | 346,500 | 1978 | 1,348 |
| **Cortlandt** town *Westchester Co.* | 76.9 | 456,600 | 1960 | 1,108 |
| **East Fishkill** town *Dutchess Co.* | 90.1 | 391,200 | 1977 | 885 |
| **East Meadow** CDP *Nassau Co.* | 86.3 | 444,400 | 1956 | 1,120 |
| **Eastchester** town *Westchester Co.* | 73.1 | 598,900 | 1951 | 1,310 |
| **Elmira** city *Chemung Co.* | 48.0 | 65,300 | before 1940 | 465 |
| **Elmont** CDP *Nassau Co.* | 72.3 | 420,000 | 1952 | 1,233 |
| **Franklin Square** CDP *Nassau Co.* | 81.0 | 464,100 | 1952 | 1,103 |
| **Freeport** village *Nassau Co.* | 67.0 | 382,100 | 1952 | 1,111 |
| **Glenville** town *Schenectady Co.* | 78.4 | 179,800 | 1957 | 696 |
| **Greece** town *Monroe Co.* | 73.3 | 123,700 | 1969 | 699 |
| **Greenburgh** town *Westchester Co.* | 72.7 | 584,600 | 1957 | 1,331 |
| **Guilderland** town *Albany Co.* | 67.9 | 235,100 | 1973 | 875 |
| **Hamburg** town *Erie Co.* | 75.4 | 133,300 | 1964 | 567 |
| **Haverstraw** town *Rockland Co.* | 62.5 | 372,600 | 1971 | 1,092 |
| **Hempstead** town *Nassau Co.* | 80.0 | 456,700 | 1952 | 1,221 |
| **Hempstead** village *Nassau Co.* | 42.1 | 365,000 | 1952 | 1,087 |
| **Henrietta** town *Monroe Co.* | 68.5 | 131,500 | 1969 | 732 |
| **Hicksville** CDP *Nassau Co.* | 84.8 | 438,300 | 1954 | 1,324 |
| **Huntington** town *Suffolk Co.* | 83.9 | 573,300 | 1961 | 1,269 |
| **Huntington Station** CDP *Suffolk Co.* | 69.5 | 419,100 | 1957 | 1,219 |
| **Irondequoit** town and CDP *Monroe Co.* | 78.1 | 111,800 | 1954 | 675 |
| **Islip** town *Suffolk Co.* | 76.4 | 395,500 | 1965 | 1,313 |
| **Ithaca** city *Tompkins Co.* | 26.4 | 171,400 | before 1940 | 743 |
| **Jamestown** city *Chautauqua Co.* | 49.2 | 63,500 | before 1940 | 402 |
| **Lancaster** town *Erie Co.* | 77.1 | 150,200 | 1967 | 542 |
| **Levittown** CDP *Nassau Co.* | 89.7 | 400,300 | 1952 | 1,524 |
| **Long Beach** city *Nassau Co.* | 55.7 | 523,900 | 1956 | 1,473 |

| Place | Homeownership Rate (%) | Median Home Value ($) | Median Year Structure Built | Median Rent ($/month) |
|---|---|---|---|---|
| Mamaroneck town Westchester Co. | 68.8 | 798,600 | 1945 | 1,375 |
| Manlius town Onondaga Co. | 78.2 | 169,900 | 1970 | 713 |
| Monroe town Orange Co. | 62.5 | 365,500 | 1983 | 874 |
| Mount Pleasant town Westchester Co. | 70.5 | 657,200 | 1953 | 1,236 |
| Mount Vernon city Westchester Co. | 38.1 | 428,400 | 1945 | 982 |
| New City CDP Rockland Co. | 89.5 | 558,100 | 1968 | 1,202 |
| New Rochelle city Westchester Co. | 51.2 | 605,500 | 1947 | 1,097 |
| New York city | 31.0 | 513,900 | 1947 | 960 |
| Newburgh city Orange Co. | 31.8 | 219,100 | before 1940 | 799 |
| Newburgh town Orange Co. | 83.9 | 304,300 | 1968 | 955 |
| Niagara Falls city Niagara Co. | 55.1 | 65,400 | 1941 | 427 |
| North Hempstead town Nassau Co. | 78.1 | 659,200 | 1953 | 1,378 |
| North Tonawanda city Niagara Co. | 66.8 | 95,000 | 1952 | 494 |
| Oceanside CDP Nassau Co. | 88.0 | 476,900 | 1955 | 1,301 |
| Orangetown town Rockland Co. | 72.1 | 528,800 | 1959 | 1,199 |
| Orchard Park town Erie Co. | 76.3 | 187,300 | 1972 | 761 |
| Ossining town Westchester Co. | 64.2 | 483,500 | 1958 | 1,185 |
| Oyster Bay town Nassau Co. | 86.9 | 517,100 | 1956 | 1,426 |
| Penfield town Monroe Co. | 82.4 | 172,300 | 1975 | 762 |
| Perinton town Monroe Co. | 79.7 | 183,100 | 1973 | 789 |
| Pittsford town Monroe Co. | 85.3 | 246,900 | 1969 | 917 |
| Port Chester village Westchester Co. | 43.2 | 472,900 | 1952 | 1,181 |
| Poughkeepsie town Dutchess Co. | 69.4 | 285,400 | 1964 | 960 |
| Poughkeepsie city Dutchess Co. | 37.3 | 263,100 | 1944 | 795 |
| Ramapo town Rockland Co. | 59.8 | 468,500 | 1971 | 1,031 |
| Riverhead town Suffolk Co. | 77.5 | 382,000 | 1979 | 1,033 |
| Rochester city Monroe Co. | 37.6 | 73,600 | before 1940 | 583 |
| Rome city Oneida Co. | 57.4 | 85,200 | 1951 | 456 |
| Rotterdam town Schenectady Co. | 79.3 | 161,500 | 1956 | 602 |
| Rye town Westchester Co. | 55.5 | 572,300 | 1955 | 1,237 |
| Salina town Onondaga Co. | 66.9 | 99,500 | 1958 | 666 |
| Schenectady city Schenectady Co. | 43.8 | 109,500 | before 1940 | 612 |
| Smithtown town Suffolk Co. | 87.3 | 511,400 | 1966 | 1,273 |
| Southampton town Suffolk Co. | 73.1 | 646,800 | 1972 | 1,359 |
| Spring Valley village Rockland Co. | 28.7 | 301,500 | 1971 | 1,004 |
| Syracuse city Onondaga Co. | 38.6 | 83,400 | before 1940 | 539 |
| Tonawanda CDP Erie Co. | 74.2 | 108,100 | 1954 | 573 |
| Tonawanda town Erie Co. | 72.6 | 106,300 | 1953 | 558 |
| Troy city Rensselaer Co. | 38.1 | 134,500 | before 1940 | 586 |
| Union town Broome Co. | 60.3 | 96,500 | 1953 | 525 |
| Utica city Oneida Co. | 47.6 | 85,300 | before 1940 | 456 |
| Valley Stream village Nassau Co. | 79.2 | 429,900 | 1949 | 1,205 |
| Warwick town Orange Co. | 79.0 | 343,200 | 1967 | 912 |
| Webster town Monroe Co. | 76.8 | 166,500 | 1978 | 756 |
| West Babylon CDP Suffolk Co. | 73.2 | 378,800 | 1961 | 1,357 |
| West Seneca CDP Erie Co. | 76.2 | 122,900 | 1963 | 570 |
| West Seneca town and CDP Erie Co. | 76.2 | 122,900 | 1963 | 570 |
| White Plains city Westchester Co. | 53.8 | 510,400 | 1956 | 1,156 |
| Yonkers city Westchester Co. | 46.2 | 428,900 | 1953 | 966 |
| Yorktown town Westchester Co. | 84.5 | 480,300 | 1967 | 1,135 |

NOTE: Homeownership Rate as of 2010; Median Rent, Median Home Value, and Median Age of Housing are 2006-2010 5-year estimates.

## Commute to Work

| Place | Automobile (%) | Public Transportation (%) | Walk (%) | Work from Home (%) |
|---|---|---|---|---|
| **Albany** city *Albany Co.* | 69.9 | 12.9 | 11.0 | 3.7 |
| **Amherst** town *Erie Co.* | 91.7 | 2.3 | 1.9 | 3.4 |
| **Babylon** town *Suffolk Co.* | 85.2 | 9.0 | 1.3 | 3.2 |
| **Bethlehem** town *Albany Co.* | 91.4 | 1.8 | 1.3 | 4.1 |
| **Binghamton** city *Broome Co.* | 81.4 | 6.5 | 5.3 | 2.9 |
| **Brentwood** CDP *Suffolk Co.* | 86.7 | 6.5 | 1.2 | 2.0 |
| **Brighton** town and CDP *Monroe Co.* | 88.3 | 2.5 | 1.5 | 5.4 |
| **Brookhaven** town *Suffolk Co.* | 91.3 | 3.9 | 1.4 | 2.7 |
| **Buffalo** city *Erie Co.* | 76.3 | 13.2 | 6.2 | 2.6 |
| **Carmel** town *Putnam Co.* | 89.7 | 4.8 | 1.2 | 3.7 |
| **Centereach** CDP *Suffolk Co.* | 93.3 | 3.1 | 0.9 | 1.9 |
| **Central Islip** CDP *Suffolk Co.* | 89.9 | 4.4 | 1.0 | 1.2 |
| **Cheektowaga** town *Erie Co.* | 94.7 | 1.3 | 1.8 | 1.6 |
| **Cheektowaga** CDP *Erie Co.* | 94.5 | 1.4 | 1.7 | 1.7 |
| **Chili** town *Monroe Co.* | 94.1 | 0.8 | 2.0 | 2.4 |
| **Cicero** town *Onondaga Co.* | 94.8 | 0.2 | 0.7 | 3.4 |
| **Clarence** town *Erie Co.* | 92.8 | 0.4 | 1.1 | 4.9 |
| **Clarkstown** town *Rockland Co.* | 86.6 | 7.3 | 1.4 | 3.8 |
| **Clay** town *Onondaga Co.* | 94.1 | 1.2 | 1.2 | 2.5 |
| **Clifton Park** town *Saratoga Co.* | 93.2 | 0.6 | 0.7 | 4.6 |
| **Colonie** town *Albany Co.* | 91.9 | 1.4 | 1.6 | 3.9 |
| **Commack** CDP *Suffolk Co.* | 88.6 | 6.4 | 0.9 | 4.1 |
| **Coram** CDP *Suffolk Co.* | 92.6 | 4.2 | 0.5 | 1.8 |
| **Cortlandt** town *Westchester Co.* | 77.4 | 16.6 | 1.1 | 3.9 |
| **East Fishkill** town *Dutchess Co.* | 90.8 | 2.9 | 0.5 | 4.9 |
| **East Meadow** CDP *Nassau Co.* | 83.8 | 10.3 | 1.9 | 3.2 |
| **Eastchester** town *Westchester Co.* | 63.7 | 25.6 | 4.2 | 6.1 |
| **Elmira** city *Chemung Co.* | 84.3 | 1.8 | 7.8 | 4.5 |
| **Elmont** CDP *Nassau Co.* | 75.2 | 18.1 | 2.8 | 1.8 |
| **Franklin Square** CDP *Nassau Co.* | 83.6 | 12.3 | 2.0 | 1.7 |
| **Freeport** village *Nassau Co.* | 75.2 | 17.0 | 4.7 | 1.4 |
| **Glenville** town *Schenectady Co.* | 95.9 | 0.2 | 1.2 | 1.9 |
| **Greece** town *Monroe Co.* | 95.0 | 0.4 | 1.1 | 2.5 |
| **Greenburgh** town *Westchester Co.* | 68.1 | 20.5 | 3.3 | 6.6 |
| **Guilderland** town *Albany Co.* | 92.4 | 1.9 | 1.6 | 3.5 |
| **Hamburg** town *Erie Co.* | 94.7 | 1.1 | 1.4 | 1.9 |
| **Haverstraw** town *Rockland Co.* | 85.1 | 9.2 | 2.1 | 2.3 |
| **Hempstead** town *Nassau Co.* | 77.0 | 16.3 | 2.7 | 2.8 |
| **Hempstead** village *Nassau Co.* | 66.2 | 23.4 | 5.3 | 1.5 |
| **Henrietta** town *Monroe Co.* | 86.3 | 1.0 | 8.5 | 2.2 |
| **Hicksville** CDP *Nassau Co.* | 81.2 | 12.5 | 1.5 | 3.4 |
| **Huntington** town *Suffolk Co.* | 82.2 | 9.8 | 1.4 | 5.8 |
| **Huntington Station** CDP *Suffolk Co.* | 82.9 | 9.0 | 2.5 | 4.4 |
| **Irondequoit** town and CDP *Monroe Co.* | 92.7 | 1.8 | 1.9 | 3.1 |
| **Islip** town *Suffolk Co.* | 88.7 | 5.8 | 1.1 | 2.7 |
| **Ithaca** city *Tompkins Co.* | 38.4 | 11.8 | 40.1 | 7.1 |
| **Jamestown** city *Chautauqua Co.* | 86.1 | 0.2 | 9.1 | 2.3 |
| **Lancaster** town *Erie Co.* | 94.5 | 0.4 | 2.0 | 1.8 |
| **Levittown** CDP *Nassau Co.* | 87.4 | 8.9 | 0.6 | 2.4 |
| **Long Beach** city *Nassau Co.* | 69.2 | 19.9 | 4.9 | 4.6 |

| Place | Automobile (%) | Public Transportation (%) | Walk (%) | Work from Home (%) |
|---|---|---|---|---|
| Mamaroneck town *Westchester Co.* | 55.2 | 31.0 | 4.3 | 7.1 |
| Manlius town *Onondaga Co.* | 92.0 | 0.5 | 2.1 | 3.9 |
| Monroe town *Orange Co.* | 74.9 | 11.3 | 8.1 | 3.6 |
| Mount Pleasant town *Westchester Co.* | 72.4 | 17.7 | 5.2 | 3.8 |
| Mount Vernon city *Westchester Co.* | 65.0 | 21.1 | 8.0 | 2.6 |
| New City CDP *Rockland Co.* | 85.6 | 7.8 | 1.2 | 4.7 |
| New Rochelle city *Westchester Co.* | 62.7 | 19.3 | 9.1 | 6.3 |
| New York city | 28.4 | 55.2 | 10.2 | 3.8 |
| Newburgh city *Orange Co.* | 74.4 | 4.2 | 8.7 | 2.9 |
| Newburgh town *Orange Co.* | 89.7 | 5.5 | 0.7 | 2.9 |
| Niagara Falls city *Niagara Co.* | 88.0 | 2.8 | 5.7 | 0.8 |
| North Hempstead town *Nassau Co.* | 72.2 | 19.5 | 3.2 | 4.1 |
| North Tonawanda city *Niagara Co.* | 94.7 | 1.1 | 1.6 | 1.8 |
| Oceanside CDP *Nassau Co.* | 77.7 | 15.7 | 2.3 | 3.6 |
| Orangetown town *Rockland Co.* | 78.6 | 8.1 | 5.1 | 7.0 |
| Orchard Park town *Erie Co.* | 94.2 | 0.1 | 1.3 | 3.2 |
| Ossining town *Westchester Co.* | 73.2 | 17.0 | 3.3 | 4.7 |
| Oyster Bay town *Nassau Co.* | 80.3 | 13.1 | 1.5 | 4.2 |
| Penfield town *Monroe Co.* | 94.3 | 0.2 | 1.2 | 3.5 |
| Perinton town *Monroe Co.* | 92.0 | 0.7 | 1.3 | 5.0 |
| Pittsford town *Monroe Co.* | 87.6 | 0.5 | 4.2 | 6.5 |
| Port Chester village *Westchester Co.* | 62.3 | 17.0 | 9.0 | 1.0 |
| Poughkeepsie town *Dutchess Co.* | 84.9 | 2.3 | 7.5 | 4.2 |
| Poughkeepsie city *Dutchess Co.* | 78.1 | 8.9 | 6.2 | 3.5 |
| Ramapo town *Rockland Co.* | 76.4 | 11.1 | 5.8 | 4.2 |
| Riverhead town *Suffolk Co.* | 91.8 | 2.1 | 1.4 | 3.5 |
| Rochester city *Monroe Co.* | 80.2 | 8.4 | 6.2 | 2.9 |
| Rome city *Oneida Co.* | 91.9 | 1.9 | 2.3 | 2.4 |
| Rotterdam town *Schenectady Co.* | 96.7 | 0.2 | 0.7 | 2.3 |
| Rye town *Westchester Co.* | 64.8 | 18.0 | 6.8 | 2.6 |
| Salina town *Onondaga Co.* | 93.6 | 0.6 | 2.6 | 2.1 |
| Schenectady city *Schenectady Co.* | 82.3 | 5.8 | 6.9 | 3.0 |
| Smithtown town *Suffolk Co.* | 89.8 | 5.1 | 1.0 | 3.8 |
| Southampton town *Suffolk Co.* | 84.1 | 4.6 | 3.5 | 5.7 |
| Spring Valley village *Rockland Co.* | 70.6 | 18.4 | 3.9 | 1.1 |
| Syracuse city *Onondaga Co.* | 76.4 | 7.6 | 10.7 | 3.0 |
| Tonawanda CDP *Erie Co.* | 91.4 | 2.4 | 2.0 | 2.5 |
| Tonawanda town *Erie Co.* | 91.4 | 2.5 | 2.1 | 2.2 |
| Troy city *Rensselaer Co.* | 76.6 | 8.7 | 9.8 | 3.5 |
| Union town *Broome Co.* | 89.6 | 2.6 | 4.0 | 3.3 |
| Utica city *Oneida Co.* | 86.5 | 3.6 | 6.3 | 2.1 |
| Valley Stream village *Nassau Co.* | 75.1 | 18.2 | 3.0 | 1.5 |
| Warwick town *Orange Co.* | 87.2 | 3.8 | 2.4 | 6.0 |
| Webster town *Monroe Co.* | 94.6 | 1.1 | 0.6 | 2.8 |
| West Babylon CDP *Suffolk Co.* | 86.9 | 8.3 | 0.6 | 2.8 |
| West Seneca CDP *Erie Co.* | 95.6 | 0.6 | 1.6 | 1.2 |
| West Seneca town and CDP *Erie Co.* | 95.6 | 0.6 | 1.6 | 1.2 |
| White Plains city *Westchester Co.* | 60.9 | 20.5 | 9.7 | 6.5 |
| Yonkers city *Westchester Co.* | 65.6 | 25.8 | 5.1 | 2.3 |
| Yorktown town *Westchester Co.* | 88.2 | 6.0 | 1.0 | 4.7 |

NOTE: Figures are 2006-2010 5-year estimates.

## Travel Time to Work

| Place | Less than 15 Minutes (%) | 15 to 30 Minutes (%) | 30 to 45 Minutes (%) | 45 to 60 Minutes (%) | 60 Minutes or More (%) |
|---|---|---|---|---|---|
| **Albany** city *Albany Co.* | 40.1 | 42.5 | 11.5 | 3.0 | 2.9 |
| **Amherst** town *Erie Co.* | 33.2 | 46.3 | 16.9 | 1.7 | 2.0 |
| **Babylon** town *Suffolk Co.* | 26.7 | 32.4 | 18.6 | 6.9 | 15.4 |
| **Bethlehem** town *Albany Co.* | 26.8 | 52.5 | 15.3 | 2.0 | 3.4 |
| **Binghamton** city *Broome Co.* | 52.6 | 37.5 | 5.3 | 1.7 | 3.0 |
| **Brentwood** CDP *Suffolk Co.* | 22.6 | 43.8 | 17.5 | 6.3 | 9.7 |
| **Brighton** town and CDP *Monroe Co.* | 43.1 | 49.0 | 5.0 | 1.2 | 1.6 |
| **Brookhaven** town *Suffolk Co.* | 23.0 | 33.2 | 19.9 | 9.0 | 14.9 |
| **Buffalo** city *Erie Co.* | 31.6 | 47.4 | 13.9 | 3.3 | 3.7 |
| **Carmel** town *Putnam Co.* | 20.5 | 22.9 | 24.4 | 13.6 | 18.6 |
| **Centereach** CDP *Suffolk Co.* | 23.5 | 31.5 | 21.3 | 9.4 | 14.3 |
| **Central Islip** CDP *Suffolk Co.* | 24.3 | 37.3 | 20.8 | 6.5 | 11.1 |
| **Cheektowaga** town *Erie Co.* | 31.5 | 53.1 | 11.4 | 1.6 | 2.5 |
| **Cheektowaga** CDP *Erie Co.* | 31.0 | 53.4 | 11.5 | 1.7 | 2.4 |
| **Chili** town *Monroe Co.* | 31.0 | 53.0 | 12.0 | 1.9 | 2.1 |
| **Cicero** town *Onondaga Co.* | 22.5 | 61.6 | 11.0 | 1.9 | 3.0 |
| **Clarence** town *Erie Co.* | 26.1 | 41.7 | 26.7 | 3.3 | 2.1 |
| **Clarkstown** town *Rockland Co.* | 25.6 | 28.8 | 17.4 | 11.1 | 17.1 |
| **Clay** town *Onondaga Co.* | 28.3 | 55.0 | 11.5 | 2.2 | 3.1 |
| **Clifton Park** town *Saratoga Co.* | 23.9 | 43.6 | 24.6 | 3.9 | 4.0 |
| **Colonie** town *Albany Co.* | 35.9 | 50.5 | 10.2 | 1.8 | 1.6 |
| **Commack** CDP *Suffolk Co.* | 23.8 | 32.7 | 19.5 | 7.3 | 16.8 |
| **Coram** CDP *Suffolk Co.* | 15.9 | 38.0 | 19.2 | 9.6 | 17.3 |
| **Cortlandt** town *Westchester Co.* | 18.5 | 18.5 | 24.9 | 12.0 | 26.1 |
| **East Fishkill** town *Dutchess Co.* | 20.6 | 27.3 | 17.9 | 13.5 | 20.7 |
| **East Meadow** CDP *Nassau Co.* | 21.3 | 36.7 | 18.6 | 6.7 | 16.6 |
| **Eastchester** town *Westchester Co.* | 21.7 | 26.8 | 18.8 | 12.3 | 20.3 |
| **Elmira** city *Chemung Co.* | 52.1 | 31.2 | 9.7 | 3.6 | 3.4 |
| **Elmont** CDP *Nassau Co.* | 12.2 | 27.7 | 25.1 | 13.1 | 21.8 |
| **Franklin Square** CDP *Nassau Co.* | 21.3 | 29.1 | 24.1 | 8.1 | 17.4 |
| **Freeport** village *Nassau Co.* | 23.5 | 30.7 | 21.7 | 7.0 | 17.1 |
| **Glenville** town *Schenectady Co.* | 29.9 | 36.9 | 26.3 | 4.6 | 2.2 |
| **Greece** town *Monroe Co.* | 27.6 | 54.2 | 14.7 | 1.5 | 2.0 |
| **Greenburgh** town *Westchester Co.* | 22.8 | 29.7 | 19.6 | 9.8 | 18.1 |
| **Guilderland** town *Albany Co.* | 29.1 | 47.2 | 18.1 | 3.9 | 1.7 |
| **Hamburg** town *Erie Co.* | 29.2 | 41.7 | 21.3 | 4.7 | 3.1 |
| **Haverstraw** town *Rockland Co.* | 20.7 | 37.2 | 19.9 | 10.3 | 11.9 |
| **Hempstead** town *Nassau Co.* | 20.3 | 29.7 | 21.3 | 9.1 | 19.6 |
| **Hempstead** village *Nassau Co.* | 18.3 | 31.2 | 26.6 | 8.0 | 15.9 |
| **Henrietta** town *Monroe Co.* | 40.3 | 47.3 | 9.8 | 1.5 | 1.1 |
| **Hicksville** CDP *Nassau Co.* | 23.8 | 34.2 | 17.4 | 6.7 | 17.9 |
| **Huntington** town *Suffolk Co.* | 25.0 | 30.6 | 18.9 | 8.1 | 17.4 |
| **Huntington Station** CDP *Suffolk Co.* | 31.5 | 31.9 | 20.2 | 6.3 | 10.1 |
| **Irondequoit** town and CDP *Monroe Co.* | 30.1 | 53.1 | 13.1 | 1.7 | 2.0 |
| **Islip** town *Suffolk Co.* | 26.3 | 35.9 | 19.1 | 6.2 | 12.4 |
| **Ithaca** city *Tompkins Co.* | 50.2 | 37.8 | 8.7 | 2.0 | 1.4 |
| **Jamestown** city *Chautauqua Co.* | 56.0 | 33.1 | 6.0 | 2.3 | 2.6 |
| **Lancaster** town *Erie Co.* | 26.4 | 48.3 | 21.2 | 2.2 | 1.9 |
| **Levittown** CDP *Nassau Co.* | 20.8 | 37.4 | 19.9 | 5.3 | 16.6 |
| **Long Beach** city *Nassau Co.* | 18.5 | 18.6 | 21.8 | 11.7 | 29.5 |

| Place | Less than 15 Minutes (%) | 15 to 30 Minutes (%) | 30 to 45 Minutes (%) | 45 to 60 Minutes (%) | 60 Minutes or More (%) |
|---|---|---|---|---|---|
| Mamaroneck town Westchester Co. | 20.1 | 23.9 | 19.1 | 16.9 | 19.9 |
| Manlius town Onondaga Co. | 26.6 | 58.0 | 11.6 | 2.4 | 1.3 |
| Monroe town Orange Co. | 29.2 | 19.6 | 17.4 | 10.2 | 23.6 |
| Mount Pleasant town Westchester Co. | 27.0 | 30.1 | 18.0 | 8.2 | 16.6 |
| Mount Vernon city Westchester Co. | 20.2 | 38.0 | 21.8 | 9.1 | 11.0 |
| New City CDP Rockland Co. | 24.3 | 24.7 | 17.2 | 13.1 | 20.7 |
| New Rochelle city Westchester Co. | 27.5 | 31.1 | 18.9 | 8.8 | 13.7 |
| New York city | 11.2 | 22.3 | 26.3 | 15.1 | 25.0 |
| Newburgh city Orange Co. | 36.9 | 34.4 | 18.8 | 4.1 | 5.8 |
| Newburgh town Orange Co. | 27.4 | 31.3 | 14.7 | 7.3 | 19.2 |
| Niagara Falls city Niagara Co. | 51.3 | 33.0 | 11.5 | 2.8 | 1.3 |
| North Hempstead town Nassau Co. | 23.1 | 26.6 | 19.7 | 8.8 | 21.7 |
| North Tonawanda city Niagara Co. | 30.6 | 46.0 | 18.6 | 2.8 | 1.9 |
| Oceanside CDP Nassau Co. | 22.5 | 23.8 | 20.5 | 10.8 | 22.3 |
| Orangetown town Rockland Co. | 31.4 | 28.3 | 16.2 | 8.6 | 15.4 |
| Orchard Park town Erie Co. | 23.8 | 47.2 | 22.5 | 3.7 | 2.8 |
| Ossining town Westchester Co. | 23.7 | 30.6 | 19.5 | 9.6 | 16.6 |
| Oyster Bay town Nassau Co. | 22.4 | 30.9 | 18.8 | 7.0 | 20.8 |
| Penfield town Monroe Co. | 27.4 | 58.1 | 11.7 | 1.2 | 1.6 |
| Perinton town Monroe Co. | 31.2 | 49.3 | 15.8 | 1.8 | 1.9 |
| Pittsford town Monroe Co. | 35.2 | 50.5 | 10.9 | 1.8 | 1.5 |
| Port Chester village Westchester Co. | 34.7 | 35.6 | 15.4 | 5.8 | 8.5 |
| Poughkeepsie town Dutchess Co. | 39.2 | 32.8 | 12.3 | 4.5 | 11.2 |
| Poughkeepsie city Dutchess Co. | 38.0 | 35.1 | 12.1 | 5.4 | 9.3 |
| Ramapo town Rockland Co. | 31.0 | 31.4 | 14.4 | 7.2 | 15.9 |
| Riverhead town Suffolk Co. | 29.2 | 30.8 | 20.6 | 9.0 | 10.4 |
| Rochester city Monroe Co. | 37.8 | 45.5 | 10.7 | 2.7 | 3.3 |
| Rome city Oneida Co. | 48.7 | 34.4 | 12.3 | 1.9 | 2.7 |
| Rotterdam town Schenectady Co. | 32.0 | 41.6 | 20.0 | 4.4 | 2.0 |
| Rye town Westchester Co. | 32.2 | 33.5 | 15.5 | 7.1 | 11.7 |
| Salina town Onondaga Co. | 40.1 | 50.5 | 4.9 | 1.8 | 2.7 |
| Schenectady city Schenectady Co. | 34.5 | 32.1 | 25.4 | 3.7 | 4.3 |
| Smithtown town Suffolk Co. | 23.9 | 32.9 | 21.3 | 7.3 | 14.5 |
| Southampton town Suffolk Co. | 34.3 | 28.5 | 17.4 | 6.8 | 12.9 |
| Spring Valley village Rockland Co. | 29.8 | 39.0 | 15.5 | 5.1 | 10.6 |
| Syracuse city Onondaga Co. | 43.8 | 43.2 | 7.6 | 2.7 | 2.7 |
| Tonawanda CDP Erie Co. | 35.8 | 48.7 | 11.5 | 1.5 | 2.5 |
| Tonawanda town Erie Co. | 35.4 | 48.9 | 11.5 | 1.6 | 2.5 |
| Troy city Rensselaer Co. | 35.8 | 40.6 | 13.6 | 4.8 | 5.2 |
| Union town Broome Co. | 47.8 | 42.7 | 4.9 | 1.6 | 2.9 |
| Utica city Oneida Co. | 49.2 | 37.4 | 7.6 | 1.7 | 4.1 |
| Valley Stream village Nassau Co. | 16.5 | 27.5 | 23.0 | 11.3 | 21.7 |
| Warwick town Orange Co. | 26.0 | 18.8 | 15.9 | 15.4 | 24.0 |
| Webster town Monroe Co. | 31.5 | 46.9 | 17.1 | 2.4 | 2.1 |
| West Babylon CDP Suffolk Co. | 27.3 | 34.1 | 15.3 | 5.5 | 17.8 |
| West Seneca CDP Erie Co. | 30.9 | 49.2 | 14.2 | 3.3 | 2.4 |
| West Seneca town and CDP Erie Co. | 30.9 | 49.2 | 14.2 | 3.3 | 2.4 |
| White Plains city Westchester Co. | 28.9 | 34.5 | 17.0 | 6.7 | 12.9 |
| Yonkers city Westchester Co. | 16.5 | 32.8 | 22.1 | 10.3 | 18.3 |
| Yorktown town Westchester Co. | 23.4 | 22.3 | 28.0 | 10.9 | 15.3 |

NOTE: Figures are 2006-2010 5-year estimates.

# Crime

| Place | Violent Crime Rate (crimes per 10,000 population) | Property Crime Rate (crimes per 10,000 population) |
|---|---|---|
| Albany city Albany Co. | 105.8 | 500.8 |
| Amherst town Erie Co. | 10.9 | 189.3 |
| Babylon town Suffolk Co. | n/a | n/a |
| Bethlehem town Albany Co. | 6.1 | 150.6 |
| Binghamton city Broome Co. | 61.0 | 477.9 |
| Brentwood CDP Suffolk Co. | n/a | n/a |
| Brighton town and CDP Monroe Co. | 13.4 | 311.9 |
| Brookhaven town Suffolk Co. | n/a | n/a |
| Buffalo city Erie Co. | 135.7 | 556.4 |
| Carmel town Putnam Co. | 3.5 | 79.7 |
| Centereach CDP Suffolk Co. | n/a | n/a |
| Central Islip CDP Suffolk Co. | n/a | n/a |
| Cheektowaga town Erie Co. | 20.2 | 358.4 |
| Cheektowaga CDP Erie Co. | n/a | n/a |
| Chili town Monroe Co. | n/a | n/a |
| Cicero town Onondaga Co. | 4.6 | 183.1 |
| Clarence town Erie Co. | n/a | n/a |
| Clarkstown town Rockland Co. | 11.7 | 216.9 |
| Clay town Onondaga Co. | n/a | n/a |
| Clifton Park town Saratoga Co. | n/a | n/a |
| Colonie town Albany Co. | 7.0 | 293.1 |
| Commack CDP Suffolk Co. | n/a | n/a |
| Coram CDP Suffolk Co. | n/a | n/a |
| Cortlandt town Westchester Co. | n/a | n/a |
| East Fishkill town Dutchess Co. | n/a | n/a |
| East Meadow CDP Nassau Co. | n/a | n/a |
| Eastchester town Westchester Co. | n/a | n/a |
| Elmira city Chemung Co. | 37.5 | 366.7 |
| Elmont CDP Nassau Co. | n/a | n/a |
| Franklin Square CDP Nassau Co. | n/a | n/a |
| Freeport village Nassau Co. | 49.0 | 236.1 |
| Glenville town Schenectady Co. | 6.9 | 170.3 |
| Greece town Monroe Co. | 12.9 | 276.5 |
| Greenburgh town Westchester Co. | 16.2 | 146.4 |
| Guilderland town Albany Co. | 3.4 | 299.0 |
| Hamburg town Erie Co. | 8.5 | 228.7 |
| Haverstraw town Rockland Co. | 17.3 | 116.8 |
| Hempstead town Nassau Co. | n/a | n/a |
| Hempstead village Nassau Co. | 84.6 | 196.7 |
| Henrietta town Monroe Co. | n/a | n/a |
| Hicksville CDP Nassau Co. | n/a | n/a |
| Huntington town Suffolk Co. | n/a | n/a |
| Huntington Station CDP Suffolk Co. | n/a | n/a |
| Irondequoit town and CDP Monroe Co. | 18.9 | 301.8 |
| Islip town Suffolk Co. | n/a | n/a |
| Ithaca city Tompkins Co. | 20.1 | 383.7 |
| Jamestown city Chautauqua Co. | 62.5 | 445.0 |
| Lancaster town Erie Co. | 9.0 | 216.9 |
| Levittown CDP Nassau Co. | n/a | n/a |
| Long Beach city Nassau Co. | n/a | n/a |

| Place | Violent Crime Rate (crimes per 10,000 population) | Property Crime Rate (crimes per 10,000 population) |
|---|---|---|
| Mamaroneck town *Westchester Co.* | 7.0 | 125.6 |
| Manlius town *Onondaga Co.* | 6.5 | 180.5 |
| Monroe town *Orange Co.* | n/a | n/a |
| Mount Pleasant town *Westchester Co.* | 3.4 | 70.8 |
| Mount Vernon city *Westchester Co.* | 99.6 | 232.7 |
| New City CDP *Rockland Co.* | n/a | n/a |
| New Rochelle city *Westchester Co.* | 29.5 | 165.1 |
| New York city | 58.2 | 167.5 |
| Newburgh city *Orange Co.* | 187.5 | 406.7 |
| Newburgh town *Orange Co.* | 9.9 | 402.3 |
| Niagara Falls city *Niagara Co.* | 121.2 | 581.1 |
| North Hempstead town *Nassau Co.* | n/a | n/a |
| North Tonawanda city *Niagara Co.* | 17.7 | 190.7 |
| Oceanside CDP *Nassau Co.* | n/a | n/a |
| Orangetown town *Rockland Co.* | 11.9 | 131.0 |
| Orchard Park town *Erie Co.* | 4.9 | 130.4 |
| Ossining town *Westchester Co.* | n/a | n/a |
| Oyster Bay town *Nassau Co.* | n/a | n/a |
| Penfield town *Monroe Co.* | n/a | n/a |
| Perinton town *Monroe Co.* | n/a | n/a |
| Pittsford town *Monroe Co.* | n/a | n/a |
| Port Chester village *Westchester Co.* | 18.3 | 242.7 |
| Poughkeepsie town *Dutchess Co.* | 9.2 | 312.7 |
| Poughkeepsie city *Dutchess Co.* | 136.4 | 361.6 |
| Ramapo town *Rockland Co.* | 10.3 | 97.8 |
| Riverhead town *Suffolk Co.* | 22.7 | 294.0 |
| Rochester city *Monroe Co.* | 109.4 | 580.0 |
| Rome city *Oneida Co.* | 12.1 | 196.8 |
| Rotterdam town *Schenectady Co.* | 8.7 | 260.1 |
| Rye town *Westchester Co.* | n/a | n/a |
| Salina town *Onondaga Co.* | n/a | n/a |
| Schenectady city *Schenectady Co.* | 111.8 | 557.5 |
| Smithtown town *Suffolk Co.* | n/a | n/a |
| Southampton town *Suffolk Co.* | 10.5 | 217.5 |
| Spring Valley village *Rockland Co.* | 55.7 | 249.5 |
| Syracuse city *Onondaga Co.* | 94.7 | 418.8 |
| Tonawanda CDP *Erie Co.* | n/a | n/a |
| Tonawanda town *Erie Co.* | 23.2 | 200.2 |
| Troy city *Rensselaer Co.* | 90.3 | 501.9 |
| Union town *Broome Co.* | n/a | n/a |
| Utica city *Oneida Co.* | 72.8 | 475.4 |
| Valley Stream village *Nassau Co.* | n/a | n/a |
| Warwick town *Orange Co.* | n/a | n/a |
| Webster town *Monroe Co.* | 4.5 | 126.9 |
| West Babylon CDP *Suffolk Co.* | n/a | n/a |
| West Seneca CDP *Erie Co.* | n/a | n/a |
| West Seneca town and CDP *Erie Co.* | 11.1 | 226.7 |
| White Plains city *Westchester Co.* | 19.2 | 191.1 |
| Yonkers city *Westchester Co.* | 44.9 | 143.1 |
| Yorktown town *Westchester Co.* | 6.9 | 122.6 |

NOTE: Data as of 2010.

| Place | Violent Crime Rate (crimes per 10,000 population) | Property Crime Rate (crimes per 10,000 population) |
|---|---|---|
| Mamaroneck town Westchester Co. | 7.0 | 126.6 |
| Manlius town Onondaga Co. | 6.6 | 180.5 |
| Monroe town Orange Co. | n/a | n/a |
| Mount Pleasant town Westchester Co. | 10.4 | 70.8 |
| Mount Vernon city Westchester Co. | 36.6 | 232.7 |
| New City CDP Rockland Co. | n/a | n/a |
| New Rochelle city Westchester Co. | 20.5 | 155.1 |
| New York city | 60.2 | 167.5 |
| Newburgh city Orange Co. | 187.5 | 408.7 |
| Newburgh town Orange Co. | 9.0 | 402.8 |
| Niagara Falls city Niagara Co. | 72.2 | 581.1 |
| North Hempstead town Nassau Co. | n/a | n/a |
| North Tonawanda city Niagara Co. | 17.7 | 190.7 |
| Oceanside CDP Nassau Co. | n/a | n/a |
| Orangetown town Rockland Co. | 11.9 | 131.0 |
| Orchard Park town Erie Co. | 6.9 | 130.4 |
| Ossining town Westchester Co. | n/a | n/a |
| Oyster Bay town Nassau Co. | n/a | n/a |
| Penfield town Monroe Co. | n/a | n/a |
| Perinton town Monroe Co. | n/a | n/a |
| Pittsford town Monroe Co. | n/a | n/a |
| Port Chester village Westchester Co. | 16.5 | 242.2 |
| Poughkeepsie town Dutchess Co. | 9.6 | 312.7 |
| Poughkeepsie city Dutchess Co. | 135.1 | 741.5 |
| Ramapo town Rockland Co. | 10.5 | 97.8 |
| Riverhead town Suffolk Co. | 22.7 | 204.0 |
| Rochester city Monroe Co. | 108.1 | 550.0 |
| Rome city Oneida Co. | 12.1 | 195.2 |
| Rotterdam town Schenectady Co. | 8.7 | 250.1 |
| Rye town Westchester Co. | n/a | n/a |
| Salina town Onondaga Co. | n/a | n/a |
| Schenectady city Schenectady Co. | 111.5 | 533.5 |
| Smithtown town Suffolk Co. | n/a | n/a |
| Southampton town Suffolk Co. | 10.8 | 217.5 |
| Spring Valley village Rockland Co. | 58.7 | 249.8 |
| Syracuse city Onondaga Co. | 97.7 | 748.8 |
| Tonawanda CDP Erie Co. | n/a | n/a |
| Tonawanda town Erie Co. | 23.2 | 290.2 |
| Troy city Rensselaer Co. | 93.5 | 501.8 |
| Union town Broome Co. | n/a | n/a |
| Utica city Oneida Co. | 72.8 | 476.4 |
| Valley Stream village Nassau Co. | n/a | n/a |
| Warwick town Orange Co. | n/a | n/a |
| Webster town Monroe Co. | 4.5 | 136.9 |
| West Babylon CDP Suffolk Co. | n/a | n/a |
| West Seneca CDP Erie Co. | n/a | n/a |
| West Seneca town and CDP Erie Co. | 11.1 | 226.7 |
| White Plains city Westchester Co. | 19.2 | 191.1 |
| Yonkers city Westchester Co. | 44.9 | 143.1 |
| Yorktown town Westchester Co. | 6.5 | 222.5 |

NOTE: Data as of 2010.

## New York Public School Educational Profile

# Education

| Category | Value | | Category | Value |
|---|---|---|---|---|
| Schools (2009-2010) | | | Diploma Recipients (2008-2009) | 4,730 |
| Instructional Level | | | White, Non-Hispanic | 106,832 |
| Primary | | | Black, Non-Hispanic | 2,542 |
| Middle | | | Asian/Pacific Islander, Non-Hispanic | 587 |
| High | | | American Indian/Alaskan Native, Non-Hisp. | 947 |
| Other/Not Reported | | | Hispanic | 584 |
| Curriculum | | | Staff (2009-2010) | |
| Regular | | | Teachers (FTE) | 4,561 |
| Special Education | | | Salary ($) | 105 |
| Vocational | | | Librarians/Media Specialists (FTE) | 6 |
| Alternative | | | Guidance Counselors (FTE) | 28 |
| Type | | | Ratios (2009-2010) | |
| Magnet | | | Number of Students per Teacher | |
| Charter | | | Number of Students per Librarian | |
| Title I Eligible | | | Number of Students per Guidance Counselor | 4,288 |
| School-wide Title I | | | Finances (2007-2008) | 1,896 |
| Students (2009-2010) | | | Current Expenditures ($ per student) | 2,766,082 |
| Gender (%) | | | Total | |
| Male | 50.8 | | Instruction | |
| Female | 49.2 | | Support Services | |
| Race/Ethnicity (%) | | | Other | |
| White, Non-Hispanic | 50.5 | | General Revenue ($ per student) | |
| Black, Non-Hispanic | 18.0 | | Total | |
| Asian/Pacific Islander | 7.9 | | From Federal Sources | |
| American Indian/Alaskan Native | 0.5 | | From State Sources | |
| Hispanic | 21.8 | | From Local Sources | |
| Special Programs (%) | | | Long-Term Debt ($ per student) | |
| Individual Education Program (IEP) | 16.0 | | At beginning of fiscal year | |
| English Language Learner (ELL) | 7.3 | | At end of fiscal year | |
| Eligible for Free Lunch Program | 18.9 | | College Entrance Exam Scores | |
| Eligible for Reduced-Price Lunch Program | 4.7 | | SAT Reasoning Test [†] (2011) | |
| Average Freshman Grad. Rate (%) (2008-2009) | 73.5 | | Participation Rate (%) | |
| White, Non-Hispanic | 85.4 | | Mean Critical Reading Score | |
| Black, Non-Hispanic | 58.1 | | Mean Math Score | |
| Asian/Pacific Islander, Non-Hispanic | 88.4 | | Mean Writing Score | |
| American Indian/Alaskan Native, Non-Hisp. | 60.0 | | ACT (2011) | |
| Hispanic | 57.4 | | Participation Rate (%) | |
| High School Drop-out Rate (%) (2008-2009) | 4.2 | | Mean Composite Score | |
| White, Non-Hispanic | 2.0 | | Mean English Score | |
| Black, Non-Hispanic | 7.8 | | Mean Math Score | |
| Asian/Pacific Islander, Non-Hispanic | 2.5 | | Mean Reading Score | |
| American Indian/Alaskan Native, Non-Hisp. | 8.7 | | Mean Science Score | |
| Hispanic | 7.8 | | | |

# New York Public School Educational Profile

| Category | Value | Category | Value |
|---|---|---|---|
| **Schools** *(2009-2010)* | 4,730 | **Diploma Recipients** *(2008-2009)* | 180,917 |
| Instructional Level | | White, Non-Hispanic | 105,632 |
| Primary | 2,542 | Black, Non-Hispanic | 30,441 |
| Middle | 857 | Asian/Pacific Islander, Non-Hispanic | 14,346 |
| High | 947 | American Indian/Alaskan Native, Non-Hisp. | 646 |
| Other/Not Reported | 384 | Hispanic | 29,529 |
| Curriculum | | **Staff** *(2009-2010)* | |
| Regular | 4,591 | Teachers (FTE) | 214,755.8 |
| Special Education | 105 | Salary[1] ($) | 74,449 |
| Vocational | 6 | Librarians/Media Specialists (FTE) | 2,962.8 |
| Alternative | 28 | Guidance Counselors (FTE) | 6,652.7 |
| Type | | **Ratios** *(2009-2010)* | |
| Magnet | 183 | Number of Students per Teacher | 12.9 to 1 |
| Charter | 140 | Number of Students per Librarian | 933.6 to 1 |
| Title I Eligible | 4,259 | Number of Students per Guidance Counselor | 415.8 to 1 |
| School-wide Title I | 1,595 | **Finances** *(2007-2008)* | |
| **Students** *(2009-2010)* | 2,766,052 | Current Expenditures ($ per student) | |
| Gender (%) | | Total | 16,794 |
| Male | 50.8 | Instruction | 11,572 |
| Female | 49.2 | Support Services | 4,864 |
| Race/Ethnicity (%) | | Other | 358 |
| White, Non-Hispanic | 50.5 | General Revenue ($ per student) | |
| Black, Non-Hispanic | 19.0 | Total | 19,081 |
| Asian/Pacific Islander | 7.9 | From Federal Sources | 1,144 |
| American Indian/Alaskan Native | 0.5 | From State Sources | 8,549 |
| Hispanic | 21.6 | From Local Sources | 9,388 |
| Special Programs (%) | | Long-Term Debt ($ per student) | |
| Individual Education Program (IEP) | 16.6 | At beginning of fiscal year | 10,077 |
| English Language Learner (ELL) | 7.3 | At end of fiscal year | 10,180 |
| Eligible for Free Lunch Program | 15.9 | **College Entrance Exam Scores** | |
| Eligible for Reduced-Price Lunch Program | 4.7 | SAT Reasoning Test™ *(2011)* | |
| **Average Freshman Grad. Rate** (%) *(2008-2009)* | 73.5 | Participation Rate (%) | 89 |
| White, Non-Hispanic | 85.1 | Mean Critical Reading Score | 485 |
| Black, Non-Hispanic | 58.1 | Mean Math Score | 499 |
| Asian/Pacific Islander, Non-Hispanic | 88.4 | Mean Writing Score | 476 |
| American Indian/Alaskan Native, Non-Hisp. | 60.6 | ACT *(2011)* | |
| Hispanic | 57.4 | Participation Rate (%) | 28 |
| **High School Drop-out Rate** (%) *(2008-2009)* | 4.2 | Mean Composite Score | 23.4 |
| White, Non-Hispanic | 2.0 | Mean English Score | 22.7 |
| Black, Non-Hispanic | 7.6 | Mean Math Score | 23.8 |
| Asian/Pacific Islander, Non-Hispanic | 2.5 | Mean Reading Score | 23.5 |
| American Indian/Alaskan Native, Non-Hisp. | 6.7 | Mean Science Score | 23.0 |
| Hispanic | 7.1 | | |

**Note:** *For an explanation of data, please refer to the User's Guide in the front of the book; (1) Average salary for classroom teachers in 2011-12*

## Number of Schools

| Rank | Number | District Name | City |
|---|---|---|---|
| 1 | 1,531 | New York City Public Schools | New York |
| 2 | 103 | NYC Geographic District # 2 | New York |
| 3 | 83 | NYC Geographic District #10 | Bronx |
| 4 | 70 | NYC Geographic District # 9 | Bronx |
| 5 | 65 | NYC Geographic District #31 | Staten Island |
| 6 | 62 | Rochester City SD | Rochester |
| 7 | 58 | Buffalo City SD | Buffalo |
| 8 | 57 | NYC Special Schools - District 75 | New York |
| 8 | 57 | NYC Geographic District #27 | Ozone Park |
| 10 | 56 | NYC Geographic District #11 | Bronx |
| 11 | 53 | NYC Geographic District #12 | Bronx |
| 12 | 52 | NYC Geographic District # 8 | Bronx |
| 13 | 49 | NYC Geographic District #17 | Brooklyn |
| 14 | 48 | NYC Geographic District #24 | Ridgewood |
| 15 | 46 | NYC Geographic District # 3 | New York |
| 15 | 46 | NYC Geographic District # 6 | New York |
| 17 | 45 | NYC Geographic District #13 | Brooklyn |
| 17 | 45 | NYC Geographic District #15 | Brooklyn |
| 17 | 45 | NYC Geographic District #19 | Brooklyn |
| 20 | 43 | NYC Geographic District #25 | Flushing |
| 21 | 42 | NYC Geographic District #14 | Brooklyn |
| 21 | 42 | NYC Geographic District #30 | Long Isl City |
| 23 | 41 | NYC Geographic District #21 | Brooklyn |
| 23 | 41 | NYC Geographic District #29 | Rosedale |
| 25 | 40 | NYC Geographic District #28 | Jamaica |
| 26 | 39 | NYC Geographic District # 7 | Bronx |
| 26 | 39 | NYC Geographic District #20 | Brooklyn |
| 28 | 38 | NYC Geographic District # 4 | New York |
| 28 | 38 | NYC Geographic District #22 | Brooklyn |
| 28 | 38 | Yonkers City SD | Yonkers |
| 31 | 37 | NYC Geographic District #18 | Brooklyn |
| 32 | 34 | Syracuse City SD | Syracuse |
| 33 | 31 | NYC Geographic District # 5 | New York |
| 33 | 31 | NYC Geographic District #26 | Bayside |
| 35 | 30 | NYC Geographic District # 1 | New York |
| 36 | 27 | NYC Geographic District #23 | Brooklyn |
| 36 | 27 | NYC Geographic District #32 | Brooklyn |
| 38 | 25 | NYC Geographic District #16 | Brooklyn |
| 39 | 20 | Greece Central SD | Rochester |
| 40 | 19 | Schenectady City SD | Schenectady |
| 41 | 18 | Sachem Central SD | Holbrook |
| 42 | 17 | Brentwood UFSD | Brentwood |
| 43 | 16 | Clarkstown Central SD | New City |
| 43 | 16 | Mount Vernon City SD | Mount Vernon |
| 43 | 16 | Newburgh City SD | Newburgh |
| 46 | 15 | Albany City SD | Albany |
| 46 | 15 | Wappingers Central SD | Wappingers Fls |
| 48 | 14 | Corning City SD | Painted Post |
| 48 | 14 | East Ramapo Central SD | Spring Valley |
| 48 | 14 | Kingston City SD | Kingston |
| 48 | 14 | Liverpool Central SD | Liverpool |
| 48 | 14 | Middle Country Central SD | Centereach |
| 48 | 14 | Smithtown Central SD | Smithtown |
| 54 | 13 | Arlington Central SD | Poughkeepsie |
| 54 | 13 | Elmira City SD | Elmira |
| 54 | 13 | Kenmore-Tonawanda UFSD | Buffalo |
| 54 | 13 | Williamsville Central SD | East Amherst |
| 58 | 12 | Ithaca City SD | Ithaca |
| 58 | 12 | Shenendehowa Central SD | Clifton Park |
| 58 | 12 | Utica City SD | Utica |
| 58 | 12 | West Seneca Central SD | West Seneca |
| 62 | 11 | Connetquot Central SD | Bohemia |
| 62 | 11 | Half Hollow Hills Central SD | Dix Hills |
| 62 | 11 | Niagara Falls City SD | Niagara Falls |
| 62 | 11 | North Syracuse Central SD | North Syracuse |
| 62 | 11 | Patchogue-Medford UFSD | Patchogue |
| 62 | 11 | Webster Central SD | Webster |
| 68 | 10 | Binghamton City SD | Binghamton |
| 68 | 10 | Great Neck UFSD | Great Neck |
| 68 | 10 | Jamestown City SD | Jamestown |
| 68 | 10 | Levittown UFSD | Levittown |
| 68 | 10 | Lockport City SD | Lockport |
| 68 | 10 | New Rochelle City SD | New Rochelle |
| 68 | 10 | North Rockland Central SD | Garnerville |
| 68 | 10 | Oceanside UFSD | Oceanside |
| 68 | 10 | Syosset Central SD | Syosset |
| 68 | 10 | West Irondequoit Central SD | Rochester |
| 78 | 9 | Baldwin UFSD | Baldwin |
| 78 | 9 | East Meadow UFSD | Westbury |
| 78 | 9 | Hempstead UFSD | Hempstead |
| 78 | 9 | Hicksville UFSD | Hicksville |
| 78 | 9 | Lakeland Central SD | Shrub Oak |
| 78 | 9 | Lindenhurst UFSD | Lindenhurst |
| 78 | 9 | Massapequa UFSD | Massapequa |
| 78 | 9 | North Colonie Central SD | Latham |
| 78 | 9 | Northport-East Northport UFSD | Northport |
| 78 | 9 | Pittsford Central SD | Pittsford |
| 78 | 9 | Rome City SD | Rome |
| 78 | 9 | Rush-Henrietta Central SD | Henrietta |
| 78 | 9 | West Islip UFSD | West Islip |
| 91 | 8 | Auburn City SD | Auburn |
| 91 | 8 | Baldwinsville Central SD | Baldwinsville |
| 91 | 8 | Bethlehem Central SD | Delmar |
| 91 | 8 | Central Islip UFSD | Central Islip |
| 91 | 8 | Central Square Central SD | Central Square |
| 91 | 8 | Commack UFSD | East Northport |
| 91 | 8 | Fairport Central SD | Fairport |
| 91 | 8 | Freeport UFSD | Freeport |
| 91 | 8 | Huntington UFSD | Huntington Stn |
| 91 | 8 | Indian River Central SD | Philadelphia |
| 91 | 8 | Lancaster Central SD | Lancaster |
| 91 | 8 | Niskayuna Central SD | Schenectady |
| 91 | 8 | North Tonawanda City SD | North Tonawanda |
| 91 | 8 | Plainview-Old Bethpage Central SD | Plainview |
| 91 | 8 | Poughkeepsie City SD | Poughkeepsie |
| 91 | 8 | Saratoga Spgs City SD | Saratoga Spgs |
| 91 | 8 | South Colonie Central SD | Albany |
| 91 | 8 | Three Village Central SD | Stony Brook |
| 91 | 8 | Troy City SD | Troy |
| 91 | 8 | Uniondale UFSD | Uniondale |
| 91 | 8 | Watertown City SD | Watertown |
| 91 | 8 | White Plains City SD | White Plains |
| 91 | 8 | William Floyd UFSD | Mastic Beach |
| 114 | 7 | Bay Shore UFSD | Bay Shore |
| 114 | 7 | Bedford Central SD | Bedford |
| 114 | 7 | East Greenbush Central SD | East Greenbush |
| 114 | 7 | East Islip UFSD | Islip Terrace |
| 114 | 7 | East Syracuse-Minoa Central SD | East Syracuse |
| 114 | 7 | Evans-Brant Central SD (Lake Shore) | Angola |
| 114 | 7 | Garden City UFSD | Garden City |
| 114 | 7 | Guilderland Central SD | Guilderland |
| 114 | 7 | Horseheads Central SD | Horseheads |
| 114 | 7 | Hyde Park Central SD | Hyde Park |
| 114 | 7 | Long Beach City SD | Long Beach |
| 114 | 7 | Longwood Central SD | Middle Island |
| 114 | 7 | Lynbrook UFSD | Lynbrook |
| 114 | 7 | Middletown City SD | Middletown |
| 114 | 7 | Mineola UFSD | Mineola |
| 114 | 7 | Monroe-Woodbury Central SD | Central Valley |
| 114 | 7 | North Babylon UFSD | North Babylon |
| 114 | 7 | Oneida City SD | Oneida |
| 114 | 7 | Oswego City SD | Oswego |
| 114 | 7 | Pine Bush Central SD | Pine Bush |
| 114 | 7 | Port Washington UFSD | Port Washington |
| 114 | 7 | Ramapo Central SD (Suffern) | Hillburn |
| 114 | 7 | Riverhead Central SD | Riverhead |
| 114 | 7 | Rockville Ctr UFSD | Rockville Ctr |
| 114 | 7 | Scarsdale UFSD | Scarsdale |
| 114 | 7 | Union-Endicott Central SD | Endicott |
| 114 | 7 | Valley Central SD (Montgomery) | Montgomery |
| 114 | 7 | Vestal Central SD | Vestal |
| 114 | 7 | West Babylon UFSD | West Babylon |
| 114 | 7 | West Genesee Central SD | Camillus |
| 114 | 7 | Whitesboro Central SD | Yorkville |
| 145 | 6 | Amsterdam City SD | Amsterdam |
| 145 | 6 | Averill Park Central SD | Averill Park |
| 145 | 6 | Ballston Spa Central SD | Ballston Spa |
| 145 | 6 | Beacon City SD | Beacon |
| 145 | 6 | Camden Central SD | Camden |
| 145 | 6 | Chappaqua Central SD | Chappaqua |
| 145 | 6 | Clarence Central SD | Clarence Center |
| 145 | 6 | Comsewogue School District | Port Jeff Stn |
| 145 | 6 | Cortland City SD | Cortland |
| 145 | 6 | Deer Park UFSD | Deer Park |
| 145 | 6 | Dunkirk City SD | Dunkirk |
| 145 | 6 | East Irondequoit Central SD | Rochester |
| 145 | 6 | Elmont UFSD | Elmont |
| 145 | 6 | Farmingdale UFSD | Farmingdale |
| 145 | 6 | Fayetteville-Manlius Central SD | Manlius |
| 145 | 6 | Frontier Central SD | Hamburg |
| 145 | 6 | Fulton City SD | Fulton |
| 145 | 6 | Gates-Chili Central SD | Rochester |
| 145 | 6 | Glen Cove City SD | Glen Cove |
| 145 | 6 | Glens Falls City SD | Glens Falls |
| 145 | 6 | Gloversville City SD | Gloversville |
| 145 | 6 | Greenburgh Central SD | Hartsdale |
| 145 | 6 | Hamburg Central SD | Hamburg |
| 145 | 6 | Harrison Central SD | Harrison |
| 145 | 6 | Iroquois Central SD | Elma |
| 145 | 6 | Katonah-Lewisboro UFSD | South Salem |
| 145 | 6 | Mahopac Central SD | Mahopac |
| 145 | 6 | Mamaroneck UFSD | Mamaroneck |
| 145 | 6 | Marlboro Central SD | Marlboro |
| 145 | 6 | Monticello Central SD | Monticello |
| 145 | 6 | Niagara-Wheatfield Central SD | Niagara Falls |
| 145 | 6 | North Bellmore UFSD | Bellmore |
| 145 | 6 | Olean City SD | Olean |
| 145 | 6 | Oneonta City SD | Oneonta |
| 145 | 6 | Orchard Park Central SD | Orchard Park |
| 145 | 6 | Ossining UFSD | Ossining |
| 145 | 6 | Pelham UFSD | Pelham |
| 145 | 6 | Penfield Central SD | Rochester |
| 145 | 6 | Port Chester-Rye UFSD | Port Chester |
| 145 | 6 | Saugerties Central SD | Saugerties |
| 145 | 6 | Scotia-Glenville Central SD | Scotia |
| 145 | 6 | South Country Central SD | East Patchogue |
| 145 | 6 | S Glens Fls Central SD | S Glens Fls |
| 145 | 6 | South Huntington UFSD | Huntington Stn |
| 145 | 6 | Spencerport Central SD | Spencerport |
| 145 | 6 | Sweet Home Central SD | Amherst |
| 145 | 6 | UFSD of the Tarrytowns | Sleepy Hollow |
| 145 | 6 | Warwick Valley Central SD | Warwick |
| 145 | 6 | Westbury UFSD | Old Westbury |
| 145 | 6 | Yorktown Central SD | Yorktown Hgts |
| 195 | 5 | Amityville UFSD | Amityville |
| 195 | 5 | Batavia City SD | Batavia |
| 195 | 5 | Bayport-Blue Point UFSD | Bayport |
| 195 | 5 | Bellmore-Merrick Central High SD | North Merrick |
| 195 | 5 | Bethpage UFSD | Bethpage |
| 195 | 5 | Brewster Central SD | Brewster |
| 195 | 5 | Brockport Central SD | Brockport |
| 195 | 5 | Burnt Hills-Ballston Lake CSD | Scotia |
| 195 | 5 | Carmel Central SD | Patterson |
| 195 | 5 | Carthage Central SD | Carthage |
| 195 | 5 | Chittenango Central SD | Chittenango |
| 195 | 5 | Churchville-Chili Central SD | Churchville |
| 195 | 5 | Cohoes City SD | Cohoes |
| 195 | 5 | Copiague UFSD | Copiague |
| 195 | 5 | Cornwall Central SD | Cornwall on Hdsn |
| 195 | 5 | Dryden Central SD | Dryden |
| 195 | 5 | Eastchester UFSD | Eastchester |
| 195 | 5 | Grand Island Central SD | Grand Island |
| 195 | 5 | Hauppauge UFSD | Hauppauge |
| 195 | 5 | Hendrick Hudson Central SD | Montrose |
| 195 | 5 | Herricks UFSD | New Hyde Park |
| 195 | 5 | Hewlett-Woodmere UFSD | Woodmere |
| 195 | 5 | Hilton Central SD | Hilton |
| 195 | 5 | Homer Central SD | Homer |
| 195 | 5 | Hornell City SD | Hornell |
| 195 | 5 | Hudson Falls Central SD | Fort Edward |
| 195 | 5 | Islip UFSD | Islip |
| 195 | 5 | Jamesville-Dewitt Central SD | Dewitt |
| 195 | 5 | Jericho UFSD | Jericho |
| 195 | 5 | Johnstown City SD | Johnstown |
| 195 | 5 | Kinderhook Central SD | Valatie |
| 195 | 5 | Kings Park Central SD | Kings Park |
| 195 | 5 | Lawrence UFSD | Lawrence |
| 195 | 5 | Malone Central SD | Malone |
| 195 | 5 | Massena Central SD | Massena |
| 195 | 5 | Mexico Central SD | Mexico |
| 195 | 5 | Minisink Valley Central SD | Slate Hill |
| 195 | 5 | New Hartford Central SD | New Hartford |
| 195 | 5 | Newark Central SD | Newark |
| 195 | 5 | Newfane Central SD | Burt |
| 195 | 5 | North Shore Central SD | Sea Cliff |
| 195 | 5 | Nyack UFSD | Nyack |
| 195 | 5 | Ogdensburg City SD | Ogdensburg |
| 195 | 5 | Onteora Central SD | Boiceville |
| 195 | 5 | Pearl River UFSD | Pearl River |
| 195 | 5 | Peekskill City SD | Peekskill |
| 195 | 5 | Plainedge UFSD | N Massapequa |
| 195 | 5 | Plattsburgh City SD | Plattsburgh |
| 195 | 5 | Rondout Valley Central SD | Accord |
| 195 | 5 | Roosevelt UFSD | Roosevelt |
| 195 | 5 | Roslyn UFSD | Roslyn |
| 195 | 5 | Rye City SD | Rye |
| 195 | 5 | Sayville UFSD | Sayville |
| 195 | 5 | Schalmont Central SD | Schenectady |
| 195 | 5 | Sewanhaka Central High SD | Floral Park |
| 195 | 5 | Shoreham-Wading River Central SD | Shoreham |
| 195 | 5 | South Orangetown Central SD | Blauvelt |
| 195 | 5 | Tonawanda City SD | Tonawanda |

*Note: This section only includes districts with 1,500 or more students; All categories are ranked from high to low*

| 195 | 5 | Vernon-Verona-Sherrill Central SD | Verona |
|---|---|---|---|
| 195 | 5 | Victor Central SD | Victor |
| 195 | 5 | Wallkill Central SD | Wallkill |
| 195 | 5 | Wantagh UFSD | Wantagh |
| 195 | 5 | Washingtonville Central SD | Washingtonville |
| 195 | 5 | Waterloo Central SD | Waterloo |
| 195 | 5 | Waverly Central SD | Waverly |
| 195 | 5 | Wayne Central SD | Ontario Center |
| 195 | 5 | West Hempstead UFSD | West Hempstead |
| 262 | 4 | Alden Central SD | Alden |
| 262 | 4 | Amherst Central SD | Amherst |
| 262 | 4 | Attica Central SD | Attica |
| 262 | 4 | Bath Central SD | Bath |
| 262 | 4 | Beekmantown Central SD | West Chazy |
| 262 | 4 | Brighton Central SD | Rochester |
| 262 | 4 | Broadalbin-Perth Central SD | Broadalbin |
| 262 | 4 | Byram Hills Central SD | Armonk |
| 262 | 4 | Canandaigua City SD | Canandaigua |
| 262 | 4 | Canastota Central SD | Canastota |
| 262 | 4 | Cheektowaga Central SD | Cheektowaga |
| 262 | 4 | Cheektowaga-Maryvale UFSD | Cheektowaga |
| 262 | 4 | Cheektowaga-Sloan UFSD | Sloan |
| 262 | 4 | Chenango Forks Central SD | Binghamton |
| 262 | 4 | Chenango Valley Central SD | Binghamton |
| 262 | 4 | Cobleskill-Richmondville Central SD | Cobleskill |
| 262 | 4 | Cold Spring Hrbr Central SD | Cold Spring Hrbr |
| 262 | 4 | Coxsackie-Athens Central SD | Coxsackie |
| 262 | 4 | Dansville Central SD | Dansville |
| 262 | 4 | Dover UFSD | Dover Plains |
| 262 | 4 | Eastport-South Manor CSD | Manorville |
| 262 | 4 | Elwood UFSD | Greenlawn |
| 262 | 4 | Fredonia Central SD | Fredonia |
| 262 | 4 | Geneva City SD | Geneva |
| 262 | 4 | Goshen Central SD | Goshen |
| 262 | 4 | Gouverneur Central SD | Gouverneur |
| 262 | 4 | Harborfields Central SD | Greenlawn |
| 262 | 4 | Holland Patent Central SD | Holland Patent |
| 262 | 4 | Honeoye Falls-Lima Central SD | Honeoye Falls |
| 262 | 4 | Irvington UFSD | Irvington |
| 262 | 4 | Island Trees UFSD | Levittown |
| 262 | 4 | Johnson City Central SD | Johnson City |
| 262 | 4 | Jordan-Elbridge Central SD | Elbridge |
| 262 | 4 | Lackawanna City SD | Lackawanna |
| 262 | 4 | Lansingburgh Central SD | Troy |
| 262 | 4 | Lewiston-Porter Central SD | Youngstown |
| 262 | 4 | Livonia Central SD | Livonia |
| 262 | 4 | Locust Valley Central SD | Locust Valley |
| 262 | 4 | Maine-Endwell Central SD | Endwell |
| 262 | 4 | Malverne UFSD | Malverne |
| 262 | 4 | Manhasset UFSD | Manhasset |
| 262 | 4 | Medina Central SD | Medina |
| 262 | 4 | Miller Place UFSD | Miller Place |
| 262 | 4 | Mohonasen Central SD | Schenectady |
| 262 | 4 | Mount Pleasant Central SD | Thornwood |
| 262 | 4 | Nanuet UFSD | Nanuet |
| 262 | 4 | New Hyde Pk-Garden City Pk UFSD | New Hyde Park |
| 262 | 4 | New Paltz Central SD | New Paltz |
| 262 | 4 | Norwich City SD | Norwich |
| 262 | 4 | Owego-Apalachin Central SD | Owego |
| 262 | 4 | Palmyra-Macedon Central SD | Palmyra |
| 262 | 4 | Peru Central SD | Peru |
| 262 | 4 | Phelps-Clifton Springs Central SD | Clifton Springs |
| 262 | 4 | Port Jervis City SD | Port Jervis |
| 262 | 4 | Queensbury UFSD | Queensbury |
| 262 | 4 | Ravena-Coeymans-Selkirk Ctrl SD | Selkirk |
| 262 | 4 | Red Hook Central SD | Red Hook |
| 262 | 4 | Rocky Point UFSD | Rocky Point |
| 262 | 4 | Saranac Central SD | Dannemora |
| 262 | 4 | Seaford UFSD | Seaford |
| 262 | 4 | Skaneateles Central SD | Skaneateles |
| 262 | 4 | Somers Central SD | Somers |
| 262 | 4 | South Jefferson Central SD | Adams Center |
| 262 | 4 | Spackenkill UFSD | Poughkeepsie |
| 262 | 4 | Springville-Griffith Institute CSD | Springville |
| 262 | 4 | Starpoint Central SD | Lockport |
| 262 | 4 | Susquehanna Valley Central SD | Conklin |
| 262 | 4 | Valhalla UFSD | Valhalla |
| 262 | 4 | Valley Stream 13 UFSD | Valley Stream |
| 262 | 4 | Valley Stream Central High SD | Valley Stream |
| 262 | 4 | Wayland-Cohocton Central SD | Wayland |
| 262 | 4 | Westhill Central SD | Syracuse |
| 262 | 4 | Windsor Central SD | Windsor |
| 262 | 4 | Wyandanch UFSD | Wyandanch |
| 262 | 4 | Yorkshire-Pioneer Central SD | Yorkshire |
| 337 | 3 | Akron Central SD | Akron |

| 337 | 3 | Albion Central SD | Albion |
|---|---|---|---|
| 337 | 3 | Ardsley UFSD | Ardsley |
| 337 | 3 | Babylon UFSD | Babylon |
| 337 | 3 | Blind Brook-Rye UFSD | Rye Brook |
| 337 | 3 | Briarcliff Mnr UFSD | Briarcliff Mnr |
| 337 | 3 | Bronxville UFSD | Bronxville |
| 337 | 3 | Catskill Central SD | Catskill |
| 337 | 3 | Cazenovia Central SD | Cazenovia |
| 337 | 3 | Center Moriches UFSD | Center Moriches |
| 337 | 3 | Croton-Harmon UFSD | Croton on Hdsn |
| 337 | 3 | Depew UFSD | Depew |
| 337 | 3 | East Aurora UFSD | East Aurora |
| 337 | 3 | East Hampton UFSD | East Hampton |
| 337 | 3 | East Williston UFSD | Old Westbury |
| 337 | 3 | Eden Central SD | Eden |
| 337 | 3 | Edgemont UFSD | Scarsdale |
| 337 | 3 | Ellenville Central SD | Ellenville |
| 337 | 3 | Franklin Square UFSD | Franklin Square |
| 337 | 3 | General Brown Central SD | Dexter |
| 337 | 3 | Hampton Bays UFSD | Hampton Bays |
| 337 | 3 | Hannibal Central SD | Hannibal |
| 337 | 3 | Hastings-on-Hudson UFSD | Hastings on Hdsn |
| 337 | 3 | Highland Central SD | Highland |
| 337 | 3 | Hudson City SD | Hudson |
| 337 | 3 | Ilion Central SD | Ilion |
| 337 | 3 | Liberty Central SD | Liberty |
| 337 | 3 | Marcellus Central SD | Marcellus |
| 337 | 3 | Merrick UFSD | Merrick |
| 337 | 3 | Mount Sinai UFSD | Mount Sinai |
| 337 | 3 | Oyster Bay-East Norwich Central SD | Oyster Bay |
| 337 | 3 | Penn Yan Central SD | Penn Yan |
| 337 | 3 | Phoenix Central SD | Phoenix |
| 337 | 3 | Pleasantville UFSD | Pleasantville |
| 337 | 3 | Putnam Valley Central SD | Putnam Valley |
| 337 | 3 | Royalton-Hartland Central SD | Middleport |
| 337 | 3 | Salmon River Central SD | Fort Covington |
| 337 | 3 | Sherburne-Earlville Central SD | Sherburne |
| 337 | 3 | Solvay UFSD | Solvay |
| 337 | 3 | Southampton UFSD | Southampton |
| 337 | 3 | Southwestern CSD at Jamestown | Jamestown |
| 337 | 3 | Taconic Hills Central SD | Craryville |
| 337 | 3 | Westhampton Bch UFSD | Westhampton Bch |
| 380 | 2 | Floral Park-Bellerose UFSD | Floral Park |
| 380 | 2 | Mattituck-Cutchogue UFSD | Cutchogue |
| 380 | 2 | Schuylerville Central SD | Schuylerville |
| 383 | 1 | Charter School for Applied Tech | Buffalo |

## Number of Teachers

| Rank | Number | District Name | City |
|---|---|---|---|
| 1 | 70,127.9 | New York City Public Schools | New York |
| 2 | 4,475.2 | NYC Special Schools - District 75 | New York |
| 3 | 3,907.1 | NYC Geographic District #10 | Bronx |
| 4 | 3,883.1 | NYC Geographic District # 2 | New York |
| 5 | 3,794.5 | NYC Geographic District #31 | Staten Island |
| 6 | 3,308.3 | NYC Geographic District #24 | Ridgewood |
| 7 | 3,031.7 | Buffalo City SD | Buffalo |
| 8 | 3,027.6 | NYC Geographic District #27 | Ozone Park |
| 9 | 2,806.1 | Rochester City SD | Rochester |
| 10 | 2,710.6 | NYC Geographic District #20 | Brooklyn |
| 11 | 2,664.3 | NYC Geographic District # 9 | Bronx |
| 12 | 2,571.8 | NYC Geographic District #11 | Bronx |
| 13 | 2,525.5 | NYC Geographic District #30 | Long Isl City |
| 14 | 2,379.5 | NYC Geographic District #22 | Brooklyn |
| 15 | 2,240.7 | NYC Geographic District # 8 | Bronx |
| 16 | 2,231.3 | NYC Geographic District #21 | Brooklyn |
| 17 | 2,169.9 | NYC Geographic District #28 | Jamaica |
| 18 | 2,062.5 | NYC Geographic District #25 | Flushing |
| 19 | 1,973.8 | NYC Geographic District #15 | Brooklyn |
| 20 | 1,959.4 | NYC Geographic District #17 | Brooklyn |
| 21 | 1,840.3 | NYC Geographic District #19 | Brooklyn |
| 22 | 1,838.0 | NYC Geographic District # 6 | New York |
| 23 | 1,789.9 | NYC Geographic District #26 | Bayside |
| 24 | 1,769.9 | Syracuse City SD | Syracuse |
| 25 | 1,755.4 | NYC Geographic District #29 | Rosedale |
| 26 | 1,713.3 | NYC Geographic District #12 | Bronx |
| 27 | 1,542.9 | NYC Geographic District # 3 | New York |
| 28 | 1,510.8 | NYC Geographic District # 7 | Bronx |
| 29 | 1,480.8 | NYC Geographic District #14 | Brooklyn |
| 30 | 1,454.6 | NYC Geographic District #13 | Brooklyn |
| 31 | 1,294.8 | NYC Geographic District #18 | Brooklyn |
| 32 | 1,191.7 | NYC Geographic District #32 | Brooklyn |
| 33 | 1,189.3 | Brentwood UFSD | Brentwood |
| 34 | 1,186.6 | NYC Geographic District # 4 | New York |
| 35 | 1,085.0 | Sachem Central SD | Holbrook |

| 36 | 1,040.9 | NYC Geographic District # 5 | New York |
|---|---|---|---|
| 37 | 1,032.3 | Greece Central SD | Rochester |
| 38 | 1,003.3 | Yonkers City SD | Yonkers |
| 39 | 942.1 | NYC Geographic District # 1 | New York |
| 40 | 921.5 | Newburgh City SD | Newburgh |
| 41 | 868.2 | NYC Geographic District #23 | Brooklyn |
| 42 | 814.6 | Wappingers Central SD | Wappingers Fls |
| 43 | 798.3 | Williamsville Central SD | East Amherst |
| 44 | 793.6 | Schenectady City SD | Schenectady |
| 45 | 792.5 | NYC Geographic District #16 | Brooklyn |
| 46 | 771.5 | Half Hollow Hills Central SD | Dix Hills |
| 47 | 748.3 | Smithtown Central SD | Smithtown |
| 48 | 743.4 | Utica City SD | Utica |
| 49 | 723.1 | North Syracuse Central SD | North Syracuse |
| 50 | 721.6 | New Rochelle City SD | New Rochelle |
| 51 | 699.8 | Kenmore-Tonawanda UFSD | Buffalo |
| 52 | 699.2 | Albany City SD | Albany |
| 53 | 697.3 | Middle Country Central SD | Centereach |
| 54 | 692.8 | Arlington Central SD | Poughkeepsie |
| 55 | 673.3 | Shenendehowa Central SD | Clifton Park |
| 56 | 670.5 | Webster Central SD | Webster |
| 57 | 659.1 | William Floyd UFSD | Mastic Beach |
| 58 | 658.4 | Levittown UFSD | Levittown |
| 59 | 658.0 | Clarkstown Central SD | New City |
| 60 | 654.8 | Mount Vernon City SD | Mount Vernon |
| 61 | 650.6 | Massapequa UFSD | Massapequa |
| 62 | 642.9 | Longwood Central SD | Middle Island |
| 63 | 619.5 | East Ramapo Central SD | Spring Valley |
| 64 | 613.0 | Great Neck UFSD | Great Neck |
| 65 | 602.7 | North Rockland Central SD | Garnerville |
| 66 | 598.5 | East Meadow UFSD | Westbury |
| 67 | 595.3 | Syosset Central SD | Syosset |
| 68 | 588.2 | Uniondale UFSD | Uniondale |
| 69 | 584.8 | Elmira City SD | Elmira |
| 70 | 584.1 | Liverpool Central SD | Liverpool |
| 71 | 580.3 | Three Village Central SD | Stony Brook |
| 72 | 577.2 | Northport-East Northport UFSD | Northport |
| 73 | 565.7 | Commack UFSD | East Northport |
| 74 | 560.8 | White Plains City SD | White Plains |
| 75 | 560.7 | Kingston City SD | Kingston |
| 76 | 557.6 | Sewanhaka Central High SD | Floral Park |
| 77 | 556.0 | Connetquot Central SD | Bohemia |
| 78 | 554.6 | Patchogue-Medford UFSD | Patchogue |
| 79 | 547.0 | Central Islip UFSD | Central Islip |
| 80 | 546.2 | Binghamton City SD | Binghamton |
| 81 | 545.7 | West Seneca Central SD | West Seneca |
| 82 | 535.4 | Freeport UFSD | Freeport |
| 83 | 528.9 | Lindenhurst UFSD | Lindenhurst |
| 84 | 527.9 | Monroe-Woodbury Central SD | Central Valley |
| 85 | 512.3 | Fairport Central SD | Fairport |
| 86 | 504.7 | Saratoga Spgs City SD | Saratoga Spgs |
| 87 | 503.3 | Farmingdale UFSD | Farmingdale |
| 88 | 492.3 | Middletown City SD | Middletown |
| 89 | 491.8 | Rush-Henrietta Central SD | Henrietta |
| 90 | 488.0 | Lakeland Central SD | Shrub Oak |
| 91 | 474.9 | South Huntington UFSD | Huntington Stn |
| 92 | 470.8 | Ithaca City SD | Ithaca |
| 93 | 468.9 | Bay Shore UFSD | Bay Shore |
| 94 | 468.6 | Oceanside UFSD | Oceanside |
| 95 | 466.8 | Jamestown City SD | Jamestown |
| 96 | 465.9 | Pittsford Central SD | Pittsford |
| 97 | 465.6 | Rome City SD | Rome |
| 98 | 458.5 | Niagara Falls City SD | Niagara Falls |
| 99 | 454.4 | Lancaster Central SD | Lancaster |
| 100 | 449.5 | Corning City SD | Painted Post |
| 101 | 448.7 | Lockport City SD | Lockport |
| 102 | 447.4 | South Colonie Central SD | Albany |
| 103 | 438.4 | Bellmore-Merrick Central High SD | North Merrick |
| 104 | 431.0 | Frontier Central SD | Hamburg |
| 105 | 429.6 | West Islip UFSD | West Islip |
| 106 | 421.7 | Guilderland Central SD | Guilderland |
| 107 | 419.3 | North Colonie Central SD | Latham |
| 108 | 417.0 | Hempstead UFSD | Hempstead |
| 109 | 415.5 | Baldwin UFSD | Baldwin |
| 110 | 415.3 | Hicksville UFSD | Hicksville |
| 111 | 412.9 | Pine Bush Central SD | Pine Bush |
| 112 | 404.5 | Baldwinsville Central SD | Baldwinsville |
| 113 | 394.6 | Deer Park UFSD | Deer Park |
| 114 | 392.3 | Orchard Park Central SD | Orchard Park |
| 115 | 392.1 | Scarsdale UFSD | Scarsdale |
| 116 | 391.6 | Penfield Central SD | Rochester |
| 117 | 388.8 | Mamaroneck UFSD | Mamaroneck |
| 118 | 386.2 | Valley Central SD (Montgomery) | Montgomery |
| 119 | 382.0 | Ramapo Central SD (Suffern) | Hillburn |
| 120 | 378.7 | South Country Central SD | East Patchogue |

*Note: This section only includes districts with 1,500 or more students; All categories are ranked from high to low*

| | | | |
|---|---|---|---|
| 121 | 376.4 | Mahopac Central SD | Mahopac |
| 122 | 375.2 | Bethlehem Central SD | Delmar |
| 123 | 371.1 | Clarence Central SD | Clarence Center |
| 124 | 364.5 | Hilton Central SD | Hilton |
| 124 | 364.5 | West Babylon UFSD | West Babylon |
| 126 | 364.1 | Bedford Central SD | Bedford |
| 127 | 363.5 | Auburn City SD | Auburn |
| 128 | 360.0 | East Islip UFSD | Islip Terrace |
| 129 | 357.9 | West Genesee Central SD | Camillus |
| 130 | 354.0 | Gates-Chili Central SD | Rochester |
| 131 | 351.7 | Union-Endicott Central SD | Endicott |
| 132 | 351.1 | Herricks UFSD | New Hyde Park |
| 133 | 350.7 | Chappaqua Central SD | Chappaqua |
| 134 | 349.8 | Poughkeepsie City SD | Poughkeepsie |
| 135 | 346.2 | Riverhead Central SD | Riverhead |
| 136 | 343.9 | Hamburg Central SD | Hamburg |
| 137 | 341.3 | Rockville Ctr UFSD | Rockville Ctr |
| 137 | 341.3 | Spencerport Central SD | Spencerport |
| 139 | 340.0 | North Babylon UFSD | North Babylon |
| 140 | 339.6 | East Greenbush Central SD | East Greenbush |
| 141 | 339.0 | Troy City SD | Troy |
| 142 | 338.9 | Long Beach City SD | Long Beach |
| 143 | 336.6 | Carmel Central SD | Patterson |
| 143 | 336.6 | Westbury UFSD | Old Westbury |
| 145 | 336.4 | Garden City UFSD | Garden City |
| 146 | 333.1 | Niagara-Wheatfield Central SD | Niagara Falls |
| 147 | 332.2 | Washingtonville Central SD | Washingtonville |
| 148 | 331.8 | Oswego City SD | Oswego |
| 149 | 331.5 | Ossining UFSD | Ossining |
| 150 | 328.9 | Ballston Spa Central SD | Ballston Spa |
| 150 | 328.9 | Harrison Central SD | Harrison |
| 152 | 326.6 | Copiague UFSD | Copiague |
| 153 | 324.2 | Central Square Central SD | Central Square |
| 154 | 324.0 | Fayetteville-Manlius Central SD | Manlius |
| 155 | 323.8 | East Syracuse-Minoa Central SD | East Syracuse |
| 156 | 323.2 | Churchville-Chili Central SD | Churchville |
| 157 | 315.9 | North Tonawanda City SD | North Tonawanda |
| 158 | 315.6 | Hyde Park Central SD | Hyde Park |
| 159 | 315.5 | Vestal Central SD | Vestal |
| 160 | 314.3 | Niskayuna Central SD | Schenectady |
| 161 | 314.0 | Horseheads Central SD | Horseheads |
| 162 | 313.6 | Canandaigua City SD | Canandaigua |
| 163 | 313.0 | Jericho UFSD | Jericho |
| 164 | 312.8 | Valley Stream Central High SD | Valley Stream |
| 165 | 310.9 | Katonah-Lewisboro UFSD | South Salem |
| 166 | 310.7 | Yorktown Central SD | Yorktown Hgts |
| 167 | 310.6 | Warwick Valley Central SD | Warwick |
| 168 | 310.3 | Hauppauge UFSD | Hauppauge |
| 169 | 309.4 | Watertown City SD | Watertown |
| 170 | 308.5 | Lawrence UFSD | Lawrence |
| 171 | 306.8 | Kings Park Central SD | Kings Park |
| 172 | 304.3 | Monticello Central SD | Monticello |
| 173 | 304.0 | Brighton Central SD | Rochester |
| 174 | 302.8 | Victor Central SD | Victor |
| 175 | 300.5 | Brockport Central SD | Brockport |
| 176 | 300.1 | East Irondequoit Central SD | Rochester |
| 177 | 296.8 | Amsterdam City SD | Amsterdam |
| 178 | 286.2 | Sweet Home Central SD | Amherst |
| 179 | 283.6 | Comsewogue School District | Port Jeff Stn |
| 180 | 283.2 | Brewster Central SD | Brewster |
| 181 | 283.0 | Roslyn UFSD | Roslyn |
| 182 | 282.2 | North Shore Central SD | Sea Cliff |
| 183 | 281.3 | Fulton City SD | Fulton |
| 184 | 281.2 | Eastport-South Manor CSD | Manorville |
| 185 | 277.6 | Hewlett-Woodmere UFSD | Woodmere |
| 186 | 277.2 | Port Chester-Rye UFSD | Port Chester |
| 187 | 274.6 | Queensbury UFSD | Queensbury |
| 188 | 273.7 | S Glens Fls Central SD | S Glens Fls |
| 189 | 272.9 | South Orangetown Central SD | Blauvelt |
| 190 | 270.1 | Wantagh UFSD | Wantagh |
| 191 | 268.4 | Elmont UFSD | Elmont |
| 192 | 265.0 | Mineola UFSD | Mineola |
| 193 | 263.4 | Whitesboro Central SD | Yorkville |
| 194 | 261.5 | Plainedge UFSD | N Massapequa |
| 195 | 258.3 | Averill Park Central SD | Averill Park |
| 196 | 255.9 | Indian River Central SD | Philadelphia |
| 197 | 255.4 | Manhasset UFSD | Manhasset |
| 198 | 254.7 | Islip UFSD | Islip |
| 199 | 253.2 | Nyack UFSD | Nyack |
| 200 | 252.0 | Amherst Central SD | Amherst |
| 201 | 251.8 | Somers Central SD | Somers |
| 202 | 251.7 | Glen Cove City SD | Glen Cove |
| 203 | 251.4 | Sayville UFSD | Sayville |
| 204 | 251.2 | Wallkill Central SD | Wallkill |
| 205 | 249.3 | Bethpage UFSD | Bethpage |
| 206 | 248.0 | Amityville UFSD | Amityville |
| 207 | 246.2 | Roosevelt UFSD | Roosevelt |
| 208 | 245.4 | Lynbrook UFSD | Lynbrook |
| 209 | 243.6 | Burnt Hills-Ballston Lake CSD | Scotia |
| 210 | 242.8 | Evans-Brant Central SD (Lake Shore) | Angola |
| 211 | 240.4 | Bayport-Blue Point UFSD | Bayport |
| 212 | 238.1 | Eastchester UFSD | Eastchester |
| 213 | 238.0 | Rondout Valley Central SD | Accord |
| 214 | 236.4 | Harborfields Central SD | Greenlawn |
| 214 | 236.4 | Rye City SD | Rye |
| 216 | 236.3 | Carthage Central SD | Carthage |
| 217 | 235.9 | Saugerties Central SD | Saugerties |
| 218 | 235.8 | Beacon City SD | Beacon |
| 219 | 235.0 | Jamesville-Dewitt Central SD | Dewitt |
| 220 | 233.0 | Mohonasen Central SD | Schenectady |
| 221 | 230.6 | Rocky Point UFSD | Rocky Point |
| 222 | 229.4 | Port Jervis City SD | Port Jervis |
| 222 | 229.4 | Wayne Central SD | Ontario Center |
| 224 | 228.5 | Byram Hills Central SD | Armonk |
| 225 | 227.1 | Cortland City SD | Cortland |
| 226 | 226.3 | Grand Island Central SD | Grand Island |
| 227 | 226.0 | Gloversville City SD | Gloversville |
| 228 | 225.0 | Maine-Endwell Central SD | Endwell |
| 229 | 222.1 | Scotia-Glenville Central SD | Scotia |
| 230 | 221.6 | Batavia City SD | Batavia |
| 231 | 220.8 | Cornwall Central SD | Cornwall on Hdsn |
| 232 | 219.9 | Miller Place UFSD | Miller Place |
| 233 | 218.8 | Starpoint Central SD | Lockport |
| 234 | 216.9 | Dunkirk City SD | Dunkirk |
| 235 | 216.8 | Goshen Central SD | Goshen |
| 236 | 216.5 | Pelham UFSD | Pelham |
| 237 | 215.9 | Island Trees UFSD | Levittown |
| 238 | 215.0 | Peekskill City SD | Peekskill |
| 239 | 214.9 | Hendrick Hudson Central SD | Montrose |
| 240 | 214.4 | Iroquois Central SD | Elma |
| 241 | 213.5 | Seaford UFSD | Seaford |
| 242 | 212.8 | Johnson City Central SD | Johnson City |
| 243 | 211.5 | Camden Central SD | Camden |
| 244 | 208.8 | Malone Central SD | Malone |
| 245 | 208.5 | Massena Central SD | Massena |
| 246 | 205.1 | Geneva City SD | Geneva |
| 247 | 203.2 | UFSD of the Tarrytowns | Sleepy Hollow |
| 248 | 202.2 | Shoreham-Wading River Central SD | Shoreham |
| 249 | 201.8 | Newark Central SD | Newark |
| 250 | 201.1 | Lansingburgh Central SD | Troy |
| 251 | 200.9 | Yorkshire-Pioneer Central SD | Yorkshire |
| 252 | 199.6 | New Hartford Central SD | New Hartford |
| 253 | 199.0 | Beekmantown Central SD | West Chazy |
| 254 | 198.3 | Ravena-Coeymans-Selkirk Ctrl SD | Selkirk |
| 255 | 197.6 | Pearl River UFSD | Pearl River |
| 256 | 196.8 | Locust Valley Central SD | Locust Valley |
| 257 | 195.8 | Nanuet UFSD | Nanuet |
| 258 | 195.2 | Ardsley UFSD | Ardsley |
| 258 | 195.2 | Plattsburgh City SD | Plattsburgh |
| 260 | 194.0 | Mexico Central SD | Mexico |
| 261 | 193.8 | Olean City SD | Olean |
| 262 | 193.7 | Honeoye Falls-Lima Central SD | Honeoye Falls |
| 263 | 192.2 | Palmyra-Macedon Central SD | Palmyra |
| 264 | 190.6 | Glens Falls City SD | Glens Falls |
| 265 | 189.9 | Lewiston-Porter Central SD | Youngstown |
| 266 | 189.3 | Norwich City SD | Norwich |
| 267 | 187.3 | Hudson City SD | Hudson |
| 267 | 187.3 | New Paltz Central SD | New Paltz |
| 269 | 186.7 | Oneida City SD | Oneida |
| 270 | 184.8 | Phoenix Central SD | Phoenix |
| 271 | 184.0 | Peru Central SD | Peru |
| 272 | 183.6 | West Hempstead UFSD | West Hempstead |
| 273 | 183.1 | North Bellmore UFSD | Bellmore |
| 274 | 182.8 | East Hampton UFSD | East Hampton |
| 275 | 182.5 | Homer Central SD | Homer |
| 276 | 182.0 | Elwood UFSD | Greenlawn |
| 277 | 180.0 | Cheektowaga Central SD | Cheektowaga |
| 277 | 180.0 | Cohoes City SD | Cohoes |
| 279 | 179.8 | Cobleskill-Richmondville Central SD | Cobleskill |
| 280 | 177.0 | Owego-Apalachin Central SD | Owego |
| 281 | 174.0 | Hudson Falls Central SD | Fort Edward |
| 282 | 173.5 | Greenburgh Central SD | Hartsdale |
| 283 | 173.2 | Kinderhook Central SD | Valatie |
| 284 | 172.6 | Chittenango Central SD | Chittenango |
| 285 | 172.5 | Cheektowaga-Maryvale UFSD | Cheektowaga |
| 285 | 172.5 | Westhampton Bch UFSD | Westhampton Bch |
| 287 | 172.2 | Red Hook Central SD | Red Hook |
| 288 | 171.8 | Mount Sinai UFSD | Mount Sinai |
| 289 | 171.3 | Albion Central SD | Albion |
| 290 | 171.0 | Southampton UFSD | Southampton |
| 291 | 170.7 | Mount Pleasant Central SD | Thornwood |
| 292 | 170.2 | Cold Spring Hrbr Central SD | Cold Spring Hrbr |
| 293 | 169.9 | Penn Yan Central SD | Penn Yan |
| 294 | 169.6 | Springville-Griffith Institute CSD | Springville |
| 295 | 169.5 | Depew UFSD | Depew |
| 296 | 169.4 | Tonawanda City SD | Tonawanda |
| 297 | 168.4 | Valley Stream 13 UFSD | Valley Stream |
| 298 | 168.1 | Malverne UFSD | Malverne |
| 299 | 167.4 | Lackawanna City SD | Lackawanna |
| 300 | 166.6 | Marlboro Central SD | Marlboro |
| 301 | 165.1 | Oneonta City SD | Oneonta |
| 302 | 163.9 | Livonia Central SD | Livonia |
| 303 | 163.4 | Wyandanch UFSD | Wyandanch |
| 304 | 163.1 | Onteora Central SD | Boiceville |
| 305 | 162.7 | Susquehanna Valley Central SD | Conklin |
| 306 | 159.3 | Dryden Central SD | Dryden |
| 307 | 158.5 | Oyster Bay-East Norwich Central SD | Oyster Bay |
| 308 | 158.1 | Vernon-Verona-Sherrill Central SD | Verona |
| 309 | 157.6 | East Williston UFSD | Old Westbury |
| 310 | 156.3 | Phelps-Clifton Springs Central SD | Clifton Springs |
| 311 | 155.3 | Briarcliff Mnr UFSD | Briarcliff Mnr |
| 311 | 155.3 | Irvington UFSD | Irvington |
| 313 | 155.0 | Westhill Central SD | Syracuse |
| 314 | 154.9 | Sherburne-Earlville Central SD | Sherburne |
| 315 | 154.1 | Pleasantville UFSD | Pleasantville |
| 315 | 154.1 | Schalmont Central SD | Schenectady |
| 315 | 154.1 | Spackenkill UFSD | Poughkeepsie |
| 318 | 153.9 | Edgemont UFSD | Scarsdale |
| 318 | 153.9 | Windsor Central SD | Windsor |
| 320 | 153.5 | South Jefferson Central SD | Adams Center |
| 321 | 152.0 | Hampton Bays UFSD | Hampton Bays |
| 322 | 151.2 | Waterloo Central SD | Waterloo |
| 323 | 151.1 | Marcellus Central SD | Marcellus |
| 323 | 151.1 | Merrick UFSD | Merrick |
| 325 | 150.9 | Ogdensburg City SD | Ogdensburg |
| 326 | 150.2 | Salmon River Central SD | Fort Covington |
| 327 | 149.3 | Solvay UFSD | Solvay |
| 328 | 148.4 | Dansville Central SD | Dansville |
| 329 | 147.8 | Schuylerville Central SD | Schuylerville |
| 330 | 147.3 | Babylon UFSD | Babylon |
| 331 | 147.1 | Taconic Hills Central SD | Craryville |
| 332 | 146.9 | Saranac Central SD | Dannemora |
| 333 | 146.7 | East Aurora UFSD | East Aurora |
| 333 | 146.7 | Newfane Central SD | Burt |
| 335 | 144.6 | Liberty Central SD | Liberty |
| 336 | 144.3 | Catskill Central SD | Catskill |
| 337 | 143.1 | Attica Central SD | Attica |
| 337 | 143.1 | Bath Central SD | Bath |
| 339 | 142.7 | Highland Central SD | Highland |
| 340 | 142.5 | Alden Central SD | Alden |
| 341 | 142.1 | Hastings-on-Hudson UFSD | Hastings on Hdsn |
| 342 | 140.3 | Ellenville Central SD | Ellenville |
| 343 | 138.6 | Hornell City SD | Hornell |
| 344 | 136.8 | Valhalla UFSD | Valhalla |
| 345 | 136.5 | Putnam Valley Central SD | Putnam Valley |
| 346 | 136.1 | Cheektowaga-Sloan UFSD | Sloan |
| 347 | 135.0 | Jordan-Elbridge Central SD | Elbridge |
| 348 | 134.8 | Bronxville UFSD | Bronxville |
| 349 | 134.2 | Wayland-Cohocton Central SD | Wayland |
| 350 | 133.2 | Franklin Square UFSD | Franklin Square |
| 351 | 133.1 | Croton-Harmon UFSD | Croton on Hdsn |
| 351 | 133.1 | Fredonia Central SD | Fredonia |
| 353 | 132.7 | Broadalbin-Perth Central SD | Broadalbin |
| 354 | 132.1 | Mattituck-Cutchogue UFSD | Cutchogue |
| 355 | 131.2 | Chenango Valley Central SD | Binghamton |
| 356 | 130.5 | Cazenovia Central SD | Cazenovia |
| 357 | 130.2 | Holland Patent Central SD | Holland Patent |
| 358 | 129.7 | New Hyde Pk-Garden City Pk UFSD | New Hyde Park |
| 359 | 128.8 | Coxsackie-Athens Central SD | Coxsackie |
| 360 | 128.4 | Ilion Central SD | Ilion |
| 361 | 127.9 | Eden Central SD | Eden |
| 362 | 126.6 | Chenango Forks Central SD | Binghamton |
| 363 | 125.8 | Southwestern CSD at Jamestown | Jamestown |
| 364 | 125.5 | Johnstown City SD | Johnstown |
| 365 | 123.1 | Blind Brook-Rye UFSD | Rye Brook |
| 366 | 122.6 | Center Moriches UFSD | Center Moriches |
| 367 | 122.4 | Waverly Central SD | Waverly |
| 368 | 121.6 | Canastota Central SD | Canastota |
| 369 | 120.3 | Akron Central SD | Akron |
| 370 | 116.9 | Dover UFSD | Dover Plains |
| 371 | 115.1 | Hannibal Central SD | Hannibal |
| 372 | 115.0 | Gouverneur Central SD | Gouverneur |
| 373 | 114.4 | Royalton-Hartland Central SD | Middleport |
| 374 | 110.8 | Charter School for Applied Tech | Buffalo |
| 375 | 106.2 | Floral Park-Bellerose UFSD | Floral Park |

*Note: This section only includes districts with 1,500 or more students; All categories are ranked from high to low*

| | | | |
|---|---|---|---|
| 376 | 105.6 | General Brown Central SD | Dexter |
| 377 | 61.4 | Huntington UFSD | Huntington Stn |
| 378 | 0.0 | Skaneateles Central SD | Skaneateles |
| n/a | n/a | Medina Central SD | Medina |
| n/a | n/a | Minisink Valley Central SD | Slate Hill |
| n/a | n/a | Plainview-Old Bethpage Central SD | Plainview |
| n/a | n/a | Port Washington UFSD | Port Washington |
| n/a | n/a | West Irondequoit Central SD | Rochester |

## Number of Students

| Rank | Number | District Name | City |
|---|---|---|---|
| 1 | 1,014,020 | New York City Public Schools | New York |
| 2 | 63,090 | NYC Geographic District #31 | Staten Island |
| 3 | 60,687 | NYC Geographic District # 2 | New York |
| 4 | 56,222 | NYC Geographic District #10 | Bronx |
| 5 | 51,213 | NYC Geographic District #24 | Ridgewood |
| 6 | 46,477 | NYC Geographic District #20 | Brooklyn |
| 7 | 45,929 | NYC Geographic District #27 | Ozone Park |
| 8 | 39,122 | NYC Geographic District #30 | Long Isl City |
| 9 | 38,520 | NYC Geographic District #11 | Bronx |
| 10 | 38,405 | NYC Geographic District #22 | Brooklyn |
| 11 | 37,779 | NYC Geographic District #21 | Brooklyn |
| 12 | 37,049 | NYC Geographic District #26 | Bayside |
| 13 | 35,907 | NYC Geographic District #28 | Jamaica |
| 14 | 35,155 | NYC Geographic District # 9 | Bronx |
| 15 | 34,526 | Buffalo City SD | Buffalo |
| 16 | 32,937 | NYC Geographic District #25 | Flushing |
| 17 | 32,753 | NYC Geographic District # 8 | Bronx |
| 18 | 32,516 | Rochester City SD | Rochester |
| 19 | 27,631 | NYC Geographic District #29 | Rosedale |
| 20 | 27,445 | NYC Geographic District #17 | Brooklyn |
| 21 | 26,355 | NYC Geographic District #19 | Brooklyn |
| 22 | 26,304 | NYC Geographic District #15 | Brooklyn |
| 23 | 25,451 | NYC Geographic District #13 | Brooklyn |
| 24 | 25,280 | NYC Geographic District # 6 | New York |
| 25 | 24,956 | Yonkers City SD | Yonkers |
| 26 | 22,856 | NYC Geographic District # 3 | New York |
| 27 | 22,825 | NYC Geographic District #12 | Bronx |
| 28 | 21,871 | NYC Special Schools - District 75 | New York |
| 29 | 21,320 | Syracuse City SD | Syracuse |
| 30 | 20,174 | NYC Geographic District #14 | Brooklyn |
| 31 | 19,136 | NYC Geographic District # 7 | Bronx |
| 32 | 18,746 | NYC Geographic District #18 | Brooklyn |
| 33 | 16,517 | Brentwood UFSD | Brentwood |
| 34 | 16,195 | NYC Geographic District #32 | Brooklyn |
| 35 | 14,760 | Sachem Central SD | Holbrook |
| 36 | 14,501 | NYC Geographic District # 4 | New York |
| 37 | 13,391 | NYC Geographic District # 5 | New York |
| 38 | 12,513 | Greece Central SD | Rochester |
| 39 | 12,407 | Wappingers Central SD | Wappingers Fls |
| 40 | 12,253 | NYC Geographic District #23 | Brooklyn |
| 41 | 12,094 | Newburgh City SD | Newburgh |
| 42 | 12,056 | NYC Geographic District # 1 | New York |
| 43 | 10,929 | Middle Country Central SD | Centereach |
| 44 | 10,862 | Smithtown Central SD | Smithtown |
| 45 | 10,850 | New Rochelle City SD | New Rochelle |
| 46 | 10,511 | Williamsville Central SD | East Amherst |
| 47 | 10,305 | NYC Geographic District #16 | Brooklyn |
| 48 | 10,041 | Arlington Central SD | Poughkeepsie |
| 49 | 10,037 | Half Hollow Hills Central SD | Dix Hills |
| 50 | 9,903 | Schenectady City SD | Schenectady |
| 51 | 9,854 | Shenendehowa Central SD | Clifton Park |
| 52 | 9,741 | North Syracuse Central SD | North Syracuse |
| 53 | 9,398 | William Floyd UFSD | Mastic Beach |
| 54 | 9,390 | Utica City SD | Utica |
| 55 | 9,196 | Clarkstown Central SD | New City |
| 56 | 9,154 | Longwood Central SD | Middle Island |
| 57 | 8,904 | Mount Vernon City SD | Mount Vernon |
| 58 | 8,732 | Webster Central SD | Webster |
| 59 | 8,571 | Patchogue-Medford UFSD | Patchogue |
| 60 | 8,449 | Sewanhaka Central High SD | Floral Park |
| 61 | 8,423 | Albany City SD | Albany |
| 62 | 8,132 | Massapequa UFSD | Massapequa |
| 63 | 8,128 | Kenmore-Tonawanda UFSD | Buffalo |
| 64 | 8,116 | East Ramapo Central SD | Spring Valley |
| 65 | 7,959 | North Rockland Central SD | Garnerville |
| 66 | 7,671 | Commack UFSD | East Northport |
| 67 | 7,669 | Liverpool Central SD | Liverpool |
| 68 | 7,625 | Levittown UFSD | Levittown |
| 69 | 7,572 | Three Village Central SD | Stony Brook |
| 70 | 7,400 | Monroe-Woodbury Central SD | Central Valley |
| 71 | 7,372 | East Meadow UFSD | Westbury |
| 72 | 7,263 | Niagara Falls City SD | Niagara Falls |
| 73 | 7,198 | West Seneca Central SD | West Seneca |
| 74 | 7,120 | Kingston City SD | Kingston |
| 75 | 7,104 | White Plains City SD | White Plains |
| 76 | 7,086 | Elmira City SD | Elmira |
| 77 | 6,810 | Lindenhurst UFSD | Lindenhurst |
| 78 | 6,807 | Saratoga Spgs City SD | Saratoga Spgs |
| 79 | 6,767 | Middletown City SD | Middletown |
| 80 | 6,757 | Connetquot Central SD | Bohemia |
| 81 | 6,666 | Syosset Central SD | Syosset |
| 82 | 6,635 | Fairport Central SD | Fairport |
| 83 | 6,532 | Freeport UFSD | Freeport |
| 84 | 6,526 | Great Neck UFSD | Great Neck |
| 85 | 6,500 | Central Islip UFSD | Central Islip |
| 86 | 6,439 | Lakeland Central SD | Shrub Oak |
| 87 | 6,358 | Uniondale UFSD | Uniondale |
| 88 | 6,333 | Northport-East Northport UFSD | Northport |
| 89 | 6,263 | Lancaster Central SD | Lancaster |
| 90 | 6,100 | Farmingdale UFSD | Farmingdale |
| 91 | 6,086 | Bellmore-Merrick Central High SD | North Merrick |
| 92 | 6,052 | Oceanside UFSD | Oceanside |
| 93 | 6,037 | Hempstead UFSD | Hempstead |
| 94 | 6,019 | South Huntington UFSD | Huntington Stn |
| 95 | 5,991 | Pine Bush Central SD | Pine Bush |
| 96 | 5,969 | Pittsford Central SD | Pittsford |
| 97 | 5,911 | Binghamton City SD | Binghamton |
| 98 | 5,815 | Baldwinsville Central SD | Baldwinsville |
| 99 | 5,756 | Bay Shore UFSD | Bay Shore |
| 100 | 5,596 | Rush-Henrietta Central SD | Henrietta |
| 101 | 5,569 | Rome City SD | Rome |
| 102 | 5,527 | North Colonie Central SD | Latham |
| 103 | 5,465 | Hicksville UFSD | Hicksville |
| 104 | 5,451 | West Islip UFSD | West Islip |
| 105 | 5,418 | Corning City SD | Painted Post |
| 106 | 5,413 | South Colonie Central SD | Albany |
| 107 | 5,374 | Ithaca City SD | Ithaca |
| 108 | 5,326 | Frontier Central SD | Hamburg |
| 109 | 5,274 | Guilderland Central SD | Guilderland |
| 110 | 5,264 | Lockport City SD | Lockport |
| 111 | 5,244 | Baldwin UFSD | Baldwin |
| 112 | 5,238 | Orchard Park Central SD | Orchard Park |
| 113 | 5,168 | Jamestown City SD | Jamestown |
| 114 | 5,116 | Bethlehem Central SD | Delmar |
| 115 | 5,112 | Mahopac Central SD | Mahopac |
| 116 | 5,101 | Clarence Central SD | Clarence Center |
| 117 | 5,097 | Plainview-Old Bethpage Central SD | Plainview |
| 118 | 5,050 | Mamaroneck UFSD | Mamaroneck |
| 119 | 5,017 | West Genesee Central SD | Camillus |
| 120 | 4,974 | Port Washington UFSD | Port Washington |
| 121 | 4,876 | East Islip UFSD | Islip Terrace |
| 122 | 4,853 | Valley Central SD (Montgomery) | Montgomery |
| 123 | 4,840 | North Babylon UFSD | North Babylon |
| 124 | 4,816 | Riverhead Central SD | Riverhead |
| 125 | 4,718 | Scarsdale UFSD | Scarsdale |
| 126 | 4,663 | Copiague UFSD | Copiague |
| 127 | 4,641 | Ramapo Central SD (Suffern) | Hillburn |
| 128 | 4,634 | Central Square Central SD | Central Square |
| 129 | 4,630 | Carmel Central SD | Patterson |
| 129 | 4,630 | Washingtonville Central SD | Washingtonville |
| 131 | 4,612 | Penfield Central SD | Rochester |
| 132 | 4,602 | Valley Stream Central High SD | Valley Stream |
| 133 | 4,600 | South Country Central SD | East Patchogue |
| 134 | 4,588 | Fayetteville-Manlius Central SD | Manlius |
| 135 | 4,559 | Hilton Central SD | Hilton |
| 136 | 4,547 | Gates-Chili Central SD | Rochester |
| 137 | 4,543 | Minisink Valley Central SD | Slate Hill |
| 138 | 4,500 | Poughkeepsie City SD | Poughkeepsie |
| 139 | 4,484 | West Babylon UFSD | West Babylon |
| 140 | 4,482 | East Greenbush Central SD | East Greenbush |
| 141 | 4,450 | Ossining UFSD | Ossining |
| 142 | 4,445 | Huntington UFSD | Huntington Stn |
| 143 | 4,386 | Deer Park UFSD | Deer Park |
| 144 | 4,378 | Auburn City SD | Auburn |
| 145 | 4,362 | Bedford Central SD | Bedford |
| 146 | 4,326 | Horseheads Central SD | Horseheads |
| 147 | 4,314 | Westbury UFSD | Old Westbury |
| 148 | 4,309 | Victor Central SD | Victor |
| 149 | 4,301 | Oswego City SD | Oswego |
| 150 | 4,300 | Ballston Spa Central SD | Ballston Spa |
| 151 | 4,283 | Warwick Valley Central SD | Warwick |
| 152 | 4,224 | Niskayuna Central SD | Schenectady |
| 153 | 4,175 | Garden City UFSD | Garden City |
| 154 | 4,167 | Watertown City SD | Watertown |
| 155 | 4,166 | Chappaqua Central SD | Chappaqua |
| 156 | 4,156 | Churchville-Chili Central SD | Churchville |
| 157 | 4,116 | Hyde Park Central SD | Hyde Park |
| 158 | 4,092 | Union-Endicott Central SD | Endicott |
| 159 | 4,076 | Hauppauge UFSD | Hauppauge |
| 160 | 4,057 | Port Chester-Rye UFSD | Port Chester |
| 161 | 4,050 | Niagara-Wheatfield Central SD | Niagara Falls |
| 162 | 4,044 | Herricks UFSD | New Hyde Park |
| 163 | 4,041 | North Tonawanda City SD | North Tonawanda |
| 164 | 4,040 | Troy City SD | Troy |
| 165 | 4,019 | Hamburg Central SD | Hamburg |
| 166 | 4,018 | Spencerport Central SD | Spencerport |
| 167 | 4,005 | Brockport Central SD | Brockport |
| 167 | 4,005 | Long Beach City SD | Long Beach |
| 169 | 3,987 | Elmont UFSD | Elmont |
| 170 | 3,969 | Canandaigua City SD | Canandaigua |
| 171 | 3,963 | Comsewogue School District | Port Jeff Stn |
| 172 | 3,955 | Kings Park Central SD | Kings Park |
| 173 | 3,940 | Yorktown Central SD | Yorktown Hgts |
| 174 | 3,897 | Eastport-South Manor CSD | Manorville |
| 175 | 3,868 | Katonah-Lewisboro UFSD | South Salem |
| 176 | 3,818 | West Irondequoit Central SD | Rochester |
| 177 | 3,767 | Amsterdam City SD | Amsterdam |
| 177 | 3,767 | Indian River Central SD | Philadelphia |
| 177 | 3,767 | Vestal Central SD | Vestal |
| 180 | 3,692 | Queensbury UFSD | Queensbury |
| 181 | 3,683 | Fulton City SD | Fulton |
| 182 | 3,664 | Harborfields Central SD | Greenlawn |
| 183 | 3,602 | Wantagh UFSD | Wantagh |
| 184 | 3,545 | Rockville Ctr UFSD | Rockville Ctr |
| 185 | 3,531 | Whitesboro Central SD | Yorkville |
| 186 | 3,524 | East Syracuse-Minoa Central SD | East Syracuse |
| 187 | 3,520 | Harrison Central SD | Harrison |
| 188 | 3,519 | South Orangetown Central SD | Blauvelt |
| 189 | 3,497 | Brewster Central SD | Brewster |
| 190 | 3,491 | Wallkill Central SD | Wallkill |
| 191 | 3,488 | Sweet Home Central SD | Amherst |
| 192 | 3,477 | Brighton Central SD | Rochester |
| 193 | 3,437 | Carthage Central SD | Carthage |
| 193 | 3,437 | Plainedge UFSD | N Massapequa |
| 195 | 3,434 | Cornwall Central SD | Cornwall on Hdsn |
| 196 | 3,433 | Islip UFSD | Islip |
| 196 | 3,433 | Rocky Point UFSD | Rocky Point |
| 198 | 3,431 | Beacon City SD | Beacon |
| 199 | 3,422 | Somers Central SD | Somers |
| 200 | 3,403 | Roslyn UFSD | Roslyn |
| 201 | 3,379 | Burnt Hills-Ballston Lake CSD | Scotia |
| 202 | 3,367 | Averill Park Central SD | Averill Park |
| 203 | 3,335 | Sayville UFSD | Sayville |
| 204 | 3,266 | S Glens Fls Central SD | S Glens Fls |
| 205 | 3,226 | Monticello Central SD | Monticello |
| 206 | 3,201 | Grand Island Central SD | Grand Island |
| 207 | 3,166 | Gloversville City SD | Gloversville |
| 208 | 3,153 | East Irondequoit Central SD | Rochester |
| 209 | 3,114 | Eastchester UFSD | Eastchester |
| 210 | 3,105 | Manhasset UFSD | Manhasset |
| 211 | 3,098 | Miller Place UFSD | Miller Place |
| 212 | 3,095 | Rye City SD | Rye |
| 213 | 3,094 | Jericho UFSD | Jericho |
| 214 | 3,092 | Lawrence UFSD | Lawrence |
| 215 | 3,083 | Saugerties Central SD | Saugerties |
| 216 | 3,079 | Mohonasen Central SD | Schenectady |
| 217 | 3,075 | Hewlett-Woodmere UFSD | Woodmere |
| 218 | 3,072 | Bethpage UFSD | Bethpage |
| 219 | 3,064 | Port Jervis City SD | Port Jervis |
| 220 | 3,039 | Glen Cove City SD | Glen Cove |
| 221 | 2,973 | Goshen Central SD | Goshen |
| 222 | 2,965 | Amherst Central SD | Amherst |
| 223 | 2,949 | Lynbrook UFSD | Lynbrook |
| 224 | 2,919 | Nyack UFSD | Nyack |
| 225 | 2,905 | Peekskill City SD | Peekskill |
| 226 | 2,868 | Jamesville-Dewitt Central SD | Dewitt |
| 227 | 2,866 | North Shore Central SD | Sea Cliff |
| 228 | 2,857 | Massena Central SD | Massena |
| 229 | 2,850 | Evans-Brant Central SD (Lake Shore) | Angola |
| 230 | 2,826 | Amityville UFSD | Amityville |
| 231 | 2,795 | Byram Hills Central SD | Armonk |
| 232 | 2,780 | Pelham UFSD | Pelham |
| 233 | 2,766 | Roosevelt UFSD | Roosevelt |
| 234 | 2,757 | Starpoint Central SD | Lockport |
| 235 | 2,745 | Scotia-Glenville Central SD | Scotia |
| 236 | 2,716 | Mineola UFSD | Mineola |
| 237 | 2,709 | Cortland City SD | Cortland |
| 238 | 2,701 | Hendrick Hudson Central SD | Montrose |
| 239 | 2,692 | Shoreham-Wading River Central SD | Shoreham |
| 240 | 2,664 | Pearl River UFSD | Pearl River |
| 241 | 2,653 | UFSD of the Tarrytowns | Sleepy Hollow |
| 242 | 2,635 | Iroquois Central SD | Elma |

*Note: This section only includes districts with 1,500 or more students; All categories are ranked from high to low*

| | | | |
|---|---|---|---|
| 243 | 2,622 | New Hartford Central SD | New Hartford |
| 244 | 2,616 | Elwood UFSD | Greenlawn |
| 245 | 2,609 | Mount Sinai UFSD | Mount Sinai |
| 246 | 2,594 | Maine-Endwell Central SD | Endwell |
| 247 | 2,582 | Honeoye Falls-Lima Central SD | Honeoye Falls |
| 248 | 2,578 | Johnson City Central SD | Johnson City |
| 249 | 2,574 | Island Trees UFSD | Levittown |
| 250 | 2,567 | Seaford UFSD | Seaford |
| 251 | 2,515 | Yorkshire-Pioneer Central SD | Yorkshire |
| 252 | 2,502 | Bayport-Blue Point UFSD | Bayport |
| 253 | 2,501 | Olean City SD | Olean |
| 254 | 2,485 | Camden Central SD | Camden |
| 255 | 2,477 | Wayne Central SD | Ontario Center |
| 256 | 2,455 | Malone Central SD | Malone |
| 257 | 2,430 | Batavia City SD | Batavia |
| 257 | 2,430 | Oneida City SD | Oneida |
| 259 | 2,426 | Lansingburgh Central SD | Troy |
| 260 | 2,372 | Cheektowaga Central SD | Cheektowaga |
| 261 | 2,316 | Rondout Valley Central SD | Accord |
| 262 | 2,309 | Lewiston-Porter Central SD | Youngstown |
| 263 | 2,299 | Nanuet UFSD | Nanuet |
| 264 | 2,295 | Newark Central SD | Newark |
| 265 | 2,290 | New Paltz Central SD | New Paltz |
| 266 | 2,285 | West Hempstead UFSD | West Hempstead |
| 267 | 2,281 | Cheektowaga-Maryvale UFSD | Cheektowaga |
| 267 | 2,281 | Mexico Central SD | Mexico |
| 269 | 2,280 | Glens Falls City SD | Glens Falls |
| 270 | 2,268 | Albion Central SD | Albion |
| 271 | 2,264 | Hudson Falls Central SD | Fort Edward |
| 272 | 2,239 | Phoenix Central SD | Phoenix |
| 273 | 2,231 | Red Hook Central SD | Red Hook |
| 274 | 2,228 | Chittenango Central SD | Chittenango |
| 275 | 2,211 | Locust Valley Central SD | Locust Valley |
| 276 | 2,210 | Geneva City SD | Geneva |
| 277 | 2,184 | Vernon-Verona-Sherrill Central SD | Verona |
| 278 | 2,175 | Norwich City SD | Norwich |
| 279 | 2,156 | Valley Stream 13 UFSD | Valley Stream |
| 280 | 2,148 | North Bellmore UFSD | Bellmore |
| 280 | 2,148 | Owego-Apalachin Central SD | Owego |
| 282 | 2,141 | Wyandanch UFSD | Wyandanch |
| 283 | 2,139 | Homer Central SD | Homer |
| 284 | 2,130 | Ardsley UFSD | Ardsley |
| 285 | 2,098 | Springville-Griffith Institute CSD | Springville |
| 286 | 2,079 | Peru Central SD | Peru |
| 287 | 2,078 | Depew UFSD | Depew |
| 288 | 2,070 | Ravena-Coeymans-Selkirk Ctrl SD | Selkirk |
| 289 | 2,064 | Cobleskill-Richmondville Central SD | Cobleskill |
| 290 | 2,051 | Marlboro Central SD | Marlboro |
| 291 | 2,037 | Palmyra-Macedon Central SD | Palmyra |
| 292 | 2,036 | South Jefferson Central SD | Adams Center |
| 293 | 2,025 | Beekmantown Central SD | West Chazy |
| 294 | 2,024 | Cohoes City SD | Cohoes |
| 295 | 2,018 | Cold Spring Hrbr Central SD | Cold Spring Hrbr |
| 296 | 1,999 | Dunkirk City SD | Dunkirk |
| 297 | 1,998 | Tonawanda City SD | Tonawanda |
| 298 | 1,988 | Marcellus Central SD | Marcellus |
| 299 | 1,987 | Kinderhook Central SD | Valatie |
| 300 | 1,977 | Mount Pleasant Central SD | Thornwood |
| 301 | 1,973 | Schalmont Central SD | Schenectady |
| 302 | 1,964 | East Aurora UFSD | East Aurora |
| 303 | 1,960 | Broadalbin-Perth Central SD | Broadalbin |
| 304 | 1,958 | Franklin Square UFSD | Franklin Square |
| 305 | 1,953 | Hudson City SD | Hudson |
| 306 | 1,947 | Lackawanna City SD | Lackawanna |
| 307 | 1,940 | Edgemont UFSD | Scarsdale |
| 308 | 1,937 | Windsor Central SD | Windsor |
| 309 | 1,929 | Highland Central SD | Highland |
| 310 | 1,916 | Hampton Bays UFSD | Hampton Bays |
| 310 | 1,916 | Plattsburgh City SD | Plattsburgh |
| 312 | 1,915 | Livonia Central SD | Livonia |
| 313 | 1,912 | Chenango Valley Central SD | Binghamton |
| 314 | 1,911 | Johnstown City SD | Johnstown |
| 314 | 1,911 | Newfane Central SD | Burt |
| 316 | 1,904 | Medina Central SD | Medina |
| 317 | 1,886 | Oneonta City SD | Oneonta |
| 318 | 1,884 | Westhill Central SD | Syracuse |
| 319 | 1,865 | Alden Central SD | Alden |
| 320 | 1,835 | Putnam Valley Central SD | Putnam Valley |
| 321 | 1,834 | Pleasantville UFSD | Pleasantville |
| 322 | 1,833 | Phelps-Clifton Springs Central SD | Clifton Springs |
| 323 | 1,822 | Ellenville Central SD | Ellenville |
| 324 | 1,818 | East Hampton UFSD | East Hampton |
| 325 | 1,807 | Babylon UFSD | Babylon |
| 325 | 1,807 | Susquehanna Valley Central SD | Conklin |
| 325 | 1,807 | Waterloo Central SD | Waterloo |

| | | | |
|---|---|---|---|
| 328 | 1,805 | Hornell City SD | Hornell |
| 329 | 1,799 | Irvington UFSD | Irvington |
| 330 | 1,798 | East Williston UFSD | Old Westbury |
| 331 | 1,796 | Catskill Central SD | Catskill |
| 332 | 1,794 | Schuylerville Central SD | Schuylerville |
| 333 | 1,786 | Greenburgh Central SD | Hartsdale |
| 333 | 1,786 | Westhampton Bch UFSD | Westhampton Bch |
| 335 | 1,778 | Dryden Central SD | Dryden |
| 336 | 1,759 | Bath Central SD | Bath |
| 337 | 1,749 | Croton-Harmon UFSD | Croton on Hdsn |
| 338 | 1,747 | Ogdensburg City SD | Ogdensburg |
| 339 | 1,739 | Dansville Central SD | Dansville |
| 340 | 1,726 | Merrick UFSD | Merrick |
| 341 | 1,724 | Waverly Central SD | Waverly |
| 342 | 1,716 | Penn Yan Central SD | Penn Yan |
| 343 | 1,703 | Chenango Forks Central SD | Binghamton |
| 344 | 1,700 | Malverne UFSD | Malverne |
| 345 | 1,699 | Eden Central SD | Eden |
| 346 | 1,697 | Gouverneur Central SD | Gouverneur |
| 347 | 1,670 | Cazenovia Central SD | Cazenovia |
| 348 | 1,664 | Briarcliff Mnr UFSD | Briarcliff Mnr |
| 348 | 1,664 | Skaneateles Central SD | Skaneateles |
| 350 | 1,662 | Oyster Bay-East Norwich Central SD | Oyster Bay |
| 351 | 1,652 | Ilion Central SD | Ilion |
| 352 | 1,651 | Onteora Central SD | Boiceville |
| 353 | 1,650 | Fredonia Central SD | Fredonia |
| 354 | 1,647 | Holland Patent Central SD | Holland Patent |
| 354 | 1,647 | Spackenkill UFSD | Poughkeepsie |
| 356 | 1,625 | Saranac Central SD | Dannemora |
| 357 | 1,621 | New Hyde Pk-Garden City Pk UFSD | New Hyde Park |
| 358 | 1,617 | Hannibal Central SD | Hannibal |
| 359 | 1,613 | Charter School for Applied Tech | Buffalo |
| 360 | 1,608 | Floral Park-Bellerose UFSD | Floral Park |
| 361 | 1,604 | Attica Central SD | Attica |
| 362 | 1,593 | Center Moriches UFSD | Center Moriches |
| 363 | 1,590 | Southampton UFSD | Southampton |
| 364 | 1,583 | Taconic Hills Central SD | Craryville |
| 365 | 1,581 | Wayland-Cohocton Central SD | Wayland |
| 366 | 1,577 | Dover UFSD | Dover Plains |
| 366 | 1,577 | Salmon River Central SD | Fort Covington |
| 368 | 1,576 | Royalton-Hartland Central SD | Middleport |
| 369 | 1,571 | Solvay UFSD | Solvay |
| 370 | 1,570 | Cheektowaga-Sloan UFSD | Sloan |
| 371 | 1,567 | Hastings-on-Hudson UFSD | Hastings on Hdsn |
| 372 | 1,554 | Jordan-Elbridge Central SD | Elbridge |
| 373 | 1,542 | Canastota Central SD | Canastota |
| 373 | 1,542 | Coxsackie-Athens Central SD | Coxsackie |
| 375 | 1,541 | Liberty Central SD | Liberty |
| 376 | 1,538 | General Brown Central SD | Dexter |
| 377 | 1,531 | Akron Central SD | Akron |
| 378 | 1,526 | Bronxville UFSD | Bronxville |
| 379 | 1,524 | Blind Brook-Rye UFSD | Rye Brook |
| 380 | 1,519 | Valhalla UFSD | Valhalla |
| 381 | 1,518 | Sherburne-Earlville Central SD | Sherburne |
| 382 | 1,516 | Mattituck-Cutchogue UFSD | Cutchogue |
| 383 | 1,501 | Southwestern CSD at Jamestown | Jamestown |

## Male Students

| Rank | Percent | District Name | City |
|---|---|---|---|
| 1 | 73.5 | NYC Special Schools - District 75 | New York |
| 2 | 55.7 | Roosevelt UFSD | Roosevelt |
| 3 | 54.8 | Greenburgh Central SD | Hartsdale |
| 4 | 54.7 | West Hempstead UFSD | West Hempstead |
| 5 | 54.5 | Hudson City SD | Hudson |
| 6 | 54.1 | NYC Geographic District # 7 | Bronx |
| 7 | 54.0 | Roslyn UFSD | Roslyn |
| 8 | 53.8 | Dunkirk City SD | Dunkirk |
| 9 | 53.7 | Southampton UFSD | Southampton |
| 10 | 53.6 | Deer Park UFSD | Deer Park |
| 11 | 53.5 | Fredonia Central SD | Fredonia |
| 11 | 53.5 | Malverne UFSD | Malverne |
| 13 | 53.3 | NYC Geographic District #24 | Ridgewood |
| 13 | 53.3 | Westhampton Bch UFSD | Westhampton Bch |
| 15 | 53.2 | Ogdensburg City SD | Ogdensburg |
| 16 | 53.1 | Hornell City SD | Hornell |
| 16 | 53.1 | Mineola UFSD | Mineola |
| 16 | 53.1 | Valley Stream 13 UFSD | Valley Stream |
| 19 | 53.0 | Brewster Central SD | Brewster |
| 19 | 53.0 | NYC Geographic District #14 | Brooklyn |
| 19 | 53.0 | North Tonawanda City SD | North Tonawanda |
| 22 | 52.9 | Floral Park-Bellerose UFSD | Floral Park |
| 22 | 52.9 | Glen Cove City SD | Glen Cove |
| 22 | 52.9 | NYC Geographic District #11 | Bronx |
| 22 | 52.9 | Shoreham-Wading River Central SD | Shoreham |
| 26 | 52.8 | Half Hollow Hills Central SD | Dix Hills |
| 27 | 52.7 | Farmingdale UFSD | Farmingdale |
| 27 | 52.7 | South Huntington UFSD | Huntington Stn |
| 29 | 52.6 | East Islip UFSD | Islip Terrace |
| 29 | 52.6 | Lawrence UFSD | Lawrence |
| 29 | 52.6 | NYC Geographic District #16 | Brooklyn |
| 29 | 52.6 | Sweet Home Central SD | Amherst |
| 29 | 52.6 | Troy City SD | Troy |
| 34 | 52.5 | Ballston Spa Central SD | Ballston Spa |
| 34 | 52.5 | Chenango Forks Central SD | Binghamton |
| 34 | 52.5 | Syosset Central SD | Syosset |
| 37 | 52.4 | Brentwood UFSD | Brentwood |
| 37 | 52.4 | Holland Patent Central SD | Holland Patent |
| 37 | 52.4 | Huntington UFSD | Huntington Stn |
| 37 | 52.4 | Lindenhurst UFSD | Lindenhurst |
| 37 | 52.4 | Owego-Apalachin Central SD | Owego |
| 42 | 52.3 | Center Moriches UFSD | Center Moriches |
| 42 | 52.3 | Honeoye Falls-Lima Central SD | Honeoye Falls |
| 42 | 52.3 | Malone Central SD | Malone |
| 42 | 52.3 | Minisink Valley Central SD | Slate Hill |
| 42 | 52.3 | North Babylon UFSD | North Babylon |
| 42 | 52.3 | Oswego City SD | Oswego |
| 42 | 52.3 | Phoenix Central SD | Phoenix |
| 42 | 52.3 | Poughkeepsie City SD | Poughkeepsie |
| 42 | 52.3 | Scotia-Glenville Central SD | Scotia |
| 42 | 52.3 | Sherburne-Earlville Central SD | Sherburne |
| 52 | 52.2 | Alden Central SD | Alden |
| 52 | 52.2 | Eastchester UFSD | Eastchester |
| 52 | 52.2 | Elmira City SD | Elmira |
| 52 | 52.2 | New Rochelle City SD | New Rochelle |
| 52 | 52.2 | Newfane Central SD | Burt |
| 52 | 52.2 | Webster Central SD | Webster |
| 52 | 52.2 | William Floyd UFSD | Mastic Beach |
| 59 | 52.1 | Chappaqua Central SD | Chappaqua |
| 59 | 52.1 | Connetquot Central SD | Bohemia |
| 59 | 52.1 | Dryden Central SD | Dryden |
| 59 | 52.1 | Lackawanna City SD | Lackawanna |
| 59 | 52.1 | Lansingburgh Central SD | Troy |
| 59 | 52.1 | Miller Place UFSD | Miller Place |
| 59 | 52.1 | North Colonie Central SD | Latham |
| 59 | 52.1 | Palmyra-Macedon Central SD | Palmyra |
| 59 | 52.1 | Queensbury UFSD | Queensbury |
| 59 | 52.1 | Riverhead Central SD | Riverhead |
| 59 | 52.1 | Wappingers Central SD | Wappingers Fls |
| 70 | 52.0 | Amherst Central SD | Amherst |
| 70 | 52.0 | Bath Central SD | Bath |
| 70 | 52.0 | Bethlehem Central SD | Delmar |
| 70 | 52.0 | Canandaigua City SD | Canandaigua |
| 70 | 52.0 | Eden Central SD | Eden |
| 70 | 52.0 | Longwood Central SD | Middle Island |
| 70 | 52.0 | Orchard Park Central SD | Orchard Park |
| 70 | 52.0 | Ossining UFSD | Ossining |
| 70 | 52.0 | Schuylerville Central SD | Schuylerville |
| 79 | 51.9 | Beekmantown Central SD | West Chazy |
| 79 | 51.9 | Clarkstown Central SD | New City |
| 79 | 51.9 | Coxsackie-Athens Central SD | Coxsackie |
| 79 | 51.9 | Hastings-on-Hudson UFSD | Hastings on Hdsn |
| 79 | 51.9 | Medina Central SD | Medina |
| 79 | 51.9 | NYC Geographic District #19 | Brooklyn |
| 79 | 51.9 | Rondout Valley Central SD | Accord |
| 79 | 51.9 | Rye City SD | Rye |
| 87 | 51.8 | Central Square Central SD | Central Square |
| 87 | 51.8 | General Brown Central SD | Dexter |
| 87 | 51.8 | Herricks UFSD | New Hyde Park |
| 87 | 51.8 | Ilion Central SD | Ilion |
| 87 | 51.8 | Marcellus Central SD | Marcellus |
| 87 | 51.8 | New Paltz Central SD | New Paltz |
| 87 | 51.8 | Peru Central SD | Peru |
| 87 | 51.8 | Phelps-Clifton Springs Central SD | Clifton Springs |
| 87 | 51.8 | Putnam Valley Central SD | Putnam Valley |
| 87 | 51.8 | Salmon River Central SD | Fort Covington |
| 87 | 51.8 | Starpoint Central SD | Lockport |
| 87 | 51.8 | West Islip UFSD | West Islip |
| 87 | 51.8 | Westhill Central SD | Syracuse |
| 100 | 51.7 | Cornwall Central SD | Cornwall on Hdsn |
| 100 | 51.7 | Dover UFSD | Dover Plains |
| 100 | 51.7 | East Williston UFSD | Old Westbury |
| 100 | 51.7 | Middle Country Central SD | Centereach |
| 100 | 51.7 | NYC Geographic District #27 | Ozone Park |
| 100 | 51.7 | Newburgh City SD | Newburgh |
| 100 | 51.7 | Rockville Ctr UFSD | Rockville Ctr |
| 100 | 51.7 | Sayville UFSD | Sayville |
| 100 | 51.7 | Southwestern CSD at Jamestown | Jamestown |
| 100 | 51.7 | Susquehanna Valley Central SD | Conklin |

*Note: This section only includes districts with 1,500 or more students; All categories are ranked from high to low*

| | | | |
|---|---|---|---|
| 100 | 51.7 | Union-Endicott Central SD | Endicott |
| 111 | 51.6 | Batavia City SD | Batavia |
| 111 | 51.6 | Bedford Central SD | Bedford |
| 111 | 51.6 | Churchville-Chili Central SD | Churchville |
| 111 | 51.6 | Freeport UFSD | Freeport |
| 111 | 51.6 | Hewlett-Woodmere UFSD | Woodmere |
| 111 | 51.6 | Ithaca City SD | Ithaca |
| 111 | 51.6 | Jericho UFSD | Jericho |
| 111 | 51.6 | NYC Geographic District # 6 | New York |
| 111 | 51.6 | Niagara-Wheatfield Central SD | Niagara Falls |
| 111 | 51.6 | North Rockland Central SD | Garnerville |
| 111 | 51.6 | Northport-East Northport UFSD | Northport |
| 111 | 51.6 | Ravena-Coeymans-Selkirk Ctrl SD | Selkirk |
| 111 | 51.6 | Seaford UFSD | Seaford |
| 111 | 51.6 | Shenendehowa Central SD | Clifton Park |
| 111 | 51.6 | Wallkill Central SD | Wallkill |
| 111 | 51.6 | Yonkers City SD | Yonkers |
| 127 | 51.5 | Baldwin UFSD | Baldwin |
| 127 | 51.5 | Bellmore-Merrick Central High SD | North Merrick |
| 127 | 51.5 | Brockport Central SD | Brockport |
| 127 | 51.5 | Catskill Central SD | Catskill |
| 127 | 51.5 | Cheektowaga-Maryvale UFSD | Cheektowaga |
| 127 | 51.5 | Fairport Central SD | Fairport |
| 127 | 51.5 | Franklin Square UFSD | Franklin Square |
| 127 | 51.5 | Gates-Chili Central SD | Rochester |
| 127 | 51.5 | Great Neck UFSD | Great Neck |
| 127 | 51.5 | Hampton Bays UFSD | Hampton Bays |
| 127 | 51.5 | Hicksville UFSD | Hicksville |
| 127 | 51.5 | Homer Central SD | Homer |
| 127 | 51.5 | Hyde Park Central SD | Hyde Park |
| 127 | 51.5 | Lakeland Central SD | Shrub Oak |
| 127 | 51.5 | Monroe-Woodbury Central SD | Central Valley |
| 127 | 51.5 | North Syracuse Central SD | North Syracuse |
| 127 | 51.5 | Three Village Central SD | Stony Brook |
| 144 | 51.4 | Amityville UFSD | Amityville |
| 144 | 51.4 | Briarcliff Mnr UFSD | Briarcliff Mnr |
| 144 | 51.4 | Canastota Central SD | Canastota |
| 144 | 51.4 | Carmel Central SD | Patterson |
| 144 | 51.4 | East Irondequoit Central SD | Rochester |
| 144 | 51.4 | East Syracuse-Minoa Central SD | East Syracuse |
| 144 | 51.4 | Evans-Brant Central SD (Lake Shore) | Angola |
| 144 | 51.4 | Hauppauge UFSD | Hauppauge |
| 144 | 51.4 | Islip UFSD | Islip |
| 144 | 51.4 | Kinderhook Central SD | Valatie |
| 144 | 51.4 | Levittown UFSD | Levittown |
| 144 | 51.4 | Monticello Central SD | Monticello |
| 144 | 51.4 | Pine Bush Central SD | Pine Bush |
| 144 | 51.4 | Saranac Central SD | Dannemora |
| 144 | 51.4 | Spencerport Central SD | Spencerport |
| 144 | 51.4 | Watertown City SD | Watertown |
| 144 | 51.4 | Wayne Central SD | Ontario Center |
| 144 | 51.4 | West Genesee Central SD | Camillus |
| 144 | 51.4 | Windsor Central SD | Windsor |
| 163 | 51.3 | Auburn City SD | Auburn |
| 163 | 51.3 | Broadalbin-Perth Central SD | Broadalbin |
| 163 | 51.3 | Bronxville UFSD | Bronxville |
| 163 | 51.3 | Byram Hills Central SD | Armonk |
| 163 | 51.3 | Jamestown City SD | Jamestown |
| 163 | 51.3 | Lewiston-Porter Central SD | Youngstown |
| 163 | 51.3 | Long Beach City SD | Long Beach |
| 163 | 51.3 | Lynbrook UFSD | Lynbrook |
| 163 | 51.3 | Mamaroneck UFSD | Mamaroneck |
| 163 | 51.3 | Massapequa UFSD | Massapequa |
| 163 | 51.3 | Mattituck-Cutchogue UFSD | Cutchogue |
| 163 | 51.3 | NYC Geographic District #28 | Jamaica |
| 163 | 51.3 | Penfield Central SD | Rochester |
| 163 | 51.3 | Pleasantville UFSD | Pleasantville |
| 163 | 51.3 | South Orangetown Central SD | Blauvelt |
| 163 | 51.3 | Vestal Central SD | Vestal |
| 163 | 51.3 | Warwick Valley Central SD | Warwick |
| 180 | 51.2 | Albion Central SD | Albion |
| 180 | 51.2 | Cazenovia Central SD | Cazenovia |
| 180 | 51.2 | Chenango Valley Central SD | Binghamton |
| 180 | 51.2 | Clarence Central SD | Clarence Center |
| 180 | 51.2 | Copiague UFSD | Copiague |
| 180 | 51.2 | Corning City SD | Painted Post |
| 180 | 51.2 | Fulton City SD | Fulton |
| 180 | 51.2 | Gloversville City SD | Gloversville |
| 180 | 51.2 | Gouverneur Central SD | Gouverneur |
| 180 | 51.2 | Hudson Falls Central SD | Fort Edward |
| 180 | 51.2 | Jordan-Elbridge Central SD | Elbridge |
| 180 | 51.2 | Kenmore-Tonawanda UFSD | Buffalo |
| 180 | 51.2 | Middletown City SD | Middletown |
| 180 | 51.2 | NYC Geographic District #18 | Brooklyn |
| 180 | 51.2 | Red Hook Central SD | Red Hook |
| 180 | 51.2 | Sewanhaka Central High SD | Floral Park |
| 180 | 51.2 | Victor Central SD | Victor |
| 180 | 51.2 | West Seneca Central SD | West Seneca |
| 198 | 51.1 | Attica Central SD | Attica |
| 198 | 51.1 | Baldwinsville Central SD | Baldwinsville |
| 198 | 51.1 | Cold Spring Hrbr Central SD | Cold Spring Hrbr |
| 198 | 51.1 | Elmont UFSD | Elmont |
| 198 | 51.1 | Garden City UFSD | Garden City |
| 198 | 51.1 | Glens Falls City SD | Glens Falls |
| 198 | 51.1 | Hempstead UFSD | Hempstead |
| 198 | 51.1 | Island Trees UFSD | Levittown |
| 198 | 51.1 | NYC Geographic District # 9 | Bronx |
| 198 | 51.1 | NYC Geographic District #29 | Rosedale |
| 198 | 51.1 | Oneida City SD | Oneida |
| 198 | 51.1 | Port Chester-Rye UFSD | Port Chester |
| 198 | 51.1 | South Colonie Central SD | Albany |
| 198 | 51.1 | Yorkshire-Pioneer Central SD | Yorkshire |
| 212 | 51.0 | Burnt Hills-Ballston Lake CSD | Scotia |
| 212 | 51.0 | Dansville Central SD | Dansville |
| 212 | 51.0 | East Ramapo Central SD | Spring Valley |
| 212 | 51.0 | Edgemont UFSD | Scarsdale |
| 212 | 51.0 | Olean City SD | Olean |
| 212 | 51.0 | Onteora Central SD | Boiceville |
| 212 | 51.0 | Pelham UFSD | Pelham |
| 212 | 51.0 | Plainview-Old Bethpage Central SD | Plainview |
| 212 | 51.0 | Rome City SD | Rome |
| 212 | 51.0 | Springville-Griffith Institute CSD | Springville |
| 212 | 51.0 | Syracuse City SD | Syracuse |
| 212 | 51.0 | Utica City SD | Utica |
| 212 | 51.0 | Valley Stream Central High SD | Valley Stream |
| 212 | 51.0 | Waverly Central SD | Waverly |
| 226 | 50.9 | Albany City SD | Albany |
| 226 | 50.9 | Averill Park Central SD | Averill Park |
| 226 | 50.9 | Central Islip UFSD | Central Islip |
| 226 | 50.9 | Cheektowaga-Sloan UFSD | Sloan |
| 226 | 50.9 | Commack UFSD | East Northport |
| 226 | 50.9 | East Hampton UFSD | East Hampton |
| 226 | 50.9 | Horseheads Central SD | Horseheads |
| 226 | 50.9 | Mahopac Central SD | Mahopac |
| 226 | 50.9 | Merrick UFSD | Merrick |
| 226 | 50.9 | Mount Sinai UFSD | Mount Sinai |
| 226 | 50.9 | Norwich City SD | Norwich |
| 226 | 50.9 | Rochester City SD | Rochester |
| 226 | 50.9 | Rush-Henrietta Central SD | Henrietta |
| 226 | 50.9 | Saratoga Spgs City SD | Saratoga Spgs |
| 226 | 50.9 | Whitesboro Central SD | Yorkville |
| 241 | 50.8 | Bayport-Blue Point UFSD | Bayport |
| 241 | 50.8 | Binghamton City SD | Binghamton |
| 241 | 50.8 | Harrison Central SD | Harrison |
| 241 | 50.8 | Iroquois Central SD | Elma |
| 241 | 50.8 | Oceanside UFSD | Oceanside |
| 241 | 50.8 | Penn Yan Central SD | Penn Yan |
| 241 | 50.8 | Schalmont Central SD | Schenectady |
| 241 | 50.8 | Somers Central SD | Somers |
| 241 | 50.8 | Yorktown Central SD | Yorktown Hgts |
| 250 | 50.7 | Akron Central SD | Akron |
| 250 | 50.7 | Bay Shore UFSD | Bay Shore |
| 250 | 50.7 | Bethpage UFSD | Bethpage |
| 250 | 50.7 | Cortland City SD | Cortland |
| 250 | 50.7 | Hilton Central SD | Hilton |
| 250 | 50.7 | Peekskill City SD | Peekskill |
| 250 | 50.7 | Wyandanch UFSD | Wyandanch |
| 257 | 50.6 | Ardsley UFSD | Ardsley |
| 257 | 50.6 | Arlington Central SD | Poughkeepsie |
| 257 | 50.6 | Eastport-South Manor CSD | Manorville |
| 257 | 50.6 | Ellenville Central SD | Ellenville |
| 257 | 50.6 | Fayetteville-Manlius Central SD | Manlius |
| 257 | 50.6 | Frontier Central SD | Hamburg |
| 257 | 50.6 | Jamesville-Dewitt Central SD | Dewitt |
| 257 | 50.6 | NYC Geographic District # 1 | New York |
| 257 | 50.6 | NYC Geographic District #10 | Bronx |
| 257 | 50.6 | NYC Geographic District #25 | Flushing |
| 257 | 50.6 | NYC Geographic District #32 | Brooklyn |
| 257 | 50.6 | Nyack UFSD | Nyack |
| 257 | 50.6 | Smithtown Central SD | Smithtown |
| 257 | 50.6 | S Glens Fls Central SD | S Glens Fls |
| 257 | 50.6 | Tonawanda City SD | Tonawanda |
| 257 | 50.6 | Wayland-Cohocton Central SD | Wayland |
| 257 | 50.6 | Williamsville Central SD | East Amherst |
| 274 | 50.5 | Brighton Central SD | Rochester |
| 274 | 50.5 | Cohoes City SD | Cohoes |
| 274 | 50.5 | Greece Central SD | Rochester |
| 274 | 50.5 | Guilderland Central SD | Guilderland |
| 274 | 50.5 | Highland Central SD | Highland |
| 274 | 50.5 | Lancaster Central SD | Lancaster |
| 274 | 50.5 | Manhasset UFSD | Manhasset |
| 274 | 50.5 | Nanuet UFSD | Nanuet |
| 274 | 50.5 | NYC Geographic District #30 | Long Isl City |
| 274 | 50.5 | Newark Central SD | Newark |
| 274 | 50.5 | Niagara Falls City SD | Niagara Falls |
| 274 | 50.5 | Patchogue-Medford UFSD | Patchogue |
| 274 | 50.5 | Schenectady City SD | Schenectady |
| 274 | 50.5 | Uniondale UFSD | Uniondale |
| 274 | 50.5 | West Babylon UFSD | West Babylon |
| 289 | 50.4 | Carthage Central SD | Carthage |
| 289 | 50.4 | Cheektowaga Central SD | Cheektowaga |
| 289 | 50.4 | Cobleskill-Richmondville Central SD | Cobleskill |
| 289 | 50.4 | Hamburg Central SD | Hamburg |
| 289 | 50.4 | Kingston City SD | Kingston |
| 289 | 50.4 | Mohonasen Central SD | Schenectady |
| 289 | 50.4 | Scarsdale UFSD | Scarsdale |
| 289 | 50.4 | Washingtonville Central SD | Washingtonville |
| 289 | 50.4 | Waterloo Central SD | Waterloo |
| 298 | 50.3 | Camden Central SD | Camden |
| 298 | 50.3 | Elwood UFSD | Greenlawn |
| 298 | 50.3 | Grand Island Central SD | Grand Island |
| 298 | 50.3 | Kings Park Central SD | Kings Park |
| 298 | 50.3 | Liverpool Central SD | Liverpool |
| 298 | 50.3 | New York City Public Schools | New York |
| 298 | 50.3 | Niskayuna Central SD | Schenectady |
| 298 | 50.3 | Oneonta City SD | Oneonta |
| 298 | 50.3 | Plattsburgh City SD | Plattsburgh |
| 298 | 50.3 | Saugerties Central SD | Saugerties |
| 298 | 50.3 | South Jefferson Central SD | Adams Center |
| 298 | 50.3 | Vernon-Verona-Sherrill Central SD | Verona |
| 310 | 50.2 | East Meadow UFSD | Westbury |
| 310 | 50.2 | Indian River Central SD | Philadelphia |
| 310 | 50.2 | Katonah-Lewisboro UFSD | South Salem |
| 310 | 50.2 | Lockport City SD | Lockport |
| 310 | 50.2 | NYC Geographic District #12 | Bronx |
| 310 | 50.2 | Port Washington UFSD | Port Washington |
| 310 | 50.2 | Ramapo Central SD (Suffern) | Hillburn |
| 310 | 50.2 | Rocky Point UFSD | Rocky Point |
| 310 | 50.2 | Valley Central SD (Montgomery) | Montgomery |
| 310 | 50.2 | Wantagh UFSD | Wantagh |
| 320 | 50.1 | Blind Brook-Rye UFSD | Rye Brook |
| 320 | 50.1 | Harborfields Central SD | Greenlawn |
| 320 | 50.1 | Pittsford Central SD | Pittsford |
| 320 | 50.1 | Sachem Central SD | Holbrook |
| 324 | 50.0 | Beacon City SD | Beacon |
| 324 | 50.0 | NYC Geographic District #23 | Brooklyn |
| 326 | 49.9 | Depew UFSD | Depew |
| 326 | 49.9 | Livonia Central SD | Livonia |
| 326 | 49.9 | Massena Central SD | Massena |
| 326 | 49.9 | New Hartford Central SD | New Hartford |
| 326 | 49.9 | North Shore Central SD | Sea Cliff |
| 326 | 49.9 | Oyster Bay-East Norwich Central SD | Oyster Bay |
| 326 | 49.9 | White Plains City SD | White Plains |
| 333 | 49.8 | Amsterdam City SD | Amsterdam |
| 333 | 49.8 | Buffalo City SD | Buffalo |
| 333 | 49.8 | Chittenango Central SD | Chittenango |
| 333 | 49.8 | Goshen Central SD | Goshen |
| 333 | 49.8 | Hannibal Central SD | Hannibal |
| 333 | 49.8 | Johnson City Central SD | Johnson City |
| 333 | 49.8 | Mount Vernon City SD | Mount Vernon |
| 333 | 49.8 | NYC Geographic District #15 | Brooklyn |
| 333 | 49.8 | North Bellmore UFSD | Bellmore |
| 333 | 49.8 | Skaneateles Central SD | Skaneateles |
| 333 | 49.8 | West Irondequoit Central SD | Rochester |
| 344 | 49.7 | Irvington UFSD | Irvington |
| 344 | 49.7 | Marlboro Central SD | Marlboro |
| 344 | 49.7 | Mount Pleasant Central SD | Thornwood |
| 344 | 49.7 | NYC Geographic District # 5 | New York |
| 344 | 49.7 | Port Jervis City SD | Port Jervis |
| 344 | 49.7 | Solvay UFSD | Solvay |
| 350 | 49.6 | East Greenbush Central SD | East Greenbush |
| 350 | 49.6 | Liberty Central SD | Liberty |
| 350 | 49.6 | Plainedge UFSD | N Massapequa |
| 350 | 49.6 | UFSD of the Tarrytowns | Sleepy Hollow |
| 354 | 49.5 | Babylon UFSD | Babylon |
| 354 | 49.5 | Comsewogue School District | Port Jeff Stn |
| 354 | 49.5 | East Aurora UFSD | East Aurora |
| 357 | 49.4 | Geneva City SD | Geneva |
| 357 | 49.4 | Hendrick Hudson Central SD | Montrose |
| 357 | 49.4 | Johnstown City SD | Johnstown |
| 357 | 49.4 | NYC Geographic District # 8 | Bronx |
| 357 | 49.4 | Royalton-Hartland Central SD | Middleport |
| 357 | 49.4 | Taconic Hills Central SD | Craryville |
| 363 | 49.3 | Maine-Endwell Central SD | Endwell |
| 363 | 49.3 | Pearl River UFSD | Pearl River |

*Note: This section only includes districts with 1,500 or more students; All categories are ranked from high to low*

| | | | |
|---|---|---|---|
| 363 | 49.3 | Spackenkill UFSD | Poughkeepsie |
| 363 | 49.3 | Westbury UFSD | Old Westbury |
| 367 | 49.1 | South Country Central SD | East Patchogue |
| 368 | 49.0 | Mexico Central SD | Mexico |
| 368 | 49.0 | New Hyde Pk-Garden City Pk UFSD | New Hyde Park |
| 370 | 48.9 | Locust Valley Central SD | Locust Valley |
| 371 | 48.6 | NYC Geographic District # 4 | New York |
| 372 | 48.2 | NYC Geographic District #17 | Brooklyn |
| 373 | 48.1 | NYC Geographic District #20 | Brooklyn |
| 373 | 48.1 | NYC Geographic District #31 | Staten Island |
| 375 | 48.0 | Charter School for Applied Tech | Buffalo |
| 376 | 47.9 | NYC Geographic District #22 | Brooklyn |
| 377 | 47.3 | NYC Geographic District # 2 | New York |
| 378 | 47.1 | Croton-Harmon UFSD | Croton on Hdsn |
| 378 | 47.1 | Valhalla UFSD | Valhalla |
| 380 | 46.8 | NYC Geographic District # 3 | New York |
| 381 | 46.3 | NYC Geographic District #21 | Brooklyn |
| 382 | 45.7 | NYC Geographic District #13 | Brooklyn |
| 383 | 44.0 | NYC Geographic District #26 | Bayside |

## Female Students

| Rank | Percent | District Name | City |
|---|---|---|---|
| 1 | 56.0 | NYC Geographic District #26 | Bayside |
| 2 | 54.3 | NYC Geographic District #13 | Brooklyn |
| 3 | 53.7 | NYC Geographic District #21 | Brooklyn |
| 4 | 53.2 | NYC Geographic District # 3 | New York |
| 5 | 52.9 | Croton-Harmon UFSD | Croton on Hdsn |
| 5 | 52.9 | Valhalla UFSD | Valhalla |
| 7 | 52.7 | NYC Geographic District # 2 | New York |
| 8 | 52.1 | NYC Geographic District #22 | Brooklyn |
| 9 | 52.0 | Charter School for Applied Tech | Buffalo |
| 10 | 51.9 | NYC Geographic District #20 | Brooklyn |
| 10 | 51.9 | NYC Geographic District #31 | Staten Island |
| 12 | 51.8 | NYC Geographic District #17 | Brooklyn |
| 13 | 51.4 | NYC Geographic District # 4 | New York |
| 14 | 51.1 | Locust Valley Central SD | Locust Valley |
| 15 | 51.0 | Mexico Central SD | Mexico |
| 15 | 51.0 | New Hyde Pk-Garden City Pk UFSD | New Hyde Park |
| 17 | 50.9 | South Country Central SD | East Patchogue |
| 18 | 50.7 | Maine-Endwell Central SD | Endwell |
| 18 | 50.7 | Pearl River UFSD | Pearl River |
| 18 | 50.7 | Spackenkill UFSD | Poughkeepsie |
| 18 | 50.7 | Westbury UFSD | Old Westbury |
| 22 | 50.6 | Geneva City SD | Geneva |
| 22 | 50.6 | Hendrick Hudson Central SD | Montrose |
| 22 | 50.6 | Johnstown City SD | Johnstown |
| 22 | 50.6 | NYC Geographic District # 8 | Bronx |
| 22 | 50.6 | Royalton-Hartland Central SD | Middleport |
| 22 | 50.6 | Taconic Hills Central SD | Craryville |
| 28 | 50.5 | Babylon UFSD | Babylon |
| 28 | 50.5 | Comsewogue School District | Port Jeff Stn |
| 28 | 50.5 | East Aurora UFSD | East Aurora |
| 31 | 50.4 | East Greenbush Central SD | East Greenbush |
| 31 | 50.4 | Liberty Central SD | Liberty |
| 31 | 50.4 | Plainedge UFSD | N Massapequa |
| 31 | 50.4 | UFSD of the Tarrytowns | Sleepy Hollow |
| 35 | 50.3 | Irvington UFSD | Irvington |
| 35 | 50.3 | Marlboro Central SD | Marlboro |
| 35 | 50.3 | Mount Pleasant Central SD | Thornwood |
| 35 | 50.3 | NYC Geographic District # 5 | New York |
| 35 | 50.3 | Port Jervis City SD | Port Jervis |
| 35 | 50.3 | Solvay UFSD | Solvay |
| 41 | 50.2 | Amsterdam City SD | Amsterdam |
| 41 | 50.2 | Buffalo City SD | Buffalo |
| 41 | 50.2 | Chittenango Central SD | Chittenango |
| 41 | 50.2 | Goshen Central SD | Goshen |
| 41 | 50.2 | Hannibal Central SD | Hannibal |
| 41 | 50.2 | Johnson City Central SD | Johnson City |
| 41 | 50.2 | Mount Vernon City SD | Mount Vernon |
| 41 | 50.2 | NYC Geographic District #15 | Brooklyn |
| 41 | 50.2 | North Bellmore UFSD | Bellmore |
| 41 | 50.2 | Skaneateles Central SD | Skaneateles |
| 41 | 50.2 | West Irondequoit Central SD | Rochester |
| 52 | 50.1 | Depew UFSD | Depew |
| 52 | 50.1 | Livonia Central SD | Livonia |
| 52 | 50.1 | Massena Central SD | Massena |
| 52 | 50.1 | New Hartford Central SD | New Hartford |
| 52 | 50.1 | North Shore Central SD | Sea Cliff |
| 52 | 50.1 | Oyster Bay-East Norwich Central SD | Oyster Bay |
| 52 | 50.1 | White Plains City SD | White Plains |
| 59 | 50.0 | Beacon City SD | Beacon |
| 59 | 50.0 | NYC Geographic District #23 | Brooklyn |
| 61 | 49.9 | Blind Brook-Rye UFSD | Rye Brook |
| 61 | 49.9 | Harborfields Central SD | Greenlawn |
| 61 | 49.9 | Pittsford Central SD | Pittsford |
| 61 | 49.9 | Sachem Central SD | Holbrook |
| 65 | 49.8 | East Meadow UFSD | Westbury |
| 65 | 49.8 | Indian River Central SD | Philadelphia |
| 65 | 49.8 | Katonah-Lewisboro UFSD | South Salem |
| 65 | 49.8 | Lockport City SD | Lockport |
| 65 | 49.8 | NYC Geographic District #12 | Bronx |
| 65 | 49.8 | Port Washington UFSD | Port Washington |
| 65 | 49.8 | Ramapo Central SD (Suffern) | Hillburn |
| 65 | 49.8 | Rocky Point UFSD | Rocky Point |
| 65 | 49.8 | Valley Central SD (Montgomery) | Montgomery |
| 65 | 49.8 | Wantagh UFSD | Wantagh |
| 75 | 49.7 | Camden Central SD | Camden |
| 75 | 49.7 | Elwood UFSD | Greenlawn |
| 75 | 49.7 | Grand Island Central SD | Grand Island |
| 75 | 49.7 | Kings Park Central SD | Kings Park |
| 75 | 49.7 | Liverpool Central SD | Liverpool |
| 75 | 49.7 | New York City Public Schools | New York |
| 75 | 49.7 | Niskayuna Central SD | Schenectady |
| 75 | 49.7 | Oneonta City SD | Oneonta |
| 75 | 49.7 | Plattsburgh City SD | Plattsburgh |
| 75 | 49.7 | Saugerties Central SD | Saugerties |
| 75 | 49.7 | South Jefferson Central SD | Adams Center |
| 75 | 49.7 | Vernon-Verona-Sherrill Central SD | Verona |
| 87 | 49.6 | Carthage Central SD | Carthage |
| 87 | 49.6 | Cheektowaga Central SD | Cheektowaga |
| 87 | 49.6 | Cobleskill-Richmondville Central SD | Cobleskill |
| 87 | 49.6 | Hamburg Central SD | Hamburg |
| 87 | 49.6 | Kingston City SD | Kingston |
| 87 | 49.6 | Mohonasen Central SD | Schenectady |
| 87 | 49.6 | Scarsdale UFSD | Scarsdale |
| 87 | 49.6 | Washingtonville Central SD | Washingtonville |
| 87 | 49.6 | Waterloo Central SD | Waterloo |
| 96 | 49.5 | Brighton Central SD | Rochester |
| 96 | 49.5 | Cohoes City SD | Cohoes |
| 96 | 49.5 | Greece Central SD | Rochester |
| 96 | 49.5 | Guilderland Central SD | Guilderland |
| 96 | 49.5 | Highland Central SD | Highland |
| 96 | 49.5 | Lancaster Central SD | Lancaster |
| 96 | 49.5 | Manhasset UFSD | Manhasset |
| 96 | 49.5 | Nanuet UFSD | Nanuet |
| 96 | 49.5 | NYC Geographic District #30 | Long Isl City |
| 96 | 49.5 | Newark Central SD | Newark |
| 96 | 49.5 | Niagara Falls City SD | Niagara Falls |
| 96 | 49.5 | Patchogue-Medford UFSD | Patchogue |
| 96 | 49.5 | Schenectady City SD | Schenectady |
| 96 | 49.5 | Uniondale UFSD | Uniondale |
| 96 | 49.5 | West Babylon UFSD | West Babylon |
| 111 | 49.4 | Ardsley UFSD | Ardsley |
| 111 | 49.4 | Arlington Central SD | Poughkeepsie |
| 111 | 49.4 | Eastport-South Manor CSD | Manorville |
| 111 | 49.4 | Ellenville Central SD | Ellenville |
| 111 | 49.4 | Fayetteville-Manlius Central SD | Manlius |
| 111 | 49.4 | Frontier Central SD | Hamburg |
| 111 | 49.4 | Jamesville-Dewitt Central SD | Dewitt |
| 111 | 49.4 | NYC Geographic District # 1 | New York |
| 111 | 49.4 | NYC Geographic District #10 | Bronx |
| 111 | 49.4 | NYC Geographic District #25 | Flushing |
| 111 | 49.4 | NYC Geographic District #32 | Brooklyn |
| 111 | 49.4 | Nyack UFSD | Nyack |
| 111 | 49.4 | Smithtown Central SD | Smithtown |
| 111 | 49.4 | S Glens Fls Central SD | S Glens Fls |
| 111 | 49.4 | Tonawanda City SD | Tonawanda |
| 111 | 49.4 | Wayland-Cohocton Central SD | Wayland |
| 111 | 49.4 | Williamsville Central SD | East Amherst |
| 128 | 49.3 | Akron Central SD | Akron |
| 128 | 49.3 | Bay Shore UFSD | Bay Shore |
| 128 | 49.3 | Bethpage UFSD | Bethpage |
| 128 | 49.3 | Cortland City SD | Cortland |
| 128 | 49.3 | Hilton Central SD | Hilton |
| 128 | 49.3 | Peekskill City SD | Peekskill |
| 128 | 49.3 | Wyandanch UFSD | Wyandanch |
| 135 | 49.2 | Bayport-Blue Point UFSD | Bayport |
| 135 | 49.2 | Binghamton City SD | Binghamton |
| 135 | 49.2 | Harrison Central SD | Harrison |
| 135 | 49.2 | Iroquois Central SD | Elma |
| 135 | 49.2 | Oceanside UFSD | Oceanside |
| 135 | 49.2 | Penn Yan Central SD | Penn Yan |
| 135 | 49.2 | Schalmont Central SD | Schenectady |
| 135 | 49.2 | Somers Central SD | Somers |
| 135 | 49.2 | Yorktown Central SD | Yorktown Hgts |
| 144 | 49.1 | Albany City SD | Albany |
| 144 | 49.1 | Averill Park Central SD | Averill Park |
| 144 | 49.1 | Central Islip UFSD | Central Islip |
| 144 | 49.1 | Cheektowaga-Sloan UFSD | Sloan |
| 144 | 49.1 | Commack UFSD | East Northport |
| 144 | 49.1 | East Hampton UFSD | East Hampton |
| 144 | 49.1 | Horseheads Central SD | Horseheads |
| 144 | 49.1 | Mahopac Central SD | Mahopac |
| 144 | 49.1 | Merrick UFSD | Merrick |
| 144 | 49.1 | Mount Sinai UFSD | Mount Sinai |
| 144 | 49.1 | Norwich City SD | Norwich |
| 144 | 49.1 | Rochester City SD | Rochester |
| 144 | 49.1 | Rush-Henrietta Central SD | Henrietta |
| 144 | 49.1 | Saratoga Spgs City SD | Saratoga Spgs |
| 144 | 49.1 | Whitesboro Central SD | Yorkville |
| 159 | 49.0 | Burnt Hills-Ballston Lake CSD | Scotia |
| 159 | 49.0 | Dansville Central SD | Dansville |
| 159 | 49.0 | East Ramapo Central SD | Spring Valley |
| 159 | 49.0 | Edgemont UFSD | Scarsdale |
| 159 | 49.0 | Olean City SD | Olean |
| 159 | 49.0 | Onteora Central SD | Boiceville |
| 159 | 49.0 | Pelham UFSD | Pelham |
| 159 | 49.0 | Plainview-Old Bethpage Central SD | Plainview |
| 159 | 49.0 | Rome City SD | Rome |
| 159 | 49.0 | Springville-Griffith Institute CSD | Springville |
| 159 | 49.0 | Syracuse City SD | Syracuse |
| 159 | 49.0 | Utica City SD | Utica |
| 159 | 49.0 | Valley Stream Central High SD | Valley Stream |
| 159 | 49.0 | Waverly Central SD | Waverly |
| 173 | 48.9 | Attica Central SD | Attica |
| 173 | 48.9 | Baldwinsville Central SD | Baldwinsville |
| 173 | 48.9 | Cold Spring Hrbr Central SD | Cold Spring Hrbr |
| 173 | 48.9 | Elmont UFSD | Elmont |
| 173 | 48.9 | Garden City UFSD | Garden City |
| 173 | 48.9 | Glens Falls City SD | Glens Falls |
| 173 | 48.9 | Hempstead UFSD | Hempstead |
| 173 | 48.9 | Island Trees UFSD | Levittown |
| 173 | 48.9 | NYC Geographic District # 9 | Bronx |
| 173 | 48.9 | NYC Geographic District #29 | Rosedale |
| 173 | 48.9 | Oneida City SD | Oneida |
| 173 | 48.9 | Port Chester-Rye UFSD | Port Chester |
| 173 | 48.9 | South Colonie Central SD | Albany |
| 173 | 48.9 | Yorkshire-Pioneer Central SD | Yorkshire |
| 187 | 48.8 | Albion Central SD | Albion |
| 187 | 48.8 | Cazenovia Central SD | Cazenovia |
| 187 | 48.8 | Chenango Valley Central SD | Binghamton |
| 187 | 48.8 | Clarence Central SD | Clarence Center |
| 187 | 48.8 | Copiague UFSD | Copiague |
| 187 | 48.8 | Corning City SD | Painted Post |
| 187 | 48.8 | Fulton City SD | Fulton |
| 187 | 48.8 | Gloversville City SD | Gloversville |
| 187 | 48.8 | Gouverneur Central SD | Gouverneur |
| 187 | 48.8 | Hudson Falls Central SD | Fort Edward |
| 187 | 48.8 | Jordan-Elbridge Central SD | Elbridge |
| 187 | 48.8 | Kenmore-Tonawanda UFSD | Buffalo |
| 187 | 48.8 | Middletown City SD | Middletown |
| 187 | 48.8 | NYC Geographic District #18 | Brooklyn |
| 187 | 48.8 | Red Hook Central SD | Red Hook |
| 187 | 48.8 | Sewanhaka Central High SD | Floral Park |
| 187 | 48.8 | Victor Central SD | Victor |
| 187 | 48.8 | West Seneca Central SD | West Seneca |
| 205 | 48.7 | Auburn City SD | Auburn |
| 205 | 48.7 | Broadalbin-Perth Central SD | Broadalbin |
| 205 | 48.7 | Bronxville UFSD | Bronxville |
| 205 | 48.7 | Byram Hills Central SD | Armonk |
| 205 | 48.7 | Jamestown City SD | Jamestown |
| 205 | 48.7 | Lewiston-Porter Central SD | Youngstown |
| 205 | 48.7 | Long Beach City SD | Long Beach |
| 205 | 48.7 | Lynbrook UFSD | Lynbrook |
| 205 | 48.7 | Mamaroneck UFSD | Mamaroneck |
| 205 | 48.7 | Massapequa UFSD | Massapequa |
| 205 | 48.7 | Mattituck-Cutchogue UFSD | Cutchogue |
| 205 | 48.7 | NYC Geographic District #28 | Jamaica |
| 205 | 48.7 | Penfield Central SD | Rochester |
| 205 | 48.7 | Pleasantville UFSD | Pleasantville |
| 205 | 48.7 | South Orangetown Central SD | Blauvelt |
| 205 | 48.7 | Vestal Central SD | Vestal |
| 205 | 48.7 | Warwick Valley Central SD | Warwick |
| 222 | 48.6 | Amityville UFSD | Amityville |
| 222 | 48.6 | Briarcliff Mnr UFSD | Briarcliff Mnr |
| 222 | 48.6 | Canastota Central SD | Canastota |
| 222 | 48.6 | Carmel Central SD | Patterson |
| 222 | 48.6 | East Irondequoit Central SD | Rochester |
| 222 | 48.6 | East Syracuse-Minoa Central SD | East Syracuse |
| 222 | 48.6 | Evans-Brant Central SD (Lake Shore) | Angola |
| 222 | 48.6 | Hauppauge UFSD | Hauppauge |
| 222 | 48.6 | Islip UFSD | Islip |
| 222 | 48.6 | Kinderhook Central SD | Valatie |

*Note: This section only includes districts with 1,500 or more students; All categories are ranked from high to low*

| | | | |
|---|---|---|---|
| 222 | 48.6 | Levittown UFSD | Levittown |
| 222 | 48.6 | Monticello Central SD | Monticello |
| 222 | 48.6 | Pine Bush Central SD | Pine Bush |
| 222 | 48.6 | Saranac Central SD | Dannemora |
| 222 | 48.6 | Spencerport Central SD | Spencerport |
| 222 | 48.6 | Watertown City SD | Watertown |
| 222 | 48.6 | Wayne Central SD | Ontario Center |
| 222 | 48.6 | West Genesee Central SD | Camillus |
| 222 | 48.6 | Windsor Central SD | Windsor |
| 241 | 48.5 | Baldwin UFSD | Baldwin |
| 241 | 48.5 | Bellmore-Merrick Central High SD | North Merrick |
| 241 | 48.5 | Brockport Central SD | Brockport |
| 241 | 48.5 | Catskill Central SD | Catskill |
| 241 | 48.5 | Cheektowaga-Maryvale UFSD | Cheektowaga |
| 241 | 48.5 | Fairport Central SD | Fairport |
| 241 | 48.5 | Franklin Square UFSD | Franklin Square |
| 241 | 48.5 | Gates-Chili Central SD | Rochester |
| 241 | 48.5 | Great Neck UFSD | Great Neck |
| 241 | 48.5 | Hampton Bays UFSD | Hampton Bays |
| 241 | 48.5 | Hicksville UFSD | Hicksville |
| 241 | 48.5 | Homer Central SD | Homer |
| 241 | 48.5 | Hyde Park Central SD | Hyde Park |
| 241 | 48.5 | Lakeland Central SD | Shrub Oak |
| 241 | 48.5 | Monroe-Woodbury Central SD | Central Valley |
| 241 | 48.5 | North Syracuse Central SD | North Syracuse |
| 241 | 48.5 | Three Village Central SD | Stony Brook |
| 258 | 48.4 | Batavia City SD | Batavia |
| 258 | 48.4 | Bedford Central SD | Bedford |
| 258 | 48.4 | Churchville-Chili Central SD | Churchville |
| 258 | 48.4 | Freeport UFSD | Freeport |
| 258 | 48.4 | Hewlett-Woodmere UFSD | Woodmere |
| 258 | 48.4 | Ithaca City SD | Ithaca |
| 258 | 48.4 | Jericho UFSD | Jericho |
| 258 | 48.4 | NYC Geographic District # 6 | New York |
| 258 | 48.4 | Niagara-Wheatfield Central SD | Niagara Falls |
| 258 | 48.4 | North Rockland Central SD | Garnerville |
| 258 | 48.4 | Northport-East Northport UFSD | Northport |
| 258 | 48.4 | Ravena-Coeymans-Selkirk Ctrl SD | Selkirk |
| 258 | 48.4 | Seaford UFSD | Seaford |
| 258 | 48.4 | Shenendehowa Central SD | Clifton Park |
| 258 | 48.4 | Wallkill Central SD | Wallkill |
| 258 | 48.4 | Yonkers City SD | Yonkers |
| 274 | 48.3 | Cornwall Central SD | Cornwall on Hdsn |
| 274 | 48.3 | Dover UFSD | Dover Plains |
| 274 | 48.3 | East Williston UFSD | Old Westbury |
| 274 | 48.3 | Middle Country Central SD | Centereach |
| 274 | 48.3 | NYC Geographic District #27 | Ozone Park |
| 274 | 48.3 | Newburgh City SD | Newburgh |
| 274 | 48.3 | Rockville Ctr UFSD | Rockville Ctr |
| 274 | 48.3 | Sayville UFSD | Sayville |
| 274 | 48.3 | Southwestern CSD at Jamestown | Jamestown |
| 274 | 48.3 | Susquehanna Valley Central SD | Conklin |
| 274 | 48.3 | Union-Endicott Central SD | Endicott |
| 285 | 48.2 | Central Square Central SD | Central Square |
| 285 | 48.2 | General Brown Central SD | Dexter |
| 285 | 48.2 | Herricks UFSD | New Hyde Park |
| 285 | 48.2 | Ilion Central SD | Ilion |
| 285 | 48.2 | Marcellus Central SD | Marcellus |
| 285 | 48.2 | New Paltz Central SD | New Paltz |
| 285 | 48.2 | Peru Central SD | Peru |
| 285 | 48.2 | Phelps-Clifton Springs Central SD | Clifton Springs |
| 285 | 48.2 | Putnam Valley Central SD | Putnam Valley |
| 285 | 48.2 | Salmon River Central SD | Fort Covington |
| 285 | 48.2 | Starpoint Central SD | Lockport |
| 285 | 48.2 | West Islip UFSD | West Islip |
| 285 | 48.2 | Westhill Central SD | Syracuse |
| 298 | 48.1 | Beekmantown Central SD | West Chazy |
| 298 | 48.1 | Clarkstown Central SD | New City |
| 298 | 48.1 | Coxsackie-Athens Central SD | Coxsackie |
| 298 | 48.1 | Hastings-on-Hudson UFSD | Hastings on Hdsn |
| 298 | 48.1 | Medina Central SD | Medina |
| 298 | 48.1 | NYC Geographic District #19 | Brooklyn |
| 298 | 48.1 | Rondout Valley Central SD | Accord |
| 298 | 48.1 | Rye City SD | Rye |
| 306 | 48.0 | Amherst Central SD | Amherst |
| 306 | 48.0 | Bath Central SD | Bath |
| 306 | 48.0 | Bethlehem Central SD | Delmar |
| 306 | 48.0 | Canandaigua City SD | Canandaigua |
| 306 | 48.0 | Eden Central SD | Eden |
| 306 | 48.0 | Longwood Central SD | Middle Island |
| 306 | 48.0 | Orchard Park Central SD | Orchard Park |
| 306 | 48.0 | Ossining UFSD | Ossining |
| 306 | 48.0 | Schuylerville Central SD | Schuylerville |
| 315 | 47.9 | Chappaqua Central SD | Chappaqua |
| 315 | 47.9 | Connetquot Central SD | Bohemia |
| 315 | 47.9 | Dryden Central SD | Dryden |
| 315 | 47.9 | Lackawanna City SD | Lackawanna |
| 315 | 47.9 | Lansingburgh Central SD | Troy |
| 315 | 47.9 | Miller Place UFSD | Miller Place |
| 315 | 47.9 | North Colonie Central SD | Latham |
| 315 | 47.9 | Palmyra-Macedon Central SD | Palmyra |
| 315 | 47.9 | Queensbury UFSD | Queensbury |
| 315 | 47.9 | Riverhead Central SD | Riverhead |
| 315 | 47.9 | Wappingers Central SD | Wappingers Fls |
| 326 | 47.8 | Alden Central SD | Alden |
| 326 | 47.8 | Eastchester UFSD | Eastchester |
| 326 | 47.8 | Elmira City SD | Elmira |
| 326 | 47.8 | New Rochelle City SD | New Rochelle |
| 326 | 47.8 | Newfane Central SD | Burt |
| 326 | 47.8 | Webster Central SD | Webster |
| 326 | 47.8 | William Floyd UFSD | Mastic Beach |
| 333 | 47.7 | Center Moriches UFSD | Center Moriches |
| 333 | 47.7 | Honeoye Falls-Lima Central SD | Honeoye Falls |
| 333 | 47.7 | Malone Central SD | Malone |
| 333 | 47.7 | Minisink Valley Central SD | Slate Hill |
| 333 | 47.7 | North Babylon UFSD | North Babylon |
| 333 | 47.7 | Oswego City SD | Oswego |
| 333 | 47.7 | Phoenix Central SD | Phoenix |
| 333 | 47.7 | Poughkeepsie City SD | Poughkeepsie |
| 333 | 47.7 | Scotia-Glenville Central SD | Scotia |
| 333 | 47.7 | Sherburne-Earlville Central SD | Sherburne |
| 343 | 47.6 | Brentwood UFSD | Brentwood |
| 343 | 47.6 | Holland Patent Central SD | Holland Patent |
| 343 | 47.6 | Huntington UFSD | Huntington Stn |
| 343 | 47.6 | Lindenhurst UFSD | Lindenhurst |
| 343 | 47.6 | Owego-Apalachin Central SD | Owego |
| 348 | 47.5 | Ballston Spa Central SD | Ballston Spa |
| 348 | 47.5 | Chenango Forks Central SD | Binghamton |
| 348 | 47.5 | Syosset Central SD | Syosset |
| 351 | 47.4 | East Islip UFSD | Islip Terrace |
| 351 | 47.4 | Lawrence UFSD | Lawrence |
| 351 | 47.4 | NYC Geographic District #16 | Brooklyn |
| 351 | 47.4 | Sweet Home Central SD | Amherst |
| 351 | 47.4 | Troy City SD | Troy |
| 356 | 47.3 | Farmingdale UFSD | Farmingdale |
| 356 | 47.3 | South Huntington UFSD | Huntington Stn |
| 358 | 47.2 | Half Hollow Hills Central SD | Dix Hills |
| 359 | 47.1 | Floral Park-Bellerose UFSD | Floral Park |
| 359 | 47.1 | Glen Cove City SD | Glen Cove |
| 359 | 47.1 | NYC Geographic District #11 | Bronx |
| 359 | 47.1 | Shoreham-Wading River Central SD | Shoreham |
| 363 | 47.0 | Brewster Central SD | Brewster |
| 363 | 47.0 | NYC Geographic District #14 | Brooklyn |
| 363 | 47.0 | North Tonawanda City SD | North Tonawanda |
| 366 | 46.9 | Hornell City SD | Hornell |
| 366 | 46.9 | Mineola UFSD | Mineola |
| 366 | 46.9 | Valley Stream 13 UFSD | Valley Stream |
| 369 | 46.8 | Ogdensburg City SD | Ogdensburg |
| 370 | 46.7 | NYC Geographic District #24 | Ridgewood |
| 370 | 46.7 | Westhampton Bch UFSD | Westhampton Bch |
| 372 | 46.5 | Fredonia Central SD | Fredonia |
| 372 | 46.5 | Malverne UFSD | Malverne |
| 374 | 46.4 | Deer Park UFSD | Deer Park |
| 375 | 46.3 | Southampton UFSD | Southampton |
| 376 | 46.2 | Dunkirk City SD | Dunkirk |
| 377 | 46.0 | Roslyn UFSD | Roslyn |
| 378 | 45.9 | NYC Geographic District # 7 | Bronx |
| 379 | 45.5 | Hudson City SD | Hudson |
| 380 | 45.3 | West Hempstead UFSD | West Hempstead |
| 381 | 45.2 | Greenburgh Central SD | Hartsdale |
| 382 | 44.3 | Roosevelt UFSD | Roosevelt |
| 383 | 26.5 | NYC Special Schools - District 75 | New York |

## Individual Education Program Students

| Rank | Percent | District Name | City |
|---|---|---|---|
| 1 | 30.6 | Lawrence UFSD | Lawrence |
| 2 | 26.3 | NYC Geographic District # 7 | Bronx |
| 3 | 26.2 | NYC Geographic District #16 | Brooklyn |
| 4 | 25.7 | Lackawanna City SD | Lackawanna |
| 5 | 25.1 | NYC Geographic District # 5 | New York |
| 6 | 24.9 | East Ramapo Central SD | Spring Valley |
| 7 | 24.8 | Buffalo City SD | Buffalo |
| 8 | 24.5 | NYC Geographic District # 4 | New York |
| 9 | 24.3 | Hewlett-Woodmere UFSD | Woodmere |
| 9 | 24.3 | NYC Geographic District # 8 | Bronx |
| 11 | 24.1 | Hudson City SD | Hudson |
| 12 | 23.9 | NYC Geographic District #12 | Bronx |
| 13 | 23.8 | NYC Geographic District #11 | Bronx |
| 14 | 23.1 | Albany City SD | Albany |
| 15 | 22.9 | Syracuse City SD | Syracuse |
| 16 | 22.6 | NYC Geographic District # 9 | Bronx |
| 17 | 22.4 | NYC Geographic District #23 | Brooklyn |
| 18 | 22.2 | Poughkeepsie City SD | Poughkeepsie |
| 19 | 22.1 | Kenmore-Tonawanda UFSD | Buffalo |
| 20 | 22.0 | Ravena-Coeymans-Selkirk Ctrl SD | Selkirk |
| 21 | 21.7 | NYC Geographic District #31 | Staten Island |
| 22 | 21.5 | NYC Geographic District #14 | Brooklyn |
| 23 | 21.4 | Lansingburgh Central SD | Troy |
| 24 | 21.1 | Troy City SD | Troy |
| 25 | 20.8 | NYC Geographic District #17 | Brooklyn |
| 25 | 20.8 | Rochester City SD | Rochester |
| 27 | 20.7 | Rondout Valley Central SD | Accord |
| 28 | 20.6 | Kingston City SD | Kingston |
| 28 | 20.6 | NYC Geographic District #15 | Brooklyn |
| 28 | 20.6 | Union-Endicott Central SD | Endicott |
| 31 | 20.4 | Utica City SD | Utica |
| 32 | 20.3 | Glens Falls City SD | Glens Falls |
| 32 | 20.3 | NYC Geographic District #21 | Brooklyn |
| 34 | 20.2 | Gloversville City SD | Gloversville |
| 34 | 20.2 | NYC Geographic District #10 | Bronx |
| 34 | 20.2 | Niagara Falls City SD | Niagara Falls |
| 37 | 20.0 | Dryden Central SD | Dryden |
| 37 | 20.0 | North Babylon UFSD | North Babylon |
| 39 | 19.8 | NYC Geographic District #22 | Brooklyn |
| 39 | 19.8 | Plattsburgh City SD | Plattsburgh |
| 41 | 19.7 | Onteora Central SD | Boiceville |
| 41 | 19.7 | Saranac Central SD | Dannemora |
| 43 | 19.6 | NYC Geographic District #19 | Brooklyn |
| 43 | 19.6 | Owego-Apalachin Central SD | Owego |
| 45 | 19.4 | Malverne UFSD | Malverne |
| 45 | 19.4 | Sherburne-Earlville Central SD | Sherburne |
| 47 | 19.3 | Malone Central SD | Malone |
| 47 | 19.3 | NYC Geographic District # 1 | New York |
| 47 | 19.3 | NYC Geographic District #27 | Ozone Park |
| 47 | 19.3 | Peru Central SD | Peru |
| 51 | 19.2 | Beekmantown Central SD | West Chazy |
| 52 | 19.1 | Glen Cove City SD | Glen Cove |
| 52 | 19.1 | Schenectady City SD | Schenectady |
| 54 | 19.0 | Hyde Park Central SD | Hyde Park |
| 54 | 19.0 | Oneonta City SD | Oneonta |
| 56 | 18.9 | Mineola UFSD | Mineola |
| 56 | 18.9 | New York City Public Schools | New York |
| 58 | 18.8 | Ithaca City SD | Ithaca |
| 58 | 18.8 | Peekskill City SD | Peekskill |
| 60 | 18.7 | Lakeland Central SD | Shrub Oak |
| 60 | 18.7 | NYC Geographic District #20 | Brooklyn |
| 62 | 18.6 | Amsterdam City SD | Amsterdam |
| 62 | 18.6 | Liverpool Central SD | Liverpool |
| 62 | 18.6 | NYC Geographic District #29 | Rosedale |
| 65 | 18.5 | Penn Yan Central SD | Penn Yan |
| 66 | 18.4 | Amityville UFSD | Amityville |
| 66 | 18.4 | Maine-Endwell Central SD | Endwell |
| 66 | 18.4 | NYC Geographic District #18 | Brooklyn |
| 66 | 18.4 | Rocky Point UFSD | Rocky Point |
| 70 | 18.3 | Ogdensburg City SD | Ogdensburg |
| 70 | 18.3 | West Islip UFSD | West Islip |
| 72 | 18.2 | Waterloo Central SD | Waterloo |
| 73 | 18.1 | Plainview-Old Bethpage Central SD | Plainview |
| 73 | 18.1 | Rome City SD | Rome |
| 75 | 18.0 | Connetquot Central SD | Bohemia |
| 75 | 18.0 | Mount Pleasant Central SD | Thornwood |
| 75 | 18.0 | Ramapo Central SD (Suffern) | Hillburn |
| 78 | 17.9 | West Hempstead UFSD | West Hempstead |
| 79 | 17.8 | Gouverneur Central SD | Gouverneur |
| 79 | 17.8 | NYC Geographic District #32 | Brooklyn |
| 81 | 17.7 | Catskill Central SD | Catskill |
| 81 | 17.7 | Hudson Falls Central SD | Fort Edward |
| 81 | 17.7 | Kinderhook Central SD | Valatie |
| 81 | 17.7 | Levittown UFSD | Levittown |
| 81 | 17.7 | Monticello Central SD | Monticello |
| 81 | 17.7 | NYC Geographic District # 6 | New York |
| 81 | 17.7 | Wyandanch UFSD | Wyandanch |
| 88 | 17.6 | Geneva City SD | Geneva |
| 89 | 17.5 | Frontier Central SD | Hamburg |
| 89 | 17.5 | Mahopac Central SD | Mahopac |
| 89 | 17.5 | Yorkshire-Pioneer Central SD | Yorkshire |
| 92 | 17.4 | Carmel Central SD | Patterson |
| 92 | 17.4 | Kings Park Central SD | Kings Park |
| 92 | 17.4 | NYC Geographic District #28 | Jamaica |
| 95 | 17.3 | Canastota Central SD | Canastota |
| 95 | 17.3 | East Syracuse-Minoa Central SD | East Syracuse |
| 95 | 17.3 | Ilion Central SD | Ilion |
| 95 | 17.3 | Scotia-Glenville Central SD | Scotia |

*Note: This section only includes districts with 1,500 or more students; All categories are ranked from high to low*

| | | | |
|---|---|---|---|
| 95 | 17.3 | Valley Central SD (Montgomery) | Montgomery |
| 100 | 17.2 | NYC Geographic District # 3 | New York |
| 100 | 17.2 | Olean City SD | Olean |
| 102 | 17.1 | Gates-Chili Central SD | Rochester |
| 102 | 17.1 | Manhasset UFSD | Manhasset |
| 102 | 17.1 | North Tonawanda City SD | North Tonawanda |
| 102 | 17.1 | Saugerties Central SD | Saugerties |
| 106 | 17.0 | Hornell City SD | Hornell |
| 106 | 17.0 | Katonah-Lewisboro UFSD | South Salem |
| 106 | 17.0 | Long Beach City SD | Long Beach |
| 106 | 17.0 | Mount Vernon City SD | Mount Vernon |
| 106 | 17.0 | North Shore Central SD | Sea Cliff |
| 111 | 16.9 | Homer Central SD | Homer |
| 111 | 16.9 | Johnson City Central SD | Johnson City |
| 113 | 16.8 | Depew UFSD | Depew |
| 113 | 16.8 | Marlboro Central SD | Marlboro |
| 113 | 16.8 | Port Washington UFSD | Port Washington |
| 116 | 16.7 | Arlington Central SD | Poughkeepsie |
| 116 | 16.7 | Brighton Central SD | Rochester |
| 116 | 16.7 | East Irondequoit Central SD | Rochester |
| 116 | 16.7 | Ellenville Central SD | Ellenville |
| 116 | 16.7 | Greenburgh Central SD | Hartsdale |
| 116 | 16.7 | Lindenhurst UFSD | Lindenhurst |
| 116 | 16.7 | Lockport City SD | Lockport |
| 116 | 16.7 | NYC Geographic District # 2 | New York |
| 116 | 16.7 | North Bellmore UFSD | Bellmore |
| 125 | 16.6 | Corning City SD | Painted Post |
| 125 | 16.6 | East Greenbush Central SD | East Greenbush |
| 125 | 16.6 | Longwood Central SD | Middle Island |
| 125 | 16.6 | Yonkers City SD | Yonkers |
| 129 | 16.5 | Cheektowaga-Sloan UFSD | Sloan |
| 130 | 16.4 | Chenango Forks Central SD | Binghamton |
| 130 | 16.4 | Hamburg Central SD | Hamburg |
| 130 | 16.4 | Huntington UFSD | Huntington Stn |
| 130 | 16.4 | Tonawanda City SD | Tonawanda |
| 134 | 16.3 | Hampton Bays UFSD | Hampton Bays |
| 134 | 16.3 | Hicksville UFSD | Hicksville |
| 134 | 16.3 | NYC Geographic District #25 | Flushing |
| 134 | 16.3 | Norwich City SD | Norwich |
| 138 | 16.2 | Averill Park Central SD | Averill Park |
| 138 | 16.2 | Holland Patent Central SD | Holland Patent |
| 138 | 16.2 | Mexico Central SD | Mexico |
| 138 | 16.2 | Solvay UFSD | Solvay |
| 138 | 16.2 | Watertown City SD | Watertown |
| 143 | 16.1 | Comsewogue School District | Port Jeff Stn |
| 143 | 16.1 | Indian River Central SD | Philadelphia |
| 143 | 16.1 | Phelps-Clifton Springs Central SD | Clifton Springs |
| 143 | 16.1 | Wappingers Central SD | Wappingers Fls |
| 147 | 16.0 | Horseheads Central SD | Horseheads |
| 147 | 16.0 | Ossining UFSD | Ossining |
| 147 | 16.0 | Pine Bush Central SD | Pine Bush |
| 150 | 15.9 | Cohoes City SD | Cohoes |
| 150 | 15.9 | Fulton City SD | Fulton |
| 150 | 15.9 | Middle Country Central SD | Centereach |
| 150 | 15.9 | NYC Geographic District #24 | Ridgewood |
| 150 | 15.9 | NYC Geographic District #30 | Long Isl City |
| 150 | 15.9 | Oyster Bay-East Norwich Central SD | Oyster Bay |
| 150 | 15.9 | Salmon River Central SD | Fort Covington |
| 150 | 15.9 | Warwick Valley Central SD | Warwick |
| 150 | 15.9 | Westbury UFSD | Old Westbury |
| 150 | 15.9 | Yorktown Central SD | Yorktown Hgts |
| 160 | 15.8 | Copiague UFSD | Copiague |
| 160 | 15.8 | Merrick UFSD | Merrick |
| 160 | 15.8 | Port Chester-Rye UFSD | Port Chester |
| 160 | 15.8 | Shoreham-Wading River Central SD | Shoreham |
| 160 | 15.8 | Somers Central SD | Somers |
| 165 | 15.7 | Bay Shore UFSD | Bay Shore |
| 165 | 15.7 | Beacon City SD | Beacon |
| 165 | 15.7 | Brewster Central SD | Brewster |
| 165 | 15.7 | Brockport Central SD | Brockport |
| 165 | 15.7 | Cheektowaga Central SD | Cheektowaga |
| 165 | 15.7 | Minisink Valley Central SD | Slate Hill |
| 165 | 15.7 | Port Jervis City SD | Port Jervis |
| 172 | 15.6 | Canandaigua City SD | Canandaigua |
| 172 | 15.6 | Jamesville-Dewitt Central SD | Dewitt |
| 172 | 15.6 | Locust Valley Central SD | Locust Valley |
| 172 | 15.6 | Middletown City SD | Middletown |
| 172 | 15.6 | Monroe-Woodbury Central SD | Central Valley |
| 172 | 15.6 | New Paltz Central SD | New Paltz |
| 172 | 15.6 | Vestal Central SD | Vestal |
| 172 | 15.6 | William Floyd UFSD | Mastic Beach |
| 180 | 15.5 | Brentwood UFSD | Brentwood |
| 180 | 15.5 | Lancaster Central SD | Lancaster |
| 180 | 15.5 | Newark Central SD | Newark |
| 183 | 15.4 | Jericho UFSD | Jericho |
| 183 | 15.4 | Johnstown City SD | Johnstown |
| 183 | 15.4 | Three Village Central SD | Stony Brook |
| 186 | 15.3 | Deer Park UFSD | Deer Park |
| 186 | 15.3 | Guilderland Central SD | Guilderland |
| 186 | 15.3 | Oneida City SD | Oneida |
| 186 | 15.3 | Seaford UFSD | Seaford |
| 190 | 15.2 | Alden Central SD | Alden |
| 190 | 15.2 | Center Moriches UFSD | Center Moriches |
| 190 | 15.2 | Dover UFSD | Dover Plains |
| 190 | 15.2 | Hannibal Central SD | Hannibal |
| 194 | 15.1 | Briarcliff Mnr UFSD | Briarcliff Mnr |
| 194 | 15.1 | Farmingdale UFSD | Farmingdale |
| 194 | 15.1 | Half Hollow Hills Central SD | Dix Hills |
| 194 | 15.1 | Phoenix Central SD | Phoenix |
| 198 | 15.0 | Ballston Spa Central SD | Ballston Spa |
| 198 | 15.0 | Camden Central SD | Camden |
| 198 | 15.0 | Jamestown City SD | Jamestown |
| 198 | 15.0 | Lewiston-Porter Central SD | Youngstown |
| 198 | 15.0 | Newburgh City SD | Newburgh |
| 203 | 14.9 | Binghamton City SD | Binghamton |
| 203 | 14.9 | Hempstead UFSD | Hempstead |
| 203 | 14.9 | Liberty Central SD | Liberty |
| 203 | 14.9 | Medina Central SD | Medina |
| 203 | 14.9 | Northport-East Northport UFSD | Northport |
| 203 | 14.9 | Oswego City SD | Oswego |
| 203 | 14.9 | South Orangetown Central SD | Blauvelt |
| 203 | 14.9 | Syosset Central SD | Syosset |
| 203 | 14.9 | Windsor Central SD | Windsor |
| 212 | 14.8 | Clarkstown Central SD | New City |
| 212 | 14.8 | Evans-Brant Central SD (Lake Shore) | Angola |
| 212 | 14.8 | Orchard Park Central SD | Orchard Park |
| 212 | 14.8 | Taconic Hills Central SD | Craryville |
| 212 | 14.8 | UFSD of the Tarrytowns | Sleepy Hollow |
| 217 | 14.7 | Burnt Hills-Ballston Lake CSD | Scotia |
| 217 | 14.7 | Central Islip UFSD | Central Islip |
| 217 | 14.7 | Central Square Central SD | Central Square |
| 217 | 14.7 | Croton-Harmon UFSD | Croton on Hdsn |
| 217 | 14.7 | Elmira City SD | Elmira |
| 217 | 14.7 | Freeport UFSD | Freeport |
| 217 | 14.7 | Highland Central SD | Highland |
| 217 | 14.7 | North Syracuse Central SD | North Syracuse |
| 217 | 14.7 | Wantagh UFSD | Wantagh |
| 226 | 14.6 | Commack UFSD | East Northport |
| 226 | 14.6 | Harrison Central SD | Harrison |
| 226 | 14.6 | South Country Central SD | East Patchogue |
| 229 | 14.5 | Baldwin UFSD | Baldwin |
| 229 | 14.5 | Bayport-Blue Point UFSD | Bayport |
| 229 | 14.5 | Churchville-Chili Central SD | Churchville |
| 229 | 14.5 | Clarence Central SD | Clarence Center |
| 229 | 14.5 | East Hampton UFSD | East Hampton |
| 229 | 14.5 | East Williston UFSD | Old Westbury |
| 229 | 14.5 | Shenendehowa Central SD | Clifton Park |
| 229 | 14.5 | Wallkill Central SD | Wallkill |
| 237 | 14.4 | North Colonie Central SD | Latham |
| 237 | 14.4 | Westhill Central SD | Syracuse |
| 239 | 14.3 | Attica Central SD | Attica |
| 239 | 14.3 | Mohonasen Central SD | Schenectady |
| 239 | 14.3 | Palmyra-Macedon Central SD | Palmyra |
| 239 | 14.3 | Whitesboro Central SD | Yorkville |
| 243 | 14.2 | Auburn City SD | Auburn |
| 243 | 14.2 | Chenango Valley Central SD | Binghamton |
| 243 | 14.2 | East Meadow UFSD | Westbury |
| 243 | 14.2 | Nyack UFSD | Nyack |
| 243 | 14.2 | Queensbury UFSD | Queensbury |
| 243 | 14.2 | Roosevelt UFSD | Roosevelt |
| 243 | 14.2 | Valhalla UFSD | Valhalla |
| 250 | 14.1 | Amherst Central SD | Amherst |
| 250 | 14.1 | Batavia City SD | Batavia |
| 250 | 14.1 | Herricks UFSD | New Hyde Park |
| 250 | 14.1 | South Jefferson Central SD | Adams Center |
| 254 | 14.0 | Carthage Central SD | Carthage |
| 254 | 14.0 | Cortland City SD | Cortland |
| 254 | 14.0 | Fairport Central SD | Fairport |
| 254 | 14.0 | Riverhead Central SD | Riverhead |
| 254 | 14.0 | Spackenkill UFSD | Poughkeepsie |
| 259 | 13.9 | Baldwinsville Central SD | Baldwinsville |
| 259 | 13.9 | Eden Central SD | Eden |
| 259 | 13.9 | Great Neck UFSD | Great Neck |
| 259 | 13.9 | Mattituck-Cutchogue UFSD | Cutchogue |
| 259 | 13.9 | Newfane Central SD | Burt |
| 259 | 13.9 | North Rockland Central SD | Garnerville |
| 259 | 13.9 | Rockville Ctr UFSD | Rockville Ctr |
| 259 | 13.9 | South Huntington UFSD | Huntington Stn |
| 267 | 13.8 | Hastings-on-Hudson UFSD | Hastings on Hdsn |
| 267 | 13.8 | Miller Place UFSD | Miller Place |
| 267 | 13.8 | Smithtown Central SD | Smithtown |
| 270 | 13.7 | South Colonie Central SD | Albany |
| 271 | 13.6 | Goshen Central SD | Goshen |
| 271 | 13.6 | Mamaroneck UFSD | Mamaroneck |
| 271 | 13.6 | Susquehanna Valley Central SD | Conklin |
| 274 | 13.5 | Bethpage UFSD | Bethpage |
| 274 | 13.5 | East Islip UFSD | Islip Terrace |
| 274 | 13.5 | Edgemont UFSD | Scarsdale |
| 274 | 13.5 | Harborfields Central SD | Greenlawn |
| 274 | 13.5 | New Rochelle City SD | New Rochelle |
| 274 | 13.5 | Pearl River UFSD | Pearl River |
| 274 | 13.5 | White Plains City SD | White Plains |
| 281 | 13.4 | Eastport-South Manor CSD | Manorville |
| 282 | 13.3 | Bethlehem Central SD | Delmar |
| 282 | 13.3 | Southampton UFSD | Southampton |
| 282 | 13.3 | Valley Stream 13 UFSD | Valley Stream |
| 285 | 13.2 | Babylon UFSD | Babylon |
| 285 | 13.2 | Nanuet UFSD | Nanuet |
| 287 | 13.1 | Ardsley UFSD | Ardsley |
| 287 | 13.1 | Cheektowaga-Maryvale UFSD | Cheektowaga |
| 287 | 13.1 | Massena Central SD | Massena |
| 287 | 13.1 | Putnam Valley Central SD | Putnam Valley |
| 287 | 13.1 | Sewanhaka Central High SD | Floral Park |
| 287 | 13.1 | West Babylon UFSD | West Babylon |
| 287 | 13.1 | West Genesee Central SD | Camillus |
| 294 | 13.0 | Bath Central SD | Bath |
| 294 | 13.0 | Elmont UFSD | Elmont |
| 294 | 13.0 | Grand Island Central SD | Grand Island |
| 294 | 13.0 | Hendrick Hudson Central SD | Montrose |
| 294 | 13.0 | Starpoint Central SD | Lockport |
| 299 | 12.9 | Broadalbin-Perth Central SD | Broadalbin |
| 299 | 12.9 | Iroquois Central SD | Elma |
| 299 | 12.9 | Oceanside UFSD | Oceanside |
| 299 | 12.9 | Patchogue-Medford UFSD | Patchogue |
| 299 | 12.9 | Sachem Central SD | Holbrook |
| 299 | 12.9 | Wayland-Cohocton Central SD | Wayland |
| 305 | 12.8 | Dansville Central SD | Dansville |
| 305 | 12.8 | Garden City UFSD | Garden City |
| 305 | 12.8 | General Brown Central SD | Dexter |
| 305 | 12.8 | Greece Central SD | Rochester |
| 305 | 12.8 | S Glens Fls Central SD | S Glens Fls |
| 310 | 12.7 | Chittenango Central SD | Chittenango |
| 310 | 12.7 | Dunkirk City SD | Dunkirk |
| 310 | 12.7 | Floral Park-Bellerose UFSD | Floral Park |
| 310 | 12.7 | Plainedge UFSD | N Massapequa |
| 310 | 12.7 | West Seneca Central SD | West Seneca |
| 315 | 12.6 | Byram Hills Central SD | Armonk |
| 315 | 12.6 | Niagara-Wheatfield Central SD | Niagara Falls |
| 317 | 12.5 | Mount Sinai UFSD | Mount Sinai |
| 317 | 12.5 | Pleasantville UFSD | Pleasantville |
| 317 | 12.5 | Red Hook Central SD | Red Hook |
| 317 | 12.5 | Washingtonville Central SD | Washingtonville |
| 317 | 12.5 | Webster Central SD | Webster |
| 322 | 12.4 | Hauppauge UFSD | Hauppauge |
| 322 | 12.4 | Irvington UFSD | Irvington |
| 322 | 12.4 | Lynbrook UFSD | Lynbrook |
| 322 | 12.4 | Valley Stream Central High SD | Valley Stream |
| 326 | 12.3 | Williamsville Central SD | East Amherst |
| 327 | 12.2 | Chappaqua Central SD | Chappaqua |
| 327 | 12.2 | Sayville UFSD | Sayville |
| 327 | 12.2 | Schalmont Central SD | Schenectady |
| 330 | 12.1 | Franklin Square UFSD | Franklin Square |
| 330 | 12.1 | Island Trees UFSD | Levittown |
| 330 | 12.1 | Vernon-Verona-Sherrill Central SD | Verona |
| 333 | 12.0 | Cornwall Central SD | Cornwall on Hdsn |
| 333 | 12.0 | Rush-Henrietta Central SD | Henrietta |
| 335 | 11.9 | Bellmore-Merrick Central High SD | North Merrick |
| 335 | 11.9 | Roslyn UFSD | Roslyn |
| 335 | 11.9 | Waverly Central SD | Waverly |
| 338 | 11.8 | Spencerport Central SD | Spencerport |
| 339 | 11.7 | Islip UFSD | Islip |
| 339 | 11.7 | Marcellus Central SD | Marcellus |
| 341 | 11.6 | Albion Central SD | Albion |
| 341 | 11.6 | NYC Geographic District #13 | Brooklyn |
| 341 | 11.6 | NYC Geographic District #26 | Bayside |
| 341 | 11.6 | Westhampton Bch UFSD | Westhampton Bch |
| 345 | 11.5 | Bronxville UFSD | Bronxville |
| 345 | 11.5 | Massapequa UFSD | Massapequa |
| 345 | 11.5 | Southwestern CSD at Jamestown | Jamestown |
| 348 | 11.4 | Cobleskill-Richmondville Central SD | Cobleskill |
| 348 | 11.4 | Elwood UFSD | Greenlawn |
| 348 | 11.4 | New Hyde Pk-Garden City Pk UFSD | New Hyde Park |
| 351 | 11.3 | Akron Central SD | Akron |
| 351 | 11.3 | Niskayuna Central SD | Schenectady |
| 351 | 11.3 | Pelham UFSD | Pelham |

*Note: This section only includes districts with 1,500 or more students; All categories are ranked from high to low*

| | | | |
|---|---|---|---|
| 351 | 11.3 | Penfield Central SD | Rochester |
| 351 | 11.3 | Schuylerville Central SD | Schuylerville |
| 351 | 11.3 | Springville-Griffith Institute CSD | Springville |
| 357 | 11.1 | East Aurora UFSD | East Aurora |
| 357 | 11.1 | Wayne Central SD | Ontario Center |
| 359 | 11.0 | Honeoye Falls-Lima Central SD | Honeoye Falls |
| 360 | 10.8 | Fredonia Central SD | Fredonia |
| 361 | 10.7 | Cold Spring Hrbr Central SD | Cold Spring Hrbr |
| 361 | 10.7 | Uniondale UFSD | Uniondale |
| 363 | 10.6 | Eastchester UFSD | Eastchester |
| 363 | 10.6 | Livonia Central SD | Livonia |
| 365 | 10.5 | Fayetteville-Manlius Central SD | Manlius |
| 366 | 10.4 | Cazenovia Central SD | Cazenovia |
| 366 | 10.4 | New Hartford Central SD | New Hartford |
| 368 | 10.2 | Jordan-Elbridge Central SD | Elbridge |
| 369 | 10.0 | Hilton Central SD | Hilton |
| 369 | 10.0 | Pittsford Central SD | Pittsford |
| 371 | 9.9 | Coxsackie-Athens Central SD | Coxsackie |
| 372 | 9.8 | Blind Brook-Rye UFSD | Rye Brook |
| 372 | 9.8 | Saratoga Spgs City SD | Saratoga Spgs |
| 374 | 9.6 | Bedford Central SD | Bedford |
| 374 | 9.6 | Royalton-Hartland Central SD | Middleport |
| 374 | 9.6 | West Irondequoit Central SD | Rochester |
| 377 | 9.4 | Skaneateles Central SD | Skaneateles |
| 378 | 8.6 | Sweet Home Central SD | Amherst |
| 379 | 8.5 | Rye City SD | Rye |
| 379 | 8.5 | Scarsdale UFSD | Scarsdale |
| 381 | 8.0 | Victor Central SD | Victor |
| 382 | 0.0 | Charter School for Applied Tech | Buffalo |
| 382 | 0.0 | NYC Special Schools - District 75 | New York |

## English Language Learner Students

| Rank | Percent | District Name | City |
|---|---|---|---|
| 1 | 35.9 | NYC Geographic District # 6 | New York |
| 2 | 30.1 | Westbury UFSD | Old Westbury |
| 3 | 29.1 | Hempstead UFSD | Hempstead |
| 4 | 26.6 | Port Chester-Rye UFSD | Port Chester |
| 5 | 25.8 | NYC Geographic District #24 | Ridgewood |
| 6 | 25.2 | Central Islip UFSD | Central Islip |
| 7 | 25.1 | NYC Geographic District # 9 | Bronx |
| 8 | 24.2 | Brentwood UFSD | Brentwood |
| 9 | 23.3 | NYC Geographic District #20 | Brooklyn |
| 10 | 22.7 | NYC Geographic District #30 | Long Isl City |
| 11 | 21.5 | NYC Geographic District #10 | Bronx |
| 12 | 19.1 | NYC Geographic District #32 | Brooklyn |
| 13 | 18.8 | NYC Geographic District #12 | Bronx |
| 14 | 18.4 | NYC Geographic District # 7 | Bronx |
| 14 | 18.4 | NYC Geographic District #25 | Flushing |
| 16 | 18.1 | Roosevelt UFSD | Roosevelt |
| 17 | 17.0 | Huntington UFSD | Huntington Stn |
| 18 | 16.8 | UFSD of the Tarrytowns | Sleepy Hollow |
| 19 | 15.8 | Wyandanch UFSD | Wyandanch |
| 20 | 15.7 | NYC Geographic District #15 | Brooklyn |
| 21 | 15.4 | Freeport UFSD | Freeport |
| 22 | 14.8 | Copiague UFSD | Copiague |
| 22 | 14.8 | Uniondale UFSD | Uniondale |
| 24 | 14.7 | Hampton Bays UFSD | Hampton Bays |
| 25 | 14.3 | NYC Geographic District #21 | Brooklyn |
| 26 | 14.0 | New York City Public Schools | New York |
| 26 | 14.0 | Peekskill City SD | Peekskill |
| 28 | 13.5 | Glen Cove City SD | Glen Cove |
| 29 | 13.3 | East Hampton UFSD | East Hampton |
| 29 | 13.3 | Yonkers City SD | Yonkers |
| 31 | 12.9 | Dunkirk City SD | Dunkirk |
| 32 | 12.8 | Utica City SD | Utica |
| 33 | 12.5 | East Ramapo Central SD | Spring Valley |
| 33 | 12.5 | NYC Geographic District #19 | Brooklyn |
| 35 | 12.4 | NYC Geographic District # 4 | New York |
| 36 | 12.2 | NYC Geographic District #14 | Brooklyn |
| 37 | 12.0 | Newburgh City SD | Newburgh |
| 38 | 11.8 | Middletown City SD | Middletown |
| 38 | 11.8 | NYC Geographic District # 1 | New York |
| 40 | 11.6 | Amityville UFSD | Amityville |
| 40 | 11.6 | NYC Geographic District # 8 | Bronx |
| 42 | 11.4 | South Huntington UFSD | Huntington Stn |
| 43 | 11.3 | NYC Geographic District # 2 | New York |
| 44 | 11.2 | NYC Geographic District # 5 | New York |
| 45 | 10.7 | NYC Geographic District #28 | Jamaica |
| 46 | 10.5 | NYC Geographic District #11 | Bronx |
| 47 | 10.3 | Riverhead Central SD | Riverhead |
| 47 | 10.3 | Southampton UFSD | Southampton |
| 49 | 9.7 | NYC Geographic District #27 | Ozone Park |
| 49 | 9.7 | Syracuse City SD | Syracuse |
| 51 | 9.6 | Lawrence UFSD | Lawrence |
| 51 | 9.6 | Patchogue-Medford UFSD | Patchogue |
| 53 | 9.5 | New Rochelle City SD | New Rochelle |
| 53 | 9.5 | NYC Geographic District #22 | Brooklyn |
| 53 | 9.5 | Rochester City SD | Rochester |
| 56 | 9.4 | Buffalo City SD | Buffalo |
| 57 | 9.2 | Poughkeepsie City SD | Poughkeepsie |
| 58 | 9.0 | Ossining UFSD | Ossining |
| 59 | 8.9 | NYC Geographic District #17 | Brooklyn |
| 60 | 8.8 | NYC Geographic District # 3 | New York |
| 61 | 8.3 | Hicksville UFSD | Hicksville |
| 62 | 8.0 | Mount Vernon City SD | Mount Vernon |
| 62 | 8.0 | Port Washington UFSD | Port Washington |
| 64 | 7.8 | Mineola UFSD | Mineola |
| 65 | 7.1 | NYC Geographic District #26 | Bayside |
| 66 | 7.0 | NYC Geographic District #29 | Rosedale |
| 67 | 6.8 | New Hyde Pk-Garden City Pk UFSD | New Hyde Park |
| 68 | 6.7 | Greenburgh Central SD | Hartsdale |
| 69 | 6.4 | Harrison Central SD | Harrison |
| 70 | 6.1 | Lackawanna City SD | Lackawanna |
| 71 | 5.9 | Albany City SD | Albany |
| 72 | 5.7 | Bedford Central SD | Bedford |
| 73 | 5.6 | NYC Geographic District #31 | Staten Island |
| 74 | 5.5 | South Country Central SD | East Patchogue |
| 75 | 5.3 | Hudson City SD | Hudson |
| 76 | 5.2 | NYC Geographic District #18 | Brooklyn |
| 77 | 5.1 | Bay Shore UFSD | Bay Shore |
| 77 | 5.1 | Valley Stream 13 UFSD | Valley Stream |
| 79 | 4.9 | Eastchester UFSD | Eastchester |
| 79 | 4.9 | West Hempstead UFSD | West Hempstead |
| 81 | 4.8 | Nyack UFSD | Nyack |
| 82 | 4.6 | Great Neck UFSD | Great Neck |
| 83 | 4.5 | Nanuet UFSD | Nanuet |
| 84 | 4.2 | Elmont UFSD | Elmont |
| 84 | 4.2 | Ithaca City SD | Ithaca |
| 84 | 4.2 | Monticello Central SD | Monticello |
| 87 | 4.1 | Brewster Central SD | Brewster |
| 87 | 4.1 | Long Beach City SD | Long Beach |
| 89 | 4.0 | Herricks UFSD | New Hyde Park |
| 89 | 4.0 | Hewlett-Woodmere UFSD | Woodmere |
| 91 | 3.8 | Liberty Central SD | Liberty |
| 91 | 3.8 | NYC Geographic District #13 | Brooklyn |
| 91 | 3.8 | NYC Geographic District #16 | Brooklyn |
| 91 | 3.8 | NYC Geographic District #23 | Brooklyn |
| 95 | 3.7 | Comsewogue School District | Port Jeff Stn |
| 95 | 3.7 | Rush-Henrietta Central SD | Henrietta |
| 95 | 3.7 | Rye City SD | Rye |
| 98 | 3.6 | Amsterdam City SD | Amsterdam |
| 98 | 3.6 | Longwood Central SD | Middle Island |
| 100 | 3.4 | Deer Park UFSD | Deer Park |
| 100 | 3.4 | Islip UFSD | Islip |
| 100 | 3.4 | Lindenhurst UFSD | Lindenhurst |
| 100 | 3.4 | Oceanside UFSD | Oceanside |
| 100 | 3.4 | Oyster Bay-East Norwich Central SD | Oyster Bay |
| 100 | 3.4 | William Floyd UFSD | Mastic Beach |
| 106 | 3.3 | Baldwin UFSD | Baldwin |
| 106 | 3.3 | East Meadow UFSD | Westbury |
| 106 | 3.3 | Geneva City SD | Geneva |
| 106 | 3.3 | Johnson City Central SD | Johnson City |
| 110 | 3.2 | East Irondequoit Central SD | Rochester |
| 110 | 3.2 | Goshen Central SD | Goshen |
| 110 | 3.2 | Jamestown City SD | Jamestown |
| 110 | 3.2 | Locust Valley Central SD | Locust Valley |
| 110 | 3.2 | Valhalla UFSD | Valhalla |
| 115 | 3.1 | Franklin Square UFSD | Franklin Square |
| 115 | 3.1 | Mamaroneck UFSD | Mamaroneck |
| 115 | 3.1 | Middle Country Central SD | Centereach |
| 115 | 3.1 | Roslyn UFSD | Roslyn |
| 119 | 3.0 | Dover UFSD | Dover Plains |
| 119 | 3.0 | Hendrick Hudson Central SD | Montrose |
| 119 | 3.0 | North Babylon UFSD | North Babylon |
| 119 | 3.0 | Westhampton Bch UFSD | Westhampton Bch |
| 123 | 2.9 | Edgemont UFSD | Scarsdale |
| 123 | 2.9 | Monroe-Woodbury Central SD | Central Valley |
| 123 | 2.9 | Schenectady City SD | Schenectady |
| 126 | 2.8 | Farmingdale UFSD | Farmingdale |
| 127 | 2.7 | Charter School for Applied Tech | Buffalo |
| 128 | 2.6 | Beacon City SD | Beacon |
| 128 | 2.6 | Indian River Central SD | Philadelphia |
| 128 | 2.6 | Scarsdale UFSD | Scarsdale |
| 128 | 2.6 | Valley Stream Central High SD | Valley Stream |
| 132 | 2.5 | Clarkstown Central SD | New City |
| 132 | 2.5 | Kingston City SD | Kingston |
| 132 | 2.5 | Ramapo Central SD (Suffern) | Hillburn |
| 135 | 2.4 | Brighton Central SD | Rochester |
| 135 | 2.4 | Center Moriches UFSD | Center Moriches |
| 135 | 2.4 | Cohoes City SD | Cohoes |
| 135 | 2.4 | Greece Central SD | Rochester |
| 135 | 2.4 | Hastings-on-Hudson UFSD | Hastings on Hdsn |
| 135 | 2.4 | Island Trees UFSD | Levittown |
| 135 | 2.4 | Sewanhaka Central High SD | Floral Park |
| 135 | 2.4 | Solvay UFSD | Solvay |
| 143 | 2.3 | Cheektowaga Central SD | Cheektowaga |
| 143 | 2.3 | Elwood UFSD | Greenlawn |
| 143 | 2.3 | Kinderhook Central SD | Valatie |
| 143 | 2.3 | South Orangetown Central SD | Blauvelt |
| 143 | 2.3 | Watertown City SD | Watertown |
| 143 | 2.3 | Yorktown Central SD | Yorktown Hgts |
| 149 | 2.2 | Carmel Central SD | Patterson |
| 149 | 2.2 | Floral Park-Bellerose UFSD | Floral Park |
| 149 | 2.2 | Mattituck-Cutchogue UFSD | Cutchogue |
| 149 | 2.2 | Rocky Point UFSD | Rocky Point |
| 149 | 2.2 | West Babylon UFSD | West Babylon |
| 154 | 2.1 | Croton-Harmon UFSD | Croton on Hdsn |
| 154 | 2.1 | Guilderland Central SD | Guilderland |
| 154 | 2.1 | Irvington UFSD | Irvington |
| 154 | 2.1 | Jamesville-Dewitt Central SD | Dewitt |
| 154 | 2.1 | North Colonie Central SD | Latham |
| 159 | 2.0 | Gates-Chili Central SD | Rochester |
| 159 | 2.0 | Red Hook Central SD | Red Hook |
| 161 | 1.9 | Ellenville Central SD | Ellenville |
| 161 | 1.9 | Mount Pleasant Central SD | Thornwood |
| 161 | 1.9 | New Paltz Central SD | New Paltz |
| 161 | 1.9 | Newark Central SD | Newark |
| 161 | 1.9 | Rockville Ctr UFSD | Rockville Ctr |
| 161 | 1.9 | Sweet Home Central SD | Amherst |
| 167 | 1.8 | Albion Central SD | Albion |
| 167 | 1.8 | Bethpage UFSD | Bethpage |
| 167 | 1.8 | Mahopac Central SD | Mahopac |
| 167 | 1.8 | Syosset Central SD | Syosset |
| 171 | 1.7 | Hyde Park Central SD | Hyde Park |
| 171 | 1.7 | Jericho UFSD | Jericho |
| 171 | 1.7 | Levittown UFSD | Levittown |
| 174 | 1.6 | Half Hollow Hills Central SD | Dix Hills |
| 174 | 1.6 | Marlboro Central SD | Marlboro |
| 174 | 1.6 | Rondout Valley Central SD | Accord |
| 174 | 1.6 | Troy City SD | Troy |
| 174 | 1.6 | Williamsville Central SD | East Amherst |
| 179 | 1.5 | Wallkill Central SD | Wallkill |
| 179 | 1.5 | Webster Central SD | Webster |
| 181 | 1.4 | Babylon UFSD | Babylon |
| 181 | 1.4 | Cheektowaga-Maryvale UFSD | Cheektowaga |
| 181 | 1.4 | Harborfields Central SD | Greenlawn |
| 181 | 1.4 | North Bellmore UFSD | Bellmore |
| 181 | 1.4 | North Shore Central SD | Sea Cliff |
| 181 | 1.4 | Spencerport Central SD | Spencerport |
| 181 | 1.4 | Vestal Central SD | Vestal |
| 188 | 1.3 | Bethlehem Central SD | Delmar |
| 188 | 1.3 | Catskill Central SD | Catskill |
| 188 | 1.3 | East Williston UFSD | Old Westbury |
| 188 | 1.3 | Fredonia Central SD | Fredonia |
| 188 | 1.3 | Lynbrook UFSD | Lynbrook |
| 188 | 1.3 | Somers Central SD | Somers |
| 188 | 1.3 | Spackenkill UFSD | Poughkeepsie |
| 195 | 1.2 | Ardsley UFSD | Ardsley |
| 195 | 1.2 | Blind Brook-Rye UFSD | Rye Brook |
| 195 | 1.2 | East Islip UFSD | Islip Terrace |
| 195 | 1.2 | Grand Island Central SD | Grand Island |
| 195 | 1.2 | Lakeland Central SD | Shrub Oak |
| 195 | 1.2 | Liverpool Central SD | Liverpool |
| 195 | 1.2 | Niskayuna Central SD | Schenectady |
| 195 | 1.2 | Pleasantville UFSD | Pleasantville |
| 203 | 1.1 | Arlington Central SD | Poughkeepsie |
| 203 | 1.1 | Fairport Central SD | Fairport |
| 203 | 1.1 | Hauppauge UFSD | Hauppauge |
| 203 | 1.1 | Manhasset UFSD | Manhasset |
| 203 | 1.1 | Miller Place UFSD | Miller Place |
| 203 | 1.1 | Niagara Falls City SD | Niagara Falls |
| 203 | 1.1 | Northport-East Northport UFSD | Northport |
| 203 | 1.1 | Onteora Central SD | Boiceville |
| 203 | 1.1 | Oswego City SD | Oswego |
| 203 | 1.1 | Pearl River UFSD | Pearl River |
| 203 | 1.1 | Penfield Central SD | Rochester |
| 203 | 1.1 | Pine Bush Central SD | Pine Bush |
| 203 | 1.1 | Plainedge UFSD | N Massapequa |
| 203 | 1.1 | Sachem Central SD | Holbrook |
| 203 | 1.1 | Valley Central SD (Montgomery) | Montgomery |
| 203 | 1.1 | West Irondequoit Central SD | Rochester |
| 219 | 1.0 | Churchville-Chili Central SD | Churchville |
| 219 | 1.0 | Connetquot Central SD | Bohemia |

*Note: This section only includes districts with 1,500 or more students; All categories are ranked from high to low*

| | | | |
|---|---|---|---|
| 219 | 1.0 | Kenmore-Tonawanda UFSD | Buffalo |
| 219 | 1.0 | Merrick UFSD | Merrick |
| 219 | 1.0 | Putnam Valley Central SD | Putnam Valley |
| 219 | 1.0 | Rome City SD | Rome |
| 219 | 1.0 | Wappingers Central SD | Wappingers Fls |
| 226 | 0.9 | Chappaqua Central SD | Chappaqua |
| 226 | 0.9 | Ravena-Coeymans-Selkirk Ctrl SD | Selkirk |
| 226 | 0.9 | South Colonie Central SD | Albany |
| 229 | 0.8 | Bronxville UFSD | Bronxville |
| 229 | 0.8 | Cornwall Central SD | Cornwall on Hdsn |
| 229 | 0.8 | Dansville Central SD | Dansville |
| 229 | 0.8 | Dryden Central SD | Dryden |
| 229 | 0.8 | Lockport City SD | Lockport |
| 229 | 0.8 | Maine-Endwell Central SD | Endwell |
| 229 | 0.8 | Medina Central SD | Medina |
| 229 | 0.8 | Minisink Valley Central SD | Slate Hill |
| 229 | 0.8 | Mount Sinai UFSD | Mount Sinai |
| 229 | 0.8 | North Syracuse Central SD | North Syracuse |
| 229 | 0.8 | Oneonta City SD | Oneonta |
| 229 | 0.8 | Owego-Apalachin Central SD | Owego |
| 229 | 0.8 | Penn Yan Central SD | Penn Yan |
| 229 | 0.8 | Plainview-Old Bethpage Central SD | Plainview |
| 229 | 0.8 | Shoreham-Wading River Central SD | Shoreham |
| 229 | 0.8 | Whitesboro Central SD | Yorkville |
| 245 | 0.7 | Amherst Central SD | Amherst |
| 245 | 0.7 | Brockport Central SD | Brockport |
| 245 | 0.7 | Carthage Central SD | Carthage |
| 245 | 0.7 | East Greenbush Central SD | East Greenbush |
| 245 | 0.7 | Lansingburgh Central SD | Troy |
| 245 | 0.7 | Shenendehowa Central SD | Clifton Park |
| 245 | 0.7 | Three Village Central SD | Stony Brook |
| 245 | 0.7 | Westhill Central SD | Syracuse |
| 253 | 0.6 | Coxsackie-Athens Central SD | Coxsackie |
| 253 | 0.6 | Depew UFSD | Depew |
| 253 | 0.6 | Eastport-South Manor CSD | Manorville |
| 253 | 0.6 | Fayetteville-Manlius Central SD | Manlius |
| 253 | 0.6 | Highland Central SD | Highland |
| 253 | 0.6 | Hilton Central SD | Hilton |
| 253 | 0.6 | Katonah-Lewisboro UFSD | South Salem |
| 253 | 0.6 | Mohonasen Central SD | Schenectady |
| 253 | 0.6 | New Hartford Central SD | New Hartford |
| 253 | 0.6 | Pelham UFSD | Pelham |
| 253 | 0.6 | Port Jervis City SD | Port Jervis |
| 253 | 0.6 | Smithtown Central SD | Smithtown |
| 253 | 0.6 | Taconic Hills Central SD | Craryville |
| 253 | 0.6 | Union-Endicott Central SD | Endicott |
| 253 | 0.6 | Victor Central SD | Victor |
| 253 | 0.6 | Washingtonville Central SD | Washingtonville |
| 269 | 0.5 | Auburn City SD | Auburn |
| 269 | 0.5 | Batavia City SD | Batavia |
| 269 | 0.5 | Cazenovia Central SD | Cazenovia |
| 269 | 0.5 | Commack UFSD | East Northport |
| 269 | 0.5 | Corning City SD | Painted Post |
| 269 | 0.5 | North Tonawanda City SD | North Tonawanda |
| 269 | 0.5 | Phelps-Clifton Springs Central SD | Clifton Springs |
| 269 | 0.5 | Pittsford Central SD | Pittsford |
| 269 | 0.5 | Seaford UFSD | Seaford |
| 269 | 0.5 | Warwick Valley Central SD | Warwick |
| 269 | 0.5 | West Islip UFSD | West Islip |
| 269 | 0.5 | West Seneca Central SD | West Seneca |
| 281 | 0.4 | Baldwinsville Central SD | Baldwinsville |
| 281 | 0.4 | Byram Hills Central SD | Armonk |
| 281 | 0.4 | Chenango Valley Central SD | Binghamton |
| 281 | 0.4 | Gloversville City SD | Gloversville |
| 281 | 0.4 | Horseheads Central SD | Horseheads |
| 281 | 0.4 | Massapequa UFSD | Massapequa |
| 281 | 0.4 | Niagara-Wheatfield Central SD | Niagara Falls |
| 281 | 0.4 | Palmyra-Macedon Central SD | Palmyra |
| 281 | 0.4 | West Genesee Central SD | Camillus |
| 281 | 0.4 | Windsor Central SD | Windsor |
| 291 | 0.3 | Averill Park Central SD | Averill Park |
| 291 | 0.3 | Bayport-Blue Point UFSD | Bayport |
| 291 | 0.3 | Briarcliff Mnr UFSD | Briarcliff Mnr |
| 291 | 0.3 | Clarence Central SD | Clarence Center |
| 291 | 0.3 | Cobleskill-Richmondville Central SD | Cobleskill |
| 291 | 0.3 | Cold Spring Hrbr Central SD | Cold Spring Hrbr |
| 291 | 0.3 | Holland Patent Central SD | Holland Patent |
| 291 | 0.3 | Homer Central SD | Homer |
| 291 | 0.3 | Hudson Falls Central SD | Fort Edward |
| 291 | 0.3 | Johnstown City SD | Johnstown |
| 291 | 0.3 | Kings Park Central SD | Kings Park |
| 291 | 0.3 | Livonia Central SD | Livonia |
| 291 | 0.3 | Massena Central SD | Massena |
| 291 | 0.3 | Norwich City SD | Norwich |
| 291 | 0.3 | Oneida City SD | Oneida |
| 291 | 0.3 | Orchard Park Central SD | Orchard Park |
| 291 | 0.3 | Queensbury UFSD | Queensbury |
| 291 | 0.3 | Saratoga Spgs City SD | Saratoga Spgs |
| 291 | 0.3 | Schalmont Central SD | Schenectady |
| 291 | 0.3 | Southwestern CSD at Jamestown | Jamestown |
| 291 | 0.3 | Wayne Central SD | Ontario Center |
| 312 | 0.2 | Alden Central SD | Alden |
| 312 | 0.2 | Ballston Spa Central SD | Ballston Spa |
| 312 | 0.2 | Bellmore-Merrick Central High SD | North Merrick |
| 312 | 0.2 | Burnt Hills-Ballston Lake CSD | Scotia |
| 312 | 0.2 | Camden Central SD | Camden |
| 312 | 0.2 | Canandaigua City SD | Canandaigua |
| 312 | 0.2 | East Aurora UFSD | East Aurora |
| 312 | 0.2 | Elmira City SD | Elmira |
| 312 | 0.2 | Ilion Central SD | Ilion |
| 312 | 0.2 | Iroquois Central SD | Elma |
| 312 | 0.2 | Lancaster Central SD | Lancaster |
| 312 | 0.2 | Lewiston-Porter Central SD | Youngstown |
| 312 | 0.2 | Peru Central SD | Peru |
| 312 | 0.2 | Phoenix Central SD | Phoenix |
| 312 | 0.2 | Plattsburgh City SD | Plattsburgh |
| 312 | 0.2 | Wantagh UFSD | Wantagh |
| 312 | 0.2 | Waterloo Central SD | Waterloo |
| 312 | 0.2 | Yorkshire-Pioneer Central SD | Yorkshire |
| 330 | 0.1 | Bath Central SD | Bath |
| 330 | 0.1 | Cheektowaga-Sloan UFSD | Sloan |
| 330 | 0.1 | Chenango Forks Central SD | Binghamton |
| 330 | 0.1 | Fulton City SD | Fulton |
| 330 | 0.1 | General Brown Central SD | Dexter |
| 330 | 0.1 | Glens Falls City SD | Glens Falls |
| 330 | 0.1 | Gouverneur Central SD | Gouverneur |
| 330 | 0.1 | Hamburg Central SD | Hamburg |
| 330 | 0.1 | Honeoye Falls-Lima Central SD | Honeoye Falls |
| 330 | 0.1 | Hornell City SD | Hornell |
| 330 | 0.1 | Jordan-Elbridge Central SD | Elbridge |
| 330 | 0.1 | Marcellus Central SD | Marcellus |
| 330 | 0.1 | Royalton-Hartland Central SD | Middleport |
| 330 | 0.1 | Saranac Central SD | Dannemora |
| 330 | 0.1 | Sayville UFSD | Sayville |
| 330 | 0.1 | Scotia-Glenville Central SD | Scotia |
| 330 | 0.1 | Skaneateles Central SD | Skaneateles |
| 330 | 0.1 | S Glens Fls Central SD | S Glens Fls |
| 330 | 0.1 | South Jefferson Central SD | Adams Center |
| 330 | 0.1 | Susquehanna Valley Central SD | Conklin |
| 330 | 0.1 | Tonawanda City SD | Tonawanda |
| 330 | 0.1 | Vernon-Verona-Sherrill Central SD | Verona |
| 330 | 0.1 | Wayland-Cohocton Central SD | Wayland |
| 353 | 0.0 | Akron Central SD | Akron |
| 353 | 0.0 | Attica Central SD | Attica |
| 353 | 0.0 | Beekmantown Central SD | West Chazy |
| 353 | 0.0 | Binghamton City SD | Binghamton |
| 353 | 0.0 | Broadalbin-Perth Central SD | Broadalbin |
| 353 | 0.0 | Canastota Central SD | Canastota |
| 353 | 0.0 | Central Square Central SD | Central Square |
| 353 | 0.0 | Chittenango Central SD | Chittenango |
| 353 | 0.0 | Cortland City SD | Cortland |
| 353 | 0.0 | East Syracuse-Minoa Central SD | East Syracuse |
| 353 | 0.0 | Eden Central SD | Eden |
| 353 | 0.0 | Evans-Brant Central SD (Lake Shore) | Angola |
| 353 | 0.0 | Frontier Central SD | Hamburg |
| 353 | 0.0 | Garden City UFSD | Garden City |
| 353 | 0.0 | Hannibal Central SD | Hannibal |
| 353 | 0.0 | Malone Central SD | Malone |
| 353 | 0.0 | Malverne UFSD | Malverne |
| 353 | 0.0 | Mexico Central SD | Mexico |
| 353 | 0.0 | NYC Special Schools - District 75 | New York |
| 353 | 0.0 | Newfane Central SD | Burt |
| 353 | 0.0 | North Rockland Central SD | Garnerville |
| 353 | 0.0 | Ogdensburg City SD | Ogdensburg |
| 353 | 0.0 | Olean City SD | Olean |
| 353 | 0.0 | Salmon River Central SD | Fort Covington |
| 353 | 0.0 | Saugerties Central SD | Saugerties |
| 353 | 0.0 | Schuylerville Central SD | Schuylerville |
| 353 | 0.0 | Sherburne-Earlville Central SD | Sherburne |
| 353 | 0.0 | Springville-Griffith Institute CSD | Springville |
| 353 | 0.0 | Starpoint Central SD | Lockport |
| 353 | 0.0 | Waverly Central SD | Waverly |
| 353 | 0.0 | White Plains City SD | White Plains |

## Students Eligible for Free Lunch

| Rank | Percent | District Name | City |
|---|---|---|---|
| 1 | 78.6 | Rochester City SD | Rochester |
| 2 | 70.2 | Buffalo City SD | Buffalo |
| 3 | 68.0 | Poughkeepsie City SD | Poughkeepsie |
| 4 | 67.6 | Wyandanch UFSD | Wyandanch |
| 5 | 67.0 | Syracuse City SD | Syracuse |
| 6 | 65.8 | Westbury UFSD | Old Westbury |
| 7 | 64.8 | Roosevelt UFSD | Roosevelt |
| 8 | 64.1 | Yonkers City SD | Yonkers |
| 9 | 63.8 | Utica City SD | Utica |
| 10 | 63.0 | Lackawanna City SD | Lackawanna |
| 11 | 60.0 | Hempstead UFSD | Hempstead |
| 12 | 58.9 | Mount Vernon City SD | Mount Vernon |
| 13 | 58.0 | Charter School for Applied Tech | Buffalo |
| 14 | 57.1 | Schenectady City SD | Schenectady |
| 15 | 53.8 | Middletown City SD | Middletown |
| 16 | 53.7 | Troy City SD | Troy |
| 17 | 53.3 | Jamestown City SD | Jamestown |
| 18 | 53.1 | Salmon River Central SD | Fort Covington |
| 19 | 52.6 | Central Islip UFSD | Central Islip |
| 20 | 52.1 | Newburgh City SD | Newburgh |
| 21 | 51.7 | Binghamton City SD | Binghamton |
| 22 | 50.9 | Gloversville City SD | Gloversville |
| 23 | 50.8 | Niagara Falls City SD | Niagara Falls |
| 24 | 50.4 | Liberty Central SD | Liberty |
| 25 | 50.2 | Amityville UFSD | Amityville |
| 26 | 50.0 | Albany City SD | Albany |
| 27 | 49.3 | Port Chester-Rye UFSD | Port Chester |
| 28 | 48.7 | Elmira City SD | Elmira |
| 29 | 48.6 | Brentwood UFSD | Brentwood |
| 30 | 47.5 | Cohoes City SD | Cohoes |
| 31 | 47.3 | East Ramapo Central SD | Spring Valley |
| 32 | 47.2 | Geneva City SD | Geneva |
| 33 | 46.0 | Dunkirk City SD | Dunkirk |
| 34 | 45.4 | Hornell City SD | Hornell |
| 34 | 45.4 | Hudson City SD | Hudson |
| 36 | 44.1 | Johnson City Central SD | Johnson City |
| 37 | 44.0 | Lansingburgh Central SD | Troy |
| 38 | 43.7 | Fulton City SD | Fulton |
| 39 | 43.2 | Ogdensburg City SD | Ogdensburg |
| 40 | 42.7 | Peekskill City SD | Peekskill |
| 41 | 42.4 | Beekmantown Central SD | West Chazy |
| 42 | 42.2 | Port Jervis City SD | Port Jervis |
| 43 | 41.8 | Cheektowaga-Sloan UFSD | Sloan |
| 44 | 41.6 | Copiague UFSD | Copiague |
| 45 | 41.4 | Hannibal Central SD | Hannibal |
| 46 | 40.5 | Norwich City SD | Norwich |
| 47 | 40.3 | Monticello Central SD | Monticello |
| 48 | 39.8 | Canastota Central SD | Canastota |
| 49 | 39.5 | Watertown City SD | Watertown |
| 50 | 39.2 | Camden Central SD | Camden |
| 51 | 38.7 | Bath Central SD | Bath |
| 51 | 38.7 | Freeport UFSD | Freeport |
| 53 | 38.3 | Olean City SD | Olean |
| 54 | 38.1 | Penn Yan Central SD | Penn Yan |
| 55 | 37.9 | Malone Central SD | Malone |
| 56 | 37.5 | Ellenville Central SD | Ellenville |
| 57 | 37.2 | Batavia City SD | Batavia |
| 58 | 36.8 | Catskill Central SD | Catskill |
| 58 | 36.8 | Rome City SD | Rome |
| 60 | 34.9 | Dryden Central SD | Dryden |
| 60 | 34.9 | East Irondequoit Central SD | Rochester |
| 60 | 34.9 | Gouverneur Central SD | Gouverneur |
| 63 | 34.7 | Elmont UFSD | Elmont |
| 63 | 34.7 | Sherburne-Earlville Central SD | Sherburne |
| 65 | 34.6 | Medina Central SD | Medina |
| 66 | 34.5 | Albion Central SD | Albion |
| 67 | 34.4 | Amsterdam City SD | Amsterdam |
| 68 | 34.2 | Massena Central SD | Massena |
| 68 | 34.2 | Solvay UFSD | Solvay |
| 70 | 34.0 | Hudson Falls Central SD | Fort Edward |
| 71 | 33.9 | Lockport City SD | Lockport |
| 72 | 33.7 | Plattsburgh City SD | Plattsburgh |
| 73 | 33.6 | Bay Shore UFSD | Bay Shore |
| 74 | 33.5 | New Rochelle City SD | New Rochelle |
| 75 | 33.3 | UFSD of the Tarrytowns | Sleepy Hollow |
| 76 | 33.1 | Cheektowaga Central SD | Cheektowaga |
| 76 | 33.1 | Waverly Central SD | Waverly |
| 78 | 32.6 | Dansville Central SD | Dansville |
| 78 | 32.6 | Uniondale UFSD | Uniondale |
| 80 | 32.4 | Cortland City SD | Cortland |
| 80 | 32.4 | Glen Cove City SD | Glen Cove |
| 82 | 32.3 | Ilion Central SD | Ilion |
| 82 | 32.3 | White Plains City SD | White Plains |
| 84 | 32.1 | William Floyd UFSD | Mastic Beach |
| 84 | 32.1 | Yorkshire-Pioneer Central SD | Yorkshire |
| 86 | 32.0 | Phoenix Central SD | Phoenix |
| 86 | 32.0 | Waterloo Central SD | Waterloo |

*Note: This section only includes districts with 1,500 or more students; All categories are ranked from high to low*

| | | | |
|---|---|---|---|
| 88 | 31.8 | Mexico Central SD | Mexico |
| 89 | 31.5 | Oneida City SD | Oneida |
| 90 | 31.3 | South Jefferson Central SD | Adams Center |
| 91 | 31.2 | Kingston City SD | Kingston |
| 92 | 30.3 | Taconic Hills Central SD | Craryville |
| 93 | 30.1 | Greenburgh Central SD | Hartsdale |
| 94 | 30.0 | South Country Central SD | East Patchogue |
| 95 | 29.8 | Newark Central SD | Newark |
| 96 | 29.7 | Riverhead Central SD | Riverhead |
| 97 | 29.5 | Lawrence UFSD | Lawrence |
| 98 | 29.4 | Auburn City SD | Auburn |
| 98 | 29.4 | Oswego City SD | Oswego |
| 100 | 29.3 | Carthage Central SD | Carthage |
| 100 | 29.3 | Ossining UFSD | Ossining |
| 102 | 28.8 | Wayland-Cohocton Central SD | Wayland |
| 103 | 28.2 | Susquehanna Valley Central SD | Conklin |
| 104 | 27.7 | Ithaca City SD | Ithaca |
| 105 | 27.2 | Owego-Apalachin Central SD | Owego |
| 105 | 27.2 | South Huntington UFSD | Huntington Stn |
| 105 | 27.2 | Union-Endicott Central SD | Endicott |
| 108 | 26.3 | Glens Falls City SD | Glens Falls |
| 109 | 26.0 | Longwood Central SD | Middle Island |
| 110 | 25.8 | Corning City SD | Painted Post |
| 110 | 25.8 | Marlboro Central SD | Marlboro |
| 112 | 25.7 | Greece Central SD | Rochester |
| 112 | 25.7 | Johnstown City SD | Johnstown |
| 114 | 25.5 | Cobleskill-Richmondville Central SD | Cobleskill |
| 115 | 25.0 | Windsor Central SD | Windsor |
| 116 | 24.8 | Evans-Brant Central SD (Lake Shore) | Angola |
| 116 | 24.8 | Huntington UFSD | Huntington Stn |
| 118 | 24.4 | Depew UFSD | Depew |
| 119 | 24.3 | Sweet Home Central SD | Amherst |
| 120 | 24.1 | Chenango Forks Central SD | Binghamton |
| 120 | 24.1 | Indian River Central SD | Philadelphia |
| 120 | 24.1 | Rondout Valley Central SD | Accord |
| 123 | 24.0 | Hyde Park Central SD | Hyde Park |
| 124 | 23.7 | Patchogue-Medford UFSD | Patchogue |
| 125 | 23.6 | Gates-Chili Central SD | Rochester |
| 126 | 23.5 | North Rockland Central SD | Garnerville |
| 127 | 23.4 | Central Square Central SD | Central Square |
| 128 | 23.1 | Tonawanda City SD | Tonawanda |
| 129 | 23.0 | Oneonta City SD | Oneonta |
| 130 | 22.9 | Vernon-Verona-Sherrill Central SD | Verona |
| 131 | 22.6 | Chenango Valley Central SD | Binghamton |
| 132 | 22.4 | Ravena-Coeymans-Selkirk Ctrl SD | Selkirk |
| 133 | 22.3 | Dover UFSD | Dover Plains |
| 133 | 22.3 | Malverne UFSD | Malverne |
| 135 | 22.2 | Peru Central SD | Peru |
| 136 | 22.1 | Liverpool Central SD | Liverpool |
| 137 | 21.7 | Palmyra-Macedon Central SD | Palmyra |
| 137 | 21.7 | Saranac Central SD | Dannemora |
| 139 | 21.6 | Long Beach City SD | Long Beach |
| 140 | 21.5 | Kenmore-Tonawanda UFSD | Buffalo |
| 141 | 21.4 | Brockport Central SD | Brockport |
| 141 | 21.4 | Newfane Central SD | Burt |
| 143 | 21.3 | Hampton Bays UFSD | Hampton Bays |
| 143 | 21.3 | Homer Central SD | Homer |
| 145 | 20.8 | Fredonia Central SD | Fredonia |
| 145 | 20.8 | North Tonawanda City SD | North Tonawanda |
| 147 | 20.7 | Pine Bush Central SD | Pine Bush |
| 148 | 20.6 | Coxsackie-Athens Central SD | Coxsackie |
| 149 | 20.3 | Attica Central SD | Attica |
| 149 | 20.3 | Phelps-Clifton Springs Central SD | Clifton Springs |
| 149 | 20.3 | Wallkill Central SD | Wallkill |
| 152 | 20.1 | Jordan-Elbridge Central SD | Elbridge |
| 153 | 19.9 | Rush-Henrietta Central SD | Henrietta |
| 154 | 19.4 | Niagara-Wheatfield Central SD | Niagara Falls |
| 155 | 19.3 | Akron Central SD | Akron |
| 155 | 19.3 | Saugerties Central SD | Saugerties |
| 157 | 18.7 | West Seneca Central SD | West Seneca |
| 158 | 18.6 | Broadalbin-Perth Central SD | Broadalbin |
| 159 | 18.4 | Deer Park UFSD | Deer Park |
| 159 | 18.4 | Wayne Central SD | Ontario Center |
| 161 | 18.3 | Cheektowaga-Maryvale UFSD | Cheektowaga |
| 161 | 18.3 | North Syracuse Central SD | North Syracuse |
| 163 | 18.2 | East Syracuse-Minoa Central SD | East Syracuse |
| 163 | 18.2 | Onteora Central SD | Boiceville |
| 165 | 17.9 | Southwestern CSD at Jamestown | Jamestown |
| 166 | 17.8 | General Brown Central SD | Dexter |
| 166 | 17.8 | Highland Central SD | Highland |
| 168 | 17.7 | North Babylon UFSD | North Babylon |
| 169 | 17.6 | Mohonasen Central SD | Schenectady |
| 169 | 17.6 | West Hempstead UFSD | West Hempstead |
| 171 | 17.4 | Horseheads Central SD | Horseheads |
| 172 | 17.0 | Chittenango Central SD | Chittenango |
| 172 | 17.0 | Valley Central SD (Montgomery) | Montgomery |
| 174 | 16.9 | Springville-Griffith Institute CSD | Springville |
| 175 | 16.8 | Alden Central SD | Alden |
| 175 | 16.8 | Beacon City SD | Beacon |
| 177 | 16.7 | Amherst Central SD | Amherst |
| 178 | 16.3 | Southampton UFSD | Southampton |
| 179 | 16.1 | Royalton-Hartland Central SD | Middleport |
| 180 | 15.8 | West Babylon UFSD | West Babylon |
| 181 | 15.5 | Holland Patent Central SD | Holland Patent |
| 181 | 15.5 | Spencerport Central SD | Spencerport |
| 183 | 14.8 | Ballston Spa Central SD | Ballston Spa |
| 184 | 14.5 | Livonia Central SD | Livonia |
| 185 | 14.4 | Center Moriches UFSD | Center Moriches |
| 186 | 14.3 | Lindenhurst UFSD | Lindenhurst |
| 187 | 14.2 | Middle Country Central SD | Centereach |
| 188 | 14.0 | Canandaigua City SD | Canandaigua |
| 189 | 13.9 | Hicksville UFSD | Hicksville |
| 190 | 13.8 | New Paltz Central SD | New Paltz |
| 191 | 13.7 | Frontier Central SD | Hamburg |
| 191 | 13.7 | Islip UFSD | Islip |
| 193 | 13.6 | Nyack UFSD | Nyack |
| 194 | 13.0 | South Colonie Central SD | Albany |
| 195 | 12.7 | Schuylerville Central SD | Schuylerville |
| 195 | 12.7 | Whitesboro Central SD | Yorkville |
| 197 | 12.6 | Kinderhook Central SD | Valatie |
| 198 | 12.4 | Washingtonville Central SD | Washingtonville |
| 199 | 12.3 | Queensbury UFSD | Queensbury |
| 200 | 12.2 | Churchville-Chili Central SD | Churchville |
| 201 | 11.9 | Sewanhaka Central High SD | Floral Park |
| 202 | 11.8 | S Glens Fls Central SD | S Glens Fls |
| 203 | 11.7 | Comsewogue School District | Port Jeff Stn |
| 204 | 11.6 | Rocky Point UFSD | Rocky Point |
| 205 | 11.5 | Hilton Central SD | Hilton |
| 206 | 11.3 | Minisink Valley Central SD | Slate Hill |
| 207 | 11.1 | Goshen Central SD | Goshen |
| 208 | 11.0 | Farmingdale UFSD | Farmingdale |
| 208 | 11.0 | Hendrick Hudson Central SD | Montrose |
| 210 | 10.7 | Eden Central SD | Eden |
| 210 | 10.7 | Scotia-Glenville Central SD | Scotia |
| 212 | 10.6 | Saratoga Spgs City SD | Saratoga Spgs |
| 213 | 10.4 | Spackenkill UFSD | Poughkeepsie |
| 213 | 10.4 | West Genesee Central SD | Camillus |
| 215 | 10.3 | Grand Island Central SD | Grand Island |
| 216 | 10.1 | Mineola UFSD | Mineola |
| 217 | 10.0 | East Hampton UFSD | East Hampton |
| 217 | 10.0 | Valley Stream 13 UFSD | Valley Stream |
| 219 | 9.9 | Elwood UFSD | Greenlawn |
| 220 | 9.8 | Oyster Bay-East Norwich Central SD | Oyster Bay |
| 221 | 9.7 | Hamburg Central SD | Hamburg |
| 221 | 9.7 | Lewiston-Porter Central SD | Youngstown |
| 223 | 9.6 | Baldwinsville Central SD | Baldwinsville |
| 223 | 9.6 | Red Hook Central SD | Red Hook |
| 225 | 9.5 | Jamesville-Dewitt Central SD | Dewitt |
| 225 | 9.5 | West Irondequoit Central SD | Rochester |
| 227 | 9.4 | Lancaster Central SD | Lancaster |
| 227 | 9.4 | Wappingers Central SD | Wappingers Fls |
| 229 | 9.1 | Carmel Central SD | Patterson |
| 229 | 9.1 | Cazenovia Central SD | Cazenovia |
| 229 | 9.1 | East Greenbush Central SD | East Greenbush |
| 229 | 9.1 | Mattituck-Cutchogue UFSD | Cutchogue |
| 233 | 9.0 | Ramapo Central SD (Suffern) | Hillburn |
| 233 | 9.0 | Schalmont Central SD | Schenectady |
| 235 | 8.9 | Starpoint Central SD | Lockport |
| 236 | 8.6 | Sachem Central SD | Holbrook |
| 237 | 8.4 | Babylon UFSD | Babylon |
| 238 | 8.3 | Lakeland Central SD | Shrub Oak |
| 238 | 8.3 | Monroe-Woodbury Central SD | Central Valley |
| 240 | 8.0 | Fairport Central SD | Fairport |
| 241 | 7.8 | Rockville Ctr UFSD | Rockville Ctr |
| 241 | 7.8 | Westhampton Bch UFSD | Westhampton Bch |
| 243 | 7.6 | Honeoye Falls-Lima Central SD | Honeoye Falls |
| 244 | 7.4 | Arlington Central SD | Poughkeepsie |
| 244 | 7.4 | Williamsville Central SD | East Amherst |
| 246 | 7.3 | Connetquot Central SD | Bohemia |
| 247 | 7.1 | Averill Park Central SD | Averill Park |
| 247 | 7.1 | Nanuet UFSD | Nanuet |
| 247 | 7.1 | Vestal Central SD | Vestal |
| 250 | 7.0 | Mamaroneck UFSD | Mamaroneck |
| 250 | 7.0 | Putnam Valley Central SD | Putnam Valley |
| 252 | 6.8 | New Hyde Pk-Garden City Pk UFSD | New Hyde Park |
| 252 | 6.8 | Port Washington UFSD | Port Washington |
| 252 | 6.8 | Webster Central SD | Webster |
| 255 | 6.7 | Bedford Central SD | Bedford |
| 255 | 6.7 | Half Hollow Hills Central SD | Dix Hills |
| 255 | 6.7 | Penfield Central SD | Rochester |
| 258 | 6.6 | Locust Valley Central SD | Locust Valley |
| 258 | 6.6 | Shenendehowa Central SD | Clifton Park |
| 258 | 6.6 | Victor Central SD | Victor |
| 261 | 6.5 | North Colonie Central SD | Latham |
| 261 | 6.5 | Roslyn UFSD | Roslyn |
| 263 | 6.4 | Brewster Central SD | Brewster |
| 263 | 6.4 | East Islip UFSD | Islip Terrace |
| 263 | 6.4 | Harrison Central SD | Harrison |
| 263 | 6.4 | Island Trees UFSD | Levittown |
| 267 | 6.3 | Iroquois Central SD | Elma |
| 267 | 6.3 | Marcellus Central SD | Marcellus |
| 269 | 6.2 | Brighton Central SD | Rochester |
| 270 | 6.1 | Levittown UFSD | Levittown |
| 271 | 5.9 | Hewlett-Woodmere UFSD | Woodmere |
| 272 | 5.7 | Cornwall Central SD | Cornwall on Hdsn |
| 272 | 5.7 | Great Neck UFSD | Great Neck |
| 272 | 5.7 | Oceanside UFSD | Oceanside |
| 272 | 5.7 | Valhalla UFSD | Valhalla |
| 272 | 5.7 | Valley Stream Central High SD | Valley Stream |
| 277 | 5.6 | North Bellmore UFSD | Bellmore |
| 278 | 5.5 | Maine-Endwell Central SD | Endwell |
| 279 | 5.3 | East Meadow UFSD | Westbury |
| 280 | 5.2 | Franklin Square UFSD | Franklin Square |
| 281 | 5.1 | South Orangetown Central SD | Blauvelt |
| 282 | 5.0 | East Aurora UFSD | East Aurora |
| 282 | 5.0 | Eastport-South Manor CSD | Manorville |
| 282 | 5.0 | Harborfields Central SD | Greenlawn |
| 282 | 5.0 | Niskayuna Central SD | Schenectady |
| 286 | 4.8 | Westhill Central SD | Syracuse |
| 287 | 4.6 | Bethpage UFSD | Bethpage |
| 287 | 4.6 | New Hartford Central SD | New Hartford |
| 289 | 4.5 | Plainedge UFSD | N Massapequa |
| 289 | 4.5 | Skaneateles Central SD | Skaneateles |
| 289 | 4.5 | Warwick Valley Central SD | Warwick |
| 292 | 4.3 | Guilderland Central SD | Guilderland |
| 293 | 4.2 | Clarkstown Central SD | New City |
| 293 | 4.2 | Miller Place UFSD | Miller Place |
| 295 | 3.9 | Burnt Hills-Ballston Lake CSD | Scotia |
| 295 | 3.9 | Clarence Central SD | Clarence Center |
| 295 | 3.9 | West Islip UFSD | West Islip |
| 298 | 3.7 | Fayetteville-Manlius Central SD | Manlius |
| 298 | 3.7 | Orchard Park Central SD | Orchard Park |
| 300 | 3.6 | Bayport-Blue Point UFSD | Bayport |
| 300 | 3.6 | Bethlehem Central SD | Delmar |
| 300 | 3.6 | Pearl River UFSD | Pearl River |
| 300 | 3.6 | Sayville UFSD | Sayville |
| 304 | 3.5 | Hastings-on-Hudson UFSD | Hastings on Hdsn |
| 304 | 3.5 | Hauppauge UFSD | Hauppauge |
| 304 | 3.5 | Pelham UFSD | Pelham |
| 307 | 3.4 | North Shore Central SD | Sea Cliff |
| 308 | 3.2 | Herricks UFSD | New Hyde Park |
| 308 | 3.2 | Somers Central SD | Somers |
| 310 | 3.1 | Northport-East Northport UFSD | Northport |
| 310 | 3.1 | Seaford UFSD | Seaford |
| 310 | 3.1 | Three Village Central SD | Stony Brook |
| 313 | 3.0 | Kings Park Central SD | Kings Park |
| 313 | 3.0 | Mount Sinai UFSD | Mount Sinai |
| 315 | 2.9 | Floral Park-Bellerose UFSD | Floral Park |
| 316 | 2.8 | Mount Pleasant Central SD | Thornwood |
| 317 | 2.7 | Mahopac Central SD | Mahopac |
| 317 | 2.7 | Pleasantville UFSD | Pleasantville |
| 319 | 2.6 | Irvington UFSD | Irvington |
| 320 | 2.5 | Manhasset UFSD | Manhasset |
| 320 | 2.5 | Pittsford Central SD | Pittsford |
| 320 | 2.5 | Rye City SD | Rye |
| 323 | 2.4 | Smithtown Central SD | Smithtown |
| 324 | 2.3 | Commack UFSD | East Northport |
| 325 | 2.1 | Plainview-Old Bethpage Central SD | Plainview |
| 326 | 1.9 | Lynbrook UFSD | Lynbrook |
| 326 | 1.9 | Yorktown Central SD | Yorktown Hgts |
| 328 | 1.7 | Bellmore-Merrick Central High SD | North Merrick |
| 329 | 1.6 | Massapequa UFSD | Massapequa |
| 329 | 1.6 | Shoreham-Wading River Central SD | Shoreham |
| 331 | 1.3 | East Williston UFSD | Old Westbury |
| 331 | 1.3 | Jericho UFSD | Jericho |
| 333 | 1.0 | Briarcliff Mnr UFSD | Briarcliff Mnr |
| 333 | 1.0 | Katonah-Lewisboro UFSD | South Salem |
| 333 | 1.0 | Wantagh UFSD | Wantagh |
| 336 | 0.8 | Ardsley UFSD | Ardsley |
| 336 | 0.8 | Chappaqua Central SD | Chappaqua |
| 338 | 0.7 | Baldwin UFSD | Baldwin |
| 338 | 0.7 | Byram Hills Central SD | Armonk |
| 340 | 0.6 | Syosset Central SD | Syosset |
| 341 | 0.3 | Blind Brook-Rye UFSD | Rye Brook |
| 342 | 0.2 | Garden City UFSD | Garden City |

*Note: This section only includes districts with 1,500 or more students; All categories are ranked from high to low*

| | | | |
|---|---|---|---|
| 343 | 0.0 | Bronxville UFSD | Bronxville |
| 343 | 0.0 | Cold Spring Hrbr Central SD | Cold Spring Hrbr |
| 343 | 0.0 | Croton-Harmon UFSD | Croton on Hdsn |
| 343 | 0.0 | Eastchester UFSD | Eastchester |
| 343 | 0.0 | Edgemont UFSD | Scarsdale |
| 343 | 0.0 | Merrick UFSD | Merrick |
| 343 | 0.0 | Scarsdale UFSD | Scarsdale |
| n/a | n/a | NYC Special Schools - District 75 | New York |
| n/a | n/a | NYC Geographic District # 1 | New York |
| n/a | n/a | NYC Geographic District # 2 | New York |
| n/a | n/a | NYC Geographic District # 3 | New York |
| n/a | n/a | NYC Geographic District # 4 | New York |
| n/a | n/a | NYC Geographic District # 5 | New York |
| n/a | n/a | NYC Geographic District # 6 | New York |
| n/a | n/a | NYC Geographic District # 7 | Bronx |
| n/a | n/a | NYC Geographic District # 8 | Bronx |
| n/a | n/a | NYC Geographic District # 9 | Bronx |
| n/a | n/a | NYC Geographic District #10 | Bronx |
| n/a | n/a | NYC Geographic District #11 | Bronx |
| n/a | n/a | NYC Geographic District #12 | Bronx |
| n/a | n/a | NYC Geographic District #13 | Brooklyn |
| n/a | n/a | NYC Geographic District #14 | Brooklyn |
| n/a | n/a | NYC Geographic District #15 | Brooklyn |
| n/a | n/a | NYC Geographic District #16 | Brooklyn |
| n/a | n/a | NYC Geographic District #17 | Brooklyn |
| n/a | n/a | NYC Geographic District #18 | Brooklyn |
| n/a | n/a | NYC Geographic District #19 | Brooklyn |
| n/a | n/a | NYC Geographic District #20 | Brooklyn |
| n/a | n/a | NYC Geographic District #21 | Brooklyn |
| n/a | n/a | NYC Geographic District #22 | Brooklyn |
| n/a | n/a | NYC Geographic District #23 | Brooklyn |
| n/a | n/a | NYC Geographic District #24 | Ridgewood |
| n/a | n/a | NYC Geographic District #25 | Flushing |
| n/a | n/a | NYC Geographic District #26 | Bayside |
| n/a | n/a | NYC Geographic District #27 | Ozone Park |
| n/a | n/a | NYC Geographic District #28 | Jamaica |
| n/a | n/a | NYC Geographic District #29 | Rosedale |
| n/a | n/a | NYC Geographic District #30 | Long Isl City |
| n/a | n/a | NYC Geographic District #31 | Staten Island |
| n/a | n/a | NYC Geographic District #32 | Brooklyn |
| n/a | n/a | New York City Public Schools | New York |

## Students Eligible for Reduced-Price Lunch

| Rank | Percent | District Name | City |
|---|---|---|---|
| 1 | 21.6 | Cheektowaga-Sloan UFSD | Sloan |
| 1 | 21.6 | Indian River Central SD | Philadelphia |
| 3 | 17.1 | Sherburne-Earlville Central SD | Sherburne |
| 4 | 17.0 | Dansville Central SD | Dansville |
| 5 | 16.9 | Middletown City SD | Middletown |
| 6 | 16.8 | Carthage Central SD | Carthage |
| 7 | 16.7 | Brentwood UFSD | Brentwood |
| 8 | 16.5 | Camden Central SD | Camden |
| 9 | 16.1 | Beekmantown Central SD | West Chazy |
| 10 | 15.8 | Ogdensburg City SD | Ogdensburg |
| 11 | 15.2 | Yorkshire-Pioneer Central SD | Yorkshire |
| 12 | 15.0 | Lackawanna City SD | Lackawanna |
| 13 | 14.6 | Elmont UFSD | Elmont |
| 14 | 14.5 | Wayland-Cohocton Central SD | Wayland |
| 15 | 14.4 | Johnstown City SD | Johnstown |
| 16 | 14.2 | Charter School for Applied Tech | Buffalo |
| 17 | 13.9 | Depew UFSD | Depew |
| 18 | 13.6 | South Jefferson Central SD | Adams Center |
| 19 | 13.2 | Central Islip UFSD | Central Islip |
| 20 | 13.0 | Taconic Hills Central SD | Craryville |
| 21 | 12.6 | East Irondequoit Central SD | Rochester |
| 22 | 12.5 | Gouverneur Central SD | Gouverneur |
| 22 | 12.5 | Port Chester-Rye UFSD | Port Chester |
| 22 | 12.5 | Roosevelt UFSD | Roosevelt |
| 25 | 12.4 | Corning City SD | Painted Post |
| 26 | 12.3 | Hudson Falls Central SD | Fort Edward |
| 26 | 12.3 | Schenectady City SD | Schenectady |
| 26 | 12.3 | Troy City SD | Troy |
| 29 | 12.2 | Attica Central SD | Attica |
| 30 | 12.1 | Dover UFSD | Dover Plains |
| 30 | 12.1 | Mexico Central SD | Mexico |
| 30 | 12.1 | Port Jervis City SD | Port Jervis |
| 33 | 12.0 | Olean City SD | Olean |
| 34 | 11.9 | Chenango Forks Central SD | Binghamton |
| 34 | 11.9 | Ilion Central SD | Ilion |
| 34 | 11.9 | Waterloo Central SD | Waterloo |
| 37 | 11.8 | Glen Cove City SD | Glen Cove |
| 37 | 11.8 | Mount Vernon City SD | Mount Vernon |
| 37 | 11.8 | Windsor Central SD | Windsor |
| 40 | 11.6 | Cobleskill-Richmondville Central SD | Cobleskill |
| 40 | 11.6 | General Brown Central SD | Dexter |
| 40 | 11.6 | Hannibal Central SD | Hannibal |
| 40 | 11.6 | Poughkeepsie City SD | Poughkeepsie |
| 44 | 11.5 | Greece Central SD | Rochester |
| 44 | 11.5 | Hornell City SD | Hornell |
| 44 | 11.5 | Hudson City SD | Hudson |
| 44 | 11.5 | Newark Central SD | Newark |
| 48 | 11.4 | Gates-Chili Central SD | Rochester |
| 48 | 11.4 | Pine Bush Central SD | Pine Bush |
| 50 | 11.3 | Albion Central SD | Albion |
| 50 | 11.3 | East Ramapo Central SD | Spring Valley |
| 50 | 11.3 | Gloversville City SD | Gloversville |
| 53 | 11.2 | Medina Central SD | Medina |
| 53 | 11.2 | Newburgh City SD | Newburgh |
| 53 | 11.2 | Ossining UFSD | Ossining |
| 53 | 11.2 | Peekskill City SD | Peekskill |
| 53 | 11.2 | Salmon River Central SD | Fort Covington |
| 53 | 11.2 | Westbury UFSD | Old Westbury |
| 59 | 11.1 | Copiague UFSD | Copiague |
| 59 | 11.1 | Susquehanna Valley Central SD | Conklin |
| 61 | 11.0 | Bath Central SD | Bath |
| 61 | 11.0 | Brockport Central SD | Brockport |
| 61 | 11.0 | Marlboro Central SD | Marlboro |
| 64 | 10.9 | Alden Central SD | Alden |
| 64 | 10.9 | West Seneca Central SD | West Seneca |
| 66 | 10.8 | Johnson City Central SD | Johnson City |
| 66 | 10.8 | Kenmore-Tonawanda UFSD | Buffalo |
| 66 | 10.8 | Liberty Central SD | Liberty |
| 66 | 10.8 | Malone Central SD | Malone |
| 66 | 10.8 | Uniondale UFSD | Uniondale |
| 71 | 10.7 | Greenburgh Central SD | Hartsdale |
| 71 | 10.7 | Newfane Central SD | Burt |
| 73 | 10.6 | Cohoes City SD | Cohoes |
| 73 | 10.6 | Highland Central SD | Highland |
| 73 | 10.6 | Owego-Apalachin Central SD | Owego |
| 76 | 10.5 | Bay Shore UFSD | Bay Shore |
| 76 | 10.5 | Penn Yan Central SD | Penn Yan |
| 78 | 10.4 | Niagara Falls City SD | Niagara Falls |
| 78 | 10.4 | Phelps-Clifton Springs Central SD | Clifton Springs |
| 78 | 10.4 | Royalton-Hartland Central SD | Middleport |
| 81 | 10.3 | Amityville UFSD | Amityville |
| 81 | 10.3 | Holland Patent Central SD | Holland Patent |
| 81 | 10.3 | Hyde Park Central SD | Hyde Park |
| 81 | 10.3 | Tonawanda City SD | Tonawanda |
| 85 | 10.2 | Evans-Brant Central SD (Lake Shore) | Angola |
| 85 | 10.2 | Malverne UFSD | Malverne |
| 85 | 10.2 | Rome City SD | Rome |
| 85 | 10.2 | Watertown City SD | Watertown |
| 89 | 10.1 | Bedford Central SD | Bedford |
| 90 | 10.0 | Chittenango Central SD | Chittenango |
| 90 | 10.0 | Massena Central SD | Massena |
| 90 | 10.0 | Saugerties Central SD | Saugerties |
| 93 | 9.9 | Dunkirk City SD | Dunkirk |
| 93 | 9.9 | Fulton City SD | Fulton |
| 93 | 9.9 | Norwich City SD | Norwich |
| 93 | 9.9 | UFSD of the Tarrytowns | Sleepy Hollow |
| 97 | 9.8 | Ellenville Central SD | Ellenville |
| 97 | 9.8 | Geneva City SD | Geneva |
| 99 | 9.7 | Freeport UFSD | Freeport |
| 99 | 9.7 | Monticello Central SD | Monticello |
| 101 | 9.6 | Dryden Central SD | Dryden |
| 101 | 9.6 | Utica City SD | Utica |
| 103 | 9.4 | Liverpool Central SD | Liverpool |
| 103 | 9.4 | Onteora Central SD | Boiceville |
| 103 | 9.4 | Rush-Henrietta Central SD | Henrietta |
| 106 | 9.3 | Akron Central SD | Akron |
| 106 | 9.3 | Jamestown City SD | Jamestown |
| 106 | 9.3 | Middle Country Central SD | Centereach |
| 106 | 9.3 | Sweet Home Central SD | Amherst |
| 110 | 9.1 | Canastota Central SD | Canastota |
| 110 | 9.1 | Horseheads Central SD | Horseheads |
| 110 | 9.1 | Lansingburgh Central SD | Troy |
| 110 | 9.1 | North Tonawanda City SD | North Tonawanda |
| 110 | 9.1 | Vernon-Verona-Sherrill Central SD | Verona |
| 115 | 9.0 | Catskill Central SD | Catskill |
| 115 | 9.0 | Cheektowaga Central SD | Cheektowaga |
| 115 | 9.0 | Frontier Central SD | Hamburg |
| 115 | 9.0 | Kingston City SD | Kingston |
| 115 | 9.0 | Lawrence UFSD | Lawrence |
| 115 | 9.0 | Patchogue-Medford UFSD | Patchogue |
| 115 | 9.0 | Waverly Central SD | Waverly |
| 122 | 8.9 | Lockport City SD | Lockport |
| 123 | 8.8 | Batavia City SD | Batavia |
| 123 | 8.8 | Chenango Valley Central SD | Binghamton |
| 123 | 8.8 | East Syracuse-Minoa Central SD | East Syracuse |
| 123 | 8.8 | New Rochelle City SD | New Rochelle |
| 123 | 8.8 | Peru Central SD | Peru |
| 123 | 8.8 | Phoenix Central SD | Phoenix |
| 129 | 8.7 | Cheektowaga-Maryvale UFSD | Cheektowaga |
| 129 | 8.7 | Deer Park UFSD | Deer Park |
| 131 | 8.6 | Albany City SD | Albany |
| 131 | 8.6 | Elmira City SD | Elmira |
| 131 | 8.6 | Longwood Central SD | Middle Island |
| 134 | 8.5 | Binghamton City SD | Binghamton |
| 134 | 8.5 | Riverhead Central SD | Riverhead |
| 136 | 8.4 | Broadalbin-Perth Central SD | Broadalbin |
| 136 | 8.4 | Central Square Central SD | Central Square |
| 136 | 8.4 | Springville-Griffith Institute CSD | Springville |
| 136 | 8.4 | Syracuse City SD | Syracuse |
| 140 | 8.2 | Churchville-Chili Central SD | Churchville |
| 140 | 8.2 | Oneida City SD | Oneida |
| 142 | 8.1 | Saranac Central SD | Dannemora |
| 142 | 8.1 | Spencerport Central SD | Spencerport |
| 142 | 8.1 | West Babylon UFSD | West Babylon |
| 145 | 8.0 | Palmyra-Macedon Central SD | Palmyra |
| 145 | 8.0 | Rondout Valley Central SD | Accord |
| 147 | 7.9 | Beacon City SD | Beacon |
| 147 | 7.9 | Wayne Central SD | Ontario Center |
| 149 | 7.8 | Solvay UFSD | Solvay |
| 150 | 7.7 | Hampton Bays UFSD | Hampton Bays |
| 150 | 7.7 | Yonkers City SD | Yonkers |
| 152 | 7.6 | Cortland City SD | Cortland |
| 152 | 7.6 | Schuylerville Central SD | Schuylerville |
| 152 | 7.6 | Union-Endicott Central SD | Endicott |
| 152 | 7.6 | William Floyd UFSD | Mastic Beach |
| 156 | 7.5 | Hilton Central SD | Hilton |
| 156 | 7.5 | Valley Central SD (Montgomery) | Montgomery |
| 158 | 7.4 | Fredonia Central SD | Fredonia |
| 158 | 7.4 | Glens Falls City SD | Glens Falls |
| 158 | 7.4 | Islip UFSD | Islip |
| 158 | 7.4 | Oneonta City SD | Oneonta |
| 162 | 7.3 | South Colonie Central SD | Albany |
| 162 | 7.3 | S Glens Fls Central SD | S Glens Fls |
| 162 | 7.3 | West Hempstead UFSD | West Hempstead |
| 165 | 7.2 | Coxsackie-Athens Central SD | Coxsackie |
| 165 | 7.2 | Mohonasen Central SD | Schenectady |
| 167 | 7.1 | Buffalo City SD | Buffalo |
| 167 | 7.1 | North Rockland Central SD | Garnerville |
| 169 | 7.0 | Grand Island Central SD | Grand Island |
| 169 | 7.0 | Homer Central SD | Homer |
| 169 | 7.0 | North Syracuse Central SD | North Syracuse |
| 169 | 7.0 | Ravena-Coeymans-Selkirk Ctrl SD | Selkirk |
| 169 | 7.0 | South Country Central SD | East Patchogue |
| 174 | 6.9 | Auburn City SD | Auburn |
| 174 | 6.9 | Jordan-Elbridge Central SD | Elbridge |
| 174 | 6.9 | Minisink Valley Central SD | Slate Hill |
| 177 | 6.8 | Center Moriches UFSD | Center Moriches |
| 177 | 6.8 | Niagara-Wheatfield Central SD | Niagara Falls |
| 177 | 6.8 | White Plains City SD | White Plains |
| 180 | 6.7 | East Greenbush Central SD | East Greenbush |
| 180 | 6.7 | Lindenhurst UFSD | Lindenhurst |
| 180 | 6.7 | North Babylon UFSD | North Babylon |
| 180 | 6.7 | Southwestern CSD at Jamestown | Jamestown |
| 184 | 6.6 | Hempstead UFSD | Hempstead |
| 185 | 6.4 | Lancaster Central SD | Lancaster |
| 185 | 6.4 | Sewanhaka Central High SD | Floral Park |
| 187 | 6.3 | Hamburg Central SD | Hamburg |
| 187 | 6.3 | Plattsburgh City SD | Plattsburgh |
| 187 | 6.3 | South Huntington UFSD | Huntington Stn |
| 190 | 6.2 | Eden Central SD | Eden |
| 190 | 6.2 | Rochester City SD | Rochester |
| 192 | 6.1 | Oswego City SD | Oswego |
| 192 | 6.1 | Washingtonville Central SD | Washingtonville |
| 194 | 6.0 | Rocky Point UFSD | Rocky Point |
| 194 | 6.0 | Scotia-Glenville Central SD | Scotia |
| 194 | 6.0 | Wallkill Central SD | Wallkill |
| 197 | 5.9 | Canandaigua City SD | Canandaigua |
| 198 | 5.8 | Ithaca City SD | Ithaca |
| 198 | 5.8 | Livonia Central SD | Livonia |
| 200 | 5.7 | East Hampton UFSD | East Hampton |
| 200 | 5.7 | Iroquois Central SD | Elma |
| 202 | 5.6 | Whitesboro Central SD | Yorkville |
| 203 | 5.5 | Kinderhook Central SD | Valatie |
| 203 | 5.5 | Lewiston-Porter Central SD | Youngstown |
| 205 | 5.4 | Amherst Central SD | Amherst |
| 205 | 5.4 | West Irondequoit Central SD | Rochester |
| 207 | 5.3 | Amsterdam City SD | Amsterdam |
| 207 | 5.3 | Hicksville UFSD | Hicksville |

*Note: This section only includes districts with 1,500 or more students; All categories are ranked from high to low*

| | | | |
|---|---|---|---|
| 207 | 5.3 | New Paltz Central SD | New Paltz |
| 207 | 5.3 | Southampton UFSD | Southampton |
| 211 | 5.2 | Ballston Spa Central SD | Ballston Spa |
| 211 | 5.2 | Mineola UFSD | Mineola |
| 211 | 5.2 | Wyandanch UFSD | Wyandanch |
| 214 | 5.1 | Great Neck UFSD | Great Neck |
| 214 | 5.1 | Long Beach City SD | Long Beach |
| 214 | 5.1 | Spackenkill UFSD | Poughkeepsie |
| 214 | 5.1 | Starpoint Central SD | Lockport |
| 218 | 5.0 | Schalmont Central SD | Schenectady |
| 219 | 4.9 | Queensbury UFSD | Queensbury |
| 220 | 4.8 | Baldwinsville Central SD | Baldwinsville |
| 220 | 4.8 | East Islip UFSD | Islip Terrace |
| 220 | 4.8 | New Hyde Pk-Garden City Pk UFSD | New Hyde Park |
| 220 | 4.8 | Red Hook Central SD | Red Hook |
| 224 | 4.7 | Valley Stream 13 UFSD | Valley Stream |
| 225 | 4.6 | Connetquot Central SD | Bohemia |
| 226 | 4.5 | Goshen Central SD | Goshen |
| 226 | 4.5 | Huntington UFSD | Huntington Stn |
| 226 | 4.5 | West Genesee Central SD | Camillus |
| 229 | 4.4 | Hendrick Hudson Central SD | Montrose |
| 229 | 4.4 | Plainedge UFSD | N Massapequa |
| 229 | 4.4 | Wappingers Central SD | Wappingers Fls |
| 232 | 4.3 | Averill Park Central SD | Averill Park |
| 233 | 4.2 | East Meadow UFSD | Westbury |
| 233 | 4.2 | Levittown UFSD | Levittown |
| 235 | 4.1 | Carmel Central SD | Patterson |
| 235 | 4.1 | Franklin Square UFSD | Franklin Square |
| 235 | 4.1 | Sachem Central SD | Holbrook |
| 238 | 4.0 | Cornwall Central SD | Cornwall on Hdsn |
| 238 | 4.0 | Harrison Central SD | Harrison |
| 238 | 4.0 | Saratoga Spgs City SD | Saratoga Spgs |
| 241 | 3.9 | Maine-Endwell Central SD | Endwell |
| 241 | 3.9 | Marcellus Central SD | Marcellus |
| 241 | 3.9 | Putnam Valley Central SD | Putnam Valley |
| 241 | 3.9 | Williamsville Central SD | East Amherst |
| 245 | 3.8 | Arlington Central SD | Poughkeepsie |
| 245 | 3.8 | Island Trees UFSD | Levittown |
| 245 | 3.8 | Nyack UFSD | Nyack |
| 245 | 3.8 | Webster Central SD | Webster |
| 249 | 3.7 | Brewster Central SD | Brewster |
| 249 | 3.7 | Comsewogue School District | Port Jeff Stn |
| 251 | 3.6 | Elwood UFSD | Greenlawn |
| 251 | 3.6 | Penfield Central SD | Rochester |
| 251 | 3.6 | Port Washington UFSD | Port Washington |
| 251 | 3.6 | Victor Central SD | Victor |
| 255 | 3.5 | Oyster Bay-East Norwich Central SD | Oyster Bay |
| 255 | 3.5 | Vestal Central SD | Vestal |
| 255 | 3.5 | Westhampton Bch UFSD | Westhampton Bch |
| 258 | 3.4 | Lakeland Central SD | Shrub Oak |
| 258 | 3.4 | Mattituck-Cutchogue UFSD | Cutchogue |
| 260 | 3.3 | Farmingdale UFSD | Farmingdale |
| 260 | 3.3 | Roslyn UFSD | Roslyn |
| 260 | 3.3 | Warwick Valley Central SD | Warwick |
| 263 | 3.2 | Babylon UFSD | Babylon |
| 263 | 3.2 | Brighton Central SD | Rochester |
| 263 | 3.2 | Burnt Hills-Ballston Lake CSD | Scotia |
| 263 | 3.2 | Monroe-Woodbury Central SD | Central Valley |
| 267 | 3.1 | Honeoye Falls-Lima Central SD | Honeoye Falls |
| 267 | 3.1 | Nanuet UFSD | Nanuet |
| 269 | 3.0 | Fairport Central SD | Fairport |
| 269 | 3.0 | Half Hollow Hills Central SD | Dix Hills |
| 269 | 3.0 | Westhill Central SD | Syracuse |
| 272 | 2.9 | Clarence Central SD | Clarence Center |
| 272 | 2.9 | New Hartford Central SD | New Hartford |
| 272 | 2.9 | North Colonie Central SD | Latham |
| 272 | 2.9 | Shenendehowa Central SD | Clifton Park |
| 276 | 2.8 | North Bellmore UFSD | Bellmore |
| 276 | 2.8 | Rockville Ctr UFSD | Rockville Ctr |
| 278 | 2.7 | Hewlett-Woodmere UFSD | Woodmere |
| 278 | 2.7 | Ramapo Central SD (Suffern) | Hillburn |
| 280 | 2.6 | West Islip UFSD | West Islip |
| 281 | 2.5 | Jamesville-Dewitt Central SD | Dewitt |
| 282 | 2.4 | Bethpage UFSD | Bethpage |
| 282 | 2.4 | Locust Valley Central SD | Locust Valley |
| 282 | 2.4 | Mamaroneck UFSD | Mamaroneck |
| 282 | 2.4 | Miller Place UFSD | Miller Place |
| 286 | 2.3 | Clarkstown Central SD | New City |
| 286 | 2.3 | Guilderland Central SD | Guilderland |
| 288 | 2.2 | Hauppauge UFSD | Hauppauge |
| 288 | 2.2 | Valley Stream Central High SD | Valley Stream |
| 290 | 2.1 | Herricks UFSD | New Hyde Park |
| 290 | 2.1 | Sayville UFSD | Sayville |
| 292 | 2.0 | Bethlehem Central SD | Delmar |
| 292 | 2.0 | Eastport-South Manor CSD | Manorville |
| 292 | 2.0 | Fayetteville-Manlius Central SD | Manlius |
| 292 | 2.0 | North Shore Central SD | Sea Cliff |
| 292 | 2.0 | Pelham UFSD | Pelham |
| 297 | 1.9 | Cazenovia Central SD | Cazenovia |
| 297 | 1.9 | Floral Park-Bellerose UFSD | Floral Park |
| 297 | 1.9 | Oceanside UFSD | Oceanside |
| 297 | 1.9 | Plainview-Old Bethpage Central SD | Plainview |
| 297 | 1.9 | Valhalla UFSD | Valhalla |
| 302 | 1.8 | East Aurora UFSD | East Aurora |
| 302 | 1.8 | Harborfields Central SD | Greenlawn |
| 302 | 1.8 | Kings Park Central SD | Kings Park |
| 302 | 1.8 | Niskayuna Central SD | Schenectady |
| 306 | 1.7 | Mount Pleasant Central SD | Thornwood |
| 306 | 1.7 | Pearl River UFSD | Pearl River |
| 306 | 1.7 | Skaneateles Central SD | Skaneateles |
| 309 | 1.6 | Mahopac Central SD | Mahopac |
| 309 | 1.6 | Northport-East Northport UFSD | Northport |
| 309 | 1.6 | Orchard Park Central SD | Orchard Park |
| 312 | 1.5 | Commack UFSD | East Northport |
| 312 | 1.5 | Massapequa UFSD | Massapequa |
| 314 | 1.4 | Pleasantville UFSD | Pleasantville |
| 314 | 1.4 | South Orangetown Central SD | Blauvelt |
| 316 | 1.3 | Pittsford Central SD | Pittsford |
| 316 | 1.3 | Three Village Central SD | Stony Brook |
| 318 | 1.2 | Bellmore-Merrick Central High SD | North Merrick |
| 318 | 1.2 | Smithtown Central SD | Smithtown |
| 320 | 1.1 | Hastings-on-Hudson UFSD | Hastings on Hdsn |
| 321 | 1.0 | Seaford UFSD | Seaford |
| 322 | 0.9 | Bayport-Blue Point UFSD | Bayport |
| 322 | 0.9 | Wantagh UFSD | Wantagh |
| 324 | 0.8 | Ardsley UFSD | Ardsley |
| 325 | 0.7 | Manhasset UFSD | Manhasset |
| 325 | 0.7 | Yorktown Central SD | Yorktown Hgts |
| 327 | 0.6 | Briarcliff Mnr UFSD | Briarcliff Mnr |
| 327 | 0.6 | Irvington UFSD | Irvington |
| 327 | 0.6 | Katonah-Lewisboro UFSD | South Salem |
| 327 | 0.6 | Mount Sinai UFSD | Mount Sinai |
| 331 | 0.5 | East Williston UFSD | Old Westbury |
| 331 | 0.5 | Syosset Central SD | Syosset |
| 333 | 0.4 | Jericho UFSD | Jericho |
| 333 | 0.4 | Lynbrook UFSD | Lynbrook |
| 333 | 0.4 | Shoreham-Wading River Central SD | Shoreham |
| 336 | 0.3 | Chappaqua Central SD | Chappaqua |
| 336 | 0.3 | Somers Central SD | Somers |
| 338 | 0.2 | Rye City SD | Rye |
| 339 | 0.1 | Blind Brook-Rye UFSD | Rye Brook |
| 339 | 0.1 | Cold Spring Hrbr Central SD | Cold Spring Hrbr |
| 339 | 0.1 | Garden City UFSD | Garden City |
| 342 | 0.0 | Baldwin UFSD | Baldwin |
| 342 | 0.0 | Bronxville UFSD | Bronxville |
| 342 | 0.0 | Byram Hills Central SD | Armonk |
| 342 | 0.0 | Croton-Harmon UFSD | Croton on Hdsn |
| 342 | 0.0 | Eastchester UFSD | Eastchester |
| 342 | 0.0 | Edgemont UFSD | Scarsdale |
| 342 | 0.0 | Merrick UFSD | Merrick |
| 342 | 0.0 | Scarsdale UFSD | Scarsdale |
| n/a | n/a | NYC Special Schools - District 75 | New York |
| n/a | n/a | NYC Geographic District # 1 | New York |
| n/a | n/a | NYC Geographic District # 2 | New York |
| n/a | n/a | NYC Geographic District # 3 | New York |
| n/a | n/a | NYC Geographic District # 4 | New York |
| n/a | n/a | NYC Geographic District # 5 | New York |
| n/a | n/a | NYC Geographic District # 6 | New York |
| n/a | n/a | NYC Geographic District # 7 | Bronx |
| n/a | n/a | NYC Geographic District # 8 | Bronx |
| n/a | n/a | NYC Geographic District # 9 | Bronx |
| n/a | n/a | NYC Geographic District #10 | Bronx |
| n/a | n/a | NYC Geographic District #11 | Bronx |
| n/a | n/a | NYC Geographic District #12 | Bronx |
| n/a | n/a | NYC Geographic District #13 | Brooklyn |
| n/a | n/a | NYC Geographic District #14 | Brooklyn |
| n/a | n/a | NYC Geographic District #15 | Brooklyn |
| n/a | n/a | NYC Geographic District #16 | Brooklyn |
| n/a | n/a | NYC Geographic District #17 | Brooklyn |
| n/a | n/a | NYC Geographic District #18 | Brooklyn |
| n/a | n/a | NYC Geographic District #19 | Brooklyn |
| n/a | n/a | NYC Geographic District #20 | Brooklyn |
| n/a | n/a | NYC Geographic District #21 | Brooklyn |
| n/a | n/a | NYC Geographic District #22 | Brooklyn |
| n/a | n/a | NYC Geographic District #23 | Brooklyn |
| n/a | n/a | NYC Geographic District #24 | Ridgewood |
| n/a | n/a | NYC Geographic District #25 | Flushing |
| n/a | n/a | NYC Geographic District #26 | Bayside |
| n/a | n/a | NYC Geographic District #27 | Ozone Park |
| n/a | n/a | NYC Geographic District #28 | Jamaica |
| n/a | n/a | NYC Geographic District #29 | Rosedale |
| n/a | n/a | NYC Geographic District #30 | Long Isl City |
| n/a | n/a | NYC Geographic District #31 | Staten Island |
| n/a | n/a | NYC Geographic District #32 | Brooklyn |
| n/a | n/a | New York City Public Schools | New York |

## Student/Teacher Ratio

(number of students per teacher)

| Rank | Number | District Name | City |
|---|---|---|---|
| 1 | 4.9 | NYC Special Schools - District 75 | New York |
| 2 | 9.2 | Dunkirk City SD | Dunkirk |
| 3 | 9.3 | Southampton UFSD | Southampton |
| 4 | 9.7 | Rondout Valley Central SD | Accord |
| 5 | 9.8 | Plattsburgh City SD | Plattsburgh |
| 5 | 9.8 | Sherburne-Earlville Central SD | Sherburne |
| 7 | 9.9 | East Hampton UFSD | East Hampton |
| 7 | 9.9 | Jericho UFSD | Jericho |
| 9 | 10.0 | Lawrence UFSD | Lawrence |
| 10 | 10.1 | Malverne UFSD | Malverne |
| 10 | 10.1 | Onteora Central SD | Boiceville |
| 10 | 10.1 | Penn Yan Central SD | Penn Yan |
| 13 | 10.2 | Beekmantown Central SD | West Chazy |
| 13 | 10.2 | Mineola UFSD | Mineola |
| 13 | 10.2 | North Shore Central SD | Sea Cliff |
| 16 | 10.3 | Greenburgh Central SD | Hartsdale |
| 17 | 10.4 | Bayport-Blue Point UFSD | Bayport |
| 17 | 10.4 | Hudson City SD | Hudson |
| 17 | 10.4 | Ravena-Coeymans-Selkirk Ctrl SD | Selkirk |
| 17 | 10.4 | Rockville Ctr UFSD | Rockville Ctr |
| 17 | 10.4 | Westhampton Bch UFSD | Westhampton Bch |
| 22 | 10.5 | East Irondequoit Central SD | Rochester |
| 22 | 10.5 | Oyster Bay-East Norwich Central SD | Oyster Bay |
| 22 | 10.5 | Salmon River Central SD | Fort Covington |
| 22 | 10.5 | Solvay UFSD | Solvay |
| 26 | 10.6 | Great Neck UFSD | Great Neck |
| 26 | 10.6 | Monticello Central SD | Monticello |
| 26 | 10.6 | Palmyra-Macedon Central SD | Palmyra |
| 29 | 10.7 | Briarcliff Mnr UFSD | Briarcliff Mnr |
| 29 | 10.7 | Harrison Central SD | Harrison |
| 29 | 10.7 | Liberty Central SD | Liberty |
| 29 | 10.7 | Spackenkill UFSD | Poughkeepsie |
| 33 | 10.8 | Binghamton City SD | Binghamton |
| 33 | 10.8 | Geneva City SD | Geneva |
| 33 | 10.8 | Taconic Hills Central SD | Craryville |
| 33 | 10.8 | Uniondale UFSD | Uniondale |
| 33 | 10.8 | Wayne Central SD | Ontario Center |
| 38 | 10.9 | Ardsley UFSD | Ardsley |
| 38 | 10.9 | East Syracuse-Minoa Central SD | East Syracuse |
| 40 | 11.0 | Batavia City SD | Batavia |
| 40 | 11.0 | Hastings-on-Hudson UFSD | Hastings on Hdsn |
| 40 | 11.0 | Northport-East Northport UFSD | Northport |
| 43 | 11.1 | Deer Park UFSD | Deer Park |
| 43 | 11.1 | Hewlett-Woodmere UFSD | Woodmere |
| 43 | 11.1 | Jamestown City SD | Jamestown |
| 43 | 11.1 | Saranac Central SD | Dannemora |
| 43 | 11.1 | Susquehanna Valley Central SD | Conklin |
| 43 | 11.1 | Valhalla UFSD | Valhalla |
| 49 | 11.2 | Attica Central SD | Attica |
| 49 | 11.2 | Cohoes City SD | Cohoes |
| 49 | 11.2 | Dryden Central SD | Dryden |
| 49 | 11.2 | Locust Valley Central SD | Locust Valley |
| 49 | 11.2 | Roosevelt UFSD | Roosevelt |
| 49 | 11.2 | Syosset Central SD | Syosset |
| 55 | 11.3 | Bronxville UFSD | Bronxville |
| 55 | 11.3 | Peru Central SD | Peru |
| 57 | 11.4 | Amityville UFSD | Amityville |
| 57 | 11.4 | Brighton Central SD | Rochester |
| 57 | 11.4 | Buffalo City SD | Buffalo |
| 57 | 11.4 | East Williston UFSD | Old Westbury |
| 57 | 11.4 | Ithaca City SD | Ithaca |
| 57 | 11.4 | Merrick UFSD | Merrick |
| 57 | 11.4 | Newark Central SD | Newark |
| 57 | 11.4 | Oneonta City SD | Oneonta |
| 57 | 11.4 | Rush-Henrietta Central SD | Henrietta |
| 66 | 11.5 | Cheektowaga-Sloan UFSD | Sloan |
| 66 | 11.5 | Cobleskill-Richmondville Central SD | Cobleskill |
| 66 | 11.5 | Herricks UFSD | New Hyde Park |
| 66 | 11.5 | Jordan-Elbridge Central SD | Elbridge |
| 66 | 11.5 | Kinderhook Central SD | Valatie |
| 66 | 11.5 | Maine-Endwell Central SD | Endwell |
| 66 | 11.5 | Mattituck-Cutchogue UFSD | Cutchogue |
| 66 | 11.5 | Norwich City SD | Norwich |
| 66 | 11.5 | Nyack UFSD | Nyack |

*Note: This section only includes districts with 1,500 or more students; All categories are ranked from high to low*

| | | | |
|---|---|---|---|
| 75 | 11.6 | Irvington UFSD | Irvington |
| 75 | 11.6 | Kenmore-Tonawanda UFSD | Buffalo |
| 75 | 11.6 | Lackawanna City SD | Lackawanna |
| 75 | 11.6 | Levittown UFSD | Levittown |
| 75 | 11.6 | Mount Pleasant Central SD | Thornwood |
| 75 | 11.6 | Ogdensburg City SD | Ogdensburg |
| 75 | 11.6 | Rochester City SD | Rochester |
| 75 | 11.6 | Union-Endicott Central SD | Endicott |
| 83 | 11.7 | Camden Central SD | Camden |
| 83 | 11.7 | Dansville Central SD | Dansville |
| 83 | 11.7 | Evans-Brant Central SD (Lake Shore) | Angola |
| 83 | 11.7 | Hamburg Central SD | Hamburg |
| 83 | 11.7 | Homer Central SD | Homer |
| 83 | 11.7 | Livonia Central SD | Livonia |
| 83 | 11.7 | Lockport City SD | Lockport |
| 83 | 11.7 | Nanuet UFSD | Nanuet |
| 83 | 11.7 | North Bellmore UFSD | Bellmore |
| 83 | 11.7 | Phelps-Clifton Springs Central SD | Clifton Springs |
| 93 | 11.8 | Amherst Central SD | Amherst |
| 93 | 11.8 | Long Beach City SD | Long Beach |
| 93 | 11.8 | Malone Central SD | Malone |
| 93 | 11.8 | Mexico Central SD | Mexico |
| 93 | 11.8 | Penfield Central SD | Rochester |
| 93 | 11.8 | Spencerport Central SD | Spencerport |
| 93 | 11.8 | Tonawanda City SD | Tonawanda |
| 93 | 11.8 | Wayland-Cohocton Central SD | Wayland |
| 101 | 11.9 | Central Islip UFSD | Central Islip |
| 101 | 11.9 | Chappaqua Central SD | Chappaqua |
| 101 | 11.9 | Cold Spring Hrbr Central SD | Cold Spring Hrbr |
| 101 | 11.9 | Cortland City SD | Cortland |
| 101 | 11.9 | Island Trees UFSD | Levittown |
| 101 | 11.9 | Pleasantville UFSD | Pleasantville |
| 101 | 11.9 | S Glens Fls Central SD | S Glens Fls |
| 101 | 11.9 | Southwestern CSD at Jamestown | Jamestown |
| 101 | 11.9 | Troy City SD | Troy |
| 101 | 11.9 | Vestal Central SD | Vestal |
| 111 | 12.0 | Albany City SD | Albany |
| 111 | 12.0 | Auburn City SD | Auburn |
| 111 | 12.0 | Bedford Central SD | Bedford |
| 111 | 12.0 | Coxsackie-Athens Central SD | Coxsackie |
| 111 | 12.0 | Glens Falls City SD | Glens Falls |
| 111 | 12.0 | Lynbrook UFSD | Lynbrook |
| 111 | 12.0 | Rome City SD | Rome |
| 111 | 12.0 | Roslyn UFSD | Roslyn |
| 111 | 12.0 | Scarsdale UFSD | Scarsdale |
| 111 | 12.0 | Seaford UFSD | Seaford |
| 111 | 12.0 | Syracuse City SD | Syracuse |
| 111 | 12.0 | Waterloo Central SD | Waterloo |
| 123 | 12.1 | Corning City SD | Painted Post |
| 123 | 12.1 | Elmira City SD | Elmira |
| 123 | 12.1 | Farmingdale UFSD | Farmingdale |
| 123 | 12.1 | Glen Cove City SD | Glen Cove |
| 123 | 12.1 | Greece Central SD | Rochester |
| 123 | 12.1 | Johnson City Central SD | Johnson City |
| 123 | 12.1 | Lansingburgh Central SD | Troy |
| 123 | 12.1 | Owego-Apalachin Central SD | Owego |
| 123 | 12.1 | Phoenix Central SD | Phoenix |
| 123 | 12.1 | Ramapo Central SD (Suffern) | Hillburn |
| 123 | 12.1 | Schuylerville Central SD | Schuylerville |
| 123 | 12.1 | South Colonie Central SD | Albany |
| 123 | 12.1 | South Country Central SD | East Patchogue |
| 136 | 12.2 | Byram Hills Central SD | Armonk |
| 136 | 12.2 | Connetquot Central SD | Bohemia |
| 136 | 12.2 | Freeport UFSD | Freeport |
| 136 | 12.2 | Jamesville-Dewitt Central SD | Dewitt |
| 136 | 12.2 | Lewiston-Porter Central SD | Youngstown |
| 136 | 12.2 | Manhasset UFSD | Manhasset |
| 136 | 12.2 | New Paltz Central SD | New Paltz |
| 136 | 12.2 | NYC Geographic District # 4 | New York |
| 136 | 12.2 | Niagara-Wheatfield Central SD | Niagara Falls |
| 136 | 12.2 | Sweet Home Central SD | Amherst |
| 136 | 12.2 | Westhill Central SD | Syracuse |
| 147 | 12.3 | Babylon UFSD | Babylon |
| 147 | 12.3 | Bath Central SD | Bath |
| 147 | 12.3 | Bay Shore UFSD | Bay Shore |
| 147 | 12.3 | Bethpage UFSD | Bethpage |
| 147 | 12.3 | Brewster Central SD | Brewster |
| 147 | 12.3 | Depew UFSD | Depew |
| 147 | 12.3 | East Meadow UFSD | Westbury |
| 147 | 12.3 | Iroquois Central SD | Elma |
| 147 | 12.3 | Marlboro Central SD | Marlboro |
| 147 | 12.3 | West Babylon UFSD | West Babylon |
| 157 | 12.4 | Blind Brook-Rye UFSD | Rye Brook |
| 157 | 12.4 | Catskill Central SD | Catskill |
| 157 | 12.4 | Fredonia Central SD | Fredonia |
| 157 | 12.4 | Frontier Central SD | Hamburg |
| 157 | 12.4 | Garden City UFSD | Garden City |
| 157 | 12.4 | Katonah-Lewisboro UFSD | South Salem |
| 157 | 12.4 | Scotia-Glenville Central SD | Scotia |
| 157 | 12.4 | Springville-Griffith Institute CSD | Springville |
| 157 | 12.4 | West Hempstead UFSD | West Hempstead |
| 166 | 12.5 | Guilderland Central SD | Guilderland |
| 166 | 12.5 | Hilton Central SD | Hilton |
| 166 | 12.5 | Massapequa UFSD | Massapequa |
| 166 | 12.5 | New Hyde Pk-Garden City Pk UFSD | New Hyde Park |
| 166 | 12.5 | Schenectady City SD | Schenectady |
| 166 | 12.5 | Yorkshire-Pioneer Central SD | Yorkshire |
| 172 | 12.6 | Baldwin UFSD | Baldwin |
| 172 | 12.6 | Edgemont UFSD | Scarsdale |
| 172 | 12.6 | Hampton Bays UFSD | Hampton Bays |
| 172 | 12.6 | Hendrick Hudson Central SD | Montrose |
| 172 | 12.6 | Holland Patent Central SD | Holland Patent |
| 172 | 12.6 | Starpoint Central SD | Lockport |
| 172 | 12.6 | Utica City SD | Utica |
| 172 | 12.6 | Valley Central SD (Montgomery) | Montgomery |
| 172 | 12.6 | Windsor Central SD | Windsor |
| 181 | 12.7 | Akron Central SD | Akron |
| 181 | 12.7 | Amsterdam City SD | Amsterdam |
| 181 | 12.7 | Canandaigua City SD | Canandaigua |
| 181 | 12.7 | Canastota Central SD | Canastota |
| 181 | 12.7 | Kingston City SD | Kingston |
| 181 | 12.7 | NYC Geographic District # 7 | Bronx |
| 181 | 12.7 | South Huntington UFSD | Huntington Stn |
| 181 | 12.7 | West Islip UFSD | West Islip |
| 181 | 12.7 | White Plains City SD | White Plains |
| 181 | 12.7 | Yorktown Central SD | Yorktown Hgts |
| 191 | 12.8 | Cazenovia Central SD | Cazenovia |
| 191 | 12.8 | Gates-Chili Central SD | Rochester |
| 191 | 12.8 | NYC Geographic District # 1 | New York |
| 191 | 12.8 | North Tonawanda City SD | North Tonawanda |
| 191 | 12.8 | Pelham UFSD | Pelham |
| 191 | 12.8 | Pittsford Central SD | Pittsford |
| 191 | 12.8 | Schalmont Central SD | Schenectady |
| 191 | 12.8 | Valley Stream 13 UFSD | Valley Stream |
| 191 | 12.8 | Westbury UFSD | Old Westbury |
| 200 | 12.9 | Chittenango Central SD | Chittenango |
| 200 | 12.9 | Churchville-Chili Central SD | Churchville |
| 200 | 12.9 | Ilion Central SD | Ilion |
| 200 | 12.9 | Kings Park Central SD | Kings Park |
| 200 | 12.9 | Lindenhurst UFSD | Lindenhurst |
| 200 | 12.9 | NYC Geographic District # 5 | New York |
| 200 | 12.9 | Oceanside UFSD | Oceanside |
| 200 | 12.9 | Olean City SD | Olean |
| 200 | 12.9 | Poughkeepsie City SD | Poughkeepsie |
| 200 | 12.9 | South Orangetown Central SD | Blauvelt |
| 210 | 13.0 | Averill Park Central SD | Averill Park |
| 210 | 13.0 | Center Moriches UFSD | Center Moriches |
| 210 | 13.0 | Ellenville Central SD | Ellenville |
| 210 | 13.0 | Fairport Central SD | Fairport |
| 210 | 13.0 | Half Hollow Hills Central SD | Dix Hills |
| 210 | 13.0 | Hornell City SD | Hornell |
| 210 | 13.0 | Hudson Falls Central SD | Fort Edward |
| 210 | 13.0 | Hyde Park Central SD | Hyde Park |
| 210 | 13.0 | Mamaroneck UFSD | Mamaroneck |
| 210 | 13.0 | NYC Geographic District #16 | Brooklyn |
| 210 | 13.0 | Newfane Central SD | Burt |
| 210 | 13.0 | Oneida City SD | Oneida |
| 210 | 13.0 | Oswego City SD | Oswego |
| 210 | 13.0 | Red Hook Central SD | Red Hook |
| 210 | 13.0 | Three Village Central SD | Stony Brook |
| 210 | 13.0 | Webster Central SD | Webster |
| 226 | 13.1 | Alden Central SD | Alden |
| 226 | 13.1 | Ballston Spa Central SD | Ballston Spa |
| 226 | 13.1 | Croton-Harmon UFSD | Croton on Hdsn |
| 226 | 13.1 | East Ramapo Central SD | Spring Valley |
| 226 | 13.1 | Eastchester UFSD | Eastchester |
| 226 | 13.1 | Fulton City SD | Fulton |
| 226 | 13.1 | Hauppauge UFSD | Hauppauge |
| 226 | 13.1 | Liverpool Central SD | Liverpool |
| 226 | 13.1 | New Hartford Central SD | New Hartford |
| 226 | 13.1 | Newburgh City SD | Newburgh |
| 226 | 13.1 | Plainedge UFSD | N Massapequa |
| 226 | 13.1 | Rye City SD | Rye |
| 226 | 13.1 | Saugerties Central SD | Saugerties |
| 226 | 13.1 | UFSD of the Tarrytowns | Sleepy Hollow |
| 226 | 13.1 | Wyandanch UFSD | Wyandanch |
| 241 | 13.2 | Albion Central SD | Albion |
| 241 | 13.2 | Cheektowaga Central SD | Cheektowaga |
| 241 | 13.2 | Cheektowaga-Maryvale UFSD | Cheektowaga |
| 241 | 13.2 | East Greenbush Central SD | East Greenbush |
| 241 | 13.2 | Hicksville UFSD | Hicksville |
| 241 | 13.2 | Lakeland Central SD | Shrub Oak |
| 241 | 13.2 | Marcellus Central SD | Marcellus |
| 241 | 13.2 | Mohonasen Central SD | Schenectady |
| 241 | 13.2 | NYC Geographic District # 9 | Bronx |
| 241 | 13.2 | North Colonie Central SD | Latham |
| 241 | 13.2 | North Rockland Central SD | Garnerville |
| 241 | 13.2 | West Seneca Central SD | West Seneca |
| 241 | 13.2 | Williamsville Central SD | East Amherst |
| 254 | 13.3 | Brockport Central SD | Brockport |
| 254 | 13.3 | Eden Central SD | Eden |
| 254 | 13.3 | Honeoye Falls-Lima Central SD | Honeoye Falls |
| 254 | 13.3 | NYC Geographic District #12 | Bronx |
| 254 | 13.3 | NYC Geographic District #15 | Brooklyn |
| 254 | 13.3 | Sayville UFSD | Sayville |
| 254 | 13.3 | Shoreham-Wading River Central SD | Shoreham |
| 254 | 13.3 | South Jefferson Central SD | Adams Center |
| 254 | 13.3 | Wantagh UFSD | Wantagh |
| 263 | 13.4 | East Aurora UFSD | East Aurora |
| 263 | 13.4 | Niskayuna Central SD | Schenectady |
| 263 | 13.4 | Orchard Park Central SD | Orchard Park |
| 263 | 13.4 | Ossining UFSD | Ossining |
| 263 | 13.4 | Port Jervis City SD | Port Jervis |
| 263 | 13.4 | Putnam Valley Central SD | Putnam Valley |
| 263 | 13.4 | Queensbury UFSD | Queensbury |
| 263 | 13.4 | Whitesboro Central SD | Yorkville |
| 271 | 13.5 | Chenango Forks Central SD | Binghamton |
| 271 | 13.5 | Dover UFSD | Dover Plains |
| 271 | 13.5 | East Islip UFSD | Islip Terrace |
| 271 | 13.5 | Highland Central SD | Highland |
| 271 | 13.5 | Islip UFSD | Islip |
| 271 | 13.5 | North Syracuse Central SD | North Syracuse |
| 271 | 13.5 | Pearl River UFSD | Pearl River |
| 271 | 13.5 | Peekskill City SD | Peekskill |
| 271 | 13.5 | Saratoga Spgs City SD | Saratoga Spgs |
| 271 | 13.5 | Watertown City SD | Watertown |
| 281 | 13.6 | Bethlehem Central SD | Delmar |
| 281 | 13.6 | Commack UFSD | East Northport |
| 281 | 13.6 | Mahopac Central SD | Mahopac |
| 281 | 13.6 | Mount Vernon City SD | Mount Vernon |
| 281 | 13.6 | NYC Geographic District #14 | Brooklyn |
| 281 | 13.6 | NYC Geographic District #32 | Brooklyn |
| 281 | 13.6 | Sachem Central SD | Holbrook |
| 281 | 13.6 | Somers Central SD | Somers |
| 289 | 13.7 | Clarence Central SD | Clarence Center |
| 289 | 13.7 | Goshen Central SD | Goshen |
| 289 | 13.7 | Massena Central SD | Massena |
| 289 | 13.7 | Middletown City SD | Middletown |
| 293 | 13.8 | Carmel Central SD | Patterson |
| 293 | 13.8 | Horseheads Central SD | Horseheads |
| 293 | 13.8 | Lancaster Central SD | Lancaster |
| 293 | 13.8 | NYC Geographic District # 6 | New York |
| 293 | 13.8 | Royalton-Hartland Central SD | Middleport |
| 293 | 13.8 | Vernon-Verona-Sherrill Central SD | Verona |
| 293 | 13.8 | Warwick Valley Central SD | Warwick |
| 300 | 13.9 | Bellmore-Merrick Central High SD | North Merrick |
| 300 | 13.9 | Brentwood UFSD | Brentwood |
| 300 | 13.9 | Burnt Hills-Ballston Lake CSD | Scotia |
| 300 | 13.9 | Eastport-South Manor CSD | Manorville |
| 300 | 13.9 | Riverhead Central SD | Riverhead |
| 300 | 13.9 | Wallkill Central SD | Wallkill |
| 300 | 13.9 | Washingtonville Central SD | Washingtonville |
| 307 | 14.0 | Clarkstown Central SD | New City |
| 307 | 14.0 | Comsewogue School District | Port Jeff Stn |
| 307 | 14.0 | Gloversville City SD | Gloversville |
| 307 | 14.0 | Hannibal Central SD | Hannibal |
| 307 | 14.0 | Monroe-Woodbury Central SD | Central Valley |
| 307 | 14.0 | NYC Geographic District #17 | Brooklyn |
| 307 | 14.0 | West Genesee Central SD | Camillus |
| 314 | 14.1 | Grand Island Central SD | Grand Island |
| 314 | 14.1 | Miller Place UFSD | Miller Place |
| 314 | 14.1 | NYC Geographic District #23 | Brooklyn |
| 314 | 14.1 | Waverly Central SD | Waverly |
| 318 | 14.2 | Fayetteville-Manlius Central SD | Manlius |
| 318 | 14.2 | Longwood Central SD | Middle Island |
| 318 | 14.2 | North Babylon UFSD | North Babylon |
| 318 | 14.2 | Victor Central SD | Victor |
| 322 | 14.3 | Central Square Central SD | Central Square |
| 322 | 14.3 | Copiague UFSD | Copiague |
| 322 | 14.3 | NYC Geographic District #19 | Brooklyn |
| 322 | 14.3 | William Floyd UFSD | Mastic Beach |
| 326 | 14.4 | Baldwinsville Central SD | Baldwinsville |
| 326 | 14.4 | Elwood UFSD | Greenlawn |
| 326 | 14.4 | NYC Geographic District #10 | Bronx |
| 329 | 14.5 | Arlington Central SD | Poughkeepsie |

*Note: This section only includes districts with 1,500 or more students; All categories are ranked from high to low*

| | | | |
|---|---|---|---|
| 329 | 14.5 | Carthage Central SD | Carthage |
| 329 | 14.5 | Hempstead UFSD | Hempstead |
| 329 | 14.5 | NYC Geographic District #18 | Brooklyn |
| 329 | 14.5 | New York City Public Schools | New York |
| 329 | 14.5 | Pine Bush Central SD | Pine Bush |
| 329 | 14.5 | Smithtown Central SD | Smithtown |
| 336 | 14.6 | Beacon City SD | Beacon |
| 336 | 14.6 | Charter School for Applied Tech | Buffalo |
| 336 | 14.6 | Chenango Valley Central SD | Binghamton |
| 336 | 14.6 | General Brown Central SD | Dexter |
| 336 | 14.6 | NYC Geographic District # 8 | Bronx |
| 336 | 14.6 | Port Chester-Rye UFSD | Port Chester |
| 336 | 14.6 | Shenendehowa Central SD | Clifton Park |
| 343 | 14.7 | Franklin Square UFSD | Franklin Square |
| 343 | 14.7 | Indian River Central SD | Philadelphia |
| 343 | 14.7 | Valley Stream Central High SD | Valley Stream |
| 346 | 14.8 | Broadalbin-Perth Central SD | Broadalbin |
| 346 | 14.8 | Gouverneur Central SD | Gouverneur |
| 346 | 14.8 | NYC Geographic District # 3 | New York |
| 349 | 14.9 | Elmont UFSD | Elmont |
| 349 | 14.9 | Rocky Point UFSD | Rocky Point |
| 351 | 15.0 | New Rochelle City SD | New Rochelle |
| 351 | 15.0 | NYC Geographic District #11 | Bronx |
| 353 | 15.1 | Floral Park-Bellerose UFSD | Floral Park |
| 354 | 15.2 | Johnstown City SD | Johnstown |
| 354 | 15.2 | Mount Sinai UFSD | Mount Sinai |
| 354 | 15.2 | NYC Geographic District #27 | Ozone Park |
| 354 | 15.2 | Sewanhaka Central High SD | Floral Park |
| 354 | 15.2 | Wappingers Central SD | Wappingers Fls |
| 359 | 15.5 | Harborfields Central SD | Greenlawn |
| 359 | 15.5 | NYC Geographic District #24 | Ridgewood |
| 359 | 15.5 | NYC Geographic District #30 | Long Isl City |
| 359 | 15.5 | Patchogue-Medford UFSD | Patchogue |
| 363 | 15.6 | Cornwall Central SD | Cornwall on Hdsn |
| 363 | 15.6 | NYC Geographic District # 2 | New York |
| 365 | 15.7 | Middle Country Central SD | Centereach |
| 365 | 15.7 | NYC Geographic District #29 | Rosedale |
| 367 | 15.8 | Niagara Falls City SD | Niagara Falls |
| 368 | 16.0 | NYC Geographic District #25 | Flushing |
| 369 | 16.1 | NYC Geographic District #22 | Brooklyn |
| 370 | 16.5 | NYC Geographic District #28 | Jamaica |
| 371 | 16.6 | NYC Geographic District #31 | Staten Island |
| 372 | 16.9 | NYC Geographic District #21 | Brooklyn |
| 373 | 17.1 | NYC Geographic District #20 | Brooklyn |
| 374 | 17.5 | NYC Geographic District #13 | Brooklyn |
| 375 | 20.7 | NYC Geographic District #26 | Bayside |
| 376 | 24.9 | Yonkers City SD | Yonkers |
| 377 | 72.4 | Huntington UFSD | Huntington Stn |
| n/a | n/a | Medina Central SD | Medina |
| n/a | n/a | Minisink Valley Central SD | Slate Hill |
| n/a | n/a | Plainview-Old Bethpage Central SD | Plainview |
| n/a | n/a | Port Washington UFSD | Port Washington |
| n/a | n/a | Skaneateles Central SD | Skaneateles |
| n/a | n/a | West Irondequoit Central SD | Rochester |

## Student/Librarian Ratio

(number of students per librarian)

| Rank | Number | District Name | City |
|---|---|---|---|
| 1 | 373.8 | Oneida City SD | Oneida |
| 2 | 377.2 | Oneonta City SD | Oneonta |
| 3 | 406.3 | Saranac Central SD | Dannemora |
| 4 | 411.8 | Spackenkill UFSD | Poughkeepsie |
| 5 | 412.8 | Onteora Central SD | Boiceville |
| 6 | 414.2 | Camden Central SD | Camden |
| 7 | 416.9 | Southwestern CSD at Jamestown | Jamestown |
| 8 | 429.6 | North Bellmore UFSD | Bellmore |
| 9 | 436.8 | Ogdensburg City SD | Ogdensburg |
| 10 | 439.2 | Iroquois Central SD | Elma |
| 11 | 442.2 | Locust Valley Central SD | Locust Valley |
| 12 | 446.5 | Greenburgh Central SD | Hartsdale |
| 13 | 447.8 | Ithaca City SD | Ithaca |
| 14 | 449.0 | Catskill Central SD | Catskill |
| 15 | 455.0 | Vernon-Verona-Sherrill Central SD | Verona |
| 16 | 457.5 | Scotia-Glenville Central SD | Scotia |
| 17 | 463.2 | Rondout Valley Central SD | Accord |
| 18 | 469.3 | Niskayuna Central SD | Schenectady |
| 19 | 470.9 | Vestal Central SD | Vestal |
| 20 | 471.0 | Westhill Central SD | Syracuse |
| 21 | 476.8 | New Hyde Pk-Garden City Pk UFSD | New Hyde Park |
| 22 | 478.8 | Livonia Central SD | Livonia |
| 23 | 482.3 | Liverpool Central SD | Liverpool |
| 24 | 491.5 | Lynbrook UFSD | Lynbrook |
| 25 | 495.4 | Wayne Central SD | Ontario Center |
| 26 | 499.1 | Byram Hills Central SD | Armonk |
| 27 | 499.5 | Tonawanda City SD | Tonawanda |
| 28 | 500.4 | Bayport-Blue Point UFSD | Bayport |
| 29 | 503.6 | Oyster Bay-East Norwich Central SD | Oyster Bay |
| 30 | 506.3 | Valhalla UFSD | Valhalla |
| 31 | 507.1 | North Colonie Central SD | Latham |
| 32 | 509.3 | Palmyra-Macedon Central SD | Palmyra |
| 33 | 512.8 | Marlboro Central SD | Marlboro |
| 34 | 513.8 | Saugerties Central SD | Saugerties |
| 35 | 514.0 | Canastota Central SD | Canastota |
| 35 | 514.0 | Coxsackie-Athens Central SD | Coxsackie |
| 37 | 515.7 | Jericho UFSD | Jericho |
| 38 | 517.5 | Ravena-Coeymans-Selkirk Ctrl SD | Selkirk |
| 39 | 518.0 | Jordan-Elbridge Central SD | Elbridge |
| 40 | 519.8 | Peru Central SD | Peru |
| 41 | 523.3 | Cheektowaga-Sloan UFSD | Sloan |
| 42 | 523.7 | Solvay UFSD | Solvay |
| 43 | 524.2 | Scarsdale UFSD | Scarsdale |
| 44 | 524.4 | New Hartford Central SD | New Hartford |
| 45 | 525.5 | East Irondequoit Central SD | Rochester |
| 46 | 529.2 | Cobleskill-Richmondville Central SD | Cobleskill |
| 47 | 530.6 | Great Neck UFSD | Great Neck |
| 48 | 534.8 | Homer Central SD | Homer |
| 49 | 537.0 | Owego-Apalachin Central SD | Owego |
| 50 | 537.4 | Binghamton City SD | Binghamton |
| 51 | 539.0 | Valley Stream 13 UFSD | Valley Stream |
| 52 | 540.0 | Batavia City SD | Batavia |
| 53 | 541.8 | Corning City SD | Painted Post |
| 54 | 542.2 | East Syracuse-Minoa Central SD | East Syracuse |
| 55 | 543.2 | Mineola UFSD | Mineola |
| 56 | 543.8 | Norwich City SD | Norwich |
| 57 | 547.3 | Auburn City SD | Auburn |
| 58 | 552.1 | Springville-Griffith Institute CSD | Springville |
| 59 | 552.2 | Bedford Central SD | Bedford |
| 60 | 552.5 | Geneva City SD | Geneva |
| 61 | 552.9 | Cortland City SD | Cortland |
| 62 | 554.7 | Briarcliff Mnr UFSD | Briarcliff Mnr |
| 63 | 555.7 | Jamestown City SD | Jamestown |
| 64 | 556.7 | Cazenovia Central SD | Cazenovia |
| 65 | 557.0 | Chittenango Central SD | Chittenango |
| 66 | 557.8 | Red Hook Central SD | Red Hook |
| 67 | 560.5 | Whitesboro Central SD | Yorkville |
| 68 | 562.5 | Poughkeepsie City SD | Poughkeepsie |
| 69 | 563.2 | Burnt Hills-Ballston Lake CSD | Scotia |
| 70 | 563.7 | Schalmont Central SD | Schenectady |
| 71 | 564.4 | Kenmore-Tonawanda UFSD | Buffalo |
| 72 | 566.7 | Malverne UFSD | Malverne |
| 73 | 567.7 | Chenango Forks Central SD | Binghamton |
| 74 | 567.9 | Southampton UFSD | Southampton |
| 75 | 568.4 | Bethlehem Central SD | Delmar |
| 76 | 571.3 | West Hempstead UFSD | West Hempstead |
| 77 | 571.8 | Beacon City SD | Beacon |
| 78 | 572.5 | New Paltz Central SD | New Paltz |
| 79 | 573.2 | North Shore Central SD | Sea Cliff |
| 80 | 573.6 | Jamesville-Dewitt Central SD | Dewitt |
| 81 | 575.3 | Merrick UFSD | Merrick |
| 82 | 576.5 | Penfield Central SD | Rochester |
| 83 | 578.0 | Uniondale UFSD | Uniondale |
| 84 | 579.3 | Central Square Central SD | Central Square |
| 85 | 579.7 | Dansville Central SD | Dansville |
| 85 | 579.7 | East Ramapo Central SD | Spring Valley |
| 87 | 581.3 | Sweet Home Central SD | Amherst |
| 88 | 582.9 | Gates-Chili Central SD | Rochester |
| 89 | 583.0 | Croton-Harmon UFSD | Croton on Hdsn |
| 90 | 583.8 | Nyack UFSD | Nyack |
| 91 | 588.0 | Hyde Park Central SD | Hyde Park |
| 92 | 591.7 | Penn Yan Central SD | Penn Yan |
| 93 | 593.5 | Cold Spring Hrbr Central SD | Cold Spring Hrbr |
| 94 | 595.1 | Chappaqua Central SD | Chappaqua |
| 95 | 595.3 | Westhampton Bch UFSD | Westhampton Bch |
| 96 | 599.3 | East Williston UFSD | Old Westbury |
| 97 | 599.7 | Irvington UFSD | Irvington |
| 98 | 601.4 | South Colonie Central SD | Albany |
| 99 | 602.3 | Babylon UFSD | Babylon |
| 100 | 602.4 | Massapequa UFSD | Massapequa |
| 101 | 605.7 | East Greenbush Central SD | East Greenbush |
| 102 | 606.0 | Syosset Central SD | Syosset |
| 103 | 607.2 | Hicksville UFSD | Hicksville |
| 103 | 607.2 | Sherburne-Earlville Central SD | Sherburne |
| 105 | 607.3 | Ellenville Central SD | Ellenville |
| 106 | 611.0 | Phelps-Clifton Springs Central SD | Clifton Springs |
| 107 | 613.8 | Fulton City SD | Fulton |
| 108 | 618.0 | Horseheads Central SD | Horseheads |
| 109 | 618.8 | Rome City SD | Rome |
| 110 | 621.7 | Alden Central SD | Alden |
| 111 | 621.8 | Pittsford Central SD | Pittsford |
| 112 | 622.2 | Herricks UFSD | New Hyde Park |
| 113 | 622.8 | Eastchester UFSD | Eastchester |
| 113 | 622.8 | West Babylon UFSD | West Babylon |
| 115 | 623.9 | Albany City SD | Albany |
| 116 | 626.3 | Lancaster Central SD | Lancaster |
| 117 | 629.3 | Eden Central SD | Eden |
| 118 | 630.2 | Utica City SD | Utica |
| 119 | 631.9 | Fairport Central SD | Fairport |
| 120 | 633.3 | Northport-East Northport UFSD | Northport |
| 121 | 638.7 | Hampton Bays UFSD | Hampton Bays |
| 121 | 638.7 | Plattsburgh City SD | Plattsburgh |
| 123 | 640.2 | Grand Island Central SD | Grand Island |
| 124 | 641.8 | Seaford UFSD | Seaford |
| 125 | 643.0 | Highland Central SD | Highland |
| 126 | 644.7 | Katonah-Lewisboro UFSD | South Salem |
| 127 | 645.5 | Honeoye Falls-Lima Central SD | Honeoye Falls |
| 128 | 646.1 | Syracuse City SD | Syracuse |
| 129 | 646.7 | Edgemont UFSD | Scarsdale |
| 130 | 647.3 | Kingston City SD | Kingston |
| 131 | 648.5 | Maine-Endwell Central SD | Endwell |
| 132 | 652.7 | Franklin Square UFSD | Franklin Square |
| 133 | 653.2 | S Glens Fls Central SD | S Glens Fls |
| 134 | 654.7 | East Aurora UFSD | East Aurora |
| 135 | 655.0 | Pleasantville UFSD | Pleasantville |
| 136 | 655.4 | Fayetteville-Manlius Central SD | Manlius |
| 137 | 656.7 | Yorktown Central SD | Yorktown Hgts |
| 138 | 658.0 | Lockport City SD | Lockport |
| 139 | 658.2 | Olean City SD | Olean |
| 140 | 658.6 | Greece Central SD | Rochester |
| 141 | 659.0 | Mount Pleasant Central SD | Thornwood |
| 142 | 659.3 | Guilderland Central SD | Guilderland |
| 143 | 660.5 | Comsewogue School District | Port Jeff Stn |
| 144 | 662.7 | Marcellus Central SD | Marcellus |
| 145 | 664.5 | Elmont UFSD | Elmont |
| 146 | 664.8 | West Islip UFSD | West Islip |
| 147 | 668.5 | Hewlett-Woodmere UFSD | Woodmere |
| 148 | 669.7 | Spencerport Central SD | Spencerport |
| 149 | 671.5 | Orchard Park Central SD | Orchard Park |
| 150 | 673.0 | Shoreham-Wading River Central SD | Shoreham |
| 151 | 673.4 | Averill Park Central SD | Averill Park |
| 152 | 674.2 | Rush-Henrietta Central SD | Henrietta |
| 153 | 674.7 | Cohoes City SD | Cohoes |
| 154 | 675.0 | Niagara-Wheatfield Central SD | Niagara Falls |
| 155 | 675.3 | Glen Cove City SD | Glen Cove |
| 155 | 675.3 | Hendrick Hudson Central SD | Montrose |
| 157 | 678.9 | Smithtown Central SD | Smithtown |
| 158 | 680.6 | Roslyn UFSD | Roslyn |
| 159 | 680.7 | Saratoga Spgs City SD | Saratoga Spgs |
| 160 | 684.4 | Somers Central SD | Somers |
| 161 | 684.9 | Amsterdam City SD | Amsterdam |
| 161 | 684.9 | Commack UFSD | East Northport |
| 163 | 686.8 | Cornwall Central SD | Cornwall on Hdsn |
| 164 | 687.4 | Plainedge UFSD | N Massapequa |
| 165 | 687.8 | Rye City SD | Rye |
| 166 | 689.3 | Starpoint Central SD | Lockport |
| 167 | 691.4 | North Babylon UFSD | North Babylon |
| 168 | 691.5 | Roosevelt UFSD | Roosevelt |
| 169 | 691.8 | Rochester City SD | Rochester |
| 170 | 692.7 | Churchville-Chili Central SD | Churchville |
| 170 | 692.7 | Depew UFSD | Depew |
| 172 | 693.3 | Valley Central SD (Montgomery) | Montgomery |
| 173 | 695.8 | Garden City UFSD | Garden City |
| 174 | 698.3 | Beekmantown Central SD | West Chazy |
| 175 | 699.4 | Brewster Central SD | Brewster |
| 176 | 703.9 | Shenendehowa Central SD | Clifton Park |
| 177 | 704.2 | Longwood Central SD | Middle Island |
| 178 | 706.2 | Sachem Central SD | Holbrook |
| 179 | 710.0 | Ardsley UFSD | Ardsley |
| 180 | 712.5 | Evans-Brant Central SD (Lake Shore) | Angola |
| 181 | 712.7 | West Seneca Central SD | West Seneca |
| 182 | 715.0 | Island Trees UFSD | Levittown |
| 183 | 715.8 | Elmira City SD | Elmira |
| 184 | 716.7 | Ballston Spa Central SD | Ballston Spa |
| 185 | 717.2 | Arlington Central SD | Poughkeepsie |
| 186 | 720.4 | Wantagh UFSD | Wantagh |
| 187 | 720.5 | Oceanside UFSD | Oceanside |
| 188 | 726.3 | Peekskill City SD | Peekskill |
| 189 | 726.9 | Baldwinsville Central SD | Baldwinsville |
| 190 | 727.3 | Hempstead UFSD | Hempstead |
| 191 | 729.5 | Port Jervis City SD | Port Jervis |
| 192 | 736.6 | Johnson City Central SD | Johnson City |
| 193 | 737.2 | East Meadow UFSD | Westbury |
| 194 | 740.0 | Monroe-Woodbury Central SD | Central Valley |
| 195 | 741.3 | Amherst Central SD | Amherst |

*Note: This section only includes districts with 1,500 or more students; All categories are ranked from high to low*

| | | | |
|---|---|---|---|
| 196 | 743.3 | Goshen Central SD | Goshen |
| 197 | 744.0 | Union-Endicott Central SD | Endicott |
| 198 | 744.3 | Hamburg Central SD | Hamburg |
| 199 | 744.6 | Schenectady City SD | Schenectady |
| 200 | 746.3 | Phoenix Central SD | Phoenix |
| 201 | 747.4 | Elwood UFSD | Greenlawn |
| 202 | 750.8 | Connetquot Central SD | Bohemia |
| 203 | 753.4 | Indian River Central SD | Philadelphia |
| 204 | 754.7 | Hudson Falls Central SD | Fort Edward |
| 205 | 754.8 | Hauppauge UFSD | Hauppauge |
| 206 | 756.0 | Albion Central SD | Albion |
| 207 | 757.0 | Mattituck-Cutchogue UFSD | Cutchogue |
| 208 | 758.5 | Patchogue-Medford UFSD | Patchogue |
| 209 | 760.0 | Glens Falls City SD | Glens Falls |
| 210 | 760.3 | Cheektowaga-Maryvale UFSD | Cheektowaga |
| 211 | 762.0 | Blind Brook-Rye UFSD | Rye Brook |
| 212 | 763.0 | Bronxville UFSD | Bronxville |
| 213 | 765.0 | Newark Central SD | Newark |
| 214 | 765.5 | Akron Central SD | Akron |
| 215 | 766.3 | Nanuet UFSD | Nanuet |
| 216 | 766.7 | South Country Central SD | East Patchogue |
| 217 | 767.5 | Bay Shore UFSD | Bay Shore |
| 218 | 768.0 | Bethpage UFSD | Bethpage |
| 219 | 769.0 | General Brown Central SD | Dexter |
| 220 | 769.8 | Mohonasen Central SD | Schenectady |
| 221 | 770.5 | Liberty Central SD | Liberty |
| 222 | 772.7 | Webster Central SD | Webster |
| 223 | 772.8 | Clarkstown Central SD | New City |
| 224 | 773.5 | Ramapo Central SD (Suffern) | Hillburn |
| 225 | 776.3 | Manhasset UFSD | Manhasset |
| 226 | 783.5 | Hastings-on-Hudson UFSD | Hastings on Hdsn |
| 227 | 785.7 | Waterloo Central SD | Waterloo |
| 228 | 788.0 | Royalton-Hartland Central SD | Middleport |
| 229 | 788.5 | Salmon River Central SD | Fort Covington |
| 230 | 790.5 | Wayland-Cohocton Central SD | Wayland |
| 231 | 790.7 | Cheektowaga Central SD | Cheektowaga |
| 232 | 791.0 | Kings Park Central SD | Kings Park |
| 233 | 791.5 | Taconic Hills Central SD | Craryville |
| 234 | 792.8 | Lawrence UFSD | Lawrence |
| 235 | 795.7 | Newburgh City SD | Newburgh |
| 236 | 796.5 | Center Moriches UFSD | Center Moriches |
| 237 | 801.0 | Brockport Central SD | Brockport |
| 237 | 801.0 | Long Beach City SD | Long Beach |
| 239 | 802.0 | Attica Central SD | Attica |
| 240 | 802.7 | Riverhead Central SD | Riverhead |
| 241 | 804.0 | Floral Park-Bellerose UFSD | Floral Park |
| 242 | 804.9 | Lakeland Central SD | Shrub Oak |
| 243 | 808.2 | North Tonawanda City SD | North Tonawanda |
| 244 | 808.5 | Williamsville Central SD | East Amherst |
| 245 | 811.8 | North Syracuse Central SD | North Syracuse |
| 246 | 812.5 | Central Islip UFSD | Central Islip |
| 247 | 813.3 | Farmingdale UFSD | Farmingdale |
| 248 | 816.5 | Freeport UFSD | Freeport |
| 249 | 817.4 | Rocky Point UFSD | Rocky Point |
| 250 | 818.3 | Malone Central SD | Malone |
| 251 | 825.0 | Fredonia Central SD | Fredonia |
| 252 | 827.1 | Wappingers Central SD | Wappingers Fls |
| 253 | 836.2 | West Genesee Central SD | Camillus |
| 254 | 841.7 | Mamaroneck UFSD | Mamaroneck |
| 255 | 844.9 | Sewanhaka Central High SD | Floral Park |
| 256 | 845.2 | Port Chester-Rye UFSD | Port Chester |
| 257 | 847.2 | Levittown UFSD | Levittown |
| 258 | 848.5 | Gouverneur Central SD | Gouverneur |
| 259 | 850.2 | Clarence Central SD | Clarence Center |
| 260 | 851.3 | Lindenhurst UFSD | Lindenhurst |
| 261 | 855.9 | Pine Bush Central SD | Pine Bush |
| 262 | 856.6 | Warwick Valley Central SD | Warwick |
| 263 | 859.9 | South Huntington UFSD | Huntington Stn |
| 264 | 860.2 | Oswego City SD | Oswego |
| 265 | 862.8 | Westbury UFSD | Old Westbury |
| 266 | 867.2 | Yorkshire-Pioneer Central SD | Yorkshire |
| 267 | 869.3 | Brentwood UFSD | Brentwood |
| 268 | 869.7 | Mount Sinai UFSD | Mount Sinai |
| 269 | 877.2 | Deer Park UFSD | Deer Park |
| 270 | 879.8 | South Orangetown Central SD | Blauvelt |
| 271 | 880.0 | Harrison Central SD | Harrison |
| 272 | 887.7 | Frontier Central SD | Hamburg |
| 273 | 888.0 | Pearl River UFSD | Pearl River |
| 274 | 889.0 | Dryden Central SD | Dryden |
| 275 | 890.4 | Mount Vernon City SD | Mount Vernon |
| 276 | 897.0 | Schuylerville Central SD | Schuylerville |
| 277 | 902.5 | Hornell City SD | Hornell |
| 278 | 903.2 | Kinderhook Central SD | Valatie |
| 279 | 904.2 | Half Hollow Hills Central SD | Dix Hills |
| 280 | 909.0 | East Hampton UFSD | East Hampton |
| 281 | 911.8 | Hilton Central SD | Hilton |
| 282 | 916.0 | Harborfields Central SD | Greenlawn |
| 283 | 917.5 | Putnam Valley Central SD | Putnam Valley |
| 284 | 923.0 | Queensbury UFSD | Queensbury |
| 285 | 925.5 | North Rockland Central SD | Garnerville |
| 286 | 926.7 | Pelham UFSD | Pelham |
| 287 | 927.1 | Lackawanna City SD | Lackawanna |
| 288 | 932.6 | Copiague UFSD | Copiague |
| 289 | 939.8 | William Floyd UFSD | Mastic Beach |
| 290 | 942.0 | Amityville UFSD | Amityville |
| 291 | 947.2 | White Plains City SD | White Plains |
| 292 | 952.3 | Massena Central SD | Massena |
| 293 | 955.5 | Newfane Central SD | Burt |
| 294 | 956.0 | Chenango Valley Central SD | Binghamton |
| 295 | 966.7 | Middletown City SD | Middletown |
| 296 | 974.3 | Eastport-South Manor CSD | Manorville |
| 297 | 976.5 | Hudson City SD | Hudson |
| 298 | 980.0 | Broadalbin-Perth Central SD | Broadalbin |
| 299 | 982.0 | Carthage Central SD | Carthage |
| 300 | 1,010.0 | Troy City SD | Troy |
| 301 | 1,012.5 | Buffalo City SD | Buffalo |
| 302 | 1,018.0 | South Jefferson Central SD | Adams Center |
| 303 | 1,032.7 | Miller Place UFSD | Miller Place |
| 304 | 1,041.8 | Watertown City SD | Watertown |
| 305 | 1,070.5 | Wyandanch UFSD | Wyandanch |
| 306 | 1,075.3 | Monticello Central SD | Monticello |
| 307 | 1,077.3 | Victor Central SD | Victor |
| 308 | 1,081.7 | Three Village Central SD | Stony Brook |
| 309 | 1,085.0 | New Rochelle City SD | New Rochelle |
| 310 | 1,092.9 | Middle Country Central SD | Centereach |
| 311 | 1,111.7 | Sayville UFSD | Sayville |
| 312 | 1,112.5 | Ossining UFSD | Ossining |
| 313 | 1,113.9 | NYC Geographic District #23 | Brooklyn |
| 314 | 1,140.5 | Mexico Central SD | Mexico |
| 315 | 1,144.3 | Islip UFSD | Islip |
| 316 | 1,150.5 | Valley Stream Central High SD | Valley Stream |
| 317 | 1,154.5 | Lewiston-Porter Central SD | Youngstown |
| 318 | 1,159.0 | Brighton Central SD | Rochester |
| 319 | 1,217.2 | Bellmore-Merrick Central High SD | North Merrick |
| 320 | 1,219.0 | East Islip UFSD | Islip Terrace |
| 321 | 1,282.6 | NYC Geographic District # 1 | New York |
| 322 | 1,286.1 | Washingtonville Central SD | Washingtonville |
| 323 | 1,323.0 | Canandaigua City SD | Canandaigua |
| 324 | 1,326.5 | UFSD of the Tarrytowns | Sleepy Hollow |
| 325 | 1,338.3 | NYC Geographic District #16 | Brooklyn |
| 326 | 1,367.9 | NYC Geographic District #30 | Long Isl City |
| 327 | 1,384.4 | NYC Geographic District #15 | Brooklyn |
| 328 | 1,542.4 | NYC Geographic District #32 | Brooklyn |
| 329 | 1,577.0 | Dover UFSD | Dover Plains |
| 330 | 1,583.0 | Gloversville City SD | Gloversville |
| 331 | 1,607.0 | NYC Geographic District #19 | Brooklyn |
| 332 | 1,608.1 | NYC Geographic District # 7 | Bronx |
| 333 | 1,617.0 | Hannibal Central SD | Hannibal |
| 334 | 1,647.0 | Holland Patent Central SD | Holland Patent |
| 335 | 1,652.0 | Ilion Central SD | Ilion |
| 336 | 1,667.2 | NYC Geographic District # 2 | New York |
| 337 | 1,724.0 | Waverly Central SD | Waverly |
| 338 | 1,745.5 | Wallkill Central SD | Wallkill |
| 339 | 1,748.0 | Baldwin UFSD | Baldwin |
| 340 | 1,759.0 | Bath Central SD | Bath |
| 341 | 1,772.5 | Rockville Ctr UFSD | Rockville Ctr |
| 342 | 1,807.0 | Susquehanna Valley Central SD | Conklin |
| 343 | 1,812.6 | NYC Geographic District # 4 | New York |
| 344 | 1,815.8 | Niagara Falls City SD | Niagara Falls |
| 345 | 1,828.8 | NYC Geographic District #22 | Brooklyn |
| 346 | 1,855.5 | NYC Geographic District #10 | Bronx |
| 347 | 1,885.4 | NYC Geographic District #14 | Brooklyn |
| 348 | 1,911.0 | Johnstown City SD | Johnstown |
| 349 | 1,913.0 | NYC Geographic District # 5 | New York |
| 350 | 1,957.8 | NYC Geographic District #13 | Brooklyn |
| 351 | 1,970.7 | NYC Geographic District #26 | Bayside |
| 352 | 1,994.8 | NYC Geographic District #28 | Jamaica |
| 353 | 1,999.0 | Dunkirk City SD | Dunkirk |
| 354 | 2,035.8 | New York City Public Schools | New York |
| 355 | 2,044.8 | Mahopac Central SD | Mahopac |
| 356 | 2,096.9 | NYC Geographic District # 3 | New York |
| 357 | 2,111.2 | NYC Geographic District #17 | Brooklyn |
| 358 | 2,125.5 | NYC Geographic District #29 | Rosedale |
| 359 | 2,198.0 | NYC Geographic District #24 | Ridgewood |
| 360 | 2,222.5 | Huntington UFSD | Huntington Stn |
| 361 | 2,277.5 | NYC Geographic District # 6 | New York |
| 362 | 2,315.0 | Carmel Central SD | Patterson |
| 363 | 2,332.3 | Yonkers City SD | Yonkers |
| 364 | 2,339.5 | NYC Geographic District # 8 | Bronx |
| 365 | 2,352.6 | NYC Geographic District #25 | Flushing |
| 366 | 2,359.2 | NYC Geographic District #20 | Brooklyn |
| 367 | 2,391.1 | NYC Geographic District #21 | Brooklyn |
| 368 | 2,404.7 | NYC Geographic District #27 | Ozone Park |
| 369 | 2,424.5 | NYC Geographic District # 9 | Bronx |
| 370 | 2,426.0 | Lansingburgh Central SD | Troy |
| 371 | 2,536.1 | NYC Geographic District #12 | Bronx |
| 372 | 2,934.4 | NYC Geographic District #31 | Staten Island |
| 373 | 2,936.9 | West Irondequoit Central SD | Rochester |
| 374 | 3,124.3 | NYC Geographic District #18 | Brooklyn |
| 375 | 3,645.2 | NYC Special Schools - District 75 | New York |
| 376 | 4,054.7 | NYC Geographic District #11 | Bronx |
| 377 | 4,974.0 | Port Washington UFSD | Port Washington |
| n/a | n/a | Charter School for Applied Tech | Buffalo |
| n/a | n/a | Medina Central SD | Medina |
| n/a | n/a | Minisink Valley Central SD | Slate Hill |
| n/a | n/a | Plainview-Old Bethpage Central SD | Plainview |
| n/a | n/a | Skaneateles Central SD | Skaneateles |
| n/a | n/a | Windsor Central SD | Windsor |

## Student/Counselor Ratio

(number of students per counselor)

| Rank | Number | District Name | City |
|---|---|---|---|
| 1 | 180.5 | NYC Special Schools - District 75 | New York |
| 2 | 181.8 | East Hampton UFSD | East Hampton |
| 3 | 188.6 | Oneonta City SD | Oneonta |
| 4 | 192.6 | Liberty Central SD | Liberty |
| 5 | 193.0 | Rondout Valley Central SD | Accord |
| 6 | 198.8 | Southampton UFSD | Southampton |
| 7 | 200.6 | Hornell City SD | Hornell |
| 8 | 206.4 | Wayne Central SD | Ontario Center |
| 9 | 207.8 | Depew UFSD | Depew |
| 10 | 212.1 | Gouverneur Central SD | Gouverneur |
| 11 | 215.1 | Waterloo Central SD | Waterloo |
| 12 | 220.9 | Batavia City SD | Batavia |
| 13 | 221.2 | Sewanhaka Central High SD | Floral Park |
| 14 | 224.3 | Schuylerville Central SD | Schuylerville |
| 15 | 224.8 | East Williston UFSD | Old Westbury |
| 16 | 232.3 | Bellmore-Merrick Central High SD | North Merrick |
| 17 | 235.2 | Dunkirk City SD | Dunkirk |
| 18 | 235.5 | Evans-Brant Central SD (Lake Shore) | Angola |
| 19 | 236.0 | Valley Stream Central High SD | Valley Stream |
| 20 | 236.7 | Ardsley UFSD | Ardsley |
| 21 | 241.7 | Norwich City SD | Norwich |
| 22 | 242.1 | Windsor Central SD | Windsor |
| 23 | 244.6 | Vestal Central SD | Vestal |
| 24 | 245.6 | Geneva City SD | Geneva |
| 25 | 248.4 | Dansville Central SD | Dansville |
| 26 | 252.1 | Plattsburgh City SD | Plattsburgh |
| 27 | 252.6 | Olean City SD | Olean |
| 28 | 254.0 | Blind Brook-Rye UFSD | Rye Brook |
| 29 | 254.3 | Bronxville UFSD | Bronxville |
| 30 | 255.8 | Jamestown City SD | Jamestown |
| 31 | 258.8 | Ravena-Coeymans-Selkirk Ctrl SD | Selkirk |
| 31 | 258.8 | Southwestern CSD at Jamestown | Jamestown |
| 33 | 262.8 | Salmon River Central SD | Fort Covington |
| 34 | 263.9 | Hudson City SD | Hudson |
| 35 | 269.3 | Troy City SD | Troy |
| 36 | 270.9 | Solvay UFSD | Solvay |
| 37 | 271.1 | East Syracuse-Minoa Central SD | East Syracuse |
| 38 | 272.1 | Massena Central SD | Massena |
| 39 | 272.8 | Malone Central SD | Malone |
| 40 | 273.6 | Elmira City SD | Elmira |
| 41 | 274.5 | Penfield Central SD | Rochester |
| 42 | 274.8 | Westhampton Bch UFSD | Westhampton Bch |
| 43 | 275.7 | Rome City SD | Rome |
| 44 | 277.3 | Briarcliff Mnr UFSD | Briarcliff Mnr |
| 45 | 281.3 | Valhalla UFSD | Valhalla |
| 46 | 282.4 | Mount Pleasant Central SD | Thornwood |
| 47 | 283.2 | Plainview-Old Bethpage Central SD | Plainview |
| 48 | 283.5 | Albion Central SD | Albion |
| 49 | 283.9 | Kinderhook Central SD | Valatie |
| 50 | 286.0 | Island Trees UFSD | Levittown |
| 50 | 286.0 | Penn Yan Central SD | Penn Yan |
| 52 | 289.3 | Beekmantown Central SD | West Chazy |
| 53 | 290.7 | Cobleskill-Richmondville Central SD | Cobleskill |
| 54 | 294.7 | Brighton Central SD | Rochester |
| 55 | 296.3 | Dryden Central SD | Dryden |
| 56 | 297.1 | Chittenango Central SD | Chittenango |
| 57 | 297.6 | Chappaqua Central SD | Chappaqua |
| 58 | 299.7 | Springville-Griffith Institute CSD | Springville |
| 59 | 300.4 | North Colonie Central SD | Latham |
| 60 | 301.0 | Corning City SD | Painted Post |
| 61 | 301.8 | Mineola UFSD | Mineola |

*Note: This section only includes districts with 1,500 or more students; All categories are ranked from high to low*

| | | | |
|---|---|---|---|
| 62 | 302.6 | Niagara Falls City SD | Niagara Falls |
| 63 | 303.0 | Greece Central SD | Rochester |
| 64 | 303.6 | Sherburne-Earlville Central SD | Sherburne |
| 65 | 305.5 | Phelps-Clifton Springs Central SD | Clifton Springs |
| 66 | 305.9 | Fayetteville-Manlius Central SD | Manlius |
| 67 | 306.0 | Newark Central SD | Newark |
| 68 | 306.6 | Saranac Central SD | Dannemora |
| 69 | 307.5 | Hewlett-Woodmere UFSD | Woodmere |
| 70 | 308.1 | Westbury UFSD | Old Westbury |
| 71 | 308.7 | Sweet Home Central SD | Amherst |
| 72 | 309.4 | Roslyn UFSD | Roslyn |
| 73 | 310.2 | Irvington UFSD | Irvington |
| 74 | 312.8 | Bayport-Blue Point UFSD | Bayport |
| 75 | 313.4 | Hastings-on-Hudson UFSD | Hastings on Hdsn |
| 76 | 313.8 | Kenmore-Tonawanda UFSD | Buffalo |
| 77 | 314.0 | Westhill Central SD | Syracuse |
| 78 | 315.3 | East Irondequoit Central SD | Rochester |
| 79 | 316.2 | Wayland-Cohocton Central SD | Wayland |
| 80 | 316.7 | Northport-East Northport UFSD | Northport |
| 81 | 317.1 | Lynbrook UFSD | Lynbrook |
| 82 | 317.5 | Pittsford Central SD | Pittsford |
| 83 | 318.6 | Camden Central SD | Camden |
| 84 | 318.7 | Jamesville-Dewitt Central SD | Dewitt |
| 85 | 319.2 | Livonia Central SD | Livonia |
| 86 | 319.8 | Peru Central SD | Peru |
| 87 | 320.7 | Mohonasen Central SD | Schenectady |
| 88 | 321.4 | Spencerport Central SD | Spencerport |
| 89 | 322.3 | Katonah-Lewisboro UFSD | South Salem |
| 90 | 322.5 | Port Jervis City SD | Port Jervis |
| 91 | 322.6 | Monticello Central SD | Monticello |
| 92 | 322.8 | Honeoye Falls-Lima Central SD | Honeoye Falls |
| 93 | 325.0 | Liverpool Central SD | Liverpool |
| 94 | 325.7 | Glens Falls City SD | Glens Falls |
| 95 | 326.4 | West Hempstead UFSD | West Hempstead |
| 96 | 329.4 | Holland Patent Central SD | Holland Patent |
| 96 | 329.4 | Spackenkill UFSD | Poughkeepsie |
| 98 | 331.9 | Center Moriches UFSD | Center Moriches |
| 99 | 332.4 | Oyster Bay-East Norwich Central SD | Oyster Bay |
| 100 | 333.0 | Great Neck UFSD | Great Neck |
| 101 | 333.5 | Canandaigua City SD | Canandaigua |
| 102 | 333.8 | Brockport Central SD | Brockport |
| 103 | 334.0 | Cazenovia Central SD | Cazenovia |
| 104 | 335.6 | Queensbury UFSD | Queensbury |
| 105 | 337.6 | Hendrick Hudson Central SD | Montrose |
| 106 | 337.7 | Glen Cove City SD | Glen Cove |
| 107 | 339.3 | South Jefferson Central SD | Adams Center |
| 108 | 339.5 | Palmyra-Macedon Central SD | Palmyra |
| 109 | 339.6 | Pleasantville UFSD | Pleasantville |
| 110 | 339.7 | Hauppauge UFSD | Hauppauge |
| 111 | 340.0 | Malverne UFSD | Malverne |
| 112 | 343.5 | NYC Geographic District #16 | Brooklyn |
| 113 | 343.8 | Freeport UFSD | Freeport |
| 114 | 344.6 | Starpoint Central SD | Lockport |
| 114 | 344.6 | Williamsville Central SD | East Amherst |
| 116 | 347.5 | Pelham UFSD | Pelham |
| 117 | 348.4 | West Genesee Central SD | Camillus |
| 118 | 349.1 | Niskayuna Central SD | Schenectady |
| 119 | 349.4 | Byram Hills Central SD | Armonk |
| 120 | 349.8 | Croton-Harmon UFSD | Croton on Hdsn |
| 120 | 349.8 | Gates-Chili Central SD | Rochester |
| 122 | 351.9 | Shenendehowa Central SD | Clifton Park |
| 123 | 352.2 | Niagara-Wheatfield Central SD | Niagara Falls |
| 124 | 353.3 | Amityville UFSD | Amityville |
| 125 | 353.9 | Eastchester UFSD | Eastchester |
| 126 | 356.2 | Middletown City SD | Middletown |
| 127 | 357.7 | Lakeland Central SD | Shrub Oak |
| 128 | 358.5 | Half Hollow Hills Central SD | Dix Hills |
| 129 | 358.8 | Hamburg Central SD | Hamburg |
| 130 | 360.7 | Mamaroneck UFSD | Mamaroneck |
| 131 | 361.4 | Babylon UFSD | Babylon |
| 131 | 361.4 | Susquehanna Valley Central SD | Conklin |
| 133 | 364.1 | Long Beach City SD | Long Beach |
| 134 | 364.4 | Ellenville Central SD | Ellenville |
| 135 | 368.0 | NYC Geographic District # 7 | Bronx |
| 136 | 368.5 | Locust Valley Central SD | Locust Valley |
| 137 | 368.9 | East Ramapo Central SD | Spring Valley |
| 138 | 371.8 | Red Hook Central SD | Red Hook |
| 139 | 372.5 | Gloversville City SD | Gloversville |
| 140 | 373.1 | Rush-Henrietta Central SD | Henrietta |
| 141 | 373.2 | Phoenix Central SD | Phoenix |
| 142 | 374.2 | Nyack UFSD | Nyack |
| 143 | 376.7 | Amsterdam City SD | Amsterdam |
| 144 | 377.7 | East Aurora UFSD | East Aurora |
| 145 | 378.7 | Manhasset UFSD | Manhasset |
| 146 | 379.9 | Hilton Central SD | Hilton |
| 147 | 380.2 | Somers Central SD | Somers |
| 148 | 380.6 | Oceanside UFSD | Oceanside |
| 149 | 381.3 | Levittown UFSD | Levittown |
| 150 | 381.4 | Islip UFSD | Islip |
| 151 | 381.6 | Cornwall Central SD | Cornwall on Hdsn |
| 152 | 382.4 | Bath Central SD | Bath |
| 153 | 382.8 | Akron Central SD | Akron |
| 154 | 383.2 | Nanuet UFSD | Nanuet |
| 155 | 384.0 | Bethpage UFSD | Bethpage |
| 156 | 384.2 | Tonawanda City SD | Tonawanda |
| 157 | 384.5 | General Brown Central SD | Dexter |
| 158 | 384.8 | Lewiston-Porter Central SD | Youngstown |
| 159 | 385.5 | Coxsackie-Athens Central SD | Coxsackie |
| 160 | 386.5 | Lawrence UFSD | Lawrence |
| 161 | 386.9 | Rye City SD | Rye |
| 162 | 387.3 | North Shore Central SD | Sea Cliff |
| 163 | 387.5 | NYC Geographic District # 2 | New York |
| 164 | 388.0 | East Meadow UFSD | Westbury |
| 164 | 388.0 | Edgemont UFSD | Scarsdale |
| 166 | 388.2 | White Plains City SD | White Plains |
| 167 | 388.6 | Brewster Central SD | Brewster |
| 167 | 388.6 | Copiague UFSD | Copiague |
| 169 | 389.4 | Warwick Valley Central SD | Warwick |
| 170 | 391.1 | Harrison Central SD | Harrison |
| 171 | 391.3 | New Hartford Central SD | New Hartford |
| 172 | 391.4 | NYC Geographic District # 1 | New York |
| 173 | 392.1 | Scotia-Glenville Central SD | Scotia |
| 174 | 393.1 | Onteora Central SD | Boiceville |
| 175 | 393.2 | Scarsdale UFSD | Scarsdale |
| 176 | 393.5 | Bethlehem Central SD | Delmar |
| 177 | 393.9 | Rockville Ctr UFSD | Rockville Ctr |
| 178 | 394.0 | Royalton-Hartland Central SD | Middleport |
| 179 | 394.3 | Dover UFSD | Dover Plains |
| 180 | 394.6 | Schalmont Central SD | Schenectady |
| 181 | 395.8 | Taconic Hills Central SD | Craryville |
| 182 | 396.5 | Bedford Central SD | Bedford |
| 183 | 397.6 | Marcellus Central SD | Marcellus |
| 184 | 398.5 | Three Village Central SD | Stony Brook |
| 185 | 401.4 | Mount Sinai UFSD | Mount Sinai |
| 186 | 401.6 | Arlington Central SD | Poughkeepsie |
| 187 | 403.6 | Cold Spring Hrbr Central SD | Cold Spring Hrbr |
| 188 | 404.4 | Herricks UFSD | New Hyde Park |
| 189 | 404.5 | Ossining UFSD | Ossining |
| 190 | 406.7 | South Huntington UFSD | Huntington Stn |
| 191 | 406.9 | Clarkstown Central SD | New City |
| 192 | 408.3 | S Glens Fls Central SD | S Glens Fls |
| 193 | 410.2 | Marlboro Central SD | Marlboro |
| 194 | 411.1 | Bay Shore UFSD | Bay Shore |
| 195 | 412.5 | Fredonia Central SD | Fredonia |
| 196 | 414.0 | Wantagh UFSD | Wantagh |
| 197 | 414.2 | Longwood Central SD | Middle Island |
| 197 | 414.2 | Rochester City SD | Rochester |
| 199 | 414.7 | Mexico Central SD | Mexico |
| 199 | 414.7 | Yorktown Central SD | Yorktown Hgts |
| 201 | 416.6 | Syosset Central SD | Syosset |
| 202 | 418.6 | Indian River Central SD | Philadelphia |
| 203 | 419.2 | Yorkshire-Pioneer Central SD | Yorkshire |
| 204 | 419.5 | Baldwin UFSD | Baldwin |
| 205 | 420.9 | Averill Park Central SD | Averill Park |
| 205 | 420.9 | Carmel Central SD | Patterson |
| 205 | 420.9 | Washingtonville Central SD | Washingtonville |
| 208 | 422.9 | NYC Geographic District #17 | Brooklyn |
| 209 | 424.7 | Goshen Central SD | Goshen |
| 210 | 425.1 | NYC Geographic District #18 | Brooklyn |
| 211 | 425.8 | Chenango Forks Central SD | Binghamton |
| 212 | 426.0 | Mahopac Central SD | Mahopac |
| 213 | 426.2 | Commack UFSD | East Northport |
| 214 | 427.8 | Homer Central SD | Homer |
| 215 | 428.2 | Wyandanch UFSD | Wyandanch |
| 216 | 429.1 | Rocky Point UFSD | Rocky Point |
| 217 | 429.6 | Plainedge UFSD | N Massapequa |
| 218 | 430.1 | NYC Geographic District #14 | Brooklyn |
| 218 | 430.1 | Oswego City SD | Oswego |
| 220 | 432.3 | Maine-Endwell Central SD | Endwell |
| 221 | 432.6 | Horseheads Central SD | Horseheads |
| 222 | 432.7 | Lackawanna City SD | Lackawanna |
| 223 | 432.9 | Churchville-Chili Central SD | Churchville |
| 224 | 434.1 | Sachem Central SD | Holbrook |
| 225 | 434.7 | Brentwood UFSD | Brentwood |
| 226 | 435.7 | Farmingdale UFSD | Farmingdale |
| 227 | 436.9 | Ithaca City SD | Ithaca |
| 228 | 437.8 | Auburn City SD | Auburn |
| 229 | 438.6 | Deer Park UFSD | Deer Park |
| 230 | 439.2 | Iroquois Central SD | Elma |
| 231 | 440.0 | Cohoes City SD | Cohoes |
| 231 | 440.0 | Union-Endicott Central SD | Endicott |
| 233 | 440.6 | Canastota Central SD | Canastota |
| 234 | 441.4 | Whitesboro Central SD | Yorkville |
| 235 | 442.0 | Jericho UFSD | Jericho |
| 236 | 444.0 | Pearl River UFSD | Pearl River |
| 237 | 446.2 | NYC Geographic District #10 | Bronx |
| 238 | 446.3 | Ramapo Central SD (Suffern) | Hillburn |
| 239 | 446.4 | NYC Geographic District # 5 | New York |
| 240 | 446.5 | Greenburgh Central SD | Hartsdale |
| 241 | 447.8 | Binghamton City SD | Binghamton |
| 242 | 449.0 | Catskill Central SD | Catskill |
| 242 | 449.0 | North Tonawanda City SD | North Tonawanda |
| 244 | 449.5 | NYC Geographic District #11 | Bronx |
| 245 | 450.8 | Port Chester-Rye UFSD | Port Chester |
| 246 | 452.1 | New Rochelle City SD | New Rochelle |
| 247 | 452.8 | Hudson Falls Central SD | Fort Edward |
| 248 | 454.1 | Uniondale UFSD | Uniondale |
| 249 | 456.2 | Cheektowaga-Maryvale UFSD | Cheektowaga |
| 250 | 457.3 | Grand Island Central SD | Grand Island |
| 251 | 457.4 | Ballston Spa Central SD | Ballston Spa |
| 252 | 458.0 | New Paltz Central SD | New Paltz |
| 253 | 458.4 | Seaford UFSD | Seaford |
| 254 | 458.8 | Putnam Valley Central SD | Putnam Valley |
| 255 | 460.8 | Pine Bush Central SD | Pine Bush |
| 256 | 461.0 | Roosevelt UFSD | Roosevelt |
| 257 | 463.4 | Central Square Central SD | Central Square |
| 258 | 467.4 | Massapequa UFSD | Massapequa |
| 259 | 468.7 | Johnson City Central SD | Johnson City |
| 260 | 469.5 | Utica City SD | Utica |
| 261 | 471.7 | Syracuse City SD | Syracuse |
| 262 | 471.9 | Orchard Park Central SD | Orchard Park |
| 263 | 472.0 | Webster Central SD | Webster |
| 264 | 473.8 | North Rockland Central SD | Garnerville |
| 265 | 473.9 | Fairport Central SD | Fairport |
| 266 | 474.4 | Cheektowaga Central SD | Cheektowaga |
| 267 | 474.7 | Kingston City SD | Kingston |
| 268 | 476.0 | Medina Central SD | Medina |
| 269 | 476.4 | Sayville UFSD | Sayville |
| 270 | 477.3 | Owego-Apalachin Central SD | Owego |
| 271 | 477.8 | Johnstown City SD | Johnstown |
| 271 | 477.8 | Newfane Central SD | Burt |
| 273 | 478.0 | Chenango Valley Central SD | Binghamton |
| 274 | 478.5 | Lockport City SD | Lockport |
| 275 | 479.0 | South Colonie Central SD | Albany |
| 276 | 479.5 | Guilderland Central SD | Guilderland |
| 277 | 479.9 | North Syracuse Central SD | North Syracuse |
| 278 | 480.6 | Baldwinsville Central SD | Baldwinsville |
| 279 | 482.0 | NYC Geographic District #32 | Brooklyn |
| 280 | 482.3 | Highland Central SD | Highland |
| 281 | 482.6 | Connetquot Central SD | Bohemia |
| 282 | 482.7 | Burnt Hills-Ballston Lake CSD | Scotia |
| 283 | 483.2 | Beacon City SD | Beacon |
| 284 | 484.2 | Peekskill City SD | Peekskill |
| 285 | 485.4 | Eden Central SD | Eden |
| 286 | 485.8 | Clarence Central SD | Clarence Center |
| 287 | 487.1 | Eastport-South Manor CSD | Manorville |
| 288 | 489.4 | NYC Geographic District #13 | Brooklyn |
| 289 | 489.9 | NYC Geographic District #19 | Brooklyn |
| 290 | 492.5 | Cortland City SD | Cortland |
| 291 | 493.1 | NYC Geographic District # 9 | Bronx |
| 292 | 495.3 | NYC Geographic District #25 | Flushing |
| 293 | 495.5 | Albany City SD | Albany |
| 293 | 495.5 | West Islip UFSD | West Islip |
| 295 | 495.8 | NYC Geographic District # 3 | New York |
| 296 | 496.8 | Middle Country Central SD | Centereach |
| 297 | 497.6 | East Islip UFSD | Islip Terrace |
| 298 | 498.7 | Wallkill Central SD | Wallkill |
| 299 | 502.7 | South Orangetown Central SD | Blauvelt |
| 300 | 504.7 | Mattituck-Cutchogue UFSD | Cutchogue |
| 301 | 506.5 | New York City Public Schools | New York |
| 302 | 506.9 | Riverhead Central SD | Riverhead |
| 303 | 509.3 | East Greenbush Central SD | East Greenbush |
| 304 | 512.3 | Buffalo City SD | Buffalo |
| 305 | 512.7 | Wappingers Central SD | Wappingers Fls |
| 306 | 514.5 | Hyde Park Central SD | Hyde Park |
| 307 | 516.3 | Miller Place UFSD | Miller Place |
| 308 | 517.1 | Frontier Central SD | Hamburg |
| 309 | 517.2 | Smithtown Central SD | Smithtown |
| 310 | 518.0 | Jordan-Elbridge Central SD | Elbridge |
| 311 | 521.9 | Garden City UFSD | Garden City |
| 312 | 522.1 | William Floyd UFSD | Mastic Beach |
| 313 | 523.2 | Elwood UFSD | Greenlawn |
| 314 | 523.3 | Cheektowaga-Sloan UFSD | Sloan |
| 315 | 523.4 | Harborfields Central SD | Greenlawn |
| 316 | 526.1 | Fulton City SD | Fulton |

*Note: This section only includes districts with 1,500 or more students; All categories are ranked from high to low*

| | | | |
|---|---|---|---|
| 317 | 527.3 | NYC Geographic District #28 | Jamaica |
| 318 | 528.4 | Comsewogue School District | Port Jeff Stn |
| 319 | 528.6 | Monroe-Woodbury Central SD | Central Valley |
| 320 | 532.9 | Ilion Central SD | Ilion |
| 321 | 537.8 | North Babylon UFSD | North Babylon |
| 322 | 538.4 | Shoreham-Wading River Central SD | Shoreham |
| 323 | 539.1 | Lansingburgh Central SD | Troy |
| 324 | 539.2 | Valley Central SD (Montgomery) | Montgomery |
| 325 | 541.7 | Central Islip UFSD | Central Islip |
| 326 | 542.3 | NYC Geographic District # 8 | Bronx |
| 327 | 544.8 | Lindenhurst UFSD | Lindenhurst |
| 328 | 548.8 | Hempstead UFSD | Hempstead |
| 329 | 549.3 | Kings Park Central SD | Kings Park |
| 330 | 550.2 | Schenectady City SD | Schenectady |
| 331 | 560.5 | West Babylon UFSD | West Babylon |
| 332 | 562.1 | NYC Geographic District #15 | Brooklyn |
| 333 | 567.3 | Saratoga Spgs City SD | Saratoga Spgs |
| 334 | 568.7 | NYC Geographic District # 4 | New York |
| 335 | 574.5 | Mount Vernon City SD | Mount Vernon |
| 336 | 575.8 | West Seneca Central SD | West Seneca |
| 337 | 577.5 | Hannibal Central SD | Hannibal |
| 338 | 582.3 | NYC Geographic District #12 | Bronx |
| 338 | 582.3 | Ogdensburg City SD | Ogdensburg |
| 338 | 582.3 | Victor Central SD | Victor |
| 341 | 588.3 | NYC Geographic District #30 | Long Isl City |
| 342 | 588.8 | NYC Geographic District #27 | Ozone Park |
| 343 | 594.0 | NYC Geographic District #21 | Brooklyn |
| 344 | 595.3 | Watertown City SD | Watertown |
| 345 | 607.2 | Hicksville UFSD | Hicksville |
| 346 | 607.5 | Oneida City SD | Oneida |
| 347 | 607.7 | NYC Geographic District # 6 | New York |
| 348 | 616.6 | Saugerties Central SD | Saugerties |
| 349 | 621.8 | Port Washington UFSD | Port Washington |
| 350 | 626.3 | Lancaster Central SD | Lancaster |
| 351 | 628.4 | NYC Geographic District #23 | Brooklyn |
| 352 | 634.8 | NYC Geographic District #22 | Brooklyn |
| 353 | 642.9 | Poughkeepsie City SD | Poughkeepsie |
| 354 | 644.6 | Amherst Central SD | Amherst |
| 355 | 651.6 | NYC Geographic District #24 | Ridgewood |
| 356 | 659.2 | NYC Geographic District #26 | Bayside |
| 357 | 661.0 | Carthage Central SD | Carthage |
| 358 | 663.3 | UFSD of the Tarrytowns | Sleepy Hollow |
| 359 | 671.9 | Newburgh City SD | Newburgh |
| 360 | 682.5 | Vernon-Verona-Sherrill Central SD | Verona |
| 361 | 689.1 | NYC Geographic District #29 | Rosedale |
| 362 | 704.2 | NYC Geographic District #20 | Brooklyn |
| 363 | 757.2 | Minisink Valley Central SD | Slate Hill |
| 364 | 766.7 | South Country Central SD | East Patchogue |
| 365 | 779.2 | Patchogue-Medford UFSD | Patchogue |
| 366 | 788.6 | NYC Geographic District #31 | Staten Island |
| 367 | 802.0 | Attica Central SD | Attica |
| 368 | 832.0 | Skaneateles Central SD | Skaneateles |
| 369 | 862.0 | Waverly Central SD | Waverly |
| 370 | 958.0 | Hampton Bays UFSD | Hampton Bays |
| 371 | 959.8 | Yonkers City SD | Yonkers |
| 372 | 980.0 | Broadalbin-Perth Central SD | Broadalbin |
| 373 | 1,111.3 | Huntington UFSD | Huntington Stn |
| 374 | 1,695.5 | Alden Central SD | Alden |
| 375 | 4,772.5 | West Irondequoit Central SD | Rochester |
| n/a | n/a | Charter School for Applied Tech | Buffalo |
| n/a | n/a | Elmont UFSD | Elmont |
| n/a | n/a | Floral Park-Bellerose UFSD | Floral Park |
| n/a | n/a | Franklin Square UFSD | Franklin Square |
| n/a | n/a | Merrick UFSD | Merrick |
| n/a | n/a | New Hyde Pk-Garden City Pk UFSD | New Hyde Park |
| n/a | n/a | North Bellmore UFSD | Bellmore |
| n/a | n/a | Valley Stream 13 UFSD | Valley Stream |

## Current Expenditures per Student

| Rank | Dollars | District Name | City |
|---|---|---|---|
| 1 | 29,085 | Lawrence UFSD | Lawrence |
| 2 | 28,458 | Jericho UFSD | Jericho |
| 3 | 28,083 | Southampton UFSD | Southampton |
| 4 | 27,849 | Greenburgh Central SD | Hartsdale |
| 5 | 26,688 | Wyandanch UFSD | Wyandanch |
| 6 | 26,552 | East Hampton UFSD | East Hampton |
| 7 | 26,384 | Mineola UFSD | Mineola |
| 8 | 26,145 | Locust Valley Central SD | Locust Valley |
| 9 | 26,094 | Oyster Bay-East Norwich Central SD | Oyster Bay |
| 10 | 26,070 | Harrison Central SD | Harrison |
| 11 | 25,918 | Great Neck UFSD | Great Neck |
| 12 | 25,772 | North Shore Central SD | Sea Cliff |
| 13 | 25,748 | East Ramapo Central SD | Spring Valley |
| 14 | 25,183 | Briarcliff Mnr UFSD | Briarcliff Mnr |
| 15 | 24,828 | Long Beach City SD | Long Beach |
| 16 | 24,640 | Hewlett-Woodmere UFSD | Woodmere |
| 17 | 24,575 | Bronxville UFSD | Bronxville |
| 18 | 24,507 | Central Islip UFSD | Central Islip |
| 19 | 24,475 | Onteora Central SD | Boiceville |
| 20 | 24,447 | Manhasset UFSD | Manhasset |
| 21 | 24,301 | Valhalla UFSD | Valhalla |
| 22 | 24,203 | White Plains City SD | White Plains |
| 23 | 24,042 | Roslyn UFSD | Roslyn |
| 24 | 23,976 | Hempstead UFSD | Hempstead |
| 25 | 23,972 | Syosset Central SD | Syosset |
| 26 | 23,951 | Bedford Central SD | Bedford |
| 27 | 23,884 | Katonah-Lewisboro UFSD | South Salem |
| 28 | 23,494 | East Williston UFSD | Old Westbury |
| 29 | 23,459 | Malverne UFSD | Malverne |
| 30 | 23,238 | Amityville UFSD | Amityville |
| 31 | 23,173 | Peekskill City SD | Peekskill |
| 32 | 23,137 | Huntington UFSD | Huntington Stn |
| 33 | 22,869 | Scarsdale UFSD | Scarsdale |
| 34 | 22,814 | Port Washington UFSD | Port Washington |
| 35 | 22,765 | Uniondale UFSD | Uniondale |
| 36 | 22,578 | Mount Pleasant Central SD | Thornwood |
| 37 | 22,526 | Westbury UFSD | Old Westbury |
| 38 | 22,301 | Hendrick Hudson Central SD | Montrose |
| 39 | 22,294 | Chappaqua Central SD | Chappaqua |
| 40 | 22,153 | Nanuet UFSD | Nanuet |
| 41 | 22,110 | Cold Spring Hrbr Central SD | Cold Spring Hrbr |
| 42 | 22,022 | Rockville Ctr UFSD | Rockville Ctr |
| 43 | 21,997 | Roosevelt UFSD | Roosevelt |
| 44 | 21,866 | Byram Hills Central SD | Armonk |
| 45 | 21,769 | Plainview-Old Bethpage Central SD | Plainview |
| 46 | 21,764 | Hastings-on-Hudson UFSD | Hastings on Hdsn |
| 47 | 21,707 | Ardsley UFSD | Ardsley |
| 48 | 21,578 | Herricks UFSD | New Hyde Park |
| 49 | 21,564 | Irvington UFSD | Irvington |
| 50 | 21,525 | Westhampton Bch UFSD | Westhampton Bch |
| 51 | 21,465 | UFSD of the Tarrytowns | Sleepy Hollow |
| 52 | 21,294 | Ossining UFSD | Ossining |
| 53 | 21,270 | Nyack UFSD | Nyack |
| 54 | 21,100 | Brewster Central SD | Brewster |
| 55 | 21,082 | Liberty Central SD | Liberty |
| 56 | 21,060 | Ramapo Central SD (Suffern) | Hillburn |
| 57 | 20,856 | Levittown UFSD | Levittown |
| 58 | 20,847 | Albany City SD | Albany |
| 59 | 20,724 | Mamaroneck UFSD | Mamaroneck |
| 60 | 20,695 | West Hempstead UFSD | West Hempstead |
| 61 | 20,679 | Riverhead Central SD | Riverhead |
| 62 | 20,608 | Blind Brook-Rye UFSD | Rye Brook |
| 63 | 20,532 | Eastchester UFSD | Eastchester |
| 64 | 20,462 | Ellenville Central SD | Ellenville |
| 65 | 20,449 | Bay Shore UFSD | Bay Shore |
| 66 | 20,375 | Glen Cove City SD | Glen Cove |
| 67 | 20,269 | Rondout Valley Central SD | Accord |
| 68 | 20,210 | South Huntington UFSD | Huntington Stn |
| 69 | 20,150 | Somers Central SD | Somers |
| 70 | 20,089 | Copiague UFSD | Copiague |
| 71 | 20,051 | Farmingdale UFSD | Farmingdale |
| 72 | 19,932 | Center Moriches UFSD | Center Moriches |
| 72 | 19,932 | Edgemont UFSD | Scarsdale |
| 74 | 19,871 | Sayville UFSD | Sayville |
| 75 | 19,841 | Carmel Central SD | Patterson |
| 76 | 19,837 | Troy City SD | Troy |
| 77 | 19,827 | North Rockland Central SD | Garnerville |
| 78 | 19,767 | Lakeland Central SD | Shrub Oak |
| 79 | 19,711 | Bethpage UFSD | Bethpage |
| 80 | 19,682 | Rye City SD | Rye |
| 81 | 19,632 | Salmon River Central SD | Fort Covington |
| 82 | 19,608 | Putnam Valley Central SD | Putnam Valley |
| 83 | 19,600 | Northport-East Northport UFSD | Northport |
| 84 | 19,587 | South Orangetown Central SD | Blauvelt |
| 85 | 19,586 | Croton-Harmon UFSD | Croton on Hdsn |
| 86 | 19,536 | Mount Vernon City SD | Mount Vernon |
| 87 | 19,535 | Yonkers City SD | Yonkers |
| 88 | 19,489 | Bayport-Blue Point UFSD | Bayport |
| 89 | 19,478 | Freeport UFSD | Freeport |
| 90 | 19,463 | Shoreham-Wading River Central SD | Shoreham |
| 91 | 19,461 | South Country Central SD | East Patchogue |
| 92 | 19,410 | Lynbrook UFSD | Lynbrook |
| 93 | 19,385 | Monticello Central SD | Monticello |
| 94 | 19,378 | Yorktown Central SD | Yorktown Hgts |
| 95 | 19,360 | Longwood Central SD | Middle Island |
| 96 | 19,359 | Hauppauge UFSD | Hauppauge |
| 97 | 19,235 | Babylon UFSD | Babylon |
| 98 | 19,218 | Hudson City SD | Hudson |
| 99 | 19,112 | Hampton Bays UFSD | Hampton Bays |
| 100 | 19,071 | Merrick UFSD | Merrick |
| 101 | 19,043 | Garden City UFSD | Garden City |
| 102 | 18,992 | Marlboro Central SD | Marlboro |
| 103 | 18,900 | Pleasantville UFSD | Pleasantville |
| 104 | 18,888 | New Rochelle City SD | New Rochelle |
| 105 | 18,847 | New Paltz Central SD | New Paltz |
| 106 | 18,799 | Connetquot Central SD | Bohemia |
| 107 | 18,752 | Hicksville UFSD | Hicksville |
| 108 | 18,733 | New York City Public Schools | New York |
| 109 | 18,715 | Spackenkill UFSD | Poughkeepsie |
| 110 | 18,654 | Mahopac Central SD | Mahopac |
| 111 | 18,648 | Baldwin UFSD | Baldwin |
| 112 | 18,635 | Valley Stream Central High SD | Valley Stream |
| 113 | 18,632 | East Meadow UFSD | Westbury |
| 114 | 18,578 | Pelham UFSD | Pelham |
| 115 | 18,565 | Lackawanna City SD | Lackawanna |
| 116 | 18,531 | Oceanside UFSD | Oceanside |
| 117 | 18,500 | North Babylon UFSD | North Babylon |
| 118 | 18,493 | Buffalo City SD | Buffalo |
| 119 | 18,277 | Three Village Central SD | Stony Brook |
| 120 | 18,258 | Deer Park UFSD | Deer Park |
| 121 | 18,239 | Massapequa UFSD | Massapequa |
| 122 | 18,145 | Brentwood UFSD | Brentwood |
| 123 | 18,138 | Island Trees UFSD | Levittown |
| 124 | 18,127 | Pearl River UFSD | Pearl River |
| 125 | 18,073 | Goshen Central SD | Goshen |
| 126 | 18,023 | Seaford UFSD | Seaford |
| 127 | 17,939 | Mattituck-Cutchogue UFSD | Cutchogue |
| 128 | 17,868 | North Bellmore UFSD | Bellmore |
| 129 | 17,850 | Plattsburgh City SD | Plattsburgh |
| 130 | 17,793 | Dunkirk City SD | Dunkirk |
| 131 | 17,744 | Ravena-Coeymans-Selkirk Ctrl SD | Selkirk |
| 132 | 17,698 | Commack UFSD | East Northport |
| 133 | 17,672 | Mexico Central SD | Mexico |
| 134 | 17,644 | Bellmore-Merrick Central High SD | North Merrick |
| 135 | 17,624 | Kingston City SD | Kingston |
| 136 | 17,585 | West Babylon UFSD | West Babylon |
| 137 | 17,536 | William Floyd UFSD | Mastic Beach |
| 138 | 17,469 | Half Hollow Hills Central SD | Dix Hills |
| 139 | 17,447 | Newburgh City SD | Newburgh |
| 140 | 17,445 | Lindenhurst UFSD | Lindenhurst |
| 141 | 17,407 | Schalmont Central SD | Schenectady |
| 142 | 17,372 | Mount Sinai UFSD | Mount Sinai |
| 143 | 17,296 | Monroe-Woodbury Central SD | Central Valley |
| 144 | 17,251 | Rochester City SD | Rochester |
| 145 | 17,182 | Plainedge UFSD | N Massapequa |
| 146 | 17,141 | Syracuse City SD | Syracuse |
| 147 | 17,091 | Geneva City SD | Geneva |
| 148 | 17,025 | Poughkeepsie City SD | Poughkeepsie |
| 149 | 17,017 | Comsewogue School District | Port Jeff Stn |
| 150 | 16,965 | Catskill Central SD | Catskill |
| 151 | 16,908 | East Islip UFSD | Islip Terrace |
| 152 | 16,871 | Port Jervis City SD | Port Jervis |
| 153 | 16,865 | Elwood UFSD | Greenlawn |
| 154 | 16,848 | Ogdensburg City SD | Ogdensburg |
| 155 | 16,821 | Niagara Falls City SD | Niagara Falls |
| 156 | 16,794 | Port Chester-Rye UFSD | Port Chester |
| 157 | 16,769 | East Syracuse-Minoa Central SD | East Syracuse |
| 158 | 16,728 | Rocky Point UFSD | Rocky Point |
| 159 | 16,711 | Islip UFSD | Islip |
| 160 | 16,634 | Miller Place UFSD | Miller Place |
| 161 | 16,512 | Ithaca City SD | Ithaca |
| 162 | 16,462 | Sewanhaka Central High SD | Floral Park |
| 163 | 16,452 | Middletown City SD | Middletown |
| 164 | 16,448 | Sachem Central SD | Holbrook |
| 165 | 16,404 | Batavia City SD | Batavia |
| 166 | 16,369 | Smithtown Central SD | Smithtown |
| 167 | 16,353 | West Islip UFSD | West Islip |
| 168 | 16,294 | Rush-Henrietta Central SD | Henrietta |
| 169 | 16,286 | Taconic Hills Central SD | Craryville |
| 170 | 16,229 | Valley Stream 13 UFSD | Valley Stream |
| 171 | 16,209 | Harborfields Central SD | Greenlawn |
| 172 | 16,192 | Kings Park Central SD | Kings Park |
| 173 | 16,162 | Red Hook Central SD | Red Hook |
| 174 | 16,078 | Penn Yan Central SD | Penn Yan |
| 175 | 16,057 | Clarkstown Central SD | New City |
| 176 | 16,033 | Eastport-South Manor CSD | Manorville |
| 177 | 15,996 | New Hyde Pk-Garden City Pk UFSD | New Hyde Park |
| 178 | 15,923 | Rome City SD | Rome |
| 179 | 15,920 | Peru Central SD | Peru |
| 180 | 15,873 | Highland Central SD | Highland |
| 181 | 15,859 | Johnson City Central SD | Johnson City |
| 182 | 15,816 | Wantagh UFSD | Wantagh |
| 183 | 15,790 | Hyde Park Central SD | Hyde Park |

*Note: This section only includes districts with 1,500 or more students; All categories are ranked from high to low*

| | | | |
|---|---|---|---|
| 184 | 15,782 | Liverpool Central SD | Liverpool |
| 185 | 15,744 | Patchogue-Medford UFSD | Patchogue |
| 186 | 15,700 | Warwick Valley Central SD | Warwick |
| 187 | 15,579 | Brighton Central SD | Rochester |
| 188 | 15,497 | Phoenix Central SD | Phoenix |
| 189 | 15,480 | East Greenbush Central SD | East Greenbush |
| 190 | 15,458 | Owego-Apalachin Central SD | Owego |
| 191 | 15,453 | Middle Country Central SD | Centereach |
| 192 | 15,435 | East Irondequoit Central SD | Rochester |
| 193 | 15,385 | Glens Falls City SD | Glens Falls |
| 194 | 15,337 | Saranac Central SD | Dannemora |
| 195 | 15,315 | Saugerties Central SD | Saugerties |
| 196 | 15,314 | Pine Bush Central SD | Pine Bush |
| 197 | 15,312 | Sherburne-Earlville Central SD | Sherburne |
| 198 | 15,305 | Dryden Central SD | Dryden |
| 199 | 15,283 | Gates-Chili Central SD | Rochester |
| 200 | 15,264 | Penfield Central SD | Rochester |
| 201 | 15,233 | Lewiston-Porter Central SD | Youngstown |
| 202 | 15,205 | Cohoes City SD | Cohoes |
| 203 | 15,187 | Oneonta City SD | Oneonta |
| 204 | 15,153 | Cheektowaga-Sloan UFSD | Sloan |
| 205 | 15,129 | Phelps-Clifton Springs Central SD | Clifton Springs |
| 206 | 15,124 | Sweet Home Central SD | Amherst |
| 207 | 15,112 | Cobleskill-Richmondville Central SD | Cobleskill |
| 208 | 15,090 | Elmont UFSD | Elmont |
| 209 | 15,045 | Susquehanna Valley Central SD | Conklin |
| 210 | 15,031 | Depew UFSD | Depew |
| 211 | 15,029 | Fulton City SD | Fulton |
| 212 | 15,025 | Hornell City SD | Hornell |
| 213 | 14,953 | Franklin Square UFSD | Franklin Square |
| 214 | 14,928 | Vestal Central SD | Vestal |
| 215 | 14,898 | Malone Central SD | Malone |
| 216 | 14,869 | Evans-Brant Central SD (Lake Shore) | Angola |
| 217 | 14,868 | Maine-Endwell Central SD | Endwell |
| 218 | 14,843 | Beekmantown Central SD | West Chazy |
| 219 | 14,841 | Union-Endicott Central SD | Endicott |
| 220 | 14,804 | Windsor Central SD | Windsor |
| 221 | 14,803 | Gouverneur Central SD | Gouverneur |
| 222 | 14,790 | Yorkshire-Pioneer Central SD | Yorkshire |
| 223 | 14,783 | Wallkill Central SD | Wallkill |
| 224 | 14,781 | Washingtonville Central SD | Washingtonville |
| 225 | 14,715 | Oswego City SD | Oswego |
| 226 | 14,675 | Cheektowaga-Maryvale UFSD | Cheektowaga |
| 227 | 14,654 | Pittsford Central SD | Pittsford |
| 227 | 14,654 | Schenectady City SD | Schenectady |
| 229 | 14,597 | Arlington Central SD | Poughkeepsie |
| 229 | 14,597 | New Hartford Central SD | New Hartford |
| 231 | 14,561 | Cornwall Central SD | Cornwall on Hdsn |
| 232 | 14,554 | Dover UFSD | Dover Plains |
| 233 | 14,548 | Schuylerville Central SD | Schuylerville |
| 234 | 14,529 | Kenmore-Tonawanda UFSD | Buffalo |
| 235 | 14,507 | Valley Central SD (Montgomery) | Montgomery |
| 236 | 14,506 | Chenango Valley Central SD | Binghamton |
| 237 | 14,495 | Kinderhook Central SD | Valatie |
| 238 | 14,342 | Horseheads Central SD | Horseheads |
| 239 | 14,325 | Norwich City SD | Norwich |
| 240 | 14,303 | Fredonia Central SD | Fredonia |
| 241 | 14,278 | Solvay UFSD | Solvay |
| 242 | 14,254 | Binghamton City SD | Binghamton |
| 243 | 14,250 | Homer Central SD | Homer |
| 244 | 14,242 | Minisink Valley Central SD | Slate Hill |
| 245 | 14,241 | Chenango Forks Central SD | Binghamton |
| 246 | 14,162 | Ballston Spa Central SD | Ballston Spa |
| 247 | 14,160 | Guilderland Central SD | Guilderland |
| 248 | 14,144 | Brockport Central SD | Brockport |
| 249 | 14,133 | Niagara-Wheatfield Central SD | Niagara Falls |
| 250 | 14,129 | Springville-Griffith Institute CSD | Springville |
| 251 | 14,121 | South Colonie Central SD | Albany |
| 252 | 14,090 | Carthage Central SD | Carthage |
| 253 | 14,067 | Cortland City SD | Cortland |
| 254 | 14,047 | Utica City SD | Utica |
| 255 | 13,994 | Newark Central SD | Newark |
| 256 | 13,957 | Jamesville-Dewitt Central SD | Dewitt |
| 257 | 13,952 | Jordan-Elbridge Central SD | Elbridge |
| 258 | 13,938 | Wayland-Cohocton Central SD | Wayland |
| 259 | 13,919 | Palmyra-Macedon Central SD | Palmyra |
| 260 | 13,895 | Olean City SD | Olean |
| 261 | 13,887 | Corning City SD | Painted Post |
| 262 | 13,882 | Auburn City SD | Auburn |
| 263 | 13,870 | Beacon City SD | Beacon |
| 264 | 13,868 | Coxsackie-Athens Central SD | Coxsackie |
| 265 | 13,854 | Bethlehem Central SD | Delmar |
| 266 | 13,836 | Scotia-Glenville Central SD | Scotia |
| 267 | 13,835 | Lockport City SD | Lockport |
| 268 | 13,818 | Elmira City SD | Elmira |
| 269 | 13,809 | Bath Central SD | Bath |
| 270 | 13,784 | Oneida City SD | Oneida |
| 271 | 13,778 | Skaneateles Central SD | Skaneateles |
| 272 | 13,749 | Churchville-Chili Central SD | Churchville |
| 273 | 13,711 | Webster Central SD | Webster |
| 274 | 13,698 | Averill Park Central SD | Averill Park |
| 275 | 13,678 | Hudson Falls Central SD | Fort Edward |
| 276 | 13,642 | Wappingers Central SD | Wappingers Fls |
| 277 | 13,634 | Niskayuna Central SD | Schenectady |
| 278 | 13,632 | Holland Patent Central SD | Holland Patent |
| 279 | 13,630 | Medina Central SD | Medina |
| 280 | 13,604 | Camden Central SD | Camden |
| 281 | 13,536 | Alden Central SD | Alden |
| 282 | 13,495 | Spencerport Central SD | Spencerport |
| 283 | 13,494 | Wayne Central SD | Ontario Center |
| 284 | 13,482 | Westhill Central SD | Syracuse |
| 285 | 13,481 | Dansville Central SD | Dansville |
| 286 | 13,471 | West Irondequoit Central SD | Rochester |
| 287 | 13,468 | North Tonawanda City SD | North Tonawanda |
| 288 | 13,453 | Attica Central SD | Attica |
| 289 | 13,422 | Gloversville City SD | Gloversville |
| 290 | 13,412 | Fairport Central SD | Fairport |
| 291 | 13,398 | Greece Central SD | Rochester |
| 292 | 13,365 | Burnt Hills-Ballston Lake CSD | Scotia |
| 293 | 13,322 | Cheektowaga Central SD | Cheektowaga |
| 294 | 13,319 | Newfane Central SD | Burt |
| 295 | 13,264 | Livonia Central SD | Livonia |
| 296 | 13,237 | Baldwinsville Central SD | Baldwinsville |
| 297 | 13,222 | Waterloo Central SD | Waterloo |
| 298 | 13,214 | Shenendehowa Central SD | Clifton Park |
| 299 | 13,211 | Saratoga Spgs City SD | Saratoga Spgs |
| 300 | 13,197 | Jamestown City SD | Jamestown |
| 301 | 13,155 | Indian River Central SD | Philadelphia |
| 302 | 13,149 | Floral Park-Bellerose UFSD | Floral Park |
| 303 | 13,139 | Canandaigua City SD | Canandaigua |
| 304 | 13,088 | Royalton-Hartland Central SD | Middleport |
| 305 | 13,081 | Massena Central SD | Massena |
| 306 | 13,043 | Tonawanda City SD | Tonawanda |
| 307 | 13,039 | Grand Island Central SD | Grand Island |
| 308 | 13,032 | Akron Central SD | Akron |
| 309 | 13,020 | Amsterdam City SD | Amsterdam |
| 310 | 12,976 | Hilton Central SD | Hilton |
| 311 | 12,955 | Hannibal Central SD | Hannibal |
| 312 | 12,950 | North Colonie Central SD | Latham |
| 313 | 12,918 | Lansingburgh Central SD | Troy |
| 314 | 12,910 | Orchard Park Central SD | Orchard Park |
| 315 | 12,909 | Chittenango Central SD | Chittenango |
| 316 | 12,878 | Whitesboro Central SD | Yorkville |
| 317 | 12,846 | S Glens Fls Central SD | S Glens Fls |
| 318 | 12,836 | Johnstown City SD | Johnstown |
| 319 | 12,826 | Williamsville Central SD | East Amherst |
| 320 | 12,803 | Fayetteville-Manlius Central SD | Manlius |
| 321 | 12,789 | North Syracuse Central SD | North Syracuse |
| 322 | 12,767 | Honeoye Falls-Lima Central SD | Honeoye Falls |
| 323 | 12,735 | Albion Central SD | Albion |
| 324 | 12,692 | Canastota Central SD | Canastota |
| 325 | 12,680 | Amherst Central SD | Amherst |
| 326 | 12,678 | Vernon-Verona-Sherrill Central SD | Verona |
| 327 | 12,642 | Southwestern CSD at Jamestown | Jamestown |
| 328 | 12,542 | Cazenovia Central SD | Cazenovia |
| 329 | 12,537 | East Aurora UFSD | East Aurora |
| 330 | 12,466 | Iroquois Central SD | Elma |
| 331 | 12,313 | Central Square Central SD | Central Square |
| 332 | 12,300 | Marcellus Central SD | Marcellus |
| 333 | 12,298 | West Seneca Central SD | West Seneca |
| 334 | 12,260 | Starpoint Central SD | Lockport |
| 335 | 12,076 | Queensbury UFSD | Queensbury |
| 336 | 11,988 | Frontier Central SD | Hamburg |
| 337 | 11,960 | West Genesee Central SD | Camillus |
| 338 | 11,922 | South Jefferson Central SD | Adams Center |
| 339 | 11,835 | Ilion Central SD | Ilion |
| 340 | 11,813 | Eden Central SD | Eden |
| 341 | 11,782 | Watertown City SD | Watertown |
| 342 | 11,768 | Hamburg Central SD | Hamburg |
| 343 | 11,708 | Broadalbin-Perth Central SD | Broadalbin |
| 344 | 11,704 | Waverly Central SD | Waverly |
| 345 | 11,470 | Victor Central SD | Victor |
| 346 | 11,360 | Mohonasen Central SD | Schenectady |
| 347 | 11,322 | Lancaster Central SD | Lancaster |
| 348 | 11,187 | Clarence Central SD | Clarence Center |
| 349 | 10,781 | General Brown Central SD | Dexter |
| n/a | n/a | Charter School for Applied Tech | Buffalo |
| n/a | n/a | NYC Special Schools - District 75 | New York |
| n/a | n/a | NYC Geographic District # 1 | New York |
| n/a | n/a | NYC Geographic District # 2 | New York |
| n/a | n/a | NYC Geographic District # 3 | New York |
| n/a | n/a | NYC Geographic District # 4 | New York |
| n/a | n/a | NYC Geographic District # 5 | New York |
| n/a | n/a | NYC Geographic District # 6 | New York |
| n/a | n/a | NYC Geographic District # 7 | Bronx |
| n/a | n/a | NYC Geographic District # 8 | Bronx |
| n/a | n/a | NYC Geographic District # 9 | Bronx |
| n/a | n/a | NYC Geographic District #10 | Bronx |
| n/a | n/a | NYC Geographic District #11 | Bronx |
| n/a | n/a | NYC Geographic District #12 | Bronx |
| n/a | n/a | NYC Geographic District #13 | Brooklyn |
| n/a | n/a | NYC Geographic District #14 | Brooklyn |
| n/a | n/a | NYC Geographic District #15 | Brooklyn |
| n/a | n/a | NYC Geographic District #16 | Brooklyn |
| n/a | n/a | NYC Geographic District #17 | Brooklyn |
| n/a | n/a | NYC Geographic District #18 | Brooklyn |
| n/a | n/a | NYC Geographic District #19 | Brooklyn |
| n/a | n/a | NYC Geographic District #20 | Brooklyn |
| n/a | n/a | NYC Geographic District #21 | Brooklyn |
| n/a | n/a | NYC Geographic District #22 | Brooklyn |
| n/a | n/a | NYC Geographic District #23 | Brooklyn |
| n/a | n/a | NYC Geographic District #24 | Ridgewood |
| n/a | n/a | NYC Geographic District #25 | Flushing |
| n/a | n/a | NYC Geographic District #26 | Bayside |
| n/a | n/a | NYC Geographic District #27 | Ozone Park |
| n/a | n/a | NYC Geographic District #28 | Jamaica |
| n/a | n/a | NYC Geographic District #29 | Rosedale |
| n/a | n/a | NYC Geographic District #30 | Long Isl City |
| n/a | n/a | NYC Geographic District #31 | Staten Island |
| n/a | n/a | NYC Geographic District #32 | Brooklyn |

## Total General Revenue per Student

| Rank | Dollars | District Name | City |
|---|---|---|---|
| 1 | 37,780 | Lawrence UFSD | Lawrence |
| 2 | 34,936 | Bronxville UFSD | Bronxville |
| 3 | 32,363 | Roosevelt UFSD | Roosevelt |
| 4 | 32,010 | Greenburgh Central SD | Hartsdale |
| 5 | 31,932 | Southampton UFSD | Southampton |
| 6 | 30,552 | Jericho UFSD | Jericho |
| 7 | 29,659 | East Hampton UFSD | East Hampton |
| 8 | 29,469 | Mineola UFSD | Mineola |
| 9 | 29,168 | North Shore Central SD | Sea Cliff |
| 10 | 28,872 | Hewlett-Woodmere UFSD | Woodmere |
| 11 | 28,451 | Briarcliff Mnr UFSD | Briarcliff Mnr |
| 12 | 28,344 | Locust Valley Central SD | Locust Valley |
| 13 | 28,309 | Oyster Bay-East Norwich Central SD | Oyster Bay |
| 14 | 28,248 | Great Neck UFSD | Great Neck |
| 15 | 28,214 | Harrison Central SD | Harrison |
| 16 | 27,390 | Roslyn UFSD | Roslyn |
| 17 | 27,076 | Long Beach City SD | Long Beach |
| 18 | 26,719 | Katonah-Lewisboro UFSD | South Salem |
| 19 | 26,639 | Wyandanch UFSD | Wyandanch |
| 20 | 26,497 | Manhasset UFSD | Manhasset |
| 21 | 26,180 | East Ramapo Central SD | Spring Valley |
| 22 | 26,054 | Onteora Central SD | Boiceville |
| 23 | 26,029 | Byram Hills Central SD | Armonk |
| 24 | 26,017 | Central Islip UFSD | Central Islip |
| 25 | 26,000 | Peekskill City SD | Peekskill |
| 26 | 25,909 | Scarsdale UFSD | Scarsdale |
| 27 | 25,729 | Syosset Central SD | Syosset |
| 28 | 25,663 | Hempstead UFSD | Hempstead |
| 29 | 25,622 | Bedford Central SD | Bedford |
| 30 | 25,601 | White Plains City SD | White Plains |
| 31 | 25,288 | Malverne UFSD | Malverne |
| 32 | 25,120 | Nanuet UFSD | Nanuet |
| 33 | 25,102 | Chappaqua Central SD | Chappaqua |
| 34 | 25,047 | Irvington UFSD | Irvington |
| 35 | 25,004 | Amityville UFSD | Amityville |
| 36 | 24,918 | Valhalla UFSD | Valhalla |
| 37 | 24,904 | Port Washington UFSD | Port Washington |
| 38 | 24,892 | East Williston UFSD | Old Westbury |
| 39 | 24,870 | Cold Spring Hrbr Central SD | Cold Spring Hrbr |
| 40 | 24,859 | North Rockland Central SD | Garnerville |
| 41 | 24,853 | Hastings-on-Hudson UFSD | Hastings on Hdsn |
| 42 | 24,850 | Uniondale UFSD | Uniondale |
| 43 | 24,799 | Mount Pleasant Central SD | Thornwood |
| 44 | 24,648 | Westbury UFSD | Old Westbury |
| 45 | 24,577 | Liberty Central SD | Liberty |
| 46 | 24,486 | Ardsley UFSD | Ardsley |
| 47 | 24,379 | Huntington UFSD | Huntington Stn |
| 48 | 24,184 | Plainview-Old Bethpage Central SD | Plainview |
| 49 | 24,102 | Westhampton Bch UFSD | Westhampton Bch |
| 50 | 23,916 | Albany City SD | Albany |

*Note: This section only includes districts with 1,500 or more students; All categories are ranked from high to low*

| | | | |
|---|---|---|---|
| 51 | 23,827 | Buffalo City SD | Buffalo |
| 52 | 23,746 | Ramapo Central SD (Suffern) | Hillburn |
| 53 | 23,624 | UFSD of the Tarrytowns | Sleepy Hollow |
| 54 | 23,560 | Ossining UFSD | Ossining |
| 55 | 23,543 | Blind Brook-Rye UFSD | Rye Brook |
| 56 | 23,379 | Mamaroneck UFSD | Mamaroneck |
| 57 | 23,233 | Glen Cove City SD | Glen Cove |
| 58 | 23,116 | Rockville Ctr UFSD | Rockville Ctr |
| 59 | 22,941 | Nyack UFSD | Nyack |
| 60 | 22,925 | Edgemont UFSD | Scarsdale |
| 61 | 22,868 | Croton-Harmon UFSD | Croton on Hdsn |
| 62 | 22,779 | Brewster Central SD | Brewster |
| 63 | 22,699 | Somers Central SD | Somers |
| 64 | 22,604 | Bayport-Blue Point UFSD | Bayport |
| 65 | 22,548 | Ellenville Central SD | Ellenville |
| 66 | 22,537 | Hendrick Hudson Central SD | Montrose |
| 67 | 22,520 | Putnam Valley Central SD | Putnam Valley |
| 68 | 22,469 | Farmingdale UFSD | Farmingdale |
| 69 | 22,422 | Riverhead Central SD | Riverhead |
| 69 | 22,422 | Rondout Valley Central SD | Accord |
| 71 | 22,386 | Rye City SD | Rye |
| 72 | 22,381 | Babylon UFSD | Babylon |
| 73 | 22,286 | Troy City SD | Troy |
| 74 | 22,273 | Bethpage UFSD | Bethpage |
| 75 | 22,207 | South Orangetown Central SD | Blauvelt |
| 76 | 22,169 | Hampton Bays UFSD | Hampton Bays |
| 77 | 22,159 | Herricks UFSD | New Hyde Park |
| 78 | 22,157 | Levittown UFSD | Levittown |
| 79 | 22,078 | Lakeland Central SD | Shrub Oak |
| 80 | 21,908 | Bay Shore UFSD | Bay Shore |
| 81 | 21,899 | Monticello Central SD | Monticello |
| 82 | 21,785 | West Hempstead UFSD | West Hempstead |
| 83 | 21,780 | Carmel Central SD | Patterson |
| 84 | 21,772 | Longwood Central SD | Middle Island |
| 85 | 21,608 | Mattituck-Cutchogue UFSD | Cutchogue |
| 86 | 21,506 | Hauppauge UFSD | Hauppauge |
| 87 | 21,471 | Garden City UFSD | Garden City |
| 88 | 21,458 | Eastchester UFSD | Eastchester |
| 89 | 21,373 | Center Moriches UFSD | Center Moriches |
| 90 | 21,360 | Marlboro Central SD | Marlboro |
| 91 | 21,347 | Pleasantville UFSD | Pleasantville |
| 92 | 21,314 | South Huntington UFSD | Huntington Stn |
| 93 | 21,311 | South Country Central SD | East Patchogue |
| 94 | 21,295 | Sayville UFSD | Sayville |
| 95 | 21,215 | Northport-East Northport UFSD | Northport |
| 96 | 21,181 | Freeport UFSD | Freeport |
| 97 | 21,091 | Yorktown Central SD | Yorktown Hgts |
| 98 | 21,025 | New Paltz Central SD | New Paltz |
| 99 | 21,019 | Deer Park UFSD | Deer Park |
| 100 | 20,969 | Pelham UFSD | Pelham |
| 101 | 20,925 | Connetquot Central SD | Bohemia |
| 102 | 20,907 | Yonkers City SD | Yonkers |
| 103 | 20,858 | Copiague UFSD | Copiague |
| 104 | 20,857 | Lackawanna City SD | Lackawanna |
| 105 | 20,844 | North Babylon UFSD | North Babylon |
| 106 | 20,742 | Schalmont Central SD | Schenectady |
| 107 | 20,728 | Pearl River UFSD | Pearl River |
| 108 | 20,712 | Lynbrook UFSD | Lynbrook |
| 109 | 20,710 | East Meadow UFSD | Westbury |
| 110 | 20,605 | Plainedge UFSD | N Massapequa |
| 111 | 20,598 | Hicksville UFSD | Hicksville |
| 112 | 20,592 | New Rochelle City SD | New Rochelle |
| 113 | 20,533 | Baldwin UFSD | Baldwin |
| 114 | 20,485 | Valley Stream Central High SD | Valley Stream |
| 115 | 20,376 | Merrick UFSD | Merrick |
| 116 | 20,323 | Salmon River Central SD | Fort Covington |
| 117 | 20,299 | Mount Vernon City SD | Mount Vernon |
| 118 | 20,089 | Plattsburgh City SD | Plattsburgh |
| 119 | 20,088 | New York City Public Schools | New York |
| 120 | 20,039 | Seaford UFSD | Seaford |
| 121 | 20,038 | Middletown City SD | Middletown |
| 121 | 20,038 | Three Village Central SD | Stony Brook |
| 123 | 19,956 | Spackenkill UFSD | Poughkeepsie |
| 124 | 19,881 | Mount Sinai UFSD | Mount Sinai |
| 125 | 19,872 | Dunkirk City SD | Dunkirk |
| 126 | 19,853 | Catskill Central SD | Catskill |
| 127 | 19,817 | Massapequa UFSD | Massapequa |
| 128 | 19,811 | William Floyd UFSD | Mastic Beach |
| 129 | 19,808 | Goshen Central SD | Goshen |
| 130 | 19,778 | Ravena-Coeymans-Selkirk Ctrl SD | Selkirk |
| 131 | 19,730 | Oceanside UFSD | Oceanside |
| 132 | 19,592 | Island Trees UFSD | Levittown |
| 133 | 19,512 | Hudson City SD | Hudson |
| 134 | 19,457 | Half Hollow Hills Central SD | Dix Hills |
| 135 | 19,388 | Mahopac Central SD | Mahopac |
| 136 | 19,271 | Smithtown Central SD | Smithtown |
| 137 | 19,192 | Commack UFSD | East Northport |
| 138 | 19,189 | Rochester City SD | Rochester |
| 139 | 19,125 | Brentwood UFSD | Brentwood |
| 140 | 19,124 | Rome City SD | Rome |
| 141 | 19,095 | North Bellmore UFSD | Bellmore |
| 142 | 19,051 | East Islip UFSD | Islip Terrace |
| 143 | 19,013 | Lindenhurst UFSD | Lindenhurst |
| 144 | 18,998 | Geneva City SD | Geneva |
| 145 | 18,980 | West Babylon UFSD | West Babylon |
| 146 | 18,954 | Taconic Hills Central SD | Craryville |
| 147 | 18,950 | New Hyde Pk-Garden City Pk UFSD | New Hyde Park |
| 148 | 18,943 | Kingston City SD | Kingston |
| 149 | 18,913 | Niagara Falls City SD | Niagara Falls |
| 150 | 18,900 | Monroe-Woodbury Central SD | Central Valley |
| 151 | 18,799 | Phelps-Clifton Springs Central SD | Clifton Springs |
| 152 | 18,697 | Port Jervis City SD | Port Jervis |
| 153 | 18,696 | Sachem Central SD | Holbrook |
| 154 | 18,647 | East Syracuse-Minoa Central SD | East Syracuse |
| 155 | 18,630 | Syracuse City SD | Syracuse |
| 156 | 18,623 | East Irondequoit Central SD | Rochester |
| 157 | 18,621 | Port Chester-Rye UFSD | Port Chester |
| 158 | 18,564 | Cheektowaga-Sloan UFSD | Sloan |
| 159 | 18,549 | Eastport-South Manor CSD | Manorville |
| 160 | 18,514 | Newburgh City SD | Newburgh |
| 161 | 18,488 | Peru Central SD | Peru |
| 162 | 18,473 | Valley Stream 13 UFSD | Valley Stream |
| 163 | 18,372 | Rush-Henrietta Central SD | Henrietta |
| 164 | 18,348 | Comsewogue School District | Port Jeff Stn |
| 165 | 18,300 | Hyde Park Central SD | Hyde Park |
| 166 | 18,281 | Poughkeepsie City SD | Poughkeepsie |
| 167 | 18,272 | Cobleskill-Richmondville Central SD | Cobleskill |
| 168 | 18,244 | Ithaca City SD | Ithaca |
| 169 | 18,214 | Red Hook Central SD | Red Hook |
| 170 | 18,162 | East Greenbush Central SD | East Greenbush |
| 171 | 18,123 | Rocky Point UFSD | Rocky Point |
| 172 | 18,117 | Dryden Central SD | Dryden |
| 173 | 18,031 | Bellmore-Merrick Central High SD | North Merrick |
| 174 | 17,978 | Batavia City SD | Batavia |
| 175 | 17,931 | Ogdensburg City SD | Ogdensburg |
| 176 | 17,927 | Highland Central SD | Highland |
| 177 | 17,923 | Sweet Home Central SD | Amherst |
| 178 | 17,903 | Patchogue-Medford UFSD | Patchogue |
| 179 | 17,863 | Sherburne-Earlville Central SD | Sherburne |
| 180 | 17,801 | Islip UFSD | Islip |
| 181 | 17,793 | Harborfields Central SD | Greenlawn |
| 182 | 17,730 | Miller Place UFSD | Miller Place |
| 183 | 17,722 | Cohoes City SD | Cohoes |
| 184 | 17,711 | Evans-Brant Central SD (Lake Shore) | Angola |
| 185 | 17,686 | Penn Yan Central SD | Penn Yan |
| 186 | 17,680 | West Islip UFSD | West Islip |
| 187 | 17,624 | Pittsford Central SD | Pittsford |
| 188 | 17,599 | Johnson City Central SD | Johnson City |
| 189 | 17,593 | Elwood UFSD | Greenlawn |
| 190 | 17,568 | Newark Central SD | Newark |
| 191 | 17,484 | Warwick Valley Central SD | Warwick |
| 192 | 17,448 | Liverpool Central SD | Liverpool |
| 193 | 17,445 | Owego-Apalachin Central SD | Owego |
| 194 | 17,413 | Brighton Central SD | Rochester |
| 195 | 17,332 | Malone Central SD | Malone |
| 196 | 17,294 | Oneonta City SD | Oneonta |
| 197 | 17,261 | Sewanhaka Central High SD | Floral Park |
| 198 | 17,259 | Susquehanna Valley Central SD | Conklin |
| 199 | 17,232 | Waterloo Central SD | Waterloo |
| 200 | 17,215 | Middle Country Central SD | Centereach |
| 201 | 17,198 | Mexico Central SD | Mexico |
| 202 | 17,088 | Kings Park Central SD | Kings Park |
| 203 | 17,034 | Solvay UFSD | Solvay |
| 204 | 17,028 | Dansville Central SD | Dansville |
| 205 | 16,995 | Depew UFSD | Depew |
| 206 | 16,973 | Jordan-Elbridge Central SD | Elbridge |
| 207 | 16,907 | Hornell City SD | Hornell |
| 208 | 16,897 | Penfield Central SD | Rochester |
| 209 | 16,896 | Camden Central SD | Camden |
| 210 | 16,881 | Yorkshire-Pioneer Central SD | Yorkshire |
| 211 | 16,878 | Dover UFSD | Dover Plains |
| 212 | 16,860 | Gates-Chili Central SD | Rochester |
| 213 | 16,848 | Vestal Central SD | Vestal |
| 214 | 16,840 | Glens Falls City SD | Glens Falls |
| 215 | 16,835 | Schuylerville Central SD | Schuylerville |
| 216 | 16,834 | Saugerties Central SD | Saugerties |
| 217 | 16,796 | Windsor Central SD | Windsor |
| 218 | 16,760 | Beacon City SD | Beacon |
| 219 | 16,754 | Lewiston-Porter Central SD | Youngstown |
| 220 | 16,751 | Phoenix Central SD | Phoenix |
| 221 | 16,750 | Elmont UFSD | Elmont |
| 222 | 16,744 | Washingtonville Central SD | Washingtonville |
| 223 | 16,698 | Beekmantown Central SD | West Chazy |
| 224 | 16,694 | Niagara-Wheatfield Central SD | Niagara Falls |
| 225 | 16,650 | Brockport Central SD | Brockport |
| 226 | 16,629 | Attica Central SD | Attica |
| 227 | 16,621 | Shoreham-Wading River Central SD | Shoreham |
| 228 | 16,615 | Wantagh UFSD | Wantagh |
| 229 | 16,579 | Gouverneur Central SD | Gouverneur |
| 230 | 16,573 | Schenectady City SD | Schenectady |
| 231 | 16,567 | Clarkstown Central SD | New City |
| 232 | 16,563 | Ballston Spa Central SD | Ballston Spa |
| 233 | 16,560 | Skaneateles Central SD | Skaneateles |
| 234 | 16,496 | Wallkill Central SD | Wallkill |
| 235 | 16,480 | Wayne Central SD | Ontario Center |
| 236 | 16,438 | Homer Central SD | Homer |
| 237 | 16,390 | Union-Endicott Central SD | Endicott |
| 238 | 16,387 | Kenmore-Tonawanda UFSD | Buffalo |
| 239 | 16,378 | Wayland-Cohocton Central SD | Wayland |
| 240 | 16,335 | Saranac Central SD | Dannemora |
| 241 | 16,332 | Chenango Forks Central SD | Binghamton |
| 242 | 16,241 | Minisink Valley Central SD | Slate Hill |
| 243 | 16,201 | Springville-Griffith Institute CSD | Springville |
| 244 | 16,199 | Palmyra-Macedon Central SD | Palmyra |
| 245 | 16,194 | Cornwall Central SD | Cornwall on Hdsn |
| 246 | 16,191 | Fulton City SD | Fulton |
| 247 | 16,190 | Newfane Central SD | Burt |
| 248 | 16,187 | Maine-Endwell Central SD | Endwell |
| 249 | 16,128 | Elmira City SD | Elmira |
| 250 | 16,124 | Oswego City SD | Oswego |
| 251 | 16,103 | Pine Bush Central SD | Pine Bush |
| 252 | 16,101 | Kinderhook Central SD | Valatie |
| 253 | 16,099 | Medina Central SD | Medina |
| 254 | 16,098 | Holland Patent Central SD | Holland Patent |
| 255 | 16,077 | Churchville-Chili Central SD | Churchville |
| 256 | 16,059 | Chenango Valley Central SD | Binghamton |
| 257 | 16,039 | South Colonie Central SD | Albany |
| 258 | 15,991 | Akron Central SD | Akron |
| 259 | 15,973 | Averill Park Central SD | Averill Park |
| 260 | 15,960 | Fredonia Central SD | Fredonia |
| 261 | 15,955 | Jamesville-Dewitt Central SD | Dewitt |
| 262 | 15,936 | Spencerport Central SD | Spencerport |
| 263 | 15,929 | Coxsackie-Athens Central SD | Coxsackie |
| 264 | 15,928 | Guilderland Central SD | Guilderland |
| 265 | 15,919 | Bath Central SD | Bath |
| 266 | 15,901 | New Hartford Central SD | New Hartford |
| 267 | 15,898 | Alden Central SD | Alden |
| 268 | 15,880 | Arlington Central SD | Poughkeepsie |
| 269 | 15,872 | Jamestown City SD | Jamestown |
| 270 | 15,864 | Massena Central SD | Massena |
| 271 | 15,806 | Binghamton City SD | Binghamton |
| 272 | 15,802 | Bethlehem Central SD | Delmar |
| 273 | 15,777 | Horseheads Central SD | Horseheads |
| 274 | 15,756 | Valley Central SD (Montgomery) | Montgomery |
| 275 | 15,737 | Chittenango Central SD | Chittenango |
| 276 | 15,722 | Scotia-Glenville Central SD | Scotia |
| 277 | 15,702 | Gloversville City SD | Gloversville |
| 278 | 15,694 | Hudson Falls Central SD | Fort Edward |
| 279 | 15,608 | Franklin Square UFSD | Franklin Square |
| 280 | 15,601 | Saratoga Spgs City SD | Saratoga Spgs |
| 281 | 15,552 | Baldwinsville Central SD | Baldwinsville |
| 282 | 15,551 | S Glens Fls Central SD | S Glens Fls |
| 283 | 15,503 | Norwich City SD | Norwich |
| 284 | 15,493 | West Irondequoit Central SD | Rochester |
| 285 | 15,472 | Niskayuna Central SD | Schenectady |
| 286 | 15,457 | Olean City SD | Olean |
| 287 | 15,453 | Westhill Central SD | Syracuse |
| 288 | 15,443 | Burnt Hills-Ballston Lake CSD | Scotia |
| 289 | 15,417 | Auburn City SD | Auburn |
| 290 | 15,416 | Carthage Central SD | Carthage |
| 291 | 15,411 | Fairport Central SD | Fairport |
| 292 | 15,410 | Grand Island Central SD | Grand Island |
| 293 | 15,392 | Canandaigua City SD | Canandaigua |
| 294 | 15,376 | Corning City SD | Painted Post |
| 295 | 15,364 | Hannibal Central SD | Hannibal |
| 296 | 15,327 | Cheektowaga Central SD | Cheektowaga |
| 297 | 15,305 | Utica City SD | Utica |
| 298 | 15,301 | Southwestern CSD at Jamestown | Jamestown |
| 299 | 15,249 | Greece Central SD | Rochester |
| 300 | 15,240 | Webster Central SD | Webster |
| 301 | 15,193 | Fayetteville-Manlius Central SD | Manlius |
| 302 | 15,168 | Livonia Central SD | Livonia |
| 303 | 15,132 | North Tonawanda City SD | North Tonawanda |
| 304 | 14,977 | Shenendehowa Central SD | Clifton Park |
| 305 | 14,936 | Indian River Central SD | Philadelphia |

*Note: This section only includes districts with 1,500 or more students; All categories are ranked from high to low*

| | | | |
|---|---|---|---|
| 306 | 14,932 | Cheektowaga-Maryvale UFSD | Cheektowaga |
| 307 | 14,888 | Starpoint Central SD | Lockport |
| 308 | 14,880 | Tonawanda City SD | Tonawanda |
| 309 | 14,863 | Lockport City SD | Lockport |
| 310 | 14,840 | Williamsville Central SD | East Amherst |
| 311 | 14,725 | Canastota Central SD | Canastota |
| 312 | 14,710 | Cortland City SD | Cortland |
| 313 | 14,685 | Honeoye Falls-Lima Central SD | Honeoye Falls |
| 314 | 14,657 | Hilton Central SD | Hilton |
| 315 | 14,625 | North Colonie Central SD | Latham |
| 316 | 14,623 | Lansingburgh Central SD | Troy |
| 317 | 14,622 | Oneida City SD | Oneida |
| 318 | 14,502 | Royalton-Hartland Central SD | Middleport |
| 319 | 14,360 | Floral Park-Bellerose UFSD | Floral Park |
| 320 | 14,351 | Vernon-Verona-Sherrill Central SD | Verona |
| 321 | 14,288 | Amsterdam City SD | Amsterdam |
| 322 | 14,271 | Cazenovia Central SD | Cazenovia |
| 323 | 14,259 | Marcellus Central SD | Marcellus |
| 324 | 14,202 | Ilion Central SD | Ilion |
| 325 | 14,140 | Albion Central SD | Albion |
| 326 | 14,091 | Orchard Park Central SD | Orchard Park |
| 327 | 14,039 | West Seneca Central SD | West Seneca |
| 328 | 14,002 | North Syracuse Central SD | North Syracuse |
| 329 | 13,993 | Victor Central SD | Victor |
| 330 | 13,985 | Iroquois Central SD | Elma |
| 331 | 13,955 | Whitesboro Central SD | Yorkville |
| 332 | 13,917 | Wappingers Central SD | Wappingers Fls |
| 333 | 13,898 | Johnstown City SD | Johnstown |
| 334 | 13,799 | Queensbury UFSD | Queensbury |
| 335 | 13,786 | Amherst Central SD | Amherst |
| 336 | 13,752 | Eden Central SD | Eden |
| 337 | 13,686 | Watertown City SD | Watertown |
| 338 | 13,441 | West Genesee Central SD | Camillus |
| 339 | 13,416 | Broadalbin-Perth Central SD | Broadalbin |
| 340 | 13,404 | Clarence Central SD | Clarence Center |
| 341 | 13,268 | East Aurora UFSD | East Aurora |
| 342 | 13,261 | Mohonasen Central SD | Schenectady |
| 343 | 13,205 | Central Square Central SD | Central Square |
| 344 | 13,178 | South Jefferson Central SD | Adams Center |
| 345 | 13,165 | Waverly Central SD | Waverly |
| 346 | 13,101 | Frontier Central SD | Hamburg |
| 347 | 12,814 | Hamburg Central SD | Hamburg |
| 348 | 12,731 | Lancaster Central SD | Lancaster |
| 349 | 12,141 | General Brown Central SD | Dexter |
| n/a | n/a | Charter School for Applied Tech | Buffalo |
| n/a | n/a | NYC Special Schools - District 75 | New York |
| n/a | n/a | NYC Geographic District # 1 | New York |
| n/a | n/a | NYC Geographic District # 2 | New York |
| n/a | n/a | NYC Geographic District # 3 | New York |
| n/a | n/a | NYC Geographic District # 4 | New York |
| n/a | n/a | NYC Geographic District # 5 | New York |
| n/a | n/a | NYC Geographic District # 6 | New York |
| n/a | n/a | NYC Geographic District # 7 | Bronx |
| n/a | n/a | NYC Geographic District # 8 | Bronx |
| n/a | n/a | NYC Geographic District # 9 | Bronx |
| n/a | n/a | NYC Geographic District #10 | Bronx |
| n/a | n/a | NYC Geographic District #11 | Bronx |
| n/a | n/a | NYC Geographic District #12 | Bronx |
| n/a | n/a | NYC Geographic District #13 | Brooklyn |
| n/a | n/a | NYC Geographic District #14 | Brooklyn |
| n/a | n/a | NYC Geographic District #15 | Brooklyn |
| n/a | n/a | NYC Geographic District #16 | Brooklyn |
| n/a | n/a | NYC Geographic District #17 | Brooklyn |
| n/a | n/a | NYC Geographic District #18 | Brooklyn |
| n/a | n/a | NYC Geographic District #19 | Brooklyn |
| n/a | n/a | NYC Geographic District #20 | Brooklyn |
| n/a | n/a | NYC Geographic District #21 | Brooklyn |
| n/a | n/a | NYC Geographic District #22 | Brooklyn |
| n/a | n/a | NYC Geographic District #23 | Brooklyn |
| n/a | n/a | NYC Geographic District #24 | Ridgewood |
| n/a | n/a | NYC Geographic District #25 | Flushing |
| n/a | n/a | NYC Geographic District #26 | Bayside |
| n/a | n/a | NYC Geographic District #27 | Ozone Park |
| n/a | n/a | NYC Geographic District #28 | Jamaica |
| n/a | n/a | NYC Geographic District #29 | Rosedale |
| n/a | n/a | NYC Geographic District #30 | Long Isl City |
| n/a | n/a | NYC Geographic District #31 | Staten Island |
| n/a | n/a | NYC Geographic District #32 | Brooklyn |

## Long-Term Debt per Student (end of FY)

| Rank | Dollars | District Name | City |
|---|---|---|---|
| 1 | 37,582 | Roosevelt UFSD | Roosevelt |
| 2 | 31,631 | North Rockland Central SD | Garnerville |
| 3 | 28,675 | Waterloo Central SD | Waterloo |
| 4 | 28,377 | Irvington UFSD | Irvington |
| 5 | 27,686 | Hampton Bays UFSD | Hampton Bays |
| 6 | 27,625 | Buffalo City SD | Buffalo |
| 7 | 27,461 | Westhampton Bch UFSD | Westhampton Bch |
| 8 | 27,088 | Byram Hills Central SD | Armonk |
| 9 | 22,468 | Eastport-South Manor CSD | Manorville |
| 10 | 22,078 | Phelps-Clifton Springs Central SD | Clifton Springs |
| 11 | 21,121 | Mattituck-Cutchogue UFSD | Cutchogue |
| 12 | 20,844 | Peekskill City SD | Peekskill |
| 13 | 20,565 | East Hampton UFSD | East Hampton |
| 14 | 20,497 | Norwich City SD | Norwich |
| 15 | 20,179 | Bethlehem Central SD | Delmar |
| 16 | 19,754 | Gloversville City SD | Gloversville |
| 17 | 19,414 | UFSD of the Tarrytowns | Sleepy Hollow |
| 18 | 19,034 | Nanuet UFSD | Nanuet |
| 19 | 18,980 | Somers Central SD | Somers |
| 20 | 18,979 | Bath Central SD | Bath |
| 21 | 18,745 | Blind Brook-Rye UFSD | Rye Brook |
| 22 | 18,739 | Catskill Central SD | Catskill |
| 23 | 18,709 | Croton-Harmon UFSD | Croton on Hdsn |
| 24 | 18,419 | Cobleskill-Richmondville Central SD | Cobleskill |
| 25 | 18,041 | Briarcliff Mnr UFSD | Briarcliff Mnr |
| 26 | 18,015 | Dansville Central SD | Dansville |
| 27 | 17,969 | Geneva City SD | Geneva |
| 28 | 17,852 | Solvay UFSD | Solvay |
| 29 | 17,484 | Bedford Central SD | Bedford |
| 30 | 17,451 | Taconic Hills Central SD | Craryville |
| 31 | 17,372 | Marlboro Central SD | Marlboro |
| 32 | 17,298 | Pittsford Central SD | Pittsford |
| 33 | 17,159 | Broadalbin-Perth Central SD | Broadalbin |
| 34 | 17,135 | Skaneateles Central SD | Skaneateles |
| 35 | 17,119 | Bronxville UFSD | Bronxville |
| 36 | 16,808 | Minisink Valley Central SD | Slate Hill |
| 37 | 16,772 | Sweet Home Central SD | Amherst |
| 38 | 16,536 | Bayport-Blue Point UFSD | Bayport |
| 39 | 16,512 | Oyster Bay-East Norwich Central SD | Oyster Bay |
| 40 | 16,435 | Patchogue-Medford UFSD | Patchogue |
| 41 | 16,287 | Mount Pleasant Central SD | Thornwood |
| 42 | 16,272 | South Country Central SD | East Patchogue |
| 43 | 16,253 | Niagara Falls City SD | Niagara Falls |
| 44 | 16,197 | Niagara-Wheatfield Central SD | Niagara Falls |
| 45 | 16,121 | Cold Spring Hrbr Central SD | Cold Spring Hrbr |
| 46 | 16,054 | New Hyde Pk-Garden City Pk UFSD | New Hyde Park |
| 47 | 15,684 | Southwestern CSD at Jamestown | Jamestown |
| 48 | 15,653 | Johnson City Central SD | Johnson City |
| 49 | 15,647 | Batavia City SD | Batavia |
| 50 | 15,485 | Pleasantville UFSD | Pleasantville |
| 51 | 15,395 | Hannibal Central SD | Hannibal |
| 51 | 15,395 | Schalmont Central SD | Schenectady |
| 53 | 15,235 | Southampton UFSD | Southampton |
| 54 | 15,214 | Ramapo Central SD (Suffern) | Hillburn |
| 55 | 15,213 | Bay Shore UFSD | Bay Shore |
| 56 | 15,117 | Hudson Falls Central SD | Fort Edward |
| 57 | 15,020 | Scarsdale UFSD | Scarsdale |
| 58 | 14,888 | Starpoint Central SD | Lockport |
| 59 | 14,514 | Beacon City SD | Beacon |
| 60 | 14,450 | North Shore Central SD | Sea Cliff |
| 61 | 14,346 | Putnam Valley Central SD | Putnam Valley |
| 62 | 14,325 | Ardsley UFSD | Ardsley |
| 63 | 14,160 | Cheektowaga-Sloan UFSD | Sloan |
| 64 | 14,114 | Niskayuna Central SD | Schenectady |
| 65 | 14,099 | Sachem Central SD | Holbrook |
| 66 | 14,077 | Hendrick Hudson Central SD | Montrose |
| 67 | 13,989 | Fredonia Central SD | Fredonia |
| 68 | 13,838 | Camden Central SD | Camden |
| 69 | 13,789 | Peru Central SD | Peru |
| 70 | 13,778 | Mamaroneck UFSD | Mamaroneck |
| 71 | 13,631 | Center Moriches UFSD | Center Moriches |
| 72 | 13,604 | Attica Central SD | Attica |
| 73 | 13,318 | Akron Central SD | Akron |
| 74 | 13,284 | Cornwall Central SD | Cornwall on Hdsn |
| 75 | 13,201 | Smithtown Central SD | Smithtown |
| 76 | 13,178 | Commack UFSD | East Northport |
| 77 | 13,049 | Chappaqua Central SD | Chappaqua |
| 78 | 13,006 | Plainedge UFSD | N Massapequa |
| 79 | 12,988 | Port Washington UFSD | Port Washington |
| 80 | 12,964 | Jamestown City SD | Jamestown |
| 81 | 12,905 | Katonah-Lewisboro UFSD | South Salem |
| 82 | 12,861 | Rye City SD | Rye |
| 83 | 12,790 | East Islip UFSD | Islip Terrace |
| 84 | 12,615 | William Floyd UFSD | Mastic Beach |
| 85 | 12,595 | Valhalla UFSD | Valhalla |
| 86 | 12,553 | Newark Central SD | Newark |
| 87 | 12,529 | Livonia Central SD | Livonia |
| 88 | 12,478 | Jordan-Elbridge Central SD | Elbridge |
| 89 | 12,423 | Ilion Central SD | Ilion |
| 90 | 12,384 | Dryden Central SD | Dryden |
| 91 | 12,328 | North Babylon UFSD | North Babylon |
| 92 | 12,265 | Mount Vernon City SD | Mount Vernon |
| 93 | 12,250 | Chenango Valley Central SD | Binghamton |
| 94 | 12,243 | Connetquot Central SD | Bohemia |
| 95 | 12,242 | Owego-Apalachin Central SD | Owego |
| 96 | 12,181 | Pearl River UFSD | Pearl River |
| 97 | 11,985 | Vestal Central SD | Vestal |
| 98 | 11,968 | Homer Central SD | Homer |
| 99 | 11,918 | Middletown City SD | Middletown |
| 100 | 11,917 | Babylon UFSD | Babylon |
| 101 | 11,885 | East Irondequoit Central SD | Rochester |
| 102 | 11,846 | Chittenango Central SD | Chittenango |
| 103 | 11,827 | Clarence Central SD | Clarence Center |
| 104 | 11,691 | New York City Public Schools | New York |
| 105 | 11,668 | East Greenbush Central SD | East Greenbush |
| 106 | 11,569 | Harborfields Central SD | Greenlawn |
| 107 | 11,469 | Ravena-Coeymans-Selkirk Ctrl SD | Selkirk |
| 108 | 11,449 | Newfane Central SD | Burt |
| 109 | 11,422 | White Plains City SD | White Plains |
| 110 | 11,406 | Glens Falls City SD | Glens Falls |
| 111 | 11,394 | Marcellus Central SD | Marcellus |
| 112 | 11,225 | Hilton Central SD | Hilton |
| 113 | 11,140 | Lakeland Central SD | Shrub Oak |
| 114 | 11,132 | Medina Central SD | Medina |
| 115 | 11,077 | Spencerport Central SD | Spencerport |
| 116 | 11,014 | Longwood Central SD | Middle Island |
| 117 | 10,984 | Carthage Central SD | Carthage |
| 118 | 10,891 | Pelham UFSD | Pelham |
| 119 | 10,876 | Queensbury UFSD | Queensbury |
| 120 | 10,874 | West Irondequoit Central SD | Rochester |
| 121 | 10,845 | Monticello Central SD | Monticello |
| 122 | 10,782 | Elmira City SD | Elmira |
| 123 | 10,654 | Highland Central SD | Highland |
| 124 | 10,549 | Tonawanda City SD | Tonawanda |
| 125 | 10,471 | Victor Central SD | Victor |
| 126 | 10,383 | Sayville UFSD | Sayville |
| 127 | 10,338 | Alden Central SD | Alden |
| 128 | 10,335 | Port Chester-Rye UFSD | Port Chester |
| 129 | 10,227 | Averill Park Central SD | Averill Park |
| 130 | 10,190 | East Syracuse-Minoa Central SD | East Syracuse |
| 131 | 10,154 | Warwick Valley Central SD | Warwick |
| 132 | 10,150 | Manhasset UFSD | Manhasset |
| 133 | 10,129 | Canandaigua City SD | Canandaigua |
| 134 | 9,841 | Malone Central SD | Malone |
| 135 | 9,797 | Beekmantown Central SD | West Chazy |
| 136 | 9,790 | Plattsburgh City SD | Plattsburgh |
| 137 | 9,787 | Hornell City SD | Hornell |
| 138 | 9,753 | Chenango Forks Central SD | Binghamton |
| 139 | 9,723 | Greece Central SD | Rochester |
| 140 | 9,667 | Evans-Brant Central SD (Lake Shore) | Angola |
| 140 | 9,667 | Gates-Chili Central SD | Rochester |
| 142 | 9,615 | Rome City SD | Rome |
| 143 | 9,572 | Mineola UFSD | Mineola |
| 144 | 9,495 | Lewiston-Porter Central SD | Youngstown |
| 145 | 9,401 | Monroe-Woodbury Central SD | Central Valley |
| 146 | 9,303 | New Paltz Central SD | New Paltz |
| 147 | 9,237 | Wayland-Cohocton Central SD | Wayland |
| 148 | 9,179 | Bethpage UFSD | Bethpage |
| 149 | 9,160 | South Orangetown Central SD | Blauvelt |
| 150 | 9,090 | Saugerties Central SD | Saugerties |
| 151 | 9,073 | Massena Central SD | Massena |
| 152 | 8,968 | Ballston Spa Central SD | Ballston Spa |
| 153 | 8,965 | Brewster Central SD | Brewster |
| 154 | 8,885 | South Jefferson Central SD | Adams Center |
| 155 | 8,867 | Saratoga Spgs City SD | Saratoga Spgs |
| 156 | 8,842 | West Genesee Central SD | Camillus |
| 157 | 8,781 | Edgemont UFSD | Scarsdale |
| 158 | 8,745 | Indian River Central SD | Philadelphia |
| 159 | 8,714 | Central Islip UFSD | Central Islip |
| 160 | 8,699 | Jamesville-Dewitt Central SD | Dewitt |
| 161 | 8,690 | Oneonta City SD | Oneonta |
| 162 | 8,661 | Red Hook Central SD | Red Hook |
| 163 | 8,652 | Auburn City SD | Auburn |
| 164 | 8,651 | Merrick UFSD | Merrick |
| 165 | 8,624 | Eden Central SD | Eden |
| 166 | 8,600 | Sherburne-Earlville Central SD | Sherburne |
| 167 | 8,553 | West Islip UFSD | West Islip |
| 168 | 8,443 | S Glens Fls Central SD | S Glens Fls |
| 169 | 8,355 | Vernon-Verona-Sherrill Central SD | Verona |
| 170 | 8,306 | Watertown City SD | Watertown |
| 171 | 8,232 | Johnstown City SD | Johnstown |
| 172 | 8,221 | Locust Valley Central SD | Locust Valley |

*Note: This section only includes districts with 1,500 or more students; All categories are ranked from high to low*

| | | | |
|---|---|---|---|
| 173 | 8,208 | Lancaster Central SD | Lancaster |
| 174 | 8,075 | Guilderland Central SD | Guilderland |
| 175 | 8,040 | Islip UFSD | Islip |
| 175 | 8,040 | Oneida City SD | Oneida |
| 177 | 8,012 | Half Hollow Hills Central SD | Dix Hills |
| 178 | 8,004 | Union-Endicott Central SD | Endicott |
| 179 | 7,975 | Honeoye Falls-Lima Central SD | Honeoye Falls |
| 180 | 7,937 | Elwood UFSD | Greenlawn |
| 181 | 7,896 | East Williston UFSD | Old Westbury |
| 182 | 7,891 | Cheektowaga Central SD | Cheektowaga |
| 183 | 7,856 | Shenendehowa Central SD | Clifton Park |
| 184 | 7,832 | Syosset Central SD | Syosset |
| 185 | 7,828 | Penn Yan Central SD | Penn Yan |
| 186 | 7,810 | Lansingburgh Central SD | Troy |
| 187 | 7,784 | Eastchester UFSD | Eastchester |
| 188 | 7,753 | Syracuse City SD | Syracuse |
| 189 | 7,745 | Arlington Central SD | Poughkeepsie |
| 190 | 7,726 | Scotia-Glenville Central SD | Scotia |
| 191 | 7,722 | Mount Sinai UFSD | Mount Sinai |
| 192 | 7,617 | Coxsackie-Athens Central SD | Coxsackie |
| 193 | 7,588 | Amsterdam City SD | Amsterdam |
| 194 | 7,581 | Holland Patent Central SD | Holland Patent |
| 195 | 7,546 | Burnt Hills-Ballston Lake CSD | Scotia |
| 196 | 7,526 | Rondout Valley Central SD | Accord |
| 197 | 7,524 | Ellenville Central SD | Ellenville |
| 198 | 7,459 | Susquehanna Valley Central SD | Conklin |
| 199 | 7,458 | Roslyn UFSD | Roslyn |
| 200 | 7,439 | Troy City SD | Troy |
| 201 | 7,359 | New Rochelle City SD | New Rochelle |
| 202 | 7,312 | Great Neck UFSD | Great Neck |
| 203 | 7,289 | North Syracuse Central SD | North Syracuse |
| 204 | 7,245 | Westhill Central SD | Syracuse |
| 205 | 7,210 | North Colonie Central SD | Latham |
| 206 | 7,133 | Franklin Square UFSD | Franklin Square |
| 207 | 7,122 | Lackawanna City SD | Lackawanna |
| 208 | 7,111 | Windsor Central SD | Windsor |
| 209 | 7,074 | Yorktown Central SD | Yorktown Hgts |
| 210 | 7,027 | Central Square Central SD | Central Square |
| 211 | 7,015 | Albion Central SD | Albion |
| 212 | 6,995 | Rocky Point UFSD | Rocky Point |
| 213 | 6,984 | Churchville-Chili Central SD | Churchville |
| 214 | 6,976 | Garden City UFSD | Garden City |
| 215 | 6,948 | Brockport Central SD | Brockport |
| 216 | 6,946 | Hewlett-Woodmere UFSD | Woodmere |
| 217 | 6,936 | Clarkstown Central SD | New City |
| 218 | 6,912 | Westbury UFSD | Old Westbury |
| 219 | 6,820 | East Meadow UFSD | Westbury |
| 220 | 6,801 | Liverpool Central SD | Liverpool |
| 221 | 6,766 | Carmel Central SD | Patterson |
| 222 | 6,692 | Mohonasen Central SD | Schenectady |
| 223 | 6,639 | Comsewogue School District | Port Jeff Stn |
| 224 | 6,596 | Dover UFSD | Dover Plains |
| 225 | 6,589 | Ossining UFSD | Ossining |
| 226 | 6,554 | Fayetteville-Manlius Central SD | Manlius |
| 227 | 6,521 | Baldwin UFSD | Baldwin |
| 228 | 6,492 | Washingtonville Central SD | Washingtonville |
| 229 | 6,456 | Middle Country Central SD | Centereach |
| 230 | 6,444 | West Seneca Central SD | West Seneca |
| 231 | 6,429 | New Hartford Central SD | New Hartford |
| 232 | 6,415 | Massapequa UFSD | Massapequa |
| 233 | 6,347 | Springville-Griffith Institute CSD | Springville |
| 234 | 6,327 | Hastings-on-Hudson UFSD | Hastings on Hdsn |
| 235 | 6,311 | South Huntington UFSD | Huntington Stn |
| 236 | 6,268 | Wayne Central SD | Ontario Center |
| 237 | 6,229 | Mahopac Central SD | Mahopac |
| 238 | 6,165 | South Colonie Central SD | Albany |
| 239 | 6,126 | Yonkers City SD | Yonkers |
| 240 | 6,092 | Herricks UFSD | New Hyde Park |
| 241 | 6,064 | Cohoes City SD | Cohoes |
| 242 | 6,054 | Kenmore-Tonawanda UFSD | Buffalo |
| 243 | 5,996 | West Babylon UFSD | West Babylon |
| 244 | 5,984 | Baldwinsville Central SD | Baldwinsville |
| 245 | 5,983 | Rockville Ctr UFSD | Rockville Ctr |
| 246 | 5,816 | Goshen Central SD | Goshen |
| 247 | 5,802 | Salmon River Central SD | Fort Covington |
| 248 | 5,784 | Utica City SD | Utica |
| 249 | 5,647 | Pine Bush Central SD | Pine Bush |
| 250 | 5,633 | Lindenhurst UFSD | Lindenhurst |
| 251 | 5,567 | Canastota Central SD | Canastota |
| 252 | 5,562 | Brentwood UFSD | Brentwood |
| 253 | 5,543 | Mexico Central SD | Mexico |
| 254 | 5,527 | Newburgh City SD | Newburgh |
| 255 | 5,519 | Poughkeepsie City SD | Poughkeepsie |
| 256 | 5,503 | Albany City SD | Albany |
| 257 | 5,496 | Amityville UFSD | Amityville |
| 258 | 5,457 | Schenectady City SD | Schenectady |
| 259 | 5,385 | Elmont UFSD | Elmont |
| 260 | 5,352 | Cazenovia Central SD | Cazenovia |
| 261 | 5,326 | Northport-East Northport UFSD | Northport |
| 262 | 5,268 | Grand Island Central SD | Grand Island |
| 263 | 5,249 | Hicksville UFSD | Hicksville |
| 264 | 5,244 | Royalton-Hartland Central SD | Middleport |
| 265 | 5,215 | Spackenkill UFSD | Poughkeepsie |
| 266 | 5,203 | Brighton Central SD | Rochester |
| 267 | 5,108 | Hauppauge UFSD | Hauppauge |
| 268 | 5,036 | Jericho UFSD | Jericho |
| 269 | 5,028 | Plainview-Old Bethpage Central SD | Plainview |
| 270 | 4,983 | Webster Central SD | Webster |
| 271 | 4,957 | Farmingdale UFSD | Farmingdale |
| 272 | 4,922 | Hyde Park Central SD | Hyde Park |
| 273 | 4,885 | Nyack UFSD | Nyack |
| 274 | 4,750 | Freeport UFSD | Freeport |
| 275 | 4,702 | West Hempstead UFSD | West Hempstead |
| 276 | 4,695 | Olean City SD | Olean |
| 277 | 4,694 | Oceanside UFSD | Oceanside |
| 278 | 4,681 | Kinderhook Central SD | Valatie |
| 279 | 4,645 | Ogdensburg City SD | Ogdensburg |
| 280 | 4,578 | Hempstead UFSD | Hempstead |
| 280 | 4,578 | Rochester City SD | Rochester |
| 282 | 4,572 | Wallkill Central SD | Wallkill |
| 283 | 4,555 | Gouverneur Central SD | Gouverneur |
| 284 | 4,551 | Levittown UFSD | Levittown |
| 285 | 4,533 | Kings Park Central SD | Kings Park |
| 286 | 4,519 | Three Village Central SD | Stony Brook |
| 287 | 4,511 | Island Trees UFSD | Levittown |
| 288 | 4,387 | Liberty Central SD | Liberty |
| 289 | 4,360 | Wantagh UFSD | Wantagh |
| 290 | 4,306 | Binghamton City SD | Binghamton |
| 291 | 4,294 | Corning City SD | Painted Post |
| 292 | 4,153 | General Brown Central SD | Dexter |
| 293 | 4,045 | Valley Stream Central High SD | Valley Stream |
| 294 | 4,007 | Horseheads Central SD | Horseheads |
| 295 | 3,983 | Miller Place UFSD | Miller Place |
| 296 | 3,812 | Palmyra-Macedon Central SD | Palmyra |
| 297 | 3,780 | Riverhead Central SD | Riverhead |
| 298 | 3,725 | Maine-Endwell Central SD | Endwell |
| 299 | 3,711 | Schuylerville Central SD | Schuylerville |
| 300 | 3,628 | Onteora Central SD | Boiceville |
| 301 | 3,625 | Valley Central SD (Montgomery) | Montgomery |
| 302 | 3,619 | Cheektowaga-Maryvale UFSD | Cheektowaga |
| 303 | 3,611 | Copiague UFSD | Copiague |
| 304 | 3,588 | Saranac Central SD | Dannemora |
| 305 | 3,478 | Amherst Central SD | Amherst |
| 306 | 3,453 | Harrison Central SD | Harrison |
| 307 | 3,418 | East Aurora UFSD | East Aurora |
| 308 | 3,411 | Fairport Central SD | Fairport |
| 309 | 3,406 | Wyandanch UFSD | Wyandanch |
| 310 | 3,306 | North Tonawanda City SD | North Tonawanda |
| 311 | 3,292 | Hudson City SD | Hudson |
| 312 | 3,130 | Depew UFSD | Depew |
| 313 | 3,091 | Fulton City SD | Fulton |
| 314 | 3,060 | Iroquois Central SD | Elma |
| 315 | 3,012 | Orchard Park Central SD | Orchard Park |
| 316 | 2,788 | Dunkirk City SD | Dunkirk |
| 317 | 2,750 | Cortland City SD | Cortland |
| 318 | 2,736 | Williamsville Central SD | East Amherst |
| 319 | 2,730 | Frontier Central SD | Hamburg |
| 320 | 2,724 | East Ramapo Central SD | Spring Valley |
| 321 | 2,698 | Deer Park UFSD | Deer Park |
| 322 | 2,598 | Whitesboro Central SD | Yorkville |
| 323 | 2,541 | Greenburgh Central SD | Hartsdale |
| 324 | 2,504 | Ithaca City SD | Ithaca |
| 325 | 2,471 | Glen Cove City SD | Glen Cove |
| 326 | 2,456 | Uniondale UFSD | Uniondale |
| 327 | 2,350 | Oswego City SD | Oswego |
| 328 | 2,275 | Hamburg Central SD | Hamburg |
| 329 | 2,199 | Port Jervis City SD | Port Jervis |
| 330 | 1,908 | Wappingers Central SD | Wappingers Fls |
| 331 | 1,879 | Lynbrook UFSD | Lynbrook |
| 332 | 1,871 | Huntington UFSD | Huntington Stn |
| 333 | 1,831 | Malverne UFSD | Malverne |
| 334 | 1,721 | Shoreham-Wading River Central SD | Shoreham |
| 335 | 1,567 | Phoenix Central SD | Phoenix |
| 336 | 1,429 | Waverly Central SD | Waverly |
| 337 | 1,391 | Yorkshire-Pioneer Central SD | Yorkshire |
| 338 | 1,390 | Lockport City SD | Lockport |
| 339 | 1,349 | Rush-Henrietta Central SD | Henrietta |
| 340 | 1,090 | Seaford UFSD | Seaford |
| 341 | 975 | Penfield Central SD | Rochester |
| 342 | 954 | Floral Park-Bellerose UFSD | Floral Park |
| 343 | 851 | Kingston City SD | Kingston |
| 344 | 453 | North Bellmore UFSD | Bellmore |
| 345 | 330 | Long Beach City SD | Long Beach |
| 346 | 192 | Valley Stream 13 UFSD | Valley Stream |
| 347 | 95 | Lawrence UFSD | Lawrence |
| 348 | 0 | Bellmore-Merrick Central High SD | North Merrick |
| 348 | 0 | Sewanhaka Central High SD | Floral Park |
| n/a | n/a | Charter School for Applied Tech | Buffalo |
| n/a | n/a | NYC Special Schools - District 75 | New York |
| n/a | n/a | NYC Geographic District # 1 | New York |
| n/a | n/a | NYC Geographic District # 2 | New York |
| n/a | n/a | NYC Geographic District # 3 | New York |
| n/a | n/a | NYC Geographic District # 4 | New York |
| n/a | n/a | NYC Geographic District # 5 | New York |
| n/a | n/a | NYC Geographic District # 6 | New York |
| n/a | n/a | NYC Geographic District # 7 | Bronx |
| n/a | n/a | NYC Geographic District # 8 | Bronx |
| n/a | n/a | NYC Geographic District # 9 | Bronx |
| n/a | n/a | NYC Geographic District #10 | Bronx |
| n/a | n/a | NYC Geographic District #11 | Bronx |
| n/a | n/a | NYC Geographic District #12 | Bronx |
| n/a | n/a | NYC Geographic District #13 | Brooklyn |
| n/a | n/a | NYC Geographic District #14 | Brooklyn |
| n/a | n/a | NYC Geographic District #15 | Brooklyn |
| n/a | n/a | NYC Geographic District #16 | Brooklyn |
| n/a | n/a | NYC Geographic District #17 | Brooklyn |
| n/a | n/a | NYC Geographic District #18 | Brooklyn |
| n/a | n/a | NYC Geographic District #19 | Brooklyn |
| n/a | n/a | NYC Geographic District #20 | Brooklyn |
| n/a | n/a | NYC Geographic District #21 | Brooklyn |
| n/a | n/a | NYC Geographic District #22 | Brooklyn |
| n/a | n/a | NYC Geographic District #23 | Brooklyn |
| n/a | n/a | NYC Geographic District #24 | Ridgewood |
| n/a | n/a | NYC Geographic District #25 | Flushing |
| n/a | n/a | NYC Geographic District #26 | Bayside |
| n/a | n/a | NYC Geographic District #27 | Ozone Park |
| n/a | n/a | NYC Geographic District #28 | Jamaica |
| n/a | n/a | NYC Geographic District #29 | Rosedale |
| n/a | n/a | NYC Geographic District #30 | Long Isl City |
| n/a | n/a | NYC Geographic District #31 | Staten Island |
| n/a | n/a | NYC Geographic District #32 | Brooklyn |

## Number of Diploma Recipients

| Rank | Number | District Name | City |
|---|---|---|---|
| 1 | 56,654 | New York City Public Schools | New York |
| 2 | 7,360 | NYC Geographic District # 2 | New York |
| 3 | 3,657 | NYC Geographic District #26 | Bayside |
| 4 | 3,595 | NYC Geographic District #10 | Bronx |
| 5 | 3,536 | NYC Geographic District #31 | Staten Island |
| 6 | 2,751 | NYC Geographic District #28 | Jamaica |
| 7 | 2,444 | NYC Geographic District #24 | Ridgewood |
| 8 | 2,279 | NYC Geographic District #22 | Brooklyn |
| 9 | 2,273 | NYC Geographic District #21 | Brooklyn |
| 10 | 2,148 | NYC Geographic District #13 | Brooklyn |
| 11 | 2,116 | NYC Geographic District #20 | Brooklyn |
| 12 | 2,091 | NYC Geographic District # 3 | New York |
| 13 | 1,943 | NYC Geographic District #27 | Ozone Park |
| 14 | 1,798 | NYC Geographic District #11 | Bronx |
| 15 | 1,762 | NYC Geographic District # 8 | Bronx |
| 16 | 1,737 | NYC Geographic District #30 | Long Isl City |
| 17 | 1,716 | NYC Geographic District #17 | Brooklyn |
| 18 | 1,568 | NYC Geographic District #25 | Flushing |
| 19 | 1,538 | Buffalo City SD | Buffalo |
| 20 | 1,406 | Rochester City SD | Rochester |
| 21 | 1,403 | Sewanhaka Central High SD | Floral Park |
| 22 | 1,361 | Yonkers City SD | Yonkers |
| 23 | 1,325 | NYC Geographic District # 9 | Bronx |
| 24 | 1,190 | Sachem Central SD | Holbrook |
| 25 | 1,062 | NYC Geographic District #19 | Brooklyn |
| 26 | 1,029 | Brentwood UFSD | Brentwood |
| 27 | 1,017 | NYC Geographic District #15 | Brooklyn |
| 28 | 993 | NYC Geographic District #14 | Brooklyn |
| 29 | 973 | Bellmore-Merrick Central High SD | North Merrick |
| 30 | 970 | NYC Geographic District # 7 | Bronx |
| 31 | 926 | Williamsville Central SD | East Amherst |
| 32 | 915 | Wappingers Central SD | Wappingers Fls |
| 33 | 889 | Greece Central SD | Rochester |
| 34 | 852 | NYC Geographic District #12 | Bronx |
| 35 | 847 | Syracuse City SD | Syracuse |
| 36 | 842 | Middle Country Central SD | Centereach |
| 37 | 839 | NYC Geographic District # 6 | New York |
| 38 | 825 | NYC Geographic District #18 | Brooklyn |
| 39 | 785 | Valley Stream Central High SD | Valley Stream |

*Note: This section only includes districts with 1,500 or more students; All categories are ranked from high to low*

| | | | |
|---|---|---|---|
| 40 | 779 | Webster Central SD | Webster |
| 41 | 769 | Arlington Central SD | Poughkeepsie |
| 42 | 761 | Smithtown Central SD | Smithtown |
| 43 | 746 | North Syracuse Central SD | North Syracuse |
| 44 | 716 | NYC Geographic District # 4 | New York |
| 45 | 715 | Newburgh City SD | Newburgh |
| 46 | 714 | Half Hollow Hills Central SD | Dix Hills |
| 47 | 712 | William Floyd UFSD | Mastic Beach |
| 48 | 692 | Longwood Central SD | Middle Island |
| 49 | 685 | Clarkstown Central SD | New City |
| 50 | 681 | NYC Geographic District # 1 | New York |
| 51 | 677 | New Rochelle City SD | New Rochelle |
| 51 | 677 | NYC Geographic District # 5 | New York |
| 53 | 676 | Kenmore-Tonawanda UFSD | Buffalo |
| 54 | 665 | Patchogue-Medford UFSD | Patchogue |
| 55 | 640 | Levittown UFSD | Levittown |
| 56 | 632 | Shenendehowa Central SD | Clifton Park |
| 57 | 624 | Three Village Central SD | Stony Brook |
| 58 | 623 | Massapequa UFSD | Massapequa |
| 59 | 615 | NYC Geographic District #29 | Rosedale |
| 60 | 614 | East Meadow UFSD | Westbury |
| 61 | 607 | Fairport Central SD | Fairport |
| 62 | 592 | Lindenhurst UFSD | Lindenhurst |
| 63 | 591 | Commack UFSD | East Northport |
| 64 | 581 | North Rockland Central SD | Garnerville |
| 65 | 558 | Monroe-Woodbury Central SD | Central Valley |
| 66 | 553 | Syosset Central SD | Syosset |
| 67 | 550 | West Seneca Central SD | West Seneca |
| 68 | 537 | Connetquot Central SD | Bohemia |
| 69 | 534 | East Ramapo Central SD | Spring Valley |
| 70 | 524 | Great Neck UFSD | Great Neck |
| 71 | 521 | Liverpool Central SD | Liverpool |
| 71 | 521 | NYC Geographic District #32 | Brooklyn |
| 73 | 516 | Mount Vernon City SD | Mount Vernon |
| 73 | 516 | Northport-East Northport UFSD | Northport |
| 75 | 511 | Utica City SD | Utica |
| 76 | 507 | Schenectady City SD | Schenectady |
| 77 | 491 | White Plains City SD | White Plains |
| 78 | 488 | Oceanside UFSD | Oceanside |
| 79 | 486 | Farmingdale UFSD | Farmingdale |
| 80 | 483 | NYC Geographic District #16 | Brooklyn |
| 81 | 481 | Lancaster Central SD | Lancaster |
| 82 | 478 | Middletown City SD | Middletown |
| 83 | 477 | Lakeland Central SD | Shrub Oak |
| 84 | 474 | South Colonie Central SD | Albany |
| 85 | 473 | Kingston City SD | Kingston |
| 86 | 471 | Pittsford Central SD | Pittsford |
| 87 | 457 | West Islip UFSD | West Islip |
| 88 | 456 | Niagara Falls City SD | Niagara Falls |
| 89 | 449 | Baldwinsville Central SD | Baldwinsville |
| 89 | 449 | Rush-Henrietta Central SD | Henrietta |
| 91 | 443 | Saratoga Spgs City SD | Saratoga Spgs |
| 92 | 442 | South Huntington UFSD | Huntington Stn |
| 93 | 441 | Bay Shore UFSD | Bay Shore |
| 93 | 441 | Mahopac Central SD | Mahopac |
| 93 | 441 | Orchard Park Central SD | Orchard Park |
| 96 | 433 | Elmira City SD | Elmira |
| 96 | 433 | Freeport UFSD | Freeport |
| 96 | 433 | Frontier Central SD | Hamburg |
| 99 | 430 | West Genesee Central SD | Camillus |
| 100 | 426 | Guilderland Central SD | Guilderland |
| 101 | 421 | Albany City SD | Albany |
| 102 | 415 | Corning City SD | Painted Post |
| 103 | 413 | Gates-Chili Central SD | Rochester |
| 103 | 413 | Uniondale UFSD | Uniondale |
| 105 | 408 | Baldwin UFSD | Baldwin |
| 106 | 405 | Pine Bush Central SD | Pine Bush |
| 107 | 401 | Hicksville UFSD | Hicksville |
| 108 | 400 | Washingtonville Central SD | Washingtonville |
| 109 | 398 | East Islip UFSD | Islip Terrace |
| 110 | 394 | Port Washington UFSD | Port Washington |
| 111 | 389 | Bethlehem Central SD | Delmar |
| 112 | 379 | Lockport City SD | Lockport |
| 112 | 379 | Ramapo Central SD (Suffern) | Hillburn |
| 114 | 378 | Fayetteville-Manlius Central SD | Manlius |
| 115 | 376 | Plainview-Old Bethpage Central SD | Plainview |
| 116 | 375 | Copiague UFSD | Copiague |
| 117 | 368 | Carmel Central SD | Patterson |
| 118 | 367 | Clarence Central SD | Clarence Center |
| 119 | 366 | Chappaqua Central SD | Chappaqua |
| 119 | 366 | Penfield Central SD | Rochester |
| 121 | 363 | Niagara-Wheatfield Central SD | Niagara Falls |
| 121 | 363 | Scarsdale UFSD | Scarsdale |
| 123 | 362 | Mamaroneck UFSD | Mamaroneck |
| 124 | 361 | Hilton Central SD | Hilton |
| 125 | 360 | Rome City SD | Rome |
| 126 | 356 | East Greenbush Central SD | East Greenbush |
| 126 | 356 | Valley Central SD (Montgomery) | Montgomery |
| 128 | 353 | West Babylon UFSD | West Babylon |
| 129 | 351 | Ithaca City SD | Ithaca |
| 130 | 347 | Churchville-Chili Central SD | Churchville |
| 130 | 347 | Deer Park UFSD | Deer Park |
| 132 | 345 | Brockport Central SD | Brockport |
| 133 | 343 | Niskayuna Central SD | Schenectady |
| 134 | 342 | Riverhead Central SD | Riverhead |
| 135 | 341 | North Babylon UFSD | North Babylon |
| 136 | 338 | Herricks UFSD | New Hyde Park |
| 137 | 335 | Minisink Valley Central SD | Slate Hill |
| 137 | 335 | North Tonawanda City SD | North Tonawanda |
| 139 | 332 | Canandaigua City SD | Canandaigua |
| 140 | 330 | Brighton Central SD | Rochester |
| 140 | 330 | Yorktown Central SD | Yorktown Hgts |
| 142 | 328 | Binghamton City SD | Binghamton |
| 143 | 327 | Union-Endicott Central SD | Endicott |
| 144 | 325 | Hyde Park Central SD | Hyde Park |
| 145 | 322 | Jamestown City SD | Jamestown |
| 145 | 322 | Kings Park Central SD | Kings Park |
| 145 | 322 | Long Beach City SD | Long Beach |
| 145 | 322 | Spencerport Central SD | Spencerport |
| 149 | 318 | Warwick Valley Central SD | Warwick |
| 150 | 317 | Oswego City SD | Oswego |
| 151 | 316 | Horseheads Central SD | Horseheads |
| 152 | 307 | West Irondequoit Central SD | Rochester |
| 153 | 305 | Central Square Central SD | Central Square |
| 153 | 305 | Hamburg Central SD | Hamburg |
| 153 | 305 | NYC Geographic District #23 | Brooklyn |
| 156 | 304 | Hauppauge UFSD | Hauppauge |
| 157 | 303 | Auburn City SD | Auburn |
| 157 | 303 | Queensbury UFSD | Queensbury |
| 159 | 302 | Bedford Central SD | Bedford |
| 160 | 300 | Central Islip UFSD | Central Islip |
| 160 | 300 | Katonah-Lewisboro UFSD | South Salem |
| 162 | 297 | Sweet Home Central SD | Amherst |
| 163 | 295 | Ballston Spa Central SD | Ballston Spa |
| 164 | 294 | Vestal Central SD | Vestal |
| 165 | 291 | Whitesboro Central SD | Yorkville |
| 166 | 287 | Jericho UFSD | Jericho |
| 167 | 286 | Ossining UFSD | Ossining |
| 168 | 284 | Comsewogue School District | Port Jeff Stn |
| 169 | 281 | Eastport-South Manor CSD | Manorville |
| 169 | 281 | Islip UFSD | Islip |
| 171 | 280 | Hewlett-Woodmere UFSD | Woodmere |
| 172 | 279 | East Irondequoit Central SD | Rochester |
| 173 | 277 | Garden City UFSD | Garden City |
| 174 | 276 | Burnt Hills-Ballston Lake CSD | Scotia |
| 174 | 276 | Plainedge UFSD | N Massapequa |
| 176 | 274 | Cornwall Central SD | Cornwall on Hdsn |
| 176 | 274 | Grand Island Central SD | Grand Island |
| 178 | 273 | Harborfields Central SD | Greenlawn |
| 179 | 272 | Averill Park Central SD | Averill Park |
| 180 | 271 | East Syracuse-Minoa Central SD | East Syracuse |
| 180 | 271 | Sayville UFSD | Sayville |
| 182 | 269 | Brewster Central SD | Brewster |
| 183 | 268 | Huntington UFSD | Huntington Stn |
| 183 | 268 | Lawrence UFSD | Lawrence |
| 185 | 266 | Roslyn UFSD | Roslyn |
| 186 | 264 | Rockville Ctr UFSD | Rockville Ctr |
| 187 | 262 | Wantagh UFSD | Wantagh |
| 188 | 261 | South Country Central SD | East Patchogue |
| 189 | 257 | Bethpage UFSD | Bethpage |
| 189 | 257 | Wallkill Central SD | Wallkill |
| 191 | 255 | Lynbrook UFSD | Lynbrook |
| 192 | 253 | Troy City SD | Troy |
| 193 | 251 | Hempstead UFSD | Hempstead |
| 193 | 251 | Victor Central SD | Victor |
| 195 | 250 | West Hempstead UFSD | West Hempstead |
| 196 | 247 | Saugerties Central SD | Saugerties |
| 197 | 243 | Miller Place UFSD | Miller Place |
| 198 | 240 | Fulton City SD | Fulton |
| 199 | 238 | Mohonasen Central SD | Schenectady |
| 200 | 236 | Iroquois Central SD | Elma |
| 201 | 233 | Somers Central SD | Somers |
| 202 | 232 | Harrison Central SD | Harrison |
| 202 | 232 | Rocky Point UFSD | Rocky Point |
| 202 | 232 | Westbury UFSD | Old Westbury |
| 205 | 231 | S Glens Fls Central SD | S Glens Fls |
| 206 | 230 | Goshen Central SD | Goshen |
| 207 | 228 | South Orangetown Central SD | Blauvelt |
| 208 | 226 | Poughkeepsie City SD | Poughkeepsie |
| 209 | 224 | Shoreham-Wading River Central SD | Shoreham |
| 210 | 223 | Port Chester-Rye UFSD | Port Chester |
| 211 | 221 | East Hampton UFSD | East Hampton |
| 211 | 221 | Hendrick Hudson Central SD | Montrose |
| 213 | 219 | Amityville UFSD | Amityville |
| 213 | 219 | Massena Central SD | Massena |
| 213 | 219 | Westhampton Bch UFSD | Westhampton Bch |
| 216 | 217 | Maine-Endwell Central SD | Endwell |
| 217 | 215 | Monticello Central SD | Monticello |
| 218 | 214 | Amherst Central SD | Amherst |
| 218 | 214 | Seaford UFSD | Seaford |
| 218 | 214 | Wayne Central SD | Ontario Center |
| 221 | 213 | Beacon City SD | Beacon |
| 221 | 213 | New Hartford Central SD | New Hartford |
| 221 | 213 | Scotia-Glenville Central SD | Scotia |
| 221 | 213 | Starpoint Central SD | Lockport |
| 225 | 212 | Watertown City SD | Watertown |
| 226 | 211 | Carthage Central SD | Carthage |
| 226 | 211 | Port Jervis City SD | Port Jervis |
| 228 | 208 | Byram Hills Central SD | Armonk |
| 228 | 208 | Island Trees UFSD | Levittown |
| 228 | 208 | Jamesville-Dewitt Central SD | Dewitt |
| 228 | 208 | Nyack UFSD | Nyack |
| 232 | 207 | Lewiston-Porter Central SD | Youngstown |
| 233 | 206 | Evans-Brant Central SD (Lake Shore) | Angola |
| 234 | 205 | Cheektowaga-Maryvale UFSD | Cheektowaga |
| 235 | 204 | Mount Sinai UFSD | Mount Sinai |
| 236 | 203 | Locust Valley Central SD | Locust Valley |
| 237 | 202 | Rondout Valley Central SD | Accord |
| 238 | 201 | UFSD of the Tarrytowns | Sleepy Hollow |
| 239 | 199 | Eastchester UFSD | Eastchester |
| 239 | 199 | Mexico Central SD | Mexico |
| 241 | 197 | Honeoye Falls-Lima Central SD | Honeoye Falls |
| 242 | 196 | Phoenix Central SD | Phoenix |
| 243 | 195 | Cortland City SD | Cortland |
| 243 | 195 | New Paltz Central SD | New Paltz |
| 245 | 193 | Indian River Central SD | Philadelphia |
| 245 | 193 | North Shore Central SD | Sea Cliff |
| 245 | 193 | Pearl River UFSD | Pearl River |
| 248 | 192 | Elwood UFSD | Greenlawn |
| 249 | 191 | Camden Central SD | Camden |
| 249 | 191 | Rye City SD | Rye |
| 251 | 190 | Amsterdam City SD | Amsterdam |
| 251 | 190 | Depew UFSD | Depew |
| 251 | 190 | Newark Central SD | Newark |
| 254 | 189 | Nanuet UFSD | Nanuet |
| 254 | 189 | Pelham UFSD | Pelham |
| 256 | 186 | Manhasset UFSD | Manhasset |
| 257 | 182 | Johnson City Central SD | Johnson City |
| 258 | 181 | Mineola UFSD | Mineola |
| 258 | 181 | Putnam Valley Central SD | Putnam Valley |
| 260 | 180 | Ardsley UFSD | Ardsley |
| 261 | 179 | Briarcliff Mnr UFSD | Briarcliff Mnr |
| 262 | 177 | Vernon-Verona-Sherrill Central SD | Verona |
| 263 | 176 | Cold Spring Hrbr Central SD | Cold Spring Hrbr |
| 264 | 175 | Albion Central SD | Albion |
| 265 | 174 | East Aurora UFSD | East Aurora |
| 266 | 173 | Batavia City SD | Batavia |
| 266 | 173 | Cheektowaga Central SD | Cheektowaga |
| 266 | 173 | Lansingburgh Central SD | Troy |
| 266 | 173 | Yorkshire-Pioneer Central SD | Yorkshire |
| 270 | 172 | Bayport-Blue Point UFSD | Bayport |
| 271 | 170 | Chittenango Central SD | Chittenango |
| 271 | 170 | Marlboro Central SD | Marlboro |
| 273 | 169 | Broadalbin-Perth Central SD | Broadalbin |
| 274 | 168 | Palmyra-Macedon Central SD | Palmyra |
| 274 | 168 | Peekskill City SD | Peekskill |
| 276 | 167 | East Williston UFSD | Old Westbury |
| 276 | 167 | Oneida City SD | Oneida |
| 278 | 166 | Westhill Central SD | Syracuse |
| 279 | 165 | Gloversville City SD | Gloversville |
| 280 | 164 | Chenango Forks Central SD | Binghamton |
| 281 | 163 | Alden Central SD | Alden |
| 281 | 163 | Glen Cove City SD | Glen Cove |
| 281 | 163 | Livonia Central SD | Livonia |
| 281 | 163 | Marcellus Central SD | Marcellus |
| 281 | 163 | Ravena-Coeymans-Selkirk Ctrl SD | Selkirk |
| 286 | 161 | Chenango Valley Central SD | Binghamton |
| 286 | 161 | Springville-Griffith Institute CSD | Springville |
| 288 | 159 | Kinderhook Central SD | Valatie |
| 289 | 158 | Schalmont Central SD | Schenectady |
| 290 | 156 | Geneva City SD | Geneva |
| 291 | 155 | Onteora Central SD | Boiceville |
| 292 | 154 | Glens Falls City SD | Glens Falls |
| 292 | 154 | Irvington UFSD | Irvington |
| 292 | 154 | Malone Central SD | Malone |

*Note: This section only includes districts with 1,500 or more students; All categories are ranked from high to low*

| 295 | 152 | Holland Patent Central SD | Holland Patent |
|---|---|---|---|
| 296 | 151 | Owego-Apalachin Central SD | Owego |
| 296 | 151 | Southwestern CSD at Jamestown | Jamestown |
| 298 | 150 | Southampton UFSD | Southampton |
| 299 | 148 | Beekmantown Central SD | West Chazy |
| 299 | 148 | Dunkirk City SD | Dunkirk |
| 299 | 148 | Gouverneur Central SD | Gouverneur |
| 299 | 148 | Plattsburgh City SD | Plattsburgh |
| 299 | 148 | Red Hook Central SD | Red Hook |
| 304 | 147 | Homer Central SD | Homer |
| 304 | 147 | Norwich City SD | Norwich |
| 304 | 147 | Saranac Central SD | Dannemora |
| 304 | 147 | Waterloo Central SD | Waterloo |
| 308 | 146 | Roosevelt UFSD | Roosevelt |
| 309 | 145 | Babylon UFSD | Babylon |
| 309 | 145 | Cobleskill-Richmondville Central SD | Cobleskill |
| 309 | 145 | Cohoes City SD | Cohoes |
| 309 | 145 | Susquehanna Valley Central SD | Conklin |
| 309 | 145 | Windsor Central SD | Windsor |
| 314 | 143 | Tonawanda City SD | Tonawanda |
| 315 | 142 | Eden Central SD | Eden |
| 315 | 142 | Fredonia Central SD | Fredonia |
| 317 | 140 | Edgemont UFSD | Scarsdale |
| 318 | 139 | Bath Central SD | Bath |
| 318 | 139 | Lackawanna City SD | Lackawanna |
| 318 | 139 | Newfane Central SD | Burt |
| 321 | 137 | Attica Central SD | Attica |
| 321 | 137 | Dover UFSD | Dover Plains |
| 321 | 137 | Mount Pleasant Central SD | Thornwood |
| 321 | 137 | South Jefferson Central SD | Adams Center |
| 325 | 134 | Hornell City SD | Hornell |
| 325 | 134 | Oneonta City SD | Oneonta |
| 325 | 134 | Taconic Hills Central SD | Craryville |
| 328 | 133 | Akron Central SD | Akron |
| 328 | 133 | Highland Central SD | Highland |
| 328 | 133 | Phelps-Clifton Springs Central SD | Clifton Springs |
| 328 | 133 | Wayland-Cohocton Central SD | Wayland |
| 332 | 131 | Cazenovia Central SD | Cazenovia |
| 332 | 131 | Hudson Falls Central SD | Fort Edward |
| 332 | 131 | Skaneateles Central SD | Skaneateles |
| 332 | 131 | Spackenkill UFSD | Poughkeepsie |
| 336 | 129 | Johnstown City SD | Johnstown |
| 336 | 129 | Pleasantville UFSD | Pleasantville |
| 338 | 127 | Jordan-Elbridge Central SD | Elbridge |
| 339 | 126 | Dryden Central SD | Dryden |
| 339 | 126 | Greenburgh Central SD | Hartsdale |
| 341 | 125 | Hastings-on-Hudson UFSD | Hastings on Hdsn |
| 342 | 124 | General Brown Central SD | Dexter |
| 342 | 124 | Medina Central SD | Medina |
| 344 | 123 | Coxsackie-Athens Central SD | Coxsackie |
| 345 | 122 | Mattituck-Cutchogue UFSD | Cutchogue |
| 346 | 120 | Peru Central SD | Peru |
| 347 | 119 | Croton-Harmon UFSD | Croton on Hdsn |
| 348 | 118 | Malverne UFSD | Malverne |
| 348 | 118 | Penn Yan Central SD | Penn Yan |
| 350 | 117 | Hampton Bays UFSD | Hampton Bays |
| 350 | 117 | Solvay UFSD | Solvay |
| 352 | 115 | Ellenville Central SD | Ellenville |
| 352 | 115 | Sherburne-Earlville Central SD | Sherburne |
| 352 | 115 | Waverly Central SD | Waverly |
| 355 | 114 | Olean City SD | Olean |
| 356 | 113 | Canastota Central SD | Canastota |
| 356 | 113 | Schuylerville Central SD | Schuylerville |
| 358 | 110 | Hudson City SD | Hudson |
| 359 | 109 | Bronxville UFSD | Bronxville |
| 360 | 106 | Cheektowaga-Sloan UFSD | Sloan |
| 361 | 105 | Dansville Central SD | Dansville |
| 362 | 104 | Ilion Central SD | Ilion |
| 362 | 104 | Royalton-Hartland Central SD | Middleport |
| 364 | 103 | Ogdensburg City SD | Ogdensburg |
| 365 | 101 | Wyandanch UFSD | Wyandanch |
| 366 | 95 | Blind Brook-Rye UFSD | Rye Brook |
| 367 | 93 | Hannibal Central SD | Hannibal |
| 368 | 92 | Catskill Central SD | Catskill |
| 369 | 90 | Center Moriches UFSD | Center Moriches |
| 369 | 90 | Valhalla UFSD | Valhalla |
| 371 | 89 | Liberty Central SD | Liberty |
| 371 | 89 | Oyster Bay-East Norwich Central SD | Oyster Bay |
| 373 | 86 | Salmon River Central SD | Fort Covington |
| 374 | 85 | Charter School for Applied Tech | Buffalo |
| n/a | n/a | Elmont UFSD | Elmont |
| n/a | n/a | Floral Park-Bellerose UFSD | Floral Park |
| n/a | n/a | Franklin Square UFSD | Franklin Square |
| n/a | n/a | Merrick UFSD | Merrick |
| n/a | n/a | NYC Special Schools - District 75 | New York |
| n/a | n/a | New Hyde Pk-Garden City Pk UFSD | New Hyde Park |
| n/a | n/a | North Bellmore UFSD | Bellmore |
| n/a | n/a | North Colonie Central SD | Latham |
| n/a | n/a | Valley Stream 13 UFSD | Valley Stream |

## High School Drop-out Rate

| Rank | Percent | District Name | City |
|---|---|---|---|
| 1 | 18.0 | NYC Geographic District #18 | Brooklyn |
| 2 | 14.2 | Hempstead UFSD | Hempstead |
| 3 | 13.6 | NYC Geographic District #16 | Brooklyn |
| 4 | 12.7 | NYC Geographic District # 8 | Bronx |
| 5 | 11.6 | NYC Geographic District #32 | Brooklyn |
| 6 | 11.5 | NYC Geographic District #27 | Ozone Park |
| 7 | 11.3 | Rochester City SD | Rochester |
| 8 | 11.0 | Syracuse City SD | Syracuse |
| 9 | 10.3 | Poughkeepsie City SD | Poughkeepsie |
| 10 | 10.0 | Lackawanna City SD | Lackawanna |
| 11 | 9.8 | NYC Geographic District # 7 | Bronx |
| 12 | 9.7 | NYC Geographic District #12 | Bronx |
| 12 | 9.7 | NYC Geographic District #15 | Brooklyn |
| 14 | 9.4 | NYC Geographic District #19 | Brooklyn |
| 15 | 9.3 | Buffalo City SD | Buffalo |
| 16 | 9.0 | NYC Geographic District #25 | Flushing |
| 17 | 8.3 | NYC Geographic District #11 | Bronx |
| 17 | 8.3 | NYC Geographic District #30 | Long Isl City |
| 19 | 8.1 | NYC Geographic District #23 | Brooklyn |
| 20 | 7.9 | Newburgh City SD | Newburgh |
| 21 | 7.6 | NYC Geographic District #10 | Bronx |
| 22 | 7.3 | Elmira City SD | Elmira |
| 22 | 7.3 | NYC Geographic District # 1 | New York |
| 22 | 7.3 | NYC Geographic District # 9 | Bronx |
| 25 | 7.2 | Albany City SD | Albany |
| 25 | 7.2 | NYC Geographic District # 2 | New York |
| 27 | 7.1 | NYC Geographic District #17 | Brooklyn |
| 27 | 7.1 | Roosevelt UFSD | Roosevelt |
| 29 | 7.0 | Gloversville City SD | Gloversville |
| 30 | 6.9 | NYC Geographic District # 3 | New York |
| 31 | 6.6 | NYC Geographic District # 5 | New York |
| 32 | 6.5 | NYC Geographic District #22 | Brooklyn |
| 33 | 6.4 | NYC Geographic District #21 | Brooklyn |
| 33 | 6.4 | NYC Geographic District #24 | Ridgewood |
| 35 | 6.3 | NYC Geographic District #20 | Brooklyn |
| 36 | 5.9 | Ellenville Central SD | Ellenville |
| 37 | 5.8 | Amityville UFSD | Amityville |
| 37 | 5.8 | Kingston City SD | Kingston |
| 37 | 5.8 | NYC Geographic District #31 | Staten Island |
| 40 | 5.6 | Evans-Brant Central SD (Lake Shore) | Angola |
| 40 | 5.6 | Middletown City SD | Middletown |
| 40 | 5.6 | NYC Geographic District #14 | Brooklyn |
| 43 | 5.5 | Monticello Central SD | Monticello |
| 43 | 5.5 | Mount Vernon City SD | Mount Vernon |
| 43 | 5.5 | NYC Geographic District # 4 | New York |
| 43 | 5.5 | Schenectady City SD | Schenectady |
| 47 | 5.4 | Mexico Central SD | Mexico |
| 47 | 5.4 | NYC Geographic District #28 | Jamaica |
| 47 | 5.4 | Utica City SD | Utica |
| 50 | 5.3 | Amsterdam City SD | Amsterdam |
| 50 | 5.3 | Newark Central SD | Newark |
| 50 | 5.3 | Port Jervis City SD | Port Jervis |
| 53 | 5.2 | Beacon City SD | Beacon |
| 54 | 5.1 | NYC Geographic District # 6 | New York |
| 54 | 5.1 | NYC Geographic District #29 | Rosedale |
| 56 | 4.9 | Bath Central SD | Bath |
| 56 | 4.9 | Hudson City SD | Hudson |
| 58 | 4.8 | Liberty Central SD | Liberty |
| 58 | 4.8 | Port Chester-Rye UFSD | Port Chester |
| 60 | 4.7 | Hornell City SD | Hornell |
| 60 | 4.7 | Salmon River Central SD | Fort Covington |
| 60 | 4.7 | Yonkers City SD | Yonkers |
| 63 | 4.6 | East Ramapo Central SD | Spring Valley |
| 64 | 4.4 | Catskill Central SD | Catskill |
| 64 | 4.4 | Huntington UFSD | Huntington Stn |
| 66 | 4.3 | Geneva City SD | Geneva |
| 66 | 4.3 | Medina Central SD | Medina |
| 68 | 4.2 | Gouverneur Central SD | Gouverneur |
| 69 | 4.1 | Central Islip UFSD | Central Islip |
| 69 | 4.1 | Norwich City SD | Norwich |
| 71 | 4.0 | Dover UFSD | Dover Plains |
| 71 | 4.0 | South Country Central SD | East Patchogue |
| 73 | 3.9 | Cheektowaga Central SD | Cheektowaga |
| 73 | 3.9 | Hampton Bays UFSD | Hampton Bays |
| 73 | 3.9 | Horseheads Central SD | Horseheads |
| 76 | 3.8 | Auburn City SD | Auburn |
| 76 | 3.8 | Binghamton City SD | Binghamton |
| 76 | 3.8 | Cheektowaga-Maryvale UFSD | Cheektowaga |
| 76 | 3.8 | Massena Central SD | Massena |
| 76 | 3.8 | Southwestern CSD at Jamestown | Jamestown |
| 81 | 3.7 | Dunkirk City SD | Dunkirk |
| 81 | 3.7 | Freeport UFSD | Freeport |
| 81 | 3.7 | Hannibal Central SD | Hannibal |
| 81 | 3.7 | Hudson Falls Central SD | Fort Edward |
| 81 | 3.7 | Johnstown City SD | Johnstown |
| 81 | 3.7 | North Tonawanda City SD | North Tonawanda |
| 81 | 3.7 | Riverhead Central SD | Riverhead |
| 81 | 3.7 | Tonawanda City SD | Tonawanda |
| 81 | 3.7 | Waterloo Central SD | Waterloo |
| 81 | 3.7 | Watertown City SD | Watertown |
| 91 | 3.6 | Olean City SD | Olean |
| 91 | 3.6 | Penn Yan Central SD | Penn Yan |
| 93 | 3.5 | NYC Geographic District #26 | Bayside |
| 93 | 3.5 | Patchogue-Medford UFSD | Patchogue |
| 95 | 3.4 | Cortland City SD | Cortland |
| 95 | 3.4 | Jamestown City SD | Jamestown |
| 95 | 3.4 | Peekskill City SD | Peekskill |
| 95 | 3.4 | Schalmont Central SD | Schenectady |
| 95 | 3.4 | Taconic Hills Central SD | Craryville |
| 100 | 3.3 | Corning City SD | Painted Post |
| 100 | 3.3 | Ilion Central SD | Ilion |
| 100 | 3.3 | Kinderhook Central SD | Valatie |
| 100 | 3.3 | NYC Geographic District #13 | Brooklyn |
| 100 | 3.3 | Phelps-Clifton Springs Central SD | Clifton Springs |
| 100 | 3.3 | Wyandanch UFSD | Wyandanch |
| 106 | 3.2 | Mohonasen Central SD | Schenectady |
| 106 | 3.2 | Ogdensburg City SD | Ogdensburg |
| 108 | 3.1 | Carthage Central SD | Carthage |
| 108 | 3.1 | Cohoes City SD | Cohoes |
| 108 | 3.1 | Dansville Central SD | Dansville |
| 108 | 3.1 | Highland Central SD | Highland |
| 108 | 3.1 | Longwood Central SD | Middle Island |
| 108 | 3.1 | Niagara Falls City SD | Niagara Falls |
| 108 | 3.1 | Waverly Central SD | Waverly |
| 108 | 3.1 | Yorkshire-Pioneer Central SD | Yorkshire |
| 116 | 3.0 | Akron Central SD | Akron |
| 116 | 3.0 | Chittenango Central SD | Chittenango |
| 116 | 3.0 | Saranac Central SD | Dannemora |
| 116 | 3.0 | Saugerties Central SD | Saugerties |
| 116 | 3.0 | Wappingers Central SD | Wappingers Fls |
| 121 | 2.9 | Batavia City SD | Batavia |
| 121 | 2.9 | Fredonia Central SD | Fredonia |
| 121 | 2.9 | Glens Falls City SD | Glens Falls |
| 121 | 2.9 | Hyde Park Central SD | Hyde Park |
| 121 | 2.9 | Uniondale UFSD | Uniondale |
| 126 | 2.8 | North Syracuse Central SD | North Syracuse |
| 126 | 2.8 | Onteora Central SD | Boiceville |
| 126 | 2.8 | Oswego City SD | Oswego |
| 126 | 2.8 | Pine Bush Central SD | Pine Bush |
| 126 | 2.8 | Union-Endicott Central SD | Endicott |
| 131 | 2.7 | Arlington Central SD | Poughkeepsie |
| 131 | 2.7 | Hamburg Central SD | Hamburg |
| 131 | 2.7 | Hicksville UFSD | Hicksville |
| 131 | 2.7 | North Rockland Central SD | Garnerville |
| 131 | 2.7 | Ossining UFSD | Ossining |
| 136 | 2.6 | Cobleskill-Richmondville Central SD | Cobleskill |
| 136 | 2.6 | Ithaca City SD | Ithaca |
| 136 | 2.6 | Malone Central SD | Malone |
| 136 | 2.6 | Troy City SD | Troy |
| 140 | 2.5 | Broadalbin-Perth Central SD | Broadalbin |
| 140 | 2.5 | Coxsackie-Athens Central SD | Coxsackie |
| 140 | 2.5 | East Greenbush Central SD | East Greenbush |
| 140 | 2.5 | East Hampton UFSD | East Hampton |
| 140 | 2.5 | Marlboro Central SD | Marlboro |
| 140 | 2.5 | Palmyra-Macedon Central SD | Palmyra |
| 140 | 2.5 | Westhampton Bch UFSD | Westhampton Bch |
| 147 | 2.4 | Bay Shore UFSD | Bay Shore |
| 147 | 2.4 | Cheektowaga-Sloan UFSD | Sloan |
| 147 | 2.4 | Dryden Central SD | Dryden |
| 147 | 2.4 | Greece Central SD | Rochester |
| 147 | 2.4 | Homer Central SD | Homer |
| 147 | 2.4 | Owego-Apalachin Central SD | Owego |
| 147 | 2.4 | Rondout Valley Central SD | Accord |
| 147 | 2.4 | Scotia-Glenville Central SD | Scotia |
| 147 | 2.4 | Valley Central SD (Montgomery) | Montgomery |
| 156 | 2.3 | Beekmantown Central SD | West Chazy |
| 156 | 2.3 | Middle Country Central SD | Centereach |
| 156 | 2.3 | Royalton-Hartland Central SD | Middleport |
| 156 | 2.3 | South Jefferson Central SD | Adams Center |
| 156 | 2.3 | Spencerport Central SD | Spencerport |
| 161 | 2.2 | Albion Central SD | Albion |
| 161 | 2.2 | East Irondequoit Central SD | Rochester |

*Note: This section only includes districts with 1,500 or more students; All categories are ranked from high to low*

| | | | |
|---|---|---|---|
| 161 | 2.2 | Peru Central SD | Peru |
| 161 | 2.2 | Phoenix Central SD | Phoenix |
| 161 | 2.2 | Schuylerville Central SD | Schuylerville |
| 166 | 2.1 | Johnson City Central SD | Johnson City |
| 166 | 2.1 | Oyster Bay-East Norwich Central SD | Oyster Bay |
| 166 | 2.1 | Ravena-Coeymans-Selkirk Ctrl SD | Selkirk |
| 169 | 2.0 | Baldwin UFSD | Baldwin |
| 169 | 2.0 | Brentwood UFSD | Brentwood |
| 169 | 2.0 | Depew UFSD | Depew |
| 169 | 2.0 | Frontier Central SD | Hamburg |
| 169 | 2.0 | Lindenhurst UFSD | Lindenhurst |
| 169 | 2.0 | Solvay UFSD | Solvay |
| 169 | 2.0 | West Babylon UFSD | West Babylon |
| 169 | 2.0 | Whitesboro Central SD | Yorkville |
| 177 | 1.9 | Livonia Central SD | Livonia |
| 177 | 1.9 | Niagara-Wheatfield Central SD | Niagara Falls |
| 177 | 1.9 | Oneida City SD | Oneida |
| 177 | 1.9 | Plattsburgh City SD | Plattsburgh |
| 177 | 1.9 | Rocky Point UFSD | Rocky Point |
| 177 | 1.9 | Sweet Home Central SD | Amherst |
| 183 | 1.8 | General Brown Central SD | Dexter |
| 183 | 1.8 | Grand Island Central SD | Grand Island |
| 183 | 1.8 | Greenburgh Central SD | Hartsdale |
| 183 | 1.8 | Lockport City SD | Lockport |
| 183 | 1.8 | Minisink Valley Central SD | Slate Hill |
| 183 | 1.8 | Rush-Henrietta Central SD | Henrietta |
| 183 | 1.8 | Seaford UFSD | Seaford |
| 183 | 1.8 | Southampton UFSD | Southampton |
| 183 | 1.8 | UFSD of the Tarrytowns | Sleepy Hollow |
| 183 | 1.8 | Wayland-Cohocton Central SD | Wayland |
| 183 | 1.8 | White Plains City SD | White Plains |
| 194 | 1.7 | Camden Central SD | Camden |
| 194 | 1.7 | Canandaigua City SD | Canandaigua |
| 194 | 1.7 | Copiague UFSD | Copiague |
| 194 | 1.7 | Marcellus Central SD | Marcellus |
| 194 | 1.7 | Oneonta City SD | Oneonta |
| 194 | 1.7 | Rome City SD | Rome |
| 194 | 1.7 | Sachem Central SD | Holbrook |
| 194 | 1.7 | South Colonie Central SD | Albany |
| 202 | 1.6 | Alden Central SD | Alden |
| 202 | 1.6 | Cazenovia Central SD | Cazenovia |
| 202 | 1.6 | Comsewogue School District | Port Jeff Stn |
| 202 | 1.6 | Connetquot Central SD | Bohemia |
| 202 | 1.6 | Glen Cove City SD | Glen Cove |
| 202 | 1.6 | Malverne UFSD | Malverne |
| 202 | 1.6 | New Rochelle City SD | New Rochelle |
| 209 | 1.5 | Ballston Spa Central SD | Ballston Spa |
| 209 | 1.5 | Brewster Central SD | Brewster |
| 209 | 1.5 | Gates-Chili Central SD | Rochester |
| 209 | 1.5 | Indian River Central SD | Philadelphia |
| 209 | 1.5 | Lancaster Central SD | Lancaster |
| 209 | 1.5 | Sherburne-Earlville Central SD | Sherburne |
| 209 | 1.5 | Susquehanna Valley Central SD | Conklin |
| 216 | 1.4 | Center Moriches UFSD | Center Moriches |
| 216 | 1.4 | Cornwall Central SD | Cornwall on Hdsn |
| 216 | 1.4 | Fulton City SD | Fulton |
| 216 | 1.4 | Jordan-Elbridge Central SD | Elbridge |
| 216 | 1.4 | Kenmore-Tonawanda UFSD | Buffalo |
| 216 | 1.4 | Lansingburgh Central SD | Troy |
| 216 | 1.4 | Springville-Griffith Institute CSD | Springville |
| 223 | 1.3 | Central Square Central SD | Central Square |
| 223 | 1.3 | Deer Park UFSD | Deer Park |
| 223 | 1.3 | East Islip UFSD | Islip Terrace |
| 223 | 1.3 | Guilderland Central SD | Guilderland |
| 223 | 1.3 | Lawrence UFSD | Lawrence |
| 223 | 1.3 | Penfield Central SD | Rochester |
| 223 | 1.3 | Ramapo Central SD (Suffern) | Hillburn |
| 223 | 1.3 | Vernon-Verona-Sherrill Central SD | Verona |
| 223 | 1.3 | West Genesee Central SD | Camillus |
| 232 | 1.2 | Babylon UFSD | Babylon |
| 232 | 1.2 | Eastport-South Manor CSD | Manorville |
| 232 | 1.2 | Queensbury UFSD | Queensbury |
| 232 | 1.2 | Saratoga Spgs City SD | Saratoga Spgs |
| 232 | 1.2 | Shenendehowa Central SD | Clifton Park |
| 232 | 1.2 | Wayne Central SD | Ontario Center |
| 232 | 1.2 | William Floyd UFSD | Mastic Beach |
| 239 | 1.1 | Brockport Central SD | Brockport |
| 239 | 1.1 | East Aurora UFSD | East Aurora |
| 239 | 1.1 | North Shore Central SD | Sea Cliff |
| 239 | 1.1 | Nyack UFSD | Nyack |
| 239 | 1.1 | S Glens Fls Central SD | S Glens Fls |
| 239 | 1.1 | Starpoint Central SD | Lockport |
| 239 | 1.1 | Washingtonville Central SD | Washingtonville |
| 239 | 1.1 | Windsor Central SD | Windsor |
| 247 | 1.0 | Amherst Central SD | Amherst |
| 247 | 1.0 | East Meadow UFSD | Westbury |
| 247 | 1.0 | East Syracuse-Minoa Central SD | East Syracuse |
| 247 | 1.0 | Lewiston-Porter Central SD | Youngstown |
| 247 | 1.0 | Monroe-Woodbury Central SD | Central Valley |
| 247 | 1.0 | North Babylon UFSD | North Babylon |
| 247 | 1.0 | Spackenkill UFSD | Poughkeepsie |
| 247 | 1.0 | West Seneca Central SD | West Seneca |
| 247 | 1.0 | Westbury UFSD | Old Westbury |
| 256 | 0.9 | Bedford Central SD | Bedford |
| 256 | 0.9 | Goshen Central SD | Goshen |
| 256 | 0.9 | Hilton Central SD | Hilton |
| 256 | 0.9 | Liverpool Central SD | Liverpool |
| 256 | 0.9 | Mamaroneck UFSD | Mamaroneck |
| 256 | 0.9 | New Paltz Central SD | New Paltz |
| 256 | 0.9 | Northport-East Northport UFSD | Northport |
| 256 | 0.9 | Orchard Park Central SD | Orchard Park |
| 256 | 0.9 | Shoreham-Wading River Central SD | Shoreham |
| 256 | 0.9 | Webster Central SD | Webster |
| 256 | 0.9 | Yorktown Central SD | Yorktown Hgts |
| 267 | 0.8 | Averill Park Central SD | Averill Park |
| 267 | 0.8 | Brighton Central SD | Rochester |
| 267 | 0.8 | Canastota Central SD | Canastota |
| 267 | 0.8 | Churchville-Chili Central SD | Churchville |
| 267 | 0.8 | Island Trees UFSD | Levittown |
| 267 | 0.8 | Jamesville-Dewitt Central SD | Dewitt |
| 267 | 0.8 | Long Beach City SD | Long Beach |
| 267 | 0.8 | Maine-Endwell Central SD | Endwell |
| 267 | 0.8 | Mattituck-Cutchogue UFSD | Cutchogue |
| 267 | 0.8 | Newfane Central SD | Burt |
| 267 | 0.8 | Three Village Central SD | Stony Brook |
| 267 | 0.8 | Warwick Valley Central SD | Warwick |
| 279 | 0.7 | Attica Central SD | Attica |
| 279 | 0.7 | Baldwinsville Central SD | Baldwinsville |
| 279 | 0.7 | Carmel Central SD | Patterson |
| 279 | 0.7 | Chenango Forks Central SD | Binghamton |
| 279 | 0.7 | Clarence Central SD | Clarence Center |
| 279 | 0.7 | Croton-Harmon UFSD | Croton on Hdsn |
| 279 | 0.7 | Farmingdale UFSD | Farmingdale |
| 279 | 0.7 | Harrison Central SD | Harrison |
| 279 | 0.7 | Hauppauge UFSD | Hauppauge |
| 279 | 0.7 | Iroquois Central SD | Elma |
| 279 | 0.7 | Miller Place UFSD | Miller Place |
| 279 | 0.7 | Mount Pleasant Central SD | Thornwood |
| 279 | 0.7 | Port Washington UFSD | Port Washington |
| 279 | 0.7 | West Irondequoit Central SD | Rochester |
| 279 | 0.7 | West Islip UFSD | West Islip |
| 294 | 0.6 | Bethlehem Central SD | Delmar |
| 294 | 0.6 | Fairport Central SD | Fairport |
| 294 | 0.6 | Lakeland Central SD | Shrub Oak |
| 294 | 0.6 | Mahopac Central SD | Mahopac |
| 294 | 0.6 | New Hartford Central SD | New Hartford |
| 294 | 0.6 | Putnam Valley Central SD | Putnam Valley |
| 294 | 0.6 | Red Hook Central SD | Red Hook |
| 294 | 0.6 | Sayville UFSD | Sayville |
| 294 | 0.6 | West Hempstead UFSD | West Hempstead |
| 294 | 0.6 | Westhill Central SD | Syracuse |
| 304 | 0.5 | Clarkstown Central SD | New City |
| 304 | 0.5 | Fayetteville-Manlius Central SD | Manlius |
| 304 | 0.5 | Great Neck UFSD | Great Neck |
| 304 | 0.5 | Honeoye Falls-Lima Central SD | Honeoye Falls |
| 304 | 0.5 | Islip UFSD | Islip |
| 304 | 0.5 | Kings Park Central SD | Kings Park |
| 304 | 0.5 | Lynbrook UFSD | Lynbrook |
| 304 | 0.5 | Mineola UFSD | Mineola |
| 304 | 0.5 | Mount Sinai UFSD | Mount Sinai |
| 304 | 0.5 | Pearl River UFSD | Pearl River |
| 304 | 0.5 | Pelham UFSD | Pelham |
| 304 | 0.5 | Sewanhaka Central High SD | Floral Park |
| 304 | 0.5 | South Huntington UFSD | Huntington Stn |
| 304 | 0.5 | Valley Stream Central High SD | Valley Stream |
| 318 | 0.4 | Bellmore-Merrick Central High SD | North Merrick |
| 318 | 0.4 | Burnt Hills-Ballston Lake CSD | Scotia |
| 318 | 0.4 | Hendrick Hudson Central SD | Montrose |
| 318 | 0.4 | Massapequa UFSD | Massapequa |
| 318 | 0.4 | Somers Central SD | Somers |
| 318 | 0.4 | South Orangetown Central SD | Blauvelt |
| 318 | 0.4 | Vestal Central SD | Vestal |
| 318 | 0.4 | Williamsville Central SD | East Amherst |
| 326 | 0.3 | Ardsley UFSD | Ardsley |
| 326 | 0.3 | Commack UFSD | East Northport |
| 326 | 0.3 | Half Hollow Hills Central SD | Dix Hills |
| 326 | 0.3 | Herricks UFSD | New Hyde Park |
| 326 | 0.3 | Levittown UFSD | Levittown |
| 326 | 0.3 | Oceanside UFSD | Oceanside |
| 326 | 0.3 | Pittsford Central SD | Pittsford |
| 326 | 0.3 | Plainview-Old Bethpage Central SD | Plainview |
| 326 | 0.3 | Smithtown Central SD | Smithtown |
| 326 | 0.3 | Victor Central SD | Victor |
| 336 | 0.1 | Hewlett-Woodmere UFSD | Woodmere |
| 337 | 0.0 | Charter School for Applied Tech | Buffalo |
| n/a | n/a | Bethpage UFSD | Bethpage |
| n/a | n/a | Briarcliff Mnr UFSD | Briarcliff Mnr |
| n/a | n/a | Bronxville UFSD | Bronxville |
| n/a | n/a | Byram Hills Central SD | Armonk |
| n/a | n/a | Chappaqua Central SD | Chappaqua |
| n/a | n/a | Cold Spring Hrbr Central SD | Cold Spring Hrbr |
| n/a | n/a | Edgemont UFSD | Scarsdale |
| n/a | n/a | Garden City UFSD | Garden City |
| n/a | n/a | Jericho UFSD | Jericho |
| n/a | n/a | Nanuet UFSD | Nanuet |
| n/a | n/a | New York City Public Schools | New York |
| n/a | n/a | Rye City SD | Rye |
| n/a | n/a | Scarsdale UFSD | Scarsdale |
| n/a | n/a | Skaneateles Central SD | Skaneateles |
| n/a | n/a | Wallkill Central SD | Wallkill |
| n/a | n/a | Wantagh UFSD | Wantagh |
| n/a | n/a | Elmont UFSD | Elmont |
| n/a | n/a | Floral Park-Bellerose UFSD | Floral Park |
| n/a | n/a | Franklin Square UFSD | Franklin Square |
| n/a | n/a | Merrick UFSD | Merrick |
| n/a | n/a | NYC Special Schools - District 75 | New York |
| n/a | n/a | New Hyde Pk-Garden City Pk UFSD | New Hyde Park |
| n/a | n/a | North Bellmore UFSD | Bellmore |
| n/a | n/a | North Colonie Central SD | Latham |
| n/a | n/a | Valley Stream 13 UFSD | Valley Stream |
| n/a | n/a | Bayport-Blue Point UFSD | Bayport |
| n/a | n/a | Blind Brook-Rye UFSD | Rye Brook |
| n/a | n/a | Chenango Valley Central SD | Binghamton |
| n/a | n/a | East Williston UFSD | Old Westbury |
| n/a | n/a | Eastchester UFSD | Eastchester |
| n/a | n/a | Eden Central SD | Eden |
| n/a | n/a | Elwood UFSD | Greenlawn |
| n/a | n/a | Harborfields Central SD | Greenlawn |
| n/a | n/a | Hastings-on-Hudson UFSD | Hastings on Hdsn |
| n/a | n/a | Holland Patent Central SD | Holland Patent |
| n/a | n/a | Irvington UFSD | Irvington |
| n/a | n/a | Katonah-Lewisboro UFSD | South Salem |
| n/a | n/a | Locust Valley Central SD | Locust Valley |
| n/a | n/a | Manhasset UFSD | Manhasset |
| n/a | n/a | Niskayuna Central SD | Schenectady |
| n/a | n/a | Plainedge UFSD | N Massapequa |
| n/a | n/a | Pleasantville UFSD | Pleasantville |
| n/a | n/a | Rockville Ctr UFSD | Rockville Ctr |
| n/a | n/a | Roslyn UFSD | Roslyn |
| n/a | n/a | Syosset Central SD | Syosset |
| n/a | n/a | Valhalla UFSD | Valhalla |

## Average Freshman Graduation Rate

| Rank | Percent | District Name | City |
|---|---|---|---|
| 1 | 100.0 | Alden Central SD | Alden |
| 1 | 100.0 | Bethpage UFSD | Bethpage |
| 1 | 100.0 | Briarcliff Mnr UFSD | Briarcliff Mnr |
| 1 | 100.0 | Cold Spring Hrbr Central SD | Cold Spring Hrbr |
| 1 | 100.0 | East Aurora UFSD | East Aurora |
| 1 | 100.0 | East Hampton UFSD | East Hampton |
| 1 | 100.0 | East Williston UFSD | Old Westbury |
| 1 | 100.0 | Edgemont UFSD | Scarsdale |
| 1 | 100.0 | Great Neck UFSD | Great Neck |
| 1 | 100.0 | Harborfields Central SD | Greenlawn |
| 1 | 100.0 | Herricks UFSD | New Hyde Park |
| 1 | 100.0 | Iroquois Central SD | Elma |
| 1 | 100.0 | Locust Valley Central SD | Locust Valley |
| 1 | 100.0 | Mount Pleasant Central SD | Thornwood |
| 1 | 100.0 | New Hartford Central SD | New Hartford |
| 1 | 100.0 | NYC Geographic District # 1 | New York |
| 1 | 100.0 | NYC Geographic District # 3 | New York |
| 1 | 100.0 | NYC Geographic District #26 | Bayside |
| 1 | 100.0 | North Shore Central SD | Sea Cliff |
| 1 | 100.0 | Pittsford Central SD | Pittsford |
| 1 | 100.0 | Plainedge UFSD | N Massapequa |
| 1 | 100.0 | Plainview-Old Bethpage Central SD | Plainview |
| 1 | 100.0 | Port Washington UFSD | Port Washington |
| 1 | 100.0 | Putnam Valley Central SD | Putnam Valley |
| 1 | 100.0 | Rockville Ctr UFSD | Rockville Ctr |
| 1 | 100.0 | Rye City SD | Rye |
| 1 | 100.0 | Sayville UFSD | Sayville |
| 1 | 100.0 | Somers Central SD | Somers |
| 1 | 100.0 | UFSD of the Tarrytowns | Sleepy Hollow |
| 1 | 100.0 | Valley Stream Central High SD | Valley Stream |

*Note: This section only includes districts with 1,500 or more students; All categories are ranked from high to low*

| | | | |
|---|---|---|---|
| 1 | 100.0 | Westhampton Bch UFSD | Westhampton Bch |
| 32 | 99.8 | Syosset Central SD | Syosset |
| 33 | 99.6 | West Hempstead UFSD | West Hempstead |
| 34 | 99.3 | Jericho UFSD | Jericho |
| 34 | 99.3 | Roslyn UFSD | Roslyn |
| 36 | 99.2 | Croton-Harmon UFSD | Croton on Hdsn |
| 37 | 99.1 | Levittown UFSD | Levittown |
| 38 | 99.0 | Hamburg Central SD | Hamburg |
| 39 | 98.9 | Center Moriches UFSD | Center Moriches |
| 39 | 98.9 | Webster Central SD | Webster |
| 41 | 98.7 | Bellmore-Merrick Central High SD | North Merrick |
| 42 | 98.6 | Lewiston-Porter Central SD | Youngstown |
| 42 | 98.6 | Scarsdale UFSD | Scarsdale |
| 42 | 98.6 | Williamsville Central SD | East Amherst |
| 45 | 98.5 | Pleasantville UFSD | Pleasantville |
| 45 | 98.5 | Wantagh UFSD | Wantagh |
| 45 | 98.5 | West Islip UFSD | West Islip |
| 48 | 98.3 | Islip UFSD | Islip |
| 49 | 98.2 | Hewlett-Woodmere UFSD | Woodmere |
| 50 | 98.1 | Chappaqua Central SD | Chappaqua |
| 50 | 98.1 | Massapequa UFSD | Massapequa |
| 52 | 98.0 | New Paltz Central SD | New Paltz |
| 53 | 97.8 | Commack UFSD | East Northport |
| 53 | 97.8 | Smithtown Central SD | Smithtown |
| 53 | 97.8 | Washingtonville Central SD | Washingtonville |
| 56 | 97.5 | Northport-East Northport UFSD | Northport |
| 57 | 97.4 | Half Hollow Hills Central SD | Dix Hills |
| 57 | 97.4 | Niskayuna Central SD | Schenectady |
| 59 | 97.3 | Babylon UFSD | Babylon |
| 59 | 97.3 | NYC Geographic District #13 | Brooklyn |
| 61 | 97.2 | Byram Hills Central SD | Armonk |
| 62 | 97.0 | Fairport Central SD | Fairport |
| 62 | 97.0 | Lynbrook UFSD | Lynbrook |
| 64 | 96.9 | Hastings-on-Hudson UFSD | Hastings on Hdsn |
| 65 | 96.5 | Katonah-Lewisboro UFSD | South Salem |
| 65 | 96.5 | Orchard Park Central SD | Orchard Park |
| 67 | 96.4 | Nanuet UFSD | Nanuet |
| 68 | 96.2 | Burnt Hills-Ballston Lake CSD | Scotia |
| 68 | 96.2 | Farmingdale UFSD | Farmingdale |
| 70 | 96.1 | Cornwall Central SD | Cornwall on Hdsn |
| 70 | 96.1 | Shoreham-Wading River Central SD | Shoreham |
| 72 | 96.0 | Niagara-Wheatfield Central SD | Niagara Falls |
| 73 | 95.9 | Chenango Forks Central SD | Binghamton |
| 73 | 95.9 | Clarkstown Central SD | New City |
| 73 | 95.9 | Livonia Central SD | Livonia |
| 73 | 95.9 | Three Village Central SD | Stony Brook |
| 77 | 95.8 | Chenango Valley Central SD | Binghamton |
| 78 | 95.7 | Oceanside UFSD | Oceanside |
| 79 | 95.6 | Holland Patent Central SD | Holland Patent |
| 79 | 95.6 | NYC Geographic District # 2 | New York |
| 81 | 95.3 | Mount Sinai UFSD | Mount Sinai |
| 81 | 95.3 | South Huntington UFSD | Huntington Stn |
| 83 | 95.2 | Eastchester UFSD | Eastchester |
| 83 | 95.2 | Honeoye Falls-Lima Central SD | Honeoye Falls |
| 83 | 95.2 | Malverne UFSD | Malverne |
| 86 | 95.1 | Pearl River UFSD | Pearl River |
| 86 | 95.1 | Rush-Henrietta Central SD | Henrietta |
| 86 | 95.1 | Sachem Central SD | Holbrook |
| 89 | 95.0 | Blind Brook-Rye UFSD | Rye Brook |
| 89 | 95.0 | Comsewogue School District | Port Jeff Stn |
| 91 | 94.9 | Southampton UFSD | Southampton |
| 92 | 94.8 | Grand Island Central SD | Grand Island |
| 92 | 94.8 | Hicksville UFSD | Hicksville |
| 92 | 94.8 | Sewanhaka Central High SD | Floral Park |
| 92 | 94.8 | Yorktown Central SD | Yorktown Hgts |
| 96 | 94.7 | Valhalla UFSD | Valhalla |
| 97 | 94.5 | Bayport-Blue Point UFSD | Bayport |
| 97 | 94.5 | Garden City UFSD | Garden City |
| 97 | 94.5 | Island Trees UFSD | Levittown |
| 100 | 94.4 | Hendrick Hudson Central SD | Montrose |
| 100 | 94.4 | Southwestern CSD at Jamestown | Jamestown |
| 102 | 94.3 | Brighton Central SD | Rochester |
| 102 | 94.3 | Fayetteville-Manlius Central SD | Manlius |
| 104 | 94.1 | Hauppauge UFSD | Hauppauge |
| 105 | 93.9 | Amherst Central SD | Amherst |
| 105 | 93.9 | Maine-Endwell Central SD | Endwell |
| 107 | 93.8 | Horseheads Central SD | Horseheads |
| 107 | 93.8 | Miller Place UFSD | Miller Place |
| 109 | 93.6 | Kings Park Central SD | Kings Park |
| 109 | 93.6 | Mahopac Central SD | Mahopac |
| 111 | 93.4 | Baldwin UFSD | Baldwin |
| 111 | 93.4 | Seaford UFSD | Seaford |
| 111 | 93.4 | South Orangetown Central SD | Blauvelt |
| 114 | 93.3 | Irvington UFSD | Irvington |
| 115 | 93.2 | Attica Central SD | Attica |
| 115 | 93.2 | Cheektowaga-Maryvale UFSD | Cheektowaga |
| 115 | 93.2 | General Brown Central SD | Dexter |
| 118 | 93.1 | Gouverneur Central SD | Gouverneur |
| 119 | 93.0 | Guilderland Central SD | Guilderland |
| 119 | 93.0 | Lakeland Central SD | Shrub Oak |
| 121 | 92.9 | Lindenhurst UFSD | Lindenhurst |
| 121 | 92.9 | Windsor Central SD | Windsor |
| 123 | 92.8 | Eden Central SD | Eden |
| 123 | 92.8 | Harrison Central SD | Harrison |
| 125 | 92.7 | Eastport-South Manor CSD | Manorville |
| 125 | 92.7 | Westhill Central SD | Syracuse |
| 127 | 92.6 | Pelham UFSD | Pelham |
| 127 | 92.6 | Victor Central SD | Victor |
| 129 | 92.5 | Manhasset UFSD | Manhasset |
| 130 | 92.4 | Bronxville UFSD | Bronxville |
| 130 | 92.4 | Connetquot Central SD | Bohemia |
| 132 | 92.3 | Ardsley UFSD | Ardsley |
| 132 | 92.3 | Mamaroneck UFSD | Mamaroneck |
| 132 | 92.3 | Spackenkill UFSD | Poughkeepsie |
| 135 | 92.2 | Clarence Central SD | Clarence Center |
| 136 | 92.0 | Lancaster Central SD | Lancaster |
| 137 | 91.9 | Elwood UFSD | Greenlawn |
| 137 | 91.9 | Monroe-Woodbury Central SD | Central Valley |
| 139 | 91.8 | Depew UFSD | Depew |
| 139 | 91.8 | Ramapo Central SD (Suffern) | Hillburn |
| 141 | 91.6 | East Meadow UFSD | Westbury |
| 142 | 91.5 | Bedford Central SD | Bedford |
| 143 | 91.3 | Carthage Central SD | Carthage |
| 143 | 91.3 | Penfield Central SD | Rochester |
| 145 | 91.2 | Gates-Chili Central SD | Rochester |
| 146 | 91.1 | Kenmore-Tonawanda UFSD | Buffalo |
| 146 | 91.1 | Marcellus Central SD | Marcellus |
| 148 | 91.0 | Frontier Central SD | Hamburg |
| 148 | 91.0 | Skaneateles Central SD | Skaneateles |
| 150 | 90.9 | Brewster Central SD | Brewster |
| 150 | 90.9 | Chittenango Central SD | Chittenango |
| 152 | 90.7 | Middle Country Central SD | Centereach |
| 152 | 90.7 | Phoenix Central SD | Phoenix |
| 154 | 90.6 | Deer Park UFSD | Deer Park |
| 155 | 90.5 | Bethlehem Central SD | Delmar |
| 155 | 90.5 | Minisink Valley Central SD | Slate Hill |
| 155 | 90.5 | Vestal Central SD | Vestal |
| 155 | 90.5 | West Babylon UFSD | West Babylon |
| 159 | 90.4 | Charter School for Applied Tech | Buffalo |
| 159 | 90.4 | Churchville-Chili Central SD | Churchville |
| 159 | 90.4 | East Greenbush Central SD | East Greenbush |
| 159 | 90.4 | Springville-Griffith Institute CSD | Springville |
| 159 | 90.4 | White Plains City SD | White Plains |
| 164 | 90.3 | Starpoint Central SD | Lockport |
| 165 | 90.2 | Goshen Central SD | Goshen |
| 166 | 90.0 | Hilton Central SD | Hilton |
| 166 | 90.0 | Sweet Home Central SD | Amherst |
| 168 | 89.9 | NYC Geographic District #14 | Brooklyn |
| 169 | 89.7 | Cazenovia Central SD | Cazenovia |
| 169 | 89.7 | East Irondequoit Central SD | Rochester |
| 169 | 89.7 | Ossining UFSD | Ossining |
| 172 | 89.6 | East Islip UFSD | Islip Terrace |
| 173 | 89.5 | Canandaigua City SD | Canandaigua |
| 174 | 89.4 | Brockport Central SD | Brockport |
| 174 | 89.4 | Queensbury UFSD | Queensbury |
| 176 | 89.3 | Copiague UFSD | Copiague |
| 176 | 89.3 | Shenendehowa Central SD | Clifton Park |
| 178 | 89.1 | Mattituck-Cutchogue UFSD | Cutchogue |
| 179 | 89.0 | West Genesee Central SD | Camillus |
| 180 | 88.9 | Averill Park Central SD | Averill Park |
| 181 | 88.7 | Akron Central SD | Akron |
| 181 | 88.7 | NYC Geographic District # 4 | New York |
| 183 | 88.5 | West Irondequoit Central SD | Rochester |
| 184 | 88.4 | NYC Geographic District #17 | Brooklyn |
| 184 | 88.4 | South Colonie Central SD | Albany |
| 186 | 88.3 | Schalmont Central SD | Schenectady |
| 186 | 88.3 | Schuylerville Central SD | Schuylerville |
| 188 | 88.2 | Carmel Central SD | Patterson |
| 189 | 88.1 | Highland Central SD | Highland |
| 190 | 87.9 | Mineola UFSD | Mineola |
| 191 | 87.8 | Jamesville-Dewitt Central SD | Dewitt |
| 192 | 87.7 | East Syracuse-Minoa Central SD | East Syracuse |
| 193 | 87.6 | Patchogue-Medford UFSD | Patchogue |
| 194 | 86.9 | Bath Central SD | Bath |
| 194 | 86.9 | Cheektowaga Central SD | Cheektowaga |
| 194 | 86.9 | Whitesboro Central SD | Yorkville |
| 197 | 86.8 | Camden Central SD | Camden |
| 197 | 86.8 | Vernon-Verona-Sherrill Central SD | Verona |
| 199 | 86.7 | Hampton Bays UFSD | Hampton Bays |
| 199 | 86.7 | Lawrence UFSD | Lawrence |
| 201 | 86.6 | Palmyra-Macedon Central SD | Palmyra |
| 202 | 86.5 | Corning City SD | Painted Post |
| 203 | 86.3 | Arlington Central SD | Poughkeepsie |
| 203 | 86.3 | Marlboro Central SD | Marlboro |
| 203 | 86.3 | Spencerport Central SD | Spencerport |
| 206 | 86.2 | Wappingers Central SD | Wappingers Fls |
| 207 | 86.1 | Middletown City SD | Middletown |
| 208 | 86.0 | Coxsackie-Athens Central SD | Coxsackie |
| 208 | 86.0 | Saranac Central SD | Dannemora |
| 210 | 85.9 | Wayne Central SD | Ontario Center |
| 211 | 85.6 | North Syracuse Central SD | North Syracuse |
| 211 | 85.6 | Nyack UFSD | Nyack |
| 213 | 85.5 | Baldwinsville Central SD | Baldwinsville |
| 213 | 85.5 | NYC Geographic District # 9 | Bronx |
| 215 | 85.4 | Huntington UFSD | Huntington Stn |
| 215 | 85.4 | Long Beach City SD | Long Beach |
| 215 | 85.4 | West Seneca Central SD | West Seneca |
| 218 | 85.0 | Fredonia Central SD | Fredonia |
| 218 | 85.0 | NYC Geographic District #23 | Brooklyn |
| 218 | 85.0 | NYC Geographic District #32 | Brooklyn |
| 221 | 84.7 | Johnson City Central SD | Johnson City |
| 222 | 84.6 | Kinderhook Central SD | Valatie |
| 223 | 84.5 | Bay Shore UFSD | Bay Shore |
| 223 | 84.5 | Broadalbin-Perth Central SD | Broadalbin |
| 223 | 84.5 | Wallkill Central SD | Wallkill |
| 226 | 84.1 | Tonawanda City SD | Tonawanda |
| 227 | 84.0 | Greenburgh Central SD | Hartsdale |
| 227 | 84.0 | North Rockland Central SD | Garnerville |
| 229 | 83.9 | Amityville UFSD | Amityville |
| 230 | 83.3 | Albion Central SD | Albion |
| 230 | 83.3 | Ellenville Central SD | Ellenville |
| 232 | 83.2 | Oyster Bay-East Norwich Central SD | Oyster Bay |
| 232 | 83.2 | Warwick Valley Central SD | Warwick |
| 234 | 83.1 | Canastota Central SD | Canastota |
| 235 | 82.9 | Greece Central SD | Rochester |
| 236 | 82.7 | Hornell City SD | Hornell |
| 236 | 82.7 | Longwood Central SD | Middle Island |
| 238 | 82.5 | New Rochelle City SD | New Rochelle |
| 239 | 82.4 | NYC Geographic District # 6 | New York |
| 240 | 82.3 | Ravena-Coeymans-Selkirk Ctrl SD | Selkirk |
| 241 | 82.2 | Red Hook Central SD | Red Hook |
| 241 | 82.2 | Union-Endicott Central SD | Endicott |
| 243 | 82.1 | Geneva City SD | Geneva |
| 244 | 82.0 | Riverhead Central SD | Riverhead |
| 245 | 81.9 | Royalton-Hartland Central SD | Middleport |
| 245 | 81.9 | Saratoga Spgs City SD | Saratoga Spgs |
| 247 | 81.8 | Beekmantown Central SD | West Chazy |
| 248 | 81.6 | Lansingburgh Central SD | Troy |
| 249 | 81.4 | Massena Central SD | Massena |
| 250 | 81.3 | Plattsburgh City SD | Plattsburgh |
| 251 | 81.2 | William Floyd UFSD | Mastic Beach |
| 252 | 81.0 | Saugerties Central SD | Saugerties |
| 253 | 80.9 | Jamestown City SD | Jamestown |
| 254 | 80.8 | Lockport City SD | Lockport |
| 254 | 80.8 | Rocky Point UFSD | Rocky Point |
| 254 | 80.8 | Westbury UFSD | Old Westbury |
| 257 | 80.6 | Mexico Central SD | Mexico |
| 257 | 80.6 | NYC Geographic District #29 | Rosedale |
| 257 | 80.6 | Susquehanna Valley Central SD | Conklin |
| 260 | 80.3 | Newfane Central SD | Burt |
| 261 | 80.2 | Ballston Spa Central SD | Ballston Spa |
| 261 | 80.2 | Rondout Valley Central SD | Accord |
| 261 | 80.2 | S Glens Fls Central SD | S Glens Fls |
| 264 | 80.1 | Yorkshire-Pioneer Central SD | Yorkshire |
| 265 | 79.9 | Hyde Park Central SD | Hyde Park |
| 266 | 79.8 | Liverpool Central SD | Liverpool |
| 267 | 79.6 | Port Chester-Rye UFSD | Port Chester |
| 267 | 79.6 | Solvay UFSD | Solvay |
| 267 | 79.6 | Valley Central SD (Montgomery) | Montgomery |
| 270 | 79.5 | Dansville Central SD | Dansville |
| 270 | 79.5 | Scotia-Glenville Central SD | Scotia |
| 272 | 79.4 | NYC Geographic District #10 | Bronx |
| 273 | 79.1 | North Babylon UFSD | North Babylon |
| 273 | 79.1 | Oneida City SD | Oneida |
| 275 | 79.0 | Malone Central SD | Malone |
| 275 | 79.0 | Medina Central SD | Medina |
| 277 | 78.9 | Ithaca City SD | Ithaca |
| 277 | 78.9 | Jordan-Elbridge Central SD | Elbridge |
| 277 | 78.9 | Pine Bush Central SD | Pine Bush |
| 280 | 78.3 | Cortland City SD | Cortland |
| 281 | 78.2 | Fulton City SD | Fulton |
| 281 | 78.2 | Wayland-Cohocton Central SD | Wayland |
| 283 | 78.1 | North Tonawanda City SD | North Tonawanda |
| 284 | 78.0 | NYC Geographic District #12 | Bronx |
| 285 | 77.9 | Oneonta City SD | Oneonta |

*Note: This section only includes districts with 1,500 or more students; All categories are ranked from high to low*

| 286 | 77.8 | Dover UFSD | Dover Plains |
| 287 | 77.7 | Sherburne-Earlville Central SD | Sherburne |
| 288 | 77.2 | Lackawanna City SD | Lackawanna |
| 289 | 77.1 | Rome City SD | Rome |
| 290 | 76.9 | Beacon City SD | Beacon |
| 290 | 76.9 | Evans-Brant Central SD (Lake Shore) | Angola |
| 292 | 76.8 | Mohonasen Central SD | Schenectady |
| 293 | 76.6 | NYC Geographic District #30 | Long Isl City |
| 294 | 76.3 | Cohoes City SD | Cohoes |
| 295 | 76.1 | South Country Central SD | East Patchogue |
| 296 | 75.9 | Cobleskill-Richmondville Central SD | Cobleskill |
| 297 | 75.7 | Cheektowaga-Sloan UFSD | Sloan |
| 297 | 75.7 | NYC Geographic District # 7 | Bronx |
| 299 | 75.6 | Phelps-Clifton Springs Central SD | Clifton Springs |
| 300 | 75.5 | Owego-Apalachin Central SD | Owego |
| 301 | 75.4 | Homer Central SD | Homer |
| 302 | 75.1 | Indian River Central SD | Philadelphia |
| 302 | 75.1 | Oswego City SD | Oswego |
| 304 | 75.0 | Johnstown City SD | Johnstown |
| 305 | 74.8 | Ilion Central SD | Ilion |
| 305 | 74.8 | Uniondale UFSD | Uniondale |
| 307 | 74.2 | Batavia City SD | Batavia |
| 307 | 74.2 | Newark Central SD | Newark |
| 309 | 74.1 | Glen Cove City SD | Glen Cove |
| 310 | 74.0 | Taconic Hills Central SD | Craryville |
| 311 | 73.9 | Elmira City SD | Elmira |
| 311 | 73.9 | Norwich City SD | Norwich |
| 313 | 73.7 | Dryden Central SD | Dryden |
| 313 | 73.7 | South Jefferson Central SD | Adams Center |
| 315 | 73.3 | Dunkirk City SD | Dunkirk |
| 316 | 73.2 | East Ramapo Central SD | Spring Valley |
| 317 | 73.1 | Brentwood UFSD | Brentwood |
| 318 | 72.9 | Salmon River Central SD | Fort Covington |
| 319 | 72.8 | Onteora Central SD | Boiceville |

| 319 | 72.8 | Penn Yan Central SD | Penn Yan |
| 321 | 72.6 | Binghamton City SD | Binghamton |
| 322 | 72.4 | NYC Geographic District #11 | Bronx |
| 323 | 72.3 | NYC Geographic District #15 | Brooklyn |
| 324 | 71.7 | Troy City SD | Troy |
| 324 | 71.7 | Waterloo Central SD | Waterloo |
| 326 | 70.8 | Olean City SD | Olean |
| 327 | 70.7 | Kingston City SD | Kingston |
| 328 | 70.6 | Waverly Central SD | Waverly |
| 329 | 69.8 | Peru Central SD | Peru |
| 330 | 69.7 | Auburn City SD | Auburn |
| 331 | 69.4 | Glens Falls City SD | Glens Falls |
| 332 | 69.3 | Freeport UFSD | Freeport |
| 333 | 69.2 | Port Jervis City SD | Port Jervis |
| 334 | 68.8 | Central Square Central SD | Central Square |
| 334 | 68.8 | Niagara Falls City SD | Niagara Falls |
| 334 | 68.8 | Utica City SD | Utica |
| 337 | 68.5 | NYC Geographic District #27 | Ozone Park |
| 338 | 68.4 | Hannibal Central SD | Hannibal |
| 339 | 68.0 | Newburgh City SD | Newburgh |
| 340 | 67.6 | Catskill Central SD | Catskill |
| 341 | 66.5 | Hudson Falls Central SD | Fort Edward |
| 342 | 66.2 | Monticello Central SD | Monticello |
| 343 | 65.5 | Gloversville City SD | Gloversville |
| 344 | 64.9 | Roosevelt UFSD | Roosevelt |
| 345 | 64.8 | Ogdensburg City SD | Ogdensburg |
| 346 | 64.3 | Yonkers City SD | Yonkers |
| 347 | 62.2 | Liberty Central SD | Liberty |
| 348 | 61.8 | Hudson City SD | Hudson |
| 349 | 61.4 | Buffalo City SD | Buffalo |
| 350 | 60.5 | Amsterdam City SD | Amsterdam |
| 351 | 60.0 | Peekskill City SD | Peekskill |
| 352 | 59.7 | Watertown City SD | Watertown |
| 353 | 59.6 | Mount Vernon City SD | Mount Vernon |

| 354 | 59.1 | Wyandanch UFSD | Wyandanch |
| 355 | 58.3 | Schenectady City SD | Schenectady |
| 356 | 55.2 | Central Islip UFSD | Central Islip |
| 357 | 54.2 | Poughkeepsie City SD | Poughkeepsie |
| 358 | 52.3 | Syracuse City SD | Syracuse |
| 359 | 50.8 | Albany City SD | Albany |
| 360 | 45.2 | NYC Geographic District #16 | Brooklyn |
| 361 | 43.9 | Rochester City SD | Rochester |
| 362 | 41.4 | Hempstead UFSD | Hempstead |
| n/a | n/a | Elmont UFSD | Elmont |
| n/a | n/a | Floral Park-Bellerose UFSD | Floral Park |
| n/a | n/a | Franklin Square UFSD | Franklin Square |
| n/a | n/a | Merrick UFSD | Merrick |
| n/a | n/a | NYC Special Schools - District 75 | New York |
| n/a | n/a | New Hyde Pk-Garden City Pk UFSD | New Hyde Park |
| n/a | n/a | NYC Geographic District # 5 | New York |
| n/a | n/a | NYC Geographic District # 8 | Bronx |
| n/a | n/a | NYC Geographic District #18 | Brooklyn |
| n/a | n/a | NYC Geographic District #19 | Brooklyn |
| n/a | n/a | NYC Geographic District #20 | Brooklyn |
| n/a | n/a | NYC Geographic District #21 | Brooklyn |
| n/a | n/a | NYC Geographic District #22 | Brooklyn |
| n/a | n/a | NYC Geographic District #24 | Ridgewood |
| n/a | n/a | NYC Geographic District #25 | Flushing |
| n/a | n/a | NYC Geographic District #28 | Jamaica |
| n/a | n/a | NYC Geographic District #31 | Staten Island |
| n/a | n/a | New York City Public Schools | New York |
| n/a | n/a | North Bellmore UFSD | Bellmore |
| n/a | n/a | North Colonie Central SD | Latham |
| n/a | n/a | Valley Stream 13 UFSD | Valley Stream |

*Note: This section only includes districts with 1,500 or more students; All categories are ranked from high to low*

**New York**
**Grade 4**
**Public Schools**

## Overall Results

- In 2011, the average score of fourth-grade students in New York was 238. This was lower than the average score of 240 for public school students in the nation.
- The average score for students in New York in 2011 (238) was lower than their average score in 2009 (241) and was higher than their average score in 1992 (218).
- In 2011, the score gap between students in New York at the 75th percentile and students at the 25th percentile was 38 points. This performance gap was not significantly different from that of 1992 (43 points).
- The percentage of students in New York who performed at or above the NAEP *Proficient* level was 36 percent in 2011. This percentage was smaller than that in 2009 (40 percent) and was greater than that in 1992 (17 percent).
- The percentage of students in New York who performed at or above the NAEP *Basic* level was 80 percent in 2011. This percentage was smaller than that in 2009 (83 percent) and was greater than that in 1992 (57 percent).

### Achievement-Level Percentages and Average Score Results

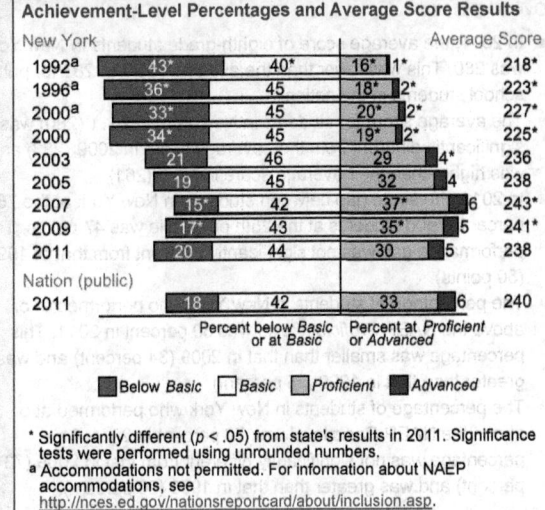

\* Significantly different (*p* < .05) from state's results in 2011. Significance tests were performed using unrounded numbers.
a Accommodations not permitted. For information about NAEP accommodations, see http://nces.ed.gov/nationsreportcard/about/inclusion.asp.

NOTE: Detail may not sum to totals because of rounding.

### Compare the Average Score in 2011 to Other States/Jurisdictions

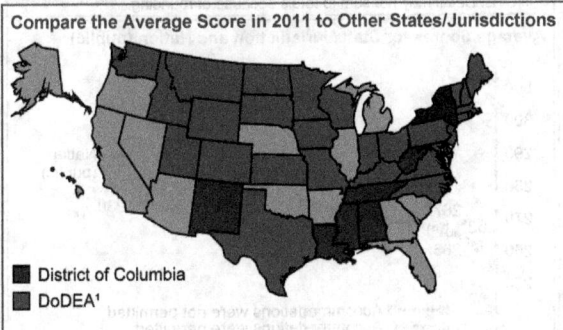

- District of Columbia
- DoDEA[1]

[1] Department of Defense Education Activity (overseas and domestic schools).

In 2011, the average score in New York (238) was
- lower than those in 30 states/jurisdictions
- higher than those in 7 states/jurisdictions
- not significantly different from those in 14 states/jurisdictions

### Average Scores for State/Jurisdiction and Nation (public)

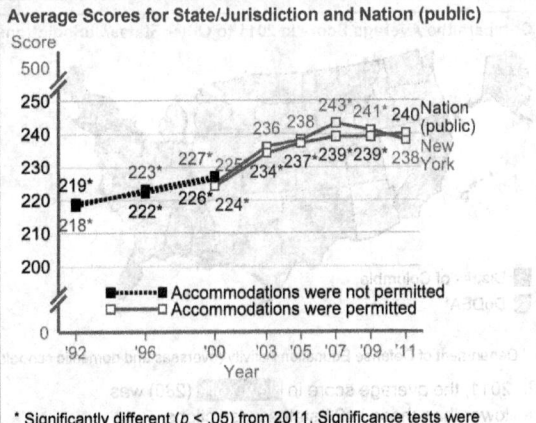

\* Significantly different (*p* < .05) from 2011. Significance tests were performed using unrounded numbers.

NOTE: For information about NAEP accommodations, see http://nces.ed.gov/nationsreportcard/about/inclusion.asp.

### Results for Student Groups in 2011

| Reporting groups | Percent of students | Avg. score | Percentages at or above Basic | Proficient | Percent at Advanced |
|---|---|---|---|---|---|
| **Race/Ethnicity** | | | | | |
| White | 48 | 245 | 89 | 46 | 7 |
| Black | 20 | 224 | 65 | 17 | 1 |
| Hispanic | 21 | 226 | 69 | 20 | 1 |
| Asian | 10 | 252 | 88 | 58 | 17 |
| American Indian/Alaska Native | 1 | ‡ | ‡ | ‡ | ‡ |
| Native Hawaiian/Pacific Islander | # | ‡ | ‡ | ‡ | ‡ |
| Two or more races | # | ‡ | ‡ | ‡ | ‡ |
| **Gender** | | | | | |
| Male | 51 | 238 | 80 | 37 | 6 |
| Female | 49 | 237 | 80 | 34 | 4 |
| **National School Lunch Program** | | | | | |
| Eligible | 55 | 229 | 71 | 25 | 3 |
| Not eligible | 43 | 248 | 90 | 49 | 8 |

# Rounds to zero.   ‡ Reporting standards not met.

NOTE: Detail may not sum to totals because of rounding, and because the "Information not available" category for the National School Lunch Program, which provides free/reduced-price lunches, is not displayed. Black includes African American and Hispanic includes Latino. Race categories exclude Hispanic origin.

### Score Gaps for Student Groups

- In 2011, Black students had an average score that was 22 points lower than White students. This performance gap was narrower than that in 1992 (31 points).
- In 2011, Hispanic students had an average score that was 19 points lower than White students. This performance gap was narrower than that in 1992 (32 points).
- In 2011, male students in New York had an average score that was not significantly different from female students.
- In 2011, students who were eligible for free/reduced-price school lunch, an indicator of low family income, had an average score that was 18 points lower than students who were not eligible for free/reduced-price school lunch. This performance gap was narrower than that in 1996 (30 points).

NOTE: Statistical comparisons are calculated on the basis of unrounded scale scores or percentages.
SOURCE: U.S. Department of Education, Institute of Education Sciences, National Center for Education Statistics, National Assessment of Educational Progress (NAEP), various years, 1992–2011 Mathematics Assessments.

**The Nation's Report Card**  **Mathematics**
2011 State Snapshot Report

New York
Grade 8
Public Schools

## Overall Results

- In 2011, the average score of eighth-grade students in New York was 280. This was lower than the average score of 283 for public school students in the nation.
- The average score for students in New York in 2011 (280) was not significantly different from their average score in 2009 (283) and was higher than their average score in 1990 (261).
- In 2011, the score gap between students in New York at the 75th percentile and students at the 25th percentile was 47 points. This performance gap was not significantly different from that of 1990 (50 points).
- The percentage of students in New York who performed at or above the NAEP *Proficient* level was 30 percent in 2011. This percentage was smaller than that in 2009 (34 percent) and was greater than that in 1990 (15 percent).
- The percentage of students in New York who performed at or above the NAEP *Basic* level was 70 percent in 2011. This percentage was not significantly different from that in 2009 (73 percent) and was greater than that in 1990 (50 percent).

## Achievement-Level Percentages and Average Score Results

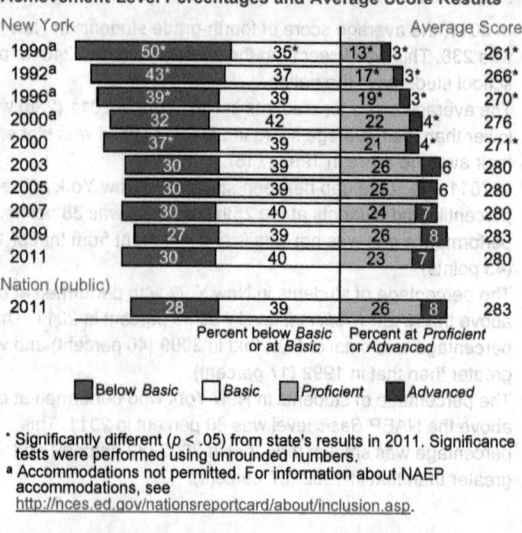

| New York | | | | | Average Score |
|---|---|---|---|---|---|
| 1990ᵃ | 50* | 35* | 13* | 3* | 261* |
| 1992ᵃ | 43* | 37 | 17* | 3* | 266* |
| 1996ᵃ | 39* | 39 | 19* | 3* | 270* |
| 2000ᵃ | 32 | 42 | 22 | 4* | 276 |
| 2000 | 37* | 39 | 21 | 4* | 271* |
| 2003 | 30 | 39 | 26 | 6 | 280 |
| 2005 | 30 | 39 | 25 | 6 | 280 |
| 2007 | 30 | 40 | 24 | 7 | 280 |
| 2009 | 27 | 39 | 26 | 8 | 283 |
| 2011 | 30 | 40 | 23 | 7 | 280 |
| Nation (public) | | | | | |
| 2011 | 28 | 39 | 26 | 8 | 283 |

Percent below *Basic* or at *Basic*    Percent at *Proficient* or *Advanced*

▇ Below *Basic*   ☐ *Basic*   ▨ *Proficient*   ▇ *Advanced*

* Significantly different (*p* < .05) from state's results in 2011. Significance tests were performed using unrounded numbers.
ᵃ Accommodations not permitted. For information about NAEP accommodations, see http://nces.ed.gov/nationsreportcard/about/inclusion.asp.

NOTE: Detail may not sum to totals because of rounding.

## Compare the Average Score in 2011 to Other States/Jurisdictions

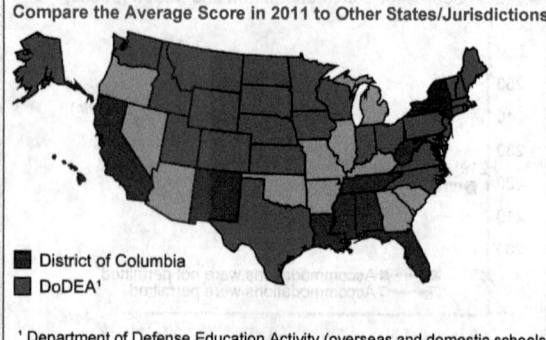

▇ District of Columbia
▇ DoDEA¹

¹ Department of Defense Education Activity (overseas and domestic schools).

In 2011, the average score in New York (280) was
- lower than those in 29 states/jurisdictions
- higher than those in 10 states/jurisdictions
- not significantly different from those in 12 states/jurisdictions

## Average Scores for State/Jurisdiction and Nation (public)

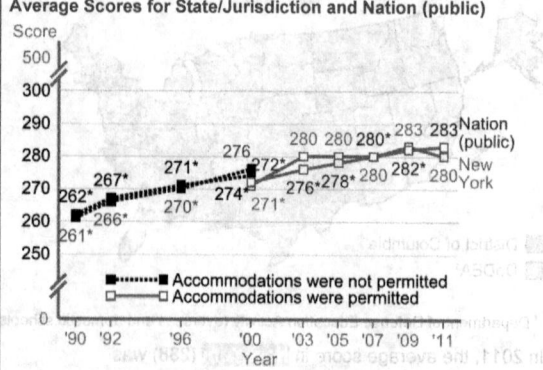

Nation (public): 280, 280, 280*, 283, 283
New York: 262*, 267*, 271*, 276, 272*, 276*, 278*, 280, 282*, 280
261*, 266*, 270*, 274, 271*

- - - ■ Accommodations were not permitted
——— □ Accommodations were permitted

'90 '92 '96 '00 '03 '05 '07 '09 '11
Year

* Significantly different (*p* < .05) from 2011. Significance tests were performed using unrounded numbers.

NOTE: For information about NAEP accommodations, see http://nces.ed.gov/nationsreportcard/about/inclusion.asp.

## Results for Student Groups in 2011

| Reporting groups | Percent of students | Avg. score | Percentages at or above Basic | Percentages at or above Proficient | Percent at Advanced |
|---|---|---|---|---|---|
| **Race/Ethnicity** | | | | | |
| White | 51 | 291 | 82 | 40 | 9 |
| Black | 19 | 264 | 53 | 13 | 1 |
| Hispanic | 22 | 263 | 51 | 13 | 1 |
| Asian | 8 | 302 | 86 | 55 | 21 |
| American Indian/Alaska Native | # | ‡ | ‡ | ‡ | ‡ |
| Native Hawaiian/Pacific Islander | # | ‡ | ‡ | ‡ | ‡ |
| Two or more races | # | ‡ | ‡ | ‡ | ‡ |
| **Gender** | | | | | |
| Male | 51 | 280 | 70 | 30 | 7 |
| Female | 49 | 281 | 70 | 30 | 7 |
| **National School Lunch Program** | | | | | |
| Eligible | 51 | 269 | 57 | 18 | 3 |
| Not eligible | 49 | 293 | 84 | 43 | 10 |

\# Rounds to zero.       ‡ Reporting standards not met.

NOTE: Detail may not sum to totals because of rounding, and because the "Information not available" category for the National School Lunch Program, which provides free/reduced-price lunches, is not displayed. Black includes African American and Hispanic includes Latino. Race categories exclude Hispanic origin.

## Score Gaps for Student Groups

- In 2011, Black students had an average score that was 26 points lower than White students. This performance gap was narrower than that in 1990 (39 points).
- In 2011, Hispanic students had an average score that was 28 points lower than White students. This performance gap was not significantly different from that in 1990 (35 points).
- In 2011, female students in New York had an average score that was not significantly different from male students.
- In 2011, students who were eligible for free/reduced-price school lunch, an indicator of low family income, had an average score that was 24 points lower than students who were not eligible for free/reduced-price school lunch. This performance gap was not significantly different from that in 1996 (29 points).

NOTE: Statistical comparisons are calculated on the basis of unrounded scale scores or percentages.
SOURCE: U.S. Department of Education, Institute of Education Sciences, National Center for Education Statistics, National Assessment of Educational Progress (NAEP), various years, 1990–2011 Mathematics Assessments.

**New York**
**Grade 4**
**Public Schools**

## Overall Results

- In 2011, the average score of fourth-grade students in New York was 222. This was higher than the average score of 220 for public school students in the nation.
- The average score for students in New York in 2011 (222) was not significantly different from their average score in 2009 (224) and was higher than their average score in 1992 (215).
- In 2011, the score gap between students in New York at the 75th percentile and students at the 25th percentile was 47 points. This performance gap was not significantly different from that of 1992 (46 points).
- The percentage of students in New York who performed at or above the NAEP *Proficient* level was 35 percent in 2011. This percentage was not significantly different from that in 2009 (36 percent) and was greater than that in 1992 (27 percent).
- The percentage of students in New York who performed at or above the NAEP *Basic* level was 68 percent in 2011. This percentage was not significantly different from that in 2009 (71 percent) and was greater than that in 1992 (61 percent).

### Achievement-Level Percentages and Average Score Results

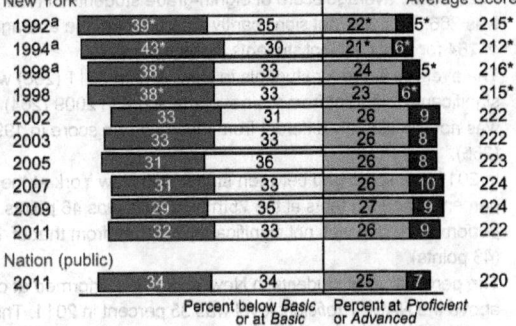

| New York | Below Basic | Basic | Proficient | Advanced | Average Score |
|---|---|---|---|---|---|
| 1992[a] | 39* | 35 | 22* | 5* | 215* |
| 1994[a] | 43* | 30 | 21* | 6* | 212* |
| 1998[a] | 38* | 33 | 24 | 5* | 216* |
| 1998 | 38* | 33 | 23* | 6* | 215* |
| 2002 | 33 | 31 | 26 | 9 | 222 |
| 2003 | 33 | 33 | 26 | 8 | 222 |
| 2005 | 31 | 36 | 26 | 8 | 223 |
| 2007 | 31 | 33 | 26 | 10 | 224 |
| 2009 | 29 | 35 | 27 | 9 | 224 |
| 2011 | 32 | 33 | 26 | 9 | 222 |

| Nation (public) | | | | | |
|---|---|---|---|---|---|
| 2011 | 34 | 34 | 25 | 7 | 220 |

Percent below *Basic* or at *Basic* ← → Percent at *Proficient* or *Advanced*

■ Below *Basic* □ *Basic* ▨ *Proficient* ■ *Advanced*

\* Significantly different (*p* < .05) from state's results in 2011. Significance tests were performed using unrounded numbers.
[a] Accommodations not permitted. For information about NAEP accommodations, see http://nces.ed.gov/nationsreportcard/about/inclusion.asp.

NOTE: Detail may not sum to totals because of rounding.

### Compare the Average Score in 2011 to Other States/Jurisdictions

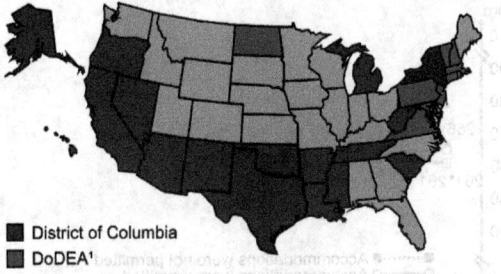

■ District of Columbia
■ DoDEA[1]

[1] Department of Defense Education Activity (overseas and domestic schools).

In 2011, the average score in New York (222) was
- lower than those in 10 states/jurisdictions
- higher than those in 17 states/jurisdictions
- not significantly different from those in 24 states/jurisdictions

### Average Scores for State/Jurisdiction and Nation (public)

New York: 215*, 212*, 216*, 215*, 222, 222, 223, 224, 224, 222
Nation (public): 215*, 212*, 215*, 213*, 217*, 216*, 217*, 220, 220, 220

■---■ Accommodations were not permitted
□—□ Accommodations were permitted

Year: '92 '94 '98 '02 '03 '05 '07 '09 '11

\* Significantly different (*p* < .05) from 2011. Significance tests were performed using unrounded numbers.

NOTE: For information about NAEP accommodations, see http://nces.ed.gov/nationsreportcard/about/inclusion.asp.

### Results for Student Groups in 2011

| Reporting groups | Percent of students | Avg. score | Percentages at or above Basic | Percentages at or above Proficient | Percent at Advanced |
|---|---|---|---|---|---|
| **Race/Ethnicity** | | | | | |
| White | 48 | 232 | 79 | 46 | 12 |
| Black | 20 | 208 | 52 | 18 | 3 |
| Hispanic | 20 | 209 | 54 | 20 | 3 |
| Asian | 10 | 235 | 80 | 49 | 17 |
| American Indian/Alaska Native | 1 | ‡ | ‡ | ‡ | ‡ |
| Native Hawaiian/Pacific Islander | # | ‡ | ‡ | ‡ | ‡ |
| Two or more races | 1 | ‡ | ‡ | ‡ | ‡ |
| **Gender** | | | | | |
| Male | 50 | 219 | 65 | 32 | 8 |
| Female | 50 | 226 | 71 | 38 | 10 |
| **National School Lunch Program** | | | | | |
| Eligible | 55 | 212 | 57 | 23 | 4 |
| Not eligible | 43 | 236 | 82 | 49 | 14 |

\# Rounds to zero.   ‡ Reporting standards not met.

NOTE: Detail may not sum to totals because of rounding, and because the "Information not available" category for the National School Lunch Program, which provides free/reduced-price lunches, is not displayed. Black includes African American and Hispanic includes Latino. Race categories exclude Hispanic origin.

### Score Gaps for Student Groups

- In 2011, Black students had an average score that was 24 points lower than White students. This performance gap was not significantly different from that in 1992 (27 points).
- In 2011, Hispanic students had an average score that was 24 points lower than White students. This performance gap was narrower than that in 1992 (42 points).
- In 2011, female students in New York had an average score that was higher than male students by 6 points.
- In 2011, students who were eligible for free/reduced-price school lunch, an indicator of low family income, had an average score that was 24 points lower than students who were not eligible for free/reduced-price school lunch. This performance gap was narrower than that in 1998 (35 points).

NOTE: Statistical comparisons are calculated on the basis of unrounded scale scores or percentages.
SOURCE: U.S. Department of Education, Institute of Education Sciences, National Center for Education Statistics, National Assessment of Educational Progress (NAEP), various years, 1992–2011 Reading Assessments.

New York
Grade 8
Public Schools

The Nation's Report Card — Reading — 2011 State Snapshot Report

## Overall Results

- In 2011, the average score of eighth-grade students in New York was 266. This was not significantly different from the average score of 264 for public school students in the nation.
- The average score for students in New York in 2011 (266) was not significantly different from their average score in 2009 (264) and was not significantly different from their average score in 1998 (265).
- In 2011, the score gap between students in New York at the 75th percentile and students at the 25th percentile was 46 points. This performance gap was not significantly different from that of 1998 (43 points).
- The percentage of students in New York who performed at or above the NAEP *Proficient* level was 35 percent in 2011. This percentage was not significantly different from that in 2009 (33 percent) and was not significantly different from that in 1998 (32 percent).
- The percentage of students in New York who performed at or above the NAEP *Basic* level was 76 percent in 2011. This percentage was not significantly different from that in 2009 (75 percent) and was not significantly different from that in 1998 (76 percent).

### Achievement-Level Percentages and Average Score Results

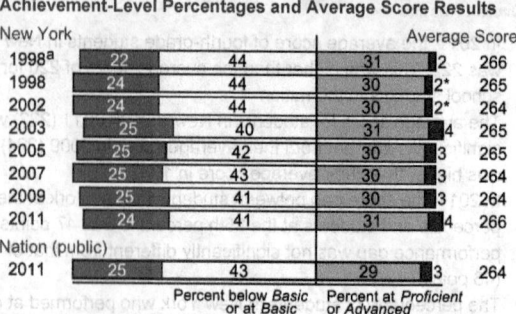

| New York | below Basic | at Basic | Proficient | Advanced | Average Score |
|---|---|---|---|---|---|
| 1998[a] | 22 | 44 | 31 | 2 | 266 |
| 1998 | 24 | 44 | 30 | 2* | 265 |
| 2002 | 24 | 44 | 30 | 2* | 264 |
| 2003 | 25 | 40 | 31 | 4 | 265 |
| 2005 | 25 | 42 | 30 | 3 | 265 |
| 2007 | 25 | 43 | 30 | 3 | 264 |
| 2009 | 25 | 41 | 30 | 3 | 264 |
| 2011 | 24 | 41 | 31 | 4 | 266 |
| Nation (public) |  |  |  |  |  |
| 2011 | 25 | 43 | 29 | 3 | 264 |

Percent below *Basic* or at *Basic*    Percent at *Proficient* or *Advanced*

■ Below *Basic*    □ *Basic*    ▨ *Proficient*    ■ *Advanced*

\* Significantly different (*p* < .05) from state's results in 2011. Significance tests were performed using unrounded numbers.
[a] Accommodations not permitted. For information about NAEP accommodations, see http://nces.ed.gov/nationsreportcard/about/inclusion.asp.

NOTE: Detail may not sum to totals because of rounding.

## Compare the Average Score in 2011 to Other States/Jurisdictions

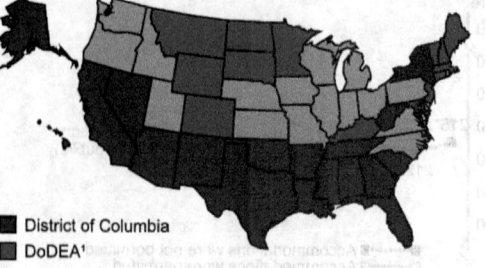

■ District of Columbia
▨ DoDEA[1]

[1] Department of Defense Education Activity (overseas and domestic schools).

In 2011, the average score in New York (266) was
- lower than those in 15 states/jurisdictions
- higher than those in 18 states/jurisdictions
- not significantly different from those in 18 states/jurisdictions

## Average Scores for State/Jurisdiction and Nation (public)

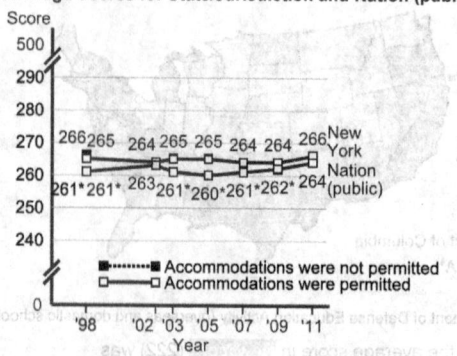

| Score | New York | Nation (public) |
|---|---|---|
| '98 | 266 | 261* |
| '02 | 265 | 261* |
| '03 | 264 | 263 |
| '05 | 265 | 261* |
| '07 | 265 | 260* |
| '09 | 264 | 261* |
| '11 | 264 / 266 | 262* / 264 |

----■---- Accommodations were not permitted
——□—— Accommodations were permitted

\* Significantly different (*p* < .05) from 2011. Significance tests were performed using unrounded numbers.

NOTE: For information about NAEP accommodations, see http://nces.ed.gov/nationsreportcard/about/inclusion.asp.

## Results for Student Groups in 2011

| Reporting groups | Percent of students | Avg. score | Percentages at or above Basic | Percentages at or above Proficient | Percent at Advanced |
|---|---|---|---|---|---|
| **Race/Ethnicity** | | | | | |
| White | 51 | 276 | 86 | 46 | 6 |
| Black | 19 | 251 | 63 | 18 | 1 |
| Hispanic | 21 | 251 | 62 | 20 | 1 |
| Asian | 8 | 277 | 83 | 50 | 6 |
| American Indian/Alaska Native | # | ‡ | ‡ | ‡ | ‡ |
| Native Hawaiian/Pacific Islander | # | ‡ | ‡ | ‡ | ‡ |
| Two or more races | # | ‡ | ‡ | ‡ | ‡ |
| **Gender** | | | | | |
| Male | 51 | 261 | 72 | 30 | 3 |
| Female | 49 | 270 | 81 | 40 | 5 |
| **National School Lunch Program** | | | | | |
| Eligible | 50 | 255 | 66 | 24 | 2 |
| Not eligible | 49 | 277 | 87 | 47 | 6 |

# Rounds to zero.          ‡ Reporting standards not met.

NOTE: Detail may not sum to totals because of rounding, and because the "Information not available" category for the National School Lunch Program, which provides free/reduced-price lunches, is not displayed. Black includes African American and Hispanic includes Latino. Race categories exclude Hispanic origin.

## Score Gaps for Student Groups

- In 2011, Black students had an average score that was 25 points lower than White students. This performance gap was not significantly different from that in 1998 (28 points).
- In 2011, Hispanic students had an average score that was 25 points lower than White students. This performance gap was not significantly different from that in 1998 (28 points).
- In 2011, female students in New York had an average score that was higher than male students by 9 points.
- In 2011, students who were eligible for free/reduced-price school lunch, an indicator of low family income, had an average score that was 22 points lower than students who were not eligible for free/reduced-price school lunch. This performance gap was not significantly different from that in 1998 (25 points).

 NATIONAL CENTER FOR EDUCATION STATISTICS
Institute of Education Sciences

NOTE: Statistical comparisons are calculated on the basis of unrounded scale scores or percentages.
SOURCE: U.S. Department of Education, Institute of Education Sciences, National Center for Education Statistics, National Assessment of Educational Progress (NAEP), various years, 1998–2011 Reading Assessments.

The Nation's Report Card
State **Writing** 2002
Snapshot Report

New York
Grade 4
Public School

NCES 2003-532NY4

The writing assessment of the National Assessment of Educational Progress (NAEP) measures narrative, informative, and persuasive writing–three purposes identified in the NAEP framework. The NAEP writing scale ranges from 0 to 300.

## Overall Writing Results for New York

- The average scale score for fourth-grade students in New York was 163.
- New York's average score (163) was higher[1] than that of the nation's public schools (153).
- Students' average scale scores in New York were higher than those in 42 jurisdictions[2], not significantly different from those in 3 jurisdictions, and lower than those in 2 jurisdictions.
- The percentage of students who performed at or above the NAEP *Proficient* level was 37 percent. The percentage of students who performed at or above the *Basic* level was 91 percent.

## Student Percentage at Each Achievement Level

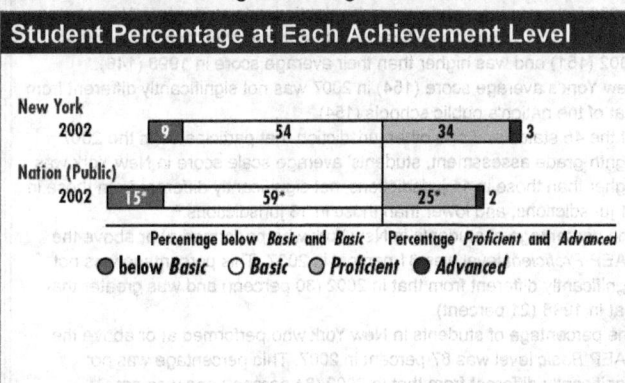

| | below *Basic* | *Basic* | *Proficient* | *Advanced* |

New York 2002: 9 | 54 | 34 | 3
Nation (Public) 2002: 15* | 59* | 25* | 2

Percentage below *Basic* and *Basic*     Percentage *Proficient* and *Advanced*

## Performance of NAEP Reporting Groups in New York

| Reporting groups | Percentage of students | Average Score | Percentage of students at | | | |
|---|---|---|---|---|---|---|
| | | | Below *Basic* | *Basic* | *Proficient* | *Advanced* |
| Male | 51 | 156 ↑ | 12 ↓ | 58 | 28 ↑ | 2 |
| Female | 49 | 170 ↑ | 6 ↓ | 50 ↓ | 40 ↑ | 4 |
| White | 54 | 172 ↑ | 4 ↓ | 49 ↓ | 42 ↑ | 4 |
| Black | 19 | 148 ↑ | 16 ↓ | 63 | 20 ↑ | 1 |
| Hispanic | 21 | 149 | 16 | 61 | 22 ↑ | 1 |
| Asian/Pacific Islander | 6 | 176 | 4 | 44 | 47 | 5 |
| American Indian/Alaska Native | # | --- | --- | --- | --- | --- |
| Free/reduced-priced school lunch | | | | | | |
|   Eligible | 44 | 150 ↑ | 16 ↓ | 61 | 22 ↑ | 1 |
|   Not eligible | 49 | 172 ↑ | 4 ↓ | 49 ↓ | 43 ↑ | 4 |
|   Information not available | 7 | 175 ↑ | 5 ↓ | 43 | 46 ↑ | 6 |

## Average Score Gaps Between Selected Groups

- Female students in New York had an average score that was higher than that of male students (14 points). This performance gap was not significantly different from that of the Nation (18 points).
- White students had an average score that was higher than that of Black students (24 points). This performance gap was not significantly different from that of the Nation (20 points).
- White students had an average score that was higher than that of Hispanic students (23 points). This performance gap was not significantly different from that of the Nation (19 points).
- Students who were not eligible for free/reduced-price school lunch had an average score that was higher than that of students who were eligible (22 points). This performance gap was not significantly different from that of the Nation (22 points).

## Writing Scale Scores at Selected Percentiles

**Scale Score Distribution**

| | 25th Percentile | 50th Percentile | 75th Percentile |
|---|---|---|---|
| **New York** | 139 ↑ | 164 ↑ | 187 ↑ |
| **Nation (Public)** | 128 | 153 | 178 |

An examination of scores at different percentiles on the 0-300 NAEP writing scale at each grade indicates how well students at lower, middle, and higher levels of the distribution performed. For example, the data above shows that 75 percent of students in public schools nationally scored below *178*, while 75 percent of students in New York scored below *187*.

# Percentage rounds to zero.                --- Reporting standards not met; sample size insufficient to permit a reliable estimate.
\* Significantly different from New York.        ↑ Significantly higher than, ↓ lower than appropriate subgroup in the nation (public).
[1] Comparisons (higher/lower/not different) are based on statistical tests. The .05 level was used for testing statistical significance.
[2] "Jurisdictions" includes participating states and other jurisdictions (such as Guam or the District of Columbia).
NOTE: Detail may not sum to totals because of rounding. Score gaps are calculated based on differences between unrounded average scale scores.
Visit http://nces.ed.gov/nationsreportcard/states/ for additional results and detailed information.
SOURCE: U.S. Department of Education, Institute of Education Sciences, National Center for Education Statistics, National Assessment of Educational Progress (NAEP), 2002 Writing Assessment.

**ies** NATIONAL CENTER FOR EDUCATION STATISTICS
Institute of Education Sciences
NCES 2008-470NY8

The Nation's Report Card

**Writing 2007**
State Snapshot Report

New York
Grade 8
Public Schools

The National Assessment of Educational Progress (NAEP) assesses writing for three purposes identified in the NAEP framework: narrative, informative, and persuasive. The NAEP writing scale ranges from 0 to 300.

## Overall Writing Results for New York

- In 2007, the average scale score for eighth-grade students in New York was 154. This was not significantly different from their average score in 2002 (151) and was higher than their average score in 1998 (146).[1]
- New York's average score (154) in 2007 was not significantly different from that of the nation's public schools (154).
- Of the 45 states and one other jurisdiction that participated in the 2007 eighth-grade assessment, students' average scale score in New York was higher than those in 11 jurisdictions, not significantly different from those in 21 jurisdictions, and lower than those in 13 jurisdictions.[2]
- The percentage of students in New York who performed at or above the NAEP *Proficient* level was 31 percent in 2007. This percentage was not significantly different from that in 2002 (30 percent) and was greater than that in 1998 (21 percent).
- The percentage of students in New York who performed at or above the NAEP *Basic* level was 87 percent in 2007. This percentage was not significantly different from that in 2002 (84 percent) and was not significantly different from that in 1998 (84 percent).

## Percentages at NAEP Achievement Levels and Average Score

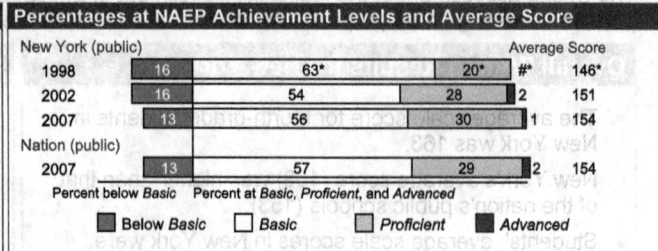

New York (public)                                        Average Score
1998    16    63*    20*    #*    146*
2002    16    54    28    2    151
2007    13    56    30    1    154
Nation (public)
2007    13    57    29    2    154

Percent below *Basic*    Percent at *Basic*, *Proficient*, and *Advanced*

■ Below *Basic*    ☐ Basic    ▨ Proficient    ■ Advanced

NOTE: The NAEP grade 8 writing achievement levels correspond to the following scale points: Below *Basic*, 113 or lower; *Basic*, 114–172; *Proficient*, 173–223; *Advanced*, 224 or above.

## Performance of NAEP Reporting Groups in New York: 2007

| Reporting groups | Percent of students | Average score | Percent below *Basic* | Percent of students at or above *Basic* | *Proficient* | Percent *Advanced* |
|---|---|---|---|---|---|---|
| Male | 50 | 145 | 19 | 81 | 22 | 1 |
| Female | 50 | 163 | 8 | 92 | 41 | 2 |
| White | 56 | 161 | 8 | 92 | 38 | 2 |
| Black | 19 | 140 | 20 | 80 | 15 | # |
| Hispanic | 18 | 140 | 25 | 75 | 20 | 1 |
| Asian/Pacific Islander | 7 | 170 | 9 | 91 | 52 | 5 |
| American Indian/Alaska Native | # | ‡ | ‡ | ‡ | ‡ | ‡ |
| Eligible for National School Lunch Program | 47↑ | 145↑ | 20 | 80 | 22↑ | 1 |
| Not eligible for National School Lunch Program | 51 | 164 | 7 | 93 | 40 | 2 |

## Average Score Gaps Between Selected Groups

- In 2007, male students in New York had an average score that was lower than that of female students by 18 points. This performance gap was not significantly different from that of 1998 (15 points).
- In 2007, Black students had an average score that was lower than that of White students by 21 points. This performance gap was not significantly different from that of 1998 (25 points).
- In 2007, Hispanic students had an average score that was lower than that of White students by 21 points. This performance gap was narrower than that of 1998 (31 points).
- In 2007, students who were eligible for free/reduced-price school lunch, an indicator of poverty, had an average score that was lower than that of students who were not eligible for free/reduced-price school lunch by 19 points. This performance gap was not significantly different from that of 1998 (26 points).
- In 2007, the score gap between students at the 75th percentile and students at the 25th percentile was 47 points. This performance gap was not significantly different from that of 1998 (44 points).

## Writing Scores at Selected Percentiles in New York

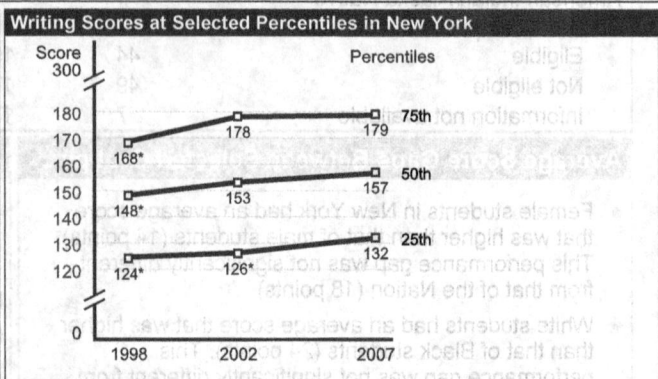

Score    Percentiles
300
180    178    179    75th
170    168*
160
150    153    157    50th
148*
140
130    126*    132    25th
120    124*
0
1998    2002    2007

NOTE: Scores at selected percentiles on the NAEP writing scale indicate how well students at lower, middle, and higher levels performed.

# Rounds to zero.                                    ‡ Reporting standards not met.
* Significantly different from 2007.                 ↑ Significantly higher than 2002. ↓ Significantly lower than 2002.

[1] Comparisons (higher/lower/narrower/wider/not different) are based on statistical tests. The .05 level with appropriate adjustments for multiple comparisons was used for testing statistical significance. Statistical comparisons are calculated on the basis of unrounded scale scores or percentages. Comparisons across jurisdictions and comparisons with the nation or within a jurisdiction across years may be affected by differences in exclusion rates for students with disabilities (SD) and English language learners (ELL). The exclusion rates for SD and ELL in New York were 2 percent and 1 percent in 2007, respectively. For more information on NAEP significance testing, see http://nces.ed.gov/nationsreportcard/writing/interpret-results.asp#statistical.

[2] "Jurisdiction" refers to states, the District of Columbia, and the Department of Defense Education Activity schools.

NOTE: Detail may not sum to totals because of rounding and because the "Information not available" category for the National School Lunch Program, which provides free and reduced-price lunches, and the "Unclassified" category for race/ethnicity are not displayed. Visit http://nces.ed.gov/nationsreportcard/states/ for additional results and detailed information.

SOURCE: U.S. Department of Education, Institute of Education Sciences, National Center for Education Statistics, National Assessment of Educational Progress (NAEP), 1998, 2002, and 2007 Writing Assessments.

The Nation's Report Card — Science 2009 — State Snapshot Report

New York
Grade 4
Public Schools

## 2009 Science Assessment Content

Guided by a new framework, the NAEP science assessment was updated in 2009 to keep the content current with key developments in science, curriculum standards, assessments, and research. The 2009 framework organizes science content into three broad content areas. **Physical science** includes concepts related to properties and changes of matter, forms of energy, energy transfer and conservation, position and motion of objects, and forces affecting motion. **Life science** includes concepts related to organization and development, matter and energy transformations, interdependence, heredity and reproduction, and evolution and diversity. **Earth and space sciences** includes concepts related to objects in the universe, the history of the Earth, properties of Earth materials, tectonics, energy in Earth systems, climate and weather, and biogeochemical cycles.

The 2009 science assessment was composed of 143 questions at grade 4, 162 at grade 8, and 179 at grade 12. Students responded to only a portion of the questions, which included both multiple-choice questions and questions that required a written response.

## Compare the Average Score in 2009 to Other States/Jurisdictions

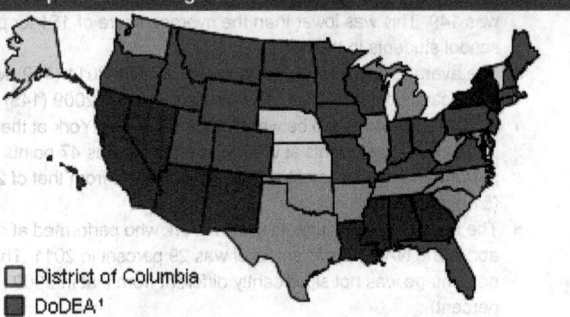

☐ District of Columbia
■ DoDEA[1]

[1] Department of Defense Education Activity (overseas and domestic schools).

In 2009, the average score in **New York** was
- lower than those in 25 states/jurisdictions
- higher than those in 9 states/jurisdictions
- not significantly different from those in 12 states/jurisdictions

- 5 states/jurisdictions did not participate

## Overall Results

- In 2009, the average score of fourth-grade students in New York was 148. This was not significantly different from the average score of 149 for public school students in the nation.
- The percentage of students in New York who performed at or above the NAEP *Proficient* level was 30 percent in 2009. This percentage was smaller than the nation (32 percent).
- The percentage of students in New York who performed at or above the NAEP *Basic* level was 70 percent in 2009. This percentage was not significantly different from the nation (71 percent).

## Achievement-Level Percentages and Average Score Results

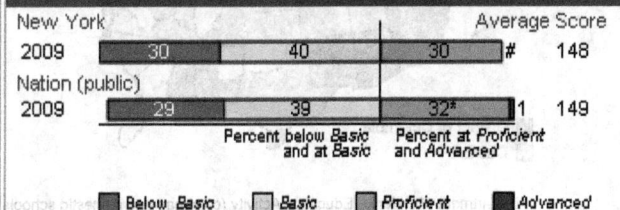

| New York | | | | Average Score |
|---|---|---|---|---|
| 2009 | 30 | 40 | 30 # | 148 |
| Nation (public) | | | | |
| 2009 | 29 | 39 | 32‡ 1 | 149 |

Percent below *Basic* and at *Basic*    Percent at *Proficient* and *Advanced*

■ Below *Basic*   ☐ *Basic*   ■ *Proficient*   ■ *Advanced*

\* Significantly different (*p* < .05) from New York. Significance tests were performed using unrounded numbers.
\# Rounds to zero.

NOTE: Detail may not sum to totals because of rounding.

## Results for Student Groups in 2009

| Reporting Groups | Percent of students | Avg. score | Percentages at or above Basic | Proficient | Percent at Advanced |
|---|---|---|---|---|---|
| **Gender** | | | | | |
| Male | 51 | 148 | 71 | 31 | 1 |
| Female | 49 | 147 | 70 | 29 | # |
| **Race/Ethnicity** | | | | | |
| White | 52 | 161 | 86 | 44 | 1 |
| Black | 19 | 127 | 45 | 9 | # |
| Hispanic | 20 | 130 | 51 | 13 | # |
| Asian/Pacific Islander | 9 | 156 | 80 | 38 | 1 |
| American Indian/Alaska Native | # | ‡ | ‡ | ‡ | ‡ |
| **National School Lunch Program** | | | | | |
| Eligible | 52 | 135 | 56 | 17 | # |
| Not eligible | 46 | 162 | 86 | 45 | 1 |

\# Rounds to zero.      ‡ Reporting standards not met.

NOTE: Detail may not sum to totals because of rounding, and because the "Information not available" category for the National School Lunch Program, which provides free/reduced-price lunches, and the "Unclassified" category for race/ethnicity are not displayed.

## Score Gaps for Student Groups

- In 2009, male students in New York had an average score that was not significantly different from female students.
- In 2009, Black students had an average score that was 34 points lower than White students. This performance gap was not significantly different from the nation (35 points).
- In 2009, Hispanic students had an average score that was 31 points lower than White students. This performance gap was not significantly different from the nation (32 points).
- In 2009, students who were eligible for free/reduced-price school lunch, an indicator of low family income, had an average score that was 27 points lower than students who were not eligible for free/reduced-price school lunch. This performance gap was not significantly different from the nation (29 points).

NOTE: Statistical comparisons are calculated on the basis of unrounded scale scores or percentages.
SOURCE: U.S. Department of Education, Institute of Education Sciences, National Center for Education Statistics, National Assessment of Educational Progress (NAEP), 2009 Science Assessment.

**New York**
**Grade 8**
**Public Schools**

The Nation's Science Report Card
2011 State Snapshot Report

## Overall Results

- In 2011, the average score of eighth-grade students in New York was 149. This was lower than the average score of 151 for public school students in the nation.
- The average score for students in New York in 2011 (149) was not significantly different from their average score in 2009 (149).
- In 2011, the score gap between students in New York at the 75th percentile and students at the 25th percentile was 47 points. This performance gap was not significantly different from that of 2009 (51 points).
- The percentage of students in New York who performed at or above the NAEP *Proficient* level was 29 percent in 2011. This percentage was not significantly different from that in 2009 (31 percent).
- The percentage of students in New York who performed at or above the NAEP *Basic* level was 62 percent in 2011. This percentage was not significantly different from that in 2009 (61 percent).

## Achievement-Level Percentages and Average Score Results

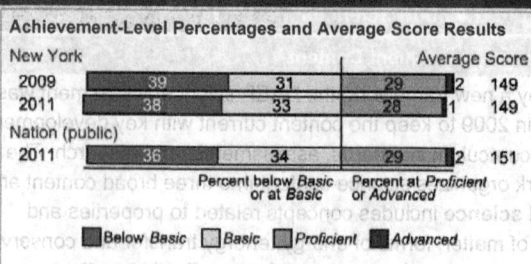

NOTE: Detail may not sum to totals because of rounding.

## Compare the Average Score in 2011 to Other States/Jurisdictions

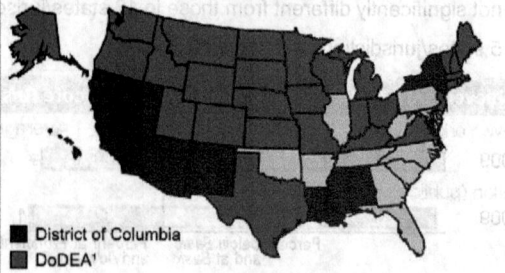

■ District of Columbia
■ DoDEA[1]

[1] Department of Defense Education Activity (overseas and domestic schools).

In 2011, the average score in New York (149) was
- lower than those in 29 states/jurisdictions
- higher than those in 9 states/jurisdictions
- not significantly different from those in 13 states/jurisdictions

## Average Scores for State/Jurisdiction and Nation (public)

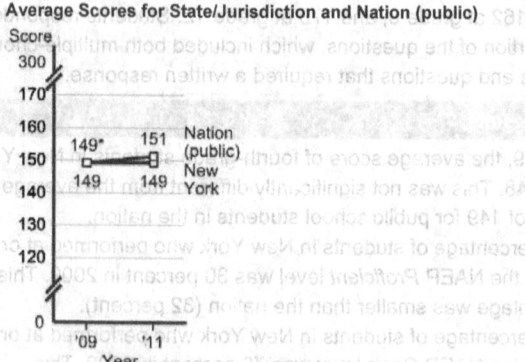

* Significantly different (*p* < .05) from 2011. Significance tests were performed using unrounded numbers.

## Results for Student Groups in 2011

| Reporting Groups | Percent of students | Avg. score | Percentages at or above Basic | Percentages at or above Proficient | Percent at Advanced |
|---|---|---|---|---|---|
| **Race/Ethnicity** | | | | | |
| White | 51 | 163 | 78 | 42 | 2 |
| Black | 19 | 130 | 38 | 11 | # |
| Hispanic | 21 | 129 | 39 | 12 | # |
| Asian | 8 | 154 | 71 | 35 | 1 |
| American Indian/Alaska Native | # | ‡ | ‡ | ‡ | ‡ |
| Native Hawaiian/Pacific Islander | # | ‡ | ‡ | ‡ | ‡ |
| Two or more races | # | ‡ | ‡ | ‡ | ‡ |
| **Gender** | | | | | |
| Male | 51 | 150 | 62 | 31 | 2 |
| Female | 49 | 147 | 61 | 27 | 1 |
| **National School Lunch Program** | | | | | |
| Eligible | 50 | 134 | 44 | 14 | 1 |
| Not eligible | 49 | 164 | 80 | 45 | 2 |

\# Rounds to zero.                    ‡ Reporting standards not met.

NOTE: Detail may not sum to totals because of rounding, and because the "Information not available" category for the National School Lunch Program, which provides free/reduced-price lunches, is not displayed. Black includes African American and Hispanic includes Latino. Race categories exclude Hispanic origin.

## Score Gaps for Student Groups

- In 2011, Black students had an average score that was 33 points lower than White students. This performance gap was narrower than that in 2009 (41 points).
- In 2011, Hispanic students had an average score that was 33 points lower than White students. This performance gap was not significantly different from that in 2009 (39 points).
- In 2011, male students in New York had an average score that was not significantly different from female students.
- In 2011, students who were eligible for free/reduced-price school lunch, an indicator of low family income, had an average score that was 31 points lower than students who were not eligible for free/reduced-price school lunch. This performance gap was not significantly different from that in 2009 (33 points).

**ies** NATIONAL CENTER FOR EDUCATION STATISTICS
Institute of Education Sciences

NOTE: Statistical comparisons are calculated on the basis of unrounded scale scores or percentages.
SOURCE: U.S. Department of Education, Institute of Education Sciences, National Center for Education Statistics, National Assessment of Educational Progress (NAEP), 2009 and 2011 Science Assessments.

# Understanding How Accountability Works in New York State

The federal No Child Left Behind (NCLB) Act requires that states develop and report on measures of student proficiency in 1) English language arts (ELA), in 2) mathematics, and on 3) a third indicator. In New York State in 2010–11, the third indicator is science at the elementary/middle level and graduation rate at the secondary level. Schools or districts that meet predefined goals on these measures are making Adequate Yearly Progress (AYP).

For more information about accountability in New York State, visit: **http://www.p12.nysed.gov/irs/accountability/**.

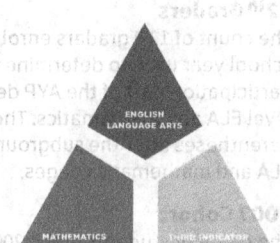

## 1 English Language Arts (ELA)

To make AYP in ELA, every accountability group must make AYP. For a group to make AYP, it must meet the participation *and* the performance criteria.

**A Participation Criterion**

At the elementary/middle level, 95 percent of Grades 3–8 students enrolled during the test administration period in each group with 40 or more students must be tested on the New York State Testing Program (NYSTP) in ELA or, if appropriate, the New York State English as a Second Language Achievement Test (NYSESLAT), or the New York State Alternate Assessment (NYSAA) in ELA. At the secondary level, 95 percent of seniors in 2010–11 in each accountability group with 40 or more students must have taken an English examination that meets the students' graduation requirement.

**B Performance Criterion**

At the elementary/middle level, the Performance Index (PI) of each group with 30 or more continuously enrolled tested students must equal or exceed its Effective Annual Measurable Objective (AMO) or the group must make Safe Harbor. (NYSESLAT is used only for participation.) At the secondary level, the PI of each group in the 2007 cohort with 30 or more members must equal or exceed its Effective AMO or the group must make Safe Harbor. To make Safe Harbor, the PI of the group must equal or exceed its Safe Harbor Target and the group must qualify for Safe Harbor using the third indicator, science or graduation rate.

## 2 Mathematics

The same criteria for making AYP in ELA apply to mathematics. At the elementary/middle level, the measures used to determine AYP are the NYSTP and the NYSAA in mathematics. At the secondary level, the measures are mathematics examinations that meet the students' graduation requirement.

## 3 Third Indicator

In addition to English language arts and mathematics, the school must also make AYP in a third area of achievement. This means meeting the criteria in science at the elementary/middle level and the criteria in graduation rate at the secondary level.

**Elementary/Middle-Level Science:** To make AYP, the All Students group must meet the participation criterion *and* the performance criterion.

**A Participation Criterion**

Eighty percent of students in Grades 4 and/or 8 enrolled during the test administration period in the All Students group, if it has 40 or more students, must be tested on an accountability measure. In Grade 4, the measures are the Grade 4 elementary-level science test and the Grade 4 NYSAA in science. In Grade 8 science, the measures are the Grade 8 middle-level science test, Regents science examinations, and the Grade 8 NYSAA in science.

**B Performance Criterion**

The PI of the All Students group, if it has 30 or more students, must equal or exceed the State Science Standard (100) or the Science Progress Target.

Qualifying for Safe Harbor in Elementary/Middle-Level ELA and Math: To qualify, the group must meet both the participation criterion and the performance criterion in science.

**Secondary-Level Graduation Rate:** For a school to make AYP in graduation rate, the percent of students in the 2006 graduation-rate total cohort in the All Students group earning a local or Regents diploma by August 31, 2010 must equal or exceed the Graduation-Rate Standard (80%) or the Graduation-Rate Progress Target.

Qualifying for Safe Harbor in Secondary-Level ELA and Math: To qualify, the percent of the 2006 graduation-rate total cohort earning a local or Regents diploma by August 31, 2010 must equal or exceed the Graduation-Rate Standard (80%) or the Graduation-Rate Progress Target for that group.

# Useful Terms for Understanding Accountability

### 12th Graders

The count of 12th graders enrolled during the 2010–11 school year used to determine the Percentage Tested for the Participation part of the AYP determination for secondary-level ELA and mathematics. These are the first numbers in the parentheses after the subgroup label on the secondary-level ELA and mathematics pages.

### 2007 Cohort

The count of students in the 2007 accountability cohort used to determine the Performance Index for the Test Performance part of the AYP determination for secondary-level ELA and mathematics. These are the second numbers in the parentheses after the subgroup label on the secondary-level ELA and mathematics pages.

### Accountability Cohort for English and Mathematics

The accountability cohort is used to determine if a school or district met the performance criterion in secondary-level ELA and mathematics. The 2007 school accountability cohort consists of all students who first entered Grade 9 anywhere in the 2007–08 school year, and all ungraded students with disabilities who reached their seventeenth birthday in the 2007–08 school year, who were enrolled on October 6, 2010 and did not transfer to a diploma granting program. Students who earned a high school equivalency diploma or were enrolled in an approved high school equivalency preparation program on June 30, 2011, are not included in the 2007 school accountability cohort. The 2007 district accountability cohort consists of all students in each school accountability cohort plus students who transferred within the district after BEDS day plus students who were placed outside the district by the Committee on Special Education or district administrators and who met the other requirements for cohort membership. Cohort is defined in Section 100.2 (p) (16) of the Commissioner's Regulations.

### Adequate Yearly Progress (AYP)

Adequate Yearly Progress (AYP) indicates satisfactory progress by a district or a school toward the goal of proficiency for all students.

### Annual Measurable Objective (AMO)

The Annual Measurable Objective (AMO) is the Performance Index value that signifies that an accountability group is making satisfactory progress toward the goal that 100 percent of students will be proficient in the State's learning standards for English language arts and mathematics by 2013–14. The AMOs for each grade level will be increased as specified in CR100.2(p) (14) and will reach 200 in 2013–14. (See Effective AMO for further information.)

### Continuous Enrollment

The count of continuously enrolled tested students used to determine the Performance Index for the Test Performance part of the AYP determination for elementary/middle-level ELA, mathematics, and science. These are the second numbers in the parentheses after the subgroup label on the elementary/middle-level ELA, mathematics, and science pages.

### Continuously Enrolled Students

At the elementary/middle level, continuously enrolled students are those enrolled in the school or district on BEDS day (usually the first Wednesday in October) of the school year until the test administration period. At the secondary level, all students who meet the criteria for inclusion in the accountability cohort are considered to be continuously enrolled.

### Effective Annual Measurable Objective (Effective AMO)

The Effective Annual Measurable Objective is the Performance Index (PI) value that each accountability group within a school or district is expected to achieve to make AYP. The Effective AMO is the lowest PI that an accountability group of a given size can achieve in a subject for the group's PI not to be considered significantly different from the AMO for that subject. If an accountability group's PI equals or exceeds the Effective AMO, it is considered to have made AYP. A more complete definition of Effective AMO and a table showing the PI values that each group size must equal or exceed to make AYP are available at **www.p12.nysed.gov/irs.**

### Graduation Rate

The Graduation Rate on the Graduation Rate page is the percentage of the 2006 cohort that earned a local or Regents diploma by August 31, 2010.

### Graduation-Rate Total Cohort

The Graduation-Rate Total Cohort, shown on the Graduation Rate page, is used to determine if a school or district made AYP in graduation rate. For the 2010–11 school year, this cohort is the 2006 graduation-rate total cohort. The 2006 total cohort consists of all students who first entered Grade 9 anywhere in the 2006–07 school year, and all ungraded students with disabilities who reached their seventeenth birthday in the 2006–07 school year, and who were enrolled in the school/district for five months or longer or who were enrolled in the school/district for less than five months but were previously enrolled in the same school/district for five months or longer between the date they first entered Grade 9 and the date they last ended enrollment. A more detailed definition of graduation-rate cohort can be found in the *SIRS Manual* at **http://www.p12.nysed.gov/irs/sirs/**.

For districts and schools with fewer than 30 graduation-rate total cohort members in the All Students group in 2010–11, data for 2009–10 and 2010–11 for accountability groups were combined to determine counts and graduation rates. Groups with fewer than 30 students in the graduation-rate total cohort are not required to meet the graduation-rate criterion.

### Limited English Proficient

For all accountability measures, if the count of LEP students is equal to or greater than 30, former LEP students are also included in the performance calculations.

### Non-Accountability Groups

Female, Male, and Migrant groups are not part of the AYP determination for any measure.

# Useful Terms for Understanding Accountability (continued)

## Participation

Accountability groups with fewer than 40 students enrolled during the test administration period (for elementary/middle-level ELA, math, and science) or fewer than 40 12th graders (for secondary-level ELA and mathematics) are not required to meet the participation criterion. If the Percentage Tested for an accountability group fell below 95 percent for ELA and math or 80 percent for science in 2010–11, the participation enrollment ("Total" or "12th Graders") shown in the tables is the sum of 2009–10 and 2010–11 participation enrollments and the "Percentage Tested" shown is the weighted average of the participation rates over those two years.

## Performance Index (PI)

A Performance Index is a value from 0 to 200 that is assigned to an accountability group, indicating how that group performed on a required State test (or approved alternative) in English language arts, mathematics, or science. Student scores on the tests are converted to four performance levels, from Level 1 to Level 4. (See performance level definitions on the Overview summary page.) At the elementary/middle level, the PI is calculated using the following equation:

100 × [(Count of Continuously Enrolled Tested Students Performing at Levels 2, 3, and 4 + the Count at Levels 3 and 4) ÷ Count of All Continuously Enrolled Tested Students]

At the secondary level, the PI is calculated using the following equation:

100 × [(Count of Cohort Members Performing at Levels 2, 3, and 4 + the Count at Levels 3 and 4) ÷ Count of All Cohort Members]

A list of tests used to measure student performance for accountability is available at **www.p12.nysed.gov/irs.**

## Progress Targets

For accountability groups below the State Standard in science or graduation rate, the Progress Target is an alternate method for making AYP or qualifying for Safe Harbor in English language arts and mathematics based on improvement over the previous year's performance.

*Science:* The current year's Science Progress Target is calculated by adding one point to the previous year's Performance Index (PI). Example: The 2010–11 Science Progress Target is calculated by adding one point to the 2009–10 PI.

*Graduation Rate:* The Graduation-rate Progress Target is calculated by determining a 20% gap reduction between the rate of the previous year's graduation-rate cohort and the state standard. Example: The 2010–11 Graduation-Rate Progress Target = [(80 − percentage of the 2005 cohort earning a local or Regents diploma by August 31, 2009) × 0.20] + percentage of the 2005 cohort earning a local or Regents diploma by August 31, 2009.

Progress Targets are provided for groups whose PI (for science) or graduation rate (for graduation rate) is below the State Standard.

## Safe Harbor Targets

Safe Harbor provides an alternate means to demonstrate AYP for accountability groups that do not achieve their EAMOs in English or mathematics. The 2010–11 safe harbor targets are calculated using the following equation:

2009–10 PI + (200 − the 2009–10 PI) × 0.10

Safe Harbor Targets are provided for groups whose PI is less than the EAMO.

## Safe Harbor Qualification (‡)

On the science page, if the group met both the participation and the performance criteria for science, the Safe Harbor Qualification column will show "Qualified." If the group did not meet one or more criteria, the column will show "Did not qualify." A "‡" symbol after the 2010–11 Safe Harbor Target on the elementary/middle- or secondary-level ELA or mathematics page indicates that the student group did not make AYP in science (elementary/middle level) or graduation rate (secondary level) and; therefore, the group did not qualify for Safe Harbor in ELA or mathematics.

## State Standard

The criterion value that represents minimally satisfactory performance (for science) or a minimally satisfactory percentage of cohort members earning a local or Regents diploma (for graduation rate). In 2010–11, the State Science Standard is a Performance Index of 100; the State Graduation-Rate Standard is 80%. The Commissioner may raise the State Standard at his discretion in future years.

## Students with Disabilities

For all measures, if the count of students with disabilities is equal to or greater than 30, former students with disabilities are also included in the performance calculations.

## Test Performance

For districts and schools with fewer than 30 continuously enrolled tested students (for elementary/middle-level ELA, math, and science) or fewer than 30 students in the 2007 cohort (for secondary-level ELA and mathematics) in the All Students group in 2010–11, data for 2009–10 and 2010–11 for accountability groups were combined to determine counts and Performance Indices. For districts and schools with 30 or more continuously enrolled students/2007 cohort members in the All Students group in 2010–11, student groups with fewer than 30 members are not required to meet the performance criterion. This is indicated by a "—" in the Test Performance column in the table.

## Total

The count of students enrolled during the test administration period used to determine the Percentage Tested for the Participation part of the AYP determination for elementary/middle-level ELA, mathematics, and science. These are the first numbers in the parentheses after the subgroup label on the elementary/middle-level ELA, mathematics, and science pages. For accountability calculations, students who were excused from testing for medical reasons in accordance with federal NCLB guidance are not included in the count.

# Summary

## On which accountability measures did the state make Adequate Yearly Progress (AYP) and which groups made AYP on each measure?

| Student Groups | Elementary/Middle Level | | | Secondary Level | | |
|---|---|---|---|---|---|---|
| | English Language Arts | Mathematics | Science | English Language Arts | Mathematics | Graduation Rate |
| **All Students** | ✔ | ✔ | ✔ | ✔ | ✔ | ✔SH |
| **Ethnicity** | | | | | | |
| American Indian or Alaska Native | ✔ | ✔ | | ✘ | ✘ | |
| Black or African American | ✔ | ✘ | | ✘ | ✘ | |
| Hispanic or Latino | ✔ | ✔ | | ✘ | ✘ | |
| Asian or Native Hawaiian/Other Pacific Islander | ✔ | ✔ | | ✔ | ✔ | |
| White | ✔ | ✔ | | ✔ | ✔ | |
| Multiracial | ✔ | | | ✔ | ✔ | |
| **Other Groups** | | | | | | |
| Students with Disabilities | ✘ | ✘ | | ✘ | ✘ | |
| Limited English Proficient | ✘ | ✘ | | ✘ | ✘ | |
| Economically Disadvantaged | ✔ | ✔ | | ✘ | ✘ | |
| **Student groups making AYP in each subject** | ✘ 8 of 10 | ✘ 7 of 10 | ✔ 1 of 1 | ✘ 3 of 10 | ✘ 4 of 10 | ✔SH 1 of 1 |

**AYP Status**

✔    Made AYP

✔SH   Made AYP Using Safe Harbor Target

✘    Did not make AYP

—    Insufficient Number of Students to Determine AYP Status

**NOTE:** See *Useful Terms for Understanding Accountability* for explanations and definitions of terms and table labels used on this page.

# Elementary/Middle-Level English Language Arts

**Accountability Measures**    8 of 10    Student groups making AYP in English language arts

✗    Did Not Make AYP

## How did students in each accountability group perform on elementary/middle-level English language arts accountability?

| Student Group (Total: Continuous Enrollment) | AYP Status | Participation Met Criterion | Participation Percentage Tested | Test Performance Met Criterion | Test Performance Performance Index | Performance Objectives Effective AMO | Safe Harbor Target 2010–11 | Safe Harbor Target 2011–12 |
|---|---|---|---|---|---|---|---|---|
| **Accountability Groups** | | | | | | | | |
| **All Students** (1,229,657:1,173,267) | ✔ | ✔ | 99% | ✔ | 144 | 121 | | |
| **Ethnicity** | | | | | | | | |
| American Indian or Alaska Native (6,126:5,710) | ✔ | ✔ | 99% | ✔ | 129 | 121 | | |
| Black or African American (232,042:217,319) | ✔ | ✔ | 99% | ✔ | 121 | 121 | | |
| Hispanic or Latino (276,155:256,947) | ✔ | ✔ | 99% | ✔ | 123 | 121 | | |
| Asian or Native Hawaiian/Other Pacific Islander (100,355:94,142) | ✔ | ✔ | 99% | ✔ | 161 | 121 | | |
| White (607,025:591,930) | ✔ | ✔ | 100% | ✔ | 159 | 121 | | |
| Multiracial (7,954:7,219) | ✔ | ✔ | 99% | ✔ | 153 | 121 | | |
| **Other Groups** | | | | | | | | |
| Students with Disabilities (207,129:204,892) | ✗ | ✔ | 98% | ✗ | 89 | 121 | 99 | 100 |
| Limited English Proficient (95,792:114,839) | ✗ | ✔ | 98% | ✗ | 98 | 121 | 108 | 108 |
| Economically Disadvantaged (665,187:623,670) | ✔ | ✔ | 99% | ✔ | 126 | 121 | | |
| **Final AYP Determination** | ✗ 8 of 10 | | | | | | | |
| **Non-Accountability Groups** | | | | | | | | |
| Female (596,744:570,924) | | | 99% | | 151 | 121 | | |
| Male (632,913:602,343) | | | 99% | | 137 | 121 | | |
| Migrant (315:267) | | | 97% | | 102 | 115 | | |

**Symbols**

✔    Made AYP

✔ SH    Made AYP Using Safe Harbor Target

✗    Did not make AYP

—    Fewer Than 40 Total/Fewer Than 30 Continuous Enrollment

‡    Did not qualify for Safe Harbor

**NOTE:** See *Useful Terms for Understanding Accountability* for explanations and definitions of terms and table labels used on this page.

# Elementary/Middle-Level Mathematics

| Accountability Measures | 7 of 10 | Student groups making AYP in mathematics |
| | ✗ | Did Not Make AYP |

## How did students in each accountability group perform on elementary/middle-level mathematics accountability measures?

| Student Group (Total: Continuous Enrollment) | AYP Status | Participation | | Test Performance | | Performance Objectives | | |
|---|---|---|---|---|---|---|---|---|
| | | Met Criterion | Percentage Tested | Met Criterion | Performance Index | Effective AMO | Safe Harbor Target 2010–11 | 2011–12 |
| **Accountability Groups** | | | | | | | | |
| All Students (1,229,983:1,179,082) | ✔ | ✔ | 99% | ✔ | 157 | 136 | | |
| **Ethnicity** | | | | | | | | |
| American Indian or Alaska Native (6,129:5,731) | ✔ | ✔ | 99% | ✔ | 144 | 136 | | |
| Black or African American (232,070:217,566) | ✗ | ✔ | 99% | ✗ | 132 | 136 | 136 | 139 |
| Hispanic or Latino (276,309:260,126) | ✔ | ✔ | 99% | ✔ | 141 | 136 | | |
| Asian or Native Hawaiian/Other Pacific Islander (100,439:95,905) | ✔ | ✔ | 100% | ✔ | 182 | 136 | | |
| White (607,085:592,531) | ✔ | ✔ | 100% | ✔ | 170 | 136 | | |
| Multiracial (7,951:7,223) | ✔ | ✔ | 99% | ✔ | 160 | 136 | | |
| **Other Groups** | | | | | | | | |
| Students with Disabilities (207,128:204,629) | ✗ | ✔ | 98% | ✗ | 110 | 136 | 116 | 119 |
| Limited English Proficient (96,000:121,307) | ✗ | ✔ | 99% | ✗ | 129 | 136 | 134 | 136 |
| Economically Disadvantaged (665,404:629,108) | ✔ | ✔ | 99% | ✔ | 143 | 136 | | |
| **Final AYP Determination** | ✗ 7 of 10 | | | | | | | |
| **Non-Accountability Groups** | | | | | | | | |
| Female (596,890:573,721) | | | 100% | | 159 | 136 | | |
| Male (633,093:605,361) | | | 99% | | 156 | 136 | | |
| Migrant (313:278) | | | 98% | | 123 | 130 | | |

**Symbols**

✔ Made AYP

✔SH Made AYP Using Safe Harbor Target

✗ Did not make AYP

— Fewer Than 40 Total/Fewer Than 30 Continuous Enrollment

‡ Did not qualify for Safe Harbor

**NOTE:** See *Useful Terms for Understanding Accountability* for explanations and definitions of terms and table labels used on this page.

# Elementary/Middle-Level Science

| Accountability Measures | 1 of 1 | Student groups making AYP in science |
| --- | --- | --- |
| | ✔ | Made AYP |

## How did students in each accountability group perform on elementary/middle-level science accountability measures?

| Student Group (Total: Continuous Enrollment) | AYP Status | Safe Harbor Qualification | Participation Met Criterion | Percentage Tested | Test Performance Met Criterion | Performance Index | Performance Objectives State Standard | Progress Target 2010–11 | Progress Target 2011–12 |
| --- | --- | --- | --- | --- | --- | --- | --- | --- | --- |
| **Accountability Groups** | | | | | | | | | |
| All Students (411,025:387,423) | ✔ | Qualified | ✔ | 98% | ✔ | 177 | 100 | | |
| **Ethnicity** | | | | | | | | | |
| American Indian or Alaska Native (2,020:1,815) | | Qualified | ✔ | 96% | ✔ | 171 | 100 | | |
| Black or African American (77,588:70,587) | | Qualified | ✔ | 96% | ✔ | 158 | 100 | | |
| Hispanic or Latino (92,027:84,539) | | Qualified | ✔ | 97% | ✔ | 162 | 100 | | |
| Asian or Native Hawaiian/Other Pacific Islander (33,425:31,643) | | Qualified | ✔ | 99% | ✔ | 185 | 100 | | |
| White (203,492:196,648) | | Qualified | ✔ | 99% | ✔ | 190 | 100 | | |
| Multiracial (2,473:2,191) | | Qualified | ✔ | 98% | ✔ | 187 | 100 | | |
| **Other Groups** | | | | | | | | | |
| Students with Disabilities (69,214:66,095) | | Qualified | ✔ | 95% | ✔ | 150 | 100 | | |
| Limited English Proficient (32,013:37,472) | | Qualified | ✔ | 97% | ✔ | 146 | 100 | | |
| Economically Disadvantaged (220,764:203,933) | | Qualified | ✔ | 97% | ✔ | 165 | 100 | | |
| **Final AYP Determination** | ✔ 1 of 1 | | | | | | | | |
| **Non-Accountability Groups** | | | | | | | | | |
| Female (199,505:188,783) | | | | 98% | | 178 | 100 | | |
| Male (211,520:198,640) | | | | 97% | | 177 | 100 | | |
| Migrant (89:83) | | | | 100% | | 163 | 100 | | |

**Symbols**

✔ Made AYP

✘ Did not make AYP

— Fewer Than 40 Total/Fewer Than 30 Continuous Enrollment

**NOTE:** See *Useful Terms for Understanding Accountability* for explanations and definitions of terms and table labels used on this page.

# Secondary-Level English Language Arts

**Accountability Measures**

| | | |
|---|---|---|
| | 3 of 10 | Student groups making AYP in English language arts |
| | ✘ | Did not make AYP |

## How did students in each accountability group perform on secondary-level English language arts accountability measures?

| Student Group (12th Graders: 2007 Cohort) | AYP Status | Participation Met Criterion | Participation Percentage Tested | Test Performance Met Criterion | Test Performance Performance Index | Performance Objectives Effective AMO | Performance Objectives Safe Harbor Target 2010–11 | Performance Objectives Safe Harbor Target 2011–12 |
|---|---|---|---|---|---|---|---|---|
| **Accountability Groups** | | | | | | | | |
| **All Students** (201,005:198,622) | ✘ | ✔ | 99% | ✘ | 181 | 182 | 182 | 183 |
| **Ethnicity** | | | | | | | | |
| American Indian or Alaska Native (862:897) | ✘ | ✔ | 99% | ✘ | 172 | 179 | 173‡ | 175 |
| Black or African American (37,249:37,012) | ✘ | ✔ | 99% | ✘ | 167 | 182 | 169‡ | 170 |
| Hispanic or Latino (38,649:38,287) | ✘ | ✔ | 99% | ✘ | 168 | 182 | 169‡ | 171 |
| Asian or Native Hawaiian/Other Pacific Islander (16,894:16,131) | ✔ | ✔ | 100% | ✔ | 187 | 182 | | |
| White (106,808:105,803) | ✔ | ✔ | 99% | ✔ | 190 | 182 | | |
| Multiracial (543:492) | ✔ | ✔ | 99% | ✔ | 187 | 178 | | |
| **Other Groups** | | | | | | | | |
| Students with Disabilities (21,318:27,376) | ✘ | ✔ | 97% | ✘ | 135 | 182 | 139‡ | 142 |
| Limited English Proficient (9,416:11,867) | ✘ | ✔ | 98% | ✘ | 139 | 182 | 145‡ | 145 |
| Economically Disadvantaged (80,905:81,891) | ✘ | ✔ | 99% | ✘ | 171 | 182 | 173 | 174 |
| **Final AYP Determination** | ✘ 3 of 10 | | | | | | | |
| **Non-Accountability Groups** | | | | | | | | |
| Female (99,992:97,933) | | | 99% | | 185 | 182 | | |
| Male (101,013:100,689) | | | 99% | | 177 | 182 | | |
| Migrant (31:34) | | | 100% | | 165 | 166 | | |

**Symbols**

✔    Made AYP

✔<sup>SH</sup>    Made AYP Using Safe Harbor Target

✘    Did not make AYP

—    Fewer Than 40 12<sup>th</sup> Graders/ Fewer Than 30 Cohort

‡    Did not qualify for Safe Harbor

**NOTE:** See *Useful Terms for Understanding Accountability* for explanations and definitions of terms and table labels used on this page.

# Secondary-Level Mathematics

| Accountability Measures | 4 of 10 | Student groups making AYP in mathematics |
|---|---|---|
| | ✗ | Did not make AYP |

## How did students in each accountability group perform on secondary-level mathematics accountability measures?

| Student Group (12th Graders: 2007 Cohort) | AYP Status | Participation | | Test Performance | | Performance Objectives | | |
|---|---|---|---|---|---|---|---|---|
| | | Met Criterion | Percentage Tested | Met Criterion | Performance Index | Effective AMO | Safe Harbor Target 2010–11 | 2011–12 |
| **Accountability Groups** | | | | | | | | |
| **All Students** (201,005:198,622) | ✔ | ✔ | 99% | ✔ | 182 | 179 | | |
| **Ethnicity** | | | | | | | | |
| American Indian or Alaska Native (862:897) | ✗ | ✔ | 98% | ✗ | 172 | 176 | 176‡ | 175 |
| Black or African American (37,249:37,012) | ✗ | ✔ | 99% | ✗ | 166 | 179 | 167‡ | 169 |
| Hispanic or Latino (38,649:38,287) | ✗ | ✔ | 98% | ✗ | 169 | 179 | 170‡ | 172 |
| Asian or Native Hawaiian/Other Pacific Islander (16,894:16,131) | ✔ | ✔ | 99% | ✔ | 192 | 179 | | |
| White (106,808:105,803) | ✔ | ✔ | 99% | ✔ | 191 | 179 | | |
| Multiracial (543:492) | ✔ | ✔ | 97% | ✔ | 184 | 175 | | |
| **Other Groups** | | | | | | | | |
| Students with Disabilities (21,318:27,376) | ✗ | ✔ | 97% | ✗ | 137 | 179 | 142‡ | 143 |
| Limited English Proficient (9,416:11,867) | ✗ | ✔ | 98% | ✗ | 159 | 179 | 161‡ | 163 |
| Economically Disadvantaged (80,905:81,891) | ✗ | ✔ | 99% | ✗ | 173 | 179 | 174 | 176 |
| **Final AYP Determination** | ✗ 4 of 10 | | | | | | | |
| **Non-Accountability Groups** | | | | | | | | |
| Female (99,992:97,933) | | | 99% | | 185 | 179 | | |
| Male (101,013:100,689) | | | 99% | | 180 | 179 | | |
| Migrant (31:34) | | | 100% | | 182 | 163 | | |

**Symbols**

✔    Made AYP

✔^SH   Made AYP Using Safe Harbor Target

✗    Did not make AYP

—    Fewer Than 40 12th Graders/ Fewer Than 30 Cohort

‡    Did not qualify for Safe Harbor

**NOTE:** See *Useful Terms for Understanding Accountability* for explanations and definitions of terms and table labels used on this page.

# Graduation Rate

**Accountability Measures**   1 of 1    Student groups making AYP in graduation rate

                              ✔ SH    Made AYP

## How did students in each accountability group perform on graduation rate accountability measures?

| Student Group | Graduation | | | Objectives | |
| --- | --- | --- | --- | --- | --- |
| (2006 Graduation-Rate Total Cohort) | AYP | Met Criterion | Graduation Rate | State Standard | Progress Target 2010–11 |
| **Accountability Groups** | | | | | |
| **All Students** (221,569) | ✔ SH | ✔ SH | 77% | 80% | 77% |
| **Ethnicity** | | | | | |
| American Indian or Alaska Native (1,038) | | ✗ | 64% | 80% | 66% |
| Black or African American (43,575) | | ✗ | 64% | 80% | 65% |
| Hispanic or Latino (42,422) | | ✗ | 63% | 80% | 64% |
| Asian or Native Hawaiian/Other Pacific Islander (16,321) | | ✔ | 86% | 80% | |
| White (117,754) | | ✔ | 86% | 80% | |
| Multiracial (459) | | ✔ SH | 79% | 80% | 72% |
| **Other Groups** | | | | | |
| Students with Disabilities (33,749) | | ✗ | 49% | 80% | 54% |
| Limited English Proficient (13,369) | | ✗ | 52% | 80% | 56% |
| Economically Disadvantaged (87,483) | | ✔ SH | 69% | 80% | 69% |
| **Final AYP Determination** | ✔ SH  1 of 1 | | | | |
| **Non-Accountability Groups** | | | | | |
| Female (108,543) | | | 81% | 80% | |
| Male (113,026) | | | 74% | 80% | |
| Migrant (25) | | | 64% | 80% | |

**Symbols**

✔    Made AYP

✗    Did not make AYP

—    Fewer than 30 Graduation-Rate Total Cohort

**NOTE:** See *Useful Terms for Understanding Accountability* for explanations and definitions of terms and table labels used on this page.

# Summary of 2010–11 Statewide Performance

Performance on the State assessments in English language arts, mathematics, and science at the elementary and middle levels is reported in terms of mean scores and the percentage of tested students scoring at or above Level 2, Level 3, and Level 4. Performance on the State assessments in ELA and mathematics at the secondary level is reported in terms of the percentage of students in a cohort scoring at these levels.

| | Percentage of students that scored at or above Level 3 | Total Tested |
|---|---|---|
| **English Language Arts** | | |
| Grade 3 | 56% | 196,575 |
| Grade 4 | 57% | 197,271 |
| Grade 5 | 54% | 200,442 |
| Grade 6 | 56% | 198,287 |
| Grade 7 | 48% | 200,307 |
| Grade 8 | 47% | 201,371 |
| **Mathematics** | | |
| Grade 3 | 60% | 198,667 |
| Grade 4 | 67% | 199,327 |
| Grade 5 | 66% | 202,595 |
| Grade 6 | 63% | 200,292 |
| Grade 7 | 65% | 202,189 |
| Grade 8 | 60% | 203,239 |
| **Science** | | |
| Grade 4 | 88% | 197,303 |
| Grade 8 | 69% | 175,068 |

| | Percentage of students that scored at or above Level 3 | 2007 Total Cohort |
|---|---|---|
| **Secondary Level** | | |
| English | 80% | 223,120 |
| Mathematics | 81% | 223,120 |

## About the Performance Level Descriptors

### English Language Arts

**Level 1: Below Standard**
Student performance does not demonstrate an understanding of the English language arts knowledge and skills expected at this grade level.

**Level 2: Meets Basic Standard**
Student performance demonstrates a partial understanding of the English language arts knowledge and skills expected at this grade level.

**Level 3: Meets Proficiency Standard**
Student performance demonstrates an understanding of the English language arts knowledge and skills expected at this grade level.

**Level 4: Exceeds Proficiency Standard**
Student performance demonstrates a thorough understanding of the English language arts knowledge and skills expected at this grade level.

### Mathematics

**Level 1: Below Standard**
Student performance does not demonstrate an understanding of the mathematics content expected at this grade level.

**Level 2: Meets Basic Standard**
Student performance demonstrates a partial understanding of the mathematics content expected at this grade level.

**Level 3: Meets Proficiency Standard**
Student performance demonstrates an understanding of the mathematics content expected at this grade level.

**Level 4: Exceeds Proficiency Standard**
Student performance demonstrates a thorough understanding of the mathematics content expected at this grade level.

# Statewide Results in Grade 3 English Language Arts

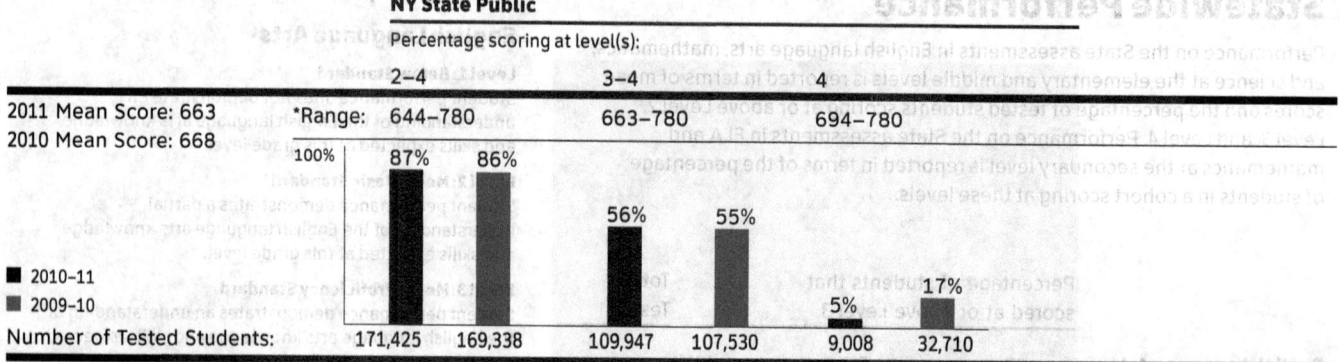

**NY State Public**

Percentage scoring at level(s):

2011 Mean Score: 663
2010 Mean Score: 668

*Range: 644–780 (2–4)    663–780 (3–4)    694–780 (4)

|  | 2–4 | 3–4 | 4 |
|---|---|---|---|
| 2010–11 | 87% | 56% | 5% |
| 2009–10 | 86% | 55% | 17% |
| Number of Tested Students: | 171,425 / 169,338 | 109,947 / 107,530 | 9,008 / 32,710 |

## Results by Student Group

| | 2010–11 School Year | | | | 2009–10 School Year | | | |
|---|---|---|---|---|---|---|---|---|
| | Total Tested | 2–4 | 3–4 | 4 | Total Tested | 2–4 | 3–4 | 4 |
| **All Students** | **196,575** | **87%** | **56%** | **5%** | **196,499** | **86%** | **55%** | **17%** |
| Female | 96,066 | 90% | 61% | 6% | 95,916 | 88% | 58% | 19% |
| Male | 100,509 | 84% | 51% | 3% | 100,583 | 84% | 52% | 15% |
| American Indian or Alaska Native | 1,092 | 82% | 46% | 2% | 966 | 82% | 47% | 11% |
| Black or African American | 36,564 | 80% | 39% | 1% | 37,178 | 77% | 39% | 9% |
| Hispanic or Latino | 45,767 | 81% | 42% | 2% | 43,665 | 80% | 41% | 10% |
| Asian or Native Hawaiian/Other Pacific Islander | 16,216 | 92% | 69% | 7% | 15,262 | 92% | 65% | 22% |
| White | 95,331 | 92% | 67% | 7% | 98,316 | 92% | 65% | 22% |
| Multiracial | 1,605 | 89% | 60% | 6% | 1,112 | 89% | 60% | 21% |
| Small Group Totals | 0 | — | — | — | 0 | — | — | — |
| General-Education Students | 167,226 | 93% | 62% | 5% | 166,506 | 92% | 61% | 19% |
| Students with Disabilities | 29,349 | 56% | 19% | 1% | 29,993 | 54% | 19% | 4% |
| English Proficient | 178,459 | 89% | 59% | 5% | 178,005 | 88% | 58% | 18% |
| Limited English Proficient | 18,116 | 66% | 22% | 0% | 18,494 | 66% | 24% | 4% |
| Economically Disadvantaged | 110,235 | 82% | 43% | 2% | 108,619 | 80% | 43% | 10% |
| Not Disadvantaged | 86,340 | 94% | 72% | 8% | 87,880 | 93% | 69% | 24% |
| Migrant | 73 | 73% | 30% | 0% | 50 | 70% | 30% | 8% |
| Not Migrant | 196,502 | 87% | 56% | 5% | 196,449 | 86% | 55% | 17% |

**NOTE**
The — symbol indicates that data for a group of students have been suppressed. If a group has fewer than five students, data for that group and the next smallest group(s) are suppressed to protect the privacy of individual students.
*These ranges are for 2010–11 data only. Ranges for the 2009–10 data are available in the 2009–10 Accountability and Overview Reports.

## Other Assessments

| | 2010–11 School Year | | | | 2009–10 School Year | | | |
|---|---|---|---|---|---|---|---|---|
| | Total Tested | 2–4 | 3–4 | 4 | Total Tested | 2–4 | 3–4 | 4 |
| | | Number scoring at level(s): | | | | Number scoring at level(s): | | |
| New York State Alternate Assessment (NYSAA): Grade 3 Equivalent | 2,500 | 2,309 | 2,154 | 1,829 | 2,515 | 2,351 | 2,162 | 1,786 |
| New York State English as a Second Language Achievement Test (NYSESLAT)†: Grade 3 | 1,629 | N/A | N/A | N/A | 1,975 | N/A | N/A | N/A |
| | Total | | | | Total | | | |
| Recently Arrived LEP Students NOT Tested on the ELA NYSTP: Grade 3 | 1,656 | N/A | N/A | N/A | 2,012 | N/A | N/A | N/A |

† These counts represent recently arrived LEP students who used the NYSESLAT to fulfill the English language arts participation requirement.

## Statewide Results in Grade 3 Mathematics

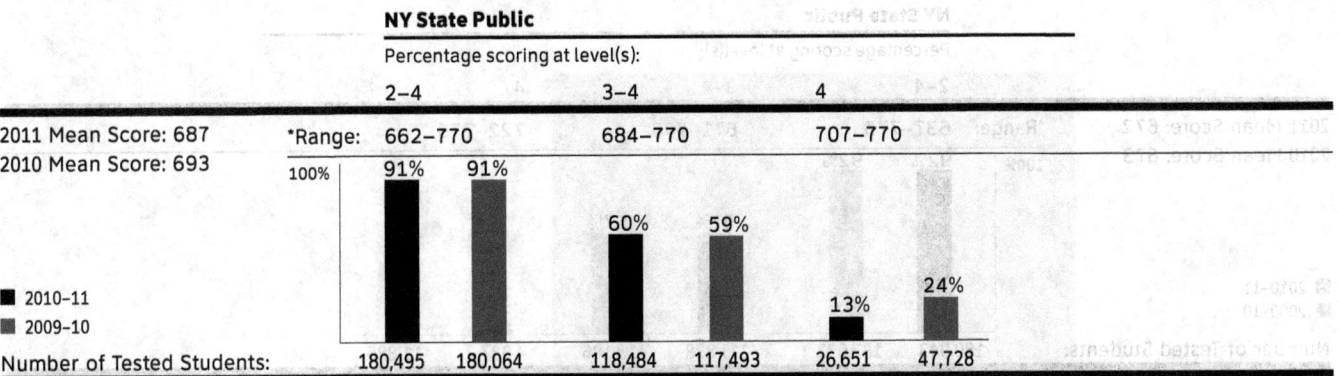

**NY State Public**

Percentage scoring at level(s):

| | 2–4 | 3–4 | 4 |
|---|---|---|---|
| *Range: | 662–770 | 684–770 | 707–770 |

2011 Mean Score: 687
2010 Mean Score: 693

- 2010–11
- 2009–10

Number of Tested Students:   180,495   180,064   118,484   117,493   26,651   47,728

## Results by Student Group

| | 2010–11 School Year | | | | 2009–10 School Year | | | |
|---|---|---|---|---|---|---|---|---|
| | | Percentage scoring at level(s): | | | | Percentage scoring at level(s): | | |
| | Total Tested | 2–4 | 3–4 | 4 | Total Tested | 2–4 | 3–4 | 4 |
| **All Students** | **198,667** | **91%** | **60%** | **13%** | **198,665** | **91%** | **59%** | **24%** |
| Female | 97,079 | 91% | 59% | 12% | 96,894 | 91% | 59% | 24% |
| Male | 101,588 | 90% | 60% | 14% | 101,771 | 90% | 59% | 24% |
| American Indian or Alaska Native | 1,102 | 88% | 51% | 8% | 976 | 88% | 47% | 16% |
| Black or African American | 36,758 | 84% | 43% | 6% | 37,425 | 83% | 42% | 13% |
| Hispanic or Latino | 46,821 | 87% | 47% | 6% | 44,688 | 87% | 48% | 16% |
| Asian or Native Hawaiian/Other Pacific Islander | 16,780 | 96% | 80% | 29% | 15,997 | 96% | 79% | 43% |
| White | 95,598 | 95% | 69% | 17% | 98,458 | 95% | 68% | 29% |
| Multiracial | 1,608 | 91% | 59% | 15% | 1,121 | 91% | 61% | 25% |
| Small Group Totals | 0 | — | — | — | 0 | — | — | — |
| General-Education Students | 169,256 | 94% | 65% | 15% | 168,567 | 94% | 65% | 27% |
| Students with Disabilities | 29,411 | 71% | 28% | 3% | 30,098 | 70% | 28% | 7% |
| English Proficient | 178,627 | 92% | 63% | 15% | 178,015 | 92% | 62% | 26% |
| Limited English Proficient | 20,040 | 78% | 33% | 3% | 20,650 | 78% | 36% | 10% |
| Economically Disadvantaged | 112,086 | 87% | 48% | 8% | 110,548 | 86% | 49% | 17% |
| Not Disadvantaged | 86,581 | 96% | 74% | 21% | 88,117 | 96% | 72% | 32% |
| Migrant | 76 | 76% | 24% | 3% | 57 | 75% | 26% | 0% |
| Not Migrant | 198,591 | 91% | 60% | 13% | 198,608 | 91% | 59% | 24% |

**NOTE**

The — symbol indicates that data for a group of students have been suppressed. If a group has fewer than five students, data for that group and the next smallest group(s) are suppressed to protect the privacy of individual students.

*These ranges are for 2010–11 data only. Ranges for the 2009–10 data are available in the 2009–10 Accountability and Overview Reports.

## Other Assessments

| | 2010–11 School Year | | | | 2009–10 School Year | | | |
|---|---|---|---|---|---|---|---|---|
| | | Number scoring at level(s): | | | | Number scoring at level(s): | | |
| | Total Tested | 2–4 | 3–4 | 4 | Total Tested | 2–4 | 3–4 | 4 |
| New York State Alternate Assessment (NYSAA): Grade 3 Equivalent | 2,500 | 2,468 | 2,275 | 1,692 | 2,518 | 2,487 | 2,202 | 1,536 |

# Statewide Results in Grade 4 English Language Arts

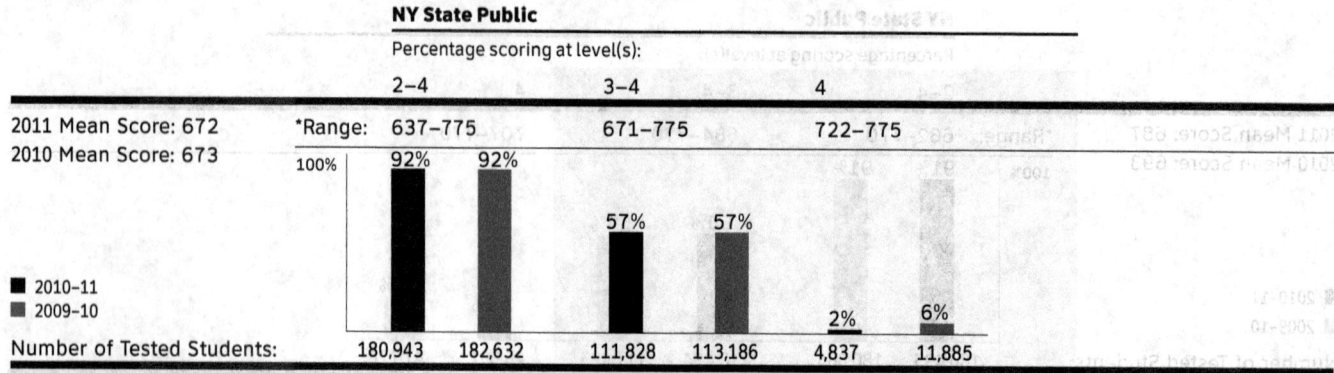

**NY State Public**

Percentage scoring at level(s):

|  | 2–4 | 3–4 | 4 |
|---|---|---|---|
| 2011 Mean Score: 672 | *Range: 637–775 | 671–775 | 722–775 |
| 2010 Mean Score: 673 | | | |

- ■ 2010–11
- ■ 2009–10

Number of Tested Students:    180,943   182,632    111,828   113,186    4,837    11,885

## Results by Student Group

|  | 2010–11 School Year | | | | 2009–10 School Year | | | |
|---|---|---|---|---|---|---|---|---|
|  | | Percentage scoring at level(s): | | | | Percentage scoring at level(s): | | |
|  | Total Tested | 2–4 | 3–4 | 4 | Total Tested | 2–4 | 3–4 | 4 |
| **All Students** | **197,271** | **92%** | **57%** | **2%** | **199,423** | **92%** | **57%** | **6%** |
| Female | 96,394 | 94% | 61% | 3% | 97,283 | 93% | 61% | 7% |
| Male | 100,877 | 90% | 52% | 2% | 102,140 | 90% | 53% | 5% |
| American Indian or Alaska Native | 968 | 90% | 46% | 1% | 938 | 90% | 45% | 4% |
| Black or African American | 36,953 | 87% | 41% | 1% | 37,731 | 85% | 37% | 2% |
| Hispanic or Latino | 44,942 | 88% | 44% | 1% | 42,742 | 87% | 40% | 2% |
| Asian or Native Hawaiian/Other Pacific Islander | 15,707 | 95% | 71% | 5% | 16,324 | 96% | 72% | 13% |
| White | 97,290 | 95% | 66% | 3% | 100,694 | 95% | 69% | 8% |
| Multiracial | 1,411 | 93% | 60% | 5% | 994 | 95% | 63% | 7% |
| Small Group Totals | 0 | — | — | — | 0 | — | — | — |
| General-Education Students | 166,146 | 96% | 64% | 3% | 168,116 | 96% | 64% | 7% |
| Students with Disabilities | 31,125 | 68% | 18% | 0% | 31,307 | 68% | 19% | 1% |
| English Proficient | 181,033 | 93% | 60% | 3% | 183,085 | 93% | 60% | 6% |
| Limited English Proficient | 16,238 | 74% | 20% | 0% | 16,338 | 75% | 20% | 0% |
| Economically Disadvantaged | 109,551 | 88% | 44% | 1% | 108,403 | 87% | 43% | 3% |
| Not Disadvantaged | 87,720 | 96% | 72% | 4% | 91,020 | 97% | 74% | 10% |
| Migrant | 46 | 70% | 30% | 0% | 54 | 87% | 31% | 2% |
| Not Migrant | 197,225 | 92% | 57% | 2% | 199,369 | 92% | 57% | 6% |

**NOTE**

The — symbol indicates that data for a group of students have been suppressed. If a group has fewer than five students, data for that group and the next smallest group(s) are suppressed to protect the privacy of individual students.

*These ranges are for 2010–11 data only. Ranges for the 2009–10 data are available in the 2009–10 Accountability and Overview Reports.

## Other Assessments

|  | 2010–11 School Year | | | | 2009–10 School Year | | | |
|---|---|---|---|---|---|---|---|---|
|  | | Number scoring at level(s): | | | | Number scoring at level(s): | | |
|  | Total Tested | 2–4 | 3–4 | 4 | Total Tested | 2–4 | 3–4 | 4 |
| New York State Alternate Assessment (NYSAA): Grade 4 Equivalent | 2,804 | 2,631 | 2,389 | 1,980 | 2,585 | 2,425 | 2,165 | 1,754 |
| New York State English as a Second Language Achievement Test (NYSESLAT)[†]: Grade 4 | 1,640 | N/A | N/A | N/A | 2,084 | N/A | N/A | N/A |
| | Total | | | | Total | | | |
| Recently Arrived LEP Students NOT Tested on the ELA NYSTP: Grade 4 | 1,668 | N/A | N/A | N/A | 2,112 | N/A | N/A | N/A |

† These counts represent recently arrived LEP students who used the NYSESLAT to fulfill the English language arts participation requirement.

# Statewide Results in Grade 4 Mathematics

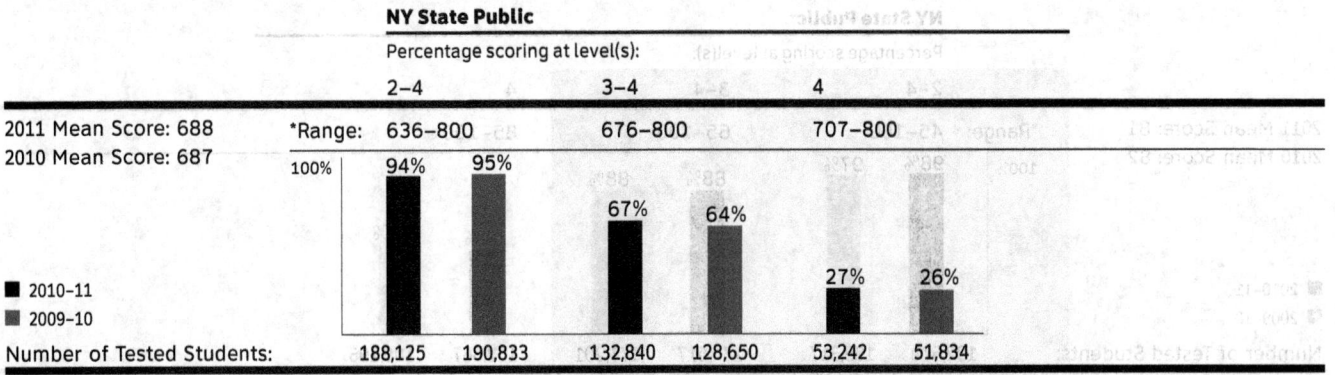

| | NY State Public | | | | | |
|---|---|---|---|---|---|---|
| | Percentage scoring at level(s): | | | | | |
| | 2–4 | | 3–4 | | 4 | |
| 2011 Mean Score: 688 | *Range: 636–800 | | 676–800 | | 707–800 | |
| 2010 Mean Score: 687 | 100% 94% | 95% | 67% | 64% | 27% | 26% |
| ■ 2010–11 | | | | | | |
| ■ 2009–10 | | | | | | |
| Number of Tested Students: | 188,125 | 190,833 | 132,840 | 128,650 | 53,242 | 51,834 |

# Results by Student Group

| | 2010–11 School Year | | | | 2009–10 School Year | | | |
|---|---|---|---|---|---|---|---|---|
| | | Percentage scoring at level(s): | | | | Percentage scoring at level(s): | | |
| | Total Tested | 2–4 | 3–4 | 4 | Total Tested | 2–4 | 3–4 | 4 |
| **All Students** | **199,327** | **94%** | **67%** | **27%** | **201,634** | **95%** | **64%** | **26%** |
| Female | 97,409 | 95% | 67% | 26% | 98,304 | 95% | 63% | 25% |
| Male | 101,918 | 94% | 66% | 27% | 103,330 | 94% | 64% | 26% |
| American Indian or Alaska Native | 977 | 93% | 57% | 18% | 942 | 93% | 54% | 16% |
| Black or African American | 37,166 | 90% | 48% | 13% | 37,968 | 90% | 45% | 12% |
| Hispanic or Latino | 46,022 | 92% | 55% | 16% | 43,740 | 92% | 51% | 15% |
| Asian or Native Hawaiian/Other Pacific Islander | 16,285 | 98% | 85% | 51% | 17,162 | 98% | 83% | 50% |
| White | 97,461 | 97% | 76% | 33% | 100,822 | 97% | 73% | 31% |
| Multiracial | 1,416 | 95% | 66% | 29% | 1,000 | 96% | 66% | 27% |
| Small Group Totals | 0 | — | — | — | 0 | — | — | — |
| General-Education Students | 168,154 | 97% | 73% | 31% | 170,285 | 97% | 70% | 29% |
| Students with Disabilities | 31,173 | 78% | 31% | 6% | 31,349 | 80% | 29% | 6% |
| English Proficient | 181,141 | 95% | 69% | 29% | 183,040 | 96% | 67% | 27% |
| Limited English Proficient | 18,186 | 84% | 39% | 8% | 18,594 | 85% | 36% | 8% |
| Economically Disadvantaged | 111,381 | 92% | 56% | 18% | 110,364 | 92% | 53% | 18% |
| Not Disadvantaged | 87,946 | 98% | 80% | 38% | 91,270 | 98% | 77% | 36% |
| Migrant | 47 | 85% | 32% | 4% | 56 | 93% | 38% | 5% |
| Not Migrant | 199,280 | 94% | 67% | 27% | 201,578 | 95% | 64% | 26% |

**NOTE**

The — symbol indicates that data for a group of students have been suppressed. If a group has fewer than five students, data for that group and the next smallest group(s) are suppressed to protect the privacy of individual students.
*These ranges are for 2010–11 data only. Ranges for the 2009–10 data are available in the 2009–10 Accountability and Overview Reports.

# Other Assessments

| | 2010–11 School Year | | | | 2009–10 School Year | | | |
|---|---|---|---|---|---|---|---|---|
| | | Number scoring at level(s): | | | | Number scoring at level(s): | | |
| | Total Tested | 2–4 | 3–4 | 4 | Total Tested | 2–4 | 3–4 | 4 |
| New York State Alternate Assessment (NYSAA): Grade 4 Equivalent | 2,801 | 2,772 | 2,454 | 1,759 | 2,584 | 2,553 | 2,223 | 1,475 |

# Statewide Results in Grade 4 Science

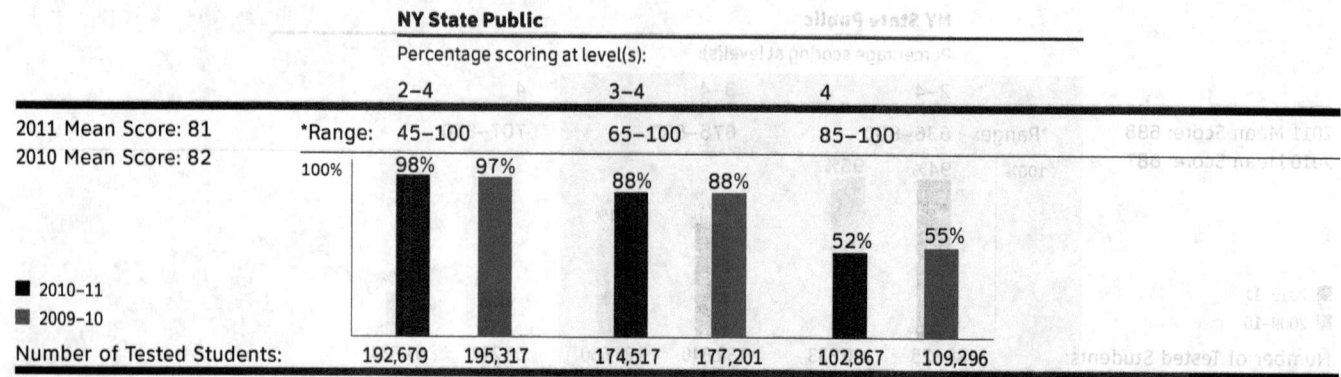

**NY State Public**

Percentage scoring at level(s):

|  | 2–4 | 3–4 | 4 |
|---|---|---|---|
| 2011 Mean Score: 81 | *Range: 45–100 | 65–100 | 85–100 |
| 2010 Mean Score: 82 | | | |

2010–11: 98%, 88%, 52%
2009–10: 97%, 88%, 55%

- ■ 2010–11
- ■ 2009–10

Number of Tested Students: 192,679   195,317   174,517   177,201   102,867   109,296

# Results by Student Group

| | 2010–11 School Year | | | | 2009–10 School Year | | | |
|---|---|---|---|---|---|---|---|---|
| | Total Tested | 2–4 | 3–4 | 4 | Total Tested | 2–4 | 3–4 | 4 |
| **All Students** | **197,303** | **98%** | **88%** | **52%** | **200,463** | **97%** | **88%** | **55%** |
| Female | 96,462 | 98% | 89% | 52% | 97,825 | 98% | 89% | 54% |
| Male | 100,841 | 97% | 88% | 52% | 102,638 | 97% | 88% | 55% |
| American Indian or Alaska Native | 965 | 97% | 86% | 43% | 938 | 98% | 86% | 47% |
| Black or African American | 36,635 | 96% | 80% | 33% | 37,603 | 95% | 79% | 35% |
| Hispanic or Latino | 45,521 | 96% | 81% | 37% | 43,429 | 96% | 81% | 38% |
| Asian or Native Hawaiian/Other Pacific Islander | 16,184 | 98% | 93% | 66% | 17,130 | 98% | 92% | 68% |
| White | 96,609 | 99% | 94% | 64% | 100,369 | 99% | 95% | 67% |
| Multiracial | 1,389 | 99% | 92% | 57% | 994 | 98% | 92% | 59% |
| Small Group Totals | 0 | — | — | — | 0 | — | — | — |
| General-Education Students | 166,670 | 99% | 92% | 58% | 169,498 | 98% | 92% | 60% |
| Students with Disabilities | 30,633 | 93% | 71% | 23% | 30,965 | 92% | 70% | 25% |
| English Proficient | 179,317 | 98% | 91% | 56% | 182,028 | 98% | 91% | 58% |
| Limited English Proficient | 17,986 | 90% | 64% | 17% | 18,435 | 89% | 65% | 20% |
| Economically Disadvantaged | 109,986 | 96% | 83% | 39% | 109,465 | 96% | 82% | 40% |
| Not Disadvantaged | 87,317 | 99% | 96% | 69% | 90,998 | 99% | 96% | 71% |
| Migrant | 47 | 96% | 81% | 28% | 57 | 95% | 75% | 28% |
| Not Migrant | 197,256 | 98% | 88% | 52% | 200,406 | 97% | 88% | 55% |

**NOTE**

The — symbol indicates that data for a group of students have been suppressed. If a group has fewer than five students, data for that group and the next smallest group(s) are suppressed to protect the privacy of individual students.

# Other Assessments

| | 2010–11 School Year | | | | 2009–10 School Year | | | |
|---|---|---|---|---|---|---|---|---|
| | Total Tested | 2–4 | 3–4 | 4 | Total Tested | 2–4 | 3–4 | 4 |
| New York State Alternate Assessment (NYSAA): Grade 4 Equivalent | 2,798 | 2,663 | 2,588 | 2,252 | 2,575 | 2,512 | 2,435 | 2,025 |

Number scoring at level(s):

# Statewide Results in Grade 5 English Language Arts

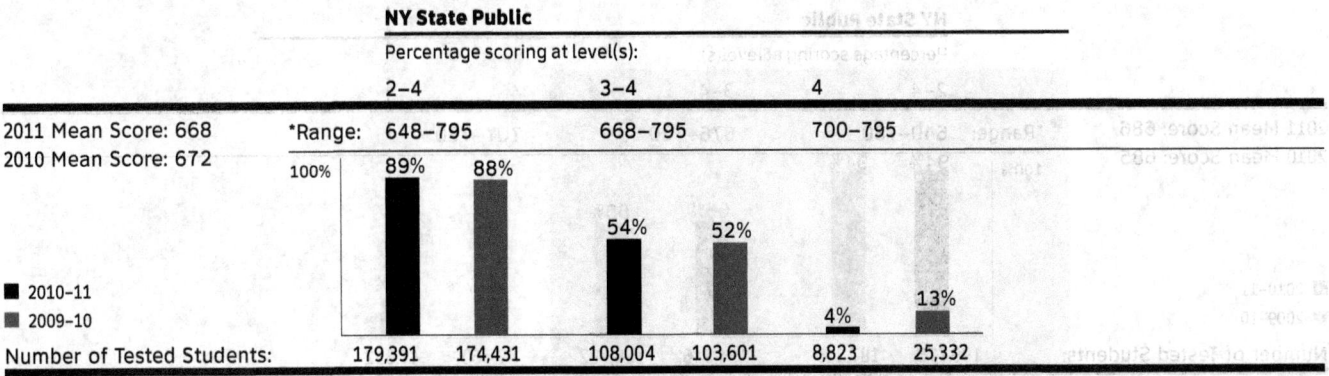

**NY State Public**

Percentage scoring at level(s):

| | 2–4 | 3–4 | 4 |
|---|---|---|---|
| 2011 Mean Score: 668 *Range: | 648–795 | 668–795 | 700–795 |
| 2010 Mean Score: 672 | 89% / 88% | 54% / 52% | 4% / 13% |

Number of Tested Students: 179,391  174,431  108,004  103,601  8,823  25,332

## Results by Student Group

| | 2010–11 School Year | | | | 2009–10 School Year | | | |
|---|---|---|---|---|---|---|---|---|
| | Total Tested | 2–4 | 3–4 | 4 | Total Tested | 2–4 | 3–4 | 4 |
| All Students | 200,442 | 89% | 54% | 4% | 197,372 | 88% | 52% | 13% |
| Female | 97,880 | 92% | 58% | 5% | 96,055 | 91% | 57% | 16% |
| Male | 102,562 | 87% | 50% | 3% | 101,317 | 86% | 48% | 10% |
| American Indian or Alaska Native | 962 | 85% | 40% | 3% | 919 | 86% | 40% | 7% |
| Black or African American | 37,399 | 83% | 37% | 2% | 37,843 | 81% | 36% | 6% |
| Hispanic or Latino | 44,156 | 85% | 40% | 2% | 41,965 | 82% | 39% | 7% |
| Asian or Native Hawaiian/Other Pacific Islander | 16,830 | 94% | 71% | 10% | 15,194 | 94% | 70% | 25% |
| White | 99,739 | 93% | 63% | 5% | 100,582 | 93% | 62% | 16% |
| Multiracial | 1,356 | 90% | 59% | 6% | 869 | 91% | 58% | 15% |
| Small Group Totals | 0 | — | — | — | 0 | — | — | — |
| General-Education Students | 168,455 | 95% | 61% | 5% | 165,573 | 94% | 59% | 15% |
| Students with Disabilities | 31,987 | 61% | 16% | 0% | 31,799 | 60% | 17% | 2% |
| English Proficient | 186,617 | 91% | 57% | 5% | 184,262 | 90% | 55% | 14% |
| Limited English Proficient | 13,825 | 64% | 13% | 0% | 13,110 | 63% | 15% | 1% |
| Economically Disadvantaged | 109,231 | 85% | 42% | 3% | 105,847 | 83% | 40% | 8% |
| Not Disadvantaged | 91,211 | 95% | 69% | 7% | 91,525 | 95% | 67% | 19% |
| Migrant | 42 | 81% | 33% | 2% | 55 | 67% | 29% | 0% |
| Not Migrant | 200,400 | 89% | 54% | 4% | 197,317 | 88% | 52% | 13% |

**NOTE**
The — symbol indicates that data for a group of students have been suppressed. If a group has fewer than five students, data for that group and the next smallest group(s) are suppressed to protect the privacy of individual students.
*These ranges are for 2010–11 data only. Ranges for the 2009–10 data are available in the 2009–10 Accountability and Overview Reports.

## Other Assessments

| | 2010–11 School Year | | | | 2009–10 School Year | | | |
|---|---|---|---|---|---|---|---|---|
| | Total Tested | 2–4 | 3–4 | 4 | Total Tested | 2–4 | 3–4 | 4 |
| New York State Alternate Assessment (NYSAA): Grade 5 Equivalent | 2,696 | 2,593 | 2,430 | 1,727 | 2,615 | 2,522 | 2,352 | 1,612 |
| New York State English as a Second Language Achievement Test (NYSESLAT)[†]: Grade 5 | 1,631 | N/A | N/A | N/A | 2,041 | N/A | N/A | N/A |
| | Total | | | | Total | | | |
| Recently Arrived LEP Students NOT Tested on the ELA NYSTP: Grade 5 | 1,664 | N/A | N/A | N/A | 2,077 | N/A | N/A | N/A |

† These counts represent recently arrived LEP students who used the NYSESLAT to fulfill the English language arts participation requirement.

# Statewide Results in Grade 5 Mathematics

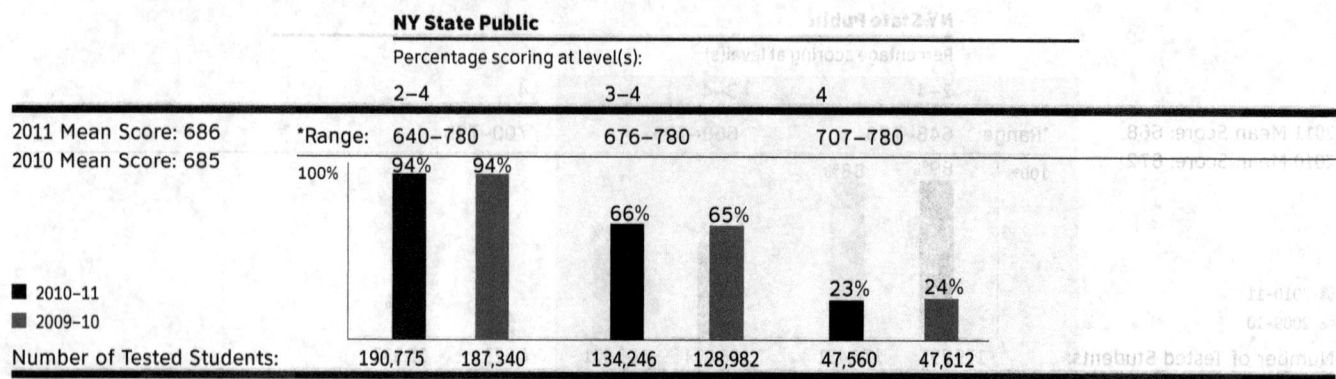

**NY State Public**

Percentage scoring at level(s):

| | 2–4 | 3–4 | 4 |
|---|---|---|---|
| 2011 Mean Score: 686 | *Range: 640–780 | 676–780 | 707–780 |
| 2010 Mean Score: 685 | 94% 94% | 66% 65% | 23% 24% |

■ 2010–11
■ 2009–10

Number of Tested Students:    190,775   187,340    134,246   128,982    47,560   47,612

## Results by Student Group

| | 2010–11 School Year | | | | 2009–10 School Year | | | |
|---|---|---|---|---|---|---|---|---|
| | | Percentage scoring at level(s): | | | | Percentage scoring at level(s): | | |
| | Total Tested | 2–4 | 3–4 | 4 | Total Tested | 2–4 | 3–4 | 4 |
| **All Students** | **202,595** | **94%** | **66%** | **23%** | **199,507** | **94%** | **65%** | **24%** |
| Female | 98,882 | 95% | 67% | 23% | 97,051 | 94% | 65% | 24% |
| Male | 103,713 | 94% | 66% | 24% | 102,456 | 93% | 65% | 24% |
| American Indian or Alaska Native | 971 | 91% | 53% | 13% | 927 | 93% | 55% | 13% |
| Black or African American | 37,585 | 90% | 49% | 10% | 38,088 | 89% | 46% | 11% |
| Hispanic or Latino | 45,230 | 91% | 55% | 14% | 43,040 | 91% | 53% | 15% |
| Asian or Native Hawaiian/Other Pacific Islander | 17,411 | 97% | 85% | 49% | 15,909 | 97% | 84% | 47% |
| White | 100,037 | 97% | 75% | 29% | 100,668 | 97% | 74% | 29% |
| Multiracial | 1,361 | 94% | 66% | 25% | 875 | 95% | 64% | 24% |
| Small Group Totals | 0 | — | — | — | 0 | — | — | — |
| General-Education Students | 170,564 | 97% | 73% | 27% | 167,625 | 97% | 71% | 27% |
| Students with Disabilities | 32,031 | 78% | 31% | 5% | 31,882 | 77% | 29% | 5% |
| English Proficient | 186,845 | 95% | 69% | 25% | 184,236 | 95% | 67% | 25% |
| Limited English Proficient | 15,750 | 81% | 34% | 6% | 15,271 | 81% | 34% | 7% |
| Economically Disadvantaged | 111,104 | 92% | 56% | 16% | 107,747 | 91% | 54% | 17% |
| Not Disadvantaged | 91,491 | 97% | 79% | 33% | 91,760 | 97% | 78% | 32% |
| Migrant | 46 | 89% | 48% | 9% | 59 | 83% | 39% | 2% |
| Not Migrant | 202,549 | 94% | 66% | 23% | 199,448 | 94% | 65% | 24% |

**NOTE**

The — symbol indicates that data for a group of students have been suppressed. If a group has fewer than five students, data for that group and the next smallest group(s) are suppressed to protect the privacy of individual students.

*These ranges are for 2010–11 data only. Ranges for the 2009–10 data are available in the 2009–10 Accountability and Overview Reports.

## Other Assessments

| | 2010–11 School Year | | | | 2009–10 School Year | | | |
|---|---|---|---|---|---|---|---|---|
| | | Number scoring at level(s): | | | | Number scoring at level(s): | | |
| | Total Tested | 2–4 | 3–4 | 4 | Total Tested | 2–4 | 3–4 | 4 |
| New York State Alternate Assessment (NYSAA): Grade 5 Equivalent | 2,702 | 2,622 | 2,460 | 1,819 | 2,612 | 2,521 | 2,377 | 1,649 |

# Statewide Results in Grade 6 English Language Arts

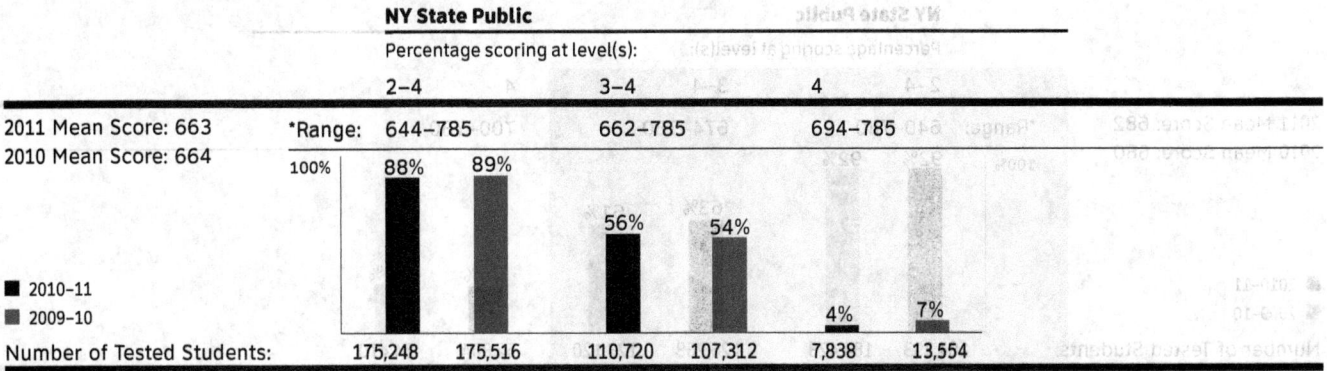

**NY State Public**

Percentage scoring at level(s):

|  | 2–4 | 3–4 | 4 |
|---|---|---|---|
| 2011 Mean Score: 663 *Range: | 644–785 | 662–785 | 694–785 |
| 2010 Mean Score: 664 | 88% / 89% | 56% / 54% | 4% / 7% |

Legend:
- 2010–11
- 2009–10

Number of Tested Students: 175,248 / 175,516 | 110,720 / 107,312 | 7,838 / 13,554

## Results by Student Group

| | **2010–11 School Year** | | | | **2009–10 School Year** | | | |
|---|---|---|---|---|---|---|---|---|
| | Total Tested | 2–4 | 3–4 | 4 | Total Tested | 2–4 | 3–4 | 4 |
| **All Students** | **198,287** | **88%** | **56%** | **4%** | **198,085** | **89%** | **54%** | **7%** |
| Female | 96,480 | 91% | 60% | 5% | 97,014 | 91% | 58% | 9% |
| Male | 101,807 | 86% | 52% | 3% | 101,071 | 87% | 50% | 5% |
| American Indian or Alaska Native | 934 | 85% | 45% | 1% | 949 | 86% | 45% | 3% |
| Black or African American | 37,703 | 82% | 37% | 1% | 38,043 | 81% | 34% | 2% |
| Hispanic or Latino | 43,305 | 80% | 38% | 1% | 41,513 | 81% | 35% | 2% |
| Asian or Native Hawaiian/Other Pacific Islander | 15,452 | 91% | 68% | 7% | 15,015 | 93% | 69% | 13% |
| White | 99,606 | 94% | 69% | 6% | 101,819 | 94% | 67% | 10% |
| Multiracial | 1,287 | 92% | 63% | 5% | 746 | 91% | 60% | 9% |
| Small Group Totals | 0 | — | — | — | 0 | — | — | — |
| General-Education Students | 166,854 | 94% | 64% | 5% | 166,100 | 94% | 62% | 8% |
| Students with Disabilities | 31,433 | 59% | 15% | 0% | 31,985 | 59% | 14% | 0% |
| English Proficient | 186,356 | 91% | 59% | 4% | 187,262 | 91% | 57% | 7% |
| Limited English Proficient | 11,931 | 48% | 6% | 0% | 10,823 | 49% | 6% | 0% |
| Economically Disadvantaged | 105,650 | 82% | 41% | 1% | 103,484 | 82% | 38% | 3% |
| Not Disadvantaged | 92,637 | 95% | 73% | 7% | 94,601 | 95% | 71% | 11% |
| Migrant | 47 | 68% | 30% | 0% | 39 | 46% | 18% | 3% |
| Not Migrant | 198,240 | 88% | 56% | 4% | 198,046 | 89% | 54% | 7% |

**NOTE**
The — symbol indicates that data for a group of students have been suppressed. If a group has fewer than five students, data for that group and the next smallest group(s) are suppressed to protect the privacy of individual students.
*These ranges are for 2010–11 data only. Ranges for the 2009–10 data are available in the 2009–10 Accountability and Overview Reports.

## Other Assessments

| | **2010–11 School Year** | | | | **2009–10 School Year** | | | |
|---|---|---|---|---|---|---|---|---|
| | Total Tested | 2–4 | 3–4 | 4 | Total Tested | 2–4 | 3–4 | 4 |
| New York State Alternate Assessment (NYSAA): Grade 6 Equivalent | 2,741 | 2,619 | 2,326 | 1,846 | 2,608 | 2,489 | 2,147 | 1,635 |
| New York State English as a Second Language Achievement Test (NYSESLAT)†: Grade 6 | 1,633 | N/A | N/A | N/A | 2,190 | N/A | N/A | N/A |
| | Total | | | | Total | | | |
| Recently Arrived LEP Students NOT Tested on the ELA NYSTP: Grade 6 | 1,678 | N/A | N/A | N/A | 2,211 | N/A | N/A | N/A |

† These counts represent recently arrived LEP students who used the NYSESLAT to fulfill the English language arts participation requirement.

# Statewide Results in Grade 6 Mathematics

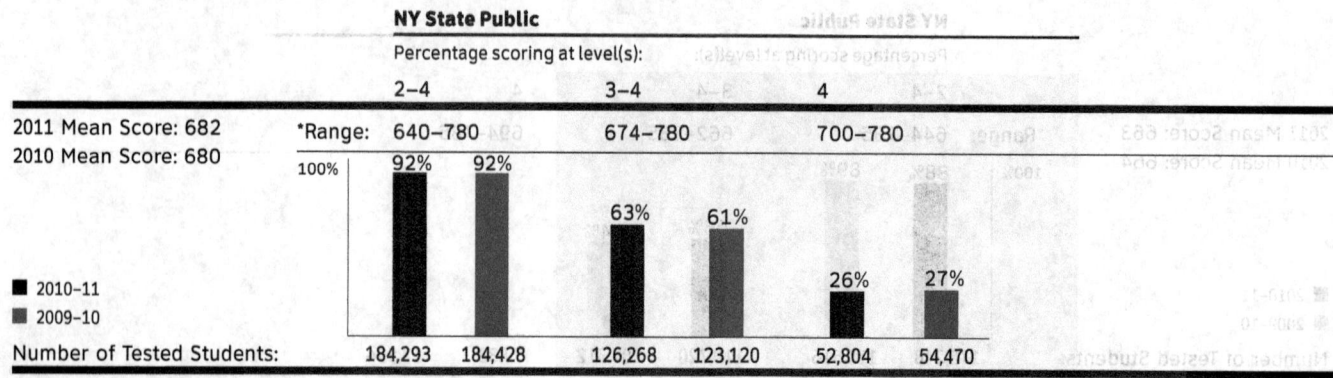

| | NY State Public | | |
|---|---|---|---|
| | Percentage scoring at level(s): | | |
| | 2–4 | 3–4 | 4 |
| 2011 Mean Score: 682 | *Range: 640–780 | 674–780 | 700–780 |

2010 Mean Score: 680

100%

92%  92%

63%  61%

26%  27%

■ 2010–11
■ 2009–10

| Number of Tested Students: | 184,293 | 184,428 | 126,268 | 123,120 | 52,804 | 54,470 |

## Results by Student Group

| | 2010–11 School Year | | | | 2009–10 School Year | | | |
|---|---|---|---|---|---|---|---|---|
| | | Percentage scoring at level(s): | | | | Percentage scoring at level(s): | | |
| | Total Tested | 2–4 | 3–4 | 4 | Total Tested | 2–4 | 3–4 | 4 |
| **All Students** | **200,292** | **92%** | **63%** | **26%** | **200,576** | **92%** | **61%** | **27%** |
| Female | 97,411 | 93% | 65% | 26% | 98,156 | 93% | 62% | 28% |
| Male | 102,881 | 91% | 62% | 26% | 102,420 | 91% | 60% | 26% |
| American Indian or Alaska Native | 943 | 89% | 52% | 16% | 958 | 90% | 53% | 19% |
| Black or African American | 37,867 | 85% | 44% | 11% | 38,373 | 85% | 41% | 12% |
| Hispanic or Latino | 44,342 | 88% | 49% | 14% | 42,633 | 87% | 47% | 16% |
| Asian or Native Hawaiian/Other Pacific Islander | 15,974 | 97% | 84% | 53% | 15,841 | 97% | 82% | 52% |
| White | 99,872 | 96% | 73% | 33% | 102,005 | 96% | 72% | 34% |
| Multiracial | 1,294 | 93% | 63% | 27% | 766 | 92% | 62% | 26% |
| Small Group Totals | 0 | — | — | — | 0 | — | — | — |
| General-Education Students | 168,855 | 96% | 70% | 30% | 168,444 | 96% | 69% | 32% |
| Students with Disabilities | 31,437 | 71% | 24% | 4% | 32,132 | 70% | 22% | 4% |
| English Proficient | 186,514 | 93% | 66% | 28% | 187,461 | 93% | 64% | 29% |
| Limited English Proficient | 13,778 | 73% | 28% | 6% | 13,115 | 72% | 23% | 6% |
| Economically Disadvantaged | 107,408 | 88% | 51% | 17% | 105,603 | 88% | 49% | 18% |
| Not Disadvantaged | 92,884 | 97% | 77% | 37% | 94,973 | 96% | 75% | 38% |
| Migrant | 50 | 84% | 50% | 10% | 42 | 74% | 19% | 5% |
| Not Migrant | 200,242 | 92% | 63% | 26% | 200,534 | 92% | 61% | 27% |

**NOTE**

The — symbol indicates that data for a group of students have been suppressed. If a group has fewer than five students, data for that group and the next smallest group(s) are suppressed to protect the privacy of individual students.

*These ranges are for 2010–11 data only. Ranges for the 2009–10 data are available in the 2009–10 Accountability and Overview Reports.

## Other Assessments

| | 2010–11 School Year | | | | 2009–10 School Year | | | |
|---|---|---|---|---|---|---|---|---|
| | | Number scoring at level(s): | | | | Number scoring at level(s): | | |
| | Total Tested | 2–4 | 3–4 | 4 | Total Tested | 2–4 | 3–4 | 4 |
| New York State Alternate Assessment (NYSAA): Grade 6 Equivalent | 2,741 | 2,697 | 2,476 | 1,956 | 2,611 | 2,565 | 2,320 | 1,728 |

# Statewide Results in Grade 7 English Language Arts

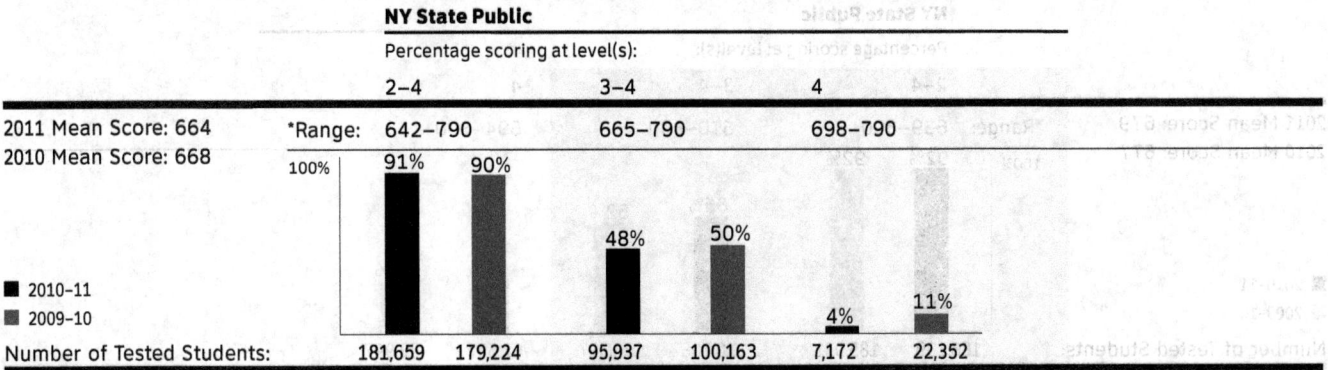

| | NY State Public | | |
|---|---|---|---|
| | Percentage scoring at level(s): | | |
| | 2–4 | 3–4 | 4 |
| 2011 Mean Score: 664 | *Range: 642–790 | 665–790 | 698–790 |
| 2010 Mean Score: 668 | 91% 2010–11 / 90% 2009–10 | 48% 2010–11 / 50% 2009–10 | 4% 2010–11 / 11% 2009–10 |
| Number of Tested Students: | 181,659 / 179,224 | 95,937 / 100,163 | 7,172 / 22,352 |

## Results by Student Group

| | 2010–11 School Year | | | | 2009–10 School Year | | | |
|---|---|---|---|---|---|---|---|---|
| | | Percentage scoring at level(s): | | | | Percentage scoring at level(s): | | |
| | Total Tested | 2–4 | 3–4 | 4 | Total Tested | 2–4 | 3–4 | 4 |
| **All Students** | **200,307** | **91%** | **48%** | **4%** | **200,062** | **90%** | **50%** | **11%** |
| Female | 98,071 | 93% | 54% | 5% | 97,534 | 92% | 56% | 14% |
| Male | 102,236 | 88% | 42% | 3% | 102,528 | 87% | 44% | 9% |
| American Indian or Alaska Native | 990 | 89% | 36% | 2% | 962 | 84% | 35% | 4% |
| Black or African American | 37,991 | 85% | 28% | 1% | 38,346 | 83% | 30% | 4% |
| Hispanic or Latino | 42,989 | 85% | 30% | 1% | 41,171 | 82% | 32% | 4% |
| Asian or Native Hawaiian/Other Pacific Islander | 15,545 | 92% | 63% | 7% | 15,294 | 93% | 65% | 20% |
| White | 101,659 | 95% | 61% | 5% | 103,586 | 95% | 63% | 16% |
| Multiracial | 1,133 | 92% | 54% | 5% | 703 | 94% | 57% | 11% |
| Small Group Totals | 0 | — | — | — | 0 | — | — | — |
| General-Education Students | 168,467 | 95% | 55% | 4% | 168,489 | 95% | 57% | 13% |
| Students with Disabilities | 31,840 | 65% | 10% | 0% | 31,573 | 63% | 12% | 1% |
| English Proficient | 189,440 | 93% | 50% | 4% | 189,681 | 92% | 53% | 12% |
| Limited English Proficient | 10,867 | 52% | 3% | 0% | 10,381 | 49% | 5% | 0% |
| Economically Disadvantaged | 104,667 | 86% | 32% | 1% | 102,458 | 84% | 34% | 5% |
| Not Disadvantaged | 95,640 | 96% | 65% | 6% | 97,604 | 96% | 66% | 18% |
| Migrant | 37 | 59% | 19% | 0% | 42 | 83% | 19% | 2% |
| Not Migrant | 200,270 | 91% | 48% | 4% | 200,020 | 90% | 50% | 11% |

**NOTE**

The — symbol indicates that data for a group of students have been suppressed. If a group has fewer than five students,
data for that group and the next smallest group(s) are suppressed to protect the privacy of individual students.
*These ranges are for 2010–11 data only. Ranges for the 2009–10 data are available in the 2009–10 Accountability and Overview Reports.

## Other Assessments

| | 2010–11 School Year | | | | 2009–10 School Year | | | |
|---|---|---|---|---|---|---|---|---|
| | | Number scoring at level(s): | | | | Number scoring at level(s): | | |
| | Total Tested | 2–4 | 3–4 | 4 | Total Tested | 2–4 | 3–4 | 4 |
| New York State Alternate Assessment (NYSAA): Grade 7 Equivalent | 2,718 | 2,688 | 2,475 | 2,189 | 2,425 | 2,401 | 2,200 | 1,912 |
| New York State English as a Second Language Achievement Test (NYSESLAT)[†]: Grade 7 | 1,697 | N/A | N/A | N/A | 2,231 | N/A | N/A | N/A |
| | Total | | | | Total | | | |
| Recently Arrived LEP Students NOT Tested on the ELA NYSTP: Grade 7 | 1,729 | N/A | N/A | N/A | 2,269 | N/A | N/A | N/A |

† These counts represent recently arrived LEP students who used the NYSESLAT to fulfill the English language arts participation requirement.

# Statewide Results in Grade 7 Mathematics

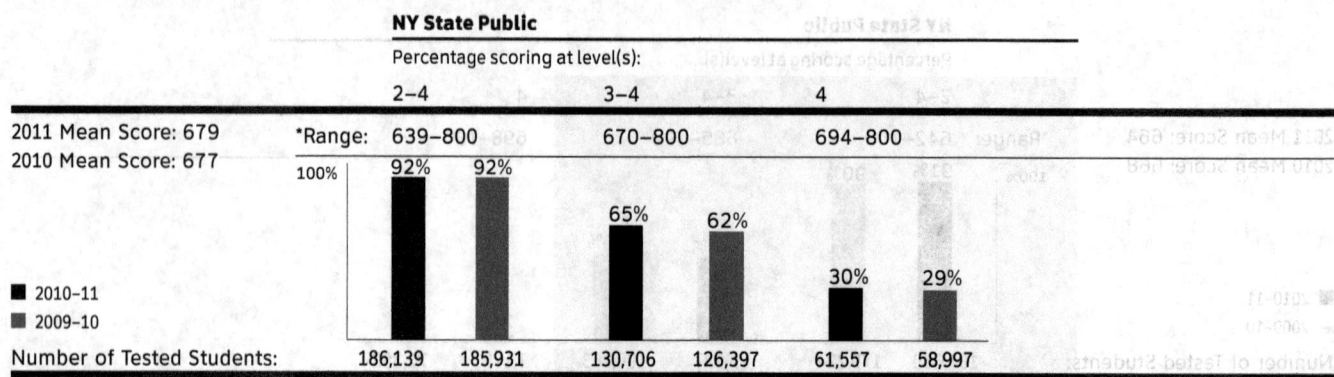

**NY State Public**

Percentage scoring at level(s):

|  | 2–4 | 3–4 | 4 |
|---|---|---|---|

2011 Mean Score: 679
2010 Mean Score: 677

*Range:  639–800   670–800   694–800

- 2010–11
- 2009–10

Number of Tested Students:   186,139   185,931   130,706   126,397   61,557   58,997

## Results by Student Group

| | 2010–11 School Year | | | | 2009–10 School Year | | | |
|---|---|---|---|---|---|---|---|---|
| | | Percentage scoring at level(s): | | | | Percentage scoring at level(s): | | |
| | Total Tested | 2–4 | 3–4 | 4 | Total Tested | 2–4 | 3–4 | 4 |
| **All Students** | **202,189** | **92%** | **65%** | **30%** | **202,488** | **92%** | **62%** | **29%** |
| Female | 98,979 | 93% | 66% | 31% | 98,675 | 93% | 64% | 30% |
| Male | 103,210 | 91% | 63% | 30% | 103,813 | 91% | 61% | 28% |
| American Indian or Alaska Native | 991 | 88% | 56% | 19% | 968 | 89% | 49% | 17% |
| Black or African American | 38,105 | 85% | 43% | 13% | 38,582 | 84% | 40% | 12% |
| Hispanic or Latino | 44,022 | 88% | 50% | 16% | 42,186 | 87% | 47% | 15% |
| Asian or Native Hawaiian/Other Pacific Islander | 16,122 | 97% | 83% | 57% | 16,224 | 96% | 82% | 55% |
| White | 101,813 | 96% | 76% | 39% | 103,808 | 96% | 74% | 37% |
| Multiracial | 1,136 | 93% | 67% | 34% | 720 | 94% | 62% | 28% |
| Small Group Totals | 0 | — | — | — | 0 | — | — | — |
| General-Education Students | 170,417 | 96% | 72% | 35% | 170,787 | 96% | 70% | 34% |
| Students with Disabilities | 31,772 | 71% | 26% | 5% | 31,701 | 70% | 23% | 5% |
| English Proficient | 189,454 | 93% | 67% | 32% | 189,809 | 93% | 65% | 31% |
| Limited English Proficient | 12,735 | 71% | 26% | 7% | 12,679 | 70% | 25% | 6% |
| Economically Disadvantaged | 106,358 | 88% | 51% | 19% | 104,507 | 87% | 49% | 18% |
| Not Disadvantaged | 95,831 | 96% | 79% | 43% | 97,981 | 96% | 77% | 41% |
| Migrant | 41 | 80% | 34% | 7% | 46 | 83% | 37% | 2% |
| Not Migrant | 202,148 | 92% | 65% | 30% | 202,442 | 92% | 62% | 29% |

**NOTE**

The — symbol indicates that data for a group of students have been suppressed. If a group has fewer than five students,
data for that group and the next smallest group(s) are suppressed to protect the privacy of individual students.

*These ranges are for 2010–11 data only. Ranges for the 2009–10 data are available in the 2009–10 Accountability and Overview Reports.

## Other Assessments

| | 2010–11 School Year | | | | 2009–10 School Year | | | |
|---|---|---|---|---|---|---|---|---|
| | | Number scoring at level(s): | | | | Number scoring at level(s): | | |
| | Total Tested | 2–4 | 3–4 | 4 | Total Tested | 2–4 | 3–4 | 4 |
| New York State Alternate Assessment (NYSAA): Grade 7 Equivalent | 2,723 | 2,560 | 2,433 | 1,671 | 2,407 | 2,199 | 2,093 | 1,392 |

# Statewide Results in Grade 8 English Language Arts

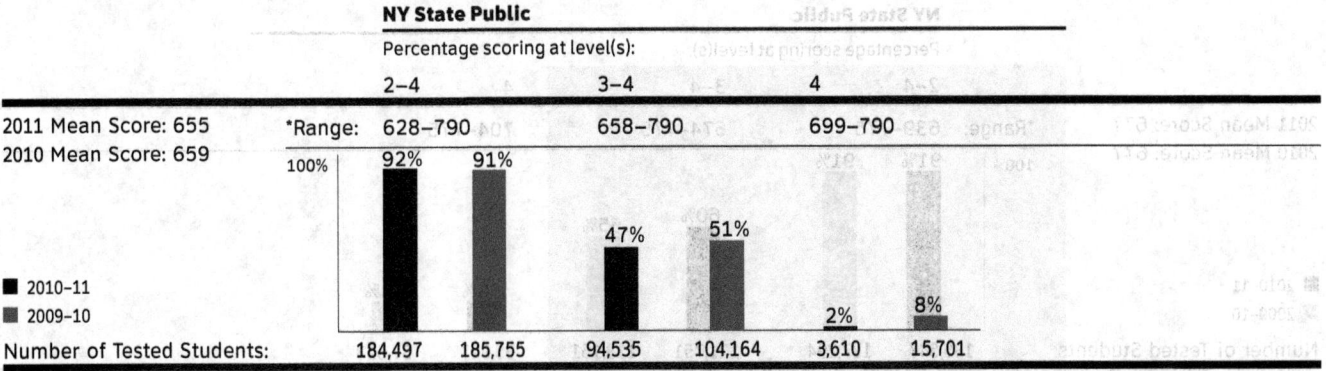

**NY State Public**

Percentage scoring at level(s):

|  | 2–4 | 3–4 | 4 |
|---|---|---|---|
| 2011 Mean Score: 655 | *Range: 628–790 | 658–790 | 699–790 |
| 2010 Mean Score: 659 | | | |

Legend: ■ 2010–11   ■ 2009–10

Bar values: 92%, 91%, 47%, 51%, 2%, 8%

| Number of Tested Students: | 184,497 | 185,755 | 94,535 | 104,164 | 3,610 | 15,701 |

## Results by Student Group

| | 2010–11 School Year | | | | 2009–10 School Year | | | |
|---|---|---|---|---|---|---|---|---|
| | Total Tested | 2–4 | 3–4 | 4 | Total Tested | 2–4 | 3–4 | 4 |
| **All Students** | **201,371** | **92%** | **47%** | **2%** | **204,148** | **91%** | **51%** | **8%** |
| Female | 98,247 | 94% | 53% | 2% | 99,420 | 93% | 57% | 10% |
| Male | 103,124 | 89% | 41% | 1% | 104,728 | 89% | 45% | 6% |
| American Indian or Alaska Native | 969 | 87% | 31% | 1% | 935 | 87% | 37% | 3% |
| Black or African American | 37,977 | 87% | 28% | 0% | 38,607 | 85% | 31% | 2% |
| Hispanic or Latino | 42,634 | 86% | 29% | 0% | 41,949 | 84% | 33% | 3% |
| Asian or Native Hawaiian/Other Pacific Islander | 16,102 | 92% | 61% | 4% | 15,661 | 92% | 66% | 15% |
| White | 102,675 | 95% | 59% | 3% | 106,384 | 96% | 63% | 11% |
| Multiracial | 1,014 | 94% | 55% | 3% | 612 | 94% | 57% | 11% |
| Small Group Totals | 0 | — | — | — | 0 | — | — | — |
| General-Education Students | 170,193 | 96% | 54% | 2% | 172,053 | 95% | 58% | 9% |
| Students with Disabilities | 31,178 | 69% | 9% | 0% | 32,095 | 67% | 11% | 0% |
| English Proficient | 190,500 | 94% | 49% | 2% | 193,961 | 93% | 54% | 8% |
| Limited English Proficient | 10,871 | 55% | 2% | 0% | 10,187 | 49% | 4% | 0% |
| Economically Disadvantaged | 103,383 | 87% | 32% | 1% | 102,450 | 86% | 35% | 3% |
| Not Disadvantaged | 97,988 | 96% | 63% | 3% | 101,698 | 96% | 67% | 12% |
| Migrant | 39 | 85% | 28% | 0% | 39 | 74% | 15% | 0% |
| Not Migrant | 201,332 | 92% | 47% | 2% | 204,109 | 91% | 51% | 8% |

**NOTE**

The — symbol indicates that data for a group of students have been suppressed. If a group has fewer than five students, data for that group and the next smallest group(s) are suppressed to protect the privacy of individual students.
*These ranges are for 2010–11 data only. Ranges for the 2009–10 data are available in the 2009–10 Accountability and Overview Reports.

## Other Assessments

| | 2010–11 School Year | | | | 2009–10 School Year | | | |
|---|---|---|---|---|---|---|---|---|
| | Total Tested | 2–4 | 3–4 | 4 | Total Tested | 2–4 | 3–4 | 4 |
| New York State Alternate Assessment (NYSAA): Grade 8 Equivalent | 2,545 | 2,519 | 2,340 | 1,982 | 2,593 | 2,561 | 2,404 | 2,041 |
| New York State English as a Second Language Achievement Test (NYSESLAT)†: Grade 8 | 1,874 | N/A | N/A | N/A | 2,370 | N/A | N/A | N/A |
| | Total | | | | Total | | | |
| Recently Arrived LEP Students NOT Tested on the ELA NYSTP: Grade 8 | 1,920 | N/A | N/A | N/A | 2,420 | N/A | N/A | N/A |

† These counts represent recently arrived LEP students who used the NYSESLAT to fulfill the English language arts participation requirement.

# Statewide Results in Grade 8 Mathematics

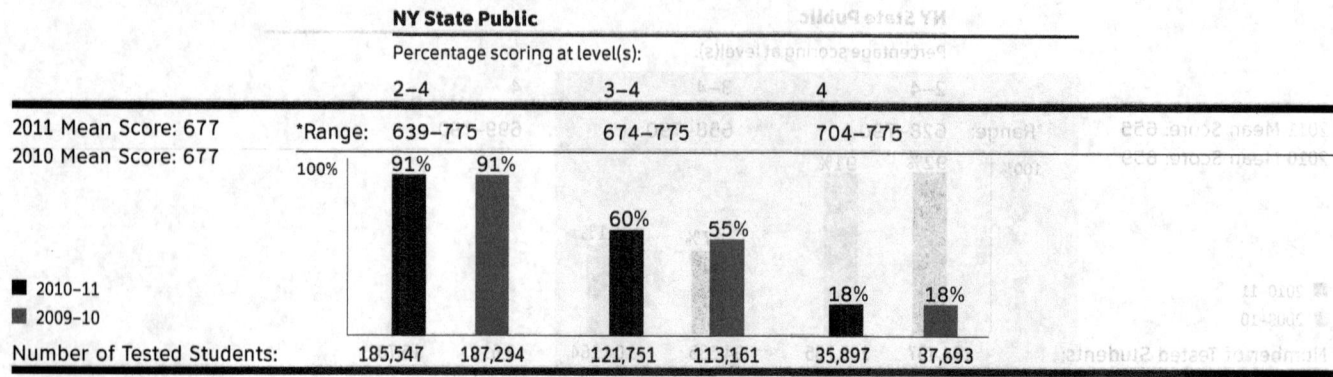

**NY State Public**

Percentage scoring at level(s):

|  | 2–4 | 3–4 | 4 |
|---|---|---|---|
| 2011 Mean Score: 677 / 2010 Mean Score: 677 | *Range: 639–775 | 674–775 | 704–775 |

2010–11 (black) / 2009–10 (gray)

| Level | 2010–11 | 2009–10 |
|---|---|---|
| 2–4 | 91% | 91% |
| 3–4 | 60% | 55% |
| 4 | 18% | 18% |

Number of Tested Students: 185,547 | 187,294 | 121,751 | 113,161 | 35,897 | 37,693

## Results by Student Group

| | 2010–11 School Year | | | | 2009–10 School Year | | | |
|---|---|---|---|---|---|---|---|---|
| | | Percentage scoring at level(s): | | | | Percentage scoring at level(s): | | |
| | Total Tested | 2–4 | 3–4 | 4 | Total Tested | 2–4 | 3–4 | 4 |
| **All Students** | **203,239** | **91%** | **60%** | **18%** | **206,417** | **91%** | **55%** | **18%** |
| Female | 99,139 | 93% | 62% | 18% | 100,479 | 92% | 58% | 20% |
| Male | 104,100 | 90% | 58% | 17% | 105,938 | 89% | 52% | 17% |
| American Indian or Alaska Native | 979 | 87% | 44% | 9% | 941 | 88% | 40% | 9% |
| Black or African American | 38,022 | 83% | 38% | 6% | 38,675 | 82% | 32% | 7% |
| Hispanic or Latino | 43,673 | 87% | 45% | 8% | 43,033 | 85% | 39% | 9% |
| Asian or Native Hawaiian/Other Pacific Islander | 16,717 | 97% | 83% | 45% | 16,567 | 97% | 80% | 44% |
| White | 102,835 | 95% | 70% | 21% | 106,561 | 95% | 66% | 22% |
| Multiracial | 1,013 | 92% | 65% | 18% | 640 | 89% | 51% | 19% |
| Small Group Totals | 0 | — | — | — | 0 | — | — | — |
| General-Education Students | 172,166 | 95% | 67% | 21% | 174,363 | 95% | 62% | 21% |
| Students with Disabilities | 31,073 | 70% | 22% | 2% | 32,054 | 68% | 17% | 2% |
| English Proficient | 190,296 | 92% | 62% | 18% | 193,828 | 92% | 57% | 19% |
| Limited English Proficient | 12,943 | 75% | 30% | 6% | 12,589 | 72% | 24% | 5% |
| Economically Disadvantaged | 105,111 | 87% | 47% | 11% | 104,436 | 86% | 41% | 12% |
| Not Disadvantaged | 98,128 | 96% | 74% | 24% | 101,981 | 96% | 69% | 25% |
| Migrant | 42 | 88% | 52% | 2% | 43 | 84% | 21% | 2% |
| Not Migrant | 203,197 | 91% | 60% | 18% | 206,374 | 91% | 55% | 18% |

**NOTE**

The — symbol indicates that data for a group of students have been suppressed. If a group has fewer than five students, data for that group and the next smallest group(s) are suppressed to protect the privacy of individual students.

*These ranges are for 2010–11 data only. Ranges for the 2009–10 data are available in the 2009–10 Accountability and Overview Reports.

## Other Assessments

| | 2010–11 School Year | | | | 2009–10 School Year | | | |
|---|---|---|---|---|---|---|---|---|
| | | Number scoring at level(s): | | | | Number scoring at level(s): | | |
| | Total Tested | 2–4 | 3–4 | 4 | Total Tested | 2–4 | 3–4 | 4 |
| New York State Alternate Assessment (NYSAA): Grade 8 Equivalent | 2,547 | 2,385 | 2,261 | 1,569 | 2,577 | 2,360 | 2,206 | 1,479 |

# Statewide Results in Grade 8 Science

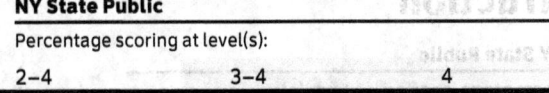

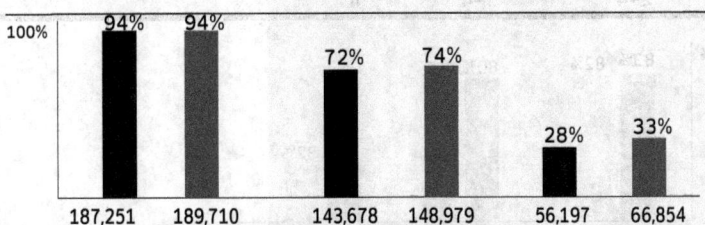

| | 2–4 | 3–4 | 4 |
|---|---|---|---|
| 2010–11 | 94% | 72% | 28% |
| 2009–10 | 94% | 74% | 33% |
| Number of Tested Students: | 187,251 / 189,710 | 143,678 / 148,979 | 56,197 / 66,854 |

## Results by Student Group

| | 2010–11 School Year | | | | 2009–10 School Year | | | |
|---|---|---|---|---|---|---|---|---|
| | Total Tested | 2–4 | 3–4 | 4 | Total Tested | 2–4 | 3–4 | 4 |
| **All Students** | **175,068** | **94%** | **69%** | **22%** | **180,503** | **93%** | **71%** | **28%** |
| Female | 84,837 | 94% | 68% | 20% | 87,277 | 94% | 70% | 26% |
| Male | 90,231 | 93% | 70% | 24% | 93,226 | 93% | 71% | 30% |
| American Indian or Alaska Native | 899 | 91% | 61% | 12% | 874 | 93% | 66% | 17% |
| Black or African American | 34,446 | 87% | 47% | 6% | 35,723 | 86% | 48% | 9% |
| Hispanic or Latino | 40,298 | 89% | 51% | 9% | 40,093 | 88% | 53% | 12% |
| Asian or Native Hawaiian/Other Pacific Islander | 14,046 | 95% | 78% | 31% | 14,013 | 95% | 80% | 38% |
| White | 84,531 | 98% | 85% | 34% | 89,276 | 98% | 86% | 41% |
| Multiracial | 848 | 96% | 78% | 29% | 524 | 93% | 69% | 30% |
| Small Group Totals | 0 | — | — | — | 0 | — | — | — |
| General-Education Students | 146,097 | 96% | 75% | 26% | 150,370 | 96% | 77% | 32% |
| Students with Disabilities | 28,971 | 82% | 39% | 5% | 30,133 | 81% | 41% | 7% |
| English Proficient | 162,756 | 95% | 72% | 24% | 168,417 | 95% | 74% | 30% |
| Limited English Proficient | 12,312 | 72% | 23% | 2% | 12,086 | 71% | 26% | 3% |
| Economically Disadvantaged | 97,456 | 90% | 56% | 12% | 97,892 | 89% | 57% | 15% |
| Not Disadvantaged | 77,612 | 98% | 86% | 36% | 82,611 | 98% | 87% | 43% |
| Migrant | 40 | 88% | 63% | 10% | 38 | 89% | 45% | 13% |
| Not Migrant | 175,028 | 94% | 69% | 22% | 180,465 | 93% | 71% | 28% |

**NOTE**
The — symbol indicates that data for a group of students have been suppressed. If a group has fewer than five students,
data for that group and the next smallest group(s) are suppressed to protect the privacy of individual students.

## Other Assessments

| | 2010–11 School Year | | | | 2009–10 School Year | | | |
|---|---|---|---|---|---|---|---|---|
| | Total Tested | 2–4 | 3–4 | 4 | Total Tested | 2–4 | 3–4 | 4 |
| New York State Alternate Assessment (NYSAA): Grade 8 Equivalent | 2,542 | 2,386 | 2,199 | 1,931 | 2,597 | 2,447 | 2,247 | 1,968 |
| Regents Science | 23,826 | 23,420 | 22,914 | 17,105 | 22,037 | 21,611 | 21,208 | 16,332 |

# Statewide Total Cohort* Results in Secondary-Level English after Four Years of Instruction

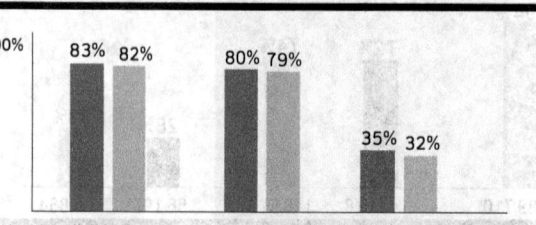

**NY State Public**

Percentage scoring at level(s):

2–4    3–4    4

100%

83% 82%    80% 79%    35% 32%

■ 2007 Cohort
■ 2006 Cohort

## Results by Student Group

| | 2007 Cohort | | | | 2006 Cohort** | | | |
|---|---|---|---|---|---|---|---|---|
| | Number of Students | Percentage scoring at level(s): | | | Number of Students | Percentage scoring at level(s): | | |
| | | 2–4 | 3–4 | 4 | | 2–4 | 3–4 | 4 |
| **All Students** | **223,120** | **83%** | **80%** | **35%** | **224,696** | **82%** | **79%** | **32%** |
| Female | 108,556 | 87% | 84% | 40% | 109,986 | 86% | 83% | 38% |
| Male | 114,564 | 80% | 77% | 29% | 114,710 | 78% | 75% | 26% |
| American Indian or Alaska Native | 1,127 | 72% | 69% | 21% | 1,078 | 68% | 64% | 19% |
| Black or African American | 44,022 | 75% | 70% | 16% | 44,597 | 72% | 67% | 14% |
| Hispanic or Latino | 45,379 | 75% | 70% | 18% | 43,320 | 72% | 68% | 15% |
| Asian or Native Hawaiian/Other Pacific Islander | 17,298 | 90% | 88% | 48% | 16,484 | 90% | 88% | 44% |
| White | 114,710 | 89% | 87% | 47% | 118,743 | 88% | 86% | 44% |
| Multiracial | 584 | 86% | 84% | 38% | 474 | 84% | 81% | 34% |
| Small Group Totals | 0 | — | — | — | 0 | — | — | — |
| General-Education Students | 190,226 | 89% | 87% | 40% | 192,010 | 88% | 86% | 37% |
| Students with Disabilities | 32,894 | 50% | 41% | 5% | 32,686 | 47% | 39% | 4% |
| English Proficient | 210,923 | 85% | 82% | 37% | 213,092 | 83% | 81% | 34% |
| Limited English Proficient | 12,197 | 55% | 46% | 3% | 11,604 | 53% | 46% | 3% |
| Economically Disadvantaged | 93,325 | 79% | 75% | 20% | 88,869 | 77% | 73% | 18% |
| Not Disadvantaged | 129,795 | 86% | 84% | 45% | 135,827 | 85% | 83% | 42% |
| Migrant | 45 | 60% | 53% | 4% | 25 | 68% | 60% | 8% |
| Not Migrant | 223,075 | 83% | 80% | 35% | 224,671 | 82% | 79% | 32% |

**NOTE**

The — symbol indicates that data for a group of students have been suppressed. If a group has fewer than five students, data for that group and the next smallest group(s) are suppressed to protect the privacy of individual students.

* A total cohort consists of all students who first entered Grade 9 in a particular year, and all ungraded students with disabilities who reached their seventeenth birthday in that year, and were enrolled in the school/district for five months. Students are excluded from the cohort if they transferred to another school district, nonpublic school, or criminal justice facility, or left the U.S. and its territories or died before the report date. Statewide total cohort also includes students who were enrolled for fewer than five months.

** 2006 cohort data are those reported in the 2009–10 *Accountability and Overview Report.*

# Statewide Total Cohort* Results in Secondary-Level Mathematics after Four Years of Instruction

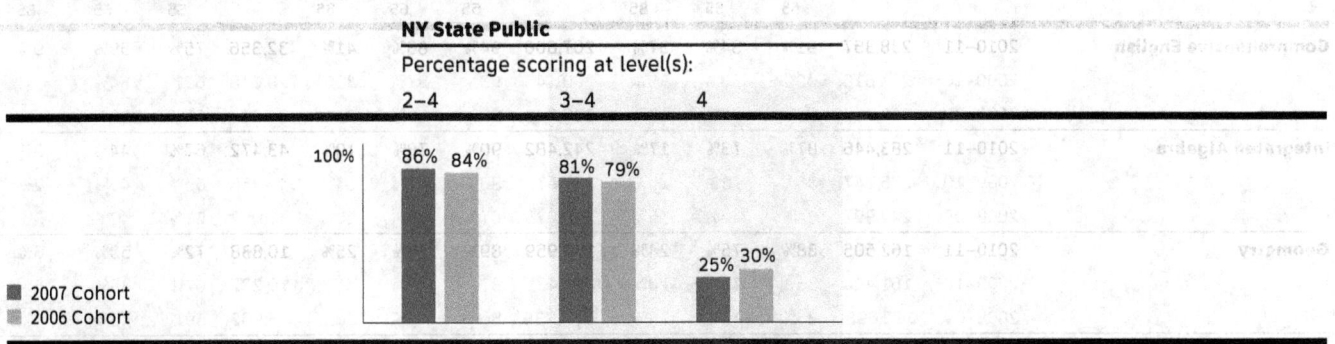

**NY State Public**

Percentage scoring at level(s):

| 2–4 | 3–4 | 4 |

- ■ 2007 Cohort
- ▨ 2006 Cohort

## Results by Student Group

| | 2007 Cohort | | | | 2006 Cohort** | | | |
|---|---|---|---|---|---|---|---|---|
| | Number of Students | \multicolumn{3}{c}{Percentage scoring at level(s):} | | Number of Students | \multicolumn{3}{c}{Percentage scoring at level(s):} | |
| | | 2–4 | 3–4 | 4 | | 2–4 | 3–4 | 4 |
| **All Students** | **223,120** | **86%** | **81%** | **25%** | **224,696** | **84%** | **79%** | **30%** |
| Female | 108,556 | 88% | 84% | 26% | 109,986 | 87% | 82% | 31% |
| Male | 114,564 | 83% | 78% | 23% | 114,710 | 82% | 76% | 28% |
| American Indian or Alaska Native | 1,127 | 77% | 70% | 10% | 1,078 | 74% | 67% | 17% |
| Black or African American | 44,022 | 77% | 68% | 6% | 44,597 | 75% | 64% | 8% |
| Hispanic or Latino | 45,379 | 78% | 70% | 8% | 43,320 | 75% | 67% | 11% |
| Asian or Native Hawaiian/Other Pacific Islander | 17,298 | 93% | 91% | 48% | 16,484 | 93% | 91% | 54% |
| White | 114,710 | 91% | 88% | 35% | 118,743 | 90% | 87% | 41% |
| Multiracial | 584 | 87% | 81% | 29% | 474 | 83% | 79% | 29% |
| Small Group Totals | 0 | — | — | — | 0 | — | — | — |
| General-Education Students | 190,226 | 92% | 88% | 28% | 192,010 | 90% | 86% | 34% |
| Students with Disabilities | 32,894 | 52% | 40% | 3% | 32,686 | 50% | 39% | 4% |
| English Proficient | 210,923 | 87% | 82% | 26% | 213,092 | 85% | 80% | 31% |
| Limited English Proficient | 12,197 | 69% | 58% | 7% | 11,604 | 66% | 55% | 8% |
| Economically Disadvantaged | 93,325 | 83% | 75% | 12% | 88,869 | 81% | 72% | 16% |
| Not Disadvantaged | 129,795 | 88% | 85% | 33% | 135,827 | 87% | 83% | 39% |
| Migrant | 45 | 76% | 64% | 9% | 25 | 68% | 64% | 16% |
| Not Migrant | 223,075 | 86% | 81% | 25% | 224,671 | 84% | 79% | 30% |

**NOTE**

The — symbol indicates that data for a group of students have been suppressed. If a group has fewer than five students, data for that group and the next smallest group(s) are suppressed to protect the privacy of individual students.

* A total cohort consists of all students who first entered Grade 9 in a particular year, and all ungraded students with disabilities who reached their seventeenth birthday in that year, and were enrolled in the school/district for five months. Students are excluded from the cohort if they transferred to another school district, nonpublic school, or criminal justice facility, or left the U.S. and its territories or died before the report date. Statewide total cohort also includes students who were enrolled for fewer than five months.

** 2006 cohort data are those reported in the 2009–10 *Accountability and Overview Report*.

# Regents Exams

| | | All Students | | | | General-Education Students | | | | Students with Disabilities | | | |
|---|---|---|---|---|---|---|---|---|---|---|---|---|---|
| | | Total Tested | Percentage of students scoring at or above: | | | Total Tested | Percentage of students scoring at or above: | | | Total Tested | Percentage of students scoring at or above: | | |
| | | | 55 | 65 | 85 | | 55 | 65 | 85 | | 55 | 65 | 85 |
| Comprehensive English | 2010–11 | 238,357 | 91% | 84% | 37% | 207,600 | 94% | 88% | 41% | 32,356 | 75% | 59% | 9% |
| | 2009–10 | 227,616 | 90% | 83% | 35% | 200,443 | 93% | 87% | 39% | 28,678 | 69% | 54% | 7% |
| | 2008–09 | 220,355 | 89% | 82% | 33% | 195,540 | 92% | 86% | 37% | 24,815 | 68% | 52% | 5% |
| Integrated Algebra | 2010–11 | 283,446 | 87% | 73% | 17% | 242,482 | 90% | 78% | 19% | 43,472 | 67% | 44% | 3% |
| | 2009–10 | 275,747 | 85% | 72% | 15% | 237,675 | 88% | 77% | 17% | 40,356 | 65% | 46% | 2% |
| | 2008–09 | 249,997 | 84% | 72% | 15% | 218,925 | 87% | 76% | 16% | 31,072 | 61% | 42% | 2% |
| Geometry | 2010–11 | 162,505 | 88% | 75% | 24% | 152,959 | 89% | 76% | 25% | 10,838 | 72% | 53% | 6% |
| | 2009–10 | 161,494 | 86% | 73% | 20% | 152,435 | 87% | 75% | 21% | 10,232 | 67% | 48% | 5% |
| | 2008–09 | 113,698 | 85% | 73% | 25% | 107,736 | 86% | 75% | 26% | 5,962 | 59% | 43% | 6% |
| Algebra 2/Trigonometry | 2010–11 | 120,387 | 76% | 64% | 23% | 117,233 | 76% | 64% | 23% | 3,802 | 62% | 47% | 10% |
| | 2009–10 | 84,947 | 75% | 65% | 27% | 82,764 | 76% | 65% | 27% | 2,626 | 59% | 45% | 11% |
| | 2008–09 | N/A | N/A | N/A | N/A | N/A | N/A | N/A | N/A | N/A | N/A | N/A | N/A |
| Global History and Geography | 2010–11 | 252,363 | 82% | 69% | 27% | 217,329 | 85% | 74% | 30% | 36,974 | 61% | 41% | 7% |
| | 2009–10 | 245,336 | 81% | 70% | 29% | 213,184 | 84% | 74% | 33% | 33,949 | 60% | 42% | 8% |
| | 2008–09 | 246,377 | 82% | 70% | 30% | 215,465 | 85% | 74% | 33% | 30,912 | 60% | 42% | 8% |
| U.S. History and Government | 2010–11 | 221,732 | 88% | 80% | 44% | 195,173 | 91% | 84% | 48% | 28,081 | 70% | 54% | 16% |
| | 2009–10 | 217,189 | 90% | 83% | 44% | 192,283 | 92% | 86% | 48% | 26,351 | 74% | 60% | 17% |
| | 2008–09 | 214,653 | 88% | 80% | 43% | 190,388 | 91% | 84% | 47% | 24,265 | 69% | 54% | 14% |
| Living Environment | 2010–11 | 236,323 | 90% | 81% | 32% | 205,095 | 93% | 85% | 35% | 33,203 | 75% | 58% | 9% |
| | 2009–10 | 237,522 | 88% | 78% | 31% | 207,829 | 91% | 82% | 34% | 31,555 | 72% | 54% | 8% |
| | 2008–09 | 241,842 | 90% | 80% | 29% | 212,950 | 92% | 83% | 32% | 28,892 | 74% | 56% | 8% |
| Physical Setting/ Earth Science | 2010–11 | 165,998 | 84% | 72% | 30% | 148,331 | 87% | 75% | 32% | 19,151 | 66% | 47% | 9% |
| | 2009–10 | 165,230 | 85% | 74% | 31% | 148,037 | 87% | 77% | 33% | 18,561 | 68% | 51% | 10% |
| | 2008–09 | 169,920 | 84% | 72% | 30% | 152,542 | 86% | 75% | 32% | 17,378 | 65% | 46% | 9% |
| Physical Setting/Chemistry | 2010–11 | 108,466 | 93% | 78% | 20% | 105,801 | 94% | 78% | 20% | 3,270 | 86% | 64% | 9% |
| | 2009–10 | 108,749 | 90% | 73% | 15% | 105,952 | 90% | 73% | 16% | 3,437 | 79% | 58% | 6% |
| | 2008–09 | 109,859 | 89% | 74% | 18% | 107,083 | 90% | 74% | 18% | 2,776 | 75% | 56% | 7% |
| Physical Setting/Physics | 2010–11 | 49,262 | 89% | 79% | 32% | 48,555 | 89% | 79% | 32% | 920 | 79% | 67% | 19% |
| | 2009–10 | 48,772 | 90% | 82% | 33% | 48,092 | 91% | 82% | 33% | 866 | 79% | 68% | 22% |
| | 2008–09 | 47,932 | 87% | 77% | 28% | 47,297 | 87% | 77% | 29% | 635 | 78% | 66% | 17% |

**NOTE**
The — symbol indicates that data for a group of students have been suppressed. If a group has fewer than five students, data for that group and the next smallest group(s) are suppressed to protect the privacy of individual students.

# Regents Exams

| | | All Students | | | | General-Education Students | | | | Students with Disabilities | | | |
|---|---|---|---|---|---|---|---|---|---|---|---|---|---|
| | | Total Tested | Percentage of students scoring at or above: | | | Total Tested | Percentage of students scoring at or above: | | | Total Tested | Percentage of students scoring at or above: | | |
| | | | 55 | 65 | 85 | | 55 | 65 | 85 | | 55 | 65 | 85 |
| Comprehensive French | 2010–11 | 17,680 | 98% | 95% | 56% | 17,392 | 98% | 96% | 57% | 362 | 94% | 87% | 28% |
| | 2009–10 | 17,298 | 98% | 95% | 54% | 17,056 | 98% | 95% | 55% | 297 | 91% | 85% | 24% |
| | 2008–09 | 17,076 | 99% | 97% | 65% | 16,832 | 99% | 97% | 65% | 244 | 96% | 91% | 36% |
| Comprehensive Italian | 2010–11 | 8,981 | 99% | 98% | 66% | 8,751 | 99% | 98% | 67% | 279 | 97% | 93% | 38% |
| | 2009–10 | 8,686 | 99% | 98% | 67% | 8,438 | 99% | 98% | 67% | 298 | 98% | 93% | 44% |
| | 2008–09 | 8,250 | 99% | 98% | 59% | 8,075 | 99% | 98% | 60% | 175 | 98% | 91% | 36% |
| Comprehensive Spanish | 2010–11 | 86,722 | 97% | 94% | 55% | 83,624 | 97% | 94% | 56% | 3,594 | 93% | 85% | 37% |
| | 2009–10 | 86,972 | 98% | 95% | 60% | 84,147 | 98% | 95% | 60% | 3,306 | 94% | 88% | 42% |
| | 2008–09 | 86,780 | 98% | 96% | 66% | 84,016 | 98% | 97% | 67% | 2,764 | 95% | 90% | 45% |

**NOTE**
The — symbol indicates that data for a group of students have been suppressed. If a group has fewer than five students, data for that group and the next smallest group(s) are suppressed to protect the privacy of individual students.

# Regents Competency Tests

| | | All Students | | General-Education Students | | Students with Disabilities | |
|---|---|---|---|---|---|---|---|
| | | Total Tested | Percent Passing | Total Tested | Percent Passing | Total Tested | Percent Passing |
| **Mathematics** | 2010–11 | 16,301 | 41% | 423 | 58% | 15,925 | 41% |
| | 2009–10 | 17,220 | 41% | 471 | 59% | 16,804 | 41% |
| | 2008–09 | 20,794 | 50% | 681 | 64% | 20,113 | 50% |
| **Science** | 2010–11 | 14,025 | 41% | 452 | 57% | 13,622 | 40% |
| | 2009–10 | 15,583 | 37% | 439 | 54% | 15,199 | 37% |
| | 2008–09 | 14,925 | 38% | 543 | 54% | 14,382 | 37% |
| **Reading** | 2010–11 | 9,180 | 44% | 360 | 57% | 8,867 | 43% |
| | 2009–10 | 11,837 | 51% | 413 | 70% | 11,473 | 51% |
| | 2008–09 | 12,360 | 47% | 436 | 66% | 11,924 | 46% |
| **Writing** | 2010–11 | 7,905 | 76% | 252 | 83% | 7,684 | 76% |
| | 2009–10 | 9,168 | 78% | 335 | 88% | 8,878 | 78% |
| | 2008–09 | 9,012 | 75% | 342 | 82% | 8,670 | 74% |
| **Global Studies** | 2010–11 | 15,481 | 33% | 804 | 43% | 14,770 | 32% |
| | 2009–10 | 15,181 | 31% | 794 | 42% | 14,490 | 31% |
| | 2008–09 | 16,039 | 32% | 845 | 39% | 15,194 | 31% |
| **U.S. History and Government** | 2010–11 | 9,780 | 43% | 554 | 55% | 9,302 | 43% |
| | 2009–10 | 8,663 | 37% | 613 | 55% | 8,107 | 36% |
| | 2008–09 | 7,503 | 34% | 400 | 45% | 7,103 | 33% |

**NOTE**

The — symbol indicates that data for a group of students have been suppressed. If a group has fewer than five students, data for that group and the next smallest group(s) are suppressed to protect the privacy of individual students.

# New York State English as a Second Language Achievement Test (NYSESLAT)

| | | All Students | | | | | General-Education Students | | | | | Students with Disabilities | | | | |
|---|---|---|---|---|---|---|---|---|---|---|---|---|---|---|---|---|
| | | Total Tested | Percent of students scoring in each performance level: | | | | Total Tested | Percent of students scoring in each performance level: | | | | Total Tested | Percent of students scoring in each performance level: | | | |
| | | | Begin. | Interm. | Adv. | Prof. | | Begin. | Interm. | Adv. | Prof. | | Begin. | Interm. | Adv. | Prof. |
| **Listening and Speaking (Grades K–1)** | 2010–11 | 51,490 | 5% | 17% | 41% | 37% | 44,509 | 5% | 16% | 40% | 39% | 6,981 | 7% | 26% | 43% | 24% |
| | 2009–10 | 51,069 | 5% | 19% | 40% | 36% | 43,948 | 5% | 17% | 40% | 38% | 7,121 | 6% | 30% | 42% | 22% |
| | 2008–09 | 50,221 | 5% | 19% | 42% | 34% | 43,529 | 5% | 17% | 42% | 36% | 6,692 | 6% | 30% | 44% | 19% |
| **Reading and Writing (Grades K–1)** | 2010–11 | 51,477 | 28% | 28% | 20% | 24% | 44,501 | 26% | 28% | 21% | 26% | 6,976 | 43% | 28% | 17% | 13% |
| | 2009–10 | 51,068 | 30% | 32% | 14% | 24% | 43,954 | 27% | 32% | 15% | 26% | 7,114 | 47% | 29% | 11% | 13% |
| | 2008–09 | 50,184 | 31% | 28% | 19% | 21% | 43,512 | 29% | 28% | 20% | 23% | 6,672 | 48% | 28% | 14% | 10% |
| **Listening and Speaking (Grades 2–4)** | 2010–11 | 60,076 | 3% | 7% | 32% | 58% | 47,312 | 4% | 7% | 29% | 60% | 12,764 | 2% | 7% | 43% | 48% |
| | 2009–10 | 62,148 | 4% | 6% | 29% | 61% | 49,078 | 5% | 6% | 25% | 64% | 13,070 | 2% | 7% | 42% | 50% |
| | 2008–09 | 60,069 | 3% | 6% | 33% | 58% | 47,527 | 3% | 6% | 30% | 61% | 12,542 | 1% | 8% | 46% | 45% |
| **Reading and Writing (Grades 2–4)** | 2010–11 | 60,060 | 14% | 28% | 39% | 19% | 47,300 | 12% | 25% | 41% | 22% | 12,760 | 21% | 38% | 33% | 8% |
| | 2009–10 | 62,143 | 14% | 29% | 38% | 20% | 49,075 | 11% | 26% | 40% | 23% | 13,068 | 21% | 41% | 29% | 8% |
| | 2008–09 | 60,033 | 13% | 29% | 41% | 17% | 47,511 | 10% | 26% | 43% | 20% | 12,522 | 23% | 40% | 30% | 7% |
| **Listening and Speaking (Grades 5–6)** | 2010–11 | 29,949 | 7% | 11% | 40% | 42% | 22,004 | 8% | 13% | 36% | 43% | 7,945 | 3% | 7% | 50% | 40% |
| | 2009–10 | 28,906 | 8% | 11% | 37% | 43% | 21,038 | 10% | 12% | 33% | 44% | 7,868 | 3% | 8% | 48% | 41% |
| | 2008–09 | 27,307 | 6% | 10% | 43% | 41% | 19,874 | 8% | 11% | 39% | 43% | 7,433 | 3% | 7% | 52% | 38% |
| **Reading and Writing (Grades 5–6)** | 2010–11 | 29,942 | 15% | 20% | 33% | 32% | 22,002 | 16% | 17% | 31% | 36% | 7,940 | 14% | 28% | 38% | 20% |
| | 2009–10 | 28,900 | 14% | 23% | 40% | 23% | 21,037 | 14% | 20% | 39% | 27% | 7,863 | 14% | 32% | 42% | 12% |
| | 2008–09 | 27,295 | 14% | 22% | 37% | 28% | 19,872 | 14% | 18% | 36% | 32% | 7,423 | 15% | 31% | 39% | 15% |
| **Listening and Speaking (Grades 7–8)** | 2010–11 | 25,734 | 7% | 16% | 29% | 48% | 19,360 | 9% | 19% | 27% | 46% | 6,374 | 3% | 7% | 34% | 56% |
| | 2009–10 | 25,632 | 8% | 16% | 26% | 50% | 19,578 | 9% | 18% | 24% | 48% | 6,054 | 3% | 7% | 32% | 58% |
| | 2008–09 | 24,143 | 7% | 15% | 30% | 49% | 18,739 | 8% | 17% | 28% | 48% | 5,404 | 3% | 9% | 37% | 51% |
| **Reading and Writing (Grades 7–8)** | 2010–11 | 25,730 | 24% | 33% | 24% | 19% | 19,356 | 25% | 31% | 23% | 21% | 6,374 | 21% | 42% | 25% | 12% |
| | 2009–10 | 25,641 | 25% | 34% | 25% | 16% | 19,580 | 26% | 31% | 25% | 18% | 6,061 | 23% | 45% | 24% | 9% |
| | 2008–09 | 24,128 | 23% | 34% | 24% | 19% | 18,736 | 23% | 31% | 24% | 22% | 5,392 | 22% | 44% | 23% | 11% |
| **Listening and Speaking (Grades 9–12)** | 2010–11 | 44,620 | 10% | 28% | 24% | 37% | 37,974 | 10% | 30% | 24% | 36% | 6,646 | 9% | 19% | 24% | 48% |
| | 2009–10 | 43,287 | 10% | 28% | 22% | 41% | 37,452 | 10% | 29% | 21% | 40% | 5,835 | 10% | 20% | 23% | 48% |
| | 2008–09 | 40,800 | 10% | 27% | 24% | 39% | 36,080 | 10% | 28% | 24% | 38% | 4,720 | 8% | 20% | 26% | 46% |
| **Reading and Writing (Grades 9–12)** | 2010–11 | 44,610 | 16% | 47% | 22% | 15% | 37,972 | 15% | 47% | 22% | 15% | 6,638 | 24% | 46% | 21% | 9% |
| | 2009–10 | 43,293 | 15% | 48% | 23% | 14% | 37,455 | 13% | 48% | 23% | 16% | 5,838 | 26% | 48% | 18% | 8% |
| | 2008–09 | 40,775 | 15% | 47% | 23% | 15% | 36,071 | 15% | 46% | 23% | 16% | 4,704 | 22% | 49% | 19% | 10% |

**NOTE**

The — symbol indicates that data for a group of students have been suppressed. If a group has fewer than five students, data for that group and the next smallest group(s) are suppressed to protect the privacy of individual students.

# High School Completers

| | | All Students | | General-Education Students | | Students with Disabilities | |
|---|---|---|---|---|---|---|---|
| | | Number of Students | Percentage of Graduates | Number of Students | Percentage of Graduates | Number of Students | Percentage of Graduates |
| **Total Graduates** | 2010–11 | 182,504 | | 164,980 | | 17,524 | |
| | 2009–10 | 183,578 | | 166,281 | | 17,297 | |
| | 2008–09 | 180,154 | | 164,147 | | 16,007 | |
| **Receiving a Regents Diploma** | 2010–11 | 157,164 | 86% | 148,543 | 90% | 8,621 | 49% |
| | 2009–10 | 152,536 | 83% | 144,267 | 87% | 8,269 | 48% |
| | 2008–09 | 146,114 | 81% | 138,406 | 84% | 7,708 | 48% |
| **Receiving a Regents Diploma with Advanced Designation** | 2010–11 | 68,782 | 38% | 67,732 | 41% | 1,050 | 6% |
| | 2009–10 | 69,998 | 38% | 68,967 | 41% | 1,031 | 6% |
| | 2008–09 | 68,159 | 38% | 67,156 | 41% | 1,003 | 6% |
| **Receiving an Individualized Education Program (IEP) Diploma** | 2010–11 | 5,465 | N/A | N/A | N/A | 5,428 | N/A |
| | 2009–10 | 5,600 | N/A | N/A | N/A | 5,566 | N/A |
| | 2008–09 | 5,842 | N/A | N/A | N/A | 5,796 | N/A |

NOTE  Students receiving Regents diplomas and Regents diplomas with advanced designation are considered graduates; recipients of IEP diplomas are not.

# High School Noncompleters

| | | All Students | | General-Education Students | | Students with Disabilities | |
|---|---|---|---|---|---|---|---|
| | | Number of Students | Percentage of Students | Number of Students | Percentage of Students | Number of Students | Percentage of Students |
| **Dropped Out** | 2010–11 | 29,226 | 2.7% | 21,473 | 2.4% | 7,753 | 4.4% |
| | 2009–10 | 29,409 | 2.7% | 21,805 | 2.4% | 7,604 | 4.3% |
| | 2008–09 | 30,081 | 2.7% | 22,599 | 2.4% | 7,482 | 4.2% |
| **Entered Approved High School Equivalency Preparation Program** | 2010–11 | 6,039 | 0.6% | 4,313 | 0.5% | 1,726 | 1.0% |
| | 2009–10 | 6,807 | 0.6% | 4,883 | 0.5% | 1,924 | 1.1% |
| | 2008–09 | 7,370 | 0.7% | 5,643 | 0.6% | 1,727 | 1.0% |
| **Total Noncompleters** | 2010–11 | 35,265 | 3.2% | 25,786 | 2.8% | 9,479 | 5.4% |
| | 2009–10 | 36,216 | 3.3% | 26,688 | 2.9% | 9,528 | 5.4% |
| | 2008–09 | 37,451 | 3.4% | 28,242 | 3.0% | 9,209 | 5.2% |

# Post-secondary Plans of 2010–11 Completers

| | All Students | | General-Education Students | | Students with Disabilities | |
|---|---|---|---|---|---|---|
| | Number of Students | Percentage of Students | Number of Students | Percentage of Students | Number of Students | Percentage of Students |
| **To 4-year College** | 86,386 | 46% | 83,171 | 50% | 3,215 | 14% |
| **To 2-year College** | 60,554 | 32% | 52,255 | 32% | 8,299 | 36% |
| **To Other Post-secondary** | 2,681 | 1% | 1,706 | 1% | 975 | 4% |
| **To the Military** | 3,446 | 2% | 2,964 | 2% | 482 | 2% |
| **To Employment** | 11,335 | 6% | 7,629 | 5% | 3,706 | 16% |
| **To Adult Services** | 1,132 | 1% | 51 | 0% | 1,081 | 5% |
| **To Other Known Plans** | 1,444 | 1% | 877 | 1% | 567 | 2% |
| **Plan Unknown** | 20,991 | 11% | 16,364 | 10% | 4,627 | 20% |

# Ancestry and Ethnicity

## New York State Profile

Population: 19,378,102

| Ancestry | Population | % |
|---|---|---|
| Afghan (9,904) | 10,755 | 0.06 |
| African, Sub-Saharan (178,451) | 240,909 | 1.25 |
| African (90,390) | 142,623 | 0.74 |
| Cape Verdean (463) | 844 | <0.01 |
| Ethiopian (4,371) | 5,107 | 0.03 |
| Ghanaian (22,113) | 23,006 | 0.12 |
| Kenyan (1,138) | 1,324 | 0.01 |
| Liberian (2,675) | 3,006 | 0.02 |
| Nigerian (25,852) | 28,991 | 0.15 |
| Senegalese (2,893) | 3,166 | 0.02 |
| Sierra Leonean (1,672) | 1,711 | 0.01 |
| Somalian (2,764) | 3,053 | 0.02 |
| South African (2,838) | 3,993 | 0.02 |
| Sudanese (1,819) | 2,137 | 0.01 |
| Ugandan (388) | 464 | <0.01 |
| Zimbabwean (607) | 646 | <0.01 |
| Other Sub-Saharan African (18,468) | 20,838 | 0.11 |
| Albanian (41,939) | 46,223 | 0.24 |
| Alsatian (202) | 882 | <0.01 |
| American (689,298) | 689,298 | 3.58 |
| Arab (103,238) | 145,746 | 0.76 |
| Arab (20,874) | 25,231 | 0.13 |
| Egyptian (21,344) | 25,478 | 0.13 |
| Iraqi (1,882) | 3,013 | 0.02 |
| Jordanian (3,956) | 4,623 | 0.02 |
| Lebanese (16,431) | 32,642 | 0.17 |
| Moroccan (9,220) | 12,364 | 0.06 |
| Palestinian (4,397) | 5,501 | 0.03 |
| Syrian (7,544) | 14,535 | 0.08 |
| Other Arab (17,590) | 22,359 | 0.12 |
| Armenian (15,331) | 24,803 | 0.13 |
| Assyrian/Chaldean/Syriac (384) | 644 | <0.01 |
| Australian (4,252) | 7,418 | 0.04 |
| Austrian (22,923) | 91,260 | 0.47 |
| Basque (570) | 1,514 | 0.01 |
| Belgian (4,380) | 13,929 | 0.07 |
| Brazilian (19,433) | 26,401 | 0.14 |
| British (29,032) | 58,548 | 0.30 |
| Bulgarian (6,409) | 8,210 | 0.04 |
| Cajun (295) | 897 | <0.01 |
| Canadian (23,228) | 50,059 | 0.26 |
| Carpatho Rusyn (474) | 741 | <0.01 |
| Celtic (1,106) | 2,324 | 0.01 |
| Croatian (15,221) | 26,607 | 0.14 |
| Cypriot (1,402) | 1,721 | 0.01 |
| Czech (13,656) | 57,264 | 0.30 |
| Czechoslovakian (9,727) | 22,547 | 0.12 |
| Danish (8,961) | 35,247 | 0.18 |
| Dutch (50,011) | 277,731 | 1.44 |
| Eastern European (82,212) | 89,540 | 0.47 |
| English (307,176) | 1,180,365 | 6.14 |
| Estonian (1,710) | 3,462 | 0.02 |
| European (142,136) | 157,939 | 0.82 |
| Finnish (5,117) | 16,941 | 0.09 |
| French, ex. Basque (93,941) | 505,680 | 2.63 |
| French Canadian (52,040) | 134,420 | 0.70 |
| German (532,432) | 2,238,521 | 11.64 |
| German Russian (196) | 587 | <0.01 |
| Greek (102,342) | 163,796 | 0.85 |
| Guyanese (109,285) | 123,809 | 0.64 |
| Hungarian (61,925) | 154,481 | 0.80 |
| Icelander (753) | 1,528 | 0.01 |
| Iranian (23,356) | 27,773 | 0.14 |
| Irish (763,450) | 2,565,928 | 13.34 |
| Israeli (25,337) | 36,808 | 0.19 |
| Italian (1,405,357) | 2,731,316 | 14.20 |
| Latvian (4,261) | 9,194 | 0.05 |
| Lithuanian (15,565) | 48,825 | 0.25 |
| Luxemburger (158) | 582 | <0.01 |
| Macedonian (6,414) | 7,783 | 0.04 |
| Maltese (3,431) | 7,645 | 0.04 |
| New Zealander (484) | 1,002 | 0.01 |
| Northern European (8,610) | 10,116 | 0.05 |

| Ancestry (cont.) | Population | % |
|---|---|---|
| Norwegian (23,292) | 85,859 | 0.45 |
| Pennsylvania German (8,537) | 13,519 | 0.07 |
| Polish (396,502) | 1,007,597 | 5.24 |
| Portuguese (28,735) | 52,967 | 0.28 |
| Romanian (28,352) | 56,605 | 0.29 |
| Russian (241,898) | 474,184 | 2.47 |
| Scandinavian (4,984) | 12,891 | 0.07 |
| Scotch-Irish (58,045) | 164,725 | 0.86 |
| Scottish (53,369) | 227,255 | 1.18 |
| Serbian (5,585) | 8,499 | 0.04 |
| Slavic (3,865) | 9,898 | 0.05 |
| Slovak (14,038) | 35,389 | 0.18 |
| Slovene (1,922) | 4,802 | 0.02 |
| Soviet Union (317) | 458 | <0.01 |
| Swedish (29,980) | 132,781 | 0.69 |
| Swiss (9,956) | 39,241 | 0.20 |
| Turkish (22,814) | 29,907 | 0.16 |
| Ukrainian (73,876) | 133,633 | 0.69 |
| Welsh (15,842) | 88,255 | 0.46 |
| West Indian, ex. Hispanic (665,395) | 790,170 | 4.11 |
| Bahamian (1,110) | 1,796 | 0.01 |
| Barbadian (22,928) | 27,200 | 0.14 |
| Belizean (5,612) | 7,037 | 0.04 |
| Bermudan (433) | 672 | <0.01 |
| British West Indian (42,984) | 49,916 | 0.26 |
| Dutch West Indian (1,177) | 1,887 | 0.01 |
| Haitian (164,815) | 179,024 | 0.93 |
| Jamaican (265,516) | 300,094 | 1.56 |
| Trinidadian/Tobagonian (76,788) | 89,490 | 0.47 |
| U.S. Virgin Islander (2,037) | 2,873 | 0.01 |
| West Indian (80,923) | 128,763 | 0.67 |
| Other West Indian (1,072) | 1,418 | 0.01 |
| Yugoslavian (20,521) | 28,253 | 0.15 |

| Hispanic Origin | Population | % |
|---|---|---|
| Hispanic or Latino (of any race) | 3,416,922 | 17.63 |
| Central American, ex. Mexican | 353,589 | 1.82 |
| Costa Rican | 11,576 | 0.06 |
| Guatemalan | 73,806 | 0.38 |
| Honduran | 71,919 | 0.37 |
| Nicaraguan | 13,006 | 0.07 |
| Panamanian | 28,200 | 0.15 |
| Salvadoran | 152,130 | 0.79 |
| Other Central American | 2,952 | 0.02 |
| Cuban | 70,803 | 0.37 |
| Dominican Republic | 674,787 | 3.48 |
| Mexican | 457,288 | 2.36 |
| Puerto Rican | 1,070,558 | 5.52 |
| South American | 513,417 | 2.65 |
| Argentinean | 24,969 | 0.13 |
| Bolivian | 7,122 | 0.04 |
| Chilean | 15,050 | 0.08 |
| Colombian | 141,879 | 0.73 |
| Ecuadorian | 228,216 | 1.18 |
| Paraguayan | 5,940 | 0.03 |
| Peruvian | 66,318 | 0.34 |
| Uruguayan | 6,021 | 0.03 |
| Venezuelan | 13,910 | 0.07 |
| Other South American | 3,992 | 0.02 |
| Other Hispanic or Latino | 276,480 | 1.43 |

| Race* | Population | % |
|---|---|---|
| African-American/Black (3,073,800) | 3,334,550 | 17.21 |
| Not Hispanic (2,783,857) | 2,946,880 | 15.21 |
| Hispanic (289,943) | 387,670 | 2.00 |
| American Indian/Alaska Native (106,906) | 221,058 | 1.14 |
| Not Hispanic (53,908) | 128,049 | 0.66 |
| Hispanic (52,998) | 93,009 | 0.48 |
| Alaska Athabascan (Ala. Nat.) (57) | 116 | <0.01 |
| Aleut (Alaska Native) (48) | 82 | <0.01 |
| Apache (337) | 1,080 | 0.01 |
| Arapaho (24) | 65 | <0.01 |
| Blackfeet (606) | 4,496 | 0.02 |
| Canadian/French Am. Ind. (530) | 1,022 | 0.01 |
| Central American Ind. (4,475) | 8,602 | 0.04 |
| Cherokee (2,714) | 16,947 | 0.09 |

| Race* (cont.) | Population | % |
|---|---|---|
| Cheyenne (47) | 163 | <0.01 |
| Chickasaw (68) | 215 | <0.01 |
| Chippewa (548) | 1,125 | 0.01 |
| Choctaw (263) | 1,052 | 0.01 |
| Colville (11) | 22 | <0.01 |
| Comanche (69) | 199 | <0.01 |
| Cree (50) | 263 | <0.01 |
| Creek (155) | 624 | <0.01 |
| Crow (52) | 181 | <0.01 |
| Delaware (598) | 1,384 | 0.01 |
| Hopi (39) | 115 | <0.01 |
| Houma (35) | 48 | <0.01 |
| Inupiat (Alaska Native) (91) | 169 | <0.01 |
| Iroquois (16,957) | 26,567 | 0.14 |
| Kiowa (24) | 44 | <0.01 |
| Lumbee (127) | 304 | <0.01 |
| Menominee (19) | 41 | <0.01 |
| Mexican American Ind. (5,344) | 7,439 | 0.04 |
| Navajo (347) | 788 | <0.01 |
| Osage (31) | 86 | <0.01 |
| Ottawa (24) | 52 | <0.01 |
| Paiute (25) | 49 | <0.01 |
| Pima (13) | 40 | <0.01 |
| Potawatomi (83) | 166 | <0.01 |
| Pueblo (556) | 1,096 | 0.01 |
| Puget Sound Salish (14) | 33 | <0.01 |
| Seminole (107) | 848 | <0.01 |
| Shoshone (22) | 96 | <0.01 |
| Sioux (628) | 1,758 | 0.01 |
| South American Ind. (6,294) | 13,078 | 0.07 |
| Spanish American Ind. (2,563) | 3,506 | 0.02 |
| Tlingit-Haida (Alaska Native) (60) | 169 | <0.01 |
| Tohono O'Odham (59) | 103 | <0.01 |
| Tsimshian (Alaska Native) (4) | 5 | <0.01 |
| Ute (13) | 36 | <0.01 |
| Yakama (8) | 18 | <0.01 |
| Yaqui (48) | 104 | <0.01 |
| Yuman (24) | 45 | <0.01 |
| Yup'ik (Alaska Native) (20) | 39 | <0.01 |
| Asian (1,420,244) | 1,579,494 | 8.15 |
| Not Hispanic (1,406,194) | 1,545,106 | 7.97 |
| Hispanic (14,050) | 34,388 | 0.18 |
| Bangladeshi (57,761) | 67,063 | 0.35 |
| Bhutanese (1,534) | 1,824 | 0.01 |
| Burmese (11,214) | 12,174 | 0.06 |
| Cambodian (4,212) | 5,114 | 0.03 |
| Chinese, ex. Taiwanese (559,516) | 598,597 | 3.09 |
| Filipino (104,287) | 126,129 | 0.65 |
| Hmong (227) | 296 | <0.01 |
| Indian (313,620) | 368,767 | 1.90 |
| Indonesian (4,568) | 6,122 | 0.03 |
| Japanese (37,780) | 51,781 | 0.27 |
| Korean (140,994) | 153,609 | 0.79 |
| Laotian (3,420) | 4,471 | 0.02 |
| Malaysian (2,537) | 3,908 | 0.02 |
| Nepalese (6,844) | 7,625 | 0.04 |
| Pakistani (63,696) | 70,622 | 0.36 |
| Sri Lankan (5,196) | 6,153 | 0.03 |
| Taiwanese (16,023) | 18,868 | 0.10 |
| Thai (9,258) | 11,763 | 0.06 |
| Vietnamese (28,764) | 34,510 | 0.18 |
| Hawaii Native/Pacific Islander (8,766) | 36,423 | 0.19 |
| Not Hispanic (5,320) | 21,768 | 0.11 |
| Hispanic (3,446) | 14,655 | 0.08 |
| Fijian (157) | 321 | <0.01 |
| Guamanian/Chamorro (2,235) | 3,407 | 0.02 |
| Marshallese (32) | 37 | <0.01 |
| Native Hawaiian (1,802) | 5,108 | 0.03 |
| Samoan (685) | 1,654 | 0.01 |
| Tongan (80) | 138 | <0.01 |
| White (12,740,974) | 13,155,274 | 67.89 |
| Not Hispanic (11,304,247) | 11,534,988 | 59.53 |
| Hispanic (1,436,727) | 1,620,286 | 8.36 |

Notes: † The Census 2010 population figure is used to calculate the percentages in the Hispanic Origin and Race categories. Ancestry percentages are based on the 2006-2010 American Community Survey population (not shown); ‡ Numbers in parentheses indicate the number of people reporting a single ancestry; * Numbers in parentheses indicate the number of persons reporting this race alone, not in combination with any other race; Please refer to the Explanation of Data for more information.

## County Profiles

### Albany County

Population: 304,204

| Ancestry | Population | % |
|---|---|---|
| Afghan (14) | 14 | <0.01 |
| African, Sub-Saharan (1,796) | 2,330 | 0.77 |
| African (1,075) | 1,506 | 0.50 |
| Cape Verdean (0) | 13 | <0.01 |
| Ethiopian (34) | 34 | 0.01 |
| Ghanaian (167) | 167 | 0.05 |
| Kenyan (101) | 101 | 0.03 |
| Liberian (0) | 0 | <0.01 |
| Nigerian (241) | 300 | 0.10 |
| Senegalese (0) | 0 | <0.01 |
| Sierra Leonean (0) | 0 | <0.01 |
| Somalian (0) | 0 | <0.01 |
| South African (9) | 32 | 0.01 |
| Sudanese (25) | 25 | 0.01 |
| Ugandan (0) | 0 | <0.01 |
| Zimbabwean (0) | 8 | <0.01 |
| Other Sub-Saharan African (144) | 144 | 0.05 |
| Albanian (934) | 1,000 | 0.33 |
| Alsatian (19) | 61 | 0.02 |
| American (8,399) | 8,399 | 2.76 |
| Arab (1,379) | 2,384 | 0.78 |
| Arab (329) | 357 | 0.12 |
| Egyptian (190) | 273 | 0.09 |
| Iraqi (0) | 0 | <0.01 |
| Jordanian (76) | 76 | 0.02 |
| Lebanese (222) | 571 | 0.19 |
| Moroccan (64) | 111 | 0.04 |
| Palestinian (207) | 312 | 0.10 |
| Syrian (102) | 451 | 0.15 |
| Other Arab (189) | 233 | 0.08 |
| Armenian (309) | 621 | 0.20 |
| Assyrian/Chaldean/Syriac (0) | 0 | <0.01 |
| Australian (68) | 126 | 0.04 |
| Austrian (202) | 1,353 | 0.45 |
| Basque (0) | 38 | 0.01 |
| Belgian (59) | 109 | 0.04 |
| Brazilian (195) | 249 | 0.08 |
| British (584) | 1,052 | 0.35 |
| Bulgarian (22) | 31 | 0.01 |
| Cajun (0) | 0 | <0.01 |
| Canadian (471) | 996 | 0.33 |
| Carpatho Rusyn (12) | 26 | 0.01 |
| Celtic (15) | 15 | <0.01 |
| Croatian (48) | 163 | 0.05 |
| Cypriot (0) | 0 | <0.01 |
| Czech (334) | 1,289 | 0.42 |
| Czechoslovakian (52) | 232 | 0.08 |
| Danish (187) | 869 | 0.29 |
| Dutch (1,770) | 11,451 | 3.77 |
| Eastern European (648) | 757 | 0.25 |
| English (5,861) | 28,025 | 9.22 |
| Estonian (0) | 0 | <0.01 |
| European (3,073) | 3,521 | 1.16 |
| Finnish (55) | 316 | 0.10 |
| French, ex. Basque (3,090) | 19,696 | 6.48 |
| French Canadian (2,042) | 5,377 | 1.77 |
| German (10,142) | 50,507 | 16.61 |
| German Russian (0) | 0 | <0.01 |
| Greek (1,010) | 2,365 | 0.78 |
| Guyanese (716) | 764 | 0.25 |
| Hungarian (553) | 2,084 | 0.69 |
| Icelander (10) | 10 | <0.01 |
| Iranian (186) | 219 | 0.07 |
| Irish (20,997) | 72,953 | 24.00 |
| Israeli (84) | 117 | 0.04 |
| Italian (20,747) | 52,353 | 17.22 |
| Latvian (111) | 198 | 0.07 |
| Lithuanian (160) | 1,067 | 0.35 |
| Luxemburger (9) | 22 | 0.01 |
| Macedonian (0) | 0 | <0.01 |
| Maltese (11) | 24 | 0.01 |
| New Zealander (0) | 0 | <0.01 |

| Ancestry | Population | % |
|---|---|---|
| Northern European (252) | 356 | 0.12 |
| Norwegian (574) | 1,786 | 0.59 |
| Pennsylvania German (52) | 88 | 0.03 |
| Polish (6,313) | 20,711 | 6.81 |
| Portuguese (208) | 613 | 0.20 |
| Romanian (81) | 470 | 0.15 |
| Russian (2,189) | 5,714 | 1.88 |
| Scandinavian (132) | 581 | 0.19 |
| Scotch-Irish (1,469) | 4,121 | 1.36 |
| Scottish (1,196) | 5,513 | 1.81 |
| Serbian (19) | 19 | 0.01 |
| Slavic (81) | 189 | 0.06 |
| Slovak (245) | 780 | 0.26 |
| Slovene (40) | 133 | 0.04 |
| Soviet Union (0) | 0 | <0.01 |
| Swedish (521) | 2,885 | 0.95 |
| Swiss (190) | 646 | 0.21 |
| Turkish (35) | 84 | 0.03 |
| Ukrainian (1,078) | 2,985 | 0.98 |
| Welsh (221) | 2,282 | 0.75 |
| West Indian, ex. Hispanic (3,212) | 4,660 | 1.53 |
| Bahamian (0) | 0 | <0.01 |
| Barbadian (14) | 45 | 0.01 |
| Belizean (0) | 0 | <0.01 |
| Bermudan (36) | 49 | 0.02 |
| British West Indian (133) | 210 | 0.07 |
| Dutch West Indian (39) | 90 | 0.03 |
| Haitian (669) | 825 | 0.27 |
| Jamaican (1,592) | 2,172 | 0.71 |
| Trinidadian/Tobagonian (215) | 329 | 0.11 |
| U.S. Virgin Islander (0) | 0 | <0.01 |
| West Indian (447) | 873 | 0.29 |
| Other West Indian (67) | 67 | 0.02 |
| Yugoslavian (245) | 282 | 0.09 |

| Hispanic Origin | Population | % |
|---|---|---|
| Hispanic or Latino (of any race) | 14,917 | 4.90 |
| Central American, ex. Mexican | 735 | 0.24 |
| Costa Rican | 84 | 0.03 |
| Guatemalan | 117 | 0.04 |
| Honduran | 114 | 0.04 |
| Nicaraguan | 57 | 0.02 |
| Panamanian | 137 | 0.05 |
| Salvadoran | 208 | 0.07 |
| Other Central American | 18 | 0.01 |
| Cuban | 548 | 0.18 |
| Dominican Republic | 1,622 | 0.53 |
| Mexican | 1,540 | 0.51 |
| Puerto Rican | 7,633 | 2.51 |
| South American | 1,278 | 0.42 |
| Argentinean | 119 | 0.04 |
| Bolivian | 25 | 0.01 |
| Chilean | 72 | 0.02 |
| Colombian | 431 | 0.14 |
| Ecuadorian | 256 | 0.08 |
| Paraguayan | 12 | <0.01 |
| Peruvian | 228 | 0.07 |
| Uruguayan | 21 | 0.01 |
| Venezuelan | 84 | 0.03 |
| Other South American | 30 | 0.01 |
| Other Hispanic or Latino | 1,561 | 0.51 |

| Race* | Population | % |
|---|---|---|
| African-American/Black (38,609) | 43,076 | 14.16 |
| Not Hispanic (36,396) | 40,017 | 13.15 |
| Hispanic (2,213) | 3,059 | 1.01 |
| American Indian/Alaska Native (654) | 2,326 | 0.76 |
| Not Hispanic (453) | 1,830 | 0.60 |
| Hispanic (201) | 496 | 0.16 |
| Alaska Athabascan (Ala. Nat.) (1) | 2 | <0.01 |
| Aleut (Alaska Native) (0) | 0 | <0.01 |
| Apache (1) | 13 | <0.01 |
| Arapaho (0) | 1 | <0.01 |
| Blackfeet (11) | 103 | 0.03 |
| Canadian/French Am. Ind. (11) | 23 | 0.01 |
| Central American Ind. (13) | 22 | 0.01 |

| Race* | Population | % |
|---|---|---|
| Cherokee (39) | 312 | 0.10 |
| Cheyenne (0) | 1 | <0.01 |
| Chickasaw (5) | 5 | <0.01 |
| Chippewa (2) | 6 | <0.01 |
| Choctaw (3) | 15 | <0.01 |
| Colville (0) | 0 | <0.01 |
| Comanche (0) | 5 | <0.01 |
| Cree (1) | 9 | <0.01 |
| Creek (0) | 7 | <0.01 |
| Crow (2) | 2 | <0.01 |
| Delaware (2) | 12 | <0.01 |
| Hopi (1) | 1 | <0.01 |
| Houma (0) | 0 | <0.01 |
| Inupiat (Alaska Native) (1) | 1 | <0.01 |
| Iroquois (80) | 278 | 0.09 |
| Kiowa (0) | 0 | <0.01 |
| Lumbee (0) | 0 | <0.01 |
| Menominee (0) | 0 | <0.01 |
| Mexican American Ind. (43) | 54 | 0.02 |
| Navajo (2) | 9 | <0.01 |
| Osage (0) | 1 | <0.01 |
| Ottawa (0) | 1 | <0.01 |
| Paiute (0) | 0 | <0.01 |
| Pima (0) | 0 | <0.01 |
| Potawatomi (1) | 3 | <0.01 |
| Pueblo (1) | 1 | <0.01 |
| Puget Sound Salish (0) | 0 | <0.01 |
| Seminole (4) | 17 | 0.01 |
| Shoshone (0) | 3 | <0.01 |
| Sioux (15) | 32 | 0.01 |
| South American Ind. (37) | 85 | 0.03 |
| Spanish American Ind. (8) | 14 | <0.01 |
| Tlingit-Haida (Alaska Native) (2) | 4 | <0.01 |
| Tohono O'Odham (0) | 0 | <0.01 |
| Tsimshian (Alaska Native) (0) | 0 | <0.01 |
| Ute (0) | 0 | <0.01 |
| Yakama (1) | 1 | <0.01 |
| Yaqui (0) | 0 | <0.01 |
| Yuman (0) | 0 | <0.01 |
| Yup'ik (Alaska Native) (2) | 2 | <0.01 |
| Asian (14,579) | 16,511 | 5.43 |
| Not Hispanic (14,500) | 16,300 | 5.36 |
| Hispanic (79) | 211 | 0.07 |
| Bangladeshi (273) | 305 | 0.10 |
| Bhutanese (62) | 62 | 0.02 |
| Burmese (313) | 342 | 0.11 |
| Cambodian (21) | 30 | 0.01 |
| Chinese, ex. Taiwanese (3,552) | 3,908 | 1.28 |
| Filipino (1,147) | 1,460 | 0.48 |
| Hmong (0) | 0 | <0.01 |
| Indian (4,600) | 5,085 | 1.67 |
| Indonesian (32) | 43 | 0.01 |
| Japanese (315) | 520 | 0.17 |
| Korean (1,329) | 1,531 | 0.50 |
| Laotian (5) | 14 | <0.01 |
| Malaysian (11) | 23 | 0.01 |
| Nepalese (70) | 78 | 0.03 |
| Pakistani (1,377) | 1,520 | 0.50 |
| Sri Lankan (68) | 75 | 0.02 |
| Taiwanese (160) | 189 | 0.06 |
| Thai (93) | 125 | 0.04 |
| Vietnamese (610) | 717 | 0.24 |
| Hawaii Native/Pacific Islander (98) | 333 | 0.11 |
| Not Hispanic (88) | 270 | 0.09 |
| Hispanic (10) | 63 | 0.02 |
| Fijian (3) | 4 | <0.01 |
| Guamanian/Chamorro (13) | 31 | 0.01 |
| Marshallese (0) | 0 | <0.01 |
| Native Hawaiian (16) | 71 | 0.02 |
| Samoan (16) | 29 | 0.01 |
| Tongan (1) | 6 | <0.01 |
| White (237,873) | 244,245 | 80.29 |
| Not Hispanic (231,152) | 236,400 | 77.71 |
| Hispanic (6,721) | 7,845 | 2.58 |

Notes: † The Census 2010 population figure is used to calculate the percentages in the Hispanic Origin and Race categories. Ancestry percentages are based on the 2006-2010 American Community Survey population (not shown); ‡ Numbers in parentheses indicate the number of people reporting a single ancestry; * Numbers in parentheses indicate the number of persons reporting this race alone, not in combination with any other race; Please refer to the Explanation of Data for more information.

## Allegany County
Population: 48,946

| Ancestry | Population | % |
|---|---|---|
| Afghan (0) | 0 | <0.01 |
| African, Sub-Saharan (22) | 37 | 0.08 |
| African (0) | 15 | 0.03 |
| Cape Verdean (0) | 0 | <0.01 |
| Ethiopian (0) | 0 | <0.01 |
| Ghanaian (0) | 0 | <0.01 |
| Kenyan (22) | 22 | 0.04 |
| Liberian (0) | 0 | <0.01 |
| Nigerian (0) | 0 | <0.01 |
| Senegalese (0) | 0 | <0.01 |
| Sierra Leonean (0) | 0 | <0.01 |
| Somalian (0) | 0 | <0.01 |
| South African (0) | 0 | <0.01 |
| Sudanese (0) | 0 | <0.01 |
| Ugandan (0) | 0 | <0.01 |
| Zimbabwean (0) | 0 | <0.01 |
| Other Sub-Saharan African (0) | 0 | <0.01 |
| Albanian (0) | 0 | <0.01 |
| Alsatian (4) | 4 | 0.01 |
| American (2,579) | 2,579 | 5.25 |
| Arab (59) | 104 | 0.21 |
| Arab (0) | 0 | <0.01 |
| Egyptian (2) | 2 | <0.01 |
| Iraqi (0) | 0 | <0.01 |
| Jordanian (0) | 0 | <0.01 |
| Lebanese (54) | 83 | 0.17 |
| Moroccan (0) | 0 | <0.01 |
| Palestinian (0) | 0 | <0.01 |
| Syrian (0) | 13 | 0.03 |
| Other Arab (3) | 6 | 0.01 |
| Armenian (3) | 3 | 0.01 |
| Assyrian/Chaldean/Syriac (0) | 0 | <0.01 |
| Australian (0) | 4 | 0.01 |
| Austrian (16) | 132 | 0.27 |
| Basque (0) | 0 | <0.01 |
| Belgian (8) | 15 | 0.03 |
| Brazilian (0) | 10 | 0.02 |
| British (101) | 249 | 0.51 |
| Bulgarian (0) | 0 | <0.01 |
| Cajun (0) | 2 | <0.01 |
| Canadian (23) | 135 | 0.27 |
| Carpatho Rusyn (0) | 0 | <0.01 |
| Celtic (19) | 19 | 0.04 |
| Croatian (0) | 39 | 0.08 |
| Cypriot (0) | 0 | <0.01 |
| Czech (34) | 138 | 0.28 |
| Czechoslovakian (34) | 63 | 0.13 |
| Danish (18) | 87 | 0.18 |
| Dutch (292) | 1,775 | 3.61 |
| Eastern European (8) | 8 | 0.02 |
| English (3,179) | 8,971 | 18.27 |
| Estonian (0) | 0 | <0.01 |
| European (191) | 255 | 0.52 |
| Finnish (0) | 59 | 0.12 |
| French, ex. Basque (258) | 1,883 | 3.83 |
| French Canadian (212) | 508 | 1.03 |
| German (3,788) | 14,728 | 29.99 |
| German Russian (0) | 0 | <0.01 |
| Greek (29) | 74 | 0.15 |
| Guyanese (0) | 18 | 0.04 |
| Hungarian (71) | 224 | 0.46 |
| Icelander (0) | 0 | <0.01 |
| Iranian (0) | 0 | <0.01 |
| Irish (2,480) | 9,350 | 19.04 |
| Israeli (0) | 9 | 0.02 |
| Italian (1,381) | 3,451 | 7.03 |
| Latvian (0) | 0 | <0.01 |
| Lithuanian (42) | 108 | 0.22 |
| Luxemburger (0) | 0 | <0.01 |
| Macedonian (0) | 0 | <0.01 |
| Maltese (12) | 27 | 0.05 |
| New Zealander (0) | 0 | <0.01 |
| Northern European (23) | 23 | 0.05 |
| Norwegian (64) | 214 | 0.44 |
| Pennsylvania German (320) | 409 | 0.83 |

| Ancestry | Population | % |
|---|---|---|
| Polish (892) | 2,591 | 5.28 |
| Portuguese (0) | 38 | 0.08 |
| Romanian (11) | 45 | 0.09 |
| Russian (48) | 234 | 0.48 |
| Scandinavian (29) | 69 | 0.14 |
| Scotch-Irish (332) | 1,044 | 2.13 |
| Scottish (411) | 1,397 | 2.84 |
| Serbian (0) | 6 | 0.01 |
| Slavic (8) | 87 | 0.18 |
| Slovak (7) | 41 | 0.08 |
| Slovene (20) | 30 | 0.06 |
| Soviet Union (0) | 0 | <0.01 |
| Swedish (178) | 789 | 1.61 |
| Swiss (55) | 225 | 0.46 |
| Turkish (0) | 0 | <0.01 |
| Ukrainian (49) | 123 | 0.25 |
| Welsh (116) | 581 | 1.18 |
| West Indian, ex. Hispanic (26) | 68 | 0.14 |
| Bahamian (0) | 0 | <0.01 |
| Barbadian (0) | 0 | <0.01 |
| Belizean (0) | 0 | <0.01 |
| Bermudan (0) | 0 | <0.01 |
| British West Indian (7) | 19 | 0.04 |
| Dutch West Indian (0) | 0 | <0.01 |
| Haitian (0) | 12 | 0.02 |
| Jamaican (0) | 12 | 0.02 |
| Trinidadian/Tobagonian (14) | 20 | 0.04 |
| U.S. Virgin Islander (0) | 0 | <0.01 |
| West Indian (5) | 5 | 0.01 |
| Other West Indian (0) | 0 | <0.01 |
| Yugoslavian (0) | 7 | 0.01 |

| Hispanic Origin | Population | % |
|---|---|---|
| Hispanic or Latino (of any race) | 670 | 1.37 |
| Central American, ex. Mexican | 47 | 0.10 |
| Costa Rican | 1 | <0.01 |
| Guatemalan | 15 | 0.03 |
| Honduran | 5 | 0.01 |
| Nicaraguan | 4 | 0.01 |
| Panamanian | 8 | 0.02 |
| Salvadoran | 14 | 0.03 |
| Other Central American | 0 | <0.01 |
| Cuban | 17 | 0.03 |
| Dominican Republic | 58 | 0.12 |
| Mexican | 182 | 0.37 |
| Puerto Rican | 203 | 0.41 |
| South American | 78 | 0.16 |
| Argentinean | 1 | <0.01 |
| Bolivian | 6 | 0.01 |
| Chilean | 5 | 0.01 |
| Colombian | 28 | 0.06 |
| Ecuadorian | 13 | 0.03 |
| Paraguayan | 1 | <0.01 |
| Peruvian | 13 | 0.03 |
| Uruguayan | 0 | <0.01 |
| Venezuelan | 4 | 0.01 |
| Other South American | 7 | 0.01 |
| Other Hispanic or Latino | 85 | 0.17 |

| Race* | Population | % |
|---|---|---|
| African-American/Black (524) | 732 | 1.50 |
| Not Hispanic (494) | 677 | 1.38 |
| Hispanic (30) | 55 | 0.11 |
| American Indian/Alaska Native (113) | 332 | 0.68 |
| Not Hispanic (97) | 295 | 0.60 |
| Hispanic (16) | 37 | 0.08 |
| Alaska Athabascan (Ala. Nat.) (0) | 0 | <0.01 |
| Aleut (Alaska Native) (0) | 0 | <0.01 |
| Apache (2) | 5 | 0.01 |
| Arapaho (0) | 0 | <0.01 |
| Blackfeet (0) | 7 | 0.01 |
| Canadian/French Am. Ind. (2) | 3 | 0.01 |
| Central American Ind. (0) | 0 | <0.01 |
| Cherokee (11) | 32 | 0.07 |
| Cheyenne (0) | 0 | <0.01 |
| Chickasaw (0) | 0 | <0.01 |
| Chippewa (2) | 4 | 0.01 |
| Choctaw (0) | 3 | 0.01 |
| Colville (0) | 0 | <0.01 |

| Race* | Population | % |
|---|---|---|
| Comanche (0) | 0 | <0.01 |
| Cree (0) | 0 | <0.01 |
| Creek (1) | 1 | <0.01 |
| Crow (1) | 2 | <0.01 |
| Delaware (0) | 3 | 0.01 |
| Hopi (0) | 0 | <0.01 |
| Houma (1) | 1 | <0.01 |
| Inupiat (Alaska Native) (0) | 0 | <0.01 |
| Iroquois (38) | 84 | 0.17 |
| Kiowa (0) | 0 | <0.01 |
| Lumbee (1) | 1 | <0.01 |
| Menominee (1) | 1 | <0.01 |
| Mexican American Ind. (2) | 3 | 0.01 |
| Navajo (0) | 3 | 0.01 |
| Osage (0) | 0 | <0.01 |
| Ottawa (0) | 0 | <0.01 |
| Paiute (0) | 0 | <0.01 |
| Pima (0) | 0 | <0.01 |
| Potawatomi (0) | 0 | <0.01 |
| Pueblo (0) | 0 | <0.01 |
| Puget Sound Salish (0) | 0 | <0.01 |
| Seminole (0) | 0 | <0.01 |
| Shoshone (0) | 0 | <0.01 |
| Sioux (0) | 1 | <0.01 |
| South American Ind. (2) | 7 | 0.01 |
| Spanish American Ind. (0) | 0 | <0.01 |
| Tlingit-Haida (Alaska Native) (0) | 0 | <0.01 |
| Tohono O'Odham (0) | 0 | <0.01 |
| Tsimshian (Alaska Native) (0) | 0 | <0.01 |
| Ute (0) | 0 | <0.01 |
| Yakama (0) | 0 | <0.01 |
| Yaqui (0) | 0 | <0.01 |
| Yuman (0) | 0 | <0.01 |
| Yup'ik (Alaska Native) (0) | 0 | <0.01 |
| Asian (452) | 603 | 1.23 |
| Not Hispanic (451) | 591 | 1.21 |
| Hispanic (1) | 12 | 0.02 |
| Bangladeshi (0) | 0 | <0.01 |
| Bhutanese (0) | 0 | <0.01 |
| Burmese (0) | 0 | <0.01 |
| Cambodian (2) | 3 | 0.01 |
| Chinese, ex. Taiwanese (172) | 205 | 0.42 |
| Filipino (22) | 58 | 0.12 |
| Hmong (0) | 0 | <0.01 |
| Indian (52) | 71 | 0.15 |
| Indonesian (3) | 3 | 0.01 |
| Japanese (59) | 88 | 0.18 |
| Korean (82) | 111 | 0.23 |
| Laotian (3) | 3 | 0.01 |
| Malaysian (0) | 0 | <0.01 |
| Nepalese (0) | 0 | <0.01 |
| Pakistani (3) | 3 | 0.01 |
| Sri Lankan (3) | 3 | 0.01 |
| Taiwanese (9) | 11 | 0.02 |
| Thai (12) | 12 | 0.02 |
| Vietnamese (12) | 22 | 0.04 |
| Hawaii Native/Pacific Islander (9) | 20 | 0.04 |
| Not Hispanic (7) | 16 | 0.03 |
| Hispanic (2) | 4 | 0.01 |
| Fijian (0) | 0 | <0.01 |
| Guamanian/Chamorro (1) | 2 | <0.01 |
| Marshallese (0) | 0 | <0.01 |
| Native Hawaiian (7) | 15 | 0.03 |
| Samoan (1) | 4 | 0.01 |
| Tongan (0) | 0 | <0.01 |
| White (47,085) | 47,605 | 97.26 |
| Not Hispanic (46,701) | 47,175 | 96.38 |
| Hispanic (384) | 430 | 0.88 |

*Notes: † The Census 2010 population figure is used to calculate the percentages in the Hispanic Origin and Race categories. Ancestry percentages are based on the 2006-2010 American Community Survey population (not shown); ‡ Numbers in parentheses indicate the number of people reporting a single ancestry; * Numbers in parentheses indicate the number of persons reporting this race alone, not in combination with any other race; Please refer to the Explanation of Data for more information.*

## Bronx County

Population: 1,385,108

| Ancestry | Population | % |
|---|---|---|
| Afghan (14) | 14 | <0.01 |
| African, Sub-Saharan (50,131) | 55,928 | 4.10 |
| African (19,345) | 22,647 | 1.66 |
| Cape Verdean (49) | 108 | 0.01 |
| Ethiopian (790) | 945 | 0.07 |
| Ghanaian (13,163) | 13,490 | 0.99 |
| Kenyan (12) | 24 | <0.01 |
| Liberian (365) | 450 | 0.03 |
| Nigerian (4,896) | 5,538 | 0.41 |
| Senegalese (956) | 1,068 | 0.08 |
| Sierra Leonean (759) | 759 | 0.06 |
| Somalian (11) | 35 | <0.01 |
| South African (29) | 68 | <0.01 |
| Sudanese (88) | 149 | 0.01 |
| Ugandan (0) | 0 | <0.01 |
| Zimbabwean (108) | 108 | 0.01 |
| Other Sub-Saharan African (9,560) | 10,539 | 0.77 |
| Albanian (7,460) | 7,835 | 0.57 |
| Alsatian (0) | 0 | <0.01 |
| American (16,297) | 16,297 | 1.19 |
| Arab (4,063) | 5,008 | 0.37 |
| Arab (1,481) | 1,719 | 0.13 |
| Egyptian (495) | 718 | 0.05 |
| Iraqi (64) | 73 | 0.01 |
| Jordanian (8) | 8 | <0.01 |
| Lebanese (229) | 347 | 0.03 |
| Moroccan (526) | 667 | 0.05 |
| Palestinian (28) | 28 | <0.01 |
| Syrian (44) | 192 | 0.01 |
| Other Arab (1,188) | 1,256 | 0.09 |
| Armenian (128) | 237 | 0.02 |
| Assyrian/Chaldean/Syriac (0) | 18 | <0.01 |
| Australian (8) | 21 | <0.01 |
| Austrian (539) | 1,868 | 0.14 |
| Basque (66) | 109 | 0.01 |
| Belgian (52) | 131 | 0.01 |
| Brazilian (276) | 397 | 0.03 |
| British (517) | 1,115 | 0.08 |
| Bulgarian (506) | 521 | 0.04 |
| Cajun (0) | 0 | <0.01 |
| Canadian (197) | 375 | 0.03 |
| Carpatho Rusyn (0) | 12 | <0.01 |
| Celtic (1) | 13 | <0.01 |
| Croatian (91) | 219 | 0.02 |
| Cypriot (12) | 38 | <0.01 |
| Czech (99) | 388 | 0.03 |
| Czechoslovakian (90) | 226 | 0.02 |
| Danish (17) | 385 | 0.03 |
| Dutch (314) | 1,920 | 0.14 |
| Eastern European (1,425) | 1,646 | 0.12 |
| English (1,821) | 7,038 | 0.52 |
| Estonian (70) | 85 | 0.01 |
| European (1,845) | 2,270 | 0.17 |
| Finnish (89) | 291 | 0.02 |
| French, ex. Basque (909) | 4,971 | 0.36 |
| French Canadian (102) | 403 | 0.03 |
| German (3,729) | 16,487 | 1.21 |
| German Russian (7) | 30 | <0.01 |
| Greek (2,499) | 3,607 | 0.26 |
| Guyanese (10,276) | 11,837 | 0.87 |
| Hungarian (966) | 2,427 | 0.18 |
| Icelander (6) | 6 | <0.01 |
| Iranian (187) | 248 | 0.02 |
| Irish (18,712) | 38,479 | 2.82 |
| Israeli (427) | 618 | 0.05 |
| Italian (38,592) | 57,527 | 4.21 |
| Latvian (92) | 103 | 0.01 |
| Lithuanian (167) | 547 | 0.04 |
| Luxemburger (0) | 0 | <0.01 |
| Macedonian (628) | 628 | 0.05 |
| Maltese (16) | 45 | <0.01 |
| New Zealander (23) | 23 | <0.01 |
| Northern European (25) | 25 | <0.01 |
| Norwegian (260) | 773 | 0.06 |
| Pennsylvania German (0) | 0 | <0.01 |

| Ancestry | Population | % |
|---|---|---|
| Polish (3,429) | 7,834 | 0.57 |
| Portuguese (474) | 1,113 | 0.08 |
| Romanian (691) | 1,164 | 0.09 |
| Russian (4,351) | 8,064 | 0.59 |
| Scandinavian (102) | 155 | 0.01 |
| Scotch-Irish (516) | 1,601 | 0.12 |
| Scottish (388) | 1,570 | 0.11 |
| Serbian (154) | 187 | 0.01 |
| Slavic (15) | 90 | 0.01 |
| Slovak (87) | 226 | 0.02 |
| Slovene (10) | 45 | <0.01 |
| Soviet Union (12) | 12 | <0.01 |
| Swedish (119) | 549 | 0.04 |
| Swiss (24) | 166 | 0.01 |
| Turkish (589) | 686 | 0.05 |
| Ukrainian (970) | 1,608 | 0.12 |
| Welsh (101) | 530 | 0.04 |
| West Indian, ex. Hispanic (93,323) | 107,527 | 7.87 |
| Bahamian (165) | 208 | 0.02 |
| Barbadian (1,285) | 1,612 | 0.12 |
| Belizean (1,253) | 1,493 | 0.11 |
| Bermudan (101) | 198 | 0.01 |
| British West Indian (5,959) | 7,136 | 0.52 |
| Dutch West Indian (127) | 172 | 0.01 |
| Haitian (3,891) | 4,652 | 0.34 |
| Jamaican (58,387) | 64,222 | 4.70 |
| Trinidadian/Tobagonian (3,695) | 4,811 | 0.35 |
| U.S. Virgin Islander (737) | 952 | 0.07 |
| West Indian (17,683) | 21,941 | 1.61 |
| Other West Indian (40) | 130 | 0.01 |
| Yugoslavian (1,275) | 1,480 | 0.11 |

| Hispanic Origin | Population | % |
|---|---|---|
| Hispanic or Latino (of any race) | 741,413 | 53.53 |
| Central American, ex. Mexican | 34,492 | 2.49 |
| Costa Rican | 1,095 | 0.08 |
| Guatemalan | 4,645 | 0.34 |
| Honduran | 17,990 | 1.30 |
| Nicaraguan | 2,342 | 0.17 |
| Panamanian | 2,372 | 0.17 |
| Salvadoran | 5,469 | 0.39 |
| Other Central American | 579 | 0.04 |
| Cuban | 8,785 | 0.63 |
| Dominican Republic | 240,987 | 17.40 |
| Mexican | 71,194 | 5.14 |
| Puerto Rican | 298,921 | 21.58 |
| South American | 35,463 | 2.56 |
| Argentinean | 1,117 | 0.08 |
| Bolivian | 227 | 0.02 |
| Chilean | 646 | 0.05 |
| Colombian | 4,635 | 0.33 |
| Ecuadorian | 23,206 | 1.68 |
| Paraguayan | 223 | 0.02 |
| Peruvian | 3,596 | 0.26 |
| Uruguayan | 148 | 0.01 |
| Venezuelan | 1,296 | 0.09 |
| Other South American | 369 | 0.03 |
| Other Hispanic or Latino | 51,571 | 3.72 |

| Race* | Population | % |
|---|---|---|
| African-American/Black (505,200) | 541,622 | 39.10 |
| Not Hispanic (416,695) | 427,134 | 30.84 |
| Hispanic (88,505) | 114,488 | 8.27 |
| American Indian/Alaska Native (18,260) | 32,011 | 2.31 |
| Not Hispanic (3,460) | 7,638 | 0.55 |
| Hispanic (14,800) | 24,373 | 1.76 |
| Alaska Athabascan (Ala. Nat.) (4) | 8 | <0.01 |
| Aleut (Alaska Native) (0) | 3 | <0.01 |
| Apache (30) | 99 | 0.01 |
| Arapaho (2) | 3 | <0.01 |
| Blackfeet (43) | 310 | 0.02 |
| Canadian/French Am. Ind. (13) | 25 | <0.01 |
| Central American Ind. (2,274) | 4,520 | 0.33 |
| Cherokee (247) | 1,312 | 0.09 |
| Cheyenne (2) | 5 | <0.01 |
| Chickasaw (6) | 16 | <0.01 |
| Chippewa (25) | 38 | <0.01 |
| Choctaw (4) | 43 | <0.01 |
| Colville (0) | 2 | <0.01 |

| | Population | % |
|---|---|---|
| Comanche (8) | 26 | <0.01 |
| Cree (1) | 16 | <0.01 |
| Creek (7) | 47 | <0.01 |
| Crow (1) | 16 | <0.01 |
| Delaware (1) | 10 | <0.01 |
| Hopi (0) | 2 | <0.01 |
| Houma (12) | 12 | <0.01 |
| Inupiat (Alaska Native) (11) | 15 | <0.01 |
| Iroquois (81) | 170 | 0.01 |
| Kiowa (1) | 1 | <0.01 |
| Lumbee (3) | 6 | <0.01 |
| Menominee (1) | 3 | <0.01 |
| Mexican American Ind. (714) | 963 | 0.07 |
| Navajo (24) | 42 | <0.01 |
| Osage (2) | 3 | <0.01 |
| Ottawa (0) | 1 | <0.01 |
| Paiute (0) | 5 | <0.01 |
| Pima (0) | 1 | <0.01 |
| Potawatomi (1) | 2 | <0.01 |
| Pueblo (177) | 382 | 0.03 |
| Puget Sound Salish (0) | 0 | <0.01 |
| Seminole (6) | 50 | <0.01 |
| Shoshone (0) | 8 | <0.01 |
| Sioux (46) | 82 | 0.01 |
| South American Ind. (1,568) | 2,938 | 0.21 |
| Spanish American Ind. (709) | 992 | 0.07 |
| Tlingit-Haida (Alaska Native) (1) | 11 | <0.01 |
| Tohono O'Odham (4) | 9 | <0.01 |
| Tsimshian (Alaska Native) (0) | 0 | <0.01 |
| Ute (2) | 5 | <0.01 |
| Yakama (3) | 3 | <0.01 |
| Yaqui (4) | 5 | <0.01 |
| Yuman (2) | 2 | <0.01 |
| Yup'ik (Alaska Native) (1) | 6 | <0.01 |
| Asian (49,609) | 59,085 | 4.27 |
| Not Hispanic (47,335) | 53,458 | 3.86 |
| Hispanic (2,274) | 5,627 | 0.41 |
| Bangladeshi (7,323) | 8,623 | 0.62 |
| Bhutanese (74) | 104 | 0.01 |
| Burmese (71) | 81 | 0.01 |
| Cambodian (1,055) | 1,188 | 0.09 |
| Chinese, ex. Taiwanese (6,644) | 8,112 | 0.59 |
| Filipino (5,576) | 6,456 | 0.47 |
| Hmong (1) | 3 | <0.01 |
| Indian (15,865) | 20,357 | 1.47 |
| Indonesian (50) | 96 | 0.01 |
| Japanese (562) | 1,027 | 0.07 |
| Korean (2,840) | 3,101 | 0.22 |
| Laotian (99) | 148 | 0.01 |
| Malaysian (11) | 30 | <0.01 |
| Nepalese (129) | 159 | 0.01 |
| Pakistani (2,399) | 2,728 | 0.20 |
| Sri Lankan (174) | 234 | 0.02 |
| Taiwanese (98) | 130 | 0.01 |
| Thai (326) | 414 | 0.03 |
| Vietnamese (3,215) | 3,526 | 0.25 |
| Hawaii Native/Pacific Islander (1,288) | 6,213 | 0.45 |
| Not Hispanic (398) | 1,854 | 0.13 |
| Hispanic (890) | 4,359 | 0.31 |
| Fijian (13) | 13 | <0.01 |
| Guamanian/Chamorro (251) | 376 | 0.03 |
| Marshallese (3) | 3 | <0.01 |
| Native Hawaiian (371) | 669 | 0.05 |
| Samoan (70) | 160 | 0.01 |
| Tongan (5) | 7 | <0.01 |
| White (386,497) | 427,659 | 30.88 |
| Not Hispanic (151,209) | 158,245 | 11.42 |
| Hispanic (235,288) | 269,414 | 19.45 |

*Notes: † The Census 2010 population figure is used to calculate the percentages in the Hispanic Origin and Race categories. Ancestry percentages are based on the 2006-2010 American Community Survey population (not shown); ‡ Numbers in parentheses indicate the number of people reporting a single ancestry; * Numbers in parentheses indicate the number of persons reporting this race alone, not in combination with any other race; Please refer to the Explanation of Data for more information.*

## Broome County

Population: 200,600

| Ancestry | Population | % |
|---|---|---|
| Afghan (0) | 0 | <0.01 |
| African, Sub-Saharan (397) | 646 | 0.32 |
| African (262) | 488 | 0.24 |
| Cape Verdean (11) | 11 | 0.01 |
| Ethiopian (0) | 0 | <0.01 |
| Ghanaian (43) | 43 | 0.02 |
| Kenyan (6) | 6 | <0.01 |
| Liberian (0) | 0 | <0.01 |
| Nigerian (17) | 17 | 0.01 |
| Senegalese (0) | 0 | <0.01 |
| Sierra Leonean (0) | 0 | <0.01 |
| Somalian (0) | 0 | <0.01 |
| South African (9) | 32 | 0.02 |
| Sudanese (0) | 0 | <0.01 |
| Ugandan (0) | 0 | <0.01 |
| Zimbabwean (0) | 0 | <0.01 |
| Other Sub-Saharan African (49) | 49 | 0.02 |
| Albanian (13) | 20 | 0.01 |
| Alsatian (0) | 13 | 0.01 |
| American (8,398) | 8,398 | 4.18 |
| Arab (1,042) | 1,422 | 0.71 |
| Arab (115) | 132 | 0.07 |
| Egyptian (106) | 155 | 0.08 |
| Iraqi (6) | 6 | <0.01 |
| Jordanian (12) | 12 | 0.01 |
| Lebanese (255) | 459 | 0.23 |
| Moroccan (0) | 8 | <0.01 |
| Palestinian (13) | 25 | 0.01 |
| Syrian (19) | 20 | 0.01 |
| Other Arab (516) | 605 | 0.30 |
| Armenian (139) | 329 | 0.16 |
| Assyrian/Chaldean/Syriac (0) | 0 | <0.01 |
| Australian (39) | 39 | 0.02 |
| Austrian (155) | 882 | 0.44 |
| Basque (0) | 0 | <0.01 |
| Belgian (15) | 133 | 0.07 |
| Brazilian (13) | 13 | 0.01 |
| British (355) | 1,018 | 0.51 |
| Bulgarian (62) | 62 | 0.03 |
| Cajun (3) | 12 | 0.01 |
| Canadian (134) | 338 | 0.17 |
| Carpatho Rusyn (64) | 126 | 0.06 |
| Celtic (30) | 67 | 0.03 |
| Croatian (21) | 68 | 0.03 |
| Cypriot (0) | 0 | <0.01 |
| Czech (788) | 2,348 | 1.17 |
| Czechoslovakian (509) | 872 | 0.43 |
| Danish (163) | 449 | 0.22 |
| Dutch (1,265) | 6,844 | 3.41 |
| Eastern European (314) | 386 | 0.19 |
| English (7,900) | 26,062 | 12.98 |
| Estonian (21) | 42 | 0.02 |
| European (1,586) | 1,795 | 0.89 |
| Finnish (10) | 181 | 0.09 |
| French, ex. Basque (644) | 6,871 | 3.42 |
| French Canadian (488) | 1,377 | 0.69 |
| German (9,379) | 36,306 | 18.08 |
| German Russian (0) | 0 | <0.01 |
| Greek (606) | 1,245 | 0.62 |
| Guyanese (171) | 251 | 0.12 |
| Hungarian (238) | 903 | 0.45 |
| Icelander (46) | 46 | 0.02 |
| Iranian (36) | 70 | 0.03 |
| Irish (12,853) | 43,809 | 21.82 |
| Israeli (0) | 26 | 0.01 |
| Italian (10,921) | 27,706 | 13.80 |
| Latvian (35) | 125 | 0.06 |
| Lithuanian (314) | 1,211 | 0.60 |
| Luxemburger (0) | 0 | <0.01 |
| Macedonian (55) | 55 | 0.03 |
| Maltese (0) | 24 | 0.01 |
| New Zealander (0) | 0 | <0.01 |
| Northern European (59) | 59 | 0.03 |
| Norwegian (303) | 987 | 0.49 |
| Pennsylvania German (541) | 938 | 0.47 |
| Polish (4,815) | 14,217 | 7.08 |
| Portuguese (77) | 128 | 0.06 |
| Romanian (214) | 387 | 0.19 |
| Russian (1,876) | 5,545 | 2.76 |
| Scandinavian (32) | 187 | 0.09 |
| Scotch-Irish (1,024) | 2,833 | 1.41 |
| Scottish (1,085) | 4,355 | 2.17 |
| Serbian (10) | 65 | 0.03 |
| Slavic (439) | 618 | 0.31 |
| Slovak (2,653) | 6,570 | 3.27 |
| Slovene (51) | 137 | 0.07 |
| Soviet Union (0) | 0 | <0.01 |
| Swedish (473) | 1,729 | 0.86 |
| Swiss (119) | 522 | 0.26 |
| Turkish (189) | 212 | 0.11 |
| Ukrainian (1,127) | 2,148 | 1.07 |
| Welsh (762) | 4,482 | 2.23 |
| West Indian, ex. Hispanic (716) | 973 | 0.48 |
| Bahamian (0) | 0 | <0.01 |
| Barbadian (0) | 0 | <0.01 |
| Belizean (5) | 5 | <0.01 |
| Bermudan (0) | 0 | <0.01 |
| British West Indian (29) | 55 | 0.03 |
| Dutch West Indian (0) | 0 | <0.01 |
| Haitian (210) | 222 | 0.11 |
| Jamaican (338) | 478 | 0.24 |
| Trinidadian/Tobagonian (54) | 54 | 0.03 |
| U.S. Virgin Islander (0) | 0 | <0.01 |
| West Indian (80) | 159 | 0.08 |
| Other West Indian (0) | 0 | <0.01 |
| Yugoslavian (273) | 310 | 0.15 |

| Hispanic Origin | Population | % |
|---|---|---|
| Hispanic or Latino (of any race) | 6,778 | 3.38 |
| Central American, ex. Mexican | 420 | 0.21 |
| Costa Rican | 44 | 0.02 |
| Guatemalan | 112 | 0.06 |
| Honduran | 87 | 0.04 |
| Nicaraguan | 31 | 0.02 |
| Panamanian | 65 | 0.03 |
| Salvadoran | 81 | 0.04 |
| Other Central American | 0 | <0.01 |
| Cuban | 322 | 0.16 |
| Dominican Republic | 505 | 0.25 |
| Mexican | 765 | 0.38 |
| Puerto Rican | 3,442 | 1.72 |
| South American | 606 | 0.30 |
| Argentinean | 92 | 0.05 |
| Bolivian | 14 | 0.01 |
| Chilean | 45 | 0.02 |
| Colombian | 181 | 0.09 |
| Ecuadorian | 128 | 0.06 |
| Paraguayan | 5 | <0.01 |
| Peruvian | 94 | 0.05 |
| Uruguayan | 9 | <0.01 |
| Venezuelan | 33 | 0.02 |
| Other South American | 5 | <0.01 |
| Other Hispanic or Latino | 718 | 0.36 |

| Race* | Population | % |
|---|---|---|
| African-American/Black (9,614) | 12,499 | 6.23 |
| Not Hispanic (8,850) | 11,278 | 5.62 |
| Hispanic (764) | 1,221 | 0.61 |
| American Indian/Alaska Native (396) | 1,664 | 0.83 |
| Not Hispanic (328) | 1,445 | 0.72 |
| Hispanic (68) | 219 | 0.11 |
| Alaska Athabascan (Ala. Nat.) (1) | 4 | <0.01 |
| Aleut (Alaska Native) (0) | 0 | <0.01 |
| Apache (7) | 34 | 0.02 |
| Arapaho (0) | 0 | <0.01 |
| Blackfeet (8) | 75 | 0.04 |
| Canadian/French Am. Ind. (4) | 10 | <0.01 |
| Central American Ind. (1) | 1 | <0.01 |
| Cherokee (37) | 248 | 0.12 |
| Cheyenne (0) | 0 | <0.01 |
| Chickasaw (0) | 1 | <0.01 |
| Chippewa (7) | 15 | 0.01 |
| Choctaw (3) | 14 | 0.01 |
| Colville (0) | 1 | <0.01 |

| | | |
|---|---|---|
| Comanche (0) | 3 | <0.01 |
| Cree (2) | 6 | <0.01 |
| Creek (2) | 7 | <0.01 |
| Crow (0) | 5 | <0.01 |
| Delaware (2) | 29 | 0.01 |
| Hopi (0) | 0 | <0.01 |
| Houma (0) | 1 | <0.01 |
| Inupiat (Alaska Native) (0) | 0 | <0.01 |
| Iroquois (74) | 254 | 0.13 |
| Kiowa (0) | 1 | <0.01 |
| Lumbee (0) | 1 | <0.01 |
| Menominee (0) | 0 | <0.01 |
| Mexican American Ind. (7) | 21 | 0.01 |
| Navajo (0) | 11 | 0.01 |
| Osage (0) | 1 | <0.01 |
| Ottawa (0) | 0 | <0.01 |
| Paiute (0) | 2 | <0.01 |
| Pima (0) | 1 | <0.01 |
| Potawatomi (1) | 3 | <0.01 |
| Pueblo (0) | 2 | <0.01 |
| Puget Sound Salish (0) | 0 | <0.01 |
| Seminole (0) | 5 | <0.01 |
| Shoshone (0) | 0 | <0.01 |
| Sioux (12) | 39 | 0.02 |
| South American Ind. (15) | 31 | 0.02 |
| Spanish American Ind. (4) | 5 | <0.01 |
| Tlingit-Haida (Alaska Native) (0) | 0 | <0.01 |
| Tohono O'Odham (0) | 0 | <0.01 |
| Tsimshian (Alaska Native) (0) | 0 | <0.01 |
| Ute (0) | 0 | <0.01 |
| Yakama (0) | 0 | <0.01 |
| Yaqui (2) | 2 | <0.01 |
| Yuman (0) | 0 | <0.01 |
| Yup'ik (Alaska Native) (0) | 0 | <0.01 |
| Asian (7,065) | 8,193 | 4.08 |
| Not Hispanic (7,019) | 8,072 | 4.02 |
| Hispanic (46) | 121 | 0.06 |
| Bangladeshi (56) | 67 | 0.03 |
| Bhutanese (0) | 0 | <0.01 |
| Burmese (12) | 14 | 0.01 |
| Cambodian (9) | 16 | 0.01 |
| Chinese, ex. Taiwanese (2,135) | 2,397 | 1.19 |
| Filipino (329) | 515 | 0.26 |
| Hmong (0) | 0 | <0.01 |
| Indian (1,487) | 1,683 | 0.84 |
| Indonesian (24) | 34 | 0.02 |
| Japanese (127) | 227 | 0.11 |
| Korean (980) | 1,117 | 0.56 |
| Laotian (541) | 667 | 0.33 |
| Malaysian (8) | 17 | 0.01 |
| Nepalese (15) | 18 | 0.01 |
| Pakistani (233) | 241 | 0.12 |
| Sri Lankan (14) | 22 | 0.01 |
| Taiwanese (82) | 103 | 0.05 |
| Thai (42) | 69 | 0.03 |
| Vietnamese (716) | 838 | 0.42 |
| Hawaii Native/Pacific Islander (82) | 243 | 0.12 |
| Not Hispanic (60) | 191 | 0.10 |
| Hispanic (22) | 52 | 0.03 |
| Fijian (0) | 3 | <0.01 |
| Guamanian/Chamorro (25) | 43 | 0.02 |
| Marshallese (0) | 0 | <0.01 |
| Native Hawaiian (16) | 48 | 0.02 |
| Samoan (6) | 12 | 0.01 |
| Tongan (1) | 1 | <0.01 |
| White (176,444) | 181,009 | 90.23 |
| Not Hispanic (173,074) | 176,969 | 88.22 |
| Hispanic (3,370) | 4,040 | 2.01 |

Notes: † The Census 2010 population figure is used to calculate the percentages in the Hispanic Origin and Race categories. Ancestry percentages are based on the 2006-2010 American Community Survey population (not shown); ‡ Numbers in parentheses indicate the number of people reporting a single ancestry; * Numbers in parentheses indicate the number of persons reporting this race alone, not in combination with any other race; Please refer to the Explanation of Data for more information.

## Cattaraugus County

Population: 80,317

| Ancestry | Population | % |
|---|---|---|
| Afghan (0) | 0 | <0.01 |
| African, Sub-Saharan (11) | 52 | 0.06 |
| African (11) | 52 | 0.06 |
| Cape Verdean (0) | 0 | <0.01 |
| Ethiopian (0) | 0 | <0.01 |
| Ghanaian (0) | 0 | <0.01 |
| Kenyan (0) | 0 | <0.01 |
| Liberian (0) | 0 | <0.01 |
| Nigerian (0) | 0 | <0.01 |
| Senegalese (0) | 0 | <0.01 |
| Sierra Leonean (0) | 0 | <0.01 |
| Somalian (0) | 0 | <0.01 |
| South African (0) | 0 | <0.01 |
| Sudanese (0) | 0 | <0.01 |
| Ugandan (0) | 0 | <0.01 |
| Zimbabwean (0) | 0 | <0.01 |
| Other Sub-Saharan African (0) | 0 | <0.01 |
| Albanian (0) | 0 | <0.01 |
| Alsatian (0) | 7 | 0.01 |
| American (3,710) | 3,710 | 4.59 |
| Arab (161) | 452 | 0.56 |
| Arab (23) | 23 | 0.03 |
| Egyptian (0) | 0 | <0.01 |
| Iraqi (0) | 0 | <0.01 |
| Jordanian (0) | 0 | <0.01 |
| Lebanese (138) | 429 | 0.53 |
| Moroccan (0) | 0 | <0.01 |
| Palestinian (0) | 0 | <0.01 |
| Syrian (0) | 0 | <0.01 |
| Other Arab (0) | 0 | <0.01 |
| Armenian (2) | 6 | 0.01 |
| Assyrian/Chaldean/Syriac (0) | 0 | <0.01 |
| Australian (0) | 0 | <0.01 |
| Austrian (28) | 215 | 0.27 |
| Basque (0) | 4 | <0.01 |
| Belgian (51) | 95 | 0.12 |
| Brazilian (6) | 6 | 0.01 |
| British (90) | 213 | 0.26 |
| Bulgarian (3) | 13 | 0.02 |
| Cajun (0) | 0 | <0.01 |
| Canadian (99) | 253 | 0.31 |
| Carpatho Rusyn (0) | 5 | 0.01 |
| Celtic (0) | 0 | <0.01 |
| Croatian (39) | 61 | 0.08 |
| Cypriot (0) | 0 | <0.01 |
| Czech (29) | 225 | 0.28 |
| Czechoslovakian (59) | 251 | 0.31 |
| Danish (37) | 157 | 0.19 |
| Dutch (265) | 2,195 | 2.72 |
| Eastern European (51) | 51 | 0.06 |
| English (2,780) | 10,168 | 12.59 |
| Estonian (3) | 3 | <0.01 |
| European (246) | 375 | 0.46 |
| Finnish (9) | 40 | 0.05 |
| French, ex. Basque (257) | 2,353 | 2.91 |
| French Canadian (241) | 614 | 0.76 |
| German (8,573) | 25,659 | 31.77 |
| German Russian (0) | 0 | <0.01 |
| Greek (60) | 178 | 0.22 |
| Guyanese (0) | 13 | 0.02 |
| Hungarian (111) | 421 | 0.52 |
| Icelander (0) | 0 | <0.01 |
| Iranian (0) | 0 | <0.01 |
| Irish (4,105) | 16,140 | 19.98 |
| Israeli (6) | 6 | 0.01 |
| Italian (3,226) | 8,276 | 10.25 |
| Latvian (0) | 0 | <0.01 |
| Lithuanian (44) | 117 | 0.14 |
| Luxemburger (0) | 4 | <0.01 |
| Macedonian (8) | 26 | 0.03 |
| Maltese (0) | 0 | <0.01 |
| New Zealander (0) | 0 | <0.01 |
| Northern European (107) | 107 | 0.13 |
| Norwegian (102) | 302 | 0.37 |
| Pennsylvania German (745) | 922 | 1.14 |

| Ancestry | Population | % |
|---|---|---|
| Polish (3,395) | 9,202 | 11.39 |
| Portuguese (24) | 72 | 0.09 |
| Romanian (38) | 88 | 0.11 |
| Russian (56) | 311 | 0.39 |
| Scandinavian (44) | 87 | 0.11 |
| Scotch-Irish (498) | 1,255 | 1.55 |
| Scottish (474) | 1,632 | 2.02 |
| Serbian (6) | 22 | 0.03 |
| Slavic (10) | 78 | 0.10 |
| Slovak (22) | 62 | 0.08 |
| Slovene (80) | 102 | 0.13 |
| Soviet Union (0) | 0 | <0.01 |
| Swedish (581) | 2,178 | 2.70 |
| Swiss (52) | 379 | 0.47 |
| Turkish (0) | 8 | 0.01 |
| Ukrainian (51) | 270 | 0.33 |
| Welsh (171) | 821 | 1.02 |
| West Indian, ex. Hispanic (45) | 73 | 0.09 |
| Bahamian (0) | 0 | <0.01 |
| Barbadian (0) | 0 | <0.01 |
| Belizean (0) | 0 | <0.01 |
| Bermudan (0) | 0 | <0.01 |
| British West Indian (0) | 0 | <0.01 |
| Dutch West Indian (0) | 0 | <0.01 |
| Haitian (11) | 11 | 0.01 |
| Jamaican (11) | 17 | 0.02 |
| Trinidadian/Tobagonian (0) | 0 | <0.01 |
| U.S. Virgin Islander (0) | 0 | <0.01 |
| West Indian (23) | 45 | 0.06 |
| Other West Indian (0) | 0 | <0.01 |
| Yugoslavian (37) | 56 | 0.07 |

| Hispanic Origin | Population | % |
|---|---|---|
| Hispanic or Latino (of any race) | 1,345 | 1.67 |
| Central American, ex. Mexican | 44 | 0.05 |
| Costa Rican | 3 | <0.01 |
| Guatemalan | 12 | 0.01 |
| Honduran | 9 | 0.01 |
| Nicaraguan | 2 | <0.01 |
| Panamanian | 5 | 0.01 |
| Salvadoran | 13 | 0.02 |
| Other Central American | 0 | <0.01 |
| Cuban | 37 | 0.05 |
| Dominican Republic | 30 | 0.04 |
| Mexican | 308 | 0.38 |
| Puerto Rican | 690 | 0.86 |
| South American | 70 | 0.09 |
| Argentinean | 8 | 0.01 |
| Bolivian | 2 | <0.01 |
| Chilean | 5 | 0.01 |
| Colombian | 21 | 0.03 |
| Ecuadorian | 12 | 0.01 |
| Paraguayan | 0 | <0.01 |
| Peruvian | 9 | 0.01 |
| Uruguayan | 1 | <0.01 |
| Venezuelan | 12 | 0.01 |
| Other South American | 0 | <0.01 |
| Other Hispanic or Latino | 166 | 0.21 |

| Race* | Population | % |
|---|---|---|
| African-American/Black (1,024) | 1,619 | 2.02 |
| Not Hispanic (966) | 1,519 | 1.89 |
| Hispanic (58) | 100 | 0.12 |
| American Indian/Alaska Native (2,443) | 3,079 | 3.83 |
| Not Hispanic (2,361) | 2,945 | 3.67 |
| Hispanic (82) | 134 | 0.17 |
| Alaska Athabascan (Ala. Nat.) (10) | 15 | 0.02 |
| Aleut (Alaska Native) (1) | 1 | <0.01 |
| Apache (1) | 4 | <0.01 |
| Arapaho (0) | 1 | <0.01 |
| Blackfeet (4) | 17 | 0.02 |
| Canadian/French Am. Ind. (9) | 15 | 0.02 |
| Central American Ind. (7) | 7 | 0.01 |
| Cherokee (17) | 46 | 0.06 |
| Cheyenne (1) | 5 | 0.01 |
| Chickasaw (0) | 0 | <0.01 |
| Chippewa (5) | 11 | 0.01 |
| Choctaw (3) | 4 | <0.01 |
| Colville (0) | 0 | <0.01 |

| Race* | Population | % |
|---|---|---|
| Comanche (0) | 0 | <0.01 |
| Cree (0) | 0 | <0.01 |
| Creek (7) | 7 | 0.01 |
| Crow (3) | 4 | <0.01 |
| Delaware (8) | 10 | 0.01 |
| Hopi (0) | 0 | <0.01 |
| Houma (0) | 0 | <0.01 |
| Inupiat (Alaska Native) (1) | 1 | <0.01 |
| Iroquois (1,961) | 2,291 | 2.85 |
| Kiowa (2) | 2 | <0.01 |
| Lumbee (4) | 7 | 0.01 |
| Menominee (2) | 2 | <0.01 |
| Mexican American Ind. (2) | 3 | <0.01 |
| Navajo (4) | 6 | 0.01 |
| Osage (0) | 0 | <0.01 |
| Ottawa (0) | 0 | <0.01 |
| Paiute (6) | 9 | 0.01 |
| Pima (0) | 0 | <0.01 |
| Potawatomi (0) | 0 | <0.01 |
| Pueblo (0) | 0 | <0.01 |
| Puget Sound Salish (0) | 0 | <0.01 |
| Seminole (0) | 5 | 0.01 |
| Shoshone (2) | 2 | <0.01 |
| Sioux (19) | 25 | 0.03 |
| South American Ind. (12) | 14 | 0.02 |
| Spanish American Ind. (0) | 0 | <0.01 |
| Tlingit-Haida (Alaska Native) (0) | 0 | <0.01 |
| Tohono O'Odham (1) | 1 | <0.01 |
| Tsimshian (Alaska Native) (0) | 0 | <0.01 |
| Ute (0) | 0 | <0.01 |
| Yakama (0) | 0 | <0.01 |
| Yaqui (1) | 1 | <0.01 |
| Yuman (0) | 0 | <0.01 |
| Yup'ik (Alaska Native) (0) | 0 | <0.01 |
| Asian (528) | 688 | 0.86 |
| Not Hispanic (524) | 675 | 0.84 |
| Hispanic (4) | 13 | 0.02 |
| Bangladeshi (1) | 1 | <0.01 |
| Bhutanese (0) | 0 | <0.01 |
| Burmese (0) | 0 | <0.01 |
| Cambodian (2) | 4 | <0.01 |
| Chinese, ex. Taiwanese (109) | 138 | 0.17 |
| Filipino (61) | 92 | 0.11 |
| Hmong (0) | 0 | <0.01 |
| Indian (171) | 205 | 0.26 |
| Indonesian (0) | 5 | 0.01 |
| Japanese (23) | 46 | 0.06 |
| Korean (42) | 61 | 0.08 |
| Laotian (13) | 21 | 0.03 |
| Malaysian (2) | 2 | <0.01 |
| Nepalese (4) | 4 | <0.01 |
| Pakistani (50) | 50 | 0.06 |
| Sri Lankan (8) | 8 | 0.01 |
| Taiwanese (2) | 2 | <0.01 |
| Thai (3) | 8 | 0.01 |
| Vietnamese (27) | 31 | 0.04 |
| Hawaii Native/Pacific Islander (15) | 36 | 0.04 |
| Not Hispanic (14) | 35 | 0.04 |
| Hispanic (1) | 1 | <0.01 |
| Fijian (0) | 5 | 0.01 |
| Guamanian/Chamorro (0) | 0 | <0.01 |
| Marshallese (0) | 0 | <0.01 |
| Native Hawaiian (7) | 18 | 0.02 |
| Samoan (0) | 1 | <0.01 |
| Tongan (0) | 0 | <0.01 |
| White (74,639) | 75,918 | 94.52 |
| Not Hispanic (73,849) | 75,003 | 93.38 |
| Hispanic (790) | 915 | 1.14 |

Notes: † The Census 2010 population figure is used to calculate the percentages in the Hispanic Origin and Race categories. Ancestry percentages are based on the 2006-2010 American Community Survey population (not shown); ‡ Numbers in parentheses indicate the number of people reporting a single ancestry; * Numbers in parentheses indicate the number of persons reporting this race alone, not in combination with any other race; Please refer to the Explanation of Data for more information.

## Cayuga County

Population: 80,026

| Ancestry | Population | % |
|---|---:|---:|
| Afghan (0) | 0 | <0.01 |
| African, Sub-Saharan (110) | 224 | 0.28 |
| African (110) | 206 | 0.26 |
| Cape Verdean (0) | 0 | <0.01 |
| Ethiopian (0) | 0 | <0.01 |
| Ghanaian (0) | 0 | <0.01 |
| Kenyan (0) | 0 | <0.01 |
| Liberian (0) | 0 | <0.01 |
| Nigerian (0) | 0 | <0.01 |
| Senegalese (0) | 0 | <0.01 |
| Sierra Leonean (0) | 0 | <0.01 |
| Somalian (0) | 0 | <0.01 |
| South African (0) | 0 | <0.01 |
| Sudanese (0) | 0 | <0.01 |
| Ugandan (0) | 0 | <0.01 |
| Zimbabwean (0) | 0 | <0.01 |
| Other Sub-Saharan African (0) | 18 | 0.02 |
| Albanian (36) | 36 | 0.04 |
| Alsatian (0) | 7 | 0.01 |
| American (3,805) | 3,805 | 4.73 |
| Arab (39) | 115 | 0.14 |
| Arab (2) | 5 | 0.01 |
| Egyptian (0) | 0 | <0.01 |
| Iraqi (0) | 0 | <0.01 |
| Jordanian (0) | 0 | <0.01 |
| Lebanese (20) | 65 | 0.08 |
| Moroccan (0) | 0 | <0.01 |
| Palestinian (0) | 0 | <0.01 |
| Syrian (7) | 35 | 0.04 |
| Other Arab (10) | 10 | 0.01 |
| Armenian (0) | 11 | 0.01 |
| Assyrian/Chaldean/Syriac (0) | 0 | <0.01 |
| Australian (0) | 10 | 0.01 |
| Austrian (57) | 197 | 0.24 |
| Basque (0) | 0 | <0.01 |
| Belgian (2) | 41 | 0.05 |
| Brazilian (37) | 40 | 0.05 |
| British (120) | 275 | 0.34 |
| Bulgarian (0) | 0 | <0.01 |
| Cajun (0) | 0 | <0.01 |
| Canadian (92) | 175 | 0.22 |
| Carpatho Rusyn (0) | 0 | <0.01 |
| Celtic (6) | 6 | 0.01 |
| Croatian (0) | 0 | <0.01 |
| Cypriot (0) | 0 | <0.01 |
| Czech (49) | 207 | 0.26 |
| Czechoslovakian (72) | 117 | 0.15 |
| Danish (65) | 201 | 0.25 |
| Dutch (736) | 3,758 | 4.67 |
| Eastern European (24) | 26 | 0.03 |
| English (4,214) | 14,572 | 18.12 |
| Estonian (0) | 0 | <0.01 |
| European (439) | 513 | 0.64 |
| Finnish (25) | 62 | 0.08 |
| French, ex. Basque (604) | 3,973 | 4.94 |
| French Canadian (555) | 1,669 | 2.08 |
| German (3,317) | 14,518 | 18.05 |
| German Russian (0) | 0 | <0.01 |
| Greek (39) | 204 | 0.25 |
| Guyanese (20) | 20 | 0.02 |
| Hungarian (39) | 187 | 0.23 |
| Icelander (0) | 3 | <0.01 |
| Iranian (0) | 0 | <0.01 |
| Irish (5,999) | 19,589 | 24.36 |
| Israeli (0) | 0 | <0.01 |
| Italian (4,906) | 11,827 | 14.70 |
| Latvian (3) | 6 | 0.01 |
| Lithuanian (30) | 71 | 0.09 |
| Luxemburger (0) | 0 | <0.01 |
| Macedonian (0) | 0 | <0.01 |
| Maltese (0) | 0 | <0.01 |
| New Zealander (0) | 0 | <0.01 |
| Northern European (42) | 42 | 0.05 |
| Norwegian (86) | 467 | 0.58 |
| Pennsylvania German (77) | 112 | 0.14 |
| Polish (1,970) | 5,462 | 6.79 |
| Portuguese (8) | 74 | 0.09 |
| Romanian (0) | 37 | 0.05 |
| Russian (179) | 482 | 0.60 |
| Scandinavian (30) | 50 | 0.06 |
| Scotch-Irish (477) | 1,048 | 1.30 |
| Scottish (433) | 1,739 | 2.16 |
| Serbian (0) | 4 | <0.01 |
| Slavic (37) | 37 | 0.05 |
| Slovak (8) | 120 | 0.15 |
| Slovene (0) | 0 | <0.01 |
| Soviet Union (0) | 0 | <0.01 |
| Swedish (100) | 712 | 0.89 |
| Swiss (53) | 429 | 0.53 |
| Turkish (0) | 20 | 0.02 |
| Ukrainian (910) | 2,400 | 2.98 |
| Welsh (214) | 839 | 1.04 |
| West Indian, ex. Hispanic (140) | 413 | 0.51 |
| Bahamian (0) | 0 | <0.01 |
| Barbadian (0) | 8 | 0.01 |
| Belizean (0) | 0 | <0.01 |
| Bermudan (0) | 0 | <0.01 |
| British West Indian (0) | 1 | <0.01 |
| Dutch West Indian (8) | 8 | 0.01 |
| Haitian (26) | 38 | 0.05 |
| Jamaican (37) | 118 | 0.15 |
| Trinidadian/Tobagonian (34) | 45 | 0.06 |
| U.S. Virgin Islander (0) | 0 | <0.01 |
| West Indian (35) | 195 | 0.24 |
| Other West Indian (0) | 0 | <0.01 |
| Yugoslavian (13) | 18 | 0.02 |

| Hispanic Origin | Population | % |
|---|---:|---:|
| Hispanic or Latino (of any race) | 1,896 | 2.37 |
| Central American, ex. Mexican | 331 | 0.41 |
| Costa Rican | 6 | 0.01 |
| Guatemalan | 249 | 0.31 |
| Honduran | 17 | 0.02 |
| Nicaraguan | 12 | 0.01 |
| Panamanian | 36 | 0.04 |
| Salvadoran | 10 | 0.01 |
| Other Central American | 1 | <0.01 |
| Cuban | 75 | 0.09 |
| Dominican Republic | 87 | 0.11 |
| Mexican | 340 | 0.42 |
| Puerto Rican | 799 | 1.00 |
| South American | 85 | 0.11 |
| Argentinean | 2 | <0.01 |
| Bolivian | 2 | <0.01 |
| Chilean | 6 | 0.01 |
| Colombian | 29 | 0.04 |
| Ecuadorian | 23 | 0.03 |
| Paraguayan | 1 | <0.01 |
| Peruvian | 10 | 0.01 |
| Uruguayan | 1 | <0.01 |
| Venezuelan | 9 | 0.01 |
| Other South American | 2 | <0.01 |
| Other Hispanic or Latino | 179 | 0.22 |

| Race* | Population | % |
|---|---:|---:|
| African-American/Black (3,195) | 4,052 | 5.06 |
| Not Hispanic (3,009) | 3,782 | 4.73 |
| Hispanic (186) | 270 | 0.34 |
| American Indian/Alaska Native (283) | 703 | 0.88 |
| Not Hispanic (252) | 636 | 0.79 |
| Hispanic (31) | 67 | 0.08 |
| Alaska Athabascan (Ala. Nat.) (0) | 0 | <0.01 |
| Aleut (Alaska Native) (1) | 1 | <0.01 |
| Apache (2) | 8 | 0.01 |
| Arapaho (0) | 1 | <0.01 |
| Blackfeet (2) | 21 | 0.03 |
| Canadian/French Am. Ind. (5) | 6 | 0.01 |
| Central American Ind. (1) | 3 | <0.01 |
| Cherokee (13) | 62 | 0.08 |
| Cheyenne (0) | 1 | <0.01 |
| Chickasaw (0) | 0 | <0.01 |
| Chippewa (3) | 13 | 0.02 |
| Choctaw (9) | 11 | 0.01 |
| Colville (0) | 0 | <0.01 |

| | Population | % |
|---|---:|---:|
| Comanche (0) | 3 | <0.01 |
| Cree (0) | 0 | <0.01 |
| Creek (1) | 1 | <0.01 |
| Crow (0) | 1 | <0.01 |
| Delaware (0) | 0 | <0.01 |
| Hopi (0) | 0 | <0.01 |
| Houma (0) | 0 | <0.01 |
| Inupiat (Alaska Native) (0) | 0 | <0.01 |
| Iroquois (107) | 224 | 0.28 |
| Kiowa (0) | 0 | <0.01 |
| Lumbee (5) | 5 | 0.01 |
| Menominee (0) | 0 | <0.01 |
| Mexican American Ind. (8) | 15 | 0.02 |
| Navajo (4) | 5 | 0.01 |
| Osage (0) | 3 | <0.01 |
| Ottawa (5) | 5 | 0.01 |
| Paiute (0) | 0 | <0.01 |
| Pima (0) | 0 | <0.01 |
| Potawatomi (0) | 0 | <0.01 |
| Pueblo (2) | 2 | <0.01 |
| Puget Sound Salish (0) | 0 | <0.01 |
| Seminole (0) | 0 | <0.01 |
| Shoshone (0) | 0 | <0.01 |
| Sioux (6) | 13 | 0.02 |
| South American Ind. (1) | 7 | 0.01 |
| Spanish American Ind. (1) | 1 | <0.01 |
| Tlingit-Haida (Alaska Native) (0) | 0 | <0.01 |
| Tohono O'Odham (0) | 0 | <0.01 |
| Tsimshian (Alaska Native) (0) | 0 | <0.01 |
| Ute (0) | 0 | <0.01 |
| Yakama (0) | 0 | <0.01 |
| Yaqui (0) | 0 | <0.01 |
| Yuman (0) | 0 | <0.01 |
| Yup'ik (Alaska Native) (0) | 0 | <0.01 |
| Asian (390) | 544 | 0.68 |
| Not Hispanic (387) | 531 | 0.66 |
| Hispanic (3) | 13 | 0.02 |
| Bangladeshi (0) | 0 | <0.01 |
| Bhutanese (0) | 0 | <0.01 |
| Burmese (10) | 10 | 0.01 |
| Cambodian (3) | 4 | <0.01 |
| Chinese, ex. Taiwanese (87) | 99 | 0.12 |
| Filipino (55) | 98 | 0.12 |
| Hmong (0) | 0 | <0.01 |
| Indian (70) | 92 | 0.11 |
| Indonesian (1) | 1 | <0.01 |
| Japanese (18) | 42 | 0.05 |
| Korean (51) | 64 | 0.08 |
| Laotian (14) | 15 | 0.02 |
| Malaysian (0) | 0 | <0.01 |
| Nepalese (0) | 0 | <0.01 |
| Pakistani (13) | 13 | 0.01 |
| Sri Lankan (0) | 0 | <0.01 |
| Taiwanese (1) | 2 | <0.01 |
| Thai (13) | 20 | 0.02 |
| Vietnamese (29) | 59 | 0.07 |
| Hawaii Native/Pacific Islander (31) | 67 | 0.08 |
| Not Hispanic (26) | 53 | 0.07 |
| Hispanic (5) | 14 | 0.02 |
| Fijian (1) | 1 | <0.01 |
| Guamanian/Chamorro (8) | 10 | 0.01 |
| Marshallese (0) | 0 | <0.01 |
| Native Hawaiian (10) | 22 | 0.03 |
| Samoan (11) | 21 | 0.03 |
| Tongan (0) | 0 | <0.01 |
| White (74,042) | 75,378 | 94.19 |
| Not Hispanic (73,098) | 74,281 | 92.82 |
| Hispanic (944) | 1,097 | 1.37 |

Notes: † The Census 2010 population figure is used to calculate the percentages in the Hispanic Origin and Race categories. Ancestry percentages are based on the 2006-2010 American Community Survey population (not shown); ‡ Numbers in parentheses indicate the number of people reporting a single ancestry; * Numbers in parentheses indicate the number of persons reporting this race alone, not in combination with any other race; Please refer to the Explanation of Data for more information.

## Chautauqua County

Population: 134,905

| Ancestry | Population | % |
|---|---|---|
| Afghan (0) | 0 | <0.01 |
| African, Sub-Saharan (28) | 147 | 0.11 |
| African (13) | 129 | 0.10 |
| Cape Verdean (0) | 0 | <0.01 |
| Ethiopian (0) | 0 | <0.01 |
| Ghanaian (0) | 0 | <0.01 |
| Kenyan (0) | 0 | <0.01 |
| Liberian (0) | 0 | <0.01 |
| Nigerian (8) | 11 | 0.01 |
| Senegalese (0) | 0 | <0.01 |
| Sierra Leonean (0) | 0 | <0.01 |
| Somalian (0) | 0 | <0.01 |
| South African (0) | 0 | <0.01 |
| Sudanese (7) | 7 | 0.01 |
| Ugandan (0) | 0 | <0.01 |
| Zimbabwean (0) | 0 | <0.01 |
| Other Sub-Saharan African (0) | 0 | <0.01 |
| Albanian (107) | 158 | 0.12 |
| Alsatian (0) | 0 | <0.01 |
| American (4,291) | 4,291 | 3.17 |
| Arab (100) | 450 | 0.33 |
| Arab (0) | 44 | 0.03 |
| Egyptian (11) | 36 | 0.03 |
| Iraqi (0) | 0 | <0.01 |
| Jordanian (0) | 0 | <0.01 |
| Lebanese (55) | 212 | 0.16 |
| Moroccan (0) | 0 | <0.01 |
| Palestinian (7) | 23 | 0.02 |
| Syrian (27) | 135 | 0.10 |
| Other Arab (0) | 0 | <0.01 |
| Armenian (23) | 32 | 0.02 |
| Assyrian/Chaldean/Syriac (0) | 0 | <0.01 |
| Australian (0) | 3 | <0.01 |
| Austrian (62) | 422 | 0.31 |
| Basque (0) | 0 | <0.01 |
| Belgian (33) | 45 | 0.03 |
| Brazilian (19) | 28 | 0.02 |
| British (140) | 373 | 0.28 |
| Bulgarian (13) | 13 | 0.01 |
| Cajun (0) | 0 | <0.01 |
| Canadian (98) | 277 | 0.20 |
| Carpatho Rusyn (0) | 0 | <0.01 |
| Celtic (0) | 31 | 0.02 |
| Croatian (97) | 210 | 0.16 |
| Cypriot (0) | 0 | <0.01 |
| Czech (88) | 400 | 0.30 |
| Czechoslovakian (43) | 151 | 0.11 |
| Danish (203) | 649 | 0.48 |
| Dutch (960) | 4,144 | 3.06 |
| Eastern European (31) | 31 | 0.02 |
| English (6,689) | 21,635 | 15.99 |
| Estonian (3) | 3 | <0.01 |
| European (588) | 620 | 0.46 |
| Finnish (16) | 163 | 0.12 |
| French, ex. Basque (460) | 3,331 | 2.46 |
| French Canadian (337) | 870 | 0.64 |
| German (10,307) | 33,780 | 24.97 |
| German Russian (0) | 0 | <0.01 |
| Greek (75) | 159 | 0.12 |
| Guyanese (0) | 0 | <0.01 |
| Hungarian (273) | 948 | 0.70 |
| Icelander (0) | 0 | <0.01 |
| Iranian (4) | 4 | <0.01 |
| Irish (5,085) | 20,147 | 14.89 |
| Israeli (0) | 16 | 0.01 |
| Italian (9,579) | 21,679 | 16.03 |
| Latvian (5) | 21 | 0.02 |
| Lithuanian (11) | 59 | 0.04 |
| Luxemburger (0) | 0 | <0.01 |
| Macedonian (50) | 50 | 0.04 |
| Maltese (0) | 0 | <0.01 |
| New Zealander (0) | 6 | <0.01 |
| Northern European (72) | 80 | 0.06 |
| Norwegian (298) | 684 | 0.51 |
| Pennsylvania German (636) | 967 | 0.71 |
| Polish (5,698) | 14,377 | 10.63 |
| Portuguese (0) | 28 | 0.02 |
| Romanian (1) | 88 | 0.07 |
| Russian (127) | 667 | 0.49 |
| Scandinavian (88) | 145 | 0.11 |
| Scotch-Irish (567) | 2,235 | 1.65 |
| Scottish (497) | 2,598 | 1.92 |
| Serbian (0) | 0 | <0.01 |
| Slavic (95) | 169 | 0.12 |
| Slovak (110) | 254 | 0.19 |
| Slovene (10) | 38 | 0.03 |
| Soviet Union (0) | 0 | <0.01 |
| Swedish (6,798) | 17,330 | 12.81 |
| Swiss (191) | 536 | 0.40 |
| Turkish (0) | 5 | <0.01 |
| Ukrainian (171) | 372 | 0.28 |
| Welsh (176) | 1,038 | 0.77 |
| West Indian, ex. Hispanic (99) | 225 | 0.17 |
| Bahamian (0) | 0 | <0.01 |
| Barbadian (0) | 3 | <0.01 |
| Belizean (0) | 6 | <0.01 |
| Bermudan (0) | 0 | <0.01 |
| British West Indian (3) | 3 | <0.01 |
| Dutch West Indian (0) | 3 | <0.01 |
| Haitian (36) | 67 | 0.05 |
| Jamaican (12) | 85 | 0.06 |
| Trinidadian/Tobagonian (23) | 31 | 0.02 |
| U.S. Virgin Islander (0) | 0 | <0.01 |
| West Indian (25) | 27 | 0.02 |
| Other West Indian (0) | 0 | <0.01 |
| Yugoslavian (28) | 79 | 0.06 |

| Hispanic Origin | Population | % |
|---|---|---|
| Hispanic or Latino (of any race) | 8,241 | 6.11 |
| Central American, ex. Mexican | 148 | 0.11 |
| Costa Rican | 14 | 0.01 |
| Guatemalan | 56 | 0.04 |
| Honduran | 20 | 0.01 |
| Nicaraguan | 7 | 0.01 |
| Panamanian | 7 | 0.01 |
| Salvadoran | 44 | 0.03 |
| Other Central American | 0 | <0.01 |
| Cuban | 101 | 0.07 |
| Dominican Republic | 167 | 0.12 |
| Mexican | 851 | 0.63 |
| Puerto Rican | 6,401 | 4.74 |
| South American | 180 | 0.13 |
| Argentinean | 26 | 0.02 |
| Bolivian | 5 | <0.01 |
| Chilean | 5 | <0.01 |
| Colombian | 70 | 0.05 |
| Ecuadorian | 30 | 0.02 |
| Paraguayan | 1 | <0.01 |
| Peruvian | 22 | 0.02 |
| Uruguayan | 3 | <0.01 |
| Venezuelan | 18 | 0.01 |
| Other South American | 0 | <0.01 |
| Other Hispanic or Latino | 393 | 0.29 |

| Race* | Population | % |
|---|---|---|
| African-American/Black (3,197) | 4,710 | 3.49 |
| Not Hispanic (2,763) | 4,006 | 2.97 |
| Hispanic (434) | 704 | 0.52 |
| American Indian/Alaska Native (689) | 1,462 | 1.08 |
| Not Hispanic (576) | 1,258 | 0.93 |
| Hispanic (113) | 204 | 0.15 |
| Alaska Athabascan (Ala. Nat.) (1) | 1 | <0.01 |
| Aleut (Alaska Native) (0) | 0 | <0.01 |
| Apache (0) | 2 | <0.01 |
| Arapaho (1) | 1 | <0.01 |
| Blackfeet (7) | 46 | 0.03 |
| Canadian/French Am. Ind. (4) | 9 | <0.01 |
| Central American Ind. (1) | 1 | <0.01 |
| Cherokee (26) | 116 | 0.09 |
| Cheyenne (0) | 2 | <0.01 |
| Chickasaw (0) | 0 | <0.01 |
| Chippewa (5) | 20 | 0.01 |
| Choctaw (1) | 1 | <0.01 |
| Colville (0) | 0 | <0.01 |
| Comanche (0) | 0 | <0.01 |
| Cree (0) | 0 | <0.01 |
| Creek (2) | 2 | <0.01 |
| Crow (1) | 1 | <0.01 |
| Delaware (4) | 5 | <0.01 |
| Hopi (0) | 0 | <0.01 |
| Houma (1) | 1 | <0.01 |
| Inupiat (Alaska Native) (5) | 6 | <0.01 |
| Iroquois (365) | 615 | 0.46 |
| Kiowa (0) | 0 | <0.01 |
| Lumbee (0) | 0 | <0.01 |
| Menominee (0) | 0 | <0.01 |
| Mexican American Ind. (22) | 27 | 0.02 |
| Navajo (3) | 3 | <0.01 |
| Osage (0) | 0 | <0.01 |
| Ottawa (0) | 0 | <0.01 |
| Paiute (0) | 0 | <0.01 |
| Pima (0) | 0 | <0.01 |
| Potawatomi (0) | 2 | <0.01 |
| Pueblo (3) | 4 | <0.01 |
| Puget Sound Salish (0) | 0 | <0.01 |
| Seminole (0) | 2 | <0.01 |
| Shoshone (0) | 0 | <0.01 |
| Sioux (3) | 6 | <0.01 |
| South American Ind. (6) | 18 | 0.01 |
| Spanish American Ind. (0) | 0 | <0.01 |
| Tlingit-Haida (Alaska Native) (0) | 0 | <0.01 |
| Tohono O'Odham (0) | 0 | <0.01 |
| Tsimshian (Alaska Native) (0) | 0 | <0.01 |
| Ute (0) | 0 | <0.01 |
| Yakama (0) | 0 | <0.01 |
| Yaqui (0) | 0 | <0.01 |
| Yuman (0) | 0 | <0.01 |
| Yup'ik (Alaska Native) (0) | 1 | <0.01 |
| Asian (688) | 945 | 0.70 |
| Not Hispanic (676) | 892 | 0.66 |
| Hispanic (12) | 53 | 0.04 |
| Bangladeshi (1) | 1 | <0.01 |
| Bhutanese (0) | 0 | <0.01 |
| Burmese (5) | 5 | <0.01 |
| Cambodian (5) | 6 | <0.01 |
| Chinese, ex. Taiwanese (169) | 203 | 0.15 |
| Filipino (105) | 176 | 0.13 |
| Hmong (1) | 1 | <0.01 |
| Indian (130) | 152 | 0.11 |
| Indonesian (5) | 15 | 0.01 |
| Japanese (33) | 71 | 0.05 |
| Korean (105) | 142 | 0.11 |
| Laotian (1) | 9 | 0.01 |
| Malaysian (0) | 3 | <0.01 |
| Nepalese (0) | 0 | <0.01 |
| Pakistani (41) | 42 | 0.03 |
| Sri Lankan (3) | 5 | <0.01 |
| Taiwanese (4) | 7 | 0.01 |
| Thai (22) | 29 | 0.02 |
| Vietnamese (36) | 49 | 0.04 |
| Hawaii Native/Pacific Islander (36) | 100 | 0.07 |
| Not Hispanic (31) | 73 | 0.05 |
| Hispanic (5) | 27 | 0.02 |
| Fijian (2) | 2 | <0.01 |
| Guamanian/Chamorro (8) | 16 | 0.01 |
| Marshallese (0) | 0 | <0.01 |
| Native Hawaiian (8) | 24 | 0.02 |
| Samoan (5) | 8 | 0.01 |
| Tongan (0) | 0 | <0.01 |
| White (124,875) | 127,434 | 94.46 |
| Not Hispanic (120,463) | 122,474 | 90.79 |
| Hispanic (4,412) | 4,960 | 3.68 |

*Notes: † The Census 2010 population figure is used to calculate the percentages in the Hispanic Origin and Race categories. Ancestry percentages are based on the 2006-2010 American Community Survey population (not shown); ‡ Numbers in parentheses indicate the number of people reporting a single ancestry; * Numbers in parentheses indicate the number of persons reporting this race alone, not in combination with any other race; Please refer to the Explanation of Data for more information.*

## Chemung County

Population: 88,830

| Ancestry | Population | % |
|---|---|---|
| Afghan (0) | 0 | <0.01 |
| African, Sub-Saharan (234) | 248 | 0.28 |
| African (172) | 186 | 0.21 |
| Cape Verdean (0) | 0 | <0.01 |
| Ethiopian (11) | 11 | 0.01 |
| Ghanaian (11) | 11 | 0.01 |
| Kenyan (39) | 39 | 0.04 |
| Liberian (0) | 0 | <0.01 |
| Nigerian (1) | 1 | <0.01 |
| Senegalese (0) | 0 | <0.01 |
| Sierra Leonean (0) | 0 | <0.01 |
| Somalian (0) | 0 | <0.01 |
| South African (0) | 0 | <0.01 |
| Sudanese (0) | 0 | <0.01 |
| Ugandan (0) | 0 | <0.01 |
| Zimbabwean (0) | 0 | <0.01 |
| Other Sub-Saharan African (0) | 0 | <0.01 |
| Albanian (0) | 0 | <0.01 |
| Alsatian (0) | 10 | 0.01 |
| American (7,001) | 7,001 | 7.89 |
| Arab (185) | 293 | 0.33 |
| Arab (0) | 0 | <0.01 |
| Egyptian (4) | 4 | <0.01 |
| Iraqi (0) | 0 | <0.01 |
| Jordanian (0) | 0 | <0.01 |
| Lebanese (151) | 245 | 0.28 |
| Moroccan (0) | 0 | <0.01 |
| Palestinian (18) | 18 | 0.02 |
| Syrian (0) | 14 | 0.02 |
| Other Arab (12) | 12 | 0.01 |
| Armenian (0) | 37 | 0.04 |
| Assyrian/Chaldean/Syriac (0) | 0 | <0.01 |
| Australian (0) | 0 | <0.01 |
| Austrian (60) | 214 | 0.24 |
| Basque (0) | 0 | <0.01 |
| Belgian (37) | 62 | 0.07 |
| Brazilian (0) | 0 | <0.01 |
| British (82) | 151 | 0.17 |
| Bulgarian (12) | 12 | 0.01 |
| Cajun (0) | 0 | <0.01 |
| Canadian (175) | 269 | 0.30 |
| Carpatho Rusyn (0) | 0 | <0.01 |
| Celtic (2) | 12 | 0.01 |
| Croatian (15) | 62 | 0.07 |
| Cypriot (0) | 0 | <0.01 |
| Czech (142) | 369 | 0.42 |
| Czechoslovakian (104) | 259 | 0.29 |
| Danish (78) | 202 | 0.23 |
| Dutch (764) | 3,692 | 4.16 |
| Eastern European (32) | 32 | 0.04 |
| English (3,931) | 12,489 | 14.08 |
| Estonian (12) | 12 | 0.01 |
| European (260) | 282 | 0.32 |
| Finnish (144) | 475 | 0.54 |
| French, ex. Basque (455) | 2,813 | 3.17 |
| French Canadian (291) | 894 | 1.01 |
| German (5,023) | 18,529 | 20.89 |
| German Russian (0) | 0 | <0.01 |
| Greek (134) | 312 | 0.35 |
| Guyanese (0) | 0 | <0.01 |
| Hungarian (110) | 267 | 0.30 |
| Icelander (0) | 0 | <0.01 |
| Iranian (12) | 12 | 0.01 |
| Irish (5,564) | 17,907 | 20.19 |
| Israeli (0) | 20 | 0.02 |
| Italian (3,852) | 10,020 | 11.30 |
| Latvian (0) | 55 | 0.06 |
| Lithuanian (78) | 183 | 0.21 |
| Luxemburger (0) | 0 | <0.01 |
| Macedonian (0) | 0 | <0.01 |
| Maltese (9) | 9 | 0.01 |
| New Zealander (0) | 0 | <0.01 |
| Northern European (13) | 13 | 0.01 |
| Norwegian (99) | 591 | 0.67 |
| Pennsylvania German (229) | 522 | 0.59 |

| Ancestry | Population | % |
|---|---|---|
| Polish (2,122) | 6,087 | 6.86 |
| Portuguese (35) | 115 | 0.13 |
| Romanian (0) | 43 | 0.05 |
| Russian (129) | 600 | 0.68 |
| Scandinavian (4) | 23 | 0.03 |
| Scotch-Irish (616) | 1,482 | 1.67 |
| Scottish (456) | 1,673 | 1.89 |
| Serbian (11) | 11 | 0.01 |
| Slavic (4) | 84 | 0.09 |
| Slovak (44) | 201 | 0.23 |
| Slovene (15) | 41 | 0.05 |
| Soviet Union (0) | 0 | <0.01 |
| Swedish (364) | 1,326 | 1.49 |
| Swiss (26) | 166 | 0.19 |
| Turkish (10) | 21 | 0.02 |
| Ukrainian (548) | 1,369 | 1.54 |
| Welsh (366) | 1,410 | 1.59 |
| West Indian, ex. Hispanic (228) | 300 | 0.34 |
| Bahamian (31) | 31 | 0.03 |
| Barbadian (26) | 26 | 0.03 |
| Belizean (0) | 0 | <0.01 |
| Bermudan (0) | 0 | <0.01 |
| British West Indian (14) | 41 | 0.05 |
| Dutch West Indian (0) | 0 | <0.01 |
| Haitian (51) | 51 | 0.06 |
| Jamaican (72) | 107 | 0.12 |
| Trinidadian/Tobagonian (0) | 0 | <0.01 |
| U.S. Virgin Islander (0) | 0 | <0.01 |
| West Indian (23) | 33 | 0.04 |
| Other West Indian (11) | 11 | 0.01 |
| Yugoslavian (139) | 193 | 0.22 |

| Hispanic Origin | Population | % |
|---|---|---|
| Hispanic or Latino (of any race) | 2,240 | 2.52 |
| Central American, ex. Mexican | 121 | 0.14 |
| Costa Rican | 18 | 0.02 |
| Guatemalan | 35 | 0.04 |
| Honduran | 15 | 0.02 |
| Nicaraguan | 5 | 0.01 |
| Panamanian | 31 | 0.03 |
| Salvadoran | 17 | 0.02 |
| Other Central American | 0 | <0.01 |
| Cuban | 82 | 0.09 |
| Dominican Republic | 100 | 0.11 |
| Mexican | 404 | 0.45 |
| Puerto Rican | 1,156 | 1.30 |
| South American | 119 | 0.13 |
| Argentinean | 15 | 0.02 |
| Bolivian | 8 | 0.01 |
| Chilean | 2 | <0.01 |
| Colombian | 26 | 0.03 |
| Ecuadorian | 23 | 0.03 |
| Paraguayan | 0 | <0.01 |
| Peruvian | 27 | 0.03 |
| Uruguayan | 3 | <0.01 |
| Venezuelan | 6 | 0.01 |
| Other South American | 9 | 0.01 |
| Other Hispanic or Latino | 258 | 0.29 |

| Race* | Population | % |
|---|---|---|
| African-American/Black (5,828) | 7,391 | 8.32 |
| Not Hispanic (5,528) | 6,946 | 7.82 |
| Hispanic (300) | 445 | 0.50 |
| American Indian/Alaska Native (233) | 812 | 0.91 |
| Not Hispanic (206) | 713 | 0.80 |
| Hispanic (27) | 99 | 0.11 |
| Alaska Athabascan (Ala. Nat.) (0) | 0 | <0.01 |
| Aleut (Alaska Native) (0) | 0 | <0.01 |
| Apache (6) | 8 | 0.01 |
| Arapaho (0) | 0 | <0.01 |
| Blackfeet (6) | 44 | 0.05 |
| Canadian/French Am. Ind. (0) | 5 | 0.01 |
| Central American Ind. (0) | 1 | <0.01 |
| Cherokee (21) | 121 | 0.14 |
| Cheyenne (0) | 0 | <0.01 |
| Chickasaw (0) | 1 | <0.01 |
| Chippewa (2) | 3 | <0.01 |
| Choctaw (0) | 0 | <0.01 |
| Colville (0) | 0 | <0.01 |

| Race* | Population | % |
|---|---|---|
| Comanche (0) | 0 | <0.01 |
| Cree (0) | 3 | <0.01 |
| Creek (0) | 1 | <0.01 |
| Crow (0) | 0 | <0.01 |
| Delaware (0) | 1 | <0.01 |
| Hopi (0) | 0 | <0.01 |
| Houma (2) | 2 | <0.01 |
| Inupiat (Alaska Native) (0) | 0 | <0.01 |
| Iroquois (74) | 153 | 0.17 |
| Kiowa (1) | 1 | <0.01 |
| Lumbee (0) | 0 | <0.01 |
| Menominee (0) | 0 | <0.01 |
| Mexican American Ind. (2) | 8 | 0.01 |
| Navajo (0) | 11 | 0.01 |
| Osage (0) | 0 | <0.01 |
| Ottawa (0) | 0 | <0.01 |
| Paiute (0) | 0 | <0.01 |
| Pima (0) | 0 | <0.01 |
| Potawatomi (0) | 1 | <0.01 |
| Pueblo (1) | 1 | <0.01 |
| Puget Sound Salish (0) | 2 | <0.01 |
| Seminole (0) | 6 | 0.01 |
| Shoshone (0) | 0 | <0.01 |
| Sioux (1) | 16 | 0.02 |
| South American Ind. (3) | 7 | 0.01 |
| Spanish American Ind. (0) | 1 | <0.01 |
| Tlingit-Haida (Alaska Native) (3) | 3 | <0.01 |
| Tohono O'Odham (0) | 1 | <0.01 |
| Tsimshian (Alaska Native) (0) | 0 | <0.01 |
| Ute (0) | 0 | <0.01 |
| Yakama (0) | 1 | <0.01 |
| Yaqui (0) | 0 | <0.01 |
| Yuman (0) | 0 | <0.01 |
| Yup'ik (Alaska Native) (0) | 0 | <0.01 |
| Asian (1,057) | 1,334 | 1.50 |
| Not Hispanic (1,041) | 1,296 | 1.46 |
| Hispanic (16) | 38 | 0.04 |
| Bangladeshi (20) | 20 | 0.02 |
| Bhutanese (0) | 0 | <0.01 |
| Burmese (0) | 0 | <0.01 |
| Cambodian (2) | 2 | <0.01 |
| Chinese, ex. Taiwanese (279) | 312 | 0.35 |
| Filipino (95) | 164 | 0.18 |
| Hmong (0) | 0 | <0.01 |
| Indian (261) | 310 | 0.35 |
| Indonesian (4) | 5 | 0.01 |
| Japanese (53) | 100 | 0.11 |
| Korean (79) | 128 | 0.14 |
| Laotian (12) | 32 | 0.04 |
| Malaysian (2) | 3 | <0.01 |
| Nepalese (3) | 3 | <0.01 |
| Pakistani (97) | 108 | 0.12 |
| Sri Lankan (11) | 12 | 0.01 |
| Taiwanese (15) | 21 | 0.02 |
| Thai (9) | 18 | 0.02 |
| Vietnamese (63) | 68 | 0.08 |
| Hawaii Native/Pacific Islander (20) | 56 | 0.06 |
| Not Hispanic (14) | 44 | 0.05 |
| Hispanic (6) | 12 | 0.01 |
| Fijian (0) | 0 | <0.01 |
| Guamanian/Chamorro (5) | 12 | 0.01 |
| Marshallese (0) | 0 | <0.01 |
| Native Hawaiian (8) | 17 | 0.02 |
| Samoan (6) | 11 | 0.01 |
| Tongan (0) | 1 | <0.01 |
| White (78,771) | 81,009 | 91.20 |
| Not Hispanic (77,643) | 79,627 | 89.64 |
| Hispanic (1,128) | 1,382 | 1.56 |

*Notes: † The Census 2010 population figure is used to calculate the percentages in the Hispanic Origin and Race categories. Ancestry percentages are based on the 2006-2010 American Community Survey population (not shown); ‡ Numbers in parentheses indicate the number of people reporting a single ancestry; * Numbers in parentheses indicate the number of persons reporting this race alone, not in combination with any other race; Please refer to the Explanation of Data for more information.*

## Chenango County

Population: 50,477

| Ancestry | Population | % |
|---|---|---|
| Afghan (0) | 0 | <0.01 |
| African, Sub-Saharan (11) | 53 | 0.10 |
| African (2) | 31 | 0.06 |
| Cape Verdean (0) | 0 | <0.01 |
| Ethiopian (0) | 0 | <0.01 |
| Ghanaian (5) | 5 | 0.01 |
| Kenyan (0) | 0 | <0.01 |
| Liberian (4) | 4 | 0.01 |
| Nigerian (0) | 13 | 0.03 |
| Senegalese (0) | 0 | <0.01 |
| Sierra Leonean (0) | 0 | <0.01 |
| Somalian (0) | 0 | <0.01 |
| South African (0) | 0 | <0.01 |
| Sudanese (0) | 0 | <0.01 |
| Ugandan (0) | 0 | <0.01 |
| Zimbabwean (0) | 0 | <0.01 |
| Other Sub-Saharan African (0) | 0 | <0.01 |
| Albanian (0) | 0 | <0.01 |
| Alsatian (0) | 13 | 0.03 |
| American (3,611) | 3,611 | 7.07 |
| Arab (39) | 94 | 0.18 |
| Arab (0) | 0 | <0.01 |
| Egyptian (2) | 2 | <0.01 |
| Iraqi (0) | 0 | <0.01 |
| Jordanian (0) | 0 | <0.01 |
| Lebanese (33) | 88 | 0.17 |
| Moroccan (0) | 0 | <0.01 |
| Palestinian (0) | 0 | <0.01 |
| Syrian (4) | 4 | 0.01 |
| Other Arab (0) | 0 | <0.01 |
| Armenian (3) | 5 | 0.01 |
| Assyrian/Chaldean/Syriac (0) | 0 | <0.01 |
| Australian (0) | 12 | 0.02 |
| Austrian (37) | 147 | 0.29 |
| Basque (0) | 0 | <0.01 |
| Belgian (0) | 7 | 0.01 |
| Brazilian (3) | 3 | 0.01 |
| British (91) | 185 | 0.36 |
| Bulgarian (0) | 0 | <0.01 |
| Cajun (0) | 0 | <0.01 |
| Canadian (47) | 133 | 0.26 |
| Carpatho Rusyn (0) | 0 | <0.01 |
| Celtic (3) | 3 | 0.01 |
| Croatian (0) | 0 | <0.01 |
| Cypriot (0) | 0 | <0.01 |
| Czech (43) | 169 | 0.33 |
| Czechoslovakian (36) | 60 | 0.12 |
| Danish (89) | 225 | 0.44 |
| Dutch (506) | 2,167 | 4.25 |
| Eastern European (109) | 109 | 0.21 |
| English (3,435) | 9,260 | 18.14 |
| Estonian (9) | 14 | 0.03 |
| European (423) | 486 | 0.95 |
| Finnish (7) | 41 | 0.08 |
| French, ex. Basque (426) | 2,237 | 4.38 |
| French Canadian (225) | 653 | 1.28 |
| German (2,635) | 8,972 | 17.58 |
| German Russian (0) | 0 | <0.01 |
| Greek (27) | 71 | 0.14 |
| Guyanese (0) | 0 | <0.01 |
| Hungarian (103) | 456 | 0.89 |
| Icelander (0) | 0 | <0.01 |
| Iranian (48) | 48 | 0.09 |
| Irish (2,193) | 8,509 | 16.67 |
| Israeli (0) | 0 | <0.01 |
| Italian (1,990) | 4,673 | 9.15 |
| Latvian (0) | 0 | <0.01 |
| Lithuanian (116) | 196 | 0.38 |
| Luxemburger (0) | 0 | <0.01 |
| Macedonian (0) | 0 | <0.01 |
| Maltese (0) | 0 | <0.01 |
| New Zealander (0) | 0 | <0.01 |
| Northern European (173) | 173 | 0.34 |
| Norwegian (108) | 432 | 0.85 |
| Pennsylvania German (24) | 86 | 0.17 |

| Ancestry (cont.) | Population | % |
|---|---|---|
| Polish (664) | 1,903 | 3.73 |
| Portuguese (56) | 98 | 0.19 |
| Romanian (2) | 18 | 0.04 |
| Russian (204) | 337 | 0.66 |
| Scandinavian (21) | 75 | 0.15 |
| Scotch-Irish (337) | 1,126 | 2.21 |
| Scottish (250) | 1,081 | 2.12 |
| Serbian (0) | 0 | <0.01 |
| Slavic (0) | 11 | 0.02 |
| Slovak (80) | 166 | 0.33 |
| Slovene (0) | 0 | <0.01 |
| Soviet Union (0) | 0 | <0.01 |
| Swedish (120) | 522 | 1.02 |
| Swiss (182) | 301 | 0.59 |
| Turkish (7) | 7 | 0.01 |
| Ukrainian (40) | 117 | 0.23 |
| Welsh (230) | 1,011 | 1.98 |
| West Indian, ex. Hispanic (39) | 50 | 0.10 |
| Bahamian (0) | 0 | <0.01 |
| Barbadian (0) | 0 | <0.01 |
| Belizean (0) | 0 | <0.01 |
| Bermudan (0) | 0 | <0.01 |
| British West Indian (0) | 0 | <0.01 |
| Dutch West Indian (3) | 6 | 0.01 |
| Haitian (0) | 3 | 0.01 |
| Jamaican (36) | 41 | 0.08 |
| Trinidadian/Tobagonian (0) | 0 | <0.01 |
| U.S. Virgin Islander (0) | 0 | <0.01 |
| West Indian (0) | 0 | <0.01 |
| Other West Indian (0) | 0 | <0.01 |
| Yugoslavian (10) | 51 | 0.10 |

| Hispanic Origin | Population | % |
|---|---|---|
| Hispanic or Latino (of any race) | 929 | 1.84 |
| Central American, ex. Mexican | 43 | 0.09 |
| Costa Rican | 6 | 0.01 |
| Guatemalan | 23 | 0.05 |
| Honduran | 7 | 0.01 |
| Nicaraguan | 0 | <0.01 |
| Panamanian | 4 | 0.01 |
| Salvadoran | 3 | 0.01 |
| Other Central American | 0 | <0.01 |
| Cuban | 44 | 0.09 |
| Dominican Republic | 27 | 0.05 |
| Mexican | 175 | 0.35 |
| Puerto Rican | 450 | 0.89 |
| South American | 55 | 0.11 |
| Argentinean | 2 | <0.01 |
| Bolivian | 0 | <0.01 |
| Chilean | 4 | 0.01 |
| Colombian | 26 | 0.05 |
| Ecuadorian | 17 | 0.03 |
| Paraguayan | 4 | 0.01 |
| Peruvian | 2 | <0.01 |
| Uruguayan | 0 | <0.01 |
| Venezuelan | 0 | <0.01 |
| Other South American | 0 | <0.01 |
| Other Hispanic or Latino | 135 | 0.27 |

| Race* | Population | % |
|---|---|---|
| African-American/Black (345) | 562 | 1.11 |
| Not Hispanic (323) | 527 | 1.04 |
| Hispanic (22) | 35 | 0.07 |
| American Indian/Alaska Native (172) | 453 | 0.90 |
| Not Hispanic (151) | 426 | 0.84 |
| Hispanic (21) | 27 | 0.05 |
| Alaska Athabascan (Ala. Nat.) (0) | 0 | <0.01 |
| Aleut (Alaska Native) (1) | 1 | <0.01 |
| Apache (1) | 5 | 0.01 |
| Arapaho (0) | 0 | <0.01 |
| Blackfeet (3) | 25 | 0.05 |
| Canadian/French Am. Ind. (0) | 0 | <0.01 |
| Central American Ind. (3) | 3 | 0.01 |
| Cherokee (12) | 43 | 0.09 |
| Cheyenne (1) | 1 | <0.01 |
| Chickasaw (0) | 0 | <0.01 |
| Chippewa (1) | 1 | <0.01 |
| Choctaw (4) | 6 | 0.01 |
| Colville (0) | 0 | <0.01 |

| Race* (cont.) | Population | % |
|---|---|---|
| Comanche (0) | 1 | <0.01 |
| Cree (1) | 1 | <0.01 |
| Creek (0) | 0 | <0.01 |
| Crow (0) | 0 | <0.01 |
| Delaware (5) | 6 | 0.01 |
| Hopi (0) | 0 | <0.01 |
| Houma (1) | 1 | <0.01 |
| Inupiat (Alaska Native) (0) | 0 | <0.01 |
| Iroquois (40) | 85 | 0.17 |
| Kiowa (0) | 0 | <0.01 |
| Lumbee (3) | 3 | 0.01 |
| Menominee (0) | 0 | <0.01 |
| Mexican American Ind. (2) | 3 | 0.01 |
| Navajo (1) | 1 | <0.01 |
| Osage (0) | 0 | <0.01 |
| Ottawa (0) | 0 | <0.01 |
| Paiute (0) | 0 | <0.01 |
| Pima (0) | 0 | <0.01 |
| Potawatomi (0) | 0 | <0.01 |
| Pueblo (1) | 2 | <0.01 |
| Puget Sound Salish (0) | 0 | <0.01 |
| Seminole (0) | 0 | <0.01 |
| Shoshone (0) | 2 | <0.01 |
| Sioux (4) | 12 | 0.02 |
| South American Ind. (0) | 3 | 0.01 |
| Spanish American Ind. (2) | 2 | <0.01 |
| Tlingit-Haida (Alaska Native) (2) | 2 | <0.01 |
| Tohono O'Odham (0) | 0 | <0.01 |
| Tsimshian (Alaska Native) (0) | 0 | <0.01 |
| Ute (0) | 0 | <0.01 |
| Yakama (0) | 0 | <0.01 |
| Yaqui (0) | 0 | <0.01 |
| Yuman (0) | 0 | <0.01 |
| Yup'ik (Alaska Native) (0) | 0 | <0.01 |
| Asian (204) | 315 | 0.62 |
| Not Hispanic (200) | 306 | 0.61 |
| Hispanic (4) | 9 | 0.02 |
| Bangladeshi (0) | 0 | <0.01 |
| Bhutanese (0) | 0 | <0.01 |
| Burmese (0) | 0 | <0.01 |
| Cambodian (0) | 0 | <0.01 |
| Chinese, ex. Taiwanese (58) | 65 | 0.13 |
| Filipino (40) | 82 | 0.16 |
| Hmong (0) | 0 | <0.01 |
| Indian (33) | 43 | 0.09 |
| Indonesian (3) | 3 | 0.01 |
| Japanese (13) | 22 | 0.04 |
| Korean (29) | 47 | 0.09 |
| Laotian (2) | 5 | 0.01 |
| Malaysian (2) | 5 | 0.01 |
| Nepalese (0) | 0 | <0.01 |
| Pakistani (0) | 0 | <0.01 |
| Sri Lankan (0) | 0 | <0.01 |
| Taiwanese (7) | 10 | 0.02 |
| Thai (3) | 6 | 0.01 |
| Vietnamese (10) | 17 | 0.03 |
| Hawaii Native/Pacific Islander (6) | 27 | 0.05 |
| Not Hispanic (4) | 24 | 0.05 |
| Hispanic (2) | 3 | 0.01 |
| Fijian (0) | 0 | <0.01 |
| Guamanian/Chamorro (0) | 3 | 0.01 |
| Marshallese (0) | 0 | <0.01 |
| Native Hawaiian (4) | 12 | 0.02 |
| Samoan (1) | 1 | <0.01 |
| Tongan (0) | 0 | <0.01 |
| White (48,896) | 49,525 | 98.11 |
| Not Hispanic (48,265) | 48,823 | 96.72 |
| Hispanic (631) | 702 | 1.39 |

Notes: † The Census 2010 population figure is used to calculate the percentages in the Hispanic Origin and Race categories. Ancestry percentages are based on the 2006-2010 American Community Survey population (not shown); ‡ Numbers in parentheses indicate the number of people reporting a single ancestry; * Numbers in parentheses indicate the number of persons reporting this race alone, not in combination with any other race; Please refer to the Explanation of Data for more information.

## Clinton County

Population: 82,128

| Ancestry | Population | % |
|---|---|---|
| Afghan (0) | 0 | <0.01 |
| African, Sub-Saharan (153) | 172 | 0.21 |
| African (85) | 104 | 0.13 |
| Cape Verdean (0) | 0 | <0.01 |
| Ethiopian (8) | 8 | 0.01 |
| Ghanaian (13) | 13 | 0.02 |
| Kenyan (0) | 0 | <0.01 |
| Liberian (0) | 0 | <0.01 |
| Nigerian (0) | 0 | <0.01 |
| Senegalese (0) | 0 | <0.01 |
| Sierra Leonean (0) | 0 | <0.01 |
| Somalian (0) | 0 | <0.01 |
| South African (0) | 0 | <0.01 |
| Sudanese (0) | 0 | <0.01 |
| Ugandan (0) | 0 | <0.01 |
| Zimbabwean (0) | 0 | <0.01 |
| Other Sub-Saharan African (47) | 47 | 0.06 |
| Albanian (70) | 70 | 0.08 |
| Alsatian (0) | 0 | <0.01 |
| American (7,652) | 7,652 | 9.29 |
| Arab (114) | 350 | 0.42 |
| Arab (12) | 18 | 0.02 |
| Egyptian (13) | 19 | 0.02 |
| Iraqi (0) | 0 | <0.01 |
| Jordanian (0) | 2 | <0.01 |
| Lebanese (59) | 257 | 0.31 |
| Moroccan (10) | 10 | 0.01 |
| Palestinian (0) | 0 | <0.01 |
| Syrian (19) | 43 | 0.05 |
| Other Arab (1) | 1 | <0.01 |
| Armenian (25) | 130 | 0.16 |
| Assyrian/Chaldean/Syriac (0) | 0 | <0.01 |
| Australian (0) | 27 | 0.03 |
| Austrian (5) | 234 | 0.28 |
| Basque (0) | 0 | <0.01 |
| Belgian (0) | 39 | 0.05 |
| Brazilian (22) | 22 | 0.03 |
| British (97) | 286 | 0.35 |
| Bulgarian (0) | 0 | <0.01 |
| Cajun (21) | 21 | 0.03 |
| Canadian (602) | 893 | 1.08 |
| Carpatho Rusyn (0) | 0 | <0.01 |
| Celtic (0) | 10 | 0.01 |
| Croatian (0) | 48 | 0.06 |
| Cypriot (0) | 0 | <0.01 |
| Czech (48) | 189 | 0.23 |
| Czechoslovakian (0) | 19 | 0.02 |
| Danish (42) | 149 | 0.18 |
| Dutch (124) | 1,267 | 1.54 |
| Eastern European (39) | 58 | 0.07 |
| English (3,020) | 9,045 | 10.98 |
| Estonian (14) | 31 | 0.04 |
| European (370) | 388 | 0.47 |
| Finnish (54) | 150 | 0.18 |
| French, ex. Basque (7,155) | 20,474 | 24.85 |
| French Canadian (4,464) | 6,631 | 8.05 |
| German (1,440) | 7,220 | 8.76 |
| German Russian (0) | 0 | <0.01 |
| Greek (76) | 174 | 0.21 |
| Guyanese (5) | 19 | 0.02 |
| Hungarian (30) | 225 | 0.27 |
| Icelander (7) | 23 | 0.03 |
| Iranian (167) | 167 | 0.20 |
| Irish (3,162) | 13,491 | 16.38 |
| Israeli (0) | 0 | <0.01 |
| Italian (2,215) | 6,104 | 7.41 |
| Latvian (0) | 2 | <0.01 |
| Lithuanian (61) | 362 | 0.44 |
| Luxemburger (0) | 0 | <0.01 |
| Macedonian (0) | 0 | <0.01 |
| Maltese (28) | 28 | 0.03 |
| New Zealander (0) | 0 | <0.01 |
| Northern European (17) | 17 | 0.02 |
| Norwegian (77) | 411 | 0.50 |
| Pennsylvania German (4) | 27 | 0.03 |

| Ancestry | Population | % |
|---|---|---|
| Polish (720) | 2,685 | 3.26 |
| Portuguese (74) | 164 | 0.20 |
| Romanian (0) | 80 | 0.10 |
| Russian (266) | 688 | 0.84 |
| Scandinavian (9) | 33 | 0.04 |
| Scotch-Irish (620) | 1,300 | 1.58 |
| Scottish (519) | 1,860 | 2.26 |
| Serbian (0) | 14 | 0.02 |
| Slavic (0) | 27 | 0.03 |
| Slovak (32) | 118 | 0.14 |
| Slovene (0) | 47 | 0.06 |
| Soviet Union (0) | 0 | <0.01 |
| Swedish (83) | 585 | 0.71 |
| Swiss (39) | 106 | 0.13 |
| Turkish (34) | 34 | 0.04 |
| Ukrainian (140) | 255 | 0.31 |
| Welsh (80) | 406 | 0.49 |
| West Indian, ex. Hispanic (140) | 248 | 0.30 |
| Bahamian (0) | 0 | <0.01 |
| Barbadian (0) | 4 | <0.01 |
| Belizean (0) | 0 | <0.01 |
| Bermudan (0) | 0 | <0.01 |
| British West Indian (43) | 56 | 0.07 |
| Dutch West Indian (0) | 0 | <0.01 |
| Haitian (0) | 14 | 0.02 |
| Jamaican (35) | 39 | 0.05 |
| Trinidadian/Tobagonian (26) | 48 | 0.06 |
| U.S. Virgin Islander (0) | 0 | <0.01 |
| West Indian (36) | 87 | 0.11 |
| Other West Indian (0) | 0 | <0.01 |
| Yugoslavian (0) | 10 | 0.01 |

| Hispanic Origin | Population | % |
|---|---|---|
| Hispanic or Latino (of any race) | 2,054 | 2.50 |
| Central American, ex. Mexican | 155 | 0.19 |
| Costa Rican | 12 | 0.01 |
| Guatemalan | 27 | 0.03 |
| Honduran | 31 | 0.04 |
| Nicaraguan | 15 | 0.02 |
| Panamanian | 25 | 0.03 |
| Salvadoran | 44 | 0.05 |
| Other Central American | 1 | <0.01 |
| Cuban | 95 | 0.12 |
| Dominican Republic | 207 | 0.25 |
| Mexican | 302 | 0.37 |
| Puerto Rican | 928 | 1.13 |
| South American | 151 | 0.18 |
| Argentinean | 10 | 0.01 |
| Bolivian | 2 | <0.01 |
| Chilean | 11 | 0.01 |
| Colombian | 58 | 0.07 |
| Ecuadorian | 24 | 0.03 |
| Paraguayan | 8 | 0.01 |
| Peruvian | 24 | 0.03 |
| Uruguayan | 2 | <0.01 |
| Venezuelan | 10 | 0.01 |
| Other South American | 2 | <0.01 |
| Other Hispanic or Latino | 216 | 0.26 |

| Race* | Population | % |
|---|---|---|
| African-American/Black (3,209) | 3,704 | 4.51 |
| Not Hispanic (2,953) | 3,383 | 4.12 |
| Hispanic (256) | 321 | 0.39 |
| American Indian/Alaska Native (286) | 747 | 0.91 |
| Not Hispanic (266) | 685 | 0.83 |
| Hispanic (20) | 62 | 0.08 |
| Alaska Athabascan (Ala. Nat.) (2) | 2 | <0.01 |
| Aleut (Alaska Native) (0) | 1 | <0.01 |
| Apache (0) | 10 | 0.01 |
| Arapaho (1) | 1 | <0.01 |
| Blackfeet (6) | 29 | 0.04 |
| Canadian/French Am. Ind. (11) | 22 | 0.03 |
| Central American Ind. (1) | 3 | <0.01 |
| Cherokee (13) | 79 | 0.10 |
| Cheyenne (0) | 1 | <0.01 |
| Chickasaw (0) | 2 | <0.01 |
| Chippewa (5) | 9 | 0.01 |
| Choctaw (2) | 2 | <0.01 |
| Colville (0) | 0 | <0.01 |

| | Population | % |
|---|---|---|
| Comanche (1) | 3 | <0.01 |
| Cree (2) | 2 | <0.01 |
| Creek (0) | 1 | <0.01 |
| Crow (1) | 3 | <0.01 |
| Delaware (0) | 0 | <0.01 |
| Hopi (0) | 0 | <0.01 |
| Houma (0) | 0 | <0.01 |
| Inupiat (Alaska Native) (2) | 2 | <0.01 |
| Iroquois (73) | 136 | 0.17 |
| Kiowa (0) | 0 | <0.01 |
| Lumbee (0) | 0 | <0.01 |
| Menominee (0) | 0 | <0.01 |
| Mexican American Ind. (2) | 4 | <0.01 |
| Navajo (0) | 1 | <0.01 |
| Osage (0) | 0 | <0.01 |
| Ottawa (0) | 0 | <0.01 |
| Paiute (0) | 0 | <0.01 |
| Pima (0) | 0 | <0.01 |
| Potawatomi (1) | 2 | <0.01 |
| Pueblo (1) | 1 | <0.01 |
| Puget Sound Salish (0) | 1 | <0.01 |
| Seminole (0) | 0 | <0.01 |
| Shoshone (0) | 0 | <0.01 |
| Sioux (12) | 22 | 0.03 |
| South American Ind. (1) | 7 | 0.01 |
| Spanish American Ind. (0) | 0 | <0.01 |
| Tlingit-Haida (Alaska Native) (0) | 0 | <0.01 |
| Tohono O'Odham (0) | 0 | <0.01 |
| Tsimshian (Alaska Native) (0) | 0 | <0.01 |
| Ute (0) | 0 | <0.01 |
| Yakama (0) | 0 | <0.01 |
| Yaqui (0) | 0 | <0.01 |
| Yuman (0) | 0 | <0.01 |
| Yup'ik (Alaska Native) (1) | 1 | <0.01 |
| Asian (898) | 1,147 | 1.40 |
| Not Hispanic (890) | 1,121 | 1.36 |
| Hispanic (8) | 26 | 0.03 |
| Bangladeshi (2) | 2 | <0.01 |
| Bhutanese (0) | 0 | <0.01 |
| Burmese (1) | 2 | <0.01 |
| Cambodian (2) | 3 | <0.01 |
| Chinese, ex. Taiwanese (238) | 273 | 0.33 |
| Filipino (114) | 185 | 0.23 |
| Hmong (0) | 0 | <0.01 |
| Indian (160) | 182 | 0.22 |
| Indonesian (0) | 3 | <0.01 |
| Japanese (91) | 125 | 0.15 |
| Korean (96) | 139 | 0.17 |
| Laotian (0) | 5 | 0.01 |
| Malaysian (2) | 4 | <0.01 |
| Nepalese (9) | 9 | 0.01 |
| Pakistani (30) | 35 | 0.04 |
| Sri Lankan (8) | 13 | 0.02 |
| Taiwanese (10) | 11 | 0.01 |
| Thai (20) | 38 | 0.05 |
| Vietnamese (66) | 74 | 0.09 |
| Hawaii Native/Pacific Islander (19) | 58 | 0.07 |
| Not Hispanic (15) | 42 | 0.05 |
| Hispanic (4) | 16 | 0.02 |
| Fijian (0) | 0 | <0.01 |
| Guamanian/Chamorro (6) | 9 | 0.01 |
| Marshallese (0) | 0 | <0.01 |
| Native Hawaiian (5) | 17 | 0.02 |
| Samoan (2) | 7 | 0.01 |
| Tongan (0) | 0 | <0.01 |
| White (75,997) | 77,099 | 93.88 |
| Not Hispanic (74,832) | 75,785 | 92.28 |
| Hispanic (1,165) | 1,314 | 1.60 |

*Notes: † The Census 2010 population figure is used to calculate the percentages in the Hispanic Origin and Race categories. Ancestry percentages are based on the 2006-2010 American Community Survey population (not shown); ‡ Numbers in parentheses indicate the number of people reporting a single ancestry; * Numbers in parentheses indicate the number of persons reporting this race alone, not in combination with any other race; Please refer to the Explanation of Data for more information.*

## Columbia County

Population: 63,096

| Ancestry | Population | % |
|---|---|---|
| Afghan (0) | 0 | <0.01 |
| African, Sub-Saharan (171) | 200 | 0.32 |
| African (102) | 130 | 0.21 |
| Cape Verdean (0) | 0 | <0.01 |
| Ethiopian (0) | 0 | <0.01 |
| Ghanaian (0) | 0 | <0.01 |
| Kenyan (0) | 0 | <0.01 |
| Liberian (16) | 16 | 0.03 |
| Nigerian (29) | 29 | 0.05 |
| Senegalese (0) | 0 | <0.01 |
| Sierra Leonean (0) | 0 | <0.01 |
| Somalian (0) | 0 | <0.01 |
| South African (24) | 25 | 0.04 |
| Sudanese (0) | 0 | <0.01 |
| Ugandan (0) | 0 | <0.01 |
| Zimbabwean (0) | 0 | <0.01 |
| Other Sub-Saharan African (0) | 0 | <0.01 |
| Albanian (0) | 0 | <0.01 |
| Alsatian (0) | 0 | <0.01 |
| American (5,649) | 5,649 | 8.93 |
| Arab (200) | 246 | 0.39 |
| Arab (127) | 127 | 0.20 |
| Egyptian (0) | 3 | <0.01 |
| Iraqi (0) | 0 | <0.01 |
| Jordanian (0) | 0 | <0.01 |
| Lebanese (17) | 32 | 0.05 |
| Moroccan (43) | 43 | 0.07 |
| Palestinian (0) | 24 | 0.04 |
| Syrian (2) | 6 | 0.01 |
| Other Arab (11) | 11 | 0.02 |
| Armenian (39) | 60 | 0.09 |
| Assyrian/Chaldean/Syriac (0) | 0 | <0.01 |
| Australian (4) | 11 | 0.02 |
| Austrian (60) | 369 | 0.58 |
| Basque (0) | 4 | 0.01 |
| Belgian (3) | 46 | 0.07 |
| Brazilian (72) | 74 | 0.12 |
| British (174) | 400 | 0.63 |
| Bulgarian (0) | 0 | <0.01 |
| Cajun (0) | 14 | 0.02 |
| Canadian (25) | 166 | 0.26 |
| Carpatho Rusyn (0) | 0 | <0.01 |
| Celtic (21) | 21 | 0.03 |
| Croatian (7) | 14 | 0.02 |
| Cypriot (0) | 0 | <0.01 |
| Czech (52) | 291 | 0.46 |
| Czechoslovakian (41) | 99 | 0.16 |
| Danish (57) | 236 | 0.37 |
| Dutch (631) | 4,629 | 7.32 |
| Eastern European (176) | 176 | 0.28 |
| English (1,608) | 6,951 | 10.99 |
| Estonian (4) | 4 | 0.01 |
| European (411) | 498 | 0.79 |
| Finnish (68) | 92 | 0.15 |
| French, ex. Basque (285) | 3,225 | 5.10 |
| French Canadian (304) | 695 | 1.10 |
| German (3,377) | 14,502 | 22.93 |
| German Russian (0) | 0 | <0.01 |
| Greek (62) | 410 | 0.65 |
| Guyanese (0) | 0 | <0.01 |
| Hungarian (217) | 681 | 1.08 |
| Icelander (0) | 0 | <0.01 |
| Iranian (18) | 44 | 0.07 |
| Irish (3,234) | 12,327 | 19.49 |
| Israeli (2) | 2 | <0.01 |
| Italian (3,909) | 10,205 | 16.14 |
| Latvian (3) | 55 | 0.09 |
| Lithuanian (123) | 309 | 0.49 |
| Luxemburger (0) | 0 | <0.01 |
| Macedonian (0) | 0 | <0.01 |
| Maltese (0) | 3 | <0.01 |
| New Zealander (0) | 0 | <0.01 |
| Northern European (20) | 20 | 0.03 |
| Norwegian (130) | 496 | 0.78 |
| Pennsylvania German (9) | 11 | 0.02 |

| Ancestry (cont.) | Population | % |
|---|---|---|
| Polish (1,145) | 3,588 | 5.67 |
| Portuguese (20) | 46 | 0.07 |
| Romanian (67) | 185 | 0.29 |
| Russian (312) | 1,220 | 1.93 |
| Scandinavian (54) | 78 | 0.12 |
| Scotch-Irish (308) | 1,127 | 1.78 |
| Scottish (333) | 1,672 | 2.64 |
| Serbian (10) | 14 | 0.02 |
| Slavic (24) | 89 | 0.14 |
| Slovak (74) | 131 | 0.21 |
| Slovene (8) | 16 | 0.03 |
| Soviet Union (0) | 0 | <0.01 |
| Swedish (112) | 872 | 1.38 |
| Swiss (44) | 227 | 0.36 |
| Turkish (20) | 26 | 0.04 |
| Ukrainian (304) | 720 | 1.14 |
| Welsh (49) | 424 | 0.67 |
| West Indian, ex. Hispanic (372) | 418 | 0.66 |
| Bahamian (0) | 0 | <0.01 |
| Barbadian (0) | 0 | <0.01 |
| Belizean (0) | 0 | <0.01 |
| Bermudan (0) | 3 | <0.01 |
| British West Indian (11) | 11 | 0.02 |
| Dutch West Indian (0) | 0 | <0.01 |
| Haitian (93) | 100 | 0.16 |
| Jamaican (256) | 277 | 0.44 |
| Trinidadian/Tobagonian (12) | 24 | 0.04 |
| U.S. Virgin Islander (0) | 0 | <0.01 |
| West Indian (0) | 3 | <0.01 |
| Other West Indian (0) | 0 | <0.01 |
| Yugoslavian (0) | 11 | 0.02 |

| Hispanic Origin | Population | % |
|---|---|---|
| Hispanic or Latino (of any race) | 2,454 | 3.89 |
| Central American, ex. Mexican | 253 | 0.40 |
| Costa Rican | 11 | 0.02 |
| Guatemalan | 112 | 0.18 |
| Honduran | 34 | 0.05 |
| Nicaraguan | 25 | 0.04 |
| Panamanian | 16 | 0.03 |
| Salvadoran | 55 | 0.09 |
| Other Central American | 0 | <0.01 |
| Cuban | 93 | 0.15 |
| Dominican Republic | 77 | 0.12 |
| Mexican | 732 | 1.16 |
| Puerto Rican | 931 | 1.48 |
| South American | 162 | 0.26 |
| Argentinean | 12 | 0.02 |
| Bolivian | 0 | <0.01 |
| Chilean | 17 | 0.03 |
| Colombian | 70 | 0.11 |
| Ecuadorian | 41 | 0.06 |
| Paraguayan | 0 | <0.01 |
| Peruvian | 9 | 0.01 |
| Uruguayan | 4 | 0.01 |
| Venezuelan | 8 | 0.01 |
| Other South American | 1 | <0.01 |
| Other Hispanic or Latino | 206 | 0.33 |

| Race* | Population | % |
|---|---|---|
| African-American/Black (2,855) | 3,570 | 5.66 |
| Not Hispanic (2,691) | 3,327 | 5.27 |
| Hispanic (164) | 243 | 0.39 |
| American Indian/Alaska Native (123) | 476 | 0.75 |
| Not Hispanic (85) | 401 | 0.64 |
| Hispanic (38) | 75 | 0.12 |
| Alaska Athabascan (Ala. Nat.) (0) | 0 | <0.01 |
| Aleut (Alaska Native) (0) | 0 | <0.01 |
| Apache (0) | 7 | 0.01 |
| Arapaho (0) | 0 | <0.01 |
| Blackfeet (0) | 25 | 0.04 |
| Canadian/French Am. Ind. (2) | 3 | <0.01 |
| Central American Ind. (0) | 0 | <0.01 |
| Cherokee (10) | 76 | 0.12 |
| Cheyenne (0) | 0 | <0.01 |
| Chickasaw (0) | 5 | 0.01 |
| Chippewa (1) | 9 | 0.01 |
| Choctaw (0) | 1 | <0.01 |
| Colville (0) | 0 | <0.01 |

| Race* (cont.) | Population | % |
|---|---|---|
| Comanche (0) | 0 | <0.01 |
| Cree (0) | 3 | <0.01 |
| Creek (0) | 1 | <0.01 |
| Crow (0) | 0 | <0.01 |
| Delaware (1) | 1 | <0.01 |
| Hopi (0) | 0 | <0.01 |
| Houma (0) | 0 | <0.01 |
| Inupiat (Alaska Native) (0) | 1 | <0.01 |
| Iroquois (21) | 61 | 0.10 |
| Kiowa (0) | 0 | <0.01 |
| Lumbee (0) | 2 | <0.01 |
| Menominee (0) | 0 | <0.01 |
| Mexican American Ind. (8) | 8 | 0.01 |
| Navajo (0) | 0 | <0.01 |
| Osage (0) | 0 | <0.01 |
| Ottawa (0) | 0 | <0.01 |
| Paiute (0) | 0 | <0.01 |
| Pima (0) | 0 | <0.01 |
| Potawatomi (1) | 3 | <0.01 |
| Pueblo (0) | 0 | <0.01 |
| Puget Sound Salish (0) | 0 | <0.01 |
| Seminole (1) | 5 | 0.01 |
| Shoshone (0) | 0 | <0.01 |
| Sioux (4) | 11 | 0.02 |
| South American Ind. (12) | 17 | 0.03 |
| Spanish American Ind. (0) | 0 | <0.01 |
| Tlingit-Haida (Alaska Native) (0) | 0 | <0.01 |
| Tohono O'Odham (0) | 0 | <0.01 |
| Tsimshian (Alaska Native) (0) | 0 | <0.01 |
| Ute (0) | 0 | <0.01 |
| Yakama (0) | 1 | <0.01 |
| Yaqui (0) | 0 | <0.01 |
| Yuman (0) | 0 | <0.01 |
| Yup'ik (Alaska Native) (0) | 0 | <0.01 |
| Asian (1,002) | 1,220 | 1.93 |
| Not Hispanic (998) | 1,192 | 1.89 |
| Hispanic (4) | 28 | 0.04 |
| Bangladeshi (248) | 279 | 0.44 |
| Bhutanese (0) | 0 | <0.01 |
| Burmese (0) | 0 | <0.01 |
| Cambodian (3) | 3 | <0.01 |
| Chinese, ex. Taiwanese (152) | 198 | 0.31 |
| Filipino (72) | 105 | 0.17 |
| Hmong (0) | 0 | <0.01 |
| Indian (256) | 315 | 0.50 |
| Indonesian (4) | 4 | 0.01 |
| Japanese (59) | 97 | 0.15 |
| Korean (65) | 82 | 0.13 |
| Laotian (0) | 1 | <0.01 |
| Malaysian (0) | 0 | <0.01 |
| Nepalese (11) | 11 | 0.02 |
| Pakistani (28) | 30 | 0.05 |
| Sri Lankan (2) | 2 | <0.01 |
| Taiwanese (0) | 2 | <0.01 |
| Thai (7) | 8 | 0.01 |
| Vietnamese (33) | 48 | 0.08 |
| Hawaii Native/Pacific Islander (18) | 45 | 0.07 |
| Not Hispanic (15) | 39 | 0.06 |
| Hispanic (3) | 6 | 0.01 |
| Fijian (1) | 1 | <0.01 |
| Guamanian/Chamorro (2) | 3 | <0.01 |
| Marshallese (0) | 0 | <0.01 |
| Native Hawaiian (2) | 12 | 0.02 |
| Samoan (3) | 8 | 0.01 |
| Tongan (0) | 0 | <0.01 |
| White (57,136) | 58,319 | 92.43 |
| Not Hispanic (55,672) | 56,690 | 89.85 |
| Hispanic (1,464) | 1,629 | 2.58 |

Notes: † The Census 2010 population figure is used to calculate the percentages in the Hispanic Origin and Race categories. Ancestry percentages are based on the 2006-2010 American Community Survey population (not shown); ‡ Numbers in parentheses indicate the number of people reporting a single ancestry; * Numbers in parentheses indicate the number of persons reporting this race alone, not in combination with any other race; Please refer to the Explanation of Data for more information.

## Cortland County

Population: 49,336

| Ancestry | Population | % |
|---|---|---|
| Afghan (0) | 0 | <0.01 |
| African, Sub-Saharan (0) | 0 | <0.01 |
| African (0) | 0 | <0.01 |
| Cape Verdean (0) | 0 | <0.01 |
| Ethiopian (0) | 0 | <0.01 |
| Ghanaian (0) | 0 | <0.01 |
| Kenyan (0) | 0 | <0.01 |
| Liberian (0) | 0 | <0.01 |
| Nigerian (0) | 0 | <0.01 |
| Senegalese (0) | 0 | <0.01 |
| Sierra Leonean (0) | 0 | <0.01 |
| Somalian (0) | 0 | <0.01 |
| South African (0) | 0 | <0.01 |
| Sudanese (0) | 0 | <0.01 |
| Ugandan (0) | 0 | <0.01 |
| Zimbabwean (0) | 0 | <0.01 |
| Other Sub-Saharan African (0) | 0 | <0.01 |
| Albanian (0) | 0 | <0.01 |
| Alsatian (0) | 0 | <0.01 |
| American (2,591) | 2,591 | 5.24 |
| Arab (86) | 252 | 0.51 |
| Arab (5) | 18 | 0.04 |
| Egyptian (0) | 0 | <0.01 |
| Iraqi (0) | 0 | <0.01 |
| Jordanian (0) | 0 | <0.01 |
| Lebanese (81) | 207 | 0.42 |
| Moroccan (0) | 0 | <0.01 |
| Palestinian (0) | 0 | <0.01 |
| Syrian (0) | 27 | 0.05 |
| Other Arab (0) | 0 | <0.01 |
| Armenian (0) | 0 | <0.01 |
| Assyrian/Chaldean/Syriac (3) | 3 | 0.01 |
| Australian (0) | 0 | <0.01 |
| Austrian (9) | 124 | 0.25 |
| Basque (0) | 0 | <0.01 |
| Belgian (16) | 19 | 0.04 |
| Brazilian (0) | 13 | 0.03 |
| British (49) | 93 | 0.19 |
| Bulgarian (0) | 0 | <0.01 |
| Cajun (0) | 0 | <0.01 |
| Canadian (72) | 149 | 0.30 |
| Carpatho Rusyn (0) | 0 | <0.01 |
| Celtic (8) | 19 | 0.04 |
| Croatian (0) | 39 | 0.08 |
| Cypriot (0) | 0 | <0.01 |
| Czech (15) | 111 | 0.22 |
| Czechoslovakian (4) | 34 | 0.07 |
| Danish (21) | 78 | 0.16 |
| Dutch (304) | 1,860 | 3.76 |
| Eastern European (30) | 30 | 0.06 |
| English (3,066) | 7,856 | 15.89 |
| Estonian (7) | 7 | 0.01 |
| European (795) | 812 | 1.64 |
| Finnish (0) | 92 | 0.19 |
| French, ex. Basque (326) | 1,886 | 3.81 |
| French Canadian (226) | 647 | 1.31 |
| German (2,599) | 8,405 | 17.00 |
| German Russian (0) | 0 | <0.01 |
| Greek (49) | 190 | 0.38 |
| Guyanese (0) | 0 | <0.01 |
| Hungarian (39) | 146 | 0.30 |
| Icelander (10) | 10 | 0.02 |
| Iranian (0) | 2 | <0.01 |
| Irish (2,679) | 8,790 | 17.77 |
| Israeli (0) | 0 | <0.01 |
| Italian (2,049) | 5,160 | 10.43 |
| Latvian (0) | 2 | <0.01 |
| Lithuanian (8) | 55 | 0.11 |
| Luxemburger (6) | 6 | 0.01 |
| Macedonian (0) | 0 | <0.01 |
| Maltese (3) | 25 | 0.05 |
| New Zealander (0) | 0 | <0.01 |
| Northern European (176) | 239 | 0.48 |
| Norwegian (51) | 265 | 0.54 |
| Pennsylvania German (70) | 97 | 0.20 |
| Polish (615) | 1,744 | 3.53 |
| Portuguese (15) | 28 | 0.06 |
| Romanian (35) | 75 | 0.15 |
| Russian (75) | 434 | 0.88 |
| Scandinavian (25) | 39 | 0.08 |
| Scotch-Irish (176) | 635 | 1.28 |
| Scottish (356) | 1,046 | 2.12 |
| Serbian (0) | 6 | 0.01 |
| Slavic (18) | 36 | 0.07 |
| Slovak (13) | 54 | 0.11 |
| Slovene (0) | 0 | <0.01 |
| Soviet Union (0) | 0 | <0.01 |
| Swedish (71) | 327 | 0.66 |
| Swiss (24) | 126 | 0.25 |
| Turkish (50) | 77 | 0.16 |
| Ukrainian (151) | 231 | 0.47 |
| Welsh (95) | 464 | 0.94 |
| West Indian, ex. Hispanic (12) | 34 | 0.07 |
| Bahamian (0) | 0 | <0.01 |
| Barbadian (0) | 0 | <0.01 |
| Belizean (0) | 0 | <0.01 |
| Bermudan (0) | 0 | <0.01 |
| British West Indian (0) | 0 | <0.01 |
| Dutch West Indian (0) | 0 | <0.01 |
| Haitian (12) | 25 | 0.05 |
| Jamaican (0) | 0 | <0.01 |
| Trinidadian/Tobagonian (0) | 9 | 0.02 |
| U.S. Virgin Islander (0) | 0 | <0.01 |
| West Indian (0) | 0 | <0.01 |
| Other West Indian (0) | 0 | <0.01 |
| Yugoslavian (6) | 13 | 0.03 |

| Hispanic Origin | Population | % |
|---|---|---|
| Hispanic or Latino (of any race) | 1,094 | 2.22 |
| Central American, ex. Mexican | 64 | 0.13 |
| Costa Rican | 3 | 0.01 |
| Guatemalan | 40 | 0.08 |
| Honduran | 4 | 0.01 |
| Nicaraguan | 1 | <0.01 |
| Panamanian | 4 | 0.01 |
| Salvadoran | 11 | 0.02 |
| Other Central American | 1 | <0.01 |
| Cuban | 60 | 0.12 |
| Dominican Republic | 66 | 0.13 |
| Mexican | 207 | 0.42 |
| Puerto Rican | 458 | 0.93 |
| South American | 94 | 0.19 |
| Argentinean | 3 | 0.01 |
| Bolivian | 4 | 0.01 |
| Chilean | 6 | 0.01 |
| Colombian | 40 | 0.08 |
| Ecuadorian | 23 | 0.05 |
| Paraguayan | 0 | <0.01 |
| Peruvian | 11 | 0.02 |
| Uruguayan | 4 | 0.01 |
| Venezuelan | 3 | 0.01 |
| Other South American | 0 | <0.01 |
| Other Hispanic or Latino | 145 | 0.29 |

| Race* | Population | % |
|---|---|---|
| African-American/Black (760) | 1,131 | 2.29 |
| Not Hispanic (705) | 1,033 | 2.09 |
| Hispanic (55) | 98 | 0.20 |
| American Indian/Alaska Native (137) | 454 | 0.92 |
| Not Hispanic (126) | 405 | 0.82 |
| Hispanic (11) | 49 | 0.10 |
| Alaska Athabascan (Ala. Nat.) (0) | 0 | <0.01 |
| Aleut (Alaska Native) (0) | 0 | <0.01 |
| Apache (1) | 1 | <0.01 |
| Arapaho (0) | 0 | <0.01 |
| Blackfeet (2) | 15 | 0.03 |
| Canadian/French Am. Ind. (2) | 10 | 0.02 |
| Central American Ind. (0) | 0 | <0.01 |
| Cherokee (4) | 47 | 0.10 |
| Cheyenne (1) | 1 | <0.01 |
| Chickasaw (0) | 0 | <0.01 |
| Chippewa (0) | 0 | <0.01 |
| Choctaw (0) | 2 | <0.01 |
| Colville (0) | 0 | <0.01 |
| Comanche (0) | 0 | <0.01 |
| Cree (1) | 2 | <0.01 |
| Creek (0) | 0 | <0.01 |
| Crow (0) | 0 | <0.01 |
| Delaware (0) | 4 | 0.01 |
| Hopi (0) | 0 | <0.01 |
| Houma (0) | 0 | <0.01 |
| Inupiat (Alaska Native) (0) | 0 | <0.01 |
| Iroquois (43) | 118 | 0.24 |
| Kiowa (0) | 0 | <0.01 |
| Lumbee (1) | 1 | <0.01 |
| Menominee (0) | 0 | <0.01 |
| Mexican American Ind. (2) | 4 | 0.01 |
| Navajo (2) | 4 | 0.01 |
| Osage (0) | 0 | <0.01 |
| Ottawa (0) | 0 | <0.01 |
| Paiute (0) | 0 | <0.01 |
| Pima (0) | 0 | <0.01 |
| Potawatomi (1) | 2 | <0.01 |
| Pueblo (0) | 0 | <0.01 |
| Puget Sound Salish (0) | 0 | <0.01 |
| Seminole (0) | 0 | <0.01 |
| Shoshone (0) | 0 | <0.01 |
| Sioux (3) | 8 | 0.02 |
| South American Ind. (1) | 1 | <0.01 |
| Spanish American Ind. (0) | 0 | <0.01 |
| Tlingit-Haida (Alaska Native) (0) | 0 | <0.01 |
| Tohono O'Odham (0) | 0 | <0.01 |
| Tsimshian (Alaska Native) (0) | 0 | <0.01 |
| Ute (0) | 0 | <0.01 |
| Yakama (0) | 0 | <0.01 |
| Yaqui (0) | 0 | <0.01 |
| Yuman (0) | 0 | <0.01 |
| Yup'ik (Alaska Native) (0) | 0 | <0.01 |
| Asian (416) | 575 | 1.17 |
| Not Hispanic (412) | 558 | 1.13 |
| Hispanic (4) | 17 | 0.03 |
| Bangladeshi (7) | 13 | 0.03 |
| Bhutanese (0) | 0 | <0.01 |
| Burmese (0) | 0 | <0.01 |
| Cambodian (1) | 1 | <0.01 |
| Chinese, ex. Taiwanese (104) | 136 | 0.28 |
| Filipino (40) | 84 | 0.17 |
| Hmong (0) | 0 | <0.01 |
| Indian (109) | 126 | 0.26 |
| Indonesian (5) | 9 | 0.02 |
| Japanese (26) | 60 | 0.12 |
| Korean (61) | 83 | 0.17 |
| Laotian (9) | 11 | 0.02 |
| Malaysian (0) | 1 | <0.01 |
| Nepalese (0) | 0 | <0.01 |
| Pakistani (6) | 6 | 0.01 |
| Sri Lankan (2) | 2 | <0.01 |
| Taiwanese (2) | 3 | 0.01 |
| Thai (1) | 3 | 0.01 |
| Vietnamese (22) | 24 | 0.05 |
| Hawaii Native/Pacific Islander (5) | 30 | 0.06 |
| Not Hispanic (3) | 23 | 0.05 |
| Hispanic (2) | 7 | 0.01 |
| Fijian (0) | 0 | <0.01 |
| Guamanian/Chamorro (2) | 2 | <0.01 |
| Marshallese (0) | 0 | <0.01 |
| Native Hawaiian (0) | 12 | 0.02 |
| Samoan (0) | 1 | <0.01 |
| Tongan (0) | 1 | <0.01 |
| White (46,901) | 47,697 | 96.68 |
| Not Hispanic (46,252) | 46,953 | 95.17 |
| Hispanic (649) | 744 | 1.51 |

*Notes: † The Census 2010 population figure is used to calculate the percentages in the Hispanic Origin and Race categories. Ancestry percentages are based on the 2006-2010 American Community Survey population (not shown); ‡ Numbers in parentheses indicate the number of people reporting a single ancestry; \* Numbers in parentheses indicate the number of persons reporting this race alone, not in combination with any other race; Please refer to the Explanation of Data for more information.*

## Delaware County

Population: 47,980

| Ancestry | Population | % |
|---|---|---|
| Afghan (0) | 0 | <0.01 |
| African, Sub-Saharan (16) | 45 | 0.09 |
| African (16) | 45 | 0.09 |
| Cape Verdean (0) | 0 | <0.01 |
| Ethiopian (0) | 0 | <0.01 |
| Ghanaian (0) | 0 | <0.01 |
| Kenyan (0) | 0 | <0.01 |
| Liberian (0) | 0 | <0.01 |
| Nigerian (0) | 0 | <0.01 |
| Senegalese (0) | 0 | <0.01 |
| Sierra Leonean (0) | 0 | <0.01 |
| Somalian (0) | 0 | <0.01 |
| South African (0) | 0 | <0.01 |
| Sudanese (0) | 0 | <0.01 |
| Ugandan (0) | 0 | <0.01 |
| Zimbabwean (0) | 0 | <0.01 |
| Other Sub-Saharan African (0) | 0 | <0.01 |
| Albanian (0) | 0 | <0.01 |
| Alsatian (0) | 0 | <0.01 |
| American (1,873) | 1,873 | 3.88 |
| Arab (15) | 15 | 0.03 |
| Arab (0) | 0 | <0.01 |
| Egyptian (0) | 0 | <0.01 |
| Iraqi (0) | 0 | <0.01 |
| Jordanian (0) | 0 | <0.01 |
| Lebanese (5) | 5 | 0.01 |
| Moroccan (0) | 0 | <0.01 |
| Palestinian (0) | 0 | <0.01 |
| Syrian (8) | 8 | 0.02 |
| Other Arab (2) | 2 | <0.01 |
| Armenian (0) | 24 | 0.05 |
| Assyrian/Chaldean/Syriac (0) | 0 | <0.01 |
| Australian (18) | 23 | 0.05 |
| Austrian (30) | 217 | 0.45 |
| Basque (0) | 0 | <0.01 |
| Belgian (5) | 19 | 0.04 |
| Brazilian (9) | 9 | 0.02 |
| British (84) | 152 | 0.32 |
| Bulgarian (0) | 3 | 0.01 |
| Cajun (0) | 0 | <0.01 |
| Canadian (40) | 139 | 0.29 |
| Carpatho Rusyn (0) | 0 | <0.01 |
| Celtic (0) | 0 | <0.01 |
| Croatian (11) | 11 | 0.02 |
| Cypriot (0) | 0 | <0.01 |
| Czech (49) | 235 | 0.49 |
| Czechoslovakian (46) | 88 | 0.18 |
| Danish (93) | 274 | 0.57 |
| Dutch (498) | 2,859 | 5.93 |
| Eastern European (53) | 69 | 0.14 |
| English (2,101) | 7,882 | 16.35 |
| Estonian (16) | 16 | 0.03 |
| European (124) | 124 | 0.26 |
| Finnish (12) | 76 | 0.16 |
| French, ex. Basque (281) | 2,275 | 4.72 |
| French Canadian (73) | 414 | 0.86 |
| German (3,517) | 13,135 | 27.24 |
| German Russian (0) | 0 | <0.01 |
| Greek (82) | 197 | 0.41 |
| Guyanese (0) | 0 | <0.01 |
| Hungarian (61) | 507 | 1.05 |
| Icelander (0) | 8 | 0.02 |
| Iranian (10) | 10 | 0.02 |
| Irish (2,940) | 10,183 | 21.12 |
| Israeli (0) | 0 | <0.01 |
| Italian (2,129) | 5,867 | 12.17 |
| Latvian (4) | 16 | 0.03 |
| Lithuanian (27) | 117 | 0.24 |
| Luxemburger (0) | 0 | <0.01 |
| Macedonian (4) | 7 | 0.01 |
| Maltese (5) | 5 | 0.01 |
| New Zealander (0) | 0 | <0.01 |
| Northern European (61) | 61 | 0.13 |
| Norwegian (144) | 542 | 1.12 |
| Pennsylvania German (6) | 43 | 0.09 |

| Ancestry (cont.) | Population | % |
|---|---|---|
| Polish (605) | 2,189 | 4.54 |
| Portuguese (22) | 108 | 0.22 |
| Romanian (77) | 113 | 0.23 |
| Russian (143) | 490 | 1.02 |
| Scandinavian (26) | 87 | 0.18 |
| Scotch-Irish (505) | 1,432 | 2.97 |
| Scottish (756) | 2,831 | 5.87 |
| Serbian (0) | 0 | <0.01 |
| Slavic (13) | 65 | 0.13 |
| Slovak (63) | 285 | 0.59 |
| Slovene (20) | 26 | 0.05 |
| Soviet Union (0) | 0 | <0.01 |
| Swedish (94) | 1,011 | 2.10 |
| Swiss (28) | 176 | 0.36 |
| Turkish (73) | 78 | 0.16 |
| Ukrainian (49) | 124 | 0.26 |
| Welsh (112) | 628 | 1.30 |
| West Indian, ex. Hispanic (113) | 189 | 0.39 |
| Bahamian (0) | 0 | <0.01 |
| Barbadian (0) | 9 | 0.02 |
| Belizean (0) | 0 | <0.01 |
| Bermudan (0) | 0 | <0.01 |
| British West Indian (0) | 29 | 0.06 |
| Dutch West Indian (0) | 0 | <0.01 |
| Haitian (30) | 33 | 0.07 |
| Jamaican (40) | 65 | 0.13 |
| Trinidadian/Tobagonian (0) | 0 | <0.01 |
| U.S. Virgin Islander (28) | 28 | 0.06 |
| West Indian (15) | 25 | 0.05 |
| Other West Indian (0) | 0 | <0.01 |
| Yugoslavian (53) | 103 | 0.21 |

| Hispanic Origin | Population | % |
|---|---|---|
| Hispanic or Latino (of any race) | 1,560 | 3.25 |
| Central American, ex. Mexican | 66 | 0.14 |
| Costa Rican | 7 | 0.01 |
| Guatemalan | 19 | 0.04 |
| Honduran | 11 | 0.02 |
| Nicaraguan | 2 | <0.01 |
| Panamanian | 9 | 0.02 |
| Salvadoran | 18 | 0.04 |
| Other Central American | 0 | <0.01 |
| Cuban | 70 | 0.15 |
| Dominican Republic | 95 | 0.20 |
| Mexican | 381 | 0.79 |
| Puerto Rican | 659 | 1.37 |
| South American | 104 | 0.22 |
| Argentinean | 18 | 0.04 |
| Bolivian | 0 | <0.01 |
| Chilean | 15 | 0.03 |
| Colombian | 38 | 0.08 |
| Ecuadorian | 14 | 0.03 |
| Paraguayan | 0 | <0.01 |
| Peruvian | 9 | 0.02 |
| Uruguayan | 4 | <0.01 |
| Venezuelan | 6 | 0.01 |
| Other South American | 0 | <0.01 |
| Other Hispanic or Latino | 185 | 0.39 |

| Race* | Population | % |
|---|---|---|
| African-American/Black (779) | 1,040 | 2.17 |
| Not Hispanic (691) | 923 | 1.92 |
| Hispanic (88) | 117 | 0.24 |
| American Indian/Alaska Native (131) | 366 | 0.76 |
| Not Hispanic (102) | 314 | 0.65 |
| Hispanic (29) | 52 | 0.11 |
| Alaska Athabascan (Ala. Nat.) (0) | 0 | <0.01 |
| Aleut (Alaska Native) (0) | 0 | <0.01 |
| Apache (0) | 0 | <0.01 |
| Arapaho (0) | 0 | <0.01 |
| Blackfeet (1) | 14 | 0.03 |
| Canadian/French Am. Ind. (0) | 0 | <0.01 |
| Central American Ind. (3) | 3 | 0.01 |
| Cherokee (7) | 49 | 0.10 |
| Cheyenne (1) | 1 | <0.01 |
| Chickasaw (0) | 0 | <0.01 |
| Chippewa (8) | 8 | 0.02 |
| Choctaw (0) | 4 | 0.01 |
| Colville (0) | 1 | <0.01 |

| Race* (cont.) | Population | % |
|---|---|---|
| Comanche (0) | 0 | <0.01 |
| Cree (0) | 1 | <0.01 |
| Creek (0) | 1 | <0.01 |
| Crow (0) | 1 | <0.01 |
| Delaware (2) | 8 | 0.02 |
| Hopi (0) | 0 | <0.01 |
| Houma (0) | 0 | <0.01 |
| Inupiat (Alaska Native) (0) | 1 | <0.01 |
| Iroquois (18) | 41 | 0.09 |
| Kiowa (0) | 2 | <0.01 |
| Lumbee (0) | 0 | <0.01 |
| Menominee (0) | 0 | <0.01 |
| Mexican American Ind. (1) | 4 | 0.01 |
| Navajo (3) | 5 | 0.01 |
| Osage (0) | 0 | <0.01 |
| Ottawa (0) | 0 | <0.01 |
| Paiute (0) | 0 | <0.01 |
| Pima (0) | 0 | <0.01 |
| Potawatomi (0) | 1 | <0.01 |
| Pueblo (0) | 0 | <0.01 |
| Puget Sound Salish (0) | 0 | <0.01 |
| Seminole (0) | 2 | <0.01 |
| Shoshone (1) | 2 | <0.01 |
| Sioux (4) | 7 | 0.01 |
| South American Ind. (4) | 7 | 0.01 |
| Spanish American Ind. (0) | 0 | <0.01 |
| Tlingit-Haida (Alaska Native) (1) | 1 | <0.01 |
| Tohono O'Odham (0) | 0 | <0.01 |
| Tsimshian (Alaska Native) (0) | 0 | <0.01 |
| Ute (0) | 0 | <0.01 |
| Yakama (0) | 0 | <0.01 |
| Yaqui (0) | 1 | <0.01 |
| Yuman (0) | 0 | <0.01 |
| Yup'ik (Alaska Native) (0) | 1 | <0.01 |
| Asian (367) | 500 | 1.04 |
| Not Hispanic (363) | 483 | 1.01 |
| Hispanic (4) | 17 | 0.04 |
| Bangladeshi (2) | 2 | <0.01 |
| Bhutanese (3) | 3 | 0.01 |
| Burmese (2) | 2 | <0.01 |
| Cambodian (2) | 2 | <0.01 |
| Chinese, ex. Taiwanese (104) | 136 | 0.28 |
| Filipino (70) | 101 | 0.21 |
| Hmong (0) | 0 | <0.01 |
| Indian (74) | 101 | 0.21 |
| Indonesian (1) | 4 | 0.01 |
| Japanese (45) | 69 | 0.14 |
| Korean (24) | 29 | 0.06 |
| Laotian (2) | 8 | 0.02 |
| Malaysian (0) | 0 | <0.01 |
| Nepalese (1) | 1 | <0.01 |
| Pakistani (9) | 9 | 0.02 |
| Sri Lankan (3) | 3 | 0.01 |
| Taiwanese (6) | 6 | 0.01 |
| Thai (1) | 1 | <0.01 |
| Vietnamese (5) | 11 | 0.02 |
| Hawaii Native/Pacific Islander (12) | 35 | 0.07 |
| Not Hispanic (6) | 24 | 0.05 |
| Hispanic (6) | 11 | 0.02 |
| Fijian (0) | 0 | <0.01 |
| Guamanian/Chamorro (6) | 8 | 0.02 |
| Marshallese (0) | 0 | <0.01 |
| Native Hawaiian (2) | 6 | 0.01 |
| Samoan (0) | 5 | 0.01 |
| Tongan (0) | 0 | <0.01 |
| White (45,675) | 46,241 | 96.38 |
| Not Hispanic (44,706) | 45,191 | 94.19 |
| Hispanic (969) | 1,050 | 2.19 |

*Notes: † The Census 2010 population figure is used to calculate the percentages in the Hispanic Origin and Race categories. Ancestry percentages are based on the 2006-2010 American Community Survey population (not shown); ‡ Numbers in parentheses indicate the number of people reporting a single ancestry; * Numbers in parentheses indicate the number of persons reporting this race alone, not in combination with any other race; Please refer to the Explanation of Data for more information.*

## Dutchess County

Population: 297,488

| Ancestry | Population | % |
|---|---|---|
| Afghan (18) | 18 | 0.01 |
| African, Sub-Saharan (1,645) | 2,652 | 0.90 |
| African (874) | 1,553 | 0.52 |
| Cape Verdean (0) | 0 | <0.01 |
| Ethiopian (0) | 0 | <0.01 |
| Ghanaian (121) | 121 | 0.04 |
| Kenyan (32) | 32 | 0.01 |
| Liberian (0) | 0 | <0.01 |
| Nigerian (383) | 632 | 0.21 |
| Senegalese (0) | 12 | <0.01 |
| Sierra Leonean (0) | 0 | <0.01 |
| Somalian (0) | 0 | <0.01 |
| South African (50) | 84 | 0.03 |
| Sudanese (0) | 0 | <0.01 |
| Ugandan (0) | 0 | <0.01 |
| Zimbabwean (0) | 0 | <0.01 |
| Other Sub-Saharan African (185) | 218 | 0.07 |
| Albanian (700) | 799 | 0.27 |
| Alsatian (0) | 10 | <0.01 |
| American (7,260) | 7,260 | 2.45 |
| Arab (1,145) | 2,373 | 0.80 |
| Arab (118) | 335 | 0.11 |
| Egyptian (43) | 131 | 0.04 |
| Iraqi (0) | 0 | <0.01 |
| Jordanian (552) | 808 | 0.27 |
| Lebanese (257) | 562 | 0.19 |
| Moroccan (65) | 65 | 0.02 |
| Palestinian (0) | 183 | 0.06 |
| Syrian (11) | 53 | 0.02 |
| Other Arab (99) | 236 | 0.08 |
| Armenian (116) | 253 | 0.09 |
| Assyrian/Chaldean/Syriac (0) | 0 | <0.01 |
| Australian (40) | 134 | 0.05 |
| Austrian (398) | 1,727 | 0.58 |
| Basque (19) | 32 | 0.01 |
| Belgian (53) | 345 | 0.12 |
| Brazilian (93) | 184 | 0.06 |
| British (511) | 1,357 | 0.46 |
| Bulgarian (106) | 139 | 0.05 |
| Cajun (30) | 61 | 0.02 |
| Canadian (222) | 656 | 0.22 |
| Carpatho Rusyn (27) | 38 | 0.01 |
| Celtic (8) | 46 | 0.02 |
| Croatian (57) | 338 | 0.11 |
| Cypriot (9) | 9 | <0.01 |
| Czech (443) | 1,985 | 0.67 |
| Czechoslovakian (129) | 515 | 0.17 |
| Danish (110) | 914 | 0.31 |
| Dutch (1,356) | 8,775 | 2.96 |
| Eastern European (414) | 596 | 0.20 |
| English (5,208) | 28,099 | 9.49 |
| Estonian (32) | 50 | 0.02 |
| European (1,482) | 1,666 | 0.56 |
| Finnish (113) | 488 | 0.16 |
| French, ex. Basque (1,230) | 9,725 | 3.28 |
| French Canadian (1,021) | 2,977 | 1.01 |
| German (9,511) | 51,637 | 17.44 |
| German Russian (0) | 0 | <0.01 |
| Greek (1,086) | 2,738 | 0.92 |
| Guyanese (233) | 263 | 0.09 |
| Hungarian (969) | 3,435 | 1.16 |
| Icelander (7) | 32 | 0.01 |
| Iranian (97) | 203 | 0.07 |
| Irish (18,790) | 70,744 | 23.89 |
| Israeli (127) | 217 | 0.07 |
| Italian (29,305) | 69,349 | 23.42 |
| Latvian (212) | 328 | 0.11 |
| Lithuanian (335) | 957 | 0.32 |
| Luxemburger (0) | 0 | <0.01 |
| Macedonian (57) | 57 | 0.02 |
| Maltese (53) | 92 | 0.03 |
| New Zealander (21) | 53 | 0.02 |
| Northern European (137) | 198 | 0.07 |
| Norwegian (521) | 2,307 | 0.78 |
| Pennsylvania German (16) | 188 | 0.06 |

| Ancestry | Population | % |
|---|---|---|
| Polish (3,538) | 14,799 | 5.00 |
| Portuguese (589) | 1,539 | 0.52 |
| Romanian (130) | 592 | 0.20 |
| Russian (1,673) | 5,793 | 1.96 |
| Scandinavian (100) | 252 | 0.09 |
| Scotch-Irish (1,448) | 4,218 | 1.42 |
| Scottish (1,334) | 5,831 | 1.97 |
| Serbian (45) | 132 | 0.04 |
| Slavic (128) | 319 | 0.11 |
| Slovak (349) | 888 | 0.30 |
| Slovene (36) | 94 | 0.03 |
| Soviet Union (0) | 0 | <0.01 |
| Swedish (627) | 3,518 | 1.19 |
| Swiss (289) | 1,231 | 0.42 |
| Turkish (67) | 226 | 0.08 |
| Ukrainian (470) | 1,586 | 0.54 |
| Welsh (180) | 1,432 | 0.48 |
| West Indian, ex. Hispanic (5,456) | 7,721 | 2.61 |
| Bahamian (0) | 0 | <0.01 |
| Barbadian (0) | 36 | 0.01 |
| Belizean (53) | 83 | 0.03 |
| Bermudan (0) | 0 | <0.01 |
| British West Indian (89) | 117 | 0.04 |
| Dutch West Indian (0) | 0 | <0.01 |
| Haitian (257) | 507 | 0.17 |
| Jamaican (4,473) | 5,581 | 1.88 |
| Trinidadian/Tobagonian (250) | 356 | 0.12 |
| U.S. Virgin Islander (7) | 55 | 0.02 |
| West Indian (327) | 986 | 0.33 |
| Other West Indian (0) | 0 | <0.01 |
| Yugoslavian (315) | 617 | 0.21 |

| Hispanic Origin | Population | % |
|---|---|---|
| Hispanic or Latino (of any race) | 31,267 | 10.51 |
| Central American, ex. Mexican | 2,115 | 0.71 |
| Costa Rican | 135 | 0.05 |
| Guatemalan | 1,032 | 0.35 |
| Honduran | 333 | 0.11 |
| Nicaraguan | 86 | 0.03 |
| Panamanian | 159 | 0.05 |
| Salvadoran | 361 | 0.12 |
| Other Central American | 9 | <0.01 |
| Cuban | 1,069 | 0.36 |
| Dominican Republic | 1,860 | 0.63 |
| Mexican | 7,575 | 2.55 |
| Puerto Rican | 11,984 | 4.03 |
| South American | 4,140 | 1.39 |
| Argentinean | 293 | 0.10 |
| Bolivian | 55 | 0.02 |
| Chilean | 179 | 0.06 |
| Colombian | 1,096 | 0.37 |
| Ecuadorian | 1,531 | 0.51 |
| Paraguayan | 48 | 0.02 |
| Peruvian | 576 | 0.19 |
| Uruguayan | 163 | 0.05 |
| Venezuelan | 149 | 0.05 |
| Other South American | 50 | 0.02 |
| Other Hispanic or Latino | 2,524 | 0.85 |

| Race* | Population | % |
|---|---|---|
| African-American/Black (29,518) | 33,599 | 11.29 |
| Not Hispanic (27,395) | 30,458 | 10.24 |
| Hispanic (2,123) | 3,141 | 1.06 |
| American Indian/Alaska Native (893) | 2,648 | 0.89 |
| Not Hispanic (465) | 1,829 | 0.61 |
| Hispanic (428) | 819 | 0.28 |
| Alaska Athabascan (Ala. Nat.) (0) | 0 | <0.01 |
| Aleut (Alaska Native) (3) | 4 | <0.01 |
| Apache (4) | 24 | 0.01 |
| Arapaho (0) | 0 | <0.01 |
| Blackfeet (20) | 109 | 0.04 |
| Canadian/French Am. Ind. (4) | 7 | <0.01 |
| Central American Ind. (9) | 32 | 0.01 |
| Cherokee (43) | 401 | 0.13 |
| Cheyenne (2) | 3 | <0.01 |
| Chickasaw (1) | 4 | <0.01 |
| Chippewa (9) | 18 | 0.01 |
| Choctaw (4) | 13 | <0.01 |
| Colville (1) | 1 | <0.01 |

| | Population | % |
|---|---|---|
| Comanche (1) | 2 | <0.01 |
| Cree (0) | 3 | <0.01 |
| Creek (4) | 13 | <0.01 |
| Crow (0) | 5 | <0.01 |
| Delaware (1) | 5 | <0.01 |
| Hopi (0) | 2 | <0.01 |
| Houma (0) | 0 | <0.01 |
| Inupiat (Alaska Native) (3) | 3 | <0.01 |
| Iroquois (72) | 215 | 0.07 |
| Kiowa (0) | 0 | <0.01 |
| Lumbee (5) | 12 | <0.01 |
| Menominee (3) | 4 | <0.01 |
| Mexican American Ind. (157) | 200 | 0.07 |
| Navajo (4) | 17 | 0.01 |
| Osage (3) | 3 | <0.01 |
| Ottawa (2) | 2 | <0.01 |
| Paiute (0) | 1 | <0.01 |
| Pima (0) | 0 | <0.01 |
| Potawatomi (0) | 2 | <0.01 |
| Pueblo (0) | 8 | <0.01 |
| Puget Sound Salish (0) | 0 | <0.01 |
| Seminole (3) | 24 | 0.01 |
| Shoshone (0) | 3 | <0.01 |
| Sioux (11) | 45 | 0.02 |
| South American Ind. (53) | 115 | 0.04 |
| Spanish American Ind. (3) | 8 | <0.01 |
| Tlingit-Haida (Alaska Native) (0) | 1 | <0.01 |
| Tohono O'Odham (2) | 4 | <0.01 |
| Tsimshian (Alaska Native) (0) | 0 | <0.01 |
| Ute (1) | 2 | <0.01 |
| Yakama (2) | 2 | <0.01 |
| Yaqui (0) | 0 | <0.01 |
| Yuman (0) | 0 | <0.01 |
| Yup'ik (Alaska Native) (0) | 0 | <0.01 |
| Asian (10,437) | 12,220 | 4.11 |
| Not Hispanic (10,330) | 11,925 | 4.01 |
| Hispanic (107) | 295 | 0.10 |
| Bangladeshi (166) | 190 | 0.06 |
| Bhutanese (0) | 0 | <0.01 |
| Burmese (51) | 54 | 0.02 |
| Cambodian (34) | 49 | 0.02 |
| Chinese, ex. Taiwanese (2,733) | 3,188 | 1.07 |
| Filipino (869) | 1,215 | 0.41 |
| Hmong (0) | 0 | <0.01 |
| Indian (3,531) | 3,939 | 1.32 |
| Indonesian (26) | 53 | 0.02 |
| Japanese (367) | 560 | 0.19 |
| Korean (1,167) | 1,331 | 0.45 |
| Laotian (37) | 44 | 0.01 |
| Malaysian (14) | 25 | 0.01 |
| Nepalese (42) | 43 | 0.01 |
| Pakistani (370) | 429 | 0.14 |
| Sri Lankan (43) | 59 | 0.02 |
| Taiwanese (127) | 144 | 0.05 |
| Thai (74) | 115 | 0.04 |
| Vietnamese (450) | 527 | 0.18 |
| Hawaii Native/Pacific Islander (108) | 356 | 0.12 |
| Not Hispanic (80) | 253 | 0.09 |
| Hispanic (28) | 103 | 0.03 |
| Fijian (0) | 1 | <0.01 |
| Guamanian/Chamorro (23) | 44 | 0.01 |
| Marshallese (0) | 1 | <0.01 |
| Native Hawaiian (26) | 79 | 0.03 |
| Samoan (7) | 17 | 0.01 |
| Tongan (3) | 8 | <0.01 |
| White (238,387) | 244,919 | 82.33 |
| Not Hispanic (221,812) | 226,434 | 76.12 |
| Hispanic (16,575) | 18,485 | 6.21 |

*Notes: † The Census 2010 population figure is used to calculate the percentages in the Hispanic Origin and Race categories. Ancestry percentages are based on the 2006-2010 American Community Survey population (not shown); ‡ Numbers in parentheses indicate the number of people reporting a single ancestry; * Numbers in parentheses indicate the number of persons reporting this race alone, not in combination with any other race; Please refer to the Explanation of Data for more information.*

## Erie County

Population: 919,040

| Ancestry | Population | % |
|---|---|---|
| Afghan (430) | 430 | 0.05 |
| African, Sub-Saharan (6,954) | 7,909 | 0.86 |
| African (4,615) | 5,206 | 0.57 |
| Cape Verdean (95) | 95 | 0.01 |
| Ethiopian (307) | 307 | 0.03 |
| Ghanaian (83) | 83 | 0.01 |
| Kenyan (74) | 136 | 0.01 |
| Liberian (92) | 107 | 0.01 |
| Nigerian (302) | 313 | 0.03 |
| Senegalese (0) | 18 | <0.01 |
| Sierra Leonean (17) | 17 | <0.01 |
| Somalian (706) | 858 | 0.09 |
| South African (79) | 92 | 0.01 |
| Sudanese (259) | 268 | 0.03 |
| Ugandan (24) | 33 | <0.01 |
| Zimbabwean (45) | 45 | <0.01 |
| Other Sub-Saharan African (256) | 331 | 0.04 |
| Albanian (515) | 763 | 0.08 |
| Alsatian (50) | 188 | 0.02 |
| American (23,171) | 23,171 | 2.52 |
| Arab (5,684) | 8,086 | 0.88 |
| Arab (2,321) | 2,545 | 0.28 |
| Egyptian (73) | 158 | 0.02 |
| Iraqi (316) | 318 | 0.03 |
| Jordanian (95) | 108 | 0.01 |
| Lebanese (1,316) | 3,012 | 0.33 |
| Moroccan (34) | 96 | 0.01 |
| Palestinian (42) | 42 | <0.01 |
| Syrian (116) | 306 | 0.03 |
| Other Arab (1,371) | 1,501 | 0.16 |
| Armenian (282) | 517 | 0.06 |
| Assyrian/Chaldean/Syriac (0) | 0 | <0.01 |
| Australian (57) | 153 | 0.02 |
| Austrian (952) | 4,008 | 0.44 |
| Basque (9) | 9 | <0.01 |
| Belgian (77) | 354 | 0.04 |
| Brazilian (323) | 370 | 0.04 |
| British (1,012) | 2,544 | 0.28 |
| Bulgarian (530) | 715 | 0.08 |
| Cajun (15) | 26 | <0.01 |
| Canadian (1,587) | 3,446 | 0.37 |
| Carpatho Rusyn (6) | 19 | <0.01 |
| Celtic (80) | 132 | 0.01 |
| Croatian (914) | 2,803 | 0.30 |
| Cypriot (17) | 17 | <0.01 |
| Czech (414) | 2,207 | 0.24 |
| Czechoslovakian (396) | 1,048 | 0.11 |
| Danish (250) | 1,162 | 0.13 |
| Dutch (1,341) | 9,750 | 1.06 |
| Eastern European (1,072) | 1,169 | 0.13 |
| English (16,244) | 70,914 | 7.70 |
| Estonian (110) | 316 | 0.03 |
| European (3,832) | 4,225 | 0.46 |
| Finnish (213) | 883 | 0.10 |
| French, ex. Basque (2,539) | 25,048 | 2.72 |
| French Canadian (1,843) | 6,635 | 0.72 |
| German (68,487) | 245,605 | 26.66 |
| German Russian (61) | 86 | 0.01 |
| Greek (1,933) | 4,465 | 0.48 |
| Guyanese (616) | 628 | 0.07 |
| Hungarian (2,785) | 9,692 | 1.05 |
| Icelander (25) | 37 | <0.01 |
| Iranian (318) | 403 | 0.04 |
| Irish (39,231) | 163,985 | 17.80 |
| Israeli (179) | 302 | 0.03 |
| Italian (65,466) | 152,676 | 16.57 |
| Latvian (130) | 237 | 0.03 |
| Lithuanian (369) | 1,275 | 0.14 |
| Luxemburger (0) | 45 | <0.01 |
| Macedonian (326) | 486 | 0.05 |
| Maltese (21) | 58 | 0.01 |
| New Zealander (11) | 37 | <0.01 |
| Northern European (318) | 441 | 0.05 |
| Norwegian (767) | 2,897 | 0.31 |
| Pennsylvania German (296) | 680 | 0.07 |

| Ancestry (cont.) | Population | % |
|---|---|---|
| Polish (80,210) | 174,651 | 18.96 |
| Portuguese (349) | 1,172 | 0.13 |
| Romanian (392) | 909 | 0.10 |
| Russian (3,531) | 8,992 | 0.98 |
| Scandinavian (71) | 489 | 0.05 |
| Scotch-Irish (3,515) | 10,370 | 1.13 |
| Scottish (2,997) | 14,392 | 1.56 |
| Serbian (785) | 1,550 | 0.17 |
| Slavic (286) | 741 | 0.08 |
| Slovak (407) | 1,584 | 0.17 |
| Slovene (86) | 261 | 0.03 |
| Soviet Union (0) | 0 | <0.01 |
| Swedish (1,594) | 8,485 | 0.92 |
| Swiss (267) | 1,342 | 0.15 |
| Turkish (457) | 687 | 0.07 |
| Ukrainian (3,183) | 7,778 | 0.84 |
| Welsh (957) | 5,167 | 0.56 |
| West Indian, ex. Hispanic (3,504) | 4,339 | 0.47 |
| Bahamian (34) | 34 | <0.01 |
| Barbadian (38) | 64 | 0.01 |
| Belizean (0) | 50 | 0.01 |
| Bermudan (0) | 0 | <0.01 |
| British West Indian (128) | 141 | 0.02 |
| Dutch West Indian (0) | 17 | <0.01 |
| Haitian (679) | 864 | 0.09 |
| Jamaican (1,863) | 2,179 | 0.24 |
| Trinidadian/Tobagonian (299) | 349 | 0.04 |
| U.S. Virgin Islander (0) | 0 | <0.01 |
| West Indian (463) | 641 | 0.07 |
| Other West Indian (0) | 0 | <0.01 |
| Yugoslavian (890) | 1,263 | 0.14 |

| Hispanic Origin | Population | % |
|---|---|---|
| Hispanic or Latino (of any race) | 41,731 | 4.54 |
| Central American, ex. Mexican | 1,034 | 0.11 |
| Costa Rican | 89 | 0.01 |
| Guatemalan | 305 | 0.03 |
| Honduran | 140 | 0.02 |
| Nicaraguan | 58 | 0.01 |
| Panamanian | 200 | 0.02 |
| Salvadoran | 224 | 0.02 |
| Other Central American | 18 | <0.01 |
| Cuban | 1,214 | 0.13 |
| Dominican Republic | 1,179 | 0.13 |
| Mexican | 3,992 | 0.43 |
| Puerto Rican | 29,400 | 3.20 |
| South American | 1,831 | 0.20 |
| Argentinean | 229 | 0.02 |
| Bolivian | 77 | 0.01 |
| Chilean | 113 | 0.01 |
| Colombian | 684 | 0.07 |
| Ecuadorian | 282 | 0.03 |
| Paraguayan | 27 | <0.01 |
| Peruvian | 245 | 0.03 |
| Uruguayan | 13 | <0.01 |
| Venezuelan | 136 | 0.01 |
| Other South American | 25 | <0.01 |
| Other Hispanic or Latino | 3,081 | 0.34 |

| Race* | Population | % |
|---|---|---|
| African-American/Black (123,931) | 133,049 | 14.48 |
| Not Hispanic (119,916) | 127,397 | 13.86 |
| Hispanic (4,015) | 5,652 | 0.61 |
| American Indian/Alaska Native (5,908) | 10,110 | 1.10 |
| Not Hispanic (5,199) | 8,799 | 0.96 |
| Hispanic (709) | 1,311 | 0.14 |
| Alaska Athabascan (Ala. Nat.) (1) | 3 | <0.01 |
| Aleut (Alaska Native) (0) | 0 | <0.01 |
| Apache (7) | 26 | <0.01 |
| Arapaho (1) | 2 | <0.01 |
| Blackfeet (22) | 188 | 0.02 |
| Canadian/French Am. Ind. (84) | 141 | 0.02 |
| Central American Ind. (14) | 24 | <0.01 |
| Cherokee (87) | 579 | 0.06 |
| Cheyenne (0) | 5 | <0.01 |
| Chickasaw (2) | 3 | <0.01 |
| Chippewa (60) | 105 | 0.01 |
| Choctaw (12) | 44 | <0.01 |
| Colville (0) | 0 | <0.01 |

| Race* (cont.) | Population | % |
|---|---|---|
| Comanche (2) | 6 | <0.01 |
| Cree (2) | 9 | <0.01 |
| Creek (8) | 23 | <0.01 |
| Crow (4) | 12 | <0.01 |
| Delaware (13) | 24 | <0.01 |
| Hopi (4) | 9 | <0.01 |
| Houma (1) | 2 | <0.01 |
| Inupiat (Alaska Native) (3) | 9 | <0.01 |
| Iroquois (3,416) | 4,481 | 0.49 |
| Kiowa (1) | 1 | <0.01 |
| Lumbee (3) | 10 | <0.01 |
| Menominee (3) | 8 | <0.01 |
| Mexican American Ind. (63) | 90 | 0.01 |
| Navajo (25) | 43 | <0.01 |
| Osage (6) | 6 | <0.01 |
| Ottawa (1) | 4 | <0.01 |
| Paiute (7) | 9 | <0.01 |
| Pima (1) | 4 | <0.01 |
| Potawatomi (8) | 16 | <0.01 |
| Pueblo (5) | 12 | <0.01 |
| Puget Sound Salish (1) | 2 | <0.01 |
| Seminole (3) | 40 | <0.01 |
| Shoshone (0) | 0 | <0.01 |
| Sioux (39) | 78 | <0.01 |
| South American Ind. (41) | 110 | 0.01 |
| Spanish American Ind. (20) | 27 | <0.01 |
| Tlingit-Haida (Alaska Native) (3) | 6 | <0.01 |
| Tohono O'Odham (3) | 5 | <0.01 |
| Tsimshian (Alaska Native) (0) | 0 | <0.01 |
| Ute (0) | 0 | <0.01 |
| Yakama (0) | 0 | <0.01 |
| Yaqui (3) | 3 | <0.01 |
| Yuman (2) | 2 | <0.01 |
| Yup'ik (Alaska Native) (1) | 3 | <0.01 |
| Asian (23,789) | 27,624 | 3.01 |
| Not Hispanic (23,621) | 27,176 | 2.96 |
| Hispanic (168) | 448 | 0.05 |
| Bangladeshi (217) | 260 | 0.03 |
| Bhutanese (298) | 370 | 0.04 |
| Burmese (2,313) | 2,414 | 0.26 |
| Cambodian (88) | 102 | 0.01 |
| Chinese, ex. Taiwanese (4,978) | 5,566 | 0.61 |
| Filipino (928) | 1,490 | 0.16 |
| Hmong (6) | 8 | <0.01 |
| Indian (6,796) | 7,576 | 0.82 |
| Indonesian (65) | 103 | 0.01 |
| Japanese (490) | 838 | 0.09 |
| Korean (2,356) | 2,775 | 0.30 |
| Laotian (369) | 445 | 0.05 |
| Malaysian (82) | 97 | 0.01 |
| Nepalese (140) | 185 | 0.02 |
| Pakistani (1,014) | 1,159 | 0.13 |
| Sri Lankan (198) | 219 | 0.02 |
| Taiwanese (241) | 285 | 0.03 |
| Thai (176) | 281 | 0.03 |
| Vietnamese (2,037) | 2,256 | 0.25 |
| Hawaii Native/Pacific Islander (219) | 714 | 0.08 |
| Not Hispanic (165) | 552 | 0.06 |
| Hispanic (54) | 162 | 0.02 |
| Fijian (6) | 6 | <0.01 |
| Guamanian/Chamorro (40) | 88 | 0.01 |
| Marshallese (1) | 1 | <0.01 |
| Native Hawaiian (46) | 185 | 0.02 |
| Samoan (45) | 112 | 0.01 |
| Tongan (3) | 4 | <0.01 |
| White (735,244) | 749,229 | 81.52 |
| Not Hispanic (714,156) | 725,671 | 78.96 |
| Hispanic (21,088) | 23,558 | 2.56 |

## Essex County

Population: 39,370

| Ancestry | Population | % |
|---|---|---|
| Afghan (0) | 0 | <0.01 |
| African, Sub-Saharan (83) | 96 | 0.24 |
| African (55) | 67 | 0.17 |
| Cape Verdean (17) | 18 | 0.05 |
| Ethiopian (11) | 11 | 0.03 |
| Ghanaian (0) | 0 | <0.01 |
| Kenyan (0) | 0 | <0.01 |
| Liberian (0) | 0 | <0.01 |
| Nigerian (0) | 0 | <0.01 |
| Senegalese (0) | 0 | <0.01 |
| Sierra Leonean (0) | 0 | <0.01 |
| Somalian (0) | 0 | <0.01 |
| South African (0) | 0 | <0.01 |
| Sudanese (0) | 0 | <0.01 |
| Ugandan (0) | 0 | <0.01 |
| Zimbabwean (0) | 0 | <0.01 |
| Other Sub-Saharan African (0) | 0 | <0.01 |
| Albanian (35) | 35 | 0.09 |
| Alsatian (0) | 0 | <0.01 |
| American (1,715) | 1,715 | 4.35 |
| Arab (110) | 330 | 0.84 |
| Arab (0) | 0 | <0.01 |
| Egyptian (0) | 0 | <0.01 |
| Iraqi (0) | 0 | <0.01 |
| Jordanian (0) | 0 | <0.01 |
| Lebanese (83) | 157 | 0.40 |
| Moroccan (21) | 56 | 0.14 |
| Palestinian (0) | 74 | 0.19 |
| Syrian (3) | 22 | 0.06 |
| Other Arab (3) | 21 | 0.05 |
| Armenian (35) | 43 | 0.11 |
| Assyrian/Chaldean/Syriac (0) | 0 | <0.01 |
| Australian (0) | 0 | <0.01 |
| Austrian (19) | 86 | 0.22 |
| Basque (0) | 0 | <0.01 |
| Belgian (0) | 18 | 0.05 |
| Brazilian (0) | 0 | <0.01 |
| British (94) | 137 | 0.35 |
| Bulgarian (0) | 0 | <0.01 |
| Cajun (0) | 0 | <0.01 |
| Canadian (156) | 231 | 0.59 |
| Carpatho Rusyn (0) | 0 | <0.01 |
| Celtic (44) | 60 | 0.15 |
| Croatian (0) | 0 | <0.01 |
| Cypriot (0) | 0 | <0.01 |
| Czech (95) | 225 | 0.57 |
| Czechoslovakian (5) | 28 | 0.07 |
| Danish (34) | 93 | 0.24 |
| Dutch (213) | 940 | 2.38 |
| Eastern European (64) | 82 | 0.21 |
| English (1,732) | 5,580 | 14.16 |
| Estonian (0) | 0 | <0.01 |
| European (206) | 216 | 0.55 |
| Finnish (4) | 15 | 0.04 |
| French, ex. Basque (2,335) | 8,236 | 20.90 |
| French Canadian (573) | 921 | 2.34 |
| German (1,511) | 5,372 | 13.63 |
| German Russian (0) | 0 | <0.01 |
| Greek (83) | 199 | 0.50 |
| Guyanese (0) | 10 | 0.03 |
| Hungarian (171) | 308 | 0.78 |
| Icelander (0) | 0 | <0.01 |
| Iranian (0) | 0 | <0.01 |
| Irish (2,945) | 8,753 | 22.21 |
| Israeli (0) | 40 | 0.10 |
| Italian (1,513) | 3,545 | 8.99 |
| Latvian (5) | 5 | 0.01 |
| Lithuanian (17) | 44 | 0.11 |
| Luxemburger (0) | 0 | <0.01 |
| Macedonian (0) | 0 | <0.01 |
| Maltese (0) | 0 | <0.01 |
| New Zealander (0) | 0 | <0.01 |
| Northern European (4) | 4 | 0.01 |
| Norwegian (33) | 268 | 0.68 |
| Pennsylvania German (0) | 11 | 0.03 |

| Ancestry | Population | % |
|---|---|---|
| Polish (383) | 1,483 | 3.76 |
| Portuguese (23) | 27 | 0.07 |
| Romanian (126) | 183 | 0.46 |
| Russian (310) | 688 | 1.75 |
| Scandinavian (9) | 41 | 0.10 |
| Scotch-Irish (249) | 998 | 2.53 |
| Scottish (340) | 1,350 | 3.43 |
| Serbian (9) | 29 | 0.07 |
| Slavic (0) | 14 | 0.04 |
| Slovak (75) | 106 | 0.27 |
| Slovene (0) | 0 | <0.01 |
| Soviet Union (0) | 0 | <0.01 |
| Swedish (112) | 634 | 1.61 |
| Swiss (13) | 108 | 0.27 |
| Turkish (0) | 0 | <0.01 |
| Ukrainian (11) | 53 | 0.13 |
| Welsh (37) | 424 | 1.08 |
| West Indian, ex. Hispanic (75) | 114 | 0.29 |
| Bahamian (0) | 0 | <0.01 |
| Barbadian (0) | 0 | <0.01 |
| Belizean (0) | 0 | <0.01 |
| Bermudan (0) | 0 | <0.01 |
| British West Indian (0) | 10 | 0.03 |
| Dutch West Indian (0) | 0 | <0.01 |
| Haitian (0) | 0 | <0.01 |
| Jamaican (17) | 17 | 0.04 |
| Trinidadian/Tobagonian (11) | 11 | 0.03 |
| U.S. Virgin Islander (0) | 0 | <0.01 |
| West Indian (47) | 76 | 0.19 |
| Other West Indian (0) | 0 | <0.01 |
| Yugoslavian (0) | 0 | <0.01 |

| Hispanic Origin | Population | % |
|---|---|---|
| Hispanic or Latino (of any race) | 993 | 2.52 |
| Central American, ex. Mexican | 92 | 0.23 |
| Costa Rican | 7 | 0.02 |
| Guatemalan | 29 | 0.07 |
| Honduran | 15 | 0.04 |
| Nicaraguan | 3 | 0.01 |
| Panamanian | 7 | 0.02 |
| Salvadoran | 31 | 0.08 |
| Other Central American | 0 | <0.01 |
| Cuban | 25 | 0.06 |
| Dominican Republic | 83 | 0.21 |
| Mexican | 355 | 0.90 |
| Puerto Rican | 296 | 0.75 |
| South American | 42 | 0.11 |
| Argentinean | 3 | 0.01 |
| Bolivian | 0 | <0.01 |
| Chilean | 4 | 0.01 |
| Colombian | 16 | 0.04 |
| Ecuadorian | 0 | <0.01 |
| Paraguayan | 0 | <0.01 |
| Peruvian | 8 | 0.02 |
| Uruguayan | 4 | 0.01 |
| Venezuelan | 7 | 0.02 |
| Other South American | 0 | <0.01 |
| Other Hispanic or Latino | 100 | 0.25 |

| Race* | Population | % |
|---|---|---|
| African-American/Black (1,073) | 1,213 | 3.08 |
| Not Hispanic (982) | 1,101 | 2.80 |
| Hispanic (91) | 112 | 0.28 |
| American Indian/Alaska Native (126) | 370 | 0.94 |
| Not Hispanic (99) | 327 | 0.83 |
| Hispanic (27) | 43 | 0.11 |
| Alaska Athabascan (Ala. Nat.) (1) | 3 | 0.01 |
| Aleut (Alaska Native) (0) | 0 | <0.01 |
| Apache (1) | 2 | 0.01 |
| Arapaho (0) | 0 | <0.01 |
| Blackfeet (4) | 19 | 0.05 |
| Canadian/French Am. Ind. (3) | 8 | 0.02 |
| Central American Ind. (0) | 1 | <0.01 |
| Cherokee (2) | 22 | 0.06 |
| Cheyenne (0) | 1 | <0.01 |
| Chickasaw (0) | 0 | <0.01 |
| Chippewa (1) | 1 | <0.01 |
| Choctaw (2) | 2 | 0.01 |
| Colville (0) | 0 | <0.01 |

| Race* | Population | % |
|---|---|---|
| Comanche (0) | 6 | 0.02 |
| Cree (0) | 6 | 0.02 |
| Creek (0) | 0 | <0.01 |
| Crow (0) | 0 | <0.01 |
| Delaware (0) | 1 | <0.01 |
| Hopi (0) | 1 | <0.01 |
| Houma (0) | 0 | <0.01 |
| Inupiat (Alaska Native) (1) | 1 | <0.01 |
| Iroquois (33) | 101 | 0.26 |
| Kiowa (0) | 0 | <0.01 |
| Lumbee (2) | 7 | 0.02 |
| Menominee (0) | 0 | <0.01 |
| Mexican American Ind. (13) | 14 | 0.04 |
| Navajo (3) | 3 | 0.01 |
| Osage (0) | 0 | <0.01 |
| Ottawa (0) | 0 | <0.01 |
| Paiute (0) | 0 | <0.01 |
| Pima (0) | 0 | <0.01 |
| Potawatomi (0) | 0 | <0.01 |
| Pueblo (0) | 0 | <0.01 |
| Puget Sound Salish (0) | 0 | <0.01 |
| Seminole (0) | 0 | <0.01 |
| Shoshone (0) | 0 | <0.01 |
| Sioux (1) | 8 | 0.02 |
| South American Ind. (0) | 1 | <0.01 |
| Spanish American Ind. (0) | 0 | <0.01 |
| Tlingit-Haida (Alaska Native) (0) | 0 | <0.01 |
| Tohono O'Odham (0) | 0 | <0.01 |
| Tsimshian (Alaska Native) (0) | 0 | <0.01 |
| Ute (0) | 0 | <0.01 |
| Yakama (0) | 0 | <0.01 |
| Yaqui (0) | 1 | <0.01 |
| Yuman (0) | 0 | <0.01 |
| Yup'ik (Alaska Native) (0) | 0 | <0.01 |
| Asian (263) | 324 | 0.82 |
| Not Hispanic (260) | 316 | 0.80 |
| Hispanic (3) | 8 | 0.02 |
| Bangladeshi (0) | 0 | <0.01 |
| Bhutanese (0) | 0 | <0.01 |
| Burmese (0) | 0 | <0.01 |
| Cambodian (5) | 5 | 0.01 |
| Chinese, ex. Taiwanese (63) | 73 | 0.19 |
| Filipino (36) | 54 | 0.14 |
| Hmong (0) | 0 | <0.01 |
| Indian (33) | 41 | 0.10 |
| Indonesian (0) | 0 | <0.01 |
| Japanese (21) | 31 | 0.08 |
| Korean (38) | 46 | 0.12 |
| Laotian (1) | 1 | <0.01 |
| Malaysian (1) | 1 | <0.01 |
| Nepalese (0) | 0 | <0.01 |
| Pakistani (29) | 30 | 0.08 |
| Sri Lankan (0) | 0 | <0.01 |
| Taiwanese (0) | 0 | <0.01 |
| Thai (3) | 6 | 0.02 |
| Vietnamese (17) | 19 | 0.05 |
| Hawaii Native/Pacific Islander (9) | 31 | 0.08 |
| Not Hispanic (8) | 28 | 0.07 |
| Hispanic (1) | 3 | 0.01 |
| Fijian (0) | 0 | <0.01 |
| Guamanian/Chamorro (1) | 3 | 0.01 |
| Marshallese (0) | 0 | <0.01 |
| Native Hawaiian (5) | 15 | 0.04 |
| Samoan (0) | 1 | <0.01 |
| Tongan (3) | 3 | 0.01 |
| White (37,100) | 37,536 | 95.34 |
| Not Hispanic (36,588) | 36,969 | 93.90 |
| Hispanic (512) | 567 | 1.44 |

Notes: † The Census 2010 population figure is used to calculate the percentages in the Hispanic Origin and Race categories. Ancestry percentages are based on the 2006-2010 American Community Survey population (not shown); ‡ Numbers in parentheses indicate the number of people reporting a single ancestry; * Numbers in parentheses indicate the number of persons reporting this race alone, not in combination with any other race; Please refer to the Explanation of Data for more information.

## Franklin County

Population: 51,599

| Ancestry | Population | % |
|---|---|---|
| Afghan (0) | 0 | <0.01 |
| African, Sub-Saharan (46) | 191 | 0.37 |
| African (46) | 182 | 0.35 |
| Cape Verdean (0) | 0 | <0.01 |
| Ethiopian (0) | 0 | <0.01 |
| Ghanaian (0) | 0 | <0.01 |
| Kenyan (0) | 0 | <0.01 |
| Liberian (0) | 0 | <0.01 |
| Nigerian (0) | 0 | <0.01 |
| Senegalese (0) | 0 | <0.01 |
| Sierra Leonean (0) | 0 | <0.01 |
| Somalian (0) | 0 | <0.01 |
| South African (0) | 9 | 0.02 |
| Sudanese (0) | 0 | <0.01 |
| Ugandan (0) | 0 | <0.01 |
| Zimbabwean (0) | 0 | <0.01 |
| Other Sub-Saharan African (0) | 0 | <0.01 |
| Albanian (74) | 74 | 0.14 |
| Alsatian (0) | 0 | <0.01 |
| American (3,069) | 3,069 | 5.94 |
| Arab (243) | 285 | 0.55 |
| Arab (12) | 12 | 0.02 |
| Egyptian (0) | 0 | <0.01 |
| Iraqi (0) | 0 | <0.01 |
| Jordanian (0) | 0 | <0.01 |
| Lebanese (59) | 82 | 0.16 |
| Moroccan (80) | 80 | 0.15 |
| Palestinian (0) | 0 | <0.01 |
| Syrian (13) | 22 | 0.04 |
| Other Arab (79) | 89 | 0.17 |
| Armenian (8) | 8 | 0.02 |
| Assyrian/Chaldean/Syriac (0) | 0 | <0.01 |
| Australian (0) | 14 | 0.03 |
| Austrian (21) | 143 | 0.28 |
| Basque (0) | 0 | <0.01 |
| Belgian (5) | 22 | 0.04 |
| Brazilian (5) | 5 | 0.01 |
| British (82) | 128 | 0.25 |
| Bulgarian (15) | 15 | 0.03 |
| Cajun (0) | 0 | <0.01 |
| Canadian (249) | 431 | 0.83 |
| Carpatho Rusyn (0) | 0 | <0.01 |
| Celtic (0) | 7 | 0.01 |
| Croatian (0) | 14 | 0.03 |
| Cypriot (0) | 0 | <0.01 |
| Czech (10) | 73 | 0.14 |
| Czechoslovakian (0) | 6 | 0.01 |
| Danish (23) | 138 | 0.27 |
| Dutch (163) | 1,095 | 2.12 |
| Eastern European (13) | 20 | 0.04 |
| English (1,709) | 5,133 | 9.93 |
| Estonian (0) | 0 | <0.01 |
| European (179) | 191 | 0.37 |
| Finnish (6) | 18 | 0.03 |
| French, ex. Basque (3,834) | 11,336 | 21.93 |
| French Canadian (1,852) | 2,810 | 5.44 |
| German (937) | 4,795 | 9.28 |
| German Russian (0) | 0 | <0.01 |
| Greek (63) | 144 | 0.28 |
| Guyanese (99) | 187 | 0.36 |
| Hungarian (32) | 205 | 0.40 |
| Icelander (0) | 0 | <0.01 |
| Iranian (0) | 0 | <0.01 |
| Irish (2,541) | 9,398 | 18.18 |
| Israeli (0) | 21 | 0.04 |
| Italian (794) | 2,508 | 4.85 |
| Latvian (0) | 0 | <0.01 |
| Lithuanian (12) | 94 | 0.18 |
| Luxemburger (0) | 6 | 0.01 |
| Macedonian (0) | 0 | <0.01 |
| Maltese (0) | 0 | <0.01 |
| New Zealander (0) | 0 | <0.01 |
| Northern European (23) | 38 | 0.07 |
| Norwegian (35) | 145 | 0.28 |
| Pennsylvania German (58) | 115 | 0.22 |

| Ancestry (cont.) | Population | % |
|---|---|---|
| Polish (407) | 1,135 | 2.20 |
| Portuguese (30) | 60 | 0.12 |
| Romanian (2) | 18 | 0.03 |
| Russian (101) | 306 | 0.59 |
| Scandinavian (22) | 38 | 0.07 |
| Scotch-Irish (293) | 865 | 1.67 |
| Scottish (326) | 1,124 | 2.17 |
| Serbian (0) | 0 | <0.01 |
| Slavic (0) | 0 | <0.01 |
| Slovak (18) | 37 | 0.07 |
| Slovene (9) | 15 | 0.03 |
| Soviet Union (0) | 0 | <0.01 |
| Swedish (40) | 285 | 0.55 |
| Swiss (59) | 159 | 0.31 |
| Turkish (16) | 22 | 0.04 |
| Ukrainian (85) | 200 | 0.39 |
| Welsh (41) | 336 | 0.65 |
| West Indian, ex. Hispanic (27) | 65 | 0.13 |
| Bahamian (0) | 0 | <0.01 |
| Barbadian (0) | 0 | <0.01 |
| Belizean (0) | 0 | <0.01 |
| Bermudan (0) | 0 | <0.01 |
| British West Indian (0) | 0 | <0.01 |
| Dutch West Indian (0) | 0 | <0.01 |
| Haitian (0) | 14 | 0.03 |
| Jamaican (19) | 35 | 0.07 |
| Trinidadian/Tobagonian (8) | 8 | 0.02 |
| U.S. Virgin Islander (0) | 0 | <0.01 |
| West Indian (0) | 8 | 0.02 |
| Other West Indian (0) | 0 | <0.01 |
| Yugoslavian (0) | 25 | 0.05 |

| Hispanic Origin | Population | % |
|---|---|---|
| Hispanic or Latino (of any race) | 1,506 | 2.92 |
| Central American, ex. Mexican | 123 | 0.24 |
| Costa Rican | 7 | 0.01 |
| Guatemalan | 25 | 0.05 |
| Honduran | 37 | 0.07 |
| Nicaraguan | 1 | <0.01 |
| Panamanian | 26 | 0.05 |
| Salvadoran | 27 | 0.05 |
| Other Central American | 0 | <0.01 |
| Cuban | 55 | 0.11 |
| Dominican Republic | 209 | 0.41 |
| Mexican | 211 | 0.41 |
| Puerto Rican | 730 | 1.41 |
| South American | 79 | 0.15 |
| Argentinean | 2 | <0.01 |
| Bolivian | 0 | <0.01 |
| Chilean | 2 | <0.01 |
| Colombian | 24 | 0.05 |
| Ecuadorian | 24 | 0.05 |
| Paraguayan | 0 | <0.01 |
| Peruvian | 18 | 0.03 |
| Uruguayan | 1 | <0.01 |
| Venezuelan | 8 | 0.02 |
| Other South American | 0 | <0.01 |
| Other Hispanic or Latino | 99 | 0.19 |

| Race* | Population | % |
|---|---|---|
| African-American/Black (3,127) | 3,262 | 6.32 |
| Not Hispanic (2,834) | 2,957 | 5.73 |
| Hispanic (293) | 305 | 0.59 |
| American Indian/Alaska Native (3,797) | 4,187 | 8.11 |
| Not Hispanic (3,753) | 4,124 | 7.99 |
| Hispanic (44) | 63 | 0.12 |
| Alaska Athabascan (Ala. Nat.) (0) | 0 | <0.01 |
| Aleut (Alaska Native) (0) | 0 | <0.01 |
| Apache (3) | 4 | 0.01 |
| Arapaho (0) | 1 | <0.01 |
| Blackfeet (0) | 6 | 0.01 |
| Canadian/French Am. Ind. (5) | 10 | 0.02 |
| Central American Ind. (0) | 0 | <0.01 |
| Cherokee (17) | 36 | 0.07 |
| Cheyenne (0) | 0 | <0.01 |
| Chickasaw (0) | 0 | <0.01 |
| Chippewa (8) | 10 | 0.02 |
| Choctaw (0) | 0 | <0.01 |
| Colville (1) | 1 | <0.01 |

| Race* (cont.) | Population | % |
|---|---|---|
| Comanche (0) | 0 | <0.01 |
| Cree (4) | 4 | 0.01 |
| Creek (1) | 2 | <0.01 |
| Crow (0) | 6 | 0.01 |
| Delaware (7) | 11 | 0.02 |
| Hopi (0) | 0 | <0.01 |
| Houma (0) | 0 | <0.01 |
| Inupiat (Alaska Native) (0) | 0 | <0.01 |
| Iroquois (2,928) | 3,130 | 6.07 |
| Kiowa (0) | 0 | <0.01 |
| Lumbee (1) | 1 | <0.01 |
| Menominee (0) | 0 | <0.01 |
| Mexican American Ind. (8) | 9 | 0.02 |
| Navajo (6) | 6 | 0.01 |
| Osage (0) | 0 | <0.01 |
| Ottawa (0) | 0 | <0.01 |
| Paiute (1) | 1 | <0.01 |
| Pima (0) | 0 | <0.01 |
| Potawatomi (0) | 0 | <0.01 |
| Pueblo (1) | 1 | <0.01 |
| Puget Sound Salish (0) | 0 | <0.01 |
| Seminole (0) | 0 | <0.01 |
| Shoshone (1) | 1 | <0.01 |
| Sioux (1) | 1 | <0.01 |
| South American Ind. (13) | 17 | 0.03 |
| Spanish American Ind. (8) | 8 | 0.02 |
| Tlingit-Haida (Alaska Native) (0) | 1 | <0.01 |
| Tohono O'Odham (0) | 0 | <0.01 |
| Tsimshian (Alaska Native) (0) | 0 | <0.01 |
| Ute (0) | 0 | <0.01 |
| Yakama (0) | 0 | <0.01 |
| Yaqui (1) | 1 | <0.01 |
| Yuman (0) | 0 | <0.01 |
| Yup'ik (Alaska Native) (1) | 1 | <0.01 |
| Asian (219) | 323 | 0.63 |
| Not Hispanic (215) | 307 | 0.59 |
| Hispanic (4) | 16 | 0.03 |
| Bangladeshi (2) | 2 | <0.01 |
| Bhutanese (0) | 0 | <0.01 |
| Burmese (0) | 0 | <0.01 |
| Cambodian (2) | 2 | <0.01 |
| Chinese, ex. Taiwanese (61) | 70 | 0.14 |
| Filipino (36) | 83 | 0.16 |
| Hmong (0) | 0 | <0.01 |
| Indian (51) | 64 | 0.12 |
| Indonesian (0) | 8 | 0.02 |
| Japanese (6) | 11 | 0.02 |
| Korean (18) | 34 | 0.07 |
| Laotian (0) | 3 | <0.01 |
| Malaysian (0) | 0 | <0.01 |
| Nepalese (0) | 0 | <0.01 |
| Pakistani (2) | 2 | <0.01 |
| Sri Lankan (0) | 0 | <0.01 |
| Taiwanese (0) | 0 | <0.01 |
| Thai (0) | 6 | 0.01 |
| Vietnamese (4) | 13 | 0.03 |
| Hawaii Native/Pacific Islander (10) | 23 | 0.04 |
| Not Hispanic (8) | 19 | 0.04 |
| Hispanic (2) | 4 | 0.01 |
| Fijian (0) | 0 | <0.01 |
| Guamanian/Chamorro (1) | 5 | 0.01 |
| Marshallese (0) | 0 | <0.01 |
| Native Hawaiian (0) | 3 | <0.01 |
| Samoan (1) | 2 | <0.01 |
| Tongan (7) | 7 | 0.01 |
| White (43,437) | 44,021 | 85.31 |
| Not Hispanic (42,640) | 43,177 | 83.68 |
| Hispanic (797) | 844 | 1.64 |

Notes: † The Census 2010 population figure is used to calculate the percentages in the Hispanic Origin and Race categories. Ancestry percentages are based on the 2006-2010 American Community Survey population (not shown); ‡ Numbers in parentheses indicate the number of people reporting a single ancestry; * Numbers in parentheses indicate the number of persons reporting this race alone, not in combination with any other race; Please refer to the Explanation of Data for more information.

## Fulton County

Population: 55,531

| Ancestry | Population | % |
|---|---|---|
| Afghan (0) | 0 | <0.01 |
| African, Sub-Saharan (23) | 23 | 0.04 |
| African (23) | 23 | 0.04 |
| Cape Verdean (0) | 0 | <0.01 |
| Ethiopian (0) | 0 | <0.01 |
| Ghanaian (0) | 0 | <0.01 |
| Kenyan (0) | 0 | <0.01 |
| Liberian (0) | 0 | <0.01 |
| Nigerian (0) | 0 | <0.01 |
| Senegalese (0) | 0 | <0.01 |
| Sierra Leonean (0) | 0 | <0.01 |
| Somalian (0) | 0 | <0.01 |
| South African (0) | 0 | <0.01 |
| Sudanese (0) | 0 | <0.01 |
| Ugandan (0) | 0 | <0.01 |
| Zimbabwean (0) | 0 | <0.01 |
| Other Sub-Saharan African (0) | 0 | <0.01 |
| Albanian (0) | 0 | <0.01 |
| Alsatian (0) | 0 | <0.01 |
| American (5,287) | 5,287 | 9.53 |
| Arab (38) | 86 | 0.15 |
| Arab (0) | 0 | <0.01 |
| Egyptian (0) | 0 | <0.01 |
| Iraqi (0) | 0 | <0.01 |
| Jordanian (0) | 0 | <0.01 |
| Lebanese (18) | 57 | 0.10 |
| Moroccan (0) | 0 | <0.01 |
| Palestinian (0) | 9 | 0.02 |
| Syrian (0) | 0 | <0.01 |
| Other Arab (20) | 20 | 0.04 |
| Armenian (37) | 88 | 0.16 |
| Assyrian/Chaldean/Syriac (0) | 0 | <0.01 |
| Australian (0) | 0 | <0.01 |
| Austrian (21) | 81 | 0.15 |
| Basque (0) | 0 | <0.01 |
| Belgian (11) | 35 | 0.06 |
| Brazilian (2) | 8 | 0.01 |
| British (61) | 162 | 0.29 |
| Bulgarian (0) | 15 | 0.03 |
| Cajun (0) | 0 | <0.01 |
| Canadian (162) | 220 | 0.40 |
| Carpatho Rusyn (0) | 0 | <0.01 |
| Celtic (0) | 0 | <0.01 |
| Croatian (0) | 0 | <0.01 |
| Cypriot (0) | 0 | <0.01 |
| Czech (67) | 239 | 0.43 |
| Czechoslovakian (74) | 146 | 0.26 |
| Danish (36) | 125 | 0.23 |
| Dutch (358) | 3,774 | 6.80 |
| Eastern European (32) | 32 | 0.06 |
| English (2,859) | 7,912 | 14.26 |
| Estonian (13) | 13 | 0.02 |
| European (146) | 153 | 0.28 |
| Finnish (13) | 26 | 0.05 |
| French, ex. Basque (486) | 3,837 | 6.91 |
| French Canadian (261) | 694 | 1.25 |
| German (2,540) | 12,273 | 22.11 |
| German Russian (0) | 0 | <0.01 |
| Greek (34) | 142 | 0.26 |
| Guyanese (0) | 0 | <0.01 |
| Hungarian (47) | 284 | 0.51 |
| Icelander (0) | 0 | <0.01 |
| Iranian (142) | 145 | 0.26 |
| Irish (2,348) | 10,129 | 18.25 |
| Israeli (0) | 0 | <0.01 |
| Italian (3,386) | 8,675 | 15.63 |
| Latvian (0) | 25 | 0.05 |
| Lithuanian (187) | 469 | 0.85 |
| Luxemburger (0) | 0 | <0.01 |
| Macedonian (0) | 0 | <0.01 |
| Maltese (0) | 0 | <0.01 |
| New Zealander (0) | 0 | <0.01 |
| Northern European (36) | 36 | 0.06 |
| Norwegian (33) | 279 | 0.50 |
| Pennsylvania German (15) | 46 | 0.08 |

| Ancestry | Population | % |
|---|---|---|
| Polish (1,314) | 4,092 | 7.37 |
| Portuguese (17) | 101 | 0.18 |
| Romanian (0) | 0 | <0.01 |
| Russian (78) | 190 | 0.34 |
| Scandinavian (0) | 6 | 0.01 |
| Scotch-Irish (155) | 653 | 1.18 |
| Scottish (226) | 1,178 | 2.12 |
| Serbian (0) | 0 | <0.01 |
| Slavic (3) | 40 | 0.07 |
| Slovak (328) | 666 | 1.20 |
| Slovene (0) | 4 | 0.01 |
| Soviet Union (0) | 0 | <0.01 |
| Swedish (84) | 410 | 0.74 |
| Swiss (0) | 131 | 0.24 |
| Turkish (0) | 15 | 0.03 |
| Ukrainian (248) | 510 | 0.92 |
| Welsh (55) | 422 | 0.76 |
| West Indian, ex. Hispanic (36) | 72 | 0.13 |
| Bahamian (0) | 0 | <0.01 |
| Barbadian (0) | 0 | <0.01 |
| Belizean (0) | 0 | <0.01 |
| Bermudan (0) | 0 | <0.01 |
| British West Indian (0) | 0 | <0.01 |
| Dutch West Indian (0) | 0 | <0.01 |
| Haitian (0) | 0 | <0.01 |
| Jamaican (27) | 36 | 0.06 |
| Trinidadian/Tobagonian (0) | 27 | 0.05 |
| U.S. Virgin Islander (0) | 0 | <0.01 |
| West Indian (9) | 9 | 0.02 |
| Other West Indian (0) | 0 | <0.01 |
| Yugoslavian (98) | 109 | 0.20 |

| Hispanic Origin | Population | % |
|---|---|---|
| Hispanic or Latino (of any race) | 1,263 | 2.27 |
| Central American, ex. Mexican | 51 | 0.09 |
| Costa Rican | 22 | 0.04 |
| Guatemalan | 5 | 0.01 |
| Honduran | 9 | 0.02 |
| Nicaraguan | 2 | <0.01 |
| Panamanian | 11 | 0.02 |
| Salvadoran | 2 | <0.01 |
| Other Central American | 0 | <0.01 |
| Cuban | 30 | 0.05 |
| Dominican Republic | 68 | 0.12 |
| Mexican | 138 | 0.25 |
| Puerto Rican | 782 | 1.41 |
| South American | 54 | 0.10 |
| Argentinean | 8 | 0.01 |
| Bolivian | 1 | <0.01 |
| Chilean | 1 | <0.01 |
| Colombian | 19 | 0.03 |
| Ecuadorian | 13 | 0.02 |
| Paraguayan | 0 | <0.01 |
| Peruvian | 11 | 0.02 |
| Uruguayan | 0 | <0.01 |
| Venezuelan | 1 | <0.01 |
| Other South American | 0 | <0.01 |
| Other Hispanic or Latino | 140 | 0.25 |

| Race* | Population | % |
|---|---|---|
| African-American/Black (1,060) | 1,433 | 2.58 |
| Not Hispanic (981) | 1,315 | 2.37 |
| Hispanic (79) | 118 | 0.21 |
| American Indian/Alaska Native (116) | 356 | 0.64 |
| Not Hispanic (104) | 331 | 0.60 |
| Hispanic (12) | 25 | 0.05 |
| Alaska Athabascan (Ala. Nat.) (0) | 0 | <0.01 |
| Aleut (Alaska Native) (0) | 0 | <0.01 |
| Apache (4) | 7 | 0.01 |
| Arapaho (0) | 0 | <0.01 |
| Blackfeet (3) | 18 | 0.03 |
| Canadian/French Am. Ind. (3) | 7 | 0.01 |
| Central American Ind. (0) | 0 | <0.01 |
| Cherokee (5) | 29 | 0.05 |
| Cheyenne (0) | 0 | <0.01 |
| Chickasaw (1) | 1 | <0.01 |
| Chippewa (0) | 4 | 0.01 |
| Choctaw (0) | 0 | <0.01 |
| Colville (0) | 0 | <0.01 |

| Race* | Population | % |
|---|---|---|
| Comanche (0) | 1 | <0.01 |
| Cree (0) | 1 | <0.01 |
| Creek (1) | 1 | <0.01 |
| Crow (0) | 0 | <0.01 |
| Delaware (1) | 2 | <0.01 |
| Hopi (0) | 0 | <0.01 |
| Houma (0) | 0 | <0.01 |
| Inupiat (Alaska Native) (0) | 0 | <0.01 |
| Iroquois (37) | 86 | 0.15 |
| Kiowa (0) | 0 | <0.01 |
| Lumbee (0) | 0 | <0.01 |
| Menominee (0) | 0 | <0.01 |
| Mexican American Ind. (3) | 3 | 0.01 |
| Navajo (3) | 6 | 0.01 |
| Osage (0) | 0 | <0.01 |
| Ottawa (0) | 0 | <0.01 |
| Paiute (0) | 0 | <0.01 |
| Pima (0) | 0 | <0.01 |
| Potawatomi (0) | 0 | <0.01 |
| Pueblo (0) | 0 | <0.01 |
| Puget Sound Salish (0) | 0 | <0.01 |
| Seminole (0) | 4 | 0.01 |
| Shoshone (0) | 0 | <0.01 |
| Sioux (0) | 5 | 0.01 |
| South American Ind. (0) | 0 | <0.01 |
| Spanish American Ind. (0) | 0 | <0.01 |
| Tlingit-Haida (Alaska Native) (0) | 0 | <0.01 |
| Tohono O'Odham (0) | 0 | <0.01 |
| Tsimshian (Alaska Native) (0) | 0 | <0.01 |
| Ute (0) | 0 | <0.01 |
| Yakama (0) | 0 | <0.01 |
| Yaqui (0) | 0 | <0.01 |
| Yuman (0) | 0 | <0.01 |
| Yup'ik (Alaska Native) (0) | 0 | <0.01 |
| Asian (321) | 454 | 0.82 |
| Not Hispanic (320) | 444 | 0.80 |
| Hispanic (1) | 10 | 0.02 |
| Bangladeshi (0) | 0 | <0.01 |
| Bhutanese (0) | 0 | <0.01 |
| Burmese (0) | 0 | <0.01 |
| Cambodian (0) | 1 | <0.01 |
| Chinese, ex. Taiwanese (71) | 88 | 0.16 |
| Filipino (44) | 80 | 0.14 |
| Hmong (0) | 0 | <0.01 |
| Indian (82) | 100 | 0.18 |
| Indonesian (3) | 7 | 0.01 |
| Japanese (32) | 47 | 0.08 |
| Korean (45) | 65 | 0.12 |
| Laotian (0) | 0 | <0.01 |
| Malaysian (1) | 2 | <0.01 |
| Nepalese (0) | 0 | <0.01 |
| Pakistani (3) | 5 | 0.01 |
| Sri Lankan (0) | 0 | <0.01 |
| Taiwanese (2) | 6 | 0.01 |
| Thai (2) | 2 | <0.01 |
| Vietnamese (20) | 29 | 0.05 |
| Hawaii Native/Pacific Islander (13) | 61 | 0.11 |
| Not Hispanic (11) | 46 | 0.08 |
| Hispanic (2) | 15 | 0.03 |
| Fijian (0) | 0 | <0.01 |
| Guamanian/Chamorro (0) | 0 | <0.01 |
| Marshallese (0) | 0 | <0.01 |
| Native Hawaiian (4) | 34 | 0.06 |
| Samoan (0) | 7 | 0.01 |
| Tongan (0) | 0 | <0.01 |
| White (52,948) | 53,684 | 96.67 |
| Not Hispanic (52,110) | 52,773 | 95.03 |
| Hispanic (838) | 911 | 1.64 |

Notes: † The Census 2010 population figure is used to calculate the percentages in the Hispanic Origin and Race categories. Ancestry percentages are based on the 2006-2010 American Community Survey population (not shown); ‡ Numbers in parentheses indicate the number of people reporting a single ancestry; * Numbers in parentheses indicate the number of persons reporting this race alone, not in combination with any other race; Please refer to the Explanation of Data for more information.

## Genesee County

Population: 60,079

| Ancestry | Population | % |
|---|---|---|
| Afghan (0) | 0 | <0.01 |
| African, Sub-Saharan (46) | 142 | 0.24 |
| African (46) | 142 | 0.24 |
| Cape Verdean (0) | 0 | <0.01 |
| Ethiopian (0) | 0 | <0.01 |
| Ghanaian (0) | 0 | <0.01 |
| Kenyan (0) | 0 | <0.01 |
| Liberian (0) | 0 | <0.01 |
| Nigerian (0) | 0 | <0.01 |
| Senegalese (0) | 0 | <0.01 |
| Sierra Leonean (0) | 0 | <0.01 |
| Somalian (0) | 0 | <0.01 |
| South African (0) | 0 | <0.01 |
| Sudanese (0) | 0 | <0.01 |
| Ugandan (0) | 0 | <0.01 |
| Zimbabwean (0) | 0 | <0.01 |
| Other Sub-Saharan African (0) | 0 | <0.01 |
| Albanian (0) | 0 | <0.01 |
| Alsatian (0) | 0 | <0.01 |
| American (2,398) | 2,398 | 4.00 |
| Arab (49) | 75 | 0.13 |
| Arab (17) | 36 | 0.06 |
| Egyptian (0) | 0 | <0.01 |
| Iraqi (0) | 0 | <0.01 |
| Jordanian (0) | 0 | <0.01 |
| Lebanese (0) | 0 | <0.01 |
| Moroccan (0) | 0 | <0.01 |
| Palestinian (22) | 22 | 0.04 |
| Syrian (0) | 0 | <0.01 |
| Other Arab (10) | 17 | 0.03 |
| Armenian (0) | 0 | <0.01 |
| Assyrian/Chaldean/Syriac (0) | 0 | <0.01 |
| Australian (0) | 0 | <0.01 |
| Austrian (53) | 141 | 0.24 |
| Basque (0) | 0 | <0.01 |
| Belgian (22) | 55 | 0.09 |
| Brazilian (0) | 0 | <0.01 |
| British (84) | 183 | 0.31 |
| Bulgarian (0) | 83 | 0.14 |
| Cajun (0) | 0 | <0.01 |
| Canadian (128) | 244 | 0.41 |
| Carpatho Rusyn (0) | 0 | <0.01 |
| Celtic (0) | 0 | <0.01 |
| Croatian (10) | 61 | 0.10 |
| Cypriot (0) | 0 | <0.01 |
| Czech (36) | 194 | 0.32 |
| Czechoslovakian (38) | 63 | 0.11 |
| Danish (47) | 85 | 0.14 |
| Dutch (172) | 1,821 | 3.04 |
| Eastern European (7) | 32 | 0.05 |
| English (2,539) | 10,461 | 17.45 |
| Estonian (0) | 0 | <0.01 |
| European (240) | 272 | 0.45 |
| Finnish (32) | 56 | 0.09 |
| French, ex. Basque (314) | 2,447 | 4.08 |
| French Canadian (213) | 453 | 0.76 |
| German (5,537) | 19,568 | 32.64 |
| German Russian (0) | 0 | <0.01 |
| Greek (151) | 285 | 0.48 |
| Guyanese (172) | 229 | 0.38 |
| Hungarian (55) | 370 | 0.62 |
| Icelander (0) | 2 | <0.01 |
| Iranian (0) | 0 | <0.01 |
| Irish (2,577) | 11,417 | 19.04 |
| Israeli (0) | 0 | <0.01 |
| Italian (4,677) | 10,953 | 18.27 |
| Latvian (0) | 0 | <0.01 |
| Lithuanian (12) | 71 | 0.12 |
| Luxemburger (0) | 0 | <0.01 |
| Macedonian (0) | 0 | <0.01 |
| Maltese (0) | 0 | <0.01 |
| New Zealander (0) | 0 | <0.01 |
| Northern European (32) | 32 | 0.05 |
| Norwegian (46) | 168 | 0.28 |
| Pennsylvania German (6) | 33 | 0.06 |
| Polish (2,200) | 6,848 | 11.42 |
| Portuguese (26) | 33 | 0.06 |
| Romanian (26) | 35 | 0.06 |
| Russian (39) | 181 | 0.30 |
| Scandinavian (7) | 14 | 0.02 |
| Scotch-Irish (365) | 1,105 | 1.84 |
| Scottish (446) | 1,321 | 2.20 |
| Serbian (0) | 19 | 0.03 |
| Slavic (9) | 30 | 0.05 |
| Slovak (73) | 123 | 0.21 |
| Slovene (0) | 9 | 0.02 |
| Soviet Union (0) | 0 | <0.01 |
| Swedish (135) | 398 | 0.66 |
| Swiss (37) | 114 | 0.19 |
| Turkish (21) | 29 | 0.05 |
| Ukrainian (75) | 230 | 0.38 |
| Welsh (81) | 480 | 0.80 |
| West Indian, ex. Hispanic (62) | 94 | 0.16 |
| Bahamian (0) | 0 | <0.01 |
| Barbadian (0) | 0 | <0.01 |
| Belizean (0) | 0 | <0.01 |
| Bermudan (0) | 0 | <0.01 |
| British West Indian (0) | 0 | <0.01 |
| Dutch West Indian (0) | 0 | <0.01 |
| Haitian (0) | 16 | 0.03 |
| Jamaican (17) | 17 | 0.03 |
| Trinidadian/Tobagonian (0) | 16 | 0.03 |
| U.S. Virgin Islander (0) | 0 | <0.01 |
| West Indian (45) | 45 | 0.08 |
| Other West Indian (0) | 0 | <0.01 |
| Yugoslavian (0) | 11 | 0.02 |

| Hispanic Origin | Population | % |
|---|---|---|
| Hispanic or Latino (of any race) | 1,616 | 2.69 |
| Central American, ex. Mexican | 66 | 0.11 |
| Costa Rican | 0 | <0.01 |
| Guatemalan | 36 | 0.06 |
| Honduran | 10 | 0.02 |
| Nicaraguan | 5 | 0.01 |
| Panamanian | 6 | 0.01 |
| Salvadoran | 9 | 0.01 |
| Other Central American | 0 | <0.01 |
| Cuban | 24 | 0.04 |
| Dominican Republic | 49 | 0.08 |
| Mexican | 683 | 1.14 |
| Puerto Rican | 620 | 1.03 |
| South American | 65 | 0.11 |
| Argentinean | 6 | 0.01 |
| Bolivian | 7 | 0.01 |
| Chilean | 5 | 0.01 |
| Colombian | 21 | 0.03 |
| Ecuadorian | 14 | 0.02 |
| Paraguayan | 0 | <0.01 |
| Peruvian | 5 | 0.01 |
| Uruguayan | 0 | <0.01 |
| Venezuelan | 7 | 0.01 |
| Other South American | 0 | <0.01 |
| Other Hispanic or Latino | 109 | 0.18 |

| Race* | Population | % |
|---|---|---|
| African-American/Black (1,612) | 2,243 | 3.73 |
| Not Hispanic (1,491) | 2,053 | 3.42 |
| Hispanic (121) | 190 | 0.32 |
| American Indian/Alaska Native (679) | 997 | 1.66 |
| Not Hispanic (661) | 949 | 1.58 |
| Hispanic (18) | 48 | 0.08 |
| Alaska Athabascan (Ala. Nat.) (0) | 0 | <0.01 |
| Aleut (Alaska Native) (0) | 0 | <0.01 |
| Apache (1) | 5 | 0.01 |
| Arapaho (0) | 0 | <0.01 |
| Blackfeet (0) | 19 | 0.03 |
| Canadian/French Am. Ind. (7) | 9 | 0.01 |
| Central American Ind. (1) | 1 | <0.01 |
| Cherokee (10) | 42 | 0.07 |
| Cheyenne (0) | 0 | <0.01 |
| Chickasaw (0) | 0 | <0.01 |
| Chippewa (5) | 8 | 0.01 |
| Choctaw (3) | 7 | 0.01 |
| Colville (0) | 0 | <0.01 |

| | Population | % |
|---|---|---|
| Comanche (1) | 1 | <0.01 |
| Cree (0) | 5 | 0.01 |
| Creek (4) | 4 | 0.01 |
| Crow (0) | 0 | <0.01 |
| Delaware (1) | 2 | <0.01 |
| Hopi (1) | 1 | <0.01 |
| Houma (0) | 0 | <0.01 |
| Inupiat (Alaska Native) (0) | 0 | <0.01 |
| Iroquois (267) | 344 | 0.57 |
| Kiowa (0) | 0 | <0.01 |
| Lumbee (0) | 0 | <0.01 |
| Menominee (0) | 0 | <0.01 |
| Mexican American Ind. (1) | 2 | <0.01 |
| Navajo (3) | 4 | 0.01 |
| Osage (0) | 4 | 0.01 |
| Ottawa (0) | 0 | <0.01 |
| Paiute (0) | 0 | <0.01 |
| Pima (0) | 0 | <0.01 |
| Potawatomi (0) | 0 | <0.01 |
| Pueblo (0) | 0 | <0.01 |
| Puget Sound Salish (0) | 0 | <0.01 |
| Seminole (0) | 10 | 0.02 |
| Shoshone (0) | 0 | <0.01 |
| Sioux (3) | 5 | 0.01 |
| South American Ind. (2) | 2 | <0.01 |
| Spanish American Ind. (0) | 0 | <0.01 |
| Tlingit-Haida (Alaska Native) (0) | 0 | <0.01 |
| Tohono O'Odham (0) | 0 | <0.01 |
| Tsimshian (Alaska Native) (0) | 0 | <0.01 |
| Ute (0) | 0 | <0.01 |
| Yakama (0) | 0 | <0.01 |
| Yaqui (0) | 5 | 0.01 |
| Yuman (0) | 0 | <0.01 |
| Yup'ik (Alaska Native) (0) | 0 | <0.01 |
| Asian (357) | 494 | 0.82 |
| Not Hispanic (355) | 481 | 0.80 |
| Hispanic (2) | 13 | 0.02 |
| Bangladeshi (2) | 4 | 0.01 |
| Bhutanese (0) | 0 | <0.01 |
| Burmese (0) | 0 | <0.01 |
| Cambodian (0) | 1 | <0.01 |
| Chinese, ex. Taiwanese (72) | 95 | 0.16 |
| Filipino (50) | 83 | 0.14 |
| Hmong (0) | 0 | <0.01 |
| Indian (84) | 103 | 0.17 |
| Indonesian (1) | 3 | <0.01 |
| Japanese (43) | 57 | 0.09 |
| Korean (52) | 76 | 0.13 |
| Laotian (14) | 17 | 0.03 |
| Malaysian (0) | 0 | <0.01 |
| Nepalese (0) | 0 | <0.01 |
| Pakistani (10) | 10 | 0.02 |
| Sri Lankan (0) | 0 | <0.01 |
| Taiwanese (0) | 0 | <0.01 |
| Thai (5) | 12 | 0.02 |
| Vietnamese (6) | 10 | 0.02 |
| Hawaii Native/Pacific Islander (4) | 27 | 0.04 |
| Not Hispanic (2) | 17 | 0.03 |
| Hispanic (2) | 10 | 0.02 |
| Fijian (0) | 0 | <0.01 |
| Guamanian/Chamorro (2) | 4 | 0.01 |
| Marshallese (0) | 0 | <0.01 |
| Native Hawaiian (2) | 12 | 0.02 |
| Samoan (0) | 1 | <0.01 |
| Tongan (0) | 0 | <0.01 |
| White (55,787) | 56,763 | 94.48 |
| Not Hispanic (54,990) | 55,842 | 92.95 |
| Hispanic (797) | 921 | 1.53 |

*Notes: † The Census 2010 population figure is used to calculate the percentages in the Hispanic Origin and Race categories. Ancestry percentages are based on the 2006-2010 American Community Survey population (not shown); ‡ Numbers in parentheses indicate the number of people reporting a single ancestry; * Numbers in parentheses indicate the number of persons reporting this race alone, not in combination with any other race; Please refer to the Explanation of Data for more information.*

## Greene County

Population: 49,221

| Ancestry | Population | % |
|---|---|---|
| Afghan (0) | 0 | <0.01 |
| African, Sub-Saharan (114) | 121 | 0.24 |
| African (57) | 64 | 0.13 |
| Cape Verdean (5) | 5 | 0.01 |
| Ethiopian (8) | 8 | 0.02 |
| Ghanaian (44) | 44 | 0.09 |
| Kenyan (0) | 0 | <0.01 |
| Liberian (0) | 0 | <0.01 |
| Nigerian (0) | 0 | <0.01 |
| Senegalese (0) | 0 | <0.01 |
| Sierra Leonean (0) | 0 | <0.01 |
| Somalian (0) | 0 | <0.01 |
| South African (0) | 0 | <0.01 |
| Sudanese (0) | 0 | <0.01 |
| Ugandan (0) | 0 | <0.01 |
| Zimbabwean (0) | 0 | <0.01 |
| Other Sub-Saharan African (0) | 0 | <0.01 |
| Albanian (80) | 85 | 0.17 |
| Alsatian (0) | 0 | <0.01 |
| American (5,920) | 5,920 | 11.98 |
| Arab (66) | 96 | 0.19 |
| Arab (0) | 0 | <0.01 |
| Egyptian (0) | 0 | <0.01 |
| Iraqi (0) | 0 | <0.01 |
| Jordanian (0) | 0 | <0.01 |
| Lebanese (11) | 30 | 0.06 |
| Moroccan (0) | 0 | <0.01 |
| Palestinian (0) | 0 | <0.01 |
| Syrian (55) | 66 | 0.13 |
| Other Arab (0) | 0 | <0.01 |
| Armenian (26) | 46 | 0.09 |
| Assyrian/Chaldean/Syriac (0) | 0 | <0.01 |
| Australian (25) | 25 | 0.05 |
| Austrian (150) | 313 | 0.63 |
| Basque (0) | 0 | <0.01 |
| Belgian (6) | 6 | 0.01 |
| Brazilian (10) | 10 | 0.02 |
| British (176) | 231 | 0.47 |
| Bulgarian (0) | 0 | <0.01 |
| Cajun (0) | 62 | 0.13 |
| Canadian (123) | 223 | 0.45 |
| Carpatho Rusyn (0) | 0 | <0.01 |
| Celtic (0) | 0 | <0.01 |
| Croatian (41) | 125 | 0.25 |
| Cypriot (0) | 0 | <0.01 |
| Czech (31) | 170 | 0.34 |
| Czechoslovakian (130) | 181 | 0.37 |
| Danish (75) | 163 | 0.33 |
| Dutch (675) | 2,970 | 6.01 |
| Eastern European (125) | 134 | 0.27 |
| English (1,220) | 4,245 | 8.59 |
| Estonian (0) | 0 | <0.01 |
| European (695) | 806 | 1.63 |
| Finnish (1) | 84 | 0.17 |
| French, ex. Basque (341) | 1,780 | 3.60 |
| French Canadian (221) | 536 | 1.08 |
| German (2,656) | 8,675 | 17.56 |
| German Russian (0) | 0 | <0.01 |
| Greek (180) | 294 | 0.60 |
| Guyanese (8) | 8 | 0.02 |
| Hungarian (183) | 448 | 0.91 |
| Icelander (0) | 0 | <0.01 |
| Iranian (15) | 15 | 0.03 |
| Irish (3,244) | 9,113 | 18.44 |
| Israeli (9) | 9 | 0.02 |
| Italian (4,020) | 8,909 | 18.03 |
| Latvian (0) | 31 | 0.06 |
| Lithuanian (48) | 98 | 0.20 |
| Luxemburger (0) | 3 | 0.01 |
| Macedonian (0) | 0 | <0.01 |
| Maltese (0) | 0 | <0.01 |
| New Zealander (0) | 0 | <0.01 |
| Northern European (10) | 16 | 0.03 |
| Norwegian (206) | 423 | 0.86 |
| Pennsylvania German (5) | 18 | 0.04 |

| Ancestry | Population | % |
|---|---|---|
| Polish (718) | 2,469 | 5.00 |
| Portuguese (32) | 148 | 0.30 |
| Romanian (67) | 83 | 0.17 |
| Russian (160) | 484 | 0.98 |
| Scandinavian (54) | 87 | 0.18 |
| Scotch-Irish (163) | 554 | 1.12 |
| Scottish (153) | 674 | 1.36 |
| Serbian (68) | 86 | 0.17 |
| Slavic (8) | 79 | 0.16 |
| Slovak (110) | 155 | 0.31 |
| Slovene (0) | 0 | <0.01 |
| Soviet Union (0) | 0 | <0.01 |
| Swedish (74) | 340 | 0.69 |
| Swiss (31) | 103 | 0.21 |
| Turkish (0) | 0 | <0.01 |
| Ukrainian (279) | 465 | 0.94 |
| Welsh (19) | 225 | 0.46 |
| West Indian, ex. Hispanic (82) | 118 | 0.24 |
| Bahamian (0) | 0 | <0.01 |
| Barbadian (0) | 0 | <0.01 |
| Belizean (0) | 0 | <0.01 |
| Bermudan (0) | 0 | <0.01 |
| British West Indian (0) | 0 | <0.01 |
| Dutch West Indian (0) | 0 | <0.01 |
| Haitian (8) | 8 | 0.02 |
| Jamaican (57) | 70 | 0.14 |
| Trinidadian/Tobagonian (17) | 17 | 0.03 |
| U.S. Virgin Islander (0) | 0 | <0.01 |
| West Indian (0) | 23 | 0.05 |
| Other West Indian (0) | 0 | <0.01 |
| Yugoslavian (36) | 106 | 0.21 |

| Hispanic Origin | Population | % |
|---|---|---|
| Hispanic or Latino (of any race) | 2,419 | 4.91 |
| Central American, ex. Mexican | 162 | 0.33 |
| Costa Rican | 10 | 0.02 |
| Guatemalan | 30 | 0.06 |
| Honduran | 22 | 0.04 |
| Nicaraguan | 5 | 0.01 |
| Panamanian | 12 | 0.02 |
| Salvadoran | 83 | 0.17 |
| Other Central American | 0 | <0.01 |
| Cuban | 74 | 0.15 |
| Dominican Republic | 148 | 0.30 |
| Mexican | 343 | 0.70 |
| Puerto Rican | 1,298 | 2.64 |
| South American | 189 | 0.38 |
| Argentinean | 17 | 0.03 |
| Bolivian | 0 | <0.01 |
| Chilean | 22 | 0.04 |
| Colombian | 72 | 0.15 |
| Ecuadorian | 28 | 0.06 |
| Paraguayan | 1 | <0.01 |
| Peruvian | 26 | 0.05 |
| Uruguayan | 4 | 0.01 |
| Venezuelan | 17 | 0.03 |
| Other South American | 2 | <0.01 |
| Other Hispanic or Latino | 205 | 0.42 |

| Race* | Population | % |
|---|---|---|
| African-American/Black (2,826) | 3,272 | 6.65 |
| Not Hispanic (2,606) | 3,010 | 6.12 |
| Hispanic (220) | 262 | 0.53 |
| American Indian/Alaska Native (145) | 406 | 0.82 |
| Not Hispanic (122) | 360 | 0.73 |
| Hispanic (23) | 46 | 0.09 |
| Alaska Athabascan (Ala. Nat.) (0) | 0 | <0.01 |
| Aleut (Alaska Native) (0) | 0 | <0.01 |
| Apache (2) | 10 | 0.02 |
| Arapaho (0) | 2 | <0.01 |
| Blackfeet (0) | 5 | 0.01 |
| Canadian/French Am. Ind. (0) | 0 | <0.01 |
| Central American Ind. (1) | 2 | <0.01 |
| Cherokee (5) | 45 | 0.09 |
| Cheyenne (0) | 0 | <0.01 |
| Chickasaw (0) | 0 | <0.01 |
| Chippewa (4) | 6 | 0.01 |
| Choctaw (2) | 6 | 0.01 |
| Colville (0) | 0 | <0.01 |

| Race* | Population | % |
|---|---|---|
| Comanche (0) | 1 | <0.01 |
| Cree (0) | 0 | <0.01 |
| Creek (0) | 2 | <0.01 |
| Crow (0) | 0 | <0.01 |
| Delaware (1) | 4 | 0.01 |
| Hopi (0) | 0 | <0.01 |
| Houma (0) | 0 | <0.01 |
| Inupiat (Alaska Native) (1) | 2 | <0.01 |
| Iroquois (19) | 46 | 0.09 |
| Kiowa (0) | 0 | <0.01 |
| Lumbee (1) | 2 | <0.01 |
| Menominee (0) | 0 | <0.01 |
| Mexican American Ind. (8) | 8 | 0.02 |
| Navajo (1) | 1 | <0.01 |
| Osage (0) | 0 | <0.01 |
| Ottawa (0) | 0 | <0.01 |
| Paiute (0) | 0 | <0.01 |
| Pima (0) | 0 | <0.01 |
| Potawatomi (0) | 0 | <0.01 |
| Pueblo (0) | 0 | <0.01 |
| Puget Sound Salish (0) | 0 | <0.01 |
| Seminole (1) | 1 | <0.01 |
| Shoshone (0) | 0 | <0.01 |
| Sioux (4) | 14 | 0.03 |
| South American Ind. (0) | 1 | <0.01 |
| Spanish American Ind. (0) | 0 | <0.01 |
| Tlingit-Haida (Alaska Native) (0) | 0 | <0.01 |
| Tohono O'Odham (1) | 2 | <0.01 |
| Tsimshian (Alaska Native) (0) | 0 | <0.01 |
| Ute (0) | 0 | <0.01 |
| Yakama (0) | 1 | <0.01 |
| Yaqui (0) | 0 | <0.01 |
| Yuman (0) | 0 | <0.01 |
| Yup'ik (Alaska Native) (0) | 0 | <0.01 |
| Asian (391) | 523 | 1.06 |
| Not Hispanic (382) | 507 | 1.03 |
| Hispanic (9) | 16 | 0.03 |
| Bangladeshi (0) | 0 | <0.01 |
| Bhutanese (0) | 0 | <0.01 |
| Burmese (5) | 5 | 0.01 |
| Cambodian (0) | 0 | <0.01 |
| Chinese, ex. Taiwanese (127) | 143 | 0.29 |
| Filipino (45) | 78 | 0.16 |
| Hmong (0) | 0 | <0.01 |
| Indian (72) | 106 | 0.22 |
| Indonesian (0) | 0 | <0.01 |
| Japanese (23) | 39 | 0.08 |
| Korean (20) | 27 | 0.05 |
| Laotian (1) | 1 | <0.01 |
| Malaysian (0) | 0 | <0.01 |
| Nepalese (6) | 6 | 0.01 |
| Pakistani (25) | 31 | 0.06 |
| Sri Lankan (0) | 3 | 0.01 |
| Taiwanese (3) | 3 | 0.01 |
| Thai (6) | 13 | 0.03 |
| Vietnamese (20) | 25 | 0.05 |
| Hawaii Native/Pacific Islander (19) | 43 | 0.09 |
| Not Hispanic (15) | 39 | 0.08 |
| Hispanic (4) | 4 | 0.01 |
| Fijian (0) | 0 | <0.01 |
| Guamanian/Chamorro (6) | 8 | 0.02 |
| Marshallese (0) | 0 | <0.01 |
| Native Hawaiian (3) | 11 | 0.02 |
| Samoan (1) | 2 | <0.01 |
| Tongan (0) | 0 | <0.01 |
| White (44,440) | 45,212 | 91.86 |
| Not Hispanic (42,857) | 43,514 | 88.41 |
| Hispanic (1,583) | 1,698 | 3.45 |

Notes: † The Census 2010 population figure is used to calculate the percentages in the Hispanic Origin and Race categories. Ancestry percentages are based on the 2006-2010 American Community Survey population (not shown); ‡ Numbers in parentheses indicate the number of people reporting a single ancestry; * Numbers in parentheses indicate the number of persons reporting this race alone, not in combination with any other race; Please refer to the Explanation of Data for more information.

## Hamilton County

Population: 4,836

| Ancestry | Population | % |
|---|---|---|
| Afghan (0) | 0 | <0.01 |
| African, Sub-Saharan (5) | 5 | 0.10 |
| African (5) | 5 | 0.10 |
| Cape Verdean (0) | 0 | <0.01 |
| Ethiopian (0) | 0 | <0.01 |
| Ghanaian (0) | 0 | <0.01 |
| Kenyan (0) | 0 | <0.01 |
| Liberian (0) | 0 | <0.01 |
| Nigerian (0) | 0 | <0.01 |
| Senegalese (0) | 0 | <0.01 |
| Sierra Leonean (0) | 0 | <0.01 |
| Somalian (0) | 0 | <0.01 |
| South African (0) | 0 | <0.01 |
| Sudanese (0) | 0 | <0.01 |
| Ugandan (0) | 0 | <0.01 |
| Zimbabwean (0) | 0 | <0.01 |
| Other Sub-Saharan African (0) | 0 | <0.01 |
| Albanian (10) | 10 | 0.20 |
| Alsatian (0) | 0 | <0.01 |
| American (263) | 263 | 5.36 |
| Arab (7) | 25 | 0.51 |
| Arab (0) | 11 | 0.22 |
| Egyptian (0) | 0 | <0.01 |
| Iraqi (0) | 0 | <0.01 |
| Jordanian (0) | 0 | <0.01 |
| Lebanese (3) | 6 | 0.12 |
| Moroccan (0) | 0 | <0.01 |
| Palestinian (0) | 0 | <0.01 |
| Syrian (4) | 8 | 0.16 |
| Other Arab (0) | 0 | <0.01 |
| Armenian (0) | 0 | <0.01 |
| Assyrian/Chaldean/Syriac (0) | 0 | <0.01 |
| Australian (5) | 10 | 0.20 |
| Austrian (0) | 18 | 0.37 |
| Basque (0) | 0 | <0.01 |
| Belgian (0) | 0 | <0.01 |
| Brazilian (0) | 0 | <0.01 |
| British (0) | 5 | 0.10 |
| Bulgarian (0) | 0 | <0.01 |
| Cajun (0) | 0 | <0.01 |
| Canadian (15) | 30 | 0.61 |
| Carpatho Rusyn (0) | 0 | <0.01 |
| Celtic (0) | 0 | <0.01 |
| Croatian (5) | 5 | 0.10 |
| Cypriot (0) | 0 | <0.01 |
| Czech (5) | 5 | 0.10 |
| Czechoslovakian (2) | 3 | 0.06 |
| Danish (0) | 5 | 0.10 |
| Dutch (64) | 275 | 5.60 |
| Eastern European (3) | 3 | 0.06 |
| English (246) | 1,011 | 20.60 |
| Estonian (0) | 0 | <0.01 |
| European (13) | 13 | 0.26 |
| Finnish (7) | 7 | 0.14 |
| French, ex. Basque (144) | 524 | 10.68 |
| French Canadian (77) | 133 | 2.71 |
| German (276) | 1,057 | 21.54 |
| German Russian (0) | 0 | <0.01 |
| Greek (4) | 9 | 0.18 |
| Guyanese (21) | 21 | 0.43 |
| Hungarian (10) | 14 | 0.29 |
| Icelander (0) | 0 | <0.01 |
| Iranian (0) | 0 | <0.01 |
| Irish (506) | 1,117 | 22.76 |
| Israeli (0) | 0 | <0.01 |
| Italian (176) | 421 | 8.58 |
| Latvian (3) | 3 | 0.06 |
| Lithuanian (2) | 10 | 0.20 |
| Luxemburger (0) | 0 | <0.01 |
| Macedonian (0) | 0 | <0.01 |
| Maltese (0) | 0 | <0.01 |
| New Zealander (0) | 0 | <0.01 |
| Northern European (21) | 21 | 0.43 |
| Norwegian (32) | 79 | 1.61 |
| Pennsylvania German (0) | 4 | 0.08 |

| Ancestry (cont.) | Population | % |
|---|---|---|
| Polish (118) | 274 | 5.58 |
| Portuguese (6) | 6 | 0.12 |
| Romanian (11) | 11 | 0.22 |
| Russian (18) | 53 | 1.08 |
| Scandinavian (0) | 2 | 0.04 |
| Scotch-Irish (50) | 114 | 2.32 |
| Scottish (70) | 286 | 5.83 |
| Serbian (0) | 0 | <0.01 |
| Slavic (6) | 6 | 0.12 |
| Slovak (7) | 7 | 0.14 |
| Slovene (0) | 0 | <0.01 |
| Soviet Union (0) | 0 | <0.01 |
| Swedish (12) | 64 | 1.30 |
| Swiss (12) | 19 | 0.39 |
| Turkish (0) | 0 | <0.01 |
| Ukrainian (2) | 13 | 0.26 |
| Welsh (19) | 57 | 1.16 |
| West Indian, ex. Hispanic (0) | 0 | <0.01 |
| Bahamian (0) | 0 | <0.01 |
| Barbadian (0) | 0 | <0.01 |
| Belizean (0) | 0 | <0.01 |
| Bermudan (0) | 0 | <0.01 |
| British West Indian (0) | 0 | <0.01 |
| Dutch West Indian (0) | 0 | <0.01 |
| Haitian (0) | 0 | <0.01 |
| Jamaican (0) | 0 | <0.01 |
| Trinidadian/Tobagonian (0) | 0 | <0.01 |
| U.S. Virgin Islander (0) | 0 | <0.01 |
| West Indian (0) | 0 | <0.01 |
| Other West Indian (0) | 0 | <0.01 |
| Yugoslavian (0) | 0 | <0.01 |

| Hispanic Origin | Population | % |
|---|---|---|
| Hispanic or Latino (of any race) | 51 | 1.05 |
| Central American, ex. Mexican | 0 | <0.01 |
| Costa Rican | 0 | <0.01 |
| Guatemalan | 0 | <0.01 |
| Honduran | 0 | <0.01 |
| Nicaraguan | 0 | <0.01 |
| Panamanian | 0 | <0.01 |
| Salvadoran | 0 | <0.01 |
| Other Central American | 0 | <0.01 |
| Cuban | 2 | 0.04 |
| Dominican Republic | 3 | 0.06 |
| Mexican | 5 | 0.10 |
| Puerto Rican | 30 | 0.62 |
| South American | 5 | 0.10 |
| Argentinean | 0 | <0.01 |
| Bolivian | 0 | <0.01 |
| Chilean | 0 | <0.01 |
| Colombian | 3 | 0.06 |
| Ecuadorian | 0 | <0.01 |
| Paraguayan | 0 | <0.01 |
| Peruvian | 0 | <0.01 |
| Uruguayan | 0 | <0.01 |
| Venezuelan | 0 | <0.01 |
| Other South American | 2 | 0.04 |
| Other Hispanic or Latino | 6 | 0.12 |

| Race* | Population | % |
|---|---|---|
| African-American/Black (35) | 40 | 0.83 |
| Not Hispanic (33) | 38 | 0.79 |
| Hispanic (2) | 2 | 0.04 |
| American Indian/Alaska Native (11) | 58 | 1.20 |
| Not Hispanic (11) | 53 | 1.10 |
| Hispanic (0) | 5 | 0.10 |
| Alaska Athabascan (Ala. Nat.) (0) | 0 | <0.01 |
| Aleut (Alaska Native) (0) | 0 | <0.01 |
| Apache (0) | 1 | 0.02 |
| Arapaho (0) | 0 | <0.01 |
| Blackfeet (0) | 2 | 0.04 |
| Canadian/French Am. Ind. (0) | 0 | <0.01 |
| Central American Ind. (0) | 0 | <0.01 |
| Cherokee (1) | 6 | 0.12 |
| Cheyenne (0) | 0 | <0.01 |
| Chickasaw (0) | 0 | <0.01 |
| Chippewa (0) | 0 | <0.01 |
| Choctaw (0) | 1 | 0.02 |
| Colville (0) | 0 | <0.01 |

| Race* (cont.) | Population | % |
|---|---|---|
| Comanche (0) | 0 | <0.01 |
| Cree (0) | 0 | <0.01 |
| Creek (0) | 0 | <0.01 |
| Crow (0) | 1 | 0.02 |
| Delaware (0) | 0 | <0.01 |
| Hopi (0) | 0 | <0.01 |
| Houma (0) | 0 | <0.01 |
| Inupiat (Alaska Native) (0) | 0 | <0.01 |
| Iroquois (5) | 17 | 0.35 |
| Kiowa (0) | 0 | <0.01 |
| Lumbee (0) | 0 | <0.01 |
| Menominee (0) | 0 | <0.01 |
| Mexican American Ind. (0) | 0 | <0.01 |
| Navajo (0) | 0 | <0.01 |
| Osage (0) | 0 | <0.01 |
| Ottawa (0) | 0 | <0.01 |
| Paiute (0) | 0 | <0.01 |
| Pima (0) | 0 | <0.01 |
| Potawatomi (0) | 0 | <0.01 |
| Pueblo (0) | 0 | <0.01 |
| Puget Sound Salish (0) | 0 | <0.01 |
| Seminole (0) | 0 | <0.01 |
| Shoshone (0) | 0 | <0.01 |
| Sioux (0) | 1 | 0.02 |
| South American Ind. (0) | 2 | 0.04 |
| Spanish American Ind. (0) | 0 | <0.01 |
| Tlingit-Haida (Alaska Native) (0) | 0 | <0.01 |
| Tohono O'Odham (0) | 0 | <0.01 |
| Tsimshian (Alaska Native) (0) | 0 | <0.01 |
| Ute (0) | 0 | <0.01 |
| Yakama (0) | 0 | <0.01 |
| Yaqui (0) | 0 | <0.01 |
| Yuman (0) | 0 | <0.01 |
| Yup'ik (Alaska Native) (0) | 0 | <0.01 |
| Asian (24) | 29 | 0.60 |
| Not Hispanic (24) | 27 | 0.56 |
| Hispanic (0) | 2 | 0.04 |
| Bangladeshi (0) | 0 | <0.01 |
| Bhutanese (0) | 0 | <0.01 |
| Burmese (0) | 0 | <0.01 |
| Cambodian (0) | 0 | <0.01 |
| Chinese, ex. Taiwanese (4) | 5 | 0.10 |
| Filipino (7) | 11 | 0.23 |
| Hmong (0) | 0 | <0.01 |
| Indian (3) | 3 | 0.06 |
| Indonesian (0) | 0 | <0.01 |
| Japanese (1) | 1 | 0.02 |
| Korean (3) | 3 | 0.06 |
| Laotian (0) | 0 | <0.01 |
| Malaysian (0) | 0 | <0.01 |
| Nepalese (0) | 0 | <0.01 |
| Pakistani (6) | 6 | 0.12 |
| Sri Lankan (0) | 0 | <0.01 |
| Taiwanese (0) | 0 | <0.01 |
| Thai (0) | 0 | <0.01 |
| Vietnamese (0) | 0 | <0.01 |
| Hawaii Native/Pacific Islander (4) | 4 | 0.08 |
| Not Hispanic (4) | 4 | 0.08 |
| Hispanic (0) | 0 | <0.01 |
| Fijian (0) | 0 | <0.01 |
| Guamanian/Chamorro (0) | 0 | <0.01 |
| Marshallese (0) | 0 | <0.01 |
| Native Hawaiian (4) | 4 | 0.08 |
| Samoan (0) | 0 | <0.01 |
| Tongan (0) | 0 | <0.01 |
| White (4,705) | 4,755 | 98.33 |
| Not Hispanic (4,664) | 4,711 | 97.42 |
| Hispanic (41) | 44 | 0.91 |

Notes: † The Census 2010 population figure is used to calculate the percentages in the Hispanic Origin and Race categories. Ancestry percentages are based on the 2006-2010 American Community Survey population (not shown); ‡ Numbers in parentheses indicate the number of people reporting a single ancestry; * Numbers in parentheses indicate the number of persons reporting this race alone, not in combination with any other race; Please refer to the Explanation of Data for more information.

## Herkimer County

Population: 64,519

| Ancestry | Population | % |
|---|---|---|
| Afghan (0) | 0 | <0.01 |
| African, Sub-Saharan (42) | 131 | 0.20 |
| African (42) | 131 | 0.20 |
| Cape Verdean (0) | 0 | <0.01 |
| Ethiopian (0) | 0 | <0.01 |
| Ghanaian (0) | 0 | <0.01 |
| Kenyan (0) | 0 | <0.01 |
| Liberian (0) | 0 | <0.01 |
| Nigerian (0) | 0 | <0.01 |
| Senegalese (0) | 0 | <0.01 |
| Sierra Leonean (0) | 0 | <0.01 |
| Somalian (0) | 0 | <0.01 |
| South African (0) | 0 | <0.01 |
| Sudanese (0) | 0 | <0.01 |
| Ugandan (0) | 0 | <0.01 |
| Zimbabwean (0) | 0 | <0.01 |
| Other Sub-Saharan African (0) | 0 | <0.01 |
| Albanian (0) | 4 | 0.01 |
| Alsatian (0) | 11 | 0.02 |
| American (3,518) | 3,518 | 5.47 |
| Arab (112) | 348 | 0.54 |
| Arab (53) | 53 | 0.08 |
| Egyptian (0) | 0 | <0.01 |
| Iraqi (0) | 0 | <0.01 |
| Jordanian (0) | 0 | <0.01 |
| Lebanese (59) | 276 | 0.43 |
| Moroccan (0) | 0 | <0.01 |
| Palestinian (0) | 0 | <0.01 |
| Syrian (0) | 19 | 0.03 |
| Other Arab (0) | 0 | <0.01 |
| Armenian (5) | 12 | 0.02 |
| Assyrian/Chaldean/Syriac (0) | 5 | 0.01 |
| Australian (0) | 26 | 0.04 |
| Austrian (66) | 243 | 0.38 |
| Basque (0) | 0 | <0.01 |
| Belgian (4) | 26 | 0.04 |
| Brazilian (0) | 0 | <0.01 |
| British (77) | 170 | 0.26 |
| Bulgarian (5) | 42 | 0.07 |
| Cajun (0) | 0 | <0.01 |
| Canadian (49) | 189 | 0.29 |
| Carpatho Rusyn (8) | 8 | 0.01 |
| Celtic (0) | 19 | 0.03 |
| Croatian (0) | 0 | <0.01 |
| Cypriot (0) | 0 | <0.01 |
| Czech (165) | 257 | 0.40 |
| Czechoslovakian (70) | 167 | 0.26 |
| Danish (103) | 365 | 0.57 |
| Dutch (443) | 2,912 | 4.53 |
| Eastern European (38) | 56 | 0.09 |
| English (2,785) | 8,608 | 13.38 |
| Estonian (0) | 36 | 0.06 |
| European (176) | 209 | 0.32 |
| Finnish (3) | 32 | 0.05 |
| French, ex. Basque (681) | 4,581 | 7.12 |
| French Canadian (802) | 1,567 | 2.44 |
| German (3,471) | 14,484 | 22.51 |
| German Russian (0) | 0 | <0.01 |
| Greek (99) | 160 | 0.25 |
| Guyanese (0) | 0 | <0.01 |
| Hungarian (47) | 187 | 0.29 |
| Icelander (0) | 6 | 0.01 |
| Iranian (0) | 0 | <0.01 |
| Irish (3,812) | 14,052 | 21.84 |
| Israeli (0) | 7 | 0.01 |
| Italian (5,689) | 11,059 | 17.19 |
| Latvian (0) | 3 | <0.01 |
| Lithuanian (102) | 219 | 0.34 |
| Luxemburger (0) | 0 | <0.01 |
| Macedonian (0) | 6 | 0.01 |
| Maltese (0) | 0 | <0.01 |
| New Zealander (0) | 0 | <0.01 |
| Northern European (27) | 27 | 0.04 |
| Norwegian (23) | 152 | 0.24 |
| Pennsylvania German (138) | 141 | 0.22 |

| | Population | % |
|---|---|---|
| Polish (1,884) | 5,302 | 8.24 |
| Portuguese (12) | 36 | 0.06 |
| Romanian (17) | 51 | 0.08 |
| Russian (242) | 562 | 0.87 |
| Scandinavian (9) | 13 | 0.02 |
| Scotch-Irish (171) | 559 | 0.87 |
| Scottish (231) | 970 | 1.51 |
| Serbian (0) | 0 | <0.01 |
| Slavic (17) | 48 | 0.07 |
| Slovak (105) | 255 | 0.40 |
| Slovene (87) | 165 | 0.26 |
| Soviet Union (0) | 0 | <0.01 |
| Swedish (89) | 356 | 0.55 |
| Swiss (155) | 302 | 0.47 |
| Turkish (0) | 0 | <0.01 |
| Ukrainian (534) | 990 | 1.54 |
| Welsh (496) | 2,032 | 3.16 |
| West Indian, ex. Hispanic (3) | 137 | 0.21 |
| Bahamian (0) | 0 | <0.01 |
| Barbadian (0) | 0 | <0.01 |
| Belizean (0) | 0 | <0.01 |
| Bermudan (0) | 0 | <0.01 |
| British West Indian (0) | 0 | <0.01 |
| Dutch West Indian (0) | 0 | <0.01 |
| Haitian (0) | 20 | 0.03 |
| Jamaican (0) | 108 | 0.17 |
| Trinidadian/Tobagonian (3) | 9 | 0.01 |
| U.S. Virgin Islander (0) | 0 | <0.01 |
| West Indian (0) | 0 | <0.01 |
| Other West Indian (0) | 0 | <0.01 |
| Yugoslavian (81) | 129 | 0.20 |

| Hispanic Origin | Population | % |
|---|---|---|
| Hispanic or Latino (of any race) | 1,040 | 1.61 |
| Central American, ex. Mexican | 51 | 0.08 |
| Costa Rican | 12 | 0.02 |
| Guatemalan | 17 | 0.03 |
| Honduran | 4 | 0.01 |
| Nicaraguan | 2 | <0.01 |
| Panamanian | 8 | 0.01 |
| Salvadoran | 8 | 0.01 |
| Other Central American | 0 | <0.01 |
| Cuban | 32 | 0.05 |
| Dominican Republic | 48 | 0.07 |
| Mexican | 180 | 0.28 |
| Puerto Rican | 514 | 0.80 |
| South American | 76 | 0.12 |
| Argentinean | 9 | 0.01 |
| Bolivian | 9 | 0.01 |
| Chilean | 7 | 0.01 |
| Colombian | 12 | 0.02 |
| Ecuadorian | 10 | 0.02 |
| Paraguayan | 0 | <0.01 |
| Peruvian | 15 | 0.02 |
| Uruguayan | 6 | 0.01 |
| Venezuelan | 3 | <0.01 |
| Other South American | 5 | 0.01 |
| Other Hispanic or Latino | 139 | 0.22 |

| Race* | Population | % |
|---|---|---|
| African-American/Black (700) | 1,079 | 1.67 |
| Not Hispanic (640) | 976 | 1.51 |
| Hispanic (60) | 103 | 0.16 |
| American Indian/Alaska Native (157) | 398 | 0.62 |
| Not Hispanic (137) | 340 | 0.53 |
| Hispanic (20) | 58 | 0.09 |
| Alaska Athabascan (Ala. Nat.) (0) | 0 | <0.01 |
| Aleut (Alaska Native) (0) | 0 | <0.01 |
| Apache (0) | 1 | <0.01 |
| Arapaho (0) | 0 | <0.01 |
| Blackfeet (2) | 6 | 0.01 |
| Canadian/French Am. Ind. (0) | 2 | <0.01 |
| Central American Ind. (1) | 1 | <0.01 |
| Cherokee (3) | 33 | 0.05 |
| Cheyenne (0) | 0 | <0.01 |
| Chickasaw (0) | 0 | <0.01 |
| Chippewa (2) | 3 | <0.01 |
| Choctaw (0) | 0 | <0.01 |
| Colville (0) | 0 | <0.01 |

| | Population | % |
|---|---|---|
| Comanche (0) | 0 | <0.01 |
| Cree (0) | 0 | <0.01 |
| Creek (2) | 2 | <0.01 |
| Crow (0) | 1 | <0.01 |
| Delaware (1) | 6 | 0.01 |
| Hopi (0) | 0 | <0.01 |
| Houma (0) | 0 | <0.01 |
| Inupiat (Alaska Native) (4) | 4 | 0.01 |
| Iroquois (40) | 89 | 0.14 |
| Kiowa (0) | 1 | <0.01 |
| Lumbee (0) | 1 | <0.01 |
| Menominee (0) | 0 | <0.01 |
| Mexican American Ind. (7) | 7 | 0.01 |
| Navajo (3) | 3 | <0.01 |
| Osage (0) | 0 | <0.01 |
| Ottawa (0) | 0 | <0.01 |
| Paiute (0) | 0 | <0.01 |
| Pima (0) | 0 | <0.01 |
| Potawatomi (3) | 3 | <0.01 |
| Pueblo (0) | 0 | <0.01 |
| Puget Sound Salish (0) | 0 | <0.01 |
| Seminole (0) | 0 | <0.01 |
| Shoshone (0) | 0 | <0.01 |
| Sioux (2) | 13 | 0.02 |
| South American Ind. (5) | 6 | 0.01 |
| Spanish American Ind. (0) | 1 | <0.01 |
| Tlingit-Haida (Alaska Native) (3) | 3 | <0.01 |
| Tohono O'Odham (1) | 1 | <0.01 |
| Tsimshian (Alaska Native) (0) | 0 | <0.01 |
| Ute (0) | 1 | <0.01 |
| Yakama (0) | 0 | <0.01 |
| Yaqui (4) | 4 | 0.01 |
| Yuman (0) | 0 | <0.01 |
| Yup'ik (Alaska Native) (0) | 0 | <0.01 |
| Asian (332) | 445 | 0.69 |
| Not Hispanic (325) | 433 | 0.67 |
| Hispanic (7) | 12 | 0.02 |
| Bangladeshi (0) | 0 | <0.01 |
| Bhutanese (0) | 0 | <0.01 |
| Burmese (0) | 0 | <0.01 |
| Cambodian (3) | 8 | 0.01 |
| Chinese, ex. Taiwanese (68) | 77 | 0.12 |
| Filipino (73) | 108 | 0.17 |
| Hmong (0) | 0 | <0.01 |
| Indian (76) | 98 | 0.15 |
| Indonesian (1) | 1 | <0.01 |
| Japanese (35) | 54 | 0.08 |
| Korean (29) | 40 | 0.06 |
| Laotian (4) | 6 | 0.01 |
| Malaysian (0) | 0 | <0.01 |
| Nepalese (0) | 0 | <0.01 |
| Pakistani (1) | 1 | <0.01 |
| Sri Lankan (0) | 0 | <0.01 |
| Taiwanese (0) | 0 | <0.01 |
| Thai (10) | 13 | 0.02 |
| Vietnamese (13) | 18 | 0.03 |
| Hawaii Native/Pacific Islander (11) | 23 | 0.04 |
| Not Hispanic (8) | 18 | 0.03 |
| Hispanic (3) | 5 | 0.01 |
| Fijian (0) | 0 | <0.01 |
| Guamanian/Chamorro (4) | 5 | 0.01 |
| Marshallese (0) | 0 | <0.01 |
| Native Hawaiian (4) | 9 | 0.01 |
| Samoan (1) | 3 | <0.01 |
| Tongan (0) | 0 | <0.01 |
| White (62,320) | 63,066 | 97.75 |
| Not Hispanic (61,690) | 62,311 | 96.58 |
| Hispanic (630) | 755 | 1.17 |

*Notes: † The Census 2010 population figure is used to calculate the percentages in the Hispanic Origin and Race categories. Ancestry percentages are based on the 2006-2010 American Community Survey population (not shown); ‡ Numbers in parentheses indicate the number of people reporting a single ancestry; * Numbers in parentheses indicate the number of persons reporting this race alone, not in combination with any other race; Please refer to the Explanation of Data for more information.*

## Jefferson County

Population: 116,229

| Ancestry | Population | % |
|---|---|---|
| Afghan (0) | 0 | <0.01 |
| African, Sub-Saharan (367) | 470 | 0.41 |
| African (316) | 409 | 0.36 |
| Cape Verdean (0) | 0 | <0.01 |
| Ethiopian (7) | 7 | 0.01 |
| Ghanaian (15) | 15 | 0.01 |
| Kenyan (0) | 0 | <0.01 |
| Liberian (0) | 0 | <0.01 |
| Nigerian (0) | 0 | <0.01 |
| Senegalese (14) | 23 | 0.02 |
| Sierra Leonean (0) | 0 | <0.01 |
| Somalian (0) | 0 | <0.01 |
| South African (15) | 16 | 0.01 |
| Sudanese (0) | 0 | <0.01 |
| Ugandan (0) | 0 | <0.01 |
| Zimbabwean (0) | 0 | <0.01 |
| Other Sub-Saharan African (0) | 0 | <0.01 |
| Albanian (0) | 3 | <0.01 |
| Alsatian (0) | 0 | <0.01 |
| American (6,079) | 6,079 | 5.28 |
| Arab (229) | 384 | 0.33 |
| Arab (0) | 0 | <0.01 |
| Egyptian (80) | 80 | 0.07 |
| Iraqi (6) | 6 | 0.01 |
| Jordanian (6) | 6 | 0.01 |
| Lebanese (18) | 129 | 0.11 |
| Moroccan (99) | 99 | 0.09 |
| Palestinian (14) | 14 | 0.01 |
| Syrian (6) | 50 | 0.04 |
| Other Arab (0) | 0 | <0.01 |
| Armenian (15) | 50 | 0.04 |
| Assyrian/Chaldean/Syriac (0) | 0 | <0.01 |
| Australian (52) | 56 | 0.05 |
| Austrian (37) | 208 | 0.18 |
| Basque (0) | 0 | <0.01 |
| Belgian (67) | 246 | 0.21 |
| Brazilian (31) | 99 | 0.09 |
| British (177) | 345 | 0.30 |
| Bulgarian (0) | 0 | <0.01 |
| Cajun (8) | 8 | 0.01 |
| Canadian (624) | 1,138 | 0.99 |
| Carpatho Rusyn (0) | 0 | <0.01 |
| Celtic (0) | 11 | 0.01 |
| Croatian (25) | 94 | 0.08 |
| Cypriot (0) | 0 | <0.01 |
| Czech (40) | 199 | 0.17 |
| Czechoslovakian (84) | 122 | 0.11 |
| Danish (54) | 172 | 0.15 |
| Dutch (642) | 3,044 | 2.65 |
| Eastern European (60) | 76 | 0.07 |
| English (4,695) | 14,861 | 12.91 |
| Estonian (0) | 0 | <0.01 |
| European (540) | 609 | 0.53 |
| Finnish (20) | 51 | 0.04 |
| French, ex. Basque (2,381) | 12,941 | 11.25 |
| French Canadian (1,909) | 4,176 | 3.63 |
| German (5,792) | 22,170 | 19.27 |
| German Russian (17) | 17 | 0.01 |
| Greek (191) | 351 | 0.31 |
| Guyanese (205) | 228 | 0.20 |
| Hungarian (305) | 700 | 0.61 |
| Icelander (0) | 0 | <0.01 |
| Iranian (9) | 9 | 0.01 |
| Irish (7,451) | 23,186 | 20.15 |
| Israeli (0) | 9 | 0.01 |
| Italian (4,621) | 12,267 | 10.66 |
| Latvian (0) | 0 | <0.01 |
| Lithuanian (18) | 114 | 0.10 |
| Luxemburger (0) | 0 | <0.01 |
| Macedonian (7) | 9 | 0.01 |
| Maltese (0) | 0 | <0.01 |
| New Zealander (0) | 0 | <0.01 |
| Northern European (64) | 73 | 0.06 |
| Norwegian (299) | 657 | 0.57 |
| Pennsylvania German (42) | 75 | 0.07 |

| Ancestry | Population | % |
|---|---|---|
| Polish (1,233) | 3,949 | 3.43 |
| Portuguese (111) | 356 | 0.31 |
| Romanian (60) | 107 | 0.09 |
| Russian (277) | 600 | 0.52 |
| Scandinavian (51) | 77 | 0.07 |
| Scotch-Irish (698) | 1,943 | 1.69 |
| Scottish (1,255) | 3,937 | 3.42 |
| Serbian (0) | 7 | 0.01 |
| Slavic (35) | 58 | 0.05 |
| Slovak (22) | 90 | 0.08 |
| Slovene (0) | 0 | <0.01 |
| Soviet Union (0) | 0 | <0.01 |
| Swedish (200) | 883 | 0.77 |
| Swiss (32) | 371 | 0.32 |
| Turkish (94) | 104 | 0.09 |
| Ukrainian (205) | 366 | 0.32 |
| Welsh (99) | 860 | 0.75 |
| West Indian, ex. Hispanic (927) | 1,171 | 1.02 |
| Bahamian (0) | 0 | <0.01 |
| Barbadian (197) | 220 | 0.19 |
| Belizean (35) | 40 | 0.03 |
| Bermudan (0) | 0 | <0.01 |
| British West Indian (2) | 2 | <0.01 |
| Dutch West Indian (0) | 74 | 0.06 |
| Haitian (154) | 158 | 0.14 |
| Jamaican (349) | 401 | 0.35 |
| Trinidadian/Tobagonian (30) | 76 | 0.07 |
| U.S. Virgin Islander (7) | 7 | <0.01 |
| West Indian (153) | 193 | 0.17 |
| Other West Indian (0) | 0 | <0.01 |
| Yugoslavian (26) | 31 | 0.03 |

| Hispanic Origin | Population | % |
|---|---|---|
| Hispanic or Latino (of any race) | 6,143 | 5.29 |
| Central American, ex. Mexican | 421 | 0.36 |
| Costa Rican | 20 | 0.02 |
| Guatemalan | 84 | 0.07 |
| Honduran | 56 | 0.05 |
| Nicaraguan | 43 | 0.04 |
| Panamanian | 143 | 0.12 |
| Salvadoran | 75 | 0.06 |
| Other Central American | 0 | <0.01 |
| Cuban | 186 | 0.16 |
| Dominican Republic | 252 | 0.22 |
| Mexican | 2,211 | 1.90 |
| Puerto Rican | 2,202 | 1.89 |
| South American | 339 | 0.29 |
| Argentinean | 17 | 0.01 |
| Bolivian | 5 | <0.01 |
| Chilean | 20 | 0.02 |
| Colombian | 115 | 0.10 |
| Ecuadorian | 84 | 0.07 |
| Paraguayan | 9 | 0.01 |
| Peruvian | 60 | 0.05 |
| Uruguayan | 1 | <0.01 |
| Venezuelan | 24 | 0.02 |
| Other South American | 4 | <0.01 |
| Other Hispanic or Latino | 532 | 0.46 |

| Race* | Population | % |
|---|---|---|
| African-American/Black (5,876) | 7,366 | 6.34 |
| Not Hispanic (5,475) | 6,724 | 5.79 |
| Hispanic (401) | 642 | 0.55 |
| American Indian/Alaska Native (586) | 1,483 | 1.28 |
| Not Hispanic (500) | 1,288 | 1.11 |
| Hispanic (86) | 195 | 0.17 |
| Alaska Athabascan (Ala. Nat.) (5) | 11 | 0.01 |
| Aleut (Alaska Native) (6) | 6 | 0.01 |
| Apache (8) | 29 | 0.02 |
| Arapaho (0) | 0 | <0.01 |
| Blackfeet (14) | 49 | 0.04 |
| Canadian/French Am. Ind. (5) | 11 | 0.01 |
| Central American Ind. (2) | 4 | <0.01 |
| Cherokee (47) | 201 | 0.17 |
| Cheyenne (0) | 1 | <0.01 |
| Chickasaw (3) | 3 | <0.01 |
| Chippewa (9) | 19 | 0.02 |
| Choctaw (15) | 34 | 0.03 |
| Colville (0) | 0 | <0.01 |

| | Population | % |
|---|---|---|
| Comanche (1) | 1 | <0.01 |
| Cree (1) | 5 | <0.01 |
| Creek (5) | 10 | 0.01 |
| Crow (0) | 1 | <0.01 |
| Delaware (2) | 7 | 0.01 |
| Hopi (0) | 1 | <0.01 |
| Houma (0) | 0 | <0.01 |
| Inupiat (Alaska Native) (6) | 8 | 0.01 |
| Iroquois (154) | 320 | 0.28 |
| Kiowa (0) | 0 | <0.01 |
| Lumbee (3) | 3 | <0.01 |
| Menominee (1) | 1 | <0.01 |
| Mexican American Ind. (11) | 23 | 0.02 |
| Navajo (25) | 42 | 0.04 |
| Osage (0) | 3 | <0.01 |
| Ottawa (0) | 0 | <0.01 |
| Paiute (0) | 0 | <0.01 |
| Pima (0) | 0 | <0.01 |
| Potawatomi (6) | 6 | <0.01 |
| Pueblo (9) | 14 | 0.01 |
| Puget Sound Salish (0) | 1 | <0.01 |
| Seminole (2) | 2 | <0.01 |
| Shoshone (0) | 0 | <0.01 |
| Sioux (15) | 40 | 0.03 |
| South American Ind. (3) | 14 | 0.01 |
| Spanish American Ind. (2) | 4 | <0.01 |
| Tlingit-Haida (Alaska Native) (0) | 2 | <0.01 |
| Tohono O'Odham (0) | 0 | <0.01 |
| Tsimshian (Alaska Native) (0) | 0 | <0.01 |
| Ute (0) | 1 | <0.01 |
| Yakama (0) | 0 | <0.01 |
| Yaqui (0) | 1 | <0.01 |
| Yuman (0) | 0 | <0.01 |
| Yup'ik (Alaska Native) (4) | 4 | <0.01 |
| Asian (1,518) | 2,253 | 1.94 |
| Not Hispanic (1,464) | 2,110 | 1.82 |
| Hispanic (54) | 143 | 0.12 |
| Bangladeshi (10) | 10 | 0.01 |
| Bhutanese (1) | 4 | <0.01 |
| Burmese (1) | 1 | <0.01 |
| Cambodian (17) | 27 | 0.02 |
| Chinese, ex. Taiwanese (171) | 242 | 0.21 |
| Filipino (496) | 777 | 0.67 |
| Hmong (2) | 4 | <0.01 |
| Indian (133) | 179 | 0.15 |
| Indonesian (3) | 11 | 0.01 |
| Japanese (71) | 190 | 0.16 |
| Korean (357) | 558 | 0.48 |
| Laotian (7) | 16 | 0.01 |
| Malaysian (0) | 0 | <0.01 |
| Nepalese (0) | 0 | <0.01 |
| Pakistani (25) | 31 | 0.03 |
| Sri Lankan (1) | 1 | <0.01 |
| Taiwanese (3) | 3 | <0.01 |
| Thai (32) | 69 | 0.06 |
| Vietnamese (82) | 125 | 0.11 |
| Hawaii Native/Pacific Islander (298) | 529 | 0.46 |
| Not Hispanic (273) | 464 | 0.40 |
| Hispanic (25) | 65 | 0.06 |
| Fijian (3) | 4 | <0.01 |
| Guamanian/Chamorro (103) | 133 | 0.11 |
| Marshallese (15) | 15 | 0.01 |
| Native Hawaiian (52) | 157 | 0.14 |
| Samoan (68) | 99 | 0.09 |
| Tongan (2) | 2 | <0.01 |
| White (103,047) | 105,977 | 91.18 |
| Not Hispanic (99,682) | 102,062 | 87.81 |
| Hispanic (3,365) | 3,915 | 3.37 |

*Notes: † The Census 2010 population figure is used to calculate the percentages in the Hispanic Origin and Race categories. Ancestry percentages are based on the 2006-2010 American Community Survey population (not shown); ‡ Numbers in parentheses indicate the number of people reporting a single ancestry; * Numbers in parentheses indicate the number of persons reporting this race alone, not in combination with any other race; Please refer to the Explanation of Data for more information.*

## Kings County
Population: 2,504,700

| Ancestry | Population | % |
|---|---|---|
| Afghan (335) | 344 | 0.01 |
| African, Sub-Saharan (30,768) | 63,004 | 2.55 |
| African (17,256) | 48,168 | 1.95 |
| Cape Verdean (106) | 153 | 0.01 |
| Ethiopian (283) | 330 | 0.01 |
| Ghanaian (3,692) | 3,898 | 0.16 |
| Kenyan (65) | 77 | <0.01 |
| Liberian (392) | 452 | 0.02 |
| Nigerian (5,499) | 6,033 | 0.24 |
| Senegalese (401) | 401 | 0.02 |
| Sierra Leonean (147) | 147 | 0.01 |
| Somalian (234) | 260 | 0.01 |
| South African (204) | 320 | 0.01 |
| Sudanese (693) | 731 | 0.03 |
| Ugandan (29) | 54 | <0.01 |
| Zimbabwean (99) | 99 | <0.01 |
| Other Sub-Saharan African (1,668) | 1,881 | 0.08 |
| Albanian (6,490) | 6,871 | 0.28 |
| Alsatian (0) | 27 | <0.01 |
| American (78,858) | 78,858 | 3.20 |
| Arab (29,346) | 34,840 | 1.41 |
| Arab (6,779) | 7,609 | 0.31 |
| Egyptian (4,705) | 5,231 | 0.21 |
| Iraqi (71) | 134 | 0.01 |
| Jordanian (714) | 752 | 0.03 |
| Lebanese (3,425) | 4,757 | 0.19 |
| Moroccan (2,156) | 2,648 | 0.11 |
| Palestinian (1,372) | 1,482 | 0.06 |
| Syrian (4,854) | 5,890 | 0.24 |
| Other Arab (5,270) | 6,337 | 0.26 |
| Armenian (1,798) | 2,300 | 0.09 |
| Assyrian/Chaldean/Syriac (22) | 44 | <0.01 |
| Australian (539) | 832 | 0.03 |
| Austrian (1,677) | 5,123 | 0.21 |
| Basque (69) | 129 | 0.01 |
| Belgian (498) | 1,012 | 0.04 |
| Brazilian (1,257) | 1,719 | 0.07 |
| British (2,002) | 4,749 | 0.19 |
| Bulgarian (970) | 1,128 | 0.05 |
| Cajun (99) | 175 | 0.01 |
| Canadian (1,814) | 3,116 | 0.13 |
| Carpatho Rusyn (46) | 53 | <0.01 |
| Celtic (16) | 32 | <0.01 |
| Croatian (488) | 998 | 0.04 |
| Cypriot (37) | 62 | <0.01 |
| Czech (759) | 3,393 | 0.14 |
| Czechoslovakian (793) | 1,684 | 0.07 |
| Danish (380) | 1,267 | 0.05 |
| Dutch (1,616) | 5,664 | 0.23 |
| Eastern European (11,912) | 12,941 | 0.52 |
| English (9,927) | 32,407 | 1.31 |
| Estonian (209) | 340 | 0.01 |
| European (25,194) | 27,499 | 1.11 |
| Finnish (303) | 692 | 0.03 |
| French, ex. Basque (3,484) | 14,137 | 0.57 |
| French Canadian (1,082) | 2,974 | 0.12 |
| German (12,299) | 52,798 | 2.14 |
| German Russian (29) | 55 | <0.01 |
| Greek (10,688) | 14,075 | 0.57 |
| Guyanese (36,322) | 38,963 | 1.58 |
| Hungarian (17,858) | 26,607 | 1.08 |
| Icelander (69) | 103 | <0.01 |
| Iranian (1,520) | 1,822 | 0.07 |
| Irish (32,255) | 84,945 | 3.44 |
| Israeli (7,062) | 9,707 | 0.39 |
| Italian (108,743) | 152,814 | 6.19 |
| Latvian (418) | 667 | 0.03 |
| Lithuanian (938) | 2,676 | 0.11 |
| Luxemburger (41) | 58 | <0.01 |
| Macedonian (389) | 498 | 0.02 |
| Maltese (197) | 362 | 0.01 |
| New Zealander (71) | 140 | 0.01 |
| Northern European (905) | 961 | 0.04 |
| Norwegian (2,042) | 5,982 | 0.24 |
| Pennsylvania German (19) | 59 | <0.01 |

| | | |
|---|---|---|
| Polish (41,882) | 66,792 | 2.71 |
| Portuguese (1,106) | 2,882 | 0.12 |
| Romanian (4,537) | 8,046 | 0.33 |
| Russian (69,188) | 88,579 | 3.59 |
| Scandinavian (512) | 882 | 0.04 |
| Scotch-Irish (1,997) | 6,090 | 0.25 |
| Scottish (2,407) | 8,809 | 0.36 |
| Serbian (288) | 520 | 0.02 |
| Slavic (289) | 564 | 0.02 |
| Slovak (1,164) | 1,826 | 0.07 |
| Slovene (55) | 160 | 0.01 |
| Soviet Union (185) | 219 | 0.01 |
| Swedish (1,240) | 5,185 | 0.21 |
| Swiss (473) | 1,491 | 0.06 |
| Turkish (4,449) | 5,164 | 0.21 |
| Ukrainian (21,703) | 25,046 | 1.02 |
| Welsh (345) | 2,606 | 0.11 |
| West Indian, ex. Hispanic (257,579) | 306,541 | 12.43 |
| Bahamian (195) | 266 | 0.01 |
| Barbadian (13,358) | 14,916 | 0.60 |
| Belizean (1,610) | 2,026 | 0.08 |
| Bermudan (16) | 16 | <0.01 |
| British West Indian (28,123) | 30,607 | 1.24 |
| Dutch West Indian (289) | 424 | 0.02 |
| Haitian (67,083) | 69,941 | 2.84 |
| Jamaican (74,216) | 80,999 | 3.28 |
| Trinidadian/Tobagonian (42,450) | 46,490 | 1.88 |
| U.S. Virgin Islander (470) | 558 | 0.02 |
| West Indian (29,404) | 59,844 | 2.43 |
| Other West Indian (365) | 454 | 0.02 |
| Yugoslavian (2,305) | 2,800 | 0.11 |

| Hispanic Origin | Population | % |
|---|---|---|
| Hispanic or Latino (of any race) | 496,285 | 19.81 |
| Central American, ex. Mexican | 46,119 | 1.84 |
| Costa Rican | 2,576 | 0.10 |
| Guatemalan | 9,160 | 0.37 |
| Honduran | 10,071 | 0.40 |
| Nicaraguan | 2,407 | 0.10 |
| Panamanian | 13,681 | 0.55 |
| Salvadoran | 7,737 | 0.31 |
| Other Central American | 487 | 0.02 |
| Cuban | 7,581 | 0.30 |
| Dominican Republic | 86,764 | 3.46 |
| Mexican | 94,585 | 3.78 |
| Puerto Rican | 176,528 | 7.05 |
| South American | 49,003 | 1.96 |
| Argentinean | 2,760 | 0.11 |
| Bolivian | 310 | 0.01 |
| Chilean | 1,026 | 0.04 |
| Colombian | 8,861 | 0.35 |
| Ecuadorian | 28,684 | 1.15 |
| Paraguayan | 230 | 0.01 |
| Peruvian | 4,222 | 0.17 |
| Uruguayan | 488 | 0.02 |
| Venezuelan | 1,916 | 0.08 |
| Other South American | 506 | 0.02 |
| Other Hispanic or Latino | 35,705 | 1.43 |

| Race* | Population | % |
|---|---|---|
| African-American/Black (860,083) | 896,165 | 35.78 |
| Not Hispanic (799,066) | 820,437 | 32.76 |
| Hispanic (61,017) | 75,728 | 3.02 |
| American Indian/Alaska Native (13,524) | 26,571 | 1.06 |
| Not Hispanic (4,638) | 12,062 | 0.48 |
| Hispanic (8,886) | 14,509 | 0.58 |
| Alaska Athabascan (Ala. Nat.) (1) | 5 | <0.01 |
| Aleut (Alaska Native) (4) | 8 | <0.01 |
| Apache (46) | 122 | <0.01 |
| Arapaho (2) | 10 | <0.01 |
| Blackfeet (89) | 531 | 0.02 |
| Canadian/French Am. Ind. (42) | 62 | <0.01 |
| Central American Ind. (616) | 1,263 | 0.05 |
| Cherokee (289) | 1,903 | 0.08 |
| Cheyenne (0) | 10 | <0.01 |
| Chickasaw (9) | 30 | <0.01 |
| Chippewa (23) | 65 | <0.01 |
| Choctaw (30) | 104 | <0.01 |
| Colville (1) | 1 | <0.01 |

| | | |
|---|---|---|
| Comanche (5) | 19 | <0.01 |
| Cree (3) | 15 | <0.01 |
| Creek (20) | 81 | <0.01 |
| Crow (5) | 19 | <0.01 |
| Delaware (5) | 35 | <0.01 |
| Hopi (7) | 12 | <0.01 |
| Houma (1) | 3 | <0.01 |
| Inupiat (Alaska Native) (7) | 21 | <0.01 |
| Iroquois (194) | 381 | 0.02 |
| Kiowa (1) | 2 | <0.01 |
| Lumbee (6) | 24 | <0.01 |
| Menominee (1) | 4 | <0.01 |
| Mexican American Ind. (1,022) | 1,363 | 0.05 |
| Navajo (41) | 93 | <0.01 |
| Osage (1) | 3 | <0.01 |
| Ottawa (2) | 5 | <0.01 |
| Paiute (0) | 1 | <0.01 |
| Pima (0) | 2 | <0.01 |
| Potawatomi (3) | 11 | <0.01 |
| Pueblo (93) | 169 | 0.01 |
| Puget Sound Salish (1) | 1 | <0.01 |
| Seminole (18) | 92 | <0.01 |
| Shoshone (6) | 23 | <0.01 |
| Sioux (29) | 121 | <0.01 |
| South American Ind. (874) | 1,855 | 0.07 |
| Spanish American Ind. (290) | 382 | 0.02 |
| Tlingit-Haida (Alaska Native) (4) | 28 | <0.01 |
| Tohono O'Odham (9) | 10 | <0.01 |
| Tsimshian (Alaska Native) (0) | 0 | <0.01 |
| Ute (0) | 4 | <0.01 |
| Yakama (1) | 3 | <0.01 |
| Yaqui (11) | 19 | <0.01 |
| Yuman (5) | 8 | <0.01 |
| Yup'ik (Alaska Native) (0) | 1 | <0.01 |
| Asian (262,276) | 284,489 | 11.36 |
| Not Hispanic (260,129) | 279,499 | 11.16 |
| Hispanic (2,147) | 4,990 | 0.20 |
| Bangladeshi (10,667) | 12,408 | 0.50 |
| Bhutanese (5) | 8 | <0.01 |
| Burmese (1,055) | 1,260 | 0.05 |
| Cambodian (613) | 751 | 0.03 |
| Chinese, ex. Taiwanese (171,214) | 178,214 | 7.12 |
| Filipino (7,930) | 10,208 | 0.41 |
| Hmong (14) | 22 | <0.01 |
| Indian (26,144) | 33,490 | 1.34 |
| Indonesian (383) | 564 | 0.02 |
| Japanese (3,938) | 5,917 | 0.24 |
| Korean (6,904) | 8,201 | 0.33 |
| Laotian (82) | 131 | 0.01 |
| Malaysian (478) | 708 | 0.03 |
| Nepalese (355) | 393 | 0.02 |
| Pakistani (18,296) | 19,840 | 0.79 |
| Sri Lankan (219) | 270 | 0.01 |
| Taiwanese (857) | 1,075 | 0.04 |
| Thai (636) | 883 | 0.04 |
| Vietnamese (3,944) | 5,041 | 0.20 |
| Hawaii Native/Pacific Islander (1,243) | 5,784 | 0.23 |
| Not Hispanic (633) | 3,463 | 0.14 |
| Hispanic (610) | 2,321 | 0.09 |
| Fijian (20) | 45 | <0.01 |
| Guamanian/Chamorro (386) | 568 | 0.02 |
| Marshallese (1) | 2 | <0.01 |
| Native Hawaiian (208) | 564 | 0.02 |
| Samoan (72) | 216 | 0.01 |
| Tongan (5) | 10 | <0.01 |
| White (1,072,041) | 1,120,592 | 44.74 |
| Not Hispanic (893,306) | 917,717 | 36.64 |
| Hispanic (178,735) | 202,875 | 8.10 |

*Notes: † The Census 2010 population figure is used to calculate the percentages in the Hispanic Origin and Race categories. Ancestry percentages are based on the 2006-2010 American Community Survey population (not shown); ‡ Numbers in parentheses indicate the number of people reporting a single ancestry; * Numbers in parentheses indicate the number of persons reporting this race alone, not in combination with any other race; Please refer to the Explanation of Data for more information.*

## Lewis County

Population: 27,087

| Ancestry | Population | % |
|---|---|---|
| Afghan (0) | 0 | <0.01 |
| African, Sub-Saharan (17) | 30 | 0.11 |
| African (17) | 26 | 0.10 |
| Cape Verdean (0) | 0 | <0.01 |
| Ethiopian (0) | 0 | <0.01 |
| Ghanaian (0) | 0 | <0.01 |
| Kenyan (0) | 0 | <0.01 |
| Liberian (0) | 0 | <0.01 |
| Nigerian (0) | 0 | <0.01 |
| Senegalese (0) | 0 | <0.01 |
| Sierra Leonean (0) | 0 | <0.01 |
| Somalian (0) | 0 | <0.01 |
| South African (0) | 4 | 0.01 |
| Sudanese (0) | 0 | <0.01 |
| Ugandan (0) | 0 | <0.01 |
| Zimbabwean (0) | 0 | <0.01 |
| Other Sub-Saharan African (0) | 0 | <0.01 |
| Albanian (25) | 25 | 0.09 |
| Alsatian (13) | 50 | 0.19 |
| American (1,155) | 1,155 | 4.28 |
| Arab (79) | 83 | 0.31 |
| Arab (0) | 0 | <0.01 |
| Egyptian (45) | 45 | 0.17 |
| Iraqi (0) | 0 | <0.01 |
| Jordanian (0) | 0 | <0.01 |
| Lebanese (13) | 13 | 0.05 |
| Moroccan (0) | 0 | <0.01 |
| Palestinian (0) | 0 | <0.01 |
| Syrian (9) | 4 | 0.01 |
| Other Arab (21) | 21 | 0.08 |
| Armenian (7) | 7 | 0.03 |
| Assyrian/Chaldean/Syriac (0) | 0 | <0.01 |
| Australian (0) | 0 | <0.01 |
| Austrian (5) | 61 | 0.23 |
| Basque (0) | 0 | <0.01 |
| Belgian (0) | 2 | 0.01 |
| Brazilian (0) | 0 | <0.01 |
| British (20) | 58 | 0.21 |
| Bulgarian (0) | 0 | <0.01 |
| Cajun (4) | 4 | 0.01 |
| Canadian (61) | 140 | 0.52 |
| Carpatho Rusyn (0) | 0 | <0.01 |
| Celtic (0) | 0 | <0.01 |
| Croatian (24) | 24 | 0.09 |
| Cypriot (0) | 0 | <0.01 |
| Czech (3) | 14 | 0.05 |
| Czechoslovakian (6) | 8 | 0.03 |
| Danish (30) | 71 | 0.26 |
| Dutch (146) | 882 | 3.26 |
| Eastern European (37) | 37 | 0.14 |
| English (757) | 2,702 | 10.00 |
| Estonian (0) | 0 | <0.01 |
| European (62) | 71 | 0.26 |
| Finnish (0) | 10 | 0.04 |
| French, ex. Basque (708) | 3,633 | 13.45 |
| French Canadian (484) | 788 | 2.92 |
| German (2,964) | 8,378 | 31.01 |
| German Russian (0) | 0 | <0.01 |
| Greek (7) | 12 | 0.04 |
| Guyanese (39) | 39 | 0.14 |
| Hungarian (212) | 307 | 1.14 |
| Icelander (0) | 0 | <0.01 |
| Iranian (9) | 9 | 0.03 |
| Irish (1,034) | 4,543 | 16.82 |
| Israeli (0) | 0 | <0.01 |
| Italian (617) | 1,963 | 7.27 |
| Latvian (0) | 0 | <0.01 |
| Lithuanian (23) | 26 | 0.10 |
| Luxemburger (0) | 0 | <0.01 |
| Macedonian (0) | 0 | <0.01 |
| Maltese (0) | 0 | <0.01 |
| New Zealander (0) | 0 | <0.01 |
| Northern European (22) | 22 | 0.08 |
| Norwegian (51) | 93 | 0.34 |
| Pennsylvania German (0) | 0 | <0.01 |

| | Population | % |
|---|---|---|
| Polish (623) | 1,338 | 4.95 |
| Portuguese (0) | 31 | 0.11 |
| Romanian (5) | 5 | 0.02 |
| Russian (44) | 98 | 0.36 |
| Scandinavian (0) | 0 | <0.01 |
| Scotch-Irish (205) | 396 | 1.47 |
| Scottish (161) | 521 | 1.93 |
| Serbian (0) | 0 | <0.01 |
| Slavic (0) | 0 | <0.01 |
| Slovak (5) | 5 | 0.02 |
| Slovene (0) | 20 | 0.07 |
| Soviet Union (0) | 0 | <0.01 |
| Swedish (52) | 137 | 0.51 |
| Swiss (202) | 630 | 2.33 |
| Turkish (0) | 0 | <0.01 |
| Ukrainian (6) | 29 | 0.11 |
| Welsh (128) | 377 | 1.40 |
| West Indian, ex. Hispanic (6) | 41 | 0.15 |
| Bahamian (0) | 0 | <0.01 |
| Barbadian (0) | 0 | <0.01 |
| Belizean (0) | 0 | <0.01 |
| Bermudan (0) | 0 | <0.01 |
| British West Indian (0) | 0 | <0.01 |
| Dutch West Indian (0) | 0 | <0.01 |
| Haitian (0) | 0 | <0.01 |
| Jamaican (0) | 35 | 0.13 |
| Trinidadian/Tobagonian (0) | 0 | <0.01 |
| U.S. Virgin Islander (0) | 0 | <0.01 |
| West Indian (6) | 6 | 0.02 |
| Other West Indian (0) | 0 | <0.01 |
| Yugoslavian (15) | 18 | 0.07 |

| Hispanic Origin | Population | % |
|---|---|---|
| Hispanic or Latino (of any race) | 357 | 1.32 |
| Central American, ex. Mexican | 22 | 0.08 |
| Costa Rican | 1 | <0.01 |
| Guatemalan | 8 | 0.03 |
| Honduran | 8 | 0.03 |
| Nicaraguan | 2 | 0.01 |
| Panamanian | 3 | 0.01 |
| Salvadoran | 0 | <0.01 |
| Other Central American | 0 | <0.01 |
| Cuban | 5 | 0.02 |
| Dominican Republic | 5 | 0.02 |
| Mexican | 171 | 0.63 |
| Puerto Rican | 98 | 0.36 |
| South American | 10 | 0.04 |
| Argentinean | 2 | 0.01 |
| Bolivian | 0 | <0.01 |
| Chilean | 1 | <0.01 |
| Colombian | 4 | 0.01 |
| Ecuadorian | 3 | 0.01 |
| Paraguayan | 0 | <0.01 |
| Peruvian | 0 | <0.01 |
| Uruguayan | 0 | <0.01 |
| Venezuelan | 0 | <0.01 |
| Other South American | 0 | <0.01 |
| Other Hispanic or Latino | 46 | 0.17 |

| Race* | Population | % |
|---|---|---|
| African-American/Black (184) | 265 | 0.98 |
| Not Hispanic (170) | 230 | 0.85 |
| Hispanic (14) | 35 | 0.13 |
| American Indian/Alaska Native (53) | 157 | 0.58 |
| Not Hispanic (44) | 146 | 0.54 |
| Hispanic (9) | 11 | 0.04 |
| Alaska Athabascan (Ala. Nat.) (0) | 0 | <0.01 |
| Aleut (Alaska Native) (4) | 4 | 0.01 |
| Apache (2) | 3 | 0.01 |
| Arapaho (0) | 0 | <0.01 |
| Blackfeet (1) | 9 | 0.03 |
| Canadian/French Am. Ind. (0) | 2 | 0.01 |
| Central American Ind. (2) | 3 | 0.01 |
| Cherokee (2) | 17 | 0.06 |
| Cheyenne (0) | 0 | <0.01 |
| Chickasaw (0) | 0 | <0.01 |
| Chippewa (0) | 2 | 0.01 |
| Choctaw (0) | 0 | <0.01 |
| Colville (0) | 0 | <0.01 |

| | Population | % |
|---|---|---|
| Comanche (0) | 0 | <0.01 |
| Cree (0) | 1 | <0.01 |
| Creek (0) | 0 | <0.01 |
| Crow (0) | 0 | <0.01 |
| Delaware (0) | 0 | <0.01 |
| Hopi (0) | 0 | <0.01 |
| Houma (0) | 0 | <0.01 |
| Inupiat (Alaska Native) (0) | 0 | <0.01 |
| Iroquois (19) | 37 | 0.14 |
| Kiowa (0) | 0 | <0.01 |
| Lumbee (0) | 2 | 0.01 |
| Menominee (0) | 0 | <0.01 |
| Mexican American Ind. (0) | 0 | <0.01 |
| Navajo (0) | 1 | <0.01 |
| Osage (0) | 0 | <0.01 |
| Ottawa (0) | 0 | <0.01 |
| Paiute (0) | 0 | <0.01 |
| Pima (0) | 0 | <0.01 |
| Potawatomi (0) | 0 | <0.01 |
| Pueblo (0) | 0 | <0.01 |
| Puget Sound Salish (0) | 0 | <0.01 |
| Seminole (0) | 1 | <0.01 |
| Shoshone (0) | 0 | <0.01 |
| Sioux (0) | 3 | 0.01 |
| South American Ind. (0) | 0 | <0.01 |
| Spanish American Ind. (0) | 0 | <0.01 |
| Tlingit-Haida (Alaska Native) (0) | 0 | <0.01 |
| Tohono O'Odham (0) | 0 | <0.01 |
| Tsimshian (Alaska Native) (0) | 0 | <0.01 |
| Ute (0) | 0 | <0.01 |
| Yakama (0) | 0 | <0.01 |
| Yaqui (0) | 0 | <0.01 |
| Yuman (0) | 0 | <0.01 |
| Yup'ik (Alaska Native) (0) | 0 | <0.01 |
| Asian (75) | 114 | 0.42 |
| Not Hispanic (72) | 107 | 0.40 |
| Hispanic (3) | 7 | 0.03 |
| Bangladeshi (0) | 0 | <0.01 |
| Bhutanese (0) | 0 | <0.01 |
| Burmese (0) | 0 | <0.01 |
| Cambodian (3) | 5 | 0.02 |
| Chinese, ex. Taiwanese (14) | 16 | 0.06 |
| Filipino (25) | 38 | 0.14 |
| Hmong (0) | 0 | <0.01 |
| Indian (8) | 13 | 0.05 |
| Indonesian (0) | 0 | <0.01 |
| Japanese (3) | 11 | 0.04 |
| Korean (14) | 22 | 0.08 |
| Laotian (0) | 0 | <0.01 |
| Malaysian (0) | 0 | <0.01 |
| Nepalese (0) | 0 | <0.01 |
| Pakistani (3) | 4 | 0.01 |
| Sri Lankan (1) | 1 | <0.01 |
| Taiwanese (0) | 0 | <0.01 |
| Thai (2) | 5 | 0.02 |
| Vietnamese (0) | 1 | <0.01 |
| Hawaii Native/Pacific Islander (16) | 30 | 0.11 |
| Not Hispanic (16) | 27 | 0.10 |
| Hispanic (0) | 3 | 0.01 |
| Fijian (0) | 0 | <0.01 |
| Guamanian/Chamorro (4) | 4 | 0.01 |
| Marshallese (0) | 0 | <0.01 |
| Native Hawaiian (0) | 7 | 0.03 |
| Samoan (1) | 3 | 0.01 |
| Tongan (0) | 0 | <0.01 |
| White (26,465) | 26,686 | 98.52 |
| Not Hispanic (26,225) | 26,416 | 97.52 |
| Hispanic (240) | 270 | 1.00 |

Notes: † The Census 2010 population figure is used to calculate the percentages in the Hispanic Origin and Race categories. Ancestry percentages are based on the 2006-2010 American Community Survey population (not shown); ‡ Numbers in parentheses indicate the number of people reporting a single ancestry; * Numbers in parentheses indicate the number of persons reporting this race alone, not in combination with any other race; Please refer to the Explanation of Data for more information.

## Livingston County

Population: 65,393

| Ancestry | Population | % |
|---|---|---|
| Afghan (0) | 0 | <0.01 |
| African, Sub-Saharan (206) | 240 | 0.37 |
| African (99) | 132 | 0.20 |
| Cape Verdean (0) | 0 | <0.01 |
| Ethiopian (27) | 27 | 0.04 |
| Ghanaian (0) | 0 | <0.01 |
| Kenyan (0) | 0 | <0.01 |
| Liberian (0) | 0 | <0.01 |
| Nigerian (0) | 0 | <0.01 |
| Senegalese (12) | 12 | 0.02 |
| Sierra Leonean (0) | 0 | <0.01 |
| Somalian (0) | 0 | <0.01 |
| South African (64) | 64 | 0.10 |
| Sudanese (0) | 0 | <0.01 |
| Ugandan (0) | 0 | <0.01 |
| Zimbabwean (0) | 0 | <0.01 |
| Other Sub-Saharan African (4) | 5 | 0.01 |
| Albanian (9) | 9 | 0.01 |
| Alsatian (0) | 0 | <0.01 |
| American (3,367) | 3,367 | 5.15 |
| Arab (33) | 163 | 0.25 |
| Arab (3) | 3 | <0.01 |
| Egyptian (0) | 0 | <0.01 |
| Iraqi (0) | 0 | <0.01 |
| Jordanian (0) | 0 | <0.01 |
| Lebanese (17) | 90 | 0.14 |
| Moroccan (0) | 0 | <0.01 |
| Palestinian (0) | 0 | <0.01 |
| Syrian (13) | 70 | 0.11 |
| Other Arab (0) | 0 | <0.01 |
| Armenian (0) | 0 | <0.01 |
| Assyrian/Chaldean/Syriac (0) | 0 | <0.01 |
| Australian (21) | 24 | 0.04 |
| Austrian (54) | 201 | 0.31 |
| Basque (0) | 0 | <0.01 |
| Belgian (65) | 105 | 0.16 |
| Brazilian (0) | 88 | 0.13 |
| British (86) | 243 | 0.37 |
| Bulgarian (0) | 0 | <0.01 |
| Cajun (0) | 0 | <0.01 |
| Canadian (135) | 235 | 0.36 |
| Carpatho Rusyn (0) | 0 | <0.01 |
| Celtic (0) | 0 | <0.01 |
| Croatian (0) | 6 | 0.01 |
| Cypriot (0) | 0 | <0.01 |
| Czech (46) | 179 | 0.27 |
| Czechoslovakian (10) | 15 | 0.02 |
| Danish (11) | 137 | 0.21 |
| Dutch (415) | 2,843 | 4.34 |
| Eastern European (71) | 71 | 0.11 |
| English (2,964) | 11,436 | 17.48 |
| Estonian (0) | 0 | <0.01 |
| European (506) | 606 | 0.93 |
| Finnish (4) | 28 | 0.04 |
| French, ex. Basque (318) | 2,864 | 4.38 |
| French Canadian (260) | 668 | 1.02 |
| German (5,115) | 19,312 | 29.51 |
| German Russian (0) | 0 | <0.01 |
| Greek (41) | 112 | 0.17 |
| Guyanese (14) | 14 | 0.02 |
| Hungarian (113) | 436 | 0.67 |
| Icelander (0) | 2 | <0.01 |
| Iranian (6) | 6 | 0.01 |
| Irish (3,826) | 15,027 | 22.96 |
| Israeli (0) | 0 | <0.01 |
| Italian (3,398) | 8,851 | 13.53 |
| Latvian (21) | 32 | 0.05 |
| Lithuanian (26) | 190 | 0.29 |
| Luxemburger (0) | 0 | <0.01 |
| Macedonian (5) | 5 | 0.01 |
| Maltese (0) | 13 | 0.02 |
| New Zealander (0) | 0 | <0.01 |
| Northern European (19) | 37 | 0.06 |
| Norwegian (60) | 173 | 0.26 |
| Pennsylvania German (103) | 162 | 0.25 |

| Ancestry | Population | % |
|---|---|---|
| Polish (973) | 3,039 | 4.64 |
| Portuguese (12) | 189 | 0.29 |
| Romanian (23) | 64 | 0.10 |
| Russian (65) | 403 | 0.62 |
| Scandinavian (44) | 124 | 0.19 |
| Scotch-Irish (465) | 1,278 | 1.95 |
| Scottish (497) | 1,873 | 2.86 |
| Serbian (0) | 20 | 0.03 |
| Slavic (0) | 2 | <0.01 |
| Slovak (48) | 168 | 0.26 |
| Slovene (0) | 12 | 0.02 |
| Soviet Union (0) | 0 | <0.01 |
| Swedish (160) | 678 | 1.04 |
| Swiss (13) | 253 | 0.39 |
| Turkish (0) | 0 | <0.01 |
| Ukrainian (198) | 491 | 0.75 |
| Welsh (97) | 523 | 0.80 |
| West Indian, ex. Hispanic (107) | 154 | 0.24 |
| Bahamian (0) | 0 | <0.01 |
| Barbadian (0) | 0 | <0.01 |
| Belizean (0) | 0 | <0.01 |
| Bermudan (0) | 0 | <0.01 |
| British West Indian (8) | 8 | 0.01 |
| Dutch West Indian (0) | 0 | <0.01 |
| Haitian (13) | 14 | 0.02 |
| Jamaican (52) | 80 | 0.12 |
| Trinidadian/Tobagonian (17) | 17 | 0.03 |
| U.S. Virgin Islander (0) | 0 | <0.01 |
| West Indian (17) | 35 | 0.05 |
| Other West Indian (0) | 0 | <0.01 |
| Yugoslavian (19) | 43 | 0.07 |

| Hispanic Origin | Population | % |
|---|---|---|
| Hispanic or Latino (of any race) | 1,802 | 2.76 |
| Central American, ex. Mexican | 86 | 0.13 |
| Costa Rican | 8 | 0.01 |
| Guatemalan | 19 | 0.03 |
| Honduran | 17 | 0.03 |
| Nicaraguan | 8 | 0.01 |
| Panamanian | 15 | 0.02 |
| Salvadoran | 19 | 0.03 |
| Other Central American | 0 | <0.01 |
| Cuban | 82 | 0.13 |
| Dominican Republic | 76 | 0.12 |
| Mexican | 327 | 0.50 |
| Puerto Rican | 1,006 | 1.54 |
| South American | 102 | 0.16 |
| Argentinean | 7 | 0.01 |
| Bolivian | 1 | <0.01 |
| Chilean | 23 | 0.04 |
| Colombian | 36 | 0.06 |
| Ecuadorian | 12 | 0.02 |
| Paraguayan | 4 | 0.01 |
| Peruvian | 13 | 0.02 |
| Uruguayan | 2 | <0.01 |
| Venezuelan | 3 | <0.01 |
| Other South American | 1 | <0.01 |
| Other Hispanic or Latino | 123 | 0.19 |

| Race* | Population | % |
|---|---|---|
| African-American/Black (1,598) | 1,932 | 2.95 |
| Not Hispanic (1,491) | 1,786 | 2.73 |
| Hispanic (107) | 146 | 0.22 |
| American Indian/Alaska Native (187) | 527 | 0.81 |
| Not Hispanic (158) | 474 | 0.72 |
| Hispanic (29) | 53 | 0.08 |
| Alaska Athabascan (Ala. Nat.) (0) | 0 | <0.01 |
| Aleut (Alaska Native) (0) | 0 | <0.01 |
| Apache (0) | 2 | <0.01 |
| Arapaho (0) | 0 | <0.01 |
| Blackfeet (3) | 17 | 0.03 |
| Canadian/French Am. Ind. (2) | 8 | 0.01 |
| Central American Ind. (0) | 0 | <0.01 |
| Cherokee (5) | 33 | 0.05 |
| Cheyenne (0) | 0 | <0.01 |
| Chickasaw (0) | 1 | <0.01 |
| Chippewa (4) | 9 | 0.01 |
| Choctaw (1) | 3 | <0.01 |
| Colville (0) | 0 | <0.01 |

| | Population | % |
|---|---|---|
| Comanche (0) | 3 | <0.01 |
| Cree (0) | 1 | <0.01 |
| Creek (0) | 1 | <0.01 |
| Crow (0) | 1 | <0.01 |
| Delaware (0) | 0 | <0.01 |
| Hopi (0) | 0 | <0.01 |
| Houma (0) | 0 | <0.01 |
| Inupiat (Alaska Native) (0) | 1 | <0.01 |
| Iroquois (66) | 166 | 0.25 |
| Kiowa (0) | 0 | <0.01 |
| Lumbee (0) | 0 | <0.01 |
| Menominee (0) | 0 | <0.01 |
| Mexican American Ind. (3) | 4 | 0.01 |
| Navajo (2) | 6 | 0.01 |
| Osage (0) | 0 | <0.01 |
| Ottawa (0) | 0 | <0.01 |
| Paiute (0) | 0 | <0.01 |
| Pima (0) | 0 | <0.01 |
| Potawatomi (0) | 0 | <0.01 |
| Pueblo (0) | 0 | <0.01 |
| Puget Sound Salish (0) | 0 | <0.01 |
| Seminole (0) | 6 | 0.01 |
| Shoshone (0) | 0 | <0.01 |
| Sioux (0) | 5 | 0.01 |
| South American Ind. (4) | 10 | 0.02 |
| Spanish American Ind. (0) | 0 | <0.01 |
| Tlingit-Haida (Alaska Native) (0) | 1 | <0.01 |
| Tohono O'Odham (0) | 0 | <0.01 |
| Tsimshian (Alaska Native) (0) | 0 | <0.01 |
| Ute (0) | 0 | <0.01 |
| Yakama (0) | 0 | <0.01 |
| Yaqui (0) | 0 | <0.01 |
| Yuman (0) | 0 | <0.01 |
| Yup'ik (Alaska Native) (0) | 0 | <0.01 |
| Asian (785) | 1,019 | 1.56 |
| Not Hispanic (780) | 991 | 1.52 |
| Hispanic (5) | 28 | 0.04 |
| Bangladeshi (1) | 1 | <0.01 |
| Bhutanese (0) | 0 | <0.01 |
| Burmese (7) | 7 | 0.01 |
| Cambodian (7) | 9 | 0.01 |
| Chinese, ex. Taiwanese (207) | 254 | 0.39 |
| Filipino (77) | 127 | 0.19 |
| Hmong (1) | 1 | <0.01 |
| Indian (84) | 115 | 0.18 |
| Indonesian (0) | 2 | <0.01 |
| Japanese (47) | 71 | 0.11 |
| Korean (170) | 226 | 0.35 |
| Laotian (16) | 31 | 0.05 |
| Malaysian (1) | 4 | 0.01 |
| Nepalese (3) | 4 | 0.01 |
| Pakistani (41) | 53 | 0.08 |
| Sri Lankan (9) | 9 | 0.01 |
| Taiwanese (6) | 7 | 0.01 |
| Thai (5) | 6 | 0.01 |
| Vietnamese (56) | 71 | 0.11 |
| Hawaii Native/Pacific Islander (18) | 53 | 0.08 |
| Not Hispanic (11) | 37 | 0.06 |
| Hispanic (7) | 16 | 0.02 |
| Fijian (0) | 1 | <0.01 |
| Guamanian/Chamorro (4) | 9 | 0.01 |
| Marshallese (0) | 0 | <0.01 |
| Native Hawaiian (7) | 25 | 0.04 |
| Samoan (0) | 3 | <0.01 |
| Tongan (0) | 0 | <0.01 |
| White (61,363) | 62,245 | 95.19 |
| Not Hispanic (60,296) | 61,067 | 93.38 |
| Hispanic (1,067) | 1,178 | 1.80 |

Notes: † The Census 2010 population figure is used to calculate the percentages in the Hispanic Origin and Race categories. Ancestry percentages are based on the 2006-2010 American Community Survey population (not shown); ‡ Numbers in parentheses indicate the number of people reporting a single ancestry; * Numbers in parentheses indicate the number of persons reporting this race alone, not in combination with any other race; Please refer to the Explanation of Data for more information.

## Madison County

Population: 73,442

| Ancestry | Population | % |
|---|---|---|
| Afghan (9) | 27 | 0.04 |
| African, Sub-Saharan (154) | 214 | 0.29 |
| African (65) | 89 | 0.12 |
| Cape Verdean (0) | 0 | <0.01 |
| Ethiopian (0) | 0 | <0.01 |
| Ghanaian (12) | 22 | 0.03 |
| Kenyan (10) | 10 | 0.01 |
| Liberian (0) | 0 | <0.01 |
| Nigerian (33) | 48 | 0.07 |
| Senegalese (0) | 0 | <0.01 |
| Sierra Leonean (12) | 12 | 0.02 |
| Somalian (0) | 0 | <0.01 |
| South African (0) | 11 | 0.02 |
| Sudanese (11) | 11 | 0.02 |
| Ugandan (11) | 11 | 0.02 |
| Zimbabwean (0) | 0 | <0.01 |
| Other Sub-Saharan African (0) | 0 | <0.01 |
| Albanian (0) | 28 | 0.04 |
| Alsatian (0) | 0 | <0.01 |
| American (10,024) | 10,024 | 13.75 |
| Arab (98) | 173 | 0.24 |
| Arab (70) | 88 | 0.12 |
| Egyptian (0) | 0 | <0.01 |
| Iraqi (0) | 0 | <0.01 |
| Jordanian (0) | 0 | <0.01 |
| Lebanese (15) | 49 | 0.07 |
| Moroccan (0) | 0 | <0.01 |
| Palestinian (0) | 0 | <0.01 |
| Syrian (13) | 28 | 0.04 |
| Other Arab (0) | 8 | 0.01 |
| Armenian (12) | 28 | 0.04 |
| Assyrian/Chaldean/Syriac (0) | 0 | <0.01 |
| Australian (8) | 19 | 0.03 |
| Austrian (10) | 266 | 0.36 |
| Basque (0) | 0 | <0.01 |
| Belgian (42) | 106 | 0.15 |
| Brazilian (0) | 0 | <0.01 |
| British (169) | 338 | 0.46 |
| Bulgarian (0) | 0 | <0.01 |
| Cajun (0) | 0 | <0.01 |
| Canadian (234) | 460 | 0.63 |
| Carpatho Rusyn (0) | 0 | <0.01 |
| Celtic (0) | 3 | <0.01 |
| Croatian (7) | 70 | 0.10 |
| Cypriot (0) | 0 | <0.01 |
| Czech (7) | 221 | 0.30 |
| Czechoslovakian (19) | 106 | 0.15 |
| Danish (57) | 298 | 0.41 |
| Dutch (520) | 2,648 | 3.63 |
| Eastern European (82) | 89 | 0.12 |
| English (3,594) | 11,718 | 16.08 |
| Estonian (9) | 9 | 0.01 |
| European (647) | 668 | 0.92 |
| Finnish (4) | 48 | 0.07 |
| French, ex. Basque (628) | 4,501 | 6.18 |
| French Canadian (573) | 1,461 | 2.00 |
| German (3,834) | 15,853 | 21.75 |
| German Russian (0) | 0 | <0.01 |
| Greek (78) | 260 | 0.36 |
| Guyanese (0) | 0 | <0.01 |
| Hungarian (117) | 282 | 0.39 |
| Icelander (0) | 0 | <0.01 |
| Iranian (0) | 0 | <0.01 |
| Irish (3,752) | 13,797 | 18.93 |
| Israeli (0) | 0 | <0.01 |
| Italian (3,492) | 8,141 | 11.17 |
| Latvian (9) | 20 | 0.03 |
| Lithuanian (64) | 201 | 0.28 |
| Luxemburger (9) | 27 | 0.04 |
| Macedonian (12) | 12 | 0.02 |
| Maltese (0) | 0 | <0.01 |
| New Zealander (0) | 0 | <0.01 |
| Northern European (69) | 69 | 0.09 |
| Norwegian (80) | 305 | 0.42 |
| Pennsylvania German (112) | 126 | 0.17 |

| Ancestry | Population | % |
|---|---|---|
| Polish (1,425) | 4,350 | 5.97 |
| Portuguese (26) | 137 | 0.19 |
| Romanian (3) | 43 | 0.06 |
| Russian (181) | 521 | 0.71 |
| Scandinavian (27) | 99 | 0.14 |
| Scotch-Irish (372) | 1,148 | 1.58 |
| Scottish (549) | 1,988 | 2.73 |
| Serbian (0) | 0 | <0.01 |
| Slavic (33) | 113 | 0.16 |
| Slovak (21) | 110 | 0.15 |
| Slovene (13) | 29 | 0.04 |
| Soviet Union (0) | 0 | <0.01 |
| Swedish (103) | 512 | 0.70 |
| Swiss (14) | 368 | 0.50 |
| Turkish (0) | 0 | <0.01 |
| Ukrainian (160) | 482 | 0.66 |
| Welsh (500) | 1,628 | 2.23 |
| West Indian, ex. Hispanic (248) | 371 | 0.51 |
| Bahamian (0) | 0 | <0.01 |
| Barbadian (0) | 0 | <0.01 |
| Belizean (0) | 0 | <0.01 |
| Bermudan (0) | 0 | <0.01 |
| British West Indian (8) | 8 | 0.01 |
| Dutch West Indian (0) | 0 | <0.01 |
| Haitian (74) | 90 | 0.12 |
| Jamaican (148) | 212 | 0.29 |
| Trinidadian/Tobagonian (0) | 43 | 0.06 |
| U.S. Virgin Islander (0) | 0 | <0.01 |
| West Indian (18) | 18 | 0.02 |
| Other West Indian (0) | 0 | <0.01 |
| Yugoslavian (116) | 192 | 0.26 |

| Hispanic Origin | Population | % |
|---|---|---|
| Hispanic or Latino (of any race) | 1,316 | 1.79 |
| Central American, ex. Mexican | 90 | 0.12 |
| Costa Rican | 11 | 0.01 |
| Guatemalan | 44 | 0.06 |
| Honduran | 1 | <0.01 |
| Nicaraguan | 4 | 0.01 |
| Panamanian | 6 | 0.01 |
| Salvadoran | 24 | 0.03 |
| Other Central American | 0 | <0.01 |
| Cuban | 92 | 0.13 |
| Dominican Republic | 88 | 0.12 |
| Mexican | 279 | 0.38 |
| Puerto Rican | 469 | 0.64 |
| South American | 132 | 0.18 |
| Argentinean | 12 | 0.02 |
| Bolivian | 1 | <0.01 |
| Chilean | 16 | 0.02 |
| Colombian | 42 | 0.06 |
| Ecuadorian | 16 | 0.02 |
| Paraguayan | 1 | <0.01 |
| Peruvian | 30 | 0.04 |
| Uruguayan | 2 | <0.01 |
| Venezuelan | 11 | 0.01 |
| Other South American | 1 | <0.01 |
| Other Hispanic or Latino | 166 | 0.23 |

| Race* | Population | % |
|---|---|---|
| African-American/Black (1,350) | 1,763 | 2.40 |
| Not Hispanic (1,260) | 1,624 | 2.21 |
| Hispanic (90) | 139 | 0.19 |
| American Indian/Alaska Native (524) | 878 | 1.20 |
| Not Hispanic (473) | 800 | 1.09 |
| Hispanic (51) | 78 | 0.11 |
| Alaska Athabascan (Ala. Nat.) (1) | 1 | <0.01 |
| Aleut (Alaska Native) (0) | 0 | <0.01 |
| Apache (0) | 0 | <0.01 |
| Arapaho (0) | 0 | <0.01 |
| Blackfeet (4) | 5 | 0.01 |
| Canadian/French Am. Ind. (4) | 5 | 0.01 |
| Central American Ind. (1) | 1 | <0.01 |
| Cherokee (13) | 55 | 0.07 |
| Cheyenne (0) | 2 | <0.01 |
| Chickasaw (0) | 0 | <0.01 |
| Chippewa (8) | 11 | 0.01 |
| Choctaw (1) | 4 | 0.01 |
| Colville (2) | 3 | <0.01 |

| | Population | % |
|---|---|---|
| Comanche (0) | 0 | <0.01 |
| Cree (0) | 1 | <0.01 |
| Creek (0) | 0 | <0.01 |
| Crow (0) | 0 | <0.01 |
| Delaware (0) | 3 | <0.01 |
| Hopi (0) | 0 | <0.01 |
| Houma (1) | 1 | <0.01 |
| Inupiat (Alaska Native) (0) | 0 | <0.01 |
| Iroquois (298) | 414 | 0.56 |
| Kiowa (0) | 1 | <0.01 |
| Lumbee (0) | 0 | <0.01 |
| Menominee (0) | 0 | <0.01 |
| Mexican American Ind. (2) | 6 | 0.01 |
| Navajo (0) | 4 | 0.01 |
| Osage (0) | 2 | <0.01 |
| Ottawa (0) | 0 | <0.01 |
| Paiute (1) | 1 | <0.01 |
| Pima (0) | 0 | <0.01 |
| Potawatomi (0) | 1 | <0.01 |
| Pueblo (0) | 1 | <0.01 |
| Puget Sound Salish (0) | 0 | <0.01 |
| Seminole (0) | 0 | <0.01 |
| Shoshone (0) | 0 | <0.01 |
| Sioux (10) | 15 | 0.02 |
| South American Ind. (12) | 14 | 0.02 |
| Spanish American Ind. (4) | 4 | 0.01 |
| Tlingit-Haida (Alaska Native) (2) | 2 | <0.01 |
| Tohono O'Odham (0) | 0 | <0.01 |
| Tsimshian (Alaska Native) (0) | 0 | <0.01 |
| Ute (0) | 0 | <0.01 |
| Yakama (0) | 0 | <0.01 |
| Yaqui (0) | 0 | <0.01 |
| Yuman (0) | 1 | <0.01 |
| Yup'ik (Alaska Native) (3) | 3 | <0.01 |
| Asian (583) | 793 | 1.08 |
| Not Hispanic (576) | 779 | 1.06 |
| Hispanic (7) | 14 | 0.02 |
| Bangladeshi (6) | 6 | 0.01 |
| Bhutanese (7) | 7 | 0.01 |
| Burmese (5) | 5 | 0.01 |
| Cambodian (6) | 9 | 0.01 |
| Chinese, ex. Taiwanese (178) | 224 | 0.31 |
| Filipino (48) | 90 | 0.12 |
| Hmong (1) | 1 | <0.01 |
| Indian (105) | 138 | 0.19 |
| Indonesian (1) | 2 | <0.01 |
| Japanese (38) | 83 | 0.11 |
| Korean (72) | 95 | 0.13 |
| Laotian (7) | 7 | <0.01 |
| Malaysian (0) | 1 | <0.01 |
| Nepalese (6) | 6 | 0.01 |
| Pakistani (5) | 8 | 0.01 |
| Sri Lankan (12) | 12 | 0.02 |
| Taiwanese (7) | 9 | 0.01 |
| Thai (15) | 15 | 0.02 |
| Vietnamese (34) | 45 | 0.06 |
| Hawaii Native/Pacific Islander (17) | 43 | 0.06 |
| Not Hispanic (11) | 32 | 0.04 |
| Hispanic (6) | 11 | 0.01 |
| Fijian (0) | 0 | <0.01 |
| Guamanian/Chamorro (7) | 12 | 0.02 |
| Marshallese (0) | 0 | <0.01 |
| Native Hawaiian (9) | 23 | 0.03 |
| Samoan (0) | 2 | <0.01 |
| Tongan (0) | 1 | <0.01 |
| White (69,740) | 70,644 | 96.19 |
| Not Hispanic (68,916) | 69,724 | 94.94 |
| Hispanic (824) | 920 | 1.25 |

Notes: † The Census 2010 population figure is used to calculate the percentages in the Hispanic Origin and Race categories. Ancestry percentages are based on the 2006-2010 American Community Survey population (not shown); ‡ Numbers in parentheses indicate the number of people reporting a single ancestry; * Numbers in parentheses indicate the number of persons reporting this race alone, not in combination with any other race; Please refer to the Explanation of Data for more information.

## Monroe County

Population: 744,344

| Ancestry | Population | % |
|---|---|---|
| Afghan (593) | 593 | 0.08 |
| African, Sub-Saharan (9,510) | 10,853 | 1.46 |
| African (6,140) | 7,288 | 0.98 |
| Cape Verdean (0) | 0 | <0.01 |
| Ethiopian (734) | 734 | 0.10 |
| Ghanaian (49) | 49 | 0.01 |
| Kenyan (9) | 9 | <0.01 |
| Liberian (89) | 109 | 0.01 |
| Nigerian (503) | 603 | 0.08 |
| Senegalese (26) | 26 | <0.01 |
| Sierra Leonean (0) | 0 | <0.01 |
| Somalian (1,018) | 1,018 | 0.14 |
| South African (156) | 179 | 0.02 |
| Sudanese (181) | 205 | 0.03 |
| Ugandan (0) | 0 | <0.01 |
| Zimbabwean (76) | 76 | 0.01 |
| Other Sub-Saharan African (529) | 557 | 0.08 |
| Albanian (375) | 445 | 0.06 |
| Alsatian (3) | 34 | <0.01 |
| American (20,394) | 20,394 | 2.75 |
| Arab (2,460) | 3,916 | 0.53 |
| Arab (591) | 865 | 0.12 |
| Egyptian (314) | 339 | 0.05 |
| Iraqi (111) | 167 | 0.02 |
| Jordanian (0) | 0 | <0.01 |
| Lebanese (539) | 1,243 | 0.17 |
| Moroccan (171) | 221 | 0.03 |
| Palestinian (80) | 140 | 0.02 |
| Syrian (126) | 231 | 0.03 |
| Other Arab (528) | 710 | 0.10 |
| Armenian (338) | 695 | 0.09 |
| Assyrian/Chaldean/Syriac (0) | 0 | <0.01 |
| Australian (161) | 304 | 0.04 |
| Austrian (484) | 2,334 | 0.31 |
| Basque (13) | 13 | <0.01 |
| Belgian (346) | 1,318 | 0.18 |
| Brazilian (223) | 312 | 0.04 |
| British (1,603) | 3,430 | 0.46 |
| Bulgarian (95) | 224 | 0.03 |
| Cajun (0) | 0 | <0.01 |
| Canadian (1,638) | 3,828 | 0.52 |
| Carpatho Rusyn (0) | 16 | <0.01 |
| Celtic (69) | 119 | 0.02 |
| Croatian (67) | 308 | 0.04 |
| Cypriot (0) | 0 | <0.01 |
| Czech (445) | 2,461 | 0.33 |
| Czechoslovakian (230) | 589 | 0.08 |
| Danish (406) | 1,719 | 0.23 |
| Dutch (3,397) | 19,639 | 2.65 |
| Eastern European (1,085) | 1,267 | 0.17 |
| English (25,417) | 94,030 | 12.68 |
| Estonian (26) | 186 | 0.03 |
| European (5,777) | 6,513 | 0.88 |
| Finnish (177) | 774 | 0.10 |
| French, ex. Basque (2,904) | 23,189 | 3.13 |
| French Canadian (2,803) | 8,059 | 1.09 |
| German (37,495) | 156,984 | 21.18 |
| German Russian (7) | 35 | <0.01 |
| Greek (2,336) | 4,548 | 0.61 |
| Guyanese (586) | 694 | 0.09 |
| Hungarian (1,031) | 3,581 | 0.48 |
| Icelander (75) | 75 | 0.01 |
| Iranian (234) | 257 | 0.03 |
| Irish (28,758) | 123,123 | 16.61 |
| Israeli (254) | 436 | 0.06 |
| Italian (71,014) | 140,596 | 18.97 |
| Latvian (208) | 456 | 0.06 |
| Lithuanian (1,049) | 2,950 | 0.40 |
| Luxemburger (43) | 101 | 0.01 |
| Macedonian (564) | 754 | 0.10 |
| Maltese (37) | 123 | 0.02 |
| New Zealander (0) | 0 | <0.01 |
| Northern European (328) | 433 | 0.06 |
| Norwegian (662) | 2,890 | 0.39 |
| Pennsylvania German (218) | 469 | 0.06 |
| Polish (11,957) | 40,211 | 5.42 |
| Portuguese (453) | 1,455 | 0.20 |
| Romanian (555) | 1,117 | 0.15 |
| Russian (3,981) | 8,944 | 1.21 |
| Scandinavian (166) | 486 | 0.07 |
| Scotch-Irish (3,160) | 9,722 | 1.31 |
| Scottish (3,214) | 15,779 | 2.13 |
| Serbian (52) | 164 | 0.02 |
| Slavic (236) | 599 | 0.08 |
| Slovak (329) | 893 | 0.12 |
| Slovene (86) | 226 | 0.03 |
| Soviet Union (0) | 0 | <0.01 |
| Swedish (1,498) | 6,462 | 0.87 |
| Swiss (294) | 2,029 | 0.27 |
| Turkish (2,064) | 2,586 | 0.35 |
| Ukrainian (5,827) | 10,628 | 1.43 |
| Welsh (841) | 5,288 | 0.71 |
| West Indian, ex. Hispanic (5,376) | 8,191 | 1.10 |
| Bahamian (58) | 218 | 0.03 |
| Barbadian (318) | 379 | 0.05 |
| Belizean (185) | 275 | 0.04 |
| Bermudan (0) | 0 | <0.01 |
| British West Indian (99) | 223 | 0.03 |
| Dutch West Indian (0) | 13 | <0.01 |
| Haitian (917) | 1,040 | 0.14 |
| Jamaican (2,942) | 4,448 | 0.60 |
| Trinidadian/Tobagonian (268) | 413 | 0.06 |
| U.S. Virgin Islander (0) | 0 | <0.01 |
| West Indian (589) | 1,182 | 0.16 |
| Other West Indian (0) | 0 | <0.01 |
| Yugoslavian (551) | 813 | 0.11 |

| Hispanic Origin | Population | % |
|---|---|---|
| Hispanic or Latino (of any race) | 54,005 | 7.26 |
| Central American, ex. Mexican | 1,513 | 0.20 |
| Costa Rican | 156 | 0.02 |
| Guatemalan | 353 | 0.05 |
| Honduran | 242 | 0.03 |
| Nicaraguan | 192 | 0.03 |
| Panamanian | 241 | 0.03 |
| Salvadoran | 320 | 0.04 |
| Other Central American | 9 | <0.01 |
| Cuban | 2,913 | 0.39 |
| Dominican Republic | 2,160 | 0.29 |
| Mexican | 3,364 | 0.45 |
| Puerto Rican | 38,907 | 5.23 |
| South American | 2,258 | 0.30 |
| Argentinean | 225 | 0.03 |
| Bolivian | 62 | 0.01 |
| Chilean | 321 | 0.04 |
| Colombian | 753 | 0.10 |
| Ecuadorian | 267 | 0.04 |
| Paraguayan | 55 | 0.01 |
| Peruvian | 358 | 0.05 |
| Uruguayan | 29 | <0.01 |
| Venezuelan | 153 | 0.02 |
| Other South American | 35 | <0.01 |
| Other Hispanic or Latino | 2,890 | 0.39 |

| Race* | Population | % |
|---|---|---|
| African-American/Black (113,171) | 124,305 | 16.70 |
| Not Hispanic (107,448) | 115,820 | 15.56 |
| Hispanic (5,723) | 8,485 | 1.14 |
| American Indian/Alaska Native (2,136) | 6,360 | 0.85 |
| Not Hispanic (1,589) | 4,952 | 0.67 |
| Hispanic (547) | 1,408 | 0.19 |
| Alaska Athabascan (Ala. Nat.) (2) | 7 | <0.01 |
| Aleut (Alaska Native) (1) | 2 | <0.01 |
| Apache (11) | 34 | <0.01 |
| Arapaho (0) | 4 | <0.01 |
| Blackfeet (21) | 184 | 0.02 |
| Canadian/French Am. Ind. (27) | 52 | 0.01 |
| Central American Ind. (23) | 41 | 0.01 |
| Cherokee (88) | 754 | 0.10 |
| Cheyenne (3) | 4 | <0.01 |
| Chickasaw (4) | 12 | <0.01 |
| Chippewa (46) | 70 | 0.01 |
| Choctaw (8) | 57 | 0.01 |
| Colville (0) | 2 | <0.01 |
| Comanche (0) | 3 | <0.01 |
| Cree (6) | 15 | <0.01 |
| Creek (7) | 28 | <0.01 |
| Crow (1) | 5 | <0.01 |
| Delaware (8) | 28 | <0.01 |
| Hopi (1) | 1 | <0.01 |
| Houma (2) | 2 | <0.01 |
| Inupiat (Alaska Native) (4) | 7 | <0.01 |
| Iroquois (686) | 1,325 | 0.18 |
| Kiowa (0) | 0 | <0.01 |
| Lumbee (1) | 5 | <0.01 |
| Menominee (0) | 0 | <0.01 |
| Mexican American Ind. (53) | 95 | 0.01 |
| Navajo (20) | 49 | 0.01 |
| Osage (1) | 5 | <0.01 |
| Ottawa (1) | 1 | <0.01 |
| Paiute (1) | 2 | <0.01 |
| Pima (0) | 3 | <0.01 |
| Potawatomi (11) | 17 | <0.01 |
| Pueblo (1) | 6 | <0.01 |
| Puget Sound Salish (1) | 1 | <0.01 |
| Seminole (3) | 63 | 0.01 |
| Shoshone (0) | 3 | <0.01 |
| Sioux (26) | 72 | 0.01 |
| South American Ind. (70) | 235 | 0.03 |
| Spanish American Ind. (18) | 22 | <0.01 |
| Tlingit-Haida (Alaska Native) (4) | 12 | <0.01 |
| Tohono O'Odham (1) | 1 | <0.01 |
| Tsimshian (Alaska Native) (0) | 0 | <0.01 |
| Ute (1) | 6 | <0.01 |
| Yakama (0) | 0 | <0.01 |
| Yaqui (0) | 0 | <0.01 |
| Yuman (3) | 3 | <0.01 |
| Yup'ik (Alaska Native) (0) | 0 | <0.01 |
| Asian (24,281) | 28,675 | 3.85 |
| Not Hispanic (24,023) | 28,047 | 3.77 |
| Hispanic (258) | 628 | 0.08 |
| Bangladeshi (79) | 98 | 0.01 |
| Bhutanese (369) | 411 | 0.06 |
| Burmese (559) | 599 | 0.08 |
| Cambodian (485) | 580 | 0.08 |
| Chinese, ex. Taiwanese (5,587) | 6,499 | 0.87 |
| Filipino (954) | 1,567 | 0.21 |
| Hmong (2) | 3 | <0.01 |
| Indian (6,146) | 6,938 | 0.93 |
| Indonesian (45) | 106 | 0.01 |
| Japanese (586) | 1,157 | 0.16 |
| Korean (2,387) | 2,997 | 0.40 |
| Laotian (1,301) | 1,551 | 0.21 |
| Malaysian (98) | 108 | 0.01 |
| Nepalese (196) | 246 | 0.03 |
| Pakistani (845) | 951 | 0.13 |
| Sri Lankan (149) | 173 | 0.02 |
| Taiwanese (340) | 438 | 0.06 |
| Thai (196) | 296 | 0.04 |
| Vietnamese (2,824) | 3,205 | 0.43 |
| Hawaii Native/Pacific Islander (227) | 874 | 0.12 |
| Not Hispanic (182) | 622 | 0.08 |
| Hispanic (45) | 252 | 0.03 |
| Fijian (9) | 9 | <0.01 |
| Guamanian/Chamorro (45) | 77 | 0.01 |
| Marshallese (0) | 1 | <0.01 |
| Native Hawaiian (62) | 208 | 0.03 |
| Samoan (44) | 88 | 0.01 |
| Tongan (5) | 6 | <0.01 |
| White (566,535) | 582,035 | 78.19 |
| Not Hispanic (542,034) | 553,986 | 74.43 |
| Hispanic (24,501) | 28,049 | 3.77 |

Notes: † The Census 2010 population figure is used to calculate the percentages in the Hispanic Origin and Race categories. Ancestry percentages are based on the 2006-2010 American Community Survey population (not shown); ‡ Numbers in parentheses indicate the number of people reporting a single ancestry; * Numbers in parentheses indicate the number of persons reporting this race alone, not in combination with any other race; Please refer to the Explanation of Data for more information.

## Montgomery County

Population: 50,219

| Ancestry | Population | % |
|---|---|---|
| Afghan (0) | 0 | <0.01 |
| African, Sub-Saharan (64) | 64 | 0.13 |
| African (49) | 49 | 0.10 |
| Cape Verdean (0) | 0 | <0.01 |
| Ethiopian (0) | 0 | <0.01 |
| Ghanaian (0) | 0 | <0.01 |
| Kenyan (0) | 0 | <0.01 |
| Liberian (0) | 0 | <0.01 |
| Nigerian (4) | 4 | 0.01 |
| Senegalese (0) | 0 | <0.01 |
| Sierra Leonean (0) | 0 | <0.01 |
| Somalian (0) | 0 | <0.01 |
| South African (11) | 11 | 0.02 |
| Sudanese (0) | 0 | <0.01 |
| Ugandan (0) | 0 | <0.01 |
| Zimbabwean (0) | 0 | <0.01 |
| Other Sub-Saharan African (0) | 0 | <0.01 |
| Albanian (11) | 25 | 0.05 |
| Alsatian (0) | 0 | <0.01 |
| American (4,301) | 4,301 | 8.61 |
| Arab (22) | 105 | 0.21 |
| Arab (0) | 18 | 0.04 |
| Egyptian (0) | 0 | <0.01 |
| Iraqi (0) | 0 | <0.01 |
| Jordanian (0) | 0 | <0.01 |
| Lebanese (22) | 67 | 0.13 |
| Moroccan (0) | 0 | <0.01 |
| Palestinian (0) | 9 | 0.02 |
| Syrian (0) | 11 | 0.02 |
| Other Arab (0) | 0 | <0.01 |
| Armenian (0) | 66 | 0.13 |
| Assyrian/Chaldean/Syriac (0) | 0 | <0.01 |
| Australian (0) | 11 | 0.02 |
| Austrian (55) | 127 | 0.25 |
| Basque (0) | 0 | <0.01 |
| Belgian (0) | 21 | 0.04 |
| Brazilian (5) | 5 | 0.01 |
| British (65) | 85 | 0.17 |
| Bulgarian (0) | 0 | <0.01 |
| Cajun (0) | 0 | <0.01 |
| Canadian (60) | 136 | 0.27 |
| Carpatho Rusyn (0) | 0 | <0.01 |
| Celtic (0) | 0 | <0.01 |
| Croatian (2) | 12 | 0.02 |
| Cypriot (0) | 0 | <0.01 |
| Czech (54) | 168 | 0.34 |
| Czechoslovakian (0) | 15 | 0.03 |
| Danish (32) | 199 | 0.40 |
| Dutch (296) | 2,858 | 5.72 |
| Eastern European (98) | 98 | 0.20 |
| English (2,674) | 6,458 | 12.93 |
| Estonian (0) | 0 | <0.01 |
| European (188) | 207 | 0.41 |
| Finnish (0) | 13 | 0.03 |
| French, ex. Basque (218) | 2,400 | 4.81 |
| French Canadian (155) | 753 | 1.51 |
| German (2,515) | 8,912 | 17.84 |
| German Russian (0) | 0 | <0.01 |
| Greek (41) | 218 | 0.44 |
| Guyanese (0) | 0 | <0.01 |
| Hungarian (30) | 95 | 0.19 |
| Icelander (0) | 0 | <0.01 |
| Iranian (0) | 0 | <0.01 |
| Irish (1,526) | 8,038 | 16.09 |
| Israeli (0) | 0 | <0.01 |
| Italian (4,249) | 9,234 | 18.49 |
| Latvian (18) | 32 | 0.06 |
| Lithuanian (336) | 636 | 1.27 |
| Luxemburger (0) | 0 | <0.01 |
| Macedonian (0) | 0 | <0.01 |
| Maltese (0) | 0 | <0.01 |
| New Zealander (0) | 0 | <0.01 |
| Northern European (13) | 13 | 0.03 |
| Norwegian (25) | 86 | 0.17 |
| Pennsylvania German (283) | 293 | 0.59 |

| Ancestry | Population | % |
|---|---|---|
| Polish (2,668) | 5,283 | 10.58 |
| Portuguese (8) | 40 | 0.08 |
| Romanian (8) | 22 | 0.04 |
| Russian (25) | 172 | 0.34 |
| Scandinavian (12) | 12 | 0.02 |
| Scotch-Irish (173) | 422 | 0.84 |
| Scottish (192) | 772 | 1.55 |
| Serbian (0) | 2 | <0.01 |
| Slavic (0) | 4 | 0.01 |
| Slovak (58) | 129 | 0.26 |
| Slovene (4) | 11 | 0.02 |
| Soviet Union (0) | 0 | <0.01 |
| Swedish (28) | 252 | 0.50 |
| Swiss (17) | 86 | 0.17 |
| Turkish (0) | 0 | <0.01 |
| Ukrainian (103) | 376 | 0.75 |
| Welsh (16) | 108 | 0.22 |
| West Indian, ex. Hispanic (65) | 149 | 0.30 |
| Bahamian (0) | 0 | <0.01 |
| Barbadian (0) | 0 | <0.01 |
| Belizean (0) | 0 | <0.01 |
| Bermudan (0) | 0 | <0.01 |
| British West Indian (0) | 0 | <0.01 |
| Dutch West Indian (0) | 0 | <0.01 |
| Haitian (5) | 5 | 0.01 |
| Jamaican (56) | 140 | 0.28 |
| Trinidadian/Tobagonian (4) | 4 | 0.01 |
| U.S. Virgin Islander (0) | 0 | <0.01 |
| West Indian (0) | 0 | <0.01 |
| Other West Indian (0) | 0 | <0.01 |
| Yugoslavian (10) | 10 | 0.02 |

| Hispanic Origin | Population | % |
|---|---|---|
| Hispanic or Latino (of any race) | 5,654 | 11.26 |
| Central American, ex. Mexican | 245 | 0.49 |
| Costa Rican | 131 | 0.26 |
| Guatemalan | 47 | 0.09 |
| Honduran | 11 | 0.02 |
| Nicaraguan | 11 | 0.02 |
| Panamanian | 10 | 0.02 |
| Salvadoran | 35 | 0.07 |
| Other Central American | 0 | <0.01 |
| Cuban | 90 | 0.18 |
| Dominican Republic | 259 | 0.52 |
| Mexican | 218 | 0.43 |
| Puerto Rican | 4,330 | 8.62 |
| South American | 160 | 0.32 |
| Argentinean | 6 | 0.01 |
| Bolivian | 1 | <0.01 |
| Chilean | 12 | 0.02 |
| Colombian | 41 | 0.08 |
| Ecuadorian | 76 | 0.15 |
| Paraguayan | 0 | <0.01 |
| Peruvian | 19 | 0.04 |
| Uruguayan | 0 | <0.01 |
| Venezuelan | 3 | 0.01 |
| Other South American | 1 | <0.01 |
| Other Hispanic or Latino | 352 | 0.70 |

| Race* | Population | % |
|---|---|---|
| African-American/Black (951) | 1,447 | 2.88 |
| Not Hispanic (712) | 1,067 | 2.12 |
| Hispanic (239) | 380 | 0.76 |
| American Indian/Alaska Native (169) | 408 | 0.81 |
| Not Hispanic (103) | 298 | 0.59 |
| Hispanic (66) | 110 | 0.22 |
| Alaska Athabascan (Ala. Nat.) (0) | 0 | <0.01 |
| Aleut (Alaska Native) (0) | 0 | <0.01 |
| Apache (0) | 3 | 0.01 |
| Arapaho (0) | 0 | <0.01 |
| Blackfeet (0) | 13 | 0.03 |
| Canadian/French Am. Ind. (0) | 1 | <0.01 |
| Central American Ind. (2) | 4 | 0.01 |
| Cherokee (7) | 37 | 0.07 |
| Cheyenne (1) | 1 | <0.01 |
| Chickasaw (0) | 0 | <0.01 |
| Chippewa (1) | 1 | <0.01 |
| Choctaw (2) | 4 | 0.01 |
| Colville (0) | 0 | <0.01 |

| Race* | Population | % |
|---|---|---|
| Comanche (0) | 0 | <0.01 |
| Cree (1) | 3 | 0.01 |
| Creek (0) | 0 | <0.01 |
| Crow (0) | 0 | <0.01 |
| Delaware (4) | 8 | 0.02 |
| Hopi (0) | 0 | <0.01 |
| Houma (0) | 0 | <0.01 |
| Inupiat (Alaska Native) (0) | 0 | <0.01 |
| Iroquois (22) | 89 | 0.18 |
| Kiowa (0) | 0 | <0.01 |
| Lumbee (1) | 3 | 0.01 |
| Menominee (0) | 0 | <0.01 |
| Mexican American Ind. (3) | 6 | 0.01 |
| Navajo (0) | 2 | <0.01 |
| Osage (0) | 1 | <0.01 |
| Ottawa (0) | 1 | <0.01 |
| Paiute (0) | 0 | <0.01 |
| Pima (0) | 0 | <0.01 |
| Potawatomi (0) | 0 | <0.01 |
| Pueblo (0) | 0 | <0.01 |
| Puget Sound Salish (0) | 0 | <0.01 |
| Seminole (0) | 1 | <0.01 |
| Shoshone (0) | 0 | <0.01 |
| Sioux (2) | 7 | 0.01 |
| South American Ind. (12) | 20 | 0.04 |
| Spanish American Ind. (2) | 5 | 0.01 |
| Tlingit-Haida (Alaska Native) (2) | 3 | 0.01 |
| Tohono O'Odham (0) | 0 | <0.01 |
| Tsimshian (Alaska Native) (0) | 0 | <0.01 |
| Ute (0) | 0 | <0.01 |
| Yakama (0) | 0 | <0.01 |
| Yaqui (0) | 0 | <0.01 |
| Yuman (0) | 0 | <0.01 |
| Yup'ik (Alaska Native) (0) | 0 | <0.01 |
| Asian (369) | 468 | 0.93 |
| Not Hispanic (356) | 435 | 0.87 |
| Hispanic (13) | 33 | 0.07 |
| Bangladeshi (0) | 0 | <0.01 |
| Bhutanese (0) | 0 | <0.01 |
| Burmese (0) | 0 | <0.01 |
| Cambodian (0) | 0 | <0.01 |
| Chinese, ex. Taiwanese (65) | 84 | 0.17 |
| Filipino (42) | 58 | 0.12 |
| Hmong (0) | 0 | <0.01 |
| Indian (136) | 149 | 0.30 |
| Indonesian (4) | 4 | 0.01 |
| Japanese (12) | 30 | 0.06 |
| Korean (45) | 61 | 0.12 |
| Laotian (0) | 0 | <0.01 |
| Malaysian (0) | 0 | <0.01 |
| Nepalese (1) | 2 | <0.01 |
| Pakistani (16) | 21 | 0.04 |
| Sri Lankan (0) | 0 | <0.01 |
| Taiwanese (1) | 1 | <0.01 |
| Thai (7) | 15 | 0.03 |
| Vietnamese (4) | 13 | 0.03 |
| Hawaii Native/Pacific Islander (19) | 56 | 0.11 |
| Not Hispanic (11) | 23 | 0.05 |
| Hispanic (8) | 33 | 0.07 |
| Fijian (0) | 0 | <0.01 |
| Guamanian/Chamorro (9) | 12 | 0.02 |
| Marshallese (0) | 0 | <0.01 |
| Native Hawaiian (4) | 9 | 0.02 |
| Samoan (3) | 3 | 0.01 |
| Tongan (2) | 2 | <0.01 |
| White (45,519) | 46,382 | 92.36 |
| Not Hispanic (42,732) | 43,292 | 86.21 |
| Hispanic (2,787) | 3,090 | 6.15 |

*Notes: † The Census 2010 population figure is used to calculate the percentages in the Hispanic Origin and Race categories. Ancestry percentages are based on the 2006-2010 American Community Survey population (not shown); ‡ Numbers in parentheses indicate the number of people reporting a single ancestry; * Numbers in parentheses indicate the number of persons reporting this race alone, not in combination with any other race; Please refer to the Explanation of Data for more information.*

## Nassau County
Population: 1,339,532

| Ancestry | Population | % |
|---|---|---|
| Afghan (938) | 1,420 | 0.11 |
| African, Sub-Saharan (5,338) | 7,241 | 0.54 |
| African (3,221) | 4,618 | 0.35 |
| Cape Verdean (12) | 12 | <0.01 |
| Ethiopian (87) | 155 | 0.01 |
| Ghanaian (356) | 423 | 0.03 |
| Kenyan (0) | 0 | <0.01 |
| Liberian (0) | 3 | <0.01 |
| Nigerian (1,144) | 1,356 | 0.10 |
| Senegalese (0) | 0 | <0.01 |
| Sierra Leonean (24) | 24 | <0.01 |
| Somalian (15) | 15 | <0.01 |
| South African (190) | 225 | 0.02 |
| Sudanese (33) | 50 | <0.01 |
| Ugandan (0) | 0 | <0.01 |
| Zimbabwean (0) | 0 | <0.01 |
| Other Sub-Saharan African (256) | 360 | 0.03 |
| Albanian (1,157) | 1,726 | 0.13 |
| Alsatian (9) | 46 | <0.01 |
| American (42,503) | 42,503 | 3.20 |
| Arab (4,560) | 7,635 | 0.57 |
| Arab (502) | 692 | 0.05 |
| Egyptian (1,361) | 1,995 | 0.15 |
| Iraqi (528) | 793 | 0.06 |
| Jordanian (66) | 66 | <0.01 |
| Lebanese (426) | 995 | 0.07 |
| Moroccan (244) | 618 | 0.05 |
| Palestinian (154) | 232 | 0.02 |
| Syrian (165) | 754 | 0.06 |
| Other Arab (1,114) | 1,490 | 0.11 |
| Armenian (2,406) | 3,535 | 0.27 |
| Assyrian/Chaldean/Syriac (7) | 40 | <0.01 |
| Australian (154) | 388 | 0.03 |
| Austrian (3,200) | 11,903 | 0.90 |
| Basque (2) | 167 | 0.01 |
| Belgian (311) | 821 | 0.06 |
| Brazilian (1,025) | 1,516 | 0.11 |
| British (1,099) | 2,526 | 0.19 |
| Bulgarian (230) | 299 | 0.02 |
| Cajun (0) | 59 | <0.01 |
| Canadian (632) | 1,951 | 0.15 |
| Carpatho Rusyn (4) | 36 | <0.01 |
| Celtic (84) | 143 | 0.01 |
| Croatian (1,742) | 2,842 | 0.21 |
| Cypriot (306) | 381 | 0.03 |
| Czech (1,112) | 4,825 | 0.36 |
| Czechoslovakian (735) | 2,195 | 0.17 |
| Danish (453) | 2,201 | 0.17 |
| Dutch (815) | 5,539 | 0.42 |
| Eastern European (13,083) | 13,843 | 1.04 |
| English (6,821) | 42,066 | 3.17 |
| Estonian (213) | 360 | 0.03 |
| European (10,190) | 11,073 | 0.83 |
| Finnish (197) | 1,079 | 0.08 |
| French, ex. Basque (1,972) | 15,598 | 1.17 |
| French Canadian (907) | 3,222 | 0.24 |
| German (29,737) | 143,597 | 10.80 |
| German Russian (0) | 43 | <0.01 |
| Greek (13,704) | 21,516 | 1.62 |
| Guyanese (3,463) | 4,442 | 0.33 |
| Hungarian (4,774) | 13,637 | 1.03 |
| Icelander (50) | 144 | 0.01 |
| Iranian (10,076) | 11,333 | 0.85 |
| Irish (73,529) | 224,843 | 16.92 |
| Israeli (4,093) | 5,327 | 0.40 |
| Italian (170,115) | 305,805 | 23.01 |
| Latvian (463) | 965 | 0.07 |
| Lithuanian (1,501) | 4,623 | 0.35 |
| Luxemburger (0) | 16 | <0.01 |
| Macedonian (41) | 51 | <0.01 |
| Maltese (496) | 1,367 | 0.10 |
| New Zealander (0) | 0 | <0.01 |
| Northern European (619) | 717 | 0.05 |
| Norwegian (1,502) | 6,174 | 0.46 |
| Pennsylvania German (121) | 182 | 0.01 |

| Ancestry | Population | % |
|---|---|---|
| Polish (24,310) | 72,081 | 5.42 |
| Portuguese (5,557) | 7,340 | 0.55 |
| Romanian (2,430) | 5,933 | 0.45 |
| Russian (26,109) | 59,061 | 4.44 |
| Scandinavian (274) | 647 | 0.05 |
| Scotch-Irish (3,219) | 8,938 | 0.67 |
| Scottish (1,993) | 8,512 | 0.64 |
| Serbian (144) | 294 | 0.02 |
| Slavic (100) | 549 | 0.04 |
| Slovak (491) | 1,528 | 0.11 |
| Slovene (98) | 277 | 0.02 |
| Soviet Union (0) | 10 | <0.01 |
| Swedish (1,026) | 7,946 | 0.60 |
| Swiss (395) | 2,316 | 0.17 |
| Turkish (1,731) | 2,980 | 0.22 |
| Ukrainian (2,820) | 5,868 | 0.44 |
| Welsh (224) | 1,755 | 0.13 |
| West Indian, ex. Hispanic (43,896) | 52,648 | 3.96 |
| Bahamian (5) | 51 | <0.01 |
| Barbadian (1,197) | 1,489 | 0.11 |
| Belizean (145) | 228 | 0.02 |
| Bermudan (52) | 65 | <0.01 |
| British West Indian (813) | 1,182 | 0.09 |
| Dutch West Indian (217) | 285 | 0.02 |
| Haitian (18,556) | 20,810 | 1.57 |
| Jamaican (16,745) | 19,674 | 1.48 |
| Trinidadian/Tobagonian (2,369) | 3,518 | 0.26 |
| U.S. Virgin Islander (15) | 45 | <0.01 |
| West Indian (3,765) | 5,269 | 0.40 |
| Other West Indian (17) | 32 | <0.01 |
| Yugoslavian (357) | 1,166 | 0.09 |

| Hispanic Origin | Population | % |
|---|---|---|
| Hispanic or Latino (of any race) | 195,355 | 14.58 |
| Central American, ex. Mexican | 69,816 | 5.21 |
| Costa Rican | 992 | 0.07 |
| Guatemalan | 7,853 | 0.59 |
| Honduran | 11,051 | 0.82 |
| Nicaraguan | 925 | 0.07 |
| Panamanian | 1,360 | 0.10 |
| Salvadoran | 47,180 | 3.52 |
| Other Central American | 455 | 0.03 |
| Cuban | 5,430 | 0.41 |
| Dominican Republic | 20,216 | 1.51 |
| Mexican | 10,535 | 0.79 |
| Puerto Rican | 29,965 | 2.24 |
| South American | 38,719 | 2.89 |
| Argentinean | 2,533 | 0.19 |
| Bolivian | 696 | 0.05 |
| Chilean | 2,945 | 0.22 |
| Colombian | 13,257 | 0.99 |
| Ecuadorian | 9,239 | 0.69 |
| Paraguayan | 406 | 0.03 |
| Peruvian | 7,853 | 0.59 |
| Uruguayan | 628 | 0.05 |
| Venezuelan | 825 | 0.06 |
| Other South American | 337 | 0.03 |
| Other Hispanic or Latino | 20,674 | 1.54 |

| Race* | Population | % |
|---|---|---|
| African-American/Black (149,049) | 159,230 | 11.89 |
| Not Hispanic (141,305) | 148,211 | 11.06 |
| Hispanic (7,744) | 11,019 | 0.82 |
| American Indian/Alaska Native (3,185) | 8,027 | 0.60 |
| Not Hispanic (1,379) | 4,240 | 0.32 |
| Hispanic (1,806) | 3,787 | 0.28 |
| Alaska Athabascan (Ala. Nat.) (0) | 1 | <0.01 |
| Aleut (Alaska Native) (2) | 3 | <0.01 |
| Apache (8) | 26 | <0.01 |
| Arapaho (0) | 0 | <0.01 |
| Blackfeet (17) | 151 | 0.01 |
| Canadian/French Am. Ind. (10) | 18 | <0.01 |
| Central American Ind. (73) | 138 | 0.01 |
| Cherokee (83) | 783 | 0.06 |
| Cheyenne (5) | 7 | <0.01 |
| Chickasaw (7) | 7 | <0.01 |
| Chippewa (14) | 28 | <0.01 |
| Choctaw (15) | 49 | <0.01 |
| Colville (1) | 1 | <0.01 |

| Race* | Population | % |
|---|---|---|
| Comanche (7) | 11 | <0.01 |
| Cree (0) | 5 | <0.01 |
| Creek (7) | 37 | <0.01 |
| Crow (0) | 3 | <0.01 |
| Delaware (9) | 24 | <0.01 |
| Hopi (1) | 5 | <0.01 |
| Houma (0) | 0 | <0.01 |
| Inupiat (Alaska Native) (2) | 5 | <0.01 |
| Iroquois (102) | 240 | 0.02 |
| Kiowa (1) | 1 | <0.01 |
| Lumbee (9) | 23 | <0.01 |
| Menominee (0) | 0 | <0.01 |
| Mexican American Ind. (157) | 239 | 0.02 |
| Navajo (4) | 16 | <0.01 |
| Osage (0) | 3 | <0.01 |
| Ottawa (1) | 1 | <0.01 |
| Paiute (0) | 0 | <0.01 |
| Pima (0) | 0 | <0.01 |
| Potawatomi (2) | 4 | <0.01 |
| Pueblo (13) | 18 | <0.01 |
| Puget Sound Salish (0) | 0 | <0.01 |
| Seminole (2) | 29 | <0.01 |
| Shoshone (2) | 5 | <0.01 |
| Sioux (22) | 57 | <0.01 |
| South American Ind. (210) | 450 | 0.03 |
| Spanish American Ind. (178) | 217 | 0.02 |
| Tlingit-Haida (Alaska Native) (3) | 6 | <0.01 |
| Tohono O'Odham (7) | 7 | <0.01 |
| Tsimshian (Alaska Native) (0) | 0 | <0.01 |
| Ute (2) | 2 | <0.01 |
| Yakama (0) | 0 | <0.01 |
| Yaqui (1) | 1 | <0.01 |
| Yuman (0) | 0 | <0.01 |
| Yup'ik (Alaska Native) (0) | 0 | <0.01 |
| Asian (102,266) | 113,831 | 8.50 |
| Not Hispanic (101,558) | 111,861 | 8.35 |
| Hispanic (708) | 1,970 | 0.15 |
| Bangladeshi (1,269) | 1,408 | 0.11 |
| Bhutanese (1) | 1 | <0.01 |
| Burmese (147) | 179 | 0.01 |
| Cambodian (89) | 120 | 0.01 |
| Chinese, ex. Taiwanese (23,026) | 25,716 | 1.92 |
| Filipino (9,881) | 11,622 | 0.87 |
| Hmong (0) | 2 | <0.01 |
| Indian (39,572) | 43,171 | 3.22 |
| Indonesian (93) | 157 | 0.01 |
| Japanese (1,967) | 2,587 | 0.19 |
| Korean (13,558) | 14,338 | 1.07 |
| Laotian (30) | 42 | <0.01 |
| Malaysian (60) | 97 | 0.01 |
| Nepalese (106) | 111 | 0.01 |
| Pakistani (6,737) | 7,382 | 0.55 |
| Sri Lankan (281) | 330 | 0.02 |
| Taiwanese (1,448) | 1,673 | 0.12 |
| Thai (436) | 555 | 0.04 |
| Vietnamese (809) | 1,071 | 0.08 |
| Hawaii Native/Pacific Islander (336) | 1,557 | 0.12 |
| Not Hispanic (197) | 1,015 | 0.08 |
| Hispanic (139) | 542 | 0.04 |
| Fijian (10) | 13 | <0.01 |
| Guamanian/Chamorro (128) | 164 | 0.01 |
| Marshallese (2) | 2 | <0.01 |
| Native Hawaiian (48) | 193 | 0.01 |
| Samoan (27) | 71 | 0.01 |
| Tongan (2) | 2 | <0.01 |
| White (977,577) | 1,000,818 | 74.71 |
| Not Hispanic (877,309) | 889,240 | 66.38 |
| Hispanic (100,268) | 111,578 | 8.33 |

Notes: † The Census 2010 population figure is used to calculate the percentages in the Hispanic Origin and Race categories. Ancestry percentages are based on the 2006-2010 American Community Survey population (not shown); ‡ Numbers in parentheses indicate the number of people reporting a single ancestry; * Numbers in parentheses indicate the number of persons reporting this race alone, not in combination with any other race; Please refer to the Explanation of Data for more information.

## New York County

Population: 1,585,873

| Ancestry | Population | % |
|---|---|---|
| Afghan (59) | 85 | 0.01 |
| African, Sub-Saharan (19,667) | 24,146 | 1.52 |
| African (10,054) | 12,839 | 0.81 |
| Cape Verdean (81) | 206 | 0.01 |
| Ethiopian (932) | 1,043 | 0.07 |
| Ghanaian (714) | 818 | 0.05 |
| Kenyan (43) | 69 | <0.01 |
| Liberian (169) | 176 | 0.01 |
| Nigerian (1,650) | 1,953 | 0.12 |
| Senegalese (1,118) | 1,216 | 0.08 |
| Sierra Leonean (422) | 422 | 0.03 |
| Somalian (125) | 125 | 0.01 |
| South African (991) | 1,372 | 0.09 |
| Sudanese (137) | 137 | 0.01 |
| Ugandan (95) | 125 | 0.01 |
| Zimbabwean (80) | 100 | 0.01 |
| Other Sub-Saharan African (3,056) | 3,545 | 0.22 |
| Albanian (1,385) | 1,618 | 0.10 |
| Alsatian (5) | 129 | 0.01 |
| American (54,694) | 54,694 | 3.45 |
| Arab (8,584) | 13,828 | 0.87 |
| Arab (1,250) | 1,720 | 0.11 |
| Egyptian (1,374) | 1,906 | 0.12 |
| Iraqi (275) | 583 | 0.04 |
| Jordanian (0) | 48 | <0.01 |
| Lebanese (1,838) | 3,331 | 0.21 |
| Moroccan (914) | 1,592 | 0.10 |
| Palestinian (626) | 794 | 0.05 |
| Syrian (518) | 1,112 | 0.07 |
| Other Arab (1,789) | 2,742 | 0.17 |
| Armenian (1,520) | 2,653 | 0.17 |
| Assyrian/Chaldean/Syriac (94) | 137 | 0.01 |
| Australian (1,965) | 2,719 | 0.17 |
| Austrian (4,202) | 14,656 | 0.93 |
| Basque (191) | 428 | 0.03 |
| Belgian (928) | 2,470 | 0.16 |
| Brazilian (2,870) | 4,541 | 0.29 |
| British (6,950) | 12,129 | 0.77 |
| Bulgarian (927) | 1,272 | 0.08 |
| Cajun (22) | 224 | 0.01 |
| Canadian (3,037) | 5,646 | 0.36 |
| Carpatho Rusyn (89) | 112 | 0.01 |
| Celtic (129) | 304 | 0.02 |
| Croatian (1,299) | 2,164 | 0.14 |
| Cypriot (139) | 216 | 0.01 |
| Czech (1,439) | 4,820 | 0.30 |
| Czechoslovakian (619) | 1,256 | 0.08 |
| Danish (1,444) | 4,095 | 0.26 |
| Dutch (2,847) | 10,414 | 0.66 |
| Eastern European (23,269) | 25,277 | 1.60 |
| English (22,270) | 77,799 | 4.91 |
| Estonian (190) | 424 | 0.03 |
| European (25,127) | 27,846 | 1.76 |
| Finnish (666) | 1,658 | 0.10 |
| French, ex. Basque (10,278) | 31,783 | 2.01 |
| French Canadian (1,692) | 5,246 | 0.33 |
| German (27,493) | 107,666 | 6.80 |
| German Russian (0) | 41 | <0.01 |
| Greek (7,557) | 13,078 | 0.83 |
| Guyanese (1,802) | 2,259 | 0.14 |
| Hungarian (4,686) | 14,667 | 0.93 |
| Icelander (246) | 382 | 0.02 |
| Iranian (3,458) | 4,256 | 0.27 |
| Irish (40,008) | 117,355 | 7.41 |
| Israeli (4,839) | 6,624 | 0.42 |
| Italian (44,498) | 98,563 | 6.22 |
| Latvian (713) | 1,822 | 0.12 |
| Lithuanian (1,597) | 5,775 | 0.36 |
| Luxemburger (23) | 68 | <0.01 |
| Macedonian (973) | 1,086 | 0.07 |
| Maltese (548) | 840 | 0.05 |
| New Zealander (243) | 405 | 0.03 |
| Northern European (1,296) | 1,485 | 0.09 |
| Norwegian (1,552) | 7,445 | 0.47 |
| Pennsylvania German (123) | 327 | 0.02 |

| | Population | % |
|---|---|---|
| Polish (20,565) | 64,078 | 4.05 |
| Portuguese (1,436) | 3,862 | 0.24 |
| Romanian (3,035) | 7,692 | 0.49 |
| Russian (36,296) | 82,983 | 5.24 |
| Scandinavian (753) | 1,731 | 0.11 |
| Scotch-Irish (4,283) | 13,158 | 0.83 |
| Scottish (4,846) | 19,553 | 1.23 |
| Serbian (1,160) | 1,526 | 0.10 |
| Slavic (177) | 400 | 0.03 |
| Slovak (812) | 2,298 | 0.15 |
| Slovene (271) | 695 | 0.04 |
| Soviet Union (28) | 54 | <0.01 |
| Swedish (3,045) | 10,408 | 0.66 |
| Swiss (1,381) | 4,962 | 0.31 |
| Turkish (2,708) | 3,703 | 0.23 |
| Ukrainian (4,361) | 8,849 | 0.56 |
| Welsh (944) | 6,000 | 0.38 |
| West Indian, ex. Hispanic (22,411) | 30,009 | 1.90 |
| Bahamian (303) | 457 | 0.03 |
| Barbadian (738) | 907 | 0.06 |
| Belizean (654) | 735 | 0.05 |
| Bermudan (86) | 127 | 0.01 |
| British West Indian (1,308) | 1,658 | 0.10 |
| Dutch West Indian (212) | 276 | 0.02 |
| Haitian (5,308) | 6,500 | 0.41 |
| Jamaican (7,099) | 9,242 | 0.58 |
| Trinidadian/Tobagonian (3,010) | 3,877 | 0.24 |
| U.S. Virgin Islander (343) | 487 | 0.03 |
| West Indian (3,296) | 5,618 | 0.35 |
| Other West Indian (54) | 125 | 0.01 |
| Yugoslavian (1,478) | 1,876 | 0.12 |

| Hispanic Origin | Population | % |
|---|---|---|
| Hispanic or Latino (of any race) | 403,577 | 25.45 |
| Central American, ex. Mexican | 13,948 | 0.88 |
| Costa Rican | 987 | 0.06 |
| Guatemalan | 2,051 | 0.13 |
| Honduran | 4,058 | 0.26 |
| Nicaraguan | 1,556 | 0.10 |
| Panamanian | 1,716 | 0.11 |
| Salvadoran | 3,419 | 0.22 |
| Other Central American | 161 | 0.01 |
| Cuban | 11,623 | 0.73 |
| Dominican Republic | 155,971 | 9.84 |
| Mexican | 41,965 | 2.65 |
| Puerto Rican | 107,774 | 6.80 |
| South American | 36,748 | 2.32 |
| Argentinean | 4,339 | 0.27 |
| Bolivian | 522 | 0.03 |
| Chilean | 1,824 | 0.12 |
| Colombian | 8,411 | 0.53 |
| Ecuadorian | 14,132 | 0.89 |
| Paraguayan | 268 | 0.02 |
| Peruvian | 3,852 | 0.24 |
| Uruguayan | 549 | 0.03 |
| Venezuelan | 2,573 | 0.16 |
| Other South American | 278 | 0.02 |
| Other Hispanic or Latino | 35,548 | 2.24 |

| Race* | Population | % |
|---|---|---|
| African-American/Black (246,687) | 272,993 | 17.21 |
| Not Hispanic (205,340) | 217,102 | 13.69 |
| Hispanic (41,347) | 55,891 | 3.52 |
| American Indian/Alaska Native (8,669) | 19,415 | 1.22 |
| Not Hispanic (2,144) | 7,395 | 0.47 |
| Hispanic (6,525) | 12,020 | 0.76 |
| Alaska Athabascan (Ala. Nat.) (11) | 18 | <0.01 |
| Aleut (Alaska Native) (4) | 7 | <0.01 |
| Apache (28) | 92 | 0.01 |
| Arapaho (3) | 5 | <0.01 |
| Blackfeet (41) | 356 | 0.02 |
| Canadian/French Am. Ind. (29) | 62 | <0.01 |
| Central American Ind. (610) | 1,090 | 0.07 |
| Cherokee (288) | 1,845 | 0.12 |
| Cheyenne (4) | 9 | <0.01 |
| Chickasaw (15) | 43 | <0.01 |
| Chippewa (36) | 99 | 0.01 |
| Choctaw (41) | 179 | 0.01 |
| Colville (4) | 5 | <0.01 |

| | Population | % |
|---|---|---|
| Comanche (13) | 22 | <0.01 |
| Cree (4) | 22 | <0.01 |
| Creek (12) | 61 | <0.01 |
| Crow (4) | 11 | <0.01 |
| Delaware (14) | 54 | <0.01 |
| Hopi (8) | 15 | <0.01 |
| Houma (0) | 3 | <0.01 |
| Inupiat (Alaska Native) (2) | 8 | <0.01 |
| Iroquois (97) | 265 | 0.02 |
| Kiowa (9) | 11 | <0.01 |
| Lumbee (10) | 21 | <0.01 |
| Menominee (2) | 3 | <0.01 |
| Mexican American Ind. (479) | 752 | 0.05 |
| Navajo (38) | 83 | 0.01 |
| Osage (7) | 12 | <0.01 |
| Ottawa (0) | 3 | <0.01 |
| Paiute (2) | 8 | <0.01 |
| Pima (2) | 4 | <0.01 |
| Potawatomi (10) | 20 | <0.01 |
| Pueblo (70) | 175 | 0.01 |
| Puget Sound Salish (2) | 5 | <0.01 |
| Seminole (6) | 110 | 0.01 |
| Shoshone (3) | 6 | <0.01 |
| Sioux (38) | 133 | 0.01 |
| South American Ind. (813) | 1,935 | 0.12 |
| Spanish American Ind. (373) | 514 | 0.03 |
| Tlingit-Haida (Alaska Native) (2) | 15 | <0.01 |
| Tohono O'Odham (11) | 15 | <0.01 |
| Tsimshian (Alaska Native) (3) | 3 | <0.01 |
| Ute (1) | 2 | <0.01 |
| Yakama (1) | 2 | <0.01 |
| Yaqui (8) | 22 | <0.01 |
| Yuman (6) | 6 | <0.01 |
| Yup'ik (Alaska Native) (0) | 2 | <0.01 |
| Asian (179,552) | 199,722 | 12.59 |
| Not Hispanic (177,624) | 194,929 | 12.29 |
| Hispanic (1,928) | 4,793 | 0.30 |
| Bangladeshi (1,672) | 2,029 | 0.13 |
| Bhutanese (26) | 26 | <0.01 |
| Burmese (240) | 317 | 0.02 |
| Cambodian (168) | 220 | 0.01 |
| Chinese, ex. Taiwanese (92,088) | 99,287 | 6.26 |
| Filipino (10,399) | 13,388 | 0.84 |
| Hmong (16) | 20 | <0.01 |
| Indian (25,857) | 29,979 | 1.89 |
| Indonesian (470) | 693 | 0.04 |
| Japanese (13,201) | 16,600 | 1.05 |
| Korean (19,683) | 21,996 | 1.39 |
| Laotian (109) | 157 | 0.01 |
| Malaysian (524) | 766 | 0.05 |
| Nepalese (240) | 281 | 0.02 |
| Pakistani (2,482) | 2,940 | 0.19 |
| Sri Lankan (450) | 563 | 0.04 |
| Taiwanese (2,789) | 3,318 | 0.21 |
| Thai (1,282) | 1,657 | 0.10 |
| Vietnamese (2,194) | 2,919 | 0.18 |
| Hawaii Native/Pacific Islander (873) | 3,727 | 0.24 |
| Not Hispanic (533) | 1,776 | 0.11 |
| Hispanic (340) | 1,951 | 0.12 |
| Fijian (29) | 73 | <0.01 |
| Guamanian/Chamorro (132) | 242 | 0.02 |
| Marshallese (3) | 4 | <0.01 |
| Native Hawaiian (185) | 608 | 0.04 |
| Samoan (87) | 183 | 0.01 |
| Tongan (18) | 33 | <0.01 |
| White (911,073) | 956,864 | 60.34 |
| Not Hispanic (761,493) | 785,299 | 49.52 |
| Hispanic (149,580) | 171,565 | 10.82 |

*Notes: † The Census 2010 population figure is used to calculate the percentages in the Hispanic Origin and Race categories. Ancestry percentages are based on the 2006-2010 American Community Survey population (not shown); ‡ Numbers in parentheses indicate the number of people reporting a single ancestry; * Numbers in parentheses indicate the number of persons reporting this race alone, not in combination with any other race; Please refer to the Explanation of Data for more information.*

## Niagara County
Population: 216,469

| Ancestry | Population | % |
|---|---|---|
| Afghan (0) | 0 | <0.01 |
| African, Sub-Saharan (371) | 625 | 0.29 |
| African (339) | 577 | 0.27 |
| Cape Verdean (0) | 0 | <0.01 |
| Ethiopian (24) | 32 | 0.01 |
| Ghanaian (0) | 0 | <0.01 |
| Kenyan (0) | 8 | <0.01 |
| Liberian (0) | 0 | <0.01 |
| Nigerian (0) | 0 | <0.01 |
| Senegalese (0) | 0 | <0.01 |
| Sierra Leonean (0) | 0 | <0.01 |
| Somalian (0) | 0 | <0.01 |
| South African (8) | 8 | <0.01 |
| Sudanese (0) | 0 | <0.01 |
| Ugandan (0) | 0 | <0.01 |
| Zimbabwean (0) | 0 | <0.01 |
| Other Sub-Saharan African (0) | 0 | <0.01 |
| Albanian (0) | 0 | <0.01 |
| Alsatian (0) | 14 | 0.01 |
| American (7,216) | 7,216 | 3.34 |
| Arab (916) | 1,832 | 0.85 |
| Arab (144) | 175 | 0.08 |
| Egyptian (24) | 61 | 0.03 |
| Iraqi (0) | 13 | 0.01 |
| Jordanian (282) | 282 | 0.13 |
| Lebanese (388) | 1,098 | 0.51 |
| Moroccan (0) | 0 | <0.01 |
| Palestinian (28) | 28 | 0.01 |
| Syrian (9) | 83 | 0.04 |
| Other Arab (41) | 92 | 0.04 |
| Armenian (164) | 269 | 0.12 |
| Assyrian/Chaldean/Syriac (0) | 0 | <0.01 |
| Australian (31) | 60 | 0.03 |
| Austrian (255) | 1,001 | 0.46 |
| Basque (0) | 0 | <0.01 |
| Belgian (38) | 97 | 0.04 |
| Brazilian (18) | 18 | 0.01 |
| British (270) | 512 | 0.24 |
| Bulgarian (0) | 10 | <0.01 |
| Cajun (0) | 0 | <0.01 |
| Canadian (707) | 1,755 | 0.81 |
| Carpatho Rusyn (14) | 14 | 0.01 |
| Celtic (0) | 27 | 0.01 |
| Croatian (196) | 353 | 0.16 |
| Cypriot (0) | 0 | <0.01 |
| Czech (63) | 422 | 0.20 |
| Czechoslovakian (86) | 245 | 0.11 |
| Danish (77) | 408 | 0.19 |
| Dutch (548) | 3,738 | 1.73 |
| Eastern European (60) | 60 | 0.03 |
| English (9,005) | 29,036 | 13.44 |
| Estonian (8) | 8 | <0.01 |
| European (960) | 978 | 0.45 |
| Finnish (0) | 44 | 0.02 |
| French, ex. Basque (1,222) | 9,233 | 4.27 |
| French Canadian (898) | 2,590 | 1.20 |
| German (18,960) | 62,469 | 28.91 |
| German Russian (16) | 16 | 0.01 |
| Greek (348) | 969 | 0.45 |
| Guyanese (43) | 43 | 0.02 |
| Hungarian (708) | 2,506 | 1.16 |
| Icelander (10) | 68 | 0.03 |
| Iranian (15) | 24 | 0.01 |
| Irish (9,618) | 39,511 | 18.29 |
| Israeli (12) | 12 | 0.01 |
| Italian (19,116) | 41,083 | 19.01 |
| Latvian (12) | 28 | 0.01 |
| Lithuanian (191) | 455 | 0.21 |
| Luxemburger (0) | 0 | <0.01 |
| Macedonian (0) | 0 | <0.01 |
| Maltese (0) | 0 | <0.01 |
| New Zealander (0) | 0 | <0.01 |
| Northern European (50) | 50 | 0.02 |
| Norwegian (257) | 1,008 | 0.47 |
| Pennsylvania German (178) | 315 | 0.15 |

| Ancestry | Population | % |
|---|---|---|
| Polish (10,633) | 26,701 | 12.36 |
| Portuguese (135) | 258 | 0.12 |
| Romanian (15) | 107 | 0.05 |
| Russian (777) | 1,533 | 0.71 |
| Scandinavian (86) | 178 | 0.08 |
| Scotch-Irish (964) | 2,795 | 1.29 |
| Scottish (1,335) | 4,977 | 2.30 |
| Serbian (0) | 27 | 0.01 |
| Slavic (129) | 382 | 0.18 |
| Slovak (142) | 461 | 0.21 |
| Slovene (28) | 65 | 0.03 |
| Soviet Union (0) | 0 | <0.01 |
| Swedish (250) | 1,940 | 0.90 |
| Swiss (67) | 236 | 0.11 |
| Turkish (10) | 41 | 0.02 |
| Ukrainian (438) | 1,138 | 0.53 |
| Welsh (301) | 1,779 | 0.82 |
| West Indian, ex. Hispanic (431) | 666 | 0.31 |
| Bahamian (0) | 0 | <0.01 |
| Barbadian (0) | 0 | <0.01 |
| Belizean (29) | 29 | 0.01 |
| Bermudan (0) | 0 | <0.01 |
| British West Indian (9) | 9 | <0.01 |
| Dutch West Indian (0) | 0 | <0.01 |
| Haitian (9) | 9 | <0.01 |
| Jamaican (346) | 409 | 0.19 |
| Trinidadian/Tobagonian (15) | 15 | 0.01 |
| U.S. Virgin Islander (0) | 0 | <0.01 |
| West Indian (23) | 195 | 0.09 |
| Other West Indian (0) | 0 | <0.01 |
| Yugoslavian (28) | 123 | 0.06 |

| Hispanic Origin | Population | % |
|---|---|---|
| Hispanic or Latino (of any race) | 4,694 | 2.17 |
| Central American, ex. Mexican | 165 | 0.08 |
| Costa Rican | 19 | 0.01 |
| Guatemalan | 50 | 0.02 |
| Honduran | 25 | 0.01 |
| Nicaraguan | 4 | <0.01 |
| Panamanian | 47 | 0.02 |
| Salvadoran | 19 | 0.01 |
| Other Central American | 1 | <0.01 |
| Cuban | 164 | 0.08 |
| Dominican Republic | 118 | 0.05 |
| Mexican | 1,107 | 0.51 |
| Puerto Rican | 2,263 | 1.05 |
| South American | 230 | 0.11 |
| Argentinean | 22 | 0.01 |
| Bolivian | 1 | <0.01 |
| Chilean | 11 | 0.01 |
| Colombian | 104 | 0.05 |
| Ecuadorian | 33 | 0.02 |
| Paraguayan | 6 | <0.01 |
| Peruvian | 31 | 0.01 |
| Uruguayan | 0 | <0.01 |
| Venezuelan | 18 | 0.01 |
| Other South American | 4 | <0.01 |
| Other Hispanic or Latino | 647 | 0.30 |

| Race* | Population | % |
|---|---|---|
| African-American/Black (14,851) | 17,632 | 8.15 |
| Not Hispanic (14,511) | 17,058 | 7.88 |
| Hispanic (340) | 574 | 0.27 |
| American Indian/Alaska Native (2,285) | 3,859 | 1.78 |
| Not Hispanic (2,135) | 3,589 | 1.66 |
| Hispanic (150) | 270 | 0.12 |
| Alaska Athabascan (Ala. Nat.) (0) | 1 | <0.01 |
| Aleut (Alaska Native) (0) | 0 | <0.01 |
| Apache (2) | 5 | <0.01 |
| Arapaho (0) | 0 | <0.01 |
| Blackfeet (6) | 49 | 0.02 |
| Canadian/French Am. Ind. (39) | 53 | 0.02 |
| Central American Ind. (9) | 13 | 0.01 |
| Cherokee (34) | 165 | 0.08 |
| Cheyenne (1) | 3 | <0.01 |
| Chickasaw (1) | 1 | <0.01 |
| Chippewa (39) | 64 | 0.03 |
| Choctaw (1) | 13 | 0.01 |
| Colville (0) | 0 | <0.01 |

| | Population | % |
|---|---|---|
| Comanche (1) | 1 | <0.01 |
| Cree (2) | 5 | <0.01 |
| Creek (0) | 6 | <0.01 |
| Crow (2) | 2 | <0.01 |
| Delaware (5) | 7 | <0.01 |
| Hopi (0) | 0 | <0.01 |
| Houma (0) | 0 | <0.01 |
| Inupiat (Alaska Native) (1) | 2 | <0.01 |
| Iroquois (1,163) | 1,751 | 0.81 |
| Kiowa (1) | 1 | <0.01 |
| Lumbee (4) | 8 | <0.01 |
| Menominee (0) | 2 | <0.01 |
| Mexican American Ind. (20) | 21 | 0.01 |
| Navajo (9) | 9 | <0.01 |
| Osage (3) | 4 | <0.01 |
| Ottawa (1) | 2 | <0.01 |
| Paiute (0) | 0 | <0.01 |
| Pima (0) | 0 | <0.01 |
| Potawatomi (0) | 0 | <0.01 |
| Pueblo (0) | 0 | <0.01 |
| Puget Sound Salish (0) | 0 | <0.01 |
| Seminole (0) | 11 | 0.01 |
| Shoshone (0) | 0 | <0.01 |
| Sioux (13) | 36 | 0.02 |
| South American Ind. (10) | 18 | 0.01 |
| Spanish American Ind. (5) | 5 | <0.01 |
| Tlingit-Haida (Alaska Native) (0) | 1 | <0.01 |
| Tohono O'Odham (0) | 0 | <0.01 |
| Tsimshian (Alaska Native) (0) | 0 | <0.01 |
| Ute (1) | 1 | <0.01 |
| Yakama (0) | 1 | <0.01 |
| Yaqui (2) | 2 | <0.01 |
| Yuman (0) | 0 | <0.01 |
| Yup'ik (Alaska Native) (0) | 0 | <0.01 |
| Asian (1,823) | 2,407 | 1.11 |
| Not Hispanic (1,807) | 2,354 | 1.09 |
| Hispanic (16) | 53 | 0.02 |
| Bangladeshi (2) | 2 | <0.01 |
| Bhutanese (0) | 0 | <0.01 |
| Burmese (13) | 13 | 0.01 |
| Cambodian (3) | 8 | <0.01 |
| Chinese, ex. Taiwanese (347) | 425 | 0.20 |
| Filipino (133) | 262 | 0.12 |
| Hmong (4) | 10 | <0.01 |
| Indian (671) | 789 | 0.36 |
| Indonesian (14) | 18 | 0.01 |
| Japanese (66) | 135 | 0.06 |
| Korean (210) | 295 | 0.14 |
| Laotian (18) | 25 | 0.01 |
| Malaysian (2) | 2 | <0.01 |
| Nepalese (0) | 0 | <0.01 |
| Pakistani (113) | 127 | 0.06 |
| Sri Lankan (6) | 16 | 0.01 |
| Taiwanese (19) | 20 | 0.01 |
| Thai (21) | 38 | 0.02 |
| Vietnamese (107) | 135 | 0.06 |
| Hawaii Native/Pacific Islander (62) | 158 | 0.07 |
| Not Hispanic (55) | 141 | 0.07 |
| Hispanic (7) | 17 | 0.01 |
| Fijian (1) | 2 | <0.01 |
| Guamanian/Chamorro (8) | 12 | 0.01 |
| Marshallese (1) | 1 | <0.01 |
| Native Hawaiian (14) | 39 | 0.02 |
| Samoan (5) | 17 | 0.01 |
| Tongan (4) | 4 | <0.01 |
| White (191,673) | 195,911 | 90.50 |
| Not Hispanic (188,907) | 192,737 | 89.04 |
| Hispanic (2,766) | 3,174 | 1.47 |

*Notes: † The Census 2010 population figure is used to calculate the percentages in the Hispanic Origin and Race categories. Ancestry percentages are based on the 2006-2010 American Community Survey population (not shown); ‡ Numbers in parentheses indicate the number of people reporting a single ancestry; * Numbers in parentheses indicate the number of persons reporting this race alone, not in combination with any other race; Please refer to the Explanation of Data for more information.*

## Oneida County

Population: 234,878

| Ancestry | Population | % |
|---|---|---|
| Afghan (42) | 42 | 0.02 |
| African, Sub-Saharan (699) | 998 | 0.43 |
| African (446) | 671 | 0.29 |
| Cape Verdean (0) | 0 | <0.01 |
| Ethiopian (20) | 79 | 0.03 |
| Ghanaian (14) | 14 | 0.01 |
| Kenyan (12) | 27 | 0.01 |
| Liberian (88) | 88 | 0.04 |
| Nigerian (2) | 2 | <0.01 |
| Senegalese (0) | 0 | <0.01 |
| Sierra Leonean (0) | 0 | <0.01 |
| Somalian (99) | 99 | 0.04 |
| South African (0) | 0 | <0.01 |
| Sudanese (0) | 0 | <0.01 |
| Ugandan (0) | 0 | <0.01 |
| Zimbabwean (0) | 0 | <0.01 |
| Other Sub-Saharan African (18) | 18 | 0.01 |
| Albanian (22) | 55 | 0.02 |
| Alsatian (0) | 29 | 0.01 |
| American (9,419) | 9,419 | 4.02 |
| Arab (2,006) | 4,287 | 1.83 |
| Arab (181) | 267 | 0.11 |
| Egyptian (149) | 189 | 0.08 |
| Iraqi (0) | 6 | <0.01 |
| Jordanian (28) | 28 | 0.01 |
| Lebanese (1,246) | 2,742 | 1.17 |
| Moroccan (41) | 50 | 0.02 |
| Palestinian (10) | 10 | <0.01 |
| Syrian (155) | 742 | 0.32 |
| Other Arab (196) | 253 | 0.11 |
| Armenian (130) | 196 | 0.08 |
| Assyrian/Chaldean/Syriac (0) | 0 | <0.01 |
| Australian (32) | 92 | 0.04 |
| Austrian (69) | 587 | 0.25 |
| Basque (0) | 0 | <0.01 |
| Belgian (8) | 75 | 0.03 |
| Brazilian (33) | 86 | 0.04 |
| British (394) | 620 | 0.26 |
| Bulgarian (0) | 5 | <0.01 |
| Cajun (0) | 0 | <0.01 |
| Canadian (288) | 644 | 0.27 |
| Carpatho Rusyn (8) | 15 | 0.01 |
| Celtic (8) | 16 | 0.01 |
| Croatian (24) | 106 | 0.05 |
| Cypriot (0) | 0 | <0.01 |
| Czech (45) | 576 | 0.25 |
| Czechoslovakian (91) | 233 | 0.10 |
| Danish (99) | 560 | 0.24 |
| Dutch (908) | 6,105 | 2.60 |
| Eastern European (180) | 200 | 0.09 |
| English (6,403) | 26,141 | 11.15 |
| Estonian (0) | 9 | <0.01 |
| European (1,134) | 1,173 | 0.50 |
| Finnish (30) | 198 | 0.08 |
| French, ex. Basque (1,786) | 13,375 | 5.70 |
| French Canadian (1,392) | 3,834 | 1.63 |
| German (9,284) | 44,884 | 19.14 |
| German Russian (0) | 0 | <0.01 |
| Greek (145) | 490 | 0.21 |
| Guyanese (54) | 68 | 0.03 |
| Hungarian (203) | 964 | 0.41 |
| Icelander (0) | 14 | 0.01 |
| Iranian (35) | 35 | 0.01 |
| Irish (11,623) | 45,802 | 19.53 |
| Israeli (0) | 0 | <0.01 |
| Italian (24,027) | 47,602 | 20.30 |
| Latvian (11) | 14 | 0.01 |
| Lithuanian (145) | 683 | 0.29 |
| Luxemburger (0) | 0 | <0.01 |
| Macedonian (21) | 21 | 0.01 |
| Maltese (0) | 0 | <0.01 |
| New Zealander (4) | 4 | <0.01 |
| Northern European (195) | 198 | 0.08 |
| Norwegian (169) | 709 | 0.30 |
| Pennsylvania German (63) | 159 | 0.07 |

| Ancestry | Population | % |
|---|---|---|
| Polish (10,228) | 26,014 | 11.09 |
| Portuguese (110) | 488 | 0.21 |
| Romanian (148) | 239 | 0.10 |
| Russian (1,169) | 2,226 | 0.95 |
| Scandinavian (32) | 161 | 0.07 |
| Scotch-Irish (737) | 2,747 | 1.17 |
| Scottish (732) | 3,742 | 1.60 |
| Serbian (0) | 82 | 0.03 |
| Slavic (13) | 30 | 0.01 |
| Slovak (135) | 249 | 0.11 |
| Slovene (9) | 11 | <0.01 |
| Soviet Union (0) | 0 | <0.01 |
| Swedish (266) | 1,098 | 0.47 |
| Swiss (294) | 1,595 | 0.68 |
| Turkish (0) | 7 | <0.01 |
| Ukrainian (1,187) | 2,419 | 1.03 |
| Welsh (1,540) | 7,279 | 3.10 |
| West Indian, ex. Hispanic (1,119) | 1,537 | 0.66 |
| Bahamian (0) | 0 | <0.01 |
| Barbadian (30) | 34 | 0.01 |
| Belizean (0) | 10 | <0.01 |
| Bermudan (0) | 0 | <0.01 |
| British West Indian (68) | 96 | 0.04 |
| Dutch West Indian (0) | 0 | <0.01 |
| Haitian (241) | 376 | 0.16 |
| Jamaican (504) | 675 | 0.29 |
| Trinidadian/Tobagonian (139) | 169 | 0.07 |
| U.S. Virgin Islander (9) | 9 | <0.01 |
| West Indian (128) | 168 | 0.07 |
| Other West Indian (0) | 0 | <0.01 |
| Yugoslavian (3,270) | 3,482 | 1.48 |

| Hispanic Origin | Population | % |
|---|---|---|
| Hispanic or Latino (of any race) | 10,819 | 4.61 |
| Central American, ex. Mexican | 551 | 0.23 |
| Costa Rican | 19 | 0.01 |
| Guatemalan | 88 | 0.04 |
| Honduran | 88 | 0.04 |
| Nicaraguan | 38 | 0.02 |
| Panamanian | 87 | 0.04 |
| Salvadoran | 221 | 0.09 |
| Other Central American | 10 | <0.01 |
| Cuban | 187 | 0.08 |
| Dominican Republic | 1,211 | 0.52 |
| Mexican | 872 | 0.37 |
| Puerto Rican | 6,538 | 2.78 |
| South American | 448 | 0.19 |
| Argentinean | 25 | 0.01 |
| Bolivian | 12 | 0.01 |
| Chilean | 20 | 0.01 |
| Colombian | 109 | 0.05 |
| Ecuadorian | 154 | 0.07 |
| Paraguayan | 3 | <0.01 |
| Peruvian | 66 | 0.03 |
| Uruguayan | 4 | <0.01 |
| Venezuelan | 49 | 0.02 |
| Other South American | 6 | <0.01 |
| Other Hispanic or Latino | 1,012 | 0.43 |

| Race* | Population | % |
|---|---|---|
| African-American/Black (14,688) | 17,445 | 7.43 |
| Not Hispanic (13,682) | 15,969 | 6.80 |
| Hispanic (1,006) | 1,476 | 0.63 |
| American Indian/Alaska Native (605) | 1,692 | 0.72 |
| Not Hispanic (499) | 1,393 | 0.59 |
| Hispanic (106) | 299 | 0.13 |
| Alaska Athabascan (Ala. Nat.) (0) | 0 | <0.01 |
| Aleut (Alaska Native) (3) | 3 | <0.01 |
| Apache (9) | 20 | 0.01 |
| Arapaho (2) | 2 | <0.01 |
| Blackfeet (3) | 41 | 0.02 |
| Canadian/French Am. Ind. (3) | 17 | 0.01 |
| Central American Ind. (9) | 13 | 0.01 |
| Cherokee (24) | 158 | 0.07 |
| Cheyenne (1) | 10 | <0.01 |
| Chickasaw (1) | 5 | <0.01 |
| Chippewa (12) | 25 | 0.01 |
| Choctaw (0) | 7 | <0.01 |
| Colville (0) | 0 | <0.01 |

| Race* | Population | % |
|---|---|---|
| Comanche (0) | 0 | <0.01 |
| Cree (2) | 8 | <0.01 |
| Creek (0) | 3 | <0.01 |
| Crow (0) | 3 | <0.01 |
| Delaware (2) | 4 | <0.01 |
| Hopi (0) | 1 | <0.01 |
| Houma (0) | 0 | <0.01 |
| Inupiat (Alaska Native) (1) | 2 | <0.01 |
| Iroquois (190) | 419 | 0.18 |
| Kiowa (1) | 3 | <0.01 |
| Lumbee (4) | 4 | <0.01 |
| Menominee (0) | 0 | <0.01 |
| Mexican American Ind. (6) | 12 | 0.01 |
| Navajo (4) | 12 | 0.01 |
| Osage (0) | 0 | <0.01 |
| Ottawa (1) | 1 | <0.01 |
| Paiute (1) | 1 | <0.01 |
| Pima (0) | 1 | <0.01 |
| Potawatomi (5) | 5 | <0.01 |
| Pueblo (3) | 5 | <0.01 |
| Puget Sound Salish (0) | 0 | <0.01 |
| Seminole (0) | 4 | <0.01 |
| Shoshone (0) | 1 | <0.01 |
| Sioux (22) | 60 | 0.03 |
| South American Ind. (8) | 28 | 0.01 |
| Spanish American Ind. (0) | 1 | <0.01 |
| Tlingit-Haida (Alaska Native) (1) | 4 | <0.01 |
| Tohono O'Odham (1) | 1 | <0.01 |
| Tsimshian (Alaska Native) (0) | 0 | <0.01 |
| Ute (0) | 0 | <0.01 |
| Yakama (0) | 0 | <0.01 |
| Yaqui (0) | 5 | <0.01 |
| Yuman (0) | 0 | <0.01 |
| Yup'ik (Alaska Native) (0) | 0 | <0.01 |
| Asian (6,565) | 7,434 | 3.17 |
| Not Hispanic (6,522) | 7,310 | 3.11 |
| Hispanic (43) | 124 | 0.05 |
| Bangladeshi (18) | 18 | 0.01 |
| Bhutanese (30) | 36 | 0.02 |
| Burmese (2,270) | 2,394 | 1.02 |
| Cambodian (435) | 513 | 0.22 |
| Chinese, ex. Taiwanese (537) | 672 | 0.29 |
| Filipino (219) | 379 | 0.16 |
| Hmong (2) | 2 | <0.01 |
| Indian (806) | 975 | 0.42 |
| Indonesian (7) | 7 | <0.01 |
| Japanese (106) | 181 | 0.08 |
| Korean (311) | 386 | 0.16 |
| Laotian (77) | 117 | 0.05 |
| Malaysian (6) | 20 | 0.01 |
| Nepalese (11) | 17 | 0.01 |
| Pakistani (137) | 152 | 0.06 |
| Sri Lankan (18) | 23 | 0.01 |
| Taiwanese (19) | 26 | 0.01 |
| Thai (104) | 149 | 0.06 |
| Vietnamese (1,032) | 1,147 | 0.49 |
| Hawaii Native/Pacific Islander (69) | 258 | 0.11 |
| Not Hispanic (49) | 194 | 0.08 |
| Hispanic (20) | 64 | 0.03 |
| Fijian (0) | 0 | <0.01 |
| Guamanian/Chamorro (12) | 30 | 0.01 |
| Marshallese (0) | 0 | <0.01 |
| Native Hawaiian (30) | 69 | 0.03 |
| Samoan (12) | 26 | 0.01 |
| Tongan (2) | 4 | <0.01 |
| White (204,679) | 208,959 | 88.96 |
| Not Hispanic (199,254) | 202,734 | 86.31 |
| Hispanic (5,425) | 6,225 | 2.65 |

Notes: † The Census 2010 population figure is used to calculate the percentages in the Hispanic Origin and Race categories. Ancestry percentages are based on the 2006-2010 American Community Survey population (not shown); ‡ Numbers in parentheses indicate the number of people reporting a single ancestry; * Numbers in parentheses indicate the number of persons reporting this race alone, not in combination with any other race; Please refer to the Explanation of Data for more information.

## Onondaga County

Population: 467,026

| Ancestry | Population | % |
|---|---|---|
| Afghan (19) | 19 | <0.01 |
| African, Sub-Saharan (2,607) | 3,016 | 0.65 |
| African (1,156) | 1,474 | 0.32 |
| Cape Verdean (0) | 23 | <0.01 |
| Ethiopian (12) | 12 | <0.01 |
| Ghanaian (187) | 187 | 0.04 |
| Kenyan (0) | 17 | <0.01 |
| Liberian (246) | 246 | 0.05 |
| Nigerian (246) | 280 | 0.06 |
| Senegalese (0) | 0 | <0.01 |
| Sierra Leonean (13) | 13 | <0.01 |
| Somalian (478) | 478 | 0.10 |
| South African (10) | 10 | <0.01 |
| Sudanese (160) | 177 | 0.04 |
| Ugandan (26) | 26 | 0.01 |
| Zimbabwean (0) | 0 | <0.01 |
| Other Sub-Saharan African (73) | 73 | 0.02 |
| Albanian (472) | 537 | 0.12 |
| Alsatian (39) | 39 | <0.01 |
| American (14,013) | 14,013 | 3.02 |
| Arab (1,701) | 3,500 | 0.75 |
| Arab (580) | 951 | 0.21 |
| Egyptian (164) | 228 | 0.05 |
| Iraqi (0) | 0 | <0.01 |
| Jordanian (28) | 28 | 0.01 |
| Lebanese (430) | 1,493 | 0.32 |
| Moroccan (60) | 86 | 0.02 |
| Palestinian (154) | 184 | 0.04 |
| Syrian (126) | 343 | 0.07 |
| Other Arab (159) | 187 | 0.04 |
| Armenian (254) | 861 | 0.19 |
| Assyrian/Chaldean/Syriac (19) | 29 | 0.01 |
| Australian (42) | 96 | 0.02 |
| Austrian (469) | 2,236 | 0.48 |
| Basque (0) | 0 | <0.01 |
| Belgian (130) | 347 | 0.07 |
| Brazilian (103) | 120 | 0.03 |
| British (664) | 1,397 | 0.30 |
| Bulgarian (34) | 56 | 0.01 |
| Cajun (24) | 34 | 0.01 |
| Canadian (872) | 1,837 | 0.40 |
| Carpatho Rusyn (0) | 0 | <0.01 |
| Celtic (18) | 91 | 0.02 |
| Croatian (60) | 239 | 0.05 |
| Cypriot (0) | 0 | <0.01 |
| Czech (311) | 1,294 | 0.28 |
| Czechoslovakian (208) | 456 | 0.10 |
| Danish (258) | 914 | 0.20 |
| Dutch (1,303) | 10,861 | 2.34 |
| Eastern European (523) | 644 | 0.14 |
| English (14,320) | 60,136 | 12.97 |
| Estonian (7) | 26 | 0.01 |
| European (2,482) | 2,761 | 0.60 |
| Finnish (235) | 699 | 0.15 |
| French, ex. Basque (3,327) | 25,406 | 5.48 |
| French Canadian (2,708) | 8,589 | 1.85 |
| German (17,906) | 90,839 | 19.59 |
| German Russian (0) | 0 | <0.01 |
| Greek (1,634) | 3,322 | 0.72 |
| Guyanese (151) | 209 | 0.05 |
| Hungarian (627) | 2,113 | 0.46 |
| Icelander (13) | 32 | 0.01 |
| Iranian (303) | 364 | 0.08 |
| Irish (28,391) | 107,847 | 23.26 |
| Israeli (145) | 184 | 0.04 |
| Italian (35,847) | 82,484 | 17.79 |
| Latvian (116) | 280 | 0.06 |
| Lithuanian (317) | 1,064 | 0.23 |
| Luxemburger (0) | 40 | 0.01 |
| Macedonian (375) | 498 | 0.11 |
| Maltese (33) | 53 | 0.01 |
| New Zealander (2) | 17 | <0.01 |
| Northern European (315) | 333 | 0.07 |
| Norwegian (417) | 1,540 | 0.33 |
| Pennsylvania German (85) | 173 | 0.04 |

| Ancestry | Population | % |
|---|---|---|
| Polish (11,929) | 35,362 | 7.63 |
| Portuguese (374) | 943 | 0.20 |
| Romanian (118) | 408 | 0.09 |
| Russian (2,120) | 5,700 | 1.23 |
| Scandinavian (175) | 394 | 0.08 |
| Scotch-Irish (2,597) | 7,595 | 1.64 |
| Scottish (2,048) | 9,589 | 2.07 |
| Serbian (76) | 144 | 0.03 |
| Slavic (64) | 322 | 0.07 |
| Slovak (287) | 948 | 0.20 |
| Slovene (53) | 229 | 0.05 |
| Soviet Union (0) | 0 | <0.01 |
| Swedish (822) | 3,763 | 0.81 |
| Swiss (401) | 1,724 | 0.37 |
| Turkish (377) | 537 | 0.12 |
| Ukrainian (3,319) | 6,832 | 1.47 |
| Welsh (699) | 4,566 | 0.98 |
| West Indian, ex. Hispanic (2,495) | 3,224 | 0.70 |
| Bahamian (0) | 0 | <0.01 |
| Barbadian (105) | 136 | 0.03 |
| Belizean (9) | 9 | <0.01 |
| Bermudan (0) | 0 | <0.01 |
| British West Indian (39) | 67 | 0.01 |
| Dutch West Indian (0) | 0 | <0.01 |
| Haitian (351) | 415 | 0.09 |
| Jamaican (1,406) | 1,928 | 0.42 |
| Trinidadian/Tobagonian (187) | 187 | 0.04 |
| U.S. Virgin Islander (0) | 0 | <0.01 |
| West Indian (398) | 482 | 0.10 |
| Other West Indian (0) | 0 | <0.01 |
| Yugoslavian (1,565) | 1,698 | 0.37 |

| Hispanic Origin | Population | % |
|---|---|---|
| Hispanic or Latino (of any race) | 18,829 | 4.03 |
| Central American, ex. Mexican | 802 | 0.17 |
| Costa Rican | 64 | 0.01 |
| Guatemalan | 346 | 0.07 |
| Honduran | 106 | 0.02 |
| Nicaraguan | 53 | 0.01 |
| Panamanian | 126 | 0.03 |
| Salvadoran | 102 | 0.02 |
| Other Central American | 5 | <0.01 |
| Cuban | 1,766 | 0.38 |
| Dominican Republic | 944 | 0.20 |
| Mexican | 2,338 | 0.50 |
| Puerto Rican | 10,246 | 2.19 |
| South American | 1,190 | 0.25 |
| Argentinean | 108 | 0.02 |
| Bolivian | 26 | 0.01 |
| Chilean | 89 | 0.02 |
| Colombian | 398 | 0.09 |
| Ecuadorian | 195 | 0.04 |
| Paraguayan | 19 | <0.01 |
| Peruvian | 204 | 0.04 |
| Uruguayan | 33 | 0.01 |
| Venezuelan | 103 | 0.02 |
| Other South American | 15 | <0.01 |
| Other Hispanic or Latino | 1,543 | 0.33 |

| Race* | Population | % |
|---|---|---|
| African-American/Black (51,220) | 58,984 | 12.63 |
| Not Hispanic (48,696) | 55,309 | 11.84 |
| Hispanic (2,524) | 3,675 | 0.79 |
| American Indian/Alaska Native (3,818) | 7,490 | 1.60 |
| Not Hispanic (3,432) | 6,695 | 1.43 |
| Hispanic (386) | 795 | 0.17 |
| Alaska Athabascan (Ala. Nat.) (0) | 5 | <0.01 |
| Aleut (Alaska Native) (1) | 2 | <0.01 |
| Apache (16) | 42 | 0.01 |
| Arapaho (2) | 2 | <0.01 |
| Blackfeet (10) | 156 | 0.03 |
| Canadian/French Am. Ind. (59) | 102 | 0.02 |
| Central American Ind. (5) | 18 | <0.01 |
| Cherokee (49) | 434 | 0.09 |
| Cheyenne (0) | 3 | <0.01 |
| Chickasaw (0) | 5 | <0.01 |
| Chippewa (32) | 53 | 0.01 |
| Choctaw (9) | 49 | 0.01 |
| Colville (0) | 1 | <0.01 |

| Race* | Population | % |
|---|---|---|
| Comanche (7) | 14 | <0.01 |
| Cree (3) | 11 | <0.01 |
| Creek (4) | 15 | <0.01 |
| Crow (0) | 2 | <0.01 |
| Delaware (8) | 14 | <0.01 |
| Hopi (0) | 5 | <0.01 |
| Houma (1) | 1 | <0.01 |
| Inupiat (Alaska Native) (5) | 9 | <0.01 |
| Iroquois (1,942) | 3,255 | 0.70 |
| Kiowa (1) | 2 | <0.01 |
| Lumbee (5) | 9 | <0.01 |
| Menominee (1) | 1 | <0.01 |
| Mexican American Ind. (53) | 75 | 0.02 |
| Navajo (8) | 12 | <0.01 |
| Osage (2) | 6 | <0.01 |
| Ottawa (1) | 4 | <0.01 |
| Paiute (0) | 0 | <0.01 |
| Pima (1) | 2 | <0.01 |
| Potawatomi (6) | 9 | <0.01 |
| Pueblo (0) | 0 | <0.01 |
| Puget Sound Salish (0) | 0 | <0.01 |
| Seminole (5) | 27 | 0.01 |
| Shoshone (1) | 3 | <0.01 |
| Sioux (29) | 64 | 0.01 |
| South American Ind. (50) | 94 | 0.02 |
| Spanish American Ind. (9) | 9 | <0.01 |
| Tlingit-Haida (Alaska Native) (1) | 2 | <0.01 |
| Tohono O'Odham (1) | 1 | <0.01 |
| Tsimshian (Alaska Native) (0) | 0 | <0.01 |
| Ute (0) | 0 | <0.01 |
| Yakama (0) | 0 | <0.01 |
| Yaqui (0) | 1 | <0.01 |
| Yuman (1) | 4 | <0.01 |
| Yup'ik (Alaska Native) (0) | 1 | <0.01 |
| Asian (14,454) | 16,875 | 3.61 |
| Not Hispanic (14,370) | 16,607 | 3.56 |
| Hispanic (84) | 268 | 0.06 |
| Bangladeshi (86) | 101 | 0.02 |
| Bhutanese (392) | 516 | 0.11 |
| Burmese (1,202) | 1,242 | 0.27 |
| Cambodian (204) | 255 | 0.05 |
| Chinese, ex. Taiwanese (2,955) | 3,411 | 0.73 |
| Filipino (703) | 1,094 | 0.23 |
| Hmong (112) | 134 | 0.03 |
| Indian (2,910) | 3,295 | 0.71 |
| Indonesian (30) | 58 | 0.01 |
| Japanese (251) | 559 | 0.12 |
| Korean (1,788) | 2,125 | 0.46 |
| Laotian (133) | 169 | 0.04 |
| Malaysian (8) | 18 | <0.01 |
| Nepalese (177) | 280 | 0.06 |
| Pakistani (343) | 388 | 0.08 |
| Sri Lankan (51) | 62 | 0.01 |
| Taiwanese (144) | 178 | 0.04 |
| Thai (134) | 195 | 0.04 |
| Vietnamese (2,133) | 2,393 | 0.51 |
| Hawaii Native/Pacific Islander (148) | 534 | 0.11 |
| Not Hispanic (120) | 432 | 0.09 |
| Hispanic (28) | 102 | 0.02 |
| Fijian (0) | 4 | <0.01 |
| Guamanian/Chamorro (41) | 53 | 0.01 |
| Marshallese (0) | 1 | <0.01 |
| Native Hawaiian (42) | 156 | 0.03 |
| Samoan (14) | 44 | 0.01 |
| Tongan (1) | 2 | <0.01 |
| White (378,885) | 390,050 | 83.52 |
| Not Hispanic (370,040) | 379,663 | 81.29 |
| Hispanic (8,845) | 10,387 | 2.22 |

*Notes: † The Census 2010 population figure is used to calculate the percentages in the Hispanic Origin and Race categories. Ancestry percentages are based on the 2006-2010 American Community Survey population (not shown); ‡ Numbers in parentheses indicate the number of people reporting a single ancestry; * Numbers in parentheses indicate the number of persons reporting this race alone, not in combination with any other race; Please refer to the Explanation of Data for more information.*

## Ontario County

Population: 107,931

| Ancestry | Population | % |
|---|---|---|
| Afghan (0) | 0 | <0.01 |
| African, Sub-Saharan (31) | 105 | 0.10 |
| African (31) | 105 | 0.10 |
| Cape Verdean (0) | 0 | <0.01 |
| Ethiopian (0) | 0 | <0.01 |
| Ghanaian (0) | 0 | <0.01 |
| Kenyan (0) | 0 | <0.01 |
| Liberian (0) | 0 | <0.01 |
| Nigerian (0) | 0 | <0.01 |
| Senegalese (0) | 0 | <0.01 |
| Sierra Leonean (0) | 0 | <0.01 |
| Somalian (0) | 0 | <0.01 |
| South African (0) | 0 | <0.01 |
| Sudanese (0) | 0 | <0.01 |
| Ugandan (0) | 0 | <0.01 |
| Zimbabwean (0) | 0 | <0.01 |
| Other Sub-Saharan African (0) | 0 | <0.01 |
| Albanian (436) | 436 | 0.41 |
| Alsatian (0) | 0 | <0.01 |
| American (5,011) | 5,011 | 4.71 |
| Arab (106) | 390 | 0.37 |
| Arab (6) | 6 | 0.01 |
| Egyptian (0) | 0 | <0.01 |
| Iraqi (0) | 0 | <0.01 |
| Jordanian (0) | 0 | <0.01 |
| Lebanese (23) | 63 | 0.06 |
| Moroccan (0) | 3 | <0.01 |
| Palestinian (0) | 14 | 0.01 |
| Syrian (77) | 304 | 0.29 |
| Other Arab (0) | 0 | <0.01 |
| Armenian (14) | 24 | 0.02 |
| Assyrian/Chaldean/Syriac (0) | 0 | <0.01 |
| Australian (0) | 5 | <0.01 |
| Austrian (78) | 251 | 0.24 |
| Basque (0) | 0 | <0.01 |
| Belgian (54) | 160 | 0.15 |
| Brazilian (0) | 11 | 0.01 |
| British (275) | 630 | 0.59 |
| Bulgarian (11) | 83 | 0.08 |
| Cajun (0) | 0 | <0.01 |
| Canadian (312) | 525 | 0.49 |
| Carpatho Rusyn (0) | 0 | <0.01 |
| Celtic (3) | 6 | 0.01 |
| Croatian (13) | 13 | 0.01 |
| Cypriot (0) | 0 | <0.01 |
| Czech (44) | 381 | 0.36 |
| Czechoslovakian (67) | 147 | 0.14 |
| Danish (237) | 1,121 | 1.05 |
| Dutch (1,459) | 7,090 | 6.67 |
| Eastern European (95) | 135 | 0.13 |
| English (5,898) | 22,292 | 20.97 |
| Estonian (0) | 0 | <0.01 |
| European (1,060) | 1,131 | 1.06 |
| Finnish (85) | 136 | 0.13 |
| French, ex. Basque (635) | 4,770 | 4.49 |
| French Canadian (419) | 1,770 | 1.67 |
| German (6,907) | 29,630 | 27.87 |
| German Russian (0) | 0 | <0.01 |
| Greek (115) | 382 | 0.36 |
| Guyanese (102) | 102 | 0.10 |
| Hungarian (213) | 399 | 0.38 |
| Icelander (0) | 10 | 0.01 |
| Iranian (0) | 0 | <0.01 |
| Irish (5,165) | 22,198 | 20.88 |
| Israeli (0) | 0 | <0.01 |
| Italian (6,590) | 16,105 | 15.15 |
| Latvian (0) | 0 | <0.01 |
| Lithuanian (109) | 270 | 0.25 |
| Luxemburger (0) | 0 | <0.01 |
| Macedonian (10) | 35 | 0.03 |
| Maltese (20) | 20 | 0.02 |
| New Zealander (0) | 0 | <0.01 |
| Northern European (92) | 98 | 0.09 |
| Norwegian (168) | 644 | 0.61 |
| Pennsylvania German (263) | 366 | 0.34 |

| Ancestry (cont.) | Population | % |
|---|---|---|
| Polish (1,315) | 5,470 | 5.15 |
| Portuguese (40) | 117 | 0.11 |
| Romanian (87) | 142 | 0.13 |
| Russian (121) | 465 | 0.44 |
| Scandinavian (145) | 381 | 0.36 |
| Scotch-Irish (620) | 1,768 | 1.66 |
| Scottish (735) | 2,962 | 2.79 |
| Serbian (21) | 66 | 0.06 |
| Slavic (0) | 51 | 0.05 |
| Slovak (101) | 273 | 0.26 |
| Slovene (0) | 5 | <0.01 |
| Soviet Union (0) | 0 | <0.01 |
| Swedish (453) | 1,399 | 1.32 |
| Swiss (105) | 371 | 0.35 |
| Turkish (3) | 20 | 0.02 |
| Ukrainian (180) | 827 | 0.78 |
| Welsh (251) | 1,231 | 1.16 |
| West Indian, ex. Hispanic (374) | 459 | 0.43 |
| Bahamian (0) | 0 | <0.01 |
| Barbadian (0) | 0 | <0.01 |
| Belizean (0) | 0 | <0.01 |
| Bermudan (0) | 0 | <0.01 |
| British West Indian (0) | 27 | 0.03 |
| Dutch West Indian (0) | 0 | <0.01 |
| Haitian (0) | 28 | 0.03 |
| Jamaican (311) | 324 | 0.30 |
| Trinidadian/Tobagonian (29) | 46 | 0.04 |
| U.S. Virgin Islander (0) | 0 | <0.01 |
| West Indian (34) | 34 | 0.03 |
| Other West Indian (0) | 0 | <0.01 |
| Yugoslavian (57) | 133 | 0.13 |

| Hispanic Origin | Population | % |
|---|---|---|
| Hispanic or Latino (of any race) | 3,679 | 3.41 |
| Central American, ex. Mexican | 180 | 0.17 |
| Costa Rican | 22 | 0.02 |
| Guatemalan | 60 | 0.06 |
| Honduran | 30 | 0.03 |
| Nicaraguan | 15 | 0.01 |
| Panamanian | 33 | 0.03 |
| Salvadoran | 20 | 0.02 |
| Other Central American | 0 | <0.01 |
| Cuban | 105 | 0.10 |
| Dominican Republic | 110 | 0.10 |
| Mexican | 837 | 0.78 |
| Puerto Rican | 2,078 | 1.93 |
| South American | 182 | 0.17 |
| Argentinean | 27 | 0.03 |
| Bolivian | 4 | <0.01 |
| Chilean | 8 | 0.01 |
| Colombian | 63 | 0.06 |
| Ecuadorian | 26 | 0.02 |
| Paraguayan | 0 | <0.01 |
| Peruvian | 35 | 0.03 |
| Uruguayan | 0 | <0.01 |
| Venezuelan | 19 | 0.02 |
| Other South American | 0 | <0.01 |
| Other Hispanic or Latino | 187 | 0.17 |

| Race* | Population | % |
|---|---|---|
| African-American/Black (2,432) | 3,342 | 3.10 |
| Not Hispanic (2,226) | 3,001 | 2.78 |
| Hispanic (206) | 341 | 0.32 |
| American Indian/Alaska Native (276) | 776 | 0.72 |
| Not Hispanic (244) | 688 | 0.64 |
| Hispanic (32) | 88 | 0.08 |
| Alaska Athabascan (Ala. Nat.) (1) | 1 | <0.01 |
| Aleut (Alaska Native) (0) | 1 | <0.01 |
| Apache (5) | 14 | 0.01 |
| Arapaho (0) | 0 | <0.01 |
| Blackfeet (3) | 19 | 0.02 |
| Canadian/French Am. Ind. (4) | 7 | 0.01 |
| Central American Ind. (1) | 1 | <0.01 |
| Cherokee (19) | 105 | 0.10 |
| Cheyenne (0) | 5 | <0.01 |
| Chickasaw (1) | 2 | <0.01 |
| Chippewa (16) | 20 | 0.02 |
| Choctaw (2) | 8 | 0.01 |
| Colville (0) | 0 | <0.01 |

| Race* (cont.) | Population | % |
|---|---|---|
| Comanche (0) | 1 | <0.01 |
| Cree (0) | 1 | <0.01 |
| Creek (0) | 0 | <0.01 |
| Crow (0) | 7 | 0.01 |
| Delaware (5) | 6 | 0.01 |
| Hopi (2) | 2 | <0.01 |
| Houma (1) | 1 | <0.01 |
| Inupiat (Alaska Native) (0) | 1 | <0.01 |
| Iroquois (84) | 190 | 0.18 |
| Kiowa (1) | 1 | <0.01 |
| Lumbee (1) | 1 | <0.01 |
| Menominee (0) | 0 | <0.01 |
| Mexican American Ind. (2) | 2 | <0.01 |
| Navajo (1) | 2 | <0.01 |
| Osage (0) | 0 | <0.01 |
| Ottawa (1) | 1 | <0.01 |
| Paiute (0) | 0 | <0.01 |
| Pima (0) | 0 | <0.01 |
| Potawatomi (0) | 0 | <0.01 |
| Pueblo (0) | 3 | <0.01 |
| Puget Sound Salish (0) | 0 | <0.01 |
| Seminole (0) | 6 | <0.01 |
| Shoshone (0) | 0 | <0.01 |
| Sioux (9) | 25 | 0.02 |
| South American Ind. (2) | 8 | 0.01 |
| Spanish American Ind. (0) | 0 | <0.01 |
| Tlingit-Haida (Alaska Native) (0) | 0 | <0.01 |
| Tohono O'Odham (0) | 0 | <0.01 |
| Tsimshian (Alaska Native) (0) | 0 | <0.01 |
| Ute (0) | 2 | <0.01 |
| Yakama (0) | 0 | <0.01 |
| Yaqui (0) | 0 | <0.01 |
| Yuman (0) | 0 | <0.01 |
| Yup'ik (Alaska Native) (1) | 1 | <0.01 |
| Asian (1,126) | 1,486 | 1.38 |
| Not Hispanic (1,111) | 1,455 | 1.35 |
| Hispanic (15) | 31 | 0.03 |
| Bangladeshi (3) | 3 | <0.01 |
| Bhutanese (0) | 0 | <0.01 |
| Burmese (7) | 7 | 0.01 |
| Cambodian (18) | 18 | 0.02 |
| Chinese, ex. Taiwanese (318) | 391 | 0.36 |
| Filipino (113) | 202 | 0.19 |
| Hmong (0) | 0 | <0.01 |
| Indian (231) | 271 | 0.25 |
| Indonesian (7) | 16 | 0.01 |
| Japanese (53) | 95 | 0.09 |
| Korean (144) | 205 | 0.19 |
| Laotian (35) | 42 | 0.04 |
| Malaysian (3) | 4 | <0.01 |
| Nepalese (3) | 4 | <0.01 |
| Pakistani (29) | 33 | 0.03 |
| Sri Lankan (5) | 5 | <0.01 |
| Taiwanese (14) | 16 | 0.01 |
| Thai (23) | 27 | 0.03 |
| Vietnamese (70) | 86 | 0.08 |
| Hawaii Native/Pacific Islander (24) | 83 | 0.08 |
| Not Hispanic (16) | 65 | 0.06 |
| Hispanic (8) | 18 | 0.02 |
| Fijian (0) | 0 | <0.01 |
| Guamanian/Chamorro (6) | 23 | 0.02 |
| Marshallese (0) | 0 | <0.01 |
| Native Hawaiian (11) | 25 | 0.02 |
| Samoan (0) | 0 | <0.01 |
| Tongan (0) | 0 | <0.01 |
| White (101,078) | 102,741 | 95.19 |
| Not Hispanic (99,119) | 100,508 | 93.12 |
| Hispanic (1,959) | 2,233 | 2.07 |

Notes: † The Census 2010 population figure is used to calculate the percentages in the Hispanic Origin and Race categories. Ancestry percentages are based on the 2006-2010 American Community Survey population (not shown); ‡ Numbers in parentheses indicate the number of people reporting a single ancestry; * Numbers in parentheses indicate the number of persons reporting this race alone, not in combination with any other race; Please refer to the Explanation of Data for more information.

## Orange County

Population: 372,813

| Ancestry | Population | % |
|---|---|---|
| Afghan (25) | 25 | 0.01 |
| African, Sub-Saharan (2,270) | 2,998 | 0.81 |
| African (1,369) | 1,938 | 0.52 |
| Cape Verdean (0) | 0 | <0.01 |
| Ethiopian (23) | 23 | 0.01 |
| Ghanaian (140) | 140 | 0.04 |
| Kenyan (0) | 0 | <0.01 |
| Liberian (0) | 22 | 0.01 |
| Nigerian (581) | 647 | 0.17 |
| Senegalese (0) | 12 | <0.01 |
| Sierra Leonean (0) | 0 | <0.01 |
| Somalian (20) | 61 | 0.02 |
| South African (14) | 22 | 0.01 |
| Sudanese (0) | 0 | <0.01 |
| Ugandan (0) | 0 | <0.01 |
| Zimbabwean (0) | 0 | <0.01 |
| Other Sub-Saharan African (123) | 133 | 0.04 |
| Albanian (231) | 545 | 0.15 |
| Alsatian (0) | 8 | <0.01 |
| American (23,068) | 23,068 | 6.23 |
| Arab (828) | 1,606 | 0.43 |
| Arab (16) | 38 | 0.01 |
| Egyptian (387) | 508 | 0.14 |
| Iraqi (0) | 15 | <0.01 |
| Jordanian (156) | 156 | 0.04 |
| Lebanese (82) | 315 | 0.09 |
| Moroccan (19) | 66 | 0.02 |
| Palestinian (0) | 0 | <0.01 |
| Syrian (20) | 330 | 0.09 |
| Other Arab (148) | 178 | 0.05 |
| Armenian (177) | 407 | 0.11 |
| Assyrian/Chaldean/Syriac (3) | 3 | <0.01 |
| Australian (42) | 182 | 0.05 |
| Austrian (528) | 2,246 | 0.61 |
| Basque (0) | 40 | 0.01 |
| Belgian (49) | 272 | 0.07 |
| Brazilian (86) | 151 | 0.04 |
| British (591) | 1,408 | 0.38 |
| Bulgarian (190) | 198 | 0.05 |
| Cajun (52) | 67 | 0.02 |
| Canadian (394) | 1,325 | 0.36 |
| Carpatho Rusyn (0) | 0 | <0.01 |
| Celtic (59) | 82 | 0.02 |
| Croatian (128) | 430 | 0.12 |
| Cypriot (13) | 13 | <0.01 |
| Czech (306) | 1,641 | 0.44 |
| Czechoslovakian (325) | 773 | 0.21 |
| Danish (89) | 596 | 0.16 |
| Dutch (2,181) | 9,116 | 2.46 |
| Eastern European (906) | 925 | 0.25 |
| English (4,565) | 24,564 | 6.64 |
| Estonian (58) | 125 | 0.03 |
| European (3,404) | 3,842 | 1.04 |
| Finnish (154) | 546 | 0.15 |
| French, ex. Basque (821) | 6,903 | 1.86 |
| French Canadian (540) | 2,032 | 0.55 |
| German (11,282) | 54,956 | 14.84 |
| German Russian (0) | 0 | <0.01 |
| Greek (825) | 2,583 | 0.70 |
| Guyanese (206) | 432 | 0.12 |
| Hungarian (3,947) | 8,222 | 2.22 |
| Icelander (23) | 124 | 0.03 |
| Iranian (50) | 108 | 0.03 |
| Irish (23,448) | 75,052 | 20.27 |
| Israeli (302) | 1,042 | 0.28 |
| Italian (26,639) | 67,312 | 18.18 |
| Latvian (107) | 332 | 0.09 |
| Lithuanian (300) | 1,081 | 0.29 |
| Luxemburger (0) | 0 | <0.01 |
| Macedonian (0) | 0 | <0.01 |
| Maltese (203) | 302 | 0.08 |
| New Zealander (0) | 35 | 0.01 |
| Northern European (67) | 95 | 0.03 |
| Norwegian (783) | 3,015 | 0.81 |
| Pennsylvania German (31) | 128 | 0.03 |

| Ancestry | Population | % |
|---|---|---|
| Polish (6,061) | 20,649 | 5.58 |
| Portuguese (473) | 1,228 | 0.33 |
| Romanian (758) | 3,000 | 0.81 |
| Russian (2,107) | 6,133 | 1.66 |
| Scandinavian (132) | 412 | 0.11 |
| Scotch-Irish (1,373) | 4,366 | 1.18 |
| Scottish (1,032) | 4,871 | 1.32 |
| Serbian (62) | 96 | 0.03 |
| Slavic (59) | 201 | 0.05 |
| Slovak (396) | 1,031 | 0.28 |
| Slovene (33) | 103 | 0.03 |
| Soviet Union (0) | 0 | <0.01 |
| Swedish (599) | 3,116 | 0.84 |
| Swiss (270) | 900 | 0.24 |
| Turkish (126) | 255 | 0.07 |
| Ukrainian (1,049) | 2,847 | 0.77 |
| Welsh (264) | 1,567 | 0.42 |
| West Indian, ex. Hispanic (4,550) | 6,861 | 1.85 |
| Bahamian (0) | 13 | <0.01 |
| Barbadian (69) | 191 | 0.05 |
| Belizean (0) | 80 | 0.02 |
| Bermudan (0) | 0 | <0.01 |
| British West Indian (395) | 708 | 0.19 |
| Dutch West Indian (10) | 48 | 0.01 |
| Haitian (1,324) | 1,665 | 0.45 |
| Jamaican (1,855) | 2,353 | 0.64 |
| Trinidadian/Tobagonian (291) | 585 | 0.16 |
| U.S. Virgin Islander (0) | 48 | 0.01 |
| West Indian (566) | 1,128 | 0.30 |
| Other West Indian (40) | 42 | 0.01 |
| Yugoslavian (75) | 369 | 0.10 |

| Hispanic Origin | Population | % |
|---|---|---|
| Hispanic or Latino (of any race) | 67,185 | 18.02 |
| Central American, ex. Mexican | 5,302 | 1.42 |
| Costa Rican | 159 | 0.04 |
| Guatemalan | 988 | 0.27 |
| Honduran | 2,659 | 0.71 |
| Nicaraguan | 112 | 0.03 |
| Panamanian | 376 | 0.10 |
| Salvadoran | 965 | 0.26 |
| Other Central American | 43 | 0.01 |
| Cuban | 1,489 | 0.40 |
| Dominican Republic | 4,293 | 1.15 |
| Mexican | 16,480 | 4.42 |
| Puerto Rican | 29,210 | 7.84 |
| South American | 6,144 | 1.65 |
| Argentinean | 654 | 0.18 |
| Bolivian | 81 | 0.02 |
| Chilean | 223 | 0.06 |
| Colombian | 1,772 | 0.48 |
| Ecuadorian | 1,426 | 0.38 |
| Paraguayan | 28 | 0.01 |
| Peruvian | 1,662 | 0.45 |
| Uruguayan | 91 | 0.02 |
| Venezuelan | 152 | 0.04 |
| Other South American | 55 | 0.01 |
| Other Hispanic or Latino | 4,267 | 1.14 |

| Race* | Population | % |
|---|---|---|
| African-American/Black (37,946) | 44,056 | 11.82 |
| Not Hispanic (33,895) | 37,986 | 10.19 |
| Hispanic (4,051) | 6,070 | 1.63 |
| American Indian/Alaska Native (1,748) | 4,451 | 1.19 |
| Not Hispanic (908) | 2,843 | 0.76 |
| Hispanic (840) | 1,608 | 0.43 |
| Alaska Athabascan (Ala. Nat.) (0) | 0 | <0.01 |
| Aleut (Alaska Native) (1) | 2 | <0.01 |
| Apache (1) | 31 | 0.01 |
| Arapaho (1) | 3 | <0.01 |
| Blackfeet (13) | 113 | 0.03 |
| Canadian/French Am. Ind. (3) | 9 | <0.01 |
| Central American Ind. (23) | 38 | 0.01 |
| Cherokee (65) | 477 | 0.13 |
| Cheyenne (1) | 3 | <0.01 |
| Chickasaw (0) | 3 | <0.01 |
| Chippewa (14) | 33 | 0.01 |
| Choctaw (8) | 13 | <0.01 |
| Colville (0) | 0 | <0.01 |

| Race* | Population | % |
|---|---|---|
| Comanche (2) | 3 | <0.01 |
| Cree (1) | 7 | <0.01 |
| Creek (2) | 10 | <0.01 |
| Crow (1) | 7 | <0.01 |
| Delaware (214) | 428 | 0.11 |
| Hopi (0) | 3 | <0.01 |
| Houma (2) | 2 | <0.01 |
| Inupiat (Alaska Native) (3) | 7 | <0.01 |
| Iroquois (144) | 302 | 0.08 |
| Kiowa (1) | 2 | <0.01 |
| Lumbee (4) | 7 | <0.01 |
| Menominee (0) | 0 | <0.01 |
| Mexican American Ind. (116) | 156 | 0.04 |
| Navajo (9) | 28 | 0.01 |
| Osage (0) | 1 | <0.01 |
| Ottawa (1) | 1 | <0.01 |
| Paiute (0) | 0 | <0.01 |
| Pima (0) | 4 | <0.01 |
| Potawatomi (2) | 6 | <0.01 |
| Pueblo (1) | 5 | <0.01 |
| Puget Sound Salish (0) | 2 | <0.01 |
| Seminole (0) | 21 | 0.01 |
| Shoshone (5) | 7 | <0.01 |
| Sioux (9) | 55 | 0.01 |
| South American Ind. (136) | 291 | 0.08 |
| Spanish American Ind. (101) | 113 | 0.03 |
| Tlingit-Haida (Alaska Native) (2) | 2 | <0.01 |
| Tohono O'Odham (1) | 15 | <0.01 |
| Tsimshian (Alaska Native) (0) | 0 | <0.01 |
| Ute (0) | 0 | <0.01 |
| Yakama (0) | 0 | <0.01 |
| Yaqui (0) | 0 | <0.01 |
| Yuman (1) | 5 | <0.01 |
| Yup'ik (Alaska Native) (1) | 1 | <0.01 |
| Asian (8,895) | 11,280 | 3.03 |
| Not Hispanic (8,685) | 10,687 | 2.87 |
| Hispanic (210) | 593 | 0.16 |
| Bangladeshi (136) | 154 | 0.04 |
| Bhutanese (2) | 2 | <0.01 |
| Burmese (26) | 28 | 0.01 |
| Cambodian (83) | 106 | 0.03 |
| Chinese, ex. Taiwanese (1,718) | 2,206 | 0.59 |
| Filipino (1,601) | 2,144 | 0.58 |
| Hmong (1) | 1 | <0.01 |
| Indian (2,621) | 3,050 | 0.82 |
| Indonesian (40) | 62 | 0.02 |
| Japanese (196) | 486 | 0.13 |
| Korean (1,005) | 1,333 | 0.36 |
| Laotian (7) | 14 | <0.01 |
| Malaysian (3) | 4 | <0.01 |
| Nepalese (7) | 10 | <0.01 |
| Pakistani (542) | 614 | 0.16 |
| Sri Lankan (47) | 56 | 0.02 |
| Taiwanese (44) | 51 | 0.01 |
| Thai (91) | 152 | 0.04 |
| Vietnamese (374) | 481 | 0.13 |
| Hawaii Native/Pacific Islander (125) | 434 | 0.12 |
| Not Hispanic (80) | 266 | 0.07 |
| Hispanic (45) | 168 | 0.05 |
| Fijian (1) | 2 | <0.01 |
| Guamanian/Chamorro (44) | 63 | 0.02 |
| Marshallese (0) | 0 | <0.01 |
| Native Hawaiian (15) | 93 | 0.02 |
| Samoan (13) | 29 | 0.01 |
| Tongan (1) | 1 | <0.01 |
| White (287,802) | 297,221 | 79.72 |
| Not Hispanic (254,259) | 260,102 | 69.77 |
| Hispanic (33,543) | 37,119 | 9.96 |

Notes: † The Census 2010 population figure is used to calculate the percentages in the Hispanic Origin and Race categories. Ancestry percentages are based on the 2006-2010 American Community Survey population (not shown); ‡ Numbers in parentheses indicate the number of people reporting a single ancestry; * Numbers in parentheses indicate the number of persons reporting this race alone, not in combination with any other race; Please refer to the Explanation of Data for more information.

## Orleans County

Population: 42,883

| Ancestry | Population | % |
|---|---|---|
| Afghan (0) | 0 | <0.01 |
| African, Sub-Saharan (8) | 37 | 0.09 |
| African (0) | 29 | 0.07 |
| Cape Verdean (0) | 0 | <0.01 |
| Ethiopian (0) | 0 | <0.01 |
| Ghanaian (0) | 0 | <0.01 |
| Kenyan (0) | 0 | <0.01 |
| Liberian (0) | 0 | <0.01 |
| Nigerian (8) | 8 | 0.02 |
| Senegalese (0) | 0 | <0.01 |
| Sierra Leonean (0) | 0 | <0.01 |
| Somalian (0) | 0 | <0.01 |
| South African (0) | 0 | <0.01 |
| Sudanese (0) | 0 | <0.01 |
| Ugandan (0) | 0 | <0.01 |
| Zimbabwean (0) | 0 | <0.01 |
| Other Sub-Saharan African (0) | 0 | <0.01 |
| Albanian (0) | 9 | 0.02 |
| Alsatian (0) | 0 | <0.01 |
| American (2,445) | 2,445 | 5.66 |
| Arab (15) | 47 | 0.11 |
| Arab (0) | 0 | <0.01 |
| Egyptian (0) | 11 | 0.03 |
| Iraqi (0) | 0 | <0.01 |
| Jordanian (0) | 0 | <0.01 |
| Lebanese (15) | 36 | 0.08 |
| Moroccan (0) | 0 | <0.01 |
| Palestinian (0) | 0 | <0.01 |
| Syrian (0) | 0 | <0.01 |
| Other Arab (0) | 0 | <0.01 |
| Armenian (0) | 0 | <0.01 |
| Assyrian/Chaldean/Syriac (0) | 0 | <0.01 |
| Australian (0) | 0 | <0.01 |
| Austrian (0) | 18 | 0.04 |
| Basque (0) | 0 | <0.01 |
| Belgian (0) | 18 | 0.04 |
| Brazilian (15) | 15 | 0.03 |
| British (59) | 114 | 0.26 |
| Bulgarian (0) | 0 | <0.01 |
| Cajun (0) | 0 | <0.01 |
| Canadian (92) | 211 | 0.49 |
| Carpatho Rusyn (0) | 0 | <0.01 |
| Celtic (0) | 0 | <0.01 |
| Croatian (0) | 69 | 0.16 |
| Cypriot (0) | 0 | <0.01 |
| Czech (4) | 52 | 0.12 |
| Czechoslovakian (0) | 0 | <0.01 |
| Danish (0) | 32 | 0.07 |
| Dutch (129) | 1,314 | 3.04 |
| Eastern European (39) | 39 | 0.09 |
| English (2,770) | 9,383 | 21.74 |
| Estonian (0) | 0 | <0.01 |
| European (123) | 128 | 0.30 |
| Finnish (0) | 0 | <0.01 |
| French, ex. Basque (198) | 2,092 | 4.85 |
| French Canadian (140) | 489 | 1.13 |
| German (3,260) | 11,665 | 27.02 |
| German Russian (0) | 0 | <0.01 |
| Greek (33) | 71 | 0.16 |
| Guyanese (0) | 0 | <0.01 |
| Hungarian (13) | 144 | 0.33 |
| Icelander (0) | 0 | <0.01 |
| Iranian (0) | 0 | <0.01 |
| Irish (1,230) | 7,575 | 17.55 |
| Israeli (0) | 0 | <0.01 |
| Italian (2,135) | 5,503 | 12.75 |
| Latvian (0) | 0 | <0.01 |
| Lithuanian (64) | 99 | 0.23 |
| Luxemburger (0) | 0 | <0.01 |
| Macedonian (0) | 0 | <0.01 |
| Maltese (0) | 0 | <0.01 |
| New Zealander (0) | 0 | <0.01 |
| Northern European (6) | 6 | 0.01 |
| Norwegian (50) | 82 | 0.19 |
| Pennsylvania German (42) | 86 | 0.20 |

| | Population | % |
|---|---|---|
| Polish (1,595) | 3,934 | 9.11 |
| Portuguese (0) | 29 | 0.07 |
| Romanian (0) | 0 | <0.01 |
| Russian (57) | 150 | 0.35 |
| Scandinavian (0) | 0 | <0.01 |
| Scotch-Irish (158) | 509 | 1.18 |
| Scottish (103) | 950 | 2.20 |
| Serbian (0) | 0 | <0.01 |
| Slavic (0) | 17 | 0.04 |
| Slovak (8) | 28 | 0.06 |
| Slovene (19) | 19 | 0.04 |
| Soviet Union (0) | 0 | <0.01 |
| Swedish (56) | 157 | 0.36 |
| Swiss (11) | 62 | 0.14 |
| Turkish (0) | 0 | <0.01 |
| Ukrainian (101) | 573 | 1.33 |
| Welsh (61) | 357 | 0.83 |
| West Indian, ex. Hispanic (158) | 207 | 0.48 |
| Bahamian (0) | 0 | <0.01 |
| Barbadian (5) | 5 | 0.01 |
| Belizean (0) | 0 | <0.01 |
| Bermudan (0) | 0 | <0.01 |
| British West Indian (0) | 0 | <0.01 |
| Dutch West Indian (0) | 0 | <0.01 |
| Haitian (13) | 19 | 0.04 |
| Jamaican (120) | 163 | 0.38 |
| Trinidadian/Tobagonian (14) | 14 | 0.03 |
| U.S. Virgin Islander (0) | 0 | <0.01 |
| West Indian (6) | 6 | 0.01 |
| Other West Indian (0) | 0 | <0.01 |
| Yugoslavian (21) | 29 | 0.07 |

| Hispanic Origin | Population | % |
|---|---|---|
| Hispanic or Latino (of any race) | 1,757 | 4.10 |
| Central American, ex. Mexican | 79 | 0.18 |
| Costa Rican | 1 | <0.01 |
| Guatemalan | 21 | 0.05 |
| Honduran | 7 | 0.02 |
| Nicaraguan | 4 | 0.01 |
| Panamanian | 31 | 0.07 |
| Salvadoran | 15 | 0.03 |
| Other Central American | 0 | <0.01 |
| Cuban | 53 | 0.12 |
| Dominican Republic | 46 | 0.11 |
| Mexican | 741 | 1.73 |
| Puerto Rican | 663 | 1.55 |
| South American | 38 | 0.09 |
| Argentinean | 0 | <0.01 |
| Bolivian | 0 | <0.01 |
| Chilean | 1 | <0.01 |
| Colombian | 19 | 0.04 |
| Ecuadorian | 8 | 0.02 |
| Paraguayan | 0 | <0.01 |
| Peruvian | 8 | 0.02 |
| Uruguayan | 1 | <0.01 |
| Venezuelan | 1 | <0.01 |
| Other South American | 0 | <0.01 |
| Other Hispanic or Latino | 137 | 0.32 |

| Race* | Population | % |
|---|---|---|
| African-American/Black (2,523) | 2,965 | 6.91 |
| Not Hispanic (2,368) | 2,771 | 6.46 |
| Hispanic (155) | 194 | 0.45 |
| American Indian/Alaska Native (247) | 527 | 1.23 |
| Not Hispanic (199) | 449 | 1.05 |
| Hispanic (48) | 78 | 0.18 |
| Alaska Athabascan (Ala. Nat.) (0) | 0 | <0.01 |
| Aleut (Alaska Native) (1) | 3 | 0.01 |
| Apache (6) | 17 | 0.04 |
| Arapaho (0) | 0 | <0.01 |
| Blackfeet (1) | 17 | 0.04 |
| Canadian/French Am. Ind. (1) | 3 | 0.01 |
| Central American Ind. (5) | 5 | 0.01 |
| Cherokee (8) | 48 | 0.11 |
| Cheyenne (0) | 1 | <0.01 |
| Chickasaw (0) | 0 | <0.01 |
| Chippewa (0) | 11 | 0.03 |
| Choctaw (1) | 5 | 0.01 |
| Colville (0) | 0 | <0.01 |

| | Population | % |
|---|---|---|
| Comanche (0) | 0 | <0.01 |
| Cree (0) | 0 | <0.01 |
| Creek (0) | 1 | <0.01 |
| Crow (0) | 1 | <0.01 |
| Delaware (10) | 14 | 0.03 |
| Hopi (0) | 0 | <0.01 |
| Houma (1) | 1 | <0.01 |
| Inupiat (Alaska Native) (0) | 0 | <0.01 |
| Iroquois (87) | 134 | 0.31 |
| Kiowa (0) | 0 | <0.01 |
| Lumbee (0) | 0 | <0.01 |
| Menominee (0) | 0 | <0.01 |
| Mexican American Ind. (9) | 21 | 0.05 |
| Navajo (1) | 2 | <0.01 |
| Osage (0) | 0 | <0.01 |
| Ottawa (0) | 0 | <0.01 |
| Paiute (0) | 0 | <0.01 |
| Pima (0) | 0 | <0.01 |
| Potawatomi (0) | 0 | <0.01 |
| Pueblo (0) | 1 | <0.01 |
| Puget Sound Salish (0) | 0 | <0.01 |
| Seminole (0) | 0 | <0.01 |
| Shoshone (0) | 8 | 0.02 |
| Sioux (2) | 4 | 0.01 |
| South American Ind. (3) | 5 | 0.01 |
| Spanish American Ind. (3) | 3 | 0.01 |
| Tlingit-Haida (Alaska Native) (0) | 0 | <0.01 |
| Tohono O'Odham (0) | 0 | <0.01 |
| Tsimshian (Alaska Native) (0) | 0 | <0.01 |
| Ute (0) | 0 | <0.01 |
| Yakama (0) | 0 | <0.01 |
| Yaqui (0) | 0 | <0.01 |
| Yuman (0) | 0 | <0.01 |
| Yup'ik (Alaska Native) (0) | 0 | <0.01 |
| Asian (179) | 259 | 0.60 |
| Not Hispanic (173) | 250 | 0.58 |
| Hispanic (6) | 9 | 0.02 |
| Bangladeshi (0) | 0 | <0.01 |
| Bhutanese (0) | 0 | <0.01 |
| Burmese (1) | 1 | <0.01 |
| Cambodian (0) | 0 | <0.01 |
| Chinese, ex. Taiwanese (31) | 41 | 0.10 |
| Filipino (39) | 63 | 0.15 |
| Hmong (0) | 0 | <0.01 |
| Indian (17) | 40 | 0.09 |
| Indonesian (0) | 0 | <0.01 |
| Japanese (6) | 17 | 0.04 |
| Korean (21) | 23 | 0.05 |
| Laotian (0) | 0 | <0.01 |
| Malaysian (0) | 0 | <0.01 |
| Nepalese (0) | 0 | <0.01 |
| Pakistani (15) | 15 | 0.03 |
| Sri Lankan (1) | 3 | 0.01 |
| Taiwanese (0) | 5 | 0.01 |
| Thai (5) | 8 | 0.02 |
| Vietnamese (2) | 5 | 0.01 |
| Hawaii Native/Pacific Islander (9) | 35 | 0.08 |
| Not Hispanic (7) | 25 | 0.06 |
| Hispanic (2) | 10 | 0.02 |
| Fijian (0) | 0 | <0.01 |
| Guamanian/Chamorro (1) | 2 | <0.01 |
| Marshallese (0) | 0 | <0.01 |
| Native Hawaiian (6) | 11 | 0.03 |
| Samoan (2) | 3 | 0.01 |
| Tongan (0) | 0 | <0.01 |
| White (38,528) | 39,297 | 91.64 |
| Not Hispanic (37,658) | 38,305 | 89.32 |
| Hispanic (870) | 992 | 2.31 |

Notes: † The Census 2010 population figure is used to calculate the percentages in the Hispanic Origin and Race categories. Ancestry percentages are based on the 2006-2010 American Community Survey population (not shown); ‡ Numbers in parentheses indicate the number of people reporting a single ancestry; * Numbers in parentheses indicate the number of persons reporting this race alone, not in combination with any other race; Please refer to the Explanation of Data for more information.

## Oswego County
Population: 122,109

| Ancestry | Population | % |
|---|---|---|
| Afghan (50) | 50 | 0.04 |
| African, Sub-Saharan (105) | 109 | 0.09 |
| African (22) | 26 | 0.02 |
| Cape Verdean (0) | 0 | <0.01 |
| Ethiopian (0) | 0 | <0.01 |
| Ghanaian (30) | 30 | 0.02 |
| Kenyan (6) | 6 | <0.01 |
| Liberian (0) | 0 | <0.01 |
| Nigerian (0) | 0 | <0.01 |
| Senegalese (19) | 19 | 0.02 |
| Sierra Leonean (0) | 0 | <0.01 |
| Somalian (0) | 0 | <0.01 |
| South African (16) | 16 | 0.01 |
| Sudanese (0) | 0 | <0.01 |
| Ugandan (0) | 0 | <0.01 |
| Zimbabwean (0) | 0 | <0.01 |
| Other Sub-Saharan African (12) | 12 | 0.01 |
| Albanian (0) | 3 | <0.01 |
| Alsatian (0) | 0 | <0.01 |
| American (6,704) | 6,704 | 5.49 |
| Arab (63) | 291 | 0.24 |
| Arab (0) | 0 | <0.01 |
| Egyptian (10) | 10 | 0.01 |
| Iraqi (0) | 0 | <0.01 |
| Jordanian (0) | 0 | <0.01 |
| Lebanese (40) | 195 | 0.16 |
| Moroccan (0) | 0 | <0.01 |
| Palestinian (0) | 0 | <0.01 |
| Syrian (13) | 74 | 0.06 |
| Other Arab (0) | 12 | 0.01 |
| Armenian (34) | 92 | 0.08 |
| Assyrian/Chaldean/Syriac (0) | 0 | <0.01 |
| Australian (0) | 0 | <0.01 |
| Austrian (62) | 235 | 0.19 |
| Basque (0) | 0 | <0.01 |
| Belgian (12) | 94 | 0.08 |
| Brazilian (17) | 17 | 0.01 |
| British (200) | 394 | 0.32 |
| Bulgarian (0) | 0 | <0.01 |
| Cajun (0) | 15 | 0.01 |
| Canadian (347) | 837 | 0.68 |
| Carpatho Rusyn (0) | 28 | 0.02 |
| Celtic (15) | 15 | 0.01 |
| Croatian (31) | 254 | 0.21 |
| Cypriot (0) | 0 | <0.01 |
| Czech (72) | 356 | 0.29 |
| Czechoslovakian (62) | 112 | 0.09 |
| Danish (82) | 255 | 0.21 |
| Dutch (661) | 4,758 | 3.89 |
| Eastern European (42) | 65 | 0.05 |
| English (5,611) | 18,945 | 15.50 |
| Estonian (0) | 0 | <0.01 |
| European (840) | 848 | 0.69 |
| Finnish (65) | 315 | 0.26 |
| French, ex. Basque (2,417) | 12,503 | 10.23 |
| French Canadian (1,857) | 4,004 | 3.28 |
| German (5,985) | 25,630 | 20.97 |
| German Russian (0) | 0 | <0.01 |
| Greek (152) | 437 | 0.36 |
| Guyanese (0) | 0 | <0.01 |
| Hungarian (139) | 441 | 0.36 |
| Icelander (20) | 20 | 0.02 |
| Iranian (0) | 0 | <0.01 |
| Irish (8,045) | 27,954 | 22.87 |
| Israeli (39) | 39 | 0.03 |
| Italian (6,436) | 17,452 | 14.28 |
| Latvian (0) | 10 | 0.01 |
| Lithuanian (148) | 359 | 0.29 |
| Luxemburger (0) | 0 | <0.01 |
| Macedonian (19) | 40 | 0.03 |
| Maltese (12) | 27 | 0.02 |
| New Zealander (0) | 0 | <0.01 |
| Northern European (94) | 94 | 0.08 |
| Norwegian (179) | 506 | 0.41 |
| Pennsylvania German (36) | 83 | 0.07 |

| Ancestry | Population | % |
|---|---|---|
| Polish (2,367) | 7,803 | 6.38 |
| Portuguese (79) | 149 | 0.12 |
| Romanian (0) | 39 | 0.03 |
| Russian (323) | 984 | 0.81 |
| Scandinavian (20) | 46 | 0.04 |
| Scotch-Irish (714) | 1,948 | 1.59 |
| Scottish (710) | 2,653 | 2.17 |
| Serbian (0) | 22 | 0.02 |
| Slavic (2) | 13 | 0.01 |
| Slovak (50) | 114 | 0.09 |
| Slovene (0) | 24 | 0.02 |
| Soviet Union (0) | 0 | <0.01 |
| Swedish (164) | 837 | 0.68 |
| Swiss (92) | 340 | 0.28 |
| Turkish (0) | 23 | 0.02 |
| Ukrainian (393) | 1,111 | 0.91 |
| Welsh (167) | 1,232 | 1.01 |
| West Indian, ex. Hispanic (98) | 226 | 0.18 |
| Bahamian (0) | 0 | <0.01 |
| Barbadian (12) | 12 | 0.01 |
| Belizean (0) | 12 | 0.01 |
| Bermudan (0) | 0 | <0.01 |
| British West Indian (0) | 15 | 0.01 |
| Dutch West Indian (0) | 0 | <0.01 |
| Haitian (73) | 73 | 0.06 |
| Jamaican (13) | 72 | 0.06 |
| Trinidadian/Tobagonian (0) | 42 | 0.03 |
| U.S. Virgin Islander (0) | 0 | <0.01 |
| West Indian (0) | 0 | <0.01 |
| Other West Indian (0) | 0 | <0.01 |
| Yugoslavian (0) | 42 | 0.03 |

| Hispanic Origin | Population | % |
|---|---|---|
| Hispanic or Latino (of any race) | 2,552 | 2.09 |
| Central American, ex. Mexican | 140 | 0.11 |
| Costa Rican | 8 | 0.01 |
| Guatemalan | 66 | 0.05 |
| Honduran | 17 | 0.01 |
| Nicaraguan | 4 | <0.01 |
| Panamanian | 18 | 0.01 |
| Salvadoran | 27 | 0.02 |
| Other Central American | 0 | <0.01 |
| Cuban | 65 | 0.05 |
| Dominican Republic | 97 | 0.08 |
| Mexican | 641 | 0.52 |
| Puerto Rican | 1,193 | 0.98 |
| South American | 155 | 0.13 |
| Argentinean | 19 | 0.02 |
| Bolivian | 3 | <0.01 |
| Chilean | 11 | 0.01 |
| Colombian | 49 | 0.04 |
| Ecuadorian | 37 | 0.03 |
| Paraguayan | 2 | <0.01 |
| Peruvian | 25 | 0.02 |
| Uruguayan | 2 | <0.01 |
| Venezuelan | 5 | <0.01 |
| Other South American | 2 | <0.01 |
| Other Hispanic or Latino | 261 | 0.21 |

| Race* | Population | % |
|---|---|---|
| African-American/Black (972) | 1,531 | 1.25 |
| Not Hispanic (862) | 1,367 | 1.12 |
| Hispanic (110) | 164 | 0.13 |
| American Indian/Alaska Native (520) | 1,200 | 0.98 |
| Not Hispanic (465) | 1,097 | 0.90 |
| Hispanic (55) | 103 | 0.08 |
| Alaska Athabascan (Ala. Nat.) (1) | 1 | <0.01 |
| Aleut (Alaska Native) (0) | 0 | <0.01 |
| Apache (1) | 9 | 0.01 |
| Arapaho (0) | 0 | <0.01 |
| Blackfeet (14) | 41 | 0.03 |
| Canadian/French Am. Ind. (18) | 26 | 0.02 |
| Central American Ind. (2) | 4 | <0.01 |
| Cherokee (19) | 77 | 0.06 |
| Cheyenne (2) | 5 | <0.01 |
| Chickasaw (1) | 2 | <0.01 |
| Chippewa (5) | 12 | 0.01 |
| Choctaw (2) | 6 | <0.01 |
| Colville (0) | 0 | <0.01 |

| Race* | Population | % |
|---|---|---|
| Comanche (0) | 0 | <0.01 |
| Cree (0) | 3 | <0.01 |
| Creek (1) | 2 | <0.01 |
| Crow (1) | 2 | <0.01 |
| Delaware (1) | 5 | <0.01 |
| Hopi (0) | 0 | <0.01 |
| Houma (0) | 0 | <0.01 |
| Inupiat (Alaska Native) (0) | 0 | <0.01 |
| Iroquois (212) | 430 | 0.35 |
| Kiowa (0) | 0 | <0.01 |
| Lumbee (0) | 0 | <0.01 |
| Menominee (0) | 0 | <0.01 |
| Mexican American Ind. (6) | 9 | 0.01 |
| Navajo (2) | 5 | <0.01 |
| Osage (0) | 0 | <0.01 |
| Ottawa (0) | 0 | <0.01 |
| Paiute (0) | 0 | <0.01 |
| Pima (0) | 0 | <0.01 |
| Potawatomi (0) | 0 | <0.01 |
| Pueblo (0) | 1 | <0.01 |
| Puget Sound Salish (0) | 0 | <0.01 |
| Seminole (0) | 2 | <0.01 |
| Shoshone (0) | 0 | <0.01 |
| Sioux (13) | 31 | 0.03 |
| South American Ind. (6) | 16 | 0.01 |
| Spanish American Ind. (2) | 2 | <0.01 |
| Tlingit-Haida (Alaska Native) (0) | 0 | <0.01 |
| Tohono O'Odham (0) | 0 | <0.01 |
| Tsimshian (Alaska Native) (0) | 0 | <0.01 |
| Ute (0) | 1 | <0.01 |
| Yakama (0) | 1 | <0.01 |
| Yaqui (0) | 0 | <0.01 |
| Yuman (0) | 0 | <0.01 |
| Yup'ik (Alaska Native) (0) | 0 | <0.01 |
| Asian (723) | 986 | 0.81 |
| Not Hispanic (709) | 947 | 0.78 |
| Hispanic (14) | 39 | 0.03 |
| Bangladeshi (2) | 2 | <0.01 |
| Bhutanese (0) | 0 | <0.01 |
| Burmese (1) | 1 | <0.01 |
| Cambodian (0) | 1 | <0.01 |
| Chinese, ex. Taiwanese (234) | 269 | 0.22 |
| Filipino (139) | 222 | 0.18 |
| Hmong (0) | 0 | <0.01 |
| Indian (100) | 137 | 0.11 |
| Indonesian (1) | 4 | <0.01 |
| Japanese (46) | 82 | 0.07 |
| Korean (104) | 134 | 0.11 |
| Laotian (0) | 0 | <0.01 |
| Malaysian (1) | 1 | <0.01 |
| Nepalese (0) | 0 | <0.01 |
| Pakistani (16) | 16 | 0.01 |
| Sri Lankan (4) | 4 | <0.01 |
| Taiwanese (1) | 6 | <0.01 |
| Thai (14) | 32 | 0.03 |
| Vietnamese (38) | 52 | 0.04 |
| Hawaii Native/Pacific Islander (16) | 65 | 0.05 |
| Not Hispanic (14) | 51 | 0.04 |
| Hispanic (2) | 14 | 0.01 |
| Fijian (0) | 0 | <0.01 |
| Guamanian/Chamorro (3) | 7 | 0.01 |
| Marshallese (0) | 0 | <0.01 |
| Native Hawaiian (5) | 18 | 0.01 |
| Samoan (0) | 4 | <0.01 |
| Tongan (0) | 0 | <0.01 |
| White (117,632) | 119,116 | 97.55 |
| Not Hispanic (116,091) | 117,378 | 96.13 |
| Hispanic (1,541) | 1,738 | 1.42 |

*Notes: † The Census 2010 population figure is used to calculate the percentages in the Hispanic Origin and Race categories. Ancestry percentages are based on the 2006-2010 American Community Survey population (not shown); ‡ Numbers in parentheses indicate the number of people reporting a single ancestry; * Numbers in parentheses indicate the number of persons reporting this race alone, not in combination with any other race; Please refer to the Explanation of Data for more information.*

## Otsego County

Population: 62,259

| Ancestry | Population | % |
|---|---|---|
| Afghan (0) | 0 | <0.01 |
| African, Sub-Saharan (131) | 151 | 0.24 |
| African (24) | 24 | 0.04 |
| Cape Verdean (0) | 0 | <0.01 |
| Ethiopian (0) | 0 | <0.01 |
| Ghanaian (0) | 0 | <0.01 |
| Kenyan (81) | 81 | 0.13 |
| Liberian (0) | 0 | <0.01 |
| Nigerian (0) | 0 | <0.01 |
| Senegalese (0) | 0 | <0.01 |
| Sierra Leonean (0) | 0 | <0.01 |
| Somalian (0) | 0 | <0.01 |
| South African (0) | 20 | 0.03 |
| Sudanese (0) | 0 | <0.01 |
| Ugandan (0) | 0 | <0.01 |
| Zimbabwean (26) | 26 | 0.04 |
| Other Sub-Saharan African (0) | 0 | <0.01 |
| Albanian (6) | 60 | 0.10 |
| Alsatian (0) | 0 | <0.01 |
| American (6,461) | 6,461 | 10.32 |
| Arab (110) | 207 | 0.33 |
| Arab (10) | 10 | 0.02 |
| Egyptian (0) | 0 | <0.01 |
| Iraqi (0) | 0 | <0.01 |
| Jordanian (0) | 0 | <0.01 |
| Lebanese (78) | 155 | 0.25 |
| Moroccan (0) | 0 | <0.01 |
| Palestinian (5) | 5 | 0.01 |
| Syrian (17) | 37 | 0.06 |
| Other Arab (0) | 0 | <0.01 |
| Armenian (59) | 62 | 0.10 |
| Assyrian/Chaldean/Syriac (0) | 0 | <0.01 |
| Australian (0) | 0 | <0.01 |
| Austrian (52) | 414 | 0.66 |
| Basque (0) | 0 | <0.01 |
| Belgian (0) | 33 | 0.05 |
| Brazilian (0) | 0 | <0.01 |
| British (163) | 234 | 0.37 |
| Bulgarian (0) | 0 | <0.01 |
| Cajun (0) | 0 | <0.01 |
| Canadian (100) | 297 | 0.47 |
| Carpatho Rusyn (0) | 0 | <0.01 |
| Celtic (0) | 5 | 0.01 |
| Croatian (27) | 82 | 0.13 |
| Cypriot (0) | 0 | <0.01 |
| Czech (31) | 230 | 0.37 |
| Czechoslovakian (31) | 37 | 0.06 |
| Danish (133) | 376 | 0.60 |
| Dutch (610) | 3,421 | 5.46 |
| Eastern European (109) | 157 | 0.25 |
| English (2,928) | 9,969 | 15.92 |
| Estonian (3) | 5 | 0.01 |
| European (511) | 543 | 0.87 |
| Finnish (32) | 94 | 0.15 |
| French, ex. Basque (345) | 3,084 | 4.93 |
| French Canadian (314) | 842 | 1.34 |
| German (2,872) | 13,660 | 21.82 |
| German Russian (0) | 0 | <0.01 |
| Greek (84) | 239 | 0.38 |
| Guyanese (12) | 12 | 0.02 |
| Hungarian (165) | 678 | 1.08 |
| Icelander (0) | 7 | 0.01 |
| Iranian (0) | 19 | 0.03 |
| Irish (3,032) | 11,787 | 18.83 |
| Israeli (13) | 13 | 0.02 |
| Italian (2,804) | 7,612 | 12.16 |
| Latvian (16) | 22 | 0.04 |
| Lithuanian (12) | 154 | 0.25 |
| Luxemburger (0) | 0 | <0.01 |
| Macedonian (0) | 0 | <0.01 |
| Maltese (0) | 0 | <0.01 |
| New Zealander (0) | 5 | 0.01 |
| Northern European (42) | 42 | 0.07 |
| Norwegian (243) | 784 | 1.25 |
| Pennsylvania German (79) | 144 | 0.23 |

| Ancestry | Population | % |
|---|---|---|
| Polish (784) | 2,833 | 4.53 |
| Portuguese (56) | 95 | 0.15 |
| Romanian (21) | 41 | 0.07 |
| Russian (299) | 1,047 | 1.67 |
| Scandinavian (51) | 115 | 0.18 |
| Scotch-Irish (366) | 1,232 | 1.97 |
| Scottish (492) | 2,493 | 3.98 |
| Serbian (11) | 15 | 0.02 |
| Slavic (55) | 118 | 0.19 |
| Slovak (78) | 143 | 0.23 |
| Slovene (57) | 146 | 0.23 |
| Soviet Union (0) | 0 | <0.01 |
| Swedish (153) | 1,004 | 1.60 |
| Swiss (30) | 206 | 0.33 |
| Turkish (0) | 0 | <0.01 |
| Ukrainian (116) | 249 | 0.40 |
| Welsh (237) | 1,116 | 1.78 |
| West Indian, ex. Hispanic (283) | 321 | 0.51 |
| Bahamian (0) | 0 | <0.01 |
| Barbadian (0) | 0 | <0.01 |
| Belizean (0) | 0 | <0.01 |
| Bermudan (0) | 0 | <0.01 |
| British West Indian (12) | 12 | 0.02 |
| Dutch West Indian (20) | 20 | 0.03 |
| Haitian (75) | 79 | 0.13 |
| Jamaican (160) | 194 | 0.31 |
| Trinidadian/Tobagonian (15) | 15 | 0.02 |
| U.S. Virgin Islander (0) | 0 | <0.01 |
| West Indian (1) | 1 | <0.01 |
| Other West Indian (0) | 0 | <0.01 |
| Yugoslavian (36) | 107 | 0.17 |

| Hispanic Origin | Population | % |
|---|---|---|
| Hispanic or Latino (of any race) | 1,921 | 3.09 |
| Central American, ex. Mexican | 122 | 0.20 |
| Costa Rican | 7 | 0.01 |
| Guatemalan | 29 | 0.05 |
| Honduran | 12 | 0.02 |
| Nicaraguan | 2 | <0.01 |
| Panamanian | 18 | 0.03 |
| Salvadoran | 53 | 0.09 |
| Other Central American | 1 | <0.01 |
| Cuban | 90 | 0.14 |
| Dominican Republic | 86 | 0.14 |
| Mexican | 306 | 0.49 |
| Puerto Rican | 798 | 1.28 |
| South American | 216 | 0.35 |
| Argentinean | 14 | 0.02 |
| Bolivian | 6 | 0.01 |
| Chilean | 22 | 0.04 |
| Colombian | 67 | 0.11 |
| Ecuadorian | 45 | 0.07 |
| Paraguayan | 1 | <0.01 |
| Peruvian | 42 | 0.07 |
| Uruguayan | 11 | 0.02 |
| Venezuelan | 6 | 0.01 |
| Other South American | 2 | <0.01 |
| Other Hispanic or Latino | 303 | 0.49 |

| Race* | Population | % |
|---|---|---|
| African-American/Black (1,066) | 1,506 | 2.42 |
| Not Hispanic (958) | 1,309 | 2.10 |
| Hispanic (108) | 197 | 0.32 |
| American Indian/Alaska Native (121) | 497 | 0.80 |
| Not Hispanic (103) | 429 | 0.69 |
| Hispanic (18) | 68 | 0.11 |
| Alaska Athabascan (Ala. Nat.) (0) | 0 | <0.01 |
| Aleut (Alaska Native) (0) | 0 | <0.01 |
| Apache (0) | 2 | <0.01 |
| Arapaho (0) | 0 | <0.01 |
| Blackfeet (1) | 16 | 0.03 |
| Canadian/French Am. Ind. (1) | 3 | <0.01 |
| Central American Ind. (0) | 0 | <0.01 |
| Cherokee (13) | 57 | 0.09 |
| Cheyenne (0) | 0 | <0.01 |
| Chickasaw (0) | 2 | <0.01 |
| Chippewa (3) | 11 | 0.02 |
| Choctaw (1) | 11 | 0.02 |
| Colville (0) | 0 | <0.01 |

| Race* | Population | % |
|---|---|---|
| Comanche (0) | 0 | <0.01 |
| Cree (0) | 0 | <0.01 |
| Creek (0) | 1 | <0.01 |
| Crow (0) | 0 | <0.01 |
| Delaware (8) | 13 | 0.02 |
| Hopi (0) | 1 | <0.01 |
| Houma (0) | 0 | <0.01 |
| Inupiat (Alaska Native) (0) | 1 | <0.01 |
| Iroquois (14) | 63 | 0.10 |
| Kiowa (0) | 2 | <0.01 |
| Lumbee (1) | 1 | <0.01 |
| Menominee (0) | 0 | <0.01 |
| Mexican American Ind. (1) | 6 | 0.01 |
| Navajo (2) | 3 | <0.01 |
| Osage (0) | 0 | <0.01 |
| Ottawa (0) | 0 | <0.01 |
| Paiute (0) | 0 | <0.01 |
| Pima (0) | 0 | <0.01 |
| Potawatomi (0) | 0 | <0.01 |
| Pueblo (0) | 0 | <0.01 |
| Puget Sound Salish (0) | 0 | <0.01 |
| Seminole (0) | 0 | <0.01 |
| Shoshone (0) | 0 | <0.01 |
| Sioux (2) | 10 | 0.02 |
| South American Ind. (3) | 8 | 0.01 |
| Spanish American Ind. (1) | 2 | <0.01 |
| Tlingit-Haida (Alaska Native) (0) | 0 | <0.01 |
| Tohono O'Odham (0) | 0 | <0.01 |
| Tsimshian (Alaska Native) (0) | 0 | <0.01 |
| Ute (0) | 0 | <0.01 |
| Yakama (0) | 0 | <0.01 |
| Yaqui (0) | 0 | <0.01 |
| Yuman (0) | 0 | <0.01 |
| Yup'ik (Alaska Native) (0) | 0 | <0.01 |
| Asian (674) | 894 | 1.44 |
| Not Hispanic (660) | 856 | 1.37 |
| Hispanic (14) | 38 | 0.06 |
| Bangladeshi (0) | 0 | <0.01 |
| Bhutanese (0) | 0 | <0.01 |
| Burmese (0) | 0 | <0.01 |
| Cambodian (0) | 0 | <0.01 |
| Chinese, ex. Taiwanese (196) | 240 | 0.39 |
| Filipino (59) | 122 | 0.20 |
| Hmong (0) | 0 | <0.01 |
| Indian (134) | 162 | 0.26 |
| Indonesian (1) | 5 | 0.01 |
| Japanese (56) | 87 | 0.14 |
| Korean (120) | 159 | 0.26 |
| Laotian (1) | 1 | <0.01 |
| Malaysian (0) | 0 | <0.01 |
| Nepalese (5) | 5 | 0.01 |
| Pakistani (31) | 34 | 0.05 |
| Sri Lankan (3) | 3 | <0.01 |
| Taiwanese (12) | 16 | 0.03 |
| Thai (15) | 21 | 0.03 |
| Vietnamese (15) | 21 | 0.03 |
| Hawaii Native/Pacific Islander (18) | 50 | 0.08 |
| Not Hispanic (16) | 40 | 0.06 |
| Hispanic (2) | 10 | 0.02 |
| Fijian (1) | 1 | <0.01 |
| Guamanian/Chamorro (2) | 3 | <0.01 |
| Marshallese (0) | 0 | <0.01 |
| Native Hawaiian (7) | 18 | 0.03 |
| Samoan (4) | 5 | 0.01 |
| Tongan (0) | 0 | <0.01 |
| White (58,935) | 59,860 | 96.15 |
| Not Hispanic (57,734) | 58,502 | 93.97 |
| Hispanic (1,201) | 1,358 | 2.18 |

Notes: † The Census 2010 population figure is used to calculate the percentages in the Hispanic Origin and Race categories. Ancestry percentages are based on the 2006-2010 American Community Survey population (not shown); ‡ Numbers in parentheses indicate the number of people reporting a single ancestry; * Numbers in parentheses indicate the number of persons reporting this race alone, not in combination with any other race; Please refer to the Explanation of Data for more information.

## Putnam County

Population: 99,710

| Ancestry | Population | % |
|---|---|---|
| Afghan (0) | 0 | <0.01 |
| African, Sub-Saharan (180) | 263 | 0.26 |
| African (90) | 137 | 0.14 |
| Cape Verdean (0) | 0 | <0.01 |
| Ethiopian (26) | 26 | 0.03 |
| Ghanaian (0) | 0 | <0.01 |
| Kenyan (0) | 0 | <0.01 |
| Liberian (0) | 0 | <0.01 |
| Nigerian (0) | 20 | 0.02 |
| Senegalese (64) | 64 | 0.06 |
| Sierra Leonean (0) | 0 | <0.01 |
| Somalian (0) | 0 | <0.01 |
| South African (0) | 16 | 0.02 |
| Sudanese (0) | 0 | <0.01 |
| Ugandan (0) | 0 | <0.01 |
| Zimbabwean (0) | 0 | <0.01 |
| Other Sub-Saharan African (0) | 0 | <0.01 |
| Albanian (924) | 980 | 0.98 |
| Alsatian (0) | 0 | <0.01 |
| American (2,598) | 2,598 | 2.61 |
| Arab (212) | 448 | 0.45 |
| Arab (0) | 61 | 0.06 |
| Egyptian (103) | 117 | 0.12 |
| Iraqi (0) | 0 | <0.01 |
| Jordanian (71) | 71 | 0.07 |
| Lebanese (38) | 138 | 0.14 |
| Moroccan (0) | 0 | <0.01 |
| Palestinian (0) | 21 | 0.02 |
| Syrian (0) | 33 | 0.03 |
| Other Arab (0) | 7 | 0.01 |
| Armenian (10) | 42 | 0.04 |
| Assyrian/Chaldean/Syriac (0) | 0 | <0.01 |
| Australian (54) | 144 | 0.14 |
| Austrian (174) | 879 | 0.88 |
| Basque (0) | 14 | 0.01 |
| Belgian (21) | 135 | 0.14 |
| Brazilian (49) | 143 | 0.14 |
| British (185) | 301 | 0.30 |
| Bulgarian (35) | 35 | 0.04 |
| Cajun (0) | 0 | <0.01 |
| Canadian (191) | 392 | 0.39 |
| Carpatho Rusyn (0) | 0 | <0.01 |
| Celtic (0) | 6 | 0.01 |
| Croatian (140) | 200 | 0.20 |
| Cypriot (0) | 0 | <0.01 |
| Czech (119) | 541 | 0.54 |
| Czechoslovakian (134) | 263 | 0.26 |
| Danish (114) | 298 | 0.30 |
| Dutch (288) | 1,529 | 1.54 |
| Eastern European (154) | 186 | 0.19 |
| English (1,140) | 7,439 | 7.47 |
| Estonian (0) | 64 | 0.06 |
| European (710) | 787 | 0.79 |
| Finnish (82) | 197 | 0.20 |
| French, ex. Basque (282) | 2,532 | 2.54 |
| French Canadian (251) | 680 | 0.68 |
| German (2,967) | 17,556 | 17.64 |
| German Russian (0) | 0 | <0.01 |
| Greek (382) | 1,015 | 1.02 |
| Guyanese (0) | 0 | <0.01 |
| Hungarian (311) | 1,309 | 1.31 |
| Icelander (0) | 0 | <0.01 |
| Iranian (125) | 125 | 0.13 |
| Irish (8,053) | 27,534 | 27.66 |
| Israeli (0) | 32 | 0.03 |
| Italian (14,946) | 31,433 | 31.58 |
| Latvian (9) | 32 | 0.03 |
| Lithuanian (57) | 546 | 0.55 |
| Luxemburger (0) | 0 | <0.01 |
| Macedonian (0) | 0 | <0.01 |
| Maltese (38) | 50 | 0.05 |
| New Zealander (0) | 0 | <0.01 |
| Northern European (85) | 125 | 0.13 |
| Norwegian (159) | 677 | 0.68 |
| Pennsylvania German (11) | 11 | 0.01 |

| | Population | % |
|---|---|---|
| Polish (1,827) | 5,597 | 5.62 |
| Portuguese (415) | 830 | 0.83 |
| Romanian (115) | 324 | 0.33 |
| Russian (793) | 2,712 | 2.72 |
| Scandinavian (107) | 193 | 0.19 |
| Scotch-Irish (506) | 1,769 | 1.78 |
| Scottish (297) | 1,829 | 1.84 |
| Serbian (0) | 13 | 0.01 |
| Slavic (27) | 66 | 0.07 |
| Slovak (183) | 439 | 0.44 |
| Slovene (13) | 45 | 0.05 |
| Soviet Union (0) | 0 | <0.01 |
| Swedish (133) | 1,061 | 1.07 |
| Swiss (16) | 140 | 0.14 |
| Turkish (16) | 31 | 0.03 |
| Ukrainian (368) | 959 | 0.96 |
| Welsh (73) | 490 | 0.49 |
| West Indian, ex. Hispanic (280) | 467 | 0.47 |
| Bahamian (0) | 0 | <0.01 |
| Barbadian (0) | 0 | <0.01 |
| Belizean (0) | 0 | <0.01 |
| Bermudan (0) | 0 | <0.01 |
| British West Indian (0) | 0 | <0.01 |
| Dutch West Indian (0) | 0 | <0.01 |
| Haitian (50) | 84 | 0.08 |
| Jamaican (56) | 160 | 0.16 |
| Trinidadian/Tobagonian (165) | 205 | 0.21 |
| U.S. Virgin Islander (0) | 0 | <0.01 |
| West Indian (9) | 18 | 0.02 |
| Other West Indian (0) | 0 | <0.01 |
| Yugoslavian (99) | 198 | 0.20 |

| Hispanic Origin | Population | % |
|---|---|---|
| Hispanic or Latino (of any race) | 11,661 | 11.69 |
| Central American, ex. Mexican | 2,565 | 2.57 |
| Costa Rican | 62 | 0.06 |
| Guatemalan | 1,909 | 1.91 |
| Honduran | 125 | 0.13 |
| Nicaraguan | 43 | 0.04 |
| Panamanian | 43 | 0.04 |
| Salvadoran | 374 | 0.38 |
| Other Central American | 9 | 0.01 |
| Cuban | 349 | 0.35 |
| Dominican Republic | 605 | 0.61 |
| Mexican | 1,023 | 1.03 |
| Puerto Rican | 3,850 | 3.86 |
| South American | 2,106 | 2.11 |
| Argentinean | 158 | 0.16 |
| Bolivian | 34 | 0.03 |
| Chilean | 89 | 0.09 |
| Colombian | 457 | 0.46 |
| Ecuadorian | 897 | 0.90 |
| Paraguayan | 53 | 0.05 |
| Peruvian | 301 | 0.30 |
| Uruguayan | 63 | 0.06 |
| Venezuelan | 43 | 0.04 |
| Other South American | 11 | 0.01 |
| Other Hispanic or Latino | 1,163 | 1.17 |

| Race* | Population | % |
|---|---|---|
| African-American/Black (2,350) | 2,967 | 2.98 |
| Not Hispanic (2,047) | 2,437 | 2.44 |
| Hispanic (303) | 530 | 0.53 |
| American Indian/Alaska Native (175) | 607 | 0.61 |
| Not Hispanic (121) | 452 | 0.45 |
| Hispanic (54) | 155 | 0.16 |
| Alaska Athabascan (Ala. Nat.) (0) | 0 | <0.01 |
| Aleut (Alaska Native) (1) | 1 | <0.01 |
| Apache (1) | 3 | <0.01 |
| Arapaho (2) | 2 | <0.01 |
| Blackfeet (2) | 31 | 0.03 |
| Canadian/French Am. Ind. (6) | 12 | 0.01 |
| Central American Ind. (14) | 19 | 0.02 |
| Cherokee (7) | 75 | 0.08 |
| Cheyenne (0) | 6 | 0.01 |
| Chickasaw (0) | 0 | <0.01 |
| Chippewa (2) | 10 | 0.01 |
| Choctaw (2) | 9 | 0.01 |
| Colville (0) | 0 | <0.01 |

| | Population | % |
|---|---|---|
| Comanche (0) | 0 | <0.01 |
| Cree (0) | 0 | <0.01 |
| Creek (1) | 5 | 0.01 |
| Crow (0) | 0 | <0.01 |
| Delaware (0) | 0 | <0.01 |
| Hopi (0) | 0 | <0.01 |
| Houma (0) | 0 | <0.01 |
| Inupiat (Alaska Native) (1) | 1 | <0.01 |
| Iroquois (18) | 37 | 0.04 |
| Kiowa (0) | 1 | <0.01 |
| Lumbee (0) | 0 | <0.01 |
| Menominee (0) | 0 | <0.01 |
| Mexican American Ind. (7) | 25 | 0.03 |
| Navajo (1) | 1 | <0.01 |
| Osage (0) | 0 | <0.01 |
| Ottawa (0) | 0 | <0.01 |
| Paiute (0) | 0 | <0.01 |
| Pima (0) | 0 | <0.01 |
| Potawatomi (0) | 1 | <0.01 |
| Pueblo (0) | 0 | <0.01 |
| Puget Sound Salish (0) | 0 | <0.01 |
| Seminole (0) | 8 | 0.01 |
| Shoshone (0) | 0 | <0.01 |
| Sioux (4) | 16 | 0.02 |
| South American Ind. (13) | 25 | 0.03 |
| Spanish American Ind. (2) | 3 | <0.01 |
| Tlingit-Haida (Alaska Native) (0) | 0 | <0.01 |
| Tohono O'Odham (0) | 0 | <0.01 |
| Tsimshian (Alaska Native) (0) | 0 | <0.01 |
| Ute (0) | 0 | <0.01 |
| Yakama (0) | 0 | <0.01 |
| Yaqui (0) | 0 | <0.01 |
| Yuman (1) | 1 | <0.01 |
| Yup'ik (Alaska Native) (0) | 0 | <0.01 |
| Asian (1,882) | 2,442 | 2.45 |
| Not Hispanic (1,832) | 2,324 | 2.33 |
| Hispanic (50) | 118 | 0.12 |
| Bangladeshi (12) | 13 | 0.01 |
| Bhutanese (0) | 0 | <0.01 |
| Burmese (1) | 1 | <0.01 |
| Cambodian (6) | 7 | 0.01 |
| Chinese, ex. Taiwanese (530) | 691 | 0.69 |
| Filipino (259) | 377 | 0.38 |
| Hmong (0) | 0 | <0.01 |
| Indian (573) | 666 | 0.67 |
| Indonesian (0) | 3 | <0.01 |
| Japanese (122) | 189 | 0.19 |
| Korean (184) | 228 | 0.23 |
| Laotian (1) | 5 | 0.01 |
| Malaysian (6) | 12 | 0.01 |
| Nepalese (13) | 16 | 0.02 |
| Pakistani (35) | 45 | 0.05 |
| Sri Lankan (4) | 6 | 0.01 |
| Taiwanese (11) | 15 | 0.02 |
| Thai (21) | 33 | 0.03 |
| Vietnamese (38) | 55 | 0.06 |
| Hawaii Native/Pacific Islander (35) | 118 | 0.12 |
| Not Hispanic (14) | 61 | 0.06 |
| Hispanic (21) | 57 | 0.06 |
| Fijian (0) | 0 | <0.01 |
| Guamanian/Chamorro (19) | 40 | 0.04 |
| Marshallese (0) | 0 | <0.01 |
| Native Hawaiian (2) | 18 | 0.02 |
| Samoan (3) | 5 | 0.01 |
| Tongan (0) | 0 | <0.01 |
| White (90,470) | 92,223 | 92.49 |
| Not Hispanic (82,709) | 83,747 | 83.99 |
| Hispanic (7,761) | 8,476 | 8.50 |

Notes: † The Census 2010 population figure is used to calculate the percentages in the Hispanic Origin and Race categories. Ancestry percentages are based on the 2006-2010 American Community Survey population (not shown); ‡ Numbers in parentheses indicate the number of people reporting a single ancestry; * Numbers in parentheses indicate the number of persons reporting this race alone, not in combination with any other race; Please refer to the Explanation of Data for more information.

## Queens County

Population: 2,230,722

| Ancestry | Population | % |
|---|---|---|
| Afghan (5,842) | 6,027 | 0.27 |
| African, Sub-Saharan (19,754) | 25,166 | 1.14 |
| African (9,764) | 14,083 | 0.64 |
| Cape Verdean (46) | 117 | 0.01 |
| Ethiopian (478) | 505 | 0.02 |
| Ghanaian (1,269) | 1,326 | 0.06 |
| Kenyan (96) | 96 | <0.01 |
| Liberian (297) | 381 | 0.02 |
| Nigerian (5,989) | 6,304 | 0.29 |
| Senegalese (84) | 84 | <0.01 |
| Sierra Leonean (127) | 127 | 0.01 |
| Somalian (52) | 98 | <0.01 |
| South African (230) | 356 | 0.02 |
| Sudanese (161) | 286 | 0.01 |
| Ugandan (65) | 77 | <0.01 |
| Zimbabwean (107) | 107 | <0.01 |
| Other Sub-Saharan African (989) | 1,219 | 0.06 |
| Albanian (6,264) | 6,624 | 0.30 |
| Alsatian (26) | 37 | <0.01 |
| American (45,604) | 45,604 | 2.07 |
| Arab (16,286) | 19,669 | 0.89 |
| Arab (1,921) | 2,283 | 0.10 |
| Egyptian (5,905) | 6,551 | 0.30 |
| Iraqi (224) | 315 | 0.01 |
| Jordanian (260) | 307 | 0.01 |
| Lebanese (1,548) | 2,228 | 0.10 |
| Moroccan (2,945) | 3,459 | 0.16 |
| Palestinian (582) | 638 | 0.03 |
| Syrian (193) | 420 | 0.02 |
| Other Arab (2,708) | 3,468 | 0.16 |
| Armenian (4,083) | 4,658 | 0.21 |
| Assyrian/Chaldean/Syriac (13) | 13 | <0.01 |
| Australian (163) | 285 | 0.01 |
| Austrian (2,702) | 7,523 | 0.34 |
| Basque (29) | 159 | 0.01 |
| Belgian (289) | 593 | 0.03 |
| Brazilian (4,871) | 6,175 | 0.28 |
| British (1,346) | 2,457 | 0.11 |
| Bulgarian (1,928) | 2,090 | 0.10 |
| Cajun (0) | 33 | <0.01 |
| Canadian (604) | 1,308 | 0.06 |
| Carpatho Rusyn (0) | 9 | <0.01 |
| Celtic (92) | 169 | 0.01 |
| Croatian (5,621) | 7,054 | 0.32 |
| Cypriot (556) | 644 | 0.03 |
| Czech (1,116) | 3,464 | 0.16 |
| Czechoslovakian (816) | 1,467 | 0.07 |
| Danish (171) | 792 | 0.04 |
| Dutch (727) | 3,516 | 0.16 |
| Eastern European (4,442) | 4,673 | 0.21 |
| English (4,389) | 20,267 | 0.92 |
| Estonian (164) | 198 | 0.01 |
| European (5,335) | 6,584 | 0.30 |
| Finnish (269) | 693 | 0.03 |
| French, ex. Basque (3,945) | 12,532 | 0.57 |
| French Canadian (552) | 2,020 | 0.09 |
| German (20,566) | 70,399 | 3.20 |
| German Russian (33) | 78 | <0.01 |
| Greek (35,368) | 41,654 | 1.89 |
| Guyanese (47,132) | 53,961 | 2.45 |
| Hungarian (4,718) | 9,470 | 0.43 |
| Icelander (10) | 26 | <0.01 |
| Iranian (3,162) | 3,707 | 0.17 |
| Irish (43,033) | 105,348 | 4.79 |
| Israeli (3,355) | 4,164 | 0.19 |
| Italian (104,251) | 159,812 | 7.27 |
| Latvian (342) | 568 | 0.03 |
| Lithuanian (1,463) | 3,131 | 0.14 |
| Luxemburger (0) | 13 | <0.01 |
| Macedonian (938) | 1,109 | 0.05 |
| Maltese (952) | 1,565 | 0.07 |
| New Zealander (0) | 16 | <0.01 |
| Northern European (370) | 512 | 0.02 |
| Norwegian (670) | 2,559 | 0.12 |
| Pennsylvania German (9) | 38 | <0.01 |

| Ancestry (cont.) | Population | % |
|---|---|---|
| Polish (37,726) | 59,757 | 2.72 |
| Portuguese (2,784) | 4,727 | 0.21 |
| Romanian (9,232) | 11,686 | 0.53 |
| Russian (29,779) | 44,676 | 2.03 |
| Scandinavian (131) | 545 | 0.02 |
| Scotch-Irish (2,079) | 4,602 | 0.21 |
| Scottish (1,567) | 5,718 | 0.26 |
| Serbian (2,176) | 2,438 | 0.11 |
| Slavic (370) | 765 | 0.03 |
| Slovak (1,161) | 1,882 | 0.09 |
| Slovene (171) | 468 | 0.02 |
| Soviet Union (12) | 71 | <0.01 |
| Swedish (511) | 2,862 | 0.13 |
| Swiss (381) | 1,260 | 0.06 |
| Turkish (3,054) | 3,767 | 0.17 |
| Ukrainian (5,770) | 8,375 | 0.38 |
| Welsh (201) | 1,666 | 0.08 |
| West Indian, ex. Hispanic (131,014) | 147,460 | 6.71 |
| Bahamian (134) | 185 | 0.01 |
| Barbadian (4,074) | 5,021 | 0.23 |
| Belizean (1,106) | 1,344 | 0.06 |
| Bermudan (142) | 177 | 0.01 |
| British West Indian (3,765) | 4,689 | 0.21 |
| Dutch West Indian (122) | 206 | 0.01 |
| Haitian (35,439) | 38,368 | 1.74 |
| Jamaican (55,278) | 59,999 | 2.73 |
| Trinidadian/Tobagonian (16,227) | 19,255 | 0.88 |
| U.S. Virgin Islander (234) | 364 | 0.02 |
| West Indian (14,052) | 17,400 | 0.79 |
| Other West Indian (441) | 452 | 0.02 |
| Yugoslavian (3,824) | 4,516 | 0.21 |

| Hispanic Origin | Population | % |
|---|---|---|
| Hispanic or Latino (of any race) | 613,750 | 27.51 |
| Central American, ex. Mexican | 52,509 | 2.35 |
| Costa Rican | 1,749 | 0.08 |
| Guatemalan | 13,700 | 0.61 |
| Honduran | 8,546 | 0.38 |
| Nicaraguan | 2,842 | 0.13 |
| Panamanian | 3,977 | 0.18 |
| Salvadoran | 21,342 | 0.96 |
| Other Central American | 353 | 0.02 |
| Cuban | 11,020 | 0.49 |
| Dominican Republic | 88,061 | 3.95 |
| Mexican | 92,835 | 4.16 |
| Puerto Rican | 102,881 | 4.61 |
| South American | 214,022 | 9.59 |
| Argentinean | 6,345 | 0.28 |
| Bolivian | 3,268 | 0.15 |
| Chilean | 3,184 | 0.14 |
| Colombian | 70,290 | 3.15 |
| Ecuadorian | 98,512 | 4.42 |
| Paraguayan | 2,775 | 0.12 |
| Peruvian | 22,886 | 1.03 |
| Uruguayan | 1,743 | 0.08 |
| Venezuelan | 3,580 | 0.16 |
| Other South American | 1,439 | 0.06 |
| Other Hispanic or Latino | 52,422 | 2.35 |

| Race* | Population | % |
|---|---|---|
| African-American/Black (426,683) | 462,351 | 20.73 |
| Not Hispanic (395,881) | 419,695 | 18.81 |
| Hispanic (30,802) | 42,656 | 1.91 |
| American Indian/Alaska Native (15,364) | 30,033 | 1.35 |
| Not Hispanic (6,490) | 15,412 | 0.69 |
| Hispanic (8,874) | 14,621 | 0.66 |
| Alaska Athabascan (Ala. Nat.) (2) | 3 | <0.01 |
| Aleut (Alaska Native) (4) | 6 | <0.01 |
| Apache (15) | 53 | <0.01 |
| Arapaho (0) | 2 | <0.01 |
| Blackfeet (45) | 342 | 0.02 |
| Canadian/French Am. Ind. (20) | 38 | <0.01 |
| Central American Ind. (419) | 733 | 0.03 |
| Cherokee (267) | 1,425 | 0.06 |
| Cheyenne (13) | 20 | <0.01 |
| Chickasaw (9) | 21 | <0.01 |
| Chippewa (14) | 37 | <0.01 |
| Choctaw (16) | 68 | <0.01 |
| Colville (1) | 1 | <0.01 |

| Race* (cont.) | Population | % |
|---|---|---|
| Comanche (3) | 6 | <0.01 |
| Cree (6) | 24 | <0.01 |
| Creek (23) | 73 | <0.01 |
| Crow (1) | 4 | <0.01 |
| Delaware (14) | 35 | <0.01 |
| Hopi (1) | 15 | <0.01 |
| Houma (0) | 4 | <0.01 |
| Inupiat (Alaska Native) (6) | 13 | <0.01 |
| Iroquois (140) | 308 | 0.01 |
| Kiowa (0) | 0 | <0.01 |
| Lumbee (7) | 30 | <0.01 |
| Menominee (0) | 0 | <0.01 |
| Mexican American Ind. (1,270) | 1,640 | 0.07 |
| Navajo (13) | 37 | <0.01 |
| Osage (0) | 5 | <0.01 |
| Ottawa (0) | 2 | <0.01 |
| Paiute (3) | 4 | <0.01 |
| Pima (0) | 0 | <0.01 |
| Potawatomi (6) | 7 | <0.01 |
| Pueblo (102) | 161 | 0.01 |
| Puget Sound Salish (2) | 5 | <0.01 |
| Seminole (15) | 79 | <0.01 |
| Shoshone (0) | 6 | <0.01 |
| Sioux (35) | 104 | <0.01 |
| South American Ind. (1,281) | 2,448 | 0.11 |
| Spanish American Ind. (468) | 659 | 0.03 |
| Tlingit-Haida (Alaska Native) (8) | 20 | <0.01 |
| Tohono O'Odham (4) | 6 | <0.01 |
| Tsimshian (Alaska Native) (0) | 1 | <0.01 |
| Ute (4) | 5 | <0.01 |
| Yakama (0) | 0 | <0.01 |
| Yaqui (3) | 7 | <0.01 |
| Yuman (2) | 5 | <0.01 |
| Yup'ik (Alaska Native) (1) | 1 | <0.01 |
| Asian (511,787) | 552,867 | 24.78 |
| Not Hispanic (508,334) | 545,389 | 24.45 |
| Hispanic (3,453) | 7,478 | 0.34 |
| Bangladeshi (33,152) | 38,341 | 1.72 |
| Bhutanese (240) | 250 | 0.01 |
| Burmese (2,132) | 2,344 | 0.11 |
| Cambodian (230) | 303 | 0.01 |
| Chinese, ex. Taiwanese (191,693) | 200,714 | 9.00 |
| Filipino (38,163) | 41,773 | 1.87 |
| Hmong (24) | 30 | <0.01 |
| Indian (117,550) | 141,147 | 6.33 |
| Indonesian (2,860) | 3,386 | 0.15 |
| Japanese (6,375) | 7,790 | 0.35 |
| Korean (64,107) | 66,124 | 2.96 |
| Laotian (137) | 210 | 0.01 |
| Malaysian (1,029) | 1,620 | 0.07 |
| Nepalese (4,930) | 5,319 | 0.24 |
| Pakistani (16,215) | 18,084 | 0.81 |
| Sri Lankan (1,293) | 1,536 | 0.07 |
| Taiwanese (7,776) | 8,962 | 0.40 |
| Thai (3,677) | 4,124 | 0.18 |
| Vietnamese (3,566) | 4,322 | 0.19 |
| Hawaii Native/Pacific Islander (1,530) | 7,691 | 0.34 |
| Not Hispanic (1,094) | 5,685 | 0.25 |
| Hispanic (436) | 2,006 | 0.09 |
| Fijian (36) | 76 | <0.01 |
| Guamanian/Chamorro (337) | 483 | 0.02 |
| Marshallese (0) | 0 | <0.01 |
| Native Hawaiian (191) | 486 | 0.02 |
| Samoan (62) | 179 | 0.01 |
| Tongan (7) | 14 | <0.01 |
| White (886,053) | 941,608 | 42.21 |
| Not Hispanic (616,727) | 638,051 | 28.60 |
| Hispanic (269,326) | 303,557 | 13.61 |

Notes: † The Census 2010 population figure is used to calculate the percentages in the Hispanic Origin and Race categories. Ancestry percentages are based on the 2006-2010 American Community Survey population (not shown); ‡ Numbers in parentheses indicate the number of people reporting a single ancestry; * Numbers in parentheses indicate the number of persons reporting this race alone, not in combination with any other race; Please refer to the Explanation of Data for more information.

## Rensselaer County

Population: 159,429

| Ancestry | Population | % |
|---|---|---|
| Afghan (0) | 0 | <0.01 |
| African, Sub-Saharan (697) | 883 | 0.56 |
| African (405) | 565 | 0.36 |
| Cape Verdean (0) | 11 | 0.01 |
| Ethiopian (0) | 0 | <0.01 |
| Ghanaian (103) | 103 | 0.06 |
| Kenyan (0) | 0 | <0.01 |
| Liberian (0) | 0 | <0.01 |
| Nigerian (8) | 8 | 0.01 |
| Senegalese (0) | 0 | <0.01 |
| Sierra Leonean (0) | 0 | <0.01 |
| Somalian (0) | 0 | <0.01 |
| South African (0) | 0 | <0.01 |
| Sudanese (28) | 28 | 0.02 |
| Ugandan (0) | 0 | <0.01 |
| Zimbabwean (0) | 0 | <0.01 |
| Other Sub-Saharan African (153) | 168 | 0.11 |
| Albanian (80) | 82 | 0.05 |
| Alsatian (13) | 13 | 0.01 |
| American (6,888) | 6,888 | 4.34 |
| Arab (537) | 1,052 | 0.66 |
| Arab (72) | 91 | 0.06 |
| Egyptian (90) | 210 | 0.13 |
| Iraqi (0) | 0 | <0.01 |
| Jordanian (0) | 0 | <0.01 |
| Lebanese (284) | 572 | 0.36 |
| Moroccan (0) | 0 | <0.01 |
| Palestinian (0) | 0 | <0.01 |
| Syrian (16) | 65 | 0.04 |
| Other Arab (75) | 114 | 0.07 |
| Armenian (412) | 992 | 0.63 |
| Assyrian/Chaldean/Syriac (0) | 0 | <0.01 |
| Australian (17) | 17 | 0.01 |
| Austrian (117) | 580 | 0.37 |
| Basque (0) | 0 | <0.01 |
| Belgian (0) | 125 | 0.08 |
| Brazilian (126) | 143 | 0.09 |
| British (258) | 500 | 0.32 |
| Bulgarian (0) | 0 | <0.01 |
| Cajun (0) | 0 | <0.01 |
| Canadian (317) | 787 | 0.50 |
| Carpatho Rusyn (0) | 0 | <0.01 |
| Celtic (0) | 40 | 0.03 |
| Croatian (89) | 113 | 0.07 |
| Cypriot (0) | 0 | <0.01 |
| Czech (115) | 607 | 0.38 |
| Czechoslovakian (116) | 305 | 0.19 |
| Danish (172) | 977 | 0.62 |
| Dutch (850) | 7,465 | 4.71 |
| Eastern European (126) | 171 | 0.11 |
| English (3,787) | 18,308 | 11.54 |
| Estonian (15) | 32 | 0.02 |
| European (1,054) | 1,508 | 0.95 |
| Finnish (32) | 195 | 0.12 |
| French, ex. Basque (2,073) | 16,113 | 10.16 |
| French Canadian (1,505) | 4,489 | 2.83 |
| German (6,342) | 31,702 | 19.98 |
| German Russian (0) | 65 | 0.04 |
| Greek (301) | 959 | 0.60 |
| Guyanese (138) | 217 | 0.14 |
| Hungarian (161) | 744 | 0.47 |
| Icelander (0) | 0 | <0.01 |
| Iranian (57) | 57 | 0.04 |
| Irish (11,871) | 43,414 | 27.37 |
| Israeli (13) | 13 | 0.01 |
| Italian (7,939) | 24,089 | 15.19 |
| Latvian (29) | 77 | 0.05 |
| Lithuanian (214) | 1,079 | 0.68 |
| Luxemburger (0) | 0 | <0.01 |
| Macedonian (0) | 0 | <0.01 |
| Maltese (0) | 3 | <0.01 |
| New Zealander (0) | 0 | <0.01 |
| Northern European (88) | 88 | 0.06 |
| Norwegian (140) | 672 | 0.42 |
| Pennsylvania German (40) | 53 | 0.03 |

| Ancestry | Population | % |
|---|---|---|
| Polish (2,632) | 10,494 | 6.62 |
| Portuguese (135) | 465 | 0.29 |
| Romanian (11) | 88 | 0.06 |
| Russian (484) | 1,724 | 1.09 |
| Scandinavian (41) | 180 | 0.11 |
| Scotch-Irish (754) | 2,400 | 1.51 |
| Scottish (872) | 3,489 | 2.20 |
| Serbian (0) | 10 | 0.01 |
| Slavic (18) | 107 | 0.07 |
| Slovak (44) | 188 | 0.12 |
| Slovene (8) | 23 | 0.01 |
| Soviet Union (0) | 0 | <0.01 |
| Swedish (342) | 1,747 | 1.10 |
| Swiss (37) | 467 | 0.29 |
| Turkish (170) | 223 | 0.14 |
| Ukrainian (746) | 2,107 | 1.33 |
| Welsh (289) | 1,378 | 0.87 |
| West Indian, ex. Hispanic (954) | 1,304 | 0.82 |
| Bahamian (0) | 0 | <0.01 |
| Barbadian (15) | 55 | 0.03 |
| Belizean (0) | 10 | 0.01 |
| Bermudan (0) | 0 | <0.01 |
| British West Indian (23) | 30 | 0.02 |
| Dutch West Indian (0) | 0 | <0.01 |
| Haitian (176) | 232 | 0.15 |
| Jamaican (316) | 440 | 0.28 |
| Trinidadian/Tobagonian (274) | 320 | 0.20 |
| U.S. Virgin Islander (0) | 0 | <0.01 |
| West Indian (150) | 204 | 0.13 |
| Other West Indian (0) | 13 | 0.01 |
| Yugoslavian (21) | 51 | 0.03 |

| Hispanic Origin | Population | % |
|---|---|---|
| Hispanic or Latino (of any race) | 6,080 | 3.81 |
| Central American, ex. Mexican | 275 | 0.17 |
| Costa Rican | 37 | 0.02 |
| Guatemalan | 58 | 0.04 |
| Honduran | 21 | 0.01 |
| Nicaraguan | 20 | 0.01 |
| Panamanian | 73 | 0.05 |
| Salvadoran | 63 | 0.04 |
| Other Central American | 3 | <0.01 |
| Cuban | 179 | 0.11 |
| Dominican Republic | 312 | 0.20 |
| Mexican | 806 | 0.51 |
| Puerto Rican | 3,498 | 2.19 |
| South American | 362 | 0.23 |
| Argentinean | 40 | 0.03 |
| Bolivian | 6 | <0.01 |
| Chilean | 31 | 0.02 |
| Colombian | 104 | 0.07 |
| Ecuadorian | 79 | 0.05 |
| Paraguayan | 7 | <0.01 |
| Peruvian | 47 | 0.03 |
| Uruguayan | 4 | <0.01 |
| Venezuelan | 39 | 0.02 |
| Other South American | 5 | <0.01 |
| Other Hispanic or Latino | 648 | 0.41 |

| Race* | Population | % |
|---|---|---|
| African-American/Black (10,338) | 12,620 | 7.92 |
| Not Hispanic (9,592) | 11,487 | 7.21 |
| Hispanic (746) | 1,133 | 0.71 |
| American Indian/Alaska Native (385) | 1,273 | 0.80 |
| Not Hispanic (283) | 1,058 | 0.66 |
| Hispanic (102) | 215 | 0.13 |
| Alaska Athabascan (Ala. Nat.) (0) | 0 | <0.01 |
| Aleut (Alaska Native) (0) | 0 | <0.01 |
| Apache (4) | 14 | 0.01 |
| Arapaho (0) | 0 | <0.01 |
| Blackfeet (5) | 74 | 0.05 |
| Canadian/French Am. Ind. (6) | 26 | 0.02 |
| Central American Ind. (1) | 3 | <0.01 |
| Cherokee (29) | 149 | 0.09 |
| Cheyenne (0) | 1 | <0.01 |
| Chickasaw (0) | 0 | <0.01 |
| Chippewa (2) | 12 | 0.01 |
| Choctaw (4) | 7 | <0.01 |
| Colville (0) | 0 | <0.01 |

| Race* | Population | % |
|---|---|---|
| Comanche (0) | 2 | <0.01 |
| Cree (2) | 4 | <0.01 |
| Creek (0) | 3 | <0.01 |
| Crow (0) | 3 | <0.01 |
| Delaware (3) | 6 | <0.01 |
| Hopi (0) | 0 | <0.01 |
| Houma (0) | 0 | <0.01 |
| Inupiat (Alaska Native) (0) | 2 | <0.01 |
| Iroquois (51) | 173 | 0.11 |
| Kiowa (0) | 0 | <0.01 |
| Lumbee (2) | 5 | <0.01 |
| Menominee (3) | 3 | <0.01 |
| Mexican American Ind. (4) | 7 | <0.01 |
| Navajo (2) | 6 | <0.01 |
| Osage (0) | 0 | <0.01 |
| Ottawa (0) | 1 | <0.01 |
| Paiute (0) | 0 | <0.01 |
| Pima (1) | 1 | <0.01 |
| Potawatomi (0) | 0 | <0.01 |
| Pueblo (0) | 0 | <0.01 |
| Puget Sound Salish (0) | 0 | <0.01 |
| Seminole (1) | 4 | <0.01 |
| Shoshone (0) | 0 | <0.01 |
| Sioux (4) | 13 | 0.01 |
| South American Ind. (19) | 30 | 0.02 |
| Spanish American Ind. (4) | 5 | <0.01 |
| Tlingit-Haida (Alaska Native) (1) | 2 | <0.01 |
| Tohono O'Odham (0) | 0 | <0.01 |
| Tsimshian (Alaska Native) (0) | 0 | <0.01 |
| Ute (0) | 0 | <0.01 |
| Yakama (0) | 0 | <0.01 |
| Yaqui (0) | 0 | <0.01 |
| Yuman (0) | 0 | <0.01 |
| Yup'ik (Alaska Native) (0) | 2 | <0.01 |
| Asian (3,517) | 4,293 | 2.69 |
| Not Hispanic (3,469) | 4,205 | 2.64 |
| Hispanic (48) | 88 | 0.06 |
| Bangladeshi (43) | 52 | 0.03 |
| Bhutanese (0) | 0 | <0.01 |
| Burmese (327) | 348 | 0.22 |
| Cambodian (6) | 19 | 0.01 |
| Chinese, ex. Taiwanese (976) | 1,120 | 0.70 |
| Filipino (228) | 380 | 0.24 |
| Hmong (2) | 5 | <0.01 |
| Indian (924) | 1,075 | 0.67 |
| Indonesian (9) | 15 | 0.01 |
| Japanese (99) | 207 | 0.13 |
| Korean (315) | 413 | 0.26 |
| Laotian (2) | 6 | <0.01 |
| Malaysian (12) | 14 | 0.01 |
| Nepalese (16) | 22 | 0.01 |
| Pakistani (193) | 217 | 0.14 |
| Sri Lankan (4) | 8 | 0.01 |
| Taiwanese (46) | 52 | 0.03 |
| Thai (32) | 49 | 0.03 |
| Vietnamese (121) | 160 | 0.10 |
| Hawaii Native/Pacific Islander (34) | 123 | 0.08 |
| Not Hispanic (25) | 100 | 0.06 |
| Hispanic (9) | 23 | 0.01 |
| Fijian (1) | 1 | <0.01 |
| Guamanian/Chamorro (7) | 13 | 0.01 |
| Marshallese (0) | 0 | <0.01 |
| Native Hawaiian (12) | 43 | 0.03 |
| Samoan (0) | 6 | <0.01 |
| Tongan (0) | 0 | <0.01 |
| White (139,529) | 143,012 | 89.70 |
| Not Hispanic (136,555) | 139,499 | 87.50 |
| Hispanic (2,974) | 3,513 | 2.20 |

Notes: † The Census 2010 population figure is used to calculate the percentages in the Hispanic Origin and Race categories. Ancestry percentages are based on the 2006-2010 American Community Survey population (not shown); ‡ Numbers in parentheses indicate the number of people reporting a single ancestry; * Numbers in parentheses indicate the number of persons reporting this race alone, not in combination with any other race; Please refer to the Explanation of Data for more information.

## Richmond County

Population: 468,730

| Ancestry | Population | % |
|---|---|---|
| Afghan (0) | 0 | <0.01 |
| African, Sub-Saharan (6,533) | 7,234 | 1.56 |
| African (3,732) | 4,164 | 0.90 |
| Cape Verdean (0) | 11 | <0.01 |
| Ethiopian (41) | 46 | 0.01 |
| Ghanaian (239) | 250 | 0.05 |
| Kenyan (78) | 78 | 0.02 |
| Liberian (515) | 532 | 0.11 |
| Nigerian (1,509) | 1,679 | 0.36 |
| Senegalese (126) | 126 | 0.03 |
| Sierra Leonean (90) | 117 | 0.03 |
| Somalian (0) | 0 | <0.01 |
| South African (0) | 0 | <0.01 |
| Sudanese (0) | 0 | <0.01 |
| Ugandan (0) | 0 | <0.01 |
| Zimbabwean (0) | 0 | <0.01 |
| Other Sub-Saharan African (203) | 231 | 0.05 |
| Albanian (7,700) | 8,108 | 1.75 |
| Alsatian (0) | 24 | 0.01 |
| American (13,977) | 13,977 | 3.02 |
| Arab (7,711) | 8,820 | 1.90 |
| Arab (1,694) | 1,829 | 0.39 |
| Egyptian (3,200) | 3,292 | 0.71 |
| Iraqi (11) | 32 | 0.01 |
| Jordanian (159) | 183 | 0.04 |
| Lebanese (784) | 1,019 | 0.22 |
| Moroccan (502) | 621 | 0.13 |
| Palestinian (443) | 479 | 0.10 |
| Syrian (209) | 584 | 0.13 |
| Other Arab (709) | 781 | 0.17 |
| Armenian (83) | 311 | 0.07 |
| Assyrian/Chaldean/Syriac (15) | 15 | <0.01 |
| Australian (24) | 49 | 0.01 |
| Austrian (343) | 1,542 | 0.33 |
| Basque (15) | 77 | 0.02 |
| Belgian (36) | 266 | 0.06 |
| Brazilian (183) | 287 | 0.06 |
| British (231) | 615 | 0.13 |
| Bulgarian (0) | 0 | <0.01 |
| Cajun (0) | 0 | <0.01 |
| Canadian (290) | 544 | 0.12 |
| Carpatho Rusyn (63) | 63 | 0.01 |
| Celtic (37) | 46 | 0.01 |
| Croatian (598) | 869 | 0.19 |
| Cypriot (0) | 0 | <0.01 |
| Czech (146) | 735 | 0.16 |
| Czechoslovakian (93) | 237 | 0.05 |
| Danish (90) | 479 | 0.10 |
| Dutch (137) | 1,637 | 0.35 |
| Eastern European (433) | 433 | 0.09 |
| English (1,973) | 9,014 | 1.94 |
| Estonian (10) | 10 | <0.01 |
| European (1,914) | 2,068 | 0.45 |
| Finnish (48) | 185 | 0.04 |
| French, ex. Basque (800) | 3,772 | 0.81 |
| French Canadian (248) | 750 | 0.16 |
| German (4,111) | 25,477 | 5.50 |
| German Russian (0) | 0 | <0.01 |
| Greek (2,403) | 4,183 | 0.90 |
| Guyanese (767) | 952 | 0.21 |
| Hungarian (1,024) | 2,288 | 0.49 |
| Icelander (55) | 55 | 0.01 |
| Iranian (121) | 171 | 0.04 |
| Irish (20,064) | 64,762 | 13.97 |
| Israeli (542) | 759 | 0.16 |
| Italian (107,263) | 156,288 | 33.72 |
| Latvian (98) | 142 | 0.03 |
| Lithuanian (178) | 645 | 0.14 |
| Luxemburger (12) | 54 | 0.01 |
| Macedonian (1,368) | 1,590 | 0.34 |
| Maltese (104) | 290 | 0.06 |
| New Zealander (0) | 0 | <0.01 |
| Northern European (60) | 60 | 0.01 |
| Norwegian (1,617) | 5,135 | 1.11 |
| Pennsylvania German (9) | 41 | 0.01 |
| Polish (9,167) | 18,430 | 3.98 |
| Portuguese (180) | 617 | 0.13 |
| Romanian (530) | 964 | 0.21 |
| Russian (11,315) | 16,388 | 3.54 |
| Scandinavian (35) | 121 | 0.03 |
| Scotch-Irish (759) | 1,886 | 0.41 |
| Scottish (718) | 2,350 | 0.51 |
| Serbian (219) | 240 | 0.05 |
| Slavic (68) | 143 | 0.03 |
| Slovak (233) | 553 | 0.12 |
| Slovene (86) | 108 | 0.02 |
| Soviet Union (51) | 63 | 0.01 |
| Swedish (253) | 1,936 | 0.42 |
| Swiss (76) | 256 | 0.06 |
| Turkish (1,267) | 1,607 | 0.35 |
| Ukrainian (3,759) | 4,836 | 1.04 |
| Welsh (68) | 417 | 0.09 |
| West Indian, ex. Hispanic (5,348) | 6,967 | 1.50 |
| Bahamian (31) | 31 | 0.01 |
| Barbadian (94) | 94 | 0.02 |
| Belizean (76) | 76 | 0.02 |
| Bermudan (0) | 0 | <0.01 |
| British West Indian (113) | 236 | 0.05 |
| Dutch West Indian (39) | 89 | 0.02 |
| Haitian (676) | 791 | 0.17 |
| Jamaican (1,463) | 2,033 | 0.44 |
| Trinidadian/Tobagonian (1,412) | 1,807 | 0.39 |
| U.S. Virgin Islander (22) | 22 | <0.01 |
| West Indian (1,392) | 1,745 | 0.38 |
| Other West Indian (30) | 43 | 0.01 |
| Yugoslavian (1,237) | 1,738 | 0.38 |

| Hispanic Origin | Population | % |
|---|---|---|
| Hispanic or Latino (of any race) | 81,051 | 17.29 |
| Central American, ex. Mexican | 4,310 | 0.92 |
| Costa Rican | 266 | 0.06 |
| Guatemalan | 864 | 0.18 |
| Honduran | 1,735 | 0.37 |
| Nicaraguan | 199 | 0.04 |
| Panamanian | 607 | 0.13 |
| Salvadoran | 592 | 0.13 |
| Other Central American | 47 | 0.01 |
| Cuban | 1,831 | 0.39 |
| Dominican Republic | 4,918 | 1.05 |
| Mexican | 18,684 | 3.99 |
| Puerto Rican | 37,517 | 8.00 |
| South American | 8,232 | 1.76 |
| Argentinean | 608 | 0.13 |
| Bolivian | 161 | 0.03 |
| Chilean | 346 | 0.07 |
| Colombian | 2,526 | 0.54 |
| Ecuadorian | 2,675 | 0.57 |
| Paraguayan | 38 | 0.01 |
| Peruvian | 1,462 | 0.31 |
| Uruguayan | 76 | 0.02 |
| Venezuelan | 254 | 0.05 |
| Other South American | 86 | 0.02 |
| Other Hispanic or Latino | 5,559 | 1.19 |

| Race* | Population | % |
|---|---|---|
| African-American/Black (49,857) | 55,014 | 11.74 |
| Not Hispanic (44,313) | 47,521 | 10.14 |
| Hispanic (5,544) | 7,493 | 1.60 |
| American Indian/Alaska Native (1,695) | 3,719 | 0.79 |
| Not Hispanic (695) | 2,034 | 0.43 |
| Hispanic (1,000) | 1,685 | 0.36 |
| Alaska Athabascan (Ala. Nat.) (1) | 3 | <0.01 |
| Aleut (Alaska Native) (0) | 2 | <0.01 |
| Apache (16) | 35 | 0.01 |
| Arapaho (1) | 1 | <0.01 |
| Blackfeet (17) | 88 | 0.02 |
| Canadian/French Am. Ind. (7) | 10 | <0.01 |
| Central American Ind. (29) | 56 | 0.01 |
| Cherokee (104) | 467 | 0.10 |
| Cheyenne (0) | 2 | <0.01 |
| Chickasaw (1) | 3 | <0.01 |
| Chippewa (7) | 13 | <0.01 |
| Choctaw (3) | 11 | <0.01 |
| Colville (0) | 0 | <0.01 |

| | Population | % |
|---|---|---|
| Comanche (2) | 3 | <0.01 |
| Cree (0) | 4 | <0.01 |
| Creek (3) | 29 | 0.01 |
| Crow (0) | 0 | <0.01 |
| Delaware (16) | 43 | 0.01 |
| Hopi (1) | 5 | <0.01 |
| Houma (1) | 1 | <0.01 |
| Inupiat (Alaska Native) (0) | 1 | <0.01 |
| Iroquois (61) | 152 | 0.03 |
| Kiowa (0) | 1 | <0.01 |
| Lumbee (1) | 8 | <0.01 |
| Menominee (0) | 0 | <0.01 |
| Mexican American Ind. (161) | 204 | 0.04 |
| Navajo (10) | 17 | <0.01 |
| Osage (0) | 0 | <0.01 |
| Ottawa (0) | 0 | <0.01 |
| Paiute (0) | 0 | <0.01 |
| Pima (2) | 2 | <0.01 |
| Potawatomi (0) | 0 | <0.01 |
| Pueblo (4) | 5 | <0.01 |
| Puget Sound Salish (0) | 0 | <0.01 |
| Seminole (7) | 26 | 0.01 |
| Shoshone (1) | 3 | <0.01 |
| Sioux (11) | 24 | 0.01 |
| South American Ind. (146) | 288 | 0.06 |
| Spanish American Ind. (31) | 47 | 0.01 |
| Tlingit-Haida (Alaska Native) (0) | 1 | <0.01 |
| Tohono O'Odham (4) | 8 | <0.01 |
| Tsimshian (Alaska Native) (0) | 0 | <0.01 |
| Ute (1) | 1 | <0.01 |
| Yakama (0) | 0 | <0.01 |
| Yaqui (1) | 1 | <0.01 |
| Yuman (0) | 1 | <0.01 |
| Yup'ik (Alaska Native) (0) | 0 | <0.01 |
| Asian (35,164) | 38,756 | 8.27 |
| Not Hispanic (34,697) | 37,689 | 8.04 |
| Hispanic (467) | 1,067 | 0.23 |
| Bangladeshi (360) | 387 | 0.08 |
| Bhutanese (0) | 0 | <0.01 |
| Burmese (116) | 130 | 0.03 |
| Cambodian (100) | 129 | 0.03 |
| Chinese, ex. Taiwanese (13,144) | 14,107 | 3.01 |
| Filipino (5,224) | 6,205 | 1.32 |
| Hmong (4) | 8 | <0.01 |
| Indian (6,793) | 7,723 | 1.65 |
| Indonesian (22) | 52 | 0.01 |
| Japanese (201) | 408 | 0.09 |
| Korean (3,207) | 3,398 | 0.72 |
| Laotian (13) | 18 | <0.01 |
| Malaysian (58) | 96 | 0.02 |
| Nepalese (27) | 35 | 0.01 |
| Pakistani (2,495) | 2,777 | 0.59 |
| Sri Lankan (1,560) | 1,766 | 0.38 |
| Taiwanese (160) | 197 | 0.04 |
| Thai (135) | 166 | 0.04 |
| Vietnamese (468) | 570 | 0.12 |
| Hawaii Native/Pacific Islander (213) | 683 | 0.15 |
| Not Hispanic (137) | 439 | 0.09 |
| Hispanic (76) | 244 | 0.05 |
| Fijian (6) | 6 | <0.01 |
| Guamanian/Chamorro (88) | 115 | 0.02 |
| Marshallese (1) | 1 | <0.01 |
| Native Hawaiian (46) | 121 | 0.03 |
| Samoan (5) | 26 | 0.01 |
| Tongan (2) | 2 | <0.01 |
| White (341,677) | 350,679 | 74.81 |
| Not Hispanic (300,169) | 305,118 | 65.09 |
| Hispanic (41,508) | 45,561 | 9.72 |

*Notes: † The Census 2010 population figure is used to calculate the percentages in the Hispanic Origin and Race categories. Ancestry percentages are based on the 2006-2010 American Community Survey population (not shown); ‡ Numbers in parentheses indicate the number of people reporting a single ancestry; * Numbers in parentheses indicate the number of persons reporting this race alone, not in combination with any other race; Please refer to the Explanation of Data for more information.*

## Rockland County

Population: 311,687

| Ancestry | Population | % |
|---|---|---|
| Afghan (172) | 172 | 0.06 |
| African, Sub-Saharan (1,590) | 2,071 | 0.68 |
| African (567) | 971 | 0.32 |
| Cape Verdean (0) | 0 | <0.01 |
| Ethiopian (27) | 44 | 0.01 |
| Ghanaian (339) | 339 | 0.11 |
| Kenyan (92) | 92 | 0.03 |
| Liberian (0) | 0 | <0.01 |
| Nigerian (207) | 262 | 0.09 |
| Senegalese (52) | 52 | 0.02 |
| Sierra Leonean (0) | 0 | <0.01 |
| Somalian (0) | 0 | <0.01 |
| South African (89) | 89 | 0.03 |
| Sudanese (0) | 0 | <0.01 |
| Ugandan (86) | 86 | 0.03 |
| Zimbabwean (0) | 0 | <0.01 |
| Other Sub-Saharan African (131) | 136 | 0.04 |
| Albanian (501) | 569 | 0.19 |
| Alsatian (0) | 3 | <0.01 |
| American (13,566) | 13,566 | 4.44 |
| Arab (1,299) | 1,848 | 0.60 |
| Arab (330) | 351 | 0.11 |
| Egyptian (344) | 377 | 0.12 |
| Iraqi (19) | 72 | 0.02 |
| Jordanian (87) | 87 | 0.03 |
| Lebanese (161) | 338 | 0.11 |
| Moroccan (216) | 301 | 0.10 |
| Palestinian (0) | 25 | 0.01 |
| Syrian (24) | 156 | 0.05 |
| Other Arab (118) | 141 | 0.05 |
| Armenian (239) | 332 | 0.11 |
| Assyrian/Chaldean/Syriac (11) | 51 | 0.02 |
| Australian (40) | 125 | 0.04 |
| Austrian (667) | 2,856 | 0.93 |
| Basque (0) | 0 | <0.01 |
| Belgian (270) | 922 | 0.30 |
| Brazilian (215) | 476 | 0.16 |
| British (457) | 879 | 0.29 |
| Bulgarian (8) | 24 | 0.01 |
| Cajun (0) | 0 | <0.01 |
| Canadian (470) | 1,139 | 0.37 |
| Carpatho Rusyn (4) | 4 | <0.01 |
| Celtic (19) | 19 | 0.01 |
| Croatian (78) | 264 | 0.09 |
| Cypriot (0) | 0 | <0.01 |
| Czech (310) | 1,346 | 0.44 |
| Czechoslovakian (489) | 955 | 0.31 |
| Danish (107) | 402 | 0.13 |
| Dutch (469) | 2,665 | 0.87 |
| Eastern European (2,769) | 3,036 | 0.99 |
| English (2,442) | 10,647 | 3.49 |
| Estonian (24) | 50 | 0.02 |
| European (9,157) | 10,292 | 3.37 |
| Finnish (50) | 191 | 0.06 |
| French, ex. Basque (590) | 3,512 | 1.15 |
| French Canadian (318) | 795 | 0.26 |
| German (5,904) | 24,634 | 8.06 |
| German Russian (12) | 12 | <0.01 |
| Greek (1,370) | 2,748 | 0.90 |
| Guyanese (387) | 482 | 0.16 |
| Hungarian (4,329) | 8,874 | 2.91 |
| Icelander (0) | 0 | <0.01 |
| Iranian (381) | 626 | 0.20 |
| Irish (22,489) | 47,471 | 15.54 |
| Israeli (1,696) | 3,753 | 1.23 |
| Italian (22,741) | 44,310 | 14.51 |
| Latvian (227) | 349 | 0.11 |
| Lithuanian (439) | 1,258 | 0.41 |
| Luxemburger (0) | 0 | <0.01 |
| Macedonian (24) | 24 | 0.01 |
| Maltese (38) | 85 | 0.03 |
| New Zealander (0) | 58 | 0.02 |
| Northern European (20) | 71 | 0.02 |
| Norwegian (405) | 962 | 0.31 |
| Pennsylvania German (20) | 38 | 0.01 |

| Ancestry | Population | % |
|---|---|---|
| Polish (5,690) | 16,940 | 5.55 |
| Portuguese (692) | 1,011 | 0.33 |
| Romanian (800) | 2,551 | 0.84 |
| Russian (6,114) | 13,933 | 4.56 |
| Scandinavian (38) | 88 | 0.03 |
| Scotch-Irish (611) | 1,605 | 0.53 |
| Scottish (672) | 2,422 | 0.79 |
| Serbian (51) | 76 | 0.02 |
| Slavic (29) | 159 | 0.05 |
| Slovak (362) | 801 | 0.26 |
| Slovene (31) | 54 | 0.02 |
| Soviet Union (0) | 0 | <0.01 |
| Swedish (298) | 1,500 | 0.49 |
| Swiss (73) | 267 | 0.09 |
| Turkish (139) | 282 | 0.09 |
| Ukrainian (1,524) | 2,602 | 0.85 |
| Welsh (78) | 620 | 0.20 |
| West Indian, ex. Hispanic (17,509) | 18,661 | 6.11 |
| Bahamian (0) | 0 | <0.01 |
| Barbadian (125) | 149 | 0.05 |
| Belizean (141) | 164 | 0.05 |
| Bermudan (0) | 3 | <0.01 |
| British West Indian (323) | 347 | 0.11 |
| Dutch West Indian (0) | 0 | <0.01 |
| Haitian (12,516) | 13,086 | 4.28 |
| Jamaican (3,254) | 3,514 | 1.15 |
| Trinidadian/Tobagonian (738) | 819 | 0.27 |
| U.S. Virgin Islander (0) | 19 | 0.01 |
| West Indian (412) | 560 | 0.18 |
| Other West Indian (0) | 0 | <0.01 |
| Yugoslavian (110) | 207 | 0.07 |

| Hispanic Origin | Population | % |
|---|---|---|
| Hispanic or Latino (of any race) | 48,783 | 15.65 |
| Central American, ex. Mexican | 9,272 | 2.97 |
| Costa Rican | 205 | 0.07 |
| Guatemalan | 5,356 | 1.72 |
| Honduran | 383 | 0.12 |
| Nicaraguan | 101 | 0.03 |
| Panamanian | 145 | 0.05 |
| Salvadoran | 3,012 | 0.97 |
| Other Central American | 70 | 0.02 |
| Cuban | 1,191 | 0.38 |
| Dominican Republic | 9,105 | 2.92 |
| Mexican | 5,358 | 1.72 |
| Puerto Rican | 12,650 | 4.06 |
| South American | 7,348 | 2.36 |
| Argentinean | 379 | 0.12 |
| Bolivian | 55 | 0.02 |
| Chilean | 203 | 0.07 |
| Colombian | 982 | 0.32 |
| Ecuadorian | 4,926 | 1.58 |
| Paraguayan | 26 | 0.01 |
| Peruvian | 562 | 0.18 |
| Uruguayan | 63 | 0.02 |
| Venezuelan | 119 | 0.04 |
| Other South American | 33 | 0.01 |
| Other Hispanic or Latino | 3,859 | 1.24 |

| Race* | Population | % |
|---|---|---|
| African-American/Black (37,058) | 40,486 | 12.99 |
| Not Hispanic (34,623) | 36,893 | 11.84 |
| Hispanic (2,435) | 3,593 | 1.15 |
| American Indian/Alaska Native (911) | 2,250 | 0.72 |
| Not Hispanic (487) | 1,366 | 0.44 |
| Hispanic (424) | 884 | 0.28 |
| Alaska Athabascan (Ala. Nat.) (1) | 1 | <0.01 |
| Aleut (Alaska Native) (1) | 1 | <0.01 |
| Apache (3) | 8 | <0.01 |
| Arapaho (0) | 0 | <0.01 |
| Blackfeet (3) | 34 | <0.01 |
| Canadian/French Am. Ind. (0) | 3 | <0.01 |
| Central American Ind. (28) | 46 | 0.01 |
| Cherokee (18) | 192 | 0.06 |
| Cheyenne (0) | 2 | <0.01 |
| Chickasaw (0) | 0 | <0.01 |
| Chippewa (1) | 2 | <0.01 |
| Choctaw (3) | 12 | <0.01 |
| Colville (0) | 0 | <0.01 |

| Race* | Population | % |
|---|---|---|
| Comanche (3) | 7 | <0.01 |
| Cree (0) | 2 | <0.01 |
| Creek (0) | 3 | <0.01 |
| Crow (1) | 1 | <0.01 |
| Delaware (113) | 236 | 0.08 |
| Hopi (0) | 0 | <0.01 |
| Houma (0) | 0 | <0.01 |
| Inupiat (Alaska Native) (0) | 0 | <0.01 |
| Iroquois (44) | 85 | 0.03 |
| Kiowa (0) | 0 | <0.01 |
| Lumbee (4) | 7 | <0.01 |
| Menominee (0) | 0 | <0.01 |
| Mexican American Ind. (72) | 107 | 0.03 |
| Navajo (0) | 5 | <0.01 |
| Osage (0) | 1 | <0.01 |
| Ottawa (0) | 0 | <0.01 |
| Paiute (1) | 1 | <0.01 |
| Pima (0) | 0 | <0.01 |
| Potawatomi (1) | 1 | <0.01 |
| Pueblo (5) | 9 | <0.01 |
| Puget Sound Salish (0) | 0 | <0.01 |
| Seminole (0) | 8 | <0.01 |
| Shoshone (0) | 0 | <0.01 |
| Sioux (4) | 18 | 0.01 |
| South American Ind. (62) | 185 | 0.06 |
| Spanish American Ind. (9) | 16 | 0.01 |
| Tlingit-Haida (Alaska Native) (2) | 8 | <0.01 |
| Tohono O'Odham (2) | 4 | <0.01 |
| Tsimshian (Alaska Native) (0) | 0 | <0.01 |
| Ute (0) | 0 | <0.01 |
| Yakama (0) | 1 | <0.01 |
| Yaqui (1) | 1 | <0.01 |
| Yuman (0) | 0 | <0.01 |
| Yup'ik (Alaska Native) (0) | 0 | <0.01 |
| Asian (19,293) | 21,506 | 6.90 |
| Not Hispanic (19,099) | 21,015 | 6.74 |
| Hispanic (194) | 491 | 0.16 |
| Bangladeshi (144) | 166 | 0.05 |
| Bhutanese (0) | 0 | <0.01 |
| Burmese (10) | 14 | <0.01 |
| Cambodian (147) | 166 | 0.05 |
| Chinese, ex. Taiwanese (2,686) | 3,154 | 1.01 |
| Filipino (4,482) | 5,049 | 1.62 |
| Hmong (30) | 32 | 0.01 |
| Indian (7,028) | 7,759 | 2.49 |
| Indonesian (30) | 52 | 0.02 |
| Japanese (277) | 410 | 0.13 |
| Korean (2,199) | 2,340 | 0.75 |
| Laotian (9) | 14 | <0.01 |
| Malaysian (5) | 16 | 0.01 |
| Nepalese (14) | 16 | 0.01 |
| Pakistani (961) | 1,080 | 0.35 |
| Sri Lankan (78) | 93 | 0.03 |
| Taiwanese (86) | 101 | 0.03 |
| Thai (185) | 220 | 0.07 |
| Vietnamese (402) | 503 | 0.16 |
| Hawaii Native/Pacific Islander (130) | 538 | 0.17 |
| Not Hispanic (43) | 295 | 0.09 |
| Hispanic (87) | 243 | 0.08 |
| Fijian (2) | 2 | <0.01 |
| Guamanian/Chamorro (48) | 65 | 0.02 |
| Marshallese (0) | 0 | <0.01 |
| Native Hawaiian (15) | 42 | 0.01 |
| Samoan (10) | 17 | 0.01 |
| Tongan (2) | 2 | <0.01 |
| White (228,295) | 234,099 | 75.11 |
| Not Hispanic (203,670) | 206,768 | 66.34 |
| Hispanic (24,625) | 27,331 | 8.77 |

*Notes:* † *The Census 2010 population figure is used to calculate the percentages in the Hispanic Origin and Race categories. Ancestry percentages are based on the 2006-2010 American Community Survey population (not shown); ‡ Numbers in parentheses indicate the number of people reporting a single ancestry; * Numbers in parentheses indicate the number of persons reporting this race alone, not in combination with any other race; Please refer to the Explanation of Data for more information.*

## Saratoga County

Population: 219,607

| Ancestry | Population | % |
|---|---|---|
| Afghan (215) | 256 | 0.12 |
| African, Sub-Saharan (91) | 164 | 0.08 |
| African (5) | 78 | 0.04 |
| Cape Verdean (0) | 0 | <0.01 |
| Ethiopian (0) | 0 | <0.01 |
| Ghanaian (61) | 61 | 0.03 |
| Kenyan (0) | 0 | <0.01 |
| Liberian (0) | 0 | <0.01 |
| Nigerian (25) | 25 | 0.01 |
| Senegalese (0) | 0 | <0.01 |
| Sierra Leonean (0) | 0 | <0.01 |
| Somalian (0) | 0 | <0.01 |
| South African (0) | 0 | <0.01 |
| Sudanese (0) | 0 | <0.01 |
| Ugandan (0) | 0 | <0.01 |
| Zimbabwean (0) | 0 | <0.01 |
| Other Sub-Saharan African (0) | 0 | <0.01 |
| Albanian (101) | 148 | 0.07 |
| Alsatian (0) | 0 | <0.01 |
| American (26,948) | 26,948 | 12.40 |
| Arab (305) | 939 | 0.43 |
| Arab (0) | 13 | 0.01 |
| Egyptian (146) | 156 | 0.07 |
| Iraqi (0) | 10 | <0.01 |
| Jordanian (0) | 0 | <0.01 |
| Lebanese (71) | 460 | 0.21 |
| Moroccan (60) | 72 | 0.03 |
| Palestinian (0) | 0 | <0.01 |
| Syrian (22) | 205 | 0.09 |
| Other Arab (6) | 23 | 0.01 |
| Armenian (142) | 458 | 0.21 |
| Assyrian/Chaldean/Syriac (13) | 13 | 0.01 |
| Australian (55) | 115 | 0.05 |
| Austrian (318) | 966 | 0.44 |
| Basque (7) | 11 | 0.01 |
| Belgian (46) | 222 | 0.10 |
| Brazilian (179) | 214 | 0.10 |
| British (535) | 886 | 0.41 |
| Bulgarian (20) | 39 | 0.02 |
| Cajun (0) | 0 | <0.01 |
| Canadian (422) | 937 | 0.43 |
| Carpatho Rusyn (0) | 0 | <0.01 |
| Celtic (11) | 19 | 0.01 |
| Croatian (112) | 198 | 0.09 |
| Cypriot (0) | 0 | <0.01 |
| Czech (190) | 848 | 0.39 |
| Czechoslovakian (167) | 387 | 0.18 |
| Danish (117) | 964 | 0.44 |
| Dutch (1,294) | 6,872 | 3.16 |
| Eastern European (261) | 287 | 0.13 |
| English (7,312) | 27,103 | 12.47 |
| Estonian (20) | 71 | 0.03 |
| European (1,477) | 1,634 | 0.75 |
| Finnish (154) | 433 | 0.20 |
| French, ex. Basque (3,190) | 21,115 | 9.72 |
| French Canadian (2,301) | 5,476 | 2.52 |
| German (7,897) | 35,201 | 16.20 |
| German Russian (0) | 26 | 0.01 |
| Greek (552) | 1,127 | 0.52 |
| Guyanese (193) | 200 | 0.09 |
| Hungarian (249) | 1,427 | 0.66 |
| Icelander (0) | 14 | 0.01 |
| Iranian (85) | 113 | 0.05 |
| Irish (15,092) | 52,194 | 24.02 |
| Israeli (113) | 127 | 0.06 |
| Italian (13,634) | 34,416 | 15.84 |
| Latvian (59) | 189 | 0.09 |
| Lithuanian (325) | 1,033 | 0.48 |
| Luxemburger (0) | 0 | <0.01 |
| Macedonian (11) | 11 | 0.01 |
| Maltese (12) | 78 | 0.04 |
| New Zealander (0) | 0 | <0.01 |
| Northern European (63) | 106 | 0.05 |
| Norwegian (591) | 1,971 | 0.91 |
| Pennsylvania German (32) | 45 | 0.02 |

| | | |
|---|---|---|
| Polish (4,777) | 16,507 | 7.60 |
| Portuguese (106) | 360 | 0.17 |
| Romanian (49) | 227 | 0.10 |
| Russian (1,235) | 3,548 | 1.63 |
| Scandinavian (100) | 250 | 0.12 |
| Scotch-Irish (1,288) | 3,641 | 1.68 |
| Scottish (1,088) | 4,810 | 2.21 |
| Serbian (42) | 63 | 0.03 |
| Slavic (72) | 236 | 0.11 |
| Slovak (219) | 911 | 0.42 |
| Slovene (44) | 63 | 0.03 |
| Soviet Union (0) | 0 | <0.01 |
| Swedish (319) | 1,884 | 0.87 |
| Swiss (95) | 442 | 0.20 |
| Turkish (99) | 113 | 0.05 |
| Ukrainian (697) | 1,955 | 0.90 |
| Welsh (285) | 1,941 | 0.89 |
| West Indian, ex. Hispanic (265) | 558 | 0.26 |
| Bahamian (0) | 13 | 0.01 |
| Barbadian (24) | 24 | 0.01 |
| Belizean (0) | 0 | <0.01 |
| Bermudan (0) | 0 | <0.01 |
| British West Indian (0) | 0 | <0.01 |
| Dutch West Indian (0) | 0 | <0.01 |
| Haitian (2) | 25 | 0.01 |
| Jamaican (132) | 353 | 0.16 |
| Trinidadian/Tobagonian (40) | 40 | 0.02 |
| U.S. Virgin Islander (9) | 9 | <0.01 |
| West Indian (58) | 94 | 0.04 |
| Other West Indian (0) | 0 | <0.01 |
| Yugoslavian (116) | 216 | 0.10 |

| Hispanic Origin | Population | % |
|---|---|---|
| Hispanic or Latino (of any race) | 5,279 | 2.40 |
| Central American, ex. Mexican | 336 | 0.15 |
| Costa Rican | 32 | 0.01 |
| Guatemalan | 90 | 0.04 |
| Honduran | 46 | 0.02 |
| Nicaraguan | 14 | 0.01 |
| Panamanian | 41 | 0.02 |
| Salvadoran | 110 | 0.05 |
| Other Central American | 3 | <0.01 |
| Cuban | 225 | 0.10 |
| Dominican Republic | 271 | 0.12 |
| Mexican | 1,331 | 0.61 |
| Puerto Rican | 1,920 | 0.87 |
| South American | 540 | 0.25 |
| Argentinean | 57 | 0.03 |
| Bolivian | 18 | 0.01 |
| Chilean | 61 | 0.03 |
| Colombian | 159 | 0.07 |
| Ecuadorian | 84 | 0.04 |
| Paraguayan | 6 | <0.01 |
| Peruvian | 80 | 0.04 |
| Uruguayan | 9 | <0.01 |
| Venezuelan | 54 | 0.02 |
| Other South American | 12 | 0.01 |
| Other Hispanic or Latino | 656 | 0.30 |

| Race* | Population | % |
|---|---|---|
| African-American/Black (3,269) | 4,700 | 2.14 |
| Not Hispanic (3,053) | 4,314 | 1.96 |
| Hispanic (216) | 386 | 0.18 |
| American Indian/Alaska Native (388) | 1,377 | 0.63 |
| Not Hispanic (325) | 1,211 | 0.55 |
| Hispanic (63) | 166 | 0.08 |
| Alaska Athabascan (Ala. Nat.) (1) | 1 | <0.01 |
| Aleut (Alaska Native) (1) | 5 | <0.01 |
| Apache (7) | 20 | 0.01 |
| Arapaho (0) | 3 | <0.01 |
| Blackfeet (8) | 56 | 0.03 |
| Canadian/French Am. Ind. (3) | 13 | <0.01 |
| Central American Ind. (2) | 7 | <0.01 |
| Cherokee (23) | 168 | 0.08 |
| Cheyenne (0) | 1 | <0.01 |
| Chickasaw (3) | 3 | <0.01 |
| Chippewa (3) | 13 | 0.01 |
| Choctaw (4) | 9 | <0.01 |
| Colville (0) | 0 | <0.01 |

| | | |
|---|---|---|
| Comanche (2) | 5 | <0.01 |
| Cree (1) | 8 | <0.01 |
| Creek (0) | 2 | <0.01 |
| Crow (1) | 1 | <0.01 |
| Delaware (2) | 6 | <0.01 |
| Hopi (0) | 0 | <0.01 |
| Houma (0) | 0 | <0.01 |
| Inupiat (Alaska Native) (0) | 1 | <0.01 |
| Iroquois (64) | 186 | 0.08 |
| Kiowa (0) | 1 | <0.01 |
| Lumbee (1) | 4 | <0.01 |
| Menominee (1) | 3 | <0.01 |
| Mexican American Ind. (17) | 22 | 0.01 |
| Navajo (16) | 28 | 0.01 |
| Osage (0) | 0 | <0.01 |
| Ottawa (0) | 0 | <0.01 |
| Paiute (0) | 0 | <0.01 |
| Pima (0) | 0 | <0.01 |
| Potawatomi (0) | 5 | <0.01 |
| Pueblo (2) | 3 | <0.01 |
| Puget Sound Salish (0) | 0 | <0.01 |
| Seminole (1) | 6 | <0.01 |
| Shoshone (0) | 0 | <0.01 |
| Sioux (4) | 20 | 0.01 |
| South American Ind. (8) | 23 | 0.01 |
| Spanish American Ind. (0) | 0 | <0.01 |
| Tlingit-Haida (Alaska Native) (0) | 2 | <0.01 |
| Tohono O'Odham (0) | 0 | <0.01 |
| Tsimshian (Alaska Native) (0) | 0 | <0.01 |
| Ute (0) | 0 | <0.01 |
| Yakama (0) | 0 | <0.01 |
| Yaqui (2) | 2 | <0.01 |
| Yuman (0) | 0 | <0.01 |
| Yup'ik (Alaska Native) (0) | 0 | <0.01 |
| Asian (3,919) | 5,079 | 2.31 |
| Not Hispanic (3,880) | 4,981 | 2.27 |
| Hispanic (39) | 98 | 0.04 |
| Bangladeshi (24) | 24 | 0.01 |
| Bhutanese (0) | 0 | <0.01 |
| Burmese (2) | 3 | <0.01 |
| Cambodian (12) | 13 | 0.01 |
| Chinese, ex. Taiwanese (1,059) | 1,280 | 0.58 |
| Filipino (275) | 500 | 0.23 |
| Hmong (0) | 0 | <0.01 |
| Indian (1,164) | 1,338 | 0.61 |
| Indonesian (6) | 20 | 0.01 |
| Japanese (184) | 346 | 0.16 |
| Korean (430) | 605 | 0.28 |
| Laotian (5) | 13 | 0.01 |
| Malaysian (7) | 9 | <0.01 |
| Nepalese (11) | 11 | 0.01 |
| Pakistani (276) | 319 | 0.15 |
| Sri Lankan (12) | 17 | 0.01 |
| Taiwanese (45) | 53 | 0.02 |
| Thai (54) | 97 | 0.04 |
| Vietnamese (187) | 223 | 0.10 |
| Hawaii Native/Pacific Islander (44) | 162 | 0.07 |
| Not Hispanic (35) | 132 | 0.06 |
| Hispanic (9) | 30 | 0.01 |
| Fijian (0) | 0 | <0.01 |
| Guamanian/Chamorro (10) | 16 | 0.01 |
| Marshallese (0) | 0 | <0.01 |
| Native Hawaiian (18) | 75 | 0.03 |
| Samoan (4) | 16 | 0.01 |
| Tongan (0) | 0 | <0.01 |
| White (207,181) | 210,587 | 95.89 |
| Not Hispanic (203,647) | 206,635 | 94.09 |
| Hispanic (3,534) | 3,952 | 1.80 |

Notes: † The Census 2010 population figure is used to calculate the percentages in the Hispanic Origin and Race categories. Ancestry percentages are based on the 2006-2010 American Community Survey population (not shown); ‡ Numbers in parentheses indicate the number of people reporting a single ancestry; * Numbers in parentheses indicate the number of persons reporting this race alone, not in combination with any other race; Please refer to the Explanation of Data for more information.

## Schenectady County
Population: 154,727

| Ancestry | Population | % |
|---|---|---|
| Afghan (318) | 318 | 0.21 |
| African, Sub-Saharan (639) | 860 | 0.56 |
| African (286) | 424 | 0.28 |
| Cape Verdean (0) | 0 | <0.01 |
| Ethiopian (0) | 0 | <0.01 |
| Ghanaian (24) | 24 | 0.02 |
| Kenyan (69) | 69 | 0.05 |
| Liberian (24) | 24 | 0.02 |
| Nigerian (131) | 186 | 0.12 |
| Senegalese (0) | 0 | <0.01 |
| Sierra Leonean (0) | 0 | <0.01 |
| Somalian (0) | 0 | <0.01 |
| South African (0) | 0 | <0.01 |
| Sudanese (0) | 0 | <0.01 |
| Ugandan (0) | 0 | <0.01 |
| Zimbabwean (0) | 0 | <0.01 |
| Other Sub-Saharan African (105) | 133 | 0.09 |
| Albanian (38) | 80 | 0.05 |
| Alsatian (0) | 0 | <0.01 |
| American (8,939) | 8,939 | 5.83 |
| Arab (231) | 473 | 0.31 |
| Arab (81) | 131 | 0.09 |
| Egyptian (13) | 13 | 0.01 |
| Iraqi (0) | 0 | <0.01 |
| Jordanian (0) | 0 | <0.01 |
| Lebanese (106) | 213 | 0.14 |
| Moroccan (0) | 0 | <0.01 |
| Palestinian (0) | 0 | <0.01 |
| Syrian (0) | 58 | 0.04 |
| Other Arab (31) | 58 | 0.04 |
| Armenian (70) | 92 | 0.06 |
| Assyrian/Chaldean/Syriac (0) | 0 | <0.01 |
| Australian (0) | 51 | 0.03 |
| Austrian (111) | 467 | 0.30 |
| Basque (0) | 0 | <0.01 |
| Belgian (7) | 28 | 0.02 |
| Brazilian (156) | 206 | 0.13 |
| British (292) | 611 | 0.40 |
| Bulgarian (0) | 0 | <0.01 |
| Cajun (0) | 6 | <0.01 |
| Canadian (206) | 511 | 0.33 |
| Carpatho Rusyn (0) | 0 | <0.01 |
| Celtic (35) | 35 | 0.02 |
| Croatian (15) | 40 | 0.03 |
| Cypriot (54) | 54 | 0.04 |
| Czech (130) | 778 | 0.51 |
| Czechoslovakian (174) | 314 | 0.20 |
| Danish (244) | 681 | 0.44 |
| Dutch (1,069) | 5,702 | 3.72 |
| Eastern European (326) | 338 | 0.22 |
| English (3,915) | 14,772 | 9.64 |
| Estonian (39) | 39 | 0.03 |
| European (1,101) | 1,173 | 0.77 |
| Finnish (15) | 32 | 0.02 |
| French, ex. Basque (1,638) | 9,023 | 5.89 |
| French Canadian (964) | 2,716 | 1.77 |
| German (4,964) | 22,454 | 14.65 |
| German Russian (0) | 0 | <0.01 |
| Greek (305) | 613 | 0.40 |
| Guyanese (1,867) | 1,999 | 1.30 |
| Hungarian (286) | 1,109 | 0.72 |
| Icelander (0) | 0 | <0.01 |
| Iranian (8) | 8 | 0.01 |
| Irish (8,174) | 26,759 | 17.46 |
| Israeli (0) | 9 | 0.01 |
| Italian (16,081) | 30,411 | 19.84 |
| Latvian (15) | 94 | 0.06 |
| Lithuanian (210) | 708 | 0.46 |
| Luxemburger (0) | 0 | <0.01 |
| Macedonian (0) | 0 | <0.01 |
| Maltese (0) | 9 | 0.01 |
| New Zealander (0) | 18 | 0.01 |
| Northern European (283) | 297 | 0.19 |
| Norwegian (149) | 570 | 0.37 |
| Pennsylvania German (10) | 35 | 0.02 |

| Ancestry | Population | % |
|---|---|---|
| Polish (5,392) | 12,827 | 8.37 |
| Portuguese (125) | 198 | 0.13 |
| Romanian (25) | 127 | 0.08 |
| Russian (561) | 1,487 | 0.97 |
| Scandinavian (35) | 108 | 0.07 |
| Scotch-Irish (666) | 1,949 | 1.27 |
| Scottish (906) | 3,064 | 2.00 |
| Serbian (0) | 24 | 0.02 |
| Slavic (54) | 84 | 0.05 |
| Slovak (198) | 543 | 0.35 |
| Slovene (0) | 9 | 0.01 |
| Soviet Union (0) | 0 | <0.01 |
| Swedish (273) | 1,002 | 0.65 |
| Swiss (204) | 517 | 0.34 |
| Turkish (94) | 123 | 0.08 |
| Ukrainian (335) | 808 | 0.53 |
| Welsh (237) | 989 | 0.65 |
| West Indian, ex. Hispanic (1,560) | 1,804 | 1.18 |
| Bahamian (0) | 0 | <0.01 |
| Barbadian (43) | 94 | 0.06 |
| Belizean (0) | 0 | <0.01 |
| Bermudan (0) | 0 | <0.01 |
| British West Indian (75) | 75 | 0.05 |
| Dutch West Indian (0) | 10 | 0.01 |
| Haitian (24) | 61 | 0.04 |
| Jamaican (766) | 817 | 0.53 |
| Trinidadian/Tobagonian (24) | 106 | 0.07 |
| U.S. Virgin Islander (0) | 0 | <0.01 |
| West Indian (628) | 641 | 0.42 |
| Other West Indian (0) | 0 | <0.01 |
| Yugoslavian (48) | 73 | 0.05 |

| Hispanic Origin | Population | % |
|---|---|---|
| Hispanic or Latino (of any race) | 8,827 | 5.70 |
| Central American, ex. Mexican | 481 | 0.31 |
| Costa Rican | 52 | 0.03 |
| Guatemalan | 101 | 0.07 |
| Honduran | 64 | 0.04 |
| Nicaraguan | 30 | 0.02 |
| Panamanian | 49 | 0.03 |
| Salvadoran | 170 | 0.11 |
| Other Central American | 15 | 0.01 |
| Cuban | 229 | 0.15 |
| Dominican Republic | 582 | 0.38 |
| Mexican | 702 | 0.45 |
| Puerto Rican | 5,442 | 3.52 |
| South American | 661 | 0.43 |
| Argentinean | 65 | 0.04 |
| Bolivian | 21 | 0.01 |
| Chilean | 35 | 0.02 |
| Colombian | 184 | 0.12 |
| Ecuadorian | 115 | 0.07 |
| Paraguayan | 10 | 0.01 |
| Peruvian | 118 | 0.08 |
| Uruguayan | 15 | 0.01 |
| Venezuelan | 55 | 0.04 |
| Other South American | 43 | 0.03 |
| Other Hispanic or Latino | 730 | 0.47 |

| Race* | Population | % |
|---|---|---|
| African-American/Black (14,710) | 17,992 | 11.63 |
| Not Hispanic (13,528) | 16,273 | 10.52 |
| Hispanic (1,182) | 1,719 | 1.11 |
| American Indian/Alaska Native (575) | 1,769 | 1.14 |
| Not Hispanic (445) | 1,465 | 0.95 |
| Hispanic (130) | 304 | 0.20 |
| Alaska Athabascan (Ala. Nat.) (1) | 1 | <0.01 |
| Aleut (Alaska Native) (0) | 0 | <0.01 |
| Apache (6) | 9 | 0.01 |
| Arapaho (1) | 1 | <0.01 |
| Blackfeet (3) | 65 | 0.04 |
| Canadian/French Am. Ind. (5) | 12 | 0.01 |
| Central American Ind. (6) | 7 | <0.01 |
| Cherokee (14) | 174 | 0.11 |
| Cheyenne (1) | 2 | <0.01 |
| Chickasaw (0) | 1 | <0.01 |
| Chippewa (6) | 17 | 0.01 |
| Choctaw (1) | 2 | <0.01 |
| Colville (0) | 0 | <0.01 |

| | Population | % |
|---|---|---|
| Comanche (0) | 0 | <0.01 |
| Cree (0) | 5 | <0.01 |
| Creek (1) | 5 | <0.01 |
| Crow (0) | 6 | <0.01 |
| Delaware (4) | 12 | 0.01 |
| Hopi (0) | 1 | <0.01 |
| Houma (0) | 0 | <0.01 |
| Inupiat (Alaska Native) (4) | 4 | <0.01 |
| Iroquois (37) | 159 | 0.10 |
| Kiowa (0) | 1 | <0.01 |
| Lumbee (2) | 4 | <0.01 |
| Menominee (0) | 0 | <0.01 |
| Mexican American Ind. (16) | 20 | 0.01 |
| Navajo (1) | 4 | <0.01 |
| Osage (0) | 0 | <0.01 |
| Ottawa (0) | 0 | <0.01 |
| Paiute (0) | 0 | <0.01 |
| Pima (1) | 5 | <0.01 |
| Potawatomi (2) | 7 | <0.01 |
| Pueblo (0) | 1 | <0.01 |
| Puget Sound Salish (0) | 0 | <0.01 |
| Seminole (2) | 11 | 0.01 |
| Shoshone (0) | 0 | <0.01 |
| Sioux (6) | 24 | 0.02 |
| South American Ind. (18) | 39 | 0.03 |
| Spanish American Ind. (1) | 7 | <0.01 |
| Tlingit-Haida (Alaska Native) (0) | 0 | <0.01 |
| Tohono O'Odham (0) | 0 | <0.01 |
| Tsimshian (Alaska Native) (0) | 0 | <0.01 |
| Ute (0) | 0 | <0.01 |
| Yakama (0) | 0 | <0.01 |
| Yaqui (0) | 0 | <0.01 |
| Yuman (0) | 0 | <0.01 |
| Yup'ik (Alaska Native) (0) | 0 | <0.01 |
| Asian (4,960) | 6,587 | 4.26 |
| Not Hispanic (4,917) | 6,436 | 4.16 |
| Hispanic (43) | 151 | 0.10 |
| Bangladeshi (13) | 20 | 0.01 |
| Bhutanese (1) | 1 | <0.01 |
| Burmese (6) | 9 | 0.01 |
| Cambodian (9) | 13 | 0.01 |
| Chinese, ex. Taiwanese (938) | 1,093 | 0.71 |
| Filipino (257) | 368 | 0.24 |
| Hmong (0) | 0 | <0.01 |
| Indian (2,597) | 3,182 | 2.06 |
| Indonesian (16) | 22 | 0.01 |
| Japanese (76) | 160 | 0.10 |
| Korean (325) | 451 | 0.29 |
| Laotian (2) | 12 | 0.01 |
| Malaysian (3) | 9 | 0.01 |
| Nepalese (12) | 17 | 0.01 |
| Pakistani (279) | 316 | 0.20 |
| Sri Lankan (21) | 26 | 0.02 |
| Taiwanese (25) | 33 | 0.02 |
| Thai (31) | 53 | 0.03 |
| Vietnamese (181) | 214 | 0.14 |
| Hawaii Native/Pacific Islander (105) | 391 | 0.25 |
| Not Hispanic (81) | 327 | 0.21 |
| Hispanic (24) | 64 | 0.04 |
| Fijian (1) | 1 | <0.01 |
| Guamanian/Chamorro (6) | 14 | 0.01 |
| Marshallese (0) | 0 | <0.01 |
| Native Hawaiian (19) | 48 | 0.03 |
| Samoan (4) | 10 | 0.01 |
| Tongan (0) | 1 | <0.01 |
| White (123,211) | 127,516 | 82.41 |
| Not Hispanic (119,409) | 123,004 | 79.50 |
| Hispanic (3,802) | 4,512 | 2.92 |

Notes: † The Census 2010 population figure is used to calculate the percentages in the Hispanic Origin and Race categories. Ancestry percentages are based on the 2006-2010 American Community Survey population (not shown); ‡ Numbers in parentheses indicate the number of people reporting a single ancestry; * Numbers in parentheses indicate the number of persons reporting this race alone, not in combination with any other race; Please refer to the Explanation of Data for more information.

## Schoharie County

Population: 32,749

| Ancestry | Population | % |
|---|---|---|
| Afghan (0) | 0 | <0.01 |
| African, Sub-Saharan (66) | 102 | 0.31 |
| African (51) | 87 | 0.27 |
| Cape Verdean (0) | 0 | <0.01 |
| Ethiopian (5) | 5 | 0.02 |
| Ghanaian (0) | 0 | <0.01 |
| Kenyan (0) | 0 | <0.01 |
| Liberian (0) | 0 | <0.01 |
| Nigerian (10) | 10 | 0.03 |
| Senegalese (0) | 0 | <0.01 |
| Sierra Leonean (0) | 0 | <0.01 |
| Somalian (0) | 0 | <0.01 |
| South African (0) | 0 | <0.01 |
| Sudanese (0) | 0 | <0.01 |
| Ugandan (0) | 0 | <0.01 |
| Zimbabwean (0) | 0 | <0.01 |
| Other Sub-Saharan African (0) | 0 | <0.01 |
| Albanian (0) | 0 | <0.01 |
| Alsatian (0) | 0 | <0.01 |
| American (3,401) | 3,401 | 10.37 |
| Arab (73) | 143 | 0.44 |
| Arab (0) | 0 | <0.01 |
| Egyptian (0) | 40 | 0.12 |
| Iraqi (46) | 46 | 0.14 |
| Jordanian (0) | 0 | <0.01 |
| Lebanese (15) | 36 | 0.11 |
| Moroccan (0) | 0 | <0.01 |
| Palestinian (0) | 0 | <0.01 |
| Syrian (12) | 21 | 0.06 |
| Other Arab (0) | 0 | <0.01 |
| Armenian (0) | 30 | 0.09 |
| Assyrian/Chaldean/Syriac (0) | 0 | <0.01 |
| Australian (0) | 20 | 0.06 |
| Austrian (31) | 187 | 0.57 |
| Basque (0) | 0 | <0.01 |
| Belgian (5) | 33 | 0.10 |
| Brazilian (0) | 10 | 0.03 |
| British (53) | 135 | 0.41 |
| Bulgarian (3) | 3 | 0.01 |
| Cajun (0) | 0 | <0.01 |
| Canadian (72) | 127 | 0.39 |
| Carpatho Rusyn (0) | 0 | <0.01 |
| Celtic (0) | 3 | 0.01 |
| Croatian (21) | 34 | 0.10 |
| Cypriot (0) | 0 | <0.01 |
| Czech (21) | 169 | 0.52 |
| Czechoslovakian (44) | 83 | 0.25 |
| Danish (29) | 118 | 0.36 |
| Dutch (510) | 2,676 | 8.16 |
| Eastern European (30) | 30 | 0.09 |
| English (1,129) | 4,576 | 13.96 |
| Estonian (0) | 24 | 0.07 |
| European (402) | 442 | 1.35 |
| Finnish (7) | 50 | 0.15 |
| French, ex. Basque (194) | 1,670 | 5.09 |
| French Canadian (152) | 546 | 1.67 |
| German (2,500) | 10,082 | 30.75 |
| German Russian (0) | 0 | <0.01 |
| Greek (44) | 95 | 0.29 |
| Guyanese (0) | 0 | <0.01 |
| Hungarian (37) | 242 | 0.74 |
| Icelander (0) | 0 | <0.01 |
| Iranian (3) | 3 | 0.01 |
| Irish (1,597) | 7,351 | 22.42 |
| Israeli (0) | 0 | <0.01 |
| Italian (1,592) | 4,233 | 12.91 |
| Latvian (6) | 6 | 0.02 |
| Lithuanian (6) | 46 | 0.14 |
| Luxemburger (0) | 0 | <0.01 |
| Macedonian (0) | 0 | <0.01 |
| Maltese (0) | 21 | 0.06 |
| New Zealander (0) | 0 | <0.01 |
| Northern European (4) | 8 | 0.02 |
| Norwegian (180) | 461 | 1.41 |
| Pennsylvania German (8) | 11 | 0.03 |

| Ancestry | Population | % |
|---|---|---|
| Polish (442) | 1,690 | 5.15 |
| Portuguese (0) | 50 | 0.15 |
| Romanian (20) | 26 | 0.08 |
| Russian (72) | 336 | 1.02 |
| Scandinavian (17) | 63 | 0.19 |
| Scotch-Irish (199) | 464 | 1.42 |
| Scottish (146) | 1,033 | 3.15 |
| Serbian (0) | 0 | <0.01 |
| Slavic (0) | 20 | 0.06 |
| Slovak (13) | 34 | 0.10 |
| Slovene (0) | 4 | 0.01 |
| Soviet Union (0) | 0 | <0.01 |
| Swedish (29) | 271 | 0.83 |
| Swiss (14) | 158 | 0.48 |
| Turkish (0) | 0 | <0.01 |
| Ukrainian (53) | 151 | 0.46 |
| Welsh (55) | 384 | 1.17 |
| West Indian, ex. Hispanic (92) | 115 | 0.35 |
| Bahamian (0) | 0 | <0.01 |
| Barbadian (0) | 0 | <0.01 |
| Belizean (0) | 0 | <0.01 |
| Bermudan (0) | 0 | <0.01 |
| British West Indian (0) | 0 | <0.01 |
| Dutch West Indian (0) | 0 | <0.01 |
| Haitian (19) | 22 | 0.07 |
| Jamaican (47) | 67 | 0.20 |
| Trinidadian/Tobagonian (14) | 14 | 0.04 |
| U.S. Virgin Islander (0) | 0 | <0.01 |
| West Indian (12) | 12 | 0.04 |
| Other West Indian (0) | 0 | <0.01 |
| Yugoslavian (0) | 13 | 0.04 |

| Hispanic Origin | Population | % |
|---|---|---|
| Hispanic or Latino (of any race) | 924 | 2.82 |
| Central American, ex. Mexican | 58 | 0.18 |
| Costa Rican | 2 | 0.01 |
| Guatemalan | 26 | 0.08 |
| Honduran | 6 | 0.02 |
| Nicaraguan | 9 | 0.03 |
| Panamanian | 5 | 0.02 |
| Salvadoran | 10 | 0.03 |
| Other Central American | 0 | <0.01 |
| Cuban | 60 | 0.18 |
| Dominican Republic | 37 | 0.11 |
| Mexican | 87 | 0.27 |
| Puerto Rican | 449 | 1.37 |
| South American | 96 | 0.29 |
| Argentinean | 9 | 0.03 |
| Bolivian | 0 | <0.01 |
| Chilean | 3 | 0.01 |
| Colombian | 38 | 0.12 |
| Ecuadorian | 20 | 0.06 |
| Paraguayan | 2 | 0.01 |
| Peruvian | 19 | 0.06 |
| Uruguayan | 1 | <0.01 |
| Venezuelan | 4 | 0.01 |
| Other South American | 0 | <0.01 |
| Other Hispanic or Latino | 137 | 0.42 |

| Race* | Population | % |
|---|---|---|
| African-American/Black (435) | 603 | 1.84 |
| Not Hispanic (394) | 541 | 1.65 |
| Hispanic (41) | 62 | 0.19 |
| American Indian/Alaska Native (70) | 273 | 0.83 |
| Not Hispanic (54) | 238 | 0.73 |
| Hispanic (16) | 35 | 0.11 |
| Alaska Athabascan (Ala. Nat.) (0) | 0 | <0.01 |
| Aleut (Alaska Native) (2) | 2 | 0.01 |
| Apache (2) | 7 | 0.02 |
| Arapaho (1) | 2 | 0.01 |
| Blackfeet (0) | 4 | 0.01 |
| Canadian/French Am. Ind. (0) | 0 | <0.01 |
| Central American Ind. (0) | 1 | <0.01 |
| Cherokee (4) | 32 | 0.10 |
| Cheyenne (0) | 1 | <0.01 |
| Chickasaw (0) | 0 | <0.01 |
| Chippewa (1) | 2 | 0.01 |
| Choctaw (0) | 0 | <0.01 |
| Colville (0) | 0 | <0.01 |

| Race* | Population | % |
|---|---|---|
| Comanche (0) | 0 | <0.01 |
| Cree (0) | 0 | <0.01 |
| Creek (0) | 0 | <0.01 |
| Crow (0) | 1 | <0.01 |
| Delaware (3) | 3 | 0.01 |
| Hopi (0) | 0 | <0.01 |
| Houma (0) | 0 | <0.01 |
| Inupiat (Alaska Native) (0) | 0 | <0.01 |
| Iroquois (11) | 42 | 0.13 |
| Kiowa (1) | 1 | <0.01 |
| Lumbee (0) | 0 | <0.01 |
| Menominee (0) | 0 | <0.01 |
| Mexican American Ind. (0) | 0 | <0.01 |
| Navajo (1) | 1 | <0.01 |
| Osage (0) | 1 | <0.01 |
| Ottawa (0) | 0 | <0.01 |
| Paiute (0) | 0 | <0.01 |
| Pima (0) | 0 | <0.01 |
| Potawatomi (0) | 0 | <0.01 |
| Pueblo (0) | 0 | <0.01 |
| Puget Sound Salish (0) | 0 | <0.01 |
| Seminole (0) | 1 | <0.01 |
| Shoshone (0) | 0 | <0.01 |
| Sioux (1) | 3 | 0.01 |
| South American Ind. (5) | 9 | 0.03 |
| Spanish American Ind. (0) | 0 | <0.01 |
| Tlingit-Haida (Alaska Native) (0) | 0 | <0.01 |
| Tohono O'Odham (0) | 0 | <0.01 |
| Tsimshian (Alaska Native) (0) | 0 | <0.01 |
| Ute (0) | 1 | <0.01 |
| Yakama (0) | 0 | <0.01 |
| Yaqui (0) | 0 | <0.01 |
| Yuman (0) | 0 | <0.01 |
| Yup'ik (Alaska Native) (0) | 0 | <0.01 |
| Asian (217) | 288 | 0.88 |
| Not Hispanic (217) | 279 | 0.85 |
| Hispanic (0) | 9 | 0.03 |
| Bangladeshi (0) | 0 | <0.01 |
| Bhutanese (0) | 0 | <0.01 |
| Burmese (0) | 0 | <0.01 |
| Cambodian (0) | 0 | <0.01 |
| Chinese, ex. Taiwanese (40) | 48 | 0.15 |
| Filipino (26) | 45 | 0.14 |
| Hmong (0) | 0 | <0.01 |
| Indian (52) | 64 | 0.20 |
| Indonesian (0) | 0 | <0.01 |
| Japanese (32) | 37 | 0.11 |
| Korean (26) | 42 | 0.13 |
| Laotian (0) | 0 | <0.01 |
| Malaysian (0) | 1 | <0.01 |
| Nepalese (3) | 4 | 0.01 |
| Pakistani (17) | 17 | 0.05 |
| Sri Lankan (3) | 4 | 0.01 |
| Taiwanese (0) | 0 | <0.01 |
| Thai (3) | 4 | 0.01 |
| Vietnamese (7) | 9 | 0.03 |
| Hawaii Native/Pacific Islander (6) | 27 | 0.08 |
| Not Hispanic (3) | 21 | 0.06 |
| Hispanic (3) | 6 | 0.02 |
| Fijian (0) | 0 | <0.01 |
| Guamanian/Chamorro (3) | 4 | 0.01 |
| Marshallese (0) | 0 | <0.01 |
| Native Hawaiian (1) | 10 | 0.03 |
| Samoan (0) | 2 | 0.01 |
| Tongan (0) | 0 | <0.01 |
| White (31,402) | 31,818 | 97.16 |
| Not Hispanic (30,742) | 31,106 | 94.98 |
| Hispanic (660) | 712 | 2.17 |

## Schuyler County
Population: 18,343

| Ancestry | Population | % |
|---|---|---|
| Afghan (0) | 0 | <0.01 |
| African, Sub-Saharan (0) | 0 | <0.01 |
| African (0) | 0 | <0.01 |
| Cape Verdean (0) | 0 | <0.01 |
| Ethiopian (0) | 0 | <0.01 |
| Ghanaian (0) | 0 | <0.01 |
| Kenyan (0) | 0 | <0.01 |
| Liberian (0) | 0 | <0.01 |
| Nigerian (0) | 0 | <0.01 |
| Senegalese (0) | 0 | <0.01 |
| Sierra Leonean (0) | 0 | <0.01 |
| Somalian (0) | 0 | <0.01 |
| South African (0) | 0 | <0.01 |
| Sudanese (0) | 0 | <0.01 |
| Ugandan (0) | 0 | <0.01 |
| Zimbabwean (0) | 0 | <0.01 |
| Other Sub-Saharan African (0) | 0 | <0.01 |
| Albanian (107) | 126 | 0.68 |
| Alsatian (0) | 0 | <0.01 |
| American (2,366) | 2,366 | 12.74 |
| Arab (43) | 45 | 0.24 |
| Arab (43) | 43 | 0.23 |
| Egyptian (0) | 0 | <0.01 |
| Iraqi (0) | 0 | <0.01 |
| Jordanian (0) | 0 | <0.01 |
| Lebanese (0) | 2 | 0.01 |
| Moroccan (0) | 0 | <0.01 |
| Palestinian (0) | 0 | <0.01 |
| Syrian (0) | 0 | <0.01 |
| Other Arab (0) | 0 | <0.01 |
| Armenian (0) | 0 | <0.01 |
| Assyrian/Chaldean/Syriac (0) | 0 | <0.01 |
| Australian (7) | 7 | 0.04 |
| Austrian (11) | 34 | 0.18 |
| Basque (0) | 0 | <0.01 |
| Belgian (10) | 39 | 0.21 |
| Brazilian (0) | 0 | <0.01 |
| British (87) | 122 | 0.66 |
| Bulgarian (0) | 0 | <0.01 |
| Cajun (0) | 0 | <0.01 |
| Canadian (33) | 50 | 0.27 |
| Carpatho Rusyn (0) | 0 | <0.01 |
| Celtic (0) | 3 | 0.02 |
| Croatian (0) | 0 | <0.01 |
| Cypriot (0) | 0 | <0.01 |
| Czech (95) | 183 | 0.99 |
| Czechoslovakian (7) | 42 | 0.23 |
| Danish (6) | 43 | 0.23 |
| Dutch (178) | 942 | 5.07 |
| Eastern European (11) | 46 | 0.25 |
| English (1,136) | 3,077 | 16.57 |
| Estonian (0) | 0 | <0.01 |
| European (74) | 85 | 0.46 |
| Finnish (12) | 101 | 0.54 |
| French, ex. Basque (110) | 694 | 3.74 |
| French Canadian (64) | 134 | 0.72 |
| German (1,125) | 3,444 | 18.55 |
| German Russian (0) | 0 | <0.01 |
| Greek (6) | 21 | 0.11 |
| Guyanese (0) | 0 | <0.01 |
| Hungarian (7) | 47 | 0.25 |
| Icelander (0) | 0 | <0.01 |
| Iranian (0) | 0 | <0.01 |
| Irish (981) | 3,340 | 17.99 |
| Israeli (0) | 0 | <0.01 |
| Italian (864) | 1,984 | 10.69 |
| Latvian (0) | 0 | <0.01 |
| Lithuanian (16) | 20 | 0.11 |
| Luxemburger (0) | 0 | <0.01 |
| Macedonian (0) | 19 | 0.10 |
| Maltese (0) | 0 | <0.01 |
| New Zealander (0) | 0 | <0.01 |
| Northern European (0) | 0 | <0.01 |
| Norwegian (50) | 119 | 0.64 |
| Pennsylvania German (38) | 83 | 0.45 |

| Ancestry (cont.) | Population | % |
|---|---|---|
| Polish (337) | 1,027 | 5.53 |
| Portuguese (0) | 19 | 0.10 |
| Romanian (0) | 11 | 0.06 |
| Russian (11) | 130 | 0.70 |
| Scandinavian (0) | 0 | <0.01 |
| Scotch-Irish (192) | 314 | 1.69 |
| Scottish (198) | 699 | 3.76 |
| Serbian (0) | 0 | <0.01 |
| Slavic (0) | 3 | 0.02 |
| Slovak (11) | 17 | 0.09 |
| Slovene (3) | 3 | 0.02 |
| Soviet Union (0) | 0 | <0.01 |
| Swedish (51) | 216 | 1.16 |
| Swiss (76) | 148 | 0.80 |
| Turkish (0) | 0 | <0.01 |
| Ukrainian (29) | 85 | 0.46 |
| Welsh (74) | 205 | 1.10 |
| West Indian, ex. Hispanic (39) | 39 | 0.21 |
| Bahamian (0) | 0 | <0.01 |
| Barbadian (0) | 0 | <0.01 |
| Belizean (0) | 0 | <0.01 |
| Bermudan (0) | 0 | <0.01 |
| British West Indian (0) | 0 | <0.01 |
| Dutch West Indian (0) | 0 | <0.01 |
| Haitian (28) | 28 | 0.15 |
| Jamaican (11) | 11 | 0.06 |
| Trinidadian/Tobagonian (0) | 0 | <0.01 |
| U.S. Virgin Islander (0) | 0 | <0.01 |
| West Indian (0) | 0 | <0.01 |
| Other West Indian (0) | 0 | <0.01 |
| Yugoslavian (0) | 7 | 0.04 |

| Hispanic Origin | Population | % |
|---|---|---|
| Hispanic or Latino (of any race) | 234 | 1.28 |
| Central American, ex. Mexican | 10 | 0.05 |
| Costa Rican | 1 | 0.01 |
| Guatemalan | 3 | 0.02 |
| Honduran | 1 | 0.01 |
| Nicaraguan | 2 | 0.01 |
| Panamanian | 0 | <0.01 |
| Salvadoran | 3 | 0.02 |
| Other Central American | 0 | <0.01 |
| Cuban | 2 | 0.01 |
| Dominican Republic | 14 | 0.08 |
| Mexican | 64 | 0.35 |
| Puerto Rican | 99 | 0.54 |
| South American | 17 | 0.09 |
| Argentinean | 5 | 0.03 |
| Bolivian | 0 | <0.01 |
| Chilean | 0 | <0.01 |
| Colombian | 3 | 0.02 |
| Ecuadorian | 1 | 0.01 |
| Paraguayan | 1 | 0.01 |
| Peruvian | 5 | 0.03 |
| Uruguayan | 0 | <0.01 |
| Venezuelan | 2 | 0.01 |
| Other South American | 0 | <0.01 |
| Other Hispanic or Latino | 28 | 0.15 |

| Race* | Population | % |
|---|---|---|
| African-American/Black (159) | 244 | 1.33 |
| Not Hispanic (143) | 216 | 1.18 |
| Hispanic (16) | 28 | 0.15 |
| American Indian/Alaska Native (47) | 161 | 0.88 |
| Not Hispanic (44) | 152 | 0.83 |
| Hispanic (3) | 9 | 0.05 |
| Alaska Athabascan (Ala. Nat.) (1) | 1 | 0.01 |
| Aleut (Alaska Native) (0) | 0 | <0.01 |
| Apache (0) | 0 | <0.01 |
| Arapaho (0) | 0 | <0.01 |
| Blackfeet (2) | 11 | 0.06 |
| Canadian/French Am. Ind. (1) | 2 | 0.01 |
| Central American Ind. (0) | 0 | <0.01 |
| Cherokee (3) | 23 | 0.13 |
| Cheyenne (0) | 0 | <0.01 |
| Chickasaw (0) | 0 | <0.01 |
| Chippewa (0) | 0 | <0.01 |
| Choctaw (0) | 2 | 0.01 |
| Colville (0) | 1 | 0.01 |

| Race* (cont.) | Population | % |
|---|---|---|
| Comanche (0) | 0 | <0.01 |
| Cree (1) | 1 | 0.01 |
| Creek (0) | 0 | <0.01 |
| Crow (0) | 0 | <0.01 |
| Delaware (1) | 2 | 0.01 |
| Hopi (1) | 2 | 0.01 |
| Houma (0) | 0 | <0.01 |
| Inupiat (Alaska Native) (0) | 0 | <0.01 |
| Iroquois (12) | 41 | 0.22 |
| Kiowa (0) | 0 | <0.01 |
| Lumbee (0) | 0 | <0.01 |
| Menominee (0) | 0 | <0.01 |
| Mexican American Ind. (0) | 0 | <0.01 |
| Navajo (0) | 4 | 0.02 |
| Osage (0) | 0 | <0.01 |
| Ottawa (0) | 0 | <0.01 |
| Paiute (0) | 0 | <0.01 |
| Pima (0) | 0 | <0.01 |
| Potawatomi (0) | 0 | <0.01 |
| Pueblo (1) | 1 | 0.01 |
| Puget Sound Salish (0) | 0 | <0.01 |
| Seminole (0) | 3 | 0.02 |
| Shoshone (0) | 0 | <0.01 |
| Sioux (1) | 2 | 0.01 |
| South American Ind. (0) | 1 | 0.01 |
| Spanish American Ind. (0) | 0 | <0.01 |
| Tlingit-Haida (Alaska Native) (0) | 0 | <0.01 |
| Tohono O'Odham (0) | 0 | <0.01 |
| Tsimshian (Alaska Native) (0) | 0 | <0.01 |
| Ute (0) | 0 | <0.01 |
| Yakama (0) | 0 | <0.01 |
| Yaqui (0) | 0 | <0.01 |
| Yuman (0) | 0 | <0.01 |
| Yup'ik (Alaska Native) (0) | 0 | <0.01 |
| Asian (53) | 88 | 0.48 |
| Not Hispanic (51) | 82 | 0.45 |
| Hispanic (2) | 6 | 0.03 |
| Bangladeshi (0) | 0 | <0.01 |
| Bhutanese (0) | 0 | <0.01 |
| Burmese (0) | 0 | <0.01 |
| Cambodian (1) | 1 | 0.01 |
| Chinese, ex. Taiwanese (9) | 12 | 0.07 |
| Filipino (6) | 15 | 0.08 |
| Hmong (0) | 0 | <0.01 |
| Indian (14) | 23 | 0.13 |
| Indonesian (1) | 2 | 0.01 |
| Japanese (7) | 11 | 0.06 |
| Korean (5) | 8 | 0.04 |
| Laotian (1) | 3 | 0.02 |
| Malaysian (0) | 0 | <0.01 |
| Nepalese (0) | 0 | <0.01 |
| Pakistani (1) | 1 | 0.01 |
| Sri Lankan (0) | 0 | <0.01 |
| Taiwanese (1) | 3 | 0.02 |
| Thai (3) | 6 | 0.03 |
| Vietnamese (0) | 1 | 0.01 |
| Hawaii Native/Pacific Islander (4) | 5 | 0.03 |
| Not Hispanic (4) | 5 | 0.03 |
| Hispanic (0) | 0 | <0.01 |
| Fijian (0) | 0 | <0.01 |
| Guamanian/Chamorro (1) | 1 | 0.01 |
| Marshallese (0) | 0 | <0.01 |
| Native Hawaiian (0) | 0 | <0.01 |
| Samoan (1) | 1 | 0.01 |
| Tongan (0) | 0 | <0.01 |
| White (17,803) | 18,035 | 98.32 |
| Not Hispanic (17,646) | 17,851 | 97.32 |
| Hispanic (157) | 184 | 1.00 |

*Notes: † The Census 2010 population figure is used to calculate the percentages in the Hispanic Origin and Race categories. Ancestry percentages are based on the 2006-2010 American Community Survey population (not shown); ‡ Numbers in parentheses indicate the number of people reporting a single ancestry; * Numbers in parentheses indicate the number of persons reporting this race alone, not in combination with any other race; Please refer to the Explanation of Data for more information.*

## Seneca County

Population: 35,251.

| Ancestry | Population | % |
|---|---|---|
| Afghan (0) | 0 | <0.01 |
| African, Sub-Saharan (54) | 82 | 0.23 |
| African (54) | 82 | 0.23 |
| Cape Verdean (0) | 0 | <0.01 |
| Ethiopian (0) | 0 | <0.01 |
| Ghanaian (0) | 0 | <0.01 |
| Kenyan (0) | 0 | <0.01 |
| Liberian (0) | 0 | <0.01 |
| Nigerian (0) | 0 | <0.01 |
| Senegalese (0) | 0 | <0.01 |
| Sierra Leonean (0) | 0 | <0.01 |
| Somalian (0) | 0 | <0.01 |
| South African (0) | 0 | <0.01 |
| Sudanese (0) | 0 | <0.01 |
| Ugandan (0) | 0 | <0.01 |
| Zimbabwean (0) | 0 | <0.01 |
| Other Sub-Saharan African (0) | 0 | <0.01 |
| Albanian (9) | 9 | 0.03 |
| Alsatian (2) | 6 | 0.02 |
| American (2,242) | 2,242 | 6.35 |
| Arab (13) | 31 | 0.09 |
| Arab (0) | 0 | <0.01 |
| Egyptian (0) | 0 | <0.01 |
| Iraqi (0) | 0 | <0.01 |
| Jordanian (0) | 0 | <0.01 |
| Lebanese (13) | 31 | 0.09 |
| Moroccan (0) | 0 | <0.01 |
| Palestinian (0) | 0 | <0.01 |
| Syrian (0) | 0 | <0.01 |
| Other Arab (0) | 0 | <0.01 |
| Armenian (0) | 0 | <0.01 |
| Assyrian/Chaldean/Syriac (0) | 0 | <0.01 |
| Australian (3) | 7 | 0.02 |
| Austrian (10) | 76 | 0.22 |
| Basque (0) | 0 | <0.01 |
| Belgian (2) | 8 | 0.02 |
| Brazilian (18) | 18 | 0.05 |
| British (43) | 121 | 0.34 |
| Bulgarian (0) | 0 | <0.01 |
| Cajun (0) | 0 | <0.01 |
| Canadian (19) | 49 | 0.14 |
| Carpatho Rusyn (0) | 0 | <0.01 |
| Celtic (0) | 0 | <0.01 |
| Croatian (39) | 43 | 0.12 |
| Cypriot (0) | 0 | <0.01 |
| Czech (10) | 99 | 0.28 |
| Czechoslovakian (28) | 53 | 0.15 |
| Danish (44) | 170 | 0.48 |
| Dutch (390) | 1,725 | 4.89 |
| Eastern European (9) | 9 | 0.03 |
| English (2,254) | 6,403 | 18.13 |
| Estonian (0) | 0 | <0.01 |
| European (129) | 155 | 0.44 |
| Finnish (49) | 65 | 0.18 |
| French, ex. Basque (391) | 1,487 | 4.21 |
| French Canadian (139) | 348 | 0.99 |
| German (2,464) | 8,012 | 22.69 |
| German Russian (0) | 0 | <0.01 |
| Greek (21) | 44 | 0.12 |
| Guyanese (8) | 8 | 0.02 |
| Hungarian (37) | 149 | 0.42 |
| Icelander (0) | 0 | <0.01 |
| Iranian (3) | 3 | 0.01 |
| Irish (1,800) | 6,509 | 18.43 |
| Israeli (0) | 0 | <0.01 |
| Italian (2,972) | 6,175 | 17.49 |
| Latvian (0) | 0 | <0.01 |
| Lithuanian (21) | 100 | 0.28 |
| Luxemburger (0) | 0 | <0.01 |
| Macedonian (0) | 0 | <0.01 |
| Maltese (0) | 0 | <0.01 |
| New Zealander (0) | 0 | <0.01 |
| Northern European (0) | 0 | <0.01 |
| Norwegian (29) | 131 | 0.37 |
| Pennsylvania German (299) | 353 | 1.00 |

| Ancestry | Population | % |
|---|---|---|
| Polish (330) | 1,065 | 3.02 |
| Portuguese (7) | 12 | 0.03 |
| Romanian (11) | 46 | 0.13 |
| Russian (84) | 155 | 0.44 |
| Scandinavian (0) | 13 | 0.04 |
| Scotch-Irish (128) | 496 | 1.40 |
| Scottish (232) | 782 | 2.21 |
| Serbian (0) | 0 | <0.01 |
| Slavic (2) | 6 | 0.02 |
| Slovak (14) | 35 | 0.10 |
| Slovene (0) | 2 | 0.01 |
| Soviet Union (0) | 0 | <0.01 |
| Swedish (79) | 213 | 0.60 |
| Swiss (151) | 371 | 1.05 |
| Turkish (0) | 0 | <0.01 |
| Ukrainian (84) | 208 | 0.59 |
| Welsh (42) | 242 | 0.69 |
| West Indian, ex. Hispanic (50) | 97 | 0.27 |
| Bahamian (0) | 0 | <0.01 |
| Barbadian (0) | 0 | <0.01 |
| Belizean (0) | 0 | <0.01 |
| Bermudan (0) | 0 | <0.01 |
| British West Indian (0) | 0 | <0.01 |
| Dutch West Indian (0) | 0 | <0.01 |
| Haitian (8) | 17 | 0.05 |
| Jamaican (25) | 55 | 0.16 |
| Trinidadian/Tobagonian (9) | 17 | 0.05 |
| U.S. Virgin Islander (0) | 0 | <0.01 |
| West Indian (8) | 8 | 0.02 |
| Other West Indian (0) | 0 | <0.01 |
| Yugoslavian (0) | 0 | <0.01 |

| Hispanic Origin | Population | % |
|---|---|---|
| Hispanic or Latino (of any race) | 952 | 2.70 |
| Central American, ex. Mexican | 68 | 0.19 |
| Costa Rican | 2 | 0.01 |
| Guatemalan | 13 | 0.04 |
| Honduran | 13 | 0.04 |
| Nicaraguan | 1 | <0.01 |
| Panamanian | 15 | 0.04 |
| Salvadoran | 21 | 0.06 |
| Other Central American | 3 | 0.01 |
| Cuban | 30 | 0.09 |
| Dominican Republic | 61 | 0.17 |
| Mexican | 154 | 0.44 |
| Puerto Rican | 527 | 1.49 |
| South American | 24 | 0.07 |
| Argentinean | 1 | <0.01 |
| Bolivian | 0 | <0.01 |
| Chilean | 0 | <0.01 |
| Colombian | 14 | 0.04 |
| Ecuadorian | 0 | <0.01 |
| Paraguayan | 1 | <0.01 |
| Peruvian | 6 | 0.02 |
| Uruguayan | 0 | <0.01 |
| Venezuelan | 2 | 0.01 |
| Other South American | 0 | <0.01 |
| Other Hispanic or Latino | 88 | 0.25 |

| Race* | Population | % |
|---|---|---|
| African-American/Black (1,607) | 1,812 | 5.14 |
| Not Hispanic (1,513) | 1,705 | 4.84 |
| Hispanic (94) | 107 | 0.30 |
| American Indian/Alaska Native (104) | 281 | 0.80 |
| Not Hispanic (96) | 269 | 0.76 |
| Hispanic (8) | 12 | 0.03 |
| Alaska Athabascan (Ala. Nat.) (0) | 0 | <0.01 |
| Aleut (Alaska Native) (0) | 0 | <0.01 |
| Apache (0) | 1 | <0.01 |
| Arapaho (0) | 2 | 0.01 |
| Blackfeet (0) | 17 | 0.05 |
| Canadian/French Am. Ind. (0) | 0 | <0.01 |
| Central American Ind. (0) | 0 | <0.01 |
| Cherokee (7) | 34 | 0.10 |
| Cheyenne (0) | 0 | <0.01 |
| Chickasaw (0) | 0 | <0.01 |
| Chippewa (2) | 5 | 0.01 |
| Choctaw (0) | 0 | <0.01 |
| Colville (0) | 0 | <0.01 |

| Race* | Population | % |
|---|---|---|
| Comanche (0) | 1 | <0.01 |
| Cree (1) | 1 | <0.01 |
| Creek (0) | 2 | 0.01 |
| Crow (0) | 0 | <0.01 |
| Delaware (0) | 3 | 0.01 |
| Hopi (0) | 0 | <0.01 |
| Houma (0) | 0 | <0.01 |
| Inupiat (Alaska Native) (0) | 0 | <0.01 |
| Iroquois (12) | 53 | 0.15 |
| Kiowa (0) | 0 | <0.01 |
| Lumbee (3) | 3 | 0.01 |
| Menominee (0) | 1 | <0.01 |
| Mexican American Ind. (5) | 7 | 0.02 |
| Navajo (0) | 0 | <0.01 |
| Osage (0) | 0 | <0.01 |
| Ottawa (0) | 2 | 0.01 |
| Paiute (0) | 0 | <0.01 |
| Pima (0) | 0 | <0.01 |
| Potawatomi (0) | 0 | <0.01 |
| Pueblo (0) | 0 | <0.01 |
| Puget Sound Salish (0) | 0 | <0.01 |
| Seminole (0) | 0 | <0.01 |
| Shoshone (0) | 1 | <0.01 |
| Sioux (7) | 9 | 0.03 |
| South American Ind. (1) | 2 | 0.01 |
| Spanish American Ind. (0) | 0 | <0.01 |
| Tlingit-Haida (Alaska Native) (0) | 0 | <0.01 |
| Tohono O'Odham (0) | 0 | <0.01 |
| Tsimshian (Alaska Native) (0) | 0 | <0.01 |
| Ute (0) | 0 | <0.01 |
| Yakama (0) | 0 | <0.01 |
| Yaqui (0) | 0 | <0.01 |
| Yuman (0) | 0 | <0.01 |
| Yup'ik (Alaska Native) (0) | 0 | <0.01 |
| Asian (244) | 291 | 0.83 |
| Not Hispanic (238) | 285 | 0.81 |
| Hispanic (6) | 6 | 0.02 |
| Bangladeshi (0) | 0 | <0.01 |
| Bhutanese (0) | 0 | <0.01 |
| Burmese (0) | 0 | <0.01 |
| Cambodian (0) | 0 | <0.01 |
| Chinese, ex. Taiwanese (42) | 49 | 0.14 |
| Filipino (20) | 31 | 0.09 |
| Hmong (0) | 0 | <0.01 |
| Indian (49) | 67 | 0.19 |
| Indonesian (0) | 0 | <0.01 |
| Japanese (12) | 19 | 0.05 |
| Korean (38) | 44 | 0.12 |
| Laotian (18) | 20 | 0.06 |
| Malaysian (0) | 0 | <0.01 |
| Nepalese (0) | 0 | <0.01 |
| Pakistani (11) | 14 | 0.04 |
| Sri Lankan (6) | 6 | 0.02 |
| Taiwanese (7) | 7 | 0.02 |
| Thai (5) | 5 | 0.01 |
| Vietnamese (15) | 15 | 0.04 |
| Hawaii Native/Pacific Islander (2) | 8 | 0.02 |
| Not Hispanic (2) | 8 | 0.02 |
| Hispanic (0) | 0 | <0.01 |
| Fijian (0) | 0 | <0.01 |
| Guamanian/Chamorro (1) | 1 | <0.01 |
| Marshallese (0) | 0 | <0.01 |
| Native Hawaiian (0) | 3 | 0.01 |
| Samoan (1) | 3 | 0.01 |
| Tongan (0) | 0 | <0.01 |
| White (32,591) | 33,034 | 93.71 |
| Not Hispanic (31,999) | 32,386 | 91.87 |
| Hispanic (592) | 648 | 1.84 |

Notes: † The Census 2010 population figure is used to calculate the percentages in the Hispanic Origin and Race categories. Ancestry percentages are based on the 2006-2010 American Community Survey population (not shown); ‡ Numbers in parentheses indicate the number of people reporting a single ancestry; * Numbers in parentheses indicate the number of persons reporting this race alone, not in combination with any other race; Please refer to the Explanation of Data for more information.

## St. Lawrence County

Population: 111,944

| Ancestry | Population | % |
|---|---|---|
| Afghan (13) | 13 | 0.01 |
| African, Sub-Saharan (105) | 182 | 0.16 |
| African (54) | 113 | 0.10 |
| Cape Verdean (0) | 0 | <0.01 |
| Ethiopian (4) | 13 | 0.01 |
| Ghanaian (0) | 0 | <0.01 |
| Kenyan (15) | 15 | 0.01 |
| Liberian (0) | 0 | <0.01 |
| Nigerian (17) | 26 | 0.02 |
| Senegalese (0) | 0 | <0.01 |
| Sierra Leonean (0) | 0 | <0.01 |
| Somalian (0) | 0 | <0.01 |
| South African (0) | 0 | <0.01 |
| Sudanese (2) | 2 | <0.01 |
| Ugandan (0) | 0 | <0.01 |
| Zimbabwean (13) | 13 | 0.01 |
| Other Sub-Saharan African (0) | 0 | <0.01 |
| Albanian (43) | 43 | 0.04 |
| Alsatian (0) | 0 | <0.01 |
| American (10,121) | 10,121 | 9.05 |
| Arab (162) | 284 | 0.25 |
| Arab (81) | 100 | 0.09 |
| Egyptian (11) | 13 | 0.01 |
| Iraqi (0) | 0 | <0.01 |
| Jordanian (21) | 21 | 0.02 |
| Lebanese (44) | 75 | 0.07 |
| Moroccan (5) | 44 | 0.04 |
| Palestinian (0) | 0 | <0.01 |
| Syrian (0) | 0 | <0.01 |
| Other Arab (0) | 31 | 0.03 |
| Armenian (13) | 22 | 0.02 |
| Assyrian/Chaldean/Syriac (0) | 0 | <0.01 |
| Australian (17) | 17 | 0.02 |
| Austrian (41) | 114 | 0.10 |
| Basque (0) | 0 | <0.01 |
| Belgian (3) | 64 | 0.06 |
| Brazilian (4) | 5 | <0.01 |
| British (289) | 476 | 0.43 |
| Bulgarian (73) | 85 | 0.08 |
| Cajun (0) | 6 | 0.01 |
| Canadian (862) | 1,468 | 1.31 |
| Carpatho Rusyn (0) | 0 | <0.01 |
| Celtic (0) | 0 | <0.01 |
| Croatian (23) | 35 | 0.03 |
| Cypriot (0) | 0 | <0.01 |
| Czech (26) | 167 | 0.15 |
| Czechoslovakian (16) | 54 | 0.05 |
| Danish (22) | 147 | 0.13 |
| Dutch (594) | 3,189 | 2.85 |
| Eastern European (26) | 71 | 0.06 |
| English (7,608) | 16,754 | 14.99 |
| Estonian (13) | 13 | 0.01 |
| European (654) | 676 | 0.60 |
| Finnish (37) | 158 | 0.14 |
| French, ex. Basque (6,347) | 18,278 | 16.35 |
| French Canadian (3,623) | 6,370 | 5.70 |
| German (2,911) | 11,355 | 10.16 |
| German Russian (0) | 0 | <0.01 |
| Greek (126) | 286 | 0.26 |
| Guyanese (19) | 19 | 0.02 |
| Hungarian (420) | 956 | 0.86 |
| Icelander (0) | 13 | 0.01 |
| Iranian (24) | 49 | 0.04 |
| Irish (6,686) | 19,743 | 17.66 |
| Israeli (30) | 34 | 0.03 |
| Italian (2,977) | 8,006 | 7.16 |
| Latvian (14) | 14 | 0.01 |
| Lithuanian (43) | 175 | 0.16 |
| Luxemburger (0) | 9 | 0.01 |
| Macedonian (0) | 7 | 0.01 |
| Maltese (0) | 14 | 0.01 |
| New Zealander (0) | 0 | <0.01 |
| Northern European (15) | 15 | 0.01 |
| Norwegian (102) | 470 | 0.42 |
| Pennsylvania German (967) | 994 | 0.89 |

| Ancestry (cont.) | Population | % |
|---|---|---|
| Polish (980) | 3,024 | 2.71 |
| Portuguese (40) | 126 | 0.11 |
| Romanian (63) | 108 | 0.10 |
| Russian (285) | 713 | 0.64 |
| Scandinavian (52) | 184 | 0.16 |
| Scotch-Irish (932) | 2,320 | 2.08 |
| Scottish (1,251) | 4,260 | 3.81 |
| Serbian (0) | 0 | <0.01 |
| Slavic (0) | 10 | 0.01 |
| Slovak (69) | 117 | 0.10 |
| Slovene (4) | 4 | <0.01 |
| Soviet Union (0) | 0 | <0.01 |
| Swedish (93) | 651 | 0.58 |
| Swiss (42) | 138 | 0.12 |
| Turkish (49) | 58 | 0.05 |
| Ukrainian (139) | 464 | 0.42 |
| Welsh (212) | 802 | 0.72 |
| West Indian, ex. Hispanic (319) | 387 | 0.35 |
| Bahamian (14) | 20 | 0.02 |
| Barbadian (7) | 13 | 0.01 |
| Belizean (0) | 0 | <0.01 |
| Bermudan (0) | 0 | <0.01 |
| British West Indian (0) | 14 | 0.01 |
| Dutch West Indian (0) | 0 | <0.01 |
| Haitian (88) | 91 | 0.08 |
| Jamaican (169) | 207 | 0.19 |
| Trinidadian/Tobagonian (0) | 0 | <0.01 |
| U.S. Virgin Islander (0) | 0 | <0.01 |
| West Indian (41) | 42 | 0.04 |
| Other West Indian (0) | 0 | <0.01 |
| Yugoslavian (24) | 83 | 0.07 |

| Hispanic Origin | Population | % |
|---|---|---|
| Hispanic or Latino (of any race) | 2,146 | 1.92 |
| Central American, ex. Mexican | 199 | 0.18 |
| Costa Rican | 21 | 0.02 |
| Guatemalan | 65 | 0.06 |
| Honduran | 27 | 0.02 |
| Nicaraguan | 3 | <0.01 |
| Panamanian | 32 | 0.03 |
| Salvadoran | 49 | 0.04 |
| Other Central American | 2 | <0.01 |
| Cuban | 67 | 0.06 |
| Dominican Republic | 205 | 0.18 |
| Mexican | 437 | 0.39 |
| Puerto Rican | 845 | 0.75 |
| South American | 137 | 0.12 |
| Argentinean | 13 | 0.01 |
| Bolivian | 2 | <0.01 |
| Chilean | 6 | 0.01 |
| Colombian | 39 | 0.03 |
| Ecuadorian | 39 | 0.03 |
| Paraguayan | 4 | <0.01 |
| Peruvian | 16 | 0.01 |
| Uruguayan | 9 | 0.01 |
| Venezuelan | 6 | 0.01 |
| Other South American | 3 | <0.01 |
| Other Hispanic or Latino | 256 | 0.23 |

| Race* | Population | % |
|---|---|---|
| African-American/Black (2,420) | 2,895 | 2.59 |
| Not Hispanic (2,259) | 2,688 | 2.40 |
| Hispanic (161) | 207 | 0.18 |
| American Indian/Alaska Native (1,135) | 1,901 | 1.70 |
| Not Hispanic (1,051) | 1,756 | 1.57 |
| Hispanic (84) | 145 | 0.13 |
| Alaska Athabascan (Ala. Nat.) (0) | 3 | <0.01 |
| Aleut (Alaska Native) (0) | 0 | <0.01 |
| Apache (2) | 3 | <0.01 |
| Arapaho (1) | 1 | <0.01 |
| Blackfeet (5) | 25 | 0.02 |
| Canadian/French Am. Ind. (12) | 32 | 0.03 |
| Central American Ind. (4) | 4 | <0.01 |
| Cherokee (15) | 88 | 0.08 |
| Cheyenne (0) | 0 | <0.01 |
| Chickasaw (0) | 1 | <0.01 |
| Chippewa (8) | 10 | 0.01 |
| Choctaw (3) | 13 | 0.01 |
| Colville (0) | 0 | <0.01 |

| Race* (cont.) | Population | % |
|---|---|---|
| Comanche (0) | 0 | <0.01 |
| Cree (0) | 3 | <0.01 |
| Creek (2) | 2 | <0.01 |
| Crow (0) | 1 | <0.01 |
| Delaware (14) | 19 | 0.02 |
| Hopi (2) | 4 | <0.01 |
| Houma (0) | 0 | <0.01 |
| Inupiat (Alaska Native) (0) | 1 | <0.01 |
| Iroquois (694) | 979 | 0.87 |
| Kiowa (1) | 1 | <0.01 |
| Lumbee (1) | 1 | <0.01 |
| Menominee (0) | 0 | <0.01 |
| Mexican American Ind. (9) | 11 | 0.01 |
| Navajo (4) | 7 | 0.01 |
| Osage (0) | 0 | <0.01 |
| Ottawa (1) | 1 | <0.01 |
| Paiute (0) | 0 | <0.01 |
| Pima (0) | 0 | <0.01 |
| Potawatomi (0) | 0 | <0.01 |
| Pueblo (0) | 4 | <0.01 |
| Puget Sound Salish (0) | 0 | <0.01 |
| Seminole (0) | 4 | <0.01 |
| Shoshone (0) | 0 | <0.01 |
| Sioux (4) | 10 | 0.01 |
| South American Ind. (13) | 19 | 0.02 |
| Spanish American Ind. (0) | 1 | <0.01 |
| Tlingit-Haida (Alaska Native) (0) | 0 | <0.01 |
| Tohono O'Odham (0) | 0 | <0.01 |
| Tsimshian (Alaska Native) (0) | 0 | <0.01 |
| Ute (0) | 0 | <0.01 |
| Yakama (0) | 0 | <0.01 |
| Yaqui (0) | 0 | <0.01 |
| Yuman (0) | 0 | <0.01 |
| Yup'ik (Alaska Native) (0) | 3 | <0.01 |
| Asian (1,085) | 1,366 | 1.22 |
| Not Hispanic (1,074) | 1,343 | 1.20 |
| Hispanic (11) | 23 | 0.02 |
| Bangladeshi (6) | 11 | 0.01 |
| Bhutanese (0) | 0 | <0.01 |
| Burmese (0) | 1 | <0.01 |
| Cambodian (5) | 5 | <0.01 |
| Chinese, ex. Taiwanese (331) | 391 | 0.35 |
| Filipino (89) | 163 | 0.15 |
| Hmong (2) | 3 | <0.01 |
| Indian (283) | 336 | 0.30 |
| Indonesian (4) | 10 | 0.01 |
| Japanese (33) | 62 | 0.06 |
| Korean (152) | 176 | 0.16 |
| Laotian (4) | 7 | 0.01 |
| Malaysian (1) | 7 | <0.01 |
| Nepalese (5) | 5 | <0.01 |
| Pakistani (39) | 42 | 0.04 |
| Sri Lankan (14) | 14 | 0.01 |
| Taiwanese (12) | 19 | 0.02 |
| Thai (13) | 15 | 0.01 |
| Vietnamese (42) | 60 | 0.05 |
| Hawaii Native/Pacific Islander (36) | 95 | 0.08 |
| Not Hispanic (26) | 65 | 0.06 |
| Hispanic (10) | 30 | 0.03 |
| Fijian (0) | 0 | <0.01 |
| Guamanian/Chamorro (4) | 8 | 0.01 |
| Marshallese (0) | 0 | <0.01 |
| Native Hawaiian (26) | 50 | 0.04 |
| Samoan (1) | 5 | <0.01 |
| Tongan (0) | 0 | <0.01 |
| White (105,064) | 106,470 | 95.11 |
| Not Hispanic (103,943) | 105,195 | 93.97 |
| Hispanic (1,121) | 1,275 | 1.14 |

*Notes: † The Census 2010 population figure is used to calculate the percentages in the Hispanic Origin and Race categories. Ancestry percentages are based on the 2006-2010 American Community Survey population (not shown); ‡ Numbers in parentheses indicate the number of people reporting a single ancestry; * Numbers in parentheses indicate the number of persons reporting this race alone, not in combination with any other race; Please refer to the Explanation of Data for more information.*

## Steuben County

Population: 98,990

| Ancestry | Population | % |
|---|---|---|
| Afghan (0) | 0 | <0.01 |
| African, Sub-Saharan (102) | 115 | 0.12 |
| African (79) | 92 | 0.09 |
| Cape Verdean (0) | 0 | <0.01 |
| Ethiopian (23) | 23 | 0.02 |
| Ghanaian (0) | 0 | <0.01 |
| Kenyan (0) | 0 | <0.01 |
| Liberian (0) | 0 | <0.01 |
| Nigerian (0) | 0 | <0.01 |
| Senegalese (0) | 0 | <0.01 |
| Sierra Leonean (0) | 0 | <0.01 |
| Somalian (0) | 0 | <0.01 |
| South African (0) | 0 | <0.01 |
| Sudanese (0) | 0 | <0.01 |
| Ugandan (0) | 0 | <0.01 |
| Zimbabwean (0) | 0 | <0.01 |
| Other Sub-Saharan African (0) | 0 | <0.01 |
| Albanian (0) | 0 | <0.01 |
| Alsatian (0) | 12 | 0.01 |
| American (8,840) | 8,840 | 8.95 |
| Arab (73) | 105 | 0.11 |
| Arab (0) | 0 | <0.01 |
| Egyptian (0) | 0 | <0.01 |
| Iraqi (0) | 0 | <0.01 |
| Jordanian (0) | 0 | <0.01 |
| Lebanese (41) | 61 | 0.06 |
| Moroccan (14) | 14 | 0.01 |
| Palestinian (0) | 0 | <0.01 |
| Syrian (18) | 30 | 0.03 |
| Other Arab (0) | 0 | <0.01 |
| Armenian (7) | 19 | 0.02 |
| Assyrian/Chaldean/Syriac (0) | 0 | <0.01 |
| Australian (0) | 4 | <0.01 |
| Austrian (28) | 211 | 0.21 |
| Basque (0) | 13 | 0.01 |
| Belgian (17) | 74 | 0.07 |
| Brazilian (11) | 19 | 0.02 |
| British (250) | 488 | 0.49 |
| Bulgarian (5) | 9 | 0.01 |
| Cajun (0) | 0 | <0.01 |
| Canadian (81) | 184 | 0.19 |
| Carpatho Rusyn (23) | 23 | 0.02 |
| Celtic (0) | 102 | 0.10 |
| Croatian (0) | 31 | 0.03 |
| Cypriot (0) | 0 | <0.01 |
| Czech (95) | 366 | 0.37 |
| Czechoslovakian (62) | 83 | 0.08 |
| Danish (106) | 229 | 0.23 |
| Dutch (886) | 4,824 | 4.89 |
| Eastern European (94) | 96 | 0.10 |
| English (5,831) | 17,210 | 17.43 |
| Estonian (5) | 5 | 0.01 |
| European (685) | 701 | 0.71 |
| Finnish (30) | 118 | 0.12 |
| French, ex. Basque (745) | 3,810 | 3.86 |
| French Canadian (323) | 859 | 0.87 |
| German (6,305) | 22,942 | 23.24 |
| German Russian (0) | 0 | <0.01 |
| Greek (115) | 200 | 0.20 |
| Guyanese (31) | 31 | 0.03 |
| Hungarian (119) | 343 | 0.35 |
| Icelander (0) | 0 | <0.01 |
| Iranian (0) | 0 | <0.01 |
| Irish (6,137) | 19,859 | 20.12 |
| Israeli (23) | 30 | 0.03 |
| Italian (2,932) | 8,609 | 8.72 |
| Latvian (6) | 42 | 0.04 |
| Lithuanian (22) | 94 | 0.10 |
| Luxemburger (5) | 5 | 0.01 |
| Macedonian (0) | 0 | <0.01 |
| Maltese (0) | 0 | <0.01 |
| New Zealander (0) | 0 | <0.01 |
| Northern European (70) | 80 | 0.08 |
| Norwegian (184) | 541 | 0.55 |
| Pennsylvania German (772) | 1,134 | 1.15 |

| Ancestry (cont.) | Population | % |
|---|---|---|
| Polish (1,810) | 5,161 | 5.23 |
| Portuguese (54) | 165 | 0.17 |
| Romanian (24) | 79 | 0.08 |
| Russian (120) | 456 | 0.46 |
| Scandinavian (37) | 82 | 0.08 |
| Scotch-Irish (681) | 1,744 | 1.77 |
| Scottish (550) | 2,433 | 2.46 |
| Serbian (3) | 13 | 0.01 |
| Slavic (9) | 21 | 0.02 |
| Slovak (60) | 161 | 0.16 |
| Slovene (0) | 18 | 0.02 |
| Soviet Union (12) | 12 | 0.01 |
| Swedish (423) | 1,367 | 1.38 |
| Swiss (122) | 317 | 0.32 |
| Turkish (25) | 46 | 0.05 |
| Ukrainian (194) | 456 | 0.46 |
| Welsh (262) | 1,328 | 1.35 |
| West Indian, ex. Hispanic (120) | 142 | 0.14 |
| Bahamian (0) | 0 | <0.01 |
| Barbadian (93) | 93 | 0.09 |
| Belizean (0) | 0 | <0.01 |
| Bermudan (0) | 0 | <0.01 |
| British West Indian (0) | 0 | <0.01 |
| Dutch West Indian (0) | 0 | <0.01 |
| Haitian (6) | 6 | 0.01 |
| Jamaican (21) | 32 | 0.03 |
| Trinidadian/Tobagonian (0) | 0 | <0.01 |
| U.S. Virgin Islander (0) | 0 | <0.01 |
| West Indian (0) | 11 | 0.01 |
| Other West Indian (0) | 0 | <0.01 |
| Yugoslavian (0) | 7 | 0.01 |

| Hispanic Origin | Population | % |
|---|---|---|
| Hispanic or Latino (of any race) | 1,371 | 1.38 |
| Central American, ex. Mexican | 109 | 0.11 |
| Costa Rican | 1 | <0.01 |
| Guatemalan | 14 | 0.01 |
| Honduran | 43 | 0.04 |
| Nicaraguan | 10 | 0.01 |
| Panamanian | 13 | 0.01 |
| Salvadoran | 28 | 0.03 |
| Other Central American | 0 | <0.01 |
| Cuban | 31 | 0.03 |
| Dominican Republic | 44 | 0.04 |
| Mexican | 432 | 0.44 |
| Puerto Rican | 500 | 0.51 |
| South American | 89 | 0.09 |
| Argentinean | 1 | <0.01 |
| Bolivian | 3 | <0.01 |
| Chilean | 8 | 0.01 |
| Colombian | 21 | 0.02 |
| Ecuadorian | 19 | 0.02 |
| Paraguayan | 7 | 0.01 |
| Peruvian | 20 | 0.02 |
| Uruguayan | 1 | <0.01 |
| Venezuelan | 5 | 0.01 |
| Other South American | 4 | <0.01 |
| Other Hispanic or Latino | 166 | 0.17 |

| Race* | Population | % |
|---|---|---|
| African-American/Black (1,540) | 2,158 | 2.18 |
| Not Hispanic (1,487) | 2,074 | 2.10 |
| Hispanic (53) | 84 | 0.08 |
| American Indian/Alaska Native (230) | 765 | 0.77 |
| Not Hispanic (193) | 683 | 0.69 |
| Hispanic (37) | 82 | 0.08 |
| Alaska Athabascan (Ala. Nat.) (0) | 0 | <0.01 |
| Aleut (Alaska Native) (0) | 0 | <0.01 |
| Apache (1) | 6 | 0.01 |
| Arapaho (0) | 0 | <0.01 |
| Blackfeet (11) | 60 | 0.06 |
| Canadian/French Am. Ind. (1) | 4 | <0.01 |
| Central American Ind. (0) | 0 | <0.01 |
| Cherokee (20) | 100 | 0.10 |
| Cheyenne (0) | 2 | <0.01 |
| Chickasaw (0) | 0 | <0.01 |
| Chippewa (2) | 4 | <0.01 |
| Choctaw (3) | 10 | 0.01 |
| Colville (0) | 0 | <0.01 |

| Race* (cont.) | Population | % |
|---|---|---|
| Comanche (0) | 0 | <0.01 |
| Cree (0) | 1 | <0.01 |
| Creek (0) | 4 | <0.01 |
| Crow (3) | 4 | <0.01 |
| Delaware (1) | 9 | 0.01 |
| Hopi (0) | 0 | <0.01 |
| Houma (0) | 0 | <0.01 |
| Inupiat (Alaska Native) (3) | 5 | 0.01 |
| Iroquois (48) | 144 | 0.15 |
| Kiowa (0) | 0 | <0.01 |
| Lumbee (0) | 0 | <0.01 |
| Menominee (0) | 0 | <0.01 |
| Mexican American Ind. (7) | 7 | 0.01 |
| Navajo (1) | 3 | <0.01 |
| Osage (0) | 0 | <0.01 |
| Ottawa (0) | 0 | <0.01 |
| Paiute (0) | 0 | <0.01 |
| Pima (0) | 0 | <0.01 |
| Potawatomi (0) | 0 | <0.01 |
| Pueblo (1) | 1 | <0.01 |
| Puget Sound Salish (0) | 0 | <0.01 |
| Seminole (0) | 3 | <0.01 |
| Shoshone (0) | 1 | <0.01 |
| Sioux (4) | 19 | 0.02 |
| South American Ind. (2) | 7 | 0.01 |
| Spanish American Ind. (1) | 4 | <0.01 |
| Tlingit-Haida (Alaska Native) (5) | 5 | 0.01 |
| Tohono O'Odham (0) | 0 | <0.01 |
| Tsimshian (Alaska Native) (0) | 0 | <0.01 |
| Ute (0) | 0 | <0.01 |
| Yakama (0) | 0 | <0.01 |
| Yaqui (0) | 0 | <0.01 |
| Yuman (0) | 0 | <0.01 |
| Yup'ik (Alaska Native) (2) | 2 | <0.01 |
| Asian (1,161) | 1,352 | 1.37 |
| Not Hispanic (1,151) | 1,332 | 1.35 |
| Hispanic (10) | 20 | 0.02 |
| Bangladeshi (12) | 12 | 0.01 |
| Bhutanese (0) | 0 | <0.01 |
| Burmese (1) | 1 | <0.01 |
| Cambodian (5) | 5 | 0.01 |
| Chinese, ex. Taiwanese (336) | 382 | 0.39 |
| Filipino (111) | 161 | 0.16 |
| Hmong (0) | 0 | <0.01 |
| Indian (392) | 438 | 0.44 |
| Indonesian (6) | 6 | 0.01 |
| Japanese (43) | 70 | 0.07 |
| Korean (82) | 108 | 0.11 |
| Laotian (12) | 14 | 0.01 |
| Malaysian (2) | 2 | <0.01 |
| Nepalese (12) | 12 | 0.01 |
| Pakistani (45) | 49 | 0.05 |
| Sri Lankan (4) | 4 | <0.01 |
| Taiwanese (28) | 28 | 0.03 |
| Thai (12) | 15 | 0.02 |
| Vietnamese (25) | 30 | 0.03 |
| Hawaii Native/Pacific Islander (17) | 48 | 0.05 |
| Not Hispanic (14) | 42 | 0.04 |
| Hispanic (3) | 6 | 0.01 |
| Fijian (2) | 2 | <0.01 |
| Guamanian/Chamorro (3) | 6 | 0.01 |
| Marshallese (2) | 2 | <0.01 |
| Native Hawaiian (8) | 24 | 0.02 |
| Samoan (0) | 1 | <0.01 |
| Tongan (0) | 0 | <0.01 |
| White (94,315) | 95,643 | 96.62 |
| Not Hispanic (93,476) | 94,659 | 95.62 |
| Hispanic (839) | 984 | 0.99 |

*Notes: † The Census 2010 population figure is used to calculate the percentages in the Hispanic Origin and Race categories. Ancestry percentages are based on the 2006-2010 American Community Survey population (not shown); ‡ Numbers in parentheses indicate the number of people reporting a single ancestry; * Numbers in parentheses indicate the number of persons reporting this race alone, not in combination with any other race; Please refer to the Explanation of Data for more information.*

## Suffolk County

Population: 1,493,350

| Ancestry | Population | % |
|---|---|---|
| Afghan (742) | 823 | 0.06 |
| African, Sub-Saharan (5,702) | 7,192 | 0.49 |
| African (3,798) | 4,984 | 0.34 |
| Cape Verdean (0) | 9 | <0.01 |
| Ethiopian (21) | 136 | 0.01 |
| Ghanaian (192) | 192 | 0.01 |
| Kenyan (0) | 0 | <0.01 |
| Liberian (309) | 318 | 0.02 |
| Nigerian (1,092) | 1,220 | 0.08 |
| Senegalese (0) | 0 | <0.01 |
| Sierra Leonean (0) | 0 | <0.01 |
| Somalian (0) | 0 | <0.01 |
| South African (84) | 102 | 0.01 |
| Sudanese (0) | 14 | <0.01 |
| Ugandan (0) | 0 | <0.01 |
| Zimbabwean (0) | 0 | <0.01 |
| Other Sub-Saharan African (206) | 217 | 0.01 |
| Albanian (614) | 824 | 0.06 |
| Alsatian (0) | 39 | <0.01 |
| American (31,772) | 31,772 | 2.14 |
| Arab (3,411) | 5,631 | 0.38 |
| Arab (547) | 751 | 0.05 |
| Egyptian (1,042) | 1,355 | 0.09 |
| Iraqi (94) | 283 | 0.02 |
| Jordanian (233) | 365 | 0.02 |
| Lebanese (210) | 787 | 0.05 |
| Moroccan (426) | 579 | 0.04 |
| Palestinian (280) | 302 | 0.02 |
| Syrian (151) | 574 | 0.04 |
| Other Arab (428) | 635 | 0.04 |
| Armenian (1,000) | 2,005 | 0.14 |
| Assyrian/Chaldean/Syriac (0) | 0 | <0.01 |
| Australian (165) | 361 | 0.02 |
| Austrian (1,961) | 9,897 | 0.67 |
| Basque (48) | 76 | 0.01 |
| Belgian (219) | 1,025 | 0.07 |
| Brazilian (1,446) | 2,033 | 0.14 |
| British (1,885) | 3,939 | 0.27 |
| Bulgarian (199) | 296 | 0.02 |
| Cajun (0) | 42 | <0.01 |
| Canadian (1,220) | 3,384 | 0.23 |
| Carpatho Rusyn (46) | 46 | <0.01 |
| Celtic (126) | 220 | 0.01 |
| Croatian (1,176) | 2,492 | 0.17 |
| Cypriot (146) | 158 | 0.01 |
| Czech (1,747) | 8,389 | 0.57 |
| Czechoslovakian (1,155) | 2,893 | 0.20 |
| Danish (865) | 3,979 | 0.27 |
| Dutch (2,110) | 12,986 | 0.88 |
| Eastern European (4,046) | 4,484 | 0.30 |
| English (15,317) | 86,937 | 5.86 |
| Estonian (193) | 470 | 0.03 |
| European (6,998) | 7,658 | 0.52 |
| Finnish (437) | 1,833 | 0.12 |
| French, ex. Basque (2,763) | 25,117 | 1.69 |
| French Canadian (2,013) | 6,822 | 0.46 |
| German (45,404) | 248,603 | 16.77 |
| German Russian (0) | 40 | <0.01 |
| Greek (8,977) | 19,268 | 1.30 |
| Guyanese (1,567) | 1,875 | 0.13 |
| Hungarian (2,826) | 12,736 | 0.86 |
| Icelander (54) | 150 | 0.01 |
| Iranian (1,181) | 1,367 | 0.09 |
| Irish (87,385) | 340,599 | 22.97 |
| Israeli (740) | 1,266 | 0.09 |
| Italian (202,824) | 427,711 | 28.85 |
| Latvian (251) | 567 | 0.04 |
| Lithuanian (1,966) | 5,680 | 0.38 |
| Luxemburger (0) | 36 | <0.01 |
| Macedonian (22) | 44 | <0.01 |
| Maltese (405) | 1,698 | 0.11 |
| New Zealander (44) | 57 | <0.01 |
| Northern European (525) | 590 | 0.04 |
| Norwegian (3,647) | 14,773 | 1.00 |
| Pennsylvania German (69) | 107 | 0.01 |

| Ancestry | Population | % |
|---|---|---|
| Polish (28,723) | 89,379 | 6.03 |
| Portuguese (4,698) | 7,670 | 0.52 |
| Romanian (1,746) | 4,330 | 0.29 |
| Russian (12,970) | 39,198 | 2.64 |
| Scandinavian (395) | 1,115 | 0.08 |
| Scotch-Irish (5,695) | 15,856 | 1.07 |
| Scottish (2,865) | 16,692 | 1.13 |
| Serbian (64) | 237 | 0.02 |
| Slavic (137) | 601 | 0.04 |
| Slovak (803) | 1,936 | 0.13 |
| Slovene (220) | 324 | 0.02 |
| Soviet Union (3) | 3 | <0.01 |
| Swedish (1,863) | 13,486 | 0.91 |
| Swiss (672) | 3,707 | 0.25 |
| Turkish (3,736) | 4,401 | 0.30 |
| Ukrainian (2,645) | 7,707 | 0.52 |
| Welsh (687) | 3,742 | 0.25 |
| West Indian, ex. Hispanic (25,884) | 31,391 | 2.12 |
| Bahamian (66) | 188 | 0.01 |
| Barbadian (189) | 308 | 0.02 |
| Belizean (35) | 47 | <0.01 |
| Bermudan (0) | 34 | <0.01 |
| British West Indian (378) | 665 | 0.04 |
| Dutch West Indian (49) | 49 | <0.01 |
| Haitian (11,652) | 12,903 | 0.87 |
| Jamaican (8,020) | 10,122 | 0.68 |
| Trinidadian/Tobagonian (2,485) | 2,971 | 0.20 |
| U.S. Virgin Islander (91) | 154 | 0.01 |
| West Indian (2,912) | 3,916 | 0.26 |
| Other West Indian (7) | 34 | <0.01 |
| Yugoslavian (475) | 1,653 | 0.11 |

| Hispanic Origin | Population | % |
|---|---|---|
| Hispanic or Latino (of any race) | 246,239 | 16.49 |
| Central American, ex. Mexican | 77,117 | 5.16 |
| Costa Rican | 1,656 | 0.11 |
| Guatemalan | 11,229 | 0.75 |
| Honduran | 9,563 | 0.64 |
| Nicaraguan | 683 | 0.05 |
| Panamanian | 1,203 | 0.08 |
| Salvadoran | 52,315 | 3.50 |
| Other Central American | 468 | 0.03 |
| Cuban | 4,310 | 0.29 |
| Dominican Republic | 21,751 | 1.46 |
| Mexican | 15,663 | 1.05 |
| Puerto Rican | 58,549 | 3.92 |
| South American | 44,731 | 3.00 |
| Argentinean | 2,260 | 0.15 |
| Bolivian | 565 | 0.04 |
| Chilean | 1,507 | 0.10 |
| Colombian | 13,846 | 0.93 |
| Ecuadorian | 17,638 | 1.18 |
| Paraguayan | 282 | 0.02 |
| Peruvian | 6,962 | 0.47 |
| Uruguayan | 474 | 0.03 |
| Venezuelan | 919 | 0.06 |
| Other South American | 278 | 0.02 |
| Other Hispanic or Latino | 24,118 | 1.62 |

| Race* | Population | % |
|---|---|---|
| African-American/Black (111,224) | 125,571 | 8.41 |
| Not Hispanic (102,117) | 112,207 | 7.51 |
| Hispanic (9,107) | 13,364 | 0.89 |
| American Indian/Alaska Native (5,366) | 12,535 | 0.84 |
| Not Hispanic (2,906) | 7,986 | 0.53 |
| Hispanic (2,460) | 4,549 | 0.30 |
| Alaska Athabascan (Ala. Nat.) (1) | 6 | <0.01 |
| Aleut (Alaska Native) (5) | 7 | <0.01 |
| Apache (24) | 65 | <0.01 |
| Arapaho (0) | 3 | <0.01 |
| Blackfeet (44) | 364 | 0.02 |
| Canadian/French Am. Ind. (20) | 43 | <0.01 |
| Central American Ind. (128) | 195 | 0.01 |
| Cherokee (246) | 1,501 | 0.10 |
| Cheyenne (2) | 12 | <0.01 |
| Chickasaw (2) | 11 | <0.01 |
| Chippewa (31) | 63 | <0.01 |
| Choctaw (13) | 90 | 0.01 |
| Colville (0) | 0 | <0.01 |

| Race* | Population | % |
|---|---|---|
| Comanche (6) | 24 | <0.01 |
| Cree (2) | 9 | <0.01 |
| Creek (5) | 58 | <0.01 |
| Crow (13) | 23 | <0.01 |
| Delaware (7) | 35 | <0.01 |
| Hopi (5) | 11 | <0.01 |
| Houma (1) | 3 | <0.01 |
| Inupiat (Alaska Native) (2) | 5 | <0.01 |
| Iroquois (160) | 388 | 0.03 |
| Kiowa (1) | 1 | <0.01 |
| Lumbee (14) | 40 | <0.01 |
| Menominee (0) | 0 | <0.01 |
| Mexican American Ind. (264) | 376 | 0.03 |
| Navajo (15) | 45 | <0.01 |
| Osage (0) | 5 | <0.01 |
| Ottawa (0) | 5 | <0.01 |
| Paiute (2) | 4 | <0.01 |
| Pima (1) | 1 | <0.01 |
| Potawatomi (9) | 13 | <0.01 |
| Pueblo (20) | 29 | <0.01 |
| Puget Sound Salish (5) | 7 | <0.01 |
| Seminole (12) | 63 | <0.01 |
| Shoshone (0) | 7 | <0.01 |
| Sioux (36) | 109 | 0.01 |
| South American Ind. (332) | 629 | 0.04 |
| Spanish American Ind. (133) | 182 | 0.01 |
| Tlingit-Haida (Alaska Native) (5) | 14 | <0.01 |
| Tohono O'Odham (0) | 1 | <0.01 |
| Tsimshian (Alaska Native) (0) | 0 | <0.01 |
| Ute (0) | 2 | <0.01 |
| Yakama (0) | 1 | <0.01 |
| Yaqui (2) | 7 | <0.01 |
| Yuman (1) | 2 | <0.01 |
| Yup'ik (Alaska Native) (0) | 0 | <0.01 |
| Asian (50,972) | 59,859 | 4.01 |
| Not Hispanic (50,295) | 57,980 | 3.88 |
| Hispanic (677) | 1,879 | 0.13 |
| Bangladeshi (1,243) | 1,469 | 0.10 |
| Bhutanese (3) | 3 | <0.01 |
| Burmese (61) | 80 | 0.01 |
| Cambodian (53) | 71 | <0.01 |
| Chinese, ex. Taiwanese (11,537) | 13,502 | 0.90 |
| Filipino (5,202) | 6,881 | 0.46 |
| Hmong (1) | 4 | <0.01 |
| Indian (15,975) | 18,167 | 1.22 |
| Indonesian (117) | 174 | 0.01 |
| Japanese (904) | 1,673 | 0.11 |
| Korean (5,627) | 6,461 | 0.43 |
| Laotian (84) | 107 | <0.01 |
| Malaysian (25) | 55 | <0.01 |
| Nepalese (69) | 72 | <0.01 |
| Pakistani (5,426) | 5,997 | 0.40 |
| Sri Lankan (149) | 183 | 0.01 |
| Taiwanese (470) | 550 | 0.04 |
| Thai (401) | 553 | 0.04 |
| Vietnamese (1,565) | 1,835 | 0.12 |
| Hawaii Native/Pacific Islander (495) | 1,606 | 0.11 |
| Not Hispanic (275) | 939 | 0.06 |
| Hispanic (220) | 667 | 0.04 |
| Fijian (3) | 16 | <0.01 |
| Guamanian/Chamorro (208) | 263 | 0.02 |
| Marshallese (1) | 1 | <0.01 |
| Native Hawaiian (105) | 331 | 0.02 |
| Samoan (25) | 59 | <0.01 |
| Tongan (5) | 5 | <0.01 |
| White (1,206,297) | 1,234,863 | 82.69 |
| Not Hispanic (1,068,728) | 1,083,973 | 72.59 |
| Hispanic (137,569) | 150,890 | 10.10 |

*Notes: † The Census 2010 population figure is used to calculate the percentages in the Hispanic Origin and Race categories. Ancestry percentages are based on the 2006-2010 American Community Survey population (not shown); ‡ Numbers in parentheses indicate the number of people reporting a single ancestry; * Numbers in parentheses indicate the number of persons reporting this race alone, not in combination with any other race; Please refer to the Explanation of Data for more information.*

## Sullivan County

Population: 77,547

| Ancestry | Population | % |
|---|---|---|
| Afghan (0) | 0 | <0.01 |
| African, Sub-Saharan (208) | 232 | 0.30 |
| African (84) | 108 | 0.14 |
| Cape Verdean (0) | 0 | <0.01 |
| Ethiopian (0) | 0 | <0.01 |
| Ghanaian (16) | 16 | 0.02 |
| Kenyan (9) | 9 | 0.01 |
| Liberian (18) | 18 | 0.02 |
| Nigerian (34) | 34 | 0.04 |
| Senegalese (0) | 0 | <0.01 |
| Sierra Leonean (0) | 0 | <0.01 |
| Somalian (0) | 0 | <0.01 |
| South African (0) | 0 | <0.01 |
| Sudanese (0) | 0 | <0.01 |
| Ugandan (0) | 0 | <0.01 |
| Zimbabwean (40) | 40 | 0.05 |
| Other Sub-Saharan African (7) | 7 | 0.01 |
| Albanian (59) | 71 | 0.09 |
| Alsatian (0) | 0 | <0.01 |
| American (4,050) | 4,050 | 5.22 |
| Arab (251) | 350 | 0.45 |
| Arab (5) | 9 | 0.01 |
| Egyptian (102) | 145 | 0.19 |
| Iraqi (0) | 0 | <0.01 |
| Jordanian (117) | 137 | 0.18 |
| Lebanese (2) | 21 | 0.03 |
| Moroccan (0) | 0 | <0.01 |
| Palestinian (0) | 0 | <0.01 |
| Syrian (12) | 25 | 0.03 |
| Other Arab (13) | 13 | 0.02 |
| Armenian (24) | 26 | 0.03 |
| Assyrian/Chaldean/Syriac (0) | 0 | <0.01 |
| Australian (17) | 81 | 0.10 |
| Austrian (130) | 374 | 0.48 |
| Basque (0) | 0 | <0.01 |
| Belgian (18) | 18 | 0.02 |
| Brazilian (53) | 86 | 0.11 |
| British (84) | 183 | 0.24 |
| Bulgarian (0) | 0 | <0.01 |
| Cajun (0) | 0 | <0.01 |
| Canadian (131) | 386 | 0.50 |
| Carpatho Rusyn (0) | 0 | <0.01 |
| Celtic (14) | 38 | 0.05 |
| Croatian (65) | 154 | 0.20 |
| Cypriot (0) | 0 | <0.01 |
| Czech (84) | 390 | 0.50 |
| Czechoslovakian (127) | 308 | 0.40 |
| Danish (65) | 251 | 0.32 |
| Dutch (428) | 2,234 | 2.88 |
| Eastern European (227) | 299 | 0.39 |
| English (1,413) | 5,957 | 7.67 |
| Estonian (8) | 16 | 0.02 |
| European (325) | 410 | 0.53 |
| Finnish (35) | 64 | 0.08 |
| French, ex. Basque (450) | 2,130 | 2.74 |
| French Canadian (120) | 393 | 0.51 |
| German (4,582) | 14,760 | 19.01 |
| German Russian (0) | 0 | <0.01 |
| Greek (285) | 449 | 0.58 |
| Guyanese (35) | 35 | 0.05 |
| Hungarian (318) | 1,183 | 1.52 |
| Icelander (0) | 0 | <0.01 |
| Iranian (94) | 100 | 0.13 |
| Irish (4,513) | 15,183 | 19.56 |
| Israeli (30) | 58 | 0.07 |
| Italian (4,173) | 10,325 | 13.30 |
| Latvian (34) | 60 | 0.08 |
| Lithuanian (158) | 381 | 0.49 |
| Luxemburger (0) | 0 | <0.01 |
| Macedonian (53) | 64 | 0.08 |
| Maltese (0) | 0 | <0.01 |
| New Zealander (0) | 18 | 0.02 |
| Northern European (33) | 66 | 0.09 |
| Norwegian (355) | 918 | 1.18 |
| Pennsylvania German (26) | 35 | 0.05 |

| Ancestry | Population | % |
|---|---|---|
| Polish (1,384) | 4,248 | 5.47 |
| Portuguese (100) | 280 | 0.36 |
| Romanian (110) | 221 | 0.28 |
| Russian (1,015) | 2,172 | 2.80 |
| Scandinavian (49) | 115 | 0.15 |
| Scotch-Irish (296) | 812 | 1.05 |
| Scottish (291) | 1,158 | 1.49 |
| Serbian (24) | 24 | 0.03 |
| Slavic (0) | 22 | 0.03 |
| Slovak (92) | 181 | 0.23 |
| Slovene (0) | 10 | 0.01 |
| Soviet Union (0) | 0 | <0.01 |
| Swedish (219) | 595 | 0.77 |
| Swiss (186) | 430 | 0.55 |
| Turkish (39) | 86 | 0.11 |
| Ukrainian (453) | 989 | 1.27 |
| Welsh (128) | 600 | 0.77 |
| West Indian, ex. Hispanic (723) | 1,131 | 1.46 |
| Bahamian (0) | 0 | <0.01 |
| Barbadian (77) | 149 | 0.19 |
| Belizean (0) | 0 | <0.01 |
| Bermudan (0) | 0 | <0.01 |
| British West Indian (16) | 16 | 0.02 |
| Dutch West Indian (0) | 55 | 0.07 |
| Haitian (73) | 73 | 0.09 |
| Jamaican (298) | 415 | 0.53 |
| Trinidadian/Tobagonian (176) | 287 | 0.37 |
| U.S. Virgin Islander (0) | 0 | <0.01 |
| West Indian (83) | 136 | 0.18 |
| Other West Indian (0) | 0 | <0.01 |
| Yugoslavian (107) | 152 | 0.20 |

| Hispanic Origin | Population | % |
|---|---|---|
| Hispanic or Latino (of any race) | 10,554 | 13.61 |
| Central American, ex. Mexican | 1,461 | 1.88 |
| Costa Rican | 46 | 0.06 |
| Guatemalan | 223 | 0.29 |
| Honduran | 575 | 0.74 |
| Nicaraguan | 45 | 0.06 |
| Panamanian | 50 | 0.06 |
| Salvadoran | 516 | 0.67 |
| Other Central American | 6 | 0.01 |
| Cuban | 297 | 0.38 |
| Dominican Republic | 448 | 0.58 |
| Mexican | 1,385 | 1.79 |
| Puerto Rican | 5,309 | 6.85 |
| South American | 866 | 1.12 |
| Argentinean | 68 | 0.09 |
| Bolivian | 9 | 0.01 |
| Chilean | 46 | 0.06 |
| Colombian | 398 | 0.51 |
| Ecuadorian | 144 | 0.19 |
| Paraguayan | 8 | 0.01 |
| Peruvian | 153 | 0.20 |
| Uruguayan | 14 | 0.02 |
| Venezuelan | 13 | 0.02 |
| Other South American | 13 | 0.02 |
| Other Hispanic or Latino | 788 | 1.02 |

| Race* | Population | % |
|---|---|---|
| African-American/Black (7,039) | 8,207 | 10.58 |
| Not Hispanic (6,349) | 7,180 | 9.26 |
| Hispanic (690) | 1,027 | 1.32 |
| American Indian/Alaska Native (354) | 950 | 1.23 |
| Not Hispanic (228) | 653 | 0.84 |
| Hispanic (126) | 297 | 0.38 |
| Alaska Athabascan (Ala. Nat.) (0) | 0 | <0.01 |
| Aleut (Alaska Native) (0) | 0 | <0.01 |
| Apache (5) | 12 | 0.02 |
| Arapaho (0) | 0 | <0.01 |
| Blackfeet (10) | 51 | 0.07 |
| Canadian/French Am. Ind. (1) | 3 | <0.01 |
| Central American Ind. (3) | 4 | 0.01 |
| Cherokee (24) | 147 | 0.19 |
| Cheyenne (0) | 0 | <0.01 |
| Chickasaw (0) | 0 | <0.01 |
| Chippewa (3) | 8 | 0.01 |
| Choctaw (1) | 7 | 0.01 |
| Colville (0) | 0 | <0.01 |

| | Population | % |
|---|---|---|
| Comanche (0) | 0 | <0.01 |
| Cree (0) | 3 | <0.01 |
| Creek (3) | 4 | 0.01 |
| Crow (1) | 3 | <0.01 |
| Delaware (30) | 60 | 0.08 |
| Hopi (0) | 0 | <0.01 |
| Houma (2) | 2 | <0.01 |
| Inupiat (Alaska Native) (1) | 1 | <0.01 |
| Iroquois (21) | 47 | 0.06 |
| Kiowa (0) | 0 | <0.01 |
| Lumbee (0) | 0 | <0.01 |
| Menominee (0) | 0 | <0.01 |
| Mexican American Ind. (24) | 35 | 0.05 |
| Navajo (2) | 4 | 0.01 |
| Osage (0) | 0 | <0.01 |
| Ottawa (0) | 0 | <0.01 |
| Paiute (0) | 0 | <0.01 |
| Pima (0) | 2 | <0.01 |
| Potawatomi (0) | 0 | <0.01 |
| Pueblo (0) | 0 | <0.01 |
| Puget Sound Salish (0) | 0 | <0.01 |
| Seminole (0) | 1 | <0.01 |
| Shoshone (0) | 0 | <0.01 |
| Sioux (1) | 4 | 0.01 |
| South American Ind. (16) | 25 | 0.03 |
| Spanish American Ind. (5) | 11 | 0.01 |
| Tlingit-Haida (Alaska Native) (0) | 0 | <0.01 |
| Tohono O'Odham (1) | 2 | <0.01 |
| Tsimshian (Alaska Native) (0) | 0 | <0.01 |
| Ute (0) | 0 | <0.01 |
| Yakama (0) | 0 | <0.01 |
| Yaqui (0) | 0 | <0.01 |
| Yuman (0) | 0 | <0.01 |
| Yup'ik (Alaska Native) (0) | 0 | <0.01 |
| Asian (1,075) | 1,395 | 1.80 |
| Not Hispanic (1,033) | 1,311 | 1.69 |
| Hispanic (42) | 84 | 0.11 |
| Bangladeshi (10) | 16 | 0.02 |
| Bhutanese (0) | 0 | <0.01 |
| Burmese (3) | 3 | <0.01 |
| Cambodian (3) | 3 | <0.01 |
| Chinese, ex. Taiwanese (223) | 278 | 0.36 |
| Filipino (142) | 212 | 0.27 |
| Hmong (0) | 0 | <0.01 |
| Indian (346) | 409 | 0.53 |
| Indonesian (5) | 8 | 0.01 |
| Japanese (34) | 66 | 0.09 |
| Korean (166) | 207 | 0.27 |
| Laotian (4) | 5 | 0.01 |
| Malaysian (0) | 0 | <0.01 |
| Nepalese (1) | 1 | <0.01 |
| Pakistani (48) | 58 | 0.07 |
| Sri Lankan (1) | 3 | <0.01 |
| Taiwanese (6) | 8 | 0.01 |
| Thai (3) | 9 | 0.01 |
| Vietnamese (24) | 35 | 0.05 |
| Hawaii Native/Pacific Islander (24) | 87 | 0.11 |
| Not Hispanic (14) | 55 | 0.07 |
| Hispanic (10) | 32 | 0.04 |
| Fijian (0) | 0 | <0.01 |
| Guamanian/Chamorro (13) | 19 | 0.02 |
| Marshallese (0) | 0 | <0.01 |
| Native Hawaiian (2) | 11 | 0.01 |
| Samoan (6) | 15 | 0.02 |
| Tongan (0) | 0 | <0.01 |
| White (63,560) | 65,476 | 84.43 |
| Not Hispanic (57,780) | 59,010 | 76.10 |
| Hispanic (5,780) | 6,466 | 8.34 |

*Notes: † The Census 2010 population figure is used to calculate the percentages in the Hispanic Origin and Race categories. Ancestry percentages are based on the 2006-2010 American Community Survey population (not shown); ‡ Numbers in parentheses indicate the number of people reporting a single ancestry; * Numbers in parentheses indicate the number of persons reporting this race alone, not in combination with any other race; Please refer to the Explanation of Data for more information.*

## Tioga County
Population: 51,125

| Ancestry | Population | % |
|---|---|---|
| Afghan (0) | 0 | <0.01 |
| African, Sub-Saharan (36) | 40 | 0.08 |
| African (11) | 15 | 0.03 |
| Cape Verdean (0) | 0 | <0.01 |
| Ethiopian (0) | 0 | <0.01 |
| Ghanaian (0) | 0 | <0.01 |
| Kenyan (0) | 0 | <0.01 |
| Liberian (0) | 0 | <0.01 |
| Nigerian (0) | 0 | <0.01 |
| Senegalese (0) | 0 | <0.01 |
| Sierra Leonean (0) | 0 | <0.01 |
| Somalian (0) | 0 | <0.01 |
| South African (25) | 25 | 0.05 |
| Sudanese (0) | 0 | <0.01 |
| Ugandan (0) | 0 | <0.01 |
| Zimbabwean (0) | 0 | <0.01 |
| Other Sub-Saharan African (0) | 0 | <0.01 |
| Albanian (0) | 0 | <0.01 |
| Alsatian (19) | 22 | 0.04 |
| American (4,114) | 4,114 | 8.01 |
| Arab (76) | 115 | 0.22 |
| Arab (0) | 0 | <0.01 |
| Egyptian (16) | 16 | 0.03 |
| Iraqi (0) | 0 | <0.01 |
| Jordanian (0) | 0 | <0.01 |
| Lebanese (60) | 99 | 0.19 |
| Moroccan (0) | 0 | <0.01 |
| Palestinian (0) | 0 | <0.01 |
| Syrian (0) | 0 | <0.01 |
| Other Arab (0) | 0 | <0.01 |
| Armenian (0) | 28 | 0.05 |
| Assyrian/Chaldean/Syriac (0) | 0 | <0.01 |
| Australian (0) | 0 | <0.01 |
| Austrian (43) | 129 | 0.25 |
| Basque (0) | 34 | 0.07 |
| Belgian (0) | 20 | 0.04 |
| Brazilian (34) | 34 | 0.07 |
| British (86) | 123 | 0.24 |
| Bulgarian (0) | 0 | <0.01 |
| Cajun (0) | 0 | <0.01 |
| Canadian (72) | 170 | 0.33 |
| Carpatho Rusyn (0) | 0 | <0.01 |
| Celtic (0) | 16 | 0.03 |
| Croatian (20) | 20 | 0.04 |
| Cypriot (0) | 0 | <0.01 |
| Czech (148) | 382 | 0.74 |
| Czechoslovakian (27) | 122 | 0.24 |
| Danish (31) | 123 | 0.24 |
| Dutch (419) | 2,091 | 4.07 |
| Eastern European (0) | 0 | <0.01 |
| English (3,529) | 9,618 | 18.72 |
| Estonian (0) | 0 | <0.01 |
| European (598) | 624 | 1.21 |
| Finnish (208) | 305 | 0.59 |
| French, ex. Basque (306) | 1,803 | 3.51 |
| French Canadian (143) | 395 | 0.77 |
| German (3,822) | 12,009 | 23.37 |
| German Russian (0) | 0 | <0.01 |
| Greek (67) | 198 | 0.39 |
| Guyanese (0) | 0 | <0.01 |
| Hungarian (241) | 430 | 0.84 |
| Icelander (0) | 0 | <0.01 |
| Iranian (0) | 0 | <0.01 |
| Irish (2,587) | 9,130 | 17.77 |
| Israeli (0) | 0 | <0.01 |
| Italian (1,844) | 4,941 | 9.62 |
| Latvian (28) | 61 | 0.12 |
| Lithuanian (35) | 235 | 0.46 |
| Luxemburger (0) | 0 | <0.01 |
| Macedonian (0) | 0 | <0.01 |
| Maltese (0) | 16 | 0.03 |
| New Zealander (0) | 0 | <0.01 |
| Northern European (110) | 110 | 0.21 |
| Norwegian (120) | 344 | 0.67 |
| Pennsylvania German (242) | 441 | 0.86 |

| Ancestry | Population | % |
|---|---|---|
| Polish (881) | 2,677 | 5.21 |
| Portuguese (26) | 67 | 0.13 |
| Romanian (20) | 50 | 0.10 |
| Russian (365) | 838 | 1.63 |
| Scandinavian (17) | 45 | 0.09 |
| Scotch-Irish (338) | 858 | 1.67 |
| Scottish (304) | 1,298 | 2.53 |
| Serbian (0) | 0 | <0.01 |
| Slavic (22) | 81 | 0.16 |
| Slovak (202) | 549 | 1.07 |
| Slovene (47) | 50 | 0.10 |
| Soviet Union (0) | 0 | <0.01 |
| Swedish (196) | 882 | 1.72 |
| Swiss (56) | 163 | 0.32 |
| Turkish (10) | 18 | 0.04 |
| Ukrainian (203) | 422 | 0.82 |
| Welsh (156) | 1,226 | 2.39 |
| West Indian, ex. Hispanic (8) | 17 | 0.03 |
| Bahamian (0) | 0 | <0.01 |
| Barbadian (0) | 0 | <0.01 |
| Belizean (0) | 0 | <0.01 |
| Bermudan (0) | 0 | <0.01 |
| British West Indian (0) | 0 | <0.01 |
| Dutch West Indian (0) | 0 | <0.01 |
| Haitian (0) | 0 | <0.01 |
| Jamaican (8) | 8 | 0.02 |
| Trinidadian/Tobagonian (0) | 0 | <0.01 |
| U.S. Virgin Islander (0) | 0 | <0.01 |
| West Indian (0) | 9 | 0.02 |
| Other West Indian (0) | 0 | <0.01 |
| Yugoslavian (0) | 13 | 0.03 |

| Hispanic Origin | Population | % |
|---|---|---|
| Hispanic or Latino (of any race) | 694 | 1.36 |
| Central American, ex. Mexican | 53 | 0.10 |
| Costa Rican | 3 | 0.01 |
| Guatemalan | 7 | 0.01 |
| Honduran | 1 | <0.01 |
| Nicaraguan | 4 | 0.01 |
| Panamanian | 11 | 0.02 |
| Salvadoran | 27 | 0.05 |
| Other Central American | 0 | <0.01 |
| Cuban | 28 | 0.05 |
| Dominican Republic | 22 | 0.04 |
| Mexican | 169 | 0.33 |
| Puerto Rican | 271 | 0.53 |
| South American | 73 | 0.14 |
| Argentinean | 4 | 0.01 |
| Bolivian | 1 | <0.01 |
| Chilean | 6 | 0.01 |
| Colombian | 19 | 0.04 |
| Ecuadorian | 24 | 0.05 |
| Paraguayan | 1 | <0.01 |
| Peruvian | 8 | 0.02 |
| Uruguayan | 4 | 0.01 |
| Venezuelan | 3 | 0.01 |
| Other South American | 3 | 0.01 |
| Other Hispanic or Latino | 78 | 0.15 |

| Race* | Population | % |
|---|---|---|
| African-American/Black (375) | 581 | 1.14 |
| Not Hispanic (349) | 532 | 1.04 |
| Hispanic (26) | 49 | 0.10 |
| American Indian/Alaska Native (86) | 306 | 0.60 |
| Not Hispanic (73) | 274 | 0.54 |
| Hispanic (13) | 32 | 0.06 |
| Alaska Athabascan (Ala. Nat.) (0) | 0 | <0.01 |
| Aleut (Alaska Native) (0) | 0 | <0.01 |
| Apache (0) | 0 | <0.01 |
| Arapaho (0) | 0 | <0.01 |
| Blackfeet (2) | 16 | 0.03 |
| Canadian/French Am. Ind. (1) | 5 | 0.01 |
| Central American Ind. (0) | 0 | <0.01 |
| Cherokee (5) | 42 | 0.08 |
| Cheyenne (0) | 2 | <0.01 |
| Chickasaw (0) | 0 | <0.01 |
| Chippewa (0) | 1 | <0.01 |
| Choctaw (0) | 1 | <0.01 |
| Colville (0) | 0 | <0.01 |

| Race* | Population | % |
|---|---|---|
| Comanche (1) | 1 | <0.01 |
| Cree (0) | 0 | <0.01 |
| Creek (0) | 4 | 0.01 |
| Crow (1) | 1 | <0.01 |
| Delaware (3) | 7 | 0.01 |
| Hopi (1) | 1 | <0.01 |
| Houma (0) | 0 | <0.01 |
| Inupiat (Alaska Native) (0) | 0 | <0.01 |
| Iroquois (15) | 61 | 0.12 |
| Kiowa (0) | 0 | <0.01 |
| Lumbee (0) | 1 | <0.01 |
| Menominee (0) | 0 | <0.01 |
| Mexican American Ind. (3) | 5 | 0.01 |
| Navajo (6) | 15 | 0.03 |
| Osage (0) | 0 | <0.01 |
| Ottawa (0) | 0 | <0.01 |
| Paiute (0) | 0 | <0.01 |
| Pima (0) | 0 | <0.01 |
| Potawatomi (0) | 0 | <0.01 |
| Pueblo (0) | 0 | <0.01 |
| Puget Sound Salish (0) | 0 | <0.01 |
| Seminole (0) | 0 | <0.01 |
| Shoshone (0) | 0 | <0.01 |
| Sioux (2) | 11 | 0.02 |
| South American Ind. (1) | 3 | 0.01 |
| Spanish American Ind. (0) | 0 | <0.01 |
| Tlingit-Haida (Alaska Native) (0) | 0 | <0.01 |
| Tohono O'Odham (1) | 1 | <0.01 |
| Tsimshian (Alaska Native) (0) | 0 | <0.01 |
| Ute (0) | 0 | <0.01 |
| Yakama (0) | 0 | <0.01 |
| Yaqui (0) | 0 | <0.01 |
| Yuman (0) | 0 | <0.01 |
| Yup'ik (Alaska Native) (0) | 0 | <0.01 |
| Asian (372) | 475 | 0.93 |
| Not Hispanic (371) | 465 | 0.91 |
| Hispanic (1) | 10 | 0.02 |
| Bangladeshi (0) | 0 | <0.01 |
| Bhutanese (0) | 0 | <0.01 |
| Burmese (0) | 0 | <0.01 |
| Cambodian (0) | 0 | <0.01 |
| Chinese, ex. Taiwanese (107) | 119 | 0.23 |
| Filipino (35) | 67 | 0.13 |
| Hmong (0) | 0 | <0.01 |
| Indian (83) | 93 | 0.18 |
| Indonesian (0) | 0 | <0.01 |
| Japanese (25) | 47 | 0.09 |
| Korean (35) | 46 | 0.09 |
| Laotian (0) | 2 | <0.01 |
| Malaysian (0) | 0 | <0.01 |
| Nepalese (0) | 0 | <0.01 |
| Pakistani (33) | 33 | 0.06 |
| Sri Lankan (0) | 0 | <0.01 |
| Taiwanese (9) | 11 | 0.02 |
| Thai (3) | 4 | 0.01 |
| Vietnamese (35) | 43 | 0.08 |
| Hawaii Native/Pacific Islander (15) | 40 | 0.08 |
| Not Hispanic (12) | 35 | 0.07 |
| Hispanic (3) | 5 | 0.01 |
| Fijian (1) | 1 | <0.01 |
| Guamanian/Chamorro (6) | 9 | 0.02 |
| Marshallese (0) | 0 | <0.01 |
| Native Hawaiian (6) | 11 | 0.02 |
| Samoan (0) | 1 | <0.01 |
| Tongan (0) | 0 | <0.01 |
| White (49,556) | 50,101 | 98.00 |
| Not Hispanic (49,105) | 49,578 | 96.97 |
| Hispanic (451) | 523 | 1.02 |

Notes: † The Census 2010 population figure is used to calculate the percentages in the Hispanic Origin and Race categories. Ancestry percentages are based on the 2006-2010 American Community Survey population (not shown); ‡ Numbers in parentheses indicate the number of people reporting a single ancestry; * Numbers in parentheses indicate the number of persons reporting this race alone, not in combination with any other race; Please refer to the Explanation of Data for more information.

## Tompkins County

Population: 101,564

| Ancestry | Population | % |
|---|---|---|
| Afghan (15) | 15 | 0.01 |
| African, Sub-Saharan (546) | 631 | 0.63 |
| African (254) | 301 | 0.30 |
| Cape Verdean (0) | 0 | <0.01 |
| Ethiopian (0) | 0 | <0.01 |
| Ghanaian (59) | 59 | 0.06 |
| Kenyan (20) | 20 | 0.02 |
| Liberian (44) | 44 | 0.04 |
| Nigerian (56) | 56 | 0.06 |
| Senegalese (0) | 0 | <0.01 |
| Sierra Leonean (22) | 22 | 0.02 |
| Somalian (0) | 0 | <0.01 |
| South African (31) | 35 | 0.03 |
| Sudanese (0) | 13 | 0.01 |
| Ugandan (24) | 24 | 0.02 |
| Zimbabwean (13) | 24 | 0.02 |
| Other Sub-Saharan African (23) | 33 | 0.03 |
| Albanian (0) | 0 | <0.01 |
| Alsatian (0) | 0 | <0.01 |
| American (4,786) | 4,786 | 4.76 |
| Arab (429) | 571 | 0.57 |
| Arab (85) | 85 | 0.08 |
| Egyptian (88) | 88 | 0.09 |
| Iraqi (0) | 0 | <0.01 |
| Jordanian (14) | 14 | 0.01 |
| Lebanese (39) | 113 | 0.11 |
| Moroccan (79) | 79 | 0.08 |
| Palestinian (72) | 72 | 0.07 |
| Syrian (52) | 92 | 0.09 |
| Other Arab (0) | 28 | 0.03 |
| Armenian (138) | 280 | 0.28 |
| Assyrian/Chaldean/Syriac (0) | 0 | <0.01 |
| Australian (24) | 30 | 0.03 |
| Austrian (53) | 496 | 0.49 |
| Basque (0) | 0 | <0.01 |
| Belgian (41) | 81 | 0.08 |
| Brazilian (58) | 116 | 0.12 |
| British (381) | 1,040 | 1.03 |
| Bulgarian (81) | 129 | 0.13 |
| Cajun (14) | 14 | 0.01 |
| Canadian (309) | 594 | 0.59 |
| Carpatho Rusyn (0) | 0 | <0.01 |
| Celtic (6) | 22 | 0.02 |
| Croatian (77) | 205 | 0.20 |
| Cypriot (0) | 16 | 0.02 |
| Czech (206) | 714 | 0.71 |
| Czechoslovakian (83) | 191 | 0.19 |
| Danish (43) | 266 | 0.26 |
| Dutch (586) | 2,655 | 2.64 |
| Eastern European (429) | 525 | 0.52 |
| English (3,791) | 13,741 | 13.66 |
| Estonian (36) | 50 | 0.05 |
| European (1,537) | 1,682 | 1.67 |
| Finnish (248) | 687 | 0.68 |
| French, ex. Basque (512) | 3,128 | 3.11 |
| French Canadian (330) | 799 | 0.79 |
| German (3,464) | 16,093 | 16.00 |
| German Russian (0) | 0 | <0.01 |
| Greek (211) | 512 | 0.51 |
| Guyanese (97) | 119 | 0.12 |
| Hungarian (383) | 1,004 | 1.00 |
| Icelander (14) | 29 | 0.03 |
| Iranian (99) | 216 | 0.21 |
| Irish (3,221) | 14,348 | 14.26 |
| Israeli (145) | 194 | 0.19 |
| Italian (3,055) | 8,635 | 8.58 |
| Latvian (0) | 70 | 0.07 |
| Lithuanian (202) | 486 | 0.48 |
| Luxemburger (10) | 24 | 0.02 |
| Macedonian (0) | 0 | <0.01 |
| Maltese (0) | 0 | <0.01 |
| New Zealander (0) | 45 | 0.04 |
| Northern European (163) | 210 | 0.21 |
| Norwegian (215) | 873 | 0.87 |
| Pennsylvania German (124) | 377 | 0.37 |

| Ancestry (cont.) | Population | % |
|---|---|---|
| Polish (1,003) | 3,827 | 3.80 |
| Portuguese (0) | 103 | 0.10 |
| Romanian (43) | 148 | 0.15 |
| Russian (1,015) | 2,382 | 2.37 |
| Scandinavian (88) | 225 | 0.22 |
| Scotch-Irish (635) | 1,729 | 1.72 |
| Scottish (505) | 2,480 | 2.46 |
| Serbian (16) | 71 | 0.07 |
| Slavic (55) | 106 | 0.11 |
| Slovak (94) | 252 | 0.25 |
| Slovene (6) | 24 | 0.02 |
| Soviet Union (0) | 0 | <0.01 |
| Swedish (245) | 1,517 | 1.51 |
| Swiss (159) | 559 | 0.56 |
| Turkish (98) | 137 | 0.14 |
| Ukrainian (291) | 595 | 0.59 |
| Welsh (183) | 1,158 | 1.15 |
| West Indian, ex. Hispanic (211) | 328 | 0.33 |
| Bahamian (0) | 0 | <0.01 |
| Barbadian (0) | 10 | 0.01 |
| Belizean (0) | 0 | <0.01 |
| Bermudan (0) | 0 | <0.01 |
| British West Indian (12) | 21 | 0.02 |
| Dutch West Indian (32) | 32 | 0.03 |
| Haitian (103) | 135 | 0.13 |
| Jamaican (27) | 72 | 0.07 |
| Trinidadian/Tobagonian (0) | 9 | 0.01 |
| U.S. Virgin Islander (0) | 0 | <0.01 |
| West Indian (37) | 49 | 0.05 |
| Other West Indian (0) | 0 | <0.01 |
| Yugoslavian (64) | 87 | 0.09 |

| Hispanic Origin | Population | % |
|---|---|---|
| Hispanic or Latino (of any race) | 4,264 | 4.20 |
| Central American, ex. Mexican | 314 | 0.31 |
| Costa Rican | 43 | 0.04 |
| Guatemalan | 115 | 0.11 |
| Honduran | 27 | 0.03 |
| Nicaraguan | 40 | 0.04 |
| Panamanian | 27 | 0.03 |
| Salvadoran | 61 | 0.06 |
| Other Central American | 1 | <0.01 |
| Cuban | 253 | 0.25 |
| Dominican Republic | 264 | 0.26 |
| Mexican | 909 | 0.90 |
| Puerto Rican | 1,167 | 1.15 |
| South American | 824 | 0.81 |
| Argentinean | 105 | 0.10 |
| Bolivian | 29 | 0.03 |
| Chilean | 88 | 0.09 |
| Colombian | 230 | 0.23 |
| Ecuadorian | 98 | 0.10 |
| Paraguayan | 8 | 0.01 |
| Peruvian | 144 | 0.14 |
| Uruguayan | 17 | 0.02 |
| Venezuelan | 94 | 0.09 |
| Other South American | 11 | 0.01 |
| Other Hispanic or Latino | 533 | 0.52 |

| Race* | Population | % |
|---|---|---|
| African-American/Black (4,020) | 5,411 | 5.33 |
| Not Hispanic (3,773) | 4,969 | 4.89 |
| Hispanic (247) | 442 | 0.44 |
| American Indian/Alaska Native (360) | 1,159 | 1.14 |
| Not Hispanic (270) | 952 | 0.94 |
| Hispanic (90) | 207 | 0.20 |
| Alaska Athabascan (Ala. Nat.) (1) | 2 | <0.01 |
| Aleut (Alaska Native) (0) | 0 | <0.01 |
| Apache (6) | 16 | 0.02 |
| Arapaho (0) | 0 | <0.01 |
| Blackfeet (7) | 53 | 0.05 |
| Canadian/French Am. Ind. (2) | 8 | 0.01 |
| Central American Ind. (4) | 9 | 0.01 |
| Cherokee (37) | 167 | 0.16 |
| Cheyenne (0) | 2 | <0.01 |
| Chickasaw (0) | 4 | <0.01 |
| Chippewa (5) | 20 | 0.02 |
| Choctaw (1) | 15 | 0.01 |
| Colville (0) | 0 | <0.01 |

| Race* (cont.) | Population | % |
|---|---|---|
| Comanche (0) | 1 | <0.01 |
| Cree (0) | 3 | <0.01 |
| Creek (3) | 11 | 0.01 |
| Crow (1) | 1 | <0.01 |
| Delaware (5) | 20 | 0.02 |
| Hopi (0) | 1 | <0.01 |
| Houma (0) | 0 | <0.01 |
| Inupiat (Alaska Native) (0) | 0 | <0.01 |
| Iroquois (52) | 159 | 0.16 |
| Kiowa (0) | 1 | <0.01 |
| Lumbee (5) | 5 | <0.01 |
| Menominee (0) | 1 | <0.01 |
| Mexican American Ind. (18) | 30 | 0.03 |
| Navajo (4) | 14 | 0.01 |
| Osage (1) | 2 | <0.01 |
| Ottawa (4) | 4 | <0.01 |
| Paiute (0) | 0 | <0.01 |
| Pima (0) | 1 | <0.01 |
| Potawatomi (1) | 1 | <0.01 |
| Pueblo (1) | 1 | <0.01 |
| Puget Sound Salish (2) | 2 | <0.01 |
| Seminole (7) | 15 | 0.01 |
| Shoshone (0) | 0 | <0.01 |
| Sioux (14) | 28 | 0.03 |
| South American Ind. (29) | 51 | 0.05 |
| Spanish American Ind. (0) | 1 | <0.01 |
| Tlingit-Haida (Alaska Native) (0) | 0 | <0.01 |
| Tohono O'Odham (0) | 0 | <0.01 |
| Tsimshian (Alaska Native) (0) | 0 | <0.01 |
| Ute (0) | 0 | <0.01 |
| Yakama (0) | 0 | <0.01 |
| Yaqui (2) | 7 | 0.01 |
| Yuman (0) | 0 | <0.01 |
| Yup'ik (Alaska Native) (0) | 1 | <0.01 |
| Asian (8,737) | 9,963 | 9.81 |
| Not Hispanic (8,680) | 9,848 | 9.70 |
| Hispanic (57) | 115 | 0.11 |
| Bangladeshi (32) | 34 | 0.03 |
| Bhutanese (0) | 0 | <0.01 |
| Burmese (126) | 133 | 0.13 |
| Cambodian (120) | 137 | 0.13 |
| Chinese, ex. Taiwanese (3,581) | 4,058 | 4.00 |
| Filipino (154) | 314 | 0.31 |
| Hmong (0) | 0 | <0.01 |
| Indian (1,435) | 1,610 | 1.59 |
| Indonesian (54) | 81 | 0.08 |
| Japanese (285) | 535 | 0.53 |
| Korean (1,722) | 1,861 | 1.83 |
| Laotian (52) | 80 | 0.08 |
| Malaysian (17) | 34 | 0.03 |
| Nepalese (34) | 39 | 0.04 |
| Pakistani (117) | 135 | 0.13 |
| Sri Lankan (24) | 32 | 0.03 |
| Taiwanese (319) | 382 | 0.38 |
| Thai (123) | 158 | 0.16 |
| Vietnamese (236) | 297 | 0.29 |
| Hawaii Native/Pacific Islander (45) | 160 | 0.16 |
| Not Hispanic (40) | 141 | 0.14 |
| Hispanic (5) | 19 | 0.02 |
| Fijian (1) | 7 | 0.01 |
| Guamanian/Chamorro (8) | 23 | 0.02 |
| Marshallese (0) | 0 | <0.01 |
| Native Hawaiian (14) | 43 | 0.04 |
| Samoan (9) | 28 | 0.03 |
| Tongan (3) | 3 | <0.01 |
| White (83,941) | 86,872 | 85.53 |
| Not Hispanic (81,490) | 84,038 | 82.74 |
| Hispanic (2,451) | 2,834 | 2.79 |

*Notes: † The Census 2010 population figure is used to calculate the percentages in the Hispanic Origin and Race categories. Ancestry percentages are based on the 2006-2010 American Community Survey population (not shown); ‡ Numbers in parentheses indicate the number of people reporting a single ancestry; * Numbers in parentheses indicate the number of persons reporting this race alone, not in combination with any other race; Please refer to the Explanation of Data for more information.*

## Ulster County

Population: 182,493

| Ancestry | Population | % |
|---|---|---|
| Afghan (29) | 29 | 0.02 |
| African, Sub-Saharan (309) | 450 | 0.25 |
| African (186) | 291 | 0.16 |
| Cape Verdean (0) | 0 | <0.01 |
| Ethiopian (37) | 73 | 0.04 |
| Ghanaian (0) | 0 | <0.01 |
| Kenyan (0) | 0 | <0.01 |
| Liberian (0) | 0 | <0.01 |
| Nigerian (75) | 75 | 0.04 |
| Senegalese (0) | 0 | <0.01 |
| Sierra Leonean (0) | 0 | <0.01 |
| Somalian (0) | 0 | <0.01 |
| South African (0) | 0 | <0.01 |
| Sudanese (0) | 0 | <0.01 |
| Ugandan (0) | 0 | <0.01 |
| Zimbabwean (0) | 0 | <0.01 |
| Other Sub-Saharan African (11) | 11 | 0.01 |
| Albanian (180) | 180 | 0.10 |
| Alsatian (0) | 20 | 0.01 |
| American (12,589) | 12,589 | 6.89 |
| Arab (209) | 460 | 0.25 |
| Arab (0) | 22 | 0.01 |
| Egyptian (96) | 165 | 0.09 |
| Iraqi (0) | 0 | <0.01 |
| Jordanian (0) | 0 | <0.01 |
| Lebanese (75) | 180 | 0.10 |
| Moroccan (0) | 0 | <0.01 |
| Palestinian (11) | 41 | 0.02 |
| Syrian (0) | 25 | 0.01 |
| Other Arab (27) | 27 | 0.01 |
| Armenian (71) | 127 | 0.07 |
| Assyrian/Chaldean/Syriac (8) | 8 | <0.01 |
| Australian (18) | 87 | 0.05 |
| Austrian (169) | 1,512 | 0.83 |
| Basque (27) | 50 | 0.03 |
| Belgian (62) | 279 | 0.15 |
| Brazilian (178) | 263 | 0.14 |
| British (319) | 898 | 0.49 |
| Bulgarian (0) | 78 | 0.04 |
| Cajun (0) | 0 | <0.01 |
| Canadian (192) | 523 | 0.29 |
| Carpatho Rusyn (0) | 10 | 0.01 |
| Celtic (25) | 50 | 0.03 |
| Croatian (147) | 234 | 0.13 |
| Cypriot (8) | 8 | <0.01 |
| Czech (213) | 801 | 0.44 |
| Czechoslovakian (98) | 286 | 0.16 |
| Danish (119) | 734 | 0.40 |
| Dutch (1,775) | 9,680 | 5.30 |
| Eastern European (808) | 877 | 0.48 |
| English (3,859) | 18,135 | 9.92 |
| Estonian (0) | 0 | <0.01 |
| European (3,396) | 3,517 | 1.92 |
| Finnish (112) | 409 | 0.22 |
| French, ex. Basque (1,080) | 7,193 | 3.94 |
| French Canadian (413) | 1,291 | 0.71 |
| German (7,795) | 35,911 | 19.65 |
| German Russian (0) | 0 | <0.01 |
| Greek (429) | 1,460 | 0.80 |
| Guyanese (185) | 185 | 0.10 |
| Hungarian (486) | 1,824 | 1.00 |
| Icelander (0) | 15 | 0.01 |
| Iranian (58) | 70 | 0.04 |
| Irish (9,720) | 38,535 | 21.08 |
| Israeli (53) | 114 | 0.06 |
| Italian (14,757) | 35,905 | 19.64 |
| Latvian (40) | 123 | 0.07 |
| Lithuanian (59) | 527 | 0.29 |
| Luxemburger (0) | 0 | <0.01 |
| Macedonian (0) | 0 | <0.01 |
| Maltese (9) | 39 | 0.02 |
| New Zealander (0) | 0 | <0.01 |
| Northern European (281) | 291 | 0.16 |
| Norwegian (683) | 2,848 | 1.56 |
| Pennsylvania German (67) | 148 | 0.08 |

| Ancestry (cont.) | Population | % |
|---|---|---|
| Polish (2,603) | 9,470 | 5.18 |
| Portuguese (145) | 604 | 0.33 |
| Romanian (259) | 440 | 0.24 |
| Russian (1,337) | 4,045 | 2.21 |
| Scandinavian (89) | 248 | 0.14 |
| Scotch-Irish (907) | 2,805 | 1.53 |
| Scottish (759) | 3,592 | 1.97 |
| Serbian (10) | 10 | 0.01 |
| Slavic (100) | 224 | 0.12 |
| Slovak (145) | 540 | 0.30 |
| Slovene (0) | 12 | 0.01 |
| Soviet Union (0) | 0 | <0.01 |
| Swedish (539) | 2,391 | 1.31 |
| Swiss (63) | 283 | 0.15 |
| Turkish (109) | 156 | 0.09 |
| Ukrainian (806) | 1,416 | 0.77 |
| Welsh (317) | 1,117 | 0.61 |
| West Indian, ex. Hispanic (1,151) | 1,576 | 0.86 |
| Bahamian (0) | 0 | <0.01 |
| Barbadian (61) | 99 | 0.05 |
| Belizean (0) | 0 | <0.01 |
| Bermudan (0) | 0 | <0.01 |
| British West Indian (30) | 62 | 0.03 |
| Dutch West Indian (0) | 0 | <0.01 |
| Haitian (69) | 219 | 0.12 |
| Jamaican (666) | 738 | 0.40 |
| Trinidadian/Tobagonian (85) | 111 | 0.06 |
| U.S. Virgin Islander (0) | 0 | <0.01 |
| West Indian (240) | 347 | 0.19 |
| Other West Indian (0) | 0 | <0.01 |
| Yugoslavian (162) | 237 | 0.13 |

| Hispanic Origin | Population | % |
|---|---|---|
| Hispanic or Latino (of any race) | 15,909 | 8.72 |
| Central American, ex. Mexican | 1,464 | 0.80 |
| Costa Rican | 34 | 0.02 |
| Guatemalan | 331 | 0.18 |
| Honduran | 228 | 0.12 |
| Nicaraguan | 17 | 0.01 |
| Panamanian | 106 | 0.06 |
| Salvadoran | 735 | 0.40 |
| Other Central American | 13 | 0.01 |
| Cuban | 438 | 0.24 |
| Dominican Republic | 813 | 0.45 |
| Mexican | 2,945 | 1.61 |
| Puerto Rican | 7,191 | 3.94 |
| South American | 1,449 | 0.79 |
| Argentinean | 142 | 0.08 |
| Bolivian | 13 | 0.01 |
| Chilean | 124 | 0.07 |
| Colombian | 520 | 0.28 |
| Ecuadorian | 267 | 0.15 |
| Paraguayan | 16 | 0.01 |
| Peruvian | 263 | 0.14 |
| Uruguayan | 34 | 0.02 |
| Venezuelan | 46 | 0.03 |
| Other South American | 24 | 0.01 |
| Other Hispanic or Latino | 1,609 | 0.88 |

| Race* | Population | % |
|---|---|---|
| African-American/Black (10,982) | 13,644 | 7.48 |
| Not Hispanic (9,982) | 12,055 | 6.61 |
| Hispanic (1,000) | 1,589 | 0.87 |
| American Indian/Alaska Native (597) | 1,975 | 1.08 |
| Not Hispanic (414) | 1,572 | 0.86 |
| Hispanic (183) | 403 | 0.22 |
| Alaska Athabascan (Ala. Nat.) (0) | 0 | <0.01 |
| Aleut (Alaska Native) (0) | 0 | <0.01 |
| Apache (6) | 26 | 0.01 |
| Arapaho (3) | 6 | <0.01 |
| Blackfeet (6) | 61 | 0.03 |
| Canadian/French Am. Ind. (5) | 13 | 0.01 |
| Central American Ind. (12) | 19 | 0.01 |
| Cherokee (59) | 321 | 0.18 |
| Cheyenne (1) | 2 | <0.01 |
| Chickasaw (1) | 2 | <0.01 |
| Chippewa (4) | 12 | 0.01 |
| Choctaw (2) | 10 | 0.01 |
| Colville (0) | 0 | <0.01 |

| Race* (cont.) | Population | % |
|---|---|---|
| Comanche (1) | 3 | <0.01 |
| Cree (0) | 5 | <0.01 |
| Creek (12) | 22 | 0.01 |
| Crow (1) | 1 | <0.01 |
| Delaware (27) | 62 | 0.03 |
| Hopi (1) | 2 | <0.01 |
| Houma (0) | 0 | <0.01 |
| Inupiat (Alaska Native) (1) | 4 | <0.01 |
| Iroquois (52) | 188 | 0.10 |
| Kiowa (0) | 0 | <0.01 |
| Lumbee (5) | 13 | 0.01 |
| Menominee (0) | 1 | <0.01 |
| Mexican American Ind. (28) | 44 | 0.02 |
| Navajo (1) | 11 | 0.01 |
| Osage (0) | 3 | <0.01 |
| Ottawa (0) | 0 | <0.01 |
| Paiute (0) | 0 | <0.01 |
| Pima (0) | 1 | <0.01 |
| Potawatomi (1) | 1 | <0.01 |
| Pueblo (6) | 6 | <0.01 |
| Puget Sound Salish (0) | 1 | <0.01 |
| Seminole (1) | 13 | 0.01 |
| Shoshone (0) | 0 | <0.01 |
| Sioux (27) | 49 | 0.03 |
| South American Ind. (26) | 57 | 0.03 |
| Spanish American Ind. (1) | 7 | <0.01 |
| Tlingit-Haida (Alaska Native) (0) | 0 | <0.01 |
| Tohono O'Odham (0) | 0 | <0.01 |
| Tsimshian (Alaska Native) (1) | 1 | <0.01 |
| Ute (0) | 0 | <0.01 |
| Yakama (0) | 0 | <0.01 |
| Yaqui (0) | 0 | <0.01 |
| Yuman (0) | 0 | <0.01 |
| Yup'ik (Alaska Native) (2) | 2 | <0.01 |
| Asian (3,106) | 4,029 | 2.21 |
| Not Hispanic (3,060) | 3,892 | 2.13 |
| Hispanic (46) | 137 | 0.08 |
| Bangladeshi (85) | 95 | 0.05 |
| Bhutanese (1) | 1 | <0.01 |
| Burmese (6) | 8 | <0.01 |
| Cambodian (10) | 16 | 0.01 |
| Chinese, ex. Taiwanese (838) | 1,039 | 0.57 |
| Filipino (277) | 456 | 0.25 |
| Hmong (0) | 0 | <0.01 |
| Indian (709) | 926 | 0.51 |
| Indonesian (15) | 27 | 0.01 |
| Japanese (197) | 344 | 0.19 |
| Korean (302) | 402 | 0.22 |
| Laotian (2) | 4 | <0.01 |
| Malaysian (5) | 16 | 0.01 |
| Nepalese (19) | 24 | 0.01 |
| Pakistani (175) | 211 | 0.12 |
| Sri Lankan (21) | 30 | 0.02 |
| Taiwanese (41) | 45 | 0.02 |
| Thai (52) | 78 | 0.04 |
| Vietnamese (118) | 163 | 0.09 |
| Hawaii Native/Pacific Islander (34) | 165 | 0.09 |
| Not Hispanic (29) | 122 | 0.07 |
| Hispanic (5) | 43 | 0.02 |
| Fijian (2) | 3 | <0.01 |
| Guamanian/Chamorro (7) | 21 | 0.01 |
| Marshallese (0) | 0 | <0.01 |
| Native Hawaiian (8) | 40 | 0.02 |
| Samoan (3) | 16 | 0.01 |
| Tongan (2) | 5 | <0.01 |
| White (158,184) | 162,629 | 89.12 |
| Not Hispanic (149,099) | 152,405 | 83.51 |
| Hispanic (9,085) | 10,224 | 5.60 |

*Notes: † The Census 2010 population figure is used to calculate the percentages in the Hispanic Origin and Race categories. Ancestry percentages are based on the 2006-2010 American Community Survey population (not shown); ‡ Numbers in parentheses indicate the number of people reporting a single ancestry; * Numbers in parentheses indicate the number of persons reporting this race alone, not in combination with any other race; Please refer to the Explanation of Data for more information.*

# Warren County

Population: 65,707

| Ancestry | Population | % |
|---|---|---|
| Afghan (0) | 9 | 0.01 |
| African, Sub-Saharan (9) | 36 | 0.05 |
| African (9) | 36 | 0.05 |
| Cape Verdean (0) | 0 | <0.01 |
| Ethiopian (0) | 0 | <0.01 |
| Ghanaian (0) | 0 | <0.01 |
| Kenyan (0) | 0 | <0.01 |
| Liberian (0) | 0 | <0.01 |
| Nigerian (0) | 0 | <0.01 |
| Senegalese (0) | 0 | <0.01 |
| Sierra Leonean (0) | 0 | <0.01 |
| Somalian (0) | 0 | <0.01 |
| South African (0) | 0 | <0.01 |
| Sudanese (0) | 0 | <0.01 |
| Ugandan (0) | 0 | <0.01 |
| Zimbabwean (0) | 0 | <0.01 |
| Other Sub-Saharan African (0) | 0 | <0.01 |
| Albanian (0) | 0 | <0.01 |
| Alsatian (0) | 0 | <0.01 |
| American (5,380) | 5,380 | 8.19 |
| Arab (174) | 318 | 0.48 |
| Arab (0) | 16 | 0.02 |
| Egyptian (0) | 0 | <0.01 |
| Iraqi (0) | 0 | <0.01 |
| Jordanian (0) | 0 | <0.01 |
| Lebanese (17) | 61 | 0.09 |
| Moroccan (0) | 0 | <0.01 |
| Palestinian (0) | 0 | <0.01 |
| Syrian (150) | 230 | 0.35 |
| Other Arab (7) | 11 | 0.02 |
| Armenian (23) | 70 | 0.11 |
| Assyrian/Chaldean/Syriac (0) | 0 | <0.01 |
| Australian (9) | 9 | 0.01 |
| Austrian (41) | 199 | 0.30 |
| Basque (0) | 0 | <0.01 |
| Belgian (7) | 24 | 0.04 |
| Brazilian (8) | 8 | 0.01 |
| British (82) | 183 | 0.28 |
| Bulgarian (20) | 32 | 0.05 |
| Cajun (0) | 0 | <0.01 |
| Canadian (419) | 607 | 0.92 |
| Carpatho Rusyn (0) | 0 | <0.01 |
| Celtic (14) | 43 | 0.07 |
| Croatian (0) | 9 | 0.01 |
| Cypriot (0) | 0 | <0.01 |
| Czech (45) | 195 | 0.30 |
| Czechoslovakian (12) | 54 | 0.08 |
| Danish (31) | 142 | 0.22 |
| Dutch (259) | 2,232 | 3.40 |
| Eastern European (149) | 149 | 0.23 |
| English (2,731) | 9,825 | 14.95 |
| Estonian (18) | 18 | 0.03 |
| European (357) | 379 | 0.58 |
| Finnish (0) | 43 | 0.07 |
| French, ex. Basque (1,964) | 8,502 | 12.94 |
| French Canadian (1,045) | 2,407 | 3.66 |
| German (2,352) | 9,279 | 14.12 |
| German Russian (0) | 16 | 0.02 |
| Greek (34) | 92 | 0.14 |
| Guyanese (17) | 17 | 0.03 |
| Hungarian (93) | 439 | 0.67 |
| Icelander (0) | 7 | 0.01 |
| Iranian (5) | 30 | 0.05 |
| Irish (4,734) | 15,493 | 23.58 |
| Israeli (15) | 15 | 0.02 |
| Italian (3,791) | 8,622 | 13.12 |
| Latvian (28) | 59 | 0.09 |
| Lithuanian (54) | 314 | 0.48 |
| Luxemburger (0) | 0 | <0.01 |
| Macedonian (0) | 0 | <0.01 |
| Maltese (0) | 0 | <0.01 |
| New Zealander (0) | 0 | <0.01 |
| Northern European (42) | 42 | 0.06 |
| Norwegian (75) | 324 | 0.49 |
| Pennsylvania German (14) | 48 | 0.07 |

| Ancestry | Population | % |
|---|---|---|
| Polish (718) | 2,771 | 4.22 |
| Portuguese (17) | 113 | 0.17 |
| Romanian (51) | 51 | 0.08 |
| Russian (212) | 669 | 1.02 |
| Scandinavian (58) | 66 | 0.10 |
| Scotch-Irish (752) | 1,489 | 2.27 |
| Scottish (585) | 1,966 | 2.99 |
| Serbian (17) | 17 | 0.03 |
| Slavic (14) | 55 | 0.08 |
| Slovak (39) | 148 | 0.23 |
| Slovene (0) | 0 | <0.01 |
| Soviet Union (0) | 0 | <0.01 |
| Swedish (258) | 910 | 1.38 |
| Swiss (19) | 137 | 0.21 |
| Turkish (0) | 4 | 0.01 |
| Ukrainian (137) | 315 | 0.48 |
| Welsh (206) | 986 | 1.50 |
| West Indian, ex. Hispanic (80) | 97 | 0.15 |
| Bahamian (0) | 0 | <0.01 |
| Barbadian (0) | 0 | <0.01 |
| Belizean (0) | 0 | <0.01 |
| Bermudan (0) | 0 | <0.01 |
| British West Indian (5) | 5 | 0.01 |
| Dutch West Indian (0) | 0 | <0.01 |
| Haitian (0) | 0 | <0.01 |
| Jamaican (70) | 70 | 0.11 |
| Trinidadian/Tobagonian (0) | 0 | <0.01 |
| U.S. Virgin Islander (0) | 0 | <0.01 |
| West Indian (5) | 22 | 0.03 |
| Other West Indian (0) | 0 | <0.01 |
| Yugoslavian (15) | 24 | 0.04 |

| Hispanic Origin | Population | % |
|---|---|---|
| Hispanic or Latino (of any race) | 1,178 | 1.79 |
| Central American, ex. Mexican | 66 | 0.10 |
| Costa Rican | 5 | 0.01 |
| Guatemalan | 15 | 0.02 |
| Honduran | 9 | 0.01 |
| Nicaraguan | 5 | 0.01 |
| Panamanian | 12 | 0.02 |
| Salvadoran | 20 | 0.03 |
| Other Central American | 0 | <0.01 |
| Cuban | 45 | 0.07 |
| Dominican Republic | 32 | 0.05 |
| Mexican | 239 | 0.36 |
| Puerto Rican | 528 | 0.80 |
| South American | 92 | 0.14 |
| Argentinean | 9 | 0.01 |
| Bolivian | 3 | <0.01 |
| Chilean | 5 | 0.01 |
| Colombian | 31 | 0.05 |
| Ecuadorian | 7 | 0.01 |
| Paraguayan | 1 | <0.01 |
| Peruvian | 23 | 0.04 |
| Uruguayan | 3 | <0.01 |
| Venezuelan | 10 | 0.02 |
| Other South American | 0 | <0.01 |
| Other Hispanic or Latino | 176 | 0.27 |

| Race* | Population | % |
|---|---|---|
| African-American/Black (590) | 949 | 1.44 |
| Not Hispanic (556) | 861 | 1.31 |
| Hispanic (34) | 88 | 0.13 |
| American Indian/Alaska Native (144) | 531 | 0.81 |
| Not Hispanic (117) | 470 | 0.72 |
| Hispanic (27) | 61 | 0.09 |
| Alaska Athabascan (Ala. Nat.) (1) | 1 | <0.01 |
| Aleut (Alaska Native) (0) | 0 | <0.01 |
| Apache (2) | 6 | 0.01 |
| Arapaho (0) | 0 | <0.01 |
| Blackfeet (6) | 26 | 0.04 |
| Canadian/French Am. Ind. (6) | 8 | 0.01 |
| Central American Ind. (1) | 1 | <0.01 |
| Cherokee (16) | 45 | 0.07 |
| Cheyenne (0) | 2 | <0.01 |
| Chickasaw (0) | 0 | <0.01 |
| Chippewa (3) | 6 | 0.01 |
| Choctaw (0) | 1 | <0.01 |
| Colville (0) | 0 | <0.01 |

| Race* | Population | % |
|---|---|---|
| Comanche (0) | 0 | <0.01 |
| Cree (0) | 2 | <0.01 |
| Creek (0) | 0 | <0.01 |
| Crow (0) | 1 | <0.01 |
| Delaware (1) | 1 | <0.01 |
| Hopi (0) | 0 | <0.01 |
| Houma (0) | 0 | <0.01 |
| Inupiat (Alaska Native) (0) | 0 | <0.01 |
| Iroquois (17) | 77 | 0.12 |
| Kiowa (0) | 0 | <0.01 |
| Lumbee (0) | 0 | <0.01 |
| Menominee (0) | 3 | <0.01 |
| Mexican American Ind. (5) | 6 | 0.01 |
| Navajo (0) | 0 | <0.01 |
| Osage (0) | 0 | <0.01 |
| Ottawa (1) | 1 | <0.01 |
| Paiute (0) | 0 | <0.01 |
| Pima (0) | 0 | <0.01 |
| Potawatomi (0) | 1 | <0.01 |
| Pueblo (0) | 0 | <0.01 |
| Puget Sound Salish (0) | 0 | <0.01 |
| Seminole (1) | 5 | 0.01 |
| Shoshone (0) | 0 | <0.01 |
| Sioux (2) | 15 | 0.02 |
| South American Ind. (4) | 5 | 0.01 |
| Spanish American Ind. (1) | 2 | <0.01 |
| Tlingit-Haida (Alaska Native) (1) | 4 | 0.01 |
| Tohono O'Odham (0) | 0 | <0.01 |
| Tsimshian (Alaska Native) (0) | 0 | <0.01 |
| Ute (0) | 0 | <0.01 |
| Yakama (0) | 0 | <0.01 |
| Yaqui (0) | 2 | <0.01 |
| Yuman (0) | 0 | <0.01 |
| Yup'ik (Alaska Native) (0) | 0 | <0.01 |
| Asian (456) | 615 | 0.94 |
| Not Hispanic (449) | 596 | 0.91 |
| Hispanic (7) | 19 | 0.03 |
| Bangladeshi (1) | 2 | <0.01 |
| Bhutanese (0) | 0 | <0.01 |
| Burmese (0) | 0 | <0.01 |
| Cambodian (0) | 1 | <0.01 |
| Chinese, ex. Taiwanese (116) | 140 | 0.21 |
| Filipino (75) | 118 | 0.18 |
| Hmong (0) | 1 | <0.01 |
| Indian (69) | 97 | 0.15 |
| Indonesian (2) | 2 | <0.01 |
| Japanese (15) | 30 | 0.05 |
| Korean (65) | 101 | 0.15 |
| Laotian (3) | 4 | 0.01 |
| Malaysian (1) | 2 | <0.01 |
| Nepalese (0) | 0 | <0.01 |
| Pakistani (27) | 34 | 0.05 |
| Sri Lankan (1) | 1 | <0.01 |
| Taiwanese (7) | 7 | 0.01 |
| Thai (13) | 16 | 0.02 |
| Vietnamese (41) | 47 | 0.07 |
| Hawaii Native/Pacific Islander (8) | 34 | 0.05 |
| Not Hispanic (5) | 25 | 0.04 |
| Hispanic (3) | 9 | 0.01 |
| Fijian (0) | 0 | <0.01 |
| Guamanian/Chamorro (1) | 6 | 0.01 |
| Marshallese (0) | 0 | <0.01 |
| Native Hawaiian (4) | 10 | 0.02 |
| Samoan (2) | 3 | <0.01 |
| Tongan (0) | 0 | <0.01 |
| White (63,391) | 64,255 | 97.79 |
| Not Hispanic (62,585) | 63,331 | 96.38 |
| Hispanic (806) | 924 | 1.41 |

*Notes: † The Census 2010 population figure is used to calculate the percentages in the Hispanic Origin and Race categories. Ancestry percentages are based on the 2006-2010 American Community Survey population (not shown); ‡ Numbers in parentheses indicate the number of people reporting a single ancestry; * Numbers in parentheses indicate the number of persons reporting this race alone, not in combination with any other race; Please refer to the Explanation of Data for more information.*

## Washington County

Population: 63,216

| Ancestry | Population | % |
|---|---|---|
| Afghan (0) | 0 | <0.01 |
| African, Sub-Saharan (40) | 66 | 0.10 |
| African (28) | 54 | 0.09 |
| Cape Verdean (0) | 0 | <0.01 |
| Ethiopian (0) | 0 | <0.01 |
| Ghanaian (0) | 0 | <0.01 |
| Kenyan (0) | 0 | <0.01 |
| Liberian (0) | 0 | <0.01 |
| Nigerian (8) | 8 | 0.01 |
| Senegalese (0) | 0 | <0.01 |
| Sierra Leonean (0) | 0 | <0.01 |
| Somalian (0) | 0 | <0.01 |
| South African (0) | 0 | <0.01 |
| Sudanese (0) | 0 | <0.01 |
| Ugandan (0) | 0 | <0.01 |
| Zimbabwean (0) | 0 | <0.01 |
| Other Sub-Saharan African (4) | 4 | 0.01 |
| Albanian (17) | 17 | 0.03 |
| Alsatian (0) | 4 | 0.01 |
| American (6,527) | 6,527 | 10.35 |
| Arab (40) | 175 | 0.28 |
| Arab (0) | 0 | <0.01 |
| Egyptian (0) | 0 | <0.01 |
| Iraqi (0) | 0 | <0.01 |
| Jordanian (0) | 0 | <0.01 |
| Lebanese (13) | 83 | 0.13 |
| Moroccan (0) | 0 | <0.01 |
| Palestinian (0) | 0 | <0.01 |
| Syrian (18) | 83 | 0.13 |
| Other Arab (9) | 9 | 0.01 |
| Armenian (29) | 113 | 0.18 |
| Assyrian/Chaldean/Syriac (0) | 0 | <0.01 |
| Australian (9) | 14 | 0.02 |
| Austrian (59) | 200 | 0.32 |
| Basque (0) | 13 | 0.02 |
| Belgian (0) | 23 | 0.04 |
| Brazilian (0) | 19 | 0.03 |
| British (106) | 174 | 0.28 |
| Bulgarian (0) | 4 | 0.01 |
| Cajun (0) | 0 | <0.01 |
| Canadian (204) | 341 | 0.54 |
| Carpatho Rusyn (0) | 0 | <0.01 |
| Celtic (7) | 7 | 0.01 |
| Croatian (0) | 0 | <0.01 |
| Cypriot (0) | 0 | <0.01 |
| Czech (65) | 117 | 0.19 |
| Czechoslovakian (118) | 258 | 0.41 |
| Danish (34) | 183 | 0.29 |
| Dutch (254) | 1,822 | 2.89 |
| Eastern European (84) | 84 | 0.13 |
| English (2,389) | 9,121 | 14.46 |
| Estonian (0) | 0 | <0.01 |
| European (209) | 209 | 0.33 |
| Finnish (25) | 47 | 0.07 |
| French, ex. Basque (1,714) | 9,148 | 14.50 |
| French Canadian (1,192) | 2,416 | 3.83 |
| German (1,476) | 7,658 | 12.14 |
| German Russian (0) | 0 | <0.01 |
| Greek (35) | 117 | 0.19 |
| Guyanese (31) | 47 | 0.07 |
| Hungarian (205) | 325 | 0.52 |
| Icelander (0) | 0 | <0.01 |
| Iranian (0) | 0 | <0.01 |
| Irish (4,128) | 13,852 | 21.96 |
| Israeli (39) | 39 | 0.06 |
| Italian (1,842) | 5,717 | 9.06 |
| Latvian (23) | 42 | 0.07 |
| Lithuanian (95) | 300 | 0.48 |
| Luxemburger (0) | 0 | <0.01 |
| Macedonian (0) | 0 | <0.01 |
| Maltese (5) | 9 | 0.01 |
| New Zealander (5) | 5 | 0.01 |
| Northern European (7) | 29 | 0.05 |
| Norwegian (79) | 279 | 0.44 |
| Pennsylvania German (5) | 8 | 0.01 |

| Ancestry | Population | % |
|---|---|---|
| Polish (811) | 2,342 | 3.71 |
| Portuguese (93) | 251 | 0.40 |
| Romanian (12) | 69 | 0.11 |
| Russian (144) | 686 | 1.09 |
| Scandinavian (15) | 21 | 0.03 |
| Scotch-Irish (983) | 1,767 | 2.80 |
| Scottish (694) | 2,905 | 4.60 |
| Serbian (0) | 13 | 0.02 |
| Slavic (8) | 20 | 0.03 |
| Slovak (74) | 201 | 0.32 |
| Slovene (9) | 18 | 0.03 |
| Soviet Union (0) | 0 | <0.01 |
| Swedish (289) | 843 | 1.34 |
| Swiss (12) | 132 | 0.21 |
| Turkish (0) | 0 | <0.01 |
| Ukrainian (88) | 299 | 0.47 |
| Welsh (336) | 1,157 | 1.83 |
| West Indian, ex. Hispanic (218) | 272 | 0.43 |
| Bahamian (9) | 9 | 0.01 |
| Barbadian (16) | 16 | 0.03 |
| Belizean (0) | 0 | <0.01 |
| Bermudan (0) | 0 | <0.01 |
| British West Indian (9) | 9 | 0.01 |
| Dutch West Indian (0) | 0 | <0.01 |
| Haitian (87) | 110 | 0.17 |
| Jamaican (33) | 60 | 0.10 |
| Trinidadian/Tobagonian (26) | 26 | 0.04 |
| U.S. Virgin Islander (0) | 0 | <0.01 |
| West Indian (38) | 42 | 0.07 |
| Other West Indian (0) | 0 | <0.01 |
| Yugoslavian (0) | 0 | <0.01 |

| Hispanic Origin | Population | % |
|---|---|---|
| Hispanic or Latino (of any race) | 1,446 | 2.29 |
| Central American, ex. Mexican | 115 | 0.18 |
| Costa Rican | 2 | <0.01 |
| Guatemalan | 53 | 0.08 |
| Honduran | 7 | 0.01 |
| Nicaraguan | 2 | <0.01 |
| Panamanian | 19 | 0.03 |
| Salvadoran | 32 | 0.05 |
| Other Central American | 0 | <0.01 |
| Cuban | 55 | 0.09 |
| Dominican Republic | 112 | 0.18 |
| Mexican | 452 | 0.72 |
| Puerto Rican | 522 | 0.83 |
| South American | 75 | 0.12 |
| Argentinean | 3 | <0.01 |
| Bolivian | 6 | 0.01 |
| Chilean | 6 | 0.01 |
| Colombian | 18 | 0.03 |
| Ecuadorian | 18 | 0.03 |
| Paraguayan | 0 | <0.01 |
| Peruvian | 12 | 0.02 |
| Uruguayan | 6 | 0.01 |
| Venezuelan | 5 | 0.01 |
| Other South American | 1 | <0.01 |
| Other Hispanic or Latino | 115 | 0.18 |

| Race* | Population | % |
|---|---|---|
| African-American/Black (1,893) | 2,149 | 3.40 |
| Not Hispanic (1,734) | 1,966 | 3.11 |
| Hispanic (159) | 183 | 0.29 |
| American Indian/Alaska Native (128) | 420 | 0.66 |
| Not Hispanic (109) | 375 | 0.59 |
| Hispanic (19) | 45 | 0.07 |
| Alaska Athabascan (Ala. Nat.) (0) | 0 | <0.01 |
| Aleut (Alaska Native) (1) | 1 | <0.01 |
| Apache (2) | 5 | 0.01 |
| Arapaho (0) | 0 | <0.01 |
| Blackfeet (2) | 29 | 0.05 |
| Canadian/French Am. Ind. (2) | 3 | <0.01 |
| Central American Ind. (1) | 1 | <0.01 |
| Cherokee (7) | 39 | 0.06 |
| Cheyenne (0) | 0 | <0.01 |
| Chickasaw (0) | 0 | <0.01 |
| Chippewa (0) | 0 | <0.01 |
| Choctaw (1) | 2 | <0.01 |
| Colville (0) | 0 | <0.01 |

| Race* | Population | % |
|---|---|---|
| Comanche (0) | 1 | <0.01 |
| Cree (0) | 3 | <0.01 |
| Creek (0) | 0 | <0.01 |
| Crow (0) | 1 | <0.01 |
| Delaware (0) | 1 | <0.01 |
| Hopi (1) | 3 | <0.01 |
| Houma (0) | 0 | <0.01 |
| Inupiat (Alaska Native) (1) | 1 | <0.01 |
| Iroquois (11) | 39 | 0.06 |
| Kiowa (0) | 0 | <0.01 |
| Lumbee (0) | 0 | <0.01 |
| Menominee (0) | 0 | <0.01 |
| Mexican American Ind. (4) | 12 | 0.02 |
| Navajo (1) | 1 | <0.01 |
| Osage (0) | 0 | <0.01 |
| Ottawa (0) | 0 | <0.01 |
| Paiute (0) | 0 | <0.01 |
| Pima (0) | 0 | <0.01 |
| Potawatomi (0) | 0 | <0.01 |
| Pueblo (0) | 0 | <0.01 |
| Puget Sound Salish (0) | 0 | <0.01 |
| Seminole (0) | 2 | <0.01 |
| Shoshone (0) | 0 | <0.01 |
| Sioux (2) | 4 | 0.01 |
| South American Ind. (0) | 0 | <0.01 |
| Spanish American Ind. (0) | 0 | <0.01 |
| Tlingit-Haida (Alaska Native) (1) | 1 | <0.01 |
| Tohono O'Odham (0) | 0 | <0.01 |
| Tsimshian (Alaska Native) (0) | 0 | <0.01 |
| Ute (0) | 0 | <0.01 |
| Yakama (0) | 0 | <0.01 |
| Yaqui (0) | 0 | <0.01 |
| Yuman (1) | 1 | <0.01 |
| Yup'ik (Alaska Native) (0) | 0 | <0.01 |
| Asian (266) | 371 | 0.59 |
| Not Hispanic (260) | 359 | 0.57 |
| Hispanic (6) | 12 | 0.02 |
| Bangladeshi (0) | 0 | <0.01 |
| Bhutanese (0) | 0 | <0.01 |
| Burmese (0) | 0 | <0.01 |
| Cambodian (11) | 14 | 0.02 |
| Chinese, ex. Taiwanese (67) | 83 | 0.13 |
| Filipino (60) | 96 | 0.15 |
| Hmong (0) | 0 | <0.01 |
| Indian (29) | 44 | 0.07 |
| Indonesian (0) | 1 | <0.01 |
| Japanese (14) | 30 | 0.05 |
| Korean (46) | 62 | 0.10 |
| Laotian (0) | 0 | <0.01 |
| Malaysian (1) | 1 | <0.01 |
| Nepalese (1) | 3 | <0.01 |
| Pakistani (0) | 1 | <0.01 |
| Sri Lankan (0) | 0 | <0.01 |
| Taiwanese (4) | 4 | 0.01 |
| Thai (7) | 10 | 0.02 |
| Vietnamese (5) | 6 | 0.01 |
| Hawaii Native/Pacific Islander (13) | 37 | 0.06 |
| Not Hispanic (11) | 32 | 0.05 |
| Hispanic (2) | 5 | 0.01 |
| Fijian (0) | 0 | <0.01 |
| Guamanian/Chamorro (0) | 4 | 0.01 |
| Marshallese (0) | 0 | <0.01 |
| Native Hawaiian (2) | 20 | 0.03 |
| Samoan (2) | 2 | <0.01 |
| Tongan (0) | 0 | <0.01 |
| White (59,815) | 60,458 | 95.64 |
| Not Hispanic (58,996) | 59,556 | 94.21 |
| Hispanic (819) | 902 | 1.43 |

*Notes: † The Census 2010 population figure is used to calculate the percentages in the Hispanic Origin and Race categories. Ancestry percentages are based on the 2006-2010 American Community Survey population (not shown); ‡ Numbers in parentheses indicate the number of people reporting a single ancestry; * Numbers in parentheses indicate the number of persons reporting this race alone, not in combination with any other race; Please refer to the Explanation of Data for more information.*

## Wayne County

Population: 93,772

| Ancestry | Population | % |
|---|---|---|
| Afghan (0) | 0 | <0.01 |
| African, Sub-Saharan (145) | 156 | 0.17 |
| African (124) | 135 | 0.14 |
| Cape Verdean (0) | 0 | <0.01 |
| Ethiopian (0) | 0 | <0.01 |
| Ghanaian (0) | 0 | <0.01 |
| Kenyan (0) | 0 | <0.01 |
| Liberian (0) | 0 | <0.01 |
| Nigerian (0) | 0 | <0.01 |
| Senegalese (0) | 0 | <0.01 |
| Sierra Leonean (0) | 0 | <0.01 |
| Somalian (0) | 0 | <0.01 |
| South African (0) | 0 | <0.01 |
| Sudanese (21) | 21 | 0.02 |
| Ugandan (0) | 0 | <0.01 |
| Zimbabwean (0) | 0 | <0.01 |
| Other Sub-Saharan African (0) | 0 | <0.01 |
| Albanian (155) | 202 | 0.22 |
| Alsatian (0) | 0 | <0.01 |
| American (5,150) | 5,150 | 5.50 |
| Arab (64) | 115 | 0.12 |
| Arab (0) | 0 | <0.01 |
| Egyptian (0) | 0 | <0.01 |
| Iraqi (0) | 0 | <0.01 |
| Jordanian (0) | 0 | <0.01 |
| Lebanese (45) | 87 | 0.09 |
| Moroccan (19) | 19 | 0.02 |
| Palestinian (0) | 0 | <0.01 |
| Syrian (0) | 0 | <0.01 |
| Other Arab (0) | 9 | 0.01 |
| Armenian (0) | 13 | 0.01 |
| Assyrian/Chaldean/Syriac (0) | 0 | <0.01 |
| Australian (0) | 57 | 0.06 |
| Austrian (52) | 174 | 0.19 |
| Basque (0) | 0 | <0.01 |
| Belgian (86) | 225 | 0.24 |
| Brazilian (0) | 24 | 0.03 |
| British (161) | 396 | 0.42 |
| Bulgarian (0) | 6 | 0.01 |
| Cajun (3) | 3 | <0.01 |
| Canadian (231) | 527 | 0.56 |
| Carpatho Rusyn (0) | 0 | <0.01 |
| Celtic (0) | 0 | <0.01 |
| Croatian (35) | 44 | 0.05 |
| Cypriot (0) | 0 | <0.01 |
| Czech (83) | 274 | 0.29 |
| Czechoslovakian (25) | 69 | 0.07 |
| Danish (133) | 267 | 0.29 |
| Dutch (3,364) | 12,028 | 12.84 |
| Eastern European (21) | 21 | 0.02 |
| English (3,997) | 15,284 | 16.32 |
| Estonian (0) | 0 | <0.01 |
| European (556) | 652 | 0.70 |
| Finnish (68) | 167 | 0.18 |
| French, ex. Basque (462) | 4,569 | 4.88 |
| French Canadian (553) | 1,649 | 1.76 |
| German (6,047) | 24,173 | 25.81 |
| German Russian (0) | 0 | <0.01 |
| Greek (350) | 402 | 0.43 |
| Guyanese (33) | 33 | 0.04 |
| Hungarian (88) | 331 | 0.35 |
| Icelander (3) | 3 | <0.01 |
| Iranian (0) | 0 | <0.01 |
| Irish (2,837) | 15,277 | 16.31 |
| Israeli (0) | 0 | <0.01 |
| Italian (5,298) | 13,414 | 14.32 |
| Latvian (7) | 81 | 0.09 |
| Lithuanian (121) | 258 | 0.28 |
| Luxemburger (0) | 0 | <0.01 |
| Macedonian (11) | 28 | 0.03 |
| Maltese (0) | 58 | 0.06 |
| New Zealander (0) | 0 | <0.01 |
| Northern European (12) | 15 | 0.02 |
| Norwegian (81) | 387 | 0.41 |
| Pennsylvania German (183) | 213 | 0.23 |

| Ancestry | Population | % |
|---|---|---|
| Polish (1,063) | 4,302 | 4.59 |
| Portuguese (62) | 149 | 0.16 |
| Romanian (24) | 43 | 0.05 |
| Russian (113) | 392 | 0.42 |
| Scandinavian (14) | 68 | 0.07 |
| Scotch-Irish (626) | 1,703 | 1.82 |
| Scottish (528) | 2,308 | 2.46 |
| Serbian (0) | 0 | <0.01 |
| Slavic (47) | 72 | 0.08 |
| Slovak (16) | 99 | 0.11 |
| Slovene (0) | 73 | 0.08 |
| Soviet Union (0) | 0 | <0.01 |
| Swedish (112) | 536 | 0.57 |
| Swiss (387) | 863 | 0.92 |
| Turkish (0) | 0 | <0.01 |
| Ukrainian (335) | 978 | 1.04 |
| Welsh (173) | 996 | 1.06 |
| West Indian, ex. Hispanic (248) | 285 | 0.30 |
| Bahamian (0) | 0 | <0.01 |
| Barbadian (0) | 0 | <0.01 |
| Belizean (0) | 0 | <0.01 |
| Bermudan (0) | 0 | <0.01 |
| British West Indian (0) | 0 | <0.01 |
| Dutch West Indian (7) | 7 | 0.01 |
| Haitian (124) | 156 | 0.17 |
| Jamaican (68) | 68 | 0.07 |
| Trinidadian/Tobagonian (0) | 0 | <0.01 |
| U.S. Virgin Islander (0) | 0 | <0.01 |
| West Indian (49) | 49 | 0.05 |
| Other West Indian (0) | 5 | 0.01 |
| Yugoslavian (45) | 96 | 0.10 |

| Hispanic Origin | Population | % |
|---|---|---|
| Hispanic or Latino (of any race) | 3,476 | 3.71 |
| Central American, ex. Mexican | 144 | 0.15 |
| Costa Rican | 5 | 0.01 |
| Guatemalan | 53 | 0.06 |
| Honduran | 57 | 0.06 |
| Nicaraguan | 3 | <0.01 |
| Panamanian | 10 | 0.01 |
| Salvadoran | 16 | 0.02 |
| Other Central American | 0 | <0.01 |
| Cuban | 51 | 0.05 |
| Dominican Republic | 85 | 0.09 |
| Mexican | 1,219 | 1.30 |
| Puerto Rican | 1,729 | 1.84 |
| South American | 64 | 0.07 |
| Argentinean | 10 | 0.01 |
| Bolivian | 4 | <0.01 |
| Chilean | 1 | <0.01 |
| Colombian | 22 | 0.02 |
| Ecuadorian | 10 | 0.01 |
| Paraguayan | 0 | <0.01 |
| Peruvian | 11 | 0.01 |
| Uruguayan | 0 | <0.01 |
| Venezuelan | 6 | 0.01 |
| Other South American | 0 | <0.01 |
| Other Hispanic or Latino | 184 | 0.20 |

| Race* | Population | % |
|---|---|---|
| African-American/Black (2,887) | 3,853 | 4.11 |
| Not Hispanic (2,743) | 3,600 | 3.84 |
| Hispanic (144) | 253 | 0.27 |
| American Indian/Alaska Native (258) | 770 | 0.82 |
| Not Hispanic (201) | 661 | 0.70 |
| Hispanic (57) | 109 | 0.12 |
| Alaska Athabascan (Ala. Nat.) (0) | 0 | <0.01 |
| Aleut (Alaska Native) (0) | 0 | <0.01 |
| Apache (2) | 6 | 0.01 |
| Arapaho (0) | 0 | <0.01 |
| Blackfeet (4) | 12 | 0.01 |
| Canadian/French Am. Ind. (3) | 9 | 0.01 |
| Central American Ind. (3) | 3 | <0.01 |
| Cherokee (16) | 102 | 0.11 |
| Cheyenne (0) | 0 | <0.01 |
| Chickasaw (0) | 0 | <0.01 |
| Chippewa (16) | 18 | 0.02 |
| Choctaw (6) | 12 | 0.01 |
| Colville (0) | 0 | <0.01 |

| Race* | Population | % |
|---|---|---|
| Comanche (2) | 2 | <0.01 |
| Cree (0) | 5 | 0.01 |
| Creek (1) | 1 | <0.01 |
| Crow (0) | 0 | <0.01 |
| Delaware (1) | 1 | <0.01 |
| Hopi (0) | 0 | <0.01 |
| Houma (0) | 0 | <0.01 |
| Inupiat (Alaska Native) (0) | 0 | <0.01 |
| Iroquois (60) | 164 | 0.17 |
| Kiowa (0) | 0 | <0.01 |
| Lumbee (1) | 8 | 0.01 |
| Menominee (0) | 0 | <0.01 |
| Mexican American Ind. (12) | 15 | 0.02 |
| Navajo (1) | 2 | <0.01 |
| Osage (0) | 1 | <0.01 |
| Ottawa (0) | 0 | <0.01 |
| Paiute (0) | 0 | <0.01 |
| Pima (2) | 2 | <0.01 |
| Potawatomi (0) | 0 | <0.01 |
| Pueblo (0) | 1 | <0.01 |
| Puget Sound Salish (0) | 0 | <0.01 |
| Seminole (0) | 7 | 0.01 |
| Shoshone (0) | 0 | <0.01 |
| Sioux (2) | 11 | 0.01 |
| South American Ind. (4) | 5 | 0.01 |
| Spanish American Ind. (1) | 2 | <0.01 |
| Tlingit-Haida (Alaska Native) (0) | 0 | <0.01 |
| Tohono O'Odham (0) | 0 | <0.01 |
| Tsimshian (Alaska Native) (0) | 0 | <0.01 |
| Ute (0) | 0 | <0.01 |
| Yakama (0) | 0 | <0.01 |
| Yaqui (0) | 0 | <0.01 |
| Yuman (0) | 0 | <0.01 |
| Yup'ik (Alaska Native) (0) | 0 | <0.01 |
| Asian (473) | 704 | 0.75 |
| Not Hispanic (465) | 685 | 0.73 |
| Hispanic (8) | 19 | 0.02 |
| Bangladeshi (1) | 1 | <0.01 |
| Bhutanese (0) | 0 | <0.01 |
| Burmese (0) | 0 | <0.01 |
| Cambodian (16) | 20 | 0.02 |
| Chinese, ex. Taiwanese (104) | 142 | 0.15 |
| Filipino (60) | 97 | 0.10 |
| Hmong (0) | 0 | <0.01 |
| Indian (51) | 93 | 0.10 |
| Indonesian (2) | 5 | 0.01 |
| Japanese (25) | 57 | 0.06 |
| Korean (74) | 110 | 0.12 |
| Laotian (47) | 53 | 0.06 |
| Malaysian (1) | 1 | <0.01 |
| Nepalese (0) | 0 | <0.01 |
| Pakistani (6) | 6 | 0.01 |
| Sri Lankan (1) | 1 | <0.01 |
| Taiwanese (0) | 0 | <0.01 |
| Thai (12) | 25 | 0.03 |
| Vietnamese (50) | 71 | 0.08 |
| Hawaii Native/Pacific Islander (24) | 59 | 0.06 |
| Not Hispanic (24) | 54 | 0.06 |
| Hispanic (0) | 5 | 0.01 |
| Fijian (0) | 0 | <0.01 |
| Guamanian/Chamorro (4) | 7 | 0.01 |
| Marshallese (1) | 1 | <0.01 |
| Native Hawaiian (3) | 25 | 0.03 |
| Samoan (1) | 4 | <0.01 |
| Tongan (0) | 1 | <0.01 |
| White (87,148) | 88,857 | 94.76 |
| Not Hispanic (85,318) | 86,736 | 92.50 |
| Hispanic (1,830) | 2,121 | 2.26 |

Notes: † The Census 2010 population figure is used to calculate the percentages in the Hispanic Origin and Race categories. Ancestry percentages are based on the 2006-2010 American Community Survey population (not shown); ‡ Numbers in parentheses indicate the number of people reporting a single ancestry; * Numbers in parentheses indicate the number of persons reporting this race alone, not in combination with any other race; Please refer to the Explanation of Data for more information.

## Westchester County

Population: 949,113

| Ancestry | Population | % |
|---|---|---|
| Afghan (12) | 12 | <0.01 |
| African, Sub-Saharan (7,149) | 9,172 | 0.98 |
| African (3,123) | 4,390 | 0.47 |
| Cape Verdean (41) | 52 | 0.01 |
| Ethiopian (391) | 470 | 0.05 |
| Ghanaian (952) | 1,063 | 0.11 |
| Kenyan (237) | 271 | 0.03 |
| Liberian (7) | 16 | <0.01 |
| Nigerian (1,135) | 1,280 | 0.14 |
| Senegalese (21) | 33 | <0.01 |
| Sierra Leonean (39) | 51 | 0.01 |
| Somalian (6) | 6 | <0.01 |
| South African (500) | 750 | 0.08 |
| Sudanese (13) | 13 | <0.01 |
| Ugandan (28) | 28 | <0.01 |
| Zimbabwean (0) | 0 | <0.01 |
| Other Sub-Saharan African (656) | 749 | 0.08 |
| Albanian (4,494) | 4,876 | 0.52 |
| Alsatian (0) | 0 | <0.01 |
| American (41,120) | 41,120 | 4.38 |
| Arab (5,524) | 7,908 | 0.84 |
| Arab (1,268) | 1,569 | 0.17 |
| Egyptian (636) | 827 | 0.09 |
| Iraqi (111) | 141 | 0.02 |
| Jordanian (971) | 1,058 | 0.11 |
| Lebanese (1,105) | 2,033 | 0.22 |
| Moroccan (407) | 657 | 0.07 |
| Palestinian (229) | 251 | 0.03 |
| Syrian (118) | 418 | 0.04 |
| Other Arab (679) | 954 | 0.10 |
| Armenian (879) | 1,450 | 0.15 |
| Assyrian/Chaldean/Syriac (176) | 265 | 0.03 |
| Australian (283) | 472 | 0.05 |
| Austrian (1,636) | 7,685 | 0.82 |
| Basque (75) | 94 | 0.01 |
| Belgian (202) | 717 | 0.08 |
| Brazilian (5,072) | 5,979 | 0.64 |
| British (2,417) | 4,054 | 0.43 |
| Bulgarian (306) | 425 | 0.05 |
| Cajun (0) | 0 | <0.01 |
| Canadian (723) | 1,750 | 0.19 |
| Carpatho Rusyn (60) | 78 | 0.01 |
| Celtic (66) | 120 | 0.01 |
| Croatian (1,470) | 2,181 | 0.23 |
| Cypriot (105) | 105 | 0.01 |
| Czech (857) | 3,626 | 0.39 |
| Czechoslovakian (610) | 1,412 | 0.15 |
| Danish (413) | 1,707 | 0.18 |
| Dutch (1,314) | 5,907 | 0.63 |
| Eastern European (11,389) | 12,279 | 1.31 |
| English (8,923) | 38,197 | 4.07 |
| Estonian (92) | 278 | 0.03 |
| European (8,977) | 10,052 | 1.07 |
| Finnish (346) | 849 | 0.09 |
| French, ex. Basque (3,407) | 15,245 | 1.62 |
| French Canadian (1,046) | 3,477 | 0.37 |
| German (15,113) | 70,010 | 7.45 |
| German Russian (14) | 27 | <0.01 |
| Greek (4,560) | 7,851 | 0.84 |
| Guyanese (1,434) | 1,848 | 0.20 |
| Hungarian (3,232) | 8,762 | 0.93 |
| Icelander (0) | 52 | 0.01 |
| Iranian (986) | 1,275 | 0.14 |
| Irish (46,713) | 124,206 | 13.22 |
| Israeli (965) | 1,392 | 0.15 |
| Italian (112,477) | 183,819 | 19.57 |
| Latvian (344) | 723 | 0.08 |
| Lithuanian (778) | 2,739 | 0.29 |
| Luxemburger (0) | 33 | <0.01 |
| Macedonian (443) | 563 | 0.06 |
| Maltese (164) | 263 | 0.03 |
| New Zealander (60) | 60 | 0.01 |
| Northern European (525) | 637 | 0.07 |
| Norwegian (1,179) | 3,840 | 0.41 |
| Pennsylvania German (33) | 67 | 0.01 |

| | Population | % |
|---|---|---|
| Polish (12,575) | 37,394 | 3.98 |
| Portuguese (6,819) | 9,618 | 1.02 |
| Romanian (1,381) | 3,301 | 0.35 |
| Russian (14,440) | 35,555 | 3.78 |
| Scandinavian (290) | 778 | 0.08 |
| Scotch-Irish (2,663) | 6,751 | 0.72 |
| Scottish (2,357) | 10,201 | 1.09 |
| Serbian (32) | 82 | 0.01 |
| Slavic (440) | 806 | 0.09 |
| Slovak (899) | 2,547 | 0.27 |
| Slovene (64) | 250 | 0.03 |
| Soviet Union (14) | 14 | <0.01 |
| Swedish (863) | 5,211 | 0.55 |
| Swiss (576) | 2,042 | 0.22 |
| Turkish (779) | 1,198 | 0.13 |
| Ukrainian (2,421) | 4,931 | 0.52 |
| Welsh (384) | 2,296 | 0.24 |
| West Indian, ex. Hispanic (31,329) | 36,267 | 3.86 |
| Bahamian (65) | 72 | 0.01 |
| Barbadian (718) | 979 | 0.10 |
| Belizean (267) | 306 | 0.03 |
| Bermudan (0) | 0 | <0.01 |
| British West Indian (935) | 1,296 | 0.14 |
| Dutch West Indian (3) | 3 | <0.01 |
| Haitian (3,480) | 3,878 | 0.41 |
| Jamaican (21,122) | 23,768 | 2.53 |
| Trinidadian/Tobagonian (1,606) | 1,812 | 0.19 |
| U.S. Virgin Islander (55) | 106 | 0.01 |
| West Indian (3,078) | 4,037 | 0.43 |
| Other West Indian (0) | 10 | <0.01 |
| Yugoslavian (717) | 977 | 0.10 |

| Hispanic Origin | Population | % |
|---|---|---|
| Hispanic or Latino (of any race) | 207,032 | 21.81 |
| Central American, ex. Mexican | 22,365 | 2.36 |
| Costa Rican | 584 | 0.06 |
| Guatemalan | 11,337 | 1.19 |
| Honduran | 3,055 | 0.32 |
| Nicaraguan | 885 | 0.09 |
| Panamanian | 686 | 0.07 |
| Salvadoran | 5,658 | 0.60 |
| Other Central American | 160 | 0.02 |
| Cuban | 5,287 | 0.56 |
| Dominican Republic | 26,573 | 2.80 |
| Mexican | 44,060 | 4.64 |
| Puerto Rican | 41,836 | 4.41 |
| South American | 50,521 | 5.32 |
| Argentinean | 1,922 | 0.20 |
| Bolivian | 749 | 0.08 |
| Chilean | 1,551 | 0.16 |
| Colombian | 10,245 | 1.08 |
| Ecuadorian | 22,460 | 2.37 |
| Paraguayan | 1,328 | 0.14 |
| Peruvian | 9,774 | 1.03 |
| Uruguayan | 1,251 | 0.13 |
| Venezuelan | 971 | 0.10 |
| Other South American | 270 | 0.03 |
| Other Hispanic or Latino | 16,390 | 1.73 |

| Race* | Population | % |
|---|---|---|
| African-American/Black (138,118) | 149,710 | 15.77 |
| Not Hispanic (126,585) | 133,406 | 14.06 |
| Hispanic (11,533) | 16,304 | 1.72 |
| American Indian/Alaska Native (3,965) | 8,854 | 0.93 |
| Not Hispanic (1,141) | 3,720 | 0.39 |
| Hispanic (2,824) | 5,134 | 0.54 |
| Alaska Athabascan (Ala. Nat.) (3) | 3 | <0.01 |
| Aleut (Alaska Native) (0) | 5 | <0.01 |
| Apache (17) | 56 | 0.01 |
| Arapaho (0) | 2 | <0.01 |
| Blackfeet (36) | 196 | 0.02 |
| Canadian/French Am. Ind. (11) | 19 | <0.01 |
| Central American Ind. (106) | 232 | 0.02 |
| Cherokee (104) | 742 | 0.08 |
| Cheyenne (4) | 15 | <0.01 |
| Chickasaw (2) | 15 | <0.01 |
| Chippewa (16) | 38 | <0.01 |
| Choctaw (11) | 45 | <0.01 |
| Colville (0) | 1 | <0.01 |

| | Population | % |
|---|---|---|
| Comanche (0) | 7 | <0.01 |
| Cree (0) | 6 | <0.01 |
| Creek (3) | 17 | <0.01 |
| Crow (2) | 5 | <0.01 |
| Delaware (8) | 28 | <0.01 |
| Hopi (1) | 8 | <0.01 |
| Houma (4) | 4 | <0.01 |
| Inupiat (Alaska Native) (8) | 11 | <0.01 |
| Iroquois (68) | 178 | 0.02 |
| Kiowa (0) | 1 | <0.01 |
| Lumbee (3) | 5 | <0.01 |
| Menominee (0) | 0 | <0.01 |
| Mexican American Ind. (396) | 619 | 0.07 |
| Navajo (11) | 28 | <0.01 |
| Osage (5) | 7 | <0.01 |
| Ottawa (1) | 3 | <0.01 |
| Paiute (0) | 0 | <0.01 |
| Pima (2) | 2 | <0.01 |
| Potawatomi (1) | 10 | <0.01 |
| Pueblo (31) | 58 | 0.01 |
| Puget Sound Salish (0) | 3 | <0.01 |
| Seminole (4) | 43 | <0.01 |
| Shoshone (0) | 1 | <0.01 |
| Sioux (24) | 75 | 0.01 |
| South American Ind. (315) | 820 | 0.09 |
| Spanish American Ind. (162) | 216 | 0.02 |
| Tlingit-Haida (Alaska Native) (1) | 2 | <0.01 |
| Tohono O'Odham (1) | 5 | <0.01 |
| Tsimshian (Alaska Native) (0) | 0 | <0.01 |
| Ute (0) | 0 | <0.01 |
| Yakama (0) | 0 | <0.01 |
| Yaqui (0) | 2 | <0.01 |
| Yuman (2) | 4 | <0.01 |
| Yup'ik (Alaska Native) (0) | 0 | <0.01 |
| Asian (51,716) | 59,734 | 6.29 |
| Not Hispanic (51,123) | 57,958 | 6.11 |
| Hispanic (593) | 1,776 | 0.19 |
| Bangladeshi (349) | 408 | 0.04 |
| Bhutanese (19) | 19 | <0.01 |
| Burmese (106) | 116 | 0.01 |
| Cambodian (104) | 135 | 0.01 |
| Chinese, ex. Taiwanese (10,224) | 12,423 | 1.31 |
| Filipino (6,441) | 7,629 | 0.80 |
| Hmong (1) | 1 | <0.01 |
| Indian (17,798) | 19,819 | 2.09 |
| Indonesian (92) | 146 | 0.02 |
| Japanese (5,719) | 6,828 | 0.72 |
| Korean (5,440) | 6,184 | 0.65 |
| Laotian (60) | 115 | 0.01 |
| Malaysian (44) | 67 | 0.01 |
| Nepalese (137) | 153 | 0.02 |
| Pakistani (1,868) | 2,111 | 0.22 |
| Sri Lankan (206) | 232 | 0.02 |
| Taiwanese (496) | 613 | 0.06 |
| Thai (633) | 796 | 0.08 |
| Vietnamese (501) | 646 | 0.07 |
| Hawaii Native/Pacific Islander (387) | 1,501 | 0.16 |
| Not Hispanic (218) | 825 | 0.09 |
| Hispanic (169) | 676 | 0.07 |
| Fijian (12) | 16 | <0.01 |
| Guamanian/Chamorro (121) | 196 | 0.02 |
| Marshallese (1) | 1 | <0.01 |
| Native Hawaiian (64) | 173 | 0.02 |
| Samoan (15) | 43 | <0.01 |
| Tongan (0) | 0 | <0.01 |
| White (646,471) | 669,460 | 70.54 |
| Not Hispanic (544,563) | 555,692 | 58.55 |
| Hispanic (101,908) | 113,768 | 11.99 |

Notes: † The Census 2010 population figure is used to calculate the percentages in the Hispanic Origin and Race categories. Ancestry percentages are based on the 2006-2010 American Community Survey population (not shown); ‡ Numbers in parentheses indicate the number of people reporting a single ancestry; * Numbers in parentheses indicate the number of persons reporting this race alone, not in combination with any other race; Please refer to the Explanation of Data for more information.

## Wyoming County

Population: 42,155

| Ancestry | Population | % |
|---|---|---|
| Afghan (0) | 0 | <0.01 |
| African, Sub-Saharan (135) | 145 | 0.34 |
| African (126) | 135 | 0.32 |
| Cape Verdean (0) | 0 | <0.01 |
| Ethiopian (0) | 0 | <0.01 |
| Ghanaian (0) | 0 | <0.01 |
| Kenyan (0) | 0 | <0.01 |
| Liberian (0) | 0 | <0.01 |
| Nigerian (9) | 10 | 0.02 |
| Senegalese (0) | 0 | <0.01 |
| Sierra Leonean (0) | 0 | <0.01 |
| Somalian (0) | 0 | <0.01 |
| South African (0) | 0 | <0.01 |
| Sudanese (0) | 0 | <0.01 |
| Ugandan (0) | 0 | <0.01 |
| Zimbabwean (0) | 0 | <0.01 |
| Other Sub-Saharan African (0) | 0 | <0.01 |
| Albanian (0) | 0 | <0.01 |
| Alsatian (0) | 2 | <0.01 |
| American (1,695) | 1,695 | 4.00 |
| Arab (20) | 53 | 0.13 |
| Arab (0) | 0 | <0.01 |
| Egyptian (0) | 9 | 0.02 |
| Iraqi (0) | 0 | <0.01 |
| Jordanian (0) | 0 | <0.01 |
| Lebanese (20) | 44 | 0.10 |
| Moroccan (0) | 0 | <0.01 |
| Palestinian (0) | 0 | <0.01 |
| Syrian (0) | 0 | <0.01 |
| Other Arab (0) | 0 | <0.01 |
| Armenian (0) | 0 | <0.01 |
| Assyrian/Chaldean/Syriac (0) | 0 | <0.01 |
| Australian (32) | 32 | 0.08 |
| Austrian (37) | 102 | 0.24 |
| Basque (0) | 0 | <0.01 |
| Belgian (29) | 174 | 0.41 |
| Brazilian (4) | 4 | 0.01 |
| British (65) | 125 | 0.30 |
| Bulgarian (0) | 16 | 0.04 |
| Cajun (0) | 9 | 0.02 |
| Canadian (18) | 144 | 0.34 |
| Carpatho Rusyn (0) | 0 | <0.01 |
| Celtic (16) | 32 | 0.08 |
| Croatian (6) | 43 | 0.10 |
| Cypriot (0) | 0 | <0.01 |
| Czech (15) | 61 | 0.14 |
| Czechoslovakian (23) | 87 | 0.21 |
| Danish (22) | 62 | 0.15 |
| Dutch (203) | 1,260 | 2.97 |
| Eastern European (0) | 0 | <0.01 |
| English (1,993) | 7,557 | 17.84 |
| Estonian (0) | 0 | <0.01 |
| European (351) | 383 | 0.90 |
| Finnish (0) | 12 | 0.03 |
| French, ex. Basque (177) | 1,615 | 3.81 |
| French Canadian (133) | 389 | 0.92 |
| German (5,087) | 14,749 | 34.81 |
| German Russian (0) | 0 | <0.01 |
| Greek (14) | 96 | 0.23 |
| Guyanese (8) | 8 | 0.02 |
| Hungarian (56) | 163 | 0.38 |
| Icelander (0) | 0 | <0.01 |
| Iranian (0) | 0 | <0.01 |
| Irish (1,451) | 6,765 | 15.97 |
| Israeli (0) | 0 | <0.01 |
| Italian (1,447) | 3,971 | 9.37 |
| Latvian (0) | 0 | <0.01 |
| Lithuanian (0) | 59 | 0.14 |
| Luxemburger (0) | 12 | 0.03 |
| Macedonian (0) | 0 | <0.01 |
| Maltese (0) | 0 | <0.01 |
| New Zealander (0) | 0 | <0.01 |
| Northern European (0) | 0 | <0.01 |
| Norwegian (32) | 138 | 0.33 |
| Pennsylvania German (106) | 163 | 0.38 |

| Ancestry | Population | % |
|---|---|---|
| Polish (1,672) | 4,223 | 9.97 |
| Portuguese (151) | 173 | 0.41 |
| Romanian (31) | 31 | 0.07 |
| Russian (138) | 232 | 0.55 |
| Scandinavian (28) | 48 | 0.11 |
| Scotch-Irish (226) | 617 | 1.46 |
| Scottish (187) | 922 | 2.18 |
| Serbian (0) | 19 | 0.04 |
| Slavic (0) | 8 | 0.02 |
| Slovak (8) | 66 | 0.16 |
| Slovene (8) | 32 | 0.08 |
| Soviet Union (0) | 0 | <0.01 |
| Swedish (38) | 411 | 0.97 |
| Swiss (57) | 271 | 0.64 |
| Turkish (0) | 0 | <0.01 |
| Ukrainian (129) | 198 | 0.47 |
| Welsh (45) | 486 | 1.15 |
| West Indian, ex. Hispanic (108) | 139 | 0.33 |
| Bahamian (0) | 0 | <0.01 |
| Barbadian (0) | 0 | <0.01 |
| Belizean (9) | 9 | 0.02 |
| Bermudan (0) | 0 | <0.01 |
| British West Indian (0) | 0 | <0.01 |
| Dutch West Indian (0) | 0 | <0.01 |
| Haitian (26) | 35 | 0.08 |
| Jamaican (47) | 52 | 0.12 |
| Trinidadian/Tobagonian (8) | 16 | 0.04 |
| U.S. Virgin Islander (10) | 10 | 0.02 |
| West Indian (8) | 17 | 0.04 |
| Other West Indian (0) | 0 | <0.01 |
| Yugoslavian (19) | 79 | 0.19 |

| Hispanic Origin | Population | % |
|---|---|---|
| Hispanic or Latino (of any race) | 1,244 | 2.95 |
| Central American, ex. Mexican | 69 | 0.16 |
| Costa Rican | 1 | <0.01 |
| Guatemalan | 29 | 0.07 |
| Honduran | 9 | 0.02 |
| Nicaraguan | 3 | 0.01 |
| Panamanian | 14 | 0.03 |
| Salvadoran | 13 | 0.03 |
| Other Central American | 0 | <0.01 |
| Cuban | 40 | 0.09 |
| Dominican Republic | 94 | 0.22 |
| Mexican | 342 | 0.81 |
| Puerto Rican | 526 | 1.25 |
| South American | 65 | 0.15 |
| Argentinean | 2 | <0.01 |
| Bolivian | 0 | <0.01 |
| Chilean | 2 | <0.01 |
| Colombian | 24 | 0.06 |
| Ecuadorian | 27 | 0.06 |
| Paraguayan | 0 | <0.01 |
| Peruvian | 7 | 0.02 |
| Uruguayan | 1 | <0.01 |
| Venezuelan | 2 | <0.01 |
| Other South American | 0 | <0.01 |
| Other Hispanic or Latino | 108 | 0.26 |

| Race* | Population | % |
|---|---|---|
| African-American/Black (2,375) | 2,492 | 5.91 |
| Not Hispanic (2,233) | 2,337 | 5.54 |
| Hispanic (142) | 155 | 0.37 |
| American Indian/Alaska Native (126) | 272 | 0.65 |
| Not Hispanic (103) | 222 | 0.53 |
| Hispanic (23) | 50 | 0.12 |
| Alaska Athabascan (Ala. Nat.) (1) | 1 | <0.01 |
| Aleut (Alaska Native) (0) | 0 | <0.01 |
| Apache (0) | 1 | <0.01 |
| Arapaho (0) | 0 | <0.01 |
| Blackfeet (0) | 5 | 0.01 |
| Canadian/French Am. Ind. (1) | 1 | <0.01 |
| Central American Ind. (1) | 1 | <0.01 |
| Cherokee (5) | 15 | 0.04 |
| Cheyenne (0) | 0 | <0.01 |
| Chickasaw (0) | 0 | <0.01 |
| Chippewa (5) | 5 | 0.01 |
| Choctaw (0) | 1 | <0.01 |
| Colville (0) | 0 | <0.01 |

| Race* | Population | % |
|---|---|---|
| Comanche (0) | 0 | <0.01 |
| Cree (0) | 0 | <0.01 |
| Creek (0) | 0 | <0.01 |
| Crow (0) | 0 | <0.01 |
| Delaware (0) | 1 | <0.01 |
| Hopi (0) | 0 | <0.01 |
| Houma (0) | 0 | <0.01 |
| Inupiat (Alaska Native) (1) | 1 | <0.01 |
| Iroquois (35) | 75 | 0.18 |
| Kiowa (0) | 0 | <0.01 |
| Lumbee (0) | 0 | <0.01 |
| Menominee (0) | 0 | <0.01 |
| Mexican American Ind. (4) | 7 | 0.02 |
| Navajo (0) | 2 | <0.01 |
| Osage (0) | 0 | <0.01 |
| Ottawa (0) | 0 | <0.01 |
| Paiute (0) | 0 | <0.01 |
| Pima (0) | 0 | <0.01 |
| Potawatomi (0) | 0 | <0.01 |
| Pueblo (0) | 0 | <0.01 |
| Puget Sound Salish (0) | 0 | <0.01 |
| Seminole (0) | 0 | <0.01 |
| Shoshone (0) | 0 | <0.01 |
| Sioux (1) | 3 | 0.01 |
| South American Ind. (6) | 6 | 0.01 |
| Spanish American Ind. (1) | 1 | <0.01 |
| Tlingit-Haida (Alaska Native) (0) | 0 | <0.01 |
| Tohono O'Odham (3) | 3 | 0.01 |
| Tsimshian (Alaska Native) (0) | 0 | <0.01 |
| Ute (0) | 0 | <0.01 |
| Yakama (0) | 0 | <0.01 |
| Yaqui (0) | 0 | <0.01 |
| Yuman (0) | 0 | <0.01 |
| Yup'ik (Alaska Native) (0) | 0 | <0.01 |
| Asian (160) | 229 | 0.54 |
| Not Hispanic (156) | 217 | 0.51 |
| Hispanic (4) | 12 | 0.03 |
| Bangladeshi (3) | 3 | 0.01 |
| Bhutanese (0) | 0 | <0.01 |
| Burmese (0) | 0 | <0.01 |
| Cambodian (1) | 1 | <0.01 |
| Chinese, ex. Taiwanese (39) | 52 | 0.12 |
| Filipino (21) | 41 | 0.10 |
| Hmong (0) | 0 | <0.01 |
| Indian (24) | 32 | 0.08 |
| Indonesian (0) | 1 | <0.01 |
| Japanese (7) | 16 | 0.04 |
| Korean (21) | 27 | 0.06 |
| Laotian (10) | 14 | 0.03 |
| Malaysian (0) | 0 | <0.01 |
| Nepalese (0) | 0 | <0.01 |
| Pakistani (7) | 8 | 0.02 |
| Sri Lankan (0) | 0 | <0.01 |
| Taiwanese (1) | 1 | <0.01 |
| Thai (2) | 5 | 0.01 |
| Vietnamese (7) | 11 | 0.03 |
| Hawaii Native/Pacific Islander (7) | 14 | 0.03 |
| Not Hispanic (7) | 12 | 0.03 |
| Hispanic (0) | 2 | <0.01 |
| Fijian (0) | 0 | <0.01 |
| Guamanian/Chamorro (0) | 0 | <0.01 |
| Marshallese (0) | 0 | <0.01 |
| Native Hawaiian (1) | 3 | 0.01 |
| Samoan (0) | 0 | <0.01 |
| Tongan (0) | 0 | <0.01 |
| White (38,602) | 38,955 | 92.41 |
| Not Hispanic (38,042) | 38,323 | 90.91 |
| Hispanic (560) | 632 | 1.50 |

Notes: † The Census 2010 population figure is used to calculate the percentages in the Hispanic Origin and Race categories. Ancestry percentages are based on the 2006-2010 American Community Survey population (not shown); ‡ Numbers in parentheses indicate the number of people reporting a single ancestry; * Numbers in parentheses indicate the number of persons reporting this race alone, not in combination with any other race; Please refer to the Explanation of Data for more information.

## Yates County
Population: 25,348

| Ancestry | Population | % |
|---|---|---|
| Afghan (0) | 0 | <0.01 |
| African, Sub-Saharan (10) | 14 | 0.06 |
| African (0) | 4 | 0.02 |
| Cape Verdean (0) | 0 | <0.01 |
| Ethiopian (0) | 0 | <0.01 |
| Ghanaian (0) | 0 | <0.01 |
| Kenyan (10) | 10 | 0.04 |
| Liberian (0) | 0 | <0.01 |
| Nigerian (0) | 0 | <0.01 |
| Senegalese (0) | 0 | <0.01 |
| Sierra Leonean (0) | 0 | <0.01 |
| Somalian (0) | 0 | <0.01 |
| South African (0) | 0 | <0.01 |
| Sudanese (0) | 0 | <0.01 |
| Ugandan (0) | 0 | <0.01 |
| Zimbabwean (0) | 0 | <0.01 |
| Other Sub-Saharan African (0) | 0 | <0.01 |
| Albanian (0) | 0 | <0.01 |
| Alsatian (0) | 0 | <0.01 |
| American (2,456) | 2,456 | 9.73 |
| Arab (3) | 17 | 0.07 |
| Arab (0) | 0 | <0.01 |
| Egyptian (0) | 0 | <0.01 |
| Iraqi (0) | 0 | <0.01 |
| Jordanian (0) | 0 | <0.01 |
| Lebanese (0) | 8 | 0.03 |
| Moroccan (0) | 0 | <0.01 |
| Palestinian (0) | 0 | <0.01 |
| Syrian (3) | 9 | 0.04 |
| Other Arab (0) | 0 | <0.01 |
| Armenian (0) | 28 | 0.11 |
| Assyrian/Chaldean/Syriac (0) | 0 | <0.01 |
| Australian (4) | 8 | 0.03 |
| Austrian (12) | 56 | 0.22 |
| Basque (0) | 0 | <0.01 |
| Belgian (3) | 15 | 0.06 |
| Brazilian (0) | 0 | <0.01 |
| British (52) | 151 | 0.60 |
| Bulgarian (0) | 0 | <0.01 |
| Cajun (0) | 0 | <0.01 |
| Canadian (29) | 88 | 0.35 |
| Carpatho Rusyn (0) | 0 | <0.01 |
| Celtic (0) | 0 | <0.01 |
| Croatian (0) | 0 | <0.01 |
| Cypriot (0) | 0 | <0.01 |
| Czech (3) | 66 | 0.26 |
| Czechoslovakian (3) | 3 | 0.01 |
| Danish (393) | 801 | 3.17 |
| Dutch (200) | 1,287 | 5.10 |
| Eastern European (19) | 19 | 0.08 |
| English (1,552) | 4,563 | 18.07 |
| Estonian (0) | 0 | <0.01 |
| European (75) | 82 | 0.32 |
| Finnish (0) | 75 | 0.30 |
| French, ex. Basque (105) | 778 | 3.08 |
| French Canadian (56) | 224 | 0.89 |
| German (2,782) | 6,401 | 25.35 |
| German Russian (0) | 0 | <0.01 |
| Greek (27) | 121 | 0.48 |
| Guyanese (0) | 0 | <0.01 |
| Hungarian (48) | 128 | 0.51 |
| Icelander (0) | 0 | <0.01 |
| Iranian (9) | 21 | 0.08 |
| Irish (1,496) | 5,291 | 20.95 |
| Israeli (0) | 6 | 0.02 |
| Italian (794) | 2,160 | 8.55 |
| Latvian (0) | 0 | <0.01 |
| Lithuanian (0) | 16 | 0.06 |
| Luxemburger (0) | 0 | <0.01 |
| Macedonian (0) | 0 | <0.01 |
| Maltese (0) | 0 | <0.01 |
| New Zealander (0) | 0 | <0.01 |
| Northern European (10) | 10 | 0.04 |
| Norwegian (19) | 106 | 0.42 |
| Pennsylvania German (408) | 471 | 1.87 |

| Ancestry | Population | % |
|---|---|---|
| Polish (256) | 915 | 3.62 |
| Portuguese (13) | 13 | 0.05 |
| Romanian (4) | 4 | 0.02 |
| Russian (50) | 123 | 0.49 |
| Scandinavian (0) | 39 | 0.15 |
| Scotch-Irish (174) | 418 | 1.66 |
| Scottish (219) | 770 | 3.05 |
| Serbian (0) | 0 | <0.01 |
| Slavic (0) | 3 | 0.01 |
| Slovak (42) | 66 | 0.26 |
| Slovene (10) | 13 | 0.05 |
| Soviet Union (0) | 0 | <0.01 |
| Swedish (58) | 207 | 0.82 |
| Swiss (501) | 719 | 2.85 |
| Turkish (0) | 0 | <0.01 |
| Ukrainian (29) | 99 | 0.39 |
| Welsh (59) | 266 | 1.05 |
| West Indian, ex. Hispanic (52) | 52 | 0.21 |
| Bahamian (0) | 0 | <0.01 |
| Barbadian (0) | 0 | <0.01 |
| Belizean (0) | 0 | <0.01 |
| Bermudan (0) | 0 | <0.01 |
| British West Indian (0) | 0 | <0.01 |
| Dutch West Indian (0) | 0 | <0.01 |
| Haitian (0) | 0 | <0.01 |
| Jamaican (8) | 8 | 0.03 |
| Trinidadian/Tobagonian (0) | 0 | <0.01 |
| U.S. Virgin Islander (0) | 0 | <0.01 |
| West Indian (44) | 44 | 0.17 |
| Other West Indian (0) | 0 | <0.01 |
| Yugoslavian (10) | 21 | 0.08 |

| Hispanic Origin | Population | % |
|---|---|---|
| Hispanic or Latino (of any race) | 421 | 1.66 |
| Central American, ex. Mexican | 15 | 0.06 |
| Costa Rican | 0 | <0.01 |
| Guatemalan | 7 | 0.03 |
| Honduran | 5 | 0.02 |
| Nicaraguan | 0 | <0.01 |
| Panamanian | 3 | 0.01 |
| Salvadoran | 0 | <0.01 |
| Other Central American | 0 | <0.01 |
| Cuban | 10 | 0.04 |
| Dominican Republic | 7 | 0.03 |
| Mexican | 152 | 0.60 |
| Puerto Rican | 159 | 0.63 |
| South American | 23 | 0.09 |
| Argentinean | 1 | <0.01 |
| Bolivian | 0 | <0.01 |
| Chilean | 3 | 0.01 |
| Colombian | 8 | 0.03 |
| Ecuadorian | 7 | 0.03 |
| Paraguayan | 3 | 0.01 |
| Peruvian | 1 | <0.01 |
| Uruguayan | 0 | <0.01 |
| Venezuelan | 0 | <0.01 |
| Other South American | 0 | <0.01 |
| Other Hispanic or Latino | 55 | 0.22 |

| Race* | Population | % |
|---|---|---|
| African-American/Black (203) | 316 | 1.25 |
| Not Hispanic (196) | 295 | 1.16 |
| Hispanic (7) | 21 | 0.08 |
| American Indian/Alaska Native (38) | 144 | 0.57 |
| Not Hispanic (35) | 127 | 0.50 |
| Hispanic (3) | 17 | 0.07 |
| Alaska Athabascan (Ala. Nat.) (0) | 0 | <0.01 |
| Aleut (Alaska Native) (0) | 0 | <0.01 |
| Apache (0) | 1 | <0.01 |
| Arapaho (0) | 1 | <0.01 |
| Blackfeet (0) | 6 | 0.02 |
| Canadian/French Am. Ind. (1) | 2 | 0.01 |
| Central American Ind. (0) | 0 | <0.01 |
| Cherokee (1) | 14 | 0.06 |
| Cheyenne (0) | 0 | <0.01 |
| Chickasaw (0) | 0 | <0.01 |
| Chippewa (0) | 4 | 0.02 |
| Choctaw (0) | 0 | <0.01 |
| Colville (0) | 0 | <0.01 |

| Race* | Population | % |
|---|---|---|
| Comanche (0) | 0 | <0.01 |
| Cree (0) | 0 | <0.01 |
| Creek (0) | 0 | <0.01 |
| Crow (0) | 0 | <0.01 |
| Delaware (0) | 0 | <0.01 |
| Hopi (0) | 0 | <0.01 |
| Houma (0) | 0 | <0.01 |
| Inupiat (Alaska Native) (0) | 0 | <0.01 |
| Iroquois (8) | 32 | 0.13 |
| Kiowa (0) | 0 | <0.01 |
| Lumbee (0) | 0 | <0.01 |
| Menominee (0) | 0 | <0.01 |
| Mexican American Ind. (0) | 0 | <0.01 |
| Navajo (0) | 0 | <0.01 |
| Osage (0) | 0 | <0.01 |
| Ottawa (0) | 0 | <0.01 |
| Paiute (0) | 0 | <0.01 |
| Pima (0) | 1 | <0.01 |
| Potawatomi (0) | 0 | <0.01 |
| Pueblo (1) | 1 | <0.01 |
| Puget Sound Salish (0) | 0 | <0.01 |
| Seminole (0) | 0 | <0.01 |
| Shoshone (0) | 0 | <0.01 |
| Sioux (1) | 5 | 0.02 |
| South American Ind. (1) | 4 | 0.02 |
| Spanish American Ind. (0) | 0 | <0.01 |
| Tlingit-Haida (Alaska Native) (0) | 0 | <0.01 |
| Tohono O'Odham (0) | 0 | <0.01 |
| Tsimshian (Alaska Native) (0) | 0 | <0.01 |
| Ute (0) | 0 | <0.01 |
| Yakama (0) | 0 | <0.01 |
| Yaqui (0) | 1 | <0.01 |
| Yuman (0) | 0 | <0.01 |
| Yup'ik (Alaska Native) (0) | 0 | <0.01 |
| Asian (97) | 124 | 0.49 |
| Not Hispanic (96) | 120 | 0.47 |
| Hispanic (1) | 4 | 0.02 |
| Bangladeshi (0) | 0 | <0.01 |
| Bhutanese (0) | 0 | <0.01 |
| Burmese (0) | 0 | <0.01 |
| Cambodian (3) | 3 | 0.01 |
| Chinese, ex. Taiwanese (30) | 42 | 0.17 |
| Filipino (8) | 10 | 0.04 |
| Hmong (0) | 0 | <0.01 |
| Indian (11) | 16 | 0.06 |
| Indonesian (0) | 0 | <0.01 |
| Japanese (9) | 26 | 0.10 |
| Korean (22) | 25 | 0.10 |
| Laotian (4) | 6 | 0.02 |
| Malaysian (0) | 0 | <0.01 |
| Nepalese (0) | 0 | <0.01 |
| Pakistani (0) | 0 | <0.01 |
| Sri Lankan (0) | 0 | <0.01 |
| Taiwanese (0) | 0 | <0.01 |
| Thai (0) | 0 | <0.01 |
| Vietnamese (1) | 2 | 0.01 |
| Hawaii Native/Pacific Islander (4) | 16 | 0.06 |
| Not Hispanic (1) | 11 | 0.04 |
| Hispanic (3) | 5 | 0.02 |
| Fijian (0) | 0 | <0.01 |
| Guamanian/Chamorro (1) | 7 | 0.03 |
| Marshallese (0) | 0 | <0.01 |
| Native Hawaiian (0) | 3 | 0.01 |
| Samoan (3) | 3 | 0.01 |
| Tongan (0) | 0 | <0.01 |
| White (24,647) | 24,903 | 98.24 |
| Not Hispanic (24,371) | 24,577 | 96.96 |
| Hispanic (276) | 326 | 1.29 |

Notes: † The Census 2010 population figure is used to calculate the percentages in the Hispanic Origin and Race categories. Ancestry percentages are based on the 2006-2010 American Community Survey population (not shown); ‡ Numbers in parentheses indicate the number of people reporting a single ancestry; * Numbers in parentheses indicate the number of persons reporting this race alone, not in combination with any other race; Please refer to the Explanation of Data for more information.

## Place Profiles

### Albany

Place Type: City
County: Albany
Population: 97,856

| Ancestry | Population | % |
|---|---|---|
| Afghan (0) | 0 | <0.01 |
| African, Sub-Saharan (1,142) | 1,533 | 1.57 |
| African (656) | 975 | 1.00 |
| Cape Verdean (0) | 13 | 0.01 |
| Ethiopian (21) | 21 | 0.02 |
| Ghanaian (143) | 143 | 0.15 |
| Kenyan (101) | 101 | 0.10 |
| Liberian (0) | 0 | <0.01 |
| Nigerian (132) | 191 | 0.19 |
| Senegalese (0) | 0 | <0.01 |
| Sierra Leonean (0) | 0 | <0.01 |
| Somalian (0) | 0 | <0.01 |
| South African (0) | 0 | <0.01 |
| Sudanese (25) | 25 | 0.03 |
| Ugandan (0) | 0 | <0.01 |
| Zimbabwean (0) | 0 | <0.01 |
| Other Sub-Saharan African (64) | 64 | 0.07 |
| Albanian (318) | 384 | 0.39 |
| Alsatian (19) | 51 | 0.05 |
| American (1,531) | 1,531 | 1.56 |
| Arab (181) | 525 | 0.54 |
| Arab (105) | 116 | 0.12 |
| Egyptian (41) | 124 | 0.13 |
| Iraqi (0) | 0 | <0.01 |
| Jordanian (0) | 0 | <0.01 |
| Lebanese (23) | 138 | 0.14 |
| Moroccan (0) | 0 | <0.01 |
| Palestinian (12) | 25 | 0.03 |
| Syrian (0) | 104 | 0.11 |
| Other Arab (0) | 18 | 0.02 |
| Armenian (26) | 75 | 0.08 |
| Assyrian/Chaldean/Syriac (0) | 0 | <0.01 |
| Australian (30) | 88 | 0.09 |
| Austrian (31) | 247 | 0.25 |
| Basque (0) | 0 | <0.01 |
| Belgian (53) | 78 | 0.08 |
| Brazilian (45) | 45 | 0.05 |
| British (132) | 255 | 0.26 |
| Bulgarian (0) | 9 | 0.01 |
| Cajun (0) | 0 | <0.01 |
| Canadian (80) | 128 | 0.13 |
| Carpatho Rusyn (12) | 12 | 0.01 |
| Celtic (0) | 0 | <0.01 |
| Croatian (32) | 54 | 0.06 |
| Cypriot (0) | 0 | <0.01 |
| Czech (153) | 392 | 0.40 |
| Czechoslovakian (11) | 35 | 0.04 |
| Danish (89) | 303 | 0.31 |
| Dutch (321) | 1,664 | 1.70 |
| Eastern European (220) | 253 | 0.26 |
| English (1,100) | 5,315 | 5.43 |
| Estonian (0) | 0 | <0.01 |
| European (1,163) | 1,362 | 1.39 |
| Finnish (0) | 35 | 0.04 |
| French, ex. Basque (458) | 3,690 | 3.77 |
| French Canadian (329) | 1,061 | 1.08 |
| German (1,888) | 10,150 | 10.36 |
| German Russian (0) | 0 | <0.01 |
| Greek (368) | 755 | 0.77 |
| Guyanese (466) | 483 | 0.49 |
| Hungarian (183) | 405 | 0.41 |
| Icelander (0) | 0 | <0.01 |
| Iranian (50) | 60 | 0.06 |
| Irish (5,251) | 17,818 | 18.19 |
| Israeli (0) | 0 | <0.01 |
| Italian (4,932) | 12,860 | 13.13 |
| Latvian (15) | 24 | 0.02 |
| Lithuanian (38) | 217 | 0.22 |
| Luxemburger (9) | 9 | 0.01 |
| Macedonian (0) | 0 | <0.01 |

| | Population | % |
|---|---|---|
| Maltese (11) | 24 | 0.02 |
| New Zealander (0) | 0 | <0.01 |
| Northern European (56) | 160 | 0.16 |
| Norwegian (146) | 406 | 0.41 |
| Pennsylvania German (0) | 12 | 0.01 |
| Polish (1,282) | 4,476 | 4.57 |
| Portuguese (116) | 266 | 0.27 |
| Romanian (0) | 182 | 0.19 |
| Russian (483) | 1,487 | 1.52 |
| Scandinavian (31) | 313 | 0.32 |
| Scotch-Irish (229) | 842 | 0.86 |
| Scottish (311) | 1,162 | 1.19 |
| Serbian (19) | 19 | 0.02 |
| Slavic (28) | 94 | 0.10 |
| Slovak (110) | 351 | 0.36 |
| Slovene (12) | 70 | 0.07 |
| Soviet Union (0) | 0 | <0.01 |
| Swedish (57) | 444 | 0.45 |
| Swiss (15) | 125 | 0.13 |
| Turkish (14) | 39 | 0.04 |
| Ukrainian (85) | 496 | 0.51 |
| Welsh (103) | 597 | 0.61 |
| West Indian, ex. Hispanic (2,407) | 3,298 | 3.37 |
| Bahamian (0) | 0 | <0.01 |
| Barbadian (14) | 29 | 0.03 |
| Belizean (0) | 0 | <0.01 |
| Bermudan (36) | 36 | 0.04 |
| British West Indian (133) | 210 | 0.21 |
| Dutch West Indian (39) | 79 | 0.08 |
| Haitian (421) | 446 | 0.46 |
| Jamaican (1,228) | 1,636 | 1.67 |
| Trinidadian/Tobagonian (193) | 219 | 0.22 |
| U.S. Virgin Islander (0) | 0 | <0.01 |
| West Indian (276) | 576 | 0.59 |
| Other West Indian (67) | 67 | 0.07 |
| Yugoslavian (36) | 48 | 0.05 |

| Hispanic Origin | Population | % |
|---|---|---|
| Hispanic or Latino (of any race) | 8,396 | 8.58 |
| Central American, ex. Mexican | 343 | 0.35 |
| Costa Rican | 35 | 0.04 |
| Guatemalan | 54 | 0.06 |
| Honduran | 70 | 0.07 |
| Nicaraguan | 28 | 0.03 |
| Panamanian | 81 | 0.08 |
| Salvadoran | 65 | 0.07 |
| Other Central American | 10 | 0.01 |
| Cuban | 298 | 0.30 |
| Dominican Republic | 1,095 | 1.12 |
| Mexican | 616 | 0.63 |
| Puerto Rican | 4,654 | 4.76 |
| South American | 626 | 0.64 |
| Argentinean | 38 | 0.04 |
| Bolivian | 5 | 0.01 |
| Chilean | 38 | 0.04 |
| Colombian | 196 | 0.20 |
| Ecuadorian | 184 | 0.19 |
| Paraguayan | 6 | 0.01 |
| Peruvian | 89 | 0.09 |
| Uruguayan | 15 | 0.02 |
| Venezuelan | 39 | 0.04 |
| Other South American | 16 | 0.02 |
| Other Hispanic or Latino | 764 | 0.78 |

| Race* | Population | % |
|---|---|---|
| African-American/Black (30,110) | 32,569 | 33.28 |
| Not Hispanic (28,479) | 30,376 | 31.04 |
| Hispanic (1,631) | 2,193 | 2.24 |
| American Indian/Alaska Native (295) | 1,120 | 1.14 |
| Not Hispanic (191) | 856 | 0.87 |
| Hispanic (104) | 264 | 0.27 |
| Alaska Athabascan (Ala. Nat.) (0) | 1 | <0.01 |
| Aleut (Alaska Native) (0) | 0 | <0.01 |
| Apache (0) | 5 | 0.01 |
| Arapaho (0) | 0 | <0.01 |
| Blackfeet (6) | 57 | 0.06 |

| | Population | % |
|---|---|---|
| Canadian/French Am. Ind. (0) | 5 | 0.01 |
| Central American Ind. (5) | 10 | 0.01 |
| Cherokee (23) | 205 | 0.21 |
| Cheyenne (0) | 0 | <0.01 |
| Chickasaw (2) | 2 | <0.01 |
| Chippewa (3) | 3 | <0.01 |
| Choctaw (2) | 8 | 0.01 |
| Colville (0) | 0 | <0.01 |
| Comanche (0) | 0 | <0.01 |
| Cree (1) | 4 | <0.01 |
| Creek (0) | 6 | 0.01 |
| Crow (0) | 0 | <0.01 |
| Delaware (2) | 11 | 0.01 |
| Hopi (0) | 0 | <0.01 |
| Houma (0) | 0 | <0.01 |
| Inupiat (Alaska Native) (1) | 1 | <0.01 |
| Iroquois (26) | 102 | 0.10 |
| Kiowa (0) | 0 | <0.01 |
| Lumbee (0) | 0 | <0.01 |
| Menominee (0) | 0 | <0.01 |
| Mexican American Ind. (10) | 13 | 0.01 |
| Navajo (1) | 2 | <0.01 |
| Osage (0) | 0 | <0.01 |
| Ottawa (0) | 1 | <0.01 |
| Paiute (0) | 0 | <0.01 |
| Pima (0) | 0 | <0.01 |
| Potawatomi (1) | 2 | <0.01 |
| Pueblo (1) | 1 | <0.01 |
| Puget Sound Salish (0) | 0 | <0.01 |
| Seminole (1) | 7 | 0.01 |
| Shoshone (0) | 1 | <0.01 |
| Sioux (5) | 11 | 0.01 |
| South American Ind. (24) | 49 | 0.05 |
| Spanish American Ind. (6) | 10 | 0.01 |
| Tlingit-Haida (Alaska Native) (1) | 3 | <0.01 |
| Tohono O'Odham (0) | 0 | <0.01 |
| Tsimshian (Alaska Native) (0) | 0 | <0.01 |
| Ute (0) | 0 | <0.01 |
| Yakama (1) | 1 | <0.01 |
| Yaqui (0) | 0 | <0.01 |
| Yuman (0) | 0 | <0.01 |
| Yup'ik (Alaska Native) (1) | 1 | <0.01 |
| Asian (4,890) | 5,588 | 5.71 |
| Not Hispanic (4,850) | 5,482 | 5.60 |
| Hispanic (40) | 106 | 0.11 |
| Bangladeshi (148) | 171 | 0.17 |
| Bhutanese (62) | 62 | 0.06 |
| Burmese (294) | 322 | 0.33 |
| Cambodian (8) | 12 | 0.01 |
| Chinese, ex. Taiwanese (1,219) | 1,349 | 1.38 |
| Filipino (645) | 746 | 0.76 |
| Hmong (0) | 0 | <0.01 |
| Indian (1,009) | 1,198 | 1.22 |
| Indonesian (10) | 12 | 0.01 |
| Japanese (109) | 200 | 0.20 |
| Korean (368) | 426 | 0.44 |
| Laotian (3) | 3 | <0.01 |
| Malaysian (2) | 8 | 0.01 |
| Nepalese (48) | 55 | 0.06 |
| Pakistani (425) | 483 | 0.49 |
| Sri Lankan (13) | 13 | 0.01 |
| Taiwanese (61) | 69 | 0.07 |
| Thai (35) | 46 | 0.05 |
| Vietnamese (197) | 231 | 0.24 |
| Hawaii Native/Pacific Islander (55) | 180 | 0.18 |
| Not Hispanic (47) | 158 | 0.16 |
| Hispanic (8) | 22 | 0.02 |
| Fijian (0) | 1 | <0.01 |
| Guamanian/Chamorro (7) | 15 | 0.02 |
| Marshallese (0) | 0 | <0.01 |
| Native Hawaiian (8) | 38 | 0.04 |
| Samoan (9) | 15 | 0.02 |
| Tongan (0) | 1 | <0.01 |
| White (55,783) | 58,605 | 59.89 |
| Not Hispanic (52,857) | 55,044 | 56.25 |
| Hispanic (2,926) | 3,561 | 3.64 |

Notes: † The Census 2010 population figure is used to calculate the percentages in the Hispanic Origin and Race categories. Ancestry percentages are based on the 2006-2010 American Community Survey population (not shown); ‡ Numbers in parentheses indicate the number of people reporting a single ancestry; * Numbers in parentheses indicate the number of persons reporting this race alone, not in combination with any other race; Please refer to the Explanation of Data for more information.

## Amherst

Place Type: Town
County: Erie
Population: 122,366

| Ancestry | Population | % |
|---|---|---|
| Afghan (144) | 144 | 0.12 |
| African, Sub-Saharan (897) | 1,095 | 0.91 |
| African (481) | 625 | 0.52 |
| Cape Verdean (0) | 0 | <0.01 |
| Ethiopian (71) | 71 | 0.06 |
| Ghanaian (15) | 15 | 0.01 |
| Kenyan (12) | 12 | 0.01 |
| Liberian (0) | 0 | <0.01 |
| Nigerian (167) | 167 | 0.14 |
| Senegalese (0) | 0 | <0.01 |
| Sierra Leonean (0) | 0 | <0.01 |
| Somalian (0) | 0 | <0.01 |
| South African (22) | 35 | 0.03 |
| Sudanese (0) | 0 | <0.01 |
| Ugandan (0) | 0 | <0.01 |
| Zimbabwean (0) | 0 | <0.01 |
| Other Sub-Saharan African (129) | 170 | 0.14 |
| Albanian (26) | 114 | 0.09 |
| Alsatian (9) | 32 | 0.03 |
| American (3,077) | 3,077 | 2.54 |
| Arab (818) | 1,530 | 1.27 |
| Arab (46) | 90 | 0.07 |
| Egyptian (8) | 8 | 0.01 |
| Iraqi (0) | 0 | <0.01 |
| Jordanian (84) | 84 | 0.07 |
| Lebanese (342) | 985 | 0.81 |
| Moroccan (13) | 13 | 0.01 |
| Palestinian (18) | 18 | 0.01 |
| Syrian (48) | 62 | 0.05 |
| Other Arab (259) | 270 | 0.22 |
| Armenian (157) | 203 | 0.17 |
| Assyrian/Chaldean/Syriac (0) | 0 | <0.01 |
| Australian (29) | 47 | 0.04 |
| Austrian (367) | 1,014 | 0.84 |
| Basque (0) | 0 | <0.01 |
| Belgian (11) | 38 | 0.03 |
| Brazilian (223) | 223 | 0.18 |
| British (194) | 438 | 0.36 |
| Bulgarian (68) | 98 | 0.08 |
| Cajun (0) | 0 | <0.01 |
| Canadian (282) | 589 | 0.49 |
| Carpatho Rusyn (0) | 0 | <0.01 |
| Celtic (10) | 10 | 0.01 |
| Croatian (114) | 393 | 0.32 |
| Cypriot (0) | 0 | <0.01 |
| Czech (105) | 255 | 0.21 |
| Czechoslovakian (46) | 82 | 0.07 |
| Danish (55) | 199 | 0.16 |
| Dutch (148) | 1,690 | 1.40 |
| Eastern European (507) | 575 | 0.48 |
| English (3,188) | 11,840 | 9.79 |
| Estonian (10) | 25 | 0.02 |
| European (915) | 981 | 0.81 |
| Finnish (35) | 196 | 0.16 |
| French, ex. Basque (438) | 3,549 | 2.93 |
| French Canadian (283) | 983 | 0.81 |
| German (8,678) | 30,579 | 25.28 |
| German Russian (0) | 0 | <0.01 |
| Greek (323) | 802 | 0.66 |
| Guyanese (43) | 43 | 0.04 |
| Hungarian (420) | 1,194 | 0.99 |
| Icelander (0) | 0 | <0.01 |
| Iranian (174) | 188 | 0.16 |
| Irish (5,285) | 22,106 | 18.28 |
| Israeli (75) | 122 | 0.10 |
| Italian (11,256) | 23,615 | 19.53 |
| Latvian (26) | 64 | 0.05 |
| Lithuanian (82) | 182 | 0.15 |
| Luxemburger (0) | 0 | <0.01 |
| Macedonian (0) | 14 | 0.01 |
| Maltese (0) | 0 | <0.01 |
| New Zealander (0) | 26 | 0.02 |
| Northern European (29) | 101 | 0.08 |

| Ancestry | Population | % |
|---|---|---|
| Norwegian (114) | 400 | 0.33 |
| Pennsylvania German (0) | 43 | 0.04 |
| Polish (6,777) | 17,104 | 14.14 |
| Portuguese (90) | 144 | 0.12 |
| Romanian (169) | 324 | 0.27 |
| Russian (1,684) | 3,468 | 2.87 |
| Scandinavian (11) | 116 | 0.10 |
| Scotch-Irish (504) | 1,527 | 1.26 |
| Scottish (333) | 1,736 | 1.44 |
| Serbian (81) | 158 | 0.13 |
| Slavic (25) | 153 | 0.13 |
| Slovak (40) | 141 | 0.12 |
| Slovene (40) | 53 | 0.04 |
| Soviet Union (0) | 0 | <0.01 |
| Swedish (139) | 902 | 0.75 |
| Swiss (67) | 222 | 0.18 |
| Turkish (138) | 164 | 0.14 |
| Ukrainian (545) | 1,074 | 0.89 |
| Welsh (218) | 798 | 0.66 |
| West Indian, ex. Hispanic (282) | 440 | 0.36 |
| Bahamian (0) | 0 | <0.01 |
| Barbadian (12) | 12 | 0.01 |
| Belizean (0) | 0 | <0.01 |
| Bermudan (0) | 0 | <0.01 |
| British West Indian (13) | 13 | 0.01 |
| Dutch West Indian (0) | 0 | <0.01 |
| Haitian (45) | 45 | 0.04 |
| Jamaican (169) | 226 | 0.19 |
| Trinidadian/Tobagonian (5) | 19 | 0.02 |
| U.S. Virgin Islander (0) | 0 | <0.01 |
| West Indian (38) | 125 | 0.10 |
| Other West Indian (0) | 0 | <0.01 |
| Yugoslavian (52) | 52 | 0.04 |

| Hispanic Origin | Population | % |
|---|---|---|
| Hispanic or Latino (of any race) | 2,870 | 2.35 |
| Central American, ex. Mexican | 189 | 0.15 |
| Costa Rican | 20 | 0.02 |
| Guatemalan | 49 | 0.04 |
| Honduran | 23 | 0.02 |
| Nicaraguan | 8 | 0.01 |
| Panamanian | 39 | 0.03 |
| Salvadoran | 49 | 0.04 |
| Other Central American | 1 | <0.01 |
| Cuban | 120 | 0.10 |
| Dominican Republic | 194 | 0.16 |
| Mexican | 478 | 0.39 |
| Puerto Rican | 1,108 | 0.91 |
| South American | 436 | 0.36 |
| Argentinean | 57 | 0.05 |
| Bolivian | 14 | 0.01 |
| Chilean | 40 | 0.03 |
| Colombian | 163 | 0.13 |
| Ecuadorian | 63 | 0.05 |
| Paraguayan | 5 | <0.01 |
| Peruvian | 52 | 0.04 |
| Uruguayan | 7 | 0.01 |
| Venezuelan | 33 | 0.03 |
| Other South American | 2 | <0.01 |
| Other Hispanic or Latino | 345 | 0.28 |

| Race* | Population | % |
|---|---|---|
| African-American/Black (7,009) | 7,946 | 6.49 |
| Not Hispanic (6,765) | 7,563 | 6.18 |
| Hispanic (244) | 383 | 0.31 |
| American Indian/Alaska Native (220) | 616 | 0.50 |
| Not Hispanic (196) | 531 | 0.43 |
| Hispanic (24) | 85 | 0.07 |
| Alaska Athabascan (Ala. Nat.) (0) | 1 | <0.01 |
| Aleut (Alaska Native) (0) | 0 | <0.01 |
| Apache (0) | 0 | <0.01 |
| Arapaho (0) | 0 | <0.01 |
| Blackfeet (2) | 14 | 0.01 |
| Canadian/French Am. Ind. (9) | 11 | 0.01 |
| Central American Ind. (0) | 1 | <0.01 |
| Cherokee (7) | 67 | 0.05 |
| Cheyenne (0) | 0 | <0.01 |
| Chickasaw (0) | 0 | <0.01 |
| Chippewa (1) | 7 | 0.01 |

| Race* | Population | % |
|---|---|---|
| Choctaw (1) | 3 | <0.01 |
| Colville (0) | 0 | <0.01 |
| Comanche (0) | 0 | <0.01 |
| Cree (0) | 0 | <0.01 |
| Creek (0) | 2 | <0.01 |
| Crow (2) | 2 | <0.01 |
| Delaware (1) | 2 | <0.01 |
| Hopi (0) | 0 | <0.01 |
| Houma (0) | 0 | <0.01 |
| Inupiat (Alaska Native) (0) | 3 | <0.01 |
| Iroquois (84) | 155 | 0.13 |
| Kiowa (0) | 0 | <0.01 |
| Lumbee (1) | 1 | <0.01 |
| Menominee (0) | 0 | <0.01 |
| Mexican American Ind. (11) | 22 | 0.02 |
| Navajo (0) | 1 | <0.01 |
| Osage (1) | 1 | <0.01 |
| Ottawa (0) | 0 | <0.01 |
| Paiute (0) | 0 | <0.01 |
| Pima (0) | 0 | <0.01 |
| Potawatomi (0) | 0 | <0.01 |
| Pueblo (2) | 5 | <0.01 |
| Puget Sound Salish (0) | 0 | <0.01 |
| Seminole (0) | 10 | 0.01 |
| Shoshone (0) | 0 | <0.01 |
| Sioux (0) | 1 | <0.01 |
| South American Ind. (4) | 13 | 0.01 |
| Spanish American Ind. (0) | 0 | <0.01 |
| Tlingit-Haida (Alaska Native) (0) | 1 | <0.01 |
| Tohono O'Odham (1) | 1 | <0.01 |
| Tsimshian (Alaska Native) (0) | 0 | <0.01 |
| Ute (0) | 0 | <0.01 |
| Yakama (0) | 0 | <0.01 |
| Yaqui (0) | 0 | <0.01 |
| Yuman (0) | 0 | <0.01 |
| Yup'ik (Alaska Native) (0) | 1 | <0.01 |
| Asian (9,675) | 10,683 | 8.73 |
| Not Hispanic (9,643) | 10,590 | 8.65 |
| Hispanic (32) | 93 | 0.08 |
| Bangladeshi (42) | 45 | 0.04 |
| Bhutanese (0) | 0 | <0.01 |
| Burmese (28) | 32 | 0.03 |
| Cambodian (16) | 17 | 0.01 |
| Chinese, ex. Taiwanese (2,925) | 3,146 | 2.57 |
| Filipino (273) | 396 | 0.32 |
| Hmong (0) | 0 | <0.01 |
| Indian (3,263) | 3,491 | 2.85 |
| Indonesian (26) | 42 | 0.03 |
| Japanese (215) | 294 | 0.24 |
| Korean (1,377) | 1,493 | 1.22 |
| Laotian (19) | 25 | 0.02 |
| Malaysian (41) | 47 | 0.04 |
| Nepalese (12) | 12 | 0.01 |
| Pakistani (515) | 592 | 0.48 |
| Sri Lankan (122) | 130 | 0.11 |
| Taiwanese (180) | 202 | 0.17 |
| Thai (36) | 52 | 0.04 |
| Vietnamese (307) | 362 | 0.30 |
| Hawaii Native/Pacific Islander (26) | 94 | 0.08 |
| Not Hispanic (26) | 86 | 0.07 |
| Hispanic (0) | 8 | 0.01 |
| Fijian (3) | 3 | <0.01 |
| Guamanian/Chamorro (8) | 10 | 0.01 |
| Marshallese (1) | 1 | <0.01 |
| Native Hawaiian (9) | 24 | 0.02 |
| Samoan (3) | 12 | 0.01 |
| Tongan (0) | 0 | <0.01 |
| White (102,558) | 104,439 | 85.35 |
| Not Hispanic (100,778) | 102,429 | 83.71 |
| Hispanic (1,780) | 2,010 | 1.64 |

*Notes: † The Census 2010 population figure is used to calculate the percentages in the Hispanic Origin and Race categories. Ancestry percentages are based on the 2006-2010 American Community Survey population (not shown); ‡ Numbers in parentheses indicate the number of people reporting a single ancestry; * Numbers in parentheses indicate the number of persons reporting this race alone, not in combination with any other race; Please refer to the Explanation of Data for more information.*

# Babylon

Place Type: Town
County: Suffolk
Population: 213,603

| Ancestry | Population | % |
|---|---|---|
| Afghan (219) | 219 | 0.10 |
| African, Sub-Saharan (1,803) | 2,217 | 1.04 |
| African (734) | 1,071 | 0.50 |
| Cape Verdean (0) | 9 | <0.01 |
| Ethiopian (0) | 11 | 0.01 |
| Ghanaian (64) | 64 | 0.03 |
| Kenyan (0) | 0 | <0.01 |
| Liberian (300) | 309 | 0.14 |
| Nigerian (670) | 707 | 0.33 |
| Senegalese (0) | 0 | <0.01 |
| Sierra Leonean (0) | 0 | <0.01 |
| Somalian (0) | 0 | <0.01 |
| South African (0) | 0 | <0.01 |
| Sudanese (0) | 0 | <0.01 |
| Ugandan (0) | 0 | <0.01 |
| Zimbabwean (0) | 0 | <0.01 |
| Other Sub-Saharan African (35) | 46 | 0.02 |
| Albanian (139) | 210 | 0.10 |
| Alsatian (0) | 0 | <0.01 |
| American (3,343) | 3,343 | 1.56 |
| Arab (595) | 842 | 0.39 |
| Arab (236) | 259 | 0.12 |
| Egyptian (30) | 79 | 0.04 |
| Iraqi (0) | 0 | <0.01 |
| Jordanian (0) | 0 | <0.01 |
| Lebanese (20) | 79 | 0.04 |
| Moroccan (142) | 209 | 0.10 |
| Palestinian (114) | 114 | 0.05 |
| Syrian (0) | 49 | 0.02 |
| Other Arab (53) | 53 | 0.02 |
| Armenian (69) | 188 | 0.09 |
| Assyrian/Chaldean/Syriac (0) | 0 | <0.01 |
| Australian (0) | 20 | 0.01 |
| Austrian (149) | 808 | 0.38 |
| Basque (15) | 15 | 0.01 |
| Belgian (22) | 41 | 0.02 |
| Brazilian (30) | 166 | 0.08 |
| British (149) | 348 | 0.16 |
| Bulgarian (8) | 20 | 0.01 |
| Cajun (0) | 0 | <0.01 |
| Canadian (80) | 581 | 0.27 |
| Carpatho Rusyn (0) | 0 | <0.01 |
| Celtic (33) | 64 | 0.03 |
| Croatian (144) | 207 | 0.10 |
| Cypriot (0) | 0 | <0.01 |
| Czech (61) | 578 | 0.27 |
| Czechoslovakian (296) | 438 | 0.21 |
| Danish (107) | 384 | 0.18 |
| Dutch (218) | 1,653 | 0.77 |
| Eastern European (253) | 270 | 0.13 |
| English (1,368) | 8,596 | 4.02 |
| Estonian (10) | 33 | 0.02 |
| European (342) | 416 | 0.19 |
| Finnish (26) | 190 | 0.09 |
| French, ex. Basque (203) | 2,679 | 1.25 |
| French Canadian (445) | 939 | 0.44 |
| German (5,375) | 31,578 | 14.78 |
| German Russian (0) | 0 | <0.01 |
| Greek (964) | 2,182 | 1.02 |
| Guyanese (602) | 747 | 0.35 |
| Hungarian (188) | 989 | 0.46 |
| Icelander (22) | 22 | 0.01 |
| Iranian (53) | 69 | 0.03 |
| Irish (10,079) | 42,364 | 19.83 |
| Israeli (28) | 172 | 0.08 |
| Italian (32,274) | 61,852 | 28.95 |
| Latvian (11) | 35 | 0.02 |
| Lithuanian (287) | 642 | 0.30 |
| Luxemburger (0) | 0 | <0.01 |
| Macedonian (11) | 33 | 0.02 |
| Maltese (61) | 378 | 0.18 |
| New Zealander (0) | 0 | <0.01 |
| Northern European (45) | 61 | 0.03 |

| Ancestry | Population | % |
|---|---|---|
| Norwegian (303) | 1,701 | 0.80 |
| Pennsylvania German (18) | 18 | 0.01 |
| Polish (5,564) | 12,444 | 5.82 |
| Portuguese (168) | 676 | 0.32 |
| Romanian (230) | 316 | 0.15 |
| Russian (845) | 3,774 | 1.77 |
| Scandinavian (17) | 48 | 0.02 |
| Scotch-Irish (570) | 1,863 | 0.87 |
| Scottish (225) | 1,548 | 0.72 |
| Serbian (16) | 19 | 0.01 |
| Slavic (6) | 64 | 0.03 |
| Slovak (134) | 367 | 0.17 |
| Slovene (14) | 14 | 0.01 |
| Soviet Union (0) | 0 | <0.01 |
| Swedish (205) | 1,400 | 0.66 |
| Swiss (57) | 361 | 0.17 |
| Turkish (826) | 939 | 0.44 |
| Ukrainian (329) | 905 | 0.42 |
| Welsh (103) | 423 | 0.20 |
| West Indian, ex. Hispanic (9,910) | 11,187 | 5.24 |
| Bahamian (35) | 88 | 0.04 |
| Barbadian (105) | 183 | 0.09 |
| Belizean (0) | 12 | 0.01 |
| Bermudan (0) | 0 | <0.01 |
| British West Indian (64) | 119 | 0.06 |
| Dutch West Indian (6) | 6 | <0.01 |
| Haitian (3,585) | 3,789 | 1.77 |
| Jamaican (4,141) | 4,758 | 2.23 |
| Trinidadian/Tobagonian (842) | 854 | 0.40 |
| U.S. Virgin Islander (0) | 0 | <0.01 |
| West Indian (1,132) | 1,378 | 0.64 |
| Other West Indian (0) | 0 | <0.01 |
| Yugoslavian (14) | 156 | 0.07 |

| Hispanic Origin | Population | % |
|---|---|---|
| Hispanic or Latino (of any race) | 35,793 | 16.76 |
| Central American, ex. Mexican | 11,096 | 5.19 |
| Costa Rican | 146 | 0.07 |
| Guatemalan | 884 | 0.41 |
| Honduran | 1,756 | 0.82 |
| Nicaraguan | 112 | 0.05 |
| Panamanian | 305 | 0.14 |
| Salvadoran | 7,805 | 3.65 |
| Other Central American | 88 | 0.04 |
| Cuban | 550 | 0.26 |
| Dominican Republic | 6,543 | 3.06 |
| Mexican | 1,145 | 0.54 |
| Puerto Rican | 7,562 | 3.54 |
| South American | 5,576 | 2.61 |
| Argentinean | 336 | 0.16 |
| Bolivian | 78 | 0.04 |
| Chilean | 226 | 0.11 |
| Colombian | 2,036 | 0.95 |
| Ecuadorian | 1,348 | 0.63 |
| Paraguayan | 37 | 0.02 |
| Peruvian | 1,313 | 0.61 |
| Uruguayan | 64 | 0.03 |
| Venezuelan | 104 | 0.05 |
| Other South American | 34 | 0.02 |
| Other Hispanic or Latino | 3,321 | 1.55 |

| Race* | Population | % |
|---|---|---|
| African-American/Black (34,881) | 37,421 | 17.52 |
| Not Hispanic (33,147) | 34,993 | 16.38 |
| Hispanic (1,734) | 2,428 | 1.14 |
| American Indian/Alaska Native (719) | 1,894 | 0.89 |
| Not Hispanic (447) | 1,351 | 0.63 |
| Hispanic (272) | 543 | 0.25 |
| Alaska Athabascan (Ala. Nat.) (0) | 0 | <0.01 |
| Aleut (Alaska Native) (2) | 2 | <0.01 |
| Apache (1) | 11 | 0.01 |
| Arapaho (0) | 0 | <0.01 |
| Blackfeet (4) | 44 | 0.02 |
| Canadian/French Am. Ind. (7) | 10 | <0.01 |
| Central American Ind. (14) | 22 | 0.01 |
| Cherokee (51) | 250 | 0.12 |
| Cheyenne (1) | 1 | <0.01 |
| Chickasaw (0) | 0 | <0.01 |
| Chippewa (6) | 7 | <0.01 |

| Race* | Population | % |
|---|---|---|
| Choctaw (1) | 5 | <0.01 |
| Colville (0) | 0 | <0.01 |
| Comanche (1) | 2 | <0.01 |
| Cree (1) | 2 | <0.01 |
| Creek (0) | 13 | 0.01 |
| Crow (0) | 1 | <0.01 |
| Delaware (2) | 2 | <0.01 |
| Hopi (3) | 5 | <0.01 |
| Houma (0) | 0 | <0.01 |
| Inupiat (Alaska Native) (0) | 1 | <0.01 |
| Iroquois (34) | 65 | 0.03 |
| Kiowa (0) | 0 | <0.01 |
| Lumbee (3) | 12 | 0.01 |
| Menominee (0) | 0 | <0.01 |
| Mexican American Ind. (15) | 25 | 0.01 |
| Navajo (1) | 6 | <0.01 |
| Osage (0) | 0 | <0.01 |
| Ottawa (0) | 0 | <0.01 |
| Paiute (0) | 0 | <0.01 |
| Pima (0) | 0 | <0.01 |
| Potawatomi (0) | 0 | <0.01 |
| Pueblo (9) | 9 | <0.01 |
| Puget Sound Salish (0) | 0 | <0.01 |
| Seminole (2) | 13 | 0.01 |
| Shoshone (0) | 0 | <0.01 |
| Sioux (8) | 16 | 0.01 |
| South American Ind. (47) | 82 | 0.04 |
| Spanish American Ind. (8) | 17 | 0.01 |
| Tlingit-Haida (Alaska Native) (0) | 1 | <0.01 |
| Tohono O'Odham (0) | 1 | <0.01 |
| Tsimshian (Alaska Native) (0) | 0 | <0.01 |
| Ute (0) | 0 | <0.01 |
| Yakama (0) | 0 | <0.01 |
| Yaqui (0) | 0 | <0.01 |
| Yuman (0) | 0 | <0.01 |
| Yup'ik (Alaska Native) (0) | 0 | <0.01 |
| Asian (6,524) | 7,919 | 3.71 |
| Not Hispanic (6,411) | 7,577 | 3.55 |
| Hispanic (113) | 342 | 0.16 |
| Bangladeshi (271) | 341 | 0.16 |
| Bhutanese (0) | 0 | <0.01 |
| Burmese (4) | 7 | <0.01 |
| Cambodian (3) | 5 | <0.01 |
| Chinese, ex. Taiwanese (1,108) | 1,357 | 0.64 |
| Filipino (765) | 1,046 | 0.49 |
| Hmong (0) | 0 | <0.01 |
| Indian (2,582) | 2,940 | 1.38 |
| Indonesian (16) | 22 | 0.01 |
| Japanese (88) | 186 | 0.09 |
| Korean (388) | 477 | 0.22 |
| Laotian (6) | 9 | <0.01 |
| Malaysian (2) | 3 | <0.01 |
| Nepalese (4) | 4 | <0.01 |
| Pakistani (678) | 739 | 0.35 |
| Sri Lankan (25) | 32 | 0.01 |
| Taiwanese (24) | 26 | 0.01 |
| Thai (41) | 67 | 0.03 |
| Vietnamese (257) | 297 | 0.14 |
| Hawaii Native/Pacific Islander (51) | 272 | 0.13 |
| Not Hispanic (31) | 153 | 0.07 |
| Hispanic (20) | 119 | 0.06 |
| Fijian (0) | 0 | <0.01 |
| Guamanian/Chamorro (11) | 22 | 0.01 |
| Marshallese (0) | 0 | <0.01 |
| Native Hawaiian (13) | 45 | 0.02 |
| Samoan (3) | 10 | <0.01 |
| Tongan (0) | 0 | <0.01 |
| White (153,067) | 157,336 | 73.66 |
| Not Hispanic (133,961) | 136,259 | 63.79 |
| Hispanic (19,106) | 21,077 | 9.87 |

Notes: † The Census 2010 population figure is used to calculate the percentages in the Hispanic Origin and Race categories. Ancestry percentages are based on the 2006-2010 American Community Survey population (not shown); ‡ Numbers in parentheses indicate the number of people reporting a single ancestry; * Numbers in parentheses indicate the number of persons reporting this race alone, not in combination with any other race; Please refer to the Explanation of Data for more information.

## Brentwood

Place Type: CDP
County: Suffolk
Population: 60,664

| Ancestry | Population | % |
|---|---|---|
| Afghan (50) | 68 | 0.12 |
| African, Sub-Saharan (301) | 336 | 0.61 |
| African (86) | 106 | 0.19 |
| Cape Verdean (0) | 0 | <0.01 |
| Ethiopian (0) | 0 | <0.01 |
| Ghanaian (45) | 45 | 0.08 |
| Kenyan (0) | 0 | <0.01 |
| Liberian (0) | 0 | <0.01 |
| Nigerian (90) | 105 | 0.19 |
| Senegalese (0) | 0 | <0.01 |
| Sierra Leonean (0) | 0 | <0.01 |
| Somalian (0) | 0 | <0.01 |
| South African (0) | 0 | <0.01 |
| Sudanese (0) | 0 | <0.01 |
| Ugandan (0) | 0 | <0.01 |
| Zimbabwean (0) | 0 | <0.01 |
| Other Sub-Saharan African (80) | 80 | 0.15 |
| Albanian (0) | 0 | <0.01 |
| Alsatian (0) | 0 | <0.01 |
| American (588) | 588 | 1.07 |
| Arab (82) | 92 | 0.17 |
| Arab (25) | 25 | 0.05 |
| Egyptian (20) | 20 | 0.04 |
| Iraqi (0) | 0 | <0.01 |
| Jordanian (0) | 0 | <0.01 |
| Lebanese (0) | 10 | 0.02 |
| Moroccan (0) | 0 | <0.01 |
| Palestinian (0) | 0 | <0.01 |
| Syrian (0) | 0 | <0.01 |
| Other Arab (37) | 37 | 0.07 |
| Armenian (0) | 0 | <0.01 |
| Assyrian/Chaldean/Syriac (0) | 0 | <0.01 |
| Australian (0) | 8 | 0.01 |
| Austrian (19) | 80 | 0.15 |
| Basque (0) | 0 | <0.01 |
| Belgian (0) | 9 | 0.02 |
| Brazilian (418) | 418 | 0.76 |
| British (46) | 78 | 0.14 |
| Bulgarian (0) | 0 | <0.01 |
| Cajun (0) | 0 | <0.01 |
| Canadian (0) | 8 | 0.01 |
| Carpatho Rusyn (0) | 0 | <0.01 |
| Celtic (0) | 0 | <0.01 |
| Croatian (0) | 0 | <0.01 |
| Cypriot (0) | 0 | <0.01 |
| Czech (0) | 38 | 0.07 |
| Czechoslovakian (8) | 25 | 0.05 |
| Danish (0) | 0 | <0.01 |
| Dutch (0) | 96 | 0.18 |
| Eastern European (0) | 0 | <0.01 |
| English (338) | 850 | 1.55 |
| Estonian (0) | 17 | 0.03 |
| European (32) | 43 | 0.08 |
| Finnish (8) | 11 | 0.02 |
| French, ex. Basque (57) | 181 | 0.33 |
| French Canadian (10) | 48 | 0.09 |
| German (310) | 1,994 | 3.64 |
| German Russian (0) | 0 | <0.01 |
| Greek (37) | 59 | 0.11 |
| Guyanese (126) | 138 | 0.25 |
| Hungarian (16) | 42 | 0.08 |
| Icelander (0) | 0 | <0.01 |
| Iranian (0) | 0 | <0.01 |
| Irish (934) | 2,578 | 4.70 |
| Israeli (0) | 0 | <0.01 |
| Italian (1,517) | 3,236 | 5.90 |
| Latvian (0) | 0 | <0.01 |
| Lithuanian (9) | 25 | 0.05 |
| Luxemburger (0) | 0 | <0.01 |
| Macedonian (0) | 0 | <0.01 |
| Maltese (17) | 17 | 0.03 |
| New Zealander (0) | 0 | <0.01 |
| Northern European (0) | 0 | <0.01 |

| Ancestry | Population | % |
|---|---|---|
| Norwegian (24) | 72 | 0.13 |
| Pennsylvania German (0) | 0 | <0.01 |
| Polish (164) | 623 | 1.14 |
| Portuguese (504) | 524 | 0.96 |
| Romanian (0) | 0 | <0.01 |
| Russian (61) | 180 | 0.33 |
| Scandinavian (7) | 29 | 0.05 |
| Scotch-Irish (39) | 161 | 0.29 |
| Scottish (20) | 92 | 0.17 |
| Serbian (0) | 10 | 0.02 |
| Slavic (0) | 0 | <0.01 |
| Slovak (8) | 8 | 0.01 |
| Slovene (0) | 0 | <0.01 |
| Soviet Union (0) | 0 | <0.01 |
| Swedish (39) | 210 | 0.38 |
| Swiss (0) | 14 | 0.03 |
| Turkish (0) | 5 | 0.01 |
| Ukrainian (0) | 10 | 0.02 |
| Welsh (0) | 0 | <0.01 |
| West Indian, ex. Hispanic (3,143) | 3,472 | 6.33 |
| Bahamian (0) | 0 | <0.01 |
| Barbadian (5) | 5 | 0.01 |
| Belizean (0) | 0 | <0.01 |
| Bermudan (0) | 0 | <0.01 |
| British West Indian (37) | 58 | 0.11 |
| Dutch West Indian (0) | 0 | <0.01 |
| Haitian (2,072) | 2,162 | 3.94 |
| Jamaican (622) | 771 | 1.41 |
| Trinidadian/Tobagonian (104) | 152 | 0.28 |
| U.S. Virgin Islander (0) | 0 | <0.01 |
| West Indian (303) | 324 | 0.59 |
| Other West Indian (0) | 0 | <0.01 |
| Yugoslavian (0) | 10 | 0.02 |

| Hispanic Origin | Population | % |
|---|---|---|
| Hispanic or Latino (of any race) | 41,529 | 68.46 |
| Central American, ex. Mexican | 19,957 | 32.90 |
| Costa Rican | 85 | 0.14 |
| Guatemalan | 1,553 | 2.56 |
| Honduran | 2,062 | 3.40 |
| Nicaraguan | 87 | 0.14 |
| Panamanian | 148 | 0.24 |
| Salvadoran | 15,946 | 26.29 |
| Other Central American | 76 | 0.13 |
| Cuban | 223 | 0.37 |
| Dominican Republic | 4,205 | 6.93 |
| Mexican | 1,193 | 1.97 |
| Puerto Rican | 6,125 | 10.10 |
| South American | 6,350 | 10.47 |
| Argentinean | 203 | 0.33 |
| Bolivian | 79 | 0.13 |
| Chilean | 153 | 0.25 |
| Colombian | 2,083 | 3.43 |
| Ecuadorian | 1,985 | 3.27 |
| Paraguayan | 36 | 0.06 |
| Peruvian | 1,610 | 2.65 |
| Uruguayan | 80 | 0.13 |
| Venezuelan | 113 | 0.19 |
| Other South American | 8 | 0.01 |
| Other Hispanic or Latino | 3,476 | 5.73 |

| Race* | Population | % |
|---|---|---|
| African-American/Black (9,934) | 11,026 | 18.18 |
| Not Hispanic (8,344) | 8,888 | 14.65 |
| Hispanic (1,590) | 2,138 | 3.52 |
| American Indian/Alaska Native (710) | 1,135 | 1.87 |
| Not Hispanic (132) | 326 | 0.54 |
| Hispanic (578) | 809 | 1.33 |
| Alaska Athabascan (Ala. Nat.) (0) | 1 | <0.01 |
| Aleut (Alaska Native) (0) | 0 | <0.01 |
| Apache (0) | 0 | <0.01 |
| Arapaho (0) | 0 | <0.01 |
| Blackfeet (5) | 6 | 0.01 |
| Canadian/French Am. Ind. (0) | 0 | <0.01 |
| Central American Ind. (27) | 36 | 0.06 |
| Cherokee (16) | 76 | 0.13 |
| Cheyenne (0) | 0 | <0.01 |
| Chickasaw (0) | 0 | <0.01 |
| Chippewa (4) | 5 | 0.01 |

| Race* | Population | % |
|---|---|---|
| Choctaw (0) | 0 | <0.01 |
| Colville (0) | 0 | <0.01 |
| Comanche (0) | 7 | 0.01 |
| Cree (0) | 0 | <0.01 |
| Creek (0) | 0 | <0.01 |
| Crow (11) | 11 | 0.02 |
| Delaware (0) | 0 | <0.01 |
| Hopi (0) | 0 | <0.01 |
| Houma (0) | 0 | <0.01 |
| Inupiat (Alaska Native) (0) | 0 | <0.01 |
| Iroquois (14) | 17 | 0.03 |
| Kiowa (0) | 0 | <0.01 |
| Lumbee (2) | 2 | <0.01 |
| Menominee (0) | 0 | <0.01 |
| Mexican American Ind. (48) | 72 | 0.12 |
| Navajo (3) | 4 | 0.01 |
| Osage (0) | 1 | <0.01 |
| Ottawa (0) | 0 | <0.01 |
| Paiute (0) | 0 | <0.01 |
| Pima (1) | 1 | <0.01 |
| Potawatomi (0) | 0 | <0.01 |
| Pueblo (4) | 5 | 0.01 |
| Puget Sound Salish (0) | 0 | <0.01 |
| Seminole (0) | 0 | <0.01 |
| Shoshone (0) | 0 | <0.01 |
| Sioux (2) | 2 | <0.01 |
| South American Ind. (63) | 87 | 0.14 |
| Spanish American Ind. (41) | 52 | 0.09 |
| Tlingit-Haida (Alaska Native) (3) | 3 | <0.01 |
| Tohono O'Odham (0) | 0 | <0.01 |
| Tsimshian (Alaska Native) (0) | 0 | <0.01 |
| Ute (0) | 0 | <0.01 |
| Yakama (0) | 0 | <0.01 |
| Yaqui (1) | 1 | <0.01 |
| Yuman (0) | 0 | <0.01 |
| Yup'ik (Alaska Native) (0) | 0 | <0.01 |
| Asian (1,193) | 1,544 | 2.55 |
| Not Hispanic (1,101) | 1,349 | 2.22 |
| Hispanic (92) | 195 | 0.32 |
| Bangladeshi (33) | 37 | 0.06 |
| Bhutanese (0) | 0 | <0.01 |
| Burmese (1) | 1 | <0.01 |
| Cambodian (5) | 5 | 0.01 |
| Chinese, ex. Taiwanese (95) | 141 | 0.23 |
| Filipino (120) | 163 | 0.27 |
| Hmong (0) | 0 | <0.01 |
| Indian (516) | 647 | 1.07 |
| Indonesian (10) | 12 | 0.02 |
| Japanese (3) | 15 | 0.02 |
| Korean (11) | 17 | 0.03 |
| Laotian (8) | 8 | 0.01 |
| Malaysian (1) | 3 | <0.01 |
| Nepalese (0) | 0 | <0.01 |
| Pakistani (246) | 268 | 0.44 |
| Sri Lankan (6) | 10 | 0.02 |
| Taiwanese (4) | 4 | 0.01 |
| Thai (30) | 38 | 0.06 |
| Vietnamese (47) | 57 | 0.09 |
| Hawaii Native/Pacific Islander (29) | 134 | 0.22 |
| Not Hispanic (11) | 59 | 0.10 |
| Hispanic (18) | 75 | 0.12 |
| Fijian (0) | 1 | <0.01 |
| Guamanian/Chamorro (8) | 8 | 0.01 |
| Marshallese (0) | 0 | <0.01 |
| Native Hawaiian (8) | 17 | 0.03 |
| Samoan (1) | 4 | 0.01 |
| Tongan (0) | 2 | <0.01 |
| White (29,344) | 31,986 | 52.73 |
| Not Hispanic (8,554) | 8,973 | 14.79 |
| Hispanic (20,790) | 23,013 | 37.94 |

*Notes: † The Census 2010 population figure is used to calculate the percentages in the Hispanic Origin and Race categories. Ancestry percentages are based on the 2006-2010 American Community Survey population (not shown); ‡ Numbers in parentheses indicate the number of people reporting a single ancestry; * Numbers in parentheses indicate the number of persons reporting this race alone, not in combination with any other race; Please refer to the Explanation of Data for more information.*

## Bronx

Place Type: Borough
County: Bronx
Population: 1,385,108

| Ancestry | Population | % |
|---|---|---|
| Afghan (14) | 14 | <0.01 |
| African, Sub-Saharan (50,131) | 55,928 | 4.10 |
| African (19,345) | 22,647 | 1.66 |
| Cape Verdean (49) | 108 | 0.01 |
| Ethiopian (790) | 945 | 0.07 |
| Ghanaian (13,163) | 13,490 | 0.99 |
| Kenyan (12) | 24 | <0.01 |
| Liberian (365) | 450 | 0.03 |
| Nigerian (4,896) | 5,538 | 0.41 |
| Senegalese (956) | 1,068 | 0.08 |
| Sierra Leonean (759) | 759 | 0.06 |
| Somalian (11) | 35 | <0.01 |
| South African (29) | 68 | <0.01 |
| Sudanese (88) | 149 | 0.01 |
| Ugandan (0) | 0 | <0.01 |
| Zimbabwean (108) | 108 | 0.01 |
| Other Sub-Saharan African (9,560) | 10,539 | 0.77 |
| Albanian (7,460) | 7,835 | 0.57 |
| Alsatian (0) | 0 | <0.01 |
| American (16,297) | 16,297 | 1.19 |
| Arab (4,063) | 5,008 | 0.37 |
| Arab (1,481) | 1,719 | 0.13 |
| Egyptian (495) | 718 | 0.05 |
| Iraqi (64) | 73 | 0.01 |
| Jordanian (8) | 8 | <0.01 |
| Lebanese (229) | 347 | 0.03 |
| Moroccan (526) | 667 | 0.05 |
| Palestinian (28) | 28 | <0.01 |
| Syrian (44) | 192 | 0.01 |
| Other Arab (1,188) | 1,256 | 0.09 |
| Armenian (128) | 237 | 0.02 |
| Assyrian/Chaldean/Syriac (0) | 18 | <0.01 |
| Australian (8) | 21 | <0.01 |
| Austrian (539) | 1,868 | 0.14 |
| Basque (66) | 109 | 0.01 |
| Belgian (52) | 131 | 0.01 |
| Brazilian (276) | 397 | 0.03 |
| British (517) | 1,115 | 0.08 |
| Bulgarian (506) | 521 | 0.04 |
| Cajun (0) | 0 | <0.01 |
| Canadian (197) | 375 | 0.03 |
| Carpatho Rusyn (0) | 12 | <0.01 |
| Celtic (1) | 13 | <0.01 |
| Croatian (91) | 219 | 0.02 |
| Cypriot (12) | 38 | <0.01 |
| Czech (99) | 388 | 0.03 |
| Czechoslovakian (90) | 226 | 0.02 |
| Danish (17) | 385 | 0.03 |
| Dutch (314) | 1,920 | 0.14 |
| Eastern European (1,425) | 1,646 | 0.12 |
| English (1,821) | 7,038 | 0.52 |
| Estonian (70) | 85 | 0.01 |
| European (1,845) | 2,270 | 0.17 |
| Finnish (89) | 291 | 0.02 |
| French, ex. Basque (909) | 4,971 | 0.36 |
| French Canadian (102) | 403 | 0.03 |
| German (3,729) | 16,487 | 1.21 |
| German Russian (7) | 30 | <0.01 |
| Greek (2,499) | 3,607 | 0.26 |
| Guyanese (10,276) | 11,837 | 0.87 |
| Hungarian (966) | 2,427 | 0.18 |
| Icelander (6) | 6 | <0.01 |
| Iranian (187) | 248 | 0.02 |
| Irish (18,712) | 38,479 | 2.82 |
| Israeli (427) | 618 | 0.05 |
| Italian (38,592) | 57,527 | 4.21 |
| Latvian (92) | 103 | 0.01 |
| Lithuanian (167) | 547 | 0.04 |
| Luxemburger (0) | 0 | <0.01 |
| Macedonian (628) | 628 | 0.05 |
| Maltese (16) | 45 | <0.01 |
| New Zealander (23) | 23 | <0.01 |
| Northern European (25) | 25 | <0.01 |

| | Population | % |
|---|---|---|
| Norwegian (260) | 773 | 0.06 |
| Pennsylvania German (0) | 0 | <0.01 |
| Polish (3,429) | 7,834 | 0.57 |
| Portuguese (474) | 1,113 | 0.08 |
| Romanian (691) | 1,164 | 0.09 |
| Russian (4,351) | 8,064 | 0.59 |
| Scandinavian (102) | 155 | 0.01 |
| Scotch-Irish (516) | 1,601 | 0.12 |
| Scottish (388) | 1,570 | 0.11 |
| Serbian (154) | 187 | 0.01 |
| Slavic (15) | 90 | 0.01 |
| Slovak (87) | 226 | 0.02 |
| Slovene (10) | 45 | <0.01 |
| Soviet Union (12) | 12 | <0.01 |
| Swedish (119) | 549 | 0.04 |
| Swiss (24) | 166 | 0.01 |
| Turkish (589) | 686 | 0.05 |
| Ukrainian (970) | 1,608 | 0.12 |
| Welsh (101) | 530 | 0.04 |
| West Indian, ex. Hispanic (93,323) | 107,527 | 7.87 |
| Bahamian (165) | 208 | 0.02 |
| Barbadian (1,285) | 1,612 | 0.12 |
| Belizean (1,253) | 1,493 | 0.11 |
| Bermudan (101) | 198 | 0.01 |
| British West Indian (5,959) | 7,136 | 0.52 |
| Dutch West Indian (127) | 172 | 0.01 |
| Haitian (3,891) | 4,652 | 0.34 |
| Jamaican (58,387) | 64,222 | 4.70 |
| Trinidadian/Tobagonian (3,695) | 4,811 | 0.35 |
| U.S. Virgin Islander (737) | 952 | 0.07 |
| West Indian (17,683) | 21,941 | 1.61 |
| Other West Indian (40) | 130 | 0.01 |
| Yugoslavian (1,275) | 1,480 | 0.11 |

| Hispanic Origin | Population | % |
|---|---|---|
| Hispanic or Latino (of any race) | 741,413 | 53.53 |
| Central American, ex. Mexican | 34,492 | 2.49 |
| Costa Rican | 1,095 | 0.08 |
| Guatemalan | 4,645 | 0.34 |
| Honduran | 17,990 | 1.30 |
| Nicaraguan | 2,342 | 0.17 |
| Panamanian | 2,372 | 0.17 |
| Salvadoran | 5,469 | 0.39 |
| Other Central American | 579 | 0.04 |
| Cuban | 8,785 | 0.63 |
| Dominican Republic | 240,987 | 17.40 |
| Mexican | 71,194 | 5.14 |
| Puerto Rican | 298,921 | 21.58 |
| South American | 35,463 | 2.56 |
| Argentinean | 1,117 | 0.08 |
| Bolivian | 227 | 0.02 |
| Chilean | 646 | 0.05 |
| Colombian | 4,635 | 0.33 |
| Ecuadorian | 23,206 | 1.68 |
| Paraguayan | 223 | 0.02 |
| Peruvian | 3,596 | 0.26 |
| Uruguayan | 148 | 0.01 |
| Venezuelan | 1,296 | 0.09 |
| Other South American | 369 | 0.03 |
| Other Hispanic or Latino | 51,571 | 3.72 |

| Race* | Population | % |
|---|---|---|
| African-American/Black (505,200) | 541,622 | 39.10 |
| Not Hispanic (416,695) | 427,134 | 30.84 |
| Hispanic (88,505) | 114,488 | 8.27 |
| American Indian/Alaska Native (18,260) | 32,011 | 2.31 |
| Not Hispanic (3,460) | 7,638 | 0.55 |
| Hispanic (14,800) | 24,373 | 1.76 |
| Alaska Athabascan (Ala. Nat.) (4) | 8 | <0.01 |
| Aleut (Alaska Native) (0) | 3 | <0.01 |
| Apache (30) | 99 | 0.01 |
| Arapaho (2) | 3 | <0.01 |
| Blackfeet (43) | 310 | 0.02 |
| Canadian/French Am. Ind. (13) | 25 | <0.01 |
| Central American Ind. (2,274) | 4,520 | 0.33 |
| Cherokee (247) | 1,312 | 0.09 |
| Cheyenne (2) | 5 | <0.01 |
| Chickasaw (6) | 16 | <0.01 |
| Chippewa (25) | 38 | <0.01 |

| | Population | % |
|---|---|---|
| Choctaw (4) | 43 | <0.01 |
| Colville (0) | 2 | <0.01 |
| Comanche (8) | 26 | <0.01 |
| Cree (1) | 16 | <0.01 |
| Creek (7) | 47 | <0.01 |
| Crow (1) | 16 | <0.01 |
| Delaware (1) | 10 | <0.01 |
| Hopi (0) | 2 | <0.01 |
| Houma (12) | 12 | <0.01 |
| Inupiat (Alaska Native) (11) | 15 | <0.01 |
| Iroquois (81) | 170 | 0.01 |
| Kiowa (1) | 1 | <0.01 |
| Lumbee (3) | 6 | <0.01 |
| Menominee (1) | 3 | <0.01 |
| Mexican American Ind. (714) | 963 | 0.07 |
| Navajo (24) | 42 | <0.01 |
| Osage (2) | 3 | <0.01 |
| Ottawa (0) | 1 | <0.01 |
| Paiute (0) | 5 | <0.01 |
| Pima (0) | 1 | <0.01 |
| Potawatomi (1) | 2 | <0.01 |
| Pueblo (177) | 382 | 0.03 |
| Puget Sound Salish (0) | 0 | <0.01 |
| Seminole (6) | 50 | <0.01 |
| Shoshone (0) | 8 | <0.01 |
| Sioux (46) | 82 | 0.01 |
| South American Ind. (1,568) | 2,938 | 0.21 |
| Spanish American Ind. (709) | 992 | 0.07 |
| Tlingit-Haida (Alaska Native) (1) | 11 | <0.01 |
| Tohono O'Odham (4) | 9 | <0.01 |
| Tsimshian (Alaska Native) (0) | 0 | <0.01 |
| Ute (2) | 5 | <0.01 |
| Yakama (3) | 3 | <0.01 |
| Yaqui (4) | 5 | <0.01 |
| Yuman (1) | 2 | <0.01 |
| Yup'ik (Alaska Native) (1) | 6 | <0.01 |
| Asian (49,609) | 59,085 | 4.27 |
| Not Hispanic (47,335) | 53,458 | 3.86 |
| Hispanic (2,274) | 5,627 | 0.41 |
| Bangladeshi (7,323) | 8,623 | 0.62 |
| Bhutanese (74) | 104 | 0.01 |
| Burmese (71) | 81 | 0.01 |
| Cambodian (1,055) | 1,188 | 0.09 |
| Chinese, ex. Taiwanese (6,644) | 8,112 | 0.59 |
| Filipino (5,576) | 6,456 | 0.47 |
| Hmong (1) | 3 | <0.01 |
| Indian (15,865) | 20,357 | 1.47 |
| Indonesian (50) | 96 | 0.01 |
| Japanese (562) | 1,027 | 0.07 |
| Korean (2,840) | 3,101 | 0.22 |
| Laotian (99) | 148 | 0.01 |
| Malaysian (11) | 30 | <0.01 |
| Nepalese (129) | 159 | 0.01 |
| Pakistani (2,399) | 2,728 | 0.20 |
| Sri Lankan (174) | 234 | 0.02 |
| Taiwanese (98) | 130 | 0.01 |
| Thai (326) | 414 | 0.03 |
| Vietnamese (3,215) | 3,526 | 0.25 |
| Hawaii Native/Pacific Islander (1,288) | 6,213 | 0.45 |
| Not Hispanic (398) | 1,854 | 0.13 |
| Hispanic (890) | 4,359 | 0.31 |
| Fijian (13) | 13 | <0.01 |
| Guamanian/Chamorro (251) | 376 | 0.03 |
| Marshallese (3) | 3 | <0.01 |
| Native Hawaiian (371) | 669 | 0.05 |
| Samoan (70) | 160 | 0.01 |
| Tongan (5) | 7 | <0.01 |
| White (386,497) | 427,659 | 30.88 |
| Not Hispanic (151,209) | 158,245 | 11.42 |
| Hispanic (235,288) | 269,414 | 19.45 |

Notes: † The Census 2010 population figure is used to calculate the percentages in the Hispanic Origin and Race categories. Ancestry percentages are based on the 2006-2010 American Community Survey population (not shown); ‡ Numbers in parentheses indicate the number of people reporting a single ancestry; * Numbers in parentheses indicate the number of persons reporting this race alone, not in combination with any other race; Please refer to the Explanation of Data for more information.

## Brookhaven

Place Type: Town
County: Suffolk
Population: 486,040

| Ancestry | Population | % |
|---|---|---|
| Afghan (0) | 0 | <0.01 |
| African, Sub-Saharan (2,475) | 2,832 | 0.59 |
| African (2,224) | 2,533 | 0.53 |
| Cape Verdean (0) | 0 | <0.01 |
| Ethiopian (0) | 0 | <0.01 |
| Ghanaian (57) | 57 | 0.01 |
| Kenyan (0) | 0 | <0.01 |
| Liberian (9) | 9 | <0.01 |
| Nigerian (163) | 179 | 0.04 |
| Senegalese (0) | 0 | <0.01 |
| Sierra Leonean (0) | 0 | <0.01 |
| Somalian (0) | 0 | <0.01 |
| South African (6) | 24 | <0.01 |
| Sudanese (0) | 14 | <0.01 |
| Ugandan (0) | 0 | <0.01 |
| Zimbabwean (0) | 0 | <0.01 |
| Other Sub-Saharan African (16) | 16 | <0.01 |
| Albanian (59) | 133 | 0.03 |
| Alsatian (0) | 12 | <0.01 |
| American (10,016) | 10,016 | 2.09 |
| Arab (797) | 1,321 | 0.28 |
| Arab (164) | 191 | 0.04 |
| Egyptian (317) | 435 | 0.09 |
| Iraqi (0) | 0 | <0.01 |
| Jordanian (100) | 178 | 0.04 |
| Lebanese (29) | 98 | 0.02 |
| Moroccan (15) | 15 | <0.01 |
| Palestinian (0) | 13 | <0.01 |
| Syrian (12) | 220 | 0.05 |
| Other Arab (160) | 171 | 0.04 |
| Armenian (254) | 643 | 0.13 |
| Assyrian/Chaldean/Syriac (0) | 0 | <0.01 |
| Australian (31) | 79 | 0.02 |
| Austrian (603) | 2,867 | 0.60 |
| Basque (9) | 23 | <0.01 |
| Belgian (61) | 401 | 0.08 |
| Brazilian (314) | 436 | 0.09 |
| British (605) | 1,235 | 0.26 |
| Bulgarian (101) | 128 | 0.03 |
| Cajun (0) | 0 | <0.01 |
| Canadian (432) | 999 | 0.21 |
| Carpatho Rusyn (0) | 0 | <0.01 |
| Celtic (0) | 31 | 0.01 |
| Croatian (317) | 588 | 0.12 |
| Cypriot (51) | 51 | 0.01 |
| Czech (697) | 3,121 | 0.65 |
| Czechoslovakian (344) | 917 | 0.19 |
| Danish (180) | 1,229 | 0.26 |
| Dutch (554) | 4,038 | 0.84 |
| Eastern European (604) | 728 | 0.15 |
| English (4,862) | 30,089 | 6.27 |
| Estonian (14) | 102 | 0.02 |
| European (1,893) | 2,098 | 0.44 |
| Finnish (144) | 706 | 0.15 |
| French, ex. Basque (933) | 8,961 | 1.87 |
| French Canadian (665) | 2,478 | 0.52 |
| German (16,000) | 89,711 | 18.69 |
| German Russian (0) | 40 | 0.01 |
| Greek (2,196) | 5,703 | 1.19 |
| Guyanese (373) | 441 | 0.09 |
| Hungarian (814) | 4,390 | 0.91 |
| Icelander (18) | 45 | 0.01 |
| Iranian (353) | 398 | 0.08 |
| Irish (29,544) | 122,200 | 25.45 |
| Israeli (355) | 545 | 0.11 |
| Italian (72,814) | 155,749 | 32.44 |
| Latvian (120) | 182 | 0.04 |
| Lithuanian (674) | 1,898 | 0.40 |
| Luxemburger (0) | 36 | 0.01 |
| Macedonian (0) | 0 | <0.01 |
| Maltese (235) | 686 | 0.14 |
| New Zealander (10) | 23 | <0.01 |
| Northern European (233) | 249 | 0.05 |

| Ancestry | Population | % |
|---|---|---|
| Norwegian (1,381) | 5,078 | 1.06 |
| Pennsylvania German (45) | 66 | 0.01 |
| Polish (7,478) | 27,233 | 5.67 |
| Portuguese (2,684) | 3,802 | 0.79 |
| Romanian (472) | 1,216 | 0.25 |
| Russian (4,331) | 12,073 | 2.51 |
| Scandinavian (127) | 388 | 0.08 |
| Scotch-Irish (1,789) | 5,102 | 1.06 |
| Scottish (1,051) | 5,703 | 1.19 |
| Serbian (0) | 0 | <0.01 |
| Slavic (22) | 91 | 0.02 |
| Slovak (304) | 690 | 0.14 |
| Slovene (5) | 76 | 0.02 |
| Soviet Union (0) | 0 | <0.01 |
| Swedish (519) | 4,045 | 0.84 |
| Swiss (319) | 1,356 | 0.28 |
| Turkish (1,572) | 1,935 | 0.40 |
| Ukrainian (779) | 2,350 | 0.49 |
| Welsh (195) | 1,189 | 0.25 |
| West Indian, ex. Hispanic (4,567) | 6,377 | 1.33 |
| Bahamian (0) | 47 | 0.01 |
| Barbadian (44) | 44 | 0.01 |
| Belizean (0) | 0 | <0.01 |
| Bermudan (0) | 34 | 0.01 |
| British West Indian (59) | 59 | 0.01 |
| Dutch West Indian (20) | 20 | <0.01 |
| Haitian (1,544) | 2,077 | 0.43 |
| Jamaican (998) | 1,546 | 0.32 |
| Trinidadian/Tobagonian (922) | 1,200 | 0.25 |
| U.S. Virgin Islander (0) | 0 | <0.01 |
| West Indian (980) | 1,323 | 0.28 |
| Other West Indian (0) | 27 | 0.01 |
| Yugoslavian (145) | 518 | 0.11 |

| Hispanic Origin | Population | % |
|---|---|---|
| Hispanic or Latino (of any race) | 60,270 | 12.40 |
| Central American, ex. Mexican | 9,259 | 1.90 |
| Costa Rican | 198 | 0.04 |
| Guatemalan | 1,411 | 0.29 |
| Honduran | 1,195 | 0.25 |
| Nicaraguan | 159 | 0.03 |
| Panamanian | 291 | 0.06 |
| Salvadoran | 5,899 | 1.21 |
| Other Central American | 106 | 0.02 |
| Cuban | 1,500 | 0.31 |
| Dominican Republic | 4,781 | 0.98 |
| Mexican | 4,926 | 1.01 |
| Puerto Rican | 21,429 | 4.41 |
| South American | 12,182 | 2.51 |
| Argentinean | 653 | 0.13 |
| Bolivian | 148 | 0.03 |
| Chilean | 363 | 0.07 |
| Colombian | 2,970 | 0.61 |
| Ecuadorian | 6,437 | 1.32 |
| Paraguayan | 50 | 0.01 |
| Peruvian | 1,074 | 0.22 |
| Uruguayan | 87 | 0.02 |
| Venezuelan | 302 | 0.06 |
| Other South American | 98 | 0.02 |
| Other Hispanic or Latino | 6,193 | 1.27 |

| Race* | Population | % |
|---|---|---|
| African-American/Black (26,639) | 31,615 | 6.50 |
| Not Hispanic (24,428) | 28,098 | 5.78 |
| Hispanic (2,211) | 3,517 | 0.72 |
| American Indian/Alaska Native (1,368) | 3,782 | 0.78 |
| Not Hispanic (847) | 2,586 | 0.53 |
| Hispanic (521) | 1,196 | 0.25 |
| Alaska Athabascan (Ala. Nat.) (1) | 4 | <0.01 |
| Aleut (Alaska Native) (2) | 3 | <0.01 |
| Apache (4) | 18 | <0.01 |
| Arapaho (0) | 1 | <0.01 |
| Blackfeet (12) | 164 | 0.03 |
| Canadian/French Am. Ind. (4) | 15 | <0.01 |
| Central American Ind. (27) | 53 | 0.01 |
| Cherokee (82) | 546 | 0.11 |
| Cheyenne (1) | 6 | <0.01 |
| Chickasaw (0) | 3 | <0.01 |
| Chippewa (8) | 19 | <0.01 |

| Race* | Population | % |
|---|---|---|
| Choctaw (7) | 34 | 0.01 |
| Colville (0) | 0 | <0.01 |
| Comanche (0) | 4 | <0.01 |
| Cree (1) | 4 | <0.01 |
| Creek (1) | 12 | <0.01 |
| Crow (0) | 1 | <0.01 |
| Delaware (3) | 12 | <0.01 |
| Hopi (0) | 1 | <0.01 |
| Houma (0) | 0 | <0.01 |
| Inupiat (Alaska Native) (1) | 2 | <0.01 |
| Iroquois (39) | 116 | 0.02 |
| Kiowa (0) | 0 | <0.01 |
| Lumbee (2) | 7 | <0.01 |
| Menominee (0) | 0 | <0.01 |
| Mexican American Ind. (37) | 64 | 0.01 |
| Navajo (3) | 15 | <0.01 |
| Osage (2) | 2 | <0.01 |
| Ottawa (0) | 3 | <0.01 |
| Paiute (2) | 4 | <0.01 |
| Pima (0) | 0 | <0.01 |
| Potawatomi (6) | 6 | <0.01 |
| Pueblo (2) | 2 | <0.01 |
| Puget Sound Salish (5) | 6 | <0.01 |
| Seminole (7) | 33 | 0.01 |
| Shoshone (0) | 4 | <0.01 |
| Sioux (16) | 42 | 0.01 |
| South American Ind. (47) | 136 | 0.03 |
| Spanish American Ind. (26) | 34 | 0.01 |
| Tlingit-Haida (Alaska Native) (0) | 5 | <0.01 |
| Tohono O'Odham (0) | 0 | <0.01 |
| Tsimshian (Alaska Native) (0) | 0 | <0.01 |
| Ute (0) | 1 | <0.01 |
| Yakama (0) | 1 | <0.01 |
| Yaqui (1) | 5 | <0.01 |
| Yuman (1) | 1 | <0.01 |
| Yup'ik (Alaska Native) (0) | 0 | <0.01 |
| Asian (19,082) | 21,849 | 4.50 |
| Not Hispanic (18,880) | 21,257 | 4.37 |
| Hispanic (202) | 592 | 0.12 |
| Bangladeshi (528) | 621 | 0.13 |
| Bhutanese (0) | 0 | <0.01 |
| Burmese (36) | 40 | 0.01 |
| Cambodian (14) | 29 | 0.01 |
| Chinese, ex. Taiwanese (5,433) | 6,107 | 1.26 |
| Filipino (2,117) | 2,705 | 0.56 |
| Hmong (1) | 4 | <0.01 |
| Indian (5,078) | 5,745 | 1.18 |
| Indonesian (38) | 63 | 0.01 |
| Japanese (339) | 605 | 0.12 |
| Korean (1,728) | 2,025 | 0.42 |
| Laotian (42) | 54 | 0.01 |
| Malaysian (9) | 18 | <0.01 |
| Nepalese (43) | 44 | 0.01 |
| Pakistani (1,867) | 2,081 | 0.43 |
| Sri Lankan (85) | 100 | 0.02 |
| Taiwanese (181) | 213 | 0.04 |
| Thai (150) | 211 | 0.04 |
| Vietnamese (544) | 620 | 0.13 |
| Hawaii Native/Pacific Islander (152) | 447 | 0.09 |
| Not Hispanic (98) | 306 | 0.06 |
| Hispanic (54) | 141 | 0.03 |
| Fijian (3) | 10 | <0.01 |
| Guamanian/Chamorro (40) | 51 | 0.01 |
| Marshallese (0) | 0 | <0.01 |
| Native Hawaiian (31) | 100 | 0.02 |
| Samoan (6) | 15 | <0.01 |
| Tongan (2) | 2 | <0.01 |
| White (410,649) | 419,725 | 86.36 |
| Not Hispanic (373,782) | 379,158 | 78.01 |
| Hispanic (36,867) | 40,567 | 8.35 |

## Brooklyn

Place Type: Borough
County: Kings
Population: 2,504,700

| Ancestry | Population | % |
|---|---|---|
| Afghan (335) | 344 | 0.01 |
| African, Sub-Saharan (30,768) | 63,004 | 2.55 |
| African (17,256) | 48,168 | 1.95 |
| Cape Verdean (106) | 153 | 0.01 |
| Ethiopian (283) | 330 | 0.01 |
| Ghanaian (3,692) | 3,898 | 0.16 |
| Kenyan (65) | 77 | <0.01 |
| Liberian (392) | 452 | 0.02 |
| Nigerian (5,499) | 6,033 | 0.24 |
| Senegalese (401) | 401 | 0.02 |
| Sierra Leonean (147) | 147 | 0.01 |
| Somalian (234) | 260 | 0.01 |
| South African (204) | 320 | 0.01 |
| Sudanese (693) | 731 | 0.03 |
| Ugandan (29) | 54 | <0.01 |
| Zimbabwean (99) | 99 | <0.01 |
| Other Sub-Saharan African (1,668) | 1,881 | 0.08 |
| Albanian (6,490) | 6,871 | 0.28 |
| Alsatian (0) | 27 | <0.01 |
| American (78,858) | 78,858 | 3.20 |
| Arab (29,346) | 34,840 | 1.41 |
| Arab (6,779) | 7,609 | 0.31 |
| Egyptian (4,705) | 5,231 | 0.21 |
| Iraqi (71) | 134 | 0.01 |
| Jordanian (714) | 752 | 0.03 |
| Lebanese (3,425) | 4,757 | 0.19 |
| Moroccan (2,156) | 2,648 | 0.11 |
| Palestinian (1,372) | 1,482 | 0.06 |
| Syrian (4,854) | 5,890 | 0.24 |
| Other Arab (5,270) | 6,337 | 0.26 |
| Armenian (1,798) | 2,300 | 0.09 |
| Assyrian/Chaldean/Syriac (22) | 44 | <0.01 |
| Australian (539) | 832 | 0.03 |
| Austrian (1,677) | 5,123 | 0.21 |
| Basque (69) | 129 | 0.01 |
| Belgian (498) | 1,012 | 0.04 |
| Brazilian (1,257) | 1,719 | 0.07 |
| British (2,002) | 4,749 | 0.19 |
| Bulgarian (970) | 1,128 | 0.05 |
| Cajun (99) | 175 | 0.01 |
| Canadian (1,814) | 3,116 | 0.13 |
| Carpatho Rusyn (46) | 53 | <0.01 |
| Celtic (16) | 32 | <0.01 |
| Croatian (488) | 998 | 0.04 |
| Cypriot (37) | 62 | <0.01 |
| Czech (759) | 3,393 | 0.14 |
| Czechoslovakian (793) | 1,684 | 0.07 |
| Danish (380) | 1,267 | 0.05 |
| Dutch (1,616) | 5,664 | 0.23 |
| Eastern European (11,912) | 12,941 | 0.52 |
| English (9,927) | 32,407 | 1.31 |
| Estonian (209) | 340 | 0.01 |
| European (25,194) | 27,499 | 1.11 |
| Finnish (303) | 692 | 0.03 |
| French, ex. Basque (3,484) | 14,137 | 0.57 |
| French Canadian (1,082) | 2,974 | 0.12 |
| German (12,299) | 52,798 | 2.14 |
| German Russian (29) | 55 | <0.01 |
| Greek (10,688) | 14,075 | 0.57 |
| Guyanese (36,322) | 38,963 | 1.58 |
| Hungarian (17,858) | 26,607 | 1.08 |
| Icelander (69) | 103 | <0.01 |
| Iranian (1,520) | 1,822 | 0.07 |
| Irish (32,255) | 84,945 | 3.44 |
| Israeli (7,062) | 9,707 | 0.39 |
| Italian (108,743) | 152,814 | 6.19 |
| Latvian (418) | 667 | 0.03 |
| Lithuanian (938) | 2,676 | 0.11 |
| Luxemburger (41) | 58 | <0.01 |
| Macedonian (389) | 498 | 0.02 |
| Maltese (197) | 362 | 0.01 |
| New Zealander (71) | 140 | 0.01 |
| Northern European (905) | 961 | 0.04 |

| Ancestry | Population | % |
|---|---|---|
| Norwegian (2,042) | 5,982 | 0.24 |
| Pennsylvania German (19) | 59 | <0.01 |
| Polish (41,882) | 66,792 | 2.71 |
| Portuguese (1,106) | 2,882 | 0.12 |
| Romanian (4,537) | 8,046 | 0.33 |
| Russian (69,188) | 88,579 | 3.59 |
| Scandinavian (512) | 882 | 0.04 |
| Scotch-Irish (1,997) | 6,090 | 0.25 |
| Scottish (2,407) | 8,809 | 0.36 |
| Serbian (288) | 520 | 0.02 |
| Slavic (289) | 564 | 0.02 |
| Slovak (1,164) | 1,826 | 0.07 |
| Slovene (55) | 160 | 0.01 |
| Soviet Union (185) | 219 | 0.01 |
| Swedish (1,240) | 5,185 | 0.21 |
| Swiss (473) | 1,491 | 0.06 |
| Turkish (4,449) | 5,164 | 0.21 |
| Ukrainian (21,703) | 25,046 | 1.02 |
| Welsh (345) | 2,606 | 0.11 |
| West Indian, ex. Hispanic (257,579) | 306,541 | 12.43 |
| Bahamian (195) | 266 | 0.01 |
| Barbadian (13,358) | 14,916 | 0.60 |
| Belizean (1,610) | 2,026 | 0.08 |
| Bermudan (16) | 16 | <0.01 |
| British West Indian (28,123) | 30,607 | 1.24 |
| Dutch West Indian (289) | 424 | 0.02 |
| Haitian (67,083) | 69,941 | 2.84 |
| Jamaican (74,216) | 80,999 | 3.28 |
| Trinidadian/Tobagonian (42,450) | 46,490 | 1.88 |
| U.S. Virgin Islander (470) | 558 | 0.02 |
| West Indian (29,404) | 59,844 | 2.43 |
| Other West Indian (365) | 454 | 0.02 |
| Yugoslavian (2,305) | 2,800 | 0.11 |

| Hispanic Origin | Population | % |
|---|---|---|
| Hispanic or Latino (of any race) | 496,285 | 19.81 |
| Central American, ex. Mexican | 46,119 | 1.84 |
| Costa Rican | 2,576 | 0.10 |
| Guatemalan | 9,160 | 0.37 |
| Honduran | 10,071 | 0.40 |
| Nicaraguan | 2,407 | 0.10 |
| Panamanian | 13,681 | 0.55 |
| Salvadoran | 7,737 | 0.31 |
| Other Central American | 487 | 0.02 |
| Cuban | 7,581 | 0.30 |
| Dominican Republic | 86,764 | 3.46 |
| Mexican | 94,585 | 3.78 |
| Puerto Rican | 176,528 | 7.05 |
| South American | 49,003 | 1.96 |
| Argentinean | 2,760 | 0.11 |
| Bolivian | 310 | 0.01 |
| Chilean | 1,026 | 0.04 |
| Colombian | 8,861 | 0.35 |
| Ecuadorian | 28,684 | 1.15 |
| Paraguayan | 230 | 0.01 |
| Peruvian | 4,222 | 0.17 |
| Uruguayan | 488 | 0.02 |
| Venezuelan | 1,916 | 0.08 |
| Other South American | 506 | 0.02 |
| Other Hispanic or Latino | 35,705 | 1.43 |

| Race* | Population | % |
|---|---|---|
| African-American/Black (860,083) | 896,165 | 35.78 |
| Not Hispanic (799,066) | 820,437 | 32.76 |
| Hispanic (61,017) | 75,728 | 3.02 |
| American Indian/Alaska Native (13,524) | 26,571 | 1.06 |
| Not Hispanic (4,638) | 12,062 | 0.48 |
| Hispanic (8,886) | 14,509 | 0.58 |
| Alaska Athabascan (Ala. Nat.) (1) | 5 | <0.01 |
| Aleut (Alaska Native) (4) | 8 | <0.01 |
| Apache (46) | 122 | <0.01 |
| Arapaho (2) | 10 | <0.01 |
| Blackfeet (89) | 531 | 0.02 |
| Canadian/French Am. Ind. (42) | 62 | <0.01 |
| Central American Ind. (616) | 1,263 | 0.05 |
| Cherokee (289) | 1,903 | 0.08 |
| Cheyenne (0) | 10 | <0.01 |
| Chickasaw (9) | 30 | <0.01 |
| Chippewa (23) | 65 | <0.01 |

| Race* | Population | % |
|---|---|---|
| Choctaw (30) | 104 | <0.01 |
| Colville (1) | 1 | <0.01 |
| Comanche (5) | 19 | <0.01 |
| Cree (3) | 15 | <0.01 |
| Creek (20) | 81 | <0.01 |
| Crow (5) | 19 | <0.01 |
| Delaware (5) | 35 | <0.01 |
| Hopi (7) | 12 | <0.01 |
| Houma (1) | 3 | <0.01 |
| Inupiat (Alaska Native) (7) | 21 | <0.01 |
| Iroquois (194) | 381 | 0.02 |
| Kiowa (1) | 2 | <0.01 |
| Lumbee (6) | 24 | <0.01 |
| Menominee (1) | 4 | <0.01 |
| Mexican American Ind. (1,022) | 1,363 | 0.05 |
| Navajo (41) | 93 | <0.01 |
| Osage (1) | 3 | <0.01 |
| Ottawa (2) | 5 | <0.01 |
| Paiute (0) | 1 | <0.01 |
| Pima (0) | 2 | <0.01 |
| Potawatomi (3) | 11 | <0.01 |
| Pueblo (93) | 169 | 0.01 |
| Puget Sound Salish (1) | 1 | <0.01 |
| Seminole (18) | 92 | <0.01 |
| Shoshone (6) | 23 | <0.01 |
| Sioux (29) | 121 | <0.01 |
| South American Ind. (874) | 1,855 | 0.07 |
| Spanish American Ind. (290) | 382 | 0.02 |
| Tlingit-Haida (Alaska Native) (4) | 28 | <0.01 |
| Tohono O'Odham (9) | 10 | <0.01 |
| Tsimshian (Alaska Native) (0) | 0 | <0.01 |
| Ute (0) | 4 | <0.01 |
| Yakama (1) | 3 | <0.01 |
| Yaqui (11) | 19 | <0.01 |
| Yuman (5) | 8 | <0.01 |
| Yup'ik (Alaska Native) (0) | 1 | <0.01 |
| Asian (262,276) | 284,489 | 11.36 |
| Not Hispanic (260,129) | 279,499 | 11.16 |
| Hispanic (2,147) | 4,990 | 0.20 |
| Bangladeshi (10,667) | 12,408 | 0.50 |
| Bhutanese (5) | 8 | <0.01 |
| Burmese (1,055) | 1,260 | 0.05 |
| Cambodian (613) | 751 | 0.03 |
| Chinese, ex. Taiwanese (171,214) | 178,214 | 7.12 |
| Filipino (7,930) | 10,208 | 0.41 |
| Hmong (14) | 22 | <0.01 |
| Indian (26,144) | 33,490 | 1.34 |
| Indonesian (383) | 564 | 0.02 |
| Japanese (3,938) | 5,917 | 0.24 |
| Korean (6,904) | 8,201 | 0.33 |
| Laotian (82) | 131 | 0.01 |
| Malaysian (478) | 708 | 0.03 |
| Nepalese (355) | 393 | 0.02 |
| Pakistani (18,296) | 19,840 | 0.79 |
| Sri Lankan (219) | 270 | 0.01 |
| Taiwanese (857) | 1,075 | 0.04 |
| Thai (636) | 883 | 0.04 |
| Vietnamese (3,944) | 5,041 | 0.20 |
| Hawaii Native/Pacific Islander (1,243) | 5,784 | 0.23 |
| Not Hispanic (633) | 3,463 | 0.14 |
| Hispanic (610) | 2,321 | 0.09 |
| Fijian (20) | 45 | <0.01 |
| Guamanian/Chamorro (386) | 568 | 0.02 |
| Marshallese (1) | 2 | <0.01 |
| Native Hawaiian (208) | 564 | 0.02 |
| Samoan (72) | 216 | 0.01 |
| Tongan (5) | 10 | <0.01 |
| White (1,072,041) | 1,120,592 | 44.74 |
| Not Hispanic (893,306) | 917,717 | 36.64 |
| Hispanic (178,735) | 202,875 | 8.10 |

## Buffalo

Place Type: City
County: Erie
Population: 261,310

| Ancestry | Population | % |
|---|---|---|
| Afghan (178) | 178 | 0.07 |
| African, Sub-Saharan (5,618) | 6,085 | 2.29 |
| African (3,925) | 4,177 | 1.57 |
| Cape Verdean (95) | 95 | 0.04 |
| Ethiopian (223) | 223 | 0.08 |
| Ghanaian (43) | 43 | 0.02 |
| Kenyan (38) | 38 | 0.01 |
| Liberian (74) | 74 | 0.03 |
| Nigerian (94) | 105 | 0.04 |
| Senegalese (0) | 0 | <0.01 |
| Sierra Leonean (17) | 17 | 0.01 |
| Somalian (706) | 858 | 0.32 |
| South African (0) | 0 | <0.01 |
| Sudanese (259) | 268 | 0.10 |
| Ugandan (24) | 33 | 0.01 |
| Zimbabwean (45) | 45 | 0.02 |
| Other Sub-Saharan African (75) | 109 | 0.04 |
| Albanian (360) | 369 | 0.14 |
| Alsatian (12) | 12 | <0.01 |
| American (6,386) | 6,386 | 2.40 |
| Arab (1,374) | 1,815 | 0.68 |
| Arab (586) | 644 | 0.24 |
| Egyptian (27) | 39 | 0.01 |
| Iraqi (286) | 288 | 0.11 |
| Jordanian (2) | 4 | <0.01 |
| Lebanese (165) | 481 | 0.18 |
| Moroccan (21) | 57 | 0.02 |
| Palestinian (0) | 0 | <0.01 |
| Syrian (17) | 32 | 0.01 |
| Other Arab (270) | 270 | 0.10 |
| Armenian (39) | 67 | 0.03 |
| Assyrian/Chaldean/Syriac (0) | 0 | <0.01 |
| Australian (0) | 14 | 0.01 |
| Austrian (244) | 799 | 0.30 |
| Basque (9) | 9 | <0.01 |
| Belgian (21) | 21 | 0.01 |
| Brazilian (25) | 25 | 0.01 |
| British (306) | 722 | 0.27 |
| Bulgarian (114) | 201 | 0.08 |
| Cajun (0) | 11 | <0.01 |
| Canadian (264) | 558 | 0.21 |
| Carpatho Rusyn (0) | 0 | <0.01 |
| Celtic (0) | 13 | <0.01 |
| Croatian (249) | 487 | 0.18 |
| Cypriot (0) | 0 | <0.01 |
| Czech (13) | 310 | 0.12 |
| Czechoslovakian (76) | 231 | 0.09 |
| Danish (41) | 152 | 0.06 |
| Dutch (224) | 1,451 | 0.55 |
| Eastern European (189) | 198 | 0.07 |
| English (2,703) | 11,203 | 4.21 |
| Estonian (0) | 11 | <0.01 |
| European (884) | 1,016 | 0.38 |
| Finnish (56) | 248 | 0.09 |
| French, ex. Basque (446) | 4,110 | 1.55 |
| French Canadian (420) | 1,376 | 0.52 |
| German (7,601) | 35,760 | 13.44 |
| German Russian (16) | 41 | 0.02 |
| Greek (305) | 769 | 0.29 |
| Guyanese (517) | 529 | 0.20 |
| Hungarian (748) | 2,201 | 0.83 |
| Icelander (0) | 0 | <0.01 |
| Iranian (82) | 125 | 0.05 |
| Irish (9,009) | 34,103 | 12.82 |
| Israeli (104) | 180 | 0.07 |
| Italian (13,524) | 30,606 | 11.51 |
| Latvian (13) | 22 | 0.01 |
| Lithuanian (121) | 358 | 0.13 |
| Luxemburger (0) | 24 | 0.01 |
| Macedonian (40) | 52 | 0.02 |
| Maltese (0) | 8 | <0.01 |
| New Zealander (0) | 0 | <0.01 |
| Northern European (31) | 31 | 0.01 |

| Ancestry | Population | % |
|---|---|---|
| Norwegian (78) | 586 | 0.22 |
| Pennsylvania German (0) | 159 | 0.06 |
| Polish (12,089) | 28,108 | 10.57 |
| Portuguese (169) | 474 | 0.18 |
| Romanian (30) | 122 | 0.05 |
| Russian (616) | 1,883 | 0.71 |
| Scandinavian (0) | 76 | 0.03 |
| Scotch-Irish (902) | 2,324 | 0.87 |
| Scottish (437) | 2,816 | 1.06 |
| Serbian (115) | 291 | 0.11 |
| Slavic (15) | 35 | 0.01 |
| Slovak (27) | 174 | 0.07 |
| Slovene (23) | 100 | 0.04 |
| Soviet Union (0) | 0 | <0.01 |
| Swedish (309) | 1,596 | 0.60 |
| Swiss (41) | 308 | 0.12 |
| Turkish (251) | 350 | 0.13 |
| Ukrainian (899) | 1,739 | 0.65 |
| Welsh (90) | 729 | 0.27 |
| West Indian, ex. Hispanic (2,330) | 2,773 | 1.04 |
| Bahamian (13) | 13 | <0.01 |
| Barbadian (18) | 44 | 0.02 |
| Belizean (0) | 0 | <0.01 |
| Bermudan (0) | 0 | <0.01 |
| British West Indian (102) | 115 | 0.04 |
| Dutch West Indian (0) | 17 | 0.01 |
| Haitian (480) | 626 | 0.24 |
| Jamaican (1,260) | 1,420 | 0.53 |
| Trinidadian/Tobagonian (196) | 200 | 0.08 |
| U.S. Virgin Islander (0) | 0 | <0.01 |
| West Indian (261) | 338 | 0.13 |
| Other West Indian (0) | 0 | <0.01 |
| Yugoslavian (187) | 282 | 0.11 |

| Hispanic Origin | Population | % |
|---|---|---|
| Hispanic or Latino (of any race) | 27,519 | 10.53 |
| Central American, ex. Mexican | 386 | 0.15 |
| Costa Rican | 27 | 0.01 |
| Guatemalan | 72 | 0.03 |
| Honduran | 76 | 0.03 |
| Nicaraguan | 25 | 0.01 |
| Panamanian | 89 | 0.03 |
| Salvadoran | 92 | 0.04 |
| Other Central American | 5 | <0.01 |
| Cuban | 795 | 0.30 |
| Dominican Republic | 707 | 0.27 |
| Mexican | 1,382 | 0.53 |
| Puerto Rican | 22,076 | 8.45 |
| South American | 679 | 0.26 |
| Argentinean | 117 | 0.04 |
| Bolivian | 35 | 0.01 |
| Chilean | 35 | 0.01 |
| Colombian | 215 | 0.08 |
| Ecuadorian | 106 | 0.04 |
| Paraguayan | 8 | <0.01 |
| Peruvian | 105 | 0.04 |
| Uruguayan | 2 | <0.01 |
| Venezuelan | 44 | 0.02 |
| Other South American | 12 | <0.01 |
| Other Hispanic or Latino | 1,494 | 0.57 |

| Race* | Population | % |
|---|---|---|
| African-American/Black (100,774) | 106,107 | 40.61 |
| Not Hispanic (97,637) | 101,817 | 38.96 |
| Hispanic (3,137) | 4,290 | 1.64 |
| American Indian/Alaska Native (2,009) | 4,019 | 1.54 |
| Not Hispanic (1,597) | 3,229 | 1.24 |
| Hispanic (412) | 790 | 0.30 |
| Alaska Athabascan (Ala. Nat.) (1) | 1 | <0.01 |
| Aleut (Alaska Native) (0) | 0 | <0.01 |
| Apache (5) | 11 | <0.01 |
| Arapaho (1) | 1 | <0.01 |
| Blackfeet (10) | 104 | 0.04 |
| Canadian/French Am. Ind. (29) | 57 | 0.02 |
| Central American Ind. (9) | 17 | 0.01 |
| Cherokee (37) | 294 | 0.11 |
| Cheyenne (0) | 0 | <0.01 |
| Chickasaw (2) | 2 | <0.01 |
| Chippewa (24) | 42 | 0.02 |

| Race* | Population | % |
|---|---|---|
| Choctaw (3) | 21 | 0.01 |
| Colville (0) | 0 | <0.01 |
| Comanche (1) | 4 | <0.01 |
| Cree (1) | 4 | <0.01 |
| Creek (0) | 7 | <0.01 |
| Crow (0) | 1 | <0.01 |
| Delaware (6) | 10 | <0.01 |
| Hopi (0) | 5 | <0.01 |
| Houma (1) | 2 | <0.01 |
| Inupiat (Alaska Native) (2) | 4 | <0.01 |
| Iroquois (935) | 1,316 | 0.50 |
| Kiowa (1) | 1 | <0.01 |
| Lumbee (1) | 1 | <0.01 |
| Menominee (2) | 2 | <0.01 |
| Mexican American Ind. (19) | 27 | 0.01 |
| Navajo (8) | 16 | 0.01 |
| Osage (0) | 0 | <0.01 |
| Ottawa (0) | 0 | <0.01 |
| Paiute (0) | 0 | <0.01 |
| Pima (1) | 1 | <0.01 |
| Potawatomi (0) | 0 | <0.01 |
| Pueblo (3) | 4 | <0.01 |
| Puget Sound Salish (0) | 0 | <0.01 |
| Seminole (3) | 23 | 0.01 |
| Shoshone (0) | 0 | <0.01 |
| Sioux (24) | 46 | 0.02 |
| South American Ind. (24) | 60 | 0.02 |
| Spanish American Ind. (11) | 14 | 0.01 |
| Tlingit-Haida (Alaska Native) (2) | 3 | <0.01 |
| Tohono O'Odham (1) | 3 | <0.01 |
| Tsimshian (Alaska Native) (0) | 0 | <0.01 |
| Ute (0) | 0 | <0.01 |
| Yakama (0) | 0 | <0.01 |
| Yaqui (2) | 2 | <0.01 |
| Yuman (1) | 1 | <0.01 |
| Yup'ik (Alaska Native) (0) | 0 | <0.01 |
| Asian (8,409) | 9,698 | 3.71 |
| Not Hispanic (8,313) | 9,459 | 3.62 |
| Hispanic (96) | 239 | 0.09 |
| Bangladeshi (167) | 206 | 0.08 |
| Bhutanese (298) | 370 | 0.14 |
| Burmese (2,267) | 2,361 | 0.90 |
| Cambodian (43) | 48 | 0.02 |
| Chinese, ex. Taiwanese (919) | 1,065 | 0.41 |
| Filipino (214) | 417 | 0.16 |
| Hmong (5) | 6 | <0.01 |
| Indian (1,576) | 1,889 | 0.72 |
| Indonesian (17) | 22 | 0.01 |
| Japanese (128) | 243 | 0.09 |
| Korean (350) | 447 | 0.17 |
| Laotian (248) | 288 | 0.11 |
| Malaysian (19) | 21 | 0.01 |
| Nepalese (115) | 160 | 0.06 |
| Pakistani (320) | 362 | 0.14 |
| Sri Lankan (45) | 54 | 0.02 |
| Taiwanese (31) | 43 | 0.02 |
| Thai (59) | 107 | 0.04 |
| Vietnamese (1,128) | 1,220 | 0.47 |
| Hawaii Native/Pacific Islander (119) | 357 | 0.14 |
| Not Hispanic (79) | 252 | 0.10 |
| Hispanic (40) | 105 | 0.04 |
| Fijian (0) | 0 | <0.01 |
| Guamanian/Chamorro (10) | 30 | 0.01 |
| Marshallese (0) | 0 | <0.01 |
| Native Hawaiian (21) | 75 | 0.03 |
| Samoan (32) | 63 | 0.02 |
| Tongan (3) | 3 | <0.01 |
| White (131,753) | 138,013 | 52.82 |
| Not Hispanic (119,801) | 124,612 | 47.69 |
| Hispanic (11,952) | 13,401 | 5.13 |

Notes: † The Census 2010 population figure is used to calculate the percentages in the Hispanic Origin and Race categories. Ancestry percentages are based on the 2006-2010 American Community Survey population (not shown); ‡ Numbers in parentheses indicate the number of people reporting a single ancestry; * Numbers in parentheses indicate the number of persons reporting this race alone, not in combination with any other race; Please refer to the Explanation of Data for more information.

## Cheektowaga

Place Type: CDP
County: Erie
Population: 75,178

| Ancestry | Population | % |
|---|---|---|
| Afghan (0) | 0 | <0.01 |
| African, Sub-Saharan (178) | 178 | 0.23 |
| African (145) | 145 | 0.19 |
| Cape Verdean (0) | 0 | <0.01 |
| Ethiopian (0) | 0 | <0.01 |
| Ghanaian (0) | 0 | <0.01 |
| Kenyan (0) | 0 | <0.01 |
| Liberian (0) | 0 | <0.01 |
| Nigerian (0) | 0 | <0.01 |
| Senegalese (0) | 0 | <0.01 |
| Sierra Leonean (0) | 0 | <0.01 |
| Somalian (0) | 0 | <0.01 |
| South African (0) | 0 | <0.01 |
| Sudanese (0) | 0 | <0.01 |
| Ugandan (0) | 0 | <0.01 |
| Zimbabwean (0) | 0 | <0.01 |
| Other Sub-Saharan African (33) | 33 | 0.04 |
| Albanian (15) | 21 | 0.03 |
| Alsatian (0) | 0 | <0.01 |
| American (1,642) | 1,642 | 2.17 |
| Arab (498) | 611 | 0.81 |
| Arab (208) | 224 | 0.30 |
| Egyptian (0) | 0 | <0.01 |
| Iraqi (30) | 30 | 0.04 |
| Jordanian (0) | 0 | <0.01 |
| Lebanese (260) | 338 | 0.45 |
| Moroccan (0) | 0 | <0.01 |
| Palestinian (0) | 0 | <0.01 |
| Syrian (0) | 13 | 0.02 |
| Other Arab (0) | 6 | 0.01 |
| Armenian (0) | 13 | 0.02 |
| Assyrian/Chaldean/Syriac (0) | 0 | <0.01 |
| Australian (0) | 0 | <0.01 |
| Austrian (33) | 202 | 0.27 |
| Basque (0) | 0 | <0.01 |
| Belgian (0) | 29 | 0.04 |
| Brazilian (0) | 0 | <0.01 |
| British (51) | 217 | 0.29 |
| Bulgarian (30) | 30 | 0.04 |
| Cajun (0) | 0 | <0.01 |
| Canadian (63) | 193 | 0.25 |
| Carpatho Rusyn (6) | 6 | 0.01 |
| Celtic (0) | 0 | <0.01 |
| Croatian (21) | 90 | 0.12 |
| Cypriot (0) | 0 | <0.01 |
| Czech (0) | 249 | 0.33 |
| Czechoslovakian (10) | 10 | 0.01 |
| Danish (0) | 53 | 0.07 |
| Dutch (59) | 763 | 1.01 |
| Eastern European (0) | 0 | <0.01 |
| English (753) | 4,258 | 5.62 |
| Estonian (78) | 78 | 0.10 |
| European (101) | 122 | 0.16 |
| Finnish (12) | 28 | 0.04 |
| French, ex. Basque (123) | 2,246 | 2.96 |
| French Canadian (122) | 608 | 0.80 |
| German (6,860) | 21,843 | 28.83 |
| German Russian (12) | 12 | 0.02 |
| Greek (116) | 188 | 0.25 |
| Guyanese (23) | 23 | 0.03 |
| Hungarian (132) | 542 | 0.72 |
| Icelander (0) | 0 | <0.01 |
| Iranian (0) | 0 | <0.01 |
| Irish (2,376) | 11,306 | 14.92 |
| Israeli (0) | 0 | <0.01 |
| Italian (5,350) | 12,314 | 16.26 |
| Latvian (16) | 16 | 0.02 |
| Lithuanian (12) | 84 | 0.11 |
| Luxemburger (0) | 0 | <0.01 |
| Macedonian (21) | 35 | 0.05 |
| Maltese (0) | 0 | <0.01 |
| New Zealander (11) | 11 | 0.01 |
| Northern European (0) | 0 | <0.01 |
| Norwegian (15) | 247 | 0.33 |
| Pennsylvania German (15) | 24 | 0.03 |
| Polish (15,029) | 26,237 | 34.63 |
| Portuguese (11) | 75 | 0.10 |
| Romanian (38) | 51 | 0.07 |
| Russian (173) | 411 | 0.54 |
| Scandinavian (0) | 15 | 0.02 |
| Scotch-Irish (268) | 861 | 1.14 |
| Scottish (183) | 788 | 1.04 |
| Serbian (82) | 100 | 0.13 |
| Slavic (11) | 45 | 0.06 |
| Slovak (71) | 229 | 0.30 |
| Slovene (0) | 16 | 0.02 |
| Soviet Union (0) | 0 | <0.01 |
| Swedish (143) | 418 | 0.55 |
| Swiss (14) | 63 | 0.08 |
| Turkish (0) | 42 | 0.06 |
| Ukrainian (268) | 499 | 0.66 |
| Welsh (8) | 327 | 0.43 |
| West Indian, ex. Hispanic (240) | 315 | 0.42 |
| Bahamian (0) | 0 | <0.01 |
| Barbadian (8) | 8 | 0.01 |
| Belizean (0) | 0 | <0.01 |
| Bermudan (0) | 0 | <0.01 |
| British West Indian (13) | 13 | 0.02 |
| Dutch West Indian (0) | 0 | <0.01 |
| Haitian (7) | 7 | 0.01 |
| Jamaican (129) | 182 | 0.24 |
| Trinidadian/Tobagonian (33) | 55 | 0.07 |
| U.S. Virgin Islander (0) | 0 | <0.01 |
| West Indian (50) | 50 | 0.07 |
| Other West Indian (0) | 0 | <0.01 |
| Yugoslavian (69) | 69 | 0.09 |

| Hispanic Origin | Population | % |
|---|---|---|
| Hispanic or Latino (of any race) | 1,672 | 2.22 |
| Central American, ex. Mexican | 55 | 0.07 |
| Costa Rican | 5 | 0.01 |
| Guatemalan | 11 | 0.01 |
| Honduran | 6 | 0.01 |
| Nicaraguan | 1 | <0.01 |
| Panamanian | 13 | 0.02 |
| Salvadoran | 14 | 0.02 |
| Other Central American | 5 | 0.01 |
| Cuban | 47 | 0.06 |
| Dominican Republic | 55 | 0.07 |
| Mexican | 244 | 0.32 |
| Puerto Rican | 1,011 | 1.34 |
| South American | 105 | 0.14 |
| Argentinean | 7 | 0.01 |
| Bolivian | 6 | 0.01 |
| Chilean | 4 | 0.01 |
| Colombian | 39 | 0.05 |
| Ecuadorian | 22 | 0.03 |
| Paraguayan | 2 | <0.01 |
| Peruvian | 10 | 0.01 |
| Uruguayan | 2 | <0.01 |
| Venezuelan | 11 | 0.01 |
| Other South American | 2 | <0.01 |
| Other Hispanic or Latino | 155 | 0.21 |

| Race* | Population | % |
|---|---|---|
| African-American/Black (6,881) | 7,619 | 10.13 |
| Not Hispanic (6,716) | 7,368 | 9.80 |
| Hispanic (165) | 251 | 0.33 |
| American Indian/Alaska Native (189) | 469 | 0.62 |
| Not Hispanic (171) | 416 | 0.55 |
| Hispanic (18) | 53 | 0.07 |
| Alaska Athabascan (Ala. Nat.) (0) | 0 | <0.01 |
| Aleut (Alaska Native) (0) | 0 | <0.01 |
| Apache (1) | 6 | 0.01 |
| Arapaho (0) | 0 | <0.01 |
| Blackfeet (0) | 12 | 0.02 |
| Canadian/French Am. Ind. (5) | 5 | 0.01 |
| Central American Ind. (1) | 1 | <0.01 |
| Cherokee (6) | 45 | 0.06 |
| Cheyenne (0) | 1 | <0.01 |
| Chickasaw (0) | 0 | <0.01 |
| Chippewa (5) | 6 | 0.01 |

| | Population | % |
|---|---|---|
| Choctaw (2) | 3 | <0.01 |
| Colville (0) | 0 | <0.01 |
| Comanche (0) | 0 | <0.01 |
| Cree (0) | 1 | <0.01 |
| Creek (1) | 1 | <0.01 |
| Crow (0) | 0 | <0.01 |
| Delaware (2) | 2 | <0.01 |
| Hopi (2) | 2 | <0.01 |
| Houma (0) | 0 | <0.01 |
| Inupiat (Alaska Native) (0) | 0 | <0.01 |
| Iroquois (95) | 179 | 0.24 |
| Kiowa (0) | 0 | <0.01 |
| Lumbee (0) | 0 | <0.01 |
| Menominee (0) | 0 | <0.01 |
| Mexican American Ind. (5) | 7 | 0.01 |
| Navajo (1) | 3 | <0.01 |
| Osage (0) | 0 | <0.01 |
| Ottawa (0) | 0 | <0.01 |
| Paiute (0) | 0 | <0.01 |
| Pima (0) | 0 | <0.01 |
| Potawatomi (0) | 0 | <0.01 |
| Pueblo (0) | 3 | <0.01 |
| Puget Sound Salish (0) | 0 | <0.01 |
| Seminole (0) | 0 | <0.01 |
| Shoshone (0) | 0 | <0.01 |
| Sioux (1) | 6 | 0.01 |
| South American Ind. (0) | 4 | 0.01 |
| Spanish American Ind. (0) | 0 | <0.01 |
| Tlingit-Haida (Alaska Native) (0) | 0 | <0.01 |
| Tohono O'Odham (0) | 0 | <0.01 |
| Tsimshian (Alaska Native) (0) | 0 | <0.01 |
| Ute (0) | 0 | <0.01 |
| Yakama (0) | 0 | <0.01 |
| Yaqui (0) | 0 | <0.01 |
| Yuman (0) | 0 | <0.01 |
| Yup'ik (Alaska Native) (0) | 0 | <0.01 |
| Asian (1,252) | 1,476 | 1.96 |
| Not Hispanic (1,249) | 1,455 | 1.94 |
| Hispanic (3) | 21 | 0.03 |
| Bangladeshi (2) | 2 | <0.01 |
| Bhutanese (0) | 0 | <0.01 |
| Burmese (6) | 8 | 0.01 |
| Cambodian (9) | 11 | 0.01 |
| Chinese, ex. Taiwanese (100) | 134 | 0.18 |
| Filipino (68) | 112 | 0.15 |
| Hmong (0) | 1 | <0.01 |
| Indian (499) | 529 | 0.70 |
| Indonesian (6) | 10 | 0.01 |
| Japanese (16) | 37 | 0.05 |
| Korean (61) | 89 | 0.12 |
| Laotian (58) | 65 | 0.09 |
| Malaysian (12) | 12 | 0.02 |
| Nepalese (5) | 5 | 0.01 |
| Pakistani (37) | 52 | 0.07 |
| Sri Lankan (0) | 2 | <0.01 |
| Taiwanese (4) | 4 | 0.01 |
| Thai (5) | 10 | 0.01 |
| Vietnamese (297) | 326 | 0.43 |
| Hawaii Native/Pacific Islander (12) | 39 | 0.05 |
| Not Hispanic (9) | 30 | 0.04 |
| Hispanic (3) | 9 | 0.01 |
| Fijian (2) | 2 | <0.01 |
| Guamanian/Chamorro (2) | 7 | 0.01 |
| Marshallese (0) | 0 | <0.01 |
| Native Hawaiian (5) | 14 | 0.02 |
| Samoan (1) | 2 | <0.01 |
| Tongan (0) | 0 | <0.01 |
| White (65,225) | 66,265 | 88.14 |
| Not Hispanic (64,288) | 65,180 | 86.70 |
| Hispanic (937) | 1,085 | 1.44 |

Notes: † The Census 2010 population figure is used to calculate the percentages in the Hispanic Origin and Race categories. Ancestry percentages are based on the 2006-2010 American Community Survey population (not shown); ‡ Numbers in parentheses indicate the number of people reporting a single ancestry; * Numbers in parentheses indicate the number of persons reporting this race alone, not in combination with any other race; Please refer to the Explanation of Data for more information.

## Cheektowaga

Place Type: Town
County: Erie
Population: 88,226

| Ancestry | Population | % |
|---|---|---|
| Afghan (0) | 0 | <0.01 |
| African, Sub-Saharan (178) | 178 | 0.20 |
| African (145) | 145 | 0.16 |
| Cape Verdean (0) | 0 | <0.01 |
| Ethiopian (0) | 0 | <0.01 |
| Ghanaian (0) | 0 | <0.01 |
| Kenyan (0) | 0 | <0.01 |
| Liberian (0) | 0 | <0.01 |
| Nigerian (0) | 0 | <0.01 |
| Senegalese (0) | 0 | <0.01 |
| Sierra Leonean (0) | 0 | <0.01 |
| Somalian (0) | 0 | <0.01 |
| South African (0) | 0 | <0.01 |
| Sudanese (0) | 0 | <0.01 |
| Ugandan (0) | 0 | <0.01 |
| Zimbabwean (0) | 0 | <0.01 |
| Other Sub-Saharan African (33) | 33 | 0.04 |
| Albanian (15) | 30 | 0.03 |
| Alsatian (0) | 0 | <0.01 |
| American (1,927) | 1,927 | 2.17 |
| Arab (768) | 905 | 1.02 |
| Arab (231) | 247 | 0.28 |
| Egyptian (0) | 0 | <0.01 |
| Iraqi (30) | 30 | 0.03 |
| Jordanian (0) | 0 | <0.01 |
| Lebanese (260) | 350 | 0.39 |
| Moroccan (0) | 0 | <0.01 |
| Palestinian (9) | 9 | 0.01 |
| Syrian (0) | 25 | 0.03 |
| Other Arab (238) | 244 | 0.27 |
| Armenian (0) | 13 | 0.01 |
| Assyrian/Chaldean/Syriac (0) | 0 | <0.01 |
| Australian (0) | 0 | <0.01 |
| Austrian (33) | 225 | 0.25 |
| Basque (0) | 0 | <0.01 |
| Belgian (0) | 29 | 0.03 |
| Brazilian (0) | 0 | <0.01 |
| British (84) | 277 | 0.31 |
| Bulgarian (73) | 73 | 0.08 |
| Cajun (0) | 0 | <0.01 |
| Canadian (72) | 202 | 0.23 |
| Carpatho Rusyn (6) | 6 | 0.01 |
| Celtic (0) | 0 | <0.01 |
| Croatian (21) | 90 | 0.10 |
| Cypriot (0) | 0 | <0.01 |
| Czech (29) | 312 | 0.35 |
| Czechoslovakian (48) | 60 | 0.07 |
| Danish (0) | 53 | 0.06 |
| Dutch (125) | 935 | 1.05 |
| Eastern European (0) | 0 | <0.01 |
| English (852) | 4,818 | 5.42 |
| Estonian (78) | 78 | 0.09 |
| European (123) | 144 | 0.16 |
| Finnish (12) | 28 | 0.03 |
| French, ex. Basque (132) | 2,577 | 2.90 |
| French Canadian (122) | 701 | 0.79 |
| German (7,899) | 26,125 | 29.39 |
| German Russian (12) | 12 | 0.01 |
| Greek (169) | 249 | 0.28 |
| Guyanese (23) | 23 | 0.03 |
| Hungarian (132) | 575 | 0.65 |
| Icelander (0) | 0 | <0.01 |
| Iranian (0) | 0 | <0.01 |
| Irish (2,677) | 13,325 | 14.99 |
| Israeli (0) | 0 | <0.01 |
| Italian (6,376) | 14,630 | 16.46 |
| Latvian (16) | 16 | 0.02 |
| Lithuanian (12) | 99 | 0.11 |
| Luxemburger (0) | 0 | <0.01 |
| Macedonian (21) | 35 | 0.04 |
| Maltese (0) | 0 | <0.01 |
| New Zealander (11) | 11 | 0.01 |
| Northern European (130) | 130 | 0.15 |

| Ancestry | Population | % |
|---|---|---|
| Norwegian (15) | 256 | 0.29 |
| Pennsylvania German (24) | 33 | 0.04 |
| Polish (18,227) | 31,456 | 35.39 |
| Portuguese (11) | 84 | 0.09 |
| Romanian (38) | 61 | 0.07 |
| Russian (182) | 430 | 0.48 |
| Scandinavian (0) | 44 | 0.05 |
| Scotch-Irish (291) | 969 | 1.09 |
| Scottish (232) | 954 | 1.07 |
| Serbian (82) | 100 | 0.11 |
| Slavic (11) | 45 | 0.05 |
| Slovak (71) | 229 | 0.26 |
| Slovene (0) | 16 | 0.02 |
| Soviet Union (0) | 0 | <0.01 |
| Swedish (228) | 542 | 0.61 |
| Swiss (26) | 85 | 0.10 |
| Turkish (0) | 42 | 0.05 |
| Ukrainian (295) | 556 | 0.63 |
| Welsh (8) | 383 | 0.43 |
| West Indian, ex. Hispanic (240) | 315 | 0.35 |
| Bahamian (0) | 0 | <0.01 |
| Barbadian (8) | 8 | 0.01 |
| Belizean (0) | 0 | <0.01 |
| Bermudan (0) | 0 | <0.01 |
| British West Indian (13) | 13 | 0.01 |
| Dutch West Indian (0) | 0 | <0.01 |
| Haitian (7) | 7 | 0.01 |
| Jamaican (129) | 182 | 0.20 |
| Trinidadian/Tobagonian (33) | 55 | 0.06 |
| U.S. Virgin Islander (0) | 0 | <0.01 |
| West Indian (50) | 50 | 0.06 |
| Other West Indian (0) | 0 | <0.01 |
| Yugoslavian (69) | 69 | 0.08 |

| Hispanic Origin | Population | % |
|---|---|---|
| Hispanic or Latino (of any race) | 1,900 | 2.15 |
| Central American, ex. Mexican | 78 | 0.09 |
| Costa Rican | 5 | 0.01 |
| Guatemalan | 21 | 0.02 |
| Honduran | 6 | 0.01 |
| Nicaraguan | 4 | <0.01 |
| Panamanian | 13 | 0.01 |
| Salvadoran | 21 | 0.02 |
| Other Central American | 8 | 0.01 |
| Cuban | 51 | 0.06 |
| Dominican Republic | 59 | 0.07 |
| Mexican | 285 | 0.32 |
| Puerto Rican | 1,138 | 1.29 |
| South American | 112 | 0.13 |
| Argentinean | 7 | 0.01 |
| Bolivian | 6 | 0.01 |
| Chilean | 4 | <0.01 |
| Colombian | 41 | 0.05 |
| Ecuadorian | 26 | 0.03 |
| Paraguayan | 2 | <0.01 |
| Peruvian | 10 | 0.01 |
| Uruguayan | 2 | <0.01 |
| Venezuelan | 12 | 0.01 |
| Other South American | 2 | <0.01 |
| Other Hispanic or Latino | 177 | 0.20 |

| Race* | Population | % |
|---|---|---|
| African-American/Black (7,069) | 7,879 | 8.93 |
| Not Hispanic (6,898) | 7,611 | 8.63 |
| Hispanic (171) | 268 | 0.30 |
| American Indian/Alaska Native (223) | 546 | 0.62 |
| Not Hispanic (200) | 482 | 0.55 |
| Hispanic (23) | 64 | 0.07 |
| Alaska Athabascan (Ala. Nat.) (0) | 0 | <0.01 |
| Aleut (Alaska Native) (0) | 0 | <0.01 |
| Apache (1) | 6 | 0.01 |
| Arapaho (1) | 1 | <0.01 |
| Blackfeet (0) | 15 | 0.02 |
| Canadian/French Am. Ind. (5) | 5 | 0.01 |
| Central American Ind. (3) | 4 | <0.01 |
| Cherokee (6) | 52 | 0.06 |
| Cheyenne (0) | 0 | <0.01 |
| Chickasaw (0) | 0 | <0.01 |
| Chippewa (5) | 6 | 0.01 |

| Race* | Population | % |
|---|---|---|
| Choctaw (2) | 3 | <0.01 |
| Colville (0) | 0 | <0.01 |
| Comanche (0) | 0 | <0.01 |
| Cree (0) | 1 | <0.01 |
| Creek (1) | 2 | <0.01 |
| Crow (0) | 0 | <0.01 |
| Delaware (2) | 2 | <0.01 |
| Hopi (2) | 2 | <0.01 |
| Houma (0) | 0 | <0.01 |
| Inupiat (Alaska Native) (0) | 0 | <0.01 |
| Iroquois (110) | 194 | 0.22 |
| Kiowa (0) | 0 | <0.01 |
| Lumbee (0) | 4 | <0.01 |
| Menominee (0) | 0 | <0.01 |
| Mexican American Ind. (7) | 9 | 0.01 |
| Navajo (1) | 3 | <0.01 |
| Osage (0) | 0 | <0.01 |
| Ottawa (0) | 0 | <0.01 |
| Paiute (0) | 0 | <0.01 |
| Pima (0) | 0 | <0.01 |
| Potawatomi (0) | 0 | <0.01 |
| Pueblo (0) | 3 | <0.01 |
| Puget Sound Salish (0) | 0 | <0.01 |
| Seminole (0) | 0 | <0.01 |
| Shoshone (0) | 0 | <0.01 |
| Sioux (1) | 6 | 0.01 |
| South American Ind. (0) | 4 | <0.01 |
| Spanish American Ind. (0) | 0 | <0.01 |
| Tlingit-Haida (Alaska Native) (0) | 0 | <0.01 |
| Tohono O'Odham (0) | 0 | <0.01 |
| Tsimshian (Alaska Native) (0) | 0 | <0.01 |
| Ute (0) | 0 | <0.01 |
| Yakama (0) | 0 | <0.01 |
| Yaqui (0) | 0 | <0.01 |
| Yuman (0) | 0 | <0.01 |
| Yup'ik (Alaska Native) (0) | 0 | <0.01 |
| Asian (1,336) | 1,598 | 1.81 |
| Not Hispanic (1,333) | 1,576 | 1.79 |
| Hispanic (3) | 22 | 0.02 |
| Bangladeshi (4) | 4 | <0.01 |
| Bhutanese (0) | 0 | <0.01 |
| Burmese (6) | 8 | 0.01 |
| Cambodian (10) | 15 | 0.02 |
| Chinese, ex. Taiwanese (111) | 146 | 0.17 |
| Filipino (77) | 128 | 0.15 |
| Hmong (1) | 1 | <0.01 |
| Indian (530) | 568 | 0.64 |
| Indonesian (6) | 10 | 0.01 |
| Japanese (17) | 38 | 0.04 |
| Korean (69) | 106 | 0.12 |
| Laotian (58) | 65 | 0.07 |
| Malaysian (13) | 13 | 0.01 |
| Nepalese (5) | 5 | 0.01 |
| Pakistani (37) | 52 | 0.06 |
| Sri Lankan (0) | 2 | <0.01 |
| Taiwanese (4) | 4 | <0.01 |
| Thai (5) | 10 | 0.01 |
| Vietnamese (315) | 344 | 0.39 |
| Hawaii Native/Pacific Islander (14) | 43 | 0.05 |
| Not Hispanic (10) | 33 | 0.04 |
| Hispanic (4) | 10 | 0.01 |
| Fijian (2) | 2 | <0.01 |
| Guamanian/Chamorro (3) | 8 | 0.01 |
| Marshallese (0) | 0 | <0.01 |
| Native Hawaiian (5) | 16 | 0.02 |
| Samoan (1) | 5 | 0.01 |
| Tongan (0) | 0 | <0.01 |
| White (77,769) | 78,958 | 89.50 |
| Not Hispanic (76,673) | 77,687 | 88.05 |
| Hispanic (1,096) | 1,271 | 1.44 |

Notes: † The Census 2010 population figure is used to calculate the percentages in the Hispanic Origin and Race categories. Ancestry percentages are based on the 2006-2010 American Community Survey population (not shown); ‡ Numbers in parentheses indicate the number of people reporting a single ancestry; * Numbers in parentheses indicate the number of persons reporting this race alone, not in combination with any other race; Please refer to the Explanation of Data for more information.

## Clarkstown

Place Type: Town
County: Rockland
Population: 84,187

| Ancestry | Population | % |
|---|---|---|
| Afghan (0) | 0 | <0.01 |
| African, Sub-Saharan (248) | 283 | 0.34 |
| African (149) | 184 | 0.22 |
| Cape Verdean (0) | 0 | <0.01 |
| Ethiopian (0) | 0 | <0.01 |
| Ghanaian (99) | 99 | 0.12 |
| Kenyan (0) | 0 | <0.01 |
| Liberian (0) | 0 | <0.01 |
| Nigerian (0) | 0 | <0.01 |
| Senegalese (0) | 0 | <0.01 |
| Sierra Leonean (0) | 0 | <0.01 |
| Somalian (0) | 0 | <0.01 |
| South African (0) | 0 | <0.01 |
| Sudanese (0) | 0 | <0.01 |
| Ugandan (0) | 0 | <0.01 |
| Zimbabwean (0) | 0 | <0.01 |
| Other Sub-Saharan African (0) | 0 | <0.01 |
| Albanian (317) | 328 | 0.39 |
| Alsatian (0) | 3 | <0.01 |
| American (4,138) | 4,138 | 4.96 |
| Arab (440) | 705 | 0.85 |
| Arab (8) | 29 | 0.03 |
| Egyptian (229) | 254 | 0.30 |
| Iraqi (7) | 24 | 0.03 |
| Jordanian (9) | 9 | 0.01 |
| Lebanese (138) | 252 | 0.30 |
| Moroccan (0) | 0 | <0.01 |
| Palestinian (0) | 0 | <0.01 |
| Syrian (88) | 88 | 0.11 |
| Other Arab (49) | 49 | 0.06 |
| Armenian (84) | 99 | 0.12 |
| Assyrian/Chaldean/Syriac (11) | 51 | 0.06 |
| Australian (12) | 18 | 0.02 |
| Austrian (199) | 827 | 0.99 |
| Basque (0) | 0 | <0.01 |
| Belgian (0) | 42 | 0.05 |
| Brazilian (69) | 203 | 0.24 |
| British (105) | 190 | 0.23 |
| Bulgarian (0) | 0 | <0.01 |
| Cajun (0) | 0 | <0.01 |
| Canadian (78) | 112 | 0.13 |
| Carpatho Rusyn (0) | 0 | <0.01 |
| Celtic (0) | 0 | <0.01 |
| Croatian (54) | 111 | 0.13 |
| Cypriot (0) | 0 | <0.01 |
| Czech (65) | 292 | 0.35 |
| Czechoslovakian (75) | 123 | 0.15 |
| Danish (20) | 91 | 0.11 |
| Dutch (130) | 487 | 0.58 |
| Eastern European (1,163) | 1,282 | 1.54 |
| English (620) | 2,751 | 3.30 |
| Estonian (0) | 0 | <0.01 |
| European (659) | 690 | 0.83 |
| Finnish (50) | 119 | 0.14 |
| French, ex. Basque (154) | 874 | 1.05 |
| French Canadian (98) | 288 | 0.35 |
| German (1,752) | 7,742 | 9.28 |
| German Russian (0) | 0 | <0.01 |
| Greek (204) | 613 | 0.74 |
| Guyanese (77) | 95 | 0.11 |
| Hungarian (301) | 1,008 | 1.21 |
| Icelander (0) | 0 | <0.01 |
| Iranian (100) | 146 | 0.18 |
| Irish (7,258) | 15,823 | 18.97 |
| Israeli (99) | 247 | 0.30 |
| Italian (9,086) | 16,766 | 20.10 |
| Latvian (64) | 87 | 0.10 |
| Lithuanian (129) | 286 | 0.34 |
| Luxemburger (0) | 0 | <0.01 |
| Macedonian (24) | 24 | 0.03 |
| Maltese (0) | 8 | 0.01 |
| New Zealander (0) | 3 | <0.01 |
| Northern European (15) | 28 | 0.03 |

| Ancestry | Population | % |
|---|---|---|
| Norwegian (214) | 464 | 0.56 |
| Pennsylvania German (0) | 0 | <0.01 |
| Polish (1,491) | 4,159 | 4.99 |
| Portuguese (165) | 216 | 0.26 |
| Romanian (167) | 544 | 0.65 |
| Russian (2,652) | 5,317 | 6.38 |
| Scandinavian (12) | 16 | 0.02 |
| Scotch-Irish (228) | 499 | 0.60 |
| Scottish (102) | 591 | 0.71 |
| Serbian (11) | 19 | 0.02 |
| Slavic (11) | 40 | 0.05 |
| Slovak (179) | 310 | 0.37 |
| Slovene (0) | 0 | <0.01 |
| Soviet Union (0) | 0 | <0.01 |
| Swedish (65) | 359 | 0.43 |
| Swiss (39) | 85 | 0.10 |
| Turkish (66) | 72 | 0.09 |
| Ukrainian (387) | 690 | 0.83 |
| Welsh (0) | 212 | 0.25 |
| West Indian, ex. Hispanic (2,635) | 2,834 | 3.40 |
| Bahamian (0) | 0 | <0.01 |
| Barbadian (10) | 10 | 0.01 |
| Belizean (9) | 9 | 0.01 |
| Bermudan (0) | 3 | <0.01 |
| British West Indian (21) | 45 | 0.05 |
| Dutch West Indian (0) | 0 | <0.01 |
| Haitian (2,003) | 2,077 | 2.49 |
| Jamaican (382) | 432 | 0.52 |
| Trinidadian/Tobagonian (90) | 117 | 0.14 |
| U.S. Virgin Islander (0) | 0 | <0.01 |
| West Indian (120) | 141 | 0.17 |
| Other West Indian (0) | 0 | <0.01 |
| Yugoslavian (43) | 53 | 0.06 |

| Hispanic Origin | Population | % |
|---|---|---|
| Hispanic or Latino (of any race) | 9,831 | 11.68 |
| Central American, ex. Mexican | 1,656 | 1.97 |
| Costa Rican | 40 | 0.05 |
| Guatemalan | 802 | 0.95 |
| Honduran | 80 | 0.10 |
| Nicaraguan | 10 | 0.01 |
| Panamanian | 41 | 0.05 |
| Salvadoran | 662 | 0.79 |
| Other Central American | 21 | 0.02 |
| Cuban | 421 | 0.50 |
| Dominican Republic | 939 | 1.12 |
| Mexican | 897 | 1.07 |
| Puerto Rican | 3,427 | 4.07 |
| South American | 1,708 | 2.03 |
| Argentinean | 113 | 0.13 |
| Bolivian | 31 | 0.04 |
| Chilean | 73 | 0.09 |
| Colombian | 281 | 0.33 |
| Ecuadorian | 1,051 | 1.25 |
| Paraguayan | 5 | 0.01 |
| Peruvian | 119 | 0.14 |
| Uruguayan | 14 | 0.02 |
| Venezuelan | 14 | 0.02 |
| Other South American | 7 | 0.01 |
| Other Hispanic or Latino | 783 | 0.93 |

| Race* | Population | % |
|---|---|---|
| African-American/Black (8,091) | 8,965 | 10.65 |
| Not Hispanic (7,598) | 8,194 | 9.73 |
| Hispanic (493) | 771 | 0.92 |
| American Indian/Alaska Native (193) | 459 | 0.55 |
| Not Hispanic (111) | 308 | 0.37 |
| Hispanic (82) | 151 | 0.18 |
| Alaska Athabascan (Ala. Nat.) (0) | 0 | <0.01 |
| Aleut (Alaska Native) (0) | 0 | <0.01 |
| Apache (0) | 2 | <0.01 |
| Arapaho (0) | 0 | <0.01 |
| Blackfeet (1) | 8 | 0.01 |
| Canadian/French Am. Ind. (0) | 0 | <0.01 |
| Central American Ind. (1) | 2 | <0.01 |
| Cherokee (1) | 42 | 0.05 |
| Cheyenne (0) | 0 | <0.01 |
| Chickasaw (0) | 0 | <0.01 |
| Chippewa (1) | 1 | <0.01 |

| Race* | Population | % |
|---|---|---|
| Choctaw (1) | 6 | 0.01 |
| Colville (0) | 0 | <0.01 |
| Comanche (0) | 0 | <0.01 |
| Cree (0) | 1 | <0.01 |
| Creek (0) | 3 | <0.01 |
| Crow (0) | 0 | <0.01 |
| Delaware (12) | 16 | 0.02 |
| Hopi (0) | 0 | <0.01 |
| Houma (0) | 0 | <0.01 |
| Inupiat (Alaska Native) (0) | 0 | <0.01 |
| Iroquois (8) | 13 | 0.02 |
| Kiowa (0) | 0 | <0.01 |
| Lumbee (2) | 2 | <0.01 |
| Menominee (0) | 0 | <0.01 |
| Mexican American Ind. (6) | 8 | 0.01 |
| Navajo (0) | 1 | <0.01 |
| Osage (0) | 0 | <0.01 |
| Ottawa (0) | 0 | <0.01 |
| Paiute (1) | 1 | <0.01 |
| Pima (0) | 0 | <0.01 |
| Potawatomi (1) | 1 | <0.01 |
| Pueblo (0) | 4 | <0.01 |
| Puget Sound Salish (0) | 0 | <0.01 |
| Seminole (0) | 4 | <0.01 |
| Shoshone (0) | 0 | <0.01 |
| Sioux (1) | 2 | <0.01 |
| South American Ind. (22) | 38 | 0.05 |
| Spanish American Ind. (0) | 0 | <0.01 |
| Tlingit-Haida (Alaska Native) (0) | 1 | <0.01 |
| Tohono O'Odham (0) | 0 | <0.01 |
| Tsimshian (Alaska Native) (0) | 0 | <0.01 |
| Ute (0) | 0 | <0.01 |
| Yakama (0) | 0 | <0.01 |
| Yaqui (0) | 0 | <0.01 |
| Yuman (0) | 0 | <0.01 |
| Yup'ik (Alaska Native) (0) | 0 | <0.01 |
| Asian (8,800) | 9,614 | 11.42 |
| Not Hispanic (8,748) | 9,462 | 11.24 |
| Hispanic (52) | 152 | 0.18 |
| Bangladeshi (73) | 85 | 0.10 |
| Bhutanese (0) | 0 | <0.01 |
| Burmese (4) | 8 | 0.01 |
| Cambodian (59) | 68 | 0.08 |
| Chinese, ex. Taiwanese (1,132) | 1,326 | 1.58 |
| Filipino (2,079) | 2,320 | 2.76 |
| Hmong (0) | 0 | <0.01 |
| Indian (3,576) | 3,874 | 4.60 |
| Indonesian (5) | 14 | 0.02 |
| Japanese (73) | 110 | 0.13 |
| Korean (994) | 1,026 | 1.22 |
| Laotian (0) | 0 | <0.01 |
| Malaysian (3) | 6 | 0.01 |
| Nepalese (2) | 2 | <0.01 |
| Pakistani (322) | 346 | 0.41 |
| Sri Lankan (43) | 55 | 0.07 |
| Taiwanese (49) | 58 | 0.07 |
| Thai (109) | 121 | 0.14 |
| Vietnamese (129) | 164 | 0.19 |
| Hawaii Native/Pacific Islander (22) | 106 | 0.13 |
| Not Hispanic (5) | 77 | 0.09 |
| Hispanic (17) | 29 | 0.03 |
| Fijian (0) | 0 | <0.01 |
| Guamanian/Chamorro (13) | 21 | 0.02 |
| Marshallese (0) | 0 | <0.01 |
| Native Hawaiian (1) | 5 | 0.01 |
| Samoan (1) | 2 | <0.01 |
| Tongan (0) | 0 | <0.01 |
| White (62,210) | 63,664 | 75.62 |
| Not Hispanic (56,369) | 57,290 | 68.05 |
| Hispanic (5,841) | 6,374 | 7.57 |

Notes: † The Census 2010 population figure is used to calculate the percentages in the Hispanic Origin and Race categories. Ancestry percentages are based on the 2006-2010 American Community Survey population (not shown); ‡ Numbers in parentheses indicate the number of people reporting a single ancestry; * Numbers in parentheses indicate the number of persons reporting this race alone, not in combination with any other race; Please refer to the Explanation of Data for more information.

## Clay

Place Type: Town
County: Onondaga
Population: 58,206

| Ancestry | Population | % |
|---|---|---|
| Afghan (0) | 0 | <0.01 |
| African, Sub-Saharan (172) | 216 | 0.37 |
| African (107) | 145 | 0.25 |
| Cape Verdean (0) | 6 | 0.01 |
| Ethiopian (0) | 0 | <0.01 |
| Ghanaian (65) | 65 | 0.11 |
| Kenyan (0) | 0 | <0.01 |
| Liberian (0) | 0 | <0.01 |
| Nigerian (0) | 0 | <0.01 |
| Senegalese (0) | 0 | <0.01 |
| Sierra Leonean (0) | 0 | <0.01 |
| Somalian (0) | 0 | <0.01 |
| South African (0) | 0 | <0.01 |
| Sudanese (0) | 0 | <0.01 |
| Ugandan (0) | 0 | <0.01 |
| Zimbabwean (0) | 0 | <0.01 |
| Other Sub-Saharan African (0) | 0 | <0.01 |
| Albanian (10) | 31 | 0.05 |
| Alsatian (0) | 0 | <0.01 |
| American (1,975) | 1,975 | 3.40 |
| Arab (153) | 417 | 0.72 |
| Arab (58) | 136 | 0.23 |
| Egyptian (7) | 7 | 0.01 |
| Iraqi (0) | 0 | <0.01 |
| Jordanian (0) | 0 | <0.01 |
| Lebanese (47) | 213 | 0.37 |
| Moroccan (0) | 0 | <0.01 |
| Palestinian (0) | 13 | 0.02 |
| Syrian (0) | 7 | 0.01 |
| Other Arab (41) | 41 | 0.07 |
| Armenian (0) | 0 | <0.01 |
| Assyrian/Chaldean/Syriac (0) | 0 | <0.01 |
| Australian (0) | 0 | <0.01 |
| Austrian (49) | 113 | 0.19 |
| Basque (0) | 0 | <0.01 |
| Belgian (57) | 68 | 0.12 |
| Brazilian (43) | 43 | 0.07 |
| British (33) | 118 | 0.20 |
| Bulgarian (0) | 0 | <0.01 |
| Cajun (0) | 0 | <0.01 |
| Canadian (176) | 345 | 0.59 |
| Carpatho Rusyn (0) | 0 | <0.01 |
| Celtic (0) | 47 | 0.08 |
| Croatian (0) | 0 | <0.01 |
| Cypriot (0) | 0 | <0.01 |
| Czech (35) | 312 | 0.54 |
| Czechoslovakian (0) | 34 | 0.06 |
| Danish (0) | 68 | 0.12 |
| Dutch (106) | 1,704 | 2.93 |
| Eastern European (25) | 40 | 0.07 |
| English (1,748) | 8,266 | 14.23 |
| Estonian (0) | 0 | <0.01 |
| European (505) | 550 | 0.95 |
| Finnish (20) | 55 | 0.09 |
| French, ex. Basque (420) | 3,175 | 5.47 |
| French Canadian (432) | 1,241 | 2.14 |
| German (2,624) | 14,237 | 24.51 |
| German Russian (0) | 0 | <0.01 |
| Greek (203) | 475 | 0.82 |
| Guyanese (17) | 17 | 0.03 |
| Hungarian (170) | 353 | 0.61 |
| Icelander (0) | 0 | <0.01 |
| Iranian (78) | 99 | 0.17 |
| Irish (3,324) | 14,197 | 24.44 |
| Israeli (0) | 0 | <0.01 |
| Italian (5,434) | 13,235 | 22.78 |
| Latvian (0) | 0 | <0.01 |
| Lithuanian (78) | 143 | 0.25 |
| Luxemburger (0) | 26 | 0.04 |
| Macedonian (177) | 185 | 0.32 |
| Maltese (0) | 0 | <0.01 |
| New Zealander (0) | 0 | <0.01 |
| Northern European (35) | 35 | 0.06 |

| Ancestry | Population | % |
|---|---|---|
| Norwegian (55) | 221 | 0.38 |
| Pennsylvania German (20) | 38 | 0.07 |
| Polish (1,694) | 4,728 | 8.14 |
| Portuguese (0) | 37 | 0.06 |
| Romanian (0) | 29 | 0.05 |
| Russian (60) | 276 | 0.48 |
| Scandinavian (8) | 8 | 0.01 |
| Scotch-Irish (380) | 1,162 | 2.00 |
| Scottish (302) | 1,377 | 2.37 |
| Serbian (0) | 9 | 0.02 |
| Slavic (8) | 93 | 0.16 |
| Slovak (78) | 150 | 0.26 |
| Slovene (0) | 9 | 0.02 |
| Soviet Union (0) | 0 | <0.01 |
| Swedish (114) | 625 | 1.08 |
| Swiss (22) | 175 | 0.30 |
| Turkish (11) | 11 | 0.02 |
| Ukrainian (136) | 650 | 1.12 |
| Welsh (52) | 496 | 0.85 |
| West Indian, ex. Hispanic (380) | 494 | 0.85 |
| Bahamian (0) | 0 | <0.01 |
| Barbadian (9) | 40 | 0.07 |
| Belizean (0) | 0 | <0.01 |
| Bermudan (0) | 0 | <0.01 |
| British West Indian (0) | 0 | <0.01 |
| Dutch West Indian (0) | 0 | <0.01 |
| Haitian (157) | 157 | 0.27 |
| Jamaican (162) | 245 | 0.42 |
| Trinidadian/Tobagonian (40) | 40 | 0.07 |
| U.S. Virgin Islander (0) | 0 | <0.01 |
| West Indian (12) | 12 | 0.02 |
| Other West Indian (0) | 0 | <0.01 |
| Yugoslavian (108) | 132 | 0.23 |

| Hispanic Origin | Population | % |
|---|---|---|
| Hispanic or Latino (of any race) | 1,472 | 2.53 |
| Central American, ex. Mexican | 94 | 0.16 |
| Costa Rican | 3 | 0.01 |
| Guatemalan | 35 | 0.06 |
| Honduran | 16 | 0.03 |
| Nicaraguan | 12 | 0.02 |
| Panamanian | 21 | 0.04 |
| Salvadoran | 7 | 0.01 |
| Other Central American | 0 | <0.01 |
| Cuban | 91 | 0.16 |
| Dominican Republic | 61 | 0.10 |
| Mexican | 283 | 0.49 |
| Puerto Rican | 633 | 1.09 |
| South American | 161 | 0.28 |
| Argentinean | 7 | 0.01 |
| Bolivian | 8 | 0.01 |
| Chilean | 16 | 0.03 |
| Colombian | 65 | 0.11 |
| Ecuadorian | 10 | 0.02 |
| Paraguayan | 6 | 0.01 |
| Peruvian | 29 | 0.05 |
| Uruguayan | 2 | <0.01 |
| Venezuelan | 16 | 0.03 |
| Other South American | 2 | <0.01 |
| Other Hispanic or Latino | 149 | 0.26 |

| Race* | Population | % |
|---|---|---|
| African-American/Black (2,524) | 3,202 | 5.50 |
| Not Hispanic (2,398) | 3,014 | 5.18 |
| Hispanic (126) | 188 | 0.32 |
| American Indian/Alaska Native (266) | 627 | 1.08 |
| Not Hispanic (228) | 557 | 0.96 |
| Hispanic (38) | 70 | 0.12 |
| Alaska Athabascan (Ala. Nat.) (0) | 0 | <0.01 |
| Aleut (Alaska Native) (0) | 0 | <0.01 |
| Apache (1) | 3 | 0.01 |
| Arapaho (0) | 0 | <0.01 |
| Blackfeet (0) | 11 | 0.02 |
| Canadian/French Am. Ind. (9) | 16 | 0.03 |
| Central American Ind. (0) | 0 | <0.01 |
| Cherokee (8) | 42 | 0.07 |
| Cheyenne (0) | 0 | <0.01 |
| Chickasaw (0) | 0 | <0.01 |
| Chippewa (5) | 11 | 0.02 |

| Race* | Population | % |
|---|---|---|
| Choctaw (1) | 5 | 0.01 |
| Colville (0) | 0 | <0.01 |
| Comanche (1) | 1 | <0.01 |
| Cree (1) | 1 | <0.01 |
| Creek (0) | 1 | <0.01 |
| Crow (0) | 0 | <0.01 |
| Delaware (0) | 1 | <0.01 |
| Hopi (0) | 2 | <0.01 |
| Houma (1) | 1 | <0.01 |
| Inupiat (Alaska Native) (0) | 1 | <0.01 |
| Iroquois (130) | 252 | 0.43 |
| Kiowa (0) | 0 | <0.01 |
| Lumbee (0) | 3 | 0.01 |
| Menominee (0) | 0 | <0.01 |
| Mexican American Ind. (5) | 9 | 0.02 |
| Navajo (3) | 4 | 0.01 |
| Osage (1) | 1 | <0.01 |
| Ottawa (1) | 1 | <0.01 |
| Paiute (0) | 0 | <0.01 |
| Pima (0) | 0 | <0.01 |
| Potawatomi (0) | 1 | <0.01 |
| Pueblo (0) | 0 | <0.01 |
| Puget Sound Salish (0) | 0 | <0.01 |
| Seminole (0) | 3 | 0.01 |
| Shoshone (0) | 0 | <0.01 |
| Sioux (2) | 4 | 0.01 |
| South American Ind. (1) | 4 | 0.01 |
| Spanish American Ind. (8) | 8 | 0.01 |
| Tlingit-Haida (Alaska Native) (0) | 0 | <0.01 |
| Tohono O'Odham (0) | 0 | <0.01 |
| Tsimshian (Alaska Native) (0) | 0 | <0.01 |
| Ute (0) | 0 | <0.01 |
| Yakama (0) | 0 | <0.01 |
| Yaqui (0) | 0 | <0.01 |
| Yuman (0) | 0 | <0.01 |
| Yup'ik (Alaska Native) (0) | 0 | <0.01 |
| Asian (1,430) | 1,754 | 3.01 |
| Not Hispanic (1,426) | 1,733 | 2.98 |
| Hispanic (4) | 21 | 0.04 |
| Bangladeshi (0) | 1 | <0.01 |
| Bhutanese (0) | 0 | <0.01 |
| Burmese (5) | 5 | 0.01 |
| Cambodian (28) | 29 | 0.05 |
| Chinese, ex. Taiwanese (259) | 299 | 0.51 |
| Filipino (123) | 192 | 0.33 |
| Hmong (61) | 75 | 0.13 |
| Indian (367) | 398 | 0.68 |
| Indonesian (1) | 2 | <0.01 |
| Japanese (21) | 66 | 0.11 |
| Korean (130) | 190 | 0.33 |
| Laotian (47) | 52 | 0.09 |
| Malaysian (0) | 1 | <0.01 |
| Nepalese (4) | 4 | 0.01 |
| Pakistani (47) | 52 | 0.09 |
| Sri Lankan (2) | 2 | <0.01 |
| Taiwanese (11) | 12 | 0.02 |
| Thai (14) | 18 | 0.03 |
| Vietnamese (246) | 265 | 0.46 |
| Hawaii Native/Pacific Islander (20) | 44 | 0.08 |
| Not Hispanic (17) | 40 | 0.07 |
| Hispanic (3) | 4 | 0.01 |
| Fijian (0) | 0 | <0.01 |
| Guamanian/Chamorro (6) | 7 | 0.01 |
| Marshallese (0) | 0 | <0.01 |
| Native Hawaiian (7) | 18 | 0.03 |
| Samoan (0) | 1 | <0.01 |
| Tongan (0) | 0 | <0.01 |
| White (52,324) | 53,514 | 91.94 |
| Not Hispanic (51,459) | 52,515 | 90.22 |
| Hispanic (865) | 999 | 1.72 |

Notes: † The Census 2010 population figure is used to calculate the percentages in the Hispanic Origin and Race categories. Ancestry percentages are based on the 2006-2010 American Community Survey population (not shown); ‡ Numbers in parentheses indicate the number of people reporting a single ancestry; * Numbers in parentheses indicate the number of persons reporting this race alone, not in combination with any other race; Please refer to the Explanation of Data for more information.

## Colonie

Place Type: Town
County: Albany
Population: 81,591

| Ancestry | Population | % |
|---|---|---|
| Afghan (0) | 0 | <0.01 |
| African, Sub-Saharan (408) | 482 | 0.59 |
| African (259) | 310 | 0.38 |
| Cape Verdean (0) | 0 | <0.01 |
| Ethiopian (13) | 13 | 0.02 |
| Ghanaian (11) | 11 | 0.01 |
| Kenyan (0) | 0 | <0.01 |
| Liberian (0) | 0 | <0.01 |
| Nigerian (80) | 80 | 0.10 |
| Senegalese (0) | 0 | <0.01 |
| Sierra Leonean (0) | 0 | <0.01 |
| Somalian (0) | 0 | <0.01 |
| South African (9) | 32 | 0.04 |
| Sudanese (0) | 0 | <0.01 |
| Ugandan (0) | 0 | <0.01 |
| Zimbabwean (0) | 0 | <0.01 |
| Other Sub-Saharan African (36) | 36 | 0.04 |
| Albanian (405) | 405 | 0.50 |
| Alsatian (0) | 0 | <0.01 |
| American (2,133) | 2,133 | 2.62 |
| Arab (561) | 863 | 1.06 |
| Arab (0) | 17 | 0.02 |
| Egyptian (125) | 125 | 0.15 |
| Iraqi (0) | 0 | <0.01 |
| Jordanian (0) | 0 | <0.01 |
| Lebanese (144) | 267 | 0.33 |
| Moroccan (64) | 111 | 0.14 |
| Palestinian (72) | 72 | 0.09 |
| Syrian (27) | 116 | 0.14 |
| Other Arab (129) | 155 | 0.19 |
| Armenian (142) | 244 | 0.30 |
| Assyrian/Chaldean/Syriac (0) | 0 | <0.01 |
| Australian (10) | 10 | 0.01 |
| Austrian (112) | 470 | 0.58 |
| Basque (0) | 0 | <0.01 |
| Belgian (0) | 25 | 0.03 |
| Brazilian (13) | 13 | 0.02 |
| British (140) | 240 | 0.29 |
| Bulgarian (9) | 9 | 0.01 |
| Cajun (0) | 0 | <0.01 |
| Canadian (114) | 321 | 0.39 |
| Carpatho Rusyn (0) | 0 | <0.01 |
| Celtic (11) | 11 | 0.01 |
| Croatian (16) | 74 | 0.09 |
| Cypriot (0) | 0 | <0.01 |
| Czech (134) | 453 | 0.56 |
| Czechoslovakian (26) | 124 | 0.15 |
| Danish (35) | 195 | 0.24 |
| Dutch (627) | 3,334 | 4.09 |
| Eastern European (46) | 83 | 0.10 |
| English (1,400) | 8,332 | 10.22 |
| Estonian (0) | 0 | <0.01 |
| European (492) | 544 | 0.67 |
| Finnish (6) | 68 | 0.08 |
| French, ex. Basque (786) | 5,795 | 7.11 |
| French Canadian (545) | 1,591 | 1.95 |
| German (2,908) | 14,495 | 17.78 |
| German Russian (0) | 0 | <0.01 |
| Greek (238) | 563 | 0.69 |
| Guyanese (116) | 137 | 0.17 |
| Hungarian (124) | 542 | 0.66 |
| Icelander (0) | 0 | <0.01 |
| Iranian (0) | 9 | 0.01 |
| Irish (6,490) | 23,049 | 28.27 |
| Israeli (42) | 42 | 0.05 |
| Italian (6,582) | 16,393 | 20.11 |
| Latvian (34) | 34 | 0.04 |
| Lithuanian (55) | 377 | 0.46 |
| Luxemburger (0) | 13 | 0.02 |
| Macedonian (0) | 0 | <0.01 |
| Maltese (0) | 0 | <0.01 |
| New Zealander (0) | 0 | <0.01 |
| Northern European (39) | 39 | 0.05 |

| Ancestry | Population | % |
|---|---|---|
| Norwegian (159) | 598 | 0.73 |
| Pennsylvania German (17) | 25 | 0.03 |
| Polish (2,206) | 6,915 | 8.48 |
| Portuguese (0) | 80 | 0.10 |
| Romanian (55) | 228 | 0.28 |
| Russian (690) | 1,626 | 1.99 |
| Scandinavian (27) | 39 | 0.05 |
| Scotch-Irish (468) | 1,261 | 1.55 |
| Scottish (263) | 1,526 | 1.87 |
| Serbian (0) | 0 | <0.01 |
| Slavic (18) | 28 | 0.03 |
| Slovak (72) | 185 | 0.23 |
| Slovene (0) | 0 | <0.01 |
| Soviet Union (0) | 0 | <0.01 |
| Swedish (217) | 944 | 1.16 |
| Swiss (17) | 145 | 0.18 |
| Turkish (10) | 10 | 0.01 |
| Ukrainian (212) | 860 | 1.05 |
| Welsh (41) | 704 | 0.86 |
| West Indian, ex. Hispanic (372) | 580 | 0.71 |
| Bahamian (0) | 0 | <0.01 |
| Barbadian (0) | 0 | <0.01 |
| Belizean (0) | 0 | <0.01 |
| Bermudan (0) | 0 | <0.01 |
| British West Indian (0) | 0 | <0.01 |
| Dutch West Indian (0) | 0 | <0.01 |
| Haitian (60) | 83 | 0.10 |
| Jamaican (235) | 373 | 0.46 |
| Trinidadian/Tobagonian (0) | 4 | <0.01 |
| U.S. Virgin Islander (0) | 0 | <0.01 |
| West Indian (77) | 120 | 0.15 |
| Other West Indian (0) | 0 | <0.01 |
| Yugoslavian (143) | 143 | 0.18 |

| Hispanic Origin | Population | % |
|---|---|---|
| Hispanic or Latino (of any race) | 2,526 | 3.10 |
| Central American, ex. Mexican | 159 | 0.19 |
| Costa Rican | 24 | 0.03 |
| Guatemalan | 25 | 0.03 |
| Honduran | 20 | 0.02 |
| Nicaraguan | 17 | 0.02 |
| Panamanian | 13 | 0.02 |
| Salvadoran | 59 | 0.07 |
| Other Central American | 1 | <0.01 |
| Cuban | 114 | 0.14 |
| Dominican Republic | 224 | 0.27 |
| Mexican | 462 | 0.57 |
| Puerto Rican | 1,001 | 1.23 |
| South American | 278 | 0.34 |
| Argentinean | 26 | 0.03 |
| Bolivian | 9 | 0.01 |
| Chilean | 12 | 0.01 |
| Colombian | 94 | 0.12 |
| Ecuadorian | 35 | 0.04 |
| Paraguayan | 3 | <0.01 |
| Peruvian | 76 | 0.09 |
| Uruguayan | 1 | <0.01 |
| Venezuelan | 19 | 0.02 |
| Other South American | 3 | <0.01 |
| Other Hispanic or Latino | 288 | 0.35 |

| Race* | Population | % |
|---|---|---|
| African-American/Black (4,288) | 5,091 | 6.24 |
| Not Hispanic (4,061) | 4,752 | 5.82 |
| Hispanic (227) | 339 | 0.42 |
| American Indian/Alaska Native (121) | 397 | 0.49 |
| Not Hispanic (79) | 318 | 0.39 |
| Hispanic (42) | 79 | 0.10 |
| Alaska Athabascan (Ala. Nat.) (1) | 1 | <0.01 |
| Aleut (Alaska Native) (0) | 0 | <0.01 |
| Apache (0) | 0 | <0.01 |
| Arapaho (0) | 0 | <0.01 |
| Blackfeet (1) | 11 | 0.01 |
| Canadian/French Am. Ind. (6) | 10 | 0.01 |
| Central American Ind. (3) | 3 | <0.01 |
| Cherokee (6) | 32 | 0.04 |
| Cheyenne (0) | 0 | <0.01 |
| Chickasaw (0) | 0 | <0.01 |
| Chippewa (0) | 1 | <0.01 |

| Race* | Population | % |
|---|---|---|
| Choctaw (0) | 1 | <0.01 |
| Colville (0) | 0 | <0.01 |
| Comanche (0) | 0 | <0.01 |
| Cree (0) | 2 | <0.01 |
| Creek (0) | 0 | <0.01 |
| Crow (1) | 1 | <0.01 |
| Delaware (0) | 0 | <0.01 |
| Hopi (0) | 0 | <0.01 |
| Houma (0) | 0 | <0.01 |
| Inupiat (Alaska Native) (0) | 0 | <0.01 |
| Iroquois (15) | 50 | 0.06 |
| Kiowa (0) | 0 | <0.01 |
| Lumbee (0) | 0 | <0.01 |
| Menominee (0) | 0 | <0.01 |
| Mexican American Ind. (28) | 29 | 0.04 |
| Navajo (0) | 1 | <0.01 |
| Osage (0) | 1 | <0.01 |
| Ottawa (0) | 0 | <0.01 |
| Paiute (0) | 0 | <0.01 |
| Pima (0) | 0 | <0.01 |
| Potawatomi (0) | 1 | <0.01 |
| Pueblo (0) | 0 | <0.01 |
| Puget Sound Salish (0) | 0 | <0.01 |
| Seminole (0) | 3 | <0.01 |
| Shoshone (0) | 0 | <0.01 |
| Sioux (3) | 7 | 0.01 |
| South American Ind. (5) | 10 | 0.01 |
| Spanish American Ind. (0) | 2 | <0.01 |
| Tlingit-Haida (Alaska Native) (1) | 1 | <0.01 |
| Tohono O'Odham (0) | 0 | <0.01 |
| Tsimshian (Alaska Native) (0) | 0 | <0.01 |
| Ute (0) | 0 | <0.01 |
| Yakama (0) | 0 | <0.01 |
| Yaqui (0) | 0 | <0.01 |
| Yuman (0) | 0 | <0.01 |
| Yup'ik (Alaska Native) (0) | 0 | <0.01 |
| Asian (5,353) | 5,892 | 7.22 |
| Not Hispanic (5,342) | 5,866 | 7.19 |
| Hispanic (11) | 26 | 0.03 |
| Bangladeshi (78) | 80 | 0.10 |
| Bhutanese (0) | 0 | <0.01 |
| Burmese (3) | 4 | <0.01 |
| Cambodian (2) | 3 | <0.01 |
| Chinese, ex. Taiwanese (1,186) | 1,284 | 1.57 |
| Filipino (306) | 397 | 0.49 |
| Hmong (0) | 0 | <0.01 |
| Indian (1,969) | 2,099 | 2.57 |
| Indonesian (11) | 13 | 0.02 |
| Japanese (58) | 90 | 0.11 |
| Korean (471) | 531 | 0.65 |
| Laotian (2) | 4 | <0.01 |
| Malaysian (3) | 5 | 0.01 |
| Nepalese (13) | 13 | 0.02 |
| Pakistani (680) | 736 | 0.90 |
| Sri Lankan (24) | 30 | 0.04 |
| Taiwanese (48) | 60 | 0.07 |
| Thai (30) | 40 | 0.05 |
| Vietnamese (313) | 360 | 0.44 |
| Hawaii Native/Pacific Islander (15) | 66 | 0.08 |
| Not Hispanic (14) | 47 | 0.06 |
| Hispanic (1) | 19 | 0.02 |
| Fijian (1) | 1 | <0.01 |
| Guamanian/Chamorro (2) | 6 | 0.01 |
| Marshallese (0) | 0 | <0.01 |
| Native Hawaiian (2) | 10 | 0.01 |
| Samoan (4) | 9 | 0.01 |
| Tongan (1) | 5 | 0.01 |
| White (69,541) | 70,917 | 86.92 |
| Not Hispanic (68,088) | 69,290 | 84.92 |
| Hispanic (1,453) | 1,627 | 1.99 |

*Notes: † The Census 2010 population figure is used to calculate the percentages in the Hispanic Origin and Race categories. Ancestry percentages are based on the 2006-2010 American Community Survey population (not shown); ‡ Numbers in parentheses indicate the number of people reporting a single ancestry; \* Numbers in parentheses indicate the number of persons reporting this race alone, not in combination with any other race; Please refer to the Explanation of Data for more information.*

## Greece

Place Type: Town
County: Monroe
Population: 96,095

| Ancestry | Population | % |
|---|---|---|
| Afghan (0) | 0 | <0.01 |
| African, Sub-Saharan (373) | 434 | 0.45 |
| African (217) | 244 | 0.26 |
| Cape Verdean (0) | 0 | <0.01 |
| Ethiopian (49) | 49 | 0.05 |
| Ghanaian (0) | 0 | <0.01 |
| Kenyan (0) | 0 | <0.01 |
| Liberian (0) | 0 | <0.01 |
| Nigerian (0) | 0 | <0.01 |
| Senegalese (0) | 0 | <0.01 |
| Sierra Leonean (0) | 0 | <0.01 |
| Somalian (0) | 0 | <0.01 |
| South African (38) | 48 | 0.05 |
| Sudanese (27) | 51 | 0.05 |
| Ugandan (0) | 0 | <0.01 |
| Zimbabwean (0) | 0 | <0.01 |
| Other Sub-Saharan African (42) | 42 | 0.04 |
| Albanian (113) | 113 | 0.12 |
| Alsatian (0) | 0 | <0.01 |
| American (2,361) | 2,361 | 2.47 |
| Arab (161) | 384 | 0.40 |
| Arab (0) | 42 | 0.04 |
| Egyptian (0) | 0 | <0.01 |
| Iraqi (0) | 0 | <0.01 |
| Jordanian (0) | 0 | <0.01 |
| Lebanese (98) | 214 | 0.22 |
| Moroccan (0) | 0 | <0.01 |
| Palestinian (0) | 31 | 0.03 |
| Syrian (63) | 97 | 0.10 |
| Other Arab (0) | 0 | <0.01 |
| Armenian (0) | 0 | <0.01 |
| Assyrian/Chaldean/Syriac (0) | 0 | <0.01 |
| Australian (29) | 87 | 0.09 |
| Austrian (36) | 225 | 0.24 |
| Basque (0) | 0 | <0.01 |
| Belgian (57) | 254 | 0.27 |
| Brazilian (23) | 23 | 0.02 |
| British (178) | 387 | 0.41 |
| Bulgarian (25) | 25 | 0.03 |
| Cajun (0) | 0 | <0.01 |
| Canadian (228) | 525 | 0.55 |
| Carpatho Rusyn (0) | 0 | <0.01 |
| Celtic (12) | 12 | 0.01 |
| Croatian (0) | 13 | 0.01 |
| Cypriot (0) | 0 | <0.01 |
| Czech (77) | 507 | 0.53 |
| Czechoslovakian (55) | 151 | 0.16 |
| Danish (40) | 144 | 0.15 |
| Dutch (571) | 2,890 | 3.03 |
| Eastern European (81) | 115 | 0.12 |
| English (3,011) | 12,568 | 13.17 |
| Estonian (0) | 40 | 0.04 |
| European (406) | 451 | 0.47 |
| Finnish (15) | 62 | 0.06 |
| French, ex. Basque (553) | 3,655 | 3.83 |
| French Canadian (346) | 1,220 | 1.28 |
| German (6,357) | 25,631 | 26.85 |
| German Russian (0) | 0 | <0.01 |
| Greek (153) | 610 | 0.64 |
| Guyanese (40) | 40 | 0.04 |
| Hungarian (85) | 397 | 0.42 |
| Icelander (0) | 0 | <0.01 |
| Iranian (14) | 14 | 0.01 |
| Irish (4,177) | 19,015 | 19.92 |
| Israeli (0) | 0 | <0.01 |
| Italian (15,156) | 26,121 | 27.36 |
| Latvian (12) | 71 | 0.07 |
| Lithuanian (183) | 543 | 0.57 |
| Luxemburger (0) | 15 | 0.02 |
| Macedonian (92) | 119 | 0.12 |
| Maltese (0) | 0 | <0.01 |
| New Zealander (0) | 0 | <0.01 |
| Northern European (0) | 0 | <0.01 |
| Norwegian (139) | 434 | 0.45 |
| Pennsylvania German (46) | 145 | 0.15 |
| Polish (1,797) | 5,879 | 6.16 |
| Portuguese (111) | 314 | 0.33 |
| Romanian (16) | 60 | 0.06 |
| Russian (229) | 654 | 0.69 |
| Scandinavian (10) | 88 | 0.09 |
| Scotch-Irish (524) | 1,469 | 1.54 |
| Scottish (452) | 1,843 | 1.93 |
| Serbian (10) | 10 | 0.01 |
| Slavic (156) | 240 | 0.25 |
| Slovak (81) | 236 | 0.25 |
| Slovene (31) | 31 | 0.03 |
| Soviet Union (0) | 0 | <0.01 |
| Swedish (31) | 447 | 0.47 |
| Swiss (16) | 116 | 0.12 |
| Turkish (489) | 561 | 0.59 |
| Ukrainian (993) | 1,758 | 1.84 |
| Welsh (36) | 564 | 0.59 |
| West Indian, ex. Hispanic (285) | 447 | 0.47 |
| Bahamian (0) | 0 | <0.01 |
| Barbadian (16) | 16 | 0.02 |
| Belizean (0) | 0 | <0.01 |
| Bermudan (0) | 0 | <0.01 |
| British West Indian (0) | 0 | <0.01 |
| Dutch West Indian (0) | 0 | <0.01 |
| Haitian (114) | 114 | 0.12 |
| Jamaican (144) | 243 | 0.25 |
| Trinidadian/Tobagonian (11) | 27 | 0.03 |
| U.S. Virgin Islander (0) | 0 | <0.01 |
| West Indian (0) | 47 | 0.05 |
| Other West Indian (0) | 0 | <0.01 |
| Yugoslavian (77) | 91 | 0.10 |

| Hispanic Origin | Population | % |
|---|---|---|
| Hispanic or Latino (of any race) | 4,625 | 4.81 |
| Central American, ex. Mexican | 159 | 0.17 |
| Costa Rican | 11 | 0.01 |
| Guatemalan | 27 | 0.03 |
| Honduran | 12 | 0.01 |
| Nicaraguan | 22 | 0.02 |
| Panamanian | 18 | 0.02 |
| Salvadoran | 68 | 0.07 |
| Other Central American | 1 | <0.01 |
| Cuban | 312 | 0.32 |
| Dominican Republic | 194 | 0.20 |
| Mexican | 338 | 0.35 |
| Puerto Rican | 3,072 | 3.20 |
| South American | 257 | 0.27 |
| Argentinean | 7 | 0.01 |
| Bolivian | 1 | <0.01 |
| Chilean | 63 | 0.07 |
| Colombian | 89 | 0.09 |
| Ecuadorian | 21 | 0.02 |
| Paraguayan | 4 | <0.01 |
| Peruvian | 33 | 0.03 |
| Uruguayan | 4 | <0.01 |
| Venezuelan | 27 | 0.03 |
| Other South American | 8 | 0.01 |
| Other Hispanic or Latino | 293 | 0.30 |

| Race* | Population | % |
|---|---|---|
| African-American/Black (5,743) | 6,728 | 7.00 |
| Not Hispanic (5,446) | 6,227 | 6.48 |
| Hispanic (297) | 501 | 0.52 |
| American Indian/Alaska Native (263) | 658 | 0.68 |
| Not Hispanic (212) | 545 | 0.57 |
| Hispanic (51) | 113 | 0.12 |
| Alaska Athabascan (Ala. Nat.) (0) | 0 | <0.01 |
| Aleut (Alaska Native) (0) | 0 | <0.01 |
| Apache (1) | 3 | <0.01 |
| Arapaho (0) | 4 | <0.01 |
| Blackfeet (1) | 9 | 0.01 |
| Canadian/French Am. Ind. (8) | 14 | 0.01 |
| Central American Ind. (5) | 6 | 0.01 |
| Cherokee (7) | 75 | 0.08 |
| Cheyenne (0) | 0 | <0.01 |
| Chickasaw (0) | 0 | <0.01 |
| Chippewa (10) | 13 | 0.01 |

| | Population | % |
|---|---|---|
| Choctaw (3) | 8 | 0.01 |
| Colville (0) | 0 | <0.01 |
| Comanche (0) | 1 | <0.01 |
| Cree (3) | 4 | <0.01 |
| Creek (2) | 2 | <0.01 |
| Crow (0) | 0 | <0.01 |
| Delaware (0) | 1 | <0.01 |
| Hopi (0) | 0 | <0.01 |
| Houma (2) | 2 | <0.01 |
| Inupiat (Alaska Native) (0) | 1 | <0.01 |
| Iroquois (114) | 181 | 0.19 |
| Kiowa (0) | 0 | <0.01 |
| Lumbee (0) | 0 | <0.01 |
| Menominee (0) | 0 | <0.01 |
| Mexican American Ind. (4) | 7 | 0.01 |
| Navajo (2) | 2 | <0.01 |
| Osage (0) | 0 | <0.01 |
| Ottawa (0) | 0 | <0.01 |
| Paiute (0) | 0 | <0.01 |
| Pima (0) | 0 | <0.01 |
| Potawatomi (0) | 0 | <0.01 |
| Pueblo (0) | 0 | <0.01 |
| Puget Sound Salish (0) | 0 | <0.01 |
| Seminole (1) | 4 | <0.01 |
| Shoshone (0) | 1 | <0.01 |
| Sioux (3) | 11 | 0.01 |
| South American Ind. (7) | 16 | 0.02 |
| Spanish American Ind. (1) | 5 | 0.01 |
| Tlingit-Haida (Alaska Native) (0) | 1 | <0.01 |
| Tohono O'Odham (0) | 0 | <0.01 |
| Tsimshian (Alaska Native) (0) | 0 | <0.01 |
| Ute (0) | 0 | <0.01 |
| Yakama (0) | 0 | <0.01 |
| Yaqui (0) | 0 | <0.01 |
| Yuman (1) | 1 | <0.01 |
| Yup'ik (Alaska Native) (0) | 0 | <0.01 |
| Asian (1,664) | 2,054 | 2.14 |
| Not Hispanic (1,643) | 2,014 | 2.10 |
| Hispanic (21) | 40 | 0.04 |
| Bangladeshi (6) | 9 | 0.01 |
| Bhutanese (0) | 0 | <0.01 |
| Burmese (0) | 0 | <0.01 |
| Cambodian (33) | 47 | 0.05 |
| Chinese, ex. Taiwanese (294) | 351 | 0.37 |
| Filipino (141) | 213 | 0.22 |
| Hmong (0) | 0 | <0.01 |
| Indian (283) | 330 | 0.34 |
| Indonesian (3) | 5 | 0.01 |
| Japanese (28) | 71 | 0.07 |
| Korean (209) | 261 | 0.27 |
| Laotian (112) | 139 | 0.14 |
| Malaysian (0) | 0 | <0.01 |
| Nepalese (3) | 3 | <0.01 |
| Pakistani (25) | 32 | 0.03 |
| Sri Lankan (5) | 5 | 0.01 |
| Taiwanese (10) | 11 | <0.01 |
| Thai (21) | 24 | 0.02 |
| Vietnamese (433) | 473 | 0.49 |
| Hawaii Native/Pacific Islander (14) | 59 | 0.06 |
| Not Hispanic (12) | 40 | 0.04 |
| Hispanic (2) | 19 | 0.02 |
| Fijian (0) | 0 | <0.01 |
| Guamanian/Chamorro (4) | 7 | 0.01 |
| Marshallese (0) | 0 | <0.01 |
| Native Hawaiian (5) | 18 | 0.02 |
| Samoan (2) | 5 | 0.01 |
| Tongan (0) | 0 | <0.01 |
| White (85,220) | 86,829 | 90.36 |
| Not Hispanic (82,634) | 83,902 | 87.31 |
| Hispanic (2,586) | 2,927 | 3.05 |

Notes: † The Census 2010 population figure is used to calculate the percentages in the Hispanic Origin and Race categories. Ancestry percentages are based on the 2006-2010 American Community Survey population (not shown); ‡ Numbers in parentheses indicate the number of people reporting a single ancestry; * Numbers in parentheses indicate the number of persons reporting this race alone, not in combination with any other race; Please refer to the Explanation of Data for more information.

## Greenburgh

Place Type: Town
County: Westchester
Population: 88,400

| Ancestry | Population | % |
|---|---|---|
| Afghan (0) | 0 | <0.01 |
| African, Sub-Saharan (642) | 914 | 1.04 |
| African (287) | 536 | 0.61 |
| Cape Verdean (0) | 0 | <0.01 |
| Ethiopian (39) | 39 | 0.04 |
| Ghanaian (16) | 16 | 0.02 |
| Kenyan (55) | 55 | 0.06 |
| Liberian (0) | 0 | <0.01 |
| Nigerian (231) | 231 | 0.26 |
| Senegalese (0) | 0 | <0.01 |
| Sierra Leonean (14) | 14 | 0.02 |
| Somalian (0) | 0 | <0.01 |
| South African (0) | 23 | 0.03 |
| Sudanese (0) | 0 | <0.01 |
| Ugandan (0) | 0 | <0.01 |
| Zimbabwean (0) | 0 | <0.01 |
| Other Sub-Saharan African (0) | 0 | <0.01 |
| Albanian (80) | 80 | 0.09 |
| Alsatian (0) | 0 | <0.01 |
| American (3,324) | 3,324 | 3.79 |
| Arab (306) | 485 | 0.55 |
| Arab (0) | 22 | 0.03 |
| Egyptian (9) | 37 | 0.04 |
| Iraqi (0) | 0 | <0.01 |
| Jordanian (45) | 45 | 0.05 |
| Lebanese (213) | 224 | 0.26 |
| Moroccan (0) | 35 | 0.04 |
| Palestinian (0) | 8 | 0.01 |
| Syrian (32) | 107 | 0.12 |
| Other Arab (7) | 7 | 0.01 |
| Armenian (109) | 175 | 0.20 |
| Assyrian/Chaldean/Syriac (15) | 29 | 0.03 |
| Australian (0) | 24 | 0.03 |
| Austrian (267) | 1,117 | 1.27 |
| Basque (0) | 8 | 0.01 |
| Belgian (21) | 93 | 0.11 |
| Brazilian (74) | 123 | 0.14 |
| British (358) | 519 | 0.59 |
| Bulgarian (54) | 54 | 0.06 |
| Cajun (0) | 0 | <0.01 |
| Canadian (53) | 282 | 0.32 |
| Carpatho Rusyn (0) | 0 | <0.01 |
| Celtic (0) | 7 | 0.01 |
| Croatian (384) | 609 | 0.69 |
| Cypriot (0) | 0 | <0.01 |
| Czech (40) | 415 | 0.47 |
| Czechoslovakian (72) | 172 | 0.20 |
| Danish (10) | 130 | 0.15 |
| Dutch (174) | 580 | 0.66 |
| Eastern European (1,840) | 2,009 | 2.29 |
| English (1,185) | 4,118 | 4.70 |
| Estonian (15) | 57 | 0.07 |
| European (1,275) | 1,360 | 1.55 |
| Finnish (34) | 85 | 0.10 |
| French, ex. Basque (225) | 1,496 | 1.71 |
| French Canadian (166) | 483 | 0.55 |
| German (1,568) | 7,526 | 8.58 |
| German Russian (0) | 13 | 0.01 |
| Greek (762) | 1,202 | 1.37 |
| Guyanese (52) | 226 | 0.26 |
| Hungarian (520) | 1,242 | 1.42 |
| Icelander (0) | 0 | <0.01 |
| Iranian (248) | 267 | 0.30 |
| Irish (4,736) | 11,358 | 12.95 |
| Israeli (172) | 225 | 0.26 |
| Italian (9,180) | 16,339 | 18.64 |
| Latvian (48) | 153 | 0.17 |
| Lithuanian (51) | 328 | 0.37 |
| Luxemburger (0) | 0 | <0.01 |
| Macedonian (24) | 24 | 0.03 |
| Maltese (0) | 11 | 0.01 |
| New Zealander (0) | 0 | <0.01 |
| Northern European (47) | 65 | 0.07 |

| Ancestry (cont.) | Population | % |
|---|---|---|
| Norwegian (204) | 530 | 0.60 |
| Pennsylvania German (0) | 0 | <0.01 |
| Polish (1,541) | 4,636 | 5.29 |
| Portuguese (534) | 718 | 0.82 |
| Romanian (234) | 489 | 0.56 |
| Russian (2,209) | 5,042 | 5.75 |
| Scandinavian (46) | 79 | 0.09 |
| Scotch-Irish (336) | 741 | 0.85 |
| Scottish (258) | 987 | 1.13 |
| Serbian (8) | 8 | 0.01 |
| Slavic (6) | 6 | 0.01 |
| Slovak (117) | 388 | 0.44 |
| Slovene (0) | 0 | <0.01 |
| Soviet Union (0) | 0 | <0.01 |
| Swedish (33) | 374 | 0.43 |
| Swiss (46) | 211 | 0.24 |
| Turkish (85) | 172 | 0.20 |
| Ukrainian (263) | 652 | 0.74 |
| Welsh (0) | 81 | 0.09 |
| West Indian, ex. Hispanic (2,889) | 3,562 | 4.06 |
| Bahamian (0) | 0 | <0.01 |
| Barbadian (143) | 155 | 0.18 |
| Belizean (10) | 19 | 0.02 |
| Bermudan (0) | 0 | <0.01 |
| British West Indian (65) | 76 | 0.09 |
| Dutch West Indian (0) | 0 | <0.01 |
| Haitian (469) | 516 | 0.59 |
| Jamaican (1,753) | 2,150 | 2.45 |
| Trinidadian/Tobagonian (159) | 201 | 0.23 |
| U.S. Virgin Islander (0) | 0 | <0.01 |
| West Indian (290) | 445 | 0.51 |
| Other West Indian (0) | 0 | <0.01 |
| Yugoslavian (123) | 130 | 0.15 |

| Hispanic Origin | Population | % |
|---|---|---|
| Hispanic or Latino (of any race) | 12,366 | 13.99 |
| Central American, ex. Mexican | 878 | 0.99 |
| Costa Rican | 34 | 0.04 |
| Guatemalan | 434 | 0.49 |
| Honduran | 90 | 0.10 |
| Nicaraguan | 50 | 0.06 |
| Panamanian | 73 | 0.08 |
| Salvadoran | 185 | 0.21 |
| Other Central American | 12 | 0.01 |
| Cuban | 565 | 0.64 |
| Dominican Republic | 1,400 | 1.58 |
| Mexican | 1,711 | 1.94 |
| Puerto Rican | 2,629 | 2.97 |
| South American | 4,004 | 4.53 |
| Argentinean | 188 | 0.21 |
| Bolivian | 48 | 0.05 |
| Chilean | 192 | 0.22 |
| Colombian | 845 | 0.96 |
| Ecuadorian | 1,434 | 1.62 |
| Paraguayan | 144 | 0.16 |
| Peruvian | 962 | 1.09 |
| Uruguayan | 65 | 0.07 |
| Venezuelan | 94 | 0.11 |
| Other South American | 32 | 0.04 |
| Other Hispanic or Latino | 1,179 | 1.33 |

| Race* | Population | % |
|---|---|---|
| African-American/Black (11,103) | 12,045 | 13.63 |
| Not Hispanic (10,377) | 11,022 | 12.47 |
| Hispanic (726) | 1,023 | 1.16 |
| American Indian/Alaska Native (201) | 630 | 0.71 |
| Not Hispanic (64) | 334 | 0.38 |
| Hispanic (137) | 296 | 0.33 |
| Alaska Athabascan (Ala. Nat.) (0) | 0 | <0.01 |
| Aleut (Alaska Native) (0) | 1 | <0.01 |
| Apache (1) | 6 | 0.01 |
| Arapaho (0) | 0 | <0.01 |
| Blackfeet (0) | 7 | 0.01 |
| Canadian/French Am. Ind. (0) | 2 | <0.01 |
| Central American Ind. (1) | 4 | <0.01 |
| Cherokee (5) | 90 | 0.10 |
| Cheyenne (0) | 5 | 0.01 |
| Chickasaw (0) | 0 | <0.01 |
| Chippewa (0) | 4 | <0.01 |

| Race* (cont.) | Population | % |
|---|---|---|
| Choctaw (0) | 3 | <0.01 |
| Colville (0) | 0 | <0.01 |
| Comanche (0) | 5 | 0.01 |
| Cree (0) | 3 | <0.01 |
| Creek (0) | 0 | <0.01 |
| Crow (0) | 0 | <0.01 |
| Delaware (3) | 5 | 0.01 |
| Hopi (0) | 0 | <0.01 |
| Houma (0) | 0 | <0.01 |
| Inupiat (Alaska Native) (1) | 1 | <0.01 |
| Iroquois (6) | 19 | 0.02 |
| Kiowa (0) | 0 | <0.01 |
| Lumbee (1) | 1 | <0.01 |
| Menominee (0) | 0 | <0.01 |
| Mexican American Ind. (10) | 25 | 0.03 |
| Navajo (0) | 3 | <0.01 |
| Osage (0) | 0 | <0.01 |
| Ottawa (0) | 0 | <0.01 |
| Paiute (0) | 0 | <0.01 |
| Pima (0) | 0 | <0.01 |
| Potawatomi (0) | 0 | <0.01 |
| Pueblo (0) | 0 | <0.01 |
| Puget Sound Salish (0) | 0 | <0.01 |
| Seminole (0) | 3 | <0.01 |
| Shoshone (0) | 0 | <0.01 |
| Sioux (1) | 8 | 0.01 |
| South American Ind. (30) | 72 | 0.08 |
| Spanish American Ind. (14) | 23 | 0.03 |
| Tlingit-Haida (Alaska Native) (0) | 0 | <0.01 |
| Tohono O'Odham (0) | 0 | <0.01 |
| Tsimshian (Alaska Native) (0) | 0 | <0.01 |
| Ute (0) | 0 | <0.01 |
| Yakama (0) | 0 | <0.01 |
| Yaqui (0) | 0 | <0.01 |
| Yuman (0) | 0 | <0.01 |
| Yup'ik (Alaska Native) (0) | 0 | <0.01 |
| Asian (9,210) | 10,180 | 11.52 |
| Not Hispanic (9,155) | 10,025 | 11.34 |
| Hispanic (55) | 155 | 0.18 |
| Bangladeshi (37) | 44 | 0.05 |
| Bhutanese (8) | 8 | 0.01 |
| Burmese (28) | 28 | 0.03 |
| Cambodian (4) | 4 | <0.01 |
| Chinese, ex. Taiwanese (1,910) | 2,225 | 2.52 |
| Filipino (826) | 959 | 1.08 |
| Hmong (0) | 0 | <0.01 |
| Indian (3,241) | 3,518 | 3.98 |
| Indonesian (18) | 24 | 0.03 |
| Japanese (1,018) | 1,230 | 1.39 |
| Korean (1,328) | 1,452 | 1.64 |
| Laotian (3) | 5 | 0.01 |
| Malaysian (6) | 11 | 0.01 |
| Nepalese (48) | 55 | 0.06 |
| Pakistani (212) | 244 | 0.28 |
| Sri Lankan (14) | 20 | 0.02 |
| Taiwanese (113) | 142 | 0.16 |
| Thai (62) | 77 | 0.09 |
| Vietnamese (81) | 95 | 0.11 |
| Hawaii Native/Pacific Islander (33) | 116 | 0.13 |
| Not Hispanic (23) | 88 | 0.10 |
| Hispanic (10) | 28 | 0.03 |
| Fijian (0) | 0 | <0.01 |
| Guamanian/Chamorro (11) | 16 | 0.02 |
| Marshallese (1) | 1 | <0.01 |
| Native Hawaiian (1) | 10 | 0.01 |
| Samoan (1) | 5 | 0.01 |
| Tongan (0) | 0 | <0.01 |
| White (61,185) | 63,005 | 71.27 |
| Not Hispanic (54,539) | 55,731 | 63.04 |
| Hispanic (6,646) | 7,274 | 8.23 |

*Notes: † The Census 2010 population figure is used to calculate the percentages in the Hispanic Origin and Race categories. Ancestry percentages are based on the 2006-2010 American Community Survey population (not shown); ‡ Numbers in parentheses indicate the number of people reporting a single ancestry; * Numbers in parentheses indicate the number of persons reporting this race alone, not in combination with any other race; Please refer to the Explanation of Data for more information.*

## Hamburg

Place Type: Town
County: Erie
Population: 56,936

| Ancestry | Population | % |
|---|---|---|
| Afghan (0) | 0 | <0.01 |
| African, Sub-Saharan (57) | 57 | 0.10 |
| African (0) | 0 | <0.01 |
| Cape Verdean (0) | 0 | <0.01 |
| Ethiopian (0) | 0 | <0.01 |
| Ghanaian (0) | 0 | <0.01 |
| Kenyan (0) | 0 | <0.01 |
| Liberian (0) | 0 | <0.01 |
| Nigerian (0) | 0 | <0.01 |
| Senegalese (0) | 0 | <0.01 |
| Sierra Leonean (0) | 0 | <0.01 |
| Somalian (0) | 0 | <0.01 |
| South African (57) | 57 | 0.10 |
| Sudanese (0) | 0 | <0.01 |
| Ugandan (0) | 0 | <0.01 |
| Zimbabwean (0) | 0 | <0.01 |
| Other Sub-Saharan African (0) | 0 | <0.01 |
| Albanian (0) | 0 | <0.01 |
| Alsatian (9) | 27 | 0.05 |
| American (1,835) | 1,835 | 3.24 |
| Arab (93) | 325 | 0.57 |
| Arab (23) | 70 | 0.12 |
| Egyptian (38) | 38 | 0.07 |
| Iraqi (0) | 0 | <0.01 |
| Jordanian (0) | 11 | 0.02 |
| Lebanese (17) | 136 | 0.24 |
| Moroccan (0) | 26 | 0.05 |
| Palestinian (15) | 15 | 0.03 |
| Syrian (0) | 0 | <0.01 |
| Other Arab (0) | 29 | 0.05 |
| Armenian (0) | 0 | <0.01 |
| Assyrian/Chaldean/Syriac (0) | 0 | <0.01 |
| Australian (0) | 0 | <0.01 |
| Austrian (35) | 216 | 0.38 |
| Basque (0) | 0 | <0.01 |
| Belgian (0) | 25 | 0.04 |
| Brazilian (0) | 0 | <0.01 |
| British (66) | 154 | 0.27 |
| Bulgarian (183) | 192 | 0.34 |
| Cajun (0) | 0 | <0.01 |
| Canadian (180) | 368 | 0.65 |
| Carpatho Rusyn (0) | 0 | <0.01 |
| Celtic (43) | 43 | 0.08 |
| Croatian (37) | 246 | 0.43 |
| Cypriot (0) | 0 | <0.01 |
| Czech (45) | 144 | 0.25 |
| Czechoslovakian (27) | 57 | 0.10 |
| Danish (32) | 66 | 0.12 |
| Dutch (69) | 660 | 1.17 |
| Eastern European (37) | 45 | 0.08 |
| English (1,093) | 5,284 | 9.34 |
| Estonian (0) | 0 | <0.01 |
| European (223) | 250 | 0.44 |
| Finnish (0) | 9 | 0.02 |
| French, ex. Basque (199) | 2,079 | 3.67 |
| French Canadian (153) | 586 | 1.04 |
| German (5,209) | 19,590 | 34.62 |
| German Russian (0) | 0 | <0.01 |
| Greek (61) | 186 | 0.33 |
| Guyanese (33) | 33 | 0.06 |
| Hungarian (200) | 761 | 1.34 |
| Icelander (0) | 0 | <0.01 |
| Iranian (44) | 44 | 0.08 |
| Irish (3,944) | 15,679 | 27.71 |
| Israeli (0) | 0 | <0.01 |
| Italian (3,775) | 10,185 | 18.00 |
| Latvian (0) | 11 | 0.02 |
| Lithuanian (26) | 63 | 0.11 |
| Luxemburger (0) | 0 | <0.01 |
| Macedonian (119) | 149 | 0.26 |
| Maltese (0) | 0 | <0.01 |
| New Zealander (0) | 0 | <0.01 |
| Northern European (0) | 0 | <0.01 |
| Norwegian (9) | 52 | 0.09 |
| Pennsylvania German (39) | 103 | 0.18 |
| Polish (5,175) | 13,189 | 23.31 |
| Portuguese (0) | 45 | 0.08 |
| Romanian (0) | 0 | <0.01 |
| Russian (39) | 385 | 0.68 |
| Scandinavian (0) | 8 | 0.01 |
| Scotch-Irish (164) | 542 | 0.96 |
| Scottish (159) | 836 | 1.48 |
| Serbian (55) | 279 | 0.49 |
| Slavic (0) | 57 | 0.10 |
| Slovak (24) | 182 | 0.32 |
| Slovene (0) | 16 | 0.03 |
| Soviet Union (0) | 0 | <0.01 |
| Swedish (188) | 948 | 1.68 |
| Swiss (17) | 57 | 0.10 |
| Turkish (0) | 0 | <0.01 |
| Ukrainian (185) | 664 | 1.17 |
| Welsh (105) | 292 | 0.52 |
| West Indian, ex. Hispanic (200) | 230 | 0.41 |
| Bahamian (21) | 21 | 0.04 |
| Barbadian (0) | 0 | <0.01 |
| Belizean (0) | 30 | 0.05 |
| Bermudan (0) | 0 | <0.01 |
| British West Indian (0) | 0 | <0.01 |
| Dutch West Indian (0) | 0 | <0.01 |
| Haitian (0) | 0 | <0.01 |
| Jamaican (144) | 144 | 0.25 |
| Trinidadian/Tobagonian (13) | 13 | 0.02 |
| U.S. Virgin Islander (0) | 0 | <0.01 |
| West Indian (22) | 22 | 0.04 |
| Other West Indian (0) | 0 | <0.01 |
| Yugoslavian (43) | 70 | 0.12 |

| Hispanic Origin | Population | % |
|---|---|---|
| Hispanic or Latino (of any race) | 1,214 | 2.13 |
| Central American, ex. Mexican | 38 | 0.07 |
| Costa Rican | 7 | 0.01 |
| Guatemalan | 20 | 0.04 |
| Honduran | 2 | <0.01 |
| Nicaraguan | 4 | 0.01 |
| Panamanian | 0 | <0.01 |
| Salvadoran | 5 | 0.01 |
| Other Central American | 0 | <0.01 |
| Cuban | 29 | 0.05 |
| Dominican Republic | 32 | 0.06 |
| Mexican | 296 | 0.52 |
| Puerto Rican | 551 | 0.97 |
| South American | 72 | 0.13 |
| Argentinean | 4 | 0.01 |
| Bolivian | 7 | 0.01 |
| Chilean | 8 | 0.01 |
| Colombian | 37 | 0.06 |
| Ecuadorian | 2 | <0.01 |
| Paraguayan | 2 | <0.01 |
| Peruvian | 10 | 0.02 |
| Uruguayan | 0 | <0.01 |
| Venezuelan | 2 | <0.01 |
| Other South American | 0 | <0.01 |
| Other Hispanic or Latino | 196 | 0.34 |

| Race* | Population | % |
|---|---|---|
| African-American/Black (433) | 664 | 1.17 |
| Not Hispanic (404) | 608 | 1.07 |
| Hispanic (29) | 56 | 0.10 |
| American Indian/Alaska Native (179) | 319 | 0.56 |
| Not Hispanic (158) | 290 | 0.51 |
| Hispanic (21) | 29 | 0.05 |
| Alaska Athabascan (Ala. Nat.) (0) | 0 | <0.01 |
| Aleut (Alaska Native) (0) | 0 | <0.01 |
| Apache (1) | 1 | <0.01 |
| Arapaho (0) | 0 | <0.01 |
| Blackfeet (1) | 2 | <0.01 |
| Canadian/French Am. Ind. (8) | 12 | 0.02 |
| Central American Ind. (0) | 0 | <0.01 |
| Cherokee (9) | 19 | 0.03 |
| Cheyenne (0) | 0 | <0.01 |
| Chickasaw (0) | 0 | <0.01 |
| Chippewa (2) | 7 | 0.01 |
| Choctaw (0) | 0 | <0.01 |
| Colville (0) | 0 | <0.01 |
| Comanche (1) | 1 | <0.01 |
| Cree (0) | 0 | <0.01 |
| Creek (0) | 0 | <0.01 |
| Crow (0) | 2 | <0.01 |
| Delaware (0) | 1 | <0.01 |
| Hopi (0) | 0 | <0.01 |
| Houma (0) | 0 | <0.01 |
| Inupiat (Alaska Native) (0) | 0 | <0.01 |
| Iroquois (100) | 159 | 0.28 |
| Kiowa (0) | 0 | <0.01 |
| Lumbee (0) | 1 | <0.01 |
| Menominee (0) | 0 | <0.01 |
| Mexican American Ind. (4) | 5 | 0.01 |
| Navajo (0) | 0 | <0.01 |
| Osage (0) | 0 | <0.01 |
| Ottawa (0) | 0 | <0.01 |
| Paiute (0) | 2 | <0.01 |
| Pima (0) | 0 | <0.01 |
| Potawatomi (0) | 0 | <0.01 |
| Pueblo (0) | 0 | <0.01 |
| Puget Sound Salish (0) | 0 | <0.01 |
| Seminole (0) | 1 | <0.01 |
| Shoshone (0) | 0 | <0.01 |
| Sioux (1) | 3 | 0.01 |
| South American Ind. (1) | 1 | <0.01 |
| Spanish American Ind. (2) | 2 | <0.01 |
| Tlingit-Haida (Alaska Native) (0) | 0 | <0.01 |
| Tohono O'Odham (0) | 0 | <0.01 |
| Tsimshian (Alaska Native) (0) | 0 | <0.01 |
| Ute (0) | 0 | <0.01 |
| Yakama (0) | 0 | <0.01 |
| Yaqui (0) | 0 | <0.01 |
| Yuman (0) | 0 | <0.01 |
| Yup'ik (Alaska Native) (0) | 0 | <0.01 |
| Asian (325) | 431 | 0.76 |
| Not Hispanic (322) | 423 | 0.74 |
| Hispanic (3) | 8 | 0.01 |
| Bangladeshi (0) | 0 | <0.01 |
| Bhutanese (0) | 0 | <0.01 |
| Burmese (0) | 0 | <0.01 |
| Cambodian (3) | 3 | 0.01 |
| Chinese, ex. Taiwanese (63) | 80 | 0.14 |
| Filipino (31) | 52 | 0.09 |
| Hmong (0) | 0 | <0.01 |
| Indian (72) | 85 | 0.15 |
| Indonesian (3) | 5 | 0.01 |
| Japanese (7) | 19 | 0.03 |
| Korean (43) | 61 | 0.11 |
| Laotian (3) | 9 | 0.02 |
| Malaysian (0) | 0 | <0.01 |
| Nepalese (0) | 0 | <0.01 |
| Pakistani (11) | 11 | 0.02 |
| Sri Lankan (0) | 0 | <0.01 |
| Taiwanese (2) | 2 | <0.01 |
| Thai (26) | 32 | 0.06 |
| Vietnamese (31) | 35 | 0.06 |
| Hawaii Native/Pacific Islander (6) | 18 | 0.03 |
| Not Hispanic (4) | 14 | 0.02 |
| Hispanic (2) | 4 | 0.01 |
| Fijian (0) | 0 | <0.01 |
| Guamanian/Chamorro (4) | 8 | 0.01 |
| Marshallese (0) | 0 | <0.01 |
| Native Hawaiian (0) | 4 | 0.01 |
| Samoan (0) | 0 | <0.01 |
| Tongan (0) | 0 | <0.01 |
| White (55,242) | 55,749 | 97.92 |
| Not Hispanic (54,366) | 54,789 | 96.23 |
| Hispanic (876) | 960 | 1.69 |

Notes: † The Census 2010 population figure is used to calculate the percentages in the Hispanic Origin and Race categories. Ancestry percentages are based on the 2006-2010 American Community Survey population (not shown); ‡ Numbers in parentheses indicate the number of people reporting a single ancestry; * Numbers in parentheses indicate the number of persons reporting this race alone, not in combination with any other race; Please refer to the Explanation of Data for more information.

## Hempstead

Place Type: Town
County: Nassau
Population: 759,757

| Ancestry | Population | % |
|---|---|---|
| Afghan (260) | 399 | 0.05 |
| African, Sub-Saharan (4,323) | 5,844 | 0.78 |
| African (2,716) | 3,879 | 0.51 |
| Cape Verdean (0) | 0 | <0.01 |
| Ethiopian (38) | 106 | 0.01 |
| Ghanaian (239) | 306 | 0.04 |
| Kenyan (0) | 0 | <0.01 |
| Liberian (0) | 0 | <0.01 |
| Nigerian (952) | 1,115 | 0.15 |
| Senegalese (0) | 0 | <0.01 |
| Sierra Leonean (11) | 11 | <0.01 |
| Somalian (15) | 15 | <0.01 |
| South African (72) | 104 | 0.01 |
| Sudanese (33) | 33 | <0.01 |
| Ugandan (0) | 0 | <0.01 |
| Zimbabwean (0) | 0 | <0.01 |
| Other Sub-Saharan African (247) | 275 | 0.04 |
| Albanian (733) | 1,052 | 0.14 |
| Alsatian (0) | 30 | <0.01 |
| American (23,869) | 23,869 | 3.17 |
| Arab (2,403) | 4,218 | 0.56 |
| Arab (232) | 319 | 0.04 |
| Egyptian (787) | 1,227 | 0.16 |
| Iraqi (149) | 284 | 0.04 |
| Jordanian (66) | 66 | 0.01 |
| Lebanese (270) | 657 | 0.09 |
| Moroccan (163) | 376 | 0.05 |
| Palestinian (64) | 113 | 0.01 |
| Syrian (103) | 512 | 0.07 |
| Other Arab (569) | 664 | 0.09 |
| Armenian (922) | 1,451 | 0.19 |
| Assyrian/Chaldean/Syriac (3) | 19 | <0.01 |
| Australian (98) | 236 | 0.03 |
| Austrian (1,518) | 4,963 | 0.66 |
| Basque (2) | 43 | 0.01 |
| Belgian (136) | 405 | 0.05 |
| Brazilian (208) | 479 | 0.06 |
| British (540) | 1,197 | 0.16 |
| Bulgarian (158) | 181 | 0.02 |
| Cajun (0) | 0 | <0.01 |
| Canadian (321) | 1,084 | 0.14 |
| Carpatho Rusyn (4) | 36 | <0.01 |
| Celtic (13) | 24 | <0.01 |
| Croatian (536) | 1,033 | 0.14 |
| Cypriot (197) | 254 | 0.03 |
| Czech (615) | 2,447 | 0.32 |
| Czechoslovakian (357) | 1,054 | 0.14 |
| Danish (150) | 1,023 | 0.14 |
| Dutch (387) | 3,142 | 0.42 |
| Eastern European (5,468) | 5,775 | 0.77 |
| English (3,407) | 21,808 | 2.89 |
| Estonian (120) | 175 | 0.02 |
| European (5,191) | 5,650 | 0.75 |
| Finnish (105) | 647 | 0.09 |
| French, ex. Basque (1,119) | 8,239 | 1.09 |
| French Canadian (440) | 1,779 | 0.24 |
| German (15,495) | 78,518 | 10.42 |
| German Russian (0) | 17 | <0.01 |
| Greek (6,061) | 10,033 | 1.33 |
| Guyanese (2,705) | 3,520 | 0.47 |
| Hungarian (2,954) | 6,992 | 0.93 |
| Icelander (19) | 92 | 0.01 |
| Iranian (290) | 539 | 0.07 |
| Irish (41,161) | 125,911 | 16.71 |
| Israeli (1,902) | 2,558 | 0.34 |
| Italian (90,988) | 164,467 | 21.82 |
| Latvian (193) | 438 | 0.06 |
| Lithuanian (826) | 2,538 | 0.34 |
| Luxemburger (0) | 0 | <0.01 |
| Macedonian (41) | 51 | 0.01 |
| Maltese (254) | 540 | 0.07 |
| New Zealander (0) | 0 | <0.01 |
| Northern European (433) | 514 | 0.07 |

| Ancestry (cont.) | Population | % |
|---|---|---|
| Norwegian (826) | 3,371 | 0.45 |
| Pennsylvania German (82) | 143 | 0.02 |
| Polish (11,210) | 35,774 | 4.75 |
| Portuguese (1,774) | 2,805 | 0.37 |
| Romanian (1,090) | 2,811 | 0.37 |
| Russian (11,619) | 26,754 | 3.55 |
| Scandinavian (171) | 360 | 0.05 |
| Scotch-Irish (1,797) | 4,788 | 0.64 |
| Scottish (822) | 3,831 | 0.51 |
| Serbian (23) | 38 | 0.01 |
| Slavic (62) | 166 | 0.02 |
| Slovak (182) | 702 | 0.09 |
| Slovene (6) | 89 | 0.01 |
| Soviet Union (0) | 10 | <0.01 |
| Swedish (601) | 3,930 | 0.52 |
| Swiss (173) | 1,183 | 0.16 |
| Turkish (820) | 1,202 | 0.16 |
| Ukrainian (1,249) | 2,806 | 0.37 |
| Welsh (84) | 865 | 0.11 |
| West Indian, ex. Hispanic (37,978) | 45,733 | 6.07 |
| Bahamian (5) | 51 | 0.01 |
| Barbadian (1,031) | 1,279 | 0.17 |
| Belizean (85) | 118 | 0.02 |
| Bermudan (52) | 52 | 0.01 |
| British West Indian (635) | 972 | 0.13 |
| Dutch West Indian (165) | 199 | 0.03 |
| Haitian (15,396) | 17,422 | 2.31 |
| Jamaican (15,060) | 17,690 | 2.35 |
| Trinidadian/Tobagonian (2,092) | 3,155 | 0.42 |
| U.S. Virgin Islander (0) | 30 | <0.01 |
| West Indian (3,440) | 4,748 | 0.63 |
| Other West Indian (17) | 17 | <0.01 |
| Yugoslavian (227) | 649 | 0.09 |

| Hispanic Origin | Population | % |
|---|---|---|
| Hispanic or Latino (of any race) | 132,154 | 17.39 |
| Central American, ex. Mexican | 49,236 | 6.48 |
| Costa Rican | 664 | 0.09 |
| Guatemalan | 5,948 | 0.78 |
| Honduran | 7,842 | 1.03 |
| Nicaraguan | 656 | 0.09 |
| Panamanian | 1,163 | 0.15 |
| Salvadoran | 32,681 | 4.30 |
| Other Central American | 282 | 0.04 |
| Cuban | 3,597 | 0.47 |
| Dominican Republic | 16,914 | 2.23 |
| Mexican | 5,000 | 0.66 |
| Puerto Rican | 20,508 | 2.70 |
| South American | 23,626 | 3.11 |
| Argentinean | 1,500 | 0.20 |
| Bolivian | 494 | 0.07 |
| Chilean | 1,415 | 0.19 |
| Colombian | 8,522 | 1.12 |
| Ecuadorian | 5,881 | 0.77 |
| Paraguayan | 185 | 0.02 |
| Peruvian | 4,510 | 0.59 |
| Uruguayan | 359 | 0.05 |
| Venezuelan | 517 | 0.07 |
| Other South American | 243 | 0.03 |
| Other Hispanic or Latino | 13,273 | 1.75 |

| Race* | Population | % |
|---|---|---|
| African-American/Black (125,724) | 133,280 | 17.54 |
| Not Hispanic (119,480) | 124,525 | 16.39 |
| Hispanic (6,244) | 8,755 | 1.15 |
| American Indian/Alaska Native (2,092) | 5,363 | 0.71 |
| Not Hispanic (913) | 2,835 | 0.37 |
| Hispanic (1,179) | 2,528 | 0.33 |
| Alaska Athabascan (Ala. Nat.) (0) | 0 | <0.01 |
| Aleut (Alaska Native) (1) | 2 | <0.01 |
| Apache (5) | 21 | <0.01 |
| Arapaho (0) | 0 | <0.01 |
| Blackfeet (16) | 117 | 0.02 |
| Canadian/French Am. Ind. (5) | 9 | <0.01 |
| Central American Ind. (36) | 87 | 0.01 |
| Cherokee (59) | 572 | 0.08 |
| Cheyenne (0) | 2 | <0.01 |
| Chickasaw (0) | 5 | <0.01 |
| Chippewa (4) | 7 | <0.01 |

| Race* (cont.) | Population | % |
|---|---|---|
| Choctaw (10) | 36 | <0.01 |
| Colville (1) | 1 | <0.01 |
| Comanche (7) | 11 | <0.01 |
| Cree (0) | 2 | <0.01 |
| Creek (6) | 29 | <0.01 |
| Crow (0) | 2 | <0.01 |
| Delaware (4) | 11 | <0.01 |
| Hopi (0) | 2 | <0.01 |
| Houma (0) | 0 | <0.01 |
| Inupiat (Alaska Native) (0) | 3 | <0.01 |
| Iroquois (66) | 145 | 0.02 |
| Kiowa (0) | 0 | <0.01 |
| Lumbee (9) | 22 | <0.01 |
| Menominee (0) | 0 | <0.01 |
| Mexican American Ind. (85) | 143 | 0.02 |
| Navajo (2) | 13 | <0.01 |
| Osage (0) | 2 | <0.01 |
| Ottawa (1) | 1 | <0.01 |
| Paiute (0) | 0 | <0.01 |
| Pima (0) | 0 | <0.01 |
| Potawatomi (0) | 0 | <0.01 |
| Pueblo (9) | 13 | <0.01 |
| Puget Sound Salish (0) | 0 | <0.01 |
| Seminole (2) | 28 | <0.01 |
| Shoshone (1) | 3 | <0.01 |
| Sioux (12) | 33 | <0.01 |
| South American Ind. (147) | 294 | 0.04 |
| Spanish American Ind. (111) | 137 | 0.02 |
| Tlingit-Haida (Alaska Native) (3) | 6 | <0.01 |
| Tohono O'Odham (7) | 7 | <0.01 |
| Tsimshian (Alaska Native) (0) | 0 | <0.01 |
| Ute (1) | 1 | <0.01 |
| Yakama (0) | 0 | <0.01 |
| Yaqui (0) | 0 | <0.01 |
| Yuman (0) | 0 | <0.01 |
| Yup'ik (Alaska Native) (0) | 0 | <0.01 |
| Asian (39,495) | 45,112 | 5.94 |
| Not Hispanic (39,084) | 43,880 | 5.78 |
| Hispanic (411) | 1,232 | 0.16 |
| Bangladeshi (530) | 582 | 0.08 |
| Bhutanese (0) | 0 | <0.01 |
| Burmese (37) | 61 | 0.01 |
| Cambodian (46) | 65 | 0.01 |
| Chinese, ex. Taiwanese (6,491) | 7,849 | 1.03 |
| Filipino (6,252) | 7,212 | 0.95 |
| Hmong (0) | 2 | <0.01 |
| Indian (15,861) | 17,802 | 2.34 |
| Indonesian (37) | 66 | 0.01 |
| Japanese (360) | 657 | 0.09 |
| Korean (2,720) | 3,074 | 0.40 |
| Laotian (21) | 32 | <0.01 |
| Malaysian (12) | 29 | <0.01 |
| Nepalese (41) | 45 | 0.01 |
| Pakistani (4,581) | 4,976 | 0.65 |
| Sri Lankan (180) | 201 | 0.03 |
| Taiwanese (367) | 438 | 0.06 |
| Thai (213) | 278 | 0.04 |
| Vietnamese (492) | 617 | 0.08 |
| Hawaii Native/Pacific Islander (229) | 1,001 | 0.13 |
| Not Hispanic (117) | 599 | 0.08 |
| Hispanic (112) | 402 | 0.05 |
| Fijian (9) | 10 | <0.01 |
| Guamanian/Chamorro (88) | 110 | 0.01 |
| Marshallese (1) | 1 | <0.01 |
| Native Hawaiian (34) | 114 | 0.02 |
| Samoan (12) | 36 | <0.01 |
| Tongan (0) | 0 | <0.01 |
| White (518,756) | 532,650 | 70.11 |
| Not Hispanic (454,883) | 460,994 | 60.68 |
| Hispanic (63,873) | 71,656 | 9.43 |

## Hempstead

Place Type: Village
County: Nassau
Population: 53,891.

| Ancestry | Population | % |
|---|---|---|
| Afghan (0) | 0 | <0.01 |
| African, Sub-Saharan (1,102) | 1,285 | 2.41 |
| African (682) | 850 | 1.59 |
| Cape Verdean (0) | 0 | <0.01 |
| Ethiopian (0) | 0 | <0.01 |
| Ghanaian (8) | 8 | 0.01 |
| Kenyan (0) | 0 | <0.01 |
| Liberian (0) | 0 | <0.01 |
| Nigerian (412) | 427 | 0.80 |
| Senegalese (0) | 0 | <0.01 |
| Sierra Leonean (0) | 0 | <0.01 |
| Somalian (0) | 0 | <0.01 |
| South African (0) | 0 | <0.01 |
| Sudanese (0) | 0 | <0.01 |
| Ugandan (0) | 0 | <0.01 |
| Zimbabwean (0) | 0 | <0.01 |
| Other Sub-Saharan African (0) | 0 | <0.01 |
| Albanian (0) | 0 | <0.01 |
| Alsatian (0) | 0 | <0.01 |
| American (471) | 471 | 0.88 |
| Arab (54) | 54 | 0.10 |
| Arab (12) | 12 | 0.02 |
| Egyptian (0) | 0 | <0.01 |
| Iraqi (0) | 0 | <0.01 |
| Jordanian (0) | 0 | <0.01 |
| Lebanese (0) | 0 | <0.01 |
| Moroccan (42) | 42 | 0.08 |
| Palestinian (0) | 0 | <0.01 |
| Syrian (0) | 0 | <0.01 |
| Other Arab (0) | 0 | <0.01 |
| Armenian (0) | 0 | <0.01 |
| Assyrian/Chaldean/Syriac (0) | 0 | <0.01 |
| Australian (9) | 9 | 0.02 |
| Austrian (28) | 64 | 0.12 |
| Basque (0) | 0 | <0.01 |
| Belgian (0) | 0 | <0.01 |
| Brazilian (0) | 41 | 0.08 |
| British (0) | 90 | 0.17 |
| Bulgarian (0) | 0 | <0.01 |
| Cajun (0) | 0 | <0.01 |
| Canadian (0) | 143 | 0.27 |
| Carpatho Rusyn (0) | 0 | <0.01 |
| Celtic (0) | 0 | <0.01 |
| Croatian (0) | 0 | <0.01 |
| Cypriot (0) | 9 | 0.02 |
| Czech (7) | 7 | 0.01 |
| Czechoslovakian (0) | 0 | <0.01 |
| Danish (0) | 0 | <0.01 |
| Dutch (6) | 6 | 0.01 |
| Eastern European (34) | 34 | 0.06 |
| English (47) | 124 | 0.23 |
| Estonian (0) | 0 | <0.01 |
| European (0) | 0 | <0.01 |
| Finnish (0) | 0 | <0.01 |
| French, ex. Basque (0) | 82 | 0.15 |
| French Canadian (0) | 9 | 0.02 |
| German (130) | 594 | 1.11 |
| German Russian (0) | 0 | <0.01 |
| Greek (203) | 231 | 0.43 |
| Guyanese (259) | 307 | 0.58 |
| Hungarian (32) | 41 | 0.08 |
| Icelander (0) | 0 | <0.01 |
| Iranian (0) | 0 | <0.01 |
| Irish (278) | 659 | 1.23 |
| Israeli (0) | 0 | <0.01 |
| Italian (333) | 641 | 1.20 |
| Latvian (0) | 6 | 0.01 |
| Lithuanian (28) | 36 | 0.07 |
| Luxemburger (0) | 0 | <0.01 |
| Macedonian (0) | 0 | <0.01 |
| Maltese (0) | 0 | <0.01 |
| New Zealander (0) | 0 | <0.01 |
| Northern European (0) | 0 | <0.01 |

| Ancestry | Population | % |
|---|---|---|
| Norwegian (0) | 0 | <0.01 |
| Pennsylvania German (0) | 0 | <0.01 |
| Polish (203) | 351 | 0.66 |
| Portuguese (13) | 69 | 0.13 |
| Romanian (0) | 0 | <0.01 |
| Russian (44) | 129 | 0.24 |
| Scandinavian (0) | 0 | <0.01 |
| Scotch-Irish (17) | 47 | 0.09 |
| Scottish (21) | 103 | 0.19 |
| Serbian (0) | 0 | <0.01 |
| Slavic (0) | 0 | <0.01 |
| Slovak (0) | 9 | 0.02 |
| Slovene (0) | 0 | <0.01 |
| Soviet Union (0) | 0 | <0.01 |
| Swedish (23) | 102 | 0.19 |
| Swiss (9) | 47 | 0.09 |
| Turkish (0) | 0 | <0.01 |
| Ukrainian (62) | 90 | 0.17 |
| Welsh (0) | 71 | 0.13 |
| West Indian, ex. Hispanic (5,489) | 6,463 | 12.11 |
| Bahamian (0) | 0 | <0.01 |
| Barbadian (153) | 153 | 0.29 |
| Belizean (0) | 0 | <0.01 |
| Bermudan (9) | 9 | 0.02 |
| British West Indian (228) | 250 | 0.47 |
| Dutch West Indian (31) | 31 | 0.06 |
| Haitian (1,796) | 2,104 | 3.94 |
| Jamaican (2,500) | 2,809 | 5.26 |
| Trinidadian/Tobagonian (203) | 322 | 0.60 |
| U.S. Virgin Islander (0) | 0 | <0.01 |
| West Indian (569) | 785 | 1.47 |
| Other West Indian (0) | 0 | <0.01 |
| Yugoslavian (0) | 0 | <0.01 |

| Hispanic Origin | Population | % |
|---|---|---|
| Hispanic or Latino (of any race) | 23,823 | 44.21 |
| Central American, ex. Mexican | 16,171 | 30.01 |
| Costa Rican | 44 | 0.08 |
| Guatemalan | 1,402 | 2.60 |
| Honduran | 3,758 | 6.97 |
| Nicaraguan | 56 | 0.10 |
| Panamanian | 138 | 0.26 |
| Salvadoran | 10,707 | 19.87 |
| Other Central American | 66 | 0.12 |
| Cuban | 174 | 0.32 |
| Dominican Republic | 1,398 | 2.59 |
| Mexican | 752 | 1.40 |
| Puerto Rican | 1,144 | 2.12 |
| South American | 1,575 | 2.92 |
| Argentinean | 25 | 0.05 |
| Bolivian | 23 | 0.04 |
| Chilean | 21 | 0.04 |
| Colombian | 506 | 0.94 |
| Ecuadorian | 641 | 1.19 |
| Paraguayan | 16 | 0.03 |
| Peruvian | 279 | 0.52 |
| Uruguayan | 4 | 0.01 |
| Venezuelan | 37 | 0.07 |
| Other South American | 23 | 0.04 |
| Other Hispanic or Latino | 2,609 | 4.84 |

| Race* | Population | % |
|---|---|---|
| African-American/Black (26,016) | 27,076 | 50.24 |
| Not Hispanic (24,724) | 25,388 | 47.11 |
| Hispanic (1,292) | 1,688 | 3.13 |
| American Indian/Alaska Native (316) | 997 | 1.85 |
| Not Hispanic (96) | 404 | 0.75 |
| Hispanic (220) | 593 | 1.10 |
| Alaska Athabascan (Ala. Nat.) (0) | 0 | <0.01 |
| Aleut (Alaska Native) (0) | 0 | <0.01 |
| Apache (2) | 5 | 0.01 |
| Arapaho (0) | 0 | <0.01 |
| Blackfeet (1) | 27 | 0.05 |
| Canadian/French Am. Ind. (0) | 0 | <0.01 |
| Central American Ind. (5) | 15 | 0.03 |
| Cherokee (17) | 109 | 0.20 |
| Cheyenne (0) | 1 | <0.01 |
| Chickasaw (0) | 0 | <0.01 |
| Chippewa (1) | 1 | <0.01 |

| | Population | % |
|---|---|---|
| Choctaw (0) | 3 | 0.01 |
| Colville (0) | 0 | <0.01 |
| Comanche (0) | 1 | <0.01 |
| Cree (0) | 0 | <0.01 |
| Creek (1) | 2 | <0.01 |
| Crow (0) | 0 | <0.01 |
| Delaware (0) | 4 | 0.01 |
| Hopi (0) | 2 | <0.01 |
| Houma (0) | 0 | <0.01 |
| Inupiat (Alaska Native) (0) | 0 | <0.01 |
| Iroquois (13) | 19 | 0.04 |
| Kiowa (0) | 0 | <0.01 |
| Lumbee (0) | 1 | <0.01 |
| Menominee (0) | 0 | <0.01 |
| Mexican American Ind. (17) | 27 | 0.05 |
| Navajo (1) | 2 | <0.01 |
| Osage (0) | 0 | <0.01 |
| Ottawa (0) | 0 | <0.01 |
| Paiute (0) | 0 | <0.01 |
| Pima (0) | 0 | <0.01 |
| Potawatomi (0) | 0 | <0.01 |
| Pueblo (4) | 6 | 0.01 |
| Puget Sound Salish (0) | 0 | <0.01 |
| Seminole (0) | 5 | 0.01 |
| Shoshone (0) | 0 | <0.01 |
| Sioux (1) | 6 | 0.01 |
| South American Ind. (9) | 18 | 0.03 |
| Spanish American Ind. (42) | 47 | 0.09 |
| Tlingit-Haida (Alaska Native) (0) | 2 | <0.01 |
| Tohono O'Odham (0) | 0 | <0.01 |
| Tsimshian (Alaska Native) (0) | 0 | <0.01 |
| Ute (0) | 0 | <0.01 |
| Yakama (0) | 0 | <0.01 |
| Yaqui (0) | 0 | <0.01 |
| Yuman (0) | 0 | <0.01 |
| Yup'ik (Alaska Native) (0) | 0 | <0.01 |
| Asian (751) | 977 | 1.81 |
| Not Hispanic (704) | 842 | 1.56 |
| Hispanic (47) | 135 | 0.25 |
| Bangladeshi (11) | 11 | 0.02 |
| Bhutanese (0) | 0 | <0.01 |
| Burmese (0) | 0 | <0.01 |
| Cambodian (0) | 0 | <0.01 |
| Chinese, ex. Taiwanese (135) | 177 | 0.33 |
| Filipino (150) | 171 | 0.32 |
| Hmong (0) | 0 | <0.01 |
| Indian (282) | 383 | 0.71 |
| Indonesian (3) | 5 | 0.01 |
| Japanese (6) | 14 | 0.03 |
| Korean (24) | 29 | 0.05 |
| Laotian (3) | 4 | 0.01 |
| Malaysian (1) | 1 | <0.01 |
| Nepalese (7) | 9 | 0.02 |
| Pakistani (48) | 60 | 0.11 |
| Sri Lankan (15) | 15 | 0.03 |
| Taiwanese (1) | 1 | <0.01 |
| Thai (5) | 10 | 0.02 |
| Vietnamese (6) | 9 | 0.02 |
| Hawaii Native/Pacific Islander (23) | 117 | 0.22 |
| Not Hispanic (13) | 57 | 0.11 |
| Hispanic (10) | 60 | 0.11 |
| Fijian (1) | 1 | <0.01 |
| Guamanian/Chamorro (9) | 13 | 0.02 |
| Marshallese (0) | 0 | <0.01 |
| Native Hawaiian (1) | 9 | 0.02 |
| Samoan (0) | 3 | 0.01 |
| Tongan (0) | 0 | <0.01 |
| White (11,788) | 13,665 | 25.36 |
| Not Hispanic (3,548) | 3,892 | 7.22 |
| Hispanic (8,240) | 9,773 | 18.13 |

Notes: † The Census 2010 population figure is used to calculate the percentages in the Hispanic Origin and Race categories. Ancestry percentages are based on the 2006-2010 American Community Survey population (not shown); ‡ Numbers in parentheses indicate the number of people reporting a single ancestry; * Numbers in parentheses indicate the number of persons reporting this race alone, not in combination with any other race; Please refer to the Explanation of Data for more information.

# Huntington

Place Type: Town
County: Suffolk
Population: 203,264

| Ancestry | Population | % |
|---|---|---|
| Afghan (314) | 314 | 0.16 |
| African, Sub-Saharan (317) | 481 | 0.24 |
| African (146) | 206 | 0.10 |
| Cape Verdean (0) | 0 | <0.01 |
| Ethiopian (21) | 125 | 0.06 |
| Ghanaian (0) | 0 | <0.01 |
| Kenyan (0) | 0 | <0.01 |
| Liberian (0) | 0 | <0.01 |
| Nigerian (87) | 87 | 0.04 |
| Senegalese (0) | 0 | <0.01 |
| Sierra Leonean (0) | 0 | <0.01 |
| Somalian (0) | 0 | <0.01 |
| South African (63) | 63 | 0.03 |
| Sudanese (0) | 0 | <0.01 |
| Ugandan (0) | 0 | <0.01 |
| Zimbabwean (0) | 0 | <0.01 |
| Other Sub-Saharan African (0) | 0 | <0.01 |
| Albanian (216) | 237 | 0.12 |
| Alsatian (0) | 9 | <0.01 |
| American (5,873) | 5,873 | 2.90 |
| Arab (721) | 1,231 | 0.61 |
| Arab (65) | 73 | 0.04 |
| Egyptian (318) | 425 | 0.21 |
| Iraqi (42) | 166 | 0.08 |
| Jordanian (11) | 11 | 0.01 |
| Lebanese (46) | 184 | 0.09 |
| Moroccan (142) | 192 | 0.09 |
| Palestinian (0) | 9 | <0.01 |
| Syrian (15) | 35 | 0.02 |
| Other Arab (82) | 136 | 0.07 |
| Armenian (368) | 525 | 0.26 |
| Assyrian/Chaldean/Syriac (0) | 0 | <0.01 |
| Australian (59) | 101 | 0.05 |
| Austrian (454) | 2,004 | 0.99 |
| Basque (6) | 20 | 0.01 |
| Belgian (30) | 115 | 0.06 |
| Brazilian (142) | 195 | 0.10 |
| British (515) | 840 | 0.42 |
| Bulgarian (44) | 65 | 0.03 |
| Cajun (0) | 19 | 0.01 |
| Canadian (356) | 743 | 0.37 |
| Carpatho Rusyn (20) | 20 | 0.01 |
| Celtic (65) | 65 | 0.03 |
| Croatian (337) | 781 | 0.39 |
| Cypriot (70) | 82 | 0.04 |
| Czech (275) | 1,271 | 0.63 |
| Czechoslovakian (89) | 435 | 0.22 |
| Danish (359) | 809 | 0.40 |
| Dutch (427) | 2,168 | 1.07 |
| Eastern European (1,918) | 2,012 | 1.00 |
| English (2,429) | 13,038 | 6.45 |
| Estonian (77) | 140 | 0.07 |
| European (1,982) | 2,177 | 1.08 |
| Finnish (21) | 178 | 0.09 |
| French, ex. Basque (400) | 3,023 | 1.50 |
| French Canadian (214) | 772 | 0.38 |
| German (6,140) | 33,758 | 16.70 |
| German Russian (0) | 0 | <0.01 |
| Greek (1,839) | 3,284 | 1.62 |
| Guyanese (124) | 180 | 0.09 |
| Hungarian (784) | 3,005 | 1.49 |
| Icelander (9) | 38 | 0.02 |
| Iranian (443) | 471 | 0.23 |
| Irish (12,700) | 45,750 | 22.63 |
| Israeli (217) | 285 | 0.14 |
| Italian (26,684) | 56,013 | 27.70 |
| Latvian (75) | 193 | 0.10 |
| Lithuanian (269) | 956 | 0.47 |
| Luxemburger (0) | 0 | <0.01 |
| Macedonian (0) | 0 | <0.01 |
| Maltese (30) | 88 | 0.04 |
| New Zealander (26) | 26 | 0.01 |
| Northern European (57) | 63 | 0.03 |

| Ancestry | Population | % |
|---|---|---|
| Norwegian (538) | 1,833 | 0.91 |
| Pennsylvania German (0) | 17 | 0.01 |
| Polish (3,447) | 13,208 | 6.53 |
| Portuguese (198) | 526 | 0.26 |
| Romanian (503) | 1,364 | 0.67 |
| Russian (3,393) | 9,499 | 4.70 |
| Scandinavian (107) | 292 | 0.14 |
| Scotch-Irish (1,045) | 2,325 | 1.15 |
| Scottish (588) | 2,306 | 1.14 |
| Serbian (17) | 80 | 0.04 |
| Slavic (28) | 97 | 0.05 |
| Slovak (109) | 225 | 0.11 |
| Slovene (27) | 37 | 0.02 |
| Soviet Union (0) | 0 | <0.01 |
| Swedish (322) | 2,237 | 1.11 |
| Swiss (118) | 632 | 0.31 |
| Turkish (438) | 502 | 0.25 |
| Ukrainian (668) | 1,742 | 0.86 |
| Welsh (126) | 533 | 0.26 |
| West Indian, ex. Hispanic (2,499) | 2,882 | 1.43 |
| Bahamian (31) | 31 | 0.02 |
| Barbadian (18) | 18 | 0.01 |
| Belizean (0) | 0 | <0.01 |
| Bermudan (0) | 0 | <0.01 |
| British West Indian (0) | 0 | <0.01 |
| Dutch West Indian (7) | 7 | <0.01 |
| Haitian (1,223) | 1,277 | 0.63 |
| Jamaican (733) | 893 | 0.44 |
| Trinidadian/Tobagonian (128) | 170 | 0.08 |
| U.S. Virgin Islander (91) | 147 | 0.07 |
| West Indian (261) | 332 | 0.16 |
| Other West Indian (7) | 7 | <0.01 |
| Yugoslavian (161) | 467 | 0.23 |

| Hispanic Origin | Population | % |
|---|---|---|
| Hispanic or Latino (of any race) | 22,362 | 11.00 |
| Central American, ex. Mexican | 9,599 | 4.72 |
| Costa Rican | 118 | 0.06 |
| Guatemalan | 1,080 | 0.53 |
| Honduran | 1,651 | 0.81 |
| Nicaraguan | 58 | 0.03 |
| Panamanian | 77 | 0.04 |
| Salvadoran | 6,563 | 3.23 |
| Other Central American | 52 | 0.03 |
| Cuban | 603 | 0.30 |
| Dominican Republic | 1,011 | 0.50 |
| Mexican | 1,440 | 0.71 |
| Puerto Rican | 4,187 | 2.06 |
| South American | 3,043 | 1.50 |
| Argentinean | 329 | 0.16 |
| Bolivian | 60 | 0.03 |
| Chilean | 252 | 0.12 |
| Colombian | 957 | 0.47 |
| Ecuadorian | 637 | 0.31 |
| Paraguayan | 91 | 0.04 |
| Peruvian | 538 | 0.26 |
| Uruguayan | 57 | 0.03 |
| Venezuelan | 87 | 0.04 |
| Other South American | 35 | 0.02 |
| Other Hispanic or Latino | 2,479 | 1.22 |

| Race* | Population | % |
|---|---|---|
| African-American/Black (9,515) | 10,864 | 5.34 |
| Not Hispanic (8,933) | 9,917 | 4.88 |
| Hispanic (582) | 947 | 0.47 |
| American Indian/Alaska Native (398) | 1,197 | 0.59 |
| Not Hispanic (187) | 785 | 0.39 |
| Hispanic (211) | 412 | 0.20 |
| Alaska Athabascan (Ala. Nat.) (0) | 0 | <0.01 |
| Aleut (Alaska Native) (0) | 0 | <0.01 |
| Apache (10) | 14 | 0.01 |
| Arapaho (0) | 0 | <0.01 |
| Blackfeet (2) | 36 | 0.02 |
| Canadian/French Am. Ind. (6) | 10 | <0.01 |
| Central American Ind. (11) | 20 | 0.01 |
| Cherokee (15) | 150 | 0.07 |
| Cheyenne (0) | 4 | <0.01 |
| Chickasaw (0) | 3 | <0.01 |
| Chippewa (2) | 10 | <0.01 |

| Race* | Population | % |
|---|---|---|
| Choctaw (0) | 13 | 0.01 |
| Colville (0) | 0 | <0.01 |
| Comanche (5) | 8 | <0.01 |
| Cree (0) | 3 | <0.01 |
| Creek (1) | 15 | 0.01 |
| Crow (2) | 5 | <0.01 |
| Delaware (1) | 12 | 0.01 |
| Hopi (0) | 0 | <0.01 |
| Houma (0) | 0 | <0.01 |
| Inupiat (Alaska Native) (0) | 0 | <0.01 |
| Iroquois (18) | 42 | 0.02 |
| Kiowa (0) | 0 | <0.01 |
| Lumbee (2) | 5 | <0.01 |
| Menominee (0) | 0 | <0.01 |
| Mexican American Ind. (18) | 26 | 0.01 |
| Navajo (3) | 8 | <0.01 |
| Osage (0) | 1 | <0.01 |
| Ottawa (0) | 2 | <0.01 |
| Paiute (0) | 0 | <0.01 |
| Pima (0) | 0 | <0.01 |
| Potawatomi (0) | 0 | <0.01 |
| Pueblo (0) | 0 | <0.01 |
| Puget Sound Salish (0) | 0 | <0.01 |
| Seminole (1) | 4 | <0.01 |
| Shoshone (0) | 0 | <0.01 |
| Sioux (1) | 9 | <0.01 |
| South American Ind. (22) | 69 | 0.03 |
| Spanish American Ind. (8) | 16 | 0.01 |
| Tlingit-Haida (Alaska Native) (0) | 1 | <0.01 |
| Tohono O'Odham (0) | 0 | <0.01 |
| Tsimshian (Alaska Native) (0) | 0 | <0.01 |
| Ute (0) | 0 | <0.01 |
| Yakama (0) | 0 | <0.01 |
| Yaqui (0) | 0 | <0.01 |
| Yuman (0) | 0 | <0.01 |
| Yup'ik (Alaska Native) (0) | 0 | <0.01 |
| Asian (10,089) | 11,684 | 5.75 |
| Not Hispanic (10,009) | 11,463 | 5.64 |
| Hispanic (80) | 221 | 0.11 |
| Bangladeshi (108) | 120 | 0.06 |
| Bhutanese (1) | 1 | <0.01 |
| Burmese (8) | 13 | 0.01 |
| Cambodian (10) | 10 | <0.01 |
| Chinese, ex. Taiwanese (2,144) | 2,546 | 1.25 |
| Filipino (637) | 905 | 0.45 |
| Hmong (0) | 0 | <0.01 |
| Indian (3,166) | 3,529 | 1.74 |
| Indonesian (11) | 18 | 0.01 |
| Japanese (218) | 338 | 0.17 |
| Korean (1,952) | 2,122 | 1.04 |
| Laotian (5) | 5 | <0.01 |
| Malaysian (6) | 13 | 0.01 |
| Nepalese (3) | 3 | <0.01 |
| Pakistani (1,149) | 1,264 | 0.62 |
| Sri Lankan (20) | 22 | 0.01 |
| Taiwanese (140) | 157 | 0.08 |
| Thai (58) | 75 | 0.04 |
| Vietnamese (151) | 186 | 0.09 |
| Hawaii Native/Pacific Islander (48) | 159 | 0.08 |
| Not Hispanic (32) | 93 | 0.05 |
| Hispanic (16) | 66 | 0.03 |
| Fijian (0) | 0 | <0.01 |
| Guamanian/Chamorro (18) | 25 | 0.01 |
| Marshallese (0) | 0 | <0.01 |
| Native Hawaiian (16) | 40 | 0.02 |
| Samoan (6) | 7 | <0.01 |
| Tongan (0) | 0 | <0.01 |
| White (171,048) | 174,612 | 85.90 |
| Not Hispanic (158,690) | 160,914 | 79.17 |
| Hispanic (12,358) | 13,698 | 6.74 |

Notes: † The Census 2010 population figure is used to calculate the percentages in the Hispanic Origin and Race categories. Ancestry percentages are based on the 2006-2010 American Community Survey population (not shown); ‡ Numbers in parentheses indicate the number of people reporting a single ancestry; * Numbers in parentheses indicate the number of persons reporting this race alone, not in combination with any other race; Please refer to the Explanation of Data for more information.

## Irondequoit

Place Type: CDP/Town
County: Monroe
Population: 51,692

| Ancestry | Population | % |
|---|---|---|
| Afghan (145) | 145 | 0.28 |
| African, Sub-Saharan (653) | 763 | 1.48 |
| African (344) | 454 | 0.88 |
| Cape Verdean (0) | 0 | <0.01 |
| Ethiopian (192) | 192 | 0.37 |
| Ghanaian (0) | 0 | <0.01 |
| Kenyan (0) | 0 | <0.01 |
| Liberian (0) | 0 | <0.01 |
| Nigerian (85) | 85 | 0.16 |
| Senegalese (0) | 0 | <0.01 |
| Sierra Leonean (0) | 0 | <0.01 |
| Somalian (0) | 0 | <0.01 |
| South African (0) | 0 | <0.01 |
| Sudanese (0) | 0 | <0.01 |
| Ugandan (0) | 0 | <0.01 |
| Zimbabwean (0) | 0 | <0.01 |
| Other Sub-Saharan African (32) | 32 | 0.06 |
| Albanian (41) | 41 | 0.08 |
| Alsatian (0) | 0 | <0.01 |
| American (1,362) | 1,362 | 2.64 |
| Arab (107) | 120 | 0.23 |
| Arab (59) | 59 | 0.11 |
| Egyptian (11) | 11 | 0.02 |
| Iraqi (0) | 0 | <0.01 |
| Jordanian (0) | 0 | <0.01 |
| Lebanese (37) | 50 | 0.10 |
| Moroccan (0) | 0 | <0.01 |
| Palestinian (0) | 0 | <0.01 |
| Syrian (0) | 0 | <0.01 |
| Other Arab (0) | 0 | <0.01 |
| Armenian (54) | 72 | 0.14 |
| Assyrian/Chaldean/Syriac (0) | 0 | <0.01 |
| Australian (0) | 12 | 0.02 |
| Austrian (25) | 176 | 0.34 |
| Basque (0) | 0 | <0.01 |
| Belgian (23) | 93 | 0.18 |
| Brazilian (52) | 71 | 0.14 |
| British (94) | 189 | 0.37 |
| Bulgarian (0) | 0 | <0.01 |
| Cajun (0) | 0 | <0.01 |
| Canadian (208) | 419 | 0.81 |
| Carpatho Rusyn (0) | 0 | <0.01 |
| Celtic (14) | 14 | 0.03 |
| Croatian (0) | 43 | 0.08 |
| Cypriot (0) | 0 | <0.01 |
| Czech (32) | 153 | 0.30 |
| Czechoslovakian (23) | 42 | 0.08 |
| Danish (14) | 111 | 0.22 |
| Dutch (161) | 1,310 | 2.54 |
| Eastern European (35) | 35 | 0.07 |
| English (2,071) | 7,215 | 13.98 |
| Estonian (0) | 0 | <0.01 |
| European (385) | 424 | 0.82 |
| Finnish (22) | 30 | 0.06 |
| French, ex. Basque (121) | 1,636 | 3.17 |
| French Canadian (191) | 465 | 0.90 |
| German (2,967) | 11,815 | 22.89 |
| German Russian (0) | 28 | 0.05 |
| Greek (199) | 335 | 0.65 |
| Guyanese (0) | 0 | <0.01 |
| Hungarian (74) | 172 | 0.33 |
| Icelander (0) | 0 | <0.01 |
| Iranian (12) | 12 | 0.02 |
| Irish (1,901) | 9,070 | 17.57 |
| Israeli (0) | 0 | <0.01 |
| Italian (8,322) | 14,566 | 28.22 |
| Latvian (12) | 26 | 0.05 |
| Lithuanian (142) | 267 | 0.52 |
| Luxemburger (24) | 24 | 0.05 |
| Macedonian (212) | 266 | 0.52 |
| Maltese (0) | 0 | <0.01 |
| New Zealander (0) | 0 | <0.01 |
| Northern European (0) | 10 | 0.02 |

| Ancestry | Population | % |
|---|---|---|
| Norwegian (33) | 157 | 0.30 |
| Pennsylvania German (7) | 32 | 0.06 |
| Polish (1,257) | 3,828 | 7.42 |
| Portuguese (34) | 113 | 0.22 |
| Romanian (59) | 71 | 0.14 |
| Russian (120) | 491 | 0.95 |
| Scandinavian (0) | 7 | 0.01 |
| Scotch-Irish (132) | 396 | 0.77 |
| Scottish (153) | 935 | 1.81 |
| Serbian (0) | 16 | 0.03 |
| Slavic (17) | 24 | 0.05 |
| Slovak (10) | 43 | 0.08 |
| Slovene (13) | 13 | 0.03 |
| Soviet Union (0) | 0 | <0.01 |
| Swedish (86) | 482 | 0.93 |
| Swiss (34) | 255 | 0.49 |
| Turkish (238) | 245 | 0.47 |
| Ukrainian (617) | 1,169 | 2.27 |
| Welsh (21) | 352 | 0.68 |
| West Indian, ex. Hispanic (97) | 143 | 0.28 |
| Bahamian (0) | 0 | <0.01 |
| Barbadian (29) | 29 | 0.06 |
| Belizean (0) | 0 | <0.01 |
| Bermudan (0) | 0 | <0.01 |
| British West Indian (0) | 0 | <0.01 |
| Dutch West Indian (0) | 0 | <0.01 |
| Haitian (58) | 58 | 0.11 |
| Jamaican (10) | 56 | 0.11 |
| Trinidadian/Tobagonian (0) | 0 | <0.01 |
| U.S. Virgin Islander (0) | 0 | <0.01 |
| West Indian (0) | 0 | <0.01 |
| Other West Indian (0) | 0 | <0.01 |
| Yugoslavian (58) | 69 | 0.13 |

| Hispanic Origin | Population | % |
|---|---|---|
| Hispanic or Latino (of any race) | 3,220 | 6.23 |
| Central American, ex. Mexican | 88 | 0.17 |
| Costa Rican | 19 | 0.04 |
| Guatemalan | 28 | 0.05 |
| Honduran | 4 | 0.01 |
| Nicaraguan | 11 | 0.02 |
| Panamanian | 7 | 0.01 |
| Salvadoran | 19 | 0.04 |
| Other Central American | 0 | <0.01 |
| Cuban | 167 | 0.32 |
| Dominican Republic | 94 | 0.18 |
| Mexican | 145 | 0.28 |
| Puerto Rican | 2,436 | 4.71 |
| South American | 146 | 0.28 |
| Argentinean | 20 | 0.04 |
| Bolivian | 0 | <0.01 |
| Chilean | 23 | 0.04 |
| Colombian | 53 | 0.10 |
| Ecuadorian | 18 | 0.03 |
| Paraguayan | 3 | 0.01 |
| Peruvian | 10 | 0.02 |
| Uruguayan | 0 | <0.01 |
| Venezuelan | 15 | 0.03 |
| Other South American | 4 | 0.01 |
| Other Hispanic or Latino | 144 | 0.28 |

| Race* | Population | % |
|---|---|---|
| African-American/Black (3,996) | 4,577 | 8.85 |
| Not Hispanic (3,741) | 4,168 | 8.06 |
| Hispanic (255) | 409 | 0.79 |
| American Indian/Alaska Native (112) | 313 | 0.61 |
| Not Hispanic (81) | 240 | 0.46 |
| Hispanic (31) | 73 | 0.14 |
| Alaska Athabascan (Ala. Nat.) (0) | 0 | <0.01 |
| Aleut (Alaska Native) (0) | 0 | <0.01 |
| Apache (1) | 3 | <0.01 |
| Arapaho (0) | 0 | <0.01 |
| Blackfeet (3) | 4 | 0.01 |
| Canadian/French Am. Ind. (2) | 6 | 0.01 |
| Central American Ind. (1) | 1 | <0.01 |
| Cherokee (0) | 16 | 0.03 |
| Cheyenne (0) | 0 | <0.01 |
| Chickasaw (0) | 0 | <0.01 |
| Chippewa (6) | 7 | 0.01 |

| Race* | Population | % |
|---|---|---|
| Choctaw (0) | 0 | <0.01 |
| Colville (0) | 1 | <0.01 |
| Comanche (0) | 0 | <0.01 |
| Cree (0) | 0 | <0.01 |
| Creek (0) | 1 | <0.01 |
| Crow (0) | 0 | <0.01 |
| Delaware (3) | 7 | 0.01 |
| Hopi (0) | 0 | <0.01 |
| Houma (0) | 0 | <0.01 |
| Inupiat (Alaska Native) (0) | 0 | <0.01 |
| Iroquois (36) | 98 | 0.19 |
| Kiowa (0) | 0 | <0.01 |
| Lumbee (0) | 0 | <0.01 |
| Menominee (0) | 0 | <0.01 |
| Mexican American Ind. (5) | 5 | 0.01 |
| Navajo (0) | 0 | <0.01 |
| Osage (0) | 0 | <0.01 |
| Ottawa (0) | 0 | <0.01 |
| Paiute (0) | 0 | <0.01 |
| Pima (0) | 1 | <0.01 |
| Potawatomi (0) | 0 | <0.01 |
| Pueblo (0) | 1 | <0.01 |
| Puget Sound Salish (0) | 0 | <0.01 |
| Seminole (0) | 2 | <0.01 |
| Shoshone (0) | 0 | <0.01 |
| Sioux (0) | 0 | <0.01 |
| South American Ind. (2) | 6 | 0.01 |
| Spanish American Ind. (7) | 7 | 0.01 |
| Tlingit-Haida (Alaska Native) (0) | 0 | <0.01 |
| Tohono O'Odham (0) | 0 | <0.01 |
| Tsimshian (Alaska Native) (0) | 0 | <0.01 |
| Ute (0) | 0 | <0.01 |
| Yakama (0) | 0 | <0.01 |
| Yaqui (0) | 0 | <0.01 |
| Yuman (0) | 0 | <0.01 |
| Yup'ik (Alaska Native) (0) | 0 | <0.01 |
| Asian (662) | 888 | 1.72 |
| Not Hispanic (648) | 851 | 1.65 |
| Hispanic (14) | 37 | 0.07 |
| Bangladeshi (0) | 1 | <0.01 |
| Bhutanese (0) | 0 | <0.01 |
| Burmese (3) | 3 | 0.01 |
| Cambodian (29) | 31 | 0.06 |
| Chinese, ex. Taiwanese (120) | 146 | 0.28 |
| Filipino (101) | 155 | 0.30 |
| Hmong (0) | 0 | <0.01 |
| Indian (78) | 100 | 0.19 |
| Indonesian (1) | 5 | 0.01 |
| Japanese (12) | 37 | 0.07 |
| Korean (73) | 107 | 0.21 |
| Laotian (94) | 109 | 0.21 |
| Malaysian (0) | 1 | <0.01 |
| Nepalese (1) | 1 | <0.01 |
| Pakistani (28) | 30 | 0.06 |
| Sri Lankan (0) | 0 | <0.01 |
| Taiwanese (3) | 3 | 0.01 |
| Thai (7) | 15 | 0.03 |
| Vietnamese (88) | 98 | 0.19 |
| Hawaii Native/Pacific Islander (12) | 42 | 0.08 |
| Not Hispanic (10) | 34 | 0.07 |
| Hispanic (2) | 8 | 0.02 |
| Fijian (1) | 1 | <0.01 |
| Guamanian/Chamorro (2) | 2 | <0.01 |
| Marshallese (0) | 0 | <0.01 |
| Native Hawaiian (5) | 11 | 0.02 |
| Samoan (0) | 0 | <0.01 |
| Tongan (1) | 1 | <0.01 |
| White (44,883) | 45,826 | 88.65 |
| Not Hispanic (43,125) | 43,832 | 84.79 |
| Hispanic (1,758) | 1,994 | 3.86 |

Notes: † The Census 2010 population figure is used to calculate the percentages in the Hispanic Origin and Race categories. Ancestry percentages are based on the 2006-2010 American Community Survey population (not shown); ‡ Numbers in parentheses indicate the number of people reporting a single ancestry; * Numbers in parentheses indicate the number of persons reporting this race alone, not in combination with any other race; Please refer to the Explanation of Data for more information.

## Islip

Place Type: Town
County: Suffolk
Population: 335,543

| Ancestry | Population | % |
| --- | --- | --- |
| Afghan (182) | 263 | 0.08 |
| African, Sub-Saharan (854) | 1,222 | 0.37 |
| African (464) | 793 | 0.24 |
| Cape Verdean (0) | 0 | <0.01 |
| Ethiopian (0) | 0 | <0.01 |
| Ghanaian (71) | 71 | 0.02 |
| Kenyan (0) | 0 | <0.01 |
| Liberian (0) | 0 | <0.01 |
| Nigerian (164) | 203 | 0.06 |
| Senegalese (0) | 0 | <0.01 |
| Sierra Leonean (0) | 0 | <0.01 |
| Somalian (0) | 0 | <0.01 |
| South African (0) | 0 | <0.01 |
| Sudanese (0) | 0 | <0.01 |
| Ugandan (0) | 0 | <0.01 |
| Zimbabwean (0) | 0 | <0.01 |
| Other Sub-Saharan African (155) | 155 | 0.05 |
| Albanian (16) | 51 | 0.02 |
| Alsatian (0) | 18 | 0.01 |
| American (5,894) | 5,894 | 1.77 |
| Arab (986) | 1,453 | 0.44 |
| Arab (51) | 177 | 0.05 |
| Egyptian (339) | 364 | 0.11 |
| Iraqi (0) | 0 | <0.01 |
| Jordanian (68) | 122 | 0.04 |
| Lebanese (86) | 185 | 0.06 |
| Moroccan (123) | 141 | 0.04 |
| Palestinian (166) | 166 | 0.05 |
| Syrian (69) | 144 | 0.04 |
| Other Arab (84) | 154 | 0.05 |
| Armenian (174) | 272 | 0.08 |
| Assyrian/Chaldean/Syriac (0) | 0 | <0.01 |
| Australian (32) | 100 | 0.03 |
| Austrian (335) | 2,019 | 0.61 |
| Basque (18) | 18 | 0.01 |
| Belgian (68) | 328 | 0.10 |
| Brazilian (683) | 895 | 0.27 |
| British (132) | 453 | 0.14 |
| Bulgarian (0) | 0 | <0.01 |
| Cajun (0) | 23 | 0.01 |
| Canadian (111) | 405 | 0.12 |
| Carpatho Rusyn (0) | 0 | <0.01 |
| Celtic (28) | 53 | 0.02 |
| Croatian (88) | 291 | 0.09 |
| Cypriot (25) | 25 | 0.01 |
| Czech (409) | 2,026 | 0.61 |
| Czechoslovakian (224) | 596 | 0.18 |
| Danish (39) | 761 | 0.23 |
| Dutch (310) | 2,191 | 0.66 |
| Eastern European (337) | 433 | 0.13 |
| English (2,211) | 13,963 | 4.18 |
| Estonian (86) | 175 | 0.05 |
| European (772) | 811 | 0.24 |
| Finnish (59) | 271 | 0.08 |
| French, ex. Basque (403) | 4,451 | 1.33 |
| French Canadian (223) | 1,160 | 0.35 |
| German (7,849) | 48,335 | 14.48 |
| German Russian (0) | 0 | <0.01 |
| Greek (1,129) | 3,126 | 0.94 |
| Guyanese (460) | 499 | 0.15 |
| Hungarian (433) | 2,067 | 0.62 |
| Icelander (0) | 29 | 0.01 |
| Iranian (111) | 170 | 0.05 |
| Irish (17,586) | 68,763 | 20.61 |
| Israeli (36) | 56 | 0.02 |
| Italian (38,447) | 84,360 | 25.28 |
| Latvian (21) | 49 | 0.01 |
| Lithuanian (294) | 799 | 0.24 |
| Luxemburger (0) | 0 | <0.01 |
| Macedonian (0) | 0 | <0.01 |
| Maltese (54) | 292 | 0.09 |
| New Zealander (8) | 8 | <0.01 |
| Northern European (63) | 63 | 0.02 |
| Norwegian (661) | 2,978 | 0.89 |
| Pennsylvania German (0) | 0 | <0.01 |
| Polish (3,602) | 14,896 | 4.46 |
| Portuguese (1,434) | 1,977 | 0.59 |
| Romanian (213) | 467 | 0.14 |
| Russian (1,589) | 5,019 | 1.50 |
| Scandinavian (55) | 183 | 0.05 |
| Scotch-Irish (960) | 3,159 | 0.95 |
| Scottish (329) | 2,852 | 0.85 |
| Serbian (0) | 46 | 0.01 |
| Slavic (29) | 109 | 0.03 |
| Slovak (46) | 280 | 0.08 |
| Slovene (27) | 27 | 0.01 |
| Soviet Union (0) | 0 | <0.01 |
| Swedish (401) | 2,528 | 0.76 |
| Swiss (81) | 619 | 0.19 |
| Turkish (281) | 384 | 0.12 |
| Ukrainian (343) | 1,272 | 0.38 |
| Welsh (102) | 552 | 0.17 |
| West Indian, ex. Hispanic (8,546) | 10,274 | 3.08 |
| Bahamian (0) | 22 | 0.01 |
| Barbadian (22) | 63 | 0.02 |
| Belizean (35) | 35 | 0.01 |
| Bermudan (0) | 0 | <0.01 |
| British West Indian (255) | 470 | 0.14 |
| Dutch West Indian (16) | 16 | <0.01 |
| Haitian (5,195) | 5,636 | 1.69 |
| Jamaican (1,961) | 2,690 | 0.81 |
| Trinidadian/Tobagonian (530) | 665 | 0.20 |
| U.S. Virgin Islander (0) | 0 | <0.01 |
| West Indian (532) | 677 | 0.20 |
| Other West Indian (0) | 0 | <0.01 |
| Yugoslavian (70) | 202 | 0.06 |

| Hispanic Origin | Population | % |
| --- | --- | --- |
| Hispanic or Latino (of any race) | 97,371 | 29.02 |
| Central American, ex. Mexican | 38,530 | 11.48 |
| Costa Rican | 297 | 0.09 |
| Guatemalan | 3,256 | 0.97 |
| Honduran | 4,232 | 1.26 |
| Nicaraguan | 253 | 0.08 |
| Panamanian | 466 | 0.14 |
| Salvadoran | 29,849 | 8.90 |
| Other Central American | 177 | 0.05 |
| Cuban | 1,113 | 0.33 |
| Dominican Republic | 8,547 | 2.55 |
| Mexican | 3,139 | 0.94 |
| Puerto Rican | 21,506 | 6.41 |
| South American | 16,012 | 4.77 |
| Argentinean | 616 | 0.18 |
| Bolivian | 220 | 0.07 |
| Chilean | 448 | 0.13 |
| Colombian | 5,156 | 1.54 |
| Ecuadorian | 5,323 | 1.59 |
| Paraguayan | 58 | 0.02 |
| Peruvian | 3,599 | 1.07 |
| Uruguayan | 216 | 0.06 |
| Venezuelan | 322 | 0.10 |
| Other South American | 54 | 0.02 |
| Other Hispanic or Latino | 8,524 | 2.54 |

| Race* | Population | % |
| --- | --- | --- |
| African-American/Black (32,024) | 35,995 | 10.73 |
| Not Hispanic (27,898) | 30,295 | 9.03 |
| Hispanic (4,126) | 5,700 | 1.70 |
| American Indian/Alaska Native (1,586) | 3,396 | 1.01 |
| Not Hispanic (520) | 1,565 | 0.47 |
| Hispanic (1,066) | 1,831 | 0.55 |
| Alaska Athabascan (Ala. Nat.) (0) | 1 | <0.01 |
| Aleut (Alaska Native) (1) | 1 | <0.01 |
| Apache (5) | 12 | <0.01 |
| Arapaho (0) | 1 | <0.01 |
| Blackfeet (12) | 77 | 0.02 |
| Canadian/French Am. Ind. (0) | 0 | <0.01 |
| Central American Ind. (52) | 73 | 0.02 |
| Cherokee (44) | 316 | 0.09 |
| Cheyenne (0) | 1 | <0.01 |
| Chickasaw (1) | 3 | <0.01 |
| Chippewa (6) | 13 | <0.01 |
| Choctaw (3) | 17 | 0.01 |
| Colville (0) | 0 | <0.01 |
| Comanche (0) | 8 | <0.01 |
| Cree (0) | 0 | <0.01 |
| Creek (1) | 7 | <0.01 |
| Crow (11) | 16 | <0.01 |
| Delaware (1) | 7 | <0.01 |
| Hopi (1) | 3 | <0.01 |
| Houma (1) | 3 | <0.01 |
| Inupiat (Alaska Native) (1) | 2 | <0.01 |
| Iroquois (36) | 92 | 0.03 |
| Kiowa (0) | 0 | <0.01 |
| Lumbee (6) | 8 | <0.01 |
| Menominee (0) | 0 | <0.01 |
| Mexican American Ind. (83) | 135 | 0.04 |
| Navajo (7) | 14 | <0.01 |
| Osage (0) | 1 | <0.01 |
| Ottawa (0) | 0 | <0.01 |
| Paiute (0) | 0 | <0.01 |
| Pima (1) | 1 | <0.01 |
| Potawatomi (1) | 1 | <0.01 |
| Pueblo (4) | 7 | <0.01 |
| Puget Sound Salish (0) | 0 | <0.01 |
| Seminole (2) | 4 | <0.01 |
| Shoshone (0) | 3 | <0.01 |
| Sioux (6) | 27 | 0.01 |
| South American Ind. (143) | 249 | 0.07 |
| Spanish American Ind. (67) | 91 | 0.03 |
| Tlingit-Haida (Alaska Native) (5) | 6 | <0.01 |
| Tohono O'Odham (0) | 0 | <0.01 |
| Tsimshian (Alaska Native) (0) | 0 | <0.01 |
| Ute (0) | 0 | <0.01 |
| Yakama (0) | 0 | <0.01 |
| Yaqui (1) | 1 | <0.01 |
| Yuman (0) | 1 | <0.01 |
| Yup'ik (Alaska Native) (0) | 0 | <0.01 |
| Asian (9,572) | 11,510 | 3.43 |
| Not Hispanic (9,358) | 10,957 | 3.27 |
| Hispanic (214) | 553 | 0.16 |
| Bangladeshi (305) | 356 | 0.11 |
| Bhutanese (0) | 0 | <0.01 |
| Burmese (9) | 15 | <0.01 |
| Cambodian (23) | 24 | 0.01 |
| Chinese, ex. Taiwanese (1,424) | 1,766 | 0.53 |
| Filipino (1,012) | 1,301 | 0.39 |
| Hmong (0) | 0 | <0.01 |
| Indian (3,680) | 4,276 | 1.27 |
| Indonesian (29) | 37 | 0.01 |
| Japanese (91) | 216 | 0.06 |
| Korean (573) | 700 | 0.21 |
| Laotian (21) | 25 | 0.01 |
| Malaysian (5) | 12 | <0.01 |
| Nepalese (13) | 13 | <0.01 |
| Pakistani (1,368) | 1,520 | 0.45 |
| Sri Lankan (13) | 21 | 0.01 |
| Taiwanese (49) | 54 | 0.02 |
| Thai (80) | 106 | 0.03 |
| Vietnamese (433) | 518 | 0.15 |
| Hawaii Native/Pacific Islander (101) | 471 | 0.14 |
| Not Hispanic (52) | 244 | 0.07 |
| Hispanic (49) | 227 | 0.07 |
| Fijian (0) | 4 | <0.01 |
| Guamanian/Chamorro (28) | 44 | 0.01 |
| Marshallese (1) | 1 | <0.01 |
| Native Hawaiian (26) | 75 | 0.02 |
| Samoan (6) | 15 | <0.01 |
| Tongan (2) | 2 | <0.01 |
| White (245,918) | 254,235 | 75.77 |
| Not Hispanic (195,283) | 198,326 | 59.11 |
| Hispanic (50,635) | 55,909 | 16.66 |

*Notes: † The Census 2010 population figure is used to calculate the percentages in the Hispanic Origin and Race categories. Ancestry percentages are based on the 2006-2010 American Community Survey population (not shown); ‡ Numbers in parentheses indicate the number of people reporting a single ancestry; * Numbers in parentheses indicate the number of persons reporting this race alone, not in combination with any other race; Please refer to the Explanation of Data for more information.*

## Levittown

Place Type: CDP
County: Nassau
Population: 51,881

| Ancestry | Population | % |
|---|---|---|
| Afghan (0) | 0 | <0.01 |
| African, Sub-Saharan (0) | 20 | 0.04 |
| African (0) | 20 | 0.04 |
| Cape Verdean (0) | 0 | <0.01 |
| Ethiopian (0) | 0 | <0.01 |
| Ghanaian (0) | 0 | <0.01 |
| Kenyan (0) | 0 | <0.01 |
| Liberian (0) | 0 | <0.01 |
| Nigerian (0) | 0 | <0.01 |
| Senegalese (0) | 0 | <0.01 |
| Sierra Leonean (0) | 0 | <0.01 |
| Somalian (0) | 0 | <0.01 |
| South African (0) | 0 | <0.01 |
| Sudanese (0) | 0 | <0.01 |
| Ugandan (0) | 0 | <0.01 |
| Zimbabwean (0) | 0 | <0.01 |
| Other Sub-Saharan African (0) | 0 | <0.01 |
| Albanian (49) | 49 | 0.09 |
| Alsatian (0) | 0 | <0.01 |
| American (1,347) | 1,347 | 2.52 |
| Arab (190) | 271 | 0.51 |
| Arab (0) | 0 | <0.01 |
| Egyptian (136) | 136 | 0.25 |
| Iraqi (0) | 0 | <0.01 |
| Jordanian (0) | 0 | <0.01 |
| Lebanese (22) | 68 | 0.13 |
| Moroccan (10) | 10 | 0.02 |
| Palestinian (0) | 0 | <0.01 |
| Syrian (0) | 35 | 0.07 |
| Other Arab (22) | 22 | 0.04 |
| Armenian (21) | 80 | 0.15 |
| Assyrian/Chaldean/Syriac (0) | 0 | <0.01 |
| Australian (14) | 14 | 0.03 |
| Austrian (66) | 307 | 0.57 |
| Basque (0) | 16 | 0.03 |
| Belgian (10) | 18 | 0.03 |
| Brazilian (8) | 8 | 0.01 |
| British (92) | 121 | 0.23 |
| Bulgarian (0) | 0 | <0.01 |
| Cajun (0) | 0 | <0.01 |
| Canadian (11) | 74 | 0.14 |
| Carpatho Rusyn (0) | 0 | <0.01 |
| Celtic (0) | 0 | <0.01 |
| Croatian (24) | 67 | 0.13 |
| Cypriot (0) | 0 | <0.01 |
| Czech (44) | 215 | 0.40 |
| Czechoslovakian (25) | 47 | 0.09 |
| Danish (10) | 110 | 0.21 |
| Dutch (11) | 340 | 0.64 |
| Eastern European (107) | 107 | 0.20 |
| English (316) | 2,076 | 3.88 |
| Estonian (0) | 0 | <0.01 |
| European (276) | 321 | 0.60 |
| Finnish (0) | 36 | 0.07 |
| French, ex. Basque (239) | 1,242 | 2.32 |
| French Canadian (74) | 206 | 0.39 |
| German (1,428) | 9,190 | 17.18 |
| German Russian (0) | 0 | <0.01 |
| Greek (630) | 1,100 | 2.06 |
| Guyanese (0) | 0 | <0.01 |
| Hungarian (158) | 781 | 1.46 |
| Icelander (9) | 52 | 0.10 |
| Iranian (23) | 79 | 0.15 |
| Irish (4,151) | 14,886 | 27.84 |
| Israeli (32) | 72 | 0.13 |
| Italian (8,524) | 17,446 | 32.62 |
| Latvian (0) | 31 | 0.06 |
| Lithuanian (73) | 314 | 0.59 |
| Luxemburger (0) | 0 | <0.01 |
| Macedonian (0) | 0 | <0.01 |
| Maltese (45) | 96 | 0.18 |
| New Zealander (0) | 0 | <0.01 |
| Northern European (0) | 0 | <0.01 |
| Norwegian (49) | 274 | 0.51 |
| Pennsylvania German (0) | 54 | 0.10 |
| Polish (535) | 2,652 | 4.96 |
| Portuguese (189) | 243 | 0.45 |
| Romanian (27) | 98 | 0.18 |
| Russian (640) | 1,993 | 3.73 |
| Scandinavian (0) | 33 | 0.06 |
| Scotch-Irish (261) | 722 | 1.35 |
| Scottish (53) | 303 | 0.57 |
| Serbian (0) | 0 | <0.01 |
| Slavic (0) | 0 | <0.01 |
| Slovak (6) | 6 | 0.01 |
| Slovene (0) | 0 | <0.01 |
| Soviet Union (0) | 0 | <0.01 |
| Swedish (13) | 287 | 0.54 |
| Swiss (55) | 105 | 0.20 |
| Turkish (112) | 181 | 0.34 |
| Ukrainian (83) | 249 | 0.47 |
| Welsh (0) | 43 | 0.08 |
| West Indian, ex. Hispanic (89) | 117 | 0.22 |
| Bahamian (0) | 0 | <0.01 |
| Barbadian (0) | 0 | <0.01 |
| Belizean (0) | 0 | <0.01 |
| Bermudan (0) | 0 | <0.01 |
| British West Indian (0) | 0 | <0.01 |
| Dutch West Indian (0) | 0 | <0.01 |
| Haitian (0) | 0 | <0.01 |
| Jamaican (20) | 36 | 0.07 |
| Trinidadian/Tobagonian (69) | 69 | 0.13 |
| U.S. Virgin Islander (0) | 0 | <0.01 |
| West Indian (0) | 12 | 0.02 |
| Other West Indian (0) | 0 | <0.01 |
| Yugoslavian (41) | 52 | 0.10 |

| Hispanic Origin | Population | % |
|---|---|---|
| Hispanic or Latino (of any race) | 5,979 | 11.52 |
| Central American, ex. Mexican | 1,200 | 2.31 |
| Costa Rican | 41 | 0.08 |
| Guatemalan | 132 | 0.25 |
| Honduran | 103 | 0.20 |
| Nicaraguan | 26 | 0.05 |
| Panamanian | 12 | 0.02 |
| Salvadoran | 876 | 1.69 |
| Other Central American | 10 | 0.02 |
| Cuban | 274 | 0.53 |
| Dominican Republic | 260 | 0.50 |
| Mexican | 214 | 0.41 |
| Puerto Rican | 1,716 | 3.31 |
| South American | 1,746 | 3.37 |
| Argentinean | 82 | 0.16 |
| Bolivian | 18 | 0.03 |
| Chilean | 112 | 0.22 |
| Colombian | 733 | 1.41 |
| Ecuadorian | 400 | 0.77 |
| Paraguayan | 19 | 0.04 |
| Peruvian | 285 | 0.55 |
| Uruguayan | 47 | 0.09 |
| Venezuelan | 23 | 0.04 |
| Other South American | 27 | 0.05 |
| Other Hispanic or Latino | 569 | 1.10 |

| Race* | Population | % |
|---|---|---|
| African-American/Black (470) | 667 | 1.29 |
| Not Hispanic (403) | 539 | 1.04 |
| Hispanic (67) | 128 | 0.25 |
| American Indian/Alaska Native (55) | 185 | 0.36 |
| Not Hispanic (43) | 134 | 0.26 |
| Hispanic (12) | 51 | 0.10 |
| Alaska Athabascan (Ala. Nat.) (0) | 0 | <0.01 |
| Aleut (Alaska Native) (0) | 0 | <0.01 |
| Apache (0) | 0 | <0.01 |
| Arapaho (0) | 0 | <0.01 |
| Blackfeet (0) | 4 | 0.01 |
| Canadian/French Am. Ind. (0) | 0 | <0.01 |
| Central American Ind. (0) | 0 | <0.01 |
| Cherokee (2) | 26 | 0.05 |
| Cheyenne (0) | 0 | <0.01 |
| Chickasaw (0) | 0 | <0.01 |
| Chippewa (1) | 1 | <0.01 |
| Choctaw (0) | 1 | <0.01 |
| Colville (0) | 0 | <0.01 |
| Comanche (7) | 7 | 0.01 |
| Cree (0) | 0 | <0.01 |
| Creek (0) | 1 | <0.01 |
| Crow (0) | 0 | <0.01 |
| Delaware (0) | 0 | <0.01 |
| Hopi (0) | 0 | <0.01 |
| Houma (0) | 0 | <0.01 |
| Inupiat (Alaska Native) (0) | 0 | <0.01 |
| Iroquois (4) | 13 | 0.03 |
| Kiowa (0) | 0 | <0.01 |
| Lumbee (3) | 6 | 0.01 |
| Menominee (0) | 0 | <0.01 |
| Mexican American Ind. (0) | 5 | 0.01 |
| Navajo (0) | 0 | <0.01 |
| Osage (0) | 1 | <0.01 |
| Ottawa (0) | 0 | <0.01 |
| Paiute (0) | 0 | <0.01 |
| Pima (0) | 0 | <0.01 |
| Potawatomi (0) | 0 | <0.01 |
| Pueblo (0) | 0 | <0.01 |
| Puget Sound Salish (0) | 0 | <0.01 |
| Seminole (1) | 3 | 0.01 |
| Shoshone (1) | 1 | <0.01 |
| Sioux (0) | 1 | <0.01 |
| South American Ind. (9) | 12 | 0.02 |
| Spanish American Ind. (0) | 1 | <0.01 |
| Tlingit-Haida (Alaska Native) (0) | 0 | <0.01 |
| Tohono O'Odham (0) | 0 | <0.01 |
| Tsimshian (Alaska Native) (0) | 0 | <0.01 |
| Ute (0) | 0 | <0.01 |
| Yakama (0) | 0 | <0.01 |
| Yaqui (0) | 0 | <0.01 |
| Yuman (0) | 0 | <0.01 |
| Yup'ik (Alaska Native) (0) | 0 | <0.01 |
| Asian (2,956) | 3,352 | 6.46 |
| Not Hispanic (2,937) | 3,298 | 6.36 |
| Hispanic (19) | 54 | 0.10 |
| Bangladeshi (65) | 70 | 0.13 |
| Bhutanese (0) | 0 | <0.01 |
| Burmese (1) | 6 | 0.01 |
| Cambodian (10) | 14 | 0.03 |
| Chinese, ex. Taiwanese (467) | 589 | 1.14 |
| Filipino (446) | 525 | 1.01 |
| Hmong (0) | 0 | <0.01 |
| Indian (1,110) | 1,212 | 2.34 |
| Indonesian (4) | 6 | 0.01 |
| Japanese (26) | 44 | 0.08 |
| Korean (358) | 380 | 0.73 |
| Laotian (3) | 3 | 0.01 |
| Malaysian (0) | 7 | 0.01 |
| Nepalese (2) | 2 | <0.01 |
| Pakistani (226) | 239 | 0.46 |
| Sri Lankan (1) | 1 | <0.01 |
| Taiwanese (22) | 25 | 0.05 |
| Thai (26) | 40 | 0.08 |
| Vietnamese (103) | 107 | 0.21 |
| Hawaii Native/Pacific Islander (10) | 47 | 0.09 |
| Not Hispanic (6) | 21 | 0.04 |
| Hispanic (4) | 26 | 0.05 |
| Fijian (0) | 0 | <0.01 |
| Guamanian/Chamorro (2) | 3 | 0.01 |
| Marshallese (0) | 0 | <0.01 |
| Native Hawaiian (0) | 3 | 0.01 |
| Samoan (5) | 7 | 0.01 |
| Tongan (0) | 0 | <0.01 |
| White (46,137) | 46,970 | 90.53 |
| Not Hispanic (41,814) | 42,268 | 81.47 |
| Hispanic (4,323) | 4,702 | 9.06 |

Notes: † The Census 2010 population figure is used to calculate the percentages in the Hispanic Origin and Race categories. Ancestry percentages are based on the 2006-2010 American Community Survey population (not shown); ‡ Numbers in parentheses indicate the number of people reporting a single ancestry; * Numbers in parentheses indicate the number of persons reporting this race alone, not in combination with any other race; Please refer to the Explanation of Data for more information.

## Manhattan

Place Type: Borough
County: New York
Population: 1,585,873

| Ancestry | Population | % |
|---|---|---|
| Afghan (59) | 85 | 0.01 |
| African, Sub-Saharan (19,667) | 24,146 | 1.52 |
| African (10,054) | 12,839 | 0.81 |
| Cape Verdean (81) | 206 | 0.01 |
| Ethiopian (932) | 1,043 | 0.07 |
| Ghanaian (714) | 818 | 0.05 |
| Kenyan (43) | 69 | <0.01 |
| Liberian (169) | 176 | 0.01 |
| Nigerian (1,650) | 1,953 | 0.12 |
| Senegalese (1,118) | 1,216 | 0.08 |
| Sierra Leonean (422) | 422 | 0.03 |
| Somalian (125) | 125 | 0.01 |
| South African (991) | 1,372 | 0.09 |
| Sudanese (137) | 137 | 0.01 |
| Ugandan (95) | 125 | 0.01 |
| Zimbabwean (80) | 100 | 0.01 |
| Other Sub-Saharan African (3,056) | 3,545 | 0.22 |
| Albanian (1,385) | 1,618 | 0.10 |
| Alsatian (5) | 129 | 0.01 |
| American (54,694) | 54,694 | 3.45 |
| Arab (8,584) | 13,828 | 0.87 |
| Arab (1,250) | 1,720 | 0.11 |
| Egyptian (1,374) | 1,906 | 0.12 |
| Iraqi (275) | 583 | 0.04 |
| Jordanian (0) | 48 | <0.01 |
| Lebanese (1,838) | 3,331 | 0.21 |
| Moroccan (914) | 1,592 | 0.10 |
| Palestinian (626) | 794 | 0.05 |
| Syrian (518) | 1,112 | 0.07 |
| Other Arab (1,789) | 2,742 | 0.17 |
| Armenian (1,520) | 2,653 | 0.17 |
| Assyrian/Chaldean/Syriac (94) | 137 | 0.01 |
| Australian (1,965) | 2,719 | 0.17 |
| Austrian (4,202) | 14,656 | 0.93 |
| Basque (191) | 428 | 0.03 |
| Belgian (928) | 2,470 | 0.16 |
| Brazilian (2,870) | 4,541 | 0.29 |
| British (6,950) | 12,129 | 0.77 |
| Bulgarian (927) | 1,272 | 0.08 |
| Cajun (22) | 224 | 0.01 |
| Canadian (3,037) | 5,646 | 0.36 |
| Carpatho Rusyn (89) | 112 | 0.01 |
| Celtic (129) | 304 | 0.02 |
| Croatian (1,299) | 2,164 | 0.14 |
| Cypriot (139) | 216 | 0.01 |
| Czech (1,439) | 4,820 | 0.30 |
| Czechoslovakian (619) | 1,256 | 0.08 |
| Danish (1,444) | 4,095 | 0.26 |
| Dutch (2,847) | 10,414 | 0.66 |
| Eastern European (23,269) | 25,277 | 1.60 |
| English (22,270) | 77,799 | 4.91 |
| Estonian (190) | 424 | 0.03 |
| European (25,127) | 27,846 | 1.76 |
| Finnish (666) | 1,658 | 0.10 |
| French, ex. Basque (10,278) | 31,783 | 2.01 |
| French Canadian (1,692) | 5,246 | 0.33 |
| German (27,493) | 107,666 | 6.80 |
| German Russian (0) | 41 | <0.01 |
| Greek (7,557) | 13,078 | 0.83 |
| Guyanese (1,802) | 2,259 | 0.14 |
| Hungarian (4,686) | 14,667 | 0.93 |
| Icelander (246) | 382 | 0.02 |
| Iranian (3,458) | 4,256 | 0.27 |
| Irish (40,008) | 117,355 | 7.41 |
| Israeli (4,839) | 6,624 | 0.42 |
| Italian (44,498) | 98,563 | 6.22 |
| Latvian (713) | 1,822 | 0.12 |
| Lithuanian (1,597) | 5,775 | 0.36 |
| Luxemburger (23) | 68 | <0.01 |
| Macedonian (973) | 1,086 | 0.07 |
| Maltese (548) | 840 | 0.05 |
| New Zealander (243) | 405 | 0.03 |
| Northern European (1,296) | 1,485 | 0.09 |

| Ancestry | Population | % |
|---|---|---|
| Norwegian (1,552) | 7,445 | 0.47 |
| Pennsylvania German (123) | 327 | 0.02 |
| Polish (20,565) | 64,078 | 4.05 |
| Portuguese (1,436) | 3,862 | 0.24 |
| Romanian (3,035) | 7,692 | 0.49 |
| Russian (36,296) | 82,983 | 5.24 |
| Scandinavian (753) | 1,731 | 0.11 |
| Scotch-Irish (4,283) | 13,158 | 0.83 |
| Scottish (4,846) | 19,553 | 1.23 |
| Serbian (1,160) | 1,526 | 0.10 |
| Slavic (177) | 400 | 0.03 |
| Slovak (812) | 2,298 | 0.15 |
| Slovene (271) | 695 | 0.04 |
| Soviet Union (28) | 54 | <0.01 |
| Swedish (3,045) | 10,408 | 0.66 |
| Swiss (1,381) | 4,962 | 0.31 |
| Turkish (2,708) | 3,703 | 0.23 |
| Ukrainian (4,361) | 8,849 | 0.56 |
| Welsh (944) | 6,000 | 0.38 |
| West Indian, ex. Hispanic (22,411) | 30,009 | 1.90 |
| Bahamian (303) | 457 | 0.03 |
| Barbadian (738) | 907 | 0.06 |
| Belizean (654) | 735 | 0.05 |
| Bermudan (86) | 127 | 0.01 |
| British West Indian (1,308) | 1,658 | 0.10 |
| Dutch West Indian (212) | 276 | 0.02 |
| Haitian (5,308) | 6,500 | 0.41 |
| Jamaican (7,099) | 9,242 | 0.58 |
| Trinidadian/Tobagonian (3,010) | 3,877 | 0.24 |
| U.S. Virgin Islander (343) | 487 | 0.03 |
| West Indian (3,296) | 5,618 | 0.35 |
| Other West Indian (54) | 125 | 0.01 |
| Yugoslavian (1,478) | 1,876 | 0.12 |

| Hispanic Origin | Population | % |
|---|---|---|
| Hispanic or Latino (of any race) | 403,577 | 25.45 |
| Central American, ex. Mexican | 13,948 | 0.88 |
| Costa Rican | 987 | 0.06 |
| Guatemalan | 2,051 | 0.13 |
| Honduran | 4,058 | 0.26 |
| Nicaraguan | 1,556 | 0.10 |
| Panamanian | 1,716 | 0.11 |
| Salvadoran | 3,419 | 0.22 |
| Other Central American | 161 | 0.01 |
| Cuban | 11,623 | 0.73 |
| Dominican Republic | 155,971 | 9.84 |
| Mexican | 41,965 | 2.65 |
| Puerto Rican | 107,774 | 6.80 |
| South American | 36,748 | 2.32 |
| Argentinean | 4,339 | 0.27 |
| Bolivian | 522 | 0.03 |
| Chilean | 1,824 | 0.12 |
| Colombian | 8,411 | 0.53 |
| Ecuadorian | 14,132 | 0.89 |
| Paraguayan | 268 | 0.02 |
| Peruvian | 3,852 | 0.24 |
| Uruguayan | 549 | 0.03 |
| Venezuelan | 2,573 | 0.16 |
| Other South American | 278 | 0.02 |
| Other Hispanic or Latino | 35,548 | 2.24 |

| Race* | Population | % |
|---|---|---|
| African-American/Black (246,687) | 272,993 | 17.21 |
| Not Hispanic (205,340) | 217,102 | 13.69 |
| Hispanic (41,347) | 55,891 | 3.52 |
| American Indian/Alaska Native (8,669) | 19,415 | 1.22 |
| Not Hispanic (2,144) | 7,395 | 0.47 |
| Hispanic (6,525) | 12,020 | 0.76 |
| Alaska Athabascan (Ala. Nat.) (11) | 18 | <0.01 |
| Aleut (Alaska Native) (4) | 7 | <0.01 |
| Apache (28) | 92 | 0.01 |
| Arapaho (3) | 5 | <0.01 |
| Blackfeet (41) | 356 | 0.02 |
| Canadian/French Am. Ind. (29) | 62 | <0.01 |
| Central American Ind. (610) | 1,090 | 0.07 |
| Cherokee (288) | 1,845 | 0.12 |
| Cheyenne (4) | 9 | <0.01 |
| Chickasaw (15) | 43 | <0.01 |
| Chippewa (36) | 99 | 0.01 |

| Race* | Population | % |
|---|---|---|
| Choctaw (41) | 179 | 0.01 |
| Colville (4) | 5 | <0.01 |
| Comanche (13) | 22 | <0.01 |
| Cree (4) | 22 | <0.01 |
| Creek (12) | 61 | <0.01 |
| Crow (4) | 11 | <0.01 |
| Delaware (14) | 54 | <0.01 |
| Hopi (8) | 15 | <0.01 |
| Houma (0) | 3 | <0.01 |
| Inupiat (Alaska Native) (2) | 8 | <0.01 |
| Iroquois (97) | 265 | 0.02 |
| Kiowa (9) | 11 | <0.01 |
| Lumbee (10) | 21 | <0.01 |
| Menominee (2) | 3 | <0.01 |
| Mexican American Ind. (479) | 752 | 0.05 |
| Navajo (38) | 83 | 0.01 |
| Osage (7) | 12 | <0.01 |
| Ottawa (0) | 3 | <0.01 |
| Paiute (2) | 8 | <0.01 |
| Pima (2) | 4 | <0.01 |
| Potawatomi (10) | 20 | <0.01 |
| Pueblo (70) | 175 | 0.01 |
| Puget Sound Salish (2) | 5 | <0.01 |
| Seminole (6) | 110 | 0.01 |
| Shoshone (3) | 6 | <0.01 |
| Sioux (38) | 133 | 0.01 |
| South American Ind. (813) | 1,935 | 0.12 |
| Spanish American Ind. (373) | 514 | 0.03 |
| Tlingit-Haida (Alaska Native) (2) | 15 | <0.01 |
| Tohono O'Odham (11) | 15 | <0.01 |
| Tsimshian (Alaska Native) (3) | 3 | <0.01 |
| Ute (1) | 2 | <0.01 |
| Yakama (1) | 2 | <0.01 |
| Yaqui (8) | 22 | <0.01 |
| Yuman (4) | 6 | <0.01 |
| Yup'ik (Alaska Native) (0) | 2 | <0.01 |
| Asian (179,552) | 199,722 | 12.59 |
| Not Hispanic (177,624) | 194,929 | 12.29 |
| Hispanic (1,928) | 4,793 | 0.30 |
| Bangladeshi (1,672) | 2,029 | 0.13 |
| Bhutanese (26) | 26 | <0.01 |
| Burmese (240) | 317 | 0.02 |
| Cambodian (168) | 220 | 0.01 |
| Chinese, ex. Taiwanese (92,088) | 99,287 | 6.26 |
| Filipino (10,399) | 13,388 | 0.84 |
| Hmong (16) | 20 | <0.01 |
| Indian (25,857) | 29,979 | 1.89 |
| Indonesian (470) | 693 | 0.04 |
| Japanese (13,201) | 16,600 | 1.05 |
| Korean (19,683) | 21,996 | 1.39 |
| Laotian (109) | 157 | 0.01 |
| Malaysian (524) | 766 | 0.05 |
| Nepalese (240) | 281 | 0.02 |
| Pakistani (2,482) | 2,940 | 0.19 |
| Sri Lankan (450) | 563 | 0.04 |
| Taiwanese (2,789) | 3,318 | 0.21 |
| Thai (1,282) | 1,657 | 0.10 |
| Vietnamese (2,194) | 2,919 | 0.18 |
| Hawaii Native/Pacific Islander (873) | 3,727 | 0.24 |
| Not Hispanic (533) | 1,776 | 0.11 |
| Hispanic (340) | 1,951 | 0.12 |
| Fijian (29) | 73 | <0.01 |
| Guamanian/Chamorro (132) | 242 | 0.02 |
| Marshallese (3) | 4 | <0.01 |
| Native Hawaiian (185) | 608 | 0.04 |
| Samoan (87) | 183 | 0.01 |
| Tongan (18) | 33 | <0.01 |
| White (911,073) | 956,864 | 60.34 |
| Not Hispanic (761,493) | 785,299 | 49.52 |
| Hispanic (149,580) | 171,565 | 10.82 |

Notes: † The Census 2010 population figure is used to calculate the percentages in the Hispanic Origin and Race categories. Ancestry percentages are based on the 2006-2010 American Community Survey population (not shown); ‡ Numbers in parentheses indicate the number of people reporting a single ancestry; * Numbers in parentheses indicate the number of persons reporting this race alone, not in combination with any other race; Please refer to the Explanation of Data for more information.

## Mount Vernon

Place Type: City
County: Westchester
Population: 67,292

| Ancestry | Population | % |
|---|---|---|
| Afghan (0) | 0 | <0.01 |
| African, Sub-Saharan (1,490) | 1,910 | 2.85 |
| African (786) | 1,162 | 1.73 |
| Cape Verdean (0) | 11 | 0.02 |
| Ethiopian (0) | 0 | <0.01 |
| Ghanaian (347) | 347 | 0.52 |
| Kenyan (0) | 0 | <0.01 |
| Liberian (0) | 9 | 0.01 |
| Nigerian (148) | 148 | 0.22 |
| Senegalese (0) | 12 | 0.02 |
| Sierra Leonean (10) | 22 | 0.03 |
| Somalian (0) | 0 | <0.01 |
| South African (0) | 0 | <0.01 |
| Sudanese (0) | 0 | <0.01 |
| Ugandan (19) | 19 | 0.03 |
| Zimbabwean (0) | 0 | <0.01 |
| Other Sub-Saharan African (180) | 180 | 0.27 |
| Albanian (303) | 303 | 0.45 |
| Alsatian (0) | 0 | <0.01 |
| American (2,069) | 2,069 | 3.08 |
| Arab (217) | 305 | 0.45 |
| Arab (0) | 0 | <0.01 |
| Egyptian (56) | 68 | 0.10 |
| Iraqi (0) | 0 | <0.01 |
| Jordanian (0) | 0 | <0.01 |
| Lebanese (0) | 12 | 0.02 |
| Moroccan (0) | 64 | 0.10 |
| Palestinian (13) | 13 | 0.02 |
| Syrian (0) | 0 | <0.01 |
| Other Arab (148) | 148 | 0.22 |
| Armenian (0) | 0 | <0.01 |
| Assyrian/Chaldean/Syriac (0) | 0 | <0.01 |
| Australian (0) | 13 | 0.02 |
| Austrian (60) | 150 | 0.22 |
| Basque (0) | 0 | <0.01 |
| Belgian (0) | 0 | <0.01 |
| Brazilian (1,938) | 2,013 | 3.00 |
| British (45) | 146 | 0.22 |
| Bulgarian (0) | 0 | <0.01 |
| Cajun (0) | 0 | <0.01 |
| Canadian (0) | 61 | 0.09 |
| Carpatho Rusyn (0) | 0 | <0.01 |
| Celtic (0) | 0 | <0.01 |
| Croatian (0) | 0 | <0.01 |
| Cypriot (0) | 0 | <0.01 |
| Czech (47) | 70 | 0.10 |
| Czechoslovakian (11) | 11 | 0.02 |
| Danish (10) | 21 | 0.03 |
| Dutch (22) | 191 | 0.28 |
| Eastern European (93) | 127 | 0.19 |
| English (260) | 843 | 1.26 |
| Estonian (21) | 45 | 0.07 |
| European (145) | 145 | 0.22 |
| Finnish (12) | 12 | 0.02 |
| French, ex. Basque (129) | 377 | 0.56 |
| French Canadian (14) | 62 | 0.09 |
| German (373) | 1,326 | 1.98 |
| German Russian (0) | 0 | <0.01 |
| Greek (100) | 185 | 0.28 |
| Guyanese (326) | 360 | 0.54 |
| Hungarian (74) | 129 | 0.19 |
| Icelander (0) | 0 | <0.01 |
| Iranian (0) | 21 | 0.03 |
| Irish (950) | 2,889 | 4.31 |
| Israeli (116) | 174 | 0.26 |
| Italian (3,462) | 5,281 | 7.87 |
| Latvian (0) | 10 | 0.01 |
| Lithuanian (13) | 57 | 0.08 |
| Luxemburger (0) | 0 | <0.01 |
| Macedonian (0) | 0 | <0.01 |
| Maltese (24) | 24 | 0.04 |
| New Zealander (0) | 0 | <0.01 |
| Northern European (0) | 0 | <0.01 |

| Ancestry | Population | % |
|---|---|---|
| Norwegian (10) | 21 | 0.03 |
| Pennsylvania German (0) | 0 | <0.01 |
| Polish (283) | 651 | 0.97 |
| Portuguese (979) | 1,149 | 1.71 |
| Romanian (123) | 123 | 0.18 |
| Russian (143) | 433 | 0.65 |
| Scandinavian (15) | 15 | 0.02 |
| Scotch-Irish (60) | 127 | 0.19 |
| Scottish (46) | 150 | 0.22 |
| Serbian (8) | 8 | 0.01 |
| Slavic (9) | 9 | 0.01 |
| Slovak (0) | 0 | <0.01 |
| Slovene (0) | 0 | <0.01 |
| Soviet Union (0) | 0 | <0.01 |
| Swedish (0) | 46 | 0.07 |
| Swiss (0) | 0 | <0.01 |
| Turkish (0) | 0 | <0.01 |
| Ukrainian (0) | 69 | 0.10 |
| Welsh (0) | 63 | 0.09 |
| West Indian, ex. Hispanic (12,148) | 13,279 | 19.80 |
| Bahamian (11) | 11 | 0.02 |
| Barbadian (190) | 208 | 0.31 |
| Belizean (118) | 118 | 0.18 |
| Bermudan (0) | 0 | <0.01 |
| British West Indian (315) | 348 | 0.52 |
| Dutch West Indian (0) | 0 | <0.01 |
| Haitian (324) | 465 | 0.69 |
| Jamaican (9,769) | 10,445 | 15.57 |
| Trinidadian/Tobagonian (370) | 397 | 0.59 |
| U.S. Virgin Islander (0) | 0 | <0.01 |
| West Indian (1,051) | 1,287 | 1.92 |
| Other West Indian (0) | 0 | <0.01 |
| Yugoslavian (9) | 9 | 0.01 |

| Hispanic Origin | Population | % |
|---|---|---|
| Hispanic or Latino (of any race) | 9,592 | 14.25 |
| Central American, ex. Mexican | 754 | 1.12 |
| Costa Rican | 64 | 0.10 |
| Guatemalan | 141 | 0.21 |
| Honduran | 233 | 0.35 |
| Nicaraguan | 35 | 0.05 |
| Panamanian | 131 | 0.19 |
| Salvadoran | 137 | 0.20 |
| Other Central American | 13 | 0.02 |
| Cuban | 231 | 0.34 |
| Dominican Republic | 1,611 | 2.39 |
| Mexican | 2,454 | 3.65 |
| Puerto Rican | 2,582 | 3.84 |
| South American | 1,205 | 1.79 |
| Argentinean | 91 | 0.14 |
| Bolivian | 18 | 0.03 |
| Chilean | 29 | 0.04 |
| Colombian | 407 | 0.60 |
| Ecuadorian | 268 | 0.40 |
| Paraguayan | 68 | 0.10 |
| Peruvian | 219 | 0.33 |
| Uruguayan | 16 | 0.02 |
| Venezuelan | 56 | 0.08 |
| Other South American | 33 | 0.05 |
| Other Hispanic or Latino | 755 | 1.12 |

| Race* | Population | % |
|---|---|---|
| African-American/Black (42,667) | 44,244 | 65.75 |
| Not Hispanic (41,226) | 42,361 | 62.95 |
| Hispanic (1,441) | 1,883 | 2.80 |
| American Indian/Alaska Native (312) | 820 | 1.22 |
| Not Hispanic (200) | 585 | 0.87 |
| Hispanic (112) | 235 | 0.35 |
| Alaska Athabascan (Ala. Nat.) (0) | 0 | <0.01 |
| Aleut (Alaska Native) (0) | 0 | <0.01 |
| Apache (0) | 0 | <0.01 |
| Arapaho (0) | 0 | <0.01 |
| Blackfeet (1) | 38 | 0.06 |
| Canadian/French Am. Ind. (0) | 0 | <0.01 |
| Central American Ind. (7) | 19 | 0.03 |
| Cherokee (27) | 116 | 0.17 |
| Cheyenne (0) | 0 | <0.01 |
| Chickasaw (2) | 4 | 0.01 |
| Chippewa (0) | 0 | <0.01 |

| Race* | Population | % |
|---|---|---|
| Choctaw (4) | 4 | 0.01 |
| Colville (0) | 0 | <0.01 |
| Comanche (0) | 0 | <0.01 |
| Cree (0) | 2 | <0.01 |
| Creek (0) | 0 | <0.01 |
| Crow (0) | 0 | <0.01 |
| Delaware (1) | 1 | <0.01 |
| Hopi (0) | 0 | <0.01 |
| Houma (0) | 0 | <0.01 |
| Inupiat (Alaska Native) (0) | 0 | <0.01 |
| Iroquois (2) | 8 | 0.01 |
| Kiowa (0) | 0 | <0.01 |
| Lumbee (0) | 0 | <0.01 |
| Menominee (0) | 0 | <0.01 |
| Mexican American Ind. (13) | 14 | 0.02 |
| Navajo (1) | 2 | <0.01 |
| Osage (0) | 0 | <0.01 |
| Ottawa (0) | 0 | <0.01 |
| Paiute (0) | 0 | <0.01 |
| Pima (0) | 0 | <0.01 |
| Potawatomi (0) | 0 | <0.01 |
| Pueblo (4) | 7 | 0.01 |
| Puget Sound Salish (0) | 0 | <0.01 |
| Seminole (0) | 9 | 0.01 |
| Shoshone (0) | 0 | <0.01 |
| Sioux (1) | 6 | 0.01 |
| South American Ind. (15) | 36 | 0.05 |
| Spanish American Ind. (0) | 4 | 0.01 |
| Tlingit-Haida (Alaska Native) (0) | 0 | <0.01 |
| Tohono O'Odham (0) | 0 | <0.01 |
| Tsimshian (Alaska Native) (0) | 0 | <0.01 |
| Ute (0) | 0 | <0.01 |
| Yakama (0) | 0 | <0.01 |
| Yaqui (0) | 0 | <0.01 |
| Yuman (0) | 0 | <0.01 |
| Yup'ik (Alaska Native) (0) | 0 | <0.01 |
| Asian (1,236) | 1,672 | 2.48 |
| Not Hispanic (1,206) | 1,587 | 2.36 |
| Hispanic (30) | 85 | 0.13 |
| Bangladeshi (7) | 11 | 0.02 |
| Bhutanese (0) | 0 | <0.01 |
| Burmese (2) | 2 | <0.01 |
| Cambodian (7) | 9 | 0.01 |
| Chinese, ex. Taiwanese (187) | 264 | 0.39 |
| Filipino (220) | 281 | 0.42 |
| Hmong (0) | 0 | <0.01 |
| Indian (529) | 711 | 1.06 |
| Indonesian (0) | 11 | 0.02 |
| Japanese (55) | 88 | 0.13 |
| Korean (72) | 92 | 0.14 |
| Laotian (5) | 12 | 0.02 |
| Malaysian (0) | 1 | <0.01 |
| Nepalese (4) | 4 | 0.01 |
| Pakistani (26) | 38 | 0.06 |
| Sri Lankan (1) | 1 | <0.01 |
| Taiwanese (10) | 10 | 0.01 |
| Thai (67) | 73 | 0.11 |
| Vietnamese (7) | 12 | 0.02 |
| Hawaii Native/Pacific Islander (36) | 156 | 0.23 |
| Not Hispanic (27) | 130 | 0.19 |
| Hispanic (9) | 26 | 0.04 |
| Fijian (0) | 1 | <0.01 |
| Guamanian/Chamorro (1) | 4 | 0.01 |
| Marshallese (0) | 0 | <0.01 |
| Native Hawaiian (5) | 13 | 0.02 |
| Samoan (1) | 3 | <0.01 |
| Tongan (0) | 0 | <0.01 |
| White (16,371) | 17,846 | 26.52 |
| Not Hispanic (12,449) | 13,354 | 19.84 |
| Hispanic (3,922) | 4,492 | 6.68 |

*Notes: † The Census 2010 population figure is used to calculate the percentages in the Hispanic Origin and Race categories. Ancestry percentages are based on the 2006-2010 American Community Survey population (not shown); ‡ Numbers in parentheses indicate the number of people reporting a single ancestry; * Numbers in parentheses indicate the number of persons reporting this race alone, not in combination with any other race; Please refer to the Explanation of Data for more information.*

## New Rochelle

Place Type: City
County: Westchester
Population: 77,062

| Ancestry | Population | % |
|---|---|---|
| Afghan (0) | 0 | <0.01 |
| African, Sub-Saharan (850) | 1,030 | 1.36 |
| African (253) | 309 | 0.41 |
| Cape Verdean (0) | 0 | <0.01 |
| Ethiopian (0) | 0 | <0.01 |
| Ghanaian (18) | 18 | 0.02 |
| Kenyan (19) | 19 | 0.03 |
| Liberian (0) | 0 | <0.01 |
| Nigerian (125) | 125 | 0.16 |
| Senegalese (0) | 0 | <0.01 |
| Sierra Leonean (15) | 15 | 0.02 |
| Somalian (0) | 0 | <0.01 |
| South African (92) | 179 | 0.24 |
| Sudanese (0) | 0 | <0.01 |
| Ugandan (0) | 0 | <0.01 |
| Zimbabwean (0) | 0 | <0.01 |
| Other Sub-Saharan African (328) | 365 | 0.48 |
| Albanian (324) | 370 | 0.49 |
| Alsatian (0) | 0 | <0.01 |
| American (2,542) | 2,542 | 3.35 |
| Arab (338) | 413 | 0.54 |
| Arab (177) | 187 | 0.25 |
| Egyptian (13) | 13 | 0.02 |
| Iraqi (0) | 0 | <0.01 |
| Jordanian (11) | 46 | 0.06 |
| Lebanese (102) | 132 | 0.17 |
| Moroccan (8) | 8 | 0.01 |
| Palestinian (0) | 0 | <0.01 |
| Syrian (0) | 0 | <0.01 |
| Other Arab (27) | 27 | 0.04 |
| Armenian (31) | 75 | 0.10 |
| Assyrian/Chaldean/Syriac (0) | 0 | <0.01 |
| Australian (33) | 33 | 0.04 |
| Austrian (104) | 547 | 0.72 |
| Basque (12) | 12 | 0.02 |
| Belgian (27) | 118 | 0.16 |
| Brazilian (580) | 728 | 0.96 |
| British (145) | 208 | 0.27 |
| Bulgarian (9) | 9 | 0.01 |
| Cajun (0) | 0 | <0.01 |
| Canadian (13) | 41 | 0.05 |
| Carpatho Rusyn (0) | 0 | <0.01 |
| Celtic (0) | 0 | <0.01 |
| Croatian (103) | 167 | 0.22 |
| Cypriot (0) | 0 | <0.01 |
| Czech (78) | 402 | 0.53 |
| Czechoslovakian (32) | 108 | 0.14 |
| Danish (0) | 55 | 0.07 |
| Dutch (38) | 257 | 0.34 |
| Eastern European (870) | 870 | 1.15 |
| English (493) | 1,832 | 2.42 |
| Estonian (9) | 16 | 0.02 |
| European (773) | 808 | 1.07 |
| Finnish (36) | 60 | 0.08 |
| French, ex. Basque (342) | 1,322 | 1.74 |
| French Canadian (62) | 152 | 0.20 |
| German (734) | 3,942 | 5.20 |
| German Russian (0) | 0 | <0.01 |
| Greek (377) | 573 | 0.76 |
| Guyanese (104) | 125 | 0.16 |
| Hungarian (231) | 684 | 0.90 |
| Icelander (0) | 0 | <0.01 |
| Iranian (12) | 33 | 0.04 |
| Irish (2,797) | 7,400 | 9.76 |
| Israeli (26) | 93 | 0.12 |
| Italian (9,697) | 14,355 | 18.93 |
| Latvian (28) | 74 | 0.10 |
| Lithuanian (130) | 228 | 0.30 |
| Luxemburger (0) | 9 | 0.01 |
| Macedonian (154) | 177 | 0.23 |
| Maltese (0) | 16 | 0.02 |
| New Zealander (0) | 0 | <0.01 |
| Northern European (25) | 25 | 0.03 |

| | Population | % |
|---|---|---|
| Norwegian (18) | 72 | 0.09 |
| Pennsylvania German (0) | 0 | <0.01 |
| Polish (1,042) | 2,744 | 3.62 |
| Portuguese (615) | 830 | 1.09 |
| Romanian (83) | 272 | 0.36 |
| Russian (917) | 3,102 | 4.09 |
| Scandinavian (0) | 0 | <0.01 |
| Scotch-Irish (92) | 326 | 0.43 |
| Scottish (166) | 563 | 0.74 |
| Serbian (0) | 0 | <0.01 |
| Slavic (116) | 171 | 0.23 |
| Slovak (0) | 116 | 0.15 |
| Slovene (0) | 0 | <0.01 |
| Soviet Union (0) | 0 | <0.01 |
| Swedish (84) | 428 | 0.56 |
| Swiss (35) | 56 | 0.07 |
| Turkish (48) | 137 | 0.18 |
| Ukrainian (13) | 146 | 0.19 |
| Welsh (17) | 129 | 0.17 |
| West Indian, ex. Hispanic (3,998) | 4,597 | 6.06 |
| Bahamian (0) | 0 | <0.01 |
| Barbadian (241) | 316 | 0.42 |
| Belizean (0) | 0 | <0.01 |
| Bermudan (0) | 0 | <0.01 |
| British West Indian (80) | 153 | 0.20 |
| Dutch West Indian (0) | 0 | <0.01 |
| Haitian (926) | 951 | 1.25 |
| Jamaican (2,245) | 2,635 | 3.48 |
| Trinidadian/Tobagonian (295) | 317 | 0.42 |
| U.S. Virgin Islander (0) | 0 | <0.01 |
| West Indian (211) | 225 | 0.30 |
| Other West Indian (0) | 0 | <0.01 |
| Yugoslavian (23) | 47 | 0.06 |

| Hispanic Origin | Population | % |
|---|---|---|
| Hispanic or Latino (of any race) | 21,452 | 27.84 |
| Central American, ex. Mexican | 2,017 | 2.62 |
| Costa Rican | 65 | 0.08 |
| Guatemalan | 1,232 | 1.60 |
| Honduran | 242 | 0.31 |
| Nicaraguan | 74 | 0.10 |
| Panamanian | 67 | 0.09 |
| Salvadoran | 330 | 0.43 |
| Other Central American | 7 | 0.01 |
| Cuban | 371 | 0.48 |
| Dominican Republic | 960 | 1.25 |
| Mexican | 10,363 | 13.45 |
| Puerto Rican | 2,779 | 3.61 |
| South American | 3,697 | 4.80 |
| Argentinean | 170 | 0.22 |
| Bolivian | 50 | 0.06 |
| Chilean | 76 | 0.10 |
| Colombian | 1,451 | 1.88 |
| Ecuadorian | 378 | 0.49 |
| Paraguayan | 49 | 0.06 |
| Peruvian | 1,297 | 1.68 |
| Uruguayan | 88 | 0.11 |
| Venezuelan | 131 | 0.17 |
| Other South American | 7 | 0.01 |
| Other Hispanic or Latino | 1,265 | 1.64 |

| Race* | Population | % |
|---|---|---|
| African-American/Black (14,847) | 15,858 | 20.58 |
| Not Hispanic (13,956) | 14,611 | 18.96 |
| Hispanic (891) | 1,247 | 1.62 |
| American Indian/Alaska Native (398) | 770 | 1.00 |
| Not Hispanic (94) | 308 | 0.40 |
| Hispanic (304) | 462 | 0.60 |
| Alaska Athabascan (Ala. Nat.) (0) | 0 | <0.01 |
| Aleut (Alaska Native) (0) | 0 | <0.01 |
| Apache (0) | 6 | 0.01 |
| Arapaho (0) | 0 | <0.01 |
| Blackfeet (5) | 25 | 0.03 |
| Canadian/French Am. Ind. (0) | 2 | <0.01 |
| Central American Ind. (7) | 20 | 0.03 |
| Cherokee (5) | 65 | 0.08 |
| Cheyenne (1) | 1 | <0.01 |
| Chickasaw (0) | 0 | <0.01 |
| Chippewa (0) | 3 | <0.01 |

| | Population | % |
|---|---|---|
| Choctaw (0) | 2 | <0.01 |
| Colville (0) | 0 | <0.01 |
| Comanche (0) | 0 | <0.01 |
| Cree (0) | 0 | <0.01 |
| Creek (0) | 1 | <0.01 |
| Crow (0) | 0 | <0.01 |
| Delaware (0) | 2 | <0.01 |
| Hopi (0) | 0 | <0.01 |
| Houma (0) | 0 | <0.01 |
| Inupiat (Alaska Native) (0) | 0 | <0.01 |
| Iroquois (5) | 11 | 0.01 |
| Kiowa (0) | 0 | <0.01 |
| Lumbee (0) | 0 | <0.01 |
| Menominee (0) | 0 | <0.01 |
| Mexican American Ind. (47) | 72 | 0.09 |
| Navajo (0) | 1 | <0.01 |
| Osage (0) | 0 | <0.01 |
| Ottawa (0) | 0 | <0.01 |
| Paiute (0) | 0 | <0.01 |
| Pima (0) | 0 | <0.01 |
| Potawatomi (0) | 0 | <0.01 |
| Pueblo (0) | 0 | <0.01 |
| Puget Sound Salish (0) | 0 | <0.01 |
| Seminole (0) | 1 | <0.01 |
| Shoshone (0) | 0 | <0.01 |
| Sioux (1) | 2 | <0.01 |
| South American Ind. (29) | 56 | 0.07 |
| Spanish American Ind. (1) | 1 | <0.01 |
| Tlingit-Haida (Alaska Native) (0) | 0 | <0.01 |
| Tohono O'Odham (0) | 0 | <0.01 |
| Tsimshian (Alaska Native) (0) | 0 | <0.01 |
| Ute (0) | 0 | <0.01 |
| Yakama (0) | 0 | <0.01 |
| Yaqui (0) | 0 | <0.01 |
| Yuman (0) | 0 | <0.01 |
| Yup'ik (Alaska Native) (0) | 0 | <0.01 |
| Asian (3,262) | 3,798 | 4.93 |
| Not Hispanic (3,212) | 3,631 | 4.71 |
| Hispanic (50) | 167 | 0.22 |
| Bangladeshi (48) | 55 | 0.07 |
| Bhutanese (2) | 2 | <0.01 |
| Burmese (6) | 8 | 0.01 |
| Cambodian (8) | 9 | 0.01 |
| Chinese, ex. Taiwanese (547) | 715 | 0.93 |
| Filipino (471) | 543 | 0.70 |
| Hmong (0) | 0 | <0.01 |
| Indian (1,352) | 1,508 | 1.96 |
| Indonesian (6) | 6 | 0.01 |
| Japanese (106) | 158 | 0.21 |
| Korean (276) | 319 | 0.41 |
| Laotian (2) | 14 | 0.02 |
| Malaysian (5) | 5 | 0.01 |
| Nepalese (5) | 5 | 0.01 |
| Pakistani (147) | 164 | 0.21 |
| Sri Lankan (75) | 83 | 0.11 |
| Taiwanese (18) | 32 | 0.04 |
| Thai (25) | 39 | 0.05 |
| Vietnamese (19) | 31 | 0.04 |
| Hawaii Native/Pacific Islander (48) | 123 | 0.16 |
| Not Hispanic (20) | 65 | 0.08 |
| Hispanic (28) | 58 | 0.08 |
| Fijian (0) | 0 | <0.01 |
| Guamanian/Chamorro (32) | 43 | 0.06 |
| Marshallese (0) | 0 | <0.01 |
| Native Hawaiian (1) | 12 | 0.02 |
| Samoan (5) | 7 | 0.01 |
| Tongan (0) | 0 | <0.01 |
| White (50,231) | 52,208 | 67.75 |
| Not Hispanic (36,948) | 37,786 | 49.03 |
| Hispanic (13,283) | 14,422 | 18.71 |

## New York

Place Type: City
Counties: Bronx, Kings, New York, Queens, and Richmond
Population: 8,175,133

| Ancestry | Population | % |
|---|---|---|
| Afghan (6,250) | 6,470 | 0.08 |
| African, Sub-Saharan (126,853) | 175,478 | 2.17 |
| African (60,151) | 101,901 | 1.26 |
| Cape Verdean (282) | 595 | 0.01 |
| Ethiopian (2,524) | 2,869 | 0.04 |
| Ghanaian (19,077) | 19,782 | 0.24 |
| Kenyan (294) | 344 | <0.01 |
| Liberian (1,738) | 1,991 | 0.02 |
| Nigerian (19,543) | 21,507 | 0.27 |
| Senegalese (2,685) | 2,895 | 0.04 |
| Sierra Leonean (1,545) | 1,572 | 0.02 |
| Somalian (422) | 518 | 0.01 |
| South African (1,454) | 2,116 | 0.03 |
| Sudanese (1,079) | 1,303 | 0.02 |
| Ugandan (189) | 256 | <0.01 |
| Zimbabwean (394) | 414 | 0.01 |
| Other Sub-Saharan African (15,476) | 17,415 | 0.22 |
| Albanian (29,299) | 31,056 | 0.38 |
| Alsatian (31) | 217 | <0.01 |
| American (209,430) | 209,430 | 2.59 |
| Arab (65,990) | 82,165 | 1.02 |
| Arab (13,125) | 15,160 | 0.19 |
| Egyptian (15,679) | 17,698 | 0.22 |
| Iraqi (645) | 1,137 | 0.01 |
| Jordanian (1,141) | 1,298 | 0.02 |
| Lebanese (7,824) | 11,682 | 0.14 |
| Moroccan (7,043) | 8,987 | 0.11 |
| Palestinian (3,051) | 3,421 | 0.04 |
| Syrian (5,818) | 8,198 | 0.10 |
| Other Arab (11,664) | 14,584 | 0.18 |
| Armenian (7,612) | 10,159 | 0.13 |
| Assyrian/Chaldean/Syriac (144) | 227 | <0.01 |
| Australian (2,699) | 3,906 | 0.05 |
| Austrian (9,463) | 30,712 | 0.38 |
| Basque (370) | 902 | 0.01 |
| Belgian (1,803) | 4,472 | 0.06 |
| Brazilian (9,457) | 13,119 | 0.16 |
| British (11,046) | 21,065 | 0.26 |
| Bulgarian (4,331) | 5,011 | 0.06 |
| Cajun (121) | 432 | 0.01 |
| Canadian (5,942) | 10,989 | 0.14 |
| Carpatho Rusyn (198) | 249 | <0.01 |
| Celtic (275) | 564 | 0.01 |
| Croatian (8,097) | 11,304 | 0.14 |
| Cypriot (744) | 960 | 0.01 |
| Czech (3,559) | 12,800 | 0.16 |
| Czechoslovakian (2,411) | 4,870 | 0.06 |
| Danish (2,102) | 7,018 | 0.09 |
| Dutch (5,641) | 23,151 | 0.29 |
| Eastern European (41,481) | 44,970 | 0.56 |
| English (40,380) | 146,525 | 1.81 |
| Estonian (643) | 1,057 | 0.01 |
| European (59,415) | 66,267 | 0.82 |
| Finnish (1,375) | 3,519 | 0.04 |
| French, ex. Basque (19,416) | 67,195 | 0.83 |
| French Canadian (3,676) | 11,393 | 0.14 |
| German (68,198) | 272,827 | 3.38 |
| German Russian (69) | 204 | <0.01 |
| Greek (58,515) | 76,597 | 0.95 |
| Guyanese (96,299) | 107,972 | 1.34 |
| Hungarian (29,252) | 55,459 | 0.69 |
| Icelander (386) | 572 | 0.01 |
| Iranian (8,448) | 10,204 | 0.13 |
| Irish (154,072) | 410,889 | 5.09 |
| Israeli (16,225) | 21,872 | 0.27 |
| Italian (403,347) | 625,004 | 7.74 |
| Latvian (1,663) | 3,302 | 0.04 |
| Lithuanian (4,343) | 12,774 | 0.16 |
| Luxemburger (76) | 193 | <0.01 |
| Macedonian (4,296) | 4,911 | 0.06 |
| Maltese (1,817) | 3,102 | 0.04 |
| New Zealander (337) | 584 | 0.01 |
| Northern European (2,656) | 3,043 | 0.04 |

| | Population | % |
|---|---|---|
| Norwegian (6,141) | 21,894 | 0.27 |
| Pennsylvania German (160) | 465 | 0.01 |
| Polish (112,769) | 216,891 | 2.68 |
| Portuguese (5,980) | 13,201 | 0.16 |
| Romanian (18,025) | 29,552 | 0.37 |
| Russian (150,929) | 240,690 | 2.98 |
| Scandinavian (1,533) | 3,434 | 0.04 |
| Scotch-Irish (9,634) | 27,337 | 0.34 |
| Scottish (9,926) | 38,000 | 0.47 |
| Serbian (3,997) | 4,911 | 0.06 |
| Slavic (919) | 1,962 | 0.02 |
| Slovak (3,457) | 6,785 | 0.08 |
| Slovene (593) | 1,476 | 0.02 |
| Soviet Union (288) | 419 | 0.01 |
| Swedish (5,168) | 20,940 | 0.26 |
| Swiss (2,335) | 8,135 | 0.10 |
| Turkish (12,067) | 14,927 | 0.18 |
| Ukrainian (36,563) | 48,714 | 0.60 |
| Welsh (1,659) | 11,219 | 0.14 |
| West Indian, ex. Hispanic (509,675) | 598,504 | 7.41 |
| Bahamian (828) | 1,147 | 0.01 |
| Barbadian (19,549) | 22,550 | 0.28 |
| Belizean (4,699) | 5,674 | 0.07 |
| Bermudan (345) | 518 | 0.01 |
| British West Indian (39,268) | 44,326 | 0.55 |
| Dutch West Indian (789) | 1,167 | 0.01 |
| Haitian (112,397) | 120,252 | 1.49 |
| Jamaican (196,443) | 216,495 | 2.68 |
| Trinidadian/Tobagonian (66,794) | 76,240 | 0.94 |
| U.S. Virgin Islander (1,806) | 2,383 | 0.03 |
| West Indian (65,827) | 106,548 | 1.32 |
| Other West Indian (930) | 1,204 | 0.01 |
| Yugoslavian (10,119) | 12,410 | 0.15 |

| Hispanic Origin | Population | % |
|---|---|---|
| Hispanic or Latino (of any race) | 2,336,076 | 28.58 |
| Central American, ex. Mexican | 151,378 | 1.85 |
| Costa Rican | 6,673 | 0.08 |
| Guatemalan | 30,420 | 0.37 |
| Honduran | 42,400 | 0.52 |
| Nicaraguan | 9,346 | 0.11 |
| Panamanian | 22,353 | 0.27 |
| Salvadoran | 38,559 | 0.47 |
| Other Central American | 1,627 | 0.02 |
| Cuban | 40,840 | 0.50 |
| Dominican Republic | 576,701 | 7.05 |
| Mexican | 319,263 | 3.91 |
| Puerto Rican | 723,621 | 8.85 |
| South American | 343,468 | 4.20 |
| Argentinean | 15,169 | 0.19 |
| Bolivian | 4,488 | 0.05 |
| Chilean | 7,026 | 0.09 |
| Colombian | 94,723 | 1.16 |
| Ecuadorian | 167,209 | 2.05 |
| Paraguayan | 3,534 | 0.04 |
| Peruvian | 36,018 | 0.44 |
| Uruguayan | 3,004 | 0.04 |
| Venezuelan | 9,619 | 0.12 |
| Other South American | 2,678 | 0.03 |
| Other Hispanic or Latino | 180,805 | 2.21 |

| Race* | Population | % |
|---|---|---|
| African-American/Black (2,088,510) | 2,228,145 | 27.26 |
| Not Hispanic (1,861,295) | 1,931,889 | 23.63 |
| Hispanic (227,215) | 296,256 | 3.62 |
| American Indian/Alaska Native (57,512) | 111,749 | 1.37 |
| Not Hispanic (17,427) | 44,541 | 0.54 |
| Hispanic (40,085) | 67,208 | 0.82 |
| Alaska Athabascan (Ala. Nat.) (19) | 37 | <0.01 |
| Aleut (Alaska Native) (12) | 26 | <0.01 |
| Apache (135) | 401 | <0.01 |
| Arapaho (8) | 21 | <0.01 |
| Blackfeet (235) | 1,627 | 0.02 |
| Canadian/French Am. Ind. (111) | 197 | <0.01 |
| Central American Ind. (3,948) | 7,662 | 0.09 |
| Cherokee (1,195) | 6,952 | 0.09 |
| Cheyenne (19) | 46 | <0.01 |
| Chickasaw (40) | 113 | <0.01 |
| Chippewa (105) | 252 | <0.01 |

| | Population | % |
|---|---|---|
| Choctaw (94) | 405 | <0.01 |
| Colville (6) | 9 | <0.01 |
| Comanche (31) | 76 | <0.01 |
| Cree (14) | 81 | <0.01 |
| Creek (65) | 291 | <0.01 |
| Crow (11) | 50 | <0.01 |
| Delaware (50) | 177 | <0.01 |
| Hopi (17) | 49 | <0.01 |
| Houma (14) | 23 | <0.01 |
| Inupiat (Alaska Native) (26) | 58 | <0.01 |
| Iroquois (573) | 1,276 | 0.02 |
| Kiowa (11) | 15 | <0.01 |
| Lumbee (27) | 89 | <0.01 |
| Menominee (4) | 10 | <0.01 |
| Mexican American Ind. (3,646) | 4,922 | 0.06 |
| Navajo (126) | 272 | <0.01 |
| Osage (10) | 23 | <0.01 |
| Ottawa (2) | 11 | <0.01 |
| Paiute (5) | 18 | <0.01 |
| Pima (4) | 9 | <0.01 |
| Potawatomi (20) | 40 | <0.01 |
| Pueblo (446) | 892 | 0.01 |
| Puget Sound Salish (5) | 11 | <0.01 |
| Seminole (52) | 357 | <0.01 |
| Shoshone (10) | 46 | <0.01 |
| Sioux (159) | 464 | 0.01 |
| South American Ind. (4,682) | 9,464 | 0.12 |
| Spanish American Ind. (1,871) | 2,594 | 0.03 |
| Tlingit-Haida (Alaska Native) (15) | 75 | <0.01 |
| Tohono O'Odham (32) | 48 | <0.01 |
| Tsimshian (Alaska Native) (3) | 4 | <0.01 |
| Ute (8) | 17 | <0.01 |
| Yakama (5) | 8 | <0.01 |
| Yaqui (27) | 54 | <0.01 |
| Yuman (12) | 22 | <0.01 |
| Yup'ik (Alaska Native) (2) | 10 | <0.01 |
| Asian (1,038,388) | 1,134,919 | 13.88 |
| Not Hispanic (1,028,119) | 1,110,964 | 13.59 |
| Hispanic (10,269) | 23,955 | 0.29 |
| Bangladeshi (53,174) | 61,788 | 0.76 |
| Bhutanese (345) | 388 | <0.01 |
| Burmese (3,614) | 4,132 | 0.05 |
| Cambodian (2,166) | 2,591 | 0.03 |
| Chinese, ex. Taiwanese (474,783) | 500,434 | 6.12 |
| Filipino (67,292) | 78,030 | 0.95 |
| Hmong (59) | 83 | <0.01 |
| Indian (192,209) | 232,696 | 2.85 |
| Indonesian (3,785) | 4,791 | 0.06 |
| Japanese (24,277) | 31,742 | 0.39 |
| Korean (96,741) | 102,820 | 1.26 |
| Laotian (440) | 664 | 0.01 |
| Malaysian (2,100) | 3,220 | 0.04 |
| Nepalese (5,681) | 6,187 | 0.08 |
| Pakistani (41,887) | 46,369 | 0.57 |
| Sri Lankan (3,696) | 4,369 | 0.05 |
| Taiwanese (11,680) | 13,682 | 0.17 |
| Thai (6,056) | 7,244 | 0.09 |
| Vietnamese (13,387) | 16,378 | 0.20 |
| Hawaii Native/Pacific Islander (5,147) | 24,098 | 0.29 |
| Not Hispanic (2,795) | 13,217 | 0.16 |
| Hispanic (2,352) | 10,881 | 0.13 |
| Fijian (104) | 213 | <0.01 |
| Guamanian/Chamorro (1,194) | 1,784 | 0.02 |
| Marshallese (8) | 10 | <0.01 |
| Native Hawaiian (1,001) | 2,448 | 0.03 |
| Samoan (296) | 764 | 0.01 |
| Tongan (37) | 66 | <0.01 |
| White (3,597,341) | 3,797,402 | 46.45 |
| Not Hispanic (2,722,904) | 2,804,430 | 34.30 |
| Hispanic (874,437) | 992,972 | 12.15 |

*Notes: † The Census 2010 population figure is used to calculate the percentages in the Hispanic Origin and Race categories. Ancestry percentages are based on the 2006-2010 American Community Survey population (not shown); ‡ Numbers in parentheses indicate the number of people reporting a single ancestry; * Numbers in parentheses indicate the number of persons reporting this race alone, not in combination with any other race; Please refer to the Explanation of Data for more information.*

## Niagara Falls

Place Type: City
County: Niagara
Population: 50,193

| Ancestry | Population | % |
|---|---|---|
| Afghan (0) | 0 | <0.01 |
| African, Sub-Saharan (318) | 520 | 1.02 |
| African (286) | 488 | 0.96 |
| Cape Verdean (0) | 0 | <0.01 |
| Ethiopian (24) | 24 | 0.05 |
| Ghanaian (0) | 0 | <0.01 |
| Kenyan (0) | 0 | <0.01 |
| Liberian (0) | 0 | <0.01 |
| Nigerian (0) | 0 | <0.01 |
| Senegalese (0) | 0 | <0.01 |
| Sierra Leonean (0) | 0 | <0.01 |
| Somalian (0) | 0 | <0.01 |
| South African (8) | 8 | 0.02 |
| Sudanese (0) | 0 | <0.01 |
| Ugandan (0) | 0 | <0.01 |
| Zimbabwean (0) | 0 | <0.01 |
| Other Sub-Saharan African (0) | 0 | <0.01 |
| Albanian (0) | 0 | <0.01 |
| Alsatian (0) | 0 | <0.01 |
| American (1,655) | 1,655 | 3.25 |
| Arab (204) | 411 | 0.81 |
| Arab (72) | 103 | 0.20 |
| Egyptian (0) | 29 | 0.06 |
| Iraqi (0) | 0 | <0.01 |
| Jordanian (0) | 0 | <0.01 |
| Lebanese (116) | 228 | 0.45 |
| Moroccan (0) | 0 | <0.01 |
| Palestinian (0) | 0 | <0.01 |
| Syrian (9) | 44 | 0.09 |
| Other Arab (7) | 7 | 0.01 |
| Armenian (96) | 156 | 0.31 |
| Assyrian/Chaldean/Syriac (0) | 0 | <0.01 |
| Australian (31) | 49 | 0.10 |
| Austrian (38) | 115 | 0.23 |
| Basque (0) | 0 | <0.01 |
| Belgian (0) | 0 | <0.01 |
| Brazilian (0) | 0 | <0.01 |
| British (29) | 64 | 0.13 |
| Bulgarian (0) | 0 | <0.01 |
| Cajun (0) | 0 | <0.01 |
| Canadian (210) | 442 | 0.87 |
| Carpatho Rusyn (14) | 14 | 0.03 |
| Celtic (0) | 0 | <0.01 |
| Croatian (73) | 85 | 0.17 |
| Cypriot (0) | 0 | <0.01 |
| Czech (37) | 92 | 0.18 |
| Czechoslovakian (0) | 6 | 0.01 |
| Danish (12) | 134 | 0.26 |
| Dutch (62) | 498 | 0.98 |
| Eastern European (0) | 0 | <0.01 |
| English (2,722) | 6,055 | 11.90 |
| Estonian (0) | 0 | <0.01 |
| European (44) | 44 | 0.09 |
| Finnish (0) | 31 | 0.06 |
| French, ex. Basque (256) | 1,555 | 3.06 |
| French Canadian (125) | 493 | 0.97 |
| German (2,324) | 8,658 | 17.01 |
| German Russian (16) | 16 | 0.03 |
| Greek (121) | 318 | 0.62 |
| Guyanese (0) | 0 | <0.01 |
| Hungarian (68) | 191 | 0.38 |
| Icelander (0) | 0 | <0.01 |
| Iranian (0) | 0 | <0.01 |
| Irish (1,933) | 7,048 | 13.85 |
| Israeli (12) | 12 | 0.02 |
| Italian (6,763) | 11,524 | 22.64 |
| Latvian (0) | 0 | <0.01 |
| Lithuanian (71) | 128 | 0.25 |
| Luxemburger (0) | 0 | <0.01 |
| Macedonian (0) | 0 | <0.01 |
| Maltese (0) | 0 | <0.01 |
| New Zealander (0) | 0 | <0.01 |
| Northern European (11) | 11 | 0.02 |

| Ancestry | Population | % |
|---|---|---|
| Norwegian (9) | 72 | 0.14 |
| Pennsylvania German (61) | 130 | 0.26 |
| Polish (1,934) | 4,962 | 9.75 |
| Portuguese (135) | 151 | 0.30 |
| Romanian (15) | 44 | 0.09 |
| Russian (140) | 312 | 0.61 |
| Scandinavian (0) | 9 | 0.02 |
| Scotch-Irish (163) | 522 | 1.03 |
| Scottish (257) | 747 | 1.47 |
| Serbian (0) | 0 | <0.01 |
| Slavic (28) | 33 | 0.06 |
| Slovak (39) | 88 | 0.17 |
| Slovene (0) | 0 | <0.01 |
| Soviet Union (0) | 0 | <0.01 |
| Swedish (51) | 395 | 0.78 |
| Swiss (6) | 19 | 0.04 |
| Turkish (0) | 18 | 0.04 |
| Ukrainian (59) | 114 | 0.22 |
| Welsh (93) | 346 | 0.68 |
| West Indian, ex. Hispanic (174) | 366 | 0.72 |
| Bahamian (0) | 0 | <0.01 |
| Barbadian (0) | 0 | <0.01 |
| Belizean (29) | 29 | 0.06 |
| Bermudan (0) | 0 | <0.01 |
| British West Indian (9) | 9 | 0.02 |
| Dutch West Indian (0) | 0 | <0.01 |
| Haitian (0) | 0 | <0.01 |
| Jamaican (121) | 167 | 0.33 |
| Trinidadian/Tobagonian (15) | 15 | 0.03 |
| U.S. Virgin Islander (0) | 0 | <0.01 |
| West Indian (0) | 146 | 0.29 |
| Other West Indian (0) | 0 | <0.01 |
| Yugoslavian (0) | 33 | 0.06 |

| Hispanic Origin | Population | % |
|---|---|---|
| Hispanic or Latino (of any race) | 1,508 | 3.00 |
| Central American, ex. Mexican | 39 | 0.08 |
| Costa Rican | 3 | 0.01 |
| Guatemalan | 15 | 0.03 |
| Honduran | 9 | 0.02 |
| Nicaraguan | 0 | <0.01 |
| Panamanian | 8 | 0.02 |
| Salvadoran | 4 | 0.01 |
| Other Central American | 0 | <0.01 |
| Cuban | 61 | 0.12 |
| Dominican Republic | 35 | 0.07 |
| Mexican | 228 | 0.45 |
| Puerto Rican | 797 | 1.59 |
| South American | 50 | 0.10 |
| Argentinean | 8 | 0.02 |
| Bolivian | 0 | <0.01 |
| Chilean | 5 | 0.01 |
| Colombian | 23 | 0.05 |
| Ecuadorian | 3 | 0.01 |
| Paraguayan | 0 | <0.01 |
| Peruvian | 4 | 0.01 |
| Uruguayan | 0 | <0.01 |
| Venezuelan | 7 | 0.01 |
| Other South American | 0 | <0.01 |
| Other Hispanic or Latino | 298 | 0.59 |

| Race* | Population | % |
|---|---|---|
| African-American/Black (10,835) | 12,203 | 24.31 |
| Not Hispanic (10,643) | 11,905 | 23.72 |
| Hispanic (192) | 298 | 0.59 |
| American Indian/Alaska Native (977) | 1,624 | 3.24 |
| Not Hispanic (930) | 1,524 | 3.04 |
| Hispanic (47) | 100 | 0.20 |
| Alaska Athabascan (Ala. Nat.) (0) | 0 | <0.01 |
| Aleut (Alaska Native) (0) | 0 | <0.01 |
| Apache (0) | 2 | <0.01 |
| Arapaho (0) | 0 | <0.01 |
| Blackfeet (1) | 16 | 0.03 |
| Canadian/French Am. Ind. (18) | 20 | 0.04 |
| Central American Ind. (8) | 11 | 0.02 |
| Cherokee (8) | 48 | 0.10 |
| Cheyenne (1) | 1 | <0.01 |
| Chickasaw (0) | 0 | <0.01 |
| Chippewa (16) | 23 | 0.05 |

| Race* | Population | % |
|---|---|---|
| Choctaw (1) | 1 | <0.01 |
| Colville (0) | 0 | <0.01 |
| Comanche (0) | 0 | <0.01 |
| Cree (2) | 3 | 0.01 |
| Creek (0) | 0 | <0.01 |
| Crow (0) | 0 | <0.01 |
| Delaware (0) | 0 | <0.01 |
| Hopi (0) | 0 | <0.01 |
| Houma (0) | 0 | <0.01 |
| Inupiat (Alaska Native) (0) | 0 | <0.01 |
| Iroquois (542) | 801 | 1.60 |
| Kiowa (0) | 0 | <0.01 |
| Lumbee (4) | 6 | 0.01 |
| Menominee (0) | 2 | <0.01 |
| Mexican American Ind. (4) | 4 | 0.01 |
| Navajo (1) | 1 | <0.01 |
| Osage (0) | 0 | <0.01 |
| Ottawa (1) | 1 | <0.01 |
| Paiute (0) | 0 | <0.01 |
| Pima (0) | 0 | <0.01 |
| Potawatomi (0) | 0 | <0.01 |
| Pueblo (0) | 0 | <0.01 |
| Puget Sound Salish (0) | 0 | <0.01 |
| Seminole (0) | 5 | 0.01 |
| Shoshone (0) | 0 | <0.01 |
| Sioux (5) | 8 | 0.02 |
| South American Ind. (1) | 2 | <0.01 |
| Spanish American Ind. (0) | 0 | <0.01 |
| Tlingit-Haida (Alaska Native) (0) | 0 | <0.01 |
| Tohono O'Odham (0) | 0 | <0.01 |
| Tsimshian (Alaska Native) (0) | 0 | <0.01 |
| Ute (0) | 0 | <0.01 |
| Yakama (0) | 0 | <0.01 |
| Yaqui (1) | 1 | <0.01 |
| Yuman (0) | 0 | <0.01 |
| Yup'ik (Alaska Native) (0) | 0 | <0.01 |
| Asian (609) | 751 | 1.50 |
| Not Hispanic (599) | 732 | 1.46 |
| Hispanic (10) | 19 | 0.04 |
| Bangladeshi (0) | 0 | <0.01 |
| Bhutanese (0) | 0 | <0.01 |
| Burmese (1) | 1 | <0.01 |
| Cambodian (1) | 1 | <0.01 |
| Chinese, ex. Taiwanese (97) | 106 | 0.21 |
| Filipino (45) | 81 | 0.16 |
| Hmong (0) | 0 | <0.01 |
| Indian (286) | 327 | 0.65 |
| Indonesian (0) | 0 | <0.01 |
| Japanese (14) | 26 | 0.05 |
| Korean (36) | 48 | 0.10 |
| Laotian (12) | 16 | 0.03 |
| Malaysian (0) | 0 | <0.01 |
| Nepalese (0) | 0 | <0.01 |
| Pakistani (58) | 64 | 0.13 |
| Sri Lankan (0) | 5 | 0.01 |
| Taiwanese (5) | 5 | 0.01 |
| Thai (4) | 15 | 0.03 |
| Vietnamese (19) | 22 | 0.04 |
| Hawaii Native/Pacific Islander (15) | 51 | 0.10 |
| Not Hispanic (10) | 43 | 0.09 |
| Hispanic (5) | 8 | 0.02 |
| Fijian (0) | 1 | <0.01 |
| Guamanian/Chamorro (5) | 5 | 0.01 |
| Marshallese (0) | 0 | <0.01 |
| Native Hawaiian (6) | 10 | 0.02 |
| Samoan (2) | 2 | <0.01 |
| Tongan (0) | 0 | <0.01 |
| White (35,394) | 37,102 | 73.92 |
| Not Hispanic (34,663) | 36,227 | 72.18 |
| Hispanic (731) | 875 | 1.74 |

*Notes: † The Census 2010 population figure is used to calculate the percentages in the Hispanic Origin and Race categories. Ancestry percentages are based on the 2006-2010 American Community Survey population (not shown); ‡ Numbers in parentheses indicate the number of people reporting a single ancestry; \* Numbers in parentheses indicate the number of persons reporting this race alone, not in combination with any other race; Please refer to the Explanation of Data for more information.*

## North Hempstead

Place Type: Town
County: Nassau
Population: 226,322

| Ancestry | Population | % |
|---|---|---|
| Afghan (88) | 203 | 0.09 |
| African, Sub-Saharan (670) | 862 | 0.39 |
| African (277) | 437 | 0.20 |
| Cape Verdean (0) | 0 | <0.01 |
| Ethiopian (49) | 49 | 0.02 |
| Ghanaian (117) | 117 | 0.05 |
| Kenyan (0) | 0 | <0.01 |
| Liberian (0) | 3 | <0.01 |
| Nigerian (145) | 154 | 0.07 |
| Senegalese (0) | 0 | <0.01 |
| Sierra Leonean (13) | 13 | 0.01 |
| Somalian (0) | 0 | <0.01 |
| South African (60) | 63 | 0.03 |
| Sudanese (0) | 17 | 0.01 |
| Ugandan (0) | 0 | <0.01 |
| Zimbabwean (0) | 0 | <0.01 |
| Other Sub-Saharan African (9) | 9 | <0.01 |
| Albanian (156) | 296 | 0.13 |
| Alsatian (9) | 9 | <0.01 |
| American (7,110) | 7,110 | 3.18 |
| Arab (1,529) | 2,078 | 0.93 |
| Arab (82) | 103 | 0.05 |
| Egyptian (404) | 529 | 0.24 |
| Iraqi (370) | 500 | 0.22 |
| Jordanian (0) | 0 | <0.01 |
| Lebanese (105) | 147 | 0.07 |
| Moroccan (34) | 85 | 0.04 |
| Palestinian (59) | 59 | 0.03 |
| Syrian (10) | 84 | 0.04 |
| Other Arab (465) | 571 | 0.26 |
| Armenian (391) | 631 | 0.28 |
| Assyrian/Chaldean/Syriac (4) | 21 | 0.01 |
| Australian (22) | 80 | 0.04 |
| Austrian (661) | 2,782 | 1.24 |
| Basque (0) | 121 | 0.05 |
| Belgian (93) | 166 | 0.07 |
| Brazilian (489) | 613 | 0.27 |
| British (233) | 705 | 0.32 |
| Bulgarian (56) | 73 | 0.03 |
| Cajun (0) | 22 | 0.01 |
| Canadian (182) | 307 | 0.14 |
| Carpatho Rusyn (0) | 0 | <0.01 |
| Celtic (0) | 48 | 0.02 |
| Croatian (478) | 672 | 0.30 |
| Cypriot (46) | 64 | 0.03 |
| Czech (150) | 636 | 0.28 |
| Czechoslovakian (205) | 493 | 0.22 |
| Danish (141) | 419 | 0.19 |
| Dutch (110) | 784 | 0.35 |
| Eastern European (3,518) | 3,769 | 1.69 |
| English (1,073) | 6,017 | 2.69 |
| Estonian (18) | 48 | 0.02 |
| European (1,809) | 2,051 | 0.92 |
| Finnish (38) | 128 | 0.06 |
| French, ex. Basque (273) | 2,191 | 0.98 |
| French Canadian (207) | 490 | 0.22 |
| German (4,524) | 18,322 | 8.19 |
| German Russian (0) | 26 | 0.01 |
| Greek (2,635) | 3,568 | 1.60 |
| Guyanese (324) | 405 | 0.18 |
| Hungarian (894) | 2,628 | 1.18 |
| Icelander (0) | 0 | <0.01 |
| Iranian (8,611) | 9,262 | 4.14 |
| Irish (10,304) | 27,339 | 12.22 |
| Israeli (1,537) | 1,853 | 0.83 |
| Italian (23,753) | 40,182 | 17.97 |
| Latvian (122) | 254 | 0.11 |
| Lithuanian (197) | 718 | 0.32 |
| Luxemburger (0) | 16 | 0.01 |
| Macedonian (0) | 0 | <0.01 |
| Maltese (125) | 248 | 0.11 |
| New Zealander (0) | 0 | <0.01 |
| Northern European (82) | 91 | 0.04 |

| Ancestry | Population | % |
|---|---|---|
| Norwegian (129) | 715 | 0.32 |
| Pennsylvania German (15) | 15 | 0.01 |
| Polish (5,076) | 13,352 | 5.97 |
| Portuguese (3,596) | 3,978 | 1.78 |
| Romanian (662) | 1,434 | 0.64 |
| Russian (6,882) | 14,712 | 6.58 |
| Scandinavian (67) | 122 | 0.05 |
| Scotch-Irish (405) | 1,188 | 0.53 |
| Scottish (369) | 1,567 | 0.70 |
| Serbian (109) | 153 | 0.07 |
| Slavic (11) | 195 | 0.09 |
| Slovak (122) | 312 | 0.14 |
| Slovene (59) | 79 | 0.04 |
| Soviet Union (0) | 0 | <0.01 |
| Swedish (179) | 1,391 | 0.62 |
| Swiss (77) | 362 | 0.16 |
| Turkish (308) | 408 | 0.18 |
| Ukrainian (488) | 1,005 | 0.45 |
| Welsh (46) | 328 | 0.15 |
| West Indian, ex. Hispanic (3,572) | 4,095 | 1.83 |
| Bahamian (0) | 0 | <0.01 |
| Barbadian (152) | 184 | 0.08 |
| Belizean (44) | 81 | 0.04 |
| Bermudan (0) | 0 | <0.01 |
| British West Indian (46) | 46 | 0.02 |
| Dutch West Indian (45) | 65 | 0.03 |
| Haitian (2,247) | 2,394 | 1.07 |
| Jamaican (723) | 868 | 0.39 |
| Trinidadian/Tobagonian (87) | 94 | 0.04 |
| U.S. Virgin Islander (0) | 0 | <0.01 |
| West Indian (228) | 363 | 0.16 |
| Other West Indian (0) | 0 | <0.01 |
| Yugoslavian (65) | 170 | 0.08 |

| Hispanic Origin | Population | % |
|---|---|---|
| Hispanic or Latino (of any race) | 29,074 | 12.85 |
| Central American, ex. Mexican | 11,455 | 5.06 |
| Costa Rican | 124 | 0.05 |
| Guatemalan | 1,193 | 0.53 |
| Honduran | 1,572 | 0.69 |
| Nicaraguan | 110 | 0.05 |
| Panamanian | 84 | 0.04 |
| Salvadoran | 8,262 | 3.65 |
| Other Central American | 110 | 0.05 |
| Cuban | 660 | 0.29 |
| Dominican Republic | 1,362 | 0.60 |
| Mexican | 3,488 | 1.54 |
| Puerto Rican | 2,705 | 1.20 |
| South American | 6,333 | 2.80 |
| Argentinean | 435 | 0.19 |
| Bolivian | 62 | 0.03 |
| Chilean | 664 | 0.29 |
| Colombian | 1,914 | 0.85 |
| Ecuadorian | 1,966 | 0.87 |
| Paraguayan | 140 | 0.06 |
| Peruvian | 925 | 0.41 |
| Uruguayan | 84 | 0.04 |
| Venezuelan | 97 | 0.04 |
| Other South American | 46 | 0.02 |
| Other Hispanic or Latino | 3,071 | 1.36 |

| Race* | Population | % |
|---|---|---|
| African-American/Black (12,587) | 13,593 | 6.01 |
| Not Hispanic (11,971) | 12,707 | 5.61 |
| Hispanic (616) | 886 | 0.39 |
| American Indian/Alaska Native (461) | 1,149 | 0.51 |
| Not Hispanic (183) | 566 | 0.25 |
| Hispanic (278) | 583 | 0.26 |
| Alaska Athabascan (Ala. Nat.) (0) | 0 | <0.01 |
| Aleut (Alaska Native) (0) | 0 | <0.01 |
| Apache (1) | 3 | <0.01 |
| Arapaho (0) | 0 | <0.01 |
| Blackfeet (0) | 0 | <0.01 |
| Canadian/French Am. Ind. (0) | 0 | <0.01 |
| Central American Ind. (9) | 16 | 0.01 |
| Cherokee (14) | 86 | 0.04 |
| Cheyenne (3) | 3 | <0.01 |
| Chickasaw (0) | 0 | <0.01 |
| Chippewa (0) | 4 | <0.01 |

| Race* | Population | % |
|---|---|---|
| Choctaw (3) | 8 | <0.01 |
| Colville (0) | 0 | <0.01 |
| Comanche (0) | 0 | <0.01 |
| Cree (0) | 0 | <0.01 |
| Creek (0) | 3 | <0.01 |
| Crow (0) | 0 | <0.01 |
| Delaware (2) | 5 | <0.01 |
| Hopi (1) | 3 | <0.01 |
| Houma (0) | 0 | <0.01 |
| Inupiat (Alaska Native) (2) | 2 | <0.01 |
| Iroquois (17) | 37 | 0.02 |
| Kiowa (0) | 0 | <0.01 |
| Lumbee (0) | 1 | <0.01 |
| Menominee (0) | 0 | <0.01 |
| Mexican American Ind. (36) | 48 | 0.02 |
| Navajo (0) | 0 | <0.01 |
| Osage (0) | 0 | <0.01 |
| Ottawa (0) | 0 | <0.01 |
| Paiute (0) | 0 | <0.01 |
| Pima (0) | 0 | <0.01 |
| Potawatomi (1) | 1 | <0.01 |
| Pueblo (0) | 0 | <0.01 |
| Puget Sound Salish (0) | 0 | <0.01 |
| Seminole (0) | 0 | <0.01 |
| Shoshone (0) | 0 | <0.01 |
| Sioux (8) | 17 | 0.01 |
| South American Ind. (32) | 79 | 0.03 |
| Spanish American Ind. (39) | 40 | 0.02 |
| Tlingit-Haida (Alaska Native) (0) | 0 | <0.01 |
| Tohono O'Odham (0) | 0 | <0.01 |
| Tsimshian (Alaska Native) (0) | 0 | <0.01 |
| Ute (0) | 0 | <0.01 |
| Yakama (0) | 0 | <0.01 |
| Yaqui (1) | 1 | <0.01 |
| Yuman (0) | 0 | <0.01 |
| Yup'ik (Alaska Native) (0) | 0 | <0.01 |
| Asian (33,889) | 36,973 | 16.34 |
| Not Hispanic (33,747) | 36,641 | 16.19 |
| Hispanic (142) | 332 | 0.15 |
| Bangladeshi (392) | 441 | 0.19 |
| Bhutanese (1) | 1 | <0.01 |
| Burmese (83) | 88 | 0.04 |
| Cambodian (11) | 14 | 0.01 |
| Chinese, ex. Taiwanese (9,631) | 10,292 | 4.55 |
| Filipino (1,567) | 1,899 | 0.84 |
| Hmong (0) | 0 | <0.01 |
| Indian (12,549) | 13,427 | 5.93 |
| Indonesian (30) | 53 | 0.02 |
| Japanese (1,094) | 1,266 | 0.56 |
| Korean (5,820) | 6,015 | 2.66 |
| Laotian (7) | 8 | <0.01 |
| Malaysian (24) | 35 | 0.02 |
| Nepalese (17) | 17 | 0.01 |
| Pakistani (904) | 1,029 | 0.45 |
| Sri Lankan (52) | 59 | 0.03 |
| Taiwanese (717) | 809 | 0.36 |
| Thai (103) | 126 | 0.06 |
| Vietnamese (132) | 186 | 0.08 |
| Hawaii Native/Pacific Islander (31) | 275 | 0.12 |
| Not Hispanic (24) | 224 | 0.10 |
| Hispanic (7) | 51 | 0.02 |
| Fijian (0) | 0 | <0.01 |
| Guamanian/Chamorro (14) | 20 | 0.01 |
| Marshallese (0) | 0 | <0.01 |
| Native Hawaiian (0) | 34 | 0.02 |
| Samoan (7) | 14 | 0.01 |
| Tongan (0) | 0 | <0.01 |
| White (161,955) | 166,538 | 73.58 |
| Not Hispanic (146,760) | 149,607 | 66.10 |
| Hispanic (15,195) | 16,931 | 7.48 |

Notes: † The Census 2010 population figure is used to calculate the percentages in the Hispanic Origin and Race categories. Ancestry percentages are based on the 2006-2010 American Community Survey population (not shown); ‡ Numbers in parentheses indicate the number of people reporting a single ancestry; * Numbers in parentheses indicate the number of persons reporting this race alone, not in combination with any other race; Please refer to the Explanation of Data for more information.

## Oyster Bay

Place Type: Town
County: Nassau
Population: 293,214

| Ancestry | Population | % |
| --- | --- | --- |
| Afghan (580) | 808 | 0.28 |
| African, Sub-Saharan (294) | 484 | 0.17 |
| African (215) | 289 | 0.10 |
| Cape Verdean (12) | 12 | <0.01 |
| Ethiopian (0) | 0 | <0.01 |
| Ghanaian (0) | 0 | <0.01 |
| Kenyan (0) | 0 | <0.01 |
| Liberian (0) | 0 | <0.01 |
| Nigerian (37) | 77 | 0.03 |
| Senegalese (0) | 0 | <0.01 |
| Sierra Leonean (0) | 0 | <0.01 |
| Somalian (0) | 0 | <0.01 |
| South African (30) | 30 | 0.01 |
| Sudanese (0) | 0 | <0.01 |
| Ugandan (0) | 0 | <0.01 |
| Zimbabwean (0) | 0 | <0.01 |
| Other Sub-Saharan African (0) | 76 | 0.03 |
| Albanian (268) | 368 | 0.13 |
| Alsatian (0) | 0 | <0.01 |
| American (9,798) | 9,798 | 3.36 |
| Arab (597) | 1,227 | 0.42 |
| Arab (177) | 245 | 0.08 |
| Egyptian (153) | 222 | 0.08 |
| Iraqi (9) | 9 | <0.01 |
| Jordanian (0) | 0 | <0.01 |
| Lebanese (51) | 191 | 0.07 |
| Moroccan (47) | 131 | 0.04 |
| Palestinian (31) | 60 | 0.02 |
| Syrian (49) | 114 | 0.04 |
| Other Arab (80) | 255 | 0.09 |
| Armenian (1,034) | 1,383 | 0.47 |
| Assyrian/Chaldean/Syriac (0) | 0 | <0.01 |
| Australian (3) | 41 | 0.01 |
| Austrian (879) | 3,412 | 1.17 |
| Basque (0) | 3 | <0.01 |
| Belgian (53) | 201 | 0.07 |
| Brazilian (328) | 370 | 0.13 |
| British (208) | 476 | 0.16 |
| Bulgarian (16) | 45 | 0.02 |
| Cajun (0) | 37 | 0.01 |
| Canadian (107) | 441 | 0.15 |
| Carpatho Rusyn (0) | 0 | <0.01 |
| Celtic (55) | 55 | 0.02 |
| Croatian (623) | 1,002 | 0.34 |
| Cypriot (63) | 63 | 0.02 |
| Czech (223) | 1,379 | 0.47 |
| Czechoslovakian (163) | 618 | 0.21 |
| Danish (126) | 573 | 0.20 |
| Dutch (288) | 1,343 | 0.46 |
| Eastern European (3,693) | 3,841 | 1.32 |
| English (1,832) | 11,799 | 4.05 |
| Estonian (68) | 130 | 0.04 |
| European (2,787) | 2,919 | 1.00 |
| Finnish (39) | 265 | 0.09 |
| French, ex. Basque (422) | 4,302 | 1.48 |
| French Canadian (238) | 807 | 0.28 |
| German (8,307) | 41,381 | 14.19 |
| German Russian (0) | 0 | <0.01 |
| Greek (4,277) | 6,908 | 2.37 |
| Guyanese (134) | 187 | 0.06 |
| Hungarian (705) | 3,138 | 1.08 |
| Icelander (31) | 52 | 0.02 |
| Iranian (1,115) | 1,464 | 0.50 |
| Irish (17,041) | 59,765 | 20.49 |
| Israeli (422) | 663 | 0.23 |
| Italian (48,450) | 88,723 | 30.43 |
| Latvian (110) | 235 | 0.08 |
| Lithuanian (378) | 1,079 | 0.37 |
| Luxemburger (0) | 0 | <0.01 |
| Macedonian (0) | 0 | <0.01 |
| Maltese (117) | 579 | 0.20 |
| New Zealander (0) | 0 | <0.01 |
| Northern European (97) | 105 | 0.04 |

| Ancestry | Population | % |
| --- | --- | --- |
| Norwegian (469) | 1,882 | 0.65 |
| Pennsylvania German (24) | 24 | 0.01 |
| Polish (6,380) | 19,395 | 6.65 |
| Portuguese (145) | 445 | 0.15 |
| Romanian (609) | 1,492 | 0.51 |
| Russian (5,986) | 14,554 | 4.99 |
| Scandinavian (24) | 144 | 0.05 |
| Scotch-Irish (832) | 2,523 | 0.87 |
| Scottish (646) | 2,493 | 0.85 |
| Serbian (12) | 103 | 0.04 |
| Slavic (27) | 173 | 0.06 |
| Slovak (164) | 442 | 0.15 |
| Slovene (10) | 55 | 0.02 |
| Soviet Union (0) | 0 | <0.01 |
| Swedish (191) | 2,325 | 0.80 |
| Swiss (114) | 686 | 0.24 |
| Turkish (520) | 1,232 | 0.42 |
| Ukrainian (859) | 1,774 | 0.61 |
| Welsh (83) | 515 | 0.18 |
| West Indian, ex. Hispanic (1,924) | 2,311 | 0.79 |
| Bahamian (0) | 0 | <0.01 |
| Barbadian (14) | 26 | 0.01 |
| Belizean (16) | 29 | 0.01 |
| Bermudan (0) | 13 | <0.01 |
| British West Indian (125) | 157 | 0.05 |
| Dutch West Indian (7) | 21 | 0.01 |
| Haitian (732) | 813 | 0.28 |
| Jamaican (818) | 972 | 0.33 |
| Trinidadian/Tobagonian (111) | 148 | 0.05 |
| U.S. Virgin Islander (15) | 15 | 0.01 |
| West Indian (86) | 102 | 0.03 |
| Other West Indian (0) | 15 | 0.01 |
| Yugoslavian (65) | 334 | 0.11 |

| Hispanic Origin | Population | % |
| --- | --- | --- |
| Hispanic or Latino (of any race) | 21,923 | 7.48 |
| Central American, ex. Mexican | 4,958 | 1.69 |
| Costa Rican | 101 | 0.03 |
| Guatemalan | 397 | 0.14 |
| Honduran | 952 | 0.32 |
| Nicaraguan | 78 | 0.03 |
| Panamanian | 88 | 0.03 |
| Salvadoran | 3,297 | 1.12 |
| Other Central American | 45 | 0.02 |
| Cuban | 906 | 0.31 |
| Dominican Republic | 1,429 | 0.49 |
| Mexican | 1,550 | 0.53 |
| Puerto Rican | 4,810 | 1.64 |
| South American | 5,752 | 1.96 |
| Argentinean | 441 | 0.15 |
| Bolivian | 110 | 0.04 |
| Chilean | 569 | 0.19 |
| Colombian | 2,035 | 0.69 |
| Ecuadorian | 1,082 | 0.37 |
| Paraguayan | 64 | 0.02 |
| Peruvian | 1,156 | 0.39 |
| Uruguayan | 134 | 0.05 |
| Venezuelan | 129 | 0.04 |
| Other South American | 32 | 0.01 |
| Other Hispanic or Latino | 2,518 | 0.86 |

| Race* | Population | % |
| --- | --- | --- |
| African-American/Black (6,657) | 7,671 | 2.62 |
| Not Hispanic (6,168) | 6,908 | 2.36 |
| Hispanic (489) | 763 | 0.26 |
| American Indian/Alaska Native (442) | 1,035 | 0.35 |
| Not Hispanic (210) | 646 | 0.22 |
| Hispanic (232) | 389 | 0.13 |
| Alaska Athabascan (Ala. Nat.) (0) | 1 | <0.01 |
| Aleut (Alaska Native) (1) | 1 | <0.01 |
| Apache (2) | 2 | <0.01 |
| Arapaho (0) | 0 | <0.01 |
| Blackfeet (0) | 17 | 0.01 |
| Canadian/French Am. Ind. (4) | 6 | <0.01 |
| Central American Ind. (13) | 16 | 0.01 |
| Cherokee (6) | 86 | 0.03 |
| Cheyenne (0) | 0 | <0.01 |
| Chickasaw (0) | 2 | <0.01 |
| Chippewa (9) | 14 | <0.01 |

| Race* | Population | % |
| --- | --- | --- |
| Choctaw (2) | 5 | <0.01 |
| Colville (0) | 0 | <0.01 |
| Comanche (0) | 0 | <0.01 |
| Cree (0) | 3 | <0.01 |
| Creek (1) | 5 | <0.01 |
| Crow (0) | 1 | <0.01 |
| Delaware (3) | 6 | <0.01 |
| Hopi (0) | 0 | <0.01 |
| Houma (0) | 0 | <0.01 |
| Inupiat (Alaska Native) (0) | 0 | <0.01 |
| Iroquois (13) | 47 | 0.02 |
| Kiowa (1) | 1 | <0.01 |
| Lumbee (0) | 0 | <0.01 |
| Menominee (0) | 0 | <0.01 |
| Mexican American Ind. (26) | 34 | 0.01 |
| Navajo (2) | 3 | <0.01 |
| Osage (0) | 1 | <0.01 |
| Ottawa (0) | 0 | <0.01 |
| Paiute (0) | 0 | <0.01 |
| Pima (0) | 0 | <0.01 |
| Potawatomi (1) | 2 | <0.01 |
| Pueblo (0) | 3 | <0.01 |
| Puget Sound Salish (0) | 0 | <0.01 |
| Seminole (0) | 0 | <0.01 |
| Shoshone (1) | 1 | <0.01 |
| Sioux (2) | 7 | <0.01 |
| South American Ind. (24) | 57 | 0.02 |
| Spanish American Ind. (21) | 25 | 0.01 |
| Tlingit-Haida (Alaska Native) (0) | 0 | <0.01 |
| Tohono O'Odham (0) | 0 | <0.01 |
| Tsimshian (Alaska Native) (0) | 0 | <0.01 |
| Ute (0) | 0 | <0.01 |
| Yakama (0) | 0 | <0.01 |
| Yaqui (0) | 0 | <0.01 |
| Yuman (0) | 0 | <0.01 |
| Yup'ik (Alaska Native) (0) | 0 | <0.01 |
| Asian (26,723) | 29,203 | 9.96 |
| Not Hispanic (26,611) | 28,910 | 9.86 |
| Hispanic (112) | 293 | 0.10 |
| Bangladeshi (331) | 365 | 0.12 |
| Bhutanese (0) | 0 | <0.01 |
| Burmese (23) | 26 | 0.01 |
| Cambodian (29) | 38 | 0.01 |
| Chinese, ex. Taiwanese (6,454) | 7,054 | 2.41 |
| Filipino (1,445) | 1,803 | 0.61 |
| Hmong (0) | 0 | <0.01 |
| Indian (10,593) | 11,289 | 3.85 |
| Indonesian (24) | 33 | 0.01 |
| Japanese (431) | 554 | 0.19 |
| Korean (4,774) | 4,977 | 1.70 |
| Laotian (2) | 2 | <0.01 |
| Malaysian (21) | 30 | 0.01 |
| Nepalese (48) | 49 | 0.02 |
| Pakistani (1,212) | 1,330 | 0.45 |
| Sri Lankan (39) | 59 | 0.02 |
| Taiwanese (346) | 401 | 0.14 |
| Thai (90) | 110 | 0.04 |
| Vietnamese (165) | 237 | 0.08 |
| Hawaii Native/Pacific Islander (34) | 174 | 0.06 |
| Not Hispanic (24) | 124 | 0.04 |
| Hispanic (10) | 50 | 0.02 |
| Fijian (0) | 2 | <0.01 |
| Guamanian/Chamorro (7) | 15 | <0.01 |
| Marshallese (0) | 0 | <0.01 |
| Native Hawaiian (9) | 29 | 0.01 |
| Samoan (3) | 10 | <0.01 |
| Tongan (1) | 1 | <0.01 |
| White (249,159) | 252,713 | 86.19 |
| Not Hispanic (234,536) | 236,944 | 80.81 |
| Hispanic (14,623) | 15,769 | 5.38 |

Notes: † The Census 2010 population figure is used to calculate the percentages in the Hispanic Origin and Race categories. Ancestry percentages are based on the 2006-2010 American Community Survey population (not shown); ‡ Numbers in parentheses indicate the number of people reporting a single ancestry; * Numbers in parentheses indicate the number of persons reporting this race alone, not in combination with any other race; Please refer to the Explanation of Data for more information.

## Queens

Place Type: Borough
County: Queens
Population: 2,230,722

| Ancestry | Population | % |
|---|---|---|
| Afghan (5,842) | 6,027 | 0.27 |
| African, Sub-Saharan (19,754) | 25,166 | 1.14 |
| African (9,764) | 14,083 | 0.64 |
| Cape Verdean (46) | 117 | 0.01 |
| Ethiopian (478) | 505 | 0.02 |
| Ghanaian (1,269) | 1,326 | 0.06 |
| Kenyan (96) | 96 | <0.01 |
| Liberian (297) | 381 | 0.02 |
| Nigerian (5,989) | 6,304 | 0.29 |
| Senegalese (84) | 84 | <0.01 |
| Sierra Leonean (127) | 127 | 0.01 |
| Somalian (52) | 98 | <0.01 |
| South African (230) | 356 | 0.02 |
| Sudanese (161) | 286 | 0.01 |
| Ugandan (65) | 77 | <0.01 |
| Zimbabwean (107) | 107 | <0.01 |
| Other Sub-Saharan African (989) | 1,219 | 0.06 |
| Albanian (6,264) | 6,624 | 0.30 |
| Alsatian (26) | 37 | <0.01 |
| American (45,604) | 45,604 | 2.07 |
| Arab (16,286) | 19,669 | 0.89 |
| Arab (1,921) | 2,283 | 0.10 |
| Egyptian (5,905) | 6,551 | 0.30 |
| Iraqi (224) | 315 | 0.01 |
| Jordanian (260) | 307 | 0.01 |
| Lebanese (1,548) | 2,228 | 0.10 |
| Moroccan (2,945) | 3,459 | 0.16 |
| Palestinian (582) | 638 | 0.03 |
| Syrian (193) | 420 | 0.02 |
| Other Arab (2,708) | 3,468 | 0.16 |
| Armenian (4,083) | 4,658 | 0.21 |
| Assyrian/Chaldean/Syriac (13) | 13 | <0.01 |
| Australian (163) | 285 | 0.01 |
| Austrian (2,702) | 7,523 | 0.34 |
| Basque (29) | 159 | 0.01 |
| Belgian (289) | 593 | 0.03 |
| Brazilian (4,871) | 6,175 | 0.28 |
| British (1,346) | 2,457 | 0.11 |
| Bulgarian (1,928) | 2,090 | 0.10 |
| Cajun (0) | 33 | <0.01 |
| Canadian (604) | 1,308 | 0.06 |
| Carpatho Rusyn (0) | 9 | <0.01 |
| Celtic (92) | 169 | 0.01 |
| Croatian (5,621) | 7,054 | 0.32 |
| Cypriot (556) | 644 | 0.03 |
| Czech (1,116) | 3,464 | 0.16 |
| Czechoslovakian (816) | 1,467 | 0.07 |
| Danish (171) | 792 | 0.04 |
| Dutch (727) | 3,516 | 0.16 |
| Eastern European (4,442) | 4,673 | 0.21 |
| English (4,389) | 20,267 | 0.92 |
| Estonian (164) | 198 | 0.01 |
| European (5,335) | 6,584 | 0.30 |
| Finnish (269) | 693 | 0.03 |
| French, ex. Basque (3,945) | 12,532 | 0.57 |
| French Canadian (552) | 2,020 | 0.09 |
| German (20,566) | 70,399 | 3.20 |
| German Russian (33) | 78 | <0.01 |
| Greek (35,368) | 41,654 | 1.89 |
| Guyanese (47,132) | 53,961 | 2.45 |
| Hungarian (4,718) | 9,470 | 0.43 |
| Icelander (10) | 26 | <0.01 |
| Iranian (3,162) | 3,707 | 0.17 |
| Irish (43,033) | 105,348 | 4.79 |
| Israeli (3,355) | 4,164 | 0.19 |
| Italian (104,251) | 159,812 | 7.27 |
| Latvian (342) | 568 | 0.03 |
| Lithuanian (1,463) | 3,131 | 0.14 |
| Luxemburger (0) | 13 | <0.01 |
| Macedonian (938) | 1,109 | 0.05 |
| Maltese (952) | 1,565 | 0.07 |
| New Zealander (0) | 16 | <0.01 |
| Northern European (370) | 512 | 0.02 |

| Ancestry | Population | % |
|---|---|---|
| Norwegian (670) | 2,559 | 0.12 |
| Pennsylvania German (9) | 38 | <0.01 |
| Polish (37,726) | 59,757 | 2.72 |
| Portuguese (2,784) | 4,727 | 0.21 |
| Romanian (9,232) | 11,686 | 0.53 |
| Russian (29,779) | 44,676 | 2.03 |
| Scandinavian (131) | 545 | 0.02 |
| Scotch-Irish (2,079) | 4,602 | 0.21 |
| Scottish (1,567) | 5,718 | 0.26 |
| Serbian (2,176) | 2,438 | 0.11 |
| Slavic (370) | 765 | 0.03 |
| Slovak (1,161) | 1,882 | 0.09 |
| Slovene (171) | 468 | 0.02 |
| Soviet Union (12) | 71 | <0.01 |
| Swedish (511) | 2,862 | 0.13 |
| Swiss (381) | 1,260 | 0.06 |
| Turkish (3,054) | 3,767 | 0.17 |
| Ukrainian (5,770) | 8,375 | 0.38 |
| Welsh (201) | 1,666 | 0.08 |
| West Indian, ex. Hispanic (131,014) | 147,460 | 6.71 |
| Bahamian (134) | 185 | 0.01 |
| Barbadian (4,074) | 5,021 | 0.23 |
| Belizean (1,106) | 1,344 | 0.06 |
| Bermudan (142) | 177 | 0.01 |
| British West Indian (3,765) | 4,689 | 0.21 |
| Dutch West Indian (122) | 206 | 0.01 |
| Haitian (35,439) | 38,368 | 1.74 |
| Jamaican (55,278) | 59,999 | 2.73 |
| Trinidadian/Tobagonian (16,227) | 19,255 | 0.88 |
| U.S. Virgin Islander (234) | 364 | 0.02 |
| West Indian (14,052) | 17,400 | 0.79 |
| Other West Indian (441) | 452 | 0.02 |
| Yugoslavian (3,824) | 4,516 | 0.21 |

| Hispanic Origin | Population | % |
|---|---|---|
| Hispanic or Latino (of any race) | 613,750 | 27.51 |
| Central American, ex. Mexican | 52,509 | 2.35 |
| Costa Rican | 1,749 | 0.08 |
| Guatemalan | 13,700 | 0.61 |
| Honduran | 8,546 | 0.38 |
| Nicaraguan | 2,842 | 0.13 |
| Panamanian | 3,977 | 0.18 |
| Salvadoran | 21,342 | 0.96 |
| Other Central American | 353 | 0.02 |
| Cuban | 11,020 | 0.49 |
| Dominican Republic | 88,061 | 3.95 |
| Mexican | 92,835 | 4.16 |
| Puerto Rican | 102,881 | 4.61 |
| South American | 214,022 | 9.59 |
| Argentinean | 6,345 | 0.28 |
| Bolivian | 3,268 | 0.15 |
| Chilean | 3,184 | 0.14 |
| Colombian | 70,290 | 3.15 |
| Ecuadorian | 98,512 | 4.42 |
| Paraguayan | 2,775 | 0.12 |
| Peruvian | 22,886 | 1.03 |
| Uruguayan | 1,743 | 0.08 |
| Venezuelan | 3,580 | 0.16 |
| Other South American | 1,439 | 0.06 |
| Other Hispanic or Latino | 52,422 | 2.35 |

| Race* | Population | % |
|---|---|---|
| African-American/Black (426,683) | 462,351 | 20.73 |
| Not Hispanic (395,881) | 419,695 | 18.81 |
| Hispanic (30,802) | 42,656 | 1.91 |
| American Indian/Alaska Native (15,364) | 30,033 | 1.35 |
| Not Hispanic (6,490) | 15,412 | 0.69 |
| Hispanic (8,874) | 14,621 | 0.66 |
| Alaska Athabascan (Ala. Nat.) (2) | 3 | <0.01 |
| Aleut (Alaska Native) (4) | 6 | <0.01 |
| Apache (15) | 53 | <0.01 |
| Arapaho (0) | 2 | <0.01 |
| Blackfeet (45) | 342 | 0.02 |
| Canadian/French Am. Ind. (20) | 38 | <0.01 |
| Central American Ind. (419) | 733 | 0.03 |
| Cherokee (267) | 1,425 | 0.06 |
| Cheyenne (13) | 20 | <0.01 |
| Chickasaw (9) | 21 | <0.01 |
| Chippewa (14) | 37 | <0.01 |

| | Population | % |
|---|---|---|
| Choctaw (16) | 68 | <0.01 |
| Colville (1) | 1 | <0.01 |
| Comanche (3) | 6 | <0.01 |
| Cree (6) | 24 | <0.01 |
| Creek (23) | 73 | <0.01 |
| Crow (1) | 4 | <0.01 |
| Delaware (14) | 35 | <0.01 |
| Hopi (1) | 15 | <0.01 |
| Houma (0) | 4 | <0.01 |
| Inupiat (Alaska Native) (6) | 13 | <0.01 |
| Iroquois (140) | 308 | 0.01 |
| Kiowa (0) | 0 | <0.01 |
| Lumbee (7) | 30 | <0.01 |
| Menominee (0) | 0 | <0.01 |
| Mexican American Ind. (1,270) | 1,640 | 0.07 |
| Navajo (13) | 37 | <0.01 |
| Osage (0) | 5 | <0.01 |
| Ottawa (0) | 2 | <0.01 |
| Paiute (3) | 4 | <0.01 |
| Pima (0) | 0 | <0.01 |
| Potawatomi (6) | 7 | <0.01 |
| Pueblo (102) | 161 | 0.01 |
| Puget Sound Salish (2) | 5 | <0.01 |
| Seminole (15) | 79 | <0.01 |
| Shoshone (0) | 6 | <0.01 |
| Sioux (35) | 104 | <0.01 |
| South American Ind. (1,281) | 2,448 | 0.11 |
| Spanish American Ind. (468) | 659 | 0.03 |
| Tlingit-Haida (Alaska Native) (8) | 20 | <0.01 |
| Tohono O'Odham (4) | 6 | <0.01 |
| Tsimshian (Alaska Native) (0) | 1 | <0.01 |
| Ute (4) | 5 | <0.01 |
| Yakama (0) | 0 | <0.01 |
| Yaqui (3) | 7 | <0.01 |
| Yuman (2) | 5 | <0.01 |
| Yup'ik (Alaska Native) (1) | 1 | <0.01 |
| Asian (511,787) | 552,867 | 24.78 |
| Not Hispanic (508,334) | 545,389 | 24.45 |
| Hispanic (3,453) | 7,478 | 0.34 |
| Bangladeshi (33,152) | 38,341 | 1.72 |
| Bhutanese (240) | 250 | 0.01 |
| Burmese (2,132) | 2,344 | 0.11 |
| Cambodian (230) | 303 | 0.01 |
| Chinese, ex. Taiwanese (191,693) | 200,714 | 9.00 |
| Filipino (38,163) | 41,773 | 1.87 |
| Hmong (24) | 30 | <0.01 |
| Indian (117,550) | 141,147 | 6.33 |
| Indonesian (2,860) | 3,386 | 0.15 |
| Japanese (6,375) | 7,790 | 0.35 |
| Korean (64,107) | 66,124 | 2.96 |
| Laotian (137) | 210 | 0.01 |
| Malaysian (1,029) | 1,620 | 0.07 |
| Nepalese (4,930) | 5,319 | 0.24 |
| Pakistani (16,215) | 18,084 | 0.81 |
| Sri Lankan (1,293) | 1,536 | 0.07 |
| Taiwanese (7,776) | 8,962 | 0.40 |
| Thai (3,677) | 4,124 | 0.18 |
| Vietnamese (3,566) | 4,322 | 0.19 |
| Hawaii Native/Pacific Islander (1,530) | 7,691 | 0.34 |
| Not Hispanic (1,094) | 5,685 | 0.25 |
| Hispanic (436) | 2,006 | 0.09 |
| Fijian (36) | 76 | <0.01 |
| Guamanian/Chamorro (337) | 483 | 0.02 |
| Marshallese (0) | 0 | <0.01 |
| Native Hawaiian (191) | 486 | 0.02 |
| Samoan (62) | 179 | 0.01 |
| Tongan (7) | 14 | <0.01 |
| White (886,053) | 941,608 | 42.21 |
| Not Hispanic (616,727) | 638,051 | 28.60 |
| Hispanic (269,326) | 303,557 | 13.61 |

Notes: † The Census 2010 population figure is used to calculate the percentages in the Hispanic Origin and Race categories. Ancestry percentages are based on the 2006-2010 American Community Survey population (not shown); ‡ Numbers in parentheses indicate the number of people reporting a single ancestry; * Numbers in parentheses indicate the number of persons reporting this race alone, not in combination with any other race; Please refer to the Explanation of Data for more information.

## Ramapo

Place Type: Town
County: Rockland
Population: 126,595

| Ancestry | Population | % |
|---|---|---|
| Afghan (111) | 111 | 0.09 |
| African, Sub-Saharan (718) | 858 | 0.70 |
| African (292) | 427 | 0.35 |
| Cape Verdean (0) | 0 | <0.01 |
| Ethiopian (0) | 0 | <0.01 |
| Ghanaian (77) | 77 | 0.06 |
| Kenyan (0) | 0 | <0.01 |
| Liberian (0) | 0 | <0.01 |
| Nigerian (207) | 207 | 0.17 |
| Senegalese (0) | 0 | <0.01 |
| Sierra Leonean (0) | 0 | <0.01 |
| Somalian (0) | 0 | <0.01 |
| South African (56) | 56 | 0.05 |
| Sudanese (0) | 0 | <0.01 |
| Ugandan (86) | 86 | 0.07 |
| Zimbabwean (0) | 0 | <0.01 |
| Other Sub-Saharan African (0) | 5 | <0.01 |
| Albanian (0) | 0 | <0.01 |
| Alsatian (0) | 0 | <0.01 |
| American (5,092) | 5,092 | 4.15 |
| Arab (608) | 781 | 0.64 |
| Arab (245) | 245 | 0.20 |
| Egyptian (16) | 24 | 0.02 |
| Iraqi (12) | 48 | 0.04 |
| Jordanian (10) | 10 | 0.01 |
| Lebanese (23) | 37 | 0.03 |
| Moroccan (216) | 291 | 0.24 |
| Palestinian (0) | 25 | 0.02 |
| Syrian (17) | 17 | 0.01 |
| Other Arab (69) | 84 | 0.07 |
| Armenian (33) | 63 | 0.05 |
| Assyrian/Chaldean/Syriac (0) | 0 | <0.01 |
| Australian (19) | 86 | 0.07 |
| Austrian (328) | 1,328 | 1.08 |
| Basque (0) | 0 | <0.01 |
| Belgian (218) | 751 | 0.61 |
| Brazilian (101) | 228 | 0.19 |
| British (179) | 396 | 0.32 |
| Bulgarian (8) | 24 | 0.02 |
| Cajun (0) | 0 | <0.01 |
| Canadian (309) | 680 | 0.55 |
| Carpatho Rusyn (0) | 0 | <0.01 |
| Celtic (19) | 19 | 0.02 |
| Croatian (0) | 16 | 0.01 |
| Cypriot (0) | 0 | <0.01 |
| Czech (174) | 565 | 0.46 |
| Czechoslovakian (355) | 654 | 0.53 |
| Danish (56) | 129 | 0.11 |
| Dutch (208) | 772 | 0.63 |
| Eastern European (1,057) | 1,144 | 0.93 |
| English (863) | 3,171 | 2.58 |
| Estonian (24) | 48 | 0.04 |
| European (7,822) | 8,814 | 7.18 |
| Finnish (0) | 17 | 0.01 |
| French, ex. Basque (183) | 954 | 0.78 |
| French Canadian (53) | 174 | 0.14 |
| German (2,191) | 7,630 | 6.22 |
| German Russian (0) | 0 | <0.01 |
| Greek (402) | 653 | 0.53 |
| Guyanese (294) | 371 | 0.30 |
| Hungarian (3,672) | 6,804 | 5.54 |
| Icelander (0) | 0 | <0.01 |
| Iranian (181) | 314 | 0.26 |
| Irish (3,209) | 8,081 | 6.59 |
| Israeli (1,511) | 3,342 | 2.72 |
| Italian (4,569) | 8,664 | 7.06 |
| Latvian (87) | 174 | 0.14 |
| Lithuanian (98) | 538 | 0.44 |
| Luxemburger (0) | 0 | <0.01 |
| Macedonian (0) | 0 | <0.01 |
| Maltese (0) | 0 | <0.01 |
| New Zealander (0) | 55 | 0.04 |
| Northern European (0) | 38 | 0.03 |
| Norwegian (64) | 140 | 0.11 |
| Pennsylvania German (10) | 17 | 0.01 |
| Polish (3,146) | 9,453 | 7.70 |
| Portuguese (120) | 252 | 0.21 |
| Romanian (524) | 1,695 | 1.38 |
| Russian (2,367) | 6,069 | 4.95 |
| Scandinavian (15) | 52 | 0.04 |
| Scotch-Irish (119) | 424 | 0.35 |
| Scottish (193) | 640 | 0.52 |
| Serbian (0) | 0 | <0.01 |
| Slavic (18) | 63 | 0.05 |
| Slovak (69) | 114 | 0.09 |
| Slovene (31) | 46 | 0.04 |
| Soviet Union (0) | 0 | <0.01 |
| Swedish (28) | 316 | 0.26 |
| Swiss (34) | 85 | 0.07 |
| Turkish (28) | 114 | 0.09 |
| Ukrainian (949) | 1,403 | 1.14 |
| Welsh (10) | 182 | 0.15 |
| West Indian, ex. Hispanic (12,117) | 12,710 | 10.36 |
| Bahamian (0) | 0 | <0.01 |
| Barbadian (10) | 34 | 0.03 |
| Belizean (12) | 35 | 0.03 |
| Bermudan (0) | 0 | <0.01 |
| British West Indian (253) | 253 | 0.21 |
| Dutch West Indian (0) | 0 | <0.01 |
| Haitian (8,747) | 8,948 | 7.29 |
| Jamaican (2,336) | 2,509 | 2.04 |
| Trinidadian/Tobagonian (550) | 604 | 0.49 |
| U.S. Virgin Islander (0) | 19 | 0.02 |
| West Indian (209) | 308 | 0.25 |
| Other West Indian (0) | 0 | <0.01 |
| Yugoslavian (42) | 78 | 0.06 |

| Hispanic Origin | Population | % |
|---|---|---|
| Hispanic or Latino (of any race) | 17,223 | 13.60 |
| Central American, ex. Mexican | 5,319 | 4.20 |
| Costa Rican | 103 | 0.08 |
| Guatemalan | 4,050 | 3.20 |
| Honduran | 182 | 0.14 |
| Nicaraguan | 29 | 0.02 |
| Panamanian | 54 | 0.04 |
| Salvadoran | 872 | 0.69 |
| Other Central American | 29 | 0.02 |
| Cuban | 279 | 0.22 |
| Dominican Republic | 1,021 | 0.81 |
| Mexican | 2,433 | 1.92 |
| Puerto Rican | 2,904 | 2.29 |
| South American | 3,759 | 2.97 |
| Argentinean | 166 | 0.13 |
| Bolivian | 9 | 0.01 |
| Chilean | 66 | 0.05 |
| Colombian | 308 | 0.24 |
| Ecuadorian | 2,915 | 2.30 |
| Paraguayan | 8 | 0.01 |
| Peruvian | 204 | 0.16 |
| Uruguayan | 16 | 0.01 |
| Venezuelan | 59 | 0.05 |
| Other South American | 8 | 0.01 |
| Other Hispanic or Latino | 1,508 | 1.19 |

| Race* | Population | % |
|---|---|---|
| African-American/Black (20,056) | 21,297 | 16.82 |
| Not Hispanic (19,173) | 20,078 | 15.86 |
| Hispanic (883) | 1,219 | 0.96 |
| American Indian/Alaska Native (430) | 963 | 0.76 |
| Not Hispanic (253) | 613 | 0.48 |
| Hispanic (177) | 350 | 0.28 |
| Alaska Athabascan (Ala. Nat.) (0) | 0 | <0.01 |
| Aleut (Alaska Native) (1) | 1 | <0.01 |
| Apache (2) | 3 | <0.01 |
| Arapaho (0) | 0 | <0.01 |
| Blackfeet (1) | 11 | 0.01 |
| Canadian/French Am. Ind. (0) | 0 | <0.01 |
| Central American Ind. (10) | 22 | 0.02 |
| Cherokee (9) | 69 | 0.05 |
| Cheyenne (0) | 1 | <0.01 |
| Chickasaw (0) | 0 | <0.01 |
| Chippewa (0) | 1 | <0.01 |
| Choctaw (1) | 1 | <0.01 |
| Colville (0) | 0 | <0.01 |
| Comanche (0) | 2 | <0.01 |
| Cree (0) | 0 | <0.01 |
| Creek (0) | 0 | <0.01 |
| Crow (0) | 0 | <0.01 |
| Delaware (93) | 167 | 0.13 |
| Hopi (0) | 0 | <0.01 |
| Houma (0) | 0 | <0.01 |
| Inupiat (Alaska Native) (0) | 0 | <0.01 |
| Iroquois (21) | 36 | 0.03 |
| Kiowa (0) | 0 | <0.01 |
| Lumbee (0) | 2 | <0.01 |
| Menominee (0) | 0 | <0.01 |
| Mexican American Ind. (52) | 74 | 0.06 |
| Navajo (0) | 4 | <0.01 |
| Osage (0) | 0 | <0.01 |
| Ottawa (0) | 0 | <0.01 |
| Paiute (0) | 0 | <0.01 |
| Pima (0) | 0 | <0.01 |
| Potawatomi (0) | 0 | <0.01 |
| Pueblo (1) | 1 | <0.01 |
| Puget Sound Salish (0) | 0 | <0.01 |
| Seminole (0) | 2 | <0.01 |
| Shoshone (0) | 0 | <0.01 |
| Sioux (0) | 2 | <0.01 |
| South American Ind. (20) | 68 | 0.05 |
| Spanish American Ind. (3) | 7 | 0.01 |
| Tlingit-Haida (Alaska Native) (2) | 7 | 0.01 |
| Tohono O'Odham (2) | 4 | <0.01 |
| Tsimshian (Alaska Native) (0) | 0 | <0.01 |
| Ute (0) | 0 | <0.01 |
| Yakama (0) | 1 | <0.01 |
| Yaqui (0) | 0 | <0.01 |
| Yuman (0) | 0 | <0.01 |
| Yup'ik (Alaska Native) (0) | 0 | <0.01 |
| Asian (5,082) | 5,750 | 4.54 |
| Not Hispanic (5,013) | 5,609 | 4.43 |
| Hispanic (69) | 141 | 0.11 |
| Bangladeshi (56) | 63 | 0.05 |
| Bhutanese (0) | 0 | <0.01 |
| Burmese (1) | 1 | <0.01 |
| Cambodian (48) | 52 | 0.04 |
| Chinese, ex. Taiwanese (606) | 730 | 0.58 |
| Filipino (1,338) | 1,472 | 1.16 |
| Hmong (0) | 0 | <0.01 |
| Indian (1,751) | 1,962 | 1.55 |
| Indonesian (18) | 23 | 0.02 |
| Japanese (98) | 136 | 0.11 |
| Korean (300) | 339 | 0.27 |
| Laotian (4) | 6 | <0.01 |
| Malaysian (2) | 8 | 0.01 |
| Nepalese (11) | 11 | 0.01 |
| Pakistani (461) | 524 | 0.41 |
| Sri Lankan (23) | 26 | 0.02 |
| Taiwanese (19) | 21 | 0.02 |
| Thai (30) | 37 | 0.03 |
| Vietnamese (112) | 148 | 0.12 |
| Hawaii Native/Pacific Islander (45) | 237 | 0.19 |
| Not Hispanic (18) | 156 | 0.12 |
| Hispanic (27) | 81 | 0.06 |
| Fijian (0) | 2 | <0.01 |
| Guamanian/Chamorro (16) | 19 | 0.02 |
| Marshallese (0) | 0 | <0.01 |
| Native Hawaiian (8) | 17 | 0.01 |
| Samoan (4) | 9 | <0.01 |
| Tongan (0) | 2 | <0.01 |
| White (90,924) | 92,843 | 73.34 |
| Not Hispanic (83,094) | 84,071 | 66.41 |
| Hispanic (7,830) | 8,772 | 6.93 |

Notes: † The Census 2010 population figure is used to calculate the percentages in the Hispanic Origin and Race categories. Ancestry percentages are based on the 2006-2010 American Community Survey population (not shown); ‡ Numbers in parentheses indicate the number of people reporting a single ancestry; * Numbers in parentheses indicate the number of persons reporting this race alone, not in combination with any other race; Please refer to the Explanation of Data for more information.

## Rochester

Place Type: City
County: Monroe
Population: 210,565

| Ancestry | Population | % |
|---|---|---|
| Afghan (0) | 0 | <0.01 |
| African, Sub-Saharan (7,095) | 7,909 | 3.73 |
| African (5,087) | 5,828 | 2.75 |
| Cape Verdean (0) | 0 | <0.01 |
| Ethiopian (227) | 227 | 0.11 |
| Ghanaian (49) | 49 | 0.02 |
| Kenyan (9) | 9 | <0.01 |
| Liberian (89) | 89 | 0.04 |
| Nigerian (151) | 203 | 0.10 |
| Senegalese (0) | 0 | <0.01 |
| Sierra Leonean (0) | 0 | <0.01 |
| Somalian (980) | 980 | 0.46 |
| South African (19) | 32 | 0.02 |
| Sudanese (107) | 107 | 0.05 |
| Ugandan (0) | 0 | <0.01 |
| Zimbabwean (76) | 76 | 0.04 |
| Other Sub-Saharan African (301) | 309 | 0.15 |
| Albanian (31) | 42 | 0.02 |
| Alsatian (0) | 0 | <0.01 |
| American (3,617) | 3,617 | 1.71 |
| Arab (785) | 1,077 | 0.51 |
| Arab (245) | 263 | 0.12 |
| Egyptian (81) | 81 | 0.04 |
| Iraqi (36) | 36 | 0.02 |
| Jordanian (0) | 0 | <0.01 |
| Lebanese (136) | 196 | 0.09 |
| Moroccan (17) | 48 | 0.02 |
| Palestinian (30) | 30 | 0.01 |
| Syrian (11) | 33 | 0.02 |
| Other Arab (229) | 390 | 0.18 |
| Armenian (84) | 105 | 0.05 |
| Assyrian/Chaldean/Syriac (0) | 0 | <0.01 |
| Australian (0) | 69 | 0.03 |
| Austrian (103) | 450 | 0.21 |
| Basque (0) | 0 | <0.01 |
| Belgian (27) | 185 | 0.09 |
| Brazilian (35) | 90 | 0.04 |
| British (259) | 606 | 0.29 |
| Bulgarian (0) | 33 | 0.02 |
| Cajun (0) | 0 | <0.01 |
| Canadian (227) | 550 | 0.26 |
| Carpatho Rusyn (0) | 0 | <0.01 |
| Celtic (13) | 40 | 0.02 |
| Croatian (12) | 61 | 0.03 |
| Cypriot (0) | 0 | <0.01 |
| Czech (77) | 484 | 0.23 |
| Czechoslovakian (30) | 44 | 0.02 |
| Danish (51) | 275 | 0.13 |
| Dutch (406) | 2,898 | 1.37 |
| Eastern European (200) | 237 | 0.11 |
| English (3,972) | 13,510 | 6.37 |
| Estonian (0) | 38 | 0.02 |
| European (893) | 1,150 | 0.54 |
| Finnish (11) | 160 | 0.08 |
| French, ex. Basque (683) | 4,083 | 1.93 |
| French Canadian (652) | 1,474 | 0.70 |
| German (5,802) | 22,972 | 10.84 |
| German Russian (0) | 0 | <0.01 |
| Greek (337) | 623 | 0.29 |
| Guyanese (348) | 381 | 0.18 |
| Hungarian (246) | 783 | 0.37 |
| Icelander (0) | 0 | <0.01 |
| Iranian (97) | 120 | 0.06 |
| Irish (5,531) | 19,595 | 9.24 |
| Israeli (37) | 57 | 0.03 |
| Italian (8,976) | 19,728 | 9.31 |
| Latvian (33) | 55 | 0.03 |
| Lithuanian (236) | 466 | 0.22 |
| Luxemburger (19) | 62 | 0.03 |
| Macedonian (0) | 10 | <0.01 |
| Maltese (34) | 100 | 0.05 |
| New Zealander (0) | 0 | <0.01 |
| Northern European (23) | 23 | 0.01 |

| Ancestry | Population | % |
|---|---|---|
| Norwegian (135) | 444 | 0.21 |
| Pennsylvania German (8) | 70 | 0.03 |
| Polish (1,583) | 5,614 | 2.65 |
| Portuguese (47) | 199 | 0.09 |
| Romanian (96) | 186 | 0.09 |
| Russian (498) | 1,342 | 0.63 |
| Scandinavian (34) | 111 | 0.05 |
| Scotch-Irish (433) | 1,614 | 0.76 |
| Scottish (526) | 3,002 | 1.42 |
| Serbian (0) | 49 | 0.02 |
| Slavic (32) | 78 | 0.04 |
| Slovak (24) | 157 | 0.07 |
| Slovene (24) | 37 | 0.02 |
| Soviet Union (0) | 0 | <0.01 |
| Swedish (403) | 1,156 | 0.55 |
| Swiss (36) | 271 | 0.13 |
| Turkish (486) | 612 | 0.29 |
| Ukrainian (727) | 1,325 | 0.63 |
| Welsh (141) | 992 | 0.47 |
| West Indian, ex. Hispanic (3,129) | 5,230 | 2.47 |
| Bahamian (58) | 218 | 0.10 |
| Barbadian (169) | 230 | 0.11 |
| Belizean (119) | 171 | 0.08 |
| Bermudan (0) | 0 | <0.01 |
| British West Indian (99) | 223 | 0.11 |
| Dutch West Indian (0) | 13 | 0.01 |
| Haitian (352) | 383 | 0.18 |
| Jamaican (1,743) | 2,834 | 1.34 |
| Trinidadian/Tobagonian (199) | 288 | 0.14 |
| U.S. Virgin Islander (0) | 0 | <0.01 |
| West Indian (390) | 870 | 0.41 |
| Other West Indian (0) | 0 | <0.01 |
| Yugoslavian (117) | 138 | 0.07 |

| Hispanic Origin | Population | % |
|---|---|---|
| Hispanic or Latino (of any race) | 34,456 | 16.36 |
| Central American, ex. Mexican | 569 | 0.27 |
| Costa Rican | 72 | 0.03 |
| Guatemalan | 85 | 0.04 |
| Honduran | 129 | 0.06 |
| Nicaraguan | 56 | 0.03 |
| Panamanian | 123 | 0.06 |
| Salvadoran | 96 | 0.05 |
| Other Central American | 8 | <0.01 |
| Cuban | 1,616 | 0.77 |
| Dominican Republic | 1,373 | 0.65 |
| Mexican | 1,168 | 0.55 |
| Puerto Rican | 27,734 | 13.17 |
| South American | 517 | 0.25 |
| Argentinean | 49 | 0.02 |
| Bolivian | 18 | 0.01 |
| Chilean | 82 | 0.04 |
| Colombian | 182 | 0.09 |
| Ecuadorian | 72 | 0.03 |
| Paraguayan | 10 | <0.01 |
| Peruvian | 68 | 0.03 |
| Uruguayan | 7 | <0.01 |
| Venezuelan | 22 | 0.01 |
| Other South American | 7 | <0.01 |
| Other Hispanic or Latino | 1,479 | 0.70 |

| Race* | Population | % |
|---|---|---|
| African-American/Black (87,897) | 94,587 | 44.92 |
| Not Hispanic (83,346) | 88,052 | 41.82 |
| Hispanic (4,551) | 6,535 | 3.10 |
| American Indian/Alaska Native (1,013) | 3,202 | 1.52 |
| Not Hispanic (666) | 2,330 | 1.11 |
| Hispanic (347) | 872 | 0.41 |
| Alaska Athabascan (Ala. Nat.) (0) | 1 | <0.01 |
| Aleut (Alaska Native) (1) | 2 | <0.01 |
| Apache (8) | 20 | 0.01 |
| Arapaho (0) | 0 | <0.01 |
| Blackfeet (16) | 134 | 0.06 |
| Canadian/French Am. Ind. (3) | 9 | <0.01 |
| Central American Ind. (15) | 29 | 0.01 |
| Cherokee (51) | 411 | 0.20 |
| Cheyenne (2) | 3 | <0.01 |
| Chickasaw (0) | 2 | <0.01 |
| Chippewa (9) | 18 | 0.01 |

| Race* | Population | % |
|---|---|---|
| Choctaw (1) | 28 | 0.01 |
| Colville (0) | 1 | <0.01 |
| Comanche (0) | 2 | <0.01 |
| Cree (1) | 2 | <0.01 |
| Creek (2) | 9 | <0.01 |
| Crow (0) | 1 | <0.01 |
| Delaware (1) | 10 | <0.01 |
| Hopi (1) | 1 | <0.01 |
| Houma (0) | 0 | <0.01 |
| Inupiat (Alaska Native) (3) | 4 | <0.01 |
| Iroquois (265) | 483 | 0.23 |
| Kiowa (0) | 0 | <0.01 |
| Lumbee (0) | 0 | <0.01 |
| Menominee (0) | 0 | <0.01 |
| Mexican American Ind. (20) | 38 | 0.02 |
| Navajo (11) | 30 | 0.01 |
| Osage (1) | 3 | <0.01 |
| Ottawa (0) | 0 | <0.01 |
| Paiute (1) | 1 | <0.01 |
| Pima (0) | 2 | <0.01 |
| Potawatomi (3) | 5 | <0.01 |
| Pueblo (0) | 2 | <0.01 |
| Puget Sound Salish (0) | 0 | <0.01 |
| Seminole (1) | 44 | 0.02 |
| Shoshone (0) | 1 | <0.01 |
| Sioux (2) | 22 | 0.01 |
| South American Ind. (45) | 144 | 0.07 |
| Spanish American Ind. (9) | 9 | <0.01 |
| Tlingit-Haida (Alaska Native) (0) | 0 | <0.01 |
| Tohono O'Odham (1) | 1 | <0.01 |
| Tsimshian (Alaska Native) (0) | 0 | <0.01 |
| Ute (0) | 4 | <0.01 |
| Yakama (0) | 0 | <0.01 |
| Yaqui (0) | 0 | <0.01 |
| Yuman (0) | 0 | <0.01 |
| Yup'ik (Alaska Native) (0) | 0 | <0.01 |
| Asian (6,493) | 7,752 | 3.68 |
| Not Hispanic (6,350) | 7,397 | 3.51 |
| Hispanic (143) | 355 | 0.17 |
| Bangladeshi (25) | 27 | 0.01 |
| Bhutanese (369) | 411 | 0.20 |
| Burmese (527) | 565 | 0.27 |
| Cambodian (342) | 381 | 0.18 |
| Chinese, ex. Taiwanese (1,195) | 1,456 | 0.69 |
| Filipino (215) | 378 | 0.18 |
| Hmong (2) | 3 | <0.01 |
| Indian (780) | 1,006 | 0.48 |
| Indonesian (13) | 27 | 0.01 |
| Japanese (127) | 301 | 0.14 |
| Korean (578) | 741 | 0.35 |
| Laotian (564) | 668 | 0.32 |
| Malaysian (8) | 10 | <0.01 |
| Nepalese (118) | 165 | 0.08 |
| Pakistani (53) | 75 | 0.04 |
| Sri Lankan (23) | 27 | 0.01 |
| Taiwanese (104) | 132 | 0.06 |
| Thai (67) | 103 | 0.05 |
| Vietnamese (942) | 1,050 | 0.50 |
| Hawaii Native/Pacific Islander (101) | 449 | 0.21 |
| Not Hispanic (77) | 284 | 0.13 |
| Hispanic (24) | 165 | 0.08 |
| Fijian (0) | 4 | <0.01 |
| Guamanian/Chamorro (12) | 26 | 0.01 |
| Marshallese (0) | 0 | <0.01 |
| Native Hawaiian (30) | 77 | 0.04 |
| Samoan (31) | 63 | 0.03 |
| Tongan (2) | 3 | <0.01 |
| White (91,951) | 98,814 | 46.93 |
| Not Hispanic (79,178) | 84,019 | 39.90 |
| Hispanic (12,773) | 14,795 | 7.03 |

*Notes: † The Census 2010 population figure is used to calculate the percentages in the Hispanic Origin and Race categories. Ancestry percentages are based on the 2006-2010 American Community Survey population (not shown); ‡ Numbers in parentheses indicate the number of people reporting a single ancestry; * Numbers in parentheses indicate the number of persons reporting this race alone, not in combination with any other race; Please refer to the Explanation of Data for more information.*

## Schenectady

Place Type: City
County: Schenectady
Population: 66,135

| Ancestry | Population | % |
|---|---|---|
| Afghan (318) | 318 | 0.49 |
| African, Sub-Saharan (554) | 770 | 1.18 |
| African (201) | 334 | 0.51 |
| Cape Verdean (0) | 0 | <0.01 |
| Ethiopian (0) | 0 | <0.01 |
| Ghanaian (24) | 24 | 0.04 |
| Kenyan (69) | 69 | 0.11 |
| Liberian (24) | 24 | 0.04 |
| Nigerian (131) | 186 | 0.28 |
| Senegalese (0) | 0 | <0.01 |
| Sierra Leonean (0) | 0 | <0.01 |
| Somalian (0) | 0 | <0.01 |
| South African (0) | 0 | <0.01 |
| Sudanese (0) | 0 | <0.01 |
| Ugandan (0) | 0 | <0.01 |
| Zimbabwean (0) | 0 | <0.01 |
| Other Sub-Saharan African (105) | 133 | 0.20 |
| Albanian (28) | 39 | 0.06 |
| Alsatian (0) | 0 | <0.01 |
| American (3,124) | 3,124 | 4.78 |
| Arab (140) | 191 | 0.29 |
| Arab (81) | 113 | 0.17 |
| Egyptian (0) | 0 | <0.01 |
| Iraqi (0) | 0 | <0.01 |
| Jordanian (0) | 0 | <0.01 |
| Lebanese (59) | 78 | 0.12 |
| Moroccan (0) | 0 | <0.01 |
| Palestinian (0) | 0 | <0.01 |
| Syrian (0) | 0 | <0.01 |
| Other Arab (0) | 0 | <0.01 |
| Armenian (19) | 19 | 0.03 |
| Assyrian/Chaldean/Syriac (0) | 0 | <0.01 |
| Australian (0) | 0 | <0.01 |
| Austrian (11) | 77 | 0.12 |
| Basque (0) | 0 | <0.01 |
| Belgian (0) | 0 | <0.01 |
| Brazilian (144) | 194 | 0.30 |
| British (100) | 187 | 0.29 |
| Bulgarian (0) | 0 | <0.01 |
| Cajun (0) | 0 | <0.01 |
| Canadian (44) | 72 | 0.11 |
| Carpatho Rusyn (0) | 0 | <0.01 |
| Celtic (20) | 20 | 0.03 |
| Croatian (0) | 0 | <0.01 |
| Cypriot (0) | 0 | <0.01 |
| Czech (50) | 236 | 0.36 |
| Czechoslovakian (68) | 167 | 0.26 |
| Danish (97) | 121 | 0.19 |
| Dutch (393) | 1,521 | 2.33 |
| Eastern European (76) | 76 | 0.12 |
| English (1,339) | 3,998 | 6.12 |
| Estonian (0) | 0 | <0.01 |
| European (205) | 263 | 0.40 |
| Finnish (15) | 26 | 0.04 |
| French, ex. Basque (658) | 2,862 | 4.38 |
| French Canadian (193) | 902 | 1.38 |
| German (1,915) | 6,846 | 10.47 |
| German Russian (0) | 0 | <0.01 |
| Greek (147) | 224 | 0.34 |
| Guyanese (1,783) | 1,915 | 2.93 |
| Hungarian (128) | 341 | 0.52 |
| Icelander (0) | 0 | <0.01 |
| Iranian (0) | 0 | <0.01 |
| Irish (2,754) | 8,655 | 13.24 |
| Israeli (0) | 9 | 0.01 |
| Italian (5,680) | 9,882 | 15.12 |
| Latvian (0) | 0 | <0.01 |
| Lithuanian (42) | 240 | 0.37 |
| Luxemburger (0) | 0 | <0.01 |
| Macedonian (0) | 0 | <0.01 |
| Maltese (0) | 0 | <0.01 |
| New Zealander (0) | 0 | <0.01 |
| Northern European (83) | 97 | 0.15 |

| | Population | % |
|---|---|---|
| Norwegian (0) | 63 | 0.10 |
| Pennsylvania German (0) | 11 | 0.02 |
| Polish (1,904) | 3,977 | 6.08 |
| Portuguese (20) | 70 | 0.11 |
| Romanian (10) | 10 | 0.02 |
| Russian (98) | 430 | 0.66 |
| Scandinavian (13) | 13 | 0.02 |
| Scotch-Irish (186) | 509 | 0.78 |
| Scottish (248) | 656 | 1.00 |
| Serbian (0) | 12 | 0.02 |
| Slavic (40) | 40 | 0.06 |
| Slovak (32) | 93 | 0.14 |
| Slovene (0) | 0 | <0.01 |
| Soviet Union (0) | 0 | <0.01 |
| Swedish (52) | 177 | 0.27 |
| Swiss (57) | 171 | 0.26 |
| Turkish (10) | 10 | 0.02 |
| Ukrainian (91) | 236 | 0.36 |
| Welsh (65) | 320 | 0.49 |
| West Indian, ex. Hispanic (1,255) | 1,477 | 2.26 |
| Bahamian (0) | 0 | <0.01 |
| Barbadian (43) | 94 | 0.14 |
| Belizean (0) | 0 | <0.01 |
| Bermudan (0) | 0 | <0.01 |
| British West Indian (7) | 7 | 0.01 |
| Dutch West Indian (0) | 10 | 0.02 |
| Haitian (24) | 61 | 0.09 |
| Jamaican (730) | 781 | 1.19 |
| Trinidadian/Tobagonian (18) | 78 | 0.12 |
| U.S. Virgin Islander (0) | 0 | <0.01 |
| West Indian (433) | 446 | 0.68 |
| Other West Indian (0) | 0 | <0.01 |
| Yugoslavian (0) | 1 | <0.01 |

| Hispanic Origin | Population | % |
|---|---|---|
| Hispanic or Latino (of any race) | 6,922 | 10.47 |
| Central American, ex. Mexican | 321 | 0.49 |
| Costa Rican | 34 | 0.05 |
| Guatemalan | 61 | 0.09 |
| Honduran | 41 | 0.06 |
| Nicaraguan | 17 | 0.03 |
| Panamanian | 31 | 0.05 |
| Salvadoran | 126 | 0.19 |
| Other Central American | 11 | 0.02 |
| Cuban | 150 | 0.23 |
| Dominican Republic | 478 | 0.72 |
| Mexican | 430 | 0.65 |
| Puerto Rican | 4,677 | 7.07 |
| South American | 346 | 0.52 |
| Argentinean | 18 | 0.03 |
| Bolivian | 5 | 0.01 |
| Chilean | 13 | 0.02 |
| Colombian | 86 | 0.13 |
| Ecuadorian | 62 | 0.09 |
| Paraguayan | 9 | 0.01 |
| Peruvian | 74 | 0.11 |
| Uruguayan | 9 | 0.01 |
| Venezuelan | 27 | 0.04 |
| Other South American | 43 | 0.07 |
| Other Hispanic or Latino | 520 | 0.79 |

| Race* | Population | % |
|---|---|---|
| African-American/Black (13,354) | 16,103 | 24.35 |
| Not Hispanic (12,258) | 14,556 | 22.01 |
| Hispanic (1,096) | 1,547 | 2.34 |
| American Indian/Alaska Native (458) | 1,372 | 2.07 |
| Not Hispanic (343) | 1,126 | 1.70 |
| Hispanic (115) | 246 | 0.37 |
| Alaska Athabascan (Ala. Nat.) (0) | 0 | <0.01 |
| Aleut (Alaska Native) (0) | 0 | <0.01 |
| Apache (2) | 5 | 0.01 |
| Arapaho (1) | 1 | <0.01 |
| Blackfeet (2) | 58 | 0.09 |
| Canadian/French Am. Ind. (3) | 9 | 0.01 |
| Central American Ind. (5) | 6 | 0.01 |
| Cherokee (9) | 145 | 0.22 |
| Cheyenne (1) | 2 | <0.01 |
| Chickasaw (0) | 0 | <0.01 |
| Chippewa (2) | 11 | 0.02 |

| | Population | % |
|---|---|---|
| Choctaw (0) | 1 | <0.01 |
| Colville (0) | 0 | <0.01 |
| Comanche (0) | 0 | <0.01 |
| Cree (0) | 4 | 0.01 |
| Creek (1) | 5 | 0.01 |
| Crow (0) | 6 | 0.01 |
| Delaware (4) | 12 | 0.02 |
| Hopi (0) | 0 | <0.01 |
| Houma (0) | 0 | <0.01 |
| Inupiat (Alaska Native) (3) | 3 | <0.01 |
| Iroquois (17) | 88 | 0.13 |
| Kiowa (0) | 1 | <0.01 |
| Lumbee (2) | 4 | 0.01 |
| Menominee (0) | 0 | <0.01 |
| Mexican American Ind. (16) | 17 | 0.03 |
| Navajo (1) | 2 | <0.01 |
| Osage (0) | 0 | <0.01 |
| Ottawa (0) | 0 | <0.01 |
| Paiute (0) | 0 | <0.01 |
| Pima (1) | 5 | 0.01 |
| Potawatomi (0) | 5 | 0.01 |
| Pueblo (0) | 1 | <0.01 |
| Puget Sound Salish (0) | 0 | <0.01 |
| Seminole (1) | 4 | 0.01 |
| Shoshone (0) | 0 | <0.01 |
| Sioux (3) | 14 | 0.02 |
| South American Ind. (17) | 33 | 0.05 |
| Spanish American Ind. (1) | 7 | 0.01 |
| Tlingit-Haida (Alaska Native) (0) | 0 | <0.01 |
| Tohono O'Odham (0) | 0 | <0.01 |
| Tsimshian (Alaska Native) (0) | 0 | <0.01 |
| Ute (0) | 0 | <0.01 |
| Yakama (0) | 0 | <0.01 |
| Yaqui (0) | 0 | <0.01 |
| Yuman (0) | 0 | <0.01 |
| Yup'ik (Alaska Native) (0) | 0 | <0.01 |
| Asian (2,396) | 3,522 | 5.33 |
| Not Hispanic (2,360) | 3,400 | 5.14 |
| Hispanic (36) | 122 | 0.18 |
| Bangladeshi (12) | 15 | 0.02 |
| Bhutanese (1) | 1 | <0.01 |
| Burmese (0) | 0 | <0.01 |
| Cambodian (7) | 8 | 0.01 |
| Chinese, ex. Taiwanese (291) | 361 | 0.55 |
| Filipino (116) | 157 | 0.24 |
| Hmong (0) | 0 | <0.01 |
| Indian (1,571) | 2,050 | 3.10 |
| Indonesian (4) | 9 | 0.01 |
| Japanese (21) | 70 | 0.11 |
| Korean (87) | 141 | 0.21 |
| Laotian (2) | 6 | 0.01 |
| Malaysian (0) | 5 | 0.01 |
| Nepalese (5) | 8 | 0.01 |
| Pakistani (80) | 86 | 0.13 |
| Sri Lankan (4) | 6 | 0.01 |
| Taiwanese (7) | 8 | 0.01 |
| Thai (6) | 15 | 0.02 |
| Vietnamese (75) | 87 | 0.13 |
| Hawaii Native/Pacific Islander (92) | 333 | 0.50 |
| Not Hispanic (68) | 272 | 0.41 |
| Hispanic (24) | 61 | 0.09 |
| Fijian (1) | 1 | <0.01 |
| Guamanian/Chamorro (6) | 14 | 0.02 |
| Marshallese (0) | 0 | <0.01 |
| Native Hawaiian (14) | 33 | 0.05 |
| Samoan (4) | 10 | 0.02 |
| Tongan (0) | 0 | <0.01 |
| White (40,592) | 43,710 | 66.09 |
| Not Hispanic (38,006) | 40,587 | 61.37 |
| Hispanic (2,586) | 3,123 | 4.72 |

*Notes: † The Census 2010 population figure is used to calculate the percentages in the Hispanic Origin and Race categories. Ancestry percentages are based on the 2006-2010 American Community Survey population (not shown); ‡ Numbers in parentheses indicate the number of people reporting a single ancestry; * Numbers in parentheses indicate the number of persons reporting this race alone, not in combination with any other race; Please refer to the Explanation of Data for more information.*

## Smithtown

Place Type: Town
County: Suffolk
Population: 117,801

| Ancestry | Population | % |
|---|---|---|
| Afghan (27) | 27 | 0.02 |
| African, Sub-Saharan (8) | 150 | 0.13 |
| African (0) | 106 | 0.09 |
| Cape Verdean (0) | 0 | <0.01 |
| Ethiopian (0) | 0 | <0.01 |
| Ghanaian (0) | 0 | <0.01 |
| Kenyan (0) | 0 | <0.01 |
| Liberian (0) | 0 | <0.01 |
| Nigerian (8) | 44 | 0.04 |
| Senegalese (0) | 0 | <0.01 |
| Sierra Leonean (0) | 0 | <0.01 |
| Somalian (0) | 0 | <0.01 |
| South African (0) | 0 | <0.01 |
| Sudanese (0) | 0 | <0.01 |
| Ugandan (0) | 0 | <0.01 |
| Zimbabwean (0) | 0 | <0.01 |
| Other Sub-Saharan African (0) | 0 | <0.01 |
| Albanian (121) | 130 | 0.11 |
| Alsatian (0) | 0 | <0.01 |
| American (3,187) | 3,187 | 2.71 |
| Arab (248) | 537 | 0.46 |
| Arab (11) | 16 | 0.01 |
| Egyptian (38) | 52 | 0.04 |
| Iraqi (52) | 89 | 0.08 |
| Jordanian (54) | 54 | 0.05 |
| Lebanese (24) | 150 | 0.13 |
| Moroccan (4) | 4 | <0.01 |
| Palestinian (0) | 0 | <0.01 |
| Syrian (39) | 89 | 0.08 |
| Other Arab (26) | 83 | 0.07 |
| Armenian (69) | 210 | 0.18 |
| Assyrian/Chaldean/Syriac (0) | 0 | <0.01 |
| Australian (19) | 23 | 0.02 |
| Austrian (205) | 930 | 0.79 |
| Basque (0) | 0 | <0.01 |
| Belgian (4) | 88 | 0.07 |
| Brazilian (22) | 32 | 0.03 |
| British (94) | 242 | 0.21 |
| Bulgarian (0) | 22 | 0.02 |
| Cajun (0) | 0 | <0.01 |
| Canadian (85) | 315 | 0.27 |
| Carpatho Rusyn (26) | 26 | 0.02 |
| Celtic (0) | 3 | <0.01 |
| Croatian (53) | 247 | 0.21 |
| Cypriot (0) | 0 | <0.01 |
| Czech (151) | 692 | 0.59 |
| Czechoslovakian (88) | 310 | 0.26 |
| Danish (76) | 314 | 0.27 |
| Dutch (199) | 983 | 0.84 |
| Eastern European (651) | 651 | 0.55 |
| English (852) | 6,551 | 5.57 |
| Estonian (0) | 0 | <0.01 |
| European (936) | 997 | 0.85 |
| Finnish (26) | 120 | 0.10 |
| French, ex. Basque (122) | 2,352 | 2.00 |
| French Canadian (233) | 648 | 0.55 |
| German (4,715) | 23,592 | 20.06 |
| German Russian (0) | 0 | <0.01 |
| Greek (1,657) | 3,078 | 2.62 |
| Guyanese (8) | 8 | 0.01 |
| Hungarian (307) | 1,257 | 1.07 |
| Icelander (5) | 16 | 0.01 |
| Iranian (199) | 237 | 0.20 |
| Irish (8,107) | 31,963 | 27.18 |
| Israeli (104) | 180 | 0.15 |
| Italian (21,409) | 45,388 | 38.60 |
| Latvian (24) | 81 | 0.07 |
| Lithuanian (141) | 627 | 0.53 |
| Luxemburger (0) | 0 | <0.01 |
| Macedonian (0) | 0 | <0.01 |
| Maltese (10) | 206 | 0.18 |
| New Zealander (0) | 0 | <0.01 |
| Northern European (4) | 4 | <0.01 |

| Ancestry | Population | % |
|---|---|---|
| Norwegian (397) | 1,686 | 1.43 |
| Pennsylvania German (6) | 6 | 0.01 |
| Polish (2,350) | 8,707 | 7.40 |
| Portuguese (47) | 247 | 0.21 |
| Romanian (196) | 707 | 0.60 |
| Russian (1,686) | 5,319 | 4.52 |
| Scandinavian (26) | 64 | 0.05 |
| Scotch-Irish (579) | 1,732 | 1.47 |
| Scottish (148) | 1,517 | 1.29 |
| Serbian (31) | 92 | 0.08 |
| Slavic (9) | 116 | 0.10 |
| Slovak (82) | 163 | 0.14 |
| Slovene (140) | 147 | 0.13 |
| Soviet Union (0) | 0 | <0.01 |
| Swedish (160) | 1,304 | 1.11 |
| Swiss (34) | 217 | 0.18 |
| Turkish (182) | 204 | 0.17 |
| Ukrainian (145) | 452 | 0.38 |
| Welsh (8) | 259 | 0.22 |
| West Indian, ex. Hispanic (160) | 341 | 0.29 |
| Bahamian (0) | 0 | <0.01 |
| Barbadian (0) | 0 | <0.01 |
| Belizean (0) | 0 | <0.01 |
| Bermudan (0) | 0 | <0.01 |
| British West Indian (0) | 0 | <0.01 |
| Dutch West Indian (0) | 0 | <0.01 |
| Haitian (100) | 100 | 0.09 |
| Jamaican (44) | 92 | 0.08 |
| Trinidadian/Tobagonian (9) | 28 | 0.02 |
| U.S. Virgin Islander (0) | 0 | <0.01 |
| West Indian (7) | 121 | 0.10 |
| Other West Indian (0) | 0 | <0.01 |
| Yugoslavian (68) | 216 | 0.18 |

| Hispanic Origin | Population | % |
|---|---|---|
| Hispanic or Latino (of any race) | 6,272 | 5.32 |
| Central American, ex. Mexican | 768 | 0.65 |
| Costa Rican | 22 | 0.02 |
| Guatemalan | 95 | 0.08 |
| Honduran | 161 | 0.14 |
| Nicaraguan | 9 | 0.01 |
| Panamanian | 37 | 0.03 |
| Salvadoran | 428 | 0.36 |
| Other Central American | 16 | 0.01 |
| Cuban | 298 | 0.25 |
| Dominican Republic | 349 | 0.30 |
| Mexican | 524 | 0.44 |
| Puerto Rican | 2,200 | 1.87 |
| South American | 1,376 | 1.17 |
| Argentinean | 159 | 0.13 |
| Bolivian | 41 | 0.03 |
| Chilean | 96 | 0.08 |
| Colombian | 503 | 0.43 |
| Ecuadorian | 258 | 0.22 |
| Paraguayan | 17 | 0.01 |
| Peruvian | 227 | 0.19 |
| Uruguayan | 28 | 0.02 |
| Venezuelan | 37 | 0.03 |
| Other South American | 10 | 0.01 |
| Other Hispanic or Latino | 757 | 0.64 |

| Race* | Population | % |
|---|---|---|
| African-American/Black (1,238) | 1,546 | 1.31 |
| Not Hispanic (1,122) | 1,350 | 1.15 |
| Hispanic (116) | 196 | 0.17 |
| American Indian/Alaska Native (91) | 317 | 0.27 |
| Not Hispanic (53) | 224 | 0.19 |
| Hispanic (38) | 93 | 0.08 |
| Alaska Athabascan (Ala. Nat.) (0) | 0 | <0.01 |
| Aleut (Alaska Native) (0) | 0 | <0.01 |
| Apache (0) | 0 | <0.01 |
| Arapaho (0) | 0 | <0.01 |
| Blackfeet (3) | 7 | 0.01 |
| Canadian/French Am. Ind. (0) | 2 | <0.01 |
| Central American Ind. (1) | 1 | <0.01 |
| Cherokee (3) | 44 | 0.04 |
| Cheyenne (0) | 0 | <0.01 |
| Chickasaw (0) | 0 | <0.01 |
| Chippewa (0) | 2 | <0.01 |

| Race* | Population | % |
|---|---|---|
| Choctaw (0) | 2 | <0.01 |
| Colville (0) | 0 | <0.01 |
| Comanche (0) | 0 | <0.01 |
| Cree (0) | 0 | <0.01 |
| Creek (0) | 7 | 0.01 |
| Crow (0) | 0 | <0.01 |
| Delaware (0) | 1 | <0.01 |
| Hopi (0) | 0 | <0.01 |
| Houma (0) | 0 | <0.01 |
| Inupiat (Alaska Native) (0) | 0 | <0.01 |
| Iroquois (19) | 36 | 0.03 |
| Kiowa (1) | 1 | <0.01 |
| Lumbee (0) | 5 | <0.01 |
| Menominee (0) | 0 | <0.01 |
| Mexican American Ind. (2) | 6 | 0.01 |
| Navajo (0) | 1 | <0.01 |
| Osage (0) | 0 | <0.01 |
| Ottawa (0) | 0 | <0.01 |
| Paiute (0) | 0 | <0.01 |
| Pima (0) | 0 | <0.01 |
| Potawatomi (0) | 0 | <0.01 |
| Pueblo (0) | 1 | <0.01 |
| Puget Sound Salish (0) | 0 | <0.01 |
| Seminole (0) | 0 | <0.01 |
| Shoshone (0) | 0 | <0.01 |
| Sioux (1) | 2 | <0.01 |
| South American Ind. (13) | 23 | 0.02 |
| Spanish American Ind. (0) | 0 | <0.01 |
| Tlingit-Haida (Alaska Native) (0) | 1 | <0.01 |
| Tohono O'Odham (0) | 0 | <0.01 |
| Tsimshian (Alaska Native) (0) | 0 | <0.01 |
| Ute (0) | 1 | <0.01 |
| Yakama (0) | 0 | <0.01 |
| Yaqui (0) | 1 | <0.01 |
| Yuman (0) | 0 | <0.01 |
| Yup'ik (Alaska Native) (0) | 0 | <0.01 |
| Asian (4,224) | 4,865 | 4.13 |
| Not Hispanic (4,197) | 4,788 | 4.06 |
| Hispanic (27) | 77 | 0.07 |
| Bangladeshi (24) | 24 | 0.02 |
| Bhutanese (2) | 2 | <0.01 |
| Burmese (2) | 2 | <0.01 |
| Cambodian (0) | 0 | <0.01 |
| Chinese, ex. Taiwanese (1,070) | 1,262 | 1.07 |
| Filipino (414) | 562 | 0.48 |
| Hmong (0) | 0 | <0.01 |
| Indian (1,206) | 1,322 | 1.12 |
| Indonesian (14) | 18 | 0.02 |
| Japanese (68) | 119 | 0.10 |
| Korean (842) | 918 | 0.78 |
| Laotian (3) | 3 | <0.01 |
| Malaysian (1) | 2 | <0.01 |
| Nepalese (4) | 4 | <0.01 |
| Pakistani (280) | 299 | 0.25 |
| Sri Lankan (5) | 6 | 0.01 |
| Taiwanese (66) | 90 | 0.08 |
| Thai (28) | 34 | 0.03 |
| Vietnamese (59) | 70 | 0.06 |
| Hawaii Native/Pacific Islander (10) | 58 | 0.05 |
| Not Hispanic (7) | 41 | 0.03 |
| Hispanic (3) | 17 | 0.01 |
| Fijian (0) | 2 | <0.01 |
| Guamanian/Chamorro (3) | 5 | <0.01 |
| Marshallese (0) | 0 | <0.01 |
| Native Hawaiian (6) | 30 | 0.03 |
| Samoan (0) | 0 | <0.01 |
| Tongan (0) | 0 | <0.01 |
| White (109,790) | 111,000 | 94.23 |
| Not Hispanic (104,976) | 105,870 | 89.87 |
| Hispanic (4,814) | 5,130 | 4.35 |

*Notes: † The Census 2010 population figure is used to calculate the percentages in the Hispanic Origin and Race categories. Ancestry percentages are based on the 2006-2010 American Community Survey population (not shown); ‡ Numbers in parentheses indicate the number of people reporting a single ancestry; \* Numbers in parentheses indicate the number of persons reporting this race alone, not in combination with any other race; Please refer to the Explanation of Data for more information.*

## Southampton

Place Type: Town
County: Suffolk
Population: 56,790

| Ancestry | Population | % |
|---|---|---|
| Afghan (0) | 0 | <0.01 |
| African, Sub-Saharan (64) | 64 | 0.11 |
| African (64) | 64 | 0.11 |
| Cape Verdean (0) | 0 | <0.01 |
| Ethiopian (0) | 0 | <0.01 |
| Ghanaian (0) | 0 | <0.01 |
| Kenyan (0) | 0 | <0.01 |
| Liberian (0) | 0 | <0.01 |
| Nigerian (0) | 0 | <0.01 |
| Senegalese (0) | 0 | <0.01 |
| Sierra Leonean (0) | 0 | <0.01 |
| Somalian (0) | 0 | <0.01 |
| South African (0) | 0 | <0.01 |
| Sudanese (0) | 0 | <0.01 |
| Ugandan (0) | 0 | <0.01 |
| Zimbabwean (0) | 0 | <0.01 |
| Other Sub-Saharan African (0) | 0 | <0.01 |
| Albanian (63) | 63 | 0.11 |
| Alsatian (0) | 0 | <0.01 |
| American (1,540) | 1,540 | 2.72 |
| Arab (52) | 130 | 0.23 |
| Arab (20) | 35 | 0.06 |
| Egyptian (0) | 0 | <0.01 |
| Iraqi (0) | 28 | 0.05 |
| Jordanian (0) | 0 | <0.01 |
| Lebanese (5) | 16 | 0.03 |
| Moroccan (0) | 18 | 0.03 |
| Palestinian (0) | 0 | <0.01 |
| Syrian (13) | 13 | 0.02 |
| Other Arab (14) | 20 | 0.04 |
| Armenian (23) | 42 | 0.07 |
| Assyrian/Chaldean/Syriac (0) | 0 | <0.01 |
| Australian (24) | 38 | 0.07 |
| Austrian (113) | 621 | 1.10 |
| Basque (0) | 0 | <0.01 |
| Belgian (34) | 34 | 0.06 |
| Brazilian (242) | 289 | 0.51 |
| British (224) | 404 | 0.71 |
| Bulgarian (29) | 29 | 0.05 |
| Cajun (0) | 0 | <0.01 |
| Canadian (96) | 153 | 0.27 |
| Carpatho Rusyn (0) | 0 | <0.01 |
| Celtic (0) | 4 | 0.01 |
| Croatian (174) | 227 | 0.40 |
| Cypriot (0) | 0 | <0.01 |
| Czech (80) | 198 | 0.35 |
| Czechoslovakian (51) | 97 | 0.17 |
| Danish (54) | 135 | 0.24 |
| Dutch (91) | 743 | 1.31 |
| Eastern European (55) | 118 | 0.21 |
| English (1,413) | 5,792 | 10.24 |
| Estonian (6) | 6 | 0.01 |
| European (518) | 523 | 0.93 |
| Finnish (53) | 206 | 0.36 |
| French, ex. Basque (250) | 1,438 | 2.54 |
| French Canadian (49) | 352 | 0.62 |
| German (1,998) | 8,313 | 14.70 |
| German Russian (0) | 0 | <0.01 |
| Greek (583) | 995 | 1.76 |
| Guyanese (0) | 0 | <0.01 |
| Hungarian (164) | 529 | 0.94 |
| Icelander (0) | 0 | <0.01 |
| Iranian (0) | 0 | <0.01 |
| Irish (4,208) | 12,998 | 22.99 |
| Israeli (0) | 28 | 0.05 |
| Italian (4,376) | 9,808 | 17.35 |
| Latvian (0) | 7 | 0.01 |
| Lithuanian (137) | 267 | 0.47 |
| Luxemburger (0) | 0 | <0.01 |
| Macedonian (11) | 11 | 0.02 |
| Maltese (15) | 33 | 0.06 |
| New Zealander (0) | 0 | <0.01 |
| Northern European (42) | 42 | 0.07 |

| Ancestry | Population | % |
|---|---|---|
| Norwegian (172) | 498 | 0.88 |
| Pennsylvania German (0) | 0 | <0.01 |
| Polish (1,918) | 4,196 | 7.42 |
| Portuguese (59) | 145 | 0.26 |
| Romanian (57) | 102 | 0.18 |
| Russian (514) | 1,517 | 2.68 |
| Scandinavian (31) | 57 | 0.10 |
| Scotch-Irish (251) | 701 | 1.24 |
| Scottish (225) | 966 | 1.71 |
| Serbian (0) | 0 | <0.01 |
| Slavic (0) | 53 | 0.09 |
| Slovak (92) | 134 | 0.24 |
| Slovene (7) | 7 | 0.01 |
| Soviet Union (0) | 0 | <0.01 |
| Swedish (152) | 598 | 1.06 |
| Swiss (37) | 231 | 0.41 |
| Turkish (75) | 75 | 0.13 |
| Ukrainian (198) | 419 | 0.74 |
| Welsh (43) | 132 | 0.23 |
| West Indian, ex. Hispanic (0) | 24 | 0.04 |
| Bahamian (0) | 0 | <0.01 |
| Barbadian (0) | 0 | <0.01 |
| Belizean (0) | 0 | <0.01 |
| Bermudan (0) | 0 | <0.01 |
| British West Indian (0) | 0 | <0.01 |
| Dutch West Indian (0) | 0 | <0.01 |
| Haitian (0) | 16 | 0.03 |
| Jamaican (0) | 0 | <0.01 |
| Trinidadian/Tobagonian (0) | 0 | <0.01 |
| U.S. Virgin Islander (0) | 0 | <0.01 |
| West Indian (0) | 8 | 0.01 |
| Other West Indian (0) | 0 | <0.01 |
| Yugoslavian (0) | 0 | <0.01 |

| Hispanic Origin | Population | % |
|---|---|---|
| Hispanic or Latino (of any race) | 11,295 | 19.89 |
| Central American, ex. Mexican | 3,715 | 6.54 |
| Costa Rican | 618 | 1.09 |
| Guatemalan | 2,081 | 3.66 |
| Honduran | 246 | 0.43 |
| Nicaraguan | 50 | 0.09 |
| Panamanian | 14 | 0.02 |
| Salvadoran | 689 | 1.21 |
| Other Central American | 17 | 0.03 |
| Cuban | 93 | 0.16 |
| Dominican Republic | 124 | 0.22 |
| Mexican | 2,856 | 5.03 |
| Puerto Rican | 593 | 1.04 |
| South American | 2,446 | 4.31 |
| Argentinean | 89 | 0.16 |
| Bolivian | 9 | 0.02 |
| Chilean | 44 | 0.08 |
| Colombian | 1,024 | 1.80 |
| Ecuadorian | 1,102 | 1.94 |
| Paraguayan | 26 | 0.05 |
| Peruvian | 97 | 0.17 |
| Uruguayan | 7 | 0.01 |
| Venezuelan | 36 | 0.06 |
| Other South American | 12 | 0.02 |
| Other Hispanic or Latino | 1,468 | 2.58 |

| Race* | Population | % |
|---|---|---|
| African-American/Black (2,929) | 3,353 | 5.90 |
| Not Hispanic (2,776) | 3,108 | 5.47 |
| Hispanic (153) | 245 | 0.43 |
| American Indian/Alaska Native (292) | 546 | 0.96 |
| Not Hispanic (136) | 344 | 0.61 |
| Hispanic (156) | 202 | 0.36 |
| Alaska Athabascan (Ala. Nat.) (0) | 0 | <0.01 |
| Aleut (Alaska Native) (0) | 0 | <0.01 |
| Apache (0) | 0 | <0.01 |
| Arapaho (0) | 0 | <0.01 |
| Blackfeet (6) | 14 | 0.02 |
| Canadian/French Am. Ind. (0) | 3 | 0.01 |
| Central American Ind. (3) | 3 | 0.01 |
| Cherokee (13) | 68 | 0.12 |
| Cheyenne (0) | 0 | <0.01 |
| Chickasaw (0) | 0 | <0.01 |
| Chippewa (7) | 7 | 0.01 |

| Race* | Population | % |
|---|---|---|
| Choctaw (1) | 2 | <0.01 |
| Colville (0) | 0 | <0.01 |
| Comanche (0) | 0 | <0.01 |
| Cree (0) | 0 | <0.01 |
| Creek (2) | 2 | <0.01 |
| Crow (0) | 0 | <0.01 |
| Delaware (0) | 0 | <0.01 |
| Hopi (0) | 1 | <0.01 |
| Houma (0) | 0 | <0.01 |
| Inupiat (Alaska Native) (0) | 0 | <0.01 |
| Iroquois (5) | 11 | 0.02 |
| Kiowa (0) | 0 | <0.01 |
| Lumbee (0) | 0 | <0.01 |
| Menominee (0) | 0 | <0.01 |
| Mexican American Ind. (76) | 83 | 0.15 |
| Navajo (0) | 0 | <0.01 |
| Osage (0) | 0 | <0.01 |
| Ottawa (0) | 0 | <0.01 |
| Paiute (0) | 0 | <0.01 |
| Pima (0) | 0 | <0.01 |
| Potawatomi (0) | 0 | <0.01 |
| Pueblo (0) | 5 | 0.01 |
| Puget Sound Salish (0) | 0 | <0.01 |
| Seminole (0) | 1 | <0.01 |
| Shoshone (0) | 0 | <0.01 |
| Sioux (2) | 3 | 0.01 |
| South American Ind. (23) | 28 | 0.05 |
| Spanish American Ind. (7) | 7 | 0.01 |
| Tlingit-Haida (Alaska Native) (0) | 0 | <0.01 |
| Tohono O'Odham (0) | 0 | <0.01 |
| Tsimshian (Alaska Native) (0) | 0 | <0.01 |
| Ute (0) | 0 | <0.01 |
| Yakama (0) | 0 | <0.01 |
| Yaqui (0) | 0 | <0.01 |
| Yuman (0) | 0 | <0.01 |
| Yup'ik (Alaska Native) (0) | 0 | <0.01 |
| Asian (633) | 869 | 1.53 |
| Not Hispanic (618) | 834 | 1.47 |
| Hispanic (15) | 35 | 0.06 |
| Bangladeshi (0) | 0 | <0.01 |
| Bhutanese (0) | 0 | <0.01 |
| Burmese (0) | 0 | <0.01 |
| Cambodian (1) | 1 | <0.01 |
| Chinese, ex. Taiwanese (133) | 177 | 0.31 |
| Filipino (146) | 197 | 0.35 |
| Hmong (0) | 0 | <0.01 |
| Indian (123) | 151 | 0.27 |
| Indonesian (5) | 6 | 0.01 |
| Japanese (40) | 97 | 0.17 |
| Korean (69) | 102 | 0.18 |
| Laotian (1) | 2 | <0.01 |
| Malaysian (1) | 2 | <0.01 |
| Nepalese (1) | 1 | <0.01 |
| Pakistani (8) | 10 | 0.02 |
| Sri Lankan (0) | 0 | <0.01 |
| Taiwanese (3) | 3 | 0.01 |
| Thai (30) | 37 | 0.07 |
| Vietnamese (38) | 51 | 0.09 |
| Hawaii Native/Pacific Islander (62) | 103 | 0.18 |
| Not Hispanic (36) | 61 | 0.11 |
| Hispanic (26) | 42 | 0.07 |
| Fijian (0) | 0 | <0.01 |
| Guamanian/Chamorro (48) | 55 | 0.10 |
| Marshallese (0) | 0 | <0.01 |
| Native Hawaiian (10) | 27 | 0.05 |
| Samoan (2) | 7 | 0.01 |
| Tongan (0) | 0 | <0.01 |
| White (47,795) | 48,682 | 85.72 |
| Not Hispanic (41,156) | 41,727 | 73.48 |
| Hispanic (6,639) | 6,955 | 12.25 |

Notes: † The Census 2010 population figure is used to calculate the percentages in the Hispanic Origin and Race categories. Ancestry percentages are based on the 2006-2010 American Community Survey population (not shown); ‡ Numbers in parentheses indicate the number of people reporting a single ancestry; * Numbers in parentheses indicate the number of persons reporting this race alone, not in combination with any other race; Please refer to the Explanation of Data for more information.

## Staten Island

Place Type: Borough
County: Richmond
Population: 468,730

| Ancestry | Population | % |
|---|---|---|
| Afghan (0) | 0 | <0.01 |
| African, Sub-Saharan (6,533) | 7,234 | 1.56 |
| African (3,732) | 4,164 | 0.90 |
| Cape Verdean (0) | 11 | <0.01 |
| Ethiopian (41) | 46 | 0.01 |
| Ghanaian (239) | 250 | 0.05 |
| Kenyan (78) | 78 | 0.02 |
| Liberian (515) | 532 | 0.11 |
| Nigerian (1,509) | 1,679 | 0.36 |
| Senegalese (126) | 126 | 0.03 |
| Sierra Leonean (90) | 117 | 0.03 |
| Somalian (0) | 0 | <0.01 |
| South African (0) | 0 | <0.01 |
| Sudanese (0) | 0 | <0.01 |
| Ugandan (0) | 0 | <0.01 |
| Zimbabwean (0) | 0 | <0.01 |
| Other Sub-Saharan African (203) | 231 | 0.05 |
| Albanian (7,700) | 8,108 | 1.75 |
| Alsatian (0) | 24 | 0.01 |
| American (13,977) | 13,977 | 3.02 |
| Arab (7,711) | 8,820 | 1.90 |
| Arab (1,694) | 1,829 | 0.39 |
| Egyptian (3,200) | 3,292 | 0.71 |
| Iraqi (11) | 32 | 0.01 |
| Jordanian (159) | 183 | 0.04 |
| Lebanese (784) | 1,019 | 0.22 |
| Moroccan (502) | 621 | 0.13 |
| Palestinian (443) | 479 | 0.10 |
| Syrian (209) | 584 | 0.13 |
| Other Arab (709) | 781 | 0.17 |
| Armenian (83) | 311 | 0.07 |
| Assyrian/Chaldean/Syriac (15) | 15 | <0.01 |
| Australian (24) | 49 | 0.01 |
| Austrian (343) | 1,542 | 0.33 |
| Basque (15) | 77 | 0.02 |
| Belgian (36) | 266 | 0.06 |
| Brazilian (183) | 287 | 0.06 |
| British (231) | 615 | 0.13 |
| Bulgarian (0) | 0 | <0.01 |
| Cajun (0) | 0 | <0.01 |
| Canadian (290) | 544 | 0.12 |
| Carpatho Rusyn (63) | 63 | 0.01 |
| Celtic (37) | 46 | 0.01 |
| Croatian (598) | 869 | 0.19 |
| Cypriot (0) | 0 | <0.01 |
| Czech (146) | 735 | 0.16 |
| Czechoslovakian (93) | 237 | 0.05 |
| Danish (90) | 479 | 0.10 |
| Dutch (137) | 1,637 | 0.35 |
| Eastern European (433) | 433 | 0.09 |
| English (1,973) | 9,014 | 1.94 |
| Estonian (10) | 10 | <0.01 |
| European (1,914) | 2,068 | 0.45 |
| Finnish (48) | 185 | 0.04 |
| French, ex. Basque (800) | 3,772 | 0.81 |
| French Canadian (248) | 750 | 0.16 |
| German (4,111) | 25,477 | 5.50 |
| German Russian (0) | 0 | <0.01 |
| Greek (2,403) | 4,183 | 0.90 |
| Guyanese (767) | 952 | 0.21 |
| Hungarian (1,024) | 2,288 | 0.49 |
| Icelander (55) | 55 | 0.01 |
| Iranian (121) | 171 | 0.04 |
| Irish (20,064) | 64,762 | 13.97 |
| Israeli (542) | 759 | 0.16 |
| Italian (107,263) | 156,288 | 33.72 |
| Latvian (98) | 142 | 0.03 |
| Lithuanian (178) | 645 | 0.14 |
| Luxemburger (12) | 54 | 0.01 |
| Macedonian (1,368) | 1,590 | 0.34 |
| Maltese (104) | 290 | 0.06 |
| New Zealander (0) | 0 | <0.01 |
| Northern European (60) | 60 | 0.01 |

| Ancestry | Population | % |
|---|---|---|
| Norwegian (1,617) | 5,135 | 1.11 |
| Pennsylvania German (9) | 41 | 0.01 |
| Polish (9,167) | 18,430 | 3.98 |
| Portuguese (180) | 617 | 0.13 |
| Romanian (530) | 964 | 0.21 |
| Russian (11,315) | 16,388 | 3.54 |
| Scandinavian (35) | 121 | 0.03 |
| Scotch-Irish (759) | 1,886 | 0.41 |
| Scottish (718) | 2,350 | 0.51 |
| Serbian (219) | 240 | 0.05 |
| Slavic (68) | 143 | 0.03 |
| Slovak (233) | 553 | 0.12 |
| Slovene (86) | 108 | 0.02 |
| Soviet Union (51) | 63 | 0.01 |
| Swedish (253) | 1,936 | 0.42 |
| Swiss (76) | 256 | 0.06 |
| Turkish (1,267) | 1,607 | 0.35 |
| Ukrainian (3,759) | 4,836 | 1.04 |
| Welsh (68) | 417 | 0.09 |
| West Indian, ex. Hispanic (5,348) | 6,967 | 1.50 |
| Bahamian (31) | 31 | 0.01 |
| Barbadian (94) | 94 | 0.02 |
| Belizean (76) | 76 | 0.02 |
| Bermudan (0) | 0 | <0.01 |
| British West Indian (113) | 236 | 0.05 |
| Dutch West Indian (39) | 89 | 0.02 |
| Haitian (676) | 791 | 0.17 |
| Jamaican (1,463) | 2,033 | 0.44 |
| Trinidadian/Tobagonian (1,412) | 1,807 | 0.39 |
| U.S. Virgin Islander (22) | 22 | <0.01 |
| West Indian (1,392) | 1,745 | 0.38 |
| Other West Indian (30) | 43 | 0.01 |
| Yugoslavian (1,237) | 1,738 | 0.38 |

| Hispanic Origin | Population | % |
|---|---|---|
| Hispanic or Latino (of any race) | 81,051 | 17.29 |
| Central American, ex. Mexican | 4,310 | 0.92 |
| Costa Rican | 266 | 0.06 |
| Guatemalan | 864 | 0.18 |
| Honduran | 1,735 | 0.37 |
| Nicaraguan | 199 | 0.04 |
| Panamanian | 607 | 0.13 |
| Salvadoran | 592 | 0.13 |
| Other Central American | 47 | 0.01 |
| Cuban | 1,831 | 0.39 |
| Dominican Republic | 4,918 | 1.05 |
| Mexican | 18,684 | 3.99 |
| Puerto Rican | 37,517 | 8.00 |
| South American | 8,232 | 1.76 |
| Argentinean | 608 | 0.13 |
| Bolivian | 161 | 0.03 |
| Chilean | 346 | 0.07 |
| Colombian | 2,526 | 0.54 |
| Ecuadorian | 2,675 | 0.57 |
| Paraguayan | 38 | 0.01 |
| Peruvian | 1,462 | 0.31 |
| Uruguayan | 76 | 0.02 |
| Venezuelan | 254 | 0.05 |
| Other South American | 86 | 0.02 |
| Other Hispanic or Latino | 5,559 | 1.19 |

| Race* | Population | % |
|---|---|---|
| African-American/Black (49,857) | 55,014 | 11.74 |
| Not Hispanic (44,313) | 47,521 | 10.14 |
| Hispanic (5,544) | 7,493 | 1.60 |
| American Indian/Alaska Native (1,695) | 3,719 | 0.79 |
| Not Hispanic (695) | 2,034 | 0.43 |
| Hispanic (1,000) | 1,685 | 0.36 |
| Alaska Athabascan (Ala. Nat.) (1) | 3 | <0.01 |
| Aleut (Alaska Native) (0) | 2 | <0.01 |
| Apache (16) | 35 | 0.01 |
| Arapaho (1) | 1 | <0.01 |
| Blackfeet (17) | 88 | 0.02 |
| Canadian/French Am. Ind. (7) | 10 | <0.01 |
| Central American Ind. (29) | 56 | 0.01 |
| Cherokee (104) | 467 | 0.10 |
| Cheyenne (0) | 2 | <0.01 |
| Chickasaw (1) | 3 | <0.01 |
| Chippewa (7) | 13 | <0.01 |

| Race* | Population | % |
|---|---|---|
| Choctaw (3) | 11 | <0.01 |
| Colville (0) | 0 | <0.01 |
| Comanche (2) | 3 | <0.01 |
| Cree (0) | 4 | <0.01 |
| Creek (3) | 29 | 0.01 |
| Crow (0) | 0 | <0.01 |
| Delaware (16) | 43 | 0.01 |
| Hopi (1) | 5 | <0.01 |
| Houma (1) | 1 | <0.01 |
| Inupiat (Alaska Native) (0) | 1 | <0.01 |
| Iroquois (61) | 152 | 0.03 |
| Kiowa (0) | 1 | <0.01 |
| Lumbee (1) | 8 | <0.01 |
| Menominee (0) | 0 | <0.01 |
| Mexican American Ind. (161) | 204 | 0.04 |
| Navajo (10) | 17 | <0.01 |
| Osage (0) | 0 | <0.01 |
| Ottawa (0) | 0 | <0.01 |
| Paiute (0) | 0 | <0.01 |
| Pima (2) | 2 | <0.01 |
| Potawatomi (0) | 0 | <0.01 |
| Pueblo (4) | 5 | <0.01 |
| Puget Sound Salish (0) | 0 | <0.01 |
| Seminole (7) | 26 | 0.01 |
| Shoshone (1) | 3 | <0.01 |
| Sioux (11) | 24 | 0.01 |
| South American Ind. (146) | 288 | 0.06 |
| Spanish American Ind. (31) | 47 | 0.01 |
| Tlingit-Haida (Alaska Native) (0) | 1 | <0.01 |
| Tohono O'Odham (4) | 8 | <0.01 |
| Tsimshian (Alaska Native) (0) | 0 | <0.01 |
| Ute (1) | 1 | <0.01 |
| Yakama (0) | 0 | <0.01 |
| Yaqui (1) | 1 | <0.01 |
| Yuman (0) | 1 | <0.01 |
| Yup'ik (Alaska Native) (0) | 0 | <0.01 |
| Asian (35,164) | 38,756 | 8.27 |
| Not Hispanic (34,697) | 37,689 | 8.04 |
| Hispanic (467) | 1,067 | 0.23 |
| Bangladeshi (360) | 387 | 0.08 |
| Bhutanese (0) | 0 | <0.01 |
| Burmese (116) | 130 | 0.03 |
| Cambodian (100) | 129 | 0.03 |
| Chinese, ex. Taiwanese (13,144) | 14,107 | 3.01 |
| Filipino (5,224) | 6,205 | 1.32 |
| Hmong (4) | 8 | <0.01 |
| Indian (6,793) | 7,723 | 1.65 |
| Indonesian (22) | 52 | 0.01 |
| Japanese (201) | 408 | 0.09 |
| Korean (3,207) | 3,398 | 0.72 |
| Laotian (13) | 18 | <0.01 |
| Malaysian (58) | 96 | 0.02 |
| Nepalese (27) | 35 | 0.01 |
| Pakistani (2,495) | 2,777 | 0.59 |
| Sri Lankan (1,560) | 1,766 | 0.38 |
| Taiwanese (160) | 197 | 0.04 |
| Thai (135) | 166 | 0.04 |
| Vietnamese (468) | 570 | 0.12 |
| Hawaii Native/Pacific Islander (213) | 683 | 0.15 |
| Not Hispanic (137) | 439 | 0.09 |
| Hispanic (76) | 244 | 0.05 |
| Fijian (6) | 6 | <0.01 |
| Guamanian/Chamorro (88) | 115 | 0.02 |
| Marshallese (1) | 1 | <0.01 |
| Native Hawaiian (46) | 121 | 0.03 |
| Samoan (5) | 26 | 0.01 |
| Tongan (2) | 2 | <0.01 |
| White (341,677) | 350,679 | 74.81 |
| Not Hispanic (300,169) | 305,118 | 65.09 |
| Hispanic (41,508) | 45,561 | 9.72 |

*Notes: † The Census 2010 population figure is used to calculate the percentages in the Hispanic Origin and Race categories. Ancestry percentages are based on the 2006-2010 American Community Survey population (not shown); ‡ Numbers in parentheses indicate the number of people reporting a single ancestry; * Numbers in parentheses indicate the number of persons reporting this race alone, not in combination with any other race; Please refer to the Explanation of Data for more information.*

## Syracuse

Place Type: City
County: Onondaga
Population: 145,170

| Ancestry | Population | % |
|---|---|---|
| Afghan (19) | 19 | 0.01 |
| African, Sub-Saharan (2,165) | 2,470 | 1.71 |
| African (898) | 1,142 | 0.79 |
| Cape Verdean (0) | 8 | 0.01 |
| Ethiopian (0) | 0 | <0.01 |
| Ghanaian (113) | 113 | 0.08 |
| Kenyan (0) | 17 | 0.01 |
| Liberian (246) | 246 | 0.17 |
| Nigerian (148) | 167 | 0.12 |
| Senegalese (0) | 0 | <0.01 |
| Sierra Leonean (13) | 13 | 0.01 |
| Somalian (478) | 478 | 0.33 |
| South African (10) | 10 | 0.01 |
| Sudanese (160) | 177 | 0.12 |
| Ugandan (26) | 26 | 0.02 |
| Zimbabwean (0) | 0 | <0.01 |
| Other Sub-Saharan African (73) | 73 | 0.05 |
| Albanian (429) | 455 | 0.31 |
| Alsatian (0) | 0 | <0.01 |
| American (3,220) | 3,220 | 2.22 |
| Arab (571) | 900 | 0.62 |
| Arab (226) | 267 | 0.18 |
| Egyptian (13) | 13 | 0.01 |
| Iraqi (0) | 0 | <0.01 |
| Jordanian (0) | 0 | <0.01 |
| Lebanese (100) | 269 | 0.19 |
| Moroccan (60) | 86 | 0.06 |
| Palestinian (58) | 66 | 0.05 |
| Syrian (57) | 114 | 0.08 |
| Other Arab (57) | 85 | 0.06 |
| Armenian (24) | 229 | 0.16 |
| Assyrian/Chaldean/Syriac (0) | 0 | <0.01 |
| Australian (42) | 54 | 0.04 |
| Austrian (81) | 372 | 0.26 |
| Basque (0) | 0 | <0.01 |
| Belgian (53) | 81 | 0.06 |
| Brazilian (30) | 42 | 0.03 |
| British (199) | 418 | 0.29 |
| Bulgarian (18) | 18 | 0.01 |
| Cajun (24) | 24 | 0.02 |
| Canadian (96) | 350 | 0.24 |
| Carpatho Rusyn (0) | 0 | <0.01 |
| Celtic (12) | 12 | 0.01 |
| Croatian (0) | 46 | 0.03 |
| Cypriot (0) | 0 | <0.01 |
| Czech (36) | 163 | 0.11 |
| Czechoslovakian (44) | 77 | 0.05 |
| Danish (36) | 109 | 0.08 |
| Dutch (174) | 2,128 | 1.47 |
| Eastern European (153) | 178 | 0.12 |
| English (2,028) | 10,153 | 7.01 |
| Estonian (0) | 12 | 0.01 |
| European (440) | 487 | 0.34 |
| Finnish (14) | 52 | 0.04 |
| French, ex. Basque (735) | 6,182 | 4.27 |
| French Canadian (804) | 1,782 | 1.23 |
| German (3,496) | 17,038 | 11.77 |
| German Russian (0) | 0 | <0.01 |
| Greek (339) | 678 | 0.47 |
| Guyanese (100) | 158 | 0.11 |
| Hungarian (88) | 540 | 0.37 |
| Icelander (0) | 10 | 0.01 |
| Iranian (65) | 105 | 0.07 |
| Irish (6,064) | 22,387 | 15.47 |
| Israeli (133) | 146 | 0.10 |
| Italian (8,625) | 18,571 | 12.83 |
| Latvian (28) | 41 | 0.03 |
| Lithuanian (72) | 309 | 0.21 |
| Luxemburger (0) | 14 | 0.01 |
| Macedonian (46) | 67 | 0.05 |
| Maltese (0) | 0 | <0.01 |
| New Zealander (0) | 13 | 0.01 |
| Northern European (71) | 71 | 0.05 |

| | Population | % |
|---|---|---|
| Norwegian (107) | 366 | 0.25 |
| Pennsylvania German (14) | 33 | 0.02 |
| Polish (2,445) | 7,273 | 5.03 |
| Portuguese (34) | 330 | 0.23 |
| Romanian (38) | 113 | 0.08 |
| Russian (596) | 1,831 | 1.27 |
| Scandinavian (49) | 98 | 0.07 |
| Scotch-Irish (639) | 1,546 | 1.07 |
| Scottish (505) | 2,233 | 1.54 |
| Serbian (0) | 26 | 0.02 |
| Slavic (12) | 45 | 0.03 |
| Slovak (46) | 158 | 0.11 |
| Slovene (15) | 85 | 0.06 |
| Soviet Union (0) | 0 | <0.01 |
| Swedish (288) | 1,044 | 0.72 |
| Swiss (91) | 286 | 0.20 |
| Turkish (169) | 279 | 0.19 |
| Ukrainian (589) | 1,095 | 0.76 |
| Welsh (155) | 1,060 | 0.73 |
| West Indian, ex. Hispanic (1,588) | 1,931 | 1.33 |
| Bahamian (0) | 0 | <0.01 |
| Barbadian (96) | 96 | 0.07 |
| Belizean (0) | 0 | <0.01 |
| Bermudan (0) | 0 | <0.01 |
| British West Indian (22) | 50 | 0.03 |
| Dutch West Indian (0) | 0 | <0.01 |
| Haitian (145) | 145 | 0.10 |
| Jamaican (908) | 1,181 | 0.82 |
| Trinidadian/Tobagonian (95) | 95 | 0.07 |
| U.S. Virgin Islander (0) | 0 | <0.01 |
| West Indian (322) | 364 | 0.25 |
| Other West Indian (0) | 0 | <0.01 |
| Yugoslavian (765) | 774 | 0.53 |

| Hispanic Origin | Population | % |
|---|---|---|
| Hispanic or Latino (of any race) | 12,036 | 8.29 |
| Central American, ex. Mexican | 348 | 0.24 |
| Costa Rican | 29 | 0.02 |
| Guatemalan | 133 | 0.09 |
| Honduran | 40 | 0.03 |
| Nicaraguan | 30 | 0.02 |
| Panamanian | 54 | 0.04 |
| Salvadoran | 59 | 0.04 |
| Other Central American | 3 | <0.01 |
| Cuban | 1,192 | 0.82 |
| Dominican Republic | 689 | 0.47 |
| Mexican | 958 | 0.66 |
| Puerto Rican | 7,594 | 5.23 |
| South American | 530 | 0.37 |
| Argentinean | 49 | 0.03 |
| Bolivian | 11 | 0.01 |
| Chilean | 35 | 0.02 |
| Colombian | 173 | 0.12 |
| Ecuadorian | 101 | 0.07 |
| Paraguayan | 3 | <0.01 |
| Peruvian | 89 | 0.06 |
| Uruguayan | 27 | 0.02 |
| Venezuelan | 39 | 0.03 |
| Other South American | 3 | <0.01 |
| Other Hispanic or Latino | 725 | 0.50 |

| Race* | Population | % |
|---|---|---|
| African-American/Black (42,770) | 48,029 | 33.08 |
| Not Hispanic (40,672) | 45,084 | 31.06 |
| Hispanic (2,098) | 2,945 | 2.03 |
| American Indian/Alaska Native (1,606) | 3,537 | 2.44 |
| Not Hispanic (1,390) | 3,067 | 2.11 |
| Hispanic (216) | 470 | 0.32 |
| Alaska Athabascan (Ala. Nat.) (0) | 3 | <0.01 |
| Aleut (Alaska Native) (0) | 1 | <0.01 |
| Apache (8) | 25 | 0.02 |
| Arapaho (2) | 2 | <0.01 |
| Blackfeet (7) | 111 | 0.08 |
| Canadian/French Am. Ind. (35) | 51 | 0.04 |
| Central American Ind. (4) | 9 | 0.01 |
| Cherokee (20) | 258 | 0.18 |
| Cheyenne (0) | 2 | <0.01 |
| Chickasaw (0) | 4 | <0.01 |
| Chippewa (11) | 18 | 0.01 |

| | Population | % |
|---|---|---|
| Choctaw (1) | 28 | 0.02 |
| Colville (0) | 0 | <0.01 |
| Comanche (6) | 12 | 0.01 |
| Cree (1) | 6 | <0.01 |
| Creek (4) | 9 | 0.01 |
| Crow (1) | 1 | <0.01 |
| Delaware (3) | 5 | <0.01 |
| Hopi (0) | 0 | <0.01 |
| Houma (0) | 0 | <0.01 |
| Inupiat (Alaska Native) (3) | 6 | <0.01 |
| Iroquois (790) | 1,373 | 0.95 |
| Kiowa (0) | 1 | <0.01 |
| Lumbee (4) | 4 | <0.01 |
| Menominee (1) | 1 | <0.01 |
| Mexican American Ind. (24) | 34 | 0.02 |
| Navajo (2) | 5 | <0.01 |
| Osage (0) | 1 | <0.01 |
| Ottawa (0) | 2 | <0.01 |
| Paiute (0) | 0 | <0.01 |
| Pima (1) | 2 | <0.01 |
| Potawatomi (1) | 2 | <0.01 |
| Pueblo (0) | 0 | <0.01 |
| Puget Sound Salish (0) | 0 | <0.01 |
| Seminole (4) | 16 | 0.01 |
| Shoshone (0) | 0 | <0.01 |
| Sioux (13) | 38 | 0.03 |
| South American Ind. (25) | 49 | 0.03 |
| Spanish American Ind. (0) | 0 | <0.01 |
| Tlingit-Haida (Alaska Native) (0) | 1 | <0.01 |
| Tohono O'Odham (1) | 1 | <0.01 |
| Tsimshian (Alaska Native) (0) | 0 | <0.01 |
| Ute (0) | 0 | <0.01 |
| Yakama (0) | 0 | <0.01 |
| Yaqui (0) | 0 | <0.01 |
| Yuman (0) | 0 | <0.01 |
| Yup'ik (Alaska Native) (0) | 1 | <0.01 |
| Asian (8,021) | 9,073 | 6.25 |
| Not Hispanic (7,971) | 8,924 | 6.15 |
| Hispanic (50) | 149 | 0.10 |
| Bangladeshi (47) | 57 | 0.04 |
| Bhutanese (392) | 516 | 0.36 |
| Burmese (1,178) | 1,218 | 0.84 |
| Cambodian (114) | 149 | 0.10 |
| Chinese, ex. Taiwanese (1,543) | 1,749 | 1.20 |
| Filipino (218) | 388 | 0.27 |
| Hmong (26) | 34 | 0.02 |
| Indian (1,216) | 1,397 | 0.96 |
| Indonesian (14) | 26 | 0.02 |
| Japanese (109) | 243 | 0.17 |
| Korean (861) | 937 | 0.65 |
| Laotian (71) | 89 | 0.06 |
| Malaysian (5) | 13 | 0.01 |
| Nepalese (160) | 262 | 0.18 |
| Pakistani (107) | 121 | 0.08 |
| Sri Lankan (13) | 17 | 0.01 |
| Taiwanese (80) | 93 | 0.06 |
| Thai (64) | 89 | 0.06 |
| Vietnamese (1,414) | 1,554 | 1.07 |
| Hawaii Native/Pacific Islander (44) | 279 | 0.19 |
| Not Hispanic (37) | 218 | 0.15 |
| Hispanic (7) | 61 | 0.04 |
| Fijian (0) | 1 | <0.01 |
| Guamanian/Chamorro (5) | 12 | 0.01 |
| Marshallese (0) | 1 | <0.01 |
| Native Hawaiian (15) | 65 | 0.04 |
| Samoan (8) | 21 | 0.01 |
| Tongan (0) | 1 | <0.01 |
| White (81,319) | 87,414 | 60.21 |
| Not Hispanic (76,653) | 81,787 | 56.34 |
| Hispanic (4,666) | 5,627 | 3.88 |

*Notes: † The Census 2010 population figure is used to calculate the percentages in the Hispanic Origin and Race categories. Ancestry percentages are based on the 2006-2010 American Community Survey population (not shown); ‡ Numbers in parentheses indicate the number of people reporting a single ancestry; * Numbers in parentheses indicate the number of persons reporting this race alone, not in combination with any other race; Please refer to the Explanation of Data for more information.*

## Tonawanda

Place Type: CDP
County: Erie
Population: 58,144

| Ancestry | Population | % |
|---|---|---|
| Afghan (108) | 108 | 0.18 |
| African, Sub-Saharan (59) | 194 | 0.33 |
| African (16) | 89 | 0.15 |
| Cape Verdean (0) | 0 | <0.01 |
| Ethiopian (0) | 0 | <0.01 |
| Ghanaian (19) | 19 | 0.03 |
| Kenyan (24) | 86 | 0.15 |
| Liberian (0) | 0 | <0.01 |
| Nigerian (0) | 0 | <0.01 |
| Senegalese (0) | 0 | <0.01 |
| Sierra Leonean (0) | 0 | <0.01 |
| Somalian (0) | 0 | <0.01 |
| South African (0) | 0 | <0.01 |
| Sudanese (0) | 0 | <0.01 |
| Ugandan (0) | 0 | <0.01 |
| Zimbabwean (0) | 0 | <0.01 |
| Other Sub-Saharan African (0) | 0 | <0.01 |
| Albanian (48) | 59 | 0.10 |
| Alsatian (0) | 24 | 0.04 |
| American (1,226) | 1,226 | 2.09 |
| Arab (293) | 502 | 0.86 |
| Arab (21) | 34 | 0.06 |
| Egyptian (0) | 8 | 0.01 |
| Iraqi (0) | 0 | <0.01 |
| Jordanian (9) | 9 | 0.02 |
| Lebanese (223) | 401 | 0.68 |
| Moroccan (0) | 0 | <0.01 |
| Palestinian (0) | 0 | <0.01 |
| Syrian (0) | 10 | 0.02 |
| Other Arab (40) | 40 | 0.07 |
| Armenian (43) | 43 | 0.07 |
| Assyrian/Chaldean/Syriac (0) | 0 | <0.01 |
| Australian (29) | 29 | 0.05 |
| Austrian (54) | 415 | 0.71 |
| Basque (0) | 0 | <0.01 |
| Belgian (0) | 13 | 0.02 |
| Brazilian (0) | 13 | 0.02 |
| British (33) | 97 | 0.17 |
| Bulgarian (0) | 0 | <0.01 |
| Cajun (0) | 0 | <0.01 |
| Canadian (144) | 288 | 0.49 |
| Carpatho Rusyn (0) | 0 | <0.01 |
| Celtic (0) | 0 | <0.01 |
| Croatian (84) | 219 | 0.37 |
| Cypriot (0) | 0 | <0.01 |
| Czech (22) | 168 | 0.29 |
| Czechoslovakian (32) | 177 | 0.30 |
| Danish (47) | 151 | 0.26 |
| Dutch (89) | 716 | 1.22 |
| Eastern European (23) | 23 | 0.04 |
| English (1,484) | 6,115 | 10.44 |
| Estonian (0) | 0 | <0.01 |
| European (354) | 354 | 0.60 |
| Finnish (49) | 95 | 0.16 |
| French, ex. Basque (188) | 2,149 | 3.67 |
| French Canadian (128) | 537 | 0.92 |
| German (4,626) | 19,292 | 32.95 |
| German Russian (0) | 0 | <0.01 |
| Greek (260) | 424 | 0.72 |
| Guyanese (0) | 0 | <0.01 |
| Hungarian (220) | 976 | 1.67 |
| Icelander (11) | 11 | 0.02 |
| Iranian (0) | 0 | <0.01 |
| Irish (2,820) | 11,980 | 20.46 |
| Israeli (0) | 0 | <0.01 |
| Italian (6,780) | 14,269 | 24.37 |
| Latvian (0) | 13 | 0.02 |
| Lithuanian (29) | 162 | 0.28 |
| Luxemburger (0) | 0 | <0.01 |
| Macedonian (0) | 18 | 0.03 |
| Maltese (8) | 26 | 0.04 |
| New Zealander (0) | 0 | <0.01 |
| Northern European (18) | 18 | 0.03 |

| Ancestry | Population | % |
|---|---|---|
| Norwegian (60) | 150 | 0.26 |
| Pennsylvania German (40) | 85 | 0.15 |
| Polish (3,451) | 9,014 | 15.40 |
| Portuguese (10) | 24 | 0.04 |
| Romanian (77) | 158 | 0.27 |
| Russian (337) | 688 | 1.18 |
| Scandinavian (15) | 15 | 0.03 |
| Scotch-Irish (309) | 989 | 1.69 |
| Scottish (328) | 1,430 | 2.44 |
| Serbian (54) | 73 | 0.12 |
| Slavic (30) | 59 | 0.10 |
| Slovak (62) | 112 | 0.19 |
| Slovene (0) | 0 | <0.01 |
| Soviet Union (0) | 0 | <0.01 |
| Swedish (77) | 584 | 1.00 |
| Swiss (44) | 109 | 0.19 |
| Turkish (0) | 0 | <0.01 |
| Ukrainian (239) | 422 | 0.72 |
| Welsh (57) | 332 | 0.57 |
| West Indian, ex. Hispanic (29) | 29 | 0.05 |
| Bahamian (0) | 0 | <0.01 |
| Barbadian (0) | 0 | <0.01 |
| Belizean (0) | 0 | <0.01 |
| Bermudan (0) | 0 | <0.01 |
| British West Indian (0) | 0 | <0.01 |
| Dutch West Indian (0) | 0 | <0.01 |
| Haitian (0) | 0 | <0.01 |
| Jamaican (12) | 12 | 0.02 |
| Trinidadian/Tobagonian (17) | 17 | 0.03 |
| U.S. Virgin Islander (0) | 0 | <0.01 |
| West Indian (0) | 0 | <0.01 |
| Other West Indian (0) | 0 | <0.01 |
| Yugoslavian (66) | 124 | 0.21 |

| Hispanic Origin | Population | % |
|---|---|---|
| Hispanic or Latino (of any race) | 1,485 | 2.55 |
| Central American, ex. Mexican | 32 | 0.06 |
| Costa Rican | 2 | <0.01 |
| Guatemalan | 19 | 0.03 |
| Honduran | 4 | 0.01 |
| Nicaraguan | 0 | <0.01 |
| Panamanian | 5 | 0.01 |
| Salvadoran | 2 | <0.01 |
| Other Central American | 0 | <0.01 |
| Cuban | 31 | 0.05 |
| Dominican Republic | 43 | 0.07 |
| Mexican | 210 | 0.36 |
| Puerto Rican | 942 | 1.62 |
| South American | 89 | 0.15 |
| Argentinean | 7 | 0.01 |
| Bolivian | 7 | 0.01 |
| Chilean | 1 | <0.01 |
| Colombian | 37 | 0.06 |
| Ecuadorian | 18 | 0.03 |
| Paraguayan | 0 | <0.01 |
| Peruvian | 14 | 0.02 |
| Uruguayan | 0 | <0.01 |
| Venezuelan | 1 | <0.01 |
| Other South American | 4 | 0.01 |
| Other Hispanic or Latino | 138 | 0.24 |

| Race* | Population | % |
|---|---|---|
| African-American/Black (1,773) | 2,226 | 3.83 |
| Not Hispanic (1,678) | 2,088 | 3.59 |
| Hispanic (95) | 138 | 0.24 |
| American Indian/Alaska Native (220) | 409 | 0.70 |
| Not Hispanic (183) | 354 | 0.61 |
| Hispanic (37) | 55 | 0.09 |
| Alaska Athabascan (Ala. Nat.) (0) | 0 | <0.01 |
| Aleut (Alaska Native) (0) | 0 | <0.01 |
| Apache (0) | 4 | 0.01 |
| Arapaho (0) | 0 | <0.01 |
| Blackfeet (2) | 5 | 0.01 |
| Canadian/French Am. Ind. (3) | 4 | 0.01 |
| Central American Ind. (0) | 0 | <0.01 |
| Cherokee (2) | 31 | 0.05 |
| Cheyenne (0) | 0 | <0.01 |
| Chickasaw (0) | 0 | <0.01 |
| Chippewa (2) | 3 | 0.01 |

| Race* | Population | % |
|---|---|---|
| Choctaw (0) | 5 | 0.01 |
| Colville (0) | 0 | <0.01 |
| Comanche (0) | 0 | <0.01 |
| Cree (0) | 0 | <0.01 |
| Creek (0) | 1 | <0.01 |
| Crow (0) | 0 | <0.01 |
| Delaware (1) | 1 | <0.01 |
| Hopi (0) | 0 | <0.01 |
| Houma (0) | 0 | <0.01 |
| Inupiat (Alaska Native) (0) | 0 | <0.01 |
| Iroquois (113) | 165 | 0.28 |
| Kiowa (0) | 0 | <0.01 |
| Lumbee (0) | 0 | <0.01 |
| Menominee (0) | 0 | <0.01 |
| Mexican American Ind. (2) | 2 | <0.01 |
| Navajo (1) | 1 | <0.01 |
| Osage (0) | 0 | <0.01 |
| Ottawa (0) | 0 | <0.01 |
| Paiute (0) | 0 | <0.01 |
| Pima (0) | 0 | <0.01 |
| Potawatomi (5) | 9 | 0.02 |
| Pueblo (0) | 0 | <0.01 |
| Puget Sound Salish (0) | 1 | <0.01 |
| Seminole (0) | 1 | <0.01 |
| Shoshone (0) | 0 | <0.01 |
| Sioux (1) | 2 | <0.01 |
| South American Ind. (8) | 14 | 0.02 |
| Spanish American Ind. (2) | 2 | <0.01 |
| Tlingit-Haida (Alaska Native) (0) | 0 | <0.01 |
| Tohono O'Odham (0) | 0 | <0.01 |
| Tsimshian (Alaska Native) (0) | 0 | <0.01 |
| Ute (0) | 0 | <0.01 |
| Yakama (0) | 0 | <0.01 |
| Yaqui (0) | 1 | <0.01 |
| Yuman (0) | 0 | <0.01 |
| Yup'ik (Alaska Native) (0) | 0 | <0.01 |
| Asian (831) | 1,029 | 1.77 |
| Not Hispanic (823) | 1,011 | 1.74 |
| Hispanic (8) | 18 | 0.03 |
| Bangladeshi (3) | 4 | 0.01 |
| Bhutanese (0) | 0 | <0.01 |
| Burmese (2) | 3 | 0.01 |
| Cambodian (1) | 1 | <0.01 |
| Chinese, ex. Taiwanese (210) | 239 | 0.41 |
| Filipino (57) | 93 | 0.16 |
| Hmong (0) | 0 | <0.01 |
| Indian (266) | 284 | 0.49 |
| Indonesian (3) | 8 | 0.01 |
| Japanese (16) | 33 | 0.06 |
| Korean (135) | 160 | 0.28 |
| Laotian (11) | 17 | 0.03 |
| Malaysian (3) | 4 | 0.01 |
| Nepalese (1) | 1 | <0.01 |
| Pakistani (5) | 7 | 0.01 |
| Sri Lankan (8) | 8 | 0.01 |
| Taiwanese (10) | 16 | 0.03 |
| Thai (11) | 23 | 0.04 |
| Vietnamese (64) | 77 | 0.13 |
| Hawaii Native/Pacific Islander (1) | 31 | 0.05 |
| Not Hispanic (1) | 21 | 0.04 |
| Hispanic (0) | 10 | 0.02 |
| Fijian (0) | 0 | <0.01 |
| Guamanian/Chamorro (0) | 3 | 0.01 |
| Marshallese (0) | 0 | <0.01 |
| Native Hawaiian (0) | 12 | 0.02 |
| Samoan (1) | 2 | <0.01 |
| Tongan (0) | 1 | <0.01 |
| White (54,151) | 54,936 | 94.48 |
| Not Hispanic (53,210) | 53,890 | 92.68 |
| Hispanic (941) | 1,046 | 1.80 |

## Tonawanda

Place Type: Town
County: Erie
Population: 73,567

| Ancestry | Population | % |
|---|---|---|
| Afghan (108) | 108 | 0.15 |
| African, Sub-Saharan (85) | 220 | 0.30 |
| African (16) | 89 | 0.12 |
| Cape Verdean (0) | 0 | <0.01 |
| Ethiopian (13) | 13 | 0.02 |
| Ghanaian (19) | 19 | 0.03 |
| Kenyan (24) | 86 | 0.12 |
| Liberian (0) | 0 | <0.01 |
| Nigerian (0) | 0 | <0.01 |
| Senegalese (0) | 0 | <0.01 |
| Sierra Leonean (0) | 0 | <0.01 |
| Somalian (0) | 0 | <0.01 |
| South African (0) | 0 | <0.01 |
| Sudanese (0) | 0 | <0.01 |
| Ugandan (0) | 0 | <0.01 |
| Zimbabwean (0) | 0 | <0.01 |
| Other Sub-Saharan African (13) | 13 | 0.02 |
| Albanian (48) | 59 | 0.08 |
| Alsatian (0) | 24 | 0.03 |
| American (1,511) | 1,511 | 2.04 |
| Arab (344) | 592 | 0.80 |
| Arab (21) | 46 | 0.06 |
| Egyptian (0) | 8 | 0.01 |
| Iraqi (0) | 0 | <0.01 |
| Jordanian (9) | 9 | 0.01 |
| Lebanese (223) | 428 | 0.58 |
| Moroccan (0) | 0 | <0.01 |
| Palestinian (0) | 0 | <0.01 |
| Syrian (12) | 22 | 0.03 |
| Other Arab (79) | 79 | 0.11 |
| Armenian (68) | 96 | 0.13 |
| Assyrian/Chaldean/Syriac (0) | 0 | <0.01 |
| Australian (0) | 29 | 0.04 |
| Austrian (54) | 459 | 0.62 |
| Basque (0) | 0 | <0.01 |
| Belgian (0) | 13 | 0.02 |
| Brazilian (0) | 13 | 0.02 |
| British (33) | 104 | 0.14 |
| Bulgarian (0) | 0 | <0.01 |
| Cajun (0) | 0 | <0.01 |
| Canadian (144) | 312 | 0.42 |
| Carpatho Rusyn (0) | 13 | 0.02 |
| Celtic (0) | 0 | <0.01 |
| Croatian (132) | 326 | 0.44 |
| Cypriot (0) | 0 | <0.01 |
| Czech (42) | 223 | 0.30 |
| Czechoslovakian (32) | 179 | 0.24 |
| Danish (60) | 179 | 0.24 |
| Dutch (104) | 872 | 1.18 |
| Eastern European (44) | 44 | 0.06 |
| English (1,746) | 7,240 | 9.77 |
| Estonian (0) | 0 | <0.01 |
| European (439) | 439 | 0.59 |
| Finnish (49) | 95 | 0.13 |
| French, ex. Basque (254) | 2,508 | 3.39 |
| French Canadian (188) | 881 | 1.19 |
| German (5,590) | 24,085 | 32.51 |
| German Russian (0) | 0 | <0.01 |
| Greek (260) | 493 | 0.67 |
| Guyanese (0) | 0 | <0.01 |
| Hungarian (294) | 1,188 | 1.60 |
| Icelander (11) | 11 | 0.01 |
| Iranian (0) | 0 | <0.01 |
| Irish (3,462) | 15,685 | 21.17 |
| Israeli (0) | 0 | <0.01 |
| Italian (9,140) | 19,213 | 25.93 |
| Latvian (15) | 28 | 0.04 |
| Lithuanian (41) | 174 | 0.23 |
| Luxemburger (0) | 0 | <0.01 |
| Macedonian (0) | 18 | 0.02 |
| Maltese (8) | 26 | 0.04 |
| New Zealander (0) | 0 | <0.01 |
| Northern European (18) | 18 | 0.02 |

| Ancestry | Population | % |
|---|---|---|
| Norwegian (60) | 150 | 0.20 |
| Pennsylvania German (53) | 98 | 0.13 |
| Polish (4,057) | 11,479 | 15.49 |
| Portuguese (10) | 24 | 0.03 |
| Romanian (77) | 158 | 0.21 |
| Russian (347) | 745 | 1.01 |
| Scandinavian (15) | 15 | 0.02 |
| Scotch-Irish (370) | 1,170 | 1.58 |
| Scottish (448) | 1,915 | 2.58 |
| Serbian (66) | 85 | 0.11 |
| Slavic (62) | 123 | 0.17 |
| Slovak (74) | 124 | 0.17 |
| Slovene (0) | 0 | <0.01 |
| Soviet Union (0) | 0 | <0.01 |
| Swedish (144) | 758 | 1.02 |
| Swiss (44) | 131 | 0.18 |
| Turkish (0) | 0 | <0.01 |
| Ukrainian (295) | 535 | 0.72 |
| Welsh (57) | 429 | 0.58 |
| West Indian, ex. Hispanic (49) | 63 | 0.09 |
| Bahamian (0) | 0 | <0.01 |
| Barbadian (0) | 0 | <0.01 |
| Belizean (0) | 0 | <0.01 |
| Bermudan (0) | 0 | <0.01 |
| British West Indian (0) | 0 | <0.01 |
| Dutch West Indian (0) | 0 | <0.01 |
| Haitian (0) | 0 | <0.01 |
| Jamaican (32) | 46 | 0.06 |
| Trinidadian/Tobagonian (17) | 17 | 0.02 |
| U.S. Virgin Islander (0) | 0 | <0.01 |
| West Indian (0) | 0 | <0.01 |
| Other West Indian (0) | 0 | <0.01 |
| Yugoslavian (75) | 133 | 0.18 |

| Hispanic Origin | Population | % |
|---|---|---|
| Hispanic or Latino (of any race) | 2,003 | 2.72 |
| Central American, ex. Mexican | 63 | 0.09 |
| Costa Rican | 9 | 0.01 |
| Guatemalan | 33 | 0.04 |
| Honduran | 5 | 0.01 |
| Nicaraguan | 3 | <0.01 |
| Panamanian | 9 | 0.01 |
| Salvadoran | 4 | 0.01 |
| Other Central American | 0 | <0.01 |
| Cuban | 39 | 0.05 |
| Dominican Republic | 51 | 0.07 |
| Mexican | 261 | 0.35 |
| Puerto Rican | 1,277 | 1.74 |
| South American | 130 | 0.18 |
| Argentinean | 12 | 0.02 |
| Bolivian | 8 | 0.01 |
| Chilean | 1 | <0.01 |
| Colombian | 49 | 0.07 |
| Ecuadorian | 27 | 0.04 |
| Paraguayan | 0 | <0.01 |
| Peruvian | 20 | 0.03 |
| Uruguayan | 1 | <0.01 |
| Venezuelan | 8 | 0.01 |
| Other South American | 4 | 0.01 |
| Other Hispanic or Latino | 182 | 0.25 |

| Race* | Population | % |
|---|---|---|
| African-American/Black (2,234) | 2,842 | 3.86 |
| Not Hispanic (2,114) | 2,658 | 3.61 |
| Hispanic (120) | 184 | 0.25 |
| American Indian/Alaska Native (312) | 575 | 0.78 |
| Not Hispanic (266) | 510 | 0.69 |
| Hispanic (46) | 65 | 0.09 |
| Alaska Athabascan (Ala. Nat.) (0) | 0 | <0.01 |
| Aleut (Alaska Native) (0) | 0 | <0.01 |
| Apache (0) | 4 | 0.01 |
| Arapaho (0) | 0 | <0.01 |
| Blackfeet (2) | 6 | 0.01 |
| Canadian/French Am. Ind. (7) | 8 | 0.01 |
| Central American Ind. (0) | 0 | <0.01 |
| Cherokee (3) | 38 | 0.05 |
| Cheyenne (0) | 0 | <0.01 |
| Chickasaw (0) | 0 | <0.01 |
| Chippewa (4) | 5 | 0.01 |

| Race* | Population | % |
|---|---|---|
| Choctaw (0) | 8 | 0.01 |
| Colville (0) | 0 | <0.01 |
| Comanche (0) | 0 | <0.01 |
| Cree (0) | 3 | <0.01 |
| Creek (0) | 1 | <0.01 |
| Crow (0) | 2 | <0.01 |
| Delaware (1) | 1 | <0.01 |
| Hopi (0) | 0 | <0.01 |
| Houma (0) | 0 | <0.01 |
| Inupiat (Alaska Native) (0) | 0 | <0.01 |
| Iroquois (164) | 256 | 0.35 |
| Kiowa (0) | 0 | <0.01 |
| Lumbee (0) | 1 | <0.01 |
| Menominee (0) | 0 | <0.01 |
| Mexican American Ind. (2) | 2 | <0.01 |
| Navajo (1) | 1 | <0.01 |
| Osage (0) | 0 | <0.01 |
| Ottawa (0) | 0 | <0.01 |
| Paiute (0) | 0 | <0.01 |
| Pima (0) | 0 | <0.01 |
| Potawatomi (5) | 9 | 0.01 |
| Pueblo (0) | 0 | <0.01 |
| Puget Sound Salish (0) | 1 | <0.01 |
| Seminole (0) | 1 | <0.01 |
| Shoshone (0) | 0 | <0.01 |
| Sioux (2) | 5 | 0.01 |
| South American Ind. (8) | 14 | 0.02 |
| Spanish American Ind. (2) | 2 | <0.01 |
| Tlingit-Haida (Alaska Native) (0) | 0 | <0.01 |
| Tohono O'Odham (0) | 0 | <0.01 |
| Tsimshian (Alaska Native) (0) | 0 | <0.01 |
| Ute (0) | 0 | <0.01 |
| Yakama (0) | 0 | <0.01 |
| Yaqui (1) | 1 | <0.01 |
| Yuman (0) | 0 | <0.01 |
| Yup'ik (Alaska Native) (0) | 0 | <0.01 |
| Asian (981) | 1,234 | 1.68 |
| Not Hispanic (972) | 1,209 | 1.64 |
| Hispanic (9) | 25 | 0.03 |
| Bangladeshi (3) | 4 | 0.01 |
| Bhutanese (0) | 0 | <0.01 |
| Burmese (2) | 3 | <0.01 |
| Cambodian (6) | 6 | 0.01 |
| Chinese, ex. Taiwanese (251) | 290 | 0.39 |
| Filipino (68) | 114 | 0.15 |
| Hmong (0) | 0 | <0.01 |
| Indian (287) | 312 | 0.42 |
| Indonesian (3) | 9 | 0.01 |
| Japanese (27) | 59 | 0.08 |
| Korean (166) | 198 | 0.27 |
| Laotian (13) | 19 | 0.03 |
| Malaysian (5) | 6 | 0.01 |
| Nepalese (2) | 2 | <0.01 |
| Pakistani (7) | 10 | 0.01 |
| Sri Lankan (8) | 8 | 0.01 |
| Taiwanese (12) | 18 | 0.02 |
| Thai (13) | 25 | 0.03 |
| Vietnamese (68) | 81 | 0.11 |
| Hawaii Native/Pacific Islander (2) | 38 | 0.05 |
| Not Hispanic (2) | 25 | 0.03 |
| Hispanic (0) | 13 | 0.02 |
| Fijian (0) | 0 | <0.01 |
| Guamanian/Chamorro (0) | 3 | <0.01 |
| Marshallese (0) | 0 | <0.01 |
| Native Hawaiian (0) | 16 | 0.02 |
| Samoan (1) | 2 | <0.01 |
| Tongan (0) | 1 | <0.01 |
| White (68,462) | 69,534 | 94.52 |
| Not Hispanic (67,172) | 68,098 | 92.57 |
| Hispanic (1,290) | 1,436 | 1.95 |

*Notes: † The Census 2010 population figure is used to calculate the percentages in the Hispanic Origin and Race categories. Ancestry percentages are based on the 2006-2010 American Community Survey population (not shown); ‡ Numbers in parentheses indicate the number of people reporting a single ancestry; * Numbers in parentheses indicate the number of persons reporting this race alone, not in combination with any other race; Please refer to the Explanation of Data for more information.*

## Troy

Place Type: City
County: Rensselaer
Population: 50,129

| Ancestry | Population | % |
|---|---|---|
| Afghan (0) | 0 | <0.01 |
| African, Sub-Saharan (643) | 773 | 1.55 |
| African (372) | 476 | 0.95 |
| Cape Verdean (0) | 11 | 0.02 |
| Ethiopian (0) | 0 | <0.01 |
| Ghanaian (91) | 91 | 0.18 |
| Kenyan (0) | 0 | <0.01 |
| Liberian (0) | 0 | <0.01 |
| Nigerian (8) | 8 | 0.02 |
| Senegalese (0) | 0 | <0.01 |
| Sierra Leonean (0) | 0 | <0.01 |
| Somalian (0) | 0 | <0.01 |
| South African (0) | 0 | <0.01 |
| Sudanese (28) | 28 | 0.06 |
| Ugandan (0) | 0 | <0.01 |
| Zimbabwean (0) | 0 | <0.01 |
| Other Sub-Saharan African (144) | 159 | 0.32 |
| Albanian (55) | 55 | 0.11 |
| Alsatian (0) | 0 | <0.01 |
| American (1,657) | 1,657 | 3.31 |
| Arab (304) | 439 | 0.88 |
| Arab (72) | 72 | 0.14 |
| Egyptian (7) | 44 | 0.09 |
| Iraqi (0) | 0 | <0.01 |
| Jordanian (0) | 0 | <0.01 |
| Lebanese (204) | 270 | 0.54 |
| Moroccan (0) | 0 | <0.01 |
| Palestinian (0) | 0 | <0.01 |
| Syrian (0) | 0 | <0.01 |
| Other Arab (21) | 53 | 0.11 |
| Armenian (270) | 418 | 0.84 |
| Assyrian/Chaldean/Syriac (0) | 0 | <0.01 |
| Australian (11) | 11 | 0.02 |
| Austrian (42) | 124 | 0.25 |
| Basque (0) | 0 | <0.01 |
| Belgian (0) | 19 | 0.04 |
| Brazilian (25) | 42 | 0.08 |
| British (97) | 207 | 0.41 |
| Bulgarian (0) | 0 | <0.01 |
| Cajun (0) | 0 | <0.01 |
| Canadian (60) | 177 | 0.35 |
| Carpatho Rusyn (0) | 0 | <0.01 |
| Celtic (0) | 23 | 0.05 |
| Croatian (0) | 0 | <0.01 |
| Cypriot (0) | 0 | <0.01 |
| Czech (9) | 182 | 0.36 |
| Czechoslovakian (20) | 38 | 0.08 |
| Danish (37) | 223 | 0.45 |
| Dutch (117) | 1,379 | 2.76 |
| Eastern European (11) | 24 | 0.05 |
| English (888) | 4,004 | 8.01 |
| Estonian (15) | 15 | 0.03 |
| European (257) | 529 | 1.06 |
| Finnish (0) | 74 | 0.15 |
| French, ex. Basque (679) | 4,862 | 9.72 |
| French Canadian (445) | 1,245 | 2.49 |
| German (926) | 6,417 | 12.83 |
| German Russian (0) | 65 | 0.13 |
| Greek (161) | 358 | 0.72 |
| Guyanese (79) | 79 | 0.16 |
| Hungarian (14) | 129 | 0.26 |
| Icelander (0) | 0 | <0.01 |
| Iranian (0) | 0 | <0.01 |
| Irish (3,757) | 12,384 | 24.76 |
| Israeli (13) | 13 | 0.03 |
| Italian (2,238) | 6,644 | 13.29 |
| Latvian (19) | 32 | 0.06 |
| Lithuanian (30) | 141 | 0.28 |
| Luxemburger (0) | 0 | <0.01 |
| Macedonian (0) | 0 | <0.01 |
| Maltese (0) | 0 | <0.01 |
| New Zealander (0) | 0 | <0.01 |
| Northern European (10) | 10 | 0.02 |

| Ancestry | Population | % |
|---|---|---|
| Norwegian (12) | 134 | 0.27 |
| Pennsylvania German (40) | 50 | 0.10 |
| Polish (733) | 2,521 | 5.04 |
| Portuguese (42) | 81 | 0.16 |
| Romanian (11) | 37 | 0.07 |
| Russian (74) | 287 | 0.57 |
| Scandinavian (8) | 8 | 0.02 |
| Scotch-Irish (239) | 784 | 1.57 |
| Scottish (304) | 848 | 1.70 |
| Serbian (0) | 0 | <0.01 |
| Slavic (0) | 38 | 0.08 |
| Slovak (0) | 52 | 0.10 |
| Slovene (0) | 0 | <0.01 |
| Soviet Union (0) | 0 | <0.01 |
| Swedish (30) | 279 | 0.56 |
| Swiss (0) | 79 | 0.16 |
| Turkish (170) | 207 | 0.41 |
| Ukrainian (299) | 819 | 1.64 |
| Welsh (67) | 432 | 0.86 |
| West Indian, ex. Hispanic (582) | 797 | 1.59 |
| Bahamian (0) | 0 | <0.01 |
| Barbadian (15) | 55 | 0.11 |
| Belizean (0) | 10 | 0.02 |
| Bermudan (0) | 0 | <0.01 |
| British West Indian (10) | 17 | 0.03 |
| Dutch West Indian (0) | 0 | <0.01 |
| Haitian (96) | 109 | 0.22 |
| Jamaican (230) | 288 | 0.58 |
| Trinidadian/Tobagonian (214) | 243 | 0.49 |
| U.S. Virgin Islander (0) | 0 | <0.01 |
| West Indian (17) | 62 | 0.12 |
| Other West Indian (0) | 13 | 0.03 |
| Yugoslavian (21) | 34 | 0.07 |

| Hispanic Origin | Population | % |
|---|---|---|
| Hispanic or Latino (of any race) | 3,984 | 7.95 |
| Central American, ex. Mexican | 153 | 0.31 |
| Costa Rican | 16 | 0.03 |
| Guatemalan | 16 | 0.03 |
| Honduran | 12 | 0.02 |
| Nicaraguan | 15 | 0.03 |
| Panamanian | 57 | 0.11 |
| Salvadoran | 37 | 0.07 |
| Other Central American | 0 | <0.01 |
| Cuban | 96 | 0.19 |
| Dominican Republic | 218 | 0.43 |
| Mexican | 400 | 0.80 |
| Puerto Rican | 2,598 | 5.18 |
| South American | 189 | 0.38 |
| Argentinean | 22 | 0.04 |
| Bolivian | 4 | 0.01 |
| Chilean | 6 | 0.01 |
| Colombian | 61 | 0.12 |
| Ecuadorian | 40 | 0.08 |
| Paraguayan | 3 | 0.01 |
| Peruvian | 29 | 0.06 |
| Uruguayan | 3 | 0.01 |
| Venezuelan | 20 | 0.04 |
| Other South American | 1 | <0.01 |
| Other Hispanic or Latino | 330 | 0.66 |

| Race* | Population | % |
|---|---|---|
| African-American/Black (8,211) | 9,646 | 19.24 |
| Not Hispanic (7,587) | 8,756 | 17.47 |
| Hispanic (624) | 890 | 1.78 |
| American Indian/Alaska Native (163) | 531 | 1.06 |
| Not Hispanic (104) | 407 | 0.81 |
| Hispanic (59) | 124 | 0.25 |
| Alaska Athabascan (Ala. Nat.) (0) | 0 | <0.01 |
| Aleut (Alaska Native) (0) | 0 | <0.01 |
| Apache (4) | 10 | 0.02 |
| Arapaho (0) | 0 | <0.01 |
| Blackfeet (3) | 22 | 0.04 |
| Canadian/French Am. Ind. (1) | 2 | <0.01 |
| Central American Ind. (0) | 1 | <0.01 |
| Cherokee (8) | 80 | 0.16 |
| Cheyenne (0) | 1 | <0.01 |
| Chickasaw (0) | 0 | <0.01 |
| Chippewa (0) | 5 | 0.01 |

| Race* | Population | % |
|---|---|---|
| Choctaw (0) | 1 | <0.01 |
| Colville (0) | 0 | <0.01 |
| Comanche (0) | 2 | <0.01 |
| Cree (0) | 0 | <0.01 |
| Creek (0) | 2 | <0.01 |
| Crow (0) | 0 | <0.01 |
| Delaware (3) | 6 | 0.01 |
| Hopi (0) | 0 | <0.01 |
| Houma (0) | 0 | <0.01 |
| Inupiat (Alaska Native) (0) | 0 | <0.01 |
| Iroquois (10) | 55 | 0.11 |
| Kiowa (0) | 0 | <0.01 |
| Lumbee (1) | 4 | 0.01 |
| Menominee (3) | 3 | 0.01 |
| Mexican American Ind. (1) | 3 | 0.01 |
| Navajo (2) | 5 | 0.01 |
| Osage (0) | 0 | <0.01 |
| Ottawa (0) | 1 | <0.01 |
| Paiute (0) | 0 | <0.01 |
| Pima (1) | 1 | <0.01 |
| Potawatomi (0) | 0 | <0.01 |
| Pueblo (0) | 0 | <0.01 |
| Puget Sound Salish (0) | 0 | <0.01 |
| Seminole (0) | 0 | <0.01 |
| Shoshone (0) | 0 | <0.01 |
| Sioux (0) | 6 | 0.01 |
| South American Ind. (8) | 16 | 0.03 |
| Spanish American Ind. (4) | 5 | 0.01 |
| Tlingit-Haida (Alaska Native) (0) | 1 | <0.01 |
| Tohono O'Odham (0) | 0 | <0.01 |
| Tsimshian (Alaska Native) (0) | 0 | <0.01 |
| Ute (0) | 0 | <0.01 |
| Yakama (0) | 0 | <0.01 |
| Yaqui (0) | 0 | <0.01 |
| Yuman (0) | 0 | <0.01 |
| Yup'ik (Alaska Native) (0) | 0 | <0.01 |
| Asian (1,721) | 2,066 | 4.12 |
| Not Hispanic (1,687) | 2,012 | 4.01 |
| Hispanic (34) | 54 | 0.11 |
| Bangladeshi (19) | 23 | 0.05 |
| Bhutanese (0) | 0 | <0.01 |
| Burmese (28) | 28 | 0.06 |
| Cambodian (3) | 7 | 0.01 |
| Chinese, ex. Taiwanese (674) | 759 | 1.51 |
| Filipino (92) | 157 | 0.31 |
| Hmong (0) | 0 | <0.01 |
| Indian (480) | 546 | 1.09 |
| Indonesian (4) | 5 | 0.01 |
| Japanese (21) | 63 | 0.13 |
| Korean (127) | 174 | 0.35 |
| Laotian (1) | 1 | <0.01 |
| Malaysian (12) | 14 | 0.03 |
| Nepalese (12) | 12 | 0.02 |
| Pakistani (72) | 81 | 0.16 |
| Sri Lankan (2) | 6 | 0.01 |
| Taiwanese (34) | 39 | 0.08 |
| Thai (10) | 15 | 0.03 |
| Vietnamese (59) | 78 | 0.16 |
| Hawaii Native/Pacific Islander (20) | 64 | 0.13 |
| Not Hispanic (15) | 50 | 0.10 |
| Hispanic (5) | 14 | 0.03 |
| Fijian (0) | 0 | <0.01 |
| Guamanian/Chamorro (4) | 5 | 0.01 |
| Marshallese (0) | 0 | <0.01 |
| Native Hawaiian (9) | 24 | 0.05 |
| Samoan (0) | 2 | <0.01 |
| Tongan (0) | 0 | <0.01 |
| White (36,555) | 38,385 | 76.57 |
| Not Hispanic (34,953) | 36,446 | 72.70 |
| Hispanic (1,602) | 1,939 | 3.87 |

Notes: † The Census 2010 population figure is used to calculate the percentages in the Hispanic Origin and Race categories. Ancestry percentages are based on the 2006-2010 American Community Survey population (not shown); ‡ Numbers in parentheses indicate the number of people reporting a single ancestry; * Numbers in parentheses indicate the number of persons reporting this race alone, not in combination with any other race; Please refer to the Explanation of Data for more information.

## Union

Place Type: Town
County: Broome
Population: 56,346

| Ancestry | Population | % |
|---|---|---|
| Afghan (0) | 0 | <0.01 |
| African, Sub-Saharan (117) | 208 | 0.37 |
| African (63) | 154 | 0.27 |
| Cape Verdean (11) | 11 | 0.02 |
| Ethiopian (0) | 0 | <0.01 |
| Ghanaian (30) | 30 | 0.05 |
| Kenyan (0) | 0 | <0.01 |
| Liberian (0) | 0 | <0.01 |
| Nigerian (13) | 13 | 0.02 |
| Senegalese (0) | 0 | <0.01 |
| Sierra Leonean (0) | 0 | <0.01 |
| Somalian (0) | 0 | <0.01 |
| South African (0) | 0 | <0.01 |
| Sudanese (0) | 0 | <0.01 |
| Ugandan (0) | 0 | <0.01 |
| Zimbabwean (0) | 0 | <0.01 |
| Other Sub-Saharan African (0) | 0 | <0.01 |
| Albanian (0) | 7 | 0.01 |
| Alsatian (0) | 0 | <0.01 |
| American (2,180) | 2,180 | 3.87 |
| Arab (175) | 231 | 0.41 |
| Arab (73) | 73 | 0.13 |
| Egyptian (57) | 69 | 0.12 |
| Iraqi (6) | 6 | 0.01 |
| Jordanian (0) | 0 | <0.01 |
| Lebanese (18) | 38 | 0.07 |
| Moroccan (0) | 0 | <0.01 |
| Palestinian (13) | 25 | 0.04 |
| Syrian (0) | 0 | <0.01 |
| Other Arab (8) | 20 | 0.04 |
| Armenian (0) | 16 | 0.03 |
| Assyrian/Chaldean/Syriac (0) | 0 | <0.01 |
| Australian (0) | 0 | <0.01 |
| Austrian (36) | 297 | 0.53 |
| Basque (0) | 0 | <0.01 |
| Belgian (0) | 31 | 0.06 |
| Brazilian (0) | 0 | <0.01 |
| British (82) | 250 | 0.44 |
| Bulgarian (0) | 0 | <0.01 |
| Cajun (3) | 12 | 0.02 |
| Canadian (46) | 153 | 0.27 |
| Carpatho Rusyn (46) | 101 | 0.18 |
| Celtic (0) | 27 | 0.05 |
| Croatian (0) | 21 | 0.04 |
| Cypriot (0) | 0 | <0.01 |
| Czech (289) | 929 | 1.65 |
| Czechoslovakian (221) | 364 | 0.65 |
| Danish (26) | 119 | 0.21 |
| Dutch (410) | 1,823 | 3.24 |
| Eastern European (61) | 83 | 0.15 |
| English (2,117) | 7,072 | 12.56 |
| Estonian (0) | 0 | <0.01 |
| European (596) | 660 | 1.17 |
| Finnish (0) | 10 | 0.02 |
| French, ex. Basque (304) | 2,044 | 3.63 |
| French Canadian (268) | 520 | 0.92 |
| German (2,612) | 10,592 | 18.81 |
| German Russian (0) | 0 | <0.01 |
| Greek (128) | 417 | 0.74 |
| Guyanese (136) | 191 | 0.34 |
| Hungarian (61) | 266 | 0.47 |
| Icelander (0) | 0 | <0.01 |
| Iranian (0) | 11 | 0.02 |
| Irish (3,292) | 12,320 | 21.88 |
| Israeli (0) | 0 | <0.01 |
| Italian (4,117) | 9,710 | 17.24 |
| Latvian (12) | 12 | 0.02 |
| Lithuanian (124) | 452 | 0.80 |
| Luxemburger (0) | 0 | <0.01 |
| Macedonian (0) | 0 | <0.01 |
| Maltese (0) | 0 | <0.01 |
| New Zealander (0) | 0 | <0.01 |
| Northern European (0) | 0 | <0.01 |

| Ancestry | Population | % |
|---|---|---|
| Norwegian (127) | 291 | 0.52 |
| Pennsylvania German (148) | 197 | 0.35 |
| Polish (1,489) | 4,619 | 8.20 |
| Portuguese (33) | 59 | 0.10 |
| Romanian (8) | 68 | 0.12 |
| Russian (582) | 1,778 | 3.16 |
| Scandinavian (9) | 18 | 0.03 |
| Scotch-Irish (171) | 712 | 1.26 |
| Scottish (158) | 1,114 | 1.98 |
| Serbian (10) | 65 | 0.12 |
| Slavic (250) | 291 | 0.52 |
| Slovak (1,272) | 3,003 | 5.33 |
| Slovene (18) | 67 | 0.12 |
| Soviet Union (0) | 0 | <0.01 |
| Swedish (158) | 406 | 0.72 |
| Swiss (12) | 76 | 0.13 |
| Turkish (92) | 103 | 0.18 |
| Ukrainian (317) | 666 | 1.18 |
| Welsh (184) | 1,372 | 2.44 |
| West Indian, ex. Hispanic (92) | 189 | 0.34 |
| Bahamian (0) | 0 | <0.01 |
| Barbadian (0) | 0 | <0.01 |
| Belizean (0) | 0 | <0.01 |
| Bermudan (0) | 0 | <0.01 |
| British West Indian (0) | 0 | <0.01 |
| Dutch West Indian (0) | 0 | <0.01 |
| Haitian (31) | 31 | 0.06 |
| Jamaican (14) | 60 | 0.11 |
| Trinidadian/Tobagonian (0) | 0 | <0.01 |
| U.S. Virgin Islander (0) | 0 | <0.01 |
| West Indian (47) | 98 | 0.17 |
| Other West Indian (0) | 0 | <0.01 |
| Yugoslavian (63) | 83 | 0.15 |

| Hispanic Origin | Population | % |
|---|---|---|
| Hispanic or Latino (of any race) | 1,802 | 3.20 |
| Central American, ex. Mexican | 120 | 0.21 |
| Costa Rican | 15 | 0.03 |
| Guatemalan | 46 | 0.08 |
| Honduran | 22 | 0.04 |
| Nicaraguan | 15 | 0.03 |
| Panamanian | 11 | 0.02 |
| Salvadoran | 11 | 0.02 |
| Other Central American | 0 | <0.01 |
| Cuban | 64 | 0.11 |
| Dominican Republic | 108 | 0.19 |
| Mexican | 247 | 0.44 |
| Puerto Rican | 928 | 1.65 |
| South American | 126 | 0.22 |
| Argentinean | 25 | 0.04 |
| Bolivian | 2 | <0.01 |
| Chilean | 4 | 0.01 |
| Colombian | 48 | 0.09 |
| Ecuadorian | 22 | 0.04 |
| Paraguayan | 0 | <0.01 |
| Peruvian | 10 | 0.02 |
| Uruguayan | 5 | 0.01 |
| Venezuelan | 9 | 0.02 |
| Other South American | 1 | <0.01 |
| Other Hispanic or Latino | 209 | 0.37 |

| Race* | Population | % |
|---|---|---|
| African-American/Black (2,499) | 3,402 | 6.04 |
| Not Hispanic (2,338) | 3,092 | 5.49 |
| Hispanic (161) | 310 | 0.55 |
| American Indian/Alaska Native (96) | 425 | 0.75 |
| Not Hispanic (75) | 363 | 0.64 |
| Hispanic (21) | 62 | 0.11 |
| Alaska Athabascan (Ala. Nat.) (0) | 0 | <0.01 |
| Aleut (Alaska Native) (0) | 0 | <0.01 |
| Apache (5) | 11 | 0.02 |
| Arapaho (0) | 0 | <0.01 |
| Blackfeet (0) | 13 | 0.02 |
| Canadian/French Am. Ind. (3) | 4 | 0.01 |
| Central American Ind. (0) | 0 | <0.01 |
| Cherokee (10) | 56 | 0.10 |
| Cheyenne (0) | 0 | <0.01 |
| Chickasaw (0) | 0 | <0.01 |
| Chippewa (2) | 2 | <0.01 |

| Race* | Population | % |
|---|---|---|
| Choctaw (1) | 4 | 0.01 |
| Colville (0) | 0 | <0.01 |
| Comanche (0) | 0 | <0.01 |
| Cree (0) | 0 | <0.01 |
| Creek (0) | 0 | <0.01 |
| Crow (0) | 1 | <0.01 |
| Delaware (1) | 5 | 0.01 |
| Hopi (0) | 0 | <0.01 |
| Houma (0) | 1 | <0.01 |
| Inupiat (Alaska Native) (0) | 0 | <0.01 |
| Iroquois (14) | 53 | 0.09 |
| Kiowa (0) | 0 | <0.01 |
| Lumbee (0) | 0 | <0.01 |
| Menominee (0) | 0 | <0.01 |
| Mexican American Ind. (2) | 6 | 0.01 |
| Navajo (0) | 2 | <0.01 |
| Osage (0) | 0 | <0.01 |
| Ottawa (0) | 0 | <0.01 |
| Paiute (0) | 0 | <0.01 |
| Pima (0) | 1 | <0.01 |
| Potawatomi (0) | 2 | <0.01 |
| Pueblo (0) | 0 | <0.01 |
| Puget Sound Salish (0) | 0 | <0.01 |
| Seminole (0) | 3 | 0.01 |
| Shoshone (0) | 0 | <0.01 |
| Sioux (3) | 8 | 0.01 |
| South American Ind. (1) | 1 | <0.01 |
| Spanish American Ind. (3) | 4 | 0.01 |
| Tlingit-Haida (Alaska Native) (0) | 0 | <0.01 |
| Tohono O'Odham (0) | 0 | <0.01 |
| Tsimshian (Alaska Native) (0) | 0 | <0.01 |
| Ute (0) | 0 | <0.01 |
| Yakama (0) | 0 | <0.01 |
| Yaqui (1) | 1 | <0.01 |
| Yuman (0) | 0 | <0.01 |
| Yup'ik (Alaska Native) (0) | 0 | <0.01 |
| Asian (1,625) | 1,958 | 3.47 |
| Not Hispanic (1,619) | 1,933 | 3.43 |
| Hispanic (6) | 25 | 0.04 |
| Bangladeshi (3) | 3 | 0.01 |
| Bhutanese (0) | 0 | <0.01 |
| Burmese (4) | 4 | 0.01 |
| Cambodian (4) | 5 | 0.01 |
| Chinese, ex. Taiwanese (333) | 405 | 0.72 |
| Filipino (90) | 143 | 0.25 |
| Hmong (0) | 0 | <0.01 |
| Indian (291) | 342 | 0.61 |
| Indonesian (10) | 12 | 0.02 |
| Japanese (22) | 55 | 0.10 |
| Korean (118) | 161 | 0.29 |
| Laotian (355) | 406 | 0.72 |
| Malaysian (2) | 7 | 0.01 |
| Nepalese (9) | 9 | 0.02 |
| Pakistani (66) | 68 | 0.12 |
| Sri Lankan (2) | 2 | <0.01 |
| Taiwanese (11) | 13 | 0.02 |
| Thai (14) | 19 | 0.03 |
| Vietnamese (215) | 248 | 0.44 |
| Hawaii Native/Pacific Islander (41) | 77 | 0.14 |
| Not Hispanic (29) | 55 | 0.10 |
| Hispanic (12) | 22 | 0.04 |
| Fijian (0) | 1 | <0.01 |
| Guamanian/Chamorro (13) | 16 | 0.03 |
| Marshallese (0) | 0 | <0.01 |
| Native Hawaiian (4) | 17 | 0.03 |
| Samoan (2) | 5 | 0.01 |
| Tongan (0) | 0 | <0.01 |
| White (50,181) | 51,487 | 91.38 |
| Not Hispanic (49,190) | 50,317 | 89.30 |
| Hispanic (991) | 1,170 | 2.08 |

*Notes: † The Census 2010 population figure is used to calculate the percentages in the Hispanic Origin and Race categories. Ancestry percentages are based on the 2006-2010 American Community Survey population (not shown); ‡ Numbers in parentheses indicate the number of people reporting a single ancestry; * Numbers in parentheses indicate the number of persons reporting this race alone, not in combination with any other race; Please refer to the Explanation of Data for more information.*

## Utica

Place Type: City
County: Oneida
Population: 62,235

| Ancestry | Population | % |
|---|---|---|
| Afghan (42) | 42 | 0.07 |
| African, Sub-Saharan (477) | 594 | 0.96 |
| African (272) | 374 | 0.60 |
| Cape Verdean (0) | 0 | <0.01 |
| Ethiopian (0) | 0 | <0.01 |
| Ghanaian (0) | 0 | <0.01 |
| Kenyan (0) | 15 | 0.02 |
| Liberian (88) | 88 | 0.14 |
| Nigerian (0) | 0 | <0.01 |
| Senegalese (0) | 0 | <0.01 |
| Sierra Leonean (0) | 0 | <0.01 |
| Somalian (99) | 99 | 0.16 |
| South African (0) | 0 | <0.01 |
| Sudanese (0) | 0 | <0.01 |
| Ugandan (0) | 0 | <0.01 |
| Zimbabwean (0) | 0 | <0.01 |
| Other Sub-Saharan African (18) | 18 | 0.03 |
| Albanian (22) | 55 | 0.09 |
| Alsatian (0) | 0 | <0.01 |
| American (1,237) | 1,237 | 2.00 |
| Arab (875) | 1,558 | 2.52 |
| Arab (170) | 198 | 0.32 |
| Egyptian (22) | 37 | 0.06 |
| Iraqi (0) | 0 | <0.01 |
| Jordanian (0) | 0 | <0.01 |
| Lebanese (506) | 947 | 1.53 |
| Moroccan (11) | 20 | 0.03 |
| Palestinian (10) | 10 | 0.02 |
| Syrian (58) | 248 | 0.40 |
| Other Arab (98) | 98 | 0.16 |
| Armenian (18) | 29 | 0.05 |
| Assyrian/Chaldean/Syriac (0) | 0 | <0.01 |
| Australian (13) | 13 | 0.02 |
| Austrian (0) | 79 | 0.13 |
| Basque (0) | 0 | <0.01 |
| Belgian (8) | 8 | 0.01 |
| Brazilian (10) | 32 | 0.05 |
| British (9) | 31 | 0.05 |
| Bulgarian (0) | 0 | <0.01 |
| Cajun (0) | 0 | <0.01 |
| Canadian (32) | 61 | 0.10 |
| Carpatho Rusyn (0) | 0 | <0.01 |
| Celtic (8) | 16 | 0.03 |
| Croatian (12) | 86 | 0.14 |
| Cypriot (0) | 0 | <0.01 |
| Czech (0) | 79 | 0.13 |
| Czechoslovakian (22) | 22 | 0.04 |
| Danish (12) | 45 | 0.07 |
| Dutch (149) | 884 | 1.43 |
| Eastern European (11) | 20 | 0.03 |
| English (812) | 3,140 | 5.08 |
| Estonian (0) | 0 | <0.01 |
| European (98) | 108 | 0.17 |
| Finnish (17) | 17 | 0.03 |
| French, ex. Basque (167) | 2,016 | 3.26 |
| French Canadian (219) | 620 | 1.00 |
| German (1,489) | 7,355 | 11.89 |
| German Russian (0) | 0 | <0.01 |
| Greek (57) | 225 | 0.36 |
| Guyanese (8) | 8 | 0.01 |
| Hungarian (37) | 118 | 0.19 |
| Icelander (0) | 14 | 0.02 |
| Iranian (23) | 23 | 0.04 |
| Irish (2,616) | 9,380 | 15.17 |
| Israeli (0) | 0 | <0.01 |
| Italian (7,837) | 14,163 | 22.90 |
| Latvian (0) | 0 | <0.01 |
| Lithuanian (43) | 76 | 0.12 |
| Luxemburger (0) | 0 | <0.01 |
| Macedonian (21) | 21 | 0.03 |
| Maltese (0) | 0 | <0.01 |
| New Zealander (0) | 0 | <0.01 |
| Northern European (0) | 0 | <0.01 |
| Norwegian (9) | 50 | 0.08 |
| Pennsylvania German (13) | 13 | 0.02 |
| Polish (2,611) | 5,408 | 8.75 |
| Portuguese (27) | 114 | 0.18 |
| Romanian (51) | 103 | 0.17 |
| Russian (655) | 862 | 1.39 |
| Scandinavian (0) | 48 | 0.08 |
| Scotch-Irish (110) | 254 | 0.41 |
| Scottish (68) | 351 | 0.57 |
| Serbian (0) | 82 | 0.13 |
| Slavic (0) | 0 | <0.01 |
| Slovak (51) | 59 | 0.10 |
| Slovene (0) | 0 | <0.01 |
| Soviet Union (0) | 0 | <0.01 |
| Swedish (0) | 89 | 0.14 |
| Swiss (32) | 74 | 0.12 |
| Turkish (0) | 0 | <0.01 |
| Ukrainian (359) | 505 | 0.82 |
| Welsh (120) | 775 | 1.25 |
| West Indian, ex. Hispanic (681) | 952 | 1.54 |
| Bahamian (0) | 0 | <0.01 |
| Barbadian (21) | 21 | 0.03 |
| Belizean (0) | 0 | <0.01 |
| Bermudan (0) | 0 | <0.01 |
| British West Indian (0) | 28 | 0.05 |
| Dutch West Indian (0) | 0 | <0.01 |
| Haitian (168) | 286 | 0.46 |
| Jamaican (325) | 420 | 0.68 |
| Trinidadian/Tobagonian (81) | 111 | 0.18 |
| U.S. Virgin Islander (0) | 0 | <0.01 |
| West Indian (86) | 86 | 0.14 |
| Other West Indian (0) | 0 | <0.01 |
| Yugoslavian (3,075) | 3,231 | 5.23 |

| Hispanic Origin | Population | % |
|---|---|---|
| Hispanic or Latino (of any race) | 6,555 | 10.53 |
| Central American, ex. Mexican | 272 | 0.44 |
| Costa Rican | 9 | 0.01 |
| Guatemalan | 8 | 0.01 |
| Honduran | 46 | 0.07 |
| Nicaraguan | 11 | 0.02 |
| Panamanian | 25 | 0.04 |
| Salvadoran | 163 | 0.26 |
| Other Central American | 10 | 0.02 |
| Cuban | 89 | 0.14 |
| Dominican Republic | 940 | 1.51 |
| Mexican | 243 | 0.39 |
| Puerto Rican | 4,220 | 6.78 |
| South American | 231 | 0.37 |
| Argentinean | 7 | 0.01 |
| Bolivian | 2 | <0.01 |
| Chilean | 7 | 0.01 |
| Colombian | 43 | 0.07 |
| Ecuadorian | 100 | 0.16 |
| Paraguayan | 1 | <0.01 |
| Peruvian | 35 | 0.06 |
| Uruguayan | 3 | <0.01 |
| Venezuelan | 31 | 0.05 |
| Other South American | 2 | <0.01 |
| Other Hispanic or Latino | 560 | 0.90 |

| Race* | Population | % |
|---|---|---|
| African-American/Black (9,501) | 11,107 | 17.85 |
| Not Hispanic (8,851) | 10,139 | 16.29 |
| Hispanic (650) | 968 | 1.56 |
| American Indian/Alaska Native (180) | 581 | 0.93 |
| Not Hispanic (123) | 432 | 0.69 |
| Hispanic (57) | 149 | 0.24 |
| Alaska Athabascan (Ala. Nat.) (0) | 0 | <0.01 |
| Aleut (Alaska Native) (1) | 1 | <0.01 |
| Apache (4) | 7 | 0.01 |
| Arapaho (0) | 0 | <0.01 |
| Blackfeet (0) | 17 | 0.03 |
| Canadian/French Am. Ind. (0) | 6 | 0.01 |
| Central American Ind. (8) | 8 | 0.01 |
| Cherokee (5) | 56 | 0.09 |
| Cheyenne (0) | 4 | 0.01 |
| Chickasaw (0) | 1 | <0.01 |
| Chippewa (2) | 8 | 0.01 |
| Choctaw (0) | 3 | <0.01 |
| Colville (0) | 0 | <0.01 |
| Comanche (0) | 0 | <0.01 |
| Cree (0) | 0 | <0.01 |
| Creek (0) | 1 | <0.01 |
| Crow (0) | 3 | <0.01 |
| Delaware (0) | 1 | <0.01 |
| Hopi (0) | 0 | <0.01 |
| Houma (0) | 0 | <0.01 |
| Inupiat (Alaska Native) (0) | 0 | <0.01 |
| Iroquois (42) | 94 | 0.15 |
| Kiowa (0) | 2 | <0.01 |
| Lumbee (1) | 1 | <0.01 |
| Menominee (0) | 0 | <0.01 |
| Mexican American Ind. (0) | 0 | <0.01 |
| Navajo (1) | 2 | <0.01 |
| Osage (0) | 0 | <0.01 |
| Ottawa (0) | 0 | <0.01 |
| Paiute (1) | 1 | <0.01 |
| Pima (0) | 1 | <0.01 |
| Potawatomi (0) | 0 | <0.01 |
| Pueblo (1) | 1 | <0.01 |
| Puget Sound Salish (0) | 0 | <0.01 |
| Seminole (0) | 0 | <0.01 |
| Shoshone (0) | 1 | <0.01 |
| Sioux (10) | 29 | 0.05 |
| South American Ind. (4) | 15 | 0.02 |
| Spanish American Ind. (0) | 0 | <0.01 |
| Tlingit-Haida (Alaska Native) (1) | 4 | 0.01 |
| Tohono O'Odham (0) | 0 | <0.01 |
| Tsimshian (Alaska Native) (0) | 0 | <0.01 |
| Ute (0) | 0 | <0.01 |
| Yakama (0) | 0 | <0.01 |
| Yaqui (0) | 0 | <0.01 |
| Yuman (0) | 0 | <0.01 |
| Yup'ik (Alaska Native) (0) | 0 | <0.01 |
| Asian (4,626) | 5,009 | 8.05 |
| Not Hispanic (4,594) | 4,936 | 7.93 |
| Hispanic (32) | 73 | 0.12 |
| Bangladeshi (0) | 0 | <0.01 |
| Bhutanese (30) | 36 | 0.06 |
| Burmese (2,198) | 2,317 | 3.72 |
| Cambodian (412) | 480 | 0.77 |
| Chinese, ex. Taiwanese (140) | 200 | 0.32 |
| Filipino (37) | 83 | 0.13 |
| Hmong (0) | 0 | <0.01 |
| Indian (273) | 368 | 0.59 |
| Indonesian (0) | 0 | <0.01 |
| Japanese (44) | 66 | 0.11 |
| Korean (107) | 133 | 0.21 |
| Laotian (42) | 72 | 0.12 |
| Malaysian (2) | 2 | <0.01 |
| Nepalese (6) | 12 | 0.02 |
| Pakistani (41) | 46 | 0.07 |
| Sri Lankan (2) | 2 | <0.01 |
| Taiwanese (1) | 2 | <0.01 |
| Thai (34) | 50 | 0.08 |
| Vietnamese (932) | 1,022 | 1.64 |
| Hawaii Native/Pacific Islander (36) | 137 | 0.22 |
| Not Hispanic (16) | 95 | 0.15 |
| Hispanic (20) | 42 | 0.07 |
| Fijian (0) | 0 | <0.01 |
| Guamanian/Chamorro (10) | 18 | 0.03 |
| Marshallese (0) | 0 | <0.01 |
| Native Hawaiian (12) | 20 | 0.03 |
| Samoan (9) | 18 | 0.03 |
| Tongan (1) | 1 | <0.01 |
| White (42,945) | 45,066 | 72.41 |
| Not Hispanic (40,164) | 41,788 | 67.15 |
| Hispanic (2,781) | 3,278 | 5.27 |

Notes: † The Census 2010 population figure is used to calculate the percentages in the Hispanic Origin and Race categories. Ancestry percentages are based on the 2006-2010 American Community Survey population (not shown); ‡ Numbers in parentheses indicate the number of people reporting a single ancestry; * Numbers in parentheses indicate the number of persons reporting this race alone, not in combination with any other race; Please refer to the Explanation of Data for more information.

## White Plains

Place Type: City
County: Westchester
Population: 56,853

| Ancestry | Population | % |
|---|---|---|
| Afghan (0) | 0 | <0.01 |
| African, Sub-Saharan (230) | 331 | 0.59 |
| African (97) | 97 | 0.17 |
| Cape Verdean (0) | 0 | <0.01 |
| Ethiopian (0) | 0 | <0.01 |
| Ghanaian (0) | 0 | <0.01 |
| Kenyan (0) | 0 | <0.01 |
| Liberian (0) | 0 | <0.01 |
| Nigerian (66) | 97 | 0.17 |
| Senegalese (0) | 0 | <0.01 |
| Sierra Leonean (0) | 0 | <0.01 |
| Somalian (0) | 0 | <0.01 |
| South African (43) | 78 | 0.14 |
| Sudanese (0) | 0 | <0.01 |
| Ugandan (9) | 9 | 0.02 |
| Zimbabwean (0) | 0 | <0.01 |
| Other Sub-Saharan African (15) | 50 | 0.09 |
| Albanian (58) | 73 | 0.13 |
| Alsatian (0) | 0 | <0.01 |
| American (2,743) | 2,743 | 4.91 |
| Arab (162) | 307 | 0.55 |
| Arab (10) | 64 | 0.11 |
| Egyptian (44) | 44 | 0.08 |
| Iraqi (0) | 0 | <0.01 |
| Jordanian (21) | 21 | 0.04 |
| Lebanese (46) | 56 | 0.10 |
| Moroccan (24) | 71 | 0.13 |
| Palestinian (7) | 7 | 0.01 |
| Syrian (0) | 7 | 0.01 |
| Other Arab (10) | 37 | 0.07 |
| Armenian (44) | 60 | 0.11 |
| Assyrian/Chaldean/Syriac (0) | 8 | 0.01 |
| Australian (0) | 0 | <0.01 |
| Austrian (201) | 572 | 1.02 |
| Basque (0) | 0 | <0.01 |
| Belgian (47) | 94 | 0.17 |
| Brazilian (409) | 440 | 0.79 |
| British (34) | 126 | 0.23 |
| Bulgarian (40) | 62 | 0.11 |
| Cajun (0) | 0 | <0.01 |
| Canadian (69) | 128 | 0.23 |
| Carpatho Rusyn (0) | 0 | <0.01 |
| Celtic (0) | 0 | <0.01 |
| Croatian (61) | 61 | 0.11 |
| Cypriot (0) | 0 | <0.01 |
| Czech (41) | 115 | 0.21 |
| Czechoslovakian (0) | 20 | 0.04 |
| Danish (9) | 48 | 0.09 |
| Dutch (64) | 313 | 0.56 |
| Eastern European (542) | 557 | 1.00 |
| English (489) | 1,818 | 3.25 |
| Estonian (0) | 0 | <0.01 |
| European (593) | 684 | 1.22 |
| Finnish (15) | 25 | 0.04 |
| French, ex. Basque (101) | 696 | 1.25 |
| French Canadian (30) | 155 | 0.28 |
| German (754) | 3,324 | 5.95 |
| German Russian (0) | 0 | <0.01 |
| Greek (102) | 279 | 0.50 |
| Guyanese (130) | 175 | 0.31 |
| Hungarian (148) | 401 | 0.72 |
| Icelander (0) | 0 | <0.01 |
| Iranian (28) | 48 | 0.09 |
| Irish (2,251) | 5,662 | 10.13 |
| Israeli (153) | 181 | 0.32 |
| Italian (5,382) | 9,116 | 16.31 |
| Latvian (7) | 7 | 0.01 |
| Lithuanian (94) | 226 | 0.40 |
| Luxemburger (0) | 0 | <0.01 |
| Macedonian (14) | 54 | 0.10 |
| Maltese (0) | 0 | <0.01 |
| New Zealander (29) | 29 | 0.05 |
| Northern European (31) | 54 | 0.10 |

| Ancestry | Population | % |
|---|---|---|
| Norwegian (42) | 134 | 0.24 |
| Pennsylvania German (0) | 0 | <0.01 |
| Polish (765) | 2,000 | 3.58 |
| Portuguese (198) | 325 | 0.58 |
| Romanian (61) | 183 | 0.33 |
| Russian (1,095) | 2,307 | 4.13 |
| Scandinavian (0) | 0 | <0.01 |
| Scotch-Irish (100) | 241 | 0.43 |
| Scottish (116) | 435 | 0.78 |
| Serbian (16) | 16 | 0.03 |
| Slavic (0) | 0 | <0.01 |
| Slovak (18) | 85 | 0.15 |
| Slovene (0) | 0 | <0.01 |
| Soviet Union (0) | 0 | <0.01 |
| Swedish (30) | 282 | 0.50 |
| Swiss (46) | 129 | 0.23 |
| Turkish (96) | 120 | 0.21 |
| Ukrainian (228) | 290 | 0.52 |
| Welsh (6) | 89 | 0.16 |
| West Indian, ex. Hispanic (1,351) | 1,555 | 2.78 |
| Bahamian (26) | 26 | 0.05 |
| Barbadian (25) | 25 | 0.04 |
| Belizean (125) | 155 | 0.28 |
| Bermudan (0) | 0 | <0.01 |
| British West Indian (34) | 57 | 0.10 |
| Dutch West Indian (0) | 0 | <0.01 |
| Haitian (386) | 397 | 0.71 |
| Jamaican (596) | 702 | 1.26 |
| Trinidadian/Tobagonian (49) | 49 | 0.09 |
| U.S. Virgin Islander (23) | 23 | 0.04 |
| West Indian (87) | 121 | 0.22 |
| Other West Indian (0) | 0 | <0.01 |
| Yugoslavian (24) | 24 | 0.04 |

| Hispanic Origin | Population | % |
|---|---|---|
| Hispanic or Latino (of any race) | 16,839 | 29.62 |
| Central American, ex. Mexican | 968 | 1.70 |
| Costa Rican | 35 | 0.06 |
| Guatemalan | 551 | 0.97 |
| Honduran | 75 | 0.13 |
| Nicaraguan | 35 | 0.06 |
| Panamanian | 56 | 0.10 |
| Salvadoran | 204 | 0.36 |
| Other Central American | 12 | 0.02 |
| Cuban | 321 | 0.56 |
| Dominican Republic | 1,177 | 2.07 |
| Mexican | 5,773 | 10.15 |
| Puerto Rican | 1,541 | 2.71 |
| South American | 5,850 | 10.29 |
| Argentinean | 189 | 0.33 |
| Bolivian | 72 | 0.13 |
| Chilean | 67 | 0.12 |
| Colombian | 1,838 | 3.23 |
| Ecuadorian | 1,001 | 1.76 |
| Paraguayan | 260 | 0.46 |
| Peruvian | 2,260 | 3.98 |
| Uruguayan | 63 | 0.11 |
| Venezuelan | 77 | 0.14 |
| Other South American | 23 | 0.04 |
| Other Hispanic or Latino | 1,209 | 2.13 |

| Race* | Population | % |
|---|---|---|
| African-American/Black (8,070) | 8,768 | 15.42 |
| Not Hispanic (7,502) | 7,918 | 13.93 |
| Hispanic (568) | 850 | 1.50 |
| American Indian/Alaska Native (394) | 890 | 1.57 |
| Not Hispanic (47) | 193 | 0.34 |
| Hispanic (347) | 697 | 1.23 |
| Alaska Athabascan (Ala. Nat.) (0) | 0 | <0.01 |
| Aleut (Alaska Native) (0) | 0 | <0.01 |
| Apache (0) | 6 | 0.01 |
| Arapaho (0) | 0 | <0.01 |
| Blackfeet (3) | 16 | 0.03 |
| Canadian/French Am. Ind. (0) | 0 | <0.01 |
| Central American Ind. (1) | 6 | 0.01 |
| Cherokee (2) | 36 | 0.06 |
| Cheyenne (0) | 0 | <0.01 |
| Chickasaw (0) | 0 | <0.01 |
| Chippewa (4) | 4 | 0.01 |

| Race* | Population | % |
|---|---|---|
| Choctaw (0) | 0 | <0.01 |
| Colville (0) | 0 | <0.01 |
| Comanche (0) | 0 | <0.01 |
| Cree (0) | 0 | <0.01 |
| Creek (2) | 3 | 0.01 |
| Crow (0) | 1 | <0.01 |
| Delaware (0) | 1 | <0.01 |
| Hopi (0) | 1 | <0.01 |
| Houma (3) | 3 | 0.01 |
| Inupiat (Alaska Native) (0) | 0 | <0.01 |
| Iroquois (1) | 12 | 0.02 |
| Kiowa (0) | 0 | <0.01 |
| Lumbee (1) | 1 | <0.01 |
| Menominee (0) | 0 | <0.01 |
| Mexican American Ind. (95) | 162 | 0.28 |
| Navajo (1) | 1 | <0.01 |
| Osage (1) | 2 | <0.01 |
| Ottawa (0) | 0 | <0.01 |
| Paiute (0) | 0 | <0.01 |
| Pima (0) | 0 | <0.01 |
| Potawatomi (0) | 0 | <0.01 |
| Pueblo (13) | 19 | 0.03 |
| Puget Sound Salish (0) | 0 | <0.01 |
| Seminole (0) | 1 | <0.01 |
| Shoshone (0) | 1 | <0.01 |
| Sioux (0) | 7 | 0.01 |
| South American Ind. (42) | 116 | 0.20 |
| Spanish American Ind. (12) | 15 | 0.03 |
| Tlingit-Haida (Alaska Native) (0) | 0 | <0.01 |
| Tohono O'Odham (0) | 0 | <0.01 |
| Tsimshian (Alaska Native) (0) | 0 | <0.01 |
| Ute (0) | 0 | <0.01 |
| Yakama (0) | 0 | <0.01 |
| Yaqui (0) | 1 | <0.01 |
| Yuman (0) | 0 | <0.01 |
| Yup'ik (Alaska Native) (0) | 0 | <0.01 |
| Asian (3,623) | 4,080 | 7.18 |
| Not Hispanic (3,587) | 3,959 | 6.96 |
| Hispanic (36) | 121 | 0.21 |
| Bangladeshi (35) | 37 | 0.07 |
| Bhutanese (0) | 0 | <0.01 |
| Burmese (9) | 9 | 0.02 |
| Cambodian (13) | 13 | 0.02 |
| Chinese, ex. Taiwanese (813) | 934 | 1.64 |
| Filipino (373) | 451 | 0.79 |
| Hmong (0) | 0 | <0.01 |
| Indian (1,281) | 1,397 | 2.46 |
| Indonesian (6) | 10 | 0.02 |
| Japanese (372) | 441 | 0.78 |
| Korean (384) | 431 | 0.76 |
| Laotian (1) | 3 | 0.01 |
| Malaysian (8) | 11 | 0.02 |
| Nepalese (7) | 7 | 0.01 |
| Pakistani (70) | 79 | 0.14 |
| Sri Lankan (10) | 17 | 0.03 |
| Taiwanese (35) | 44 | 0.08 |
| Thai (31) | 42 | 0.07 |
| Vietnamese (73) | 82 | 0.14 |
| Hawaii Native/Pacific Islander (20) | 180 | 0.32 |
| Not Hispanic (14) | 71 | 0.12 |
| Hispanic (6) | 109 | 0.19 |
| Fijian (6) | 6 | 0.01 |
| Guamanian/Chamorro (2) | 7 | 0.01 |
| Marshallese (0) | 0 | <0.01 |
| Native Hawaiian (4) | 7 | 0.01 |
| Samoan (0) | 0 | <0.01 |
| Tongan (0) | 0 | <0.01 |
| White (36,178) | 37,846 | 66.57 |
| Not Hispanic (27,805) | 28,446 | 50.03 |
| Hispanic (8,373) | 9,400 | 16.53 |

*Notes: † The Census 2010 population figure is used to calculate the percentages in the Hispanic Origin and Race categories. Ancestry percentages are based on the 2006-2010 American Community Survey population (not shown); ‡ Numbers in parentheses indicate the number of people reporting a single ancestry; * Numbers in parentheses indicate the number of persons reporting this race alone, not in combination with any other race; Please refer to the Explanation of Data for more information.*

## Yonkers

Place Type: City
County: Westchester
Population: 195,976

| Ancestry | Population | % |
|---|---|---|
| Afghan (0) | 0 | <0.01 |
| African, Sub-Saharan (2,404) | 2,939 | 1.51 |
| African (1,162) | 1,496 | 0.77 |
| Cape Verdean (41) | 41 | 0.02 |
| Ethiopian (159) | 159 | 0.08 |
| Ghanaian (489) | 585 | 0.30 |
| Kenyan (73) | 107 | 0.05 |
| Liberian (7) | 7 | <0.01 |
| Nigerian (371) | 442 | 0.23 |
| Senegalese (21) | 21 | 0.01 |
| Sierra Leonean (0) | 0 | <0.01 |
| Somalian (6) | 6 | <0.01 |
| South African (59) | 59 | 0.03 |
| Sudanese (0) | 0 | <0.01 |
| Ugandan (0) | 0 | <0.01 |
| Zimbabwean (0) | 0 | <0.01 |
| Other Sub-Saharan African (16) | 16 | 0.01 |
| Albanian (2,122) | 2,270 | 1.16 |
| Alsatian (0) | 0 | <0.01 |
| American (5,127) | 5,127 | 2.63 |
| Arab (2,696) | 3,210 | 1.65 |
| Arab (899) | 1,036 | 0.53 |
| Egyptian (243) | 243 | 0.12 |
| Iraqi (103) | 103 | 0.05 |
| Jordanian (855) | 907 | 0.47 |
| Lebanese (44) | 327 | 0.17 |
| Moroccan (103) | 110 | 0.06 |
| Palestinian (139) | 139 | 0.07 |
| Syrian (13) | 33 | 0.02 |
| Other Arab (297) | 312 | 0.16 |
| Armenian (338) | 411 | 0.21 |
| Assyrian/Chaldean/Syriac (135) | 157 | 0.08 |
| Australian (0) | 17 | 0.01 |
| Austrian (121) | 618 | 0.32 |
| Basque (0) | 0 | <0.01 |
| Belgian (0) | 12 | 0.01 |
| Brazilian (334) | 422 | 0.22 |
| British (168) | 297 | 0.15 |
| Bulgarian (10) | 10 | 0.01 |
| Cajun (0) | 0 | <0.01 |
| Canadian (111) | 182 | 0.09 |
| Carpatho Rusyn (40) | 40 | 0.02 |
| Celtic (11) | 15 | 0.01 |
| Croatian (65) | 121 | 0.06 |
| Cypriot (0) | 0 | <0.01 |
| Czech (152) | 478 | 0.25 |
| Czechoslovakian (185) | 354 | 0.18 |
| Danish (0) | 62 | 0.03 |
| Dutch (50) | 468 | 0.24 |
| Eastern European (441) | 458 | 0.24 |
| English (1,054) | 3,968 | 2.04 |
| Estonian (0) | 53 | 0.03 |
| European (325) | 391 | 0.20 |
| Finnish (50) | 84 | 0.04 |
| French, ex. Basque (245) | 1,367 | 0.70 |
| French Canadian (53) | 284 | 0.15 |
| German (1,666) | 8,502 | 4.36 |
| German Russian (14) | 14 | 0.01 |
| Greek (949) | 1,272 | 0.65 |
| Guyanese (410) | 526 | 0.27 |
| Hungarian (410) | 920 | 0.47 |
| Icelander (0) | 0 | <0.01 |
| Iranian (137) | 173 | 0.09 |
| Irish (10,811) | 22,187 | 11.38 |
| Israeli (38) | 77 | 0.04 |
| Italian (21,697) | 32,142 | 16.49 |
| Latvian (33) | 71 | 0.04 |
| Lithuanian (111) | 327 | 0.17 |
| Luxemburger (0) | 13 | 0.01 |
| Macedonian (236) | 236 | 0.12 |
| Maltese (73) | 73 | 0.04 |
| New Zealander (8) | 8 | <0.01 |
| Northern European (13) | 13 | 0.01 |

| Ancestry | Population | % |
|---|---|---|
| Norwegian (79) | 370 | 0.19 |
| Pennsylvania German (0) | 0 | <0.01 |
| Polish (2,602) | 5,453 | 2.80 |
| Portuguese (1,947) | 2,670 | 1.37 |
| Romanian (170) | 278 | 0.14 |
| Russian (1,453) | 2,804 | 1.44 |
| Scandinavian (10) | 21 | 0.01 |
| Scotch-Irish (274) | 562 | 0.29 |
| Scottish (293) | 1,047 | 0.54 |
| Serbian (0) | 11 | 0.01 |
| Slavic (185) | 237 | 0.12 |
| Slovak (274) | 590 | 0.30 |
| Slovene (10) | 10 | 0.01 |
| Soviet Union (14) | 14 | 0.01 |
| Swedish (115) | 574 | 0.29 |
| Swiss (12) | 83 | 0.04 |
| Turkish (112) | 112 | 0.06 |
| Ukrainian (943) | 1,494 | 0.77 |
| Welsh (20) | 140 | 0.07 |
| West Indian, ex. Hispanic (7,179) | 8,578 | 4.40 |
| Bahamian (0) | 0 | <0.01 |
| Barbadian (47) | 157 | 0.08 |
| Belizean (0) | 0 | <0.01 |
| Bermudan (0) | 0 | <0.01 |
| British West Indian (313) | 497 | 0.26 |
| Dutch West Indian (3) | 3 | <0.01 |
| Haitian (897) | 1,026 | 0.53 |
| Jamaican (4,479) | 5,051 | 2.59 |
| Trinidadian/Tobagonian (650) | 689 | 0.35 |
| U.S. Virgin Islander (32) | 83 | 0.04 |
| West Indian (758) | 1,072 | 0.55 |
| Other West Indian (0) | 0 | <0.01 |
| Yugoslavian (38) | 46 | 0.02 |

| Hispanic Origin | Population | % |
|---|---|---|
| Hispanic or Latino (of any race) | 67,927 | 34.66 |
| Central American, ex. Mexican | 5,822 | 2.97 |
| Costa Rican | 156 | 0.08 |
| Guatemalan | 765 | 0.39 |
| Honduran | 1,451 | 0.74 |
| Nicaraguan | 534 | 0.27 |
| Panamanian | 185 | 0.09 |
| Salvadoran | 2,691 | 1.37 |
| Other Central American | 40 | 0.02 |
| Cuban | 1,501 | 0.77 |
| Dominican Republic | 15,903 | 8.11 |
| Mexican | 13,761 | 7.02 |
| Puerto Rican | 19,875 | 10.14 |
| South American | 6,622 | 3.38 |
| Argentinean | 273 | 0.14 |
| Bolivian | 30 | 0.02 |
| Chilean | 215 | 0.11 |
| Colombian | 1,493 | 0.76 |
| Ecuadorian | 3,271 | 1.67 |
| Paraguayan | 79 | 0.04 |
| Peruvian | 946 | 0.48 |
| Uruguayan | 45 | 0.02 |
| Venezuelan | 207 | 0.11 |
| Other South American | 63 | 0.03 |
| Other Hispanic or Latino | 4,443 | 2.27 |

| Race* | Population | % |
|---|---|---|
| African-American/Black (36,572) | 40,198 | 20.51 |
| Not Hispanic (31,297) | 32,873 | 16.77 |
| Hispanic (5,275) | 7,325 | 3.74 |
| American Indian/Alaska Native (1,463) | 2,801 | 1.43 |
| Not Hispanic (382) | 995 | 0.51 |
| Hispanic (1,081) | 1,806 | 0.92 |
| Alaska Athabascan (Ala. Nat.) (1) | 1 | <0.01 |
| Aleut (Alaska Native) (0) | 0 | <0.01 |
| Apache (3) | 10 | 0.01 |
| Arapaho (0) | 0 | <0.01 |
| Blackfeet (17) | 58 | 0.03 |
| Canadian/French Am. Ind. (3) | 4 | <0.01 |
| Central American Ind. (46) | 103 | 0.05 |
| Cherokee (28) | 151 | 0.08 |
| Cheyenne (1) | 3 | <0.01 |
| Chickasaw (0) | 1 | <0.01 |
| Chippewa (6) | 8 | <0.01 |

| Race* | Population | % |
|---|---|---|
| Choctaw (1) | 12 | 0.01 |
| Colville (0) | 1 | <0.01 |
| Comanche (0) | 1 | <0.01 |
| Cree (0) | 0 | <0.01 |
| Creek (1) | 3 | <0.01 |
| Crow (1) | 2 | <0.01 |
| Delaware (2) | 6 | <0.01 |
| Hopi (1) | 5 | <0.01 |
| Houma (1) | 1 | <0.01 |
| Inupiat (Alaska Native) (3) | 5 | <0.01 |
| Iroquois (16) | 41 | 0.02 |
| Kiowa (0) | 0 | <0.01 |
| Lumbee (1) | 2 | <0.01 |
| Menominee (0) | 0 | <0.01 |
| Mexican American Ind. (99) | 171 | 0.09 |
| Navajo (7) | 7 | <0.01 |
| Osage (1) | 1 | <0.01 |
| Ottawa (0) | 0 | <0.01 |
| Paiute (0) | 0 | <0.01 |
| Pima (0) | 0 | <0.01 |
| Potawatomi (0) | 0 | <0.01 |
| Pueblo (8) | 20 | 0.01 |
| Puget Sound Salish (0) | 0 | <0.01 |
| Seminole (1) | 11 | 0.01 |
| Shoshone (0) | 0 | <0.01 |
| Sioux (5) | 13 | 0.01 |
| South American Ind. (95) | 270 | 0.14 |
| Spanish American Ind. (104) | 132 | 0.07 |
| Tlingit-Haida (Alaska Native) (0) | 1 | <0.01 |
| Tohono O'Odham (0) | 3 | <0.01 |
| Tsimshian (Alaska Native) (0) | 0 | <0.01 |
| Ute (0) | 0 | <0.01 |
| Yakama (0) | 0 | <0.01 |
| Yaqui (0) | 0 | <0.01 |
| Yuman (2) | 2 | <0.01 |
| Yup'ik (Alaska Native) (0) | 0 | <0.01 |
| Asian (11,556) | 13,253 | 6.76 |
| Not Hispanic (11,370) | 12,736 | 6.50 |
| Hispanic (186) | 517 | 0.26 |
| Bangladeshi (148) | 167 | 0.09 |
| Bhutanese (1) | 1 | <0.01 |
| Burmese (11) | 11 | 0.01 |
| Cambodian (26) | 36 | 0.02 |
| Chinese, ex. Taiwanese (872) | 1,149 | 0.59 |
| Filipino (2,584) | 2,819 | 1.44 |
| Hmong (0) | 0 | <0.01 |
| Indian (5,313) | 5,818 | 2.97 |
| Indonesian (20) | 28 | 0.01 |
| Japanese (155) | 251 | 0.13 |
| Korean (906) | 977 | 0.50 |
| Laotian (16) | 18 | 0.01 |
| Malaysian (3) | 7 | <0.01 |
| Nepalese (8) | 9 | <0.01 |
| Pakistani (783) | 874 | 0.45 |
| Sri Lankan (36) | 39 | 0.02 |
| Taiwanese (41) | 49 | 0.03 |
| Thai (248) | 268 | 0.14 |
| Vietnamese (79) | 95 | 0.05 |
| Hawaii Native/Pacific Islander (122) | 483 | 0.25 |
| Not Hispanic (58) | 211 | 0.11 |
| Hispanic (64) | 272 | 0.14 |
| Fijian (5) | 6 | <0.01 |
| Guamanian/Chamorro (27) | 52 | 0.03 |
| Marshallese (0) | 0 | <0.01 |
| Native Hawaiian (35) | 57 | 0.03 |
| Samoan (4) | 8 | <0.01 |
| Tongan (0) | 0 | <0.01 |
| White (109,351) | 114,948 | 58.65 |
| Not Hispanic (81,163) | 83,170 | 42.44 |
| Hispanic (28,188) | 31,778 | 16.22 |

*Notes: † The Census 2010 population figure is used to calculate the percentages in the Hispanic Origin and Race categories. Ancestry percentages are based on the 2006-2010 American Community Survey population (not shown); ‡ Numbers in parentheses indicate the number of people reporting a single ancestry; * Numbers in parentheses indicate the number of persons reporting this race alone, not in combination with any other race; Please refer to the Explanation of Data for more information.*

## Ancestry Group Rankings

### Afghan

#### Top 10 Places Sorted by Population
*Based on all places, regardless of total population*

| Place | Population | % |
|---|---|---|
| New York (city) | 6,470 | 0.08 |
| Queens (borough) Queens County | 6,027 | 0.27 |
| Oyster Bay (town) Nassau County | 808 | 0.28 |
| Hempstead (town) Nassau County | 399 | 0.05 |
| Brooklyn (borough) Kings County | 344 | 0.01 |
| Hicksville (cdp) Nassau County | 323 | 0.77 |
| Schenectady (city) Schenectady County | 318 | 0.49 |
| Huntington (town) Suffolk County | 314 | 0.16 |
| Huntington Station (cdp) Suffolk County | 268 | 0.85 |
| Islip (town) Suffolk County | 263 | 0.08 |

#### Top 10 Places Sorted by Percent of Total Population
*Based on all places, regardless of total population*

| Place | Population | % |
|---|---|---|
| DeRuyter (town) Madison County | 27 | 2.14 |
| Pomona (village) Rockland County | 61 | 1.73 |
| Malverne (village) Nassau County | 139 | 1.63 |
| Viola (cdp) Rockland County | 111 | 1.57 |
| Huntington Bay (village) Suffolk County | 21 | 1.47 |
| Woodbury (cdp) Nassau County | 125 | 1.38 |
| Wyandanch (cdp) Suffolk County | 123 | 1.13 |
| Jericho (cdp) Nassau County | 129 | 0.99 |
| New Hyde Park (village) Nassau County | 89 | 0.93 |
| Upper Brookville (village) Nassau County | 13 | 0.87 |

#### Top 10 Places Sorted by Percent of Total Population
*Based on places with total population of 50,000 or more*

| Place | Population | % |
|---|---|---|
| Schenectady (city) Schenectady County | 318 | 0.49 |
| Oyster Bay (town) Nassau County | 808 | 0.28 |
| Irondequoit (cdp/town) Monroe County | 145 | 0.28 |
| Queens (borough) Queens County | 6,027 | 0.27 |
| Tonawanda (cdp) Erie County | 108 | 0.18 |
| Huntington (town) Suffolk County | 314 | 0.16 |
| Tonawanda (town) Erie County | 108 | 0.15 |
| Amherst (town) Erie County | 144 | 0.12 |
| Brentwood (cdp) Suffolk County | 68 | 0.12 |
| Babylon (town) Suffolk County | 219 | 0.10 |

### African, Sub-Saharan

#### Top 10 Places Sorted by Population
*Based on all places, regardless of total population*

| Place | Population | % |
|---|---|---|
| New York (city) | 175,478 | 2.17 |
| Brooklyn (borough) Kings County | 63,004 | 2.55 |
| Bronx (borough) Bronx County | 55,928 | 4.10 |
| Queens (borough) Queens County | 25,166 | 1.14 |
| Manhattan (borough) New York County | 24,146 | 1.52 |
| Rochester (city) Monroe County | 7,909 | 3.73 |
| Staten Island (borough) Richmond County | 7,234 | 1.56 |
| Buffalo (city) Erie County | 6,085 | 2.29 |
| Hempstead (town) Nassau County | 5,844 | 0.78 |
| Yonkers (city) Westchester County | 2,939 | 1.51 |

#### Top 10 Places Sorted by Percent of Total Population
*Based on all places, regardless of total population*

| Place | Population | % |
|---|---|---|
| Linwood (cdp) Livingston County | 64 | 48.85 |
| Wheatley Heights (cdp) Suffolk County | 896 | 14.46 |
| North Bellport (cdp) Suffolk County | 737 | 6.54 |
| Gordon Heights (cdp) Suffolk County | 199 | 6.10 |
| Hobart (village) Delaware County | 29 | 5.99 |
| Pomona (village) Rockland County | 207 | 5.86 |
| South Blooming Grove (village) Orange County | 192 | 5.83 |
| Aurora (village) Cayuga County | 64 | 5.72 |
| Deferiet (village) Jefferson County | 26 | 5.53 |
| West End (cdp) Otsego County | 86 | 5.50 |

#### Top 10 Places Sorted by Percent of Total Population
*Based on places with total population of 50,000 or more*

| Place | Population | % |
|---|---|---|
| Bronx (borough) Bronx County | 55,928 | 4.10 |
| Rochester (city) Monroe County | 7,909 | 3.73 |
| Mount Vernon (city) Westchester County | 1,910 | 2.85 |
| Brooklyn (borough) Kings County | 63,004 | 2.55 |
| Hempstead (village) Nassau County | 1,285 | 2.41 |
| Buffalo (city) Erie County | 6,085 | 2.29 |
| New York (city) | 175,478 | 2.17 |
| Syracuse (city) Onondaga County | 2,470 | 1.71 |
| Albany (city) Albany County | 1,533 | 1.57 |
| Staten Island (borough) Richmond County | 7,234 | 1.56 |

### African, Sub-Saharan: African

#### Top 10 Places Sorted by Population
*Based on all places, regardless of total population*

| Place | Population | % |
|---|---|---|
| New York (city) | 101,901 | 1.26 |
| Brooklyn (borough) Kings County | 48,168 | 1.95 |
| Bronx (borough) Bronx County | 22,647 | 1.66 |
| Queens (borough) Queens County | 14,083 | 0.64 |
| Manhattan (borough) New York County | 12,839 | 0.81 |
| Rochester (city) Monroe County | 5,828 | 2.75 |
| Buffalo (city) Erie County | 4,177 | 1.57 |
| Staten Island (borough) Richmond County | 4,164 | 0.90 |
| Hempstead (town) Nassau County | 3,879 | 0.51 |
| Brookhaven (town) Suffolk County | 2,533 | 0.53 |

#### Top 10 Places Sorted by Percent of Total Population
*Based on all places, regardless of total population*

| Place | Population | % |
|---|---|---|
| North Bellport (cdp) Suffolk County | 728 | 6.46 |
| Gordon Heights (cdp) Suffolk County | 199 | 6.10 |
| Hobart (village) Delaware County | 29 | 5.99 |
| Wheatley Heights (cdp) Suffolk County | 368 | 5.94 |
| Aurora (village) Cayuga County | 64 | 5.72 |
| Great River (cdp) Suffolk County | 80 | 4.86 |
| St. Regis Mohawk Reservation Franklin County | 134 | 4.28 |
| South Blooming Grove (village) Orange County | 135 | 4.10 |
| Deferiet (village) Jefferson County | 19 | 4.04 |
| Groveland (town) Livingston County | 132 | 3.90 |

#### Top 10 Places Sorted by Percent of Total Population
*Based on places with total population of 50,000 or more*

| Place | Population | % |
|---|---|---|
| Rochester (city) Monroe County | 5,828 | 2.75 |
| Brooklyn (borough) Kings County | 48,168 | 1.95 |
| Mount Vernon (city) Westchester County | 1,162 | 1.73 |
| Bronx (borough) Bronx County | 22,647 | 1.66 |
| Hempstead (village) Nassau County | 850 | 1.59 |
| Buffalo (city) Erie County | 4,177 | 1.57 |
| New York (city) | 101,901 | 1.26 |
| Albany (city) Albany County | 975 | 1.00 |
| Niagara Falls (city) Niagara County | 488 | 0.96 |
| Troy (city) Rensselaer County | 476 | 0.95 |

### African, Sub-Saharan: Cape Verdean

#### Top 10 Places Sorted by Population
*Based on all places, regardless of total population*

| Place | Population | % |
|---|---|---|
| New York (city) | 595 | 0.01 |
| Manhattan (borough) New York County | 206 | 0.01 |
| Brooklyn (borough) Kings County | 153 | 0.01 |
| Queens (borough) Queens County | 117 | 0.01 |
| Bronx (borough) Bronx County | 108 | 0.01 |
| Buffalo (city) Erie County | 95 | 0.04 |
| Yonkers (city) Westchester County | 41 | 0.02 |
| North Elba (town) Essex County | 17 | 0.19 |
| Albany (city) Albany County | 13 | 0.01 |
| Plainview (cdp) Nassau County | 12 | 0.05 |

#### Top 10 Places Sorted by Percent of Total Population
*Based on all places, regardless of total population*

| Place | Population | % |
|---|---|---|
| Liverpool (village) Onondaga County | 9 | 0.38 |
| North Elba (town) Essex County | 17 | 0.19 |
| New Baltimore (town) Greene County | 5 | 0.15 |
| Endwell (cdp) Broome County | 11 | 0.09 |
| Plainview (cdp) Nassau County | 12 | 0.05 |
| Buffalo (city) Erie County | 95 | 0.04 |
| Copiague (cdp) Suffolk County | 9 | 0.04 |
| Jay (town) Essex County | 1 | 0.04 |
| Salina (town) Onondaga County | 9 | 0.03 |
| Yonkers (city) Westchester County | 41 | 0.02 |

#### Top 10 Places Sorted by Percent of Total Population
*Based on places with total population of 50,000 or more*

| Place | Population | % |
|---|---|---|
| Buffalo (city) Erie County | 95 | 0.04 |
| Yonkers (city) Westchester County | 41 | 0.02 |
| Mount Vernon (city) Westchester County | 11 | 0.02 |
| Troy (city) Rensselaer County | 11 | 0.02 |
| Union (town) Broome County | 11 | 0.02 |
| New York (city) | 595 | 0.01 |
| Manhattan (borough) New York County | 206 | 0.01 |
| Brooklyn (borough) Kings County | 153 | 0.01 |
| Queens (borough) Queens County | 117 | 0.01 |
| Bronx (borough) Bronx County | 108 | 0.01 |

### African, Sub-Saharan: Ethiopian

#### Top 10 Places Sorted by Population
*Based on all places, regardless of total population*

| Place | Population | % |
|---|---|---|
| New York (city) | 2,869 | 0.04 |
| Manhattan (borough) New York County | 1,043 | 0.07 |
| Bronx (borough) Bronx County | 945 | 0.07 |
| Queens (borough) Queens County | 505 | 0.02 |
| Brooklyn (borough) Kings County | 330 | 0.01 |
| Rochester (city) Monroe County | 227 | 0.11 |
| Buffalo (city) Erie County | 223 | 0.08 |
| Irondequoit (cdp/town) Monroe County | 192 | 0.37 |
| Henrietta (town) Monroe County | 177 | 0.42 |
| Yonkers (city) Westchester County | 159 | 0.08 |

#### Top 10 Places Sorted by Percent of Total Population
*Based on all places, regardless of total population*

| Place | Population | % |
|---|---|---|
| Lloyd Harbor (village) Suffolk County | 110 | 3.00 |
| Jasper (town) Steuben County | 23 | 1.84 |
| Sparta (town) Livingston County | 27 | 1.62 |
| Deferiet (village) Jefferson County | 7 | 1.49 |
| North Salem (town) Westchester County | 75 | 1.47 |
| Manhasset Hills (cdp) Nassau County | 38 | 1.03 |
| Pomona (village) Rockland County | 31 | 0.88 |
| Elmsford (village) Westchester County | 39 | 0.84 |
| Bedford (town) Westchester County | 117 | 0.67 |
| Athens (village) Greene County | 8 | 0.48 |

#### Top 10 Places Sorted by Percent of Total Population
*Based on places with total population of 50,000 or more*

| Place | Population | % |
|---|---|---|
| Irondequoit (cdp/town) Monroe County | 192 | 0.37 |
| Rochester (city) Monroe County | 227 | 0.11 |
| Buffalo (city) Erie County | 223 | 0.08 |
| Yonkers (city) Westchester County | 159 | 0.08 |
| Manhattan (borough) New York County | 1,043 | 0.07 |
| Bronx (borough) Bronx County | 945 | 0.07 |
| Huntington (town) Suffolk County | 125 | 0.06 |
| Amherst (town) Erie County | 71 | 0.06 |
| Greece (town) Monroe County | 49 | 0.05 |
| Niagara Falls (city) Niagara County | 24 | 0.05 |

## African, Sub-Saharan: Ghanaian

### Top 10 Places Sorted by Population
*Based on all places, regardless of total population*

| Place | Population | % |
|---|---|---|
| New York (city) | 19,782 | 0.24 |
| Bronx (borough) Bronx County | 13,490 | 0.99 |
| Brooklyn (borough) Kings County | 3,898 | 0.16 |
| Queens (borough) Queens County | 1,326 | 0.06 |
| Manhattan (borough) New York County | 818 | 0.05 |
| Yonkers (city) Westchester County | 585 | 0.30 |
| Mount Vernon (city) Westchester County | 347 | 0.52 |
| Hempstead (town) Nassau County | 306 | 0.04 |
| Staten Island (borough) Richmond County | 250 | 0.05 |
| Lakeview (cdp) Nassau County | 169 | 3.03 |

### Top 10 Places Sorted by Percent of Total Population
*Based on all places, regardless of total population*

| Place | Population | % |
|---|---|---|
| Lakeview (cdp) Nassau County | 169 | 3.03 |
| South Blooming Grove (village) Orange County | 57 | 1.73 |
| Coxsackie (village) Greene County | 44 | 1.54 |
| Katonah (cdp) Westchester County | 20 | 1.36 |
| West Haverstraw (village) Rockland County | 108 | 1.07 |
| Wheatley Heights (cdp) Suffolk County | 64 | 1.03 |
| Bronx (borough) Bronx County | 13,490 | 0.99 |
| Hillcrest (cdp) Rockland County | 77 | 0.94 |
| Flower Hill (village) Nassau County | 39 | 0.85 |
| SUNY Oswego (cdp) Oswego County | 30 | 0.67 |

### Top 10 Places Sorted by Percent of Total Population
*Based on places with total population of 50,000 or more*

| Place | Population | % |
|---|---|---|
| Bronx (borough) Bronx County | 13,490 | 0.99 |
| Mount Vernon (city) Westchester County | 347 | 0.52 |
| Yonkers (city) Westchester County | 585 | 0.30 |
| New York (city) | 19,782 | 0.24 |
| Troy (city) Rensselaer County | 91 | 0.18 |
| Brooklyn (borough) Kings County | 3,898 | 0.16 |
| Albany (city) Albany County | 143 | 0.15 |
| Clarkstown (town) Rockland County | 99 | 0.12 |
| Clay (town) Onondaga County | 65 | 0.11 |
| Syracuse (city) Onondaga County | 113 | 0.08 |

## African, Sub-Saharan: Kenyan

### Top 10 Places Sorted by Population
*Based on all places, regardless of total population*

| Place | Population | % |
|---|---|---|
| New York (city) | 344 | <0.01 |
| Yonkers (city) Westchester County | 107 | 0.05 |
| Albany (city) Albany County | 101 | 0.10 |
| Queens (borough) Queens County | 96 | <0.01 |
| Tonawanda (cdp) Erie County | 86 | 0.15 |
| Tonawanda (town) Erie County | 86 | 0.12 |
| West End (cdp) Otsego County | 81 | 5.18 |
| Oneonta (town) Otsego County | 81 | 1.56 |
| Staten Island (borough) Richmond County | 78 | 0.02 |
| Brooklyn (borough) Kings County | 77 | <0.01 |

### Top 10 Places Sorted by Percent of Total Population
*Based on all places, regardless of total population*

| Place | Population | % |
|---|---|---|
| West End (cdp) Otsego County | 81 | 5.18 |
| Oneonta (town) Otsego County | 81 | 1.56 |
| Houghton (cdp) Allegany County | 22 | 1.29 |
| Piermont (village) Rockland County | 32 | 1.27 |
| Caneadea (town) Allegany County | 22 | 0.86 |
| Mount Ivy (cdp) Rockland County | 50 | 0.76 |
| Horseheads (village) Chemung County | 39 | 0.61 |
| Youngstown (village) Niagara County | 8 | 0.42 |
| Hamilton (village) Madison County | 10 | 0.28 |
| Ossining (village) Westchester County | 66 | 0.27 |

### Top 10 Places Sorted by Percent of Total Population
*Based on places with total population of 50,000 or more*

| Place | Population | % |
|---|---|---|
| Tonawanda (cdp) Erie County | 86 | 0.15 |
| Tonawanda (town) Erie County | 86 | 0.12 |
| Schenectady (city) Schenectady County | 69 | 0.11 |
| Albany (city) Albany County | 101 | 0.10 |

| Greenburgh (town) Westchester County | 55 | 0.06 |
| Yonkers (city) Westchester County | 107 | 0.05 |
| New Rochelle (city) Westchester County | 19 | 0.03 |
| Staten Island (borough) Richmond County | 78 | 0.02 |
| Utica (city) Oneida County | 15 | 0.02 |
| Buffalo (city) Erie County | 38 | 0.01 |

## African, Sub-Saharan: Liberian

### Top 10 Places Sorted by Population
*Based on all places, regardless of total population*

| Place | Population | % |
|---|---|---|
| New York (city) | 1,991 | 0.02 |
| Staten Island (borough) Richmond County | 532 | 0.11 |
| Brooklyn (borough) Kings County | 452 | 0.02 |
| Bronx (borough) Bronx County | 450 | 0.03 |
| Queens (borough) Queens County | 381 | 0.02 |
| Babylon (town) Suffolk County | 309 | 0.14 |
| Wheatley Heights (cdp) Suffolk County | 251 | 4.05 |
| Syracuse (city) Onondaga County | 246 | 0.17 |
| Manhattan (borough) New York County | 176 | 0.01 |
| Rochester (city) Monroe County | 89 | 0.04 |

### Top 10 Places Sorted by Percent of Total Population
*Based on all places, regardless of total population*

| Place | Population | % |
|---|---|---|
| Wheatley Heights (cdp) Suffolk County | 251 | 4.05 |
| Copake (town) Columbia County | 16 | 0.45 |
| Wyandanch (cdp) Suffolk County | 33 | 0.30 |
| Smithville (town) Chenango County | 4 | 0.29 |
| Saddle Rock (village) Nassau County | 3 | 0.29 |
| Danby (town) Tompkins County | 9 | 0.28 |
| Port Jervis (city) Orange County | 22 | 0.25 |
| Syracuse (city) Onondaga County | 246 | 0.17 |
| Babylon (town) Suffolk County | 309 | 0.14 |
| Utica (city) Oneida County | 88 | 0.14 |

### Top 10 Places Sorted by Percent of Total Population
*Based on places with total population of 50,000 or more*

| Place | Population | % |
|---|---|---|
| Syracuse (city) Onondaga County | 246 | 0.17 |
| Babylon (town) Suffolk County | 309 | 0.14 |
| Utica (city) Oneida County | 88 | 0.14 |
| Staten Island (borough) Richmond County | 532 | 0.11 |
| Rochester (city) Monroe County | 89 | 0.04 |
| Schenectady (city) Schenectady County | 24 | 0.04 |
| Bronx (borough) Bronx County | 450 | 0.03 |
| Buffalo (city) Erie County | 74 | 0.03 |
| New York (city) | 1,991 | 0.02 |
| Brooklyn (borough) Kings County | 452 | 0.02 |

## African, Sub-Saharan: Nigerian

### Top 10 Places Sorted by Population
*Based on all places, regardless of total population*

| Place | Population | % |
|---|---|---|
| New York (city) | 21,507 | 0.27 |
| Queens (borough) Queens County | 6,304 | 0.29 |
| Brooklyn (borough) Kings County | 6,033 | 0.24 |
| Bronx (borough) Bronx County | 5,538 | 0.41 |
| Manhattan (borough) New York County | 1,953 | 0.12 |
| Staten Island (borough) Richmond County | 1,679 | 0.36 |
| Hempstead (town) Nassau County | 1,115 | 0.15 |
| Babylon (town) Suffolk County | 707 | 0.33 |
| Yonkers (city) Westchester County | 442 | 0.23 |
| Hempstead (village) Nassau County | 427 | 0.80 |

### Top 10 Places Sorted by Percent of Total Population
*Based on all places, regardless of total population*

| Place | Population | % |
|---|---|---|
| Wesley Hills (village) Rockland County | 180 | 3.30 |
| Wheatley Heights (cdp) Suffolk County | 167 | 2.70 |
| Deerpark (town) Orange County | 196 | 2.47 |
| Myers Corner (cdp) Dutchess County | 134 | 2.10 |
| Chester (village) Orange County | 66 | 1.67 |
| Wyandanch (cdp) Suffolk County | 172 | 1.57 |
| North Valley Stream (cdp) Nassau County | 212 | 1.28 |
| Orchard Park (village) Erie County | 41 | 1.26 |
| Rock Hill (cdp) Sullivan County | 20 | 1.21 |
| New Lebanon (town) Columbia County | 29 | 1.17 |

### Top 10 Places Sorted by Percent of Total Population
*Based on places with total population of 50,000 or more*

| Place | Population | % |
|---|---|---|
| Hempstead (village) Nassau County | 427 | 0.80 |
| Bronx (borough) Bronx County | 5,538 | 0.41 |
| Staten Island (borough) Richmond County | 1,679 | 0.36 |
| Babylon (town) Suffolk County | 707 | 0.33 |
| Queens (borough) Queens County | 6,304 | 0.29 |
| Schenectady (city) Schenectady County | 186 | 0.28 |
| New York (city) | 21,507 | 0.27 |
| Greenburgh (town) Westchester County | 231 | 0.26 |
| Brooklyn (borough) Kings County | 6,033 | 0.24 |
| Yonkers (city) Westchester County | 442 | 0.23 |

## African, Sub-Saharan: Senegalese

### Top 10 Places Sorted by Population
*Based on all places, regardless of total population*

| Place | Population | % |
|---|---|---|
| New York (city) | 2,895 | 0.04 |
| Manhattan (borough) New York County | 1,216 | 0.08 |
| Bronx (borough) Bronx County | 1,068 | 0.08 |
| Brooklyn (borough) Kings County | 401 | 0.02 |
| Staten Island (borough) Richmond County | 126 | 0.03 |
| Queens (borough) Queens County | 84 | <0.01 |
| Mahopac (cdp) Putnam County | 64 | 0.84 |
| Carmel (town) Putnam County | 64 | 0.19 |
| Haverstraw (village) Rockland County | 52 | 0.45 |
| Haverstraw (town) Rockland County | 52 | 0.14 |

### Top 10 Places Sorted by Percent of Total Population
*Based on all places, regardless of total population*

| Place | Population | % |
|---|---|---|
| Cattaraugus Reservation Erie County | 18 | 0.96 |
| Mahopac (cdp) Putnam County | 64 | 0.84 |
| Clayton (village) Jefferson County | 17 | 0.83 |
| Haverstraw (village) Rockland County | 52 | 0.45 |
| Sackets Harbor (village) Jefferson County | 6 | 0.44 |
| SUNY Oswego (cdp) Oswego County | 19 | 0.43 |
| Crown Heights (cdp) Dutchess County | 12 | 0.42 |
| Clayton (town) Jefferson County | 17 | 0.34 |
| Oswego (town) Oswego County | 19 | 0.24 |
| Carmel (town) Putnam County | 64 | 0.19 |

### Top 10 Places Sorted by Percent of Total Population
*Based on places with total population of 50,000 or more*

| Place | Population | % |
|---|---|---|
| Manhattan (borough) New York County | 1,216 | 0.08 |
| Bronx (borough) Bronx County | 1,068 | 0.08 |
| New York (city) | 2,895 | 0.04 |
| Staten Island (borough) Richmond County | 126 | 0.03 |
| Brooklyn (borough) Kings County | 401 | 0.02 |
| Mount Vernon (city) Westchester County | 12 | 0.02 |
| Yonkers (city) Westchester County | 21 | 0.01 |
| Queens (borough) Queens County | 84 | <0.01 |
| Albany (city) Albany County | 0 | 0.00 |
| Amherst (town) Erie County | 0 | 0.00 |

## African, Sub-Saharan: Sierra Leonean

### Top 10 Places Sorted by Population
*Based on all places, regardless of total population*

| Place | Population | % |
|---|---|---|
| New York (city) | 1,572 | 0.02 |
| Bronx (borough) Bronx County | 759 | 0.06 |
| Manhattan (borough) New York County | 422 | 0.03 |
| Brooklyn (borough) Kings County | 147 | 0.01 |
| Queens (borough) Queens County | 127 | 0.01 |
| Staten Island (borough) Richmond County | 117 | 0.03 |
| Dryden (town) Tompkins County | 22 | 0.15 |
| Mount Vernon (city) Westchester County | 22 | 0.03 |
| Buffalo (city) Erie County | 17 | 0.01 |
| New Rochelle (city) Westchester County | 15 | 0.02 |

### Top 10 Places Sorted by Percent of Total Population
*Based on all places, regardless of total population*

| Place | Population | % |
|---|---|---|
| Hamilton (village) Madison County | 12 | 0.34 |
| Hamilton (town) Madison County | 12 | 0.18 |
| Manhasset (cdp) Nassau County | 13 | 0.16 |

| Place | Population | % |
|---|---|---|
| Dryden (town) Tompkins County | 22 | 0.15 |
| Bronx (borough) Bronx County | 759 | 0.06 |
| Baldwin (cdp) Nassau County | 11 | 0.05 |
| Manhattan (borough) New York County | 422 | 0.03 |
| Staten Island (borough) Richmond County | 117 | 0.03 |
| Mount Vernon (city) Westchester County | 22 | 0.03 |
| New York (city) | 1,572 | 0.02 |

**Top 10 Places Sorted by Percent of Total Population**
*Based on places with total population of 50,000 or more*

| Place | Population | % |
|---|---|---|
| Bronx (borough) Bronx County | 759 | 0.06 |
| Manhattan (borough) New York County | 422 | 0.03 |
| Staten Island (borough) Richmond County | 117 | 0.03 |
| Mount Vernon (city) Westchester County | 22 | 0.03 |
| New York (city) | 1,572 | 0.02 |
| New Rochelle (city) Westchester County | 15 | 0.02 |
| Greenburgh (town) Westchester County | 14 | 0.02 |
| Brooklyn (borough) Kings County | 147 | 0.01 |
| Queens (borough) Queens County | 127 | 0.01 |
| Buffalo (city) Erie County | 17 | 0.01 |

## African, Sub-Saharan: Somalian

**Top 10 Places Sorted by Population**
*Based on all places, regardless of total population*

| Place | Population | % |
|---|---|---|
| Rochester (city) Monroe County | 980 | 0.46 |
| Buffalo (city) Erie County | 858 | 0.32 |
| New York (city) | 518 | 0.01 |
| Syracuse (city) Onondaga County | 478 | 0.33 |
| Brooklyn (borough) Kings County | 260 | 0.01 |
| Manhattan (borough) New York County | 125 | 0.01 |
| Utica (city) Oneida County | 99 | 0.16 |
| Queens (borough) Queens County | 98 | <0.01 |
| Perinton (town) Monroe County | 38 | 0.08 |
| Newburgh (city) Orange County | 35 | 0.12 |

**Top 10 Places Sorted by Percent of Total Population**
*Based on all places, regardless of total population*

| Place | Population | % |
|---|---|---|
| Rochester (city) Monroe County | 980 | 0.46 |
| Syracuse (city) Onondaga County | 478 | 0.33 |
| Buffalo (city) Erie County | 858 | 0.32 |
| Port Jervis (city) Orange County | 26 | 0.29 |
| Utica (city) Oneida County | 99 | 0.16 |
| Newburgh (city) Orange County | 35 | 0.12 |
| Perinton (town) Monroe County | 38 | 0.08 |
| Uniondale (cdp) Nassau County | 15 | 0.06 |
| New York (city) | 518 | 0.01 |
| Brooklyn (borough) Kings County | 260 | 0.01 |

**Top 10 Places Sorted by Percent of Total Population**
*Based on places with total population of 50,000 or more*

| Place | Population | % |
|---|---|---|
| Rochester (city) Monroe County | 980 | 0.46 |
| Syracuse (city) Onondaga County | 478 | 0.33 |
| Buffalo (city) Erie County | 858 | 0.32 |
| Utica (city) Oneida County | 99 | 0.16 |
| New York (city) | 518 | 0.01 |
| Brooklyn (borough) Kings County | 260 | 0.01 |
| Manhattan (borough) New York County | 125 | 0.01 |
| Queens (borough) Queens County | 98 | <0.01 |
| Bronx (borough) Bronx County | 35 | <0.01 |
| Hempstead (town) Nassau County | 15 | <0.01 |

## African, Sub-Saharan: South African

**Top 10 Places Sorted by Population**
*Based on all places, regardless of total population*

| Place | Population | % |
|---|---|---|
| New York (city) | 2,116 | 0.03 |
| Manhattan (borough) New York County | 1,372 | 0.09 |
| Queens (borough) Queens County | 356 | 0.02 |
| Brooklyn (borough) Kings County | 320 | 0.01 |
| New Rochelle (city) Westchester County | 179 | 0.24 |
| Hempstead (town) Nassau County | 104 | 0.01 |
| Scarsdale (town/village) Westchester County | 80 | 0.47 |
| Cortlandt (town) Westchester County | 80 | 0.20 |
| White Plains (city) Westchester County | 78 | 0.14 |
| Mount Pleasant (town) Westchester County | 77 | 0.18 |

**Top 10 Places Sorted by Percent of Total Population**
*Based on all places, regardless of total population*

| Place | Population | % |
|---|---|---|
| Linwood (cdp) Livingston County | 64 | 48.85 |
| Cape Vincent (village) Jefferson County | 15 | 2.21 |
| York (town) Livingston County | 64 | 1.89 |
| Kinderhook (village) Columbia County | 24 | 1.71 |
| Woodsburgh (village) Nassau County | 10 | 1.34 |
| Rhinebeck (village) Dutchess County | 29 | 1.05 |
| Great Neck Estates (village) Nassau County | 25 | 0.92 |
| Pomona (village) Rockland County | 30 | 0.85 |
| Pelham Manor (village) Westchester County | 43 | 0.79 |
| Orangeburg (cdp) Rockland County | 33 | 0.76 |

**Top 10 Places Sorted by Percent of Total Population**
*Based on places with total population of 50,000 or more*

| Place | Population | % |
|---|---|---|
| New Rochelle (city) Westchester County | 179 | 0.24 |
| White Plains (city) Westchester County | 78 | 0.14 |
| Hamburg (town) Erie County | 57 | 0.10 |
| Manhattan (borough) New York County | 1,372 | 0.09 |
| Ramapo (town) Rockland County | 56 | 0.05 |
| Greece (town) Monroe County | 48 | 0.05 |
| Colonie (town) Albany County | 32 | 0.04 |
| New York (city) | 2,116 | 0.03 |
| Huntington (town) Suffolk County | 63 | 0.03 |
| North Hempstead (town) Nassau County | 63 | 0.03 |

## African, Sub-Saharan: Sudanese

**Top 10 Places Sorted by Population**
*Based on all places, regardless of total population*

| Place | Population | % |
|---|---|---|
| New York (city) | 1,303 | 0.02 |
| Brooklyn (borough) Kings County | 731 | 0.03 |
| Queens (borough) Queens County | 286 | 0.01 |
| Buffalo (city) Erie County | 268 | 0.10 |
| Syracuse (city) Onondaga County | 177 | 0.12 |
| Bronx (borough) Bronx County | 149 | 0.01 |
| Manhattan (borough) New York County | 137 | 0.01 |
| Rochester (city) Monroe County | 107 | 0.05 |
| Greece (town) Monroe County | 51 | 0.05 |
| Brighton (cdp/town) Monroe County | 47 | 0.13 |

**Top 10 Places Sorted by Percent of Total Population**
*Based on all places, regardless of total population*

| Place | Population | % |
|---|---|---|
| Northeast Ithaca (cdp) Tompkins County | 13 | 0.49 |
| Morrisville (village) Madison County | 11 | 0.43 |
| Williamson (town) Wayne County | 21 | 0.30 |
| Eaton (town) Madison County | 11 | 0.21 |
| Portland (town) Chautauqua County | 7 | 0.14 |
| Brighton (cdp/town) Monroe County | 47 | 0.13 |
| Syracuse (city) Onondaga County | 177 | 0.12 |
| Russell (town) St. Lawrence County | 2 | 0.12 |
| Port Washington (cdp) Nassau County | 17 | 0.11 |
| Buffalo (city) Erie County | 268 | 0.10 |

**Top 10 Places Sorted by Percent of Total Population**
*Based on places with total population of 50,000 or more*

| Place | Population | % |
|---|---|---|
| Syracuse (city) Onondaga County | 177 | 0.12 |
| Buffalo (city) Erie County | 268 | 0.10 |
| Troy (city) Rensselaer County | 28 | 0.06 |
| Rochester (city) Monroe County | 107 | 0.05 |
| Greece (town) Monroe County | 51 | 0.05 |
| Brooklyn (borough) Kings County | 731 | 0.03 |
| Albany (city) Albany County | 25 | 0.03 |
| New York (city) | 1,303 | 0.02 |
| Queens (borough) Queens County | 286 | 0.01 |
| Bronx (borough) Bronx County | 149 | 0.01 |

## African, Sub-Saharan: Ugandan

**Top 10 Places Sorted by Population**
*Based on all places, regardless of total population*

| Place | Population | % |
|---|---|---|
| New York (city) | 256 | <0.01 |
| Manhattan (borough) New York County | 125 | 0.01 |
| Spring Valley (village) Rockland County | 86 | 0.28 |

| Place | Population | % |
|---|---|---|
| Ramapo (town) Rockland County | 86 | 0.07 |
| Queens (borough) Queens County | 77 | <0.01 |
| Brooklyn (borough) Kings County | 54 | <0.01 |
| Buffalo (city) Erie County | 33 | 0.01 |
| Syracuse (city) Onondaga County | 26 | 0.02 |
| Ithaca (town) Tompkins County | 24 | 0.12 |
| Mount Vernon (city) Westchester County | 19 | 0.03 |

**Top 10 Places Sorted by Percent of Total Population**
*Based on all places, regardless of total population*

| Place | Population | % |
|---|---|---|
| Hamilton (village) Madison County | 11 | 0.31 |
| Spring Valley (village) Rockland County | 86 | 0.28 |
| Hamilton (town) Madison County | 11 | 0.17 |
| Ithaca (town) Tompkins County | 24 | 0.12 |
| Ramapo (town) Rockland County | 86 | 0.07 |
| Mount Vernon (city) Westchester County | 19 | 0.03 |
| Syracuse (city) Onondaga County | 26 | 0.02 |
| White Plains (city) Westchester County | 9 | 0.02 |
| Manhattan (borough) New York County | 125 | 0.01 |
| Buffalo (city) Erie County | 33 | 0.01 |

**Top 10 Places Sorted by Percent of Total Population**
*Based on places with total population of 50,000 or more*

| Place | Population | % |
|---|---|---|
| Ramapo (town) Rockland County | 86 | 0.07 |
| Mount Vernon (city) Westchester County | 19 | 0.03 |
| Syracuse (city) Onondaga County | 26 | 0.02 |
| White Plains (city) Westchester County | 9 | 0.02 |
| Manhattan (borough) New York County | 125 | 0.01 |
| Buffalo (city) Erie County | 33 | 0.01 |
| New York (city) | 256 | <0.01 |
| Queens (borough) Queens County | 77 | <0.01 |
| Brooklyn (borough) Kings County | 54 | <0.01 |
| Albany (city) Albany County | 0 | 0.00 |

## African, Sub-Saharan: Zimbabwean

**Top 10 Places Sorted by Population**
*Based on all places, regardless of total population*

| Place | Population | % |
|---|---|---|
| New York (city) | 414 | 0.01 |
| Bronx (borough) Bronx County | 108 | 0.01 |
| Queens (borough) Queens County | 107 | <0.01 |
| Manhattan (borough) New York County | 100 | 0.01 |
| Brooklyn (borough) Kings County | 99 | <0.01 |
| Rochester (city) Monroe County | 76 | 0.04 |
| Buffalo (city) Erie County | 45 | 0.02 |
| Callicoon (town) Sullivan County | 40 | 1.30 |
| Oneonta (city) Otsego County | 26 | 0.19 |
| East Ithaca (cdp) Tompkins County | 24 | 1.20 |

**Top 10 Places Sorted by Percent of Total Population**
*Based on all places, regardless of total population*

| Place | Population | % |
|---|---|---|
| Callicoon (town) Sullivan County | 40 | 1.30 |
| East Ithaca (cdp) Tompkins County | 24 | 1.20 |
| Canton (village) St. Lawrence County | 13 | 0.21 |
| Oneonta (city) Otsego County | 26 | 0.19 |
| Ithaca (town) Tompkins County | 24 | 0.12 |
| Canton (town) St. Lawrence County | 13 | 0.12 |
| Rochester (city) Monroe County | 76 | 0.04 |
| Buffalo (city) Erie County | 45 | 0.02 |
| Bethlehem (town) Albany County | 8 | 0.02 |
| New York (city) | 414 | 0.01 |

**Top 10 Places Sorted by Percent of Total Population**
*Based on places with total population of 50,000 or more*

| Place | Population | % |
|---|---|---|
| Rochester (city) Monroe County | 76 | 0.04 |
| Buffalo (city) Erie County | 45 | 0.02 |
| New York (city) | 414 | 0.01 |
| Bronx (borough) Bronx County | 108 | 0.01 |
| Manhattan (borough) New York County | 100 | 0.01 |
| Queens (borough) Queens County | 107 | <0.01 |
| Brooklyn (borough) Kings County | 99 | <0.01 |
| Albany (city) Albany County | 0 | 0.00 |
| Amherst (town) Erie County | 0 | 0.00 |
| Babylon (town) Suffolk County | 0 | 0.00 |

## African, Sub-Saharan: Other

### Top 10 Places Sorted by Population
*Based on all places, regardless of total population*

| Place | Population | % |
|---|---|---|
| New York (city) | 17,415 | 0.22 |
| Bronx (borough) Bronx County | 10,539 | 0.77 |
| Manhattan (borough) New York County | 3,545 | 0.22 |
| Brooklyn (borough) Kings County | 1,881 | 0.08 |
| Queens (borough) Queens County | 1,219 | 0.06 |
| New Rochelle (city) Westchester County | 365 | 0.48 |
| Rochester (city) Monroe County | 309 | 0.15 |
| Hempstead (town) Nassau County | 275 | 0.04 |
| Staten Island (borough) Richmond County | 231 | 0.05 |
| Mount Vernon (city) Westchester County | 180 | 0.27 |

### Top 10 Places Sorted by Percent of Total Population
*Based on all places, regardless of total population*

| Place | Population | % |
|---|---|---|
| South Nyack (village) Rockland County | 105 | 1.89 |
| Pelham (village) Westchester County | 68 | 1.00 |
| Menands (village) Albany County | 36 | 0.90 |
| Woodbury (cdp) Nassau County | 76 | 0.84 |
| West Hempstead (cdp) Nassau County | 143 | 0.78 |
| Bronx (borough) Bronx County | 10,539 | 0.77 |
| Wheatley Heights (cdp) Suffolk County | 46 | 0.74 |
| Pomona (village) Rockland County | 26 | 0.74 |
| Ravena (village) Albany County | 23 | 0.69 |
| Pelham (town) Westchester County | 76 | 0.62 |

### Top 10 Places Sorted by Percent of Total Population
*Based on places with total population of 50,000 or more*

| Place | Population | % |
|---|---|---|
| Bronx (borough) Bronx County | 10,539 | 0.77 |
| New Rochelle (city) Westchester County | 365 | 0.48 |
| Troy (city) Rensselaer County | 159 | 0.32 |
| Mount Vernon (city) Westchester County | 180 | 0.27 |
| New York (city) | 17,415 | 0.22 |
| Manhattan (borough) New York County | 3,545 | 0.22 |
| Schenectady (city) Schenectady County | 133 | 0.20 |
| Rochester (city) Monroe County | 309 | 0.15 |
| Brentwood (cdp) Suffolk County | 80 | 0.15 |
| Amherst (town) Erie County | 170 | 0.14 |

## Albanian

### Top 10 Places Sorted by Population
*Based on all places, regardless of total population*

| Place | Population | % |
|---|---|---|
| New York (city) | 31,056 | 0.38 |
| Staten Island (borough) Richmond County | 8,108 | 1.75 |
| Bronx (borough) Bronx County | 7,835 | 0.57 |
| Brooklyn (borough) Kings County | 6,871 | 0.28 |
| Queens (borough) Queens County | 6,624 | 0.30 |
| Yonkers (city) Westchester County | 2,270 | 1.16 |
| Manhattan (borough) New York County | 1,618 | 0.10 |
| Hempstead (town) Nassau County | 1,052 | 0.14 |
| Yorktown (town) Westchester County | 628 | 1.75 |
| Syracuse (city) Onondaga County | 455 | 0.31 |

### Top 10 Places Sorted by Percent of Total Population
*Based on all places, regardless of total population*

| Place | Population | % |
|---|---|---|
| Yorktown Heights (cdp) Westchester County | 170 | 10.19 |
| Milton (cdp) Ulster County | 101 | 8.68 |
| Shrub Oak (cdp) Westchester County | 134 | 7.40 |
| Brewster Hill (cdp) Putnam County | 91 | 3.78 |
| Monroe (village) Orange County | 310 | 3.73 |
| Saltaire (village) Suffolk County | 2 | 3.45 |
| Farmington (town) Ontario County | 388 | 3.35 |
| Dix (town) Schuyler County | 126 | 3.20 |
| Tivoli (village) Dutchess County | 30 | 3.02 |
| Keene (town) Essex County | 23 | 2.63 |

### Top 10 Places Sorted by Percent of Total Population
*Based on places with total population of 50,000 or more*

| Place | Population | % |
|---|---|---|
| Staten Island (borough) Richmond County | 8,108 | 1.75 |
| Yonkers (city) Westchester County | 2,270 | 1.16 |
| Bronx (borough) Bronx County | 7,835 | 0.57 |
| Colonie (town) Albany County | 405 | 0.50 |

| Place | Population | % |
|---|---|---|
| New Rochelle (city) Westchester County | 370 | 0.49 |
| Mount Vernon (city) Westchester County | 303 | 0.45 |
| Albany (city) Albany County | 384 | 0.39 |
| Clarkstown (town) Rockland County | 328 | 0.39 |
| New York (city) | 31,056 | 0.38 |
| Syracuse (city) Onondaga County | 455 | 0.31 |

## Alsatian

### Top 10 Places Sorted by Population
*Based on all places, regardless of total population*

| Place | Population | % |
|---|---|---|
| New York (city) | 217 | <0.01 |
| Manhattan (borough) New York County | 129 | 0.01 |
| Albany (city) Albany County | 51 | 0.05 |
| New Bremen (town) Lewis County | 50 | 1.85 |
| Orchard Park (town) Erie County | 40 | 0.14 |
| De Witt (town) Onondaga County | 39 | 0.15 |
| Queens (borough) Queens County | 37 | <0.01 |
| Amherst (town) Erie County | 32 | 0.03 |
| Hempstead (town) Nassau County | 30 | <0.01 |
| Hamburg (town) Erie County | 27 | 0.05 |

### Top 10 Places Sorted by Percent of Total Population
*Based on all places, regardless of total population*

| Place | Population | % |
|---|---|---|
| Rifton (cdp) Ulster County | 20 | 3.31 |
| New Bremen (town) Lewis County | 50 | 1.85 |
| Pittsford (village) Monroe County | 12 | 0.85 |
| Gainesville (village) Wyoming County | 2 | 0.75 |
| Wayne (town) Steuben County | 4 | 0.41 |
| Tioga (town) Tioga County | 19 | 0.39 |
| Berne (town) Albany County | 10 | 0.36 |
| East Aurora (village) Erie County | 21 | 0.33 |
| Great Neck Estates (village) Nassau County | 9 | 0.33 |
| Varick (town) Seneca County | 6 | 0.33 |

### Top 10 Places Sorted by Percent of Total Population
*Based on places with total population of 50,000 or more*

| Place | Population | % |
|---|---|---|
| Albany (city) Albany County | 51 | 0.05 |
| Hamburg (town) Erie County | 27 | 0.05 |
| Tonawanda (cdp) Erie County | 24 | 0.04 |
| Amherst (town) Erie County | 32 | 0.03 |
| Tonawanda (town) Erie County | 24 | 0.03 |
| Manhattan (borough) New York County | 129 | 0.01 |
| Staten Island (borough) Richmond County | 24 | 0.01 |
| Islip (town) Suffolk County | 18 | 0.01 |
| New York (city) | 217 | <0.01 |
| Queens (borough) Queens County | 37 | <0.01 |

## American

### Top 10 Places Sorted by Population
*Based on all places, regardless of total population*

| Place | Population | % |
|---|---|---|
| New York (city) | 209,430 | 2.59 |
| Brooklyn (borough) Kings County | 78,858 | 3.20 |
| Manhattan (borough) New York County | 54,694 | 3.45 |
| Queens (borough) Queens County | 45,604 | 2.07 |
| Hempstead (town) Nassau County | 23,869 | 3.17 |
| Bronx (borough) Bronx County | 16,297 | 1.19 |
| Staten Island (borough) Richmond County | 13,977 | 3.02 |
| Brookhaven (town) Suffolk County | 10,016 | 2.09 |
| Oyster Bay (town) Nassau County | 9,798 | 3.36 |
| North Hempstead (town) Nassau County | 7,110 | 3.18 |

### Top 10 Places Sorted by Percent of Total Population
*Based on all places, regardless of total population*

| Place | Population | % |
|---|---|---|
| Cumminsville (cdp) Livingston County | 59 | 50.86 |
| Northumberland (town) Saratoga County | 1,519 | 30.31 |
| Durham (town) Greene County | 815 | 29.96 |
| Ashland (town) Greene County | 182 | 29.74 |
| Schuylerville (village) Saratoga County | 441 | 29.72 |
| Hadley (cdp) Saratoga County | 284 | 29.04 |
| Lodi (village) Seneca County | 137 | 28.84 |
| Victory (village) Saratoga County | 154 | 27.21 |
| Cranberry Lake (cdp) St. Lawrence County | 51 | 26.84 |
| Hadley (town) Saratoga County | 462 | 26.81 |

### Top 10 Places Sorted by Percent of Total Population
*Based on places with total population of 50,000 or more*

| Place | Population | % |
|---|---|---|
| Clarkstown (town) Rockland County | 4,138 | 4.96 |
| White Plains (city) Westchester County | 2,743 | 4.91 |
| Schenectady (city) Schenectady County | 3,124 | 4.78 |
| Ramapo (town) Rockland County | 5,092 | 4.15 |
| Union (town) Broome County | 2,180 | 3.87 |
| Greenburgh (town) Westchester County | 3,324 | 3.79 |
| Manhattan (borough) New York County | 54,694 | 3.45 |
| Clay (town) Onondaga County | 1,975 | 3.40 |
| Oyster Bay (town) Nassau County | 9,798 | 3.36 |
| New Rochelle (city) Westchester County | 2,542 | 3.35 |

## Arab: Total

### Top 10 Places Sorted by Population
*Based on all places, regardless of total population*

| Place | Population | % |
|---|---|---|
| New York (city) | 82,165 | 1.02 |
| Brooklyn (borough) Kings County | 34,840 | 1.41 |
| Queens (borough) Queens County | 19,669 | 0.89 |
| Manhattan (borough) New York County | 13,828 | 0.87 |
| Staten Island (borough) Richmond County | 8,820 | 1.90 |
| Bronx (borough) Bronx County | 5,008 | 0.37 |
| Hempstead (town) Nassau County | 4,218 | 0.56 |
| Yonkers (city) Westchester County | 3,210 | 1.65 |
| North Hempstead (town) Nassau County | 2,078 | 0.93 |
| Buffalo (city) Erie County | 1,815 | 0.68 |

### Top 10 Places Sorted by Percent of Total Population
*Based on all places, regardless of total population*

| Place | Population | % |
|---|---|---|
| Clark Mills (cdp) Oneida County | 109 | 9.71 |
| Lackawanna (city) Erie County | 1,753 | 9.61 |
| Crown Point (town) Essex County | 167 | 8.06 |
| Saddle Rock (village) Nassau County | 74 | 7.06 |
| Hewlett Bay Park (village) Nassau County | 33 | 6.36 |
| Ravena (village) Albany County | 200 | 6.03 |
| Deerfield (town) Oneida County | 230 | 5.48 |
| Tannersville (village) Greene County | 22 | 5.07 |
| Northwest Ithaca (cdp) Tompkins County | 56 | 4.85 |
| New York Mills (village) Oneida County | 161 | 4.77 |

### Top 10 Places Sorted by Percent of Total Population
*Based on places with total population of 50,000 or more*

| Place | Population | % |
|---|---|---|
| Utica (city) Oneida County | 1,558 | 2.52 |
| Staten Island (borough) Richmond County | 8,820 | 1.90 |
| Yonkers (city) Westchester County | 3,210 | 1.65 |
| Brooklyn (borough) Kings County | 34,840 | 1.41 |
| Amherst (town) Erie County | 1,530 | 1.27 |
| Colonie (town) Albany County | 863 | 1.06 |
| New York (city) | 82,165 | 1.02 |
| Cheektowaga (town) Erie County | 905 | 1.02 |
| North Hempstead (town) Nassau County | 2,078 | 0.93 |
| Queens (borough) Queens County | 19,669 | 0.89 |

## Arab: Arab

### Top 10 Places Sorted by Population
*Based on all places, regardless of total population*

| Place | Population | % |
|---|---|---|
| New York (city) | 15,160 | 0.19 |
| Brooklyn (borough) Kings County | 7,609 | 0.31 |
| Queens (borough) Queens County | 2,283 | 0.10 |
| Staten Island (borough) Richmond County | 1,829 | 0.39 |
| Manhattan (borough) New York County | 1,720 | 0.11 |
| Bronx (borough) Bronx County | 1,719 | 0.13 |
| Lackawanna (city) Erie County | 1,331 | 7.30 |
| Yonkers (city) Westchester County | 1,036 | 0.53 |
| Buffalo (city) Erie County | 644 | 0.24 |
| Henrietta (town) Monroe County | 321 | 0.76 |

### Top 10 Places Sorted by Percent of Total Population
*Based on all places, regardless of total population*

| Place | Population | % |
|---|---|---|
| Lackawanna (city) Erie County | 1,331 | 7.30 |
| Brinckerhoff (cdp) Dutchess County | 101 | 3.13 |
| Millbrook (village) Dutchess County | 48 | 2.94 |

| Place | | Population | % |
|---|---|---|---|
| Clark Mills (cdp) Oneida County | | 32 | 2.85 |
| Morristown (town) St. Lawrence County | | 71 | 2.59 |
| New Scotland (town) Albany County | | 209 | 2.41 |
| Orange (town) Schuyler County | | 43 | 2.41 |
| Cherry Valley (village) Otsego County | | 10 | 2.27 |
| Spencerport (village) Monroe County | | 72 | 2.02 |
| Hudson (city) Columbia County | | 127 | 1.85 |

### Top 10 Places Sorted by Percent of Total Population
*Based on places with total population of 50,000 or more*

| Place | Population | % |
|---|---|---|
| Yonkers (city) Westchester County | 1,036 | 0.53 |
| Staten Island (borough) Richmond County | 1,829 | 0.39 |
| Utica (city) Oneida County | 198 | 0.32 |
| Brooklyn (borough) Kings County | 7,609 | 0.31 |
| Cheektowaga (cdp) Erie County | 224 | 0.30 |
| Cheektowaga (town) Erie County | 247 | 0.28 |
| New Rochelle (city) Westchester County | 187 | 0.25 |
| Buffalo (city) Erie County | 644 | 0.24 |
| Clay (town) Onondaga County | 136 | 0.23 |
| Ramapo (town) Rockland County | 245 | 0.20 |

## Arab: Egyptian

### Top 10 Places Sorted by Population
*Based on all places, regardless of total population*

| Place | Population | % |
|---|---|---|
| New York (city) | 17,698 | 0.22 |
| Queens (borough) Queens County | 6,551 | 0.30 |
| Brooklyn (borough) Kings County | 5,231 | 0.21 |
| Staten Island (borough) Richmond County | 3,292 | 0.71 |
| Manhattan (borough) New York County | 1,906 | 0.12 |
| Hempstead (town) Nassau County | 1,227 | 0.16 |
| Bronx (borough) Bronx County | 718 | 0.05 |
| North Hempstead (town) Nassau County | 529 | 0.24 |
| Brookhaven (town) Suffolk County | 435 | 0.09 |
| Huntington (town) Suffolk County | 425 | 0.21 |

### Top 10 Places Sorted by Percent of Total Population
*Based on all places, regardless of total population*

| Place | Population | % |
|---|---|---|
| Callicoon (town) Sullivan County | 125 | 4.05 |
| Oakdale (cdp) Suffolk County | 220 | 2.87 |
| Orange Lake (cdp) Orange County | 183 | 2.68 |
| Deerfield (town) Oneida County | 110 | 2.62 |
| Northwest Ithaca (cdp) Tompkins County | 28 | 2.43 |
| Woodmere (cdp) Nassau County | 418 | 2.39 |
| Gordon Heights (cdp) Suffolk County | 76 | 2.33 |
| Woodridge (village) Sullivan County | 20 | 2.23 |
| Carlisle (town) Schoharie County | 40 | 2.15 |
| Herricks (cdp) Nassau County | 75 | 1.91 |

### Top 10 Places Sorted by Percent of Total Population
*Based on places with total population of 50,000 or more*

| Place | Population | % |
|---|---|---|
| Staten Island (borough) Richmond County | 3,292 | 0.71 |
| Queens (borough) Queens County | 6,551 | 0.30 |
| Clarkstown (town) Rockland County | 254 | 0.30 |
| Levittown (cdp) Nassau County | 136 | 0.25 |
| North Hempstead (town) Nassau County | 529 | 0.24 |
| New York (city) | 17,698 | 0.22 |
| Brooklyn (borough) Kings County | 5,231 | 0.21 |
| Huntington (town) Suffolk County | 425 | 0.21 |
| Hempstead (town) Nassau County | 1,227 | 0.16 |
| Colonie (town) Albany County | 125 | 0.15 |

## Arab: Iraqi

### Top 10 Places Sorted by Population
*Based on all places, regardless of total population*

| Place | Population | % |
|---|---|---|
| New York (city) | 1,137 | 0.01 |
| Manhattan (borough) New York County | 583 | 0.04 |
| North Hempstead (town) Nassau County | 500 | 0.22 |
| Queens (borough) Queens County | 315 | 0.01 |
| Buffalo (city) Erie County | 288 | 0.11 |
| Hempstead (town) Nassau County | 284 | 0.04 |
| Dix Hills (cdp) Suffolk County | 166 | 0.63 |
| Huntington (town) Suffolk County | 166 | 0.08 |
| Brooklyn (borough) Kings County | 134 | 0.01 |
| West Hempstead (cdp) Nassau County | 112 | 0.61 |

### Top 10 Places Sorted by Percent of Total Population
*Based on all places, regardless of total population*

| Place | Population | % |
|---|---|---|
| Saddle Rock (village) Nassau County | 46 | 4.39 |
| Kensington (village) Nassau County | 28 | 2.32 |
| Herricks (cdp) Nassau County | 86 | 2.18 |
| Water Mill (cdp) Suffolk County | 28 | 1.83 |
| Great Neck Gardens (cdp) Nassau County | 16 | 1.76 |
| Hewlett (cdp) Nassau County | 94 | 1.40 |
| Sands Point (village) Nassau County | 33 | 1.24 |
| Middleburgh (town) Schoharie County | 46 | 1.23 |
| Atlantic Beach (village) Nassau County | 21 | 1.13 |
| East Hills (village) Nassau County | 71 | 1.04 |

### Top 10 Places Sorted by Percent of Total Population
*Based on places with total population of 50,000 or more*

| Place | Population | % |
|---|---|---|
| North Hempstead (town) Nassau County | 500 | 0.22 |
| Buffalo (city) Erie County | 288 | 0.11 |
| Huntington (town) Suffolk County | 166 | 0.08 |
| Smithtown (town) Suffolk County | 89 | 0.08 |
| Yonkers (city) Westchester County | 103 | 0.05 |
| Southampton (town) Suffolk County | 28 | 0.05 |
| Manhattan (borough) New York County | 583 | 0.04 |
| Hempstead (town) Nassau County | 284 | 0.04 |
| Ramapo (town) Rockland County | 48 | 0.04 |
| Cheektowaga (cdp) Erie County | 30 | 0.04 |

## Arab: Jordanian

### Top 10 Places Sorted by Population
*Based on all places, regardless of total population*

| Place | Population | % |
|---|---|---|
| New York (city) | 1,298 | 0.02 |
| Yonkers (city) Westchester County | 907 | 0.47 |
| Brooklyn (borough) Kings County | 752 | 0.03 |
| Queens (borough) Queens County | 307 | 0.01 |
| Poughkeepsie (town) Dutchess County | 223 | 0.51 |
| Hyde Park (town) Dutchess County | 204 | 0.94 |
| Staten Island (borough) Richmond County | 183 | 0.04 |
| Brookhaven (town) Suffolk County | 178 | 0.04 |
| La Grange (town) Dutchess County | 175 | 1.12 |
| Niagara (town) Niagara County | 149 | 1.77 |

### Top 10 Places Sorted by Percent of Total Population
*Based on all places, regardless of total population*

| Place | Population | % |
|---|---|---|
| Fairview (cdp) Dutchess County | 108 | 2.32 |
| Niagara (town) Niagara County | 149 | 1.77 |
| Fremont (town) Sullivan County | 20 | 1.62 |
| Putnam Lake (cdp) Putnam County | 52 | 1.42 |
| Woodbury (village) Orange County | 126 | 1.20 |
| Liberty (town) Sullivan County | 117 | 1.18 |
| Woodbury (town) Orange County | 126 | 1.14 |
| La Grange (town) Dutchess County | 175 | 1.12 |
| Baywood (cdp) Suffolk County | 82 | 1.04 |
| Hyde Park (town) Dutchess County | 204 | 0.94 |

### Top 10 Places Sorted by Percent of Total Population
*Based on places with total population of 50,000 or more*

| Place | Population | % |
|---|---|---|
| Yonkers (city) Westchester County | 907 | 0.47 |
| Amherst (town) Erie County | 84 | 0.07 |
| New Rochelle (city) Westchester County | 46 | 0.06 |
| Smithtown (town) Suffolk County | 54 | 0.05 |
| Greenburgh (town) Westchester County | 45 | 0.05 |
| Staten Island (borough) Richmond County | 183 | 0.04 |
| Brookhaven (town) Suffolk County | 178 | 0.04 |
| Islip (town) Suffolk County | 122 | 0.04 |
| White Plains (city) Westchester County | 21 | 0.04 |
| Brooklyn (borough) Kings County | 752 | 0.03 |

## Arab: Lebanese

### Top 10 Places Sorted by Population
*Based on all places, regardless of total population*

| Place | Population | % |
|---|---|---|
| New York (city) | 11,682 | 0.14 |
| Brooklyn (borough) Kings County | 4,757 | 0.19 |
| Manhattan (borough) New York County | 3,331 | 0.21 |

| Place | | Population | % |
|---|---|---|---|
| Queens (borough) Queens County | | 2,228 | 0.10 |
| Staten Island (borough) Richmond County | | 1,019 | 0.22 |
| Amherst (town) Erie County | | 985 | 0.81 |
| Utica (city) Oneida County | | 947 | 1.53 |
| Hempstead (town) Nassau County | | 657 | 0.09 |
| Whitestown (town) Oneida County | | 495 | 2.66 |
| Buffalo (city) Erie County | | 481 | 0.18 |

### Top 10 Places Sorted by Percent of Total Population
*Based on all places, regardless of total population*

| Place | Population | % |
|---|---|---|
| Clark Mills (cdp) Oneida County | 65 | 5.79 |
| Crown Point (town) Essex County | 94 | 4.54 |
| New York Mills (village) Oneida County | 145 | 4.30 |
| Lewiston (village) Niagara County | 105 | 3.88 |
| Williamsville (village) Erie County | 177 | 3.33 |
| Yorkville (village) Oneida County | 76 | 2.83 |
| Vernon (town) Oneida County | 144 | 2.68 |
| Whitestown (town) Oneida County | 495 | 2.66 |
| Lacona (village) Oswego County | 16 | 2.63 |
| Pultneyville (cdp) Wayne County | 20 | 2.61 |

### Top 10 Places Sorted by Percent of Total Population
*Based on places with total population of 50,000 or more*

| Place | Population | % |
|---|---|---|
| Utica (city) Oneida County | 947 | 1.53 |
| Amherst (town) Erie County | 985 | 0.81 |
| Tonawanda (cdp) Erie County | 401 | 0.68 |
| Tonawanda (town) Erie County | 428 | 0.58 |
| Troy (city) Rensselaer County | 270 | 0.54 |
| Cheektowaga (cdp) Erie County | 338 | 0.45 |
| Niagara Falls (city) Niagara County | 228 | 0.45 |
| Cheektowaga (town) Erie County | 350 | 0.39 |
| Clay (town) Onondaga County | 213 | 0.37 |
| Colonie (town) Albany County | 267 | 0.33 |

## Arab: Moroccan

### Top 10 Places Sorted by Population
*Based on all places, regardless of total population*

| Place | Population | % |
|---|---|---|
| New York (city) | 8,987 | 0.11 |
| Queens (borough) Queens County | 3,459 | 0.16 |
| Brooklyn (borough) Kings County | 2,648 | 0.11 |
| Manhattan (borough) New York County | 1,592 | 0.10 |
| Bronx (borough) Bronx County | 667 | 0.05 |
| Staten Island (borough) Richmond County | 621 | 0.13 |
| Hempstead (town) Nassau County | 376 | 0.05 |
| Ramapo (town) Rockland County | 291 | 0.24 |
| Lindenhurst (village) Suffolk County | 209 | 0.76 |
| Babylon (town) Suffolk County | 209 | 0.10 |

### Top 10 Places Sorted by Percent of Total Population
*Based on all places, regardless of total population*

| Place | Population | % |
|---|---|---|
| Northwest Ithaca (cdp) Tompkins County | 28 | 2.43 |
| Philmont (village) Columbia County | 24 | 2.07 |
| Tupper Lake (village) Franklin County | 68 | 1.77 |
| South Valley Stream (cdp) Nassau County | 76 | 1.44 |
| Airmont (village) Rockland County | 109 | 1.29 |
| Brookville (village) Nassau County | 43 | 1.24 |
| Wheeler (town) Steuben County | 14 | 1.19 |
| Tupper Lake (town) Franklin County | 68 | 1.13 |
| Mechanicville (city) Saratoga County | 58 | 1.12 |
| Gouverneur (village) St. Lawrence County | 44 | 1.10 |

### Top 10 Places Sorted by Percent of Total Population
*Based on places with total population of 50,000 or more*

| Place | Population | % |
|---|---|---|
| Ramapo (town) Rockland County | 291 | 0.24 |
| Queens (borough) Queens County | 3,459 | 0.16 |
| Colonie (town) Albany County | 111 | 0.14 |
| Staten Island (borough) Richmond County | 621 | 0.13 |
| White Plains (city) Westchester County | 71 | 0.13 |
| New York (city) | 8,987 | 0.11 |
| Brooklyn (borough) Kings County | 2,648 | 0.11 |
| Manhattan (borough) New York County | 1,592 | 0.10 |
| Babylon (town) Suffolk County | 209 | 0.10 |
| Mount Vernon (city) Westchester County | 64 | 0.10 |

## Arab: Palestinian

### Top 10 Places Sorted by Population
*Based on all places, regardless of total population*

| Place | Population | % |
|---|---|---|
| New York (city) | 3,421 | 0.04 |
| Brooklyn (borough) Kings County | 1,482 | 0.06 |
| Manhattan (borough) New York County | 794 | 0.05 |
| Queens (borough) Queens County | 638 | 0.03 |
| Staten Island (borough) Richmond County | 479 | 0.10 |
| Ravena (village) Albany County | 200 | 6.03 |
| Coeymans (town) Albany County | 200 | 2.63 |
| Poughkeepsie (town) Dutchess County | 183 | 0.42 |
| Islip (town) Suffolk County | 166 | 0.05 |
| Yonkers (city) Westchester County | 139 | 0.07 |

### Top 10 Places Sorted by Percent of Total Population
*Based on all places, regardless of total population*

| Place | Population | % |
|---|---|---|
| Ravena (village) Albany County | 200 | 6.03 |
| Crown Point (town) Essex County | 70 | 3.38 |
| Coeymans (town) Albany County | 200 | 2.63 |
| Van Etten (town) Chemung County | 18 | 1.43 |
| Roslyn (village) Nassau County | 35 | 1.28 |
| Stuyvesant (town) Columbia County | 24 | 1.19 |
| Oakfield (village) Genesee County | 22 | 1.07 |
| Silver Creek (village) Chautauqua County | 23 | 0.86 |
| Farmingdale (village) Nassau County | 58 | 0.71 |
| Oakfield (town) Genesee County | 22 | 0.68 |

### Top 10 Places Sorted by Percent of Total Population
*Based on places with total population of 50,000 or more*

| Place | Population | % |
|---|---|---|
| Staten Island (borough) Richmond County | 479 | 0.10 |
| Colonie (town) Albany County | 72 | 0.09 |
| Yonkers (city) Westchester County | 139 | 0.07 |
| Brooklyn (borough) Kings County | 1,482 | 0.06 |
| Manhattan (borough) New York County | 794 | 0.05 |
| Islip (town) Suffolk County | 166 | 0.05 |
| Babylon (town) Suffolk County | 114 | 0.05 |
| Syracuse (city) Onondaga County | 66 | 0.05 |
| New York (city) | 3,421 | 0.04 |
| Union (town) Broome County | 25 | 0.04 |

## Arab: Syrian

### Top 10 Places Sorted by Population
*Based on all places, regardless of total population*

| Place | Population | % |
|---|---|---|
| New York (city) | 8,198 | 0.10 |
| Brooklyn (borough) Kings County | 5,890 | 0.24 |
| Manhattan (borough) New York County | 1,112 | 0.07 |
| Staten Island (borough) Richmond County | 584 | 0.13 |
| Hempstead (town) Nassau County | 512 | 0.07 |
| Queens (borough) Queens County | 420 | 0.02 |
| New Hartford (town) Oneida County | 351 | 1.60 |
| Utica (city) Oneida County | 248 | 0.40 |
| Brookhaven (town) Suffolk County | 220 | 0.05 |
| Bronx (borough) Bronx County | 192 | 0.01 |

### Top 10 Places Sorted by Percent of Total Population
*Based on all places, regardless of total population*

| Place | Population | % |
|---|---|---|
| Tannersville (village) Greene County | 22 | 5.07 |
| Chautauqua (cdp) Chautauqua County | 12 | 4.55 |
| Mountain Lodge Park (cdp) Orange County | 74 | 3.98 |
| Manchester (village) Ontario County | 46 | 2.86 |
| Beaver Dam Lake (cdp) Orange County | 55 | 2.01 |
| Fort Montgomery (cdp) Orange County | 17 | 1.99 |
| Taylor (town) Cortland County | 11 | 1.98 |
| West Glens Falls (cdp) Warren County | 126 | 1.90 |
| Chadwicks (cdp) Oneida County | 22 | 1.84 |
| Fillmore (cdp) Allegany County | 10 | 1.63 |

### Top 10 Places Sorted by Percent of Total Population
*Based on places with total population of 50,000 or more*

| Place | Population | % |
|---|---|---|
| Utica (city) Oneida County | 248 | 0.40 |
| Brooklyn (borough) Kings County | 5,890 | 0.24 |
| Colonie (town) Albany County | 116 | 0.14 |
| Staten Island (borough) Richmond County | 584 | 0.13 |

| Place | Population | % |
|---|---|---|
| Greenburgh (town) Westchester County | 107 | 0.12 |
| Albany (city) Albany County | 104 | 0.11 |
| Clarkstown (town) Rockland County | 88 | 0.11 |
| New York (city) | 8,198 | 0.10 |
| Greece (town) Monroe County | 97 | 0.10 |
| Niagara Falls (city) Niagara County | 44 | 0.09 |

## Arab: Other

### Top 10 Places Sorted by Population
*Based on all places, regardless of total population*

| Place | Population | % |
|---|---|---|
| New York (city) | 14,584 | 0.18 |
| Brooklyn (borough) Kings County | 6,337 | 0.26 |
| Queens (borough) Queens County | 3,468 | 0.16 |
| Manhattan (borough) New York County | 2,742 | 0.17 |
| Bronx (borough) Bronx County | 1,256 | 0.09 |
| Staten Island (borough) Richmond County | 781 | 0.17 |
| Hempstead (town) Nassau County | 664 | 0.09 |
| North Hempstead (town) Nassau County | 571 | 0.26 |
| Binghamton (city) Broome County | 521 | 1.10 |
| Lackawanna (city) Erie County | 402 | 2.20 |

### Top 10 Places Sorted by Percent of Total Population
*Based on all places, regardless of total population*

| Place | Population | % |
|---|---|---|
| Hewlett Bay Park (village) Nassau County | 26 | 5.01 |
| Gates (cdp) Monroe County | 256 | 4.76 |
| Saddle Rock (village) Nassau County | 28 | 2.67 |
| Lackawanna (city) Erie County | 402 | 2.20 |
| St. Regis Mohawk Reservation Franklin County | 65 | 2.07 |
| Depew (village) Erie County | 303 | 1.96 |
| Kings Point (village) Nassau County | 92 | 1.85 |
| Roslyn Heights (cdp) Nassau County | 107 | 1.65 |
| Mill Neck (village) Nassau County | 13 | 1.61 |
| Sands Point (village) Nassau County | 41 | 1.54 |

### Top 10 Places Sorted by Percent of Total Population
*Based on places with total population of 50,000 or more*

| Place | Population | % |
|---|---|---|
| Cheektowaga (town) Erie County | 244 | 0.27 |
| Brooklyn (borough) Kings County | 6,337 | 0.26 |
| North Hempstead (town) Nassau County | 571 | 0.26 |
| Amherst (town) Erie County | 270 | 0.22 |
| Mount Vernon (city) Westchester County | 148 | 0.22 |
| Colonie (town) Albany County | 155 | 0.19 |
| New York (city) | 14,584 | 0.18 |
| Rochester (city) Monroe County | 390 | 0.18 |
| Manhattan (borough) New York County | 2,742 | 0.17 |
| Staten Island (borough) Richmond County | 781 | 0.17 |

## Armenian

### Top 10 Places Sorted by Population
*Based on all places, regardless of total population*

| Place | Population | % |
|---|---|---|
| New York (city) | 10,159 | 0.13 |
| Queens (borough) Queens County | 4,658 | 0.21 |
| Manhattan (borough) New York County | 2,653 | 0.17 |
| Brooklyn (borough) Kings County | 2,300 | 0.09 |
| Hempstead (town) Nassau County | 1,451 | 0.19 |
| Oyster Bay (town) Nassau County | 1,383 | 0.47 |
| Brookhaven (town) Suffolk County | 643 | 0.13 |
| North Hempstead (town) Nassau County | 631 | 0.28 |
| Huntington (town) Suffolk County | 525 | 0.26 |
| Troy (city) Rensselaer County | 418 | 0.84 |

### Top 10 Places Sorted by Percent of Total Population
*Based on all places, regardless of total population*

| Place | Population | % |
|---|---|---|
| Harbor Hills (cdp) Nassau County | 67 | 13.54 |
| Tannersville (village) Greene County | 34 | 7.83 |
| Duane Lake (cdp) Schenectady County | 16 | 6.61 |
| Pine Hill (cdp) Ulster County | 13 | 5.06 |
| Pleasant Valley (cdp) Dutchess County | 41 | 4.95 |
| Boylston (town) Oswego County | 19 | 3.98 |
| Hewlett (cdp) Nassau County | 264 | 3.92 |
| Munsey Park (village) Nassau County | 103 | 3.87 |
| Pittsford (village) Monroe County | 52 | 3.70 |
| Chenango Bridge (cdp) Broome County | 106 | 3.48 |

### Top 10 Places Sorted by Percent of Total Population
*Based on places with total population of 50,000 or more*

| Place | Population | % |
|---|---|---|
| Troy (city) Rensselaer County | 418 | 0.84 |
| Oyster Bay (town) Nassau County | 1,383 | 0.47 |
| Niagara Falls (city) Niagara County | 156 | 0.31 |
| Colonie (town) Albany County | 244 | 0.30 |
| North Hempstead (town) Nassau County | 631 | 0.28 |
| Huntington (town) Suffolk County | 525 | 0.26 |
| Queens (borough) Queens County | 4,658 | 0.21 |
| Yonkers (city) Westchester County | 411 | 0.21 |
| Greenburgh (town) Westchester County | 175 | 0.20 |
| Hempstead (town) Nassau County | 1,451 | 0.19 |

## Assyrian/Chaldean/Syriac

### Top 10 Places Sorted by Population
*Based on all places, regardless of total population*

| Place | Population | % |
|---|---|---|
| New York (city) | 227 | <0.01 |
| Yonkers (city) Westchester County | 157 | 0.08 |
| Manhattan (borough) New York County | 137 | 0.01 |
| Clarkstown (town) Rockland County | 51 | 0.06 |
| Cortlandt (town) Westchester County | 45 | 0.11 |
| Brooklyn (borough) Kings County | 44 | <0.01 |
| Congers (cdp) Rockland County | 34 | 0.43 |
| Greenburgh (town) Westchester County | 29 | 0.03 |
| Peekskill (city) Westchester County | 26 | 0.11 |
| North Hempstead (town) Nassau County | 21 | 0.01 |

### Top 10 Places Sorted by Percent of Total Population
*Based on all places, regardless of total population*

| Place | Population | % |
|---|---|---|
| Tuxedo Park (village) Orange County | 3 | 0.50 |
| Congers (cdp) Rockland County | 34 | 0.43 |
| Plandome Heights (village) Nassau County | 4 | 0.38 |
| Cuyler (town) Cortland County | 3 | 0.33 |
| Fairfield (town) Herkimer County | 5 | 0.30 |
| New Paltz (village) Ulster County | 8 | 0.12 |
| East Williston (village) Nassau County | 3 | 0.12 |
| Cortlandt (town) Westchester County | 45 | 0.11 |
| Peekskill (city) Westchester County | 26 | 0.11 |
| Yonkers (city) Westchester County | 157 | 0.08 |

### Top 10 Places Sorted by Percent of Total Population
*Based on places with total population of 50,000 or more*

| Place | Population | % |
|---|---|---|
| Yonkers (city) Westchester County | 157 | 0.08 |
| Clarkstown (town) Rockland County | 51 | 0.06 |
| Greenburgh (town) Westchester County | 29 | 0.03 |
| Manhattan (borough) New York County | 137 | 0.01 |
| North Hempstead (town) Nassau County | 21 | 0.01 |
| White Plains (city) Westchester County | 8 | 0.01 |
| New York (city) | 227 | <0.01 |
| Brooklyn (borough) Kings County | 44 | <0.01 |
| Hempstead (town) Nassau County | 19 | <0.01 |
| Bronx (borough) Bronx County | 18 | <0.01 |

## Australian

### Top 10 Places Sorted by Population
*Based on all places, regardless of total population*

| Place | Population | % |
|---|---|---|
| New York (city) | 3,906 | 0.05 |
| Manhattan (borough) New York County | 2,719 | 0.17 |
| Brooklyn (borough) Kings County | 832 | 0.03 |
| Queens (borough) Queens County | 285 | 0.01 |
| Hempstead (town) Nassau County | 236 | 0.03 |
| Huntington (town) Suffolk County | 101 | 0.05 |
| Islip (town) Suffolk County | 100 | 0.03 |
| Scarsdale (town/village) Westchester County | 96 | 0.56 |
| Putnam Valley (town) Putnam County | 90 | 0.77 |
| Albany (city) Albany County | 88 | 0.09 |

### Top 10 Places Sorted by Percent of Total Population
*Based on all places, regardless of total population*

| Place | Population | % |
|---|---|---|
| Cape Vincent (village) Jefferson County | 13 | 1.91 |
| Galway (village) Saratoga County | 2 | 1.85 |
| Newport (village) Herkimer County | 9 | 1.84 |

*Please refer to the Explanation of Data in the front of the book for more detailed information.*

| Place | Population | % |
|---|---|---|
| Andes (cdp) Delaware County | 5 | 1.80 |
| Bovina (town) Delaware County | 9 | 1.76 |
| Marlboro (cdp) Ulster County | 63 | 1.57 |
| Windham (town) Greene County | 25 | 1.50 |
| Ovid (village) Seneca County | 7 | 1.47 |
| Alexandria Bay (village) Jefferson County | 14 | 1.28 |
| Hagaman (village) Montgomery County | 11 | 1.04 |

### Top 10 Places Sorted by Percent of Total Population
*Based on places with total population of 50,000 or more*

| Place | Population | % |
|---|---|---|
| Manhattan (borough) New York County | 2,719 | 0.17 |
| Niagara Falls (city) Niagara County | 49 | 0.10 |
| Albany (city) Albany County | 88 | 0.09 |
| Greece (town) Monroe County | 87 | 0.09 |
| Ramapo (town) Rockland County | 86 | 0.07 |
| Southampton (town) Suffolk County | 38 | 0.07 |
| New York (city) | 3,906 | 0.05 |
| Huntington (town) Suffolk County | 101 | 0.05 |
| Tonawanda (cdp) Erie County | 29 | 0.05 |
| North Hempstead (town) Nassau County | 80 | 0.04 |

## Austrian

### Top 10 Places Sorted by Population
*Based on all places, regardless of total population*

| Place | Population | % |
|---|---|---|
| New York (city) | 30,712 | 0.38 |
| Manhattan (borough) New York County | 14,656 | 0.93 |
| Queens (borough) Queens County | 7,523 | 0.34 |
| Brooklyn (borough) Kings County | 5,123 | 0.21 |
| Hempstead (town) Nassau County | 4,963 | 0.66 |
| Oyster Bay (town) Nassau County | 3,412 | 1.17 |
| Brookhaven (town) Suffolk County | 2,867 | 0.60 |
| North Hempstead (town) Nassau County | 2,782 | 1.24 |
| Islip (town) Suffolk County | 2,019 | 0.61 |
| Huntington (town) Suffolk County | 2,004 | 0.99 |

### Top 10 Places Sorted by Percent of Total Population
*Based on all places, regardless of total population*

| Place | Population | % |
|---|---|---|
| West Hampton Dunes (village) Suffolk County | 8 | 18.60 |
| Harbor Hills (cdp) Nassau County | 50 | 10.10 |
| Great Neck Gardens (cdp) Nassau County | 64 | 7.05 |
| Saltaire (village) Suffolk County | 4 | 6.90 |
| Palenville (cdp) Greene County | 70 | 6.17 |
| Islip Terrace (cdp) Suffolk County | 353 | 6.15 |
| Cuylerville (cdp) Livingston County | 25 | 5.76 |
| High Falls (cdp) Ulster County | 45 | 5.23 |
| Ocean Beach (village) Suffolk County | 6 | 5.22 |
| Golden's Bridge (cdp) Westchester County | 86 | 4.81 |

### Top 10 Places Sorted by Percent of Total Population
*Based on places with total population of 50,000 or more*

| Place | Population | % |
|---|---|---|
| Greenburgh (town) Westchester County | 1,117 | 1.27 |
| North Hempstead (town) Nassau County | 2,782 | 1.24 |
| Oyster Bay (town) Nassau County | 3,412 | 1.17 |
| Southampton (town) Suffolk County | 621 | 1.10 |
| Ramapo (town) Rockland County | 1,328 | 1.08 |
| White Plains (city) Westchester County | 572 | 1.02 |
| Huntington (town) Suffolk County | 2,004 | 0.99 |
| Clarkstown (town) Rockland County | 827 | 0.99 |
| Manhattan (borough) New York County | 14,656 | 0.93 |
| Amherst (town) Erie County | 1,014 | 0.84 |

## Basque

### Top 10 Places Sorted by Population
*Based on all places, regardless of total population*

| Place | Population | % |
|---|---|---|
| New York (city) | 902 | 0.01 |
| Manhattan (borough) New York County | 428 | 0.03 |
| Queens (borough) Queens County | 159 | 0.01 |
| Brooklyn (borough) Kings County | 129 | 0.01 |
| North Hempstead (town) Nassau County | 121 | 0.05 |
| Bronx (borough) Bronx County | 109 | 0.01 |
| Staten Island (borough) Richmond County | 77 | 0.02 |
| Mineola (village) Nassau County | 54 | 0.29 |
| Hempstead (town) Nassau County | 43 | 0.01 |
| Croton-on-Hudson (village) Westchester County | 42 | 0.53 |

### Top 10 Places Sorted by Percent of Total Population
*Based on all places, regardless of total population*

| Place | Population | % |
|---|---|---|
| Platekill (cdp) Ulster County | 15 | 1.09 |
| East Williston (village) Nassau County | 17 | 0.67 |
| Gardiner (town) Ulster County | 35 | 0.62 |
| Williston Park (village) Nassau County | 39 | 0.54 |
| Croton-on-Hudson (village) Westchester County | 42 | 0.53 |
| Fort Edward (village) Washington County | 13 | 0.39 |
| Mill Neck (village) Nassau County | 3 | 0.37 |
| Waterford (village) Saratoga County | 7 | 0.34 |
| Arlington (cdp) Dutchess County | 13 | 0.31 |
| Austerlitz (town) Columbia County | 4 | 0.31 |

### Top 10 Places Sorted by Percent of Total Population
*Based on places with total population of 50,000 or more*

| Place | Population | % |
|---|---|---|
| North Hempstead (town) Nassau County | 121 | 0.05 |
| Manhattan (borough) New York County | 428 | 0.03 |
| Levittown (cdp) Nassau County | 16 | 0.03 |
| Staten Island (borough) Richmond County | 77 | 0.02 |
| New Rochelle (city) Westchester County | 12 | 0.02 |
| New York (city) | 902 | 0.01 |
| Queens (borough) Queens County | 159 | 0.01 |
| Brooklyn (borough) Kings County | 129 | 0.01 |
| Bronx (borough) Bronx County | 109 | 0.01 |
| Hempstead (town) Nassau County | 43 | 0.01 |

## Belgian

### Top 10 Places Sorted by Population
*Based on all places, regardless of total population*

| Place | Population | % |
|---|---|---|
| New York (city) | 4,472 | 0.06 |
| Manhattan (borough) New York County | 2,470 | 0.16 |
| Brooklyn (borough) Kings County | 1,012 | 0.04 |
| Ramapo (town) Rockland County | 751 | 0.61 |
| Queens (borough) Queens County | 593 | 0.03 |
| Hempstead (town) Nassau County | 405 | 0.05 |
| Brookhaven (town) Suffolk County | 401 | 0.08 |
| Monsey (cdp) Rockland County | 400 | 2.66 |
| Islip (town) Suffolk County | 328 | 0.10 |
| Staten Island (borough) Richmond County | 266 | 0.06 |

### Top 10 Places Sorted by Percent of Total Population
*Based on all places, regardless of total population*

| Place | Population | % |
|---|---|---|
| DeKalb Junction (cdp) St. Lawrence County | 41 | 12.58 |
| Sheldon (town) Wyoming County | 82 | 3.77 |
| New Square (village) Rockland County | 225 | 3.48 |
| Odessa (village) Schuyler County | 18 | 3.43 |
| Wallkill (cdp) Ulster County | 75 | 3.18 |
| Westport (town) Essex County | 14 | 3.11 |
| Strykersville (cdp) Wyoming County | 14 | 2.78 |
| Cold Spring (village) Putnam County | 47 | 2.77 |
| Tuscarora Nation Reservation Niagara County | 27 | 2.68 |
| Monsey (cdp) Rockland County | 400 | 2.66 |

### Top 10 Places Sorted by Percent of Total Population
*Based on places with total population of 50,000 or more*

| Place | Population | % |
|---|---|---|
| Ramapo (town) Rockland County | 751 | 0.61 |
| Greece (town) Monroe County | 254 | 0.27 |
| Irondequoit (cdp/town) Monroe County | 93 | 0.18 |
| White Plains (city) Westchester County | 94 | 0.17 |
| Manhattan (borough) New York County | 2,470 | 0.16 |
| New Rochelle (city) Westchester County | 118 | 0.16 |
| Clay (town) Onondaga County | 68 | 0.12 |
| Greenburgh (town) Westchester County | 93 | 0.11 |
| Islip (town) Suffolk County | 328 | 0.10 |
| Rochester (city) Monroe County | 185 | 0.09 |

## Brazilian

### Top 10 Places Sorted by Population
*Based on all places, regardless of total population*

| Place | Population | % |
|---|---|---|
| New York (city) | 13,119 | 0.16 |
| Queens (borough) Queens County | 6,175 | 0.28 |
| Manhattan (borough) New York County | 4,541 | 0.29 |

| Place | Population | % |
|---|---|---|
| Mount Vernon (city) Westchester County | 2,013 | 3.00 |
| Brooklyn (borough) Kings County | 1,719 | 0.07 |
| Rye (town) Westchester County | 929 | 2.05 |
| Islip (town) Suffolk County | 895 | 0.27 |
| Port Chester (village) Westchester County | 803 | 2.81 |
| New Rochelle (city) Westchester County | 728 | 0.96 |
| North Hempstead (town) Nassau County | 613 | 0.27 |

### Top 10 Places Sorted by Percent of Total Population
*Based on all places, regardless of total population*

| Place | Population | % |
|---|---|---|
| Three Mile Bay (cdp) Jefferson County | 21 | 9.95 |
| Saddle Rock Estates (cdp) Nassau County | 33 | 6.30 |
| Sagaponack (village) Suffolk County | 11 | 4.30 |
| West Sand Lake (cdp) Rensselaer County | 101 | 3.85 |
| Mount Vernon (city) Westchester County | 2,013 | 3.00 |
| Port Chester (village) Westchester County | 803 | 2.81 |
| University at Buffalo (cdp) Erie County | 156 | 2.77 |
| Flanders (cdp) Suffolk County | 120 | 2.66 |
| Napanoch (cdp) Ulster County | 24 | 2.26 |
| Cragsmoor (cdp) Ulster County | 8 | 2.22 |

### Top 10 Places Sorted by Percent of Total Population
*Based on places with total population of 50,000 or more*

| Place | Population | % |
|---|---|---|
| Mount Vernon (city) Westchester County | 2,013 | 3.00 |
| New Rochelle (city) Westchester County | 728 | 0.96 |
| White Plains (city) Westchester County | 440 | 0.79 |
| Brentwood (cdp) Suffolk County | 418 | 0.76 |
| Southampton (town) Suffolk County | 289 | 0.51 |
| Schenectady (city) Schenectady County | 194 | 0.30 |
| Manhattan (borough) New York County | 4,541 | 0.29 |
| Queens (borough) Queens County | 6,175 | 0.28 |
| Islip (town) Suffolk County | 895 | 0.27 |
| North Hempstead (town) Nassau County | 613 | 0.27 |

## British

### Top 10 Places Sorted by Population
*Based on all places, regardless of total population*

| Place | Population | % |
|---|---|---|
| New York (city) | 21,065 | 0.26 |
| Manhattan (borough) New York County | 12,129 | 0.77 |
| Brooklyn (borough) Kings County | 4,749 | 0.19 |
| Queens (borough) Queens County | 2,457 | 0.11 |
| Brookhaven (town) Suffolk County | 1,235 | 0.26 |
| Hempstead (town) Nassau County | 1,197 | 0.16 |
| Bronx (borough) Bronx County | 1,115 | 0.08 |
| Huntington (town) Suffolk County | 840 | 0.42 |
| Buffalo (city) Erie County | 722 | 0.27 |
| North Hempstead (town) Nassau County | 705 | 0.32 |

### Top 10 Places Sorted by Percent of Total Population
*Based on all places, regardless of total population*

| Place | Population | % |
|---|---|---|
| Pierrepont Manor (cdp) Jefferson County | 28 | 22.95 |
| Salisbury Mills (cdp) Orange County | 36 | 12.33 |
| Gorham (cdp) Ontario County | 47 | 8.08 |
| Chazy (cdp) Clinton County | 34 | 6.71 |
| Montague (town) Lewis County | 6 | 6.12 |
| New Suffolk (cdp) Suffolk County | 10 | 5.32 |
| Prattsburgh (cdp) Steuben County | 29 | 4.07 |
| Old Forge (cdp) Herkimer County | 20 | 3.88 |
| Poquott (village) Suffolk County | 45 | 3.85 |
| Burke (village) Franklin County | 7 | 3.85 |

### Top 10 Places Sorted by Percent of Total Population
*Based on places with total population of 50,000 or more*

| Place | Population | % |
|---|---|---|
| Manhattan (borough) New York County | 12,129 | 0.77 |
| Southampton (town) Suffolk County | 404 | 0.71 |
| Greenburgh (town) Westchester County | 519 | 0.59 |
| Union (town) Broome County | 250 | 0.44 |
| Huntington (town) Suffolk County | 840 | 0.42 |
| Greece (town) Monroe County | 387 | 0.41 |
| Troy (city) Rensselaer County | 207 | 0.41 |
| Irondequoit (cdp/town) Monroe County | 189 | 0.37 |
| Amherst (town) Erie County | 438 | 0.36 |
| North Hempstead (town) Nassau County | 705 | 0.32 |

## Bulgarian

### Top 10 Places Sorted by Population
*Based on all places, regardless of total population*

| Place | Population | % |
|---|---|---|
| **New York** (city) | 5,011 | 0.06 |
| **Queens** (borough) Queens County | 2,090 | 0.10 |
| **Manhattan** (borough) New York County | 1,272 | 0.08 |
| **Brooklyn** (borough) Kings County | 1,128 | 0.05 |
| **Bronx** (borough) Bronx County | 521 | 0.04 |
| **Buffalo** (city) Erie County | 201 | 0.08 |
| **Hamburg** (town) Erie County | 192 | 0.34 |
| **Hempstead** (town) Nassau County | 181 | 0.02 |
| **West Hempstead** (cdp) Nassau County | 142 | 0.77 |
| **Brookhaven** (town) Suffolk County | 128 | 0.03 |

### Top 10 Places Sorted by Percent of Total Population
*Based on all places, regardless of total population*

| Place | Population | % |
|---|---|---|
| **Bedford Hills** (cdp) Westchester County | 99 | 3.04 |
| **Wales** (town) Erie County | 81 | 2.72 |
| **Fairfield** (town) Herkimer County | 42 | 2.49 |
| **Pembroke** (town) Genesee County | 83 | 1.92 |
| **Maybrook** (village) Orange County | 44 | 1.48 |
| **Crompond** (cdp) Westchester County | 26 | 1.27 |
| **Walden** (village) Orange County | 82 | 1.19 |
| **Hilton** (village) Monroe County | 69 | 1.18 |
| **Glasco** (cdp) Ulster County | 22 | 0.95 |
| **Mayfield** (village) Fulton County | 8 | 0.92 |

### Top 10 Places Sorted by Percent of Total Population
*Based on places with total population of 50,000 or more*

| Place | Population | % |
|---|---|---|
| **Hamburg** (town) Erie County | 192 | 0.34 |
| **White Plains** (city) Westchester County | 62 | 0.11 |
| **Queens** (borough) Queens County | 2,090 | 0.10 |
| **Manhattan** (borough) New York County | 1,272 | 0.08 |
| **Buffalo** (city) Erie County | 201 | 0.08 |
| **Amherst** (town) Erie County | 98 | 0.08 |
| **Cheektowaga** (town) Erie County | 73 | 0.08 |
| **New York** (city) | 5,011 | 0.06 |
| **Greenburgh** (town) Westchester County | 54 | 0.06 |
| **Brooklyn** (borough) Kings County | 1,128 | 0.05 |

## Cajun

### Top 10 Places Sorted by Population
*Based on all places, regardless of total population*

| Place | Population | % |
|---|---|---|
| **New York** (city) | 432 | 0.01 |
| **Manhattan** (borough) New York County | 224 | 0.01 |
| **Brooklyn** (borough) Kings County | 175 | 0.01 |
| **Catskill** (village) Greene County | 62 | 1.50 |
| **Catskill** (town) Greene County | 62 | 0.52 |
| **West Point** (cdp) Orange County | 54 | 0.57 |
| **Highlands** (town) Orange County | 54 | 0.43 |
| **Poughkeepsie** (city) Dutchess County | 41 | 0.13 |
| **Oyster Bay** (town) Nassau County | 37 | 0.01 |
| **Queens** (borough) Queens County | 33 | <0.01 |

### Top 10 Places Sorted by Percent of Total Population
*Based on all places, regardless of total population*

| Place | Population | % |
|---|---|---|
| **Catskill** (village) Greene County | 62 | 1.50 |
| **Madrid** (cdp) St. Lawrence County | 6 | 0.82 |
| **Brownville** (village) Jefferson County | 8 | 0.76 |
| **West Point** (cdp) Orange County | 54 | 0.57 |
| **Elma Center** (cdp) Erie County | 15 | 0.55 |
| **East Ithaca** (cdp) Tompkins County | 11 | 0.55 |
| **Catskill** (town) Greene County | 62 | 0.52 |
| **Chazy** (town) Clinton County | 21 | 0.49 |
| **West Sayville** (cdp) Suffolk County | 23 | 0.44 |
| **Kings Point** (village) Nassau County | 22 | 0.44 |

### Top 10 Places Sorted by Percent of Total Population
*Based on places with total population of 50,000 or more*

| Place | Population | % |
|---|---|---|
| **Syracuse** (city) Onondaga County | 24 | 0.02 |
| **Union** (town) Broome County | 12 | 0.02 |
| **New York** (city) | 432 | 0.01 |
| **Manhattan** (borough) New York County | 224 | 0.01 |

| Place | Population | % |
|---|---|---|
| **Brooklyn** (borough) Kings County | 175 | 0.01 |
| **Oyster Bay** (town) Nassau County | 37 | 0.01 |
| **Islip** (town) Suffolk County | 23 | 0.01 |
| **North Hempstead** (town) Nassau County | 22 | 0.01 |
| **Huntington** (town) Suffolk County | 19 | 0.01 |
| **Queens** (borough) Queens County | 33 | <0.01 |

## Canadian

### Top 10 Places Sorted by Population
*Based on all places, regardless of total population*

| Place | Population | % |
|---|---|---|
| **New York** (city) | 10,989 | 0.14 |
| **Manhattan** (borough) New York County | 5,646 | 0.36 |
| **Brooklyn** (borough) Kings County | 3,116 | 0.13 |
| **Queens** (borough) Queens County | 1,308 | 0.06 |
| **Hempstead** (town) Nassau County | 1,084 | 0.14 |
| **Brookhaven** (town) Suffolk County | 999 | 0.21 |
| **Huntington** (town) Suffolk County | 743 | 0.37 |
| **Ramapo** (town) Rockland County | 680 | 0.55 |
| **Amherst** (town) Erie County | 589 | 0.49 |
| **Babylon** (town) Suffolk County | 581 | 0.27 |

### Top 10 Places Sorted by Percent of Total Population
*Based on all places, regardless of total population*

| Place | Population | % |
|---|---|---|
| **Fishers Landing** (cdp) Jefferson County | 10 | 18.87 |
| **Natural Bridge** (cdp) Jefferson County | 58 | 14.36 |
| **La Fargeville** (cdp) Jefferson County | 99 | 14.14 |
| **Cumminsville** (cdp) Livingston County | 9 | 7.76 |
| **Orleans** (town) Jefferson County | 164 | 6.09 |
| **Chateaugay** (village) Franklin County | 31 | 5.54 |
| **Birdsall** (town) Allegany County | 17 | 5.54 |
| **Waddington** (village) St. Lawrence County | 37 | 5.13 |
| **Richville** (village) St. Lawrence County | 15 | 5.12 |
| **Machias** (cdp) Cattaraugus County | 37 | 5.08 |

### Top 10 Places Sorted by Percent of Total Population
*Based on places with total population of 50,000 or more*

| Place | Population | % |
|---|---|---|
| **Niagara Falls** (city) Niagara County | 442 | 0.87 |
| **Irondequoit** (cdp/town) Monroe County | 419 | 0.81 |
| **Hamburg** (town) Erie County | 368 | 0.65 |
| **Clay** (town) Onondaga County | 345 | 0.59 |
| **Ramapo** (town) Rockland County | 680 | 0.55 |
| **Greece** (town) Monroe County | 525 | 0.55 |
| **Amherst** (town) Erie County | 589 | 0.49 |
| **Tonawanda** (cdp) Erie County | 288 | 0.49 |
| **Tonawanda** (town) Erie County | 312 | 0.42 |
| **Colonie** (town) Albany County | 321 | 0.39 |

## Carpatho Rusyn

### Top 10 Places Sorted by Population
*Based on all places, regardless of total population*

| Place | Population | % |
|---|---|---|
| **New York** (city) | 249 | <0.01 |
| **Manhattan** (borough) New York County | 112 | 0.01 |
| **Union** (town) Broome County | 101 | 0.18 |
| **Staten Island** (borough) Richmond County | 63 | 0.01 |
| **Brooklyn** (borough) Kings County | 53 | <0.01 |
| **Yonkers** (city) Westchester County | 40 | 0.02 |
| **Johnson City** (village) Broome County | 39 | 0.26 |
| **Hempstead** (town) Nassau County | 36 | <0.01 |
| **Oswego** (town) Oswego County | 28 | 0.35 |
| **Hauppauge** (cdp) Suffolk County | 26 | 0.12 |

### Top 10 Places Sorted by Percent of Total Population
*Based on all places, regardless of total population*

| Place | Population | % |
|---|---|---|
| **Shenorock** (cdp) Westchester County | 20 | 1.02 |
| **New Hartford** (village) Oneida County | 15 | 0.78 |
| **Stewart Manor** (village) Nassau County | 13 | 0.60 |
| **Gang Mills** (cdp) Steuben County | 23 | 0.55 |
| **Oswego** (town) Oswego County | 28 | 0.35 |
| **North Salem** (town) Westchester County | 18 | 0.35 |
| **Erwin** (town) Steuben County | 23 | 0.29 |
| **Johnson City** (village) Broome County | 39 | 0.26 |
| **Fairview** (cdp) Dutchess County | 10 | 0.22 |
| **Persia** (town) Cattaraugus County | 5 | 0.20 |

### Top 10 Places Sorted by Percent of Total Population
*Based on places with total population of 50,000 or more*

| Place | Population | % |
|---|---|---|
| **Union** (town) Broome County | 101 | 0.18 |
| **Niagara Falls** (city) Niagara County | 14 | 0.03 |
| **Yonkers** (city) Westchester County | 40 | 0.02 |
| **Smithtown** (town) Suffolk County | 26 | 0.02 |
| **Tonawanda** (town) Erie County | 13 | 0.02 |
| **Manhattan** (borough) New York County | 112 | 0.01 |
| **Staten Island** (borough) Richmond County | 63 | 0.01 |
| **Huntington** (town) Suffolk County | 20 | 0.01 |
| **Albany** (city) Albany County | 12 | 0.01 |
| **Cheektowaga** (cdp) Erie County | 6 | 0.01 |

## Celtic

### Top 10 Places Sorted by Population
*Based on all places, regardless of total population*

| Place | Population | % |
|---|---|---|
| **New York** (city) | 564 | 0.01 |
| **Manhattan** (borough) New York County | 304 | 0.02 |
| **Queens** (borough) Queens County | 169 | 0.01 |
| **Hornell** (city) Steuben County | 102 | 1.18 |
| **Huntington** (town) Suffolk County | 65 | 0.03 |
| **Babylon** (town) Suffolk County | 64 | 0.03 |
| **Oyster Bay** (town) Nassau County | 55 | 0.02 |
| **Islip** (town) Suffolk County | 53 | 0.02 |
| **Williston Park** (village) Nassau County | 48 | 0.66 |
| **North Hempstead** (town) Nassau County | 48 | 0.02 |

### Top 10 Places Sorted by Percent of Total Population
*Based on all places, regardless of total population*

| Place | Population | % |
|---|---|---|
| **Napanoch** (cdp) Ulster County | 25 | 2.35 |
| **North Lynbrook** (cdp) Nassau County | 13 | 1.75 |
| **Katonah** (cdp) Westchester County | 22 | 1.50 |
| **Lewis** (town) Essex County | 18 | 1.41 |
| **St. Armand** (town) Essex County | 17 | 1.33 |
| **Cayuga** (village) Cayuga County | 6 | 1.32 |
| **Hornell** (city) Steuben County | 102 | 1.18 |
| **Clinton** (town) Dutchess County | 45 | 1.05 |
| **Chesterfield** (town) Essex County | 25 | 1.04 |
| **Delanson** (village) Schenectady County | 3 | 1.02 |

### Top 10 Places Sorted by Percent of Total Population
*Based on places with total population of 50,000 or more*

| Place | Population | % |
|---|---|---|
| **Clay** (town) Onondaga County | 47 | 0.08 |
| **Hamburg** (town) Erie County | 43 | 0.08 |
| **Union** (town) Broome County | 27 | 0.05 |
| **Troy** (city) Rensselaer County | 23 | 0.05 |
| **Huntington** (town) Suffolk County | 65 | 0.03 |
| **Babylon** (town) Suffolk County | 64 | 0.03 |
| **Schenectady** (city) Schenectady County | 20 | 0.03 |
| **Utica** (city) Oneida County | 16 | 0.03 |
| **Irondequoit** (cdp/town) Monroe County | 14 | 0.03 |
| **Manhattan** (borough) New York County | 304 | 0.02 |

## Croatian

### Top 10 Places Sorted by Population
*Based on all places, regardless of total population*

| Place | Population | % |
|---|---|---|
| **New York** (city) | 11,304 | 0.14 |
| **Queens** (borough) Queens County | 7,054 | 0.32 |
| **Manhattan** (borough) New York County | 2,164 | 0.14 |
| **Hempstead** (town) Nassau County | 1,033 | 0.14 |
| **Oyster Bay** (town) Nassau County | 1,002 | 0.34 |
| **Brooklyn** (borough) Kings County | 998 | 0.04 |
| **Staten Island** (borough) Richmond County | 869 | 0.19 |
| **Huntington** (town) Suffolk County | 781 | 0.39 |
| **North Hempstead** (town) Nassau County | 672 | 0.30 |
| **Greenburgh** (town) Westchester County | 609 | 0.69 |

### Top 10 Places Sorted by Percent of Total Population
*Based on all places, regardless of total population*

| Place | Population | % |
|---|---|---|
| **Castorland** (village) Lewis County | 21 | 5.44 |
| **North Lynbrook** (cdp) Nassau County | 30 | 4.04 |
| **Pleasantville** (village) Westchester County | 276 | 3.93 |

| Place | Population | % |
|---|---|---|
| Irvington (village) Westchester County | 245 | 3.82 |
| Halesite (cdp) Suffolk County | 78 | 3.70 |
| Rockland (town) Sullivan County | 124 | 3.22 |
| Herricks (cdp) Nassau County | 126 | 3.20 |
| Palenville (cdp) Greene County | 31 | 2.73 |
| Strykersville (cdp) Wyoming County | 13 | 2.58 |
| North Sea (cdp) Suffolk County | 133 | 2.57 |

### Top 10 Places Sorted by Percent of Total Population
*Based on places with total population of 50,000 or more*

| Place | Population | % |
|---|---|---|
| Greenburgh (town) Westchester County | 609 | 0.69 |
| Tonawanda (town) Erie County | 326 | 0.44 |
| Hamburg (town) Erie County | 246 | 0.43 |
| Southampton (town) Suffolk County | 227 | 0.40 |
| Huntington (town) Suffolk County | 781 | 0.39 |
| Tonawanda (cdp) Erie County | 219 | 0.37 |
| Oyster Bay (town) Nassau County | 1,002 | 0.34 |
| Queens (borough) Queens County | 7,054 | 0.32 |
| Amherst (town) Erie County | 393 | 0.32 |
| North Hempstead (town) Nassau County | 672 | 0.30 |

## Cypriot

### Top 10 Places Sorted by Population
*Based on all places, regardless of total population*

| Place | Population | % |
|---|---|---|
| New York (city) | 960 | 0.01 |
| Queens (borough) Queens County | 644 | 0.03 |
| Hempstead (town) Nassau County | 254 | 0.03 |
| Manhattan (borough) New York County | 216 | 0.01 |
| Oceanside (cdp) Nassau County | 90 | 0.29 |
| Huntington (town) Suffolk County | 82 | 0.04 |
| Valley Stream (village) Nassau County | 68 | 0.18 |
| Franklin Square (cdp) Nassau County | 67 | 0.23 |
| Yorktown (town) Westchester County | 65 | 0.18 |
| North Hempstead (town) Nassau County | 64 | 0.03 |

### Top 10 Places Sorted by Percent of Total Population
*Based on all places, regardless of total population*

| Place | Population | % |
|---|---|---|
| Hillside (cdp) Ulster County | 8 | 1.06 |
| Eatons Neck (cdp) Suffolk County | 12 | 0.89 |
| Clarence Center (cdp) Erie County | 17 | 0.79 |
| Hewlett Harbor (village) Nassau County | 7 | 0.60 |
| Greenlawn (cdp) Suffolk County | 56 | 0.43 |
| Laurel Hollow (village) Nassau County | 8 | 0.42 |
| Balmville (cdp) Orange County | 13 | 0.39 |
| Muttontown (village) Nassau County | 13 | 0.38 |
| Lake Grove (village) Suffolk County | 39 | 0.35 |
| Roslyn (village) Nassau County | 9 | 0.33 |

### Top 10 Places Sorted by Percent of Total Population
*Based on places with total population of 50,000 or more*

| Place | Population | % |
|---|---|---|
| Huntington (town) Suffolk County | 82 | 0.04 |
| Queens (borough) Queens County | 644 | 0.03 |
| Hempstead (town) Nassau County | 254 | 0.03 |
| North Hempstead (town) Nassau County | 64 | 0.03 |
| Oyster Bay (town) Nassau County | 63 | 0.02 |
| Hempstead (village) Nassau County | 9 | 0.02 |
| New York (city) | 960 | 0.01 |
| Manhattan (borough) New York County | 216 | 0.01 |
| Brookhaven (town) Suffolk County | 51 | 0.01 |
| Islip (town) Suffolk County | 25 | 0.01 |

## Czech

### Top 10 Places Sorted by Population
*Based on all places, regardless of total population*

| Place | Population | % |
|---|---|---|
| New York (city) | 12,800 | 0.16 |
| Manhattan (borough) New York County | 4,820 | 0.30 |
| Queens (borough) Queens County | 3,464 | 0.16 |
| Brooklyn (borough) Kings County | 3,393 | 0.14 |
| Brookhaven (town) Suffolk County | 3,121 | 0.65 |
| Hempstead (town) Nassau County | 2,447 | 0.32 |
| Islip (town) Suffolk County | 2,026 | 0.61 |
| Oyster Bay (town) Nassau County | 1,379 | 0.47 |
| Huntington (town) Suffolk County | 1,271 | 0.63 |
| Union (town) Broome County | 929 | 1.65 |

### Top 10 Places Sorted by Percent of Total Population
*Based on all places, regardless of total population*

| Place | Population | % |
|---|---|---|
| West Hampton Dunes (village) Suffolk County | 6 | 13.95 |
| Durhamville (cdp) Oneida County | 61 | 10.61 |
| Pleasant Valley (cdp) Dutchess County | 83 | 10.01 |
| Lakeville (cdp) Livingston County | 42 | 6.98 |
| Shoreham (village) Suffolk County | 45 | 6.73 |
| Andes (cdp) Delaware County | 16 | 5.76 |
| Summerhill (town) Cayuga County | 59 | 5.20 |
| Boylston (town) Oswego County | 24 | 5.03 |
| Constantia (cdp) Oswego County | 72 | 4.77 |
| Williamson (cdp) Wayne County | 103 | 4.33 |

### Top 10 Places Sorted by Percent of Total Population
*Based on places with total population of 50,000 or more*

| Place | Population | % |
|---|---|---|
| Union (town) Broome County | 929 | 1.65 |
| Brookhaven (town) Suffolk County | 3,121 | 0.65 |
| Huntington (town) Suffolk County | 1,271 | 0.63 |
| Islip (town) Suffolk County | 2,026 | 0.61 |
| Smithtown (town) Suffolk County | 692 | 0.59 |
| Colonie (town) Albany County | 453 | 0.56 |
| Clay (town) Onondaga County | 312 | 0.54 |
| Greece (town) Monroe County | 507 | 0.53 |
| New Rochelle (city) Westchester County | 402 | 0.53 |
| Oyster Bay (town) Nassau County | 1,379 | 0.47 |

## Czechoslovakian

### Top 10 Places Sorted by Population
*Based on all places, regardless of total population*

| Place | Population | % |
|---|---|---|
| New York (city) | 4,870 | 0.06 |
| Brooklyn (borough) Kings County | 1,684 | 0.07 |
| Queens (borough) Queens County | 1,467 | 0.07 |
| Manhattan (borough) New York County | 1,256 | 0.08 |
| Hempstead (town) Nassau County | 1,054 | 0.14 |
| Brookhaven (town) Suffolk County | 917 | 0.19 |
| Ramapo (town) Rockland County | 654 | 0.53 |
| Oyster Bay (town) Nassau County | 618 | 0.21 |
| Islip (town) Suffolk County | 596 | 0.18 |
| North Hempstead (town) Nassau County | 493 | 0.22 |

### Top 10 Places Sorted by Percent of Total Population
*Based on all places, regardless of total population*

| Place | Population | % |
|---|---|---|
| Smallwood (cdp) Sullivan County | 145 | 21.08 |
| Ellisburg (village) Jefferson County | 17 | 6.75 |
| Yorkshire (cdp) Cattaraugus County | 75 | 5.96 |
| Walker Valley (cdp) Ulster County | 28 | 5.22 |
| Kensington (village) Nassau County | 56 | 4.65 |
| Greenville (cdp) Greene County | 34 | 3.91 |
| Bethel (town) Sullivan County | 156 | 3.62 |
| Preston-Potter Hollow (cdp) Albany County | 9 | 3.30 |
| Freedom (town) Cattaraugus County | 75 | 3.18 |
| Pleasant Valley (cdp) Dutchess County | 26 | 3.14 |

### Top 10 Places Sorted by Percent of Total Population
*Based on places with total population of 50,000 or more*

| Place | Population | % |
|---|---|---|
| Union (town) Broome County | 364 | 0.65 |
| Ramapo (town) Rockland County | 654 | 0.53 |
| Tonawanda (cdp) Erie County | 177 | 0.30 |
| Smithtown (town) Suffolk County | 310 | 0.26 |
| Schenectady (city) Schenectady County | 167 | 0.26 |
| Tonawanda (town) Erie County | 179 | 0.24 |
| North Hempstead (town) Nassau County | 493 | 0.22 |
| Huntington (town) Suffolk County | 435 | 0.22 |
| Oyster Bay (town) Nassau County | 618 | 0.21 |
| Babylon (town) Suffolk County | 438 | 0.21 |

## Danish

### Top 10 Places Sorted by Population
*Based on all places, regardless of total population*

| Place | Population | % |
|---|---|---|
| New York (city) | 7,018 | 0.09 |
| Manhattan (borough) New York County | 4,095 | 0.26 |
| Brooklyn (borough) Kings County | 1,267 | 0.05 |

| Place | Population | % |
|---|---|---|
| Brookhaven (town) Suffolk County | 1,229 | 0.26 |
| Hempstead (town) Nassau County | 1,023 | 0.14 |
| Huntington (town) Suffolk County | 809 | 0.40 |
| Queens (borough) Queens County | 792 | 0.04 |
| Islip (town) Suffolk County | 761 | 0.23 |
| Oyster Bay (town) Nassau County | 573 | 0.20 |
| Staten Island (borough) Richmond County | 479 | 0.10 |

### Top 10 Places Sorted by Percent of Total Population
*Based on all places, regardless of total population*

| Place | Population | % |
|---|---|---|
| Thousand Island Park (cdp) Jefferson County | 16 | 14.41 |
| Pine Hill (cdp) Ulster County | 23 | 8.95 |
| Windham (cdp) Greene County | 37 | 8.53 |
| Benton (town) Yates County | 224 | 7.99 |
| Hall (cdp) Ontario County | 15 | 7.77 |
| Dresden (village) Yates County | 18 | 7.53 |
| Shokan (cdp) Ulster County | 53 | 6.85 |
| Shrub Oak (cdp) Westchester County | 111 | 6.13 |
| Duane (town) Franklin County | 10 | 5.65 |
| Birdsall (town) Allegany County | 17 | 5.54 |

### Top 10 Places Sorted by Percent of Total Population
*Based on places with total population of 50,000 or more*

| Place | Population | % |
|---|---|---|
| Troy (city) Rensselaer County | 223 | 0.45 |
| Huntington (town) Suffolk County | 809 | 0.40 |
| Albany (city) Albany County | 303 | 0.31 |
| Smithtown (town) Suffolk County | 314 | 0.27 |
| Manhattan (borough) New York County | 4,095 | 0.26 |
| Brookhaven (town) Suffolk County | 1,229 | 0.26 |
| Tonawanda (cdp) Erie County | 151 | 0.26 |
| Niagara Falls (city) Niagara County | 134 | 0.26 |
| Colonie (town) Albany County | 195 | 0.24 |
| Tonawanda (town) Erie County | 179 | 0.24 |

## Dutch

### Top 10 Places Sorted by Population
*Based on all places, regardless of total population*

| Place | Population | % |
|---|---|---|
| New York (city) | 23,151 | 0.29 |
| Manhattan (borough) New York County | 10,414 | 0.66 |
| Brooklyn (borough) Kings County | 5,664 | 0.23 |
| Brookhaven (town) Suffolk County | 4,038 | 0.84 |
| Queens (borough) Queens County | 3,516 | 0.16 |
| Colonie (town) Albany County | 3,334 | 4.09 |
| Hempstead (town) Nassau County | 3,142 | 0.42 |
| Rochester (city) Monroe County | 2,898 | 1.37 |
| Greece (town) Monroe County | 2,890 | 3.03 |
| Arcadia (town) Wayne County | 2,484 | 17.31 |

### Top 10 Places Sorted by Percent of Total Population
*Based on all places, regardless of total population*

| Place | Population | % |
|---|---|---|
| Tuscarora (cdp) Livingston County | 36 | 46.75 |
| Malden-on-Hudson (cdp) Ulster County | 104 | 32.20 |
| Livonia Center (cdp) Livingston County | 141 | 28.89 |
| Hall (cdp) Ontario County | 55 | 28.50 |
| Clymer (town) Chautauqua County | 431 | 24.83 |
| Galway (village) Saratoga County | 26 | 24.07 |
| Pultneyville (cdp) Wayne County | 183 | 23.92 |
| Pierrepont Manor (cdp) Jefferson County | 27 | 22.13 |
| Blenheim (town) Schoharie County | 64 | 19.39 |
| Cattaraugus Reservation Chautauqua County | 3 | 18.75 |

### Top 10 Places Sorted by Percent of Total Population
*Based on places with total population of 50,000 or more*

| Place | Population | % |
|---|---|---|
| Colonie (town) Albany County | 3,334 | 4.09 |
| Union (town) Broome County | 1,823 | 3.24 |
| Greece (town) Monroe County | 2,890 | 3.03 |
| Clay (town) Onondaga County | 1,704 | 2.93 |
| Troy (city) Rensselaer County | 1,379 | 2.76 |
| Irondequoit (cdp/town) Monroe County | 1,310 | 2.54 |
| Schenectady (city) Schenectady County | 1,521 | 2.33 |
| Albany (city) Albany County | 1,664 | 1.70 |
| Syracuse (city) Onondaga County | 2,128 | 1.47 |
| Utica (city) Oneida County | 884 | 1.43 |

## Eastern European

### Top 10 Places Sorted by Population
*Based on all places, regardless of total population*

| Place | Population | % |
|---|---|---|
| New York (city) | 44,970 | 0.56 |
| Manhattan (borough) New York County | 25,277 | 1.60 |
| Brooklyn (borough) Kings County | 12,941 | 0.52 |
| Hempstead (town) Nassau County | 5,775 | 0.77 |
| Queens (borough) Queens County | 4,673 | 0.21 |
| Oyster Bay (town) Nassau County | 3,841 | 1.32 |
| North Hempstead (town) Nassau County | 3,769 | 1.69 |
| Huntington (town) Suffolk County | 2,012 | 1.00 |
| Greenburgh (town) Westchester County | 2,009 | 2.29 |
| Bronx (borough) Bronx County | 1,646 | 0.12 |

### Top 10 Places Sorted by Percent of Total Population
*Based on all places, regardless of total population*

| Place | Population | % |
|---|---|---|
| Great Neck Gardens (cdp) Nassau County | 106 | 11.67 |
| Saddle Rock Estates (cdp) Nassau County | 60 | 11.45 |
| Hewlett Harbor (village) Nassau County | 109 | 9.29 |
| Harbor Hills (cdp) Nassau County | 44 | 8.89 |
| East Hills (village) Nassau County | 523 | 7.63 |
| Old Westbury (village) Nassau County | 297 | 7.54 |
| Greenvale (cdp) Nassau County | 33 | 7.35 |
| Hewlett Neck (village) Nassau County | 34 | 7.26 |
| Scarsdale (town/village) Westchester County | 1,208 | 7.06 |
| Matinecock (village) Nassau County | 54 | 7.05 |

### Top 10 Places Sorted by Percent of Total Population
*Based on places with total population of 50,000 or more*

| Place | Population | % |
|---|---|---|
| Greenburgh (town) Westchester County | 2,009 | 2.29 |
| North Hempstead (town) Nassau County | 3,769 | 1.69 |
| Manhattan (borough) New York County | 25,277 | 1.60 |
| Clarkstown (town) Rockland County | 1,282 | 1.54 |
| Oyster Bay (town) Nassau County | 3,841 | 1.32 |
| New Rochelle (city) Westchester County | 870 | 1.15 |
| Huntington (town) Suffolk County | 2,012 | 1.00 |
| White Plains (city) Westchester County | 557 | 1.00 |
| Ramapo (town) Rockland County | 1,144 | 0.93 |
| Hempstead (town) Nassau County | 5,775 | 0.77 |

## English

### Top 10 Places Sorted by Population
*Based on all places, regardless of total population*

| Place | Population | % |
|---|---|---|
| New York (city) | 146,525 | 1.81 |
| Manhattan (borough) New York County | 77,799 | 4.91 |
| Brooklyn (borough) Kings County | 32,407 | 1.31 |
| Brookhaven (town) Suffolk County | 30,089 | 6.27 |
| Hempstead (town) Nassau County | 21,808 | 2.89 |
| Queens (borough) Queens County | 20,267 | 0.92 |
| Islip (town) Suffolk County | 13,963 | 4.18 |
| Rochester (city) Monroe County | 13,510 | 6.37 |
| Huntington (town) Suffolk County | 13,038 | 6.45 |
| Greece (town) Monroe County | 12,568 | 13.17 |

### Top 10 Places Sorted by Percent of Total Population
*Based on all places, regardless of total population*

| Place | Population | % |
|---|---|---|
| Thousand Island Park (cdp) Jefferson County | 58 | 52.25 |
| Dalton (cdp) Livingston County | 165 | 51.24 |
| Dering Harbor (village) Suffolk County | 8 | 50.00 |
| Redwood (cdp) Jefferson County | 152 | 49.19 |
| Denning (town) Ulster County | 202 | 38.70 |
| Davenport Center (cdp) Delaware County | 113 | 38.18 |
| Honeoye (cdp) Ontario County | 266 | 37.62 |
| Piffard (cdp) Livingston County | 21 | 35.00 |
| Central Bridge (cdp) Schoharie County | 208 | 34.61 |
| Saltaire (village) Suffolk County | 20 | 34.48 |

### Top 10 Places Sorted by Percent of Total Population
*Based on places with total population of 50,000 or more*

| Place | Population | % |
|---|---|---|
| Clay (town) Onondaga County | 8,266 | 14.23 |
| Irondequoit (cdp/town) Monroe County | 7,215 | 13.98 |
| Greece (town) Monroe County | 12,568 | 13.17 |
| Union (town) Broome County | 7,072 | 12.56 |

| | | |
|---|---|---|
| Niagara Falls (city) Niagara County | 6,055 | 11.90 |
| Tonawanda (cdp) Erie County | 6,115 | 10.44 |
| Southampton (town) Suffolk County | 5,792 | 10.24 |
| Colonie (town) Albany County | 8,332 | 10.22 |
| Amherst (town) Erie County | 11,840 | 9.79 |
| Tonawanda (town) Erie County | 7,240 | 9.77 |

## Estonian

### Top 10 Places Sorted by Population
*Based on all places, regardless of total population*

| Place | Population | % |
|---|---|---|
| New York (city) | 1,057 | 0.01 |
| Manhattan (borough) New York County | 424 | 0.03 |
| Brooklyn (borough) Kings County | 340 | 0.01 |
| Queens (borough) Queens County | 198 | 0.01 |
| Islip (town) Suffolk County | 175 | 0.05 |
| Hempstead (town) Nassau County | 175 | 0.02 |
| Huntington (town) Suffolk County | 140 | 0.07 |
| Oyster Bay (town) Nassau County | 130 | 0.04 |
| Brookhaven (town) Suffolk County | 102 | 0.02 |
| Bronx (borough) Bronx County | 85 | 0.01 |

### Top 10 Places Sorted by Percent of Total Population
*Based on all places, regardless of total population*

| Place | Population | % |
|---|---|---|
| Redford (cdp) Clinton County | 31 | 6.47 |
| Fort Montgomery (cdp) Orange County | 55 | 6.44 |
| Warren (town) Herkimer County | 36 | 3.18 |
| Clarence (cdp) Erie County | 78 | 2.64 |
| Chenango Bridge (cdp) Broome County | 32 | 1.05 |
| Red Hook (village) Dutchess County | 18 | 0.96 |
| Preston (town) Chenango County | 9 | 0.93 |
| Orient (cdp) Suffolk County | 5 | 0.83 |
| Saranac (town) Clinton County | 31 | 0.77 |
| Yaphank (cdp) Suffolk County | 47 | 0.76 |

### Top 10 Places Sorted by Percent of Total Population
*Based on places with total population of 50,000 or more*

| Place | Population | % |
|---|---|---|
| Cheektowaga (cdp) Erie County | 78 | 0.10 |
| Cheektowaga (town) Erie County | 78 | 0.09 |
| Huntington (town) Suffolk County | 140 | 0.07 |
| Greenburgh (town) Westchester County | 57 | 0.07 |
| Mount Vernon (city) Westchester County | 45 | 0.07 |
| Islip (town) Suffolk County | 175 | 0.05 |
| Oyster Bay (town) Nassau County | 130 | 0.04 |
| Ramapo (town) Rockland County | 48 | 0.04 |
| Greece (town) Monroe County | 40 | 0.04 |
| Manhattan (borough) New York County | 424 | 0.03 |

## European

### Top 10 Places Sorted by Population
*Based on all places, regardless of total population*

| Place | Population | % |
|---|---|---|
| New York (city) | 66,267 | 0.82 |
| Manhattan (borough) New York County | 27,846 | 1.76 |
| Brooklyn (borough) Kings County | 27,499 | 1.11 |
| Ramapo (town) Rockland County | 8,814 | 7.18 |
| Queens (borough) Queens County | 6,584 | 0.30 |
| Hempstead (town) Nassau County | 5,650 | 0.75 |
| Monsey (cdp) Rockland County | 3,363 | 22.35 |
| Oyster Bay (town) Nassau County | 2,919 | 1.00 |
| Bronx (borough) Bronx County | 2,270 | 0.17 |
| Huntington (town) Suffolk County | 2,177 | 1.08 |

### Top 10 Places Sorted by Percent of Total Population
*Based on all places, regardless of total population*

| Place | Population | % |
|---|---|---|
| Kaser (village) Rockland County | 1,293 | 29.15 |
| Monsey (cdp) Rockland County | 3,363 | 22.35 |
| New Square (village) Rockland County | 1,147 | 17.76 |
| West Hampton Dunes (village) Suffolk County | 6 | 13.95 |
| Ghent (cdp) Columbia County | 70 | 11.02 |
| Adams Center (cdp) Jefferson County | 179 | 10.45 |
| Wesley Hills (village) Rockland County | 551 | 10.11 |
| Covington (town) Wyoming County | 111 | 8.80 |
| Claverack-Red Mills (cdp) Columbia County | 72 | 8.56 |
| Accord (cdp) Ulster County | 50 | 8.40 |

### Top 10 Places Sorted by Percent of Total Population
*Based on places with total population of 50,000 or more*

| Place | Population | % |
|---|---|---|
| Ramapo (town) Rockland County | 8,814 | 7.18 |
| Manhattan (borough) New York County | 27,846 | 1.76 |
| Greenburgh (town) Westchester County | 1,360 | 1.55 |
| Albany (city) Albany County | 1,362 | 1.39 |
| White Plains (city) Westchester County | 684 | 1.22 |
| Union (town) Broome County | 660 | 1.17 |
| Brooklyn (borough) Kings County | 27,499 | 1.11 |
| Huntington (town) Suffolk County | 2,177 | 1.08 |
| New Rochelle (city) Westchester County | 808 | 1.07 |
| Troy (city) Rensselaer County | 529 | 1.06 |

## Finnish

### Top 10 Places Sorted by Population
*Based on all places, regardless of total population*

| Place | Population | % |
|---|---|---|
| New York (city) | 3,519 | 0.04 |
| Manhattan (borough) New York County | 1,658 | 0.10 |
| Brookhaven (town) Suffolk County | 706 | 0.15 |
| Queens (borough) Queens County | 693 | 0.03 |
| Brooklyn (borough) Kings County | 692 | 0.03 |
| Hempstead (town) Nassau County | 647 | 0.09 |
| Bronx (borough) Bronx County | 291 | 0.02 |
| Islip (town) Suffolk County | 271 | 0.08 |
| Oyster Bay (town) Nassau County | 265 | 0.09 |
| Dryden (town) Tompkins County | 254 | 1.78 |

### Top 10 Places Sorted by Percent of Total Population
*Based on all places, regardless of total population*

| Place | Population | % |
|---|---|---|
| Van Etten (village) Chemung County | 39 | 8.71 |
| Van Etten (town) Chemung County | 109 | 8.68 |
| Freeville (village) Tompkins County | 29 | 5.80 |
| Ward (town) Allegany County | 18 | 5.34 |
| Spencer (town) Tioga County | 151 | 4.80 |
| Preston-Potter Hollow (cdp) Albany County | 12 | 4.40 |
| Hunter (village) Greene County | 21 | 4.25 |
| East Randolph (village) Cattaraugus County | 21 | 4.07 |
| Smyrna (village) Chenango County | 6 | 3.51 |
| Shelter Island (cdp) Suffolk County | 45 | 3.45 |

### Top 10 Places Sorted by Percent of Total Population
*Based on places with total population of 50,000 or more*

| Place | Population | % |
|---|---|---|
| Southampton (town) Suffolk County | 206 | 0.36 |
| Amherst (town) Erie County | 196 | 0.16 |
| Tonawanda (cdp) Erie County | 95 | 0.16 |
| Brookhaven (town) Suffolk County | 706 | 0.15 |
| Troy (city) Rensselaer County | 74 | 0.15 |
| Clarkstown (town) Rockland County | 119 | 0.14 |
| Tonawanda (town) Erie County | 95 | 0.13 |
| Manhattan (borough) New York County | 1,658 | 0.10 |
| Smithtown (town) Suffolk County | 120 | 0.10 |
| Greenburgh (town) Westchester County | 85 | 0.10 |

## French, except Basque

### Top 10 Places Sorted by Population
*Based on all places, regardless of total population*

| Place | Population | % |
|---|---|---|
| New York (city) | 67,195 | 0.83 |
| Manhattan (borough) New York County | 31,783 | 2.01 |
| Brooklyn (borough) Kings County | 14,137 | 0.57 |
| Queens (borough) Queens County | 12,532 | 0.57 |
| Brookhaven (town) Suffolk County | 8,961 | 1.87 |
| Hempstead (town) Nassau County | 8,239 | 1.09 |
| Syracuse (city) Onondaga County | 6,182 | 4.27 |
| Colonie (town) Albany County | 5,795 | 7.11 |
| Bronx (borough) Bronx County | 4,971 | 0.36 |
| Troy (city) Rensselaer County | 4,862 | 9.72 |

### Top 10 Places Sorted by Percent of Total Population
*Based on all places, regardless of total population*

| Place | Population | % |
|---|---|---|
| Witherbee (cdp) Essex County | 175 | 70.56 |
| Chazy (cdp) Clinton County | 293 | 57.79 |
| Redford (cdp) Clinton County | 255 | 53.24 |

| Place | Population | % |
|---|---|---|
| Redwood (cdp) Jefferson County | 158 | 51.13 |
| Saranac (town) Clinton County | 1,685 | 41.73 |
| Bellmont (town) Franklin County | 720 | 39.80 |
| Mooers (cdp) Clinton County | 218 | 38.86 |
| Three Mile Bay (cdp) Jefferson County | 80 | 37.91 |
| Byersville (cdp) Livingston County | 23 | 37.70 |
| Norfolk (cdp) St. Lawrence County | 461 | 37.12 |

### Top 10 Places Sorted by Percent of Total Population
Based on places with total population of 50,000 or more

| Place | Population | % |
|---|---|---|
| Troy (city) Rensselaer County | 4,862 | 9.72 |
| Colonie (town) Albany County | 5,795 | 7.11 |
| Clay (town) Onondaga County | 3,175 | 5.47 |
| Schenectady (city) Schenectady County | 2,862 | 4.38 |
| Syracuse (city) Onondaga County | 6,182 | 4.27 |
| Greece (town) Monroe County | 3,655 | 3.83 |
| Albany (city) Albany County | 3,690 | 3.77 |
| Tonawanda (cdp) Erie County | 2,149 | 3.67 |
| Hamburg (town) Erie County | 2,079 | 3.67 |
| Union (town) Broome County | 2,044 | 3.63 |

## French Canadian

### Top 10 Places Sorted by Population
Based on all places, regardless of total population

| Place | Population | % |
|---|---|---|
| New York (city) | 11,393 | 0.14 |
| Manhattan (borough) New York County | 5,246 | 0.33 |
| Brooklyn (borough) Kings County | 2,974 | 0.12 |
| Brookhaven (town) Suffolk County | 2,478 | 0.52 |
| Queens (borough) Queens County | 2,020 | 0.09 |
| Syracuse (city) Onondaga County | 1,782 | 1.23 |
| Hempstead (town) Nassau County | 1,779 | 0.24 |
| Colonie (town) Albany County | 1,591 | 1.95 |
| Rochester (city) Monroe County | 1,474 | 0.70 |
| Buffalo (city) Erie County | 1,376 | 0.52 |

### Top 10 Places Sorted by Percent of Total Population
Based on all places, regardless of total population

| Place | Population | % |
|---|---|---|
| Mooers (cdp) Clinton County | 124 | 22.10 |
| Champlain (town) Clinton County | 1,079 | 18.59 |
| Mooers (town) Clinton County | 614 | 17.16 |
| Rensselaer Falls (village) St. Lawrence County | 75 | 15.56 |
| Waverly (town) Franklin County | 157 | 15.23 |
| Tupper Lake (village) Franklin County | 581 | 15.11 |
| St. Regis Falls (cdp) Franklin County | 57 | 14.73 |
| Clinton (town) Clinton County | 114 | 14.36 |
| Schenevus (cdp) Otsego County | 39 | 14.18 |
| Salt Point (cdp) Dutchess County | 46 | 14.11 |

### Top 10 Places Sorted by Percent of Total Population
Based on places with total population of 50,000 or more

| Place | Population | % |
|---|---|---|
| Troy (city) Rensselaer County | 1,245 | 2.49 |
| Clay (town) Onondaga County | 1,241 | 2.14 |
| Colonie (town) Albany County | 1,591 | 1.95 |
| Schenectady (city) Schenectady County | 902 | 1.38 |
| Greece (town) Monroe County | 1,220 | 1.28 |
| Syracuse (city) Onondaga County | 1,782 | 1.23 |
| Tonawanda (town) Erie County | 881 | 1.19 |
| Albany (city) Albany County | 1,061 | 1.08 |
| Hamburg (town) Erie County | 586 | 1.04 |
| Utica (city) Oneida County | 620 | 1.00 |

## German

### Top 10 Places Sorted by Population
Based on all places, regardless of total population

| Place | Population | % |
|---|---|---|
| New York (city) | 272,827 | 3.38 |
| Manhattan (borough) New York County | 107,666 | 6.80 |
| Brookhaven (town) Suffolk County | 89,711 | 18.69 |
| Hempstead (town) Nassau County | 78,518 | 10.42 |
| Queens (borough) Queens County | 70,399 | 3.20 |
| Brooklyn (borough) Kings County | 52,798 | 2.14 |
| Islip (town) Suffolk County | 48,335 | 14.48 |
| Oyster Bay (town) Nassau County | 41,381 | 14.19 |
| Buffalo (city) Erie County | 35,760 | 13.44 |
| Huntington (town) Suffolk County | 33,758 | 16.70 |

### Top 10 Places Sorted by Percent of Total Population
Based on all places, regardless of total population

| Place | Population | % |
|---|---|---|
| Websters Crossing (cdp) Livingston County | 42 | 100.00 |
| Belleville (cdp) Jefferson County | 78 | 66.67 |
| South Lima (cdp) Livingston County | 132 | 65.02 |
| Farnham (village) Erie County | 148 | 62.45 |
| Corfu (village) Genesee County | 453 | 58.83 |
| Livonia Center (cdp) Livingston County | 276 | 56.56 |
| Allen (town) Allegany County | 273 | 55.38 |
| Java (town) Wyoming County | 1,212 | 54.69 |
| Machias (cdp) Cattaraugus County | 393 | 53.91 |
| Alexander (village) Genesee County | 330 | 53.23 |

### Top 10 Places Sorted by Percent of Total Population
Based on places with total population of 50,000 or more

| Place | Population | % |
|---|---|---|
| Hamburg (town) Erie County | 19,590 | 34.62 |
| Tonawanda (cdp) Erie County | 19,292 | 32.95 |
| Tonawanda (town) Erie County | 24,085 | 32.51 |
| Cheektowaga (town) Erie County | 26,125 | 29.39 |
| Cheektowaga (cdp) Erie County | 21,843 | 28.83 |
| Greece (town) Monroe County | 25,631 | 26.85 |
| Amherst (town) Erie County | 30,579 | 25.28 |
| Clay (town) Onondaga County | 14,237 | 24.51 |
| Irondequoit (cdp/town) Monroe County | 11,815 | 22.89 |
| Smithtown (town) Suffolk County | 23,592 | 20.06 |

## German Russian

### Top 10 Places Sorted by Population
Based on all places, regardless of total population

| Place | Population | % |
|---|---|---|
| New York (city) | 204 | <0.01 |
| Queens (borough) Queens County | 78 | <0.01 |
| Troy (city) Rensselaer County | 65 | 0.13 |
| Brooklyn (borough) Kings County | 55 | <0.01 |
| Buffalo (city) Erie County | 41 | 0.02 |
| Manhattan (borough) New York County | 41 | <0.01 |
| Mastic (cdp) Suffolk County | 40 | 0.28 |
| Brookhaven (town) Suffolk County | 40 | 0.01 |
| Tonawanda (city) Erie County | 33 | 0.22 |
| Bronx (borough) Bronx County | 30 | <0.01 |

### Top 10 Places Sorted by Percent of Total Population
Based on all places, regardless of total population

| Place | Population | % |
|---|---|---|
| Lake George (town) Warren County | 16 | 0.45 |
| Garden City Park (cdp) Nassau County | 26 | 0.33 |
| Mastic (cdp) Suffolk County | 40 | 0.28 |
| Tonawanda (city) Erie County | 33 | 0.22 |
| Fort Drum (cdp) Jefferson County | 17 | 0.14 |
| Troy (city) Rensselaer County | 65 | 0.13 |
| Dobbs Ferry (village) Westchester County | 13 | 0.12 |
| Haverstraw (village) Rockland County | 12 | 0.10 |
| Wantagh (cdp) Nassau County | 17 | 0.09 |
| Le Ray (town) Jefferson County | 17 | 0.08 |

### Top 10 Places Sorted by Percent of Total Population
Based on places with total population of 50,000 or more

| Place | Population | % |
|---|---|---|
| Troy (city) Rensselaer County | 65 | 0.13 |
| Irondequoit (cdp/town) Monroe County | 28 | 0.05 |
| Niagara Falls (city) Niagara County | 16 | 0.03 |
| Buffalo (city) Erie County | 41 | 0.02 |
| Cheektowaga (cdp) Erie County | 12 | 0.02 |
| Brookhaven (town) Suffolk County | 40 | 0.01 |
| North Hempstead (town) Nassau County | 26 | 0.01 |
| Yonkers (city) Westchester County | 14 | 0.01 |
| Greenburgh (town) Westchester County | 13 | 0.01 |
| Cheektowaga (town) Erie County | 12 | 0.01 |

## Greek

### Top 10 Places Sorted by Population
Based on all places, regardless of total population

| Place | Population | % |
|---|---|---|
| New York (city) | 76,597 | 0.95 |
| Queens (borough) Queens County | 41,654 | 1.89 |
| Brooklyn (borough) Kings County | 14,075 | 0.57 |

| Place | Population | % |
|---|---|---|
| Manhattan (borough) New York County | 13,078 | 0.83 |
| Hempstead (town) Nassau County | 10,033 | 1.33 |
| Oyster Bay (town) Nassau County | 6,908 | 2.37 |
| Brookhaven (town) Suffolk County | 5,703 | 1.19 |
| Staten Island (borough) Richmond County | 4,183 | 0.90 |
| Bronx (borough) Bronx County | 3,607 | 0.26 |
| North Hempstead (town) Nassau County | 3,568 | 1.60 |

### Top 10 Places Sorted by Percent of Total Population
Based on all places, regardless of total population

| Place | Population | % |
|---|---|---|
| Harbor Hills (cdp) Nassau County | 94 | 18.99 |
| Plandome Manor (village) Nassau County | 97 | 11.02 |
| Manhasset Hills (cdp) Nassau County | 328 | 8.90 |
| Old Brookville (village) Nassau County | 189 | 8.49 |
| Sparkill (cdp) Rockland County | 114 | 8.25 |
| Halcott (town) Greene County | 20 | 7.52 |
| Shinnecock Hills (cdp) Suffolk County | 133 | 7.25 |
| High Falls (cdp) Ulster County | 62 | 7.20 |
| Bellerose (village) Nassau County | 84 | 6.75 |
| Mattituck (cdp) Suffolk County | 279 | 6.73 |

### Top 10 Places Sorted by Percent of Total Population
Based on places with total population of 50,000 or more

| Place | Population | % |
|---|---|---|
| Smithtown (town) Suffolk County | 3,078 | 2.62 |
| Oyster Bay (town) Nassau County | 6,908 | 2.37 |
| Levittown (cdp) Nassau County | 1,100 | 2.06 |
| Queens (borough) Queens County | 41,654 | 1.89 |
| Southampton (town) Suffolk County | 995 | 1.76 |
| Huntington (town) Suffolk County | 3,284 | 1.62 |
| North Hempstead (town) Nassau County | 3,568 | 1.60 |
| Greenburgh (town) Westchester County | 1,202 | 1.37 |
| Hempstead (town) Nassau County | 10,033 | 1.33 |
| Brookhaven (town) Suffolk County | 5,703 | 1.19 |

## Guyanese

### Top 10 Places Sorted by Population
Based on all places, regardless of total population

| Place | Population | % |
|---|---|---|
| New York (city) | 107,972 | 1.34 |
| Queens (borough) Queens County | 53,961 | 2.45 |
| Brooklyn (borough) Kings County | 38,963 | 1.58 |
| Bronx (borough) Bronx County | 11,837 | 0.87 |
| Hempstead (town) Nassau County | 3,520 | 0.47 |
| Manhattan (borough) New York County | 2,259 | 0.14 |
| Schenectady (city) Schenectady County | 1,915 | 2.93 |
| Staten Island (borough) Richmond County | 952 | 0.21 |
| Valley Stream (village) Nassau County | 840 | 2.27 |
| Babylon (town) Suffolk County | 747 | 0.35 |

### Top 10 Places Sorted by Percent of Total Population
Based on all places, regardless of total population

| Place | Population | % |
|---|---|---|
| St. Regis Mohawk Reservation Franklin County | 162 | 5.17 |
| Greenville (town) Orange County | 161 | 3.57 |
| Hillcrest (cdp) Rockland County | 280 | 3.42 |
| Schenectady (city) Schenectady County | 1,915 | 2.93 |
| Manhasset Hills (cdp) Nassau County | 102 | 2.77 |
| Highland (cdp) Ulster County | 149 | 2.62 |
| Batavia (town) Genesee County | 172 | 2.60 |
| Queens (borough) Queens County | 53,961 | 2.45 |
| Menands (village) Albany County | 97 | 2.43 |
| Valley Stream (village) Nassau County | 840 | 2.27 |

### Top 10 Places Sorted by Percent of Total Population
Based on places with total population of 50,000 or more

| Place | Population | % |
|---|---|---|
| Schenectady (city) Schenectady County | 1,915 | 2.93 |
| Queens (borough) Queens County | 53,961 | 2.45 |
| Brooklyn (borough) Kings County | 38,963 | 1.58 |
| New York (city) | 107,972 | 1.34 |
| Bronx (borough) Bronx County | 11,837 | 0.87 |
| Hempstead (village) Nassau County | 307 | 0.58 |
| Mount Vernon (city) Westchester County | 360 | 0.54 |
| Albany (city) Albany County | 483 | 0.49 |
| Hempstead (town) Nassau County | 3,520 | 0.47 |
| Babylon (town) Suffolk County | 747 | 0.35 |

## Hungarian

### Top 10 Places Sorted by Population
*Based on all places, regardless of total population*

| Place | Population | % |
|---|---|---|
| New York (city) | 55,459 | 0.69 |
| Brooklyn (borough) Kings County | 26,607 | 1.08 |
| Manhattan (borough) New York County | 14,667 | 0.93 |
| Queens (borough) Queens County | 9,470 | 0.43 |
| Hempstead (town) Nassau County | 6,992 | 0.93 |
| Ramapo (town) Rockland County | 6,804 | 5.54 |
| Monroe (town) Orange County | 5,591 | 14.45 |
| Kiryas Joel (village) Orange County | 5,471 | 28.66 |
| Brookhaven (town) Suffolk County | 4,390 | 0.91 |
| Oyster Bay (town) Nassau County | 3,138 | 1.08 |

### Top 10 Places Sorted by Percent of Total Population
*Based on all places, regardless of total population*

| Place | Population | % |
|---|---|---|
| South Lima (cdp) Livingston County | 72 | 35.47 |
| Natural Bridge (cdp) Jefferson County | 137 | 33.91 |
| Kiryas Joel (village) Orange County | 5,471 | 28.66 |
| New Square (village) Rockland County | 1,787 | 27.67 |
| Kaser (village) Rockland County | 1,034 | 23.31 |
| Monroe (town) Orange County | 5,591 | 14.45 |
| Prattsville (cdp) Greene County | 41 | 12.85 |
| Lawrence (village) Nassau County | 746 | 11.57 |
| Monsey (cdp) Rockland County | 1,483 | 9.85 |
| Saddle Rock Estates (cdp) Nassau County | 48 | 9.16 |

### Top 10 Places Sorted by Percent of Total Population
*Based on places with total population of 50,000 or more*

| Place | Population | % |
|---|---|---|
| Ramapo (town) Rockland County | 6,804 | 5.54 |
| Tonawanda (cdp) Erie County | 976 | 1.67 |
| Tonawanda (town) Erie County | 1,188 | 1.60 |
| Huntington (town) Suffolk County | 3,005 | 1.49 |
| Levittown (cdp) Nassau County | 781 | 1.46 |
| Greenburgh (town) Westchester County | 1,242 | 1.42 |
| Hamburg (town) Erie County | 761 | 1.34 |
| Clarkstown (town) Rockland County | 1,008 | 1.21 |
| North Hempstead (town) Nassau County | 2,628 | 1.18 |
| Brooklyn (borough) Kings County | 26,607 | 1.08 |

## Icelander

### Top 10 Places Sorted by Population
*Based on all places, regardless of total population*

| Place | Population | % |
|---|---|---|
| New York (city) | 572 | 0.01 |
| Manhattan (borough) New York County | 382 | 0.02 |
| Brooklyn (borough) Kings County | 103 | <0.01 |
| Hempstead (town) Nassau County | 92 | 0.01 |
| Pittsford (town) Monroe County | 63 | 0.22 |
| Blooming Grove (town) Orange County | 62 | 0.34 |
| Wawayanda (town) Orange County | 55 | 0.77 |
| Staten Island (borough) Richmond County | 55 | 0.01 |
| Lockport (town) Niagara County | 52 | 0.26 |
| Levittown (cdp) Nassau County | 52 | 0.10 |

### Top 10 Places Sorted by Percent of Total Population
*Based on all places, regardless of total population*

| Place | Population | % |
|---|---|---|
| Northwest Ithaca (cdp) Tompkins County | 14 | 1.21 |
| Brewerton (cdp) Onondaga County | 33 | 0.81 |
| Wawayanda (town) Orange County | 55 | 0.77 |
| Meredith (town) Delaware County | 8 | 0.51 |
| West Monroe (town) Oswego County | 20 | 0.47 |
| Port Ewen (cdp) Ulster County | 15 | 0.40 |
| Sempronius (town) Cayuga County | 3 | 0.36 |
| Blooming Grove (town) Orange County | 62 | 0.34 |
| Dannemora (town) Clinton County | 16 | 0.32 |
| Homer (village) Cortland County | 10 | 0.30 |

### Top 10 Places Sorted by Percent of Total Population
*Based on places with total population of 50,000 or more*

| Place | Population | % |
|---|---|---|
| Levittown (cdp) Nassau County | 52 | 0.10 |
| Manhattan (borough) New York County | 382 | 0.02 |
| Oyster Bay (town) Nassau County | 52 | 0.02 |
| Huntington (town) Suffolk County | 38 | 0.02 |

| Utica (city) Oneida County | 14 | 0.02 |
|---|---|---|
| Tonawanda (cdp) Erie County | 11 | 0.02 |
| New York (city) | 572 | 0.01 |
| Hempstead (town) Nassau County | 92 | 0.01 |
| Staten Island (borough) Richmond County | 55 | 0.01 |
| Brookhaven (town) Suffolk County | 45 | 0.01 |

## Iranian

### Top 10 Places Sorted by Population
*Based on all places, regardless of total population*

| Place | Population | % |
|---|---|---|
| New York (city) | 10,204 | 0.13 |
| North Hempstead (town) Nassau County | 9,262 | 4.14 |
| Manhattan (borough) New York County | 4,256 | 0.27 |
| Queens (borough) Queens County | 3,707 | 0.17 |
| Great Neck (village) Nassau County | 2,382 | 24.20 |
| Kings Point (village) Nassau County | 2,070 | 41.62 |
| Brooklyn (borough) Kings County | 1,822 | 0.07 |
| Oyster Bay (town) Nassau County | 1,464 | 0.50 |
| Great Neck Plaza (village) Nassau County | 673 | 10.18 |
| Great Neck Estates (village) Nassau County | 566 | 20.72 |

### Top 10 Places Sorted by Percent of Total Population
*Based on all places, regardless of total population*

| Place | Population | % |
|---|---|---|
| Kings Point (village) Nassau County | 2,070 | 41.62 |
| Saddle Rock (village) Nassau County | 380 | 36.26 |
| Great Neck (village) Nassau County | 2,382 | 24.20 |
| Great Neck Estates (village) Nassau County | 566 | 20.72 |
| Saddle Rock Estates (cdp) Nassau County | 90 | 17.18 |
| Kensington (village) Nassau County | 180 | 14.94 |
| Great Neck Plaza (village) Nassau County | 673 | 10.18 |
| Roslyn Heights (cdp) Nassau County | 452 | 6.97 |
| North Hills (village) Nassau County | 316 | 6.40 |
| Flower Hill (village) Nassau County | 294 | 6.38 |

### Top 10 Places Sorted by Percent of Total Population
*Based on places with total population of 50,000 or more*

| Place | Population | % |
|---|---|---|
| North Hempstead (town) Nassau County | 9,262 | 4.14 |
| Oyster Bay (town) Nassau County | 1,464 | 0.50 |
| Greenburgh (town) Westchester County | 267 | 0.30 |
| Manhattan (borough) New York County | 4,256 | 0.27 |
| Ramapo (town) Rockland County | 314 | 0.26 |
| Huntington (town) Suffolk County | 471 | 0.23 |
| Smithtown (town) Suffolk County | 237 | 0.20 |
| Clarkstown (town) Rockland County | 146 | 0.18 |
| Queens (borough) Queens County | 3,707 | 0.17 |
| Clay (town) Onondaga County | 99 | 0.17 |

## Irish

### Top 10 Places Sorted by Population
*Based on all places, regardless of total population*

| Place | Population | % |
|---|---|---|
| New York (city) | 410,889 | 5.09 |
| Hempstead (town) Nassau County | 125,911 | 16.71 |
| Brookhaven (town) Suffolk County | 122,200 | 25.45 |
| Manhattan (borough) New York County | 117,355 | 7.41 |
| Queens (borough) Queens County | 105,348 | 4.79 |
| Brooklyn (borough) Kings County | 84,945 | 3.44 |
| Islip (town) Suffolk County | 68,763 | 20.61 |
| Staten Island (borough) Richmond County | 64,762 | 13.97 |
| Oyster Bay (town) Nassau County | 59,765 | 20.49 |
| Huntington (town) Suffolk County | 45,750 | 22.63 |

### Top 10 Places Sorted by Percent of Total Population
*Based on all places, regardless of total population*

| Place | Population | % |
|---|---|---|
| Oak Beach-Captree (cdp) Suffolk County | 348 | 73.26 |
| Hopewell Junction (cdp) Dutchess County | 290 | 61.97 |
| Point Lookout (cdp) Nassau County | 763 | 59.98 |
| Walker Valley (cdp) Ulster County | 319 | 59.51 |
| Pearl River (cdp) Rockland County | 7,647 | 52.46 |
| Staatsburg (cdp) Dutchess County | 274 | 52.29 |
| Bellerose (village) Nassau County | 648 | 52.09 |
| Palenville (cdp) Greene County | 584 | 51.45 |
| Winthrop (cdp) St. Lawrence County | 236 | 50.97 |
| Parc (cdp) Clinton County | 20 | 47.62 |

### Top 10 Places Sorted by Percent of Total Population
*Based on places with total population of 50,000 or more*

| Place | Population | % |
|---|---|---|
| Colonie (town) Albany County | 23,049 | 28.27 |
| Levittown (cdp) Nassau County | 14,886 | 27.84 |
| Hamburg (town) Erie County | 15,679 | 27.71 |
| Smithtown (town) Suffolk County | 31,963 | 27.18 |
| Brookhaven (town) Suffolk County | 122,200 | 25.45 |
| Troy (city) Rensselaer County | 12,384 | 24.76 |
| Clay (town) Onondaga County | 14,197 | 24.44 |
| Southampton (town) Suffolk County | 12,998 | 22.99 |
| Huntington (town) Suffolk County | 45,750 | 22.63 |
| Union (town) Broome County | 12,320 | 21.88 |

## Israeli

### Top 10 Places Sorted by Population
*Based on all places, regardless of total population*

| Place | Population | % |
|---|---|---|
| New York (city) | 21,872 | 0.27 |
| Brooklyn (borough) Kings County | 9,707 | 0.39 |
| Manhattan (borough) New York County | 6,624 | 0.42 |
| Queens (borough) Queens County | 4,164 | 0.19 |
| Ramapo (town) Rockland County | 3,342 | 2.72 |
| Hempstead (town) Nassau County | 2,558 | 0.34 |
| North Hempstead (town) Nassau County | 1,853 | 0.83 |
| Kiryas Joel (village) Orange County | 949 | 4.97 |
| Monroe (town) Orange County | 949 | 2.45 |
| Woodmere (cdp) Nassau County | 879 | 5.04 |

### Top 10 Places Sorted by Percent of Total Population
*Based on all places, regardless of total population*

| Place | Population | % |
|---|---|---|
| Saddle Rock (village) Nassau County | 153 | 14.60 |
| Kaser (village) Rockland County | 540 | 12.17 |
| Viola (cdp) Rockland County | 792 | 11.23 |
| Greenvale (cdp) Nassau County | 32 | 7.13 |
| Lake Success (village) Nassau County | 172 | 5.94 |
| South Valley Stream (cdp) Nassau County | 268 | 5.09 |
| Woodmere (cdp) Nassau County | 879 | 5.04 |
| Kiryas Joel (village) Orange County | 949 | 4.97 |
| Wesley Hills (village) Rockland County | 231 | 4.24 |
| Monsey (cdp) Rockland County | 608 | 4.04 |

### Top 10 Places Sorted by Percent of Total Population
*Based on places with total population of 50,000 or more*

| Place | Population | % |
|---|---|---|
| Ramapo (town) Rockland County | 3,342 | 2.72 |
| North Hempstead (town) Nassau County | 1,853 | 0.83 |
| Manhattan (borough) New York County | 6,624 | 0.42 |
| Brooklyn (borough) Kings County | 9,707 | 0.39 |
| Hempstead (town) Nassau County | 2,558 | 0.34 |
| White Plains (city) Westchester County | 181 | 0.32 |
| Clarkstown (town) Rockland County | 247 | 0.30 |
| New York (city) | 21,872 | 0.27 |
| Greenburgh (town) Westchester County | 225 | 0.26 |
| Mount Vernon (city) Westchester County | 174 | 0.26 |

## Italian

### Top 10 Places Sorted by Population
*Based on all places, regardless of total population*

| Place | Population | % |
|---|---|---|
| New York (city) | 625,004 | 7.74 |
| Hempstead (town) Nassau County | 164,467 | 21.82 |
| Queens (borough) Queens County | 159,812 | 7.27 |
| Staten Island (borough) Richmond County | 156,288 | 33.72 |
| Brookhaven (town) Suffolk County | 155,749 | 32.44 |
| Brooklyn (borough) Kings County | 152,814 | 6.19 |
| Manhattan (borough) New York County | 98,563 | 6.22 |
| Oyster Bay (town) Nassau County | 88,723 | 30.43 |
| Islip (town) Suffolk County | 84,360 | 25.28 |
| Babylon (town) Suffolk County | 61,852 | 28.95 |

### Top 10 Places Sorted by Percent of Total Population
*Based on all places, regardless of total population*

| Place | Population | % |
|---|---|---|
| Witherbee (cdp) Essex County | 149 | 60.08 |
| Hillside Lake (cdp) Dutchess County | 350 | 51.32 |
| North Massapequa (cdp) Nassau County | 9,384 | 50.28 |

| Place | Population | % |
|---|---|---|
| Frankfort (village) Herkimer County | 1,299 | 50.17 |
| East Kingston (cdp) Ulster County | 170 | 49.56 |
| Great River (cdp) Suffolk County | 803 | 48.78 |
| Leeds (cdp) Greene County | 151 | 47.19 |
| Fowlerville (cdp) Livingston County | 116 | 46.96 |
| Moriches (cdp) Suffolk County | 1,413 | 46.85 |
| Franklin Square (cdp) Nassau County | 13,514 | 45.54 |

### Top 10 Places Sorted by Percent of Total Population
*Based on places with total population of 50,000 or more*

| Place | Population | % |
|---|---|---|
| Smithtown (town) Suffolk County | 45,388 | 38.60 |
| Staten Island (borough) Richmond County | 156,288 | 33.72 |
| Levittown (cdp) Nassau County | 17,446 | 32.62 |
| Brookhaven (town) Suffolk County | 155,749 | 32.44 |
| Oyster Bay (town) Nassau County | 88,723 | 30.43 |
| Babylon (town) Suffolk County | 61,852 | 28.95 |
| Irondequoit (cdp/town) Monroe County | 14,566 | 28.22 |
| Huntington (town) Suffolk County | 56,013 | 27.70 |
| Greece (town) Monroe County | 26,121 | 27.36 |
| Tonawanda (town) Erie County | 19,213 | 25.93 |

## Latvian

### Top 10 Places Sorted by Population
*Based on all places, regardless of total population*

| Place | Population | % |
|---|---|---|
| New York (city) | 3,302 | 0.04 |
| Manhattan (borough) New York County | 1,822 | 0.12 |
| Brooklyn (borough) Kings County | 667 | 0.03 |
| Queens (borough) Queens County | 568 | 0.03 |
| Hempstead (town) Nassau County | 438 | 0.06 |
| North Hempstead (town) Nassau County | 254 | 0.11 |
| Oyster Bay (town) Nassau County | 235 | 0.08 |
| Huntington (town) Suffolk County | 193 | 0.10 |
| Brookhaven (town) Suffolk County | 182 | 0.04 |
| Ramapo (town) Rockland County | 174 | 0.14 |

### Top 10 Places Sorted by Percent of Total Population
*Based on all places, regardless of total population*

| Place | Population | % |
|---|---|---|
| Williamson (cdp) Wayne County | 62 | 2.61 |
| Halesite (cdp) Suffolk County | 55 | 2.61 |
| Stony Creek (town) Warren County | 24 | 2.61 |
| Bemus Point (village) Chautauqua County | 6 | 2.05 |
| Airmont (village) Rockland County | 132 | 1.57 |
| Pleasant Valley (cdp) Dutchess County | 13 | 1.57 |
| Tully (village) Onondaga County | 13 | 1.52 |
| Esperance (village) Schoharie County | 6 | 1.34 |
| LaFayette (town) Onondaga County | 65 | 1.32 |
| North Hills (village) Nassau County | 59 | 1.19 |

### Top 10 Places Sorted by Percent of Total Population
*Based on places with total population of 50,000 or more*

| Place | Population | % |
|---|---|---|
| Greenburgh (town) Westchester County | 153 | 0.17 |
| Ramapo (town) Rockland County | 174 | 0.14 |
| Manhattan (borough) New York County | 1,822 | 0.12 |
| North Hempstead (town) Nassau County | 254 | 0.11 |
| Huntington (town) Suffolk County | 193 | 0.10 |
| Clarkstown (town) Rockland County | 87 | 0.10 |
| New Rochelle (city) Westchester County | 74 | 0.10 |
| Oyster Bay (town) Nassau County | 235 | 0.08 |
| Smithtown (town) Suffolk County | 81 | 0.07 |
| Greece (town) Monroe County | 71 | 0.07 |

## Lithuanian

### Top 10 Places Sorted by Population
*Based on all places, regardless of total population*

| Place | Population | % |
|---|---|---|
| New York (city) | 12,774 | 0.16 |
| Manhattan (borough) New York County | 5,775 | 0.36 |
| Queens (borough) Queens County | 3,131 | 0.14 |
| Brooklyn (borough) Kings County | 2,676 | 0.11 |
| Hempstead (town) Nassau County | 2,538 | 0.34 |
| Brookhaven (town) Suffolk County | 1,898 | 0.40 |
| Oyster Bay (town) Nassau County | 1,079 | 0.37 |
| Huntington (town) Suffolk County | 956 | 0.47 |
| Islip (town) Suffolk County | 799 | 0.24 |
| North Hempstead (town) Nassau County | 718 | 0.32 |

### Top 10 Places Sorted by Percent of Total Population
*Based on all places, regardless of total population*

| Place | Population | % |
|---|---|---|
| Lyon Mountain (cdp) Clinton County | 61 | 16.05 |
| Wynantskill (cdp) Rensselaer County | 256 | 7.24 |
| Marion (cdp) Wayne County | 102 | 5.38 |
| Santa Clara (town) Franklin County | 21 | 5.33 |
| Leeds (cdp) Greene County | 16 | 5.00 |
| Hagaman (village) Montgomery County | 48 | 4.52 |
| Webb (town) Herkimer County | 68 | 4.38 |
| Durhamville (cdp) Oneida County | 25 | 4.35 |
| Napeague (cdp) Suffolk County | 9 | 4.31 |
| Old Forge (cdp) Herkimer County | 22 | 4.27 |

### Top 10 Places Sorted by Percent of Total Population
*Based on places with total population of 50,000 or more*

| Place | Population | % |
|---|---|---|
| Union (town) Broome County | 452 | 0.80 |
| Levittown (cdp) Nassau County | 314 | 0.59 |
| Greece (town) Monroe County | 543 | 0.57 |
| Smithtown (town) Suffolk County | 627 | 0.53 |
| Irondequoit (cdp/town) Monroe County | 267 | 0.52 |
| Huntington (town) Suffolk County | 956 | 0.47 |
| Southampton (town) Suffolk County | 267 | 0.47 |
| Colonie (town) Albany County | 377 | 0.46 |
| Ramapo (town) Rockland County | 538 | 0.44 |
| Brookhaven (town) Suffolk County | 1,898 | 0.40 |

## Luxemburger

### Top 10 Places Sorted by Population
*Based on all places, regardless of total population*

| Place | Population | % |
|---|---|---|
| New York (city) | 193 | <0.01 |
| Manhattan (borough) New York County | 68 | <0.01 |
| Rochester (city) Monroe County | 62 | 0.03 |
| Brooklyn (borough) Kings County | 58 | <0.01 |
| Staten Island (borough) Richmond County | 54 | 0.01 |
| Brookhaven (town) Suffolk County | 36 | 0.01 |
| Lenox (town) Madison County | 27 | 0.30 |
| Clay (town) Onondaga County | 26 | 0.04 |
| Ithaca (city) Tompkins County | 24 | 0.08 |
| Irondequoit (cdp/town) Monroe County | 24 | 0.05 |

### Top 10 Places Sorted by Percent of Total Population
*Based on all places, regardless of total population*

| Place | Population | % |
|---|---|---|
| Lyndon (town) Cattaraugus County | 4 | 0.70 |
| Dickinson (town) Franklin County | 6 | 0.56 |
| Sheldon (town) Wyoming County | 7 | 0.32 |
| Lenox (town) Madison County | 27 | 0.30 |
| Roslyn Heights (cdp) Nassau County | 16 | 0.25 |
| Virgil (town) Cortland County | 6 | 0.25 |
| Java (town) Wyoming County | 5 | 0.23 |
| Athens (village) Greene County | 3 | 0.18 |
| Caton (town) Steuben County | 5 | 0.17 |
| Terryville (cdp) Suffolk County | 18 | 0.15 |

### Top 10 Places Sorted by Percent of Total Population
*Based on places with total population of 50,000 or more*

| Place | Population | % |
|---|---|---|
| Irondequoit (cdp/town) Monroe County | 24 | 0.05 |
| Clay (town) Onondaga County | 26 | 0.04 |
| Rochester (city) Monroe County | 62 | 0.03 |
| Greece (town) Monroe County | 15 | 0.02 |
| Colonie (town) Albany County | 13 | 0.02 |
| Staten Island (borough) Richmond County | 54 | 0.01 |
| Brookhaven (town) Suffolk County | 36 | 0.01 |
| Buffalo (city) Erie County | 24 | 0.01 |
| North Hempstead (town) Nassau County | 16 | 0.01 |
| Syracuse (city) Onondaga County | 14 | 0.01 |

## Macedonian

### Top 10 Places Sorted by Population
*Based on all places, regardless of total population*

| Place | Population | % |
|---|---|---|
| New York (city) | 4,911 | 0.06 |
| Staten Island (borough) Richmond County | 1,590 | 0.34 |
| Queens (borough) Queens County | 1,109 | 0.05 |
| Manhattan (borough) New York County | 1,086 | 0.07 |
| Bronx (borough) Bronx County | 628 | 0.05 |
| Brooklyn (borough) Kings County | 498 | 0.02 |
| Irondequoit (cdp/town) Monroe County | 266 | 0.52 |
| Yonkers (city) Westchester County | 236 | 0.12 |
| Clay (town) Onondaga County | 185 | 0.32 |
| New Rochelle (city) Westchester County | 177 | 0.23 |

### Top 10 Places Sorted by Percent of Total Population
*Based on all places, regardless of total population*

| Place | Population | % |
|---|---|---|
| Sunset Bay (cdp) Chautauqua County | 50 | 5.55 |
| Hannibal (village) Oswego County | 15 | 2.65 |
| Cold Brook (village) Herkimer County | 6 | 1.59 |
| Village Green (cdp) Onondaga County | 56 | 1.25 |
| Chappaqua (cdp) Westchester County | 13 | 1.25 |
| Union Vale (town) Dutchess County | 57 | 1.18 |
| Riga (town) Monroe County | 61 | 1.10 |
| Angola on the Lake (cdp) Erie County | 12 | 0.86 |
| Pulaski (village) Oswego County | 19 | 0.78 |
| Hanover (town) Chautauqua County | 50 | 0.70 |

### Top 10 Places Sorted by Percent of Total Population
*Based on places with total population of 50,000 or more*

| Place | Population | % |
|---|---|---|
| Irondequoit (cdp/town) Monroe County | 266 | 0.52 |
| Staten Island (borough) Richmond County | 1,590 | 0.34 |
| Clay (town) Onondaga County | 185 | 0.32 |
| Hamburg (town) Erie County | 149 | 0.26 |
| New Rochelle (city) Westchester County | 177 | 0.23 |
| Yonkers (city) Westchester County | 236 | 0.12 |
| Greece (town) Monroe County | 119 | 0.12 |
| White Plains (city) Westchester County | 54 | 0.10 |
| Manhattan (borough) New York County | 1,086 | 0.07 |
| New York (city) | 4,911 | 0.06 |

## Maltese

### Top 10 Places Sorted by Population
*Based on all places, regardless of total population*

| Place | Population | % |
|---|---|---|
| New York (city) | 3,102 | 0.04 |
| Queens (borough) Queens County | 1,565 | 0.07 |
| Manhattan (borough) New York County | 840 | 0.05 |
| Brookhaven (town) Suffolk County | 686 | 0.14 |
| Oyster Bay (town) Nassau County | 579 | 0.20 |
| Hempstead (town) Nassau County | 540 | 0.07 |
| Babylon (town) Suffolk County | 378 | 0.18 |
| Brooklyn (borough) Kings County | 362 | 0.01 |
| Islip (town) Suffolk County | 292 | 0.09 |
| Staten Island (borough) Richmond County | 290 | 0.06 |

### Top 10 Places Sorted by Percent of Total Population
*Based on all places, regardless of total population*

| Place | Population | % |
|---|---|---|
| Tuxedo (town) Orange County | 93 | 2.59 |
| Hamptonburgh (town) Orange County | 103 | 1.89 |
| Plandome Heights (village) Nassau County | 15 | 1.42 |
| Carle Place (cdp) Nassau County | 77 | 1.38 |
| Hillside Lake (cdp) Dutchess County | 8 | 1.17 |
| Wright (town) Schoharie County | 21 | 1.11 |
| East Patchogue (cdp) Suffolk County | 220 | 1.04 |
| Milton (cdp) Ulster County | 12 | 1.03 |
| Sparkill (cdp) Rockland County | 13 | 0.94 |
| Brewerton (cdp) Onondaga County | 36 | 0.89 |

### Top 10 Places Sorted by Percent of Total Population
*Based on places with total population of 50,000 or more*

| Place | Population | % |
|---|---|---|
| Oyster Bay (town) Nassau County | 579 | 0.20 |
| Babylon (town) Suffolk County | 378 | 0.18 |
| Smithtown (town) Suffolk County | 206 | 0.18 |
| Levittown (cdp) Nassau County | 96 | 0.18 |
| Brookhaven (town) Suffolk County | 686 | 0.14 |
| North Hempstead (town) Nassau County | 248 | 0.11 |
| Islip (town) Suffolk County | 292 | 0.09 |
| Queens (borough) Queens County | 1,565 | 0.07 |
| Hempstead (town) Nassau County | 540 | 0.07 |
| Staten Island (borough) Richmond County | 290 | 0.06 |

## New Zealander

### Top 10 Places Sorted by Population
*Based on all places, regardless of total population*

| Place | Population | % |
| --- | --- | --- |
| New York (city) | 584 | 0.01 |
| Manhattan (borough) New York County | 405 | 0.03 |
| Brooklyn (borough) Kings County | 140 | 0.01 |
| Monsey (cdp) Rockland County | 55 | 0.37 |
| Ramapo (town) Rockland County | 55 | 0.04 |
| Ithaca (city) Tompkins County | 45 | 0.15 |
| Milan (town) Dutchess County | 35 | 1.38 |
| Deerpark (town) Orange County | 35 | 0.44 |
| White Plains (city) Westchester County | 29 | 0.05 |
| Eggertsville (cdp) Erie County | 26 | 0.17 |

### Top 10 Places Sorted by Percent of Total Population
*Based on all places, regardless of total population*

| Place | Population | % |
| --- | --- | --- |
| Milan (town) Dutchess County | 35 | 1.38 |
| Oriskany Falls (village) Oneida County | 4 | 0.53 |
| Deerpark (town) Orange County | 35 | 0.44 |
| Niskayuna (cdp) Schenectady County | 18 | 0.39 |
| Monsey (cdp) Rockland County | 55 | 0.37 |
| North Harmony (town) Chautauqua County | 6 | 0.28 |
| Cooperstown (village) Otsego County | 5 | 0.28 |
| Hartford (town) Washington County | 5 | 0.22 |
| Spafford (town) Onondaga County | 4 | 0.20 |
| Augusta (town) Oneida County | 4 | 0.19 |

### Top 10 Places Sorted by Percent of Total Population
*Based on places with total population of 50,000 or more*

| Place | Population | % |
| --- | --- | --- |
| White Plains (city) Westchester County | 29 | 0.05 |
| Ramapo (town) Rockland County | 55 | 0.04 |
| Manhattan (borough) New York County | 405 | 0.03 |
| Amherst (town) Erie County | 26 | 0.02 |
| New York (city) | 584 | 0.01 |
| Brooklyn (borough) Kings County | 140 | 0.01 |
| Huntington (town) Suffolk County | 26 | 0.01 |
| Syracuse (city) Onondaga County | 13 | 0.01 |
| Cheektowaga (cdp) Erie County | 11 | 0.01 |
| Cheektowaga (town) Erie County | 11 | 0.01 |

## Northern European

### Top 10 Places Sorted by Population
*Based on all places, regardless of total population*

| Place | Population | % |
| --- | --- | --- |
| New York (city) | 3,043 | 0.04 |
| Manhattan (borough) New York County | 1,485 | 0.09 |
| Brooklyn (borough) Kings County | 961 | 0.04 |
| Hempstead (town) Nassau County | 514 | 0.07 |
| Queens (borough) Queens County | 512 | 0.02 |
| Brookhaven (town) Suffolk County | 249 | 0.05 |
| Oceanside (cdp) Nassau County | 161 | 0.52 |
| Albany (city) Albany County | 160 | 0.16 |
| Depew (village) Erie County | 130 | 0.84 |
| Cheektowaga (town) Erie County | 130 | 0.15 |

### Top 10 Places Sorted by Percent of Total Population
*Based on all places, regardless of total population*

| Place | Population | % |
| --- | --- | --- |
| Duanesburg (cdp) Schenectady County | 21 | 12.00 |
| Schenevus (cdp) Otsego County | 32 | 11.64 |
| West Valley (cdp) Cattaraugus County | 33 | 7.37 |
| Newfield Hamlet (cdp) Tompkins County | 30 | 4.48 |
| Long Lake (cdp) Hamilton County | 21 | 3.92 |
| Guilford (town) Chenango County | 97 | 3.27 |
| New Suffolk (cdp) Suffolk County | 6 | 3.19 |
| Scott (town) Cortland County | 36 | 2.85 |
| Long Lake (town) Hamilton County | 21 | 2.80 |
| Laurel (cdp) Suffolk County | 30 | 2.79 |

### Top 10 Places Sorted by Percent of Total Population
*Based on places with total population of 50,000 or more*

| Place | Population | % |
| --- | --- | --- |
| Albany (city) Albany County | 160 | 0.16 |
| Cheektowaga (town) Erie County | 130 | 0.15 |
| Schenectady (city) Schenectady County | 97 | 0.15 |
| White Plains (city) Westchester County | 54 | 0.10 |

| | | |
| --- | --- | --- |
| Manhattan (borough) New York County | 1,485 | 0.09 |
| Amherst (town) Erie County | 101 | 0.08 |
| Hempstead (town) Nassau County | 514 | 0.07 |
| Greenburgh (town) Westchester County | 65 | 0.07 |
| Southampton (town) Suffolk County | 42 | 0.07 |
| Clay (town) Onondaga County | 35 | 0.06 |

## Norwegian

### Top 10 Places Sorted by Population
*Based on all places, regardless of total population*

| Place | Population | % |
| --- | --- | --- |
| New York (city) | 21,894 | 0.27 |
| Manhattan (borough) New York County | 7,445 | 0.47 |
| Brooklyn (borough) Kings County | 5,982 | 0.24 |
| Staten Island (borough) Richmond County | 5,135 | 1.11 |
| Brookhaven (town) Suffolk County | 5,078 | 1.06 |
| Hempstead (town) Nassau County | 3,371 | 0.45 |
| Islip (town) Suffolk County | 2,978 | 0.89 |
| Queens (borough) Queens County | 2,559 | 0.12 |
| Oyster Bay (town) Nassau County | 1,882 | 0.65 |
| Huntington (town) Suffolk County | 1,833 | 0.91 |

### Top 10 Places Sorted by Percent of Total Population
*Based on all places, regardless of total population*

| Place | Population | % |
| --- | --- | --- |
| Saltaire (village) Suffolk County | 8 | 13.79 |
| Stone Ridge (cdp) Ulster County | 91 | 10.48 |
| Margaretville (village) Delaware County | 52 | 9.83 |
| Great Bend (cdp) Jefferson County | 86 | 9.50 |
| Fishers Island (cdp) Suffolk County | 21 | 8.40 |
| Red House (town) Cattaraugus County | 2 | 7.69 |
| Northville (cdp) Suffolk County | 88 | 7.39 |
| Benson (town) Hamilton County | 11 | 7.24 |
| Pitcher (town) Chenango County | 48 | 7.08 |
| Shokan (cdp) Ulster County | 44 | 5.68 |

### Top 10 Places Sorted by Percent of Total Population
*Based on places with total population of 50,000 or more*

| Place | Population | % |
| --- | --- | --- |
| Smithtown (town) Suffolk County | 1,686 | 1.43 |
| Staten Island (borough) Richmond County | 5,135 | 1.11 |
| Brookhaven (town) Suffolk County | 5,078 | 1.06 |
| Huntington (town) Suffolk County | 1,833 | 0.91 |
| Islip (town) Suffolk County | 2,978 | 0.89 |
| Southampton (town) Suffolk County | 498 | 0.88 |
| Babylon (town) Suffolk County | 1,701 | 0.80 |
| Colonie (town) Albany County | 598 | 0.73 |
| Oyster Bay (town) Nassau County | 1,882 | 0.65 |
| Greenburgh (town) Westchester County | 530 | 0.60 |

## Pennsylvania German

### Top 10 Places Sorted by Population
*Based on all places, regardless of total population*

| Place | Population | % |
| --- | --- | --- |
| New York (city) | 465 | 0.01 |
| Morristown (town) St. Lawrence County | 433 | 15.79 |
| Troupsburg (town) Steuben County | 341 | 23.32 |
| Manhattan (borough) New York County | 327 | 0.02 |
| Conewango (town) Cattaraugus County | 262 | 18.04 |
| Jamestown (city) Chautauqua County | 245 | 0.79 |
| Colesville (town) Broome County | 220 | 4.18 |
| Hume (town) Allegany County | 219 | 10.74 |
| Lisbon (town) St. Lawrence County | 215 | 5.28 |
| St. Johnsville (town) Montgomery County | 209 | 7.99 |

### Top 10 Places Sorted by Percent of Total Population
*Based on all places, regardless of total population*

| Place | Population | % |
| --- | --- | --- |
| Troupsburg (town) Steuben County | 341 | 23.32 |
| Conewango (town) Cattaraugus County | 262 | 18.04 |
| Morristown (town) St. Lawrence County | 433 | 15.79 |
| De Peyster (town) St. Lawrence County | 147 | 15.34 |
| Napoli (town) Cattaraugus County | 181 | 11.95 |
| Hume (town) Allegany County | 219 | 10.74 |
| Junius (town) Seneca County | 160 | 10.12 |
| Leon (town) Cattaraugus County | 148 | 10.12 |
| Sherman (town) Chautauqua County | 166 | 8.96 |
| Cherry Creek (town) Chautauqua County | 108 | 8.52 |

### Top 10 Places Sorted by Percent of Total Population
*Based on places with total population of 50,000 or more*

| Place | Population | % |
| --- | --- | --- |
| Union (town) Broome County | 197 | 0.35 |
| Niagara Falls (city) Niagara County | 130 | 0.26 |
| Hamburg (town) Erie County | 103 | 0.18 |
| Greece (town) Monroe County | 145 | 0.15 |
| Tonawanda (cdp) Erie County | 85 | 0.15 |
| Tonawanda (town) Erie County | 98 | 0.13 |
| Levittown (cdp) Nassau County | 54 | 0.10 |
| Troy (city) Rensselaer County | 50 | 0.10 |
| Clay (town) Onondaga County | 38 | 0.07 |
| Buffalo (city) Erie County | 159 | 0.06 |

## Polish

### Top 10 Places Sorted by Population
*Based on all places, regardless of total population*

| Place | Population | % |
| --- | --- | --- |
| New York (city) | 216,891 | 2.68 |
| Brooklyn (borough) Kings County | 66,792 | 2.71 |
| Manhattan (borough) New York County | 64,078 | 4.05 |
| Queens (borough) Queens County | 59,757 | 2.72 |
| Hempstead (town) Nassau County | 35,774 | 4.75 |
| Cheektowaga (town) Erie County | 31,456 | 35.39 |
| Buffalo (city) Erie County | 28,108 | 10.57 |
| Brookhaven (town) Suffolk County | 27,233 | 5.67 |
| Cheektowaga (cdp) Erie County | 26,237 | 34.63 |
| Oyster Bay (town) Nassau County | 19,395 | 6.65 |

### Top 10 Places Sorted by Percent of Total Population
*Based on all places, regardless of total population*

| Place | Population | % |
| --- | --- | --- |
| Sloan (village) Erie County | 1,831 | 49.88 |
| Depew (village) Erie County | 5,979 | 38.69 |
| Piffard (cdp) Livingston County | 22 | 36.67 |
| Lancaster (town) Erie County | 15,025 | 36.65 |
| Cheektowaga (town) Erie County | 31,456 | 35.39 |
| Marilla (town) Erie County | 1,884 | 35.06 |
| Cheektowaga (cdp) Erie County | 26,237 | 34.63 |
| Darien (town) Genesee County | 946 | 30.30 |
| Duane Lake (cdp) Schenectady County | 73 | 30.17 |
| Lancaster (village) Erie County | 3,134 | 29.99 |

### Top 10 Places Sorted by Percent of Total Population
*Based on places with total population of 50,000 or more*

| Place | Population | % |
| --- | --- | --- |
| Cheektowaga (town) Erie County | 31,456 | 35.39 |
| Cheektowaga (cdp) Erie County | 26,237 | 34.63 |
| Hamburg (town) Erie County | 13,189 | 23.31 |
| Tonawanda (town) Erie County | 11,479 | 15.49 |
| Tonawanda (cdp) Erie County | 9,014 | 15.40 |
| Amherst (town) Erie County | 17,104 | 14.14 |
| Buffalo (city) Erie County | 28,108 | 10.57 |
| Niagara Falls (city) Niagara County | 4,962 | 9.75 |
| Utica (city) Oneida County | 5,408 | 8.75 |
| Colonie (town) Albany County | 6,915 | 8.48 |

## Portuguese

### Top 10 Places Sorted by Population
*Based on all places, regardless of total population*

| Place | Population | % |
| --- | --- | --- |
| New York (city) | 13,201 | 0.16 |
| Queens (borough) Queens County | 4,727 | 0.21 |
| North Hempstead (town) Nassau County | 3,978 | 1.78 |
| Manhattan (borough) New York County | 3,862 | 0.24 |
| Brookhaven (town) Suffolk County | 3,802 | 0.79 |
| Brooklyn (borough) Kings County | 2,882 | 0.12 |
| Hempstead (town) Nassau County | 2,805 | 0.37 |
| Yonkers (city) Westchester County | 2,670 | 1.37 |
| Mineola (village) Nassau County | 2,368 | 12.67 |
| Islip (town) Suffolk County | 1,977 | 0.59 |

### Top 10 Places Sorted by Percent of Total Population
*Based on all places, regardless of total population*

| Place | Population | % |
| --- | --- | --- |
| Freedom Plains (cdp) Dutchess County | 134 | 19.06 |
| Mineola (village) Nassau County | 2,368 | 12.67 |
| Fishers Landing (cdp) Jefferson County | 5 | 9.43 |

| Place | Population | % |
|---|---|---|
| Farmingville (cdp) Suffolk County | 1,109 | 6.92 |
| Fishers Island (cdp) Suffolk County | 16 | 6.40 |
| Carle Place (cdp) Nassau County | 318 | 5.69 |
| Fishkill (village) Dutchess County | 111 | 5.34 |
| Decatur (town) Otsego County | 15 | 4.78 |
| Davenport Center (cdp) Delaware County | 14 | 4.73 |
| Phoenicia (cdp) Ulster County | 17 | 4.66 |

### Top 10 Places Sorted by Percent of Total Population
*Based on places with total population of 50,000 or more*

| Place | Population | % |
|---|---|---|
| North Hempstead (town) Nassau County | 3,978 | 1.78 |
| Mount Vernon (city) Westchester County | 1,149 | 1.71 |
| Yonkers (city) Westchester County | 2,670 | 1.37 |
| New Rochelle (city) Westchester County | 830 | 1.09 |
| Brentwood (cdp) Suffolk County | 524 | 0.96 |
| Greenburgh (town) Westchester County | 718 | 0.82 |
| Brookhaven (town) Suffolk County | 3,802 | 0.79 |
| Islip (town) Suffolk County | 1,977 | 0.59 |
| White Plains (city) Westchester County | 325 | 0.58 |
| Levittown (cdp) Nassau County | 243 | 0.45 |

## Romanian

### Top 10 Places Sorted by Population
*Based on all places, regardless of total population*

| Place | Population | % |
|---|---|---|
| New York (city) | 29,552 | 0.37 |
| Queens (borough) Queens County | 11,686 | 0.53 |
| Brooklyn (borough) Kings County | 8,046 | 0.33 |
| Manhattan (borough) New York County | 7,692 | 0.49 |
| Hempstead (town) Nassau County | 2,811 | 0.37 |
| Monroe (town) Orange County | 2,439 | 6.31 |
| Kiryas Joel (village) Orange County | 2,293 | 12.01 |
| Ramapo (town) Rockland County | 1,695 | 1.38 |
| Oyster Bay (town) Nassau County | 1,492 | 0.51 |
| North Hempstead (town) Nassau County | 1,434 | 0.64 |

### Top 10 Places Sorted by Percent of Total Population
*Based on all places, regardless of total population*

| Place | Population | % |
|---|---|---|
| Kiryas Joel (village) Orange County | 2,293 | 12.01 |
| Kaser (village) Rockland County | 497 | 11.20 |
| Monroe (town) Orange County | 2,439 | 6.31 |
| Harbor Hills (cdp) Nassau County | 27 | 5.45 |
| University Gardens (cdp) Nassau County | 217 | 5.44 |
| Smallwood (cdp) Sullivan County | 32 | 4.65 |
| Milford (village) Otsego County | 21 | 4.12 |
| Port Henry (village) Essex County | 74 | 4.11 |
| East Norwich (cdp) Nassau County | 95 | 3.67 |
| Barker (town) Broome County | 95 | 3.48 |

### Top 10 Places Sorted by Percent of Total Population
*Based on places with total population of 50,000 or more*

| Place | Population | % |
|---|---|---|
| Ramapo (town) Rockland County | 1,695 | 1.38 |
| Huntington (town) Suffolk County | 1,364 | 0.67 |
| Clarkstown (town) Rockland County | 544 | 0.65 |
| North Hempstead (town) Nassau County | 1,434 | 0.64 |
| Smithtown (town) Suffolk County | 707 | 0.60 |
| Greenburgh (town) Westchester County | 489 | 0.56 |
| Queens (borough) Queens County | 11,686 | 0.53 |
| Oyster Bay (town) Nassau County | 1,492 | 0.51 |
| Manhattan (borough) New York County | 7,692 | 0.49 |
| New York (city) | 29,552 | 0.37 |

## Russian

### Top 10 Places Sorted by Population
*Based on all places, regardless of total population*

| Place | Population | % |
|---|---|---|
| New York (city) | 240,690 | 2.98 |
| Brooklyn (borough) Kings County | 88,579 | 3.59 |
| Manhattan (borough) New York County | 82,983 | 5.24 |
| Queens (borough) Queens County | 44,676 | 2.03 |
| Hempstead (town) Nassau County | 26,754 | 3.55 |
| Staten Island (borough) Richmond County | 16,388 | 3.54 |
| North Hempstead (town) Nassau County | 14,712 | 6.58 |
| Oyster Bay (town) Nassau County | 14,554 | 4.99 |
| Brookhaven (town) Suffolk County | 12,073 | 2.51 |
| Huntington (town) Suffolk County | 9,499 | 4.70 |

### Top 10 Places Sorted by Percent of Total Population
*Based on all places, regardless of total population*

| Place | Population | % |
|---|---|---|
| Piffard (cdp) Livingston County | 22 | 36.67 |
| Hewlett Bay Park (village) Nassau County | 155 | 29.87 |
| Great Neck Gardens (cdp) Nassau County | 258 | 28.41 |
| Hewlett Harbor (village) Nassau County | 331 | 28.22 |
| Roslyn Estates (village) Nassau County | 327 | 26.48 |
| Woodsburgh (village) Nassau County | 178 | 23.89 |
| Grand View-on-Hudson (village) Rockland County | 62 | 21.83 |
| Hewlett Neck (village) Nassau County | 97 | 20.73 |
| Russell Gardens (village) Nassau County | 199 | 20.66 |
| Scotts Corners (cdp) Westchester County | 102 | 20.28 |

### Top 10 Places Sorted by Percent of Total Population
*Based on places with total population of 50,000 or more*

| Place | Population | % |
|---|---|---|
| North Hempstead (town) Nassau County | 14,712 | 6.58 |
| Clarkstown (town) Rockland County | 5,317 | 6.38 |
| Greenburgh (town) Westchester County | 5,042 | 5.75 |
| Manhattan (borough) New York County | 82,983 | 5.24 |
| Oyster Bay (town) Nassau County | 14,554 | 4.99 |
| Ramapo (town) Rockland County | 6,069 | 4.95 |
| Huntington (town) Suffolk County | 9,499 | 4.70 |
| Smithtown (town) Suffolk County | 5,319 | 4.52 |
| White Plains (city) Westchester County | 2,307 | 4.13 |
| New Rochelle (city) Westchester County | 3,102 | 4.09 |

## Scandinavian

### Top 10 Places Sorted by Population
*Based on all places, regardless of total population*

| Place | Population | % |
|---|---|---|
| New York (city) | 3,434 | 0.04 |
| Manhattan (borough) New York County | 1,731 | 0.11 |
| Brooklyn (borough) Kings County | 882 | 0.04 |
| Queens (borough) Queens County | 545 | 0.02 |
| Brookhaven (town) Suffolk County | 388 | 0.08 |
| Hempstead (town) Nassau County | 360 | 0.05 |
| Albany (city) Albany County | 313 | 0.32 |
| Huntington (town) Suffolk County | 292 | 0.14 |
| Islip (town) Suffolk County | 183 | 0.05 |
| Bronx (borough) Bronx County | 155 | 0.01 |

### Top 10 Places Sorted by Percent of Total Population
*Based on all places, regardless of total population*

| Place | Population | % |
|---|---|---|
| Norfolk (cdp) St. Lawrence County | 85 | 6.84 |
| Pine Hill (cdp) Ulster County | 15 | 5.84 |
| Afton (village) Chenango County | 39 | 4.00 |
| Gardiner (cdp) Ulster County | 40 | 3.82 |
| Clifton (town) St. Lawrence County | 27 | 3.35 |
| Shortsville (village) Ontario County | 39 | 3.08 |
| Cairo (cdp) Greene County | 54 | 2.89 |
| Springfield (town) Otsego County | 41 | 2.85 |
| Limestone (village) Cattaraugus County | 9 | 2.85 |
| Sharon Springs (village) Schoharie County | 10 | 2.77 |

### Top 10 Places Sorted by Percent of Total Population
*Based on places with total population of 50,000 or more*

| Place | Population | % |
|---|---|---|
| Albany (city) Albany County | 313 | 0.32 |
| Huntington (town) Suffolk County | 292 | 0.14 |
| Manhattan (borough) New York County | 1,731 | 0.11 |
| Amherst (town) Erie County | 116 | 0.10 |
| Southampton (town) Suffolk County | 57 | 0.10 |
| Greece (town) Monroe County | 88 | 0.09 |
| Greenburgh (town) Westchester County | 79 | 0.09 |
| Brookhaven (town) Suffolk County | 388 | 0.08 |
| Utica (city) Oneida County | 48 | 0.08 |
| Syracuse (city) Onondaga County | 98 | 0.07 |

## Scotch-Irish

### Top 10 Places Sorted by Population
*Based on all places, regardless of total population*

| Place | Population | % |
|---|---|---|
| New York (city) | 27,337 | 0.34 |
| Manhattan (borough) New York County | 13,158 | 0.83 |
| Brooklyn (borough) Kings County | 6,090 | 0.25 |

| Place | Population | % |
|---|---|---|
| Brookhaven (town) Suffolk County | 5,102 | 1.06 |
| Hempstead (town) Nassau County | 4,788 | 0.64 |
| Queens (borough) Queens County | 4,602 | 0.21 |
| Islip (town) Suffolk County | 3,159 | 0.95 |
| Oyster Bay (town) Nassau County | 2,523 | 0.87 |
| Huntington (town) Suffolk County | 2,325 | 1.15 |
| Buffalo (city) Erie County | 2,324 | 0.87 |

### Top 10 Places Sorted by Percent of Total Population
*Based on all places, regardless of total population*

| Place | Population | % |
|---|---|---|
| Onondaga Nation Reservation Onondaga County | 8 | 53.33 |
| Laurens (village) Otsego County | 35 | 17.33 |
| Port Gibson (cdp) Ontario County | 80 | 14.98 |
| Argyle (village) Washington County | 49 | 13.61 |
| Parish (village) Oswego County | 63 | 12.91 |
| Claverack-Red Mills (cdp) Columbia County | 108 | 12.84 |
| Oxbow (cdp) Jefferson County | 9 | 12.50 |
| Piffard (cdp) Livingston County | 7 | 11.67 |
| Breesport (cdp) Chemung County | 85 | 10.81 |
| Windham (cdp) Greene County | 41 | 9.45 |

### Top 10 Places Sorted by Percent of Total Population
*Based on places with total population of 50,000 or more*

| Place | Population | % |
|---|---|---|
| Clay (town) Onondaga County | 1,162 | 2.00 |
| Tonawanda (cdp) Erie County | 989 | 1.69 |
| Tonawanda (town) Erie County | 1,170 | 1.58 |
| Troy (city) Rensselaer County | 784 | 1.57 |
| Colonie (town) Albany County | 1,261 | 1.55 |
| Greece (town) Monroe County | 1,469 | 1.54 |
| Smithtown (town) Suffolk County | 1,732 | 1.47 |
| Levittown (cdp) Nassau County | 722 | 1.35 |
| Amherst (town) Erie County | 1,527 | 1.26 |
| Union (town) Broome County | 712 | 1.26 |

## Scottish

### Top 10 Places Sorted by Population
*Based on all places, regardless of total population*

| Place | Population | % |
|---|---|---|
| New York (city) | 38,000 | 0.47 |
| Manhattan (borough) New York County | 19,553 | 1.23 |
| Brooklyn (borough) Kings County | 8,809 | 0.36 |
| Queens (borough) Queens County | 5,718 | 0.26 |
| Brookhaven (town) Suffolk County | 5,703 | 1.19 |
| Hempstead (town) Nassau County | 3,831 | 0.51 |
| Rochester (city) Monroe County | 3,002 | 1.42 |
| Islip (town) Suffolk County | 2,852 | 0.85 |
| Buffalo (city) Erie County | 2,816 | 1.06 |
| Oyster Bay (town) Nassau County | 2,493 | 0.85 |

### Top 10 Places Sorted by Percent of Total Population
*Based on all places, regardless of total population*

| Place | Population | % |
|---|---|---|
| Dering Harbor (village) Suffolk County | 5 | 31.25 |
| Rhinecliff (cdp) Dutchess County | 86 | 23.18 |
| Callicoon (cdp) Sullivan County | 21 | 18.75 |
| Colton (cdp) St. Lawrence County | 64 | 16.75 |
| Andes (town) Delaware County | 149 | 15.63 |
| Tuscarora (cdp) Livingston County | 12 | 15.58 |
| Salt Point (cdp) Dutchess County | 47 | 14.42 |
| Thousand Island Park (cdp) Jefferson County | 16 | 14.41 |
| Laurel (cdp) Suffolk County | 152 | 14.14 |
| Walton (village) Delaware County | 372 | 14.06 |

### Top 10 Places Sorted by Percent of Total Population
*Based on places with total population of 50,000 or more*

| Place | Population | % |
|---|---|---|
| Tonawanda (town) Erie County | 1,915 | 2.58 |
| Tonawanda (cdp) Erie County | 1,430 | 2.44 |
| Clay (town) Onondaga County | 1,377 | 2.37 |
| Union (town) Broome County | 1,114 | 1.98 |
| Greece (town) Monroe County | 1,843 | 1.93 |
| Colonie (town) Albany County | 1,526 | 1.87 |
| Irondequoit (cdp/town) Monroe County | 935 | 1.81 |
| Southampton (town) Suffolk County | 966 | 1.71 |
| Troy (city) Rensselaer County | 848 | 1.70 |
| Syracuse (city) Onondaga County | 2,233 | 1.54 |

*Please refer to the Explanation of Data in the front of the book for more detailed information.*

## Serbian

### Top 10 Places Sorted by Population
*Based on all places, regardless of total population*

| Place | Population | % |
|---|---|---|
| New York (city) | 4,911 | 0.06 |
| Queens (borough) Queens County | 2,438 | 0.11 |
| Manhattan (borough) New York County | 1,526 | 0.10 |
| Brooklyn (borough) Kings County | 520 | 0.02 |
| Buffalo (city) Erie County | 291 | 0.11 |
| Hamburg (town) Erie County | 279 | 0.49 |
| Orchard Park (town) Erie County | 247 | 0.86 |
| Staten Island (borough) Richmond County | 240 | 0.05 |
| Bronx (borough) Bronx County | 187 | 0.01 |
| Amherst (town) Erie County | 158 | 0.13 |

### Top 10 Places Sorted by Percent of Total Population
*Based on all places, regardless of total population*

| Place | Population | % |
|---|---|---|
| West Almond (town) Allegany County | 6 | 2.08 |
| Port Henry (village) Essex County | 29 | 1.61 |
| Ames (village) Montgomery County | 2 | 1.24 |
| Roslyn (village) Nassau County | 30 | 1.10 |
| South Nyack (village) Rockland County | 57 | 1.03 |
| Cairo (town) Greene County | 68 | 1.02 |
| Scottsville (village) Monroe County | 20 | 0.96 |
| New Albion (town) Cattaraugus County | 19 | 0.96 |
| Arcade (village) Wyoming County | 19 | 0.87 |
| Orchard Park (town) Erie County | 247 | 0.86 |

### Top 10 Places Sorted by Percent of Total Population
*Based on places with total population of 50,000 or more*

| Place | Population | % |
|---|---|---|
| Hamburg (town) Erie County | 279 | 0.49 |
| Amherst (town) Erie County | 158 | 0.13 |
| Cheektowaga (cdp) Erie County | 100 | 0.13 |
| Utica (city) Oneida County | 82 | 0.13 |
| Tonawanda (cdp) Erie County | 73 | 0.12 |
| Union (town) Broome County | 65 | 0.12 |
| Queens (borough) Queens County | 2,438 | 0.11 |
| Buffalo (city) Erie County | 291 | 0.11 |
| Cheektowaga (town) Erie County | 100 | 0.11 |
| Tonawanda (town) Erie County | 85 | 0.11 |

## Slavic

### Top 10 Places Sorted by Population
*Based on all places, regardless of total population*

| Place | Population | % |
|---|---|---|
| New York (city) | 1,962 | 0.02 |
| Queens (borough) Queens County | 765 | 0.03 |
| Brooklyn (borough) Kings County | 564 | 0.02 |
| Manhattan (borough) New York County | 400 | 0.03 |
| Union (town) Broome County | 291 | 0.52 |
| Greece (town) Monroe County | 240 | 0.25 |
| Yonkers (city) Westchester County | 237 | 0.12 |
| North Tonawanda (city) Niagara County | 209 | 0.66 |
| North Hempstead (town) Nassau County | 195 | 0.06 |
| Oyster Bay (town) Nassau County | 173 | 0.06 |

### Top 10 Places Sorted by Percent of Total Population
*Based on all places, regardless of total population*

| Place | Population | % |
|---|---|---|
| Tannersville (village) Greene County | 15 | 3.46 |
| Rhinecliff (cdp) Dutchess County | 12 | 3.23 |
| Depauville (cdp) Jefferson County | 12 | 2.70 |
| Jefferson Heights (cdp) Greene County | 40 | 2.51 |
| Harmony (town) Chautauqua County | 44 | 1.96 |
| Apalachin (cdp) Tioga County | 22 | 1.96 |
| Riverside (cdp) Suffolk County | 53 | 1.89 |
| Corfu (village) Genesee County | 13 | 1.69 |
| Hawthorne (cdp) Westchester County | 76 | 1.68 |
| Ripley (town) Chautauqua County | 35 | 1.64 |

### Top 10 Places Sorted by Percent of Total Population
*Based on places with total population of 50,000 or more*

| Place | Population | % |
|---|---|---|
| Union (town) Broome County | 291 | 0.52 |
| Greece (town) Monroe County | 240 | 0.25 |
| New Rochelle (city) Westchester County | 171 | 0.23 |
| Tonawanda (town) Erie County | 123 | 0.17 |

| Clay (town) Onondaga County | 93 | 0.16 |
| Amherst (town) Erie County | 153 | 0.13 |
| Yonkers (city) Westchester County | 237 | 0.12 |
| Smithtown (town) Suffolk County | 116 | 0.10 |
| Albany (city) Albany County | 94 | 0.10 |
| Tonawanda (cdp) Erie County | 59 | 0.10 |

## Slovak

### Top 10 Places Sorted by Population
*Based on all places, regardless of total population*

| Place | Population | % |
|---|---|---|
| New York (city) | 6,785 | 0.08 |
| Union (town) Broome County | 3,003 | 5.33 |
| Manhattan (borough) New York County | 2,298 | 0.15 |
| Queens (borough) Queens County | 1,882 | 0.09 |
| Brooklyn (borough) Kings County | 1,826 | 0.07 |
| Binghamton (city) Broome County | 1,334 | 2.81 |
| Johnson City (village) Broome County | 908 | 5.96 |
| Endwell (cdp) Broome County | 740 | 6.33 |
| Hempstead (town) Nassau County | 702 | 0.09 |
| Brookhaven (town) Suffolk County | 690 | 0.14 |

### Top 10 Places Sorted by Percent of Total Population
*Based on all places, regardless of total population*

| Place | Population | % |
|---|---|---|
| Fowlerville (cdp) Livingston County | 42 | 17.00 |
| Port Dickinson (village) Broome County | 109 | 7.68 |
| Endwell (cdp) Broome County | 740 | 6.33 |
| Maine (town) Broome County | 334 | 6.20 |
| Johnson City (village) Broome County | 908 | 5.96 |
| Apalachin (cdp) Tioga County | 60 | 5.36 |
| Union (town) Broome County | 3,003 | 5.33 |
| Endicott (village) Broome County | 634 | 4.76 |
| Hemlock (cdp) Livingston County | 11 | 4.35 |
| Lincolndale (cdp) Westchester County | 58 | 4.33 |

### Top 10 Places Sorted by Percent of Total Population
*Based on places with total population of 50,000 or more*

| Place | Population | % |
|---|---|---|
| Union (town) Broome County | 3,003 | 5.33 |
| Greenburgh (town) Westchester County | 388 | 0.44 |
| Clarkstown (town) Rockland County | 310 | 0.37 |
| Albany (city) Albany County | 351 | 0.36 |
| Hamburg (town) Erie County | 182 | 0.32 |
| Yonkers (city) Westchester County | 590 | 0.30 |
| Cheektowaga (cdp) Erie County | 229 | 0.30 |
| Cheektowaga (town) Erie County | 229 | 0.26 |
| Clay (town) Onondaga County | 150 | 0.26 |
| Greece (town) Monroe County | 236 | 0.25 |

## Slovene

### Top 10 Places Sorted by Population
*Based on all places, regardless of total population*

| Place | Population | % |
|---|---|---|
| New York (city) | 1,476 | 0.02 |
| Manhattan (borough) New York County | 695 | 0.04 |
| Queens (borough) Queens County | 468 | 0.02 |
| Brooklyn (borough) Kings County | 160 | 0.01 |
| Commack (cdp) Suffolk County | 150 | 0.41 |
| Smithtown (town) Suffolk County | 147 | 0.13 |
| Staten Island (borough) Richmond County | 108 | 0.02 |
| Buffalo (city) Erie County | 100 | 0.04 |
| Bedford (town) Westchester County | 96 | 0.55 |
| Hempstead (town) Nassau County | 89 | 0.01 |

### Top 10 Places Sorted by Percent of Total Population
*Based on all places, regardless of total population*

| Place | Population | % |
|---|---|---|
| Decatur (town) Otsego County | 15 | 4.78 |
| Bedford (cdp) Westchester County | 86 | 4.73 |
| Bovina (town) Delaware County | 20 | 3.92 |
| Worcester (cdp) Otsego County | 51 | 3.24 |
| Little Falls (town) Herkimer County | 41 | 2.88 |
| Titusville (cdp) Dutchess County | 13 | 2.72 |
| Worcester (town) Otsego County | 57 | 2.22 |
| Pavilion (cdp) Genesee County | 9 | 1.86 |
| Laurel Hollow (village) Nassau County | 32 | 1.70 |
| Horseheads North (cdp) Chemung County | 41 | 1.56 |

### Top 10 Places Sorted by Percent of Total Population
*Based on places with total population of 50,000 or more*

| Place | Population | % |
|---|---|---|
| Smithtown (town) Suffolk County | 147 | 0.13 |
| Union (town) Broome County | 67 | 0.12 |
| Albany (city) Albany County | 70 | 0.07 |
| Syracuse (city) Onondaga County | 85 | 0.06 |
| Manhattan (borough) New York County | 695 | 0.04 |
| Buffalo (city) Erie County | 100 | 0.04 |
| North Hempstead (town) Nassau County | 79 | 0.04 |
| Amherst (town) Erie County | 53 | 0.04 |
| Ramapo (town) Rockland County | 46 | 0.04 |
| Greece (town) Monroe County | 31 | 0.03 |

## Soviet Union

### Top 10 Places Sorted by Population
*Based on all places, regardless of total population*

| Place | Population | % |
|---|---|---|
| New York (city) | 419 | 0.01 |
| Brooklyn (borough) Kings County | 219 | 0.01 |
| Queens (borough) Queens County | 71 | <0.01 |
| Staten Island (borough) Richmond County | 63 | 0.01 |
| Manhattan (borough) New York County | 54 | <0.01 |
| Yonkers (city) Westchester County | 14 | 0.01 |
| Hornell (city) Steuben County | 12 | 0.14 |
| Bronx (borough) Bronx County | 12 | <0.01 |
| Oceanside (cdp) Nassau County | 10 | 0.03 |
| Hempstead (town) Nassau County | 10 | <0.01 |

### Top 10 Places Sorted by Percent of Total Population
*Based on all places, regardless of total population*

| Place | Population | % |
|---|---|---|
| Wainscott (cdp) Suffolk County | 3 | 0.69 |
| Hornell (city) Steuben County | 12 | 0.14 |
| Oceanside (cdp) Nassau County | 10 | 0.03 |
| New York (city) | 419 | 0.01 |
| Brooklyn (borough) Kings County | 219 | 0.01 |
| Staten Island (borough) Richmond County | 63 | 0.01 |
| Yonkers (city) Westchester County | 14 | 0.01 |
| East Hampton (town) Suffolk County | 3 | 0.01 |
| Queens (borough) Queens County | 71 | <0.01 |
| Manhattan (borough) New York County | 54 | <0.01 |

### Top 10 Places Sorted by Percent of Total Population
*Based on places with total population of 50,000 or more*

| Place | Population | % |
|---|---|---|
| New York (city) | 419 | 0.01 |
| Brooklyn (borough) Kings County | 219 | 0.01 |
| Staten Island (borough) Richmond County | 63 | 0.01 |
| Yonkers (city) Westchester County | 14 | 0.01 |
| Queens (borough) Queens County | 71 | <0.01 |
| Manhattan (borough) New York County | 54 | <0.01 |
| Bronx (borough) Bronx County | 12 | <0.01 |
| Hempstead (town) Nassau County | 10 | <0.01 |
| Albany (city) Albany County | 0 | 0.00 |
| Amherst (town) Erie County | 0 | 0.00 |

## Swedish

### Top 10 Places Sorted by Population
*Based on all places, regardless of total population*

| Place | Population | % |
|---|---|---|
| New York (city) | 20,940 | 0.26 |
| Manhattan (borough) New York County | 10,408 | 0.66 |
| Jamestown (city) Chautauqua County | 5,809 | 18.63 |
| Brooklyn (borough) Kings County | 5,185 | 0.21 |
| Brookhaven (town) Suffolk County | 4,045 | 0.84 |
| Hempstead (town) Nassau County | 3,930 | 0.52 |
| Queens (borough) Queens County | 2,862 | 0.13 |
| Islip (town) Suffolk County | 2,528 | 0.76 |
| Oyster Bay (town) Nassau County | 2,325 | 0.80 |
| Busti (town) Chautauqua County | 2,252 | 30.51 |

### Top 10 Places Sorted by Percent of Total Population
*Based on all places, regardless of total population*

| Place | Population | % |
|---|---|---|
| Chautauqua (cdp) Chautauqua County | 119 | 45.08 |
| Kiantone (town) Chautauqua County | 482 | 32.44 |
| Busti (town) Chautauqua County | 2,252 | 30.51 |

| Place | Population | % |
|---|---|---|
| Celoron (village) Chautauqua County | 345 | 30.45 |
| Busti (cdp) Chautauqua County | 158 | 29.81 |
| Poland (town) Chautauqua County | 614 | 27.47 |
| Frewsburg (cdp) Chautauqua County | 531 | 26.14 |
| Carroll (town) Chautauqua County | 903 | 25.67 |
| Ellicott (town) Chautauqua County | 2,238 | 25.52 |
| Lakewood (village) Chautauqua County | 773 | 25.44 |

### Top 10 Places Sorted by Percent of Total Population
*Based on places with total population of 50,000 or more*

| Place | Population | % |
|---|---|---|
| Hamburg (town) Erie County | 948 | 1.68 |
| Colonie (town) Albany County | 944 | 1.16 |
| Huntington (town) Suffolk County | 2,237 | 1.11 |
| Smithtown (town) Suffolk County | 1,304 | 1.11 |
| Clay (town) Onondaga County | 625 | 1.08 |
| Southampton (town) Suffolk County | 598 | 1.06 |
| Tonawanda (town) Erie County | 758 | 1.02 |
| Tonawanda (cdp) Erie County | 584 | 1.00 |
| Irondequoit (cdp/town) Monroe County | 482 | 0.93 |
| Brookhaven (town) Suffolk County | 4,045 | 0.84 |

## Swiss

### Top 10 Places Sorted by Population
*Based on all places, regardless of total population*

| Place | Population | % |
|---|---|---|
| New York (city) | 8,135 | 0.10 |
| Manhattan (borough) New York County | 4,962 | 0.31 |
| Brooklyn (borough) Kings County | 1,491 | 0.06 |
| Brookhaven (town) Suffolk County | 1,356 | 0.28 |
| Queens (borough) Queens County | 1,260 | 0.06 |
| Hempstead (town) Nassau County | 1,183 | 0.16 |
| Oyster Bay (town) Nassau County | 686 | 0.24 |
| Huntington (town) Suffolk County | 632 | 0.31 |
| Islip (town) Suffolk County | 619 | 0.19 |
| Galen (town) Wayne County | 390 | 9.04 |

### Top 10 Places Sorted by Percent of Total Population
*Based on all places, regardless of total population*

| Place | Population | % |
|---|---|---|
| Belleville (cdp) Jefferson County | 79 | 67.52 |
| Constableville (village) Lewis County | 36 | 11.65 |
| Barrington (town) Yates County | 184 | 10.73 |
| Jeffersonville (village) Sullivan County | 31 | 9.63 |
| Galen (town) Wayne County | 390 | 9.04 |
| Castorland (village) Lewis County | 34 | 8.81 |
| Leon (town) Cattaraugus County | 116 | 7.93 |
| Torrey (town) Yates County | 100 | 7.69 |
| Red House (town) Cattaraugus County | 2 | 7.69 |
| Benton (town) Yates County | 190 | 6.78 |

### Top 10 Places Sorted by Percent of Total Population
*Based on places with total population of 50,000 or more*

| Place | Population | % |
|---|---|---|
| Irondequoit (cdp/town) Monroe County | 255 | 0.49 |
| Southampton (town) Suffolk County | 231 | 0.41 |
| Manhattan (borough) New York County | 4,962 | 0.31 |
| Huntington (town) Suffolk County | 632 | 0.31 |
| Clay (town) Onondaga County | 175 | 0.30 |
| Brookhaven (town) Suffolk County | 1,356 | 0.28 |
| Schenectady (city) Schenectady County | 171 | 0.26 |
| Oyster Bay (town) Nassau County | 686 | 0.24 |
| Greenburgh (town) Westchester County | 211 | 0.24 |
| White Plains (city) Westchester County | 129 | 0.23 |

## Turkish

### Top 10 Places Sorted by Population
*Based on all places, regardless of total population*

| Place | Population | % |
|---|---|---|
| New York (city) | 14,927 | 0.18 |
| Brooklyn (borough) Kings County | 5,164 | 0.21 |
| Queens (borough) Queens County | 3,767 | 0.17 |
| Manhattan (borough) New York County | 3,703 | 0.23 |
| Brookhaven (town) Suffolk County | 1,935 | 0.40 |
| Staten Island (borough) Richmond County | 1,607 | 0.35 |
| Oyster Bay (town) Nassau County | 1,232 | 0.42 |
| Hempstead (town) Nassau County | 1,202 | 0.16 |
| Babylon (town) Suffolk County | 939 | 0.44 |
| Bronx (borough) Bronx County | 686 | 0.05 |

### Top 10 Places Sorted by Percent of Total Population
*Based on all places, regardless of total population*

| Place | Population | % |
|---|---|---|
| Dering Harbor (village) Suffolk County | 5 | 31.25 |
| Jeffersonville (village) Sullivan County | 15 | 4.66 |
| Orient (cdp) Suffolk County | 20 | 3.33 |
| Port Washington North (village) Nassau County | 100 | 3.29 |
| Walton (village) Delaware County | 61 | 2.31 |
| Wading River (cdp) Suffolk County | 178 | 2.18 |
| Northport (village) Suffolk County | 161 | 2.16 |
| Piermont (village) Rockland County | 50 | 1.99 |
| Bayville (village) Nassau County | 128 | 1.91 |
| East Patchogue (cdp) Suffolk County | 388 | 1.84 |

### Top 10 Places Sorted by Percent of Total Population
*Based on places with total population of 50,000 or more*

| Place | Population | % |
|---|---|---|
| Greece (town) Monroe County | 561 | 0.59 |
| Irondequoit (cdp/town) Monroe County | 245 | 0.47 |
| Babylon (town) Suffolk County | 939 | 0.44 |
| Oyster Bay (town) Nassau County | 1,232 | 0.42 |
| Troy (city) Rensselaer County | 207 | 0.41 |
| Brookhaven (town) Suffolk County | 1,935 | 0.40 |
| Staten Island (borough) Richmond County | 1,607 | 0.35 |
| Levittown (cdp) Nassau County | 181 | 0.34 |
| Rochester (city) Monroe County | 612 | 0.29 |
| Huntington (town) Suffolk County | 502 | 0.25 |

## Ukrainian

### Top 10 Places Sorted by Population
*Based on all places, regardless of total population*

| Place | Population | % |
|---|---|---|
| New York (city) | 48,714 | 0.60 |
| Brooklyn (borough) Kings County | 25,046 | 1.02 |
| Manhattan (borough) New York County | 8,849 | 0.56 |
| Queens (borough) Queens County | 8,375 | 0.38 |
| Staten Island (borough) Richmond County | 4,836 | 1.04 |
| Hempstead (town) Nassau County | 2,806 | 0.37 |
| Brookhaven (town) Suffolk County | 2,350 | 0.49 |
| Oyster Bay (town) Nassau County | 1,774 | 0.61 |
| Greece (town) Monroe County | 1,758 | 1.84 |
| Huntington (town) Suffolk County | 1,742 | 0.86 |

### Top 10 Places Sorted by Percent of Total Population
*Based on all places, regardless of total population*

| Place | Population | % |
|---|---|---|
| Washington Mills (cdp) Oneida County | 186 | 17.30 |
| Kerhonkson (cdp) Ulster County | 202 | 15.97 |
| Cragsmoor (cdp) Ulster County | 43 | 11.94 |
| Clarendon (town) Orleans County | 374 | 10.35 |
| Webster (village) Monroe County | 531 | 9.90 |
| Redwood (cdp) Jefferson County | 30 | 9.71 |
| Schuyler (town) Herkimer County | 321 | 9.46 |
| Mountain Lodge Park (cdp) Orange County | 175 | 9.41 |
| Cayuga (village) Cayuga County | 36 | 7.93 |
| Walker Valley (cdp) Ulster County | 41 | 7.65 |

### Top 10 Places Sorted by Percent of Total Population
*Based on places with total population of 50,000 or more*

| Place | Population | % |
|---|---|---|
| Irondequoit (cdp/town) Monroe County | 1,169 | 2.27 |
| Greece (town) Monroe County | 1,758 | 1.84 |
| Troy (city) Rensselaer County | 819 | 1.64 |
| Union (town) Broome County | 666 | 1.18 |
| Hamburg (town) Erie County | 664 | 1.17 |
| Ramapo (town) Rockland County | 1,403 | 1.14 |
| Clay (town) Onondaga County | 650 | 1.12 |
| Colonie (town) Albany County | 860 | 1.05 |
| Staten Island (borough) Richmond County | 4,836 | 1.04 |
| Brooklyn (borough) Kings County | 25,046 | 1.02 |

## Welsh

### Top 10 Places Sorted by Population
*Based on all places, regardless of total population*

| Place | Population | % |
|---|---|---|
| New York (city) | 11,219 | 0.14 |
| Manhattan (borough) New York County | 6,000 | 0.38 |
| Brooklyn (borough) Kings County | 2,606 | 0.11 |

| Place | Population | % |
|---|---|---|
| Queens (borough) Queens County | 1,666 | 0.08 |
| Union (town) Broome County | 1,372 | 2.44 |
| Brookhaven (town) Suffolk County | 1,189 | 0.25 |
| Syracuse (city) Onondaga County | 1,060 | 0.73 |
| Rochester (city) Monroe County | 992 | 0.47 |
| Rome (city) Oneida County | 891 | 2.63 |
| Hempstead (town) Nassau County | 865 | 0.11 |

### Top 10 Places Sorted by Percent of Total Population
*Based on all places, regardless of total population*

| Place | Population | % |
|---|---|---|
| Parc (cdp) Clinton County | 22 | 52.38 |
| Barneveld (village) Oneida County | 74 | 24.10 |
| Duanesburg (cdp) Schenectady County | 28 | 16.00 |
| Remsen (town) Oneida County | 274 | 14.13 |
| West Winfield (village) Herkimer County | 112 | 14.11 |
| Winfield (town) Herkimer County | 268 | 13.96 |
| Remsen (village) Oneida County | 76 | 13.89 |
| Holland Patent (village) Oneida County | 75 | 13.54 |
| Madison (village) Madison County | 49 | 12.47 |
| Thousand Island Park (cdp) Jefferson County | 13 | 11.71 |

### Top 10 Places Sorted by Percent of Total Population
*Based on places with total population of 50,000 or more*

| Place | Population | % |
|---|---|---|
| Union (town) Broome County | 1,372 | 2.44 |
| Utica (city) Oneida County | 775 | 1.25 |
| Colonie (town) Albany County | 704 | 0.86 |
| Troy (city) Rensselaer County | 432 | 0.86 |
| Clay (town) Onondaga County | 496 | 0.85 |
| Syracuse (city) Onondaga County | 1,060 | 0.73 |
| Irondequoit (cdp/town) Monroe County | 352 | 0.68 |
| Niagara Falls (city) Niagara County | 346 | 0.68 |
| Amherst (town) Erie County | 798 | 0.66 |
| Albany (city) Albany County | 597 | 0.61 |

## West Indian, excluding Hispanic

### Top 10 Places Sorted by Population
*Based on all places, regardless of total population*

| Place | Population | % |
|---|---|---|
| New York (city) | 598,504 | 7.41 |
| Brooklyn (borough) Kings County | 306,541 | 12.43 |
| Queens (borough) Queens County | 147,460 | 6.71 |
| Bronx (borough) Bronx County | 107,527 | 7.87 |
| Hempstead (town) Nassau County | 45,733 | 6.07 |
| Manhattan (borough) New York County | 30,009 | 1.90 |
| Mount Vernon (city) Westchester County | 13,279 | 19.80 |
| Ramapo (town) Rockland County | 12,710 | 10.36 |
| Babylon (town) Suffolk County | 11,187 | 5.24 |
| Islip (town) Suffolk County | 10,274 | 3.08 |

### Top 10 Places Sorted by Percent of Total Population
*Based on all places, regardless of total population*

| Place | Population | % |
|---|---|---|
| Hillcrest (cdp) Rockland County | 2,791 | 34.04 |
| Elmont (cdp) Nassau County | 9,499 | 27.54 |
| Spring Valley (village) Rockland County | 7,957 | 26.24 |
| North Valley Stream (cdp) Nassau County | 4,249 | 25.74 |
| North Amityville (cdp) Suffolk County | 3,825 | 21.47 |
| Uniondale (cdp) Nassau County | 5,218 | 21.30 |
| Mount Vernon (city) Westchester County | 13,279 | 19.80 |
| Lakeview (cdp) Nassau County | 1,015 | 18.22 |
| South Floral Park (village) Nassau County | 271 | 17.35 |
| Wheatley Heights (cdp) Suffolk County | 1,036 | 16.72 |

### Top 10 Places Sorted by Percent of Total Population
*Based on places with total population of 50,000 or more*

| Place | Population | % |
|---|---|---|
| Mount Vernon (city) Westchester County | 13,279 | 19.80 |
| Brooklyn (borough) Kings County | 306,541 | 12.43 |
| Hempstead (village) Nassau County | 6,463 | 12.11 |
| Ramapo (town) Rockland County | 12,710 | 10.36 |
| Bronx (borough) Bronx County | 107,527 | 7.87 |
| New York (city) | 598,504 | 7.41 |
| Queens (borough) Queens County | 147,460 | 6.71 |
| Brentwood (cdp) Suffolk County | 3,472 | 6.33 |
| Hempstead (town) Nassau County | 45,733 | 6.07 |
| New Rochelle (city) Westchester County | 4,597 | 6.06 |

*Please refer to the Explanation of Data in the front of the book for more detailed information.*

## West Indian: Bahamian, excluding Hispanic

### Top 10 Places Sorted by Population
*Based on all places, regardless of total population*

| Place | Population | % |
|---|---|---|
| New York (city) | 1,147 | 0.01 |
| Manhattan (borough) New York County | 457 | 0.03 |
| Brooklyn (borough) Kings County | 266 | 0.01 |
| Rochester (city) Monroe County | 218 | 0.10 |
| Bronx (borough) Bronx County | 208 | 0.02 |
| Queens (borough) Queens County | 185 | 0.01 |
| North Amityville (cdp) Suffolk County | 88 | 0.49 |
| Babylon (town) Suffolk County | 88 | 0.04 |
| Hempstead (town) Nassau County | 51 | 0.01 |
| Miller Place (cdp) Suffolk County | 47 | 0.38 |

### Top 10 Places Sorted by Percent of Total Population
*Based on all places, regardless of total population*

| Place | Population | % |
|---|---|---|
| North Amityville (cdp) Suffolk County | 88 | 0.49 |
| Miller Place (cdp) Suffolk County | 47 | 0.38 |
| South Floral Park (village) Nassau County | 5 | 0.32 |
| Fowler (town) St. Lawrence County | 6 | 0.24 |
| Melville (cdp) Suffolk County | 31 | 0.16 |
| West Hempstead (cdp) Nassau County | 28 | 0.15 |
| Potsdam (village) St. Lawrence County | 14 | 0.15 |
| Fort Ann (town) Washington County | 9 | 0.14 |
| Peekskill (city) Westchester County | 28 | 0.12 |
| Elmira (city) Chemung County | 31 | 0.11 |

### Top 10 Places Sorted by Percent of Total Population
*Based on places with total population of 50,000 or more*

| Place | Population | % |
|---|---|---|
| Rochester (city) Monroe County | 218 | 0.10 |
| White Plains (city) Westchester County | 26 | 0.05 |
| Babylon (town) Suffolk County | 88 | 0.04 |
| Hamburg (town) Erie County | 21 | 0.04 |
| Manhattan (borough) New York County | 457 | 0.03 |
| Bronx (borough) Bronx County | 208 | 0.02 |
| Huntington (town) Suffolk County | 31 | 0.02 |
| Mount Vernon (city) Westchester County | 11 | 0.02 |
| New York (city) | 1,147 | 0.01 |
| Brooklyn (borough) Kings County | 266 | 0.01 |

## West Indian: Barbadian, excluding Hispanic

### Top 10 Places Sorted by Population
*Based on all places, regardless of total population*

| Place | Population | % |
|---|---|---|
| New York (city) | 22,550 | 0.28 |
| Brooklyn (borough) Kings County | 14,916 | 0.60 |
| Queens (borough) Queens County | 5,021 | 0.23 |
| Bronx (borough) Bronx County | 1,612 | 0.12 |
| Hempstead (town) Nassau County | 1,279 | 0.17 |
| Manhattan (borough) New York County | 907 | 0.06 |
| Freeport (village) Nassau County | 447 | 1.05 |
| New Rochelle (city) Westchester County | 316 | 0.42 |
| Rochester (city) Monroe County | 230 | 0.11 |
| Mount Vernon (city) Westchester County | 208 | 0.31 |

### Top 10 Places Sorted by Percent of Total Population
*Based on all places, regardless of total population*

| Place | Population | % |
|---|---|---|
| Carthage (village) Jefferson County | 183 | 4.92 |
| Wilna (town) Jefferson County | 183 | 2.87 |
| South Nyack (village) Rockland County | 105 | 1.89 |
| Harriman (village) Orange County | 44 | 1.86 |
| Lakeview (cdp) Nassau County | 89 | 1.60 |
| South Valley Stream (cdp) Nassau County | 73 | 1.39 |
| Hornell (city) Steuben County | 93 | 1.08 |
| Freeport (village) Nassau County | 447 | 1.05 |
| Monticello (village) Sullivan County | 68 | 1.01 |
| Westbury (village) Nassau County | 129 | 0.87 |

### Top 10 Places Sorted by Percent of Total Population
*Based on places with total population of 50,000 or more*

| Place | Population | % |
|---|---|---|
| Brooklyn (borough) Kings County | 14,916 | 0.60 |

| | | |
|---|---|---|
| New Rochelle (city) Westchester County | 316 | 0.42 |
| Mount Vernon (city) Westchester County | 208 | 0.31 |
| Hempstead (village) Nassau County | 153 | 0.29 |
| New York (city) | 22,550 | 0.28 |
| Queens (borough) Queens County | 5,021 | 0.23 |
| Greenburgh (town) Westchester County | 155 | 0.18 |
| Hempstead (town) Nassau County | 1,279 | 0.17 |
| Schenectady (city) Schenectady County | 94 | 0.14 |
| Bronx (borough) Bronx County | 1,612 | 0.12 |

## West Indian: Belizean, excluding Hispanic

### Top 10 Places Sorted by Population
*Based on all places, regardless of total population*

| Place | Population | % |
|---|---|---|
| New York (city) | 5,674 | 0.07 |
| Brooklyn (borough) Kings County | 2,026 | 0.08 |
| Bronx (borough) Bronx County | 1,493 | 0.11 |
| Queens (borough) Queens County | 1,344 | 0.06 |
| Manhattan (borough) New York County | 735 | 0.05 |
| Rochester (city) Monroe County | 171 | 0.08 |
| White Plains (city) Westchester County | 155 | 0.28 |
| South Nyack (village) Rockland County | 120 | 2.16 |
| Orangetown (town) Rockland County | 120 | 0.25 |
| Mount Vernon (city) Westchester County | 118 | 0.18 |

### Top 10 Places Sorted by Percent of Total Population
*Based on all places, regardless of total population*

| Place | Population | % |
|---|---|---|
| South Nyack (village) Rockland County | 120 | 2.16 |
| Black River (village) Jefferson County | 22 | 1.41 |
| Panama (village) Chautauqua County | 6 | 1.26 |
| Herricks (cdp) Nassau County | 37 | 0.94 |
| Rutland (town) Jefferson County | 22 | 0.73 |
| Cattaraugus Reservation Erie County | 12 | 0.64 |
| Carthage (village) Jefferson County | 17 | 0.46 |
| Chestnut Ridge (village) Rockland County | 35 | 0.45 |
| Brookville (village) Nassau County | 13 | 0.38 |
| Chili (town) Monroe County | 85 | 0.30 |

### Top 10 Places Sorted by Percent of Total Population
*Based on places with total population of 50,000 or more*

| Place | Population | % |
|---|---|---|
| White Plains (city) Westchester County | 155 | 0.28 |
| Mount Vernon (city) Westchester County | 118 | 0.18 |
| Bronx (borough) Bronx County | 1,493 | 0.11 |
| Brooklyn (borough) Kings County | 2,026 | 0.08 |
| Rochester (city) Monroe County | 171 | 0.08 |
| New York (city) | 5,674 | 0.07 |
| Queens (borough) Queens County | 1,344 | 0.06 |
| Niagara Falls (city) Niagara County | 29 | 0.06 |
| Manhattan (borough) New York County | 735 | 0.05 |
| Hamburg (town) Erie County | 30 | 0.05 |

## West Indian: Bermudan, excluding Hispanic

### Top 10 Places Sorted by Population
*Based on all places, regardless of total population*

| Place | Population | % |
|---|---|---|
| New York (city) | 518 | 0.01 |
| Bronx (borough) Bronx County | 198 | 0.01 |
| Queens (borough) Queens County | 177 | 0.01 |
| Manhattan (borough) New York County | 127 | 0.01 |
| Hempstead (town) Nassau County | 52 | 0.01 |
| Roosevelt (cdp) Nassau County | 43 | 0.29 |
| Albany (city) Albany County | 36 | 0.04 |
| Centereach (cdp) Suffolk County | 34 | 0.11 |
| Brookhaven (town) Suffolk County | 34 | 0.01 |
| Brooklyn (borough) Kings County | 16 | <0.01 |

### Top 10 Places Sorted by Percent of Total Population
*Based on all places, regardless of total population*

| Place | Population | % |
|---|---|---|
| Green Island (town/village) Albany County | 13 | 0.51 |
| Old Westbury (village) Nassau County | 13 | 0.33 |
| Roosevelt (cdp) Nassau County | 43 | 0.29 |
| Clermont (town) Columbia County | 3 | 0.15 |
| Upper Nyack (village) Rockland County | 3 | 0.15 |
| Centereach (cdp) Suffolk County | 34 | 0.11 |
| Albany (city) Albany County | 36 | 0.04 |

| | | |
|---|---|---|
| Hempstead (village) Nassau County | 9 | 0.02 |
| New York (city) | 518 | 0.01 |
| Bronx (borough) Bronx County | 198 | 0.01 |

### Top 10 Places Sorted by Percent of Total Population
*Based on places with total population of 50,000 or more*

| Place | Population | % |
|---|---|---|
| Albany (city) Albany County | 36 | 0.04 |
| Hempstead (village) Nassau County | 9 | 0.02 |
| New York (city) | 518 | 0.01 |
| Bronx (borough) Bronx County | 198 | 0.01 |
| Queens (borough) Queens County | 177 | 0.01 |
| Manhattan (borough) New York County | 127 | 0.01 |
| Hempstead (town) Nassau County | 52 | 0.01 |
| Brookhaven (town) Suffolk County | 34 | 0.01 |
| Brooklyn (borough) Kings County | 16 | <0.01 |
| Oyster Bay (town) Nassau County | 13 | <0.01 |

## West Indian: British West Indian, excluding Hispanic

### Top 10 Places Sorted by Population
*Based on all places, regardless of total population*

| Place | Population | % |
|---|---|---|
| New York (city) | 44,326 | 0.55 |
| Brooklyn (borough) Kings County | 30,607 | 1.24 |
| Bronx (borough) Bronx County | 7,136 | 0.52 |
| Queens (borough) Queens County | 4,689 | 0.21 |
| Manhattan (borough) New York County | 1,658 | 0.10 |
| Hempstead (town) Nassau County | 972 | 0.13 |
| Yonkers (city) Westchester County | 497 | 0.26 |
| Islip (town) Suffolk County | 470 | 0.14 |
| Mount Vernon (city) Westchester County | 348 | 0.52 |
| Wallkill (town) Orange County | 296 | 1.09 |

### Top 10 Places Sorted by Percent of Total Population
*Based on all places, regardless of total population*

| Place | Population | % |
|---|---|---|
| Wawayanda (town) Orange County | 271 | 3.79 |
| Scotchtown (cdp) Orange County | 222 | 2.28 |
| Amagansett (cdp) Suffolk County | 17 | 1.90 |
| Cumberland Head (cdp) Clinton County | 25 | 1.51 |
| Brooklyn (borough) Kings County | 30,607 | 1.24 |
| Hillcrest (cdp) Rockland County | 93 | 1.13 |
| Wallkill (town) Orange County | 296 | 1.09 |
| Bay Shore (cdp) Suffolk County | 253 | 0.91 |
| Highland (cdp) Ulster County | 49 | 0.86 |
| Mechanicstown (cdp) Orange County | 63 | 0.84 |

### Top 10 Places Sorted by Percent of Total Population
*Based on places with total population of 50,000 or more*

| Place | Population | % |
|---|---|---|
| Brooklyn (borough) Kings County | 30,607 | 1.24 |
| New York (city) | 44,326 | 0.55 |
| Bronx (borough) Bronx County | 7,136 | 0.52 |
| Mount Vernon (city) Westchester County | 348 | 0.52 |
| Hempstead (village) Nassau County | 250 | 0.47 |
| Yonkers (city) Westchester County | 497 | 0.26 |
| Queens (borough) Queens County | 4,689 | 0.21 |
| Ramapo (town) Rockland County | 253 | 0.21 |
| Albany (city) Albany County | 210 | 0.21 |
| New Rochelle (city) Westchester County | 153 | 0.20 |

## West Indian: Dutch West Indian, excluding Hispanic

### Top 10 Places Sorted by Population
*Based on all places, regardless of total population*

| Place | Population | % |
|---|---|---|
| New York (city) | 1,167 | 0.01 |
| Brooklyn (borough) Kings County | 424 | 0.02 |
| Manhattan (borough) New York County | 276 | 0.02 |
| Queens (borough) Queens County | 206 | 0.01 |
| Hempstead (town) Nassau County | 199 | 0.03 |
| Bronx (borough) Bronx County | 172 | 0.01 |
| North Valley Stream (cdp) Nassau County | 134 | 0.81 |
| Staten Island (borough) Richmond County | 89 | 0.02 |
| Albany (city) Albany County | 79 | 0.08 |
| Brownville (town) Jefferson County | 71 | 1.16 |

### Top 10 Places Sorted by Percent of Total Population
*Based on all places, regardless of total population*

| Place | Population | % |
|---|---|---|
| Brownville (town) Jefferson County | 71 | 1.16 |
| Barnum Island (cdp) Nassau County | 25 | 0.95 |
| German (town) Chenango County | 3 | 0.95 |
| Hartwick (town) Otsego County | 20 | 0.83 |
| North Valley Stream (cdp) Nassau County | 134 | 0.81 |
| Mamakating (town) Sullivan County | 55 | 0.46 |
| Westbury (village) Nassau County | 65 | 0.44 |
| Lansing (village) Tompkins County | 14 | 0.40 |
| Preston (town) Chenango County | 3 | 0.31 |
| Lansing (town) Tompkins County | 32 | 0.29 |

### Top 10 Places Sorted by Percent of Total Population
*Based on places with total population of 50,000 or more*

| Place | Population | % |
|---|---|---|
| Albany (city) Albany County | 79 | 0.08 |
| Hempstead (village) Nassau County | 31 | 0.06 |
| Hempstead (town) Nassau County | 199 | 0.03 |
| North Hempstead (town) Nassau County | 65 | 0.03 |
| Brooklyn (borough) Kings County | 424 | 0.02 |
| Manhattan (borough) New York County | 276 | 0.02 |
| Staten Island (borough) Richmond County | 89 | 0.02 |
| Schenectady (city) Schenectady County | 10 | 0.02 |
| New York (city) | 1,167 | 0.01 |
| Queens (borough) Queens County | 206 | 0.01 |

## West Indian: Haitian, excluding Hispanic

### Top 10 Places Sorted by Population
*Based on all places, regardless of total population*

| Place | Population | % |
|---|---|---|
| New York (city) | 120,252 | 1.49 |
| Brooklyn (borough) Kings County | 69,941 | 2.84 |
| Queens (borough) Queens County | 38,368 | 1.74 |
| Hempstead (town) Nassau County | 17,422 | 2.31 |
| Ramapo (town) Rockland County | 8,948 | 7.29 |
| Spring Valley (village) Rockland County | 6,665 | 21.98 |
| Manhattan (borough) New York County | 6,500 | 0.41 |
| Islip (town) Suffolk County | 5,636 | 1.69 |
| Elmont (cdp) Nassau County | 5,587 | 16.20 |
| Bronx (borough) Bronx County | 4,652 | 0.34 |

### Top 10 Places Sorted by Percent of Total Population
*Based on all places, regardless of total population*

| Place | Population | % |
|---|---|---|
| Spring Valley (village) Rockland County | 6,665 | 21.98 |
| Elmont (cdp) Nassau County | 5,587 | 16.20 |
| Hillcrest (cdp) Rockland County | 1,310 | 15.98 |
| North Valley Stream (cdp) Nassau County | 1,827 | 11.07 |
| Hillburn (village) Rockland County | 88 | 9.27 |
| Wheatley Heights (cdp) Suffolk County | 545 | 8.80 |
| New Cassel (cdp) Nassau County | 1,053 | 8.38 |
| Nyack (village) Rockland County | 577 | 8.29 |
| Deferiet (village) Jefferson County | 38 | 8.09 |
| Uniondale (cdp) Nassau County | 1,927 | 7.87 |

### Top 10 Places Sorted by Percent of Total Population
*Based on places with total population of 50,000 or more*

| Place | Population | % |
|---|---|---|
| Ramapo (town) Rockland County | 8,948 | 7.29 |
| Brentwood (cdp) Suffolk County | 2,162 | 3.94 |
| Hempstead (village) Nassau County | 2,104 | 3.94 |
| Brooklyn (borough) Kings County | 69,941 | 2.84 |
| Clarkstown (town) Rockland County | 2,077 | 2.49 |
| Hempstead (town) Nassau County | 17,422 | 2.31 |
| Babylon (town) Suffolk County | 3,789 | 1.77 |
| Queens (borough) Queens County | 38,368 | 1.74 |
| Islip (town) Suffolk County | 5,636 | 1.69 |
| New York (city) | 120,252 | 1.49 |

## West Indian: Jamaican, excluding Hispanic

### Top 10 Places Sorted by Population
*Based on all places, regardless of total population*

| Place | Population | % |
|---|---|---|
| New York (city) | 216,495 | 2.68 |
| Brooklyn (borough) Kings County | 80,999 | 3.28 |

| Bronx (borough) Bronx County | 64,222 | 4.70 |
| Queens (borough) Queens County | 59,999 | 2.73 |
| Hempstead (town) Nassau County | 17,690 | 2.35 |
| Mount Vernon (city) Westchester County | 10,445 | 15.57 |
| Manhattan (borough) New York County | 9,242 | 0.58 |
| Yonkers (city) Westchester County | 5,051 | 2.59 |
| Babylon (town) Suffolk County | 4,758 | 2.23 |
| Poughkeepsie (city) Dutchess County | 3,093 | 9.53 |

### Top 10 Places Sorted by Percent of Total Population
*Based on all places, regardless of total population*

| Place | Population | % |
|---|---|---|
| Mount Vernon (city) Westchester County | 10,445 | 15.57 |
| Lakeview (cdp) Nassau County | 791 | 14.20 |
| North Amityville (cdp) Suffolk County | 2,248 | 12.62 |
| Hillcrest (cdp) Rockland County | 854 | 10.42 |
| Poughkeepsie (city) Dutchess County | 3,093 | 9.53 |
| South Floral Park (village) Nassau County | 141 | 9.03 |
| Elmont (cdp) Nassau County | 2,968 | 8.61 |
| Uniondale (cdp) Nassau County | 1,905 | 7.78 |
| North Valley Stream (cdp) Nassau County | 1,257 | 7.62 |
| Morrisville (village) Madison County | 173 | 6.83 |

### Top 10 Places Sorted by Percent of Total Population
*Based on places with total population of 50,000 or more*

| Place | Population | % |
|---|---|---|
| Mount Vernon (city) Westchester County | 10,445 | 15.57 |
| Hempstead (village) Nassau County | 2,809 | 5.26 |
| Bronx (borough) Bronx County | 64,222 | 4.70 |
| New Rochelle (city) Westchester County | 2,635 | 3.48 |
| Brooklyn (borough) Kings County | 80,999 | 3.28 |
| Queens (borough) Queens County | 59,999 | 2.73 |
| New York (city) | 216,495 | 2.68 |
| Yonkers (city) Westchester County | 5,051 | 2.59 |
| Greenburgh (town) Westchester County | 2,150 | 2.45 |
| Hempstead (town) Nassau County | 17,690 | 2.35 |

## West Indian: Trinidadian and Tobagonian, excluding Hispanic

### Top 10 Places Sorted by Population
*Based on all places, regardless of total population*

| Place | Population | % |
|---|---|---|
| New York (city) | 76,240 | 0.94 |
| Brooklyn (borough) Kings County | 46,490 | 1.88 |
| Queens (borough) Queens County | 19,255 | 0.88 |
| Bronx (borough) Bronx County | 4,811 | 0.35 |
| Manhattan (borough) New York County | 3,877 | 0.24 |
| Hempstead (town) Nassau County | 3,155 | 0.42 |
| Staten Island (borough) Richmond County | 1,807 | 0.39 |
| Brookhaven (town) Suffolk County | 1,200 | 0.25 |
| Babylon (town) Suffolk County | 854 | 0.40 |
| Yonkers (city) Westchester County | 689 | 0.35 |

### Top 10 Places Sorted by Percent of Total Population
*Based on all places, regardless of total population*

| Place | Population | % |
|---|---|---|
| Brewster (village) Putnam County | 131 | 6.53 |
| Hillcrest (cdp) Rockland County | 367 | 4.48 |
| East Marion (cdp) Suffolk County | 54 | 4.04 |
| South Floral Park (village) Nassau County | 53 | 3.39 |
| North Valley Stream (cdp) Nassau County | 551 | 3.34 |
| Rockland (town) Sullivan County | 106 | 2.75 |
| South Valley Stream (cdp) Nassau County | 110 | 2.09 |
| Greenwood Lake (village) Orange County | 67 | 2.07 |
| Goshen (village) Orange County | 111 | 2.00 |
| Brooklyn (borough) Kings County | 46,490 | 1.88 |

### Top 10 Places Sorted by Percent of Total Population
*Based on places with total population of 50,000 or more*

| Place | Population | % |
|---|---|---|
| Brooklyn (borough) Kings County | 46,490 | 1.88 |
| New York (city) | 76,240 | 0.94 |
| Queens (borough) Queens County | 19,255 | 0.88 |
| Hempstead (village) Nassau County | 322 | 0.60 |
| Mount Vernon (city) Westchester County | 397 | 0.59 |
| Ramapo (town) Rockland County | 604 | 0.49 |
| Troy (city) Rensselaer County | 243 | 0.49 |
| Hempstead (town) Nassau County | 3,155 | 0.42 |
| New Rochelle (city) Westchester County | 317 | 0.42 |
| Babylon (town) Suffolk County | 854 | 0.40 |

## West Indian: U.S. Virgin Islander, excluding Hispanic

### Top 10 Places Sorted by Population
*Based on all places, regardless of total population*

| Place | Population | % |
|---|---|---|
| New York (city) | 2,383 | 0.03 |
| Bronx (borough) Bronx County | 952 | 0.07 |
| Brooklyn (borough) Kings County | 558 | 0.02 |
| Manhattan (borough) New York County | 487 | 0.03 |
| Queens (borough) Queens County | 364 | 0.02 |
| South Huntington (cdp) Suffolk County | 147 | 1.49 |
| Huntington (town) Suffolk County | 147 | 0.07 |
| Yonkers (city) Westchester County | 83 | 0.04 |
| Poughkeepsie (city) Dutchess County | 42 | 0.13 |
| Middletown (city) Orange County | 33 | 0.12 |

### Top 10 Places Sorted by Percent of Total Population
*Based on all places, regardless of total population*

| Place | Population | % |
|---|---|---|
| South Huntington (cdp) Suffolk County | 147 | 1.49 |
| Roxbury (town) Delaware County | 28 | 1.12 |
| Brownville (village) Jefferson County | 7 | 0.67 |
| Brookville (village) Nassau County | 15 | 0.43 |
| Otisville (village) Orange County | 4 | 0.36 |
| New Hyde Park (village) Nassau County | 30 | 0.31 |
| Washingtonville (village) Orange County | 11 | 0.18 |
| Poughkeepsie (city) Dutchess County | 42 | 0.13 |
| Attica (town) Wyoming County | 10 | 0.13 |
| Middletown (city) Orange County | 33 | 0.12 |

### Top 10 Places Sorted by Percent of Total Population
*Based on places with total population of 50,000 or more*

| Place | Population | % |
|---|---|---|
| Bronx (borough) Bronx County | 952 | 0.07 |
| Huntington (town) Suffolk County | 147 | 0.07 |
| Yonkers (city) Westchester County | 83 | 0.04 |
| White Plains (city) Westchester County | 23 | 0.04 |
| New York (city) | 2,383 | 0.03 |
| Manhattan (borough) New York County | 487 | 0.03 |
| Brooklyn (borough) Kings County | 558 | 0.02 |
| Queens (borough) Queens County | 364 | 0.02 |
| Ramapo (town) Rockland County | 19 | 0.02 |
| Oyster Bay (town) Nassau County | 15 | 0.01 |

## West Indian: West Indian, excluding Hispanic

### Top 10 Places Sorted by Population
*Based on all places, regardless of total population*

| Place | Population | % |
|---|---|---|
| New York (city) | 106,548 | 1.32 |
| Brooklyn (borough) Kings County | 59,844 | 2.43 |
| Bronx (borough) Bronx County | 21,941 | 1.61 |
| Queens (borough) Queens County | 17,400 | 0.79 |
| Manhattan (borough) New York County | 5,618 | 0.35 |
| Hempstead (town) Nassau County | 4,748 | 0.63 |
| Staten Island (borough) Richmond County | 1,745 | 0.38 |
| Babylon (town) Suffolk County | 1,378 | 0.64 |
| Brookhaven (town) Suffolk County | 1,323 | 0.28 |
| Mount Vernon (city) Westchester County | 1,287 | 1.92 |

### Top 10 Places Sorted by Percent of Total Population
*Based on all places, regardless of total population*

| Place | Population | % |
|---|---|---|
| Aurora (village) Cayuga County | 76 | 6.79 |
| Rushville (village) Yates County | 44 | 6.48 |
| Fairview (cdp) Westchester County | 103 | 4.32 |
| Hillburn (village) Rockland County | 38 | 4.00 |
| Ledyard (town) Cayuga County | 76 | 3.41 |
| South Blooming Grove (village) Orange County | 105 | 3.19 |
| South Hempstead (cdp) Nassau County | 90 | 2.82 |
| Moravia (town) Cayuga County | 102 | 2.75 |
| Calcium (cdp) Jefferson County | 91 | 2.57 |
| North Valley Stream (cdp) Nassau County | 422 | 2.56 |

### Top 10 Places Sorted by Percent of Total Population
*Based on places with total population of 50,000 or more*

| Place | Population | % |
|---|---|---|
| Brooklyn (borough) Kings County | 59,844 | 2.43 |

| Place | Population | % |
|---|---|---|
| Mount Vernon (city) Westchester County | 1,287 | 1.92 |
| Bronx (borough) Bronx County | 21,941 | 1.61 |
| Hempstead (village) Nassau County | 785 | 1.47 |
| New York (city) | 106,548 | 1.32 |
| Queens (borough) Queens County | 17,400 | 0.79 |
| Schenectady (city) Schenectady County | 446 | 0.68 |
| Babylon (town) Suffolk County | 1,378 | 0.64 |
| Hempstead (town) Nassau County | 4,748 | 0.63 |
| Albany (city) Albany County | 576 | 0.59 |

## West Indian: Other, excluding Hispanic

### Top 10 Places Sorted by Population
*Based on all places, regardless of total population*

| Place | Population | % |
|---|---|---|
| New York (city) | 1,204 | 0.01 |
| Brooklyn (borough) Kings County | 454 | 0.02 |
| Queens (borough) Queens County | 452 | 0.02 |
| Bronx (borough) Bronx County | 130 | 0.01 |
| Manhattan (borough) New York County | 125 | 0.01 |
| Albany (city) Albany County | 67 | 0.07 |
| Staten Island (borough) Richmond County | 43 | 0.01 |
| Monroe (village) Orange County | 40 | 0.48 |
| Monroe (town) Orange County | 40 | 0.10 |
| Brookhaven (town) Suffolk County | 27 | 0.01 |

### Top 10 Places Sorted by Percent of Total Population
*Based on all places, regardless of total population*

| Place | Population | % |
|---|---|---|
| Unionville (village) Orange County | 2 | 0.52 |
| Monroe (village) Orange County | 40 | 0.48 |
| Horseheads (village) Chemung County | 11 | 0.17 |
| Monroe (town) Orange County | 40 | 0.10 |

| Place | Population | % |
|---|---|---|
| Stony Brook (cdp) Suffolk County | 12 | 0.09 |
| Albany (city) Albany County | 67 | 0.07 |
| Massapequa (cdp) Nassau County | 15 | 0.07 |
| Williamson (town) Wayne County | 5 | 0.07 |
| Horseheads (town) Chemung County | 11 | 0.06 |
| Centereach (cdp) Suffolk County | 15 | 0.05 |

### Top 10 Places Sorted by Percent of Total Population
*Based on places with total population of 50,000 or more*

| Place | Population | % |
|---|---|---|
| Albany (city) Albany County | 67 | 0.07 |
| Troy (city) Rensselaer County | 13 | 0.03 |
| Brooklyn (borough) Kings County | 454 | 0.02 |
| Queens (borough) Queens County | 452 | 0.02 |
| New York (city) | 1,204 | 0.01 |
| Bronx (borough) Bronx County | 130 | 0.01 |
| Manhattan (borough) New York County | 125 | 0.01 |
| Staten Island (borough) Richmond County | 43 | 0.01 |
| Brookhaven (town) Suffolk County | 27 | 0.01 |
| Oyster Bay (town) Nassau County | 15 | 0.01 |

## Yugoslavian

### Top 10 Places Sorted by Population
*Based on all places, regardless of total population*

| Place | Population | % |
|---|---|---|
| New York (city) | 12,410 | 0.15 |
| Queens (borough) Queens County | 4,516 | 0.21 |
| Utica (city) Oneida County | 3,231 | 5.23 |
| Brooklyn (borough) Kings County | 2,800 | 0.11 |
| Manhattan (borough) New York County | 1,876 | 0.12 |
| Staten Island (borough) Richmond County | 1,738 | 0.38 |
| Bronx (borough) Bronx County | 1,480 | 0.11 |

| Place | Population | % |
|---|---|---|
| Syracuse (city) Onondaga County | 774 | 0.53 |
| Hempstead (town) Nassau County | 649 | 0.09 |
| Brookhaven (town) Suffolk County | 518 | 0.11 |

### Top 10 Places Sorted by Percent of Total Population
*Based on all places, regardless of total population*

| Place | Population | % |
|---|---|---|
| Napeague (cdp) Suffolk County | 51 | 24.40 |
| Pinckney (town) Lewis County | 15 | 6.33 |
| Utica (city) Oneida County | 3,231 | 5.23 |
| Lebanon (town) Madison County | 73 | 4.93 |
| Hawthorne (cdp) Westchester County | 211 | 4.49 |
| Angola on the Lake (cdp) Erie County | 55 | 3.92 |
| Exeter (town) Otsego County | 27 | 3.11 |
| Fleischmanns (village) Delaware County | 6 | 2.91 |
| Masonville (town) Delaware County | 38 | 2.81 |
| Milan (town) Dutchess County | 71 | 2.80 |

### Top 10 Places Sorted by Percent of Total Population
*Based on places with total population of 50,000 or more*

| Place | Population | % |
|---|---|---|
| Utica (city) Oneida County | 3,231 | 5.23 |
| Syracuse (city) Onondaga County | 774 | 0.53 |
| Staten Island (borough) Richmond County | 1,738 | 0.38 |
| Huntington (town) Suffolk County | 467 | 0.23 |
| Clay (town) Onondaga County | 132 | 0.23 |
| Queens (borough) Queens County | 4,516 | 0.21 |
| Tonawanda (cdp) Erie County | 124 | 0.21 |
| Smithtown (town) Suffolk County | 216 | 0.18 |
| Colonie (town) Albany County | 143 | 0.18 |
| Tonawanda (town) Erie County | 133 | 0.18 |

# Hispanic Origin Rankings

## Hispanic or Latino (of any race)

### Top 10 Places Sorted by Population
Based on all places, regardless of total population

| Place | Population | % |
|---|---|---|
| New York (city) | 2,336,076 | 28.58 |
| Bronx (borough) Bronx County | 741,413 | 53.53 |
| Queens (borough) Queens County | 613,750 | 27.51 |
| Brooklyn (borough) Kings County | 496,285 | 19.81 |
| Manhattan (borough) New York County | 403,577 | 25.45 |
| Hempstead (town) Nassau County | 132,154 | 17.39 |
| Islip (town) Suffolk County | 97,371 | 29.02 |
| Staten Island (borough) Richmond County | 81,051 | 17.29 |
| Yonkers (city) Westchester County | 67,927 | 34.66 |
| Brookhaven (town) Suffolk County | 60,270 | 12.40 |

### Top 10 Places Sorted by Percent of Total Population
Based on all places, regardless of total population

| Place | Population | % |
|---|---|---|
| Brentwood (cdp) Suffolk County | 41,529 | 68.46 |
| Haverstraw (village) Rockland County | 7,993 | 67.11 |
| North Bay Shore (cdp) Suffolk County | 12,310 | 64.98 |
| Port Chester (village) Westchester County | 17,193 | 59.35 |
| Brewster (village) Putnam County | 1,338 | 55.98 |
| New Cassel (cdp) Nassau County | 7,577 | 53.89 |
| Bronx (borough) Bronx County | 741,413 | 53.53 |
| Central Islip (cdp) Suffolk County | 17,938 | 52.07 |
| Sleepy Hollow (village) Westchester County | 5,038 | 51.04 |
| Newburgh (city) Orange County | 13,814 | 47.86 |

### Top 10 Places Sorted by Percent of Total Population
Based on places with total population of 50,000 or more

| Place | Population | % |
|---|---|---|
| Brentwood (cdp) Suffolk County | 41,529 | 68.46 |
| Bronx (borough) Bronx County | 741,413 | 53.53 |
| Hempstead (village) Nassau County | 23,823 | 44.21 |
| Yonkers (city) Westchester County | 67,927 | 34.66 |
| White Plains (city) Westchester County | 16,839 | 29.62 |
| Islip (town) Suffolk County | 97,371 | 29.02 |
| New York (city) | 2,336,076 | 28.58 |
| New Rochelle (city) Westchester County | 21,452 | 27.84 |
| Queens (borough) Queens County | 613,750 | 27.51 |
| Manhattan (borough) New York County | 403,577 | 25.45 |

## Central American, excluding Mexican

### Top 10 Places Sorted by Population
Based on all places, regardless of total population

| Place | Population | % |
|---|---|---|
| New York (city) | 151,378 | 1.85 |
| Queens (borough) Queens County | 52,509 | 2.35 |
| Hempstead (town) Nassau County | 49,236 | 6.48 |
| Brooklyn (borough) Kings County | 46,119 | 1.84 |
| Islip (town) Suffolk County | 38,530 | 11.48 |
| Bronx (borough) Bronx County | 34,492 | 2.49 |
| Brentwood (cdp) Suffolk County | 19,957 | 32.90 |
| Hempstead (village) Nassau County | 16,171 | 30.01 |
| Manhattan (borough) New York County | 13,948 | 0.88 |
| North Hempstead (town) Nassau County | 11,455 | 5.06 |

### Top 10 Places Sorted by Percent of Total Population
Based on all places, regardless of total population

| Place | Population | % |
|---|---|---|
| Brewster (village) Putnam County | 967 | 40.46 |
| Brentwood (cdp) Suffolk County | 19,957 | 32.90 |
| New Cassel (cdp) Nassau County | 4,455 | 31.69 |
| North Bay Shore (cdp) Suffolk County | 5,763 | 30.42 |
| Hempstead (village) Nassau County | 16,171 | 30.01 |
| Inwood (cdp) Nassau County | 2,509 | 25.62 |
| Uniondale (cdp) Nassau County | 6,264 | 25.30 |
| Central Islip (cdp) Suffolk County | 8,487 | 24.64 |
| Flanders (cdp) Suffolk County | 1,034 | 23.12 |
| Roosevelt (cdp) Nassau County | 3,748 | 23.05 |

### Top 10 Places Sorted by Percent of Total Population
Based on places with total population of 50,000 or more

| Place | Population | % |
|---|---|---|
| Brentwood (cdp) Suffolk County | 19,957 | 32.90 |
| Hempstead (village) Nassau County | 16,171 | 30.01 |
| Islip (town) Suffolk County | 38,530 | 11.48 |
| Southampton (town) Suffolk County | 3,715 | 6.54 |
| Hempstead (town) Nassau County | 49,236 | 6.48 |
| Babylon (town) Suffolk County | 11,096 | 5.19 |
| North Hempstead (town) Nassau County | 11,455 | 5.06 |
| Huntington (town) Suffolk County | 9,599 | 4.72 |
| Ramapo (town) Rockland County | 5,319 | 4.20 |
| Yonkers (city) Westchester County | 5,822 | 2.97 |

## Central American: Costa Rican

### Top 10 Places Sorted by Population
Based on all places, regardless of total population

| Place | Population | % |
|---|---|---|
| New York (city) | 6,673 | 0.08 |
| Brooklyn (borough) Kings County | 2,576 | 0.10 |
| Queens (borough) Queens County | 1,749 | 0.08 |
| Bronx (borough) Bronx County | 1,095 | 0.08 |
| Manhattan (borough) New York County | 987 | 0.06 |
| Hempstead (town) Nassau County | 664 | 0.09 |
| Southampton (town) Suffolk County | 618 | 1.09 |
| Hampton Bays (cdp) Suffolk County | 406 | 2.98 |
| Islip (town) Suffolk County | 297 | 0.09 |
| Staten Island (borough) Richmond County | 266 | 0.06 |

### Top 10 Places Sorted by Percent of Total Population
Based on all places, regardless of total population

| Place | Population | % |
|---|---|---|
| Hampton Bays (cdp) Suffolk County | 406 | 2.98 |
| Tuckahoe (cdp) Suffolk County | 23 | 1.68 |
| Springs (cdp) Suffolk County | 103 | 1.56 |
| East Hampton North (cdp) Suffolk County | 53 | 1.28 |
| Bridgehampton (cdp) Suffolk County | 21 | 1.20 |
| Peconic (cdp) Suffolk County | 8 | 1.17 |
| Southampton (town) Suffolk County | 618 | 1.09 |
| East Hampton (town) Suffolk County | 216 | 1.01 |
| Shinnecock Hills (cdp) Suffolk County | 22 | 1.01 |
| Woodridge (village) Sullivan County | 8 | 0.94 |

### Top 10 Places Sorted by Percent of Total Population
Based on places with total population of 50,000 or more

| Place | Population | % |
|---|---|---|
| Southampton (town) Suffolk County | 618 | 1.09 |
| Brentwood (cdp) Suffolk County | 85 | 0.14 |
| Brooklyn (borough) Kings County | 2,576 | 0.10 |
| Mount Vernon (city) Westchester County | 64 | 0.10 |
| Hempstead (town) Nassau County | 664 | 0.09 |
| Islip (town) Suffolk County | 297 | 0.09 |
| New York (city) | 6,673 | 0.08 |
| Queens (borough) Queens County | 1,749 | 0.08 |
| Bronx (borough) Bronx County | 1,095 | 0.08 |
| Yonkers (city) Westchester County | 156 | 0.08 |

## Central American: Guatemalan

### Top 10 Places Sorted by Population
Based on all places, regardless of total population

| Place | Population | % |
|---|---|---|
| New York (city) | 30,420 | 0.37 |
| Queens (borough) Queens County | 13,700 | 0.61 |
| Brooklyn (borough) Kings County | 9,160 | 0.37 |
| Hempstead (town) Nassau County | 5,948 | 0.78 |
| Bronx (borough) Bronx County | 4,645 | 0.34 |
| Ramapo (town) Rockland County | 4,050 | 3.20 |
| Spring Valley (village) Rockland County | 3,265 | 10.42 |
| Islip (town) Suffolk County | 3,256 | 0.97 |
| Rye (town) Westchester County | 2,654 | 5.78 |
| Port Chester (village) Westchester County | 2,433 | 8.40 |

### Top 10 Places Sorted by Percent of Total Population
Based on all places, regardless of total population

| Place | Population | % |
|---|---|---|
| Brewster (village) Putnam County | 912 | 38.16 |
| Mount Kisco (town/village) Westchester County | 1,782 | 16.38 |
| Flanders (cdp) Suffolk County | 678 | 15.16 |
| Cattaraugus Reservation Chautauqua County | 5 | 13.16 |
| Greenport (village) Suffolk County | 287 | 13.06 |
| Quiogue (cdp) Suffolk County | 103 | 12.62 |
| Bedford Hills (cdp) Westchester County | 317 | 10.56 |
| Spring Valley (village) Rockland County | 3,265 | 10.42 |
| Westhampton Beach (village) Suffolk County | 178 | 10.34 |
| Riverside (cdp) Suffolk County | 273 | 9.38 |

### Top 10 Places Sorted by Percent of Total Population
Based on places with total population of 50,000 or more

| Place | Population | % |
|---|---|---|
| Southampton (town) Suffolk County | 2,081 | 3.66 |
| Ramapo (town) Rockland County | 4,050 | 3.20 |
| Hempstead (village) Nassau County | 1,402 | 2.60 |
| Brentwood (cdp) Suffolk County | 1,553 | 2.56 |
| New Rochelle (city) Westchester County | 1,232 | 1.60 |
| Islip (town) Suffolk County | 3,256 | 0.97 |
| White Plains (city) Westchester County | 551 | 0.97 |
| Clarkstown (town) Rockland County | 802 | 0.95 |
| Hempstead (town) Nassau County | 5,948 | 0.78 |
| Queens (borough) Queens County | 13,700 | 0.61 |

## Central American: Honduran

### Top 10 Places Sorted by Population
Based on all places, regardless of total population

| Place | Population | % |
|---|---|---|
| New York (city) | 42,400 | 0.52 |
| Bronx (borough) Bronx County | 17,990 | 1.30 |
| Brooklyn (borough) Kings County | 10,071 | 0.40 |
| Queens (borough) Queens County | 8,546 | 0.38 |
| Hempstead (town) Nassau County | 7,842 | 1.03 |
| Islip (town) Suffolk County | 4,232 | 1.26 |
| Manhattan (borough) New York County | 4,058 | 0.26 |
| Hempstead (village) Nassau County | 3,758 | 6.97 |
| Brentwood (cdp) Suffolk County | 2,062 | 3.40 |
| Babylon (town) Suffolk County | 1,756 | 0.82 |

### Top 10 Places Sorted by Percent of Total Population
Based on all places, regardless of total population

| Place | Population | % |
|---|---|---|
| Woodridge (village) Sullivan County | 60 | 7.08 |
| Hempstead (village) Nassau County | 3,758 | 6.97 |
| South Fallsburg (cdp) Sullivan County | 200 | 6.97 |
| New Cassel (cdp) Nassau County | 812 | 5.78 |
| Newburgh (city) Orange County | 1,545 | 5.35 |
| Huntington Station (cdp) Suffolk County | 1,260 | 3.81 |
| Brentwood (cdp) Suffolk County | 2,062 | 3.40 |
| Uniondale (cdp) Nassau County | 806 | 3.26 |
| Central Islip (cdp) Suffolk County | 1,118 | 3.25 |
| Oyster Bay (cdp) Nassau County | 212 | 3.16 |

### Top 10 Places Sorted by Percent of Total Population
Based on places with total population of 50,000 or more

| Place | Population | % |
|---|---|---|
| Hempstead (village) Nassau County | 3,758 | 6.97 |
| Brentwood (cdp) Suffolk County | 2,062 | 3.40 |
| Bronx (borough) Bronx County | 17,990 | 1.30 |
| Islip (town) Suffolk County | 4,232 | 1.26 |
| Hempstead (town) Nassau County | 7,842 | 1.03 |
| Babylon (town) Suffolk County | 1,756 | 0.82 |
| Huntington (town) Suffolk County | 1,651 | 0.81 |
| Yonkers (city) Westchester County | 1,451 | 0.74 |
| North Hempstead (town) Nassau County | 1,572 | 0.69 |
| New York (city) | 42,400 | 0.52 |

## Central American: Nicaraguan

### Top 10 Places Sorted by Population
*Based on all places, regardless of total population*

| Place | Population | % |
|---|---|---|
| New York (city) | 9,346 | 0.11 |
| Queens (borough) Queens County | 2,842 | 0.13 |
| Brooklyn (borough) Kings County | 2,407 | 0.10 |
| Bronx (borough) Bronx County | 2,342 | 0.17 |
| Manhattan (borough) New York County | 1,556 | 0.10 |
| Hempstead (town) Nassau County | 656 | 0.09 |
| Yonkers (city) Westchester County | 534 | 0.27 |
| Islip (town) Suffolk County | 253 | 0.08 |
| Staten Island (borough) Richmond County | 199 | 0.04 |
| Brookhaven (town) Suffolk County | 159 | 0.03 |

### Top 10 Places Sorted by Percent of Total Population
*Based on all places, regardless of total population*

| Place | Population | % |
|---|---|---|
| Quiogue (cdp) Suffolk County | 8 | 0.98 |
| Inwood (cdp) Nassau County | 79 | 0.81 |
| Cove Neck (village) Nassau County | 2 | 0.70 |
| Hewlett (cdp) Nassau County | 36 | 0.53 |
| North Hornell (village) Steuben County | 4 | 0.51 |
| Woodmere (cdp) Nassau County | 73 | 0.43 |
| Bellerose Terrace (cdp) Nassau County | 9 | 0.41 |
| South Fallsburg (cdp) Sullivan County | 11 | 0.38 |
| Greenport (village) Suffolk County | 8 | 0.36 |
| Cedarhurst (village) Nassau County | 23 | 0.35 |

### Top 10 Places Sorted by Percent of Total Population
*Based on places with total population of 50,000 or more*

| Place | Population | % |
|---|---|---|
| Yonkers (city) Westchester County | 534 | 0.27 |
| Bronx (borough) Bronx County | 2,342 | 0.17 |
| Brentwood (cdp) Suffolk County | 87 | 0.14 |
| Queens (borough) Queens County | 2,842 | 0.13 |
| New York (city) | 9,346 | 0.11 |
| Brooklyn (borough) Kings County | 2,407 | 0.10 |
| Manhattan (borough) New York County | 1,556 | 0.10 |
| New Rochelle (city) Westchester County | 74 | 0.10 |
| Hempstead (village) Nassau County | 56 | 0.10 |
| Hempstead (town) Nassau County | 656 | 0.09 |

## Central American: Panamanian

### Top 10 Places Sorted by Population
*Based on all places, regardless of total population*

| Place | Population | % |
|---|---|---|
| New York (city) | 22,353 | 0.27 |
| Brooklyn (borough) Kings County | 13,681 | 0.55 |
| Queens (borough) Queens County | 3,977 | 0.18 |
| Bronx (borough) Bronx County | 2,372 | 0.17 |
| Manhattan (borough) New York County | 1,716 | 0.11 |
| Hempstead (town) Nassau County | 1,163 | 0.15 |
| Staten Island (borough) Richmond County | 607 | 0.13 |
| Islip (town) Suffolk County | 466 | 0.14 |
| Babylon (town) Suffolk County | 305 | 0.14 |
| Brookhaven (town) Suffolk County | 291 | 0.06 |

### Top 10 Places Sorted by Percent of Total Population
*Based on all places, regardless of total population*

| Place | Population | % |
|---|---|---|
| Lakeview (cdp) Nassau County | 53 | 0.94 |
| Northampton (cdp) Suffolk County | 5 | 0.88 |
| Evans Mills (village) Jefferson County | 5 | 0.81 |
| Parc (cdp) Clinton County | 2 | 0.79 |
| Washington Heights (cdp) Orange County | 11 | 0.65 |
| Otego (village) Otsego County | 6 | 0.59 |
| North Valley Stream (cdp) Nassau County | 93 | 0.56 |
| Corfu (village) Genesee County | 4 | 0.56 |
| Brooklyn (borough) Kings County | 13,681 | 0.55 |
| Wyandanch (cdp) Suffolk County | 57 | 0.49 |

### Top 10 Places Sorted by Percent of Total Population
*Based on places with total population of 50,000 or more*

| Place | Population | % |
|---|---|---|
| Brooklyn (borough) Kings County | 13,681 | 0.55 |
| New York (city) | 22,353 | 0.27 |
| Hempstead (village) Nassau County | 138 | 0.26 |
| Brentwood (cdp) Suffolk County | 148 | 0.24 |

---

| Place | Population | % |
|---|---|---|
| Mount Vernon (city) Westchester County | 131 | 0.19 |
| Queens (borough) Queens County | 3,977 | 0.18 |
| Bronx (borough) Bronx County | 2,372 | 0.17 |
| Hempstead (town) Nassau County | 1,163 | 0.15 |
| Islip (town) Suffolk County | 466 | 0.14 |
| Babylon (town) Suffolk County | 305 | 0.14 |

## Central American: Salvadoran

### Top 10 Places Sorted by Population
*Based on all places, regardless of total population*

| Place | Population | % |
|---|---|---|
| New York (city) | 38,559 | 0.47 |
| Hempstead (town) Nassau County | 32,681 | 4.30 |
| Islip (town) Suffolk County | 29,849 | 8.90 |
| Queens (borough) Queens County | 21,342 | 0.96 |
| Brentwood (cdp) Suffolk County | 15,946 | 26.29 |
| Hempstead (village) Nassau County | 10,707 | 19.87 |
| North Hempstead (town) Nassau County | 8,262 | 3.65 |
| Babylon (town) Suffolk County | 7,805 | 3.65 |
| Brooklyn (borough) Kings County | 7,737 | 0.31 |
| Huntington (town) Suffolk County | 6,563 | 3.23 |

### Top 10 Places Sorted by Percent of Total Population
*Based on all places, regardless of total population*

| Place | Population | % |
|---|---|---|
| Brentwood (cdp) Suffolk County | 15,946 | 26.29 |
| New Cassel (cdp) Nassau County | 3,477 | 24.73 |
| North Bay Shore (cdp) Suffolk County | 4,530 | 23.91 |
| Uniondale (cdp) Nassau County | 4,998 | 20.19 |
| Hempstead (village) Nassau County | 10,707 | 19.87 |
| Central Islip (cdp) Suffolk County | 6,381 | 18.52 |
| Roosevelt (cdp) Nassau County | 2,891 | 17.78 |
| Huntington Station (cdp) Suffolk County | 5,233 | 15.84 |
| Inwood (cdp) Nassau County | 1,523 | 15.55 |
| Wyandanch (cdp) Suffolk County | 1,485 | 12.75 |

### Top 10 Places Sorted by Percent of Total Population
*Based on places with total population of 50,000 or more*

| Place | Population | % |
|---|---|---|
| Brentwood (cdp) Suffolk County | 15,946 | 26.29 |
| Hempstead (village) Nassau County | 10,707 | 19.87 |
| Islip (town) Suffolk County | 29,849 | 8.90 |
| Hempstead (town) Nassau County | 32,681 | 4.30 |
| North Hempstead (town) Nassau County | 8,262 | 3.65 |
| Babylon (town) Suffolk County | 7,805 | 3.65 |
| Huntington (town) Suffolk County | 6,563 | 3.23 |
| Levittown (cdp) Nassau County | 876 | 1.69 |
| Yonkers (city) Westchester County | 2,691 | 1.37 |
| Brookhaven (town) Suffolk County | 5,899 | 1.21 |

## Central American: Other Central American

### Top 10 Places Sorted by Population
*Based on all places, regardless of total population*

| Place | Population | % |
|---|---|---|
| New York (city) | 1,627 | 0.02 |
| Bronx (borough) Bronx County | 579 | 0.04 |
| Brooklyn (borough) Kings County | 487 | 0.02 |
| Queens (borough) Queens County | 353 | 0.02 |
| Hempstead (town) Nassau County | 282 | 0.04 |
| Islip (town) Suffolk County | 177 | 0.05 |
| Manhattan (borough) New York County | 161 | 0.01 |
| North Hempstead (town) Nassau County | 110 | 0.05 |
| Brookhaven (town) Suffolk County | 106 | 0.02 |
| Babylon (town) Suffolk County | 88 | 0.04 |

### Top 10 Places Sorted by Percent of Total Population
*Based on all places, regardless of total population*

| Place | Population | % |
|---|---|---|
| Mount Kisco (town/village) Westchester County | 31 | 0.29 |
| New Cassel (cdp) Nassau County | 37 | 0.26 |
| Flanders (cdp) Suffolk County | 10 | 0.22 |
| Pawling (village) Dutchess County | 5 | 0.21 |
| Amityville (village) Suffolk County | 19 | 0.20 |
| West Nyack (cdp) Rockland County | 7 | 0.20 |
| Central Islip (cdp) Suffolk County | 65 | 0.19 |
| Berne (town) Albany County | 5 | 0.18 |
| Greenvale (cdp) Nassau County | 2 | 0.18 |
| Mattituck (cdp) Suffolk County | 7 | 0.17 |

---

### Top 10 Places Sorted by Percent of Total Population
*Based on places with total population of 50,000 or more*

| Place | Population | % |
|---|---|---|
| Brentwood (cdp) Suffolk County | 76 | 0.13 |
| Hempstead (village) Nassau County | 66 | 0.12 |
| Islip (town) Suffolk County | 177 | 0.05 |
| North Hempstead (town) Nassau County | 110 | 0.05 |
| Bronx (borough) Bronx County | 579 | 0.04 |
| Hempstead (town) Nassau County | 282 | 0.04 |
| Babylon (town) Suffolk County | 88 | 0.04 |
| Huntington (town) Suffolk County | 52 | 0.03 |
| Southampton (town) Suffolk County | 17 | 0.03 |
| New York (city) | 1,627 | 0.02 |

## Cuban

### Top 10 Places Sorted by Population
*Based on all places, regardless of total population*

| Place | Population | % |
|---|---|---|
| New York (city) | 40,840 | 0.50 |
| Manhattan (borough) New York County | 11,623 | 0.73 |
| Queens (borough) Queens County | 11,020 | 0.49 |
| Bronx (borough) Bronx County | 8,785 | 0.63 |
| Brooklyn (borough) Kings County | 7,581 | 0.30 |
| Hempstead (town) Nassau County | 3,597 | 0.47 |
| Staten Island (borough) Richmond County | 1,831 | 0.39 |
| Rochester (city) Monroe County | 1,616 | 0.77 |
| Yonkers (city) Westchester County | 1,501 | 0.77 |
| Brookhaven (town) Suffolk County | 1,500 | 0.31 |

### Top 10 Places Sorted by Percent of Total Population
*Based on all places, regardless of total population*

| Place | Population | % |
|---|---|---|
| Hunt (cdp) Livingston County | 2 | 2.56 |
| Hewlett Bay Park (village) Nassau County | 10 | 2.48 |
| East Kingston (cdp) Ulster County | 6 | 2.17 |
| Tarrytown (village) Westchester County | 205 | 1.82 |
| Bellerose (village) Nassau County | 20 | 1.68 |
| South Floral Park (village) Nassau County | 23 | 1.30 |
| Sleepy Hollow (village) Westchester County | 123 | 1.25 |
| North Hudson (town) Essex County | 3 | 1.25 |
| Port Chester (village) Westchester County | 359 | 1.24 |
| Plattekill (cdp) Ulster County | 14 | 1.11 |

### Top 10 Places Sorted by Percent of Total Population
*Based on places with total population of 50,000 or more*

| Place | Population | % |
|---|---|---|
| Syracuse (city) Onondaga County | 1,192 | 0.82 |
| Rochester (city) Monroe County | 1,616 | 0.77 |
| Yonkers (city) Westchester County | 1,501 | 0.77 |
| Manhattan (borough) New York County | 11,623 | 0.73 |
| Greenburgh (town) Westchester County | 565 | 0.64 |
| Bronx (borough) Bronx County | 8,785 | 0.63 |
| White Plains (city) Westchester County | 321 | 0.56 |
| Levittown (cdp) Nassau County | 274 | 0.53 |
| New York (city) | 40,840 | 0.50 |
| Clarkstown (town) Rockland County | 421 | 0.50 |

## Dominican Republic

### Top 10 Places Sorted by Population
*Based on all places, regardless of total population*

| Place | Population | % |
|---|---|---|
| New York (city) | 576,701 | 7.05 |
| Bronx (borough) Bronx County | 240,987 | 17.40 |
| Manhattan (borough) New York County | 155,971 | 9.84 |
| Queens (borough) Queens County | 88,061 | 3.95 |
| Brooklyn (borough) Kings County | 86,764 | 3.46 |
| Hempstead (town) Nassau County | 16,914 | 2.23 |
| Yonkers (city) Westchester County | 15,903 | 8.11 |
| Islip (town) Suffolk County | 8,547 | 2.55 |
| Babylon (town) Suffolk County | 6,543 | 3.06 |
| Haverstraw (town) Rockland County | 6,277 | 17.13 |

### Top 10 Places Sorted by Percent of Total Population
*Based on all places, regardless of total population*

| Place | Population | % |
|---|---|---|
| Haverstraw (village) Rockland County | 3,847 | 32.30 |
| Sleepy Hollow (village) Westchester County | 1,831 | 18.55 |
| Bronx (borough) Bronx County | 240,987 | 17.40 |

| | | |
|---|---|---|
| Haverstraw (town) Rockland County | 6,277 | 17.13 |
| West Haverstraw (village) Rockland County | 1,667 | 16.40 |
| Freeport (village) Nassau County | 5,539 | 12.92 |
| Copiague (cdp) Suffolk County | 2,846 | 12.38 |
| Manhattan (borough) New York County | 155,971 | 9.84 |
| Yonkers (city) Westchester County | 15,903 | 8.11 |
| New York (city) | 576,701 | 7.05 |

### Top 10 Places Sorted by Percent of Total Population
*Based on places with total population of 50,000 or more*

| Place | Population | % |
|---|---|---|
| Bronx (borough) Bronx County | 240,987 | 17.40 |
| Manhattan (borough) New York County | 155,971 | 9.84 |
| Yonkers (city) Westchester County | 15,903 | 8.11 |
| New York (city) | 576,701 | 7.05 |
| Brentwood (cdp) Suffolk County | 4,205 | 6.93 |
| Queens (borough) Queens County | 88,061 | 3.95 |
| Brooklyn (borough) Kings County | 86,764 | 3.46 |
| Babylon (town) Suffolk County | 6,543 | 3.06 |
| Hempstead (village) Nassau County | 1,398 | 2.59 |
| Islip (town) Suffolk County | 8,547 | 2.55 |

## Mexican

### Top 10 Places Sorted by Population
*Based on all places, regardless of total population*

| Place | Population | % |
|---|---|---|
| New York (city) | 319,263 | 3.91 |
| Brooklyn (borough) Kings County | 94,585 | 3.78 |
| Queens (borough) Queens County | 92,835 | 4.16 |
| Bronx (borough) Bronx County | 71,194 | 5.14 |
| Manhattan (borough) New York County | 41,965 | 2.65 |
| Staten Island (borough) Richmond County | 18,684 | 3.99 |
| Yonkers (city) Westchester County | 13,761 | 7.02 |
| New Rochelle (city) Westchester County | 10,363 | 13.45 |
| Newburgh (city) Orange County | 6,181 | 21.41 |
| White Plains (city) Westchester County | 5,773 | 10.15 |

### Top 10 Places Sorted by Percent of Total Population
*Based on all places, regardless of total population*

| Place | Population | % |
|---|---|---|
| Fleischmanns (village) Delaware County | 117 | 33.33 |
| Newburgh (city) Orange County | 6,181 | 21.41 |
| Port Chester (village) Westchester County | 4,864 | 16.79 |
| Middletown (city) Orange County | 4,208 | 14.98 |
| New Rochelle (city) Westchester County | 10,363 | 13.45 |
| Tuckahoe (cdp) Suffolk County | 181 | 13.18 |
| Shinnecock Hills (cdp) Suffolk County | 282 | 12.89 |
| New Cassel (cdp) Nassau County | 1,739 | 12.37 |
| Rye (town) Westchester County | 5,313 | 11.57 |
| Dresden (village) Yates County | 34 | 11.04 |

### Top 10 Places Sorted by Percent of Total Population
*Based on places with total population of 50,000 or more*

| Place | Population | % |
|---|---|---|
| New Rochelle (city) Westchester County | 10,363 | 13.45 |
| White Plains (city) Westchester County | 5,773 | 10.15 |
| Yonkers (city) Westchester County | 13,761 | 7.02 |
| Bronx (borough) Bronx County | 71,194 | 5.14 |
| Southampton (town) Suffolk County | 2,856 | 5.03 |
| Queens (borough) Queens County | 92,835 | 4.16 |
| Staten Island (borough) Richmond County | 18,684 | 3.99 |
| New York (city) | 319,263 | 3.91 |
| Brooklyn (borough) Kings County | 94,585 | 3.78 |
| Mount Vernon (city) Westchester County | 2,454 | 3.65 |

## Puerto Rican

### Top 10 Places Sorted by Population
*Based on all places, regardless of total population*

| Place | Population | % |
|---|---|---|
| New York (city) | 723,621 | 8.85 |
| Bronx (borough) Bronx County | 298,921 | 21.58 |
| Brooklyn (borough) Kings County | 176,528 | 7.05 |
| Manhattan (borough) New York County | 107,774 | 6.80 |
| Queens (borough) Queens County | 102,881 | 4.61 |
| Staten Island (borough) Richmond County | 37,517 | 8.00 |
| Rochester (city) Monroe County | 27,734 | 13.17 |
| Buffalo (city) Erie County | 22,076 | 8.45 |
| Islip (town) Suffolk County | 21,506 | 6.41 |
| Brookhaven (town) Suffolk County | 21,429 | 4.41 |

### Top 10 Places Sorted by Percent of Total Population
*Based on all places, regardless of total population*

| Place | Population | % |
|---|---|---|
| Plattekill (cdp) Ulster County | 328 | 26.03 |
| Dunkirk (city) Chautauqua County | 2,782 | 22.14 |
| Bronx (borough) Bronx County | 298,921 | 21.58 |
| Amsterdam (city) Montgomery County | 3,923 | 21.07 |
| Ellenville (village) Ulster County | 832 | 20.12 |
| Middletown (city) Orange County | 4,533 | 16.14 |
| Monticello (village) Sullivan County | 1,073 | 15.95 |
| Washington Heights (cdp) Orange County | 261 | 15.45 |
| Scotchtown (cdp) Orange County | 1,410 | 15.31 |
| Mechanicstown (cdp) Orange County | 996 | 14.52 |

### Top 10 Places Sorted by Percent of Total Population
*Based on places with total population of 50,000 or more*

| Place | Population | % |
|---|---|---|
| Bronx (borough) Bronx County | 298,921 | 21.58 |
| Rochester (city) Monroe County | 27,734 | 13.17 |
| Yonkers (city) Westchester County | 19,875 | 10.14 |
| Brentwood (cdp) Suffolk County | 6,125 | 10.10 |
| New York (city) | 723,621 | 8.85 |
| Buffalo (city) Erie County | 22,076 | 8.45 |
| Staten Island (borough) Richmond County | 37,517 | 8.00 |
| Schenectady (city) Schenectady County | 4,677 | 7.07 |
| Brooklyn (borough) Kings County | 176,528 | 7.05 |
| Manhattan (borough) New York County | 107,774 | 6.80 |

## South American

### Top 10 Places Sorted by Population
*Based on all places, regardless of total population*

| Place | Population | % |
|---|---|---|
| New York (city) | 343,468 | 4.20 |
| Queens (borough) Queens County | 214,022 | 9.59 |
| Brooklyn (borough) Kings County | 49,003 | 1.96 |
| Manhattan (borough) New York County | 36,748 | 2.32 |
| Bronx (borough) Bronx County | 35,463 | 2.56 |
| Hempstead (town) Nassau County | 23,626 | 3.11 |
| Islip (town) Suffolk County | 16,012 | 4.77 |
| Brookhaven (town) Suffolk County | 12,182 | 2.51 |
| Staten Island (borough) Richmond County | 8,232 | 1.76 |
| Ossining (town) Westchester County | 6,825 | 18.12 |

### Top 10 Places Sorted by Percent of Total Population
*Based on all places, regardless of total population*

| Place | Population | % |
|---|---|---|
| East Hampton North (cdp) Suffolk County | 1,076 | 25.98 |
| Ossining (village) Westchester County | 6,440 | 25.70 |
| Springs (cdp) Suffolk County | 1,623 | 24.62 |
| Sleepy Hollow (village) Westchester County | 2,098 | 21.26 |
| Port Chester (village) Westchester County | 5,769 | 19.92 |
| Ossining (town) Westchester County | 6,825 | 18.12 |
| Elmsford (village) Westchester County | 812 | 17.41 |
| Peekskill (city) Westchester County | 4,041 | 17.14 |
| East Hampton (town) Suffolk County | 3,513 | 16.37 |
| Patchogue (village) Suffolk County | 1,777 | 15.06 |

### Top 10 Places Sorted by Percent of Total Population
*Based on places with total population of 50,000 or more*

| Place | Population | % |
|---|---|---|
| Brentwood (cdp) Suffolk County | 6,350 | 10.47 |
| White Plains (city) Westchester County | 5,850 | 10.29 |
| Queens (borough) Queens County | 214,022 | 9.59 |
| New Rochelle (city) Westchester County | 3,697 | 4.80 |
| Islip (town) Suffolk County | 16,012 | 4.77 |
| Greenburgh (town) Westchester County | 4,004 | 4.53 |
| Southampton (town) Suffolk County | 2,446 | 4.31 |
| New York (city) | 343,468 | 4.20 |
| Yonkers (city) Westchester County | 6,622 | 3.38 |
| Levittown (cdp) Nassau County | 1,746 | 3.37 |

## South American: Argentinean

### Top 10 Places Sorted by Population
*Based on all places, regardless of total population*

| Place | Population | % |
|---|---|---|
| New York (city) | 15,169 | 0.19 |
| Queens (borough) Queens County | 6,345 | 0.28 |
| Manhattan (borough) New York County | 4,339 | 0.27 |

| | | |
|---|---|---|
| Brooklyn (borough) Kings County | 2,760 | 0.11 |
| Hempstead (town) Nassau County | 1,500 | 0.20 |
| Bronx (borough) Bronx County | 1,117 | 0.08 |
| Brookhaven (town) Suffolk County | 653 | 0.13 |
| Islip (town) Suffolk County | 616 | 0.18 |
| Staten Island (borough) Richmond County | 608 | 0.13 |
| Oyster Bay (town) Nassau County | 441 | 0.15 |

### Top 10 Places Sorted by Percent of Total Population
*Based on all places, regardless of total population*

| Place | Population | % |
|---|---|---|
| Russell Gardens (village) Nassau County | 9 | 0.95 |
| Kiryas Joel (village) Orange County | 186 | 0.92 |
| Hobart (village) Delaware County | 4 | 0.91 |
| Northville (cdp) Suffolk County | 9 | 0.67 |
| Woodsburgh (village) Nassau County | 5 | 0.64 |
| Asharoken (village) Suffolk County | 4 | 0.61 |
| Lynbrook (village) Nassau County | 110 | 0.57 |
| Salisbury Mills (cdp) Orange County | 3 | 0.56 |
| Monroe (town) Orange County | 217 | 0.54 |
| Harbor Hills (cdp) Nassau County | 3 | 0.52 |

### Top 10 Places Sorted by Percent of Total Population
*Based on places with total population of 50,000 or more*

| Place | Population | % |
|---|---|---|
| Brentwood (cdp) Suffolk County | 203 | 0.33 |
| White Plains (city) Westchester County | 189 | 0.33 |
| Queens (borough) Queens County | 6,345 | 0.28 |
| Manhattan (borough) New York County | 4,339 | 0.27 |
| New Rochelle (city) Westchester County | 170 | 0.22 |
| Greenburgh (town) Westchester County | 188 | 0.21 |
| Hempstead (town) Nassau County | 1,500 | 0.20 |
| New York (city) | 15,169 | 0.19 |
| North Hempstead (town) Nassau County | 435 | 0.19 |
| Islip (town) Suffolk County | 616 | 0.18 |

## South American: Bolivian

### Top 10 Places Sorted by Population
*Based on all places, regardless of total population*

| Place | Population | % |
|---|---|---|
| New York (city) | 4,488 | 0.05 |
| Queens (borough) Queens County | 3,268 | 0.15 |
| Manhattan (borough) New York County | 522 | 0.03 |
| Hempstead (town) Nassau County | 494 | 0.07 |
| Rye (town) Westchester County | 375 | 0.82 |
| Port Chester (village) Westchester County | 350 | 1.21 |
| Brooklyn (borough) Kings County | 310 | 0.01 |
| Bronx (borough) Bronx County | 227 | 0.02 |
| Islip (town) Suffolk County | 220 | 0.07 |
| Staten Island (borough) Richmond County | 161 | 0.03 |

### Top 10 Places Sorted by Percent of Total Population
*Based on all places, regardless of total population*

| Place | Population | % |
|---|---|---|
| Poospatuck Reservation Suffolk County | 4 | 1.23 |
| Port Chester (village) Westchester County | 350 | 1.21 |
| Rye (town) Westchester County | 375 | 0.82 |
| Merritt Park (cdp) Dutchess County | 6 | 0.48 |
| Inwood (cdp) Nassau County | 43 | 0.44 |
| Matinecock (village) Nassau County | 3 | 0.37 |
| Friendship (cdp) Allegany County | 4 | 0.33 |
| East Rockaway (village) Nassau County | 31 | 0.32 |
| Islandia (village) Suffolk County | 10 | 0.30 |
| Cedarhurst (village) Nassau County | 18 | 0.27 |

### Top 10 Places Sorted by Percent of Total Population
*Based on places with total population of 50,000 or more*

| Place | Population | % |
|---|---|---|
| Queens (borough) Queens County | 3,268 | 0.15 |
| Brentwood (cdp) Suffolk County | 79 | 0.13 |
| White Plains (city) Westchester County | 72 | 0.13 |
| Hempstead (town) Nassau County | 494 | 0.07 |
| Islip (town) Suffolk County | 220 | 0.07 |
| New Rochelle (city) Westchester County | 50 | 0.06 |
| New York (city) | 4,488 | 0.05 |
| Greenburgh (town) Westchester County | 48 | 0.05 |
| Oyster Bay (town) Nassau County | 110 | 0.04 |
| Babylon (town) Suffolk County | 78 | 0.04 |

*Please refer to the Explanation of Data in the front of the book for more detailed information.*

## South American: Chilean

### Top 10 Places Sorted by Population
*Based on all places, regardless of total population*

| Place | Population | % |
|---|---|---|
| **New York** (city) | 7,026 | 0.09 |
| **Queens** (borough) Queens County | 3,184 | 0.14 |
| **Manhattan** (borough) New York County | 1,824 | 0.12 |
| **Hempstead** (town) Nassau County | 1,415 | 0.19 |
| **Brooklyn** (borough) Kings County | 1,026 | 0.04 |
| **North Hempstead** (town) Nassau County | 664 | 0.29 |
| **Bronx** (borough) Bronx County | 646 | 0.05 |
| **Oyster Bay** (town) Nassau County | 569 | 0.19 |
| **Islip** (town) Suffolk County | 448 | 0.13 |
| **Brookhaven** (town) Suffolk County | 363 | 0.07 |

### Top 10 Places Sorted by Percent of Total Population
*Based on all places, regardless of total population*

| Place | Population | % |
|---|---|---|
| **Manorhaven** (village) Nassau County | 234 | 3.57 |
| **Oyster Bay** (cdp) Nassau County | 179 | 2.67 |
| **Windham** (cdp) Greene County | 6 | 1.63 |
| **Sleepy Hollow** (village) Westchester County | 146 | 1.48 |
| **Forest Home** (cdp) Tompkins County | 8 | 1.40 |
| **Ames** (village) Montgomery County | 2 | 1.38 |
| **Inwood** (cdp) Nassau County | 108 | 1.10 |
| **North Lynbrook** (cdp) Nassau County | 8 | 1.01 |
| **Cedarhurst** (village) Nassau County | 65 | 0.99 |
| **Port Washington** (cdp) Nassau County | 149 | 0.94 |

### Top 10 Places Sorted by Percent of Total Population
*Based on places with total population of 50,000 or more*

| Place | Population | % |
|---|---|---|
| **North Hempstead** (town) Nassau County | 664 | 0.29 |
| **Brentwood** (cdp) Suffolk County | 153 | 0.25 |
| **Greenburgh** (town) Westchester County | 192 | 0.22 |
| **Levittown** (cdp) Nassau County | 112 | 0.22 |
| **Hempstead** (town) Nassau County | 1,415 | 0.19 |
| **Oyster Bay** (town) Nassau County | 569 | 0.19 |
| **Queens** (borough) Queens County | 3,184 | 0.14 |
| **Islip** (town) Suffolk County | 448 | 0.13 |
| **Manhattan** (borough) New York County | 1,824 | 0.12 |
| **Huntington** (town) Suffolk County | 252 | 0.12 |

## South American: Colombian

### Top 10 Places Sorted by Population
*Based on all places, regardless of total population*

| Place | Population | % |
|---|---|---|
| **New York** (city) | 94,723 | 1.16 |
| **Queens** (borough) Queens County | 70,290 | 3.15 |
| **Brooklyn** (borough) Kings County | 8,861 | 0.35 |
| **Hempstead** (town) Nassau County | 8,522 | 1.12 |
| **Manhattan** (borough) New York County | 8,411 | 0.53 |
| **Islip** (town) Suffolk County | 5,156 | 1.54 |
| **Bronx** (borough) Bronx County | 4,635 | 0.33 |
| **Brookhaven** (town) Suffolk County | 2,970 | 0.61 |
| **Staten Island** (borough) Richmond County | 2,526 | 0.54 |
| **Brentwood** (cdp) Suffolk County | 2,083 | 3.43 |

### Top 10 Places Sorted by Percent of Total Population
*Based on all places, regardless of total population*

| Place | Population | % |
|---|---|---|
| **East Hampton North** (cdp) Suffolk County | 284 | 6.86 |
| **Springs** (cdp) Suffolk County | 430 | 6.52 |
| **Bellerose Terrace** (cdp) Nassau County | 124 | 5.64 |
| **East Hampton** (town) Suffolk County | 987 | 4.60 |
| **Hampton Bays** (cdp) Suffolk County | 614 | 4.51 |
| **Elmsford** (village) Westchester County | 186 | 3.99 |
| **Shinnecock Hills** (cdp) Suffolk County | 84 | 3.84 |
| **Montauk** (cdp) Suffolk County | 119 | 3.58 |
| **Brentwood** (cdp) Suffolk County | 2,083 | 3.43 |
| **White Plains** (city) Westchester County | 1,838 | 3.23 |

### Top 10 Places Sorted by Percent of Total Population
*Based on places with total population of 50,000 or more*

| Place | Population | % |
|---|---|---|
| **Brentwood** (cdp) Suffolk County | 2,083 | 3.43 |
| **White Plains** (city) Westchester County | 1,838 | 3.23 |
| **Queens** (borough) Queens County | 70,290 | 3.15 |
| **New Rochelle** (city) Westchester County | 1,451 | 1.88 |

| | | |
|---|---|---|
| **Southampton** (town) Suffolk County | 1,024 | 1.80 |
| **Islip** (town) Suffolk County | 5,156 | 1.54 |
| **Levittown** (cdp) Nassau County | 733 | 1.41 |
| **New York** (city) | 94,723 | 1.16 |
| **Hempstead** (town) Nassau County | 8,522 | 1.12 |
| **Greenburgh** (town) Westchester County | 845 | 0.96 |

## South American: Ecuadorian

### Top 10 Places Sorted by Population
*Based on all places, regardless of total population*

| Place | Population | % |
|---|---|---|
| **New York** (city) | 167,209 | 2.05 |
| **Queens** (borough) Queens County | 98,512 | 4.42 |
| **Brooklyn** (borough) Kings County | 28,684 | 1.15 |
| **Bronx** (borough) Bronx County | 23,206 | 1.68 |
| **Manhattan** (borough) New York County | 14,132 | 0.89 |
| **Brookhaven** (town) Suffolk County | 6,437 | 1.32 |
| **Hempstead** (town) Nassau County | 5,881 | 0.77 |
| **Islip** (town) Suffolk County | 5,323 | 1.59 |
| **Ossining** (town) Westchester County | 4,988 | 13.24 |
| **Ossining** (village) Westchester County | 4,840 | 19.31 |

### Top 10 Places Sorted by Percent of Total Population
*Based on all places, regardless of total population*

| Place | Population | % |
|---|---|---|
| **Ossining** (village) Westchester County | 4,840 | 19.31 |
| **Sleepy Hollow** (village) Westchester County | 1,731 | 17.54 |
| **East Hampton North** (cdp) Suffolk County | 717 | 17.31 |
| **Springs** (cdp) Suffolk County | 1,137 | 17.25 |
| **Peekskill** (city) Westchester County | 3,490 | 14.80 |
| **Patchogue** (village) Suffolk County | 1,616 | 13.70 |
| **Ossining** (town) Westchester County | 4,988 | 13.24 |
| **East Hampton** (town) Suffolk County | 2,319 | 10.81 |
| **Port Chester** (village) Westchester County | 2,774 | 9.58 |
| **Spring Valley** (village) Rockland County | 2,681 | 8.55 |

### Top 10 Places Sorted by Percent of Total Population
*Based on places with total population of 50,000 or more*

| Place | Population | % |
|---|---|---|
| **Queens** (borough) Queens County | 98,512 | 4.42 |
| **Brentwood** (cdp) Suffolk County | 1,985 | 3.27 |
| **Ramapo** (town) Rockland County | 2,915 | 2.30 |
| **New York** (city) | 167,209 | 2.05 |
| **Southampton** (town) Suffolk County | 1,102 | 1.94 |
| **White Plains** (city) Westchester County | 1,001 | 1.76 |
| **Bronx** (borough) Bronx County | 23,206 | 1.68 |
| **Yonkers** (city) Westchester County | 3,271 | 1.67 |
| **Greenburgh** (town) Westchester County | 1,434 | 1.62 |
| **Islip** (town) Suffolk County | 5,323 | 1.59 |

## South American: Paraguayan

### Top 10 Places Sorted by Population
*Based on all places, regardless of total population*

| Place | Population | % |
|---|---|---|
| **New York** (city) | 3,534 | 0.04 |
| **Queens** (borough) Queens County | 2,775 | 0.12 |
| **Manhattan** (borough) New York County | 268 | 0.02 |
| **White Plains** (city) Westchester County | 260 | 0.46 |
| **Harrison** (town/village) Westchester County | 235 | 0.86 |
| **Brooklyn** (borough) Kings County | 230 | 0.01 |
| **Bronx** (borough) Bronx County | 223 | 0.02 |
| **Hempstead** (town) Nassau County | 185 | 0.02 |
| **Greenburgh** (town) Westchester County | 144 | 0.16 |
| **North Hempstead** (town) Nassau County | 140 | 0.06 |

### Top 10 Places Sorted by Percent of Total Population
*Based on all places, regardless of total population*

| Place | Population | % |
|---|---|---|
| **Bedford** (cdp) Westchester County | 28 | 1.53 |
| **Scotts Corners** (cdp) Westchester County | 10 | 1.41 |
| **Cove Neck** (village) Nassau County | 3 | 1.05 |
| **Fairview** (cdp) Westchester County | 28 | 0.90 |
| **Harrison** (town/village) Westchester County | 235 | 0.86 |
| **Elmsford** (village) Westchester County | 35 | 0.75 |
| **Mamaroneck** (village) Westchester County | 130 | 0.69 |
| **Hewlett Bay Park** (village) Nassau County | 2 | 0.50 |
| **Bedford Hills** (cdp) Westchester County | 14 | 0.47 |
| **White Plains** (city) Westchester County | 260 | 0.46 |

### Top 10 Places Sorted by Percent of Total Population
*Based on places with total population of 50,000 or more*

| Place | Population | % |
|---|---|---|
| **White Plains** (city) Westchester County | 260 | 0.46 |
| **Greenburgh** (town) Westchester County | 144 | 0.16 |
| **Queens** (borough) Queens County | 2,775 | 0.12 |
| **Mount Vernon** (city) Westchester County | 68 | 0.10 |
| **North Hempstead** (town) Nassau County | 140 | 0.06 |
| **New Rochelle** (city) Westchester County | 49 | 0.06 |
| **Brentwood** (cdp) Suffolk County | 36 | 0.06 |
| **Southampton** (town) Suffolk County | 26 | 0.05 |
| **New York** (city) | 3,534 | 0.04 |
| **Huntington** (town) Suffolk County | 91 | 0.04 |

## South American: Peruvian

### Top 10 Places Sorted by Population
*Based on all places, regardless of total population*

| Place | Population | % |
|---|---|---|
| **New York** (city) | 36,018 | 0.44 |
| **Queens** (borough) Queens County | 22,886 | 1.03 |
| **Hempstead** (town) Nassau County | 4,510 | 0.59 |
| **Brooklyn** (borough) Kings County | 4,222 | 0.17 |
| **Manhattan** (borough) New York County | 3,852 | 0.24 |
| **Islip** (town) Suffolk County | 3,599 | 1.07 |
| **Bronx** (borough) Bronx County | 3,596 | 0.26 |
| **White Plains** (city) Westchester County | 2,260 | 3.98 |
| **Rye** (town) Westchester County | 1,734 | 3.78 |
| **Brentwood** (cdp) Suffolk County | 1,610 | 2.65 |

### Top 10 Places Sorted by Percent of Total Population
*Based on all places, regardless of total population*

| Place | Population | % |
|---|---|---|
| **Port Chester** (village) Westchester County | 1,485 | 5.13 |
| **Island Park** (village) Nassau County | 234 | 5.03 |
| **Elmsford** (village) Westchester County | 189 | 4.05 |
| **White Plains** (city) Westchester County | 2,260 | 3.98 |
| **Rye** (town) Westchester County | 1,734 | 3.78 |
| **Glen Cove** (city) Nassau County | 883 | 3.27 |
| **Baywood** (cdp) Suffolk County | 222 | 3.02 |
| **Barnum Island** (cdp) Nassau County | 73 | 3.02 |
| **Fairview** (cdp) Westchester County | 89 | 2.87 |
| **Bellerose Terrace** (cdp) Nassau County | 60 | 2.73 |

### Top 10 Places Sorted by Percent of Total Population
*Based on places with total population of 50,000 or more*

| Place | Population | % |
|---|---|---|
| **White Plains** (city) Westchester County | 2,260 | 3.98 |
| **Brentwood** (cdp) Suffolk County | 1,610 | 2.65 |
| **New Rochelle** (city) Westchester County | 1,297 | 1.68 |
| **Greenburgh** (town) Westchester County | 962 | 1.09 |
| **Islip** (town) Suffolk County | 3,599 | 1.07 |
| **Queens** (borough) Queens County | 22,886 | 1.03 |
| **Babylon** (town) Suffolk County | 1,313 | 0.61 |
| **Hempstead** (town) Nassau County | 4,510 | 0.59 |
| **Levittown** (cdp) Nassau County | 285 | 0.55 |
| **Hempstead** (village) Nassau County | 279 | 0.52 |

## South American: Uruguayan

### Top 10 Places Sorted by Population
*Based on all places, regardless of total population*

| Place | Population | % |
|---|---|---|
| **New York** (city) | 3,004 | 0.04 |
| **Queens** (borough) Queens County | 1,743 | 0.08 |
| **Manhattan** (borough) New York County | 549 | 0.03 |
| **Brooklyn** (borough) Kings County | 488 | 0.02 |
| **Hempstead** (town) Nassau County | 359 | 0.05 |
| **Ossining** (town) Westchester County | 273 | 0.72 |
| **Ossining** (village) Westchester County | 230 | 0.92 |
| **Islip** (town) Suffolk County | 216 | 0.06 |
| **Rye** (town) Westchester County | 211 | 0.46 |
| **Port Chester** (village) Westchester County | 159 | 0.55 |

### Top 10 Places Sorted by Percent of Total Population
*Based on all places, regardless of total population*

| Place | Population | % |
|---|---|---|
| **Ossining** (village) Westchester County | 230 | 0.92 |
| **Ossining** (town) Westchester County | 273 | 0.72 |
| **Cove Neck** (village) Nassau County | 2 | 0.70 |

| Place | Population | % |
|---|---|---|
| **Buchanan** (village) Westchester County | 13 | 0.58 |
| **Port Chester** (village) Westchester County | 159 | 0.55 |
| **Hillside Lake** (cdp) Dutchess County | 6 | 0.55 |
| **Crugers** (cdp) Westchester County | 8 | 0.52 |
| **Rye** (town) Westchester County | 211 | 0.46 |
| **Islandia** (village) Suffolk County | 15 | 0.45 |
| **Chappaqua** (cdp) Westchester County | 6 | 0.42 |

### Top 10 Places Sorted by Percent of Total Population
*Based on places with total population of 50,000 or more*

| Place | Population | % |
|---|---|---|
| **Brentwood** (cdp) Suffolk County | 80 | 0.13 |
| **New Rochelle** (city) Westchester County | 88 | 0.11 |
| **White Plains** (city) Westchester County | 63 | 0.11 |
| **Levittown** (cdp) Nassau County | 47 | 0.09 |
| **Queens** (borough) Queens County | 1,743 | 0.08 |
| **Greenburgh** (town) Westchester County | 65 | 0.07 |
| **Islip** (town) Suffolk County | 216 | 0.06 |
| **Hempstead** (town) Nassau County | 359 | 0.05 |
| **Oyster Bay** (town) Nassau County | 134 | 0.05 |
| **New York** (city) | 3,004 | 0.04 |

## South American: Venezuelan

### Top 10 Places Sorted by Population
*Based on all places, regardless of total population*

| Place | Population | % |
|---|---|---|
| **New York** (city) | 9,619 | 0.12 |
| **Queens** (borough) Queens County | 3,580 | 0.16 |
| **Manhattan** (borough) New York County | 2,573 | 0.16 |
| **Brooklyn** (borough) Kings County | 1,916 | 0.08 |
| **Bronx** (borough) Bronx County | 1,296 | 0.09 |
| **Hempstead** (town) Nassau County | 517 | 0.07 |
| **Islip** (town) Suffolk County | 322 | 0.10 |
| **Brookhaven** (town) Suffolk County | 302 | 0.06 |
| **Staten Island** (borough) Richmond County | 254 | 0.05 |
| **Yonkers** (city) Westchester County | 207 | 0.11 |

### Top 10 Places Sorted by Percent of Total Population
*Based on all places, regardless of total population*

| Place | Population | % |
|---|---|---|
| **Westport** (cdp) Essex County | 6 | 1.16 |
| **Ward** (town) Allegany County | 4 | 1.09 |
| **Shinnecock Reservation** Suffolk County | 4 | 0.60 |
| **Scotts Corners** (cdp) Westchester County | 4 | 0.56 |
| **Shoreham** (village) Suffolk County | 3 | 0.56 |
| **Merritt Park** (cdp) Dutchess County | 6 | 0.48 |
| **Westport** (town) Essex County | 6 | 0.46 |
| **Mountain Lodge Park** (cdp) Orange County | 7 | 0.44 |
| **Jewett** (town) Greene County | 4 | 0.42 |
| **Washington Mills** (cdp) Oneida County | 4 | 0.34 |

### Top 10 Places Sorted by Percent of Total Population
*Based on places with total population of 50,000 or more*

| Place | Population | % |
|---|---|---|
| **Brentwood** (cdp) Suffolk County | 113 | 0.19 |
| **New Rochelle** (city) Westchester County | 131 | 0.17 |
| **Queens** (borough) Queens County | 3,580 | 0.16 |
| **Manhattan** (borough) New York County | 2,573 | 0.16 |
| **White Plains** (city) Westchester County | 77 | 0.14 |
| **New York** (city) | 9,619 | 0.12 |
| **Yonkers** (city) Westchester County | 207 | 0.11 |
| **Greenburgh** (town) Westchester County | 94 | 0.11 |
| **Islip** (town) Suffolk County | 322 | 0.10 |
| **Bronx** (borough) Bronx County | 1,296 | 0.09 |

## South American: Other South American

### Top 10 Places Sorted by Population
*Based on all places, regardless of total population*

| Place | Population | % |
|---|---|---|
| **New York** (city) | 2,678 | 0.03 |
| **Queens** (borough) Queens County | 1,439 | 0.06 |
| **Brooklyn** (borough) Kings County | 506 | 0.02 |
| **Bronx** (borough) Bronx County | 369 | 0.03 |
| **Manhattan** (borough) New York County | 278 | 0.03 |
| **Hempstead** (town) Nassau County | 243 | 0.03 |
| **Brookhaven** (town) Suffolk County | 98 | 0.02 |
| **Staten Island** (borough) Richmond County | 86 | 0.02 |
| **Yonkers** (city) Westchester County | 63 | 0.03 |
| **Islip** (town) Suffolk County | 54 | 0.02 |

### Top 10 Places Sorted by Percent of Total Population
*Based on all places, regardless of total population*

| Place | Population | % |
|---|---|---|
| **Woodsburgh** (village) Nassau County | 8 | 1.03 |
| **Quiogue** (cdp) Suffolk County | 4 | 0.49 |
| **East Hampton North** (cdp) Suffolk County | 19 | 0.46 |
| **Plattekill** (cdp) Ulster County | 5 | 0.40 |
| **Scio** (town) Allegany County | 5 | 0.27 |
| **Northwest Harbor** (cdp) Suffolk County | 8 | 0.24 |
| **Dolgeville** (village) Herkimer County | 5 | 0.23 |
| **Lakeview** (cdp) Nassau County | 12 | 0.21 |
| **Harriman** (village) Orange County | 5 | 0.21 |
| **Cold Spring** (village) Putnam County | 4 | 0.20 |

### Top 10 Places Sorted by Percent of Total Population
*Based on places with total population of 50,000 or more*

| Place | Population | % |
|---|---|---|
| **Schenectady** (city) Schenectady County | 43 | 0.07 |
| **Queens** (borough) Queens County | 1,439 | 0.06 |
| **Mount Vernon** (city) Westchester County | 33 | 0.05 |

| Place | Population | % |
|---|---|---|
| **Levittown** (cdp) Nassau County | 27 | 0.05 |
| **Greenburgh** (town) Westchester County | 32 | 0.04 |
| **Hempstead** (village) Nassau County | 23 | 0.04 |
| **White Plains** (city) Westchester County | 23 | 0.04 |
| **New York** (city) | 2,678 | 0.03 |
| **Bronx** (borough) Bronx County | 369 | 0.03 |
| **Hempstead** (town) Nassau County | 243 | 0.03 |

## Other Hispanic or Latino

### Top 10 Places Sorted by Population
*Based on all places, regardless of total population*

| Place | Population | % |
|---|---|---|
| **New York** (city) | 180,805 | 2.21 |
| **Queens** (borough) Queens County | 52,422 | 2.35 |
| **Bronx** (borough) Bronx County | 51,571 | 3.72 |
| **Brooklyn** (borough) Kings County | 35,705 | 1.43 |
| **Manhattan** (borough) New York County | 35,548 | 2.24 |
| **Hempstead** (town) Nassau County | 13,273 | 1.75 |
| **Islip** (town) Suffolk County | 8,524 | 2.54 |
| **Brookhaven** (town) Suffolk County | 6,193 | 1.27 |
| **Staten Island** (borough) Richmond County | 5,559 | 1.19 |
| **Yonkers** (city) Westchester County | 4,443 | 2.27 |

### Top 10 Places Sorted by Percent of Total Population
*Based on all places, regardless of total population*

| Place | Population | % |
|---|---|---|
| **Riverside** (cdp) Suffolk County | 348 | 11.95 |
| **Watchtower** (cdp) Ulster County | 171 | 7.18 |
| **Brentwood** (cdp) Suffolk County | 3,476 | 5.73 |
| **North Bay Shore** (cdp) Suffolk County | 967 | 5.10 |
| **Northwest Harbor** (cdp) Suffolk County | 168 | 5.06 |
| **New Cassel** (cdp) Nassau County | 699 | 4.97 |
| **Hempstead** (village) Nassau County | 2,609 | 4.84 |
| **Central Islip** (cdp) Suffolk County | 1,667 | 4.84 |
| **Inwood** (cdp) Nassau County | 467 | 4.77 |
| **Brewster** (village) Putnam County | 113 | 4.73 |

### Top 10 Places Sorted by Percent of Total Population
*Based on places with total population of 50,000 or more*

| Place | Population | % |
|---|---|---|
| **Brentwood** (cdp) Suffolk County | 3,476 | 5.73 |
| **Hempstead** (village) Nassau County | 2,609 | 4.84 |
| **Bronx** (borough) Bronx County | 51,571 | 3.72 |
| **Southampton** (town) Suffolk County | 1,468 | 2.58 |
| **Islip** (town) Suffolk County | 8,524 | 2.54 |
| **Queens** (borough) Queens County | 52,422 | 2.35 |
| **Yonkers** (city) Westchester County | 4,443 | 2.27 |
| **Manhattan** (borough) New York County | 35,548 | 2.24 |
| **New York** (city) | 180,805 | 2.21 |
| **White Plains** (city) Westchester County | 1,209 | 2.13 |

# Racial Group Rankings

## African-American/Black

### Top 10 Places Sorted by Population
Based on all places, regardless of total population

| Place | Population | % |
|---|---|---|
| New York (city) | 2,228,145 | 27.26 |
| Brooklyn (borough) Kings County | 896,165 | 35.78 |
| Bronx (borough) Bronx County | 541,622 | 39.10 |
| Queens (borough) Queens County | 462,351 | 20.73 |
| Manhattan (borough) New York County | 272,993 | 17.21 |
| Hempstead (town) Nassau County | 133,280 | 17.54 |
| Buffalo (city) Erie County | 106,107 | 40.61 |
| Rochester (city) Monroe County | 94,587 | 44.92 |
| Staten Island (borough) Richmond County | 55,014 | 11.74 |
| Syracuse (city) Onondaga County | 48,029 | 33.08 |

### Top 10 Places Sorted by Percent of Total Population
Based on all places, regardless of total population

| Place | Population | % |
|---|---|---|
| Lakeview (cdp) Nassau County | 4,757 | 84.72 |
| Wyandanch (cdp) Suffolk County | 7,865 | 67.53 |
| Mount Vernon (city) Westchester County | 44,244 | 65.75 |
| Roosevelt (cdp) Nassau County | 10,657 | 65.55 |
| North Amityville (cdp) Suffolk County | 10,971 | 61.42 |
| Fairview (cdp) Westchester County | 1,895 | 61.15 |
| South Floral Park (village) Nassau County | 1,075 | 60.94 |
| Wheatley Heights (cdp) Suffolk County | 2,960 | 57.70 |
| Hillcrest (cdp) Rockland County | 4,328 | 57.26 |
| Gordon Heights (cdp) Suffolk County | 2,294 | 56.75 |

### Top 10 Places Sorted by Percent of Total Population
Based on places with total population of 50,000 or more

| Place | Population | % |
|---|---|---|
| Mount Vernon (city) Westchester County | 44,244 | 65.75 |
| Hempstead (village) Nassau County | 27,076 | 50.24 |
| Rochester (city) Monroe County | 94,587 | 44.92 |
| Buffalo (city) Erie County | 106,107 | 40.61 |
| Bronx (borough) Bronx County | 541,622 | 39.10 |
| Brooklyn (borough) Kings County | 896,165 | 35.78 |
| Albany (city) Albany County | 32,569 | 33.28 |
| Syracuse (city) Onondaga County | 48,029 | 33.08 |
| New York (city) | 2,228,145 | 27.26 |
| Schenectady (city) Schenectady County | 16,103 | 24.35 |

## African-American/Black: Not Hispanic

### Top 10 Places Sorted by Population
Based on all places, regardless of total population

| Place | Population | % |
|---|---|---|
| New York (city) | 1,931,889 | 23.63 |
| Brooklyn (borough) Kings County | 820,437 | 32.76 |
| Bronx (borough) Bronx County | 427,134 | 30.84 |
| Queens (borough) Queens County | 419,695 | 18.81 |
| Manhattan (borough) New York County | 217,102 | 13.69 |
| Hempstead (town) Nassau County | 124,525 | 16.39 |
| Buffalo (city) Erie County | 101,817 | 38.96 |
| Rochester (city) Monroe County | 88,052 | 41.82 |
| Staten Island (borough) Richmond County | 47,521 | 10.14 |
| Syracuse (city) Onondaga County | 45,084 | 31.06 |

### Top 10 Places Sorted by Percent of Total Population
Based on all places, regardless of total population

| Place | Population | % |
|---|---|---|
| Lakeview (cdp) Nassau County | 4,534 | 80.75 |
| Wyandanch (cdp) Suffolk County | 7,550 | 64.82 |
| Mount Vernon (city) Westchester County | 42,361 | 62.95 |
| Roosevelt (cdp) Nassau County | 10,138 | 62.36 |
| North Amityville (cdp) Suffolk County | 10,434 | 58.41 |
| Fairview (cdp) Westchester County | 1,800 | 58.08 |
| South Floral Park (village) Nassau County | 1,024 | 58.05 |
| Wheatley Heights (cdp) Suffolk County | 2,821 | 54.99 |
| Hillcrest (cdp) Rockland County | 4,140 | 54.78 |
| Gordon Heights (cdp) Suffolk County | 2,073 | 51.29 |

### Top 10 Places Sorted by Percent of Total Population
Based on places with total population of 50,000 or more

| Place | Population | % |
|---|---|---|
| Mount Vernon (city) Westchester County | 42,361 | 62.95 |
| Hempstead (village) Nassau County | 25,388 | 47.11 |
| Rochester (city) Monroe County | 88,052 | 41.82 |
| Buffalo (city) Erie County | 101,817 | 38.96 |
| Brooklyn (borough) Kings County | 820,437 | 32.76 |
| Syracuse (city) Onondaga County | 45,084 | 31.06 |
| Albany (city) Albany County | 30,376 | 31.04 |
| Bronx (borough) Bronx County | 427,134 | 30.84 |
| Niagara Falls (city) Niagara County | 11,905 | 23.72 |
| New York (city) | 1,931,889 | 23.63 |

## African-American/Black: Hispanic

### Top 10 Places Sorted by Population
Based on all places, regardless of total population

| Place | Population | % |
|---|---|---|
| New York (city) | 296,256 | 3.62 |
| Bronx (borough) Bronx County | 114,488 | 8.27 |
| Brooklyn (borough) Kings County | 75,728 | 3.02 |
| Manhattan (borough) New York County | 55,891 | 3.52 |
| Queens (borough) Queens County | 42,656 | 1.91 |
| Hempstead (town) Nassau County | 8,755 | 1.15 |
| Staten Island (borough) Richmond County | 7,493 | 1.60 |
| Yonkers (city) Westchester County | 7,325 | 3.74 |
| Rochester (city) Monroe County | 6,535 | 3.10 |
| Islip (town) Suffolk County | 5,700 | 1.70 |

### Top 10 Places Sorted by Percent of Total Population
Based on all places, regardless of total population

| Place | Population | % |
|---|---|---|
| Bronx (borough) Bronx County | 114,488 | 8.27 |
| Gordon Heights (cdp) Suffolk County | 221 | 5.47 |
| Haverstraw (village) Rockland County | 574 | 4.82 |
| Middletown (city) Orange County | 1,209 | 4.30 |
| Monticello (village) Sullivan County | 283 | 4.21 |
| Washington Heights (cdp) Orange County | 68 | 4.03 |
| North Bay Shore (cdp) Suffolk County | 756 | 3.99 |
| Lakeview (cdp) Nassau County | 223 | 3.97 |
| Parc (cdp) Clinton County | 10 | 3.94 |
| Yonkers (city) Westchester County | 7,325 | 3.74 |

### Top 10 Places Sorted by Percent of Total Population
Based on places with total population of 50,000 or more

| Place | Population | % |
|---|---|---|
| Bronx (borough) Bronx County | 114,488 | 8.27 |
| Yonkers (city) Westchester County | 7,325 | 3.74 |
| New York (city) | 296,256 | 3.62 |
| Manhattan (borough) New York County | 55,891 | 3.52 |
| Brentwood (cdp) Suffolk County | 2,138 | 3.52 |
| Hempstead (village) Nassau County | 1,688 | 3.13 |
| Rochester (city) Monroe County | 6,535 | 3.10 |
| Brooklyn (borough) Kings County | 75,728 | 3.02 |
| Mount Vernon (city) Westchester County | 1,883 | 2.80 |
| Schenectady (city) Schenectady County | 1,547 | 2.34 |

## American Indian/Alaska Native

### Top 10 Places Sorted by Population
Based on all places, regardless of total population

| Place | Population | % |
|---|---|---|
| New York (city) | 111,749 | 1.37 |
| Bronx (borough) Bronx County | 32,011 | 2.31 |
| Queens (borough) Queens County | 30,033 | 1.35 |
| Brooklyn (borough) Kings County | 26,571 | 1.06 |
| Manhattan (borough) New York County | 19,415 | 1.22 |
| Hempstead (town) Nassau County | 5,363 | 0.71 |
| Buffalo (city) Erie County | 4,019 | 1.54 |
| Brookhaven (town) Suffolk County | 3,782 | 0.78 |
| Staten Island (borough) Richmond County | 3,719 | 0.79 |
| Syracuse (city) Onondaga County | 3,537 | 2.44 |

### Top 10 Places Sorted by Percent of Total Population
Based on all places, regardless of total population

| Place | Population | % |
|---|---|---|
| Tonawanda Reservation Erie County | 34 | 100.00 |
| Oil Springs Reservation Allegany County | 1 | 100.00 |
| Onondaga Nation Reservation Onondaga County | 457 | 97.65 |
| St. Regis Mohawk Reservation Franklin County | 3,131 | 97.00 |
| Tonawanda Reservation Genesee County | 463 | 95.86 |
| Cattaraugus Reservation Cattaraugus County | 294 | 93.63 |
| Cattaraugus Reservation Erie County | 1,672 | 91.22 |
| Shinnecock Reservation Suffolk County | 584 | 88.22 |
| Cattaraugus Reservation Chautauqua County | 29 | 76.32 |
| Allegany Reservation Cattaraugus County | 670 | 65.69 |

### Top 10 Places Sorted by Percent of Total Population
Based on places with total population of 50,000 or more

| Place | Population | % |
|---|---|---|
| Niagara Falls (city) Niagara County | 1,624 | 3.24 |
| Syracuse (city) Onondaga County | 3,537 | 2.44 |
| Bronx (borough) Bronx County | 32,011 | 2.31 |
| Schenectady (city) Schenectady County | 1,372 | 2.07 |
| Brentwood (cdp) Suffolk County | 1,135 | 1.87 |
| Hempstead (village) Nassau County | 997 | 1.85 |
| White Plains (city) Westchester County | 890 | 1.57 |
| Buffalo (city) Erie County | 4,019 | 1.54 |
| Rochester (city) Monroe County | 3,202 | 1.52 |
| Yonkers (city) Westchester County | 2,801 | 1.43 |

## American Indian/Alaska Native: Not Hispanic

### Top 10 Places Sorted by Population
Based on all places, regardless of total population

| Place | Population | % |
|---|---|---|
| New York (city) | 44,541 | 0.54 |
| Queens (borough) Queens County | 15,412 | 0.69 |
| Brooklyn (borough) Kings County | 12,062 | 0.48 |
| Bronx (borough) Bronx County | 7,638 | 0.55 |
| Manhattan (borough) New York County | 7,395 | 0.47 |
| Buffalo (city) Erie County | 3,229 | 1.24 |
| St. Regis Mohawk Reservation Franklin County | 3,116 | 96.53 |
| Syracuse (city) Onondaga County | 3,067 | 2.11 |
| Hempstead (town) Nassau County | 2,835 | 0.37 |
| Brookhaven (town) Suffolk County | 2,586 | 0.53 |

### Top 10 Places Sorted by Percent of Total Population
Based on all places, regardless of total population

| Place | Population | % |
|---|---|---|
| Tonawanda Reservation Erie County | 34 | 100.00 |
| Oil Springs Reservation Allegany County | 1 | 100.00 |
| St. Regis Mohawk Reservation Franklin County | 3,116 | 96.53 |
| Onondaga Nation Reservation Onondaga County | 447 | 95.51 |
| Tonawanda Reservation Genesee County | 447 | 92.55 |
| Cattaraugus Reservation Cattaraugus County | 283 | 90.13 |
| Cattaraugus Reservation Erie County | 1,613 | 88.00 |
| Shinnecock Reservation Suffolk County | 554 | 83.69 |
| Allegany Reservation Cattaraugus County | 645 | 63.24 |
| Cattaraugus Reservation Chautauqua County | 24 | 63.16 |

### Top 10 Places Sorted by Percent of Total Population
Based on places with total population of 50,000 or more

| Place | Population | % |
|---|---|---|
| Niagara Falls (city) Niagara County | 1,524 | 3.04 |
| Syracuse (city) Onondaga County | 3,067 | 2.11 |
| Schenectady (city) Schenectady County | 1,126 | 1.70 |
| Buffalo (city) Erie County | 3,229 | 1.24 |
| Rochester (city) Monroe County | 2,330 | 1.11 |
| Clay (town) Onondaga County | 557 | 0.96 |
| Albany (city) Albany County | 856 | 0.87 |
| Mount Vernon (city) Westchester County | 585 | 0.87 |
| Troy (city) Rensselaer County | 407 | 0.81 |
| Hempstead (village) Nassau County | 404 | 0.75 |

## American Indian/Alaska Native: Hispanic

### Top 10 Places Sorted by Population
*Based on all places, regardless of total population*

| Place | Population | % |
|---|---|---|
| New York (city) | 67,208 | 0.82 |
| Bronx (borough) Bronx County | 24,373 | 1.76 |
| Queens (borough) Queens County | 14,621 | 0.66 |
| Brooklyn (borough) Kings County | 14,509 | 0.58 |
| Manhattan (borough) New York County | 12,020 | 0.76 |
| Hempstead (town) Nassau County | 2,528 | 0.33 |
| Islip (town) Suffolk County | 1,831 | 0.55 |
| Yonkers (city) Westchester County | 1,806 | 0.92 |
| Staten Island (borough) Richmond County | 1,685 | 0.36 |
| Brookhaven (town) Suffolk County | 1,196 | 0.25 |

### Top 10 Places Sorted by Percent of Total Population
*Based on all places, regardless of total population*

| Place | Population | % |
|---|---|---|
| Cattaraugus Reservation Chautauqua County | 5 | 13.16 |
| Baxter Estates (village) Nassau County | 51 | 5.11 |
| Shinnecock Reservation Suffolk County | 30 | 4.53 |
| Poospatuck Reservation Suffolk County | 14 | 4.32 |
| Cattaraugus Reservation Cattaraugus County | 11 | 3.50 |
| Tonawanda Reservation Genesee County | 16 | 3.31 |
| Cattaraugus Reservation Erie County | 59 | 3.22 |
| Allegany Reservation Cattaraugus County | 25 | 2.45 |
| Onondaga Nation Reservation Onondaga County | 10 | 2.14 |
| Shinnecock Hills (cdp) Suffolk County | 46 | 2.10 |

### Top 10 Places Sorted by Percent of Total Population
*Based on places with total population of 50,000 or more*

| Place | Population | % |
|---|---|---|
| Bronx (borough) Bronx County | 24,373 | 1.76 |
| Brentwood (cdp) Suffolk County | 809 | 1.33 |
| White Plains (city) Westchester County | 697 | 1.23 |
| Hempstead (village) Nassau County | 593 | 1.10 |
| Yonkers (city) Westchester County | 1,806 | 0.92 |
| New York (city) | 67,208 | 0.82 |
| Manhattan (borough) New York County | 12,020 | 0.76 |
| Queens (borough) Queens County | 14,621 | 0.66 |
| New Rochelle (city) Westchester County | 462 | 0.60 |
| Brooklyn (borough) Kings County | 14,509 | 0.58 |

## Alaska Native: Alaska Athabascan

### Top 10 Places Sorted by Population
*Based on all places, regardless of total population*

| Place | Population | % |
|---|---|---|
| New York (city) | 37 | <0.01 |
| Manhattan (borough) New York County | 18 | <0.01 |
| Salamanca (city) Cattaraugus County | 9 | 0.15 |
| Watertown (city) Jefferson County | 8 | 0.03 |
| Bronx (borough) Bronx County | 8 | <0.01 |
| Brighton (cdp/town) Monroe County | 5 | 0.01 |
| Brooklyn (borough) Kings County | 5 | <0.01 |
| Brookhaven (town) Suffolk County | 4 | <0.01 |
| Schroon (town) Essex County | 3 | 0.18 |
| Gouverneur (town) St. Lawrence County | 3 | 0.04 |

### Top 10 Places Sorted by Percent of Total Population
*Based on all places, regardless of total population*

| Place | Population | % |
|---|---|---|
| Burdett (village) Schuyler County | 1 | 0.29 |
| Schroon (town) Essex County | 3 | 0.18 |
| Salamanca (city) Cattaraugus County | 9 | 0.15 |
| Little Valley (town) Cattaraugus County | 2 | 0.11 |
| Orwell (town) Oswego County | 1 | 0.09 |
| Randolph (town) Cattaraugus County | 2 | 0.08 |
| Napoli (town) Cattaraugus County | 1 | 0.08 |
| Randolph (village) Cattaraugus County | 1 | 0.08 |
| Orleans (town) Jefferson County | 2 | 0.07 |
| Lattingtown (village) Nassau County | 1 | 0.06 |

### Top 10 Places Sorted by Percent of Total Population
*Based on places with total population of 50,000 or more*

| Place | Population | % |
|---|---|---|
| New York (city) | 37 | <0.01 |
| Manhattan (borough) New York County | 18 | <0.01 |
| Bronx (borough) Bronx County | 8 | <0.01 |
| Brooklyn (borough) Kings County | 5 | <0.01 |

| Brookhaven (town) Suffolk County | 4 | <0.01 |
| Queens (borough) Queens County | 3 | <0.01 |
| Staten Island (borough) Richmond County | 3 | <0.01 |
| Syracuse (city) Onondaga County | 3 | <0.01 |
| Albany (city) Albany County | 1 | <0.01 |
| Amherst (town) Erie County | 1 | <0.01 |

## Alaska Native: Aleut

### Top 10 Places Sorted by Population
*Based on all places, regardless of total population*

| Place | Population | % |
|---|---|---|
| New York (city) | 26 | <0.01 |
| Brooklyn (borough) Kings County | 8 | <0.01 |
| Manhattan (borough) New York County | 7 | <0.01 |
| Queens (borough) Queens County | 6 | <0.01 |
| Wilton (town) Saratoga County | 5 | 0.03 |
| Denmark (town) Lewis County | 4 | 0.14 |
| Mamaroneck (town) Westchester County | 4 | 0.01 |
| Carlton (town) Orleans County | 3 | 0.10 |
| Champion (town) Jefferson County | 3 | 0.07 |
| Bronx (borough) Bronx County | 3 | <0.01 |

### Top 10 Places Sorted by Percent of Total Population
*Based on all places, regardless of total population*

| Place | Population | % |
|---|---|---|
| Denmark (town) Lewis County | 4 | 0.14 |
| Sempronius (town) Cayuga County | 1 | 0.11 |
| Carlton (town) Orleans County | 3 | 0.10 |
| Richmondville (town) Schoharie County | 2 | 0.08 |
| Champion (town) Jefferson County | 3 | 0.07 |
| Little Valley (town) Cattaraugus County | 1 | 0.06 |
| Morrisonville (cdp) Clinton County | 1 | 0.06 |
| Beaver Dam Lake (cdp) Orange County | 1 | 0.04 |
| Rhinebeck (village) Dutchess County | 1 | 0.04 |
| Salem (town) Washington County | 1 | 0.04 |

### Top 10 Places Sorted by Percent of Total Population
*Based on places with total population of 50,000 or more*

| Place | Population | % |
|---|---|---|
| New York (city) | 26 | <0.01 |
| Brooklyn (borough) Kings County | 8 | <0.01 |
| Manhattan (borough) New York County | 7 | <0.01 |
| Queens (borough) Queens County | 6 | <0.01 |
| Bronx (borough) Bronx County | 3 | <0.01 |
| Brookhaven (town) Suffolk County | 3 | <0.01 |
| Babylon (town) Suffolk County | 2 | <0.01 |
| Hempstead (town) Nassau County | 2 | <0.01 |
| Rochester (city) Monroe County | 2 | <0.01 |
| Staten Island (borough) Richmond County | 2 | <0.01 |

## American Indian: Apache

### Top 10 Places Sorted by Population
*Based on all places, regardless of total population*

| Place | Population | % |
|---|---|---|
| New York (city) | 401 | <0.01 |
| Brooklyn (borough) Kings County | 122 | <0.01 |
| Bronx (borough) Bronx County | 99 | 0.01 |
| Manhattan (borough) New York County | 92 | 0.01 |
| Queens (borough) Queens County | 53 | <0.01 |
| Staten Island (borough) Richmond County | 35 | 0.01 |
| Syracuse (city) Onondaga County | 25 | 0.02 |
| Hempstead (town) Nassau County | 21 | <0.01 |
| Rochester (city) Monroe County | 20 | 0.01 |
| Brookhaven (town) Suffolk County | 18 | <0.01 |

### Top 10 Places Sorted by Percent of Total Population
*Based on all places, regardless of total population*

| Place | Population | % |
|---|---|---|
| Breesport (cdp) Chemung County | 5 | 0.80 |
| Smithville Flats (cdp) Chenango County | 2 | 0.57 |
| Benson (town) Hamilton County | 1 | 0.52 |
| Waterville (village) Oneida County | 6 | 0.38 |
| Lyndonville (village) Orleans County | 3 | 0.36 |
| Ellenburg (town) Clinton County | 6 | 0.34 |
| Stone Ridge (cdp) Ulster County | 4 | 0.34 |
| Windsor (village) Broome County | 3 | 0.33 |
| Carlton (town) Orleans County | 9 | 0.30 |
| German (town) Chenango County | 1 | 0.27 |

### Top 10 Places Sorted by Percent of Total Population
*Based on places with total population of 50,000 or more*

| Place | Population | % |
|---|---|---|
| Syracuse (city) Onondaga County | 25 | 0.02 |
| Union (town) Broome County | 11 | 0.02 |
| Troy (city) Rensselaer County | 10 | 0.02 |
| Bronx (borough) Bronx County | 99 | 0.01 |
| Manhattan (borough) New York County | 92 | 0.01 |
| Staten Island (borough) Richmond County | 35 | 0.01 |
| Rochester (city) Monroe County | 20 | 0.01 |
| Huntington (town) Suffolk County | 14 | 0.01 |
| Babylon (town) Suffolk County | 11 | 0.01 |
| Yonkers (city) Westchester County | 10 | 0.01 |

## American Indian: Arapaho

### Top 10 Places Sorted by Population
*Based on all places, regardless of total population*

| Place | Population | % |
|---|---|---|
| New York (city) | 21 | <0.01 |
| Brooklyn (borough) Kings County | 10 | <0.01 |
| Manhattan (borough) New York County | 5 | <0.01 |
| Greece (town) Monroe County | 4 | <0.01 |
| Malta (town) Saratoga County | 3 | 0.02 |
| Bronx (borough) Bronx County | 3 | <0.01 |
| New Baltimore (town) Greene County | 2 | 0.06 |
| Waterloo (town) Seneca County | 2 | 0.03 |
| Philipstown (town) Putnam County | 2 | 0.02 |
| Kingston (city) Ulster County | 2 | 0.01 |

### Top 10 Places Sorted by Percent of Total Population
*Based on all places, regardless of total population*

| Place | Population | % |
|---|---|---|
| Rifton (cdp) Ulster County | 1 | 0.22 |
| New Baltimore (town) Greene County | 2 | 0.06 |
| Victory (town) Cayuga County | 1 | 0.06 |
| Boonville (village) Oneida County | 1 | 0.05 |
| Carlisle (town) Schoharie County | 1 | 0.05 |
| Berne (town) Albany County | 1 | 0.04 |
| Machias (town) Cattaraugus County | 1 | 0.04 |
| Waterloo (town) Seneca County | 2 | 0.03 |
| Montauk (cdp) Suffolk County | 1 | 0.03 |
| Saugerties (village) Ulster County | 1 | 0.03 |

### Top 10 Places Sorted by Percent of Total Population
*Based on places with total population of 50,000 or more*

| Place | Population | % |
|---|---|---|
| New York (city) | 21 | <0.01 |
| Brooklyn (borough) Kings County | 10 | <0.01 |
| Manhattan (borough) New York County | 5 | <0.01 |
| Greece (town) Monroe County | 4 | <0.01 |
| Bronx (borough) Bronx County | 3 | <0.01 |
| Queens (borough) Queens County | 2 | <0.01 |
| Syracuse (city) Onondaga County | 2 | <0.01 |
| Brookhaven (town) Suffolk County | 1 | <0.01 |
| Buffalo (city) Erie County | 1 | <0.01 |
| Cheektowaga (town) Erie County | 1 | <0.01 |

## American Indian: Blackfeet

### Top 10 Places Sorted by Population
*Based on all places, regardless of total population*

| Place | Population | % |
|---|---|---|
| New York (city) | 1,627 | 0.02 |
| Brooklyn (borough) Kings County | 531 | 0.02 |
| Manhattan (borough) New York County | 356 | 0.02 |
| Queens (borough) Queens County | 342 | 0.02 |
| Bronx (borough) Bronx County | 310 | 0.02 |
| Brookhaven (town) Suffolk County | 164 | 0.03 |
| Rochester (city) Monroe County | 134 | 0.06 |
| Hempstead (town) Nassau County | 117 | 0.02 |
| Syracuse (city) Onondaga County | 111 | 0.08 |
| Buffalo (city) Erie County | 104 | 0.04 |

### Top 10 Places Sorted by Percent of Total Population
*Based on all places, regardless of total population*

| Place | Population | % |
|---|---|---|
| Ellisburg (village) Jefferson County | 6 | 2.46 |
| Cohocton (village) Steuben County | 7 | 0.84 |
| Nassau (village) Rensselaer County | 9 | 0.79 |

| Place | Population | % |
|---|---|---|
| Cameron (town) Steuben County | 7 | 0.74 |
| Cayuta (town) Schuyler County | 4 | 0.72 |
| Dresden (village) Yates County | 2 | 0.65 |
| Theresa (village) Jefferson County | 5 | 0.58 |
| Hemlock (cdp) Livingston County | 3 | 0.54 |
| Lyons Falls (village) Lewis County | 3 | 0.53 |
| East Avon (cdp) Livingston County | 3 | 0.49 |

### Top 10 Places Sorted by Percent of Total Population
*Based on places with total population of 50,000 or more*

| Place | Population | % |
|---|---|---|
| Schenectady (city) Schenectady County | 58 | 0.09 |
| Syracuse (city) Onondaga County | 111 | 0.08 |
| Rochester (city) Monroe County | 134 | 0.06 |
| Albany (city) Albany County | 57 | 0.06 |
| Mount Vernon (city) Westchester County | 38 | 0.06 |
| Hempstead (village) Nassau County | 27 | 0.05 |
| Buffalo (city) Erie County | 104 | 0.04 |
| Troy (city) Rensselaer County | 22 | 0.04 |
| Brookhaven (town) Suffolk County | 164 | 0.03 |
| Yonkers (city) Westchester County | 58 | 0.03 |

## American Indian: Canadian/French American Indian

### Top 10 Places Sorted by Population
*Based on all places, regardless of total population*

| Place | Population | % |
|---|---|---|
| New York (city) | 197 | <0.01 |
| Brooklyn (borough) Kings County | 62 | <0.01 |
| Manhattan (borough) New York County | 62 | <0.01 |
| Buffalo (city) Erie County | 57 | 0.02 |
| Syracuse (city) Onondaga County | 51 | 0.04 |
| Queens (borough) Queens County | 38 | <0.01 |
| Bronx (borough) Bronx County | 25 | <0.01 |
| Niagara Falls (city) Niagara County | 20 | 0.04 |
| Clay (town) Onondaga County | 16 | 0.03 |
| Grand Island (town) Erie County | 15 | 0.07 |

### Top 10 Places Sorted by Percent of Total Population
*Based on all places, regardless of total population*

| Place | Population | % |
|---|---|---|
| Tonawanda Reservation Genesee County | 5 | 1.04 |
| Clare (town) St. Lawrence County | 1 | 0.95 |
| Farnham (village) Erie County | 3 | 0.79 |
| Orwell (town) Oswego County | 6 | 0.51 |
| Rifton (cdp) Ulster County | 2 | 0.44 |
| Verona (cdp) Oneida County | 3 | 0.35 |
| Sinclairville (village) Chautauqua County | 2 | 0.34 |
| East Avon (cdp) Livingston County | 2 | 0.33 |
| Bellmont (town) Franklin County | 4 | 0.28 |
| Decatur (town) Otsego County | 1 | 0.28 |

### Top 10 Places Sorted by Percent of Total Population
*Based on places with total population of 50,000 or more*

| Place | Population | % |
|---|---|---|
| Syracuse (city) Onondaga County | 51 | 0.04 |
| Niagara Falls (city) Niagara County | 20 | 0.04 |
| Clay (town) Onondaga County | 16 | 0.03 |
| Buffalo (city) Erie County | 57 | 0.02 |
| Hamburg (town) Erie County | 12 | 0.02 |
| Greece (town) Monroe County | 14 | 0.01 |
| Amherst (town) Erie County | 11 | 0.01 |
| Colonie (town) Albany County | 10 | 0.01 |
| Schenectady (city) Schenectady County | 9 | 0.01 |
| Tonawanda (town) Erie County | 8 | 0.01 |

## American Indian: Central American Indian

### Top 10 Places Sorted by Population
*Based on all places, regardless of total population*

| Place | Population | % |
|---|---|---|
| New York (city) | 7,662 | 0.09 |
| Bronx (borough) Bronx County | 4,520 | 0.33 |
| Brooklyn (borough) Kings County | 1,263 | 0.05 |
| Manhattan (borough) New York County | 1,090 | 0.07 |
| Queens (borough) Queens County | 733 | 0.03 |
| Yonkers (city) Westchester County | 103 | 0.05 |
| Hempstead (town) Nassau County | 87 | 0.01 |
| Islip (town) Suffolk County | 73 | 0.02 |
| Staten Island (borough) Richmond County | 56 | 0.01 |

| Place | Population | % |
|---|---|---|
| Brookhaven (town) Suffolk County | 53 | 0.01 |

### Top 10 Places Sorted by Percent of Total Population
*Based on all places, regardless of total population*

| Place | Population | % |
|---|---|---|
| Shelter Island (cdp) Suffolk County | 14 | 1.05 |
| Shelter Island (town) Suffolk County | 16 | 0.67 |
| Nelliston (village) Montgomery County | 3 | 0.50 |
| Mount Kisco (town/village) Westchester County | 43 | 0.40 |
| Washington Heights (cdp) Orange County | 6 | 0.36 |
| Bronx (borough) Bronx County | 4,520 | 0.33 |
| Copenhagen (village) Lewis County | 2 | 0.25 |
| Columbus (town) Chenango County | 2 | 0.21 |
| Shelter Island Heights (cdp) Suffolk County | 2 | 0.19 |
| Bolton Landing (cdp) Warren County | 1 | 0.19 |

### Top 10 Places Sorted by Percent of Total Population
*Based on places with total population of 50,000 or more*

| Place | Population | % |
|---|---|---|
| Bronx (borough) Bronx County | 4,520 | 0.33 |
| New York (city) | 7,662 | 0.09 |
| Manhattan (borough) New York County | 1,090 | 0.07 |
| Brentwood (cdp) Suffolk County | 36 | 0.06 |
| Brooklyn (borough) Kings County | 1,263 | 0.05 |
| Yonkers (city) Westchester County | 103 | 0.05 |
| Queens (borough) Queens County | 733 | 0.03 |
| New Rochelle (city) Westchester County | 20 | 0.03 |
| Mount Vernon (city) Westchester County | 19 | 0.03 |
| Hempstead (village) Nassau County | 15 | 0.03 |

## American Indian: Cherokee

### Top 10 Places Sorted by Population
*Based on all places, regardless of total population*

| Place | Population | % |
|---|---|---|
| New York (city) | 6,952 | 0.09 |
| Brooklyn (borough) Kings County | 1,903 | 0.08 |
| Manhattan (borough) New York County | 1,845 | 0.12 |
| Queens (borough) Queens County | 1,425 | 0.06 |
| Bronx (borough) Bronx County | 1,312 | 0.09 |
| Hempstead (town) Nassau County | 572 | 0.08 |
| Brookhaven (town) Suffolk County | 546 | 0.11 |
| Staten Island (borough) Richmond County | 467 | 0.10 |
| Rochester (city) Monroe County | 411 | 0.20 |
| Islip (town) Suffolk County | 316 | 0.09 |

### Top 10 Places Sorted by Percent of Total Population
*Based on all places, regardless of total population*

| Place | Population | % |
|---|---|---|
| Poospatuck Reservation Suffolk County | 11 | 3.40 |
| Shinnecock Reservation Suffolk County | 16 | 2.42 |
| Winthrop (cdp) St. Lawrence County | 11 | 2.16 |
| Bloomingburg (village) Sullivan County | 9 | 2.14 |
| North Rose (cdp) Wayne County | 11 | 1.73 |
| Phoenicia (cdp) Ulster County | 5 | 1.62 |
| Wainscott (cdp) Suffolk County | 9 | 1.38 |
| Hopewell Junction (cdp) Dutchess County | 5 | 1.33 |
| Morehouse (town) Hamilton County | 11 | 1.16 |
| Natural Bridge (cdp) Jefferson County | 4 | 1.10 |

### Top 10 Places Sorted by Percent of Total Population
*Based on places with total population of 50,000 or more*

| Place | Population | % |
|---|---|---|
| Schenectady (city) Schenectady County | 145 | 0.22 |
| Albany (city) Albany County | 205 | 0.21 |
| Rochester (city) Monroe County | 411 | 0.20 |
| Hempstead (village) Nassau County | 109 | 0.20 |
| Syracuse (city) Onondaga County | 258 | 0.18 |
| Mount Vernon (city) Westchester County | 116 | 0.17 |
| Troy (city) Rensselaer County | 80 | 0.16 |
| Brentwood (cdp) Suffolk County | 76 | 0.13 |
| Manhattan (borough) New York County | 1,845 | 0.12 |
| Babylon (town) Suffolk County | 250 | 0.12 |

## American Indian: Cheyenne

### Top 10 Places Sorted by Population
*Based on all places, regardless of total population*

| Place | Population | % |
|---|---|---|
| New York (city) | 46 | <0.01 |

| Place | Population | % |
|---|---|---|
| Queens (borough) Queens County | 20 | <0.01 |
| Brooklyn (borough) Kings County | 10 | <0.01 |
| Manhattan (borough) New York County | 9 | <0.01 |
| Kent (town) Putnam County | 6 | 0.04 |
| Brookhaven (town) Suffolk County | 6 | <0.01 |
| Greenburgh (town) Westchester County | 5 | 0.01 |
| Bronx (borough) Bronx County | 5 | <0.01 |
| Whitestown (town) Oneida County | 4 | 0.02 |
| Utica (city) Oneida County | 4 | 0.01 |

### Top 10 Places Sorted by Percent of Total Population
*Based on all places, regardless of total population*

| Place | Population | % |
|---|---|---|
| Bloomville (cdp) Delaware County | 1 | 0.47 |
| Celoron (village) Chautauqua County | 2 | 0.18 |
| Hannibal (village) Oswego County | 1 | 0.18 |
| Conewango (town) Cattaraugus County | 3 | 0.16 |
| Crompond (cdp) Westchester County | 3 | 0.13 |
| Willsboro (cdp) Essex County | 1 | 0.13 |
| Yorkville (village) Oneida County | 3 | 0.11 |
| Cameron (town) Steuben County | 1 | 0.11 |
| Nelson (town) Madison County | 2 | 0.10 |
| Allegany Reservation Cattaraugus County | 1 | 0.10 |

### Top 10 Places Sorted by Percent of Total Population
*Based on places with total population of 50,000 or more*

| Place | Population | % |
|---|---|---|
| Greenburgh (town) Westchester County | 5 | 0.01 |
| Utica (city) Oneida County | 4 | 0.01 |
| New York (city) | 46 | <0.01 |
| Queens (borough) Queens County | 20 | <0.01 |
| Brooklyn (borough) Kings County | 10 | <0.01 |
| Manhattan (borough) New York County | 9 | <0.01 |
| Brookhaven (town) Suffolk County | 6 | <0.01 |
| Bronx (borough) Bronx County | 5 | <0.01 |
| Huntington (town) Suffolk County | 4 | <0.01 |
| North Hempstead (town) Nassau County | 3 | <0.01 |

## American Indian: Chickasaw

### Top 10 Places Sorted by Population
*Based on all places, regardless of total population*

| Place | Population | % |
|---|---|---|
| New York (city) | 113 | <0.01 |
| Manhattan (borough) New York County | 43 | <0.01 |
| Brooklyn (borough) Kings County | 30 | <0.01 |
| Queens (borough) Queens County | 21 | <0.01 |
| Bronx (borough) Bronx County | 16 | <0.01 |
| Mount Kisco (town/village) Westchester County | 5 | 0.05 |
| Hempstead (town) Nassau County | 5 | <0.01 |
| Chatham (village) Columbia County | 4 | 0.23 |
| Chatham (town) Columbia County | 4 | 0.10 |
| Rockville Centre (village) Nassau County | 4 | 0.02 |

### Top 10 Places Sorted by Percent of Total Population
*Based on all places, regardless of total population*

| Place | Population | % |
|---|---|---|
| Chatham (village) Columbia County | 4 | 0.23 |
| Port Gibson (cdp) Ontario County | 1 | 0.22 |
| Chatham (town) Columbia County | 4 | 0.10 |
| Gasport (cdp) Niagara County | 1 | 0.08 |
| Philadelphia (village) Jefferson County | 1 | 0.08 |
| West Sparta (town) Livingston County | 1 | 0.08 |
| Pittsfield (town) Otsego County | 1 | 0.07 |
| Austerlitz (town) Columbia County | 1 | 0.06 |
| Cumberland Head (cdp) Clinton County | 1 | 0.06 |
| Mount Kisco (town/village) Westchester County | 5 | 0.05 |

### Top 10 Places Sorted by Percent of Total Population
*Based on places with total population of 50,000 or more*

| Place | Population | % |
|---|---|---|
| Mount Vernon (city) Westchester County | 4 | 0.01 |
| New York (city) | 113 | <0.01 |
| Manhattan (borough) New York County | 43 | <0.01 |
| Brooklyn (borough) Kings County | 30 | <0.01 |
| Queens (borough) Queens County | 21 | <0.01 |
| Bronx (borough) Bronx County | 16 | <0.01 |
| Hempstead (town) Nassau County | 5 | <0.01 |
| Syracuse (city) Onondaga County | 4 | <0.01 |
| Brookhaven (town) Suffolk County | 3 | <0.01 |
| Huntington (town) Suffolk County | 3 | <0.01 |

## American Indian: Chippewa

### Top 10 Places Sorted by Population
*Based on all places, regardless of total population*

| Place | Population | % |
|---|---|---|
| New York (city) | 252 | <0.01 |
| Manhattan (borough) New York County | 99 | 0.01 |
| Brooklyn (borough) Kings County | 65 | <0.01 |
| Buffalo (city) Erie County | 42 | 0.02 |
| Bronx (borough) Bronx County | 38 | <0.01 |
| Queens (borough) Queens County | 37 | <0.01 |
| Niagara Falls (city) Niagara County | 23 | 0.05 |
| Brookhaven (town) Suffolk County | 19 | <0.01 |
| Rochester (city) Monroe County | 18 | 0.01 |
| Syracuse (city) Onondaga County | 18 | 0.01 |

### Top 10 Places Sorted by Percent of Total Population
*Based on all places, regardless of total population*

| Place | Population | % |
|---|---|---|
| Barneveld (village) Oneida County | 3 | 1.06 |
| Milford (village) Otsego County | 3 | 0.72 |
| Poospatuck Reservation Suffolk County | 2 | 0.62 |
| Amenia (cdp) Dutchess County | 5 | 0.52 |
| Morristown (village) St. Lawrence County | 2 | 0.51 |
| Dickinson (town) Franklin County | 4 | 0.49 |
| Piffard (cdp) Livingston County | 1 | 0.45 |
| French Creek (town) Chautauqua County | 4 | 0.44 |
| Greenville (cdp) Greene County | 3 | 0.44 |
| Wampsville (village) Madison County | 2 | 0.37 |

### Top 10 Places Sorted by Percent of Total Population
*Based on places with total population of 50,000 or more*

| Place | Population | % |
|---|---|---|
| Niagara Falls (city) Niagara County | 23 | 0.05 |
| Buffalo (city) Erie County | 42 | 0.02 |
| Clay (town) Onondaga County | 11 | 0.02 |
| Schenectady (city) Schenectady County | 11 | 0.02 |
| Manhattan (borough) New York County | 99 | 0.01 |
| Rochester (city) Monroe County | 18 | 0.01 |
| Syracuse (city) Onondaga County | 18 | 0.01 |
| Greece (town) Monroe County | 13 | 0.01 |
| Utica (city) Oneida County | 8 | 0.01 |
| Amherst (town) Erie County | 7 | 0.01 |

## American Indian: Choctaw

### Top 10 Places Sorted by Population
*Based on all places, regardless of total population*

| Place | Population | % |
|---|---|---|
| New York (city) | 405 | <0.01 |
| Manhattan (borough) New York County | 179 | <0.01 |
| Brooklyn (borough) Kings County | 104 | <0.01 |
| Queens (borough) Queens County | 68 | <0.01 |
| Bronx (borough) Bronx County | 43 | <0.01 |
| Hempstead (town) Nassau County | 36 | <0.01 |
| Brookhaven (town) Suffolk County | 34 | 0.01 |
| Syracuse (city) Onondaga County | 28 | 0.02 |
| Rochester (city) Monroe County | 28 | 0.01 |
| Buffalo (city) Erie County | 21 | 0.01 |

### Top 10 Places Sorted by Percent of Total Population
*Based on all places, regardless of total population*

| Place | Population | % |
|---|---|---|
| Winthrop (cdp) St. Lawrence County | 5 | 0.98 |
| Smallwood (cdp) Sullivan County | 5 | 0.86 |
| Schaghticoke (village) Rensselaer County | 4 | 0.68 |
| Cattaraugus Reservation Cattaraugus County | 2 | 0.64 |
| Theresa (village) Jefferson County | 3 | 0.35 |
| Old Field (village) Suffolk County | 3 | 0.33 |
| Rose (town) Wayne County | 7 | 0.30 |
| Worcester (cdp) Otsego County | 3 | 0.27 |
| Leeds (cdp) Greene County | 1 | 0.27 |
| Marcellus (village) Onondaga County | 4 | 0.22 |

### Top 10 Places Sorted by Percent of Total Population
*Based on places with total population of 50,000 or more*

| Place | Population | % |
|---|---|---|
| Syracuse (city) Onondaga County | 28 | 0.02 |
| Manhattan (borough) New York County | 179 | 0.01 |
| Brookhaven (town) Suffolk County | 34 | 0.01 |
| Rochester (city) Monroe County | 28 | 0.01 |

| Place | Population | % |
|---|---|---|
| Buffalo (city) Erie County | 21 | 0.01 |
| Islip (town) Suffolk County | 17 | 0.01 |
| Huntington (town) Suffolk County | 13 | 0.01 |
| Yonkers (city) Westchester County | 12 | 0.01 |
| Albany (city) Albany County | 8 | 0.01 |
| Greece (town) Monroe County | 8 | 0.01 |

## American Indian: Colville

### Top 10 Places Sorted by Population
*Based on all places, regardless of total population*

| Place | Population | % |
|---|---|---|
| New York (city) | 9 | <0.01 |
| Manhattan (borough) New York County | 5 | <0.01 |
| Brookfield (town) Madison County | 3 | 0.12 |
| Bronx (borough) Bronx County | 2 | <0.01 |
| Sidney (village) Delaware County | 1 | 0.03 |
| St. Regis Mohawk Reservation Franklin County | 1 | 0.03 |
| Triangle (town) Broome County | 1 | 0.03 |
| Hector (town) Schuyler County | 1 | 0.02 |
| LaFayette (town) Onondaga County | 1 | 0.02 |
| Sidney (town) Delaware County | 1 | 0.02 |

### Top 10 Places Sorted by Percent of Total Population
*Based on all places, regardless of total population*

| Place | Population | % |
|---|---|---|
| Brookfield (town) Madison County | 3 | 0.12 |
| Sidney (village) Delaware County | 1 | 0.03 |
| St. Regis Mohawk Reservation Franklin County | 1 | 0.03 |
| Triangle (town) Broome County | 1 | 0.03 |
| Hector (town) Schuyler County | 1 | 0.02 |
| LaFayette (town) Onondaga County | 1 | 0.02 |
| Sidney (town) Delaware County | 1 | 0.02 |
| New York (city) | 9 | <0.01 |
| Manhattan (borough) New York County | 5 | <0.01 |
| Bronx (borough) Bronx County | 2 | <0.01 |

### Top 10 Places Sorted by Percent of Total Population
*Based on places with total population of 50,000 or more*

| Place | Population | % |
|---|---|---|
| New York (city) | 9 | <0.01 |
| Manhattan (borough) New York County | 5 | <0.01 |
| Bronx (borough) Bronx County | 2 | <0.01 |
| Brooklyn (borough) Kings County | 1 | <0.01 |
| Hempstead (town) Nassau County | 1 | <0.01 |
| Irondequoit (cdp/town) Monroe County | 1 | <0.01 |
| Queens (borough) Queens County | 1 | <0.01 |
| Rochester (city) Monroe County | 1 | <0.01 |
| Yonkers (city) Westchester County | 1 | <0.01 |
| Albany (city) Albany County | 0 | 0.00 |

## American Indian: Comanche

### Top 10 Places Sorted by Population
*Based on all places, regardless of total population*

| Place | Population | % |
|---|---|---|
| New York (city) | 76 | <0.01 |
| Bronx (borough) Bronx County | 26 | <0.01 |
| Manhattan (borough) New York County | 22 | <0.01 |
| Brooklyn (borough) Kings County | 19 | <0.01 |
| Syracuse (city) Onondaga County | 12 | 0.01 |
| Hempstead (town) Nassau County | 11 | <0.01 |
| Huntington (town) Suffolk County | 8 | <0.01 |
| Islip (town) Suffolk County | 8 | <0.01 |
| Brentwood (cdp) Suffolk County | 7 | 0.01 |
| Levittown (cdp) Nassau County | 7 | 0.01 |

### Top 10 Places Sorted by Percent of Total Population
*Based on all places, regardless of total population*

| Place | Population | % |
|---|---|---|
| Westport (cdp) Essex County | 3 | 0.58 |
| Cato (village) Cayuga County | 3 | 0.56 |
| Westport (town) Essex County | 3 | 0.23 |
| Schroon (town) Essex County | 3 | 0.18 |
| Accord (cdp) Ulster County | 1 | 0.18 |
| Ira (town) Cayuga County | 3 | 0.14 |
| Elmsford (village) Westchester County | 5 | 0.11 |
| Amenia (cdp) Dutchess County | 1 | 0.10 |
| Tyre (town) Seneca County | 1 | 0.10 |
| North Dansville (town) Livingston County | 3 | 0.05 |

### Top 10 Places Sorted by Percent of Total Population
*Based on places with total population of 50,000 or more*

| Place | Population | % |
|---|---|---|
| Syracuse (city) Onondaga County | 12 | 0.01 |
| Brentwood (cdp) Suffolk County | 7 | 0.01 |
| Levittown (cdp) Nassau County | 7 | 0.01 |
| Greenburgh (town) Westchester County | 5 | 0.01 |
| New York (city) | 76 | <0.01 |
| Bronx (borough) Bronx County | 26 | <0.01 |
| Manhattan (borough) New York County | 22 | <0.01 |
| Brooklyn (borough) Kings County | 19 | <0.01 |
| Hempstead (town) Nassau County | 11 | <0.01 |
| Huntington (town) Suffolk County | 8 | <0.01 |

## American Indian: Cree

### Top 10 Places Sorted by Population
*Based on all places, regardless of total population*

| Place | Population | % |
|---|---|---|
| New York (city) | 81 | <0.01 |
| Queens (borough) Queens County | 24 | <0.01 |
| Manhattan (borough) New York County | 22 | <0.01 |
| Bronx (borough) Bronx County | 16 | <0.01 |
| Brooklyn (borough) Kings County | 15 | <0.01 |
| Syracuse (city) Onondaga County | 6 | <0.01 |
| Elizabethtown (cdp) Essex County | 5 | 0.66 |
| Elizabethtown (town) Essex County | 5 | 0.43 |
| Pembroke (town) Genesee County | 5 | 0.12 |
| Brownville (town) Jefferson County | 5 | 0.08 |

### Top 10 Places Sorted by Percent of Total Population
*Based on all places, regardless of total population*

| Place | Population | % |
|---|---|---|
| Elizabethtown (cdp) Essex County | 5 | 0.66 |
| Elizabethtown (town) Essex County | 5 | 0.43 |
| Fonda (village) Montgomery County | 2 | 0.25 |
| Germantown (cdp) Columbia County | 2 | 0.24 |
| Port Gibson (cdp) Ontario County | 1 | 0.22 |
| Denning (town) Ulster County | 1 | 0.18 |
| Margaretville (village) Delaware County | 1 | 0.17 |
| Pembroke (town) Genesee County | 5 | 0.12 |
| St. Regis Mohawk Reservation Franklin County | 4 | 0.12 |
| Triangle (town) Broome County | 3 | 0.10 |

### Top 10 Places Sorted by Percent of Total Population
*Based on places with total population of 50,000 or more*

| Place | Population | % |
|---|---|---|
| Schenectady (city) Schenectady County | 4 | 0.01 |
| Niagara Falls (city) Niagara County | 3 | 0.01 |
| New York (city) | 81 | <0.01 |
| Queens (borough) Queens County | 24 | <0.01 |
| Manhattan (borough) New York County | 22 | <0.01 |
| Bronx (borough) Bronx County | 16 | <0.01 |
| Brooklyn (borough) Kings County | 15 | <0.01 |
| Syracuse (city) Onondaga County | 6 | <0.01 |
| Albany (city) Albany County | 4 | <0.01 |
| Brookhaven (town) Suffolk County | 4 | <0.01 |

## American Indian: Creek

### Top 10 Places Sorted by Population
*Based on all places, regardless of total population*

| Place | Population | % |
|---|---|---|
| New York (city) | 291 | <0.01 |
| Brooklyn (borough) Kings County | 81 | <0.01 |
| Queens (borough) Queens County | 73 | <0.01 |
| Manhattan (borough) New York County | 61 | <0.01 |
| Bronx (borough) Bronx County | 47 | <0.01 |
| Staten Island (borough) Richmond County | 29 | 0.01 |
| Hempstead (town) Nassau County | 29 | <0.01 |
| Huntington (town) Suffolk County | 15 | 0.01 |
| Babylon (town) Suffolk County | 13 | 0.01 |
| Brookhaven (town) Suffolk County | 12 | <0.01 |

### Top 10 Places Sorted by Percent of Total Population
*Based on all places, regardless of total population*

| Place | Population | % |
|---|---|---|
| Cattaraugus Reservation Cattaraugus County | 6 | 1.91 |
| Tonawanda Reservation Genesee County | 4 | 0.83 |
| Pamelia Center (cdp) Jefferson County | 1 | 0.38 |

| Place | Population | % |
|---|---|---|
| Milton (cdp) Ulster County | 5 | 0.36 |
| Apalachin (cdp) Tioga County | 4 | 0.35 |
| Plandome Manor (village) Nassau County | 3 | 0.34 |
| Avoca (village) Steuben County | 3 | 0.32 |
| Cattaraugus Reservation Erie County | 5 | 0.27 |
| Rapids (cdp) Niagara County | 3 | 0.18 |
| Rock Hill (cdp) Sullivan County | 3 | 0.17 |

### Top 10 Places Sorted by Percent of Total Population
*Based on places with total population of 50,000 or more*

| Place | Population | % |
|---|---|---|
| Staten Island (borough) Richmond County | 29 | 0.01 |
| Huntington (town) Suffolk County | 15 | 0.01 |
| Babylon (town) Suffolk County | 13 | 0.01 |
| Syracuse (city) Onondaga County | 9 | 0.01 |
| Smithtown (town) Suffolk County | 7 | 0.01 |
| Albany (city) Albany County | 6 | 0.01 |
| Schenectady (city) Schenectady County | 5 | 0.01 |
| White Plains (city) Westchester County | 3 | 0.01 |
| New York (city) | 291 | <0.01 |
| Brooklyn (borough) Kings County | 81 | <0.01 |

## American Indian: Crow

### Top 10 Places Sorted by Population
*Based on all places, regardless of total population*

| Place | Population | % |
|---|---|---|
| New York (city) | 50 | <0.01 |
| Brooklyn (borough) Kings County | 19 | <0.01 |
| Bronx (borough) Bronx County | 16 | <0.01 |
| Islip (town) Suffolk County | 16 | <0.01 |
| Brentwood (cdp) Suffolk County | 11 | 0.02 |
| Manhattan (borough) New York County | 11 | 0.01 |
| Schenectady (city) Schenectady County | 6 | 0.01 |
| Bombay (town) Franklin County | 5 | 0.37 |
| Huntington (town) Suffolk County | 5 | <0.01 |
| Crown Heights (cdp) Dutchess County | 4 | 0.14 |

### Top 10 Places Sorted by Percent of Total Population
*Based on all places, regardless of total population*

| Place | Population | % |
|---|---|---|
| Benson (town) Hamilton County | 1 | 0.52 |
| Bombay (town) Franklin County | 5 | 0.37 |
| Santa Clara (town) Franklin County | 1 | 0.29 |
| Valley Falls (village) Rensselaer County | 1 | 0.21 |
| East Avon (cdp) Livingston County | 1 | 0.16 |
| Crown Heights (cdp) Dutchess County | 4 | 0.14 |
| Cumberland Head (cdp) Clinton County | 2 | 0.12 |
| Manchester (village) Ontario County | 2 | 0.12 |
| Portville (village) Cattaraugus County | 1 | 0.10 |
| Gilboa (town) Schoharie County | 1 | 0.08 |

### Top 10 Places Sorted by Percent of Total Population
*Based on places with total population of 50,000 or more*

| Place | Population | % |
|---|---|---|
| Brentwood (cdp) Suffolk County | 11 | 0.02 |
| Schenectady (city) Schenectady County | 6 | 0.01 |
| New York (city) | 50 | <0.01 |
| Brooklyn (borough) Kings County | 19 | <0.01 |
| Bronx (borough) Bronx County | 16 | <0.01 |
| Islip (town) Suffolk County | 16 | <0.01 |
| Manhattan (borough) New York County | 11 | <0.01 |
| Huntington (town) Suffolk County | 5 | <0.01 |
| Queens (borough) Queens County | 4 | <0.01 |
| Utica (city) Oneida County | 3 | <0.01 |

## American Indian: Delaware

### Top 10 Places Sorted by Population
*Based on all places, regardless of total population*

| Place | Population | % |
|---|---|---|
| New York (city) | 177 | <0.01 |
| Ramapo (town) Rockland County | 167 | 0.13 |
| Hillburn (village) Rockland County | 120 | 12.62 |
| Warwick (town) Orange County | 58 | 0.18 |
| Wallkill (town) Orange County | 57 | 0.21 |
| Manhattan (borough) New York County | 54 | <0.01 |
| Blooming Grove (town) Orange County | 51 | 0.28 |
| Middletown (city) Orange County | 43 | 0.15 |
| Staten Island (borough) Richmond County | 43 | 0.01 |
| Port Jervis (city) Orange County | 39 | 0.44 |

### Top 10 Places Sorted by Percent of Total Population
*Based on all places, regardless of total population*

| Place | Population | % |
|---|---|---|
| Hillburn (village) Rockland County | 120 | 12.62 |
| Mountain Lodge Park (cdp) Orange County | 25 | 1.57 |
| Brushton (village) Franklin County | 4 | 0.84 |
| La Fargeville (cdp) Jefferson County | 5 | 0.82 |
| Wurtsboro (village) Sullivan County | 8 | 0.64 |
| Brandon (town) Franklin County | 3 | 0.52 |
| Greenwood Lake (village) Orange County | 15 | 0.48 |
| Port Jervis (city) Orange County | 39 | 0.44 |
| Chester (village) Orange County | 17 | 0.43 |
| Roseboom (town) Otsego County | 3 | 0.42 |

### Top 10 Places Sorted by Percent of Total Population
*Based on places with total population of 50,000 or more*

| Place | Population | % |
|---|---|---|
| Ramapo (town) Rockland County | 167 | 0.13 |
| Clarkstown (town) Rockland County | 16 | 0.02 |
| Schenectady (city) Schenectady County | 12 | 0.02 |
| Staten Island (borough) Richmond County | 43 | 0.01 |
| Huntington (town) Suffolk County | 12 | 0.01 |
| Albany (city) Albany County | 11 | 0.01 |
| Irondequoit (cdp/town) Monroe County | 7 | 0.01 |
| Troy (city) Rensselaer County | 6 | 0.01 |
| Greenburgh (town) Westchester County | 5 | 0.01 |
| Union (town) Broome County | 5 | 0.01 |

## American Indian: Hopi

### Top 10 Places Sorted by Population
*Based on all places, regardless of total population*

| Place | Population | % |
|---|---|---|
| New York (city) | 49 | <0.01 |
| Manhattan (borough) New York County | 15 | <0.01 |
| Queens (borough) Queens County | 15 | <0.01 |
| Brooklyn (borough) Kings County | 12 | <0.01 |
| Babylon (town) Suffolk County | 5 | <0.01 |
| Buffalo (city) Erie County | 5 | <0.01 |
| Staten Island (borough) Richmond County | 5 | <0.01 |
| Yonkers (city) Westchester County | 5 | <0.01 |
| Village Green (cdp) Onondaga County | 3 | 0.08 |
| Massena (village) St. Lawrence County | 3 | 0.03 |

### Top 10 Places Sorted by Percent of Total Population
*Based on all places, regardless of total population*

| Place | Population | % |
|---|---|---|
| Tonawanda Reservation Genesee County | 1 | 0.21 |
| Cayuta (town) Schuyler County | 1 | 0.18 |
| Shinnecock Reservation Suffolk County | 1 | 0.15 |
| Village Green (cdp) Onondaga County | 3 | 0.08 |
| North Collins (town) Erie County | 2 | 0.06 |
| Massena (village) St. Lawrence County | 3 | 0.03 |
| Shandaken (town) Ulster County | 1 | 0.03 |
| Theresa (town) Jefferson County | 1 | 0.03 |
| Cornwall (town) Orange County | 3 | 0.02 |
| Kingsbury (town) Washington County | 3 | 0.02 |

### Top 10 Places Sorted by Percent of Total Population
*Based on places with total population of 50,000 or more*

| Place | Population | % |
|---|---|---|
| New York (city) | 49 | <0.01 |
| Manhattan (borough) New York County | 15 | <0.01 |
| Queens (borough) Queens County | 15 | <0.01 |
| Brooklyn (borough) Kings County | 12 | <0.01 |
| Babylon (town) Suffolk County | 5 | <0.01 |
| Buffalo (city) Erie County | 5 | <0.01 |
| Staten Island (borough) Richmond County | 5 | <0.01 |
| Yonkers (city) Westchester County | 5 | <0.01 |
| Islip (town) Suffolk County | 3 | <0.01 |
| North Hempstead (town) Nassau County | 3 | <0.01 |

## American Indian: Houma

### Top 10 Places Sorted by Population
*Based on all places, regardless of total population*

| Place | Population | % |
|---|---|---|
| New York (city) | 23 | <0.01 |
| Bronx (borough) Bronx County | 12 | <0.01 |
| Queens (borough) Queens County | 4 | <0.01 |

| Place | Population | % |
|---|---|---|
| White Plains (city) Westchester County | 3 | 0.01 |
| Brooklyn (borough) Kings County | 3 | <0.01 |
| Islip (town) Suffolk County | 3 | <0.01 |
| Manhattan (borough) New York County | 3 | <0.01 |
| Liberty (village) Sullivan County | 2 | 0.05 |
| Firthcliffe (cdp) Orange County | 2 | 0.04 |
| West Bay Shore (cdp) Suffolk County | 2 | 0.04 |

### Top 10 Places Sorted by Percent of Total Population
*Based on all places, regardless of total population*

| Place | Population | % |
|---|---|---|
| Willing (town) Allegany County | 1 | 0.08 |
| Coventry (town) Chenango County | 1 | 0.06 |
| Liberty (village) Sullivan County | 2 | 0.05 |
| Firthcliffe (cdp) Orange County | 2 | 0.04 |
| West Bay Shore (cdp) Suffolk County | 2 | 0.04 |
| Kendall (town) Orleans County | 1 | 0.04 |
| Cornwall (town) Orange County | 2 | 0.02 |
| Liberty (town) Sullivan County | 2 | 0.02 |
| Elmira Heights (village) Chemung County | 1 | 0.02 |
| White Plains (city) Westchester County | 3 | 0.01 |

### Top 10 Places Sorted by Percent of Total Population
*Based on places with total population of 50,000 or more*

| Place | Population | % |
|---|---|---|
| White Plains (city) Westchester County | 3 | 0.01 |
| New York (city) | 23 | <0.01 |
| Bronx (borough) Bronx County | 12 | <0.01 |
| Queens (borough) Queens County | 4 | <0.01 |
| Brooklyn (borough) Kings County | 3 | <0.01 |
| Islip (town) Suffolk County | 3 | <0.01 |
| Manhattan (borough) New York County | 3 | <0.01 |
| Buffalo (city) Erie County | 2 | <0.01 |
| Greece (town) Monroe County | 2 | <0.01 |
| Clay (town) Onondaga County | 1 | <0.01 |

## Alaska Native: Inupiat (Eskimo)

### Top 10 Places Sorted by Population
*Based on all places, regardless of total population*

| Place | Population | % |
|---|---|---|
| New York (city) | 58 | <0.01 |
| Brooklyn (borough) Kings County | 21 | <0.01 |
| Bronx (borough) Bronx County | 15 | <0.01 |
| Queens (borough) Queens County | 13 | <0.01 |
| Manhattan (borough) New York County | 8 | <0.01 |
| Syracuse (city) Onondaga County | 6 | <0.01 |
| Port Chester (village) Westchester County | 5 | 0.02 |
| Rye (town) Westchester County | 5 | 0.01 |
| Yonkers (city) Westchester County | 5 | <0.01 |
| Frewsburg (cdp) Chautauqua County | 4 | 0.21 |

### Top 10 Places Sorted by Percent of Total Population
*Based on all places, regardless of total population*

| Place | Population | % |
|---|---|---|
| West Winfield (village) Herkimer County | 3 | 0.36 |
| Frewsburg (cdp) Chautauqua County | 4 | 0.21 |
| Winfield (town) Herkimer County | 3 | 0.14 |
| Mountain Lodge Park (cdp) Orange County | 2 | 0.13 |
| North Hornell (village) Steuben County | 1 | 0.13 |
| Pine Plains (town) Dutchess County | 3 | 0.12 |
| Schroon Lake (cdp) Essex County | 1 | 0.12 |
| Carroll (town) Chautauqua County | 4 | 0.11 |
| Dexter (village) Jefferson County | 1 | 0.10 |
| Rathbone (town) Steuben County | 1 | 0.09 |

### Top 10 Places Sorted by Percent of Total Population
*Based on places with total population of 50,000 or more*

| Place | Population | % |
|---|---|---|
| New York (city) | 58 | <0.01 |
| Brooklyn (borough) Kings County | 21 | <0.01 |
| Bronx (borough) Bronx County | 15 | <0.01 |
| Queens (borough) Queens County | 13 | <0.01 |
| Manhattan (borough) New York County | 8 | <0.01 |
| Syracuse (city) Onondaga County | 6 | <0.01 |
| Yonkers (city) Westchester County | 5 | <0.01 |
| Buffalo (city) Erie County | 4 | <0.01 |
| Rochester (city) Monroe County | 4 | <0.01 |
| Amherst (town) Erie County | 3 | <0.01 |

## American Indian: Iroquois

### Top 10 Places Sorted by Population
*Based on all places, regardless of total population*

| Place | Population | % |
|---|---|---|
| St. Regis Mohawk Reservation Franklin County | 2,493 | 77.23 |
| Syracuse (city) Onondaga County | 1,373 | 0.95 |
| Buffalo (city) Erie County | 1,316 | 0.50 |
| Cattaraugus Reservation Erie County | 1,295 | 70.65 |
| New York (city) | 1,276 | 0.02 |
| Salamanca (city) Cattaraugus County | 951 | 16.35 |
| Niagara Falls (city) Niagara County | 801 | 1.60 |
| Allegany Reservation Cattaraugus County | 610 | 59.80 |
| Rochester (city) Monroe County | 483 | 0.23 |
| Massena (town) St. Lawrence County | 442 | 3.43 |

### Top 10 Places Sorted by Percent of Total Population
*Based on all places, regardless of total population*

| Place | Population | % |
|---|---|---|
| St. Regis Mohawk Reservation Franklin County | 2,493 | 77.23 |
| Tonawanda Reservation Erie County | 26 | 76.47 |
| Cattaraugus Reservation Cattaraugus County | 227 | 72.29 |
| Cattaraugus Reservation Erie County | 1,295 | 70.65 |
| Allegany Reservation Cattaraugus County | 610 | 59.80 |
| Cattaraugus Reservation Chautauqua County | 20 | 52.63 |
| Tonawanda Reservation Genesee County | 168 | 34.78 |
| Onondaga Nation Reservation Onondaga County | 93 | 19.87 |
| Salamanca (city) Cattaraugus County | 951 | 16.35 |
| Bombay (town) Franklin County | 206 | 15.18 |

### Top 10 Places Sorted by Percent of Total Population
*Based on places with total population of 50,000 or more*

| Place | Population | % |
|---|---|---|
| Niagara Falls (city) Niagara County | 801 | 1.60 |
| Syracuse (city) Onondaga County | 1,373 | 0.95 |
| Buffalo (city) Erie County | 1,316 | 0.50 |
| Clay (town) Onondaga County | 252 | 0.43 |
| Tonawanda (town) Erie County | 256 | 0.35 |
| Tonawanda (cdp) Erie County | 165 | 0.28 |
| Hamburg (town) Erie County | 159 | 0.28 |
| Cheektowaga (cdp) Erie County | 179 | 0.24 |
| Rochester (city) Monroe County | 483 | 0.23 |
| Cheektowaga (town) Erie County | 194 | 0.22 |

## American Indian: Kiowa

### Top 10 Places Sorted by Population
*Based on all places, regardless of total population*

| Place | Population | % |
|---|---|---|
| New York (city) | 15 | <0.01 |
| Manhattan (borough) New York County | 11 | <0.01 |
| Middlefield (town) Otsego County | 2 | 0.09 |
| Roxbury (town) Delaware County | 2 | 0.08 |
| Brooklyn (borough) Kings County | 2 | <0.01 |
| Utica (city) Oneida County | 2 | <0.01 |
| Old Forge (cdp) Herkimer County | 1 | 0.13 |
| Tuscarora Nation Reservation Niagara County | 1 | 0.09 |
| Webb (town) Herkimer County | 1 | 0.06 |
| Carlisle (town) Schoharie County | 1 | 0.05 |

### Top 10 Places Sorted by Percent of Total Population
*Based on all places, regardless of total population*

| Place | Population | % |
|---|---|---|
| Old Forge (cdp) Herkimer County | 1 | 0.13 |
| Middlefield (town) Otsego County | 2 | 0.09 |
| Tuscarora Nation Reservation Niagara County | 1 | 0.09 |
| Roxbury (town) Delaware County | 2 | 0.08 |
| Webb (town) Herkimer County | 1 | 0.06 |
| Carlisle (town) Schoharie County | 1 | 0.05 |
| New Hartford (village) Oneida County | 1 | 0.05 |
| Triangle (town) Broome County | 1 | 0.03 |
| Elmira Heights (village) Chemung County | 1 | 0.02 |
| Old Bethpage (cdp) Nassau County | 1 | 0.02 |

### Top 10 Places Sorted by Percent of Total Population
*Based on places with total population of 50,000 or more*

| Place | Population | % |
|---|---|---|
| New York (city) | 15 | <0.01 |
| Manhattan (borough) New York County | 11 | <0.01 |
| Brooklyn (borough) Kings County | 2 | <0.01 |
| Utica (city) Oneida County | 2 | <0.01 |

---

| Place | Population | % |
|---|---|---|
| Bronx (borough) Bronx County | 1 | <0.01 |
| Buffalo (city) Erie County | 1 | <0.01 |
| Oyster Bay (town) Nassau County | 1 | <0.01 |
| Schenectady (city) Schenectady County | 1 | <0.01 |
| Smithtown (town) Suffolk County | 1 | <0.01 |
| Staten Island (borough) Richmond County | 1 | <0.01 |

## American Indian: Lumbee

### Top 10 Places Sorted by Population
*Based on all places, regardless of total population*

| Place | Population | % |
|---|---|---|
| New York (city) | 89 | <0.01 |
| Queens (borough) Queens County | 30 | <0.01 |
| Brooklyn (borough) Kings County | 24 | <0.01 |
| Hempstead (town) Nassau County | 22 | <0.01 |
| Manhattan (borough) New York County | 21 | <0.01 |
| Babylon (town) Suffolk County | 12 | 0.01 |
| Islip (town) Suffolk County | 8 | <0.01 |
| Staten Island (borough) Richmond County | 8 | <0.01 |
| Rose (town) Wayne County | 7 | 0.30 |
| Brookhaven (town) Suffolk County | 7 | <0.01 |

### Top 10 Places Sorted by Percent of Total Population
*Based on all places, regardless of total population*

| Place | Population | % |
|---|---|---|
| Limestone (village) Cattaraugus County | 3 | 0.77 |
| Shinnecock Reservation Suffolk County | 3 | 0.45 |
| Newfield Hamlet (cdp) Tompkins County | 3 | 0.40 |
| Farmersville (town) Cattaraugus County | 4 | 0.37 |
| St. Armand (town) Essex County | 5 | 0.32 |
| Rose (town) Wayne County | 7 | 0.30 |
| Hermon (village) St. Lawrence County | 1 | 0.24 |
| Carrollton (town) Cattaraugus County | 3 | 0.23 |
| Brushton (village) Franklin County | 1 | 0.21 |
| Shandaken (town) Ulster County | 6 | 0.19 |

### Top 10 Places Sorted by Percent of Total Population
*Based on places with total population of 50,000 or more*

| Place | Population | % |
|---|---|---|
| Babylon (town) Suffolk County | 12 | 0.01 |
| Levittown (cdp) Nassau County | 6 | 0.01 |
| Niagara Falls (city) Niagara County | 6 | 0.01 |
| Schenectady (city) Schenectady County | 4 | 0.01 |
| Troy (city) Rensselaer County | 4 | 0.01 |
| Clay (town) Onondaga County | 3 | 0.01 |
| New York (city) | 89 | <0.01 |
| Queens (borough) Queens County | 30 | <0.01 |
| Brooklyn (borough) Kings County | 24 | <0.01 |
| Hempstead (town) Nassau County | 22 | <0.01 |

## American Indian: Menominee

### Top 10 Places Sorted by Population
*Based on all places, regardless of total population*

| Place | Population | % |
|---|---|---|
| New York (city) | 10 | <0.01 |
| Cattaraugus Reservation Erie County | 5 | 0.27 |
| Brooklyn (borough) Kings County | 4 | <0.01 |
| Crown Heights (cdp) Dutchess County | 3 | 0.11 |
| Northumberland (town) Saratoga County | 3 | 0.06 |
| Glens Falls (city) Warren County | 3 | 0.02 |
| Poughkeepsie (town) Dutchess County | 3 | 0.01 |
| Troy (city) Rensselaer County | 3 | 0.01 |
| Bronx (borough) Bronx County | 3 | <0.01 |
| Manhattan (borough) New York County | 3 | <0.01 |

### Top 10 Places Sorted by Percent of Total Population
*Based on all places, regardless of total population*

| Place | Population | % |
|---|---|---|
| Cattaraugus Reservation Erie County | 5 | 0.27 |
| Fillmore (cdp) Allegany County | 1 | 0.17 |
| Crown Heights (cdp) Dutchess County | 3 | 0.11 |
| Pine Plains (cdp) Dutchess County | 1 | 0.07 |
| Northumberland (town) Saratoga County | 3 | 0.06 |
| Trumansburg (village) Tompkins County | 1 | 0.06 |
| Angola (village) Erie County | 1 | 0.05 |
| Hume (town) Allegany County | 1 | 0.05 |
| Pine Plains (town) Dutchess County | 1 | 0.04 |
| Glens Falls (city) Warren County | 3 | 0.02 |

---

### Top 10 Places Sorted by Percent of Total Population
*Based on places with total population of 50,000 or more*

| Place | Population | % |
|---|---|---|
| Troy (city) Rensselaer County | 3 | 0.01 |
| New York (city) | 10 | <0.01 |
| Brooklyn (borough) Kings County | 4 | <0.01 |
| Bronx (borough) Bronx County | 3 | <0.01 |
| Manhattan (borough) New York County | 3 | <0.01 |
| Buffalo (city) Erie County | 2 | <0.01 |
| Niagara Falls (city) Niagara County | 2 | <0.01 |
| Syracuse (city) Onondaga County | 1 | <0.01 |
| Albany (city) Albany County | 0 | 0.00 |
| Amherst (town) Erie County | 0 | 0.00 |

## American Indian: Mexican American Indian

### Top 10 Places Sorted by Population
*Based on all places, regardless of total population*

| Place | Population | % |
|---|---|---|
| New York (city) | 4,922 | 0.06 |
| Queens (borough) Queens County | 1,640 | 0.07 |
| Brooklyn (borough) Kings County | 1,363 | 0.05 |
| Bronx (borough) Bronx County | 963 | 0.07 |
| Manhattan (borough) New York County | 752 | 0.05 |
| Staten Island (borough) Richmond County | 204 | 0.04 |
| Yonkers (city) Westchester County | 171 | 0.09 |
| White Plains (city) Westchester County | 162 | 0.28 |
| Poughkeepsie (city) Dutchess County | 160 | 0.49 |
| Hempstead (town) Nassau County | 143 | 0.02 |

### Top 10 Places Sorted by Percent of Total Population
*Based on all places, regardless of total population*

| Place | Population | % |
|---|---|---|
| Cattaraugus Reservation Chautauqua County | 5 | 13.16 |
| Shinnecock Hills (cdp) Suffolk County | 27 | 1.23 |
| Westhampton Beach (village) Suffolk County | 13 | 0.76 |
| Flanders (cdp) Suffolk County | 29 | 0.65 |
| Phoenicia (cdp) Ulster County | 2 | 0.65 |
| Rensselaer Falls (village) St. Lawrence County | 2 | 0.60 |
| Lorraine (cdp) Jefferson County | 1 | 0.57 |
| Poughkeepsie (city) Dutchess County | 160 | 0.49 |
| Palatine Bridge (village) Montgomery County | 3 | 0.41 |
| Woodstock (cdp) Ulster County | 8 | 0.38 |

### Top 10 Places Sorted by Percent of Total Population
*Based on places with total population of 50,000 or more*

| Place | Population | % |
|---|---|---|
| White Plains (city) Westchester County | 162 | 0.28 |
| Southampton (town) Suffolk County | 83 | 0.15 |
| Brentwood (cdp) Suffolk County | 72 | 0.12 |
| Yonkers (city) Westchester County | 171 | 0.09 |
| New Rochelle (city) Westchester County | 72 | 0.09 |
| Queens (borough) Queens County | 1,640 | 0.07 |
| Bronx (borough) Bronx County | 963 | 0.07 |
| New York (city) | 4,922 | 0.06 |
| Ramapo (town) Rockland County | 74 | 0.06 |
| Brooklyn (borough) Kings County | 1,363 | 0.05 |

## American Indian: Navajo

### Top 10 Places Sorted by Population
*Based on all places, regardless of total population*

| Place | Population | % |
|---|---|---|
| New York (city) | 272 | <0.01 |
| Brooklyn (borough) Kings County | 93 | <0.01 |
| Manhattan (borough) New York County | 83 | 0.01 |
| Bronx (borough) Bronx County | 42 | <0.01 |
| Queens (borough) Queens County | 37 | <0.01 |
| Rochester (city) Monroe County | 30 | 0.01 |
| Le Ray (town) Jefferson County | 24 | 0.11 |
| Fort Drum (cdp) Jefferson County | 23 | 0.18 |
| Staten Island (borough) Richmond County | 17 | <0.01 |
| Buffalo (city) Erie County | 16 | 0.01 |

### Top 10 Places Sorted by Percent of Total Population
*Based on all places, regardless of total population*

| Place | Population | % |
|---|---|---|
| Rodman (cdp) Jefferson County | 1 | 0.65 |
| Tonawanda Reservation Genesee County | 3 | 0.62 |

| Place | Population | % |
|---|---|---|
| **Margaretville** (village) Delaware County | 3 | 0.50 |
| **Lakeville** (cdp) Livingston County | 3 | 0.40 |
| **Allegany Reservation** Cattaraugus County | 4 | 0.39 |
| **Baldwin** (town) Chemung County | 3 | 0.36 |
| **East Avon** (cdp) Livingston County | 2 | 0.33 |
| **Strykersville** (cdp) Wyoming County | 2 | 0.31 |
| **Brant** (town) Erie County | 5 | 0.24 |
| **Owego** (village) Tioga County | 9 | 0.23 |

### Top 10 Places Sorted by Percent of Total Population
*Based on places with total population of 50,000 or more*

| Place | Population | % |
|---|---|---|
| **Manhattan** (borough) New York County | 83 | 0.01 |
| **Rochester** (city) Monroe County | 30 | 0.01 |
| **Buffalo** (city) Erie County | 16 | 0.01 |
| **Troy** (city) Rensselaer County | 5 | 0.01 |
| **Brentwood** (cdp) Suffolk County | 4 | 0.01 |
| **Clay** (town) Onondaga County | 4 | 0.01 |
| **New York** (city) | 272 | <0.01 |
| **Brooklyn** (borough) Kings County | 93 | <0.01 |
| **Bronx** (borough) Bronx County | 42 | <0.01 |
| **Queens** (borough) Queens County | 37 | <0.01 |

## American Indian: Osage

### Top 10 Places Sorted by Population
*Based on all places, regardless of total population*

| Place | Population | % |
|---|---|---|
| **New York** (city) | 23 | <0.01 |
| **Manhattan** (borough) New York County | 12 | <0.01 |
| **Queens** (borough) Queens County | 5 | <0.01 |
| **Oakfield** (village) Genesee County | 4 | 0.22 |
| **Oakfield** (town) Genesee County | 4 | 0.12 |
| **Manlius** (town) Onondaga County | 4 | 0.01 |
| **Moravia** (village) Cayuga County | 3 | 0.23 |
| **Moravia** (town) Cayuga County | 3 | 0.08 |
| **Wheatfield** (town) Niagara County | 3 | 0.02 |
| **Le Ray** (town) Jefferson County | 3 | 0.01 |

### Top 10 Places Sorted by Percent of Total Population
*Based on all places, regardless of total population*

| Place | Population | % |
|---|---|---|
| **Poospatuck Reservation** Suffolk County | 1 | 0.31 |
| **Moravia** (village) Cayuga County | 3 | 0.23 |
| **Oakfield** (village) Genesee County | 4 | 0.22 |
| **Oakfield** (town) Genesee County | 4 | 0.12 |
| **Moravia** (town) Cayuga County | 3 | 0.08 |
| **North Collins** (town) Erie County | 2 | 0.06 |
| **Wolcott** (village) Wayne County | 1 | 0.06 |
| **Woodstock** (cdp) Ulster County | 1 | 0.05 |
| **Florida** (town) Montgomery County | 1 | 0.04 |
| **Cazenovia** (town) Madison County | 2 | 0.03 |

### Top 10 Places Sorted by Percent of Total Population
*Based on places with total population of 50,000 or more*

| Place | Population | % |
|---|---|---|
| **New York** (city) | 23 | <0.01 |
| **Manhattan** (borough) New York County | 12 | <0.01 |
| **Queens** (borough) Queens County | 5 | <0.01 |
| **Bronx** (borough) Bronx County | 3 | <0.01 |
| **Brooklyn** (borough) Kings County | 3 | <0.01 |
| **Rochester** (city) Monroe County | 3 | <0.01 |
| **Brookhaven** (town) Suffolk County | 2 | <0.01 |
| **Hempstead** (town) Nassau County | 2 | <0.01 |
| **White Plains** (city) Westchester County | 2 | <0.01 |
| **Amherst** (town) Erie County | 1 | <0.01 |

## American Indian: Ottawa

### Top 10 Places Sorted by Population
*Based on all places, regardless of total population*

| Place | Population | % |
|---|---|---|
| **New York** (city) | 11 | <0.01 |
| **Auburn** (city) Cayuga County | 5 | 0.02 |
| **Brooklyn** (borough) Kings County | 5 | <0.01 |
| **Newfield Hamlet** (cdp) Tompkins County | 4 | 0.53 |
| **Newfield** (town) Tompkins County | 4 | 0.08 |
| **East Aurora** (village) Erie County | 3 | 0.05 |
| **Aurora** (town) Erie County | 3 | 0.02 |
| **Setauket-East Setauket** (cdp) Suffolk County | 3 | 0.02 |
| **Brookhaven** (town) Suffolk County | 3 | <0.01 |

---

| Place | Population | % |
|---|---|---|
| **Manhattan** (borough) New York County | 3 | <0.01 |

### Top 10 Places Sorted by Percent of Total Population
*Based on all places, regardless of total population*

| Place | Population | % |
|---|---|---|
| **Newfield Hamlet** (cdp) Tompkins County | 4 | 0.53 |
| **Newfield** (town) Tompkins County | 4 | 0.08 |
| **East Aurora** (village) Erie County | 3 | 0.05 |
| **Cattaraugus Reservation** Erie County | 1 | 0.05 |
| **Seneca Falls** (village) Seneca County | 2 | 0.03 |
| **Mohawk** (town) Montgomery County | 1 | 0.03 |
| **Auburn** (city) Cayuga County | 5 | 0.02 |
| **Aurora** (town) Erie County | 3 | 0.02 |
| **Setauket-East Setauket** (cdp) Suffolk County | 3 | 0.02 |
| **Lewisboro** (town) Westchester County | 2 | 0.02 |

### Top 10 Places Sorted by Percent of Total Population
*Based on places with total population of 50,000 or more*

| Place | Population | % |
|---|---|---|
| **New York** (city) | 11 | <0.01 |
| **Brooklyn** (borough) Kings County | 5 | <0.01 |
| **Brookhaven** (town) Suffolk County | 3 | <0.01 |
| **Manhattan** (borough) New York County | 3 | <0.01 |
| **Huntington** (town) Suffolk County | 2 | <0.01 |
| **Queens** (borough) Queens County | 2 | <0.01 |
| **Syracuse** (city) Onondaga County | 2 | <0.01 |
| **Albany** (city) Albany County | 1 | <0.01 |
| **Bronx** (borough) Bronx County | 1 | <0.01 |
| **Clay** (town) Onondaga County | 1 | <0.01 |

## American Indian: Paiute

### Top 10 Places Sorted by Population
*Based on all places, regardless of total population*

| Place | Population | % |
|---|---|---|
| **New York** (city) | 18 | <0.01 |
| **Manhattan** (borough) New York County | 8 | <0.01 |
| **Perrysburg** (town) Cattaraugus County | 6 | 0.37 |
| **Cattaraugus Reservation** Erie County | 6 | 0.33 |
| **Bronx** (borough) Bronx County | 5 | <0.01 |
| **Brookhaven** (town) Suffolk County | 4 | <0.01 |
| **Queens** (borough) Queens County | 4 | <0.01 |
| **Olean** (city) Cattaraugus County | 3 | 0.02 |
| **Conklin** (town) Broome County | 2 | 0.04 |
| **Manorville** (cdp) Suffolk County | 2 | 0.01 |

### Top 10 Places Sorted by Percent of Total Population
*Based on all places, regardless of total population*

| Place | Population | % |
|---|---|---|
| **Perrysburg** (town) Cattaraugus County | 6 | 0.37 |
| **Cattaraugus Reservation** Erie County | 6 | 0.33 |
| **Upper Nyack** (village) Rockland County | 1 | 0.05 |
| **Conklin** (town) Broome County | 2 | 0.04 |
| **Gowanda** (village) Cattaraugus County | 1 | 0.04 |
| **St. Regis Mohawk Reservation** Franklin County | 1 | 0.03 |
| **Olean** (city) Cattaraugus County | 3 | 0.02 |
| **Collins** (town) Erie County | 1 | 0.02 |
| **Manorville** (cdp) Suffolk County | 2 | 0.01 |
| **Miller Place** (cdp) Suffolk County | 1 | 0.01 |

### Top 10 Places Sorted by Percent of Total Population
*Based on places with total population of 50,000 or more*

| Place | Population | % |
|---|---|---|
| **New York** (city) | 18 | <0.01 |
| **Manhattan** (borough) New York County | 8 | <0.01 |
| **Bronx** (borough) Bronx County | 5 | <0.01 |
| **Brookhaven** (town) Suffolk County | 4 | <0.01 |
| **Queens** (borough) Queens County | 4 | <0.01 |
| **Hamburg** (town) Erie County | 2 | <0.01 |
| **Brooklyn** (borough) Kings County | 1 | <0.01 |
| **Clarkstown** (town) Rockland County | 1 | <0.01 |
| **Rochester** (city) Monroe County | 1 | <0.01 |
| **Utica** (city) Oneida County | 1 | <0.01 |

## American Indian: Pima

### Top 10 Places Sorted by Population
*Based on all places, regardless of total population*

| Place | Population | % |
|---|---|---|
| **New York** (city) | 9 | <0.01 |

---

| Place | Population | % |
|---|---|---|
| **Schenectady** (city) Schenectady County | 5 | 0.01 |
| **Manhattan** (borough) New York County | 4 | <0.01 |
| **Fort Montgomery** (cdp) Orange County | 3 | 0.19 |
| **Gowanda** (village) Cattaraugus County | 3 | 0.11 |
| **Collins** (town) Erie County | 3 | 0.05 |
| **Highlands** (town) Orange County | 3 | 0.02 |
| **Fallsburg** (town) Sullivan County | 2 | 0.02 |
| **Ontario** (town) Wayne County | 2 | 0.02 |
| **Harrison** (town/village) Westchester County | 2 | 0.01 |

### Top 10 Places Sorted by Percent of Total Population
*Based on all places, regardless of total population*

| Place | Population | % |
|---|---|---|
| **Fort Montgomery** (cdp) Orange County | 3 | 0.19 |
| **Rushville** (village) Yates County | 1 | 0.15 |
| **Gowanda** (village) Cattaraugus County | 3 | 0.11 |
| **Collins** (town) Erie County | 3 | 0.05 |
| **Potter** (town) Yates County | 1 | 0.05 |
| **Highlands** (town) Orange County | 3 | 0.02 |
| **Fallsburg** (town) Sullivan County | 2 | 0.02 |
| **Ontario** (town) Wayne County | 2 | 0.02 |
| **Minisink** (town) Orange County | 1 | 0.02 |
| **Ulysses** (town) Tompkins County | 1 | 0.02 |

### Top 10 Places Sorted by Percent of Total Population
*Based on places with total population of 50,000 or more*

| Place | Population | % |
|---|---|---|
| **Schenectady** (city) Schenectady County | 5 | 0.01 |
| **New York** (city) | 9 | <0.01 |
| **Manhattan** (borough) New York County | 4 | <0.01 |
| **Brooklyn** (borough) Kings County | 2 | <0.01 |
| **Rochester** (city) Monroe County | 2 | <0.01 |
| **Staten Island** (borough) Richmond County | 2 | <0.01 |
| **Syracuse** (city) Onondaga County | 2 | <0.01 |
| **Brentwood** (cdp) Suffolk County | 1 | <0.01 |
| **Bronx** (borough) Bronx County | 1 | <0.01 |
| **Buffalo** (city) Erie County | 1 | <0.01 |

## American Indian: Potawatomi

### Top 10 Places Sorted by Population
*Based on all places, regardless of total population*

| Place | Population | % |
|---|---|---|
| **New York** (city) | 40 | <0.01 |
| **Manhattan** (borough) New York County | 20 | <0.01 |
| **Brooklyn** (borough) Kings County | 11 | <0.01 |
| **Tonawanda** (cdp) Erie County | 9 | 0.02 |
| **Tonawanda** (town) Erie County | 9 | 0.01 |
| **Queens** (borough) Queens County | 7 | <0.01 |
| **Brookhaven** (town) Suffolk County | 6 | <0.01 |
| **Fort Drum** (cdp) Jefferson County | 5 | 0.04 |
| **Le Ray** (town) Jefferson County | 5 | 0.02 |
| **Schenectady** (city) Schenectady County | 5 | 0.01 |

### Top 10 Places Sorted by Percent of Total Population
*Based on all places, regardless of total population*

| Place | Population | % |
|---|---|---|
| **Onondaga Nation Reservation** Onondaga County | 4 | 0.85 |
| **Mina** (town) Chautauqua County | 2 | 0.18 |
| **Denning** (town) Ulster County | 1 | 0.18 |
| **Merritt Park** (cdp) Dutchess County | 2 | 0.16 |
| **Russia** (town) Herkimer County | 3 | 0.12 |
| **Cuyler** (town) Cortland County | 1 | 0.10 |
| **Greenport West** (cdp) Suffolk County | 2 | 0.09 |
| **Truxton** (town) Cortland County | 1 | 0.09 |
| **Lake Erie Beach** (cdp) Erie County | 3 | 0.08 |
| **Vernon** (town) Oneida County | 3 | 0.06 |

### Top 10 Places Sorted by Percent of Total Population
*Based on places with total population of 50,000 or more*

| Place | Population | % |
|---|---|---|
| **Tonawanda** (cdp) Erie County | 9 | 0.02 |
| **Tonawanda** (town) Erie County | 9 | 0.01 |
| **Schenectady** (city) Schenectady County | 5 | 0.01 |
| **New York** (city) | 40 | <0.01 |
| **Manhattan** (borough) New York County | 20 | <0.01 |
| **Brooklyn** (borough) Kings County | 11 | <0.01 |
| **Queens** (borough) Queens County | 7 | <0.01 |
| **Brookhaven** (town) Suffolk County | 6 | <0.01 |
| **Rochester** (city) Monroe County | 5 | <0.01 |
| **Albany** (city) Albany County | 2 | <0.01 |

## American Indian: Pueblo

### Top 10 Places Sorted by Population
*Based on all places, regardless of total population*

| Place | Population | % |
|---|---|---|
| New York (city) | 892 | 0.01 |
| Bronx (borough) Bronx County | 382 | 0.03 |
| Manhattan (borough) New York County | 175 | 0.01 |
| Brooklyn (borough) Kings County | 169 | 0.01 |
| Queens (borough) Queens County | 161 | 0.01 |
| Yonkers (city) Westchester County | 20 | 0.01 |
| White Plains (city) Westchester County | 19 | 0.03 |
| Hempstead (town) Nassau County | 13 | <0.01 |
| Le Ray (town) Jefferson County | 11 | 0.05 |
| Fort Drum (cdp) Jefferson County | 10 | 0.08 |

### Top 10 Places Sorted by Percent of Total Population
*Based on all places, regardless of total population*

| Place | Population | % |
|---|---|---|
| DeKalb Junction (cdp) St. Lawrence County | 4 | 0.77 |
| Denning (town) Ulster County | 2 | 0.36 |
| Pine Hill (cdp) Ulster County | 1 | 0.36 |
| Natural Bridge (cdp) Jefferson County | 1 | 0.27 |
| De Kalb (town) St. Lawrence County | 4 | 0.16 |
| Northwest Harbor (cdp) Suffolk County | 4 | 0.12 |
| Ripley (cdp) Chautauqua County | 1 | 0.11 |
| Stone Ridge (cdp) Ulster County | 1 | 0.09 |
| Fort Drum (cdp) Jefferson County | 10 | 0.08 |
| Ripley (town) Chautauqua County | 2 | 0.08 |

### Top 10 Places Sorted by Percent of Total Population
*Based on places with total population of 50,000 or more*

| Place | Population | % |
|---|---|---|
| Bronx (borough) Bronx County | 382 | 0.03 |
| White Plains (city) Westchester County | 19 | 0.03 |
| New York (city) | 892 | 0.01 |
| Manhattan (borough) New York County | 175 | 0.01 |
| Brooklyn (borough) Kings County | 169 | 0.01 |
| Queens (borough) Queens County | 161 | 0.01 |
| Yonkers (city) Westchester County | 20 | 0.01 |
| Mount Vernon (city) Westchester County | 7 | 0.01 |
| Hempstead (village) Nassau County | 6 | 0.01 |
| Brentwood (cdp) Suffolk County | 5 | 0.01 |

## American Indian: Puget Sound Salish

### Top 10 Places Sorted by Population
*Based on all places, regardless of total population*

| Place | Population | % |
|---|---|---|
| New York (city) | 11 | <0.01 |
| Brookhaven (town) Suffolk County | 6 | <0.01 |
| Gordon Heights (cdp) Suffolk County | 5 | 0.12 |
| Manhattan (borough) New York County | 5 | <0.01 |
| Queens (borough) Queens County | 5 | <0.01 |
| Bronxville (village) Westchester County | 3 | 0.05 |
| Eastchester (town) Westchester County | 3 | 0.01 |
| East Ithaca (cdp) Tompkins County | 2 | 0.09 |
| Horseheads (village) Chemung County | 2 | 0.03 |
| Orange Lake (cdp) Orange County | 2 | 0.03 |

### Top 10 Places Sorted by Percent of Total Population
*Based on all places, regardless of total population*

| Place | Population | % |
|---|---|---|
| Gordon Heights (cdp) Suffolk County | 5 | 0.12 |
| East Ithaca (cdp) Tompkins County | 2 | 0.09 |
| Bronxville (village) Westchester County | 3 | 0.05 |
| Bellport (village) Suffolk County | 1 | 0.05 |
| Cattaraugus Reservation Erie County | 1 | 0.05 |
| Horseheads (village) Chemung County | 2 | 0.03 |
| Orange Lake (cdp) Orange County | 2 | 0.03 |
| Calcium (cdp) Jefferson County | 1 | 0.03 |
| Southold (cdp) Suffolk County | 1 | 0.02 |
| Eastchester (town) Westchester County | 3 | 0.01 |

### Top 10 Places Sorted by Percent of Total Population
*Based on places with total population of 50,000 or more*

| Place | Population | % |
|---|---|---|
| New York (city) | 11 | <0.01 |
| Brookhaven (town) Suffolk County | 6 | <0.01 |
| Manhattan (borough) New York County | 5 | <0.01 |
| Queens (borough) Queens County | 5 | <0.01 |

| Place | Population | % |
|---|---|---|
| Brooklyn (borough) Kings County | 1 | <0.01 |
| Tonawanda (cdp) Erie County | 1 | <0.01 |
| Tonawanda (town) Erie County | 1 | <0.01 |
| Albany (city) Albany County | 0 | 0.00 |
| Amherst (town) Erie County | 0 | 0.00 |
| Babylon (town) Suffolk County | 0 | 0.00 |

## American Indian: Seminole

### Top 10 Places Sorted by Population
*Based on all places, regardless of total population*

| Place | Population | % |
|---|---|---|
| New York (city) | 357 | <0.01 |
| Manhattan (borough) New York County | 110 | <0.01 |
| Brooklyn (borough) Kings County | 92 | <0.01 |
| Queens (borough) Queens County | 79 | <0.01 |
| Bronx (borough) Bronx County | 50 | <0.01 |
| Rochester (city) Monroe County | 44 | 0.02 |
| Brookhaven (town) Suffolk County | 33 | <0.01 |
| Hempstead (town) Nassau County | 28 | <0.01 |
| Staten Island (borough) Richmond County | 26 | 0.01 |
| Buffalo (city) Erie County | 23 | 0.01 |

### Top 10 Places Sorted by Percent of Total Population
*Based on all places, regardless of total population*

| Place | Population | % |
|---|---|---|
| Randolph (village) Cattaraugus County | 5 | 0.39 |
| Cuylerville (cdp) Livingston County | 1 | 0.34 |
| Wainscott (cdp) Suffolk County | 2 | 0.31 |
| Poospatuck Reservation Suffolk County | 1 | 0.31 |
| West Sparta (town) Livingston County | 3 | 0.24 |
| Randolph (town) Cattaraugus County | 5 | 0.19 |
| Haviland (cdp) Dutchess County | 5 | 0.14 |
| Greenport (village) Suffolk County | 3 | 0.14 |
| Veteran (town) Chemung County | 4 | 0.12 |
| De Kalb (town) St. Lawrence County | 3 | 0.12 |

### Top 10 Places Sorted by Percent of Total Population
*Based on places with total population of 50,000 or more*

| Place | Population | % |
|---|---|---|
| Rochester (city) Monroe County | 44 | 0.02 |
| Manhattan (borough) New York County | 110 | 0.01 |
| Brookhaven (town) Suffolk County | 33 | 0.01 |
| Staten Island (borough) Richmond County | 26 | 0.01 |
| Buffalo (city) Erie County | 23 | 0.01 |
| Syracuse (city) Onondaga County | 16 | 0.01 |
| Babylon (town) Suffolk County | 13 | 0.01 |
| Yonkers (city) Westchester County | 11 | 0.01 |
| Amherst (town) Erie County | 10 | 0.01 |
| Mount Vernon (city) Westchester County | 9 | 0.01 |

## American Indian: Shoshone

### Top 10 Places Sorted by Population
*Based on all places, regardless of total population*

| Place | Population | % |
|---|---|---|
| New York (city) | 46 | <0.01 |
| Brooklyn (borough) Kings County | 23 | <0.01 |
| Yates (town) Orleans County | 8 | 0.31 |
| Bronx (borough) Bronx County | 8 | <0.01 |
| Manhattan (borough) New York County | 6 | <0.01 |
| Queens (borough) Queens County | 6 | <0.01 |
| Middletown (city) Orange County | 4 | 0.01 |
| Brookhaven (town) Suffolk County | 4 | <0.01 |
| Bay Shore (cdp) Suffolk County | 3 | 0.01 |
| Hempstead (town) Nassau County | 3 | <0.01 |

### Top 10 Places Sorted by Percent of Total Population
*Based on all places, regardless of total population*

| Place | Population | % |
|---|---|---|
| Rhinecliff (cdp) Dutchess County | 2 | 0.47 |
| Hobart (village) Delaware County | 2 | 0.45 |
| Yates (town) Orleans County | 8 | 0.31 |
| St. Regis Falls (cdp) Franklin County | 1 | 0.22 |
| Waverly (town) Franklin County | 1 | 0.10 |
| Stamford (town) Delaware County | 2 | 0.09 |
| Covert (town) Seneca County | 1 | 0.05 |
| Minisink (town) Orange County | 2 | 0.04 |
| Afton (town) Chenango County | 1 | 0.04 |
| Rhinebeck (town) Dutchess County | 2 | 0.03 |

### Top 10 Places Sorted by Percent of Total Population
*Based on places with total population of 50,000 or more*

| Place | Population | % |
|---|---|---|
| New York (city) | 46 | <0.01 |
| Brooklyn (borough) Kings County | 23 | <0.01 |
| Bronx (borough) Bronx County | 8 | <0.01 |
| Manhattan (borough) New York County | 6 | <0.01 |
| Queens (borough) Queens County | 6 | <0.01 |
| Brookhaven (town) Suffolk County | 4 | <0.01 |
| Hempstead (town) Nassau County | 3 | <0.01 |
| Islip (town) Suffolk County | 3 | <0.01 |
| Staten Island (borough) Richmond County | 3 | <0.01 |
| Albany (city) Albany County | 1 | <0.01 |

## American Indian: Sioux

### Top 10 Places Sorted by Population
*Based on all places, regardless of total population*

| Place | Population | % |
|---|---|---|
| New York (city) | 464 | 0.01 |
| Manhattan (borough) New York County | 133 | 0.01 |
| Brooklyn (borough) Kings County | 121 | <0.01 |
| Queens (borough) Queens County | 104 | <0.01 |
| Bronx (borough) Bronx County | 82 | 0.01 |
| Buffalo (city) Erie County | 46 | 0.02 |
| Brookhaven (town) Suffolk County | 42 | 0.01 |
| Syracuse (city) Onondaga County | 38 | 0.03 |
| Hempstead (town) Nassau County | 33 | <0.01 |
| Utica (city) Oneida County | 29 | 0.05 |

### Top 10 Places Sorted by Percent of Total Population
*Based on all places, regardless of total population*

| Place | Population | % |
|---|---|---|
| Hardenburgh (town) Ulster County | 10 | 4.20 |
| Napeague (cdp) Suffolk County | 3 | 1.50 |
| Poospatuck Reservation Suffolk County | 3 | 0.93 |
| Windham (cdp) Greene County | 3 | 0.82 |
| Redfield (town) Oswego County | 4 | 0.73 |
| Plessis (cdp) Jefferson County | 1 | 0.61 |
| Allegany Reservation Cattaraugus County | 6 | 0.59 |
| Perrysburg (village) Cattaraugus County | 2 | 0.50 |
| Ashland (town) Chemung County | 7 | 0.41 |
| Calcium (cdp) Jefferson County | 14 | 0.40 |

### Top 10 Places Sorted by Percent of Total Population
*Based on places with total population of 50,000 or more*

| Place | Population | % |
|---|---|---|
| Utica (city) Oneida County | 29 | 0.05 |
| Syracuse (city) Onondaga County | 38 | 0.03 |
| Buffalo (city) Erie County | 46 | 0.02 |
| Schenectady (city) Schenectady County | 14 | 0.02 |
| Niagara Falls (city) Niagara County | 8 | 0.02 |
| New York (city) | 464 | 0.01 |
| Manhattan (borough) New York County | 133 | 0.01 |
| Bronx (borough) Bronx County | 82 | 0.01 |
| Brookhaven (town) Suffolk County | 42 | 0.01 |
| Islip (town) Suffolk County | 27 | 0.01 |

## American Indian: South American Indian

### Top 10 Places Sorted by Population
*Based on all places, regardless of total population*

| Place | Population | % |
|---|---|---|
| New York (city) | 9,464 | 0.12 |
| Bronx (borough) Bronx County | 2,938 | 0.21 |
| Queens (borough) Queens County | 2,448 | 0.11 |
| Manhattan (borough) New York County | 1,935 | 0.12 |
| Brooklyn (borough) Kings County | 1,855 | 0.07 |
| Hempstead (town) Nassau County | 294 | 0.04 |
| Staten Island (borough) Richmond County | 288 | 0.06 |
| Yonkers (city) Westchester County | 270 | 0.14 |
| Islip (town) Suffolk County | 249 | 0.07 |
| Rochester (city) Monroe County | 144 | 0.07 |

### Top 10 Places Sorted by Percent of Total Population
*Based on all places, regardless of total population*

| Place | Population | % |
|---|---|---|
| Onondaga Nation Reservation Onondaga County | 9 | 1.92 |
| Cattaraugus Reservation Cattaraugus County | 5 | 1.59 |
| Allegany Reservation Cattaraugus County | 9 | 0.88 |

*Please refer to the Explanation of Data in the front of the book for more detailed information.*

| Place | Population | % |
|---|---|---|
| **Shinnecock Hills** (cdp) Suffolk County | 18 | 0.82 |
| **Poospatuck Reservation** Suffolk County | 2 | 0.62 |
| **Roslyn Harbor** (village) Nassau County | 4 | 0.38 |
| **Fairview** (cdp) Westchester County | 11 | 0.35 |
| **East Hampton North** (cdp) Suffolk County | 13 | 0.31 |
| **St. Regis Mohawk Reservation** Franklin County | 10 | 0.31 |
| **Haverstraw** (village) Rockland County | 32 | 0.27 |

### Top 10 Places Sorted by Percent of Total Population
*Based on places with total population of 50,000 or more*

| Place | Population | % |
|---|---|---|
| **Bronx** (borough) Bronx County | 2,938 | 0.21 |
| **White Plains** (city) Westchester County | 116 | 0.20 |
| **Yonkers** (city) Westchester County | 270 | 0.14 |
| **Brentwood** (cdp) Suffolk County | 87 | 0.14 |
| **New York** (city) | 9,464 | 0.12 |
| **Manhattan** (borough) New York County | 1,935 | 0.12 |
| **Queens** (borough) Queens County | 2,448 | 0.11 |
| **Greenburgh** (town) Westchester County | 72 | 0.08 |
| **Brooklyn** (borough) Kings County | 1,855 | 0.07 |
| **Islip** (town) Suffolk County | 249 | 0.07 |

## American Indian: Spanish American Indian

### Top 10 Places Sorted by Population
*Based on all places, regardless of total population*

| Place | Population | % |
|---|---|---|
| **New York** (city) | 2,594 | 0.03 |
| **Bronx** (borough) Bronx County | 992 | 0.07 |
| **Queens** (borough) Queens County | 659 | 0.03 |
| **Manhattan** (borough) New York County | 514 | 0.03 |
| **Brooklyn** (borough) Kings County | 382 | 0.02 |
| **Hempstead** (town) Nassau County | 137 | 0.02 |
| **Yonkers** (city) Westchester County | 132 | 0.07 |
| **Newburgh** (city) Orange County | 92 | 0.32 |
| **Islip** (town) Suffolk County | 91 | 0.03 |
| **Brentwood** (cdp) Suffolk County | 52 | 0.09 |

### Top 10 Places Sorted by Percent of Total Population
*Based on all places, regardless of total population*

| Place | Population | % |
|---|---|---|
| **Shinnecock Reservation** Suffolk County | 4 | 0.60 |
| **Fort Covington Hamlet** (cdp) Franklin County | 7 | 0.54 |
| **Fort Covington** (town) Franklin County | 7 | 0.42 |
| **Newburgh** (city) Orange County | 92 | 0.32 |
| **Lebanon** (town) Madison County | 4 | 0.30 |
| **Westhampton Beach** (village) Suffolk County | 5 | 0.29 |
| **Greenport West** (cdp) Suffolk County | 6 | 0.28 |
| **South Floral Park** (village) Nassau County | 4 | 0.23 |
| **Woodstock** (cdp) Ulster County | 4 | 0.19 |
| **Canisteo** (village) Steuben County | 4 | 0.18 |

### Top 10 Places Sorted by Percent of Total Population
*Based on places with total population of 50,000 or more*

| Place | Population | % |
|---|---|---|
| **Brentwood** (cdp) Suffolk County | 52 | 0.09 |
| **Hempstead** (village) Nassau County | 47 | 0.09 |
| **Bronx** (borough) Bronx County | 992 | 0.07 |
| **Yonkers** (city) Westchester County | 132 | 0.07 |
| **New York** (city) | 2,594 | 0.03 |
| **Queens** (borough) Queens County | 659 | 0.03 |
| **Manhattan** (borough) New York County | 514 | 0.03 |
| **Islip** (town) Suffolk County | 91 | 0.03 |
| **Greenburgh** (town) Westchester County | 23 | 0.03 |
| **White Plains** (city) Westchester County | 15 | 0.03 |

## Alaska Native: Tlingit-Haida

### Top 10 Places Sorted by Population
*Based on all places, regardless of total population*

| Place | Population | % |
|---|---|---|
| **New York** (city) | 75 | <0.01 |
| **Brooklyn** (borough) Kings County | 28 | <0.01 |
| **Queens** (borough) Queens County | 20 | <0.01 |
| **Manhattan** (borough) New York County | 15 | <0.01 |
| **Bronx** (borough) Bronx County | 11 | <0.01 |
| **Ramapo** (town) Rockland County | 7 | 0.01 |
| **Hempstead** (town) Nassau County | 6 | <0.01 |
| **Islip** (town) Suffolk County | 6 | <0.01 |
| **Hilton** (village) Monroe County | 5 | 0.08 |

| Place | Population | % |
|---|---|---|
| **Parma** (town) Monroe County | 5 | 0.03 |

### Top 10 Places Sorted by Percent of Total Population
*Based on all places, regardless of total population*

| Place | Population | % |
|---|---|---|
| **Wampsville** (village) Madison County | 1 | 0.18 |
| **Lake George** (town) Warren County | 4 | 0.11 |
| **Dolgeville** (village) Herkimer County | 2 | 0.09 |
| **Poestenkill** (cdp) Rensselaer County | 1 | 0.09 |
| **Hilton** (village) Monroe County | 5 | 0.08 |
| **Gordon Heights** (cdp) Suffolk County | 3 | 0.07 |
| **Bellmont** (town) Franklin County | 1 | 0.07 |
| **Manheim** (town) Herkimer County | 2 | 0.06 |
| **Hornell** (city) Steuben County | 4 | 0.05 |
| **Hillcrest** (cdp) Rockland County | 3 | 0.04 |

### Top 10 Places Sorted by Percent of Total Population
*Based on places with total population of 50,000 or more*

| Place | Population | % |
|---|---|---|
| **Ramapo** (town) Rockland County | 7 | 0.01 |
| **Utica** (city) Oneida County | 4 | 0.01 |
| **New York** (city) | 75 | <0.01 |
| **Brooklyn** (borough) Kings County | 28 | <0.01 |
| **Queens** (borough) Queens County | 20 | <0.01 |
| **Manhattan** (borough) New York County | 15 | <0.01 |
| **Bronx** (borough) Bronx County | 11 | <0.01 |
| **Hempstead** (town) Nassau County | 6 | <0.01 |
| **Islip** (town) Suffolk County | 6 | <0.01 |
| **Brookhaven** (town) Suffolk County | 5 | <0.01 |

## American Indian: Tohono O'Odham

### Top 10 Places Sorted by Population
*Based on all places, regardless of total population*

| Place | Population | % |
|---|---|---|
| **New York** (city) | 48 | <0.01 |
| **Manhattan** (borough) New York County | 15 | <0.01 |
| **Brooklyn** (borough) Kings County | 10 | <0.01 |
| **Bronx** (borough) Bronx County | 9 | <0.01 |
| **Staten Island** (borough) Richmond County | 8 | <0.01 |
| **Hempstead** (town) Nassau County | 7 | <0.01 |
| **Middletown** (city) Orange County | 6 | 0.02 |
| **New Windsor** (town) Orange County | 6 | 0.02 |
| **Uniondale** (cdp) Nassau County | 6 | 0.02 |
| **Queens** (borough) Queens County | 6 | <0.01 |

### Top 10 Places Sorted by Percent of Total Population
*Based on all places, regardless of total population*

| Place | Population | % |
|---|---|---|
| **Hillburn** (village) Rockland County | 4 | 0.42 |
| **Covington** (town) Wyoming County | 3 | 0.24 |
| **Allegany Reservation** Cattaraugus County | 1 | 0.10 |
| **Chester** (village) Orange County | 3 | 0.08 |
| **Durham** (town) Greene County | 1 | 0.04 |
| **Chester** (town) Orange County | 3 | 0.03 |
| **Middletown** (city) Orange County | 6 | 0.02 |
| **New Windsor** (town) Orange County | 6 | 0.02 |
| **Uniondale** (cdp) Nassau County | 6 | 0.02 |
| **Poughkeepsie** (city) Dutchess County | 3 | 0.01 |

### Top 10 Places Sorted by Percent of Total Population
*Based on places with total population of 50,000 or more*

| Place | Population | % |
|---|---|---|
| **New York** (city) | 48 | <0.01 |
| **Manhattan** (borough) New York County | 15 | <0.01 |
| **Brooklyn** (borough) Kings County | 10 | <0.01 |
| **Bronx** (borough) Bronx County | 9 | <0.01 |
| **Staten Island** (borough) Richmond County | 8 | <0.01 |
| **Hempstead** (town) Nassau County | 7 | <0.01 |
| **Queens** (borough) Queens County | 6 | <0.01 |
| **Ramapo** (town) Rockland County | 4 | <0.01 |
| **Buffalo** (city) Erie County | 3 | <0.01 |
| **Yonkers** (city) Westchester County | 3 | <0.01 |

## Alaska Native: Tsimshian

### Top 10 Places Sorted by Population
*Based on all places, regardless of total population*

| Place | Population | % |
|---|---|---|
| **New York** (city) | 4 | <0.01 |

| Place | Population | % |
|---|---|---|
| **Manhattan** (borough) New York County | 3 | <0.01 |
| **Rochester** (town) Ulster County | 1 | 0.01 |
| **Queens** (borough) Queens County | 1 | <0.01 |
| **Accord** (cdp) Ulster County | 0 | 0.00 |
| **Adams** (village) Jefferson County | 0 | 0.00 |
| **Adams** (town) Jefferson County | 0 | 0.00 |
| **Adams Center** (cdp) Jefferson County | 0 | 0.00 |
| **Addison** (village) Steuben County | 0 | 0.00 |
| **Addison** (town) Steuben County | 0 | 0.00 |

### Top 10 Places Sorted by Percent of Total Population
*Based on all places, regardless of total population*

| Place | Population | % |
|---|---|---|
| **Rochester** (town) Ulster County | 1 | 0.01 |
| **New York** (city) | 4 | <0.01 |
| **Manhattan** (borough) New York County | 3 | <0.01 |
| **Queens** (borough) Queens County | 1 | <0.01 |
| **Accord** (cdp) Ulster County | 0 | 0.00 |
| **Adams** (village) Jefferson County | 0 | 0.00 |
| **Adams** (town) Jefferson County | 0 | 0.00 |
| **Adams Center** (cdp) Jefferson County | 0 | 0.00 |
| **Addison** (village) Steuben County | 0 | 0.00 |
| **Addison** (town) Steuben County | 0 | 0.00 |

### Top 10 Places Sorted by Percent of Total Population
*Based on places with total population of 50,000 or more*

| Place | Population | % |
|---|---|---|
| **New York** (city) | 4 | <0.01 |
| **Manhattan** (borough) New York County | 3 | <0.01 |
| **Queens** (borough) Queens County | 1 | <0.01 |
| **Albany** (city) Albany County | 0 | 0.00 |
| **Amherst** (town) Erie County | 0 | 0.00 |
| **Babylon** (town) Suffolk County | 0 | 0.00 |
| **Brentwood** (cdp) Suffolk County | 0 | 0.00 |
| **Bronx** (borough) Bronx County | 0 | 0.00 |
| **Brookhaven** (town) Suffolk County | 0 | 0.00 |
| **Brooklyn** (borough) Kings County | 0 | 0.00 |

## American Indian: Ute

### Top 10 Places Sorted by Population
*Based on all places, regardless of total population*

| Place | Population | % |
|---|---|---|
| **New York** (city) | 17 | <0.01 |
| **Bronx** (borough) Bronx County | 5 | <0.01 |
| **Queens** (borough) Queens County | 5 | <0.01 |
| **Brooklyn** (borough) Kings County | 4 | <0.01 |
| **Rochester** (city) Monroe County | 4 | <0.01 |
| **Farmington** (town) Ontario County | 2 | 0.02 |
| **Manhattan** (borough) New York County | 2 | <0.01 |
| **Jefferson** (town) Schoharie County | 1 | 0.07 |
| **Calcium** (cdp) Jefferson County | 1 | 0.03 |
| **Amenia** (town) Dutchess County | 1 | 0.02 |

### Top 10 Places Sorted by Percent of Total Population
*Based on all places, regardless of total population*

| Place | Population | % |
|---|---|---|
| **Jefferson** (town) Schoharie County | 1 | 0.07 |
| **Calcium** (cdp) Jefferson County | 1 | 0.03 |
| **Farmington** (town) Ontario County | 2 | 0.02 |
| **Amenia** (town) Dutchess County | 1 | 0.02 |
| **Little Falls** (city) Herkimer County | 1 | 0.02 |
| **Wilson** (town) Niagara County | 1 | 0.02 |
| **Center Moriches** (cdp) Suffolk County | 1 | 0.01 |
| **Hastings** (town) Oswego County | 1 | 0.01 |
| **Kings Park** (cdp) Suffolk County | 1 | 0.01 |
| **Lynbrook** (village) Nassau County | 1 | 0.01 |

### Top 10 Places Sorted by Percent of Total Population
*Based on places with total population of 50,000 or more*

| Place | Population | % |
|---|---|---|
| **New York** (city) | 17 | <0.01 |
| **Bronx** (borough) Bronx County | 5 | <0.01 |
| **Queens** (borough) Queens County | 5 | <0.01 |
| **Brooklyn** (borough) Kings County | 4 | <0.01 |
| **Rochester** (city) Monroe County | 4 | <0.01 |
| **Manhattan** (borough) New York County | 2 | <0.01 |
| **Brookhaven** (town) Suffolk County | 1 | <0.01 |
| **Hempstead** (town) Nassau County | 1 | <0.01 |
| **Smithtown** (town) Suffolk County | 1 | <0.01 |
| **Staten Island** (borough) Richmond County | 1 | <0.01 |

## American Indian: Yakama

### Top 10 Places Sorted by Population
*Based on all places, regardless of total population*

| Place | Population | % |
|---|---|---|
| New York (city) | 8 | <0.01 |
| Bronx (borough) Bronx County | 3 | <0.01 |
| Brooklyn (borough) Kings County | 3 | <0.01 |
| Poughkeepsie (city) Dutchess County | 2 | 0.01 |
| Manhattan (borough) New York County | 2 | <0.01 |
| Austerlitz (town) Columbia County | 1 | 0.06 |
| Coxsackie (village) Greene County | 1 | 0.04 |
| Gordon Heights (cdp) Suffolk County | 1 | 0.02 |
| Coxsackie (town) Greene County | 1 | 0.01 |
| Oswego (city) Oswego County | 1 | 0.01 |

### Top 10 Places Sorted by Percent of Total Population
*Based on all places, regardless of total population*

| Place | Population | % |
|---|---|---|
| Austerlitz (town) Columbia County | 1 | 0.06 |
| Coxsackie (village) Greene County | 1 | 0.04 |
| Gordon Heights (cdp) Suffolk County | 1 | 0.02 |
| Poughkeepsie (city) Dutchess County | 2 | 0.01 |
| Coxsackie (town) Greene County | 1 | 0.01 |
| Oswego (city) Oswego County | 1 | 0.01 |
| New York (city) | 8 | <0.01 |
| Bronx (borough) Bronx County | 3 | <0.01 |
| Brooklyn (borough) Kings County | 3 | <0.01 |
| Manhattan (borough) New York County | 2 | <0.01 |

### Top 10 Places Sorted by Percent of Total Population
*Based on places with total population of 50,000 or more*

| Place | Population | % |
|---|---|---|
| New York (city) | 8 | <0.01 |
| Bronx (borough) Bronx County | 3 | <0.01 |
| Brooklyn (borough) Kings County | 3 | <0.01 |
| Manhattan (borough) New York County | 2 | <0.01 |
| Albany (city) Albany County | 1 | <0.01 |
| Brookhaven (town) Suffolk County | 1 | <0.01 |
| Niagara Falls (city) Niagara County | 1 | <0.01 |
| Ramapo (town) Rockland County | 1 | <0.01 |
| Amherst (town) Erie County | 0 | 0.00 |
| Babylon (town) Suffolk County | 0 | 0.00 |

## American Indian: Yaqui

### Top 10 Places Sorted by Population
*Based on all places, regardless of total population*

| Place | Population | % |
|---|---|---|
| New York (city) | 54 | <0.01 |
| Manhattan (borough) New York County | 22 | <0.01 |
| Brooklyn (borough) Kings County | 19 | <0.01 |
| Queens (borough) Queens County | 7 | <0.01 |
| Groton (village) Tompkins County | 5 | 0.21 |
| Pembroke (town) Genesee County | 5 | 0.12 |
| Groton (town) Tompkins County | 5 | 0.08 |
| Kirkland (town) Oneida County | 5 | 0.05 |
| Bronx (borough) Bronx County | 5 | <0.01 |
| Brookhaven (town) Suffolk County | 5 | <0.01 |

### Top 10 Places Sorted by Percent of Total Population
*Based on all places, regardless of total population*

| Place | Population | % |
|---|---|---|
| Groton (village) Tompkins County | 5 | 0.21 |
| Lake Luzerne (cdp) Warren County | 2 | 0.16 |
| Rushville (village) Yates County | 1 | 0.15 |
| Pembroke (town) Genesee County | 5 | 0.12 |
| Schuyler (town) Herkimer County | 4 | 0.12 |
| Chateaugay (village) Franklin County | 1 | 0.12 |
| Allegany Reservation Cattaraugus County | 1 | 0.10 |
| Groton (town) Tompkins County | 5 | 0.08 |
| Lake Luzerne (town) Warren County | 2 | 0.06 |
| Kortright (town) Delaware County | 1 | 0.06 |

### Top 10 Places Sorted by Percent of Total Population
*Based on places with total population of 50,000 or more*

| Place | Population | % |
|---|---|---|
| New York (city) | 54 | <0.01 |
| Manhattan (borough) New York County | 22 | <0.01 |
| Brooklyn (borough) Kings County | 19 | <0.01 |
| Queens (borough) Queens County | 7 | <0.01 |

| Place | Population | % |
|---|---|---|
| Bronx (borough) Bronx County | 5 | <0.01 |
| Brookhaven (town) Suffolk County | 5 | <0.01 |
| Buffalo (city) Erie County | 2 | <0.01 |
| Brentwood (cdp) Suffolk County | 1 | <0.01 |
| Islip (town) Suffolk County | 1 | <0.01 |
| Niagara Falls (city) Niagara County | 1 | <0.01 |

## American Indian: Yuman

### Top 10 Places Sorted by Population
*Based on all places, regardless of total population*

| Place | Population | % |
|---|---|---|
| New York (city) | 22 | <0.01 |
| Brooklyn (borough) Kings County | 8 | <0.01 |
| Manhattan (borough) New York County | 6 | <0.01 |
| Queens (borough) Queens County | 5 | <0.01 |
| Deerpark (town) Orange County | 4 | 0.05 |
| De Witt (town) Onondaga County | 4 | 0.02 |
| Webster (village) Monroe County | 2 | 0.04 |
| Bronx (borough) Bronx County | 2 | <0.01 |
| Webster (town) Monroe County | 2 | <0.01 |
| Yonkers (city) Westchester County | 2 | <0.01 |

### Top 10 Places Sorted by Percent of Total Population
*Based on all places, regardless of total population*

| Place | Population | % |
|---|---|---|
| Deerpark (town) Orange County | 4 | 0.05 |
| Webster (village) Monroe County | 2 | 0.04 |
| Brewster (village) Putnam County | 1 | 0.04 |
| De Witt (town) Onondaga County | 4 | 0.02 |
| Lyncourt (cdp) Onondaga County | 1 | 0.02 |
| Eastchester (cdp) Westchester County | 1 | 0.01 |
| Granville (town) Washington County | 1 | 0.01 |
| Greece (cdp) Monroe County | 1 | 0.01 |
| Highlands (town) Orange County | 1 | 0.01 |
| Southeast (town) Putnam County | 1 | 0.01 |

### Top 10 Places Sorted by Percent of Total Population
*Based on places with total population of 50,000 or more*

| Place | Population | % |
|---|---|---|
| New York (city) | 22 | <0.01 |
| Brooklyn (borough) Kings County | 8 | <0.01 |
| Manhattan (borough) New York County | 6 | <0.01 |
| Queens (borough) Queens County | 5 | <0.01 |
| Bronx (borough) Bronx County | 2 | <0.01 |
| Yonkers (city) Westchester County | 2 | <0.01 |
| Brookhaven (town) Suffolk County | 1 | <0.01 |
| Buffalo (city) Erie County | 1 | <0.01 |
| Greece (town) Monroe County | 1 | <0.01 |
| Islip (town) Suffolk County | 1 | <0.01 |

## Alaska Native: Yup'ik

### Top 10 Places Sorted by Population
*Based on all places, regardless of total population*

| Place | Population | % |
|---|---|---|
| New York (city) | 10 | <0.01 |
| Bronx (borough) Bronx County | 6 | <0.01 |
| Cazenovia (town) Madison County | 3 | 0.04 |
| Canton (town) St. Lawrence County | 3 | 0.03 |
| Fort Drum (cdp) Jefferson County | 3 | 0.02 |
| Le Ray (town) Jefferson County | 3 | 0.01 |
| Stephentown (town) Rensselaer County | 2 | 0.07 |
| Colden (town) Erie County | 2 | 0.06 |
| New Paltz (village) Ulster County | 2 | 0.03 |
| New Paltz (town) Ulster County | 2 | 0.01 |

### Top 10 Places Sorted by Percent of Total Population
*Based on all places, regardless of total population*

| Place | Population | % |
|---|---|---|
| Forest Home (cdp) Tompkins County | 1 | 0.17 |
| Savona (village) Steuben County | 1 | 0.12 |
| Ripley (cdp) Chautauqua County | 1 | 0.11 |
| Rathbone (town) Steuben County | 1 | 0.09 |
| Stephentown (town) Rensselaer County | 2 | 0.07 |
| Colden (town) Erie County | 2 | 0.06 |
| Cazenovia (town) Madison County | 3 | 0.04 |
| Franklin (town) Delaware County | 1 | 0.04 |
| Green Island (town/village) Albany County | 1 | 0.04 |
| Orleans (town) Jefferson County | 1 | 0.04 |

### Top 10 Places Sorted by Percent of Total Population
*Based on places with total population of 50,000 or more*

| Place | Population | % |
|---|---|---|
| New York (city) | 10 | <0.01 |
| Bronx (borough) Bronx County | 6 | <0.01 |
| Manhattan (borough) New York County | 2 | <0.01 |
| Albany (city) Albany County | 1 | <0.01 |
| Amherst (town) Erie County | 1 | <0.01 |
| Brooklyn (borough) Kings County | 1 | <0.01 |
| Queens (borough) Queens County | 1 | <0.01 |
| Syracuse (city) Onondaga County | 1 | <0.01 |
| Babylon (town) Suffolk County | 0 | 0.00 |
| Brentwood (cdp) Suffolk County | 0 | 0.00 |

## Asian

### Top 10 Places Sorted by Population
*Based on all places, regardless of total population*

| Place | Population | % |
|---|---|---|
| New York (city) | 1,134,919 | 13.88 |
| Queens (borough) Queens County | 552,867 | 24.78 |
| Brooklyn (borough) Kings County | 284,489 | 11.36 |
| Manhattan (borough) New York County | 199,722 | 12.59 |
| Bronx (borough) Bronx County | 59,085 | 4.27 |
| Hempstead (town) Nassau County | 45,112 | 5.94 |
| Staten Island (borough) Richmond County | 38,756 | 8.27 |
| North Hempstead (town) Nassau County | 36,973 | 16.34 |
| Oyster Bay (town) Nassau County | 29,203 | 9.96 |
| Brookhaven (town) Suffolk County | 21,849 | 4.50 |

### Top 10 Places Sorted by Percent of Total Population
*Based on all places, regardless of total population*

| Place | Population | % |
|---|---|---|
| Herricks (cdp) Nassau County | 1,943 | 45.24 |
| Manhasset Hills (cdp) Nassau County | 1,483 | 41.29 |
| Searingtown (cdp) Nassau County | 2,008 | 40.85 |
| Forest Home (cdp) Tompkins County | 210 | 36.71 |
| Merritt Park (cdp) Dutchess County | 442 | 35.19 |
| Garden City Park (cdp) Nassau County | 2,698 | 34.56 |
| University Gardens (cdp) Nassau County | 1,316 | 31.14 |
| North New Hyde Park (cdp) Nassau County | 4,585 | 30.77 |
| Bellerose Terrace (cdp) Nassau County | 663 | 30.16 |
| Thomaston (village) Nassau County | 783 | 29.92 |

### Top 10 Places Sorted by Percent of Total Population
*Based on places with total population of 50,000 or more*

| Place | Population | % |
|---|---|---|
| Queens (borough) Queens County | 552,867 | 24.78 |
| North Hempstead (town) Nassau County | 36,973 | 16.34 |
| New York (city) | 1,134,919 | 13.88 |
| Manhattan (borough) New York County | 199,722 | 12.59 |
| Greenburgh (town) Westchester County | 10,180 | 11.52 |
| Clarkstown (town) Rockland County | 9,614 | 11.42 |
| Brooklyn (borough) Kings County | 284,489 | 11.36 |
| Oyster Bay (town) Nassau County | 29,203 | 9.96 |
| Amherst (town) Erie County | 10,683 | 8.73 |
| Staten Island (borough) Richmond County | 38,756 | 8.27 |

## Asian: Not Hispanic

### Top 10 Places Sorted by Population
*Based on all places, regardless of total population*

| Place | Population | % |
|---|---|---|
| New York (city) | 1,110,964 | 13.59 |
| Queens (borough) Queens County | 545,389 | 24.45 |
| Brooklyn (borough) Kings County | 279,499 | 11.16 |
| Manhattan (borough) New York County | 194,929 | 12.29 |
| Bronx (borough) Bronx County | 53,458 | 3.86 |
| Hempstead (town) Nassau County | 43,880 | 5.78 |
| Staten Island (borough) Richmond County | 37,689 | 8.04 |
| North Hempstead (town) Nassau County | 36,641 | 16.19 |
| Oyster Bay (town) Nassau County | 28,910 | 9.86 |
| Brookhaven (town) Suffolk County | 21,257 | 4.37 |

### Top 10 Places Sorted by Percent of Total Population
*Based on all places, regardless of total population*

| Place | Population | % |
|---|---|---|
| Herricks (cdp) Nassau County | 1,931 | 44.96 |
| Manhasset Hills (cdp) Nassau County | 1,476 | 41.09 |
| Searingtown (cdp) Nassau County | 2,000 | 40.69 |

| Place | Population | % |
|---|---|---|
| **Forest Home** (cdp) Tompkins County | 210 | 36.71 |
| **Merritt Park** (cdp) Dutchess County | 442 | 35.19 |
| **Garden City Park** (cdp) Nassau County | 2,670 | 34.20 |
| **University Gardens** (cdp) Nassau County | 1,309 | 30.97 |
| **North New Hyde Park** (cdp) Nassau County | 4,558 | 30.59 |
| **Bellerose Terrace** (cdp) Nassau County | 652 | 29.66 |
| **Thomaston** (village) Nassau County | 772 | 29.50 |

### Top 10 Places Sorted by Percent of Total Population
*Based on places with total population of 50,000 or more*

| Place | Population | % |
|---|---|---|
| **Queens** (borough) Queens County | 545,389 | 24.45 |
| **North Hempstead** (town) Nassau County | 36,641 | 16.19 |
| **New York** (city) | 1,110,964 | 13.59 |
| **Manhattan** (borough) New York County | 194,929 | 12.29 |
| **Greenburgh** (town) Westchester County | 10,025 | 11.34 |
| **Clarkstown** (town) Rockland County | 9,462 | 11.24 |
| **Brooklyn** (borough) Kings County | 279,499 | 11.16 |
| **Oyster Bay** (town) Nassau County | 28,910 | 9.86 |
| **Amherst** (town) Erie County | 10,590 | 8.65 |
| **Staten Island** (borough) Richmond County | 37,689 | 8.04 |

## Asian: Hispanic

### Top 10 Places Sorted by Population
*Based on all places, regardless of total population*

| Place | Population | % |
|---|---|---|
| **New York** (city) | 23,955 | 0.29 |
| **Queens** (borough) Queens County | 7,478 | 0.34 |
| **Bronx** (borough) Bronx County | 5,627 | 0.41 |
| **Brooklyn** (borough) Kings County | 4,990 | 0.20 |
| **Manhattan** (borough) New York County | 4,793 | 0.30 |
| **Hempstead** (town) Nassau County | 1,232 | 0.16 |
| **Staten Island** (borough) Richmond County | 1,067 | 0.23 |
| **Brookhaven** (town) Suffolk County | 592 | 0.12 |
| **Islip** (town) Suffolk County | 553 | 0.16 |
| **Yonkers** (city) Westchester County | 517 | 0.26 |

### Top 10 Places Sorted by Percent of Total Population
*Based on all places, regardless of total population*

| Place | Population | % |
|---|---|---|
| **Salamanca** (town) Cattaraugus County | 4 | 0.83 |
| **Nelsonville** (village) Putnam County | 5 | 0.80 |
| **North Lynbrook** (cdp) Nassau County | 6 | 0.76 |
| **Grove** (town) Allegany County | 4 | 0.73 |
| **La Fargeville** (cdp) Jefferson County | 4 | 0.66 |
| **Tonawanda Reservation** Genesee County | 3 | 0.62 |
| **Rensselaer Falls** (village) St. Lawrence County | 2 | 0.60 |
| **Tannersville** (village) Greene County | 3 | 0.56 |
| **Waterford** (village) Saratoga County | 11 | 0.55 |
| **Chautauqua** (cdp) Chautauqua County | 1 | 0.52 |

### Top 10 Places Sorted by Percent of Total Population
*Based on places with total population of 50,000 or more*

| Place | Population | % |
|---|---|---|
| **Bronx** (borough) Bronx County | 5,627 | 0.41 |
| **Queens** (borough) Queens County | 7,478 | 0.34 |
| **Brentwood** (cdp) Suffolk County | 195 | 0.32 |
| **Manhattan** (borough) New York County | 4,793 | 0.30 |
| **New York** (city) | 23,955 | 0.29 |
| **Yonkers** (city) Westchester County | 517 | 0.26 |
| **Hempstead** (village) Nassau County | 135 | 0.25 |
| **Staten Island** (borough) Richmond County | 1,067 | 0.23 |
| **New Rochelle** (city) Westchester County | 167 | 0.22 |
| **White Plains** (city) Westchester County | 121 | 0.21 |

## Asian: Bangladeshi

### Top 10 Places Sorted by Population
*Based on all places, regardless of total population*

| Place | Population | % |
|---|---|---|
| **New York** (city) | 61,788 | 0.76 |
| **Queens** (borough) Queens County | 38,341 | 1.72 |
| **Brooklyn** (borough) Kings County | 12,408 | 0.50 |
| **Bronx** (borough) Bronx County | 8,623 | 0.62 |
| **Manhattan** (borough) New York County | 2,029 | 0.13 |
| **Brookhaven** (town) Suffolk County | 621 | 0.13 |
| **Hempstead** (town) Nassau County | 582 | 0.08 |
| **North Hempstead** (town) Nassau County | 441 | 0.19 |
| **Staten Island** (borough) Richmond County | 387 | 0.08 |
| **Oyster Bay** (town) Nassau County | 365 | 0.12 |

### Top 10 Places Sorted by Percent of Total Population
*Based on all places, regardless of total population*

| Place | Population | % |
|---|---|---|
| **Hudson** (city) Columbia County | 271 | 4.04 |
| **Bellerose Terrace** (cdp) Nassau County | 44 | 2.00 |
| **Queens** (borough) Queens County | 38,341 | 1.72 |
| **Harriman** (village) Orange County | 40 | 1.65 |
| **Clintondale** (cdp) Ulster County | 22 | 1.52 |
| **Manhasset Hills** (cdp) Nassau County | 33 | 0.92 |
| **Greenvale** (cdp) Nassau County | 9 | 0.82 |
| **Deer Park** (cdp) Suffolk County | 224 | 0.81 |
| **Herricks** (cdp) Nassau County | 35 | 0.81 |
| **New York** (city) | 61,788 | 0.76 |

### Top 10 Places Sorted by Percent of Total Population
*Based on places with total population of 50,000 or more*

| Place | Population | % |
|---|---|---|
| **Queens** (borough) Queens County | 38,341 | 1.72 |
| **New York** (city) | 61,788 | 0.76 |
| **Bronx** (borough) Bronx County | 8,623 | 0.62 |
| **Brooklyn** (borough) Kings County | 12,408 | 0.50 |
| **North Hempstead** (town) Nassau County | 441 | 0.19 |
| **Albany** (city) Albany County | 171 | 0.17 |
| **Babylon** (town) Suffolk County | 341 | 0.16 |
| **Manhattan** (borough) New York County | 2,029 | 0.13 |
| **Brookhaven** (town) Suffolk County | 621 | 0.13 |
| **Levittown** (cdp) Nassau County | 70 | 0.13 |

## Asian: Bhutanese

### Top 10 Places Sorted by Population
*Based on all places, regardless of total population*

| Place | Population | % |
|---|---|---|
| **Syracuse** (city) Onondaga County | 516 | 0.36 |
| **Rochester** (city) Monroe County | 411 | 0.20 |
| **New York** (city) | 388 | <0.01 |
| **Buffalo** (city) Erie County | 370 | 0.14 |
| **Queens** (borough) Queens County | 250 | 0.01 |
| **Bronx** (borough) Bronx County | 104 | 0.01 |
| **Albany** (city) Albany County | 62 | 0.06 |
| **Utica** (city) Oneida County | 36 | 0.06 |
| **Manhattan** (borough) New York County | 26 | <0.01 |
| **Greenville** (cdp) Westchester County | 8 | 0.11 |

### Top 10 Places Sorted by Percent of Total Population
*Based on all places, regardless of total population*

| Place | Population | % |
|---|---|---|
| **Syracuse** (city) Onondaga County | 516 | 0.36 |
| **Rochester** (city) Monroe County | 411 | 0.20 |
| **Meredith** (town) Delaware County | 3 | 0.20 |
| **Buffalo** (city) Erie County | 370 | 0.14 |
| **Greenville** (cdp) Westchester County | 8 | 0.11 |
| **Albany** (city) Albany County | 62 | 0.06 |
| **Utica** (city) Oneida County | 36 | 0.06 |
| **Kerhonkson** (cdp) Ulster County | 1 | 0.06 |
| **Sullivan** (town) Madison County | 7 | 0.05 |
| **Harrison** (town/village) Westchester County | 8 | 0.03 |

### Top 10 Places Sorted by Percent of Total Population
*Based on places with total population of 50,000 or more*

| Place | Population | % |
|---|---|---|
| **Syracuse** (city) Onondaga County | 516 | 0.36 |
| **Rochester** (city) Monroe County | 411 | 0.20 |
| **Buffalo** (city) Erie County | 370 | 0.14 |
| **Albany** (city) Albany County | 62 | 0.06 |
| **Utica** (city) Oneida County | 36 | 0.06 |
| **Queens** (borough) Queens County | 250 | 0.01 |
| **Bronx** (borough) Bronx County | 104 | 0.01 |
| **Greenburgh** (town) Westchester County | 8 | 0.01 |
| **New York** (city) | 388 | <0.01 |
| **Manhattan** (borough) New York County | 26 | <0.01 |

## Asian: Burmese

### Top 10 Places Sorted by Population
*Based on all places, regardless of total population*

| Place | Population | % |
|---|---|---|
| **New York** (city) | 4,132 | 0.05 |
| **Buffalo** (city) Erie County | 2,361 | 0.90 |
| **Queens** (borough) Queens County | 2,344 | 0.11 |

| Place | Population | % |
|---|---|---|
| **Utica** (city) Oneida County | 2,317 | 3.72 |
| **Brooklyn** (borough) Kings County | 1,260 | 0.05 |
| **Syracuse** (city) Onondaga County | 1,218 | 0.84 |
| **Rochester** (city) Monroe County | 565 | 0.27 |
| **Albany** (city) Albany County | 322 | 0.33 |
| **Manhattan** (borough) New York County | 317 | 0.02 |
| **Rensselaer** (city) Rensselaer County | 316 | 3.36 |

### Top 10 Places Sorted by Percent of Total Population
*Based on all places, regardless of total population*

| Place | Population | % |
|---|---|---|
| **Utica** (city) Oneida County | 2,317 | 3.72 |
| **Rensselaer** (city) Rensselaer County | 316 | 3.36 |
| **East Ithaca** (cdp) Tompkins County | 46 | 2.06 |
| **Buffalo** (city) Erie County | 2,361 | 0.90 |
| **Syracuse** (city) Onondaga County | 1,218 | 0.84 |
| **Lakeville** (cdp) Livingston County | 4 | 0.53 |
| **Union Springs** (village) Cayuga County | 6 | 0.50 |
| **Northeast Ithaca** (cdp) Tompkins County | 12 | 0.45 |
| **Green Island** (town/village) Albany County | 11 | 0.42 |
| **Albany** (city) Albany County | 322 | 0.33 |

### Top 10 Places Sorted by Percent of Total Population
*Based on places with total population of 50,000 or more*

| Place | Population | % |
|---|---|---|
| **Utica** (city) Oneida County | 2,317 | 3.72 |
| **Buffalo** (city) Erie County | 2,361 | 0.90 |
| **Syracuse** (city) Onondaga County | 1,218 | 0.84 |
| **Albany** (city) Albany County | 322 | 0.33 |
| **Rochester** (city) Monroe County | 565 | 0.27 |
| **Queens** (borough) Queens County | 2,344 | 0.11 |
| **Troy** (city) Rensselaer County | 28 | 0.06 |
| **New York** (city) | 4,132 | 0.05 |
| **Brooklyn** (borough) Kings County | 1,260 | 0.05 |
| **North Hempstead** (town) Nassau County | 88 | 0.04 |

## Asian: Cambodian

### Top 10 Places Sorted by Population
*Based on all places, regardless of total population*

| Place | Population | % |
|---|---|---|
| **New York** (city) | 2,591 | 0.03 |
| **Bronx** (borough) Bronx County | 1,188 | 0.09 |
| **Brooklyn** (borough) Kings County | 751 | 0.03 |
| **Utica** (city) Oneida County | 480 | 0.77 |
| **Rochester** (city) Monroe County | 381 | 0.18 |
| **Queens** (borough) Queens County | 303 | 0.01 |
| **Manhattan** (borough) New York County | 220 | 0.01 |
| **Syracuse** (city) Onondaga County | 149 | 0.10 |
| **Staten Island** (borough) Richmond County | 129 | 0.03 |
| **Ithaca** (city) Tompkins County | 68 | 0.23 |

### Top 10 Places Sorted by Percent of Total Population
*Based on all places, regardless of total population*

| Place | Population | % |
|---|---|---|
| **Fowlerville** (cdp) Livingston County | 2 | 0.88 |
| **Utica** (city) Oneida County | 480 | 0.77 |
| **East Ithaca** (cdp) Tompkins County | 13 | 0.58 |
| **York Hamlet** (cdp) Livingston County | 3 | 0.55 |
| **East Nassau** (village) Rensselaer County | 3 | 0.51 |
| **Bloomingburg** (village) Sullivan County | 2 | 0.48 |
| **Lansing** (village) Tompkins County | 16 | 0.45 |
| **Andes** (cdp) Delaware County | 1 | 0.40 |
| **Parc** (cdp) Clinton County | 1 | 0.39 |
| **Argyle** (town) Washington County | 12 | 0.32 |

### Top 10 Places Sorted by Percent of Total Population
*Based on places with total population of 50,000 or more*

| Place | Population | % |
|---|---|---|
| **Utica** (city) Oneida County | 480 | 0.77 |
| **Rochester** (city) Monroe County | 381 | 0.18 |
| **Syracuse** (city) Onondaga County | 149 | 0.10 |
| **Bronx** (borough) Bronx County | 1,188 | 0.09 |
| **Clarkstown** (town) Rockland County | 68 | 0.08 |
| **Irondequoit** (cdp/town) Monroe County | 31 | 0.06 |
| **Greece** (town) Monroe County | 47 | 0.05 |
| **Clay** (town) Onondaga County | 29 | 0.05 |
| **Ramapo** (town) Rockland County | 52 | 0.04 |
| **New York** (city) | 2,591 | 0.03 |

## Asian: Chinese, except Taiwanese

### Top 10 Places Sorted by Population
*Based on all places, regardless of total population*

| Place | Population | % |
|---|---|---|
| New York (city) | 500,434 | 6.12 |
| Queens (borough) Queens County | 200,714 | 9.00 |
| Brooklyn (borough) Kings County | 178,214 | 7.12 |
| Manhattan (borough) New York County | 99,287 | 6.26 |
| Staten Island (borough) Richmond County | 14,107 | 3.01 |
| North Hempstead (town) Nassau County | 10,292 | 4.55 |
| Bronx (borough) Bronx County | 8,112 | 0.59 |
| Hempstead (town) Nassau County | 7,849 | 1.03 |
| Oyster Bay (town) Nassau County | 7,054 | 2.41 |
| Brookhaven (town) Suffolk County | 6,107 | 1.26 |

### Top 10 Places Sorted by Percent of Total Population
*Based on all places, regardless of total population*

| Place | Population | % |
|---|---|---|
| University Gardens (cdp) Nassau County | 711 | 16.82 |
| Thomaston (village) Nassau County | 398 | 15.21 |
| Lake Success (village) Nassau County | 382 | 13.02 |
| Russell Gardens (village) Nassau County | 119 | 12.59 |
| Forest Home (cdp) Tompkins County | 68 | 11.89 |
| Manhasset Hills (cdp) Nassau County | 417 | 11.61 |
| Binghamton University (cdp) Broome County | 694 | 11.24 |
| Lansing (village) Tompkins County | 375 | 10.63 |
| North Hills (village) Nassau County | 516 | 10.17 |
| University at Buffalo (cdp) Erie County | 589 | 9.71 |

### Top 10 Places Sorted by Percent of Total Population
*Based on places with total population of 50,000 or more*

| Place | Population | % |
|---|---|---|
| Queens (borough) Queens County | 200,714 | 9.00 |
| Brooklyn (borough) Kings County | 178,214 | 7.12 |
| Manhattan (borough) New York County | 99,287 | 6.26 |
| New York (city) | 500,434 | 6.12 |
| North Hempstead (town) Nassau County | 10,292 | 4.55 |
| Staten Island (borough) Richmond County | 14,107 | 3.01 |
| Amherst (town) Erie County | 3,146 | 2.57 |
| Greenburgh (town) Westchester County | 2,225 | 2.52 |
| Oyster Bay (town) Nassau County | 7,054 | 2.41 |
| White Plains (city) Westchester County | 934 | 1.64 |

## Asian: Filipino

### Top 10 Places Sorted by Population
*Based on all places, regardless of total population*

| Place | Population | % |
|---|---|---|
| New York (city) | 78,030 | 0.95 |
| Queens (borough) Queens County | 41,773 | 1.87 |
| Manhattan (borough) New York County | 13,388 | 0.84 |
| Brooklyn (borough) Kings County | 10,208 | 0.41 |
| Hempstead (town) Nassau County | 7,212 | 0.95 |
| Bronx (borough) Bronx County | 6,456 | 0.47 |
| Staten Island (borough) Richmond County | 6,205 | 1.32 |
| Yonkers (city) Westchester County | 2,819 | 1.44 |
| Brookhaven (town) Suffolk County | 2,705 | 0.56 |
| Clarkstown (town) Rockland County | 2,320 | 2.76 |

### Top 10 Places Sorted by Percent of Total Population
*Based on all places, regardless of total population*

| Place | Population | % |
|---|---|---|
| Hillcrest (cdp) Rockland County | 441 | 5.83 |
| Bellerose Terrace (cdp) Nassau County | 119 | 5.41 |
| Valley Cottage (cdp) Rockland County | 485 | 5.33 |
| Orangeburg (cdp) Rockland County | 237 | 5.19 |
| Sparkill (cdp) Rockland County | 56 | 3.58 |
| Nanuet (cdp) Rockland County | 574 | 3.21 |
| Merritt Park (cdp) Dutchess County | 37 | 2.95 |
| South Valley Stream (cdp) Nassau County | 174 | 2.92 |
| New Hempstead (village) Rockland County | 150 | 2.92 |
| Clarkstown (town) Rockland County | 2,320 | 2.76 |

### Top 10 Places Sorted by Percent of Total Population
*Based on places with total population of 50,000 or more*

| Place | Population | % |
|---|---|---|
| Clarkstown (town) Rockland County | 2,320 | 2.76 |
| Queens (borough) Queens County | 41,773 | 1.87 |
| Yonkers (city) Westchester County | 2,819 | 1.44 |
| Staten Island (borough) Richmond County | 6,205 | 1.32 |

| Place | Population | % |
|---|---|---|
| Ramapo (town) Rockland County | 1,472 | 1.16 |
| Greenburgh (town) Westchester County | 959 | 1.08 |
| Levittown (cdp) Nassau County | 525 | 1.01 |
| New York (city) | 78,030 | 0.95 |
| Hempstead (town) Nassau County | 7,212 | 0.95 |
| Manhattan (borough) New York County | 13,388 | 0.84 |

## Asian: Hmong

### Top 10 Places Sorted by Population
*Based on all places, regardless of total population*

| Place | Population | % |
|---|---|---|
| New York (city) | 83 | <0.01 |
| Clay (town) Onondaga County | 75 | 0.13 |
| Syracuse (city) Onondaga County | 34 | 0.02 |
| Orangetown (town) Rockland County | 32 | 0.07 |
| South Nyack (village) Rockland County | 31 | 0.88 |
| Queens (borough) Queens County | 30 | <0.01 |
| Brooklyn (borough) Kings County | 22 | <0.01 |
| Manhattan (borough) New York County | 20 | <0.01 |
| Cicero (town) Onondaga County | 12 | 0.04 |
| Salina (town) Onondaga County | 11 | 0.03 |

### Top 10 Places Sorted by Percent of Total Population
*Based on all places, regardless of total population*

| Place | Population | % |
|---|---|---|
| South Nyack (village) Rockland County | 31 | 0.88 |
| Newfane (cdp) Niagara County | 10 | 0.26 |
| Clay (town) Onondaga County | 75 | 0.13 |
| Newfane (town) Niagara County | 10 | 0.10 |
| Orangetown (town) Rockland County | 32 | 0.07 |
| Spafford (town) Onondaga County | 1 | 0.06 |
| Nelson (town) Madison County | 1 | 0.05 |
| Cicero (town) Onondaga County | 12 | 0.04 |
| Galeville (cdp) Onondaga County | 2 | 0.04 |
| Johnsburg (town) Warren County | 1 | 0.04 |

### Top 10 Places Sorted by Percent of Total Population
*Based on places with total population of 50,000 or more*

| Place | Population | % |
|---|---|---|
| Clay (town) Onondaga County | 75 | 0.13 |
| Syracuse (city) Onondaga County | 34 | 0.02 |
| New York (city) | 83 | <0.01 |
| Queens (borough) Queens County | 30 | <0.01 |
| Brooklyn (borough) Kings County | 22 | <0.01 |
| Manhattan (borough) New York County | 20 | <0.01 |
| Staten Island (borough) Richmond County | 8 | <0.01 |
| Buffalo (city) Erie County | 6 | <0.01 |
| Brookhaven (town) Suffolk County | 4 | <0.01 |
| Bronx (borough) Bronx County | 3 | <0.01 |

## Asian: Indian

### Top 10 Places Sorted by Population
*Based on all places, regardless of total population*

| Place | Population | % |
|---|---|---|
| New York (city) | 232,696 | 2.85 |
| Queens (borough) Queens County | 141,147 | 6.33 |
| Brooklyn (borough) Kings County | 33,490 | 1.34 |
| Manhattan (borough) New York County | 29,979 | 1.89 |
| Bronx (borough) Bronx County | 20,357 | 1.47 |
| Hempstead (town) Nassau County | 17,802 | 2.34 |
| North Hempstead (town) Nassau County | 13,427 | 5.93 |
| Oyster Bay (town) Nassau County | 11,289 | 3.85 |
| Staten Island (borough) Richmond County | 7,723 | 1.65 |
| Yonkers (city) Westchester County | 5,818 | 2.97 |

### Top 10 Places Sorted by Percent of Total Population
*Based on all places, regardless of total population*

| Place | Population | % |
|---|---|---|
| Herricks (cdp) Nassau County | 1,036 | 24.12 |
| Manhasset Hills (cdp) Nassau County | 690 | 19.21 |
| Garden City Park (cdp) Nassau County | 1,487 | 19.05 |
| Searingtown (cdp) Nassau County | 935 | 19.02 |
| New Hyde Park (village) Nassau County | 1,682 | 17.32 |
| North New Hyde Park (cdp) Nassau County | 2,547 | 17.10 |
| Merritt Park (cdp) Dutchess County | 208 | 16.56 |
| Muttontown (village) Nassau County | 569 | 16.27 |
| Albertson (cdp) Nassau County | 690 | 13.32 |
| Bellerose Terrace (cdp) Nassau County | 277 | 12.60 |

### Top 10 Places Sorted by Percent of Total Population
*Based on places with total population of 50,000 or more*

| Place | Population | % |
|---|---|---|
| Queens (borough) Queens County | 141,147 | 6.33 |
| North Hempstead (town) Nassau County | 13,427 | 5.93 |
| Clarkstown (town) Rockland County | 3,874 | 4.60 |
| Greenburgh (town) Westchester County | 3,518 | 3.98 |
| Oyster Bay (town) Nassau County | 11,289 | 3.85 |
| Schenectady (city) Schenectady County | 2,050 | 3.10 |
| Yonkers (city) Westchester County | 5,818 | 2.97 |
| New York (city) | 232,696 | 2.85 |
| Amherst (town) Erie County | 3,491 | 2.85 |
| Colonie (town) Albany County | 2,099 | 2.57 |

## Asian: Indonesian

### Top 10 Places Sorted by Population
*Based on all places, regardless of total population*

| Place | Population | % |
|---|---|---|
| New York (city) | 4,791 | 0.06 |
| Queens (borough) Queens County | 3,386 | 0.15 |
| Manhattan (borough) New York County | 693 | 0.04 |
| Brooklyn (borough) Kings County | 564 | 0.02 |
| Bronx (borough) Bronx County | 96 | 0.01 |
| Hempstead (town) Nassau County | 66 | 0.01 |
| Brookhaven (town) Suffolk County | 63 | 0.01 |
| North Hempstead (town) Nassau County | 53 | 0.02 |
| Staten Island (borough) Richmond County | 52 | 0.01 |
| Amherst (town) Erie County | 42 | 0.03 |

### Top 10 Places Sorted by Percent of Total Population
*Based on all places, regardless of total population*

| Place | Population | % |
|---|---|---|
| Forest Home (cdp) Tompkins County | 11 | 1.92 |
| Grand View-on-Hudson (village) Rockland County | 2 | 0.70 |
| Colton (cdp) St. Lawrence County | 2 | 0.58 |
| Lyndon (town) Cattaraugus County | 4 | 0.57 |
| Lansing (village) Tompkins County | 11 | 0.31 |
| Adams Center (cdp) Jefferson County | 4 | 0.26 |
| Kensington (village) Nassau County | 3 | 0.26 |
| South Hempstead (cdp) Nassau County | 7 | 0.22 |
| Port Gibson (cdp) Ontario County | 1 | 0.22 |
| Hillburn (village) Rockland County | 2 | 0.21 |

### Top 10 Places Sorted by Percent of Total Population
*Based on places with total population of 50,000 or more*

| Place | Population | % |
|---|---|---|
| Queens (borough) Queens County | 3,386 | 0.15 |
| New York (city) | 4,791 | 0.06 |
| Manhattan (borough) New York County | 693 | 0.04 |
| Amherst (town) Erie County | 42 | 0.03 |
| Greenburgh (town) Westchester County | 24 | 0.03 |
| Brooklyn (borough) Kings County | 564 | 0.02 |
| North Hempstead (town) Nassau County | 53 | 0.02 |
| Syracuse (city) Onondaga County | 26 | 0.02 |
| Ramapo (town) Rockland County | 23 | 0.02 |
| Smithtown (town) Suffolk County | 18 | 0.02 |

## Asian: Japanese

### Top 10 Places Sorted by Population
*Based on all places, regardless of total population*

| Place | Population | % |
|---|---|---|
| New York (city) | 31,742 | 0.39 |
| Manhattan (borough) New York County | 16,600 | 1.05 |
| Queens (borough) Queens County | 7,790 | 0.35 |
| Brooklyn (borough) Kings County | 5,917 | 0.24 |
| North Hempstead (town) Nassau County | 1,266 | 0.56 |
| Harrison (town/village) Westchester County | 1,239 | 4.51 |
| Greenburgh (town) Westchester County | 1,230 | 1.39 |
| Bronx (borough) Bronx County | 1,027 | 0.07 |
| Eastchester (town) Westchester County | 903 | 2.79 |
| Hempstead (town) Nassau County | 657 | 0.09 |

### Top 10 Places Sorted by Percent of Total Population
*Based on all places, regardless of total population*

| Place | Population | % |
|---|---|---|
| Manorhaven (village) Nassau County | 368 | 5.61 |
| Hartsdale (cdp) Westchester County | 246 | 4.65 |
| Harrison (town/village) Westchester County | 1,239 | 4.51 |

| Place | Population | % |
|---|---|---|
| Tuckahoe (village) Westchester County | 210 | 3.24 |
| Greenville (cdp) Westchester County | 223 | 3.13 |
| Eastchester (cdp) Westchester County | 610 | 3.12 |
| Rye (city) Westchester County | 482 | 3.07 |
| Eastchester (town) Westchester County | 903 | 2.79 |
| Scarsdale (town/village) Westchester County | 428 | 2.49 |
| Fishkill (village) Dutchess County | 52 | 2.40 |

### Top 10 Places Sorted by Percent of Total Population
*Based on places with total population of 50,000 or more*

| Place | Population | % |
|---|---|---|
| Greenburgh (town) Westchester County | 1,230 | 1.39 |
| Manhattan (borough) New York County | 16,600 | 1.05 |
| White Plains (city) Westchester County | 441 | 0.78 |
| North Hempstead (town) Nassau County | 1,266 | 0.56 |
| New York (city) | 31,742 | 0.39 |
| Queens (borough) Queens County | 7,790 | 0.35 |
| Brooklyn (borough) Kings County | 5,917 | 0.24 |
| Amherst (town) Erie County | 294 | 0.24 |
| New Rochelle (city) Westchester County | 158 | 0.21 |
| Albany (city) Albany County | 200 | 0.20 |

## Asian: Korean

### Top 10 Places Sorted by Population
*Based on all places, regardless of total population*

| Place | Population | % |
|---|---|---|
| New York (city) | 102,820 | 1.26 |
| Queens (borough) Queens County | 66,124 | 2.96 |
| Manhattan (borough) New York County | 21,996 | 1.39 |
| Brooklyn (borough) Kings County | 8,201 | 0.33 |
| North Hempstead (town) Nassau County | 6,015 | 2.66 |
| Oyster Bay (town) Nassau County | 4,977 | 1.70 |
| Staten Island (borough) Richmond County | 3,398 | 0.72 |
| Bronx (borough) Bronx County | 3,101 | 0.22 |
| Hempstead (town) Nassau County | 3,074 | 0.40 |
| Huntington (town) Suffolk County | 2,122 | 1.04 |

### Top 10 Places Sorted by Percent of Total Population
*Based on all places, regardless of total population*

| Place | Population | % |
|---|---|---|
| Lake Success (village) Nassau County | 290 | 9.88 |
| Forest Home (cdp) Tompkins County | 54 | 9.44 |
| University Gardens (cdp) Nassau County | 383 | 9.06 |
| Fishkill (village) Dutchess County | 179 | 8.25 |
| Thomaston (village) Nassau County | 209 | 7.99 |
| Jericho (cdp) Nassau County | 1,078 | 7.95 |
| Searingtown (cdp) Nassau County | 380 | 7.73 |
| North Hills (village) Nassau County | 383 | 7.55 |
| Manorhaven (village) Nassau County | 457 | 6.97 |
| Lansing (village) Tompkins County | 237 | 6.72 |

### Top 10 Places Sorted by Percent of Total Population
*Based on places with total population of 50,000 or more*

| Place | Population | % |
|---|---|---|
| Queens (borough) Queens County | 66,124 | 2.96 |
| North Hempstead (town) Nassau County | 6,015 | 2.66 |
| Oyster Bay (town) Nassau County | 4,977 | 1.70 |
| Greenburgh (town) Westchester County | 1,452 | 1.64 |
| Manhattan (borough) New York County | 21,996 | 1.39 |
| New York (city) | 102,820 | 1.26 |
| Amherst (town) Erie County | 1,493 | 1.22 |
| Clarkstown (town) Rockland County | 1,026 | 1.22 |
| Huntington (town) Suffolk County | 2,122 | 1.04 |
| Smithtown (town) Suffolk County | 918 | 0.78 |

## Asian: Laotian

### Top 10 Places Sorted by Population
*Based on all places, regardless of total population*

| Place | Population | % |
|---|---|---|
| Rochester (city) Monroe County | 668 | 0.32 |
| New York (city) | 664 | 0.01 |
| Union (town) Broome County | 406 | 0.72 |
| Buffalo (city) Erie County | 288 | 0.11 |
| Johnson City (village) Broome County | 278 | 1.83 |
| Henrietta (town) Monroe County | 235 | 0.55 |
| Binghamton (city) Broome County | 211 | 0.45 |
| Queens (borough) Queens County | 210 | 0.01 |
| Manhattan (borough) New York County | 157 | 0.01 |
| Bronx (borough) Bronx County | 148 | 0.01 |

### Top 10 Places Sorted by Percent of Total Population
*Based on all places, regardless of total population*

| Place | Population | % |
|---|---|---|
| Fowlerville (cdp) Livingston County | 5 | 2.20 |
| Johnson City (village) Broome County | 278 | 1.83 |
| Union (town) Broome County | 406 | 0.72 |
| Interlaken (village) Seneca County | 4 | 0.66 |
| Henrietta (town) Monroe County | 235 | 0.55 |
| Smithfield (town) Madison County | 7 | 0.54 |
| Chautauqua (cdp) Chautauqua County | 1 | 0.52 |
| York (town) Livingston County | 16 | 0.47 |
| Binghamton (city) Broome County | 211 | 0.45 |
| Endicott (village) Broome County | 54 | 0.40 |

### Top 10 Places Sorted by Percent of Total Population
*Based on places with total population of 50,000 or more*

| Place | Population | % |
|---|---|---|
| Union (town) Broome County | 406 | 0.72 |
| Rochester (city) Monroe County | 668 | 0.32 |
| Irondequoit (cdp/town) Monroe County | 109 | 0.21 |
| Greece (town) Monroe County | 139 | 0.14 |
| Utica (city) Oneida County | 72 | 0.12 |
| Buffalo (city) Erie County | 288 | 0.11 |
| Cheektowaga (cdp) Erie County | 65 | 0.09 |
| Clay (town) Onondaga County | 52 | 0.09 |
| Cheektowaga (town) Erie County | 65 | 0.07 |
| Syracuse (city) Onondaga County | 89 | 0.06 |

## Asian: Malaysian

### Top 10 Places Sorted by Population
*Based on all places, regardless of total population*

| Place | Population | % |
|---|---|---|
| New York (city) | 3,220 | 0.04 |
| Queens (borough) Queens County | 1,620 | 0.07 |
| Manhattan (borough) New York County | 766 | 0.05 |
| Brooklyn (borough) Kings County | 708 | 0.03 |
| Staten Island (borough) Richmond County | 96 | 0.02 |
| Henrietta (town) Monroe County | 70 | 0.16 |
| Amherst (town) Erie County | 47 | 0.04 |
| North Hempstead (town) Nassau County | 35 | 0.02 |
| Oyster Bay (town) Nassau County | 30 | 0.01 |
| Bronx (borough) Bronx County | 30 | <0.01 |

### Top 10 Places Sorted by Percent of Total Population
*Based on all places, regardless of total population*

| Place | Population | % |
|---|---|---|
| Forest Home (cdp) Tompkins County | 5 | 0.87 |
| Grand View-on-Hudson (village) Rockland County | 1 | 0.35 |
| Portage (town) Livingston County | 3 | 0.34 |
| University at Buffalo (cdp) Erie County | 15 | 0.25 |
| Brocton (village) Chautauqua County | 3 | 0.20 |
| Washington Mills (cdp) Oneida County | 2 | 0.17 |
| Henrietta (town) Monroe County | 70 | 0.16 |
| Breesport (cdp) Chemung County | 1 | 0.16 |
| New Berlin (town) Chenango County | 4 | 0.15 |
| Wainscott (cdp) Suffolk County | 1 | 0.15 |

### Top 10 Places Sorted by Percent of Total Population
*Based on places with total population of 50,000 or more*

| Place | Population | % |
|---|---|---|
| Queens (borough) Queens County | 1,620 | 0.07 |
| Manhattan (borough) New York County | 766 | 0.05 |
| New York (city) | 3,220 | 0.04 |
| Amherst (town) Erie County | 47 | 0.04 |
| Brooklyn (borough) Kings County | 708 | 0.03 |
| Troy (city) Rensselaer County | 14 | 0.03 |
| Staten Island (borough) Richmond County | 96 | 0.02 |
| North Hempstead (town) Nassau County | 35 | 0.02 |
| Cheektowaga (cdp) Erie County | 12 | 0.02 |
| White Plains (city) Westchester County | 11 | 0.02 |

## Asian: Nepalese

### Top 10 Places Sorted by Population
*Based on all places, regardless of total population*

| Place | Population | % |
|---|---|---|
| New York (city) | 6,187 | 0.08 |
| Queens (borough) Queens County | 5,319 | 0.24 |
| Brooklyn (borough) Kings County | 393 | 0.02 |

| Place | Population | % |
|---|---|---|
| Manhattan (borough) New York County | 281 | 0.02 |
| Syracuse (city) Onondaga County | 262 | 0.18 |
| Rochester (city) Monroe County | 165 | 0.08 |
| Buffalo (city) Erie County | 160 | 0.06 |
| Bronx (borough) Bronx County | 159 | 0.01 |
| Albany (city) Albany County | 55 | 0.06 |
| Greenburgh (town) Westchester County | 55 | 0.06 |

### Top 10 Places Sorted by Percent of Total Population
*Based on all places, regardless of total population*

| Place | Population | % |
|---|---|---|
| Windham (cdp) Greene County | 6 | 1.63 |
| Forest Home (cdp) Tompkins County | 3 | 0.52 |
| Merritt Park (cdp) Dutchess County | 6 | 0.48 |
| Windham (town) Greene County | 6 | 0.35 |
| Nelliston (village) Montgomery County | 2 | 0.34 |
| Argyle (village) Washington County | 1 | 0.33 |
| Northeast Ithaca (cdp) Tompkins County | 8 | 0.30 |
| Brewster (village) Putnam County | 7 | 0.29 |
| Elmsford (village) Westchester County | 12 | 0.26 |
| Queens (borough) Queens County | 5,319 | 0.24 |

### Top 10 Places Sorted by Percent of Total Population
*Based on places with total population of 50,000 or more*

| Place | Population | % |
|---|---|---|
| Queens (borough) Queens County | 5,319 | 0.24 |
| Syracuse (city) Onondaga County | 262 | 0.18 |
| New York (city) | 6,187 | 0.08 |
| Rochester (city) Monroe County | 165 | 0.08 |
| Buffalo (city) Erie County | 160 | 0.06 |
| Albany (city) Albany County | 55 | 0.06 |
| Greenburgh (town) Westchester County | 55 | 0.06 |
| Brooklyn (borough) Kings County | 393 | 0.02 |
| Manhattan (borough) New York County | 281 | 0.02 |
| Oyster Bay (town) Nassau County | 49 | 0.02 |

## Asian: Pakistani

### Top 10 Places Sorted by Population
*Based on all places, regardless of total population*

| Place | Population | % |
|---|---|---|
| New York (city) | 46,369 | 0.57 |
| Brooklyn (borough) Kings County | 19,840 | 0.79 |
| Queens (borough) Queens County | 18,084 | 0.81 |
| Hempstead (town) Nassau County | 4,976 | 0.65 |
| Manhattan (borough) New York County | 2,940 | 0.19 |
| Staten Island (borough) Richmond County | 2,777 | 0.59 |
| Bronx (borough) Bronx County | 2,728 | 0.20 |
| Brookhaven (town) Suffolk County | 2,081 | 0.43 |
| Islip (town) Suffolk County | 1,520 | 0.45 |
| Oyster Bay (town) Nassau County | 1,330 | 0.45 |

### Top 10 Places Sorted by Percent of Total Population
*Based on all places, regardless of total population*

| Place | Population | % |
|---|---|---|
| Bellerose Terrace (cdp) Nassau County | 103 | 4.69 |
| South Valley Stream (cdp) Nassau County | 249 | 4.18 |
| North Valley Stream (cdp) Nassau County | 425 | 2.56 |
| Herricks (cdp) Nassau County | 85 | 1.98 |
| Elmont (cdp) Nassau County | 650 | 1.96 |
| Valley Stream (village) Nassau County | 733 | 1.95 |
| East Meadow (cdp) Nassau County | 708 | 1.86 |
| Garden City Park (cdp) Nassau County | 124 | 1.59 |
| Muttontown (village) Nassau County | 50 | 1.43 |
| North Bellmore (cdp) Nassau County | 278 | 1.39 |

### Top 10 Places Sorted by Percent of Total Population
*Based on places with total population of 50,000 or more*

| Place | Population | % |
|---|---|---|
| Colonie (town) Albany County | 736 | 0.90 |
| Queens (borough) Queens County | 18,084 | 0.81 |
| Brooklyn (borough) Kings County | 19,840 | 0.79 |
| Hempstead (town) Nassau County | 4,976 | 0.65 |
| Huntington (town) Suffolk County | 1,264 | 0.62 |
| Staten Island (borough) Richmond County | 2,777 | 0.59 |
| New York (city) | 46,369 | 0.57 |
| Albany (city) Albany County | 483 | 0.49 |
| Amherst (town) Erie County | 592 | 0.48 |
| Levittown (cdp) Nassau County | 239 | 0.46 |

*Please refer to the Explanation of Data in the front of the book for more detailed information.*

## Asian: Sri Lankan

### Top 10 Places Sorted by Population
*Based on all places, regardless of total population*

| Place | Population | % |
|---|---|---|
| New York (city) | 4,369 | 0.05 |
| Staten Island (borough) Richmond County | 1,766 | 0.38 |
| Queens (borough) Queens County | 1,536 | 0.07 |
| Manhattan (borough) New York County | 563 | 0.04 |
| Brooklyn (borough) Kings County | 270 | 0.01 |
| Bronx (borough) Bronx County | 234 | 0.02 |
| Hempstead (town) Nassau County | 201 | 0.03 |
| Amherst (town) Erie County | 130 | 0.11 |
| Brookhaven (town) Suffolk County | 100 | 0.02 |
| New Rochelle (city) Westchester County | 83 | 0.11 |

### Top 10 Places Sorted by Percent of Total Population
*Based on all places, regardless of total population*

| Place | Population | % |
|---|---|---|
| Poquott (village) Suffolk County | 6 | 0.63 |
| Bellerose Terrace (cdp) Nassau County | 10 | 0.45 |
| Watchtower (cdp) Ulster County | 10 | 0.42 |
| Fishers Island (cdp) Suffolk County | 1 | 0.42 |
| Staten Island (borough) Richmond County | 1,766 | 0.38 |
| Forestburgh (town) Sullivan County | 3 | 0.37 |
| South Floral Park (village) Nassau County | 6 | 0.34 |
| Bedford (cdp) Westchester County | 6 | 0.33 |
| Harbor Isle (cdp) Nassau County | 4 | 0.31 |
| Garden City Park (cdp) Nassau County | 22 | 0.28 |

### Top 10 Places Sorted by Percent of Total Population
*Based on places with total population of 50,000 or more*

| Place | Population | % |
|---|---|---|
| Staten Island (borough) Richmond County | 1,766 | 0.38 |
| Amherst (town) Erie County | 130 | 0.11 |
| New Rochelle (city) Westchester County | 83 | 0.11 |
| Queens (borough) Queens County | 1,536 | 0.07 |
| Clarkstown (town) Rockland County | 55 | 0.07 |
| New York (city) | 4,369 | 0.05 |
| Manhattan (borough) New York County | 563 | 0.04 |
| Colonie (town) Albany County | 30 | 0.04 |
| Hempstead (town) Nassau County | 201 | 0.03 |
| North Hempstead (town) Nassau County | 59 | 0.03 |

## Asian: Taiwanese

### Top 10 Places Sorted by Population
*Based on all places, regardless of total population*

| Place | Population | % |
|---|---|---|
| New York (city) | 13,682 | 0.17 |
| Queens (borough) Queens County | 8,962 | 0.40 |
| Manhattan (borough) New York County | 3,318 | 0.21 |
| Brooklyn (borough) Kings County | 1,075 | 0.04 |
| North Hempstead (town) Nassau County | 809 | 0.36 |
| Hempstead (town) Nassau County | 438 | 0.06 |
| Oyster Bay (town) Nassau County | 401 | 0.14 |
| Ithaca (city) Tompkins County | 214 | 0.71 |
| Brookhaven (town) Suffolk County | 213 | 0.04 |
| Amherst (town) Erie County | 202 | 0.17 |

### Top 10 Places Sorted by Percent of Total Population
*Based on all places, regardless of total population*

| Place | Population | % |
|---|---|---|
| Russell Gardens (village) Nassau County | 23 | 2.43 |
| Forest Home (cdp) Tompkins County | 13 | 2.27 |
| Thomaston (village) Nassau County | 47 | 1.80 |
| University Gardens (cdp) Nassau County | 63 | 1.49 |
| East Ithaca (cdp) Tompkins County | 33 | 1.48 |
| North Hills (village) Nassau County | 56 | 1.10 |
| Lansing (village) Tompkins County | 36 | 1.02 |
| Harbor Hills (cdp) Nassau County | 5 | 0.87 |
| Lake Success (village) Nassau County | 25 | 0.85 |
| Saddle Rock (village) Nassau County | 7 | 0.84 |

### Top 10 Places Sorted by Percent of Total Population
*Based on places with total population of 50,000 or more*

| Place | Population | % |
|---|---|---|
| Queens (borough) Queens County | 8,962 | 0.40 |
| North Hempstead (town) Nassau County | 809 | 0.36 |
| Manhattan (borough) New York County | 3,318 | 0.21 |
| New York (city) | 13,682 | 0.17 |

| | Population | % |
|---|---|---|
| Amherst (town) Erie County | 202 | 0.17 |
| Greenburgh (town) Westchester County | 142 | 0.16 |
| Oyster Bay (town) Nassau County | 401 | 0.14 |
| Huntington (town) Suffolk County | 157 | 0.08 |
| Smithtown (town) Suffolk County | 90 | 0.08 |
| White Plains (city) Westchester County | 44 | 0.08 |

## Asian: Thai

### Top 10 Places Sorted by Population
*Based on all places, regardless of total population*

| Place | Population | % |
|---|---|---|
| New York (city) | 7,244 | 0.09 |
| Queens (borough) Queens County | 4,124 | 0.18 |
| Manhattan (borough) New York County | 1,657 | 0.10 |
| Brooklyn (borough) Kings County | 883 | 0.04 |
| Bronx (borough) Bronx County | 414 | 0.03 |
| Hempstead (town) Nassau County | 278 | 0.04 |
| Yonkers (city) Westchester County | 268 | 0.14 |
| Brookhaven (town) Suffolk County | 211 | 0.04 |
| Staten Island (borough) Richmond County | 166 | 0.04 |
| North Hempstead (town) Nassau County | 126 | 0.06 |

### Top 10 Places Sorted by Percent of Total Population
*Based on all places, regardless of total population*

| Place | Population | % |
|---|---|---|
| Forest Home (cdp) Tompkins County | 8 | 1.40 |
| Watchtower (cdp) Ulster County | 20 | 0.84 |
| Greenvale (cdp) Nassau County | 9 | 0.82 |
| Lyon Mountain (cdp) Clinton County | 3 | 0.71 |
| Tribes Hill (cdp) Montgomery County | 7 | 0.70 |
| Quiogue (cdp) Suffolk County | 5 | 0.61 |
| Cooperstown (village) Otsego County | 11 | 0.59 |
| West Nyack (cdp) Rockland County | 18 | 0.52 |
| Middlefield (town) Otsego County | 11 | 0.52 |
| Lansing (village) Tompkins County | 16 | 0.45 |

### Top 10 Places Sorted by Percent of Total Population
*Based on places with total population of 50,000 or more*

| Place | Population | % |
|---|---|---|
| Queens (borough) Queens County | 4,124 | 0.18 |
| Yonkers (city) Westchester County | 268 | 0.14 |
| Clarkstown (town) Rockland County | 121 | 0.14 |
| Mount Vernon (city) Westchester County | 73 | 0.11 |
| Manhattan (borough) New York County | 1,657 | 0.10 |
| New York (city) | 7,244 | 0.09 |
| Greenburgh (town) Westchester County | 77 | 0.09 |
| Utica (city) Oneida County | 50 | 0.08 |
| Levittown (cdp) Nassau County | 40 | 0.08 |
| White Plains (city) Westchester County | 42 | 0.07 |

## Asian: Vietnamese

### Top 10 Places Sorted by Population
*Based on all places, regardless of total population*

| Place | Population | % |
|---|---|---|
| New York (city) | 16,378 | 0.20 |
| Brooklyn (borough) Kings County | 5,041 | 0.20 |
| Queens (borough) Queens County | 4,322 | 0.19 |
| Bronx (borough) Bronx County | 3,526 | 0.25 |
| Manhattan (borough) New York County | 2,919 | 0.18 |
| Syracuse (city) Onondaga County | 1,554 | 1.07 |
| Buffalo (city) Erie County | 1,220 | 0.47 |
| Rochester (city) Monroe County | 1,050 | 0.50 |
| Utica (city) Oneida County | 1,022 | 1.64 |
| Brookhaven (town) Suffolk County | 620 | 0.13 |

### Top 10 Places Sorted by Percent of Total Population
*Based on all places, regardless of total population*

| Place | Population | % |
|---|---|---|
| Byersville (cdp) Livingston County | 2 | 4.26 |
| North Gates (cdp) Monroe County | 183 | 1.92 |
| Utica (city) Oneida County | 1,022 | 1.64 |
| Salt Point (cdp) Dutchess County | 3 | 1.58 |
| Gates (town) Monroe County | 411 | 1.45 |
| Gates (cdp) Monroe County | 71 | 1.45 |
| Websters Crossing (cdp) Livingston County | 1 | 1.45 |
| Galeville (cdp) Onondaga County | 62 | 1.34 |
| Pamelia Center (cdp) Jefferson County | 3 | 1.14 |
| Syracuse (city) Onondaga County | 1,554 | 1.07 |

### Top 10 Places Sorted by Percent of Total Population
*Based on places with total population of 50,000 or more*

| Place | Population | % |
|---|---|---|
| Utica (city) Oneida County | 1,022 | 1.64 |
| Syracuse (city) Onondaga County | 1,554 | 1.07 |
| Rochester (city) Monroe County | 1,050 | 0.50 |
| Greece (town) Monroe County | 473 | 0.49 |
| Buffalo (city) Erie County | 1,220 | 0.47 |
| Clay (town) Onondaga County | 265 | 0.46 |
| Colonie (town) Albany County | 360 | 0.44 |
| Union (town) Broome County | 248 | 0.44 |
| Cheektowaga (cdp) Erie County | 326 | 0.43 |
| Cheektowaga (town) Erie County | 344 | 0.39 |

## Hawaii Native/Pacific Islander

### Top 10 Places Sorted by Population
*Based on all places, regardless of total population*

| Place | Population | % |
|---|---|---|
| New York (city) | 24,098 | 0.29 |
| Queens (borough) Queens County | 7,691 | 0.34 |
| Bronx (borough) Bronx County | 6,213 | 0.45 |
| Brooklyn (borough) Kings County | 5,784 | 0.23 |
| Manhattan (borough) New York County | 3,727 | 0.24 |
| Hempstead (town) Nassau County | 1,001 | 0.13 |
| Staten Island (borough) Richmond County | 683 | 0.15 |
| Yonkers (city) Westchester County | 483 | 0.25 |
| Islip (town) Suffolk County | 471 | 0.14 |
| Rochester (city) Monroe County | 449 | 0.21 |

### Top 10 Places Sorted by Percent of Total Population
*Based on all places, regardless of total population*

| Place | Population | % |
|---|---|---|
| Philadelphia (village) Jefferson County | 25 | 2.00 |
| Fort Drum (cdp) Jefferson County | 226 | 1.74 |
| Quiogue (cdp) Suffolk County | 13 | 1.59 |
| Burke (village) Franklin County | 3 | 1.42 |
| Le Ray (town) Jefferson County | 286 | 1.31 |
| Philadelphia (town) Jefferson County | 25 | 1.28 |
| Herrings (village) Jefferson County | 1 | 1.11 |
| Brewster (village) Putnam County | 24 | 1.00 |
| Speculator (village) Hamilton County | 3 | 0.93 |
| Calcium (cdp) Jefferson County | 32 | 0.92 |

### Top 10 Places Sorted by Percent of Total Population
*Based on places with total population of 50,000 or more*

| Place | Population | % |
|---|---|---|
| Schenectady (city) Schenectady County | 333 | 0.50 |
| Bronx (borough) Bronx County | 6,213 | 0.45 |
| Queens (borough) Queens County | 7,691 | 0.34 |
| White Plains (city) Westchester County | 180 | 0.32 |
| New York (city) | 24,098 | 0.29 |
| Yonkers (city) Westchester County | 483 | 0.25 |
| Manhattan (borough) New York County | 3,727 | 0.24 |
| Brooklyn (borough) Kings County | 5,784 | 0.23 |
| Mount Vernon (city) Westchester County | 156 | 0.23 |
| Utica (city) Oneida County | 137 | 0.22 |

## Hawaii Native/Pacific Islander: Not Hispanic

### Top 10 Places Sorted by Population
*Based on all places, regardless of total population*

| Place | Population | % |
|---|---|---|
| New York (city) | 13,217 | 0.16 |
| Queens (borough) Queens County | 5,685 | 0.25 |
| Brooklyn (borough) Kings County | 3,463 | 0.14 |
| Bronx (borough) Bronx County | 1,854 | 0.13 |
| Manhattan (borough) New York County | 1,776 | 0.11 |
| Hempstead (town) Nassau County | 599 | 0.08 |
| Staten Island (borough) Richmond County | 439 | 0.09 |
| Brookhaven (town) Suffolk County | 306 | 0.06 |
| Rochester (city) Monroe County | 284 | 0.13 |
| Schenectady (city) Schenectady County | 272 | 0.41 |

### Top 10 Places Sorted by Percent of Total Population
*Based on all places, regardless of total population*

| Place | Population | % |
|---|---|---|
| Quiogue (cdp) Suffolk County | 13 | 1.59 |
| Fort Drum (cdp) Jefferson County | 196 | 1.51 |

| Place | Population | % |
|---|---|---|
| **Philadelphia** (village) Jefferson County | 18 | 1.44 |
| **Le Ray** (town) Jefferson County | 244 | 1.12 |
| **Herrings** (village) Jefferson County | 1 | 1.11 |
| **Burke** (village) Franklin County | 2 | 0.95 |
| **Speculator** (village) Hamilton County | 3 | 0.93 |
| **Philadelphia** (town) Jefferson County | 18 | 0.92 |
| **Constableville** (village) Lewis County | 2 | 0.83 |
| **La Fargeville** (cdp) Jefferson County | 5 | 0.82 |

### Top 10 Places Sorted by Percent of Total Population
*Based on places with total population of 50,000 or more*

| Place | Population | % |
|---|---|---|
| **Schenectady** (city) Schenectady County | 272 | 0.41 |
| **Queens** (borough) Queens County | 5,685 | 0.25 |
| **Mount Vernon** (city) Westchester County | 130 | 0.19 |
| **New York** (city) | 13,217 | 0.16 |
| **Albany** (city) Albany County | 158 | 0.16 |
| **Syracuse** (city) Onondaga County | 218 | 0.15 |
| **Utica** (city) Oneida County | 95 | 0.15 |
| **Brooklyn** (borough) Kings County | 3,463 | 0.14 |
| **Bronx** (borough) Bronx County | 1,854 | 0.13 |
| **Rochester** (city) Monroe County | 284 | 0.13 |

## Hawaii Native/Pacific Islander: Hispanic

### Top 10 Places Sorted by Population
*Based on all places, regardless of total population*

| Place | Population | % |
|---|---|---|
| **New York** (city) | 10,881 | 0.13 |
| **Bronx** (borough) Bronx County | 4,359 | 0.31 |
| **Brooklyn** (borough) Kings County | 2,321 | 0.09 |
| **Queens** (borough) Queens County | 2,006 | 0.09 |
| **Manhattan** (borough) New York County | 1,951 | 0.12 |
| **Hempstead** (town) Nassau County | 402 | 0.05 |
| **Yonkers** (city) Westchester County | 272 | 0.05 |
| **Staten Island** (borough) Richmond County | 244 | 0.05 |
| **Islip** (town) Suffolk County | 227 | 0.07 |
| **Rochester** (city) Monroe County | 165 | 0.08 |

### Top 10 Places Sorted by Percent of Total Population
*Based on all places, regardless of total population*

| Place | Population | % |
|---|---|---|
| **Brewster** (village) Putnam County | 23 | 0.96 |
| **Philadelphia** (village) Jefferson County | 7 | 0.56 |
| **Haverstraw** (village) Rockland County | 66 | 0.55 |
| **Aquebogue** (cdp) Suffolk County | 13 | 0.53 |
| **Woodridge** (village) Sullivan County | 4 | 0.47 |
| **Burke** (village) Franklin County | 1 | 0.47 |
| **Philadelphia** (town) Jefferson County | 7 | 0.36 |
| **Tivoli** (village) Dutchess County | 4 | 0.36 |
| **Bronx** (borough) Bronx County | 4,359 | 0.31 |
| **Sleepy Hollow** (village) Westchester County | 31 | 0.31 |

### Top 10 Places Sorted by Percent of Total Population
*Based on places with total population of 50,000 or more*

| Place | Population | % |
|---|---|---|
| **Bronx** (borough) Bronx County | 4,359 | 0.31 |
| **White Plains** (city) Westchester County | 109 | 0.19 |
| **Yonkers** (city) Westchester County | 272 | 0.14 |
| **New York** (city) | 10,881 | 0.13 |
| **Manhattan** (borough) New York County | 1,951 | 0.12 |
| **Brentwood** (cdp) Suffolk County | 75 | 0.12 |
| **Hempstead** (village) Nassau County | 60 | 0.11 |
| **Brooklyn** (borough) Kings County | 2,321 | 0.09 |
| **Queens** (borough) Queens County | 2,006 | 0.09 |
| **Schenectady** (city) Schenectady County | 61 | 0.09 |

## Hawaii Native/Pacific Islander: Fijian

### Top 10 Places Sorted by Population
*Based on all places, regardless of total population*

| Place | Population | % |
|---|---|---|
| **New York** (city) | 213 | <0.01 |
| **Queens** (borough) Queens County | 76 | <0.01 |
| **Manhattan** (borough) New York County | 73 | <0.01 |
| **Brooklyn** (borough) Kings County | 45 | <0.01 |
| **Bronx** (borough) Bronx County | 13 | <0.01 |
| **Brookhaven** (town) Suffolk County | 10 | <0.01 |
| **Hempstead** (town) Nassau County | 10 | <0.01 |
| **Sound Beach** (cdp) Suffolk County | 6 | 0.08 |
| **Woodmere** (cdp) Nassau County | 6 | 0.04 |

| Place | Population | % |
|---|---|---|
| **White Plains** (city) Westchester County | 6 | 0.01 |

### Top 10 Places Sorted by Percent of Total Population
*Based on all places, regardless of total population*

| Place | Population | % |
|---|---|---|
| **Salamanca** (city) Cattaraugus County | 5 | 0.09 |
| **Sound Beach** (cdp) Suffolk County | 6 | 0.08 |
| **Woodmere** (cdp) Nassau County | 6 | 0.04 |
| **Florida** (village) Orange County | 1 | 0.04 |
| **Fairmount** (cdp) Onondaga County | 3 | 0.03 |
| **Pelham** (village) Westchester County | 2 | 0.03 |
| **South Hill** (cdp) Tompkins County | 2 | 0.03 |
| **Westmere** (cdp) Albany County | 2 | 0.03 |
| **Lansing** (village) Tompkins County | 1 | 0.03 |
| **Spencer** (town) Tioga County | 1 | 0.03 |

### Top 10 Places Sorted by Percent of Total Population
*Based on places with total population of 50,000 or more*

| Place | Population | % |
|---|---|---|
| **White Plains** (city) Westchester County | 6 | 0.01 |
| **New York** (city) | 213 | <0.01 |
| **Queens** (borough) Queens County | 76 | <0.01 |
| **Manhattan** (borough) New York County | 73 | <0.01 |
| **Brooklyn** (borough) Kings County | 45 | <0.01 |
| **Bronx** (borough) Bronx County | 13 | <0.01 |
| **Brookhaven** (town) Suffolk County | 10 | <0.01 |
| **Hempstead** (town) Nassau County | 10 | <0.01 |
| **Staten Island** (borough) Richmond County | 6 | <0.01 |
| **Yonkers** (city) Westchester County | 6 | <0.01 |

## Hawaii Native/Pacific Islander: Guamanian or Chamorro

### Top 10 Places Sorted by Population
*Based on all places, regardless of total population*

| Place | Population | % |
|---|---|---|
| **New York** (city) | 1,784 | 0.02 |
| **Brooklyn** (borough) Kings County | 568 | 0.02 |
| **Queens** (borough) Queens County | 483 | 0.02 |
| **Bronx** (borough) Bronx County | 376 | 0.03 |
| **Manhattan** (borough) New York County | 242 | 0.02 |
| **Staten Island** (borough) Richmond County | 115 | 0.02 |
| **Hempstead** (town) Nassau County | 110 | 0.01 |
| **Le Ray** (town) Jefferson County | 88 | 0.40 |
| **Fort Drum** (cdp) Jefferson County | 70 | 0.54 |
| **Southampton** (town) Suffolk County | 55 | 0.10 |

### Top 10 Places Sorted by Percent of Total Population
*Based on all places, regardless of total population*

| Place | Population | % |
|---|---|---|
| **Quiogue** (cdp) Suffolk County | 13 | 1.59 |
| **Burke** (village) Franklin County | 2 | 0.95 |
| **Brewster** (village) Putnam County | 22 | 0.92 |
| **Fort Drum** (cdp) Jefferson County | 70 | 0.54 |
| **Aquebogue** (cdp) Suffolk County | 13 | 0.53 |
| **Port Gibson** (cdp) Ontario County | 2 | 0.44 |
| **Le Ray** (town) Jefferson County | 88 | 0.40 |
| **Southold** (cdp) Suffolk County | 22 | 0.38 |
| **Adams Center** (cdp) Jefferson County | 6 | 0.38 |
| **Pamelia Center** (cdp) Jefferson County | 1 | 0.38 |

### Top 10 Places Sorted by Percent of Total Population
*Based on places with total population of 50,000 or more*

| Place | Population | % |
|---|---|---|
| **Southampton** (town) Suffolk County | 55 | 0.10 |
| **New Rochelle** (city) Westchester County | 43 | 0.06 |
| **Bronx** (borough) Bronx County | 376 | 0.03 |
| **Yonkers** (city) Westchester County | 52 | 0.03 |
| **Utica** (city) Oneida County | 18 | 0.03 |
| **Union** (town) Broome County | 16 | 0.03 |
| **New York** (city) | 1,784 | 0.02 |
| **Brooklyn** (borough) Kings County | 568 | 0.02 |
| **Queens** (borough) Queens County | 483 | 0.02 |
| **Manhattan** (borough) New York County | 242 | 0.02 |

## Hawaii Native/Pacific Islander: Marshallese

### Top 10 Places Sorted by Population
*Based on all places, regardless of total population*

| Place | Population | % |
|---|---|---|
| **New York** (city) | 10 | <0.01 |
| **Le Ray** (town) Jefferson County | 6 | 0.03 |
| **Carthage** (village) Jefferson County | 5 | 0.13 |
| **Wilna** (town) Jefferson County | 5 | 0.08 |
| **Fort Drum** (cdp) Jefferson County | 5 | 0.04 |
| **Philadelphia** (village) Jefferson County | 4 | 0.32 |
| **Philadelphia** (town) Jefferson County | 4 | 0.21 |
| **Manhattan** (borough) New York County | 4 | <0.01 |
| **Bronx** (borough) Bronx County | 3 | <0.01 |
| **Hornell** (city) Steuben County | 2 | 0.02 |

### Top 10 Places Sorted by Percent of Total Population
*Based on all places, regardless of total population*

| Place | Population | % |
|---|---|---|
| **Philadelphia** (village) Jefferson County | 4 | 0.32 |
| **Philadelphia** (town) Jefferson County | 4 | 0.21 |
| **Carthage** (village) Jefferson County | 5 | 0.13 |
| **Wilna** (town) Jefferson County | 5 | 0.08 |
| **Huron** (town) Wayne County | 1 | 0.05 |
| **Fort Drum** (cdp) Jefferson County | 5 | 0.04 |
| **Le Ray** (town) Jefferson County | 6 | 0.03 |
| **Hornell** (city) Steuben County | 2 | 0.02 |
| **Hartland** (town) Niagara County | 1 | 0.02 |
| **Hartsdale** (cdp) Westchester County | 1 | 0.02 |

### Top 10 Places Sorted by Percent of Total Population
*Based on places with total population of 50,000 or more*

| Place | Population | % |
|---|---|---|
| **New York** (city) | 10 | <0.01 |
| **Manhattan** (borough) New York County | 4 | <0.01 |
| **Bronx** (borough) Bronx County | 3 | <0.01 |
| **Brooklyn** (borough) Kings County | 2 | <0.01 |
| **Amherst** (town) Erie County | 1 | <0.01 |
| **Greenburgh** (town) Westchester County | 1 | <0.01 |
| **Hempstead** (town) Nassau County | 1 | <0.01 |
| **Islip** (town) Suffolk County | 1 | <0.01 |
| **Staten Island** (borough) Richmond County | 1 | <0.01 |
| **Syracuse** (city) Onondaga County | 1 | <0.01 |

## Hawaii Native/Pacific Islander: Native Hawaiian

### Top 10 Places Sorted by Population
*Based on all places, regardless of total population*

| Place | Population | % |
|---|---|---|
| **New York** (city) | 2,448 | 0.03 |
| **Bronx** (borough) Bronx County | 669 | 0.05 |
| **Manhattan** (borough) New York County | 608 | 0.04 |
| **Brooklyn** (borough) Kings County | 564 | 0.02 |
| **Queens** (borough) Queens County | 486 | 0.02 |
| **Staten Island** (borough) Richmond County | 121 | 0.03 |
| **Hempstead** (town) Nassau County | 114 | 0.02 |
| **Brookhaven** (town) Suffolk County | 100 | 0.02 |
| **Rochester** (city) Monroe County | 77 | 0.04 |
| **Buffalo** (city) Erie County | 75 | 0.03 |

### Top 10 Places Sorted by Percent of Total Population
*Based on all places, regardless of total population*

| Place | Population | % |
|---|---|---|
| **Speculator** (village) Hamilton County | 3 | 0.93 |
| **Felts Mills** (cdp) Jefferson County | 3 | 0.81 |
| **Hemlock** (cdp) Livingston County | 4 | 0.72 |
| **Waterville** (village) Oneida County | 8 | 0.51 |
| **Philadelphia** (village) Jefferson County | 6 | 0.48 |
| **Ischua** (town) Cattaraugus County | 4 | 0.47 |
| **Tivoli** (village) Dutchess County | 5 | 0.45 |
| **Calcium** (cdp) Jefferson County | 15 | 0.43 |
| **Plandome Heights** (village) Nassau County | 4 | 0.40 |
| **Fort Drum** (cdp) Jefferson County | 49 | 0.38 |

### Top 10 Places Sorted by Percent of Total Population
*Based on places with total population of 50,000 or more*

| Place | Population | % |
|---|---|---|
| **Bronx** (borough) Bronx County | 669 | 0.05 |

| Place | Population | % |
|---|---|---|
| **Schenectady** (city) Schenectady County | 33 | 0.05 |
| **Southampton** (town) Suffolk County | 27 | 0.05 |
| **Troy** (city) Rensselaer County | 24 | 0.05 |
| **Manhattan** (borough) New York County | 608 | 0.04 |
| **Rochester** (city) Monroe County | 77 | 0.04 |
| **Syracuse** (city) Onondaga County | 65 | 0.04 |
| **Albany** (city) Albany County | 38 | 0.04 |
| **New York** (city) | 2,448 | 0.03 |
| **Staten Island** (borough) Richmond County | 121 | 0.03 |

## Hawaii Native/Pacific Islander: Samoan

### Top 10 Places Sorted by Population
*Based on all places, regardless of total population*

| Place | Population | % |
|---|---|---|
| **New York** (city) | 764 | 0.01 |
| **Brooklyn** (borough) Kings County | 216 | 0.01 |
| **Manhattan** (borough) New York County | 183 | 0.01 |
| **Queens** (borough) Queens County | 179 | 0.01 |
| **Bronx** (borough) Bronx County | 160 | 0.01 |
| **Rochester** (city) Monroe County | 63 | 0.03 |
| **Buffalo** (city) Erie County | 63 | 0.02 |
| **Le Ray** (town) Jefferson County | 53 | 0.24 |
| **Fort Drum** (cdp) Jefferson County | 49 | 0.38 |
| **Hempstead** (town) Nassau County | 36 | <0.01 |

### Top 10 Places Sorted by Percent of Total Population
*Based on all places, regardless of total population*

| Place | Population | % |
|---|---|---|
| **Philadelphia** (village) Jefferson County | 12 | 0.96 |
| **Constableville** (village) Lewis County | 2 | 0.83 |
| **La Fargeville** (cdp) Jefferson County | 4 | 0.66 |
| **Philadelphia** (town) Jefferson County | 12 | 0.62 |
| **Staatsburg** (cdp) Dutchess County | 2 | 0.53 |
| **Fremont** (town) Sullivan County | 6 | 0.43 |
| **Fort Drum** (cdp) Jefferson County | 49 | 0.38 |
| **Caroline** (town) Tompkins County | 12 | 0.37 |
| **Sagaponack** (village) Suffolk County | 1 | 0.32 |
| **Worcester** (cdp) Otsego County | 3 | 0.27 |

### Top 10 Places Sorted by Percent of Total Population
*Based on places with total population of 50,000 or more*

| Place | Population | % |
|---|---|---|
| **Rochester** (city) Monroe County | 63 | 0.03 |
| **Utica** (city) Oneida County | 18 | 0.03 |
| **Buffalo** (city) Erie County | 63 | 0.02 |
| **Albany** (city) Albany County | 15 | 0.02 |
| **Schenectady** (city) Schenectady County | 10 | 0.02 |
| **New York** (city) | 764 | 0.01 |
| **Brooklyn** (borough) Kings County | 216 | 0.01 |
| **Manhattan** (borough) New York County | 183 | 0.01 |
| **Queens** (borough) Queens County | 179 | 0.01 |
| **Bronx** (borough) Bronx County | 160 | 0.01 |

## Hawaii Native/Pacific Islander: Tongan

### Top 10 Places Sorted by Population
*Based on all places, regardless of total population*

| Place | Population | % |
|---|---|---|
| **New York** (city) | 66 | <0.01 |
| **Manhattan** (borough) New York County | 33 | <0.01 |
| **Queens** (borough) Queens County | 14 | <0.01 |
| **Brooklyn** (borough) Kings County | 10 | <0.01 |
| **Bronx** (borough) Bronx County | 7 | <0.01 |
| **Chateaugay** (village) Franklin County | 6 | 0.72 |
| **Chateaugay** (town) Franklin County | 6 | 0.28 |
| **Colonie** (town) Albany County | 5 | 0.01 |
| **Stone Ridge** (cdp) Ulster County | 4 | 0.34 |
| **Cambria** (town) Niagara County | 4 | 0.07 |

### Top 10 Places Sorted by Percent of Total Population
*Based on all places, regardless of total population*

| Place | Population | % |
|---|---|---|
| **Chateaugay** (village) Franklin County | 6 | 0.72 |
| **Staatsburg** (cdp) Dutchess County | 2 | 0.53 |
| **Elizabethtown** (cdp) Essex County | 3 | 0.40 |
| **Stone Ridge** (cdp) Ulster County | 4 | 0.34 |

| Place | Population | % |
|---|---|---|
| **Chateaugay** (town) Franklin County | 6 | 0.28 |
| **Elizabethtown** (town) Essex County | 3 | 0.26 |
| **Fort Plain** (village) Montgomery County | 2 | 0.09 |
| **Franklin** (town) Franklin County | 1 | 0.09 |
| **Washington Mills** (cdp) Oneida County | 1 | 0.08 |
| **Cambria** (town) Niagara County | 4 | 0.07 |

### Top 10 Places Sorted by Percent of Total Population
*Based on places with total population of 50,000 or more*

| Place | Population | % |
|---|---|---|
| **Colonie** (town) Albany County | 5 | 0.01 |
| **New York** (city) | 66 | <0.01 |
| **Manhattan** (borough) New York County | 33 | <0.01 |
| **Queens** (borough) Queens County | 14 | <0.01 |
| **Brooklyn** (borough) Kings County | 10 | <0.01 |
| **Bronx** (borough) Bronx County | 7 | <0.01 |
| **Buffalo** (city) Erie County | 3 | <0.01 |
| **Rochester** (city) Monroe County | 3 | <0.01 |
| **Brentwood** (cdp) Suffolk County | 2 | <0.01 |
| **Brookhaven** (town) Suffolk County | 2 | <0.01 |

## White

### Top 10 Places Sorted by Population
*Based on all places, regardless of total population*

| Place | Population | % |
|---|---|---|
| **New York** (city) | 3,797,402 | 46.45 |
| **Brooklyn** (borough) Kings County | 1,120,592 | 44.74 |
| **Manhattan** (borough) New York County | 956,864 | 60.34 |
| **Queens** (borough) Queens County | 941,608 | 42.21 |
| **Hempstead** (town) Nassau County | 532,650 | 70.11 |
| **Bronx** (borough) Bronx County | 427,659 | 30.88 |
| **Brookhaven** (town) Suffolk County | 419,725 | 86.36 |
| **Staten Island** (borough) Richmond County | 350,679 | 74.81 |
| **Islip** (town) Suffolk County | 254,235 | 75.77 |
| **Oyster Bay** (town) Nassau County | 252,713 | 86.19 |

### Top 10 Places Sorted by Percent of Total Population
*Based on all places, regardless of total population*

| Place | Population | % |
|---|---|---|
| **Putnam** (town) Washington County | 609 | 100.00 |
| **Odessa** (village) Schuyler County | 591 | 100.00 |
| **DeKalb Junction** (cdp) St. Lawrence County | 519 | 100.00 |
| **Cold Brook** (village) Herkimer County | 329 | 100.00 |
| **Pinckney** (town) Lewis County | 329 | 100.00 |
| **West Union** (town) Steuben County | 312 | 100.00 |
| **Madison** (village) Madison County | 305 | 100.00 |
| **Gainesville** (village) Wyoming County | 229 | 100.00 |
| **Osceola** (town) Lewis County | 229 | 100.00 |
| **Pierrepont Manor** (cdp) Jefferson County | 228 | 100.00 |

### Top 10 Places Sorted by Percent of Total Population
*Based on places with total population of 50,000 or more*

| Place | Population | % |
|---|---|---|
| **Hamburg** (town) Erie County | 55,749 | 97.92 |
| **Tonawanda** (town) Erie County | 69,534 | 94.52 |
| **Tonawanda** (cdp) Erie County | 54,936 | 94.48 |
| **Smithtown** (town) Suffolk County | 111,000 | 94.23 |
| **Clay** (town) Onondaga County | 53,514 | 91.94 |
| **Union** (town) Broome County | 51,487 | 91.38 |
| **Levittown** (cdp) Nassau County | 46,970 | 90.53 |
| **Greece** (town) Monroe County | 86,829 | 90.36 |
| **Cheektowaga** (town) Erie County | 78,958 | 89.50 |
| **Irondequoit** (cdp/town) Monroe County | 45,826 | 88.65 |

## White: Not Hispanic

### Top 10 Places Sorted by Population
*Based on all places, regardless of total population*

| Place | Population | % |
|---|---|---|
| **New York** (city) | 2,804,430 | 34.30 |
| **Brooklyn** (borough) Kings County | 917,717 | 36.64 |
| **Manhattan** (borough) New York County | 785,299 | 49.52 |
| **Queens** (borough) Queens County | 638,051 | 28.60 |
| **Hempstead** (town) Nassau County | 460,994 | 60.68 |
| **Brookhaven** (town) Suffolk County | 379,158 | 78.01 |
| **Staten Island** (borough) Richmond County | 305,118 | 65.09 |

| Place | Population | % |
|---|---|---|
| **Oyster Bay** (town) Nassau County | 236,944 | 80.81 |
| **Islip** (town) Suffolk County | 198,326 | 59.11 |
| **Huntington** (town) Suffolk County | 160,914 | 79.17 |

### Top 10 Places Sorted by Percent of Total Population
*Based on all places, regardless of total population*

| Place | Population | % |
|---|---|---|
| **Osceola** (town) Lewis County | 229 | 100.00 |
| **Birdsall** (town) Allegany County | 221 | 100.00 |
| **Oxbow** (cdp) Jefferson County | 108 | 100.00 |
| **Morehouse** (town) Hamilton County | 86 | 100.00 |
| **Woodsville** (cdp) Livingston County | 80 | 100.00 |
| **Linwood** (cdp) Livingston County | 74 | 100.00 |
| **Tuscarora** (cdp) Livingston County | 74 | 100.00 |
| **Red House** (town) Cattaraugus County | 38 | 100.00 |
| **Saltaire** (village) Suffolk County | 37 | 100.00 |
| **Thousand Island Park** (cdp) Jefferson County | 31 | 100.00 |

### Top 10 Places Sorted by Percent of Total Population
*Based on places with total population of 50,000 or more*

| Place | Population | % |
|---|---|---|
| **Hamburg** (town) Erie County | 54,789 | 96.23 |
| **Tonawanda** (cdp) Erie County | 53,890 | 92.68 |
| **Tonawanda** (town) Erie County | 68,098 | 92.57 |
| **Clay** (town) Onondaga County | 52,515 | 90.22 |
| **Smithtown** (town) Suffolk County | 105,870 | 89.87 |
| **Union** (town) Broome County | 50,317 | 89.30 |
| **Cheektowaga** (town) Erie County | 77,687 | 88.05 |
| **Greece** (town) Monroe County | 83,902 | 87.31 |
| **Cheektowaga** (cdp) Erie County | 65,180 | 86.70 |
| **Colonie** (town) Albany County | 69,290 | 84.92 |

## White: Hispanic

### Top 10 Places Sorted by Population
*Based on all places, regardless of total population*

| Place | Population | % |
|---|---|---|
| **New York** (city) | 992,972 | 12.15 |
| **Queens** (borough) Queens County | 303,557 | 13.61 |
| **Bronx** (borough) Bronx County | 269,414 | 19.45 |
| **Brooklyn** (borough) Kings County | 202,875 | 8.10 |
| **Manhattan** (borough) New York County | 171,565 | 10.82 |
| **Hempstead** (town) Nassau County | 71,656 | 9.43 |
| **Islip** (town) Suffolk County | 55,909 | 16.66 |
| **Staten Island** (borough) Richmond County | 45,561 | 9.72 |
| **Brookhaven** (town) Suffolk County | 40,567 | 8.35 |
| **Yonkers** (city) Westchester County | 31,778 | 16.22 |

### Top 10 Places Sorted by Percent of Total Population
*Based on all places, regardless of total population*

| Place | Population | % |
|---|---|---|
| **Brewster** (village) Putnam County | 993 | 41.55 |
| **Brentwood** (cdp) Suffolk County | 23,013 | 37.94 |
| **North Bay Shore** (cdp) Suffolk County | 6,358 | 33.56 |
| **Haverstraw** (village) Rockland County | 3,914 | 32.86 |
| **Port Chester** (village) Westchester County | 9,507 | 32.82 |
| **Central Islip** (cdp) Suffolk County | 9,372 | 27.20 |
| **Springs** (cdp) Suffolk County | 1,608 | 24.39 |
| **Sleepy Hollow** (village) Westchester County | 2,406 | 24.38 |
| **East Hampton North** (cdp) Suffolk County | 999 | 24.12 |
| **Rye** (town) Westchester County | 11,021 | 24.00 |

### Top 10 Places Sorted by Percent of Total Population
*Based on places with total population of 50,000 or more*

| Place | Population | % |
|---|---|---|
| **Brentwood** (cdp) Suffolk County | 23,013 | 37.94 |
| **Bronx** (borough) Bronx County | 269,414 | 19.45 |
| **New Rochelle** (city) Westchester County | 14,422 | 18.71 |
| **Hempstead** (village) Nassau County | 9,773 | 18.13 |
| **Islip** (town) Suffolk County | 55,909 | 16.66 |
| **White Plains** (city) Westchester County | 9,400 | 16.53 |
| **Yonkers** (city) Westchester County | 31,778 | 16.22 |
| **Queens** (borough) Queens County | 303,557 | 13.61 |
| **Southampton** (town) Suffolk County | 6,955 | 12.25 |
| **New York** (city) | 992,972 | 12.15 |

# Climate

Climate

# New York State Physical Features and Climate Narrative

PHYSICAL FEATURES. New York State contains 49,576 square miles, inclusive of 1,637 square miles of inland water, but exclusive of the boundary-water areas of Long Island Sound, New York Harbor, Lake Ontario, and Lake Erie. The major portion of the State lies generally between latitudes 42° and 45° N. and between longitudes 73° 30' and 79° 45' W. However, in the extreme southeast, a triangular portion extends southward to about latitude 40° 30' N., while Long Island lies eastward to about longitude 72° W.

The principal highland regions of the State are the Adirondacks in the northeast and the Appalachian Plateau (Southern Plateau) in the south. A minor highland region occurs in southeastern New York where the Hudson River has cut a valley between the Palisades on the west, near the New Jersey border, and the Taconic Mountains on the east, along the Connecticut and Massachusetts border. Just west of the Adirondacks and the upper Black River Valley in Lewis County is another minor highland known as Tug Hill. Much of the eastern border of the State consists of a long, narrow lowland region which is occupied by Lake Champlain, Lake George, and the middle and lower portions of the Hudson Valley.

Approximately 40 percent of New York State has an elevation of more than 1,000 feet above sea level. In northwestern Essex County are a number of peaks with an elevation of between 4,000 to 5,000 feet. The highest point, Mount Marcy, reaches a height of 5,344 feet above sea level. The Appalachian Plateau merges variously into the Great Lakes Plain of western New York with gradual- to steep-sloping terrain. This Plateau is penetrated by the valleys of the Finger Lakes which extend southward from the Great Lakes Plain. Other prominent lakes plus innumerable smaller lakes and ponds dot the landscape, with more than 1,500 in the Adirondack region alone.

GENERAL CLIMATE. The climate of New York State is broadly representative of the humid continental type which prevails in the Northeastern United States, but its diversity is not usually encountered in an area of comparable size. The geographical position of the State and the usual course of air masses, governed by the large-scale patterns of atmospheric circulation, provide general climatic controls. Differences in latitude, character of the topography, and proximity to large bodies of water have pronounced effects on the climate.

Lengthy periods of either abnormally cold or warm weather result from the movement of great high pressure (anticyclonic) systems into and through the Eastern United States. Cold winter temperatures prevail over New York whenever Arctic air masses, under high barometric pressure, flow southward from central Canada or from Hudson Bay. High pressure systems often move just off the Atlantic coast, become more or less stagnant for several days, and then a persistent air flow from the southwest or south affects the State. This circulation brings the very warm, often humid weather of the summer season and the mild, more pleasant temperatures during the fall, winter, and spring seasons.

TEMPERATURE. Many atmospheric and physiographic controls on the climate result in a considerable variation of temperature conditions over New York State. The average annual mean temperature ranges from about 40°F. in the Adirondacks to near 55°F. in the New York City area. The winters are long and cold in the Plateau Divisions of the State. Winter temperatures are moderated considerably in the Great Lakes Plain of western New York. The moderating influence of Lakes Erie and Ontario is comparable to that produced by the Atlantic Ocean in the southern portion of the Hudson Valley.

The summer climate is cool in the Adirondacks, Catskills, and higher elevations of the Southern Plateau. The New York City area and lower portions of the Hudson Valley have rather warm summers by comparison, with some periods of high, uncomfortable humidity. The remainder of New York State enjoys pleasantly warm summers, marred by only occasional, brief intervals of sultry conditions. Summer daytime temperatures usually range from the upper 70s to mid-80s over much of the State. The moderating effect of Lakes Erie and Ontario on temperatures assumes practical importance during the spring and fall seasons. The lake waters warm slowly in the spring, the effect of which is to reduce the warming of the atmosphere over adjacent land areas. In the fall season, the lake waters cool more slowly than the land areas and thus serve as a heat source.

PRECIPITATION. Moisture for precipitation in New York State is transported primarily from the Gulf of Mexico and Atlantic Ocean through circulation patterns and storm systems of the atmosphere. Distribution of precipitation within the State is greatly influenced by topography and proximity to the Great Lakes or Atlantic Ocean. Average annual amounts in excess of 50 inches occur in the western Adirondacks, Tug Hill area, and the Catskills, while slightly less than that amount is noted in the higher elevations of the Western Plateau southeast of Lake Erie. Areas of least rainfall, with average accumulations of about 30 inches, occur near Lake Ontario in the extreme western counties, in the lower half of the Genesee River Valley, and in the vicinity of Lake Champlain.

New York State has a fairly uniform distribution of precipitation during the year. There are no distinctly dry or wet seasons which are regularly repeated on an annual basis. Minimum precipitation occurs in the winter season. Maximum amounts are noted in the summer season throughout the State except along the Great Lakes where slight peaks of similar magnitude occur in both the spring and fall seasons.

SNOWFALL. The climate of New York State is marked by abundant snowfall. With the exception of the Coastal Division, the State receives an average seasonal amount of 40 inches or more. The average snowfall is greater than 70 inches over some 60 percent of New York's area. The moderating influence of the Atlantic Ocean reduces the snow accumulation to 25 to 35 inches in the New York City area and on Long Island. About one-third of the winter season precipitation in the Coastal Division occurs from storms which also yield at least one inch of snow. The great bulk of the winter precipitation in upstate New York comes as snow.

A durable snow cover generally begins to develop in the Adirondacks and northern lowlands by late November and remains on the ground until various times in April, depending upon late winter snowfall and early spring temperatures. The Southern Plateau, Great Lakes Plain in southern portions of western upstate New York, and the Hudson Valley experience a continuous snow cover from about mid-December to mid-March, with maximum depths usually occurring in February. Bare ground may occur briefly in the lower elevations of these regions during some winters. From late December or early January through February, the Atlantic coastal region of the State experiences alternating periods of measurable snow cover and bare ground.

FLOODS. Although major floods are relatively infrequent, the greatest potential and frequency for floods occur in the early spring when substantial rains combine with rapid snowmelting to produce a heavy runoff. Damaging floods are caused at other times of the year by prolonged periods of heavy rainfall.

WINDS AND STORMS. The prevailing wind is generally from the west in New York State. A southwest component becomes evident in winds during the warmer months while a northwest component is characteristic of the colder one-half of the year. Thunderstorms occur on an average of about 30 days in a year throughout the State. Destructive winds and lightning strikes in local areas are common with the more vigorous warm-season thunderstorms. Locally, hail occurs with more severe thunderstorms. Tornadoes are not common. About 3 or 4 of these storms strike limited, localized areas of New York State in most years. Tornadoes occur generally between late May and late August. Storms of freezing rain occur on one or more occasions during the winter season and often affect a wide area of the State in any one incident. Such storms are usually limited to a thin but dangerous coating of ice on exposed surfaces. Hurricanes and tropical storms periodically cause serious and heavy losses in the vicinity of Long Island and southeastern upstate New York. The greatest storm hazard in terms of area affected is heavy snow. Coastal northeaster storms occur with some frequency in most winters. Blizzard conditions of heavy snow, high winds, and rapidly falling temperature occur occasionally, but are much less characteristic of New York's climate than in the plains of Midwestern United States.

OTHER CLIMATIC ELEMENTS. The climate of the State features much cloudy weather during the months of November, December, and January in upstate New York. From June through September, however, about 60 to 70 percent of the possible sunshine hours is received. In the Atlantic coastal region, the sunshine hours increases from 50 percent of possible in the winter to about 65 percent of possible in the summer. The occurrence of heavy dense fog is variable over the State. The valleys and ridges of the Southern Plateau are most subject to periods of fog, with occurrences averaging about 50 days in a year. In the Great Lakes Plain and northern valleys, the frequency decreases to only 10 to 20 days annually. In those portions of the State with greater maritime influence, the frequency of dense fog in a year ranges from about 35 days on the south shore of Long Island to 25 days in the Hudson Valley.

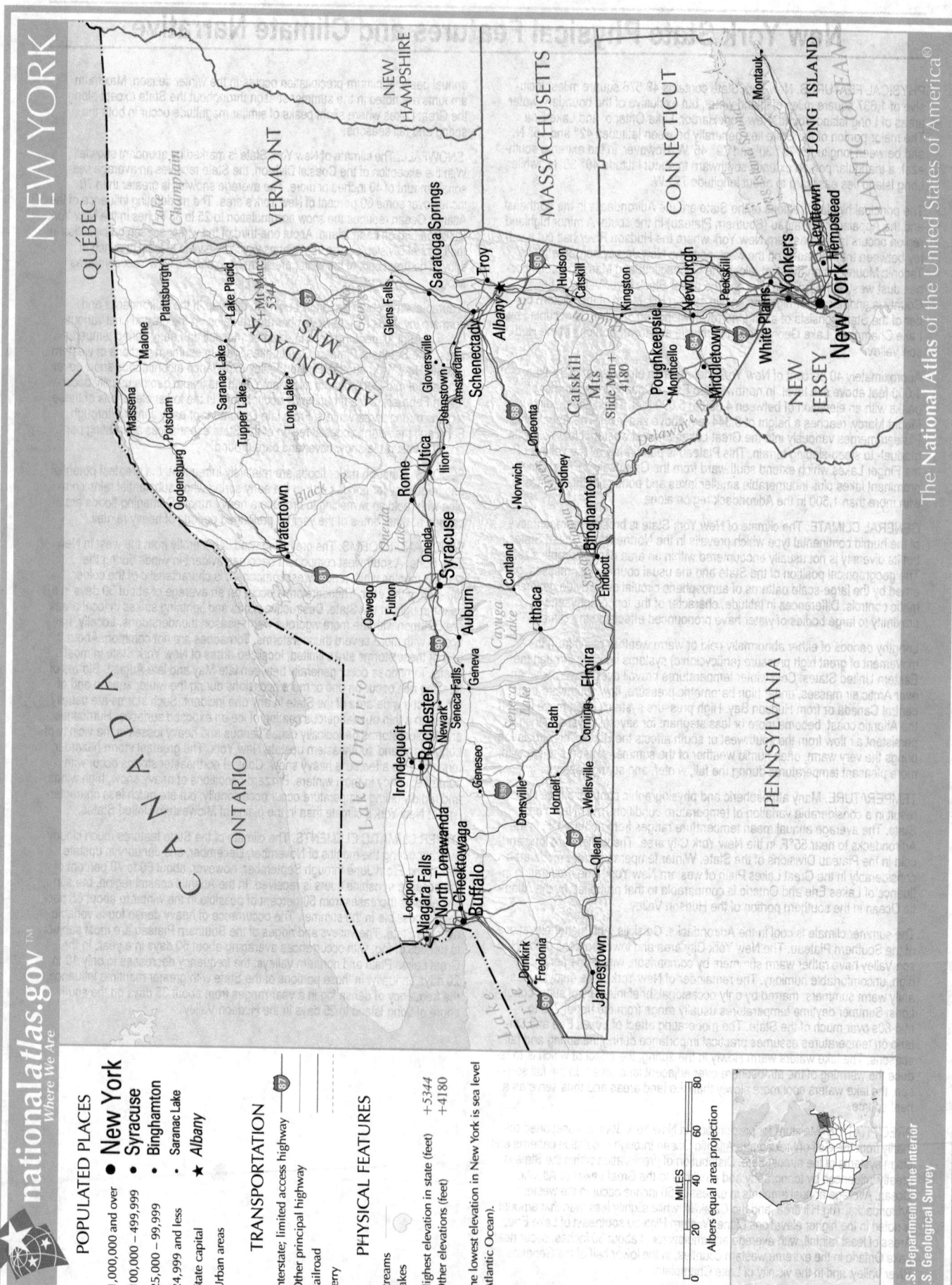

Elevation in Feet
10000 - 20320
9500 - 9999
9000 - 9499
8500 - 8999
8000 - 8499
7500 - 7999
7000 - 7499
6500 - 6999
6000 - 6499
5500 - 5999
5000 - 5499
4500 - 4999
4000 - 4499
3500 - 3999
3000 - 3499
2500 - 2999
2000 - 2499
1500 - 1999
1000 - 1499
500 - 999
250 - 499
1 - 249
-282 - 0
Water

44° 14' 27" North
69° 47' 46" West
79° 11' 56" West
46° 23' 25" North
80° 49' 45" West
41° 44' 33" North
39° 47' 20" North
72° 01' 07" West

Montpelier
Concord
Boston
Providence
Hartford
Albany
New York

Lambert Azimuthal Equal-Area
Projection

National Atlas of the United States

http://nationalatlas.gov
02-Dec-10 01:29PM

Miles    25    50    75

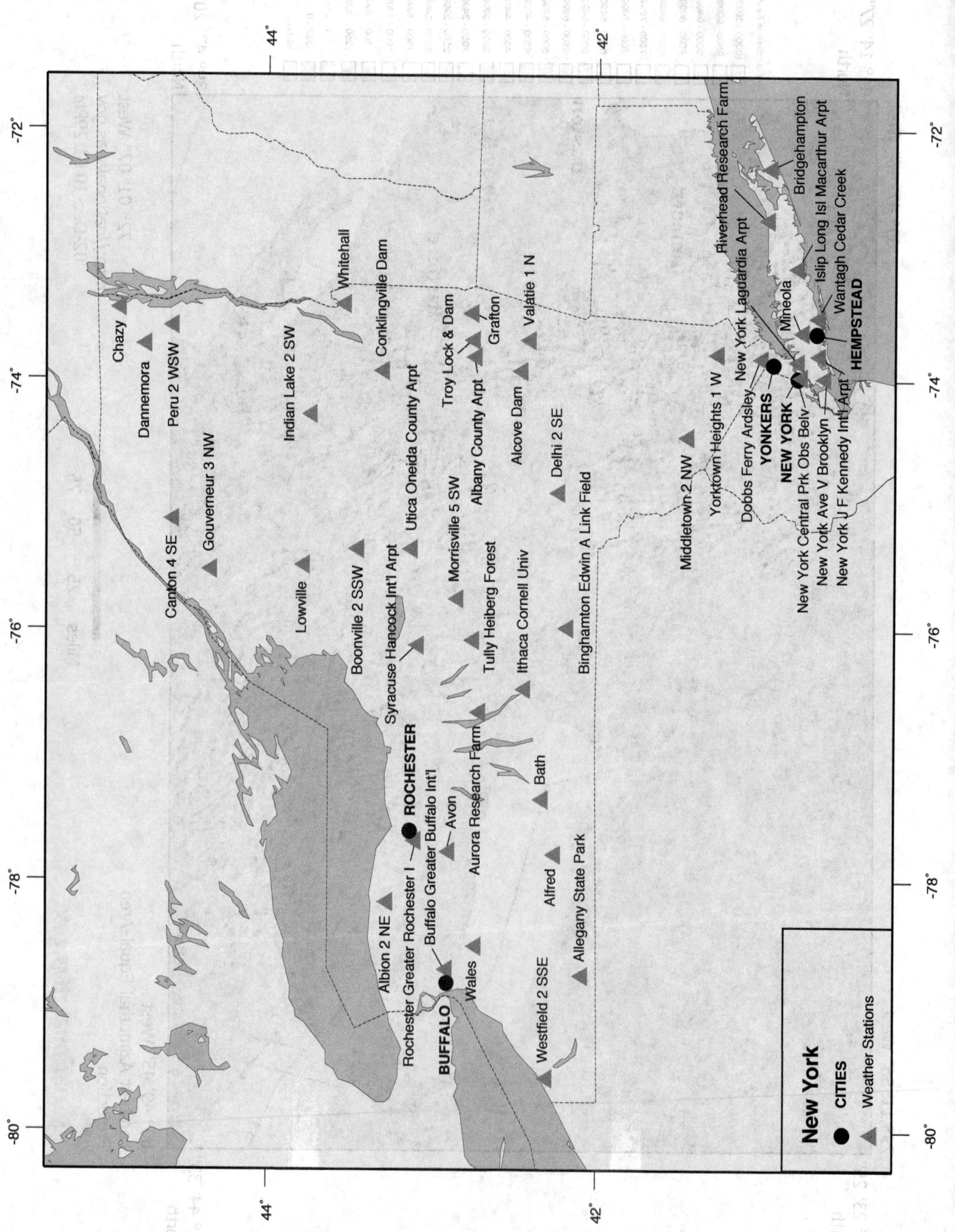

New York

CITIES

Weather Stations

# New York Weather Stations by County

| County | Station Name |
|---|---|
| Albany | Albany County Arpt |
| | Alcove Dam |
| Allegany | Alfred |
| Broome | Binghamton Edwin A Link Field |
| Cattaraugus | Allegany State Park |
| Cayuga | Aurora Research Farm |
| Chautauqua | Westfield 2 SSE |
| Clinton | Chazy |
| | Dannemora |
| | Peru 2 WSW |
| Columbia | Valatie 1 N |
| Cortland | Tully Heiberg Forest |
| Delaware | Delhi 2 SE |
| Erie | Buffalo Greater Buffalo Int'l |
| | Wales |
| Hamilton | Indian Lake 2 SW |
| Kings | New York Ave V Brooklyn |
| Lewis | Lowville |
| Livingston | Avon |
| Madison | Morrisville 5 SW |
| Monroe | Rochester Intl Arpt |
| Nassau | Mineola |
| | Wantagh Cedar Creek |
| New York | New York Central Park Observ |
| Oneida | Boonville 2 SSW |
| | Utica Oneida County Arpt |
| Onondaga | Syracuse Hancock Int'l Arpt |
| Orange | Middletown 2 NW |
| Orleans | Albion 2 NE |
| Queens | New York J F Kennedy Int'l Arpt |
| | New York Laguardia Arpt |
| Rensselaer | Grafton |
| | Troy Lock and Dam |
| Saratoga | Conklingville Dam |
| St. Lawrence | Canton 4 SE |
| | Gouverneur 3 NW |
| Steuben | Bath |

| County | Station Name |
|---|---|
| Suffolk | Bridgehampton |
| | Islip-Macarthur Arpt |
| | Riverhead Research Farm |
| Tompkins | Ithaca Cornell Univ |
| Washington | Whitehall |
| Westchester | Dobbs Ferry Ardsley |
| | Yorktown Heights 1 W |

# New York Weather Stations by City

| City | Station Name | Miles |
|------|-------------|-------|
| Albany | Albany County Arpt | 6.2 |
| | Alcove Dam | 15.4 |
| | Grafton | 18.3 |
| | Troy Lock and Dam | 8.1 |
| | Valatie 1 N | 16.5 |
| Amherst | Buffalo Greater Buffalo Int'l | 4.5 |
| | Wales | 21.1 |
| Babylon | Islip-Macarthur Arpt | 14.7 |
| | Mineola | 13.2 |
| | New York J F Kennedy Int'l Arpt | 23.2 |
| | Wantagh Cedar Creek | 8.3 |
| Brentwood | Islip-Macarthur Arpt | 7.5 |
| | Mineola | 19.8 |
| | Wantagh Cedar Creek | 16.2 |
| Bronx | Essex Fells Serv Bldg, NJ | 21.0 |
| | Newark Intl Arpt, NJ | 18.3 |
| | Dobbs Ferry Ardsley | 10.7 |
| | Mineola | 16.1 |
| | New York Ave V Brooklyn | 18.1 |
| | New York Central Park Observ | 6.4 |
| | New York J F Kennedy Int'l Arpt | 14.5 |
| | New York Laguardia Arpt | 4.6 |
| | Wantagh Cedar Creek | 24.3 |
| Brookhaven | Bridgeport Sikorsky Memorial, CT | 24.2 |
| | Islip-Macarthur Arpt | 7.6 |
| | Riverhead Research Farm | 16.3 |
| Brooklyn | Canoe Brook, NJ | 21.8 |
| | Cranford, NJ | 18.1 |
| | Essex Fells Serv Bldg, NJ | 21.4 |
| | Newark Intl Arpt, NJ | 12.8 |
| | Plainfield, NJ | 23.6 |
| | Mineola | 18.6 |
| | New York Ave V Brooklyn | 3.8 |
| | New York Central Park Observ | 9.2 |
| | New York J F Kennedy Int'l Arpt | 8.1 |
| | New York Laguardia Arpt | 9.9 |
| | Wantagh Cedar Creek | 23.8 |
| Buffalo | Buffalo Greater Buffalo Int'l | 6.0 |
| | Wales | 20.1 |
| Cheektowaga | Buffalo Greater Buffalo Int'l | 2.1 |
| | Wales | 16.1 |
| Clarkstown | Stamford 5 N, CT | 22.6 |
| | Charlotteburg Reservoir, NJ | 24.3 |
| | Dobbs Ferry Ardsley | 11.7 |
| | New York Central Park Observ | 23.7 |
| | New York Laguardia Arpt | 24.3 |
| | Yorktown Heights 1 W | 13.6 |
| Clay | Syracuse Hancock Int'l Arpt | 5.2 |
| Colonie | Albany County Arpt | 1.5 |
| | Alcove Dam | 19.7 |
| | Grafton | 16.7 |
| | Troy Lock and Dam | 5.4 |
| | Valatie 1 N | 21.2 |

| City | Station Name | Miles |
|------|-------------|-------|
| Greece | Albion 2 NE | 24.6 |
| | Avon | 22.3 |
| | Rochester Intl Arpt | 8.2 |
| Greenburgh | Stamford 5 N, CT | 16.0 |
| | Dobbs Ferry Ardsley | 2.1 |
| | Mineola | 23.5 |
| | New York Central Park Observ | 18.4 |
| | New York Laguardia Arpt | 17.3 |
| | Yorktown Heights 1 W | 16.4 |
| Hamburg | Buffalo Greater Buffalo Int'l | 14.0 |
| | Wales | 16.8 |
| Hempstead | Dobbs Ferry Ardsley | 24.8 |
| | Mineola | 3.6 |
| | New York Ave V Brooklyn | 19.9 |
| | New York Central Park Observ | 19.6 |
| | New York J F Kennedy Int'l Arpt | 9.7 |
| | New York Laguardia Arpt | 15.6 |
| | Wantagh Cedar Creek | 6.6 |
| Huntington | Stamford 5 N, CT | 20.7 |
| | Islip-Macarthur Arpt | 14.9 |
| | Mineola | 15.1 |
| | Wantagh Cedar Creek | 15.4 |
| Islip | Islip-Macarthur Arpt | 5.2 |
| | Mineola | 22.1 |
| | Wantagh Cedar Creek | 17.7 |
| Levittown | Islip-Macarthur Arpt | 22.0 |
| | Mineola | 5.5 |
| | New York Central Park Observ | 24.1 |
| | New York J F Kennedy Int'l Arpt | 15.9 |
| | New York Laguardia Arpt | 19.8 |
| | Wantagh Cedar Creek | 5.2 |
| Manhattan | Canoe Brook, NJ | 20.3 |
| | Cranford, NJ | 19.7 |
| | Essex Fells Serv Bldg, NJ | 17.1 |
| | Newark Intl Arpt, NJ | 12.2 |
| | Dobbs Ferry Ardsley | 16.7 |
| | Mineola | 18.5 |
| | New York Ave V Brooklyn | 12.5 |
| | New York Central Park Observ | 0.2 |
| | New York J F Kennedy Int'l Arpt | 12.5 |
| | New York Laguardia Arpt | 4.3 |
| Mount Vernon | Stamford 5 N, CT | 20.4 |
| | Essex Fells Serv Bldg, NJ | 24.2 |
| | Newark Intl Arpt, NJ | 22.8 |
| | Dobbs Ferry Ardsley | 6.0 |
| | Mineola | 16.7 |
| | New York Ave V Brooklyn | 23.0 |
| | New York Central Park Observ | 11.4 |
| | New York J F Kennedy Int'l Arpt | 18.2 |
| | New York Laguardia Arpt | 9.3 |
| | Yorktown Heights 1 W | 24.5 |
| New Rochelle | Stamford 5 N, CT | 18.2 |
| | Dobbs Ferry Ardsley | 6.0 |
| | Mineola | 15.7 |

| City | Station Name | Miles |
|---|---|---|
| New Rochelle (cont.) | New York Ave V Brooklyn | 24.5 |
| | New York Central Park Observ | 13.5 |
| | New York J F Kennedy Int'l Arpt | 18.8 |
| | New York Laguardia Arpt | 10.8 |
| | Wantagh Cedar Creek | 24.0 |
| | Yorktown Heights 1 W | 23.9 |
| New York | Canoe Brook, NJ | 22.5 |
| | Cranford, NJ | 20.5 |
| | Essex Fells Serv Bldg, NJ | 20.4 |
| | Newark Intl Arpt, NJ | 13.7 |
| | Dobbs Ferry Ardsley | 19.6 |
| | Mineola | 15.9 |
| | New York Ave V Brooklyn | 9.2 |
| | New York Central Park Observ | 4.7 |
| | New York J F Kennedy Int'l Arpt | 8.2 |
| | New York Laguardia Arpt | 4.5 |
| | Wantagh Cedar Creek | 22.7 |
| Niagara Falls | Buffalo Greater Buffalo Int'l | 18.2 |
| North Hempstead | Stamford 5 N, CT | 24.1 |
| | Dobbs Ferry Ardsley | 17.6 |
| | Mineola | 4.1 |
| | New York Ave V Brooklyn | 20.7 |
| | New York Central Park Observ | 15.7 |
| | New York J F Kennedy Int'l Arpt | 11.3 |
| | New York Laguardia Arpt | 11.4 |
| | Wantagh Cedar Creek | 12.5 |
| Oyster Bay | Stamford 5 N, CT | 24.8 |
| | Dobbs Ferry Ardsley | 24.1 |
| | Islip-Macarthur Arpt | 20.8 |
| | Mineola | 6.5 |
| | New York Central Park Observ | 24.6 |
| | New York J F Kennedy Int'l Arpt | 17.6 |
| | New York Laguardia Arpt | 20.3 |
| | Wantagh Cedar Creek | 7.6 |
| Queens | Cranford, NJ | 24.9 |
| | Essex Fells Serv Bldg, NJ | 24.8 |
| | Newark Intl Arpt, NJ | 18.3 |
| | Dobbs Ferry Ardsley | 19.2 |
| | Mineola | 11.4 |
| | New York Ave V Brooklyn | 11.5 |
| | New York Central Park Observ | 8.2 |
| | New York J F Kennedy Int'l Arpt | 5.3 |
| | New York Laguardia Arpt | 5.0 |
| | Wantagh Cedar Creek | 18.2 |
| Ramapo | Charlotteburg Reservoir, NJ | 19.7 |
| | Essex Fells Serv Bldg, NJ | 22.7 |
| | Dobbs Ferry Ardsley | 15.1 |
| | New York Central Park Observ | 24.1 |
| | Yorktown Heights 1 W | 17.4 |
| Rochester | Avon | 18.5 |
| | Rochester Intl Arpt | 4.9 |
| Schenectady | Albany County Arpt | 7.5 |
| | Alcove Dam | 23.3 |
| | Grafton | 23.5 |
| | Troy Lock and Dam | 13.0 |
| Smithtown | Bridgeport Sikorsky Memorial, CT | 22.7 |

| City | Station Name | Miles |
|---|---|---|
| Smithtown (cont.) | Stamford 5 N, CT | 24.9 |
| | Islip-Macarthur Arpt | 8.0 |
| | Mineola | 22.7 |
| | Wantagh Cedar Creek | 20.8 |
| Southampton | Bridgehampton | 11.7 |
| | Riverhead Research Farm | 12.1 |
| Staten Island | Canoe Brook, NJ | 15.8 |
| | Cranford, NJ | 9.6 |
| | Essex Fells Serv Bldg, NJ | 18.6 |
| | Newark Intl Arpt, NJ | 9.2 |
| | New Brunswick 3 SE, NJ | 17.7 |
| | Plainfield, NJ | 13.8 |
| | New York Ave V Brooklyn | 8.1 |
| | New York Central Park Observ | 16.1 |
| | New York J F Kennedy Int'l Arpt | 18.2 |
| | New York Laguardia Arpt | 18.9 |
| Syracuse | Syracuse Hancock Int'l Arpt | 5.5 |
| | Tully Heiberg Forest | 19.3 |
| Tonawanda | Buffalo Greater Buffalo Int'l | 7.0 |
| | Wales | 23.4 |
| Union | Binghamton Edwin A Link Field | 6.2 |
| | Montrose, PA | 19.3 |
| Utica | Utica Oneida County Arpt | 8.5 |
| White Plains | Stamford 5 N, CT | 12.8 |
| | Dobbs Ferry Ardsley | 4.0 |
| | Mineola | 21.6 |
| | New York Central Park Observ | 19.8 |
| | New York Laguardia Arpt | 17.9 |
| | Yorktown Heights 1 W | 16.7 |
| Yonkers | Stamford 5 N, CT | 20.9 |
| | Essex Fells Serv Bldg, NJ | 22.6 |
| | Newark Intl Arpt, NJ | 22.2 |
| | Dobbs Ferry Ardsley | 4.8 |
| | Mineola | 19.5 |
| | New York Ave V Brooklyn | 24.0 |
| | New York Central Park Observ | 11.7 |
| | New York J F Kennedy Int'l Arpt | 20.2 |
| | New York Laguardia Arpt | 10.7 |
| | Yorktown Heights 1 W | 23.1 |

*Note: Miles is the distance between the geographic center of the city and the weather station.*

# New York Weather Stations by Elevation

| Feet | Station Name |
|---|---|
| 1,898 | Tully Heiberg Forest |
| 1,770 | Alfred |
| 1,660 | Indian Lake 2 SW |
| 1,600 | Binghamton Edwin A Link Field |
| 1,580 | Boonville 2 SSW |
| 1,560 | Grafton |
| 1,500 | Allegany State Park |
| 1,439 | Delhi 2 SE |
| 1,339 | Dannemora |
| 1,299 | Morrisville 5 SW |
| 1,120 | Bath |
| 1,089 | Wales |
| 959 | Ithaca Cornell Univ |
| 859 | Lowville |
| 830 | Aurora Research Farm |
| 808 | Conklingville Dam |
| 711 | Utica Oneida County Arpt |
| 707 | Westfield 2 SSE |
| 705 | Buffalo Greater Buffalo Int'l |
| 700 | Middletown 2 NW |
| 669 | Yorktown Heights 1 W |
| 606 | Alcove Dam |
| 600 | Rochester Intl Arpt |
| 544 | Avon |
| 509 | Peru 2 WSW |
| 439 | Albion 2 NE |
| 439 | Canton 4 SE |
| 419 | Gouverneur 3 NW |
| 410 | Syracuse Hancock Int'l Arpt |
| 299 | Valatie 1 N |
| 274 | Albany County Arpt |
| 200 | Dobbs Ferry Ardsley |
| 169 | Chazy |
| 131 | New York Central Park Observ |
| 119 | Whitehall |
| 100 | Riverhead Research Farm |
| 96 | Mineola |
| 83 | Islip-Macarthur Arpt |
| 60 | Bridgehampton |
| 23 | Troy Lock and Dam |
| 20 | New York Ave V Brooklyn |
| 16 | New York J F Kennedy Int'l Arpt |
| 11 | New York Laguardia Arpt |
| 9 | Wantagh Cedar Creek |

*See User Guide for station inclusion criteria.*

# Albany County Airport

Albany is located on the west bank of the Hudson River some 150 miles north of New York City, and 8 miles south of the confluence of the Mohawk and Hudson Rivers. The river-front portion of the city is only a few feet above sea level, and there is a tidal effect upstream to Troy. Eleven miles west of Albany the Helderberg hill range rises to 1,800 feet. Between it and the Hudson River the valley floor is gently rolling, ranging some 200 to 500 feet above sea level. East of the city there is more rugged terrain 5 or 6 miles wide with elevations of 300 to 600 feet. Farther to the east the terrain rises more sharply. It reaches a north-south range of hills 12 miles east of Albany with elevations ranging to 2,000 feet.

The climate at Albany is primarily continental in character, but is subjected to some modification by the Atlantic Ocean. The moderating effect on temperatures is more pronounced during the warmer months than in winter when outbursts of cold air sweep down from Canada. In the warmer seasons, temperatures rise rapidly in the daytime. However, temperatures also fall rapidly after sunset so that the nights are relatively cool. Occasionally there are extended periods of oppressive heat up to a week or more in duration.

Winters are usually cold and sometimes fairly severe. Maximum temperatures during the colder winters are often below freezing and nighttime lows are frequently below 10 degrees. Sub-zero readings occur about 12 times a year. Snowfall throughout the area is quite variable and snow flurries are quite frequent during the winter. Precipitation is sufficient to serve the economy of the region in most years, and only occasionally do periods of drought exist. Most of the rainfall in the summer is from thunderstorms. Tornadoes are quite rare and hail is not usually of any consequence.

Wind velocities are moderate. The north-south Hudson River Valley has a marked effect on the lighter winds and in the warm months, average wind direction is usually southerly. Destructive winds rarely occur.

The area enjoys one of the highest percentages of sunshine in the entire state. Seldom does the area experience long periods of cloudy days and long periods of smog are rare.

Based on the 1951-1980 period, the average first occurrence of 32 degrees Fahrenheit in the fall is September 29 and the average last occurrence in the spring is May 7.

## Albany County Airport  *Albany County*    Elevation: 274 ft.    Latitude: 42° 45' N    Longitude: 73° 48' W

|  | JAN | FEB | MAR | APR | MAY | JUN | JUL | AUG | SEP | OCT | NOV | DEC | YEAR |
|---|---|---|---|---|---|---|---|---|---|---|---|---|---|
| Mean Maximum Temp. (°F) | 31.1 | 34.9 | 44.3 | 58.3 | 69.6 | 77.9 | 82.3 | 80.5 | 72.4 | 60.0 | 48.2 | 36.1 | 58.0 |
| Mean Temp. (°F) | 22.8 | 25.9 | 34.8 | 47.6 | 58.2 | 67.0 | 71.6 | 70.0 | 61.8 | 49.8 | 39.8 | 28.4 | 48.2 |
| Mean Minimum Temp. (°F) | 14.5 | 16.8 | 25.2 | 36.9 | 46.8 | 56.1 | 60.9 | 59.5 | 51.2 | 39.4 | 31.3 | 20.8 | 38.3 |
| Extreme Maximum Temp. (°F) | 71 | 68 | 89 | 92 | 94 | 96 | 99 | 97 | 92 | 86 | 81 | 71 | 99 |
| Extreme Minimum Temp. (°F) | -23 | -18 | -6 | 13 | 28 | 36 | 44 | 34 | 28 | 18 | 6 | -20 | -23 |
| Days Maximum Temp. ≥ 90°F | 0 | 0 | 0 | 0 | 0 | 2 | 4 | 2 | 0 | 0 | 0 | 0 | 8 |
| Days Maximum Temp. ≤ 32°F | 17 | 11 | 4 | 0 | 0 | 0 | 0 | 0 | 0 | 0 | 1 | 10 | 43 |
| Days Minimum Temp. ≤ 32°F | 29 | 26 | 24 | 9 | 1 | 0 | 0 | 0 | 0 | 7 | 18 | 27 | 141 |
| Days Minimum Temp. ≤ 0°F | 5 | 2 | 1 | 0 | 0 | 0 | 0 | 0 | 0 | 0 | 0 | 1 | 9 |
| Heating Degree Days (base 65°F) | 1,301 | 1,099 | 929 | 519 | 231 | 51 | 6 | 19 | 138 | 469 | 749 | 1,127 | 6,638 |
| Cooling Degree Days (base 65°F) | 0 | 0 | 1 | 4 | 27 | 117 | 217 | 183 | 50 | 4 | 0 | 0 | 603 |
| Mean Precipitation (in.) | 2.54 | 2.09 | 3.26 | 3.22 | 3.58 | 3.80 | 4.11 | 3.62 | 3.26 | 3.52 | 3.27 | 2.87 | 39.14 |
| Maximum Precipitation (in.)* | 6.4 | 5.0 | 5.9 | 7.9 | 9.0 | 7.4 | 7.0 | 7.3 | 7.9 | 8.8 | 8.1 | 6.7 | 47.2 |
| Minimum Precipitation (in.)* | 0.4 | 0.2 | 0.3 | 1.1 | 1.0 | 0.6 | 0.5 | 0.7 | 0.4 | 0.2 | 0.6 | 0.6 | 21.5 |
| Extreme Maximum Daily Precip. (in.) | 1.78 | 1.60 | 2.02 | 2.26 | 2.16 | 3.30 | 3.49 | 2.78 | 5.60 | 2.82 | 2.21 | 2.79 | 5.60 |
| Days With ≥ 0.1" Precipitation | 6 | 5 | 7 | 7 | 8 | 8 | 7 | 7 | 6 | 6 | 7 | 7 | 81 |
| Days With ≥ 0.5" Precipitation | 2 | 1 | 2 | 2 | 3 | 3 | 3 | 2 | 2 | 2 | 2 | 2 | 26 |
| Days With ≥ 1.0" Precipitation | 0 | 0 | 1 | 1 | 0 | 1 | 1 | 1 | 1 | 1 | 1 | 0 | 8 |
| Mean Snowfall (in.) | 17.7 | 11.5 | 11.4 | 2.3 | 0.1 | trace | trace | 0.0 | trace | 0.3 | 3.2 | 13.7 | 60.2 |
| Maximum Snowfall (in.)* | 48 | 35 | 35 | 18 | 2 | 0 | 0 | 0 | 0 | 7 | 25 | 58 | 107 |
| Maximum 24-hr. Snowfall (in.)* | 13 | 17 | 22 | 17 | 2 | 0 | 0 | 0 | 0 | 7 | 22 | 14 | 22 |
| Maximum Snow Depth (in.) | 24 | 20 | 28 | 13 | trace | trace | trace | 0 | trace | 2 | 10 | 16 | 28 |
| Days With ≥ 1.0" Snow Depth | 19 | 16 | 9 | 1 | 0 | 0 | 0 | 0 | 0 | 0 | 2 | 12 | 59 |
| Thunderstorm Days* | < 1 | < 1 | 1 | 1 | 3 | 5 | 6 | 5 | 2 | 1 | < 1 | < 1 | 24 |
| Foggy Days* | 10 | 9 | 11 | 9 | 12 | 13 | 14 | 17 | 17 | 15 | 13 | 12 | 152 |
| Predominant Sky Cover* | OVR | OVR | OVR | OVR | OVR | OVR | OVR | OVR | OVR | OVR | OVR | OVR | OVR |
| Mean Relative Humidity 7am (%)* | 77 | 77 | 76 | 72 | 74 | 77 | 80 | 85 | 88 | 86 | 82 | 80 | 80 |
| Mean Relative Humidity 4pm (%)* | 64 | 59 | 54 | 48 | 50 | 53 | 53 | 55 | 57 | 56 | 64 | 67 | 57 |
| Mean Dewpoint (°F)* | 14 | 15 | 23 | 33 | 45 | 55 | 60 | 59 | 52 | 41 | 31 | 20 | 38 |
| Prevailing Wind Direction* | WNW | WNW | WNW | WNW | S | S | S | S | S | S | WNW | WNW | S |
| Prevailing Wind Speed (mph)* | 15 | 15 | 15 | 15 | 10 | 9 | 8 | 8 | 9 | 9 | 14 | 14 | 12 |
| Maximum Wind Gust (mph)* | 62 | 67 | 61 | 58 | 67 | 59 | 77 | 62 | 64 | 60 | 67 | 63 | 77 |

Note: (*) Period of record is 1946-1995

# Binghamton Edwin A. Link Field

Binghamton, in south central New York lies in a comparatively narrow valley at the confluence of the Susquehanna and Chenango Rivers. Within a radius of 5 miles, hills rise to elevations of 1,400-1,600 feet above mean sea level. In the spring, melting snow, sometimes supplemented by rainfall, occasionally causes flooding in the city and along the streams.

The climate of Binghamton is representative of the humid area of the north-eastern United States and is primarily continental in type. The area, being adjacent to the so-called St. Lawrence Valley storm track, and also subject to cold air masses approaching from the west and north, has a variable climate, characterized by frequent and rapid changes. Furthermore, diurnal and seasonal changes assist in the production of an invigorating climate. As a rule, the temperature rises rapidly to moderate daytime levels with readings of 90 degrees or above only a few days in any month summer nights provide favorable sleeping conditions.

Winters are usually cold, but not commonly severe. Highest daytime temperatures average in the high 20s to low 30s, while the lowest nighttime readings average from the mid-teens to low 20s. Ordinarily a few sub-zero readings may be expected in January and February, with a lesser number in November, December, and March. The transitional seasons, spring and autumn, are the most variable of the year.

Most of the precipitation in the Binghamton area derives from moisture laden air transported from the Gulf of Mexico and cyclonic systems moving northward along the Atlantic coast. The annual rainfall is rather evenly distributed over the year. However, the greatest average monthly amounts occur during the growing season, April through September. As a rule, rainfall is ample for good crop growth and comes mostly in the form of thunderstorms. Annual snowfall is around 50 inches in Binghamton and above 85 inches at Edwin A. Link Field, some 10 miles to the NNW, and about 700 feet higher in elevation. Most of the snow falls during the normal winter months. However, heavy snows can occur as early as November and as late as April. Being adjacent to the track of storms that move through the St. Lawrence Valley, and being under the influence of winds that sweep across Lakes Erie and Ontario to the interior of the state, the area is subject to much cloudiness and winter snow flurries.

For the most part, the winds at Binghamton have northerly and westerly components. Tornadoes, although rare, have struck in the Binghamton area.

Based on the 1951-1980 period, the growing season averages 150 to 160 days. Usually the last spring frost occurs during early May, and the first frost in autumn during early October.

**Binghamton Edwin A. Link Field** *Broome County*   Elevation: 1,600 ft.   Latitude: 42° 12' N   Longitude: 75° 59' W

| | JAN | FEB | MAR | APR | MAY | JUN | JUL | AUG | SEP | OCT | NOV | DEC | YEAR |
|---|---|---|---|---|---|---|---|---|---|---|---|---|---|
| Mean Maximum Temp. (°F) | 29.4 | 32.5 | 41.3 | 54.6 | 66.0 | 74.2 | 78.3 | 77.0 | 69.1 | 57.2 | 45.4 | 33.8 | 54.9 |
| Mean Temp. (°F) | 22.6 | 25.0 | 33.0 | 45.3 | 56.2 | 64.7 | 69.0 | 67.8 | 59.9 | 48.7 | 38.5 | 27.5 | 46.5 |
| Mean Minimum Temp. (°F) | 15.8 | 17.4 | 24.6 | 36.0 | 46.2 | 55.1 | 59.7 | 58.4 | 50.8 | 40.2 | 31.5 | 21.2 | 38.1 |
| Extreme Maximum Temp. (°F) | 63 | 63 | 82 | 89 | 89 | 92 | 98 | 95 | 91 | 82 | 77 | 65 | 98 |
| Extreme Minimum Temp. (°F) | -15 | -10 | -7 | 9 | 28 | 33 | 44 | 38 | 27 | 19 | 8 | -18 | -18 |
| Days Maximum Temp. ≥ 90°F | 0 | 0 | 0 | 0 | 0 | 0 | 1 | 1 | 0 | 0 | 0 | 0 | 2 |
| Days Maximum Temp. ≤ 32°F | 19 | 15 | 7 | 0 | 0 | 0 | 0 | 0 | 0 | 0 | 3 | 14 | 58 |
| Days Minimum Temp. ≤ 32°F | 29 | 26 | 24 | 11 | 1 | 0 | 0 | 0 | 0 | 6 | 18 | 27 | 142 |
| Days Minimum Temp. ≤ 0°F | 3 | 1 | 0 | 0 | 0 | 0 | 0 | 0 | 0 | 0 | 0 | 1 | 5 |
| Heating Degree Days (base 65°F) | 1,307 | 1,124 | 987 | 588 | 290 | 85 | 20 | 35 | 180 | 500 | 790 | 1,154 | 7,060 |
| Cooling Degree Days (base 65°F) | 0 | 0 | 1 | 4 | 22 | 82 | 152 | 128 | 35 | 2 | 0 | 0 | 426 |
| Mean Precipitation (in.) | 2.38 | 2.29 | 3.09 | 3.53 | 3.53 | 4.33 | 3.67 | 3.37 | 3.55 | 3.30 | 3.29 | 2.81 | 39.14 |
| Maximum Precipitation (in.)* | 6.4 | 4.4 | 6.0 | 8.6 | 6.5 | 9.5 | 7.4 | 7.5 | 9.7 | 9.4 | 7.5 | 6.1 | 48.0 |
| Minimum Precipitation (in.)* | 0.8 | 0.4 | 0.7 | 1.0 | 0.8 | 1.0 | 0.8 | 0.6 | 0.6 | 0.3 | 1.0 | 0.9 | 29.9 |
| Extreme Maximum Daily Precip. (in.) | 1.64 | 1.80 | 1.83 | 2.86 | 2.91 | 4.05 | 1.70 | 2.73 | 3.50 | 2.94 | 2.35 | 2.66 | 4.05 |
| Days With ≥ 0.1" Precipitation | 6 | 6 | 7 | 8 | 8 | 8 | 7 | 7 | 7 | 6 | 7 | 7 | 84 |
| Days With ≥ 0.5" Precipitation | 1 | 1 | 2 | 2 | 2 | 3 | 3 | 2 | 2 | 2 | 2 | 2 | 24 |
| Days With ≥ 1.0" Precipitation | 0 | 0 | 0 | 1 | 1 | 1 | 1 | 1 | 1 | 1 | 1 | 0 | 8 |
| Mean Snowfall (in.) | 21.7 | 15.9 | 15.5 | 4.3 | 0.1 | trace | 0.0 | trace | trace | 1.1 | 7.0 | 17.2 | 82.8 |
| Maximum Snowfall (in.)* | 44 | 44 | 38 | 23 | 3 | 0 | 0 | 0 | trace | 12 | 29 | 60 | 138 |
| Maximum 24-hr. Snowfall (in.)* | 18 | 21 | 19 | 12 | 3 | 0 | 0 | 0 | trace | 7 | 11 | 14 | 21 |
| Maximum Snow Depth (in.)* | 32 | 19 | 35 | 9 | 1 | trace | 0 | trace | trace | 3 | 13 | 15 | 35 |
| Days With ≥ 1.0" Snow Depth | 23 | 20 | 13 | 2 | 0 | 0 | 0 | 0 | 0 | 0 | 5 | 16 | 79 |
| Thunderstorm Days* | < 1 | < 1 | 1 | 2 | 4 | 6 | 7 | 5 | 3 | 1 | < 1 | < 1 | 29 |
| Foggy Days* | 11 | 10 | 13 | 12 | 14 | 15 | 16 | 19 | 17 | 15 | 14 | 13 | 169 |
| Predominant Sky Cover* | OVR | OVR | OVR | OVR | OVR | OVR | OVR | OVR | OVR | OVR | OVR | OVR | OVR |
| Mean Relative Humidity 7am (%)* | 80 | 79 | 79 | 76 | 78 | 83 | 85 | 89 | 90 | 85 | 82 | 82 | 82 |
| Mean Relative Humidity 4pm (%)* | 69 | 65 | 60 | 54 | 54 | 57 | 57 | 59 | 62 | 60 | 68 | 72 | 61 |
| Mean Dewpoint (°F)* | 15 | 16 | 23 | 32 | 44 | 54 | 59 | 58 | 51 | 40 | 31 | 20 | 37 |
| Prevailing Wind Direction* | WNW | NW | NW | NW | NW | SW | SW | SW | SW | S | SW | WNW | NW |
| Prevailing Wind Speed (mph)* | 14 | 14 | 14 | 13 | 12 | 9 | 8 | 8 | 9 | 9 | 10 | 14 | 12 |
| Maximum Wind Gust (mph)* | 61 | 56 | 58 | 64 | 54 | 60 | 74 | 63 | 48 | 51 | 58 | 54 | 74 |

*Note: (*) Period of record is 1948-1995*

# Buffalo Int'l Airport

The country surrounding Buffalo is comparatively low and level to the west. To the east and south the land is gently rolling, rising to pronounced hills within 12 to 18 miles, and to 1,000 feet above the level of Lake Erie about 35 miles south-southeast of the city. A steep slope of 50 to 100 feet lies east-west one and a half miles to the north. The eastern end of Lake Erie is nine miles to the west-southwest, while Lake Ontario lies 25 miles to the north, the two being connected by the Niagara River, which flows north-northwestward from the end of Lake Erie.

Buffalo is located near the mean position of the polar front. Its weather is varied and changeable, characteristic of the latitude. Wide seasonal swings of temperature from hot to cold are tempered appreciably by the proximity of Lakes Erie and Ontario. Lake Erie lies to the southwest, the direction of the prevailing wind. Wind flow throughout the year is somewhat higher due to this exposure. The vigorous interplay of warm and cold air masses during the winter and early spring months causes one or more windstorms. Precipitation is moderate and fairly evenly divided throughout the twelve months.

The spring season is more cloudy and cooler than points not affected by the cold lake. Spring growth of vegetation is retarded, protecting it from late spring frosts. With heavy winter ice accumulations in the lake, typical spring conditions are delayed until late May or early June.

Summer comes suddenly in mid-June. Lake breezes temper the extreme heat of the summer season. Temperatures of 90 degrees and above are infrequent. There is more summer sunshine here than in any other section of the state. Due to the stabilizing effects of Lake Erie, thunderstorms are relatively infrequent. Most of them are caused by frontal action. To the north and south of the city thunderstorms occur more often.

Autumn has long, dry periods and is frost free usually until mid-October. Cloudiness increases in November, continuing mostly cloudy throughout the winter and early spring. Snow flurries off the lake begin in mid-November or early December. Outbreaks of Arctic air in December and throughout the winter months produce locally heavy snowfalls from the lake. At the same time, temperatures of well below zero over Canada and the midwest are raised 10 to 30 degrees in crossing the lakes. Only on rare occasions do polar air masses drop southward from eastern Hudson Bay across Lake Ontario without appreciable warming.

**Buffalo Int'l Airport** *Erie County*    Elevation: 705 ft.    Latitude: 42° 56' N    Longitude: 78° 44' W

| | JAN | FEB | MAR | APR | MAY | JUN | JUL | AUG | SEP | OCT | NOV | DEC | YEAR |
|---|---|---|---|---|---|---|---|---|---|---|---|---|---|
| Mean Maximum Temp. (°F) | 31.8 | 33.6 | 42.1 | 55.2 | 66.7 | 75.5 | 80.1 | 78.7 | 71.4 | 59.3 | 47.8 | 36.5 | 56.6 |
| Mean Temp. (°F) | 25.3 | 26.5 | 34.0 | 46.0 | 57.1 | 66.4 | 71.3 | 69.9 | 62.5 | 51.1 | 41.0 | 30.3 | 48.5 |
| Mean Minimum Temp. (°F) | 18.8 | 19.3 | 25.9 | 36.9 | 47.5 | 57.2 | 62.4 | 61.0 | 53.5 | 42.9 | 34.2 | 24.1 | 40.3 |
| Extreme Maximum Temp. (°F) | 68 | 71 | 79 | 94 | 91 | 96 | 97 | 96 | 92 | 86 | 73 | 74 | 97 |
| Extreme Minimum Temp. (°F) | -16 | -6 | -7 | 12 | 31 | 38 | 46 | 38 | 32 | 25 | 11 | -10 | -16 |
| Days Maximum Temp. ≥ 90°F | 0 | 0 | 0 | 0 | 0 | 1 | 1 | 1 | 0 | 0 | 0 | 0 | 3 |
| Days Maximum Temp. ≤ 32°F | 16 | 14 | 7 | 1 | 0 | 0 | 0 | 0 | 0 | 0 | 2 | 11 | 51 |
| Days Minimum Temp. ≤ 32°F | 27 | 25 | 23 | 9 | 0 | 0 | 0 | 0 | 0 | 3 | 13 | 25 | 125 |
| Days Minimum Temp. ≤ 0°F | 2 | 1 | 0 | 0 | 0 | 0 | 0 | 0 | 0 | 0 | 0 | 1 | 4 |
| Heating Degree Days (base 65°F) | 1,223 | 1,083 | 953 | 566 | 261 | 61 | 7 | 16 | 126 | 430 | 713 | 1,069 | 6,508 |
| Cooling Degree Days (base 65°F) | 0 | 0 | 0 | 3 | 25 | 109 | 208 | 175 | 57 | 5 | 0 | 0 | 582 |
| Mean Precipitation (in.) | 3.13 | 2.47 | 2.94 | 3.03 | 3.41 | 3.58 | 3.24 | 3.32 | 3.95 | 3.57 | 3.97 | 3.88 | 40.49 |
| Maximum Precipitation (in.)* | 6.9 | 5.9 | 6.0 | 5.9 | 7.2 | 8.4 | 8.9 | 10.7 | 9.0 | 9.1 | 9.8 | 8.7 | 53.5 |
| Minimum Precipitation (in.)* | 1.0 | 0.8 | 1.2 | 1.3 | 1.2 | 0.1 | 0.9 | 1.1 | 0.8 | 0.3 | 1.5 | 1.7 | 28.5 |
| Extreme Maximum Daily Precip. (in.) | 1.83 | 1.74 | 1.39 | 1.66 | 3.41 | 5.01 | 2.19 | 2.41 | 3.55 | 2.42 | 2.31 | 1.66 | 5.01 |
| Days With ≥ 0.1" Precipitation | 9 | 7 | 8 | 8 | 8 | 8 | 6 | 7 | 7 | 8 | 9 | 10 | 95 |
| Days With ≥ 0.5" Precipitation | 1 | 1 | 2 | 2 | 2 | 2 | 2 | 2 | 3 | 3 | 2 | 2 | 24 |
| Days With ≥ 1.0" Precipitation | 0 | 0 | 0 | 0 | 1 | 1 | 1 | 1 | 1 | 1 | 1 | 0 | 7 |
| Mean Snowfall (in.) | 24.4 | 17.2 | 13.4 | 2.8 | 0.3 | trace | trace | trace | trace | 0.9 | 8.1 | 26.9 | 94.0 |
| Maximum Snowfall (in.)* | 68 | 54 | 29 | 15 | 8 | 0 | 0 | 0 | trace | 3 | 31 | 68 | 176 |
| Maximum 24-hr. Snowfall (in.)* | 18 | 18 | 15 | 6 | 8 | 0 | 0 | 0 | trace | 3 | 19 | 34 | 34 |
| Maximum Snow Depth (in.) | 30 | 20 | 20 | 6 | 4 | trace | trace | trace | trace | 22 | 25 | 44 | 44 |
| Days With ≥ 1.0" Snow Depth | 21 | 19 | 11 | 1 | 0 | 0 | 0 | 0 | 0 | 0 | 4 | 15 | 71 |
| Thunderstorm Days* | < 1 | < 1 | 1 | 2 | 3 | 5 | 6 | 6 | 4 | 2 | 1 | < 1 | 30 |
| Foggy Days* | 12 | 12 | 14 | 13 | 14 | 13 | 13 | 15 | 13 | 13 | 13 | 13 | 158 |
| Predominant Sky Cover* | OVR | OVR | OVR | OVR | OVR | OVR | SCT | OVR | OVR | OVR | OVR | OVR | OVR |
| Mean Relative Humidity 7am (%)* | 79 | 80 | 80 | 77 | 76 | 77 | 79 | 83 | 83 | 81 | 80 | 80 | 79 |
| Mean Relative Humidity 4pm (%)* | 73 | 70 | 65 | 57 | 55 | 54 | 54 | 56 | 59 | 60 | 69 | 73 | 62 |
| Mean Dewpoint (°F)* | 18 | 18 | 25 | 34 | 44 | 54 | 59 | 59 | 52 | 42 | 33 | 23 | 39 |
| Prevailing Wind Direction* | WSW | WSW | SW | SW | SW | SW | SW | SW | SW | SW | W | W | SW |
| Prevailing Wind Speed (mph)* | 18 | 17 | 16 | 15 | 14 | 14 | 13 | 13 | 13 | 15 | 15 | 15 | 15 |
| Maximum Wind Gust (mph)* | 71 | 82 | 73 | 74 | 64 | 79 | 59 | 81 | 62 | 63 | 73 | 69 | 82 |

*Note: (*) Period of record is 1946-1995*

# Islip Macarthur Airport

Long Island is the terminal moraine marking the southernmost advance of the ice sheet along the Atlantic Coast during the last ice age. The terrain is generally flat, with only a gradual rise in elevation from Long Island Sound on the northern shore and from the Atlantic Ocean on the southern shore toward the middle of the island. Islip is located about half-way out Long Island on the southern coast. The airport is located about seven miles to the northeast of the city. Islip is protected from flooding during periods of high tides by Fire Island, a natural barrier located about three miles offshore. Most of the air masses affecting Islip are continental in origin, however the ocean has a pronounced influence on the climate of the area.

A cool sea breeze blowing off the ocean during the summer months helps to alleviate the afternoon heat. There are an average of 7 days between June and September when the afternoon temperature exceeds 90 degrees, while farther inland there are 10 to 15 such days.

It is uncommon for the eye of a tropical storm to pass directly over Long Island. Tropical weather systems moving along the Atlantic Coast, however, are capable of producing episodes of heavy rain and strong winds in the late summer or fall.

The winter season is relatively mild. Below zero temperatures are reported on only one or two days in about half the winters. Temperatures of 10 degrees below zero or colder are extremely rare. The seasonal snowfall averages about 29 inches. Almost all of this snow falls between December and March. Coastal low pressure systems, Northeasters, are the principle source of this snow. These weather systems will occasionally produce a heavy snowfall. There are usually extended periods during the winter when the ground is bare of snow.

Based on the 1951-1980 period, the average date of the last spring temperature of 32 degrees is April 27 and the average first fall occurrence is October 21. Inland locations would expect a shorter freeze-free season.

## Islip Macarthur Airport *Suffolk County*   Elevation: 83 ft.   Latitude: 40° 47' N   Longitude: 73° 06' W

| | JAN | FEB | MAR | APR | MAY | JUN | JUL | AUG | SEP | OCT | NOV | DEC | YEAR |
|---|---|---|---|---|---|---|---|---|---|---|---|---|---|
| Mean Maximum Temp. (°F) | 39.5 | 41.0 | 47.8 | 58.0 | 67.9 | 77.2 | 82.0 | 81.1 | 74.2 | 63.5 | 53.8 | 43.9 | 60.8 |
| Mean Temp. (°F) | 31.9 | 33.0 | 39.5 | 49.3 | 58.8 | 68.7 | 74.1 | 73.3 | 65.9 | 54.6 | 45.5 | 36.2 | 52.6 |
| Mean Minimum Temp. (°F) | 24.4 | 24.9 | 31.2 | 40.6 | 49.6 | 60.2 | 66.1 | 65.4 | 57.6 | 45.5 | 37.2 | 28.5 | 44.3 |
| Extreme Maximum Temp. (°F) | 69 | 67 | 82 | 94 | 98 | 96 | 102 | 100 | 92 | 88 | 78 | 77 | 102 |
| Extreme Minimum Temp. (°F) | -7 | 2 | 5 | 23 | 32 | 42 | 50 | 50 | 38 | 29 | 11 | 5 | -7 |
| Days Maximum Temp. ≥ 90°F | 0 | 0 | 0 | 0 | 1 | 2 | 3 | 2 | 0 | 0 | 0 | 0 | 8 |
| Days Maximum Temp. ≤ 32°F | 7 | 5 | 1 | 0 | 0 | 0 | 0 | 0 | 0 | 0 | 0 | 4 | 17 |
| Days Minimum Temp. ≤ 32°F | 25 | 23 | 18 | 3 | 0 | 0 | 0 | 0 | 0 | 1 | 10 | 21 | 101 |
| Days Minimum Temp. ≤ 0°F | 0 | 0 | 0 | 0 | 0 | 0 | 0 | 0 | 0 | 0 | 0 | 0 | 0 |
| Heating Degree Days (base 65°F) | 1,017 | 898 | 782 | 467 | 211 | 32 | 1 | 2 | 59 | 327 | 579 | 886 | 5,261 |
| Cooling Degree Days (base 65°F) | 0 | 0 | 0 | 3 | 24 | 151 | 290 | 266 | 94 | 11 | 0 | 0 | 839 |
| Mean Precipitation (in.) | 3.79 | 2.99 | 4.37 | 4.25 | 3.80 | 4.08 | 3.29 | 4.34 | 3.83 | 4.01 | 3.59 | 4.19 | 46.53 |
| Maximum Precipitation (in.)* | 6.3 | 5.5 | 5.5 | 5.1 | 10.1 | 7.9 | 8.4 | 13.8 | 5.1 | 8.7 | 8.0 | 6.1 | 65.3 |
| Minimum Precipitation (in.)* | 1.3 | 1.1 | 1.3 | 1.3 | 0.7 | 0.6 | 1.2 | 0.5 | 0.8 | 0.3 | 1.3 | 0.9 | 34.4 |
| Extreme Maximum Daily Precip. (in.) | 3.61 | 2.32 | 3.25 | 4.63 | 4.01 | 4.87 | 3.34 | 6.74 | 2.85 | 5.38 | 2.63 | 2.65 | 6.74 |
| Days With ≥ 0.1" Precipitation | 7 | 6 | 7 | 7 | 7 | 6 | 6 | 6 | 6 | 6 | 6 | 7 | 77 |
| Days With ≥ 0.5" Precipitation | 3 | 2 | 3 | 3 | 2 | 2 | 2 | 3 | 3 | 3 | 3 | 3 | 32 |
| Days With ≥ 1.0" Precipitation | 1 | 1 | 1 | 1 | 1 | 1 | 1 | 1 | 1 | 1 | 1 | 1 | 12 |
| Mean Snowfall (in.) | na | na | na | na | na | na | na | na | na | na | na | na | na |
| Maximum Snowfall (in.)* | 14 | 20 | 13 | 3 | 0 | 0 | 0 | 0 | 0 | 0 | 8 | 10 | 34 |
| Maximum 24-hr. Snowfall (in.)* | 6 | 7 | 8 | 3 | 0 | 0 | 0 | 0 | 0 | 0 | 8 | 9 | 9 |
| Maximum Snow Depth (in.) | na | na | na | na | na | na | na | na | na | na | na | na | na |
| Days With ≥ 1.0" Snow Depth | na | na | na | na | na | na | na | na | na | na | na | na | na |
| Thunderstorm Days* | < 1 | < 1 | 1 | 2 | 3 | 5 | 6 | 4 | 2 | 1 | 1 | < 1 | 25 |
| Foggy Days* | 15 | 14 | 16 | 16 | 18 | 16 | 22 | 19 | 17 | 15 | 14 | 14 | 196 |
| Predominant Sky Cover* | OVR | OVR | OVR | OVR | OVR | SCT | OVR | SCT | OVR | CLR | OVR | OVR | OVR |
| Mean Relative Humidity 7am (%)* | 76 | 76 | 77 | 76 | 76 | 77 | 81 | 84 | 85 | 85 | 80 | 76 | 79 |
| Mean Relative Humidity 4pm (%)* | 62 | 59 | 57 | 58 | 59 | 59 | 63 | 63 | 63 | 62 | 62 | 60 | 61 |
| Mean Dewpoint (°F)* | 22 | 22 | 28 | 38 | 48 | 58 | 65 | 64 | 57 | 46 | 36 | 26 | 43 |
| Prevailing Wind Direction* | WNW | NW | NW | SW | SW | SW | SW | SW | SW | SW | SW | WNW | SW |
| Prevailing Wind Speed (mph)* | 13 | 13 | 13 | 10 | 10 | 10 | 10 | 9 | 10 | 10 | 10 | 12 | 12 |
| Maximum Wind Gust (mph)* | na | na | na | na | na | na | na | na | na | na | na | na | na |

Note: (*) Period of record is 1984-1995

# New York Central Park Observatory

New York City, in area exceeding 300 square miles, is located on the Atlantic coastal plain at the mouth of the Hudson River. The terrain is laced with numerous waterways, all but one of the five boroughs in the city are situated on islands. Elevations range from less than 50 feet over most of Manhattan, Brooklyn, and Queens to almost 300 feet in northern Manhattan and the Bronx, and over 400 feet in Staten Island.

The New York Metropolitan area is close to the path of most storm and frontal systems which move across the North American continent. Therefore, weather conditions affecting the city most often approach from a westerly direction, resulting in higher temperatures in summer and lower ones in winter than would otherwise be expected in a coastal area. However, the frequent passage of weather systems often helps reduce the length of extremes.

Although continental influence predominates, oceanic influence is by no means absent. During the summer local sea breezes, winds blowing onshore from the cool water surface, often moderate the afternoon heat. The effect of the sea breeze diminishes inland. On winter mornings, ocean temperatures which are warm relative to the land reinforce the effect of the city heat island and low temperatures are often 10-20 degrees lower in the inland suburbs than in the central city. The relatively warm water temperatures also delay the advent of winter snows. Conversely, the lag in warming of water temperatures keeps spring temperatures relatively cool.

Precipitation is moderate and distributed fairly evenly throughout the year. Most of the rainfall from May through October comes from thunderstorms, usually of brief duration and sometimes intense. Heavy rains of long duration associated with tropical storms occur infrequently in late summer or fall. For the other seasons precipitation is associated with widespread storm areas, producing day-long rain or snow. Coastal storms, occurring most often in the fall and winter months, produce on occasion considerable amounts of precipitation, record rains, snows, and high winds.

The average annual precipitation is reasonably uniform within the city but higher in the suburbs and less on eastern Long Island. Annual snowfall totals also show a consistent increase to the north and west of the city with lesser amounts along the south shores and the eastern end of Long Island.

Local Climatological Data is published for three locations in New York City, Central Park, La Guardia Airport, and John°F. Kennedy International Airport.

Based on the 1951-1980 period, the average first occurrence of 32 degrees Fahrenheit in the fall is November 11 and the average last occurrence in the spring is April 1.

**New York Central Park Observatory** *New York County*   Elevation: 131 ft.   Latitude: 40° 47' N   Longitude: 73° 58' W

| | JAN | FEB | MAR | APR | MAY | JUN | JUL | AUG | SEP | OCT | NOV | DEC | YEAR |
|---|---|---|---|---|---|---|---|---|---|---|---|---|---|
| Mean Maximum Temp. (°F) | 39.2 | 42.2 | 50.3 | 61.9 | 71.6 | 79.9 | 84.8 | 83.5 | 76.0 | 64.5 | 54.5 | 43.8 | 62.7 |
| Mean Temp. (°F) | 33.1 | 35.5 | 42.7 | 53.3 | 62.8 | 71.7 | 76.8 | 75.8 | 68.4 | 57.2 | 48.0 | 37.9 | 55.3 |
| Mean Minimum Temp. (°F) | 26.9 | 28.7 | 35.0 | 44.8 | 54.0 | 63.5 | 68.8 | 68.0 | 60.8 | 49.9 | 41.4 | 31.9 | 47.8 |
| Extreme Maximum Temp. (°F) | 72 | 75 | 86 | 96 | 97 | 98 | 102 | 103 | 99 | 87 | 80 | 75 | 103 |
| Extreme Minimum Temp. (°F) | -2 | 4 | 10 | 21 | 40 | 47 | 53 | 50 | 43 | 31 | 18 | -1 | -2 |
| Days Maximum Temp. ≥ 90°F | 0 | 0 | 0 | 0 | 1 | 3 | 7 | 5 | 1 | 0 | 0 | 0 | 17 |
| Days Maximum Temp. ≤ 32°F | 8 | 4 | 1 | 0 | 0 | 0 | 0 | 0 | 0 | 0 | 0 | 4 | 17 |
| Days Minimum Temp. ≤ 32°F | 21 | 19 | 11 | 1 | 0 | 0 | 0 | 0 | 0 | 0 | 3 | 15 | 70 |
| Days Minimum Temp. ≤ 0°F | 0 | 0 | 0 | 0 | 0 | 0 | 0 | 0 | 0 | 0 | 0 | 0 | 0 |
| Heating Degree Days (base 65°F) | 983 | 829 | 687 | 355 | 124 | 15 | 0 | 1 | 36 | 254 | 505 | 833 | 4,622 |
| Cooling Degree Days (base 65°F) | 0 | 0 | 2 | 12 | 64 | 223 | 374 | 343 | 145 | 20 | 1 | 0 | 1,184 |
| Mean Precipitation (in.) | 3.59 | 2.92 | 4.13 | 4.35 | 4.16 | 4.51 | 4.73 | 4.24 | 4.21 | 4.36 | 4.00 | 3.88 | 49.08 |
| Maximum Precipitation (in.)* | 10.5 | 6.0 | 10.4 | 8.3 | 10.2 | 9.3 | 11.8 | 12.4 | 9.3 | 7.8 | 12.4 | 10.0 | 67.0 |
| Minimum Precipitation (in.)* | 0.6 | 0.5 | 0.9 | 1.3 | 0.6 | 1.2 | 1.3 | 0.2 | 1.3 | 0.1 | 0.3 | 0.6 | 26.1 |
| Extreme Maximum Daily Precip. (in.) | 2.73 | 1.94 | 3.10 | 7.56 | 2.40 | 3.07 | 3.75 | 4.64 | 5.02 | 4.35 | 3.60 | 2.41 | 7.56 |
| Days With ≥ 0.1" Precipitation | 6 | 6 | 7 | 7 | 7 | 7 | 7 | 6 | 6 | 6 | 6 | 7 | 78 |
| Days With ≥ 0.5" Precipitation | 3 | 2 | 3 | 3 | 3 | 3 | 3 | 3 | 3 | 3 | 3 | 3 | 35 |
| Days With ≥ 1.0" Precipitation | 1 | 1 | 1 | 1 | 1 | 1 | 1 | 1 | 1 | 1 | 1 | 1 | 12 |
| Mean Snowfall (in.) | 7.0 | 7.6 | 3.8 | 0.6 | trace | 0.0 | trace | 0.0 | 0.0 | trace | 0.3 | 4.3 | 23.6 |
| Maximum Snowfall (in.)* | 20 | 26 | 17 | 10 | trace | 0 | 0 | 0 | 0 | trace | 5 | 12 | 53 |
| Maximum 24-hr. Snowfall (in.)* | 12 | 16 | 10 | 10 | trace | 0 | 0 | 0 | 0 | trace | 4 | 7 | 16 |
| Maximum Snow Depth (in.) | *14* | *na* | *9* | *9* | *trace* | *0* | *trace* | *0* | *0* | *0* | *5* | *10* | *na* |
| Days With ≥ 1.0" Snow Depth | *8* | *na* | *3* | *0* | *0* | *0* | *0* | *0* | *0* | *0* | *0* | *2* | *na* |
| Thunderstorm Days* | < 1 | < 1 | 1 | 1 | 3 | 4 | 5 | 4 | 1 | 1 | < 1 | < 1 | 20 |
| Foggy Days* | 0 | 0 | 0 | 0 | 0 | 0 | 0 | 0 | 0 | 0 | 0 | < 1 | 1 |
| Predominant Sky Cover* | OVR | OVR | OVR | OVR | OVR | SCT | SCT | SCT | OVR | CLR | OVR | OVR | OVR |
| Mean Relative Humidity 7am (%)* | 67 | 67 | 66 | 64 | 72 | 74 | 74 | 76 | 78 | 75 | 72 | 69 | 71 |
| Mean Relative Humidity 4pm (%)* | 55 | 53 | 50 | 45 | 52 | 55 | 53 | 54 | 56 | 55 | 58 | 59 | 54 |
| Mean Dewpoint (°F)* | 18 | 19 | 26 | 34 | 47 | 57 | 62 | 62 | 56 | 44 | 34 | 25 | 40 |
| Prevailing Wind Direction* | NW | NW | NW | NW | NE | SW | SW | SW | SW | W | W | NW | NW |
| Prevailing Wind Speed (mph)* | 12 | 12 | 13 | 12 | 10 | 8 | 8 | 8 | 8 | 9 | 9 | 12 | 10 |
| Maximum Wind Gust (mph)* | 52 | 51 | 63 | 46 | 44 | 41 | 46 | 43 | 52 | 46 | 58 | 64 | 64 |

*Note: (\*) Period of record is 1965-1995*

# New York JFK Int'l Airport

New York City, in area exceeding 300 square miles, is located on the Atlantic coastal plain at the mouth of the Hudson River. The terrain is laced with numerous waterways, all but one of the five boroughs in the city are situated on islands. Elevations range from less than 50 feet over most of Manhattan, Brooklyn, and Queens to almost 300 feet in northern Manhattan and the Bronx, and over 400 feet in Staten Island.

The New York Metropolitan area is close to the path of most storm and frontal systems which move across the North American continent. Therefore, weather conditions affecting the city most often approach from a westerly direction, resulting in higher temperatures in summer and lower ones in winter than would otherwise be expected in a coastal area. However, the frequent passage of weather systems often helps reduce the length of extremes.

Although continental influence predominates, oceanic influence is by no means absent. During the summer local sea breezes, winds blowing onshore from the cool water surface, often moderate the afternoon heat. The effect of the sea breeze diminishes inland. On winter mornings, ocean temperatures which are warm relative to the land reinforce the effect of the city heat island and low temperatures are often 10-20 degrees lower in the inland suburbs than in the central city. The relatively warm water temperatures also delay the advent of winter snows. Conversely, the lag in warming of water temperatures keeps spring temperatures relatively cool.

Precipitation is moderate and distributed fairly evenly throughout the year. Most of the rainfall from May through October comes from thunderstorms, usually of brief duration and sometimes intense. Heavy rains of long duration associated with tropical storms occur infrequently in late summer or fall. For the other seasons precipitation is associated with widespread storm areas, producing day-long rain or snow. Coastal storms, occurring most often in the fall and winter months, produce on occasion considerable amounts of precipitation, record rains, snows, and high winds.

The average annual precipitation is reasonably uniform within the city but higher in the suburbs and less on eastern Long Island. Annual snowfall totals also show a consistent increase to the north and west of the city with lesser amounts along the south shores and the eastern end of Long Island.

Local Climatological Data is published for three locations in New York City, Central Park, La Guardia Airport, and John°F. Kennedy International Airport.

Based on the 1951-1980 period, the average first occurrence of 32 degrees Fahrenheit in the fall is November 11 and the average last occurrence in the spring is April 1.

**New York JFK Int'l Airport** *Queens County*   Elevation: 16 ft.   Latitude: 40° 39' N   Longitude: 73° 48' W

| | JAN | FEB | MAR | APR | MAY | JUN | JUL | AUG | SEP | OCT | NOV | DEC | YEAR |
|---|---|---|---|---|---|---|---|---|---|---|---|---|---|
| Mean Maximum Temp. (°F) | 39.1 | 41.7 | 48.8 | 58.8 | 68.4 | 77.7 | 82.9 | 82.0 | 75.4 | 64.4 | 54.3 | 44.1 | 61.5 |
| Mean Temp. (°F) | 32.8 | 34.8 | 41.4 | 51.2 | 60.6 | 70.2 | 75.7 | 75.0 | 68.2 | 57.1 | 47.5 | 37.9 | 54.4 |
| Mean Minimum Temp. (°F) | 26.3 | 27.9 | 34.0 | 43.6 | 52.8 | 62.5 | 68.5 | 68.0 | 60.9 | 49.7 | 40.8 | 31.5 | 47.2 |
| Extreme Maximum Temp. (°F) | 71 | 71 | 85 | 90 | 95 | 98 | 102 | 100 | 98 | 90 | 77 | 75 | 102 |
| Extreme Minimum Temp. (°F) | -2 | 7 | 8 | 20 | 37 | 48 | 56 | 51 | 43 | 31 | 19 | 2 | -2 |
| Days Maximum Temp. ≥ 90°F | 0 | 0 | 0 | 0 | 0 | 2 | 4 | 3 | 1 | 0 | 0 | 0 | 10 |
| Days Maximum Temp. ≤ 32°F | 7 | 4 | 1 | 0 | 0 | 0 | 0 | 0 | 0 | 0 | 0 | 3 | 15 |
| Days Minimum Temp. ≤ 32°F | 22 | 20 | 12 | 1 | 0 | 0 | 0 | 0 | 0 | 0 | 3 | 16 | 74 |
| Days Minimum Temp. ≤ 0°F | 0 | 0 | 0 | 0 | 0 | 0 | 0 | 0 | 0 | 0 | 0 | 0 | 0 |
| Heating Degree Days (base 65°F) | 993 | 846 | 725 | 410 | 162 | 19 | 0 | 1 | 33 | 255 | 518 | 834 | 4,796 |
| Cooling Degree Days (base 65°F) | 0 | 0 | 0 | 0 | 3 | 33 | 180 | 341 | 319 | 135 | 15 | 0 | 1,026 |
| Mean Precipitation (in.) | 3.15 | 2.42 | 3.77 | 4.01 | 3.97 | 3.93 | 4.13 | 3.61 | 3.39 | 3.57 | 3.37 | 3.32 | 42.64 |
| Maximum Precipitation (in.)* | 8.3 | 4.9 | 8.2 | 9.5 | 10.7 | 8.1 | 8.5 | 8.3 | 9.6 | 6.6 | 9.5 | 6.7 | 59.1 |
| Minimum Precipitation (in.)* | 0.5 | 1.0 | 0.9 | 1.4 | 0.6 | trace | 0.5 | 0.2 | 1.0 | 0.9 | 0.3 | 0.6 | 25.4 |
| Extreme Maximum Daily Precip. (in.) | 3.78 | 1.62 | 2.56 | 3.15 | 2.70 | 6.27 | 3.51 | 4.10 | 3.42 | 4.66 | 2.45 | 2.55 | 6.27 |
| Days With ≥ 0.1" Precipitation | 6 | 5 | 7 | 7 | 7 | 6 | 6 | 6 | 5 | 5 | 6 | 6 | 72 |
| Days With ≥ 0.5" Precipitation | 2 | 2 | 3 | 3 | 3 | 3 | 3 | 2 | 2 | 3 | 3 | 3 | 31 |
| Days With ≥ 1.0" Precipitation | 1 | 1 | 1 | 1 | 1 | 1 | 1 | 1 | 1 | 1 | 1 | 1 | 12 |
| Mean Snowfall (in.) | 6.4 | 7.4 | 3.6 | 0.8 | trace | 0.0 | trace | 0.0 | 0.0 | trace | 0.3 | 4.2 | 22.7 |
| Maximum Snowfall (in.)* | 20 | 25 | 16 | 8 | 0 | 0 | 0 | 0 | 0 | trace | 4 | 22 | 49 |
| Maximum 24-hr. Snowfall (in.)* | 13 | 20 | 9 | 8 | 0 | 0 | 0 | 0 | 0 | trace | 3 | 18 | 20 |
| Maximum Snow Depth (in.) | 22 | 28 | 8 | 8 | trace | 0 | trace | 0 | 0 | trace | 4 | 14 | 28 |
| Days With ≥ 1.0" Snow Depth | 7 | 5 | 3 | 0 | 0 | 0 | 0 | 0 | 0 | 0 | 0 | 3 | 18 |
| Thunderstorm Days* | < 1 | < 1 | 1 | 2 | 3 | 4 | 5 | 5 | 2 | 1 | 1 | < 1 | 24 |
| Foggy Days* | 10 | 9 | 11 | 11 | 13 | 12 | 13 | 12 | 11 | 10 | 11 | 10 | 133 |
| Predominant Sky Cover* | OVR | OVR | OVR | OVR | OVR | OVR | SCT | SCT | OVR | CLR | OVR | OVR | OVR |
| Mean Relative Humidity 7am (%)* | 71 | 71 | 71 | 70 | 73 | 74 | 75 | 78 | 79 | 78 | 76 | 73 | 74 |
| Mean Relative Humidity 4pm (%)* | 61 | 59 | 57 | 58 | 61 | 63 | 63 | 63 | 62 | 60 | 61 | 62 | 61 |
| Mean Dewpoint (°F)* | 21 | 22 | 28 | 37 | 48 | 58 | 64 | 63 | 57 | 46 | 36 | 26 | 42 |
| Prevailing Wind Direction* | NW | NW | NW | S | S | S | S | S | S | WSW | NW | NW | S |
| Prevailing Wind Speed (mph)* | 16 | 17 | 17 | 13 | 13 | 12 | 12 | 12 | 12 | 10 | 15 | 16 | 14 |
| Maximum Wind Gust (mph)* | 59 | 60 | 68 | 61 | 71 | 56 | 54 | 68 | 60 | 62 | 67 | 61 | 71 |

*Note: (*) Period of record is 1948-1995*

# New York Laguardia Airport

New York City, in area exceeding 300 square miles, is located on the Atlantic coastal plain at the mouth of the Hudson River. The terrain is laced with numerous waterways, all but one of the five boroughs in the city are situated on islands. Elevations range from less than 50 feet over most of Manhattan, Brooklyn, and Queens to almost 300 feet in northern Manhattan and the Bronx, and over 400 feet in Staten Island.

The New York Metropolitan area is close to the path of most storm and frontal systems which move across the North American continent. Therefore, weather conditions affecting the city most often approach from a westerly direction, resulting in higher temperatures in summer and lower ones in winter than would otherwise be expected in a coastal area. However, the frequent passage of weather systems often helps reduce the length of extremes.

Although continental influence predominates, oceanic influence is by no means absent. During the summer local sea breezes, winds blowing onshore from the cool water surface, often moderate the afternoon heat. The effect of the sea breeze diminishes inland. On winter mornings, ocean temperatures which are warm relative to the land reinforce the effect of the city heat island and low temperatures are often 10-20 degrees lower in the inland suburbs than in the central city. The relatively warm water temperatures also delay the advent of winter snows. Conversely, the lag in warming of water temperatures keeps spring temperatures relatively cool.

Precipitation is moderate and distributed fairly evenly throughout the year. Most of the rainfall from May through October comes from thunderstorms, usually of brief duration and sometimes intense. Heavy rains of long duration associated with tropical storms occur infrequently in late summer or fall. For the other seasons precipitation is associated with widespread storm areas, producing day-long rain or snow. Coastal storms, occurring most often in the fall and winter months, produce on occasion considerable amounts of precipitation, record rains, snows, and high winds.

The average annual precipitation is reasonably uniform within the city but higher in the suburbs and less on eastern Long Island. Annual snowfall totals also show a consistent increase to the north and west of the city with lesser amounts along the south shores and the eastern end of Long Island.

Local Climatological Data is published for three locations in New York City, Central Park, La Guardia Airport, and John°F. Kennedy International Airport.

Based on the 1951-1980 period, the average first occurrence of 32 degrees Fahrenheit in the fall is November 11 and the average last occurrence in the spring is April 1.

## New York Laguardia Airport  *Queens County*   Elevation: 11 ft.   Latitude: 40° 47' N   Longitude: 73° 53' W

| | JAN | FEB | MAR | APR | MAY | JUN | JUL | AUG | SEP | OCT | NOV | DEC | YEAR |
|---|---|---|---|---|---|---|---|---|---|---|---|---|---|
| Mean Maximum Temp. (°F) | 39.1 | 42.0 | 49.4 | 60.5 | 71.0 | 80.1 | 85.0 | 83.5 | 76.1 | 64.9 | 54.4 | 44.2 | 62.5 |
| Mean Temp. (°F) | 33.3 | 35.6 | 42.3 | 52.8 | 62.8 | 72.3 | 77.6 | 76.6 | 69.4 | 58.3 | 48.4 | 38.4 | 55.6 |
| Mean Minimum Temp. (°F) | 27.4 | 29.1 | 35.1 | 45.1 | 54.6 | 64.4 | 70.1 | 69.6 | 62.6 | 51.6 | 42.4 | 32.6 | 48.7 |
| Extreme Maximum Temp. (°F) | 72 | 73 | 83 | 94 | 97 | 100 | 103 | 104 | 96 | 89 | 80 | 75 | 104 |
| Extreme Minimum Temp. (°F) | -3 | 4 | 8 | 22 | 38 | 49 | 56 | 51 | 45 | 34 | 20 | -1 | -3 |
| Days Maximum Temp. ≥ 90°F | 0 | 0 | 0 | 0 | 1 | 4 | 7 | 5 | 1 | 0 | 0 | 0 | 18 |
| Days Maximum Temp. ≤ 32°F | 8 | 5 | 1 | 0 | 0 | 0 | 0 | 0 | 0 | 0 | 0 | 4 | 18 |
| Days Minimum Temp. ≤ 32°F | 21 | 18 | 10 | 1 | 0 | 0 | 0 | 0 | 0 | 0 | 3 | 14 | 67 |
| Days Minimum Temp. ≤ 0°F | 0 | 0 | 0 | 0 | 0 | 0 | 0 | 0 | 0 | 0 | 0 | 0 | 0 |
| Heating Degree Days (base 65°F) | 976 | 825 | 698 | 366 | 124 | 13 | 0 | 1 | 29 | 227 | 491 | 816 | 4,566 |
| Cooling Degree Days (base 65°F) | 0 | 0 | 1 | 8 | 62 | 238 | 395 | 366 | 166 | 25 | 1 | 0 | 1,262 |
| Mean Precipitation (in.) | 3.18 | 2.62 | 3.94 | 4.13 | 3.77 | 4.00 | 4.57 | 4.09 | 3.67 | 3.73 | 3.49 | 3.47 | 44.66 |
| Maximum Precipitation (in.)* | 8.7 | 5.7 | 8.7 | 11.5 | 9.3 | 8.1 | 12.3 | 16.0 | 9.6 | 7.3 | 9.9 | 7.7 | 60.8 |
| Minimum Precipitation (in.)* | 0.5 | 0.7 | 0.9 | 1.0 | 0.4 | trace | 0.7 | 0.1 | 1.0 | 0.1 | 0.3 | 0.3 | 22.2 |
| Extreme Maximum Daily Precip. (in.) | 2.60 | 1.63 | 2.83 | 6.69 | 2.57 | 4.00 | 3.53 | 3.54 | 4.63 | 4.39 | 2.91 | 2.74 | 6.69 |
| Days With ≥ 0.1" Precipitation | 6 | 5 | 7 | 7 | 7 | 7 | 7 | 6 | 5 | 5 | 6 | 7 | 75 |
| Days With ≥ 0.5" Precipitation | 2 | 2 | 3 | 2 | 3 | 3 | 3 | 3 | 2 | 3 | 3 | 3 | 32 |
| Days With ≥ 1.0" Precipitation | 1 | 1 | 1 | 1 | 1 | 1 | 1 | 1 | 1 | 1 | 1 | 1 | 12 |
| Mean Snowfall (in.) | 7.5 | 8.2 | 4.5 | 0.6 | trace | 0.0 | trace | trace | 0.0 | trace | 0.3 | 4.8 | 25.9 |
| Maximum Snowfall (in.)* | 18 | 26 | 19 | 8 | trace | 0 | 0 | 0 | 0 | 1 | 6 | 22 | 60 |
| Maximum 24-hr. Snowfall (in.)* | 11 | 17 | 14 | 8 | trace | 0 | 0 | 0 | 0 | 1 | 6 | 16 | 17 |
| Maximum Snow Depth (in.) | 25 | 22 | 9 | 8 | trace | 0 | trace | trace | 0 | trace | 6 | 15 | 25 |
| Days With ≥ 1.0" Snow Depth | 7 | 6 | 3 | 0 | 0 | 0 | 0 | 0 | 0 | 0 | 0 | 3 | 19 |
| Thunderstorm Days* | < 1 | < 1 | 1 | 2 | 3 | 4 | 5 | 5 | 2 | 1 | < 1 | < 1 | 23 |
| Foggy Days* | 10 | 9 | 10 | 10 | 11 | 9 | 8 | 8 | 8 | 8 | 9 | 10 | 110 |
| Predominant Sky Cover* | OVR | OVR | OVR | OVR | OVR | OVR | SCT | SCT | OVR | OVR | OVR | OVR | OVR |
| Mean Relative Humidity 7am (%)* | 67 | 67 | 67 | 67 | 71 | 71 | 73 | 75 | 76 | 74 | 71 | 68 | 71 |
| Mean Relative Humidity 4pm (%)* | 57 | 55 | 52 | 51 | 53 | 53 | 54 | 56 | 56 | 55 | 57 | 59 | 55 |
| Mean Dewpoint (°F)* | 20 | 21 | 27 | 36 | 48 | 57 | 63 | 62 | 56 | 45 | 35 | 25 | 41 |
| Prevailing Wind Direction* | NW | WNW | NW | NW | S | S | S | S | S | SW | WNW | WNW | NW |
| Prevailing Wind Speed (mph)* | 17 | 17 | 17 | 16 | 12 | 12 | 12 | 12 | 10 | 12 | 15 | 16 | 14 |
| Maximum Wind Gust (mph)* | 61 | 67 | 71 | 63 | 56 | 56 | 59 | 73 | 64 | 71 | 76 | 77 | 77 |

*Note: (\*) Period of record is 1947-1995*

# Rochester Int'l Airport

Rochester is located at the mouth of the Genesee River at about the mid point of the south shore of Lake Ontario. The river flows northward from northwest Pennsylvania and empties into Lake Ontario. The land slopes from a lakeshore elevation of 246 feet to over 1,000 feet some 20 miles south. The airport is located just south of the city.

Lake Ontario plays a major role in the Rochester weather. In the summer its cooling effect inhibits the temperature from rising much above the low to mid 90s. In the winter the modifying temperature effect prevents temperatures from falling below -15 degrees most of the time, although temperatures at locations more than 15 miles inland do drop below -30 degrees.

The lake plays a major role in winter snowfall distribution. Well inland from the lake and toward the airport, the seasonal snowfall is usually less than in the area north of the airport and toward the lakeshore where wide variations occur. This is due to what is called the lake effect. Snowfalls of one to two feet or more in 24 hours are common near the lake in winter due the lake effect alone. The lake rarely freezes over because of its depth. The area is also prone to other heavy snowstorms and blizzards because of its proximity to the paths of low pressure systems coming up the east coast, out of the Ohio Valley.

Precipitation is rather evenly distributed throughout the year. Excessive rains occur infrequently but may be caused by slowly moving thunderstorms, slowly moving or stalled major low pressure systems, or by hurricanes and tropical storms that move inland. Hail occurs occasionally and heavy fog is rare.

The growing season averages 150 to 180 days. The years first frost usually occurs in late September and the last frost typically occurs in mid-May.

**Rochester Int'l Airport** *Monroe County*   Elevation: 600 ft.   Latitude: 43° 07' N   Longitude: 77° 41' W

| | JAN | FEB | MAR | APR | MAY | JUN | JUL | AUG | SEP | OCT | NOV | DEC | YEAR |
|---|---|---|---|---|---|---|---|---|---|---|---|---|---|
| Mean Maximum Temp. (°F) | 32.0 | 34.2 | 42.8 | 56.0 | 67.8 | 76.8 | 81.2 | 79.4 | 72.0 | 59.8 | 48.2 | 36.8 | 57.3 |
| Mean Temp. (°F) | 24.9 | 26.4 | 34.2 | 46.4 | 57.2 | 66.4 | 71.0 | 69.6 | 62.1 | 50.8 | 40.7 | 30.2 | 48.3 |
| Mean Minimum Temp. (°F) | 17.8 | 18.6 | 25.6 | 36.7 | 46.5 | 55.9 | 60.8 | 59.7 | 52.1 | 41.7 | 33.2 | 23.5 | 39.3 |
| Extreme Maximum Temp. (°F) | 68 | 73 | 83 | 93 | 94 | 95 | 98 | 97 | 95 | 85 | 75 | 72 | 98 |
| Extreme Minimum Temp. (°F) | -17 | -8 | -7 | 13 | 30 | 36 | 45 | 38 | 30 | 21 | 9 | -12 | -17 |
| Days Maximum Temp. ≥ 90°F | 0 | 0 | 0 | 0 | 0 | 1 | 3 | 2 | 0 | 0 | 0 | 0 | 6 |
| Days Maximum Temp. ≤ 32°F | 16 | 13 | 6 | 0 | 0 | 0 | 0 | 0 | 0 | 0 | 1 | 10 | 46 |
| Days Minimum Temp. ≤ 32°F | 28 | 25 | 23 | 10 | 1 | 0 | 0 | 0 | 0 | 4 | 15 | 25 | 131 |
| Days Minimum Temp. ≤ 0°F | 3 | 1 | 0 | 0 | 0 | 0 | 0 | 0 | 0 | 0 | 0 | 0 | 4 |
| Heating Degree Days (base 65°F) | 1,236 | 1,084 | 948 | 556 | 265 | 64 | 10 | 20 | 135 | 440 | 723 | 1,072 | 6,553 |
| Cooling Degree Days (base 65°F) | 0 | 0 | 0 | 0 | 29 | 112 | 204 | 170 | 55 | 6 | 0 | 0 | 581 |
| Mean Precipitation (in.) | 2.37 | 1.90 | 2.55 | 2.76 | 2.83 | 3.36 | 3.20 | 3.49 | 3.39 | 2.73 | 2.92 | 2.62 | 34.12 |
| Maximum Precipitation (in.)* | 5.8 | 5.1 | 5.0 | 4.1 | 6.6 | 6.8 | 6.0 | 6.0 | 6.3 | 7.8 | 7.0 | 4.6 | 40.5 |
| Minimum Precipitation (in.)* | 0.7 | 0.7 | 0.5 | 1.2 | 0.4 | 0.2 | 0.6 | 0.8 | 0.3 | 0.2 | 0.4 | 0.6 | 22.4 |
| Extreme Maximum Daily Precip. (in.) | 1.77 | 1.59 | 1.44 | 1.79 | 2.12 | 2.19 | 3.33 | 2.51 | 3.08 | 2.94 | 1.83 | 1.46 | 3.33 |
| Days With ≥ 0.1" Precipitation | 7 | 6 | 7 | 7 | 6 | 7 | 6 | 6 | 7 | 6 | 7 | 8 | 80 |
| Days With ≥ 0.5" Precipitation | 1 | 1 | 1 | 2 | 2 | 2 | 2 | 2 | 2 | 2 | 2 | 1 | 20 |
| Days With ≥ 1.0" Precipitation | 0 | 0 | 0 | 0 | 0 | 1 | 1 | 1 | 1 | 0 | 0 | 0 | 4 |
| Mean Snowfall (in.) | 27.0 | 21.3 | 17.0 | 3.9 | 0.4 | trace | trace | 0.0 | trace | 0.1 | 7.6 | 22.1 | 99.4 |
| Maximum Snowfall (in.)* | 60 | 65 | 40 | 20 | 11 | 0 | 0 | 0 | trace | 3 | 23 | 46 | 152 |
| Maximum 24-hr. Snowfall (in.)* | 18 | 18 | 18 | 10 | 11 | 0 | 0 | 0 | trace | 3 | 12 | 18 | 18 |
| Maximum Snow Depth (in.) | 28 | 17 | 34 | 7 | 4 | trace | trace | 0 | trace | trace | 10 | 13 | 34 |
| Days With ≥ 1.0" Snow Depth | 21 | 20 | 12 | 1 | 0 | 0 | 0 | 0 | 0 | 0 | 4 | 15 | 73 |
| Thunderstorm Days* | < 1 | < 1 | 1 | 2 | 3 | 5 | 6 | 6 | 3 | 1 | < 1 | < 1 | 27 |
| Foggy Days* | 8 | 9 | 10 | 10 | 10 | 10 | 11 | 13 | 12 | 11 | 11 | 10 | 125 |
| Predominant Sky Cover* | OVR | OVR | OVR | OVR | OVR | OVR | SCT | OVR | OVR | OVR | OVR | OVR | OVR |
| Mean Relative Humidity 7am (%)* | 79 | 80 | 80 | 78 | 77 | 79 | 82 | 86 | 88 | 85 | 82 | 81 | 81 |
| Mean Relative Humidity 4pm (%)* | 71 | 69 | 63 | 56 | 53 | 53 | 52 | 55 | 59 | 60 | 69 | 73 | 61 |
| Mean Dewpoint (°F)* | 18 | 18 | 25 | 35 | 45 | 55 | 60 | 59 | 53 | 42 | 33 | 23 | 39 |
| Prevailing Wind Direction* | WSW | WSW | WSW | WSW | WSW | WSW | SW | SW | SW | WSW | WSW | WSW | WSW |
| Prevailing Wind Speed (mph)* | 16 | 15 | 15 | 14 | 13 | 12 | 8 | 8 | 8 | 12 | 14 | 14 | 13 |
| Maximum Wind Gust (mph)* | 63 | 70 | 68 | 71 | 64 | 52 | 56 | 62 | 51 | 60 | 67 | 55 | 71 |

*Note: (\*) Period of record is 1948-1995*

# Syracuse Hancock Int'l Airport

Syracuse is located approximately at the geographical center of the state. Gently rolling terrain stretches northward for about 30 miles to the eastern end of Lake Ontario. Oneida Lake is about 8 miles northeast of Syracuse. Approximately five miles south of the city, hills rise to 1,500 feet. Immediately to the west, the terrain is gently rolling with elevations 500 to 800 feet above sea level.

The climate of Syracuse is primarily continental in character and comparatively humid. Nearly all cyclonic systems moving from the interior of the country through the St. Lawrence Valley will affect the Syracuse area. Seasonal and diurnal changes are marked and produce an invigorating climate.

In the summer and in portions of the transitional seasons, temperatures usually rise rapidly during the daytime to moderate levels and as a rule fall rapidly after sunset. The nights are relatively cool and comfortable. There are only a few days in a year when atmospheric humidity causes great personal discomfort.

Winters are usually cold and are sometimes severe in part. Daytime temperatures average in the low 30s with nighttime lows in the teens. Low winter temperatures below -25 degrees have been recorded. The autumn, winter, and spring seasons display marked variability.

Based on the 1951-1980 period, the average first occurrence of 32 degrees Fahrenheit in the fall is October 16 and the average last occurrence in the spring is April 28.

Precipitation in the Syracuse area is derived principally from cyclonic storms which pass from the interior of the country through the St. Lawrence Valley. Lake Ontario provides the source of significant winter precipitation. The lake is quite deep and never freezes so cold air flowing over the lake is quickly saturated and produces the cloudiness and snow squalls which are a well-known feature of winter weather in the Syracuse area.

The precipitation is uncommonly well distributed, averaging about 3 inches per month throughout the year. Snowfall is moderately heavy with an average just over 100 inches. There are about 30 days per year with thunderstorms.

Wind velocities are moderate, but during the winter months there are numerous days with sufficient winds to cause blowing and drifting snow.

During December, January, and February there is much cloudiness. Syracuse receives only about one-third of possible sunshine during winter months. Approximately two-thirds of possible sunshine is received during the warm months.

**Syracuse Hancock Int'l Airport** *Onondaga County*    Elevation: 410 ft.    Latitude: 43° 07' N    Longitude: 76° 06' W

| | JAN | FEB | MAR | APR | MAY | JUN | JUL | AUG | SEP | OCT | NOV | DEC | YEAR |
|---|---|---|---|---|---|---|---|---|---|---|---|---|---|
| Mean Maximum Temp. (°F) | 31.7 | 34.2 | 43.0 | 57.1 | 68.9 | 77.5 | 81.7 | 80.2 | 72.3 | 59.9 | 48.2 | 36.5 | 57.6 |
| Mean Temp. (°F) | 23.8 | 25.7 | 33.9 | 46.8 | 57.6 | 66.6 | 71.3 | 69.9 | 62.1 | 50.5 | 40.5 | 29.3 | 48.2 |
| Mean Minimum Temp. (°F) | 15.8 | 17.3 | 24.8 | 36.5 | 46.3 | 55.7 | 60.9 | 59.5 | 51.8 | 41.0 | 32.7 | 22.0 | 38.7 |
| Extreme Maximum Temp. (°F) | 70 | 69 | 87 | 92 | 93 | 97 | 98 | 101 | 95 | 85 | 76 | 72 | 101 |
| Extreme Minimum Temp. (°F) | -25 | -15 | -15 | 12 | 27 | 36 | 46 | 42 | 28 | 22 | 6 | -22 | -25 |
| Days Maximum Temp. ≥ 90°F | 0 | 0 | 0 | 0 | 0 | 2 | 4 | 2 | 0 | 0 | 0 | 0 | 8 |
| Days Maximum Temp. ≤ 32°F | 16 | 13 | 6 | 0 | 0 | 0 | 0 | 0 | 0 | 0 | 2 | 11 | 48 |
| Days Minimum Temp. ≤ 32°F | 28 | 26 | 24 | 10 | 0 | 0 | 0 | 0 | 0 | 5 | 15 | 26 | 134 |
| Days Minimum Temp. ≤ 0°F | 4 | 2 | 1 | 0 | 0 | 0 | 0 | 0 | 0 | 0 | 0 | 1 | 8 |
| Heating Degree Days (base 65°F) | 1,272 | 1,103 | 957 | 543 | 249 | 59 | 7 | 19 | 134 | 446 | 729 | 1,100 | 6,618 |
| Cooling Degree Days (base 65°F) | 0 | 0 | 1 | 5 | 27 | 114 | 209 | 177 | 53 | 4 | 0 | 0 | 590 |
| Mean Precipitation (in.) | 2.46 | 2.04 | 3.00 | 3.27 | 3.17 | 3.24 | 3.72 | 3.40 | 3.62 | 3.40 | 3.52 | 3.06 | 37.90 |
| Maximum Precipitation (in.)* | 5.8 | 5.4 | 6.8 | 8.1 | 7.4 | 12.3 | 9.5 | 8.4 | 8.8 | 8.3 | 6.8 | 5.5 | 57.9 |
| Minimum Precipitation (in.)* | 1.0 | 0.6 | 1.0 | 1.2 | 0.8 | 1.0 | 0.9 | 1.3 | 0.8 | 0.2 | 1.3 | 0.8 | 27.1 |
| Extreme Maximum Daily Precip. (in.) | 1.41 | 1.62 | 1.33 | 1.60 | 1.69 | 2.86 | 4.29 | 2.98 | 2.59 | 2.98 | 3.56 | 1.48 | 4.29 |
| Days With ≥ 0.1" Precipitation | 7 | 6 | 8 | 8 | 8 | 7 | 7 | 7 | 7 | 8 | 9 | 8 | 90 |
| Days With ≥ 0.5" Precipitation | 1 | 1 | 2 | 2 | 2 | 2 | 3 | 2 | 2 | 2 | 2 | 2 | 23 |
| Days With ≥ 1.0" Precipitation | 0 | 0 | 0 | 0 | 0 | 1 | 1 | 1 | 1 | 1 | 1 | 0 | 4 |
| Mean Snowfall (in.) | 34.9 | 26.2 | 18.7 | 3.8 | 0.1 | trace | trace | trace | trace | 0.4 | 9.7 | 30.7 | 124.5 |
| Maximum Snowfall (in.)* | 72 | 73 | 54 | 16 | 2 | 0 | 0 | trace | trace | 6 | 34 | 65 | 208 |
| Maximum 24-hr. Snowfall (in.)* | 22 | 21 | 22 | 7 | 2 | 0 | 0 | trace | trace | 3 | 12 | 16 | 22 |
| Maximum Snow Depth (in.) | 26 | 33 | 35 | 6 | 1 | trace | trace | trace | trace | trace | 10 | 20 | 35 |
| Days With ≥ 1.0" Snow Depth | 23 | 21 | 13 | 1 | 0 | 0 | 0 | 0 | 0 | 0 | 4 | 16 | 78 |
| Thunderstorm Days* | < 1 | < 1 | 1 | 2 | 3 | 5 | 6 | 5 | 3 | 1 | 1 | < 1 | 27 |
| Foggy Days* | 10 | 9 | 11 | 10 | 11 | 11 | 12 | 13 | 14 | 12 | 12 | 11 | 136 |
| Predominant Sky Cover* | OVR | OVR | OVR | OVR | OVR | OVR | OVR | OVR | OVR | OVR | OVR | OVR | OVR |
| Mean Relative Humidity 7am (%)* | 77 | 78 | 78 | 76 | 76 | 77 | 79 | 85 | 86 | 84 | 80 | 79 | 80 |
| Mean Relative Humidity 4pm (%)* | 69 | 67 | 60 | 52 | 53 | 54 | 54 | 57 | 60 | 60 | 68 | 72 | 60 |
| Mean Dewpoint (°F)* | 16 | 17 | 24 | 34 | 45 | 55 | 60 | 59 | 53 | 42 | 32 | 22 | 38 |
| Prevailing Wind Direction* | WSW | WSW | WNW | WNW | WNW | WNW | WSW | WSW | WSW | WSW | WSW | WSW | WSW |
| Prevailing Wind Speed (mph)* | 15 | 14 | 14 | 14 | 12 | 12 | 9 | 9 | 9 | 10 | 13 | 14 | 12 |
| Maximum Wind Gust (mph)* | 58 | 56 | 61 | 63 | 76 | 67 | 66 | 49 | 48 | 60 | 58 | 63 | 76 |

*Note: (\*) Period of record is 1945-1995*

## Albion 2 NE *Orleans County*    Elevation: 439 ft.    Latitude: 43° 17' N    Longitude: 78° 10' W

|  | JAN | FEB | MAR | APR | MAY | JUN | JUL | AUG | SEP | OCT | NOV | DEC | YEAR |
|---|---|---|---|---|---|---|---|---|---|---|---|---|---|
| Mean Maximum Temp. (°F) | 32.3 | 34.6 | 43.5 | 57.1 | 68.9 | 78.0 | 82.1 | 80.4 | 73.2 | 60.7 | 48.5 | 37.1 | 58.0 |
| Mean Temp. (°F) | 25.4 | 26.9 | 34.8 | 47.1 | 57.9 | 67.4 | 72.0 | 70.5 | 63.5 | 51.8 | 41.3 | 30.6 | 49.1 |
| Mean Minimum Temp. (°F) | 18.4 | 19.2 | 26.0 | 36.9 | 46.9 | 56.8 | 61.8 | 60.5 | 53.7 | 42.9 | 33.9 | 24.0 | 40.1 |
| Extreme Maximum Temp. (°F) | 67 | 74 | 80 | 87 | 91 | 96 | 101 | 98 | 93 | 84 | 74 | 75 | 101 |
| Extreme Minimum Temp. (°F) | -15 | -6 | -5 | 13 | 28 | 35 | 45 | 39 | 32 | 22 | 11 | -10 | -15 |
| Days Maximum Temp. ≥ 90°F | 0 | 0 | 0 | 0 | 0 | 2 | 4 | 2 | 0 | 0 | 0 | 0 | 8 |
| Days Maximum Temp. ≤ 32°F | 16 | 13 | 6 | 0 | 0 | 0 | 0 | 0 | 0 | 0 | 1 | 10 | 46 |
| Days Minimum Temp. ≤ 32°F | 28 | 25 | 23 | 10 | 1 | 0 | 0 | 0 | 0 | 3 | 14 | 25 | 129 |
| Days Minimum Temp. ≤ 0°F | 2 | 1 | 0 | 0 | 0 | 0 | 0 | 0 | 0 | 0 | 0 | 0 | 3 |
| Heating Degree Days (base 65°F) | 1,222 | 1,070 | 931 | 537 | 245 | 53 | 6 | 15 | 110 | 409 | 706 | 1,061 | 6,365 |
| Cooling Degree Days (base 65°F) | 0 | 0 | 1 | 5 | 32 | 132 | 229 | 192 | 71 | 7 | 0 | 0 | 669 |
| Mean Precipitation (in.) | 2.68 | 2.04 | 2.77 | 3.01 | 2.99 | 3.14 | 3.01 | 3.04 | 3.57 | 3.13 | 3.22 | 2.95 | 35.55 |
| Extreme Maximum Daily Precip. (in.) | 2.00 | 1.36 | 1.90 | 1.85 | 2.15 | 3.79 | 2.31 | 3.06 | 3.28 | 2.28 | 2.16 | 1.96 | 3.79 |
| Days With ≥ 0.1" Precipitation | 8 | 6 | 7 | 8 | 7 | 7 | 6 | 6 | 7 | 7 | 9 | 8 | 87 |
| Days With ≥ 0.5" Precipitation | 1 | 1 | 2 | 2 | 2 | 2 | 2 | 2 | 2 | 2 | 2 | 1 | 21 |
| Days With ≥ 1.0" Precipitation | 0 | 0 | 0 | 0 | 0 | 1 | 1 | 1 | 1 | 1 | 0 | 0 | 5 |
| Mean Snowfall (in.) | 19.5 | 13.6 | 11.1 | 2.1 | 0.3 | 0.0 | 0.0 | 0.0 | 0.0 | 0.2 | 4.5 | 15.1 | 66.4 |
| Maximum Snow Depth (in.) | 30 | 25 | 19 | 5 | 6 | 0 | 0 | 0 | 0 | 2 | 9 | 12 | 30 |
| Days With ≥ 1.0" Snow Depth | 15 | 11 | 6 | 1 | 0 | 0 | 0 | 0 | 0 | 0 | 3 | 11 | 47 |

## Alcove Dam *Albany County*    Elevation: 606 ft.    Latitude: 42° 28' N    Longitude: 73° 56' W

|  | JAN | FEB | MAR | APR | MAY | JUN | JUL | AUG | SEP | OCT | NOV | DEC | YEAR |
|---|---|---|---|---|---|---|---|---|---|---|---|---|---|
| Mean Maximum Temp. (°F) | 31.3 | 34.6 | 42.4 | 56.3 | 67.7 | 75.8 | 80.0 | 78.9 | 71.0 | 58.9 | 47.3 | 35.9 | 56.7 |
| Mean Temp. (°F) | 21.5 | 24.1 | 32.0 | 45.1 | 55.9 | 64.6 | 69.1 | 67.9 | 59.8 | 48.0 | 38.3 | 27.2 | 46.1 |
| Mean Minimum Temp. (°F) | 11.6 | 13.6 | 21.6 | 33.9 | 44.1 | 53.4 | 58.1 | 56.8 | 48.6 | 37.1 | 29.2 | 18.6 | 35.5 |
| Extreme Maximum Temp. (°F) | 71 | 70 | 86 | 91 | 90 | 96 | 100 | 96 | 98 | 83 | 81 | 73 | 100 |
| Extreme Minimum Temp. (°F) | -29 | -16 | -13 | 10 | 26 | 32 | 39 | 35 | 28 | 18 | 6 | -24 | -29 |
| Days Maximum Temp. ≥ 90°F | 0 | 0 | 0 | 0 | 0 | 1 | 2 | 2 | 0 | 0 | 0 | 0 | 5 |
| Days Maximum Temp. ≤ 32°F | 16 | 12 | 6 | 0 | 0 | 0 | 0 | 0 | 0 | 0 | 1 | 11 | 47 |
| Days Minimum Temp. ≤ 32°F | 30 | 27 | 27 | 14 | 2 | 0 | 0 | 0 | 1 | 10 | 21 | 28 | 160 |
| Days Minimum Temp. ≤ 0°F | 6 | 3 | 1 | 0 | 0 | 0 | 0 | 0 | 0 | 0 | 0 | 2 | 12 |
| Heating Degree Days (base 65°F) | 1,343 | 1,150 | 1,017 | 592 | 291 | 83 | 20 | 36 | 180 | 521 | 794 | 1,163 | 7,190 |
| Cooling Degree Days (base 65°F) | 0 | 0 | 0 | 2 | 16 | 78 | 153 | 131 | 31 | 1 | 0 | 0 | 412 |
| Mean Precipitation (in.) | 2.43 | 2.05 | 3.54 | 3.77 | 3.48 | 4.46 | 3.84 | 3.54 | 3.71 | 3.45 | 3.48 | 2.81 | 40.56 |
| Extreme Maximum Daily Precip. (in.) | 2.15 | 1.80 | 5.38 | 3.95 | 2.25 | 4.28 | 3.42 | 2.84 | 6.89 | 3.51 | 3.38 | 2.05 | 6.89 |
| Days With ≥ 0.1" Precipitation | 5 | 5 | 6 | 7 | 7 | 8 | 7 | 7 | 6 | 6 | 6 | 6 | 76 |
| Days With ≥ 0.5" Precipitation | 2 | 1 | 3 | 3 | 2 | 3 | 3 | 2 | 2 | 2 | 2 | 1 | 28 |
| Days With ≥ 1.0" Precipitation | 0 | 0 | 1 | 1 | 1 | 1 | 1 | 1 | 1 | 1 | 1 | 1 | 10 |
| Mean Snowfall (in.) | na | na | na | 0.4 | trace | 0.0 | 0.0 | 0.0 | 0.0 | 0.1 | 0.4 | na | na |
| Maximum Snow Depth (in.) | na | na | na | na | na | na | na | na | na | na | na | na | na |
| Days With ≥ 1.0" Snow Depth | na | na | na | 0 | 0 | 0 | 0 | 0 | 0 | 0 | 0 | na | na |

## Alfred *Allegany County*    Elevation: 1,770 ft.    Latitude: 42° 16' N    Longitude: 77° 47' W

|  | JAN | FEB | MAR | APR | MAY | JUN | JUL | AUG | SEP | OCT | NOV | DEC | YEAR |
|---|---|---|---|---|---|---|---|---|---|---|---|---|---|
| Mean Maximum Temp. (°F) | 31.4 | 34.8 | 43.6 | 56.7 | 68.2 | 76.3 | 80.1 | 78.5 | 70.7 | 59.1 | 47.0 | 36.1 | 56.9 |
| Mean Temp. (°F) | 22.0 | 24.1 | 31.9 | 44.0 | 54.3 | 63.0 | 67.1 | 65.5 | 58.2 | 47.2 | 37.4 | 27.3 | 45.2 |
| Mean Minimum Temp. (°F) | 12.6 | 13.4 | 20.4 | 31.3 | 40.3 | 49.8 | 54.1 | 52.5 | 45.7 | 35.3 | 27.8 | 18.6 | 33.5 |
| Extreme Maximum Temp. (°F) | 63 | 65 | 83 | 91 | 93 | 93 | 96 | 98 | 94 | 84 | 77 | 68 | 98 |
| Extreme Minimum Temp. (°F) | -25 | -15 | -16 | 5 | 22 | 28 | 37 | 27 | 20 | 15 | 4 | -21 | -25 |
| Days Maximum Temp. ≥ 90°F | 0 | 0 | 0 | 0 | 0 | 1 | 2 | 1 | 0 | 0 | 0 | 0 | 4 |
| Days Maximum Temp. ≤ 32°F | 17 | 13 | 5 | 0 | 0 | 0 | 0 | 0 | 0 | 0 | 2 | 11 | 48 |
| Days Minimum Temp. ≤ 32°F | 29 | 27 | 27 | 17 | 7 | 0 | 0 | 0 | 2 | 12 | 21 | 28 | 170 |
| Days Minimum Temp. ≤ 0°F | 6 | 5 | 2 | 0 | 0 | 0 | 0 | 0 | 0 | 0 | 0 | 2 | 15 |
| Heating Degree Days (base 65°F) | 1,325 | 1,151 | 1,019 | 624 | 339 | 114 | 38 | 60 | 219 | 545 | 821 | 1,161 | 7,416 |
| Cooling Degree Days (base 65°F) | 0 | 0 | 0 | 2 | 14 | 62 | 110 | 83 | 22 | 1 | 0 | 0 | 294 |
| Mean Precipitation (in.) | 2.15 | 1.71 | 2.66 | 2.99 | 3.32 | 4.25 | 3.91 | 3.63 | 3.73 | 3.30 | 3.29 | 2.55 | 37.49 |
| Extreme Maximum Daily Precip. (in.) | 1.75 | 1.29 | 1.62 | 1.70 | 2.23 | 3.33 | 2.46 | 1.96 | 2.43 | 2.92 | 2.10 | 1.10 | 3.33 |
| Days With ≥ 0.1" Precipitation | 6 | 6 | 7 | 8 | 8 | 8 | 8 | 7 | 7 | 8 | 8 | 7 | 88 |
| Days With ≥ 0.5" Precipitation | 1 | 1 | 2 | 2 | 2 | 3 | 3 | 2 | 2 | 2 | 2 | 1 | 23 |
| Days With ≥ 1.0" Precipitation | 0 | 0 | 0 | 0 | 0 | 1 | 1 | 1 | 1 | 1 | 0 | 0 | 6 |
| Mean Snowfall (in.) | 20.8 | 16.7 | 17.1 | 4.0 | 0.3 | 0.0 | 0.0 | 0.0 | 0.0 | 0.5 | 8.6 | 19.6 | 87.6 |
| Maximum Snow Depth (in.) | na | na | na | 8 | trace | 0 | 0 | 0 | 0 | 2 | 8 | na | na |
| Days With ≥ 1.0" Snow Depth | na | na | na | 1 | 0 | 0 | 0 | 0 | 0 | 0 | 2 | na | na |

## Allegany State Park *Cattaraugus County*    Elevation: 1,500 ft.    Latitude: 42° 06' N    Longitude: 78° 45' W

|  | JAN | FEB | MAR | APR | MAY | JUN | JUL | AUG | SEP | OCT | NOV | DEC | YEAR |
|---|---|---|---|---|---|---|---|---|---|---|---|---|---|
| Mean Maximum Temp. (°F) | 30.3 | 32.9 | 41.8 | 54.7 | 66.7 | 74.6 | 77.9 | 76.3 | 69.0 | 57.2 | 46.1 | 34.6 | 55.2 |
| Mean Temp. (°F) | 21.8 | 23.4 | 31.1 | 43.2 | 53.8 | 62.2 | 66.0 | 64.9 | 57.9 | 46.6 | 37.6 | 27.1 | 44.6 |
| Mean Minimum Temp. (°F) | 13.3 | 13.9 | 20.4 | 31.5 | 40.9 | 49.8 | 54.0 | 53.4 | 46.7 | 36.0 | 29.1 | 19.5 | 34.0 |
| Extreme Maximum Temp. (°F) | 63 | 68 | 80 | 89 | 90 | 92 | 97 | 93 | 89 | 80 | 75 | 70 | 97 |
| Extreme Minimum Temp. (°F) | -22 | -18 | -17 | 11 | 21 | 24 | 29 | 31 | 26 | 14 | -1 | -16 | -22 |
| Days Maximum Temp. ≥ 90°F | 0 | 0 | 0 | 0 | 0 | 0 | 1 | 0 | 0 | 0 | 0 | 0 | 1 |
| Days Maximum Temp. ≤ 32°F | 18 | 14 | 7 | 1 | 0 | 0 | 0 | 0 | 0 | 0 | 3 | 13 | 56 |
| Days Minimum Temp. ≤ 32°F | 28 | 26 | 26 | 17 | 6 | 1 | 0 | 0 | 1 | 11 | 20 | 27 | 163 |
| Days Minimum Temp. ≤ 0°F | 5 | 4 | 2 | 0 | 0 | 0 | 0 | 0 | 0 | 0 | 0 | 2 | 13 |
| Heating Degree Days (base 65°F) | 1,330 | 1,169 | 1,045 | 651 | 351 | 127 | 52 | 70 | 226 | 562 | 816 | 1,168 | 7,567 |
| Cooling Degree Days (base 65°F) | 0 | 0 | 0 | 0 | 11 | 50 | 89 | 73 | 19 | 1 | 0 | 0 | 244 |
| Mean Precipitation (in.) | 3.03 | 2.34 | 3.05 | 3.53 | 3.78 | 4.92 | 4.55 | 4.08 | 4.07 | 3.81 | 3.88 | 3.43 | 44.47 |
| Extreme Maximum Daily Precip. (in.) | 2.08 | 1.64 | 1.84 | 2.15 | 2.30 | 4.00 | 2.62 | 3.38 | 3.75 | 2.55 | 2.05 | 1.45 | 4.00 |
| Days With ≥ 0.1" Precipitation | 9 | 7 | 8 | 9 | 8 | 9 | 9 | 7 | 8 | 10 | 9 | 10 | 103 |
| Days With ≥ 0.5" Precipitation | 1 | 1 | 2 | 2 | 3 | 3 | 3 | 2 | 3 | 2 | 2 | 2 | 26 |
| Days With ≥ 1.0" Precipitation | 0 | 0 | 0 | 0 | 1 | 1 | 1 | 1 | 1 | 0 | 0 | 0 | 5 |
| Mean Snowfall (in.) | na | na | 10.5 | 2.1 | trace | 0.0 | 0.0 | 0.0 | 0.0 | 0.1 | 4.3 | na | na |
| Maximum Snow Depth (in.) | 24 | 21 | 25 | 9 | trace | 0 | 0 | 0 | 0 | 5 | 16 | 24 | 25 |
| Days With ≥ 1.0" Snow Depth | 26 | 24 | 18 | 2 | 0 | 0 | 0 | 0 | 0 | 6 | 19 |  | 95 |

*The period of record for all cooperative weather station data is 1980 – 2009. See User Guide for detailed explanation of data.*

## Aurora Research Farm *Cayuga County*  Elevation: 830 ft.  Latitude: 42° 44' N  Longitude: 76° 39' W

| | JAN | FEB | MAR | APR | MAY | JUN | JUL | AUG | SEP | OCT | NOV | DEC | YEAR |
|---|---|---|---|---|---|---|---|---|---|---|---|---|---|
| Mean Maximum Temp. (°F) | 31.9 | 34.4 | 42.1 | 55.8 | 67.7 | 76.9 | 81.3 | 80.1 | 72.7 | 59.9 | 48.2 | 36.8 | 57.3 |
| Mean Temp. (°F) | 24.4 | 26.2 | 33.5 | 46.1 | 57.1 | 66.6 | 71.0 | 69.6 | 62.5 | 50.7 | 40.7 | 30.0 | 48.2 |
| Mean Minimum Temp. (°F) | 16.9 | 18.0 | 24.9 | 36.4 | 46.5 | 56.3 | 60.6 | 59.1 | 52.2 | 41.5 | 33.2 | 23.1 | 39.0 |
| Extreme Maximum Temp. (°F) | 67 | 67 | 85 | 93 | 94 | 96 | 101 | 97 | 98 | 87 | 81 | 69 | 101 |
| Extreme Minimum Temp. (°F) | -21 | -15 | -11 | 10 | 28 | 34 | 45 | 40 | 27 | 23 | 10 | -15 | -21 |
| Days Maximum Temp. ≥ 90°F | 0 | 0 | 0 | 0 | 0 | 2 | 4 | 2 | 1 | 0 | 0 | 0 | 9 |
| Days Maximum Temp. ≤ 32°F | 16 | 12 | 7 | 0 | 0 | 0 | 0 | 0 | 0 | 0 | 1 | 10 | 46 |
| Days Minimum Temp. ≤ 32°F | 28 | 25 | 24 | 11 | 1 | 0 | 0 | 0 | 0 | 4 | 14 | 25 | 132 |
| Days Minimum Temp. ≤ 0°F | 3 | 1 | 0 | 0 | 0 | 0 | 0 | 0 | 0 | 0 | 0 | 1 | 5 |
| Heating Degree Days (base 65°F) | 1,252 | 1,091 | 970 | 566 | 270 | 70 | 15 | 24 | 132 | 442 | 722 | 1,079 | 6,633 |
| Cooling Degree Days (base 65°F) | 0 | 0 | 1 | 7 | 32 | 125 | 207 | 174 | 63 | 6 | 0 | 0 | 615 |
| Mean Precipitation (in.) | 1.85 | 1.68 | 2.57 | 3.26 | 3.18 | 3.83 | 3.53 | 3.12 | 4.10 | 3.36 | 3.22 | 2.31 | 36.01 |
| Extreme Maximum Daily Precip. (in.) | 1.75 | 1.44 | 1.83 | 1.91 | 1.36 | 1.91 | 2.85 | 2.98 | 3.03 | 1.85 | 2.73 | 1.34 | 3.03 |
| Days With ≥ 0.1" Precipitation | 5 | 5 | 7 | 8 | 8 | 8 | 8 | 8 | 7 | 7 | 7 | 6 | 82 |
| Days With ≥ 0.5" Precipitation | 1 | 1 | 1 | 2 | 2 | 2 | 2 | 2 | 3 | 2 | 2 | 1 | 21 |
| Days With ≥ 1.0" Precipitation | 0 | 0 | 0 | 0 | 0 | 1 | 1 | 1 | 1 | 1 | 1 | 0 | 5 |
| Mean Snowfall (in.) | 14.5 | 11.8 | 12.1 | 3.9 | 0.2 | 0.0 | 0.0 | 0.0 | 0.0 | 0.2 | 4.9 | 11.3 | 58.9 |
| Maximum Snow Depth (in.) | 25 | 28 | 43 | 16 | 4 | 0 | 0 | 0 | 0 | 3 | 17 | 17 | 43 |
| Days With ≥ 1.0" Snow Depth | 21 | 19 | 12 | 2 | 0 | 0 | 0 | 0 | 0 | 0 | 4 | 13 | 71 |

## Avon *Livingston County*  Elevation: 544 ft.  Latitude: 42° 55' N  Longitude: 77° 45' W

| | JAN | FEB | MAR | APR | MAY | JUN | JUL | AUG | SEP | OCT | NOV | DEC | YEAR |
|---|---|---|---|---|---|---|---|---|---|---|---|---|---|
| Mean Maximum Temp. (°F) | 32.5 | 34.5 | 42.6 | 55.9 | 68.1 | 77.3 | 81.3 | 79.7 | 72.5 | 60.6 | 48.8 | 37.0 | 57.6 |
| Mean Temp. (°F) | 24.6 | 25.8 | 33.1 | 45.3 | 56.5 | 66.3 | 70.4 | 68.7 | 61.4 | 50.2 | 40.4 | 29.8 | 47.7 |
| Mean Minimum Temp. (°F) | 16.7 | 17.0 | 23.5 | 34.7 | 44.8 | 55.2 | 59.4 | 57.6 | 50.2 | 39.7 | 31.9 | 22.6 | 37.8 |
| Extreme Maximum Temp. (°F) | 67 | 72 | 84 | 91 | 93 | 95 | 99 | 97 | 93 | 87 | 77 | 71 | 99 |
| Extreme Minimum Temp. (°F) | -24 | -13 | -9 | 11 | 28 | 35 | 45 | 37 | 28 | 21 | 9 | -7 | -24 |
| Days Maximum Temp. ≥ 90°F | 0 | 0 | 0 | 0 | 0 | 2 | 3 | 2 | 0 | 0 | 0 | 0 | 7 |
| Days Maximum Temp. ≤ 32°F | 16 | 12 | 7 | 0 | 0 | 0 | 0 | 0 | 0 | 0 | 1 | 10 | 46 |
| Days Minimum Temp. ≤ 32°F | 28 | 26 | 25 | 14 | 1 | 0 | 0 | 0 | 0 | 6 | 17 | 26 | 143 |
| Days Minimum Temp. ≤ 0°F | 4 | 2 | 1 | 0 | 0 | 0 | 0 | 0 | 0 | 0 | 0 | 1 | 8 |
| Heating Degree Days (base 65°F) | 1,246 | 1,102 | 982 | 587 | 284 | 67 | 13 | 29 | 150 | 456 | 733 | 1,083 | 6,732 |
| Cooling Degree Days (base 65°F) | 0 | 0 | 0 | 4 | 26 | 113 | 187 | 150 | 48 | 5 | 0 | 0 | 533 |
| Mean Precipitation (in.) | 1.79 | 1.56 | 2.42 | 2.72 | 2.78 | 3.25 | 3.31 | 3.35 | 3.35 | 2.65 | 2.72 | 2.09 | 31.99 |
| Extreme Maximum Daily Precip. (in.) | 3.04 | 1.91 | 1.95 | 1.35 | 1.71 | 1.85 | 1.92 | 5.20 | 3.12 | 2.60 | 1.57 | 1.23 | 5.20 |
| Days With ≥ 0.1" Precipitation | 5 | 4 | 5 | 6 | 7 | 7 | 7 | 7 | 7 | 7 | 7 | 6 | 75 |
| Days With ≥ 0.5" Precipitation | 1 | 1 | 1 | 2 | 2 | 2 | 2 | 2 | 2 | 1 | 2 | 1 | 19 |
| Days With ≥ 1.0" Precipitation | 0 | 0 | 0 | 0 | 0 | 1 | 1 | 1 | 1 | 0 | 0 | 0 | 4 |
| Mean Snowfall (in.) | 13.3 | 10.5 | 10.7 | 2.1 | 0.2 | 0.0 | 0.0 | 0.0 | 0.0 | trace | 3.7 | 11.4 | 51.9 |
| Maximum Snow Depth (in.) | 18 | 14 | 27 | 7 | 4 | 0 | 0 | 0 | 0 | 1 | 10 | 10 | 27 |
| Days With ≥ 1.0" Snow Depth | 21 | 19 | 11 | 1 | 0 | 0 | 0 | 0 | 0 | 0 | 3 | 15 | 70 |

## Bath *Steuben County*  Elevation: 1,120 ft.  Latitude: 42° 21' N  Longitude: 77° 21' W

| | JAN | FEB | MAR | APR | MAY | JUN | JUL | AUG | SEP | OCT | NOV | DEC | YEAR |
|---|---|---|---|---|---|---|---|---|---|---|---|---|---|
| Mean Maximum Temp. (°F) | 31.5 | 34.9 | 42.7 | 55.9 | 68.2 | 76.6 | 80.7 | 79.3 | 72.2 | 59.7 | 47.4 | 36.4 | 57.1 |
| Mean Temp. (°F) | 22.1 | 24.6 | 31.7 | 44.0 | 54.7 | 63.5 | 67.8 | 66.5 | 59.2 | 47.6 | 38.0 | 27.8 | 45.6 |
| Mean Minimum Temp. (°F) | 12.7 | 14.2 | 20.6 | 32.0 | 41.3 | 50.5 | 54.9 | 53.7 | 46.1 | 35.3 | 28.6 | 19.2 | 34.1 |
| Extreme Maximum Temp. (°F) | 64 | 69 | 84 | 92 | 94 | 93 | 101 | 100 | 94 | 85 | 77 | 70 | 101 |
| Extreme Minimum Temp. (°F) | -24 | -13 | -18 | 8 | 24 | 28 | 39 | 28 | 25 | 16 | 1 | -16 | -24 |
| Days Maximum Temp. ≥ 90°F | 0 | 0 | 0 | 0 | 0 | 1 | 3 | 2 | 0 | 0 | 0 | 0 | 6 |
| Days Maximum Temp. ≤ 32°F | 16 | 12 | 6 | 0 | 0 | 0 | 0 | 0 | 0 | 0 | 2 | 10 | 46 |
| Days Minimum Temp. ≤ 32°F | 29 | 27 | 27 | 17 | 5 | 0 | 0 | 0 | 2 | 13 | 21 | 28 | 169 |
| Days Minimum Temp. ≤ 0°F | 5 | 4 | 1 | 0 | 0 | 0 | 0 | 0 | 0 | 0 | 0 | 2 | 12 |
| Heating Degree Days (base 65°F) | 1,314 | 1,137 | 1,026 | 626 | 325 | 106 | 33 | 50 | 200 | 534 | 804 | 1,146 | 7,301 |
| Cooling Degree Days (base 65°F) | 0 | 0 | 0 | 3 | 14 | 68 | 127 | 104 | 30 | 1 | 0 | 0 | 347 |
| Mean Precipitation (in.) | 1.69 | 1.48 | 2.09 | 2.79 | 2.86 | 3.75 | 3.19 | 2.84 | 3.37 | 2.46 | 2.67 | 2.05 | 31.24 |
| Extreme Maximum Daily Precip. (in.) | 3.00 | 1.25 | 1.55 | 1.73 | 2.20 | 4.67 | 2.30 | 2.90 | 2.40 | 2.05 | 2.06 | 1.30 | 4.67 |
| Days With ≥ 0.1" Precipitation | 4 | 4 | 6 | 7 | 7 | 7 | 7 | 6 | 6 | 6 | 6 | 5 | 71 |
| Days With ≥ 0.5" Precipitation | 1 | 1 | 1 | 2 | 2 | 2 | 2 | 2 | 2 | 1 | 1 | 1 | 18 |
| Days With ≥ 1.0" Precipitation | 0 | 0 | 0 | 0 | 0 | 1 | 0 | 1 | 1 | 0 | 0 | 0 | 3 |
| Mean Snowfall (in.) | 11.1 | 9.1 | 10.3 | 1.5 | trace | trace | 0.0 | 0.0 | 0.0 | trace | 3.6 | 9.2 | 44.8 |
| Maximum Snow Depth (in.) | 23 | 28 | 36 | 9 | trace | trace | 0 | 0 | 0 | trace | 14 | 14 | 36 |
| Days With ≥ 1.0" Snow Depth | 19 | 18 | 12 | 1 | 0 | 0 | 0 | 0 | 0 | 0 | 4 | 13 | 67 |

## Boonville 2 SSW *Oneida County*  Elevation: 1,580 ft.  Latitude: 43° 27' N  Longitude: 75° 21' W

| | JAN | FEB | MAR | APR | MAY | JUN | JUL | AUG | SEP | OCT | NOV | DEC | YEAR |
|---|---|---|---|---|---|---|---|---|---|---|---|---|---|
| Mean Maximum Temp. (°F) | 24.7 | 27.9 | 36.1 | 50.5 | 63.0 | 71.3 | 74.9 | 73.9 | 65.9 | 53.9 | 41.4 | 29.8 | 51.1 |
| Mean Temp. (°F) | 16.5 | 19.1 | 27.5 | 41.2 | 53.1 | 61.6 | 65.8 | 64.7 | 56.9 | 45.3 | 34.4 | 22.6 | 42.4 |
| Mean Minimum Temp. (°F) | 8.3 | 10.2 | 18.8 | 31.9 | 43.0 | 52.0 | 56.7 | 55.4 | 47.8 | 36.6 | 27.4 | 15.3 | 33.6 |
| Extreme Maximum Temp. (°F) | 57 | 55 | 77 | 86 | 88 | 89 | 94 | 90 | 89 | 79 | 68 | 62 | 94 |
| Extreme Minimum Temp. (°F) | -31 | -22 | -18 | 0 | 22 | 29 | 33 | 38 | 25 | 17 | 0 | -33 | -33 |
| Days Maximum Temp. ≥ 90°F | 0 | 0 | 0 | 0 | 0 | 0 | 0 | 0 | 0 | 0 | 0 | 0 | 0 |
| Days Maximum Temp. ≤ 32°F | 24 | 19 | 12 | 2 | 0 | 0 | 0 | 0 | 0 | 0 | 6 | 19 | 82 |
| Days Minimum Temp. ≤ 32°F | 30 | 27 | 28 | 17 | 3 | 0 | 0 | 0 | 1 | 11 | 22 | 29 | 168 |
| Days Minimum Temp. ≤ 0°F | 9 | 7 | 3 | 0 | 0 | 0 | 0 | 0 | 0 | 0 | 0 | 4 | 23 |
| Heating Degree Days (base 65°F) | 1,498 | 1,291 | 1,157 | 709 | 373 | 140 | 53 | 74 | 253 | 604 | 910 | 1,307 | 8,369 |
| Cooling Degree Days (base 65°F) | 0 | 0 | 0 | 0 | 10 | 46 | 86 | 71 | 16 | 0 | 0 | 0 | 230 |
| Mean Precipitation (in.) | 4.99 | 3.95 | 4.48 | 4.49 | 4.52 | 4.69 | 4.37 | 4.69 | 5.50 | 5.57 | 5.37 | 5.46 | 58.08 |
| Extreme Maximum Daily Precip. (in.) | 3.11 | 2.65 | 1.90 | 3.18 | 2.66 | 3.11 | 3.67 | 3.01 | 4.86 | 3.08 | 3.15 | 1.97 | 4.86 |
| Days With ≥ 0.1" Precipitation | 12 | 10 | 10 | 9 | 9 | 9 | 8 | 8 | 10 | 10 | 9 | 12 | 116 |
| Days With ≥ 0.5" Precipitation | 3 | 2 | 3 | 3 | 3 | 3 | 3 | 3 | 4 | 4 | 3 | 3 | 37 |
| Days With ≥ 1.0" Precipitation | 1 | 1 | 1 | 1 | 1 | 1 | 1 | 1 | 2 | 1 | 1 | 1 | 13 |
| Mean Snowfall (in.) | 52.9 | 39.8 | 31.4 | 8.5 | 0.2 | trace | 0.0 | 0.0 | trace | 2.2 | 17.8 | 44.7 | 197.5 |
| Maximum Snow Depth (in.) | 51 | 48 | 57 | 48 | 2 | trace | 0 | 0 | trace | 9 | 21 | 35 | 57 |
| Days With ≥ 1.0" Snow Depth | 29 | 28 | 29 | 10 | 0 | 0 | 0 | 0 | 0 | 1 | 11 | 26 | 134 |

*The period of record for all cooperative weather station data is 1980 – 2009. See User Guide for detailed explanation of data.*

### Bridgehampton *Suffolk County*   Elevation: 60 ft.   Latitude: 40° 57' N   Longitude: 72° 18' W

| | JAN | FEB | MAR | APR | MAY | JUN | JUL | AUG | SEP | OCT | NOV | DEC | YEAR |
|---|---|---|---|---|---|---|---|---|---|---|---|---|---|
| Mean Maximum Temp. (°F) | 38.7 | 40.4 | 46.6 | 56.1 | 65.9 | 75.1 | 80.9 | 80.2 | 73.6 | 63.2 | 53.5 | 43.8 | 59.8 |
| Mean Temp. (°F) | 31.0 | 32.6 | 38.5 | 47.6 | 56.8 | 66.3 | 72.1 | 71.4 | 64.4 | 53.8 | 45.2 | 35.9 | 51.3 |
| Mean Minimum Temp. (°F) | 23.2 | 24.8 | 30.3 | 39.0 | 47.6 | 57.4 | 63.3 | 62.7 | 55.2 | 44.4 | 36.8 | 27.9 | 42.7 |
| Extreme Maximum Temp. (°F) | 67 | 63 | 79 | 92 | 93 | 95 | 102 | 98 | 93 | 83 | 75 | 70 | 102 |
| Extreme Minimum Temp. (°F) | -11 | 0 | 6 | 14 | 29 | 39 | 48 | 41 | 35 | 24 | 10 | -5 | -11 |
| Days Maximum Temp. ≥ 90°F | 0 | 0 | 0 | 0 | 0 | 1 | 2 | 2 | 0 | 0 | 0 | 0 | 5 |
| Days Maximum Temp. ≤ 32°F | 8 | 5 | 1 | 0 | 0 | 0 | 0 | 0 | 0 | 0 | 0 | 3 | 17 |
| Days Minimum Temp. ≤ 32°F | 26 | 23 | 19 | 5 | 0 | 0 | 0 | 0 | 0 | 3 | 11 | 22 | 109 |
| Days Minimum Temp. ≤ 0°F | 0 | 0 | 0 | 0 | 0 | 0 | 0 | 0 | 0 | 0 | 0 | 0 | 0 |
| Heating Degree Days (base 65°F) | 1,047 | 908 | 815 | 518 | 260 | 51 | 4 | 7 | 80 | 347 | 589 | 897 | 5,523 |
| Cooling Degree Days (base 65°F) | 0 | 0 | 0 | 1 | 11 | 97 | 232 | 214 | 70 | 7 | 0 | 0 | 632 |
| Mean Precipitation (in.) | 3.99 | 3.52 | 4.86 | 4.65 | 3.73 | 4.18 | 3.41 | 3.95 | 4.44 | 4.19 | 4.41 | 4.32 | 49.65 |
| Extreme Maximum Daily Precip. (in.) | 2.35 | 2.49 | 3.96 | 3.46 | 3.25 | 6.61 | 3.55 | 7.04 | 5.87 | 5.69 | 3.19 | 3.27 | 7.04 |
| Days With ≥ 0.1" Precipitation | 7 | 6 | 7 | 8 | 7 | 6 | 5 | 5 | 6 | 6 | 7 | 8 | 78 |
| Days With ≥ 0.5" Precipitation | 3 | 2 | 3 | 3 | 2 | 3 | 2 | 2 | 3 | 3 | 3 | 3 | 32 |
| Days With ≥ 1.0" Precipitation | 1 | 1 | 1 | 1 | 1 | 1 | 1 | 1 | 1 | 1 | 1 | 1 | 12 |
| Mean Snowfall (in.) | 7.7 | 7.9 | 5.3 | 0.9 | 0.0 | 0.0 | 0.0 | 0.0 | 0.0 | trace | 0.7 | 4.0 | 26.5 |
| Maximum Snow Depth (in.) | 27 | 24 | 13 | 8 | 0 | 0 | 0 | 0 | 0 | trace | 7 | 18 | 27 |
| Days With ≥ 1.0" Snow Depth | 8 | 6 | 3 | 0 | 0 | 0 | 0 | 0 | 0 | 0 | 0 | 3 | 20 |

### Canton 4 SE *St. Lawrence County*   Elevation: 439 ft.   Latitude: 44° 34' N   Longitude: 75° 07' W

| | JAN | FEB | MAR | APR | MAY | JUN | JUL | AUG | SEP | OCT | NOV | DEC | YEAR |
|---|---|---|---|---|---|---|---|---|---|---|---|---|---|
| Mean Maximum Temp. (°F) | 26.2 | 29.4 | 38.7 | 53.3 | 65.7 | 74.4 | 79.0 | 77.5 | 69.4 | 56.8 | 44.8 | 32.3 | 54.0 |
| Mean Temp. (°F) | 15.8 | 18.6 | 28.5 | 43.1 | 54.9 | 64.0 | 68.7 | 66.8 | 58.6 | 46.8 | 36.4 | 23.2 | 43.8 |
| Mean Minimum Temp. (°F) | 5.3 | 7.7 | 18.4 | 32.8 | 44.1 | 53.6 | 58.4 | 56.1 | 47.7 | 36.7 | 27.9 | 14.1 | 33.6 |
| Extreme Maximum Temp. (°F) | 66 | 65 | 92 | 89 | 90 | 93 | 93 | 97 | 93 | 82 | 76 | 69 | 97 |
| Extreme Minimum Temp. (°F) | -40 | -37 | -26 | 6 | 23 | 29 | 35 | 33 | 22 | 15 | -5 | -37 | -40 |
| Days Maximum Temp. ≥ 90°F | 0 | 0 | 0 | 0 | 0 | 0 | 1 | 1 | 0 | 0 | 0 | 0 | 2 |
| Days Maximum Temp. ≤ 32°F | 20 | 17 | 10 | 1 | 0 | 0 | 0 | 0 | 0 | 0 | 3 | 15 | 66 |
| Days Minimum Temp. ≤ 32°F | 30 | 26 | 27 | 15 | 3 | 0 | 0 | 0 | 2 | 11 | 20 | 28 | 162 |
| Days Minimum Temp. ≤ 0°F | 12 | 10 | 3 | 0 | 0 | 0 | 0 | 0 | 0 | 0 | 0 | 6 | 31 |
| Heating Degree Days (base 65°F) | 1,521 | 1,308 | 1,124 | 653 | 323 | 102 | 30 | 59 | 218 | 559 | 851 | 1,287 | 8,035 |
| Cooling Degree Days (base 65°F) | 0 | 0 | 0 | 2 | 17 | 80 | 153 | 122 | 33 | 3 | 0 | 0 | 410 |
| Mean Precipitation (in.) | 2.10 | 1.79 | 2.13 | 2.90 | 3.11 | 3.26 | 3.86 | 3.67 | 4.03 | 3.86 | 3.37 | 2.56 | 36.64 |
| Extreme Maximum Daily Precip. (in.) | 1.30 | 1.58 | 1.17 | 1.43 | 1.86 | 1.75 | 4.10 | 2.85 | 3.20 | 2.35 | 2.68 | 1.46 | 4.10 |
| Days With ≥ 0.1" Precipitation | 6 | 5 | 6 | 7 | 8 | 7 | 7 | 7 | 8 | 8 | 8 | 6 | 83 |
| Days With ≥ 0.5" Precipitation | 1 | 1 | 1 | 2 | 2 | 2 | 2 | 2 | 3 | 2 | 2 | 1 | 21 |
| Days With ≥ 1.0" Precipitation | 0 | 0 | 0 | 0 | 0 | 0 | 1 | 1 | 1 | 1 | 0 | 0 | 4 |
| Mean Snowfall (in.) | 20.1 | 16.9 | 12.4 | 3.6 | trace | 0.0 | 0.0 | 0.0 | trace | 0.6 | 5.8 | 18.5 | 77.9 |
| Maximum Snow Depth (in.) | 30 | 33 | 38 | 11 | 1 | 0 | 0 | 0 | trace | 8 | 8 | 24 | 38 |
| Days With ≥ 1.0" Snow Depth | 25 | 23 | 17 | 2 | 0 | 0 | 0 | 0 | 0 | 0 | 6 | 19 | 92 |

### Chazy *Clinton County*   Elevation: 169 ft.   Latitude: 44° 53' N   Longitude: 73° 26' W

| | JAN | FEB | MAR | APR | MAY | JUN | JUL | AUG | SEP | OCT | NOV | DEC | YEAR |
|---|---|---|---|---|---|---|---|---|---|---|---|---|---|
| Mean Maximum Temp. (°F) | 27.4 | 30.4 | 40.1 | 55.4 | 67.8 | 76.3 | 80.4 | 78.7 | 70.1 | 57.2 | 44.8 | 32.9 | 55.1 |
| Mean Temp. (°F) | 17.7 | 20.2 | 30.1 | 44.7 | 56.3 | 65.2 | 69.8 | 68.0 | 59.8 | 48.0 | 37.0 | 24.5 | 45.1 |
| Mean Minimum Temp. (°F) | 8.0 | 10.0 | 20.2 | 34.0 | 44.8 | 54.1 | 59.1 | 57.3 | 49.5 | 38.6 | 29.2 | 16.1 | 35.1 |
| Extreme Maximum Temp. (°F) | 61 | 60 | 79 | 91 | 91 | 97 | 96 | 100 | 95 | 85 | 74 | 66 | 100 |
| Extreme Minimum Temp. (°F) | -44 | -41 | -28 | 6 | 27 | 30 | 38 | 36 | 22 | 17 | -2 | -26 | -44 |
| Days Maximum Temp. ≥ 90°F | 0 | 0 | 0 | 0 | 0 | 1 | 1 | 1 | 0 | 0 | 0 | 0 | 3 |
| Days Maximum Temp. ≤ 32°F | 20 | 16 | 7 | 0 | 0 | 0 | 0 | 0 | 0 | 0 | 3 | 14 | 60 |
| Days Minimum Temp. ≤ 32°F | 29 | 26 | 26 | 14 | 2 | 0 | 0 | 0 | 1 | 9 | 19 | 27 | 153 |
| Days Minimum Temp. ≤ 0°F | 10 | 8 | 3 | 0 | 0 | 0 | 0 | 0 | 0 | 0 | 0 | 4 | 25 |
| Heating Degree Days (base 65°F) | 1,460 | 1,260 | 1,074 | 604 | 275 | 73 | 16 | 36 | 181 | 523 | 833 | 1,249 | 7,584 |
| Cooling Degree Days (base 65°F) | 0 | 0 | 0 | 3 | 14 | 84 | 170 | 136 | 32 | 2 | 0 | 0 | 441 |
| Mean Precipitation (in.) | 0.78 | na | 0.85 | 2.25 | 2.94 | 3.46 | 3.53 | 3.81 | 3.23 | 3.05 | 2.21 | 0.81 | na |
| Extreme Maximum Daily Precip. (in.) | 1.30 | na | 1.80 | 2.10 | 1.65 | 2.66 | 1.76 | 2.98 | 2.80 | 2.85 | 4.27 | 1.30 | na |
| Days With ≥ 0.1" Precipitation | 2 | 2 | 2 | 5 | 7 | 7 | 7 | 7 | 6 | 6 | 4 | 2 | 57 |
| Days With ≥ 0.5" Precipitation | 0 | 0 | 0 | 2 | 2 | 2 | 3 | 3 | 2 | 2 | 1 | 1 | 18 |
| Days With ≥ 1.0" Precipitation | 0 | 0 | 0 | 0 | 0 | 1 | 1 | 1 | 1 | 1 | 0 | 0 | 5 |
| Mean Snowfall (in.) | 13.7 | 12.7 | 11.1 | 2.9 | 0.1 | 0.0 | 0.0 | 0.0 | 0.0 | 0.3 | 4.6 | 11.2 | 56.6 |
| Maximum Snow Depth (in.) | 30 | 31 | 50 | 15 | 0 | 0 | 0 | 0 | 0 | 0 | 12 | 20 | 50 |
| Days With ≥ 1.0" Snow Depth | 22 | 21 | 16 | 2 | 0 | 0 | 0 | 0 | 0 | 0 | 4 | 16 | 81 |

### Conklingville Dam *Saratoga County*   Elevation: 808 ft.   Latitude: 43° 19' N   Longitude: 73° 56' W

| | JAN | FEB | MAR | APR | MAY | JUN | JUL | AUG | SEP | OCT | NOV | DEC | YEAR |
|---|---|---|---|---|---|---|---|---|---|---|---|---|---|
| Mean Maximum Temp. (°F) | 29.4 | 33.1 | 41.1 | 54.3 | 66.3 | 74.1 | 78.3 | 76.6 | 69.1 | 57.8 | 45.8 | 33.4 | 54.9 |
| Mean Temp. (°F) | 19.4 | 22.3 | 31.1 | 43.7 | 55.4 | 64.0 | 68.4 | 66.9 | 59.3 | 48.1 | 37.8 | 25.2 | 45.1 |
| Mean Minimum Temp. (°F) | 9.4 | 11.5 | 20.9 | 33.1 | 44.6 | 53.7 | 58.4 | 57.2 | 49.4 | 38.3 | 29.7 | 17.0 | 35.3 |
| Extreme Maximum Temp. (°F) | 60 | 61 | 80 | 87 | 89 | 92 | 95 | 91 | 88 | 80 | 75 | 67 | 95 |
| Extreme Minimum Temp. (°F) | -29 | -22 | -13 | 7 | 27 | 30 | 44 | 35 | 28 | 22 | 8 | -22 | -29 |
| Days Maximum Temp. ≥ 90°F | 0 | 0 | 0 | 0 | 0 | 0 | 1 | 0 | 0 | 0 | 0 | 0 | 1 |
| Days Maximum Temp. ≤ 32°F | 18 | 12 | 5 | 0 | 0 | 0 | 0 | 0 | 0 | 0 | 1 | 12 | 48 |
| Days Minimum Temp. ≤ 32°F | 29 | 25 | 26 | 14 | 1 | 0 | 0 | 0 | 0 | 7 | 18 | 27 | 147 |
| Days Minimum Temp. ≤ 0°F | 8 | 5 | 1 | 0 | 0 | 0 | 0 | 0 | 0 | 0 | 0 | 3 | 17 |
| Heating Degree Days (base 65°F) | 1,408 | 1,202 | 1,046 | 633 | 302 | 89 | 19 | 39 | 189 | 519 | 809 | 1,228 | 7,483 |
| Cooling Degree Days (base 65°F) | 0 | 0 | 0 | 1 | 13 | 64 | 131 | 105 | 24 | 1 | 0 | 0 | 339 |
| Mean Precipitation (in.) | 3.35 | 2.77 | 3.96 | 3.69 | 4.06 | 4.06 | 4.19 | 4.02 | 3.76 | 3.71 | 3.84 | 3.75 | 45.16 |
| Extreme Maximum Daily Precip. (in.) | 2.53 | 1.71 | 2.70 | 2.97 | 2.67 | 2.25 | 2.85 | 2.25 | 4.01 | 2.83 | 2.90 | 2.38 | 4.01 |
| Days With ≥ 0.1" Precipitation | 7 | 6 | 7 | 7 | 8 | 8 | 7 | 6 | 6 | 7 | 7 | 7 | 83 |
| Days With ≥ 0.5" Precipitation | 2 | 2 | 3 | 2 | 3 | 3 | 3 | 3 | 2 | 2 | 2 | 2 | 29 |
| Days With ≥ 1.0" Precipitation | 1 | 1 | 1 | 1 | 1 | 1 | 1 | 1 | 1 | 1 | 1 | 1 | 12 |
| Mean Snowfall (in.) | 19.9 | 13.8 | 13.8 | 2.6 | trace | 0.0 | 0.0 | 0.0 | 0.0 | 0.1 | 3.7 | 16.5 | 70.4 |
| Maximum Snow Depth (in.) | 39 | 37 | 45 | 20 | 1 | 0 | 0 | 0 | 0 | trace | 16 | 23 | 45 |
| Days With ≥ 1.0" Snow Depth | 24 | 25 | 20 | 3 | 0 | 0 | 0 | 0 | 0 | 0 | 3 | 19 | 94 |

*The period of record for all cooperative weather station data is 1980 – 2009. See User Guide for detailed explanation of data.*

## Dannemora  *Clinton County*  Elevation: 1,339 ft.  Latitude: 44° 43' N  Longitude: 73° 43' W

| | JAN | FEB | MAR | APR | MAY | JUN | JUL | AUG | SEP | OCT | NOV | DEC | YEAR |
|---|---|---|---|---|---|---|---|---|---|---|---|---|---|
| Mean Maximum Temp. (°F) | 25.7 | 29.5 | 38.4 | 52.6 | 65.4 | 74.0 | 78.0 | 76.1 | 68.5 | 55.7 | 42.5 | 31.0 | 53.1 |
| Mean Temp. (°F) | 16.9 | 20.4 | 29.3 | 43.0 | 55.0 | 64.0 | 68.2 | 66.4 | 58.6 | 46.9 | 35.1 | 23.1 | 43.9 |
| Mean Minimum Temp. (°F) | 8.1 | 11.3 | 20.2 | 33.3 | 44.5 | 53.9 | 58.5 | 56.7 | 48.8 | 38.0 | 27.7 | 15.1 | 34.7 |
| Extreme Maximum Temp. (°F) | 64 | 62 | 77 | 87 | 88 | 94 | 96 | 93 | 93 | 79 | 70 | 65 | 96 |
| Extreme Minimum Temp. (°F) | -34 | -23 | -22 | 2 | 18 | 32 | 42 | 33 | 25 | 17 | 0 | -28 | -34 |
| Days Maximum Temp. ≥ 90°F | 0 | 0 | 0 | 0 | 0 | 1 | 1 | 0 | 0 | 0 | 0 | 0 | 2 |
| Days Maximum Temp. ≤ 32°F | 22 | 18 | 10 | 1 | 0 | 0 | 0 | 0 | 0 | 0 | 5 | 17 | 73 |
| Days Minimum Temp. ≤ 32°F | 30 | 27 | 27 | 14 | 2 | 0 | 0 | 0 | 1 | 9 | 21 | 29 | 160 |
| Days Minimum Temp. ≤ 0°F | 9 | 6 | 2 | 0 | 0 | 0 | 0 | 0 | 0 | 0 | 0 | 4 | 21 |
| Heating Degree Days (base 65°F) | 1,485 | 1,255 | 1,098 | 657 | 319 | 97 | 23 | 49 | 210 | 556 | 890 | 1,294 | 7,933 |
| Cooling Degree Days (base 65°F) | 0 | 0 | 0 | 2 | 15 | 73 | 131 | 100 | 25 | 1 | 0 | 0 | 347 |
| Mean Precipitation (in.) | 2.45 | 2.12 | 2.53 | 3.32 | 3.63 | 3.98 | 4.18 | 4.40 | 3.85 | 3.94 | 3.61 | 2.92 | 40.93 |
| Extreme Maximum Daily Precip. (in.) | 2.79 | 2.10 | 1.78 | 2.30 | 1.62 | 1.95 | 3.01 | 2.80 | 4.55 | 3.09 | 3.64 | 2.41 | 4.55 |
| Days With ≥ 0.1" Precipitation | 6 | 6 | 8 | 8 | 9 | 9 | 9 | 9 | 8 | 9 | 8 | 8 | 97 |
| Days With ≥ 0.5" Precipitation | 2 | 1 | 1 | 2 | 2 | 3 | 3 | 3 | 3 | 3 | 2 | 2 | 27 |
| Days With ≥ 1.0" Precipitation | 0 | 0 | 0 | 0 | 0 | 1 | 1 | 1 | 1 | 1 | 1 | 0 | 6 |
| Mean Snowfall (in.) | na | na | na | trace | 0.0 | 0.0 | 0.0 | 0.0 | 0.0 | trace | 1.0 | na | na |
| Maximum Snow Depth (in.) | na | na | na | na | na | na | na | na | na | na | na | na | na |
| Days With ≥ 1.0" Snow Depth | na | na | na | 0 | 0 | 0 | 0 | 0 | 0 | 0 | na | na | na |

## Delhi 2 SE  *Delaware County*  Elevation: 1,439 ft.  Latitude: 42° 15' N  Longitude: 74° 54' W

| | JAN | FEB | MAR | APR | MAY | JUN | JUL | AUG | SEP | OCT | NOV | DEC | YEAR |
|---|---|---|---|---|---|---|---|---|---|---|---|---|---|
| Mean Maximum Temp. (°F) | 31.1 | 34.3 | 42.3 | 55.4 | 66.7 | 75.1 | 79.2 | 78.3 | 70.7 | 59.4 | 47.3 | 35.7 | 56.3 |
| Mean Temp. (°F) | 20.9 | 23.4 | 31.4 | 43.6 | 53.9 | 62.7 | 66.7 | 65.7 | 58.3 | 47.1 | 37.8 | 26.7 | 44.8 |
| Mean Minimum Temp. (°F) | 10.6 | 12.4 | 20.5 | 31.8 | 41.0 | 50.3 | 54.2 | 53.1 | 45.8 | 34.7 | 28.2 | 17.7 | 33.3 |
| Extreme Maximum Temp. (°F) | 65 | 64 | 83 | 91 | 91 | 91 | 97 | 96 | 90 | 83 | 77 | 66 | 97 |
| Extreme Minimum Temp. (°F) | -32 | -24 | -18 | 8 | 20 | 26 | 33 | 32 | 23 | 11 | -1 | -25 | -32 |
| Days Maximum Temp. ≥ 90°F | 0 | 0 | 0 | 0 | 0 | 1 | 1 | 1 | 0 | 0 | 0 | 0 | 3 |
| Days Maximum Temp. ≤ 32°F | 16 | 12 | 6 | 0 | 0 | 0 | 0 | 0 | 0 | 0 | 2 | 12 | 48 |
| Days Minimum Temp. ≤ 32°F | 29 | 27 | 26 | 17 | 6 | 0 | 0 | 0 | 2 | 14 | 21 | 28 | 170 |
| Days Minimum Temp. ≤ 0°F | 8 | 5 | 2 | 0 | 0 | 0 | 0 | 0 | 0 | 0 | 0 | 3 | 18 |
| Heating Degree Days (base 65°F) | 1,362 | 1,170 | 1,035 | 637 | 349 | 121 | 48 | 60 | 218 | 551 | 811 | 1,180 | 7,542 |
| Cooling Degree Days (base 65°F) | 0 | 0 | 0 | 2 | 11 | 60 | 106 | 89 | 24 | 1 | 0 | 0 | 293 |
| Mean Precipitation (in.) | 3.23 | 2.49 | 3.54 | 3.94 | 4.24 | 4.60 | 4.55 | 3.64 | 4.38 | 4.02 | 3.90 | 3.45 | 45.98 |
| Extreme Maximum Daily Precip. (in.) | 2.05 | 2.00 | 2.17 | 2.46 | 2.77 | 4.31 | 2.91 | 3.40 | 4.49 | 3.15 | 3.62 | 2.54 | 4.49 |
| Days With ≥ 0.1" Precipitation | 8 | 6 | 8 | 8 | 9 | 9 | 8 | 7 | 7 | 8 | 8 | 8 | 94 |
| Days With ≥ 0.5" Precipitation | 2 | 1 | 2 | 2 | 3 | 3 | 3 | 3 | 3 | 3 | 3 | 2 | 30 |
| Days With ≥ 1.0" Precipitation | 0 | 0 | 0 | 1 | 1 | 1 | 1 | 1 | 1 | 1 | 1 | 0 | 8 |
| Mean Snowfall (in.) | 18.2 | 12.4 | 11.2 | 3.8 | 0.1 | 0.0 | 0.0 | 0.0 | 0.0 | 0.6 | 4.3 | 14.8 | 65.4 |
| Maximum Snow Depth (in.) | 25 | 23 | 28 | 17 | 3 | 0 | 0 | 0 | 0 | 7 | 9 | 31 | 31 |
| Days With ≥ 1.0" Snow Depth | 23 | 20 | 13 | 2 | 0 | 0 | 0 | 0 | 0 | 0 | 4 | 16 | 78 |

## Dobbs Ferry Ardsley  *Westchester County*  Elevation: 200 ft.  Latitude: 41° 00' N  Longitude: 73° 50' W

| | JAN | FEB | MAR | APR | MAY | JUN | JUL | AUG | SEP | OCT | NOV | DEC | YEAR |
|---|---|---|---|---|---|---|---|---|---|---|---|---|---|
| Mean Maximum Temp. (°F) | 38.7 | 42.3 | 50.5 | 62.4 | 72.4 | 80.6 | 85.2 | 83.6 | 76.4 | 65.3 | 54.3 | 43.3 | 62.9 |
| Mean Temp. (°F) | 30.9 | 33.5 | 40.7 | 51.4 | 61.1 | 69.8 | 74.8 | 73.6 | 66.2 | 55.1 | 45.4 | 35.6 | 53.2 |
| Mean Minimum Temp. (°F) | 23.1 | 24.6 | 30.8 | 40.4 | 49.6 | 58.9 | 64.3 | 63.5 | 55.9 | 44.9 | 36.4 | 27.8 | 43.4 |
| Extreme Maximum Temp. (°F) | 72 | 75 | 86 | 96 | 97 | 98 | 104 | 100 | 98 | 88 | 81 | 77 | 104 |
| Extreme Minimum Temp. (°F) | -10 | -2 | 2 | 17 | 29 | 38 | 49 | 44 | 34 | 27 | 12 | -4 | -10 |
| Days Maximum Temp. ≥ 90°F | 0 | 0 | 0 | 0 | 1 | 4 | 7 | 5 | 1 | 0 | 0 | 0 | 18 |
| Days Maximum Temp. ≤ 32°F | 8 | 4 | 1 | 0 | 0 | 0 | 0 | 0 | 0 | 0 | 0 | 4 | 17 |
| Days Minimum Temp. ≤ 32°F | 26 | 23 | 18 | 5 | 0 | 0 | 0 | 0 | 0 | 0 | 2 | 10 | 22 | 106 |
| Days Minimum Temp. ≤ 0°F | 1 | 0 | 0 | 0 | 0 | 0 | 0 | 0 | 0 | 0 | 0 | 0 | 1 |
| Heating Degree Days (base 65°F) | 1,049 | 884 | 748 | 408 | 160 | 24 | 1 | 3 | 64 | 312 | 582 | 905 | 5,140 |
| Cooling Degree Days (base 65°F) | 0 | 0 | 1 | 6 | 45 | 175 | 312 | 277 | 106 | 13 | 0 | 0 | 935 |
| Mean Precipitation (in.) | 3.78 | 3.03 | 4.45 | 4.74 | 4.47 | 4.39 | 4.64 | 4.23 | 4.64 | 4.48 | 4.39 | 4.25 | 51.49 |
| Extreme Maximum Daily Precip. (in.) | 3.11 | 2.85 | 2.97 | 5.34 | 2.80 | 4.49 | 3.22 | 3.30 | 7.62 | 3.27 | 3.25 | 3.07 | 7.62 |
| Days With ≥ 0.1" Precipitation | 7 | 6 | 7 | 8 | 7 | 7 | 7 | 6 | 6 | 6 | 7 | 7 | 81 |
| Days With ≥ 0.5" Precipitation | 3 | 2 | 3 | 3 | 3 | 3 | 3 | 3 | 3 | 3 | 3 | 3 | 35 |
| Days With ≥ 1.0" Precipitation | 1 | 1 | 1 | 1 | 1 | 1 | 1 | 2 | 1 | 1 | 1 | 1 | 13 |
| Mean Snowfall (in.) | 9.0 | 8.4 | 5.7 | 0.9 | trace | 0.0 | 0.0 | 0.0 | 0.0 | 0.1 | 0.7 | 5.8 | 30.6 |
| Maximum Snow Depth (in.) | 26 | 20 | 17 | 10 | trace | 0 | 0 | 0 | 0 | 2 | 4 | 14 | 26 |
| Days With ≥ 1.0" Snow Depth | 12 | 11 | 5 | 0 | 0 | 0 | 0 | 0 | 0 | 0 | 0 | 6 | 34 |

## Gouverneur 3 NW  *St. Lawrence County*  Elevation: 419 ft.  Latitude: 44° 21' N  Longitude: 75° 31' W

| | JAN | FEB | MAR | APR | MAY | JUN | JUL | AUG | SEP | OCT | NOV | DEC | YEAR |
|---|---|---|---|---|---|---|---|---|---|---|---|---|---|
| Mean Maximum Temp. (°F) | 27.3 | 30.6 | 39.8 | 54.8 | 66.9 | 75.8 | 80.1 | 78.8 | 71.0 | 57.7 | 45.4 | 32.9 | 55.1 |
| Mean Temp. (°F) | 16.5 | 19.3 | 28.9 | 43.6 | 54.6 | 64.0 | 68.3 | 66.7 | 58.8 | 46.9 | 36.6 | 23.6 | 44.0 |
| Mean Minimum Temp. (°F) | 5.7 | 7.9 | 17.9 | 32.3 | 42.1 | 52.1 | 56.5 | 54.6 | 46.5 | 36.0 | 27.7 | 14.2 | 32.8 |
| Extreme Maximum Temp. (°F) | 65 | 64 | 81 | 87 | 88 | 96 | 95 | 98 | 94 | 81 | 73 | 70 | 98 |
| Extreme Minimum Temp. (°F) | -45 | -37 | -27 | 4 | 23 | 29 | 36 | 32 | 22 | 15 | -10 | -37 | -45 |
| Days Maximum Temp. ≥ 90°F | 0 | 0 | 0 | 0 | 0 | 1 | 1 | 1 | 0 | 0 | 0 | 0 | 3 |
| Days Maximum Temp. ≤ 32°F | 19 | 16 | 8 | 1 | 0 | 0 | 0 | 0 | 0 | 0 | 3 | 14 | 61 |
| Days Minimum Temp. ≤ 32°F | 30 | 27 | 27 | 16 | 4 | 0 | 0 | 0 | 2 | 11 | 20 | 29 | 166 |
| Days Minimum Temp. ≤ 0°F | 12 | 10 | 4 | 0 | 0 | 0 | 0 | 0 | 0 | 0 | 0 | 6 | 32 |
| Heating Degree Days (base 65°F) | 1,498 | 1,288 | 1,114 | 638 | 327 | 96 | 29 | 51 | 209 | 556 | 846 | 1,278 | 7,930 |
| Cooling Degree Days (base 65°F) | 0 | 0 | 0 | 2 | 10 | 72 | 138 | 111 | 29 | 2 | 0 | 0 | 364 |
| Mean Precipitation (in.) | 2.30 | 1.97 | 2.24 | 3.00 | 3.09 | 3.26 | 3.60 | 3.44 | 3.94 | 4.04 | 3.72 | 2.72 | 37.32 |
| Extreme Maximum Daily Precip. (in.) | 1.56 | 1.45 | 1.68 | 1.95 | 1.72 | 2.48 | 4.18 | 2.50 | 4.51 | 2.06 | 2.70 | 1.72 | 4.51 |
| Days With ≥ 0.1" Precipitation | 6 | 5 | 6 | 7 | 7 | 7 | 7 | 7 | 8 | 8 | 9 | 7 | 84 |
| Days With ≥ 0.5" Precipitation | 1 | 1 | 1 | 2 | 2 | 2 | 3 | 2 | 3 | 2 | 2 | 1 | 22 |
| Days With ≥ 1.0" Precipitation | 0 | 0 | 0 | 0 | 0 | 1 | 1 | 1 | 1 | 1 | 1 | 0 | 6 |
| Mean Snowfall (in.) | 21.9 | 18.2 | 13.6 | 3.9 | trace | trace | 0.0 | 0.0 | trace | 1.0 | 6.8 | 19.2 | 84.6 |
| Maximum Snow Depth (in.) | 30 | 30 | 30 | 8 | trace | 0 | 0 | 0 | 0 | trace | 12 | 19 | 30 |
| Days With ≥ 1.0" Snow Depth | 26 | 25 | 19 | 2 | 0 | 0 | 0 | 0 | 0 | 1 | 5 | 20 | 97 |

*The period of record for all cooperative weather station data is 1980 – 2009. See User Guide for detailed explanation of data.*

### Grafton *Rensselaer County*   Elevation: 1,560 ft.   Latitude: 42° 47' N   Longitude: 73° 28' W

| | JAN | FEB | MAR | APR | MAY | JUN | JUL | AUG | SEP | OCT | NOV | DEC | YEAR |
|---|---|---|---|---|---|---|---|---|---|---|---|---|---|
| Mean Maximum Temp. (°F) | 28.2 | 32.5 | 41.0 | 54.4 | 66.4 | 73.6 | 77.9 | 75.9 | 68.1 | 56.7 | 44.5 | 33.3 | 54.4 |
| Mean Temp. (°F) | 20.2 | 23.8 | 31.9 | 44.4 | 55.8 | 63.5 | 68.1 | 66.5 | 58.9 | 47.9 | 36.9 | 25.9 | 45.3 |
| Mean Minimum Temp. (°F) | 12.1 | 15.0 | 22.7 | 34.3 | 45.2 | 53.4 | 58.2 | 57.1 | 49.8 | 39.1 | 29.3 | 18.5 | 36.2 |
| Extreme Maximum Temp. (°F) | 61 | 62 | 83 | 88 | 86 | 90 | 93 | 94 | 89 | 79 | 76 | 65 | 94 |
| Extreme Minimum Temp. (°F) | -26 | -21 | -11 | 5 | 26 | 32 | 40 | 32 | 27 | 18 | 4 | -23 | -26 |
| Days Maximum Temp. ≥ 90°F | 0 | 0 | 0 | 0 | 0 | 0 | 0 | 0 | 0 | 0 | 0 | 0 | 0 |
| Days Maximum Temp. ≤ 32°F | 21 | 15 | 7 | 0 | 0 | 0 | 0 | 0 | 0 | 0 | 4 | 15 | 62 |
| Days Minimum Temp. ≤ 32°F | 30 | 26 | 26 | 14 | 1 | 0 | 0 | 0 | 0 | 8 | 20 | 28 | 153 |
| Days Minimum Temp. ≤ 0°F | 6 | 4 | 1 | 0 | 0 | 0 | 0 | 0 | 0 | 0 | 0 | 2 | 13 |
| Heating Degree Days (base 65°F) | 1,383 | 1,161 | 1,020 | 613 | 293 | 100 | 24 | 47 | 201 | 524 | 835 | 1,205 | 7,406 |
| Cooling Degree Days (base 65°F) | 0 | 0 | 0 | 2 | 14 | 62 | 128 | 102 | 26 | 1 | 0 | 0 | 335 |
| Mean Precipitation (in.) | 2.88 | 2.57 | 3.56 | 3.87 | 4.53 | 4.15 | 4.51 | 4.46 | 4.19 | 3.98 | 4.00 | 3.21 | 45.91 |
| Extreme Maximum Daily Precip. (in.) | 1.50 | 2.60 | 1.95 | 2.14 | 2.06 | 2.52 | 3.75 | 3.50 | 3.58 | 4.75 | 2.65 | 2.56 | 4.75 |
| Days With ≥ 0.1" Precipitation | 7 | 6 | 9 | 9 | 9 | 8 | 8 | 8 | 7 | 8 | 9 | 8 | 96 |
| Days With ≥ 0.5" Precipitation | 2 | 2 | 3 | 3 | 3 | 3 | 3 | 3 | 3 | 3 | 3 | 3 | 33 |
| Days With ≥ 1.0" Precipitation | 0 | 0 | 1 | 1 | 1 | 1 | 1 | 1 | 1 | 1 | 1 | 1 | 10 |
| Mean Snowfall (in.) | 20.6 | 14.9 | 15.4 | 5.9 | 0.2 | 0.0 | 0.0 | 0.0 | trace | 1.2 | 7.2 | 17.8 | 83.2 |
| Maximum Snow Depth (in.) | 37 | 31 | 32 | 23 | trace | 0 | 0 | 0 | trace | 22 | 14 | 23 | 37 |
| Days With ≥ 1.0" Snow Depth | 24 | 24 | 18 | 3 | 0 | 0 | 0 | 0 | 0 | 0 | 5 | 20 | 94 |

### Indian Lake 2 SW *Hamilton County*   Elevation: 1,660 ft.   Latitude: 43° 45' N   Longitude: 74° 17' W

| | JAN | FEB | MAR | APR | MAY | JUN | JUL | AUG | SEP | OCT | NOV | DEC | YEAR |
|---|---|---|---|---|---|---|---|---|---|---|---|---|---|
| Mean Maximum Temp. (°F) | 25.5 | 28.7 | 36.6 | 49.8 | 62.5 | 70.7 | 74.2 | 73.1 | 65.8 | 53.7 | 41.6 | 30.3 | 51.0 |
| Mean Temp. (°F) | 15.3 | 17.5 | 25.7 | 39.1 | 50.8 | 59.8 | 63.8 | 62.6 | 55.3 | 43.7 | 33.5 | 21.4 | 40.7 |
| Mean Minimum Temp. (°F) | 5.0 | 6.3 | 14.8 | 28.4 | 39.0 | 48.8 | 53.4 | 52.1 | 44.7 | 33.6 | 25.4 | 12.6 | 30.3 |
| Extreme Maximum Temp. (°F) | 55 | 57 | 74 | 85 | 85 | 90 | 91 | 90 | 89 | 78 | 68 | 64 | 91 |
| Extreme Minimum Temp. (°F) | -35 | -30 | -25 | -1 | 21 | 29 | 35 | 31 | 23 | 15 | -2 | -27 | -35 |
| Days Maximum Temp. ≥ 90°F | 0 | 0 | 0 | 0 | 0 | 0 | 0 | 0 | 0 | 0 | 0 | 0 | 0 |
| Days Maximum Temp. ≤ 32°F | 22 | 18 | 11 | 1 | 0 | 0 | 0 | 0 | 0 | 0 | 5 | 18 | 75 |
| Days Minimum Temp. ≤ 32°F | 30 | 28 | 29 | 21 | 8 | 0 | 0 | 0 | 2 | 15 | 23 | 30 | 186 |
| Days Minimum Temp. ≤ 0°F | 12 | 11 | 5 | 0 | 0 | 0 | 0 | 0 | 0 | 0 | 0 | 6 | 34 |
| Heating Degree Days (base 65°F) | 1,537 | 1,338 | 1,211 | 770 | 437 | 178 | 85 | 111 | 295 | 653 | 938 | 1,343 | 8,896 |
| Cooling Degree Days (base 65°F) | 0 | 0 | 0 | 0 | 4 | 28 | 55 | 44 | 9 | 0 | 0 | 0 | 140 |
| Mean Precipitation (in.) | 2.83 | 2.34 | 2.92 | 3.20 | 3.59 | 3.70 | 3.85 | 3.62 | 3.73 | 4.22 | 3.33 | 2.86 | 40.19 |
| Extreme Maximum Daily Precip. (in.) | 1.70 | 2.10 | 2.40 | 2.09 | 2.03 | 3.00 | 2.42 | 2.58 | 3.43 | 3.34 | 2.90 | 1.70 | 3.43 |
| Days With ≥ 0.1" Precipitation | 7 | 6 | 7 | 7 | 8 | 8 | 8 | 8 | 7 | 8 | 7 | 7 | 88 |
| Days With ≥ 0.5" Precipitation | 2 | 1 | 2 | 2 | 2 | 2 | 2 | 3 | 3 | 2 | 2 | 2 | 25 |
| Days With ≥ 1.0" Precipitation | 0 | 0 | 1 | 1 | 1 | 1 | 1 | 1 | 1 | 1 | 1 | 0 | 9 |
| Mean Snowfall (in.) | na | na | na | 3.0 | 0.1 | 0.0 | 0.0 | 0.0 | 0.0 | 0.7 | na | na | na |
| Maximum Snow Depth (in.) | na | na | na | na | na | na | na | na | na | na | na | na | na |
| Days With ≥ 1.0" Snow Depth | na | na | na | 4 | 0 | 0 | 0 | 0 | 0 | 1 | na | na | na |

### Ithaca Cornell Univ *Tompkins County*   Elevation: 959 ft.   Latitude: 42° 27' N   Longitude: 76° 27' W

| | JAN | FEB | MAR | APR | MAY | JUN | JUL | AUG | SEP | OCT | NOV | DEC | YEAR |
|---|---|---|---|---|---|---|---|---|---|---|---|---|---|
| Mean Maximum Temp. (°F) | 31.2 | 33.6 | 41.4 | 54.8 | 67.0 | 75.5 | 79.5 | 78.6 | 71.2 | 58.9 | 47.3 | 35.8 | 56.2 |
| Mean Temp. (°F) | 23.0 | 24.7 | 32.2 | 44.6 | 55.4 | 64.4 | 68.7 | 67.7 | 60.3 | 48.8 | 39.3 | 28.5 | 46.5 |
| Mean Minimum Temp. (°F) | 14.7 | 15.7 | 22.9 | 34.3 | 43.8 | 53.4 | 57.7 | 56.7 | 49.3 | 38.6 | 31.4 | 21.1 | 36.6 |
| Extreme Maximum Temp. (°F) | 66 | 67 | 83 | 91 | 93 | 94 | 98 | 97 | 92 | 84 | 78 | 69 | 98 |
| Extreme Minimum Temp. (°F) | -24 | -18 | -17 | 11 | 25 | 31 | 40 | 34 | 24 | 18 | 2 | -19 | -24 |
| Days Maximum Temp. ≥ 90°F | 0 | 0 | 0 | 0 | 0 | 1 | 2 | 1 | 0 | 0 | 0 | 0 | 4 |
| Days Maximum Temp. ≤ 32°F | 17 | 13 | 7 | 1 | 0 | 0 | 0 | 0 | 0 | 0 | 2 | 12 | 52 |
| Days Minimum Temp. ≤ 32°F | 29 | 26 | 25 | 13 | 4 | 0 | 0 | 0 | 1 | 8 | 17 | 27 | 150 |
| Days Minimum Temp. ≤ 0°F | 5 | 3 | 1 | 0 | 0 | 0 | 0 | 0 | 0 | 0 | 0 | 2 | 11 |
| Heating Degree Days (base 65°F) | 1,297 | 1,132 | 1,011 | 609 | 309 | 96 | 30 | 42 | 175 | 500 | 763 | 1,126 | 7,090 |
| Cooling Degree Days (base 65°F) | 0 | 0 | 0 | 4 | 20 | 86 | 150 | 133 | 41 | 3 | 0 | 0 | 438 |
| Mean Precipitation (in.) | 1.99 | 1.83 | 2.76 | 3.27 | 3.16 | 3.91 | 3.86 | 3.54 | 3.69 | 3.29 | 3.16 | 2.32 | 36.78 |
| Extreme Maximum Daily Precip. (in.) | 1.87 | 1.52 | 2.06 | 2.13 | 2.25 | 2.04 | 2.08 | 3.30 | 3.90 | 5.08 | 4.02 | 1.87 | 5.08 |
| Days With ≥ 0.1" Precipitation | 6 | 5 | 6 | 8 | 8 | 9 | 8 | 7 | 7 | 7 | 7 | 6 | 84 |
| Days With ≥ 0.5" Precipitation | 1 | 1 | 1 | 2 | 2 | 2 | 3 | 2 | 2 | 2 | 2 | 1 | 21 |
| Days With ≥ 1.0" Precipitation | 0 | 0 | 0 | 0 | 0 | 1 | 1 | 1 | 1 | 1 | 1 | 0 | 5 |
| Mean Snowfall (in.) | 17.3 | 12.7 | 12.2 | 3.6 | 0.0 | 0.0 | 0.0 | 0.0 | 0.0 | 0.4 | 4.8 | 12.9 | 63.9 |
| Maximum Snow Depth (in.) | 19 | 20 | 28 | 14 | 0 | 0 | 0 | 0 | 0 | 5 | 12 | 11 | 28 |
| Days With ≥ 1.0" Snow Depth | 21 | 20 | 12 | 2 | 0 | 0 | 0 | 0 | 0 | 0 | 4 | 15 | 74 |

### Lowville *Lewis County*   Elevation: 859 ft.   Latitude: 43° 48' N   Longitude: 75° 29' W

| | JAN | FEB | MAR | APR | MAY | JUN | JUL | AUG | SEP | OCT | NOV | DEC | YEAR |
|---|---|---|---|---|---|---|---|---|---|---|---|---|---|
| Mean Maximum Temp. (°F) | 26.2 | 29.1 | 37.5 | 52.4 | 65.0 | 73.6 | 77.9 | 76.7 | 68.7 | 56.1 | 43.7 | 31.6 | 53.2 |
| Mean Temp. (°F) | 16.7 | 19.1 | 28.1 | 42.4 | 53.9 | 62.9 | 67.2 | 65.8 | 57.7 | 46.3 | 35.7 | 23.4 | 43.3 |
| Mean Minimum Temp. (°F) | 7.2 | 9.1 | 18.6 | 32.4 | 42.7 | 52.2 | 56.5 | 54.8 | 46.7 | 36.5 | 27.6 | 15.0 | 33.3 |
| Extreme Maximum Temp. (°F) | 62 | 59 | 80 | 87 | 88 | 97 | 94 | 96 | 92 | 81 | 72 | 67 | 97 |
| Extreme Minimum Temp. (°F) | -35 | -28 | -25 | 5 | 23 | 28 | 39 | 32 | 24 | 18 | -1 | -29 | -35 |
| Days Maximum Temp. ≥ 90°F | 0 | 0 | 0 | 0 | 0 | 1 | 1 | 1 | 0 | 0 | 0 | 0 | 3 |
| Days Maximum Temp. ≤ 32°F | 21 | 17 | 10 | 1 | 0 | 0 | 0 | 0 | 0 | 0 | 4 | 15 | 68 |
| Days Minimum Temp. ≤ 32°F | 30 | 27 | 27 | 17 | 3 | 0 | 0 | 0 | 2 | 11 | 21 | 29 | 167 |
| Days Minimum Temp. ≤ 0°F | 10 | 9 | 3 | 0 | 0 | 0 | 0 | 0 | 0 | 0 | 0 | 5 | 27 |
| Heating Degree Days (base 65°F) | 1,491 | 1,292 | 1,138 | 673 | 349 | 119 | 40 | 65 | 235 | 573 | 873 | 1,285 | 8,133 |
| Cooling Degree Days (base 65°F) | 0 | 0 | 0 | 0 | 2 | 11 | 63 | 116 | 23 | 1 | 0 | 0 | 311 |
| Mean Precipitation (in.) | 3.16 | 2.49 | 2.73 | 3.23 | 3.34 | 3.35 | 3.63 | 3.70 | 3.96 | 4.09 | 3.92 | 3.64 | 41.24 |
| Extreme Maximum Daily Precip. (in.) | 2.35 | 2.03 | 2.12 | 2.27 | 2.45 | 2.10 | 2.25 | 3.05 | 4.78 | 2.60 | 3.30 | 2.02 | 4.78 |
| Days With ≥ 0.1" Precipitation | 8 | 7 | 7 | 7 | 8 | 7 | 7 | 7 | 8 | 9 | 9 | 10 | 94 |
| Days With ≥ 0.5" Precipitation | 2 | 1 | 2 | 2 | 2 | 2 | 2 | 2 | 3 | 3 | 3 | 2 | 25 |
| Days With ≥ 1.0" Precipitation | 0 | 0 | 0 | 2 | 1 | 1 | 1 | 1 | 1 | 1 | 1 | 0 | 8 |
| Mean Snowfall (in.) | 33.0 | 25.7 | 14.9 | 4.7 | 0.1 | 0.0 | 0.0 | 0.0 | trace | 0.8 | 9.3 | 32.9 | 121.4 |
| Maximum Snow Depth (in.) | 33 | 26 | 27 | 16 | 1 | 0 | 0 | 0 | trace | 8 | 11 | 28 | 33 |
| Days With ≥ 1.0" Snow Depth | 27 | 26 | 20 | 4 | 0 | 0 | 0 | 0 | 0 | 0 | 7 | 23 | 107 |

*The period of record for all cooperative weather station data is 1980 – 2009. See User Guide for detailed explanation of data.*

## Middletown 2 NW *Orange County*    Elevation: 700 ft.    Latitude: 41° 28' N    Longitude: 74° 27' W

|  | JAN | FEB | MAR | APR | MAY | JUN | JUL | AUG | SEP | OCT | NOV | DEC | YEAR |
|---|---|---|---|---|---|---|---|---|---|---|---|---|---|
| Mean Maximum Temp. (°F) | 35.4 | 39.2 | 48.1 | 61.1 | 71.5 | 79.4 | 83.4 | 82.1 | 74.9 | 63.4 | 51.4 | 39.7 | 60.8 |
| Mean Temp. (°F) | 27.0 | 29.8 | 37.9 | 50.2 | 60.4 | 68.9 | 73.2 | 71.9 | 64.6 | 53.2 | 42.9 | 32.1 | 51.0 |
| Mean Minimum Temp. (°F) | 18.5 | 20.4 | 27.7 | 39.3 | 49.2 | 58.3 | 63.0 | 61.6 | 54.3 | 43.0 | 34.3 | 24.5 | 41.2 |
| Extreme Maximum Temp. (°F) | 66 | 71 | 85 | 91 | 92 | 93 | 101 | 97 | 94 | 87 | 78 | 71 | 101 |
| Extreme Minimum Temp. (°F) | -23 | -8 | -7 | 17 | 26 | 40 | 47 | 41 | 27 | 19 | 12 | -10 | -23 |
| Days Maximum Temp. ≥ 90°F | 0 | 0 | 0 | 0 | 0 | 2 | 4 | 3 | 1 | 0 | 0 | 0 | 10 |
| Days Maximum Temp. ≤ 32°F | 12 | 7 | 2 | 0 | 0 | 0 | 0 | 0 | 0 | 0 | 0 | 7 | 28 |
| Days Minimum Temp. ≤ 32°F | 28 | 25 | 21 | 5 | 0 | 0 | 0 | 0 | 0 | 3 | 14 | 25 | 121 |
| Days Minimum Temp. ≤ 0°F | 2 | 1 | 0 | 0 | 0 | 0 | 0 | 0 | 0 | 0 | 0 | 0 | 3 |
| Heating Degree Days (base 65°F) | 1,172 | 990 | 832 | 443 | 177 | 30 | 3 | 7 | 85 | 364 | 658 | 1,012 | 5,773 |
| Cooling Degree Days (base 65°F) | 0 | 0 | 0 | 6 | 40 | 153 | 265 | 227 | 80 | 7 | 0 | 0 | 778 |
| Mean Precipitation (in.) | 2.66 | 2.34 | 3.14 | 4.03 | 4.13 | 4.47 | 3.98 | 3.98 | 4.15 | 3.76 | 3.58 | 3.14 | 43.36 |
| Extreme Maximum Daily Precip. (in.) | 2.00 | 2.52 | 2.45 | 3.46 | 2.51 | 2.95 | 2.49 | 5.00 | 3.00 | 4.12 | 1.94 | 2.87 | 5.00 |
| Days With ≥ 0.1" Precipitation | 6 | 5 | 6 | 7 | 8 | 8 | 7 | 6 | 6 | 6 | 6 | 6 | 77 |
| Days With ≥ 0.5" Precipitation | 2 | 2 | 2 | 3 | 3 | 3 | 3 | 3 | 3 | 3 | 3 | 2 | 32 |
| Days With ≥ 1.0" Precipitation | 0 | 0 | 1 | 1 | 1 | 1 | 1 | 1 | 1 | 1 | 1 | 1 | 10 |
| Mean Snowfall (in.) | na | na | na | trace | 0.0 | 0.0 | 0.0 | 0.0 | 0.0 | 0.0 | 0.2 | na | na |
| Maximum Snow Depth (in.) | na | na | na | na | na | na | na | na | na | na | na | na | na |
| Days With ≥ 1.0" Snow Depth | na | na | na | 0 | 0 | 0 | 0 | 0 | 0 | 0 | 0 | na | na |

## Mineola *Nassau County*    Elevation: 96 ft.    Latitude: 40° 44' N    Longitude: 73° 37' W

|  | JAN | FEB | MAR | APR | MAY | JUN | JUL | AUG | SEP | OCT | NOV | DEC | YEAR |
|---|---|---|---|---|---|---|---|---|---|---|---|---|---|
| Mean Maximum Temp. (°F) | 39.1 | 42.2 | 49.4 | 59.4 | 69.2 | 78.8 | 83.7 | 82.4 | 75.1 | 64.4 | 55.1 | 44.3 | 61.9 |
| Mean Temp. (°F) | 32.4 | 34.7 | 41.4 | 50.6 | 59.7 | 69.5 | 74.8 | 73.7 | 66.5 | 56.0 | 47.5 | 37.6 | 53.7 |
| Mean Minimum Temp. (°F) | 25.7 | 27.3 | 33.2 | 41.8 | 50.2 | 60.2 | 65.9 | 64.9 | 57.8 | 47.3 | 39.8 | 30.8 | 45.4 |
| Extreme Maximum Temp. (°F) | 71 | 73 | 85 | 94 | 97 | 101 | 103 | 105 | 95 | 89 | 79 | 76 | 105 |
| Extreme Minimum Temp. (°F) | -4 | 3 | 5 | 13 | 34 | 43 | 50 | 46 | 38 | 29 | 18 | -1 | -4 |
| Days Maximum Temp. ≥ 90°F | 0 | 0 | 0 | 0 | 1 | 3 | 6 | 4 | 1 | 0 | 0 | 0 | 15 |
| Days Maximum Temp. ≤ 32°F | 8 | 4 | 1 | 0 | 0 | 0 | 0 | 0 | 0 | 0 | 0 | 3 | 16 |
| Days Minimum Temp. ≤ 32°F | 23 | 20 | 14 | 2 | 0 | 0 | 0 | 0 | 0 | 0 | 5 | 18 | 82 |
| Days Minimum Temp. ≤ 0°F | 0 | 0 | 0 | 0 | 0 | 0 | 0 | 0 | 0 | 0 | 0 | 0 | 0 |
| Heating Degree Days (base 65°F) | 1,002 | 850 | 725 | 430 | 190 | 23 | 1 | 4 | 56 | 287 | 519 | 844 | 4,931 |
| Cooling Degree Days (base 65°F) | 0 | 0 | 0 | 4 | 34 | 167 | 313 | 279 | 107 | 14 | 0 | 0 | 918 |
| Mean Precipitation (in.) | 3.49 | 2.72 | 4.28 | 4.37 | 3.99 | 3.90 | 4.36 | 3.65 | 3.81 | 4.01 | 3.78 | 3.72 | 46.08 |
| Extreme Maximum Daily Precip. (in.) | 4.05 | 2.05 | 3.11 | 3.72 | 2.87 | 4.30 | 3.82 | 4.04 | 3.52 | 4.02 | 2.92 | 2.95 | 4.30 |
| Days With ≥ 0.1" Precipitation | 6 | 5 | 7 | 7 | 7 | 6 | 6 | 6 | 5 | 6 | 6 | 7 | 74 |
| Days With ≥ 0.5" Precipitation | 2 | 2 | 3 | 3 | 3 | 3 | 3 | 2 | 3 | 3 | 3 | 3 | 33 |
| Days With ≥ 1.0" Precipitation | 1 | 1 | 1 | 1 | 1 | 1 | 1 | 1 | 1 | 1 | 1 | 1 | 12 |
| Mean Snowfall (in.) | 4.9 | 6.4 | 3.6 | 0.6 | 0.0 | 0.0 | 0.0 | 0.0 | 0.0 | 0.0 | 0.1 | 4.2 | 19.8 |
| Maximum Snow Depth (in.) | 12 | 20 | 8 | 9 | 0 | 0 | 0 | 0 | 0 | 0 | 3 | 14 | 20 |
| Days With ≥ 1.0" Snow Depth | 7 | 6 | 2 | 0 | 0 | 0 | 0 | 0 | 0 | 0 | 0 | 3 | 18 |

## Morrisville 5 SW *Madison County*    Elevation: 1,299 ft.    Latitude: 42° 50' N    Longitude: 75° 44' W

|  | JAN | FEB | MAR | APR | MAY | JUN | JUL | AUG | SEP | OCT | NOV | DEC | YEAR |
|---|---|---|---|---|---|---|---|---|---|---|---|---|---|
| Mean Maximum Temp. (°F) | 28.7 | 32.0 | 39.9 | 53.9 | 65.8 | 73.8 | 77.5 | 76.0 | 69.1 | 56.6 | 44.8 | 33.6 | 54.3 |
| Mean Temp. (°F) | 20.0 | 22.6 | 30.2 | 43.5 | 54.6 | 63.0 | 67.0 | 65.6 | 58.8 | 47.0 | 37.1 | 26.2 | 44.6 |
| Mean Minimum Temp. (°F) | 11.4 | 13.1 | 20.4 | 33.1 | 43.4 | 52.2 | 56.3 | 55.3 | 48.5 | 37.3 | 29.3 | 18.7 | 34.9 |
| Extreme Maximum Temp. (°F) | 60 | 60 | 82 | 87 | 87 | 89 | 92 | 90 | 89 | 80 | 75 | 64 | 92 |
| Extreme Minimum Temp. (°F) | -27 | -25 | -21 | 4 | 24 | 30 | 36 | 35 | 24 | 16 | 1 | -30 | -30 |
| Days Maximum Temp. ≥ 90°F | 0 | 0 | 0 | 0 | 0 | 0 | 0 | 0 | 0 | 0 | 0 | 0 | 0 |
| Days Maximum Temp. ≤ 32°F | 19 | 15 | 9 | 1 | 0 | 0 | 0 | 0 | 0 | 0 | 3 | 15 | 62 |
| Days Minimum Temp. ≤ 32°F | 29 | 26 | 26 | 15 | 3 | 0 | 0 | 0 | 1 | 9 | 20 | 28 | 157 |
| Days Minimum Temp. ≤ 0°F | 7 | 5 | 2 | 0 | 0 | 0 | 0 | 0 | 0 | 0 | 0 | 2 | 16 |
| Heating Degree Days (base 65°F) | 1,388 | 1,192 | 1,074 | 641 | 325 | 108 | 36 | 57 | 203 | 551 | 830 | 1,196 | 7,601 |
| Cooling Degree Days (base 65°F) | 0 | 0 | 0 | 2 | 10 | 57 | 104 | 84 | 25 | 1 | 0 | 0 | 283 |
| Mean Precipitation (in.) | 3.15 | 2.99 | 3.38 | 3.66 | 4.09 | 4.48 | 4.02 | 3.57 | 4.32 | 4.08 | 3.94 | 3.88 | 45.56 |
| Extreme Maximum Daily Precip. (in.) | 1.65 | 2.39 | 1.55 | 2.15 | 3.39 | 2.80 | 2.08 | 2.36 | 4.11 | 2.10 | 2.89 | 1.67 | 4.11 |
| Days With ≥ 0.1" Precipitation | 10 | 8 | 9 | 8 | 9 | 8 | 7 | 7 | 8 | 9 | 9 | 11 | 103 |
| Days With ≥ 0.5" Precipitation | 1 | 2 | 2 | 2 | 3 | 3 | 3 | 2 | 3 | 3 | 2 | 2 | 28 |
| Days With ≥ 1.0" Precipitation | 0 | 0 | 0 | 0 | 1 | 1 | 1 | 1 | 1 | 1 | 0 | 0 | 7 |
| Mean Snowfall (in.) | 30.5 | 25.7 | 21.1 | 5.6 | 0.2 | 0.0 | 0.0 | 0.0 | trace | 1.5 | 12.0 | 27.5 | 124.1 |
| Maximum Snow Depth (in.) | 45 | 51 | 44 | 29 | 4 | 0 | 0 | 0 | trace | 17 | 16 | 30 | 51 |
| Days With ≥ 1.0" Snow Depth | 27 | 27 | 22 | 5 | 0 | 0 | 0 | 0 | 0 | 1 | 9 | 24 | 115 |

## New York Ave V Brooklyn *Kings County*    Elevation: 20 ft.    Latitude: 40° 36' N    Longitude: 73° 59' W

|  | JAN | FEB | MAR | APR | MAY | JUN | JUL | AUG | SEP | OCT | NOV | DEC | YEAR |
|---|---|---|---|---|---|---|---|---|---|---|---|---|---|
| Mean Maximum Temp. (°F) | 39.5 | 42.3 | 49.6 | 60.2 | 70.4 | 79.5 | 84.5 | 83.3 | 76.1 | 64.8 | 54.6 | 43.6 | 62.4 |
| Mean Temp. (°F) | 33.4 | 35.7 | 42.3 | 52.4 | 62.3 | 71.7 | 77.1 | 76.1 | 68.9 | 57.6 | 48.1 | 37.8 | 55.3 |
| Mean Minimum Temp. (°F) | 27.2 | 29.0 | 34.9 | 44.5 | 54.2 | 63.8 | 69.7 | 68.9 | 61.7 | 50.3 | 41.5 | 31.9 | 48.2 |
| Extreme Maximum Temp. (°F) | 70 | 73 | 83 | 91 | 96 | 97 | 103 | 101 | 98 | 86 | 79 | 75 | 103 |
| Extreme Minimum Temp. (°F) | -4 | 6 | 10 | 19 | 40 | 48 | 57 | 51 | 44 | 36 | 23 | -1 | -4 |
| Days Maximum Temp. ≥ 90°F | 0 | 0 | 0 | 0 | 1 | 3 | 6 | 4 | 1 | 0 | 0 | 0 | 15 |
| Days Maximum Temp. ≤ 32°F | 7 | 4 | 1 | 0 | 0 | 0 | 0 | 0 | 0 | 0 | 0 | 4 | 16 |
| Days Minimum Temp. ≤ 32°F | 21 | 18 | 11 | 1 | 0 | 0 | 0 | 0 | 0 | 0 | 3 | 15 | 69 |
| Days Minimum Temp. ≤ 0°F | 0 | 0 | 0 | 0 | 0 | 0 | 0 | 0 | 0 | 0 | 0 | 0 | 0 |
| Heating Degree Days (base 65°F) | 973 | 822 | 697 | 378 | 130 | 13 | 0 | 1 | 29 | 241 | 501 | 836 | 4,621 |
| Cooling Degree Days (base 65°F) | 0 | 0 | 0 | 6 | 54 | 220 | 382 | 353 | 153 | 18 | 1 | 0 | 1,187 |
| Mean Precipitation (in.) | 3.54 | 2.66 | 4.22 | 4.36 | 4.19 | 3.92 | 4.83 | 3.68 | 3.73 | 3.73 | 3.78 | 3.32 | 45.96 |
| Extreme Maximum Daily Precip. (in.) | 3.13 | 1.68 | 2.92 | 5.46 | 2.36 | 2.91 | 4.62 | 2.85 | 4.44 | 4.29 | 2.68 | 2.49 | 5.46 |
| Days With ≥ 0.1" Precipitation | 7 | 6 | 7 | 7 | 7 | 7 | 7 | 6 | 6 | 6 | 3 | 3 | 77 |
| Days With ≥ 0.5" Precipitation | 3 | 2 | 3 | 2 | 3 | 3 | 3 | 3 | 3 | 5 | 3 | 3 | 32 |
| Days With ≥ 1.0" Precipitation | 1 | 1 | 1 | 1 | 1 | 1 | 2 | 1 | 1 | 1 | 1 | 1 | 13 |
| Mean Snowfall (in.) | 6.6 | 7.3 | 3.9 | 0.7 | 0.0 | 0.0 | 0.0 | 0.0 | 0.0 | trace | 0.3 | 3.5 | 22.3 |
| Maximum Snow Depth (in.) | 23 | 20 | 10 | 9 | 0 | 0 | 0 | 0 | 0 | trace | 4 | 12 | 23 |
| Days With ≥ 1.0" Snow Depth | 7 | 6 | 3 | 0 | 0 | 0 | 0 | 0 | 0 | 0 | 0 | 2 | 18 |

*The period of record for all cooperative weather station data is 1980 - 2009. See User Guide for detailed explanation of data.*

### Peru 2 WSW *Clinton County*    Elevation: 509 ft.    Latitude: 44° 34' N    Longitude: 73° 34' W

| | JAN | FEB | MAR | APR | MAY | JUN | JUL | AUG | SEP | OCT | NOV | DEC | YEAR |
|---|---|---|---|---|---|---|---|---|---|---|---|---|---|
| Mean Maximum Temp. (°F) | 27.9 | 31.7 | 41.0 | 55.7 | 68.4 | 77.2 | 81.4 | 79.4 | 71.0 | 57.9 | 45.4 | 33.3 | 55.8 |
| Mean Temp. (°F) | 18.6 | 21.9 | 31.1 | 44.7 | 56.5 | 65.7 | 70.2 | 68.0 | 59.9 | 48.0 | 37.3 | 25.1 | 45.6 |
| Mean Minimum Temp. (°F) | 9.2 | 12.1 | 21.2 | 33.8 | 44.6 | 54.2 | 58.9 | 56.5 | 48.7 | 37.9 | 29.1 | 16.8 | 35.3 |
| Extreme Maximum Temp. (°F) | 65 | 63 | 83 | 92 | 93 | 98 | 98 | 98 | 95 | 84 | 75 | 69 | 98 |
| Extreme Minimum Temp. (°F) | -34 | -30 | -17 | 5 | 25 | 29 | 40 | 37 | 24 | 18 | 1 | -26 | -34 |
| Days Maximum Temp. ≥ 90°F | 0 | 0 | 0 | 0 | 0 | 1 | 3 | 2 | 0 | 0 | 0 | 0 | 6 |
| Days Maximum Temp. ≤ 32°F | 20 | 15 | 7 | 0 | 0 | 0 | 0 | 0 | 0 | 0 | 3 | 14 | 59 |
| Days Minimum Temp. ≤ 32°F | 29 | 26 | 26 | 14 | 2 | 0 | 0 | 0 | 1 | 9 | 19 | 28 | 154 |
| Days Minimum Temp. ≤ 0°F | 8 | 6 | 2 | 0 | 0 | 0 | 0 | 0 | 0 | 0 | 0 | 4 | 20 |
| Heating Degree Days (base 65°F) | 1,434 | 1,212 | 1,043 | 604 | 276 | 70 | 13 | 37 | 182 | 523 | 825 | 1,231 | 7,450 |
| Cooling Degree Days (base 65°F) | 0 | 0 | 0 | 3 | 21 | 98 | 180 | 136 | 35 | 2 | 0 | 0 | 475 |
| Mean Precipitation (in.) | 1.37 | 1.29 | 1.71 | 2.56 | 2.73 | 3.62 | 3.49 | 3.51 | 2.81 | 3.00 | 2.67 | 1.96 | 30.72 |
| Extreme Maximum Daily Precip. (in.) | 1.12 | 1.26 | 1.50 | 1.85 | 2.40 | 4.10 | 3.27 | 3.11 | 4.08 | 2.41 | 4.80 | 1.85 | 4.80 |
| Days With ≥ 0.1" Precipitation | 4 | 3 | 4 | 6 | 7 | 7 | 7 | 7 | 5 | 6 | 6 | 4 | 66 |
| Days With ≥ 0.5" Precipitation | 1 | 1 | 1 | 2 | 2 | 2 | 3 | 2 | 2 | 2 | 2 | 1 | 21 |
| Days With ≥ 1.0" Precipitation | 0 | 0 | 0 | 0 | 0 | 1 | 1 | 1 | 1 | 1 | 1 | 0 | 6 |
| Mean Snowfall (in.) | 11.3 | 10.4 | 11.1 | 2.9 | 0.0 | 0.0 | 0.0 | 0.0 | 0.0 | 0.5 | 3.2 | 12.6 | 52.0 |
| Maximum Snow Depth (in.) | na | na | na | na | na | na | na | na | na | na | na | na | na |
| Days With ≥ 1.0" Snow Depth | na | na | na | 0 | 0 | 0 | 0 | 0 | 0 | 0 | 0 | na | na |

### Riverhead Research Farm *Suffolk County*    Elevation: 100 ft.    Latitude: 40° 58' N    Longitude: 72° 43' W

| | JAN | FEB | MAR | APR | MAY | JUN | JUL | AUG | SEP | OCT | NOV | DEC | YEAR |
|---|---|---|---|---|---|---|---|---|---|---|---|---|---|
| Mean Maximum Temp. (°F) | 39.6 | 41.5 | 48.6 | 59.8 | 70.5 | 79.3 | 84.0 | 82.5 | 75.7 | 64.8 | 54.5 | 44.5 | 62.1 |
| Mean Temp. (°F) | 32.3 | 34.0 | 40.3 | 50.3 | 60.3 | 69.5 | 74.8 | 73.7 | 67.1 | 56.3 | 47.1 | 37.3 | 53.6 |
| Mean Minimum Temp. (°F) | 25.0 | 26.4 | 32.0 | 40.8 | 50.0 | 59.7 | 65.5 | 64.8 | 58.4 | 47.8 | 39.5 | 30.1 | 45.0 |
| Extreme Maximum Temp. (°F) | 68 | 67 | 80 | 92 | 96 | 97 | 100 | 99 | 97 | 85 | 78 | 76 | 100 |
| Extreme Minimum Temp. (°F) | -8 | 4 | 9 | 18 | 32 | 42 | 47 | 45 | 37 | 28 | 17 | 1 | -8 |
| Days Maximum Temp. ≥ 90°F | 0 | 0 | 0 | 0 | 1 | 2 | 5 | 3 | 0 | 0 | 0 | 0 | 11 |
| Days Maximum Temp. ≤ 32°F | 7 | 4 | 1 | 0 | 0 | 0 | 0 | 0 | 0 | 0 | 0 | 3 | 15 |
| Days Minimum Temp. ≤ 32°F | 25 | 21 | 17 | 3 | 0 | 0 | 0 | 0 | 0 | 1 | 6 | 19 | 92 |
| Days Minimum Temp. ≤ 0°F | 0 | 0 | 0 | 0 | 0 | 0 | 0 | 0 | 0 | 0 | 0 | 0 | 0 |
| Heating Degree Days (base 65°F) | 1,006 | 870 | 758 | 436 | 172 | 22 | 0 | 2 | 42 | 274 | 532 | 851 | 4,965 |
| Cooling Degree Days (base 65°F) | 0 | 0 | 0 | 3 | 33 | 165 | 310 | 280 | 111 | 12 | 0 | 0 | 914 |
| Mean Precipitation (in.) | 3.71 | 3.14 | 4.48 | 4.49 | 3.86 | 4.12 | 3.21 | 3.90 | 3.84 | 4.22 | 4.27 | 4.01 | 47.25 |
| Extreme Maximum Daily Precip. (in.) | 3.10 | 2.34 | 3.06 | 3.18 | 3.01 | 5.27 | 3.38 | 6.34 | 3.84 | 5.58 | 2.90 | 3.62 | 6.34 |
| Days With ≥ 0.1" Precipitation | 7 | 6 | 7 | 7 | 7 | 7 | 5 | 6 | 6 | 6 | 7 | 7 | 78 |
| Days With ≥ 0.5" Precipitation | 3 | 2 | 3 | 3 | 3 | 3 | 2 | 3 | 3 | 3 | 3 | 3 | 34 |
| Days With ≥ 1.0" Precipitation | 1 | 1 | 1 | 1 | 1 | 1 | 1 | 1 | 1 | 1 | 1 | 1 | 12 |
| Mean Snowfall (in.) | 8.4 | 7.6 | 5.1 | 0.7 | 0.0 | 0.0 | 0.0 | 0.0 | 0.0 | 0.0 | 0.5 | 4.7 | 27.0 |
| Maximum Snow Depth (in.) | 20 | 16 | 14 | 6 | 0 | 0 | 0 | 0 | 0 | 0 | 7 | 20 | 20 |
| Days With ≥ 1.0" Snow Depth | 9 | 6 | 3 | 0 | 0 | 0 | 0 | 0 | 0 | 0 | 0 | 3 | 21 |

### Troy Lock and Dam *Rensselaer County*    Elevation: 23 ft.    Latitude: 42° 45' N    Longitude: 73° 41' W

| | JAN | FEB | MAR | APR | MAY | JUN | JUL | AUG | SEP | OCT | NOV | DEC | YEAR |
|---|---|---|---|---|---|---|---|---|---|---|---|---|---|
| Mean Maximum Temp. (°F) | 31.7 | 35.3 | 44.3 | 58.6 | 70.4 | 78.7 | 83.5 | 82.2 | 74.3 | 61.6 | 49.4 | 37.1 | 58.9 |
| Mean Temp. (°F) | 23.2 | 25.9 | 34.7 | 48.0 | 59.2 | 68.2 | 73.1 | 71.6 | 63.5 | 51.3 | 40.9 | 29.6 | 49.1 |
| Mean Minimum Temp. (°F) | 14.6 | 16.5 | 25.0 | 37.4 | 47.9 | 57.7 | 62.6 | 60.9 | 52.6 | 40.9 | 32.4 | 22.1 | 39.2 |
| Extreme Maximum Temp. (°F) | 66 | 67 | 84 | 92 | 92 | 96 | 101 | 99 | 93 | 86 | 81 | 69 | 101 |
| Extreme Minimum Temp. (°F) | -23 | -14 | -7 | 15 | 27 | 39 | 48 | 40 | 31 | 23 | 10 | -15 | -23 |
| Days Maximum Temp. ≥ 90°F | 0 | 0 | 0 | 0 | 0 | 3 | 5 | 4 | 1 | 0 | 0 | 0 | 13 |
| Days Maximum Temp. ≤ 32°F | 15 | 11 | 4 | 0 | 0 | 0 | 0 | 0 | 0 | 0 | 1 | 9 | 40 |
| Days Minimum Temp. ≤ 32°F | 28 | 26 | 24 | 8 | 0 | 0 | 0 | 0 | 0 | 5 | 16 | 26 | 133 |
| Days Minimum Temp. ≤ 0°F | 5 | 2 | 1 | 0 | 0 | 0 | 0 | 0 | 0 | 0 | 0 | 1 | 9 |
| Heating Degree Days (base 65°F) | 1,290 | 1,098 | 933 | 506 | 204 | 40 | 3 | 12 | 107 | 423 | 716 | 1,090 | 6,422 |
| Cooling Degree Days (base 65°F) | 0 | 0 | 0 | 4 | 30 | 142 | 260 | 224 | 68 | 5 | 0 | 0 | 733 |
| Mean Precipitation (in.) | 2.23 | 1.88 | 2.98 | 3.26 | 3.74 | 4.22 | 4.42 | 4.09 | 3.32 | 3.65 | 3.09 | 2.58 | 39.46 |
| Extreme Maximum Daily Precip. (in.) | 1.80 | 1.71 | 3.00 | 2.20 | 2.40 | 2.68 | 2.70 | 2.71 | 3.00 | 2.22 | 2.62 | 2.50 | 3.00 |
| Days With ≥ 0.1" Precipitation | 5 | 5 | 6 | 7 | 8 | 7 | 8 | 7 | 6 | 7 | 6 | 6 | 78 |
| Days With ≥ 0.5" Precipitation | 1 | 1 | 2 | 2 | 3 | 3 | 3 | 3 | 2 | 3 | 2 | 2 | 27 |
| Days With ≥ 1.0" Precipitation | 0 | 0 | 1 | 1 | 1 | 1 | 1 | 1 | 1 | 1 | 1 | 0 | 9 |
| Mean Snowfall (in.) | 12.7 | 8.0 | 7.5 | 1.3 | 0.0 | 0.0 | 0.0 | 0.0 | 0.0 | 0.1 | 1.8 | 7.2 | 38.6 |
| Maximum Snow Depth (in.) | 38 | 39 | 30 | 16 | 0 | 0 | 0 | 0 | 0 | 0 | 10 | 19 | 39 |
| Days With ≥ 1.0" Snow Depth | 19 | 16 | 8 | 1 | 0 | 0 | 0 | 0 | 0 | 0 | 1 | 10 | 55 |

### Tully Heiberg Forest *Cortland County*    Elevation: 1,898 ft.    Latitude: 42° 46' N    Longitude: 76° 05' W

| | JAN | FEB | MAR | APR | MAY | JUN | JUL | AUG | SEP | OCT | NOV | DEC | YEAR |
|---|---|---|---|---|---|---|---|---|---|---|---|---|---|
| Mean Maximum Temp. (°F) | 27.2 | 29.8 | 37.5 | 50.6 | 63.0 | 71.6 | 75.9 | 74.7 | 66.9 | 54.9 | 43.1 | 31.9 | 52.3 |
| Mean Temp. (°F) | 19.5 | 21.3 | 28.9 | 41.5 | 53.1 | 61.9 | 66.4 | 65.2 | 57.6 | 46.1 | 35.7 | 24.7 | 43.5 |
| Mean Minimum Temp. (°F) | 11.6 | 12.8 | 20.3 | 32.2 | 43.2 | 52.2 | 56.9 | 55.7 | 48.2 | 37.2 | 28.2 | 17.5 | 34.7 |
| Extreme Maximum Temp. (°F) | 61 | 58 | 80 | 85 | 88 | 89 | 93 | 92 | 89 | 80 | 74 | 65 | 93 |
| Extreme Minimum Temp. (°F) | -21 | -19 | -11 | 5 | 24 | 30 | 41 | 33 | 25 | 17 | 3 | -29 | -29 |
| Days Maximum Temp. ≥ 90°F | 0 | 0 | 0 | 0 | 0 | 0 | 0 | 0 | 0 | 0 | 0 | 0 | 0 |
| Days Maximum Temp. ≤ 32°F | 21 | 17 | 11 | 2 | 0 | 0 | 0 | 0 | 0 | 0 | 5 | 16 | 72 |
| Days Minimum Temp. ≤ 32°F | 30 | 27 | 27 | 16 | 3 | 0 | 0 | 0 | 1 | 10 | 21 | 29 | 164 |
| Days Minimum Temp. ≤ 0°F | 6 | 5 | 1 | 0 | 0 | 0 | 0 | 0 | 0 | 0 | 0 | 2 | 14 |
| Heating Degree Days (base 65°F) | 1,406 | 1,228 | 1,113 | 702 | 374 | 141 | 50 | 69 | 238 | 580 | 872 | 1,241 | 8,014 |
| Cooling Degree Days (base 65°F) | 0 | 0 | 0 | 2 | 11 | 53 | 101 | 83 | 21 | 1 | 0 | 0 | 272 |
| Mean Precipitation (in.) | 2.85 | 2.67 | 3.33 | 3.96 | 3.99 | 4.85 | 4.00 | 4.04 | 4.80 | 3.97 | 4.00 | 3.28 | 45.74 |
| Extreme Maximum Daily Precip. (in.) | 1.91 | 1.30 | 2.22 | 2.23 | 1.85 | 3.22 | 2.30 | 4.24 | 4.98 | 3.56 | 3.56 | 2.68 | 4.98 |
| Days With ≥ 0.1" Precipitation | 7 | 7 | 9 | 9 | 9 | 10 | 8 | 8 | 8 | 9 | 9 | 8 | 103 |
| Days With ≥ 0.5" Precipitation | 1 | 1 | 2 | 2 | 3 | 3 | 2 | 3 | 3 | 2 | 3 | 2 | 27 |
| Days With ≥ 1.0" Precipitation | 0 | 0 | 1 | 1 | 1 | 1 | 1 | 1 | 1 | 1 | 1 | 0 | 8 |
| Mean Snowfall (in.) | 26.3 | 23.3 | 21.1 | 7.6 | 0.4 | trace | 0.0 | 0.0 | trace | 1.8 | 11.9 | 23.4 | 115.8 |
| Maximum Snow Depth (in.) | 47 | 43 | 60 | 36 | 5 | 0 | 0 | 0 | trace | 9 | 17 | 34 | 60 |
| Days With ≥ 1.0" Snow Depth | 28 | 27 | 26 | 8 | 0 | 0 | 0 | 0 | 0 | 1 | 10 | 24 | 124 |

*The period of record for all cooperative weather station data is 1980 – 2009. See User Guide for detailed explanation of data.*

## Utica Oneida County Arpt *Oneida County*    Elevation: 711 ft.    Latitude: 43° 09' N    Longitude: 75° 23' W

| | JAN | FEB | MAR | APR | MAY | JUN | JUL | AUG | SEP | OCT | NOV | DEC | YEAR |
|---|---|---|---|---|---|---|---|---|---|---|---|---|---|
| Mean Maximum Temp. (°F) | 29.4 | 32.3 | 40.9 | 55.0 | 67.6 | 75.9 | 80.4 | 78.7 | 70.6 | 58.1 | 46.0 | 34.0 | 55.7 |
| Mean Temp. (°F) | 21.9 | 24.1 | 32.4 | 45.3 | 56.8 | 65.4 | 70.2 | 68.6 | 60.8 | 49.0 | 38.8 | 27.0 | 46.7 |
| Mean Minimum Temp. (°F) | 14.3 | 15.9 | 23.9 | 35.6 | 46.0 | 54.9 | 59.9 | 58.4 | 50.9 | 39.9 | 31.5 | 20.1 | 37.6 |
| Extreme Maximum Temp. (°F) | 65 | 63 | 85 | 91 | 91 | 94 | 96 | 97 | 92 | 82 | 79 | 69 | 97 |
| Extreme Minimum Temp. (°F) | -27 | -17 | -12 | 9 | 27 | 33 | 45 | 40 | 25 | 21 | 1 | -23 | -27 |
| Days Maximum Temp. ≥ 90°F | 0 | 0 | 0 | 0 | 0 | 1 | 2 | 1 | 0 | 0 | 0 | 0 | 4 |
| Days Maximum Temp. ≤ 32°F | 18 | 15 | 7 | 0 | 0 | 0 | 0 | 0 | 0 | 0 | 2 | 13 | 55 |
| Days Minimum Temp. ≤ 32°F | 28 | 26 | 24 | 11 | 1 | 0 | 0 | 0 | 0 | 6 | 17 | 27 | 140 |
| Days Minimum Temp. ≤ 0°F | 5 | 3 | 1 | 0 | 0 | 0 | 0 | 0 | 0 | 0 | 0 | 2 | 11 |
| Heating Degree Days (base 65°F) | 1,328 | 1,149 | 1,005 | 586 | 269 | 77 | 12 | 29 | 162 | 492 | 780 | 1,170 | 7,059 |
| Cooling Degree Days (base 65°F) | 0 | 0 | 1 | 3 | 22 | 95 | 181 | 148 | 42 | 2 | 0 | 0 | 494 |
| Mean Precipitation (in.) | 2.94 | 2.38 | 3.15 | 3.47 | 3.90 | 4.28 | 3.86 | 3.88 | 4.10 | 3.66 | 3.91 | 3.37 | 42.90 |
| Extreme Maximum Daily Precip. (in.) | 1.64 | 1.88 | 2.31 | 1.96 | 2.75 | 2.98 | 3.24 | 2.80 | 4.14 | 1.88 | 2.35 | 2.11 | 4.14 |
| Days With ≥ 0.1" Precipitation | 8 | 7 | 8 | 9 | 9 | 8 | 7 | 7 | 7 | 8 | 10 | 9 | 97 |
| Days With ≥ 0.5" Precipitation | 1 | 1 | 2 | 2 | 2 | 3 | 3 | 3 | 3 | 2 | 2 | 1 | 25 |
| Days With ≥ 1.0" Precipitation | 0 | 0 | 1 | 0 | 1 | 1 | 1 | 1 | 1 | 1 | 1 | 0 | 8 |
| Mean Snowfall (in.) | na | na | na | na | na | na | na | na | na | na | na | na | na |
| Maximum Snow Depth (in.) | 33 | na | na | na | na | na | na | na | na | na | na | na | na |
| Days With ≥ 1.0" Snow Depth | 24 | na | na | na | na | na | na | na | na | na | na | na | na |

## Valatie 1 N *Columbia County*    Elevation: 299 ft.    Latitude: 42° 26' N    Longitude: 73° 41' W

| | JAN | FEB | MAR | APR | MAY | JUN | JUL | AUG | SEP | OCT | NOV | DEC | YEAR |
|---|---|---|---|---|---|---|---|---|---|---|---|---|---|
| Mean Maximum Temp. (°F) | 32.2 | 35.9 | 44.2 | 57.7 | 69.4 | 77.5 | 82.2 | 80.9 | 73.4 | 61.1 | 49.2 | 37.2 | 58.4 |
| Mean Temp. (°F) | 22.6 | 26.1 | 34.2 | 46.6 | 57.6 | 66.2 | 70.7 | 69.6 | 61.7 | 49.6 | 39.9 | 28.3 | 47.8 |
| Mean Minimum Temp. (°F) | 13.0 | 16.2 | 24.0 | 35.3 | 45.7 | 54.9 | 59.2 | 58.2 | 49.9 | 38.1 | 30.6 | 19.5 | 37.1 |
| Extreme Maximum Temp. (°F) | 71 | 69 | 86 | 93 | 92 | 97 | 100 | 97 | 94 | 87 | 81 | 69 | 100 |
| Extreme Minimum Temp. (°F) | -25 | -13 | -9 | 10 | 27 | 34 | 43 | 35 | 28 | 19 | 2 | -20 | -25 |
| Days Maximum Temp. ≥ 90°F | 0 | 0 | 0 | 0 | 0 | 2 | 4 | 3 | 1 | 0 | 0 | 0 | 10 |
| Days Maximum Temp. ≤ 32°F | 15 | 11 | 4 | 0 | 0 | 0 | 0 | 0 | 0 | 0 | 1 | 9 | 40 |
| Days Minimum Temp. ≤ 32°F | 29 | 26 | 25 | 12 | 2 | 0 | 0 | 0 | 0 | 9 | 18 | 27 | 148 |
| Days Minimum Temp. ≤ 0°F | 6 | 2 | 1 | 0 | 0 | 0 | 0 | 0 | 0 | 0 | 0 | 2 | 11 |
| Heating Degree Days (base 65°F) | 1,308 | 1,094 | 950 | 550 | 250 | 65 | 13 | 25 | 142 | 474 | 747 | 1,129 | 6,747 |
| Cooling Degree Days (base 65°F) | 0 | 0 | 1 | 3 | 27 | 109 | 197 | 173 | 48 | 3 | 0 | 0 | 561 |
| Mean Precipitation (in.) | 2.05 | 1.90 | 2.82 | 3.74 | 4.07 | 4.50 | 4.06 | 4.14 | 3.96 | 3.91 | 3.29 | 2.55 | 40.99 |
| Extreme Maximum Daily Precip. (in.) | 1.28 | 1.15 | 3.89 | 3.65 | 3.00 | 2.68 | 3.87 | 3.51 | 5.10 | 2.94 | 2.16 | 2.25 | 5.10 |
| Days With ≥ 0.1" Precipitation | 5 | 5 | 6 | 8 | 8 | 8 | 7 | 7 | 7 | 7 | 6 | 6 | 80 |
| Days With ≥ 0.5" Precipitation | 2 | 1 | 2 | 2 | 3 | 3 | 3 | 3 | 3 | 3 | 2 | 2 | 29 |
| Days With ≥ 1.0" Precipitation | 0 | 0 | 1 | 1 | 1 | 1 | 1 | 1 | 1 | 1 | 1 | 0 | 9 |
| Mean Snowfall (in.) | 10.8 | 8.2 | 6.4 | 2.2 | 0.0 | 0.0 | 0.0 | 0.0 | 0.0 | 0.3 | 2.4 | 11.1 | 41.4 |
| Maximum Snow Depth (in.) | 33 | 24 | 18 | 14 | 0 | 0 | 0 | 0 | 0 | 6 | 9 | 17 | 33 |
| Days With ≥ 1.0" Snow Depth | 18 | 15 | 8 | 1 | 0 | 0 | 0 | 0 | 0 | 0 | 1 | 10 | 53 |

## Wales *Erie County*    Elevation: 1,089 ft.    Latitude: 42° 45' N    Longitude: 78° 31' W

| | JAN | FEB | MAR | APR | MAY | JUN | JUL | AUG | SEP | OCT | NOV | DEC | YEAR |
|---|---|---|---|---|---|---|---|---|---|---|---|---|---|
| Mean Maximum Temp. (°F) | 31.3 | 32.5 | 41.2 | 54.6 | 65.5 | 74.0 | 77.4 | 76.3 | 69.5 | 57.9 | 46.9 | 35.2 | 55.2 |
| Mean Temp. (°F) | 23.6 | 23.6 | 31.6 | 44.0 | 54.4 | 63.8 | 67.4 | 66.1 | 59.3 | 48.4 | 38.9 | 28.2 | 45.8 |
| Mean Minimum Temp. (°F) | 15.9 | 14.7 | 22.0 | 33.4 | 43.3 | 53.7 | 57.4 | 55.9 | 48.9 | 38.8 | 30.9 | 21.1 | 36.3 |
| Extreme Maximum Temp. (°F) | 65 | 71 | 82 | 89 | 88 | 92 | 95 | 94 | 90 | 83 | 73 | 68 | 95 |
| Extreme Minimum Temp. (°F) | -18 | -14 | -12 | 12 | 27 | 31 | 40 | 35 | 26 | 21 | 7 | -19 | -19 |
| Days Maximum Temp. ≥ 90°F | 0 | 0 | 0 | 0 | 0 | 0 | 0 | 0 | 0 | 0 | 0 | 0 | 0 |
| Days Maximum Temp. ≤ 32°F | 17 | 14 | 9 | 1 | 0 | 0 | 0 | 0 | 0 | 0 | 3 | 12 | 56 |
| Days Minimum Temp. ≤ 32°F | 28 | 26 | 26 | 16 | 3 | 0 | 0 | 1 | 8 | 18 | 27 | 153 | |
| Days Minimum Temp. ≤ 0°F | 4 | 4 | 1 | 0 | 0 | 0 | 0 | 0 | 0 | 0 | 0 | 1 | 10 |
| Heating Degree Days (base 65°F) | 1,275 | 1,163 | 1,027 | 625 | 337 | 103 | 38 | 55 | 195 | 513 | 776 | 1,135 | 7,242 |
| Cooling Degree Days (base 65°F) | 0 | 0 | 0 | 1 | 17 | 75 | 120 | 96 | 29 | 4 | 0 | 0 | 345 |
| Mean Precipitation (in.) | 3.49 | 2.55 | 3.00 | 3.35 | 3.36 | 4.17 | 3.90 | 3.71 | 4.26 | 3.72 | 3.68 | 3.80 | 42.99 |
| Extreme Maximum Daily Precip. (in.) | 2.47 | 2.30 | 1.76 | 1.64 | 1.54 | 5.33 | 2.97 | 3.22 | 3.09 | 1.89 | 2.35 | 1.43 | 5.33 |
| Days With ≥ 0.1" Precipitation | 11 | 8 | 8 | 8 | 8 | 8 | 8 | 8 | 8 | 8 | 9 | 11 | 103 |
| Days With ≥ 0.5" Precipitation | 2 | 1 | 2 | 2 | 2 | 3 | 3 | 3 | 3 | 3 | 2 | 2 | 29 |
| Days With ≥ 1.0" Precipitation | 0 | 0 | 0 | 0 | 0 | 1 | 1 | 1 | 1 | 1 | 0 | 0 | 5 |
| Mean Snowfall (in.) | 32.7 | 19.0 | 15.9 | 4.8 | 0.3 | 0.0 | 0.0 | 0.0 | 0.0 | 0.3 | 10.1 | 27.7 | 110.8 |
| Maximum Snow Depth (in.) | 34 | 28 | 29 | 11 | 6 | 0 | 0 | 0 | 0 | 2 | 20 | 19 | 34 |
| Days With ≥ 1.0" Snow Depth | 25 | 23 | 16 | 3 | 0 | 0 | 0 | 0 | 0 | 0 | 6 | 20 | 93 |

## Wantagh Cedar Creek *Nassau County*    Elevation: 9 ft.    Latitude: 40° 39' N    Longitude: 73° 30' W

| | JAN | FEB | MAR | APR | MAY | JUN | JUL | AUG | SEP | OCT | NOV | DEC | YEAR |
|---|---|---|---|---|---|---|---|---|---|---|---|---|---|
| Mean Maximum Temp. (°F) | 38.3 | 40.2 | 47.1 | 56.4 | 65.9 | 76.1 | 81.4 | 81.2 | 74.4 | 64.0 | 54.0 | 43.4 | 60.2 |
| Mean Temp. (°F) | 32.3 | 33.8 | 40.3 | 49.3 | 58.4 | 68.7 | 74.0 | 73.8 | 66.7 | 56.3 | 47.0 | 37.4 | 53.2 |
| Mean Minimum Temp. (°F) | 26.2 | 27.3 | 33.4 | 41.9 | 50.9 | 61.2 | 66.7 | 66.4 | 59.0 | 48.5 | 40.0 | 31.3 | 46.1 |
| Extreme Maximum Temp. (°F) | 69 | 67 | 81 | 89 | 95 | 97 | 103 | 103 | 92 | 90 | 78 | 77 | 103 |
| Extreme Minimum Temp. (°F) | -3 | 0 | 5 | 19 | 29 | 34 | 45 | 48 | 38 | 28 | 15 | 3 | -3 |
| Days Maximum Temp. ≥ 90°F | 0 | 0 | 0 | 0 | 0 | 1 | 3 | 2 | 0 | 0 | 0 | 0 | 6 |
| Days Maximum Temp. ≤ 32°F | 8 | 5 | 1 | 0 | 0 | 0 | 0 | 0 | 0 | 0 | 0 | 4 | 18 |
| Days Minimum Temp. ≤ 32°F | 22 | 21 | 14 | 2 | 0 | 0 | 0 | 0 | 0 | 0 | 6 | 18 | 83 |
| Days Minimum Temp. ≤ 0°F | 0 | 0 | 0 | 0 | 0 | 0 | 0 | 0 | 0 | 0 | 0 | 0 | 0 |
| Heating Degree Days (base 65°F) | 1,008 | 876 | 760 | 466 | 220 | 32 | 7 | 3 | 51 | 279 | 534 | 847 | 5,083 |
| Cooling Degree Days (base 65°F) | 0 | 0 | 0 | 2 | 23 | 149 | 295 | 283 | 109 | 16 | 1 | 0 | 878 |
| Mean Precipitation (in.) | 3.32 | 2.62 | 4.00 | 4.22 | 3.60 | 3.57 | 3.60 | 3.29 | 3.50 | 3.67 | 3.46 | 3.55 | 42.40 |
| Extreme Maximum Daily Precip. (in.) | 4.91 | 2.19 | 2.47 | 4.64 | 2.44 | 3.32 | 3.90 | 3.89 | 3.73 | 5.43 | 2.21 | 2.36 | 5.43 |
| Days With ≥ 0.1" Precipitation | 6 | 5 | 7 | 7 | 6 | 6 | 6 | 5 | 5 | 5 | 6 | 7 | 71 |
| Days With ≥ 0.5" Precipitation | 2 | 1 | 3 | 3 | 2 | 2 | 3 | 2 | 3 | 3 | 3 | 3 | 28 |
| Days With ≥ 1.0" Precipitation | 1 | 0 | 1 | 1 | 1 | 1 | 1 | 1 | 1 | 1 | 1 | 1 | 11 |
| Mean Snowfall (in.) | na | na | na | 0.0 | 0.0 | 0.0 | 0.0 | 0.0 | 0.0 | 0.0 | 0.0 | na | na |
| Maximum Snow Depth (in.) | na | na | na | na | na | na | na | na | na | na | na | na | na |
| Days With ≥ 1.0" Snow Depth | na | na | na | 0 | 0 | 0 | 0 | 0 | 0 | 0 | 0 | na | na |

*The period of record for all cooperative weather station data is 1980 – 2009. See User Guide for detailed explanation of data.*

### Westfield 2 SSE *Chautauqua County*   Elevation: 707 ft.   Latitude: 42° 18' N   Longitude: 79° 35' W

| | JAN | FEB | MAR | APR | MAY | JUN | JUL | AUG | SEP | OCT | NOV | DEC | YEAR |
|---|---|---|---|---|---|---|---|---|---|---|---|---|---|
| Mean Maximum Temp. (°F) | 32.8 | 35.3 | 43.1 | 55.6 | 67.3 | 76.1 | 80.3 | 78.2 | 71.0 | 59.7 | 48.2 | 37.4 | 57.1 |
| Mean Temp. (°F) | 26.4 | 28.0 | 35.0 | 46.8 | 58.3 | 67.2 | 71.8 | 70.1 | 63.1 | 52.2 | 41.8 | 31.5 | 49.3 |
| Mean Minimum Temp. (°F) | 19.9 | 20.5 | 26.9 | 37.9 | 49.2 | 58.1 | 63.3 | 62.0 | 55.2 | 44.6 | 35.4 | 25.6 | 41.6 |
| Extreme Maximum Temp. (°F) | 66 | 70 | 82 | 90 | 91 | 97 | 96 | 99 | 92 | 83 | 74 | 72 | 99 |
| Extreme Minimum Temp. (°F) | -16 | -7 | -13 | 14 | 29 | 37 | 49 | 41 | 36 | 27 | 16 | -8 | -16 |
| Days Maximum Temp. ≥ 90°F | 0 | 0 | 0 | 0 | 0 | 2 | 2 | 1 | 0 | 0 | 0 | 0 | 5 |
| Days Maximum Temp. ≤ 32°F | 15 | 12 | 6 | 0 | 0 | 0 | 0 | 0 | 0 | 0 | 1 | 10 | 44 |
| Days Minimum Temp. ≤ 32°F | 27 | 25 | 23 | 9 | 0 | 0 | 0 | 0 | 0 | 1 | 11 | 24 | 120 |
| Days Minimum Temp. ≤ 0°F | 1 | 1 | 0 | 0 | 0 | 0 | 0 | 0 | 0 | 0 | 0 | 0 | 2 |
| Heating Degree Days (base 65°F) | 1,191 | 1,041 | 924 | 546 | 241 | 60 | 7 | 14 | 119 | 398 | 690 | 1,032 | 6,263 |
| Cooling Degree Days (base 65°F) | 0 | 0 | 1 | 7 | 40 | 131 | 226 | 180 | 70 | 7 | 0 | 0 | 662 |
| Mean Precipitation (in.) | 2.50 | 2.20 | 2.90 | 3.40 | 3.82 | 4.14 | 4.16 | 3.96 | 4.89 | 4.88 | 4.32 | 3.42 | 44.59 |
| Extreme Maximum Daily Precip. (in.) | 1.38 | 2.09 | 1.11 | 1.76 | 2.17 | 4.29 | 3.36 | 2.41 | 2.85 | 2.52 | 3.38 | 1.65 | 4.29 |
| Days With ≥ 0.1" Precipitation | 7 | 7 | 8 | 8 | 8 | 8 | 7 | 7 | 9 | 10 | 10 | 9 | 98 |
| Days With ≥ 0.5" Precipitation | 1 | 1 | 2 | 2 | 2 | 2 | 3 | 3 | 4 | 4 | 3 | 2 | 29 |
| Days With ≥ 1.0" Precipitation | 0 | 0 | 0 | 0 | 1 | 1 | 1 | 1 | 1 | 1 | 0 | 0 | 7 |
| Mean Snowfall (in.) | 21.2 | 14.0 | 12.7 | 2.7 | 0.4 | 0.0 | 0.0 | 0.0 | trace | 0.4 | 8.7 | 24.4 | 84.5 |
| Maximum Snow Depth (in.) | 23 | 22 | 17 | 9 | na | 0 | 0 | 0 | trace | na | 11 | 25 | na |
| Days With ≥ 1.0" Snow Depth | 25 | 20 | 12 | 1 | 0 | 0 | 0 | 0 | 0 | 0 | 5 | 17 | 80 |

### Whitehall *Washington County*   Elevation: 119 ft.   Latitude: 43° 33' N   Longitude: 73° 24' W

| | JAN | FEB | MAR | APR | MAY | JUN | JUL | AUG | SEP | OCT | NOV | DEC | YEAR |
|---|---|---|---|---|---|---|---|---|---|---|---|---|---|
| Mean Maximum Temp. (°F) | 30.1 | 34.4 | 44.3 | 58.6 | 70.8 | 79.7 | 84.0 | 81.8 | 73.1 | 60.6 | 47.5 | 35.1 | 58.3 |
| Mean Temp. (°F) | 21.0 | 24.1 | 34.1 | 47.5 | 59.1 | 68.2 | 72.6 | 70.9 | 62.4 | 50.6 | 39.7 | 27.4 | 48.1 |
| Mean Minimum Temp. (°F) | 11.8 | 13.7 | 23.9 | 36.2 | 47.0 | 56.6 | 61.2 | 60.1 | 51.7 | 40.6 | 31.8 | 19.7 | 37.9 |
| Extreme Maximum Temp. (°F) | 64 | 63 | 84 | 94 | 92 | 102 | 100 | 96 | 94 | 83 | 75 | 68 | 102 |
| Extreme Minimum Temp. (°F) | -36 | -33 | -14 | 13 | 23 | 36 | 45 | 37 | 28 | 19 | 4 | -25 | -36 |
| Days Maximum Temp. ≥ 90°F | 0 | 0 | 0 | 0 | 0 | 3 | 4 | 3 | 0 | 0 | 0 | 0 | 10 |
| Days Maximum Temp. ≤ 32°F | 17 | 11 | 4 | 0 | 0 | 0 | 0 | 0 | 0 | 0 | 1 | 12 | 45 |
| Days Minimum Temp. ≤ 32°F | 29 | 26 | 24 | 11 | 1 | 0 | 0 | 0 | 0 | 6 | 17 | 27 | 141 |
| Days Minimum Temp. ≤ 0°F | 7 | 5 | 1 | 0 | 0 | 0 | 0 | 0 | 0 | 0 | 0 | 2 | 15 |
| Heating Degree Days (base 65°F) | 1,360 | 1,150 | 952 | 523 | 204 | 38 | 3 | 13 | 132 | 442 | 755 | 1,158 | 6,730 |
| Cooling Degree Days (base 65°F) | 0 | 0 | 0 | 5 | 29 | 141 | 246 | 204 | 62 | 3 | 0 | 0 | 690 |
| Mean Precipitation (in.) | 3.01 | 2.52 | 2.95 | 3.22 | 3.67 | 3.89 | 4.46 | 4.16 | 3.68 | 3.72 | 3.55 | 3.22 | 42.05 |
| Extreme Maximum Daily Precip. (in.) | 1.96 | 2.40 | 2.02 | 2.23 | 1.85 | 2.96 | 3.45 | 4.01 | 4.25 | 2.62 | 2.59 | 2.89 | 4.25 |
| Days With ≥ 0.1" Precipitation | 6 | 5 | 6 | 7 | 8 | 7 | 7 | 7 | 6 | 7 | 7 | 6 | 79 |
| Days With ≥ 0.5" Precipitation | 2 | 2 | 2 | 2 | 2 | 3 | 3 | 3 | 2 | 2 | 3 | 2 | 28 |
| Days With ≥ 1.0" Precipitation | 1 | 0 | 1 | 1 | 1 | 1 | 1 | 1 | 1 | 1 | 1 | 1 | 11 |
| Mean Snowfall (in.) | 16.6 | 12.0 | 12.5 | 2.1 | 0.0 | 0.0 | 0.0 | 0.0 | 0.0 | trace | 2.7 | 13.6 | 59.5 |
| Maximum Snow Depth (in.) | na | na | na | 2 | 0 | 0 | 0 | 0 | 0 | na | na | na | na |
| Days With ≥ 1.0" Snow Depth | na | na | na | 0 | 0 | 0 | 0 | 0 | 0 | 0 | 0 | na | na |

### Yorktown Heights 1 W *Westchester County*   Elevation: 669 ft.   Latitude: 41° 16' N   Longitude: 73° 48' W

| | JAN | FEB | MAR | APR | MAY | JUN | JUL | AUG | SEP | OCT | NOV | DEC | YEAR |
|---|---|---|---|---|---|---|---|---|---|---|---|---|---|
| Mean Maximum Temp. (°F) | 34.5 | 38.4 | 46.8 | 59.1 | 69.4 | 77.5 | 82.0 | 80.7 | 73.5 | 62.1 | 51.2 | 39.6 | 59.6 |
| Mean Temp. (°F) | 26.6 | 29.7 | 37.5 | 49.2 | 59.2 | 67.9 | 72.7 | 71.4 | 63.9 | 52.6 | 43.1 | 32.3 | 50.5 |
| Mean Minimum Temp. (°F) | 18.7 | 21.0 | 28.2 | 39.2 | 48.8 | 58.2 | 63.3 | 62.1 | 54.4 | 43.1 | 35.0 | 24.9 | 41.4 |
| Extreme Maximum Temp. (°F) | 67 | 73 | 85 | 95 | 94 | 95 | 100 | 100 | 95 | 87 | 78 | 73 | 100 |
| Extreme Minimum Temp. (°F) | -15 | -5 | 0 | 14 | 33 | 39 | 49 | 39 | 32 | 25 | 13 | -9 | -15 |
| Days Maximum Temp. ≥ 90°F | 0 | 0 | 0 | 0 | 0 | 2 | 3 | 2 | 1 | 0 | 0 | 0 | 8 |
| Days Maximum Temp. ≤ 32°F | 13 | 8 | 3 | 0 | 0 | 0 | 0 | 0 | 0 | 0 | 1 | 7 | 32 |
| Days Minimum Temp. ≤ 32°F | 28 | 25 | 21 | 5 | 0 | 0 | 0 | 0 | 0 | 3 | 12 | 25 | 119 |
| Days Minimum Temp. ≤ 0°F | 2 | 0 | 0 | 0 | 0 | 0 | 0 | 0 | 0 | 0 | 0 | 0 | 2 |
| Heating Degree Days (base 65°F) | 1,183 | 991 | 846 | 474 | 208 | 43 | 4 | 11 | 96 | 385 | 650 | 1,008 | 5,899 |
| Cooling Degree Days (base 65°F) | 0 | 0 | 1 | 6 | 33 | 136 | 249 | 217 | 71 | 7 | 0 | 0 | 720 |
| Mean Precipitation (in.) | 3.59 | 2.97 | 3.96 | 4.60 | 4.35 | 4.76 | 4.82 | 4.41 | 4.53 | 4.53 | 4.39 | 3.88 | 50.79 |
| Extreme Maximum Daily Precip. (in.) | 2.48 | 2.22 | 4.60 | 5.15 | 3.35 | 2.82 | 3.44 | 4.04 | 10.95 | 4.64 | 2.97 | 3.00 | 10.95 |
| Days With ≥ 0.1" Precipitation | 7 | 6 | 7 | 8 | 8 | 8 | 7 | 7 | 6 | 6 | 7 | 6 | 83 |
| Days With ≥ 0.5" Precipitation | 3 | 2 | 3 | 3 | 3 | 3 | 3 | 3 | 3 | 3 | 3 | 3 | 35 |
| Days With ≥ 1.0" Precipitation | 1 | 1 | 1 | 1 | 1 | 1 | 2 | 1 | 1 | 1 | 1 | 1 | 13 |
| Mean Snowfall (in.) | 11.0 | 10.3 | 7.7 | 2.1 | 0.0 | 0.0 | 0.0 | 0.0 | 0.0 | trace | 1.3 | 7.6 | 40.0 |
| Maximum Snow Depth (in.) | 29 | 29 | 19 | 17 | 0 | 0 | 0 | 0 | 0 | trace | 5 | 15 | 29 |
| Days With ≥ 1.0" Snow Depth | 18 | 15 | 9 | 1 | 0 | 0 | 0 | 0 | 0 | 0 | 1 | 10 | 54 |

*The period of record for all cooperative weather station data is 1980 – 2009. See User Guide for detailed explanation of data.*

# New York Weather Station Rankings

## Annual Extreme Maximum Temperature

| | Highest | | | Lowest | |
|---|---|---|---|---|---|
| **Rank** | **Station Name** | **°F** | **Rank** | **Station Name** | **°F** |
| 1 | Mineola | 105 | 1 | Indian Lake 2 SW | 91 |
| 2 | Dobbs Ferry Ardsley | 104 | 2 | Morrisville 5 SW | 92 |
| 2 | New York Laguardia Arpt | 104 | 3 | Tully Heiberg Forest | 93 |
| 4 | New York Central Park Observ | 103 | 4 | Boonville 2 SSW | 94 |
| 4 | New York Ave V Brooklyn | 103 | 4 | Grafton | 94 |
| 4 | Wantagh Cedar Creek | 103 | 6 | Conklingville Dam | 95 |
| 7 | Bridgehampton | 102 | 6 | Wales | 95 |
| 7 | Islip-Macarthur Arpt | 102 | 8 | Dannemora | 96 |
| 7 | New York J F Kennedy Int'l Arpt | 102 | 9 | Allegany State Park | 97 |
| 7 | Whitehall | 102 | 9 | Buffalo Greater Buffalo Int'l | 97 |
| 11 | Albion 2 NE | 101 | 9 | Canton 4 SE | 97 |
| 11 | Aurora Research Farm | 101 | 9 | Delhi 2 SE | 97 |
| 11 | Bath | 101 | 9 | Lowville | 97 |
| 11 | Middletown 2 NW | 101 | 9 | Utica Oneida County Arpt | 97 |
| 11 | Syracuse Hancock Int'l Arpt | 101 | 15 | Alfred | 98 |
| 11 | Troy Lock and Dam | 101 | 15 | Binghamton Edwin A Link Field | 98 |
| 17 | Alcove Dam | 100 | 15 | Gouverneur 3 NW | 98 |
| 17 | Chazy | 100 | 15 | Ithaca Cornell Univ | 98 |
| 17 | Riverhead Research Farm | 100 | 15 | Peru 2 WSW | 98 |
| 17 | Valatie 1 N | 100 | 15 | Rochester Intl Arpt | 98 |
| 17 | Yorktown Heights 1 W | 100 | 21 | Albany County Arpt | 99 |
| 22 | Albany County Arpt | 99 | 21 | Avon | 99 |
| 22 | Avon | 99 | 21 | Westfield 2 SSE | 99 |
| 22 | Westfield 2 SSE | 99 | 24 | Alcove Dam | 100 |
| 25 | Alfred | 98 | 24 | Chazy | 100 |

## Annual Mean Maximum Temperature

| | Highest | | | Lowest | |
|---|---|---|---|---|---|
| **Rank** | **Station Name** | **°F** | **Rank** | **Station Name** | **°F** |
| 1 | Dobbs Ferry Ardsley | 62.9 | 1 | Indian Lake 2 SW | 51.0 |
| 2 | New York Central Park Observ | 62.7 | 2 | Boonville 2 SSW | 51.1 |
| 3 | New York Laguardia Arpt | 62.5 | 3 | Tully Heiberg Forest | 52.3 |
| 4 | New York Ave V Brooklyn | 62.4 | 4 | Dannemora | 53.1 |
| 5 | Riverhead Research Farm | 62.1 | 5 | Lowville | 53.2 |
| 6 | Mineola | 61.9 | 6 | Canton 4 SE | 54.0 |
| 7 | New York J F Kennedy Int'l Arpt | 61.5 | 7 | Morrisville 5 SW | 54.3 |
| 8 | Islip-Macarthur Arpt | 60.8 | 8 | Grafton | 54.4 |
| 8 | Middletown 2 NW | 60.8 | 9 | Binghamton Edwin A Link Field | 54.9 |
| 10 | Wantagh Cedar Creek | 60.2 | 9 | Conklingville Dam | 54.9 |
| 11 | Bridgehampton | 59.8 | 11 | Chazy | 55.1 |
| 12 | Yorktown Heights 1 W | 59.6 | 11 | Gouverneur 3 NW | 55.1 |
| 13 | Troy Lock and Dam | 58.9 | 13 | Allegany State Park | 55.2 |
| 14 | Valatie 1 N | 58.4 | 13 | Wales | 55.2 |
| 15 | Whitehall | 58.3 | 15 | Utica Oneida County Arpt | 55.7 |
| 16 | Albion 2 NE | 58.1 | 16 | Peru 2 WSW | 55.9 |
| 17 | Albany County Arpt | 58.0 | 17 | Ithaca Cornell Univ | 56.2 |
| 18 | Avon | 57.6 | 18 | Delhi 2 SE | 56.3 |
| 18 | Syracuse Hancock Int'l Arpt | 57.6 | 19 | Buffalo Greater Buffalo Int'l | 56.6 |
| 20 | Aurora Research Farm | 57.3 | 20 | Alcove Dam | 56.7 |
| 20 | Rochester Intl Arpt | 57.3 | 21 | Alfred | 56.9 |
| 22 | Bath | 57.1 | 22 | Bath | 57.1 |
| 22 | Westfield 2 SSE | 57.1 | 22 | Westfield 2 SSE | 57.1 |
| 24 | Alfred | 56.9 | 24 | Aurora Research Farm | 57.3 |
| 25 | Alcove Dam | 56.7 | 24 | Rochester Intl Arpt | 57.3 |

*Rankings include 25 highest/lowest stations. If state has less than 25 stations, all stations are included. The period of record is 1980–2009. See User Guide for detailed explanation of data.*

## Annual Mean Temperature

| Highest | | | Lowest | | |
|---|---|---|---|---|---|
| Rank | Station Name | °F | Rank | Station Name | °F |
| 1 | New York Laguardia Arpt | 55.6 | 1 | Indian Lake 2 SW | 40.7 |
| 2 | New York Central Park Observ | 55.3 | 2 | Boonville 2 SSW | 42.4 |
| 2 | New York Ave V Brooklyn | 55.3 | 3 | Lowville | 43.3 |
| 4 | New York J F Kennedy Int'l Arpt | 54.4 | 4 | Tully Heiberg Forest | 43.5 |
| 5 | Mineola | 53.7 | 5 | Canton 4 SE | 43.8 |
| 6 | Riverhead Research Farm | 53.6 | 6 | Dannemora | 43.9 |
| 7 | Dobbs Ferry Ardsley | 53.2 | 7 | Gouverneur 3 NW | 44.0 |
| 7 | Wantagh Cedar Creek | 53.2 | 8 | Allegany State Park | 44.6 |
| 9 | Islip-Macarthur Arpt | 52.6 | 8 | Morrisville 5 SW | 44.6 |
| 10 | Bridgehampton | 51.3 | 10 | Delhi 2 SE | 44.8 |
| 11 | Middletown 2 NW | 51.0 | 11 | Chazy | 45.1 |
| 12 | Yorktown Heights 1 W | 50.5 | 11 | Conklingville Dam | 45.1 |
| 13 | Westfield 2 SSE | 49.4 | 13 | Alfred | 45.2 |
| 14 | Albion 2 NE | 49.1 | 14 | Grafton | 45.3 |
| 14 | Troy Lock and Dam | 49.1 | 15 | Bath | 45.6 |
| 16 | Buffalo Greater Buffalo Int'l | 48.5 | 15 | Peru 2 WSW | 45.6 |
| 17 | Rochester Intl Arpt | 48.3 | 17 | Wales | 45.8 |
| 18 | Albany County Arpt | 48.2 | 18 | Alcove Dam | 46.1 |
| 18 | Aurora Research Farm | 48.2 | 19 | Binghamton Edwin A Link Field | 46.5 |
| 18 | Syracuse Hancock Int'l Arpt | 48.2 | 19 | Ithaca Cornell Univ | 46.5 |
| 21 | Whitehall | 48.1 | 21 | Utica Oneida County Arpt | 46.7 |
| 22 | Valatie 1 N | 47.8 | 22 | Avon | 47.7 |
| 23 | Avon | 47.7 | 23 | Valatie 1 N | 47.8 |
| 24 | Utica Oneida County Arpt | 46.7 | 24 | Whitehall | 48.1 |
| 25 | Binghamton Edwin A Link Field | 46.5 | 25 | Albany County Arpt | 48.2 |

## Annual Mean Minimum Temperature

| Highest | | | Lowest | | |
|---|---|---|---|---|---|
| Rank | Station Name | °F | Rank | Station Name | °F |
| 1 | New York Laguardia Arpt | 48.7 | 1 | Indian Lake 2 SW | 30.3 |
| 2 | New York Ave V Brooklyn | 48.2 | 2 | Gouverneur 3 NW | 32.8 |
| 3 | New York Central Park Observ | 47.8 | 3 | Lowville | 33.3 |
| 4 | New York J F Kennedy Int'l Arpt | 47.2 | 4 | Delhi 2 SE | 33.4 |
| 5 | Wantagh Cedar Creek | 46.1 | 5 | Alfred | 33.5 |
| 6 | Mineola | 45.4 | 6 | Boonville 2 SSW | 33.6 |
| 7 | Riverhead Research Farm | 45.0 | 6 | Canton 4 SE | 33.6 |
| 8 | Islip-Macarthur Arpt | 44.3 | 8 | Allegany State Park | 34.0 |
| 9 | Dobbs Ferry Ardsley | 43.4 | 9 | Bath | 34.1 |
| 10 | Bridgehampton | 42.7 | 10 | Dannemora | 34.7 |
| 11 | Westfield 2 SSE | 41.6 | 10 | Tully Heiberg Forest | 34.7 |
| 12 | Yorktown Heights 1 W | 41.4 | 12 | Morrisville 5 SW | 34.9 |
| 13 | Middletown 2 NW | 41.2 | 13 | Chazy | 35.1 |
| 14 | Buffalo Greater Buffalo Int'l | 40.3 | 14 | Conklingville Dam | 35.3 |
| 15 | Albion 2 NE | 40.1 | 14 | Peru 2 WSW | 35.3 |
| 16 | Rochester Intl Arpt | 39.3 | 16 | Alcove Dam | 35.5 |
| 17 | Troy Lock and Dam | 39.2 | 17 | Grafton | 36.2 |
| 18 | Aurora Research Farm | 39.1 | 18 | Wales | 36.3 |
| 19 | Syracuse Hancock Int'l Arpt | 38.7 | 19 | Ithaca Cornell Univ | 36.6 |
| 20 | Albany County Arpt | 38.3 | 20 | Valatie 1 N | 37.1 |
| 21 | Binghamton Edwin A Link Field | 38.1 | 21 | Utica Oneida County Arpt | 37.6 |
| 22 | Whitehall | 37.9 | 22 | Avon | 37.8 |
| 23 | Avon | 37.8 | 23 | Whitehall | 37.9 |
| 24 | Utica Oneida County Arpt | 37.6 | 24 | Binghamton Edwin A Link Field | 38.1 |
| 25 | Valatie 1 N | 37.1 | 25 | Albany County Arpt | 38.3 |

*Rankings include 25 highest/lowest stations. If state has less than 25 stations, all stations are included. The period of record is 1980–2009. See User Guide for detailed explanation of data.*

## Annual Extreme Minimum Temperature

| | Highest | | | | Lowest | |
|---|---|---|---|---|---|---|
| Rank | Station Name | °F | | Rank | Station Name | °F |
| 1 | New York Central Park Observ | -2 | | 1 | Gouverneur 3 NW | -45 |
| 1 | New York J F Kennedy Int'l Arpt | -2 | | 2 | Chazy | -44 |
| 3 | New York Laguardia Arpt | -3 | | 3 | Canton 4 SE | -40 |
| 3 | Wantagh Cedar Creek | -3 | | 4 | Whitehall | -36 |
| 5 | Mineola | -4 | | 5 | Indian Lake 2 SW | -35 |
| 5 | New York Ave V Brooklyn | *-4* | | 5 | Lowville | -35 |
| 7 | Islip-Macarthur Arpt | *-7* | | 7 | Dannemora | -34 |
| 8 | Riverhead Research Farm | -8 | | 7 | Peru 2 WSW | -34 |
| 9 | Dobbs Ferry Ardsley | -10 | | 9 | Boonville 2 SSW | -33 |
| 10 | Bridgehampton | -11 | | 10 | Delhi 2 SE | -32 |
| 11 | Albion 2 NE | -15 | | 11 | Morrisville 5 SW | *-30* |
| 11 | Yorktown Heights 1 W | -15 | | 12 | Alcove Dam | -29 |
| 13 | Buffalo Greater Buffalo Int'l | -16 | | 12 | Conklingville Dam | -29 |
| 13 | Westfield 2 SSE | *-16* | | 12 | Tully Heiberg Forest | *-29* |
| 15 | Rochester Intl Arpt | -17 | | 15 | Utica Oneida County Arpt | *-27* |
| 16 | Binghamton Edwin A Link Field | -18 | | 16 | Grafton | *-26* |
| 17 | Wales | *-19* | | 17 | Alfred | -25 |
| 18 | Aurora Research Farm | -21 | | 17 | Syracuse Hancock Int'l Arpt | -25 |
| 19 | Allegany State Park | *-22* | | 17 | Valatie 1 N | *-25* |
| 20 | Albany County Arpt | -23 | | 20 | Avon | -24 |
| 20 | Middletown 2 NW | -23 | | 20 | Bath | *-24* |
| 20 | Troy Lock and Dam | -23 | | 20 | Ithaca Cornell Univ | -24 |
| 23 | Avon | -24 | | 23 | Albany County Arpt | -23 |
| 23 | Bath | *-24* | | 23 | Middletown 2 NW | -23 |
| 23 | Ithaca Cornell Univ | -24 | | 23 | Troy Lock and Dam | -23 |

## July Mean Maximum Temperature

| | Highest | | | | Lowest | |
|---|---|---|---|---|---|---|
| Rank | Station Name | °F | | Rank | Station Name | °F |
| 1 | Dobbs Ferry Ardsley | 85.2 | | 1 | Indian Lake 2 SW | 74.2 |
| 2 | New York Laguardia Arpt | 85.0 | | 2 | Boonville 2 SSW | 74.9 |
| 3 | New York Central Park Observ | 84.8 | | 3 | Tully Heiberg Forest | 75.9 |
| 4 | New York Ave V Brooklyn | 84.5 | | 4 | Wales | *77.4* |
| 5 | Riverhead Research Farm | 84.0 | | 5 | Morrisville 5 SW | *77.5* |
| 5 | Whitehall | 84.0 | | 6 | Allegany State Park | 77.9 |
| 7 | Mineola | 83.7 | | 6 | Grafton | *77.9* |
| 8 | Troy Lock and Dam | 83.5 | | 6 | Lowville | 77.9 |
| 9 | Middletown 2 NW | 83.4 | | 9 | Dannemora | 78.0 |
| 10 | New York J F Kennedy Int'l Arpt | 82.9 | | 10 | Conklingville Dam | *78.3* |
| 11 | Albany County Arpt | 82.3 | | 11 | Binghamton Edwin A Link Field | 78.4 |
| 12 | Valatie 1 N | *82.2* | | 12 | Canton 4 SE | 79.0 |
| 13 | Albion 2 NE | 82.1 | | 13 | Delhi 2 SE | 79.2 |
| 14 | Islip-Macarthur Arpt | *82.0* | | 14 | Ithaca Cornell Univ | 79.5 |
| 14 | Yorktown Heights 1 W | 82.0 | | 15 | Alcove Dam | 80.0 |
| 16 | Syracuse Hancock Int'l Arpt | 81.7 | | 16 | Alfred | 80.1 |
| 17 | Peru 2 WSW | 81.4 | | 16 | Buffalo Greater Buffalo Int'l | 80.1 |
| 17 | Wantagh Cedar Creek | 81.4 | | 16 | Gouverneur 3 NW | 80.1 |
| 19 | Aurora Research Farm | 81.3 | | 19 | Westfield 2 SSE | *80.3* |
| 19 | Avon | 81.3 | | 20 | Chazy | 80.4 |
| 21 | Rochester Intl Arpt | 81.2 | | 20 | Utica Oneida County Arpt | 80.4 |
| 22 | Bridgehampton | 80.9 | | 22 | Bath | *80.7* |
| 23 | Bath | *80.7* | | 23 | Bridgehampton | 80.9 |
| 24 | Chazy | 80.4 | | 24 | Rochester Intl Arpt | 81.2 |
| 24 | Utica Oneida County Arpt | 80.4 | | 25 | Aurora Research Farm | 81.3 |

*Rankings include 25 highest/lowest stations. If state has less than 25 stations, all stations are included. The period of record is 1980–2009. See User Guide for detailed explanation of data.*

## January Mean Minimum Temperature

| | Highest | | | | Lowest | |
|---|---|---|---|---|---|---|
| Rank | Station Name | °F | | Rank | Station Name | °F |
| 1 | New York Laguardia Arpt | 27.4 | | 1 | Indian Lake 2 SW | 5.0 |
| 2 | New York Ave V Brooklyn | 27.2 | | 2 | Canton 4 SE | 5.3 |
| 3 | New York Central Park Observ | 26.9 | | 3 | Gouverneur 3 NW | 5.7 |
| 4 | New York J F Kennedy Int'l Arpt | 26.3 | | 4 | Lowville | 7.2 |
| 5 | Wantagh Cedar Creek | 26.2 | | 5 | Chazy | 8.0 |
| 6 | Mineola | 25.7 | | 6 | Dannemora | 8.1 |
| 7 | Riverhead Research Farm | 25.0 | | 7 | Boonville 2 SSW | 8.3 |
| 8 | Islip-Macarthur Arpt | 24.4 | | 8 | Peru 2 WSW | 9.2 |
| 9 | Bridgehampton | 23.2 | | 9 | Conklingville Dam | 9.4 |
| 10 | Dobbs Ferry Ardsley | 23.1 | | 10 | Delhi 2 SE | 10.6 |
| 11 | Westfield 2 SSE | 19.9 | | 11 | Morrisville 5 SW | 11.4 |
| 12 | Buffalo Greater Buffalo Int'l | 18.8 | | 12 | Alcove Dam | 11.6 |
| 13 | Yorktown Heights 1 W | 18.7 | | 13 | Tully Heiberg Forest | 11.7 |
| 14 | Middletown 2 NW | 18.5 | | 14 | Whitehall | 11.8 |
| 15 | Albion 2 NE | 18.4 | | 15 | Grafton | 12.1 |
| 16 | Rochester Intl Arpt | 17.8 | | 16 | Alfred | 12.7 |
| 17 | Aurora Research Farm | 16.9 | | 16 | Bath | 12.7 |
| 18 | Avon | 16.7 | | 18 | Valatie 1 N | 13.0 |
| 19 | Wales | 15.9 | | 19 | Allegany State Park | 13.4 |
| 20 | Binghamton Edwin A Link Field | 15.8 | | 20 | Utica Oneida County Arpt | 14.3 |
| 20 | Syracuse Hancock Int'l Arpt | 15.8 | | 21 | Albany County Arpt | 14.5 |
| 22 | Ithaca Cornell Univ | 14.7 | | 22 | Troy Lock and Dam | 14.6 |
| 23 | Troy Lock and Dam | 14.6 | | 23 | Ithaca Cornell Univ | 14.7 |
| 24 | Albany County Arpt | 14.5 | | 24 | Binghamton Edwin A Link Field | 15.8 |
| 25 | Utica Oneida County Arpt | 14.3 | | 24 | Syracuse Hancock Int'l Arpt | 15.8 |

## Number of Days Annually Maximum Temperature ≥ 90°F

| | Highest | | | | Lowest | |
|---|---|---|---|---|---|---|
| Rank | Station Name | Days | | Rank | Station Name | Days |
| 1 | Dobbs Ferry Ardsley | 18 | | 1 | Boonville 2 SSW | 0 |
| 1 | New York Laguardia Arpt | 18 | | 1 | Grafton | 0 |
| 3 | New York Central Park Observ | 17 | | 1 | Indian Lake 2 SW | 0 |
| 4 | Mineola | 15 | | 1 | Morrisville 5 SW | 0 |
| 4 | New York Ave V Brooklyn | 15 | | 1 | Tully Heiberg Forest | 0 |
| 6 | Troy Lock and Dam | 13 | | 1 | Wales | 0 |
| 7 | Riverhead Research Farm | 11 | | 7 | Allegany State Park | 1 |
| 8 | Middletown 2 NW | 10 | | 7 | Conklingville Dam | 1 |
| 8 | New York J F Kennedy Int'l Arpt | 10 | | 9 | Binghamton Edwin A Link Field | 2 |
| 8 | Valatie 1 N | 10 | | 9 | Canton 4 SE | 2 |
| 8 | Whitehall | 10 | | 9 | Dannemora | 2 |
| 12 | Aurora Research Farm | 9 | | 12 | Buffalo Greater Buffalo Int'l | 3 |
| 13 | Albany County Arpt | 8 | | 12 | Chazy | 3 |
| 13 | Albion 2 NE | 8 | | 12 | Delhi 2 SE | 3 |
| 13 | Islip-Macarthur Arpt | 8 | | 12 | Gouverneur 3 NW | 3 |
| 13 | Syracuse Hancock Int'l Arpt | 8 | | 12 | Lowville | 3 |
| 13 | Yorktown Heights 1 W | 8 | | 17 | Alfred | 4 |
| 18 | Avon | 7 | | 17 | Ithaca Cornell Univ | 4 |
| 19 | Bath | 6 | | 17 | Utica Oneida County Arpt | 4 |
| 19 | Peru 2 WSW | 6 | | 20 | Alcove Dam | 5 |
| 19 | Rochester Intl Arpt | 6 | | 20 | Bridgehampton | 5 |
| 19 | Wantagh Cedar Creek | 6 | | 20 | Westfield 2 SSE | 5 |
| 23 | Alcove Dam | 5 | | 23 | Bath | 6 |
| 23 | Bridgehampton | 5 | | 23 | Peru 2 WSW | 6 |
| 23 | Westfield 2 SSE | 5 | | 23 | Rochester Intl Arpt | 6 |

*Rankings include 25 highest/lowest stations. If state has less than 25 stations, all stations are included. The period of record is 1980–2009. See User Guide for detailed explanation of data.*

## Number of Days Annually Maximum Temperature ≤ 32°F

| | Highest | | | | Lowest | |
|---|---|---|---|---|---|---|
| Rank | Station Name | Days | | Rank | Station Name | Days |
| 1 | Boonville 2 SSW | 82 | | 1 | New York J F Kennedy Int'l Arpt | 15 |
| 2 | Indian Lake 2 SW | 75 | | 1 | Riverhead Research Farm | 15 |
| 3 | Dannemora | 73 | | 3 | Mineola | 16 |
| 4 | Tully Heiberg Forest | 72 | | 3 | New York Ave V Brooklyn | 16 |
| 5 | Lowville | 68 | | 5 | Bridgehampton | 17 |
| 6 | Canton 4 SE | 66 | | 5 | Dobbs Ferry Ardsley | 17 |
| 7 | Grafton | 62 | | 5 | Islip-Macarthur Arpt | 17 |
| 7 | Morrisville 5 SW | 62 | | 5 | New York Central Park Observ | 17 |
| 9 | Gouverneur 3 NW | 61 | | 9 | New York Laguardia Arpt | 18 |
| 10 | Chazy | 60 | | 9 | Wantagh Cedar Creek | 18 |
| 11 | Peru 2 WSW | 59 | | 11 | Middletown 2 NW | 28 |
| 12 | Binghamton Edwin A Link Field | 58 | | 12 | Yorktown Heights 1 W | 32 |
| 13 | Allegany State Park | 56 | | 13 | Troy Lock and Dam | 40 |
| 13 | Wales | 56 | | 13 | Valatie 1 N | 40 |
| 15 | Utica Oneida County Arpt | 55 | | 15 | Albany County Arpt | 43 |
| 16 | Ithaca Cornell Univ | 52 | | 16 | Westfield 2 SSE | 44 |
| 17 | Buffalo Greater Buffalo Int'l | 51 | | 17 | Whitehall | 45 |
| 18 | Alfred | 48 | | 18 | Albion 2 NE | 46 |
| 18 | Conklingville Dam | 48 | | 18 | Aurora Research Farm | 46 |
| 18 | Delhi 2 SE | 48 | | 18 | Avon | 46 |
| 18 | Syracuse Hancock Int'l Arpt | 48 | | 18 | Bath | 46 |
| 22 | Alcove Dam | 47 | | 18 | Rochester Intl Arpt | 46 |
| 23 | Albion 2 NE | 46 | | 23 | Alcove Dam | 47 |
| 23 | Aurora Research Farm | 46 | | 24 | Alfred | 48 |
| 23 | Avon | 46 | | 24 | Conklingville Dam | 48 |

## Number of Days Annually Minimum Temperature ≤ 32°F

| | Highest | | | | Lowest | |
|---|---|---|---|---|---|---|
| Rank | Station Name | Days | | Rank | Station Name | Days |
| 1 | Indian Lake 2 SW | 186 | | 1 | New York Laguardia Arpt | 67 |
| 2 | Alfred | 170 | | 2 | New York Ave V Brooklyn | 69 |
| 2 | Delhi 2 SE | 170 | | 3 | New York Central Park Observ | 70 |
| 4 | Bath | 169 | | 4 | New York J F Kennedy Int'l Arpt | 74 |
| 5 | Boonville 2 SSW | 168 | | 5 | Mineola | 82 |
| 6 | Lowville | 167 | | 6 | Wantagh Cedar Creek | 83 |
| 7 | Gouverneur 3 NW | 166 | | 7 | Riverhead Research Farm | 92 |
| 8 | Tully Heiberg Forest | 164 | | 8 | Islip-Macarthur Arpt | 101 |
| 9 | Allegany State Park | 163 | | 9 | Dobbs Ferry Ardsley | 106 |
| 10 | Canton 4 SE | 162 | | 10 | Bridgehampton | 109 |
| 11 | Alcove Dam | 160 | | 11 | Yorktown Heights 1 W | 119 |
| 11 | Dannemora | 160 | | 12 | Westfield 2 SSE | 120 |
| 13 | Morrisville 5 SW | 157 | | 13 | Middletown 2 NW | 121 |
| 14 | Peru 2 WSW | 154 | | 14 | Buffalo Greater Buffalo Int'l | 125 |
| 15 | Chazy | 153 | | 15 | Albion 2 NE | 129 |
| 15 | Grafton | 153 | | 16 | Rochester Intl Arpt | 131 |
| 15 | Wales | 153 | | 17 | Aurora Research Farm | 132 |
| 18 | Ithaca Cornell Univ | 150 | | 18 | Troy Lock and Dam | 133 |
| 19 | Valatie 1 N | 148 | | 19 | Syracuse Hancock Int'l Arpt | 134 |
| 20 | Conklingville Dam | 147 | | 20 | Utica Oneida County Arpt | 140 |
| 21 | Avon | 143 | | 21 | Albany County Arpt | 141 |
| 22 | Binghamton Edwin A Link Field | 142 | | 21 | Whitehall | 141 |
| 23 | Albany County Arpt | 141 | | 23 | Binghamton Edwin A Link Field | 142 |
| 23 | Whitehall | 141 | | 24 | Avon | 143 |
| 25 | Utica Oneida County Arpt | 140 | | 25 | Conklingville Dam | 147 |

*Rankings include 25 highest/lowest stations. If state has less than 25 stations, all stations are included. The period of record is 1980–2009. See User Guide for detailed explanation of data.*

## Number of Days Annually Minimum Temperature ≤ 0°F

| | Highest | | | | Lowest | |
|---|---|---|---|---|---|---|
| Rank | Station Name | Days | | Rank | Station Name | Days |
| 1 | Indian Lake 2 SW | 34 | | 1 | Bridgehampton | 0 |
| 2 | Gouverneur 3 NW | 32 | | 1 | Islip-Macarthur Arpt | 0 |
| 3 | Canton 4 SE | 31 | | 1 | Mineola | 0 |
| 4 | Lowville | 27 | | 1 | New York Central Park Observ | 0 |
| 5 | Chazy | 25 | | 1 | New York J F Kennedy Int'l Arpt | 0 |
| 6 | Boonville 2 SSW | 23 | | 1 | New York Laguardia Arpt | 0 |
| 7 | Dannemora | 21 | | 1 | New York Ave V Brooklyn | 0 |
| 8 | Peru 2 WSW | 20 | | 1 | Riverhead Research Farm | 0 |
| 9 | Delhi 2 SE | 18 | | 1 | Wantagh Cedar Creek | 0 |
| 10 | Conklingville Dam | 17 | | 10 | Dobbs Ferry Ardsley | 1 |
| 11 | Morrisville 5 SW | 16 | | 11 | Westfield 2 SSE | 2 |
| 12 | Alfred | 15 | | 11 | Yorktown Heights 1 W | 2 |
| 12 | Whitehall | 15 | | 13 | Albion 2 NE | 3 |
| 14 | Tully Heiberg Forest | 14 | | 13 | Middletown 2 NW | 3 |
| 15 | Allegany State Park | 13 | | 15 | Buffalo Greater Buffalo Int'l | 4 |
| 15 | Grafton | 13 | | 15 | Rochester Intl Arpt | 4 |
| 17 | Alcove Dam | 12 | | 17 | Aurora Research Farm | 5 |
| 17 | Bath | 12 | | 17 | Binghamton Edwin A Link Field | 5 |
| 19 | Ithaca Cornell Univ | 11 | | 19 | Avon | 8 |
| 19 | Utica Oneida County Arpt | 11 | | 19 | Syracuse Hancock Int'l Arpt | 8 |
| 19 | Valatie 1 N | 11 | | 21 | Albany County Arpt | 9 |
| 22 | Wales | 10 | | 21 | Troy Lock and Dam | 9 |
| 23 | Albany County Arpt | 9 | | 23 | Wales | 10 |
| 23 | Troy Lock and Dam | 9 | | 24 | Ithaca Cornell Univ | 11 |
| 25 | Avon | 8 | | 24 | Utica Oneida County Arpt | 11 |

## Number of Annual Heating Degree Days

| | Highest | | | | Lowest | |
|---|---|---|---|---|---|---|
| Rank | Station Name | Num. | | Rank | Station Name | Num. |
| 1 | Indian Lake 2 SW | 8,896 | | 1 | New York Laguardia Arpt | 4,566 |
| 2 | Boonville 2 SSW | 8,369 | | 2 | New York Ave V Brooklyn | 4,621 |
| 3 | Lowville | 8,133 | | 3 | New York Central Park Observ | 4,622 |
| 4 | Canton 4 SE | 8,035 | | 4 | New York J F Kennedy Int'l Arpt | 4,796 |
| 5 | Tully Heiberg Forest | 8,014 | | 5 | Mineola | 4,931 |
| 6 | Dannemora | 7,933 | | 6 | Riverhead Research Farm | 4,965 |
| 7 | Gouverneur 3 NW | 7,930 | | 7 | Wantagh Cedar Creek | 5,083 |
| 8 | Morrisville 5 SW | 7,601 | | 8 | Dobbs Ferry Ardsley | 5,140 |
| 9 | Chazy | 7,584 | | 9 | Islip-Macarthur Arpt | 5,261 |
| 10 | Allegany State Park | 7,567 | | 10 | Bridgehampton | 5,523 |
| 11 | Delhi 2 SE | 7,542 | | 11 | Middletown 2 NW | 5,773 |
| 12 | Conklingville Dam | 7,483 | | 12 | Yorktown Heights 1 W | 5,899 |
| 13 | Peru 2 WSW | 7,450 | | 13 | Westfield 2 SSE | 6,263 |
| 14 | Alfred | 7,416 | | 14 | Albion 2 NE | 6,365 |
| 15 | Grafton | 7,406 | | 15 | Troy Lock and Dam | 6,422 |
| 16 | Bath | 7,301 | | 16 | Buffalo Greater Buffalo Int'l | 6,508 |
| 17 | Wales | 7,242 | | 17 | Rochester Intl Arpt | 6,553 |
| 18 | Alcove Dam | 7,190 | | 18 | Syracuse Hancock Int'l Arpt | 6,618 |
| 19 | Ithaca Cornell Univ | 7,090 | | 19 | Aurora Research Farm | 6,633 |
| 20 | Binghamton Edwin A Link Field | 7,060 | | 20 | Albany County Arpt | 6,638 |
| 21 | Utica Oneida County Arpt | 7,059 | | 21 | Whitehall | 6,730 |
| 22 | Valatie 1 N | 6,747 | | 22 | Avon | 6,732 |
| 23 | Avon | 6,732 | | 23 | Valatie 1 N | 6,747 |
| 24 | Whitehall | 6,730 | | 24 | Utica Oneida County Arpt | 7,059 |
| 25 | Albany County Arpt | 6,638 | | 25 | Binghamton Edwin A Link Field | 7,060 |

*Rankings include 25 highest/lowest stations. If state has less than 25 stations, all stations are included. The period of record is 1980–2009. See User Guide for detailed explanation of data.*

## Number of Annual Cooling Degree Days

| | Highest | | | Lowest | |
|---|---|---|---|---|---|
| Rank | Station Name | Num. | Rank | Station Name | Num. |
| 1 | New York Laguardia Arpt | 1,262 | 1 | Indian Lake 2 SW | 140 |
| 2 | New York Ave V Brooklyn | 1,187 | 2 | Boonville 2 SSW | 230 |
| 3 | New York Central Park Observ | 1,184 | 3 | Allegany State Park | 244 |
| 4 | New York J F Kennedy Int'l Arpt | 1,026 | 4 | Tully Heiberg Forest | 272 |
| 5 | Dobbs Ferry Ardsley | 935 | 5 | Morrisville 5 SW | 283 |
| 6 | Mineola | 918 | 6 | Delhi 2 SE | 293 |
| 7 | Riverhead Research Farm | 914 | 7 | Alfred | 294 |
| 8 | Wantagh Cedar Creek | 878 | 8 | Lowville | 311 |
| 9 | Islip-Macarthur Arpt | 839 | 9 | Grafton | 335 |
| 10 | Middletown 2 NW | 778 | 10 | Conklingville Dam | 339 |
| 11 | Troy Lock and Dam | 733 | 11 | Wales | 345 |
| 12 | Yorktown Heights 1 W | 720 | 12 | Bath | 347 |
| 13 | Whitehall | 690 | 12 | Dannemora | 347 |
| 14 | Albion 2 NE | 669 | 14 | Gouverneur 3 NW | 364 |
| 15 | Westfield 2 SSE | 662 | 15 | Canton 4 SE | 410 |
| 16 | Bridgehampton | 632 | 16 | Alcove Dam | 412 |
| 17 | Aurora Research Farm | 615 | 17 | Binghamton Edwin A Link Field | 426 |
| 18 | Albany County Arpt | 603 | 18 | Ithaca Cornell Univ | 438 |
| 19 | Syracuse Hancock Int'l Arpt | 590 | 19 | Chazy | 441 |
| 20 | Buffalo Greater Buffalo Int'l | 582 | 20 | Peru 2 WSW | 475 |
| 21 | Rochester Intl Arpt | 581 | 21 | Utica Oneida County Arpt | 494 |
| 22 | Valatie 1 N | 561 | 22 | Avon | 533 |
| 23 | Avon | 533 | 23 | Valatie 1 N | 561 |
| 24 | Utica Oneida County Arpt | 494 | 24 | Rochester Intl Arpt | 581 |
| 25 | Peru 2 WSW | 475 | 25 | Buffalo Greater Buffalo Int'l | 582 |

## Annual Precipitation

| | Highest | | | Lowest | |
|---|---|---|---|---|---|
| Rank | Station Name | Inches | Rank | Station Name | Inches |
| 1 | Boonville 2 SSW | 58.08 | 1 | Peru 2 WSW | 30.72 |
| 2 | Dobbs Ferry Ardsley | 51.49 | 2 | Bath | 31.24 |
| 3 | Yorktown Heights 1 W | 50.79 | 3 | Avon | 31.99 |
| 4 | Bridgehampton | 49.65 | 4 | Rochester Intl Arpt | 34.12 |
| 5 | New York Central Park Observ | 49.08 | 5 | Albion 2 NE | 35.55 |
| 6 | Riverhead Research Farm | 47.25 | 6 | Aurora Research Farm | 36.01 |
| 7 | Islip-Macarthur Arpt | 46.53 | 7 | Canton 4 SE | 36.64 |
| 8 | Mineola | 46.08 | 8 | Ithaca Cornell Univ | 36.78 |
| 9 | Delhi 2 SE | 45.98 | 9 | Gouverneur 3 NW | 37.32 |
| 10 | New York Ave V Brooklyn | 45.96 | 10 | Alfred | 37.49 |
| 11 | Grafton | 45.91 | 11 | Syracuse Hancock Int'l Arpt | 37.90 |
| 12 | Tully Heiberg Forest | 45.74 | 12 | Albany County Arpt | 39.14 |
| 13 | Morrisville 5 SW | 45.56 | 12 | Binghamton Edwin A Link Field | 39.14 |
| 14 | Conklingville Dam | 45.16 | 14 | Troy Lock and Dam | 39.46 |
| 15 | New York Laguardia Arpt | 44.66 | 15 | Indian Lake 2 SW | 40.19 |
| 16 | Westfield 2 SSE | 44.59 | 16 | Buffalo Greater Buffalo Int'l | 40.49 |
| 17 | Allegany State Park | 44.47 | 17 | Alcove Dam | 40.56 |
| 18 | Middletown 2 NW | 43.36 | 18 | Dannemora | 40.93 |
| 19 | Wales | 42.99 | 19 | Valatie 1 N | 40.99 |
| 20 | Utica Oneida County Arpt | 42.90 | 20 | Lowville | 41.24 |
| 21 | New York J F Kennedy Int'l Arpt | 42.64 | 21 | Whitehall | 42.05 |
| 22 | Wantagh Cedar Creek | 42.40 | 22 | Wantagh Cedar Creek | 42.40 |
| 23 | Whitehall | 42.05 | 23 | New York J F Kennedy Int'l Arpt | 42.64 |
| 24 | Lowville | 41.24 | 24 | Utica Oneida County Arpt | 42.90 |
| 25 | Valatie 1 N | 40.99 | 25 | Wales | 42.99 |

*Rankings include 25 highest/lowest stations. If state has less than 25 stations, all stations are included. The period of record is 1980–2009. See User Guide for detailed explanation of data.*

## Annual Extreme Maximum Daily Precipitation

| | Highest | | | | Lowest | |
|---|---|---|---|---|---|---|
| Rank | Station Name | Inches | | Rank | Station Name | Inches |
| 1 | Yorktown Heights 1 W | 10.95 | | 1 | Troy Lock and Dam | 3.00 |
| 2 | Dobbs Ferry Ardsley | 7.62 | | 2 | Aurora Research Farm | 3.03 |
| 3 | New York Central Park Observ | 7.56 | | 3 | Alfred | 3.33 |
| 4 | Bridgehampton | 7.04 | | 3 | Rochester Intl Arpt | 3.33 |
| 5 | Alcove Dam | 6.89 | | 5 | Indian Lake 2 SW | 3.43 |
| 6 | Islip-Macarthur Arpt | 6.74 | | 6 | Albion 2 NE | 3.79 |
| 7 | New York Laguardia Arpt | 6.69 | | 7 | Allegany State Park | 4.00 |
| 8 | Riverhead Research Farm | 6.34 | | 8 | Conklingville Dam | 4.01 |
| 9 | New York J F Kennedy Int'l Arpt | 6.27 | | 9 | Binghamton Edwin A Link Field | 4.05 |
| 10 | Albany County Arpt | 5.60 | | 10 | Canton 4 SE | 4.10 |
| 11 | New York Ave V Brooklyn | 5.46 | | 11 | Morrisville 5 SW | 4.11 |
| 12 | Wantagh Cedar Creek | 5.43 | | 12 | Utica Oneida County Arpt | 4.14 |
| 13 | Wales | 5.33 | | 13 | Whitehall | 4.25 |
| 14 | Avon | 5.20 | | 14 | Syracuse Hancock Int'l Arpt | 4.29 |
| 15 | Valatie 1 N | 5.10 | | 14 | Westfield 2 SSE | 4.29 |
| 16 | Ithaca Cornell Univ | 5.08 | | 16 | Mineola | 4.30 |
| 17 | Buffalo Greater Buffalo Int'l | 5.01 | | 17 | Delhi 2 SE | 4.49 |
| 18 | Middletown 2 NW | 5.00 | | 18 | Gouverneur 3 NW | 4.51 |
| 19 | Tully Heiberg Forest | 4.98 | | 19 | Dannemora | 4.55 |
| 20 | Boonville 2 SSW | 4.86 | | 20 | Bath | 4.67 |
| 21 | Peru 2 WSW | 4.80 | | 21 | Grafton | 4.75 |
| 22 | Lowville | 4.78 | | 22 | Lowville | 4.78 |
| 23 | Grafton | 4.75 | | 23 | Peru 2 WSW | 4.80 |
| 24 | Bath | 4.67 | | 24 | Boonville 2 SSW | 4.86 |
| 25 | Dannemora | 4.55 | | 25 | Tully Heiberg Forest | 4.98 |

## Number of Days Annually With ≥ 0.1 Inches of Precipitation

| | Highest | | | | Lowest | |
|---|---|---|---|---|---|---|
| Rank | Station Name | Days | | Rank | Station Name | Days |
| 1 | Boonville 2 SSW | 116 | | 1 | Chazy | 57 |
| 2 | Allegany State Park | 103 | | 2 | Peru 2 WSW | 66 |
| 2 | Morrisville 5 SW | 103 | | 3 | Bath | 71 |
| 2 | Tully Heiberg Forest | 103 | | 3 | Wantagh Cedar Creek | 71 |
| 2 | Wales | 103 | | 5 | New York J F Kennedy Int'l Arpt | 72 |
| 6 | Westfield 2 SSE | 98 | | 6 | Mineola | 74 |
| 7 | Dannemora | 97 | | 7 | Avon | 75 |
| 7 | Utica Oneida County Arpt | 97 | | 7 | New York Laguardia Arpt | 75 |
| 9 | Grafton | 96 | | 9 | Alcove Dam | 76 |
| 10 | Buffalo Greater Buffalo Int'l | 95 | | 10 | Islip-Macarthur Arpt | 77 |
| 11 | Delhi 2 SE | 94 | | 10 | Middletown 2 NW | 77 |
| 11 | Lowville | 94 | | 10 | New York Ave V Brooklyn | 77 |
| 13 | Syracuse Hancock Int'l Arpt | 90 | | 13 | Bridgehampton | 78 |
| 14 | Alfred | 88 | | 13 | New York Central Park Observ | 78 |
| 14 | Indian Lake 2 SW | 88 | | 13 | Riverhead Research Farm | 78 |
| 16 | Albion 2 NE | 87 | | 13 | Troy Lock and Dam | 78 |
| 17 | Binghamton Edwin A Link Field | 84 | | 17 | Whitehall | 79 |
| 17 | Gouverneur 3 NW | 84 | | 18 | Rochester Intl Arpt | 80 |
| 17 | Ithaca Cornell Univ | 84 | | 18 | Valatie 1 N | 80 |
| 20 | Canton 4 SE | 83 | | 20 | Albany County Arpt | 81 |
| 20 | Conklingville Dam | 83 | | 20 | Dobbs Ferry Ardsley | 81 |
| 20 | Yorktown Heights 1 W | 83 | | 22 | Aurora Research Farm | 82 |
| 23 | Aurora Research Farm | 82 | | 23 | Canton 4 SE | 83 |
| 24 | Albany County Arpt | 81 | | 23 | Conklingville Dam | 83 |
| 24 | Dobbs Ferry Ardsley | 81 | | 23 | Yorktown Heights 1 W | 83 |

*Rankings include 25 highest/lowest stations. If state has less than 25 stations, all stations are included. The period of record is 1980–2009. See User Guide for detailed explanation of data.*

## Number of Days Annually With ≥ 0.5 Inches of Precipitation

| Highest | | | | Lowest | | |
|---|---|---|---|---|---|---|
| **Rank** | **Station Name** | | **Days** | **Rank** | **Station Name** | **Days** |
| 1 | Boonville 2 SSW | | 37 | 1 | Bath | *18* |
| 2 | Dobbs Ferry Ardsley | | 35 | 1 | Chazy | *18* |
| 2 | New York Central Park Observ | | 35 | 3 | Avon | 19 |
| 2 | Yorktown Heights 1 W | | 35 | 4 | Rochester Intl Arpt | 20 |
| 5 | Riverhead Research Farm | | 34 | 5 | Albion 2 NE | 21 |
| 6 | Grafton | | *33* | 5 | Aurora Research Farm | 21 |
| 6 | Mineola | | 33 | 5 | Canton 4 SE | 21 |
| 8 | Bridgehampton | | 32 | 5 | Ithaca Cornell Univ | 21 |
| 8 | Islip-Macarthur Arpt | | *32* | 5 | Peru 2 WSW | 21 |
| 8 | Middletown 2 NW | | 32 | 10 | Gouverneur 3 NW | 22 |
| 8 | New York Laguardia Arpt | | 32 | 11 | Alfred | 23 |
| 8 | New York Ave V Brooklyn | | *32* | 11 | Syracuse Hancock Int'l Arpt | 23 |
| 13 | New York J F Kennedy Int'l Arpt | | 31 | 13 | Binghamton Edwin A Link Field | 24 |
| 14 | Delhi 2 SE | | 30 | 13 | Buffalo Greater Buffalo Int'l | 24 |
| 15 | Conklingville Dam | | 29 | 15 | Indian Lake 2 SW | 25 |
| 15 | Valatie 1 N | | *29* | 15 | Lowville | 25 |
| 15 | Wales | | *29* | 15 | Utica Oneida County Arpt | *25* |
| 15 | Westfield 2 SSE | | 29 | 18 | Albany County Arpt | 26 |
| 19 | Alcove Dam | | 28 | 18 | Allegany State Park | 26 |
| 19 | Morrisville 5 SW | | 28 | 20 | Dannemora | 27 |
| 19 | Wantagh Cedar Creek | | 28 | 20 | Troy Lock and Dam | 27 |
| 19 | Whitehall | | 28 | 20 | Tully Heiberg Forest | *27* |
| 23 | Dannemora | | 27 | 23 | Alcove Dam | 28 |
| 23 | Troy Lock and Dam | | 27 | 23 | Morrisville 5 SW | 28 |
| 23 | Tully Heiberg Forest | | *27* | 23 | Wantagh Cedar Creek | 28 |

## Number of Days Annually With ≥ 1.0 Inches of Precipitation

| Highest | | | | Lowest | | |
|---|---|---|---|---|---|---|
| **Rank** | **Station Name** | | **Days** | **Rank** | **Station Name** | **Days** |
| 1 | Boonville 2 SSW | | 13 | 1 | Bath | *3* |
| 1 | Dobbs Ferry Ardsley | | 13 | 2 | Avon | 4 |
| 1 | New York Ave V Brooklyn | | *13* | 2 | Canton 4 SE | 4 |
| 1 | Yorktown Heights 1 W | | 13 | 2 | Rochester Intl Arpt | 4 |
| 5 | Bridgehampton | | 12 | 2 | Syracuse Hancock Int'l Arpt | 4 |
| 5 | Conklingville Dam | | 12 | 6 | Albion 2 NE | 5 |
| 5 | Islip-Macarthur Arpt | | *12* | 6 | Allegany State Park | 5 |
| 5 | Mineola | | 12 | 6 | Aurora Research Farm | 5 |
| 5 | New York Central Park Observ | | 12 | 6 | Chazy | *5* |
| 5 | New York J F Kennedy Int'l Arpt | | 12 | 6 | Ithaca Cornell Univ | 5 |
| 5 | New York Laguardia Arpt | | 12 | 6 | Wales | *5* |
| 5 | Riverhead Research Farm | | 12 | 12 | Alfred | 6 |
| 13 | Wantagh Cedar Creek | | 11 | 12 | Dannemora | 6 |
| 13 | Whitehall | | 11 | 12 | Gouverneur 3 NW | 6 |
| 15 | Alcove Dam | | 10 | 12 | Peru 2 WSW | 6 |
| 15 | Grafton | | *10* | 16 | Buffalo Greater Buffalo Int'l | 7 |
| 15 | Middletown 2 NW | | 10 | 16 | Morrisville 5 SW | 7 |
| 18 | Indian Lake 2 SW | | 9 | 16 | Westfield 2 SSE | *7* |
| 18 | Troy Lock and Dam | | 9 | 19 | Albany County Arpt | 8 |
| 18 | Valatie 1 N | | *9* | 19 | Binghamton Edwin A Link Field | 8 |
| 21 | Albany County Arpt | | 8 | 19 | Delhi 2 SE | 8 |
| 21 | Binghamton Edwin A Link Field | | 8 | 19 | Lowville | 8 |
| 21 | Delhi 2 SE | | 8 | 19 | Tully Heiberg Forest | *8* |
| 21 | Lowville | | 8 | 19 | Utica Oneida County Arpt | *8* |
| 21 | Tully Heiberg Forest | | *8* | 25 | Indian Lake 2 SW | 9 |

*Rankings include 25 highest/lowest stations. If state has less than 25 stations, all stations are included. The period of record is 1980–2009. See User Guide for detailed explanation of data.*

## Annual Snowfall

| | Highest | | | | Lowest | |
|---|---|---|---|---|---|---|
| Rank | Station Name | Inches | | Rank | Station Name | Inches |
| 1 | Boonville 2 SSW | 197.5 | | 1 | Mineola | 19.8 |
| 2 | Syracuse Hancock Int'l Arpt | 124.5 | | 2 | New York Ave V Brooklyn | 22.3 |
| 3 | Morrisville 5 SW | 124.1 | | 3 | New York J F Kennedy Int'l Arpt | 22.7 |
| 4 | Lowville | 121.4 | | 4 | New York Central Park Observ | 23.6 |
| 5 | Tully Heiberg Forest | 115.8 | | 5 | New York Laguardia Arpt | 25.9 |
| 6 | Wales | 110.8 | | 6 | Bridgehampton | 26.5 |
| 7 | Rochester Intl Arpt | 99.4 | | 7 | Riverhead Research Farm | 27.0 |
| 8 | Buffalo Greater Buffalo Int'l | 94.0 | | 8 | Dobbs Ferry Ardsley | 30.6 |
| 9 | Alfred | 87.6 | | 9 | Troy Lock and Dam | 38.6 |
| 10 | Gouverneur 3 NW | 84.6 | | 10 | Yorktown Heights 1 W | 40.0 |
| 11 | Westfield 2 SSE | 84.5 | | 11 | Valatie 1 N | 41.4 |
| 12 | Grafton | 83.2 | | 12 | Bath | 44.8 |
| 13 | Binghamton Edwin A Link Field | 82.8 | | 13 | Avon | 51.9 |
| 14 | Canton 4 SE | 77.9 | | 14 | Peru 2 WSW | 52.0 |
| 15 | Conklingville Dam | 70.4 | | 15 | Chazy | 56.6 |
| 16 | Albion 2 NE | 66.4 | | 16 | Aurora Research Farm | 58.9 |
| 17 | Delhi 2 SE | 65.4 | | 17 | Whitehall | 59.5 |
| 18 | Ithaca Cornell Univ | 63.9 | | 18 | Albany County Arpt | 60.2 |
| 19 | Albany County Arpt | 60.2 | | 19 | Ithaca Cornell Univ | 63.9 |
| 20 | Whitehall | 59.5 | | 20 | Delhi 2 SE | 65.4 |
| 21 | Aurora Research Farm | 58.9 | | 21 | Albion 2 NE | 66.4 |
| 22 | Chazy | 56.6 | | 22 | Conklingville Dam | 70.4 |
| 23 | Peru 2 WSW | 52.0 | | 23 | Canton 4 SE | 77.9 |
| 24 | Avon | 51.9 | | 24 | Binghamton Edwin A Link Field | 82.8 |
| 25 | Bath | 44.8 | | 25 | Grafton | 83.2 |

## Annual Maximum Snow Depth

| | Highest | | | | Lowest | |
|---|---|---|---|---|---|---|
| Rank | Station Name | Inches | | Rank | Station Name | Inches |
| 1 | Tully Heiberg Forest | 60 | | 1 | Mineola | 20 |
| 2 | Boonville 2 SSW | 57 | | 1 | Riverhead Research Farm | 20 |
| 3 | Morrisville 5 SW | 51 | | 3 | New York Ave V Brooklyn | 23 |
| 4 | Chazy | 50 | | 4 | Allegany State Park | 25 |
| 5 | Conklingville Dam | 45 | | 4 | New York Laguardia Arpt | 25 |
| 6 | Buffalo Greater Buffalo Int'l | 44 | | 6 | Dobbs Ferry Ardsley | 26 |
| 7 | Aurora Research Farm | 43 | | 7 | Avon | 27 |
| 8 | Troy Lock and Dam | 39 | | 7 | Bridgehampton | 27 |
| 9 | Canton 4 SE | 38 | | 9 | Albany County Arpt | 28 |
| 10 | Grafton | 37 | | 9 | Ithaca Cornell Univ | 28 |
| 11 | Bath | 36 | | 9 | New York J F Kennedy Int'l Arpt | 28 |
| 12 | Binghamton Edwin A Link Field | 35 | | 12 | Yorktown Heights 1 W | 29 |
| 12 | Syracuse Hancock Int'l Arpt | 35 | | 13 | Albion 2 NE | 30 |
| 14 | Rochester Intl Arpt | 34 | | 13 | Gouverneur 3 NW | 30 |
| 14 | Wales | 34 | | 15 | Delhi 2 SE | 31 |
| 16 | Lowville | 33 | | 16 | Lowville | 33 |
| 16 | Valatie 1 N | 33 | | 16 | Valatie 1 N | 33 |
| 18 | Delhi 2 SE | 31 | | 18 | Rochester Intl Arpt | 34 |
| 19 | Albion 2 NE | 30 | | 18 | Wales | 34 |
| 19 | Gouverneur 3 NW | 30 | | 20 | Binghamton Edwin A Link Field | 35 |
| 21 | Yorktown Heights 1 W | 29 | | 20 | Syracuse Hancock Int'l Arpt | 35 |
| 22 | Albany County Arpt | 28 | | 22 | Bath | 36 |
| 22 | Ithaca Cornell Univ | 28 | | 23 | Grafton | 37 |
| 22 | New York J F Kennedy Int'l Arpt | 28 | | 24 | Canton 4 SE | 38 |
| 25 | Avon | 27 | | 25 | Troy Lock and Dam | 39 |

*Rankings include 25 highest/lowest stations. If state has less than 25 stations, all stations are included. The period of record is 1980–2009. See User Guide for detailed explanation of data.*

## Number of Days Annually With ≥ 1.0 Inch Snow Depth

| | Highest | | | Lowest | |
|---|---|---|---|---|---|
| Rank | Station Name | Days | Rank | Station Name | Days |
| 1 | Boonville 2 SSW | 134 | 1 | Mineola | 18 |
| 2 | Tully Heiberg Forest | 124 | 1 | New York J F Kennedy Int'l Arpt | 18 |
| 3 | Morrisville 5 SW | 115 | 1 | New York Ave V Brooklyn | 18 |
| 4 | Lowville | 107 | 4 | New York Laguardia Arpt | 19 |
| 5 | Gouverneur 3 NW | 97 | 5 | Bridgehampton | 20 |
| 6 | Allegany State Park | 95 | 6 | Riverhead Research Farm | 21 |
| 7 | Conklingville Dam | 94 | 7 | Dobbs Ferry Ardsley | 34 |
| 7 | Grafton | 94 | 8 | Albion 2 NE | 47 |
| 9 | Wales | 93 | 9 | Valatie 1 N | 53 |
| 10 | Canton 4 SE | 92 | 10 | Yorktown Heights 1 W | 54 |
| 11 | Chazy | 81 | 11 | Troy Lock and Dam | 55 |
| 12 | Westfield 2 SSE | 80 | 12 | Albany County Arpt | 59 |
| 13 | Binghamton Edwin A Link Field | 79 | 13 | Bath | 67 |
| 14 | Delhi 2 SE | 78 | 14 | Avon | 70 |
| 14 | Syracuse Hancock Int'l Arpt | 78 | 15 | Aurora Research Farm | 71 |
| 16 | Ithaca Cornell Univ | 74 | 15 | Buffalo Greater Buffalo Int'l | 71 |
| 17 | Rochester Intl Arpt | 73 | 17 | Rochester Intl Arpt | 73 |
| 18 | Aurora Research Farm | 71 | 18 | Ithaca Cornell Univ | 74 |
| 18 | Buffalo Greater Buffalo Int'l | 71 | 19 | Delhi 2 SE | 78 |
| 20 | Avon | 70 | 19 | Syracuse Hancock Int'l Arpt | 78 |
| 21 | Bath | 67 | 21 | Binghamton Edwin A Link Field | 79 |
| 22 | Albany County Arpt | 59 | 22 | Westfield 2 SSE | 80 |
| 23 | Troy Lock and Dam | 55 | 23 | Chazy | 81 |
| 24 | Yorktown Heights 1 W | 54 | 24 | Canton 4 SE | 92 |
| 25 | Valatie 1 N | 53 | 25 | Wales | 93 |

*Rankings include 25 highest/lowest stations. If state has less than 25 stations, all stations are included. The period of record is 1980–2009. See User Guide for detailed explanation of data.*

## Significant Storm Events in New York: 2000 – 2009

| Location or County | Date | Type | Mag. | Deaths | Injuries | Property Damage ($mil.) | Crop Damage ($mil.) |
|---|---|---|---|---|---|---|---|
| Buffalo Metro Area, Western Southern Tier | 11/20/00 | Heavy Snow | na | 0 | 0 | 46.5 | 0.0 |
| New York City Metro Area | 02/17/03 | Heavy Snow | na | 0 | 0 | 20.0 | 0.0 |
| Northwest New York | 04/04/03 | Ice Storm | na | 1 | 0 | 28.5 | 8.5 |
| Northwestern Central New York | 04/04/03 | Ice Storm | na | 0 | 0 | 28.5 | 0.0 |
| Broome | 06/13/03 | Flash Flood | na | 5 | 0 | 0.1 | 0.0 |
| Sullivan | 08/30/04 | Flash Flood | na | 0 | 0 | 20.0 | 0.0 |
| Delaware | 06/27/06 | Flash Flood | na | 2 | 0 | 250.0 | 0.0 |
| Broome | 06/27/06 | Flash Flood | na | 0 | 0 | 200.0 | 0.0 |
| Tioga | 06/27/06 | Flash Flood | na | 0 | 0 | 100.0 | 0.0 |
| Sullivan | 06/27/06 | Flash Flood | na | 1 | 0 | 100.0 | 0.0 |
| Oneida | 06/27/06 | Flash Flood | na | 0 | 0 | 50.0 | 0.0 |
| Chenango | 06/27/06 | Flood | na | 0 | 0 | 50.0 | 0.0 |
| Otsego | 06/27/06 | Flash Flood | na | 0 | 0 | 50.0 | 0.0 |
| Broome | 06/27/06 | Flood | na | 0 | 0 | 50.0 | 0.0 |
| Chenango | 06/27/06 | Flash Flood | na | 1 | 0 | 50.0 | 0.0 |
| Madison | 06/27/06 | Flash Flood | na | 0 | 0 | 25.0 | 0.0 |
| Southeast New York | 08/01/06 | Excessive Heat | na | 42 | 0 | 0.0 | 0.0 |
| Southwest Suffolk County | 04/16/07 | Coastal Flood | na | 0 | 0 | 26.0 | 0.0 |
| Delaware | 06/19/07 | Flash Flood | na | 4 | 0 | 30.0 | 0.0 |
| Cattaraugus | 08/09/09 | Flash Flood | na | 1 | 1 | 45.0 | 0.0 |
| Chautauqua | 08/09/09 | Flash Flood | na | 0 | 0 | 30.0 | 0.0 |
| Jefferson and Lewis Counties | 12/09/09 | High Wind | 58 mph | 0 | 0 | 100.0 | 0.0 |

Note: Deaths, injuries, and damages are date and location specific.

# Grey House Publishing
# 2012 Title List

Visit **www.greyhouse.com** for Product Information, Table of Contents and Sample Pages

## General Reference

America's College Museums
American Environmental Leaders: From Colonial Times to the Present
An African Biographical Dictionary
An Encyclopedia of Human Rights in the United States
Encyclopedia of African-American Writing
Encyclopedia of Gun Control & Gun Rights
Encyclopedia of Invasions & Conquests
Encyclopedia of Prisoners of War & Internment
Encyclopedia of Religion & Law in America
Encyclopedia of Rural America
Encyclopedia of the United States Cabinet, 1789-2010
Encyclopedia of War Journalism
Encyclopedia of Warrior Peoples & Fighting Groups
From Suffrage to the Senate: America's Political Women
Nations of the World
Political Corruption in America
Speakers of the House of Representatives, 1789-2009
The Environmental Debate: A Documentary History
The Evolution Wars: A Guide to the Debates
The Religious Right: A Reference Handbook
The Value of a Dollar: 1860-2009
The Value of a Dollar: Colonial Era
US Land & Natural Resource Policy
Weather America
Working Americans 1770-1869 Vol. IX: Revol. War to the Civil War
Working Americans 1880-1999 Vol. I: The Working Class
Working Americans 1880-1999 Vol. II: The Middle Class
Working Americans 1880-1999 Vol. III: The Upper Class
Working Americans 1880-1999 Vol. IV: Their Children
Working Americans 1880-2003 Vol. V: At War
Working Americans 1880-2005 Vol. VI: Women at Work
Working Americans 1880-2006 Vol. VII: Social Movements
Working Americans 1880-2007 Vol. VIII: Immigrants
Working Americans 1880-2009 Vol. X: Sports & Recreation
Working Americans 1880-2010 Vol. XI: Inventors & Entrepreneurs
Working Americans 1880-2011 Vol. XII: Our History through Music
World Cultural Leaders of the 20th & 21st Centuries

## Business Information

Directory of Business Information Resources
Directory of Mail Order Catalogs
Directory of Venture Capital & Private Equity Firms
Environmental Resource Handbook
Food & Beverage Market Place
Grey House Homeland Security Directory
Grey House Performing Arts Directory
Hudson's Washington News Media Contacts Directory
New York State Directory
Sports Market Place Directory
The Rauch Guides – Industry Market Research Reports
Sweets Directory by McGraw Hill Construction

## Statistics & Demographics

America's Top-Rated Cities
America's Top-Rated Small Towns & Cities
America's Top-Rated Smaller Cities
Comparative Guide to American Hospitals
Comparative Guide to American Suburbs
Profiles of... Series – State Handbooks

## Health Information

Comparative Guide to American Hospitals
Complete Directory for Pediatric Disorders
Complete Directory for People with Chronic Illness
Complete Directory for People with Disabilities
Complete Mental Health Directory
Directory of Health Care Group Purchasing Organizations
Directory of Hospital Personnel
HMO/PPO Directory
Medical Device Register
Older Americans Information Directory

## Education Information

Charter School Movement
Comparative Guide to American Elementary & Secondary Schools
Complete Learning Disabilities Directory
Educators Resource Directory
Special Education

## Financial Ratings Series

TheStreet.com Ratings Guide to Bond & Money Market Mutual Funds
TheStreet.com Ratings Guide to Common Stocks
TheStreet.com Ratings Guide to Exchange-Traded Funds
TheStreet.com Ratings Guide to Stock Mutual Funds
TheStreet.com Ratings Ultimate Guided Tour of Stock Investing
Weiss Ratings Consumer Box Set
Weiss Ratings Guide to Banks & Thrifts
**Weiss** Ratings Guide to Credit Unions
Weiss Ratings Guide to Health Insurers
Weiss Ratings Guide to Life & Annuity Insurers
Weiss Ratings Guide to Property & Casualty Insurers

## Bowker's Books In Print® Titles

Books In Print®
Books In Print® Supplement
American Book Publishing Record® Annual
American Book Publishing Record® Monthly
Books Out Loud™
Bowker's Complete Video Directory™
Children's Books In Print®
Complete Directory of Large Print Books & Serials™
El-Hi Textbooks & Serials In Print®
Forthcoming Books®
Law Books & Serials In Print™
Medical & Health Care Books In Print™
Publishers, Distributors & Wholesalers of the US™
Subject Guide to Books In Print®
Subject Guide to Children's Books In Print®

## Canadian General Reference

Associations Canada
Canadian Almanac & Directory
Canadian Environmental Resource Guide
Canadian Parliamentary Guide
Financial Services Canada
Governments Canada
Libraries Canada
The History of Canada

**Grey House Publishing**
4919 Route 22, PO Box 56, Amenia NY 12501-0056 | (800) 562-2139 | www.greyhouse.com | books@greyhouse.com